FAR EAST
CHINESE-ENGLISH
DICTIONARY

遠東漢英大辭典

（原主編人　梁實秋）

簡明本

主　編

張　芳　杰

總審定　朱良箴　總編輯　鄧樂然

遠東圖書公司印行

部　首　表

部 首 表

目　錄

字	字號	字	字號	字	字號	字	字號	字	字號
獎	946	麼	7242	褒	5441	縣	4402	藝	5456
犛	1047	鼻	7298	蜵	5487	穀	4403	穀	5510
辮	1093	齊	7303	豎	5717	雚	4506	膾	5648
對	1166	**十五　　畫**		輝	5997	羲	4530	賽	5652
幕	1335	單字　　字號		靚	6724	翰	4558	豁	5709
斡	2162	賤	443	靠	6729	舱	4768	闔	5733
暢	2273	奭	947	養	6868	學	4784	贖	5805
揭	2313	弊	1414	魯	7063	融	5294	輿	6015
靽	2541	慕	1693	鷹	7126	衡	5372	轂	6016
縠	2542	憂	1694	蓹	7236	褰	5446	隷	6653
毓	2730	慶	1696	麾	7243	豫	5730	韓	6768
爾	3296	暮	2274	黎	7248	賴	5800	鹹	6917
疑	3589	樊	2579	齒	7307	赭	5825	鼇	7072
蓮	3590	滕	3028	**十六　　畫**		賴	5826	黏	7249
戰	3712	蔡	3066	單字　　字號		辦	6042	歡	7273
睿	3794	漿	3067	冀	321	辨	6043	齋	7304
寧	3788	穎	3068	冪	333	覷	6732	龠	7329
罰	4501	瑩	3476	器	751	龍	7325	**十八　　畫**	
署	4502	畿	3583	麗	752	龜	7328	單字　　字號	
罳	4503	皺	3713	奮	948	**十七　　畫**		叢	526
聚	4602	穀	4018	贏	1064	單字　　字號		彝	1446
聞	4603	縣	4400	整	2145	孻	1067	斃	2148
臧	4762	罵	4504	暨	2281	尷	1178	歸	2690
臺	4771	龍	4505	曆	2282	幫	1345	爵	3289
舞	4796	翫	4555	曌	2287	龜	2734	瞿	3819
裹	5427	膚	4724	歷	2689	營	3264	舊	4785
賓	5785	興	4783	燕	3258	變	3272	覆	5476
赫	5824	號	5190	薨	3531	臨	4763	豐	5719
辣	6041	蝕	5270	盧	3735	艱	4825	蹟	5925
衙	6378	衝	5368	暜	3805	蘄	5191	鼇	6309
韶	6777	衚	5369	穌	4026	褒	5453	隳	6651
鳳	7119	衛	5370	穎	4027	襄	5455	雙	6673

燼 ⋯⋯⋯6676	韻 ⋯⋯⋯6778	辯 ⋯⋯⋯6046	蠱 ⋯⋯⋯5348	鹽 ⋯⋯⋯7215
蹟 ⋯⋯⋯6770	麗 ⋯⋯⋯7228	轢 ⋯⋯⋯6848	躅 ⋯⋯⋯5349	籛 ⋯⋯⋯7246
馥 ⋯⋯⋯6919	麴 ⋯⋯⋯7239	魘 ⋯⋯⋯7058	變 ⋯⋯⋯5695	**廿六　　畫**
魏 ⋯⋯⋯7055	黼 ⋯⋯⋯7274	骰 ⋯⋯⋯7184	鑵 ⋯⋯⋯5697	單字　　字號
十九　　畫	**二十　　畫**	竇 ⋯⋯⋯7305	驕 ⋯⋯⋯6734	閻 ⋯⋯⋯7043
單字　　字號	單字　　字號	**廿二　　畫**	徽 ⋯⋯⋯7268	驥 ⋯⋯⋯7270
衢 ⋯⋯⋯769	嚴 ⋯⋯⋯772	單字　　字號	齋 ⋯⋯⋯7306	**廿七　　畫**
龐 ⋯⋯⋯1403	璺 ⋯⋯⋯3821	襄 ⋯⋯⋯780	**廿四　　畫**	單字　　字號
爇 ⋯⋯⋯3279	競 ⋯⋯⋯4084	懿 ⋯⋯⋯1746	單字　　字號	鑾 ⋯⋯⋯6526
瓣 ⋯⋯⋯3520	耀 ⋯⋯⋯4567	疊 ⋯⋯⋯3586	罷 ⋯⋯⋯3823	**廿八　　畫**
疆 ⋯⋯⋯3584	贏 ⋯⋯⋯5814	耀 ⋯⋯⋯4272	蠹 ⋯⋯⋯4473	單字　　字號
繭 ⋯⋯⋯4453	辮 ⋯⋯⋯6045	罅 ⋯⋯⋯4510	羈 ⋯⋯⋯4511	豔 ⋯⋯⋯5721
羆 ⋯⋯⋯4508	馨 ⋯⋯⋯6920	聽 ⋯⋯⋯4612	蠶 ⋯⋯⋯5351	鑿 ⋯⋯⋯6527
羅 ⋯⋯⋯4509	騰 ⋯⋯⋯6965	巒 ⋯⋯⋯6034	衢 ⋯⋯⋯5373	**廿九　　畫**
獸 ⋯⋯⋯4533	**廿一　　畫**	響 ⋯⋯⋯6779	贛 ⋯⋯⋯5820	單字　　字號
贏 ⋯⋯⋯4534	單字　　字號	覊 ⋯⋯⋯7047	鑷 ⋯⋯⋯6719	爨 ⋯⋯⋯3283
嬴 ⋯⋯⋯5336	覺 ⋯⋯⋯777	龕 ⋯⋯⋯7326	**廿五　　畫**	鬱 ⋯⋯⋯7045
繫 ⋯⋯⋯5477	屬 ⋯⋯⋯4535	龕 ⋯⋯⋯7327	單字　　字號	**卅二　　畫**
贖 ⋯⋯⋯5810	贏 ⋯⋯⋯4754	**廿三　　畫**	耀 ⋯⋯⋯4274	單字　　字號
辭 ⋯⋯⋯6044	藥 ⋯⋯⋯5168	單字　　字號	釁 ⋯⋯⋯6300	籲 ⋯⋯⋯4232
靡 ⋯⋯⋯6730	譽 ⋯⋯⋯5690	蘗 ⋯⋯⋯4273	饗 ⋯⋯⋯6721	

梁 序

　　這一部漢英辭典是爲適應現代大衆需要而編的，所以單字收入雖不太多，包括常見常用的字約八千字之數，但是收入短辭、成語卻不在少數。過於典雅的與過於粗鄙的詞語，以及過於專門性的術語，則均割愛。深信在資料的選擇上，這部辭典可以滿足一般讀者的要求。

　　單字排列沒有萬全的辦法，我們採取部首的編排是因爲這可能是最大多數讀者所熟習的。附有索引，或以筆畫部首爲準，或以國語注音符號爲準，或以威妥瑪式羅馬拼音爲準，以增加讀者檢字的便利。

　　單字與詞一概加注注音符號，這是我們特別致力的項目之一，讀者於檢求英文解釋之餘，可以因此得到正確的讀音。爲篇幅所限，只能以國語注音符號爲主。事實上國語注音符號是最簡便而又最準確的一套工具，欲求發音正確，讀者無分中外，皆宜通曉國語注音符號。

　　這樣一部辭典之最重要的一部分，當然是在英文解釋方面。我們使用的英文是現代流行的淺顯的英文。這些字詞，無妨一字對一字的直譯；有些只能以意義相當的字詞譯之；更有些不能不出於較冗長之解釋。我們的主旨是盡力使讀者在理解上得到便利。

　　我們編輯這部辭典，參考了我們所能獲得的不少的中外辭典，尤其是坊間早已出版的幾種類似的漢英辭典。在取材上、在翻譯上、在編排上，見仁見智，各有其獨特之處，我們不敢自詡後來居上，但是我們能從前此已有之成就汲取經驗，轉益多師，卻是不能不表示感激的。凡是字典均需隨時修訂，方能延長其壽命。我們誠懇的歡迎讀者指示其疏誤，以便陸續補正。

　　這部辭典的編輯，中文部分是由鍾露昇先生主其事，英文部分由朱良箴先生、董昭輝先生、邵廓清先生分別擔任。而全稿之綜閱、校戡、修改，則由朱良箴先生獨任其艱鉅。稿成之後，遠東圖書公司編輯部同人除悉心校對外，亦常提供意見，使這部辭典減少缺陷。這都是我們應該表示謝意的。

梁實秋

六十年五月

—1—

張 序

　　遠東圖書公司敦請梁實秋先生主編的最新實用漢英辭典，於一九七一年五月間世後，行銷中外，深受歡迎。十餘年來中英新詞語不斷增加。外人學習中文者日多，國人從事中譯英工作者亦眾。隨時代演變，中外讀者莫不殷切期待一部內容更新、更豐富的漢英辭典。遠東圖書公司主人浦家麟先生有鑑於此，遂於一九八四年初就商於梁實秋先生擬將最新實用漢英辭典擴編並增加新詞、新義等以應讀者需要，後經約集編審委員會同仁數度商議，研討擴編細則，由余綜理其事，並聘請遠東英漢大辭典總編輯兼英文中國日報總主筆朱良箴先生為總審定，聘請鄧樂然先生為總編輯，成立擴編小組。計畫既定，立即展開工作。

　　擴編小組主要成員包括張振生、謝文男、鄭明哲、范國生、嚴偉行等諸位教授外並約請台大、師大、政大、輔大、東吳、淡江、文化等校優秀同學（名單另詳於後）及蘇全福老師等百餘位參加查證、核對、審訂工作，並參考各種中英文辭典、英漢辭典、百科全書、專用名詞辭典、中國歷代名著英譯本、當代中英文刊物，據以擴充詞語，增加例句。凡字詞適用於白話者，以白話為例句；適用於文言者，以文言者為例句；可用於白話亦可用於文言者，酌加白話例句及文言例句，並儘量納入科技新詞語、流行的口語、俚語等。一九八七年十一月梁實秋先生逝世後，浦家麟先生將擴編小組擴大為編審小組，加速進行。其後增聘海峽兩岸及留美十餘位學者專家參加審訂工作以資妥善。

　　整個擴編過程中，我們特別感謝鄧樂然先生的奉獻，他督導先後一百餘位成員，鍥而不捨，日夜加班，倍極辛勞。他們逐字逐詞複查原稿後，尚須查證辭句出處，故而每字每詞皆經過二十餘次核校，始可發排，工作至艱至鉅。此外，擴編工作歷經六載，其間物價波動，經費較原訂計畫超出數倍，幸賴遠東圖書公司經理部鼎力支援，一一克服遭遇到的諸多困難，其堅毅不撓，精益求精的精神，令人欽佩。

　　本辭典經擴編後，堪稱規模最大的一部漢英辭典，計彙集常用單字約八千之數，短詞、成語達十餘萬條，例句數萬條。取材標準著重現代化與實用性。為求儘量幫助讀者，本辭典採用三種注音符號，備有五種索引。惟近來科技發展迅速，中文電腦排版逐漸取代手工排版。漢字若干字體、字彙正用俗用在電腦系統中筆畫慣例在技術上仍未臻完善，電腦磁片輸入尚待克服，故在本書中有若干字彙正用俗用互相調用。儘管如此，由於工作量浩瀚，動員了百餘位專業人士，同仁等雖竭盡所能，猶恐力有未逮，疏漏之處難免，尚祈海內外學者、專家、以及所有讀者不吝指正。

張若生謹識
一九九一年十月

本辭典編審委員會編校小組

助　理

校　對

體 例

一、字彙：本辭典收集常用單字七千三百餘字，短詞、成語達十二萬餘條。取材範圍包括中英文辭典、中國經典、新舊文藝作品、報章雜誌及日常談話。取材標準著重現代化與實用性，典雅的、俚俗的、以及常見的科學詞語，一併收羅，深信足供一般中外讀者參考之用。

二、字體：本辭典所列單字，以正體爲準。俗寫與訛體則加註於本字之後，或單獨列入並加註本字正體。

三、排列：

(甲) 單字的排列是根據部首（見部首表），同一部首之單字，則依筆畫多寡排列。每一單字均編列號碼，以便檢字，如單字「一」的號碼是「1」，單字「中」的號碼是「21」。

　　一單字如有二種或二種以上的讀音，且意義因而變異的，則分開排列。如「中」字在「中間」坐ㄨㄥˉ ㄐㄧㄢ與「中毒」坐ㄨㄥˋ ㄉㄨˊ兩個詞語裏讀音不同，解釋也不同，故分列爲「中」坐ㄨㄥˉ與「中」坐ㄨㄥˋ，但其編號則同爲一個號碼，即「中」坐ㄨㄥˉ與「中」坐ㄨㄥˋ均爲「21」號。

　　一個單字如果祇是讀音不同而不影響其意義時，則不分列，僅在變異的讀音後註明「又讀」字樣。

(乙) 詞語的排列是按照國語注音符號的順序來決定先後。例如「打鼓」與「打草驚蛇」兩個詞語，是按「鼓」《ㄨˇ與「草」ㄘㄠˇ在注音符號表上的順序來決定排列的先後。

　　每一個單字下的詞語，一律以該單字開始。例如在「文」字下的每一個詞語的第一個字，一律是「文」。讀者如要查「以文會友」這個成語，不要查「文」字，而要查「以」字。

四、注音：本辭典採用三種注音符號：國語注音符號、國語羅馬字、聯合國華語注音符號（漢語拼音）。每一個單字與每一個詞語的後面都加註國語注音符號，後兩者則僅列於單字之後以節省篇幅。

五、英解：本辭典之英文解釋，可分別爲兩大類：1.直接翻譯，2.解釋。前者適用於中英文可以直接對譯的情形（如：跑—to run，書—a book 等），後者用在無法對譯時使用（如：且角—a female role in Chinese opera）。本辭典英解方面之體例如下：

1. 一個詞語如有兩個或兩個以上截然不同的解釋，它的英文解釋是分開排列而冠以阿拉伯數字。例如「歲暮」的英解是 ① the late season of a year ② the closing years of one's life。

2. 許多中文成語、諺語的英解方式，是先直譯爲英文，然後在破折號後面再加引伸的意義。目的是使外國讀者對這些成語、諺語有較深切的體會。

3. 書名與拉丁文的專門名詞，一律用斜體字排印。

六、索引：本辭典共有五種索引：1.部首索引。2.筆畫索引。3.國語注音符號索引。4.國語羅馬字索引。5.聯合國注音符號（漢語拼音）索引。

七、附錄：詳見本辭典目錄表。

INTRODUCTION

Vocabulary   Between the covers of this dictionary are collected 7,331 Chinese characters, under which are to be found some 120,000 entries. They were selected from a vast wealth of source materials, including dictionaries, Chinese classics, works of old and modern literature, newspapers, periodicals, legal documents and daily conversations. Inasmuch as this dictionary is intended as a useful tool for present-day readers seeking general but not encyclopedic information, the selection of the entries was made with the emphasis on *wide application* and *current usage*. Language being what it is, a lexicographer would be faulted for allowing his personal preference to influence his judgment in this respect. Among the entries of this dictionary one will find, side by side with what is "classic" or "highbrow", scientific and technological terms, familiar journalistic expressions, idioms and even slang, which may appear slightly repulsive to those with a refined taste.

Form of Characters   Many characters in the Chinese language are interchangeable. Some characters have a standard form and a popular form. In addition, there are simplified forms and corrupt forms. The problem is further compounded by the fact that many "standard forms" have sunk into oblivion, while what were originally considered "corrupt forms" have been accepted as legitimate through long usage. To solve this problem, the compilers of this dictionary have chosen for inclusion those forms that are treated as "standard" by the majority of Chinese dictionaries in circulation. Popular forms and the most commonly seen corrupt forms are also listed, either separately or right beside the pertinent standard forms, and are included in the Radical Index for easy reference.

Arrangement of Entries   Individual characters in this dictionary are arranged according to their radicals in keeping with Chinese tradition. Each radical is shown in the Radical Table with a page number. Characters with the same radical are arranged according to the number of strokes in the ascending order.

Some Chinese characters have more than one pronunciation, with each pronunciation representing a totally different meaning. Characters of the category are listed separately. For example, the character "中" is pronounced ㄓㄨㄥ in "中間" (in the middle) and ㄓㄨㄥ in "中毒" (to be poisoned). Therefore, the same character "中" is treated as two separate characters. No such distinction is made with those characters whose meaning is not affected by difference in pronunciation. For example, the character "微" can be pronounced ㄨㄟ or ㄨㄟ without change in meaning. Characters of this nature are treated as a single entity with the different pronunciations indicated behind each.

Entries under each character are arranged according to the order of the Mandarin Phonetic Symbols (國語注音符號). For example, the expression "打草驚蛇" ㄉㄚ ㄘㄠ ㄐㄧㄥ ㄕㄜ is listed after

"打鼓" ㄉㄚˇ ㄍㄨˇ.

All entries under each character begin with that particular character. For example, the entries under the character "文" all begin with "文". If one wants to find the expression "以文會友", he must look for it under the character "以".

Pronunciation Guide   Three kinds of pronunciation guide are adopted in this dictionary. They are the Mandarin Phonetic Symbols (國語注音符號), the Gwoyeu Romatzyh (國語羅馬字), and the United Nations Mandarin Phonetic Symbols (HAN YU PIN YIN)(聯合國華語注音符號[漢語拼音]).

English Definitions   Woe to those who attempt to make a *perfect* translation between Chinese and English, two languages that have few common denominators. The primary objective of this dictionary is to give the Chinese characters and phrases their *equivalent* meaning in English, on the assumption that the majority of them have English counterparts with identical or similar meaning. In cases where this is not true, the Chinese character or phrase in question is merely *explained* in English with no equivalent given. The late Mr. Yen Fu laid down three cardinal principles for the guidance of translators: *fidelity, readability* and *literary elegance.* The compilers of this dictionary have done their best to meet at least the first two of the three requirements, hoping that the deficiency in the last will be made up by the learned user himself.

The following rules are observed in giving the English definitions.

1. If one entry has two or more definitions totally different, they are listed separately and introduced by Arabic numerals in the ascending order with the more popular ones placed first. For example, the phrase "歲暮" has two definitions: (1) the late season of a year and (2) the closing years of one's life.

2. To enable non-Chinese speaking readers to savor the beauty of some Chinese proverbs and expressions, this dictionary usually gives a literal translation first and then the inferred meaning after a dash.

3. Latin words and titles of books which appear in the English definitions are printed in italics.

Indices   Five indices are attached to this dictionary. They are: (1) Radical Index, (2) Stroke Number Index, (3) Mandarin Phonetic Symbol Index, (4) Gwoyeu Romatzyh Index, and (5) United Nations Mandarin Phonetic Symbol (HAN YU PIN YIN) Index. With these indices no one can fail to find in this dictionary the character or any of the entries he is looking for.

Appendix   See the Table of Contents.

部首筆畫與索引頁碼對照表

部首筆畫索引

部首筆畫索引

編 法： 本索引係按單字之部首編列。其屬同一部首者，再以單字筆畫
多寡爲序。單字後註明單字編號。

用 法： 檢查時先查出單字所屬之部首，按筆畫（除去部首筆畫數）在
索引中查出單字，再根據單字編號，查出書內單字及這一單字
爲首所組成的詞語。

RADICAL INDEX

In this index the characters are listed under their respective
radicals. Characters with the same radical are arranged in the
ascending order according to the number of strokes used in writing
them. The figure to the right of each character is its identification
number under which the character can be found in the body of
the dictionary.

The first step in looking for a character is to find out the radical under which it is listed. The next step is to look for the character in the index according to the number of strokes (i.e. the total
number of strokes used in writing the whole character minus the
number of strokes used in writing the radical) which is indicated
with Chinese numerals in the column to the left of the characters.
With the identification number as a guide, one can locate in the
dictionary the character and the entries beneath it.

人（續）

筆畫	單字	字號
	們	198
	倒	199
	倔	200
	倖	201
	倘	202
	候	203
	倚	204
	偶	205
	借	206
	倡	207
	値	208
	倦	209
	倨	210
	倩	211
	倪	212
	倫	213
	倭	214
九	偓	215
	假	216
	偈	217
	偉	218
	偌	219
	偎	220
	偏	221
	偓	222
	偕	223
	做	224
	停	226
	健	226
	偬	227
	側	228
	偵	229
	偶	230
	偷	231
一〇	傢	232
	傀	233
	傅	234
	傍	235
	傑	236
	傖	237

筆畫	單字	字號
	傘	238
	備	239
	傚	240
	傜(猺)	3378
一一	催	241
	傭	242
	傲	243
	傳	244
	傴	245
	債	246
	傷	247
	傺	248
	傾	249
	僂	250
	僅	251
	僉	252
	傯	253
	傻	276
	(傻)	
→二	像	254
	僑	255
	僕	256
	僔	257
	僚	258
	僞	259
	僥	260
	僦	261
	僧	262
	僭	263
	僮	264
	僵	265
一三	僻	266
	價	267
	儁	268
	儀	269
	儂	270
	儇	271
	儆	272
	儈	273

筆畫	單字	字號
	儉	274
	儋	275
	儐	276
一四	儐	277
	儒	278
	儔	279
	儕	280
	儘	281
一五	償	282
	儡	283
	優	284
一六	儲	285
一九	儺	286
二〇	儼	287

儿

筆畫	單字	字號
一	兀	288
二	允	289
	元	290
三	兄	291
	充	292
四	充(充)	
	兆	293
	兇	294
	先	295
五	光	296
	克	297
	兌	298
	免	299
	兔	301
六	(兔)	
	兒	300
	兒	301
七	兗	302
九	兜	304
一二	兢	305

入

筆畫	單字	字號
	入	306
二	內	307
四	全	308
六	兩	309
七	兪	310

八

筆畫	單字	字號
	八	311
二	公	312
	六	313
	兮	314
四	共	315
五	兵	316
六	其	317
	具	318
	典	319
八	兼	320
一四	冀	321

冂

筆畫	單字	字號
三	冉	322
	册	323
四	再	324
七	冑	325
	冓	326
八	冕	327
九	冕	328

冖

筆畫	單字	字號
七	冠	329
八	冤	330
	冥	331
	冢	332
一四	冪	333

冫

筆畫	單字	字號
三	冬	334
四	冰	335
	決	2786
	(決)	
	沖	2801
五	(沖)	
	冶	336
	冷	337
	況	2821
六	(況)	
	冽	338
八	准	339
	清	340
	凋	341
	凌	342
	凍	343
九	湊	2977
	(湊)	
一三	凜	344
一四	凝	345

几

筆畫	單字	字號
	几	346
一	凡	347
九	鳳	348
一〇	凱	349
一二	凳	350

凵

筆畫	單字	字號
二	凶	351
三	凸	352
	凹	353
	出	354
六	函	355

刀

筆畫	單字	字號
	刀	356
	刁	357
一二	刃	358
	分	359
	切	360
	刈	361
三	刊	362
四	刎	363
	刑	364
	划	365
	刓	366
	刖	367
	列	368
五	初	369
	刪	370
	判	371
	別	372
	刨	373
	利	374
	刧(劫)	423
六	刮	375
	券	376
	到	377
	剁	379
	剌	380
	制	381
	刷	382
	刺	383
	刻	384
七	剎	379
	(剎)	
	則	385
	剃	386
	剄	387
	剉	388

刀(刂)部（續）

筆畫	單字	字號
	削	389
	剋	390
	剌	391
	前	392
八	剔	393
	剖	394
	剮	395
	剛	396
	剜	397
九	剝	398
	副	399
一〇	剪	400
	剩	401
	割	402
	剴	403
	創	404
一一	剿	405
	剷	406
	剽	407
一二	剳	408
	劃	409
一三	劇	410
	劈	411
	劉	412
	劊	413
	劍	414
一四	剸	415
	剹	416

力部

筆畫	單字	字號
	力	417
三	功	418
	加	419
四	劣	420
五	助	421
	努	422
	劫	423
	劬	424
	劭	425
六	劾	426
	效	2123
	(效)	427
七	勃	428
	勑	429
	勇	430
	勉	431
九	勒	432
	動	433
	勗	434
	勖	434
	(勖)	
	勘	435
	務	436
一〇	勝	437
	勞	438
一一	勦	405
	(剿)	
	勢	439
	募	440
	勤	441
	勣	442
一三	勰	443
一四	勳	444
一五	勱	445
一八	勸	446

勹部

筆畫	單字	字號
一	勺	447
二	勻	448
	勾	449
	勿	450
三	包	451
	匆	1549
	(匆)	
四	匈	452
七	匍	453
九	匏	454
	匐	455

匕部

筆畫	單字	字號
	匕	456
二	化	457
三	北	458
九	匙	459

匚部

筆畫	單字	字號
三	匜	460
	匝	461
四	匠	462
	匡	463
五	匣	464
八	匭	465
九	匪	466
	匯	467
一二	匱	468
一三	匲	469

匸部

筆畫	單字	字號
二	匹	470
九	匾	471
	匽	472
	區	473

十部

筆畫	單字	字號
	十	474
二	千	475
	升	476
	午	477
	卅	478
三	半	479
	卌	480
	卉	481
	(卉)	
四	卉	481
六	卑	482
	卒	483
	卓	484
	協	485
七	南	486
一〇	博	487

卜部

筆畫	單字	字號
	卜	488
二	卞	489
	占	490
	卡	491
五	卣	492
六	卦	493

卩部

筆畫	單字	字號
三	卮	494
	卯	495
四	印	496
	危	497
五	卵	498
	却	503
	(卻)	
	即	504
	(即)	
六	卷	499
	卸	500
	卹	501
	卺	502
七	卻	503
	卽	504
	卿	505

厂部

筆畫	單字	字號
二	厄	506
七	厓	507
	厚	508
八	原	509
	厝	510
一〇	厥	511
一二	厭	512
一三	厲	513

厶部

筆畫	單字	字號
三	去	514
九	參	515

又部

筆畫	單字	字號
	又	516
二	叉	517
	及	518
	友	519
	反	520
六	叔	521
	取	522
	受	523
七	叛	524
	叙	2125
	(敘)	
八	叜	525
	(叟)	
	疊	3586
	(疊)	
一六	叢	526

口部

筆畫	單字	字號
	口	527
二	叨	528
	叼	529
	古	530
	句	531
	另	532
	叩	533
	只	534
	叫	535
	召	536
	叭	537
	叮	538
	可	539
	台	540
	叱	541
	史	542
	右	543
	叵	544
	叶	545
	司	546
三	合	547
	吁	548
	吃	549
	各	550
	吉	551
	吋	552
	同	553
	吲	554
	吒	555
	名	556
	后	557
	吐	558
	向	559
	吏	560
	吊	1420
	(弔)	
四	君	561
	吝	562
	吞	563
	吟	564
	吠	565
	否	566
	吩	567
	含	568
	吮	569
	呈	570
	吳	571

五 吵	572		呑	610		(脣)			喊	684	一一	嗽	722		噪	756
呐	573		咪	611	八	售	647		喋	685		嗸	722		嗾	757
吸	574		呸	612		唯	648		喏	686		(嗷)			歔	758
吹	575		咬	613		唱	649		喑	687		嘩	723		噯	759
吻	576		咯	614		唾	650		喔	688		嗽	724		噹	760
吼	577		咱	615		啡	651		喘	689		嗾	725		嘖	761
吱	578		咳	616		啡	652		喙	690		嘅	726	一四	壞	762
吾	579		咸	617		啁	653		喚	691		嘈	727		嚅	763
告	580		咽	618		啄	654		喜	692		嘉	728		嚆	764
呀	581		咿	619		啇	655		喝	693		嘍	729		嚇	765
呃	582		哀	620		問	656		喞	694		嘏	730		嚏	767
呂	583		品	621		啊	657		喟	695		嘔	731		嚨	767
呆	584		哂	622		啤	658		喧	696		嘖	732	一五	嚕	768
呎	585		哄	623		啐	659		唡	697		嘗	733		嚐	7317
吧	586		哆	624		啓	660		喩	698		嘆	2668		(嚐)	
五 呢	587		哇	625		唳	661		喪	699		(歎)		一六	嚮	769
周	588		哈	626		唎	662		喬	700	一二	嘮	661		嚦	770
咒	589		哉	627		唷	663		單	701		(唠)			嚨	771
咨	590		哎	628		啦	664		喳	702		嘩	734	一七	嚴	772
呱	591	七	員	629		啞	665	一〇	嗄	703		噓	735		嚶	773
味	592		哥	630		唒	666		嗅	704		嘮	736	一八	嚼	774
呵	593		哦	631		唬	667		嗆	705		嘴	737		嚼	775
咕	594		哨	632		啄	668		嗇	706		嘰	738		嚳	776
咂	595		哩	633		唸	669		喋	707		嘲	739		嚶	777
咚	596		哭	634		啥	670		嗜	708		嘴	740		嚶	778
呻	597		哮	635		啜	671		嗎	709		嘶	741	十九	囁	779
呼	598		哲	636	九	啜	549		嗒	710		嘽	742		囊	780
命	599		哺	637		(吃)			嗓	711		喉	743	二一	囋	781
咀	600		哼	638		啻	672		嗩	712		嘻	744		囓	7317
咄	601		哽	639		啼	673		嗚	713		嘸	745		(嚙)	
咆	602		唁	640		啾	674		嗜	714		嘻	746			
咋	603		唆	641		喀	675		嗝	715		默	747			
和	604		唉	642		啈	676		嗯	716		噍	748			
咖	605		唏	643		喂	677		嗟	717		嘬	749			
咐	606		唐	644		喃	678		嗣	718		嗜	750			
咏	5549		哪	645		善	679	一三	嗷	719		器	751			
(詠)			哞	646		嘍	680		嗡	720		嘍	752			
六 咧	607		唧	694		喇	681		嗤	721		噴	753			
咤	608		(唧)			喈	682		嗾	726		噹	754			
咦	609		唇	4677		喉	683					噸	755			

囗		
筆畫	單字	字號
二	囚	782
	四	783
三	回	784
	囟	785
	因	786
四	困	787
	囿	788

囗（續）

筆畫	單字	字號
	囫	789
	圐	790
五	圂	791
	圇	792
	固	793
六	囿	794
七	圃	795
	圉	796
八	國	797
	圄	798
	圈	799
九	圍	800
一〇	園	801
	圓	802
一一	圖	803
	團	804

土

筆畫	單字	字號
	土	805
三	在	806
	圬	807
	圭	808
	圯	809
	地	810
四	坊	811
	圾	812
	址	813
	坂	814
	均	815
	坍	816
	坎	817
	坐	818
	坑	819
五	坡	820
	坤	821
	坦	822
	坷	823
	坯	824
	坳	825
	垂	826
	垃	827
	坪	828
六	坩	829
	垓	830
	垢	831
	型	832
	垮	833
七	埋	834
	城	835
	垠	836
	埃	837
	埔	838
八	培	839
	域	840
	埠	841
	埤	842
	執	843
	基	844
	堂	845
	堅	846
	堆	847
	埽(掃)	1912
九	報	848
	堡	849
	堪	850
	堯	851
	堰	852
	場	853
	堵(隄)	6624
	堤(隄)	6626
一〇	塊	855
	塋	856
	塌	857
	塚	858
	塑	859
	塔	860
	塗	861
	塘	862
	塞	863
	填	864
	塢	865
一一	墓	866
	塵	867
	塹	868
	墊	869
	境	870
	墅	871
	墉	872
	塼(磚)	3530
	塲(鏝)	6486
一二	墟	874
	墀	875
	墜	876
	增	877
	墨	878
	墩	879
	墳	880
一三	墳	881
	壁	882
	壅	883
	壇	884
	壇(壃)	885
一四	壓	886
	壎	887
	墼	888
	壤	889
一五	壜	890
	壘	891
一六	罎	892
	壞	893
一七	壩	894
二一	壩	895

士

筆畫	單字	字號
	士	896
三	壬	897
四	壯	898
	壳(殼)	2719
九	壻	899
	壹	900
	壺	901
一〇	壼	902
二一	壽	903

夂

筆畫	單字	字號
七	夏	904
一二	夔	905
一八	夒	906

夕

筆畫	單字	字號
	夕	907
二	外	908
三	多	909
	夙	910
五	夜	911
	夐	3300
	夠	912
	夠(夠)	912
一一	夢	913
	夤	914
	夥	915

大

筆畫	單字	字號
	大	916
一	天	917
	太	918
	夫	919
	央	920
	夭	921
二	失	922
	央	923
	夯	924
三	夸	925
	夷	926
四	夾	927
五	奄	928
	奇	929
	奈	930
	奉	931
	奔	932
六	奔(奔)	932
	奎	933
	奏	934
	奐	935
	契	936
七	奕	937
	奘	938
	套	939
	奢	940
	奚	941
九	奠	942
	奢	943
一〇	奧	944
一一	奩(奩)	469
	奪	945
一二	奬	946
	奭	947
一三	奮	948

女

筆畫	單字	字號
	女	949
二	奴	950
	奶	951
三	奸	952
	她	953
	好	954
	妁	955
	如	956
	妃	957
	妄	958
	妊(姙)	997
四	妓	959
	妊	960
	妒	961
	妖	962
	妞	963
	妙	964
	妝	965
	姒	966
	妤	967
	妥	968
	妨	969
	妍(妍)	996
五	姑	961
	妒(妒)	
	姐	970
	妮	971
	妯	972
	妹	973
	妻	974
	妾	975
	姆	976
	姉	977
	姍	977
	姊(姊)	
	始	978
	姍	979
	姐	980

女

單字	字號
姑	981
妣	982
姓	983
委	984
妳	985
六	
姚	986
姜	987
姝	988
妓	989
姤	990
姥	991
姦	992
媄	993
姪	994
娉	995
奸	996
姹	997
姻	998
姿	999
威	1000
娃	1001
妍	1018
(姘)	
七	
娓	1002
娉	1003
娌	1004
姬	1005
娑	1006
娘	1007
娛	1008
娜	1009
娟	1010
娠	1011
娣	1012
娥	1013
娩	1014
八	
婆	1015
婀	1016
娶	1017
姘	1018
婁	1019
婉	1020
婕	1021
婚	1022
婢	1023
婦	1024
娶	1025
婬	1026
婭	1027
婊	1028
婗	1029
九	
婿(壻)	899
婷	1030
媟	1031
媒	1032
媚	1033
媛	1034
媧	1035
媄	1036
一〇	
嫁	1037
媸	1038
媳	1039
媵	1040
媸	1041
嫗	1042
媽	1043
媾	1044
嫉	1045
嫌	1046
嫋	1065
一一	
媿(愧)	1654
嫠	1047
嫖	1048
嫘	1049
嫚	1050
嫡	1051
嫣	1052
嫦	1053
嫩	1054
嫵(娬)	1029
一二	
嬉	1055
嫻	1056
嫻(嫻)	1056
一三	
嬋	1057
嬌	1058
嬖	1059
嬙	1060
嬗	1061
嬈	1062
嬡	1063
嬴	1064
一四	
嬰	1066
嬲	1067
嬪	1068
一五・一七	
嬸	1069
孃(娘)	1007
一七	
嬤	1070
孅	1071
十九	
孌	1072

子

筆畫	單字	字號
	子	1073
	孑	1074
	孓	1075
一	孔	1076
二	孕	1077
三	字	1078
	存	1079
四	孚	1080
	孛	1081
	孜	1082
	孝	1083
五	孟	1084
	季	1085
	孥	1086
	孤	1087
六	孩	1088
七	孫	1089
八	孰	1090
九	孱	1091
一一	孳	1092
一三	孵	1093
一四	學	1094
一六	孺	1095
	孿(孼)	1096
	孽	5161
	孿(孼)	1096
一九	孿	1097

宀

筆畫	單字	字號
二	宄	1098
	宂	1099
	宁	1100
	宅	1101
三	宅	1102
	字	1103
	守	1104
	安	1105
四	宋	1106
	完	1107
	宏	1108
五	宕	1109
	宓	1110
	宗	1111
	官	1112
	宙	1113
	定	1114
	宛	1115
	宜	1116
六	客	1117
	宣	1118
	室	1119
	宥	1120
	宦	1121
七	宮	1122
	宰	1123
	害	1124
	宴	1125
	宵	1126
	家	1127
	宸	1128
	容	1129
	宽(宽)	330
八	密	1130
	宿	1131
	寂	1132
	寄	1133
	寅	1134
	寇	1135
九	富	1136
	寐	1137
	寒	1138
	寓	1139
一〇	寘	1140
一一	寞	1141
	察	1142
	寧	1143
	寡	1144
	寢	1145
	寤	1146
	寥	1147
	實	1148
	寨	1149
一二	審	1150
	寫	1151
	寬	1152
	寮	1153
一三	寰	1154
一六	寵	1155
	寶(寳)	
	(寶)	
一七	寶	1156

寸

筆畫	單字	字號
	寸	1157
三	寺	1158
六	封	1159
七	射	1160
八	專	1161
	將	1162
	尉	1163
九	尊	1164
	尋	1165
一一	對	1166
一三	導	1167

小

筆畫	單字	字號
	小	1168
一	少	1169
三	尖	1170
五	尚	1171
六	尞	1172
一〇	尠	1173
	尟(尠)	1173

尢

筆畫	單字	字號
一	尤	1174
四	尨	1175
	尬	1176
九	就	1177
一四	尷	1178

尸

尸

筆畫	單字	字號
	尸	1179
一	尺	1180
	尹	1181
二	尻	1182
	尼	1183
四	尾	1184
	尿	1185
	局	1186
	屁	1187
五	居	1188
	屆	1189
	屈	1190
	屍	1191
	屄(雁)	1199
六	屋	1192
	屍	1193
	屎	1194
七	展	1195
	屐	1196
	屑	1197
八	屏	1198
	肩	1200
九	屠	1201
一一	屜	1202
	屢	1203
一二	層	1204
	履	1205
一四	屩	1206
一八	屬	1207

屮

筆畫	單字	字號
一	屯	1208

山

筆畫	單字	字號
	山	1209
三	屹	1210
	屺	1211
四	岌	1212
	岐	1214
	岑	1215
五	岡	1216
	岫	1217
	岬	1218
	岭	1219
	岱	1220
	岳	1221
	岷	1222
	岸	1223
	岩	1224
六	峋	1225
	峒	1226
	峙	1227
七	峨	1228
	峭	1229
	峯	1230
	峴	1231
	島	1232
	峻	1233
	峽	1234
	峪	1235
	崇	1236
八	崎	1237
	崑	1238
	崔	1239
	崖	1240
	崗	1241
	崙	1242
	崛	1243
	崝	1244
	崝	1245
	崩	1246
	崧	1247
	崒	1248
	崌	1249
	崺	1250
	嵷	1251
九	嵲	1252
	嵺	1253
	嵆	1254
	嵇	1255
	嵋	1256
	嵌	1257
	嵐	1258
	嵎	1259
	崿	1260
一〇	嵩	1261
	嵬	1262
	嵊	1263
	嵯	1264
一一	嶇	1265
	嶂	1266
	嶄	1267
一二	嶢	1268
	嶒	1269
	嶓	1270
	嶝	1271
	嶠	1272
	嶙	1273
	嵾	1274
一三	嶧	1275
	嶮	1276
	嶴	1277
	嶺	1278
	嶼	1279
	嶽	1280
一七	嶸	1281
	嶷	1282
	嶧	1283
一八	巍	1284
一九	巒	1285
	巔	1286
二〇	巖	1287
	巘	1288

巛

筆畫	單字	字號
三	川	1289
	州	1290
	巡	1291
	(巡)	6053
	巡(巡)	1291
四	巡	1291
八	巢	1292

工

筆畫	單字	字號
	工	1293
二	左	1294
	巧	1295
	巨	1296
四	巫	1297
七	差	1298

己

筆畫	單字	字號
	己	1299
	已	1300
	巳	1301
	巴	1302
一	巷	1303
六	異	1304
九		

巾

筆畫	單字	字號
	巾	1305
二	市	1306
	布	1307
三	帆	1308
	帆(帆)	1308
四	希	1309
五	帔	1310
	帑	1311
	帕	1312
	帖	1313
	帔	1314
	帚	1315
	帙	1316
	帶	1317
	帛	1318
六	帥	1319
	帝	
七	帨	1321
	師	1322
	席	1323
	帬(帬)	1345
八	帳	1324
	帶	1325
	帷	1326
	常	1327
九	幅	1328
	帽	1329
	幀	1330
	幃	1331
	幄	1332
一〇	幌	1333
	幔	1334
	幕	1335
	幗	1336
	幘	1337
	幛	1338
一二	幟	1339
	幞	1340
	幡	1341
	幢	1342
	幣	1343
一四	幬	1344
	幫	1345
	幬	1346
一五	幭	1347

干

筆畫	單字	字號
	干	1348
二	平	1349
三	年	1350
五	并	1351
	幸	1352
一〇	幹	1353

幺

筆畫	單字	字號
	幺	1354
一	幻	1355
二	幼	1356
六	幽	1357
九	幾	1358

广

筆畫	單字	字號
二	庀	1359
三	庄	1360
四	庇	1361
	庋	1362
	序	1363
	床	3297
	(牀)	
五	底	1364
	庖	1365
	店	1366
	庚	1367
	府	1368
六	度	1369
	庠	1370
	庥	1371
七	座	1372
	庫	1373
	庭	1374
八	庵	1375
	庶	1376

广（續）

筆畫	單字	字號
	康	1377
	庸	1378
	度	1379
九	庾	1380
	廁	1381
	廂	1382
一〇	廈	1383
	廉	1384
	廊	1385
	廋	1386
一一	廋	1387
	廖	1388
	廔	1389
	廓	1390
	廕	1391
一二	廚	1392
	廛	1393
	廝	1394
	廟	1395
	廠	1396
	廡	1397
	廢	1398
	廣	1399
一三	廩	1400
	廬	1401
一六	龐	1402
	廱	1403
一八	廰	1404
	廳	1405

廴

筆畫	單字	字號
三	巡	1291
	（巡）	6053
	（巡）	
四	延	1406
	廷	1407
五	廸	6067
	（廸）	6068
	（迫）	
六	建	1408
	廻	6072
	（迴）	

廾

筆畫	單字	字號
一	廿	1409
二	弁	1410
四	弄	1411
	弃	2476
	（棄）	
六	拿	1412
	弈	1413
一二	弊	1414

弋

筆畫	單字	字號
	弋	1415
三	式	1416
一〇	弒	1417

弓

筆畫	單字	字號
	弓	1418
一	引	1419
	弔	1420
二	弗	1421
	弘	1422
三	弛	1423
四	弟	1424
五	弦	1425
	弧	1426
	弢	1427
	弨	1428
六	弭	1429
	弮	1430
七	弱	1431
	弱	1432
八	張	1433
	強	1434
九	強	1434
	（強）	
	弼	1435
	彀	1436
一〇	彈	1437
	彇	1438
	彊	1434
一三	彊	1434
	（強）	
一四	彌	1439
一九	彎	1440

彐

筆畫	單字	字號
五	彔	1441
六	彖	1442
八	彗	1443
九	彘	1444
一〇	彙	1445
一三	彝	1446
	（彝）	
一五	彝	1446

彡

筆畫	單字	字號
四	形	1447
	形	1448
六	形	1448
	（彤）	
	彥	1449
七	彧	1450
八	彪	1451
	彩	1452
	彬	1453
	彫	1454
九	彭	1455
一一	彰	1456
一二	影	1457

彳

筆畫	單字	字號
	彳	1458
四	彷	1459
	役	1460
五	彼	1461
	往	1462
	征	1463
	徂	1464
	彿	1465
六	待	1466
	徇	1467
	很	1468
	徉	1469
	徊	1470
	律	1471
	後	1472
七	徐	1473
	徑	1474
	徒	1475
八	得	1476
	徘	1477
	徜	1478
	徙	1479
	從	1480
	徠	1481
	御	1482
九	徧	1483
	徨	1484
	復	1485
	循	1486
一〇	徬	1487
	徭	1488
	徯	1489
	微	1490
一一	徵	1491
	徹	1492
	德	1493
一三	徼	1494
一四	徽	1495

心

筆畫	單字	字號
	心	1496
一	必	1497
二	忉	1498
三	忌	1499
	忍	1500
	忒	1501
	志	1502
	忐	1503
	忘	1504
	忘	1505
	忙	1506
	忖	1507
	忡	1508
四	忤	1509
	快	1510
	忮	1511
	忭	1512
	忱	1513
	忸	1514
	忻	1515
	忪	1516
	忠	1517
	念	1518
	忽	1519
	忿	1520
	忝	1521
五	怍	1523
	怏	1524
	怖	1525
	怕	1526
	怙	1527
	怛	1528
	怦	1529
	怡	1530
	性	1531
	怩	1532
	怫	1533
	怯	1534
	怪	1535
	怰	1536
	怔	1537
	恰	1538
	怓	1539
	怗	1540
	怊	1541
	怎	1542
	怒	1543
	思	1544
	怠	1545
	急	1546
	怨	1547
	恖	1548
	恝	1549
六	恂	1550
	恆	1551
	恒	1551
	（恆）	
	恃	1552
	恌	1553
	恓	1554
	恍	1555
	恟	1556
	恢	1557
	恨	1558
	恤	1559
	恪	1560
	恫	1561
	恇	1562
	恬	1563
	恰	1564
	恊	1565
	恖	1566
	恐	1567
	恕	1568
	恚	1569

字	字號		字	字號		字	字號		字	字號		字	字號		字	字號		字	字號
忿	1570		惓	1610		意	1650		慭	1686		憶	1720			戈	1751
恚	1571		惘	1611		愚	1651		慾	1687		憺	1721	一	戊	1752
恋	1572		惚	1612		感	1652		憖	1688		憸	1722		戉	1753
恖	1573		惙	1613		愛	1653		憇	1688		懂	1723	二	戍	1754
恧	1574		惛	1614		愬	5345		(憇)			懆	1724		戌	1755
息	1575		惆	1615		(蠢)			慧	1689		懈	1725	三	戎	1756
恭	1576		惦	1616	一〇	愧	1654		慜	1690		懊	1726		成	1757
恥	1577		惜	1617		愴	1655		慙	1691		懍	1727		戒	1758
恉	1578		惟	1618		愫	1656		(慼)	1691		懌	1728		我	1759
七	悃	1579		悶	1619		慍	1657		(慼)			應	1729	四	或	1760
	悁	1580	九	惄	1620		愷	1658		慾	1692	一四	懃	1730		戕	1761
	悄	1581		惑	1621		愾	1659		慕	1693		懇	1731		戔	1762
	悅	1582		悲	1622		慄	1660		憂	1694		懋	1732	七	戚	1763
	悌	1583		惠	1623		慎	1661		慮	1695		憶	1733		戛	1764
	悔	1584		惡	1624		慊	1662		慶	1696		懦	1734	八	(戞)	1764
	悒	1585	九	惰	1625		慌	1663		慜	1713		懟	1735		(戞)	
	悍	1586		惱	1626		慆	1664		(憙)			(懟)	1735		戟	1765
	悚	1587		惴	1627	一二	慵	1665		憍	1697		懣	1736		(戟)	1765
	悛	1588		惶	1628		慈	1666		憐	1698		懲	1737	九	戡	1766
	悖	1589		惲	1629		遝	1667		憎	1699		懆	1741		戥	1767
	悟	1590		惷	1630		態	1668		憔	1700		(憯)			戤	1768
	悝	1591		愒	1631		慇	1669		憚	1701	一五	懲	1738	一〇	戧	1769
	悠	1592		愔	1632		恩	1670		憧	1702	一六	懷	1739		截	1770
	悉	1593		愕	1633		(恩)	1670	一五	憬	1703		懶	1740		戧	1771
	患	1594		愣	1634		(恩)		一六	憤	1704		懵	1741	一一	戮	1772
	悤	1595		愀	1635		愿	1671		憫	1705		懸	1742		戯	1774
	您	1596		惺	1636		應	1672		憮	1706		懿	1746		(戲)	
八	悱	1597		愀	1637	一一	慘	1673		憐	1707		(懿)		一二	戰	1773
	悵	1598		惻	1638		慢	1674		憯	1708		懽	1743	一三	戴	1775
	悸	1599		愎	1639		慣	1675		憒	1709	一七	懼	1744	一四	戳	1776
	悴	1600		愉	1640		慥	1676		憑	1710	一八	懾	1745			
	悴	1601		愴	1641		慟	1677		憋	1711		懿	1746	戶		
	悼	1602		愊	1642		慨	1678		憊	1712		懺	1747	筆畫	單字	字號
	悾	1603		愜	1643		慷	1679		憩	1713	一九	戀	1748		戶	1777
	悽	1604		想	1644		慳	1680		憲	1714	二〇	戄	1749		戹	1778
	惆	1605		惹	1645		慵	1681		憝	1715	二四	戀	1750	一	戾	1779
	惜	1606		愁	1646		慴	1682		憨	1716				四	扁	1780
	惇	1607		愍	1647		傮	1683		憖	1717	戈				房	1781
	惋	1608		愆	1648		慘	1684		憾	1718	筆畫	單字	字號			
	惕	1609		愈	1649	一三	慝	1685		憒	1719						

筆畫	單字	字號															
	所	1782	投	1819	拚	1853	挽	1883	披	1923	揚	1955
五	扁	1783	抗	1820	抿	1854	挺	1884	拼	1924	揀	1956
	扃	1784	抖	1821	招	1855	捃	1885	掙	1925	搵	1957
六	晨	1785	折	1822	拜	1856	捆	1886	捹	1926	換	1958
	扇	1786	抑	1823	拳	1874	持	1887	掠	1927	握	1959
七	扈	1787	扼	1824	(拿)		捉	1888	掛	1928	揣	1960
八	扉	1788	承	1825	担	2059	挾	1889	採	1929	揩	1961
			抛	1840	(擔)		捍	1890	探	1930	揪	1962

手																	
筆畫	單字	字號		抬	2073	捌	1891	控	1931	揫	1962
	手	1789	扼	1824	(擡)		捕	1892	接	1932	(揪)	
	才	1790	(扼)		六	拭	1857	捐	1893	推	1933	揮	1964
一	扎	1791	抱	1826	拮	1858	捎	1894	措	1934	揭	1964
二	扑	1792	抨	1827	拯	1859	捏	1895	掩	1935	援	1965
	扒	1793	披	1828	括	1860	揭	1896	搧	1936	揲	1966
	打	1794	抵	1829	拱	1861	八	捨	1897	掏	1937	揸	1967
	扔	1795	抹	1830	拴	1862	捧	1898	捶	1938	揶	1968
三	扦	1796	抽	1831	拶	1863	振	1899	掘	1939	揍	1969
	扣	1797	押	1832	拾	1864	捭	1900	掌	1940	揹	1970
	扛	1798	挂	1833	持	1865	捫	1901	掣	1941	揎	1971
	托	1799	拂	1834	按	1866	据	1902	捵	1942	揣	1972
	扦	1800	拇	1835	指	1867	捱	1903	掔	1943	搘	1973
	扷	1801	拈	1836	挑	1868	換	1904	挃	3879	揻	1974
四	扭	1802	拆	1837	拽	1869	捺	1905	(碰)		損	1975
	扮	1803	拉	1838	挖	1870	捽	1906	九	揑	1895	搆	1976
	扶	1804	拊	1839	拷	1871	捲	1907	(捏)		搏	1977
	扯	1805	抛	1840	托	1872	捻	1908	捷	1909	搔	1978
	扳	1806	拌	1841	拳	1873	捷	1909	(捷)		搾	1979
	扱	1807	拐	1842	拿	1874	掂	1910	揀	1944	搓	1980
	批	1808	拑	1843	挈	1875	掀	1911	揄	1945	搽	1981
	找	1809	拍	1844	拼	1924	掃	1912	揆	1946	搞	1982
	扐	1810	拎	1845	(拼)		授	1913	揉	1948	搖	1983
	技	1811	拒	1846	挂	1928	掇	1914	描	1949	搢	1984
	抄	1812	拓	1847	(掛)		掄	1915	搂	1950	搥	1986
	抉	1813	拔	1848	七	挨	1876	掎	1916	提	1951	搜	1987
	扷	1814	拗	1849	挪	1877	掏	1917	揕	1952	搭	1988
	抒	1815	拖	1850	抄	1878	掐	1918	揖	1953	搶	1989
	抓	1816	扼	1850	挫	1879	培	1919	插	1954	搗	1990
	抔	1817	(拖)		振	1880	掉	1920	插	1954	搨	1991
	把	1818	拙	1851	按	1881	排	1921	(插)		搋	1992
			拘	1852	揭	1882	掘	1922				

手（續）

單字	字號		單字	字號		單字	字號		單字	字號
搬	1993		撤	2029		撿	2067	一八	擴	2099
搭	1994		撒	2030		擭	2068		攝	2100
搖	1995		撥	2031		擊	2069		攜	2101
搯	1996		撅	2032		擘	2070	一九	攢	2102
搵	1997		撓	2033		擎	2071		攤	2103
搧	1998		撦	2034		攜	2100		攔	2104
搁	1999		撙	2035		(攜)			攙	2105
搗	2000		撢	2036		攜	2100		攀	2106
搵	2001		撚	2037		(攜)		二〇	攩	2107
搴	2002	一四	撕	2038	一四	擠	2072		攪	2108
搞	2003		撞	2039		擡	2073		攫	2109
携	2100		撟	2040		擢	2074		攆	2110
(攜)			撦	2041		擣	2075	二一	攬	2111
摘	2004		撫	2042		擬	2076	二二	攤	2112
摑	2005		播	2043		擯	2077			
摜	2006		撩	2044		擦	2078			
摋	2007		撬	2045		擱	2079			
摒	2008		撲	2046		擭	2080			
搞	2009		撰	2047		揚	2081			
捽	2010		撮	2048		擰	2082			
掝	2011		撟	2049		壓	2083			
摧	2012		撢	2050		擥	2111			
搏	2013		撣	2050		(攬)				
摎	2014		(撢)			舉	4784			
摎	2015	一三	撻	2051		(舉)				
摺	2016		撼	2052	一五	擲	2084			
摸	2017		撾	2053		擷	2085			
摽	2018		擂	2054		擴	2086			
撟	2019		擄	2055		擺	2087			
撢	2020		擁	2056		擾	2088			
摺	2021		擅	2057		擿	2089			
摩	2022		操	2058		擻	2090			
摯	2023		擔	2059		攄	2091			
摰	2024		擇	2060		撐	2092			
擎	2025		擋	2061		攀	2093			
撨	2026		擒	2062	一六	攔	2094			
撑	2027	一七	擎	2063	一七	攖	2095			
撑	2027		辯	2064		攫	2096			
(撐)			辮	2065		攙	2097			
撈	2028		撰	2066		攛	2098			

支

筆畫	單字	字號
八	攲	2113

攴

筆畫	單字	字號
二	收	2115
	攷	4569
	(考)	
三	攸	2116
	改	2117
	攻	2118
四	放	2119
	攽	2120
五	政	2121
	故	2122
六	效	2123
	敉	2124
七	啟	660
	(啓)	
	敍	2125
	敘	2125
	(敍)	
	教	2126
	敏	2127
	救	2128
	敕	2129
	救	2130
	敗	2131
	敔	2132
八	敏	2133
	敝	2134
	啟	2135
	敢	2136
	散	2137
	敦	2138
九	敬	2139
一〇	敲	2140
一一	敵	2141
	敷	2142
	數	2143
	敺	2144
一二	整	2145
一三	斁	2146
	斂	2147
一四	斃	2148
一六	斅	2149

文

筆畫	單字	字號
	文	2150
六	斎	7304
	(齋)	
八	斌	2151
	斐	2152
	斑	2153
九	斒	2154
一七	斕	2155

斗

筆畫	單字	字號
	斗	2156
六	料	2157
七	斜	2158
	斜	2159
八	斠	2160
九	斡	2161
一〇	斢	2162
	斠	2163

斤

筆畫	單字	字號
	斤	2164
一	斥	2165
四	斧	2166
五	斫	2167
七	斬	2168
八	斷	2169
	斯	2170
九	新	2171
一〇	斳	2172
一三	斲	2172
	(斷)	
一四	斷	2173

方

筆畫	單字	字號
	方	2174
四	於	2175
	斞	2178
	(旁)	
五	施	2176
	斿	2177
六	旁	2178
	旅	2179
	旆	2180
	施	2181
	旎	2182
	旅	2183
七	旋	2184
	旌	2185
	旎	2186
	族	2187
八	旋	2188

字	頁	字	頁	字	頁	字	頁	字	頁	字	頁
柔	2397	案	2435	梳	2473	(碗)		樺	2543	樺	2577
柑	2398	桌	2436	桿	2474	九 楠	2367	樹	2544	槫	2578
柳	2399	桑	2437	梨	2475	(相)	2507	樺	2545	樊	2579
柘	2400	栽	2438	(梨)		(椶)		樿	2546	標	2580
柙	2401	桂	2439	八 梁	2475	椹	2508	榜	2547	標	2581
柚	2402	桃	2440	棄	2476	椥	2509	榑	2548	樛	2582
柜	2403	桄	2441	棉	2477	械	2510	榻	2549	樞	2583
柞	2404	桅	2442	棋	2478	椽	2511	榴	2550	模	2584
柝	2405	框	2443	基	2478	椰	2512	榮	2551	樣	2585
柢	2406	桎	2444	(棋)		椿	2513	槃	2552	樢	2586
柩	2407	桐	2445	棍	2479	楂	2514	栗	2553	一二 樸	2587
柯	2408	桓	2446	棒	2480	楓	2515	槁	2554	樵	2588
柱	2409	桔	2447	棗	2481	楊	2516	(橋)		樺	2589
柬	2410	栲	2448	棘	2482	楔	2517	構	2555	樨	2590
查	2411	柏	2449	根	2483	楙	2518	植	2556	橔	2591
柰	2412	栱	2450	棧	2484	桔	2519	槍	2557	樲	2592
柴	2413	梳	2473	棟	2485	楞	2520	槐	2558	檜	2593
柷	2414	(梳)		棚	2486	楡	2521	槎	2559	橐	2594
柚	2415	七 桴	2451	棣	2487	楝	2522	槓	2560	樹	2595
柵	2416	杪	2452	棠	2488	楢	2523	権	2561	橇	2596
柶	2417	梧	2453	棨	2489	楔	2524	槤	2562	橾	2597
柁	2418	桶	2454	棻	2490	楚	2525	槽	2563	橘	2598
枰	2419	桷	2455	棐	2491	業	2526	榼	2564	橙	2599
柏	2420	梁	2456	棼	2492	楣	2527	槨	2504	橘	2600
柜	2461	梃	2457	森	2493	(楣)		(槨)		橢	2601
(櫃)		梅	2458	椒	2494	一一 榦	2528	楙	2565	橛	2602
六 栓	2421	梓	2459	械	2495	楫	2529	槭	2566	橦	2603
栱	2422	梏	2460	棬	2496	楬	2530	栖	2567	橾	2604
栖	2423	梔	2461	椵	2497	極	2531	概	2568	機	2605
栝	2424	梗	2462	棺	2498	楮	2532	槊	2568	橫	2606
栩	2425	條	2463	棵	2499	楷	2533	(槑)		樹	2633
栗	2426	梟	2464	植	2500	楸	2534	(橅)		(橺)	
株	2427	梵	2465	椎	2501	楹	2535	一三 槳	2569	一三 檀	2607
核	2428	梯	2466	椁	2502	楯	2536	槳	2570	檄	2608
校	2429	械	2467	椅	2503	梗	2537	樂	2571	檜	2609
栲	2430	梲	2468	椁	2504	一○ 榕	2538	槲	2572	檔	2610
根	2431	梏	2469	椏	2505	榔	2539	権	2573	檉	2611
桁	2432	梢	2470	椋	2506	榛	2540	槽	2574	檜	2612
格	2433	梭	2471	棕	2507	榦	2541	椿	2575	橘	2613
桀	2434	梆	2472	椀	3886	槃	2542	樅	2576	檟	2614

筆畫	單字	字號
	檢	2615
	櫩	2616
	檬	2617
	橄	2618
	橢	2619
	橢	2630
	(櫜)	
一四	橈	350
	(㮣)	
	檸	2620
	檎	2621
	檣	2622
	檻	2623
	櫃	2624
	㻪	2625
	槓	2626
	櫂	2627
	樸	3691
	(㮞)	
一五	櫚	2628
	櫟	2629
	櫓	2630
	櫛	2631
	橫	2632
	櫨	2633
一六	櫺	2634
	櫬	2635
	櫨	2636
	櫨	2637
	櫞	2637
	(㰀)	
	欒	2638
	欒	2639
一七	欄	2640
	欄	2641
	櫻	2642
	欅	2643
	欐	2644
	欂	2645
	欒	2646

筆畫	單字	字號
一八	權	2647
一九	欒	2648
二一	欖	2649

欠

筆畫	單字	字號
	欠	2650
二	次	2651
二四	欣	2652
六	欬	2653
七	欲	2654
	欸	2655
	欷	2656
	欹	2657
	(款)	
八	款	2657
	欽	2658
	欺	2659
	欻	2660
	欲	2661
	歆	2662
九	歇	2663
	歃	2664
	歉	2665
一〇	歌	2666
	歐	2667
一一	歔	2668
	歙	2669
	歛	2670
	(歛)	
一二	歟	2671
	歡	2672
	歠	2673
	歎	2674
一三	歔	2675
	歜	2676
	歛	2677
一四	歟	2678
一五	歡	2679
一八	歠	2680

止

筆畫	單字	字號
	止	2681
一	正	2682
二	此	2683
三	步	2684
四	歧	2685
	武	2686
	歪	2687
五	歲	2688
九	歷	2689
一四	歸	2690

歹

筆畫	單字	字號
	歹	2691
	歺	2691
	(歹)	
二	死	2692
四	歿	2693
	殁	2693
	(殁)	
	歼	2694
五	殆	2695
	殄	2696
	殃	2697
	殂	2698
六	殉	2699
	殊	2700
七	殍	2701
八	殖	2702
	殘	2703
九	殫	2704
一〇	殞	2705
一一	殫	2706
	殤	2707
	殯	2708
	殮	2709
一二	殯	2709
	殫	2710

筆畫	單字	字號
一三	殪	2711
	殮	2712
一四	殯	2713
一七	殲	2714

殳

筆畫	單字	字號
	殳	2715
五	段	2716
六	殷	2717
	殽	2719
	(殻)	
七	殺	2718
八	殼	2719
	殳	2720
九	殿	2721
	毀	2722
一	毅	2723
	殿	2724

毋

筆畫	單字	字號
	毋	2725
一	母	2726
三	每	2727
	毒	2728
四	毓	2729
九	毓	2730

比

筆畫	單字	字號
	比	2731
五	毖	2732
	毗	2733
一三	毚	2734

毛

筆畫	單字	字號
	毛	2735
五	毡	2745

筆畫	單字	字號
	(毧)	
六	毰	2736
七	毫	2737
	毬	2738
八	毯	2739
	毱	2740
九	毽	2741
一一	毵	2742
一二	毾	2743
	氈	2744
一三	氍	2745
	氆	2745
	(氌)	

氏

筆畫	單字	字號
	氏	2746
一	氐	2747
	民	2748
四	氓	2749

气

筆畫	單字	字號
	气	2750
二	氛	2751
五	氟	2752
六	氣	2753
	氦	2754
	氧	2755
	氨	2756
七	氫	2757
八	氬	2758
	氮	2759
一〇	氰	2760

水

筆畫	單字	字號
	水	2761
一	永	2762
二	氽	2763

筆畫	單字	字號
	氾	2764
	汁	2765
	汀	2766
	求	2767
三	汆	2768
	汎	2769
	汕	2770
	汐	2771
	汗	2772
	池	2773
	汜	2774
	汝	2775
	江	2776
	汛	2777
	汞	2778
	污	2779
	汙	2779
	(汚)	
	污	2779
	(洿)	
四	汨	2780
	汩	2781
	汭	2782
	汰	2784
	汪	2785
	汲	2785
	決	2786
	汶	2787
	汴	2788
	汾	2789
	沁	2790
	沂	2791
	沃	2792
	汽	2793
	沈	2794
	沈	2795
	沉	2796
	沌	2797
	沙	2798
	沔	2798

	(沈)			泛	2838		潰	2876		涼	2916		(涅)			湢	2994
	沐	2799		波	2839		洸	2877		淅	2917		渙	2955		潰	2995
	沔	2800		泣	2840	七	浙	2878		清	2918		渚	2956		漳	2996
	冲	2801		泡	2841		浚	2879		洪	2919		渟	2957		湉	2997
	沙	2802		泥	2842		浜	2880		淘	2920		渝	2958		溫	2998
	沒	2803		泮	2843		浮	2881		淖	2921		減	2959		(溫)	
	沚	2804		泯	2844		浣	2882		淑	2922		渡	2960	一〇	溫	2998
	泃	2805		注	2845		浩	2883		淒	2923		渣	2961		源	2999
	查	2806		決	2846		浯	2884		淋	2924		渠	2962		溘	3000
	沛	2807		泳	2847		浦	2885		淘	2925		渤	2963		溟	3001
五	沫	2808		泉	2848		涅	2886		淚	2926		渥	2964		溝	3002
	沬	2809		泰	2849		浪	2887		淝	2927		渦	2965		溜	3003
	沮	2810		泪	2926		浸	2888		淙	2928		渭	2966		準	3004
	沆	2811		(淚)			浴	2889		洴	2929		港	2967		溢	3005
	沱	2812	六	洄	2850		浮	2890		淞	2930		渲	2968		溥	3006
	沴	2813		洎	2851		海	2891		淡	2931		測	2969		溧	3007
	沸	2814		洑	2852		浸	2892		淤	2932		渴	2970		溯	3008
	油	2815		洌	2853		涎	2893		淦	2933		湃	2971		溪	3009
	河	2816		洋	2854		涇	2894		淥	2934		湢	2972		溲	3010
	沼	2817		洒	2855		涅	2895		淩	2935		渺	2973		溴	3011
	沽	2818		洗	2856		涉	2896		淪	2936		游	2974		溷	3012
	治	2819		洙	2857		消	2897		淨	2937		渾	2975		溺	3013
	沾	2820		洟	2858		涑	2898		淬	2938		湄	2976		溶	3014
	況	2821		洞	2859		涓	2899		淮	2939		湊	2977		溳	3015
	泂	2822		洛	2860		涎	2900		淫	2940		湢	2978		滁	3016
	沿	2823		津	2861		涔	2901		淳	2941		湍	2979		滄	3017
	泄	2824		洧	2862		涕	2902		淵	2942		溢	2980		滂	3018
	泫	2825		洫	2863		涂	2903		深	2943		湔	2981		滄	3019
	泐	2826		洩	2864		涖	2904		淶	2944		湜	2982		滅	3020
	泊	2827		洪	2865		涅	2905		混	2945		湧	2983		滇	3021
	泗	2828		洱	2866		涪	2906		清	2946		湖	2984		滋	3022
	泌	2829		洳	2867		涌	2907		淺	2947		湘	2985		滑	3023
	泔	2830		洲	2868	八	涯	2908		淹	2948		湛	2986		滔	3024
	泓	2831		洮	2869		液	2909		添	2949		渾	2987		滓	3025
	法	2832		洵	2870		涪	2910		淲	2950		湫	2988		滎	3026
	泗	2833		洶	2871		涵	2911		淇	2951		湯	2989		淮	3027
	泖	2834		洽	2872		涸	2912		淵	2952		湟	2990		滕	3028
	泚	2835		活	2873		涿	2913		淰	2953		漢	2991		滾	3036
	泝	2836		派	2874		淀	2914		淼	2954		湲	2992		(濱)	
	泠	2837		流	2875		淄	2915	九	湼	2895		湒	2993		滢	3133

水

字	字號		字	字號		字	字號		字	字號
	(濕)		潁	3068		澤	3106		瀨	3146
一一			潑	3069		澱	3107		瀚	3147
漚	3029	一二	澣	3070		澳	3108		瀝	3148
滌	3030		潔	3071		澥	3109		瀟	3149
滯	3031		潑	3072		澮	3110		瀘	3150
滲	3032		潛	3073		澶	3111		瀾	3151
滴	3033		潘	3074		激	3112		瀧	3152
漳	3034		潟	3075		濁	3113		瀣	3153
滸	3035		潞	3076		濂	3114		瀦	3154
滾	3036		潢	3077		濃	3115		瀛	3155
滿	3037		潤	3078		濆	3116	一七	瀰	3156
漁	3038		潦	3079		澣	3117		瀹	3157
漅	3039		潤	3080		澣	3118		瀾	3158
漂	3040		潭	3081	一四	濘	3119		瀲	3159
漂	3041		潮	3082		濛	3120	一八	灃	2832
漆	3042		潯	3083		濕	3121		(法)	
漏	3043		潼	3084		濟	3122		灄	3160
漓	3044		潑	3085		濟	3123		灉	3161
壺	3045		潸	3086		濤	3124		灌	3162
漚	3046		潰	3087		濡	3125	一九	灑	3163
演	3047		澄	3088		濫	3126		灘	3164
漕	3048		澈	3089		濯	3127	二一	灣	3165
漢	3049		澎	3090		濮	3128		灔	3166
漣	3050		澍	3091		濰	3129	二二	灖	3167
漩	3051		潠	3092		濺	3130	二三	灤	3168
漩	3052		澶	3093		濱	3131	二四	灢	3169
漢	3053		澇	3094		濠	3132		灨	3170
漫	3054		潟	3095		濫	3133	二八	(灨)	
漬	3055		澌	3096	一五	濺	3134		灩	3170
漯	3056		澈	3097		濼	3135			
漱	3057		澠	3098		濆	3136			
滋	3058		潡	3099		濾	3137			
漳	3059	一三	澗	3100		瀑	3138			
漲	3060		澥	3101		瀉	3139			
溪	3061		澡	3102		瀋	3140			
漸	3062		澧	3103		瀏	3141			
澄	3063		澮	3104		瀅	3142			
滷	3064		遴	3105		瀣	3143			
漲	3065		(澀)	3121		濆	3144			
漅	3066				一六	瀘	3145			
漅	3067									

火

筆畫	單字	字號
	火	3171
二	灰	3172
三	灸	3173
	灼	3174
	災	3175
	灾	3175
	(灾)	

字	字號		字	字號
灶	4071	八	焙	3208
(竈)			焌	3209
四			焯	3210
炎	3176		焚	3211
炊	3177		焱	3212
炕	3178		焦	3213
炖	3179		無	3214
炘	3180		然	3215
炙	3181		焰	3216
炒	3182	九	煇	3217
五			煉	3218
炫	3183		煒	3219
炬	3184		煖	3220
炮	3185		煜	3221
炱	3185		煙	3222
(炮)			煤	3223
炯	3186		煥	3224
炳	3187		煨	3225
炷	3188		煩	3226
炸	3189		煬	3227
炭	3190		煮	3228
炤	3191		煲	3228
為	3192		(煮)	
烖	3175		煎	3229
(災)			煞	3230
六			煦	3231
烏	3193		照	3232
烈	3194		煢	3233
烝	3195		煅	6441
烊	3196		(鍛)	
烘	3197	一〇	熙	3234
烤	3198		熊	3235
烟	3199		熏	3236
烙	3200		熄	3237
七			熗	3238
烔	3186		熘	3239
(烔)			熔	3240
烽	3201		熒	3241
烹	3202	一一	熠	3242
焄	3203		熟	3243
焉	3204			
烺	3205			
烷	3206			
烯	3207			

熬	3244		爐	3275	筆畫	單字	字號		犄	3328	猊	3364		獷	3399
熱	3245		爛	3276		片	3301		犉	3329	猙	3365		獸	3400
栖	3246	一五	爆	3277	四畫	版	3302		犇	3330	猛	3366	一六	獺	3401
㮱	3246		㸼	3278	八畫	牌	3303	九	犍	3331	猜	3367		獻	3402
(栖)			爇	3279		牋	4138		犏	3332	猓	3368	一七	玀	3403
熨	3247	一六	爐	3280				一一	犖	3333	猝	3369	一九	玁	3404
熏	3248	一七	爛	3281	九畫	牒	3304		犗	3334	猋	3370	二〇	玁	3405
㶊	3216	一八	爛	3282	一〇	牓	3305	一五	犢	3335	猢	3371			
(焰)		二五	爨	3283	一一	牖	3306	一六	犧	3336	猶	3373	**玄**		
熾	3249					牕	4053		犫	3337	猩	3374	筆畫	單字	字號
燈	3250	**爪**				(窗)				猓	3375		玄	3406
燃	3251	筆畫	單字	字號	一五	牘	3307	**犬**		猴	3376	六	率	3407
燎	3252		爪	3284				筆畫	單字	字號	獃	3377			
燉	3253				**牙**				犬	3338	猨	3379	**玉**		
燒	3254	四	爬	3285	筆畫	單字	字號		友	3339			筆畫	單字	字號
燐	3255		爭	3286		牙	3308	一二三	犯	3340	獅	3380		玉	3408
燔	3256	五	爰	3287	八	穿	3309		狂	3341	猾	3381		王	3409
熹	3257	八	為	3288				四	狀	3342	猻	3382	二三	玎	3410
㷊	3257	一四	爵	3289	**牛**				狂	3343	獄	3383		玕	3411
(熹)					筆畫	單字	字號		狄	3344	獄	3384		玖	3412
燕	3258	**父**				牛	3310		狁	3345	獒	3385	四	玫	3413
燙	3259	筆畫	單字	字號	二	牝	3311		狃	3346	獎	3386		玦	3414
燊	3260		父	3290		牟	3312	五	狎	3347	獐	3387		玩	3415
燋	3261	四	爸	3291	三	牡	3313		狗	3348	獠	3388		玨	3416
燜	3262	六	爹	3292		牠	3314		狐	3349	獘	3390		玠	3417
燁	3263	九	爺	3293		牢	3315		狒	3350	獨	3391	五	珏	3416
營	3264				四	牧	3316		狙	3351	獝	3392		(珏)	
燦	3265	**爻**				物	3317	六	狠	3352	獬	3393		玲	3418
燠	3266	筆畫	單字	字號	五	牯	3318		狡	3353	猻	3405		玷	3419
燥	3267		爻	3294		牲	3319		狩	3354	(獼)			玳	3420
燬	3268	七	爽	3295		牴	3320	七	狴	3355				珉	3421
燥	3269	一〇	爾	3296	六	特	3321		狼	3356	一四	獲	3394		珂	3422
燴	3270					牷	3322		狽	3357		獮	3395		珈	3423
燭	3271	**爿**			七	牸	3323		猗	3358		獯	3396		珊	3424
燾	3272	筆畫	單字	字號		犁	3324		狸	3359		獰	3397		珍	3425
燻	3236	四	牀	3297		牾	3325		狹	3360	一五	獷	3398		玻	3426
(熏)		五	牁	3298		犂	3326		猖	3361				珀	3427
燹	3273	六	牂	3299		(犁)			猖	3362				珈	3428
爇	3274	一三	牆	3300	八	犂	3326	八	猗	3363			六	珙	3429
						犀	3327							珥	3430
													珞	3431

玉（續）

筆畫	單字	字號
	珠	3432
	珩	3433
	班	3434
	珪	3435
	珣	3436
	珮	3437
	琉	3438
七	現	3439
	球	3440
	理	3441
	琅	3442
	邪	3443
八	琖	3444
	琛	3445
	琢	3446
	琚	3447
	琤	3448
	琦	3449
	琨	3450
	琪	3451
	琥	3452
	琺	3453
	琬	3454
	琮	3455
	琴	3456
	琵	3457
	琶	3458
	琳	3459
	琭	3460
	琯	3461
九	瑟	3462
	瑁	3463
	瑋	3464
	瑧	3465
	瑑	3466
	瑕	3467
	瑙	3468
	瑛	3469
	瑜	3470
	瑞	3471
	瑚	3472
	琿	3473
	瑗	3474
	瑪	3475
一〇	瑩	3476
	瑤	3477
	瑣	3478
	瑯	3479
	瑰	3480
	璊	3481
	瑪	3482
	瑳	3483
	瑨	3484
	瑨	3485
一一	璇	3486
	璡	3487
	璀	3488
	璇	3489
	璃	3490
	璉	3491
	璈	3492
	璋	3493
	璗	3494
一二	環	3495
	璘	3496
	璜	3497
	璞	3498
	璣	3499
	璠	3500
	璢	3501
一三	璦	3502
	璧	3503
	環	3504
	璨	3505
	璿	3506
	璵	3507
一四	璽	3508
	瓔	3509
	瓏	3510
	瓅	3511
一五	瓊	3512
一六	瓏	3513
	瓔	3514
一七	瓚	3515

瓜

筆畫	單字	字號
	瓜	3516
五	瓞	3517
六	瓠	3518
	瓢	3519
一四	瓣	3520
一七	瓤	3521

瓦

筆畫	單字	字號
	瓦	3522
五	瓴	3523
六	瓷	3524
	瓶	3526
	(瓶)	
八	甄	3525
	瓿	3526
九	甌	3527
	甃	3528
一一	甈	3529
	甎	3530
	甍	3531
一二	甑	3532
一三	甕	3533
	甓	3534
一六	甗	3535

甘

筆畫	單字	字號
	甘	3536
四	甚	3537
六	甜	3538

生

筆畫	單字	字號
	生	3539
五	甡	3540
六	產	3541
七	甥	3542
	甦	3543
	甤	3544

用

筆畫	單字	字號
	用	3545
	甩	3546
二	甫	3547
	甬	3548
四	甯	3549
七	甯	3550

田

筆畫	單字	字號
	田	3551
	由	3552
	甲	3553
	申	3554
二	男	3555
	甸	3556
	町	3557
三	甼	3558
	畀	3559
四	界	3560
	畏	3561
	畋	3562
	畎	3563
五	畔	3564
	畛	3565
	畚	3566
	畜	3567
	畝	3568
	留	3569
六	畦	3570
	畤	3571
	略	3572
	畧	3572
	(略)	
	畢	3573
七	異	3574
	畱	3569
	(留)	
	異	3574
	(異)	
	番	3575
	畬	3576
	畲	3577
	畫	3578
	畯	3579
八	畹	3580
	畸	3581
	當	3582
一〇	畿	3583
一四	疆	3584
	疇	3585
一七	疊	3586

疋

筆畫	單字	字號
	疋	3587
六	疏	3588
七	疎	3588
	(疏)	
	疏	3588
	(疏)	
九	疑	3589
	疐	3590

疒

筆畫	單字	字號
二	疔	3591
三	疙	3592
	疚	3593
	疝	3594
四	疤	3595
	疥	3596
	疫	3597
	疣	3598
五	疲	3599
	疳	3600
	疽	3601
	疴	3602
	疹	3603
	疸	3604
	疼	3605
	疾	3606
	病	3607
	症	3608
	痉	3609
	痂	3610
	痄	3611
	疱	3612
	痁	3613
	痊	3614
	(痱)	
六	疵	3615
	痌	3616
	痍	3617
	痊	3618
	痏	3620
	痕	3621
	痔	3677
	痒	3622
	(瘝)	
七	痛	3622
	痘	3623
	痙	3624
	痢	3625
	痧	3626
	悲	3627
	痡	3629

疒（續）

筆畫	單字	字號
八	痤	3630
	痤	3631
八	痛	3602
(痫)		
	痰	3632
	痱	3633
	痲	3634
	痳	3635
	痹	3636
	痼	3637
	瘀	3638
	痿	3639
	瘁	3640
	痴	3641
九	瘍	3642
	瘟	3643
	瘓	3644
	瘔	3645
	瘌	3646
	瘉	3647
	瘩	3648
一〇	瘝	3649
	瘟	3650
	瘡	3651
	瘦	3652
	瘠	3653
	瘛	3654
	瘥	3655
	瘩	3656
	瘞	3657
	瘤	3658
	瘴	3659
一一	瘳	3660
	療	3661
	瘻	3662
	癇	3663
	瘼	3664
一二	瘤	3658
(瘤)		
	癆	3665
	癤	3666
	癌	3667
	癆	3668
	癇	3669
	癉	3671
一三	癖	3672
	癘	3673
	癒	3674
一四	癟	3675
	癢	3676
	癥	3677
一五	癤	3678
	癥	3679
一六	癲	3680
一七	瘰	3681
	癱	3682
	癬	3683
一八	癰	3684
	癱	3685
一九	顛	3686
	癱	3687
二三	癮	3675
(癱)		

癶

筆畫	單字	字號
四	癸	3688
七	登	3689
	發	3690
九	癹	3691

白

筆畫	單字	字號
	白	3692
一	百	3693
	皁	3694
二	皂	3695
	的	3696
四	皆	3697
	皇	3698
	皈	3699
五	皋	3700
六	皐	3700
(皐)		
	皎	3701
七	皓	3702
	皖	3703
	皕	3704
八	皙	3705
一〇	皚	3706
	皤	3707
一二	皤	3708

皮

筆畫	單字	字號
	皮	3709
五	皰	3710
七	皴	3711
九	皸	3712
一〇	皺	3713

皿

筆畫	單字	字號
	皿	3714
三	盂	3715
	盅	3716
四	盆	3717
	盈	3718
五	盃	3719
	益	3720
	盍	3721
	盌	3722
	盋	3723
	盉	6353
(鉢)		
六	盒	3724
	盔	3725
(蓋)		
七	盛	3726
	盜	3727
八	盞	3728
	盟	3729
九	盡	3730
	監	3731
一〇	盤	3732
一一	盥	3733
	盦	3734
	盧	3735
一二	盩	3736
	盪	3737
一四	鹽	3738

目

筆畫	單字	字號
	目	3739
二	盯	3740
三	盱	3741
	盲	3742
	直	3743
四	相	3744
	盻	3745
	盼	3746
	盹	3747
五	眇	3748
	眈	3749
	眊	3750
	眍	3751
	盾	3752
	省	3753
	眉	3754
	看	3755
六	眙	3756
	眏	3757
	眛	3758
	眠	3759
	眩	3760
	眨	3761
	眞	3762
	真	3762
(眞)		
	青	3763
六	眥	3764
	眦	3764
(眥)		
	眯	3765
	眵	3766
	眶	3767
	眸	3768
	眼	3770
	眺	3770
	眵	3771
	眾	3772
	眷	3773
七	睇	3774
	睏	3775
	着	3776
	睛	3777
八	睞	3778
	睡	3779
	睢	3780
	睜	3781
	睥	3782
	睨	3783
	睦	3784
	睫	3785
	睬	3786
	督	3787
	睪	3788
	睠	3789
九	睾	3788
(睪)		
	睹	3790
	睽	3791
	睎	3792
	瞄	3793
	睿	3794
	瞀	3795
一〇	瞋	3796
	瞎	3797
	瞍	3798
	瞑	3799
	瞳	3800
	瞇	3801
一一	瞞	3802
	瞟	3803
	瞠	3804
	瞢	3805
	瞥	3806
一二	瞬	3807
	瞰	3808
	瞼	3809
	瞪	3810
	瞭	3811
	瞧	3812
	瞩	3813
	瞵	3814
	瞽	3815
一三	瞻	3816
	臉	3817
	瞽	3818
	瞿	3819
一四	矇	3820
一五	矍	3821
一六	矓	3822
一九	矗	3823
二〇	矚	3824
二一	矙	3825

矛

筆畫	單字	字號
	矛	3826
四	矜	3827
七	矞	3828

矢

筆畫	單字	字號
	矢	3829

矢

筆畫	單字	字號
二	矣	3830
三	知	3831
四	矧	3832
	矦	3833
五	矩	3834
七	矬	3835
	短	3836
八	矮	3837
一二	矯	3838
	矰	3839
一四	矱	3840

石

筆畫	單字	字號
	石	3841
三	矽	3842
	砉	3843
四	舂	3844
	砂	3845
	砌	3846
	砍	3847
	砒	3848
	研	3864
	(研)	
五	砥	3849
	砧	3850
	砭	3851
	砰	3852
	砝	3853
	破	3854
	砷	3855
	砸	3856
	砮	3857
	砦	3858
	砲	3859
六	硃	3860
	硌	3861
	硐	3862
	硫	3863
	硏	3864
七	硫	
	(硫)	
	硬	3865
	硝	3866
	硤	3867
	硯	3868
	硜	3869
	确	3870
八	硼	3871
	硼	3872
	碌	3873
	碑	3874
	碎	3875
	碉	3876
	碓	3877
	碇	3878
	碗	3879
	碚	3880
	碘	3881
	碏	3882
	碏	3883
	碁	3884
	碍	3885
	碗	3886
九	碧	3887
	碣	3888
	碩	3889
	碳	3890
	碴	3891
	碟	3892
○	碻	3893
	碾	3894
	碼	3895
	磁	3896
	磋	3897
	磅	3898
	磔	3899
	磊	3900
	磐	3901
	磑	3902
一一	磯	3903
	磨	3904
	磬	3905
	磧	3906
	磚	3907
一二	磯	3908
	磢	3909
	磲	3910
	磺	3911
	磽	3912
	磴	3913
一三	礎	3914
一四	礙	3915
一五	礫	3916
	礪	3917
	礜	3918
一六	礦	3919
	礮	3920
一七	礴	3921
	礵	3922

示

筆畫	單字	字號
	示	3923
二	礿	3924
三	社	3925
	祁	3926
	祀	3927
四	祆	3928
	祅	3929
	祇	3930
	祈	3931
	祉	3932
五	祐	3933
	祓	3934
	祔	3935
	祕	3936
	祖	3937
	祇	3938
	祜	3939
	祛	3940
	祚	3941
	祝	3942
	祠	3943
	崇	3944
	祟	3945
六	祥	3946
	祧	3947
	票	3948
	祭	3949
七	祲	3950
八	祺	3951
	祿	3952
	祼	3953
	禁	3954
九	禍	3955
	福	3956
	禋	3957
	禔	3958
	禖	3959
	禎	3960
	禕	3961
	禘	3962
○	禡	3963
	禛	3964
	禟	3965
一	禧	3966
	禪	3967
	禨	3968
	禫	3969
一三	禮	3970
一四	禰	3971
	禱	3972
七	禳	3973
	襘	3974

内

筆畫	單字	字號
四	禹	3975
	禺	3976
八	禽	3977

禾

筆畫	單字	字號
	禾	3978
二	禿	3979
	禿	3979
	(禿)	
	秀	3980
	私	3981
三	秉	3982
四	秋	3983
	秌	3983
	(秋)	
	科	3984
	秒	3985
	秕	3986
	秔	3987
五	杭	3988
	祕	3936
	(祕)	
	秦	3989
	租	3990
	秧	3991
	秤	3992
	秩	3993
	秫	3994
	秭	3995
	秬	3996
	桃	3997
六	移	3998
七	稉	3988
	(杭)	
	稍	3999
	稀	4000
	稅	4001
	稊	4002
	稃	4003
	稈	4004
	程	4005
	稌	4006
八	稑	4007
	稔	4008
	稚	4009
	稜	4010
	稗	4011
	稠	4012
	稞	4013
九	種	4014
	稱	4015
	稭	4016
	稬	4017
	(糯)	4269
	穀	4018
	稿	4019
	稟	4019
	(稾)	
	稯	4020
	稼	4021
	稻	4022
	稽	4023
	稷	4024
一一	穈	4025
	穌	4026
	穎	4027
	穆	4028
	積	4029
	穄	4030
一二	穉	4009
	(稚)	
	穗	4031
一三	穡	4032
	穢	4033
	穟	4034
一四	穩	4035
	穠	4036
	穭	4269

	(糯)	
一七	穤	4037

穴

筆畫	單字	字號
	穴	4038
二	究	4039
三	穼	4040
	穿	4041
	空	4042
四	穿	4043
	突	4044
	窀	4045
五	窅	4046
	窈	4047
	窄	4048
	窆	4049
六	窒	4050
	窕	4051
	窓	4053
	(窗)	
七	窖	4052
	窗	4053
	窘	4054
八	窟	4055
	窠	4056
九	窩	4057
	窪	4058
	窨	4059
	窬	4060
一〇	窮	4061
	窯	4062
	窰	4062
	(窯)	
	窳	4063
一一	窻	4053
	(窗)	
	窺	4064
	窶	4065
一三	竅	4066

	窿	4067
一三	窸	4068
	竀	4069
一五	竇	4070
一六	竈	4071
一七	竊	4072

立

筆畫	單字	字號
	立	4073
五	站	4074
	竚	4075
	竝	4076
六	竟	4077
	章	4078
七	童	4079
	竣	4080
	竦	4081
九	竭	4082
	端	4083
一五	競	4084

竹

筆畫	單字	字號
	竹	4085
二	竺	4086
三	竿	4087
	竽	4088
四	笆	4089
	笕	4090
	笏	4091
	笈	4092
	笑	4093
	笋	4112
	(筍)	
	笄	4121
	(笄)	
五	笙	4094
	笠	4095
	笛	4096

	笨	4097
	笞	4098
	笥	4099
	第	4100
	符	4101
	笰	4102
	笳	4103
	笯	4104
	笴	4105
	笘	4106
六	笮	4107
	范	4108
	筆	4109
	筌	4111
	筍	4112
	等	4113
	筏	4114
	筑	4115
	筐	4116
	筒	4117
	筋	4118
	答	4119
	筈	4120
七	筅	4121
	策	4122
	筊	4123
	筥	4125
	筮	4126
	箐	4127
	筷	4128
	筋	4129
	筱	4130
	筲	4131
	筷	4132
	筳	4133
	筵	4134
	筚	4135
	筷	4136

八	筧	4137
	筬	4138
	筆	4139
	箑	4140
	箝	4141
	箔	4142
	箕	4143
	算	4144
	箑	4145
	算	4146
	箜	4147
	箝	4148
	管	4149
	箚	4150
	箬	4151
	箇	4152
	箊	4174
	(箊)	
九	箬	4153
	箱	4154
	箭	4155
	箯	4156
	箸	4157
	箴	4158
	節	4159
	箪	4160
	範	4161
	篁	4162
	篆	4163
	篋	4164
	篌	4165
一〇	築	4166
	篝	4167
	篚	4168
	篡	4169
	篤	4170
	篥	4171
	節	4172
一三	篦	4173
	篾	4174

	簁	4175
	箱	4176
	篪	4177
	篛	4178
	篾	4179
	篦	4183
	(篾)	
	篠	4180
	篳	4181
	篾	4182
	篷	4184
	簌	4185
	簏	4186
	簇	4187
	簃	4188
	簀	4189
	簋	4190
	簠	4191
	簣	4192
	簍	4193
一二	節	4194
	簡	4195
	簰	4196
	簨	4197
	簞	4198
	簟	4199
	簡	4200
	(簡)	
	簣	4201
	簦	4202
	簋	4203
	簪	4204
	簧	4205
	簧	4206
	簿	4207
	簫	4208
一三	簣	4209
	簸	4210

	簽	4211
	簾	4212
	籅	4213
	簿	4214
	簳	4215
	籀	4216
一四	籃	4217
	籌	4218
	籍	4219
一五	籀	4216
	(籓)	
	簾	4220
	籛	4226
	(籙)	
一六	籙	4221
	籜	4222
	籟	4223
	籠	4224
	籤	4225
一七	籛	4226
	籥	4228
	簫	4228
一九	簿	4229
	籬	4230
	籮	4231
二六	籲	4232

米

筆畫	單字	字號
	米	4233
三	籽	4234
四	粉	4235
五	粗	4236
	粒	4237
	粕	4238
	粘	4239
六	粟	4240
	粢	4241
	粥	4242

糸（續）

筆畫	單字	字號
	繽	4458
	繼	4459
	繡	4460
	纁	4461
一五	纊	4462
	纉	4463
	續	4464
	纆	4465
	纍	4466
	纇	4467
一六	纏	4468
一七	纓	4469
	纓	4470
	纊	4471
	織	4472
一八	纛	4473
一九	纘	4474
二一	纜	4475

缶

筆畫	單字	字號
	缶	4476
三	缸	4477
四	缺	4478
五	缽	6353
	(鉢)	
八	缾	4479
一〇	罌	4480
	罄	4481
	罅	4482
一一	罇	4483
	罈	4484
一三	罍	4485
一四	罌	4486
一五	罍	4487
一六	罎	4488
	罏	4489
一八	罐	4490

网

筆畫	單字	字號
三	罔	4491
	罕	4492
四	罘	4493
五	罡	4494
	罟	4495
	罝	4496
六	罩	4497
八	罩	4498
	罪	4499
	置	4500
九	罰	4501
	署	4502
	罳	4503
一〇	罵	4504
	罷	4505
一一	羅	4506
一二	羈	4507
一四	羆	4508
	羅	4509
一七	羇	4510
二九	羈	4511

羊

筆畫	單字	字號
	羊	4512
	羋	4513
二	羌	4514
三	美	4515
	羑	4516
	羌	4517
四	羔	4514
	(羌)	
	羔	4518
	羖	4519
	羓	4520
	粉	4521
	瓶	4522
	羚	4523
五	羞	4524

六	戕	4525
七	羣	4526
	群	4526
	(羣)	
	羨	4527
	義	4528
九	羯	4529
一〇	羲	4530
一一	羹	4531
一二	羵	4532
	羹	4533
	羸	4534
一五	羼	4535

羽

筆畫	單字	字號
	羽	4536
三	羿	4537
四	翁	4538
	翅	4539
	翅	4540
五	翎	4541
	翊	4542
	翌	4543
	習	4544
六	翔	4545
	翕	4546
八	翟	4547
	翠	4548
	翡	4549
	翟	4550
九	翦	4551
	翥	4552
	翬	4553
	翩	4554
	翫	4555
一〇	翱	4556
	翩	4557
	翰	4558
	翯	4559

	翼	4560
一二	翹	4561
	翻	4562
	翻	4563
一三	翻	4564
	翻	4565
一四	耀	4566
	耀	4567

老

筆畫	單字	字號
	老	4568
	考	4569
四	耄	4570
	耆	4571
五	者	4572
	耇	4573
	耇	4573
	(耈)	
六	耆	4574

而

筆畫	單字	字號
	而	4575
三	耐	4576
	耍	4577
	耑	4578

耒

筆畫	單字	字號
	耒	4579
三	耔	4580
四	耙	4581
	耕	4582
	耘	4583
	耗	4584
五	耜	4585
七	耡	4586
九	耦	4587
一〇	耨	4588

一五	耰	4589

耳

筆畫	單字	字號
	耳	4590
	耶	4591
三	聿	4592
四	耽	4593
	耿	4594
	聃	4595
	耻	4596
五	聘	4595
	(聃)	
	聆	4597
	聊	4598
六	聒	4599
七	聖	4600
	聘	4601
八	聚	4602
	聞	4603
	聝	6917
	(馘)	
一一	聯	4604
	聰	4605
	聲	4606
	聳	4607
	聱	4608
一二	職	4609
	聵	4610
	聶	4611
一六	聽	4612
	聾	4613

聿

筆畫	單字	字號
	聿	4614
七	肆	4615
	肄	4616
	肅	4617
八	肇	4618

肉

筆畫	單字	字號
	肉	4619
一	肌	4620
二	肋	4621
	肌	4622
	肐	4637
	(肯)	
三	肖	4623
	肘	4624
	肓	4625
	肚	4626
	肛	4627
	肝	4628
	肜	4629
	肟	4630
四	股	4631
	肢	4632
	肥	4633
	肩	4634
	肪	4635
	肬	4636
	肯	4637
	肓	4637
	(肯)	
	肱	4638
	育	4640
	肴	4640
	胖	4641
五	肺	4642
	胥	4643
	胃	4644
	胄	4645
	背	4646
	胎	4647
	胖	4648
	胙	4649
	胛	4650
	胚	4651

單字	字號
胞	4652
肮	4653
胡	4654
胤	4655
胸	4656
胗	4657
胘	4658
脉(脈)	4671
胆(膽)	4736

筆畫	單字	字號
六	胭	4659
	胯	4660
	脢	4661
	胱	4662
	胴	4663
	胸	4664
	匈(胸)	4664
	胱	4665
	能	4666
	䏗	4667
	脂	4668
	脆	4669
	脆(脆)	4669
	脅	4670
	脈	4671
	脊	4672
	胇	4673
	胳	4674
	胼(胼)	4689
七	脘	4675
	脛	4676
	脣	4677
	脩	4678
	脫	4679
	脯	4680
	脬	4681

單字	字號
脼	4682
胜	4683
脤	4684
脖	4685
脂	4686
脝	4687

筆畫	單字	字號
八	脤	4688
	胼	4689
	胰	4690
	腋	4691
	腌	4692
	脺	4693
	腎	4695
	腐	4695
	腑	4696
	腔	4697
	腕	4698
九	脾	4699
	腊	4700
	腓	4701
	腠	4702
	腥	4703
	腦	4704
	腫	4705
	腰	4706
	腳	4707
	腱	4708
	腴	4709
	腸	4710
	腹	4711
	腩	4712
	腺	4713
	胸	4714
十	腭	4715
	腿	4716
	腿	4717
	膀	4718
	膂	4719
	膈	4720
	膏	4721

單字	字號
膊	4722
膊	4723

筆畫	單字	字號
一一	膚	4724
	膜	4725
	膝	4726
	膣	4727
	膠	4728
	膛	4729
	膣	4730
	(膣)	4751
一二	膝(臍)	4693
	膨(脖)	4731
	膩	4732
	膳	4733
	膰	4734
一三	膿	4735
	膽	4736
	膾	4737
	膺	4738
	腎(臀)	4739
	臂	4740
	臃	4741
	膽	4742
	臉	4743
	臊	4744
	臍	4745
	臏	4746
一四	臑	4747
	臏	4748
	臘	4749
一五	臙	4750
	臚	4751
一六	臟	4752
	臟	4753
一七	臝	4754
	臟	4755
一八	臢	4756
一九	臠	4757

單字	字號
臠	4758

臣

筆畫	單字	字號
	臣	4759
	臣	4760
二	臥	4761
八	臧	4762
一一	臨	4763

自

筆畫	單字	字號
	自	4764
四	臬	4765
	臭	4766
六	鼻	4767
一〇	皪	4768

至

筆畫	單字	字號
	至	4769
三	致	4770
四	致(致)	4770
八	臺	4771
一〇	臻	4772

臼

筆畫	單字	字號
	臼	4773
一	臼	4774
二	臾	4775
三	舀	4776
四	舁	4777
	舀	4778
五	舂	4779
六	舄	4780
	鳥(舄)	4780
七	舅	4781

單字	字號
與	4782

筆畫	單字	字號
九	興	4783
一〇	舉	4784
一二	舊	4785

舌

筆畫	單字	字號
	舌	4786
二	舍	4787
四	舐	4788
六	舒	4789
八	舔	4790
九	舖	4791
一〇	舘	4792

舛

筆畫	單字	字號
	舛	4793
六	舜	4794
七	舝	4795
八	舞	4796

舟

筆畫	單字	字號
	舟	4797
	舠	4798
二三	舡	4799
	紅	4800
四	航	4801
	般	4802
	舫	4803
	舨	4804
五	舲	4805
	舳	4806
	舴	4807
	舵	4808
	舶	4809
	舷	4810
	舸	4811

筆畫	單字	字號
七	船	4812
	艇	4813
	艄	4814
	艋	4815
八	艘	4816
一〇	艙	4817
一二	艤	4818
	艦	4819
一四	艦	4820
	艨	4821
一六	艫	4822

艮

筆畫	單字	字號
	艮	4823
一	良	4824
一一	艱	4825

色

筆畫	單字	字號
	色	4826
五	艴	4827
一八	艷	4828

艸

筆畫	單字	字號
	艸	4829
二	艾	4830
	芎	4831
	芃	4832
三	芫	4833
	芋	4834
	芊	4835
	芍	4836
	芎	4837
	芒	4838
四	芙	4840
	芝	4841
	芟	4842

茉	4843	苴	4882	茜	4922	菊	4958	萬	4996	蒙	5034
芥	4844	苻	4883	荽	4923	菌	4959	萱	4997	蒜	5035
芋	4845	苾	4884	荃	4924	菜	4960	萵	4998	蒯	5036
芩	4846	茁	4885	荇	4925	菖	4961	萼	4999	蒲	5037
芫	4847	茂	4886	荐	4926	菉	4962	落	5000	蒸	5039
芬	4848	范	4887	一(荊)	4994	菜	4963	葉	5001	蓁	5040
芘	4849	茄	4888			菜	4964	葑	5002	蒺	5041
芭	4850	茅	4889	七 荷	4927	菠	4965	著	5003	蒼	5042
芯	4851	茆	4890	荽	4928	華	4966	葚	5004	蒿	5043
芮	4852	茌	4891	荏	4929	菇	4967	葛	5005	蓧	5044
芟	4853	苙	4892	荻	4930	菰	4968	葡	5006	蒹	5045
花	4854	苣	4893	茶	4931	菁	4969	葭	5007	蓄	5046
芳	4855	苺	4894	薈	4932	菲	4970	董	5008	蓆	5047
芷	4856	苿	4895	莊	4933	菸	4971	葦	5009	蓉	5048
芸	4857	茇	4896	莒	4934	菹	4972	葳	5010	蓋	5049
芹	4858	茉	4897	莓	4935	菽	4973	葩	5011	蔴	5050
芼	4859	苟	4898	莖	4936	萁	4974	葫	5012	蓑	5051
芽	4860	苶	4899	莘	4937	萃	4975	葬	5013	蓓	5052
芾	4861	苑	4900	莞	4938	萄	4976	葭	5014	蒔	5053
芴	4862	苣	4901	莠	4939	萋	4977	葷	5015	蒲	5054
五 苑	4863	六 茗	4902	莢	4940	莉	4978	葳	5016	蒻	5055
苒	4864	荔	4903	莧	4941	萊	4979	葵	5017	蓊	5056
苓	4865	茼	4904	莩	4942	萎	4980	葦	5018	蓍	5057
苔	4866	茨	4905	莪	4943	萌	4981	蔥	5019	蒡	5058
苕	4867	茫	4906	莫	4944	萍	4982	茸	5020	蓏	5059
苗	4868	茯	4907	莆	4945	萎	4983	萎	5021	蓏	5060
苛	4869	茲	4908	莉	4946	菌	4984	葆	5022	蓐	5061
苜	4870	茴	4909	莽	4947	菪	4985	葒	5023	蓊	5062
苞	4871	茴	4910	莎	4948	菩	4986	葽	5024	蓂	5068
苡	4872	茵	4911	莐	4949	菱	4987	萳	5025	(蓂)	
若	4873	茶	4912	莩	4950	菴	4988	葵	5026	十一	
苦	4874	茸	4913	菡	4951	草	4989	蔥	5027	蓬	5063
苧	4875	茹	4914	莛	4952	菓	4990	蒂	5028	蔻	5064
苫	4876	荀	4915	莨	4953	菔	4991	蓋	5029	蔲	5065
英	4877	茭	4916	荳	4954	萵	4992	葯	5030	蓼	5066
苴	4878	草	4917	八 莽(莽)	4947	菫	4993	葅	5031	蒨	5067
茶	4879	茬	4918	莵	4955	荊	4994	韭	5032	蔑	5068
苯	4880	荑	4919	莬	4956	菓	4995	蓤	5007	蔓	5069
苹	4881	荒	4920	菅	4957	九 菑(菑)	4961	(葵)		蔕	5070
		荳	4921			菑	5033			蔗	5071

蔚	5072	薄	5112	蘊(蘊)	5163	虜	5187	蛔	5222	蜾	5262
蔡	5073	蕷	5113			號	5188	蛛	5223	蜿	5263
蔣	5074	蕾	5114	一六　闌	5152	八　虡	5189	蛟	5224	蝀	5264
蔥	5075	蕵	5115	蘑	5153	九　號	5190	蛤	5225	蜻	5265
蔦	5076	薇	5116	蘄	5154	一一　虧	5191	蛩	5226	蜺	5266
蔬	5077	薈	5117	藹	5155			蛭	5227	蝍	5267
蓴	5078	薊	5118	藻	5156	**虫**		蛐	5228	(蝪)	5304
蕐	5079	薐	5119	蘆	5157	筆畫　單字　字號		蛘	5229		
蕤	5080	薏	5120	蘐	5158	一　虬	5192	七　蛺	5230	九　蝙	5268
蒟	5081	薐	5121	蘅	5159	二　虯	5193	蛸	5231	蝌	5269
蕢	5082	薑	5122	蘆	5160	虱	5194	蛹	5232	蝕	5270
蔪	5083	薔	5123	蘗	5161	三　虹	5195	蛻	5233	蝗	5271
蔭	5084	薙	5124	蘇	5162	虺	5196	蛾	5234	蝘	5272
蔯	5085	薛	5125	蘊	5163	虼	5197	蜀	5235	蝎	5273
蔜	5086	薤	5126	蘋	5164	虻	5198	蜂	5236	蝴	5274
蓯	5087	薦	5127	蘚	5165	虵(蛇)	5218	蜃	5237	蝠	5275
蔴	5088	薨	5128	龍	5166			蜆	5238	蝟	5276
一二　蔽	5089	一七　薪	5129	一七　蘧	5167	四　蚌	5199	蜑	5239	蝣	5277
蕃	5090	薉	5130	蘽	5168	蚊	5200	蜊	5240	蝤	5278
蕆	5091	薛	5131	蘿	5169	蚪	5201	蜓	5241	蝥	5279
蕉	5092	一四　薩	5132	薛	5170	蚋	5202	蜒	5242	蝦	5280
蕋	5093	薯	5133	蘩	5171	蚍	5203	蜋	5243	蝻	5281
蕭	5094	薰	5134	蘭	5172	蚓	5204	蜉	5244	蝨	5282
蕘	5095	薺	5135	蔽	5173	蚖	5205	蜍	5245	蝮	5283
蕘	5096	薷	5136	一九　蘸	5174	蚤	5206	蜋	5246	蝡	5284
蕙	5097	藍	5137	蘺	5175	蚩	5207	蜚	5247	蝴	5285
蕢	5098	薘	5138	蘿	5176	蚨	5208	八　蜥	5248	蝶	5286
蕓	5099	藏	5139	蘿	5177	蚣	5209	蜘	5249	蝸	5287
蕡	5100	藐	5140	虉	5178	蚜	5210	蜚	5250	蝲	5288
蕨	5101	藕	5141	二一　蔂	5179	五　蚯	5211	蜜	5251	蝘	5289
蕭	5102	一五　藕	5142	**虍**		蚰	5212	蜡	5252	蝪	5290
蕬	5103	藜	5143	筆畫　單字　字號		蚱	5213	蝘	5253	一〇　蝥	5291
蕩	5104	藝	5144	二　虎	5180	蚶	5214	蝱	5254	蝻	5292
蕁	5105	蘦	5145	三　虐	5181	蛀	5215	蜿	5255	蝻	5293
蕈	5106	薄	5146	四　虔	5182	蛄	5216	蜩	5256	融	5294
蕉	5107	藤	5147	五　處	5183	蛆	5217	蜩	5257	螓	5295
蕅	5108	藥	5148	虖	5184	蛇	5218	蜮	5258	螞	5296
蕰	5109	藩	5149	六　虛	5185	蛉	5219	蜴	5259	螟	5297
蕢	5110	藪	5150	七　虞	5186	蛋	5220	蜷	5260	螢	5298
一三　薄	5111	蔿	5151			六　蛙	5221	蜻	5261		

虫（續）

筆畫	單字	字號
一一	螯	5299
	螂	5300
	螫	5301
	螬	5302
	螞	5303
	蝓	5304
	螯	5305
	螳	5306
	螺	5307
	螻	5308
	蟊	5309
	蟄	5310
	蟀	5311
	螣	5312
	螟	5313
	蜩	5314
	蟋	5315
	蟑	5316
一二	螽	5317
	蟥	5318
	蟒	5319
	蟠	5320
	蟢	5321
	蟻	5322
	蟪	5323
	蟬	5324
	蟲	5325
	蟯	5326
	蟠	5327
一三	蟹	5328
	蠏	5328
	(蟹)	
	螳	5329
	蠰	5330
	蟻	5331
	蠐	5332
	蠅	5333
	蠹	5334
	蠍	5335
	蠃	5336
一四	蠑	5337
	蠑	5338
	蠛	5339
	蠣	5340
	蠕	5341
	蠔	5342
一五	蠟	5343
	蠡	5344
	蠱	5345
	蠨	5346
	蠶	5347
	蠹	5353
	(蠹)	
一七	蠢	5348
	蠲	5349
一八	蠻	5350
	蠮	5351
	蠹	5352
	蠱	5353
一九	蠶	5354
二〇	蠻	5355

血

筆畫	單字	字號
	血	5356
四	衄	5357
六	衇	4671
	(脈)	
	衆	5358
一五	衊	5359

行

筆畫	單字	字號
	行	5360
三	衍	5361
五	術	5362
	術	5363
六	衖	5364
	衕	5365
	街	5366
七	衝	5367
九	衝	5368
	衚	5369
	衛	5370
一〇	衡	5371
	衡	5372
一八	衢	5373

衣

筆畫	單字	字號
	衣	5374
三	表	5375
	衫	5376
	衩	5377
四	衰	5378
	衲	5379
	衵	5380
	袒	5381
	衷	5382
	衾	5383
	衽	5384
	衿	5385
	衿	5386
	袁	5387
	袂	5388
五	裂	5389
	袖	5390
	袋	5391
	袍	5392
	袓	5393
	袪	5394
	袤	5395
六	袪	5396
	被	5397
	袞	5398
	袴	5399
	袱	5400
	袷	5401
	裁	5402
	裂	5403
	裉	5404
七	祛	5405
	袅	5406
	袓	5407
	裙	5408
	裎	5409
	裏	5410
	裡	5410
	(裏)	
八	裏	5411
	裔	5412
	裕	5413
	裘	5414
	補	5415
	裝	5416
	裟	5417
	裏	5418
	袷	5419
	裸	5420
	褪	5421
	裨	5422
	裯	5423
	裱	5424
	裳	5425
	裴	5426
	裹	5427
	褐	5428
	製	5429
	褌	5430
	褂	5431
九	複	5432
	褊	5433
	褌	5434
	褐	5435
	褓	5436
	褌	5437
	褟	5438
	褶	5439
	褕	5440
一〇	褒	5441
	褥	5442
	褫	5443
	褪	5444
	褫	5445
	褻	5446
	褡	5447
一一	褔	5448
	補	5449
	褵	5450
	褶	5451
	褸	5452
	褻	5453
	襄	5454
	襄	5455
	襞	5456
	襋	5456
	(襞)	
一二	褳	5457
	襁	5454
	(襁)	
一三	襠	5458
	襞	5459
	襜	5460
	襟	5461
	襖	5462
	襦	5463
一四	襤	5464
	襺	5465
一五	襪	5466
	襬	5467
一六	襯	5468
	襲	5469
一七	襬	5470
一八	襪	5471
一九	襤	5472

西

筆畫	單字	字號
	西	5473
三	要	5474
六	覃	5475
一二	覆	5476
一三	覈	5477
	覇	5478
一七	覊	5479
一九	覉	5480

見

筆畫	單字	字號
	見	5481
四	規	5482
	覓	5483
	覔	5483
	(覓)	
五	覘	5484
	視	5485
七	覞	5486
八	覡	5487
九	覣	5488
	覩	5489
	親	5490
一〇	覬	5491
	覯	5492
一一	覦	5493
	覲	5494
一二	覦	5494
	(覦)	
	覯	5495
一三	覦	5494
	(覦)	
	覺	5496
一四	覲	5495
	(覯)	
	覼	5497
一五	覽	5498
一八	觀	5499

角

筆畫	單字	字號
	角	5500
二	觔	5501

豕

筆畫	單字	字號
七	蒙	5728
	豨	5729
九	豫	5730
	豬	5731
	豬	5732
一〇	圂	5733
一八	羅(羅)	5746

豸

筆畫	單字	字號
	豸	5734
三	豹	5735
	豺	5736
	犴	5737
五	貂	5738
六	貅	5739
	貉	5740
	貊	5740
	(貉)	
七	貌	5741
	狸	5742
九	貓	5743
一〇	貚	5744
	貘	5745
一八	貛	5746

貝

筆畫	單字	字號
	貝	5747
二	負	5748
	貞	5749
三	貢	5750
	財	5751
	貤	5752
四	貧	5753
	貨	5754
	販	5755
	貪	5756
	貫	5757
	責	5758
五	貯	5759
	貰	5760
	貲	5761
	貳	5762
	貴	5763
	貶	5764
	買	5765
	貸	5766
	貺	5767
	費	5768
	貼	5769
	貽	5770
	貿	5771
六	貸	5772
	賁	5773
	貰	5774
	賂	5775
	賄	5776
	資	5777
	賅	5778
	賈	5779
	賊	5780
	賖	5781
	賍	5782
七	賑	5783
	賒	5784
	賓	5785
	(賓)	
八	賕	5786
	賦	5787
	賙	5788
	賜	5789
	賞	5790
	賠	5791
	賡	5792
	賢	5793
	賣	5794
	賤	5795
	賦	5796
	質	5797
	賬	5798
	賷	7305
九	賭	5799
	賴	5800
一〇	賺	5801
	賻	5802
	購	5803
	賽	5804
	膽	5805
	賷	7305
一一	贅	5806
	贄	5807
一二	贋	5808
	贈	5809
	贉	5810
	贊	5811
	贇	5812
一三	贍	5813
	贏	5814
一四	贓	5815
	贐	5816
	質	5817
一五	贖	5818
	贇	5819
一七	贛	5820

赤

筆畫	單字	字號
	赤	5821
四	赦	5822
五	赧	5823
七	赫	5824
九	赭	5825
	赬	5826

走

筆畫	單字	字號
	走	5827
二	赳	5828
	赴	5829
三	起	5830
	赸	5831
五	趁	5832
	(趂)	5832
	趙	5833
	超	5834
	越	5835
六	趑	5836
	趄	5837
七	趙	5838
	趕	5839
八	趣	5840
	趟	5841
一〇	趨	5842
一九	趲	5843

足

筆畫	單字	字號
	足	5844
	趴	5845
二	趵	5846
三	趾	5847
四	跌	5848
	趺	5849
	跔	5850
	跰(跰)	5861
五	跋	5851
	跌	5852
	跎	5853
	跑	5854
	距	5855
	跗	5856
	踢	5857
	跛	5858
	距	5859
六	跨	5860
	跰	5861
	跟	5862
	跡	5863
	距	5864
	跣	5865
	跌	5866
	跪	5867
	跫	5868
	跬	5869
	跲	5870
	路	5871
	跳	5872
	踩	5873
	踐	5874
	跤	5875
	跼	5876
	踉	5877
	跟	5878
	踅	5879
	踊	5880
八	踐	5881
	踠	5882
	踏	5883
	踝	5884
	踞	5885
	踟	5886
	踏	5887
	踢	5888
	踦	5889
	踆	5890
	踧	5891
	踔	5892
	踔	5893
	踩	5894
	踦	5895
	踪	5896
九	踰	5897
	踱	5898
	踵	5899
	踴	5900
	踝	5901
	蹃	5902
	踩	5903
	蹄	5904
	踹	5905
	蹀	5906
一〇	蹈	5907
	蹇	5908
	蹉	5909
	蹊	5910
	蹋	5911
	蹌	5912
	蹐	5913
	蹏	5914
	蹠	5915
一一	蹕	5916
	蹙	5917
	蹬	5918
	蹤	5919
	踸	5920
	蹣	5921
	蹦	5922
	蹢	5923
	蹭	5924
	蹟	5925
	暫	5926
	蹴	5927
一二	蹲	5928
	蹙	5929
	蹬	5930
	蹭	5931
	蹯	5932
	蹴	5933
	蹶	5934
	蹺	5935
	蹻	5936
	蹼	5937
	蹾	5938
	蹴	5939

部	字	號	部	字	號	部	字	號	部	字	號	部	字	號	部	字	號
	蹣	5940		軟	5974	一〇	輮	6014	三	辱	6048		逈	6084		運	6122
一三	躓	5941	五	軫	5975		輿	6015	六	農	6049		酒	6085		逼	6123
	躁	5942		軨	5976		轂	6016					迸	6106		過	6124
	躅	5943		軸	5977		轄	6017	**辵**				(迸)			逿	6125
	躋	5944		軺	5978		轅	6018	部	字	號	七	逍	6086		邊	6126
	躉	5945		軹	5979	一一	轉	6019	三	迂	6050		逝	6087		退	6127
	躂	5946		軻	5980		轆	6020		迄	6051		逋	6088		遒	6128
	蹕	5947		軼	5981		轍	6021		迅	6052		透	6089		道	6129
一四	躊	5948		軜	5982		轇	6022		巡	6053		逐	6090		達	6130
	躓	5949	六	較	5983	一二	轍	6023		迆	6054		逑	6091		違	6131
一五	躍	5950		軾	5984		轎	6024	四	迎	6055		逡	6092	一〇	遜	6132
	躐	5951		輅	5985		轔	6025		近	6056		途	6093		遘	6133
	躑	5952		軿	5986	一三	鞭	6026		迎	6057		逖	6094		遙	6134
	躓	5953		載	5987		轖	6027		返	6058		逗	6095		運	6135
	躚	5954		輕	5988		轗	6028		迕	6059		這	6096		遞	6136
一六	躡	5955	七	輒	5989		轘	6029		迍	6060		通	6097		遠	6138
一七	躩	5956		輓	5990	一四	轟	6030		迓	6061		逛	6098		遢	6139
一八	躐	5957		輔	5991		轝	6031	五	迢	6062		逞	6099		遝	6140
	躥	5958		輊	5992		轞	6032		迤	6063		速	6100		遣	6141
二〇	躪	5959	八	輻	5993	一五	轢	6033		迵	6064		造	6101		遢	6142
身				輗	5994		轤	6034		迦	6065		逢	6102		遨	6143
部	字	號		輘	5995	一六	轥	6035		迫	6066		連	6103		適	6144
	身	5960		輛	5996		轤	6036		迪	6067		逭	6104		遮	6145
三	躬	5961		輝	5997	**辛**				迫	6068	八	逬	6106		遜	6146
四	軀	5962		輞	5998	部	字	號		迭	6069		逮	6107	一二	遭	6147
六	躲	5963		輟	5999		辛	6037		迤	6070		週	6108		遵	6148
八	躺	5964		肇	6000	五	辜	6038	六	迴	6071		進	6109		遲	6149
一一	軆	5965		耕	6001	六	辟	6039		迷	6072		逶	6110		遷	6151
車				輦	6002		辠	6040		迷	6073		逸	6112		選	6152
部	字	號		輪	6003	七	辣	6041		迹	6074		道	6113		遺	6153
	車	5966		輬	6004	九	辦	6042		追	6075		達	6114		遼	6154
一	軋	5967		輮	6005		辨	6043		退	6076	九	逾	6115		遵	6155
二	軌	5968	九	輯	6006	一二	辭	6044		送	6077		遍	6116		避	6156
	軍	5969		輳	6007	一三	辯	6045		適	6078		逼	6117		邀	6157
三	軒	5970		輶	6008	一四	辮	6046		逃	6079		逢	6118		邀	6158
	軔	5971		輸	6009	**辰**				逅	6080		遄	6119		邁	6159
	軛	5972		輻	6010	部	字	號		逆	6081		遇	6120		邂	6160
四	軣	5973		縏	6011		辰	6047		逑	6082		遊	6121		還	6161
				輼	6012					逢	6083						
				輹	6013												

筆畫	單字	字號
	遒	6162
一四	遍	6163
	遂	6164
	邊	6165
一五	邊	6166
一九	邐	6167
	邏	6168
邑		
筆畫	單字	字號
	邑	6169
三	邝	6170
	邛	6171
	邕	6172
四	邪	6173
	那	6174
	邦	6175
	邪	6176
	邢	6177
	邨	6178
五	邵	6179
	邯	6180
	邰	6181
	邱	6182
	邲	6183
	邴	6184
	邶	6185
	邺	6186
	邸	6187
六	郁	6188
	邢	6189
	郅	6190
	郇	6191
	郊	6192
	郎	6193
	邦	6194
	郃	6195
七	郭	6196
	郫	6197
	郝	6198
	郎	6199
	郑	6200
	郡	6201
	郎	6202
	郗	6203
	郤	6204
	部	6205
八	部	6206
	郵	6207
	郭	6208
	郑	6209
	郴	6210
	郾	6211
	郑	6212
	都	6213
九	都	6214
	郿	6215
	鄂	6216
	鄆	6217
	圖	6218
	鄒	6219
一〇	鄗	6220
	鄉	6221
	鄒	6222
	鄔	6223
一一	鄙	6224
	鄞	6225
	鄢	6226
	鄠	6227
	鄯	6228
	鄣	6229
一二	鄰	6230
	鄭	6231
	鄫	6232
	鄴	6233
	鄱	6234
	鄲	6235
	鄦	6236
一三	鄰	6237
	鄶	6238
一四	鄂	6239
一五	鄭	6240
一七	鄙	6241
一八	鄲	6242
一九	鄲	6243
	鄲	6244
西		
筆畫	單字	字號
	西	6245
二	酊	6246
	酋	6247
三	酌	6248
	配	6249
	酒	6250
四	酖	6251
	酣	6252
五	酢	6253
	酣	6254
	酤	6255
	酥	6256
六	酪	6257
	酩	6258
	酯	6259
	酬	6260
	酮	6261
七	醒	6262
	醇	6263
	醋	6264
	酸	6265
	醉	6266
	醡	6267
	醉	6268
八	醃	6269
	醋	6270
	醇	6271
	醉	6272
	醱	6273
	醋	6274
	醉	6275
九	醒	6276
	醍	6277
	醐	6278
一〇	醜	6279
	醞	6280
	醚	6281
	醛	6282
	醡	6283
	醢	6284
一一	醫	6285
	醨	6286
	醪	6287
	醬	6288
	醱	6289
一二	醱	6290
	醮	6291
	醱	6292
一三	醴	6293
	醸	6294
	醲	6295
一四	醲	6296
一七	釀	6297
	醼	6298
	釁	6299
一八	釃	6300
二〇	釀	6301
釆		
筆畫	單字	字號
二	釆	6302
五	釉	6303
一三	釋	6304
里		
筆畫	單字	字號
	里	6305
二	重	6306
四	野	6307
五	量	6308
一	釐	6309
金		
筆畫	單字	字號
	金	6310
一	釓	6311
	釚	6312
二	釘	6313
	釜	6314
	釙	6315
	針	6316
	釕	6317
	釘	6318
三	釧	6319
	釣	6320
	釦	6321
	釵	6322
	釘	6323
	釧	6324
	釵	6325
	釤	6326
	釬	6411
	(釬)	
四	釺	6327
	釴	6328
	釱	6329
	鈦	6330
	鈔	6331
	鈇	6332
	鈉	6333
	鈍	6334
	鈐	6335
	鈕	6336
	鈞	6337
	鈣	6338
	鈎	6339
五	鈸	6340
	鈴	6341
	鈿	6342
	鈾	6343
	鉧	6344
	鉅	6345
	鉉	6346
	鉋	6347
	鉏	6348
	鉑	6349
	鉗	6350
	鉛	6351
	鐵	6352
	鉢	6353
	鉤	6354
	鉦	6355
	鈺	6356
	鉥	6357
	鈷	6358
	鉈	6359
	鉕	6360
	鉍	6361
	鈹	6362
	鉬	6363
	鉏	6364
	鈳	6365
	鈒	6366
	鐘	6367
六	銀	6368
	銨	6369
	銑	6370
	銅	6371
	銃	6372
	銓	6373
	銖	6374
	銘	6375
	銚	6376
	銛	6377
	銜	6378
	鉦	6379
	銬	6380
	銥	6381
	鉰	6382
	銑	6383

筆畫	單字	字號		單字	字號		單字	字號		單字	字號
	銪	6384		錠	6424		鎬	6464		鐵	6504
	鉿	6385		錡	6425		鎮	6465		鐶	6505
	絪	6386		錢	6426		鎰	6466		鐸	6506
	鉋	6387		錦	6427		鎳	6467		鐺	6507
	銈	6388		錫	6428		鎢	6468	五	鐳	6508
	鉻	6389		錕	6429		鎘	6469		鐽	6509
	釦	6390		錭	6430		鎌	6470	一四	鑄	6510
七	銳	6391		錯	6431		鎷	6471	六	鑊	6511
	銷	6392		錳	6432		鎘	6472		鑑	6512
	銻	6393		錶	6433		錴	6473		鑒	6513
	鈇	6394		銈	6434	一一	鏺	6474	一五	鑔	6347
	銀	6395	九	鍊	6435		鏃	6475		(鉋)	
	鋰	6396		錨	6436		鍛	6476		鑠	6514
	鋯	6397		鍋	6437		鏦	6477	七	鑣	6515
	鋨	6398		鍍	6438		鏈	6478		鑢	6516
	鋁	6399		鍔	6439		鏊	6479		鑞	6517
	銫	6400		鍘	6440		鏑	6480		鑪	6518
	鋅	6401		鍛	6441		鏖	6481	八	鑪	6519
	鋌	6402		鍥	6442		鏗	6482		鑫	6520
	鋏	6403		鎣	6443	一七	鏘	6483	一七	鑰	6521
	鋒	6404		鍪	6444		鏇	6484		鑲	6522
	鋯	6405		鍰	6445		鏜	6485		鑱	6523
	鋤	6406		鍵	6446	一八	鏝	6486	九	鑼	6524
	鋐	6407		鍼	6447		鏟	6487		鑽	6525
	鋊	6408		鍾	6448		鏡	6488		鑾	6526
	銼	6409		鎂	6449		鏢	6489	二〇	鑿	6527
	鋪	6410		鍺	6450		鏤	6490			
	銲	6411		鍶	6451		鏨	6491			
	銹	6412		鍒	6452		鏹	6492			
八	鋸	6413	一二	鍇	6453	一二	鐘	6493			
	鋼	6414		鍬	6454		鐃	6494			
	鋤	6415	一〇	鎖	6455		鐐	6495			
	鋏	6416		鎡	6456		鐙	6496			
	鋼	6417		鎣	6457		鐳	6497			
	錄	6418		鎧	6458		鐦	6498			
	鋼	6419		鎈	6459		鐋	6499			
	錐	6420		鎔	6460		鐝	6500			
	錘	6421		鎛	6461		鐍	6501			
	鎦	6422		鎛	6462		鐲	6502			
	錚	6423		鎧	6463		鐮	6503			

長

筆畫	單字	字號
	長	6528

門

筆畫	單字	字號
	門	6529
一	閂	6530
二	閃	6531
三	閉	6532
四	開	6533
	閈	6534
	閎	6535

筆畫	單字	字號
	閏	6536
	閑	6537
	閒	6538
	閔	6539
五	閞	6540
	閣	6541
六	閡	6542
	閣	6543
	閤	6544
	閥	6545
	閨	6546
	閩	6547
七	閫	6548
	閬	6549
	閭	6550
	閱	6551
八	閾	6552
	閽	6553
	閼	6554
	閻	6555
	閹	6556
	閶	6557
九	闈	6558
	闉	6559
	闊	6560
	闋	6561
	闌	6562
	闐	6563
	闑	6564
	闒	6565
	闓	6566
一〇	闔	6567
	闕	6568
	闖	6569
	闘	6570
	闙	6571
一一	關	6572
	闚	6573
	闛	6574
	闝	6575

筆畫	單字	字號
一二	闞	6576
	闟	6577
	闠	6578
一三	闢	6579
	闤	6580
	闥	6581

阜

筆畫	單字	字號
	阜	6582
三	阡	6583
	阢	6584
四	阬	6585
	阨	6586
	阪	6587
	阮	6588
	阱	6589
	防	6590
	阯	6591
五	阻	6592
	阼	6593
	阿	6594
	陀	6595
	陂	6596
	附	6597
	阽	6598
六	陋	6599
	陌	6600
	降	6601
	限	6602
	陔	6603
七	陘	6604
	陛	6605
	陸	6606
	陬	6607
	陡	6608
	院	6609
	陳	6610
	除	6611
	陝	6612

八	陪	6613
	陬	6614
	陰	6615
	陲	6616
	陳	6617
	陣	6618
	陵	6619
	陶	6620
	陷	6621
九	陸	6622
	陽	6623
	陞	6624
	隃	6625
	隄	6626
	隅	6627
	隆	6628
	限	6629
	陧	6630
	隋	6631
	隊	6632
	階	6633
一〇	隔	6634
	隕	6635
	隖	6636
	隘	6637
	陳	6638
	隗	6639
一一	隙	6638
	(隙)	6640
	際	6641
	障	6642
一二	隣	6643
一三	隨	6644
	隩	6645
	隩	6646
	險	6647
一四	隱	6648
	隰	6649
	隘	6650

| 一五 | 驪 | 6651 |
| 一六 | 驨 | 6652 |

隶

筆畫	單字	字號
九	隸	6653

佳

筆畫	單字	字號
	佳	6654
二	隻	6655
	隼	6656
三	雀	6657
四	雄	6658
	雁	6659
	雅	6660
	集	6661
	雇	6662
五	雍	6663
	雉	6664
	雊	6665
	雌	6666
	雋	6667
	雎	6668
六	雒	6669
八	雕	6670
	雔	6671
九	雛	6672
	雙	6673
	雜	6674
	雜	6675
	雟	6676
	雞	6677
一一	離	6678
	離	6679
	難	6680

雨

筆畫	單字	字號
	雨	6681
三	雩	6682
	雪	6683
四	雯	6684
	雰	6685
	雱	6686
	雲	6687
五	零	6688
	雷	6689
	電	6690
	電	6691
六	需	6692
七	震	6693
	霄	6694
	霆	6695
	霈	6696
	霍	6697
八	霎	6698
	霙	6699
	霏	6700
	霑	6701
	霓	6702
	霖	6703
九	霜	6704
	霞	6705
	霝	6706
十	霤	6710
	(霤)	
一一	霧	6707
	霪	6708
	霰	6709
一二	霸	6710
	霹	6711
	霽	6712
一三	霾	6713
	霽	6714
一四	霽	6715
	霾	6716
一六	靂	6717
	靈	6718

	鞬	6719
	靆	6720
七	靅	6721

青

筆畫	單字	字號
	青	6722
五	靖	6723
七	靦	6724
八	靜	6725
	靛	6726
一〇	靨	6727

非

筆畫	單字	字號
	非	6728
七	靠	6729
一一	靡	6730

面

筆畫	單字	字號
	面	6731
七	靦	6732
一二	靧	6733
一四	靨	6734

革

筆畫	單字	字號
	革	6735
二	靪	6736
四	靳	6737
	靴	6738
	靶	6739
	靷	6740
	靸	6741
五	鞅	6742
	靺	6743
	靼	6744
六	鞍	6745

	鞋	6746
	鞏	6747
七	鞘	6748
八	鞠	6749
九	鞭	6750
	鞦	6751
	鞳	6752
	鞨	6753
	鞫	6754
	鞬	6755
一〇	鞲	6756
	鞴	6757
	鞴	6758
	鞶	6759
一一	韁	6760
一三	韃	6761
	韁	6762
一五	韉	6763
一七	韆	6764

章

筆畫	單字	字號
	韋	6765
三	韌	6766
五	韍	6767
八	韓	6768
	韔	6769
九	韙	6770
一〇	韜	6771
	韞	6772

韭

筆畫	單字	字號
	韭	6773

音

筆畫	單字	字號
	音	6774
四	韵	6775

	欽	6776
五	韶	6777
一〇	韻	6778
一三	響	6779

頁

筆畫	單字	字號
	頁	6780
二	頂	6781
	頃	6782
三	項	6783
	順	6784
	預	6785
	須	6786
四	頌	6787
	頏	6788
	頎	6789
	預	6790
	頑	6791
	頒	6792
	頓	6793
五	領	6794
	頗	6795
	頤	6796
六	頡	6797
	頦	6798
	頪	6799
	頦	6800
七	潁	4027
	(穎)	
	頤	6802
	頭	6803
	頰	6804
	頦	6805
	頹	6806
	頸	6807
	頽	6808
	頰	6809
八	顆	6810

頁（續）

筆畫	單字	字號
九	頷	6811
	頟	6812
	頸	6813
	頴	6814
	頦	6815
	顏	6816
	顇	6817
	顈	6818
一〇	頭	6819
	頹	6820
	頰	6821
	頯	6822
	頲	6823
	頜	6824
一一	顋	6825
一二	顠	6826
	顤	6827
	顢	6828
	顣	6829
一三	顬	6830
一四	顯	6831
	顳	6832
一五	顰	6833
一六	顴	6834
一八	顱	6835
	顲	6836

風

筆畫	單字	字號
	風	6837
五	颯	6838
	颭	6839
六	颱	6840
八	颶	6841
九	颼	6842
一〇	颺	6843
	颻	6844
一一	飄	6845
一二	飆	6846
	飀	6846

（飆）

飛

筆畫	單字	字號
	飛	6847
一二	飜	6848

食

筆畫	單字	字號
	食	6849
二	飢	6850
	飣	6851
	飧	6852
三	飩	6853
四	飪	6853

（飥）

筆畫	單字	字號
	飩	6854
	飪	6855
	飫	6856
	飲	6857
	飫	6858
五	飯	6859
	飼	6860
	飴	6861
	飽	6862
	飾	6863
六	餂	6864
	餁	6865
	養	6866
	餉	6867
	餌	6868
	餈	6869
	餃	6870
七	餅	6871
	餑	6872
	餕	6873
	餖	6874
	餓	6875
	餔	6876

筆畫	單字	字號
	餖	6877
	餗	6878
	餘	6879
八	餅	6880
	餚	6881
	餛	6882
	餞	6883
	餡	6884
	餟	6885
	館	6886
	餜	6887
	餞	6888
九	餮	6889
	餱	6890
	餬	6891
	餳	6892
	餲	6893
一〇	餺	6894
	餼	6895
	餾	6896
	餹	6897
	饁	6898
	饅	6899
	饈	6900
	饉	6901
	饍	6913

（饍）

筆畫	單字	字號
一二	饋	6902
	饌	6903
	饒	6904
	饒	6905
	饖	6906
	饘	6907
一三	饔	6908
	饗	6909
	饗	6910
	體	6911
一四	饜	6912
一六	饞	6913
一七	饢	6914

首

筆畫	單字	字號
	首	6915
二	馗	6916
八	馘	6917

香

筆畫	單字	字號
	香	6918
九	馥	6919
一一	馨	6920

馬

筆畫	單字	字號
	馬	6921
二	馭	6922
	馮	6923
三	馱	6924
	馳	6925
	馴	6926
	馼	6927
四	駁	6928
	駃	6929
五	駐	6930
	駕	6931
	駒	6932
	駔	6933
	駑	6934
	駘	6935
	駙	6936
	駛	6937
	駝	6938
	駟	6939
六	駱	6940
	駭	6941
	駢	6942
	駿	6943
	駪	6944
七	騁	6945

筆畫	單字	字號
	駿	6946
	騂	6947
	騃	6948
	騄	6949
	騑	6950
八	騎	6951
	騏	6952
	騌	6953
	騍	6954
	騅	6955
	騐	6956
九	騖	6957
	騙	6958
	騣	6959
	騤	6960
	騠	6961
	騧	6962
一〇	騫	6963
	騰	6964
	騵	6965
	騮	6966
	騪	6967
	騶	6968
	騾	6969
	驁	6970
	驂	6971
	騶	6972
	驃	6973
	驄	6974
一二	騙	6975
	驊	6976
	驌	6977
	驍	6978
	驒	6979
	驏	6980
一三	驗	6981
	驚	6982
	驛	6983
	驟	6984
一四	驥	6985

筆畫	單字	字號
	驢	6986
一七	驤	6987
一八	驪	6988
一九	驫	6989

骨

筆畫	單字	字號
	骨	6990
三	骭	6991
	骱	6992
四	骰	6993
	骯	6994
五	骷	6995
六	骸	6996
	骹	6997
	骼	6998
七	骾	6999
八	髀	7000
	髁	7001
	體	7002
一三	髒	7003
	髓	7004
	髑	7005
	髖	7006
一四	髕	7007

高

筆畫	單字	字號
	高	7008

髟

筆畫	單字	字號
三	髡	7009
	髦	7010
四	髣	7011
	髯	7012
	髻	7013
	髭	7014
五	髽	7015
	髹	7016

單字	字號
髻	7017
髭	7018
髽	7019
六	
鬃	7020
七	
鬋	7021
鬆	7022
八	
鬆	7023
鬐	7024
鬅	7025
九	
鬈	7026
鬍	7027
一〇	
鬑	7028
鬒	7029
鬘	7030
一一	
鬚	7031
一二	鬢 7032
一三	鬣 7033
一四	鬟 7034
一五	鬢 7035

鬥

筆畫	單字	字號
	鬥	7036
四	鬨	7037
五	鬧	7038
六	鬩	7039
八	鬪	7040
一〇	鬬	7041
一四	鬮	7042
一六	鬮	7043

鬯

筆畫	單字	字號
	鬯	7044
一九	鬱	7045

鬲

筆畫	單字	字號
	鬲	7046
一二	鬶	7047

鬼

筆畫	單字	字號
	鬼	7048
四	魁	7049
	魂	7050
五	魅	7051
	魅	7052
八	魍	7053
	魎	7054
	魏	7055
一一	魑	7056
	魔	7057
	魘	7058
一四	魘	7059

魚

筆畫	單字	字號
	魚	7060
三	魟	7061
四	魷	7062
	魯	7063
	魴	7064
五	鮎	7065
	鮑	7066
	鮒	7067
六	鮫	7068
	鮪	7069
	鮭	7070
	鮮	7071
	鮺	7072
七	鯀	7073
	鮸	7074
	鯁	7075
	鯉	7076
	鯇	7077
	鯀	7078
	鯡	7079
八	鯖	7080
	鯛	7081

單字	字號
鯨	7082
鯪	7083
鯢	7084
九	
鯽	7085
鰈	7086
鯿	7087
鮹	7088
鰒	7089
鰍	7090
鰓	7091
一〇	
鰐	7092
鰜	7093
鰮	7094
鰭	7095
鰤	7096
鰲	7097
一一	
鰻	7098
鱈	7099
鰵	7100
鱘	7101
鱒	7102
鱔	7103
一二	
鰹	7104
鱗	7105
鱝	7106
鱚	7107
鱘	7108
鱉	7281 (黽)
一三	
鱟	7109
鱠	7110
一五	鱤 7111
一六	鱸 7112
	鱷 7113
二二	龠 7114

鳥

筆畫	單字	字號
	鳥	7115
二	鳧	7116

單字	字號
三	
鳩	7117
鳰	7118
鳳	7119
鳴	7120
四	
鳶	7121
鳲	7122
鴇	7123
鴉	7124
鴣	7125
鴃	7125 (鴂)
鴈	7126
五	
鴿	7127
鴕	7128
鴦	7129
鴨	7130
鴟	7131
鴣	7132
鴦	7133
鴨	7134
鴯	7135
鴰	7136
六	
鴿	7137
鴻	7138
鴻	7139
鵑	7140
鵝	7141
鵠	7142
鵒	7143
鵜	7144
鵡	7145
七	
鵬	7146
鵬	7147
鵪	7148
鵲	7149
餘	7150
鶉	7151
鵝	7152
鷙	7152

單字	字號
鯖	7152
(鶺)	
鶻	7153
鶵	7154
八	
鵬	7155
鶹	7156
鶴	7157
鶼	7158
鶿	7159
鷉	7160
鶺	7161
(鶃)	
鷁	7162
鷂	7163
鷃	7164
鷓	7165
九	
鵬	7166
鷟	7167
鶿	7168
鷳	7169
鷺	7170
鷦	7171
一〇	
鷸	7173
鷭	7174
鷲	7175
鷴	7176
鷺	7176
(鷟)	
鷯	7177
鷽	7178
鷸	7179
鷹	7180
鷿	7181
鸇	7182
鸛	7183
鷇	7184
鸚	7185
一一	鸌 7186
鸞	7187
鸝	7188

單字	字號
鷙	7189
鸞	7190
一二	
鸕	7191
鸝	7192
鸛	7193
鸞	7194
鸝	7195
鸞	7196
鸛	7197
鸞	7198
一三	
鸙	7199
鸝	7200
鸘	7201
鸝	7202
鷹	7203
一六	鸞 7204
一七	鸝 7205
一八	鸚 7206
	鸛 7207
一九	鸝 7208
	鸞 7209

鹵

筆畫	單字	字號
	鹵	7210
九	鹹	7211
一〇	鹺	7212
	鹼	7213
一三	鹽	7214
一四	鹾	7215

鹿

筆畫	單字	字號
	鹿	7216
二	麂	7217
	麀	7218
四	麇	7219
五	麈	7220
	麇	7221
六	麋	7222

筆畫部首索引

編　法：本索引係按單字筆畫多寡編列。其筆畫相同者，再按部首順
序。單字後註明單字編號。

用　法：檢字時先計算單字筆畫，按筆畫在索引中查出單字，再根據單
字編號，查出書內單字及這一單字為首所組成的詞語。

STROKE NUMBER INDEX

In this index the characters are arranged in the ascending
order according to the number of strokes used in writing them.
Characters with the same number of strokes and under the same
radical are grouped together, the radicals being indicated in the
column to the left of the characters. The figure to the right of each
character is its identification number under which the character
can be found in the body of the dictionary.

The first step in looking for a character is to count the number
of strokes used in writing it. The next step is to find the character
in the index according to its number of strokes. With the identification number as a guide, one can locate in the dictionary the character and the entries beneath it.

一畫

部首	單字	字號
一	一	1
乙	乙	37

二畫

部首	單字	字號
一	丁	2
	七	3
丿	乃	28
乙	乜	38
	九	39
亅	了	46
二	二	49
人	人	71
入	入	306
八	八	311
几	几	346
刀	刀	356
	刁	357
力	力	417
匕	匕	456
十	十	474
卜	卜	488
又	又	516

三畫

部首	單字	字號
一	丈	4
	三	5
	上	6
	下	7
	万(萬)	4996
丨	丫	20
丶	丸	24
	久	29
	之	30
乙	乞	40
	也	41
二	亍	50
	于	51
亠	亡	60
儿	兀	288
几	凡	347
刀	刃	358
勹	勺	447
十	千	517
又	叉	527
口	口	805
土	土	896
士	士	907
夕	夕	916
大	大	949
女	女	1073
子	子	1074
	孑	1075
寸	寸	1157
小	小	1168
尸	尸	1179
山	山	1209
巛	巛	1289
工	工	1293
己	己	1299
	已	1301
巾	巾	1305
干	干	1348
幺	幺	1354
	么(幺)	1354
弋	弋	1415
弓	弓	1418
彳	彳	1458
手	才	1790

四畫

部首	單字	字號
一	不	8
	丏	9
	丐	10
	丑	11
丨	中	22
	丰	25
丿	予	47
二	云	52
	互	53
	五	55
人	什	72
	仁	73
	仃	74
	仆	75
	仄	76
	仇	77
	仉	78
	今	79
	介	80
	仍	81
	从(從)	1480
儿	允	289
入	內	307
八	公	312
	六	313
	兮	314
凵	凶	351
刀	分	359
	切	360
	刈	361
勹	勻	448
	勾	449
	勿	450
匕	化	457
匚	匹	470
十	升	476
	午	477
	卅	478
卜	卞	489
厂	厄	506
又	及	518
	友	519
	反	520
士	壬	897
大	天	917
	太	918
	夫	919
	夬	920
	夭	921
子	孔	1076
小	少	1169
尢	尤	1174
尸	尺	1180
	尹	1181
屮	屯	1208
巳	巴	1302
幺	幻	1355
廾	廿	1409
弓	引	1419
	弔	1420
心	心	1496
戈	戈	1751
戶	戶	1777
手	手	1789
	扎	1791
支	支	2113
文	文	2150
斗	斗	2156
斤	斤	2164
方	方	2174
无	无	2195
日	日	2198
曰	曰	2301
月	月	2314
木	木	2330
欠	欠	2650
止	止	2681
歹	歹	2691
殳	殳	2715
毋	毋	2725
比	比	2731
氏	氏	2735
水	水	2746
火	火	2761
爪	爪	3171
父	父	3284
爻	爻	3290
片	片	3294
牙	牙	3301
牛	牛	3308
犬	犬	3310
王	王	3338
玉	玉	3409

五畫

部首	單字	字號
一	且	12
	丕	13
	世	14
	丘	15
	丙	16
丶	主	26
丿	乍	31
	乎	
	乏	
人	仔	82
	仕	83
	他	84
	仗	85
	付	87
	仙	88
	仞	89
	亿	90
	代	91
	令	92
	以	93
	仝	94
	仟	95
儿	兄	291
	充	292
冂	冊	334
冫	冬	352
凵	凹	353
	出	354
刀	刊	362
力	功	418
	加	419
勹	包	451
	匆(怱)	1549
匕	北	458
匚	匝	460
	匜	461
十	半	479
	卅	480
	卉	481
卜	占	490
	卡	491
卩	卮	494
	卯	495
厶	去	514
口	叨	528
	叼	530
	古	531
	句	532
	另	533
	叩	534
	叭	535

五畫（續）

部首	單字	字號
	召	536
	叩	537
	叮	538
	可	539
	台	540
	叱	541
	史	542
	右	543
	叵	544
	叶	545
	司	546
囗	四	782
	四	783
夕	外	908
大	失	922
	央	923
	夯	924
女	奴	950
	奶	951
子	孕	1077
宀	宄	1098
	它	1099
	宁	1100
	宂	1101
尸	尻	1182
	尼	1183
工	左	1294
	巧	1295
	巨	1296
巾	市	1306
	布	1307
干	平	1349
幺	幼	1356
广	庀	1359
廾	弁	1410
弓	弗	1421
	弘	1422
心	忉	1497
	忉	1498
戈	戊	1752

部首	單字	字號
	戊	1753
戶	戾	1778
手	扑	1792
	扒	1793
	打	1794
	扔	1795
斤	斥	2165
无	旡	2196
日	旦	2199
木	末	2331
	末	2332
	本	2333
	札	2334
	朮	2335
止	正	2682
歹	歺	2691
毋	母	2726
氏	氐	2747
	民	2748
水	永	2762
	氾	2764
	汁	2765
	汀	2766
犬	犯	3339
玄	玄	3406
玉	玉	3408
瓜	瓜	3516
瓦	瓦	3522
甘	甘	3536
用	用	3545
	甩	3546
田	田	3551
	由	3552
	甲	3553
疋	疋	3587
白	白	3692

部首	單字	字號
皮	皮	3709
皿	皿	3714
目	矛	3826
矢	矢	3829
石	石	3841
示	示	3923
禾	禾	3978
穴	穴	4038
立	立	4073
肉	肋	4620

六畫

部首	單字	字號
一	丞	17
	丟	18
丿	乒	27
乙	乩	42
二	互	56
亠	交	62
	亥	63
	亦	64
人	仰	96
	仲	97
	份	98
	件	99
	伃	100
	任	101
	仿	103
	企	103
	伉	104
	伊	105
	伋	106
	伍	107
	伎	108
	伏	109
	伐	110
	休	111
	伙	112

部首	單字	字號
	充（充）	292
儿	兆	293
	兕	294
	先	295
	光	296
入	全	308
八	共	315
冂	再	324
冫	冰	335
	决（決）	2786
	沖（沖）	2801

部首	單字	字號
刀	冽	363
	刑	364
	划	365
	刉	366
	删	367
	列	368
力	劣	420
	匈	452
匚	匠	462
	匡	463
十	卉	481
卩	印	496
	危	497
口	合	547
	吁	548
	吃	549
	各	550
	吉	551
	吋	552
	同	553
	吣	554
	吒	555
	名	556
	后	557
	吐	558
	向	559

部首	單字	字號
	吏	560
	吊（吊）	1420
囗	回	784
	囚	785
	因	786
土	在	806
	圬	807
	圭	808
	圯	809
	地	810
夕	多	909
	夙	910
大	夷	925
	夸	926
女	奸	952
	她	953
	好	954
	妁	955
	如	956
	妃	957
	妄	958
	妊（妊）（蛇）	997
子	字	1078
	存	1079
宀	宅	1102
	字	1103
	守	1104
	安	1105
寸	尋	1158
小	尖	1170
山	屹	1210
	屺	1211
巛	州	1290
	巡	1291
	（巡）	
	巡	6053
	（巡）	
巾	帆	1308

部首	單字	字號
	帆（帆）	1308
	年	1350
广	庄	1360
廴	巡	1291
	（巡）	
	巡	6053
	（巡）	
弋	式	1416
弓	弛	1423
心	忙	1506
	忖	1507
戈	戍	1754
	戌	1755
	戎	1756
手	扦	1796
	扣	1797
	扛	1798
	托	1799
	扡	1800
	扱	1801
支	收	2115
攴	攷	4569
	（考）	
日	旨	2200
	早	2201
	旬	2202
	旭	2203
	旮	2204
	晃	2205
曰	曲	2303
	曳	2315
月	有	2336
木	朱	2337
	朴	2338
	朽	2339
	朵（朵）	2339
欠	次	2651

止	此	2683
歹	死	2692
气	氖	2750
水	汆	2763
	汍	2768
	汛	2769
	汕	2770
	汐	2771
	汗	2772
	池	2773
	汜	2774
	汝	2775
	江	2776
	汎	2777
	污	2779
	汗	2779
	(污)	
	污	2779
	(洿)	
火	灰	3172
牛	牝	3311
	牟	3312
犬	狂	3341
王	玎	3410
白	百	3693
竹	竺	4085
米	米	4233
缶	缶	4476
羊	羊	4512
羽	羽	4536
老	老	4568
	考	4569
而	而	4575
耒	耒	4579
耳	耳	4590
聿	聿	4614
肉	肉	4619
	肋	4021
	肌	4622
	肓	4637

	(肯)	
臣	臣	4759
自	自	4764
至	至	4769
臼	臼	4773
舌	舌	4786
舛	舛	4793
舟	舟	4797
艮	艮	4823
色	色	4826
艸	艸	4829
	艾	4830
	芎	4831
血	血	5356
行	行	5360
衣	衣	5374
両	西	5473
邑	邨	6170
	邛	6171
阜	阡	6583
	阢	6584

七畫

部首	單字	字號
丨	串	23
二	些	57
一	亟	65
人	伯	113
	佔	114
	你	115
	伴	116
	伶	117
	伸	118
	伺	119
	似	120
	伽	121
	佃	122
	但	123
	佇	124
	佈	125

位	126
低	127
住	128
佐	129
佑	130
佔	131
何	132
佗	133
佘	134
余	135
佚	136
佛	137
作	138
佞	139
佟	140

八	克	297
	兌	298
	兔	299
	兔	301
	(兔)	
八	兵	316
冫	冶	336
	冷	337
	況	2821
刀	初	369
	刪	370
	判	371
	別	372
	刨	373
	利	374
力	助	421
	努	422
	劫	423
	劬	424
	劭	425
匚	匣	464
卜	卣	492
卩	卵	498
	却	503

	(卻)	
	即	504
	(卲)	
口	君	561
	吝	562
	吞	563
	吟	564
	吠	565
	否	566
	吩	567
	含	569
	呪	570
	呈	571
	吳	572
	吵	573
	吶	574
	吸	575
	吻	576
	吼	577
	吱	578
	吾	579
	告	580
	呀	581
	呃	582
	呂	583
	呆	584
	呎	585
	吧	586
囗	困	787
	囤	788
	囪	789
	囫	790
土	坊	811
	圾	812
	址	813
	坂	814
	均	815
	坍	816
	坎	817

坐	818
坑	819
壯	898
壳	2719
(殼)	

大	夾	927
女	妓	959
	妊	960
	妒	961
	妖	962
	妞	963
	妙	964
	妝	965
	姒	966
	好	967
	妥	968
	妨	969
	妍	996
	(姸)	
子	孚	1080
	孛	1081
	孜	1082
	孝	1083
宀	宋	1106
	完	1107
	宏	1175
尤	尨	1175
	尬	1176
尸	尾	1184
	尿	1185
	局	1186
	屁	1187
山	岔	1212
	岌	1213
	岐	1214
	岑	1215
巛	巡	1291
工	巫	1297
巾	希	1309
广	庇	1361
	庋	1362
	序	1363

床	3297
(牀)	

廴	延	1406
	廷	1407
廾	弄	1411
	弇	2476
弓	弟	1447
彡	形	1448
彳	役	1459
	彷	1460
心	忍	1499
	忒	1500
	志	1501
	忐	1502
	忑	1503
	忘	1504
	忡	1505
	忤	1509
	忭	1510
	快	1511
	忮	1511
	忸	1512
	忱	1513
	忉	1514
	忻	1515
	忪	1516
戈	戒	1737
	戒	1758
	我	1759
手	扭	1802
	扮	1803
	扶	1804
	扯	1805
	扳	1806
	扱	1807
	批	1808
	找	1809
	抔	1810
	技	1811
	抄	1812
	抉	1813

扻	1814	汪	2784	田		男	3555

主要索引（按欄排列）

第一欄（手／支／日／木／止／毋／水 部）

字	字號
扻	1814
抒	1815
抓	1816
抔	1817
把	1818
投	1819
抗	1820
抖	1821
折	1822
抑	1823
拒	1824
抛	1840
支 攸	2116
(改) 攺	2117
攻	2118
日 旰	2206
旱	2207
日 木 更	2304
李	2340
杉	2341
杈	2342
杌	2343
杏	2344
杓	2345
材	2346
村	2347
杕	2348
杜	2349
杞	2350
束	2351
杠	2352
杆	2353
杙	2354
止 步	2684
毋 每	2727
毒	2767
水 求	2767
汆	2778
汩	2780
汨	2781
汭	2782
汰	2783

第二欄（水／火／牛／犬／王／用 部）

字	字號
汪	2784
汲	2785
冹 決	2786
汶 汴	2787
汾	2788
汢	2789
沁	2790
沂	2791
沅 沉	2792
沃 汽	2793
沄	2794
沈	2795
沇 沌	2796
沌	2797
沈	2798
(沈) 沉	2798
沐	2799
沔 泅	2800
沖	2801
沙	2802
沒	2803
沘 沚	2804
沏 洫	2805
沛	2807
火 灸	3173
灼	3174
災	3175
(災) 灾	3175
(竈) 灶	4071
牛 牡	3313
牠 牝	3314
牟 牢	3315
犬 狂	3343
狄	3344
犰	3345
狃	3346
王 玕	3411
玖	3412
甫	3547
用 甬	3548

第三欄（田／疒／白／目／矢／示／禾／穴／糸／罕／羊／肉／臣／臼／艮／艸／虫／見／角／言／谷／豆 部）

字	字號
田 男	3555
甸 町	3556
甼	3557
疒 疔	3591
白 皂	3694
皁	3695
目 盯	3740
矢 矧	3830
示 祄	3924
禾 禿	3979
禿	3979
(禿) 秀	3980
私	3981
穴 究	4039
糸 系	4275
糾	4276
罕	4492
羊 羋	4513
肉 肖	4623
肘	2624
肓	4625
肚	4626
肛	4627
肝	4628
肗	4629
肜	4630
臣 臥	4760
臼	4774
艮 良	4824
芃	4832
芄	4833
芋	4834
芋	4835
芍	4836
莒	4837
芒	4838
虫 虬	5192
見 見	5481
角 角	5500
言 言	5514
谷 谷	5706
豆 豆	5710

第四欄（豕／貝／赤／走／足／身／車／辛／辰／辵／邑／酉／里／阜 部）

字	字號
豕 豖	5722
豝	5734
貝 貝	5747
赤 赤	5821
走 走	5827
足 足	5844
身 身	5960
車 車	5966
辛 辛	6037
辰 辰	6047
辵 迂	6050
迄	6051
迅	6052
巡	6053
迤	6054
邑 邪	6169
邞	6173
那	6174
邦	6175
邪	6176
邢	6177
邱	6178
酉 酉	6245
里 里	6305
阜 阢	6585
陀	6586
阪	6587
阮	6588
阱	6589
防	6590
阯	6591

八畫

部首	單字	字號
一	並	19
丿	乖	35
乙	乳	43
	事	48
二	亞	58
亠	享	66
	京	67
人	佩	141
	伻	142

第五欄（人／儿／入／八／冂／刀／力 部）

字	字號
佳	143
佻	144
佼	145
佾	146
使	147
侃	148
侈	149
侉	150
例	151
侍	152
侏	153
侑	154
佺	155
供	156
依	157
佶	158
(併)	189
儿 兒	300
兔	301
兒	302
兩	309
其	317
具	318
典	319
冂 凵 函	355
刀 刮	375
券	376
到	377
刳	379
刹	380
制	381
刷	382
刺	383
刻	384
(劫) 刬	423
力 劾	426
劼	2123
(效) 卑	482

第六欄（卜／卩／又／口／囗／土 部）

字	字號
卒	483
卓	484
協	485
卜 卩 卦	493
卷	499
卸	501
卲	502
又 叔	521
取	522
受	523
口 呢	587
周	588
咒	589
呰	590
呱	591
味	592
呵	593
咕	594
呫	595
咚	596
呻	597
呼	598
命	599
咀	600
咄	601
咆	602
咋	603
和	604
咖	605
咐	606
(詠) 咏	5549
囗 圉	791
圄	792
固	793
土 坡	820
坤	821
坦	822
坷	823
坼	824
坳	825
垂	826

第一欄

部首	字	頁
土	垃	827
	坪	828
夕	夜	911
大	奄	928
	奇	929
	奈	930
	奉	931
	奔	932
女	妳	961
	(妌)	
	姐	970
	妮	971
	妯	972
	妹	973
	妻	974
	妾	975
	姆	976
	姊	977
	姉	977
	(姊)	
	始	978
	姍	979
	姐	980
	姑	981
	姒	982
	姓	983
	委	984
	妳	985
子	孟	1084
	季	1085
	孥	1086
	孤	1087
宀	宕	1109
	宓	1110
	宗	1111
	宙	1112
	定	1113
	宛	1114
	宜	1115
尸	尚	1171
	居	1188
小	屆	1189

第二欄

部首	字	頁
	屈	1190
	屍	1191
	屖	1199
	(屝)	
山	岡	1216
	岫	1217
	岬	1218
	岭	1219
	岱	1220
	岳	1221
	岷	1222
	岸	1223
	岩	1224
巾	帔	1310
	帑	1311
	帕	1312
	帖	1313
	帔	1314
	帚	1315
	帙	1316
	帶	1317
	帛	1318
干	并	1351
	幸	1352
广	底	1364
	庖	1365
	店	1366
	庚	1367
	府	1368
辶	廸	6067
	(迪)	
	廻	6068
	(迫)	
弓	弦	1425
	弧	1426
	弩	1427
	弩	1428
ヨ	彔	1441
彳	彼	1461
	往	1462
	征	1463
	徂	1464
	彿	1465

第三欄

部首	字	頁
心	忠	1517
	念	1518
	忽	1519
	忿	1520
	忝	1521
	怍	1522
	怍	1523
	快	1524
	怖	1525
	怕	1526
	怙	1527
	怛	1528
	怦	1529
	怡	1530
	性	1531
	怩	1532
	怫	1533
	怯	1534
	怪	1535
	悅	1536
	怔	1537
	怜	1538
	愍	1539
	怗	1540
	恍	1541
戈	或	1760
	戕	1761
	戔	1762
戶	戾	1779
	扉	1780
	房	1781
	所	1824
手	(把)	
	承	1825
	抱	1826
	抔	1827
	拔	1828
	抵	1829
	抹	1830
	抽	1831
	押	1832
	拄	1833

第四欄

部首	字	頁
	拂	1834
	拇	1835
	拈	1836
	拆	1837
	拉	1838
	拊	1839
	拋	1840
	拌	1841
	拐	1842
	拑	1843
	拍	1844
	拾	1845
	拒	1846
	拓	1847
	拔	1848
	拗	1849
	拖	1850
	(拖)	
	拙	1851
	拘	1852
	拚	1853
	抿	1854
	招	1855
	担	2059
	(擔)	
	抬	2073
	(擡)	
支	放	2119
	攻	2120
斤方	斥	2166
	斧	2175
	於	2178
	(旁)	

第五欄

部首	字	頁
日	明	2217
	昏	2218
	易	2219
	昔	2220
	昕	2221
	昀	2222
	昝 (時)	2240
月	朋	2316
	服	2317
木	杭	2355
	杯	2356
	杲	2357
	杳	2358
	東	2359
	杵	2360
	枇	2361
	杷	2362
	杼	2363
	枋	2364
	板	2365
	松	2366
	枏	2367
	枉	2368
	枌	2369
	枋	2370
	析	2371
	柯	2372
	枕	2373
	柄	2374
	林	2375
	枝	2376
	果	2377
	枚	2378
	杰	2379

第六欄

部首	字	頁
日	旺	2208
	旻	2209
	昂	2210
	昃	2211
	昆	2212
	昇	2213
	昉	2214
	昊	2215
	昌	2216
欠	欣	2652
止	歧	2685
	武	2686
歹	殁	2693
殳	殳	2693
	(殳)	
	殃	2694
毋	毒	2729

第七欄

部首	字	頁
氏	氒	2749
气	氖	2751
水	沓	2806
	沫	2808
	沫	2809
	沮	2810
	流	2811
	沱	2812
	滲	2813
	沸	2814
	油	2815
	河	2816
	沼	2817
	沽	2818
	治	2819
	沾	2820
	況	2821
	洞	2822
	沿	2823
	泄	2824
	泱	2825
	泐	2826
	泊	2827
	泅	2828
	泌	2829
	泔	2830
	泓	2831
	法	2832
	泗	2833
	泖	2834
	洌	2835
	泝	2836
	泠	2837
	泛	2838
	波	2839
	泣	2840
	泡	2841
	泥	2842
	泮	2843
	泯	2844
	注	2845
	泱	2846
	泳	2847

泪(淚)	2926	
火　炎	3176	
炊	3177	
炕	3178	
炖	3179	
炘	3180	
炙	3181	
炒	3182	
爪　爬	3285	
爭	3286	
爸	3291	
爿　牀	3297	
片　版	3302	
牛　牧	3316	
物	3317	
犬　狀	3342	
狎	3342	
狗	3348	
狐	3349	
狒	3350	
狙	3351	
玉　玫	3413	
玦	3414	
玩	3415	
玕	3416	
玠	3417	
田　畀	3558	
畍	3559	
疒　疙	3592	
疚	3593	
疝	3593	
白　的	3696	
皿　盂	3715	
目　盱	3741	
盲	3742	
直	3743	
矢　知	3831	
石　矽	3842	
砒	3843	
示　社	3925	
祁	3926	
祀	3927	

禾　秉	3982	
秒	4040	
穴　穹	4041	
空	4042	
竹　竺	4086	
糸　糾	4277	
网　罔	4491	
羊　羌	4514	
肉　股	4631	
肢	4632	
肥	4633	
肩	4634	
肪	4635	
肫	4636	
肯	4637	
宵	4637	
(肯)		
肱	4638	
育	4639	
肴	4640	
胖	4641	
臣　臥	4761	
舌　舍	4775	
與	4775	
舟　舠	4798	
艸　芙	4839	
芝	4840	
芨	4841	
茇	4842	
茉	4843	
芥	4844	
芋	4845	
芩	4846	
芫	4847	
芬	4848	
苊	4849	
芭	4850	
芯	4851	
芮	4852	
菱	4853	
花	4854	
芳	4855	
芷	4856	

芸	4857	
芹	4858	
苣	4859	
芽	4860	
苒	4861	
虍　虎	5180	
虫　蚓	5193	
虱	5193	
衣　表	5375	
衫	5376	
衩	5377	
車　軋	5967	
辵　迎	6055	
近	6056	
迅	6057	
返	6058	
迕	6059	
迓	6060	
迍	6061	
邑　邵	6179	
邯	6180	
邰	6181	
邱	6182	
邲	6183	
邳	6184	
邶	6185	
鄆	6186	
邸	6187	
釆　采	6302	
金　金	6310	
長　長	6528	
門　門	6529	
阜　阜	6582	
阻	6592	
阼	6593	
阿	6594	
陀	6595	
陵	6596	
附	6597	
陞	6598	
隹　雨	6654	
雨	6681	
青　青	6722	

非　非	6728

九畫

部首	單字	字號
二(亠)	亟	59
	亭	68
	亮	69
人	侮	159
	侯	160
	侶	161
	侵	162
	侗	163
	便	164
	係	165
	促	166
	俄	167
	俊	168
	俎	169
	俏	170
	俐	171
	俑	172
	俗	173
	俘	174
	俚	175
	保	176
	俟	177
	俠	178
	信	179
儿	兗	303
入	兪	310
	冒	325
	冑	326
	冠	329
刀	剎	379
(刔)		
	則	385
	剃	386
	剄	387
	剉	388
	削	389
	剋	390
	剌	391
	前	392

力	勁	427
	勃	428
	勅	429
	勇	430
	勉	431
勹	匍	453
十	南	486
卩	卸	503
	卽	504
厂	厎	507
	厚	508
又	叛	524
	叙	2125
	(敍)	
口	咧	607
	咤	608
	咦	609
	咨	610
	咪	611
	咫	612
	咬	613
	咯	614
	咱	615
	咳	616
	咸	617
	咽	618
	咿	619
	哀	620
	品	621
	哂	622
	哄	623
	哆	624
	哇	625
	哈	626
	哉	627
	咥	628
	圄	794
土	垠	829
	坰	830
	垢	831
	型	832
	垮	833
大	奔	932

	(奔)	933
	奏	934
	奐	935
	契	936
	奕	937
女	姚	986
	姜	987
	姝	988
	姣	989
	姤	990
	姥	991
	姦	992
	姪	993
	姪	994
	姱	995
	姍	996
	姹	997
	姻	998
	姿	999
	威	1000
	娃	1001
	姘	1018
	(姘)	
子	孩	1088
宀	客	1117
	宣	1118
	室	1119
	宥	1120
	宦	1121
寸	封	1159
尸	屋	1193
	屍	1194
	屎	1194
山	崎	1225
	峒	1226
	峙	1227
己	巷	1303
巾	帥	1319
	帝	1320
幺	幽	1357
广	度	1369
	庫	1370

麻	1371	恰	1564	昂	2231	柱	2409	洲	2867	珈	3428
辶 建	1408	協	1565	昶	2232	東	2410	洮	2868	甚	3537
廻	6072	惜	1578	昫	2233	查	2411	洴	2869	甫	3549
(迴)		戶 扁	1783	昳	2234	柰	2412	洶	2870	田 界	3560
卅 弇	1412	手 局	1784	督	2235	柴	2413	洵	2871	畏	3561
弓 弈	1413	拜	1856	昪	2236	柷	2414	洽	2872	畋	3562
彐 弭	1429	拭	1857	昺	2237	柚	2415	活	2873	畎	3563
彡 弱	1430	拮	1858	(昺)		柵	2416	派	2874	广 疤	3595
象	1442	拯	1859	易	2238	柶	2417	流	2875	疥	3596
形	1448	括	1860	昵	2278	柁	2418	洒	2876	疫	3597
(形)		拱	1861	(暱)		枰	2419	洗	2877	疣	3598
彡 彦	1449	拴	1862	日 易	2305	枱	2420	火 炫	3183	皮 皆	3688
彳 待	1466	挬	1863	月 朏	2318	柷	2461	炮	3184	白 皇	3697
徇	1467	拾	1864	木 枯	2380	(椏)		炰	3185	皈	3698
很	1468	持	1865	枳	2381	止 歪	2687	烖	3185	皇	3699
徉	1469	按	1866	枴	2382	歹 殆	2695	(炮)		皿 盅	3716
徊	1470	指	1867	枵	2383	殄	2696	炯	3186	盆	3717
律	1471	挑	1868	枲	2384	殃	2697	炳	3187	盈	3718
後	1472	拽	1869	架	2385	殂	2698	烊	3188	盃	3719
心 怎	1542	挖	1870	枷	2386	殳 段	2716	炸	3189	目 相	3744
怒	1543	拷	1871	柿	2387	毋 毖	2732	炭	3190	盼	3745
思	1544	拕	1872	枸	2388	毗	2733	炤	3191	盻	3746
怠	1545	拏	1874	枹	2389	毛 毡	2745	為	3192	眄	3747
急	1546	(拿)		柒	2390	(氈)		爪 爰	3287	眇	3748
怨	1547	拼	1924	枻	2391	气 氟	2752	爿 牁	3298	眈	3749
態	1548	(拼)		柑	2392	泉	2848	牛 牯	3318	眊	3750
怱	1549	挂	1928	柄	2393	水 洄	2851	牲	3319	盹	3751
恂	1550	(掛)		柏	2394	洎	2851	牴	3320	盾	3752
恆	1551	支 政	2121	某	2395	洠	2852	犬 狠	3352	省	3753
恒	1551	故	2122	染	2396	洌	2853	狡	3353	眉	3754
(恆)		斤 斫	2167	柔	2397	洋	2855	狩	3354	看	3755
恃	1552	方 施	2176	柑	2398	酒	2855	玉 珏	3416	矛 矜	3827
恌	1553	斿	2177	柳	2399	洗	2856	(珏)		矢 矧	3832
恓	1554	无 既	2197	柘	2400	洙	2857	玲	3418	矣	3833
恍	1555	(旣)		柙	2401	潢	2858	珐	3419	石 春	3844
恟	1556	日 星	2223	柚	2402	洞	2859	玳	3420	砂	3845
恢	1557	映	2224	柜	2403	洛	2860	珉	3421	砌	3846
恨	1558	春	2225	柞	2404	津	2861	珂	3422	砍	3847
恤	1559	昧	2226	柝	2405	洧	2862	珑	3423	砒	3848
恪	1560	昨	2227	柢	2406	洫	2863	珊	3424	研	3864
恫	1561	昭	2228	柩	2407	洩	2864	珍	3425	(研)	
惺	1562	是	2229	柯	2408	洪	2865	玻	3426	示 祆	3928
恬	1563	昱	2230			洱	2866	珀	3427	祅	3929

土	埋	834		峪	1235	手	拳	1873	晒		2300	毛	(殻)			(殻)	2736		烘	3197
	城	835		差	1298		拿	1874	(曬)			气	毯	2736		氣	2753		烤	3198
	埂	836	工巾	帨	1321		挈	1875	日	書	2306					氫	2754		烟	3199
	埃	837		師	1322		挨	1876	月	朔	2319					氧	2755	父	烙	3200
	埔	838		席	1323		挪	1877		朕	2320	水				氦	2756		爹	3292
夊	夏	904		帮	1345		抄	1878		朓	2321					浙	2878	片	牉	3299
大	奘	938					挫	1879	木	栓	2421					浚	2879	牛	牷	3321
	套	939	广	座	1372		振	1880		栱	2422					浜	2880		牷	3322
	奢	940		庫	1373		按	1881		栖	2423					浮	2881		牸	3323
	奚	941		庭	1374		挹	1882		栝	2424					浣	2882	犬	猛	3355
女	娌	1002	弓	弱	1431		挽	1883		栵	2425					浩	2883		狼	3356
	娉	1003		弭	1432		挺	1884		栗	2427					浥	2884		狽	3357
	娌	1004	彳	徐	1450		挶	1885		株	2427					浦	2885		狷	3358
	姬	1005		徑	1473		捆	1886		核	2428					浬	2886		狸	3359
	娑	1006		徒	1474		持	1887		校	2429					浪	2887		狹	3360
	娘	1007	心	徒	1475		捉	1888		栲	2430					浹	2888		狺	3361
	娛	1008		恁	1566		挾	1889		根	2431					浴	2889	玉	珥	3429
	娜	1009		恐	1567		捍	1890		桁	2432					浮	2890		珙	3430
	娟	1010		恝	1568		捌	1891		格	2433					海	2891		珞	3431
	娠	1011		患	1569		捕	1892		桀	2434					浸	2892		珠	3432
	娣	1012		恕	1570		捐	1893		案	2436					浼	2893		珩	3433
	娥	1013		恙	1571		捎	1894		桌	2436					涇	2894		班	3434
	娩	1014		态	1572		捏	1895		桑	2437					涅	2895		珪	3435
子	孫	1089		恩	1573		捂	1896		栽	2438					涉	2896		珣	3436
宀	宮	1122		愿	1574	支	效	2123		桂	2439					消	2897		珊	3437
	宰	1123		息	1575		敉	2124		桃	2440					涑	2898		珧	3438
	害	1124		恭	1576	文	斋	7304		栬	2441					消	2899	瓜	瓞	3517
	宴	1125		恥	1577		(齋)			桅	2442					涎	2900	瓦	瓴	3523
	宵	1126		悃	1579	斗	料	2157		框	2443					涕	2901	生	甡	3540
	家	1127		悄	1580	方	旁	2178		桎	2444					涕	2902	田	畔	3564
	宸	1128		悄	1581		旂	2179		桐	2445					涔	2903		畛	3565
	容	1129		悅	1582		旆	2180		桓	2446					泿	2904		畚	3566
寸	射	1160		悌	1583		旃	2181		桔	2447					泿	2905		畜	3567
尸	展	1195		悔	1584		旄	2182		栝	2448					涌	2907		畝	3568
	屐	1196		悒	1585		旅	2183		柏	2449	火	烖	3175					留	3569
	屑	1197		悍	1586	日	晏	2240		栱	2450		(災)					广	疲	3599
山	峨	1228		悚	1587		時	2240		梳	2473		烏	3193					疳	3601
	峭	1229		悛	1588		晉	2241		(梘)			烈	3194					疸	3602
	峯	1230		悖	1589		晉	2241	欠	歁	2653		烝	3195					痂	3603
	峴	1231		悟	1590		(晉)		歹	殉	2699		烊	3196					疹	3604
	島	1232		悝	1591		晃	2242		殊	2700								疼	3605
	峻	1233	户	扆	1785		晃	2243	殳	殷	2717								疾	3606
	峽	1234		扇	1786		晌	2244		毀	2719									

病	3607	砦	3859	納	4288	朕	4661	茹	4914	訊	5522
症	3608	祐	3933	紐	4289	胱	4662	荀	4915	訌	5523
疢	3609	祓	3934	純	4290	胴	4663	荌	4916	訓	5524
痾	3610	祙	3935	紓	4291	胸	4664	草	4917	訕	5525
痲	3611	祕	3936	紕	4292	脅	4664	荏	4918	訖	5526
疱	3612	祖	3937	紘	4293	(胸)		荑	4919	託	5527
痁	3613	祇	3938	紗	4294	朓	4665	荒	4920	記	5528
痒	3614	祜	3939	紙	4295	能	4666	茛	4921	訑	5529
疵	3615	祛	3940	紜	4296	脂	4668	茜	4922	訒	5530
痛	3633	祚	3941	紝	4297	脆	4669	茭	4923	訐	5531
(痱)		祝	3942	級	4298	胺	4669	荃	4924	豈	5711
皋	3700	神	3943	紛	4299	(脆)		荇	4925	豇	5712
臯	3710	祠	3944	紡	4300	脊	4670	荠	4926	豹	5735
益	3720	祟	3945	素	4301	脈	4671	荊	4994	豺	5736
盍	3721	秘	3936	索	4302	脅	4672	(荆)		豻	5737
盇	3722	(祕)		紮	4303	脒	4673	虔	5182	貢	5750
盌	3723	秦	3989	綮	4304	胳	4674	蚌	5199	財	5751
盉	6353	租	3990	(紮)		胼	4689	蚊	5200	貤	5752
(鉢)		秧	3991	缺	4478	(胼)		蚪	5201	赸	5830
眙	3756	秤	3992	罡	4494	臬	4765	蚋	5202	赹	5831
胅	3757	秩	3993	罟	4495	臭	4766	蚍	5203	赳	5846
眜	3758	秫	3994	買	4496	致	4770	蚓	5204	趵	5961
眼	3759	秭	3995	羔	4514	(致)		蚜	5205	軒	5970
眩	3760	秬	3996	(羌)		異	4777	蚤	5207	軔	5971
眨	3761	秸	3997	羕	4518	舀	4778	蚨	5208	軏	5972
眞	3762	窅	4046	殺	4519	舐	4788	蚩	5209	辱	6048
真	3762	窈	4047	粑	4520	舫	4801	蚗	5357	迴	6072
(眞)		窄	4048	粉	4521	般	4802	衰	5378	迷	6074
眚	3763	窆	4049	翁	4538	舭	4803	衷	5382	迹	6074
眥	3764	站	4074	翅	4539	舨	4804	衾	5383	迫	6075
眈	3764	竚	4075	翃	4540	舨	4862	衾	5385	退	6076
(眥)		竛	4076	耄	4570	茗	4902	袁	5387	送	6077
矩	3834	笆	4089	耆	4571	荔	4903	衮	5388	适	6078
砥	3849	竿	4090	耙	4581	茼	4904	袖	5390	逃	6079
砧	3850	笏	4091	耕	4582	茨	4905	袍	5392	追	6080
砭	3851	笈	4092	耘	4583	茫	4906	祖	5393	逆	6081
砰	3852	笑	4093	耗	4584	茯	4907	袜	5394	逐	6082
砝	3853	笋	4112	耽	4593	茱	4908	祛	5396	逢	6083
破	3854	(筍)		耿	4594	茲	4909	被	5397	逈	6084
砷	3855	笄	4121	聅	4595	茴	4910	討	5520	逾	6085
砸	3856	(笲)		恥	4596	茵	4911	訐	5521	逬	6106
砮	3857	粉	4235	胭	4659	茶	4912			(逬)	
砲	3858	紋	4287	脖	4660	茸	4913			邕	6172

部首標記：白 皮 皿（皋）・目（眙）・矢 石（矩）・示（祐）・禾（秦）・穴（窅）・立（站）・竹（笆）・米（粉）・糸（紋）・缶 网（缺）・羊（羔）・羽（翁）・老（耄）・耒（耙）・耳（耽）・肉（胭）・自（臬）・至（致）・白（異）・舌 舟（舐・舫）・艸（茗）・声 虫（虔）・血 衣（衰）・言（討）・豆（豈）・豸（豹）・貝（貢）・走（赸）・足 身 車（趵）・辰 辵（辱）・邑（邕）

部首	單字	字號
	郊	6196
	部	6197
	郝	6198
	郎	6199
	郟	6200
	郡	6201
	郭	6202
	都	6203
	鄙	6204
	鄉	6205
酉	酌	6248
	配	6249
金	酒	6250
	釘	6313
	釜	6314
	釗	6315
	針	6316
	釙	6317
	釘	6318
門	閃	6531
阜	陛	6604
	陸	6605
	陵	6606
	陬	6607
	陡	6608
	院	6609
	陣	6610
	除	6611
	陝	6612
隹	隻	6655
	隼	6656
馬	馬	6921
骨	骨	6990
高	高	7008
鬥	鬥	7036
鬯	鬯	7044
鬲	鬲	7046
鬼	鬼	7048

十一畫

部首	單字	字號
乙	乾	44
人	偃	215

部首	單字	字號
	假	216
	偈	217
	偉	218
	偌	219
	偎	220
	偏	221
	偓	222
	偕	223
	做	224
	停	225
	健	226
	偬	227
	側	228
	偵	229
	偶	230
	偷	231
儿	兜	304
	晷	328
	湊	2977
	(湊)	
几	凰	348
刀	副	399
	剪	400
力	勒	432
	動	433
	勗	434
	勖	434
	(勖)	
	勘	435
	務	436
勹	匍	454
	匐	455
	匙	459
匚	匭	466
	區	471
	匿	472
	匾	473
厶	參	515
口	售	647
	唯	648
	唱	649
	唉	650
	唾	651

部首	單字	字號
	啡	652
	唰	653
	啄	654
	蔄	655
	問	656
	啊	657
	啤	658
	啐	659
	啓	660
	唳	661
	唰	662
	啍	663
	啦	664
	啞	665
	唷	666
	唬	667
	喙	668
	唸	669
	啥	670
	啜	671

部首	單字	字號
口	國	797
	圖	798
	圈	799
土	培	839
	域	840
	埠	841
	埤	842
	執	843
	基	844
	堂	845
	堆	846
	埽	1912
	(掃)	
夕	夠	912
	够	912
	(夠)	
女	婆	1015
	婀	1016
	娶	1017
	妍	1018
	婊	1019
	婉	1020

部首	單字	字號
	婕	1021
	婚	1022
	婢	1023
	婦	1024
	婪	1025
	娼	1026
	婭	1027
	婊	1028
	婌	1029
子	孰	1090
	寃	330
	(冤)	
宀	密	1130
	宿	1131
	寂	1132
	寄	1133
	寅	1134
	寇	1135
寸	專	1161
	將	1162
	尉	1163
尸	屏	1198
	屜	1199
	屙	1200
山	崇	1236
	崎	1237
	崒	1238
	崔	1239
	崖	1240
	崗	1241
	崙	1242
	崛	1244
	崢	1244
	崤	1245
	崧	1246
	崩	1247
	崍	1248
	崑	1249
	崚	1250
	崕	1251
巛	巢	1292
巾	帳	1324
	帶	1325

部首	單字	字號
	帷	1326
	常	1327
广	庵	1375
	庶	1376
	康	1377
	庸	1378
	庹	1379
弓	張	1433
	強	1434
	彗	1443
彡	影	1451
	彩	1452
	彬	1453
	彪	1454
彳	得	1476
	徘	1477
	徜	1478
	徙	1479
	從	1480
	徠	1481
	御	1482
心	悠	1592
	悉	1593
	患	1594
	悤	1595
	您	1596
	悱	1597
	悵	1598
	悸	1599
	悴	1600
	悴	1601
	悼	1602
	悾	1603
	悽	1604
	惆	1605
	情	1606
	悻	1607
	惋	1608
	惕	1609
	惓	1610
	惘	1611
	惚	1612
	惙	1613

部首	單字	字號
	慆	1614
	惆	1615
	恬	1616
	惜	1617
	惟	1618
戈	戚	1763
	戛	1764
戶	扈	1787
手	捨	1897
	捧	1898
	捩	1899
	捫	1900
	捫	1901
	据	1902
	捱	1903
	捥	1904
	捺	1905
	捽	1906
	捲	1907
	捻	1908
	捷	1909
	捭	1910
	掀	1911
	掃	1913
	授	1914
	掇	1915
	掎	1916
	掏	1917
	掐	1918
	掊	1919
	掉	1920
	排	1921
	掘	1922
	披	1923
	拼	1924
	捭	1925
	掞	1926
	掠	1927
	掛	1928
	採	1929
	探	1930
	控	1931

	接	1932	木	桫	2451		淄	2915		煮	3203		恃	3621		第	4102
	推	1933		桫	2452		涼	2916		焉	3204		瘴(瘴)	3677		笳	4103
	摺	1934		梧	2453		淅	2917		焌	3205		(瘴)			笯	4104
	掩	1935		桶	2454		洴	2918		烷	3206	白	皐	3700		笱	4105
	捬	1936		梅	2455		淯	2919		烯	3207		(皋)			笪	4106
	掏	1937		梁	2456		淌	2920	爻牛	爽	3295	皿	皎	3701		笮	4107
	捶	1938		梃	2457		淖	2921		牽	3324		盒	3724		笵	4108
	摋	1939		梅	2458		淑	2922		牾	3325		盔	3725	米	粒	4236
	捵	3879		梓	2459		淒	2923		犂	3326		盖	5049		粗	4237
	(㪣)			梏	2460		淋	2924		(犁)			(蓋)			粕	4238
文	啓	660		梔	2461		淘	2925	犬	猖	3362	目	眯	3765		粘	4239
	(启)			梗	2462		淚	2926		猗	3363		眵	3766	糸	絜	4304
	敘	2125		條	2463		淫	2927		猊	3364		眶	3767		絇	4305
	敍	2125		梟	2464		淙	2928		猙	3365		眸	3768		紫	4306
	(敘)			梵	2465		淟	2929		猛	3366		眼	3769		累	4307
	教	2126		梯	2466		淞	2930		猜	3367		眺	3770		紬	4308
	敏	2127		械	2467		淡	2931		猓	3368		眵	3771		細	4309
	救	2128		梲	2468		涿	2932		猝	3369		眾	3772		紱	4310
	敕	2129		梧	2469		淦	2933		率	3407		眷	3773		紳	4311
	敚	2130		棺	2470		淳	2934	玄玉	現	3439	石	硃	3860		紹	4312
	敗	2131		梭	2471		淩	2935		球	3440		硌	3861		紼	4313
	敔	2132		梆	2472		淪	2936		理	3441		硒	3862		紾	4314
斗	斜	2158		梳	2473		淨	2937		琅	3442		硫	3863		絀	4315
	斜	2159		桿	2474		淬	2938		邪	3443		研	3864		紵	4316
斤	斬	2168		梨	2475		淮	2939	瓜瓦	瓠	3518	示	祥	3946		紺	4317
方	旋	2184		(棃)			淫	2940		瓷	3524		祧	3947		絃	4318
	旌	2185	欠	欲	2654		淳	2941		瓶	3526		票	3948		終	4319
	旎	2186		欸	2655		淵	2942		(瓶)			祭	3949		組	4320
	族	2187		欷	2656		深	2943	甘生田	甜	3538	禾穴	移	3998		絆	4321
无	既	2197		欸	2657		淶	2944		產	3541		窒	4050		絅	4322
日	晟	2245		(款)			混	2945		畦	3570		窕	4051		紽	4323
	晚	2246	歹	殍	2701		清	2946		時	3571		窓	4053		紩	4324
	晝	2247	殳	殺	2718		淺	2947		略	3572		(窗)			絁	4325
	晞	2248	毛	毫	2737		淹	2948		畧	3572	立	竟	4077		絀	4329
	晡	2249		毬	2738		添	2949		(略)			章	4078		(綫)	
	晤	2250	气	氫	2757		淉	2950		畢	3573	竹	笙	4094	缶	缽	6353
	晦	2251	水	涯	2908		淇	2951		異	3574		笠	4095		(鉢)	
	晧	2252		液	2909		淜	2952	疋广	疏	3588		笛	4096	网羊	罩	4497
	晨	2253		涪	2910		淲	2953		痾	3616		笨	4097		羝	4522
日	曹	2307		涵	2911	火	烟	3186		痩	3617		笞	4098		羚	4523
	曼	2308		涸	2912		(烔)			痊	3618		笥	4099		羕	4524
月	朗	2322		淥	2913		烽	3201		痏	3619		第	4100	羽	翊	4541
	望	2323		淀	2914		烹	3202		痕	3620		符	4101		翎	4542

部首	單字	字號
老	翌	4543
	習	4544
	耆	4573
	耄	4573
	(耆)	
耒	耜	4585
	耡	4595
	(耡)	
耳	聆	4597
	聊	4598
肉	脘	4675
	脛	4676
	脣	4677
	脩	4678
	脫	4679
	脯	4680
	脬	4681
	脏	4682
	脞	4683
	脤	4684
	脬	4685
	脂	4686
	脚	4687
臼	舂	4779
舟	舲	4805
	舳	4806
	舴	4807
	舵	4808
	舶	4809
	舷	4810
	舸	4811
	船	4812
	舲	4827
色		
艸	荷	4927
	菱	4928
	菇	4929
	荻	4930
	茶	4931
	著	4932
	莊	4933
	菖	4934
	莓	4935
	菫	4936
	莘	4937
	莞	4938
	莠	4939
	莢	4940
	莧	4941
	莩	4942
	莪	4943
	莫	4944
	莆	4945
	莉	4946
	莽	4947
	莎	4948
	莎	4949
	莩	4950
	葆	4951
	莖	4952
	莨	4953
	菫	4954
虍	處	5183
	虛	5184
虫	蚯	5211
	蚰	5212
	蚱	5213
	蚶	5214
	蛀	5215
	蛄	5216
	蛆	5217
	蛇	5218
	蛤	5219
	蛋	5220
行	衒	5362
	術	5363
衣	袈	5389
	袋	5391
	袤	5395
	袬	5398
	袴	5399
	袱	5400
	袷	5401
	裉	5404
	袿	5405
見	規	5482
	覓	5483

部首	單字	字號
	覓	5483
	(覓)	
角 言	觖	5502
	訟	5532
	訛	5533
	訝	5534
	訴	5535
	訣	5536
	訥	5537
	訩	5538
	訪	5539
	設	5540
	許	5541
豆 豕	豉	5713
貝	豚	5723
	犯	5724
	貧	5753
	貨	5754
	販	5755
	貪	5756
	貫	5757
	責	5758
赤 足	赦	5822
	趾	5847
	趺	5848
	跋	5849
	跎	5850
	跰	5861
	(跰)	
身 車	躭	5962
	軛	5973
	軟	5974
足	逍	6086
	逝	6087
	逋	6088
	透	6089
	逐	6090
	逑	6091
	途	6092
	逖	6093
	逛	6094
	逗	6095

部首	單字	字號
辵 辶	逭	6096
	通	6097
	逛	6098
	逞	6099
	速	6100
	造	6101
	逢	6103
	連	6104
	逌	6105
邑	部	6206
	郫	6207
	郭	6208
	郯	6209
	郴	6210
	郪	6211
	郫	6212
	郵	6213
酉	酖	6251
	酗	6252
里 金	野	6307
	釩	6319
	釣	6320
	釱	6321
	釹	6322
	釦	6323
	釧	6324
	釵	6325
	釣	6326
	釬	6411
	(鋅)	
門 阜	閉	6532
	陪	6613
	陳	6614
	陰	6615
	陲	6616
	陴	6617
	陣	6618
	陵	6619
	陶	6620
	陷	6621
	陸	6622
隹	雀	6657

部首	單字	字號
雨	雰	6682
	雪	6683
革 頁	釘	6736
	頂	6781
食	頃	6782
	飢	6850
	釘	6851
	飡	6852
首 魚	魚	6916
鳥 鹵	鳥	7060
鹿 麥	鹵	7115
麻	鹿	7216
	麥	7234
	麻	7241

十二畫

部首	單字	字號
乙	乾	44
	(乾)	
人	像	232
	傀	233
	傅	234
	傍	235
	傑	236
	僋	237
	傘	238
	備	239
	傲	240
	傖	3378
	(傜)	
几 刀	凱	349
	剩	401
	割	402
	剴	403
	創	404
力	勝	437
	勞	438
	博	487
卜卩	卿	505
厂口	厥	511
	喫(吃)	549

部首	單字	字號
	窨	672
	啼	673
	啾	674
	喀	675
	喁	676
	喂	677
	喃	678
	善	679
	嗖	680
	喇	681
	喈	682
	喉	683
	喊	684
	喋	685
	喏	686
	喑	687
	喔	688
	喘	689
	喙	690
	喚	691
	喜	692
	喝	693
	卿	694
	喟	695
	喧	696
	喨	697
	嗑	698
	喪	699
	喬	700
	單	701
	喳	702
	喊(喫)	726
口 土	圍	800
	報	848
	堡	849
	堪	850
	堯	851
	堰	852
	場	853
	堵	854
	堙	6624
	(隂)	

	堤	6626	广	庾	1380	手	捏	1895		殳	2135		棠	2488	減	2959

土 / 大 / 女 / 子 / 宀 / 寸 / 小 / 尢 / 尸 / 山 / 己 / 巾 / 幺 欄

字	頁
堤(隄)	6626
土 增	899
壹	900
壺	901
大 奡	942
奢	943
婿(壻)	899
女 婷	1030
媄	1031
媒	1032
媚	1033
媛	1034
媧	1035
媟	1036
子 孱	1091
孳	1092
宀 富	1136
寐	1137
寒	1138
寓	1138
寸 尊	1164
尋	1165
小 寮	1172
尢 就	1177
尸 屠	1201
山 崴	1252
崼	1253
崽	1254
嵇	1255
嵋	1256
嵌	1257
嵐	1258
嵎	1259
嵏	1304
己 巽	1304
巾 幅	1328
帽	1329
幀	1330
幃	1331
幄	1332
幺 幾	1358

广 / 弓 / ヨ彐彡 / 彳 / 心 / 戈 / 戶 欄

字	頁
广 庾	1380
廁	1381
廂	1382
弓 強(强)	1434
弼	1435
ヨ彐彡 彘	1444
彳 徧	1483
徨	1484
復	1485
循	1486
心 惑	1619
惑	1620
悲	1621
悲	1622
惠	1623
惡	1624
情	1625
愜	1626
惴	1627
愕	1628
惲	1629
惶	1630
愒	1631
愐	1632
愕	1633
愣	1634
惇	1635
惺	1636
愀	1637
惻	1638
愎	1639
愉	1640
愔	1641
惰	1642
愛	1643
戈 戞	1764
戟	1765
戡(戟)	1765
戶 扉	1788

手 / 支 / 支 欄

字	頁
手 捏(捏)	1895
逮(捷)	1909
掌	1940
掔	1941
掰	1942
掔	1943
揀	1944
揄	1945
揍	1946
搽	1947
揉	1948
描	1949
搂	1950
提	1951
揕	1952
揖	1953
插	1954
插(插)	1954
揚	1955
揀	1956
擺	1957
換	1958
揑	1959
揣	1960
揩	1961
揪	1962
揫(揪)	1962
揮	1963
揭	1964
援	1965
揲	1966
揸	1967
揶	1968
揎	1969
揞	1970
揎	1971
支 攲	2114
支 敝	2133
敨	2134

殳 / 文 / 斗 / 斤 / 方 / 日 / 月 / 木 欄

字	頁
毀	2135
敢	2136
散	2137
敦	2138
文 斌	2151
斐	2152
斑	2153
斗 斝	2160
斤 斮	2169
斯	2170
方 旐	2188
晬	2254
普	2255
景	2256
晰	2257
晢	2258
晴	2259
晶	2260
晷	2261
智	2262
晾	2263
日 曾	2309
替	2310
最	2311
月 朝	2324
期	2325
朞(期)	2325
木 椁	2475
棄	2476
棉	2477
棊(棋)	2478
棍	2479
棒	2480
棗	2481
棘	2482
根	2483
棧	2484
棟	2485
棚	2486
棣	2487

木(續) / 欠 / 歹 / 殳 / 毛 / 气 / 水 欄

字	頁
棠	2488
棨	2489
棻	2490
棐	2491
棼	2492
森	2493
椒	2494
械	2495
椗	2496
棲	2497
棺	2498
棵	2499
植	2500
椎	2501
棹	2502
椅	2503
椁	2504
椏	2505
椋	2506
棕	2507
椀(碗)	3886
欠 款	2657
欽	2658
欺	2659
欻	2660
歊	2661
歆	2662
歹 殖	2702
殘	2703
殳 殼	2719
毀	2720
毛 毯	2739
毳	2740
气 氩	2758
氮	2759
水 涅(湦)	2895
淼	2954
渙	2955
渚	2956
淳	2957
渝	2958

水(續) / 火 欄

字	頁
減	2959
渡	2960
渣	2961
渠	2962
渤	2963
渥	2964
渦	2965
渭	2966
港	2967
渲	2968
測	2969
渴	2970
湃	2971
湣	2972
游	2973
游	2974
渾	2975
湄	2976
湊	2977
湎	2978
湍	2979
溢	2980
湔	2981
湜	2982
湧	2983
湖	2984
湘	2985
湛	2986
湮	2987
湫	2988
湯	2989
湟	2990
潶	2991
湲	2992
渻	2993
湢	2994
浪	2995
渟	2996
活	2997
溫(溫)	2998
火 焙	3208
焜	3209

第一欄

部首	字	號碼
	焯	3210
	焚	3211
	焱	3212
	焦	3213
	無	3214
	然	3215
	焰	3216
	爲	3288
爪 片	牌	3303
	牋	4138
	(箋)	
牙 牛	犛	3309
	犀	3326
	犄	3327
	犉	3328
	犇	3329
犬	犇	3330
	猢	3371
	猨	3372
	猶	3373
	猩	3374
	猱	3375
	猴	3376
	猨	3379
	(猿)	
	猫	5743
	(貓)	
五	琠	3444
	琛	3445
	琢	3446
	瑁	3447
	琤	3448
	琦	3449
	琨	3450
	琪	3451
	琥	3452
	琺	3453
	琬	3454
	琮	3455
	琴	3456
	琵	3457
	琶	3458

第二欄

部首	字	號碼
	琳	3459
	琰	3460
	琯	3461
生	甥	3542
	甦	3543
	甤	3544
用 田	甯	3550
	畱	3569
	(留)	
	異	3574
	(異)	
	番	3575
	畬	3576
	畫	3577
	畯	3578
	畷	3579
疋	疏	3588
	(疏)	
	疎	3588
	(疏)	
广	痛	3622
	痘	3623
	痙	3624
	痢	3625
	痎	3626
	痣	3627
	痰	3628
	痼	3629
	痞	3630
	痤	3631
癶	登	3689
	發	3690
白	皓	3702
	皖	3703
	皕	3704
皮 皿	皺	3711
	盛	3726
	盜	3727
目	睞	3774
	睏	3775
	睫	3776
矛 矢	矞	3828
	矬	3835

第三欄

部首	字	號碼
	短	3836
石	硫	3863
	(硫)	
	硜	3865
	硬	3866
	硝	3867
	硯	3868
	硭	3869
	确	3870
示 禾	裰	3950
	稉	3988
	稊	3999
	稀	4000
	稅	4001
	稈	4002
	稈	4003
	稂	4004
	程	4005
	稌	4006
穴	窖	4052
	窗	4053
	窘	4054
立	童	4079
	竣	4080
	竦	4081
竹	筆	4109
	筍	4110
	筌	4111
	筒	4112
	等	4113
	筏	4114
	筑	4115
	筐	4116
	筒	4117
	筋	4118
	答	4119
	筈	4120
	筓	4121
	策	4122
	筆	4123
米	粟	4240
	粢	4241

第四欄

部首	字	號碼
	粥	4242
	粵	4243
	粧	4244
糸	紙	4297
	(紝)	
	結	4326
	絓	4327
	絕	4328
	綖	4329
	絞	4330
	絡	4331
	絢	4332
	給	4333
	絨	4334
	綱	4335
	經	4336
	統	4337
	絳	4338
	絲	4339
	絮	4340
	絜	4341
	絝	5399
	(絝)	
羊	羢	4525
羽	翔	4545
	翕	4574
老 耳	聒	4599
	耋	4617
肀 肉	耾	4667
	肷	4688
	胼	4689
	腆	4690
	胺	4691
	腕	4692
	脺	4693
	腎	4694
	腑	4696
	腔	4697
	腕	4698
	脾	4699
	腊	4700
	腓	4701

第五欄

部首	字	號碼
自 白	皋	4767
	舄	4780
	鳥	4780
	(舄)	
舌 舛 艸	舒	4789
	舜	4794
	莽	4947
	(莽)	
	菟	4955
	菀	4956
	萱	4957
	菊	4958
	菌	4959
	菜	4960
	菑	4961
	菔	4962
	菖	4963
	萊	4964
	菠	4965
	華	4966
	菇	4967
	菰	4968
	菁	4969
	菲	4970
	菸	4971
	萑	4972
	菽	4973
	萁	4974
	萃	4975
	葡	4976
	萇	4977
	萄	4978
	萊	4979
	萋	4980
	萌	4981
	萍	4982
	菌	4984
	苕	4985
	菩	4986
	菱	4987
	菴	4988
	萆	4989

第六欄

部首	字	號碼
	墓	4990
	苞	4991
	苕	4992
	董	4993
	荊	4994
	菓	4995
庐	虛	5185
虫	蛔	5222
	蛛	5223
	蛟	5225
	蛤	5226
	蛭	5227
	蜑	5228
	蚰	5229
血	鯡	4671
	(脈)	
	衆	5358
行	衛	5364
	衙	5365
	街	5366
衣	裁	5402
	裂	5403
	袒	5407
	裙	5408
	裎	5409
	裡	5410
	(裏)	
	裕	5413
	補	5415
	裌	5419
覀 見	覃	5475
	覘	5484
	覗	5485
角 言	觚	5503
	觛	5504
	觶	5542
	訴	5543
	訶	5544
	診	5545
	註	5546
	詁	5547

十二畫（續）

字	字號
謐	5548
詈	5549
詠	5550
詎	5551
詐	5552
詒	5553
詔	5554
誖	5555
詖	5556
詛	5557
詞	5558
詘	5559
詵	5560
証	5561

豕・豸 · 貝

字	字號
象	5725
豼	5726
貂	5738
貯	5759
貫	5760
賁	5761
貳	5762
貴	5763
貶	5764
買	5765
貧	5766
貺	5767
費	5768
貼	5769
貽	5770
賀	5771
貿	5772
賈	5773

赤・走・足

字	字號
趁	5823
趀	5832
（趄）	5832
趙	5833
超	5834
越	5835
跋	5851
跌	5852
跎	5853
跑	5854
跙	5855
跗	5856
跚	5857
跛	5858
距	5859

車

字	字號
輇	5975
輪	5976
軸	5977
軺	5978
軹	5979
軻	5980
軼	5981
軝	5982

辛・走・辵

字	字號
迸	6106
建	6107
週	6108
進	6109
達	6110
逮	6111
逸	6112
道	6113
逯	6114

邑

字	字號
都	6214
鄆	6215
鄂	6216
鄄	6217
鄖	6218
鄃	6219

酉・里・金

字	字號
酢	6253
酤	6254
酟	6255
酥	6256
釉	6303
量	6308
鈗	6327
鈇	6328
鈀	6329
鈦	6330
鈔	6331
鉄	6332
鈉	6333
鈍	6334
鈴	6335
鈕	6336
鈞	6337
鈣	6338
鈞	6339

門

字	字號
開	6533
閒	6534
閦	6535
閨	6536
閖	6537
開	6538
閔	6539

阜

字	字號
陽	6623
匯	6624
隘	6625
隄	6626
隅	6627
隆	6628
隒	6629
隉	6630
隋	6631
隊	6632
階	6633

隹・雨

字	字號
雄	6658
雁	6659
雅	6660
集	6661
雇	6662
雯	6684
雰	6685
雱	6686
雲	6687

韋・頁・食・馬・黃・黍・黑

字	字號
韌	6766
項	6783
順	6784
須	6785
須	6786
飩	6922
馮	6923
黃	7244
黍	7247
黑	7250
脩	7272
帶	7272

十三畫

部首	單字	字號
乙	亂	45
人	催	241
	傭	242
	傲	243
	傳	244
	傴	245
	債	246
	傷	247
	僳	248
	傾	249
	僂	250
	僅	251
	僉	252
	傺	253
	傻	276
	（傻）	
刀	剷	405
	剸	406
	剽	407
	（剽）	405
力	勤	405
	勢	439
	募	440
	勤	441
	勠	442
匚	匯	467
又	叠	3586
	（疊）	
口	嗄	703
	嗅	704
	嗆	705
	嗇	706
	嗹	707
	嗩	708
	嗎	709
	嗒	710
	嗓	711
	嗔	712
	嗚	713
	嗜	714
	嗝	715
	嗯	716
	嗥	717
	嗣	718
	嗤	719
	嗡	720
	嗟	721
囗	園	801
	圓	802
	塊	855
土	塋	856
	塌	857
	塚	858
	塑	859
	塔	860
	塗	861
	塘	862
	塞	863
	填	864
	塢	865
	塏	902
	奧	944
士 大 女	嫁	1037
	嫂	1038
	媳	1039
	媵	1040
	嫄	1041
	媼	1042
	媽	1043
	媾	1044
	嫉	1045
	嫌	1046
	嫋	1065
	（孃）	
	媿	1654
	（愧）	
宀 小	寘	1140
	尠	1173
	尟	1173
	（尟）	
山	嵩	1261
	嵬	1262
	嶸	1263
	嵯	1264
巾 干 广	幌	1333
	幹	1353
	廈	1383
	廉	1384
	廊	1385
	廋	1386
弋 弓 彐 彳	弒	1417
	彀	1436
	彙	1445
	徬	1487
	徭	1488
	徯	1489
	微	1490
心	想	1644
	惹	1645
	愁	1646
	愍	1647
	愻	1648
	愆	1649
	意	1650
	愚	1651
	感	1652
	愛	1653
	愧	1654
	愴	1655
	愫	1656
	慍	1657
	愷	1658
	愾	1659
	慄	1660
	慎	1661
	慊	1662
	慌	1663
	慆	1664
	慉	1665
	惱	1670
	（惱）	
	（愿）	
	（惷）	5345
	（愛）	
戈	戡	1766
	戢	1767

火										
滗	3065	(睪)睹	3790	箬	4148	网 罰	4501	蓋	5049	複 5432
澤	3069	睽	3791	管	4149	署	4502	蓐	5050	褔 5433
火 熙	3234	瞅	3792	箭	4150	罳	4503	蒼	5051	褌 5434
熊	3235	瞄	3793	箙	4151	羽 翟	4547	蓓	5052	褐 5435
熏	3236	睿	3794	箇	4152	翠	4548	蒔	5053	褓 5436
熄	3237	瞽	3795	(筧)	4174	翠	4549	蒨	5054	褘 5437
燴	3238	石 碧	3887	(箴)米 精	4249	翡	4550	蔫	5055	褙 5438
熵	3239	碣	3888	粹	4250	耳 聚	4602	蔾	5056	褚 5439
熔	3240	碩	3889	粺	4251	聞	4603	蓍	5057	褕 5440
熒	3241	碳	3890	粽	4253	賕(膩)	6917	蓲	5058	見 覡 5486
爻 爾	3296	碴	3891	(糉)糸 綜	4353	肀肉 肇	4618	蒓	5059	角言 觫 5507
片 膡	3305	碟	3892	綠	4354	腿	4695	蕊	5060	認 5583
牛 犒	3332	禍	3955	綱	4355	膁	4717	蔗	5061	誌 5584
犖	3333	示 福	3956	綯	4356	膀	4718	蔛	5062	証 5585
犬 獄	3383	禋	3957	綬	4357	臀	4719	(蔑)	5068	誓 5586
獒	3384	禊	3958	維	4358	膈	4720	虍 虞	5189	誑 5587
獏	3386	禎	3959	綰	4359	膏	4721	虫 蝲	5248	誘 5588
獐	3387	禕	3960	網	4360	膝	4722	蜘	5249	誚 5589
玉 瑤	3477	禘	3961	綱	4361	膊	4723	蜇	5250	誠 5590
瑣	3478	種	3962	綴	4362	臣 臧	4762	蜜	5251	語 5591
瑯	3479	禾 種	4014	綵	4363	至 臺	4771	蜡	5252	誠 5592
瑰	3480	稱	4015	綹	4364	舌 舔	4790	蜾	5253	誣 5593
璉	3481	稭	4016	綸	4365	舛舟 舞	4796	蜢	5254	誤 5594
瑪	3482	稫	4017	綺	4366	艸 艋	4815	蜕	5255	誥 5595
瑳	3483	(糯)稬	4029	綻	4367	(蔆)蓤	5007	蜩	5256	誦 5596
瑲	3484	穴 窩	4057	綽	4368	蒐	5033	蜩	5257	誨 5597
瑨	3485	窪	4058	綾	4369	蒙	5034	蜮	5258	說 5598
瓦 甄	3527	窨	4059	緇	4370	蒜	5035	蜴	5259	誒 5599
甍	3528	窬	4060	緄	4371	蓟	5036	蜷	5260	豕 豪 5728
疋 疑	3589	立 竭	4082	綿	4372	蒲	5037	蜻	5261	豨 5729
疐	3590	端	4083	綦	4373	蒸	5038	蜱	5262	豸 貌 5741
疒 瘍	3642	竹 箋	4138	綮	4374	蒹	5039	蜿	5263	貍 5742
瘋	3643	箏	4139	緊	4375	蒺	5040	蜾	5264	貝 賑 5783
瘓	3644	箠	4140	緋	4376	蒌	5041	蜻	5265	賒 5785
瘖	3645	箝	4141	(緌)綬	4377	蒿	5042	蜱	5266	賓 5785
瘌	3646	箔	4142	綫	4378	蒿	5043	蟮	5304	(貲)寶 5785
瘡	3648	箕	4143	(緒)緔	4386	蓀	5044	(蜎)		賕 5786
癶 癛	3691	算	4144	(綳)綳	4433	蓁	5045	衣 裳	5425	赤 赫 5824
皮 皸	3712	箄	4145	(綳)		蓄	5046	裝	5426	走 趙 5838
血 盡	3730	箅	4146	綳	4479	蓆	5047	裹	5427	趕 5839
監	3731	箜	4147			蓉	5048	製	5429	足 踽 5876
目 睿	3788									踹 5877

部首	單字	字號	部首	單字	字號	部首	單字	字號	部首	單字	字號	部首	單字	字號	部首	單字	字號
	跟	5878		銹	6380	門	鬧	7037		嘲	739		幢	1342		慫	1713
	踵	5879		鉞	6381	鬼	魁	7049		嘴	740		幣	1343		(憩)	
車	踊	5880		鋼	6382	魚	魂	7050		嘶	741	广	廚	1392	戈	戮	1772
	輒	5989		鉋	6383	鳥	魟	7061		嘷	742		廛	1393		戲	1774
	輓	5990		銷	6384	麻	鴈	7118		嘹	743		廝	1394		(戲)	
	輔	5991		鋁	6385		鳳	7119		嘻	744		廟	1395	手	摩	2022
	輕	5992		鋇	6386		鳴	7120		嘸	745		廠	1396		摯	2023
辛	辣	6041		鋩	6387		鳶	7121		噎	746		廡	1397		擊	2024
走	遜	6132		鋙	6388	麻	麼	7242		嘿	747		廢	1398		摹	2025
	遭	6133		鉻	6389		麽	7242		噍	748		廣	1399		撫	2026
	遙	6134		鉚	6390		(麼)			嘬	749	廾	弊	1414		撐	2027
	遛	6135	門	閤	6542	鼻	鼻	7298	土	墟	874	弓	彈	1437		撐	2027
	還	6136		閨	6543	齊	齊	7303		墀	875		彉	1438		(撐)	
	遮	6137		閣	6544					墮	876	彡	影	1457		撈	2028
	遠	6138		閥	6545		**十五畫**			增	877	彳	徵	1491		撒	2029
	遢	6139		閩	6546	部首	單字	字號		墨	878		徹	1492		撇	2030
	潬	6140		閬	6547	人	僵	266		墩	879		德	1493		撥	2031
	遣	6141	阜	隙	6638		價	267		墜	880	心	慝	1685		撙	2032
邑	鄙	6224		(隙)			僻	268	大	奭	947		憨	1686		撝	2033
	鄒	6225		際	6640		儀	269	女	嫵	1029		慫	1687		撤	2034
	鄘	6226		障	6641		儂	270		(嫵)			憨	1688		撓	2035
	郯	6227	隹	雒	6669		億	271		嬉	1055		(憨)			撙	2036
	鄞	6228	雨	需	6692		儆	272		嫻	1056		慧	1689		撚	2037
	鄣	6229	革	靺	6742		儈	273		嫺	1056		慰	1690		撕	2038
酉	醒	6262		鞊	6743		儉	274		(嫺)			感	1691		撞	2039
	醇	6263		鞓	6744		儌	275		嬋	1057		慾	1692		撟	2040
	酷	6264	韋	韍	6767		僾	276		嬌	1058		慕	1693		撋	2041
	酸	6265	音	韶	6777	刂	漢	344	宀	審	1150		憂	1694		播	2042
	醋	6266	頁	領	6795	刀	劇	410		寫	1151		慮	1695		撩	2043
	醃	6267		顆	6796		劈	411		寬	1152		慶	1696		撩	2044
	醅	6268	風	颯	6838		劉	412		寮	1153		憍	1697		撲	2045
金	銀	6368		颱	6839		創	413	尸	層	1204		憐	1698		撬	2046
	銥	6369	食	飼	6860		劍	414		履	1205		憎	1699		撰	2047
	銃	6370		飴	6861		劌	443	山	嶙	1268		憔	1700		撮	2048
	銅	6371		飽	6862	匚	匱	469		嶒	1269		憚	1701		搞	2049
	銑	6372		飾	6863	厂	厲	513		嶓	1270		憧	1702		撣	2050
	銓	6373	馬	馭	6928	口	噉	661		嶝	1271		憬	1703		撢	2050
	銖	6374		駃	6929		(啖)			嶠	1272		憒	1704	支	敵	2141
	銘	6375	骨	骰	6993		嘩	734		嶢	1273		憫	1705		敷	2142
	銚	6376		骯	6994		噓	735		嶷	1274		憮	1706		數	2143
	銛	6377	髟	髣	7011		嘮	736	巾	幟	1339		憒	1707		毆	2144
	銜	6378		髥	7012		嘰	737		幞	1340		憭	1708	日	暮	2274
	銼	6379		髦	7013		嘰	738		幡	1341		憚	1709			

	暫 2275	潁 3068	臆 4053	磅 3898	緅 4384	蔓 5069

行衣見角言		走足身車走邑		西金門阜雨		青非革頁風食馬骨彡門鬼魚		鳥鹿麥麻黍黑鼎齒		
行 衝	5368	質	5797	鄰	6232	需	6696	鳥 鳿	7122	
衞	5369	賬	5798	鄹	6233	霉	6697	鳷	7123	
衡	5370	賫	7305	鄶	6234	青 靚	6724	鴉	7124	
衣 褐	5441	走 趣	5840	鄲	6235	非 靠	6729	鳩	7125	
襬	5442	趙	5841	鄺	6236	革 鞍	6745	鴃	7125	
褪	5443	足 踐	5881	西 醃	6269	鞌	6746	(鳩)	3300	
襪	5444	踠	5882	醋	6270	鞏	6747	鷹	7126	
褡	5445	踏	5883	醇	6271	頁 頡	6797	鹿 麋	7219	大
褥	5447	踝	5884	醉	6272	頫	6798	麥 麩	7235	女
褲	5448	踞	5885	醆	6273	頦	6799	麴	7236	
見 褲	5449	踟	5886	醋	6274	頜	6800	麻 麾	7243	
覷	5487	金 踥	5887	醁	6275	頯	6801	黍 黎	7248	子
角 觭	5508	踢	5888	金 銳	6391	風 颺	6840	黑 黕	7251	宀
言 課	5600	踣	5889	銷	6392	食 餂	6864	鼐	7284	寸
誰	5601	踧	5890	鋅	6393	餃	6865	鼏	7285	山
誶	5602	踦	5891	鋨	6394	餐	6866	齒 齒	7307	
誹	5603	踖	5892	銅	6395	餉	6867			广
誼	5604	踔	5893	鋰	6396	餓	6868	**十六畫**		弓
調	5605	踩	5894	鋯	6397	餌	6869	部首 單字 字號		彐
諂	5606	踦	5895	鐵	6398	飪	6870	人 儐	277	彳
諄	5607	踪	5896	鋁	6399	餅	6871	儒	278	心
談	5608	身 輞	5964	銀	6400	馬 駐	6930	儔	279	
諉	5609	車 輻	5993	鋅	6401	駑	6931	償	280	
請	5610	輗	5994	鋱	6402	駒	6932	儘	281	
諍	5611	輘	5995	鋏	6403	駔	6933	八 冀	333	
諏	5612	輪	5996	鋒	6404	駕	6934	冫 凝	345	
諑	5613	輝	5997	鋼	6405	駘	6935	刀 劑	415	
諒	5614	輞	5998	鋯	6406	駙	6936	劂	416	
論	5615	輵	5999	鋤	6407	駛	6937	力 勳	444	
諗	5616	輦	6000	鋑	6408	駝	6938	口 噤	750	
諆	5617	耕	6001	鋞	6409	駟	6939	器	751	
豆 豌	5716	耩	6002	鋪	6410	骨 骷	6995	噦	752	
豎	5717	輪	6003	鋩	6411	髟 骻	7014	噪	753	
貝 賫	5787	輨	6004	銹	6412	髮	7015	噫	754	
賙	5788	輮	6005	門 閬	6548	髯	7016	噬	755	
賜	5789	走 遭	6142	閭	6549	髫	7017	噥	756	
賞	5790	遨	6143	閫	6550	髭	7018	噲	757	
賠	5791	適	6144	閱	6551	門 鬼 魄	7051	噥	758	
賡	5792	遮	6145	阜 隤	6642	魅	7052	噯	759	
賢	5793	遯	6146	隣	6643	魚 魷	7062	噹	760	
賣	5794	邑 鄧	6230	雨 震	6693	魯	7063	噴	761	
賤	5795	鄭	6231	霄	6694	魴	7064	土 墳	881	
賦	5796			霆	6695					

大 女 子 宀 寸 山 广 弓 彐 彳 心	
壁	882
墼	883
壅	884
壇	885
墻(牆)	3300
大 奮	948
女 嬰	1059
嬋	1060
嬙	1061
嬡	1062
嬴	1063
嬝	1064
嬛	1065
子 學	1094
寸 導	1154
宀 寰	1167
山 嶧	1275
嶮	1276
嶰	1400
广 廩	1401
弓 彊	1434
(強)	
彐 彈	1446
(彊)	
彳 徼	1494
心 憑	1710
憨	1711
憩	1712
憊	1713
憲	1714
憝	1715
憖	1716
憨	1717
憲	1718
憤	1719
憶	1720
憾	1721
憒	1723
懂	1724
懈	1725
懊	1726

諧	5629	輳	6012	閣	6555		骸	6997		勝	1067	日 暖 2289
諫	5630	輹	6013	閤	6556		骼	6998		嬪	1068	曧 2290
諸	5631	辛 辨	6042	闊	6557	彭	髻	7019	子	孺	1095	木 檀 2607
諱	5632	辨	6043	阜		隨	6644	尤	髦	7020	尷	1178	檄 2608
諳	5633	辵 遲	6147	隆	6645	門	閼	7039	尸	屢	1206	檜 2609
諝	5634	遵	6148	陸	6646	魚	鮎	7065	山	嶸	1277	檔 2610
諟	5635	避	6149	隹	雕	6670	鮑	7066		嶺	1278	檉 2611
諷	5636	遷	6150	雖	6671	鮒	7067		嶼	1279	檜 2612
諸	5637	遷	6151	雨 霍	6698	鳥	鴒	7127	嶽	1280	檎 2613
諼	5638	選	6152	霙	6699	鴕	7128	巾	幬	1344	檟 2614
諾	5639	遯	6153	霏	6700	鴛	7129	幫	1345	檢 2615
諜	5640	遺	6154	霓	6701	鴉	7130	幪	1346	檣 2616
謁	5641	遼	6155	霜	6702	鴝	7131	弓 彌	1439	檏 2617
謂	5642	邑 鄭	6237	霖	6703	鵠	7132	彳 徽	1495	檨 2618
諲	5643	鄙	6238	青 靜	6725	鴦	7133	心 應	1729	檵 2619
諲	5644	酉 醒	6276	靛	6726	鴨	7134	懋	1730	檖 2630
諴	5645	醍	6277	面 靦	6732	鳧	7135	懇	1731	(檥)
諲	5646	醐	6278	革 鞘	6748	鴟	7136	懑	1732	欠 歙 2675
謙	5647	金 鋸	6413	頁 頴	4207	鹿 麈	7220	懦	1733	歔 2676
豕 豭	5731	鋼	6414	(穎)		麇	7221	懦	1734	欽 2677
豬	5732	鉥	6415	頭	6802	黑 黔	7252	懜	1735	歹 殭 2711
貝 貓	5743	鍊	6416	頭	6803	默	7253	(懞)		殮 2712
賭	5799	銅	6417	頰	6804	鼎 鼐	7286	懌	1741	毛 氈 2734
賴	5800	錄	6418	頷	6805	龍 龍	7325	(懨)		氌 2745
赭	5825	鋪	6419	頹	6806	龜	7328	戈 戲	1774	毽 2745
赬	5826	錐	6420	頸	6807				手 擊	2069	(毽)
足 蹂	5897	錘	6421	頻	6808	**十七畫**		擎	2070	水 澤 3119
蹠	5898	鋸	6422	頻	6809	部首	單字	字號	擘	2071	濛 3120
蹟	5899	錚	6423	食 餐	6872	人	償	282	擠	2072	澀 3121
蹕	5900	錠	6424	餚	6873		僵	283	擡	2073	濠 3122
蹀	5901	錡	6425	餞	6874		優	284	擢	2074	濟 3123
蹄	5902	錢	6426	餓	6875	力	勱	445	擣	2075	濤 3124
蹂	5903	錦	6427	餔	6876	口	嚎	762	擬	2076	濡 3125
蹄	5904	鋸	6428	餖	6877		嚅	763	擯	2077	濫 3126
蹋	5905	錮	6429	餗	6878		嚦	764	擦	2078	濯 3127
蹐	5906	錮	6430	餘	6879		嚀	765	擱	2079	濩 3128
車 輯	6006	錯	6431	馬 駭	6940		嚇	766	擭	2080	濱 3129
轇	6007	錳	6432	駱	6941		嚏	767	搗	2081	濰 3130
輻	6008	錢	6433	駰	6942	土	壓	886	撐	2082	濱 3131
輪	6009	門 閻	6552	駮	6943		壖	887	支 斂	2146	濩 3132
輻	6010	閭	6553	駢	6944		壑	888	斤 斷	2127	濕 3133
輮	6011	閼	6554	骨 骼	6996	女	壕 嬰	889 1066	(斷)		火 營 3264 / 燧 3265

部首	字	號
火	燠	3266
	燦	3267
	燬	3268
	燥	3269
	燴	3270
	燭	3271
	爕	3272
爿	牆	3300
犬	獲	3394
	獮	3395
	獯	3396
	獰	3397
玉	璦	3502
	環	3504
	璪	3505
	璐	3506
	璨	3507
瓦	甑	3532
疒	癤	3658
	(瘤)	
	療	3665
	癆	3666
	癌	3667
	癍	3668
	癇	3669
	癉	3670
	癟	3671
白	皤	3708
皿	盩	3736
	盪	3737
目	瞬	3807
	瞰	3808
	瞳	3809
	瞪	3810
	瞭	3811
	瞶	3812
	瞧	3813
	瞼	3814
	瞥	3815
矢	矯	3838
	短	3839
石	磺	3908
	磴	3909

部首	字	號
	磷	3910
	磧	3911
	磽	3912
	礁	3913
示	禧	3967
	禪	3968
	禨	3969
禾	穉	4009
	(稚)	
	穗	4031
穴	窾	4066
	窿	4067
竹	篠	4180
	篳	4181
	笾	4182
	篾	4183
	篷	4184
	簌	4185
	簏	4186
	簇	4187
	篸	4188
	簀	4189
	簋	4190
	簁	4191
	簣	4192
	簍	4193
	節	4194
	簎	4195
	簿	4196
	簜	4197
米	糜	4259
	糞	4260
	糙	4261
	糝	4262
	糟	4263
	糠	4264
	糗	4265
	糧	4266
	(糧)	
糸	縫	4416
	縞	4417
	縱	4418

部首	字	號
	縮	4419
	縵	4420
	縹	4421
	繂	4422
	縷	4423
	縹	4424
	總	4425
	縶	4426
	縻	4427
	繁	4428
	縈	4429
	縣	4430
	績	4431
	繅	4432
	綳	4433
	繆	4434
	縴	4435
缶	罃	4481
	罇	4482
网	罥	4507
羽	翳	4559
	翼	4560
耳	聯	4604
	聰	4605
	聲	4606
	聳	4607
	聱	4608
肉	膿	4735
	膾	4736
	膾	4737
	膚	4738
	臀	4739
	臂	4740
	臁	4741
	臆	4742
	臉	4743
	膝	4744
	膿	4745
	膴	4746
	膻	4747
臣	臨	4763
艮	艱	4825
艸	薄	5111

部首	字	號
	蕁	5112
	薊	5113
	薔	5114
	薐	5115
	薇	5116
	蕇	5117
	薊	5118
	薤	5119
	蕙	5120
	稜	5121
	薑	5122
	薔	5123
	薙	5124
	薛	5125
	薀	5126
	薦	5127
	薨	5128
	薪	5129
	截	5130
	薛	5131
虍	虧	5191
虫	螫	5301
	蟥	5302
	蟎	5303
	螵	5304
	螯	5305
	螳	5306
	螺	5307
	螻	5308
	蟊	5309
	螶	5310
	蟀	5311
	蟄	5312
	蟆	5313
	蟈	5314
	蟋	5315
	蟑	5316
	孟	5317
衣	褒	5453
	褔	5454
	(褘)	
	襄	5455
	褻	5456

部首	字	號
	褻	5456
	(褻)	
	襠	5458
見	覬	5491
	覯	5492
	覷	5510
角言	謎	5648
	謄	5649
	謊	5650
	諡	5651
	謇	5652
	謖	5653
	謐	5654
	謗	5655
	謙	5656
	講	5657
	謝	5658
	謠	5659
	謨	5660
	謅	5661
	謐	5662
谷	谿	5707
	谿	5708
	豁	5709
豆	豌	5718
豕	豭	5733
豸	貌	5744
貝	賺	5801
	賻	5802
	購	5803
	賽	5804
	賸	5805
	賮	5811
	賰	5812
	蟎	5813
走	趨	5842
足	蹈	5907
	蹇	5908
	蹉	5909
	蹊	5910
	蹋	5911
	蹌	5912
	蹐	5913
	蹁	5914

部首	字	號
車	輾	6014
	輿	6015
	轂	6016
	轄	6017
	轅	6018
	轀	6019
足	避	6156
	邃	6157
	邂	6158
	邁	6159
	邋	6160
	還	6161
	邅	6162
邑西	鄹	6239
	醜	6279
	醞	6280
	醚	6281
	醛	6282
	醣	6283
	醢	6284
金	鍊	6435
	錨	6436
	鍋	6437
	鍍	6438
	鍔	6439
	鍘	6440
	鍛	6441
	鎂	6442
	鎣	6443
	鍳	6444
	鍰	6445
	鍵	6446
	鍼	6447
	鍾	6448
	鎊	6449
	鍺	6450
	鍶	6451
	鎄	6452
	鎇	6453
	鍬	6454
門	闈	6558
	闊	6559
	闆	6560

部首	單字	字號		部首	單字	字號
門	闋	6561		髟	鬖	7072
	闊	6562		鳥	鴿	7137
	闌	6563			鵁	7138
	闈	6564			鴻	7139
	闉	6565			鴰	7140
	闆	6566			鵝	7141
卓	隱	6648			鴛	7142
	隱	6649			鷙	7143
	陰	6650			鴰	7144
隶	隸	6653			鴟	7145
隹	雔	6672		鹿	麋	7222
雨	霜	6704		麥	麴	7237
	霆	6705			麩	7238
	霝	6706		黃	黏	7245
革	鞠	6749		黍	黎	7249
韋	韓	6768		黑	點	7254
	韔	6769			黛	7255
頁	顆	6810			黜	7256
	領	6811			黝	7257
風	颿			黹	黻	7273
食	餅	6880		黽	黿	7276
	餉	6881		鼻	鼾	7299
	餛	6882		齊	齋	7304
	餞	6883		齒	齙	7308
	餡	6884		龠	龠	7329
	餧	6885				

十八畫

部首	單字	字號
	館	6886
	課	6887
	餲	6888
首	餴	6917
馬	驅	6945
	駿	6946
	騂	6947
	駸	6948
	駬	6949
	駍	6950
骨	骭	6999
髟	黔	7021
	髻	
魚	鮫	7068
	鮪	7069
	鮭	7070
	鮮	7071

部首	單字	字號
人	儲	285
又	叢	526
口	嚕	768
	嚙	7317
	(醫)	
土	壙	890
	壘	891
女	嬪	1069
巾	幬	1347
ヨ	彝	1446
心	懟	1735
	懣	1736
	懟	1737
戈	戴	1775
	戳	1776

部首	單字	字號		部首	單字	字號
手	擥	2083		木	檬	350
	擲	2084			檸	2620
	擷	2085			檣	2621
	擴	2086			櫅	2622
	擺	2087			檻	2623
	擾	2088			櫃	2624
	鏑	2089			檔	2625
	擻	2090			檳	2626
	攄	2091			櫂	2627
	擋	2092			檯	3691
	(擥)			欠	歟	2678
	擧(舉)	4784			歸	2690
支	斃	2148		止	殯	2713
斤	斷	2173		水	瀋	3134
方	旛	2192			濼	3135
日	曜	2291			濱	3136
	曚	2292			瀆	3137
	曨	2293			瀑	3138
	曚	2294			瀉	3139
月	朦	2328				

部首	單字	字號		部首	單字	字號
水	瀟	3140		竹	簣	4206
	瀏	3141			簿	4207
	瀅	3142			簫	4208
	瀍	3143		米	糧	4267
	瀘	3144		糸	繒	4436
火	燻(燻)	3236			織	4437
	燮	3273			繕	4438
	燾	3274			繚	4439
	爐	3275			繳	4440
	燼	3276			繙	4441
爪	爵	3289			繞	4442
犬	獷	3398			繢	4443
	獵	3399			繟	4444
玉	璧	3503			繩	4483
	璦	3509		缶	罈	4484
	璿	3510		羊	羹	4531
瓦	甕	3533		羽	翹	4561
	甏	3534			翻	4562
广	癖	3672			翺	4563
	癘	3673		耳	職	4609
	癒	3674			聰	4610
目	瞼	3816			聶	4611
	瞼	3817			聵	4748
	瞽	3818		肉	臍	4749
	瞿	3819		臼	舊	4785
石	礎	3914		舟	艟	4818
示	禮	3970		艸	薩	5132
禾	穡	4032			薯	5133
	穢	4033			薰	5134
	穠	4034			薺	5135
穴	竄	4068			藉	5136
	竅	4069			藍	5137
竹	簞	4198			薹	5138
	簡	4199			藏	5139
	簦	4200			藐	5140
	(簡)	4200			藕	5141
	簧	4201		虫	蟣	5318
	簦	4202			蟒	5319
	簠	4203			蟠	5320
	簣	4204			蟢	5321
	簪	4205			蟥	5322
					蟪	5323
					蟬	5324

部首	單字	字號
虫	蟲	5325
	蟟	5326
	蟮	5327
衣	襠	5460
	襟	5461
	襖	5462
	襜	5463
	覆	5476
見	覲	5493
	覷	5494
	覰	5511
角	觴	5663
言	謦	5664
	謦	5665
	謨	5666
	謫	5667
	謬	5668
	謳	5669
	謹	5670
	謾	5671
豆	豐	5719
豕	貕	5745
貝	贄	5806
	贅	5807
足	蹕	5915
	蹕	5916
	蹙	5917
	蹣	5918
	蹠	591
	蹤	591
	蹢	592
	蹜	592
	蹡	592
	蹟	592
	蹣	592
身	軀	596
車	轉	602
	轆	602
	轇	602
辵	邇	616

邑	遵 6164
	邈 6165
邑	鄺 6240
西	醫 6285
	醯 6286
	醪 6287
	醬 6288
	醴 6289
里	釐 6309
金	鎖 6455
	鎰 6456
	鎊 6457
	鎛 6458
	鎔 6459
	鎗 6460
	鎦 6461
	鎛 6462
	鎧 6463
	鎬 6464
	鎳 6465
	鎰 6466
	鎳 6467
	鎢 6468
	鎩 6469
	鎌 6470
	鎡 6471
	鍋 6472
	鎵 6473
門	闈 6567
	闉 6568
	闌 6569
	闊 6570
	闋 6571
	闍 6572
	闐 6573
阜	隳 6651
隹	雙 6673
	雛 6674
	雜 6675
	雞 6676
	雞 6677
	雜 6678
雨	霤 6710

	(雷)
青	靜 6727
革	鞭 6750
	鞦 6751
	鞳 6752
	鞨 6753
	鞫 6754
	鞬 6755
	鞮 6770
韋	額 6812
頁	題 6813
	題 6814
	顎 6815
	顏 6816
	顒 6817
	顓 6818
風	颺 6842
食	饕 6889
	饒 6890
	餼 6891
	餿 6892
	餽 6893
香	馦 6919
馬	騎 6951
	駢 6952
	騅 6954
	騄 6955
	騇 6956
骨	骿 7000
	髁 7001
	髀 7023
彡	鬃 7024
	鬈 7025
鬥	鬩 7040
鬼	魍 7053
	魑 7054
	魏 7055
	魅 7056
魚	鯀 7073
	鮸 7074
	鯁 7075
	鯉 7076

| 紫 7077 |
鳥	鴿 7146
	鵬 7147
	鵠 7148
	鵒 7149
	鵨 7150
	鵪 7151
	鵝 7152
	鶩 7152
	(鵝)
	鵨 7152
	(鵝)
	鵠 7153
	鵰 7154
鹿	麌 7223
	麋 7224
黑	點 7258
	黝 7259
黽	黿 7277
鼓	鼕 7288
鼠	鼬 7292
	鼣 7293
齒	齕 7309

十九畫

部首	單字	字號
口	嚮	769
	嚥	770
	嚦	771
土	嚨	892
	壞	893
子	擘	1096
	(孼)	
宀	孽	5161
	寵	1155
	寶	1156
	(寶)	
广	廬	1402
	龐	1403
心	懲	1738
	懷	1739
	懶	1740

	憻 1741
手	攀 2093
	攏 2094
方	旞 2193
日	曠 2295
	曝 2296
木	櫚 2628
	櫟 2629
	櫓 2630
	櫚 2631
	櫝 2632
	櫓 2633
欠	歠 2679
水	瀘 3145
	瀕 3146
	瀦 3147
	瀝 3148
	瀟 3149
	瀠 3150
	瀨 3151
	瀧 3152
	瀣 3153
	瀜 3154
	瀛 3155

火	爆 3277
	爍 3278
	爇 3279
片	牘 3307
牛	犢 3335
犬	獸 3400
	獺 3401
玉	璽 3508
	璧 3511
	瓊 3512
	璧 3520
瓜	瓣 3584
	瓣 3585
田	疇 3675
疒	癟 3675
	癡 3676
皿	鹽 3738
目	矇 3820
矢	矱 3840
石	礙 3915

示	禰 3971
	禱 3972
禾	穢 4035
	穗 4036
	穧 4269
竹	(穧)
	簫 4209
	簸 4210
	簽 4211
	簾 4212
	簞 4213
	簫 4215
	簜 4216
米	櫱 4268
糸	繩 4445
	繪 4446
	繮 4447
	繯 4448
	繳 4449
	繴 4450
	繹 4451
	繫 4452
	繭 4453
	繰 4454

缶	罌 4508
网	罷 4509
羊	羶 4532
	羹 4533
羽	翻 4564
	翽 4565
肉	臘 4750
	臚 4751
舟	艤 4819
艸	藕 5142
	藜 5143
	藝 5144
	藍 5145
	薄 5146
	藤 5147
	藥 5148

	藩 5149
	藪 5150
	蕾 5151
	蘊 5163
	(蘊)
虫	蟹 5328
	蟀 5328
	(蟹)
	蠅 5329
	蟺 5330
	蟻 5331
	蟾 5332
	蠅 5333
	蟲 5334
	蠍 5335
	蠃 5336
	蠆 5459
衣	蠔 5464
	蠕 5465
襾	蠢 5477
	蟈 5478
見	蠖 5494
	(艤)
	覷 5495
言	譏 5672
	譁 5673
	證 5674
	譖 5675
	譜 5676
	識 5677
	譙 5678
	譚 5679
	譊 5680
	譜 5681
	譞 5682
貝	贗 5808
	贈 5809
	贊 5810
	贇 5811
	贋 5812
足	蹲 5928
	蹩 5929
	蹬 5930

部首	單字	字號	部首	單字	字號	部首	單字	字號
	蹭	5931	非	靡	6730		鵒	7162
	蹛	5932	革	鞲	6756		鶂	7163
	蹴	5933		鞳	6757		鶊	7164
	蹶	5934		鞴	6758		鷗	7165
	蹺	5935		鞶	6759	鹿	麠	7225
	蹻	5936	韋	韜	6771		麒	7226
	蹼	5937		韞	6772		麑	7227
	躄	5938	音	韻	6778		麗	7228
	躑	5939	頁	頤	6819		麗	7229
	躅	5940		願	6820	麥	麵	7239
車	轍	6023		顆	6821		黼	7274
	轎	6024		顙	6822		黿	7278
辛	辭	6044		類	6823		鼓	7289
走	邊	6166		領	6824		鼩	7300
酉	醮	6290	風	颶	6843		齗	7310
	醱	6291		飆	6844			
	醲	6292	食	餿	6894	**二十畫**		
金	鏃	6474		鼠	6895	部首	單字	字號
	鏇	6475		餾	6896	力	勸	446
	鍛	6476		餵	6897	口	嚴	772
	鏒	6477		餽	6898		嚷	773
	鏈	6478	馬	騖	6957	土	壤	894
	鑒	6479		騙	6958	女	孃	1007
	鏑	6480		騣	6959	（娘）		
	鏖	6481		騤	6960		孀	1070
	鏗	6482		騧	6961		孃	1071
	鏘	6483		騜	6962		孽	1096
	鏹	6484	彡	鬜	7026		寶	1156
	鏜	6485	魚	鯤	7027	子	巇	1282
	鏝	6486		鯡	7078	山	巉	1283
	鏞	6487		鯖	7079		懸	1742
	鏡	6488		鯛	7080	心	懺	1743
	鏢	6489		鯢	7081		懵	1746
	鏷	6490		鯨	7082	（懺）		
	鏨	6491		鯪	7083	手	攔	2095
	鏤	6492		鮣	7084		攙	2096
門	關	6574	鳥	鵬	7155		攘	2097
	闒	6575		鵰	7156		攖	2098
阜	隴	6652		鶉	7157	支	敵	2149
	隳	6679		鵳	7158	方	旟	2194
	雞	6680		鵲	7159	日	曦	2297
雨	霧	6707		鵼	7160		曨	2298
	霪	6708		鶇	7161			

部首	單字	字號	部首	單字	字號	部首	單字	字號
月	朧	2329	羽	翻	4566		躊	5944
木	櫪	2634		耀	4567		躋	5945
	櫟	2635	肉	臚	4752		躂	5946
	櫨	2636		朧	4753		躍	5947
	櫸	2637	舟	艦	4820	車	轓	6025
（櫳）	櫳	2637		艨	4821		轔	6026
	櫼	2638	艸	蘭	5152		轕	6027
	櫱	2639		蘗	5153		轗	6028
水	瀾	3156		蘄	5154		轘	6029
	瀹	3157		蘸	5155	辛	辭	6241
	瀼	3158		藻	5156	酉	醴	6293
	瀲	3159		藿	5157		醲	6294
火	爐	3280		蘋	5158		醳	6295
牛	犠	3336		蘅	5159	釆	釋	6304
	犨	3337		蘆	5160	金	鐃	6493
犬	獻	3402		蘗	5161		鐋	6494
	獺	3403		蘇	5162		鐐	6495
玉	瓏	3513		蘊	5163		鐙	6496
	瓔	3514		蘋	5164		鐦	6497
疒	癢	3677		藉	5165		鐧	6498
	癥	3678		蘢	5166		錯	6499
	癩	3679	虫	蟶	5337		鐲	6500
目	矍	3821		蠖	5338	門	闞	6576
石	礫	3916		蠕	5339		闟	6577
	礩	3917		蠔	5340		闠	6578
	礬	3918		蠐	5341	雨	霰	6709
	礦	3919		蠑	5342		霤	6710
穴	竇	4070	衣	褫	5466		露	6711
立	競	4084		襦	5467	革	鞹	6825
竹	籃	4217		褻	5494	頁	顥	6825
	籌	4218	見	覷	5494	風	飄	6845
	籍	4219	（覰）			食	饅	6899
	糯	4269		覺	5496		饉	6900
	糲	4270	角	觸	5512		饊	6901
糸	辮	4455	言	議	5683		饋	6913
	纂	4456		譟	5684	（饝）		
	纈	4457		警	5685	香	馨	6920
	纊	4458		譬	5686	馬	騫	6963
	繼	4459		譯	5687		驁	6964
	纈	4460	貝	贍	5813		騰	6965
	纁	4461		贏	5814		騷	6966
缶	罌	4486	足	躄	5941		騮	6967
				躇	5942			
				躅	5943			

部首	單字	字號
彡	髏	6968
髟	鬢	7028
	鬘	7029
	鬈	7030
門	鬧	7041
魚	鯽	7085
	鰈	7086
	鰌	7087
	鰒	7088
	鰍	7089
	鰌	7090
	鰓	7091
鳥	鶖	7166
	鶩	7167
	鶚	7168
	鶡	7169
	鶿	7170
	鶉	7171
	鶗	7172
鹵	鹹	7211
麥	麵	7240
黑	黥	7260
	黧	7261
	黨	7262
	黮	7263
	黤	7264
鼎	鼯	7294
	鼱	7311
	齟	7312
	齡	7313
	齣	7314
	齦	7315

二十一畫

部首	單字	字號
人	儹	286
口	嚽	774
	嚾	775
	嚿	776
	嚴	777
夊	夒	906
尸	屬	1207
山	巍	1284

部首	單字	字號
广	龎	1404
心	懼	1744
	懾	1745
手	攜	1747
	攝	2099
	攛	2100
	攘	2101
文	斕	2155
日	曩	2299
木	欄	2640
	櫻	2641
	欅	2642
	欃	2643
	欂	2644
	槊	2645
	殲	2646
歹	殲	2714
水	瀺	2832
(法)		
	瀹	3160
	瀼	3161
	灌	3162
火	爛	3281
玉	瓔	3515
瓦	甒	3535
广	癩	3680
目	矙	3822
石	礬	3920
	礦	3921
穴	竇	4071
竹	籍	4216
(籀)		
	籐	4220
	籤	4226
米	糲	4271
糸	纈	4462
	纊	4463
	續	4464
	纏	4465
	纍	4466
	纇	4467
缶	罍	4487

部首	單字	字號
羊	羼	4535
	羺	4754
艸	蘕	5167
	蘗	5168
	薛	5169
	藜	5170
	蘭	5171
	蘭	5172
	蘇	5173
虫	蠟	5343
	蠢	5344
	蠡	5345
	蠣	5346
	蟻	5359
血	衊	5468
衣	襯	5495
見	(覷)	
	覽	5497
言	護	5688
	譴	5689
	譬	5690
貝	贓	5815
	贖	5816
	贇	5817
	躊	5949
足	躍	5950
車	轟	6030
	轡	6031
	轞	6032
辛	辯	6046
邑	鄹	6242
酉	醴	6296
金	鐲	6501
	鐫	6502
	鐵	6503
	鐶	6504
	鐸	6505
	鐺	6506
	鐳	6507
	鐽	6508
	鐽	6509

部首	單字	字號
門	闢	6579
	闡	6580
	闥	6581
雨	霹	6712
	霸	6713
	雩	6714
	殰	6733
面	靧	6826
頁	顧	6826
	顥	6827
	顬	6828
	顦	6829
風	颿	6846
	飆	6846
	(飆)	
飛	飜	6848
食	饋	6902
	饌	6903
	饖	6904
	饒	6905
	饘	6906
	饐	6907
馬	驊	6969
	鷙	6970
	驀	6971
	驂	6972
	驃	6973
	驄	6974
	驅	6975
骨	髏	7002
彡	鬘	7031
鬼	魑	7057
	魔	7058
魚	鰱	7092
	鰳	7093
	鰮	7094
	鰭	7095
	鰷	7096
	鮧	7097
鳥	鶴	7173
	鶹	7174
	鶼	7175
	鷉	7176
	鶿	7176

部首	單字	字號
(鶿)		
	鶴	7177
	鶺	7178
	鶲	7179
	鶵	7180
	鷁	7181
	鶺	7182
	雞	7183
	縠	7184
	鶏	7185
鹵	鹺	7212
	鹻	7213
鹿	麝	7230
黑	黯	7265
	黰	7266
	黱	7279
	鼕	7290
鼓	鼙	7305
齊	齏	7316
齒	齦	7317
	齩	7318

二十二畫

部首	單字	字號
人	儼	287
口	囓	778
	囔	779
	囊	780
女	孌	1072
子	孿	1097
山	巒	1285
	巓	1286
弓	彎	1440
心	懿	1746
手	攤	2102
	攢	2103
	攤	2104
	攝	2105
木	權	2647
欠	歟	2680
水	灑	3163
	灘	3164
火	爝	3282

部首	單字	字號
犬	玀	3404
瓜	甕	3521
田	疊	3586
广	癰	3681
	癱	3682
	癬	3683
石	礴	3922
示	禳	3973
	禴	3974
禾	穰	4037
穴	竄	4221
竹	籜	4222
	籟	4223
	籠	4224
	籙	4225
米	糴	4272
	糵	4273
(粱)		
糸	纓	4468
	纔	4488
	纕	4489
网	羈	4510
耳	聽	4612
	聾	4613
肉	臟	4755
舟	艫	4822
虫	蠨	5347
	蠱	5355
衣	襲	5469
	襴	5470
見	覬	5498
言	讀	5691
	讌	5692
	讎	5693
	讒	5694
貝	贖	5818
	贐	5819
足	躑	5951
	躒	5952
	躓	5953
	躔	5954

二十二畫（承前頁）

部首	單字	字號
車	欒	6033
	欏	6034
邑	酈	6243
	鄺	6244
金	鑊	6510
	鑄	6511
	鑑	6512
	鑒	6513
雨	霽	6715
	霾	6716
革	韁	6761
	韃	6762
音	響	6779
頁	顥	6830
食	饔	6908
	饕	6909
	饗	6910
	體	6911
馬	驍	6976
	驊	6977
	驌	6978
	驖	6979
	驔	6980
	驒	7032
彡	鬚	7047
鬥	鬨	7098
魚	鱷	7099
	鱉	7100
	鰱	7101
	鱐	7102
	鰽	7103
	鰹	7104
鳥	鷦	7186
	鷥	7187
	鷫	7188
	鷲	7189
	鷺	7190
鹿	麒	7231
鼠	鼱	7295
齒	齯	7319
	齰	7320
龍	襲	7326

部首	單字	字號
金	鑫	7327
龠	龢	7330

部首	單字	字號
讌		5696
讔		5697
讕		5697
足	躜	5955
車	轤	6035
	轣	6036
辵	邐	6167
	邏	6168
金	鑠	6347
(鉋)		
	鑢	6514
	鑣	6515
	鑥	6516
	鑤	6517
	鑧	6518
面	靨	6734
頁	顬	6831
	顯	6832
食	饜	6912
馬	驗	6981
	驚	6982
	驛	6983
骨	髓	7003
	髑	7004
	髐	7005
	髏	7006
彡	鬢	7033
魚	鱔	7105
	鱖	7106
	鱗	7107
	鱒	7108
	鱣	7281
鳥	鷺	7191
	鷯	7192
	鷳	7193
	鷲	7194
	鷸	7195
	鷥	7196

部首	單字	字號
鷫		7197
鸑		7198
鹿	麟	7232
黑	黟	7267
	黴	7268
鼠	鼷	7296
	鼸	7297
齊	齏	7306

部首	單字	字號
金	鑪	6519
	鑫	6520
雨	靂	6717
	靄	6718
	靆	6719
	靈	6720
革	韉	6763
馬	驟	6984
骨	髕	7007
彡	鬟	7034
鬥	鬮	7042
鬼	魘	7059
魚	鱨	7109
	鱧	7110
	鱮	7199
	鱭	7200
	鱯	7201
	鱲	7202
	鷹	7203
齒	齲	7214
	齷	7280
鼻	齉	7301
齒	齶	7322
	齵	7323

部首	單字	字號
肉	臠	4756
	臡	4758
艸	虆	5179
虫	蠼	5354
襾	覊	5480
見	觀	5499
角	觿	5513
言	讞	5702
	讜	5746
(讟)		
足	躪	5957
	躡	5958
酉	釁	6300
金	鑼	6521
	鑽	6522
雨	靆	6721
頁	顱	6834
食	饢	6913
彡	鬣	7035
齒	齼	7215
黃	黌	7246
黑	黷	7269
	黶	7281
	黸	7282
齒	齻	7324

二十三畫

部首	單字	字號
山	巖	1287
	巘	1288
心	戀	1748
	戁	1749
手	攪	2106
	攦	2107
	攥	2108
	攢	2109
	攩	2110
日	曬	2300
木	欒	2648
犬	玁	3405
广	癰	3684
	癱	3685
竹	籤	4226
	籣	4227
	籬	4228
米	糵	4273
糸	纞	4469
	纓	4470
	纘	4471
	纖	4472
肉	臙	4757
艸	蘸	5174
	蘺	5175
	薜	5176
	蘿	5177
	虀	5178
虫	蠱	5348
	蠲	5349
	蠵	5350
衣	襴	5471
	襳	5479
言	變	5695

二十四畫

部首	單字	字號
口	囑	781
	囔	7317
(醫)		
土	壩	895
手	攬	2111
水	灘	3165
	灟	3166
广	癲	3686
	癱	3687
目	矗	3823
糸	纛	4473
缶	罐	4490
网	羈	4511
色	艷	4828
虫	蠹	5351
	蠻	5352
	蠶	5353
行	衢	5372
衣	襯	5373
言	讓	5698
	讒	5699
	讖	5700
	讔	5701
豆	豔	5720
貝	贛	5820
足	躞	6297
酉	釀	6297
	釃	6298
	釅	6299

二十五畫

部首	單字	字號
广	廳	1405
木	欖	2649
手	攮	2112
水	灣	3167
目	矚	3825
竹	籩	4229
	籬	4230
	籭	4231
米	糶	4274
糸	纜	4474

二十六畫

部首	單字	字號
水	灤	3168
目	矚	3825
虫	蠼	5355
言	讟	5703
走	趲	5843
酉	釂	6301
金	鑿	6523
革	韉	6764
食	饢	6914
馬	驪	6985

一部

ㄧ i yī

【一】 （雙調 〔 yí yī
〔 yih yī ）

1. union; uniformity; uniform
2. one; unit
3. single; alone
4. whole; all; throughout
5. a; an; the
6. to unify; to unite
7. once; as soon as: 他一聽到消息就立刻動身了。He started as soon as he received the news.
8. each; per; every time

一巴掌（ㄧ ㄅㄚ ㄓㄤˇ）
(to give someone) a slap

一把（ㄧ ㄅㄚˇ）
a handful; a bundle; a bunch

一把抓（ㄧ ㄅㄚˇ ㄓㄨㄚ）
to grasp all the power or authority(of an organization); authoritarian; dictatorial

一把手（ㄧ ㄅㄚˇ ㄕㄡˇ）
a good hand; an expert: 他幹農活可真是一把手。He is really good at farm work.

一波三折（ㄧ ㄅㄛ ㄙㄢ ㄓㄜˊ）
meeting repeated difficulties; hitting one snag after another

一波未平一波又起（ㄧ ㄅㄛ ㄨㄟˋ ㄆㄧㄥˊ ㄧ ㄅㄛ ㄧㄡˋ ㄑㄧˇ）
Hardly has one wave subsided when another rises.—One trouble follows another.

一百（ㄧ ㄅㄞˇ）
one hundred

一百週年（ㄧ ㄅㄞˇ ㄓㄡ ㄋㄧㄢˊ）
a centenary; a centennial

一敗塗地（ㄧ ㄅㄞˋ ㄊㄨˊ ㄉㄧˋ）
a crushing defeat; a complete failure

一杯（ㄧ ㄅㄟ）
a cup of; a glass of

一輩（ㄧ ㄅㄟˋ）
a generation

一輩子（ㄧ ㄅㄟˋ ˙ㄗ）
throughout one's life; as long as one lives; a lifetime: 我一輩子也忘不了。I won't forget as long as I live.

一包（ㄧ ㄅㄠ）
a parcel; a package; a pack

一抱（ㄧ ㄅㄠˋ）
an armful

一班（ㄧ ㄅㄢ）
a class (of students); a squad (of foot soldiers)

一般（ㄧ ㄅㄢ）
①common; general; commonly; generally; as a rule ②same as; just like: 這倆兄弟一般高。The two brothers are of the same height.

一般見識（ㄧ ㄅㄢ ㄐㄧㄢˋ ㄕˋ）
to hold the same kind of view (usually in a derogatory sense)

一般性（ㄧ ㄅㄢ ㄒㄧㄥˋ）
a common quality; generality

一板一眼（ㄧ ㄅㄢˇ ㄧ ㄧㄢˇ）
①(to sing) in an expert manner ② methodically ③ following a prescribed pattern in speech or action

一半（ㄧ ㄅㄢˋ）or 一半兒（ㄧ ㄅㄢˋㄦ）
a half; half; in part

一本（ㄧ ㄅㄣˇ）
a volume

一本正經（ㄧ ㄅㄣˇ ㄓㄥˋ ㄐㄧㄥ）
①in a serious manner ② (irony) sanctimonious: 他看起來一本正經的樣子。He looks sanctimonious.

一本萬利（ㄧ ㄅㄣˇ ㄨㄢˋ ㄌㄧˋ）
to gain enormous profit out of small capital investment; to make handsome profits with a small capital

一幫（ㄧ ㄅㄤ）
a gang; a clique; a group of people devoted to a common cause (usually an unworthy one)

一榜（ㄧ ㄅㄤˇ）
(imperial China) a group of scholars who passed the same government-administered civil service examination and whose names were announced in the same official notice

一蹦一跳（ㄧ ㄅㄥˋ ㄧ ㄊㄧㄠˋ）
skipping and hopping

一鼻孔出氣（ㄧ ㄅㄧˊ ㄎㄨㄥˇ ㄔㄨ ㄑㄧˋ）
to hold identical opinions; to conspire or be in league with somebody; to sing the same tune: 他們一個鼻孔出氣。They say exactly the same thing.

一鼻子灰（ㄧ ㄅㄧˊ ˙ㄗ ㄏㄨㄟ）
to meet rejection, humiliation or frustration

一筆（ㄧ ㄅㄧˇ）
①one stroke (in Chinese painting or calligraphic work) ② a sum (of money); a (debt, account, etc.)

一筆抹殺（ㄧ ㄅㄧˇ ㄇㄛˇ ㄕㄚ）
to blot out at one stroke; to condemn out of hand; totally negate

一筆勾消（ㄧ ㄅㄧˇ ㄍㄡ ㄒㄧㄠ）
①to undo something by a single stroke; all cancelled ② to settle an account once (and) for all

一臂之力（ㄧ ㄅㄧˋ ㄓ ㄌㄧˋ）
help; assistance: 請助我們一臂之力。Please lend us a hand.

一碧萬頃（ㄧ ㄅㄧˋ ㄨㄢˋ ㄑㄧㄥˇ）
(said of vast lakes, seas or oceans) boundless; vast; watery blue reaching far beyond the horizon

一表人材（ㄧ ㄅㄧㄠˇ ㄖㄣˊ ㄘㄞˊ）
handsome or dashing

一邊（ㄧ ㄅㄧㄢ）or 一邊兒（ㄧ ㄅㄧㄢㄦ）
on one side; by the side

一邊倒（ㄧ ㄅㄧㄢ ㄉㄠˇ）
①to fall on one side; to side with somebody without reservation ② to predominate; to enjoy overpowering superiority

一併（ㄧ ㄅㄧㄥˋ）
all; wholly; at the same time; together with

一病不起（ㄧ ㄅㄧㄥˋ ㄅㄨˋ ㄑㄧˇ）
to die of illness

一不做二不休（ㄧ ㄅㄨˋ ㄗㄨㄛˋ ㄦˋ ㄅㄨˋ ㄒㄧㄡ）
①to do something by hook or by crook ② not to stop half way once a thing is started

一部（ㄧ ㄅㄨˋ）
a (book, motion picture, etc.); a volume

〔一部〕

一部分 or 一部份 (ㄧ ㄅㄨ ㄈㄣ)
a part; a portion; partially

一步登天 (ㄧ ㄅㄨ ㄉㄥ ㄊㄧㄢ)
a meteoric rise to fame; fast advancement in one's career, etc.

一拍即合 (ㄧ ㄆㄞ ㄐㄧ ㄏㄜ)
to become good friends or partners after brief contact

一派 (ㄧ ㄆㄞ)
a school (of thought, etc.); a faction; a group of people sharing the same ideals or interests

一派胡言 (ㄧ ㄆㄞ ㄏㄨˊ ㄧㄢ)
complete nonsense

一砲而紅 (ㄧ ㄆㄠˋ ㄦ ㄏㄨㄥˊ)
to have a meteoric rise to fame; to become famous all at once

一抔黃土 (ㄧ ㄆㄡˊ ㄏㄨㄤ ㄊㄨ)
a handful of yellow earth—a grave

一盤散沙 (ㄧ ㄆㄢˊ ㄙㄢ ㄕㄚ)
a plate of loose sand—utterly lacking cohesion; disunited

一盆 (ㄧ ㄆㄣˊ)
a plate or tray (of food); a pot (of flower); a basin (of water)

一旁 (ㄧ ㄆㄤˊ)
one side; on the sideline

一捧 (ㄧ ㄆㄥˇ)
the amount held by two half-stretched hands linked together with palms up

一匹 (ㄧ ㄆㄧˇ)
① (ㄧ ㄆㄧˇ) a (horse, etc.)
② (ㄧ ㄆㄧ) 參看「一疋」

一批 (ㄧ ㄆㄧ)
a batch; a shipment (of goods)

一疋 or 一匹 (ㄧ ㄆㄧ)
a roll (of cloth about 100 feet in length)

一瞥 (ㄧ ㄆㄧㄝ)
a glimpse; a glance

一篇 (ㄧ ㄆㄧㄢ)
a literary article; a chapter (of a book)

一偏之見 (ㄧ ㄆㄧㄢ ㄓ ㄐㄧㄢ)
a one-sided view

一片 (ㄧ ㄆㄧㄢˋ)
a denominative adjective for any object which is flat and thin

一片痴心 (ㄧ ㄆㄧㄢˋ ㄔ ㄒㄧㄣ)
strong affection, usually one-sided, for a member of the opposite sex

一貧如洗 (ㄧ ㄆㄧㄣˊ ㄖㄨˊ ㄒㄧˇ)
as poor as a church mouse; penniless; in utter destitution

一顰一笑 (ㄧ ㄆㄧㄣˊ ㄧ ㄒㄧㄠˋ)
① every facial expression of a VIP ② affected coquetry of a prostitute

一品 (ㄧ ㄆㄧㄣˇ)
the highest rank in officialdom in feudal Chinese courts (usually the prime minister)

一品夫人 (ㄧ ㄆㄧㄣˇ ㄈㄨ ㄖㄣˊ)
the wife of the highest-ranking official in ancient China

一品紅 (ㄧ ㄆㄧㄣˇ ㄏㄨㄥˊ)
a poinsettia 亦作「聖誕紅」

一暴十寒 (ㄧ ㄆㄨˋ ㄕˊ ㄏㄢˊ)
to do something by fits and starts

一馬當先 (ㄧ ㄇㄚˇ ㄉㄤ ㄒㄧㄢ)
to be the first to take on the enemy or to do work

一抹 (ㄧ ㄇㄛˇ)
a faint trace of something

一脈相傳 (ㄧ ㄇㄞˋ ㄒㄧㄤ ㄔㄨㄢˊ)
(said of lineage, philosophy, etc.) derived from the same origin

一枚 (ㄧ ㄇㄟˊ)
a (coin, medal, etc.)

一毛 (ㄧ ㄇㄠˊ)
① a hair ② one dime or ten cents ③ an insignificant thing

一毛不拔 (ㄧ ㄇㄠˊ ㄅㄨˋ ㄅㄚˊ)
(literally) unwilling to sacrifice even a single hair (for the sake of others)—parsimonious; very stingy

一門 (ㄧ ㄇㄣˊ)
① a course in a curriculum ② a family (of patriotic people, heroes, etc.) ③ a (big gun); a (cannon)

一面 (ㄧ ㄇㄧㄢˋ)
① one side; an aspect ② a (mirror) ③ at the same time

一面倒 (ㄧ ㄇㄧㄢˋ ㄉㄠˇ)
excessively dependent upon something or somebody

一面之交 (ㄧ ㄇㄧㄢˋ ㄓ ㄐㄧㄠ) or 一面

之緣 (ㄧ ㄇㄧㄢˋ ㄓ ㄩㄢˊ)
to have met but once; a nodding acquaintance

一面之詞 (ㄧ ㄇㄧㄢˋ ㄓ ㄘˊ)
one-sided statements

一鳴驚人 (ㄧ ㄇㄧㄥˊ ㄐㄧㄥ ㄖㄣˊ)
to become famous overnight; to achieve enormous success at the very first try

一命歸陰 (ㄧ ㄇㄧㄥˋ ㄍㄨㄟ ㄧㄣ)
to die 亦作「一命歸西」

一命嗚呼 (ㄧ ㄇㄧㄥˋ ㄨ ㄏㄨ)
to die

一模一樣 (ㄧ ㄇㄛˊ ㄧ ㄧㄤˋ)
exactly the same; identical

一木難支 (ㄧ ㄇㄨˋ ㄋㄢˊ ㄓ)
(literally) A single post cannot support a mansion.——One person alone cannot accomplish a difficult task.

一目了然 (ㄧ ㄇㄨˋ ㄌㄧㄠˇ ㄖㄢˊ)
(said of clarity in presentation) to understand fully at a glance

一目十行 (ㄧ ㄇㄨˋ ㄕˊ ㄏㄤˊ)
(said of the ability to read very fast) to read ten lines at one glance

一發 (ㄧ ㄈㄚ)
① a round (of ammunition) ② outbreak (of crisis, etc.)

一髮千鈞 (ㄧ ㄈㄚˇ ㄑㄧㄢ ㄐㄩㄣ)
(literally) A thing which weighs one thousand chiun (鈞) hangs on a hair.—a desperate or critical situation; a close shave

一番 (ㄧ ㄈㄢ)
① a kind, type, style, etc. ② once ③ a (silver dollar)

一番好意 (ㄧ ㄈㄢ ㄏㄠˇ ㄧˋ)
good will; well-intentioned

一帆風順 (ㄧ ㄈㄢˊ ㄈㄥ ㄕㄨㄣˋ)
(literally) May you have favorable winds in your sails!—to proceed smoothly without a hitch

一反常態 (ㄧ ㄈㄢˇ ㄔㄤˊ ㄊㄞˋ)
to act out of one's normal behavior; to act out of one's character

一飯千金 (ㄧ ㄈㄢˋ ㄑㄧㄢ ㄐㄧㄣ)
to reward a benefactor handsomely for the favor or help one has received from him

一分高下 (ㄧ ㄈㄣ ㄍㄠ ㄒㄧㄚˋ)

to decide who is the better or stronger of two individuals or groups

一分耕耘，一分收穫(ㄧ ㄈㄣ《ㄥ ㄩㄣ，ㄧ ㄈㄣ ㄕㄡ ㄏㄨㄛ)
One reaps no more than what he has sown. 或 As a man sows, so shall he reap.

一分(價)錢，一分貨(ㄧ ㄈㄣ(ㄐㄧㄚˋ) ㄑㄧㄢ，ㄧ ㄈㄣ ㄏㄨㄛˋ)
The higher the price, the better the quality of the merchandise.

一分為二(ㄧ ㄈㄣ ㄨㄟˊ ㄦˋ)
(philosophy) one dividing into two

一份(兒)(ㄧ ㄈㄣˋ)
a part, portion or share

一方(ㄧ ㄈㄤ)
①an area or region ②a party (in contract, etc.)

一方面(ㄧ ㄈㄤ ㄇㄧㄢˋ)
①one side ②on the one hand…, on the other hand…; for one thing…, for another…

一方之寄(ㄧ ㄈㄤ ㄓ ㄐㄧˋ)or一方之任(ㄧ ㄈㄤ ㄓ ㄖㄣˋ)
a responsible government position which carries considerable authority

一封(ㄧ ㄈㄥ)
a (letter)

一夫當關(ㄧ ㄈㄨ ㄉㄤ 《ㄨㄢ)
to hold or defend a key position single-handedly

一夫多妻(ㄧ ㄈㄨ ㄉㄨㄛ ㄑㄧ)
polygamy

一夫一妻(ㄧ ㄈㄨ ㄧ ㄑㄧ)
monogamy

一服(ㄧ ㄈㄨˊ)
a dose (of medicine)

一幅(ㄧ ㄈㄨˊ)
a (painting, scroll, etc.)

一副(ㄧ ㄈㄨˋ)
①a pair; a set ②a (facial expression)

一傅眾咻(ㄧ ㄈㄨˋ ㄓㄨㄥˋ ㄒㄧㄡ)
Too many detractors can undo the teachings of the wise.

一打(ㄧ ㄉㄚˊ)
a dozen

一刀兩斷(ㄧ ㄉㄠ ㄌㄧㄤˇ ㄉㄨㄢˋ)
to sever relations by one stroke; to be through with

一道(ㄧ ㄉㄠˋ)
①together ②a (problem, etc.) ③on the same path

一旦(ㄧ ㄉㄢˋ)
①once; whenever ②someday ③a day

一黨專政(ㄧ ㄉㄤˇ ㄓㄨㄢ ㄓㄥˋ)
one-party dictatorship

一登龍門，身價百倍(ㄧ ㄉㄥ ㄌㄨㄥˊ ㄇㄣˊ，ㄕㄣ ㄐㄧㄚˋ ㄅㄞˇ ㄅㄟˋ)
to rocket into fame after one's literary or artistic work won the praise of a master; to vault into the high society after winning the patronage of an influential or powerful person

一等(ㄧ ㄉㄥˇ)
top-notch; first-class; first-rate

一吊(ㄧ ㄉㄧㄠˋ)
a string (of coins)

一點(ㄧ ㄉㄧㄢˇ)
①a point ②a little bit

一點兒(ㄧ ㄉㄧㄢˇㄦ)or一丁點兒(ㄧ ㄉㄧㄥ ㄉㄧㄢˇㄦ)or一零兒(ㄧ ㄌㄧㄥˊㄦ)
①a little bit; small amount ②somewhat

一點一滴(ㄧ ㄉㄧㄢˇ ㄧ ㄉㄧ)
every drop; every bit; every little bit

一頂(ㄧ ㄉㄧㄥˇ)
a (hat, cap, or sedan chair)

一定(ㄧ ㄉㄧㄥˋ)
①fixed; specified; regular: 他沒有一定的職業。He has no regular work. ②certainly; surely; necessarily: 我們一定能夠達到我們的目標。Our goal can unquestionably be attained. ③given; particular; certain: 在一定程度上a certain degree

一度(ㄧ ㄉㄨˋ)
once; on one occasion; for a time: 我因病一度休學。I stopped going to school for a time on account of illness.

一度燒傷(ㄧ ㄉㄨˋ ㄕㄠ ㄕㄤ)
first-degree burn

一肚子(ㄧ ㄉㄨˋ ㄗ)
a stomachful (of grudge, food, etc.)

一朵(ㄧ ㄉㄨㄛˇ)
a (flower or cloud)

a pile or heap

一隊(ㄧ ㄉㄨㄟˋ)
a detachment or contingent (of soldiers, policemen, boy scouts, etc.); a (musical band)

一對(ㄧ ㄉㄨㄟˋ)or一對兒(ㄧ ㄉㄨㄟˋㄦ)
a pair; a couple; a brace

一對璧人(ㄧ ㄉㄨㄟˋ ㄅㄧˋ ㄖㄣˊ)
(said of newlyweds) an ideal couple

一端(ㄧ ㄉㄨㄢ)
①one end ②one aspect

一段(ㄧ ㄉㄨㄢˋ)or一段兒(ㄧ ㄉㄨㄢˋㄦ)
①one paragraph, passage or stanza ②a section; a length of…

一頓(ㄧ ㄉㄨㄣˋ)
①a pause (in reading) ②a (meal) ③a (beating or dressing down)

一冬(ㄧ ㄉㄨㄥ)
one winter season

一動(ㄧ ㄉㄨㄥˋ)
①a move; a jerk; a jolt ②to move once

一動不如一靜(ㄧ ㄉㄨㄥˋ ㄅㄨˋ ㄖㄨˊ ㄧ ㄐㄧㄥˋ)
Unless one is absolutely sure that he can succeed in doing something, he should not try it.

一棟(ㄧ ㄉㄨㄥˋ)
a (house or building): 我買了一棟房子。I have bought a house.

一塌糊塗(ㄧ ㄊㄚˋ ㄏㄨˊ ㄊㄨˊ)
in a great mess; topsy-turvy; in an awful state: 他把事情弄得一塌糊塗。He has made a mess of the job.

一榻橫陳(ㄧ ㄊㄚˋ ㄏㄥˊ ㄔㄣˊ)
to lie in bed

一臺(ㄧ ㄊㄞˊ)
a (theatrical performance)

一套(ㄧ ㄊㄠˋ)
①a suit; a set ②phony promise; trick; flattery; insincere gesture, etc.

一頭(ㄧ ㄊㄡˊ)or一頭兒(ㄧ ㄊㄡˊㄦ)
①a head (covered with gray hair, dust, skin ailments, etc.) ②(said of cattle, hogs, mules, etc.) a head ③a jerky motion of the head ④to come face to face with someone unexpectedly

〔一部〕

一頭霧水(ㄧ ㄊㄡ ㄨˋ ㄕㄨㄟˇ)
(slang) in bewilderment or confusion; not knowing what's the matter

一灘(ㄧ ㄊㄢ)
a puddle (of water, blood, oil, etc.)

一堂(ㄧ ㄊㄤˊ)
in the same hall; under the same roof

一堂課(ㄧ ㄊㄤˊ ㄎㄜˋ)
a period of teaching and learning at school

一趟(ㄧ ㄊㄤˋ)
a trip; a ride

一體(ㄧ ㄊㄧˇ)
①an organic (or integral) whole: 融成一體 to merge into an organic whole ②all people concerned; to a man

一貼(ㄧ ㄊㄧㄝ)
①to paste or glue ②a piece (of adhesive balm)

一帖藥(ㄧ ㄊㄧㄝ ㄧㄠˋ)
herbal medicines listed in a prescription for a particular ailment

一條(ㄧ ㄊㄧㄠˊ)
①a (rope, whip, snake, etc.) ②an article (of a law) ③a carton (of cigarettes)

一條心(ㄧ ㄊㄧㄠˊ ㄒㄧㄣ)
to be of one mind; to be at one

一天(ㄧ ㄊㄧㄢ)
①a whole day ②one day (any day in the past or in the future)

一天到晚(ㄧ ㄊㄧㄢ ㄉㄠˋ ㄨㄢˇ)
from morning till night; from dawn to dusk; all day long: 他一天到晚無所事事。 He has been doing nothing all day long.

一天星斗(ㄧ ㄊㄧㄢ ㄒㄧㄥ ㄉㄡˇ)
to exaggerate

一團和氣(ㄧ ㄊㄨㄢˊ ㄏㄜˊ ㄑㄧˋ)
full of goodwill toward one another; amicable; good-natured; harmonious, etc.

一團漆黑(ㄧ ㄊㄨㄢˊ ㄑㄧ ㄏㄟ)
pitch-dark—utterly hopeless; an utter failure

一團糟(ㄧ ㄊㄨㄢˊ ㄗㄠ)
in a hopeless mess

一通(ㄧ ㄊㄨㄥ)
a (telegram, etc.)

一通百通(ㄧ ㄊㄨㄥ ㄅㄞˇ ㄊㄨㄥ)
Grasp this one thing and you'll grasp everything.

一同(ㄧ ㄊㄨㄥˊ)
together with; in the company of

一統(ㄧ ㄊㄨㄥˇ)
①unification; unity ②to unify

一統江山(ㄧ ㄊㄨㄥˇ ㄐㄧㄤ ㄕㄢ)
territories under one sovereign

一男半女(ㄧ ㄋㄢˊ ㄅㄢˋ ㄋㄩˇ)
a few children (connoting one's longing for children after marriage): 他們想要有個一男半女。 They wish to have a few children.

一年半載(ㄧ ㄋㄧㄢˊ ㄅㄢˋ ㄗㄞˇ)
from six months to a year — a relatively short time

一年到頭(ㄧ ㄋㄧㄢˊ ㄉㄠˋ ㄊㄡˊ)
all (the) year round

一年之計在於春(ㄧ ㄋㄧㄢˊ ㄓ ㄐㄧˋ ㄗㄞˋ ㄩˊ ㄔㄨㄣ)
Spring is the best time to do the year's work.

一年四季(ㄧ ㄋㄧㄢˊ ㄙˋ ㄐㄧˋ)
throughout the four seasons of the year; all the year round

一年一度(ㄧ ㄋㄧㄢˊ ㄧ ㄉㄨˋ)
once a year; annual(ly)

一念之差(ㄧ ㄋㄧㄢˋ ㄓ ㄔㄚ)
a false step (which brings untold woes); a wrong decision made in a moment of weakness

一怒而去(ㄧ ㄋㄨˋ ㄦˊ ㄑㄩˋ)
to go away in a temper; to leave in anger

一諾千金(ㄧ ㄋㄨㄛˋ ㄑㄧㄢ ㄐㄧㄣ)
a solemn promise: 他們一諾千金。 They keep a solemn promise.

一樂也(ㄧ ㄌㄜˋ ㄧㄝˇ)
a great delight or blessing

一來(ㄧ ㄌㄞˊ)
①on the one hand ②as soon as (someone) arrives

一類(ㄧ ㄌㄟˋ)
of the same class, category or species

一勞永逸(ㄧ ㄌㄠˊ ㄩㄥˇ ㄧˋ)
to make a great effort to accomplish something once (and) for all

一覽(ㄧ ㄌㄢˇ)
a general survey

一覽表(ㄧ ㄌㄢˇ ㄅㄧㄠˇ)
a table list, or chart

一覽無餘(ㄧ ㄌㄢˇ ㄨˊ ㄩˊ)
(literally) A single glance takes in all.—a panoramic view

一愣(ㄧ ㄌㄥˋ)or 一愣兒(ㄧ ㄌㄥˋㄦ)
taken aback

一力成全(ㄧ ㄌㄧˋ ㄔㄥˊ ㄑㄩㄢˊ)
to spare no effort in helping somebody to accomplish something

一了百了(ㄧ ㄌㄧㄠˇ ㄅㄞˇ ㄌㄧㄠˇ)
(literally) The solution of one problem leads to the solution of all other problems.—To solve the key issue will expedite the solution of the whole problem.

一流(ㄧ ㄌㄧㄡˊ)
①first-rate ②of the same class

一溜煙(ㄧ ㄌㄧㄡ ㄧㄢ)or 一溜煙兒(ㄧ ㄌㄧㄡ ㄧㄢㄦ)
(to vanish) like smoke; (to get away) quickly: 小男孩一溜煙兒就不見了。 The little boy disappeared in a flash.

一連(ㄧ ㄌㄧㄢˊ)
①successively; consecutively; in a row: 一連下了三天雨。 It rained for three days in a row. ②a company (of foot soldiers)

一連串(ㄧ ㄌㄧㄢˊ ㄔㄨㄢˋ)
a series of

一鱗半爪(ㄧ ㄌㄧㄣˊ ㄅㄢˋ ㄓㄠˇ)
fragments (of antiques, ancient ruins, etc.)

一輛(ㄧ ㄌㄧㄤˋ)
a (car, truck, carriage, etc.)

一令(ㄧ ㄌㄧㄥˋ)
a ream (of paper)

一路(ㄧ ㄌㄨˋ)
①all the way; through the journey: 他們一路上說說笑笑。 They chatted cheerfully all the way. ②to go the same way; to take the same route ③single file

一路貨(ㄧ ㄌㄨˋ ㄏㄨㄛˋ)
of the same ilk 亦作「一路貨色」

一落千丈(ㄧ ㄌㄨㄛˋ ㄑㄧㄢ ㄓㄤˋ)
(said of prestige, fortune,

etc.) to nose-dive or decline
drastically

一輪明月 (ㄧ ㄌㄨㄣˊ ㄇㄧㄥˊ ㄩㄝˋ)
the full bright moon

一龍一豬 (ㄧ ㄌㄨㄥˊ ㄧ ㄓㄨ)
One is very capable, while
the other is extremely incompetent.

一律 (ㄧ ㄌㄩˋ)
uniformly; equally; without
exception (or discrimina-
tion)

一個 (ㄧˊ ˙ㄍㄜ)
one; a; an

一個巴掌拍不響 (ㄧˊ ˙ㄍㄜ ㄅㄚ ㄓㄤˇ
ㄆㄞ ㄅㄨˋ ㄒㄧㄤˇ)
One hand alone can't clap.
—It takes two to make a
quarrel.

一個個 (ㄧˊ ˙ㄍㄜ ˙ㄍㄜ)
① one by one ② each and
every one

一個夠 (ㄧˊ ˙ㄍㄜ ㄍㄡˋ)
to one's heart's content: 他開
懷痛飲一個夠。He drinks to
his heart's content.

一個勁兒 (ㄧˊ ˙ㄍㄜ ㄐㄧㄥˋ)
full of zest or enthusiasm;
persistently

一個心眼兒 (ㄧˊ ˙ㄍㄜ ㄒㄧㄣ ㄧㄢˇ)
① to have one's heart set on
something; devotedly ② to
be of one mind

一個樣 (ㄧˊ ˙ㄍㄜ ㄧㄤˋ) or 一個樣兒
(ㄧˊ ˙ㄍㄜ ㄧㄤˋ)
alike; in the same manner;
of the same sort

一概 (ㄧ ㄍㄞˋ)
all; without exception;
totally

一概而論 (ㄧ ㄍㄞˋ ㄦˊ ㄌㄨㄣˋ)
discussed or regarded in the
same frame of mind or in an
indiscriminating manner

一干人犯 (ㄧ ㄍㄢ ㄖㄣˊ ㄈㄢˋ)
a bunch of criminals

一乾二淨 (ㄧ ㄍㄢ ㄦˋ ㄐㄧㄥˋ)
① thoroughly cleaned-up ②
completely

一根 (ㄧ ㄍㄣ)
a (stick, hair, club, flag pole
or other objects which are
long and slender)

一骨碌 (ㄧ ㄍㄨˊ ㄌㄨˊ)
to get up (from bed) hastily
(as a result of a fire alarm,
exciting news, or the arrival

of some important person-
age or dear one)

一股 (ㄧ ㄍㄨˇ)
① a streak; a strand ② one
share (in stockholding) ③ a
band (of bandits): 一股匪徒
在我們鎮上出現。A band of
robbers appeared in our
town. ④ a (strong smell) ⑤
full of (spirit, zest, etc.)

一股傻勁 (ㄧ ㄍㄨˇ ㄕㄚˇ ㄐㄧㄣˋ)
great enthusiasm; single-
mindedness

一古腦兒 (ㄧ ㄍㄨˇ ㄋㄠˇ)
(dialect) completely; thoroughly

一鼓作氣 (ㄧ ㄍㄨˇ ㄗㄨㄛˋ ㄑㄧˋ)
to brace oneself (for a challenge, a difficult task, etc.);
to get something done in
one tremendous effort

一鼓而下 (ㄧ ㄍㄨˇ ㄦˊ ㄒㄧㄚˋ)
to conquer (a city or strategic point) in an overpowering attack

一國三公 (ㄧ ㄍㄨㄛˊ ㄙㄢ ㄍㄨㄥ)
too many leaders in a country or organization

一官半職 (ㄧ ㄍㄨㄢ ㄅㄢˋ ㄓˊ)
one of official positions in
general

一貫 (ㄧ ㄍㄨㄢˋ)
from beginning to end; consistent; unswerving

一貫道 (ㄧ ㄍㄨㄢˋ ㄉㄠˋ)
a religious sect with a combination of Confucianist,
Buddhist and Taoist fea-
tures

一貫作風 (ㄧ ㄍㄨㄢˋ ㄗㄨㄛˋ ㄈㄥ)
the consistent way of doing
things

一貫作業 (ㄧ ㄍㄨㄢˋ ㄗㄨㄛˋ ㄧㄝˋ)
(said of factories) integrat-
ed operation

一工 (ㄧ ㄍㄨㄥ)
a day's work done by a
laborer

一共 (ㄧ ㄍㄨㄥˋ)
altogether; in all; all told

一棵 (ㄧ ㄎㄜ)
a (tree); a head (of cab-
bage)

一顆 (ㄧ ㄎㄜ)
a piece (of candy); a (heart,
seal, diamond, star, mole,
etc.)

一刻 (ㄧ ㄎㄜˋ)
① fifteen minutes; a quarter
② a moment

一刻千金 (ㄧ ㄎㄜˋ ㄑㄧㄢ ㄐㄧㄣ)
(literally) One moment is
worth a thousand pieces of
gold.—(said of newlyweds
during their honeymoon)
Time is precious. 或 Every
minute is precious.

一客不煩二主 (ㄧ ㄎㄜˋ ㄅㄨˋ ㄈㄢˊ ㄦˋ ㄓㄨˇ)
(literally) One guest should
not bother two hosts.—Since
you have already helped me,
please help me finish the
task.

一口 (ㄧ ㄎㄡˇ)
① a mouthful; a bite ② (to
promise or grant a favor)
without hesitation ③ to
insist (often falsely that
somebody has done some-
thing bad) ④ a (well or bell)
⑤ an individual

一口答應 (ㄧ ㄎㄡˇ ㄉㄚ ㄧㄥˋ)
to promise without hesitation

一口氣 (ㄧ ㄎㄡˇ ㄑㄧˋ)
① in one breath; without
stop ② breath: 讓我鬆一口氣
吧! Let me catch my breath.
③ honor, face, etc. 參看「爭一
口氣」

一口咬定 (ㄧ ㄎㄡˇ ㄧㄠˇ ㄉㄧㄥˋ)
to stick to one's statement;
to insist on saying some-
thing

一塊兒 (ㄧ ㄎㄨㄞˋ)
together; altogether

一塊 (ㄧ ㄎㄨㄞˋ)
a piece; a block

一捆 (ㄧ ㄎㄨㄣˇ)
a bundle of

一匡天下 (ㄧ ㄎㄨㄤ ㄊㄧㄢ ㄒㄧㄚˋ)
to unite the whole empire
under one government

一孔之見 (ㄧ ㄎㄨㄥˇ ㄓ ㄐㄧㄢˋ)
a very limited outlook; a
narrow view

一行 (ㄧ ㄒㄧㄥˊ)
a row; a line; a single file

一呼百諾 (ㄧ ㄏㄨ ㄅㄞˇ ㄋㄨㄛˋ)
(said of a wealthy or powerful person with a large number of attendants) One command draws a hundred
answers.

〔一部〕

一忽兒(ㄧ ㄏㄨㄦ)
in a moment

一壺千金(ㄧ ㄏㄨ ㄑㄧㄢ ㄐㄧㄣ)
Things that are ordinarily worthless become very valuable when they are needed.

一狐之腋(ㄧ ㄏㄨ ㄓ ㄧㄝ)
the best part of something

一夥(ㄧ ㄏㄨㄛ)
a group; a gang

一會兒(ㄧ ㄏㄨㄟㄦ)
①a short while; presently; in a moment ②now…now…; one moment…the next…

一揮而就(ㄧ ㄏㄨㄟ ㄦ ㄐㄧㄡ)
to finish writing an article or drawing a painting very quickly

一回(ㄧ ㄏㄨㄟ)
①an occasion; a round (in boxing) ②once

一回事(ㄧ ㄏㄨㄟ ㄕ)
①one and the same (thing) ②one thing

一回生二回熟(ㄧ ㄏㄨㄟ ㄕㄥ ㄦ ㄏㄨㄟ ㄕㄨ)
①awkward at first but skilful later on ②strangers at the first meeting but friends at the second

還一報(ㄧ ㄏㄨㄢ ㄧ ㄅㄠ)
tit for tat; an eye for an eye

一晃兒
①(ㄧ ㄏㄨㄤ) to flash ②(ㄧ ㄏㄨㄤㄦ) in an instant; a short period

一哄而起(ㄧ ㄏㄨㄥ ㄦ ㄑㄧ)
(said of crowds) to rush headlong into mass action

一哄而散(ㄧ ㄏㄨㄥ ㄦ ㄙㄢ)
(said of crowds) to disperse in a hubbub

一己之私(ㄧ ㄐㄧ ㄓ ㄙ)
one's own selfish interests

一紀(ㄧ ㄐㄧ)
twelve years

一技之長(ㄧ ㄐㄧ ㄓ ㄔㄤ)
proficiency in a particular line (or field); professional skill; speciality

一家(ㄧ ㄐㄧㄚ)
the same family

一家言(ㄧ ㄐㄧㄚ ㄧㄢ)
a school of thought; an authority in a certain field (mostly in the humanities)

一甲子(ㄧ ㄐㄧㄚˇ ㄗ)
a cycle of sixty years

一截(ㄧ ㄐㄧㄝ)
a section; a length

一節(ㄧ ㄐㄧㄝ)
a section or passage (of a written work)

一介(ㄧ ㄐㄧㄝ)
a (scholar, etc.)

一介不取(ㄧ ㄐㄧㄝ ㄅㄨ ㄑㄩ)
said of the integrity of a public servant who does not take a single penny unrightfully

一腳(ㄧ ㄐㄧㄠ)
①a kick ②to take part in something (often unsolicited)

一…就…(ㄧ … ㄐㄧㄡ …)
no sooner…; the moment…; as soon as; once: 我一接到通知就動身了。I started off as soon as I got the message.

一間(ㄧ ㄐㄧㄢ)
a (room)

一肩行李兩袖清風(ㄧ ㄐㄧㄢ ㄒㄧㄥ ㄌㄧˇ ㄌㄧㄤˇ ㄒㄧㄡˋ ㄑㄧㄥ ㄈㄥ)
(said of an honest official on retirement) to possess nothing but one's personal belongings

一見鍾情(ㄧ ㄐㄧㄢ ㄓㄨㄥ ㄑㄧㄥ)
to fall in love at first sight

一見如故(ㄧ ㄐㄧㄢ ㄖㄨ ㄍㄨ)
to become intimate at the first meeting

一箭之地(ㄧ ㄐㄧㄢ ㄓ ㄉㄧ)
(literally) as far as the arrow flies—a short distance

一箭雙鵰(ㄧ ㄐㄧㄢ ㄕㄨㄤ ㄉㄧㄠ)
(literally) to kill two birds with one arrow—①to win the affection of two beauties at the same time ②to kill two birds with one stone

一斤(ㄧ ㄐㄧㄣ)
one catty

一將功成萬骨枯(ㄧ ㄐㄧㄤ ㄍㄨㄥ ㄔㄥ ㄨㄢ ㄍㄨˇ ㄎㄨ)
(literally) One general achieves renown over the dead bodies of 10,000 soldiers. —War is cruel.

一局(ㄧ ㄐㄩ)
①a game (of chess) ②(baseball) an inning

一舉(ㄧ ㄐㄩ)

---

with one action; at a blow; at one fell swoop: 他一舉成名。He became famous overnight.

一舉得男(ㄧ ㄐㄩ ㄉㄜˊ ㄋㄢˊ)
to get a son as one's first child

一舉兩得(ㄧ ㄐㄩ ㄌㄧㄤˇ ㄉㄜˊ)
to attain two objectives or gain two advantages by a single move; to kill two birds with one stone

一舉一動(ㄧ ㄐㄩ ㄧ ㄉㄨㄥˋ)
every movement and every action; behavior

一絕(ㄧ ㄐㄩㄝˊ)
a special skill; a unique talent or accomplishment

一蹶不振(ㄧ ㄐㄩㄝˊ ㄅㄨ ㄓㄣ)
unable to recover from a failure or after a decline

一決雌雄(ㄧ ㄐㄩㄝˊ ㄘ ㄒㄩㄥˊ)
to fight it out; to compete for championship

一妻多夫(ㄧ ㄑㄧ ㄉㄨㄛ ㄈㄨ)
polyandry

一齊(ㄧ ㄑㄧˊ)
at the same time; simultaneously; in unison

一起(ㄧ ㄑㄧˇ)
①in the same place ②together; in company

一徑(ㄧ ㄑㄧㄥˋ)
①without stop; at a stretch ②to get angry

一氣呵成(ㄧ ㄑㄧˋ ㄏㄜ ㄔㄥˊ)
①to complete in one breath (said of a literary piece, painting, etc. so that it is characterized by unity in style and coherence in thought) ②to get something done at one go

一氣之下(ㄧ ㄑㄧˋ ㄓ ㄒㄧㄚˋ)
in a huff; in a fit of anger

一切(ㄧ ㄑㄧㄝˋ)
all; everything: 金錢對他重於一切。Money is everything to him.

一竅不通(ㄧ ㄑㄧㄠˋ ㄅㄨ ㄊㄨㄥ)
completely ignorant; utterly stupid; very poor (writing)

一秋(ㄧ ㄑㄧㄡ)
one autumnal season

一丘之貉(ㄧ ㄑㄧㄡ ㄓ ㄏㄜˊ)
people of the same ilk

一錢不值(ㄧ ㄑㄧㄢ ㄅㄨ ㄓˊ) or 一文

一部

不值(ㄅㄨˋ ㄓˊ)
not worth a penny; completely worthless; mere trash: 它一文不值。It isn't worth a penny.

一錢如命(ㄧˋ ㄑㄧㄢˊ ㄖㄨˊ ㄇㄧㄥˋ)
niggardly

親芳澤(ㄑㄧㄣ ㄈㄤ ㄗㄜˊ)
to caress, kiss, or sleep with a woman

琴一鶴(ㄑㄧㄣˊ ㄧˋ ㄏㄜˋ)
(said of a government official) very honest; incorruptible

一曲(ㄧˋ ㄑㄩ)
a song

一去不復返(ㄧˋ ㄑㄩˋ ㄅㄨˊ ㄈㄨˋ ㄈㄢˇ)
gone for ever; gone never to return

一去不回(ㄧˋ ㄑㄩˋ ㄅㄨˋ ㄏㄨㄟˊ)
to leave for good

一瘸一拐(ㄧˋ ㄑㄩㄝˊ ㄧˋ ㄍㄨㄞˇ)
to limp; to walk jerkily and unevenly

一圈(ㄧˋ ㄑㄩㄢ)
① a circle ② one round (in a mah-jong game)

一犬吠形，百犬吠聲(ㄧˋ ㄑㄩㄢˇ ㄈㄟˋ ㄒㄧㄥˊ，ㄅㄞˇ ㄑㄩㄢˇ ㄈㄟˋ ㄕㄥ)
to repeat after what others are saying without knowing why

一羣(ㄧˋ ㄑㄩㄣˊ)
a group; a crowd; a herd; a pack; a flock

一窮二白(ㄧˋ ㄑㄩㄥˊ ㄦˋ ㄅㄞˊ)
grinding poverty

一襲(ㄧˋ ㄒㄧˊ)
a piece of (garment)

一席話(ㄧˋ ㄒㄧˊ ㄏㄨㄚˋ)
a speech (usually referring to enlightening statements)

一息尚存(ㄧˋ ㄒㄧˊ ㄕㄤˋ ㄘㄨㄣˊ)
so long as one is alive (often followed by a vow to do something)

一系列(ㄧˋ ㄒㄧˋ ㄌㄧㄝˋ)
a series of

一夕數驚(ㄧˋ ㄒㄧˋ ㄕㄨˋ ㄐㄧㄥ)
(said of people in troubled times) in constant fear

一下(ㄧˋ ㄒㄧㄚˋ)
once

一下子(ㄧˋ ㄒㄧㄚˋ ·ㄗ)
① at once ② at one stroke

一夏(ㄧˋ ㄒㄧㄚˋ)
a summer season

一些(ㄧˋ ㄒㄧㄝ)or **一些個**(ㄧˋ ㄒㄧㄝ ·ㄍㄜ)
① some; a few ② somewhat

一蟹不如一蟹(ㄧˊ ㄒㄧㄝˋ ㄅㄨˋ ㄖㄨˊ ㄧˊ ㄒㄧㄝˋ)
Each one is worse than the last.

一瀉千里(ㄧˊ ㄒㄧㄝˋ ㄑㄧㄢ ㄌㄧˇ)
① (descriptive of water in a giant river which) flows a thousand li at one plunge ② (said of the ability) to write fast and in a fluent style

一小撮(ㄧˋ ㄒㄧㄠˇ ㄘㄨㄛˋ)
a handful

一笑千金(ㄧˊ ㄒㄧㄠˋ ㄑㄧㄢ ㄐㄧㄣ)
A smile (of a beautiful woman) is worth a thousand pieces of gold.—an enchanting smile

一笑置之(ㄧˊ ㄒㄧㄠˋ ㄓˋ ㄓ)
to dismiss with a laugh; to laugh off

一宿(ㄧˋ ㄒㄧㄡˇ)or **一宿兒**(ㄧˋ ㄒㄧㄡˇ ㄦ)
one night; an overnight stay

一線(ㄧˊ ㄒㄧㄢˋ)
a thread; a ray

一線希望(ㄧˊ ㄒㄧㄢˋ ㄒㄧ ㄨㄤˋ)
a gleam of hope; a silver lining

一新(ㄧˋ ㄒㄧㄣ)
a new look or fresh look

一心(ㄧˋ ㄒㄧㄣ)
① wholeheartedly; heart and soul ② of one mind; at one: 萬眾一心。Millions of people are all of one mind.

一心一意(ㄧˋ ㄒㄧㄣ ㄧˋ ㄧˋ)
① of one heart and mind ② bent on (doing something)

一心一德(ㄧˋ ㄒㄧㄣ ㄧˋ ㄉㄜˊ)
to be of one heart and one mind

一廂情願(ㄧˋ ㄒㄧㄤ ㄑㄧㄥˊ ㄩㄢˋ)
unilateral willingness; wishful thinking

一向(ㄧˋ ㄒㄧㄤˋ)
① hitherto; up to now ② always; consistently: 他一向為人正直。He is always upright.

一星半點兒(ㄧˋ ㄒㄧㄥ ㄅㄢˋ ㄉㄧㄢˇㄦ)
just a little

一行(ㄧˋ ㄒㄧㄥˊ)
a group of (officials, businessmen, etc. during a trip)

一枝(ㄧˋ ㄓ)
① a (flower, pen, cigarette, etc.); a piece of (chalk) ② a branch

一枝獨秀(ㄧˋ ㄓ ㄉㄨˊ ㄒㄧㄡˋ)
(literally) One branch of the tree is particularly thriving. —to outshine others

一枝之棲(ㄧˋ ㄓ ㄓ ㄑㄧ)
a shelter or a minor position (for people out of luck)

一知半解(ㄧˋ ㄓ ㄅㄢˋ ㄐㄧㄝˇ)
a smack of knowledge; incomplete comprehension

一之為甚(ㄧˋ ㄓ ㄨㄟˊ ㄕㄣˋ)
One mistake is enough.

一直(ㄧˋ ㄓˊ)
① always; constantly; on end; all along: 我們一直是朋友。We've been friends all along. ② (to go) straight forward

一擲千金(ㄧˊ ㄓˊ ㄑㄧㄢ ㄐㄧㄣ)
to spend money recklessly

一紙(ㄧˋ ㄓˇ)
a (document); a (letter)

一紙具文(ㄧˋ ㄓˇ ㄐㄩˋ ㄨㄣˊ)
(said of a treaty, contract, or law that has been violated) a piece of worthless paper

一致(ㄧˋ ㄓˋ)
unanimously; one and all; consistent

一折(ㄧˋ ㄓㄜˊ)
① a 90 per cent discount ② one fold

一着(ㄧˋ ㄓㄠ)
a move; a gambit

一着不慎，滿盤皆輸(ㄧˋ ㄓㄠ ㄅㄨˊ ㄕㄣˋ，ㄇㄢˇ ㄆㄢˊ ㄐㄧㄝ ㄕㄨ)
A careless move, and the whole game is lost.

一朝(ㄧˋ ㄓㄠ)
① in one day: 他企盼一朝成名。He expects to become famous in one day. ② once

一朝千古(ㄧˋ ㄓㄠ ㄑㄧㄢ ㄍㄨˇ)
to die suddenly

一朝之忿(ㄧˋ ㄓㄠ ㄓ ㄈㄣˋ)

〔一部〕

a sudden outburst of anger

一朝一夕(ㄧ ㄓㄠ ㄧ ㄒㄧˋ)
a short period of time

一週(ㄓㄡ)
①a week ②a revolution, circle or cycle

一盞(ㄓㄢˇ)
a (lamp); a (cup)

一針見血(ㄧ ㄓㄣ ㄐㄧㄢˋ ㄒㄧㄝˇ)
exactly right; to the point 亦作「一語中的」

一陣(ㄓㄣˋ)
a sudden gust (of wind, laughter, etc.)

一陣子(ㄧ ㄓㄣˋ ˙ㄗ)
for a while

一章(ㄓㄤ)
a chapter (of a book)

一張(ㄓㄤ)
a sheet (of paper); a (table, desk, painting or calligraphic work)

一張一弛(ㄧ ㄓㄤ ㄧ ㄔˊ)
①off and on ②tension and lull

一丈(ㄧ ㄓㄤˋ)
a unit in Chinese lineal measurement slightly longer than ten feet

一株(ㄓㄨ)
a (tree, weed, flower, etc.)

一柱擎天(ㄧ ㄓㄨˋ ㄑㄧㄥˊ ㄊㄧㄢ)
to lead the nation safely through a crisis single-handed; to be the only man capable of saving the nation in time of trouble

一桌(ㄓㄨㄛ)
①a (banquet or feast) ②8 to 12 people (seated around a table partaking of a feast)

一樁(ㄓㄨㄤ)
an (affair); a (matter)

一種(ㄓㄨㄥˇ)
①one kind or type ②a species: 在他的花園裏有一種珍貴的玫瑰。 There is a rare species of rose in his garden.

一尺(ㄧ ㄔˇ)
a unit in Chinese lineal measurement slightly longer than one foot, which equals to one tenth of a 一丈

一差二錯(ㄧ ㄔㄚ ㄦˋ ㄔㄨㄛˋ)
mistakes or errors which one is likely to make

一剎那(ㄧ ㄔㄚˋ ㄋㄚˋ)
in a moment; in the twinkling of an eye: 一剎那, 它便完成了。 It was done in a moment.

一朝天子一朝臣(ㄧ ㄓㄠ ㄊㄧㄢ ㄗˇ ㄧ ㄓㄠ ㄔㄣˊ)
(literally) When a new king is crowned he brings to the court his own favorites and expels those of his predecessor. 或 Every new sovereign brings his own courtiers.—the tenuous nature of official positions

一籌莫展(ㄧ ㄔㄡˊ ㄇㄛˋ ㄓㄢˇ)
knowing not what to do; at one's wit's end; helpless

一塵不染(ㄧ ㄔㄣˊ ㄅㄨˋ ㄖㄢˇ)
①immaculate; spotless ②(figuratively) uncontaminated

一場(ㄧ ㄔㄤˊ)or(ㄧ ㄔㄤˇ)
①a performance ②a (long period of association) ③a (dream) ④a (period of happiness, grief, etc.)

一場空(ㄧ ㄔㄤˊ ㄎㄨㄥ)
all in vain; futile

一倡百和(ㄧ ㄔㄤˋ ㄅㄞˇ ㄏㄜˋ)
One person proposes and a hundred others respond.

一唱三歎(ㄧ ㄔㄤˋ ㄙㄢ ㄊㄢˋ)
(literally) one singing and three sighs—an expression to describe a deeply touching literary work

一唱一和(ㄧ ㄔㄤˋ ㄧ ㄏㄜˋ)
(said of two persons on the same side of an argument, etc.) One echoes the other.

一成(ㄧ ㄔㄥˊ)
10 percent

一成不變(ㄧ ㄔㄥˊ ㄅㄨˋ ㄅㄧㄢˋ)
fixed; conservative; unchangeable; invariable; inflexible

一程(ㄧ ㄔㄥˊ)
a short distance

一齣戲(ㄧ ㄔㄨ ㄒㄧˋ)
a play; a theatrical performance

一出一入(ㄧ ㄔㄨ ㄧ ㄖㄨˋ)or一出一進(ㄧ ㄔㄨ ㄧ ㄐㄧㄣˋ)
(the difference between) addition and deduction

一觸即發(ㄧ ㄔㄨˋ ㄐㄧˊ ㄈㄚ)
(literally) One slight touch and off it goes.—imminent

一傳十, 十傳百(ㄧ ㄔㄨㄢˊ ㄕˊ ㄕˊ ㄔㄨㄢˊ ㄅㄞˇ)
(said of rumors, gossips, etc.) to travel fast

一串(ㄧ ㄔㄨㄢˋ)
a string (of coins, pearls, etc.)

一牀(ㄧ ㄔㄨㄤˊ)
a (coverlet or comforter)

一失足成千古恨(ㄧ ㄕ ㄗㄨˊ ㄔㄥˊ ㄑㄧㄢ ㄍㄨˇ ㄏㄣˋ)
One pitfall leads to endless misery and regret.

一時(ㄧ ㄕˊ)
①for a moment ②a period of time: 此一時彼一時。 Times have changed. ③accidentally

一時半刻(ㄧ ㄕˊ ㄅㄢˋ ㄎㄜˋ)
a short time; a little while:

一時一刻(ㄧ ㄕˊ ㄧ ㄎㄜˋ)
for a single moment

一時瑜亮(ㄧ ㄕˊ ㄩˊ ㄌㄧㄤˋ)
two equally talented or outstanding contemporaries

一世(ㄧ ㄕˋ)
①an epoch; an age ②a lifetime ③I (used after the name of an emperor such as Napoleon I)

一世之雄(ㄧ ㄕˋ ㄓ ㄒㄩㄥˊ)
a great hero of his time

一事無成(ㄧ ㄕˋ ㄨˊ ㄔㄥˊ)
to accomplish nothing; to get nowhere

一視同仁(ㄧ ㄕˋ ㄊㄨㄥˊ ㄖㄣˊ)
impartial; without discrimination

一手(ㄧ ㄕㄡˇ)
①single-handedly; all by oneself ②good at: 他對於數字計算很有一手。 He is good at figures.

一手包辦(ㄧ ㄕㄡˇ ㄅㄠ ㄅㄢˋ)
①dictatorial; arbitrary ②to do something all by oneself

一手拍難疾無聲(ㄧ ㄕㄡˇ ㄆㄞ ㄋㄢˊ ㄇㄨˋ ㄨˊ ㄕㄥ)
No matter how capable one is, he needs the help of others to do more or better work.

一手交錢一手交貨(ㄧ ㄕㄡˇ ㄐㄧㄠ ㄑㄧㄢˊ ㄧ ㄕㄡˇ ㄐㄧㄠ ㄏㄨㄛˋ)
cash on delivery

一手遮天（ㄧ ㄕㄡ ㄓㄜ ㄊㄧㄢ）
(literally) to shut out the heavens with one hand—to hide the truth from the masses; to hoodwink the public

一手造成（ㄧ ㄕㄡ ㄗㄠˋ ㄔㄥˊ）
to be solely responsible for (a bad situation, etc.)

一手掩盡天下人耳目（ㄧ ㄕㄡ ㄧㄢˇ ㄐㄧㄣˋ ㄊㄧㄢ ㄒㄧㄚˋ ㄖㄣˊ ㄦˇ ㄇㄨˋ）
to try to hide from public knowledge mistakes committed by one person or a few persons

一閃念（ㄧ ㄕㄢˇ ㄋㄧㄢˋ）
a fleeting thought

一扇（ㄧ ㄕㄢˋ）
a (door, window, etc.)

一身（ㄧ ㄕㄣ）
①a suit ②the whole body; all over the body ③a solitary person: 他孑然一身。He is solitary.

一身是病（ㄧ ㄕㄣ ㄕˋ ㄅㄧㄥˋ）
to be afflicted by several ailments or diseases

一身是膽（ㄧ ㄕㄣ ㄕˋ ㄉㄢˇ）
to have plenty of guts; very brave

一身是債（ㄧ ㄕㄣ ㄕˋ ㄓㄞˋ）
(said of individuals) to be deep in debt

一神教（ㄧ ㄕㄣˊ ㄐㄧㄠˋ）
monotheism

一晌（ㄧ ㄕㄤˇ）
a short moment

一升（ㄧ ㄕㄥ）
a unit in Chinese cubic measurement slightly less than a liter

一生（ㄧ ㄕㄥ）
a lifetime

一生受用不盡（ㄧ ㄕㄥ ㄕㄡˋ ㄩㄥˋ ㄅㄨˋ ㄐㄧㄣˋ）
to enjoy the benefit or reward all one's life

一聲不響（ㄧ ㄕㄥ ㄅㄨˋ ㄒㄧㄤˇ）
do not say a word; do not utter a sound

一聲令下（ㄧ ㄕㄥ ㄌㄧㄥˋ ㄒㄧㄚˋ）
as soon as the order (to attack) is given (everyone will rush forward to engage the enemy)

一樹百穫（ㄧ ㄕㄨˋ ㄅㄞˇ ㄏㄨㄛˋ）
To encourage or patronize

the talented will be rewarded manifold.

一說（ㄧ ㄕㄨㄛ）
①according to one version, theory, etc. ②brief explanation

一瞬（ㄧ ㄕㄨㄣˋ）or 一眨眼（ㄧ ㄓㄚˇ ㄧㄢˇ）
the twinkling of an eye; in an instant

一雙（ㄧ ㄕㄨㄤ）
a couple; a pair

一日（ㄧ ㄖˋ）
one day; such a day: 總有一日你會達到你的目的。There'll be one day when you will achieve your purpose.

一日千里（ㄧ ㄖˋ ㄑㄧㄢ ㄌㄧˇ）
(literally) a thousand li a day—to make progress or improvement at a tremendous pace

一日之計在於晨（ㄧ ㄖˋ ㄓ ㄐㄧˋ ㄗㄞˋ ㄩˊ ㄔㄣˊ）
Morning hours are the best time of the day to work.

一日之長（ㄧ ㄖˋ ㄓ ㄔㄤˊ）
①（ㄧ ㄖˋ ㄓ ㄓㄤˇ）a little older in age
②（ㄧ ㄖˋ ㄓ ㄔㄤˊ）slightly superior in learning

一日之雅（ㄧ ㄖˋ ㄓ ㄧㄚˇ）
only slightly acquainted with (a person)

一日三秋（ㄧ ㄖˋ ㄙㄢ ㄑㄧㄡ）
(literally) A single day seems as long as three years.—longing for loved ones or close friends far away

一日為師終身為父（ㄧ ㄖˋ ㄨㄟˊ ㄕ ㄓㄨㄥ ㄕㄣ ㄨㄟˊ ㄈㄨˋ）
One should respect his teacher as if the teacher were his own father, even if the teacher-student relationship has existed for only a single day.

一人得道，雞犬升天（ㄧ ㄖㄣˊ ㄉㄜˊ ㄉㄠˋ，ㄐㄧ ㄑㄩㄢˇ ㄕㄥ ㄊㄧㄢ）
(literally) When one attains the Tao, even his chickens and dogs ascend to heaven.—When one gets to the highest position, all his friends and relatives get there with him.

一任（ㄧ ㄖㄣˋ）
a tour, term, or tenure (of duty)

一仍舊貫（ㄧ ㄖㄥˊ ㄐㄧㄡˋ ㄍㄨㄢˋ）
to stick to the old customs; to follow the old routine

一如既往（ㄧ ㄖㄨˊ ㄐㄧˋ ㄨㄤˇ）
just as in the past; as before; as always

一字褒貶（ㄧ ㄗˋ ㄅㄠ ㄅㄧㄢˇ）
to praise or criticize with a single word

一字千金（ㄧ ㄗˋ ㄑㄧㄢ ㄐㄧㄣ）
(said of superb writings) A single word is worth a thousand pieces of gold.

一字之差（ㄧ ㄗˋ ㄓ ㄔㄚ）
the change of one word (which would make a great deal of difference)

一字兒（ㄧ ㄗˋ ㄦ）
in a row; in a line

一字一淚（ㄧ ㄗˋ ㄧ ㄌㄟˋ）
(said of sentimental writings) a teardrop for every word

一則（ㄧ ㄗㄜˊ）
①one item ②on the one hand

一再（ㄧ ㄗㄞˋ）
repeatedly; over and over; again and again

一早（ㄧ ㄗㄠˇ）or 一早兒（ㄧ ㄗㄠˇㄦ）
in the early morning

一走了之（ㄧ ㄗㄡˇ ㄌㄧㄠˇ ㄓ）
to evade the solution of a problem by walking away from where it exists

一組（ㄧ ㄗㄨˇ）
a set; a group

一座（ㄧ ㄗㄨㄛˋ）
a (bridge, mountain, statue, etc.)

一尊（ㄧ ㄗㄨㄣ）
①a (fieldpiece, or Buddha statue) ②a jug (of wine)

一此為足（ㄧ ㄘˇ ㄨㄟˊ ㄗㄨˊ）
Once is enough.

一次（ㄧ ㄘˋ）
once

一次方程式（ㄧ ㄘˋ ㄈㄤ ㄔㄥˊ ㄕˋ）
(mathematics) a linear equation, or an equation of the first degree

一餐（ㄧ ㄘㄢ）
a meal

一
部】

〔一部〕

一層(ㄧ ㄘㄥ)
①one story or floor (of a multistory building) ②a stratum

一蹴而幾(ㄧ ㄘㄨ ㄦ ㄐㄧ)
to succeed in doing something at the first try

一寸(ㄧ ㄘㄨㄣ)
a unit in Chinese lineal measurement slightly longer than an inch

一絲不掛(ㄧ ㄙ ㄅㄨˋ ㄍㄨㄚˋ)
to have not a stitch on; stark-naked

一絲不苟(ㄧ ㄙ ㄅㄨˋ ㄍㄡˇ)
No detail is overlooked. 或 to do things carefully and seriously

一絲一毫(ㄧ ㄙ ㄧ ㄏㄠˊ)
a tiny bit; an iota; a trace: 沒有一絲一毫的差別 without the least difference

一死了之(ㄧ ㄙˇ ㄌㄧㄠˇ ㄓ)
to end one's troubles or worries by death

一色(ㄧ ㄙㄜˋ)
①of one color; of the same color: 海天一色。The sea melts into the sky. ②of the same type

一掃而空(ㄧ ㄙㄠˇ ㄦ ㄎㄨㄥ)
(worries, doubts) completely removed

一所(ㄧ ㄙㄨㄛˇ)
a (school, charity institute, etc.)

一索得男(ㄧ ㄙㄨㄛˇ ㄉㄜˊ ㄋㄢˊ)
to produce a male heir by a woman in her first child-birth

一而再再而三(ㄧ ㄦˊ ㄗㄞˋ ㄗㄞˋ ㄦˊ ㄙㄢ)
to happen repeatedly; to repeat or try again and again despite failure

一二(ㄧ ㄦˋ)
a little; a few

一一(ㄧ ㄧ)
one by one; each separately; each one

一衣帶水(ㄧ ㄧ ㄉㄞˋ ㄕㄨㄟˇ)
a narrow water course; a strip of water

一以當十(ㄧ ㄧˇ ㄉㄤ ㄕˊ)
One fights against ten. (said of brave soldiers taking on an enemy force enjoying overwhelming numerical superiority)

一意孤行(ㄧ ㄧˋ ㄍㄨ ㄒㄧㄥˊ)
to do something against the advice of others; self-willed; self-opinionated

一頁(ㄧ ㄧㄝˋ)
one page

一葉扁舟(ㄧ ㄧㄝˋ ㄆㄧㄢ ㄓㄡ)
a small boat

一葉知秋(ㄧ ㄧㄝˋ ㄓ ㄑㄧㄡ)
(literally) A single fallen leaf tells of the oncoming autumn.— any sign foretelling things to come或A small sign can indicate a great trend.

一言不發(ㄧ ㄧㄢˊ ㄅㄨˋ ㄈㄚ)
to keep one's mouth shut

一言不合(ㄧ ㄧㄢˊ ㄅㄨˋ ㄏㄜˊ)
A single jarring note in conversation (between two persons is immediately followed by a quarrel, fist fight, etc.)

一言難盡(ㄧ ㄧㄢˊ ㄋㄢˊ ㄐㄧㄣˋ)
It is a long story.

一言既出駟馬難追(ㄧ ㄧㄢˊ ㄐㄧˋ ㄔㄨ ㄙˋ ㄇㄚˇ ㄋㄢˊ ㄓㄨㄟ)
A promise cannot be taken back once it is made.

一言九鼎(ㄧ ㄧㄢˊ ㄐㄧㄡˇ ㄉㄧㄥˇ)
a solemn promise or pledge

一言興邦(ㄧ ㄧㄢˊ ㄒㄧㄥ ㄅㄤ)
A timely warning may avert a national crisis.

一言喪邦(ㄧ ㄧㄢˊ ㄙㄤˋ ㄅㄤ)
A single wrong statement may bring disaster to the nation.

一言以蔽之(ㄧ ㄧㄢˊ ㄧˇ ㄅㄧˋ ㄓ)
to sum up; to make a long story short

一言一行(ㄧ ㄧㄢˊ ㄧ ㄒㄧㄥˊ)
every word and deed

一言為定(ㄧ ㄧㄢˊ ㄨㄟˊ ㄉㄧㄥˋ)
to reach a binding agreement verbally

一眼看去(ㄧ ㄧㄢˇ ㄎㄢˋ ㄑㄩˋ)
①to take a sweeping look ②at first glance

一飲而盡(ㄧ ㄧㄣˇ ㄦ ㄐㄧㄣˋ)
to empty the glass at one gulp

一飲一啄(ㄧ ㄧㄣˇ ㄧ ㄓㄨㄛˊ)
One does not try to get what is denied him by destiny.

一氧化碳(ㄧ ㄧㄤˇ ㄏㄨㄚˋ ㄊㄢˋ)
carbon monoxide (CO)

一樣(ㄧ ㄧㄤˋ)
①alike; in the same manner ②an (object, item or article)

一應俱全(ㄧ ㄧㄥ ㄐㄩˋ ㄑㄩㄢˊ)
complete with everything

一無是處(ㄧ ㄨˊ ㄕˋ ㄔㄨˋ)
without a single redeeming feature; devoid of any merit

一無所得(ㄧ ㄨˊ ㄙㄨㄛˇ ㄉㄜˊ)
Nothing is gained.

一無所獲(ㄧ ㄨˊ ㄙㄨㄛˇ ㄏㄨㄛˋ)
to achieve or gain nothing (after all the efforts made)

一無所知(ㄧ ㄨˊ ㄙㄨㄛˇ ㄓ)
to know nothing at all; completely unaware; not have the least inkling of; to be absolutely ignorant of

一無所長(ㄧ ㄨˊ ㄙㄨㄛˇ ㄔㄤˊ)
do not have a single skill or merit; to be a Jack of all trades

一無所有(ㄧ ㄨˊ ㄙㄨㄛˇ ㄧㄡˇ)
to own nothing at all

一五一十(ㄧ ㄨˇ ㄧ ㄕˊ)
to enumerate or to narrate in detail; to tell something exactly as it happened

一物降一物(ㄧ ㄨˋ ㄒㄧㄤˊ ㄧ ㄨˋ)
There is always one thing to conquer another. 或 Everything has its nemesis.

一誤再誤(ㄧ ㄨˋ ㄗㄞˋ ㄨˋ)
①to commit one mistake after another ②to make things worse by repeated delays

一窩(ㄧ ㄨㄛ)or 一窩兒(ㄧ ㄨㄛㄦ)
a nest

一窩蜂(ㄧ ㄨㄛ ㄈㄥ)
(literally) a swarm of bees or hornets—①(said of a crowd of people) to swarm ②to follow the herd instinct

一尾(ㄧ ㄨㄟˇ)
a (fish)

一味(ㄧ ㄨㄟˋ)
habitually; invariably: 他一味地固執成見。He invariably sticks to his own view.

一位(ㄧ ㄨㄟˋ)
a (guest, gentleman, lady, hero, VIP, etc.)

一文不值(ㄧ ㄨㄣˊ ㄅㄨˋ ㄓˊ)or 一錢不

值(ㄓˊㄑㄧㄢㄅㄨˋㄓㄧ)
not worth a penny; worthless

一問三不知(ㄧㄨㄣˋㄙㄢㄅㄨˋㄓㄧ)
to say "I don't know" to every question—① do not know a thing; to be entirely ignorant ② to keep one's mouth tightly shut

一網打盡(ㄧㄨㄤˇㄉㄚˇㄐㄧㄣˋ)
(literally) to catch all the fish in one net—to round up all (the criminals, rebels or other undesirable elements)

一往情深(ㄧㄨㄤˇㄑㄧㄥˊㄕㄣ)
to fall deeply in love

一往直前(ㄧㄨㄤˇㄓˊㄑㄧㄢˊ)
to go ahead bravely without looking back

一望而知(ㄧㄨㄤˋㄦˊㄓㄧ)
to know all at a single glance

一望無際(ㄧㄨㄤˋㄨˊㄐㄧˋ)
(said of open space or vast plain) to spread out far beyond the horizon

一隅(ㄧˊㄩˊ)
a corner

一語破的(ㄧˇㄩˇㄆㄛˋㄉㄧ)
to hit the mark with a single comment

一語道破(ㄧˇㄩˇㄉㄠˋㄆㄛˋ)
to hit the nail on the head; to expose someone's ulterior motive or secret design by a single remark

一語成讖(ㄧˇㄩˇㄔㄥˊㄔㄣˋ)
a casual remark that turned out to be prophetic in a tragedy

一雨成秋(ㄧˇㄩˇㄔㄥˊㄑㄧㄡ)
(said of weather in late summer or early autumn) A sudden shower turns the lingering heat into the brisk cool air of autumn.

一月(ㄧˊㄩㄝˋ)
① January ② one month

一員(ㄧˊㄩㄢˊ)
a member; a (field commander or top lieutenant)

一元方程式(ㄧˊㄩㄢˊㄈㄤㄔㄥˊㄕˋ)
the equation with one unknown

一元化(ㄧˊㄩㄢˊㄏㄨㄚˋ)
centralized; unified

一院制(ㄧˊㄩㄢˋㄓˋ)

the unicameral system (of a parliament)

一擁而上(ㄧㄩㄥㄦˊㄕㄤˋ)
to rush up in a crowd

一畫

【丁】 2
1. ㄉㄧㄥ ding ding
1. the fourth of the Ten Celestial Stems (天干)
2. population
3. attendants
4. fourth: 丁等 grade D
5. small cubes of meat or vegetable
6. a Chinese family name

丁賦(ㄉㄧㄥㄈㄨˋ)
poll tax

丁當(ㄉㄧㄥㄉㄤ)
the sound of "ding dang"

丁點兒(ㄉㄧㄥㄉㄧㄢㄦˇ)
(dialect) a tiny bit

丁東(ㄉㄧㄥㄉㄨㄥ)
the sound of "ting tung"

丁男(ㄉㄧㄥㄋㄢˊ)
a male adult

丁年(ㄉㄧㄥㄋㄧㄢˊ)
the age of 16 which was the age of adulthood in ancient China

丁寧(ㄉㄧㄥㄋㄧㄥˊ)
to give repeated injunctions 亦作「叮嚀」

丁口(ㄉㄧㄥㄎㄡˇ)
people; population

丁錢(ㄉㄧㄥㄑㄧㄢˊ)or 丁稅(ㄉㄧㄥㄕㄨㄟˋ)
poll tax

丁香(ㄉㄧㄥㄒㄧㄤ)
a clove

丁香花(ㄉㄧㄥㄒㄧㄤㄏㄨㄚ)
lilac

丁字鐵(ㄉㄧㄥㄗˋㄊㄧㄝˇ)
a T-beam; a T-bar

丁字街(ㄉㄧㄥㄗˋㄐㄧㄝ)
T-shaped road junction

丁字尺(ㄉㄧㄥㄗˋㄔˇ)
a T-square

丁財兩旺(ㄉㄧㄥㄘㄞˊㄌㄧㄤˇㄨㄤˋ)
to be blessed with many male children and great wealth (a congratulatory expression in old China)

丁役(ㄉㄧㄥㄧˋ)
a male adult undergoing

labor service for the country or community

丁夜(ㄉㄧㄥㄧㄝˋ)
the fourth watch of the night— (i.e. 2:00 AM)

丁徭(ㄉㄧㄥㄧㄠˊ)
poll tax; military service

丁憂(ㄉㄧㄥㄧㄡ)or 丁艱(ㄉㄧㄥ)
bereavement of parents

丁銀(ㄉㄧㄥㄧㄣˊ)
poll tax money

【丁】 2
2. ㄓㄥ jeng zheng
sound: 伐木丁丁,鳥鳴嚶嚶。(詩經·小雅·伐木) On the trees go the blows jeng-jeng,/ And the birds cry out ying-ying.

【七】 3
ㄑㄧ chi qi
(變調)ㄑㄧˊ chyi qi)
the number seven

七八成(ㄑㄧㄅㄚㄔㄥˊ)or 七八成兒(ㄑㄧㄅㄚㄔㄥˊㄦ)
① seventy or eighty per cent ② very likely

七步成詩(ㄑㄧㄅㄨˋㄔㄥˊㄕ)
(said of a literary genius) to compose a poem within the time required for taking seven steps

七拼八湊(ㄑㄧㄆㄧㄣㄅㄚㄘㄡˋ)
① to raise money from different sources (usually implies financial stringency) ② to cannibalize (said of machines when supply of spare parts has run out) ③ to piece together

七平八穩(ㄑㄧㄆㄧㄥㄅㄚㄨㄣˇ)
balanced; stable

七大小(ㄑㄧㄉㄚˋㄒㄧㄠˇ)
objects of various sizes thrown together

七顛八倒(ㄑㄧㄉㄧㄢㄅㄚㄉㄠˇ)
topsy-turvy; in great confusion

七通八達(ㄑㄧㄊㄨㄥㄅㄚㄉㄚˊ)
very erudite; to know everything

七扭八歪(ㄑㄧㄋㄧㄡˇㄅㄚㄨㄞ)
(said of smashed or ruined objects) out of shape

七零八落(ㄑㄧㄌㄧㄥˊㄅㄚㄌㄨㄛˋ)
scattered here and there; in confusion

七律(ㄑㄧㄌㄩˋ)

【一部】

a poem composed of eight seven-character lines with a strict tonal pattern and rhyme scheme

七高八低(ㄑㄧ ㄍㄠ ㄅㄚ ㄉㄧ)
bumpy (roads); rough (terrain)

七國(ㄑㄧ ㄍㄨㄛ)or 七雄(ㄑㄧ ㄒㄩㄥ)
the seven states—Chin(秦), Chu(楚), Yen(燕), Chao(趙), Han(韓), Wei(魏), Chi(齊)—in the Epoch of Warring States (403-221 B.C.)

七級浮屠(ㄑㄧ ㄐㄧ ㄈㄨ ㄊㄨ)
a seven-storied pagoda

七角形(ㄑㄧ ㄐㄧㄠ ㄒㄧㄥ)
a heptagon

七件事(ㄑㄧ ㄐㄧㄢˋ ㄕ)
the seven necessities—fuel, rice, oil, salt, soy sauce, vinegar and tea

七絕(ㄑㄧ ㄐㄩㄝ)
a verse of four lines with seven characters to a line

七七(ㄑㄧ ㄑㄧ)
the seven-week period after a person's death, during which funeral rites are observed

七七事變(ㄑㄧ ㄑㄧ ㄕˋ ㄅㄧㄢˋ)
the Marco Polo Bridge Incident (July 7, 1937), which triggered the War of Resistance Against Japanese Aggression (1937-1945)

七巧板(ㄑㄧ ㄑㄧㄠˇ ㄅㄢˇ)
the seven-pieced puzzle; a tangram; the magic square (The pieces are cut from a square and may be put together to form a large number of shapes and designs.)

七竅(ㄑㄧ ㄑㄧㄠˋ)
the seven apertures in the human head, i.e. eyes, ears, nostrils and mouth

七竅流血(ㄑㄧ ㄑㄧㄠˋ ㄌㄧㄡ ㄒㄧㄝˇ)
bleeding from the seven apertures on the head

七竅生煙(ㄑㄧ ㄑㄧㄠˋ ㄕㄥ ㄧㄢ)
(literally) Smoke belches out from the seven apertures on the head.—in a state of great fury

七擒七縱(ㄑㄧ ㄑㄧㄣˊ ㄑㄧ ㄗㄨㄥˋ)
to capture an enemy seven

times and release him after each capture (with the intention to win his heart and submission forever)

七情六慾(ㄑㄧ ㄑㄧㄥˊ ㄌㄧㄡˋ ㄩˋ)
(Buddhism) the seven emotions—happiness (喜), anger (怒), sorrow (憂), fear (懼), love (愛), hate (憎), and desire (慾)—and the six sensory pleasures derived from the eyes, ears, nose, tongue, body and mind

七夕(ㄑㄧ ㄒㄧ)
the seventh night of the seventh lunar month when the legendary Cowherd and Weaving Maid meet each other for their once-a-year tryst over a bridge formed by sympathetic magpies over the Milky Way (The day is a festival for girls and young lovers.)

七絃琴(ㄑㄧ ㄒㄧㄢˊ ㄑㄧㄣˊ)
a seven-stringed Chinese musical instrument

七折八扣(ㄑㄧ ㄓㄜˊ ㄅㄚ ㄎㄡˋ)
①big discounts (in a bargain sale) ②to make allowance for inaccuracy, exaggeration, etc. in a statement or report

七尺之軀(ㄑㄧ ㄔˇ ㄓ ㄑㄩ)
men's average height (referring to a full-grown man); the human adult body

七長八短(ㄑㄧ ㄔㄤˊ ㄅㄚ ㄉㄨㄢˇ)
of various lengths

七穿八洞(ㄑㄧ ㄔㄨㄢ ㄅㄚ ㄉㄨㄥˋ)
full of holes; riddled with bullets

七重奏(ㄑㄧ ㄔㄨㄥˊ ㄗㄡˋ)
a septet

七十至七十九歲的人(ㄑㄧ ㄕˊ ㄓˋ ㄑㄧ ㄕˊ ㄐㄧㄡˇ ㄙㄨㄟˋ·ㄉㄜ ㄖㄣˊ)
a septuagenarian

七十二烈士(ㄑㄧ ㄕˊ ㄦˋ ㄌㄧㄝˋ ㄕˋ)
the 72 martyrs who sacrificed their lives in an abortive uprising against the Manchus which took place in Canton on March 29, 1911

七十二賢人(ㄑㄧ ㄕˊ ㄦˋ ㄒㄧㄢˊ ㄖㄣˊ)
the 72 most prominent scholars among the 3,000 students of Confucius

七手八腳(ㄑㄧ ㄕㄡˇ ㄅㄚ ㄐㄧㄠˇ)

many people doing something simultaneously in a disorganized manner 或 Too many cooks spoil the broth.

七上八下(ㄑㄧ ㄕㄤˋ ㄅㄚ ㄒㄧㄚˋ)
an unsettled state of mind

七聲(ㄑㄧ ㄕㄥ)or 七音(ㄑㄧ ㄧㄣ)
the seven-notes of the scale—five main notes (宮, 商, 角, 徵, 羽) and two modified notes (變徵 fa and 變宮 si)

七嘴八舌(ㄑㄧ ㄗㄨㄟˇ ㄅㄚ ㄕㄜˊ)
everybody talking at the same time: 老師離開後, 大家就七嘴八舌談了起來。After the teacher left, everyone talked freely.

七死八活(ㄑㄧ ㄙˇ ㄅㄚ ㄏㄨㄛˊ)
on the verge of death (after hard work, severe beating, etc.)

七色(ㄑㄧ ㄙㄜˋ)
the seven colors of the spectrum

七言八語(ㄑㄧ ㄧㄢˊ ㄅㄚ ㄩˇ)
gossip; all sorts of opinions

七言詩(ㄑㄧ ㄧㄢˊ ㄕ)
verses with seven characters to a line

七月(ㄑㄧ ㄩㄝˋ)
①July ②the seventh month of the lunar year; the seventh moon

二畫

【丈】 [4] ㄓㄤˋ janq zhòng
1. a unit in Chinese lineal measurement slightly longer than 10 feet
2. an elder; a senior
3. to measure; to survey

丈母娘(ㄓㄤˋ ㄇㄨˇ ㄋㄧㄤˊ)
a mother-in-law

丈夫(ㄓㄤˋ ㄈㄨ)
①a husband ②a man

丈夫氣概(ㄓㄤˋ ㄈㄨ ㄑㄧˋ ㄍㄞˋ)
manliness; manliness

丈量(ㄓㄤˋ ㄌㄧㄤˊ)
to measure; to survey

丈人(ㄓㄤˋ ㄖㄣˊ)
a father-in-law

【三】 [5] ㄙㄢ san sān
three; third; thrice: 孟子曰:
「諸侯之寶三: 土地、人民、政

事。」(孟子・盡心下) Mencius said, "The precious things of a prince are three:—the territory, the people, the government and its business."

三八節 (ㄙㄢ ㄅㄚ ㄐㄧㄝ)
Women's Day on March the 8th

三八主義 (ㄙㄢ ㄅㄚ ㄓㄨ ㄧˋ)
the three "8" system under which a 24-hour day is divided into 8 hours of work, 8 hours of recreation and 8 hours of sleep

三百六十行 (ㄙㄢ ㄅㄞˇ ㄌㄧㄡˋ ㄕˊ ㄏㄤˊ)
all trades and professions

三胞胎 (ㄙㄢ ㄅㄠ ㄊㄞ)
triplets

三寶 (ㄙㄢ ㄅㄠˇ)
(Buddhism) Triratna—the triad of the Buddha, the dharma, and the sangha

三保太監 (ㄙㄢ ㄅㄠˇ ㄊㄞˋ ㄐㄧㄢ)
Cheng Ho (鄭和), a powerful eunuch in the early Ming Dynasty, who led a large fleet to call at the various ports of the South China Sea and the ports on the eastern African coast during seven expeditions between 1405 and 1423

三不幸 (ㄙㄢ ㄅㄨˋ ㄒㄧㄥˋ)
the three greatest misfortunes—death of one's father in youth, widowhood in middle age, and to have no son in old age

三不管 (ㄙㄢ ㄅㄨˋ ㄍㄨㄢˇ)
① referring to a lazy man who does not look after his own and his family's clothing, food and housing ② a district not within the jurisdiction of any of the neighboring magistrates

三不朽 (ㄙㄢ ㄅㄨˋ ㄒㄧㄡˇ)
the three imperishable —one's virtue, achievements and teachings (立德, 立功, 立言)

三不知 (ㄙㄢ ㄅㄨˋ ㄓ)
to be ignorant of the beginning, the middle, and the end of a matter; complete ignorance (sometimes pretended) 參看「一問三不知」

三部曲 (ㄙㄢ ㄅㄨˋ ㄑㄩˇ)
a trilogy

三昧 (ㄙㄢ ㄇㄟˋ)
① the key to a problem; the best method to do something (originally, in Buddhism, *samadhi* meaning "intent contemplation") ② a secret; a knack: 他深得其中三昧。He has mastered the secrets of the art.

三民主義 (ㄙㄢ ㄇㄧㄣˊ ㄓㄨ ㄧˋ)
The Three Principles of the People—nationalism (民族), democracy (民權) and livelihood (民生)—by Dr. Sun Yat-sen, father of the Republic of China

三明治 (ㄙㄢ ㄇㄧㄥˊ ㄓˋ)
a sandwich

三番五次 (ㄙㄢ ㄈㄢ ㄨˇ ㄘˋ) or 三番兩次 (ㄙㄢ ㄈㄢ ㄌㄧㄤˇ ㄘˋ)
time and again; over and over again; repeatedly: 我三番兩次告訴他不可這樣。I have told him over and over again not to do that.

三藩 (ㄙㄢ ㄈㄢˊ)
the three princes—Wu San-kuei (吳三桂), Shang Ke-hsi (尚可喜) and Keng Chung-ming (耿仲明)—They were generals of the Ming Dynasty who surrendered to the Manchus when the latter invaded the Ming Empire. The Manchus rewarded them with the title of king for their surrender.

三藩市 (ㄙㄢ ㄈㄢˊ ㄕˋ)
San Francisco

三分人材，七分打扮 (ㄙㄢ ㄈㄣ ㄖㄣˊ ㄘㄞˊ, ㄑㄧ ㄈㄣ ㄉㄚˇ ㄅㄢˋ)
three-tenths natural figure and seven-tenths make-up

三分鼎足 (ㄙㄢ ㄈㄣ ㄉㄧㄥˇ ㄗㄨˊ)
(said of warlords or rivaling princes) to hold the different parts of a country and vie for hegemony in a three-way tie

三伏天 (ㄙㄢ ㄈㄨˊ ㄊㄧㄢ)
dog days

三復斯言 (ㄙㄢ ㄈㄨˋ ㄙㄨ ㄧㄢˊ)
to think over or ponder on my advice (an expression used in speaking to a junior)

三達德 (ㄙㄢ ㄉㄚˊ ㄉㄜˊ)
the three virtues—wisdom, benevolence and courage (智, 仁, 勇)

三大發明 (ㄙㄢ ㄉㄚˋ ㄈㄚ ㄇㄧㄥˊ)
the three major inventions by the Chinese—gunpowder, printing and compass

三大洋 (ㄙㄢ ㄉㄚˋ ㄧㄤˊ)
the three big oceans—the Pacific Ocean, the Atlantic Ocean and the Indian Ocean

三代 (ㄙㄢ ㄉㄞˋ)
① three generations ② the three ancient Chinese dynasties—Hsia, Shang and Chou

三代同堂 (ㄙㄢ ㄉㄞˋ ㄊㄨㄥˊ ㄊㄤˊ)
three generations living under the same roof (under the big family system in old China)

三島 (ㄙㄢ ㄉㄠˇ)
① the British Isles—England, Scotland and Ireland ② the three major islands of Japan—Honshu, Shikoku and Kyushu

三到 (ㄙㄢ ㄉㄠˋ)
to use three organs—ears, eyes and mouth—simultaneously (in study)

三等 (ㄙㄢ ㄉㄥˇ)
① three grades or classes ② the third grade; inferior

三點裝 (ㄙㄢ ㄉㄧㄢˇ ㄓㄨㄤ)
a bikini suit

三點水 (ㄙㄢ ㄉㄧㄢˇ ㄕㄨㄟˇ)
three points which make up the radical "氵" in Chinese characters

三讀 (ㄙㄢ ㄉㄨˊ)
the third reading of a bill in a legislative session

三度空間 (ㄙㄢ ㄉㄨˋ ㄎㄨㄥ ㄐㄧㄢ)
three-dimensional space: 直線為一度空間, 平面為二度空間, 立體為三度空間. A line has one dimension, a plane has two dimensions, and a cube has three dimensions.

三多 (ㄙㄢ ㄉㄨㄛ)
three abundances—blessing, longevity and male offspring (多福, 多壽, 多男子)—which the people of old China considered the ingredients of a

［一部］

happy life

三對六面 (ㄙㄢ ㄉㄨㄟˋ ㄌㄧㄡˋ ㄇㄧㄢˋ)
All the interested parties are present.

三段論法 (ㄙㄢ ㄉㄨㄢˋ ㄌㄨㄣˊ ㄈㄚˇ)
syllogism

三態 (ㄙㄢ ㄊㄞˋ)
(physics) the three states of matter—solid, liquid and gas

三頭 (ㄙㄢ ㄊㄡˊ)
(in phrases) three-headed

三頭馬車 (ㄙㄢ ㄊㄡˊ ㄇㄚˇ ㄔㄜ)
a troika 亦作「三駕馬車」

三頭六臂 (ㄙㄢ ㄊㄡˊ ㄌㄧㄡˋ ㄅㄧˋ)
a resourceful and capable man who, figuratively speaking, has three heads and six arms to use

三頭政治 (ㄙㄢ ㄊㄡˊ ㄓㄥˋ ㄓˋ)
the triumvirate

三潭印月 (ㄙㄢ ㄊㄢˊ ㄧㄣˋ ㄩㄝˋ)
a scenic attraction in the West Lake, Hangchow, where the moon leaves three images in the water

三歎 (ㄙㄢ ㄊㄢˋ)
deep sighs and regrets (over an unhappy experience, a tragic accidents, etc.)

三天打魚，兩天曬網 (ㄙㄢ ㄊㄧㄢ ㄉㄚˇ ㄩˊ, ㄌㄧㄤˇ ㄊㄧㄢ ㄕㄞˋ ㄨㄤˇ)
to go fishing for three days and dry the nets for two —(figuratively) to work off and on

三天兩頭兒 (ㄙㄢ ㄊㄧㄢ ㄌㄧㄤˇ ㄊㄡˊ ㄦ)
frequently; every other day; almost every day

三年蓄艾 (ㄙㄢ ㄋㄧㄢˊ ㄒㄩˋ ㄞˋ)
to make thorough preparations beforehand; to stock-pile supplies or build up a manpower pool in anticipation of demand

三年有成 (ㄙㄢ ㄋㄧㄢˊ ㄧㄡˇ ㄔㄥˊ)
Three years' hard work is crowned with success.

三年五載 (ㄙㄢ ㄋㄧㄢˊ ㄨˇ ㄗㄞˇ)
three to five years

三聯單 (ㄙㄢ ㄌㄧㄢˊ ㄉㄢ)
three-sectional tax forms, invoices, etc.; triplicate forms

三令五申 (ㄙㄢ ㄌㄧㄥˋ ㄨˇ ㄕㄣ)
①to give repeated orders and injunctions ②repeated orders and injunctions

---

三輪車 (ㄙㄢ ㄌㄨㄣˊ ㄔㄜ) or 三輪兒 (ㄙㄢ ㄌㄨㄣˊ ㄦ)
a pedicab; a tricycle

三個臭皮匠，合成一個諸葛亮 (ㄙㄢ ㄍㄜˋ ㄔㄡˋ ㄆㄧˊ ㄐㄧㄤˋ, ㄏㄜˊ ㄔㄥˊ ㄧˊ ㄍㄜˋ ㄓㄨ ㄍㄜˇ ㄌㄧㄤˋ)
Three cobblers with their wits combined are a match for Chu-Ko Liang the genius. The wisdom of the masses exceeds that of the wisest individual. 亦作「三個臭皮匠，勝過諸葛亮」

三綱五常 (ㄙㄢ ㄍㄤ ㄨˇ ㄔㄤˊ)
the three bonds in human relations (prince and minister, father and son, husband and wife) and the five constant virtues (father's righteousness, mother's benevolence, elder brother's love, younger brother's respect, and son's filial piety)

三更半夜 (ㄙㄢ ㄍㄥ ㄅㄢˋ ㄧㄝˋ)
late at night (usually after midnight)

三姑六婆 (ㄙㄢ ㄍㄨ ㄌㄧㄡˋ ㄆㄛˊ)
women whose professions are either illegitimate or disreputable such as 尼姑, 道姑, 卦姑, 牙婆, 媒婆, 師婆, 虔婆, 藥婆, 穩婆 (a reference to despicable women in general)

三顧茅廬 (ㄙㄢ ㄍㄨˋ ㄇㄠˊ ㄌㄨˊ)
to make three calls at the thatched cottage—a historical allusion dating back to the Epoch of the Three Kingdoms, now used to describe a man in power who tries to obtain the service of the capable and the virtuous by showing his utmost sincerity and eagerness

三國 (ㄙㄢ ㄍㄨㄛˊ)
the Three Kingdoms—Wei (魏), Shu(蜀) and Wu(吳)—which existed in China simultaneously from A.D. 222 to 265

三國志 (ㄙㄢ ㄍㄨㄛˊ ㄓˋ)
The History of the Three Kingdoms by Chen Shou (陳壽)

三國演義 (ㄙㄢ ㄍㄨㄛˊ ㄧㄢˇ ㄧˋ)
The Romance of the Three Kingdoms by Lo Kuan-

---

chung (羅貫中), a very popular novel mixing facts with fiction about the Epoch of the Three Kingdoms

三跪九叩 (ㄙㄢ ㄍㄨㄟˇ ㄐㄧㄡˇ ㄎㄡˋ)
to kneel three times with the head touching the ground nine times, an ancient ritual performed by a subject during an audience with the emperor

三光政策 (ㄙㄢ ㄍㄨㄤ ㄓㄥˋ ㄘㄜˋ)
(said of invading troops) to kill all the civilians, to burn down all the houses, and to take away all that is movable—the policy once pursued by the Japanese invaders in China

三公 (ㄙㄢ ㄍㄨㄥ)
the three highest-ranking officials in the imperial court of ancient China

三宮六苑 (ㄙㄢ ㄍㄨㄥ ㄌㄧㄡˋ ㄩㄢˋ)
the emperor's harem

三K黨 (ㄙㄢ ㄎㄟ ㄉㄤˇ)
the Ku Klux Klan

三合板 (ㄙㄢ ㄏㄜˊ ㄅㄢˇ)
a three-ply board; plywood

三合土 (ㄙㄢ ㄏㄜˊ ㄊㄨˇ)
mortar

三合會 (ㄙㄢ ㄏㄜˊ ㄏㄨㄟˋ)
the Triad Society (a secret society during the Ching Dynasty dedicated to the overthrow of the Manchus and the restoration of the Ming Dynasty)

三呼萬歲 (ㄙㄢ ㄏㄨ ㄨㄢˋ ㄙㄨㄟˋ)
to shout "Long Live the Emperor" three times

三花臉 (ㄙㄢ ㄏㄨㄚ ㄌㄧㄢˇ)
a clown in Chinese opera

三皇五帝 (ㄙㄢ ㄏㄨㄤˊ ㄨˇ ㄉㄧˋ)
the three sage kings and five virtuous emperors of China at the dawn of human civilization

三級跳遠 (ㄙㄢ ㄐㄧˊ ㄊㄧㄠˋ ㄩㄢˇ)
hop, step (or skip), and jump

三家村 (ㄙㄢ ㄐㄧㄚ ㄘㄨㄣ)
a small village

三街六巷 (ㄙㄢ ㄐㄧㄝ ㄌㄧㄡˋ ㄒㄧㄤˋ)
the whole town or city

三節 (ㄙㄢ ㄐㄧㄝˊ)
the three important festivals

of the year—端午節 the Dragon-Boat Festival, 5th of 5th lunar month, 中秋節 Mid-Autumn Festival, 15th of 8th lunar month, and 新年 the Lunar New Year

三角 (ㄙㄢ ㄐㄧㄠ)
① trigonometry ② three angles

三角板 (ㄙㄢ ㄐㄧㄠ ㄅㄢ)
a set square

三角貿易 (ㄙㄢ ㄐㄧㄠ ㄇㄠ ㄧ)
triangular trade

三角鐵 (ㄙㄢ ㄐㄧㄠ ㄊㄧㄝ)
(construction) angle iron

三角戀愛 (ㄙㄢ ㄐㄧㄠ ㄌㄧㄢ ㄞ)
a love triangle

三角褲 (ㄙㄢ ㄐㄧㄠ ㄎㄨ)
panties; briefs

三角函數 (ㄙㄢ ㄐㄧㄠ ㄏㄢ ㄕㄨ)
trigonometric function

三角形 (ㄙㄢ ㄐㄧㄠ ㄒㄧㄥ)
a triangle

三角洲 (ㄙㄢ ㄐㄧㄠ ㄓㄡ)
a delta

三腳貓 (ㄙㄢ ㄐㄧㄠ ㄇㄠ)
a person who can do many odd things but specializes in nothing

三腳架 (ㄙㄢ ㄐㄧㄠ ㄐㄧㄚ)
a tripod

三教 (ㄙㄢ ㄐㄧㄠ)
Confucianism, Taoism and Buddhism

三教九流 (ㄙㄢ ㄐㄧㄠ ㄐㄧㄡ ㄌㄧㄡ)
(literally) the three religions (Confucianism, Buddhism and Taoism) and the nine schools (Confucianist, Taoist, Astrologist, Legalist, Nominalist, Mohist, Diplomatist, Miscellanist and Agriculturist)—people of all walks of life

三緘其口 (ㄙㄢ ㄐㄧㄢ ㄑㄧ ㄎㄡ)
to remain silent; to be very reluctant to make comments or voice one's opinions: 你最好三緘其口。 You had better be silent.

三晉 (ㄙㄢ ㄐㄧㄣ)
the states of Han (韓), Wei (魏), and Chao (趙) during the Epoch of Warring States, which constituted the state of Tsin in the preceding Spring and Autumn era

三句不離本行 (ㄙㄢ ㄐㄩ ㄅㄨ ㄌㄧ ㄅㄣ ㄏㄤ)
to talk shop frequently when conversing with people outside one's own profession

三軍 (ㄙㄢ ㄐㄩㄣ)
the three armies; the armed forces

三七二十一 (ㄙㄢ ㄑㄧ ㄦ ㄕ ㄧ)
① Three sevens are twenty-one; ② the true story of a matter or happening

三七五減租 (ㄙㄢ ㄑㄧ ㄨ ㄐㄧㄢ ㄗㄨ)
the 37.5% rental reduction policy, the first step taken in Taiwan's land reform program in 1949, under which the ceiling of farm rental was fixed at 37.5% of the crop yield

三秋 (ㄙㄢ ㄑㄧㄡ)
① three falls—three years ② the three months of autumn

三缺一 (ㄙㄢ ㄑㄩㄝ ㄧ)
(mah-jong) one more player still needed

三拳不敵四手 (ㄙㄢ ㄑㄩㄢ ㄅㄨ ㄉㄧ ㄙ ㄕㄡ)
(literally) Three fists are no match for four hands.—outnumbered

三權分立 (ㄙㄢ ㄑㄩㄢ ㄈㄣ ㄌㄧ)
separation of the legislative, executive and judicial functions of a government

三峽 (ㄙㄢ ㄒㄧㄚ)
the Three Gorges of the Yangtze River on the border of Szechwan and Hupei

三鮮 (ㄙㄢ ㄒㄧㄢ)
a Chinese dish composed of any three kinds of fresh delicacies

三絃 (ㄙㄢ ㄒㄧㄢ)
a Chinese musical instrument with three strings played by fingers

三心二意 (ㄙㄢ ㄒㄧㄣ ㄦ ㄧ)
① hesitating; irresolute; vacillating ② halfhearted

三薰三沐 (ㄙㄢ ㄒㄩㄣ ㄙㄢ ㄇㄨ)
to show the highest respect to someone

三隻手 (ㄙㄢ ㄓ ㄕㄡ)
a pickpocket

三朝 (ㄙㄢ ㄓㄠ)
① the third day of baby's

birth ② a bride's homecoming on the third day after matrimony

三戰兩勝 (ㄙㄢ ㄓㄢ ㄌㄧㄤ ㄕㄥ)
the best of three games

三振 (ㄙㄢ ㄓㄣ) or 三振出局 (ㄙㄢ ㄓㄣ ㄔㄨ ㄐㄩ)
to strike out; a strikeout

三徵七辟 (ㄙㄢ ㄓ ㄑㄧ ㄅㄧ)
(said of emperors in ancient China) to issue repeated invitations to the virtuous and capable for public service

三尺童子 (ㄙㄢ ㄔ ㄊㄨㄥ ㄗ)
a lad

三叉路口 (ㄙㄢ ㄔㄚ ㄌㄨ ㄎㄡ)
a junction where three roads meet

三朝元老 (ㄙㄢ ㄔㄠ ㄩㄢ ㄌㄠ)
① a veteran statesman who had served under three emperors in a row ② (in modern usage) the most senior employee in a government organization

三長兩短 (ㄙㄢ ㄔㄤ ㄌㄧㄤ ㄉㄨㄢ)
unforeseen disasters or accidents (usually referring to death): 萬一他有個三長兩短，那我們怎麼辦呢? If an unforeseen accident should happen to him, what should we do?

三十六行 (ㄙㄢ ㄕ ㄌㄧㄡ ㄏㄤ)
all trades and professions

三十六計，走為上計 (ㄙㄢ ㄕ ㄌㄧㄡ ㄐㄧ，ㄗㄡ ㄨㄟ ㄕㄤ ㄐㄧ)
Of the thirty-six stratagems, the best one is to go away. —The best thing to do now is to go away. 亦作「三十六策，走為上策」

三十六著 (ㄙㄢ ㄕ ㄌㄧㄡ ㄓㄠ) or 三十六計 (ㄙㄢ ㄕ ㄌㄧㄡ ㄐㄧ) or 三十六策 (ㄙㄢ ㄕ ㄌㄧㄡ ㄘㄜ)
all the possible schemes or stratagems

三而立 (ㄙㄢ ㄦ ㄌㄧ)
thirty years of age when a man should stand on his own feet

三十二開 (ㄙㄢ ㄕ ㄦ ㄎㄞ)
thirty-two mo; 32 mo

三牲 (ㄙㄢ ㄕㄥ)
three sacrificial offerings —ox, sheep and hog—used

〔一〕部

in worship

三生有幸 (ㄙㄢ ㄕㄥ ㄧ ㄡ ㄒㄧㄥˋ)
the greatest fortune in three incarnations (to make friends with worthy persons or to marry a virtuous and beautiful wife, etc.); lucky indeed

三人行必有我師 (ㄙㄢ ㄖㄣˊ ㄒㄧㄥˊ ㄅㄧˋ ㄧㄡˇ ㄨㄛˇ ㄕ)
If three of us are walking together, at least one of the other two is good enough to be my teacher. (an expression to show one's open-mindedness)

三人成虎 (ㄙㄢ ㄖㄣˊ ㄔㄥˊ ㄏㄨˇ)
A lie, if repeated often enough, will be accepted as truth.

三字經 (ㄙㄢ ㄗˋ ㄐㄧㄥ)
①the *Three-Character Classic* or the *Trimetrical Classic*, formerly the first primer in schools ②a four-letter word; an expletive

三災八難 (ㄙㄢ ㄗㄞ ㄅㄚ ㄋㄢˋ)
(said of children) to suffer from one ailment after another

三族 (ㄙㄢ ㄗㄨˊ)
①parents, brothers, and wife and children ②relatives of father, of mother and of wife ③three generations of grandfather, father and son ④paternal uncles, brothers, and sons

三次方程式 (ㄙㄢ ㄘˋ ㄈㄤ ㄔㄥˊ ㄕˋ)
an equation of the third degree or a cubic equation

三才 (ㄙㄢ ㄘㄞˊ)
the three powers—heaven, earth and man

三餐 (ㄙㄢ ㄘㄢ)
three meals—breakfast, lunch and supper

三寸 (ㄙㄢ ㄘㄨㄣˋ)
a very small short person

三寸金蓮 (ㄙㄢ ㄘㄨㄣˋ ㄐㄧㄣ ㄌㄧㄢˊ)
three-inch golden lilies (women's feet deformed by foot-binding, which were considered beautiful in ancient China)

三寸之舌 (ㄙㄢ ㄘㄨㄣˋ ㄓ ㄕㄜˊ)
the three-inch tongue (said of a persuasive person who

can talk others into doing something, about which the listener at first holds reservations)

三從四德 (ㄙㄢ ㄘㄨㄥˊ ㄙˋ ㄉㄜˊ)
three obediences and four virtues of women (In ancient China a woman was required to obey her father before marriage, her husband during married life, and her sons in widowhood. (在家從父，出嫁從夫，夫死從子) The four virtues are fidelity, physical charm, propriety in speech and efficiency in needlework. (婦德，婦容，婦言，婦工))

三色 (ㄙㄢ ㄙㄜˋ)
the three basic colors—yellow, blue and red

三色版 (ㄙㄢ ㄙㄜˋ ㄅㄢˇ)
(printing) a three-color halftone

三色紫羅蘭 (ㄙㄢ ㄙㄜˋ ㄗˇ ㄌㄨㄛˊ ㄌㄢˊ)
pansy 亦作「三色菫」

三兩 (ㄙㄢ ㄌㄧㄤˇ)
by twos and threes; in twos and threes

三三制 (ㄙㄢ ㄙㄢ ㄓˋ)
the education system which prescribes three years for junior high school and three years for senior high school

三三五五 (ㄙㄢ ㄙㄢ ㄨˇ ㄨˇ)
small groups of people scattered here and there

三言兩語 (ㄙㄢ ㄧㄢˊ ㄌㄧㄤˇ ㄩˇ)
a brief talk, discussion, conversation, description, etc.

三陽開泰 (ㄙㄢ ㄧㄤˊ ㄎㄞ ㄊㄞˋ)
a surge of good luck

三五成群 (ㄙㄢ ㄨˇ ㄔㄥˊ ㄑㄩㄣˊ)
in groups of three or five

三圍 (ㄙㄢ ㄨㄟˊ)
the vital statistics, or the three measurements, of a woman

三位一體 (ㄙㄢ ㄨㄟˋ ㄧ ㄊㄧˇ)
the Trinity; three-in-one

三溫暖 (ㄙㄢ ㄨㄣ ㄋㄨㄢˇ)
sauna bath 亦作「蒸氣浴」

三月 (ㄙㄢ ㄩㄝˋ)
①March ②the third moon

of the lunar calendar ③ three months

【上】 6
1. ㄕㄤˋ shàng shǎng
1. above
2. upper; upward; up
3. better; superior
4. previous; before
5. top; summit; on
6. to ascend; to mount; to board
7. to go to court

上輩 (ㄕㄤˋ ㄅㄟˋ) or 上輩兒 (ㄕㄤˋ ㄅㄟˋ ㄦ)
the earlier generation; one's seniors

上報 (ㄕㄤˋ ㄅㄠˋ)
①to be published in newspapers ②to report to a higher body; to report to one's boss

上班 (ㄕㄤˋ ㄅㄢ) or 上班兒 (ㄕㄤˋ ㄅㄢ ㄦ)
to go to office; to go on duty

上半天 (ㄕㄤˋ ㄅㄢˋ ㄊㄧㄢ) or 上半天兒 (ㄕㄤˋ ㄅㄢˋ ㄊㄧㄢ ㄦ)
the morning; the forenoon

上半場 (ㄕㄤˋ ㄅㄢˋ ㄔㄤˇ)
first half (of a game): 上半場比哪一隊贏? Which team won at the first half of the game?

上半身 (ㄕㄤˋ ㄅㄢˋ ㄕㄣ)
the upper part of the body; above the waist

上半夜 (ㄕㄤˋ ㄅㄢˋ ㄧㄝˋ)
before midnight; the first half of the night

上半月 (ㄕㄤˋ ㄅㄢˋ ㄩㄝˋ)
the first half of a month

上榜 (ㄕㄤˋ ㄅㄤˇ)
to have one's name included in the name list of successful candidates of an examination

上幣 (ㄕㄤˋ ㄅㄧˋ)
gold and jade as currency

上臂 (ㄕㄤˋ ㄅㄧˋ)
the upper arm

上邊 (ㄕㄤˋ ㄅㄧㄢ)
①the upper side ②up there

上賓 (ㄕㄤˋ ㄅㄧㄣ)
distinguished guests

上不去 (ㄕㄤˋ ㄅㄨˋ ㄑㄩˋ)
cannot ascend it; cannot go up

上不上(ㄕㄤˋ ㄅㄨˋ ㄕㄤˋ)
(said of tools, instruments, etc.) cannot fix it

上不來(ㄕㄤˋ ㄅㄨˋ ㄌㄞˊ)
cannot come up

上部(ㄕㄤˋ ㄅㄨˋ)
①the upper portion; the first part ②the first volume (of a two-volume book)

上坡(ㄕㄤˋ ㄆㄛ)
to climb a slope

上坡路(ㄕㄤˋ ㄆㄛ ㄌㄨˋ)
an ascending road or path; an uphill road; an upward slope

上片(ㄕㄤˋ ㄆㄧㄢˋ)
to start showing a movie (in a movie theater)

上品(ㄕㄤˋ ㄆㄧㄣˇ)
goods of superior quality

上鋪(ㄕㄤˋ ㄆㄨˋ)
the upper berth

上馬(ㄕㄤˋ ㄇㄚˇ)
to mount a horse

上門(ㄕㄤˋ ㄇㄣˊ)or 上門兒(ㄕㄤˋ ㄇㄣˊ ㄦ)
to visit; to call

上面(ㄕㄤˋ ㄇㄧㄢˋ)or 上面兒(ㄕㄤˋ ㄇㄧㄢˋ ㄦ)
①the upper surface; the top; above ②the higher authorities ③aspect; respect

上發條(ㄕㄤˋ ㄈㄚ ㄊㄧㄠˊ)
to wind a watch, clock, mechanical toy, etc.

上墳(ㄕㄤˋ ㄈㄣˊ)
to visit somebody's grave

上方(ㄕㄤˋ ㄈㄤ)
①the place above ②the celestial realm

上房(ㄕㄤˋ ㄈㄤˊ)
①the position of a lawfully wedded wife—in contrast to the position of the concubines ②main rooms (usually facing south, within a courtyard)

上風(ㄕㄤˋ ㄈㄥ)
①the upper hand; advantage ②windward

上峰(ㄕㄤˋ ㄈㄥ)
the upper echelon; the higher-up

上伏塔(ㄕㄤˋ ㄈㄨˊ ㄊㄚˇ)
Upper Volta

上達(ㄕㄤˋ ㄉㄚˊ)
to reach the higher authorities

上德(ㄕㄤˋ ㄉㄜˊ)
the highest virtue

上代(ㄕㄤˋ ㄉㄞˋ)
the previous generation

上當(ㄕㄤˋ ㄉㄤˋ)
to be taken in; to be a fool; to be fooled: 同這種人打交道, 你會上當。Dealing with such a person, you will be taken in.

上燈(ㄕㄤˋ ㄉㄥ)
to light the lamp; to light up

上等(ㄕㄤˋ ㄉㄥˇ)
first-class; superior quality

上等兵(ㄕㄤˋ ㄉㄥˇ ㄅㄧㄥ)
private first class (PFC)

上帝(ㄕㄤˋ ㄉㄧˋ)
God: 願上帝幫助你。God help you!

上吊(ㄕㄤˋ ㄉㄧㄠˋ)or 上弔(ㄕㄤˋ ㄉㄧㄠˋ)
to commit suicide by hanging; to hang oneself

上端(ㄕㄤˋ ㄉㄨㄢ)
the upper end

上臺(ㄕㄤˋ ㄊㄞˊ)
①to go on the stage ②(said of high-ranking officials) to assume office

上套兒(ㄕㄤˋ ㄊㄠˋ ㄦ)
①to put the bit on a horse ②to be imposed upon

上頭(ㄕㄤˋ ㄊㄡˊ)
①the top; above; up ②the authorities

上膛(ㄕㄤˋ ㄊㄤˊ)
(said of a gun) to be loaded: 子彈上膛了。The gun is loaded.

上天(ㄕㄤˋ ㄊㄧㄢ)
①Heaven; Providence; God ②to go up to the sky

上天下地(ㄕㄤˋ ㄊㄧㄢ ㄒㄧㄚˋ ㄉㄧˋ)
(literally) to ascend the heaven or to descend to earth—①everywhere ②to leave no stone unturned; to spare no efforts

上天無路入地無門(ㄕㄤˋ ㄊㄧㄢ ㄨˊ ㄌㄨˋ ㄖㄨˋ ㄉㄧˋ ㄨˊ ㄇㄣˊ)
There is no road to heaven and no door into the earth. — (figuratively) no way of escape; at the end of the rope; in a desperate situation; at the end of the line;

at the end of the road

上哪兒去?(ㄕㄤˋ ㄋㄚˇ ㄦ ㄑㄩˋ)
Where to go? 或Where are you going?

上年(ㄕㄤˋ ㄋㄧㄢˊ)
last year

上年紀(ㄕㄤˋ ㄋㄧㄢˊ ㄐㄧˋ)or 上了年紀(ㄕㄤˋ ㄌㄜ ㄋㄧㄢˊ ㄐㄧˋ)
getting on in years; getting along in years

上蠟(ㄕㄤˋ ㄌㄚˋ)
(textile and dyeing) waxing

上來(ㄕㄤˋ ㄌㄞˊ)
Come up! 或Come out!

上壘(ㄕㄤˋ ㄌㄟˇ)
(baseball) to touch the base

上樓(ㄕㄤˋ ㄌㄡˊ)
to go upstairs

上列(ㄕㄤˋ ㄌㄧㄝˋ)
the above-listed; the above-mentioned

上流(ㄕㄤˋ ㄌㄧㄡˊ)
①the upper part of a stream ②belonging to the upper circles

上流社會(ㄕㄤˋ ㄌㄧㄡˊ ㄕㄜˋ ㄏㄨㄟˋ)
the upper class; the high society

上聯(ㄕㄤˋ ㄌㄧㄢˊ)
the first line of a couplet on a scroll

上梁(ㄕㄤˋ ㄌㄧㄤˊ)
(said of buildings) the main beam

上梁不正下梁歪(ㄕㄤˋ ㄌㄧㄤˊ ㄅㄨˋ ㄓㄥˋ ㄒㄧㄚˋ ㄌㄧㄤˊ ㄨㄞ)
When the higher-ups (or parents) do not set a good example, the subordinates (or children) cannot be expected to behave well.

上路(ㄕㄤˋ ㄌㄨˋ)
①to start a journey ②(slang) good; well-behaved

上略(ㄕㄤˋ ㄌㄩㄝˋ)
the above or preceding part omitted

上鈎(ㄕㄤˋ ㄍㄡ)
①(fishing) to be caught by the hook ②to fall into the snare; to be tricked into doing something

上古(ㄕㄤˋ ㄍㄨˇ)
prehistoric times; ancient times

上軌道(ㄕㄤˋ ㄍㄨㄟˇ ㄉㄠˋ)

to get on the right track—to begin to work smoothly: 我們的工作已上軌道。Our work goes on smoothly.

上官(ㄕㄤˋ ㄍㄨㄢ)
① one's direct superior in office ② a compound surname

上工(ㄕㄤˋ ㄍㄨㄥ)
to begin work

上供(ㄕㄤˋ ㄍㄨㄥ)
① to offer sacrifices in worship ② taxes which went directly to the imperial treasury in the Tang Dynasty

上客(ㄕㄤˋ ㄎㄜˋ)
distinguished or esteemed guests

上課(ㄕㄤˋ ㄎㄜˋ)
(said of students) to attend class; (said of teachers) to conduct class

上口(ㄕㄤˋ ㄎㄡˇ)
easy to speak or read; euphonious

上款(ㄕㄤˋ ㄎㄨㄢˇ)
the address of the recipient, including his given name and position, etc., of a painting or calligraphic work

上空(ㄕㄤˋ ㄎㄨㄥ)
in the sky; overhead

上空裝(ㄕㄤˋ ㄎㄨㄥ ㄓㄨㄤ)
a topless suit

上海(ㄕㄤˋ ㄏㄞˇ)
Shanghai

上好(ㄕㄤˋ ㄏㄠˇ)
superior; excellent; the best

上戶(ㄕㄤˋ ㄏㄨˋ)
a wealthy family

上火(ㄕㄤˋ ㄏㄨㄛˇ)
①(dialect) to get angry ②(Chinese medicine) to suffer from too much internal heat (with such symptoms as constipation, conjunctivitis and inflammation of the nasal and oral cavities)

上貨(ㄕㄤˋ ㄏㄨㄛˋ)
to load (ships, trucks, etc.)

上回(ㄕㄤˋ ㄏㄨㄟˊ)
on a previous occasion; last time

上會(ㄕㄤˋ ㄏㄨㄟˋ)
to attend a temporary association for mutual loan money, decided monthly by

the highest bidder for interest, or by dice

上級(ㄕㄤˋ ㄐㄧˊ)
higher-ups; superiors

上計(ㄕㄤˋ ㄐㄧˋ)
the best plan

上街(ㄕㄤˋ ㄐㄧㄝ)
① to go into (or on) the street ② to go shopping

上屆(ㄕㄤˋ ㄐㄧㄝˋ)
the previous (election, congress, conference, tour of duty, etc.)

上界(ㄕㄤˋ ㄐㄧㄝˋ)
heaven

上繳(ㄕㄤˋ ㄐㄧㄠˇ)
to transfer (revenues, etc.) to the higher authorities

上進(ㄕㄤˋ ㄐㄧㄣˋ)
to make progress; to advance

上勁(ㄕㄤˋ ㄐㄧㄣˋ)
energetically; with gusto; with great vigor: 他工作比別人更上勁。He works more energetically than others.

上江(ㄕㄤˋ ㄐㄧㄤ)
the upper Yangtze

上漿(ㄕㄤˋ ㄐㄧㄤ)
to starch (laundries, etc.); (textile and dyeing) to size; sizing

上將(ㄕㄤˋ ㄐㄧㄤˋ)
(army, marine, and air force) full general; (navy) full admiral

上鏡頭(ㄕㄤˋ ㄐㄧㄥˋ ㄊㄡˊ)
① photogenic ② to appear in a movie

上氣不接下氣(ㄕㄤˋ ㄑㄧˋ ㄅㄨˋ ㄐㄧㄝ ㄒㄧㄚˋ ㄑㄧˋ)
to be out of breath: 他跑得太快，因而上氣不接下氣。He ran so fast that he was out of breath.

上前(ㄕㄤˋ ㄑㄧㄢˊ)
to come forward

上去(ㄕㄤˋ ㄑㄩ)
to go up; to ascend

上下(ㄕㄤˋ ㄒㄧㄚˋ)
① above and below; up and down ② superior and inferior; ruler and subjects; senior and junior; high and low ③ about; more or less ④ heaven and earth ⑤ to go up and come down: 山上修了

公路，我們上下很方便。With the completion of the freeway up the mountain, we can easily go up and come down.

上下交征利(ㄕㄤˋ ㄒㄧㄚˋ ㄐㄧㄠ ㄓㄥ ㄌㄧˋ)
Everybody (in a country) is greedy.

上下其手(ㄕㄤˋ ㄒㄧㄚˋ ㄑㄧˊ ㄕㄡˇ)
to distort facts to suit one's private ends

上下四方(ㄕㄤˋ ㄒㄧㄚˋ ㄙˋ ㄈㄤ)
in all directions

上下一心(ㄕㄤˋ ㄒㄧㄚˋ ㄧ ㄒㄧㄣ)
of one heart and mind 或 The leadership and the rank and file are of one heart and mind. 亦作「上下一條心」

上下文(ㄕㄤˋ ㄒㄧㄚˋ ㄨㄣˊ)
the context

上校(ㄕㄤˋ ㄒㄧㄠˋ)
(army, marine, and air force) colonel; (navy) captain

上弦(ㄕㄤˋ ㄒㄧㄢˊ)
the first quarter of the moon

上限(ㄕㄤˋ ㄒㄧㄢˋ)
the upper limit

上香(ㄕㄤˋ ㄒㄧㄤ)
to offer incense (to ancestors, Buddhist deities or Taoist deities)

上詳(ㄕㄤˋ ㄒㄧㄤˊ)
to report to a superior

上像(ㄕㄤˋ ㄒㄧㄤˋ)
to come out well in a photograph; to be photogenic 參看「上鏡頭」

上刑(ㄕㄤˋ ㄒㄧㄥˊ)
to apply the third degree; to torture

上行(ㄕㄤˋ ㄒㄧㄥˊ)
to go up to the north

上行下效(ㄕㄤˋ ㄒㄧㄥˊ ㄒㄧㄚˋ ㄒㄧㄠˋ)
The doings of superiors are imitated by inferiors. 或 The subordinates will follow the example set by their superiors.

上行車(ㄕㄤˋ ㄒㄧㄥˊ ㄔㄜ)
the up train

上學(ㄕㄤˋ ㄒㄩㄝˊ)
to go to school

上選(ㄕㄤˋ ㄒㄩㄢˇ)
the choicest

上旬(ㄕㄤˋ ㄒㄩㄣˊ)

the first ten days of a month

上肢(ㄕㄤˋㄓ)
the upper limbs

上智 or 上知(ㄕㄤˋㄓ)
the sage; the wisest; the most intelligent

上週(ㄕㄤˋㄓㄡ) or 上禮拜(ㄕㄤˋㄌㄧˇㄅㄞˋ) or 上星期(ㄕㄤˋㄒㄧㄥ ㄑㄧˊ)
last week

上陣(ㄕㄤˋㄓㄣˋ)
①to pitch into the work ②to go to battle

上漲(ㄕㄤˋㄓㄤˇ)
(said of commodity prices or flood waters) to rise: 物價上漲. The prices are going up.

上賬 or 上帳(ㄕㄤˋㄓㄤˋ)
to put a purchase on credit; to make an entry in an account book

上裝(ㄕㄤˋㄓㄨㄤ)
to make up (for a theatrical performance); to dress up (as an actor or a bride)

上車(ㄕㄤˋㄔㄜ)
to get on or into (a car, truck, bus or train)

上朝(ㄕㄤˋㄔㄠˊ)
to go to the imperial court

上場(ㄕㄤˋㄔㄤˇ) or (ㄕㄤˋㄔㄤˋ)
①(drama)to go on stage; to enter ②(sports) to enter the court or field

上船(ㄕㄤˋㄔㄨㄢˊ)
to board a ship; to embark

上床(ㄕㄤˋㄔㄨㄤˊ)
to go to bed

上士(ㄕㄤˋㄕˋ)
(military rank) first sergeant

上市(ㄕㄤˋㄕˋ)
(said of seasonal goods or new products) to go on the market

上世(ㄕㄤˋㄕˋ)
the primeval times; the pre-historic times

上首(ㄕㄤˋㄕㄡˇ)
① the honored one ②the seat of honor 亦作「上座」

上壽(ㄕㄤˋㄕㄡˋ)
①advanced age ②to drink a toast for longevity

上山(ㄕㄤˋㄕㄢ)
to go up a hill; to go to the

mountains

上身(ㄕㄤˋㄕㄣ)or上身兒(ㄕㄤˋㄕㄣㄦ)
①the torso; the upper part of the body ②an upper outer garment; a blouse; a jacket ③to wear ④ to contract a disease; to incur some misfortune

上上(ㄕㄤˋㄕㄤˋ)
the very best

上上大吉(ㄕㄤˋㄕㄤˋㄉㄚˋㄐㄧˊ)
most auspicious (a phrase usually used in divination)

上上下下(ㄕㄤˋㄕㄤˋㄒㄧㄚˋㄒㄧㄚˋ)
①above and below; up and down ②all; the whole

上升 or 上昇(ㄕㄤˋㄕㄥ)
to soar or rise

上乘(ㄕㄤˋㄔㄥˊ)
①a carriage drawn by a team of four horses ②(Buddhism) the Great Conveyance ③the best in quality

上書(ㄕㄤˋㄕㄨ)
to present a petition; to make a presentation in writing

上述(ㄕㄤˋㄕㄨˋ)
the aforesaid or afore-mentioned; what has been mentioned before

上疏(ㄕㄤˋㄕㄨ)
to submit an appeal or a memorial to the emperor

上水(ㄕㄤˋㄕㄨㄟˇ)
①to add water (to a kettle) ②to sail against the current ③to feed water to a stream engine, radiator (of an auto-mobile) ④to sprinkle water on vegetables or fruit

上稅(ㄕㄤˋㄕㄨㄟˋ)
to levy taxes or duties

上日(ㄕㄤˋㄖˋ)
①the first day of the lunar month ②a beautiful or fes-tive day

上人(ㄕㄤˋㄖㄣˊ)
(a courteous address) a monk

上任(ㄕㄤˋㄖㄣˋ)
to take up an official appointment; to enter upon office

上祖(ㄕㄤˋㄗㄨˇ)
remote ancestors

上座(ㄕㄤˋㄗㄨㄛˋ)or上座兒(ㄕㄤˋㄗㄨㄛˋㄦ)

ㄗㄨㄛˋㄦ)
the seat at the head of the table reserved for the guest of honor; the seat of honor

上次(ㄕㄤˋㄘˋ)
last time; the previous occa-sion

上策(ㄕㄤˋㄘㄜˋ)
the best stratagem; the best plan; the best way

上菜(ㄕㄤˋㄘㄞˋ)
①the best dishes ②to place dishes on the table

上操(ㄕㄤˋㄘㄠ)
to drill; to do physical exer-cises

上蒼(ㄕㄤˋㄘㄤ)
Heaven; God

上層(ㄕㄤˋㄘㄥˊ)
the upper layer, level or stratum

上竄下跳(ㄕㄤˋㄘㄨㄢˋㄒㄧㄚˋㄊㄧㄠˋ)
to run around on sinister errands

上司(ㄕㄤˋㄙ)
a boss; a superior official

上駟(ㄕㄤˋㄙˋ)
a thoroughbred horse

上色(ㄕㄤˋㄙㄜˋ)
①best-quality; top-grade ②to color (a picture, map, etc.)

上訴(ㄕㄤˋㄙㄨˋ)
①to appeal to a higher court ②to state one's case to a superior

上鎖(ㄕㄤˋㄙㄨㄛˇ)
to lock

上歲數(ㄕㄤˋㄙㄨㄟˋㄕㄨˋ)
to be getting on in years

上算(ㄕㄤˋㄙㄨㄢˋ)
a profitable deal; economi-cal

上顎(ㄕㄤˋㄜˋ)
the palate

上衣(ㄕㄤˋㄧ)
upper garments; jackets

上議院(ㄕㄤˋㄧˋㄩㄢˋ)
the Upper House; the Senate

上油(ㄕㄤˋㄧㄡˊ)
to apply lubricant; to replen-ish lubricating oil

上游(ㄕㄤˋㄧㄡˊ)
①the upper reaches (of a river)②advanced position: 他力爭上游. He strived for

（一部）

the best.

上言(ㄕㄤˋ 一ㄢˊ)
to submit (request, etc.) respectfully

上眼(ㄕㄤˋ 一ㄢˇ)
to be worth looking at

上演(ㄕㄤˋ 一ㄢˇ)
to perform; to stage (a play)

上癮(ㄕㄤˋ 一ㄣˇ)
to become addicted to a certain drug or habit; habit-forming 這種藥吃多了會上癮。
This medicine is habit-forming.

上映(ㄕㄤˋ 一ㄥˋ)
to show (a movie)

上午(ㄕㄤˋ ㄨˇ)
forenoon; A.M.

上位(ㄕㄤˋ ㄨㄟˋ)
① a top seat ② a person occupying a leading position

上尉(ㄕㄤˋ ㄨㄟˋ)
(navy) lieutenant; (army, marine and air force) captain

上文(ㄕㄤˋ ㄨㄣˊ)
the foregoing paragraphs or chapters; preceding part of the text; the preceding context

上愚(ㄕㄤˋ ㄩˊ)
the most stupid

上諭(ㄕㄤˋ ㄩˋ)
an imperial edict

上月(ㄕㄤˋ ㄩㄝˋ)or 上個月(ㄕㄤˋ ㄍㄜˋ ㄩㄝˋ)
last month

上元(ㄕㄤˋ ㄩㄢˊ)
the fifteenth of the first lunar month (which is the Lantern Festival in China)

上苑(ㄕㄤˋ ㄩㄢˋ)
the royal garden

【上】 6
2. ㄕㄤˇ shaang shǎng

上聲(ㄕㄤˇ ㄕㄥ)
falling-rising tone, one of the four tones in classical Chinese and the third tone in modern standard Chinese phonetics

【下】 7
ㄒㄧㄚˋ shiah xià

1. to put down
2. to lay
3. to fall

4. to descend
5. to begin
6. below; under: 現在溫度在冰點以下。The temperature is now below freezing point.
7. inferior; lower
8. next

下巴(ㄒㄧㄚˋ ㄅㄚ)or 下巴頦(ㄒㄧㄚˋ ·ㄅㄚ ㄎㄜ)or 下巴頦兒(ㄒㄧㄚˋ ·ㄅㄚ ㄎㄜㄦ)
the chin; the lower jaw

下膊(ㄒㄧㄚˋ ㄅㄛˊ)
the lower arm

下擺(ㄒㄧㄚˋ ㄅㄞˇ)
the lower part of a Chinese gown

下拜(ㄒㄧㄚˋ ㄅㄞˋ)
to bow

下輩(ㄒㄧㄚˋ ㄅㄟˋ)or 下輩兒(ㄒㄧㄚˋ ㄅㄟㄦ)
the next generation; the younger generation of a family

下輩子(ㄒㄧㄚˋ ㄅㄟˋ ·ㄗ)
the next life; the next incarnation

下班(ㄒㄧㄚˋ ㄅㄢ)
to leave office (or factory) after working hours; to knock off

下半輩(ㄒㄧㄚˋ ㄅㄢˋ ㄅㄟˋ)
the latter half of one's life; the rest of one's life

下半天(ㄒㄧㄚˋ ㄅㄢˋ ㄊㄧㄢ)
the last half day; afternoon

下半旗(ㄒㄧㄚˋ ㄅㄢˋ ㄑㄧˊ)
to fly a flag at half-mast

下半場(ㄒㄧㄚˋ ㄅㄢˋ ㄔㄤˇ)
the second half (of a game)

下半晌(ㄒㄧㄚˋ ㄅㄢˋ ㄕㄤˇ)
afternoon

下半夜(ㄒㄧㄚˋ ㄅㄢˋ 一ㄝˋ)
after midnight; the wee hours

下半月(ㄒㄧㄚˋ ㄅㄢˋ ㄩㄝˋ)
the last half month; after the 15th of a month

下筆(ㄒㄧㄚˋ ㄅㄧˇ)
to start writing

下筆成章(ㄒㄧㄚˋ ㄅㄧˇ ㄔㄥˊ ㄓㄤ)
to write quickly and skilfully; to have literary acumen

下邊(ㄒㄧㄚˋ ㄅㄧㄢ)or 下邊兒(ㄒㄧㄚˋ ㄅㄧㄢㄦ)
as follows; following; below; under

下部(ㄒㄧㄚˋ ㄅㄨˋ)

① the lower part ② the private parts

下不了臺(ㄒㄧㄚˋ ㄅㄨˋ ㄌㄧㄠˇ ㄊㄞˊ)
① cannot bring to a conclusion ② to put someone in an awkward position; to be put on the spot

下不爲例(ㄒㄧㄚˋ ㄅㄨˋ ㄨㄟˊ ㄌㄧˋ)
This does not constitute a precedent. 或 Don't do it again! 或 Just this once.

下不來(ㄒㄧㄚˋ ㄅㄨˋ ㄌㄞˊ)
① cannot get down ② to be embarrassed

下不去(ㄒㄧㄚˋ ㄅㄨˋ ㄑㄩˋ)
to go against; to harass; to cause someone to lose face

下坡路(ㄒㄧㄚˋ ㄆㄛ ㄌㄨˋ)
a descending road or foot path

下片(ㄒㄧㄚˋ ㄆㄧㄢˋ)
to stop showing a movie (after attendance tapers off)

下品(ㄒㄧㄚˋ ㄆㄧㄣˇ)
low-grade; inferior

下聘(ㄒㄧㄚˋ ㄆㄧㄣˋ)
to present betrothal gifts

下舖(ㄒㄧㄚˋ ㄆㄨˋ)
the lower berth

下馬(ㄒㄧㄚˋ ㄇㄚˇ)
to dismount from a horse

下馬威(ㄒㄧㄚˋ ㄇㄚˇ ㄨㄟ)
to warn against insubordination, etc. by enforcing strict disciplinary action when one first takes office

下麵(ㄒㄧㄚˋ ㄇㄧㄢˋ)
to cook noodles

下面(ㄒㄧㄚˋ ·ㄇㄧㄢ)or 下面兒(ㄒㄧㄚˋ ㄇㄧㄢㄦ)
① underneath; below ② following; ③ lower levels; subordinates 請瞭解下面情況。Please find out about how things are at the lower levels.

下命令(ㄒㄧㄚˋ ㄇㄧㄥˋ ㄌㄧㄥˋ)
to give orders 亦作「下令」

下凡(ㄒㄧㄚˋ ㄈㄢˊ)
(said of supernatural beings or gods in mythology) to descend to earth from heaven

下飯(ㄒㄧㄚˋ ㄈㄢˋ)
(said of dishes) to go along with rice

下方(ㄒㄧㄚˋ ㄈㄤ)

① south and west ② below;
under ③ below the earth

下房(ㄒㄧㄚˋ ㄈㄤˊ)
the servant's quarters

下放(ㄒㄧㄚˋ ㄈㄤˋ)
to transfer to a lower level:
他把權力下放。He transfered
his power to a lower level.

下風(ㄒㄧㄚˋ ㄈㄥ)
① in an inferior position; at
a disadvantage ② leeward

下蛋(ㄒㄧㄚˋ ㄉㄢˋ)
to lay eggs

下等(ㄒㄧㄚˋ ㄉㄥˇ)
①low-grade②mean; depraved

下地(ㄒㄧㄚˋ ㄉㄧˋ)
① to go to the fields ② to
leave a sickbed

下地獄(ㄒㄧㄚˋ ㄉㄧˋ ㄩˋ)
to go to hell

下定(ㄒㄧㄚˋ ㄉㄧㄥˋ)
to send betrothal gifts or
money

下定義(ㄒㄧㄚˋ ㄉㄧㄥˋ ㄧˋ)
to define; to give a definition

下毒(ㄒㄧㄚˋ ㄉㄨˊ)
to poison; to put poison into
something

下毒手(ㄒㄧㄚˋ ㄉㄨˊ ㄕㄡˇ)
to lay violent hands on
someone

下榻(ㄒㄧㄚˋ ㄊㄚˋ)
to take up abode; to stay

下臺(ㄒㄧㄚˋ ㄊㄞˊ)
① to get off stage ② to be
relieved from office; to go
out of power

下列(ㄒㄧㄚˋ ㄌㄧㄝˋ)
as follows; below; under

下堂(ㄒㄧㄚˋ ㄊㄤˊ)
to leave or to be divorced
by one's husband

下體(ㄒㄧㄚˋ ㄊㄧˇ)
the privates; the genitals

下帖(ㄒㄧㄚˋ ㄊㄧㄝˇ)
to send an invitation

下條子(ㄒㄧㄚˋ ㄊㄧㄠˊ ㄗˇ)
to send notes or memos to
one's subordinates

下田(ㄒㄧㄚˋ ㄊㄧㄢˊ)
to work on farmland; to cultivate the land

下土(ㄒㄧㄚˋ ㄊㄨˇ)
① the earth; the world ② the
countryside

下同(ㄒㄧㄚˋ ㄊㄨㄥˊ)
similarly hereinafter; the
same below

下女(ㄒㄧㄚˋ ㄋㄩˇ)
a maid

下來(ㄒㄧㄚˋ ·ㄌㄞ)
to come down

下樓(ㄒㄧㄚˋ ㄌㄡˊ)
to descend the stairs; to go
(or come) downstairs

下禮(ㄒㄧㄚˋ ㄌㄧˇ)
to send gifts

下里巴人(ㄒㄧㄚˋ ㄌㄧˇ ㄅㄚ ㄖㄣˊ)
simple and crude folk songs

下列(ㄒㄧㄚˋ ㄌㄧㄝˋ)or 下開(ㄒㄧㄚˋ
ㄎㄞ)
① as follows ② what are
listed below: 注意下列幾點。
Pay attention to the following points.

下流(ㄒㄧㄚˋ ㄌㄧㄡˊ)
① downstream ② to flow
down ③ low; nasty; mean;
scurrilous

下流話(ㄒㄧㄚˋ ㄌㄧㄡˊ ㄏㄨㄚˋ)
obscene (or dirty, foul) language; obscenities

下聯(ㄒㄧㄚˋ ㄌㄧㄢˊ)
the second line of a couplet

下令(ㄒㄧㄚˋ ㄌㄧㄥˋ)
to give orders; to order

下落(ㄒㄧㄚˋ ㄌㄨㄛˋ)
whereabouts: 有一幅古畫現在
下落不明。 The whereabouts
of one of the ancient paintings is unknown.

下略(ㄒㄧㄚˋ ㄌㄩㄝˋ)
What follows is omitted.

下崗(ㄒㄧㄚˋ ㄍㄤˇ)
to come or go off sentry
duty

下國(ㄒㄧㄚˋ ㄍㄨㄛˊ)
my humble country

下跪(ㄒㄧㄚˋ ㄍㄨㄟˋ)
to kneel down: 教堂中每個人
都下跪祈禱。 Everyone in the
church knelt in prayer.

下工(ㄒㄧㄚˋ ㄍㄨㄥ)
to leave when one's work is
done; to stop working

下工夫(ㄒㄧㄚˋ ㄍㄨㄥ·ㄈㄨ)
to devote much time and
energy to a task

下課(ㄒㄧㄚˋ ㄎㄜˋ)
to get out of class; to finish
class

下款(ㄒㄧㄚˋ ㄎㄨㄢˇ)
the signature of an artist on
a painting or calligraphic
work presented to someone
as a gift

下海(ㄒㄧㄚˋ ㄏㄞˇ)
① to turn professional (usually referring to show personalities) ② to go to sea

下頦(ㄒㄧㄚˋ ㄏㄞˊ)
the lower jaw; the mandible

下懷(ㄒㄧㄚˋ ㄏㄨㄞˊ)
one's desire; one's concern:
正中下懷 to be exactly what
one wants

下回(ㄒㄧㄚˋ ㄏㄨㄟˊ)
next time

下級(ㄒㄧㄚˋ ㄐㄧˊ)
① lower levels ② subordi-
nates

下嫁(ㄒㄧㄚˋ ㄐㄧㄚˋ)
to marry someone beneath
her station

下屆(ㄒㄧㄚˋ ㄐㄧㄝˋ)
next (term, election, etc.)

下界(ㄒㄧㄚˋ ㄐㄧㄝˋ)
the earth (in the eyes of
supernatural beings who are
supposed to dwell in the
heavens above); the world of
mortals

下腳(ㄒㄧㄚˋ ㄐㄧㄠˇ)
① to get a foothold; to make
a short stay ② residual raw
materials; scraps

下酒(ㄒㄧㄚˋ ㄐㄧㄡˇ)
(said of food) to go with
wine or liquor

下酒菜(ㄒㄧㄚˋ ㄐㄧㄡˇ ㄘㄞˋ)
a dish that goes with wine

下賤(ㄒㄧㄚˋ ㄐㄧㄢˋ)
low; cheap; degrading

下降(ㄒㄧㄚˋ ㄐㄧㄤˋ)
to descend; to drop: 氣溫驟然
下降。There was a sudden
drop in the temperature.

下決心(ㄒㄧㄚˋ ㄐㄩㄝˊ ㄒㄧㄣ)
to make a resolution

下棋(ㄒㄧㄚˋ ㄑㄧˊ)
to play chess

下旗歸國(ㄒㄧㄚˋ ㄑㄧˊ ㄍㄨㄟ ㄍㄨㄛˊ)
(said of diplomats) to close
diplomatic mission and
return home after severance
or suspension of official ties

下氣(ㄒㄧㄚˋ ㄑㄧˋ)
① calm; to keep calm ②

（二）
部】

(Chinese medicine) to emit gas

下妾(ㄒㄧㄚˋ ㄑㄧㄝˋ)
(formerly, the wife's self-reference) your wife

下情(ㄒㄧㄚˋ ㄑㄧㄥˊ)
the opinion of the masses; the difficulties or problems encountered by a subordinate

下去(ㄒㄧㄚˋ ㄑㄩˋ)
①to go down 到站了，快下去。Here we are. Let's get off at once. ②to go on: 你這樣工作下去必會累垮。If you go on working like this, you'll certainly crack up.

下弦(ㄒㄧㄚˋ ㄒㄧㄢˊ)
the last quarter of the moon usually on the 22nd or 23rd day of a month in the Chinese lunar calendar

下限(ㄒㄧㄚˋ ㄒㄧㄢˋ)
lower limit; prescribed minimum; floor level

下鄉(ㄒㄧㄚˋ ㄒㄧㄤ)
to go to the country; to rusticate

下行(ㄒㄧㄚˋ ㄒㄧㄥˊ)
(train) traveling away from the starting point of a line, usually southward

下行車(ㄒㄧㄚˋ ㄒㄧㄥˊ ㄔㄜ)
the down train

下學(ㄒㄧㄚˋ ㄒㄩㄝˊ)
to leave for home after school

下學期(ㄒㄧㄚˋ ㄒㄩㄝˊ ㄑㄧ)
next semester; the coming term

下雪(ㄒㄧㄚˋ ㄒㄩㄝˇ)
to snow

下旬(ㄒㄧㄚˋ ㄒㄩㄣˊ)
the last ten days of a month

下肢(ㄒㄧㄚˋ ㄓ)
the lower limbs

下詔(ㄒㄧㄚˋ ㄓㄠˋ)
to issue imperial orders or instructions

下戰書(ㄒㄧㄚˋ ㄓㄢˋ ㄕㄨ)
to deliver a challenge in writing

下逐客令(ㄒㄧㄚˋ ㄓㄨˊ ㄎㄜˋ ㄌㄧㄥˋ)
to ask an unwelcome guest or visitor to leave; to throw out a guest after he has overstayed his welcome

下注(ㄒㄧㄚˋ ㄓㄨˋ)
to put stake; to stake a wager; to wager

下箸(ㄒㄧㄚˋ ㄓㄨˋ)
to start eating

下墜(ㄒㄧㄚˋ ㄓㄨㄟˋ)
to fall

下裝(ㄒㄧㄚˋ ㄓㄨㄤ)
to take off one's costume (especially referring to performers)

下種(ㄒㄧㄚˋ ㄓㄨㄥˇ)
to sow seed

下茶(ㄒㄧㄚˋ ㄔㄚˊ)
to send a gift of tea as a token of betrothal

下車(ㄒㄧㄚˋ ㄔㄜ)
①to get off (trains or vehicles, etc.) ②to take up new office

下沉(ㄒㄧㄚˋ ㄔㄣˊ)
to sink; to subside; to submerge

下場(ㄒㄧㄚˋ ㄔㄤˇ)or(ㄒㄧㄚˋ ㄔㄤˊ)
①the conclusion; the end: 他的下場可惡。He met with a miserable fate. ②to get to the playground to compete, play ball, etc. ③an exit on the stage

下廚(ㄒㄧㄚˋ ㄔㄨˊ)
to go to the kitchen; to prepare food

下處(ㄒㄧㄚˋ ㄔㄨˋ)
one's temporary lodging during a trip; a lodging for the night

下垂(ㄒㄧㄚˋ ㄔㄨㄟˊ)
①to hang down; to droop ②(medicine) prolapse

下船(ㄒㄧㄚˋ ㄔㄨㄢˊ)
to go ashore

下牀(ㄒㄧㄚˋ ㄔㄨㄤˊ)
to get up

下士(ㄒㄧㄚˋ ㄕˋ)
①(military rank) corporal ②a fool ③an ordinary person

下室(ㄒㄧㄚˋ ㄕˋ)
a bedroom

下手(ㄒㄧㄚˋ ㄕㄡˇ)
①to start doing something: 我不知從何處下手。I don't know where to start. ②to commit a crime ③an inferior attendant; a helper; an assistant

下首(ㄒㄧㄚˋ ㄕㄡˇ)
the right-hand seat

下山(ㄒㄧㄚˋ ㄕㄢ)
to go down a mountain

下身(ㄒㄧㄚˋ ㄕㄣ)or下身兒(ㄒㄧㄚˋ ㄕㄜㄦ)
①the lower part of the body ②the privates

下書(ㄒㄧㄚˋ ㄕㄨ)
to deliver a letter

下屬(ㄒㄧㄚˋ ㄕㄨˇ)
subordinates

下水(ㄒㄧㄚˋ ㄕㄨㄟˇ)
①(ㄒㄧㄚˋ ㄕㄨㄟˇ) to launch a boat: 這艘新船下水了。This new ship was launched. ②(ㄒㄧㄚˋ ㄕㄨㄟˇ) internal organs of animals (especially poultry)

下水道(ㄒㄧㄚˋ ㄕㄨㄟˇ ㄉㄠˋ)
sewers; the sewerage system

下水禮(ㄒㄧㄚˋ ㄕㄨㄟˇ ㄌㄧˇ)
the ceremony of launching a ship

下人(ㄒㄧㄚˋ ㄖㄣˊ)
servants

下葬(ㄒㄧㄚˋ ㄗㄤˋ)
to bury: 他昨天下葬。He was buried yesterday.

下座(ㄒㄧㄚˋ ㄗㄨㄛˋ)
inferior seats or ranks

下作(ㄒㄧㄚˋ ㄗㄨㄛˋ)
①low; vulgar; nasty ②greedy; gluttonous

下罪(ㄒㄧㄚˋ ㄗㄨㄟˋ)
to convict

下次(ㄒㄧㄚˋ ㄘˋ)
next time

下策(ㄒㄧㄚˋ ㄘㄜˋ)
a bad strategy, measure or policy

下層(ㄒㄧㄚˋ ㄘㄥˊ)
①a lower stratum, layer or deck ②low-ranking

下三爛(ㄒㄧㄚˋ ㄙㄢ ㄌㄢˋ)
a bum

下頦(ㄒㄧㄚˋ ㄎㄜ)
the lower jaw; the mandible

下意識(ㄒㄧㄚˋ ㄧˋ ㄕˋ)
subconscious

下議院(ㄒㄧㄚˋ ㄧˋ ㄩㄢˋ)
the Lower House

下野(ㄒㄧㄚˋ ㄧㄝˇ)
to quit or resign from official posts or politics (referring to top-ranking offi-

下藥（ㄒㄧㄚˋ ㄧㄠˋ）
①(said of doctors) to write a prescription ②to put in poison

下游（ㄒㄧㄚˋ ㄧㄡˊ）
downstream

下嚥（ㄒㄧㄚˋ ㄧㄢˋ）
to swallow

下午（ㄒㄧㄚˋ ㄨˇ）
afternoon

下霧（ㄒㄧㄚˋ ㄨˋ）
to mist; foggy

下文（ㄒㄧㄚˋ ㄨㄣˊ）
①the statement that follows; the words that follow ②further development or information; sequel 這案子未了, 尚有下文哩。The case is not over; there is still further development.

下問（ㄒㄧㄚˋ ㄨㄣˋ）
to learn from one's inferior

下愚（ㄒㄧㄚˋ ㄩˊ）
a fool; an imbecile

下餘（ㄒㄧㄚˋ ㄩˊ）
the remnant

下雨（ㄒㄧㄚˋ ㄩˇ）
to rain

下雨天（ㄒㄧㄚˋ ㄩˇ ㄊㄧㄢ）
a rainy day

下獄（ㄒㄧㄚˋ ㄩˋ）
to put behind bars; to imprison

下月（ㄒㄧㄚˋ ㄩㄝˋ）
next month

下元（ㄒㄧㄚˋ ㄩㄢˊ）
the 15th day of the 10th month in the Chinese lunar calendar

三畫

【不】 ㄅㄨˋ buh bù
（變調 ㄅㄨˊ bwu bú）
no; not; negative: 他不走了。He's not going.

不白之冤（ㄅㄨˋ ㄅㄞˊ ㄓ ㄩㄢ）
①a wrong that has not been righted ②falsely accused

不敗之地（ㄅㄨˋ ㄅㄞˋ ㄓ ㄉㄧˋ）
an invincible position

不卑不亢（ㄅㄨˋ ㄅㄟ ㄅㄨˋ ㄎㄤˋ）
(literally) neither humble nor arrogant — to conduct

oneself properly

不備（ㄅㄨˋ ㄅㄟˋ）
not ready; by surprise; unawares; unprepared

不比（ㄅㄨˋ ㄅㄧˇ）
unlike

不必（ㄅㄨˋ ㄅㄧˋ）
not necessary; unnecessary; not have to

不避艱險（ㄅㄨˋ ㄅㄧˋ ㄐㄧㄢ ㄒㄧㄢˇ）
to shrink (or draw back) from no difficulty or danger

不便（ㄅㄨˋ ㄅㄧㄢˋ）
inconvenience; inconvenient；

不辨菽麥（ㄅㄨˋ ㄅㄧㄢˋ ㄕㄨˊ ㄇㄞˋ）
(said of a person) unable to distinguish beans from wheat — devoid of common sense; ignorant

不怕（ㄅㄨˋ ㄆㄚˋ）
not afraid

不破不立（ㄅㄨˋ ㄆㄛˋ ㄅㄨˋ ㄌㄧˋ）
No destruction, No construction.

不配（ㄅㄨˋ ㄆㄟˋ）
①mismatch；misfit ②unequal to; not qualified

不偏不倚（ㄅㄨˋ ㄆㄧㄢ ㄅㄨˋ ㄧˇ）
①exact；just ②fair；unbiased

不平（ㄅㄨˋ ㄆㄧㄥˊ）
①complain; a grudge ②unjust

不平等條約（ㄅㄨˋ ㄆㄧㄥˊ ㄉㄥˇ ㄊㄧㄠˊ ㄩㄝ）
an unequal treaty

不平則鳴（ㄅㄨˋ ㄆㄧㄥˊ ㄗㄜˊ ㄇㄧㄥˊ）
Those who are discriminated against will complain.

不美（ㄅㄨˋ ㄇㄟˇ）
unbeautiful; not pretty

不毛之地（ㄅㄨˋ ㄇㄠˊ ㄓ ㄉㄧˋ）
①barren land ②an uncivilized area

不謀而合（ㄅㄨˋ ㄇㄡˊ ㄦˊ ㄏㄜˊ）
to agree without prior consultation; to be coincident

不滿（ㄅㄨˋ ㄇㄢˇ）
discontent; dissatisfaction

不蔓不枝（ㄅㄨˋ ㄇㄢˋ ㄅㄨˋ ㄓ）
(said of writing) succinct and to the point

不忙（ㄅㄨˋ ㄇㄤˊ）
not in a hurry; to take one's time

不妙（ㄅㄨˋ ㄇㄧㄠˋ）

Something is wrong or going badly.

不眠不休（ㄅㄨˋ ㄇㄧㄢˊ ㄅㄨˋ ㄒㄧㄡ）
without rest; tireless; indefatigable

不免（ㄅㄨˋ ㄇㄧㄢˇ）
have to; must; invariably; unavoidable: 人不免一死。Man must die.

不敏（ㄅㄨˋ ㄇㄧㄣˇ）
not intelligent (a modest term referring to oneself)

不明（ㄅㄨˋ ㄇㄧㄥˊ）
not clear; nebulous; unknown

不明飛行物體（ㄅㄨˋ ㄇㄧㄥˊ ㄈㄟ ㄒㄧㄥˊ ㄨˋ ㄊㄧˇ）
unidentified flying object (UFO) 亦作「幽浮」

不明底蘊（ㄅㄨˋ ㄇㄧㄥˊ ㄉㄧˇ ㄩㄣˋ）
ignorant of the true picture

不名一錢（ㄅㄨˋ ㄇㄧㄥˊ ㄧ ㄑㄧㄢˊ）
penniless 亦作「不名一文」

不名譽（ㄅㄨˋ ㄇㄧㄥˊ ㄩˋ）
disreputable; scandalous

不乏（ㄅㄨˋ ㄈㄚˊ）
there is no lack of; not rare: 不乏先例。There is no lack of precedents

不法（ㄅㄨˋ ㄈㄚˇ）
unlawful; illegal

不法之徒（ㄅㄨˋ ㄈㄚˇ ㄓ ㄊㄨˊ）
lawless elements

不費吹灰之力（ㄅㄨˋ ㄈㄟˋ ㄔㄨㄟ ㄏㄨㄟ ㄓ ㄌㄧˋ）
as easy as blowing dust off — do not need the slightest effort

不凡（ㄅㄨˋ ㄈㄢˊ）
extraordinary；outstanding; unusual

不分彼此（ㄅㄨˋ ㄈㄣ ㄅㄧˇ ㄘˇ）
exchange of goods and services between close friends without asking for payment

不分高下（ㄅㄨˋ ㄈㄣ ㄍㄠ ㄒㄧㄚˋ）
a draw; a tie; well-matched

不分青紅皂白（ㄅㄨˋ ㄈㄣ ㄑㄧㄥ ㄏㄨㄥˊ ㄗㄠˋ ㄅㄞˊ）
indiscriminately 參看「不分皂白」

不分軒輕（ㄅㄨˋ ㄈㄣ ㄒㄩㄢ ㄑㄧㄥ）
a draw; a tie; well-matched

不分晝夜（ㄅㄨˋ ㄈㄣ ㄓㄡˋ ㄧㄝˋ）
(to work) day and night

不分畛域（ㄅㄨˋ ㄈㄣ ㄓㄣˇ ㄩˋ）

〔一部〕

regardless of geographical difference

不分首從(ㄅㄨ ㄈㄣ ㄕㄡ ㄘㄨㄥ)
(All offenders will be punished) whether they are ringleaders or accomplices.

不分勝負(ㄅㄨ ㄈㄣ ㄕㄥ ㄈㄨ)
to tie; to draw; to come out even

不分皂白(ㄅㄨ ㄈㄣ ㄗㄠ ㄅㄞ)
impetuous; indiscriminately

不妨(ㄅㄨ ㄈㄤ)
no harm in (trying, doing, etc.); might as well

不防(ㄅㄨ ㄈㄤ)
by surprise; not ready or prepared; unawares

不符(ㄅㄨ ㄈㄨ)
do not tally; to be inconsistent

不服(ㄅㄨ ㄈㄨ)
to recalcitrate; to rebel; to disobey; to resist; to refuse to accept

不服氣(ㄅㄨ ㄈㄨ ㄑㄧ)
recalcitrant; unwilling to submit; rebellious; disobedient

不服輸(ㄅㄨ ㄈㄨ ㄕㄨ)
to refuse to concede defeat

不服水土(ㄅㄨ ㄈㄨ ㄕㄨㄟ ㄊㄨ)
(said of a stranger) not get used to the climate of a new place; not acclimatized

不孚眾望(ㄅㄨ ㄈㄨ ㄓㄨㄥ ㄨㄤ)
not popular with the masses

不負所託(ㄅㄨ ㄈㄨ ㄙㄨㄛ ㄊㄨㄛ)
to merit someone's trust

不打不相識(ㄅㄨ ㄉㄚ ㄅㄨ ㄒㄧㄤ ㄕ)
Friendship results from an exchange of blows. 或 No discord, no concord.

不打緊(ㄅㄨ ㄉㄚ ㄐㄧㄣ)
do not matter; not important

不打自招(ㄅㄨ ㄉㄚ ㄗ ㄓㄠ)
to make a confession without being pressed

不得(ㄅㄨ ㄉㄜ)
don't; no; must not

不得不(ㄅㄨ ㄉㄜ ㄅㄨ)
to have to; must

不得了(ㄅㄨ ㄉㄜ ㄌㄧㄠ)
①Good heavens! ②It's serious! ③ disastrous ④ extremely

不得勁(ㄅㄨ ㄉㄜ ㄐㄧㄣ)or 不得勁

兒(ㄅㄨ ㄉㄜ ㄐㄧㄥ ㄦ)
listless; uncomfortable

不得其法(ㄅㄨ ㄉㄜ ㄑㄧ ㄈㄚ)
do not know the right way (to do something)

不得人心(ㄅㄨ ㄉㄜ ㄖㄣ ㄒㄧㄣ)
not enjoy popular support; to be unpopular

不得而知(ㄅㄨ ㄉㄜ ㄦ ㄓ)
do not know; still unknown

不得已(ㄅㄨ ㄉㄜ ㄧ)
cannot help but…; no alternative but…

不得要領(ㄅㄨ ㄉㄜ ㄧㄠ ㄌㄧㄥ)
①cannot get the gist; pointless; irrelevant ②don't know the right way (to do something)

不待說(ㄅㄨ ㄉㄞ ㄕㄨㄛ)
needless to say; it goes without saying

不導體(ㄅㄨ ㄉㄠ ㄊㄧ)
a nonconductor

不倒翁(ㄅㄨ ㄉㄠ ㄨㄥ)
①a tumbler ②a politician who deftly manages to survive many political crises; a political tightrope walker

不道德(ㄅㄨ ㄉㄠ ㄉㄜ)
immoral; unethical

不到(ㄅㄨ ㄉㄠ)
insufficient; less than

不到黃河心不死(ㄅㄨ ㄉㄠ ㄏㄨㄤ ㄏㄜ ㄒㄧㄣ ㄅㄨ ㄙ)
not stop until one reaches the Yellow River—to refuse to give up until one reaches one's goal

不丹(ㄅㄨ ㄉㄢ)
Bhutan

不單(ㄅㄨ ㄉㄢ)
①not the only ②not merely; not simply

不但(ㄅㄨ ㄉㄢ)
not only…

不憚煩(ㄅㄨ ㄉㄢ ㄈㄢ)
to spare no effort; do not shrink from trouble

不當(ㄅㄨ ㄉㄤ)
unsuitable; improper; inappropriate;這件案子他們處理不當。They handled this case improperly.

不登大雅之堂(ㄅㄨ ㄉㄥ ㄉㄚ ㄧㄚ ㄓ ㄊㄤ)
do not appeal to refined taste; to be unpresentable

不等(ㄅㄨ ㄉㄥ)
not uniform; to vary

不敵(ㄅㄨ ㄉㄧ)
no match for; to be defeated

不抵抗主義(ㄅㄨ ㄉㄧ ㄎㄤ ㄓㄨ ㄧ)
the principle of non-resistance

不第(ㄅㄨ ㄉㄧ)
①to fail in a civil service examination ②not only

不定(ㄅㄨ ㄉㄧㄥ)
①not certain; uncertain ②indefinite

不定冠詞(ㄅㄨ ㄉㄧㄥ ㄍㄨㄢ ㄘ)
indefinite article

不定期(ㄅㄨ ㄉㄧㄥ ㄑㄧ)
without a fixed schedule; irregular

不獨(ㄅㄨ ㄉㄨ)
not only

不對(ㄅㄨ ㄉㄨㄟ)
not right; wrong

不對頭(ㄅㄨ ㄉㄨㄟ ㄊㄡ)
①incorrect; wrong ②amiss; abnormal

不對勁(ㄅㄨ ㄉㄨㄟ ㄐㄧㄣ)or 不對勁兒(ㄅㄨ ㄉㄨㄟ ㄐㄧㄥ ㄦ)
not in harmony; feeling not up to par; listless

不端(ㄅㄨ ㄉㄨㄢ)
improper; dishonorable: 品行不端 dishonorable behavior

不短(ㄅㄨ ㄉㄨㄢ)
not lacking; just right

不斷(ㄅㄨ ㄉㄨㄢ)
unceasing; uninterrupted; continuous; constant

不動(ㄅㄨ ㄉㄨㄥ)
motionless

不動腦筋(ㄅㄨ ㄉㄨㄥ ㄋㄠ ㄐㄧㄣ)
don't use one's brain(s); do not take the trouble to think

不動心(ㄅㄨ ㄉㄨㄥ ㄒㄧㄣ)
showing no interest

不動產(ㄅㄨ ㄉㄨㄥ ㄔㄢ)
real estate; immovable assets

不動聲色(ㄅㄨ ㄉㄨㄥ ㄕㄥ ㄙㄜ)
not showing any feeling or emotion; with composure

不凍港(ㄅㄨ ㄉㄨㄥ ㄍㄤ)
an ice-free port; an open port

不透明(ㄅㄨ ㄊㄡ ㄇㄧㄥ)
opaque

不透風(ㄅㄨ ㄊㄡ ㄈㄥ)

stuffy

不透氣(ㄅㄨ ㄊㄡ ㄑㄧˋ)
hermetic; airtight

不透水(ㄅㄨ ㄊㄡ ㄕㄨㄟˇ)
waterproof; watertight; impermeable

不透熱(ㄅㄨ ㄊㄡ ㄖㄜˋ)
athermanous

不腆之儀(ㄅㄨ ㄊㄧㄢˇ ㄓ ㄧˊ)
(my) small gift or negligible present

不停(ㄅㄨ ㄊㄧㄥˊ)
without stop

不圖(ㄅㄨ ㄊㄨˊ)
① contrary to one's expectation; unexpectedly ② do not intend

不妥(ㄅㄨ ㄊㄨㄛˇ)
not the right way; improper; not proper; amiss. 我覺得有點不妥。I feel that something is amiss.

不通(ㄅㄨ ㄊㄨㄥ)
① (said of writings) poor; illogical; inarticulate ② blocked; not passable: 管子不通。The pipe is blocked.

不同(ㄅㄨ ㄊㄨㄥˊ)
different; distinct

不同凡響(ㄅㄨ ㄊㄨㄥˊ ㄈㄢˊ ㄒㄧㄤˇ)
extraordinary; remarkable

不同意(ㄅㄨ ㄊㄨㄥˊ ㄧˋ)
to disagree

不痛不癢(ㄅㄨ ㄊㄨㄥˋ ㄅㄨ ㄧㄤˇ)
① not grasping the main points; pointless; playing with words ② indecisive ③ superficial; perfunctory

不耐煩(ㄅㄨ ㄋㄞˋ ㄈㄢˊ)
impatient

不男不女(ㄅㄨ ㄋㄢˊ ㄅㄨ ㄋㄩˇ)
(a disapproving description of someone's manner, dress, make-up, etc.) neither a male nor a female—grotesque

不能(ㄅㄨ ㄋㄥˊ)
cannot; unable

不能不(ㄅㄨ ㄋㄥˊ ㄅㄨ)
to have to; must; cannot but

不能夠(ㄅㄨ ㄋㄥˊ ㄍㄡˋ)
cannot; unable

不念舊惡(ㄅㄨ ㄋㄧㄢˋ ㄐㄧㄡˋ ㄜˋ)
to forget past grudges; to let bygones be bygones

不寧唯是(ㄅㄨ ㄋㄧㄥˊ ㄨㄟˊ ㄕˋ)

not only

不佞(ㄅㄨ ㄋㄧㄥˊ)
my humble self

不樂仕進(ㄅㄨ ㄌㄜˋ ㄕˋ ㄐㄧㄣˋ)
unwilling to enter government service

不賴(ㄅㄨ ㄌㄞˋ)
not bad; good; fine

不勞而獲(ㄅㄨ ㄌㄠˊ ㄦˊ ㄏㄨㄛˋ)
to gain without effort; to get undeserved credit

不根不秀(ㄅㄨ ㄍㄣ ㄅㄨ ㄒㄧㄡˋ)or 不郎不秀(ㄅㄨ ㄌㄤˊ ㄅㄨ ㄒㄧㄡˋ)
(said of a person) good for nothing

不冷不熱(ㄅㄨ ㄌㄥˇ ㄅㄨ ㄖㄜˋ)
lukewarm

不理(ㄅㄨ ㄌㄧˇ)
in disregard of; to ignore; don't pay attention to

不理睬(ㄅㄨ ㄌㄧˇ ㄘㄞˇ)
to refuse to talk to somebody; to give someone the silent treatment

不理會(ㄅㄨ ㄌㄧˇ ㄏㄨㄟˋ)
inattentive; unmindful; to pay no attention to

不力(ㄅㄨ ㄌㄧˋ)
(said of the performance of duties) half-heartedly; perfunctorily

不利(ㄅㄨ ㄌㄧˋ)
① not going smoothly; unsuccessful ② bad; adverse; harmful

不列顛(ㄅㄨ ㄌㄧㄝˋ ㄉㄧㄢ)
Britain

不列顛國協(ㄅㄨ ㄌㄧㄝˋ ㄉㄧㄢ ㄍㄨㄛˊ ㄒㄧㄝˊ)
the British Commonwealth of Nations

不了了之(ㄅㄨ ㄌㄧㄠˇ ㄌㄧㄠˇ ㄓ)
to conclude without concrete result or decision; to leave in the status quo; to end up with nothing definite

不了解(ㄅㄨ ㄌㄧㄠˇ ㄐㄧㄝˇ)
do not understand; not familiar with

不料(ㄅㄨ ㄌㄧㄠˋ)
unexpectedly; never thought

不留(ㄅㄨ ㄌㄧㄡˊ)
① do not keep ② do not leave behind; do not spare ③ do not stay

不留情面(ㄅㄨ ㄌㄧㄡˊ ㄑㄧㄥˊ ㄇㄧㄢˋ)

to be very strict; to disregard another's "face" or feelings

不留餘地(ㄅㄨ ㄌㄧㄡˊ ㄩˊ ㄉㄧˋ)or 不留心(ㄅㄨ ㄌㄧㄡˊ ㄒㄧㄣ)
careless

不留餘地(ㄅㄨ ㄌㄧㄡˊ ㄩˊ ㄉㄧˋ)
① without leaving leeway or elbowroom ② to pursue to the brutal end

不吝(ㄅㄨ ㄌㄧㄣˋ)
not stingy; without sparing; do not stint

不吝珠玉(ㄅㄨ ㄌㄧㄣˋ ㄓㄨ ㄩˋ)
Please make frank comments (on my performance).

不良(ㄅㄨ ㄌㄧㄤˊ)
bad; harmful; unhealthy

不良分子(ㄅㄨ ㄌㄧㄤˊ ㄈㄣˋ ㄗˇ)
undesirables; scums

不良導體(ㄅㄨ ㄌㄧㄤˊ ㄉㄠˋ ㄊㄧˇ)
a nonconductor

不良適應(ㄅㄨ ㄌㄧㄤˊ ㄕˋ ㄧㄥˋ)
maladjustment

不良少年(ㄅㄨ ㄌㄧㄤˊ ㄕㄠˋ ㄋㄧㄢˊ)
juvenile delinquents

不良影響(ㄅㄨ ㄌㄧㄤˊ ㄧㄥˇ ㄒㄧㄤˇ)
harmful or adverse effects

不良於行(ㄅㄨ ㄌㄧㄤˊ ㄩˊ ㄒㄧㄥˊ)
to have difficulty in walking

不量力(ㄅㄨ ㄌㄧㄤˋ ㄌㄧˋ)
do not consider one's own strength, ability, resources, etc. in doing a job

不靈(ㄅㄨ ㄌㄧㄥˊ)
① awkwardly; ineffectively ② do not work

不露聲色(ㄅㄨ ㄌㄨˋ ㄕㄥ ㄙㄜˋ)
do not show one's feelings, intentions, motives, etc.

不落窠臼(ㄅㄨ ㄌㄨㄛˋ ㄎㄜ ㄐㄧㄡˋ)
do not follow a beaten track; to have a unique style

不倫不類(ㄅㄨ ㄌㄨㄣˊ ㄅㄨ ㄌㄟˋ)
grotesque; incongruous; unfit

不論(ㄅㄨ ㄌㄨㄣˋ)
no matter; regardless

不苟(ㄅㄨ ㄍㄡˇ)
in a serious manner; solemn; strict; upright: 他做事一絲不苟。He works in a serious manner.

不苟言笑(ㄅㄨ ㄍㄡˇ ㄧㄢˊ ㄒㄧㄠˋ)
strictly adhere to propriety in one's behavior; serious; not given to talking and

laughing

不夠(ㄅㄨˋㄍㄡˋ)
not enough; insufficient; inadequate

不夠本(ㄅㄨˋㄍㄡˋㄅㄣˇ)
below cost; unable to cover the cost

不夠資格(ㄅㄨˋㄍㄡˋㄗㄐㄛˊ)
not qualified

不甘(ㄅㄨˋㄍㄢ)
unreconciled to; not resigned to; unwilling; dissatisfied; chagrined: 他不甘於自己的厄運。He is unreconciled to his misfortune.

不甘落後(ㄅㄨˋㄍㄢㄌㄨㄛˋㄏㄡˋ)
unwilling to lag behind

不甘寂寞(ㄅㄨˋㄍㄢㄐㄧˊㄇㄛˋ)
unwilling to remain out of the limelight; eager to seek publicity

不甘示弱(ㄅㄨˋㄍㄢㄕˋㄖㄨㄛˋ)
unwilling to let the other fellow hold the center stage; not to be outdone

不甘雌服(ㄅㄨˋㄍㄢㄘㄈㄨˊ)
unwilling to lie low; eager to prove one's worth

不乾不淨(ㄅㄨˋㄍㄢㄅㄨˋㄐㄧㄥˋ)
not clean; filthy

不敢(ㄅㄨˋㄍㄢˇ)
dare not

不敢當(ㄅㄨˋㄍㄢˇㄉㄤ)
(a polite expression in reply to a compliment) I don't deserve it. 或 I am flattered. 或 I am unworthy.

不領敢(ㄅㄨˋㄍㄢˇㄌㄧㄥˇㄐㄧㄠ)
too bad to be accepted (bought, etc.)

不敢越雷池一步(ㄅㄨˋㄍㄢˇㄩㄝˋㄌㄟˊㄔˊㄧㄅㄨˋ)
dare no go one step beyond the commanded limit

不根之談(ㄅㄨˋㄍㄣㄓㄊㄢˊ)
mere talk; unfounded statements or remarks 參看「不經之談」

不更事(ㄅㄨˋㄍㄥˋㄕˋ)
inexperienced

不顧(ㄅㄨˋㄍㄨˋ)
in disregard of; don't take into consideration; despite; in spite of; regardless of

不過(ㄅㄨˋㄍㄨㄛˋ)
①only; merely ②but; nevertheless

不過如此(ㄅㄨˋㄍㄨㄛˋㄖㄨˊㄘˇ)or不過爾爾(ㄅㄨˋㄍㄨㄛˋㄦˇㄦˇ)
so-so; tolerably passable; barely acceptable; merely mediocre

不過意(ㄅㄨˋㄍㄨㄛˋㄧˋ)
to feel that one does not deserve a favor or gift given; to be sorry

不規則(ㄅㄨˋㄍㄨㄟㄗㄜˊ)
irregular

不規則動詞(ㄅㄨˋㄍㄨㄟㄗㄜˊㄉㄨㄥˋㄘˊ)
irregular verbs

不軌(ㄅㄨˋㄍㄨㄟˇ)
conspiracy, plots, etc.: 他們圖謀不軌。They are engaging in conspiracy.

不關痛癢(ㄅㄨˋㄍㄨㄢㄊㄨㄥˋㄧㄤˇ)
irrelevant; insignificant

不管(ㄅㄨˋㄍㄨㄢˇ)
in disregard of; no matter

不管三七二十一(ㄅㄨˋㄍㄨㄢˇㄙㄢㄑㄧㄦˋㄕˊㄧ)
casting all caution to the winds; regardless of consequences; reckless of results

不公(ㄅㄨˋㄍㄨㄥ)
unjust; unfair

不恭(ㄅㄨˋㄍㄨㄥ)
disrespectful

不攻自破(ㄅㄨˋㄍㄨㄥㄗˋㄆㄛˋ)
to collapse of itself

不共戴天(ㄅㄨˋㄍㄨㄥˋㄉㄞˋㄊㄧㄢ)
won't live under the same sky (with an archenemy); absolutely irreconcilable

不可(ㄅㄨˋㄎㄜˇ)
①no; negative ②not allowed; forbidden ③cannot

不可磨滅(ㄅㄨˋㄎㄜˇㄇㄛˊㄇㄧㄝˋ)
indelible

不可名狀(ㄅㄨˋㄎㄜˇㄇㄧㄥˊㄓㄨㄤˋ)
indescribable 亦作「不可言狀」

不可多得(ㄅㄨˋㄎㄜˇㄉㄨㄛㄉㄜˊ)
hard to come by; scarce; rare

不可理喻(ㄅㄨˋㄎㄜˇㄌㄧˇㄩˋ)
unreasonable; not subject to reason

不可告人(ㄅㄨˋㄎㄜˇㄍㄠˋㄖㄣˊ)
not to be divulged; hidden; ulterior; confidential; secret or shameful (act, etc.)

不可估量(ㄅㄨˋㄎㄜˇㄍㄨㄍㄨㄟˊ)
inestimable; incalculable

不可抗力(ㄅㄨˋㄎㄜˇㄎㄤˋㄌㄧˋ)
irresistible (natural) force

不可究詰(ㄅㄨˋㄎㄜˇㄐㄧㄡㄐㄧㄝˊ)
cannot explain or find out why (because it's too confused or shifting so fast)

不可救藥(ㄅㄨˋㄎㄜˇㄐㄧㄡˋㄧㄠˋ)
incurable; beyond hope; incorrigible

不可限量(ㄅㄨˋㄎㄜˇㄒㄧㄢˋㄌㄧㄤˋ)
limitless (opportunities); very promising

不可捉摸(ㄅㄨˋㄎㄜˇㄓㄨㄛㄇㄛˊ·ㄇㄛ)
uncanny; unpredictable; unfathomable

不可收拾(ㄅㄨˋㄎㄜˇㄕㄡㄕˊ)
pandemonium; wild disorder or confusion; hopeless (situation, etc.); out of control

不可勝數(ㄅㄨˋㄎㄜˇㄕㄥㄕㄨˇ)
countless; innumerable

不可思議(ㄅㄨˋㄎㄜˇㄙㄧˋ)
uncanny; mysterious; unimaginable; beyond comprehension; inconceivable

不可一世(ㄅㄨˋㄎㄜˇㄧㄕˋ)
to consider oneself unrivaled in the world; to be extremely arrogant

不可以道里計(ㄅㄨˋㄎㄜˇㄧˇㄉㄠˋㄌㄧˇㄐㄧˋ)
(impossible to make a comparison because) the difference is too great

不可逾越(ㄅㄨˋㄎㄜˇㄩˊㄩㄝˋ)
impassable; insurmountable; insuperable

不克(ㄅㄨˋㄎㄜˋ)
①can not; unable: 他不克前來。He can not come. ②unable to win (in a fight, etc.)

不客氣(ㄅㄨˋㄎㄜˋㄑㄧˋ)
①impolite; rude; blunt: 讓我說句不客氣的話。Let me put it bluntly. ②(a term used in reply to another's "thanks") You are welcome. 或 Don't mention it. 或 Not at all. ③(a term used in expressing one's gratitude for another's kind act) Please don't bother yourself about it. 或 I'll help myself.

不堪(ㄅㄨˋㄎㄢ)
cannot suffer or bear; unendurable

不堪回首(ㄅㄨˋㄎㄢㄏㄨㄟˊㄕㄡˇ)
cannot recall without pain;

cannot bear to look back

不堪設想(ㄅㄨˋㄎㄢㄕㄜˋㄒㄧㄤˇ)
(said of consequences) serious or unthinkable

不堪一擊(ㄅㄨˋㄎㄢ一ㄐㄧˊ)
too weak to stand competition or attack; cannot withstand a single blow

不刊之論(ㄅㄨˋㄎㄢ ㄓ ㄌㄨㄣˋ)
an imperishable statement

不亢不卑(ㄅㄨˋㄎㄤˋㄅㄨˋㄅㄟ)
with perfect propriety; neither proud nor obsequious; to carry oneself with dignity; neither haughty nor humble

不快(ㄅㄨˋㄎㄨㄞˋ)
① unhappy; uncomfortable
② slow

不愧(ㄅㄨˋㄎㄨㄟˋ)
to be worthy of; to deserve to be; to prove oneself to be

不愧屋漏(ㄅㄨˋㄎㄨㄟˋㄨ ㄌㄡˋ)
to be strictly honest under all circumstances

不和(ㄅㄨˋㄏㄜˊ)
at loggerheads; not on good terms; do not get along well; to be at odds

不和諧(ㄅㄨˋㄏㄜˊㄒㄧㄝˊ)
disharmony; discord; incompatibility

不合(ㄅㄨˋㄏㄜˊ)
unsuitable; in disagreement with (rules, etc.); not up to (standard, etc.); to disagree;
你的作品不合標準。Your work is not up to standard.

不合邏輯(ㄅㄨˋㄏㄜˊㄌㄨㄛˊㄐㄧˊ)
illogical

不合格(ㄅㄨˋㄏㄜˊㄍㄜˊ)
not qualified; below standard

不合時宜(ㄅㄨˋㄏㄜˊㄕˊ一ˊ)
bad timing; out of fashion; anachronistic; to be incompatible with present needs

不合適(ㄅㄨˋㄏㄜˊㄕˋ)
not suitable; improper; inappropriate

不合身(ㄅㄨˋㄏㄜˊㄕㄣ)
(said of a garment) ill-fitting

不合作(ㄅㄨˋㄏㄜˊㄗㄨㄛˋ)
non-cooperative

不好(ㄅㄨˋㄏㄠˇ)
① not good ② to be spoiled;

to become worse

不好過(ㄅㄨˋㄏㄠˇㄍㄨㄛˋ)
feeling miserable (because of financial difficulties, mental or physical discomforts)

不好惹(ㄅㄨˋㄏㄠˇㄖㄜˇ)
not to be trifled with; not to be pushed around

不好意思(ㄅㄨˋㄏㄠˇ一ˋㄙ)
① to feel ashamed, shy, bashful or embarrassed ② to find it embarrassing (to do something)

不合糊(ㄅㄨˋㄏㄜˊㄏㄨˊ)
①(something) solid; with good foundation; very good
② to mince no words

不寒而慄(ㄅㄨˋㄏㄢˊㄦˊㄌㄧˋ)
trembling with fear; terrified

不惑(ㄅㄨˋㄏㄨㄛˋ)
① without doubt; with full self-confidence ② the age of 40: 他已屆不惑之年。He is aged forty.

不懷好意(ㄅㄨˋㄏㄨㄞˊㄏㄠˇ一ˋ)
with evil intention; to harbor evil designs

不諱(ㄅㄨˋㄏㄨㄟˋ)
① without concealing anything ② to die; to pass away

不會(ㄅㄨˋㄏㄨㄟˋ)
unable; can not; will not; do not know how

不會吧(ㄅㄨˋㄏㄨㄟˋ·ㄅㄚ)
not necessarily so; may not turn out that way

不歡而散(ㄅㄨˋㄏㄨㄢㄦˊㄙㄢˋ)
to part on bad terms; (said of a meeting, etc.) to break up in disagreement

不慌不忙(ㄅㄨˋㄏㄨㄤㄅㄨˋㄇㄤˊ)
① leisurely; unhurried ② with full composure

不遑(ㄅㄨˋㄏㄨㄤˊ)
too busy to…

不羈(ㄅㄨˋㄐㄧ)
carefree; not bound by social etiquette, customs, etc.

不及(ㄅㄨˋㄐㄧˊ)
not so (good, tall, early, etc.) as…; to be inferior to (someone or something in…)

不及格(ㄅㄨˋㄐㄧˊㄍㄜˊ)
to fail to pass (examinations); disqualified

不及物動詞(ㄅㄨˋㄐㄧˊㄨˋㄉㄨㄥˋㄘˊ)

an intransitive verb

不即不離(ㄅㄨˋㄐㄧˊㄅㄨˋㄌㄧˊ)
to keep someone at arm's length; keeping the right distance

不急之務(ㄅㄨˋㄐㄧˊㄓ ㄨˋ)
not an urgent matter; a matter of no great urgency

不濟(ㄅㄨˋㄐㄧˋ)
unsuccessful; ineffective; not good; not help

不濟於事(ㄅㄨˋㄐㄧˋㄩˊㄕˋ)
to no avail; of no use; no good

不記名投票(ㄅㄨˋㄐㄧˋㄇㄧㄥˊㄊㄡˊㄆㄧㄠˋ)
secret ballots; secret votes

不計其數(ㄅㄨˋㄐㄧˋㄑㄧˊㄕㄨˋ)
countless; innumerable

不假辭色(ㄅㄨˋㄐㄧㄚˇㄘˊㄙㄜˋ)
to be very stern; to show no kindness

不假思索(ㄅㄨˋㄐㄧㄚˇㄙㄙㄨㄛˇ)
without thinking; without hesitation; readily 亦作「不加思索」

不假外出(ㄅㄨˋㄐㄧㄚˇㄨㄞˋㄔㄨ)
absent without leave

不結盟(ㄅㄨˋㄐㄧㄝˊㄇㄥˊ)
nonalignment

不結盟國家(ㄅㄨˋㄐㄧㄝˊㄇㄥˊㄍㄨㄛˊㄐㄧㄚ)
nonaligned nations

不櫛進士(ㄅㄨˋㄐㄧㄝˊㄐㄧㄣˋㄕˋ)
a learned woman

不解(ㄅㄨˋㄐㄧㄝˇ)
① do not understand ② indissoluble

不解風情(ㄅㄨˋㄐㄧㄝˇㄈㄥㄑㄧㄥˊ)
do not understand implications in love affair

不介意(ㄅㄨˋㄐㄧㄝˋ一ˋ)
do not mind

不教而誅(ㄅㄨˋㄐㄧㄠˋㄦˊㄓㄨ)
to punish an offender who has not been told what is the right thing to do and what is not

不久(ㄅㄨˋㄐㄧㄡˇ)
within a short time; soon; shortly afterward

不咎既往(ㄅㄨˋㄐㄧㄡˋㄐㄧˋㄨㄤˇ)
Let bygones be bygones.

不簡單(ㄅㄨˋㄐㄧㄢˇㄉㄢ)
① not simple; rather complicated ② remarkable; marvel-

ous

不見得(ㄅㄨ ㄐㄧㄢˋ ˙ㄉㄜ)
not likely; not necessarily so; do not think so; to doubt the probability of…

不見天日(ㄅㄨ ㄐㄧㄢˋ ㄊㄧㄢ ㄖˋ)
①in total darkness ②injustice

不見了(ㄅㄨ ㄐㄧㄢˋ ˙ㄌㄜ)
missing; disappeared

不見棺材不落淚(ㄅㄨ ㄐㄧㄢˋ ㄍㄨㄢ ㄘㄞˊ ㄅㄨ ㄌㄨㄛˋ ㄌㄟˋ)
One does not shed tears until one sees the coffin.—One refuses to be convinced until one faces the grim reality.

不見可欲使心不亂(ㄅㄨ ㄐㄧㄢˋ ㄎㄜˇ ㄩˋ ㄕˇ ㄒㄧㄣ ㄅㄨ ㄌㄨㄢˋ)
To avoid temptation helps one retain one's presence of mind.

不見經傳(ㄅㄨ ㄐㄧㄢˋ ㄐㄧㄥ ㄓㄨㄢˋ)
①(something) not supported by historical fact ②(somebody) of no consequence; a nobody

不禁(ㄅㄨ ㄐㄧㄣ)
cannot help…

不今不古(ㄅㄨ ㄐㄧㄣ ㄅㄨ ㄍㄨˇ)
neither modern nor ancient—a sarcastic reference to a pedant or pedantry

不矜細行(ㄅㄨ ㄐㄧㄣ ㄒㄧˋ ㄒㄧㄥˊ)
to pay no attention to trivial matters

不僅(ㄅㄨ ㄐㄧㄣˇ)
not only

不盡然(ㄅㄨ ㄐㄧㄣˋ ㄖㄢˊ)
not exactly so; not necessarily so

不近人情(ㄅㄨ ㄐㄧㄣˋ ㄖㄣˊ ㄑㄧㄥˊ)
unreasonable; inconsiderate; disregarding others' feelings

不進則退(ㄅㄨ ㄐㄧㄣˋ ㄗㄜˊ ㄊㄨㄟˋ)
(said of a boat sailing against the current) either to keep progressing or retrogressing

不經濟(ㄅㄨ ㄐㄧㄥ ㄐㄧˋ)
not economical

不經之談(ㄅㄨ ㄐㄧㄥ ㄓ ㄊㄢˊ)
an absurd statement; a cock-and-bull story 參看「不根之談」

不經事(ㄅㄨ ㄐㄧㄥ ㄕˋ)
inexperienced

不經一事, 不長一智(ㄅㄨ ㄐㄧㄥ ㄧˊ ㄕˋ, ㄅㄨ ㄓㄤˇ ㄧˊ ㄓˋ)
One learns from experience. 或 Wisdom comes from experience.

不經意(ㄅㄨ ㄐㄧㄥ ㄧˋ)
inattentive(ly); careless(ly)

不景氣(ㄅㄨ ㄐㄧㄥˇ ㄑㄧˋ)
(economics) depression

不脛而走(ㄅㄨ ㄐㄧㄥˋ ㄦˊ ㄗㄡˇ)
(said of news, etc.) to travel fast; to spread far and wide

不拘(ㄅㄨ ㄐㄩ)
①no limit; not to be bound ②whatever

不拘小節(ㄅㄨ ㄐㄩ ㄒㄧㄠˇ ㄐㄧㄝˊ)
to disregard trifles, niceties, etc.

不拘一格(ㄅㄨ ㄐㄩ ㄧˋ ㄍㄜˊ)
to follow no set pattern

不具(ㄅㄨ ㄐㄩˋ)
①not encompassing or complete enough (usually used at the end of a letter) ②crippled

不覺技癢(ㄅㄨ ㄐㄩㄝˊ ㄐㄧˋ ㄧㄤˇ)
cannot suppress the desire to show off one's ability or skill

不絕如縷(ㄅㄨ ㄐㄩㄝˊ ㄖㄨˊ ㄌㄩˇ)
(said of a situation) critical

不倦(ㄅㄨ ㄐㄩㄢˋ)
tireless; indefatigable

不欺暗室(ㄅㄨ ㄑㄧ ㄢˋ ㄕˋ)
to be scrupulously honest even when there is no one around

不期然而然(ㄅㄨ ㄑㄧˊ ㄖㄢˊ ㄦˊ ㄖㄢˊ)
It happened naturally and out of one's anticipation. 或 It happened unexpectedly.

不期而遇(ㄅㄨ ㄑㄧˊ ㄦˊ ㄩˋ)
to meet by chance; to encounter someone unexpectedly

不起(ㄅㄨ ㄑㄧˇ)
①very ill ②to die

不棄菲才(ㄅㄨ ㄑㄧˋ ㄈㄟ ㄘㄞˊ)
do not discard one because of one's inability

不洽輿情(ㄅㄨ ㄑㄧㄚˋ ㄩˊ ㄑㄧㄥˊ)
to act against public opinion; not popular with the public

不切實際(ㄅㄨ ㄑㄧㄝˋ ㄕˊ ㄐㄧˋ)
impractical

不巧(ㄅㄨ ㄑㄧㄠˇ)
unfortunately; as luck would have it

不求甚解(ㄅㄨ ㄑㄧㄡˊ ㄕㄣˋ ㄐㄧㄝˇ)
to read casually; do not seek to understand things thoroughly

不求聞達(ㄅㄨ ㄑㄧㄡˊ ㄨㄣˊ ㄉㄚˊ)
having no desire to enter government service; to be uninterested in fame or prestige

不遷怒(ㄅㄨ ㄑㄧㄢ ㄋㄨˋ)
not blame others for one's own failure, mistake, etc.

不屈(ㄅㄨ ㄑㄩ)
unyielding; unbending

不屈不撓(ㄅㄨ ㄑㄩ ㄅㄨ ㄋㄠˊ)
①not to be bent or cowed; unswerving; indomitable; unyielding ②to fight to the very end; do not give up

不羣(ㄅㄨ ㄑㄩㄣˊ)
outstanding; foremost

不惜(ㄅㄨ ㄒㄧˊ)
to be ready to go to extreme lengths; do not hesitate to do something

不惜工本(ㄅㄨ ㄒㄧˊ ㄍㄨㄥ ㄅㄣˇ)
to spare neither energy nor money; to spare no expense

不惜一戰(ㄅㄨ ㄒㄧˊ ㄧˊ ㄓㄢˋ)
to be prepared to go to war (unless demand is met)

不暇(ㄅㄨ ㄒㄧㄚˊ)
to have no time (for something); to be too busy (to do something)

不下(ㄅㄨ ㄒㄧㄚˋ)
①not less than ②unable to capture (a city or position)

不下於(ㄅㄨ ㄒㄧㄚˋ ㄩˊ)
①as many as; no less than ②not inferior to; as good as

不屑(ㄅㄨ ㄒㄧㄝˋ)
do not condescend (or deign) to do something (for the sake of one's own dignity); to disdain

不謝(ㄅㄨ ㄒㄧㄝˋ)
Don't mention it. 或 Not at all.

不懈(ㄅㄨ ㄒㄧㄝˋ)
untiring; indefatigable

不曉得(ㄅㄨ ㄒㄧㄠˇ ˙ㄉㄜ)
do not know; ignorant of; to know nothing about

不肖(ㄅㄨ ㄒㄧㄠˋ)
①a son who is not so good as his father ②good-for-nothing; unworthy

不孝(ㄅㄨ ㄒㄧㄠˋ)
①not in accordance with filial piety ②a term referring to oneself in the obituary announcing the death of one's parent

不孝有三(ㄅㄨ ㄒㄧㄠˋ ㄧㄡˇ ㄙㄢ)
There are three major offenses against filial piety. (do not support parents when they are alive, do not give them a decent burial upon their death, and do not produce an heir——the last of which is the gravest offense)

不休(ㄅㄨ ㄒㄧㄡ)
endlessly; ceaselessly

不修邊幅(ㄅㄨ ㄒㄧㄡ ㄅㄧㄢ ㄈㄨˊ)
do not care about details (especially in clothing); unmindful of social conventions; slovenly; sloppy

不朽(ㄅㄨ ㄒㄧㄡˇ)
immortal; immortality

不銹鋼(ㄅㄨ ㄒㄧㄡˋ ㄍㄤ)
stainless steel

不先不後(ㄅㄨ ㄒㄧㄢ ㄅㄨ ㄏㄡˋ)
(It happens) just at the right time

不嫌詞費(ㄅㄨ ㄒㄧㄢˊ ㄘˊ ㄈㄟˋ)
to speak voluminously; to dwell on (a topic); to talk at length

不相干(ㄅㄨ ㄒㄧㄤ ㄍㄢ)
irrelevant; to have nothing to do with

不相下(ㄅㄨ ㄒㄧㄤ ㄒㄧㄚˋ)
(said of two sides engaged in a fight) in a state of stalemate

不相稱(ㄅㄨ ㄒㄧㄤ ㄔㄥ)
ill-matched; inharmonious

不相識(ㄅㄨ ㄒㄧㄤ ㄕˋ)
do not know

不相上下(ㄅㄨ ㄒㄧㄤ ㄕㄤˋ ㄒㄧㄚˋ)
about the same (in strength, quality, etc.); equal; equally matched

不相容(ㄅㄨ ㄒㄧㄤ ㄖㄨㄥˊ)
incompatible

不相聞問(ㄅㄨ ㄒㄧㄤ ㄨㄣˊ ㄨㄣˋ)
not on speaking terms; complete severance of relations (between individuals)

不祥(ㄅㄨ ㄒㄧㄤˊ)
ominous; unlucky; inauspicious

不祥之兆(ㄅㄨ ㄒㄧㄤˊ ㄓ ㄓㄠˋ)
a bad (or an ill) omen

不詳(ㄅㄨ ㄒㄧㄤˊ)
①unknown ②not detailed enough

不想(ㄅㄨ ㄒㄧㄤˇ)
do not want

不像話(ㄅㄨ ㄒㄧㄤˋ ㄏㄨㄚˋ)
absurd or ludicrous (talks, acts, etc.); unreasonable; too ridiculous

不像樣(ㄅㄨ ㄒㄧㄤˋ ㄧㄤˋ)or 不像樣兒(ㄅㄨ ㄒㄧㄤˋ ㄧㄤㄦˋ)
①improper (behavior); disreputable (conduct) ②beyond recognition

不行(ㄅㄨ ㄒㄧㄥˊ)
①not allowed; nothing doing ②unsuccessful; to no avail ③not qualified ④do not work

不行了(ㄅㄨ ㄒㄧㄥˊ ·ㄌㄜ)
on the point of death

不省人事(ㄅㄨ ㄒㄧㄥˇ ㄖㄣˊ ㄕˋ)
in a coma; unconscious

不幸(ㄅㄨ ㄒㄧㄥˋ)
misfortune; adversity; unfortunate; unfortunately; bad luck; sad

不幸中之大幸(ㄅㄨ ㄒㄧㄥˋ ㄓㄨㄥ ㄓ ㄉㄚˋ ㄒㄧㄥˋ)
a lucky occurrence in the course of a disaster, such as a priceless painting saved from a fire

不須(ㄅㄨ ㄒㄩ)
need not

不需(ㄅㄨ ㄒㄩ)
do not need

不虛此行(ㄅㄨ ㄒㄩ ㄘˇ ㄒㄧㄥˊ)
One gains much on the trip. 或 The trip has not been made in vain. 或 It's been a worthwhile trip.

不許(ㄅㄨ ㄒㄩˇ)
not allowed; must not; prohibited

不學無術(ㄅㄨ ㄒㄩㄝˊ ㄨˊ ㄕㄨˋ)
unlearned; ignorant

不宣而戰(ㄅㄨ ㄒㄩㄢ ㄦˊ ㄓㄢˋ)
to fight without a declaration of war; to attack without prior notice

不旋踵(ㄅㄨ ㄒㄩㄢˊ ㄓㄨㄥˇ)
(literally) in less time than it takes to turn one's heels—a very brief moment

不遜(ㄅㄨ ㄒㄩㄣˋ)
not polite; rude; impertinent

不支(ㄅㄨ ㄓ)
unable to hang on; exhausted

不知不覺(ㄅㄨ ㄓ ㄅㄨˋ ㄐㄩㄝˊ)
imperceptibly; unnoticed; without knowing it; unconsciously: 不知不覺地四個月已經過去了。Four months has passed imperceptibly.

不知道(ㄅㄨ ㄓ ㄉㄠˋ)
do not know; to be unconscious: 他不知自己的錯誤。He was unconscious of his own mistake.

不知天高地厚(ㄅㄨ ㄓ ㄊㄧㄢ ㄍㄠ ㄉㄧˋ ㄏㄡˋ)
do not know the height of the heaven and the thickness of the earth——to think too much of one's abilities

不知甘苦(ㄅㄨ ㄓ ㄍㄢ ㄎㄨˇ)
do not know how difficult it is to make a living, to earn money, etc.

不知好歹(ㄅㄨ ㄓ ㄏㄠˇ ㄉㄞˇ)
①unable to tell good from bad; unappreciative; do not know what's good for one ②stubborn

不知底裏(ㄅㄨ ㄓ ㄉㄧˇ ㄌㄧˇ)
do not know the inside story

不知進退(ㄅㄨ ㄓ ㄐㄧㄣˋ ㄊㄨㄟˋ)
do not know whether to advance or retreat; muddled or mixed-up

不知輕重(ㄅㄨ ㄓ ㄑㄧㄥ ㄓㄨㄥˋ)
muddled or mixed-up; unable to tell the significance of a situation

不知情(ㄅㄨ ㄓ ㄑㄧㄥˊ)
to know nothing about…; to be ignorant of…

不知去向(ㄅㄨ ㄓ ㄑㄩˋ ㄒㄧㄤˋ)
to disappear without a trace

不知自量(ㄅㄨ ㄓ ㄗˋ ㄌㄧㄤˋ)
to do something beyond one's ability

不知自愛(ㄅㄨ ㄓ ㄗˋ ㄞˋ)
to act without self-respect; to behave ungenteelly

(一部)

〔一部〕

不知足(ㄅㄨ ㄓ ㄗㄨˊ)
insatiable; greedy

不知死活(ㄅㄨ ㄓ ㄙˇ ㄏㄨㄛˊ)
muddled or mixed-up (characterized by rashness or recklessness)

不知所措(ㄅㄨ ㄓ ㄙㄨㄛˇ ㄘㄨㄛˋ)
stunned into inaction or stoppage of mental activity; to be at a loss: 我全然不知所措。I am quite at a loss what to do.

不知所云(ㄅㄨ ㄓ ㄙㄨㄛˇ ㄩㄣˊ)
(said of statements) unintelligible; do not know what someone is driving at

不值得(ㄅㄨ ㄓˊ ㄉㄜˊ)
not worth it; unworthy of

不值一錢(ㄅㄨ ㄓˊ ㄧ ㄑㄧㄢˊ)
worthless

不值一笑(ㄅㄨ ㄓˊ ㄧ ㄒㄧㄠˋ)
not worth even a laugh; extremely ridiculous

不止(ㄅㄨ ㄓˇ)
①do not stop ②not only… ③more than…; over

不只(ㄅㄨ ㄓˇ)
not only; not merely

不治(ㄅㄨ ㄓˋ)
to die of illness or injury despite medical help

不治之症(ㄅㄨ ㄓˋ ㄓ ㄓㄥˋ)
an incurable disease

不置可否(ㄅㄨ ㄓˋ ㄎㄜˇ ㄈㄡˇ)
without giving an affirmative or negative answer; noncommittal; to make no comment; to hedge; to evade (the point, issue, etc.)

不技不求(ㄅㄨ ㄓ ㄅㄨˋ ㄑㄧㄡˊ)
generous to others and lacking greediness

不至於(ㄅㄨ ㄓˋ ㄩˊ)
will not go so far as…; will not be so serious as…; to be unlikely: 她不至於連這點道理也不懂。She must have more sense than that.

不折不扣(ㄅㄨ ㄓㄜˊ ㄅㄨˋ ㄎㄡˋ)
①without any discount; net cost ②absolute; out-and-out

不周延(ㄅㄨ ㄓㄡ ㄧㄢˊ)
(logic) undistributed

不戰而勝(ㄅㄨ ㄓㄢˋ ㄦˊ ㄕㄥˋ)
to win without fighting a battle

不長進(ㄅㄨ ㄓㄤˇ ㄐㄧㄣˋ)

①without improvement or progress ②good-for-nothing

不爭氣(ㄅㄨ ㄓㄥ ㄑㄧˋ)
to submit to defeat or failure without putting up a fight; to be easily discouraged; to fail to live up to one's expectations; to let someone down

不主故常(ㄅㄨ ㄓㄨˇ ㄍㄨˋ ㄔㄤˊ)
to be flexible; to be ready to adapt to circumstances

不住(ㄅㄨ ㄓㄨˋ)
continuously; incessantly

不著邊際(ㄅㄨ ㄓㄨㄛˊ ㄅㄧㄢ ㄐㄧˋ)
far-fetched; far off the beam; totally beside the point

不著痕跡(ㄅㄨ ㄓㄨㄛˊ ㄏㄣˊ ㄐㄧ)
without trace; ingeniously secret

不准(ㄅㄨ ㄓㄨㄣˇ)
not allowed; forbidden

不中聽(ㄅㄨ ㄓㄨㄥ ㄊㄧㄥ)
(referring to unpleasant words or remarks) not worth listening; grating

不中意(ㄅㄨ ㄓㄨㄥ ㄧˋ)
not quite up to one's idea (or expectation); not desirable; not suitable; not to one's liking

不中用(ㄅㄨ ㄓㄨㄥ ㄩㄥˋ)
useless; good-for-nothing; without any talent or ability; no good

不齒(ㄅㄨ ㄔˇ)
to condemn; to despise; condemnable; to hold a person in contempt

不恥下問(ㄅㄨ ㄔˇ ㄒㄧㄚˋ ㄨㄣˋ)
not ashamed to learn (or ask for information) from one's inferiors (or subordinates)

不啻(ㄅㄨ ㄔˋ)
①equivalent to ②not less than ③as; like

不差累黍(ㄅㄨ ㄔㄚ ㄌㄟˇ ㄕㄨˇ)or不差毫髮(ㄅㄨ ㄔㄚ ㄏㄠˊ ㄈㄚˇ)
exactly the same; to fit like hand in glove; not an iota less or more

不瞅不睬(ㄅㄨ ㄔㄡ ㄅㄨˋ ㄘㄞˇ)or不理不睬(ㄅㄨ ㄌㄧˇ ㄅㄨˋ ㄘㄞˇ)
to give someone a cold shoulder; to ignore completely

不稱意(ㄅㄨ ㄔㄣˋ ㄧˋ)
Things do not match one's hope.

不成(ㄅㄨ ㄔㄥˊ)
①not going to succeed; will not do ②an expression used at the end of a question

不成體統(ㄅㄨ ㄔㄥˊ ㄊㄧˇ ㄊㄨㄥˇ)
(acting or talking) wildly; without regard to common practice or propriety

不成話(ㄅㄨ ㄔㄥˊ ㄏㄨㄚˋ)
(acting or talking) wildly; unreasonable; absurd; ridiculous

不成敬意(ㄅㄨ ㄔㄥˊ ㄐㄧㄥˋ ㄧˋ)
(an expression used in presenting a gift to a friend or a superior) just a little token to show my respect to you

不成器(ㄅㄨ ㄔㄥˊ ㄑㄧˋ)
good-for-nothing; without promise of achievement

不成材(ㄅㄨ ㄔㄥˊ ㄘㄞˊ)
useless; good-for-nothing; worthless

不成文法(ㄅㄨ ㄔㄥˊ ㄨㄣˊ ㄈㄚˇ)
(law) unwritten law; lex non scripta

不逞之徒(ㄅㄨ ㄔㄥˇ ㄓ ㄊㄨˊ)
lawbreakers; lawless elements; outlaws

不出所料(ㄅㄨ ㄔㄨ ㄙㄨㄛˇ ㄌㄧㄠˋ)
just as expected

不揣(ㄅㄨ ㄔㄨㄞˇ)
ignorant of one's own meager strength (usually used as a self-depreciative expression)

不揣冒昧(ㄅㄨ ㄔㄨㄞˇ ㄇㄠˋ ㄇㄟˋ)
to venture; to presume; to take the liberty of

不失時機(ㄅㄨ ㄕ ㄕˊ ㄐㄧ)
to take one's opportunity; to lose no time

不失爲(ㄅㄨ ㄕ ㄨㄟˊ)
can yet be regarded as; may after all be accepted as

不時(ㄅㄨ ㄕˊ)
①frequently; often ②at any time; always

不時之需(ㄅㄨ ㄕˊ ㄓ ㄒㄩ)
occasional needs; may be needed any time; a possible period of want

不是(ㄅㄨ ㄕˋ)

①no; not right ②if…not ③
in the wrong; to be to
blame: 這是我的不是。It's my
fault. 或 I'm to blame.

不是玩兒的(ㄅㄨ ㄕ ㄨㄢˊ ·ㄦㄉ)
no joke

不適(ㄅㄨ ㄕˋ)
ill; indisposed; unwell

不識大體(ㄅㄨ ㄕˊ ㄉㄚˋ ㄊㄧˇ)
to fail to see the important
points; to ignore the whole
interest

不識擡舉(ㄅㄨ ㄕˊ ㄊㄞˊ ㄐㄩˇ)
unappreciative; ungrateful;
to fail to appreciate someone's kindness

不識泰山(ㄅㄨ ㄕˊ ㄊㄞˋ ㄕㄢ)
to fail to recognize a
famous personage when
meeting him face to face

不識相(ㄅㄨ ㄕˊ ㄒㄧㄤˋ)
impervious to an obvious
situation; unable to see the
fitness of things

不識之無(ㄅㄨ ㄕˊ ㄓ ㄨˊ)
unable to read and write; illiterate

不識時務(ㄅㄨ ㄕˊ ㄕˊ ㄨˋ)
ignorant of the changes of
the times or failing to make
use of available chances; to
show no understanding of
times

不識字(ㄅㄨ ㄕˊ ㄗˋ)
illiterate; cannot read

不識一丁(ㄅㄨ ㄕˊ ㄧ ㄉㄧㄥ)
illiterate

不世之才(ㄅㄨ ㄕˋ ㄓ ㄘㄞˊ)
a rare talent; a genius

不世出(ㄅㄨ ㄕˋ ㄔㄨ)
(said of a man of unusual
ability) not to be found in
every age

不受理(ㄅㄨ ㄕㄡˋ ㄌㄧˇ)
①(law) to reject (a com-
plaint); not entertained ②
(diplomacy) to refuse to
entertain (a proposal)

不受歡迎的人(ㄅㄨ ㄕㄡˋ ㄏㄨㄢ ㄧㄥˊ ㄉㄜ
·ㄖㄣˊ)
(diplomacy) *persona non
grata*; a nuisance

不衫不履(ㄅㄨ ㄕㄢ ㄅㄨ ㄌㄩˇ)
to dress slovenly; to disregard outward appearance

不善(ㄅㄨ ㄕㄢˋ)
①bad; ill ②improper(ly);

not proper(ly) ③not good
at: 我們的老板是個不善管理的
人。Our boss is a man not
good at management.

不上不下(ㄅㄨ ㄕㄤˋ ㄅㄨ ㄒㄧㄚˋ)
①on a spot; in an impasse
②inappropriate

不上算(ㄅㄨ ㄕㄤˋ ㄙㄨㄢˋ)
a bad bargain; not profitable

不勝(ㄅㄨ ㄕㄥ)
①cannot bear (or stand); to
be unequal to ②very; ex-
tremely; overwhelmed: 她不勝
悲傷。She was overwhelmed
by grief.

不勝枚舉(ㄅㄨ ㄕㄥ ㄇㄟˊ ㄐㄩˇ)
too numerous to recount;
too many to cite; too numerous to mention individually

不勝其煩(ㄅㄨ ㄕㄥ ㄑㄧˊ ㄈㄢˊ)
cannot stand the harass-
ment, nuisance, etc.

不聲不響(ㄅㄨ ㄕㄥ ㄅㄨ ㄒㄧㄤˇ)
stealthily; furtively

不服(ㄅㄨ ㄈㄨˊ ·ㄈㄨ)
unwell; not feeling well; uncomfortable; indisposed

不淑(ㄅㄨ ㄕㄨˊ)
unprincipled; (said of a
mate) ill

不順服(ㄅㄨ ㄕㄨㄣˋ ㄈㄨˊ)
incurring dislike or vexation; disagreeable

不爽(ㄅㄨ ㄕㄨㄤˇ)
①out of sorts; in a bad
mood ②without discrep-
ancy; accurate

不爽快(ㄅㄨ ㄕㄨㄤˇ ㄎㄨㄞˋ)
not frank

不日(ㄅㄨ ㄖˋ)
soon; in a few days; within
the next few days

不然(ㄅㄨ ㄖㄢˊ)
①not so ②otherwise; or

不仁(ㄅㄨ ㄖㄣˊ)
①not benevolent; hard-
hearted ②paralyzed; numbed

不人道(ㄅㄨ ㄖㄣˊ ㄉㄠˋ)
inhuman

不忍(ㄅㄨ ㄖㄣˇ)or 不忍心(ㄅㄨ ㄖㄣˇ
ㄒㄧㄣ)
disturbed (characterized by
pity); cannot bear to…; cannot stand the sight of…

不忍之心(ㄅㄨ ㄖㄣˇ ㄓ ㄒㄧㄣ)
a heart of mercy

不讓鬚眉(ㄅㄨ ㄖㄤˋ ㄒㄩ ㄇㄟˊ)
(in terms of ability, vision,
valor, etc.) to compare
favorably with men; to be a
match for men

不如(ㄅㄨ ㄖㄨˊ)or 不若
①not equal to; can do no
better than; inferior to ②
might as well; it would be
better to

不如歸去(ㄅㄨ ㄖㄨˊ 《ㄨㄟ ㄑㄩˋ)
It's better to retire or quit.
—a term connoting frustration, disappointment, etc.

不入虎穴，焉得虎子(ㄅㄨ ㄖㄨˋ
ㄏㄨˇ ㄒㄩㄝˋ，ㄧㄢ ㄉㄜˊ ㄏㄨˇ ㄗˇ)
(literally) How can one get
the cubs without entering
the tiger's den?—Nothing
venture, nothing gain (or
have).

不入耳(ㄅㄨ ㄖㄨˋ ㄦˇ)
unpleasant to the ear; not
worth listening to

不辱使命(ㄅㄨ ㄖㄨˇ ㄕˇ ㄇㄧㄥˋ)
to have succeeded in carrying out an assignment

不容(ㄅㄨ ㄖㄨㄥˊ)
①do not tolerate; do not
allow; do not brook ②do
not welcome

不容分説(ㄅㄨ ㄖㄨㄥˊ ㄈㄣ ㄕㄨㄛ)
do not wait for an explanation

不容置喙(ㄅㄨ ㄖㄨㄥˊ ㄓˋ ㄏㄨㄟˋ)
to refuse to let others talk,
explain, etc.

不貲(ㄅㄨ ㄗ)
immeasurable; incalculable

不自量(ㄅㄨ ㄗˋ ㄌㄧㄤˋ)
without considering one's
own capability; overconfi-
dent; to overrate one's own
abilities

不自在(ㄅㄨ ㄗˋ ·ㄗㄞ)
feeling uneasy or uncomfortable

不自愛(ㄅㄨ ㄗˋ ㄞˋ)
(said of a person who acts
in total disregard of others)
do not have self-respect

不自由，毋寧死(ㄅㄨ ㄗˋ ㄧㄡˊ，ㄨˊ
ㄋㄧㄥˊ ㄙˇ)
"Give me liberty, or give me
death."—Liberty is more
important than life.

不擇手段(ㄅㄨ ㄗㄜˊ ㄕㄡˇ ㄉㄨㄢˋ)

（一部）

by fair means or foul; by hook or by crook; unscrupulously

不在(ㄅㄨˋ ㄗㄞˋ)
①dead ②not in; absent

不在乎(ㄅㄨˋ ㄗㄞˋ ·ㄏㄨ)
do not care; do not mind

不在話下(ㄅㄨˋ ㄗㄞˋ ㄏㄨㄚˋ ㄒㄧㄚˋ)
nothing difficult; an easy thing

不在其位，不謀其政(ㄅㄨˋ ㄗㄞˋ ㄑㄧˊ ㄨㄟˋ，ㄅㄨˋ ㄇㄡˊ ㄑㄧˊ ㄓㄥˋ)
unwilling to comment on something which is not one's own concern

不在此限(ㄅㄨˋ ㄗㄞˋ ㄘˇ ㄒㄧㄢˋ)
not subject to the limits or restrictions

不在意(ㄅㄨˋ ㄗㄞˋ ㄧˋ)
①to take no notice of; to pay no attention to ②inattentive; careless; negligent

不贊一辭(ㄅㄨˋ ㄗㄢˋ ㄧˋ ㄘˊ)
to keep silent; to make no comment

不怎麼(ㄅㄨˋ ㄗㄣˇ ·ㄇㄜ)
not very; not particularly

不怎麼樣(ㄅㄨˋ ㄗㄣˇ ·ㄇㄜ ㄧㄤˋ)
not up to much; very indifferent

不足(ㄅㄨˋ ㄗㄨˊ)
①not deserving ②insufficient; not enough

不足道(ㄅㄨˋ ㄗㄨˊ ㄉㄠˋ)
do not deserve mentioning; insignificant; of no consequence

不足掛齒(ㄅㄨˋ ㄗㄨˊ ㄍㄨㄚˋ ㄔˇ)
(What little I have done for you) does not deserve mentioning. 或not worth mentioning

不足輕重(ㄅㄨˋ ㄗㄨˊ ㄑㄧㄥ ㄓㄨㄥˋ)
of little value; of little importance; carrying little weight

不足採信(ㄅㄨˋ ㄗㄨˊ ㄘㄞˇ ㄒㄧㄣˋ)
①(law) unacceptable as evidence ②can not be considered as reliable

不足為奇(ㄅㄨˋ ㄗㄨˊ ㄨㄟˊ ㄑㄧˊ)
nothing strange, extraordinary or remarkable about it; not at all surprising

不足為訓(ㄅㄨˋ ㄗㄨˊ ㄨㄟˊ ㄒㄩㄣˋ)
not to be taken as a guide; not to be taken as an exam-

ple; not to be taken as authoritative

不足為外人道(ㄅㄨˋ ㄗㄨˊ ㄨㄟˊ ㄨㄞˋ ㄖㄣˊ ㄉㄠˋ)
no need to let others know (because it's purely a personal matter)

不作美(ㄅㄨˋ ㄗㄨㄛˋ ㄇㄟˇ)
do not help (a happy occasion or marriage), such as rain on a wedding day

不作第二人想(ㄅㄨˋ ㄗㄨㄛˋ ㄉㄧˋ ㄦˋ ㄖㄣˊ ㄒㄧㄤˇ)
not content with playing second fiddle

不作聲(ㄅㄨˋ ㄗㄨㄛˋ ㄕㄥ)
to keep silence; to say nothing

不作此想(ㄅㄨˋ ㄗㄨㄛˋ ㄘˇ ㄒㄧㄤˇ)
to have no intention or desire to do something

不辭辛苦(ㄅㄨˋ ㄘˊ ㄒㄧㄣ ㄎㄨˇ)
to work with all-out effort; to leave no stone unturned; to make nothing of hardships

不辭而別(ㄅㄨˋ ㄘˊ ㄦˊ ㄅㄧㄝˊ)
to leave without bidding (or saying) goodbye; to take French leave

不測(ㄅㄨˋ ㄘㄜˋ)
①unpredictable; unfathomable ②misfortune; disaster; accident

不才(ㄅㄨˋ ㄘㄞˊ)
(usually a polite, self-depreciative term referring to oneself) without capability

不保 或 不睬(ㄅㄨˋ ㄘㄞˇ)
to ignore (someone)

不曾(ㄅㄨˋ ㄘㄥˊ)
to have never done something

不錯(ㄅㄨˋ ㄘㄨㄛˋ)
①to be right: 一點也不錯。It is quite right. ②granted that; to be sure that; yes ③not bad; pretty good

不存芥蒂(ㄅㄨˋ ㄘㄨㄣˊ ㄐㄧㄝˋ ㄉㄧˋ)
do not harbor previous grievances (between good friends)

不存心(ㄅㄨˋ ㄘㄨㄣˊ ㄒㄧㄣ)
not intended; unintentional; do not intend

不存在(ㄅㄨˋ ㄘㄨㄣˊ ㄗㄞˋ)

nonexistent

不死心(ㄅㄨˋ ㄙˇ ㄒㄧㄣ)
unwilling to give up

不三不四(ㄅㄨˋ ㄙㄢ ㄅㄨˋ ㄙˋ)
grotesque; incongruous; neither fish nor fowl

不俗(ㄅㄨˋ ㄙㄨˊ)
original; uncommon; not hackneyed or stereotyped

不速之客(ㄅㄨˋ ㄙㄨˋ ㄓ ㄎㄜˋ)
an uninvited guest; an unexpected guest; an unwelcome person

不遂(ㄅㄨˋ ㄙㄨㄟˋ)
①unsuccessful ②paralyzed

不送(ㄅㄨˋ ㄙㄨㄥˋ)
don't bother to see me out

不礙(ㄅㄨˋ ㄞˋ)or 不礙事(ㄅㄨˋ ㄞˋ ㄕˋ)
It doesn't matter. 或 There is no harm in (trying, etc.)

不安(ㄅㄨˋ ㄢ)
①uneasy; disturbed ②intranquil

不安於室(ㄅㄨˋ ㄢ ㄩˊ ㄕˋ)
(said of women) having extramarital affairs

不安於位(ㄅㄨˋ ㄢ ㄩˊ ㄨㄟˋ)
do not discharge official duties conscientiously

不貳過(ㄅㄨˋ ㄦˋ ㄍㄨㄛˋ)
not to repeat a previous mistake

不二法門(ㄅㄨˋ ㄦˋ ㄈㄚˇ ㄇㄣˊ)
the only way

不二價(ㄅㄨˋ ㄦˋ ㄐㄧㄚˋ)
a uniform price; a fixed price

不二色(ㄅㄨˋ ㄦˋ ㄙㄜˋ)
(said of men) consistent in love; loyal to one woman only

不依(ㄅㄨˋ ㄧ)
①do not comply; do not go along with ②not let off easily; not let somebody get away with it

不一(ㄅㄨˋ ㄧ)
to vary; to differ; to disagree: 這些繩子長短不一。These ropes differ in length.

不一而足(ㄅㄨˋ ㄧ ㄦˊ ㄗㄨˊ)
many; a large variety (used in a contemptuous sense); numerous

不一定(ㄅㄨˋ ㄧ ㄉㄧㄥˋ)
uncertain; not sure; not nec-

不宜(ㄅㄨˋ ㄧˊ)
not suitable; inadvisable: 不
宜操之過急。It's no good
being overhasty.

不遺在遠(ㄅㄨˋ ㄧˊ ㄗㄞˋ ㄩㄢˇ)
(an expression used in correspondence) Please don't
forget me because I'm far
away.

不遺餘力(ㄅㄨˋ ㄧˊ ㄩˊ ㄌㄧˋ)
to spare no effort; to spare
no pains; to do one's best
(or utmost)

不已(ㄅㄨˋ ㄧˇ)
continuously; endlessly;
incessantly

不以爲然(ㄅㄨˋ ㄧˇ ㄨㄟˊ ㄖㄢˊ)
to object to; to take exception to; do not approve

不意(ㄅㄨˋ ㄧˋ)
unexpectedly

不亦樂乎(ㄅㄨˋ ㄧˋ ㄌㄜˋ ㄏㄨ)
①What a delight it would
be if… ②extremely;
awfully: 我忙得不亦樂乎。I
am awfully busy.

不易之論(ㄅㄨˋ ㄧˋ ㄓ ㄌㄨㄣˋ)
a sound or irrefutable statement; unalterable truth

不義之財(ㄅㄨˋ ㄧˋ ㄓ ㄘㄞˊ)
dirty money; loot; wealth
acquired illicitly; ill-gotten
wealth

不翼而飛(ㄅㄨˋ ㄧˋ ㄦˊ ㄈㄟ)
missing inexplicably; stolen

不雅觀(ㄅㄨˋ ㄧㄚˇ ㄍㄨㄢ)
ungraceful; do not look nice
or proper; unbecoming

不亞於(ㄅㄨˋ ㄧㄚˋ ㄩˊ)or 不遜於(ㄅㄨˋ
ㄒㄩㄣˋ ㄩˊ)
not worse than; as good as;
as well as

不夜城(ㄅㄨˋ ㄧㄝˋ ㄔㄥˊ)
(literally) a city with lights
turned on all night—a big
city with gay night life

不要(ㄅㄨˋ ㄧㄠˋ)
①don't ②don't want

不要臉(ㄅㄨˋ ㄧㄠˋ ㄌㄧㄢˇ)
shameless; brazen; to have
no sense of shame

不要緊(ㄅㄨˋ ㄧㄠˋ ㄐㄧㄣˇ)
①unimportant; not serious
②never mind

不藥而愈(ㄅㄨˋ ㄧㄠˋ ㄦˊ ㄩˋ)
to recover (from illness)

without medical help

不由分說(ㄅㄨˋ ㄧㄡˊ ㄈㄣ ㄕㄨㄛ)
not waiting for an explanation; unreasonable

不由得(ㄅㄨˋ ㄧㄡˊ ㄉㄜ˙)
cannot help; cannot but…

不由自主(ㄅㄨˋ ㄧㄡˊ ㄗˋ ㄓㄨˇ)
can't help; involuntarily

不言而喩(ㄅㄨˋ ㄧㄢˊ ㄦˊ ㄩˋ)
understood; self-evident; to
understand without explanation

不厭(ㄅㄨˋ ㄧㄢˋ)
do not mind doing some-
thing; do not tire of

不厭其煩(ㄅㄨˋ ㄧㄢˋ ㄑㄧˊ ㄈㄢˊ)
do not mind taking all the
trouble; to be very patient

不厭求詳(ㄅㄨˋ ㄧㄢˋ ㄑㄧㄡˊ ㄒㄧㄤˊ)
to omit no details

不揚(ㄅㄨˋ ㄧㄤˊ)
(said of one's looks) plain

不無(ㄅㄨˋ ㄨˊ)
not without

不無可取(ㄅㄨˋ ㄨˊ ㄎㄜˇ ㄑㄩˇ)
more or less laudable or
commendable

不無可疑(ㄅㄨˋ ㄨˊ ㄎㄜˇ ㄧˊ)
not above suspicion

不無小補(ㄅㄨˋ ㄨˊ ㄒㄧㄠˇ ㄅㄨˇ)
It might be of some small
help.

不務正業(ㄅㄨˋ ㄨˋ ㄓㄥˋ ㄧㄝˋ)
①(said of a playboy, etc.)
do not have a legitimate
business or profession ②do
not attend to one's proper
duties

不外(ㄅㄨˋ ㄨㄞˋ)
invariably; most likely; no
other than; nothing more
than; only

不惟(ㄅㄨˋ ㄨㄟˊ)
not only

不違農時(ㄅㄨˋ ㄨㄟˊ ㄋㄨㄥˊ ㄕˊ)
(said of government meas-
ure) do not interfere with
farming; do not miss the
farming season

不爲已甚(ㄅㄨˋ ㄨㄟˊ ㄧˇ ㄕㄣˋ)
do not push (an advantage,
victory, etc.) to the extreme

不爲所動(ㄅㄨˋ ㄨㄟˊ ㄙㄨㄛˇ ㄉㄨㄥˋ)
to remain unmoved (by
promises of reward, etc.)

不聞不問(ㄅㄨˋ ㄨㄣˊ ㄅㄨˋ ㄨㄣˋ)

to care nothing about; to cut
off all intercourse; indifferent to: 朋友有困難，我們不能
不聞不問。We can't remain
indifferent when any friend
is in difficulty.

不穩(ㄅㄨˋ ㄨㄣˇ)
unsteady; unstable (market,
position)

不問(ㄅㄨˋ ㄨㄣˋ)
①to pay no attention to; to
disregard; to ignore ②to let
go unpunished

不忘溝壑(ㄅㄨˋ ㄨㄤˋ ㄍㄡ ㄏㄨㄛˋ)
do not forget the ditch and
the stream—(figuratively)
to be determined to die for
one's country

不渝(ㄅㄨˋ ㄩˊ)
not to change; to remain
faithful

不虞(ㄅㄨˋ ㄩˊ)
①unexpected: 不虞之譽 un-
expected praise ②eventual-
ity; contingency ③do not
worry about ④an untoward
event

不予考慮(ㄅㄨˋ ㄩˇ ㄎㄠˇ ㄌㄩˋ)
do not consider

不豫(ㄅㄨˋ ㄩˋ)
①to be unprepared ②dis-
pleased

不育(ㄅㄨˋ ㄩˋ)
sterility

不約而同(ㄅㄨˋ ㄩㄝ ㄦˊ ㄊㄨㄥˊ)
to accord without consulting
each other

不悅(ㄅㄨˋ ㄩㄝˋ)
unhappy; displeased

不用(ㄅㄨˋ ㄩㄥˋ)
①not necessary ②need not

不用功(ㄅㄨˋ ㄩㄥˋ ㄍㄨㄥ)
do not work or study diligently

不用說(ㄅㄨˋ ㄩㄥˋ ㄕㄨㄛ)or 不待說
(ㄅㄨˋ ㄉㄞˋ ㄕㄨㄛ)
it goes without saying; needless to say

【丏】 ⁹ ㄇㄧㄢˇ mean miǎn
1. the curtain to ward off
arrows
2. hidden

【丐】 ¹⁰ 《ㄞˋ gay gài
1. to beg for alms
2. a beggar

〔一
部〕

3. to give

丐頭（«ㄞˋ ㄊㄡˊ）
the leader of (a group of) beggars

丐助（«ㄞˋ ㄓㄨˋ）
to ask for help

丐養（«ㄞˋ ㄧㄤˇ）
to adopt a child or children

【丑】 11
ㄔㄡˇ choou chŏu
1. the second of the twelve "Terrestrial Branches" (地支)
2. the period of the day from 1 to 3 a.m.
3. a clown
4. a Chinese family name

丑表功（ㄔㄡˇ ㄅㄧㄠˇ ㄍㄨㄥ）
to claim an undeserved credit; to brag shamelessly about one's deeds

丑旦（ㄔㄡˇ ㄉㄢˋ）or 丑婆子（ㄔㄡˇ ㄆㄛˊ ㄗ）
a woman clown or comedienne

丑角（ㄔㄡˇ ㄐㄩㄝˊ）or 丑角兒（ㄔㄡˇ ㄐㄩㄝˊㄦ）or 丑兒（ㄔㄡˇㄦ）
a comedian; a clown; a buffoon

四畫

【且】 12
ㄑㄧㄝˇ chiee qiě
1. moreover; still; further
2. just; for the time being: 且等一下。Just wait a moment.
3. even
4. both…and…

且不（ㄑㄧㄝˇ ㄅㄨˋ）
not for the time being; not going to

且慢（ㄑㄧㄝˇ ㄇㄢˋ）
Hold it! 或 Wait a minute.

且…且…（ㄑㄧㄝˇ…ㄑㄧㄝˇ…）
while; as

且住（ㄑㄧㄝˇ ㄓㄨˋ）
Hold it! 或 Stop it!

且說（ㄑㄧㄝˇ ㄕㄨㄛ）
(usually used at the beginning of a narrative) Let us now talk about....或 moreover

【丕】 13
ㄆㄧ pi pī
1. great; distinguished
2. in observance of (a ruling, etc.)

不烈（ㄆㄧ ㄌㄧㄝˋ）
unusual achievements, merits or contribution

不基（ㄆㄧ ㄐㄧ）
the imperial throne; a great heritage

不績（ㄆㄧ ㄐㄧ）
grand achievements

不顯（ㄆㄧ ㄒㄧㄢˇ）
great and distinguished; splendid; glorious

不業（ㄆㄧ ㄧㄝˋ）
(especially referring to the throne) great career

【世】 14
ㄕˋ shyh shì
1. a generation
2. a person's life span
3. an age
4. the world

世伯（ㄕˋ ㄅㄛˊ）
a designation for the male friends of one's father

世面（ㄕˋ ㄇㄧㄢˋ）
the various facets of human activities; state of the world

世法（ㄕˋ ㄈㄚˇ）
①tradition; traditional practices ②(Buddhism) common or ordinary dharmas, i.e. truths, laws, things, etc.

世風不古（ㄕˋ ㄈㄥ ㄅㄨˋ ㄍㄨˇ）
Public morals are no longer what they were in the good old days.

世風澆薄（ㄕˋ ㄈㄥ ㄐㄧㄠ ㄅㄛˊ）
There are scarcely public morals to speak of these days.

世風日下（ㄕˋ ㄈㄥ ㄖˋ ㄒㄧㄚˋ）
The moral degeneration of the world is getting worse day by day. 或 The world is declining in its moral values.

世德（ㄕˋ ㄉㄜˊ）
traditional morals; moral principles upheld by one's ancestors

世代（ㄕˋ ㄉㄞˋ）
①a generation ②the times ③from generation to generation: 世代相傳 to pass on from generation to generation

世代交替（ㄕˋ ㄉㄞˋ ㄐㄧㄠ ㄊㄧˋ）
(biology) metagenesis; alter-

nation of generations

世道（ㄕˋ ㄉㄠˋ）
the ways of the world

世道人心（ㄕˋ ㄉㄠˋ ㄖㄣˊ ㄒㄧㄣ）
the ways of the world and the time; the manners and morals of the time

世弟（ㄕˋ ㄉㄧˋ）
a son of one's father's friend, younger than oneself

世態炎涼（ㄕˋ ㄊㄞˋ ㄧㄢˊ ㄌㄧㄤˊ）
snobbish; inconstancy of human relationships

世路（ㄕˋ ㄌㄨˋ）
the ways and state of the world

世祿（ㄕˋ ㄌㄨˋ）
hereditary honors such as rank and wealth

世故（ㄕˋ ㄍㄨˋ）
①the ways of the world ② shrewd; worldly

世紀（ㄕˋ ㄐㄧˋ）
a century

世家（ㄕˋ ㄐㄧㄚ）
a family holding official ranks for generations

世家子弟（ㄕˋ ㄐㄧㄚ ㄗˇ ㄉㄧˋ）
youngsters of 「世家」

世界（ㄕˋ ㄐㄧㄝˋ）
the world

世界博覽會（ㄕˋ ㄐㄧㄝˋ ㄅㄛˊ ㄌㄢˇ ㄏㄨㄟˋ）
a world's fair; a world expo

世界末日（ㄕˋ ㄐㄧㄝˋ ㄇㄛˋ ㄖˋ）
the end of the world; doomsday

世界大同（ㄕˋ ㄐㄧㄝˋ ㄉㄚˋ ㄊㄨㄥˊ）
universal brotherhood

世界大戰（ㄕˋ ㄐㄧㄝˋ ㄉㄚˋ ㄓㄢˋ）
a world war; a global war

世界觀（ㄕˋ ㄐㄧㄝˋ ㄍㄨㄢ）
a philosophical view (or concept) of the world; a world view

世界氣象組織（ㄕˋ ㄐㄧㄝˋ ㄑㄧˋ ㄒㄧㄤˋ ㄗㄨˇ ㄓ）
the World Meteorological Organization (WMO)

世界主義（ㄕˋ ㄐㄧㄝˋ ㄓㄨˇ ㄧˋ）
cosmopolitanism

世界潮流（ㄕˋ ㄐㄧㄝˋ ㄔㄠˊ ㄌㄧㄡˊ）
world trends

世界人權宣言（ㄕˋ ㄐㄧㄝˋ ㄖㄣˊ ㄑㄩㄢˊ ㄒㄩㄢ ㄧㄢˊ）
the Universal Declaration of Human Rights

世界衛生組織(ㄕㄐㄧㄝㄨㄟㄕㄥㄗㄨㄓ)
the World Health Organization (WHO)

世界語(ㄕㄐㄧㄝㄩ)
Esperanto; the universal language

世交(ㄕㄐㄧㄠ)
families closely related or associated for generations; long-standing friendship between two families

世間(ㄕㄐㄧㄢ)
on earth; in the world

世襲(ㄕㄒㄧ)
hereditary (title, rank, etc.)

世系(ㄕㄒㄧ)
a family tree; a pedigree; lineage; a genealogy

世兄(ㄕㄒㄩㄥ)
a designation for the son of one's father's friend or the son of one's teacher

世姪(ㄕㄓ)
one's close friend's son

世職(ㄕㄓ)
a hereditary official rank

世主(ㄕㄓㄨ)
the ruler of the times

世仇(ㄕㄔㄡ)
①family feud; blood feud ②a mortal enemy in family feud

世傳(ㄕㄔㄨㄢ)
hereditary; to be handed down through generations

世事(ㄕㄕ)
the affairs of the world

世世代代(ㄕㄕㄉㄞㄉㄞ)
generation after generation; from generation to generation

世上(ㄕㄕㄤ)
on earth; in the world

世叔(ㄕㄕㄨ)
a younger friend of one's father

世人(ㄕㄖㄣ)
people of the world; (in the Bible) men or women; common people

世子(ㄕㄗ)
the crown prince

世族(ㄕㄗㄨ)
a powerful family that has great political influence for generations

世尊(ㄕㄗㄨㄣ)
(Buddhism) the Revered One of the World——Buddha

世俗(ㄕㄙㄨ)
①customs and traditions; common practices; social conventions ②secular; worldly

世俗之見(ㄕㄙㄨㄓㄐㄧㄢ)
a very vulgar or commonplace point of view; common views

世誼(ㄕㄧ)
long-standing friendship between two families 亦作「世交」

世業(ㄕㄧㄝ)
trade or property inherited from one's ancestors; hereditary profession in the family

世務(ㄕㄨ)
affairs of the world; worldly affairs

世外桃源(ㄕㄨㄞㄊㄠㄩㄢ)
an imaginary, ideal world; a secluded paradise; Shangri-la

世味(ㄕㄨㄟ)
the various phases and tastes of the world

世緣(ㄕㄩㄢ)
(Buddhism) secular ties and affairs

世運(ㄕㄩㄣ)
①the Olympiad; the Olympic Games ②trends or vicissitudes of the world

【丘】 15
　ㄑㄧㄡ chiou qiū
1. a hillock or mound
2. big; elder
3. empty
4. first name of Confucius
5. a surname

丘八(ㄑㄧㄡㄅㄚ)
an anagram for "soldier" (often used in contemptuous sense)

丘墳(ㄑㄧㄡㄈㄣ)
a grave in the form of an earthen mound

丘里(ㄑㄧㄡㄌㄧ)
a native village

丘陵(ㄑㄧㄡㄌㄧㄥ)
mounds; craggy terrains; hills

丘陵地帶(ㄑㄧㄡㄌㄧㄉㄧㄉㄞ)
the hilly country

丘壑(ㄑㄧㄡㄏㄨㄜ)
(literary) hills and ravines ——a wooded place for retirement

丘墟(ㄑㄧㄡㄒㄩ)
empty land; wasteland

丘山(ㄑㄧㄡㄕㄢ)
①hills and mountains ②the wild country

丘野(ㄑㄧㄡㄧㄝ)
the rural country

丘園(ㄑㄧㄡㄩㄢ)
a garden in the hills

【丙】 16
　ㄅㄧㄥ biing bǐng
1. the third of the ten "Celestial Stems" (天干)
2. another name for fire
3. the tail of a fish
4. a Chinese family name

丙等(ㄅㄧㄥㄉㄥ)
roughly equivalent to the "C" grade; the third grade

丙酮(ㄅㄧㄥㄊㄨㄥ)
(chemistry) acetone

五畫

【承】 17
　ㄔㄥ cherng chéng
1. to aid; to assist
2. a deputy to an official

丞相(ㄔㄥㄒㄧㄤ)
the prime minister (in ancient China)

【丟】 18
　ㄉㄧㄡ diou diū
1. to throw: 把球丟給我。Throw me the ball.
2. to lose
3. to put (or lay) aside: 他們把工作丟在一邊。They lay their work aside.

丟面子(ㄉㄧㄡㄇㄧㄢ˙ㄗ)
to lose face

丟掉(ㄉㄧㄡㄉㄧㄠ)
①to lose ②to cast away; to throw away

丟臉(ㄉㄧㄡㄌㄧㄢ)or丟人(ㄉㄧㄡㄖㄣ)
to lose face; to disgrace

丟開(ㄉㄧㄡㄎㄞ)
①to leave it off; not to mention; to forget for a

while ② to throw away

丟盔卸甲(ㄉㄧㄡ ㄎㄨㄟ ㄒㄧㄝˋ ㄐㄧㄚˇ)
(descriptive of defeated troops) to throw away one's helmet and coat of mail

丟去(ㄉㄧㄡ ㄑㄩˋ)or 丟棄(ㄉㄧㄡ ㄑㄧˋ)
to get rid of; to cast away

丟下(ㄉㄧㄡ ㄒㄧㄚˋ)
to throw down; to lay aside

丟醜(ㄉㄧㄡ ㄔㄡˇ)
to disgrace oneself; to make oneself a laughingstock

丟失(ㄉㄧㄡ ㄕ)
to lose

丟三落四(ㄉㄧㄡ ㄙㄢ ㄌㄚˋ ㄙˋ)
forgetful; scatterbrained; to miss this and that

丟眼色(ㄉㄧㄡ ㄧㄢˇ ㄙㄜˋ)
to give somebody a wink

七畫

【並】 19
ㄅㄧㄥˋ bìng bìng
1. and; also; at the same time
2. on the same level with; even; equal
3. entirely; completely

並不(ㄅㄧㄥˋ ㄅㄨˋ)
really not

並排(ㄅㄧㄥˋ ㄆㄞˊ)
side by side; in a row; in the same row

並非(ㄅㄧㄥˋ ㄈㄟ)
by no means

並蒂(ㄅㄧㄥˋ ㄉㄧˋ)
①two blossoms on one stalk ②united in love

並立(ㄅㄧㄥˋ ㄌㄧˋ)
①to stand together; to stand side by side ②to exist simultaneously

並列(ㄅㄧㄥˋ ㄌㄧㄝˋ)
to stand side by side; to juxtapose

並聯(ㄅㄧㄥˋ ㄌㄧㄢˊ)
parallel connection: 並聯電路 parallel circuit

並駕齊驅(ㄅㄧㄥˋ ㄐㄧㄚˋ ㄑㄧˊ ㄑㄩ)
to ride bridle to bridle; to keep abreast of; to be equal; to run neck to neck

並肩(ㄅㄧㄥˋ ㄐㄧㄢ)
shoulder to shoulder; side by side; abreast: 他們並肩而行。They walked side by side.

並進(ㄅㄧㄥˋ ㄐㄧㄣˋ)

to advance together; to advance at the same time

並舉(ㄅㄧㄥˋ ㄐㄩˇ)
to develop simultaneously

並且(ㄅㄧㄥˋ ㄑㄧㄝˇ)
moreover; furthermore; and; in addition; to boot

並行不悖(ㄅㄧㄥˋ ㄒㄧㄥˊ ㄅㄨˋ ㄅㄟˋ)
to proceed together or simultaneously without interfering with each other; compatible

並重(ㄅㄧㄥˋ ㄓㄨㄥˋ)
to lay equal stress on; to pay equal attention to: 我們應該經濟與教育並重。We should pay equal attention to both economy and education.

並世無雙(ㄅㄧㄥˋ ㄕˋ ㄨˊ ㄕㄨㄤ)
peerless; foremost

並無不當(ㄅㄧㄥˋ ㄨˊ ㄅㄨˋ ㄉㄤˋ)
There is nothing wrong or improper about it.

丿 部
ㄍㄨㄣ goen gǔn

二畫

【丫】 20
ㄧㄚ ia yā
something that branches or forks upward

丫頭(ㄧㄚ ㄊㄡˊ)
①(in ancient China) a slave girl; a bought maid; a maid ②(in modern usage) a small girl, especially one's own daughter

丫鬟(ㄧㄚ ˙ㄏㄨㄢˊ)
參看「丫頭①」

三畫

【中】 21
ㄓㄨㄥ jong zhōng
1. the middle; among; within; between: 她站在男孩們之中。She stood among the boys.
2. China or Chinese; Sino-

中波(ㄓㄨㄥ ㄅㄛ)
(radio) medium wave

中飽(ㄓㄨㄥ ㄅㄠˇ)
to squeeze; to embezzle; to pocket money to which one has no claim

中班(ㄓㄨㄥ ㄅㄢ)
①the middle shift; the swing shift ②the middle class in a kindergarten

中部(ㄓㄨㄥ ㄅㄨˋ)
the central part; the middle part

中篇小說(ㄓㄨㄥ ㄆㄧㄢ ㄒㄧㄠˇ ㄕㄨㄛ)
a medium-length novel; a novelette

中頻(ㄓㄨㄥ ㄆㄧㄣˊ)
intermediate frequency

中美(ㄓㄨㄥ ㄇㄟˇ)
① Central America ②China and U. S. A.; Sino-American

中美洲(ㄓㄨㄥ ㄇㄟˇ ㄓㄡ)
Central America

中飯(ㄓㄨㄥ ㄈㄢˋ)
lunch; luncheon

中非(ㄓㄨㄥ ㄈㄟ)
① Sino-African ② Central Africa

中非共和國(ㄓㄨㄥ ㄈㄟ ㄍㄨㄥˋ ㄏㄜˊ ㄍㄨㄛˊ)
Central African Republic

中鋒(ㄓㄨㄥ ㄈㄥ)
the center (in basketball, soccer, military operations, etc.)

中道(ㄓㄨㄥ ㄉㄠˋ)
①the middle course ②halfway

中道而廢(ㄓㄨㄥ ㄉㄠˋ ㄦˊ ㄈㄟˋ)
to stop halfway

中等(ㄓㄨㄥ ㄉㄥˇ)
middle-class; medium; mediocre; so-so

中等階級(ㄓㄨㄥ ㄉㄥˇ ㄐㄧㄝ ㄐㄧˊ)or 中產階級(ㄓㄨㄥ ㄔㄢˇ ㄐㄧㄝ ㄐㄧˊ)
the middle class; the bourgeois; white-collar workers

中等教育(ㄓㄨㄥ ㄉㄥˇ ㄐㄧㄠˋ ㄩˋ)
secondary education

中隊(ㄓㄨㄥ ㄉㄨㄟˋ)
①a military unit corresponding to a company; a squadron ②a unit composed of several groups

中斷(ㄓㄨㄥ ㄉㄨㄢˋ)
suspension; interruption; to suspend; to discontinue; to interrupt: 電信中斷了好幾個小

時。Telecommunication was suspended for a few hours.

中東(ㄓㄨㄥ ㄉㄨㄥ)
the Middle East (Asia)

中唐(ㄓㄨㄥ ㄊㄤ)
the mid-Tang Dynasty

中堂(ㄓㄨㄥ ㄊㄤ)
①a large scroll of painting or calligraphy hung vertically in the parlor ②the Grand Secretary in the Ming and Ching Dynasties

中提琴(ㄓㄨㄥ ㄊㄧ ㄑㄧㄣ)
a viola

中停(ㄓㄨㄥ ㄊㄧㄥ)
to stop in the middle; to interrupt or suspend

中途(ㄓㄨㄥ ㄊㄨ)
midway; halfway; on the way: 我們中途停下來用餐。We stopped midway for a meal.

中途島(ㄓㄨㄥ ㄊㄨ ㄉㄠ)
the Midway Islands

中土(ㄓㄨㄥ ㄊㄨ)
①China; Cathay ②the Central Plains—the downstream regions of the Yellow River

中南半島(ㄓㄨㄥ ㄋㄢ ㄅㄢ ㄉㄠ)
Indochina

中年(ㄓㄨㄥ ㄋㄧㄢ)
middle age

中欄(ㄓㄨㄥ ㄌㄢ)
middle hurdles (in track and field)

中立(ㄓㄨㄥ ㄌㄧ)
neutral; neutrality: 他們總是保持中立。They always remain neutral.

中立國(ㄓㄨㄥ ㄌㄧ ㄍㄨㄛ)
neutral nations

中立區(ㄓㄨㄥ ㄌㄧ ㄑㄩ)
a neutral zone

中立主義(ㄓㄨㄥ ㄌㄧ ㄓㄨ ㄧ)
neutralism

中流(ㄓㄨㄥ ㄌㄧㄡ)
①the middle of the stream ②average

中流砥柱(ㄓㄨㄥ ㄌㄧㄡ ㄉㄧ ㄓㄨ)
①one who stands firm amid adversities; a man of perseverance or independence ②a main supporter or support; a mainstay

中量級(ㄓㄨㄥ ㄌㄧㄤ ㄐㄧ)
(sports)middle weight

中落(ㄓㄨㄥ ㄌㄨㄛ)

a sudden fall of one's family fortune; to decline

中古(ㄓㄨㄥ ㄍㄨ)
the Middle Ages; medieval

中國(ㄓㄨㄥ ㄍㄨㄛ)
①China; Cathay ②the Middle Kingdom

中國民主社會黨(ㄓㄨㄥ ㄍㄨㄛ ㄇㄧㄣ ㄓㄨ ㄕㄜ ㄏㄨㄟ ㄉㄤ)
China Democratic Socialist Party

中國電影製片廠(ㄓㄨㄥ ㄍㄨㄛ ㄉㄧㄢ ㄧㄥ ㄓ ㄆㄧㄢ ㄔㄤ)
the China Movie Studio

中國國民黨(ㄓㄨㄥ ㄍㄨㄛ ㄍㄨㄛ ㄇㄧㄣ ㄉㄤ)
Kuomintang (the Chinese Nationalist Party)

中國共產黨(ㄓㄨㄥ ㄍㄨㄛ ㄍㄨㄥ ㄔㄢ ㄉㄤ)
Communist Party of China; the Chinese Communist Party

中國海(ㄓㄨㄥ ㄍㄨㄛ ㄏㄞ)
the China Sea

中國話(ㄓㄨㄥ ㄍㄨㄛ ㄏㄨㄚ)
the Chinese language; Chinese

中國畫(ㄓㄨㄥ ㄍㄨㄛ ㄏㄨㄚ)
Chinese painting

中國青年黨(ㄓㄨㄥ ㄍㄨㄛ ㄑㄧㄥ ㄋㄧㄢ ㄉㄤ)
Young China Party

中國城(ㄓㄨㄥ ㄍㄨㄛ ㄔㄥ)
Chinatown

中國銀行(ㄓㄨㄥ ㄍㄨㄛ ㄧㄣ ㄏㄤ)
Bank of China

中國猿人(ㄓㄨㄥ ㄍㄨㄛ ㄩㄢ ㄖㄣ)
Sinanthropus 參看「北京人」

中共(ㄓㄨㄥ ㄍㄨㄥ)
Communist Party of China (中國共產黨)

中饋(ㄓㄨㄥ ㄎㄨㄟ)
①the wife's job ②a wife

中饋猶虛(ㄓㄨㄥ ㄎㄨㄟ ㄧㄡ ㄒㄩ)
(said of men) still unmarried

中和(ㄓㄨㄥ ㄏㄜ)
①justice and peace ②(chemistry) to neutralize: 一種毒品常能中和另一種毒品。One poison often neutralizes another. ③to lessen the effect; to modify ④Chungho, a suburban district of Taipei

中和作用(ㄓㄨㄥ ㄏㄜ ㄗㄨㄛ ㄩㄥ)
neutralization

中華(ㄓㄨㄥ ㄏㄨㄚ)
(originally, the region along the Yellow River where the Chinese people thrived) the Chinese nation; the Chinese people

中華民國(ㄓㄨㄥ ㄏㄨㄚ ㄇㄧㄣ ㄍㄨㄛ)
the Republic of China

中華民族(ㄓㄨㄥ ㄏㄨㄚ ㄇㄧㄣ ㄗㄨ)
a name for the ethnic groups that constitute the Chinese nation; the Chinese nation

中華革命黨(ㄓㄨㄥ ㄏㄨㄚ ㄍㄜ ㄇㄧㄥ ㄉㄤ)
Chinese Revolutionary Party (the forerunner of Kuomingtang)

中華日報(ㄓㄨㄥ ㄏㄨㄚ ㄖ ㄅㄠ)
the China Daily News

中級(ㄓㄨㄥ ㄐㄧ)
middle rank; intermediate

中繼站(ㄓㄨㄥ ㄐㄧ ㄓㄢ)
a relay station 亦作「轉播站」

中介(ㄓㄨㄥ ㄐㄧㄝ)
intermediary; medium

中堅(ㄓㄨㄥ ㄐㄧㄢ)
①the main force (of an army); crack troops ②a cadre; underpinning; the core; the backbone

中堅分子(ㄓㄨㄥ ㄐㄧㄢ ㄈㄣ ㄗ)
the hard core; the salt of the earth; the people most concerned at the center of an activity, especially when opposed to some other group

中間(ㄓㄨㄥ ㄐㄧㄢ)or 中間兒(ㄓㄨㄥ ㄐㄧㄢ ㄦ)
in the middle; in the center

中間派(ㄓㄨㄥ ㄐㄧㄢ ㄆㄞ)
the middle-of-the-roaders; the neutral faction; the straddlers or fence-sitters

中間產品(ㄓㄨㄥ ㄐㄧㄢ ㄔㄢ ㄆㄧㄣ)
intermediate products

中將(ㄓㄨㄥ ㄐㄧㄤ)
(army, marine and air force) lieutenant general; (navy) vice-admiral

中距離(ㄓㄨㄥ ㄐㄩ ㄌㄧ)
middle distance

中絕(ㄓㄨㄥ ㄐㄩㄝ)
to stop midway; to perish or

（一部）

vanish before reaching a conclusion

中軍(ㄓㄨㄥ ㄐㄩㄣ)
the central column; the main army

中秋節(ㄓㄨㄥ ㄑㄧㄡ ㄐㄧㄝ)
the Mid-Autumn Festival or the Moon Festival (the 15th day of the 8th lunar month)

中西(ㄓㄨㄥ ㄒㄧ)
Chinese and Western

中西合璧(ㄓㄨㄥ ㄒㄧ ㄏㄜ ㄅㄧˋ)
a (good) combination or blending of Chinese and Western (fashion, style, etc.)

中西文化(ㄓㄨㄥ ㄒㄧ ㄨㄣˊ ㄏㄨㄚˋ)
Chinese and Western civilizations; Chinese and Western culture

中夏(ㄓㄨㄥ ㄒㄧㄚˋ)
China

中宵(ㄓㄨㄥ ㄒㄧㄠ)
middle of the night; midnight

中校(ㄓㄨㄥ ㄒㄧㄠˋ)
(army, marine and air force) lieutenant colonel; (navy) commander

中線(ㄓㄨㄥ ㄒㄧㄢˋ)
(sports) the center line; half-way line

中心(ㄓㄨㄥ ㄒㄧㄣ)
①center ②central point ③persons holding important positions

中心人物(ㄓㄨㄥ ㄒㄧㄣ ㄖㄣˊ ㄨˋ)
the central figure; the key figure

中心思想(ㄓㄨㄥ ㄒㄧㄣ ㄙ ㄒㄧㄤˇ)
a central idea or thought (of a principle or philosophy); the gist

中興(ㄓㄨㄥ ㄒㄧㄥ)
revival (of a nation or family); to rise after decline; rejuvenation; resurgence

中型(ㄓㄨㄥ ㄒㄧㄥˊ)
medium-sized; middle-sized

中性(ㄓㄨㄥ ㄒㄧㄥˋ)
①(chemistry) neutral or neutrality ②(grammar) the neuter gender

中學(ㄓㄨㄥ ㄒㄩㄝˊ)or 中等學校
(ㄓㄨㄥ ㄉㄥˇ ㄒㄩㄝˊ ㄒㄧㄠˋ)
middle school; high school; secondary school

中旬(ㄓㄨㄥ ㄒㄩㄣˊ)
the middle part of a month; the middle ten days of a month

中止(ㄓㄨㄥ ㄓˇ)
to suspend; suspension; to interrupt; interruption

中指(ㄓㄨㄥ ㄓˇ)
the middle finger

中正(ㄓㄨㄥ ㄓㄥˋ)
just; fair; unbiased; impartial; not prejudiced

中裝(ㄓㄨㄥ ㄓㄨㄤ)
traditional Chinese clothing

中產階級(ㄓㄨㄥ ㄔㄢˇ ㄐㄧㄝ ㄐㄧˊ)
the middle class; bourgeois

中程(ㄓㄨㄥ ㄔㄥˊ)
intermediate range; medium-range

中程飛彈(ㄓㄨㄥ ㄔㄥˊ ㄈㄟ ㄉㄢˋ)
an intermediate range missile; a medium-range missile

中輟(ㄓㄨㄥ ㄔㄨㄛˋ)
to stop in the middle of something; to give up half-way

中式(ㄓㄨㄥ ㄕˋ)
the Chinese style or fashion; the Chinese way

中士(ㄓㄨㄥ ㄕˋ)
a sergeant

中世(ㄓㄨㄥ ㄕˋ)or 中世紀(ㄓㄨㄥ ㄕˋ ㄐㄧˋ)
the Middle Ages

中沙群島(ㄓㄨㄥ ㄕㄚ ㄑㄩㄣˊ ㄉㄠˇ)
the Zhongsha Islands

中山(ㄓㄨㄥ ㄕㄢ)
the courtesy name of Dr. Sun Yat-sen (孫逸仙), father of the Republic of China (often used as name of roads, schools, etc.)

中山堂(ㄓㄨㄥ ㄕㄢ ㄊㄤˊ)
any building named after Dr. Sun Yat-sen (often used as a city hall, community center, etc.)

中山樓(ㄓㄨㄥ ㄕㄢ ㄌㄡˊ)
the Chungshan Building (at Yangmingshan near Taipei)

中山狼(ㄓㄨㄥ ㄕㄢ ㄌㄤˊ)
a perfidious person

中山陵(ㄓㄨㄥ ㄕㄢ ㄌㄧㄥˊ)
the Dr. Sun Yat-sen Mausoleum (in Nanking)

中山裝(ㄓㄨㄥ ㄕㄢ ㄓㄨㄤ)or 中山服
(ㄓㄨㄥ ㄕㄢ ㄈㄨˊ)
the dress like a military uniform with closed collar; the style of man's jacket with closed collar without tie

中生代(ㄓㄨㄥ ㄕㄥ ㄉㄞˋ)
the Mesozoic (Era)

中樞(ㄓㄨㄥ ㄕㄨ)
①the central administration ②(physiology) the center

中書省(ㄓㄨㄥ ㄕㄨ ㄕㄥˇ)
(the Tang Dynasty) cabinet of ministers

中日戰爭(ㄓㄨㄥ ㄖˋ ㄓㄢˋ ㄓㄥ)
the Sino-Japanese War, 1894; the Sino-Japanese War—the War of Resistance Against Japanese Aggression, 1937-1945

中人(ㄓㄨㄥ ㄖㄣˊ)or 中間人(ㄓㄨㄥ ㄐㄧㄢ ㄖㄣˊ)
a middleman; a go-between; an agent; a mediator

中人之姿(ㄓㄨㄥ ㄖㄣˊ ㄓ ㄗ)
homely

中子(ㄓㄨㄥ ㄗˇ)
neutron

中材(ㄓㄨㄥ ㄘㄞˊ)
a person of ordinary talent

中菜(ㄓㄨㄥ ㄘㄞˋ)
Chinese dishes

中菜西吃(ㄓㄨㄥ ㄘㄞˋ ㄒㄧ ㄔ)
to eat Chinese food in the Western way (by dividing it into shares with one share for each)

中餐(ㄓㄨㄥ ㄘㄢ)
①a midday meal ②Chinese meal; Chinese food

中歐(ㄓㄨㄥ ㄡ)
the central part of Europe

中耳(ㄓㄨㄥ ㄦˇ)
the middle ear

中醫(ㄓㄨㄥ ㄧ)
①a Chinese herb doctor ②traditional Chinese medical science

中亞(ㄓㄨㄥ ㄧㄚˋ)
Central Asia

中葉(ㄓㄨㄥ ㄧㄝˋ)
the middle decades of a century; the middle period (of a dynasty, century, reign)

中藥(ㄓㄨㄥ ㄧㄠˋ)
Chinese medicine (mostly herbs)

中游(ㄓㄨㄥ ㄧㄡˊ)

〔一
部〕

① middle reaches (of a river) ② the state of being middling: 他甘居中游。He is content to stay middling.

中央(ㄓㄨㄥ ㄧㄤ)
the center; the middle

中央電影公司(ㄓㄨㄥ ㄧㄤ ㄉㄧㄢ ㄧㄥ ㄍㄨㄥ ㄙ)
Central Motion Picture Corporation

中央通訊社(ㄓㄨㄥ ㄧㄤ ㄊㄨㄥ ㄒㄩㄣ ㄕㄜ)
Central News Agency (CNA)

中央集權(ㄓㄨㄥ ㄧㄤ ㄐㄧ ㄑㄩㄢ)
a centralized government; centralization of authority

中央情報局(ㄓㄨㄥ ㄧㄤ ㄑㄧㄥ ㄅㄠ ㄐㄩ)
Central Intelligence Agency (CIA)

中央系統空氣調節(ㄓㄨㄥ ㄧㄤ ㄒㄧ ㄊㄨㄥ ㄎㄨㄥ ㄑㄧ ㄊㄧㄠ ㄐㄧㄝ)
central system air conditioning

中央信託局(ㄓㄨㄥ ㄧㄤ ㄒㄧㄣ ㄊㄨㄛ ㄐㄩ)
Central Trust of China

中央政府(ㄓㄨㄥ ㄧㄤ ㄓㄥ ㄈㄨ)
the Central Government; the National Government

中央日報(ㄓㄨㄥ ㄧㄤ ㄖ ㄅㄠ)
Central Daily News

中央研究院(ㄓㄨㄥ ㄧㄤ ㄧㄢ ㄐㄧㄡ ㄩㄢ)
Academia Sinica

中央銀行(ㄓㄨㄥ ㄧㄤ ㄧㄣ ㄏㄤ)
Central Bank of China

中央委員(ㄓㄨㄥ ㄧㄤ ㄨㄟ ㄩㄢ)
a member of the central committee of a political party

中央預算(ㄓㄨㄥ ㄧㄤ ㄩ ㄙㄨㄢ)
the central budget

中午(ㄓㄨㄥ ㄨ)
noon; high noon; midday

中外(ㄓㄨㄥ ㄨㄞ)
Chinese and foreign; in China and abroad

中外一理(ㄓㄨㄥ ㄨㄞ ㄧ ㄌㄧ)
Truth, human nature, and so on are the same everywhere.

中外野手(ㄓㄨㄥ ㄨㄞ ㄧㄝ ㄕㄡ)
(baseball) a center fielder

中尉(ㄓㄨㄥ ㄨㄟ)
(army, marine and air force) first lieutenant;

(navy) lieutenant (j.g.)

中文(ㄓㄨㄥ ㄨㄣ)
the Chinese language; Chinese

中文打字電報機(ㄓㄨㄥ ㄨㄣ ㄉㄚ ㄗ ㄉㄧㄢ ㄅㄠ ㄐㄧ)
a Chinese teletype

中文電腦(ㄓㄨㄥ ㄨㄣ ㄉㄧㄢ ㄋㄠ)
a Chinese language programmable computer

中原(ㄓㄨㄥ ㄩㄢ)
① the Central Plains—the downstream regions of the Yellow River ② the midst of a plain

中原逐鹿(ㄓㄨㄥ ㄩㄢ ㄓㄨ ㄌㄨ)
to fight for hegemony (among contending princes, warlords, etc.)

中元節(ㄓㄨㄥ ㄩㄢ ㄐㄧㄝ)
the Ghost Festival on the 15th day of the seventh lunar month

中庸(ㄓㄨㄥ ㄩㄥ)
① the golden mean of the Confucian school ② the Doctrine of the Mean—one of the Four Books ③ of ordinary talent; common; mediocre

【中】 21
2. ㄓㄨㄥ jonq zhòng
1. to hit (the target); to attain (a goal)
2. to be hit by; to be affected by: 他被落石擊中。He was hit by a falling stone.

中風(ㄓㄨㄥ ㄈㄥ)
to suffer from a stroke of paralysis or apoplexy

中伏(ㄓㄨㄥ ㄈㄨ)
to be ambushed

中彈(ㄓㄨㄥ ㄉㄢ)
to be struck by a bullet; to get shot

中的(ㄓㄨㄥ ㄉㄧ)
to hit the bull's-eye; to hit the right point; to hit the target

中第(ㄓㄨㄥ ㄉㄧ)
to pass the civil examination

中毒(ㄓㄨㄥ ㄉㄨ)
to be poisoned; toxicosis

中聽(ㄓㄨㄥ ㄊㄧㄥ)
pleasant to the ear

中看(ㄓㄨㄥ ㄎㄢ)

good to look at

中肯(ㄓㄨㄥ ㄎㄣ)
to the point; fair; relevant: 他的回答簡短而中肯。His reply was brief and to the point.

中寒(ㄓㄨㄥ ㄏㄢ)
to catch cold; to be attacked by cold

中計(ㄓㄨㄥ ㄐㄧ)
to walk into a trap; to fall into a trap; to be trapped; to be victimized by a scheme

中節(ㄓㄨㄥ ㄐㄧㄝ)
① in rhythm ② proper and just

中舉(ㄓㄨㄥ ㄐㄩ)
to pass the provincial civil service examination under the old Chinese examination system

中籤(ㄓㄨㄥ ㄑㄧㄢ)
to be chosen by lot

中選(ㄓㄨㄥ ㄒㄩㄢ)
to be chosen; to be selected

中吃(ㄓㄨㄥ ㄔ)
good to eat; tasty

中傷(ㄓㄨㄥ ㄕㄤ)
to hurt somebody insidiously; to say damaging things about others before a third party; to malign; to vilify; to slander: 有人在報上中傷他。He was vilified in newspapers.

中暑(ㄓㄨㄥ ㄕㄨ)
to have (or take) a sunstroke (or heatstroke)

中彩(ㄓㄨㄥ ㄘㄞ)or中獎(ㄓㄨㄥ ㄐㄧㄤ)
to win a (lottery) prize

中意(ㄓㄨㄥ ㄧ)
to suit one's fancy; agreeable; satisfied; to one's liking: 這些書，我一本中意。None of these books is to my liking.

中用(ㄓㄨㄥ ㄩㄥ)
useful; serviceable

【丰】 22
ㄈㄥ feng fēng
1. good-looking; buxom
2. appearance and carriage of a person

丰標(ㄈㄥ ㄅㄧㄠ)
looks; appearances

丰容(ㄈㄥ ㄖㄨㄥ)

(to address a lady) your face

手姿(ㄕㄡ ㄗ)

appearances of a person (usually indicating grace and charm)

手采(ㄕㄡ ㄘㄞˇ)

good-looking; dashing appearances

手韻(ㄕㄡ ㄩㄣˋ)

charming appearances or carriage; graceful poise

六畫

【串】²³ ㄔㄨㄢˋ chuann chuàn

1. to string together
2. a string (of coins, etc.)
3. to pour into

串騙(ㄔㄨㄢˋ ㄆㄧㄢˋ)

to swindle; to collaborate for such a purpose

串門子(ㄔㄨㄢˋ ㄇㄣˊ ˙ㄗ)or 串門兒(ㄔㄨㄢˋ ㄇㄣㄦˊ)

to visit or gossip from door to door: 她有空就來串門子。 She visits from door to door when she's free.

串通(ㄔㄨㄢˋ ㄊㄨㄥ)

to collude or to conspire

串同(ㄔㄨㄢˋ ㄊㄨㄥˊ)

to band together (to do something evil); to gang up

串聯(ㄔㄨㄢˋ ㄌㄧㄢˊ)

series connection

串鈴(ㄔㄨㄢˋ ㄌㄧㄥˊ)

a string of bells used by peddlers to attract customers

串供(ㄔㄨㄢˋ ㄍㄨㄥˋ)

collusion among witnesses or suspects for false confessions; to act in collusion

串戲(ㄔㄨㄢˋ ㄒㄧˋ)

to take part in a play; to act in a play as an amateur

串珠(ㄔㄨㄢˋ ㄓㄨ)or 串珠兒(ㄔㄨㄢˋ ㄓㄨㄦ)

a string of pearls or beads

串演(ㄔㄨㄢˋ ㄧㄢˇ)

to play respective roles in an opera or a play

、 部
ㄓㄨˇ juu zhǔ

二畫

【丸】²⁴ ㄨㄢˊ wan wán

1. a pellet; a small ball; a pill
2. an egg
3. used in Japanese indicating completion or completeness

丸劑(ㄨㄢˊ ㄐㄧˋ)

a medical pill

丸子(ㄨㄢˊ ˙ㄗ)

①a meat ball; fish balls ②a medical pill

丸藥(ㄨㄢˊ ㄧㄠˋ)

medicine in pill form

三畫

【丹】²⁵ ㄉㄢ dan dān

1. cinnabar
2. red; scarlet
3. a sophisticated decoction
4. a medical pill, ointment and powder

丹砥(ㄉㄢ ㄓˊ)

amber

丹麥(ㄉㄢ ㄇㄞˋ)

Denmark

丹麥人(ㄉㄢ ㄇㄞˋ ㄖㄣˊ)

a Dane; the Danes

丹麥語(ㄉㄢ ㄇㄞˋ ㄩˇ)

Danish

丹方(ㄉㄢ ㄈㄤ)

a prescription; a folk prescription

丹毒(ㄉㄢ ㄉㄨˊ)

erysipelas; an inflammatory disease with redness of skin

丹田(ㄉㄢ ㄊㄧㄢˊ)

the lower part of abdomen; (Taoism) the region three inches below the navel

丹鉛(ㄉㄢ ㄑㄧㄢ)

a mixture of cinnabar and white lead powder formerly used for writing or painting purpose—the business of proofreading or revision,

---

from practice of using red ink

丹青(ㄉㄢ ㄑㄧㄥ)

①painting ②history; annals

丹闕(ㄉㄢ ㄑㄩㄝˋ)

the red gate of a palace—a palace

丹心(ㄉㄢ ㄒㄧㄣ)

sincere heart; the bottom of one's heart

丹竹(ㄉㄢ ㄓㄨˊ)

the red bamboo

丹忱(ㄉㄢ ㄔㄣˊ)

sincere loyalty

丹誠(ㄉㄢ ㄔㄥˊ)

loyalty; devotion

丹砂(ㄉㄢ ㄕㄚ)

cinnabar; material for red color

丹書(ㄉㄢ ㄕㄨ)or 丹詔(ㄉㄢ ㄓㄠˋ)

the imperial edict written in red

四畫

【主】²⁶ ㄓㄨˇ juu zhǔ

1. a master; a leader; a chief; a host
2. Jesus Christ; God; Lord
3. to officiate at; to preside over; to take charge of
4. main; chief; primary; principal

主辦(ㄓㄨˇ ㄅㄢˋ)

to sponsor; to take charge of

主筆(ㄓㄨˇ ㄅㄧˇ)

an editorial writer of a newspaper

主編(ㄓㄨˇ ㄅㄧㄢ)

a senior editor who edits a specific page or section of a newspaper; an editor-in-chief

主賓席(ㄓㄨˇ ㄅㄧㄣ ㄒㄧˊ)

the head table (at a banquet, etc.); the seat for the guest of honor

主僕(ㄓㄨˇ ㄆㄨˊ)

master and servant

主謀(ㄓㄨˇ ㄇㄡˊ)

①the mastermind; the stringpuller ②to head a conspiracy; to be the chief plotter

主犯(ㄓㄨˇ ㄈㄢˋ)

the leader of a racket; the principal criminal; the main

culprit

主峯(ㄓㄨ ㄈㄥ)
the main peak of a mountain; the highest peak in a mountain range

主婦(ㄓㄨ ㄈㄨˋ)
a housewife; a hostess; the mistress of the house

主導(ㄓㄨ ㄉㄠˇ)
leading; dominant; guiding

主動(ㄓㄨ ㄉㄨㄥˋ)
to take the initiative; of one's own accord

主動脈(ㄓㄨ ㄉㄨㄥˋ ㄇㄞˋ)
(anatomy) the aorta

主動式(ㄓㄨ ㄉㄨㄥˋ ㄕˋ)
(grammar) the active voice

主題(ㄓㄨ ㄊㄧˊ)
the main theme (of an essay or a musical piece); the main points; the central thought; the gist

主體(ㄓㄨ ㄊㄧˇ)
①the subjective (as against the objective) ②the main body or the most important part of something

主腦(ㄓㄨ ㄋㄠˇ)
the mastermind; the chief; the leader

主奴(ㄓㄨ ㄋㄨˊ)
master and servant

主力(ㄓㄨ ㄌㄧˋ)
the main force; the main body of an army

主力艦(ㄓㄨ ㄌㄧˋ ㄐㄧㄢˋ)
a battleship; a capital ship

主力軍(ㄓㄨ ㄌㄧˋ ㄐㄩㄣ)
the main force; the principal force

主流(ㄓㄨ ㄌㄧㄡˊ)
①the mainstream; the main current; the mother current ②the essential or main aspect; the main trend

主糧(ㄓㄨ ㄌㄧㄤˊ)
the staple food grain

主格(ㄓㄨ ㄍㄜˊ)
(grammar) the subjective case

主稿(ㄓㄨ ㄍㄠˇ)
the chief writer; a person who organizes material presented by others for writings

主幹(ㄓㄨ ㄍㄢˋ)
①the trunk ②the main

force; the mainstay

主顧(ㄓㄨ ㄍㄨˋ)
a customer; a client

主觀(ㄓㄨ ㄍㄨㄢ)
the subjective point of view

主管(ㄓㄨ ㄍㄨㄢˇ)
①the boss; the chief ②to take charge of: 他將主管這件工作。He will be in charge of this job.

主管機關(ㄓㄨ ㄍㄨㄢˇ ㄐㄧ ㄍㄨㄢ)
the authorities concerned; the agency which is in charge of (a program, etc.)

主攻(ㄓㄨ ㄍㄨㄥ)
the main attack

主客(ㄓㄨ ㄎㄜˋ)
the guest of honor

主考(ㄓㄨ ㄎㄠˇ)
①to be in charge of a competitive examination ②(in ancient China) the official in charge of a civil service examination

主和(ㄓㄨ ㄏㄜˊ)
to advocate peace

主和派(ㄓㄨ ㄏㄜˊ ㄆㄞˋ)
the doves

主婚(ㄓㄨ ㄏㄨㄣ)
to preside over a wedding ceremony

主婚人(ㄓㄨ ㄏㄨㄣ ㄖㄣˊ)
the parents (or guardians) of the marrying couple at a wedding ceremony

主機(ㄓㄨ ㄐㄧ)
①the main engine ②(air force) the lead plane; the leader ③the host computer

主祭(ㄓㄨ ㄐㄧˋ)
①to officiate at a religious rite or service ②a person officiating at such a service

主計室(ㄓㄨ ㄐㄧˋ ㄕˋ)
the auditing department; the accounting department

主記憶體(ㄓㄨ ㄐㄧˋ ㄧˋ ㄊㄧˇ)
(computers) the main memory

主教(ㄓㄨ ㄐㄧㄠˋ)
a bishop

主見(ㄓㄨ ㄐㄧㄢˋ)
the ideas or thoughts of one's own: 他這人很有主見。He knows his own mind.

主講(ㄓㄨ ㄐㄧㄤˇ)
①to lecture; to speak on a

special subject ②the main speaker

主將(ㄓㄨ ㄐㄧㄤˋ)
①the commanding general ②the most important athlete in a sports team

主句(ㄓㄨ ㄐㄩˋ)
a main clause; a principal clause

主角(ㄓㄨ ㄐㄩㄝˊ)or主角兒(ㄓㄨ ㄐㄩㄝˊ ㄦ)
the leading player; the leading role; the main actor or actress; the protagonist; the lead

主權(ㄓㄨ ㄑㄩㄢˊ)
①sovereignty ②the right of autonomy

主權國(ㄓㄨ ㄑㄩㄢˊ ㄍㄨㄛˊ)
a sovereign state (or country)

主席(ㄓㄨ ㄒㄧˊ)
a chairman; a president

主席團(ㄓㄨ ㄒㄧˊ ㄊㄨㄢˊ)
the presidium

主修(ㄓㄨ ㄒㄧㄡ)
①to specialize (in a subject); to major ②to be responsible for the repair or overhaul (of a machine)

主旨(ㄓㄨ ㄓˇ)
the gist, substance, purport, or the main points (of a speech, statement, etc.)

主治(ㄓㄨ ㄓˋ)
①the major functions of a drug ②a physician in charge of a patient or patients

主治醫師(ㄓㄨ ㄓˋ ㄧ ㄕ)
a physician in charge of a case

主戰(ㄓㄨ ㄓㄢˋ)
to advocate war

主戰派(ㄓㄨ ㄓㄢˋ ㄆㄞˋ)
the hawks

主張(ㄓㄨ ㄓㄤ)
①an opinion or idea ②to hold a view; to advocate: 我主張釋放那犯人。I advocate the release of the prisoner.

主政(ㄓㄨ ㄓㄥˋ)
①to head the administration ②the person in charge

主終端機(ㄓㄨ ㄓㄨㄥ ㄉㄨㄢ ㄐㄧ)
(computers) the master terminal

【丿部】

主持 (ㄓㄨˇ ㄔˊ)
to officiate at; to preside over; to take charge of; to supervise: 張先生主持會議。Mr. Chang presided over the meeting.

主持正義 (ㄓㄨˇ ㄔˊ ㄓㄥˋ ㄧˋ)
to uphold justice; to champion the cause of justice

主程式 (ㄓㄨˇ ㄔㄥˊ ㄕˋ)
(computers) the main program

主食 (ㄓㄨˇ ㄕˊ)
the principal food items; staple food

主使 (ㄓㄨˇ ㄕˇ)
①a mastermind; a behind-the-scene operator; a ringleader ②to incite; to instigate

主試官 (ㄓㄨˇ ㄕˋ ㄍㄨㄢ)
(in ancient China) the official in charge of a civil service examination

主帥 (ㄓㄨˇ ㄕㄨㄞˋ)
an address to the commander in chief

主日 (ㄓㄨˇ ㄖˋ)
Sunday

主日學校 (ㄓㄨˇ ㄖˋ ㄒㄩㄝˊ ㄒㄧㄠˋ)
Sunday school

主人 (ㄓㄨˇ ㄖㄣˊ)
①an owner ②a host ③a master

主人翁 (ㄓㄨˇ ㄖㄣˊ ㄨㄥ)
①a respectful term for a host ②a master: 年輕的一代是新社會的主人翁。The younger generation is the master of the new society.

主任 (ㄓㄨˇ ㄖㄣˋ)
the head of an office; the person in charge (of an undertaking, committee, etc.)

主子 (ㄓㄨˇ ˙ㄗ)
①the emperor ②one's master; one's boss

主宰 (ㄓㄨˇ ㄗㄞˇ)
①the man in charge; a man with supreme powers ②a god

主座 (ㄓㄨˇ ㄗㄨㄛˋ)
the seat of honor; the person occupying it

主從 (ㄓㄨˇ ㄗㄨㄥˊ)
①the master and his servant (or servants) ②the principal and the secondary (criminals)

主詞 (ㄓㄨˇ ㄘˊ)
(grammar) the subject

entrée; the principal dish

主隨客便 (ㄓㄨˇ ㄙㄨㄟˊ ㄎㄜˋ ㄅㄧㄢˋ)
A host respects his guest's wishes.

主意
an idea; a suggestion: 那真是個好主意。It's a good idea.

主義 (ㄓㄨˇ ㄧˋ)
a principle; a doctrine

主要 (ㄓㄨˇ ㄧㄠˋ)
essential; important; major; chief; principal

主祐 (ㄓㄨˇ ㄧㄡˋ)
blessed or protected by God

主演 (ㄓㄨˇ ㄧㄢˇ)
to star; to play the leading role in a play or a motion picture

主因 (ㄓㄨˇ ㄧㄣ)
the major cause; the principal cause

主位 (ㄓㄨˇ ㄨㄟˋ)
the seat of the host

主語 (ㄓㄨˇ ㄩˇ)
(grammar) the subject of a sentence

五畫

【兵】 27
(ㄅㄧㄤ pang pāng)
used for the sound 參看「乒乓」. 門在他身後砰然地關上。The door banged after him.

丿 部

(ㄆㄧㄝˇ ㄆㄧㄝ piee piě)

一畫

【乃】 28
(ㄋㄞˇ nae nǎi)
1. to be: 需要乃發明之根源。Necessity is the mother of invention.
2. but; however
3. and also; moreover

4. so; therefore
5. you; your
6. then
7. if

乃至 (ㄋㄞˇ ㄓˋ)
①so that; so… as to; leading to ②hence; consequently ③even: 乃至如此。It even came to such a pass.

乃是 (ㄋㄞˇ ㄕˋ)
①but ②which is…; to be; really is (are): 失敗乃是成功之母。Failure is the mother of success.

乃祖 (ㄋㄞˇ ㄗㄨˇ)
your grandfather

乃翁 (ㄋㄞˇ ㄨㄥ)or 乃父 (ㄋㄞˇ ㄈㄨˋ)
your father

二畫

【久】 29
(ㄐㄧㄡˇ jeou jiǔ)
1. long
2. for a long time: 由來久矣! It's been so for a long time.
3. to detain someone long

久別 (ㄐㄧㄡˇ ㄅㄧㄝˊ)
long separated; long separation

久病成良醫 (ㄐㄧㄡˇ ㄅㄧㄥˋ ㄔㄥˊ ㄌㄧㄤˊ ㄧ)
Long illness makes the patient a good doctor.

久聞 (ㄐㄧㄡˇ ㄨㄣˊ)
I have heard of you for a long time.—a conventional phrase for greeting somebody one has just been introduced to

久佃成業 (ㄐㄧㄡˇ ㄉㄧㄢˋ ㄔㄥˊ ㄧㄝˋ)
A long-term tenant regards the land he tills as his own.

久歷風塵 (ㄐㄧㄡˇ ㄌㄧˋ ㄈㄥ ㄔㄣˊ)
(said of women) to have led a life of sin for a long time

久留 (ㄐㄧㄡˇ ㄌㄧㄡˊ)
to stay for a long time

久客 (ㄐㄧㄡˇ ㄎㄜˋ)
to be a guest for an extended period of time; to be a wanderer away from home for a long time

久困 (ㄐㄧㄡˇ ㄎㄨㄣˋ)
to stay in an unpleasant situation or on a lowly job for a long time

久候 (ㄐㄧㄡˇ ㄏㄡˋ)

to wait for a long time

久旱逢甘霖(ㄐㄧㄡˇㄏㄢˋㄈㄥˊㄍㄢ
ㄌㄧㄣˊ)
(literally) to have a sweet
shower after a long drought
—to get something urgently
needed after being deprived
of it for a long time

久計(ㄐㄧㄡˇㄐㄧˋ)
a long-range plan

久假不歸(ㄐㄧㄡˇㄐㄧㄚˇㄅㄨˋㄍㄨㄟ)
to fail to return (something)
after having borrowed it for
a long time; to put off indefinitely returning something
one has borrowed

久久(ㄐㄧㄡˇㄐㄧㄡˇ)
for a long, long time

久經風霜(ㄐㄧㄡˇㄐㄧㄥㄈㄥㄕㄨㄤ)
to have experienced all sorts
of hardships

久居人下(ㄐㄧㄡˇㄐㄩㄖㄣˊㄒㄧㄚˋ)
to remain in a subordinate
position for a long period

久屈(ㄐㄧㄡˇㄑㄩ)
(said of a talented person)
to occupy a lowly position
for a long time

久蟄思動(ㄐㄧㄡˇㄓㄜˊㄙㄉㄨㄥˋ)
to be eager to enter the
limelight again after a long
period of retirement or inactivity

久長(ㄐㄧㄡˇㄔㄤˊ)
for a long time; an extended
period of time

久長之策(ㄐㄧㄡˇㄔㄤˊㄓㄘㄜˋ)
a long-range plan

久而久之(ㄐㄧㄡˇㄦˊㄐㄧㄡˇㄓ)
over a long period of time

久仰(ㄐㄧㄡˇㄧㄤˇ)
(literally) I have heard of
your illustrious name for a
long time.—Glad to meet
you.

久仰大名(ㄐㄧㄡˇㄧㄤˇㄉㄚˋㄇㄧㄥˊ)
I've heard of your illustrious
name for a long time. 亦作
「久聞大名」

久違(ㄐㄧㄡˇㄨㄟˊ)
the literary form of "Long
time no see." 或 I have not
seen you for a long time.

久遠(ㄐㄧㄡˇㄩㄢˇ)
a long time; forever; long
and far-reaching; perpetual;
ages ago; remote

三畫

【之】 ㄓ jy zhī
1. to go to; to leave for; to
arrive at
2. zigzag; winding
3. an expletive
4. third person objective case
(it; her; them)
5. this; that; these; those
6. (possessive particle) or: 鐘鼓
之聲 the sound of drums and
bells

之內(ㄓㄋㄟˋ)
within; inside; including; included

之後(ㄓㄏㄡˋ)
after this; afterward: 他走之
後，我們就吃飯。After he goes,
we shall eat.

之乎者也(ㄓㄏㄨㄓㄜˇㄧㄝˇ)
①pedantry; archaisms ②
auxiliary characters used to
embellish the literary style

之前(ㄓㄑㄧㄢˊ)
before this; before; prior to:
睡 覺之前請服這藥。Please
take the medicine before
bedtime.

之上(ㄓㄕㄤˋ)
above; over; on

之子于歸(ㄓㄗˇㄩㄍㄨㄟ)
(said of women) to marry 或
The maiden goes to her
future (or new) home.

之字路(ㄓㄗˋㄌㄨˋ)
a zigzag road (or path); an
S-shaped road

之死靡它(ㄓㄙˇㄇㄧˇㄊㄚ)
(said of a widow) to refuse
to remarry

之無(ㄓㄨˊ)
the simplest and most common characters

之外(ㄓㄨㄞˋ)
besides this; in addition

四畫

【乍】 ㄓㄚˋ jah zhà
1. at first; for the first time: 乍
看起來她很美麗。At first
glance she looks beautiful.
2. suddenly; unexpectedly;
abruptly; inadvertently

乍富(ㄓㄚˋㄈㄨˋ)
from rags to riches; sudden
wealth; *nouveau riche*

乍到(ㄓㄚˋㄉㄠˋ)
①to arrive at some place
unexpectedly and suddenly
②to have just arrived at
some place

乍冷乍熱(ㄓㄚˋㄌㄥˇㄓㄚˋㄖㄜˋ)
now cold. now hot (refer-
ring to changeable weather):
天氣乍冷乍熱。The tempera-
ture changes abruptly.

乍見(ㄓㄚˋㄐㄧㄢˋ)
①to meet for the first time
②to see suddenly

乍晴乍雨(ㄓㄚˋㄑㄧㄥˊㄓㄚˋㄩˇ)
sudden change from rain to
shine

乍然(ㄓㄚˋㄖㄢˊ)
abruptly; unexpectedly

乍聞(ㄓㄚˋㄨㄣˊ)
suddenly learn for the first
time

部

【乎】 ㄏㄨ hu hū
1. at; in; from; than: 我認爲這
不合乎道理。I don't think it's
in accord with reason.
2. an interrogative particle
3. an exclamatory particle

【乏】 ㄈㄚˊ far fá
1. in want of; deficient; lack
2. exhausted; tired
3. poor; poverty-stricken

乏力(ㄈㄚˊㄌㄧˋ)
to feel exhausted; to lack
strength or vitality

乏趣(ㄈㄚˊㄑㄩˋ)
lacking in interest

乏善可陳(ㄈㄚˊㄕㄢˋㄎㄜˇㄔㄣˊ)
to have nothing good or unusual to report

乏人照應(ㄈㄚˊㄖㄣˊㄓㄠˋㄧㄥˋ)
in need of people to look
after

乏味(ㄈㄚˊㄨㄟˋ)
monotonous; dull; insipid;
tasteless

五畫

【乒】 ㄆㄧㄥ ping pīng
used for the sound: 我聽到乒
的一聲槍響。I heard the crack
of a gun.

乒乓〈ㄆㄧㄥ ㄆㄤ〉
ping-pong (used for the sound)

乒乓球〈ㄆㄧㄥ ㄆㄤ ㄑㄧㄡˊ〉
①table tennis ②a table tennis ball

〔乙
部〕

七畫

【乖】 35
〈ㄍㄨㄞ guai guāi〉
1. to oppose; to contradict; to be at variance
2. perverse; obstinate; untoward; sulky
3. obedient; well-behaved: 他是個乖孩子。He is an obedient child.
4. cunning; artful; crafty; wily

乖僻〈ㄍㄨㄞ ㄆㄧˋ〉
unreasonable; perverse; eccentric

乖謬〈ㄍㄨㄞ ㄇㄧㄡˋ〉
absurd; fallacious

乖戾〈ㄍㄨㄞ ㄌㄧˋ〉
cantankerous; perverse

乖乖〈ㄍㄨㄞ ㄍㄨㄞ〉or 乖乖兒的〈ㄍㄨㄞ ㄍㄨㄞㄦ˙ㄉㄜ〉
①submissive; docile; obedient ②an endearing name for children

乖覺〈ㄍㄨㄞ ㄐㄩㄝˊ〉
shrewd and capable

乖巧〈ㄍㄨㄞ ㄑㄧㄠˇ〉
clever; ingenious: 這小孩甚爲乖巧。The child is very clever.

乖張〈ㄍㄨㄞ ㄓㄤ〉
recalcitrant; stubbornly persisting in doing something wrong

乖異〈ㄍㄨㄞ ㄧˋ〉
strange; odd; eccentric; intractable: 她的性情乖異。She has an intractable temper.

乖違〈ㄍㄨㄞ ㄨㄟˊ〉
①contradictory; conflicting ②separate

九畫

【乘】 36
1. ㄔㄥˊ cherng chéng
1. to ride; to mount
2. to avail oneself of; to take advantage of; to seize a chance or an opportunity
3. to multiply

乘便〈ㄔㄥˊ ㄅㄧㄢˋ〉
①to take advantage of the chance ②at your convenience

乘馬〈ㄔㄥˊ ㄇㄚˇ〉
to ride a horse

乘冪〈ㄔㄥˊ ㄇㄧˋ〉or 乘方〈ㄔㄥˊ ㄈㄤ〉
(mathematics) power

乘法〈ㄔㄥˊ ㄈㄚˇ〉
(arithmetic) multiplication

乘風破浪〈ㄔㄥˊ ㄈㄥ ㄆㄛˋ ㄌㄤˋ〉
(literally) to ride the wind and weather the storm—great ambition

乘涼〈ㄔㄥˊ ㄌㄧㄤˊ〉
to cool oneself in the shade or in the breeze; to enjoy the cool air; to relax in a cool place

乘龍快婿〈ㄔㄥˊ ㄌㄨㄥˊ ㄎㄨㄞˋ ㄒㄩˋ〉
an ideal son-in-law

乘客〈ㄔㄥˊ ㄎㄜˋ〉
a passenger

乘空〈ㄔㄥˊ ㄎㄨㄥˋ〉or 乘空兒〈ㄔㄥˊ ㄎㄨㄥˋㄦ〉
to do something while one has plenty of time on hand

乘號〈ㄔㄥˊ ㄏㄠˋ〉
the sign of multiplication

乘積〈ㄔㄥˊ ㄐㄧ〉
(arithmetic) the product

乘機〈ㄔㄥˊ ㄐㄧ〉
①to avail oneself of an opportunity; to seize the right time; to embrace a chance ②to ride an airplane

乘堅策肥〈ㄔㄥˊ ㄐㄧㄢ ㄘㄜˋ ㄈㄟˊ〉
(said of a wealthy person) to ride a sturdy carriage and mount a well-fed horse

乘間〈ㄔㄥˊ ㄐㄧㄢˋ〉or 乘隙〈ㄔㄥˊ ㄒㄧˋ〉
to seize a fleeting chance

乘間竊發〈ㄔㄥˊ ㄐㄧㄢˋ ㄑㄧㄝˋ ㄈㄚ〉
to seize an opportunity to start doing something

乘興〈ㄔㄥˊ ㄒㄧㄥˋ〉
on the spur of the moment: 我們乘興往海邊走去。We headed for the beach on the spur of the moment.

乘興而往，敗興而歸〈ㄔㄥˊ ㄒㄧㄥˋ ㄦˊ ㄨㄤˇ ㄅㄞˋ ㄒㄧㄥˋ ㄦˊ ㄍㄨㄟ〉
to go with great enthusiasm and return disappointed or disillusioned

乘虛而入〈ㄔㄥˊ ㄒㄩ ㄦˊ ㄖㄨˋ〉
to take advantage of a weak point; to act when somebody is off guard

乘除〈ㄔㄥˊ ㄔㄨˊ〉
(literally) multiplication and division—wax and wane

乘勢〈ㄔㄥˊ ㄕˋ〉
to act when a good chance is available; to take advantage of circumstances

乘勝追擊〈ㄔㄥˊ ㄕㄥˋ ㄓㄨㄟ ㄐㄧˊ〉
to pursue enemy troops in retreat

乘數〈ㄔㄥˊ ㄕㄨˋ〉
multiplicator or multiplier

乘人之危〈ㄔㄥˊ ㄖㄣˊ ㄓ ㄨㄟ〉
to take advantage of somebody when he is not in a position to resist

【乘】 36
2. ㄕㄥˋ shenq shèng
1. historical records: 這事件記載在史乘中。This event is carried in historical records.
2. an ancient carriage
3. Buddhist teaching—a conveyance to bring the truth to men and help them
4. a team of four horses

乙 部
ㄧˇ yii yǐ

【乙】 37
ㄧˇ yii yǐ
1. the second of the Ten Celestial Stems
2. one
3. someone
4. an ancient Chinese family name

乙榜〈ㄧˇ ㄅㄤˇ〉
the candidate who passed the provincial civil service examination in old China

乙醚〈ㄧˇ ㄇㄧˊ〉
ether

乙炔〈ㄧˇ ㄑㄩㄝ〉
acetylene; ethyne

乙烯〈ㄧˇ ㄒㄧ〉
ethylene

乙種〈ㄧˇ ㄓㄨㄥˇ〉
Category B

乙醇〈ㄧˇ ㄔㄨㄣˊ〉

ethanol; alcohol

一畫

【乜】 38
　1. ㄇㄧㄝ mhie miě
乜斜(ㄇㄧㄝ ㄒㄧㄝ)
to glance sideways: 她乜斜着
眼睛看他。 She glanced side-
ways at him.

【乜】 38
　2. ㄋㄧㄝ nieh niè
a very rare Chinese family
name

【九】 39
　ㄐㄧㄡˇ jeou jiǔ
nine; ninth: 他十次有九次忘
記。 Nine times out of ten he
forgot.

九邊形(ㄐㄧㄡˇ ㄅㄧㄢ ㄒㄧㄥˊ)or 九角
形(ㄐㄧㄡˇ ㄐㄧㄠˇ ㄒㄧㄥˊ)
a nonagon; nonagonal: 這圖
案是九邊形的。 The shape of
this design is a nonagonal
one.

九品(ㄐㄧㄡˇ ㄆㄧㄣˇ)
① (in ancient China) the
nine grades of official rank
② the ninth official rank

九大行星(ㄐㄧㄡˇ ㄉㄚˋ ㄒㄧㄥˊ ㄒㄧㄥ)
the nine planets in the solar
system—Mercury, Venus,
Earth, Mars, Jupiter, Saturn,
Uranus, Neptune, and Pluto

九頭鳥(ㄐㄧㄡˇ ㄊㄡˊ ㄋㄧㄠˇ)
a legendary bird with nine
heads, now used in reference
to a crafty fellow

九天(ㄐㄧㄡˇ ㄊㄧㄢ)
① the highest heavens ② the
heaven of the Taoists

九牛二虎(ㄐㄧㄡˇ ㄋㄧㄡˊ ㄦˋ ㄏㄨˇ)
(literally) the combined
strength of nine oxen and
two tigers—a herculean
effort

九牛一毛(ㄐㄧㄡˇ ㄋㄧㄡˊ ㄧ ㄇㄠˊ)
(literally) one hair from
nine oxen—an iota from a
vast quantity

九鍊成鋼(ㄐㄧㄡˇ ㄌㄧㄢˋ ㄔㄥˊ ㄍㄤ)
Mastery is the result of long
practice or training.

九宮格(ㄐㄧㄡˇ ㄍㄨㄥ ㄍㄜˊ)
(calligraphy) squares into
which each page of a copybook is divided

九九表(ㄐㄧㄡˇ ㄐㄧㄡˇ ㄅㄧㄠˇ)
the multiplication table up
to nine times nine

九九歸原(ㄐㄧㄡˇ ㄐㄧㄡˇ ㄍㄨㄟ ㄩㄢˊ)
(said of argument, etc.) to
return to where it started

九江(ㄐㄧㄡˇ ㄐㄧㄤ)
Chiuchiang, a city in Kiangsi on the northern bank of
the Yangtze

九竅(ㄐㄧㄡˇ ㄑㄧㄠˋ)
the orifices of the body

九泉(ㄐㄧㄡˇ ㄑㄩㄢˊ)
Hades; the underworld

九泉地下(ㄐㄧㄡˇ ㄑㄩㄢˊ ㄉㄧˋ ㄒㄧㄚˋ)
in the grave; the under-
world; under the earth;
Hades

九霄雲外(ㄐㄧㄡˇ ㄒㄧㄠ ㄩㄣˊ ㄨㄞˋ)
beyond the farthest limits of
the sky—far, far away

九州(ㄐㄧㄡˇ ㄓㄡ)
① another name for ancient
China ② Kyushu, an island
of Japan

九成(ㄐㄧㄡˇ ㄔㄥˊ)
ninety percent

九成宮(ㄐㄧㄡˇ ㄔㄥˊ ㄍㄨㄥ)
① name of a palace in Shensi Province ② a distinctive
style of Chinese calligraphy
started by Ou-Yang Hsün
(歐陽詢), a famous calligra-
pher of the Tang Dynasty

九重天(ㄐㄧㄡˇ ㄔㄨㄥˊ ㄊㄧㄢ)
① the nine divisions of the
celestial sphere, i.e., the four
cardinal points, the four
intermediate points, and the
center ② the Taoist Heaven

九重葛(ㄐㄧㄡˇ ㄔㄨㄥˊ ㄍㄜˊ)
(botany) bougainvillea

九十歲至九十九歲的人(ㄐㄧㄡˇ ㄕˊ
ㄙㄨㄟˋ ㄓˋ ㄐㄧㄡˇ ㄕˊ ㄐㄧㄡˇ ㄙㄨㄟˋ ·ㄉㄜ
ㄖㄣˊ)
a nonagenarian

九日(ㄐㄧㄡˇ ㄖˋ)
the ninth day of the ninth
moon, a festival on the
lunar calendar

九族(ㄐㄧㄡˇ ㄗㄨˊ)
the nine degrees of kindred

九死一生(ㄐㄧㄡˇ ㄙˇ ㄧ ㄕㄥ)
a very narrow escape from
death; grave danger

九一八事變(ㄐㄧㄡˇ ㄧ ㄅㄚ ㄕˋ ㄅㄧㄢˋ)
the Mukden Incident on Sep-

tember 18, 1931, which led to
the Japanese occupation of
Manchuria and the creation
of the puppet Manchukuo

九月(ㄐㄧㄡˇ ㄩㄝˋ)
① September ② the ninth
month of the lunar calendar
③ nine months

二畫

【乞】 40
　ㄑㄧˇ chii qǐ
to ask for alms; to beg; to
entreat; to pray humbly

乞和(ㄑㄧˇ ㄏㄜˊ)
① to sue for peace ② (said
of rulers) to pray before the
deity

乞免(ㄑㄧˇ ㄇㄧㄢˇ)
to beg for exception (from
taxation, punishment, etc.)

乞命(ㄑㄧˇ ㄇㄧㄥˋ)
to beg for life

乞貸(ㄑㄧˇ ㄉㄞˋ)or 乞借(ㄑㄧˇ ㄐㄧㄝˋ)
to beg for a loan

乞討(ㄑㄧˇ ㄊㄠˇ)
to beg for food, money, etc.

乞憐(ㄑㄧˇ ㄌㄧㄢˊ)
to beg for pity and charity

乞靈(ㄑㄧˇ ㄌㄧㄥˊ)
to seek help (from herbs,
divine beings, etc.)

乞丐(ㄑㄧˇ ㄍㄞˋ)
a beggar

乞假(ㄑㄧˇ ㄐㄧㄚˋ)
to ask for a leave of
absence

乞巧(ㄑㄧˇ ㄑㄧㄠˇ)
to pray for divine instructions for improvement of
needlework on the 7th night
of the 7th lunar month when
the Weaving Maid meets the
Cowherd across the Milky
Way (The occasion is a sort
of festival to unmarried
girls.)

乞求(ㄑㄧˇ ㄑㄧㄡˊ)
to beg for; to supplicate; to
implore

乞降(ㄑㄧˇ ㄒㄧㄤˊ)
to negotiate for surrender
on the part of the defeated

乞師(ㄑㄧˇ ㄕ)
to ask for military help or
troop reinforcements

乙部

乞兒(くゴル)
a beggar

乞援(くゴロ)
to ask for assistance; to beg for aid

【乙部】

【也】 41
(ㄧㄝˇ) yee yě
1. and; also; besides; either; too
2. still
3. even
4. an expletive in Chinese writing

也罷(ㄧㄝˇ ㄅㄚ)
Never mind. 或 Let it pass. 或 That's all right. (This expression is used to show the speaker's reluctance.)

也門(ㄧㄝˇ ㄇㄣˊ)
Yemen 亦作「葉門」

也可以(ㄧㄝˇ ㄎㄜˇ ㄧˇ)
① may also ② It makes no difference. 或 It's okay.

也好(ㄧㄝˇ ㄏㄠˇ)
That's fine.

也就(ㄧㄝˇ ㄐㄧㄡˋ)
… and then…

也行(ㄧㄝˇ ㄒㄧㄥˊ)
All right! 或 That will do too.

也許(ㄧㄝˇ ㄒㄩˇ)
perhaps; probably: 也許要下雨. It will probably rain.

也是(ㄧㄝˇ ㄕˋ)
also the same

也有(ㄧㄝˇ ㄧㄡˇ)
① There are in addition…. ② There are others (who or which)….

也未可知(ㄧㄝˇ ㄨㄟˋ ㄎㄜˇ ㄓ)
Who knows but that…. 或 perhaps; maybe

五畫

【占】 42
ㄓ ㄐㄧ jī ji
to divine; to resolve doubts by an application to spiritual beings

七畫

【乳】 43
ㄖㄨˇ ruu rǔ
1. breasts; the nipple
2. milk

3. any milk-like liquid
4. the young of animals, birds, etc.
5. to give birth
6. to triturate

乳白(ㄖㄨˇ ㄅㄞˊ)
milky white; cream color

乳哺(ㄖㄨˇ ㄅㄨˇ)
to feed with milk or chewed food

乳糜(ㄖㄨˇ ㄇㄧˊ)
chyle

乳名(ㄖㄨˇ ㄇㄧㄥˊ)
a pet name given to a child

乳母(ㄖㄨˇ ㄇㄨˇ)or 乳娘(ㄖㄨˇ ㄋㄧㄤˊ)
a wet nurse

乳房(ㄖㄨˇ ㄈㄤˊ)
the udders; the breasts

乳頭(ㄖㄨˇ ㄊㄡˊ)
a nipple; a teat

乳糖(ㄖㄨˇ ㄊㄤˊ)
lactose; milk sugar

乳牛(ㄖㄨˇ ㄋㄧㄡˊ)
the dairy cattle; a milch cow

乳場(ㄖㄨˇ ㄋㄧㄡˊ ㄔㄤˇ)
a dairy farm

乳酪(ㄖㄨˇ ㄌㄠˋ)
junket; curds

乳化(ㄖㄨˇ ㄏㄨㄚˋ)
emulsification

乳化劑(ㄖㄨˇ ㄏㄨㄚˋ ㄐㄧˋ)
an emulsifying agent; an emulsifier

乳劑(ㄖㄨˇ ㄐㄧˋ)
emulsion: 感光乳劑 (photograph) sensitive emulsion

乳膠液(ㄖㄨˇ ㄐㄧㄠ ㄧㄝˋ)
emulsion

乳酒(ㄖㄨˇ ㄐㄧㄡˇ)
milk-white wine

乳氣(ㄖㄨˇ ㄑㄧˋ)
childishness; childish

乳臭未乾(ㄖㄨˇ ㄒㄧㄡˋ ㄨㄟˋ ㄍㄢ)
very young and inexperienced like a sucking child

乳腺(ㄖㄨˇ ㄒㄧㄢˋ)
mammary glands

乳腺炎(ㄖㄨˇ ㄒㄧㄢˋ ㄧㄢˊ)
mastitis

乳香(ㄖㄨˇ ㄒㄧㄤ)
frankincense

乳汁(ㄖㄨˇ ㄓ)
milk

乳脂(ㄖㄨˇ ㄓ)
butter

乳製品(ㄖㄨˇ ㄓˋ ㄆㄧㄣˇ)
dairy products

乳罩(ㄖㄨˇ ㄓㄠˋ)
a brassiere; a bra

乳狀液(ㄖㄨˇ ㄓㄨㄤˋ ㄧㄝˋ)
milklike liquid

乳齒(ㄖㄨˇ ㄔˇ)
milk teeth; deciduous teeth

乳酸(ㄖㄨˇ ㄙㄨㄢ)
lactic acid

乳酸菌(ㄖㄨˇ ㄙㄨㄢ ㄐㄩㄣ)
(bacteriology) lactobacillus

乳媼(ㄖㄨˇ ㄠˇ)
a wet nurse

乳兒(ㄖㄨˇ ㄦˊ)
a sucking child

乳癌(ㄖㄨˇ ㄞˊ)
cancer of the breast; mastocarcinoma

乳媼(ㄖㄨˇ ㄨㄥ)
a wet nurse

乳暈(ㄖㄨˇ ㄩㄣ)
mammary areola

十畫

【乾】 44
1. (乾) ㄍㄢ gan gān
1. clean: 他的手是乾淨的. His hands are clean.
2. dry; dried: 乾柴可燃. Dry wood will burn.
3. exhausted

乾爸爸(ㄍㄢ ㄅㄚˋ ·ㄅㄚ)or 乾爹(ㄍㄢ ㄉㄧㄝ)
a man whose position is roughly equivalent to a foster father and godfather in Western countries without religious or legal complications

乾巴巴(ㄍㄢ ·ㄅㄚ)or 乾巴巴的(ㄍㄢ ·ㄅㄚ ·ㄅㄚ ·ㄉㄜ)
dry; deficient in moisture

乾杯(ㄍㄢ ㄅㄟ)
to toast 或 Bottoms up!

乾貝 or 干貝(ㄍㄢ ㄅㄟˋ)
a dried scallop

乾癟(ㄍㄢ ㄅㄧㄝˇ)
dry and withered; shrunken

乾冰(ㄍㄢ ㄅㄧㄥ)
dry ice

乾媽(ㄍㄢ ㄇㄚˊ)or 乾娘(ㄍㄢ ㄋㄧㄤˊ)
a woman whose position is roughly equivalent to a foster mother and godmother in Western countries without religious or legal com-

plications

乾麵《ㄍㄢ ㄇㄧㄢˋ》
dry noodles

乾飯《ㄍㄢ ㄈㄢˋ》
cooked rice without gravy

乾粉《ㄍㄢ ㄈㄣˇ》
vermicelli made from flour,
not yet soaked in water

乾打雷，不下雨《ㄍㄢ ㄉㄚˇ ㄌㄟˊ，ㄅㄨˋ ㄒㄧㄚˋ ㄩˇ》
thunder without rain—much
noise without action

乾瞪眼《ㄍㄢ ㄉㄥˋ ㄧㄢˇ》
to stand by anxiously without doing anything; unable
to help; to look on in
despair

乾電池《ㄍㄢ ㄉㄧㄢˋ ㄔˊ》
a dry battery or cell

乾女兒《ㄍㄢ ㄋㄩˇ ㄦ˙》
a nominal foster daughter

乾酪《ㄍㄢ ㄌㄠˋ》
cheese

乾冷《ㄍㄢ ㄌㄥˇ》
dry and cold (weather)

乾裂《ㄍㄢ ㄌㄧㄝˋ》
dry and cracked (wood,
soil)

乾糧《ㄍㄢ ㄌㄧㄤˊ》
dry provisions; canned or
packed food ready to serve

乾果《ㄍㄢ ㄍㄨㄛˇ》
dried or preserved fruit

乾咳《ㄍㄢ ㄎㄜˊ》
to cough without producing
sputum

乾枯《ㄍㄢ ㄎㄨ》
dried up; withered

乾涸《ㄍㄢ ㄏㄜˊ》
(said of water) to dry up: 河
道乾涸。The river dried up.

乾旱《ㄍㄢ ㄏㄢˋ》
drought

乾貨《ㄍㄢ ㄏㄨㄛˋ》
dried food and nuts (as merchandise)

乾淨《ㄍㄢ ㄐㄧㄥˋ》or 乾乾淨淨《ㄍㄢ
ㄍㄢ ㄐㄧㄥˋ ㄐㄧㄥˋ》
①clean ②entirely; all gone

乾淨俐落《ㄍㄢ ㄐㄧㄥˋ ㄌㄧˋ ㄌㄨㄛˋ》
neat and tidy; neat; efficient:
這一仗打得乾淨俐落。The bat-
tle was neatly won.

乾親《ㄍㄢ ㄑㄧㄣ》
nominal kinship

乾洗《ㄍㄢ ㄒㄧˇ》
dry cleaning

乾笑《ㄍㄢ ㄒㄧㄠˋ》
to laugh without mirth

乾癬《ㄍㄢ ㄒㄧㄢˇ》
ringworm skin disease, with
discolored patches covered
with scales

乾薪《ㄍㄢ ㄒㄧㄣ》
a salary for a sinecure

乾著急《ㄍㄢ ㄓㄜ˙ ㄐㄧˊ》
to sit fretting and fuming
when in trouble, but taking
no action (sometimes
because nothing can be
done)

乾柴烈火《ㄍㄢ ㄔㄞˊ ㄌㄧㄝˋ ㄏㄨㄛˇ》
(literally) a chance meeting between dry firewood
and blazing flames — (said
of romance between a man
and a woman, often illegal
liaison) instantaneous response to each other

乾濕表《ㄍㄢ ㄕ ㄅㄧㄠˇ》
a psychrometer

乾熱《ㄍㄢ ㄖㄜˋ》
(weather) dry heat; scorching hot

乾燥《ㄍㄢ ㄗㄠˋ》
dry

乾燥機《ㄍㄢ ㄗㄠˋ ㄐㄧ》
a drier

乾燥劑《ㄍㄢ ㄗㄠˋ ㄐㄧˋ》
a desiccant; a drying agent

乾草《ㄍㄢ ㄘㄠˇ》
hay

乾脆《ㄍㄢ ㄘㄨㄟˋ》
straightforward; clear-cut

乾嘔《ㄍㄢ ㄡˇ》
to retch

乾兒(子)《ㄍㄢ ㄦ (˙ㄗ)》
a nominal foster son

【乾】 44
2. 《ㄑㄧㄢˊ》chyan qián
1. the first of the Eight Diagrams (八卦)
2. heaven; male; a father; a
sovereign

乾道《ㄑㄧㄢˊ ㄉㄠˋ》
ways of heaven; natural law

乾隆《ㄑㄧㄢˊ ㄌㄨㄥˊ》
reigning title of Emperor
Kao Tsung of the Ching
Dynasty, whose reign lasted
from 1736 to 1796

乾綱《ㄑㄧㄢˊ ㄍㄤ》
①emperorship ②the author-

ity of a husband to his wife

乾坤《ㄑㄧㄢˊ ㄎㄨㄣ》
two of the Eight Diagrams
of the *Book of Changes*
——(figuratively) male and
female, heaven and earth,
sun and moon, etc.

乾象《ㄑㄧㄢˊ ㄒㄧㄤˋ》
celestial phenomena

乾元《ㄑㄧㄢˊ ㄩㄢˊ》
the beginning of the Heav-
en's creation

十二畫

【亂】 45
ㄌㄨㄢˋ luann luàn
1. chaos; anarchy; distraction;
confusion: 地震後這城市甚為
混亂。The city was in great
chaos after the earthquake.
2. rebellion; revolt; insurrection: 叛亂很快就被平定了。The
insurrection was easily suppressed.
3. confused; perplexed; agitated; disarranged; raveled
4. out of order; out of sorts; to
throw into disorder; to confuse; to confound

亂兵《ㄌㄨㄢˋ ㄅㄧㄥ》
rebels; soldiers on the rampage (in the absence of
effective control)

亂蓬蓬《ㄌㄨㄢˋ ㄆㄥˊ ㄆㄥˊ》
disheveled; tangled; jumbled

亂民《ㄌㄨㄢˋ ㄇㄧㄣˊ》
rioters; mobsters

亂命《ㄌㄨㄢˋ ㄇㄧㄥˋ》
orders or instructions given
when the giver is not in a
healthy state of mind due to
illness, etc.

亂罰《ㄌㄨㄢˋ ㄈㄚˊ》
to mete out unjustified punishment

亂紛紛《ㄌㄨㄢˋ ㄈㄣ ㄈㄣ》
disorderly; confused; chaotic;
tumultuous

亂風《ㄌㄨㄢˋ ㄈㄥ》
degenerate social customs
and practices

亂黨《ㄌㄨㄢˋ ㄉㄤˇ》
a rebel party or faction

亂點鴛鴦《ㄌㄨㄢˋ ㄉㄧㄢˇ ㄩㄢ ㄧㄤ》or
亂點鴛鴦譜《ㄌㄨㄢˋ ㄉㄧㄢˇ ㄩㄢ ㄧㄤ ㄆㄨˇ》

【亅部】

to cause an exchange of partners by mistake between two couples engaged to marry

亂彈 (ㄌㄨㄢˋ ㄊㄢˊ)
name of a dramatic tune played with a few different instruments

亂來 (ㄌㄨㄢˋ ㄌㄞˊ)
to act foolishly or recklessly; to do something without following proper procedure or methods

亂離 (ㄌㄨㄢˋ ㄌㄧˊ)
involuntary separation in troubled times

亂流 (ㄌㄨㄢˋ ㄌㄧㄡˊ)
a turbulent flow

亂倫 (ㄌㄨㄢˋ ㄌㄨㄣˊ)
incest

亂搞一氣 (ㄌㄨㄢˋ ㄍㄠˇ ㄧ ㄑㄧˋ)
to do something without knowing how

亂喊亂叫 (ㄌㄨㄢˋ ㄏㄢˇ ㄌㄨㄢˋ ㄐㄧㄠˋ)
to clamor; to talk wildly

亂花亂用 (ㄌㄨㄢˋ ㄏㄨㄚ ㄌㄨㄢˋ ㄩㄥˋ)
to spend money recklessly

亂婚 (ㄌㄨㄢˋ ㄏㄨㄣ)
incestuous marriage; marriage between blood relatives

亂烘烘 (ㄌㄨㄢˋ ㄏㄨㄥ ㄏㄨㄥ)
noisy and disorderly

亂七八糟 (ㄌㄨㄢˋ ㄑㄧ ㄅㄚ ㄗㄠ)
in confusion; topsy-turvy: 大城市的交通亂七八糟。Traffic in big cities is in confusion.

亂性 (ㄌㄨㄢˋ ㄒㄧㄥˋ)
to upset the presence of mind

亂眞 (ㄌㄨㄢˋ ㄓㄣ)
an imitation or forgery so skillfully made that one often takes it as the original or genuine object

亂針繡 (ㄌㄨㄢˋ ㄓㄣ ㄒㄧㄡˋ)
a form of embroidery which features overlapping threads in different directions

亂吃 (ㄌㄨㄢˋ ㄔ)
to eat without caution

亂臣賊子 (ㄌㄨㄢˋ ㄔㄣˊ ㄗㄟˊ ㄗˇ)
ministers or generals who rebel against their monarch or collaborate with the enemy

亂成一團 (ㄌㄨㄢˋ ㄔㄥˊ ㄧ ㄊㄨㄢˊ)

中欄

in great confusion; topsy-turvy

亂世 (ㄌㄨㄢˋ ㄕˋ)
times of anarchy and disorder

亂視 (ㄌㄨㄢˋ ㄕˋ)
(ophthalmology) astigmatism 亦作「散光」

亂說 (ㄌㄨㄢˋ ㄕㄨㄛ) or 亂道 (ㄌㄨㄢˋ ㄉㄠˋ)
①to say what should not be said ②to lie

亂嚷 (ㄌㄨㄢˋ ㄖㄤˇ)
to clamor

亂子 (ㄌㄨㄢˋ ㄗ)
disturbance; trouble

亂糟糟 (ㄌㄨㄢˋ ㄗㄠ ㄗㄠ)
①chaotic; in a mess ②confused; perturbed

亅 部
ㄐㄩㄝˊ jyue jué

一畫

【了】 46
1. ㄌㄧㄠˇ leau liǎo
1. to finish; to end; to complete
2. intelligent; remarkable
3. entirely; wholly
4. to understand

了不得 (ㄌㄧㄠˇ ·ㄅㄨ ·ㄉㄜ)
①Wonderful! 或 Excellent! ②at the worst; should the worst come to happen

了不了 (ㄌㄧㄠˇ ·ㄅㄨ ㄌㄧㄠˇ)
cannot be brought to an end

了不起 (ㄌㄧㄠˇ ·ㄅㄨ ㄑㄧˇ)
Wonderful! 參看「了不得①」

了得 (ㄌㄧㄠˇ ·ㄉㄜ)
very good; excellent (said of performance or demonstration of skill)

了得 (ㄌㄧㄠˇ ·ㄉㄜ ㄌㄧㄠˇ)
can be solved or settled

了當 (ㄌㄧㄠˇ ㄉㄤˋ)
appropriate

了斷 (ㄌㄧㄠˇ ㄉㄨㄢˋ)
①to settle (a case) ②to commit suicide

了了 (ㄌㄧㄠˇ ㄌㄧㄠˇ)

intelligent; bright

了結 (ㄌㄧㄠˇ ㄐㄧㄝˊ)
to get through with; to bring to conclusion; to settle

了解 (ㄌㄧㄠˇ ㄐㄧㄝˇ)
to understand or comprehend

了局 (ㄌㄧㄠˇ ㄐㄩˊ)
the end; the result; the final settlement; the conclusion

了部 (ㄌㄧㄠˇ ㄅㄨˋ)
to finish

了債 (ㄌㄧㄠˇ ㄓㄞˋ)
to pay off one's debts

了賬 (ㄌㄧㄠˇ ㄓㄤˋ)
to settle an account

了事 (ㄌㄧㄠˇ ㄕˋ)
to finish up a matter

了然 (ㄌㄧㄠˇ ㄖㄢˊ)
to understand clearly

了如指掌 (ㄌㄧㄠˇ ㄖㄨˊ ㄓˇ ㄓㄤˇ)
to know something like the palm of one's hand

了此殘生 (ㄌㄧㄠˇ ㄘˇ ㄘㄢˊ ㄕㄥ)
to end this miserable life

了案 (ㄌㄧㄠˇ ㄢˋ)
to conclude a case; to close a case

了無痕 (ㄌㄧㄠˇ ㄨˊ ㄏㄣˊ)
without a trace

了無長進 (ㄌㄧㄠˇ ㄨˊ ㄓㄤˇ ㄐㄧㄣˋ)
(said of a good-for-nothing fellow) having made no progress or improvement in the least

了悟 (ㄌㄧㄠˇ ㄨˋ)
to comprehend; to understand; to wake up to; to realize

【了】 46
2. ·ㄌㄜ ·le le
an expletive in the Chinese language: 他的病痊癒了。His sickness is wholly cured.

三畫

【予】 47
1. ㄩˊ yu yú
I; me

予取予求 (ㄩˊ ㄑㄩˇ ㄩˊ ㄑㄧㄡˊ)
to make repeated demands of somebody

予智自雄 (ㄩˊ ㄓˋ ㄗˋ ㄒㄩㄥˊ)
conceited

【予】 47
2. ㄩˇ yeu yǔ

to give: 予人口實 to give people a cause for discussion

七畫

【事】 48
ㄕ shyh shì
1. an affair; a matter; business
2. a job; an occupation; a task
3. a service: 電話是公用事業. The telephone is a public service.
4. duties; functions
5. a subject
6. to serve; to attend
7. to manage a business

事倍功半(ㄕㄅㄟㄍㄨㄥㄅㄢ)
to achieve little result despite herculean effort

事半功倍(ㄕㄅㄢㄍㄨㄥㄅㄟ)
half the work with double the result; to achieve maximum results with little effort

事必躬親(ㄕㄅㄧㄍㄨㄥㄑㄧㄣ)
to attend to everything personally

事變(ㄕㄅㄧㄢ)
an incident

事不宜遲(ㄕㄅㄨㄧˊㄔ)
One must lose no time in doing something.

事非得已(ㄕㄈㄟㄉㄜˊㄧ)
There is no other choice.

事非經過不知難
(ㄕㄈㄟㄐㄧㄥ
ㄍㄨㄛㄅㄨㄓㄋㄢˊ)
One does not realize the difficulty of an undertaking unless he has experienced it before.

事到臨頭(ㄕㄉㄠㄌㄧㄣˊㄊㄡˊ)
when a thing comes to a critical moment; at the last moment

事到如今(ㄕㄉㄠㄖㄨˊㄐㄧㄣ)
as things have come to such a pass

事端(ㄕㄉㄨㄢ)
a trouble

事態(ㄕㄊㄞ)
the state of affairs; the situation

事體(ㄕㄊㄧˇ)
systems of matters

事理(ㄕㄌㄧˇ)
the principle of action; facts and principles involved; the way of doing business

事例(ㄕㄌㄧ)
an example; a precedent

事略(ㄕㄌㄩㄝ)
a brief biography

事故(ㄕㄍㄨ)
a troublesome incident; an accident

事過境遷(ㄕㄍㄨㄛㄐㄧㄥˋㄑㄧㄢ)
Things change with the passage of time.

事後(ㄕㄏㄡ)
after an event; afterward

事迹(ㄕㄐㄧ)
the trace (of a past event); a vestige

事機(ㄕㄐㄧ)
① a chance; an opportunity ② a secret or plot

事蹟(ㄕㄐㄧ)
the accomplishments, exploits, etc. of a person during his or her lifetime

事假(ㄕㄐㄧㄚˇ)
private affair leave: 他請一天事假. He asked for one day's private affair leave.

事件(ㄕㄐㄧㄢ)
an individual matter; an incident; an event

事前(ㄕㄑㄧㄢˊ)or 事先(ㄕㄒㄧㄢ)
before an event; beforehand: 事先準備一切. Get everything ready beforehand.

事親至孝(ㄕㄑㄧㄣㄓㄒㄧㄠ)
to treat one's parents with great respect and tender affection

事情(ㄕㄑㄧㄥ˙)
a matter; business; circumstances; an event; an affair; an incident

事項(ㄕㄒㄧㄤ)
an individual matter (as part of a whole); an item

事主(ㄕㄓㄨˇ)
① the principal person concerned in any matter; a client ② the victim in a criminal case

事出有因(ㄕㄔㄨㄧㄡˇㄧㄣ)
not entirely devoid of truth

事實(ㄕㄕˊ)
a fact; truth; reality

事實上(ㄕㄕˊㄕㄤ)
in fact; in reality

事實勝於雄辯(ㄕㄕˊㄕㄥˋㄩˊㄒㄩㄥˊ
ㄅㄧㄢ)
Facts are more convincing than eloquent theories.

事事(ㄕㄕ)
everything: 他事事親躬. He does everything himself.

事勢(ㄕㄕ)
the trend of things in general; general course of events

事在人為(ㄕㄗㄞㄖㄣˊㄨㄟˊ)
Human effort can achieve everything.

事兒(dialect) an affair, or a matter

事宜(ㄕㄧˊ)
① affairs; matters ② the necessary arrangements

事已如此(ㄕㄧˇㄖㄨˊㄘˇ)
things being so

事業(ㄕㄧㄝ)
① an enterprise; an undertaking ② a career; a pursuit

事由(ㄕㄧㄡˊ)
① the origin of a matter ② the subject (of a business letter)

事物(ㄕㄨ)
things; articles; objects

事務(ㄕㄨ)
business (in the sense of any serious, often monotonous, work one has to do); work; general affairs (of an office, organization, etc.)

事務官(ㄕㄨㄍㄨㄢ)
government officials whose duties require professional expertise

事務所(ㄕㄨㄙㄨㄛˇ)
an office (especially of a lawyer, accountant, political candidate, etc.)

事務員(ㄕㄨㄩㄢˊ)
an office clerk

事與願違(ㄕㄩˇㄩㄢˋㄨㄟˊ)
Things do not turn out as one wishes.

二 部
ㄦ ell er

【二】⁴⁹ ㄦ ell èr

two; second; twice

二八年華(ㄦ ㄅㄚ ㄋㄧㄢˊ ㄏㄨㄚˊ)
(said of a girl) sixteen
years of age

二八佳人(ㄦ ㄅㄚ ㄐㄧㄚ ㄖㄣˊ)
a sixteen-year-old beauty

二百五(ㄦ ㄅㄞˇ ㄨˇ)
(abuse) a simpleton, a
blockhead

二部制(ㄦ ㄅㄨˋ ㄓˋ)
the two-shift system (of
schools)

二拇指(ㄦ ㄇㄨˇ ㄓˇ)
the index finger

二分明月(ㄦ ㄈㄣ ㄇㄧㄥˊ ㄩㄝˋ)
the prosperity of Yangchow
in former times

二分法(ㄦ ㄈㄣ ㄈㄚˇ)
dichotomy

二房(ㄦ ㄈㄤˊ)
a concubine

二房東(ㄦ ㄈㄤˊ ㄉㄨㄥ)
a person who sublets a
house rented from another

二副(ㄦ ㄈㄨˋ)
(navigation) a second mate

二等(ㄦ ㄉㄥˇ)
(said of trains, ocean liners,
etc.) economy class; second
grade

二地主(ㄦ ㄉㄧˋ ㄓㄨˇ)
a sub-landlord

二度梅(ㄦ ㄉㄨˋ ㄇㄟˊ)
(said of women) married
for the second time

二度燒傷(ㄦ ㄉㄨˋ ㄕㄠ ㄕㄤ)
second-degree burn

二老(ㄦ ㄌㄠˇ)
one's father and mother

二郎腿(ㄦ ㄌㄤˊ ㄊㄨㄟˇ)
(to sit) cross-legged: 別蹺起
二郎腿。Don't sit cross-
legged.

二郎神(ㄦ ㄌㄤˊ ㄕㄣˊ)
(mythology) a Chinese god
who is good at fighting
demons

二愣(ㄦ ㄌㄥ)
① stunned ② scared stiff

二愣子(ㄦ ㄌㄥˋ ㄗ˙)
a rash fellow

二路兒(ㄦ ㄌㄨˋ ㄦˊ)
second-rate (goods)

二鍋頭(ㄦ ㄍㄨㄛ ㄊㄡˊ)

---

a kind of strong alcoholic
drink usually made from
sorghum

二胡(ㄦ ㄏㄨˊ)
a two-stringed Chinese musical instrument

二花臉(ㄦ ㄏㄨㄚ ㄌㄧㄢˇ)
(Chinese opera) a number
two actor with a painted
face 亦作「副淨」

二簧(ㄦ ㄏㄨㄤˊ)
name of a tune in Peking
opera

二級風(ㄦ ㄐㄧˊ ㄈㄥ)
force 2 wind; light breeze

二喬(ㄦ ㄑㄧㄠˊ)
the Chiao sisters, who were
famous beauties in the state
of Wu during the Epoch of
Three Kingdoms

二親(ㄦ ㄑㄧㄣ)
one's father and mother

二心(ㄦ ㄒㄧㄣ)
disloyalty; disloyal: 他對主人
有二心。He is disloyal to his
master.

二姓(ㄦ ㄒㄧㄥˋ)
① two families of different
clans united in marriage ②
two ruling houses of different surnames

二臣(ㄦ ㄔㄣˊ)
a turncoat

二程子(ㄦ ㄔㄥˊ ㄗˇ)
the Cheng brothers (referring to Cheng Hao (程顥)
and Cheng Yi (程頤), both
renowned Confucian scholars
of the Sung Dynasty)

二重國籍(ㄦ ㄔㄨㄥˊ ㄍㄨㄛˊ ㄐㄧˊ)
dual nationality 亦作「雙重國
籍」: 他有二重國籍。He has
dual nationality.

二重唱(ㄦ ㄔㄨㄥˊ ㄔㄤˋ)
(vocal) a duet

二重奏(ㄦ ㄔㄨㄥˊ ㄗㄡˋ)
a duet performance on the
piano

二重人格(ㄦ ㄔㄨㄥˊ ㄖㄣˊ ㄍㄜˊ)
dual personality 亦作「雙重人
格」

二十八宿(ㄦ ㄕˊ ㄅㄚ ㄒㄧㄡˋ)
(astronomy) the lunar man-
sions

二十四孝(ㄦ ㄕˊ ㄙˋ ㄒㄧㄠˋ)
the 24 examples of filial
piety (selected by Kuo Chu-

---

ching (郭居敬) of the Yüan
Dynasty)—虞舜, 漢文帝, 曾參,
閔損, 仲由, 董永, 郯子, 江革,
陸績, 唐夫人, 吳猛, 王祥, 郭
巨, 楊香, 朱壽昌, 庾黔婁, 老
萊子, 蔡順, 黃香, 姜詩, 王裒,
丁蘭, 孟宗, 黃庭堅。

二十四史(ㄦ ㄕˊ ㄙˋ ㄕˇ)
The Twenty-Four Books of
History (an official history
of China up to the end of
the Ming Dynasty consisting
of 24 books, authorized by
Emperor Kao Tsung of the
Ching Dynasty)

二十一條(ㄦ ㄕˊ ㄧ ㄊㄧㄠˊ)
the Twenty-One Demands,
which Japan forced Yüan
Shih-kai to accept in 1915

二十五史(ㄦ ㄕˊ ㄨˇ ㄕˇ)
The Twenty-Five Books of
History (The Twenty-Four
Books of History plus an
additional book, the New
History of Yüan)

二世(ㄦ ㄕˋ)
II (used after the name of an
emperor such as 秦二世 or
James II)

二手貨(ㄦ ㄕㄡˇ ㄏㄨㄛˋ)
a used item; a secondhand
commodity

二豎為疾(ㄦ ㄕㄨˋ ㄨㄟˊ ㄐㄧˊ)
to suffer from illness

二水貨(ㄦ ㄕㄨㄟˇ ㄏㄨㄛˋ)
used goods; secondhand
goods 亦作「二手貨」

二次方程式(ㄦ ㄘˋ ㄈㄤ ㄔㄥˊ ㄕˋ)
a quadratic equation

二次革命(ㄦ ㄘˋ ㄍㄜˊ ㄇㄧㄥˋ)
the Second Revolution (the
revolution of the Kuomin-
tang against Yüan Shih-kai
in 1913 after the revolution
against the Manchu government)

二三其德(ㄦ ㄙㄢ ㄑㄧˊ ㄉㄜˊ)
inconsistent

二氧化碳(ㄦ ㄧㄤˇ ㄏㄨㄚˋ ㄊㄢˋ)
carbon dioxide

二月(ㄦ ㄩㄝˋ)
① February ② the second
moon of the lunar calendar
③ two months

二月革命(ㄦ ㄩㄝˋ ㄍㄜˊ ㄇㄧㄥˋ)
February Revolution (of
February 22-24, 1848) in

French history

二元方程式(ルロムこたぇロム)
an equation with two unknowns

二元論(ル山ちカメら)
dualism

一畫

【丁】50
ルㄧ chuh chū
a step with the right foot

【于】51
山ㄧ yu yú

1.(a particle in literary use) in; at; by; to: 光榮歸于勝利者。Glory goes to the victors.

2.(a verb in literary use) to go or proceed; to take

于飛之樂(ㄩㄈㄟㄓㄌㄜ)
the happiness of a married couple deeply in love

于歸(ㄩㄍㄨㄟ)
(said of a girl) to enter into matrimony

于今(ㄩㄐㄧㄣ)
①up to the present; since: 自君別後，于今兩年。It has been two years since you left. ②nowadays

于是(ㄩㄕ)
hence; consequently; thereupon

于思(ㄩㄙㄞ)
a long and thick beard and mustache (after days without shaving)

二畫

【云】52
ㄩㄣ yun yún
to say; to speak: 不要人云亦云。Don't say what everybody says.

云云(ㄩㄣㄩㄣ)
so and so; and so forth; and so on

【互】53
ㄏㄨ huh hù
each other; mutually; reciprocally

互保(ㄏㄨㄅㄠ)
to give guarantee for each other

互補角色(ㄏㄨㄅㄨㄐㄩㄝㄙㄜ)
(sociology) complementary role

互補色(ㄏㄨㄅㄨㄙㄜ)
complementary colors

互不侵犯(ㄏㄨㄅㄨㄑㄧㄣㄈㄢ)
to refrain from invading each other

互不侵犯條約(ㄏㄨㄅㄨㄑㄧㄣㄈㄢㄊㄧㄠㄩㄝ)
a nonaggression treaty (or pact)

互訪(ㄏㄨㄈㄤ)
to exchange visits

互通有無(ㄏㄨㄊㄨㄥㄧㄡㄨ)
to give mutual help financially; to supply each other's needs

互利(ㄏㄨㄌㄧ)
mutually beneficial

互惠(ㄏㄨㄏㄨㄟ)
mutually beneficial; reciprocal

互惠條約(ㄏㄨㄏㄨㄟㄊㄧㄠㄩㄝ)
a bilateral treaty in which the signatories grant favored nation status to each other

互惠關稅(ㄏㄨㄏㄨㄟㄍㄨㄢㄕㄨㄟ)
a mutually preferential tariff

互換(ㄏㄨㄏㄨㄢ)
to exchange

互相(ㄏㄨㄒㄧㄤ)
mutually; reciprocally; each other; one another

互相標榜(ㄏㄨㄒㄧㄤㄅㄧㄠㄅㄤ)
to eulogize each other

互相切磋(ㄏㄨㄒㄧㄤㄑㄧㄝㄘㄨㄛ)
to improve each other by active discussion

互選(ㄏㄨㄒㄩㄢ)
an election in which a voter may elect any other voter

互爭雄長(ㄏㄨㄓㄥㄒㄩㄥㄓㄤ)
to fight for leadership or hegemony

互助(ㄏㄨㄓㄨ)
to help each other; mutual help

互市(ㄏㄨㄕ)
mutual trade

互為因果(ㄏㄨㄨㄟㄧㄣㄍㄨㄛ)
to interact as both cause and effect

【五】54
ㄨ wuu wǔ
five; fifth: 他家有五個小孩。There are five children in

his family.

五霸(ㄨㄅㄚ)
the Five Powers—Chi (齊), Sung (宋), Tsin (晉), Chin (秦), and Chu (楚)—in the late Chou Dynasty

五倍子(ㄨㄅㄟㄗ)
gallnuts

五胞胎(ㄨㄅㄠㄊㄞ)
quintuplets

五邊形(ㄨㄅㄧㄢㄒㄧㄥ)
a pentagon

五面體(ㄨㄇㄧㄢㄊㄧ)
a pentahedron

五分(ㄨㄈㄣ)
fifty percent

五分鐘熱度(ㄨㄈㄣㄓㄨㄥㄖㄜㄉㄨ)
short-lived enthusiasm

五方(ㄨㄈㄤ)
the five directions (east, west, south, north and center)

五服(ㄨㄈㄨ)
the five grades of mourning (according to kinship) —for parents or husbands, three years; for grandparents, twelve months; for brothers, etc., nine months; for uncles, aunts, etc., five months; for distant relatives, three months

五福(ㄨㄈㄨ)
the five blessings—longevity, wealth, health, love of virtue, and natural death (壽, 富, 康寧, 攸好德, 考終命)

五大湖(ㄨㄉㄚㄏㄨ)
Great Lakes

五大洲(ㄨㄉㄚㄓㄡ)
the five continents—Asia, Africa, Europe, the Americas, and Oceania

五大洋(ㄨㄉㄚㄧㄤ)
the five oceans—Pacific, Atlantic, Indian, Arctic and Antarctic

五代(ㄨㄉㄞ)
the (Earlier) Five Dynasties (before the Tang Dynasty), 420-618 A.D.; the (Later) Five Dynasties (after the Tang Dynasty), 907-959 A.D.

五代同堂(ㄨㄉㄞㄊㄨㄥㄊㄤ)or 五世同堂(ㄨㄕㄊㄨㄥㄊㄤ)
five generations living under the same roof

〔二部〕

五代史 (ㄨ ㄉㄞˋ ㄕˇ)
The History of the (Later) Five Dynasties—with two versions, new and old, both included in The Twenty-Four Books of History

五斗米折腰 (ㄨˇ ㄉㄡˇ ㄇㄧˇ ㄓㄜˊ ㄧㄠ)
to compromise one's principles for some scanty material reward

五等 (ㄨˇ ㄉㄥˇ)
the five ranks of the nobility corresponding to duke, marquis, count, viscount, baron (公、侯、伯、子、男)

五帝 (ㄨˇ ㄉㄧˋ)
the Five Emperors of the legendary period (太昊、炎帝、黃帝、少昊、顓頊)

五體投地 (ㄨˇ ㄊㄧˇ ㄊㄡˊ ㄉㄧˋ)
①to prostrate oneself ②to admire someone with the utmost sincerity

五內 (ㄨˇ ㄋㄟˋ) or 五臟 (ㄨˇ ㄗㄤˋ)
the five viscera—the heart, the lungs, the liver, the kidneys, and the spleen

五內如焚 (ㄨˇ ㄋㄟˋ ㄖㄨˊ ㄈㄣˊ)
(literally) The five viscera are on fire.—① very anxious ② grief-stricken: 他的失敗使他五內如焚。His failure made him grief-stricken.

五里霧中 (ㄨˇ ㄌㄧˇ ㄨˋ ㄓㄨㄥ)
utter bewilderment: 他的話使她如墮五里霧中。His words caused her to fall in utter bewilderment.

五柳先生 (ㄨˇ ㄌㄧㄡˇ ㄒㄧㄢ ㄕㄥ)
Mr. Five Willows, a name assumed by poet Tao Chien (陶潛, 365-427 A.D.)

五陵少年 (ㄨˇ ㄌㄧㄥˊ ㄕㄠˋ ㄋㄧㄢˊ)
rich and handsome young men

五嶺 (ㄨˇ ㄌㄧㄥˇ)
the five mountain ranges (which formed the southern boundary of the empire during the Chin Dynasty)

五倫 (ㄨˇ ㄌㄨㄣˊ)
the five human relationships—between sovereign and subjects, father and sons, husband and wife, among brothers, and among friends

五律 (ㄨˇ ㄌㄩˋ)
the five-character verse (with five characters to each of the eight lines)

五更 (ㄨˇ ㄍㄥ)
the fifth watch of the night which is about 4 a.m. (by the former time system which divided the period from nightfall to daybreak into five watches)

五穀 (ㄨˇ ㄍㄨˇ)
(literally) the five major grains (variously listed)—grains of all sorts

五官 (ㄨˇ ㄍㄨㄢ)
① the five organs—the ear, the eye, the mouth, the nose and the heart ② the five senses—visual, auditory, olfactory, gustatory and tactile senses

五官端正 (ㄨˇ ㄍㄨㄢ ㄉㄨㄢ ㄓㄥˋ)
a pleasant-looking face with the five organs in normal shape and position

五光十色 (ㄨˇ ㄍㄨㄤ ㄕˊ ㄙㄜˋ)
resplendent with variegated coloration: 湖面上的風景五光十色。The scenery on the lake is resplendent with variegated coloration.

五口通商 (ㄨˇ ㄎㄡˇ ㄊㄨㄥ ㄕㄤ)
the opening of five ports—Shanghai, Canton, Ningpo, Foochow and Amoy—in 1842 to European traders

五口之家 (ㄨˇ ㄎㄡˇ ㄓ ㄐㄧㄚ)
a family of five persons

五胡 (ㄨˇ ㄏㄨˊ)
the five barbarian tribes from the North (who invaded China in the 5th century A.D.)—匈奴, 鮮卑, 羯, 氐, 羌

五胡亂華 (ㄨˇ ㄏㄨˊ ㄌㄨㄢˋ ㄏㄨㄚˊ)
the invasion of China by the northern barbarians (in the 5th century A.D.)

五胡十六國 (ㄨˇ ㄏㄨˊ ㄕˊ ㄌㄧㄡˋ ㄍㄨㄛˊ)
the five nomadic tribes (匈奴, 鮮卑, 羯, 氐, 羌) and three Han generals who founded in China 16 states (前涼, 後涼, 南涼, 北涼, 西涼, 前趙, 後趙, 前秦, 後秦, 西秦, 前燕, 後燕, 南燕, 北燕, 夏, 成漢) at one time or another between A.D. 304 and 439

五湖四海 (ㄨˇ ㄏㄨˊ ㄙˋ ㄏㄞˇ)
everywhere in the world

五花八門 (ㄨˇ ㄏㄨㄚ ㄅㄚ ㄇㄣˊ)
rich in variety; unpredictable as to the variations manifested

五花肉 (ㄨˇ ㄏㄨㄚ ㄖㄡˋ)
streaky pork

五加皮 (ㄨˇ ㄐㄧㄚ ㄆㄧˊ)
the bark of Acanthopanax gracilistylus (used as medicine)

五戒 (ㄨˇ ㄐㄧㄝˋ)
the Five Precepts (of Buddhism)—slay not, steal not, lust not, lie not, taste not intoxicants and meat

五角大廈 (ㄨˇ ㄐㄧㄠˇ ㄉㄚˋ ㄒㄧㄚˋ)
① the Pentagon, which houses most U. S. Defense Department offices ② the United States Department of Defense

五角形 (ㄨˇ ㄐㄧㄠˇ ㄒㄧㄥˊ)
a pentagon

五金 (ㄨˇ ㄐㄧㄣ)
① the five metals—gold, silver, copper, iron, and tin ② metals in general ③ hardware

五金店 (ㄨˇ ㄐㄧㄣ ㄉㄧㄢˋ)
a hardware store

五經 (ㄨˇ ㄐㄧㄥ)
The Five Classics—the Confucian canon including The Book of Changes (易經), The Book of Odes (詩經), The Book of History (書經), The Book of Rites (禮記), and The Spring and Autumn Annals (春秋)

五絕 (ㄨˇ ㄐㄩㄝˊ)
a poem of four lines having five characters to each line

五權憲法 (ㄨˇ ㄑㄩㄢˊ ㄒㄧㄢˋ ㄈㄚˇ)
the five-power constitution of the Republic of China outlined by Dr. Sun Yat-sen (which provides that the government administration shall be composed of executive, legislative, judiciary, examination and supervisory or control powers)

五線譜 (ㄨˇ ㄒㄧㄢˋ ㄆㄨˇ)
(music) a staff; a musical score using the staff notation

五香 (ㄨˇ ㄒㄧㄤ)
a kind of blended spice used in Chinese cooking

五項運動 (ㄨˇ ㄒㄧㄤˋ ㄩㄣˋ ㄉㄨㄥˋ)
(sports) pentathlon

五星 (ㄨˇ ㄒㄧㄥ)
the five planets—Venus, Jupiter, Mercury, Mars, and Saturn

五星上將 (ㄨˇ ㄒㄧㄥ ㄕㄤˋ ㄐㄧㄤˋ)
a five-star general or admiral

五刑 (ㄨˇ ㄒㄧㄥˊ)
the five penalties—branding, cutting off the nose, cutting off the feet, castration, and death (in ancient classification 古代); or death, life imprisonment, imprisonment for a limited term, detention, and fines (in later classification 現代: 死刑, 無期徒刑, 有期徒刑, 拘留, 罰鍰)

五行 (ㄨˇ ㄒㄧㄥˊ)
① the five primary elements—metal, wood, water, fire and earth (金, 木, 水, 火, 土) ② the five constant virtues—benevolence, righteousness, propriety, knowledge, and faith (仁, 義, 禮, 智, 信)

五指 (ㄨˇ ㄓˇ)
the five fingers—the thumb, the index finger, the middle finger, the ring finger, the little finger

五常 (ㄨˇ ㄔㄤˊ)
the five constant virtues—① benevolence, righteousness, propriety, knowledge and faith (仁, 義, 禮, 智, 信) ② father's righteousness, mother's benevolence, elder brother's love, younger brother's respect, and son's filial piety (父義, 母慈, 兄友, 弟恭, 子孝)

五畜 (ㄨˇ ㄔㄨˋ)
① the five domestic animals—cattle, sheep, swine, dogs, fowls ② livestock in general

五十步笑百步 (ㄨˇ ㄕˊ ㄅㄨˋ ㄒㄧㄠˋ ㄅㄞˇ ㄅㄨˋ)
to deride or denounce another's fault which the denouncer himself also has, though in a smaller degree

或 The pot calls the kettle black.

五十肩 (ㄨˇ ㄕˊ ㄐㄧㄢ)
frozen shoulder 亦作〔冰凍肩〕

五世其昌 (ㄨˇ ㄕˋ ㄑㄧˊ ㄔㄤ)
May you be blessed with many children and grandchildren! (The expression is usually used in congratulatory messages to the newly-weds at their wedding.)

五日京兆 (ㄨˇ ㄖˋ ㄐㄧㄥ ㄓㄠˋ)
office held for a short time only

五子棋 (ㄨˇ ㄗˇ ㄑㄧˊ)
gobang

五臟 (ㄨˇ ㄗㄤˋ)
(Chinese medicine) the five internal organs—the heart, liver, spleen, lungs and kidneys

五族 (ㄨˇ ㄗㄨˊ)
the five ethnic groups which make up the Chinese nation—Han, Manchu, Mongol, Mohammedan and Tibetan (漢, 滿, 蒙, 回, 藏)

五彩 (ㄨˇ ㄘㄞˇ)
blue, yellow, red, white and black

五四運動 (ㄨˇ ㄙˋ ㄩㄣˋ ㄉㄨㄥˋ)
The May Fourth Movement (the student demonstrations in Peking on May 4, 1919, in protest of government's surrender to the Twenty-One Demands from Japan, touching off subsequent literary and other reforms)

五卅事件 (ㄨˇ ㄙㄚˋ ㄕˋ ㄐㄧㄢˋ)
The May 30 Incident (the incident on May 30, 1925, in which a number of Chinese were shot to death by the British in the International Settlement, Shanghai)

五一勞動節 (ㄨˇ ㄧ ㄌㄠˊ ㄉㄨㄥˋ ㄐㄧㄝˊ)
May Day; Labor Day

五顏六色 (ㄨˇ ㄧㄢˊ ㄌㄧㄡˋ ㄙㄜˋ)
of variegated colors

五言詩 (ㄨˇ ㄧㄢˊ ㄕ)
verse with five characters to each line

五音 (ㄨˇ ㄧㄣ)
① the five classes of initials (in ancient Chinese phonology, corresponding to glot-

tals, palatals, dentals, labials and velars in modern phonology) ② the five notes of traditional Chinese music (宮, 商, 角, 徵, 羽)

五味 (ㄨˇ ㄨㄟˋ)
the five flavors—sweet, sour, bitter, pungent, salty (甜, 酸, 苦, 辣, 鹹)

五嶽 (ㄨˇ ㄩㄝˋ)
the Five Sacred Mountains—the Eastern Mountain located in Shantung, the Southern Mountain in Hunan, the Western Mountain in Shensi, the Northern Mountain in Hopei, and the Central Mountain in Honan (東嶽泰山, 南嶽衡山, 西嶽華山, 北嶽恒山, 中嶽嵩山)

五月 (ㄨˇ ㄩㄝˋ)
① May ② the fifth moon of the lunar calendar ③ five months

五月花號 (ㄨˇ ㄩㄝˋ ㄏㄨㄚ ㄏㄠˋ)
Mayflower

五月節 (ㄨˇ ㄩㄝˋ ㄐㄧㄝˊ)
the Dragon Boat Festival, which comes on the fifth day of the fifth lunar month

五院 (ㄨˇ ㄩㄢˋ)
the five yuan (of the government of the Republic of China)—the Executive Yuan, the Judicial Yuan, the Legislative Yuan, the Control Yuan, the Examination Yuan (行政院, 司法院, 立法院, 監察院, 考試院)

【井】 55 ㄐㄧㄥˇ jǐng jing
a well: 在鄉村中人們掘井取水。In the village people dug wells for water.

井底蛙 (ㄐㄧㄥˇ ㄉㄧˇ ㄨㄚ)
(literally) a frog in a well—a person of very limited outlook and experience

井田 (ㄐㄧㄥˇ ㄊㄧㄢˊ)
the system of land division in the Chou Dynasty in which a 900-mu plot was divided into nine portions like the character 井, with the eight outlying portions separately cultivated and owned by eight families, which jointly cultivated the

〔二部〕

central portion for the state

井欄 (ㄐㄧㄥˇ ㄌㄢˊ)
① the railings around a well
② a framework used as a tool for attacking city walls

井臼親操 (ㄐㄧㄥˇ ㄐㄧㄡˋ ㄑㄧㄣ ㄘㄠ)
(said of housewives) to do domestic chores personally

井井有條 (ㄐㄧㄥˇ ㄐㄧㄥˇ ㄧㄡˇ ㄊㄧㄠˊ)
systematic (in handling things); orderly; methodical

井水不犯河水 (ㄐㄧㄥˇ ㄕㄨㄟˇ ㄅㄨˋ ㄈㄢˋ ㄏㄜˊ ㄕㄨㄟˇ)
Well water and river water leave each other alone.—not to interfere with each other's affairs

井然 (ㄐㄧㄥˇ ㄖㄢˊ)
orderly

井鹽 (ㄐㄧㄥˇ ㄧㄢˊ)
well salt (extracted from brine out of wells, as in Szechwan)

四畫

【亙】 [56] ㄍㄣˋ genn gèn
(又讀 ㄍㄥˋ genq gèng)
1. to extend (over space or time)
2. a Chinese family name

亙古未有 (ㄍㄣˋ ㄍㄨˇ ㄨㄟˋ ㄧㄡˇ)
unprecedented 或 There has been nothing like it since time immemorial.

五畫

【些】 [57] ㄒㄧㄝ shie xiē
a small quantity or number; a little; a few; some

些兒 (ㄒㄧㄝ ㄦˊ)
① a little while ② a little bit

些個 (ㄒㄧㄝ ㄍㄜˊ)
a little

些些 (ㄒㄧㄝ ㄒㄧㄝ)
a little

些須 (ㄒㄧㄝ ㄒㄩ)
a little 參看「些個」這個他懂得些須。He understands it a little.

些微 (ㄒㄧㄝ ㄨㄟ)
① very little ② slightly: 他有些微近視。He is slightly near-sighted.

六畫

【亞】 [58] ㄧㄚˇ yah yǎ
(又讀 ㄧㄚˋ yea yà)
1. second (in excellence): 他不亞於任何人。He is second to none.
2. Asia

亞伯拉罕 (ㄧㄚˇ ㄅㄛˊ ㄌㄚ ㄏㄢˇ)
Abraham, the first patriarch and ancestor of the Hebrews

亞麻 (ㄧㄚˇ ㄇㄚˊ)
Linum usitatissimum; flax

亞麻仁油 (ㄧㄚˇ ㄇㄚˊ ㄖㄣˊ ㄧㄡˊ)
linseed oil

亞馬遜河 (ㄧㄚˇ ㄇㄚˇ ㄒㄩㄣˋ ㄏㄜˊ)
the Amazon River in South America

亞美尼亞 (ㄧㄚˇ ㄇㄟˇ ㄋㄧˊ ㄧㄚˇ)
Armenia

亞美利加 (ㄧㄚˇ ㄇㄟˇ ㄌㄧˋ ㄐㄧㄚ)
America

亞得里亞海 (ㄧㄚˇ ㄉㄜˊ ㄌㄧˇ ㄧㄚˇ ㄏㄞˇ)
the Adriatic Sea

亞當 (ㄧㄚˇ ㄉㄤ)
Adam

亞當斯 (ㄧㄚˇ ㄉㄤ ㄙ)
transliteration of Adams

亞丁 (ㄧㄚˇ ㄉㄧㄥ)
Aden, in southwestern Arabia

亞理斯多德 (ㄧㄚˇ ㄌㄧˇ ㄙ ㄉㄨㄛ ㄉㄜˊ)
Aristotle, 384-322 B.C., Greek philosopher

亞歷山大大帝 (ㄧㄚˇ ㄌㄧˋ ㄕㄢ ㄉㄚˋ ㄉㄚˋ ㄉㄧˋ)
Alexander the Great, 356-323 B.C.

亞歷山大城 (ㄧㄚˇ ㄌㄧˋ ㄕㄢ ㄔㄥˊ) or 亞力山卓 (ㄧㄚˇ ㄌㄧˋ ㄕㄢ ㄓㄨㄛˊ)
Alexandria, a port city in North Africa

亞利桑那州 (ㄧㄚˇ ㄌㄧˋ ㄙㄤ ㄋㄚˋ ㄓㄡ)
the state of Arizona, U.S.A.

亞軍 (ㄧㄚˇ ㄐㄩㄣ)
the runner-up

亞西司 (ㄧㄚˇ ㄒㄧ ㄙ)
Department of West Asia (of the Ministry of Foreign Affairs)

亞洲 (ㄧㄚˇ ㄓㄡ) or 亞細亞洲 (ㄧㄚˇ ㄒㄧˋ ㄧㄚˇ ㄓㄡ)
Asia

亞洲開發銀行 (ㄧㄚˇ ㄓㄡ ㄎㄞ ㄈㄚ ㄧㄣˊ ㄏㄤˊ)

(ㄏㄤˊ)
Asian Development Bank

亞聖 (ㄧㄚˇ ㄕㄥˋ)
the Lesser Sage—Mencius, next to the Sage Confucius

亞述 (ㄧㄚˇ ㄕㄨˋ)
Assyria

亞熱帶 (ㄧㄚˇ ㄖㄜˋ ㄉㄞˋ)
the subtropical zone

七畫

【亟】 [59] ㄐㄧˊ jyi jí
urgently; pressingly

亟欲 (ㄐㄧˊ ㄩˋ)
very anxious to do something

亠 部
ㄊㄡˊ　tour　tóu

一畫

【亡】 [60] ㄨㄤˊ wang wáng
1. to perish
2. to flee
3. lost; dead
4. the late (applicable only to deceased blood relatives or friends)

亡命 (ㄨㄤˊ ㄇㄧㄥˋ)
to go into exile; to escape (from justice) to a place far away from home

亡命之徒 (ㄨㄤˊ ㄇㄧㄥˋ ㄓ ㄊㄨˊ)
lawless elements; criminals

亡故 (ㄨㄤˊ ㄍㄨˋ)
dead; died

亡國 (ㄨㄤˊ ㄍㄨㄛˊ)
① a conquered country; a subjugated nation ② fall of a nation; national doom

亡國奴 (ㄨㄤˊ ㄍㄨㄛˊ ㄋㄨˊ)
subjugated people; conquered people

亡國之音 (ㄨㄤˊ ㄍㄨㄛˊ ㄓ ㄧㄣ)
degenerate or decadent music (presaging national ruin)

亡魂 (ㄨㄤˊ ㄏㄨㄣˊ)
the spirit of the dead

亡羊補牢(ㄨㄤˊ ㄧㄤˊ ㄅㄨˇ ㄌㄠˊ)
to mend the sheepfold after losing the sheep—to take precaution after suffering a loss: 亡羊補牢, 未爲晚也。It is still not too late to mend the sheepfold after a sheep is lost.

亡羊得牛(ㄨㄤˊ ㄧㄤˊ ㄉㄜˊ ㄋㄧㄡˊ)
The gain more than compensates for the loss.

二畫

【亢】 61 ㄎㄤˋ kanq kàng
1. proud
2. indomitable
3. excessive

亢奮(ㄎㄤˋ ㄈㄣˋ)
stimulated; excited

亢旱(ㄎㄤˋ ㄏㄢˋ)
drought

亢直(ㄎㄤˋ ㄓˊ)
righteous(ness)

四畫

【交】 62 ㄐㄧㄠ jiau jiāo
1. to submit; to hand in or over
2. to meet
3. to exchange
4. to intersect

交白卷(ㄐㄧㄠ ㄅㄞˊ ㄐㄩㄢˋ)or 交白卷兒(ㄐㄧㄠ ㄅㄞˊ ㄐㄩㄢˋㄦ)
to turn in a blank examination paper

交拜(ㄐㄧㄠ ㄅㄞˋ)
to exchange bows (especially between bride and bridegroom at the wedding)

交杯酒(ㄐㄧㄠ ㄅㄟ ㄐㄧㄡˇ)
the rite of drinking from nuptial cups by bride and bridegroom in the old-fashioned wedding

交保(ㄐㄧㄠ ㄅㄠˇ)
to release (a suspect) on bail

交班(ㄐㄧㄠ ㄅㄢ)
to hand over to the next shift

交臂(ㄐㄧㄠ ㄅㄧˋ)
very close or near

交兵(ㄐㄧㄠ ㄅㄧㄥ)
to fight (between nations); to wage war

交迫(ㄐㄧㄠ ㄆㄛˋ)
to be pressed from more than one direction; beleaguered; beset

交配(ㄐㄧㄠ ㄆㄟˋ)
①(biology) copulation ②to mate

交鋒(ㄐㄧㄠ ㄈㄥ)
to wage war; to engage in battle

交付(ㄐㄧㄠ ㄈㄨˋ)
①to hand over ②to make payment

交代(ㄐㄧㄠ ㄉㄞˋ)
①to hand over responsibility ②to give an explanation or excuse; the explanation or excuse given

交道(ㄐㄧㄠ ㄉㄠˋ)
social communication; social intercourse

交點(ㄐㄧㄠ ㄉㄧㄢˇ)or 交叉點(ㄐㄧㄠ ㄔㄚ ㄉㄧㄢˇ)
a point of intersection

交桃花運(ㄐㄧㄠ ㄊㄠˊ ㄏㄨㄚ ㄩㄣˋ)
to be successful in romantic affairs

交頭接耳(ㄐㄧㄠ ㄊㄡˊ ㄐㄧㄝ ㄦˇ)or 交耳(ㄐㄧㄠ ㄦˇ)
to whisper in each other's ears

交談(ㄐㄧㄠ ㄊㄢˊ)
to converse

交替(ㄐㄧㄠ ㄊㄧˋ)
to alternate

交通(ㄐㄧㄠ ㄊㄨㄥ)
①traffic ②communication

交通部(ㄐㄧㄠ ㄊㄨㄥ ㄅㄨˋ)
Ministry of Communications

交通大學(ㄐㄧㄠ ㄊㄨㄥ ㄉㄚˋ ㄒㄩㄝˊ)
National Chiao Tung University

交通警察(ㄐㄧㄠ ㄊㄨㄥ ㄐㄧㄥˇ ㄔㄚˊ)
traffic police

交通銀行(ㄐㄧㄠ ㄊㄨㄥ ㄧㄣˊ ㄏㄤˊ)
Bank of Communications

交通網(ㄐㄧㄠ ㄊㄨㄥ ㄨㄤˇ)
a communication network; the communication system

交流(ㄐㄧㄠ ㄌㄧㄡˊ)
to flow across each other

交流道(ㄐㄧㄠ ㄌㄧㄡˊ ㄉㄠˋ)
(traffic) an interchange

交流電(ㄐㄧㄠ ㄌㄧㄡˊ ㄉㄧㄢˋ)
an alternating current or A.C.

交割(ㄐㄧㄠ ㄍㄜ)
a business transaction

交給(ㄐㄧㄠ ㄍㄟˇ)
to hand to; to give to

交媾(ㄐㄧㄠ ㄍㄡˋ)
sexual intercourse; sexual union

交感經(ㄐㄧㄠ ㄍㄢˇ ㄕㄣ ㄐㄧㄥ)
the sympathetic nerve

交口稱讚(ㄐㄧㄠ ㄎㄡˇ ㄔㄥ ㄗㄢˋ)
to praise somebody or something unanimously

交困(ㄐㄧㄠ ㄎㄨㄣˋ)
multiple distress

交好運(ㄐㄧㄠ ㄏㄠˇ ㄩㄣˋ)
to have good luck; lucky

交互(ㄐㄧㄠ ㄏㄨˋ)
mutually; reciprocally

交互作用(ㄐㄧㄠ ㄏㄨˋ ㄗㄨㄛˋ ㄩㄥˋ)
interaction; interplay

交貨(ㄐㄧㄠ ㄏㄨㄛˋ)
to deliver goods; delivery

交歡(ㄐㄧㄠ ㄏㄨㄢ)
to get along with each other very friendly

交還(ㄐㄧㄠ ㄏㄨㄢˊ)
to hand back; to return

交換(ㄐㄧㄠ ㄏㄨㄢˋ)
to exchange

交集(ㄐㄧㄠ ㄐㄧˊ)
(said of different feelings) to be mixed

交際(ㄐㄧㄠ ㄐㄧˋ)
social intercourse

交際費(ㄐㄧㄠ ㄐㄧˋ ㄈㄟˋ)
entertainment fees

交際花(ㄐㄧㄠ ㄐㄧˋ ㄏㄨㄚ)
a derogatory term referring to women who are very active in social functions

交際草(ㄐㄧㄠ ㄐㄧˋ ㄘㄠˇ)
a reference to promiscuous women in general

交際舞(ㄐㄧㄠ ㄐㄧˋ ㄨˇ)
a social dance

交加(ㄐㄧㄠ ㄐㄧㄚ)
to act upon (something) or to hit (someone) simultaneously by two or more forces

交接(ㄐㄧㄠ ㄐㄧㄝ)
①to make contact with each other ②to adjoin each other ③to hand over and to

部
(一)

【二部】

take over (duties)

交結(ㄐㄧㄠ ㄐㄧㄝˊ)
to associate (with a person)

交睫(ㄐㄧㄠ ㄐㄧㄝˊ)
to close eyes

交界(ㄐㄧㄠ ㄐㄧㄝˋ)
a border (between two areas)

交角(ㄐㄧㄠ ㄐㄧㄠˇ)
(mathematics) angle of intersection

交頸(ㄐㄧㄠ ㄐㄧㄥˇ)
to fondle each other; to neck

交卷(ㄐㄧㄠ ㄐㄩㄢˇ)or 交卷兒(ㄐㄧㄠ ㄐㄩㄢㄦ)
①to hand in the examination paper ②to complete an assignment

交淺言深(ㄐㄧㄠ ㄑㄧㄢˇ ㄧㄢˊ ㄕㄣ)
intimate in conversation though not intimate in association

交情(ㄐㄧㄠ ㄑㄧㄥˊ)
friendship; association in private life

交卸(ㄐㄧㄠ ㄒㄧㄝˋ)
to leave office to a successor

交心(ㄐㄧㄠ ㄒㄧㄣ)
to lay one's heart bare; to be frank with others

交響樂(ㄐㄧㄠ ㄒㄧㄤˇ ㄌㄜˋ)
a symphony; symphonic music

交響樂團(ㄐㄧㄠ ㄒㄧㄤˇ ㄌㄜˋ ㄊㄨㄢˊ)or 交響樂隊(ㄐㄧㄠ ㄒㄧㄤˇ ㄌㄜˋ ㄉㄨㄟˋ)
an orchestra; a symphony orchestra

交織(ㄐㄧㄠ ㄓ)
to interlace; to interweave

交戰(ㄐㄧㄠ ㄓㄢˋ)
(said of nations) to wage war against each other

交戰國(ㄐㄧㄠ ㄓㄢˋ ㄍㄨㄛˊ)
a belligerent state

交叉(ㄐㄧㄠ ㄔㄚ)
to cross each other; to intersect

交叉火網(ㄐㄧㄠ ㄔㄚ ㄏㄨㄛˇ ㄨㄤˇ)
cross fire

交差(ㄐㄧㄠ ㄔㄞ)
to report what one has done in the line of duty

交出(ㄐㄧㄠ ㄔㄨ)
to surrender; to hand over: 他們交出武器。 They surren-

dered their weapons.

交涉(ㄐㄧㄠ ㄕㄜˋ)
to negotiate; negotiation

交手(ㄐㄧㄠ ㄕㄡˇ)
to exchange blows (in a fight)

交融(ㄐㄧㄠ ㄖㄨㄥˊ)
to blend; to mingle

交錯(ㄐㄧㄠ ㄘㄨㄛˋ)
to interlock

交椅(ㄐㄧㄠ ㄧˇ)
a chair; an armchair

交易(ㄐㄧㄠ ㄧˋ)
a trade; business transaction

交易所(ㄐㄧㄠ ㄧˋ ㄙㄨㄛˇ)
a stock exchange; a bourse

交易物品(ㄐㄧㄠ ㄧˋ ㄨˋ ㄆㄧㄣˇ)
a barter

交誼(ㄐㄧㄠ ㄧˋ)or(ㄐㄧㄠ ㄧˊ)
friendly relations; amity

交遊(ㄐㄧㄠ ㄧㄡˊ)
①to have friendly contact with ②people with whom one has friendly contacts; friends: 他的交遊甚廣。He has a large circle of friends.

交遊不慎(ㄐㄧㄠ ㄧㄡˊ ㄅㄨˋ ㄕㄣˋ)
to be indiscriminate in making friends

交友(ㄐㄧㄠ ㄧㄡˇ)
to make friends

交惡(ㄐㄧㄠ ㄜˋ)or(ㄐㄧㄠ ㄨˋ)
to be on unfriendly terms; to become hostile to each other

交尾(ㄐㄧㄠ ㄨㄟˇ)
(said of birds or fish) to mate

交往(ㄐㄧㄠ ㄨㄤˇ)
to have friendly relations

交運(ㄐㄧㄠ ㄩㄣˋ)
to have everything going one's way; to be favored by Lady Luck

【亥】 63
ㄏㄞˇ hay hài
1. the last of the twelve Terrestrial Branches
2. the hours between 9 and 11 p.m.

亥豕(ㄏㄞˋ ㄕˇ)
errors in handwriting, or typographical errors due to confusion of similar words

【亦】 64
ㄧˋ yih yì
also; too

亦步亦趨(ㄧˋ ㄅㄨˋ ㄧˋ ㄑㄩ)

to follow the example of another person at each move; slavish imitation

亦即(ㄧˋ ㄐㄧˊ)
that is; i.e.; namely; viz.

亦且(ㄧˋ ㄑㄧㄝˇ)
and also; as well

亦然(ㄧˋ ㄖㄢˊ)
also; too; similarly

五畫

【享】 65
ㄏㄥ heng hēng
to go through smoothly; 他的事業亨通。He runs his business smoothly.

亨利(ㄏㄥ ㄌㄧˋ)
transliteration of Henry

亨通(ㄏㄥ ㄊㄨㄥ)
to go well; to proceed smoothly

六畫

【享】 66
ㄒㄧㄤˇ sheang xiǎng
1. to enjoy; to receive
2. to offer
3. to entertain

享福(ㄒㄧㄤˇ ㄈㄨˊ)
to enjoy happiness and prosperity; to have a blessing

享堂(ㄒㄧㄤˇ ㄊㄤˊ)or 享堂(ㄒㄧㄤˇ ㄊㄤˊ)
a sanctuary (for worship of ancestors or deities)

享年(ㄒㄧㄤˇ ㄋㄧㄢˊ)or 享壽(ㄒㄧㄤˇ ㄕㄡˋ)
the number of years lived (by one who dies old)

享樂(ㄒㄧㄤˇ ㄌㄜˋ)
to seek pleasure; to make merry

享樂主義(ㄒㄧㄤˇ ㄌㄜˋ ㄓㄨˇ ㄧˋ)
hedonism

享國(ㄒㄧㄤˇ ㄍㄨㄛˊ)
the number of years of the reign (by a sovereign)

享受(ㄒㄧㄤˇ ㄕㄡˋ)
to enjoy; to indulge oneself in (some pleasant pursuit)

享有(ㄒㄧㄤˇ ㄧㄡˇ)
to possess; to have in possession: 他享有很多特權。He possesses many privileges.

享用(ㄒㄧㄤˇ ㄩㄥˋ)

to enjoy the use of

【京】 67 ㄐㄧㄥ jīng jìng
1. the capital (of a country); a metropolis
2. great; greatness

京派(ㄐㄧㄥ ㄆㄞˋ)
the Peking style or school (as opposed to the Shanghai style)

京調(ㄐㄧㄥ ㄉㄧㄠˋ)
the Peking style (of music in Chinese opera)

京都(ㄐㄧㄥ ㄉㄨ)
①the national capital ②Kyoto, Japan

京官(ㄐㄧㄥ ㄍㄨㄢ)
an official who works in the capital

京胡(ㄐㄧㄥ ㄏㄨˊ)
a Chinese violin

京滬鐵路(ㄐㄧㄥ ㄏㄨˋ ㄊㄧㄝˇ ㄌㄨˋ)
the Nanking-Shanghai Railway

京話(ㄐㄧㄥ ㄏㄨㄚˋ)
Pekinese or Mandarin

京畿(ㄐㄧㄥ ㄐㄧ)
the capital and vicinity

京劇(ㄐㄧㄥ ㄐㄩˋ)or 京劇(ㄐㄧㄥ ㄐㄩˋ)
Peking opera

京兆尹(ㄐㄧㄥ ㄓㄠˋ ㄧㄣˇ)
the mayor of the national capital (in ancient China)

京城(ㄐㄧㄥ ㄔㄥˊ)
the capital (of the country)

京油子(ㄐㄧㄥ ㄧㄡˊ ˙ㄗ)
the oily Pekinese (a derogatory term describing their sophistication)

京韻大鼓(ㄐㄧㄥ ㄩㄣˋ ㄉㄚˋ ㄍㄨˇ)
storytelling in the Peking dialect accompanied by drum-beating

七畫

【亭】 68 ㄊㄧㄥˊ tyng tíng
1. a booth; a pavilion; a garden house or rest house: 公園中有一座八角亭。There is an octagonal pavilion in the park.
2. slim and erect
3. exactly during

亭臺樓閣(ㄊㄧㄥˊ ㄊㄞˊ ㄌㄡˊ ㄍㄜˊ)
a general reference to the

---

elaborate Chinese architecture

亭亭玉立(ㄊㄧㄥˊ ㄊㄧㄥˊ ㄩˋ ㄌㄧˋ)
(said of women, especially young ladies) slim and graceful

亭候(ㄊㄧㄥˊ ㄏㄡˋ)
a military station in ancient China

亭長(ㄊㄧㄥˊ ㄓㄤˇ)
a village constable (of the Chin and Han dynasties)

亭子(ㄊㄧㄥˊ ˙ㄗ)
a pavilion

亭午(ㄊㄧㄥˊ ㄨˇ)
high noon

【亮】 69 ㄌㄧㄤˋ liang liàng
1. bright; lustrous; brilliant; luminous; radiant; clear
2. to display; to show

亮牌(ㄌㄧㄤˋ ㄆㄞˊ)
to lay one's cards on the table—(figuratively) to have a showdown

亮度(ㄌㄧㄤˋ ㄉㄨˋ)
brightness; light intensity; radiance; luminosity

亮光(ㄌㄧㄤˋ ㄍㄨㄤ)
bright light; flash

亮話(ㄌㄧㄤˋ ㄏㄨㄚˋ)
frank remarks; outspoken speech

亮節(ㄌㄧㄤˋ ㄐㄧㄝˊ)
integrity (of character); uprightness

亮晶晶(ㄌㄧㄤˋ ㄐㄧㄥ ㄐㄧㄥ)
bright; brilliant; dazzling; glaring; glistening; glittering; glowing; luminous; lustrous; radiant; resplendent; shining; sparkling; splendid

亮相(ㄌㄧㄤˋ ㄒㄧㄤˋ)or 亮像兒(ㄌㄧㄤˋ ㄒㄧㄤˋ ㄦ)
to pose for the audience's admiration on the stage (originally said of Peking opera players)

亮察(ㄌㄧㄤˋ ㄔㄚˊ)
to understand (another's difficulty)

八畫

【亳】 70 ㄅㄛˊ boh bó
the seat of government dur-

---

ing the Shang Dynasty, located in today's Shangchiu County, Honan Province

人 部
ㄖㄣˊ ren rén

【人】 71 ㄖㄣˊ ren rén
a human being; a person; people

人保(ㄖㄣˊ ㄅㄠˇ)
a personal guarantor

人本主義(ㄖㄣˊ ㄅㄣˇ ㄓㄨˇ ㄧˋ)or 人文主義(ㄖㄣˊ ㄨㄣˊ ㄓㄨˇ ㄧˋ)
(philosophy) humanism

人不可貌相(ㄖㄣˊ ㄅㄨˋ ㄎㄜˇ ㄇㄠˋ ㄒㄧㄤˋ)
A man's worth cannot be measured by his looks.

人不知鬼不覺(ㄖㄣˊ ㄅㄨˋ ㄓ ㄍㄨㄟˇ ㄅㄨˋ ㄐㄩㄝˊ)
without the knowledge of anybody else

人不為己，天誅地滅(ㄖㄣˊ ㄅㄨˋ ㄨㄟˋ ㄐㄧˇ，ㄊㄧㄢ ㄓㄨ ㄉㄧˋ ㄇㄧㄝˋ)
If a person did not look out for himself, Heaven and Earth will destroy him.

人怕出名豬怕肥(ㄖㄣˊ ㄆㄚˋ ㄔㄨ ㄇㄧㄥˊ ㄓㄨ ㄆㄚˋ ㄈㄟˊ)
Men are afraid of becoming famous while pigs of getting fat.—(figuratively) Fame portends trouble for people.

人品(ㄖㄣˊ ㄆㄧㄣˇ)
character (of a person); personality

人馬(ㄖㄣˊ ㄇㄚˇ)
①a person and the horse he rides; a crowd of people and horses ②traffic (consisting of people and horses) ③troops (consisting of soldiers and horses)

人馬宮(ㄖㄣˊ ㄇㄚˇ ㄍㄨㄥ)or 人馬座(ㄖㄣˊ ㄇㄚˇ ㄗㄨㄛˋ)
(astronomy) Sagittarius

人滿之患(ㄖㄣˊ ㄇㄢˇ ㄓ ㄏㄨㄢˋ)
trouble of overpopulation or overcrowdedness

人面桃花(ㄖㄣˊ ㄇㄧㄢˋ ㄊㄠˊ ㄏㄨㄚ)
①memory of an old sweetheart ②name of a Peking opera play

〔人部〕

人面獅身(ㄖㄣˊㄇㄧㄢˋㄕㄕㄣ)
a sphinx

人面獸心(ㄖㄣˊㄇㄧㄢˋㄕㄡˋㄒㄧㄣ)
gentle in appearance but cruel at heart; a wolf in sheep's clothing

人民(ㄖㄣˊㄇㄧㄣˊ)
people (as opposed to the ruler or the government)

人民代表大會(ㄖㄣˊㄇㄧㄣˊㄉㄞˋㄅㄧㄠˇㄉㄚˋㄏㄨㄟˋ)
the National People's Congress in mainland China

人民團體(ㄖㄣˊㄇㄧㄣˊㄊㄨㄢˊㄊㄧˇ)
a civic organization or civic body

人民公社(ㄖㄣˊㄇㄧㄣˊㄍㄨㄥㄕㄜˋ)
people's commune (in mainland China)

人民陣線(ㄖㄣˊㄇㄧㄣˊㄓㄣˋㄒㄧㄢˋ)
the popular front

人命關天(ㄖㄣˊㄇㄧㄥˋㄍㄨㄢㄊㄧㄢ)
Human life is of utmost importance.

人命攸關(ㄖㄣˊㄇㄧㄥˋㄧㄡㄍㄨㄢ)
a matter of life and death

人非木石(ㄖㄣˊㄈㄟㄇㄨˋㄕˊ)
Man is a sentimental creature.

人犯(ㄖㄣˊㄈㄢˋ)
a criminal; a suspect (in a criminal case)

人販子(ㄖㄣˊㄈㄢˋㄗˇ)
a trader in human beings

人浮於事(ㄖㄣˊㄈㄨˊㄩˊㄕˋ)
There are more job-hunters than there are jobs.

人大心大(ㄖㄣˊㄉㄚˋㄒㄧㄣㄉㄚˋ)
to grow in independence of mind, or insubordination, with growth in body (usually said of girls)

人道(ㄖㄣˊㄉㄠˋ)
① humanitarianism; philanthropy; charity; humanity ② sexual union

人地生疏(ㄖㄣˊㄉㄧˋㄕㄥㄕㄨ)
to have trouble getting about in a strange land because of unfamiliarity with the local people and their customs

人丁(ㄖㄣˊㄉㄧㄥ)
① an adult ② population: 此村人丁不足一千。 The population of this village is less than 1,000.

人定勝天(ㄖㄣˊㄉㄧㄥˋㄕㄥˋㄊㄧㄢ)
Man's determination will conquer nature.

人多嘴雜(ㄖㄣˊㄉㄨㄛㄗㄨㄟˇㄗㄚˊ)
① Agreement is difficult if there are too many people. ② Secrecy is difficult if too many people share it.

人頭稅(ㄖㄣˊㄊㄡˊㄕㄨㄟˋ)
poll tax

人體(ㄖㄣˊㄊㄧˇ)
a human body

人同此心, 心同此理(ㄖㄣˊㄊㄨㄥˊㄘˇㄒㄧㄣ, ㄒㄧㄣㄊㄨㄥˊㄘˇㄌㄧˇ)
The sense of justice and rationality is the same in everybody.

人籟(ㄖㄣˊㄌㄞˋ)
hubbub or noises of human habitation

人類(ㄖㄣˊㄌㄟˋ)
man; mankind; the human race: 一個人應立志為全人類謀幸福。 One should make up one's mind to benefit all mankind.

人類學(ㄖㄣˊㄌㄟˋㄒㄩㄝˊ)
anthropology

人力(ㄖㄣˊㄌㄧˋ)
human power, strength or efforts

人力車(ㄖㄣˊㄌㄧˋㄔㄜ)
a rickshaw, ricksha or jinrikisha

人力資源(ㄖㄣˊㄌㄧˋㄗㄩㄢˊ)
human resources

人倫(ㄖㄣˊㄌㄨㄣˊ)
principles of human relationships

人格(ㄖㄣˊㄍㄜˊ)
character; personality

人格分裂(ㄖㄣˊㄍㄜˊㄈㄣㄌㄧㄝˋ)
split personality

人工(ㄖㄣˊㄍㄨㄥ)
① human labor ② man-made

人孵化(ㄖㄣˊㄍㄨㄥㄈㄨˋㄏㄨㄚˋ)
artificial incubation

人工港(ㄖㄣˊㄍㄨㄥㄍㄤˇ)
an artificial harbor

人工呼吸(ㄖㄣˊㄍㄨㄥㄏㄨㄒㄧ)
artificial respiration

人工湖(ㄖㄣˊㄍㄨㄥㄏㄨˊ)
an artificial lake

人工受孕(ㄖㄣˊㄍㄨㄥㄕㄡˋㄩㄣˋ)
artificial insemination

人口(ㄖㄣˊㄎㄡˇ)
population

人口普查(ㄖㄣˊㄎㄡˇㄆㄨˇㄔㄚˊ)
a population census

人口密度(ㄖㄣˊㄎㄡˇㄇㄧˋㄉㄨˋ)
density of population

人口統計(ㄖㄣˊㄎㄡˇㄊㄨㄥˇㄐㄧˋ)
demographic statistics; population statistics

人口論(ㄖㄣˊㄎㄡˇㄌㄨㄣˋ)
The Principle of Population by Thomas Robert Malthus

人口過剩(ㄖㄣˊㄎㄡˇㄍㄨㄛˋㄕㄥˋ)
overpopulation

人口學(ㄖㄣˊㄎㄡˇㄒㄩㄝˊ)
demography

人口政策(ㄖㄣˊㄎㄡˇㄓㄥˋㄘㄜˋ)
population policy

人口問題(ㄖㄣˊㄎㄡˇㄨㄣˋㄊㄧˊ)
population problems

人困馬乏(ㄖㄣˊㄎㄨㄣˋㄇㄚˇㄈㄚˊ)
Both the horse and the rider are exhausted.

人和(ㄖㄣˊㄏㄜˊ)
popularity or harmony with the people, colleagues, constituents, etc.

人海(ㄖㄣˊㄏㄞˇ)
huge crowds

人海浮沈(ㄖㄣˊㄏㄞˇㄈㄨˊㄔㄣˊ)
the vicissitudes of life

人海戰術(ㄖㄣˊㄏㄞˇㄓㄢˋㄕㄨˋ)
human-sea tactics; human-wave sweep

人話(ㄖㄣˊㄏㄨㄚˋ)
reasonable statement (as opposed to nonsense)

人寰(ㄖㄣˊㄏㄨㄢˊ)
the world; the earth

人迹(ㄖㄣˊㄐㄧˋ)
signs or traces indicating human presence

人際關係(ㄖㄣˊㄐㄧˋㄍㄨㄢㄒㄧˋ)
human relation

人家(ㄖㄣˊㄐㄧㄚ)
① a human abode or residence; a home ② other people

人傑地靈(ㄖㄣˊㄐㄧㄝˊㄉㄧˋㄌㄧㄥˊ)
The birth (or presence) of heroes brings glory to a place.

人間(ㄖㄣˊㄐㄧㄢ)
the world of mortals

人間地獄(ㄖㄣˊㄐㄧㄢㄉㄧˋㄩˋ)
pandemonium; a hell away from Hell

人間何世(ㄖㄣ ㄐㄧㄢ ㄏㄜˊ ㄕˋ)
What a world is this?!

人見人愛(ㄖㄣˊ ㄐㄧㄢˋ ㄖㄣˊ ㄞˋ)
loved by all; everybody's
darling

人盡可夫(ㄖㄣˊ ㄐㄧㄣˋ ㄎㄜˇ ㄈㄨ)
(said of women) promiscu-
ous

人盡其才(ㄖㄣˊ ㄐㄧㄣˋ ㄑㄧˊ ㄘㄞˊ)
No talent is to be wasted.

人君(ㄖㄣˊ ㄐㄩㄣ)
a sovereign; a king

人棄我取(ㄖㄣˊ ㄑㄧˋ ㄨㄛˇ ㄑㄩˇ)
I will take whatever others
don't want.

人情(ㄖㄣˊ ㄑㄧㄥˊ)
① human sentiment, emotion
or feeling ② favors asked or
done ③ good will (expressed
in the form of gifts, invitation to dinners, etc.)

人情世故(ㄖㄣˊ ㄑㄧㄥˊ ㄕˋ ㄍㄨˋ)
the ways of the world: 他 不
懂人情世故。 He does not
know the ways of the world.

人情味(ㄖㄣˊ ㄑㄧㄥˊ ㄨㄟˋ)
human touch; friendliness;
hospitality

人去樓空(ㄖㄣˊ ㄑㄩˋ ㄌㄡˊ ㄎㄨㄥ)
After the occupants have
gone, the building is empty.
或 Old sights recall to mind
the memory of old friends.

人權(ㄖㄣˊ ㄑㄩㄢˊ)
human rights

人權宣言(ㄖㄣˊ ㄑㄩㄢˊ ㄒㄩㄢ ㄧㄢˊ)
the declaration of human
rights

人羣(ㄖㄣˊ ㄑㄩㄣˊ)
a crowd, throng or multi-
tude (of people)

人窮志短(ㄖㄣˊ ㄑㄩㄥˊ ㄓˋ ㄉㄨㄢˇ)
Poverty stifles ambition.

人小鬼大(ㄖㄣˊ ㄒㄧㄠˇ ㄍㄨㄟˇ ㄉㄚˋ)
young but tricky; young but
ambitious

人心(ㄖㄣˊ ㄒㄧㄣ)
human heart, will, feeling or
emotion; morale

人心不同，各如其面(ㄖㄣˊ ㄒㄧㄣ
ㄅㄨˋ ㄊㄨㄥˊ，ㄍㄜˋ ㄖㄨˊ ㄑㄧˊ ㄇㄧㄢˋ)
Individual thinking is as
varied as individual looks.

人心不古(ㄖㄣˊ ㄒㄧㄣ ㄅㄨˋ ㄍㄨˇ)
Public morality is not what
it used to be. 或 Public

morality has degenerated.

人心皇皇(ㄖㄣˊ ㄒㄧㄣ ㄏㄨㄤˊ ㄏㄨㄤˊ)
(said of people in time of
war or social upheaval) jittery or panicky

人心思漢(ㄖㄣˊ ㄒㄧㄣ ㄙ ㄏㄢˋ)
The people living under the
control of a usurper or foreign invaders long for the
return of the legitimate government.

人像(ㄖㄣˊ ㄒㄧㄤˋ)
a portrait; an image

人行道(ㄖㄣˊ ㄒㄧㄥˊ ㄉㄠˋ)
a sidewalk; a footpath

人行穿越道(ㄖㄣˊ ㄒㄧㄥˊ ㄔㄨㄢ ㄩㄝˋ
ㄉㄠˋ)
a pedestrian crosswalk; a
pedestrian crossing

人性(ㄖㄣˊ ㄒㄧㄥˋ)
human nature; normal
human feelings; reason

人選(ㄖㄣˊ ㄒㄩㄢˇ)
candidates (for certain jobs)

人之常情(ㄖㄣˊ ㄓ ㄔㄤˊ ㄑㄧㄥˊ)
the way of the world; what
is natural in human relationships

人治(ㄖㄣˊ ㄓˋ)
enlightened government
brought about by virtuous
rulers or administrators (as
distinguished from what
results from the rule of law)

人質(ㄖㄣˊ ㄓˋ)
a hostage

人證(ㄖㄣˊ ㄓㄥˋ)
① witnesses ② testimony
given by witnesses

人主(ㄖㄣˊ ㄓㄨˇ)
a sovereign; a king

人中(ㄖㄣˊ ㄓㄨㄥ)
(physiognomy) philtrum

人種(ㄖㄣˊ ㄓㄨㄥˇ)
human races

人種學(ㄖㄣˊ ㄓㄨㄥˇ ㄒㄩㄝˊ)
ethnology

人臣(ㄖㄣˊ ㄔㄣˊ)
a vassal

人稱(ㄖㄣˊ ㄔㄥ)
①(grammar) the first, second or third person ②a
nickname by which one is
known

人稱代詞(ㄖㄣˊ ㄔㄥ ㄉㄞˋ ㄘˊ)
a personal pronoun

人師(ㄖㄣˊ ㄕ)
a paragon (of virtue or/and
learning)

人士(ㄖㄣˊ ㄕˋ)
personages (usually plural)

人氏(ㄖㄣˊ ㄕˋ)
persons born of a particular
place: 他 是本地人氏。 He is a
native here.

人世(ㄖㄣˊ ㄕˋ)
① human life; life ② the
world

人事(ㄖㄣˊ ㄕˋ)
① human affairs; human
customs ② personnel affairs
(of an organization) ③
human endeavors

人事關係(ㄖㄣˊ ㄕˋ ㄍㄨㄢ ㄒㄧˋ)
personal connections

人事管理(ㄖㄣˊ ㄕˋ ㄍㄨㄢˇ ㄌㄧˇ)
personnel administration

人手(ㄖㄣˊ ㄕㄡˇ)
① manpower ② a human
hand

人手一册(ㄖㄣˊ ㄕㄡˇ ㄧ ㄘㄜˋ)
Everyone has a copy.(referring to a popular book)

人壽保險(ㄖㄣˊ ㄕㄡˋ ㄅㄠˇ ㄒㄧㄢˇ)
life insurance

人山人海(ㄖㄣˊ ㄕㄢ ㄖㄣˊ ㄏㄞˇ)
a large crowd

人身(ㄖㄣˊ ㄕㄣ)
①a human body ②(law)
personal (liberty)

人參(ㄖㄣˊ ㄕㄣ)
ginseng

人生(ㄖㄣˊ ㄕㄥ)
human life; life

人生觀(ㄖㄣˊ ㄕㄥ ㄍㄨㄢ)
a view of life; an outlook on
life; the philosophy of life

人生朝露(ㄖㄣˊ ㄕㄥ ㄓㄠ ㄌㄨˋ)
Life is ephemeral (like the
morning dew).

人生如夢(ㄖㄣˊ ㄕㄥ ㄖㄨˊ ㄇㄥˋ)
Life is but a dream.

人生如寄(ㄖㄣˊ ㄕㄥ ㄖㄨˊ ㄐㄧˋ)
(literally) Man living in the
world is like a sojourner in
a hotel.—Life is short.

人肉市場(ㄖㄣˊ ㄖㄡˋ ㄕˋ ㄔㄤˇ)or 人
市(ㄖㄣˊ ㄕˋ)
the sex market; houses of ill
fame

人人(ㄖㄣˊ ㄖㄣˊ)
everybody

〔人
部〕

人人自危(ㄖㄣˊ ㄖㄣˊ ㄗ ㄨㄟ)
Everyone feels insecure.

人瑞(ㄖㄣˊ ㄖㄨㄟˋ)
a very old man or woman, considered a happy omen for the whole human race

人造(ㄖㄣˊ ㄗㄠˋ)
man-made; artificial; imitation

人造寶石(ㄖㄣˊ ㄗㄠˋ ㄅㄠˇ ㄕˊ)
an imitation jewel

人造冰(ㄖㄣˊ ㄗㄠˋ ㄅㄧㄥ)
manufactured ice; artificial ice

人造棉(ㄖㄣˊ ㄗㄠˋ ㄇㄧㄢˊ)
staple rayon

人造肥料(ㄖㄣˊ ㄗㄠˋ ㄈㄟˊ ㄌㄧㄠˋ)or人造牛油(ㄖㄣˊ ㄗㄠˋ ㄋㄧㄡˊ ㄧㄡˊ)
margarine

人造纖維(ㄖㄣˊ ㄗㄠˋ ㄒㄧㄢ ㄨㄟˊ)
man-made fiber

人造心臟(ㄖㄣˊ ㄗㄠˋ ㄒㄧㄣ ㄗㄤˋ)
an artificial heart

人造絲(ㄖㄣˊ ㄗㄠˋ ㄙ)
synthetic silk; rayon

人造衛星(ㄖㄣˊ ㄗㄠˋ ㄨㄟˋ ㄒㄧㄥ)
an artificial satellite; a satellite

人造雨(ㄖㄣˊ ㄗㄠˋ ㄩˇ)
artificial rain; rain caused by cloud seeding

人造語言(ㄖㄣˊ ㄗㄠˋ ㄩˇ ㄧㄢˊ)
an artificial language

人贓並獲(ㄖㄣˊ ㄗㄤ ㄅㄧㄥˋ ㄏㄨㄛˋ)
(a thief or robber) caught together with the loot

人才(ㄖㄣˊ ㄘㄞˊ)
a man of talent; a talent; a man of ability

人才輩出(ㄖㄣˊ ㄘㄞˊ ㄅㄟˋ ㄔㄨ)
Great talents appear successively (or continuously).

人才濟濟(ㄖㄣˊ ㄘㄞˊ ㄐㄧˇ ㄐㄧˇ)
There is a wealth of talents.

人才外流(ㄖㄣˊ ㄘㄞˊ ㄨㄞˋ ㄌㄧㄡˊ)
the brain drain

人存政舉，人亡政息(ㄖㄣˊ ㄘㄨㄣˊ ㄓㄥˋ ㄐㄩˇ, ㄖㄣˊ ㄨㄤˊ ㄓㄥˋ ㄒㄧˊ)
The policies and regulations of an organization shift with the change of the person in charge.

人一己百(ㄖㄣˊ ㄧ ㄐㄧˇ ㄅㄞˇ)
If others can do it, I must

exert myself a hundred times harder(because I am less talented than they are) in order to do the same.

人妖(ㄖㄣˊ ㄧㄠ)
①a man disguised as a woman or vice versa who engages in evil activities under the disguise ②a hermaphrodite

人煙(ㄖㄣˊ ㄧㄢ)
signs of a human settlement; human habitation

人言(ㄖㄣˊ ㄧㄢˊ)
①human speech ②public opinion; the words of people

人言可畏(ㄖㄣˊ ㄧㄢˊ ㄎㄜˇ ㄨㄟˋ)
Criticisms should be feared.

人言嘖嘖(ㄖㄣˊ ㄧㄢˊ ㄗㄜˊ ㄗㄜˊ)
There are plenty of criticisms.

人仰馬翻(ㄖㄣˊ ㄧㄤˇ ㄇㄚˇ ㄈㄢ)
to suffer an utter defeat

人樣兒(ㄖㄣˊ ㄧㄤˋ ㄦ)
the proper human appearance

人影(ㄖㄣˊ ㄧㄥˇ)or人影兒(ㄖㄣˊ ㄧㄥˇ ㄦ)
a human shadow

人無遠慮，必有近憂(ㄖㄣˊ ㄨˊ ㄩㄢˇ ㄌㄩˋ, ㄅㄧˋ ㄧㄡˇ ㄐㄧㄣˋ ㄧㄡ)
Those who do not plan for the future will find trouble at their doorsteps.

人物(ㄖㄣˊ ㄨˋ)
①a personage or figure (usually referring to famous persons) ②people and things

人物畫(ㄖㄣˊ ㄨˋ ㄏㄨㄚˋ)
portrait painting

人微言輕(ㄖㄣˊ ㄨㄟˊ ㄧㄢˊ ㄑㄧㄥ)
(a self-depreciatory expression) Words from a man of lowly position(like me) carry little weight.

人為(ㄖㄣˊ ㄨㄟˊ)
man-made; artificial

人為刀俎，我為魚肉(ㄖㄣˊ ㄨㄟˊ ㄉㄠ ㄗㄨˇ, ㄨㄛˇ ㄨㄟˊ ㄩˊ ㄖㄡˋ)
(literally) to be meat on somebody's chopping board —to be at the mercy of somebody

人為萬物之靈(ㄖㄣˊ ㄨㄟˊ ㄨㄢˋ ㄨˋ ㄓ ㄌㄧㄥˊ)
The human being is the most intelligent among crea-

tures. 或 Man is the lord of creation.

人文(ㄖㄣˊ ㄨㄣˊ)
①humanities; culture ②human affairs

人文地理(ㄖㄣˊ ㄨㄣˊ ㄉㄧˋ ㄌㄧˇ)
human geography

人文科學(ㄖㄣˊ ㄨㄣˊ ㄎㄜ ㄒㄩㄝˊ)
the humanities; humane studies

人文薈萃(ㄖㄣˊ ㄨㄣˊ ㄏㄨㄟˋ ㄘㄨㄟˋ)
(said of culture centers) gathering of talents

人文主義(ㄖㄣˊ ㄨㄣˊ ㄓㄨˇ ㄧˋ)
humanism

人亡物在(ㄖㄣˊ ㄨㄤˊ ㄨˋ ㄗㄞˋ)
the relics of the dead (heightening the grief of the living)

人望(ㄖㄣˊ ㄨㄤˋ)
popularity

人慾(ㄖㄣˊ ㄩˋ)
desires; passions

人慾橫流(ㄖㄣˊ ㄩˋ ㄏㄥˊ ㄌㄧㄡˊ)
mass indulgence in decadent life

人員(ㄖㄣˊ ㄩㄢˊ)
the personnel; the staff

人猿(ㄖㄣˊ ㄩㄢˊ)
an ape

人緣(ㄖㄣˊ ㄩㄢˊ)or人緣兒(ㄖㄣˊ ㄩㄢˊ ㄦ)
relations with others; personality(as an impression upon others)

人云亦云(ㄖㄣˊ ㄩㄣˊ ㄧˋ ㄩㄣˊ)
to parrot what others say; me-tooism; me-too

二畫

【什】⁷²
1. ㄕˊ shyr shí
1. sundry; miscellaneous
2. ten
3. a squad (of ten soldiers, in former times)

什錦(ㄕˊ ㄐㄧㄣˇ)
multiple ingredients (for a dish); assorted

什器(ㄕˊ ㄑㄧˋ)
miscellaneous utensils

什襲珍藏(ㄕˊ ㄒㄧˊ ㄓㄣ ㄘㄤˊ)
to store away like treasure

什一(ㄕˊ ㄧ)
one tenth

〔人部〕

什物(ㄕ ㄨ)
miscellaneous goods; sundry items

【什】 72
2.(甚) ㄕㄜ´ sher shé
什麼 在什麼

什麼(ㄕㄜ´ ·ㄇㄜ)
what (used either in question or as an exclamation)

什麼東西(ㄕㄜ´ ·ㄇㄜ ㄉㄨㄥ ·ㄒㄧ)
①What is this (or that)?②
What does he think he is?

什麼話(ㄕㄜ´ ·ㄇㄜ ㄏㄨㄚˋ)
How can you say that!? 或
How can you do this!?

【仁】 73
ㄖㄣ´ ren rén
1. benevolence; humanity; mercy; kindness; charity
2. kernel

仁民(ㄖㄣ´ ㄇㄧㄣ´)
to be benevolent to the common people; to be philanthropic

仁民愛物(ㄖㄣ´ ㄇㄧㄣ´ ㄞˋ ㄨ)
to love all people and animals

仁風(ㄖㄣ´ ㄈㄥ)
benevolence (as prevailing effect)

仁德(ㄖㄣ´ ㄉㄜ´)
benevolence; magnanimity; charity; humanity; kindness

仁弟(ㄖㄣ´ ㄉㄧˋ)
dear little brother (a designation for a younger brother, or one's student)

仁厚(ㄖㄣ´ ㄏㄡˋ)
benevolent and generous

仁君(ㄖㄣ´ ㄐㄩㄣ)
your (or his) lordship

仁心(ㄖㄣ´ ㄒㄧㄣ)
kindheartedness; charity; kindness

仁心仁術(ㄖㄣ´ ㄒㄧㄣ ㄖㄣ´ ㄕㄨˋ)
benevolence entertained at heart and practiced in deeds (usually used as a eulogy to medical practitioners)

仁兄(ㄖㄣ´ ㄒㄩㄥ)
dear elder brother (a designation for a friend of the same standing as oneself)

仁至義盡(ㄖㄣ´ ㄓˋ ㄧˋ ㄐㄧㄣˋ)
Everything is to be expected in the light of benevolence and duty has been done.

仁者壽(ㄖㄣ´ ㄓㄜˇ ㄕㄡˋ)
The kind live long.

仁者見仁，智者見智(ㄖㄣ´ ㄓㄜˇ
ㄐㄧㄢˋ ㄖㄣ´，ㄓˋ ㄓㄜˇ ㄐㄧㄢˋ ㄓˋ)
The virtuous see virtue and the wise see wisdom.—Different people have different views.

仁政(ㄖㄣ´ ㄓㄥˋ)
humanitarian rule; good administration

仁人(ㄖㄣ´ ㄖㄣ´)
a kind-hearted person

仁人君子(ㄖㄣ´ ㄖㄣ´ ㄐㄩㄣ ㄗˇ)
kind-hearted gentlemen; good people; philanthropists

仁人志士(ㄖㄣ´ ㄖㄣ´ ㄓˋ ㄕˋ)
a person with lofty ideals

仁慈(ㄖㄣ´ ㄘ´)
benevolence; magnanimity; charity; humanity; kindness; love

仁愛(ㄖㄣ´ ㄞˋ)
humanity; philanthropy; kindness; benevolence; love

仁義(ㄖㄣ´ ㄧˋ)
love and justice

仁義道德(ㄖㄣ´ ㄧˋ ㄉㄠˋ ㄉㄜ´)
benevolence, justice and virtue; virtue and morality

【仂】 74
ㄌㄜˋ leh lè
a fraction (of number)

【仃】 75
ㄉㄧㄥ ding dīng
lonely; solitary

【仄】 76
ㄗㄜˋ tzeh zè
1. oblique
2. said of the three tones other than the even tone (in ancient Chinese phonology)
3. narrow
4. uneasy

仄聲(ㄗㄜˋ ㄕㄥ)
an oblique tone (any of the three tones other than the even tone, i.e., rising tone, going tone, and entering tone)

仄韻(ㄗㄜˋ ㄩㄣˋ)
poetry rhyming with the characters of 仄聲

【仆】 77
ㄆㄨ´ pu pú
(又讀 ㄈㄨ´ fuh fú)
1. to prostrate
2. to fall

【仇】 78
1.(讎) ㄔㄡ´ chour chóu
1. a foe; an enemy; a rival; an adversary
2. hatred; enmity; antagonism; hostility; feud
3. to hate: 她容易仇視別人。She hates easily.

仇敵(ㄔㄡ´ ㄉㄧ´)
an enemy, a foe, or an antagonist

仇恨(ㄔㄡ´ ㄏㄣˋ)
①hatred; spite; animosity; enmity; hostility; feud; ill will; resentment; bitterness; rancor ②to hate; to bear a grudge against

仇家(ㄔㄡ´ ㄐㄧㄚ)
a personal enemy

仇隙(ㄔㄡ´ ㄒㄧˋ)
a breach (of friendly relations); feud; a quarrel

仇視(ㄔㄡ´ ㄕˋ)
to regard with hostility or enmity

仇殺(ㄔㄡ´ ㄕㄚ)
a murder committed out of grudge or vendetta

仇人(ㄔㄡ´ ㄖㄣ´) or 仇家(ㄔㄡ´ ㄐㄧㄚ)
an enemy; a foe; a rival; an opponent; an adversary; an antagonist

【仇】 78
2. ㄑㄧㄡ´ chyou qiú
1. a Chinese family name
2. a spouse

仇偶(ㄑㄧㄡ´ ㄡˇ)
one's spouse

【今】 79
ㄐㄧㄣ jin jīn
1. present; recent; modern
2. now; currently; presently; nowadays
3. immediately; right away

今非昔比(ㄐㄧㄣ ㄈㄟ ㄒㄧ´ ㄅㄧˇ)
Time has changed and the good old days are gone.

今體(ㄐㄧㄣ ㄊㄧˇ)
(said of literary works) the modern style

今天(ㄐㄧㄣ ㄊㄧㄢ) or 今兒(ㄐㄧㄣ ㄦ)
or 今兒個(ㄐㄧㄣ ㄦ ·ㄍㄜ)
today

今年(ㄐㄧㄣ ㄋㄧㄢ´)
this year

今後(ㄐㄧㄣ ㄏㄡˋ)
hereafter; henceforward;

henceforth; from now on

今昔(ㄐㄧㄣ ㄒㄧ)
the present and the past

今昔之感(ㄐㄧㄣ ㄒㄧ ㄓ ㄍㄢˇ)
an expression to convey a
sense of loss when the present situation is definitely
worse than what it used to
be

今朝(ㄐㄧㄣ ㄓㄠ)
today; this morning

今朝有酒今朝醉(ㄐㄧㄣ ㄓㄠ ㄧㄡˇ
ㄐㄧㄡˇ ㄐㄧㄣ ㄓㄠ ㄗㄨㄟˋ)
to enjoy while one can;
carpe diem

今晨(ㄐㄧㄣ ㄔㄣˊ)
this morning

今世(ㄐㄧㄣ ㄕˋ)
①the present era ②life on
this side of the grave; this
present life

今是昨非(ㄐㄧㄣ ㄕˋ ㄗㄨㄛˊ ㄈㄟ)
(said of repentance and
reformation) to step onto
the right path as of today
and to say good-bye to the
wrongdoings of the past

今生(ㄐㄧㄣ ㄕㄥ)
this present life (as distinct
from past and future lives
by the concept of life and
death as a never-ending
cycle)

今日(ㄐㄧㄣ ㄖˋ)
①today ②nowadays

今人(ㄐㄧㄣ ㄖㄣˊ)
a now living person; a contemporary

今譯(ㄐㄧㄣ ㄧˋ)
the modern language ver-
sion

今夜(ㄐㄧㄣ ㄧㄝˋ)or 今夕(ㄐㄧㄣ ㄒㄧ)
or 今晚(ㄐㄧㄣ ㄨㄢˇ)or 今宵(ㄐㄧㄣ
ㄒㄧㄠ)
tonight

今音(ㄐㄧㄣ ㄧㄣ)
modern pronunciation (of
words pronounced differently in the past)

【介】 80
　　　ㄐㄧㄝˋ jieh jiè
1. a shelled aquatic animal
2. to lie between
3. (said of one's character) upright
4. great and honorable
5. to aid; to benefit

6. tiny

介弟(ㄐㄧㄝˋ ㄉㄧˋ)
your younger brother (in
formal speech)

介殼(ㄐㄧㄝˋ ㄎㄜˊ)
the shell (of an insect or
animal)

介居(ㄐㄧㄝˋ ㄐㄩ)
to live in between

介蟲(ㄐㄧㄝˋ ㄔㄨㄥˊ)
a shelled aquatic animal
(like the crab, the shrimp,
etc.); the crustacean

介士(ㄐㄧㄝˋ ㄕˋ)
a man of principle; an
upright man

介紹(ㄐㄧㄝˋ ㄕㄠˋ)
to introduce (a person to
another)

介紹人(ㄐㄧㄝˋ ㄕㄠˋ ㄖㄣˊ)
an introducer; a match-
maker

介壽(ㄐㄧㄝˋ ㄕㄡˋ)
to benefit one's longevity —
birthday congratulations

介入(ㄐㄧㄝˋ ㄖㄨˋ)
to get involved; to interfere
with

介詞(ㄐㄧㄝˋ ㄘˊ)
a preposition

介意(ㄐㄧㄝˋ ㄧˋ)or 介懷(ㄐㄧㄝˋ ㄏㄨㄞˊ)
to mind; to heed: 不要介意他
人怎麼說, Don't mind what
other people say.

介於(ㄐㄧㄝˋ ㄩˊ)
to lie in between; to be situated between

【仍】 81
　　　ㄖㄥˊ reng réng
still; yet: 我回來的時候, 他仍
會在這兒嗎? Will he still be
here when I get back?

仍舊(ㄖㄥˊ ㄐㄧㄡˋ)or 仍然(ㄖㄥˊ ㄖㄢˊ)
still; yet

仍是(ㄖㄥˊ ㄕˋ)
still is (what it used to be);
still was (what it had been):
王小姐仍是學生嗎? Is Miss
Wang still a student?

三畫

【仔】 82
　　　1. ㄗˇ tzyy zǐ
careful

仔細(ㄗˇ ㄒㄧˋ)
careful; punctilious; minute;

attentive

【仔】 82
　　　2. ㄗㄞˇ tzae zǎi
1. young animals
2. one who tends cattle

仔畜(ㄗㄞˇ ㄔㄨˋ)
a newborn animal; a young
animal

【仕】 83
　　　ㄕˋ shyh shì
1. an official
2. to enter government service;
to serve the government; to
be an official; to fill an
office

仕版(ㄕˋ ㄅㄢˇ)
a register of officials

仕途(ㄕˋ ㄊㄨˊ)or 仕塗(ㄕˋ ㄊㄨˊ)
the career in government
service; a political career

仕女(ㄕˋ ㄋㄩˇ)or 士女(ㄕˋ ㄋㄩˇ)
①young men and women ②
a painting portraying beautiful women

仕路(ㄕˋ ㄌㄨˋ)
an official career

仕宦(ㄕˋ ㄏㄨㄢˋ)
to be an official; to enter
government service; to serve
the government

仕進(ㄕˋ ㄐㄧㄣˋ)
to advance into government
service

【他】 84
　　　ㄊㄚ ta tā
1. he; him
2. other; another
3. future

他們(ㄊㄚ ·ㄇㄣ)
they; them

他們倆(ㄊㄚ ·ㄇㄣ ㄌㄧㄚˇ)
they two; them two: 他們倆
是兄弟. They two are
brothers.

他方(ㄊㄚ ㄈㄤ)
①the other party (to a
transaction, dispute, etc.) ②
other places

他動詞(ㄊㄚ ㄉㄨㄥˋ ㄘˊ)
a transitive verb 亦作「及物動
詞」

他圖(ㄊㄚ ㄊㄨˊ)
a different scheme or plan;
another plot

他年(ㄊㄚ ㄋㄧㄢˊ)
another year; some time in
the future

他力(ㄊㄚ ㄌㄧˋ)

somebody else's power (as opposed to one's own)

他故(ㄊㄚ ㄍㄨ)
another cause

他國(ㄊㄚ ㄍㄨㄜ)
other countries

他計(ㄊㄚ ㄐㄧ)
another plan; a different plan

他家(ㄊㄚ ㄐㄧㄚ)
other people's homes; somebody else's home

他就(ㄊㄚ ㄐㄧㄡ)
to accept another job

他心(ㄊㄚ ㄒㄧㄣ)
dishonesty; insincerity; treachery; unfaithfulness

他鄉(ㄊㄚ ㄒㄧㄤ)
other lands or strange lands; a land away from home

他鄉遇故知(ㄊㄚ ㄒㄧㄤ ㄩˋ ㄍㄨˋ ㄓ)
to run across an old friend in a distant land

他志(ㄊㄚ ㄓ)
other ambitions; other (disloyal) ideas: 他翻然他志。He suddenly had other (disloyal) ideas.

他處(ㄊㄚ ㄔㄨ)
elsewhere

他事(ㄊㄚ ㄕ)
other matters, things, or business

他殺(ㄊㄚ ㄕㄚ)
homicide (as opposed to suicide)

他山之石，可以攻玉(ㄊㄚ ㄕㄢ ㄓ ㄕ，ㄎㄜˇ ㄧˇ ㄍㄨㄥ ㄩˋ)
The stones of those hills may be used to polish gems. —Advice from others may help one overcome one's defects. 或 to remedy one's defects by means of others' good quality or suggestion

他日(ㄊㄚ ㄖˋ)
① another day; some time in the future ② some time in the past

他人(ㄊㄚ ㄖㄣ)
others; other people; somebody else; another person

他意(ㄊㄚ ㄧ)
another intention (different from the professed one)

【仗】 85 ㄓㄤ　jang zhàng

1. weaponry
2. to lean upon; to rely upon; to depend on
3. battle; war: 他去打仗。He went to war.

仗氣(ㄓㄤ ㄑㄧ)
to rely on emotion

仗著本事(ㄓㄤ ˙ㄓㄜ ㄅㄣˇ ㄕ)
to rely on one's own skill or ability

仗恃(ㄓㄤ ㄕ)
to rely on (an advantage or someone's power)

仗勢欺人(ㄓㄤ ㄕˋ ㄑㄧ ㄖㄣ)
to bully the weaker on one's strength or power, or connection with powerful people

仗義(ㄓㄤ ㄧ)
to rely on a sense of justice

仗義執言(ㄓㄤ ㄧ ㄓ ㄧㄢ)
to speak in accordance with justice

仗義疏財(ㄓㄤ ㄧ ㄕㄨ ㄘㄞ)
to think little of one's fortune in one's enthusiasm for charity, etc.

【付】 86 ㄈㄨˋ fuh fù

1. to pay (money)
2. to deliver (goods); to consign

付託(ㄈㄨ ㄊㄨㄜ)
to entrust; to commission; to charge

付管(ㄈㄨ ㄍㄨㄢ)
to entrust the care of someone to another

付款(ㄈㄨ ㄎㄨㄢ)or 付錢(ㄈㄨ ㄑㄧㄢ)
to make payments; to pay (money); to shell out

付給(ㄈㄨ ㄐㄧ)
to pay; to deliver

付訖(ㄈㄨ ㄑㄧ)or 付清(ㄈㄨ ㄑㄧㄥ)
(said of a bill, tax, etc.) paid; all paid

付息(ㄈㄨ ㄒㄧ)
to pay interest

付現(ㄈㄨ ㄒㄧㄢ)
to pay in cash

付之一炬(ㄈㄨ ㄓ ㄧ ㄐㄩ)or 付丙(ㄈㄨ ㄅㄧㄥˇ)
to reduce to ashes; to burn; to burn down

付之一笑(ㄈㄨ ㄓ ㄧ ㄒㄧㄠ)
to laugh it away (or off)

付賬 or 付帳(ㄈㄨ ㄓㄤ)
to pay a bill

付諸東流(ㄈㄨ ㄓㄨ ㄉㄨㄥ ㄌㄧㄡ)or 付之流水(ㄈㄨ ㄓ ㄌㄧㄡ ㄕㄨㄟ)
(efforts) wasted; (accomplishments) undone or ruined; (hope) busted; irrevocably lost

付諸實施(ㄈㄨ ㄓㄨ ㄕ ㄕ)
to put into effect

付出(ㄈㄨ ㄔㄨ)
① to pay ② to give

付以重任(ㄈㄨ ㄧ ㄓㄨㄥ ㄖㄣ)
to entrust with an important post

付郵(ㄈㄨ ㄧㄡ)
to post (a letter)：to mail (a parcel)

付印(ㄈㄨ ㄧㄣ)or 付刊(ㄈㄨ ㄎㄢ)or 付梓(ㄈㄨ ㄗˇ)
① to send to (the) press for publication ② to turn over to the printing shop (after proofreading)

【仙】 87 ㄒㄧㄢ　shian xiān

1. a god; an immortal; a fairy
2. divine

仙方兒(ㄒㄧㄢ ㄈㄤ ㄦ)
a divine prescription—effective medicine

仙風道骨(ㄒㄧㄢ ㄈㄥ ㄉㄠˋ ㄍㄨ)
divine poise or bearing

仙丹(ㄒㄧㄢ ㄉㄢ)or 仙藥(ㄒㄧㄢ ㄧㄠ)
a divine pill; a panacea; a cure-all; an elixir

仙丹花(ㄒㄧㄢ ㄉㄢ ㄏㄨㄚ)
red ixora

仙桃(ㄒㄧㄢ ㄊㄠ)
a divine peach 參看「蟠桃②」

仙童(ㄒㄧㄢ ㄊㄨㄥ)
a fairy messenger boy

仙女(ㄒㄧㄢ ㄋㄩˇ)
a fairy; a· woman of divine beauty

仙姑(ㄒㄧㄢ ㄍㄨ)
① a fairy; an immortal lady ② a woman Taoist

仙鶴(ㄒㄧㄢ ㄏㄜˋ)
the crane (as a divine bird)

仙界(ㄒㄧㄢ ㄐㄧㄝ)
the land of the divine; a paradise; a fairyland

仙境(ㄒㄧㄢ ㄐㄧㄥˋ)
① a fairyland 參看「仙界」②
② a place of exquisite natural beauty

〔人部〕

仙居(ㄒㄧㄢ ㄐㄩ)
a divine abode

仙鄉(ㄒㄧㄢ ㄒㄧㄤ)
①a fairyland 參看「仙界」②
your hometown (an honorific term); 仙鄉何處? Where is your hometown?

仙逝(ㄒㄧㄢ ㄕ)or仙去(ㄒㄧㄢ ㄑㄩ)
to die (a euphemistic expression); to pass away

仙山(ㄒㄧㄢ ㄕㄢ)
a mountain inhabited by the immortals

仙術(ㄒㄧㄢ ㄕㄨ)
the supernatural feat of the immortals

仙人(ㄒㄧㄢ ㄖㄣ)
①an immortal ②a very beautiful woman

仙人跳(ㄒㄧㄢ ㄖㄣ ㄊㄧㄠ)
a badger game

仙人掌(ㄒㄧㄢ ㄖㄣ ㄓㄤ)
a prickly pear; a kind of cactus

仙姿(ㄒㄧㄢ ㄗ)
a fairylike look, appearance, or figure

仙子(ㄒㄧㄢ ㄗ)
a fairy (in the sense of a beautiful woman); an immortal

【仞】 88
ㄖㄣˋ renn rèn
1. a measure of length (approximately eight feet)
2. to measure depth

【仟】 89
ㄑㄧㄢ chian qiān
1. leader of one thousand men
2. thousand

【仡】 90
ㄧˋ yih yì
1. gallant; valiant
2. stately; majestic
3. upright

仡然(ㄧˋ ㄖㄢˊ)
standing upright

【代】 91
ㄉㄞˋ day dài
1. a generation
2. a dynasty
3. an era
4. to be a substitute or an equivalent; to take the place of

代辦(ㄉㄞˋ ㄅㄢˋ)
①to manage on behalf of another; to act for another

②a chargé d'affaires

代筆(ㄉㄞˋ ㄅㄧˇ)
to write for another; to be a ghost writer

代表(ㄉㄞˋ ㄅㄧㄠˇ)
①to represent (another person, an organization, etc.); to stand for (something) ②a representative; a delegate; a proxy

代表大會(ㄉㄞˋ ㄅㄧㄠˇ ㄉㄚˋ ㄏㄨㄟˋ)
a congress; a representative assembly (or conference)

代表團(ㄉㄞˋ ㄅㄧㄠˇ ㄊㄨㄢˊ)
a delegation (to a conference)

代表權(ㄉㄞˋ ㄅㄧㄠˇ ㄑㄩㄢˊ)
representation

代作(ㄉㄞˋ ㄗㄨㄛˋ)
representative works (of art, literature, etc.)

代步(ㄉㄞˋ ㄅㄨˋ)
the means of transportation

代庖(ㄉㄞˋ ㄆㄠˊ)
to work on behalf of another; to act in somebody's place

代名詞(ㄉㄞˋ ㄇㄧㄥˊ ㄘˊ)
a pronoun; 它是代名詞。"It" is a pronoun.

代打(ㄉㄞˋ ㄉㄚˇ)
to pinch-hit

代電(ㄉㄞˋ ㄉㄧㄢˋ)
correspondence between government agencies which do not have direct connection in the administrative chain of command

代墊(ㄉㄞˋ ㄉㄧㄢˋ)
to advance money for another

代替(ㄉㄞˋ ㄊㄧˋ)
to take the place of; to stand proxy for; to substitute

代勞(ㄉㄞˋ ㄌㄠˊ)
to labor on behalf of another (usually used as a polite expression when asking someone to do something for oneself)

代理(ㄉㄞˋ ㄌㄧˇ)
①an agent (of a business firm, organization, etc.) ②to serve as agent of; to act as the deputy of; to act for

代理貿易(ㄉㄞˋ ㄌㄧˇ ㄇㄠˋ ㄧˋ)

commission agency

代理商(ㄉㄞˋ ㄌㄧˇ ㄕㄤ)
a business agent; an agent

代理人(ㄉㄞˋ ㄌㄧˇ ㄖㄣˊ)
(legal) a representative; an agent; an attorney

代理業務(ㄉㄞˋ ㄌㄧˇ ㄧㄝˋ ㄨˋ)
to act as the deputy of another in charge of business

代溝(ㄉㄞˋ ㄍㄡ)
the generation gap

代購(ㄉㄞˋ ㄍㄡˋ)
to buy on behalf of somebody; to act as a purchasing agent

代管(ㄉㄞˋ ㄍㄨㄢˇ)
to manage, govern, or administer on behalf of another

代課(ㄉㄞˋ ㄎㄜˋ)
to teach on behalf of another teacher

代號(ㄉㄞˋ ㄏㄠˋ)
a code name

代換(ㄉㄞˋ ㄏㄨㄢˋ)
to replace

代價(ㄉㄞˋ ㄐㄧㄚˋ)
price; cost; reward: 我將付出甚麼樣的代價? What will the cost be to me?

代簽(ㄉㄞˋ ㄑㄧㄢ)
(accounting) procuration indorsement

代謝(ㄉㄞˋ ㄒㄧㄝˋ)
①to express thanks to someone on behalf of others ②to metabolize; metabolism

代銷(ㄉㄞˋ ㄒㄧㄠ)
to sell on consignment; to be commissioned to sell something; to act as a commission agent

代銷店(ㄉㄞˋ ㄒㄧㄠ ㄉㄧㄢˋ)
a commission agent

代銷商(ㄉㄞˋ ㄒㄧㄠ ㄕㄤ)
a consignee

代行職權(ㄉㄞˋ ㄒㄧㄥˊ ㄓˊ ㄑㄩㄢˊ)
to do something in an acting capacity

代序(ㄉㄞˋ ㄒㄩˋ)
an article used in lieu of a preface

代售(ㄉㄞˋ ㄕㄡˋ)
to be commissioned to sell something

代書(ㄉㄞˋ ㄕㄨ)
one who writes legal documents for others

代贖(ㄉㄞˋ ㄕㄨˊ)
redemption

代數學(ㄉㄞˋ ㄕㄨˋ ㄒㄩㄝˊ)
algebra

代人受過(ㄉㄞˋ ㄖㄣˊ ㄕㄡˋ ㄍㄨㄛˋ)
to take the blame for others

代罪羔羊(ㄉㄞˋ ㄗㄨㄟˋ ㄍㄠ ㄧㄤˊ)
a scapegoat: 他當他朋友的代罪羔羊。 He was made the scapegoat for his friend.

代議制(ㄉㄞˋ ㄧˋ ㄓˋ)
the parliamentary system

代議政治(ㄉㄞˋ ㄧˋ ㄓㄥˋ ㄓˋ)
representative government

代議士(ㄉㄞˋ ㄧˋ ㄕˋ)
a parliamentarian

代有傳人(ㄉㄞˋ ㄧㄡˇ ㄔㄨㄢˊ ㄖㄣˊ)
There are people who carry on in every generation.

代言(ㄉㄞˋ ㄧㄢˊ)
to be a spokesman; to speak in behalf of

代言人(ㄉㄞˋ ㄧㄢˊ ㄖㄣˊ)
a spokesman; a mouthpiece

代為辦理(ㄉㄞˋ ㄨㄟˊ ㄅㄢˋ ㄌㄧˇ)
to do something for another

代為說項(ㄉㄞˋ ㄨㄟˊ ㄕㄨㄛ ㄒㄧㄤˋ)
to intercede or intervene for another person; to use one's good office for the sake of another person

代遠年湮(ㄉㄞˋ ㄩㄢˇ ㄋㄧㄢˊ ㄧㄢ)
The exact year (in which a given event took place) cannot be ascertained because it happened long long ago.

代用(ㄉㄞˋ ㄩㄥˋ)
to substitute for something; to use in place of something

代用品(ㄉㄞˋ ㄩㄥˋ ㄆㄧㄣˇ)
a substitute; an ersatz

代用教員(ㄉㄞˋ ㄩㄥˋ ㄐㄧㄠˋ ㄩㄢˊ)
a substitute teacher (who has no teaching certificate)

【令】 92
1. ㄌㄧㄥˋ ling ling
1. a directive; an order
2. to order
3. to cause; to make
4. nice; good; excellent

令妹(ㄌㄧㄥˋ ㄇㄟˋ)
your younger sister (used in formal speech)

令名(ㄌㄧㄥˋ ㄇㄧㄥˊ) or 令聞(ㄌㄧㄥˋ ㄨㄣˊ) or 令望(ㄌㄧㄥˋ ㄨㄤˋ) or 令譽(ㄌㄧㄥˋ ㄩˋ)
good reputation; fame

令德(ㄌㄧㄥˋ ㄉㄜˊ)
excellent virtue

令弟(ㄌㄧㄥˋ ㄉㄧˋ)
your younger brother (used in formal speech)

令堂(ㄌㄧㄥˋ ㄊㄤˊ)
your mother (used in formal speech)

令郎(ㄌㄧㄥˋ ㄌㄤˊ) or 令嗣(ㄌㄧㄥˋ ㄙˋ)
your son (used in formal speech)

令姊(ㄌㄧㄥˋ ㄐㄧㄝˇ)
your elder sister (used in formal speech)

令箭(ㄌㄧㄥˋ ㄐㄧㄢˋ)
an arrow used as a token of authority (by field commanders in old China)

令親(ㄌㄧㄥˋ ㄑㄧㄣ)
your relative (used in formal speech)

令兄(ㄌㄧㄥˋ ㄒㄩㄥ)
your elder brother (used in formal speech)

令出如山(ㄌㄧㄥˋ ㄔㄨ ㄖㄨˊ ㄕㄢ)
(literally) Every order is as firm as a mountain.—Orders must be obeyed implicitly.

令人噴飯(ㄌㄧㄥˋ ㄖㄣˊ ㄆㄣ ㄈㄢˋ)
(said of clownish acts, witty remarks, etc.) to make people laugh

令人滿意(ㄌㄧㄥˋ ㄖㄣˊ ㄇㄢˇ ㄧˋ)
to make people contented; satisfactory

令人髮指(ㄌㄧㄥˋ ㄖㄣˊ ㄈㄚˇ ㄓˇ)
(said of enemy atrocities, heinous crimes, etc.) to make one's blood boil

令人懷疑(ㄌㄧㄥˋ ㄖㄣˊ ㄏㄨㄞˊ ㄧˊ)
to cause suspicion

令人喜歡(ㄌㄧㄥˋ ㄖㄣˊ ㄒㄧˇ ㄏㄨㄢ)
to be liked by most people

令尊(ㄌㄧㄥˋ ㄗㄨㄣ)
your father (used in formal speech)

令嬡(ㄌㄧㄥˋ ㄞˋ) or 令媛(ㄌㄧㄥˋ ㄩㄢˊ)
your daughter (used in formal speech)

令岳(ㄌㄧㄥˋ ㄩㄝˋ)
your father-in-law (used in formal speech)

【令】 92
2. ㄌㄧㄥˊ ling ling
a ream (of paper)

【以】 93
ㄧˇ yiˇ yiˇ
by means of; because of

以博一粲(ㄧˇ ㄅㄛˊ ㄧˋ ㄘㄢˋ)
for your entertainment

以備(ㄧˇ ㄅㄟˋ)
to be ready for

以備萬一(ㄧˇ ㄅㄟˋ ㄨㄢˋ ㄧ)
to provide against any accidental happenings

以暴易暴(ㄧˇ ㄅㄠˋ ㄧˋ ㄅㄠˋ)
to displace violence with violence; to replace evil with evil

以便(ㄧˇ ㄅㄧㄢˋ)
① so as to; in order to ② for the convenience of

以不變應萬變(ㄧˇ ㄅㄨˋ ㄅㄧㄢˋ ㄧㄥˋ ㄨㄢˋ ㄅㄧㄢˋ)
to cope with shifting events by sticking to a fundamental principle or policy

以偏概全(ㄧˇ ㄆㄧㄢ ㄍㄞˋ ㄑㄩㄢˊ)
(literally) to take the part for the whole—to make sweeping comments

以貌取人(ㄧˇ ㄇㄠˋ ㄑㄩˇ ㄖㄣˊ)
to judge a person by his appearance or looks

以免(ㄧˇ ㄇㄧㄢˇ)
in order to avoid; so as not to

以大欺小(ㄧˇ ㄉㄚˋ ㄑㄧ ㄒㄧㄠˇ)
to bully the weak

以德報怨(ㄧˇ ㄉㄜˊ ㄅㄠˋ ㄩㄢˋ)
to repay injury with kindness; to return good for evil

以德服人(ㄧˇ ㄉㄜˊ ㄈㄨˊ ㄖㄣˊ)
to win popular following by dint of one's virtue

以毒攻毒(ㄧˇ ㄉㄨˊ ㄍㄨㄥ ㄉㄨˊ)
to fight evil with evil; to use poison as an antidote for poison; to fight fire with fire

以杜後患(ㄧˇ ㄉㄨˋ ㄏㄡˋ ㄏㄨㄢˋ)
to forestall future trouble

以多為勝(ㄧˇ ㄉㄨㄛ ㄨㄟˊ ㄕㄥˋ)
to crush an enemy by numerical superiority

以太(ㄧˇ ㄊㄞˋ)
(physics) ether

以退為進(ㄧˇ ㄊㄨㄟˋ ㄨㄟˊ ㄐㄧㄣˋ)
(literally) to retreat in order to advance—to make

〔人部〕

【人部】

concessions in order to gain advantages

以內 (ㄧˇ ㄋㄟˋ)
within

以農立國 (ㄧˇ ㄋㄨㄥˊ ㄌㄧˋ ㄍㄨㄛˊ)
a nation based on agricultural economy

以來 (ㄧˇ ㄌㄞˊ)
since (a given point of time in the past)

以淚洗面 (ㄧˇ ㄌㄟˋ ㄒㄧˇ ㄇㄧㄢˋ)
to cry with abandon

以理服人 (ㄧˇ ㄌㄧˇ ㄈㄨˊ ㄖㄣˊ)
to convince a person by reasoning

以禮相待 (ㄧˇ ㄌㄧˇ ㄒㄧㄤ ㄉㄞˋ)
to treat somebody with due respect

以利民生 (ㄧˇ ㄌㄧˋ ㄇㄧㄣˊ ㄕㄥ)
for the benefit of people's livelihood

以鄰爲壑 (ㄧˇ ㄌㄧㄣˊ ㄨㄟˊ ㄏㄨㄛˋ)
to profit oneself at the expense of others

以卵投石 (ㄧˇ ㄌㄨㄢˇ ㄊㄡˊ ㄕˊ)
to hurl eggs against a stone — to fight a hopeless battle

以古非今 (ㄧˇ ㄍㄨˇ ㄈㄟ ㄐㄧㄣ)
to belittle the present by extolling the past

以寡敵衆 (ㄧˇ ㄍㄨㄚˇ ㄉㄧˊ ㄓㄨㄥˋ)
to fight a numerically superior enemy

以廣招徠 (ㄧˇ ㄍㄨㄤˇ ㄓㄠ ㄌㄞˊ)
in order to promote patronage or sales

以工代賑 (ㄧˇ ㄍㄨㄥ ㄉㄞˋ ㄓㄣˋ)
to relieve people in disaster areas by giving them employment instead of outright grant

以攻爲守 (ㄧˇ ㄍㄨㄥ ㄨㄟˊ ㄕㄡˇ)
to take the offensive in a basically defensive operation

以匡不逮 (ㄧˇ ㄎㄨㄤ ㄅㄨˋ ㄉㄞˋ)
to correct one's mistakes or make up one's shortcomings (usually used when soliciting advice)

以空間爭取時間 (ㄧˇ ㄎㄨㄥ ㄐㄧㄢ ㄓㄥ ㄑㄩˇ ㄕˊ ㄐㄧㄢ)
to trade space for time (as a military strategy)

以後 (ㄧˇ ㄏㄡˋ)
after (a given point or a period of time); afterward

以及 (ㄧˇ ㄐㄧˊ)
and; including; as well as

以己度人 (ㄧˇ ㄐㄧˇ ㄉㄨㄛˋ ㄖㄣˊ)
to assume that other people think the same way as oneself

以假亂眞 (ㄧˇ ㄐㄧㄚˇ ㄌㄨㄢˋ ㄓㄣ)
to mix the spurious with the genuine

以解倒懸 (ㄧˇ ㄐㄧㄝˇ ㄉㄠˋ ㄒㄩㄢˊ)
to save one from a crisis or to help weather a critical situation (usually used in asking for help)

以介眉壽 (ㄧˇ ㄐㄧㄝˋ ㄇㄟˊ ㄕㄡˋ)
Many happy returns of the day. (a cliché in offering birthday congratulations)

以救燃眉 (ㄧˇ ㄐㄧㄡˋ ㄖㄢˊ ㄇㄟˊ)
to meet a pressing need

以進爲退 (ㄧˇ ㄐㄧㄣˋ ㄨㄟˊ ㄊㄨㄟˋ)
to pretend to move ahead in order to hide the intention to retreat

以儆效尤 (ㄧˇ ㄐㄧㄥˇ ㄒㄧㄠˋ ㄧㄡˊ)
to warn others against making the same mistake

以竟全功 (ㄧˇ ㄐㄧㄥˋ ㄑㄩㄢˊ ㄍㄨㄥ)
to bring a task to a successful conclusion

以其人之道，還治其人之身 (ㄧˇ ㄑㄧˊ ㄖㄣˊ ㄓ ㄉㄠˋ，ㄏㄨㄢˊ ㄓˋ ㄑㄧˊ ㄖㄣˊ ㄓ ㄕㄣ)
Pay someone (back) in his own coin. 或 Deal with a man as he deals with you.

以前 (ㄧˇ ㄑㄧㄢˊ)
before (a given point or a period of time); previously

以勤補拙 (ㄧˇ ㄑㄧㄣˊ ㄅㄨˇ ㄓㄨㄛˊ)
to amend stupidity by diligence

以下 (ㄧˇ ㄒㄧㄚˋ)
below (a given point or line)

以饗讀者 (ㄧˇ ㄒㄧㄤˇ ㄉㄨˊ ㄓㄜˇ)
to offer to the reader

以直報怨 (ㄧˇ ㄓˊ ㄅㄠˋ ㄩㄢˋ)
justice in return for injustice; to repay injustice with justice

以至 (ㄧˇ ㄓˋ)
① up to (a given point); until ② so…that

以致 (ㄧˇ ㄓˋ)
so that; with the result that

以正視聽 (ㄧˇ ㄓㄥˋ ㄕˋ ㄊㄧㄥ)
in order to ensure a right understanding of the facts

以珠彈雀 (ㄧˇ ㄓㄨ ㄊㄢˊ ㄑㄩㄝˋ)
to make big investment for small returns

以衆暴寡 (ㄧˇ ㄓㄨㄥˋ ㄅㄠˋ ㄍㄨㄚˇ)
to bully the minority

以示公平 (ㄧˇ ㄕˋ ㄍㄨㄥ ㄆㄧㄥˊ)
to show fairness or impartiality

以釋群疑 (ㄧˇ ㄕˋ ㄑㄩㄣˊ ㄧˊ)
to allay doubt in the public's mind

以手加額 (ㄧˇ ㄕㄡˇ ㄐㄧㄚ ㄜˊ)
to exhibit gratification

以身相許 (ㄧˇ ㄕㄣ ㄒㄧㄤ ㄒㄩˇ)
(said of girls) to pledge to marry somebody

以身殉職 (ㄧˇ ㄕㄣ ㄒㄩㄣˋ ㄓˊ)
to die at one's post

以身試法 (ㄧˇ ㄕㄣ ㄕˋ ㄈㄚˇ)
to defy the law; to dare to violate the law

以身作則 (ㄧˇ ㄕㄣ ㄗㄨㄛˋ ㄗㄜˊ)
(said of people holding responsible positions or the head of a family) to set examples by one's own action

以上 (ㄧˇ ㄕㄤˋ)
above (a given point or line)

以升量石 (ㄧˇ ㄕㄥ ㄌㄧㄤˊ ㄉㄢˋ)
A little man cannot understand the ways of a true gentleman.

以柔克剛 (ㄧˇ ㄖㄡˊ ㄎㄜˋ ㄍㄤ)
Soft and fair goes far. 或 Willows are weak, yet they bend other wood.

以人廢言 (ㄧˇ ㄖㄣˊ ㄈㄟˋ ㄧㄢˊ)
to dismiss someone's statement as untrue or unimportant because of his ill reputation

以子之矛，攻子之盾 (ㄧˇ ㄗˇ ㄓ ㄇㄠˊ，ㄍㄨㄥ ㄗˇ ㄓ ㄉㄨㄣˋ)
to attack someone by exploiting his weakness

以奏膚功 (ㄧˇ ㄗㄡˋ ㄈㄨ ㄍㄨㄥ)
to complete a monumental task

以詞害意 (ㄧˇ ㄘˊ ㄏㄞˋ ㄧˋ)
to sacrifice clarity in the use of wrong words for expression

以此 (ㄧˇ ㄘˇ)
for this reason; on this account

以此類推 (ㄧˇ ㄘˇ ㄌㄟˋ ㄊㄨㄟ)
The rest can be done in the same manner. 或 The rest can be deduced accordingly.

以此為戒 (ㄧˇ ㄘˇ ㄨㄟˊ ㄐㄧㄝˋ)
to take this as a lesson

以次 (ㄧˇ ㄘˋ)
in turn; in due order

以色列 (ㄧˇ ㄙㄜˋ ㄌㄧㄝˋ)
Israel

以色列人 (ㄧˇ ㄙㄜˋ ㄌㄧㄝˋ ㄖㄣˊ)
Israelis; Israelites

以訛傳訛 (ㄧˇ ㄜˊ ㄔㄨㄢˊ ㄜˊ)
(said of rumors) to convey incorrectly what is already incorrect

以一當十 (ㄧˇ ㄧ ㄉㄤ ㄕˊ)
to pit one against ten

以一警百 (ㄧˇ ㄧ ㄐㄧㄥˇ ㄅㄞˇ)
to punish one as a warning to the others

以夷制夷 (ㄧˇ ㄧˊ ㄓˋ ㄧˊ)
to play off one foreign power against another (so as to prevent them from invading one's own country)

以逸待勞 (ㄧˇ ㄧˋ ㄉㄞˋ ㄌㄠˊ)
to wait in comfort for an exhausted enemy; to conserve strength while the enemy tires himself through a long march

以牙還牙 (ㄧˇ ㄧㄚˊ ㄏㄨㄢˊ ㄧㄚˊ)
an eye for an eye, a tooth for a tooth; to repay evil with evil

以有易無 (ㄧˇ ㄧㄡˇ ㄧˋ ㄨˊ)
to trade what one has in abundance for what one does not have; to barter

以外 (ㄧˇ ㄨㄞˋ)
①other than; besides; in addition: 除我以外沒人知道。No one knows besides me. ②outside; without; beyond

以為 (ㄧˇ ㄨㄟˊ)
to take …for (or to be); to regard…as; to think; to consider

以文會友 (ㄧˇ ㄨㄣˊ ㄏㄨㄟˋ ㄧㄡˇ)
to gather friends together for literary activities

以往 (ㄧˇ ㄨㄤˇ)
in the past; formerly

以怨報德 (ㄧˇ ㄩㄢˋ ㄅㄠˋ ㄉㄜˊ)
to bite the hand that feeds one

【仨】 94 ㄙㄚ sā
three (Peking colloquialism)

【仝】 95 (同) ㄊㄨㄥˊ torng tóng
a Chinese family name

四畫

【仰】 96 ㄧㄤˇ yeang yǎng
1. to look up
2. to admire, admire or revere
3. to lean or rely upon
4. to swallow

仰不愧天 (ㄧㄤˇ ㄅㄨˋ ㄎㄨㄟˋ ㄊㄧㄢ)
to feel no shame before God

仰面朝天 (ㄧㄤˇ ㄇㄧㄢˋ ㄔㄠˊ ㄊㄧㄢ)
to lie on one's back

仰慕 (ㄧㄤˇ ㄇㄨˋ)
to adore; to regard with admiration; to admire and respect

仰藥 (ㄧㄤˇ ㄧㄠˋ) or 仰藥 (ㄧㄤˇ ㄧㄠˋ)
to swallow or take poison

仰天長歎 (ㄧㄤˇ ㄊㄧㄢ ㄔㄤˊ ㄊㄢˋ)
to sigh deeply

仰天長嘯 (ㄧㄤˇ ㄊㄧㄢ ㄔㄤˊ ㄒㄧㄠˋ)
to make a long cry into the air

仰能合意 (ㄧㄤˇ ㄋㄥˊ ㄏㄜˊ ㄧˋ)
to hope it is what you want

仰賴 (ㄧㄤˇ ㄌㄞˋ)
to look to (somebody for help); to rely upon

仰光 (ㄧㄤˇ ㄍㄨㄤ)
Rangoon, capital of Burma

仰給 (ㄧㄤˇ ㄐㄧˇ)
to depend on

仰角 (ㄧㄤˇ ㄐㄧㄠˇ)
(mathematics) an angle of elevation

仰求 (ㄧㄤˇ ㄑㄧㄡˊ)
to be dependent on someone; to turn to someone for help, favor, etc.

仰止 (ㄧㄤˇ ㄓˇ)
admiration

仰仗 (ㄧㄤˇ ㄓㄤˋ)
to rely on (other's influence, power, etc.)

仰食於人 (ㄧㄤˇ ㄕˊ ㄩˊ ㄖㄣˊ)
to depend on another person for living

仰事俯畜 (ㄧㄤˇ ㄕˋ ㄈㄨˇ ㄒㄩˋ)
to support parents as well as wife and children

仰人鼻息 (ㄧㄤˇ ㄖㄣˊ ㄅㄧˊ ㄒㄧˊ)
to rely on others and have to watch their every expression; to be dependent on another's whims and pleasures

仰臥 (ㄧㄤˇ ㄨㄛˋ)
to lie on the back

仰臥起坐 (ㄧㄤˇ ㄨㄛˋ ㄑㄧˇ ㄗㄨㄛˋ)
(sports) sit-up

仰望 (ㄧㄤˇ ㄨㄤˋ)
①to hope ②to rely upon (someone for support, help, etc.)

仰泳 (ㄧㄤˇ ㄩㄥˇ)
a backstroke

【仲】 97 ㄓㄨㄥˋ jonq zhòng
1. in the middle; between two entities
2. the second in order of birth

仲冬 (ㄓㄨㄥˋ ㄉㄨㄥ)
the second of the winter months (i.e., the eleventh moon); midwinter

仲尼 (ㄓㄨㄥˋ ㄋㄧˊ)
another name of Confucius

仲秋 (ㄓㄨㄥˋ ㄑㄧㄡ)
the second of the autumn months (i.e., the eighth moon); midautumn

仲夏 (ㄓㄨㄥˋ ㄒㄧㄚˋ)
the second of the summer months (i.e., the fifth moon); midsummer

仲春 (ㄓㄨㄥˋ ㄔㄨㄣ)
the second of the spring months (i.e., the second moon); midspring

仲裁 (ㄓㄨㄥˋ ㄘㄞˊ)
to arbitrate; arbitration

【仳】 98 ㄆㄧˇ pii pǐ
to part company

仳離 (ㄆㄧˇ ㄌㄧˊ)
to part (from one's spouse); to divorce

【仵】 99 ㄨˇ wuu wǔ
opposing; wrong

仵作 (ㄨˇ ㄗㄨㄛˋ)
a coroner

【件】 100 ㄐㄧㄢˋ jiann jiàn
an auxiliary noun applied to things, clothes, etc.

件件 (ㄐㄧㄢˋ ㄐㄧㄢˋ) or 件件兒 (ㄐㄧㄢˋ)

〔人部〕

［人部］

ㄐㄧㄢㄦ

all (of the things or items in question)

件數(ㄐㄧㄢ ㄕㄨˋ)or件數兒(ㄐㄧㄢ ㄕㄨˋ)

the number of things, items, suits, etc.

【任】 101　1. ㄖㄣˋ　renn rèn

1. a duty

2. to let (one act at will): 不要任小孩外出。Don't let the child go out.

3. to employ (one for a job): 這女子在郵局任職。This girl is employed at the post office.

4. to bear (a burden)

5. an official post; office

任便(ㄖㄣˋ ㄅㄧㄢˋ)

as you please; as you see fit: 你來不來任便。You may come or not as you please.

任憑(ㄖㄣˋ ㄆㄧㄥˊ)

without restriction; (to allow someone to do something) at will; despite

任免(ㄖㄣˋ ㄇㄧㄢˇ)

hiring and firing; employment and discharge

任命(ㄖㄣˋ ㄇㄧㄥˋ)

to appoint (someone to an office); appointment

任命狀(ㄖㄣˋ ㄇㄧㄥˋ ㄓㄨㄤˋ)

a letter (or certificate) of appointment

任達(ㄖㄣˋ ㄉㄚˊ)

(said of one's disposition) unrestrained

任勞任怨(ㄖㄣˋ ㄌㄠˊ ㄖㄣˋ ㄩㄢˋ)

to do something without complaint despite hardships and criticisms

任課(ㄖㄣˋ ㄎㄜˋ)

to teach a course (at school)

任何(ㄖㄣˋ ㄏㄜˊ)

any; whatever

任期(ㄖㄣˋ ㄑㄧˊ)

a term of office; the tenure of office; a tour of duty

任俠(ㄖㄣˋ ㄒㄧㄚˊ)

to be generous and chivalrous

任性(ㄖㄣˋ ㄒㄧㄥˋ)

doing as one pleases; unrestrained; uninhibited

任職(ㄖㄣˋ ㄓˊ)

to hold a post; to be in office

任重道遠(ㄖㄣˋ ㄓㄨㄥˋ ㄉㄠˋ ㄩㄢˇ)

The load is heavy, while the way is long.

任人(ㄖㄣˋ ㄖㄣˊ)

to let people (do something without restriction)

任人唯賢(ㄖㄣˋ ㄖㄣˊ ㄨㄟˊ ㄒㄧㄢˊ)

to appoint a person according to his virtue and ability; to choose a person for an office according to his merits

任從(ㄖㄣˋ ㄘㄨㄥˊ)

to let (one do something as he pleases)

任意(ㄖㄣˋ ㄧˋ)

arbitrary; at will

任務(ㄖㄣˋ ㄨˋ)

duty; responsibility

任用(ㄖㄣˋ ㄩㄥˋ)

to employ; to hire; to engage

【任】 101　2. ㄖㄣˊ　ren rén

a Chinese family name

【仿】 102　(倣) ㄈㄤˇ　faang fǎng

to imitate; to copy

仿單(ㄈㄤˇ ㄉㄢ)

advertising literature attached to merchandise

仿古(ㄈㄤˇ ㄍㄨˇ)

to imitate the ancient style

仿效(ㄈㄤˇ ㄒㄧㄠˋ)

to imitate; to copy; to follow the example of

仿製(ㄈㄤˇ ㄓˋ)or仿造(ㄈㄤˇ ㄗㄠˋ)

to manufacture an imitation of something already in market

仿製品(ㄈㄤˇ ㄓˋ ㄆㄧㄣˇ)

an imitation

仿照(ㄈㄤˇ ㄓㄠˋ)

after the example of; to pattern after

仿宋(ㄈㄤˇ ㄙㄨㄥˋ)

the imitation of the style of Chinese characters prevalent in the Sung Dynasty

仿宋本(ㄈㄤˇ ㄙㄨㄥˋ ㄅㄣˇ)

the reprint (of a book) in imitation of the Sung edition

仿宋體(ㄈㄤˇ ㄙㄨㄥˋ ㄊㄧˇ)

a kind of printing type in imitation of the style of Chinese characters prevalent

during the Sung Dynasty

【企】 103　ㄑㄧˇ　chii qǐ

1. to stand on tiptoe

2. to hope; to long; to expect

企盼(ㄑㄧˇ ㄆㄢˋ)or企望(ㄑㄧˇ ㄨㄤˋ)

to expect or hope with eagerness

企慕(ㄑㄧˇ ㄇㄨˋ)

to admire greatly

企圖(ㄑㄧˇ ㄊㄨˊ)

①to intend; to plan; to scheme; to attempt ②an intention; a plan; a scheme

企圖心(ㄑㄧˇ ㄊㄨˊ ㄒㄧㄣ)

enterprising spirit; aggressiveness

企管(ㄑㄧˇ ㄍㄨㄢˇ)

business management

企劃(ㄑㄧˇ ㄏㄨㄚˋ)

to make a scheme for; to design; to lay out; to plan

企求(ㄑㄧˇ ㄑㄧㄡˊ)

to desire; to seek for; to hanker for

企踵(ㄑㄧˇ ㄓㄨㄥˇ)

to stand on tiptoe

企鵝(ㄑㄧˇ ㄜˊ)

a penguin

企業(ㄑㄧˇ ㄧㄝˋ)

a business enterprise; an enterprise

企業家(ㄑㄧˇ ㄧㄝˋ ㄐㄧㄚ)

an entrepreneur

企望(ㄑㄧˇ ㄨㄤˋ)

to hope for; to look forward to

【伉】 104　ㄎㄤˋ　kanq kàng

a spouse

伉儷(ㄎㄤˋ ㄌㄧˋ)

a married couple (in formal speech)

【伊】 105　ㄧ　i yī

1. he; she

2. a Chinese family name

伊伯利安牛島(ㄧ ㄅㄛˊ ㄌㄧˋ ㄢ ㄋㄧㄡˊ ㄉㄠˇ)

the Iberian Peninsula

伊凡(ㄧ ㄈㄢˊ)

transliteration of Ivan

伊底帕斯(ㄧ ㄉㄧˇ ㄆㄚˋ ㄙ)

Oedipus

伊甸樂園(ㄧ ㄉㄧㄢˋ ㄌㄜˋ ㄩㄢˊ)

the Garden of Eden

伊拉克(ㄧ ㄌㄚ ㄎㄜˋ)

〔人部〕

Iraq
伊拉瓦底江(ㄧㄎㄚ ㄨㄚ ㄉㄧ ㄐㄧㄤ)
the Irawadi River

伊朗(ㄧ ㄌㄤ)
Iran

伊犂(ㄧ ㄌㄧˊ)
Ili, an important town in western Sinkiang

伊利諾斯(ㄧ ㄌㄧˋ ㄋㄨㄛˋ ㄙ)
Illinois, U.S.A.

伊利湖(ㄧ ㄌㄧˋ ㄏㄨˊ)
the Erie Lake

伊利莎白(ㄧ ㄌㄧˋ ㄕㄚ ㄅㄞˊ)
transliteration of Elizabeth

伊人(ㄧ ㄖㄣˊ)
that man (in poetry or song)

伊斯坦堡(ㄧ ㄙ ㄊㄢˇ ㄅㄠˇ)
Istanbul, a Turkish city

伊斯蘭(ㄧ ㄙ ㄌㄢˊ)
Islam

伊斯蘭教徒(ㄧ ㄙ ㄌㄢˊ ㄐㄧㄠˋ ㄊㄨˊ)
a Moslem

伊索寓言(ㄧ ㄙㄨㄛˇ ㄩˋ ㄧㄢˊ)
Aesop's Fables

伊于胡底(ㄧ ㄩˊ ㄏㄨˊ ㄉㄧˇ)
(not knowing) when it will stop or where it will lead to

伊鬱(ㄧ ㄩˋ)
melancholy; dejection; depression; despondence; gloom

【伋】 106 ㄐㄧˊ jyi jí
1. deceptive
2. name of Tzu-szu (子思), grandson of Confucius

伋伋(ㄐㄧˊ ㄐㄧˊ)
deceptive

【伍】 107 ㄨˇ wuu wǔ
1. a military unit of five soldiers (in the Chou Dynasty)
2. as in 行伍——the army
3. a Chinese family name
4. to associate (with a person): 大家都不願意與他為伍。 Everyone is unwilling to associate with him.
5. five

伍長(ㄨˇ ㄓㄤˇ)
a leader of a military unit of five soldiers (in former times)

【伎】 108 ㄐㄧˋ jih jì
talent; ability; skill

伎倆(ㄐㄧˋ ㄌㄧㄤˇ)
skill; dexterity; craft

伎藝(ㄐㄧˋ ㄧˋ)
① mechanical arts ② expert skill

【伏】 109 ㄈㄨˊ fwu fú
1. to prostrate; to yield
2. to hide; to lie in ambush

伏筆(ㄈㄨˊ ㄅㄧˇ)
a remark in writing made with a view to preparing the reader for what is to follow

伏兵(ㄈㄨˊ ㄅㄧㄥ)
an ambush

伏法(ㄈㄨˊ ㄈㄚˇ) or 伏誅(ㄈㄨˊ ㄓㄨ)
to plead guilty and be executed

伏地挺身(ㄈㄨˊ ㄉㄧˋ ㄊㄧㄥˇ ㄕㄣ)
push-up

伏特(ㄈㄨˊ ㄊㄜˋ)
(electricity) a volt

伏特計(ㄈㄨˊ ㄊㄜˋ ㄐㄧˋ)
a voltmeter

伏特加(ㄈㄨˊ ㄊㄜˋ ㄐㄧㄚ)
(spirits) vodka

伏貼(ㄈㄨˊ ㄊㄧㄝ)
① comfortable; fitting ② to acknowledge someone's merits, etc. sincerely

伏櫪(ㄈㄨˊ ㄌㄧˋ)
to be in the stable—(figuratively) obedient: 老驥伏櫪，志在千里。 The old horse in the stable is yet ambitious to achieve heroic deeds.

伏流(ㄈㄨˊ ㄌㄧㄡˊ)
(geography) subterranean drainage; an underground stream

伏擊(ㄈㄨˊ ㄐㄧˊ)
to attack from ambush

伏祈(ㄈㄨˊ ㄑㄧˊ)
to beg (used in letters to one's elders or superiors)

伏氣(ㄈㄨˊ ㄑㄧˋ)
to yield or submit willingly

伏羲(ㄈㄨˊ ㄒㄧ)
Fu-hsi, a legendary Chinese ruler credited with the introduction of farming, fishing and animal husbandry

伏尸遍野(ㄈㄨˊ ㄕ ㄅㄧㄢˋ ㄧㄝˇ)
The battlefield is littered with the (enemy) dead.

伏輸(ㄈㄨˊ ㄕㄨ)
to concede (an election, a game, etc.); to admit defeat

伏罪(ㄈㄨˊ ㄗㄨㄟˋ)
① to admit guilt ② to be executed

伏藏(ㄈㄨˊ ㄘㄤˊ)
to lie in ambush; to hide

伏案(ㄈㄨˊ ㄢˋ)
absorbed in work at one's desk

【伐】 110 ㄈㄚ fa fā
(又讀 ㄈㄚˊ far fá)
1. to cut (wood)
2. to attack; to smite

伐木(ㄈㄚˊ ㄇㄨˋ)
to fell trees

伐柯(ㄈㄚˊ ㄎㄜ)
① to hew the wood for an axe-handle ② (figuratively) to be a go-between

伐罪(ㄈㄚˊ ㄗㄨㄟˋ)
to punish the guilty

【休】 111 ㄒㄧㄡ shiou xiū
1. rest; to rest
2. to stop; to cease
3. happiness; joy; weal: 他們休戚與共。 They share weal and woe.

休兵(ㄒㄧㄡ ㄅㄧㄥ) or 休戰(ㄒㄧㄡ ㄓㄢˋ)
① to stop fighting; to cease fire ② a truce; an armistice

休眠(ㄒㄧㄡ ㄇㄧㄢˊ)
(biology) dormancy

休提(ㄒㄧㄡ ㄊㄧˊ)
do not mention

休倫湖(ㄒㄧㄡ ㄌㄨㄣˊ ㄏㄨˊ)
the Huron Lake

休怪(ㄒㄧㄡ ㄍㄨㄞˋ)
① to stop blaming ② to stop wondering

休克(ㄒㄧㄡ ㄎㄜˋ)
shock (in medical science)

休火山(ㄒㄧㄡ ㄏㄨㄛˇ ㄕㄢ)
a dormant volcano

休會(ㄒㄧㄡ ㄏㄨㄟˋ)
to adjourn a meeting; adjournment

休假(ㄒㄧㄡ ㄐㄧㄚˋ)
a holiday; to have a holiday

休咎(ㄒㄧㄡ ㄐㄧㄡˋ)
good fortune and ill

休妻(ㄒㄧㄡ ㄑㄧ)
to divorce one's wife

休戚(ㄒㄧㄡ ㄑㄧ)
weal and woe; for better and worse

【人部】

休戚相關(ㄒㄧㄡ ㄑㄧ ㄒㄧㄤ ㄍㄨㄢ)
to share joys and sorrows with each other

休息(ㄒㄧㄡ ㄒㄧ)
to have a rest; to rest

休息(ㄒㄧㄡ ㄒㄧ)
to rest from work; to take a rest; rest

休息(ㄒㄧㄡ ㄒㄧ)
①to stop for rest; to take a rest ②to take a nap

休閒(ㄒㄧㄡ ㄒㄧㄢˊ)
leisure; relaxation; ease

休閒服(ㄒㄧㄡ ㄒㄧㄢˊ ㄈㄨˊ)
casual wear; sports wear

休想(ㄒㄧㄡ ㄒㄧㄤˇ)
to stop thinking (about something); to stop dreaming: 你休想逃脫。Stop thinking you can get away.

休學(ㄒㄧㄡ ㄒㄩㄝˊ)
a leave of absence (for a considerable period of time) from school

休止(ㄒㄧㄡ ㄓˇ)
to stop; to cease

休止符(ㄒㄧㄡ ㄓˇ ㄈㄨˊ)
a sign of rests in staff notation

休戰(ㄒㄧㄡ ㄓㄢˋ)
to stop fighting; a truce

休書(ㄒㄧㄡ ㄕㄨ)
a divorce paper (signed by the husband in old China)

休業(ㄒㄧㄡ ㄧㄝˋ)
to suspend business; to close the store (for a holiday)

休業式(ㄒㄧㄡ ㄧㄝˋ ㄕˋ)
a semester closing ceremony

休養(ㄒㄧㄡ ㄧㄤˇ)
to rest; to recuperate: 他在病後到海濱休養。He went to the seaside to recuperate after his illness.

休養生息(ㄒㄧㄡ ㄧㄤˇ ㄕㄥ ㄒㄧˊ)
(said of a nation) to recuperate and multiply; to rest and build up strength

【伙】 112
ㄏㄨㄛˇ huoo huǒ

1 a companion; a colleague
2. household goods

伙伴(ㄏㄨㄛˇ ㄅㄢˋ)or伙伴兒(ㄏㄨㄛˇ ㄅㄢˋ ㄦˊ)
a companion; a colleague

伙房(ㄏㄨㄛˇ ㄈㄤˊ)
a kitchen (in a school, factory, etc.)

伙夫(ㄏㄨㄛˇ ㄈㄨ)or伙頭軍(ㄏㄨㄛˇ ㄊㄡˊ ㄐㄩㄣ)
a cook (in military barracks or troops); kitchen police

伙同(ㄏㄨㄛˇ ㄊㄨㄥˊ)
in league with

伙計(ㄏㄨㄛˇ ㄐㄧˋ)
a shop clerk

伙食(ㄏㄨㄛˇ ㄕˊ)
meals

五畫

【伯】 113
ㄅㄛˊ bor bó
(又讀 ㄅㄞˇ bae bǎi)

1. one's father's elder brother; an uncle
2. a rank of the nobility—a count

伯伯(ㄅㄛˊ ·ㄅㄛ)
an uncle (one's father's elder brother)

伯明罕(ㄅㄛˊ ㄇㄧㄥˊ ㄏㄢˇ)
Birmingham, an industrial city in England

伯母(ㄅㄛˊ ㄇㄨˇ)
an aunt (the wife of one's father's elder brother)

伯父(ㄅㄛˊ ㄈㄨˋ)
an uncle (one's father's elder brother)

伯樂(ㄅㄛˊ ㄌㄜˋ)
a man in the Chou Dynasty, who was famous for his being good at examining the qualities of horses

伯勞(ㄅㄛˊ ㄌㄠˊ)
the shrike

伯利恆(ㄅㄛˊ ㄌㄧˋ ㄏㄥˊ)
Bethlehem, a town in Palestine where Jesus Christ was born

伯爵(ㄅㄛˊ ㄐㄩㄝˊ)
a rank of the nobility—a count

伯爵夫人(ㄅㄛˊ ㄐㄩㄝˊ ㄈㄨ ㄖㄣˊ)
a countess

伯仲之間(ㄅㄛˊ ㄓㄨㄥˋ ㄓ ㄐㄧㄢ)
about the same (in terms of competence, quality, etc.)

伯仲叔季(ㄅㄛˊ ㄓㄨㄥˋ ㄕㄨ ㄐㄧˋ)
the eldest, second, third and youngest of brothers—order of seniority among brothers

伯爾尼(ㄅㄛˊ ㄦˇ ㄋㄧˊ)
Bern, capital of Switzerland

伯爾格來德(ㄅㄛˊ ㄦˇ ㄍㄜˊ ㄌㄞˊ ㄉㄜˊ)
Belgrade, capital of Yugoslavia

【估】 114
1. ㄍㄨ gu gū
to estimate; to calculate; to evaluate

估量(ㄍㄨ ㄌㄧㄤˊ)or估計(ㄍㄨ ㄐㄧˋ)
to estimate; to make an estimate; to calculate; to reckon; to conjecture

估價(ㄍㄨ ㄐㄧㄚˋ)
to estimate cost or value; to evaluate; to appraise

估價單(ㄍㄨ ㄐㄧㄚˋ ㄉㄢ)
a list of cost estimate (prepared for the prospective customer, client, etc.)

估稅(ㄍㄨ ㄕㄨㄟˋ)
sales tax 亦作「貨物稅」or「銷售稅」

【估】 114
2. ㄍㄨˋ guh gù
to sell (used clothing)

估衣鋪(ㄍㄨˋ ㄧ ㄆㄨˋ)
a secondhand clothes store

【你】 115
ㄋㄧˇ nii nǐ
you (singular)

你們(ㄋㄧˇ ·ㄇㄣ)
you (plural)

你老(ㄋㄧˇ ㄌㄠˇ)
you (in addressing an elder)

你好(ㄋㄧˇ ㄏㄠˇ)
How do you do? 或 How are you?

你死我活(ㄋㄧˇ ㄙˇ ㄨㄛˇ ㄏㄨㄛˊ)
(to fight) to the bitter end; (to fight) until either of the combatants is killed; to fight *à outrance*

【伴】 116
ㄅㄢˋ bann bàn
1. a companion
2. to accompany

伴娘(ㄅㄢˋ ㄋㄧㄤˊ)
the maid of honor

伴郎(ㄅㄢˋ ㄌㄤˊ)
the best man

伴侶(ㄅㄢˋ ㄌㄩˇ)or伴兒(ㄅㄢˋ ㄦˊ)
a companion; a pal; a buddy; a chum

伴君如伴虎(ㄅㄢˋ ㄐㄩㄣ ㄖㄨˊ ㄅㄢˋ ㄏㄨˇ)
To be in the king's company is tantamount to living with

a tiger (which makes one feel apprehensive all the time)

伴唱(ㄅㄢ ㄔㄤ)
①a vocal accompaniment ② to accompany (a singer)

伴奏(ㄅㄢ ㄗㄡ)
to accompany (a soloist); to play an accompaniment

伴宿(ㄅㄢ ㄙㄨ)
①to keep vigil at a funeral ②(said of a prostitute) to pass the night with a person

伴隨(ㄅㄢ ㄙㄨㄟ)
to accompany; to follow

伴送(ㄅㄢ ㄙㄨㄥ)
to escort; 我常伴送她回家。I often escort her home.

伴舞(ㄅㄢ ㄨ)
to be a dancing partner

【伶】 117　ㄌㄧㄥ ling líng
1. a drama performer; a theatrical performer; an actor; an actress
2. lonely; solitary
3. clever; intelligent

伶仃(ㄌㄧㄥ ㄉㄧㄥ)
lonely; solitary

伶俐(ㄌㄧㄥ ㄌㄧ)
clever; intelligent; cute; sharp; bright; smart

伶人(ㄌㄧㄥ ㄖㄣˊ)
a theatrical performer; a drama performer; an actor; an actress

伶牙利齒(ㄌㄧㄥ ㄧㄚˊ ㄌㄧˋ ㄔˇ)
eloquent

【伸】 118　ㄕㄣ shen shēn
1. to stretch; to extend; to straighten
2. to report

伸頭探腦(ㄕㄣ ㄊㄡˊ ㄊㄢˋ ㄋㄠˇ)
to crane, or stretch the neck in an effort to find out

伸腿(ㄕㄣ ㄊㄨㄟˇ)
①to stretch one's legs ② (figuratively) to die ③ to step in (to gain an advantage)

伸腿瞪眼(ㄕㄣ ㄊㄨㄟˇ ㄉㄥˋ ㄧㄢˇ)
(said of human beings) dead

伸懶腰(ㄕㄣ ㄌㄢˇ ㄧㄠ)
to stretch oneself or one's muscles; to stretch and yawn

伸開(ㄕㄣ ㄎㄞ)
to stretch out; to extend; to spread

伸直(ㄕㄣ ㄓˊ)
to straighten; to stretch out (so as to make straight)

伸志(ㄕㄣ ㄓˋ)
to have one's ambition fulfilled

伸展(ㄕㄣ ㄓㄢˇ)
to stretch; to spread out; to extend

伸展台(ㄕㄣ ㄓㄢˇ ㄊㄞˊ)
a ramp or runway used in a beauty pageant, fashion show, etc.

伸張(ㄕㄣ ㄓㄤ)
to expand (power)

伸張正義(ㄕㄣ ㄓㄤ ㄓㄥˋ ㄧˋ)
to be a champion of justice

伸長(ㄕㄣ ㄔㄤˊ)
to stretch so as to make or become longer; to elongate; to lengthen

伸出(ㄕㄣ ㄔㄨ)
to stretch outward; to stretch out; to reach out; to jut out

伸舌頭(ㄕㄣ ㄕㄜˊ ㄊㄡ)
to stick out the tongue (to express horror, often in jest)

伸手(ㄕㄣ ㄕㄡˇ)
to reach out, hold out, or stretch out one's hand

伸訴(ㄕㄣ ㄙㄨˋ)
to present a complaint; to air a grievance

伸縮(ㄕㄣ ㄙㄨㄛ)
to expand and contract; to distend and shrink

伸縮性(ㄕㄣ ㄙㄨㄛ ㄒㄧㄥˋ)
flexibility; elasticity

伸腰兒(ㄕㄣ ㄧㄠ儿)
①to stretch oneself ②(figuratively) to be successful in one's career

伸冤(ㄕㄣ ㄩㄢ)
to clear up a false charge; to right a wrong

【伺】 119　ㄙˋ syh sì
to spy; to reconnoiter; to watch

伺探(ㄙˋ ㄊㄢˋ)or 伺諜(ㄙˋ ㄉㄧㄝˊ)
to investigate secretly; to spy

伺機(ㄙˋ ㄐㄧ)
to wait for one's chance

伺機而動(ㄙˋ ㄐㄧ ㄦˊ ㄉㄨㄥˋ)
to wait for a favorable moment to make a move

伺隙(ㄙˋ ㄒㄧˋ)
to watch for a chance or opening (to do something evil)

伺察(ㄙˋ ㄔㄚˊ)
to spy; to investigate; to trace secretly

【伺】 119　ㄘˋ tsyh cì
to serve

伺候(ㄘˋ ㄏㄡ)
to wait, or attend upon; to serve

【似】 120　ㄙˋ syh sì
1. to resemble; to seem: 她酷似她的母親。She strongly resembles her mother.
2. like; as if

似的(ㄙˋ ㄉㄜ)
to give the impression that

似通非通(ㄙˋ ㄊㄨㄥ ㄈㄟ ㄊㄨㄥ)
(said of writing, argument, etc.) plausible

似乎(ㄙˋ ㄏㄨ)
it seems or appears that; it seems, appears, or looks as if or as though

似笑非笑(ㄙˋ ㄒㄧㄠˋ ㄈㄟ ㄒㄧㄠˋ)
(One) looks smiling but (one) actually doesn't smile

似是而非(ㄙˋ ㄕˋ ㄦˊ ㄈㄟ)
seemingly correct but really incorrect; having the semblance of what it is not

【伽】 121　ㄑㄧㄝˊ chye qié
(the character is not used alone)

伽藍(ㄑㄧㄝˊ ㄌㄢˊ)
①a Buddhist temple ②a Buddhist deity (Sangharama or Sanghagara)

【伽】 121　ㄐㄧㄚ jia jiā

伽瑪(ㄐㄧㄚ ㄇㄚˇ)
gamma

伽瑪射線(ㄐㄧㄚ ㄇㄚˇ ㄕㄜˋ ㄒㄧㄢˋ)
(physics)gamma rays

伽利略(ㄐㄧㄚ ㄌㄧˋ ㄌㄩㄝˋ)
Galileo, 1564-1642, Italian physicist, astronomer, and mathematician

〔人部〕

【佃】 [122] ㄉㄧㄢˋ diann diàn
1. a tenant farmer
2. to tenant a farm
3. hunting

佃農 (ㄉㄧㄢˋ ㄋㄨㄥˊ)
a tenant farmer or share-cropper

佃戶 (ㄉㄧㄢˋ ㄏㄨˋ)
a tenant (of a farm)

佃契 (ㄉㄧㄢˋ ㄑㄧˋ)
a land lease; a renting contract or agreement (between the tenant farmer and the landlord)

佃租 (ㄉㄧㄢˋ ㄗㄨ)
land rent

【但】 [123] ㄉㄢˋ dann dàn
but; however; yet

但凡 (ㄉㄢˋ ㄈㄢˊ)
whoever; whenever; whatever; all

但丁 (ㄉㄢˋ ㄉㄧㄥ)
Dante, 1265-1321, Italian poet

但求無過 (ㄉㄢˋ ㄑㄧㄡˊ ㄨˊ ㄍㄨㄛˋ)
Just try to avoid making mistakes.

但是 (ㄉㄢˋ ㄕˋ)
but; however; yet

但書 (ㄉㄢˋ ㄕㄨ)
a proviso; a condition; a qualifying clause

但說無妨 (ㄉㄢˋ ㄕㄨㄛ ㄨˊ ㄈㄤˊ)
Just speak out what is in your mind.

但澤 (ㄉㄢˋ ㄗㄜˊ)
Danzig, inlet of the Baltic Sea in northern Poland

但坐無妨 (ㄉㄢˋ ㄗㄨㄛˋ ㄨˊ ㄈㄤˊ)
Just sit down as you please.

但願 (ㄉㄢˋ ㄩㄢˋ)
to wish; to hope: 但願你成功。 I wish you success.

【佇】 [124] ㄓㄨˋ juh zhù
1. to stand (for a long time)
2. to expect

佇立 (ㄓㄨˋ ㄌㄧˋ)
to stand still; to stand motionless

佇候 (ㄓㄨˋ ㄏㄡˋ)
to stand and wait; to look forward to: 佇候佳音。 I look forward to hearing your good message.

【佈】 [125] ㄅㄨˋ buh bù
1. to announce; to declare 參看「佈」
2. to arrange: 那軍隊佈好陣勢以備戰。 The army is arranged for battle.

佈滿 (ㄅㄨˋ ㄇㄢˇ)
to be covered with: 野花佈滿了田野。 The field is covered with wild flowers.

佈防 (ㄅㄨˋ ㄈㄤˊ)
to organize the defense; to deploy troops in anticipation of an enemy attack

佈覆 or 布覆 (ㄅㄨˋ ㄈㄨˋ)
to reply (used in letter writing): 謹此佈覆。I hereby reply to your letter.

佈達 or 布達 (ㄅㄨˋ ㄉㄚˊ)
to notify: 謹此佈達。I hereby notify you.

佈達式 (ㄅㄨˋ ㄉㄚˊ ㄕˋ)
(military) a change-of-command ceremony

佈道 (ㄅㄨˋ ㄉㄠˋ)
to preach the gospel; to evangelize

佈雷 (ㄅㄨˋ ㄌㄟˊ)
to lay mines

佈告 (ㄅㄨˋ ㄍㄠˋ)
① a bulletin ② to make public announcement

佈崗 (ㄅㄨˋ ㄍㄤˇ)
to post sentries; to mount guards

佈阱 (ㄅㄨˋ ㄐㄧㄥˇ)
to lay a trap

佈景 (ㄅㄨˋ ㄐㄧㄥˇ)
scenery (for the stage)

佈局 (ㄅㄨˋ ㄐㄩˊ)
the layout (of a literary writing, painting, etc.)

佈置 (ㄅㄨˋ ㄓˋ)
① to make arrangement ② to arrange (furniture); to decorate (a living room, convention hall, etc.)

佈施 (ㄅㄨˋ ㄕ)
to make a contribution to a relief fund; to give money or materials to the poor

【位】 [126] ㄨㄟˋ wey wèi
1. position; rank
2. location

位分 (ㄨㄟˋ ㄈㄣˋ)
one's social status

位極人臣 (ㄨㄟˋ ㄐㄧˊ ㄖㄣˊ ㄔㄣˊ)
(in ancient China) to become prime minister

位居津要 (ㄨㄟˋ ㄐㄩ ㄐㄧㄣ ㄧㄠˋ)
to hold a sensitive post; to occupy a key position

位置 (ㄨㄟˋ ㄓˋ)
① position (in space); location ② position (in an organization)

位子 (ㄨㄟˋ ·ㄗ)
a seat

位次 (ㄨㄟˋ ㄘˋ)
① rank ② seating order

位於 (ㄨㄟˋ ㄩˊ)
situated at; located at

位元 (ㄨㄟˋ ㄩㄢˊ)
(computers) a bit

【低】 [127] ㄉㄧ di dī
1. low
2. to lower

低眉 (ㄉㄧ ㄇㄟˊ)
① kindness ② obedience; compliance

低迷 (ㄉㄧ ㄇㄧˊ)
(said of the sky, clouds, etc.) turbid

低等動物 (ㄉㄧ ㄉㄥˇ ㄉㄨㄥˋ ㄨˋ)
lower animals

低地 (ㄉㄧ ㄉㄧˋ)
lowlands

低調 (ㄉㄧ ㄉㄧㄠˋ)
(music) low-key

低頭 (ㄉㄧ ㄊㄡˊ)
to bow one's head; to lower one's head (in shame): 他們低頭禱告。 They bowed their heads in prayer.

低能兒 (ㄉㄧ ㄋㄥˊ ㄦˊ)
a mentally retarded child

低欄 (ㄉㄧ ㄌㄢˊ)
(sports) low hurdles

低劣 (ㄉㄧ ㄌㄧㄝˋ)
poor in quality

低廉 (ㄉㄧ ㄌㄧㄢˊ)
cheap; low

低落 (ㄉㄧ ㄌㄨㄛˋ)
low; downcast

低估 (ㄉㄧ ㄍㄨ)
to underestimate: 不要低估敵人的力量。 Don't underestimate the enemy's strength.

低空 (ㄉㄧ ㄎㄨㄥ)
the atmosphere near the

earth

低迴(ㄉㄧ ㄏㄨㄟˊ)
to leave, or part reluctantly; to show reluctance to go

低級(ㄉㄧ ㄐㄧˊ)
① elementary; rudimentary ② vulgar; low

低級趣味(ㄉㄧ ㄐㄧˊ ㄑㄩˋ ㄨㄟˋ)
bad taste; vulgar interests

低賤(ㄉㄧ ㄐㄧㄢˋ)
① cheap in price ② low-class

低氣壓(ㄉㄧ ㄑㄧˋ ㄧㄚ)
low atmospheric pressure; atmospheric depression

低下(ㄉㄧ ㄒㄧㄚˋ)
low; lowly

低消耗(ㄉㄧ ㄒㄧㄠ ㄏㄠˋ)
low consumption (of raw materials, fuel, etc.)

低血糖(ㄉㄧ ㄒㄩㄝˋ ㄊㄤˊ)
(medicine) hypoglycemia

低潮(ㄉㄧ ㄔㄠˊ)
a low tide; a low ebb

低產(ㄉㄧ ㄔㄢˇ)
a low yield

低沈(ㄉㄧ ㄔㄣˊ)
low and heavy (spirit, tone, etc.)

低垂(ㄉㄧ ㄔㄨㄟˊ)
to hang low

低濕(ㄉㄧ ㄕ)
(said of places) low and moist; low in elevation and high in humidity

低首(ㄉㄧ ㄕㄡˇ)
to bend one's head

低首下心(ㄉㄧ ㄕㄡˇ ㄒㄧㄚˋ ㄒㄧㄣ)
to submit; to yield; to give oneself up

低聲(ㄉㄧ ㄕㄥ)
in a low voice; under one's breath

低聲下氣(ㄉㄧ ㄕㄥ ㄒㄧㄚˋ ㄑㄧˋ)
to be meek and timid; to be submissive

低姿態(ㄉㄧ ㄗ ㄊㄞˋ)
a low profile

低三下四(ㄉㄧ ㄙㄢ ㄒㄧㄚˋ ㄙˋ)
lowly; mean

低昂(ㄉㄧ ㄤˊ)
rises and falls; fluctuation in height

低壓(ㄉㄧ ㄧㄚ)
① (physics) low pressure ② (electricity) low voltage ③

(meteorology) low pressure

低音(ㄉㄧ ㄧㄣ)
① a low-pitched sound ② (female) contralto; (male) bass

低窪(ㄉㄧ ㄨㄚ)
low-lying (ground)

低微(ㄉㄧ ㄨㄟˊ)
① mean; base; menial; ignoble ② humble (origin)

低溫(ㄉㄧ ㄨㄣ)
① low temperature ② (meteorology) microtherm ③ (medicine) hypothermia

低溫殺菌(ㄉㄧ ㄨㄣ ㄕㄚ ㄐㄩㄣ)
low temperature sterilization

【住】 128 ㄓㄨˋ juh zhù
1. to dwell; to inhabit; to live: 他想居住在鄉間。He wants to live in the country.
2. to stop: 風住了。The wind has stopped.
3. used after verb to complement its meaning: 拿住! Hold it fast!

住不下(ㄓㄨˋ ㄅㄨˋ ㄒㄧㄚˋ)
cannot accommodate (because of limitation of space)

住民(ㄓㄨˋ ㄇㄧㄣˊ)
an inhabitant; a resident

住口(ㄓㄨˋ ㄎㄡˇ) or **住嘴**(ㄓㄨˋ ㄗㄨㄟˇ)
① to stop talking ② Shut up!

住戶(ㄓㄨˋ ㄏㄨˋ)
a resident family

住家(ㄓㄨˋ ㄐㄧㄚ)
① a residence; a home ② (said of a married woman) to visit her parents' home

住址(ㄓㄨˋ ㄓˇ)
address: 在信封上寫姓名與住址。Write the name and address on the envelope.

住宅(ㄓㄨˋ ㄓㄞˊ)
a residence; a dwelling; a house

住宅區(ㄓㄨˋ ㄓㄞˊ ㄑㄩ)
a residential area, district or quarter

住持(ㄓㄨˋ ㄔˊ)
an abbot; the head monk (of a temple)

住處(ㄓㄨˋ ㄔㄨˋ)
a residence; a dwelling; lodging; quarters

住手(ㄓㄨˋ ㄕㄡˇ)

① Stop! ② to stop an action; to halt; to hold

住宿(ㄓㄨˋ ㄙㄨˋ)
to stay overnight; to lodge

住所(ㄓㄨˋ ㄙㄨㄛˇ)
a dwelling place; a home; a residence; a domicile

住院(ㄓㄨˋ ㄩㄢˋ)
to be hospitalized

住院總醫師(ㄓㄨˋ ㄩㄢˋ ㄗㄨㄥˇ ㄧ ㄕ)
a chief resident

住院醫師(ㄓㄨˋ ㄩㄢˋ ㄧ ㄕ)
a resident (in a hospital)

【佐】 129 ㄗㄨㄛˇ tzuoo zuǒ
to assist; to aid; to second

佐命(ㄗㄨㄛˇ ㄇㄧㄥˋ)
to help a prince to gain the throne and establish a new dynasty

佐拉(ㄗㄨㄛˇ ㄌㄚ), Émile Zola, 1840–1902, French novelist

佐理(ㄗㄨㄛˇ ㄌㄧˇ)
to assist

佐證(ㄗㄨㄛˇ ㄓㄥˋ)
the evidence

佐世保(ㄗㄨㄛˇ ㄕˋ ㄅㄠˇ)
Sasebo, a naval base in Japan

佐膳(ㄗㄨㄛˇ ㄕㄢˋ)
side dishes (as distinct from the staple food)

佐餐(ㄗㄨㄛˇ ㄘㄢ)
to be eaten together with rice; to go with rice

【佑】 130 ㄧㄡˋ yow yòu
to help; to protect; to aid; to bless: 求上天保佑這家人。Heaven bless this family.

佑助(ㄧㄡˋ ㄓㄨˋ)
to help; to aid; to assist

【佔】 131 ㄓㄢˋ jann zhàn
to seize; to usurp; to occupy; to take by force: 敵人佔據了我們的堡壘。The enemy occupied our fort.

佔便宜(ㄓㄢˋ ㄆㄧㄢˊ ㄧ˙)
① to be in an advantageous position ② to take advantage (of a person)

佔領(ㄓㄢˋ ㄌㄧㄥˇ)
to occupy (a foreign territory); to capture or take (an enemy position)

佔領軍(ㄓㄢ ㄌㄧㄥˇ ㄐㄩㄣ)
occupation troops

佔據(ㄓㄢ ㄐㄩ)
to occupy; to take possession of

佔先(ㄓㄢ ㄒㄧㄢ)
to lead (in a game or contest)

佔線(ㄓㄢ ㄒㄧㄢˋ)
(telephone) The line's busy (or engaged).

佔上風(ㄓㄢ ㄕㄤˋ ㄈㄥ)
to have the upper hand (in a struggle or contest)

佔有(ㄓㄢ ㄧㄡˇ)
① to own; to possess; to have ② to occupy; to hold; 商業在台灣經濟中佔有重要地位。Commerce occupies an important place in the economy of Taiwan.

【何】 132
ㄏㄜˊ her hé
1. what; how; where; why; 為何不可? Why not?
2. a Chinese family name

何必(ㄏㄜˊ ㄅㄧˋ)or何須(ㄏㄜˊ ㄒㄩ)
why should; why must; why is it necessary; not necessary …; there is no need: 他只是開開玩笑，何必當眞? He is only joking. Why take it so seriously?

何不(ㄏㄜˊ ㄅㄨˋ)
why not: 何不早說? Why didn't you say it earlier?

何妨(ㄏㄜˊ ㄈㄤˊ)or(ㄏㄜˊ ㄈㄤˋ)
There is no harm (trying, doing, etc.) also might as well: 何妨一試? Why not have a try?

何等(ㄏㄜˊ ㄉㄥˇ)
① how (in exclamatory expressions) ② what sort of; what kind of: 你知道他是何等人物? Do you know what sort of person he is?

何獨(ㄏㄜˊ ㄉㄨˊ)
Why…only?

何樂不爲(ㄏㄜˊ ㄌㄜˋ ㄅㄨˋ ㄨㄟˊ)
Why not do it gladly?

何干(ㄏㄜˊ ㄍㄢ)
What has that got to do with…?

何敢(ㄏㄜˊ ㄍㄢˇ)
How dare…?

何故(ㄏㄜˊ ㄍㄨˋ)

why; for what reason

何可勝數(ㄏㄜˊ ㄎㄜˇ ㄕㄥ ㄕㄨˇ)
countless; numerous

何苦(ㄏㄜˊ ㄎㄨˇ)
Why take the trouble? 或 for what earthly reason

何況(ㄏㄜˊ ㄎㄨㄤˋ)
much less; not to mention; let alone: 他連伙食錢都不夠，何況娛樂。He hasn't enough money for food, let alone amusements.

何濟於事(ㄏㄜˊ ㄐㄧˋ ㄩˊ ㄕˋ)
Of what avail is it?

何去何從(ㄏㄜˊ ㄑㄩˋ ㄏㄜˊ ㄘㄨㄥˊ)
choice (of action); what course to follow

何須(ㄏㄜˊ ㄒㄩ)
unnecessary; why is it necessary…

何許人(ㄏㄜˊ ㄒㄩˇ ㄖㄣˊ)
who (used to indicate ignorance of someone's background)

何止(ㄏㄜˊ ㄓˇ)
far more than

何至於(ㄏㄜˊ ㄓˋ ㄩˊ)
How could it have turned out (like that)? 或How come?

何者(ㄏㄜˊ ㄓㄜˇ)
which one

何啻(ㄏㄜˊ ㄔˋ)
not different from; to be the same as

何愁(ㄏㄜˊ ㄔㄡˊ)
Why worry about it?

何嘗(ㄏㄜˊ ㄔㄤˊ)
How (could it be an exception)? 或 not that…; never

何處(ㄏㄜˊ ㄔㄨˋ)
where; in what place

何時(ㄏㄜˊ ㄕˊ)
when; at what time

何事(ㄏㄜˊ ㄕˋ)
What (do you want)? 或 What (is the trouble)? or for what: 何事令你如此不安? What makes you so anxious?

何首烏(ㄏㄜˊ ㄕㄡˇ ㄨ)
(herb medicine) Polygonum multiflorum

何如(ㄏㄜˊ ㄖㄨˊ)
① What about it? ② Wouldn't it be better? ③ What do you think…?

何在(ㄏㄜˊ ㄗㄞˋ)
① Where is (that particular thing)? ② What is (that particular reason)?

何足掛齒(ㄏㄜˊ ㄗㄨˊ ㄍㄨㄚˋ ㄔˇ)
Don't mention it. (used in formal speech)

何曾(ㄏㄜˊ ㄘㄥˊ)
Has it ever happened?

何以(ㄏㄜˊ ㄧˇ)
why; wherefore; how: 何以見得? How do you think so?

何以自處(ㄏㄜˊ ㄧˇ ㄗˋ ㄔㄨˇ)
how to explain (what one has done has caused trouble or harm to others)

何由見得(ㄏㄜˊ ㄧㄡˊ ㄐㄧㄢˋ ㄉㄜˊ)
What makes you think so?

何謂(ㄏㄜˊ ㄨㄟˋ)
what is meant by

何用(ㄏㄜˊ ㄩㄥˋ)
of what use

【佗】 133
　　1. ㄊㄨㄛˊ two tuó
a load

【佗】 133
　　2. ㄊㄨㄛ tuo tuó
1. he
2. a Chinese family name

【余】 134
ㄕㄜˊ sher shé
a Chinese family name

【余】 135
ㄩˊ yu yú
1. (informal speech) I; me
2. a Chinese family name

【佚】 136
ㄧˋ yih yì
idleness; comfort

【佛】 137
ㄈㄛˊ for fó
1. Buddha (Sakyamuni 釋迦牟尼)
2. of Buddhism

佛門(ㄈㄛˊ ㄇㄣˊ)
Buddhism; the Buddhist faith; the school of Buddhism

佛門弟子(ㄈㄛˊ ㄇㄣˊ ㄉㄧˋ ㄗˇ)
Buddhist monks and nuns; Buddhists

佛法(ㄈㄛˊ ㄈㄚˇ)
the Buddhist doctrines (Buddhadharma); the law of Buddha

佛法僧(ㄈㄛˊ ㄈㄚˇ ㄙㄥ)
Buddha-dharma-sangha

佛法無邊(ㄈㄛˊ ㄈㄚˇ ㄨˊ ㄅㄧㄢ)

The greatness of Buddhism is immeasurable.

佛誕日(ㄈㄜˊ ㄉㄢˋ ㄖˋ)
Buddha's Birthday (There are two versions: the 8th day of the 4th moon, and the 8th day of the 2nd moon. The former is preferred in China.)

佛堂(ㄈㄜˊ ㄊㄤˊ)
a Buddhist sanctuary; the hall for worshipping Buddha or with the statue of Buddha

佛徒(ㄈㄜˊ ㄊㄨˊ)
a Buddhist disciple; a Buddhist

佛陀(ㄈㄜˊ ㄊㄨㄛˊ)
Buddha—a title applied by Buddhists to someone regarded as embodying divine wisdom and virtue

佛老(ㄈㄜˊ ㄌㄠˇ)
① Buddha and Lao-tzu ② Buddhism and Taoism

佛蘭克林(ㄈㄜˊ ㄌㄢˊ ㄎㄜˋ ㄌㄧㄣˊ)
Benjamin Franklin, 1706-1790, American statesman, writer and inventor

佛羅里達(ㄈㄜˊ ㄌㄨㄛˊ ㄌㄧˇ ㄉㄚˊ)
Florida, U. S. A.

佛倫斯(ㄈㄜˊ ㄌㄨㄣˊ ㄙ)
Florence, a city in Italy

佛骨(ㄈㄜˊ ㄍㄨˇ)
the remains of Buddha

佛國(ㄈㄜˊ ㄍㄨㄛˊ)
① India, the country where Buddha was born (*Buddhaksetra*) ② the land purified by Buddha

佛口蛇心(ㄈㄜˊ ㄎㄡˇ ㄕㄜˊ ㄒㄧㄣ)
the mouth of Buddha and the heart of a serpent—(figuratively) descriptive of an evil person who speaks sweet words but does evil things

佛龕(ㄈㄜˊ ㄎㄢ)
a Buddhist altar; a niche for Buddha

佛海(ㄈㄜˊ ㄏㄞˇ)
(the all-encompassing) teachings of Buddha; Buddha's ocean (the realm of Buddha as boundless as the sea)

佛會(ㄈㄜˊ ㄏㄨㄟˋ)
the celebration of Buddhist festivals

佛家(ㄈㄜˊ ㄐㄧㄚ)
a Buddhist; the Buddhist faithful; a Buddhist follower

佛教(ㄈㄜˊ ㄐㄧㄠˋ)
Buddhism; the Buddhist religion

佛經(ㄈㄜˊ ㄐㄧㄥ)
the Sutras; the Buddhist scriptures; the Buddhist canon

佛像(ㄈㄜˊ ㄒㄧㄤˋ)
a figure of Buddha; a statue of Buddha

佛性(ㄈㄜˊ ㄒㄧㄥˋ)
Buddhata; a nature like that of Buddha (believed to be present in every living thing)

佛學(ㄈㄜˊ ㄒㄩㄝˊ)
Buddhistic study; Buddhism

佛事(ㄈㄜˊ ㄕˋ)
Buddhist rituals; Buddhist religious service

佛手(ㄈㄜˊ ㄕㄡˇ)
①(botany)bergamot; *Citrus medica* ② Buddha's hand

佛祖(ㄈㄜˊ ㄗㄨˇ)
① Buddha ② Buddhist patriarchs

佛寺(ㄈㄜˊ ㄙˋ)
a Buddhist temple

佛爺(ㄈㄜˊ ·ㄧㄝ)
Buddha

【作】 138
1. ㄗㄨㄛˋ tzuoh zuò
1. to do; to make
2. the works (of a writer, etc.)
3. to rise up
4. to pretend; to affect
5. to regard…as; to take… for
6. to write; to compose

作罷(ㄗㄨㄛˋ ㄅㄚˋ)
to drop; to give up

作保(ㄗㄨㄛˋ ㄅㄠˇ)
to guarantee; to vouch for; to be a guarantor; to stand guarantee

作伴(ㄗㄨㄛˋ ㄅㄢˋ)
to keep (someone) company; to serve as a companion for

作弊(ㄗㄨㄛˋ ㄅㄧˋ)
to cheat (especially in examinations); to indulge in corrupt practices

作壁上觀(ㄗㄨㄛˋ ㄅㄧˋ ㄕㄤˋ ㄍㄨㄢ)
to watch (a fight, quarrel, etc.) with detachment

作別(ㄗㄨㄛˋ ㄅㄧㄝˊ)
to bid farewell; to take one's leave

作陪(ㄗㄨㄛˋ ㄆㄟˊ)
to accompany; to escort; to be invited (to a reception, etc.) as company to the guest of honor

作品(ㄗㄨㄛˋ ㄆㄧㄣˇ)
the works (of a writer, artist, etc.); a literary or artistic work

作媒(ㄗㄨㄛˋ ㄇㄟˊ)
to act as a go-between in marriage

作美(ㄗㄨㄛˋ ㄇㄟˇ)
(of weather, etc.) to help; to cooperate; to make things better for somebody: 如果天公作美，我們明天去新公園野餐。If Heaven makes things better for us, we'll go on a picnic in New Park tomorrow.

作夢(ㄗㄨㄛˋ ㄇㄥˋ)
① to dream ② to imagine as in a dream; to have daydreams

作伐(ㄗㄨㄛˋ ㄈㄚ)or(ㄗㄨㄛˋ ㄈㄚˊ)
to be a matchmaker; to act as a go-between in marriage

作法(ㄗㄨㄛˋ ㄈㄚˇ)
① a way of doing or handling things; course of action ② a method of making, preparing, manufacturing, or cooking ③ to exercise magic powers ④ to legislate; to make laws

作法自斃(ㄗㄨㄛˋ ㄈㄚˇ ㄗˋ ㄅㄧˋ)
to get into trouble through one's own scheme; a scheme that boomerangs; to be caught by one's own device

作事(ㄗㄨㄛˋ ㄈㄛˊ)
(said of Buddhist monks) to recite passages from the Sutras to worship Buddha

作廢(ㄗㄨㄛˋ ㄈㄟˋ)
to nullify; to make void; to cancel; to declare invalid

作風(ㄗㄨㄛˋ ㄈㄥ)
①(literary or artistic) style ② one's way of doing things

作歹(ㄗㄨㄛˋ ㄉㄞˇ)

〔人部〕

〔人部〕

to do evil; to act criminally

作對(ㄗㄨㄛˋ ㄉㄨㄟˋ)
①to oppose; to act against; to choose to be someone's rival or opponent 亦作「作對頭」②to match with another in marriage

作東(ㄗㄨㄛˋ ㄉㄨㄥ)
to stand treat

作態(ㄗㄨㄛˋ ㄊㄞˋ)
①(especially referring to a woman trying to please a man) to act pretentiously ②to take on a certain expression; to feign; to strike an attitude

作孽(ㄗㄨㄛˋ ㄋㄧㄝˋ)
to do evil; to do something that causes harm to others

作弄(ㄗㄨㄛˋ ㄋㄨㄥˋ)
to tease; to make a fool of; to play a trick on

作樂(ㄗㄨㄛˋ ㄌㄜˋ)
to make merry; to have fun; to enjoy

作亂(ㄗㄨㄛˋ ㄌㄨㄢˋ)
to rebel; to start an uprising; to turn against the authorities

作梗(ㄗㄨㄛˋ ㄍㄥˇ)
to obstruct or to oppose secretly; to impede; to create difficulties; to hamper; to hinder

作古(ㄗㄨㄛˋ ㄍㄨˇ)
to die; to pass away

作怪(ㄗㄨㄛˋ ㄍㄨㄞˋ)
mischievous; to act mischievously; to make trouble; to play tricks on 別作怪。Don't play dirty tricks on me.

作官(ㄗㄨㄛˋ ㄍㄨㄢ)
to be a government official; to hold a government post

作工(ㄗㄨㄛˋ ㄍㄨㄥ)
to labor; to work

作客(ㄗㄨㄛˋ ㄎㄜˋ)
①to be a guest ②to stay outside of one's hometown; to sojourn in a strange place

作闊(ㄗㄨㄛˋ ㄎㄨㄛˋ)
to show off; to make a vain display: 他愛作闊。He is fond of showing off.

作活(ㄗㄨㄛˋ ㄏㄨㄛˊ)
to work (for one's living)

作家(ㄗㄨㄛˋ ㄐㄧㄚ)
a writer; an author

作假(ㄗㄨㄛˋ ㄐㄧㄚˇ)or 作偽(ㄗㄨㄛˋ ㄨㄟˋ)
to pretend; to be an impostor; to cheat; to make an imitation copy

作嫁(ㄗㄨㄛˋ ㄐㄧㄚˋ)
to sew somebody else's trousseau—to earn a living by working for others: 我們總是為人作嫁。We always busy ourselves in helping other people.

作姦犯科(ㄗㄨㄛˋ ㄐㄧㄢ ㄈㄢˋ ㄎㄜ)
to do evil; to break the law; to act criminally

作繭自縛(ㄗㄨㄛˋ ㄐㄧㄢˇ ㄗˋ ㄈㄨˊ)
(said of a silkworm) to spin a cocoon and imprison itself in it—(figuratively) to tie oneself up with duties; to get into trouble by one's own schemes

作曲(ㄗㄨㄛˋ ㄑㄩ)
to write a song; to set a song to music; to compose

作曲家(ㄗㄨㄛˋ ㄑㄩ ㄐㄧㄚ)
a composer

作秀(ㄗㄨㄛˋ ㄒㄧㄡˋ)
(informal) ①to appear in a stage show ②to grandstand; grandstanding; showboating

作者(ㄗㄨㄛˋ ㄓㄜˇ)
a writer (of a composition, novel, etc.); an author

作戰(ㄗㄨㄛˋ ㄓㄢˋ)
to go to battle; to fight against; to make war

作證(ㄗㄨㄛˋ ㄓㄥˋ)
to act as a witness in court; to bear witness

作主(ㄗㄨㄛˋ ㄓㄨˇ)
to take up responsibility for making a decision; to make the final decision: 這件事由他作主。He made the final decision on this matter.

作長工(ㄗㄨㄛˋ ㄔㄤˊ ㄍㄨㄥ)
to be a regular laborer on a farm; to be a farm hand

作成(ㄗㄨㄛˋ ㄔㄥˊ)
to arrange or complete (a job); to help succeed (in an undertaking, etc.)

作詩(ㄗㄨㄛˋ ㄕ)
to write poems; to versify

作勢(ㄗㄨㄛˋ ㄕˋ)

to put on airs; to pretend

作舍道傍(ㄗㄨㄛˋ ㄕㄜˇ ㄉㄠˋ ㄅㄤˋ)
difficult to succeed

作壽(ㄗㄨㄛˋ ㄕㄡˋ)
to celebrate a birthday

作善(ㄗㄨㄛˋ ㄕㄢˋ)
to do good turns

作聲(ㄗㄨㄛˋ ㄕㄥ)
to make noise; to speak; to break silence

作殊死戰(ㄗㄨㄛˋ ㄕㄨ ㄙˇ ㄓㄢˋ)
to fight to the bitter end

作人(ㄗㄨㄛˋ ㄖㄣˊ)
①to get along with other people ②to be pleasant in manner or personality; to behave oneself properly

作色(ㄗㄨㄛˋ ㄙㄜˋ)
to change facial expression (usually to show anger)

作祟(ㄗㄨㄛˋ ㄙㄨㄟˋ)
①(said of spirits) to haunt ②(said of people) to make mischief; to cause trouble: 這些都是利己主義作祟。All these troubles are caused by egoism.

作惡(ㄗㄨㄛˋ ㄜˋ)ⓐ to indulge in evildoings ⓑ gloomy; sullen; melancholy

作惡(ㄗㄨㄛˋ ㄜˇ) to vomit

作惡多端(ㄗㄨㄛˋ ㄜˋ ㄉㄨㄛ ㄉㄨㄢ)
to indulge in all sorts of evildoing; to commit many crimes

作嘔(ㄗㄨㄛˋ ㄡˇ)
①to nauseate; nauseating (usually referring to poor writings, unflavoring utterances, conceited manner, etc.) ②to feel resentment or detest ③to sicken

作案(ㄗㄨㄛˋ ㄢˋ)
to commit a crime

作押(ㄗㄨㄛˋ ㄧㄚ)
to offer something as a pledge; to mortgage

作業(ㄗㄨㄛˋ ㄧㄝˋ)
①students' homework ②the job of a person ③main fields of operation of a firm, etc.

作業系統(ㄗㄨㄛˋ ㄧㄝˋ ㄒㄧˋ ㄊㄨㄥˇ)
(computers) the operating system

作豐生(ㄗㄨㄛˋ ㄧˋ ㄕㄥ)

to work for a living

作物(ㄗㄨㄛˋ ㄨˋ)
①crops ②literary or artistic compositions

作威作福(ㄗㄨㄛˋ ㄨㄟ ㄗㄨㄛˋ ㄈㄨˊ)
bossy; to throw one's weight around freely; to overexert one's power and position by acting impudently

作爲(ㄗㄨㄛˋ ㄨㄟˊ)
①conduct; behavior; action ②to accomplish; a promising future ③to serve as; to look upon as; to regard as

作文(ㄗㄨㄛˋ ㄨㄣˊ)
①to write a composition ② a composition

作樂(ㄗㄨㄛˋ ㄩㄝˋ)
①to play music ② to write scores

作俑(ㄗㄨㄛˋ ㄩㄥˇ)
to make wooden images—to originate an immoral (or vicious) practice

作用(ㄗㄨㄛˋ ㄩㄥˋ)
①functions; uses; usefulness ②effect: 這藥對病人沒有什麼作用。The drug has no effect on patients. ③objective; purpose: 你這麼說有何作用? What is your purpose to have said so?

作用點(ㄗㄨㄛˋ ㄩㄥˋ ㄉㄧㄢˇ)
(physics) a point of application

【作】 138
2. ㄗㄨㄛ tzuo zuō

作坊(ㄗㄨㄛ ·ㄈㄤ)
a small workshop

作揖(ㄗㄨㄛ ㄧ)
a Chinese gesture in greeting, with the greeter holding his hands together in an up-and-down motion

作寃(ㄗㄨㄛ ㄩㄢ)
to get trapped by oneself

【作】 138
3. ㄗㄨㄛˋ tzwo zuò

作料(ㄗㄨㄛˋ ㄌㄧㄠˋ)or作料兒(ㄗㄨㄛˋ ㄌㄧㄠˋㄦ)
ingredients of a recipe; dressing; seasoning; materials

作踐(ㄗㄨㄛˋ ㄐㄧㄢ)
to abuse; to waste; to ill-use; to trample; to treat harshly

作興(ㄗㄨㄛˋ ·ㄒㄧㄥ)

①allowable ②to be in good spirits ③in vogue ④to hold in high regard ⑤perhaps; likely

【佞】 139
ㄋㄧㄥˋ ning nìng
1. eloquent; persuasive; gifted with a glib tongue
2. obsequious; fawning
3. to believe (in superstition)
4. one given to flattery

佞佛(ㄋㄧㄥˋ ㄈㄛˊ)
to worship Buddha ingratiatingly

佞婦(ㄋㄧㄥˋ ㄈㄨˋ)
a glib-tongued woman

佞黨(ㄋㄧㄥˋ ㄉㄤˇ)
a clique of traitors

佞口(ㄋㄧㄥˋ ㄎㄡˇ)
a person who is glib-tongued and good at flattery

佞幸(ㄋㄧㄥˋ ㄒㄧㄥˋ)
flattering

佞臣(ㄋㄧㄥˋ ㄔㄣˊ)
a flattering courtier

佞人(ㄋㄧㄥˋ ㄖㄣˊ)
an obsequious person who flatters others by his glib tongue in order to gain favors; a bootlicker

【佟】 140
ㄊㄨㄥˊ torng tóng
a Chinese family name

六畫

【佩】 141
ㄆㄟˋ pey pèi
1. to wear; to carry: 他佩佩手槍。He carried a pistol in his belt.
2. to admire; to adore
3. to be grateful
4. something worn on a girdle or clothing; a pendant

佩服(ㄆㄟˋ ·ㄈㄨ)
to admire; to respect: 你的機智與勇氣，令我們佩服。We must admire your resourcefulness and courage.

佩帶(ㄆㄟˋ ㄉㄞˋ)
to wear; to carry

佩刀(ㄆㄟˋ ㄉㄠ)
to wear a knife or sword at the waist; a knife thus worn

佩劍(ㄆㄟˋ ㄐㄧㄢˋ)
to wear a sword at the waist; a sword one carries

佩勳章(ㄆㄟˋ ㄒㄩㄣ ㄓㄤ)
to wear medals

佩玉(ㄆㄟˋ ㄩˋ)
a jade ornament

【佯】 142
ㄧㄤˊ yang yáng
1. to pretend; to feign; to sham
2. false; deceitful; feigning

佯病(ㄧㄤˊ ㄅㄧㄥˋ)
to pretend to be ill

佯狂(ㄧㄤˊ ㄎㄨㄤˊ)
to feign madness; feigned madness

佯作不知(ㄧㄤˊ ㄗㄨㄛˋ ㄅㄨˋ ㄓ)
to feign ignorance; to pretend not to know

佯死(ㄧㄤˊ ㄙˇ)
to feign death; to pretend to be dead

【佳】 143
ㄐㄧㄚ jia jiā
1. beautiful; good; fine
2. auspicious
3. distinguished

佳賓(ㄐㄧㄚ ㄅㄧㄣ)
distinguished or honored guests

佳釀(ㄐㄧㄚ ㄋㄧㄤˋ)
excellent wine or liquor

佳麗(ㄐㄧㄚ ㄌㄧˋ)
a beautiful woman; a beauty

佳客(ㄐㄧㄚ ㄎㄜˋ)
a good visitor or guest; an honored guest

佳話(ㄐㄧㄚ ㄏㄨㄚˋ)
①(usually a romance) an interesting story or a story that has been popular for a period of time ②a deed worthy of praising far and wide

佳節(ㄐㄧㄚ ㄐㄧㄝˊ)
a festival; a carnival

佳景(ㄐㄧㄚ ㄐㄧㄥˇ)
beautiful scenery

佳境(ㄐㄧㄚ ㄐㄧㄥˋ)
①delightful regions ②wonderful circumstances; a favorable condition

佳句(ㄐㄧㄚ ㄐㄩˋ)
a quotable quote; a beautiful line; a well-turned verse

佳期(ㄐㄧㄚ ㄑㄧˊ)
① the wedding or nuptial day ②the date of a rendezvous with a beautiful wom-

〔人部〕

an
佳趣 (ㄐㄧㄚ ㄑㄩ)
(of) a delightful and intriguing flavor; matters of intense interest
佳婿 (ㄐㄧㄚ ㄒㄧㄝ)
a good or favorite son-in-law
佳城 (ㄐㄧㄚ ㄔㄥ)
a tomb or a grave
佳士 (ㄐㄧㄚ ㄕ)
a scholar of virtue and ability
佳人 (ㄐㄧㄚ ㄖㄣ)
① a beauty; a pretty woman ② a handsome young man
佳作 (ㄐㄧㄚ ㄗㄨㄛ)
an excellent (literary) work; a fine piece of writing
佳偶 (ㄐㄧㄚ ㄡ)
a happily married couple; a fine couple
佳偶天成 (ㄐㄧㄚ ㄡ ㄊㄧㄢ ㄔㄥ)
an ideal couple; a wonderful match
佳餚 (ㄐㄧㄚ ㄧㄠ)
a delicacy
佳餚美酒 (ㄐㄧㄚ ㄧㄠ ㄇㄟ ㄐㄧㄡ)
good food and excellent wine; a sumptuous feast
佳言 (ㄐㄧㄚ ㄧㄢ)
good words; a quotable quote
佳音 (ㄐㄧㄚ ㄧㄣ)
good news; welcome news; good tidings

【佻】 144 ㄊㄧㄠ tyau tiāo
1. frivolous; imprudent
2. to steal; stealthily; to act in a furtive manner
3. to delay; dilatory; slow
4. to provoke
佻薄 (ㄊㄧㄠ ㄅㄛ) or 佻儇 (ㄊㄧㄠ ㄒㄩㄢ)
frivolous; not dignified
佻脫 (ㄊㄧㄠ ㄊㄨㄛ)
frivolous and careless
佻巧 (ㄊㄧㄠ ㄑㄧㄠ)
frivolous and tricky

【佼】 145 ㄐㄧㄠ jeau jiǎo
1. beautiful; handsome; attractive; charming
2. outstanding
佼好 (ㄐㄧㄠ ㄏㄠ)
pretty; pleasant
佼佼 (ㄐㄧㄠ ㄐㄧㄠ)

① stunningly beautiful; handsome; good-looking ② above the average; remarkable; outstanding
佼佼者 (ㄐㄧㄠ ㄐㄧㄠ ㄓㄜ)
an outstanding person
佼人 (ㄐㄧㄠ ㄖㄣ)
a beauty

【佾】 146 ㄧ yih yì
a row or file of dancers, especially referring to those in ancient dances at sacrifices or other rites; a dance squad
佾生 (ㄧ ㄕㄥ)
young boy dancers at the court or temple on ceremonial occasions, etc.
佾舞 (ㄧ ㄨ)
rows of ceremonial dancers, a dance now performed especially on Confucius' birthday at the sage's shrine

【使】 147 ㄕ shyy shǐ
1. to use; to employ; to apply
2. to make; to act
3. to indulge in
4. to send as diplomatic personnel; diplomatic envoys
5. if
使絆兒 (ㄕㄅㄢㄦ)
① (in Chinese wrestling) to trip the opponent with a leg trick ② to injure others by devious (often stealthy) means
使不得 (ㄕ ㄅㄨ ㄉㄜ)
① useless; unserviceable; 鋼筆壞了, 使不得了。The pen is broken; it is useless. ② impermissible; undesirable
使不慣 (ㄕ ㄅㄨ ㄍㄨㄢ)
not used to; not familiar with the use of
使不上 (ㄕ ㄅㄨ ㄕㄤ)
not usable; unfit to be used
使脾氣 (ㄕ ㄆㄧ ㄑㄧ)
to lose one's temper
使民以時 (ㄕ ㄇㄧㄣ ㄧ ㄕ)
to employ the people in the proper season (i.e., when they are not busy farming)
使命 (ㄕ ㄇㄧㄥ)
a mission; a job
使命感 (ㄕ ㄇㄧㄥ ㄍㄢ)
a sense of calling

使得 (ㄕ ㄉㄜ)
① all right; can be done or used ② to make (somebody mad, sad, happy, etc.); to cause; to render
usable; employable; can be used; useful
使女 (ㄕ ㄋㄩ)
a maidservant; a housemaid; a chambermaid
使壞 (ㄕ ㄏㄨㄞ)
① to be up to mischief; to play a dirty trick ② to destroy
使喚 (ㄕ ㄏㄨㄢ)
① to answer the beck and call of; to run errands for ② to order others to do something
使勁 (ㄕ ㄐㄧㄣ) or 使勁兒 (ㄕ ㄐㄧㄣㄦ)
to use or apply (greater) force; to exert effort; to strain: 他們使勁是高嗓子。They strained their voice.
使氣 (ㄕ ㄑㄧ)
to be influenced by sentiment or emotion in handling things
使性子 (ㄕ ㄒㄧㄥ ㄗ)
to lose one's temper; to indulge in one's temper: 別使性子。Don't indulge in your temper.
使出 (ㄕ ㄔㄨ)
to exert
使出渾身解數 (ㄕ ㄔㄨ ㄏㄨㄣ ㄕㄣ ㄐㄧㄝ ㄕㄨ)
to do one's best (in order to please or impress somebody); to bring forth all the talent one has
使眼色 (ㄕ ㄧㄢ ㄙㄜ)
to say something with eyes; to make eyes at; to wink: 她向男友使眼色。She made eyes at her boy friend.
使用 (ㄕ ㄩㄥ)
to use; to employ; to resort to: 她使用新的教學法。She employs a new teaching method.
使用年限 (ㄕ ㄩㄥ ㄋㄧㄢ ㄒㄧㄢ)
the tenure of use
使用價值 (ㄕ ㄩㄥ ㄐㄧㄚ ㄓ)
① (economics) utility ② the value of something being

utilized

使用權(ㄕ ㄩㄥ ㄑㄩㄢ)
(law) the right of use (or using); the right to use something

【使】 147
ㄕ shyh shì
(或讀 ㄕ shyy shǐ)
1. to be appointed as a diplomatic envoy; to be an ambassador to
2. an envoy; an emissary; a minister

使徒(ㄕ ㄊㄨˊ)
(in the Bible) the Apostle or Apostles

使團(ㄕ ㄊㄨㄢˊ)or 使節團(ㄕ ㄐㄧㄝˊ ㄊㄨㄢˊ)
①a diplomatic mission ② the diplomatic corps

使領館(ㄕ ㄌㄧㄥˇ ㄍㄨㄢˇ)
embassies and consulates

使館(ㄕ ㄍㄨㄢˇ)
a legation; an embassy

使節(ㄕ ㄐㄧㄝˊ)
an envoy; an official mission abroad

使者有婦(ㄕ ㄓㄜˇ ㄧㄡˇ ㄈㄨˋ)
a married man

使者(ㄕ ㄓㄜˇ)
an envoy; an emissary; a messenger

使臣(ㄕ ㄔㄣˊ)
an envoy; a representative of a country abroad

【侃】 148
ㄎㄢˇ kaan kǎn
1. straightforward; frank; bold; open
2. amiable; pleasant
3. with confidence and composure

侃侃而談(ㄎㄢˇ ㄎㄢˇ ㄦˊ ㄊㄢˊ)
to talk with confidence and composure

侃直(ㄎㄢˇ ㄓˊ)
resolute and honest

【來】 149
ㄌㄞˊ lai lái
1. to come; coming; to arrive: 他昨天來這裡。He came here yesterday.
2. used in place of a verb: 讓我自己來吧! Let me do it myself.
3. to return; to come back; returning: 他還沒回來。He has not come back.

4. future; later on; next: 來春 next spring
5. ever since: 別來無恙乎? How have you been since we separated?
6. (used after a number) a little more than; about: 他大約四十來歲。He is about forty years old.
7. used after one, two, to explain: 一來路太遠, 二來沒時間。I haven't been to see her for a long time now. For one thing, she lives too far away; for another, I've been rather busy.
8. used after or before a verb to complement its meaning: 大家來想辦法。Let's try our best and see what to do. 我們合不來。We are not able to get along with each other.
9. a Chinese family name

來比錫(ㄌㄞˊ ㄅㄧˇ ㄒㄧ)
Leipzig, a city in the east of Germany

來賓(ㄌㄞˊ ㄅㄧㄣ)
①a guest; a visitor ②name of a county in Kwangsi Province

來賓席(ㄌㄞˊ ㄅㄧㄣ ㄒㄧˊ)
seats for guests

來不及(ㄌㄞˊ ㄅㄨˋ ㄐㄧˊ)
unable to make it in time; not enough time left to do it; too late to do something

來犯(ㄌㄞˊ ㄈㄢˋ)
to come to attack us; to invade our territory: 我們決心消滅膽敢來犯的敵人。We resolutely wipe out any enemy that dares to invade our territory.

來訪(ㄌㄞˊ ㄈㄤˇ)
to come to visit; to come to call

來福槍(ㄌㄞˊ ㄈㄨˊ ㄑㄧㄤ)
a rifle

來附(ㄌㄞˊ ㄈㄨˋ)
to flock to; to submit as vassals

來得(ㄌㄞˊ ㄉㄜ˙)
①to be able to; competent: 我父親很能來得一兩杯。My father is able to drink quite a few cups. ②to act or

speak with great force: 他這幾句話來得利害。His words are most telling. ③to happen; to come: 那些事情來得不巧。Those matters happened at the wrong (or unfortunate) moment. ④to emerge (from a comparison) as, to come out as

來得及(ㄌㄞˊ ㄉㄜ˙ ㄐㄧˊ)
①to be able to make it in time; there is time for…: 趕快走還來得及。Go at once while there's (still) time. ②to be able to accomplish or manage

來到(ㄌㄞˊ ㄉㄠˋ)
to arrive; to come: 雨季來到了。The rainy season has come.

來電(ㄌㄞˊ ㄉㄧㄢˋ)
①an incoming telegram (or telephone); your message: 五月五日來電悉。Your message of May 5 received. ②to telephone; to send a telegram here: 請來電告知。Please telephone me.

來頭(ㄌㄞˊ ㄊㄡˊ)or 來頭兒(ㄌㄞˊ ㄊㄡˊ ㄦ)
①background; personal connections ②fun in doing anything: 這種遊戲還有什麼來頭兒? What's the fun with this kind of game?

來頭大(ㄌㄞˊ ㄊㄡˊ ㄉㄚˋ)or 來頭不小(ㄌㄞˊ ㄊㄡˊ ㄅㄨˋ ㄒㄧㄠˇ)
of an impressive background, connections, etc.; very influential socially or politically; not to be taken lightly: 他們的來頭不小。They have an impressive background.

來年(ㄌㄞˊ ㄋㄧㄢˊ)
the next year; the years to come

來來往往(ㄌㄞˊ ㄌㄞˊ ㄨㄤˇ ㄨㄤˇ)
coming and going in great numbers

來歷(ㄌㄞˊ ㄌㄧˋ)
past history; origin; background

來歷不明(ㄌㄞˊ ㄌㄧˋ ㄅㄨˋ ㄇㄧㄥˊ)
of questionable antecedents, source, origin, background, etc.: 他的來歷不明。He is a man of obscure origin.

〔人部〕

來臨(ㄌㄞˊ ㄌㄧㄣˊ)
to arrive; to come; to approach

來路(ㄌㄞˊ ㄌㄨˋ)
①source; origin; (personal) background ②incoming road; approach

來路不正(ㄌㄞˊ ㄌㄨˋ ㄅㄨˋ ㄓㄥˋ)or 來路不明(ㄌㄞˊ ㄌㄨˋ ㄅㄨˋ ㄇㄧㄥˊ)
of questionable origin; of dubious background

來路貨(ㄌㄞˊ ㄌㄨˋ ㄏㄨㄛˋ)
imported goods

來龍去脈(ㄌㄞˊ ㄌㄨㄥˊ ㄑㄩˋ ㄇㄞˋ)
the beginning and subsequent development of (an incident, etc.); cause and effect: 我們必須弄清此事的來龍去脈。We must find out the cause and effect of the incident.

來稿(ㄌㄞˊ ㄍㄠˇ)
(often used by newspaper editors or publishing houses) your manuscript; incoming manuscripts

來客(ㄌㄞˊ ㄎㄜˋ)
a visitor; a guest

來函(ㄌㄞˊ ㄏㄢˊ)or 來信(ㄌㄞˊ ㄒㄧㄣˋ) or 來札(ㄌㄞˊ ㄓㄚˊ)or 來翰(ㄌㄞˊ ㄏㄢˋ)
your letter (to me or us)

來亨鷄(ㄌㄞˊ ㄏㄥ ㄐㄧ)
the Leghorn

來貨(ㄌㄞˊ ㄏㄨㄛˋ)
the goods sent here

來回(ㄌㄞˊ ㄏㄨㄟˊ)
①coming and going; to come and go; back and forth; to and fro: 他在房裏來回走動。He paced to and fro the room. ②to make a return journey

來回票(ㄌㄞˊ ㄏㄨㄟˊ ㄆㄧㄠˋ)
a round-trip ticket

來件(ㄌㄞˊ ㄐㄧㄢˋ)
the communication (or the parcel) received

來勁(ㄌㄞˊ ㄐㄧㄣˋ)
(dialect) ①full of enthusiasm; in high spirits ②exciting; thrilling ③to annoy; to offend: 你別跟我來勁。Don't offend me.

…來…去(ㄌㄞˊ …ㄑㄩ)
back and forth; over and over again: 鳥飛來飛去。Birds

fly back and forth.

來信(ㄌㄞˊ ㄒㄧㄣˋ)
①your letter ②to send a letter here: 到了那裏就請來信。Please write to us as soon as you get there.

來之不易(ㄌㄞˊ ㄓ ㄅㄨˋ ㄧˋ)
It has not come easily. 或It is hard-earned. 我們的勝利來之不易。Our victory was hard-earned.

來者(ㄌㄞˊ ㄓㄜˇ)
①anything in the future ②anyone who has come

來者不拒(ㄌㄞˊ ㄓㄜˇ ㄅㄨˋ ㄐㄩˋ)
to grant favors to whoever asks for it

來者不善,善者不來(ㄌㄞˊ ㄓㄜˇ ㄅㄨˋ ㄕㄢˋ, ㄕㄢˋ ㄓㄜˇ ㄅㄨˋ ㄌㄞˊ)
Those who have come are surely strong. 或Those who have come, come with ill intentions.

來者可追(ㄌㄞˊ ㄓㄜˇ ㄎㄜˇ ㄓㄨㄟ)
There is still time to mend.

來世(ㄌㄞˊ ㄕˋ)
①later generations ②(Buddhism)the future life

來勢(ㄌㄞˊ ㄕˋ)
oncoming force: 這場雨來勢很猛。The oncoming force of the rainstorm is violent.

來勢洶洶(ㄌㄞˊ ㄕˋ ㄒㄩㄥ ㄒㄩㄥ)
to move threateningly towards

來沙兒(ㄌㄞˊ ㄕㄚ ㄦ)or 來沙爾(ㄌㄞˊ ㄕㄚ ㄦˇ)
(medicine) lysol

來生(ㄌㄞˊ ㄕㄥ)
the future life; the next life or incarnation

來日(ㄌㄞˊ ㄖˋ)
①tomorrow ②the future

來日方長(ㄌㄞˊ ㄖˋ ㄈㄤ ㄔㄤˊ)
There is a long time ahead (so there is no need to be in a hurry).

來人(ㄌㄞˊ ㄖㄣˊ)
①the person or persons who came or are coming ②the incoming envoy, messenger, etc.: 收據請交來人帶回。Please give the receipt to the messenger.

來意(ㄌㄞˊ ㄧˋ)
the purpose of a personal call; the objectives of a visit:

他正想說明來意。He is trying to make clear what he has come for.

來由(ㄌㄞˊ ㄧㄡˊ)
reason; cause (of something or some happening): 我在尋思其來由。I'm trying to find out its cause.

來茵河(ㄌㄞˊ ㄧㄣ ㄏㄜˊ)or 萊茵河(ㄌㄞˊ ㄧㄣ ㄏㄜˊ)
the Rhine

來文(ㄌㄞˊ ㄨㄣˊ)
incoming documents, letters, etc.; document(s) received

來往(ㄌㄞˊ ㄨㄤˇ)
①social intercourse or connection: 我跟他從未有任何來往。I've never had any intercourse with him. ②coming and going: 街上來往的人很多。There are many people coming and going on the streets.

來往存款(ㄌㄞˊ ㄨㄤˇ ㄘㄨㄣˊ ㄎㄨㄢˇ)
a current account

來月(ㄌㄞˊ ㄩㄝˋ)
the following month; months to come

來源(ㄌㄞˊ ㄩㄢˊ)
the source; the origin

【侈】 150
ㄔ chyy chǐ
1. wasteful; luxurious; lavish; extravagant
2. to exaggerate; bragging
3. evildoing
4. excessive

侈靡(ㄔ ㄇㄧˊ)
extravagance and excesses; extravagant; wasteful

侈論(ㄔ ㄌㄨㄣˋ)or 侈談(ㄔ ㄊㄢˊ)
①exaggerated talk ②to speak boastingly; to talk glibly about; to prate about

侈言(ㄔ ㄧㄢˊ)
①exaggerated talk ②to exaggerate; to swagger

【例】 151
ㄌㄧˋ lih lì
1. a regulation; a rule; a custom; something with which to compare; a practice: 我的慣例是早餐前散步。My rule is to have a walk before breakfast.
2. a precedent: 你要我做的事有前例可援嗎? Is there a precedent for what you want me to do?
3. an example; an instance

〔人部〕

4. regular; routine

例題 (ㄌ丨ㄊ丨)
(in a textbook) a question or problem for which an answer or a solution is provided for the student; an example

例規 (ㄌ丨 ㄍㄨㄟ)
regulations; a usual practice

例話 (ㄌ丨 ㄏㄨㄚ)
systematic exemplification of moral teachings

例會 (ㄌ丨 ㄏㄨㄟ)
a regular meeting

例假 (ㄌ丨 ㄐ丨ㄚ)
a statutory holiday; a customary holiday; a legal holiday

例句 (ㄌ丨 ㄐㄩ)
a sentence serving as an example (in a textbook, etc.) to show proper structure, arrangement of words, etc.; an illustrative sentence

例行公事 (ㄌ丨 ㄒ丨ㄥ ㄍㄨㄥ ㄕ)
official routine; routine: 這些不過是例行公事。These are done as a matter of routine.

例證 (ㄌ丨 ㄓㄥ)
an antecedent used to clarify or explain a point; illustration; a case in point; proof of a given proposition or theorem

例如 (ㄌ丨 ㄖㄨ)
for example; for instance; such as

例子 (ㄌ丨˙ㄗ)
an example; an instance

例言 (ㄌ丨 丨ㄢ)
an introduction to a book; introductory remarks

例外 (ㄌ丨 ㄨㄞ)
an exception: 每一原則都有一些例外。There is no rule without exception.

【侍】 152
ㄕ shyh shì
1. to serve; to wait upon.
2. to accompany one's elder or superior
3. a designation for oneself when addressing an elder or a senior
4. an attendant

侍婢 (ㄕ ㄅ丨)
a personal attendant maid; a

maidservant

侍奉 (ㄕ ㄈㄥ)
to serve; to attend on

侍女 (ㄕ ㄋㄩ)
a maid; a maidservant

侍候 (ㄕ ㄏㄡ)
to wait upon; to serve; to attend: 他們是侍候國王的。They were in attendance on the king.

侍妾 (ㄕ ㄑ丨ㄝ)
a concubine

侍親 (ㄕ ㄑ丨ㄣ)
to attend one's parents (tenderly and dutifully)

侍者 (ㄕ ㄓㄜ)
① attendants, waiters, etc.
② Buddhist monks — as attendants to Buddha

侍臣 (ㄕ ㄔㄣ)
a courtier

侍役 (ㄕ 丨ㄝ˙ㄗ)
attendants; servants; retinue

侍應生 (ㄕ 丨ㄥ ㄕㄥ)
an attendant; a waiter or waitress

侍衛 (ㄕ ㄨㄟ)
bodyguards

【侏】 153
ㄓㄨ ju zhū
1. short
2. a pigmy or dwarf

侏儒 (ㄓㄨ ㄖㄨˊ)
① a dwarf ② a court jester

【侑】 154
丨ㄡ yow yòu
1. to help
2. to urge (or press) somebody to eat or drink
3. to repay other's kindness

【侘】 155
ㄔㄚ chah chà
1. to boast
2. disappointed

侘傺 (ㄔㄚ ㄔ)
disappointed; frustrated

侘傺不安 (ㄔㄚ ㄔ ㄅㄨ ㄢ)
uneasy

【供】 156
ㄍㄨㄥ gong gōng
to supply; to contribute to

供不應求 (ㄍㄨㄥ ㄅㄨ 丨ㄥ ㄑ丨ㄡ)
The supply is unable to meet the demand. 或 The demand exceeds the supply.

供電 (ㄍㄨㄥ ㄉ丨ㄢ)
power supply

供過於求 (ㄍㄨㄥ ㄍㄨㄛ ㄩ ㄑ丨ㄡ)
The supply has outstripped the demand.

供給 (ㄍㄨㄥ ㄐ丨)
to supply; to equip; to provide

供求 (ㄍㄨㄥ ㄑ丨ㄡ)
supply and demand

供求律 (ㄍㄨㄥ ㄑ丨ㄡ ㄌㄩ)
the law of supply and demand

供銷 (ㄍㄨㄥ ㄒ丨ㄠ)
supply and marketing

供應 (ㄍㄨㄥ 丨ㄥ)
① to supply; to furnish ② supply; support: 他出錢供應我讀書。He gave me financial support for my studies.

【供】 2. ㄍㄨㄥ gonq gòng
1. to give a statement or an account of a criminal act; to give evidence; to confess: 他供出主犯。He gave the name of the chief culprit.
2. to offer in worship
3. articles of sacrifice; offerings
4. testimony of a prisoner; confession
5. supplies

供品 (ㄍㄨㄥ ㄆ丨ㄣ)
offerings

供佛 (ㄍㄨㄥ ㄈㄛ)
to make offerings to Buddha

供奉 (ㄍㄨㄥ ㄈㄥ)
① to provide for one's elders (especially parents) ② to offer sacrifices in worshiping

供職 (ㄍㄨㄥ ㄓ)
to hold office

供桌 (ㄍㄨㄥ ㄓㄨㄛ)
the table on which sacrificial offerings are placed

供狀 (ㄍㄨㄥ ㄓㄨㄤ)
(law) an affidavit

供認 (ㄍㄨㄥ ㄖㄣ)
to confess; a confession

供詞 (ㄍㄨㄥ ㄘ)
a confession to a criminal act; verbal depositions

供養 (ㄍㄨㄥ 丨ㄤ)
① to offer provisions (especially to one's elders) ② to bring up one's children: 他供養三個小孩。He brought up

three children. ③ provisions offered to one's elders

【依】 157
ㄧ　ī yī

1. to depend on; to lean to: 他們倆相依為命。They depend on each other for existence.
2. to follow; to comply with; to consent; to yield to
3. to be tolerant to; to forgive
4. according to; in the light of; judging by: 依我看來, 他會贏。According to my opinion, he will win.

依傍(ㄧ ㄅㄤ)
①to depend on ②to pattern after; to imitate ; to model after

依仗(ㄧ ㄓㄤˋ)
to rely on; to depend on

依法(ㄧ ㄈㄚˇ)
according to law

依附(ㄧ ㄈㄨˋ)
①to depend on ②to submit to

依託(ㄧ ㄊㄨㄛ)
to trust; to depend on

依賴(ㄧ ㄌㄞˋ)
to depend on

依賴性(ㄧ ㄌㄞˋ ㄒㄧㄥˋ)
the habit of relying upon others

依留申(ㄧ ㄌㄧㄡˊ ㄕㄣ)
Ilyushin (a type of Russian planes)

依戀(ㄧ ㄌㄧㄢˋ)
to be reluctant to leave; to feel attachment to someone

依靠(ㄧ ㄎㄠˋ)
①to rely on; to depend on: 他依靠自己的力量。He depends on his own strength. ②someone or something to fall back on; support; backing: 他尋找依靠。He seeks support.

依舊(ㄧ ㄐㄧㄡˋ)
as usual; as before; in the usual way or manner

依據(ㄧ ㄐㄩˋ)
①according to; in accordance with; on the strength of; based on ②a basis; foundation: 當時我們沒有任何遵循的依據。We didn't have any basis to go by at that time.

依稀(ㄧ ㄒㄧ)

unclear; uncertain; not distinct

依照(ㄧ ㄓㄠˋ)
in accordance with; in compliance with

依從(ㄧ ㄘㄨㄥˊ)
①someone or something to fall back upon ②to rely on or count on (influence, wealth, etc.): 他依從權勢。He relies on his power and position.

依順(ㄧ ㄕㄨㄣˋ)
to be obedient

依然(ㄧ ㄖㄢˊ)
as before; as usual; still

依然故我(ㄧ ㄖㄢˊ ㄍㄨˋ ㄨㄛˇ)
I am still what I used to be.

依此類推(ㄧ ㄘˇ ㄌㄟˋ ㄊㄨㄟ)
The rest may be deduced by analogy. 或 and so on; and so forth

依次(ㄧ ㄘˋ)
in order (in proper sequence or position); one by one

依存(ㄧ ㄘㄨㄣˊ)
interdependent; to depend on somebody or something for existence: 他們相互依存。They are interdependent.

依從(ㄧ ㄘㄨㄥˊ)
to comply with; to follow; to submit or listen to (suggestion, etc.)

依隨(ㄧ ㄙㄨㄟˊ)
to follow (a person, a wish); to comply with

依依不捨(ㄧ ㄧ ㄅㄨˋ ㄕㄜˇ)
unwilling to part (with the loved ones): 他們依依不捨。They are unwilling to part with each other.

依樣(畫)葫蘆(ㄧ ㄧㄤˋ (ㄏㄨㄚˋ) ㄏㄨˊ ㄌㄨˊ)
to imitate others or to follow the beaten path without questioning; to copy mechanically

依違兩可(ㄧ ㄨㄟˊ ㄌㄧㄤˇ ㄎㄜˇ)
shilly-shally; to be undecided; to be unable to make up one's mind

依約(ㄧ ㄩㄝ)
①to follow conventions and

traditions ②indistinct; obscure ③in accordance with the promise

【佬】 158
ㄌㄠˇ lao lǎo

1. a fellow; a man; a guy
2. a vulgar person; a hillbilly

七畫

【侮】 159
ㄨˇ wuu wǔ

1. to bully
2. to disgrace; to insult; to humiliate
3. an insult; a bully

侮罵(ㄨˇ ㄇㄚˋ)
to insult with words

侮慢(ㄨˇ ㄇㄢˋ)
①to insult ②haughty and rude

侮蔑(ㄨˇ ㄇㄧㄝˋ)
to disgrace; to slight

侮弄(ㄨˇ ㄋㄨㄥˋ)
to make a fool of

侮辱(ㄨˇ ㄖㄨˇ)
to insult; to humiliate; an insult

【侯】 160
ㄏㄡˊ hour hóu

1. (in ancient China) the second of the five grades of the nobility
2. the target in archery
3. a marquis; a nobleman or a high official
4. a Chinese family name

侯門如海(ㄏㄡˊ ㄇㄣˊ ㄖㄨˊ ㄏㄞˇ)
①(said of women of humble origin married to the nobility) Once inside the marquis's door there's no turning back. ② A rich man's mansion is inaccessible to the common people.

侯國(ㄏㄡˊ ㄍㄨㄛˊ)
a principality

侯爵(ㄏㄡˊ ㄐㄩㄝˊ)
a marquis

侯爵夫人(ㄏㄡˊ ㄐㄩㄝˊ ㄈㄨ ㄖㄣˊ)
a marchioness

【侶】 161
ㄌㄩˇ leu lǚ

1. a companion; a mate
2. to associate with

【侵】 162
ㄑㄧㄣ chin qīn

1. to raid; to aggress; to

invade: 敵人侵略我們的國家。
The enemy invaded our country.
2. to encroach upon; to use force stealthily
3. to proceed gradually
4. a bad year; a year of famine or disaster

侵犯(ㄑㄧㄣ ㄈㄢˋ)
(law) to encroach upon other's rights; to violate; to invade; to infringe upon (rights)

侵奪(ㄑㄧㄣ ㄉㄨㄛˊ)
to seize by force

侵吞(ㄑㄧㄣ ㄊㄨㄣ)
to misappropriate (public funds, etc. for private ends); to embezzle; to take by illegal means; to annex: 貪官侵吞公款. Corrupt officials embezzle public funds.

侵擾(ㄑㄧㄣ ㄖㄠˇ)
to raid and humiliate; to intimidate

侵略(ㄑㄧㄣ ㄌㄩㄝˋ)
① to invade ② aggression; encroachment

侵掠(ㄑㄧㄣ ㄌㄩㄝˋ)
to invade; to harass and loot

侵害(ㄑㄧㄣ ㄏㄞˋ)
to infringe or encroach upon (the rights, etc. of another); to violate

侵襲(ㄑㄧㄣ ㄒㄧˊ)
to attack stealthily; to make a sneaking attack on; to encroach upon

侵佔 or 侵占(ㄑㄧㄣ ㄓㄢˋ)
to occupy or take (the land, the property, etc. of another) illegally; misappropriation; to seize

侵佔罪 or 侵占罪(ㄑㄧㄣ ㄓㄢˋ ㄗㄨㄟˋ)
(law) an offense of misappropriation; embezzlement

侵晨(ㄑㄧㄣ ㄔㄣˊ)
early morning

侵蝕(ㄑㄧㄣ ㄕˊ)
erosion; to encroach; to erode; to eat into gradually: 土壤侵蝕 soil erosion

侵擾(ㄑㄧㄣ ㄖㄠˇ)
to trespass and cause disorder or trouble; to harass

侵人犯規(ㄑㄧㄣ ㄖㄣˊ ㄈㄢˋ ㄍㄨㄟ)
(sports) a personal foul

侵入(ㄑㄧㄣ ㄖㄨˋ)
to intrude; to invade; to make incursions into: 他們侵入別國領土. They intruded into another country's territory.

【侷】 163
ㄐㄩˊ jyu jú
narrow; cramped; confined

侷促一隅(ㄐㄩˊ ㄘㄨˋ ㄧ ㄩˊ)
to be confined to a small place or corner

侷促(ㄐㄩˊ ㄘㄨˋ)
① cramped; confined ② fidgeting; restless

侷促不安(ㄐㄩˊ ㄘㄨˋ ㄅㄨˋ ㄢ)
restless; fidgeting; nervous; uneasy

【便】 164
1. ㄅㄧㄢˋ biann biàn
1. expedient; convenient; handy: 這本字典便於帶在口袋中. This dictionary is convenient for carrying in one's pocket.
2. fitting; appropriate
3. in that case; even if: 便有不是, 也得原諒他. Even if he is wrong, you shall ' forgive him.
4. then: 你不去, 他便得去. If you do not go, then he has to.
5. advantageous
6. excrement and urine; to relieve oneself
7. informal; at ease; plain; ordinary

便步(ㄅㄧㄢˋ ㄅㄨˋ)
(military drill) to walk at ease as contrasted to goose stepping

便帽(ㄅㄧㄢˋ ㄇㄠˋ) or 便帽兒(ㄅㄧㄢˋ ㄇㄠˋ ㄦ)
a cap or hat for ordinary wear

便門(ㄅㄧㄢˋ ㄇㄣˊ) or 便門兒(ㄅㄧㄢˋ ㄇㄣˊ ㄦ)
a side door; a wicket

便祕(ㄅㄧㄢˋ ㄇㄧˋ)
constipation

便民(ㄅㄧㄢˋ ㄇㄧㄣˊ)
to offer greater convenience to the people (by reducing red tape)

便飯(ㄅㄧㄢˋ ㄈㄢˋ)
a meal; potluck; an ordinary meal (as distinguished from a feast); a simple meal

便服(ㄅㄧㄢˋ ㄈㄨˊ)

---

ordinary clothing; everyday dress; informal dress

便道(ㄅㄧㄢˋ ㄉㄠˋ)
① a shortcut; a snap course ② sidewalks; paths flanking the main road ③ to do something on the way

便當
① (ㄅㄧㄢˋ ㄉㄤ) a box lunch one takes to school, office, etc. in the morning
② (ㄅㄧㄢˋ·ㄉㄤ) easy; convenient

便條(ㄅㄧㄢˋ ㄊㄧㄠˊ) or 便條兒(ㄅㄧㄢˋ ㄊㄧㄠˊ ㄦ)
a note; a memo; an informal letter, etc.

便桶(ㄅㄧㄢˋ ㄊㄨㄥˇ)
a deep container for emptying the bowels; a pail for stool

便溺(ㄅㄧㄢˋ ㄋㄧˋ)
to empty the bowels and to urinate

便覽(ㄅㄧㄢˋ ㄌㄢˇ)
a pocket-size book or pamphlet for convenient reading

便利(ㄅㄧㄢˋ ㄌㄧˋ)
convenience; expediency; facility; convenient; expedient

便了(ㄅㄧㄢˋ·ㄌㄜ)
an expletive used at the end of a sentence (usually found in songs): 這樣做去便了. Just do it like this.

便路(ㄅㄧㄢˋ ㄌㄨˋ)
a shortcut; a bypath

便函(ㄅㄧㄢˋ ㄏㄢˊ)
an informal letter

便壺(ㄅㄧㄢˋ ㄏㄨˊ)
a night-pot for urination; a chamber pot

便捷(ㄅㄧㄢˋ ㄐㄧㄝˊ)
easy and convenient; convenience; facility

便箋(ㄅㄧㄢˋ ㄐㄧㄢ)
notepaper; a memo; a memo pad

便徑(ㄅㄧㄢˋ ㄐㄧㄥˋ)
a quick route; a shortcut

便橋(ㄅㄧㄢˋ ㄑㄧㄠˊ)
a temporary bridge; a makeshift bridge

便鞋(ㄅㄧㄢˋ ㄒㄧㄝˊ)
① cloth shoes ② slippers

便酌(ㄅㄧㄢˋ ㄓㄨㄛˊ)

（人 部）

an informal feast; an informal dinner

便中（ㄅㄧㄢˋ ㄓㄨㄥ）
at (your) convenience

便池（ㄅㄧㄢˋ ㄔˊ）
a urinal

便士（ㄅㄧㄢˋ ㄕˋ）
penny

便菜（ㄅㄧㄢˋ ㄘㄞˋ）
an ordinary dish; an everyday dish

便簣（ㄅㄧㄢˋ ㄈㄢˋ）
an informal and ordinary meal

便所（ㄅㄧㄢˋ ㄙㄨㄛˇ）
a toilet; a lavatory; a privy; a rest room

便衣（ㄅㄧㄢˋ ㄧ）
①ordinary clothes; plain clothes ② a plainclothesman

便宜行事（ㄅㄧㄢˋ ㄧˊ ㄒㄧㄥˊ ㄕˋ）
to act as circumstances may require without asking for approval from superiors

便於（ㄅㄧㄢˋ ㄩˊ）
easy to; convenient for

【便】 164
ㄅㄧㄢˋ、ㄆㄧㄢˊ pyan pian
1. cheap; inexpensive
2. a Chinese family name

便嬖（ㄆㄧㄢˊ ㄅㄧˋ）
a sycophant

便辟（ㄆㄧㄢˊ ㄅㄧˋ）
a man of specious airs

便佞（ㄆㄧㄢˊ ㄋㄧㄥˋ）
a glib-tongued man

便宜（ㄆㄧㄢˊ ㄧˊ）
①cheap; inexpensive ②to gain advantage ③ advantage; profit ④to let someone off lightly

【係】 165
ㄒㄧˋ shih xi
1. to bind; to belong to; to attach to; to connect with
2. relationship; consequences
3. to be
4. a Chinese family name

係數（ㄒㄧˋ ㄕㄨˋ）
(mathematics) coefficient

【促】 166
ㄘㄨˋ tsuh cù
1. close; crowded; near
2. to urge; to hurry; to promote
3. hurried; urgent

促迫（ㄘㄨˋ ㄆㄛˋ）

to urge; to hurry; pressing

促忙（ㄘㄨˋ ㄇㄤˊ）
in a hurry

促進（ㄘㄨˋ ㄐㄧㄣˋ）
to urge to proceed; to press forward; to promote; promotion

促膝談心（ㄘㄨˋ ㄒㄧ ㄊㄢˊ ㄒㄧㄣ）
to talk intimately; to have a heart-to-heart talk; to cross the knees and talk over things as close friends; to sit side by side and talk intimately

促狹鬼（ㄘㄨˋ ㄒㄧㄚˊ ㄍㄨㄟˇ）
a mischievous fellow; a person who likes to play jokes on others; a practical joker; a mean and spiteful fellow

促銷（ㄘㄨˋ ㄒㄧㄠ）
sales promotion

促織（ㄘㄨˋ ㄓ）
another name for the cricket

促成（ㄘㄨˋ ㄔㄥˊ）
to help to materialize; to help to bring about

促使（ㄘㄨˋ ㄕˇ）
to impel; to urge; to spur

【俄】 167
ㄜˊ er é
1. suddenly; sudden; momentarily

俄頃（ㄜˊ ㄑㄧㄥˇ）
shortly afterward; soon; in a short moment; momentarily

俄而（ㄜˊ ㄦˊ）
instantly; soon

【俄】 167
ㄜˋ eh è
俄勒岡（ㄜˋ ㄌㄜˋ ㄍㄤ）
Oregon, U. S. A.

俄羅斯族（ㄜˋ ㄌㄨㄛˊ ㄙ ㄗㄨˊ）
①the Eluosi (Russian) nationality ②the Russians (of the U.S.S.R.)

俄國（ㄜˋ ㄍㄨㄛˊ）or 俄羅斯（ㄜˋ ㄌㄨㄛˊ ㄙ）
Russia

俄國的（ㄜˋ ㄍㄨㄛˊ ˙ㄉㄜ）
Russian

俄國人（ㄜˋ ㄍㄨㄛˊ ㄖㄣˊ）
a Russian

俄亥俄（ㄜˋ ㄏㄞˋ ㄜˋ）
Ohio, U. S. A.

俄語（ㄜˋ ㄩˇ）or 俄文（ㄜˋ ㄨㄣˊ）
Russian (language)

【俊】 168
ㄐㄩㄣˋ jiunn jùn
1. talented; capable; superior; refined; smart; bright
2. handsome; good-looking
3. big; huge

俊拔（ㄐㄩㄣˋ ㄅㄚˊ）
uncommon

俊邁（ㄐㄩㄣˋ ㄇㄞˋ）
excelling in grace and elegance

俊美（ㄐㄩㄣˋ ㄇㄟˇ）
good-looking; handsome

俊傑（ㄐㄩㄣˋ ㄐㄧㄝˊ）
a brave and superior person; a person of extraordinary talent; an individual of distinction and mark

俊俏（ㄐㄩㄣˋ ㄑㄧㄠˋ）
elegant; graceful; good-looking and smart; lovely; charming

俊秀（ㄐㄩㄣˋ ㄒㄧㄡˋ）
talented and superior; handsome and refined

俊才（ㄐㄩㄣˋ ㄘㄞˊ）
a talented person

俊雅（ㄐㄩㄣˋ ㄧㄚˇ）
handsome, elegant and refined

俊偉（ㄐㄩㄣˋ ㄨㄟˇ）
superior and great

【俎】 169
ㄗㄨˇ tzuu zǔ
1. a painted wooden stand used in offering rites
2. a chopping board
3. a small table or stand
4. a Chinese family name

俎豆（ㄗㄨˇ ㄉㄡˋ）
sacrificial stand and pot —sacrificial rites

俎上肉（ㄗㄨˇ ㄕㄤˋ ㄖㄡˋ）
(literally) meat on a chopping board—a helpless victim

【俏】 170
ㄑㄧㄠˋ chiaw qiào
1. like; similar; to resemble; to be like
2. pretty and cute; good-looking; smart; handsome: 她是位俏女郎。 She is a pretty girl.
3. (commodities) enjoying brisk sale at higher prices; in great demand
4. (said of stocks) bullish

俏皮（く１ㄠ·ㄆ１）
① pretty and cute; winsome; 他年輕又俏皮。He is young and winsome. ② sarcastic; witty; to make sarcastic remarks at

俏皮話（く１ㄠ·ㄆ１ ㄏㄨㄚˋ）
a wisecrack; a jibe; a clever retort; a witty remark; a sarcastic remark

俏俏（く１ㄠˋ）
beautiful; good-looking

俏似（く１ㄠˋ ㄙˋ）
to resemble; to be like: 人生俏似一場夢。Life is just like a dream.

俏冤家（く１ㄠˋ ㄩㄢ ㄐ１ㄚ）
(my) pretty but naughty lover

【例】171 ㄌ１ˋ lih lì
1. facile; easy and quick
2. sharp; clever
3. in good order; tidy; neat

例落（ㄌ１ˋ ㄌㄨㄛˋ）
well-executed 亦作「利落」

【俑】172 ㄩㄥˇ yeong yǒng
(in ancient China) wooden or earthen figures of men and women buried with the dead; a tomb figure; a figurine

【俗】173 ㄙㄨˊ swu sú
1. customs or customary
2. vulgar; unrefined
3. common; popular
4. lay (as distinguished from clerical); worldly; secular
5. tasteless; trite

俗不可耐（ㄙㄨˊ ㄅㄨˋ ㄎㄜˇ ㄋㄞˋ）
unbearably vulgar

俗民文化（ㄙㄨˊ ㄇㄧㄣˊ ㄨㄣˊ ㄏㄨㄚˋ）
folk culture

俗套（ㄙㄨˊ ㄊㄠˋ）
social conventions; conventional patterns

俗念（ㄙㄨˊ ㄋㄧㄢˋ）
worldly thoughts; a layman's ideas

俗累（ㄙㄨˊ ㄌㄟˋ）
worldly troubles

俗例（ㄙㄨˊ ㄌㄧˋ）
common practices; customary rules

the common lot of people; the layman

俗骨（ㄙㄨˊ ㄍㄨˇ）
(a self-depreciatory expression) vulgar to the bone; vulgar bones

俗話（ㄙㄨˊ ㄏㄨㄚˋ）
a common saying; a proverb: 俗話說時間就是金錢。A proverb says that time is money.

俗家（ㄙㄨˊ ㄐ１ㄚ）
① the layman; the common lot of people ② the home of a monk or nun before taking the tonsure

俗氣（ㄙㄨˊ ·くㄧ）
① vulgarity; vulgar; in poor taste ② hackneyed

俗稱（ㄙㄨˊ ㄔㄥ）
① the secular name of a monk, etc. before consecration ② commonly called …; commonly known as…

俗事（ㄙㄨˊ ㄕˋ）or 俗事兒（ㄙㄨˊ ㄕˋㄦ）
mundane affairs; everyday matters; daily routine; worldly affairs

俗世（ㄙㄨˊ ㄕˋ）
earthly life

俗尚（ㄙㄨˊ ㄕㄤˋ）
customs; customary; common beliefs; common conventions; the current

俗人（ㄙㄨˊ ㄖㄣˊ）
① a layman as opposed to the clergy ② an ordinary person; a vulgarian

俗儒（ㄙㄨˊ ㄖㄨˊ）
a scholar of shallow learning

俗字（ㄙㄨˊ ㄗˋ）
① a non-classical word; a vulgar word ② the popular or simplified form of a Chinese character

俗眼（ㄙㄨˊ ㄧㄢˇ）
(in) the eyes of a commoner, layman, ordinary person, etc.; mortal eyes

俗諺（ㄙㄨˊ ㄧㄢˋ）
a common saying; a popular saying; a proverb 參看「俗語」

俗物（ㄙㄨˊ ㄨˋ）
unrefined persons or things; philistines; a vulgar

俗務（ㄙㄨˊ ㄨˋ）
chores; routines; everyday matters or business; worldly cares

俗語（ㄙㄨˊ ㄩˇ）
There is a common saying….

俗文學（ㄙㄨˊ ㄨㄣˊ ㄒㄩㄝˊ）
popular literature (ballads, songs, novels, etc.)

俗緣（ㄙㄨˊ ㄩㄢˊ）
worldly relations, ties, obligations, etc. (of a Buddhist monk or nun)

【俘】174 ㄈㄨˊ fwu fú
1. prisoners of war
2. to capture; to take prisoner: 首領已被俘。The chief was captured.

俘虜（ㄈㄨˊ ㄌㄨˇ）
① to take prisoner: 他被敵人俘擄。He was taken prisoner by the enemy. ② a prisoner of war

俘虜營（ㄈㄨˊ ㄌㄨˇ ㄧㄥˊ）
a concentration camp for prisoners of war

俘獲（ㄈㄨˊ ㄏㄨㄛˋ）
to capture (weapons, documents, etc. from the enemy)

【俚】175 ㄌㄧˇ lii lǐ
1. vulgar; rustic; unpolished; unrefined
2. a small town or village; a tribe (aborigines, etc.)

俚歌（ㄌㄧˇ ㄍㄜ）
folk songs; country songs

俚俗（ㄌㄧˇ ㄙㄨˊ）
vulgar; unrefined

俚語（ㄌㄧˇ ㄩˇ）
slang; rustic expressions; vulgar expressions

【保】176 ㄅㄠˇ bao bǎo
1. to guard; to shelter; to protect; to defend: 英勇的軍人保家衛國。Brave soldiers protect our homes and defend our country.
2. to be responsible; to guarantee; to insure
3. a waiter or tender
4. to care for
5. to keep; to maintain
6. to stand guarantor or surety for someone: 我為他作保。I stand guarantor for him.
7. an official post in ancient

China

保鏢(ㄅㄠˇ ㄅㄧㄠ)
①a bodyguard; an armed escort (for passengers or cargo) ②to act as a bodyguard

保不住(ㄅㄠˇ·ㄅㄨ ㄓㄨˋ)
①cannot be defended ②most likely; more likely than not; may well: 保不住明天會下雨。 Most likely it's going to rain tomorrow.

保密(ㄅㄠˇ ㄇㄧˋ)
to keep the secret

保密防諜(ㄅㄠˇ ㄇㄧˋ ㄈㄤˊ ㄉㄧㄝˊ)
to keep the secret and prevent espionage

保姆(ㄅㄠˇ ㄇㄨˇ)
a nurse who looks after small children

保防工作(ㄅㄠˇ ㄈㄤˊ ㄍㄨㄥ ㄗㄨㄛˋ)
security measures

保單(ㄅㄠˇ ㄉㄢ)
①a formal note or document of guaranty ②an insurance policy

保定(ㄅㄠˇ ㄉㄧㄥˋ)
Paoting, a city in Hopen Province

保留(ㄅㄠˇ ㄌㄧㄡˊ)
①to preserve; to reserve; with reservations; to hold back: 他無保留地同意。 He agreed without reservation. ②to defer discussion for the future

保留地(ㄅㄠˇ ㄌㄧㄡˊ ㄉㄧˋ)
①the land reserved for a certain purpose ②a reservation (as the territory set apart for a certain class of people, like aborigines)

保齡球(ㄅㄠˇ ㄌㄧㄥˊ ㄑㄧㄡˊ)
bowling

保齡球場(ㄅㄠˇ ㄌㄧㄥˊ ㄑㄧㄡˊ ㄔㄤˇ)or (ㄅㄠˇ ㄌㄧㄥˊ ㄑㄧㄡˊ ㄔㄤˇ)
a building or enclosed area containing a number of bowling alleys

保羅(ㄅㄠˇ ㄌㄨㄛˊ)
a transliteration of Paul

保管(ㄅㄠˇ ㄍㄨㄢˇ)
①to safeguard; to safekeep; to put something under one's custody ②certainly; surely

保管費(ㄅㄠˇ ㄍㄨㄢˇ ㄈㄟˋ)
storage charges

保管室(ㄅㄠˇ ㄍㄨㄢˇ ㄕˋ)
a storeroom

保護(ㄅㄠˇ ㄏㄨˋ)
to protect; to guard; protection: 我們應保護環境防止汙染。We should protect the environment against pollution.

保護貿易政策(ㄅㄠˇ ㄏㄨˋ ㄇㄠˋ ㄧˋ ㄓㄥˋ ㄘㄜˋ)
the policy of protection

保護國(ㄅㄠˇ ㄏㄨˋ ㄍㄨㄛˊ)
a protectorate

保護(關)稅(ㄅㄠˇ ㄏㄨˋ (ㄍㄨㄢ) ㄕㄨㄟˋ)
a protective tariff

保護區(ㄅㄠˇ ㄏㄨˋ ㄑㄩ)
a protected area

保護主義(ㄅㄠˇ ㄏㄨˋ ㄓㄨˇ ㄧˋ)
protectionism

保護人(ㄅㄠˇ ㄏㄨˋ ㄖㄣˊ)
a guardian

保護組織(ㄅㄠˇ ㄏㄨˋ ㄗㄨˇ ㄓ)
(biology) protected tissue

保護色(ㄅㄠˇ ㄏㄨˋ ㄙㄜˋ)
protective coloration

保皇黨(ㄅㄠˇ ㄏㄨㄤˊ ㄉㄤˇ)
The Royalist Party

保加利亞(ㄅㄠˇ ㄐㄧㄚ ㄌㄧˋ ㄧㄚˇ)
Bulgaria

保家衛國(ㄅㄠˇ ㄐㄧㄚ ㄨㄟˋ ㄍㄨㄛˊ)
to defend the home and the country

保甲(ㄅㄠˇ ㄐㄧㄚˇ)
the Tithing System, devised by Prime Minister Wang An-shih (1021-1086) of the Sung Dynasty to maintain internal security and strengthen national defense

保駕(ㄅㄠˇ ㄐㄧㄚˋ)
①to protect or escort the royalty ②to protect an important person, guest, etc.

保結(ㄅㄠˇ ㄐㄧㄝˊ)
a document signed by one to the authorities to prove or guarantee the identity or good conduct of another person

保薦(ㄅㄠˇ ㄐㄧㄢˋ)
to recommend (somebody for a job, etc.)

保健(ㄅㄠˇ ㄐㄧㄢˋ)
health protection; health care

保健館(ㄅㄠˇ ㄐㄧㄢˋ ㄍㄨㄢˇ)
①a health center ②a gymnasium

保健工作(ㄅㄠˇ ㄐㄧㄢˋ ㄍㄨㄥ ㄗㄨㄛˋ)
public health work

保健箱(ㄅㄠˇ ㄐㄧㄢˋ ㄒㄧㄤ)
a medical kit

保健站(ㄅㄠˇ ㄐㄧㄢˋ ㄓㄢˋ)
a health station (or center)

保全(ㄅㄠˇ ㄑㄩㄢˊ)
to assure the safety of

保全公司(ㄅㄠˇ ㄑㄩㄢˊ ㄍㄨㄥ ㄙ)
a company that offers protection of life and property by rendering such services as guards, patrols and burglar alarms

保修(ㄅㄠˇ ㄒㄧㄡ)
to guarantee to keep something in good repair: 這台收音機保修一年。This radio is guaranteed in good repair for a year.

保險(ㄅㄠˇ ㄒㄧㄢˇ)
①insurance ②to guarantee ③a protective device, especially on a firearm, to prevent accidental discharge ④safe: 開快車可不保險。 It's not safe to drive too fast.

保險費(ㄅㄠˇ ㄒㄧㄢˇ ㄈㄟˋ)
the premium of an insurance policy; insurance premiums

保險帶(ㄅㄠˇ ㄒㄧㄢˇ ㄉㄞˋ)
a safety belt 亦作「安全帶」

保險單(ㄅㄠˇ ㄒㄧㄢˇ ㄉㄢ)
an insurance policy

保險套(ㄅㄠˇ ㄒㄧㄢˇ ㄊㄠˋ)
a condom; a sheath

保險槓(ㄅㄠˇ ㄒㄧㄢˇ ㄍㄤˋ)
a bumper (of an automobile)

保險公司(ㄅㄠˇ ㄒㄧㄢˇ ㄍㄨㄥ ㄙ)
an insurance company

保險開關(ㄅㄠˇ ㄒㄧㄢˇ ㄎㄞ ㄍㄨㄢ)
a cut-out switch

保險活門(ㄅㄠˇ ㄒㄧㄢˇ ㄏㄨㄛˊ ㄇㄣˊ)
a safety valve

保險基金(ㄅㄠˇ ㄒㄧㄢˇ ㄐㄧ ㄐㄧㄣ)
an insurance fund

保險金額(ㄅㄠˇ ㄒㄧㄢˇ ㄐㄧㄣ ㄜˊ)
amount insured

保險箱(ㄅㄠˇ ㄒㄧㄢˇ ㄒㄧㄤ)
a safe; a strongbox; a bank's vault

保險事業(ㄅㄠˇ ㄒㄧㄢˇ ㄕˋ ㄧㄝˋ)
insurance business

保險人(ㄅㄠ ㄒㄧㄢ ㄖㄣ)
an insurer; an underwriter

保險絲(ㄅㄠ ㄒㄧㄢ ㄙ)
a fuse wire

保值(ㄅㄠ ㄓ)
to preserve the value (of currency)

保障(ㄅㄠ ㄓㄤ)
to safeguard; to protect; to ensure; to guarantee: 憲法保障人民的言論自由。 The constitution guarantees people's freedom of speech.

保證(ㄅㄠ ㄓㄥ)
to guarantee; to assure; to assume full responsibility for another person's financial undertaking, etc.; a guaranty

保證金(ㄅㄠ ㄓㄥ ㄐㄧㄣ)
security deposit; guaranty money

保證書(ㄅㄠ ㄓㄥ ㄕㄨ)
a deed of security; a letter of guaranty

保證人(ㄅㄠ ㄓㄥ ㄖㄣ)
a guarantor; a guarantee

保重(ㄅㄠ ㄓㄨㄥ)
(usually used at the end of a letter or when parting) Please take good care of yourself.

保持(ㄅㄠ ㄔ)
to maintain; to keep: 這兩國保持友好關係。 The two countries maintain friendly relations.

保持現場(ㄅㄠ ㄔ ㄒㄧㄢ ㄔㄤ)
to preserve the scene of a crime

保釋(ㄅㄠ ㄕ)
to release on bail: 他被捕不到十小時就被保釋出來。 He was released on bail within ten hours of his arrest.

保釋金(ㄅㄠ ㄕ ㄐㄧㄣ)
bail

保守(ㄅㄠ ㄕㄡ)
①conservative: 老年人通常比年輕人保守。 Old people are usually more conservative than young people. ②to keep; to guard

保守派(ㄅㄠ ㄕㄡ ㄆㄞ)
an Old Guard 亦作「守舊元老」

保守黨(ㄅㄠ ㄕㄡ ㄉㄤ)
The Conservative Party

保守主義(ㄅㄠ ㄕㄡ ㄓㄨ ㄧ)
conservatism

保身(ㄅㄠ ㄕㄣ)
to save one's own skin

保稅倉庫(ㄅㄠ ㄕㄨㄟ ㄘㄤ ㄎㄨ)
a bonded godown

保人(ㄅㄠ ㄖㄣ)
a guarantor

保存(ㄅㄠ ㄘㄨㄣ)
①to safeguard; safekeeping ②to maintain; to preserve: 這批古畫保存很完整。 These ancient paintings are well preserved.

保存期限(ㄅㄠ ㄘㄨㄣ ㄑㄧ ㄒㄧㄢ)
①the shelf life of a commodity ②the period for keeping official papers on file

保送(ㄅㄠ ㄙㄨㄥ)
①to send a student to school or college without an entrance examination, usually for his high scholastic qualifications ②(baseball) to walk; a walk; bases on balls

保安(ㄅㄠ ㄢ)
①to ensure local security ②to ensure the workers' safety ③public security

保安隊(ㄅㄠ ㄢ ㄉㄨㄟ)
a public security corps, etc.; a unit of public security policemen

保安林(ㄅㄠ ㄢ ㄌㄧㄣ)
a shelter forest

保安處分(ㄅㄠ ㄢ ㄔㄨ ㄈㄣ)
(law) Peace Preservation Measures

保安人員(ㄅㄠ ㄢ ㄖㄣ ㄩㄢ)
security personnel

保安措施(ㄅㄠ ㄢ ㄘㄨㄛ ㄕ)
security measures

保有(ㄅㄠ ㄧㄡ)
possession

保佑(ㄅㄠ ㄧㄡ)
①to protect or bless ②a blessing

保養(ㄅㄠ ㄧㄤ)
①maintenance (of a car, ship, etc.) ②to take care (of health) ③to maintain; to keep in good repair

保養費(ㄅㄠ ㄧㄤ ㄈㄟ)
maintenance cost; upkeep

to defend; to guard against

保溫(ㄅㄠ ㄨㄣ)
①heat preservation ②to preserve heat; to keep (water, etc.) hot

保溫杯(ㄅㄠ ㄨㄣ ㄅㄟ)
a thermos cup or container

保育(ㄅㄠ ㄩ)
to raise (a kid)

保育院(ㄅㄠ ㄩ ㄩㄢ)
①a nursery ②an orphanage

〔人部〕

【俟】 177
ㄙ syh sì
1. to wait for; to await
2. until; as soon as

俟候(ㄙ ㄏㄡ)
to wait for

俟駕(ㄙ ㄐㄧㄚ)
①to wait for the emperor's arrival ②to wait for your arrival

俟時(ㄙ ㄕ)
to wait for an opportunity

【俠】 178
ㄒㄧㄚˊ shya xiá
1. a person adept in martial arts and dedicated to helping the poor and weak; one who fights rather than submit to injustice
2. chivalry
3. a Chinese family name

俠盜(ㄒㄧㄚˊ ㄉㄠ)
a robber, burglar, bandit, etc. who robs the rich only to help the poor

俠烈(ㄒㄧㄚˊ ㄌㄧㄝ)
chivalrous

俠骨(ㄒㄧㄚˊ ㄍㄨ)
chivalrous spirit

俠客(ㄒㄧㄚˊ ㄎㄜ)or 俠士(ㄒㄧㄚˊ ㄕ)
a person dedicated to the cause of justice, fairness, etc. by fighting for the poor and the oppressed; a man who has a strong sense of justice

俠氣(ㄒㄧㄚˊ ㄑㄧ)
chivalry

俠義(ㄒㄧㄚˊ ㄧ)
chivalry; honor and gallantry; a strong sense of justice

【信】 179
ㄒㄧㄣ shinn xìn
1. honesty; truthfulness; faith;

〔人 部〕

confidence; trust: 政府應取信於民。The government should win the people's confidence (or trust).
2. believing; true
3. to believe or trust
4. an envoy; an emissary; a messenger
5. news; a message; information; word
6. a letter; mail
7. credentials; evidence; a pledge; a token; a sign
8. to let (others do what they choose); free; easy; aimless; at will; at random; without a plan
9. regular periodical appearance

信筆(ㄒㄧㄣ ㄅㄧ)
to write without much thought; to write freely or aimlessly

信步(ㄒㄧㄣ ㄅㄨ)
to wander; to stroll aimlessly: 他信步街頭。He wandered the streets.

信不過(ㄒㄧㄣ ㄅㄨ ㄍㄨㄛ)
incredible; to have no trust in

信馬由韁(ㄒㄧㄣ ㄇㄚ ㄧㄡ ㄐㄧㄤ)
to give free rein to (imagination, etc.); to have no fixed opinion; to be easily influenced by the circumstances of the moment

信封(ㄒㄧㄣ ㄈㄥ)or 信封兒(ㄒㄧㄣ ㄈㄥ ㄦ)
an envelope

信風(ㄒㄧㄣ ㄈㄥ)
trade wind; seasonal wind

信風帶(ㄒㄧㄣ ㄈㄥ ㄉㄞ)
the trade wind zone

信奉(ㄒㄧㄣ ㄈㄥ)
to believe in (a religion, etc.)

信服(ㄒㄧㄣ ㄈㄨ)
to believe in; to trust; to be convinced; to admire

信得過(ㄒㄧㄣ ㄉㄜ ㄍㄨㄛ)
can be believed, credible

信條(ㄒㄧㄣ ㄊㄧㄠ)
a creed or code; a dogma; a precept

信徒(ㄒㄧㄣ ㄊㄨ)
a believer (of a religion, etc.); a follower; an adherent: 他是基督教的信徒。He is

a believer in Christianity.

信託(ㄒㄧㄣ ㄊㄨㄛ)
trust; to trust

信託公司(ㄒㄧㄣ ㄊㄨㄛ ㄍㄨㄥ ㄙ)
a trust company

信託局(ㄒㄧㄣ ㄊㄨㄛ ㄐㄩ)
the Trust Bureau

信筒(ㄒㄧㄣ ㄊㄨㄥ)
a letter box; a mailbox; a postbox

信念(ㄒㄧㄣ ㄋㄧㄢ)
a belief; a conviction

信女(ㄒㄧㄣ ㄋㄩ)
(Buddhism) a female believer

信賴(ㄒㄧㄣ ㄌㄞ)
trust; to trust

信鴿(ㄒㄧㄣ ㄍㄜ)
a carrier pigeon

信稿(ㄒㄧㄣ ㄍㄠ)
the draft of a letter

信口開河 or 信口開合(ㄒㄧㄣ ㄎㄡ ㄎㄞ ㄏㄜ)
to talk at random (often devoid of truth); to talk without forethought; to brag; to talk irresponsibly

信口胡說(ㄒㄧㄣ ㄎㄡ ㄏㄨ ㄕㄨㄛ)
to talk nonsense

信口雌黃(ㄒㄧㄣ ㄎㄡ ㄘ ㄏㄨㄤ)
to make irresponsible remarks; to criticize without grounds; to criticize wildly

信號(ㄒㄧㄣ ㄏㄠ)
a signal (with flags, lamps, etc.): 紅燈是危險的信號。A red light is a signal of danger.

信號彈(ㄒㄧㄣ ㄏㄠ ㄉㄢ)
a signal shot; a signal bullet; a flare

信號燈(ㄒㄧㄣ ㄏㄠ ㄉㄥ)
a semaphore; a signal lamp

信號槍(ㄒㄧㄣ ㄏㄠ ㄑㄧㄤ)
a signal pistol; a flare pistol

信教(ㄒㄧㄣ ㄐㄧㄠ)
to believe in a religion

信箋(ㄒㄧㄣ ㄐㄧㄢ)
letter paper

信件(ㄒㄧㄣ ㄐㄧㄢ)
mail or letters (collectively)

信息(ㄒㄧㄣ ㄒㄧ)
news; information; a message

信心(ㄒㄧㄣ ㄒㄧㄣ)
faith; confidence: 我對這計畫的信心不大。I haven't much

faith in this plan.

信箱(ㄒㄧㄣ ㄒㄧㄤ)
a postbox; a letter box; a post office box (P.O.B)

信紙(ㄒㄧㄣ ㄓ)
letter paper

信札(ㄒㄧㄣ ㄓㄚ)
mail or letters (collectively)

信插(ㄒㄧㄣ ㄔㄚ)
a mail rack

信差(ㄒㄧㄣ ㄔㄞ)
a mailman; a postman

信實(ㄒㄧㄣ ㄕ)
good faith; honesty; trustworthiness; reliable

信史(ㄒㄧㄣ ㄕ)
authentic historical records

信誓(ㄒㄧㄣ ㄕ)
faithful oaths; faithful pledges

信守(ㄒㄧㄣ ㄕㄡ)
to abide by; to keep (a promise): 我們必須信守諾言。We must keep our promises.

信手(ㄒㄧㄣ ㄕㄡ)
without a previous plan; at random: 他信手抽一本書。He picked out a book at random.

信手拈來(ㄒㄧㄣ ㄕㄡ ㄋㄧㄢ ㄌㄞ)
to pick at random; to take without forethought; to get without effort

賞罰必酬(ㄒㄧㄣ ㄕㄤ ㄅㄧ ㄔㄡ)
to give rewards or punishments strictly and impartially; awards and punishments rigorously carried out

信任(ㄒㄧㄣ ㄖㄣ)
①to trust; to have faith in ②trust: 你可以信任他。You can put your trust in him.

信任投票(ㄒㄧㄣ ㄖㄣ ㄊㄡ ㄆㄧㄠ)
a vote of confidence

信從(ㄒㄧㄣ ㄘㄨㄥ)
to trust and follow (a person's advice, etc.); to listen to

信義(ㄒㄧㄣ ㄧ)
honesty

信仰(ㄒㄧㄣ ㄧㄤ)
(religious or political) belief; to admire; to believe in

信物(ㄒㄧㄣ ㄨ)
an authenticating object; a token of promise; a pledge

信譽(ㄒㄧㄣˋ ㄩˋ)
　credit and reputation

信用(ㄒㄧㄣˋ ㄩㄥˋ)
　credit

信用卡(ㄒㄧㄣˋ ㄩㄥˋ ㄎㄚˇ)
　a credit card

信用合作社(ㄒㄧㄣˋ ㄩㄥˋ ㄏㄜˊ ㄗㄨㄛˋ ㄕㄜˋ)
　a credit cooperative

信用交易(ㄒㄧㄣˋ ㄩㄥˋ ㄐㄧㄠ ㄧˋ)
　margin trading or margin transaction

信用狀(ㄒㄧㄣˋ ㄩㄥˋ ㄓㄨㄤˋ)or信用證
(ㄒㄧㄣˋ ㄩㄥˋ ㄓㄥˋ)
　a letter of credit

八畫

【修】 180
ㄒㄧㄡ shiou xiū

1. to repair; to mend
2. to adorn; to decorate
3. to construct; to build
4. long; slender
5. to prune; to cut; to sharpen; to trim
6. to study; to cultivate
7. to write; to compile; to edit

修補(ㄒㄧㄡ ㄅㄨˇ)
　to repair; to mend: 修補破洞
　to repair a puncture

修配(ㄒㄧㄡ ㄆㄟˋ)
　to repair and supply replacements

修面(ㄒㄧㄡ ㄇㄧㄢˋ)
　to shave one's face

修明(ㄒㄧㄡ ㄇㄧㄥˊ)
　(said of political administration) enlightened and orderly

修睦(ㄒㄧㄡ ㄇㄨˋ)
　to cultivate friendship with neighbors

修墓(ㄒㄧㄡ ㄇㄨˋ)
　to renovate or keep ancestral graves

修福(ㄒㄧㄡ ㄈㄨˊ)
　to do good deeds in order to win blessings

修復(ㄒㄧㄡ ㄈㄨˋ)
　to complete a repair job; to make as good as new

修復舊觀(ㄒㄧㄡ ㄈㄨˋ ㄐㄧㄡˋ ㄍㄨㄢ)
　to restore to original shape and appearance

修道(ㄒㄧㄡ ㄉㄠˋ)
　to cultivate oneself according to a religious doctrine; to practice Buddhist or Taoist rules

修道院(ㄒㄧㄡ ㄉㄠˋ ㄩㄢˋ)
　①a monastery ②a nunnery; a convent

修訂(ㄒㄧㄡ ㄉㄧㄥˋ)
　to revise

修訂版(ㄒㄧㄡ ㄉㄧㄥˋ ㄅㄢˇ)or修訂本
(ㄒㄧㄡ ㄉㄧㄥˋ ㄅㄣˇ)
　a revision; the revised edition: 此書的修訂本將於明年出版。A revision of this book will be published next year.

修女(ㄒㄧㄡ ㄋㄩˇ)
　a Catholic nun; a sister

修理(ㄒㄧㄡ ㄌㄧˇ)
　①to repair; repair; mend: 這部機器正在修理中。The machine is under repair. ②(slang) to torture

修理費(ㄒㄧㄡ ㄌㄧˇ ㄈㄟˋ)
　(accounting) repairs

修煉(ㄒㄧㄡ ㄌㄧㄢˋ)
　①to practice asceticism ②(Taoism) to cultivate one's physical and mental capabilities according to Taoist rules; to go into religious self-discipline

修路(ㄒㄧㄡ ㄌㄨˋ)
　①to repair roads ②to build roads

修路機(ㄒㄧㄡ ㄌㄨˋ ㄐㄧ)
　a steam (or gasoline or diesel) roller for surfacing roads; a road-roller

修改(ㄒㄧㄡ ㄍㄞˇ)
　to correct; to alter; to revise; to modify

修和(ㄒㄧㄡ ㄏㄜˊ)
　to conciliate and unite

修好(ㄒㄧㄡ ㄏㄠˇ)
　①to cultivate friendship with other states, etc. ②to do good deeds in order to win blessings

修函(ㄒㄧㄡ ㄏㄢˊ)
　to write a letter

修脚(ㄒㄧㄡ ㄐㄧㄠˇ)
　to pare toenails (a typical trade in a Chinese bathhouse); pedicure

修脚刀兒(ㄒㄧㄡ ㄐㄧㄠˇ ㄉㄠ ㄦ)
　a tiny blade for paring toenails

修剪(ㄒㄧㄡ ㄐㄧㄢˇ)
　to trim, cut, clip, or prune

修建(ㄒㄧㄡ ㄐㄧㄢˋ)
　to repair and build

修濬(ㄒㄧㄡ ㄐㄩㄣˋ)
　to dredge a river

修葺(ㄒㄧㄡ ㄑㄧˋ)
　to repair; to renovate: 此屋修葺一新。This house is completely renovated.

修橋補路(ㄒㄧㄡ ㄑㄧㄠˊ ㄅㄨˇ ㄌㄨˋ)
　(literally) to repair bridges and mend roads—to do many good deeds

修補補(ㄒㄧㄡ ㄅㄨˇ ㄅㄨˇ)
　to patch up; to tinker

修仙(ㄒㄧㄡ ㄒㄧㄢ)
　to train, shape, cultivate oneself to attain divinity; to train by self-discipline to become an immortal

修行(ㄒㄧㄡ ㄒㄧㄥˊ)
　①to practice Buddhist or Taoist rules (often strict and ascetic in nature) ②to practice moral teachings

修指甲(ㄒㄧㄡ ㄓˇ ㄐㄧㄚˊ)
　to manicure fingernails; to trim fingernails

修治(ㄒㄧㄡ ㄓˋ)
　to repair and adjust

修整(ㄒㄧㄡ ㄓㄥˇ)
　①to repair and maintain ②to prune; to trim

修正(ㄒㄧㄡ ㄓㄥˋ)
　to correct

修正主義(ㄒㄧㄡ ㄓㄥˋ ㄓㄨˇ ㄧˋ)
　revisionism

修築(ㄒㄧㄡ ㄓㄨˊ)
　to build (especially a road or bridge); to construct

修撰(ㄒㄧㄡ ㄓㄨㄢˋ)
　①to edit; to compile ②the title of an official in the Tang Dynasty whose job was to revise historical records; a court historian

修長(ㄒㄧㄡ ㄔㄤˊ)
　tall and thin; slender

修士(ㄒㄧㄡ ㄕˋ)
　a monk; a brother (of the Roman Catholic or Greek Orthodox church); a friar

修飾(ㄒㄧㄡ ㄕˋ)
　①to take care of one's appearance; to doll up; to beautify ②to redecorate or

〔人部〕

refurnish

修繕(ㄒㄧㄡㄕㄢˋ)
to repair; to renovate

修身(ㄒㄧㄡㄕㄣ)
to cultivate one's moral culture

【人部】

修身齊家(ㄒㄧㄡㄕㄣㄑㄧˊㄐㄧㄚ)
to cultivate oneself and put family in order

修身自省(ㄒㄧㄡㄕㄣㄗˋㄒㄧㄥˇ)
to look after one's conduct by self-examination

修書(ㄒㄧㄡㄕㄨ)
to write a letter

修容(ㄒㄧㄡㄖㄨㄥˊ)
to make up one's features

修造(ㄒㄧㄡㄗㄠˋ)
to repair and build

修辭(ㄒㄧㄡㄘˊ)
rhetoric; diction; the use of proper words

修辭學(ㄒㄧㄡㄘˊㄒㄩㄝˊ)
rhetoric (as a subject of study)

修業(ㄒㄧㄡㄧㄝˋ)
to pursue academic studies; to go to school

修陰功(ㄒㄧㄡㄧㄣ ㄍㄨㄥ)or 修陰德(ㄒㄧㄡㄧㄣㄉㄜˊ)
to do a good deed secretly

修養(ㄒㄧㄡㄧㄤˇ)
①to seek perfection in scholastic or ethical pursuits ②man's moral culture as the result of training; possession of profound knowledge and a sense of morality

【俯】 181. ㄈㄨˇ fuu fǔ
1. to face down; to come down; to bow down; to stoop
2. to condescend; to deign

俯拜(ㄈㄨˇㄅㄞˋ)
to do obeisance to

俯伏(ㄈㄨˇㄈㄨˊ)
to prostrate; to make obeisance to

俯念(ㄈㄨˇㄋㄧㄢˋ)
Please condescend to consider (my position, situation, etc.)—an expression used in a written request to one's superior

俯瞰(ㄈㄨˇㄎㄢˋ)
to look down at; to overlook

① to adapt (usually by lowering) oneself to… ②to condescend to accept a job

俯惟(ㄈㄨˇㄨㄟˊ)
to give (your) gracious approval

俯衝(ㄈㄨˇㄔㄨㄥ)
a dive; to dive

俯拾即是(ㄈㄨˇㄕˊㄐㄧˊㄕˋ)
①just to stoop and gather—It's everywhere.或extremely common ②a very easy thing to do or get

俯視(ㄈㄨˇㄕˋ)
to look down at; to overlook

俯首(ㄈㄨˇㄕㄡˇ)
to bend one's head; to bow (usually referring to submission or admission of wrong-doing)

俯首帖耳(ㄈㄨˇㄕㄡˇㄊㄧㄝ ㄦˇ)
servile; submissive

俯首聽命(ㄈㄨˇㄕㄡˇㄊㄧㄥˋㄇㄧㄥˋ)
to obey submissively

俯首就範(ㄈㄨˇㄕㄡˇㄐㄧㄡˋㄈㄢˋ)
to submit; to surrender

俯首無言(ㄈㄨˇㄕㄡˇㄨˊㄧㄢˊ)
to bend one's head in silence—to admit one's fault or crime without protest

俯仰(ㄈㄨˇㄧㄤˇ)
①a bending or lifting of the head ②one's everyday life at home ③(figuratively) a very short time

俯仰之間(ㄈㄨˇㄧㄤˇㄓ ㄐㄧㄢ)
in the twinkling of an eye; in an instant; a very short time

俯仰由人(ㄈㄨˇㄧㄤˇㄧㄡˊㄖㄣˊ)
to be at somebody's beck and call 亦作「隨人俯仰」

俯仰無愧(ㄈㄨˇㄧㄤˇㄨˊㄎㄨㄟˋ)
to have done nothing to make one feel ashamed

俯允(ㄈㄨˇㄩㄣˇ)
to grant (your) gracious permission

【俱】 182. ㄐㄩˋ jiuh jù (又讀 ㄐㄩ jiu jū)
1. altogether; all
2. to accompany
3. a Chinese family name

俱備(ㄐㄩˋㄅㄟˋ)
all made ready; all complete

俱發罪(ㄐㄩˋㄈㄚ ㄗㄨㄟˋ)

concurrent offenses

俱樂部(ㄐㄩˋㄌㄜˋㄅㄨˋ)
a club (as a country club, golf club, etc.)

俱盡(ㄐㄩˋㄐㄧㄣˋ)
all finished; nothing left

俱全(ㄐㄩˋㄑㄩㄢˊ)
to be available in all varieties

俱在(ㄐㄩˋㄗㄞˋ)
all present

俱已齊備(ㄐㄩˋㄧˇㄑㄧˊㄅㄟˋ)
Everything is ready.

【俳】 183. ㄆㄞˊ pair pái
1. a variety show; a vaudeville
2. insincere; not serious
3. to walk to and fro

俳賦(ㄆㄞˊㄈㄨˋ)
a light, ornate literary form popular in ancient China

俳體詩(ㄆㄞˊㄊㄧˇㄕ)
light, comic poetry

俳徊(ㄆㄞˊㄏㄨㄞˊ)
to walk to and fro

俳句(ㄆㄞˊㄐㄩ)
a Japanese form of light poetry consisting of three sentences (17 words in all)

俳諧(ㄆㄞˊㄒㄧㄝˊ)
funny talk; comic

俳優(ㄆㄞˊㄧㄡ)
①a variety show; a vaudeville ②a player in a variety show; a comedian

【俶】 184. 1. ㄔㄨˋ chuh chù
1. to begin; a beginning
2. to arrange the baggage for travel
3. to build

【俶】 2. ㄊㄧˋ tih tì
not bound by conventions

俶儻(ㄊㄧˋㄊㄤˇ)
to behave merrily and freely, regardless of conventions

【俸】 185. ㄈㄥˋ fenq fèng
emoluments; a salary from the government

俸祿(ㄈㄥˋㄌㄨˋ)or 俸給(ㄈㄥˋㄐㄧˇ)
emoluments; a government salary

【俺】 186. ㄢˇ aan ǎn
the personal pronoun I, used

especially in Shantung Province

俺們〔ㄢ˙ㄇㄣ〕
we

俺家〔ㄢˇㄐㄧㄚ〕
I

俺家的〔ㄢˇㄐㄧㄚ·ㄉㄜ〕
my husband

【俾】187 〔ㄅㄧˇ bǐh bǐ〕
1. to cause; to enable
2. that; so that; in order that

俾倪〔ㄅㄧˋㄋㄧˊ〕
to glance sideways

俾資挹注〔ㄅㄧˇㄗ ㄧˋㄓㄨˋ〕
so as to help make both ends meet

俾斯麥〔ㄅㄧˇㄙㄇㄞˋ〕
Prince Otto Eduard Leopold von Bismarck (1815-1898), German prime minister

【倀】188 〔ㄔㄤ chang chāng〕
1. (mythology) a ghost controlled by the tiger
2. wild; rash

【併】189 〔(併) ㄅㄧㄥˋ bìng bìng〕
1. on a level with; even; equal; to go side by side
2. all; entire
3. together
4. to combine; to annex

併滅〔ㄅㄧㄥˋㄇㄧㄝˋ〕
to destroy

併發〔ㄅㄧㄥˋㄈㄚ〕
to begin, explode, erupt, attack, occur, etc. at the same time

併發症〔ㄅㄧㄥˋㄈㄚ ㄓㄥˋ〕
(medicine) a complication; an epiphenomenon; a syndrome

併吞〔ㄅㄧㄥˋㄊㄨㄣ〕
to swallow up entirely; to annex and absorb (a neighboring country)

併攏〔ㄅㄧㄥˋㄌㄨㄥˇ〕
to draw close to each other

併合〔ㄅㄧㄥˋㄏㄜˊ〕
to unite; to integrate

併肩〔ㄅㄧㄥˋㄐㄧㄢ〕
shoulder to shoulder

併案〔ㄅㄧㄥˋㄢˋ〕
①an arrangement to group similar cases under a single heading for quicker or better processing, treatment, etc. ②a package deal

【倆】190 〔ㄌㄧㄤˇ leang liǎng〕
craft; ability

【倆】190 〔ㄌㄧㄚˇ lea liǎ〕
two; a pair; a couple

倆口子〔ㄌㄧㄚˇㄎㄡˇ·ㄗ〕
husband and wife

倆錢兒〔ㄌㄧㄚˇㄑㄧㄢˊㄦ〕
not much money; a little money

倆人〔ㄌㄧㄚˇㄖㄣˊ〕
two persons, usually referring to a couple in love

倆月〔ㄌㄧㄚˇㄩㄝˋ〕
a couple of months

【倉】191 〔ㄘㄤ tsang cāng〕
1. a granary; a storehouse; a warehouse
2. a cabin, as in the ship
3. green
4. a Chinese family name

倉房〔ㄘㄤ ㄈㄤˊ〕
a storage for food; a granary; a storehouse

倉廩〔ㄘㄤ ㄌㄧㄣˇ〕
a granary

倉庫〔ㄘㄤ ㄎㄨˋ〕
a warehouse; a godown; a storehouse

倉皇〔ㄘㄤ ㄏㄨㄤˊ〕
in haste; hurriedly (especially in panic): 敵人倉皇撤退. The enemy retreated in haste.

倉頡〔ㄘㄤ ㄐㄧㄝˊ〕
Tsang Chieh, a legendary figure credited with the invention of the written Chinese language

倉儲〔ㄘㄤ ㄔㄨˊ〕
to keep grain, goods, etc. in a storehouse

倉促 or 倉卒〔ㄘㄤ ㄘㄨˋ〕
in a hurry: 他倉促下結論. He jumped to a conclusion.

【個】192 〔(箇) 《ㄜˋ geh gè〕
1. a numeray adjunct: 一個包子 one steamed dumpling
2. piece
3. single
4. roughly
5. an adjunct to an indefinite pronoun, as this, that

個把〔《ㄜˋㄅㄚˇ〕
a few; one or two: 多個把人也住得下. There is enough room to put up one or two more people.

個把月〔《ㄜˋㄅㄚˇㄩㄝˋ〕
a month or two: 再個把月就可做完了. It can easily be finished in a month or two.

個別〔《ㄜˋㄅㄧㄝˊ〕
individual; individually; separately: 老師找他個別談話. The teacher had a private talk with him.

個體〔《ㄜˋㄊㄧˇ〕
a matter, etc. having an independent and distinct quality; the individual as contrasted with the group; an entity

個體戶〔《ㄜˋㄊㄧˇㄏㄨˋ〕
an individual business or shop

個個〔《ㄜˋ《ㄜˋ〕or 個個兒〔《ㄜˋ《ㄜˋㄦ〕
(each and) every one

個性〔《ㄜˋㄒㄧㄥˋ〕
personality; individuality

個中〔《ㄜˋㄓㄨㄥ〕
within; inside

個人〔《ㄜˋㄖㄣˊ〕
①the individual as contrasted with the group ②oneself ③personal; personally: 我個人認為他是好人. In my personal opinion he is a good man.

個人主義〔《ㄜˋㄖㄣˊㄓㄨˇㄧˋ〕
individualism; egoism

個子〔《ㄜˋ·ㄗ〕
physical size of a person; build

個兒〔《ㄜˋㄦ〕
①size; height; stature ②persons or things taken singly

個案〔《ㄜˋㄢˋ〕
an individual case; an isolated case; a special case

個位〔《ㄜˋㄨㄟˋ〕
(mathematics) a unit; a digit; a unit place

【倌】193 〔《ㄨㄢ guan guān〕
1. a boy or an assistant in the employ of a teahouse, tavern or restaurant

【人部】

2. a euphemism for a prostitute
3. the groom

倡人 (《ㄔㄤ ㄖㄣˊ)
①an officer in charge of royal chariots ② (formerly) a prostitute

【倍】 194 ㄅㄟˋ bey bèi
1. double; to double
2. (joined to a numeral) -times; -fold
3. to rebel; to be insubordinate

倍塔 (ㄅㄟˋ ㄊㄚˇ)
beta

倍塔射線 (ㄅㄟˋ ㄊㄚˇ ㄕㄜˋ ㄒㄧㄢˋ)
a beta ray

倍率 (ㄅㄟˋ ㄌㄩˋ)
percentage

倍加 (ㄅㄟˋ ㄐㄧㄚ)
to double; double

倍蓰 (ㄅㄟˋ ㄒㄧˇ)
one to five times; very many

倍數 (ㄅㄟˋ ㄕㄨˋ)
a multiple: 14 是 7 的倍數。 Fourteen is a multiple of seven.

倍增 (ㄅㄟˋ ㄗㄥ)
double; double

【倞】 195 ㄐㄧㄥˋ jìng jìng
strong

【倞】 195 ㄌㄧㄤˋ liàng liàng
1. far
2. to request

【倏】 196 ㄕㄨˋ shuh shù
hastily; suddenly

倏忽 (ㄕㄨˋ ㄏㄨ)
all of a sudden; very suddenly; quickly

倏瞬 (ㄕㄨˋ ㄕㄨㄣˋ)
a brief glimpse; time for a brief glimpse

【倕】 197 ㄔㄨㄟˊ chwei chuí
name of an expert craftsman in ancient China

【們】 198 ㄇㄣˊ men mén
(語音 •ㄇㄣ •men men)
(usually said of persons) an adjunct to a pronoun or noun to indicate plurality: 朋友們 friends 同胞們 fellow citizens

【倒】 199 ㄉㄠˇ dao dǎo
to fall down; to lie down

倒班 (ㄉㄠˇ ㄅㄢ)
to work in shifts; to work by turns: 我們晝夜倒班。 We work in shifts around the clock.

倒閉 (ㄉㄠˇ ㄅㄧˋ) or 倒店 (ㄉㄠˇ ㄉㄧㄢˋ)
to close down a shop; to go bankrupt or insolvent: 去年有許多企業倒閉。 Many enterprises went bankrupt last year.

倒斃 (ㄉㄠˇ ㄅㄧˋ)
to fall dead

倒賣 (ㄉㄠˇ ㄇㄞˋ)
to resell at a profit

倒楣 (ㄉㄠˇ ㄇㄟˊ)
to be out of luck; an unlucky break

倒鳳顛鸞 (ㄉㄠˇ ㄈㄥˋ ㄉㄧㄢ ㄌㄨㄢˊ) or 顛鸞倒鳳 (ㄉㄧㄢ ㄌㄨㄢˊ ㄉㄠˇ ㄈㄥˋ)
to have sexual intercourse

倒塌 (ㄉㄠˇ ㄊㄚ)
(especially said of a building) to collapse; to cave in

倒臺 (ㄉㄠˇ ㄊㄞˊ)
to fall from power

倒頭便睡 (ㄉㄠˇ ㄊㄡˊ ㄅㄧㄢˋ ㄕㄨㄟˋ)
to fall asleep as soon as one goes to bed (sometimes connoting a sense of carefreeness or indifference)

倒閣 (ㄉㄠˇ ㄍㄜˊ)
the resignation of the cabinet (in the face of a political crisis)

倒換 (ㄉㄠˇ ㄏㄨㄢˋ)
①to rotate; to take turns ② to exchange; to substitute; to replace

倒嚼 (ㄉㄠˇ ㄐㄩㄝˊ)
to chew the cud; to ruminate

倒賬 or 倒帳 (ㄉㄠˇ ㄓㄤˋ)
①bad debts ②to refuse to pay loans under various excuses

倒嗓(子) (ㄉㄠˇ ㄙㄤˇ •ㄗ)
an ailment of the vocal cords caused by over-tensing them with constant singing or shouting

倒胃口 (ㄉㄠˇ ㄨㄟˋ ㄎㄡˇ)
to spoil one's appetite

倒運 (ㄉㄠˇ ㄩㄣˋ)
to be out of luck; unlucky:

他是個倒運的作家。 He is an unlucky writer.

【倒】 199 2. ㄉㄠˋ daw dào
1. to inverse; to place upside down; in reverse order or the wrong direction
2. to pour out; to empty: 倒垃圾 to pour out garbage
3. on the contrary
4. after all: 老師倒底說得不錯。 What the teacher said was not wrong after all.
5. but; and yet: 說是她, 倒不是她。You think it is she, but it isn't.

倒背如流 (ㄉㄠˋ ㄅㄟˋ ㄖㄨˊ ㄌㄧㄡˊ)
can even recite (an article, etc.) backwards fluently—to understand something thoroughly by heart

倒不如 (ㄉㄠˋ ㄅㄨˋ ㄖㄨˊ)
①would rather: 倒不如死了乾淨。 I would rather die. ② not better than; even worse than

倒貼 (ㄉㄠˋ ㄊㄧㄝ)
to have to pay—after expecting to receive (usually referring to money)

倒片 (ㄉㄠˋ ㄆㄧㄢˋ)
(movie) to rewind

倒飛 (ㄉㄠˋ ㄈㄟ)
inverted flight

倒反 (ㄉㄠˋ ㄈㄢˇ)
unexpectedly; contrary to what one expects

倒貼 (ㄉㄠˋ ㄊㄧㄝ)
(said of an unfaithful wife, wealthy widow or concubine) to pay for the upkeep of a lover

倒退 (ㄉㄠˋ ㄊㄨㄟˋ)
①to retreat; to go backwards; to fall back ②to retrospect; to review

倒立 (ㄉㄠˋ ㄌㄧˋ)
①to stand upside down ②a handstand

倒流 (ㄉㄠˋ ㄌㄧㄡˊ)
to flow backward

倒戈 (ㄉㄠˋ ㄍㄜ)
to apostatize or tergiversate; to desert to the enemy camp; mutiny

倒掛 (ㄉㄠˋ ㄍㄨㄚˋ)
①to hang upside down ② the lovebird of Taiwan and

Kwangsi Provinces, resembling a parakeet

倒果爲因(ㄉㄠ ㄍㄨㄛ ㄨㄟ ㄧㄣ)
to mistake the effect for the cause

倒灌(ㄉㄠ ㄍㄨㄢ)
(said of a flood which spills over river banks or dikes onto the adjoining land) to flow backward

倒屣(ㄉㄠ ㄒㄧˇ)
in a big hurry to welcome a guest

倒行逆施(ㄉㄠ ㄒㄧㄥˊ ㄋㄧˋ ㄕ)
to go against commonsense rules; to adopt measures beyond reasonable comprehension; perverse acts

倒敍(ㄉㄠ ㄒㄩˋ)
to narrate an incident in inverted order chronologically; the flashback

倒懸(ㄉㄠ ㄒㄩㄢˊ)
hanging upside down—great suffering; deep affliction

倒置(ㄉㄠ ㄓˋ)
to place (things, etc.) in wrong order; to place emphasis on the wrong point; to put the cart before the horse

倒轉(ㄉㄠ ㄓㄨㄢˇ)
①to turn the other way round ②contrary to reason or one's expectation

倒裝(ㄉㄠ ㄓㄨㄤ)
①to place things in inverted order ②(rhetoric) hyperbaton

倒持泰阿 or 倒持太阿(ㄉㄠ ㄔˊ ㄊㄞˋ ㄜ)
(literally) to hold the sword at the wrong end—to relegate one's power to a subordinate unwisely and suffer the consequences thereof; to allow one's powers to fall into another's hands

倒揷(ㄉㄠ ㄔㄚ)
①to insert something or plant a tree upside down ②in writing or narration, a reversal of the normal order or sequence of sentences, paragraphs, etc.

倒車(ㄉㄠ ㄔㄜ)
to back up a car, locomotive, etc.; to move a vehicle backward

倒抽一口氣(ㄉㄠ ㄔㄡ ㄧ ㄎㄡˇ ㄑㄧˋ)
to hold one's breath; to give a gasp of astonishment; to be in fear or disappointment, etc.

倒是(ㄉㄠ ㄕˋ)
actually; really

倒數(ㄉㄠ ㄕㄨˋ)
to count from bottom to top; to count backward; to count from rear to front: 倒數第五行 the fifth line from the bottom

倒數計時(ㄉㄠ ㄕㄨˋ ㄐㄧˋ ㄕˊ)
to count down; countdown (as in rocket launching)

倒栽葱(ㄉㄠ ㄗㄞ ㄘㄨㄥ)
to fall headlong; to fall head over heels

倒彩(ㄉㄠ ㄘㄞˇ)
(Chinese opera) to applaud when a performer slips

倒也罷了(ㄉㄠ ㄧㄝˇ ㄅㄚˋ ㄌㄜ)
It would have been better if....

倒因爲果(ㄉㄠ ㄧㄣ ㄨㄟ ㄍㄨㄛˇ)
to reverse cause and effect; to take the cause for effect

倒影(ㄉㄠ ㄧㄥˇ)
the reflection of something in the water; the upside-down image of an object in the viewfinder of a camera; inverted images

【倔】200
1. ㄐㄩㄝˊ jyue jué
intransigent; hard; obstinate; stubborn

倔強(ㄐㄩㄝˊ ㄐㄧㄤˋ)
intransigent; intransigence; obstinate; stubborn: 這個老人相當倔強。The old man is as stubborn as a mule.

倔起(ㄐㄩㄝˊ ㄑㄧˇ)
(said of a nation) to rise suddenly

【倔】200
2. ㄐㄩㄝˊ jiueh jué
gruff; rude; rude in manner or speech

【倖】201
ㄒㄧㄥˋ shing xìng
1. good luck; lucky; by luck or chance; fortunate
2. to dote on; to spoil

倖免(ㄒㄧㄥˋ ㄇㄧㄢˇ)
to escape (punishment) by luck; to survive luckily

倖進(ㄒㄧㄥˋ ㄐㄧㄣˋ)
to attain (a position, etc.) by luck; to be promoted by luck

倖臣(ㄒㄧㄥˋ ㄔㄣˊ)
a favorite courtier

倖存(ㄒㄧㄥˋ ㄘㄨㄣˊ)
to survive by good luck

【倘】202
ㄊㄤˇ taang tǎng
if; supposing; in the event of

倘來之物(ㄊㄤˇ ㄌㄞˊ ㄓ ㄨˋ)
an unexpected or undeserved gain

倘使(ㄊㄤˇ ㄕˇ)
if

倘如(ㄊㄤˇ ㄖㄨˊ)
if

倘若(ㄊㄤˇ ㄖㄨㄛˋ)
if; in the event of; in case

【候】203
ㄏㄡˋ how hòu
1. to wait; to expect: 請稍候。Please wait a moment.
2. a period; time; a season
3. a situation; a condition
4. to pay (bills); to take care of the bill: 這筆賬他候過鈔了。He has paid the bill.
5. to greet; to inquire after: 他問候你。He inquired after you.

候補(ㄏㄡˋ ㄅㄨˇ)
waiting to fill a vacancy, such as an alternate member of a committee, etc.; to be a candidate

候脈(ㄏㄡˋ ㄇㄞˋ)
to feel the pulse

候鳥(ㄏㄡˋ ㄋㄧㄠˇ)
migratory birds

候光(ㄏㄡˋ ㄍㄨㄤ)
to request (someone's) company at a dinner, etc.; to await the honor of your presence (at a dinner party)

候機室(ㄏㄡˋ ㄐㄧ ㄕˋ)
a lounge or waiting room (at an airport terminal building)

候駕(ㄏㄡˋ ㄐㄧㄚˋ)
to await (your) gracious presence—an expression usually used in an invitation: 隨時候駕。You are welcome

人部

〔人部〕

any time.

候教(ㄏㄡ ㄐㄧㄠˋ)
to await (your) gracious teaching—a common usage in an invitation, etc.

候選人(ㄏㄡˋ ㄒㄩㄢˇ ㄖㄣˊ)
a candidate (especially in elections)

候診(ㄏㄡˋ ㄓㄣˇ)
to wait to see the doctor

候車亭(ㄏㄡˋ ㄔㄜ ㄊㄧㄥˊ)
a bus stop with an eaves-like roof

候車室(ㄏㄡˋ ㄔㄜ ㄕˋ)
a waiting room (at a railway station or bus terminal)

候示(ㄏㄡˋ ㄕˋ)
to await (your) further instructions

候審(ㄏㄡˋ ㄕㄣˇ)
(law) to await trial

【倚】²⁰⁴ (ㄧˇ yǐ)
1. to rely on; to depend on
2. to lean toward; to rest on
3. biased; partial: 不偏不倚 unbiased; impartial

倚傍(ㄧˇ ㄅㄤ)
to pattern after; to emulate

倚馬可待(ㄧˇ ㄇㄚˇ ㄎㄜˇ ㄉㄞˋ)
a writer's ability to write an article very fast

倚門賣笑(ㄧˇ ㄇㄣˊ ㄇㄞˋ ㄒㄧㄠˋ)or 倚門賣俏(ㄧˇ ㄇㄣˊ ㄇㄞˋ ㄑㄧㄠˋ)
(said of coquettish women) to invite attention of passers-by; love for sale; to be a prostitute; to flirt near the door with passers-by

倚門倚閭(ㄧˇ ㄇㄣˊ ㄧˇ ㄌㄩˊ)
to await the return of one's son eagerly

倚托(ㄧˇ ㄊㄨㄛ)
to rely on; to depend on

倚賴(ㄧˇ ㄌㄞˋ)
①to depend on; to rely on (others): 小孩的衣食都倚賴父母, Children depend on their parents for food and clothing. ②to presume on authority to browbeat others

倚老賣老(ㄧˇ ㄌㄠˇ ㄇㄞˋ ㄌㄠˇ)
to presume on age to despise the youth; to take advantage of one's seniority or old age (to ignore manners, regulations, etc.)

倚靠(ㄧˇ ㄎㄠˋ)
①to lean against ②to rely on; to trust to; to depend on; to lean on ③support

倚著(ㄧˇ ㄓㄜˋ)
to count on support; someone or something to depend on

倚仗(ㄧˇ ㄓㄤˋ)
to presume on (one's position, authority, etc.)

倚仗權勢(ㄧˇ ㄓㄤˋ ㄑㄩㄢˊ ㄕˋ)
to rely on one's power and position; to count on one's powerful connections

倚重(ㄧˇ ㄓㄨㄥˋ)
to entrust a person with heavy responsibility

倚恃(ㄧˇ ㄕˋ)
to depend on; to rely on

倚勢凌人(ㄧˇ ㄕˋ ㄌㄧㄥˊ ㄖㄣˊ)or 倚勢欺人(ㄧˇ ㄕˋ ㄑㄧ ㄖㄣˊ)
to take advantage of one's position to bully people

【偶】²⁰⁵ (ㄊㄧˇ tǐ)
1. to raise high
2. unrestrained; unoccupied

偶儻 or 倜儻(ㄊㄧˋ ㄊㄤˇ)
elegant in a casual way; free and easy of manner; unconventional

倜儻不羈(ㄊㄧˋ ㄊㄤˇ ㄅㄨˋ ㄐㄧ)
untrammeled; free; unconventional

【借】²⁰⁶ (ㄐㄧㄝˋ jieh jiè)
1. to lend: 借我筆好嗎? Could you lend me your pen?
2. to borrow
3. to avail oneself of; to make use of; to resort to
4. to make a pretext of
5. if; supposing

借貸(ㄐㄧㄝˋ ㄉㄞˋ)
①to ask for a loan; to borrow money ②debit and credit sides

借刀殺人(ㄐㄧㄝˋ ㄉㄠ ㄕㄚ ㄖㄣˊ)
to kill one's enemy by another's hands; to instigate (or trick) others to commit a crime to serve one's own purpose

借道(ㄐㄧㄝˋ ㄉㄠˋ)
①(said of an invading army) to reach the target country through the territory of a third nation ②(said of burglars, robbers, etc.) to reach the target house by way of a neighboring residence

借讓(ㄐㄧㄝˋ ㄖㄤˋ)
to transfer temporarily; loan

借讀(ㄐㄧㄝˋ ㄉㄨˊ)
to study at a school on a temporary basis

借端(ㄐㄧㄝˋ ㄉㄨㄢ)
on the pretext of

借題發揮(ㄐㄧㄝˋ ㄊㄧˊ ㄈㄚ ㄏㄨㄟ)
to make an issue of; to capitalize on; to seize a pretext (to air one's own complaints, to attack others, etc.)

借古諷今(ㄐㄧㄝˋ ㄍㄨˇ ㄈㄥˇ ㄐㄧㄣ)
to use the past to disparage the present

借故(ㄐㄧㄝˋ ㄍㄨˋ)
to find an excuse

借故推托(ㄐㄧㄝˋ ㄍㄨˋ ㄊㄨㄟ ㄊㄨㄛ)
to find an excuse to refuse

借光(ㄐㄧㄝˋ ㄍㄨㄤ)
①(a polite expression) Please let me pass. 或 Will you please tell me…? ②to be given favors, assistance, help, etc.

借錢(ㄐㄧㄝˋ ㄑㄧㄢˊ)
to borrow money; to ask for a loan; a loan

借花獻佛(ㄐㄧㄝˋ ㄏㄨㄚ ㄒㄧㄢˋ ㄈㄛˊ)
(literally) to borrow flowers to offer to Buddha—to get things from another person to entertain one's own guest

借火兒(ㄐㄧㄝˋ ㄏㄨㄛˇㄦ)
Please give me a light. 或 to borrow matches or a lighted cigarette; to ask for a light

借酒澆愁(ㄐㄧㄝˋ ㄐㄧㄡˇ ㄐㄧㄠ ㄔㄡˊ)
to drown one's worries or anxieties by drinking

借鑒(ㄐㄧㄝˋ ㄐㄧㄢˋ)or 借鏡(ㄐㄧㄝˋ ㄐㄧㄥˋ)
to learn a lesson from another person's experience; to benefit by another person's past experience

借據(ㄐㄧㄝˋ ㄐㄩˋ)
an I.O.U.; a written acknowledgment of indebtedness; a certificate of indebtedness

借支(ㄐㄧㄝˋ ㄓ)

to request an advance on one's pay

借債（ㄐㄧㄝˋ ㄓㄞˋ）
to borrow money; to raise a loan

借主（ㄐㄧㄝˋ ㄓㄨˇ）
the creditor

借住（ㄐㄧㄝˋ ㄓㄨˋ）
to stay in another's house

借助（ㄐㄧㄝˋ ㄓㄨˋ）
to have the aid of; to draw support from

借箸代籌（ㄐㄧㄝˋ ㄓㄨˋ ㄉㄞˋ ㄔㄡˊ）
to propose or suggest; to make a plan for others

借重（ㄐㄧㄝˋ ㄓㄨㄥˋ）
to rely on; to seek the assistance (of)

借屍還魂（ㄐㄧㄝˋ ㄕ ㄏㄨㄢˊ ㄏㄨㄣˊ）
①(Chinese folklore) A dead person comes to life again by reposing his or her spirit in the body of another dead person. ②(said of something evil) to revive in a new guise

借書證（ㄐㄧㄝˋ ㄕㄨ ㄓㄥˋ）
a library card

借宿（ㄐㄧㄝˋ ㄙㄨˋ）
to stay overnight in another's place (or hotel, etc.)

借以（ㄐㄧㄝˋ ㄧˇ）
so as to; for the purpose of

借問（ㄐㄧㄝˋ ㄨㄣˋ）
Will you please tell me…?

借喻（ㄐㄧㄝˋ ㄩˋ）
to use an analogy 亦作「比喻」

借用（ㄐㄧㄝˋ ㄩㄥˋ）
to borrow; to use something for another purpose: 借用一下你的字典好嗎？May I use your dictionary?

【倡】 207
ㄔㄤ chang chāng
1. a prostitute
2. wild and unrestrained

倡狂（ㄔㄤ ㄎㄨㄤˊ）
profligate

倡優（ㄔㄤ ㄧㄡ）
①a prostitute ②actress（倡）and actor（優）; a musician; an entertainer

【倡】 207
ㄔㄤˋ chang chàng
to lead; to introduce; to initiate; to advocate: 首倡 the

first to propose or lead

倡導（ㄔㄤˋ ㄉㄠˇ）
to lead; to advocate; to promote

倡議（ㄔㄤˋ ㄧˋ）
to make a motion; to advocate; to advance a cause

倡言（ㄔㄤˋ ㄧㄢˊ）
to be the first to propose or promote publicly; to initiate

【值】 208
ㄓˊ jyr zhí
1. prices of commodities; value; cost; to cost; to be worth
2. at the time of…
3. to meet; to happen: 他上次來訪,正值她外出。She happened to be out when he called.

值班（ㄓˊ ㄅㄢ）or 值班兒（ㄓˊ ㄅㄚㄦ）
to be on duty; to be on the shift

值得（ㄓˊ ㄉㄜˊ）
to be worth of; to deserve: 這本小說值得一讀。This novel is well worth reading.

值錢（ㄓˊ ㄑㄧㄢˊ）
valuable; expensive

值勤（ㄓˊ ㄑㄧㄣˊ）
(said of soldiers, policemen, etc.) to be on duty

值星（ㄓˊ ㄒㄧㄥ）
(said of army officers) to be on duty for the week

值日（ㄓˊ ㄖˋ）
to be one's turn to be on duty; to be on duty for the day

值日生（ㄓˊ ㄖˋ ㄕㄥ）
the student on duty

【倦】 209
ㄐㄩㄢˋ jiuann juàn
tired; weary

倦怠（ㄐㄩㄢˋ ㄉㄞˋ）
to be tired; worn out; languor

倦鳥知還（ㄐㄩㄢˋ ㄋㄧㄠˇ ㄓ ㄏㄨㄢˊ）
(literally) The weary bird always returns to its nest. —to return home after years of wandering far away

倦勤（ㄐㄩㄢˋ ㄑㄧㄣˊ）
wanting to resign from a high position; to be tired of work

倦遊（ㄐㄩㄢˋ ㄧㄡˊ）
①to be weary of wandering

or traveling ②to be weary of official duties; to be weary of a public life

【倨】 210
ㄐㄩˋ jiuh jù
1. haughty; rude; arrogant
2. slightly bent

倨傲（ㄐㄩˋ ㄠˋ）
haughty; rude; supercilious; conceited

【倩】 211
ㄑㄧㄢˋ chiann qiàn
1. pretty dimples of a smiling woman
2. handsome
3. a son-in-law
4. to ask somebody to do something for oneself; to solicit the service of a ghost writer, etc.

倩兮（ㄑㄧㄢˋ ㄒㄧ）
How graceful she looks!

倩粧（ㄑㄧㄢˋ ㄓㄨㄤ）
beautiful make-up and becoming clothes

倩影（ㄑㄧㄢˋ ㄧㄥˇ）
the beautiful image of a woman

【倪】 212
ㄋㄧˊ ni ní
1. young and weak
2. division
3. a beginning
4. a limit; bounds
5. a Chinese family name

【倫】 213
ㄌㄨㄣˊ luen lún
1. normal relationships among people
2. comparison; a peer; a match: 無與倫比 beyond comparison
3. classification
4. order; logic
5. regular; ordinary
6. to choose; choice

倫比（ㄌㄨㄣˊ ㄅㄧˇ）
comparable; equal

倫敦（ㄌㄨㄣˊ ㄉㄨㄣ）
London

倫理（ㄌㄨㄣˊ ㄌㄧˇ）
moral principles; ethics

倫理學（ㄌㄨㄣˊ ㄌㄧˇ ㄒㄩㄝˊ）
ethics

倫常（ㄌㄨㄣˊ ㄔㄤˊ）
normal and accepted ways and relationships of people

倫次（ㄌㄨㄣˊ ㄘˋ）

〔人部〕

the normal order of things, reasons, evidence, etc.; an orderly presentation of such: 他說話語無倫次。 He spoke incoherently.

〔人部〕

【倭】 214
1. ㄨㄛ uo wǒ
name of a human race; an old name for Japan

倭奴(ㄨㄛ ㄋㄨˊ)
①(used in ancient times) the Japanese ②(in modern usage, derogatively) the Japs

倭國(ㄨㄛ ㄍㄨㄛˊ)
an ancient name for Japan

倭寇(ㄨㄛ ㄎㄡˋ)
(ancient usage) the dwarf pirates; the Japs; Japanese corsairs (in the Ming Dynasty)

【倭】 214
2. ㄨㄟ uei wei
參看「倭遲」

倭遲(ㄨㄟ ㄔˊ)
winding; circuitous ; meandering

九畫

【偃】 215
| ㄧㄢˇ yean yǎn
1. to cease; to be at rest; to stop; to suppress; to lay off
2. to lie on one's back
3. an embankment; an earthen bank or dyke
4. a Chinese family name

偃兵(ㄧㄢˇ ㄅㄧㄥ)
to stop a military action

偃仆(ㄧㄢˇ ㄆㄨˊ)
to fall down flat; to fall on one's back

偃旗息鼓(ㄧㄢˇ ㄑㄧˊ ㄒㄧˊ ㄍㄨˇ)
①to stop the fanfare; to halt the noisy show ②(said of opposing armies) to stop fighting; to lower the banners and muffle the drums —to cease all activities

偃武修文(ㄧㄢˇ ㄨˇ ㄒㄧㄡ ㄨㄣˊ)
(literally) to cease military activities or preparations and promote culture—to emphasize cultural pursuits; (after conquest) to disband troops and attend to civilian affairs

偃臥(ㄧㄢˇ ㄨㄛˋ)
to lie (or sleep) on one's back

偃月刀(ㄧㄢˇ ㄩㄝˋ ㄉㄠ)
a big crescent knife with a long shaft (especially the one used by General Kuan Yü (關羽) in the Epoch of the Three Kingdoms)

【假】 216
1. ㄐㄧㄚˇ jea jiǎ
1. false; not real; phoney; artificial; fake; bogus; sham
2. supposing; if
3. to borrow; to avail oneself of
4. a Chinese family name

假扮(ㄐㄧㄚˇ ㄅㄢˋ)
to disguise; to masquerade

假寐(ㄐㄧㄚˇ ㄇㄟˋ)
to sleep without taking off one's clothes; to take a nap; a catnap; a doze; a siesta

假冒(ㄐㄧㄚˇ ㄇㄠˋ)
① to counterfeit ② to assume the identity of somebody else

假面具(ㄐㄧㄚˇ ㄇㄧㄢˋ ㄐㄩˋ)
a mask—a false front

假名(ㄐㄧㄚˇ ㄇㄧㄥˊ)
①a false name; a pseudonym; an alias ②kana (the Japanese syllabary)

假髮(ㄐㄧㄚˇ ㄈㄚˇ)
a wig

假分數(ㄐㄧㄚˇ ㄈㄣ ㄕㄨˋ)
(arithmetic) an improper fraction

假貸(ㄐㄧㄚˇ ㄉㄞˋ)
to borrow (money, etc.)

假貸顏色(ㄐㄧㄚˇ ㄉㄞˋ ㄧㄢˊ ㄙㄜˋ)
to tolerate; to bear

假道(ㄐㄧㄚˇ ㄉㄠˋ)
via; by way of

假道學(ㄐㄧㄚˇ ㄉㄠˋ ㄒㄩㄝˊ)
a sanctimonious person; a hypocrite

假定(ㄐㄧㄚˇ ㄉㄧㄥˋ)
① if; assuming; supposing; a supposition; a hypothesis; an assumption ②(mathematics) a postulate

假動作(ㄐㄧㄚˇ ㄉㄨㄥˋ ㄗㄨㄛˋ)
(sports) dummy play; a deceiving move

假託(ㄐㄧㄚˇ ㄊㄨㄛ)
①an excuse; a pretext; a

subterfuge ②by means of ③ under someone else's name

假退役(ㄐㄧㄚˇ ㄊㄨㄟˋ ㄧˋ)
semi-retirement from the military service, which permits the person concerned to take up civilian jobs while still drawing part of his military pay

假老實(ㄐㄧㄚˇ ㄌㄠˇ ㄕˊ)
double-dealing; double-faced

假公濟私(ㄐㄧㄚˇ ㄍㄨㄥ ㄐㄧˋ ㄙ)
to attain private or personal ends in the name of official duties; to gain private ends in public cause or by public money

假扣押(ㄐㄧㄚˇ ㄎㄡˋ ㄧㄚˊ)
(law) provisional seizure

假花(ㄐㄧㄚˇ ㄏㄨㄚ)
an artificial flower

假話(ㄐㄧㄚˇ ㄏㄨㄚˋ)
a lie; a falsehood

假借(ㄐㄧㄚˇ ㄐㄧㄝˋ)
①to borrow ②"phonetic loan characters"—one of the six classes of the Chinese characters (A character under this category is used with the sense which properly belongs to another of the same sound but different form.)

假借名義(ㄐㄧㄚˇ ㄐㄧㄝˋ ㄇㄧㄥˊ ㄧˋ)
under the guise of; in the name of

假戲真做(ㄐㄧㄚˇ ㄒㄧˋ ㄓㄣ ㄗㄨㄛˋ)
to do something seriously after starting it as a joke, ruse, etc.

假想(ㄐㄧㄚˇ ㄒㄧㄤˇ)
①an imagination; a hypothesis; a supposition ②imaginary; hypothetical; fictitious

假想敵(ㄐㄧㄚˇ ㄒㄧㄤˇ ㄉㄧˊ)
a hypothetical enemy; an imaginary enemy

假象(ㄐㄧㄚˇ ㄒㄧㄤˋ)
①false appearances or impressions: 他製造假象。He created a false impression. ②(geology) a pseudomorph

假惺惺(ㄐㄧㄚˇ ㄒㄧㄥ ㄒㄧㄥ)
to pretend; to shed crocodile tears: 他假惺惺表示願意支持你。He pretended to express his willingness to support

you.

假裝天花(ㄐㄧㄚˇ ㄒㄧㄤ ㄊㄧㄢ ㄏㄨㄚ) or 假痘(ㄐㄧㄚˇ ㄉㄡ)
varioloid

假性近視(ㄐㄧㄚˇ ㄒㄧㄥ ㄐㄧㄣˋ ㄕˋ)
pseudo-myopia

假執行(ㄐㄧㄚˇ ㄓˊ ㄒㄧㄥˊ)
(law) a false execution; to sequestrate

假正經(ㄐㄧㄚˇ ㄓㄥˋ ㄐㄧㄥ)
hypocritical

假裝(ㄐㄧㄚˇ ㄓㄨㄤ)
to pretend; to assume the appearance of

假裝分子(ㄐㄧㄚˇ ㄒㄧㄤ ㄈㄣ ㄗˇ)
provisional measures

假充(ㄐㄧㄚˇ ㄔㄨㄥ)
to counterfeit; to pretend

假充內行(ㄐㄧㄚˇ ㄔㄨㄥ ㄋㄟˋ ㄏㄤˊ)
to pretend to know what one does not

假使(ㄐㄧㄚˇ ㄕˇ)
if; in case; supposing: 假使他不能來, 誰做這項工作? Supposing he can't come, who will do the work?

假釋(ㄐㄧㄚˇ ㄕˋ)
to parole; parole; conditional release; to free (a prisoner) on probation

假設(ㄐㄧㄚˇ ㄕㄜˋ)
a hypothesis; a supposition; an assumption: 科學假設 a scientific hypothesis

假設法(ㄐㄧㄚˇ ㄕㄜˋ ㄈㄚˇ) or 假設語氣(ㄐㄧㄚˇ ㄕㄜˋ ㄩˇ ㄑㄧˋ)
(grammar) the subjunctive mood

假手(ㄐㄧㄚˇ ㄕㄡˇ)
to do something by means of (an agent)

假手他人(ㄐㄧㄚˇ ㄕㄡˇ ㄊㄚ ㄖㄣˊ)
to do something (usually evil) by another's hand; to make somebody else do the work

假山(ㄐㄧㄚˇ ㄕㄢ)
a small artificial hill (used as decoration in a Chinese garden); a rockery

假聲(ㄐㄧㄚˇ ㄕㄥ)
(music) falsetto

假說(ㄐㄧㄚˇ ㄕㄨㄛ)
a postulate; a hypothesis

假仁假義(ㄐㄧㄚˇ ㄖㄣˊ ㄐㄧㄚˇ ㄧˋ)
to be a wolf in sheep's cloth-

ing; to shed crocodile tears; pretended benevolence and righteousness; hypocrisy

假如(ㄐㄧㄚˇ ㄖㄨˊ)
supposing; in case; if

假若(ㄐㄧㄚˇ ㄖㄨㄛˋ)
if; supposing; in case

假造(ㄐㄧㄚˇ ㄗㄠˋ)
①to forge; to counterfeit: 那張鈔票是假造的。That bank note is a forgery. ②to invent; to fabricate

假造罪名(ㄐㄧㄚˇ ㄗㄠˋ ㄗㄨㄟˋ ㄇㄧㄥˊ)
to cook up a false charge against; to frame up

假慈悲(ㄐㄧㄚˇ ㄘˊ ㄅㄟ)
pretending to be kindhearted

假死(ㄐㄧㄚˇ ㄙˇ)
①(medicine) suspended animation ②to play dead; to feign death; sham death

假以時日(ㄐㄧㄚˇ ㄧˇ ㄕˊ ㄖˋ)
to give sufficient time

假意(ㄐㄧㄚˇ ㄧˋ)
①false intent; insincerity; hypocrisy ②to pretend

假意奉承(ㄐㄧㄚˇ ㄧˋ ㄈㄥˋ ㄔㄥˊ)
false flattery

假牙(ㄐㄧㄚˇ ㄧㄚˊ)
a false tooth; a denture

【假】216
2. ㄐㄧㄚˋ jiah jià
a holiday

假條(ㄐㄧㄚˋ ㄊㄧㄠˊ)
①an application for leave
②a leave permit

假期(ㄐㄧㄚˋ ㄑㄧˊ)
a vacation; a holiday

假日(ㄐㄧㄚˋ ㄖˋ)
a holiday

【偈】217
ㄐㄧㄝˋ jye jiè
1. brave; martial
2. hasty; scudding

【偉】218
ㄨㄟˇ woei wěi
1.extraordinary; great; big; gigantic: 他身體魁偉 He is gigantic in stature.
2. a Chinese family name

偉大(ㄨㄟˇ ㄉㄚˋ)
great; extraordinary: 貝多芬是一個偉大的音樂家。Beethoven was a great musician.

偉績(ㄨㄟˇ ㄐㄧ)
great achievements

偉器(ㄨㄟˇ ㄑㄧˋ)

a man of great capability

偉人(ㄨㄟˇ ㄖㄣˊ)
a great man

偉岸(ㄨㄟˇ ㄢˋ)
tall and robust

偉業(ㄨㄟˇ ㄧㄝˋ)
a great career; monumental accomplishments

【偌】219
ㄖㄨㄛˋ ruoh ruò
so (used as an adverb to modify an adjective)

偌大(ㄖㄨㄛˋ ㄉㄚˋ)
so; big: 你見過偌大的地方? Have you seen such a big place?

【偎】220
ㄨㄟ uei wēi
1. to cuddle; to embrace
2. intimate; very dear to
3. to lean on

偎傍(ㄨㄟ ㄅㄤˋ)
to stay close together

偎貼(ㄨㄟ ㄊㄧㄝ)
to snuggle close to

偎臉(ㄨㄟ ㄌㄧㄢˇ)
to put cheek and cheek together

偎紅倚翠(ㄨㄟ ㄏㄨㄥˊ ㄧˇ ㄘㄨㄟˋ)
to frequent brothels

偎愛(ㄨㄟ ㄞˋ)
to be intimately in love

偎倚(ㄨㄟ ㄧˇ) or 偎依(ㄨㄟ ㄧ)
to cuddle or curl up; to snuggle up to; to lean close to: 嬰兒偎倚在母親的懷裏。The baby snuggled up in his mother's arms.

【偏】221
ㄆㄧㄢ pian piān
1. biased; not fair; prejudiced; partial
2. leaning; inclined to one side
3. an auxiliary verb indicating a sense of contrariness or determination

偏頗(ㄆㄧㄢ ㄆㄛˇ)
partial; biased; not fair

偏旁(ㄆㄧㄢ ㄆㄤˊ) or 偏旁兒(ㄆㄧㄢ ㄆㄤˊ ㄦ)
a radical on one side of a character

偏僻(ㄆㄧㄢ ㄆㄧˋ)
(said of a place) out-of-the-way; not easily accessible; secluded: 那是一個偏僻的小村莊。That is an out-of-the-way

〔人部〕

village.

偏偏(ㄆㄧㄢ ㄆㄧㄢ)
① unfortunately it happened that… 不該他去。他偏偏要去。He was not supposed to go, but he insisted on going.

偏廢(ㄆㄧㄢ ㄈㄟˋ)
① crippled ② to emphasize one thing and neglect others

偏方(ㄆㄧㄢ ㄈㄤ)or 偏方兒(ㄆㄧㄢ ㄈㄤㄦ)
(Chinese medicine) an informal recipe or prescription; a folk prescription

偏房(ㄆㄧㄢ ㄈㄤˊ)
a concubine

偏鋒(ㄆㄧㄢ ㄈㄥ)
① (said of writings or paintings) an oblique stroke of the brush ② (figuratively) an unorthodox way of doing things

偏頭痛(ㄆㄧㄢ ㄊㄡˊ ㄊㄨㄥˋ)
(medicine) hemicrania; migraine

偏袒(ㄆㄧㄢ ㄊㄢˇ)
partiality; partial: 做父母的不應偏袒任何一個孩子。A parent should not be partial to any of his children.

偏疼(ㄆㄧㄢ ㄊㄥˊ)
undue partiality (as of a parent to a child)

偏題(ㄆㄧㄢ ㄊㄧˊ)
a catch question (in an examination)

偏聽偏信(ㄆㄧㄢ ㄊㄧㄥ ㄆㄧㄢ ㄒㄧㄣˋ)
to heed and believe only one side—to favor one side too much; to be prejudiced; to be biased

偏勞(ㄆㄧㄢ ㄌㄠˊ)
① to let one person take on the work of the whole team: 我們只好偏勞他了。We cannot but let him take on the whole job. ② (usually from a boss to an employee) "Thanks for the good work."

偏離(ㄆㄧㄢ ㄌㄧˊ)
to deviate; to diverge: 他的談話偏離題論。His talk deviated from the subject under discussion.

偏枯(ㄆㄧㄢ ㄎㄨ)
① paralysed on one side ② uneven or unfair distribution of something, such as benefit, etc. ③ a theory about calligraphy

偏狂(ㄆㄧㄢ ㄎㄨㄤˊ)
monomania

偏好(ㄆㄧㄢ ㄏㄠˋ)
a hobby

偏護(ㄆㄧㄢ ㄏㄨˋ)
partial; to favor one side against the other; to give undue protection to; to screen or shelter

偏諱(ㄆㄧㄢ ㄏㄨㄟˋ)
to avoid using either of the two characters in the emperor's or one's parent's name

偏激(ㄆㄧㄢ ㄐㄧ)
extreme; radical: 他的想法偏激。He has radical ideas.

偏激分子(ㄆㄧㄢ ㄐㄧ ㄈㄣˋ ㄗˇ)
a radical

偏見(ㄆㄧㄢ ㄐㄧㄢˋ)
prejudice; bias: 他對我懷有偏見。He has a prejudice against me.

偏巧(ㄆㄧㄢ ㄑㄧㄠˇ)
it so happened; as luck would have it: 那天偏巧是一個晴天。It happened to be a fine day.

偏斜(ㄆㄧㄢ ㄒㄧㄝˊ)
to slant

偏心(ㄆㄧㄢ ㄒㄧㄣ)
partiality; bias: 她絲毫不偏心。She is free from any bias.

偏向(ㄆㄧㄢ ㄒㄧㄤˋ)
to lean or to be inclined toward

偏執(ㄆㄧㄢ ㄓˊ)
stubbornly biased; strong inclination toward

偏轉(ㄆㄧㄢ ㄓㄨㄢˇ)
(physics) deflection

偏重(ㄆㄧㄢ ㄓㄨㄥˋ)
① to give undue emphasis to: 我們研究科學不應只偏重理論而忽視實驗。In studying science, we shouldn't stress theory at the expense of experiment. ② to lean heavily toward; to have extraordinary faith in (somebody)

偏差(ㄆㄧㄢ ㄔㄚ)
errors; deviation

偏食(ㄆㄧㄢ ㄕˊ)
(said of children) to eat certain dishes only

偏蝕(ㄆㄧㄢ ㄕˊ)
a partial eclipse (of the sun or moon)

偏才(ㄆㄧㄢ ㄘㄞˊ)
clever in petty matters; talents in a petty way

偏私(ㄆㄧㄢ ㄙ)
biased; favoritism: 受雇者認為大部分的加薪都偏私。The employees think that most pay raises are based on favoritism.

偏阿(ㄆㄧㄢ ㄜ)
biased; prejudiced

偏愛(ㄆㄧㄢ ㄞˋ)
to love someone or something in particular; personal favorites or hobbies: 孩子們常常偏愛糖果。Children love candy in particular.

偏安(ㄆㄧㄢ ㄢ)
(the authority of the emperor) to be confined to a (usually small) portion of his empire (due to rebellion or foreign invasion)

偏倚(ㄆㄧㄢ ㄧˇ)
to lean on

偏要(ㄆㄧㄢ ㄧㄠˋ)
bent on having (in disregard of difficulties involved or others' opposition); to positively choose, take, etc.: 這男孩子偏要惡作劇。The boy is bent on mischief.

偏遠(ㄆㄧㄢ ㄩㄢˇ)
remote; faraway

【偓】 222
ㄨㄛˋ woh wò
1. narrow-mindedness
2. a Chinese family name

【偕】 223
ㄒㄧㄝˊ shye xié
(又讀 ㄐㄧㄝ jie jiē)
1. to accompany
2. together

偕同(ㄒㄧㄝˊ ㄊㄨㄥˊ)
in company with; along with

偕老(ㄒㄧㄝˊ ㄌㄠˇ)
to grow old together as man and wife

【做】 224
ㄗㄨㄛˋ tzuoh zuò
1. to work; to make; to do: 她

在做巧克力蛋糕。She is making a chocolate cake.
2. to act as
3. to pretend to be
4. to give (a party, reception, etc.)
5. to enter (a profession)
6. to become: 後來她做了褓姆。Later she became a babysitter.

做伴(ㄗㄨㄜ ㄅㄢˋ)
to keep somebody company

做不得(ㄗㄨㄜ ·ㄅㄨ ·ㄉㄜ)
Don't do it!

做不了(ㄗㄨㄜ ·ㄅㄨ ㄌㄧㄠˇ)
cannot do it

做不好(ㄗㄨㄜ ·ㄅㄨ ㄏㄠˇ)
cannot do it well

做媒(ㄗㄨㄜ ㄇㄟˊ)
to be a matchmaker

做夢(ㄗㄨㄜ ㄇㄥˋ)
①to have a dream; to dream: 我昨晚做了個惡夢。I had a bad dream last night. ②to have a pipe dream; to daydream: 她的從影計畫不過是在做夢罷了。Her plans for a movie career are just a pipe dream.

做面子(ㄗㄨㄜ ㄇㄧㄢˋ·ㄗ)
to render eye-service; to put up a pleasant front; to do something for the sake of appearance

做法(ㄗㄨㄜ ㄈㄚˇ)
way of doing a thing; practice: 他慣做的做法是利用別人。His usual way of doing things is to take advantage of others.

做飯(ㄗㄨㄜ ㄈㄢˋ)
to prepare food; to prepare a meal

做大(ㄗㄨㄜ ㄉㄚˋ)
to arrogate to oneself a high rank; to put on airs

做得了(ㄗㄨㄜ ·ㄉㄜ ㄌㄧㄠˇ)
can be done

做到(ㄗㄨㄜ ㄉㄠˋ)
to accomplish; to achieve: 你應該說到做到。You should accomplish what you promise.

做東(ㄗㄨㄜ ㄉㄨㄥ)
to play the host; to host

做頭髮(ㄗㄨㄜ ㄊㄡˊ ㄈㄚˇ)
to have one's hair done at a beauty parlor

做禮拜(ㄗㄨㄜ ㄌㄧˇ ㄅㄞˋ)
to go to church; to be at church

做弄(ㄗㄨㄜ ㄋㄨㄥˋ)
to make fun of; to play jokes upon

做官(ㄗㄨㄜ ㄍㄨㄢ)
to become an official; to secure oneself an official position; to join government service: 有些人一though做官,就想發財。Some people wish to become rich once they become officials.

做工(ㄗㄨㄜ ㄍㄨㄥ)
①to work: 他在電算機工廠做工。He works in a computer factory. ②the acting part in Chinese opera, etc.

做客(ㄗㄨㄜ ㄎㄜˋ)
to be a guest: 我爸爸昨晚到一個老朋友家真去做客。My father was a guest at an old friend's last night.

做闊(ㄗㄨㄜ ㄎㄨㄛˋ)
to show off one's wealth; to make a display of one's riches

做和向(ㄗㄨㄜ ㄏㄜˊ ㄕㄤˋ)
to become a Buddhist monk

做好事(ㄗㄨㄜ ㄏㄠˇ ㄕˋ)
①to do a good deed; to help the needy ②to perform religious rites for the repose of the dead

做好人(ㄗㄨㄜ ㄏㄠˇ ㄖㄣˊ)
to play the role of a good guy (often insincerely)

做好歹(ㄗㄨㄜ ㄏㄠˇ ㄗㄨㄜ ㄉㄞˇ)
to play the good or crook (to get something done)

做活(ㄗㄨㄜ ㄏㄨㄛˊ)or做活兒(ㄗㄨㄜ ㄏㄨㄛˊㄦ)
①to earn a living; to work: 我們一塊兒在田裏做活兒。We worked together in the fields. ②(said of women)to do needlework

做假(ㄗㄨㄜ ㄐㄧㄚˇ)
to cheat

做絕(ㄗㄨㄜ ㄐㄩㄝˊ)
①to leave no room for a maneuver; to leave no avenue of retreat: 他把事情做絕了。He left himself no avenue of retreat. ②to do to the utmost: 這流氓壞事做絕了。

The hoodlum has done villainies to the utmost.

做小(ㄗㄨㄜ ㄒㄧㄠˇ)
to be someone's concubine

做主(ㄗㄨㄜ ㄓㄨˇ)
to take charge of; to be responsible for; to decide

做莊(ㄗㄨㄜ ㄓㄨㄤ)
(gambling) to be the banker

做事(ㄗㄨㄜ ㄕˋ)
①to handle affairs; to do a deed: 我們應該熱心為大衆做事。We should handle the public affairs heartily. ②to work; to have a job: 我在鋼廠做事。I work in a steel mill.

做手脚(ㄗㄨㄜ ㄕㄡˇ ㄐㄧㄠˇ)
to tamper something with the intention to cheat or to hurt somebody

做聲(ㄗㄨㄜ ㄕㄥ)
to make a sound; to speak: 別做聲! Keep quiet! 或Don't speak!

做生日(ㄗㄨㄜ ㄕㄥ ㄖˋ)or做壽(ㄗㄨㄜ ㄕㄡˋ)
to give a birthday party; to celebrate one's birthday

做生意(ㄗㄨㄜ ㄕㄥ ˙ㄧ)
to do business transactions; to be a businessman

做人(ㄗㄨㄜ ㄖㄣˊ)
①to conduct oneself; to behave: 他懂得如何做人處世。He knows how to conduct himself in society. ②to be an upright person. 他想要重新做人。He wishes to be an upright person again.

做人情(ㄗㄨㄜ ㄖㄣˊ ㄑㄧㄥˊ)
to do something as a favor; to do someone a favor of doing something; to do someone a special favor

做賊心虛(ㄗㄨㄜ ㄗㄟˊ ㄒㄧㄣ ㄒㄩ)
(literally) The Thief has a guilty conscience.—One who has done something bad secretly cannot look others in the eye. 或The evildoer has a guilty conscience.

做作(ㄗㄨㄜ ㄗㄨㄛˋ)
①affectation; pretentiousness; affected; pretentious ②to affect; to behave unnaturally

【入部】

做愛（ㄗㄨㄛˋ ㄞˋ）
to make love

做衣服（ㄗㄨㄛˋ ㄧ ㄈㄨˊ）
to tailor; to have a dress made

做一天和尚撞一天鐘（ㄗㄨㄛˋ ㄧ ㄊㄧㄢ ㄏㄜˊ ㄕㄤˋ ㄓㄨㄤˋ ㄧ ㄊㄧㄢ ㄓㄨㄥ）
to keep tolling the bell as long as one is a monk; to take a passive attitude towards one's duty

做樣子（ㄗㄨㄛˋ ㄧㄤˋ ·ㄗ）
to go through the motion of doing something; to pretend to do something

做文章（ㄗㄨㄛˋ ㄨㄣˊ ㄓㄤ）
① to write an essay ② to make an issue of

【停】 ㄊㄧㄥˊ tyng tíng 225
1. to stop; to pause; to halt; to stay; to park: 雨已經停了。
The rain has stopped.
2. to suspend; to delay
3. percentage

停泊（ㄊㄧㄥˊ ㄅㄛˊ）
to anchor; to berth; to dock: 船停泊著。The ship was at anchor.

停擺（ㄊㄧㄥˊ ㄅㄞˇ）
(literally) The pendulum stops.—to suspend work: 鬧鐘停擺了。The alarm clock has stopped.

停辦（ㄊㄧㄥˊ ㄅㄢˋ）
to suspend (a business or school); to stop handling something

停飛（ㄊㄧㄥˊ ㄈㄟ）
the grounding of aircraft: 飛機因霧而停飛。The airplanes were grounded by the fog.

停放（ㄊㄧㄥˊ ㄈㄤˋ）
to park; to place

停付（ㄊㄧㄥˊ ㄈㄨˋ）
to stop payment (of checks, salaries, etc.)

停當（ㄊㄧㄥˊ ㄉㄤˋ）
ready; all set

停電（ㄊㄧㄥˊ ㄉㄧㄢˋ）
① power failure; blackout ② to cut off power supply

停頓（ㄊㄧㄥˊ ㄉㄨㄣˋ）
to grind to a halt; to suspend: 罷工使工業逐漸停頓。The strikes brought industry grinding to a halt.

停妥（ㄊㄧㄥˊ ㄊㄨㄛˇ）
① ready; all set; in A-1 condition ② (said of a vehicle, etc.) to have been parked in a proper place

停留（ㄊㄧㄥˊ ㄌㄧㄡˊ）
to stay; to stop or remain (at a certain stage)

停擱（ㄊㄧㄥˊ ㄍㄜ）
to stop and shelve (a project, etc.)

停工（ㄊㄧㄥˊ ㄍㄨㄥ）
to suspend work

停課（ㄊㄧㄥˊ ㄎㄜˋ）
to suspend class: 昨天學校停課了。Classes were suspended yesterday.

停靠（ㄊㄧㄥˊ ㄎㄠˋ）
① (said of a train) to stop ② (said of a ship) to berth

停刊（ㄊㄧㄥˊ ㄎㄢ）
(said of a newspaper, magazine, etc.) to stop publication

停航（ㄊㄧㄥˊ ㄏㄤˊ）
to suspend air or shipping service: 班機因暴風雨而停航。The regular flight is suspended on account of the storm.

停火（ㄊㄧㄥˊ ㄏㄨㄛˇ）
to cease fire

停機坪（ㄊㄧㄥˊ ㄐㄧ ㄆㄧㄥˊ）
an apron (at an airfield)

停經期（ㄊㄧㄥˊ ㄐㄧㄥ ㄑㄧ）
menopause

停妻再娶（ㄊㄧㄥˊ ㄑㄧ ㄗㄞˋ ㄑㄩˇ）
to commit bigamy

停息（ㄊㄧㄥˊ ㄒㄧˊ）
to stop; to cease: 暴風雨終於停息了。At last the storm has ceased.

停歇（ㄊㄧㄥˊ ㄒㄧㄝ）
to stop for a rest

停薪（ㄊㄧㄥˊ ㄒㄧㄣ）
to stop or suspend payment to an employee

停學（ㄊㄧㄥˊ ㄒㄩㄝˊ）
to rusticate (a student); rustication

停職（ㄊㄧㄥˊ ㄓˊ）
to suspend a person from office

停止（ㄊㄧㄥˊ ㄓˇ）
to stop; to cease: 比賽因雨停止。The game was stopped

by rain.

停滯（ㄊㄧㄥˊ ㄓˋ）
① to stop or be held up (at a certain stage, etc.): 會議停滯不前。The meeting has stopped. ② indigestion

停戰（ㄊㄧㄥˊ ㄓㄢˋ）
① to stop fighting ② a truce; suspension of hostilities: 兩軍之間宣布停戰。A truce was declared between the two armies.

停戰協定（ㄊㄧㄥˊ ㄓㄢˋ ㄒㄧㄝˊ ㄉㄧㄥˋ）
a truce; an armistice

停車（ㄊㄧㄥˊ ㄔㄜ）
to park a car

停車場（ㄊㄧㄥˊ ㄔㄜ ㄔㄤˇ）or（ㄊㄧㄥˊ ㄔㄜ ㄔㄤ）
a parking lot

停產（ㄊㄧㄥˊ ㄔㄢˇ）
to stop production

停屍間（ㄊㄧㄥˊ ㄕ ㄐㄧㄢ）
a mortuary

停水（ㄊㄧㄥˊ ㄕㄨㄟˇ）
to cut off the water supply

停業（ㄊㄧㄥˊ ㄧㄝˋ）
to stop doing business; to close down 亦作「歇業」

【健】 ㄐㄧㄢˋ jiann jiàn 226
1. healthy; strong
2. vigorous; capable
3. fond of; inclined to; liable to
4. to strengthen; to toughen

健步（ㄐㄧㄢˋ ㄅㄨˋ）
① to walk fast: 那老人健步如飛。The old man walked as if on wings. ② capable of walking a long way

健美（ㄐㄧㄢˋ ㄇㄟˇ）
① (said of a man) healthy and handsome; tall, dark and handsome ② (said of a woman) healthy and pretty; having a nice figure; beautiful in an athletic way ③ vigorous and graceful

健談（ㄐㄧㄢˋ ㄊㄢˊ）
brilliant conversation: 她的健談很令人激賞。Her brilliant conversation is much appreciated.

健康（ㄐㄧㄢˋ ㄎㄤ）
① health: 他身體一向很健康。He has always had good health. ② healthy: 孩子們有起來非常健康。The children

looked very healthy.

健康教育（ㄐㄧㄢ ㄎㄤ ㄐㄧㄠ ㄩ）
health education

健康證明書（ㄐㄧㄢ ㄎㄤ ㄓㄥ ㄇㄧㄥ ㄕㄨ）
a health certificate

健将（ㄐㄧㄢ ㄐㄧㄤ）
①one who plays a leading role in an activity ②one who is good at a sport or sports; a top-notch player: 他是足球健将。 He is a top-notch footballer.

健全（ㄐㄧㄢ ㄑㄩㄢ）
①in good condition; in good order; flawless (usually referring to a system, an institution, etc.) ②to strengthen; to perfect

健行（ㄐㄧㄢ ㄒㄧㄥ）
to hike; hiking

健壯（ㄐㄧㄢ ㄓㄨㄤ）
healthy and robust; strong and vigorous: 他是一位健壯的小伙子。 He is a robust young man.

健身房（ㄐㄧㄢ ㄕㄣ ㄈㄤ）
a gymnasium; a gym

健身操（ㄐㄧㄢ ㄕㄣ ㄘㄠ）
calisthenics

健在（ㄐㄧㄢ ㄗㄞ）
to be in good health; alive

健素糖（ㄐㄧㄢ ㄙㄨ ㄊㄤ）
sugar-coated yeast pills

健兒（ㄐㄧㄢ ㄦ）
(said of friendly forces) soldiers

健胃散（ㄐㄧㄢ ㄨㄟ ㄙㄢ）
a medicine which expedites food digestion and is consequently conducive to the health of stomach

健旺（ㄐㄧㄢ ㄨㄤ）
to be in wonderful health; robust and vigorous; energetic: 那老人依然精力健旺有朝氣。 The old man is still vigorous and lively.

健忘（ㄐㄧㄢ ㄨㄤ）
forgetful; liable to forget: 老年人有時很健忘。 Old people are sometimes forgetful.

健忘症（ㄐㄧㄢ ㄨㄤ ㄓㄥ）
(pathology) amnesia

【傯】227
ㄗㄨㄥ tzoong zǒng
1. urgent; having no leisure;

busy
2. to be in (financial, etc.) straits

傯傯（ㄈㄨㄥ ㄈㄨㄥ）
in a hurry

【側】228
ㄘㄜ tseh cè
1. the side; sideways: 道路兩側種着楓樹。 Maples are planted on both sides of the road.
2. to slant; to incline towards: 我側身和他談話。 I was inclining to talk to him.
3. low and narrow-minded; prejudiced

側門（ㄘㄜ ㄇㄣˊ）
a side door

側面（ㄘㄜ ㄇㄧㄢˋ）
the side; the flank

側面圖（ㄘㄜ ㄇㄧㄢˋ ㄊㄨˊ）
a profile

側面消息（ㄘㄜ ㄇㄧㄢˋ ㄒㄧㄠ ㄒㄧˊ）
sidelights

側目（ㄘㄜ ㄇㄨˋ）
①a sidelong glance; to look askance: 我們全都側目視之。We all looked upon it askance. ②to cause raised eyebrows

側光（ㄘㄜ ㄍㄨㄤ）
sidelight; light coming from the side

側擊（ㄘㄜ ㄐㄧ）
①a flank attack; to make a flank attack ②to make oblique remarks

側重（ㄘㄜ ㄓㄨㄥˋ）
to place particular emphasis on; to be partial: 我重做污染宣傳工作。 My job is to place particular emphasis on anti-pollution propaganda.

側出（ㄘㄜ ㄔㄨ）
①to get out (launch, shoot, etc.) from the side ②to be born of a concubine

側身（ㄘㄜ ㄕㄣ）
①to live cautiously in apprehension ②to sidle; on one's side; sideways ③(a modest expression) to be in (a profession, career, etc.)

側耳傾聽（ㄘㄜ ㄦˇ ㄑㄧㄥ ㄊㄧㄥ）
to listen attentively; to be all ears

側翼（ㄘㄜ ㄧˋ）
(military) a flank

側影（ㄘㄜ ㄧㄥˇ）
a silhouette; a profile

側臥（ㄘㄜ ㄨㄛˋ）
to lie on the side

側聞（ㄘㄜ ㄨㄣˊ）
to learn of something from others

【偵】229
ㄓㄣ jen zhēn
1. to detect; to spy; to scout: 我們偵探敵人的行動。 We spy upon the enemy's movements.
2. a scout; a spy; a detective: 他們派遣偵探到我國來。 They sent out a spy to our country.

偵破（ㄓㄣ ㄆㄛˋ）
to bust a crime; to crack a criminal case

偵探（ㄓㄣ ㄊㄢˋ）
① a detective; a private eye ② to investigate

偵探小說（ㄓㄣ ㄊㄢˋ ㄒㄧㄠˇ ㄕㄨㄛ）
detective stories; whodunits

偵聽（ㄓㄣ ㄊㄧㄥ）
(military) to intercept (enemy) radio communications); to monitor

偵緝（ㄓㄣ ㄑㄧ）
to track down and arrest

偵詢（ㄓㄣ ㄒㄩㄣˊ）
to examine a suspect or someone concerned to gather information

偵查（ㄓㄣ ㄔㄚˊ）
to investigate

偵察（ㄓㄣ ㄔㄚˊ）
reconnaissance; to reconnoiter

偵察敵情（ㄓㄣ ㄔㄚˊ ㄉㄧˊ ㄑㄧㄥˊ）
to gather intelligence about the enemy

偵察機（ㄓㄣ ㄔㄚˊ ㄐㄧ）
a reconnaissance plane

【偶】230
ㄡ oou ǒu
1. an idol; an image
2. coincidentally; accidentally
3. once in a while; occasionally: 他偶一為之。 He does it once in a while.
4. not to be taken for granted
5. an even number
6. a counterpart: 無獨有偶。 It is not a unique instance, but has its counterpart.
7. a mate; to mate

〔人
部〕

8. one's company; fellows; buddies

偶發(ㄡ ㄈㄚ)
to happen accidentally; to happen by chance ; to happen occasionally

偶犯(ㄡ ㄈㄢ)
① a casual offense ② a casual offender

偶感(ㄡ ㄍㄢ)
to feel suddenly; to feel occasionally

偶合(ㄡ ㄏㄜ)
by coincidence; coincidental; coincidentally; accidental

偶或(ㄡ ㄏㄨㄛ)
by chance

偶戲(ㄡ ㄒㄧ)
a marionette show; a puppet show

偶像(ㄡ ㄒㄧㄤ)
an idol; an image

偶數(ㄡ ㄕㄨ)
an even number

偶然(ㄡ ㄖㄢ)
① unexpectedly ② accidentally; by chance: 我偶然遇見一個老朋友。I met an old friend by chance.

偶爾(ㄡ ㄦ) or 偶而(ㄡ ㄦ)
occasionally

【偷】 ㄊㄡ tou tōu   231
1. to steal; to filch; to burglarize; to pilfer
2. to do something without others' knowledge; stealthily; surreptitiously
3. to while away time without purpose
4. to have an ex-marital activity

偷盜(ㄊㄡ ㄉㄠ)
to steal; stealing; burglary; to pilfer

偷渡(ㄊㄡ ㄉㄨ)
to steal into another country by hiding oneself aboard a train, ship, airplane, etc.; to stow away

偷渡者(ㄊㄡ ㄉㄨ ㄓㄜ)
a stowaway

偷偷(ㄊㄡ ㄊㄡ) or 偷偷地(ㄊㄡ ㄊㄡ ㄉㄧ)
stealthily; secretly; covertly; on the sly (or quiet); quietly; without others' knowl-

edge; surreptitiously: 我偷偷告訴他那個秘密。I told him the secret on the sly.

偷偷摸摸(ㄊㄡ ㄊㄡ ㄇㄛ ㄇㄛ)
stealthily; surreptitiously; to do something stealthily

偷天換日(ㄊㄡ ㄊㄧㄢ ㄏㄨㄢ ㄖ)
to steal the sky and put up a sham sun—to perpetrate a gigantic fraud; to commit a big cheat, fraud, etc.; to pull off a monumental hoax

偷聽(ㄊㄡ ㄊㄧㄥ)
to eavesdrop; eavesdropping; to bug; bugging; to tap; tapping

偷懶(ㄊㄡ ㄌㄢ)
to loaf on a job; to be lazy

偷工減料(ㄊㄡ ㄍㄨㄥ ㄐㄧㄢ ㄌㄧㄠ)
to do less work and use less or inferior materials than agreed upon (especially in a building job); to jerry-build; to scamp work and stint material

偷看(ㄊㄡ ㄎㄢ)
① to act Peeping Tom; to steal a look; to steal a glance: 他偷看了她一眼。He stole a glance at her. ② to cheat (in an examination)

偷空(ㄊㄡ ㄎㄨㄥ) or 偷空兒(ㄊㄡ ㄎㄨㄥ ㄦ)
to avail oneself of a leisure moment; to snatch a moment; to take time off: 他偷空睡了一小時。He snatched an hour's sleep.

偷漢子(ㄊㄡ ㄏㄢˋ ㄗ)
(said of a married woman) to have an affair with a man other than her own husband; to have a lover

偷活(ㄊㄡ ㄏㄨㄛˊ) or 偷生(ㄊㄡ ㄕㄥ)
to live without much purpose; to while away one's life span aimlessly; to live in disgrace: 他苟且偷生。He lives without ambition.

偷雞不著蝕一把米(ㄊㄡ ㄐㄧ ㄅㄨ ㄓㄠˊ ㄕˊ ㄧ ㄅㄚˇ ㄇㄧˇ)
(literally) The chicken thief failed to catch a chicken after losing a handful of rice which he used as a bait.—to fail to gain an advantage and incur a loss to oneself in the process; to go for

wool and come home shorn

偷雞摸狗(ㄊㄡ ㄐㄧ ㄇㄛ ㄍㄡˇ)
① to steal ② an unprincipled person ③ to engage in under-the-table dealings ④ a thief

偷竊(ㄊㄡ ㄑㄧㄝˋ)
to steal; to pilfer; to filch; to thieve

偷巧(ㄊㄡ ㄑㄧㄠˇ)
to finesse; to take a shortcut

偷情(ㄊㄡ ㄑㄧㄥ)
to make love; to carry on a clandestine love affair

偷襲(ㄊㄡ ㄒㄧ)
to attack by surprise; a surprise attack; a sneak attack; a sneak raid

偷閒(ㄊㄡ ㄒㄧㄢˊ)
to steal a moment of leisure; to avail oneself of a leisure moment: 他忙裡偷閒。He snatched a little leisure from a busy life.

偷香竊玉(ㄊㄡ ㄒㄧㄤ ㄑㄧㄝˋ ㄩˋ)
(said of a man) to have illicit relation with a woman

偷生怕死(ㄊㄡ ㄕㄥ ㄆㄚˋ ㄙˇ)
cowardly; to be afraid to die or eager to save one's skin

偷嘴(ㄊㄡ ㄗㄨㄟˇ)
to take food stealthily; to steal food

偷安(ㄊㄡ ㄢ)
① (said of a person) to seek temporary ease; to live in complacency on barely sufficient or insecure means: 他終日苟且偷安。He seeks only temporary ease and comfort all day. ② (said of a state) to exist in precarious peace without trying to improve the situation

偷兒(ㄊㄡ ㄦ)
a thief

十畫

【傢】 ㄐㄧㄚ jia jiā   232
1. furniture
2. a tool or tools

傢伙(ㄐㄧㄚ ㄏㄨㄛˇ)
(in a comical sense) a character; a jerk; a son of a gun; a fellow; a guy

像具 or 家具 (ㄐㄧㄚˋ ㄐㄩˋ)
furniture: 床、椅子、書桌皆是像具。Beds, chairs, and desks are furniture.

【傀】 233
ㄎㄨㄟˇ koei kuǐ
a puppet

傀儡 (ㄎㄨㄟˇ ㄌㄟˇ)
a puppet

傀儡戲 (ㄎㄨㄟˇ ㄌㄟˇ ㄒㄧˋ)
a puppet show

【傀】 233
ㄍㄨㄟ guei guī
great; wonderful

傀異 (ㄍㄨㄟ ㄧˋ)
rare and strange

傀偉 (ㄍㄨㄟ ㄨㄟˇ)
great and imposing

【傅】 234
ㄈㄨˋ fuh fù
1. a teacher; to teach
2. to go together with; to add to; to be attached to
3. a Chinese family name

【傍】 235
1. (旁) ㄆㄤˊ parng páng
beside; by the side of

傍邊 (ㄆㄤˊ ㄅㄧㄢ)
beside

傍聽 (ㄆㄤˊ ㄊㄧㄥ)
to audit (at a college class)

傍聽生 (ㄆㄤˊ ㄊㄧㄥ ㄕㄥ)
an auditor (in a school class)

傍觀 (ㄆㄤˊ ㄍㄨㄢ)
to watch on the sideline

傍偟 (ㄆㄤˊ ㄏㄨㄤˊ)
vacillating

傍敲側擊 (ㄆㄤˊ ㄑㄧㄠ ㄘㄜˋ ㄐㄧˊ)
to ask questions slyly (with a view to finding out a secret or an answer to something seemingly having nothing to do with the questions asked); to talk in a round-about way; to make oblique references

傍系 (ㄆㄤˊ ㄒㄧˋ)
blood relatives not on the direct lineal line such as brothers, uncles, nephews, nieces, etc.

傍人 (ㄆㄤˊ ㄖㄣˊ)
other people

傍若無人 (ㄆㄤˊ ㄖㄨㄛˋ ㄨˊ ㄖㄣˊ)
to act audaciously or unin-

hibitively as if there were no other persons around

【傍】 235
2. ㄅㄤˋ bang bàng
near; approaching

傍午 (ㄅㄤˋ ㄨˇ)
near noontime; shortly before noon

傍晚 (ㄅㄤˋ ㄨㄢˇ)
dusk; twilight; nightfall: 我將在傍晚時歸來。I shall be back by nightfall.

【傍】 235
3. ㄅㄤˋ bang bàng
1. to depend on
2. to draw near; to be close to: 船傍了岸。The boat drew alongside the bank.

傍戶而立 (ㄅㄤˋ ㄏㄨˋ ㄦˊ ㄌㄧˋ)
to stand close to the door

傍人門戶 (ㄅㄤˋ ㄖㄣˊ ㄇㄣˊ ㄏㄨˋ)
to depend on another or others; to follow in the steps of someone, as a disciple

【傑】 236
ㄐㄧㄝˊ jye jié
1. outstanding; remarkable; extraordinary
2. a hero

傑出 (ㄐㄧㄝˊ ㄔㄨ)
outstanding; eminent; extraordinary

傑作 (ㄐㄧㄝˊ ㄗㄨㄛˋ)
a masterpiece

【傖】 237
ㄘㄤ tsang cāng
1. (said of persons) vulgar; cheap; lowly
2. confused; disorderly

傖夫俗子 (ㄘㄤ ㄈㄨ ㄙㄨˊ ㄗˇ)
a vulgar person

傖俗 (ㄘㄤ ㄙㄨˊ)
vulgar

【傘】 238
ㄙㄢˇ saan sǎn
1. an umbrella: 我要帶雨傘以防下雨。I'll take my umbrella in case it rains.
2. a parachute

傘兵 (ㄙㄢˇ ㄅㄧㄥ)
paratroopers

傘骨 (ㄙㄢˇ ㄍㄨˇ)
the ribs of an umbrella

【備】 239
ㄅㄟˋ bey bèi
1. a sense of completeness; perfection
2. to be equipped with

3. to get ready
4. to prepare against
5. fully; in every possible way

備辦 (ㄅㄟˋ ㄅㄢˋ)
to prepare; to provide; to get things ready

備補 (ㄅㄟˋ ㄅㄨˇ)
awaiting to fill a vacancy (as a runner-up in a contest who will get the top spot if the winner is disqualified, etc.); the next choice; a stand-in or understudy

備馬 (ㄅㄟˋ ㄇㄚˇ)
to saddle a horse for riding

備胎 (ㄅㄟˋ ㄊㄞ)
a spare tire

備考 (ㄅㄟˋ ㄎㄠˇ)
①for reference ② an appendix for reference

備荒 (ㄅㄟˋ ㄏㄨㄤ)
to prepare against natural disasters: 他們儲糧以備荒。They store foodstuffs to prepare against natural disasters.

備件 (ㄅㄟˋ ㄐㄧㄢˋ)
spare parts

備取 (ㄅㄟˋ ㄑㄩˇ)
those candidates who have passed the qualification examination held by a school or organization but are put on the waiting list because the quota of enrollment or recruitment has been filled up by other candidates who score higher marks in the same examination; candidates on the waiting list for admission to a school

備悉 (ㄅㄟˋ ㄒㄧ)
to learn completely; to know the whole story

備細 (ㄅㄟˋ ㄒㄧˋ)
in detail; all the details (of an incident, etc.)

備至 (ㄅㄟˋ ㄓˋ)
to the utmost; in every possible way: 他們對我關懷備至。They are considerate to me in every possible way.

備戰 (ㄅㄟˋ ㄓㄢˋ)
①to prepare for war ②to be prepared against war

備註 (ㄅㄟˋ ㄓㄨˋ)
①remarks or footnotes ②

〔人部〕

【入部】

備查（ㄅㄟ ㄔㄚ）
space reserved for footnotes
for reference

備嘗辛苦（ㄅㄟ ㄔㄤ ㄒㄧㄣ ㄎㄨˇ）
to undergo all the hardships

備述（ㄅㄟ ㄕㄨˋ）
to narrate or report completely

備案（ㄅㄟ ㄢˋ）
to serve as a record; to keep on record; to file or lodge an application and go ahead with a project before formal approval is granted

備而不用（ㄅㄟ ㄦˊ ㄅㄨˋ ㄩㄥˋ）
It's better to get ready for nothing than caught unprepared. 或 to have something ready just in case; to keep something for possible future use

備位（ㄅㄟ ㄨㄟˋ）
to be a "filler" for an opening

備忘錄（ㄅㄟ ㄨㄤˋ ㄌㄨˋ）
a memorandum

備員（ㄅㄟ ㄩㄢˊ）
a polite and modest term referring to oneself as just a "filler" for an opening

備用（ㄅㄟ ㄩㄥˋ）
reserve; spare; alternate

【傚】 240
（ㄒㄧㄠˋ shiaw xiào）
to model after; to imitate; to emulate; to copy

傚尤（ㄒㄧㄠˋ ㄧㄡˊ）or 傚仿（ㄒㄧㄠˋ ㄈㄤˇ）
emulation (of bad example)

十一畫

【催】 241
（ㄘㄨㄟ tsuei cuī）
to hasten; to urge; to press; to hurry

催逼（ㄘㄨㄟ ㄅㄧ）
to hasten; to press (for payment of a debt) 亦作「催追」

催眠（ㄘㄨㄟ ㄇㄧㄢˊ）
to hypnotize; to mesmerize

催眠術（ㄘㄨㄟ ㄇㄧㄢˊ ㄕㄨˋ）
hypnotism

催命符（ㄘㄨㄟ ㄇㄧㄥˋ ㄈㄨˊ）
a written Taoistic spell which is supposed to hasten a person's death; hence, anything having such an effect

催討（ㄘㄨㄟ ㄊㄠˇ）
to press for repayment of a debt

催涙彈（ㄘㄨㄟ ㄌㄟˋ ㄉㄢˋ）
a tear gas bomb; a tear gas grenade

催趕（ㄘㄨㄟ ㄍㄢˇ）
①to urge someone to come or go ②to hasten to a destination

催化（ㄘㄨㄟ ㄏㄨㄚˋ）
(chemistry) catalysis

催化劑（ㄘㄨㄟ ㄏㄨㄚˋ ㄐㄧˋ）
(chemistry) a catalyst

催請（ㄘㄨㄟ ㄑㄧㄥˇ）
to urge; to urge the guest of honor in a party to be present so that the function can begin in time

催生（ㄘㄨㄟ ㄕㄥ）
①a present from the parental home of the expectant mother usually one month before the childbirth ②a drug to hasten the birth of a child

催生針（ㄘㄨㄟ ㄕㄥ ㄓㄣ）
pituitary extract

催熟（ㄘㄨㄟ ㄕㄡˊ）
(agriculture) to accelerate the ripening (of fruit)

催租（ㄘㄨㄟ ㄗㄨ）
to dun or press for the payment of a rental

催促（ㄘㄨㄟ ㄘㄨˋ）
to hasten; to urge; to press: 他們催促我盡快去紐約。They urged me to go to New York as soon as possible.

【傭】 242
（ㄩㄥ yong yōng）
（又讀 ㄩㄥˋ iong yòng）
1. to hire
2. a servant; a domestic help

傭保（ㄩㄥ ㄅㄠˇ）
hired labor; an employee

傭兵（ㄩㄥ ㄅㄧㄥ）
mercenaries

傭工（ㄩㄥ ㄍㄨㄥ）
①to hire laborers ②hired laborers or servants: 傭工們贊成每日工作七小時。Hired laborers favor a seven-hour day.

傭介紹所（ㄩㄥ ㄐㄧㄝˋ ㄕㄠˋ ㄙㄨㄛˇ）
an agency handling the hir-ing of servants for clients at a fee

【傲】 243
（ㄠˋ aw ào）
1. proud; haughty; overbearing
2. to disdain; to despise; to look down upon
3. rash and impatient

傲慢（ㄠˋ ㄇㄢˋ）
haughty and overbearing; impudent; 貴族往生傲慢輕蔑地對待平民。The nobles used to treat the common people with haughty contempt.

傲睨（ㄠˋ ㄋㄧˋ）
to look down upon; to despise

傲骨（ㄠˋ ㄍㄨˇ）
self-esteem; lofty character

傲氣（ㄠˋ ㄑㄧˋ）
an air of arrogance; haughtiness: 他這個人一向傲氣十足。He is always full of arrogance.

傲性（ㄠˋ ㄒㄧㄥˋ）
a proud temperament

傲世（ㄠˋ ㄕˋ）
to look down upon the world; to be lofty-minded

傲視（ㄠˋ ㄕˋ）
to turn up one's nose at; to show disdain for

傲岸（ㄠˋ ㄢˋ）
proud; haughty; 她是個生性傲岸的女人。She is a woman of a haughty nature.

傲物（ㄠˋ ㄨˋ）
overbearing; insolent; rude; haughty

【傳】 244
（ㄔㄨㄢˊ chwan chuán）
1. ㄔㄨㄢˊ
1. to pass (a ball, an order, learning, etc.) on to
2. to propagate; to disseminate
3. to summon: 債務人被傳出庭。The debtor was summoned to appear in court.
4. to preach

傳播（ㄔㄨㄢˊ ㄅㄛ）
to disseminate (news, information, etc.); to spread; dissemination

傳播媒體（ㄔㄨㄢˊ ㄅㄛ ㄇㄟˊ ㄊㄧˇ）
a news medium; a mass medium

傳播界（ㄔㄨㄢˊ ㄅㄛ ㄐㄧㄝˋ）
the media; journalistic circles

傳布 or 傳佈(ㄔㄨㄢ ㄅㄨ)
①to disseminate; to spread ②to preach: 那傳教士去山區傳佈福音。The missionary went to the mountain area to preach the gospel.

傳票(ㄔㄨㄢ ㄆㄧㄠ)
①(bookkeeping) a voucher ②(law) a summons for appearance in court; a subpoena

傳達(ㄔㄨㄢ ㄉㄚ)
①to forward (a message) ②to inform, or notify ③ a messenger

傳達室(ㄔㄨㄢ ㄉㄚ ㄕ)
a small office for messengers; an information office at the door of a government organization to announce the arrival of a caller; a reception office; a janitor's room

傳代(ㄔㄨㄢ ㄉㄞ)
to hand on from generation to generation

傳導(ㄔㄨㄢ ㄉㄠ)
to conduct (heat, electricity); conduction

傳道(ㄔㄨㄢ ㄉㄠ)
①to preach a religion (especially Christianity) ②to propagate doctrines of the ancient sages

傳單(ㄔㄨㄢ ㄉㄢ)
handbills; leaflets

傳遞(ㄔㄨㄢ ㄉㄧ)
①to forward (information, letters, etc.); to deliver; to transmit; to transfer: 我們彼此傳遞信息。We transmit messages to each other. ②to cheat by passing slips of paper containing answers in an examination

傳動(ㄔㄨㄢ ㄉㄨㄥ)
transmission; drive

傳統(ㄔㄨㄢ ㄊㄨㄥ)
tradition; convention; traditional

傳令(ㄔㄨㄢ ㄌㄧㄥ)
①to deliver or give orders ②a person delivering orders

傳令兵(ㄔㄨㄢ ㄌㄧㄥ ㄅㄧㄥ)
a soldier-messenger; a dispatch rider

傳國璽(ㄔㄨㄢ ㄍㄨㄛ ㄒㄧ)
the imperial seal in a heredi-

tary monarchy, handed down by the founder of the dynasty to his heirs as a symbol of royal authority

傳觀(ㄔㄨㄢ ㄍㄨㄢ)or 傳閱(ㄔㄨㄢ ㄩㄝ)
to pass on for a look or reading: 那封信由在座的人傳閱。The letter was passed round the table.

傳話(ㄔㄨㄢ ㄏㄨㄚ)
to pass on a message

傳喚(ㄔㄨㄢ ㄏㄨㄢ)
to summon

傳家寶(ㄔㄨㄢ ㄐㄧㄚ ㄅㄠ)
a family treasure; an heirloom: 我們一定要把中國文化當作傳家寶,世代代傳下去。We must cherish Chinese culture as our precious heirloom, and hand it on from generation to generation.

傳教(ㄔㄨㄢ ㄐㄧㄠ)
to preach a religion (especially Christianity)

傳教士(ㄔㄨㄢ ㄐㄧㄠ ㄕ)
a missionary: 那傳教士到非洲去使非洲人改信基督教。The missionary went to Africa to convert people to Christianity.

傳經(ㄔㄨㄢ ㄐㄧㄥ)
①to hand down the classics or sacred books ②the exogenous febrile disease passing from one channel to another

傳奇(ㄔㄨㄢ ㄑㄧ)
a legend, saga, romance, etc.

傳情(ㄔㄨㄢ ㄑㄧㄥ)
to flirt; to play at love; to coquet

傳習(ㄔㄨㄢ ㄒㄧ)
to teach and learn

傳寫(ㄔㄨㄢ ㄒㄧㄝ)
to copy down a masterpiece for study or appreciation

傳薪(ㄔㄨㄢ ㄒㄧㄣ)
to pass on the torch of learning

傳信(ㄔㄨㄢ ㄒㄧㄣ)
①to communicate one's belief to another ②to deliver letters

傳宣(ㄔㄨㄢ ㄒㄩㄢ)
to summon someone to the imperial audience

傳訊(ㄔㄨㄢ ㄒㄩㄣ)
(law) to summon (someone) for interrogation; to command someone to appear in a court of law

傳旨(ㄔㄨㄢ ㄓ)
(in old China) the transmission of imperial orders or edicts

傳真(ㄔㄨㄢ ㄓㄣ)
①a lifelike portrait by a painter ②to transmit photos, printed matter, etc. (by electronic devices); to facsimile

傳真機(ㄔㄨㄢ ㄓㄣ ㄐㄧ)
a facsimile machine or fax machine

傳種(ㄔㄨㄢ ㄓㄨㄥ)
①to propagate the species ②to have sons and grandsons to carry on the family name

傳抄(ㄔㄨㄢ ㄔㄠ)
to copy privately (a manuscript, document, etc.)

傳示(ㄔㄨㄢ ㄕ)
to show around

傳世(ㄔㄨㄢ ㄕ)
①(said of great books, etc.) to pass on to the world ②to hand down from generation to generation

傳授(ㄔㄨㄢ ㄕㄡ)
to teach; to teach by demonstration (especially in the art of hand-to-hand combat): 大師傳授我們如何攝影。The master teaches us how to take a good picture.

傳神(ㄔㄨㄢ ㄕㄣ)
a vivid portrayal (of a person or thing by writing or drawing)

傳神之筆(ㄔㄨㄢ ㄕㄣ ㄓ ㄅㄧ)
a vivid touch

傳聲筒(ㄔㄨㄢ ㄕㄥ ㄊㄨㄥ)
①a person who passes to others remarks supposed to be confidential ②a megaphone

傳說(ㄔㄨㄢ ㄕㄨㄛ)
hearsay; legends; unconfirmed reports

傳熱(ㄔㄨㄢ ㄖㄜ)
①heat conduction ②to communicate heat: 火爐傳熱

〔人部〕

到室內。A stove communicates heat to a room.

傳染(ㄔㄨㄢˊ ㄖㄢˇ)
to infect; to be contagious

傳染病(ㄔㄨㄢˊ ㄖㄢˇ ㄅㄧㄥˋ)
infectious diseases

傳宗接代(ㄔㄨㄢˊ ㄗㄨㄥ ㄐㄧㄝ ㄉㄞˋ)
to continue the family line by producing a male heir; 他的使命就是傳宗接代。His mission is to produce a son to continue the family.

傳送(ㄔㄨㄢˊ ㄙㄨㄥˋ)
to convey; to deliver

傳誦(ㄔㄨㄢˊ ㄙㄨㄥˋ)
①to pass from mouth to mouth (especially good poems); 當地居民傳誦着英雄事跡。The heroic deeds are continually on the lips of the local inhabitants. ②to be admired and appreciated by all; popular

傳訛(ㄔㄨㄢˊ ㄜˊ)
to pass on wrong reports

傳衣鉢(ㄔㄨㄢˊ ㄧ ㄅㄛˋ)
to hand one's trade on to disciples; to teach one's students all one knows (especially about academic endeavors and the fine arts)

傳言(ㄔㄨㄢˊ ㄧㄢˊ)
①hearsay; rumor: 那只是傳言罷了。It's merely hearsay. ②to pass on a message

傳揚(ㄔㄨㄢˊ ㄧㄤˊ)
to spread (from mouth to mouth): 他的美名已傳揚四方。His good reputation has spread far and wide.

傳為佳話(ㄔㄨㄢˊ ㄨㄟˊ ㄐㄧㄚ ㄏㄨㄚˋ)
to become a favorite tale or fond memory

傳聞(ㄔㄨㄢˊ ㄨㄣˊ)
hearsay; unconfirmed reports; 據傳聞他已經大學畢業了。According to unconfirmed reports, he has graduated from college.

傳閱(ㄔㄨㄢˊ ㄩㄝˋ)
(said of a public notice or circular) to be passed around for perusal; to be circulated

【傳】 244
2. ㄓㄨㄢˋ juann zhuàn
a biography

傳略(ㄓㄨㄢˋ ㄌㄩㄝˋ)
a brief biography; a biographical sketch

傳記(ㄓㄨㄢˋ ㄐㄧˋ)
a biography

傳記小說(ㄓㄨㄢˋ ㄐㄧˋ ㄒㄧㄠˇ ㄕㄨㄛ)
a saga novel; *roman-fleuve*

傳注(ㄓㄨㄢˋ ㄓㄨˋ)
a remark on a classic

傳疏(ㄓㄨㄢˋ ㄕㄨ)
a commentary and further interpretation of a said annotation

傳贊(ㄓㄨㄢˋ ㄗㄢˋ)
commentaries on a biography

傳驛(ㄓㄨㄢˋ ㄧˋ)
a courier station

【傴】 245
ㄩˇ yeu yǔ
hunchbacked

傴僂(ㄩˇ ㄌㄡˊ)
①hunchbacked ②an attitude of reverence

【債】 246
ㄓㄞˋ jay zhài
a debt; an obligation: 我還了債。I paid my debt.

債臺(ㄓㄞˋ ㄉㄞˋ)
a bond

債多不愁(ㄓㄞˋ ㄉㄨㄛ ㄅㄨˋ ㄔㄡˊ)
(literally) When debts are too many, one won't worry. —Too many obligations will numb a person's sense of responsibility.

債臺高築(ㄓㄞˋ ㄊㄞˊ ㄍㄠ ㄓㄨˊ)
to be deep in debt; to be up to one's ears in debt; to be heavily in debt; to be debt-ridden

債款(ㄓㄞˋ ㄎㄨㄢˇ)
a loan

債戶(ㄓㄞˋ ㄏㄨˋ)or 債務人(ㄓㄞˋ ㄨˋ ㄖㄣˊ)
a debtor

債券(ㄓㄞˋ ㄑㄩㄢˋ)
bonds issued by a government or debentures issued by a company

債主(ㄓㄞˋ ㄓㄨˇ)or 債權人(ㄓㄞˋ ㄑㄩㄢˊ ㄖㄣˊ)
a creditor

債務(ㄓㄞˋ ㄨˋ)
debt or obligation

【傷】 247
ㄕㄤ shang shāng

1. a cut, wound, or injury
2. to cut or injure: 工作過度傷健康。Overwork injures one's health.
3. grief; to grieve; distressed
4. to impede; an impediment
5. to hurt (feelings)
6. to make sick

傷疤(ㄕㄤ ㄅㄚ)
a scar

傷悲(ㄕㄤ ㄅㄟ)
grief; distress

傷兵(ㄕㄤ ㄅㄧㄥ)
wounded soldiers

傷風(ㄕㄤ ㄈㄥ)
to catch cold; to have a cold

傷風敗俗(ㄕㄤ ㄈㄥ ㄅㄞˋ ㄙㄨˊ)
to act immorally; a breach of morality; to offend public decency; to corrupt public morals

傷悼(ㄕㄤ ㄉㄠˋ)
to mourn over the loss of a dear one

傷天害理(ㄕㄤ ㄊㄧㄢ ㄏㄞˋ ㄌㄧˇ)
to commit crimes

傷痛(ㄕㄤ ㄊㄨㄥˋ)
to mourn

傷腦筋(ㄕㄤ ㄋㄠˇ ㄐㄧㄣ)
①to beat one's brains; to have a nut to crack ②troublesome

傷感(ㄕㄤ ㄍㄢˇ)
distress; distressed; to be deeply moved or touched; to be sick at heart; sentimental

傷感情(ㄕㄤ ㄍㄢˇ ㄑㄧㄥˊ)
①to hurt the feelings ②(colloquial) to have a nut to crack

傷口(ㄕㄤ ㄎㄡˇ)
a wound: 護士清洗那病人的傷口。The nurse bathed that patient's wound.

傷害(ㄕㄤ ㄏㄞˋ)
to hurt; to injure; to harm

傷害罪(ㄕㄤ ㄏㄞˋ ㄗㄨㄟˋ)
(law) injury

傷寒(ㄕㄤ ㄏㄢˊ)
①typhoid fever; typhus ②(Chinese medicine) diseases due to cold factors; the exogenous febrile diseases

傷痕(ㄕㄤ ㄏㄣˊ)
a scar; a bruise

傷痕文學(ㄕㄤ ㄏㄣˊ ㄨㄣˊ ㄒㄩㄝˊ)
scar literature (a body of

literature describing the excesses of the Cultural Revolution Period in Mainland China, which appeared in the early 1980s)

傷懷(ㄕㄤ ㄏㄨㄞˊ)
a distressing mood; grief

傷患(ㄕㄤ ㄏㄨㄢˋ)
the sick and wounded

傷心(ㄕㄤ ㄒㄧㄣ)
① to hurt one's feelings; to break one's heart ② very sad: 她為她父親的過世而傷心。 She is very sad for her father's death.

傷心慘目(ㄕㄤ ㄒㄧㄣ ㄘㄢˇ ㄇㄨˋ)
① to be too ghastly to look at ② tragic (scenes); pitiful (sights)

傷處(ㄕㄤ ㄔㄨˋ)
a wound

傷時感事(ㄕㄤ ㄕˊ ㄍㄢˇ ㄕˋ)
deeply worried about national crises, political corruption, moral decadence, etc.

傷逝(ㄕㄤ ㄕˋ)
to mourn over the loss of a dear person

傷勢(ㄕㄤ ㄕˋ)
the condition of an injury (or a wound)

傷身(ㄕㄤ ㄕㄣ)
to be injurious to health

傷神(ㄕㄤ ㄕㄣˊ)
① to beat one's brains out; to overtax one's nerves; to be nerve-racking ② deeply hurt

傷生(ㄕㄤ ㄕㄥ)
① to bring injury to one's life ② to impair one's vitality

傷人(ㄕㄤ ㄖㄣˊ)
① to hurt people (by verbal attacks, etc.) ② to inflict physical injury on another ③ harmful to health

傷財(ㄕㄤ ㄘㄞˊ)
to lose money; to waste money

傷殘(ㄕㄤ ㄘㄢˊ)
the wounded and disabled

傷亡(ㄕㄤ ㄨㄤˊ)
casualties: 入侵者傷亡慘重。 The invaders suffered heavy casualties.

【傺】 248
ㄔˋ chyh chì
1. to hinder
2. to be disappointed

【傾】 249
1. ㄑㄧㄥ ching qīng
1. to slant; to bend: 他身子向前傾。 He was bending forward.
2. to collapse; to fall flat; to upset; to subvert
3. to pour out
4. to exhaust (one's wealth, etc.); to exert oneself to do (something)
5. to admire; to be fascinated or intrigued

傾盆大雨(ㄑㄧㄥ ㄆㄣˊ ㄉㄚˋ ㄩˇ)
a pouring rain; to rain hard; to rain cats and dogs; to be pelting with rain: 昨晚一直下著傾盆大雨。 It was raining cats and dogs last night.

傾圮(ㄑㄧㄥ ㄆㄧˇ)
(said of buildings) to collapse; in dilapidated condition

傾慕(ㄑㄧㄥ ㄇㄨˋ)
to admire; admiration

傾覆(ㄑㄧㄥ ㄈㄨˋ)
① to topple (a kingdom); the fall of a state ② to overturn; to capsize: 地震使房屋傾覆。 The earthquake overturned houses.

傾倒(ㄑㄧㄥ ㄉㄠˇ)
①ⓐ to fall for (a woman); to be infatuated with (a woman); to be overwhelmed with admiration for (a woman) ⓑ to collapse
②(ㄑㄧㄥ ㄉㄠˋ) to dump; to empty the contents of

傾動一時(ㄑㄧㄥ ㄉㄨㄥˋ ㄧˋ ㄕˊ)
to affect the times or generation overwhelmingly ② to have convulsive effect on one's mind

傾談(ㄑㄧㄥ ㄊㄢˊ)
to have a good, heart-to-heart talk

傾聽(ㄑㄧㄥ ㄊㄧㄥ)
to listen carefully; to be all ears for

傾吐(ㄑㄧㄥ ㄊㄨˇ)
to pour out one's heart; to unburden oneself to someone; to get (something) off

---

one's chest

傾囊相助(ㄑㄧㄥ ㄋㄤˊ ㄒㄧㄤ ㄓㄨˋ)
to exhaust (or give) all one has to help; to give one's all to help; to empty one's purse to help; to give generous financial support

傾匱倒篋(ㄑㄧㄥ ㄎㄨㄟˋ ㄉㄠˇ ㄑㄧㄝˋ)
① to empty the coffers; to exhaust all one has ② to leave no stone unturned; to try one's best

傾家蕩產(ㄑㄧㄥ ㄐㄧㄚ ㄉㄤˋ ㄔㄢˇ)
to exhaust one's wealth—to go bankrupt; to lose a family fortune

傾斜(ㄑㄧㄥ ㄒㄧㄝˊ)
① to slant ② (geology) the angle formed by a stratum with the level; to slope

傾瀉(ㄑㄧㄥ ㄒㄧㄝˋ)
to come down in torrents

傾銷(ㄑㄧㄥ ㄒㄧㄠ)
a cutthroat sale; dumping; to dump

傾心(ㄑㄧㄥ ㄒㄧㄣ)
① to be all for; to admire wholeheartedly ② heart-to-heart: 我們傾心交談。 We have a heart-to-heart talk.

傾向(ㄑㄧㄥ ㄒㄧㄤˋ)
① to be inclined to; to side with ② a tendency; a trend

傾注(ㄑㄧㄥ ㄓㄨˋ)
① to pour into: 他將開水傾注到水壺裏。 He poured boiled water into a kettle. ② to throw (energy, etc.) into

傾巢(ㄑㄧㄥ ㄔㄠˊ)
(of the enemy or bandits) to turn out in full force: 敵軍傾巢而出。 The enemy turned out in full strength.

傾巢來犯(ㄑㄧㄥ ㄔㄠˊ ㄌㄞˊ ㄈㄢˋ)
(said of bandits or enemy forces) to invade in full force

傾城傾國(ㄑㄧㄥ ㄔㄥˊ ㄑㄧㄥ ㄍㄨㄛˊ)
an exceptionally beautiful woman, for whose sake a city is ruined or a country is lost 亦用作「傾國傾城」

傾座(ㄑㄧㄥ ㄗㄨㄛˋ)
Everyone present is moved. 或 to win the admiration of all present; to bring the house down

〔人部〕

傾訴(くｌㄥㄙㄨˋ)
to pour out(one's heart, troubles, etc.)

傾吐衷腸(くｌㄥㄊㄨˇㄓㄨㄥㄔㄤˊ)
to reveal one's innermost feelings

傾耳而聽(くｌㄥㄦˇㄦˊㄊｌㄥ)
to listen attentively

傾軋(くｌㄥㄧㄚˋ)
to fight for power; intramural jostling; to jostle against each other

傾危(くｌㄥㄨㄟ)
① mean, treacherous or crooked ② precarious; highly dangerous

【傾】 249
2. ㄎㄥ keng kēng
參看「傾人」

傾人(ㄎㄥㄖㄣˊ)
to frame or implicate a person

【僂】 250
ㄌㄡˊ lou lóu
1. hunchbacked; deformed
2. bent
3. a Chinese family name

傴僂(ㄩˇㄌㄡˊ)
a bandit's lackey or fellower
亦作「嘍囉」

【僅】 251
ㄐｌㄣˇ jiin jǐn
1. only: 僅一人出席。Only one is present.
2. barely; scarcely; almost: 他僅免於死。He barely escaped death.

僅夠(ㄐｌㄣˇㄍㄡˋ)
barely enough

僅可(ㄐｌㄣˇㄎㄜˇ)
only for (coping with a specific situation); barely enough for

僅僅(ㄐｌㄣˇㄐｌㄣˇ)
only; hardly enough; barely: 這僅僅是開始。This is only the beginning.

僅容旋馬(ㄐｌㄣˇㄖㄨㄥˊㄒㄩㄢˊㄇㄚˇ)
space only big enough for turning a horse－narrow space

僅存(ㄐｌㄣˇㄘㄨㄣˊ)
only (things or persons)

僅以身免(ㄐｌㄣˇｌˇㄕㄣㄇｌㄢˇ)
barely able to escape alive

僅有(ㄐｌㄣˇｌㄡˇ)
to have only...; there is

(or are) only...

【僉】 252
くｌㄢ chian qiān
all; the whole

【僇】 253
ㄌㄨˋ luh lù
1. to kill; to massacre
2. to disgrace; to shame
3. to collaborate; to pool strength together

十二畫

【像】 254
ㄒｌㄤˋ shiang xiàng
1. an image; a portrait: 神像 images of gods
2. to resemble; resemblance
3. like; as

像片(ㄒｌㄤˋㄆｌㄢˋ)
a personal photograph

像貌(ㄒｌㄤˋㄇㄠˋ)
a person's looks

像貌非凡(ㄒｌㄤˋㄇㄠˋㄈㄟㄈㄢˊ)
a distinguished appearance

像模像樣(ㄒｌㄤˋㄇㄛˊㄒｌㄤˋｌㄤˋ)
① (with) all sincerity ② to look respectable

像話(ㄒｌㄤˋㄏㄨㄚˋ)
to appeal to reason, logic, accepted practice, etc.

像是(ㄒｌㄤˋㄕˋ)
to look like; to seem: 天像是要下雨。It looks like rain.

像煞有介事(ㄒｌㄤˋㄕㄚˊｌㄡˇㄐｌㄝˋㄕˋ)
(Shanghai dialect) to act as if one's going to handle a big deal; pretentious; to make a big fuss

像樣(ㄒｌㄤˋｌㄤˋ)
proper in appearance; presentable; decent

【僑】 255
くｌㄠˊ chyau qiáo
to sojourn; a sojourn

僑胞(くｌㄠˊㄅㄠ)
overseas Chinese

僑民(くｌㄠˊㄇｌㄣˊ)
persons who reside in a country other than their own; alien residents

僑聯(くｌㄠˊㄌｌㄢˊ)
the Federation of Overseas Chinese Associations

僑領(くｌㄠˊㄌｌㄥˇ)
leaders of overseas Chinese

僑匯(くｌㄠˊㄏㄨㄟˋ)

remittance sent back home by emigrants

僑教(くｌㄠˊㄐｌㄠˋ)
the education of overseas Chinese

僑居(くｌㄠˊㄐㄩ)
to reside in a town or country other than one's own

僑眷(くｌㄠˊㄐㄩㄢˋ)
dependents of overseas Chinese

僑校(くｌㄠˊㄒｌㄠˋ)
schools run for overseas Chinese or their children

僑生(くｌㄠˊㄕㄥ)
children of overseas Chinese who attend schools in China; overseas Chinese students in China

僑資(くｌㄠˊㄗ)
overseas Chinese capital

僑務(くｌㄠˊㄨˋ)
affairs concerning nationals living abroad

僑務委員會(くｌㄠˊㄨˋㄨㄟˇㄩㄢˊㄏㄨㄟˋ)
the Overseas Chinese Affairs Commission

【僕】 256
ㄆㄨˊ pwu pú
1. a servant
2. a modest term referring to oneself
3. (formerly) to act as a driver; to drive

僕僕風塵(ㄆㄨˊㄆㄨˊㄈㄥㄔㄣˊ)
to travel around a lot; to be constantly on the run; to be travel-stained; to endure the hardships of a long journey; to be travel-worn and weary

僕人(ㄆㄨˊㄖㄣˊ)
① a servant ② a modest term referring to oneself (used in a formal letter or praying to God)

僕從(ㄆㄨˊㄘㄨㄥˊ)
retinue; a group of retainers

僕歐(ㄆㄨˊㄡ)
a boy or waiter (especially in a restaurant, cabaret)

僕役(ㄆㄨˊｌˋ)
servants

【僖】 257
ㄒｌ shi xī
1. joy; joyful
2. a Chinese family name

【僚】 258
ㄌｌㄠˊ liau liáo

1. a companion; a friend
2. a colleague; subordinates
3. officials

僚屬 (ㄌㄧㄠˊ ㄕㄨˇ)
subordinates; staff

僚友 (ㄌㄧㄠˊ ㄧㄡˇ)
colleagues

【偽】 259 ㄨㄟˇ wey wěi
(語音 ㄨㄟ̌ woei wèi)

1. false; counterfeit
2. simulated; artificial
3. illegal; not legally constituted

偽幣 (ㄨㄟˇ ㄅㄧˋ)
①counterfeit money; a purious coin ② money issued by a puppet government

偽滿 (ㄨㄟˇ ㄇㄢˇ)
Manchukuo (a puppet state set up by the Japanese in Manchuria between 1931 and 1945)

偽蒙 (ㄨㄟˇ ㄇㄥˊ)
Mongolia when under a puppet rule

偽托 (ㄨㄟˇ ㄊㄨㄛ)
①to forge ancient literary or art works ②to pass off counterfeit works as ancient ones

偽國 (ㄨㄟˇ ㄍㄨㄛˊ)
an illegal state

偽君子 (ㄨㄟˇ ㄐㄩㄣ ˙ㄗ)
a hypocrite

偽證 (ㄨㄟˇ ㄓㄥˋ)
perjury

偽政府 (ㄨㄟˇ ㄓㄥˋ ㄈㄨˇ)
a bogus government; a government dominated by a usurper or traitor

偽裝 (ㄨㄟˇ ㄓㄨㄤ)
disguise or camouflage; to disguise or camouflage; to mask

偽鈔 (ㄨㄟˇ ㄔㄠ)
a counterfeit bank note

偽善 (ㄨㄟˇ ㄕㄢˋ)
hypocrisy; hypocritical

偽造 (ㄨㄟˇ ㄗㄠˋ)
to forge; to falsify; to fabricate; to counterfeit

偽造文書 (ㄨㄟˇ ㄗㄠˋ ㄨㄣˊ ㄕㄨ)
a forgery; counterfeit documents

偽組織 (ㄨㄟˇ ㄗㄨˇ ㄓ)
the quisling government

【僥】 260 ㄐㄧㄠˇ jeau jiǎo
luck; lucky

僥倖 (ㄐㄧㄠˇ ㄒㄧㄥˋ)
by luck or chance

【僦】 261 ㄐㄧㄡˋ jiow jiù
to rent; to hire

僦居 (ㄐㄧㄡˋ ㄐㄩ)
to rent (a house)

【僧】 262 ㄙㄥ seng sēng

1. a Buddhist; a priest; a monk: 他是一位虔誠的僧人。He is a pious monk.
2. a Chinese family name

僧多粥少 (ㄙㄥ ㄉㄨㄛ ㄓㄡ ㄕㄠˇ)
The monks are many and the gruel is meagre.—not enough (posts, positions, etc.) to go around because there are too many people on the waiting list 亦作「粥少僧多」

僧徒 (ㄙㄥ ㄊㄨˊ) or 僧侶 (ㄙㄥ ㄌㄩˇ)
Buddhist monks; the Buddhist hierarchy; the monks as a group

僧尼 (ㄙㄥ ㄋㄧˊ)
Buddhist monks and nuns

僧人 (ㄙㄥ ㄖㄣˊ)
a monk

僧寺 (ㄙㄥ ㄙˋ)
a Buddhist temple

僧院 (ㄙㄥ ㄩㄢˋ)
a monastery

【僭】 263 ㄐㄧㄢˋ jiann jiàn
to assume; to usurp; to overstep one's authority

僭號 (ㄐㄧㄢˋ ㄏㄠˋ)
usurpation of the title of a king by his subject; to adopt an illegal title

僭竊 (ㄐㄧㄢˋ ㄑㄧㄝˋ)
to usurp (the throne, authority, title, etc.)

僭位 (ㄐㄧㄢˋ ㄨㄟˋ)
to usurp the throne

僭越 (ㄐㄧㄢˋ ㄩㄝˋ)
to assume (a title or powers); to overstep one's authority

【僮】 264 1. ㄊㄨㄥˊ torng tóng

1. a servant
2. a boy
3. a Chinese family name

僮僕 (ㄊㄨㄥˊ ㄆㄨˊ)
servants

【僮】 2. ㄓㄨㄤ juang zhuang

參看「僮族」

僮族 (ㄓㄨㄤ ㄗㄨˊ)
the name of a small tribe in southwestern China 亦作「壯族」

【僱】 265 ㄍㄨˋ guh gù
to hire; to engage; to employ

僱工 (ㄍㄨˋ ㄍㄨㄥ)
a hired hand

僱主 (ㄍㄨˋ ㄓㄨˇ)
an employer

僱員 or 雇員 (ㄍㄨˋ ㄩㄢˊ)
①a government employee who is not on the official payroll of the employing agency and, as such, can be hired or fired without going through the prescribed procedure ② an employee

僱傭 (ㄍㄨˋ ㄩㄥ)
a person employed by another

to engage (a person): 我僱用了一個學生當嚮導。I engaged a student as a guide.

十三畫

【僵】 266 ㄐㄧㄤ jiang jiāng

1. to lie flat
2. to be inactive; stiff; rigid; numb: 我的手指頭幾乎凍僵了。My fingers were nearly numb with cold.
3. to be at a stalemate; deadlocked: 她把事情弄僵了。She's brought things to a deadlock.

僵立 (ㄐㄧㄤ ㄌㄧˋ)
to stand rigidly

僵化 (ㄐㄧㄤ ㄏㄨㄚˋ)
①heading toward a deadlock ②to become rigid; to ossify

僵局 (ㄐㄧㄤ ㄐㄩˊ)
a deadlock; a stalemate; an impasse: 兩派因勢均力敵而陷於僵局。The two parties are at a deadlock.

【入部】

僵持(ㄐㅣ�九ㄔ)
to come to a deadlock; to be at a stalemate; to refuse to budge: 雇主和罷工者僵持不下。Employers and strikers have come to a deadlock.

僵屍 or 殭屍(ㄐㅣ九ㄕ)
①a stiff corpse ②a vampire

僵死(ㄐㅣ九ㄙˇ)
dead; ossified

僵硬(ㄐㅣ九ㄧㄥˋ)
rigid; stiff: 他覺得四肢僵硬。He felt stiff in the limbs.

僵臥(ㄐㅣ九ㄨㄛˋ)
to lie still at full length

【價】 267 ㄐㅣㄚˋ jiah jià
1. prices; cost; value: 美德乃無價之寶。Virtue is beyond price.
2. (chemistry) valence: 氫是一價的元素。Hydrogen is a one-valence element.

價兒(ㄐㅣㄚˋㄦˊ)
the price of a commodity

價目(ㄐㅣㄚˋㄇㄨˋ)
prices; quotations

價單(ㄐㅣㄚˋㄉㄢ)
a price (or quotation) list

價廉物美(ㄐㅣㄚˋㄌㄧㄢˊㄨˋㄇㄟˇ)
(literally) excellent quality at low prices—a bargain buy; a good bargain

價格(ㄐㅣㄚˋㄍㄜˊ)or 價錢(ㄐㅣㄚˋㄑㄧㄢˊ)
prices: 水果價格正在上漲。The prices of fruits are going up.

價值(ㄐㅣㄚˋㄓˊ)
①(economics) value: 這項產品的剩餘價值高。The surplus value of this product is plentiful. ② worth; value: 這個線索對我們很有價值。This clue is of great value to us.

價值標準(ㄐㅣㄚˋㄓˊㄅㄧㄠ ㄓㄨㄣˇ)
standard of value: 每個人都有自己的價值標準。Everybody has his own standard of value.

價值判斷(ㄐㅣㄚˋㄓˊㄆㄢˋㄉㄨㄢˋ)
value judgment

價值連城(ㄐㅣㄚˋㄓˊㄌㄧㄢˊㄔㄥˊ)
invaluable; priceless

【僻】 268 ㄆㄧˋ pih pì
1. biased
2. not easily accessible; out-of-the-way; secluded
3. not common; not ordinary; unusual

僻道(ㄆㄧˋㄉㄠˋ)
a seldom-traveled road

僻典(ㄆㄧˋㄉㄧㄢˇ)
a quotation of an ambiguous or nebulous source

僻陬(ㄆㄧˋㄗㄡ)
an out-of-the-way place

僻靜(ㄆㄧˋㄐㄧㄥˋ)
out-of-the-way; secluded: 他住在一個僻靜的地方。He lived in a secluded place.

僻巷(ㄆㄧˋㄒㄧㄤˋ)
a side-lane; a narrow, out-of-the-way lane

僻處(ㄆㄧˋㄔㄨˋ)
to live in an out-of-the-way or secluded place

僻壤(ㄆㄧˋㄖㄤˇ)
an out-of-the-way village, town, etc.

僻遠(ㄆㄧˋㄩㄢˇ)
distant and out-of-the-way

【儀】 269 ㄧˊ yi yí
1. appearance; deportment; manners; looks; demeanor
2. ceremonies; rites
3. a rule, regulation, form or standard
4. customs
5. instruments; apparatus
6. a Chinese family name

儀表(ㄧˊㄅㄧㄠˇ)
①appearance and deportment; a man's personal look: 她的儀表大方。Her appearance is poised and graceful. ②a rule; a model

儀隊(ㄧˊㄉㄨㄟˋ)
an honor guard

儀態(ㄧˊㄊㄞˋ)
bearing; deportment; demeanor: 這個女孩有一種嫻靜而謙遜的儀態。The girl had a quiet, modest demeanor.

儀態萬方(ㄧˊㄊㄞˋㄨㄢˋㄈㄤ)
(usually said of girls) charming poises and exquisite bearing; regal bearing

儀器(ㄧˊㄑㄧˋ)
(laboratory, medical, etc.) instruments; apparatus

儀仗(ㄧˊㄓㄤˋ)
flags, weapons, etc. carried by a guard of honor

儀式(ㄧˊㄕˋ)
ceremonies; rites: 開幕和閉幕都是以隆重的儀式完成的。Openings and closings were all accomplished with majestic ceremonies.

儀容(ㄧˊㄖㄨㄥˊ)
appearance and deportment; looks; demeanor

【儂】 270 ㄋㄨㄥˊ nong nóng
1. (in old usage) I; me
2. (Shanghai dialect) you
3. he; she
4. a Chinese family name

【億】 271 ㄧˋ yih yì
1. a hundred million
2. tranquility; repose
3. (according to) estimates

億兆(ㄧˋㄓㄠˋ)
①astronomical in number; countless; numberless ②the people; the masses

hundreds of millions; millions upon millions

億萬富翁(ㄧˋㄨㄢˋㄈㄨˋㄨㄥ)
a billionaire

【儆】 272 ㄐㄧㄥˇ jiing jǐng
1. to be on guard; to get ready (for an attack, etc.)
2. to warn; to caution: 死刑用來儆一儆百。Sentence of death is used to punish one to warn a hundred.

儆戒(ㄐㄧㄥˇㄐㄧㄝˋ)
to warn; to caution; warning; caution

儆儆(ㄐㄧㄥˇㄐㄧㄥˇ)
uneasy; wary

【儈】 273 ㄎㄨㄞˋ kuay kuài
a middleman; a go-between; a broker

【儉】 274 ㄐㄧㄢˇ jean jiǎn
(又讀 ㄐㄧㄢˋ jiann jiàn)
1. frugal; economical; thrift
2. meager
3. a poor harvest

儉薄(ㄐㄧㄢˇㄅㄛˊ)
lacking the necessities of life

儉樸(ㄐㄧㄢˇㄆㄨˇ)
to be thrifty in daily spend-

ing; simple in dressing: 成功
的農夫大都是儉樸的。Successful
farmers are thrifty.

儉省(ㄐㄧㄢˇ ㄕㄥˇ)
thrift; frugal; economical

儉以養廉(ㄐㄧㄢˇ ㄧˇ ㄧㄤˇ ㄌㄧㄢˊ)
Frugality makes honesty.

儉約(ㄐㄧㄢˇ ㄩㄝ)
thrifty and temperate;
practicing austerity

儉用(ㄐㄧㄢˇ ㄩㄥˋ)
to be careful with one's
spending; frugal; thrifty; careful in spending

【儋】 275
ㄉㄢ　dan dàn
1. to shoulder or bear a burden
2. a load of two piculs (especially of rice or grains)

【傻】 276
(傻) ㄕㄚˇ shaa shǎ
1. stupid; foolish; dumb
2. naive
3. stunned; stupefied; terrified
4. to think or work mechanically

傻頭傻腦(ㄕㄚˇ ㄊㄡˊ ㄕㄚˇ ㄋㄠˇ)
①foolish-looking ②muddle-
headed

傻裏傻氣(ㄕㄚˇ ·ㄌㄧ ㄕㄚˇ ·ㄑㄧ)
foolish-looking or acting
foolishly

傻瓜(ㄕㄚˇ ㄍㄨㄚ)
a fool; a silly; a blockhead;
a simpleton: 他很可能是個傻
瓜。He's very likely a fool.

傻呵呵(ㄕㄚˇ ㄏㄜ ㄏㄜ)
likable but stupid; silly
appearance; simple-minded:
別看他傻呵呵的，他可是滿腹經
綸。Maybe he does not look
very clever, but he is actually very much learned.

傻話(ㄕㄚˇ ㄏㄨㄚˋ)
foolish talk; nonsense

傻勁兒(ㄕㄚˇ ㄐㄧㄣˋ ㄦ)
①stupidity; foolishness ②
sheer enthusiasm; dogged-
ness: 他做事總有股傻勁兒。He
always works with dogged-
ness.

傻氣(ㄕㄚˇ ·ㄑㄧ)
silly manners; dumb-looking

傻小子(ㄕㄚˇ ㄒㄧㄠˇ ·ㄗ)
(usually used in a comical
sense) a young fool; a silly
boy

傻笑(ㄕㄚˇ ㄒㄧㄠˋ)
to smirk; to laugh for no
conceivable reason; a silly
smile; a smirk: 他對過路的每
個人傻笑。He smirked at
everyone that passes.

傻子(ㄕㄚˇ ·ㄗ)
a bloody fool; an idiot or
imbecile; a nincompoop; a
blockhead

傻眼(ㄕㄚˇ ㄧㄢˇ)
to be dumbfounded; to be
stunned: 看到此番美景，我們不
禁傻眼了。All of us were
dumbfounded by the beauty
of the scene.

十四畫

【儐】 277
ㄅㄧㄣ　binn bìn
(語音 ㄅㄧㄣ bīn bìn)
1. to entertain guests
2. to arrange; to set in order
3. to guide

儐相(ㄅㄧㄣ ㄒㄧㄤˋ)
①the best man of a bride-
groom ②a bridesmaid

【儒】 278
ㄖㄨˊ ru rú
1. the learned; scholars collectively
2. Confucian; Confucianism
3. weak; shrinking from hardship

儒門(ㄖㄨˊ ㄇㄣˊ)
①scholars following Con-
fucian thoughts; Confu-
cianists ②the name of a
fort to the north of Taming
County in Hopeh Province

儒風(ㄖㄨˊ ㄈㄥ)
the style, ways, etc. of Confucian scholars

儒林(ㄖㄨˊ ㄌㄧㄣˊ)
①the circle of Confucians ②
the circle of scholars

儒林外史(ㄖㄨˊ ㄌㄧㄣˊ ㄨㄞˋ ㄕˇ)
the title of a sarcastic novel
lampooning Chinese scholars
of the late Ming and early
Ching dynasties by Wu
Ching-tze (吳敬梓) in the
early Ching Dynasty

儒家(ㄖㄨˊ ㄐㄧㄚ)
scholars following Confucian
thoughts; Confucianists; the
Confucian school

儒教(ㄖㄨˊ ㄐㄧㄠˋ)
Confucianism

儒將(ㄖㄨˊ ㄐㄧㄤˋ)
a general who is also an
accomplished scholar

儒學(ㄖㄨˊ ㄒㄩㄝˊ)
① the teachings of Con-
fucius② (in old China) education officials on various
governmental levels

儒生(ㄖㄨˊ ㄕㄥ)
①a scholar ②a scholar of
the Confucian school; a Confucian scholar

儒宗(ㄖㄨˊ ㄗㄨㄥ)
one who is admired and respected by the scholastic
community

儒雅(ㄖㄨˊ ㄧㄚˇ)
scholarly and refined; elegant; (with) style: 他的舉止
溫文儒雅。He has elegant
manners.

【儔】 279
ㄔㄡˊ chour chóu
1.a companion or companions
2. a class

儔匹(ㄔㄡˊ ㄆㄧˇ)
a companion

儔類(ㄔㄡˊ ㄌㄟˋ)
①a class ②persons of the
same class

【儕】 280
ㄔㄞˊ chair chái
1. a class; company
2. an adjunct to show plurality
3. to match (as man and wife)

儕輩(ㄔㄞˊ ㄅㄟˋ)
persons (especially friends
or companions) of the same
generation

【儘】 281
ㄐㄧㄣˇ jiin jǐn
1. the utmost; the extreme
2. to let (someone do it)

儘量(ㄐㄧㄣˇ ㄌㄧㄤˋ)
as (much, soon, strong, etc.)
as possible: 你年輕時應儘量多
讀點書。You should read as
many books as possible
when young.

儘夠(ㄐㄧㄣˇ ㄍㄡˋ)
quite enough; more than
enough

儘管(ㄐㄧㄣˇ ㄍㄨㄢˇ)
①even if; no matter; despite;
in spite of ②not hesitate
to: 有什麼問題儘管問他。If

〔人部〕

you have any questions, don't hesitate to ask him.

儘可能(ㄐㄧㄣ ㄎㄜˇ ㄋㄥˊ)
as far as possible; to the best of one's ability: 儘可能快。Be as quick as possible.

儘快(ㄐㄧㄣ ㄎㄨㄞˋ)
as quickly (or soon) as possible: 我將儘快來。I will come as soon as I possibly can.

儘其所有(ㄐㄧㄣ ㄑㄧˊ ㄙㄨㄛˇ ㄧㄡˇ)
to exhaust all one has

儘情享受(ㄐㄧㄣˇ ㄑㄧㄥˊ ㄒㄧㄤˇ ㄕㄡˋ)
to seek pleasure to one's heart's content

儘先(ㄐㄧㄣˇ ㄒㄧㄢ)
①the very first: 我們應該儘先照顧孩子們。We ought to look after the children first. ②(to give) first priority (to)

儘着(ㄐㄧㄣˇ ·ㄓㄜ)
to the greatest possible extent; to do one's best

儘上頭(ㄐㄧㄣˇ ㄕㄤˋ ·ㄊㄡ)
the uppermost; the highest spot

儘讓(ㄐㄧㄣˇ ㄖㄤˋ)
to let (others try, choose, etc.) first; to be as humble and yielding as possible

儘早(ㄐㄧㄣˇ ㄗㄠˇ)
as early as possible

十五畫

【償】 282 ㄔㄤˊ charng cháng
1. to repay
2. to compensate; to make restitution
3. to fulfill (a wish): 他得償夙願。He has fulfilled his long-cherished wish.
4. to offset

償付(ㄔㄤˊ ㄈㄨˋ)
to pay back; to pay

償還(ㄔㄤˊ ㄏㄨㄢˊ)
redemption; to repay (what one owes)

償清(ㄔㄤˊ ㄑㄧㄥ)
to clear off: 我已償清我的債務。I have cleared off my debts.

償債(ㄔㄤˊ ㄓㄞˋ)
to repay a debt; to pay (or discharge) a debt

償願(ㄔㄤˊ ㄩㄢˋ)
to fulfill one's wish; to get what one desires

【傀】 283 ㄎㄨㄟˇ leei lei
1. a puppet: 他們在征服地區建立一傀儡政府。They set up a puppet government in the conquered territory.
2. sickly and thin
3. dilapidated

【優】 284 ㄧㄡ iou yōu
1. good; excellent: 他因英文particular 優而得獎。He received a prize for excellence in English.
2. abundant; plenty
3. players (as in an opera)
4. victory; winning
5. soft
6. a Chinese family name

優美(ㄧㄡ ㄇㄟˇ)
①good; wonderful; graceful; fine: 我很喜歡優美的風景。I enjoy fine scenery very much. ②anything that inspires a sense of joy

優孟衣冠(ㄧㄡ ㄇㄥˋ ㄧ ㄍㄨㄢ)
to act on the stage

優待(ㄧㄡ ㄉㄞˋ)
favorable treatment; to give special treatment: 我們政府優待軍眷。Our government gives special treatment to servicemen's families.

優待券(ㄧㄡ ㄉㄞˋ ㄑㄩㄢˋ)
①a discount ticket (for shopping in a certain store) ②a free ticket (for a show, etc.); a complimentary ticket

優等(ㄧㄡ ㄉㄥˇ)
an excellent grade; the best class; first-rate

優點(ㄧㄡ ㄉㄧㄢˇ)
①merits: 他的個性有優點和缺點。His character has merits and demerits (or virtues and defects). ②good qualities ③advantages: 住在大都市裡有許多優點。Living in a big city has many advantages.

優劣(ㄧㄡ ㄌㄧㄝˋ)
①good and bad ②bright and dull ③fit and unfit

優良(ㄧㄡ ㄌㄧㄤˊ)
fine; good: 他的成績優良。He got good marks.

優伶(ㄧㄡ ㄌㄧㄥˊ)
professional actors or actresses

優厚(ㄧㄡ ㄏㄡˋ)
munificent; liberal; favorable: 這個工作待遇優厚。This job has liberal wages and benefits.

優惠(ㄧㄡ ㄏㄨㄟˋ)
preferential; favorable

優惠待遇(ㄧㄡ ㄏㄨㄟˋ ㄉㄞˋ ㄩˋ)
preferential treatment

優惠國(ㄧㄡ ㄏㄨㄟˋ ㄍㄨㄛˊ)
(international treaty) a favored nation

優惠稅率(ㄧㄡ ㄏㄨㄟˋ ㄕㄨㄟˋ ㄌㄩˋ)
(reduced) import tariff rates for goods imported from a favored nation

優境學(ㄧㄡ ㄐㄧㄥˋ ㄒㄩㄝˊ)
euthenics

優秀(ㄧㄡ ㄒㄧㄡˋ)
outstanding; foremost; remarkable: 她是一個優秀的學生。She is an outstanding student.

優秀份子(ㄧㄡ ㄒㄧㄡˋ ㄈㄣˋ ㄗˇ)
the elite

優先(ㄧㄡ ㄒㄧㄢ)
priority; to have priority; to take precedence

優先股(ㄧㄡ ㄒㄧㄢ ㄍㄨˇ)
preferred stocks; preference shares

優先權(ㄧㄡ ㄒㄧㄢ ㄑㄩㄢˊ)
priority

優閒(ㄧㄡ ㄒㄧㄢˊ)
carefree; leisure; free and content

優質(ㄧㄡ ㄓˊ)
high (or top) quality

優勢(ㄧㄡ ㄕˋ)
supremacy; superiority; advantage; the upper hand

優勢行為(ㄧㄡ ㄕˋ ㄒㄧㄥˊ ㄨㄟˊ)
dominance behavior

優生學(ㄧㄡ ㄕㄥ ㄒㄩㄝˊ)
eugenics

優勝(ㄧㄡ ㄕㄥˋ)
winning; superior

優勝劣敗(ㄧㄡ ㄕㄥˋ ㄌㄧㄝˋ ㄅㄞˋ)
survival of the fittest

優勝獎(ㄧㄡ ㄕㄥˋ ㄐㄧㄤˇ)

a winning prize

優勝者〔一ㄡㄕㄥ ㄓㄜˇ〕
a winner; a champion: 他是
我們鎮上的網球優勝者。He is
the tennis champion of our
town.

優柔寡斷〔一ㄡ ㄖㄡˊ ㄍㄨㄚˇ ㄉㄨㄢˋ〕
to be peaceable and easy-
going but lacking the
strength of making quick
decisions

優〔一ㄡ ㄖㄣˊ〕
an actor

優哉游哉〔一ㄡ ㄗㄞ 一ㄡˊ ㄗㄞ〕
living a life of ease and leisure; leisurely and carefree

優異〔一ㄡ 一ˋ〕
excellent; remarkable; extraordinary; brilliant

優游〔一ㄡ 一ㄡˊ〕
①carefree 亦作「優遊」: 他度
過了優游的歲月。He passed
his days in carefree leisure.
②indecisive; unable to make
decisions ③ to leave one's
life to fate

優游林下〔一ㄡ 一ㄡˊ ㄌ一ㄣˊ ㄒ一ㄚˋ〕
to live in the countryside leisurely and happily after
retirement

優厚〔一ㄡ ㄏㄡˋ〕
handsome (pay, gifts, etc.);
munificent

優裕〔一ㄡ ㄩˋ〕
well-to-do; wealthy; comfortable (financial standing);
excellent (pay); affluent: 他
們生活優裕。They lived in
affluence.

優遇〔一ㄡ ㄩˋ〕
to treat well

優越〔一ㄡ ㄩㄝˋ〕
superior; outstanding: 他的寫
作技巧比我優越。His skill in
writing is superior to mine.

優越感〔一ㄡ ㄩㄝˋ ㄍㄢˇ〕
a sense of superiority; superiority complex

十六畫

【儲】²⁸⁵ ㄔㄨˊ chwu chú
（又讀 ㄔㄨˇ chuu chǔ）
1. to save; to store; saving
2. a deputy; an alternate
3. a Chinese family name

儲備〔ㄔㄨˊ ㄅㄟˋ〕
savings and/or reserves

儲量〔ㄔㄨˊ ㄌ一ㄤˋ〕
(mineral) reserves

儲宮〔ㄔㄨˊ ㄍㄨㄥ〕
the crown prince 亦作「儲君」
or「儲貳」or「儲嗣」

儲蓄〔ㄔㄨˊ ㄒㄩˋ〕
to save money (in the
bank); savings

儲款以待〔ㄔㄨˊ ㄎㄨㄢˇ 一ˇ ㄉㄞˋ〕
to get the money ready

儲戶〔ㄔㄨˊ ㄏㄨˋ〕
a person or organization
that has a savings account
in the bank; a depositor

儲積〔ㄔㄨˊ ㄐ一〕
to store; to stockpile; to
save up

儲金〔ㄔㄨˊ ㄐ一ㄣ〕
savings

儲氣〔ㄔㄨˊ ㄑ一ˋ〕
gas storage

儲蓄〔ㄔㄨˊ ㄒㄩˋ〕
①to save (money): 我們必
須儲蓄，以備不時之需。We
must save for a rainy day.
②savings: 她失去了所有的儲
蓄。She lost all her savings.

儲蓄銀行〔ㄔㄨˊ ㄒㄩˋ 一ㄣˊ ㄏㄤˊ〕
a savings bank

儲藏〔ㄔㄨˊ ㄘㄤˊ〕
①to store up; to hoard; to
save and preserve: 松鼠儲藏
堅果過冬。A squirrel hoards
nuts for the winter. ② a
deposit: 我國有豐富的煤和石
油儲藏。Our country abounds
in coal and petroleum de-
posits.

儲藏室〔ㄔㄨˊ ㄘㄤˊ ㄕˋ〕
a storeroom

儲存〔ㄔㄨˊ ㄘㄨㄣˊ〕
①storage; saving ②to store
or stockpile; to lay in; to lay
up

儲油〔ㄔㄨˊ 一ㄡˊ〕
(petroleum) oil storage

十九畫

【儷】²⁸⁶ ㄌ一ˋ lih lì
1. a pair; a couple
2. husband and wife; a married couple

儷辭〔ㄌ一ˋ ㄘˊ〕
a form of literary writing in
which sentences or words
come in couplets

儷影〔ㄌ一ˋ 一ㄥˇ〕
the heart-warming sight of a
couple in love; a married
couple appearing in a photograph

二十畫

【儼】²⁸⁷ 一ㄢˇ yean yǎn
1. majestic; respectable
2. (to act, talk, appear) as if;
like

儼然〔一ㄢˇ ㄖㄢˊ〕
①dignified-looking; solemn;
stern ②neat-looking (house,
etc.) ③just like: 他說起話來
儼然是個專家。He speaks just
like an expert.

儼如〔一ㄢˇ ㄖㄨˊ〕or儼若〔一ㄢˇ ㄖㄨㄛˋ〕
just like 參看「儼然③」

儿 部
ㄖㄣˊ ren rén

〔儿部〕

一畫

【兀】²⁸⁸ ㄨ wuh wù
1. to cut off the feet
2. high and flat on the top
3. this
4. ignorant-looking

兀立〔ㄨ ㄌ一ˋ〕
to stand rigidly without
motion

兀自〔ㄨ ㄗˋ〕
still

兀傲〔ㄨ ㄠˋ〕
proud

兀鷹〔ㄨ 一ㄥ〕
a vulture (Gyps fulvus)

二畫

【允】²⁸⁹ ㄩㄣˇ yeun yǔn
1. to allow; to consent; to
grant
2. appropriate; proper

〔儿 部〕

3. sincere; loyal; faithful; truly

允當(ㄩㄣ ㄉㄤ)
appropriate; suitable; fit; proper; to put just right

允洽(ㄩㄣ ㄒㄧㄚ)
proper; fair; well settled

允許(ㄩㄣ ㄒㄩ)or 允諾(ㄩㄣ ㄋㄨㄛˋ)
to assent; to consent; to grant; to permit; to give permission; to allow: 請允許我代表全家向你們致謝。Allow me to thank you on behalf of my family.

允准(ㄩㄣ ㄓㄨㄣˇ)
to approve; to grant; to consent: 他允准讓他的女兒單獨去旅行。He consented to let his daughter travel alone.

允從(ㄩㄣ ㄘㄨㄥˊ)
to follow (one's advice, etc.); to consent to; to comply with; to promise to follow (one's suggestion)

允文允武(ㄩㄣ ㄨㄣˊ ㄩㄣˊ ㄨˇ)
to be good at wielding both pen and weapon; to be well versed both in learning and military affairs; both good in civil and in military affairs

【元】 290
ㄩㄢˊ yuan yuán
1. the beginning; the first; original
2. the head
3. a dollar: 一百分等於一元。One hundred cents make a dollar.
4. the eldest; chief; big
5. (Chinese astrology) 60 years
6. the Yüan Dynasty (1279-1367)
7. a Chinese family name

元寶(ㄩㄢˊ ㄅㄠˇ)
①a silver or gold ingot weighing about 55 ounces, used in old China ②a mock ingot of tinfoil paper of similar shape to be burnt in ancestor-worshipping as an offering)

元本(ㄩㄢˊ ㄅㄣˇ)
①the origin 亦作「原本」②capital (for business) ③a Yüan Dynasty edition

元配(ㄩㄢˊ ㄆㄟˋ)
a man's first wife

元旦(ㄩㄢˊ ㄉㄢˋ)
New Year's Day

元太祖(ㄩㄢˊ ㄊㄞˋ ㄗㄨˇ)
Genghis Khan, 1162-1227, Mongol conqueror of Central Asia

元年(ㄩㄢˊ ㄋㄧㄢˊ)
the first year of a reign, dynasty, etc.

元老(ㄩㄢˊ ㄌㄠˇ)
an elder person who has held high positions for long period of time and is highly respected by the nation; a veteran statesman; a senior statesman

元老院(ㄩㄢˊ ㄌㄠˇ ㄩㄢˋ)
the Senate (of the Roman Empire)

元氣(ㄩㄢˊ ㄑㄧˋ)
vitality and constitution; stamina; strength; vigor: 一夜的安睡使他恢復元氣。A good night's rest makes him regain his strength.

元曲(ㄩㄢˊ ㄑㄩˇ)
a form of dramatic literature prospered in the Yüan Dynasty

元宵(ㄩㄢˊ ㄒㄧㄠ)
①the Lantern Festival (on the 15th day of the first moon in the Chinese lunar calendar, marking the end of New Year's festivities) ②small rice-flour dumplings eaten on the Lantern Festival

元勳(ㄩㄢˊ ㄒㄩㄣ)
①great achievements ②persons of great achievements; a founding father

元兇(ㄩㄢˊ ㄒㄩㄥ)
the chief culprit; a ringleader (of a crime); an arch-criminal

元世祖(ㄩㄢˊ ㄕˋ ㄗㄨˇ)
Kublai Khan, 1216 - 1294, grandson of Genghis Khan and founder of the Yüan Dynasty

元首(ㄩㄢˊ ㄕㄡˇ)
①the chief of state; the king; the president, etc. ②the beginning

元帥(ㄩㄢˊ ㄕㄨㄞˋ)
a field marshal; a five-star general or admiral; the commander in chief

元戎(ㄩㄢˊ ㄖㄨㄥˊ)
①the commander in chief ②a large war chariot

元素(ㄩㄢˊ ㄙㄨˋ)
(chemistry) the elements

元惡(ㄩㄢˊ ㄜˋ)
the chief culprit

元音(ㄩㄢˊ ㄧㄣ)
the equivalent of vowels in Chinese phonetics

元月(ㄩㄢˊ ㄩㄝˋ)
①the first month of the lunar calendar ②January

三畫

【兄】 291
ㄒㄩㄥ shiong xiōng
1. one's elder brother
2. a term used in addressing a senior of the same generation to show respect: 老兄,這件事就委託你了。And so, brother, I'll leave the matter to you.

兄弟(ㄒㄩㄥ ㄉㄧˋ)
①(ㄒㄩㄥ ㄉㄧˋ) brothers
②(ㄒㄩㄥ ㄉㄧˇ) ⓐ one's younger brother ⓑ a designation for juniors of the same generation among one's relatives ⓒ I (a modest term); 兄弟不敢推辭。I, your younger brother, dare not decline.

兄弟鬩牆(ㄒㄩㄥ ㄉㄧˋ ㄒㄧˋ ㄑㄧㄤˊ)
brothers fighting among themselves; an intramural fight

兄長(ㄒㄩㄥ ㄓㄤˇ)
an elder brother

兄友弟恭(ㄒㄩㄥ ㄧㄡˇ ㄉㄧˋ ㄍㄨㄥ)
to show love and respect as good brothers should

【充】 292
(充)ㄔㄨㄥ chong chōng
1. full; sufficient: 我們有充分的供應。We have sufficient supplies.
2. to fill
3. to fake; to cheat; to pretend: 你別充內行了。Don't pretend to be an expert.
4. a Chinese family name

充沛(ㄔㄨㄥ ㄆㄟˋ)
brimming (with energy)

充滿(ㄔㄨㄥ ㄇㄢˇ)

充(ㄔㄨㄥ)
to fill up; to resound; full of;
filled with; replete with: 她眼
中充滿了眼淚。Tears filled
her eyes.

充分(ㄔㄨㄥ ㄈㄣ)
fully; sufficient; enough

充分條件(ㄔㄨㄥ ㄈㄣ ㄊㄧㄠˊ ㄐㄧㄢˋ)
(logic) sufficient condition

充當(ㄔㄨㄥ ㄉㄤ)
to serve as; to act as; to
play the part of: 她充當翻譯
員。She acted as an inter-
preter.

充電(ㄔㄨㄥ ㄉㄧㄢˋ)
to recharge (a battery)

充電器(ㄔㄨㄥ ㄉㄧㄢˋ ㄑㄧˋ)
a charger

充公(ㄔㄨㄥ ㄍㄨㄥ)
to confiscate: 政府將所有叛國
者的財產充公。The govern-
ment confiscated the property of all traitors.

充好漢(ㄔㄨㄥ ㄏㄠˇ ㄏㄢˋ)
to play the hero: 你別充好漢。
Don't pose as a hero.

充行家(ㄔㄨㄥ ㄏㄤˊ ㄐㄧㄚ)
to pretend to be a professional or specialist

充飢(ㄔㄨㄥ ㄐㄧ)
to satisfy (or appease) one's
hunger (usually with poor
food)

充軍(ㄔㄨㄥ ㄐㄩㄣ)
to exile a criminal (or prisoner) to a distant place for
military service, as a penalty in old China

充其量(ㄔㄨㄥ ㄑㄧˊ ㄌㄧㄤˋ)
at most; at best: 這點糧食充
其量只夠維持十天。The provi-
sions can last ten days at
most.

充斥(ㄔㄨㄥ ㄔˋ)
numerous; filled with; rife;
everywhere: 走私貨到處充斥。
Smuggled goods are every-
where.

充實(ㄔㄨㄥ ㄕˊ)
①rich; substantial; abun-
dant ②to fill out ③(said of
knowledge, facilities, etc.) to
strengthen or improve

充數(ㄔㄨㄥ ㄕㄨˋ)
(just) to complete the number; to fill a vacancy with
an incompetent person; to
use a substitute of inferior
quality

充任(ㄔㄨㄥ ㄖㄣˋ)
to fill the post of; to hold
the position of

充足(ㄔㄨㄥ ㄗㄨˊ)
plenty; abundance; suffi-
ciency; plentiful; abundant;
sufficient

充塞(ㄔㄨㄥ ㄙㄜˋ)
full of; filled with

充耳不聞(ㄔㄨㄥ ㄦˇ ㄅㄨˋ ㄨㄣˊ)
to turn a deaf ear to; to
ignore what is said

充盈(ㄔㄨㄥ ㄧㄥˊ)
plentiful; full

充裕(ㄔㄨㄥ ㄩˋ)
abundance; sufficiency;
abundant; sufficient; rich;
substantial

四畫

【兆】 ²⁹³
ㄓㄠˋ jaw zhào
1. a sign (in fortune-telling)
2. to portend; to foretell: 瑞雪
兆豐年。A timely snow por-
tends a good harvest.
3. an omen
4. a trillion (1,000,000,000,000);
a billion
5. to begin; beginning
6. a Chinese family name

兆民(ㄓㄠˋ ㄇㄧㄣˊ)
the people; the masses

兆頭(ㄓㄠˋ ˙ㄊㄡ)
a sign; an omen; a portent

【兇】 ²⁹⁴
ㄒㄩㄥ shiong xiōng
1. fierce; violent; cruel; ferocious: 他臉上有兇惡的表情。
He has a fierce look on his
face.
2. truculent; inhuman

兇暴(ㄒㄩㄥ ㄅㄠˋ)
cruel and violent

兇猛(ㄒㄩㄥ ㄇㄥˇ)
fierce; ferocious: 那隻老虎非
常兇猛。The tiger is very
ferocious.

兇犯(ㄒㄩㄥ ㄈㄢˋ)
a criminal; a murderer

兇漢(ㄒㄩㄥ ㄏㄢˋ)or兇徒(ㄒㄩㄥ ㄊㄨˊ)
a hoodlum; a gangster; a
violent person

兇悍(ㄒㄩㄥ ㄏㄢˋ)or兇狠(ㄒㄩㄥ ㄏㄣˇ)
or兇橫(ㄒㄩㄥ ㄏㄥˋ)
truculent, savage, ferocious,
fierce, etc.

兇器(ㄒㄩㄥ ㄑㄧˋ)
the murderous weapon

兇殺(ㄒㄩㄥ ㄕㄚ)
murder; homicide; manslaughter

兇手(ㄒㄩㄥ ㄕㄡˇ)
the murderer; the killer

兇惡(ㄒㄩㄥ ㄜˋ)
evil; wicked; malignant;
ferocious: 他是個兇惡的傢伙。
He is a ferocious fellow.

【先】 ²⁹⁵
ㄒㄧㄢ shian xiān
1. first; foremost: 他首先發言。
He spoke first.
2. before; earlier; in advance:
我比他先到。I arrived earlier
than he did.
3. the late...; the deceased...
4. one's forebears
5. the abbreviation for Mister
or Sir
6. a Chinese family name

先輩(ㄒㄧㄢ ㄅㄟˋ)
the seniors; members of a
former generation; the
senior generation

先民(ㄒㄧㄢ ㄇㄧㄣˊ)
ancients; the former men

先母(ㄒㄧㄢ ㄇㄨˇ)or先慈(ㄒㄧㄢ ㄘˊ)or
先妣(ㄒㄧㄢ ㄅㄧˇ)
my late mother

先發制人(ㄒㄧㄢ ㄈㄚ ㄓˋ ㄖㄣˊ)
to attack first (in order to
cripple the opponent's
defenses); to take the initiative: 他採取先發制人的手段。
He took preemptive mea-
sures.

先鋒(ㄒㄧㄢ ㄈㄥ)or先驅(ㄒㄧㄢ ㄑㄩ)
a vanguard; a forerunner; a
trailblazer; a pioneer; a harbinger: 知更鳥是春天的先鋒。
The robin is a harbinger of
spring.

先夫(ㄒㄧㄢ ㄈㄨ)
my late husband

先父(ㄒㄧㄢ ㄈㄨˋ)or先考(ㄒㄧㄢ ㄎㄠˇ)
or先嚴(ㄒㄧㄢ ㄧㄢˊ)
my late father

先導(ㄒㄧㄢ ㄉㄠˇ)
①to lead the way ②a
model; a mentor; a teacher

〔ㄦ
部〕

③a guide; a forerunner; a precursor: 失敗常常是成功的先導。Failure is often the precursor of what is successful.

〔儿部〕

先帝(ㄒㄧㄢ ㄉㄧˋ)
the late emperor

先睹爲快(ㄒㄧㄢ ㄉㄨˇ ㄨㄟˊ ㄎㄨㄞˋ)
to eagerly await a look at (something) ahead of others; to consider it a pleasure to be among the first to read (a poem, article, etc.)

先頭(ㄒㄧㄢ ㄊㄡˊ)
①ahead; in front; in advance: 我們走在最前頭。We walk ahead of all other people. ②before; formerly; in the past: 他先頭沒說過這事。He didn't mention this before.

先頭部隊(ㄒㄧㄢ ㄊㄡˊ ㄅㄨˋ ㄉㄨㄟˋ)或先遣部隊(ㄒㄧㄢ ㄑㄧㄢˋ ㄅㄨˋ ㄉㄨㄟˋ)
the vanguard; the advance detachment

先天(ㄒㄧㄢ ㄊㄧㄢ)
①natural physical endowments ②congenital; innate; inherent

先天不足(ㄒㄧㄢ ㄊㄧㄢ ㄅㄨˋ ㄗㄨˊ)
inborn deficiency; inherited weakness

先來後到(ㄒㄧㄢ ㄌㄞˊ ㄏㄡˋ ㄉㄠˋ)
the order of arrival 或 First come, first served.

先禮後兵(ㄒㄧㄢ ㄌㄧˇ ㄏㄡˋ ㄅㄧㄥ)
diplomacy (or courtesy) before the use of force

先例(ㄒㄧㄢ ㄌㄧˋ)
a precedent; a former example: 此事有先例可援。This matter has a precedent to go by.

先烈(ㄒㄧㄢ ㄌㄧㄝˋ)
the national martyrs

先令(ㄒㄧㄢ ㄌㄧㄥˋ)
(the British monetary system) a shilling

先乾爲敬(ㄒㄧㄢ ㄍㄢ ㄨㄟˊ ㄐㄧㄥˋ)
(in toasting someone) I empty my glass first to show my respect to you.

先河(ㄒㄧㄢ ㄏㄜˊ)
the beginning of something; a harbinger; a forerunner

先後(ㄒㄧㄢ ㄏㄡˋ)
①the order (of things

placed, narrated, etc.) ②the ins and outs of an incident

先見(ㄒㄧㄢ ㄐㄧㄢˋ)
foresight; forethought; prophetic vision

先見之明(ㄒㄧㄢ ㄐㄧㄢˋ ㄓ ㄇㄧㄥˊ)
the ability to discern what is coming

先進(ㄒㄧㄢ ㄐㄧㄣˋ)
predecessors; seniors

先進國(ㄒㄧㄢ ㄐㄧㄣˋ ㄍㄨㄛˊ)
advanced nations; civilized nations; developed powers

先覺(ㄒㄧㄢ ㄐㄩㄝˊ)
a prophet

先決條件(ㄒㄧㄢ ㄐㄩㄝˊ ㄊㄧㄠˊ ㄐㄧㄢˋ)
a prerequisite; a precondition; an antecedent condition

先決問題(ㄒㄧㄢ ㄐㄩㄝˊ ㄨㄣˋ ㄊㄧˊ)
problems that demand a priority in solution

先君(ㄒㄧㄢ ㄐㄩㄣ)
my late father

先期(ㄒㄧㄢ ㄑㄧˊ)
before the appointed time; beforehand

先前(ㄒㄧㄢ ㄑㄧㄢˊ)
before ; previously: 這孩子比先前高多了。The child is much taller than before.

先秦時代(ㄒㄧㄢ ㄑㄧㄣ ㄕˊ ㄉㄞˋ)
the era before Shih Huang Ti of the Chin Dynasty (221-207 B.C.) when Chinese culture blossomed

先驅(ㄒㄧㄢ ㄑㄩ)
a vanguard; a forerunner; a pioneer

先下手爲強(ㄒㄧㄢ ㄒㄧㄚˋ ㄕㄡˇ ㄨㄟˊ ㄑㄧㄤˊ)
It's always advantageous to make the first move (or take the initiative).

先小人後君子(ㄒㄧㄢ ㄒㄧㄠˇ ㄖㄣˊ ㄏㄡˋ ㄐㄩㄣ ㄗˇ)
(especially in business negotiations) to specify terms clearly at first and use a good deal of courtesy later

先修班(ㄒㄧㄢ ㄒㄧㄡ ㄅㄢ)
a preparatory class

先賢(ㄒㄧㄢ ㄒㄧㄢˊ)或先哲(ㄒㄧㄢ ㄓㄜˊ)
ancient saints and sages

先行(ㄒㄧㄢ ㄒㄧㄥˊ)
①to go ahead of the rest; to

start off before the others ②beforehand; in advance: 他先行通知我。He let me know it in advance.

先行者(ㄒㄧㄢ ㄒㄧㄥˊ ㄓㄜˇ)
a forerunner: 紀念偉大的革命先行者孫中山先生! Let's pay tribute to our great revolutionary forerunner, Dr. Sun Yat-sen!

先知(ㄒㄧㄢ ㄓ)
①a prophet ②a person of foresight or forethought

先知先覺(ㄒㄧㄢ ㄓ ㄒㄧㄢ ㄐㄩㄝˊ)
①a person of foresight or forethought ②having foresight

先兆(ㄒㄧㄢ ㄓㄠˋ)
an omen; a portent; a sign; an indication: 燕子是夏天的先兆。The swallow is a sign of summer.

先斬後奏(ㄒㄧㄢ ㄓㄢˇ ㄏㄡˋ ㄗㄡˋ)
①(in old China) to order execution of criminals before reporting the case to the emperor ②(in a modern sense) to take action before reporting to one's superior

先師(ㄒㄧㄢ ㄕ)
①Confucius ②my late teacher

先世(ㄒㄧㄢ ㄕˋ)
①the preceding generation ②forebears; ancestors; forefathers

先室(ㄒㄧㄢ ㄕˋ)
my late wife

先手(ㄒㄧㄢ ㄕㄡˇ)
(in chess) on the offensive

先聲(ㄒㄧㄢ ㄕㄥ)
first signs; a herald; a harbinger

先聲奪人(ㄒㄧㄢ ㄕㄥ ㄉㄨㄛˊ ㄖㄣˊ)
to start doing something with such a brilliant performance as to inspire awe among others; with an impressive start; to forestall one's opponent by a show of strength; to overawe others by displaying one's strength

先聖(ㄒㄧㄢ ㄕㄥˋ)
①Confucius ②ancient sages

先生(ㄒㄧㄢ ．ㄕㄥ)
①an honorable title for a teacher ②a name for the

elderly and learned ③ Mister; Sir ④ a husband

先人 (ㄒㄧㄢ ㄖㄣˊ)
①previous generations ② forebears

先入之見 (ㄒㄧㄢ ㄖㄨˋ ㄓ ㄐㄧㄢˋ)
a preconception; a preconceived idea, a prejudice

先入為主 (ㄒㄧㄢ ㄖㄨˋ ㄨㄟˊ ㄓㄨˇ)
One is often most impressed by the very first idea entering his mind. 或 One usually favors the very first idea entering his mind. 或 First impressions are most lasting.

先澤 (ㄒㄧㄢ ㄗㄜˊ)
kindness and charity from one's ancestors

先意承志 (ㄒㄧㄢ ㄧˋ ㄔㄥˊ ㄓˋ)
①to do what one's parents would like one to do ②to anticipate others' intention and do it without being told (in order to please them)

先憂後樂 (ㄒㄧㄢ ㄧㄡ ㄏㄡˋ ㄌㄜˋ)
①(said of a capable ruler or statesman) to worry and plan ahead of his subjects and enjoy himself only after they are assured of peace and happiness②Forethought brings happiness.

先嚴 (ㄒㄧㄢ ㄧㄢˊ)
my deceased father

先驗 (ㄒㄧㄢ ㄧㄢˋ)
a priori

先務之急 (ㄒㄧㄢ ㄨˋ ㄓ ㄐㄧˊ)
first things first

先王 (ㄒㄧㄢ ㄨㄤˊ)
①the late king ②ancient sage sovereigns

【光】 296
（ㄍㄨㄤ guang guāng）
1. light; brightness; light rays
2. glossy; smooth
3. glory; glorious; honor: 我們的棒球隊為國爭光。Our baseball team won honor for our country.
4. to exhaust; to use up: 他用光了所有的錢。He has used up all the money.
5. alone; only: 光剩下你一人在家。You alone remain at home.
6. bare; to bare; naked
7. a Chinese family name

光被四表 (ㄍㄨㄤ ㄅㄟˋ ㄙˋ ㄅㄧㄠˇ)
The benefit (of your enlightened administration) reaches far and wide.

光膀子 (ㄍㄨㄤ ㄅㄤˇ ˙ㄗ)
stripped to the waist; barebreasted

光波 (ㄍㄨㄤ ㄅㄛ)
light waves

光屁股 (ㄍㄨㄤ ㄆㄧˋ ˙ㄍㄨ)
stark-naked; in the nude; without a single stitch on

光譜 (ㄍㄨㄤ ㄆㄨˇ)
a spectrum

光芒 (ㄍㄨㄤ ㄇㄤˊ)
rays of light; brilliant rays; radiance

光芒萬丈 (ㄍㄨㄤ ㄇㄤˊ ㄨㄢˋ ㄓㄤˋ)
shining in all directions; radiance; radiant; resplendent: 那光芒萬丈的燈塔，照耀着我們勝利前進。The radiant lighthouse guides us in our victorious march forward.

光面 (ㄍㄨㄤ ㄇㄧㄢˋ)
a glossy surface

光明 (ㄍㄨㄤ ㄇㄧㄥˊ)
①light ②bright; promising: 我們的前途是光明的。Our future is bright. ③openhearted; guileless

光明磊落 (ㄍㄨㄤ ㄇㄧㄥˊ ㄌㄟˇ ㄌㄨㄛˋ)
straightforward and upright; open and aboveboard

光明正大 (ㄍㄨㄤ ㄇㄧㄥˊ ㄓㄥˋ ㄉㄚˋ)
honest, just and upright

光復 (ㄍㄨㄤ ㄈㄨˋ)
to recover (a lost land); retrocession

光大 (ㄍㄨㄤ ㄉㄚˋ)
①glorious and majestic ②to make great; to glorify

光蛋 (ㄍㄨㄤ ㄉㄢˋ)
a person reduced to complete poverty

光碟 (ㄍㄨㄤ ㄉㄧㄝˊ)
a compact disk

光電 (ㄍㄨㄤ ㄉㄧㄢˋ)
photoelectricity

光電子 (ㄍㄨㄤ ㄉㄧㄢˋ ㄗˇ)
photoelectrons

光度 (ㄍㄨㄤ ㄉㄨˋ)
the intensity of light

光度計 (ㄍㄨㄤ ㄉㄨˋ ㄐㄧˋ)
a photometer

光頭 (ㄍㄨㄤ ㄊㄡˊ)

a baldhead; baldheaded

光天化日 (ㄍㄨㄤ ㄊㄧㄢ ㄏㄨㄚˋ ㄖˋ)
(in) broad daylight; the light of day

光禿禿 (ㄍㄨㄤ ㄊㄨ ㄊㄨ)
bare; bald

光年 (ㄍㄨㄤ ㄋㄧㄢˊ)
a light-year

光溜溜 (ㄍㄨㄤ ㄌㄧㄡ ㄌㄧㄡ)
①bare; naked; bald ②smooth and glossy

光臨 (ㄍㄨㄤ ㄌㄧㄣˊ)
(usually used in an invitation) Please grace our place with your presence. 歡迎光臨台灣! Welcome to Taiwan!

光亮 (ㄍㄨㄤ ㄌㄧㄤˋ)
brightness; bright; radiance; radiant; light; shiny

光桿兒 (ㄍㄨㄤ ㄍㄢˇ ㄦ)
①a bare trunk or stalk ②a man who has lost his family ③a person without a following

光顧 (ㄍㄨㄤ ㄍㄨˋ)
to patronize; to honor with one's presence: 許多顧客光顧這個新開張的超級市場。Many customers patronize the newly-opened supermarket.

光怪陸離 (ㄍㄨㄤ ㄍㄨㄞˋ ㄌㄨˋ ㄌㄧˊ)
grotesque; strange-looking; fantastic

光棍
①（ㄍㄨㄤ ㄍㄨㄣˋ）ⓐ a ruffian; a hoodlum ⓑ a bachelor or unmarried man 亦作「光棍兒」②（ㄍㄨㄤ ㄍㄨㄣˋ）a tough guy; a brave man: 他總是光光棍。He always pretends to be a brave man.

光光 (ㄍㄨㄤ ㄍㄨㄤ)
①radiant ②glossy ③(said of money, goods, etc.) exhausted ④naked

光合作用 (ㄍㄨㄤ ㄏㄜˊ ㄗㄨㄛˋ ㄩㄥˋ)
photosynthesis

光華 (ㄍㄨㄤ ㄏㄨㄚˊ)
brilliance; splendor

光滑 (ㄍㄨㄤ ㄏㄨㄚˊ)
smooth and glossy

光火 (ㄍㄨㄤ ㄏㄨㄛˇ)
①angry ②to anger

光輝 (ㄍㄨㄤ ㄏㄨㄟ)
radiance; brightness; 烏雲擋住太陽的光輝。The dark cloud shut out the radiance

of the sun.

光環（ㄍㄨㄤ ㄏㄨㄢˊ）
(astronomy) a corona; a halo

光潔（ㄍㄨㄤ ㄐㄧㄝˊ）
bright and clean

光脚（ㄍㄨㄤ ㄐㄧㄠˇ）
bare feet; barefooted

光景（ㄍㄨㄤ ㄐㄧㄥˇ）
① a situation; circumstances ② about; around: 離這裡大約有十公里光景。It's about 10 kilometers away from here.

光球（ㄍㄨㄤ ㄑㄧㄡˊ）
a photosphere

光前裕後（ㄍㄨㄤ ㄑㄧㄢˊ ㄩˋ ㄏㄡˋ）
(said of one attaining a high position) to glorify the forebears and to provide for the descendants

光圈（ㄍㄨㄤ ㄑㄩㄢ）
the diaphragm of a camera

光鮮（ㄍㄨㄤ ㄒㄧㄢ）
fresh and bright

光線（ㄍㄨㄤ ㄒㄧㄢˋ）
a ray of light

光緒皇帝（ㄍㄨㄤ ㄒㄩˋ ㄏㄨㄤˊ ㄉㄧˋ）
the reigning title of Emperor Te Tsung of the Ching Dynasty, whose reign lasted from 1875 to 1908

光學（ㄍㄨㄤ ㄒㄩㄝˊ）
optics

光學儀器（ㄍㄨㄤ ㄒㄩㄝˊ ㄧˊ ㄑㄧˋ）
optical instruments

光手（ㄍㄨㄤ ㄕㄡˇ）
barehanded

光身人兒（ㄍㄨㄤ ㄕㄣ ㄖㄣˊ ㄦˊ）
① a single man ② a person with no valuable possession

光束（ㄍㄨㄤ ㄕㄨˋ）
(physics) a light beam

光潤（ㄍㄨㄤ ㄖㄨㄣˋ）
smooth and glossy

光榮（ㄍㄨㄤ ㄖㄨㄥˊ）
glory; honor; glorious; honorable: 他曾經在戰場上贏得光榮。He had won glory on the field of battle.

光澤（ㄍㄨㄤ ㄗㄜˊ）
luster: 那顆珍珠有美麗的光澤。It is a pearl with beautiful luster.

光宗耀祖（ㄍㄨㄤ ㄗㄨㄥ ㄧㄠˋ ㄗㄨˇ）
to glorify one's forebears (by one's great achieve-

ments)

光彩（ㄍㄨㄤ ㄘㄞˇ）
① luster; splendor; radiance: 光彩絢麗的冰雕吸引了許多觀光客。The brilliant luster of the ice carving attracted many tourists. ② honorable; glorious: 我認爲做科學家是很光彩的。I think it is honorable to be a scientist.

光彩奪目（ㄍㄨㄤ ㄘㄞˇ ㄉㄨㄛˊ ㄇㄨˋ）
the luster that dazzles the eyes: 她的鑽戒光彩奪目。Her diamond ring dazzled with brilliancy.

光速（ㄍㄨㄤ ㄙㄨˋ）
(physics) the speed of light

光耀（ㄍㄨㄤ ㄧㄠˋ）
① brilliant light; brilliance ② glorious; honorable

光焰（ㄍㄨㄤ ㄧㄢˋ）
radiance; flare

光陰（ㄍㄨㄤ ㄧㄣ）
time

光陰似箭（ㄍㄨㄤ ㄧㄣ ㄙˋ ㄐㄧㄢˋ）
Time passes as fast as a flying arrow.

光源（ㄍㄨㄤ ㄩㄢˊ）
(physics) a light source

五畫

【克】 297
ㄎㄜˋ keh kè

1. to be able to: 他不克分身。He was unable to leave what he was doing at the moment.
2. to win; to overcome; to conquer: 在大戰中他們戰無不克。In the war, they won every battle they were engaged in.
3. love of superiority
4. a gram
5. to limit

克服（ㄎㄜˋ ㄈㄨˊ）
①to overcome (difficulties, etc.): 他克服了許多障礙。He overcame many obstacles. ② to put up with (inconveniences, etc.)

克復（ㄎㄜˋ ㄈㄨˋ）
to recapture or recover (a fallen city, etc.)

克敵致勝（ㄎㄜˋ ㄉㄧˊ ㄓˋ ㄕㄥˋ）
to defeat the enemy and win the battle; to vanquish the enemy

克難（ㄎㄜˋ ㄋㄢˊ）

to overcome difficulties

克拉（ㄎㄜˋ ㄌㄚ）
a carat

克里米亞（ㄎㄜˋ ㄌㄧˇ ㄇㄧˇ ㄧㄚˋ）
Crimea

克里姆林宮（ㄎㄜˋ ㄌㄧˇ ㄇㄨˇ ㄌㄧㄣˊ ㄍㄨㄥ）
the Kremlin

克林威爾（ㄎㄜˋ ㄌㄧㄣˊ ㄨㄟ ㄦˇ）
Oliver Cromwell, 1599-1658, British statesman

克格勃（ㄎㄜˋ ㄍㄜˊ ㄅㄛˊ）
KGB (Soviet State Security Committee) 亦作「格別烏」

克己（ㄎㄜˋ ㄐㄧˇ）
① to overcome one's own desires ② reasonable (price)

克己奉公（ㄎㄜˋ ㄐㄧˇ ㄈㄥˋ ㄍㄨㄥ）
to place public interests above one's own; wholehearted devotion to public duty

克勤克儉（ㄎㄜˋ ㄑㄧㄣˊ ㄎㄜˋ ㄐㄧㄢˇ）
diligent and frugal

克制（ㄎㄜˋ ㄓˋ）
to restrain; to control (one's emotions, desires, etc.); to exercise restraint: 我認爲你不需克制自己的感情。I think you don't have to restrain your passion.

克什米爾（ㄎㄜˋ ㄕˊ ㄇㄧˇ ㄦˇ）
Kashmir

克紹箕裘（ㄎㄜˋ ㄕㄠˋ ㄐㄧ ㄑㄧㄡˊ）
to be able to follow in the footsteps of one's father; to be able to inherit a business, trade, career, etc. and make good

【兌】 298
ㄉㄨㄟˋ duey duì

1. to exchange; to barter
2. (said of wine, etc.) to water; to weaken by adding water

兌付（ㄉㄨㄟˋ ㄈㄨˋ）
to pay; to advance money; to cash

兌換（ㄉㄨㄟˋ ㄏㄨㄢˋ）
exchange; to exchange (currencies); to convert: 他把英磅兌換成美元。He exchanged pounds for dollars.

兌換率（ㄉㄨㄟˋ ㄏㄨㄢˋ ㄌㄩˋ）
the rate of exchange (between two currencies); exchange rates

兌換紙幣（ㄉㄨㄟˋ ㄏㄨㄢˋ ㄓˇ ㄅㄧˋ）

convertible paper money

兌現(ㄉㄨㄟˋㄒㄧㄢˋ)
①to cash (a check, etc.): 我在銀行把支票兌現。I get my checks cashed at the bank.
②to fulfill (a promise); to carry out

【免】 299 (免)ㄇㄧㄢˇ mean mian
1. to avoid; to escape; to evade
2. to forego; to spare; to excuse; to exempt
3. to dismiss (from office)

免不了(ㄇㄧㄢˇ·ㄅㄨˋㄌㄧㄠˇ)
unavoidable; to have to

免票(ㄇㄧㄢˇㄆㄧㄠˋ)
①a free ticket; a free pass
②free of charge

免費(ㄇㄧㄢˇㄈㄟˋ)
free of charge; gratuitous; gratis：美術館在星期六免費開放。The gallery is open free on Saturdays.

免得(ㄇㄧㄢˇ·ㄉㄜ)
to save (the trouble of); to avoid; so as not to：她靜悄悄地走進房間,免得吵醒小孩。She came into the room quietly so that she might not wake her child.

免談(ㄇㄧㄢˇㄊㄢˊ)
You might just as well save your breath.

免禮(ㄇㄧㄢˇㄌㄧˇ)
(usually ordered by a superior) to forego formalities (especially a salute, etc.)

免官(ㄇㄧㄢˇㄍㄨㄢ)
to dismiss from office 參看「免職」

免尊口(ㄇㄧㄢˇㄗㄨㄣㄎㄡˇ)
You might as well save your breath.

免稅(ㄇㄧㄢˇㄕㄨㄟˋ)
to exempt from payment or taxation

免刑(ㄇㄧㄢˇㄒㄧㄥˊ)
to be exempted from punishment

免職(ㄇㄧㄢˇㄓˊ)
to be dismissed from office (sometimes for a new assignment)：部長受到免職處分。The minister was dismissed from his office in disgrace.

免戰牌(ㄇㄧㄢˇㄓㄢˋㄆㄞˊ)
a tablet of truce (In old China when one warring party hung the tablet high up the camp, it indicated the party's unwillingness to engage in battle temporarily for some reason which was often respected by the other party.)

免除(ㄇㄧㄢˇㄔㄨˊ)
①to prevent; to avoid ②to exempt (from obligations, etc.); to exonerate

免試升學(ㄇㄧㄢˇㄕˋㄕㄥ ㄒㄩㄝˊ)
to enter a school without taking an entrance examination

免稅(ㄇㄧㄢˇㄕㄨㄟˋ)
exemption of tax; free of duty; duty-free; to be exempted from taxation

免稅商店(ㄇㄧㄢˇㄕㄨㄟˋㄕㄤ ㄉㄧㄢˋ)
a duty-free shop

免罪(ㄇㄧㄢˇㄗㄨㄟˋ)
to be acquitted; exonerated; to be exempted from punishment

免俗(ㄇㄧㄢˇㄙㄨˊ)
to forego customary routines, formalities, etc.

免役(ㄇㄧㄢˇㄧˋ)
exemption from military service

免疫(ㄇㄧㄢˇㄧˋ)
immunity (from disease)

免疫性(ㄇㄧㄢˇㄧˋㄒㄧㄥˋ)
immunity from infection

免驗(ㄇㄧㄢˇㄧㄢˋ)
①to forego inspection ②to be exempt from customs examination

六畫

【兒】 300 ㄦˊ erl ér
1. a child; a baby
2. a son：他有兩個兒子。He has two sons.
3. referring to oneself when addressing parents
4. As a particle after noun, pronoun, adjective, adverb, and verb, 兒 is pronounced (ㄦ). 屋裡有燈兒。There's a lamp in the room.

children

兒童電視劇(ㄦˊㄊㄨㄥˊㄉㄧㄢˋㄕˋㄐㄩˋ)
children's TV show; a TV show for children

兒童讀物(ㄦˊㄊㄨㄥˊㄉㄨˊㄨˋ)
juvenile publications; children's books; children's reading material

兒童樂園(ㄦˊㄊㄨㄥˊㄌㄜˋㄩㄢˊ)
an amusement park catering to children

兒童廣播(ㄦˊㄊㄨㄥˊㄍㄨㄤˇㄅㄛˋ)
a radio play for children

兒童節(ㄦˊㄊㄨㄥˊㄐㄧㄝˊ)
Children's Day (April 4)

兒童節目(ㄦˊㄊㄨㄥˊㄐㄧㄝˊㄇㄨˋ)
children's programs：所有的兒童節目都很合人愉快。All the children's programs are delightful.

兒童教育(ㄦˊㄊㄨㄥˊㄐㄧㄠˋㄩˋ)
education for children; primary education; children's education：兒童教育是一件重要的事情。Education for children is an important thing.

兒童戲院(ㄦˊㄊㄨㄥˊㄒㄧˋㄩㄢˋ)
①The Children's Theater (in Taipei) ②a theater for kids

兒童心理學(ㄦˊㄊㄨㄥˊㄒㄧㄣ ㄌㄧˇㄒㄩㄝˊ)
child psychology

兒童醫院(ㄦˊㄊㄨㄥˊㄧ ㄩㄢˋ)
a children's hospital

兒童文學(ㄦˊㄊㄨㄥˊㄨㄣˊㄒㄩㄝˊ)
literary writings for children; tales for children; children's literature

兒女(ㄦˊㄋㄩˇ)
①sons and daughters; children：他們的兒女都已長大。Their children have all grown up. ②young men and women

兒女情長(ㄦˊㄋㄩˇㄑㄧㄥˊㄔㄤˊ)
Long is the love between a man and a woman.

兒女債(ㄦˊㄋㄩˇㄓㄞˋ)
the obligations of parents to their children

兒歌(ㄦˊㄍㄜ)
children's songs; nursery rhymes

兒科(ㄦˊㄎㄜ)
pediatrics

兒媳(ㄦㄒㄧˊ)or 兒媳婦(ㄦㄒㄧ ㄈㄨˋ)
a daughter-in-law

兒戲(ㄦㄒㄧˋ)or 兒嬉(ㄦㄒㄧ)
① child's play ② a plaything; a trifling matter: 這樣重要的工作可不能當兒戲。Such important work should not be regarded as a trifling matter. ③ to treat lightly

兒時(ㄦˊㄕ)
childhood

兒子(ㄦˊ·ㄗ)or(·ㄗ)
a son or sons

兒孫(ㄦˊㄙㄨㄣ)
① children and grandchildren ② offspring; descendants

兒孫自有兒孫福(ㄦˊㄙㄨㄣ ㄗˋ ㄧㄡˇ ㄦˊ ㄙㄨㄣ ㄈㄨˊ)
The children can take care of themselves when they grow up. (Therefore, the parents don't have to work too hard for their children's future.)

【兔】301 (兎) ㄊㄨˋ tuh tù
1. a hare; a rabbit
2. a young boy kept for sexual perversion

兔脫(ㄊㄨˋㄊㄨㄛ)
to escape fast

兔起鶻落(ㄊㄨˋㄑㄧˇㄏㄨˊㄌㄨㄛˋ)
(said of calligraphic works) bold and agile

兔唇(ㄊㄨˋ ㄔㄨㄣˊ)
a harelip, or a cleft lip

兔子(ㄊㄨˋ·ㄗ)
① a hare; a rabbit ② a young boy kept for sexual perversion

兔子不吃窩邊草(ㄊㄨˋ·ㄗ ㄅㄨˋ ㄔ ㄨㄛ ㄅㄧㄢ ㄘㄠˇ)
A rabbit doesn't eat the grass near its own burrow. —(figuratively) A villain does not harm his next-door neighbors.

兔崽子(ㄊㄨˋ ㄗㄞˇ·ㄗ)
a brat; a bastard

兔死狗烹(ㄊㄨˋ ㄙˇ ㄍㄡˇ ㄆㄥ)
(literally) The hounds are killed for cooking food once all the hares are bagged. — Trusted aides are eliminated when they have outlived their usefulness. 或

(usually referring to the first emperor of a dynasty) to get rid of all the brave and meritorious comrades-in-arms after they had helped him win the throne and were no longer useful to him

兔死狐悲(ㄊㄨˋ ㄙˇ ㄏㄨˊ ㄅㄟ)
(literally) When the hare dies, the fox is sad.—sympathy with one of its kind

【兕】302 ㄙ syh sì
a female rhinoceros

七畫

【兗】303 ㄧㄢˇ yean yǎn
(in ancient China) one of the Nine Divisions of the Empire under Yü the Great including parts of Shantung and Hopeh provinces

九畫

【兜】304 ㄉㄡ dou dōu
1. a head-covering; a helmet
2. overalls
3. to solicit
4. to go for a drive around; to move around
5. to surround; to wrap up
6. a small pocket in clothes

兜捕(ㄉㄡ ㄅㄨˇ)
to surround and seize

兜風(ㄉㄡ ㄈㄥ)
to go joyriding; to have a drive to enjoy countryside; to take the air; to go for a ride: 坐我的新車去兜風吧! Let's go for a ride in my new car.

兜肚(ㄉㄡ·ㄉㄨ)
an undergarment covering the chest and abdomen 亦作「兜兜」or「兜子」

兜攬(ㄉㄡ ㄌㄢˇ)
① to befriend another person with a view to winning him over ② to solicit

兜圈子(ㄉㄡ ㄑㄩㄢ·ㄗ)
① to take a stroll ② to circle: 敵機在我們頭上兜圈子。The enemy's planes circled

round and round above our heads. ③ circumlocutory; to beat about the bush

兜紗(ㄉㄡ ㄕㄚ)
(in old China) a head-covering for the bride at a wedding

兜售(ㄉㄡ ㄕㄡˋ)
to peddle

兜兒(ㄉㄡ ㄦ)
a small pocket

十二畫

【兢】305 ㄐㄧㄥ jing jīng
to fear; to dread; apprehensive; cautious

兢兢業業(ㄐㄧㄥ ㄐㄧㄥ ㄧㄝˋ ㄧㄝˋ)
with caution and fear; cautious and attentive

入 部
ㄖㄨˋ ruh rù

【入】306 ㄖㄨˋ ruh rù
1. to enter; to come into: 他進入屋子裡。He entered the house.
2. to join; to come into the company of: 他加入了網球俱樂部。He joined a tennis club.
3. to arrive at; to reach: 他已進入成人階段。He has arrived at manhood.
4. to put in: 她打開錢包放入一些錢。She opened her purse and put in some money.
5. receipts; income: 我們必須要量入為出。We should regulate expenses according to income.
6. to get out of sight; to disappear
7. to get (inside, picked, elected, etc.)
8. to agree with; to conform to
9. one of the four tones of a character 參看「入聲」

入不敷出(ㄖㄨˋ ㄅㄨˋ ㄈㄨ ㄔㄨ)
expenditure exceeding income; cannot make both ends meet; to live beyond

（入部）

one's means 或 One's income cannot cover one's spending.

入魔(ㄖㄨˋ ㄇㄛˊ)
① to be deeply fascinated; to be captivated; to be infatuated ② bedeviled; bewitched; spellbound

入門(ㄖㄨˋ ㄇㄣˊ)
① to have an elementary knowledge of (a subject); to initiate into; to get ready for more profound study (of a subject) ② a primer (for chess, bridge, etc.)

入夢(ㄖㄨˋ ㄇㄥˋ)
① to fall asleep ② to appear in one's dream

入迷(ㄖㄨˋ ㄇㄧˊ)
to be captivated or fascinated; to be bewitched; to be enchanted: 那美麗的舞者叫我們看得入迷了。 We were all bewitched by the pretty dancer.

入木三分(ㄖㄨˋ ㄇㄨˋ ㄙㄢ ㄈㄣ)
① (said of Chinese calligraphy) a forceful style ② (comments, analyses, etc.) incisive; penetrating; sharp; profound: 他的分析真是入木三分。 His analysis was really penetrating.

入黨(ㄖㄨˋ ㄉㄤˇ)
to join a political party; to become a member of a political party

入定(ㄖㄨˋ ㄉㄧㄥˋ)
(Buddhism) to enter into meditation by tranquilizing the body, mouth (i.e. lips), and mind

入肚(ㄖㄨˋ ㄉㄨˋ)
to enter the stomach—to eat

入土(ㄖㄨˋ ㄊㄨˇ)
to bury; to be buried

入列(ㄖㄨˋ ㄌㄧㄝˋ)
to take one's place in the ranks; to fall in

入流(ㄖㄨˋ ㄌㄧㄡˊ)
① to be in fashion ② to attain a certain level ③ (in old China) within the Nine Official Ranks

入殮(ㄖㄨˋ ㄌㄧㄢˋ)
to put a corpse in a coffin; to coffin

入閣(ㄖㄨˋ ㄍㄜˊ)
(in old China) to get inside the imperial cabinet; to be appointed a minister

入彀(ㄖㄨˋ ㄍㄡˋ)
to be trapped, harnessed, controlled, etc.

入港(ㄖㄨˋ ㄍㄤˇ)
① to enter a harbor (or port) ② (said of conversation) agreeable, amicable and interesting

入股(ㄖㄨˋ ㄍㄨˇ)
to become a shareholder; to buy a share

入骨(ㄖㄨˋ ㄍㄨˇ)
deep (hatred, love, etc.); to the marrow: 她恨他入骨。 She hates him to the marrow.

入貢(ㄖㄨˋ ㄍㄨㄥˋ)
(said of protectorates or tributary nations) to offer tributes to the emperor

入口(ㄖㄨˋ ㄎㄡˇ)
① an entrance ② to import (commodities, etc.) ③ to enter the mouth

入寇(ㄖㄨˋ ㄎㄡˋ)
to invade; intrusion

入扣兒(ㄖㄨˋ ㄎㄡˋ)
to be completely engrossed

入庫(ㄖㄨˋ ㄎㄨˋ)
① to confiscate; to be confiscated ② to enter (cargo) into a public warehouse before shipment to a final destination

入海口(ㄖㄨˋ ㄏㄞˇ ㄎㄡˇ)
an estuary

入畫(ㄖㄨˋ ㄏㄨㄚˋ)
suitable for a painting; picturesque: 花蓮景緻處處可以入畫。 Every bit of Hualien scenery is picturesque.

入伙(ㄖㄨˋ ㄏㄨㄛˇ)
① to join in an enterprise (or a gang) ② to join a mess

入夥(ㄖㄨˋ ㄏㄨㄛˇ)
① to join a gang (especially of bandits, etc.) ② to join in an undertaking or enterprise

入會(ㄖㄨˋ ㄏㄨㄟˋ)
to join a society, club, organization, etc.; to become a member

入籍(ㄖㄨˋ ㄐㄧˊ)
to naturalize; to be natural-ized

入教(ㄖㄨˋ ㄐㄧㄠˋ)
to become a follower or believer of a religion

入境(ㄖㄨˋ ㄐㄧㄥˋ)
to entry a country

入境證(ㄖㄨˋ ㄐㄧㄥˋ ㄓㄥˋ)
an entry permit

入境問禁(ㄖㄨˋ ㄐㄧㄥˋ ㄨㄣˋ ㄐㄧㄣˋ)
to learn the taboos of the local people after arriving at a strange place; to keep oneself informed of what things are forbidden in the country one is entering

入境隨俗(ㄖㄨˋ ㄐㄧㄥˋ ㄙㄨㄟˊ ㄙㄨˊ)
to learn the customs of a new place when one goes there 或 When in Rome, do as the Romans do.

入侵(ㄖㄨˋ ㄑㄧㄣ)
to invade; to intrude; to make an incursion; to make inroads: 敵人再次入侵。 The enemy made another intrusion.

入情入理(ㄖㄨˋ ㄑㄧㄥˊ ㄖㄨˋ ㄌㄧˇ)
fair and reasonable

入席(ㄖㄨˋ ㄒㄧˊ)
to be properly seated at a gathering, meeting or feast; to take one's seat at a banquet, ceremony, etc.

入學(ㄖㄨˋ ㄒㄩㄝˊ)
to enter school (usually referring to primary school); to start school: 新生明天入學。 The new students will enter school tomorrow.

入學考試(ㄖㄨˋ ㄒㄩㄝˊ ㄎㄠˇ ㄕˋ)
an entrance examination (of a school)

入選(ㄖㄨˋ ㄒㄩㄢˇ)
to be selected; to be chosen

入帳(ㄖㄨˋ ㄓㄤˋ)
to enter an item in an account

入主出奴(ㄖㄨˋ ㄓㄨˇ ㄔㄨ ㄋㄨˊ)
(said of academic schools, political philosophies, etc.) bigotry

入贅(ㄖㄨˋ ㄓㄨㄟˋ)
to marry into the family of one's wife—children thus born will bear her family name

入超(ㄖㄨˋ ㄔㄠ)

〔入部〕

an unfavorable balance of trade; trade deficit 亦作「貿易逆差」

入場(ㄖㄨˋㄔㄤˇ)or(ㄖㄨˋㄔㄤˊ)
①to enter a meeting place ②to take part in an examination

入場券(ㄖㄨˋㄔㄤˇㄐㄩㄢˋ)or(ㄖㄨˋㄔㄤˊㄐㄩㄢˋ)
an admission ticket

入時(ㄖㄨˋㄕˊ)
fashionable; to keep up with the times

入室(ㄖㄨˋㄕˋ)
to attain profundity in scholastic pursuits; to become a real expert (or specialist)

入室弟子(ㄖㄨˋㄕˋㄉ丨ˋㄗˇ)
one who learns an art directly from a master

入室操戈(ㄖㄨˋㄕˋㄘㄠ ㄍㄜ)
to attack somebody with his own writings or statements

入手(ㄖㄨˋㄕㄡˇ)
to begin; to start; to put one's hand to

入山(ㄖㄨˋㄕㄢ)
to go to the mountain—to become a hermit; to live the life of a recluse; to decline offers of official ranks, etc.

入神(ㄖㄨˋㄕㄣˊ)
with ecstasy; captivated; bewitched; fascinated; spellbound: 他聽音樂聽得入神。He listened to the music with ecstasy.

入聲(ㄖㄨˋㄕㄥ)
(traditional Chinese phonetics) the fourth tone

入聖(ㄖㄨˋㄕㄥˋ)
(Buddhism) to become an arhat (a saint)

入睡(ㄖㄨˋㄕㄨㄟˋ)
to go to sleep; to fall asleep

入座(ㄖㄨˋㄗㄨㄛˋ)
properly seated (especially in a feast)

入耳(ㄖㄨˋㄦˇ)
①to hear ②pleasing to the ear

入夜(ㄖㄨˋ丨ㄝˋ)
at night; in the evening; at nightfall: 入夜時分, 城裡燈火通明。When night falls, the city is ablaze with light.

入眼(ㄖㄨˋ丨ㄢˇ)

pleasing to the eye; agreeable to look at; to one's liking

入營(ㄖㄨˋ丨ㄥˊ)
to enter the barracks—to join the army

入伍(ㄖㄨˋㄨˇ)
to become a soldier (usually under the conscription system); to enlist in the armed forces; to join up: 他入伍從軍為國而戰。He joined up to fight for his country.

入圍(ㄖㄨˋㄨㄟˊ)
①to be selected or elected as one of the few; to enter the final contest ②to enter a circle, or a trapped area

入闈(ㄖㄨˋㄨㄟˊ)
①(said of a teacher) to enter a tightly guarded building to write test papers and stay there until the examination is over ②(in imperial China) to take the civil service examination in a cubicle of a tightly guarded building

入味(ㄖㄨˋㄨㄟˋ)
①tasty: 這湯很入味。The soup is very tasty. ②interesting

入獄(ㄖㄨˋㄩˋ)
to be imprisoned; to be put in prison; to be sent to jail; to put behind bars

入院(ㄖㄨˋㄩㄢˋ)
①to be hospitalized; to be admitted to hospital: 他昨天入院就醫。He was hospitalized yesterday. ②(Buddhism) to enter a monastery; to become a monk

二畫

【內】 307
ㄋㄟˋ ney nèi
1. inside; within; inner; interior: 屋子內外都很整潔。The house is clean inside and out.
2. wife
3. the palace of an emperor

內部(ㄋㄟˋㄅㄨˋ)
the interior; the internal parts; inside; within: 他油漆房子內部。He painted the

inside of the house.

內布拉斯加(ㄋㄟˋㄅㄨ ㄌㄚ ㄙ ㄐ丨ㄚ)
the state of Nebraska, U.S.A.

內蒙古(ㄋㄟˋㄇㄥˊㄍㄨˇ)
Inner Mongolia (Jehol, Chahar and Suiyüan)

內幕(ㄋㄟˋㄇㄨˋ)
an inside story

內幕消息(ㄋㄟˋㄇㄨˋㄒ丨ㄠ ㄒ丨ˊ)
inside information; inside skinny 亦作「內幕傳出」

內犯(ㄋㄟˋㄈㄢˋ)
intrusion by (bandits, enemy troops, etc.)

內分泌(ㄋㄟˋㄈㄣ ㄇ丨ˋ)
glandular excretion; internal secretion; endocrines

內服藥(ㄋㄟˋㄈㄨˊ丨ㄠˋ)
drugs taken orally or internally; drugs for oral administration

內附(ㄋㄟˋㄈㄨˋ)
enclosed herewith

內弟(ㄋㄟˋㄉ丨ˋ)
younger brothers of one's wife

內地(ㄋㄟˋㄉ丨ˋ)
the hinterland; the inland; a land area behind the border or coast

內地會(ㄋㄟˋㄉ丨ˋㄏㄨㄟˋ)
China Inland Mission

內定(ㄋㄟˋㄉ丨ㄥˋ)
(said of official appointment) to have already decided, but yet to be officially announced

內動詞(ㄋㄟˋㄉㄨㄥˋㄘˊ)
linking verbs

內奴外主(ㄋㄟˋㄋㄨˊㄨㄞˋㄓㄨˇ)
(said of a bad government) to treat one's own people as slaves but to regard foreign powers as masters

內陸(ㄋㄟˋㄌㄨˋ)
inland; interior

內陸國(ㄋㄟˋㄌㄨˋㄍㄨㄛˊ)
a landlocked country

內亂(ㄋㄟˋㄌㄨㄢˋ)
rebellion; a civil war; civil strife; internal disorders

內亂罪(ㄋㄟˋㄌㄨㄢˋㄗㄨㄟˋ)
treason

內閣(ㄋㄟˋㄍㄜˊ)
the cabinet

內閣制(ㄋㄟ ㄍㄜ ㄓ)
the cabinet system

內閣總理(ㄋㄟ ㄍㄜ ㄗㄨㄥ ㄌㄧ)
the premier; the prime minister; the chancellor

內顧(ㄋㄟ ㄍㄨ)
to look after home or domestic affairs

內顧之憂(ㄋㄟ ㄍㄨ ㄓ ㄧㄡ)
worries for trouble at home

內功(ㄋㄟ ㄍㄨㄥ)
(Chinese boxing) the exercise and training of internal organs to develop uncanny strength, feats, endurance, etc.

內科(ㄋㄟ ㄎㄜ)
internal medicine; general medicine

內科醫生(ㄋㄟ ㄎㄜ ㄧ ㄕㄥ)
a physician (as distinguished from a surgeon)

內開(ㄋㄟ ㄎㄞ)
what is listed therein (used in documents)

內庫(ㄋㄟ ㄎㄨ)
the treasury within the palace

內河(ㄋㄟ ㄏㄜ)
rivers in the hinterland; inland rivers

內海(ㄋㄟ ㄏㄞ)
inland seas; continental seas

內含(ㄋㄟ ㄏㄢ)
to contain

內涵(ㄋㄟ ㄏㄢ)
(logic) intension; connotation

內行(ㄋㄟ ㄏㄤ)
a professional; a specialist; an expert

內華達(ㄋㄟ ㄏㄨㄚ ㄉㄚ)
the state of Nevada, U. S. A.

內訌(ㄋㄟ ㄏㄨㄥ)
an internal squabble; an intramural fight; internal strife (or dissension)

內角(ㄋㄟ ㄐㄧㄠ)
(mathematics) an interior angle

內疚(ㄋㄟ ㄐㄧㄡ)
deep regret; remorse; compunction; a guilty conscience

內奸(ㄋㄟ ㄐㄧㄢ)
a spy within; a traitor

內景(ㄋㄟ ㄐㄧㄥ)
(motion pictures) scenes within the sound stage; studio scenes; indoor scenes (or settings)

內舉不避親(ㄋㄟ ㄐㄩ ㄅㄨ ㄅㄧ ㄑㄧㄣ)
to promote or appoint a relative to a post on the basis of personal merit

內眷(ㄋㄟ ㄐㄩㄢ)
female members of a family

內切圓(ㄋㄟ ㄑㄧㄝ ㄩㄢ)
(mathematics) an inscribed circle

內親(ㄋㄟ ㄑㄧㄣ)
relatives of one's wife

內勤(ㄋㄟ ㄑㄧㄣ)
desk work; working inside an office

內情(ㄋㄟ ㄑㄧㄥ)
an inside story

內銷(ㄋㄟ ㄒㄧㄠ)
(said of local products) for domestic sale or market

內線(ㄋㄟ ㄒㄧㄢ)
inside contacts; a stool pigeon

內心(ㄋㄟ ㄒㄧㄣ)
heart; the bottom of one's heart: 他是個內心仁慈的人。He is a man with a kind heart.

內詳(ㄋㄟ ㄒㄧㄤ)
the name and address of the sender enclosed

內向(ㄋㄟ ㄒㄧㄤ)
introversion; introverted

內省(ㄋㄟ ㄒㄧㄥ)
self-examination; to search one's heart

內兄(ㄋㄟ ㄒㄩㄥ)
elder brothers of one's wife

內姪(ㄋㄟ ㄓ)
nephews of one's wife

內姪女(ㄋㄟ ㄓ ㄋㄩ)
nieces of one's wife

內痔(ㄋㄟ ㄓ)
internal hemorrhoids

內宅(ㄋㄟ ㄓㄞ)
the inner quarters of a house (usually occupied by the female members)

內債(ㄋㄟ ㄓㄞ)
internal debts

內戰(ㄋㄟ ㄓㄢ)
a civil war

內政(ㄋㄟ ㄓㄥ)
home administration; internal (or domestic) affairs: 他們主張互不干涉內政。They insist on noninterference in each other's internal affairs.

內政部(ㄋㄟ ㄓㄥ ㄅㄨ)
the Ministry of the Interior

內助(ㄋㄟ ㄓㄨ)
wife (a complimentary term)

內重外輕(ㄋㄟ ㄓㄨㄥ ㄨㄞ ㄑㄧㄥ)
over-concentration of power in the central government

內出血(ㄋㄟ ㄔㄨ ㄒㄩㄝ)
internal bleeding

內侍(ㄋㄟ ㄕ)
eunuchs and palace attendants

內傷(ㄋㄟ ㄕㄤ)
①internal injury ②(Chinese medicine) disorder of internal organs

內聖外王(ㄋㄟ ㄕㄥ ㄨㄞ ㄨㄤ)
sagely within and kingly without—a learning both sound in theory and practice

內燃機(ㄋㄟ ㄖㄢ ㄐㄧ)
an internal-combustion engine

內人(ㄋㄟ ㄖㄣ) or 內子(ㄋㄟ ㄗ)
my wife

內容(ㄋㄟ ㄖㄨㄥ)
①content ②the meaning, theme, etc. of a literary or artistic work

內則無虧(ㄋㄟ ㄗㄜ ㄨ ㄎㄨㄟ)
(said of a housewife) dutiful and virtuous

內在(ㄋㄟ ㄗㄞ)
inherent; intrinsic; internal; inner

內在美(ㄋㄟ ㄗㄞ ㄇㄟ)
inner beauty (as contrasted with physical charms); the beauty of spirit

內臟(ㄋㄟ ㄗㄤ)
internal organs; viscera

內才(ㄋㄟ ㄘㄞ)
talent; scholastic achievements; learning

內耳(ㄋㄟ ㄦ)
the inner ear

內衣(ㄋㄟ ㄧ)
underwear; undergarments

內憂外患(ㄋㄟ ㄧㄡ ㄨㄞ ㄏㄨㄢ)
(said of countries) troubles within and without

〔入部〕

〔入部〕

內應 (ㄋㄟˋ ㄧㄥ)
an inside help; a planted agent

內務 (ㄋㄟˋ ㄨˋ)
①domestic affairs; internal affairs ②(in ancient China) affairs within the palace ③ family affairs

內外 (ㄋㄟˋ ㄨㄞˋ)
①inside and outside: 這道牆的內外都是藍色。Both sides of the wall are blue. ②domestic and foreign; home and abroad: 這個國家內外交困。This country is beset with difficulties both at home and abroad. ③around; about: 他的年紀在六十歲內外。His age is about sixty.

內外夾攻 (ㄋㄟˋ ㄨㄞˋ ㄐㄧㄚ ㄍㄨㄥ)
to attack (an enemy) simultaneously from within and without; subjected to synchronized attack from within and without

內圓 (ㄋㄟˋ ㄩㄢˊ)
(geometry) an internal circle

四畫

【全】 308
(ㄑㄩㄢˊ) chyuan quán
1. perfect
2. complete; whole; total; intact; all; entire; absolute: 上星期我全家人都去台南。My whole family went to Tainan last week.
3. to keep whole or intact
4. a Chinese family name

全豹 (ㄑㄩㄢˊ ㄅㄠˋ)
the complete picture; the entire thing: 我們有幸得窺全豹。We are fortunate to see the entire thing.

全班 (ㄑㄩㄢˊ ㄅㄢ)
the whole class; the whole squad

全本 (ㄑㄩㄢˊ ㄅㄣˇ)
(Chinese opera) the staging of the whole story in a single show

全部 (ㄑㄩㄢˊ ㄅㄨˋ)
the whole; completely; fully; total: 他以全部的心力去做這件工作。He did the work with his whole heart.

全盤 (ㄑㄩㄢˊ ㄆㄢˊ)
total; overall; all-out; entire; wholesale; complete: 我們將做全盤考慮。We will give overall consideration to it.

全盤計劃 (ㄑㄩㄢˊ ㄆㄢˊ ㄐㄧˋ ㄏㄨㄚˋ)
an overall program or plan

全貌 (ㄑㄩㄢˊ ㄇㄠˋ)
the overall picture or appearance

全面 (ㄑㄩㄢˊ ㄇㄧㄢˋ)
overall; comprehensive; all-round

全面攻擊 (ㄑㄩㄢˊ ㄇㄧㄢˋ ㄍㄨㄥ ㄐㄧ)
an all-out offensive

全面戰爭 (ㄑㄩㄢˊ ㄇㄧㄢˋ ㄓㄢˋ ㄓㄥ)
a total war; a full-scale war

全民 (ㄑㄩㄢˊ ㄇㄧㄣˊ)
the whole (or entire) people; all the people

全民皆兵 (ㄑㄩㄢˊ ㄇㄧㄣˊ ㄐㄧㄝ ㄅㄧㄥ)
an entire nation in arms; every citizen as a soldier

全民政治 (ㄑㄩㄢˊ ㄇㄧㄣˊ ㄓㄥˋ ㄓˋ)
democracy; government by all the people

全副 (ㄑㄩㄢˊ ㄈㄨˋ)
the whole set

全副武裝 (ㄑㄩㄢˊ ㄈㄨˋ ㄨˇ ㄓㄨㄤ)
to be armed to the teeth; with all the equipment (issued to a soldier such as ammunition, a rifle, a sack, a shovel, etc.); fully armed; in full battle array

全部 (ㄑㄩㄢˊ ㄅㄨˋ)
all; altogether; everyone: 去年栽的花全都開了。All the flowers planted last year have bloomed.

全等 (ㄑㄩㄢˊ ㄉㄥˇ)
identically equal; congruent

全套 (ㄑㄩㄢˊ ㄊㄠˋ)
the whole set; the complete set: 這實驗室擁有全套設備。This laboratory has a complete set of equipment.

全體 (ㄑㄩㄢˊ ㄊㄧˇ)
all; the whole body; everybody; plenary (assembly): 全體贊成他的提議。All approved of his suggestion.

全天候 (ㄑㄩㄢˊ ㄊㄧㄢ ㄏㄡˋ)
all-weather; capable of operating under all weather conditions

全能 (ㄑㄩㄢˊ ㄋㄥˊ)
①omnipotence ②all-round: 他是個全能運動員。He's an all-round sportsman.

全能運動 (ㄑㄩㄢˊ ㄋㄥˊ ㄩㄣˋ ㄉㄨㄥˋ)
(for men) the decathlon; (for women) the pentathlon

全年 (ㄑㄩㄢˊ ㄋㄧㄢˊ)
the whole year; throughout the year; all the year round

全壘打 (ㄑㄩㄢˊ ㄌㄟˇ ㄉㄚˇ)
(baseball) a home run

全力 (ㄑㄩㄢˊ ㄌㄧˋ)
(with) all-out effort; (with) wholehearted dedication

全力以赴 (ㄑㄩㄢˊ ㄌㄧˋ ㄧˇ ㄈㄨˋ)
to spare no efforts: 我們全力以赴以挽回局勢。We spare no efforts to save the situation.

全國 (ㄑㄩㄢˊ ㄍㄨㄛˊ)
the whole country or nation; national; nationwide; throughout the nation

全國性 (ㄑㄩㄢˊ ㄍㄨㄛˊ ㄒㄧㄥˋ)
nationwide; countrywide; national

全國人口普查 (ㄑㄩㄢˊ ㄍㄨㄛˊ ㄖㄣˊ ㄎㄡˇ ㄆㄨˇ ㄔㄚˊ)
a nationwide census

全規 (ㄑㄩㄢˊ ㄍㄨㄟ)
standard-sized; full-size

全集 (ㄑㄩㄢˊ ㄐㄧˊ)
①the complete works of (Shakespeare, etc.) ②the whole set of books of an author dealing with a single subject

全家 (ㄑㄩㄢˊ ㄐㄧㄚ)
the whole family

全家福 (ㄑㄩㄢˊ ㄐㄧㄚ ㄈㄨˊ)
a family photo

全景 (ㄑㄩㄢˊ ㄐㄧㄥˇ)
a panoramic view; a panorama; a full view; a whole scene: 西湖的全景很美。The full view of the West Lake is very beautiful.

全局 (ㄑㄩㄢˊ ㄐㄩˊ)
the situation as a whole; the overall situation

全軍 (ㄑㄩㄢˊ ㄐㄩㄣ)
the whole (or entire) army

全軍覆沒 (ㄑㄩㄢˊ ㄐㄩㄣ ㄈㄨˋ ㄇㄛˋ)
The whole army was lost. 或 The army was totally annihilated.

〔入部〕

全球〈ㄑㄩㄢˊ ㄑㄧㄡˊ〉
around the globe; the globe; the world

全權代表〈ㄑㄩㄢˊ ㄑㄩㄢˊ ㄉㄞˋ ㄅㄧㄠˇ〉
an envoy plenipotentiary; a representative vested with full authority; a delegate with full powers

全席〈ㄑㄩㄢˊ ㄒㄧˊ〉
a whole feast; a whole banquet (without omission of any dishes listed in a Chinese menu)

全休〈ㄑㄩㄢˊ ㄒㄧㄡ〉
a complete rest

全線〈ㄑㄩㄢˊ ㄒㄧㄢˋ〉
all fronts; the whole line: 我們將全線出擊。We will launch an attack on all fronts.

全心全意〈ㄑㄩㄢˊ ㄒㄧㄣ ㄑㄩㄢˊ ㄧˋ〉
wholeheartedly: 她決定全心全意爲窮人服務。She decided to serve the poor wholeheartedly.

全脂奶粉〈ㄑㄩㄢˊ ㄓ ㄋㄞˇ ㄈㄣˇ〉
whole milk powder

全知全能〈ㄑㄩㄢˊ ㄓ ㄑㄩㄢˊ ㄋㄥˊ〉
omniscient and omnipotent

全場〈ㄑㄩㄢˊ ㄔㄤˇ〉
①the whole audience; all those present: 全場掌聲雷動。The audience applauded thunderously. ②(basketball) full-court; all-court

全程〈ㄑㄩㄢˊ ㄔㄥˊ〉
the whole journey; the whole course: 賽車比賽全程五百公里。The whole course of the automobile race is 500 kilometers.

全屍〈ㄑㄩㄢˊ ㄕ〉
a corpse with no part missing, a reference to execution by hanging or poisoning instead of decapitation or mutilation in imperial China

全蝕〈ㄑㄩㄢˊ ㄕˊ〉
a total eclipse

全壽〈ㄑㄩㄢˊ ㄕㄡˋ〉
to live one's full life span; to die of natural cause

全身〈ㄑㄩㄢˊ ㄕㄣ〉
the whole body

全神貫注〈ㄑㄩㄢˊ ㄕㄣˊ ㄍㄨㄢˋ ㄓㄨˋ〉
to pay undivided attention to; to concentrate on: 他不能全神貫注於學術工作。He is unable to concentrate on academic work.

全勝〈ㄑㄩㄢˊ ㄕㄥˋ〉
a total victory; a complete victory

全盛〈ㄑㄩㄢˊ ㄕㄥˋ〉
flourishing; in full bloom; at the peak of development

全盛時代〈ㄑㄩㄢˊ ㄕㄥˋ ㄕˊ ㄉㄞˋ〉or 全盛時期〈ㄑㄩㄢˊ ㄕㄥˋ ㄕˊ ㄑㄧˊ〉
the heyday; the zenith; the prime

全數〈ㄑㄩㄢˊ ㄕㄨˋ〉
the whole amount; the total number; the sum total

全然〈ㄑㄩㄢˊ ㄖㄢˊ〉
completely (ignorant, etc.); totally: 他全然不知道這件事。He is totally ignorant of it.

全人〈ㄑㄩㄢˊ ㄖㄣˊ〉
a sage; a perfect person

全自動化〈ㄑㄩㄢˊ ㄗˋ ㄉㄨㄥˋ ㄏㄨㄚˋ〉
automation

全才〈ㄑㄩㄢˊ ㄘㄞˊ〉
an all-round talent; a master of all trades; a versatile person

全速〈ㄑㄩㄢˊ ㄙㄨˋ〉
full (or maximum) speed: 這部車以全速行駛。The car was running at full speed.

全無心肝〈ㄑㄩㄢˊ ㄨˊ ㄒㄧㄣ ㄍㄢ〉
totally heartless; totally unconscionable; absolutely ungrateful

全武行〈ㄑㄩㄢˊ ㄨˇ ㄏㄤˊ〉
a brawl; a free-for-all

全文〈ㄑㄩㄢˊ ㄨㄣˊ〉
a full text

全愈〈ㄑㄩㄢˊ ㄩˋ〉
to have completely recovered (from illness, injury, etc.)

六畫

【兩】 309 ㄌㄧㄤˇ leang liǎng

1. two; a pair; a couple: 他們只有兩人沒有通過考試。Only two of them failed in the examination.

2. both; either: 那兩所房子都是白的。Both (the) houses are white.

3. a tael (a unit of weight)

4. (in ancient China) a piece of cloth, etc. of about 44 feet

5. (in ancient China) a group of 25 soldiers

兩敗俱傷〈ㄌㄧㄤˇ ㄅㄞˋ ㄐㄩˋ ㄕㄤ〉
Both are hurt. 或 Nobody wins.

兩倍〈ㄌㄧㄤˇ ㄅㄟˋ〉
double; twice: 十是五的兩倍。Ten is the double of five.

兩半〈ㄌㄧㄤˇ ㄅㄢˋ〉
two halves: 她把蘋果切成兩半。She cut the apple in two.

兩邊〈ㄌㄧㄤˇ ㄅㄧㄢ〉or 兩旁〈ㄌㄧㄤˇ ㄆㄤˊ〉
both sides; two sides; two directions: 人群向兩邊散開了。The crowd scattered in two directions.

兩邊倒〈ㄌㄧㄤˇ ㄅㄧㄢ ㄉㄠˇ〉
(said of fence-sitting opportunists) to lean now to one side, now to the other; to sway; to waver

兩邊討好〈ㄌㄧㄤˇ ㄅㄧㄢ ㄊㄠˇ ㄏㄠˇ〉
to please both sides by saying bad things about one side in the presence of the other and vice versa

兩便〈ㄌㄧㄤˇ ㄅㄧㄢˋ〉
①to suit both parties; to be convenient to both; to profit both official and private ends ②to go Dutch

兩碼事〈ㄌㄧㄤˇ ㄇㄚˇ ㄕˋ〉
two different matters 參看「兩回事」

兩面〈ㄌㄧㄤˇ ㄇㄧㄢˋ〉or 兩面兒〈ㄌㄧㄤˇ ㄇㄧㄢˋ ㄦ〉
①two sides (of a story, etc.) ②straddling; unprincipled; double or dual (character)

兩面夾攻〈ㄌㄧㄤˇ ㄇㄧㄢˋ ㄐㄧㄚ ㄍㄨㄥ〉
to make a pincers drive

兩面作戰〈ㄌㄧㄤˇ ㄇㄧㄢˋ ㄗㄨㄛˋ ㄓㄢˋ〉
to fight on two fronts

兩黨制〈ㄌㄧㄤˇ ㄉㄤˇ ㄓˋ〉
the two-party system; the bipartisan system

兩抵〈ㄌㄧㄤˇ ㄉㄧˇ〉
to balance or cancel each other: 功過兩抵。Merits and demerits balance each other.

兩端〈ㄌㄧㄤˇ ㄉㄨㄢ〉
①from end to end; from beginning to end; the two extremities ②excess and insufficience ③vacillation; in-

〔入〕
部

decision

兩頭蛇(ㄌㄧㄤ ㄊㄡˊ ㄕㄜˊ)
①a two-headed snake ②
one who tries to hurt or
please either of two contending parties when it suits his
purpose

兩頭兒(ㄌㄧㄤ ㄊㄡˊ ㄦˊ)
both ends; either end

兩條心(ㄌㄧㄤ ㄊㄧㄠˊ ㄒㄧㄣ)
disagreement between the
two; not of one mind

兩難(ㄌㄧㄤ ㄋㄢˊ)
(literally) between two difficulties — indecisive; to be
in a dilemma

兩立(ㄌㄧㄤ ㄌㄧˋ)
to coexist; coexistence

兩姑之間難為婦(ㄌㄧㄤ ㄍㄨ ㄓ ㄐㄧㄢ
ㄋㄢˊ ㄨㄟˊ ㄈㄨˋ)
It's difficult to serve under
two bosses. 或(said of a
small nation) It's difficult to
exist between two powers.

兩廣(ㄌㄧㄤ ㄍㄨㄤˇ)or 兩粵(ㄌㄧㄤ
ㄩㄝˋ)
Kwangtung and Kwangsi

兩可(ㄌㄧㄤ ㄎㄜˇ)
two alternatives; indecisive;
indecision 或 Both (or
Either) will do.

兩口子(ㄌㄧㄤ ㄎㄡˇ ㄗ˙)or 兩口兒
(ㄌㄧㄤ ㄎㄡˇ ㄦˊ)
①a married couple; hus-
band and wife ②two per-
sons living under the same
roof

兩害相權取其輕(ㄌㄧㄤ ㄏㄞˋ ㄒㄧㄤ
ㄑㄩㄢˊ ㄑㄩˇ ㄑㄧˊ ㄑㄧㄥ)
to accept the lesser of two
evils

兩漢(ㄌㄧㄤ ㄏㄢˋ)
(history) the Former and
Later Han Dynasties

兩湖(ㄌㄧㄤ ㄏㄨˊ)
Hunan and Hupeh Provinces

兩虎相鬥必有一傷(ㄌㄧㄤ ㄏㄨˇ
ㄒㄧㄤ ㄉㄡˋ ㄅㄧˋ ㄧㄡˇ ㄧ ㄕㄤ)
When two tigers fight, one
is going to get hurt. —When
two powers battle, one is
going to get hurt.

兩淮(ㄌㄧㄤ ㄏㄨㄞˊ)
referring to areas north and
south of the Huai River

兩回事(ㄌㄧㄤ ㄏㄨㄟˊ ㄕˋ)

two entirely different things;
two different matters

兩極(ㄌㄧㄤ ㄐㄧˊ)
the opposing poles; two
extremes

兩截(ㄌㄧㄤ ㄐㄧㄝˊ)or 兩截兒(ㄌㄧㄤ
ㄐㄧㄝˊ ㄦˊ)
two pieces; in two pieces

兩腳規(ㄌㄧㄤ ㄐㄧㄠˇ ㄍㄨㄟ)or 圓規
(ㄩㄢˊ ㄍㄨㄟ)
compasses; dividers

兩腳書櫥(ㄌㄧㄤ ㄐㄧㄠˇ ㄕㄨ ㄔㄨˊ)
①a two-legged bookcase ②
a bookworm; a person who
cannot profit by what he
reads

兩晉(ㄌㄧㄤ ㄐㄧㄣˋ)
(history) the Western Tsin
and the Eastern Tsin
Dynasties

兩江(ㄌㄧㄤ ㄐㄧㄤ)
(Ching Dynasty) the area
covering the present-day
Kiangsu, Anhwei and Kiangsi

兩棲(ㄌㄧㄤ ㄑㄧ)
amphibious

兩棲部隊(ㄌㄧㄤ ㄑㄧ ㄅㄨˋ ㄉㄨㄟˋ)
amphibious force; amphibious troops; amphibious units

兩棲類(ㄌㄧㄤ ㄑㄧ ㄌㄟˋ)
the amphibian

兩棲作戰(ㄌㄧㄤ ㄑㄧ ㄗㄨㄛˋ ㄓㄢˋ)
amphibious operations

兩歧(ㄌㄧㄤ ㄑㄧˊ)
(said of two things) do not
tally

兩訖(ㄌㄧㄤ ㄑㄧˋ)or 兩清(ㄌㄧㄤ
ㄑㄧㄥ)
(said of a purchase) paid
and delivered; (said of an
account) both sides clear

兩情繾綣(ㄌㄧㄤ ㄑㄧㄥˊ ㄑㄧㄢˇ ㄑㄩㄢˇ)
deeply in love with each
other

兩全(ㄌㄧㄤ ㄑㄩㄢˊ)
to be satisfactory to both
parties: 這是個兩全的辦法。
This is a measure satisfactory to both sides.

兩全其美(ㄌㄧㄤ ㄑㄩㄢˊ ㄑㄧˊ ㄇㄟˇ)
to profit both parties or
attain two objectives by a
single act

兩權分立(ㄌㄧㄤ ㄑㄩㄢˊ ㄈㄣ ㄌㄧˋ)
a political system under
which the legislative and

executive branches are independent of each other

兩下子(ㄌㄧㄤ ㄒㄧㄚˋ ㄗ˙)
①in a few minutes ②a few
tricks of the trade

兩小無猜(ㄌㄧㄤ ㄒㄧㄠˇ ㄨˊ ㄘㄞ)
(said of a young boy and a
little girl) living and playing
together in childhood innocence 或 Two innocent ones,
a boy and a girl, grew up
together.

兩袖清風(ㄌㄧㄤ ㄒㄧㄡˋ ㄑㄧㄥ ㄈㄥ)
(usually said of an honest
public servant) to attain
high official ranks without
money in the bank

兩性(ㄌㄧㄤ ㄒㄧㄥˋ)
①both sexes ②amphoteric

兩性花(ㄌㄧㄤ ㄒㄧㄥˋ ㄏㄨㄚ)
a bisexual flower; a her-
maphrodite flower

兩相好(ㄌㄧㄤ ㄒㄧㄤ ㄏㄠˇ)
two lovers

兩相情願(ㄌㄧㄤ ㄒㄧㄤ ㄑㄧㄥˊ ㄩㄢˋ)
Both parties are willing.

兩浙(ㄌㄧㄤ ㄓㄜˋ)
the eastern and western
parts of Chekiang Province

兩重(ㄌㄧㄤ ㄔㄨㄥˊ)
double; dual; twofold: 他有兩
重性格。He has a dual
nature.

兩手(ㄌㄧㄤ ㄕㄡˇ)
dual tactics

兩造(ㄌㄧㄤ ㄗㄠˋ)
the plaintiff and the defendant; parties to a contract or
lawsuit

兩側(ㄌㄧㄤ ㄘㄜˋ)
two sides

兩耳不聞窗外事(ㄌㄧㄤ ㄦˇ ㄅㄨˋ ㄨㄣˊ
ㄔㄨㄤ ㄨㄞˋ ㄕˋ)
to care nothing outside one's
window—One does not care
what is going on beyond
one's own surroundings.

兩儀(ㄌㄧㄤ ㄧˊ)
the yin (陰) and the yang
(陽), the two polarities

兩翼(ㄌㄧㄤ ㄧˋ)
(a military term) two flanks
or wings

兩樣(ㄌㄧㄤ ㄧㄤˋ)
①two kinds; two different
things ② different: 兩樣作法
產生兩種結果。Two different

methods produce two different results.

兩院制 (ㄌㄧㄢˇ ㄩㄢˋ ㄓˋ)
the bicameral system (of a parliament)

兩用 (ㄌㄧㄤˇ ㄩㄥˋ)
① (said of an instrument, a gadget, etc.) serving two purposes; a dual purpose ② (said of a coat) reversible:
兩用夾克 a reversible jacket

七畫

【兪】310 (ㄩˊ yú yù)

1. to answer in the affirmative
2. to make a boat by hollowing the log
3. a Chinese family name
兪允 (ㄩˊ ㄩㄣˇ)
to consent; to approve

八 部
ㄅㄚ ba bā

【八】311 ㄅㄚ ba bā
(變讀 ㄅㄚ bar bā)
eight

八百羅漢 (ㄅㄚ ㄅㄞ ㄌㄨㄛˊ ㄏㄢˋ)
the eight hundred Buddhist saints

八拜之交 (ㄅㄚ ㄅㄞ ㄓ ㄐㄧㄠ)
sworn brotherhood

八寶飯 (ㄅㄚ ㄅㄠˇ ㄈㄢ)
rice cooked with eight ingredients

八病 (ㄅㄚ ㄅㄧㄥˋ)
the eight taboos of poetry listed by Shen Yüeh (沈約) of the Liang Dynasty

八面體 (ㄅㄚ ㄇㄧㄢˋ ㄊㄧˇ)
an octahedron

八面玲瓏 (ㄅㄚ ㄇㄧㄢˋ ㄌㄧㄥˊ ㄌㄨㄥˊ)
to be pleasant all round; well polished and elegant throughout; to be a perfect mixer in any company

八面威風 (ㄅㄚ ㄇㄧㄢˋ ㄨㄟ ㄈㄥ)
influential in every quarter; having an awe-inspiring reputation everywhere; to make an magnificent appearance

八方 (ㄅㄚ ㄈㄤ) or 八區 (ㄅㄚ ㄑㄩ)
the eight points of the compass; all directions

八大行星 (ㄅㄚ ㄉㄚˋ ㄒㄧㄥˊ ㄒㄧㄥ)
the eight major planets of the solar system — Mercury, Venus, Earth, Mars, Jupiter, Saturn, Uranus, and Neptune

八大山人 (ㄅㄚ ㄉㄚˋ ㄕㄢ ㄖㄣˊ)
the pseudonym of Chu Ta (朱耷), a famous painter of the late Ming Dynasty

八代之衰 (ㄅㄚ ㄉㄞˋ ㄓ ㄕㄨㄞ)
(literally) the decline of the eight dynasties from Eastern Han (東漢) to Sui (隋) — the dark age in Chinese literature

八斗之才 (ㄅㄚ ㄉㄡˇ ㄓ ㄘㄞˊ)
(literally) a person with eight bushels of talent — a very talented or gifted person

八哥 (ㄅㄚ ㄍㄜ) or 八哥兒 (ㄅㄚ ㄍㄜ ㄦ)
a mynah

八股 (ㄅㄚ ㄍㄨˇ)
corny; lacking in originality

八股文 (ㄅㄚ ㄍㄨˇ ㄨㄣˊ)
the eight-legged essay (originally, a style of rigid literary writing during the era of Imperial Examination; hence, writings that reek of pedantry or triteness)

八卦 (ㄅㄚ ㄍㄨㄚˋ)
the Eight Diagrams, consisting of an arrangement of single and divided lines in eight groups of three lines each as specified in the *Book of Changes* — 乾(☰), 兌(☱), 離(☲), 震(☳), 巽(☴), 坎(☵), 艮(☶), 坤(☷)

八國聯軍 (ㄅㄚ ㄍㄨㄛˊ ㄌㄧㄢˊ ㄐㄩㄣ)
the joint forces of the eight powers which occupied Peking in the wake of the Boxer Movement in 1900

八開 (ㄅㄚ ㄎㄞ)
octavo (books, paper, etc.)

八行書 (ㄅㄚ ㄏㄤˊ ㄕㄨ)
a letter of eight lines — a formal letter to recommend someone for a post; a letter of recommendation

八紘一宇 (ㄅㄚ ㄏㄨㄥˊ ㄧ ㄩˇ)
to unite the whole world under one sovereign by force of arms

八戒 (ㄅㄚ ㄐㄧㄝˋ)
(Buddhism) the first eight of the Ten Prohibitions

八角 (ㄅㄚ ㄐㄧㄠˇ)
Japanese star anise, a kind of spice

八角形 (ㄅㄚ ㄐㄧㄠˇ ㄒㄧㄥˊ)
an octagon

八九不離十 (ㄅㄚ ㄐㄧㄡˇ ㄅㄨˋ ㄌㄧˊ ㄕˊ)
pretty close; very near; about right

八旗 (ㄅㄚ ㄑㄧˊ)
the eight banners (of the Manchu troops identified by the color of the banner — each banner roughly corresponding to a modern division)

八仙 (ㄅㄚ ㄒㄧㄢ)
the Eight Immortals of Taoism (namely, 漢鍾離, 張果老, 韓湘子, 曹國舅, 李鐵拐, 藍采和, 呂洞賓, 何仙姑)

八仙桌 (ㄅㄚ ㄒㄧㄢ ㄓㄨㄛ)
a square dining table for eight persons

八陣圖 (ㄅㄚ ㄓㄣˋ ㄊㄨˊ)
a military tactics worked out by Chu-Ko Kung-ming (諸葛孔明), a military genius during the period of the Three Kingdoms

八成 (ㄅㄚ ㄔㄥˊ)
(literally) eighty per cent — nearly; almost; very likely; most probably: 事情有八成了. It's almost settled.

八十至八十九歲的人 (ㄅㄚ ㄕˊ ㄓˋ ㄅㄚ ㄕˊ ㄐㄧㄡˇ ㄙㄨㄟˋ ㄉㄜ ㄖㄣˊ)
an octogenarian

八字 (ㄅㄚ ㄗˋ) or 八字兒 (ㄅㄚ ㄗˋ ㄦ)
a general term for the Celestial Stems and the Terrestrial Branches (干支), denoting the time, date, month and year of a person's birth; now used by fortuneteller as a reference to see if the betrothed are well matched; the horoscope

八字鬍 (ㄅㄚ ㄗˋ ㄏㄨˊ)
mustaches shaped roughly like the character 八

八音 (ㄅㄚ ㄧㄣ)

〔八部〕

〔八部〕

eight kinds of musical sounds—produced from the calabash, earthenware, stretched hides, wood, stone, metal, silk strings and bamboo

八音盒(ㄅㄚ ㄧㄣ ㄏㄜˊ)
a music box

八王之亂(ㄅㄚ ㄨㄤˊ ㄓ ㄌㄨㄢˋ)
The Upheaval of the Eight Princes—during the West Tsin Dynasty (265-313 A.D.), when major feudal lords rose and fought each other

八月(ㄅㄚ ㄩㄝˋ)
① August ② eight months ③ the eighth month of the lunar calendar

二畫

【公】 312
(ㄍㄨㄥ gong gōng)
1. unselfish; unbiased; fair
2. to make public; open to all
3. public
4. the first of old China's five-grades of the nobility; an old Chinese official rank
5. the father of one's husband (one's husband's father); one's father-in-law
6. one's grandfather
7. a respectful salutation
8. the male (of animals)
9. office; official duties: 他因公出差。He took an offical trip.
10. a Chinese family name

公倍數(ㄍㄨㄥ ㄅㄟˋ ㄕㄨˋ)
(mathematics) a common multiple

公保(ㄍㄨㄥ ㄅㄠˇ)
government insurance for public servants

公報(ㄍㄨㄥ ㄅㄠˋ)
an official bulletin; a gazette; a communiqué

公報私仇(ㄍㄨㄥ ㄅㄠˋ ㄙ ㄔㄡˊ)
to avenge oneself on one's enemies in the name of public interests

公布 or 公佈(ㄍㄨㄥ ㄅㄨˋ)
to make public; to promulgate; to announce

公婆(ㄍㄨㄥ ㄆㄛˊ)
the parents of one's husband

公平(ㄍㄨㄥ ㄆㄧㄥˊ)
fair; unbiased; just

公僕(ㄍㄨㄥ ㄆㄨˊ)
a public servant; an official

公馬(ㄍㄨㄥ ㄇㄚˇ)
a stallion (not castrated); a gelding (castrated)

公賣品(ㄍㄨㄥ ㄇㄞˋ ㄆㄧㄣˇ)
a government monopoly

公賣局(ㄍㄨㄥ ㄇㄞˋ ㄐㄩˊ)
a government monopoly bureau

公貓(ㄍㄨㄥ ㄇㄠ)
a tom; a tomcat

公民(ㄍㄨㄥ ㄇㄧㄣˊ)
citizens

公民投票(ㄍㄨㄥ ㄇㄧㄣˊ ㄊㄡˊ ㄆㄧㄠˋ)
the referendum; the plebiscite

公民科(ㄍㄨㄥ ㄇㄧㄣˊ ㄎㄜ)
civics

公民權(ㄍㄨㄥ ㄇㄧㄣˊ ㄑㄩㄢˊ)
civil rights—including election, recall, referendum and initiative

公畝(ㄍㄨㄥ ㄇㄡˇ)
an area of 100 meters square

公墓(ㄍㄨㄥ ㄇㄨˋ)
①a public cemetery ②(in ancient China) tombs or graveyards of kings or the nobility

公法(ㄍㄨㄥ ㄈㄚˇ)
public law

公費(ㄍㄨㄥ ㄈㄟˋ)
public funds; government funds; government scholarships

公分(ㄍㄨㄥ ㄈㄣ)
①a centimeter (cm.) ② a gram (g.)

公分母(ㄍㄨㄥ ㄈㄣ ㄇㄨˇ)
a common denominator

公分子(ㄍㄨㄥ ㄈㄣ ㄗˇ)
a common numerator

公憤(ㄍㄨㄥ ㄈㄣˋ)
public indignation

公德(ㄍㄨㄥ ㄉㄜˊ)
social morality; social ethics

公德心(ㄍㄨㄥ ㄉㄜˊ ㄒㄧㄣ)
regard for public welfare; public-mindedness

公道(ㄍㄨㄥ ㄉㄠˋ)
①justice ②reasonable (prices); just; fair; impartial

公斗(ㄍㄨㄥ ㄉㄡˇ)
a decaliter

公石(ㄍㄨㄥ ㄉㄢˋ)
a hectoliter

公擔(ㄍㄨㄥ ㄉㄢˋ)
a quintal

公敵(ㄍㄨㄥ ㄉㄧˊ)
a public enemy

公牘(ㄍㄨㄥ ㄉㄨˊ)
official documents; official letters or correspondence

公噸(ㄍㄨㄥ ㄉㄨㄣˋ)
a metric ton

公攤(ㄍㄨㄥ ㄊㄢ)
to share (expenditures, capital investment, etc.) equally

公堂(ㄍㄨㄥ ㄊㄤˊ)
a court of law

公天下(ㄍㄨㄥ ㄊㄧㄢ ㄒㄧㄚˋ)
the world belongs to all the people

公聽會(ㄍㄨㄥ ㄊㄧㄥ ㄏㄨㄟˋ)
a public hearing

公兔(ㄍㄨㄥ ㄊㄨˋ)
a buck

公推(ㄍㄨㄥ ㄊㄨㄟ)
to recommend by general acclaim

公牛(ㄍㄨㄥ ㄋㄧㄡˊ)
a bull; a bullock; an ox

公老虎(ㄍㄨㄥ ㄌㄠˇ ㄏㄨˇ)
a tiger

公狼(ㄍㄨㄥ ㄌㄤˊ)
a he-wolf

公釐(ㄍㄨㄥ ㄌㄧˊ)
① a millimeter ② an area of one square meter

公里(ㄍㄨㄥ ㄌㄧˇ)
a kilometer

公理(ㄍㄨㄥ ㄌㄧˇ)
①a universal principle; generally accepted truth; right; justice ②(mathematics) an axiom

公立學校(ㄍㄨㄥ ㄌㄧˋ ㄒㄩㄝˊ ㄒㄧㄠˋ)
public schools

公兩(ㄍㄨㄥ ㄌㄧㄤˇ)
100 grams

公鹿(ㄍㄨㄥ ㄌㄨˋ)
a stag; a hart; a buck

公路(ㄍㄨㄥ ㄌㄨˋ)
a highway

公論(ㄍㄨㄥ ㄌㄨㄣˋ)
public opinion: 是非曲直自有公論。Public opinion is the best judge.

公合(ㄍㄨㄥ ㄍㄜˊ)
a deciliter

公告《ㄍㄨㄥ ㄍㄠˋ》
① a proclamation; a public announcement ② to make an announcement

公告地價《ㄍㄨㄥ ㄍㄠˋ ㄉㄧˋ ㄐㄧㄚˋ》
a government-assessed land price

公狗《ㄍㄨㄥ ㄍㄡˇ》
a dog

公幹《ㄍㄨㄥ ㄍㄢˋ》
an official assignment or duty; official business

公館《ㄍㄨㄥ ㄍㄨㄢˇ》
① an official residence ② a residence (a polite reference to other's residence); a mansion ③ Kungkuan, a suburban district of Taipei ④ Kungkuan in central Taiwan, the site of a big air base

公共《ㄍㄨㄥ ㄍㄨㄥˋ》
public (relations, health, etc.); owned and shared by all

公共電視《ㄍㄨㄥ ㄍㄨㄥˋ ㄉㄧㄢˋ ㄕˋ》
public television

公共投資《ㄍㄨㄥ ㄍㄨㄥˋ ㄊㄡˊ ㄗ》
public investment

公共利益《ㄍㄨㄥ ㄍㄨㄥˋ ㄌㄧˋ ㄧˋ》
public interests

公共關係《ㄍㄨㄥ ㄍㄨㄥˋ ㄍㄨㄢ ㄒㄧˋ》
public relations (PR)

公共汽車《ㄍㄨㄥ ㄍㄨㄥˋ ㄑㄧˋ ㄔㄜ》
a bus; an omnibus

公共行政《ㄍㄨㄥ ㄍㄨㄥˋ ㄒㄧㄥˊ ㄓㄥˋ》
public administration

公共秩序《ㄍㄨㄥ ㄍㄨㄥˋ ㄓˋ ㄒㄩˋ》
public order; public peace and order

公共事業《ㄍㄨㄥ ㄍㄨㄥˋ ㄕˋ ㄧㄝˋ》
public utilities

公共租界《ㄍㄨㄥ ㄍㄨㄥˋ ㄗㄨ ㄐㄧㄝˋ》
the International Settlement in Shanghai

公共財產《ㄍㄨㄥ ㄍㄨㄥˋ ㄘㄞˊ ㄔㄢˇ》
public property

公共衛生《ㄍㄨㄥ ㄍㄨㄥˋ ㄨㄟˋ ㄕㄥ》
public health; public sanitation; public hygiene

公公《ㄍㄨㄥ ㄍㄨㄥ》
① one's grandfather ② the father of one's husband ③ a respectful designation for an elder ④ a eunuch

公克《ㄍㄨㄥ ㄎㄜˋ》
a gram

公開《ㄍㄨㄥ ㄎㄞ》
to make known to the public; to make public; open (letters, etc.); to exhibit; openly; publicly: 他做了公開演講。He gave a public lecture.

公款《ㄍㄨㄥ ㄎㄨㄢˇ》
public funds; public money

公海《ㄍㄨㄥ ㄏㄞˇ》
the high seas

公害《ㄍㄨㄥ ㄏㄞˋ》
social effects of pollution; environmental pollution; a public nuisance

公毫《ㄍㄨㄥ ㄏㄠˊ》
a centigram

公函《ㄍㄨㄥ ㄏㄢˊ》
an official letter

公衡《ㄍㄨㄥ ㄏㄥˊ》
ten kilograms

公會《ㄍㄨㄥ ㄏㄨㄟˋ》
a union, league, society, federation, etc. of a certain trade, as lawyers, medical practitioners, etc.

公雞《ㄍㄨㄥ ㄐㄧ》
a cock; a rooster

公祭《ㄍㄨㄥ ㄐㄧˋ》
a public memorial ceremony

公家《ㄍㄨㄥ ㄐㄧㄚ》
the nation, government, state, public, etc. as distinct from the private

公價《ㄍㄨㄥ ㄐㄧㄚˋ》
an official or controlled price

公教人員《ㄍㄨㄥ ㄐㄧㄠˋ ㄖㄣˊ ㄩㄢˊ》
government employees and staffs of public schools

公斤《ㄍㄨㄥ ㄐㄧㄣ》
a kilogram (kg)

公決《ㄍㄨㄥ ㄐㄩㄝˊ》
a common decision; to decide by majority

公爵《ㄍㄨㄥ ㄐㄩㄝˊ》
a duke

公爵夫人《ㄍㄨㄥ ㄐㄩㄝˊ ㄈㄨ ㄖㄣˊ》
a duchess

公錢《ㄍㄨㄥ ㄑㄧㄢˊ》
a decagram

公卿《ㄍㄨㄥ ㄑㄧㄥ》
(in ancient China) officials of higher ranks; high-ranking officials

公頃《ㄍㄨㄥ ㄑㄧㄥˇ》
a hectare (ha)

公權《ㄍㄨㄥ ㄑㄩㄢˊ》
civil rights; civic rights

公休《ㄍㄨㄥ ㄒㄧㄡ》
① an official holiday ② a holiday for a particular trade

公信力《ㄍㄨㄥ ㄒㄧㄣˋ ㄌㄧˋ》
government credibility

公象《ㄍㄨㄥ ㄒㄧㄤˋ》
a male elephant; a bull elephant

公職《ㄍㄨㄥ ㄓˊ》
government offices; official posts or ranks; (under) government employment

公制《ㄍㄨㄥ ㄓˋ》
the metric system

公債《ㄍㄨㄥ ㄓㄞˋ》
① government bonds ② the public debt

公丈《ㄍㄨㄥ ㄓㄤˋ》
a decameter

公正《ㄍㄨㄥ ㄓㄥˋ》
justice; fairness; just; impartial

公證《ㄍㄨㄥ ㄓㄥˋ》
to legalize an act or document by a notary public; to notarize

公證結婚《ㄍㄨㄥ ㄓㄥˋ ㄐㄧㄝˊ ㄏㄨㄣ》
marriages before the justice of the peace; a court wedding

公證人《ㄍㄨㄥ ㄓㄥˋ ㄖㄣˊ》
a notary public; a witness

公豬《ㄍㄨㄥ ㄓㄨ》
a boar

公諸同好《ㄍㄨㄥ ㄓㄨ ㄊㄨㄥˊ ㄏㄠˋ》
to make (a recipe, manufacturing process, etc.) public for the benefit of kindred spirits; to share what one cherishes with those of the same taste

公主《ㄍㄨㄥ ㄓㄨˇ》
a princess

公轉《ㄍㄨㄥ ㄓㄨㄢˇ》
(said of the earth or other major planets) to revolve around the sun

公忠體國《ㄍㄨㄥ ㄓㄨㄥ ㄊㄧˇ ㄍㄨㄛˊ》
to be loyal to one's country

公眾《ㄍㄨㄥ ㄓㄨㄥˋ》
the public; the general pub-

lic; the community

公尺(《ㄨㄥ ㄔˇ)
a meter

公差
①(《ㄨㄥ ㄔ万)official assignments (usually involving travel)
②(《ㄨㄥ ㄔㄚ)(mathematics) common difference

〔八部〕

公產(《ㄨㄥ ㄔㄢˇ)
government or public property

公娼(《ㄨㄥ ㄔㄤ)
a licensed prostitute; licensed prostitution

公出(《ㄨㄥ ㄔㄨ)
to be away on official duties or business

公獅(《ㄨㄥ ㄕ)
a lion

公使(《ㄨㄥ ㄕˇ)
(diplomacy) a minister; an envoy

公使館(《ㄨㄥ ㄕˇ 《ㄨㄢˇ)
a legation

公式(《ㄨㄥ ㄕˋ)
a formula

公式化(《ㄨㄥ ㄕˋ ㄏㄨㄚˋ)
stereotyped; formulistic; to put in formulas

公事(《ㄨㄥ ㄕˋ)
official business; public affairs

公事包(《ㄨㄥ ㄕˋ ㄅㄠ)
an attaché case; a briefcase

公事房(《ㄨㄥ ㄕˋ ㄈㄤˊ)
an office

公事公辦(《ㄨㄥ ㄕˋ 《ㄨㄥ ㄅㄢˋ)
to discharge official duties strictly according to rules

公示催告(《ㄨㄥ ㄕˋ ㄘㄨㄟ 《ㄠˋ)
(law) a public summons

公示送達(《ㄨㄥ ㄕˋ ㄙㄨㄥˋ ㄉㄚˊ)
(law) service by public notification

公社(《ㄨㄥ ㄕㄜˋ)
a commune

公設辯護人(《ㄨㄥ ㄕㄜˋ ㄅㄧㄢˋ ㄏㄨˋ ㄖㄣˊ)
a public defense counsel

公山羊(《ㄨㄥ ㄕㄢ ㄧㄤˊ)
a he-goat

公審(《ㄨㄥ ㄕㄣˇ)
a public trial

公升(《ㄨㄥ ㄕㄥ)
a liter

公署(《ㄨㄥ ㄕㄨˇ)
a government office

公說公有理，婆說婆有理(《ㄨㄥ ㄕㄨㄛ 《ㄨㄥ ㄧㄡˇ ㄌㄧˇ，ㄆㄛˊ ㄕㄨㄛ ㄆㄛˊ ㄧㄡˇ ㄌㄧˇ)
In the presence of a superior, umpire, etc., each of two quarreling parties insists that he is right.

公然(《ㄨㄥ ㄖㄢˊ)
openly; in public

公認(《ㄨㄥ ㄖㄣˋ)
generally recognized; universally accepted; established

公子(《ㄨㄥ ㄗˇ)
①(in ancient China) sons of a duke or a ranking official
②a polite designation for another's son or sons

公子哥兒(《ㄨㄥ ㄗˇ 《ㄜ ㄦ)
sons of the rich or powerful; dandies; playboys

公子王孫(《ㄨㄥ ㄗˇ ㄨㄤˊ ㄙㄨㄣ)
sons of the rich or powerful

公廁(《ㄨㄥ ㄘㄜˋ)
a public lavatory

公寸(《ㄨㄥ ㄘㄨㄣˋ)
a decimeter

公絲(《ㄨㄥ ㄙ)
a milligram

公司(《ㄨㄥ ㄙ)
a company; a corporation

公司法(《ㄨㄥ ㄙ ㄈㄚˇ)
company law

公私不分(《ㄨㄥ ㄙ ㄅㄨˋ ㄈㄣ)
to make no distinction between public and private interests

公私分明(《ㄨㄥ ㄙ ㄈㄣ ㄇㄧㄥˊ)
to be scrupulous in separating public from private interests

公私兩便(《ㄨㄥ ㄙ ㄌㄧㄤˇ ㄅㄧㄢˋ)
advantageous to both public and private interests

公私合營(《ㄨㄥ ㄙ ㄏㄜˊ ㄧㄥˊ)
state and private joint ownership

公訴(《ㄨㄥ ㄙㄨˋ)
public prosecution; public indictment

公算(《ㄨㄥ ㄙㄨㄢˋ)
the law of probability

公孫(《ㄨㄥ ㄙㄨㄣ)
a Chinese family name

公鵝(《ㄨㄥ ㄜˊ)
a gander

公安(《ㄨㄥ ㄢ)
public security

公安局(《ㄨㄥ ㄢ ㄐㄩˊ)
a police department

公案(《ㄨㄥ ㄢˋ)
①a case of law ②office desks ③official business

公爾忘私(《ㄨㄥ ㄦˇ ㄨㄤˋ ㄙ)or 公而忘私(《ㄨㄥ ㄦˊ ㄨㄤˋ ㄙ)
to forget oneself in the discharge of official duties; selfless

公益(《ㄨㄥ ㄧˋ)
public interests or welfare; public good; community benefit

公議(《ㄨㄥ ㄧˋ)
① public discussion ② discussion of national or public affairs ③ open negotiations (for prices, terms, specifications, etc.) as contrasted to a tender

公鴨(《ㄨㄥ ㄧㄚ)
a drake

公有(《ㄨㄥ ㄧㄡˇ)
publicly-owned; public

公有土地(《ㄨㄥ ㄧㄡˇ ㄊㄨˇ ㄉㄧˋ)or 公地(《ㄨㄥ ㄉㄧˋ)
public land

公演(《ㄨㄥ ㄧㄢˇ)
to stage shows for public viewing; to perform in public

公宴(《ㄨㄥ ㄧㄢˋ)
to honor a celebrity at a dinner party or luncheon hosted by a club, government organization, etc.

公引(《ㄨㄥ ㄧㄣˇ)
a hectometer

公羊(《ㄨㄥ ㄧㄤˊ)
①a ram ②a Chinese family name

公羊傳(《ㄨㄥ ㄧㄤˊ ㄓㄨㄢˋ)
Spring and Autumn Annals with Commentary by Kung-Yang Kao (公羊高), one of the three expansions of Confucius' Spring and Autumn Annals (春秋)

公營(《ㄨㄥ ㄧㄥˊ)
publicly-owned

公營事業(《ㄨㄥ ㄧㄥˊ ㄕˋ ㄧㄝˋ)
public enterprises; govern-

ment-owned enterprises

公物《《ㄍㄨㄥ ㄨ》
public or government property

公務《ㄍㄨㄥ ㄨ》
public business; official matters, business, duties, etc.

公務員《ㄍㄨㄥ ㄨ ㄩㄢ》
government employees; civil servants

公務員懲誡委員會《ㄍㄨㄥ ㄨ ㄩㄢ ㄔㄥ ㄐㄧㄝˋ ㄨㄟˇ ㄩㄢˊ ㄏㄨㄟˋ》
the Committee on the Discipline of Public Functionaries

公文《ㄍㄨㄥ ㄨㄣˊ》
official documents

公餘《ㄍㄨㄥ ㄩˊ》
after office hours

公寓《ㄍㄨㄥ ㄩˋ》
an apartment house

公約《ㄍㄨㄥ ㄩㄝ》
① a treaty; a covenant; a convention; a pact ② joint pledge

公約數《ㄍㄨㄥ ㄩㄝ ㄕㄨˋ》
(mathematics) a common factor

公元《ㄍㄨㄥ ㄩㄢˊ》
in the year of our Lord…; the Christian era

公園《ㄍㄨㄥ ㄩㄢˊ》
a park; a public garden

公允《ㄍㄨㄥ ㄩㄣˇ》
fair and proper; just and sound

公用《ㄍㄨㄥ ㄩㄥˋ》
public (telephones, etc.); for public use

公用電話《ㄍㄨㄥ ㄩㄥˋ ㄉㄧㄢˋ ㄏㄨㄚˋ》
a public telephone

公用事業《ㄍㄨㄥ ㄩㄥˋ ㄕˋ ㄧㄝˋ》
public utilities

313
【六】 ㄌㄧㄡˋ liow liù
（讀音 ㄌㄨˋ luh lù)
six

六邊形《ㄌㄧㄡˋ ㄅㄧㄢ ㄒㄧㄥˊ》
a hexagon

六轡在手《ㄌㄧㄡˋ ㄆㄟˋ ㄗㄞˋ ㄕㄡˇ》
to hold all the trump cards; to have complete power over others

六面體《ㄌㄧㄡˋ ㄇㄧㄢˋ ㄊㄧˇ》
a hexahedron

六法全書《ㄌㄧㄡˋ ㄈㄚˇ ㄑㄩㄢˊ ㄕㄨ》
The Complete Volume of Six Laws—an omnibus of modern Chinese laws

六分儀《ㄌㄧㄡˋ ㄈㄣ ㄧˊ》
a sextant

六大洲《ㄌㄧㄡˋ ㄉㄚˋ ㄓㄡ》
the six continents of the world

六根《ㄌㄧㄡˋ ㄍㄣ》
(Buddhism) the six senses —eyes, ears, nose, tongue, body and mind

六根清淨《ㄌㄧㄡˋ ㄍㄣ ㄑㄧㄥ ㄐㄧㄥˋ》
the purification of the six indriyas or sense organs—(said of a Buddha) free from human desires and passions

六國《ㄌㄧㄡˋ ㄍㄨㄛˊ》
six of the seven major kingdoms during the Warring States Period annexed by the state of Chin (秦)

六宮《ㄌㄧㄡˋ ㄍㄨㄥ》
Six Palaces — a general name for the palaces where the queen and other wives of the emperor lived; the imperial harems

六合《ㄌㄧㄡˋ ㄏㄜˊ》
① the Six Realms (north, south, east, west, up and down)—(in) the whole wide world ② name of a subprefecture in Kiangsu Province

六角形《ㄌㄧㄡˋ ㄐㄧㄠˇ ㄒㄧㄥˊ》
a hexagon

六經《ㄌㄧㄡˋ ㄐㄧㄥ》
the Six Books of Chinese classics—the *Book of Poetry* (詩), the *Book of History* (書), the *Book of Changes* (易), the *Book of Rites* (禮), the *Book of Music* (樂), the *Spring and Autumn Annals* (春秋)

六親《ㄌㄧㄡˋ ㄑㄧㄣ》
the six relations —father, mother, elder brothers, younger brothers, wife, children

六親不認《ㄌㄧㄡˋ ㄑㄧㄣ ㄅㄨˋ ㄖㄣˋ》
not to recognize one's own closest relatives—cold and arrogant

六親無靠《ㄌㄧㄡˋ ㄑㄧㄣ ㄨˊ ㄎㄠˋ》

nobody to turn to

六情《ㄌㄧㄡˋ ㄑㄧㄥˊ》
the six emotions or feelings of a person—joy, anger, sorrow, happiness, love and hatred

六宅不安《ㄌㄧㄡˋ ㄓㄞˊ ㄅㄨˋ ㄢ》
successive family misfortunes

六尺之孤《ㄌㄧㄡˋ ㄔˇ ㄓ ㄍㄨ》
orphaned boys and girls under 15 years of age

六朝《ㄌㄧㄡˋ ㄔㄠˊ》
the Six Dynasties (222—589), which successively made Nanking their capital—Wu (吳), Eastern Tsin (東晉), Sung (宋), Chi (齊), Liang (梁), Chen (陳)

六畜《ㄌㄧㄡˋ ㄔㄨˋ》
the six domestic animals —horse, cattle, sheep, chicken, dog, and hog

六十四開《ㄌㄧㄡˋ ㄕˊ ㄙˋ ㄎㄞ》
sixty-fourmo; 64mo

六神《ㄌㄧㄡˋ ㄕㄣˊ》
the source of energy controlling the six organs (六臟)

六神無主《ㄌㄧㄡˋ ㄕㄣˊ ㄨˊ ㄓㄨˇ》
shocked; stunned out of one's wits; to be in a state of utter stupefaction

六書《ㄌㄧㄡˋ ㄕㄨ》
the six classes into which Chinese characters are divided—pictograph (象形), picture of action (指事), ideograph (會意), figurative extension of meaning (轉注), determinative-phonetics (形聲), making one form stand for another word (假借)

六一居士《ㄌㄧㄡˋ ㄧ ㄐㄩ ㄕˋ》
an alias of Ou-Yang Hsiu (歐陽修), a famous scholar of the Sung Dynasty

六藝《ㄌㄧㄡˋ ㄧˋ》
the six arts—rites (禮), music (樂), archery (射), driving of the chariot (御), learning (書), mathematics (數)—which ancient Chinese scholars were required to master

六問三推《ㄌㄧㄡˋ ㄨㄣˋ ㄙㄢ ㄊㄨㄟ》
to interrogate a criminal

〔八部〕

suspect or prisoner of war again and again

〔八部〕

六欲 or 六慾（ㄌㄧㄡˋㄩˋ）
(Buddhism) the desires originated from the six senses—eyes, ears, nose, tongue, body and mind; the six sexual attractions arising from color, form, carriage, voice, softness, and features 參看「七情六慾」

六月（ㄌㄧㄡˋㄩㄝˋ）
① June ② the sixth month of the lunar calendar ③ six months

【兮】 314
ㄒㄧ shi xī
1. an adjunct with no independent meaning, roughly equivalent to "Oh" or "Ah" in English
2. a particle of pause used in ancient poetry and still used in eulogies

四畫

【共】 315
《ㄍㄨㄥˋ gòng gòng
1. common; same
2. all; collectively
3. to share; to work together: 我與他們甘苦與共。I shared joys and sorrows with them.
4. together: 我們設法同來解決這問題吧! Let's try to get together on this problem.
5. an abbreviation of the word "Communism" or "Communist"

共謀（《ㄍㄨㄥˋㄇㄡˊ）
to scheme together; to plan together; to collaborate; to collude; collusion

共勉（《ㄍㄨㄥˋㄇㄧㄢˇ）
to encourage each other: 願共勉之。Let's encourage each other in our endeavors.

共鳴（《ㄍㄨㄥˋㄇㄧㄥˊ）
①(physics) resonance or sympathetic vibration ②(to inspire) the same feeling in others; sympathetic response or understanding

共犯（《ㄍㄨㄥˋㄈㄢˋ）
① collusion; collaboration in an act of crime ②a joint offender; an accomplice; a

confederate

共赴國難（《ㄍㄨㄥˋㄈㄨˋ《ㄨㄛˊㄋㄢˋ）
to work together to save the country in time of a national crisis

共通（《ㄍㄨㄥˋㄊㄨㄥ）
applicable to both or all

共同（《ㄍㄨㄥˋㄊㄨㄥˊ）
common; shared by all; to cooperate in (an undertaking, etc.)

共同市場（《ㄍㄨㄥˋㄊㄨㄥˊㄕˋㄔㄤˇ）
a common market; 歐洲共同市場 the European Economic Community

共同生活（《ㄍㄨㄥˋㄊㄨㄥˊㄕㄥㄏㄨㄛˊ）
to live together; collective life

共管（《ㄍㄨㄥˋ《ㄨㄢˇ）
(a state, region, etc.) under the joint control of two or more authorities

共和（《ㄍㄨㄥˋㄏㄜˊ）
a republic; the republican form of government

共和黨（《ㄍㄨㄥˋㄏㄜˊㄉㄤˇ）
the Republican Party

共和國（《ㄍㄨㄥˋㄏㄜˊ《ㄨㄛˊ）
a republic

共計（《ㄍㄨㄥˋㄐㄧˋ）
the sum total; to come to; to total; to add up to

共襄盛舉（《ㄍㄨㄥˋㄒㄧㄤˊㄕㄥˋㄐㄩˇ）
Let's all work together for this worthy project.

共享（《ㄍㄨㄥˋㄒㄧㄤˇ）
to enjoy together; to share

共振（《ㄍㄨㄥˋㄓㄣˋ）
resonance

共產黨（《ㄍㄨㄥˋㄔㄢˇㄉㄤˇ）
the Communist Party

共產國際（《ㄍㄨㄥˋㄔㄢˇ《ㄨㄛˊㄐㄧˋ）
the Communist International; the Comintern

共產主義（《ㄍㄨㄥˋㄔㄢˇㄓㄨˇㄧˋ）
Communism

共處（《ㄍㄨㄥˋㄔㄨˇ）
to coexist

共事（《ㄍㄨㄥˋㄕˋ）
①to work together; to work in the same office; to be colleagues ②(said of women) to share the same husband; to be the wives of one man

共識（《ㄍㄨㄥˋㄕˊ）

common consensus

共商（《ㄍㄨㄥˋㄕㄤ）
to discuss together; to hold a joint discussion

共存（《ㄍㄨㄥˋㄘㄨㄣˊ）
to coexist; coexistent; co-existence

共存亡（《ㄍㄨㄥˋㄘㄨㄣˊㄨㄤˊ）
(to defend a city or place) to the last man; to live or die together

共有（《ㄍㄨㄥˋㄧㄡˇ）
owned by all; owned by both; common (traits, customs, etc.)

共營（《ㄍㄨㄥˋㄧㄥˊ）
joint operation

五畫

【兵】 316
ㄅㄧㄥ bing bing
1. arms; weapons
2. a soldier; a serviceman; the military
3. to strike; to attack
4. a piece in Chinese chess—a pawn

兵變（ㄅㄧㄥㄅㄧㄢˋ）
mutiny; troops in mutiny

兵不血刃（ㄅㄧㄥㄅㄨˋㄒㄩㄝˋㄖㄣˋ）
(to achieve military objective) without firing a shot in anger or without bloodshed; to win victory without firing a shot

兵不厭詐（ㄅㄧㄥㄅㄨˋㄧㄢˋㄓㄚˋ）
Trickery is no vice in military operations. 或All is fair in war.

兵不由將（ㄅㄧㄥㄅㄨˋㄧㄡˊㄐㄧㄤˋ）
disobedient soldiers; troops that do not obey orders

兵馬（ㄅㄧㄥㄇㄚˇ）
troops and horses—armaments

兵馬未動，糧草先行（ㄅㄧㄥㄇㄚˇㄨㄟˋㄉㄨㄥˋㄌㄧㄤˊㄘㄠˇㄒㄧㄢㄒㄧㄥˊ）
Provisions and fodder should go before troops and horses.—We should make preparations before we embark on anything.

兵馬俑（ㄅㄧㄥㄇㄚˇㄩㄥˇ）
wood or clay figures of soldiers and horses buried with the dead

兵法(ㄅㄧㄥ ㄈㄚˇ)or 兵略(ㄅㄧㄥ ㄌㄩㄝˋ)
military tactics and strategy

兵符(ㄅㄧㄥ ㄈㄨˊ)
a commander's seal

兵多將廣(ㄅㄧㄥ ㄉㄨㄛ ㄐㄧㄤ ㄍㄨㄤˇ)
(said of military troops) to enjoy numerical superiority

兵團(ㄅㄧㄥ ㄊㄨㄢˊ)
a large (military) unit; corps; a legion

兵力(ㄅㄧㄥ ㄌㄧˋ)
military strength

兵連禍結(ㄅㄧㄥ ㄌㄧㄢˊ ㄏㄨㄛˋ ㄐㄧㄝˊ)
continuous war ravages; constantly ravaged by war

兵臨城下(ㄅㄧㄥ ㄌㄧㄣˊ ㄔㄥˊ ㄒㄧㄚˋ)
The attacking army has reached the city gates.

兵貴神速(ㄅㄧㄥ ㄍㄨㄟˋ ㄕㄣˊ ㄙㄨˋ)
Mobility is the most important thing in fighting a war. 或 Speed is precious in war.

兵工廠(ㄅㄧㄥ ㄍㄨㄥ ㄔㄤˇ)
an arsenal; an ammunition works

兵工署(ㄅㄧㄥ ㄍㄨㄥ ㄕㄨˇ)
the Ordnance Department (under the Logistic Command of the Chinese Army)

兵荒馬亂(ㄅㄧㄥ ㄏㄨㄤ ㄇㄚˇ ㄌㄨㄢˋ)
disorder caused by continuous military operations; the ravages of war; war rapine

兵家(ㄅㄧㄥ ㄐㄧㄚ)
① a person specialized in military operations; a strategist ② military; one of old China's nine categories of professions

兵家常事(ㄅㄧㄥ ㄐㄧㄚ ㄔㄤˊ ㄕˋ)
a commonplace in military operations; 勝敗乃兵家常事。Victory or defeat is a commonplace in military operations.

兵器(ㄅㄧㄥ ㄑㄧˋ)
weapons; arms

兵強馬壯(ㄅㄧㄥ ㄑㄧㄤˊ ㄇㄚˇ ㄓㄨㄤˋ)
strong soldiers and sturdy horses—well-equipped and well-trained troops with high morale; a well-trained and powerful army

兵權(ㄅㄧㄥ ㄑㄩㄢˊ)
authority to make military decisions; military power or leadership

兵燹(ㄅㄧㄥ ㄒㄧㄢˇ)or 兵禍(ㄅㄧㄥ ㄏㄨㄛˋ)
the ravages of soldiery; fire, havoc, disturbance caused by war

兵餉(ㄅㄧㄥ ㄒㄧㄤˇ)
① a soldier's pay ② generally, military expenses and provisions

兵學(ㄅㄧㄥ ㄒㄩㄝˊ)
military science

兵凶戰危(ㄅㄧㄥ ㄒㄩㄥ ㄓㄢˋ ㄨㄟ)
In war everybody is a loser.

兵制(ㄅㄧㄥ ㄓˋ)
the military system

兵種(ㄅㄧㄥ ㄓㄨㄥˇ)
intra-service classification of military units according to their equipment and functions

兵士(ㄅㄧㄥ ㄕˋ)
a soldier; a foot soldier

兵書(ㄅㄧㄥ ㄕㄨ)
a book on military strategy

兵戎(ㄅㄧㄥ ㄖㄨㄥˊ)
① arms; weapons ② warfare

兵戎相見(ㄅㄧㄥ ㄖㄨㄥˊ ㄒㄧㄤ ㄐㄧㄢˋ)
to resort to arms; to appeal to force

兵蟻(ㄅㄧㄥ ㄧˇ)
a dinergate; a soldier ant

兵役(ㄅㄧㄥ ㄧˋ)
(compulsory) military service

兵役法(ㄅㄧㄥ ㄧˋ ㄈㄚˇ)
conscription law; military service law

兵營(ㄅㄧㄥ ㄧㄥˊ)or 兵舍(ㄅㄧㄥ ㄕㄜˋ)
barracks; a military camp

兵源(ㄅㄧㄥ ㄩㄢˊ)
manpower as a source of conscription

六畫

【其】 *317*
(ㄑㄧˊ) chyi chí
1. a pronoun—he, she, it; they; his, her, its, their
2. this; that; the
3. an interrogative used to introduce a question

其貌不揚(ㄑㄧˊ ㄇㄠˋ ㄅㄨˋ ㄧㄤˊ)
physically unattractive; ugly in appearance

其他(ㄑㄧˊ ㄊㄚ)
the others; the rest

其他費用(ㄑㄧˊ ㄊㄚ ㄈㄟˋ ㄩㄥˋ)
other expenses

其內(ㄑㄧˊ ㄋㄟˋ)
inside

其樂無窮(ㄑㄧˊ ㄌㄜˋ ㄨˊ ㄑㄩㄥˊ)
The joy is boundless.

其來有自(ㄑㄧˊ ㄌㄞˊ ㄧㄡˇ ㄗˋ)
It did not happen by accident. 或 It may be traced to a cause or source.

其間(ㄑㄧˊ ㄐㄧㄢ)
in; among; in between; between

其情可憫(ㄑㄧˊ ㄑㄧㄥˊ ㄎㄜˇ ㄇㄧㄣˇ)
(said of one's conduct, actions, etc.) deserving sympathetic understanding or compassion

其心可誅(ㄑㄧˊ ㄒㄧㄣ ㄎㄜˇ ㄓㄨ)
devious or condemnable in intention

其中(ㄑㄧˊ ㄓㄨㄥ)
in; among; in the midst

其實(ㄑㄧˊ ㄕˊ)
in fact; as a matter of fact; actually

其人其事(ㄑㄧˊ ㄖㄣˊ ㄑㄧˊ ㄕˋ)
the man and his deeds; a biographic sketch

其次(ㄑㄧˊ ㄘˋ)
secondly; the next in order; besides

其一(ㄑㄧˊ ㄧ)
first or firstly

其餘(ㄑㄧˊ ㄩˊ)
the others; the rest; the remainder

【具】 *318*
(ㄐㄩˋ) jiuh jù
1. an appliance, implement, utensil, tool, etc.
2. talent; capability
3. to prepare; to equip
4. complete; all; the whole
5. a Chinese family name

具備(ㄐㄩˋ ㄅㄟˋ)or 具足(ㄐㄩˋ ㄗㄨˊ)
① all complete; all ready ② to have (qualifications or advantages); 她具備了當祕書的資格。She has all the qualifications for a secretary.

具保(ㄐㄩˋ ㄅㄠˇ)
(said of a defendant in a lawsuit) to complete all arrangements and proce-

dures for release on bail

具報(ㄐㄩˋ ㄅㄠˋ)
to present or prepare a complete report

具名(ㄐㄩˋ ㄇㄧㄥˊ)
①to sign ②to publish a writing, letter, etc. with a byline

具體(ㄐㄩˋ ㄊㄧˇ)
concrete (measures, results, etc.), as opposed to abstract

具體而微(ㄐㄩˋ ㄊㄧˇ ㄦˊ ㄨㄟ)
similar in shape but smaller in proportions

具結(ㄐㄩˋ ㄐㄧㄝˊ)
①to enter into a bond; to submit a pledge or guarantee to a government office for fulfilling of all obligations agreed upon ②(law) to sign a bond to tell the truth; to sign an affidavit

具有(ㄐㄩˋ ㄧㄡˇ)
to be provided with; to be supplied with

具文(ㄐㄩˋ ㄨㄣˊ)
①to prepare a document, etc. for presenting to higher authorities ②(said of agreements, pledges, contracts, etc. which are not carried out) empty words

【典】 319
ㄉㄧㄢˇ dean diǎn
1. a rule; a statute; a law; a canon
2. a tale or story from the classics; an allusion: 他的文章裏用典甚多。His writings are filled with allusions.
3. to pawn; to mortgage
4. to take charge of: 他是典試委員之一。He is a member of the committee in charge of examination affairs.

典舖(ㄉㄧㄢˇ ㄆㄨˋ)
a pawnshop

典賣(ㄉㄧㄢˇ ㄇㄞˋ)
to mortgage

典範(ㄉㄧㄢˇ ㄈㄢˋ)
a model to be followed; an example; a paragon

典當(ㄉㄧㄢˇ ㄉㄤˋ)
①to pawn ②a pawnshop

典禮(ㄉㄧㄢˇ ㄌㄧˇ)
a ceremony; a rite

典故(ㄉㄧㄢˇ ㄍㄨˋ)
an allusion (from history, old classics, etc.); an origin (of a proverb, aphorism, etc.)

典籍(ㄉㄧㄢˇ ㄐㄧˊ)
ancient books, statute-records, etc.

典刑(ㄉㄧㄢˇ ㄒㄧㄥˊ)
laws; penalties

典型(ㄉㄧㄢˇ ㄒㄧㄥˊ)
a model; a pattern; a typical example

典當(ㄉㄧㄢˇ ㄉㄤˋ)
to mortgage; to pawn

典制(ㄉㄧㄢˇ ㄓˋ)or典章(ㄉㄧㄢˇ ㄓㄤ)
laws and institutions (of a society)

典試委員會(ㄉㄧㄢˇ ㄕˋ ㄨㄟˇ ㄩㄢˊ ㄏㄨㄟˋ)
a committee in charge of examination affairs

典押(ㄉㄧㄢˇ ㄧㄚ)
to mortgage

典雅(ㄉㄧㄢˇ ㄧㄚˇ)
refined (writing); elegant (style)

典要(ㄉㄧㄢˇ ㄧㄠˋ)
①refined and succinct ②a standard; a model

典獄官(ㄉㄧㄢˇ ㄩˋ ㄍㄨㄢ)
prison officials

典獄長(ㄉㄧㄢˇ ㄩˋ ㄓㄤˇ)
the warden (of a penitentiary)

八畫

【兼】 320
ㄐㄧㄢ jian jiān
1. to unite in one; to connect; to annex
2. and; also; together with; both; equally; concurrently

兼備(ㄐㄧㄢ ㄅㄟˋ)
to be in possession of both

兼辦(ㄐㄧㄢ ㄅㄢˋ)
to manage or handle simultaneously

兼併(ㄐㄧㄢ ㄅㄧㄥˋ)
to annex (another country, etc.)

兼祧(ㄐㄧㄢ ㄊㄧㄠ)
to be the heir to two branches of a family

兼顧(ㄐㄧㄢ ㄍㄨˋ)
to look after both sides; to take care of the needs, etc. of both parties

兼管(ㄐㄧㄢ ㄍㄨㄢˇ)
to also look after; to also have charge of

兼課(ㄐㄧㄢ ㄎㄜˋ)
①to do some teaching besides one's main occupation ②to hold two or more teaching jobs concurrently

兼薪(ㄐㄧㄢ ㄒㄧㄣ)
to get pay from two or more employers or organizations

兼旬(ㄐㄧㄢ ㄒㄩㄣˊ)
twenty days: 他別後瞬已兼旬。Very quickly it has been twenty days since he left us.

兼之(ㄐㄧㄢ ㄓ)
furthermore; besides

兼職(ㄐㄧㄢ ㄓˊ)
to take two or more jobs concurrently; to hold a concurrent post; a side job; a part-time job

兼差(ㄐㄧㄢ ㄔㄞ)
to take two or more jobs concurrently; to moonlight; a side job; a part-time job

兼籌並顧(ㄐㄧㄢ ㄔㄡˊ ㄅㄧㄥˋ ㄍㄨˋ)
to plan and care for both duties

兼程(ㄐㄧㄢ ㄔㄥˊ)
to proceed on one's trip on the double

兼善天下(ㄐㄧㄢ ㄕㄢˋ ㄊㄧㄢ ㄒㄧㄚˋ)
to benefit all the people in the world

兼人之量(ㄐㄧㄢ ㄖㄣˊ ㄓ ㄌㄧㄤˋ)
to have the capacity of two persons combined

兼任(ㄐㄧㄢ ㄖㄣˋ)
to serve concurrently as (a secretary, etc.); to have a side job

兼任教師(ㄐㄧㄢ ㄖㄣˋ ㄐㄧㄠˋ ㄕ)
a part-time teacher

兼容並蓄(ㄐㄧㄢ ㄖㄨㄥˊ ㄅㄧㄥˋ ㄒㄩˋ)
tolerant; open-minded

兼愛(ㄐㄧㄢ ㄞˋ)
love without distinction; fraternity

兼而有之(ㄐㄧㄢ ㄦˊ ㄧㄡˇ ㄓ)
to have both (merits and defects, advantages and disadvantages, etc.)

十四畫

【冀】 321
ㄐㄧˋ jih jì

1. to hope
2. another name for Hopeh Province
3. a Chinese family name

口 部
ㄐㄩㄥ jiong jiōng

三畫

【再】 322
ㄖㄢˇ raan rǎn

1. gradually
2. tender; weak
3. the outer edge of a turtle's shell
4. a Chinese family name

冉冉(ㄖㄢˇ ㄖㄢˇ)
gradually; imperceptibly

冉冉上升(ㄖㄢˇ ㄖㄢˇ ㄕㄤˋ ㄕㄥ)
to rise gradually

【册】 323
ㄘㄜˋ tseh cè

1. (in ancient China) a register; a book or books in general; volumes
2. a list; statistical tables; to record; records
3. an order to confer nobility titles

册封(ㄘㄜˋ ㄈㄥ)
(in ancient China) to confer titles of nobility on the emperor's wives or princes

册立(ㄘㄜˋ ㄌㄧˋ)
to crown an empress

册子(ㄘㄜˋ ˙ㄗ)
a book; a pamphlet

四畫

【再】 324
ㄗㄞˋ tzay zài

1. again; repeated
2. still; further; then

再拜(ㄗㄞˋ ㄅㄞˋ)
(literally) to bow twice—a courteous expression in letters, especially those addressed to a superior

再保險(ㄗㄞˋ ㄅㄠˇ ㄒㄧㄢˇ)
reinsurance

再版(ㄗㄞˋ ㄅㄢˇ)
the second printing or edition (of a book)

再發(ㄗㄞˋ ㄈㄚ)
to have a relapse

再犯(ㄗㄞˋ ㄈㄢˋ)
①to repeat an offense ②a second-time offender

再度(ㄗㄞˋ ㄉㄨˋ)
once more; a second time; once again

再談(ㄗㄞˋ ㄊㄢˊ)
to discuss (something) later

再來(ㄗㄞˋ ㄌㄞˊ)
①to come again: 失去的機會不再來。 The lost chance will never come again. ② to encore ③to request for or order a repetition

再過幾天(ㄗㄞˋ ㄍㄨㄛˋ ㄐㄧˇ ㄊㄧㄢ)
in a few more days

再會(ㄗㄞˋ ㄏㄨㄟˋ)
Good-bye. 或 See you again.

再婚(ㄗㄞˋ ㄏㄨㄣ)
to remarry after the annulment of a former marriage; digamy

再嫁(ㄗㄞˋ ㄐㄧㄚˋ)or 再醮(ㄗㄞˋ ㄐㄧㄠˋ)
(usually said of a widow) to remarry

再接再勵(ㄗㄞˋ ㄐㄧㄝ ㄗㄞˋ ㄌㄧˋ) or 再接再厲
to forge ahead in disregard of obstructions or failures; to make a determined effort undismayed

再見(ㄗㄞˋ ㄐㄧㄢˋ)
Good-bye. 或 See you again. 參看「再會」

再起(ㄗㄞˋ ㄑㄧˇ)
①to rise again; to stage a comeback ②to assume public office again

再娶(ㄗㄞˋ ㄑㄩˇ)
(said of a man) to remarry

再現(ㄗㄞˋ ㄒㄧㄢˋ)
①reappearance ②(geology) the reappearance of an earth stratum or lode ③reenactment

再製鹽(ㄗㄞˋ ㄓˋ ㄧㄢˊ)
refined salt

再者(ㄗㄞˋ ㄓㄜˇ)
furthermore; in addition

再審(ㄗㄞˋ ㄕㄣˇ)
a retrial

再生(ㄗㄞˋ ㄕㄥ)
①to be a second so-and-so (a well-known figure already dead) ②regeneration; to regenerate

再生父母(ㄗㄞˋ ㄕㄥ ㄈㄨˋ ㄇㄨˇ)
second parents—an expression of deep gratitude to benefactors for great help rendered

再說(ㄗㄞˋ ㄕㄨㄛ)
①please repeat (what you said)② furthermore; besides

再衰三竭(ㄗㄞˋ ㄕㄨㄞ ㄙㄢ ㄐㄧㄝˊ)
to be nearing exhaustion; to be weakened and demoralized

再造(ㄗㄞˋ ㄗㄠˋ)
born a second time—an expression of gratitude

再次(ㄗㄞˋ ㄘˋ)
once more; a second time; once again: 再次感謝各位的光臨。 Thank you once again for your coming.

再三(ㄗㄞˋ ㄙㄢ)
again and again; time and again; repeatedly

再三再四(ㄗㄞˋ ㄙㄢ ㄗㄞˋ ㄙˋ)
repeatedly; over and over again

再議(ㄗㄞˋ ㄧˋ)
to talk about or discuss (a subject, etc.) again or later

再也不(ㄗㄞˋ ㄧㄝˇ ㄅㄨˋ)
never again

七畫

【冒】 325
ㄇㄠˋ maw mào

1. incautious; imprudent; rash
2. to risk; to brave; to be exposed to (hardships)
3. to put forth; to issue forth; to go up (as fire, smoke, etc.)
4. a Chinese family name

冒牌(ㄇㄠˋ ㄆㄞˊ)or冒牌兒(ㄇㄠˋ ㄆㄞˊ ㄦ)
(literally) a product using the brand name or trademark of the same product by another manufacturer—a fake; an imitation; a counterfeit

冒昧(ㄇㄠˋ ㄇㄟˋ)
to make bold; presumptuous;

口
部

〔门部〕

to presume (usually used as a polite expression)

冒失(ㄇㄠˋ ㄕ) rash; imprudent; hasty; reckless

冒名(ㄇㄠˋ ㄇㄧㄥˊ) to assume another's name

冒名頂替(ㄇㄠˋ ㄇㄧㄥˊ ㄉㄧㄥˇ ㄊㄧˋ) to assume the identity of another person

冒犯(ㄇㄠˋ ㄈㄢˋ) to offend (a superior, elder, etc.)

冒瀆(ㄇㄠˋ ㄉㄨˊ) to bother or annoy (a superior)

冒頭(ㄇㄠˋ ㄊㄡˊ) to begin to crop up

冒天下之大不韙(ㄇㄠˋ ㄊㄧㄢ ㄒㄧㄚˋ ㄓ ㄉㄚˋ ㄅㄨˋ ㄨㄟˇ) to defy world opinion; to take the chances of universal condemnation; to ignore the will of the people

冒領(ㄇㄠˋ ㄌㄧㄥˇ) to get or take something by posing as someone else for whom it is intended

冒口(ㄇㄠˋ ㄎㄡˇ) (machinery) a rising head; a riser

冒號(ㄇㄠˋ ㄏㄠˋ) the colon

冒火(ㄇㄠˋ ㄏㄨㄛˇ) to blow one's top; to become angry

冒進(ㄇㄠˋ ㄐㄧㄣˋ) premature advance; rash advance

冒險(ㄇㄠˋ ㄒㄧㄢˇ) to take risks; to brave dangers

冒險犯難(ㄇㄠˋ ㄒㄧㄢˇ ㄈㄢˋ ㄋㄢˊ) to do something despite the dangers and difficulties involved

冒稱(ㄇㄠˋ ㄔㄥ) to claim falsely; to make false claims

冒充(ㄇㄠˋ ㄔㄨㄥ) to pretend to be somebody else; to use a substitute (of inferior quality) in place of the genuine item

冒失(ㄇㄠˋ ㄕ) hasty; reckless; rash: 你這麼做真是太冒失了。 It's rash of you to do so.

冒失鬼(ㄇㄠˋ ㄕ ㄍㄨㄟˇ) a rash fellow; a reckless guy

冒然(ㄇㄠˋ ㄖㄢˊ) recklessly; reckless; rashly; rash 參看「冒然」

冒死(ㄇㄠˋ ㄙˇ) to risk death

冒煙(ㄇㄠˋ ㄧㄢ) Smoke rises. 或 to belch smoke

冒雨(ㄇㄠˋ ㄩˇ) to brave the rain: 他們冒雨來訪我們。 They braved the rain to visit us.

【冑】 326
ㄓㄡˋ jow zhòu
a helmet: 參看肉部「冑」4645

冑甲(ㄓㄡˋ ㄐㄧㄚˇ) a helmet and armor

八畫

【篝】 327
ㄍㄡ gow gōu
a secluded place in a palace; a secret cabinet

九畫

【冕】 328
ㄇㄧㄢˇ mean miǎn
1. a ceremonial cap for high ministers in ancient China
2. a crown

一 部

ㄇㄧˋ　mih　mì

七畫

【冠】 329
1. a cap
2. the comb or crest of a bird
3. a Chinese family name

冠冕(ㄍㄨㄢ ㄇㄧㄢˇ) ① the hat ② the high official position

冠冕堂皇(ㄍㄨㄢ ㄇㄧㄢˇ ㄊㄤˊ ㄏㄨㄤˊ) ① elegant and stately; officially or publicly ② high-sounding: 他有冠冕堂皇的理

由。His excuses are high sounding.

冠帶之國(ㄍㄨㄢ ㄉㄞˋ ㄓ ㄍㄨㄛˊ) a civilized nation; a nation with a highly developed culture

冠蓋相望(ㄍㄨㄢ ㄍㄞˋ ㄒㄧㄤ ㄨㄤˋ) constant exchange of visits of ranking officials between nations

冠蓋雲集(ㄍㄨㄢ ㄍㄞˋ ㄩㄣˊ ㄐㄧˊ) (usually said of a meeting or gathering) where ranking officials congregate; a gathering of dignitaries

【冠】 329
2. ㄍㄨㄢˋ guann guàn
1. at 20 when a young man is capped
2. first-rate
3. to wear a cap

冠禮(ㄍㄨㄢˋ ㄌㄧˇ) (in ancient China) a capping ceremony for a young man when he reaches 20

冠軍(ㄍㄨㄢˋ ㄐㄩㄣ) a champion; an outstanding person

冠詞(ㄍㄨㄢˋ ㄘˊ) (grammar) the article ("a", "an", or "the")

八畫

【冤】 330
(寃)ㄩㄢ iuan yuān
1. oppression; injustice; a grievance; a wrong
2. feud; animosity; enmity
3. to cheat; to lie
4. to spend money recklessly; to waste money
5. to make false accusations

冤大頭(ㄩㄢ ㄉㄚˋ ㄊㄡˊ) a person played for a big fool; a fathead

冤擊(ㄩㄢ ㄐㄧ) a foreordained enemy; a person's stumbling block

冤鬼(ㄩㄢ ㄍㄨㄟˇ) a wronged soul; the ghost of a person who died of injustice

冤魂(ㄩㄢ ㄏㄨㄣˊ) the ghost of a person who was wrongly put to death or murdered

冤家(ㄩㄢ ㄐㄧㄚ)

部

ㄅ

an enemy (but also used for lovers)

寇家路窄(ㄎㄡ ㄐㄧㄚ ㄌㄨ ㄓㄞˇ)
(literally) The road is narrow for enemies.—Enemies often cross each other's path.

寃情(ㄩㄢ ㄑㄧㄥˊ)
the details of a grievance or wrong

寃屈(ㄩㄢ ㄑㄩ)
a grievance; a wrong; victimized by a frame-up

寃仇(ㄩㄢ ㄔㄡˊ)
feud; enmity; animus

寃枉(ㄩㄢ ㄨㄤˇ)
to wrong; to accuse a person with a false charge; a wrong; a grievance; to do someone injustice

寃獄(ㄩㄢ ㄩˋ)
miscarriage of justice

寃賠償法(ㄩㄢ ㄆㄟˊ ㄔㄤˊ ㄈㄚˇ)
Law of Compensation for Wrongful Detentions and Executions

【冥】 331
ㄇㄧㄥˊ ming ming
1. dark; obscure; dim; dusk
2. stupid; stupid: 他秉性冥頑不靈. He has a stupid and stubborn character.
3. far and high
4. deep; profound: 他陷於冥想中. He was deep in thought.
5. the unseen world; Hades
6. night
7. a Chinese family name

冥報(ㄇㄧㄥˊ ㄅㄠˋ)
① a mysterious retribution; a retribution executed by unseen hands ②to return (someone's kindness) in Hades

冥冥之中(ㄇㄧㄥˊ ㄇㄧㄥˊ ㄓ ㄓㄨㄥ)
(said of divine influence) imperceptibly but inexorably

冥府(ㄇㄧㄥˊ ㄈㄨˇ)
the underworld; Hades

冥河(ㄇㄧㄥˊ ㄏㄜˊ)
(mythology) the Styx

冥婚(ㄇㄧㄥˊ ㄏㄨㄣ)
a marriage ceremony for persons already dead

冥器(ㄇㄧㄥˊ ㄑㄧˋ)
paper-made household articles to be burnt for the dead

冥錢(ㄇㄧㄥˊ ㄑㄧㄢˊ)
paper money to be burnt for the dead

冥想(ㄇㄧㄥˊ ㄒㄧㄤˇ)
deep meditation

冥紙(ㄇㄧㄥˊ ㄓˇ)
參看「冥錢」

冥壽(ㄇㄧㄥˊ ㄕㄡˋ)
a birth anniversary of a person already dead

冥思苦想(ㄇㄧㄥˊ ㄙ ㄎㄨˇ ㄒㄧㄤˇ)
to think long and hard; to cudgel one's brains

冥衣(ㄇㄧㄥˊ ㄧ)
paper clothes to be burnt for the dead

冥佑(ㄇㄧㄥˊ ㄧㄡˋ)
protection of the gods

冥頑不靈(ㄇㄧㄥˊ ㄨㄢˊ ㄅㄨˋ ㄌㄧㄥˊ)
stupid and stubborn; foolhardy

冥王星(ㄇㄧㄥˊ ㄨㄤˊ ㄒㄧㄥ)
the planet Pluto

【冢】 332
ㄓㄨㄥˇ joong zhǒng
1. a high grave
2. a peak; a summit
3. the eldest
4. great; supreme; prime (all referring to official ranks)

十四畫

【冪】 333
ㄇㄧˋ mih mì
1. to cover with cloth
2. a cloth cover; a veil
3. (mathematics) power

冫 部
ㄅㄧㄥ bing bīng

三畫

【冬】 334
ㄉㄨㄥ dong dōng
1. winter: 有些候鳥在南方過冬. Some birds pass the winter in the south.
2. (the lunar calendar) the period from the 10th to the 12th month

冬眠(ㄉㄨㄥ ㄇㄧㄢˊ)
to hibernate; hibernation: 有些熊能冬眠. Some bears hibernate.

冬防(ㄉㄨㄥ ㄈㄤˊ)
the winter curfew (imposed annually to guard against undesirable elements)

冬天(ㄉㄨㄥ ㄊㄧㄢ)or 冬令(ㄉㄨㄥ ㄌㄧㄥˋ)
winter

冬暖夏涼(ㄉㄨㄥ ㄋㄨㄢˇ ㄒㄧㄚˋ ㄌㄧㄤˊ)
cool in summer and warm in winter

冬令救濟(ㄉㄨㄥ ㄌㄧㄥˋ ㄐㄧㄡˋ ㄐㄧˋ)
relief of the poor during winter months

冬菇(ㄉㄨㄥ ㄍㄨ)
a mushroom

冬瓜(ㄉㄨㄥ ㄍㄨㄚ)
a white gourd; a wax gourd

冬烘(ㄉㄨㄥ ㄏㄨㄥ)
(used in a contemptuous sense) a pedant or a pedagogue

冬季(ㄉㄨㄥ ㄐㄧˋ)
the winter season

冬青(ㄉㄨㄥ ㄑㄧㄥ)
(botany) holly

冬汛(ㄉㄨㄥ ㄒㄩㄣˋ)
the winter fishing season

冬至(ㄉㄨㄥ ㄓˋ)
the winter solstice, (for the Northern Hemisphere) the time when the sun is farthest south from the equator, on or about December 22

冬至線(ㄉㄨㄥ ㄓˋ ㄒㄧㄢˋ)
the tropic of Capricorn 亦作「南回歸線」

冬裝(ㄉㄨㄥ ㄓㄨㄤ)
winter dress

冬菜(ㄉㄨㄥ ㄘㄞˋ)
preserved, dried cabbages

冬筍(ㄉㄨㄥ ㄙㄨㄣˇ)
winter sprouts of bamboos

四畫

【冰】 335
ㄅㄧㄥ bing bīng
1. ice; icicles
2. cold; frost

冰雹(ㄅㄧㄥ ㄅㄠˊ)
hail; a hailstone

冰棒(ㄅㄧㄥ ㄅㄤˋ)

【冫部】

a flavored popsicle

冰片(ㄅㄧㄥ ㄆㄧㄢˋ)
borneol

冰封(ㄅㄧㄥ ㄈㄥ)
icebound

冰刀(ㄅㄧㄥ ㄉㄠ)
the blades of ice skates

冰島(ㄅㄧㄥ ㄉㄠˇ)
Iceland

冰點(ㄅㄧㄥ ㄉㄧㄢˇ)
the freezing point

冰凍(ㄅㄧㄥ ㄉㄨㄥˋ)
to freeze

冰凍三尺非一日之寒(ㄅㄧㄥ ㄉㄨㄥˋ ㄙㄢ ㄔˇ ㄈㄟ ㄧˊ ㄖˋ ㄓ ㄏㄢˊ)
(literally) Ice sheet of three feet in thickness takes more than one cold day to form. —The grudge or animosity has its deep root.

冰炭(ㄅㄧㄥ ㄊㄢˋ)
as incompatible as ice and burning charcoal

冰糖(ㄅㄧㄥ ㄊㄤˊ)
rock candy

冰天雪地(ㄅㄧㄥ ㄊㄧㄢ ㄒㄩㄝˇ ㄉㄧˋ)
frozen and snow-covered land

冰囊(ㄅㄧㄥ ㄋㄤˊ)or 冰袋(ㄅㄧㄥ ㄉㄞˋ)
an ice bag

冰冷(ㄅㄧㄥ ㄌㄥˇ)
①icy cold; cold as ice ②cold or frosty (expressions, etc.)

冰涼(ㄅㄧㄥ ㄌㄧㄤˊ)
icy cold; very cold

冰輪(ㄅㄧㄥ ㄌㄨㄣˊ)or 冰鏡(ㄅㄧㄥ ㄐㄧㄥˋ)or 冰盤(ㄅㄧㄥ ㄆㄢˊ)
the cool moon

冰菓店(ㄅㄧㄥ ㄍㄨㄛˇ ㄉㄧㄢˋ)
a cold drink shop

冰塊(ㄅㄧㄥ ㄎㄨㄞˋ)
lumps of ice; ice cubes; ice blocks

冰河(ㄅㄧㄥ ㄏㄜˊ)
a glacier

冰河時期(ㄅㄧㄥ ㄏㄜˊ ㄕˊ ㄑㄧ)
the glacial epoch; the ice age

冰肌玉骨(ㄅㄧㄥ ㄐㄧ ㄩˋ ㄍㄨˇ)
(literally) flesh of ice and bones of jade—a Chinese description of beautiful women

冰窖(ㄅㄧㄥ ㄐㄧㄠˋ)
an icehouse; a glacial vault

冰淇淋(ㄅㄧㄥ ㄑㄧˊ ㄌㄧㄣˊ)
ice cream

冰橇(ㄅㄧㄥ ㄑㄧㄠ)
a sled; a sledge; a sleigh

冰球(ㄅㄧㄥ ㄑㄧㄡˊ)
(ice hockey) a puck

冰球戲(ㄅㄧㄥ ㄑㄧㄡˊ ㄒㄧˋ)
ice hockey 亦作「冰上曲棍球」

冰清玉潔(ㄅㄧㄥ ㄑㄧㄥ ㄩˋ ㄐㄧㄝˊ)
(said of one's character) incorruptible

冰鞋(ㄅㄧㄥ ㄒㄧㄝˊ)
ice skates

冰消瓦解(ㄅㄧㄥ ㄒㄧㄠ ㄨㄚˇ ㄐㄧㄝˇ)
total dissolution or disintegration like melting ice

冰心(ㄅㄧㄥ ㄒㄧㄣ)
①chaste; chastity; virtuous ②not enthusiastic; to be somewhat indifferent

冰箱(ㄅㄧㄥ ㄒㄧㄤ)
an icebox; a refrigerator

冰雪聰明(ㄅㄧㄥ ㄒㄩㄝˇ ㄘㄨㄥ ㄇㄧㄥˊ)
very clever; remarkably bright; brilliant

冰鎮(ㄅㄧㄥ ㄓㄣˋ)
to preserve on ice; to cool food with ice

冰柱(ㄅㄧㄥ ㄓㄨˋ)
icicles

冰磚(ㄅㄧㄥ ㄓㄨㄢ)
ice blocks; frozen cream

冰川(ㄅㄧㄥ ㄔㄨㄢ)or 冰河(ㄅㄧㄥ ㄏㄜˊ)
a glacier

冰蝕(ㄅㄧㄥ ㄕˊ)
(geology) glacial erosion

冰釋(ㄅㄧㄥ ㄕˋ)
solved; to disappear without a trace

冰山(ㄅㄧㄥ ㄕㄢ)
an iceberg

冰上運動(ㄅㄧㄥ ㄕㄤˋ ㄩㄣˋ ㄉㄨㄥˋ)
ice sports

冰水(ㄅㄧㄥ ㄕㄨㄟˇ)
ice water

冰霜(ㄅㄧㄥ ㄕㄨㄤ)
①cold and severe ②incorruptible

冰人(ㄅㄧㄥ ㄖㄣˊ)
a matchmaker

冰原(ㄅㄧㄥ ㄩㄢˊ)
an ice field

五畫

【冶】336 ㄧㄝˇ yee yě
1. to smelt; to fuse metals
2. seductive; fascinating

冶煉(ㄧㄝˇ ㄌㄧㄢˋ)
to smelt

冶工(ㄧㄝˇ ㄍㄨㄥ)
a blacksmith

冶金學(ㄧㄝˇ ㄐㄧㄣ ㄒㄩㄝˊ)
metallurgy

冶遊(ㄧㄝˇ ㄧㄡˊ)
to frequent brothels

冶艷(ㄧㄝˇ ㄧㄢˋ)
beautiful; beauty; charms

【冷】337 ㄌㄥˇ leeng lěng
1. cold
2. (said of business, farming etc.) off-season
3. a Chinese family name

冷板凳(ㄌㄥˇ ㄅㄢˇ ㄉㄥˋ)
①a post which has little or no authority ②a cold reception

冷冰冰(ㄌㄥˇ ㄅㄧㄥ ㄅㄧㄥ)
icy cold; cold as ice

冷不防(ㄌㄥˇ ㄅㄨˋ ㄈㄤˊ)
a bolt from the blue; unexpectedly

冷盤(ㄌㄥˇ ㄆㄢˊ)or 冷碟(ㄌㄥˇ ㄉㄧㄝˊ)
a dish of assorted cold meats

冷僻(ㄌㄥˇ ㄆㄧˋ)
①out-of-the-way or secluded (places) ②big or hard (words or expressions)

冷漠(ㄌㄥˇ ㄇㄛˋ)
cool and detached; indifferent; apathetic

冷門(ㄌㄥˇ ㄇㄣˊ)
①(said of a commodity, academic course, etc.) not popular or not in great demand ②(said of appointments or nominations) unexpected

冷面(ㄌㄥˇ ㄇㄧㄢˋ)
a poker face

冷鋒(ㄌㄥˇ ㄈㄥ)
a cold front

冷敷(ㄌㄥˇ ㄈㄨ)
(medicine) a cold compress

冷淡(ㄌㄥˇ ㄉㄢˋ)
cold (expressions); indifferent (attitudes)

冷調(ㄌㄥˇ ㄉㄧㄠˋ)
cool color-tone; cool tone

冷凍(ㄌㄥˇ ㄉㄨㄥˋ)

freezing

冷凍庫(カㄥ カㄨㄥ ㄎㄨ)
a freezer

冷凍劑(カㄥ カㄨㄥ ㄐㄧ)
a coolant agent; a refrigerant

冷凍食品(カㄥ カㄨㄥ ㄕ ㄆㄧㄣ)
frozen foods

凝結(カㄥ ㄐㄧㄝ)
(physics) condensation

冷凝器(カㄥ ㄋㄧㄥ ㄑㄧ)
a condenser

冷暖(カㄥ ㄋㄨㄢ)
the degree of cold or heat

冷暖自知(カㄥ ㄋㄨㄢ ㄗ ㄓ)
One knows what it's like without being told.

冷冷清清(カㄥ カㄥ ㄑㄧㄥ ㄑㄧㄥ)
(said of a place) deserted and quiet; desolate; lonely

冷落(カㄥ カㄨㄛ)
①cold and lonely ②cold reception; to cold-shoulder

冷宮(カㄥ ㄍㄨㄥ)
a palace to confine the emperor's concubines after they lost his favor

冷酷(カㄥ ㄎㄨ)
merciless; heartless

冷汗(カㄥ ㄏㄢ)
①a cold sweat (as in great fright, etc.) ②(Chinese medicine) clammy perspiration

冷話(カㄥ ㄏㄨㄚ)
cool, sarcastic remarks

冷箭(カㄥ ㄐㄧㄢ)
(literally) an arrow shot from an ambush—an unexpected attack or a pot shot

冷靜(カㄥ ㄐㄧㄥ)
①clear (mind, thinking, etc.); calm or composed: 她冷靜下來回信。She composed herself to answer the letter. ②secluded or quiet (place, etc.)

冷氣(カㄥ ㄑㄧ)
air conditioning

冷氣機(カㄥ ㄑㄧ ㄐㄧ)
an air-conditioner

冷氣設備(カㄥ ㄑㄧ ㄕㄜ ㄅㄟ)
air-conditioning equipment or facilities

冷槍(カㄥ ㄑㄧㄤ)
a sniper's shot

冷清(カㄥ ㄑㄧㄥ)
desolate; lonely; deserted

冷却(カㄥ ㄑㄩㄝ)
to get cold; to cool off

冷却劑(カㄥ ㄑㄩㄝ ㄐㄧ)
a coolant

冷血(カㄥ ㄒㄧㄝ)
cold-blooded; hardcarted

冷血動物(カㄥ ㄒㄧㄝ ㄉㄨㄥ ㄨ)
①cold-blooded animals ②a heartless or ruthless person

冷笑(カㄥ ㄒㄧㄠ)
a sarcastic smile or grin

冷戰(カㄥ ㄓㄢ)
①(カㄥ ㄓㄢ) cold war ②(カㄥ ㄓㄢ) to shiver with cold 亦作「冷顫」

冷嘲熱諷(カㄥ ㄔㄠ ㄖㄜ ㄈㄥ)
sarcasm and mockery

冷場(カㄥ ㄔㄤ)
temporary suspension of a show, party, etc. occasioned by inefficient management; a stage wait

冷食(カㄥ ㄕ)
cold drinks and snacks

冷水(カㄥ ㄕㄨㄟ)
cold water; unboiled water

冷水澆頭(カㄥ ㄕㄨㄟ ㄐㄧㄠ ㄊㄡ)
(literally) splashing the head with cold water—a sudden and harsh disappointment or discouragement

冷水浴(カㄥ ㄕㄨㄟ ㄩ)
a cold shower; a cold bath

冷霜(カㄥ ㄕㄨㄤ)
cold cream

冷熱病(カㄥ ㄖㄜ ㄅㄧㄥ)
①malaria ②sudden waxing and waning of enthusiasm

冷若冰霜(カㄥ ㄖㄨㄛ ㄅㄧㄥ ㄕㄨㄤ)
(usually said of women) as cold as an iceberg—aloof

冷字(カㄥ ㄗ)
a rarely used word

冷餐(カㄥ ㄘㄢ)
a buffet

冷藏(カㄥ ㄘㄤ)
to preserve by means of refrigeration

冷色(カㄥ ㄙㄜ)
cool colors

冷颼颼(カㄥ ㄙㄡ ㄙㄡ)
frosty; chilly; cold and windy

冷言冷語(カㄥ ㄧㄢ カㄥ ㄩ)
sarcastic remarks

冷眼(カㄥ ㄧㄢ)
to look at (something) without prejudice; to look on as a disinterested bystander

冷眼旁觀(カㄥ ㄧㄢ ㄆㄤ ㄍㄨㄢ)
①to look on coldly ②to look on with a critical eye

冷飲(カㄥ ㄧㄣ)
cold drinks

六畫

【冽】 338
ㄌㄧㄝ lieh lie
crystal-clear (water or wine)

八畫

【准】 339
ㄓㄨㄣ joen zhǔn
1. to approve; to permit; to grant; to authorize
2. in accordance with; accordingly
3. equivalent; equal

准將(ㄓㄨㄣ ㄐㄧㄤ)
a brigadier general

准許(ㄓㄨㄣ ㄒㄩ)
to approve; to permit; to allow; approval; permission

准尉(ㄓㄨㄣ ㄨㄟ)
a warrant officer

准予(ㄓㄨㄣ ㄩ)
to permit; to authorize

【凊】 340
ㄐㄧㄥ jing jìng
cold; cool; chilly

【凋】 341
ㄉㄧㄠ diāo diāo
1. withered; faded
2. exhausted; emaciated

凋敝(ㄉㄧㄠ ㄅㄧ)
emaciated; destitute; exhausted; injured; ridden by illness

凋兵(ㄉㄧㄠ ㄅㄧㄥ)
tired and weary soldiers; demoralized troops

凋零(ㄉㄧㄠ ㄌㄧㄥ)
①withered ②(said of persons) to pass away

凋落(ㄉㄧㄠ カㄨㄛ)or凋謝(ㄉㄧㄠ ㄒㄧㄝ)
①fallen; withered ②(said of

ㄧ 部

persons) to pass away

凋殘(ㄉㄧㄠ ㄘㄢˊ)
①(said of business) declining ②(said of cities) deserted

凋萎(ㄉㄧㄠ ㄨㄟˇ)
①(said of flowers, etc.) withered; faded ②(said of a great person) passing away

【凌】 342 ㄌㄧㄥˊ ling líng
1. accumulated ice
2. to insult; to maltreat to throw one's weight around
3. to rise; to ride; to soar
4. to traverse
5. a Chinese family name

凌波(ㄌㄧㄥˊ ㄅㄛ)
to ride the waves; to walk over ripples — a term used to describe the grace of a beauty's walking

凌波仙子(ㄌㄧㄥˊ ㄅㄛ ㄒㄧㄢ ㄗˇ)
①fairies walking over ripples ②another name for daffodils

凌厲(ㄌㄧㄥˊ ㄌㄧˋ)
relentless (said of the military offensive, implementation of orders, etc.)

凌亂(ㄌㄧㄥˊ ㄌㄨㄢˋ)
in total disorder or disarray; messy; disheveled; untidy

凌駕(ㄌㄧㄥˊ ㄐㄧㄚˋ)
to ride high; to rise above others; to outstrip

凌霄(ㄌㄧㄥˊ ㄒㄧㄠ)
to ride the clouds; to rise up to the skies; to soar to the skies

凌遲(ㄌㄧㄥˊ ㄔˊ)
(in ancient China) a slow death by torture (usually by dismemberment)

凌晨(ㄌㄧㄥˊ ㄔㄣˊ)
the wee hours; very early in the morning

凌辱(ㄌㄧㄥˊ ㄖㄨˇ)
①to insult; to maltreat ②to assault (a woman)

凌雲(ㄌㄧㄥˊ ㄩㄣˊ)
to ride the high clouds — (usually said of a person's ambition or aspiration) to aim high

【凍】 343 ㄉㄨㄥˋ dong dòng
1. to freeze

2. cold; icy
3. a Chinese family name

凍餒(ㄉㄨㄥˋ ㄋㄟˇ)
to suffer from cold and hunger

凍裂(ㄉㄨㄥˋ ㄌㄧㄝˋ)
to crack as a result of freezing or cold

凍結(ㄉㄨㄥˋ ㄐㄧㄝˊ)
to freeze (an account, etc.)

凍僵(ㄉㄨㄥˋ ㄐㄧㄤ)
to be benumbed with cold; to be frozen stiff

凍瘡(ㄉㄨㄥˋ ㄔㄨㄤ)
frostbite; chilblains

凍傷(ㄉㄨㄥˋ ㄕㄤ)
to suffer injuries or illness as a result of long exposure to cold weather

凍子(ㄉㄨㄥˋ ㄗˇ)
jelly; coagulation (of meat broth, etc.)

凍死(ㄉㄨㄥˋ ㄙˇ)
to freeze to death; to die of frost

十三畫

【凜】 344 ㄌㄧㄣˇ liin lín
1. cold; bleak
2. to be apprehensive; to shiver with cold or fear
3. imposing; awe-inspiring

凜冽(ㄌㄧㄣˇ ㄌㄧㄝˋ)
very cold; cold to the marrow

凜凜(ㄌㄧㄣˇ ㄌㄧㄣˇ)
①very cold; icy ②(said of manners) forbidding

凜凜如生(ㄌㄧㄣˇ ㄌㄧㄣˇ ㄖㄨˊ ㄕㄥ)
(said of a portrait) to seem alive

凜然(ㄌㄧㄣˇ ㄖㄢˊ)
a stern, repellent appearance arousing fear, reverence

凜若冰霜(ㄌㄧㄣˇ ㄖㄨㄛˋ ㄅㄧㄥ ㄕㄨㄤ)
(said of a woman) to be cold as ice

凜遵(ㄌㄧㄣˇ ㄗㄨㄣ)
to respectfully comply with; to obey in fear

十四畫

【凝】 345 ㄋㄧㄥˊ ning níng

1. to freeze
2. to congeal; to coagulate
3. to form; to take shape
4. to concentrate; to cohere

凝眸(ㄋㄧㄥˊ ㄇㄡˊ)
to fix one's eyes on

凝凍(ㄋㄧㄥˊ ㄉㄨㄥˋ)
to freeze

凝鍊(ㄋㄧㄥˊ ㄌㄧㄢˋ)
concise; condensed

凝固(ㄋㄧㄥˊ ㄍㄨˋ)
(said of liquid) to congeal; to solidify

凝固點(ㄋㄧㄥˊ ㄍㄨˋ ㄉㄧㄢˇ)
the freezing point; the point of solidification

凝結(ㄋㄧㄥˊ ㄐㄧㄝˊ)
to condense (from gas to liquid); to solidify or congeal (from liquid to solid); to curdle

凝結器(ㄋㄧㄥˊ ㄐㄧㄝˊ ㄑㄧˋ)
a condenser

凝聚(ㄋㄧㄥˊ ㄐㄩˋ)
to concentrate; to curdle

凝聚力(ㄋㄧㄥˊ ㄐㄩˋ ㄌㄧˋ)
cohesion; cohesive force

凝想(ㄋㄧㄥˊ ㄒㄧㄤˇ)
to concentrate one's thought; to meditate; deep in thought

凝脂(ㄋㄧㄥˊ ㄓ)
congealed fat—(usually said of a woman's skin) smooth, soft, and glossy

凝滯(ㄋㄧㄥˊ ㄓˋ)
frozen at a point; delayed; stagnant; stalemated

凝妝(ㄋㄧㄥˊ ㄓㄨㄤ)
(usually said of a woman) to be fully dressed; to dress up; to doll up

凝重(ㄋㄧㄥˊ ㄓㄨㄥˋ)
dignified

凝視(ㄋㄧㄥˊ ㄕˋ)
to gaze (lovingly); to fix one's gaze on; a fixed gaze

凝神(ㄋㄧㄥˊ ㄕㄣˊ)
to concentrate

凝神諦聽(ㄋㄧㄥˊ ㄕㄣˊ ㄉㄧˋ ㄊㄧㄥ)
to listen attentively

凝霜(ㄋㄧㄥˊ ㄕㄨㄤ)
to frost

凝思(ㄋㄧㄥˊ ㄙ)
to concentrate one's thought on; to be deep in thought; meditation; deep thinking

几 部
ㄐㄧˇ jii jǐ

【几】 346
ㄐㄧˇ jii jǐ
(語音 ㄐㄧ ji jī)
1. a small table
2. a simplified form of the character "幾"
几席(ㄐㄧ ㄒㄧˊ)
a small table with a few mats around it
几案(ㄐㄧˋ)
① an office desk ② a small table

一畫

【凡】 347
ㄈㄢ farn fán
1. common; ordinary; dull: 她是一位平凡的畫家。 She is a common painter.
2. worldly; mortal; earthly: 凡人不免死亡。 The mortal life has an end.
3. generally; every; whenever; wherever
4. altogether: 全書凡十卷。 The set consists of ten volumes altogether.
凡人俗子(ㄈㄢ ㄖㄣˊ ㄙㄨˊ ㄗˇ)
the masses; ordinary people
凡例(ㄈㄢˊ ㄌㄧˋ)
the introduction of a book
凡骨(ㄈㄢ ㄍㄨˇ)
(literally) mortal bones—ordinary endowments; an ordinary person
凡間(ㄈㄢ ㄐㄧㄢ)
the material world
凡心(ㄈㄢ ㄒㄧㄣ)
worldly desires; desires of the flesh
凡事(ㄈㄢˊ ㄕˋ)
everything
凡是(ㄈㄢˊ ㄕˋ)
all (who are present, etc.); all (which are black, heavy, etc.)
凡士林(ㄈㄢ ㄕˋ ㄌㄧㄣˊ)
Vaseline; petrolatum
凡人(ㄈㄢˊ ㄖㄣˊ)
an ordinary person; one of the masses; a layman
凡爾賽(ㄈㄢˊ ㄦˇ ㄙㄞˋ)
Versailles, French city and site of the Versailles Palace built by Louis XIV
凡眼(ㄈㄢˊ ㄧㄢˇ)
mortal eyes; mortal eyesight
凡庸(ㄈㄢˊ ㄩㄥ)
commonplace; ordinary

九畫

【凰】 348
ㄏㄨㄤˊ hwang huáng
the female phoenix, a legendary bird in Chinese mythology

十畫

【凱】 349
ㄎㄞˇ kae kǎi
1. peace; joy
2. balmy; soothing; tender
3. a victory—a triumphant return of an army
凱風(ㄎㄞˇ ㄈㄥ)
the south wind
凱歌(ㄎㄞˇ ㄍㄜ)
a song of victory or triumph
凱旋(ㄎㄞˇ ㄒㄩㄢˊ)
a triumphant return of an army; to return in triumph
凱旋門(ㄎㄞˇ ㄒㄩㄢˊ ㄇㄣˊ)
① the Arc of Triumph (in Paris, France) ② a triumphal arch
凱撒(ㄎㄞˇ ㄙㄚˋ)
Gaius Julius Caesar
凱樂(ㄎㄞˇ ㄌㄜˋ)
music of triumph

十二畫

【凳】 350
(櫈)ㄉㄥˋ denq dèng
a stool; a bench
凳子(ㄉㄥˋ ˙ㄗ)
a stool; a bench

凵 部
ㄑㄩ chiu qū

二畫

【凶】 351
ㄒㄩㄥ shiong xiōng
1. evil; bad
2. famine
3. unlucky; unfortunate
4. fear; fearsome
5. very; excessive; excess
凶暴(ㄒㄩㄥ ㄅㄠˋ)
fierce and brutal
凶猛(ㄒㄩㄥ ㄇㄥˇ)
violent; ferocious
凶夢(ㄒㄩㄥ ㄇㄥˋ)
a bad dream; a nightmare
凶服(ㄒㄩㄥ ㄈㄨˊ)
mourning dress
凶多吉少(ㄒㄩㄥ ㄉㄨㄛ ㄐㄧˊ ㄕㄠˇ)
to bode ill rather than well
凶徒(ㄒㄩㄥ ㄊㄨˊ)
a villain; an evildoer
凶年(ㄒㄩㄥ ㄋㄧㄢˊ)or 凶歲(ㄒㄩㄥ ㄙㄨㄟˋ)
a year of famine; a year of misfortune
凶耗(ㄒㄩㄥ ㄏㄠˋ)
bad news; a death notice
凶悍(ㄒㄩㄥ ㄏㄢˋ)
fierce and tough
凶狠(ㄒㄩㄥ ㄏㄣˇ)
fierce and malicious
凶橫(ㄒㄩㄥ ㄏㄥˋ)
fierce and arrogant
凶氣(ㄒㄩㄥ ㄑㄧˋ)
the fearsome air (of a person)
凶器(ㄒㄩㄥ ㄑㄧˋ)
a tool or weapon for criminal purposes; a lethal weapon
凶險(ㄒㄩㄥ ㄒㄧㄢˇ)
danger; dangerous
凶相(ㄒㄩㄥ ㄒㄧㄤˋ)
ferocious features; fierce looks
凶宅(ㄒㄩㄥ ㄓㄞˊ)
① a house where murders, etc. took place ② a haunted

house
凶兆(ㄒㄩㄥ ㄓㄠˋ)
a bad omen
凶事(ㄒㄩㄥ ㄕˋ)
① unlucky incidents—deaths, killings, etc. ② war; armed clashes
凶殺(ㄒㄩㄥ ㄕㄚ)
homicide; murder
凶煞(ㄒㄩㄥ ㄕㄚ)
the evil spirit that causes illness, death, etc.
凶手(ㄒㄩㄥ ㄕㄡˇ)
a murderer; an assassin
凶神惡煞(ㄒㄩㄥ ㄕㄣˊ ㄜˋ ㄕㄚ)
devils; fiends
凶殘(ㄒㄩㄥ ㄘㄢˊ)
bloodthirsty; merciless
凶惡(ㄒㄩㄥ ㄜˋ)
brutish; fearful; ferocious

三畫

【凸】 352
　　ㄊㄨ twu tú
1. protuberant; convex
2. to protrude; to jut
凸版(ㄊㄨ ㄅㄢˇ)
a relief printing plate
凸面(ㄊㄨ ㄇㄧㄢˋ)
convex
凸透鏡(ㄊㄨ ㄊㄡˋ ㄐㄧㄥˋ)
a convex lens
凸鏡(ㄊㄨ ㄐㄧㄥˋ)or 凸面鏡(ㄊㄨ ㄇㄧㄢˋ ㄐㄧㄥˋ)
a convex mirror
凸出(ㄊㄨ ㄔㄨ)
bulging out; to protrude

【凹】 353
　　ㄠ au ào
1. indented; an indention
2. hollow; concave
凹版(ㄠ ㄅㄢˇ)
intaglio; gravure
凹版印刷(ㄠ ㄅㄢˇ ㄧㄣˋ ㄕㄨㄚ)
intaglio printing
凹面(ㄠ ㄇㄧㄢˋ)
concave
凹面鏡(ㄠ ㄇㄧㄢˋ ㄐㄧㄥˋ)
a concave mirror 亦作「凹鏡」
凹地(ㄠ ㄉㄧˋ)
hollow ground
凹透鏡(ㄠ ㄊㄡˋ ㄐㄧㄥˋ)
a concave lens
凹鏡(ㄠ ㄐㄧㄥˋ)
a concave mirror

凹陷(ㄠ ㄒㄧㄢˋ)
(said of a place) a hollow or depression

【出】 354
　　ㄔㄨ chu chū
1. to go out; to come out: 她出門購物。She went out shopping.
2. to produce; to reproduce: 這工廠出產汽車。This factory produces cars.
3. to beget
4. to happen or occur; to incur
5. to put forth; to bud
6. to divorce (a wife, etc.)
7. to chase away; to banish
8. to expend; to pay out
9. to escape; to leave (one's home, etc.): 我們從敵人手中逃出。We escaped from the enemy.
10. to appear: 他突然出現在我們面前。He suddenly appeared before us.
11. to take office
12. to vent (one's anger, etc.)
出版(ㄔㄨ ㄅㄢˇ)
to publish
出版法(ㄔㄨ ㄅㄢˇ ㄈㄚˇ)
publication law
出版家(ㄔㄨ ㄅㄢˇ ㄐㄧㄚ)or 出版者(ㄔㄨ ㄅㄢˇ ㄓㄜˇ)
a publisher
出版自由(ㄔㄨ ㄅㄢˇ ㄗˋ ㄧㄡˊ)
freedom of publication: 在民主社會中有出版自由。In a democratic society there is freedom of publication.
出版物(ㄔㄨ ㄅㄢˇ ㄨˋ)
publications
出奔(ㄔㄨ ㄅㄣ)
to escape; to leave one's home and live in exile
出榜(ㄔㄨ ㄅㄤˇ)or 放榜(ㄈㄤˋ ㄅㄤˇ)
① to publish or announce the result of successful candidates or examinees ② to put up a notice
出殯(ㄔㄨ ㄅㄧㄣˋ)
to carry a coffin to the grave for burial; a funeral procession
出兵(ㄔㄨ ㄅㄧㄥ)
to dispatch troops; to send military forces: 當局出兵鎮壓叛亂。The authorities dispatched troops to quell the rebellion.

出品(ㄔㄨ ㄆㄧㄣˇ)
products (of a certain company, etc.)
出馬(ㄔㄨ ㄇㄚˇ)
① to go out and face something ② to take office
出沒無常(ㄔㄨ ㄇㄛˋ ㄨˊ ㄔㄤˊ)
(usually said of guerrilla bands or bandits) to appear and disappear at unpredictable places and times
出賣(ㄔㄨ ㄇㄞˋ)
① to sell ② to betray; betrayal
出毛病(ㄔㄨ ㄇㄠˊ ㄅㄧㄥˋ)
to be or go out of order; to go wrong
出門(ㄔㄨ ㄇㄣˊ)or 出門兒(ㄔㄨ ㄇㄣˊ ㄦ)
to leave one's home; to take a trip
出門子(ㄔㄨ ㄇㄣˊ ˙ㄗ)
(said of a girl) to get married; to leave her parental home for marriage
出面(ㄔㄨ ㄇㄧㄢˋ)
to assume the responsibility (in mediation, negotiations, etc.); to act on someone else's behalf
出名(ㄔㄨ ㄇㄧㄥˊ)
to become famous; famous: 一大群人向那出名的英雄歡呼。A great crowd of people greeted the famous hero.
出發(ㄔㄨ ㄈㄚ)
to set out; to leave for (a destination)
出發點(ㄔㄨ ㄈㄚ ㄉㄧㄢˇ)
① the point from which one sets out; the starting point ② (in argument, discussion, etc.) premises; a basis ③ a motive
出分子(ㄔㄨ ㄈㄣˋ ˙ㄗ)
to offer money as a gift or condolence
出風頭(ㄔㄨ ㄈㄥ ˙ㄊㄡ)
to be in the spotlight; to be very popular; to steal the show; to seek publicity
出婦(ㄔㄨ ㄈㄨˋ)
① a divorced woman ② to divorce one's wife 亦作「出妻」
出點子(ㄔㄨ ㄉㄧㄢˇ ˙ㄗ)
to offer advice

出動(ㄔㄨ ㄉㄨㄥˋ)
to dispatch or send out (especially troops, armored units, reinforcements, etc.)

出頭(ㄔㄨ ㄊㄡˊ)
(said of people of humble origin) to make good or to succeed

出頭露面(ㄔㄨ ㄊㄡˊ ㄌㄨˋ ㄇㄧㄢˋ)
to appear in public

出題(ㄔㄨ ㄊㄧˊ)
①to set a theme (especially in composing poems or writings) ②to set questions (for an examination, etc.)

出天花(ㄔㄨ ㄊㄧㄢ ㄏㄨㄚ)
to have smallpox

出庭(ㄔㄨ ㄊㄧㄥˊ)
to appear in court

出土(ㄔㄨ ㄊㄨˇ)
(said of antiques, etc.) to be unearthed; to come out of earth

出脫(ㄔㄨ ㄊㄨㄛ)
①to vindicate (someone from charges, etc.) ②to sell

出納(ㄔㄨ ㄋㄚˋ)
a teller or treasurer

出來(ㄔㄨ ㄌㄞ·)
①to come out; to appear: 星星出來了。The stars came out. ②to make out ③to bring to pass

出類拔萃(ㄔㄨ ㄌㄟˋ ㄅㄚˊ ㄘㄨㄟˋ)
outstanding; eminent; remarkable

出漏子 or 出樓子(ㄔㄨ ㄌㄡˋ·ㄗ) or 出亂子(ㄔㄨ ㄌㄨㄢˋ·ㄗ) or 出岔子(ㄔㄨ ㄔㄚˋ·ㄗ)
in trouble; to get into trouble

出力(ㄔㄨ ㄌㄧˋ)
to devote one's efforts to (an undertaking, etc.)

出列(ㄔㄨ ㄌㄧㄝˋ)
to leave one's place in the ranks

出獵(ㄔㄨ ㄌㄧㄝˋ)
to go hunting; to hunt

出路(ㄔㄨ ㄌㄨˋ)
① the prospects (of a career, etc.) ②an outlet

出落(ㄔㄨ ㄌㄨㄛˋ)
to grow (prettier, etc.)

出籠(ㄔㄨ ㄌㄨㄥˊ)
to become current; to appear in the market

出格(ㄔㄨ ㄍㄜˊ)
to step out of line; to behave disorderly

出閣(ㄔㄨ ㄍㄜˊ)
(said of a girl) to get married

出港(ㄔㄨ ㄍㄤˇ)
①(said of a vessel) to leave (a) port ②to send (goods) abroad; to export

出國(ㄔㄨ ㄍㄨㄛˊ)
to go abroad

出乖露醜(ㄔㄨ ㄍㄨㄞ ㄌㄨˋ ㄔㄡˇ)
to make oneself a laughing-stock in public

出軌(ㄔㄨ ㄍㄨㄟˇ)
①to derail ② to behave contrary to a normal pattern

出恭(ㄔㄨ ㄍㄨㄥ)
to empty the bowels

出口(ㄔㄨ ㄎㄡˇ)
①to export ②to utter; to speak ③an exit (in a theater, etc.)

出口貿易(ㄔㄨ ㄎㄡˇ ㄇㄠˋ ㄧˋ)
export trade

出口貨(ㄔㄨ ㄎㄡˇ ㄏㄨㄛˋ)
exports; goods for export

出口成章(ㄔㄨ ㄎㄡˇ ㄔㄥˊ ㄓㄤ)
One's tongue is the pen of a ready writer.

出口傷人(ㄔㄨ ㄎㄡˇ ㄕㄤ ㄖㄣˊ)
to make insulting remarks

出口稅(ㄔㄨ ㄎㄡˇ ㄕㄨㄟˋ)
export duties

出海(ㄔㄨ ㄏㄞˇ)
to leave (a) port; to go to sea; to put (out) to sea

出海口(ㄔㄨ ㄏㄞˇ ㄎㄡˇ)
an estuary

出汗(ㄔㄨ ㄏㄢˋ)
to perspire; to sweat

出航(ㄔㄨ ㄏㄤˊ)
①to set out on a voyage; to set sail ②to set out on a flight

出乎(ㄔㄨ ㄏㄨ)
to come from

出乎意外(ㄔㄨ ㄏㄨ ㄧˋ ㄨㄞˋ)
unexpectedly

出貨(ㄔㄨ ㄏㄨㄛˋ)
①to produce goods ②to get delivered goods ③to contribute money

部
口

出擊(ㄔㄨ ㄐㄧˊ)
to leave (a base, camp, position, etc.) to attack or raid (the enemy)

出家(ㄔㄨ ㄐㄧㄚ)
(Buddhism) to leave home and become a monk or nun

出家人(ㄔㄨ ㄐㄧㄚ ㄖㄣˊ)
a monk or nun

出價(ㄔㄨ ㄐㄧㄚˋ)
to bid; to offer a price

出嫁(ㄔㄨ ㄐㄧㄚˋ)
(said of a woman) to get married

出結(ㄔㄨ ㄐㄧㄝ)
to guarantee in writing

出界(ㄔㄨ ㄐㄧㄝˋ)
(sports) out-of-bounds; out-side

出借(ㄔㄨ ㄐㄧㄝˋ)
to lend

出教(ㄔㄨ ㄐㄧㄠ)
to be excommunicated

出尖(ㄔㄨ ㄐㄧㄢ)or 出尖兒(ㄔㄨ ㄐㄧㄢ)
①outstanding; remarkable ②to heap a container (with grains, etc.)

出金(ㄔㄨ ㄐㄧㄣ)
(Japanese) to draw money (from a bank or an investment company)

出進(ㄔㄨ ㄐㄧㄣˋ)
incomings and outgoings; receipts and expenditures

出將入相(ㄔㄨ ㄐㄧㄤ ㄖㄨˋ ㄒㄧㄤ)
(literally) to be as good a general as a minister—well versed in both politics and military tactics

出境(ㄔㄨ ㄐㄧㄥˋ)
to leave a place or country: 他已辦好出境手續。He has gone through all formalities to leave the country.

出境證(ㄔㄨ ㄐㄧㄥˋ ㄓㄥˋ)
an exit permit

出局(ㄔㄨ ㄐㄩˊ)
(baseball) out

出妻(ㄔㄨ ㄑㄧ)
(in ancient China) to divorce one's wife

出奇(ㄔㄨ ㄑㄧˊ)
①extraordinary; extraordinarily: 今年多天冷得出奇。It is extraordinarily cold this winter. ② (to win) by sur-

［口部］

prise
出奇制勝(ㄔㄨㄑㄧㄓˋㄕㄥˋ)
to win by surprise

出其不意(ㄔㄨㄑㄧˊㄅㄨˋㄧˋ)
to take (someone) un-
awares; to take by surprise;
to catch (someone) off-
guard

出氣(ㄔㄨㄑㄧˋ)
to vent one's anger

出氣筒(ㄔㄨㄑㄧˋㄊㄨㄥˇ)
(in a colloquial expression)
one who serves as a vent to
somebody's anger and, as
such, is often scolded without provocation

出氣口(ㄔㄨㄑㄧˋㄎㄡˇ)
①a gas outlet ②an air vent

出錢(ㄔㄨㄑㄧㄢˊ)
to provide the funds

出勤(ㄔㄨㄑㄧㄣˊ)
to take a business trip

出去(ㄔㄨㄑㄩˋ)
①to go out; to be out ②
Get out!

出缺(ㄔㄨㄑㄩㄝ)
a vacancy created by illness,
death, etc.

出席(ㄔㄨㄒㄧˊ)
to attend or to be present at
(a meeting, etc.): 我必須出席
這次的會議。I must attend the
meeting.

出息(ㄔㄨㄒㄧˊ)
①promising (kids, etc.) ②
profit

出血(ㄔㄨㄒㄧㄝˇ)
bleeding; hemorrhage

出現(ㄔㄨㄒㄧㄢˋ)
to appear; to emerge: 船出現
在水平線上。The ship ap-
peared on the horizon.

出行(ㄔㄨㄒㄧㄥˊ)
to leave for a long journey

出巡(ㄔㄨㄒㄩㄣˊ)
to go on an inspection trip

出診(ㄔㄨㄓㄣˇ)
(said of a physician) to be
on house call

出疹子(ㄔㄨㄓㄣˇ‧ㄗ)
to get the measles

出陣(ㄔㄨㄓㄣˋ)
(usually said of a general in
ancient times) to go out and
confront the enemy

出征(ㄔㄨㄓㄥ)

to go out to battle

出主意(ㄔㄨㄓㄨˇㄧˋ)
①to scheme; to cook up
something; to provide an
idea ②to incite or instigate

出贅(ㄔㄨㄓㄨㄟˋ)
(said of a man) to marry
into the family of one's wife

出眾(ㄔㄨㄓㄨㄥˋ)
outstanding; foremost

出車禍(ㄔㄨㄔㄜㄏㄨㄛˋ)
to have a car accident

出差(ㄔㄨㄔㄞ)
(said of subordinate officials) to go out of town on
business

出超(ㄔㄨㄔㄠ)
a favorable balance of trade
亦作「貿易順差」

出醜(ㄔㄨㄔㄡˇ)
to make a scene; to lose
face; to look or sound ridiculous; to make a fool of oneself

出產(ㄔㄨㄔㄢˇ)
to produce or grow (espe-
cially said of agricultural
products)

出塵(ㄔㄨㄔㄣˊ)
out-of-the-world

出場(ㄔㄨㄔㄤˇ)or(ㄔㄨㄔㄤˊ)
①(said of a player) to go
on the stage ②(said of an
athlete, etc.) to enter the
stadium or go on to the
playground

出廠(ㄔㄨㄔㄤˇ)
(said of a product) to leave
the factory

出處(
①(ㄔㄨㄔㄨˋ) ⓐ background (of
a person) ⓑ the source of
an allusion or a quotation
② (ㄔㄨㄔㄨˋ) to leave and to
take office

出師(ㄔㄨㄕ)
①to move soldiers forward
for attack; to mobilize
troops for offensive ②to
complete one's apprenticeship in a trade and make a
debut as a professional

出師不利(ㄔㄨㄕㄅㄨˋㄌㄧˋ)
①to suffer a defeat at the
very first battle ②to meet a
setback at the start of an
undertaking

出使(ㄔㄨㄕˇ)or(ㄔㄨㄕˋ)
to be appointed as a diplomatic envoy; to be an
ambassador to

出仕(ㄔㄨㄕˋ)
to be an official; to take a
government position

出世(ㄔㄨㄕˋ)
(Buddhism) ①appearance
in the world, e.g. the Buddha's appearance ②to leave
the mundane world (as a
monk or nun) ③beyond or
outside this world; not of
this world; of nirvana character ④to come into the
world; to be born

出示(ㄔㄨㄕˋ)
to show (something to someone)

出事(ㄔㄨㄕˋ)
to be in trouble; to have an
accident

出手(ㄔㄨㄕㄡˇ)
①to sell; to part with ②to
take on a job or work ③an
offer; to offer ④to reach
out with one's hand

出手大方(ㄔㄨㄕㄡˇㄉㄚˋㄈㄤ)
to spend money freely; very
generous

出售(ㄔㄨㄕㄡˋ)
to sell

出山(ㄔㄨㄕㄢ)
to leave retirement and take
a government post

出身(ㄔㄨㄕㄣ)
(personal) backgrounds;
qualifications

出神(ㄔㄨㄕㄣˊ)
①absorbed in ②absent-
minded

出神入化(ㄔㄨㄕㄣˊㄖㄨˋㄏㄨㄚˋ)
uncanny (feats, skill, etc.);
superb; out-of-this-world
(performances, etc.)

出聲(ㄔㄨㄕㄥ)or出聲兒(ㄔㄨ
ㄕㄥㄦ)
to utter (a sound); to make
a sound; to speak

出生(ㄔㄨㄕㄥ)
to be born

出生率(ㄔㄨㄕㄥㄌㄩˋ)
birthrate

出生紙(ㄔㄨㄕㄥㄓˇ)or出生證書
(ㄔㄨㄕㄥㄓㄥˋㄕㄨ)
a birth certificate

出生入死 (ㄔㄨ ㄕㄥ ㄖㄨˋ ㄙˇ)
to risk one's life; to brave untold dangers

出書
to publish books

出人頭地 (ㄔㄨ ㄖㄣˊ ㄊㄡˊ ㄉㄧˋ)
to be somebody; to stand out among one's fellows; to make good

出人意表 (ㄔㄨ ㄖㄣˊ ㄧˋ ㄅㄧㄠˇ)
beyond expectation; to come as a surprise

出任 (ㄔㄨ ㄖㄣˋ)
to take up the post of

出售 (ㄔㄨ ㄕㄡˋ)
to sell; for sale

出入 (ㄔㄨ ㄖㄨˋ)
① to come and go ② receipts and expenditures ③ discrepancy; inconsistency

出資 (ㄔㄨ ㄗ)
to put up capital (for a business venture, etc.)

出走 (ㄔㄨ ㄗㄡˇ)
to run away from one's home; to desert one's family

出租 (ㄔㄨ ㄗㄨ) or 出賃 (ㄔㄨ ㄖㄣˋ)
to let (a house, equipment, etc.)

出操 (ㄔㄨ ㄘㄠ)
to drill; to train (soldiers, etc.): 本隊今天下午出操。Our team will have drill this afternoon.

出錯 (ㄔㄨ ㄘㄨㄛˋ)
to make mistakes: 她做事很少出錯。She seldom makes a mistake in her work.

出色 (ㄔㄨ ㄙㄜˋ)
outstanding; remarkable

出塞 (ㄔㄨ ㄙㄞˋ)
(in ancient China) to go far out of the frontiers; to cross the frontier

出賽 (ㄔㄨ ㄙㄞˋ)
to contend with; to contest

出爾反爾 (ㄔㄨ ㄦˇ ㄈㄢˇ ㄦˇ)
to renege on one's promise; to act contrary to one's word

出以公心 (ㄔㄨ ㄧˇ ㄍㄨㄥ ㄒㄧㄣ)
to do something impartially; to act without any selfish considerations

出芽 (ㄔㄨ ㄧㄚˊ) or 出芽兒 (ㄔㄨ ㄧㄚˊㄦ)
(said of a plant) to sprout

出遊 (ㄔㄨ ㄧㄡˊ)
to go on an excursion

出言不遜 (ㄔㄨ ㄧㄢˊ ㄅㄨˋ ㄒㄩㄣˋ)
to utter insulting remarks; to insult

出洋 (ㄔㄨ ㄧㄤˊ)
to go abroad

出洋相 (ㄔㄨ ㄧㄤˊ ㄒㄧㄤˋ)
to make a fool of oneself (especially in public)

出迎 (ㄔㄨ ㄧㄥˊ)
to go or come out to receive

出外 (ㄔㄨ ㄨㄞˋ)
to leave for a distant place

出亡 (ㄔㄨ ㄨㄤˊ)
to escape; to go into exile

出於 or 出于 (ㄔㄨ ㄩˊ)
to start from; to proceed from; to stem from

出於無意 (ㄔㄨ ㄩˊ ㄨˊ ㄧˋ)
unintentional; unintentionally

出院 (ㄔㄨ ㄩㄢˋ)
to leave the hospital: 他病癒出院了。He left the hospital after recovery.

六畫

【函】 355 (ㄏㄢˊ harn hán)
1. a letter; correspondence
2. armor
3. to contain; to envelop
4. a sheath, as for a sword or a knife
5. an envelope

函購 (ㄏㄢˊ ㄍㄡˋ)
to purchase by mail order

函件 (ㄏㄢˊ ㄐㄧㄢˋ)
letters; correspondence

函授 (ㄏㄢˊ ㄕㄡˋ)
teaching by mail or correspondence

函授學校 (ㄏㄢˊ ㄕㄡˋ ㄒㄩㄝˊ ㄒㄧㄠˋ)
a correspondence school

函數 (ㄏㄢˊ ㄕㄨˋ)
(mathematics) function

函索即寄 (ㄏㄢˊ ㄙㄨㄛˇ ㄐㄧˊ ㄐㄧˋ)
to send (samples, etc.) upon request by mail

函約 (ㄏㄢˊ ㄩㄝ)
to make an appointment by letter

刀 部
ㄉㄠ dau dāo

【刀】 356 (ㄉㄠ dau dāo)
1. a knife; a blade; a sword
2. knife-shaped coins of ancient China

刀把兒 or 刀靶兒 (ㄉㄠ ㄅㄚˇㄦ)
① the handle of a knife ② power ③ a hold that may be used against somebody 亦作「刀把子」

刀背 (ㄉㄠ ㄅㄟˋ)
① the back of a knife ② an occasion on which the money spent is wasted

刀筆吏 (ㄉㄠ ㄅㄧˇ ㄌㄧˋ)
(in ancient China) a literary hack who specialized in drawing up indictments and other legal documents for a fee

刀片 (ㄉㄠ ㄆㄧㄢˋ)
a razor blade

刀馬旦 (ㄉㄠ ㄇㄚˇ ㄉㄢˋ)
(Peking opera) the role of a female warrior

刀鋒 (ㄉㄠ ㄈㄥ)
the blade or edge of a knife

刀斧手 (ㄉㄠ ㄈㄨˇ ㄕㄡˇ)
an executioner

刀光劍影 (ㄉㄠ ㄍㄨㄤ ㄐㄧㄢˋ ㄧㄥˇ)
engaged in hot battle; a heated combat (usually between individual swordsmen)

刀口 (ㄉㄠ ㄎㄡˇ) or 刀刃 (ㄉㄠ ㄖㄣˋ)
① the blade or edge of a knife ② an occasion on which money can be spent to advantage

刀匠 (ㄉㄠ ㄐㄧㄤˋ)
a bladesmith

刀鞘 (ㄉㄠ ㄑㄧㄠˋ)
a sheath

刀槍 (ㄉㄠ ㄑㄧㄤ)
swords and spears; weapons

刀下留人 (ㄉㄠ ㄒㄧㄚˋ ㄌㄧㄡˊ ㄖㄣˊ)
Hold the execution! (The exclamation was used in former times when a criminal about to be beheaded on the

刀 部

【刀部】

execution ground won a last-minute pardon or when the case was suddenly reversed.)

刀叉(カ ㄉ ㄚ ㄔ)
knives and forks (used in Western meals)

刀山火海(カ ㄉ ㄕㄢ ㄏㄨㄛ ㄏㄞˇ)
a mountain of swords and a sea of flames—most dangerous places

刀傷(カ ㄉ ㄕㄤ)
① knife wound ② to inflict a wound or injury with a knife

刀子(カ ㄉ ·ㄗ)
a small knife; a dagger

刀俎(カ ㄉ ㄗㄨˇ)
a knife and chopping board

刀魚(カ ㄉ ㄩˊ)
Chinese herring

【刁】 357 ㄉ ㄧㄠ diau diāo
1. low and cunning; crafty; wicked; artful; knavish
2. a Chinese family name

刁蠻(ㄉ ㄧㄠ ㄇㄢˊ)
obstinate

刁斗(ㄉ ㄧㄠ ㄉㄡˇ)
a pot made of copper used by the army

刁斗森嚴(ㄉ ㄧㄠ ㄉㄡˇ ㄙㄣ ㄧㄢˊ)
strict army discipline

刁難(ㄉ ㄧㄠ ㄋㄢˊ)
to (deliberately) make things difficult for others

刁悍(ㄉ ㄧㄠ ㄏㄢˋ)
cunning and fierce

刁猾(ㄉ ㄧㄠ ㄏㄨㄚˊ)
cunning; low and cunning

刁詐(ㄉ ㄧㄠ ㄓㄚˋ)
knavish; crafty

刁鑽(ㄉ ㄧㄠ ㄗㄨㄢ)
wily; cunning

刁鑽古怪(ㄉ ㄧㄠ ㄗㄨㄢ ㄍㄨˇ ㄍㄨㄞˋ)
perverse; mischievous; cranky

一畫

【刃】 358 ㄖㄣˋ renn rèn
1. the blade or edge of a knife
2. to kill

刃兒(ㄖㄣˋ ㄦ)
the edge or blade of a knife

二畫

【分】 359 1. ㄈㄣ fen fēn
1. to divide
2. to part
3. to share
4. to distribute
5. to distinguish
6. one minute
7. one cent
8. one hundredth of a tael
9. a centimeter
10. located separately; a branch

分貝(ㄈㄣ ㄅㄟˋ)
a decibel

分班(ㄈㄣ ㄅㄢ)
to divide (students) into classes

分謗(ㄈㄣ ㄅㄤˋ)
to share blame; to be the target of the same slander (as that which is directed to another person)

分崩離析(ㄈㄣ ㄅㄥ ㄌㄧˊ ㄒㄧ)
to disintegrate and decompose; to lose unity

分別(ㄈㄣ ㄅㄧㄝˊ)
① to part (from a person) ② to distinguish or tell apart ③ separately; to separate

分辨(ㄈㄣ ㄅㄧㄢˋ)
to distinguish; to tell apart

分辯(ㄈㄣ ㄅㄧㄢˋ)
to make excuses; to explain

分兵進攻(ㄈㄣ ㄅㄧㄥ ㄐㄧㄣˋ ㄍㄨㄥ)
to divide the forces to attack

分布 or 分佈(ㄈㄣ ㄅㄨˋ)
to be scattered (over an area); to spread

分派(ㄈㄣ ㄆㄞˋ)
to assign; to allot; to apportion

分配(ㄈㄣ ㄆㄟˋ)
① to distribute; to portion out; to share out; to deal out; to allocate ② distribution

分批(ㄈㄣ ㄆㄧ)
in batches; in turn

分袂(ㄈㄣ ㄇㄟˋ)
(said of friends) to part; to separate

分門別類(ㄈㄣ ㄇㄣˊ ㄅㄧㄝˊ ㄌㄟˋ)
to classify systematically

分米(ㄈㄣ ㄇㄧˇ)
a decimeter

分泌(ㄈㄣ ㄇㄧˋ)
(biology) to secrete; secretion

分秒必爭(ㄈㄣ ㄇㄧㄠˇ ㄅㄧˋ ㄓㄥ)
to seize every minute and second; to make the best of one's time

分娩(ㄈㄣ ㄇㄧㄢˇ)
to lie in; to give birth; childbirth

分明(ㄈㄣ ㄇㄧㄥˊ)
clear; distinct; unambiguous; unmistakable

分母(ㄈㄣ ㄇㄨˇ)
the denominator of a fraction

分發(ㄈㄣ ㄈㄚ)
① to issue or distribute (articles) ② to assign or appoint (to a post or duty)

分肥(ㄈㄣ ㄈㄟˊ)
to divide or share spoils, embezzled money, etc.

分封(ㄈㄣ ㄈㄥ)
to confer (on each vassal) a title to a feudal state

分付(ㄈㄣ ㄈㄨˋ)
to pay or shell out separately

分赴(ㄈㄣ ㄈㄨˋ)
to leave for different destinations

分道揚鑣(ㄈㄣ ㄉㄠˋ ㄧㄤˊ ㄅㄧㄠ)
① (for two persons) to engage in different pursuits ② to quit partnership, association, etc.

分擔(ㄈㄣ ㄉㄢ)
to undertake different portions of or share the responsibility for (the same task, duty, etc.)

分等(ㄈㄣ ㄉㄥˇ)
to grade; to classify

分隊(ㄈㄣ ㄉㄨㄟˋ)
a unit of soldiers or policemen corresponding to the platoon or squad

分頭辦理(ㄈㄣ ㄊㄡˊ ㄅㄢˋ ㄌㄧˇ)
to manage or handle separately for the same goal

分攤(ㄈㄣ ㄊㄢ)
to share (a financial burden), stocks, etc.)

分庭抗禮(ㄈㄣㄊㄧㄥㄎㄤㄌㄧ)
to function as rivals; to
rival each other; to be in
competing positions; to compete on equal terms

分途(ㄈㄣㄊㄨ)
to take different paths; to
diverge; to separate

分類(ㄈㄣㄌㄟ)
① to classify; to sort ② classification; taxonomy

分類廣告(ㄈㄣㄌㄟㄍㄨㄤㄍㄠ)
classified ads

分勞(ㄈㄣㄌㄠ)
to help someone do work

分離(ㄈㄣㄌㄧ)
to separate; to part; to
divide; to disconnect; to dis-
sociate; to detach; to cut off;
to segregate

分離派(ㄈㄣㄌㄧㄆㄞ)
secessionists

分力(ㄈㄣㄌㄧ)
(physics) components of
force

分利(ㄈㄣㄌㄧ)
to share benefit

分裂(ㄈㄣㄌㄧㄝ)
to break up; to split; to disunite

分路(ㄈㄣㄌㄨ)
① along separate routes; to
take different paths ②(electricity) a shunt

分割(ㄈㄣㄍㄜ)
① to divide up; to cut apart
② segmentation

分隔(ㄈㄣㄍㄜ)
to partition

分光鏡(ㄈㄣㄍㄨㄤㄐㄧㄥ)
a spectroscope

分光儀(ㄈㄣㄍㄨㄤㄧ)
a spectrometer

分工(ㄈㄣㄍㄨㄥ)
to divide the work; division
of labor

分工合作(ㄈㄣㄍㄨㄥㄏㄜㄗㄨㄛ)
to share out the work and
cooperate with one another

分科(ㄈㄣㄎㄜ)
(education) to divide students into groups, each ma-
joring in a different field of
studies

分開(ㄈㄣㄎㄞ)
to separate; to set apart; to

segregate; to isolate

分合(ㄈㄣㄏㄜ)
union and division; synthesis
and analysis; fusion and fission

分毫(ㄈㄣㄏㄠ)
a modicum; a bit; a trifle; a
whit

分號(ㄈㄣㄏㄠ)
① the semicolon ② a branch
store

分行(ㄈㄣㄏㄤ)
a branch office; a branch
store

分化(ㄈㄣㄏㄨㄚ)
①(biology) differentiation
② to disunite; disunion or
dissension; to sow discord

分會(ㄈㄣㄏㄨㄟ)
a branch association; a
chapter (of an organization)

分紅(ㄈㄣㄏㄨㄥ)
(business) to distribute a
dividend

分機(ㄈㄣㄐㄧ)
(telephone) an extension

分級(ㄈㄣㄐㄧ)
to grade; to classify

分家(ㄈㄣㄐㄧㄚ)
(for brothers) to divide family property (so as to set up
separate households)

分解(ㄈㄣㄐㄧㄝ)
① to resolve; to decompose
② to dissolve ③ to analyze

分解熱(ㄈㄣㄐㄧㄝㄖㄜ)
heat of decomposition

分界(ㄈㄣㄐㄧㄝ)
① to have as the boundary;
to be demarcated by ② a
line of demarcation

分界線(ㄈㄣㄐㄧㄝㄒㄧㄢ)
a boundary; a borderline; a
line of demarcation

分進合擊(ㄈㄣㄐㄧㄣㄏㄜㄐㄧ)
(military) a concerted
attack by converging col-
umns

分疆畫界(ㄈㄣㄐㄧㄤㄏㄨㄚㄐㄧㄝ)
to mark boundaries

分居(ㄈㄣㄐㄩ)
to separate without a legal
divorce; to live apart

分局(ㄈㄣㄐㄩ)
a police precinct office

分句(ㄈㄣㄐㄩ)

(grammar) a clause

分歧(ㄈㄣㄑㄧ)
① difference; divergence;
discrepancy ② to diverge; to
differ; to disagree

分期付款(ㄈㄣㄑㄧㄈㄨㄎㄨㄢ)
payment in installments; the
installment plan

分區(ㄈㄣㄑㄩ)
to divide into districts; to
zone

分權(ㄈㄣㄑㄩㄢ)
division of power or authority

分析(ㄈㄣㄒㄧ)
to analyze; to study; to
investigate; analysis; study;
investigation

分析法(ㄈㄣㄒㄧㄈㄚ)
an analytical method

分析師(ㄈㄣㄒㄧㄕ)
an analyst

分銷(ㄈㄣㄒㄧㄠ)
to retail (goods)

分曉(ㄈㄣㄒㄧㄠ)
the result (of a developing
event); the answer (to a
puzzle, riddle, etc.)

分校(ㄈㄣㄒㄧㄠ)
a branch of a school (away
from the school's main campus)

分心(ㄈㄣㄒㄧㄣ)or 分神(ㄈㄣㄕㄣ)
① to give some attention; to
give a thought ② to fail to
pay full attention; to fail to
concentrate oneself ③ distraction

分享(ㄈㄣㄒㄧㄤ)
to share (joys, rights, etc.);
to take part in: 讓我們分享成
功的喜悅。Let us share the
joys of success.

分支(ㄈㄣㄓ)
a branch; a division

分針(ㄈㄣㄓㄣ)
the minute hand

分社(ㄈㄣㄕㄜ)
① a branch office ② a news
bureau

分手(ㄈㄣㄕㄡ)
to part; to separate; to cease
associating: 我們是在火車站
分手的。We separated at the
railway station.

分身(ㄈㄣㄕㄣ)
to divide attention; to han-

〔**刀**
部〕

〔刀部〕

dle more than one thing at the same time

分身乏術(ㄈㄣ ㄕㄣ ㄈㄚˊ ㄕㄨˋ)
unable to show up at all the places where one is needed; unable to do all the things one has to do

分數(ㄈㄣ ㄕㄨˋ)
① a fraction (as distinct from a whole number) ② grades or percentage (in an examination); scores (in sports competitions)

分說(ㄈㄣ ㄕㄨㄛ)
to make excuses; to explain

分水嶺(ㄈㄣ ㄕㄨㄟˇ ㄌㄧㄥˇ)
a watershed (in the sense of a ridge)

分潤(ㄈㄣ ㄖㄨㄣˋ)
to share or have a share of (a fortune, profit, etc.)

分子(ㄈㄣ ㄗˇ)
① (mathematics) a numerator (as opposed to a denominator) ② (physics) a molecule

分子力(ㄈㄣ ㄗˇ ㄌㄧˋ)
molecular force

分子量(ㄈㄣ ㄗˇ ㄌㄧㄤˋ)
molecular weight

分子式(ㄈㄣ ㄗˇ ㄕˋ)
a molecular formula

分贓(ㄈㄣ ㄗㄤ)
to share or get a share of loot or bribes

分組(ㄈㄣ ㄗㄨˇ)
to divide into groups

分詞(ㄈㄣ ㄘˊ)
(grammar) a participle

分冊(ㄈㄣ ㄘㄜˋ)
a fascicle

分層負責(ㄈㄣ ㄘㄥˊ ㄈㄨˋ ㄗㄜˊ)
delegation of the right authority to the right level of officials (as distinct from concentration of authority in the hands of the boss)

分寸(ㄈㄣ ㄘㄨㄣˋ)
judgment for propriety in speech, behavior, etc.); 說話應有分寸。One should talk with propriety.

分散(ㄈㄣ ㄙㄢˋ)
to scatter; to disperse; to dissipate; to divert

分送(ㄈㄣ ㄙㄨㄥˋ)
to distribute

分野(ㄈㄣ ㄧㄝˇ)
demarcation; a borderline; a boundary

分憂(ㄈㄣ ㄧㄡ)
to share sorrows, worries, etc.

分陰(ㄈㄣ ㄧㄣ)
a very short while; a moment

分文不取(ㄈㄣ ㄨㄣˊ ㄅㄨˋ ㄑㄩˇ)
do not charge a single cent

【分】 359
2. (份) ㄈㄣˋ fenn fèn
1. a role or part (played by a person in life)
2. a part or portion (of a whole); a component: 這章稿的一部分不易辨識。A portion of the manuscript is illegible.

分內之事(ㄈㄣˋ ㄋㄟˋ ㄓ ㄕˋ)
one's due task; a duty

分量(ㄈㄣˋ ㄌㄧㄤˋ)
① an amount ② (said of statements) weight or impact

分子(ㄈㄣˋ ㄗˇ)
a member (of some organization)

分外(ㄈㄣˋ ㄨㄞˋ)
① particularly; especially ② undeserved; beyond the scope of duty or position

分外之物(ㄈㄣˋ ㄨㄞˋ ㄓ ㄨˋ)
undue gain, luxury, etc.

【切】 360
1. ㄑㄧㄝ chie qiē
to cut; to mince; to slice; to carve

切片(ㄑㄧㄝ ㄆㄧㄢˋ)
① microtome section ② to cut into slices

切片檢查(ㄑㄧㄝ ㄆㄧㄢˋ ㄐㄧㄢˇ ㄔㄚˊ)
the microscopic examination of the affected tissue cut into very thin pieces

切面(ㄑㄧㄝ ㄇㄧㄢˋ)
a tangent surface or tangent plane

切麵(ㄑㄧㄝ ㄇㄧㄢˋ)
chopped band noodles

切腹自殺(ㄑㄧㄝ ㄈㄨˋ ㄗˋ ㄕㄚ)
to commit hara-kiri (a ritual suicide under the Japanese samurai code of honor)

切斷(ㄑㄧㄝ ㄉㄨㄢˋ)
to sever; to cut asunder: 他用刀子切斷繩子。He cut the

rope asunder with a knife.

切開(ㄑㄧㄝ ㄎㄞ)
to cut open

切塊(ㄑㄧㄝ ㄎㄨㄞˋ)
stripping and slicing

切線(ㄑㄧㄝ ㄒㄧㄢˋ)
a tangent (line)

切除(ㄑㄧㄝ ㄔㄨˊ)
① to cut out; to resect ② excision; resection

切磋(ㄑㄧㄝ ㄘㄨㄛ)
to improve oneself through discussions with another; to learn from each other by exchanging views

切圓(ㄑㄧㄝ ㄩㄢˊ)
tangent circles

【切】 360
2. ㄑㄧㄝˋ chieh qiè
to be close to: 譯文需切原意。The translation should be close in meaning to the original.

切莫(ㄑㄧㄝˋ ㄇㄛˋ)
by no means

切脈(ㄑㄧㄝˋ ㄇㄛˋ)
to feel a patient's pulse

切膚(ㄑㄧㄝˋ ㄈㄨ)or **切己**(ㄑㄧㄝˋ ㄐㄧˇ)
very close to oneself; keenly felt

切膚之痛(ㄑㄧㄝˋ ㄈㄨ ㄓ ㄊㄨㄥˋ)
① keenly felt pain ② a personal loss

切當(ㄑㄧㄝˋ ㄉㄤˋ)or **切合**(ㄑㄧㄝˋ ㄏㄜˊ)
to the point; apposite; appropriate; fitting; apt

切題(ㄑㄧㄝˋ ㄊㄧˊ)
to the point

切骨(ㄑㄧㄝˋ ㄍㄨˇ)
(said of hatred, etc.) strongly felt; deep; intense; bitter

切口(ㄑㄧㄝˋ ㄎㄡˇ)
professional jargons

切忌(ㄑㄧㄝˋ ㄐㄧˋ)
to be sure to avoid; to forbid

切記(ㄑㄧㄝˋ ㄐㄧˋ)
to be sure to remember; to keep in mind; to bear in mind

切近(ㄑㄧㄝˋ ㄐㄧㄣˋ)
close; closely related

切切(ㄑㄧㄝˋ ㄑㄧㄝˋ)
① urgent; important ② pathetic; pathetic sounds ③ soft sounds (or voices)

刀切實實（くlㄠ くlㄝ ㄕ ㄕ）or 切實（くlㄝ ㄕ）
① real; sure; certain ② thoroughly; strictly; thorough

切齒（くlㄝ ㄔ）
to grind the teeth in anger, with hatred, etc.

切身（くlㄝ ㄕㄣ）
personal (interests); directly affecting a person

切要（くlㄝ lㄠ）
very important; of vital importance

切勿（くlㄝ ㄨˋ）
do not by any means: 切勿自以為是。Do not be presumptuous and opinionated by any means.

【刈】 361 | ㄧˋ yih yì
to mow; to reap

刈草機（ㄧˋ ㄘㄠˇ ㄐl）
a lawn mower; a mowing machine; a mower

三畫

【刊】 362 ㄎㄢ kan kān
1. to hew; to cut
2. to engrave
3. a publication
4. to publish

刊本（ㄎㄢ ㄅㄣˇ）
an edition (of a book)

刊譯（ㄎㄢ ㄇlˋ）or 刊誤（ㄎㄢ ㄨˋ）
to correct errors in printing

刊登（ㄎㄢ ㄉㄥ）or 刊載（ㄎㄢ ㄗㄞˋ）
①(for a writer) to publish (an article in a periodical) ②(for a periodical) to carry (an article)

刊頭（ㄎㄢ ㄊㄡˊ）
the masthead of a newspaper or magazine

刊行（ㄎㄢ ㄒlㄥˊ）
to publish for sale

刊印（ㄎㄢ lㄣˋ）
to print for publication

刊物（ㄎㄢ ㄨˋ）
a periodical; a publication

刊誤表 or 勘誤表（ㄎㄢ ㄨˋ ㄅlㄠˇ）
a list of corrections attached to a publication; errata

四畫

【刎】 363 ㄨㄣˇ woen wěn
to cut the throat

刎頸之交（ㄨㄣˇ ㄐlㄥˇ ㄓ ㄐlㄠ）
ties between friends willing to sacrifice even life for each other; profound mutual devotion between friends

【刑】 364 ㄒlㄥˊ shyng xíng
penalty; punishment

刑不上大夫（ㄒlㄥˊ ㄅㄨˋ ㄕㄤˋ ㄉㄚˋ ㄈㄨ）
(in feudal China) High officials are exempt from the penalties prescribed the law.

刑部（ㄒlㄥˊ ㄅㄨˋ）
the Ministry of Justice (one of the six major government branches in former times)

刑名（ㄒlㄥˊ ㄇlㄥˊ）
laws

刑名之學（ㄒlㄥˊ ㄇlㄥˊ ㄓ ㄒㄩㄝˊ）
the philosophy of the Legalist School in the period of Warring States

刑罰（ㄒlㄥˊ ㄈㄚˊ）
penalty; punishment

刑法（ㄒlㄥˊ ㄈㄚˇ）
criminal law; the criminal code; the penal code: 別觸犯刑法。Don't violate criminal law.

刑典（ㄒlㄥˊ ㄉlㄢˇ）
the criminal code; the penal code

刑戮（ㄒlㄥˊ ㄌㄨˋ）
to kill as penalty

刑具（ㄒlㄥˊ ㄐㄩˋ）
an instrument of torture

刑期（ㄒlㄥˊ くl）
a term of imprisonment

刑求（ㄒlㄥˊ くlㄡˊ）
to exact confession by means of torture

刑杖（ㄒlㄥˊ ㄓㄤˋ）
a club, or rod, for torture

刑場（ㄒlㄥˊ ㄔㄤˇ）or 刑地（ㄒlㄥˊ ㄉlˋ）
an execution ground

刑事（ㄒlㄥˊ ㄕˋ）
criminal; penal

刑事犯（ㄒlㄥˊ ㄕˋ ㄈㄢˋ）
a criminal; a criminal suspect

刑事訴訟法（ㄒlㄥˊ ㄕˋ ㄙㄨˋ ㄙㄨㄥˋ ㄈㄚˇ）
the code of criminal procedure

刑網（ㄒlㄥˊ ㄨㄤˇ）
the criminal code

【划】 365 ㄏㄨㄚˊ hwa huá
to oar; to row

划拳（ㄏㄨㄚˊ くㄩㄢˊ）
①a finger-guessing game—a drinking game at feasts ②to play the finger guessing game, each putting out one hand and guessing the total of the two parties 亦作「豁拳」

划船（ㄏㄨㄚˊ ㄔㄨㄢˊ）
to row a boat

划子（ㄏㄨㄚˊ ㄗˇ）
a small boat

划算（ㄏㄨㄚˊ ㄙㄨㄢˋ）
①to calculate; to weigh ②profitable; advantageous

【刓】 366 ㄨㄢˊ wan wán
to round off; to trim

【刖】 367 ㄩㄝˋ yueh yuè
to cut off the feet as a punishment

【列】 368 ㄌlㄝˋ lieh liè
1. to arrange in a line; to line up: 將軍整列他的隊伍。The general lined up his troops.
2. to enumerate
3. to display
4. a line; a series: 沿着池塘有一列柳樹。Along the pond there is a line of willows.
5. a Chinese family name

列表（ㄌlㄝˋ ㄅlㄠˇ）
to prepare a list or chart

列名（ㄌlㄝˋ ㄇlㄥˊ）
to appear on a name list

列島（ㄌlㄝˋ ㄉㄠˇ）
a chain of islands; an archipelago

列土分疆（ㄌlㄝˋ ㄊㄨˇ ㄈㄣ ㄐlㄤ）
(said of the first emperor of a dynasty) to award fiefs to the chief lieutenants

列寧（ㄌlㄝˋ ㄋlㄥˊ）
Nikolai Lenin, 1870-1924, Russian revolutionary

列寧格勒（ㄌlㄝˋ ㄋlㄥˊ ㄍㄜˊ ㄌㄜˋ）
Leningrad

列國（ㄌlㄝˋ ㄍㄨㄛˊ）
the various states or nations

列舉（ㄌlㄝˋ ㄐㄩˇ）
to enumerate; to cite or mention item by item

〔刀部〕

列強(ㄌㄧㄝˋ ㄑㄧㄤˊ)
the various powers; an array of powerful nations

列清單(ㄌㄧㄝˋ ㄑㄧㄥ ㄉㄢ)
to list in detail

列席(ㄌㄧㄝˋ ㄒㄧˊ)
to be present (at a meeting as an observer); to attend a meeting with no voting right

列傳(ㄌㄧㄝˋ ㄓㄨㄢˋ)
collected biographies; a collection of biographies

列車(ㄌㄧㄝˋ ㄔㄜ)
a train

列入(ㄌㄧㄝˋ ㄖㄨˋ)
to be included in; to be incorporated in

列子(ㄌㄧㄝˋ ㄗˇ)
a book in philosophy written by Lieh Yü-kou (列禦寇) of the Chou Dynasty, some time right after Confucius, considered as a Taoist classic

列祖列宗(ㄌㄧㄝˋ ㄗㄨˇ ㄌㄧㄝˋ ㄗㄨㄥ)
an array of ancestors

列為(ㄌㄧㄝˋ ㄨㄟˊ)
listed as

列位(ㄌㄧㄝˋ ㄨㄟˋ)
all the ladies and gentlemen present (on this occasion)

五畫

【初】 369
ㄔㄨ chu chū
1. first
2. original: 最初的計畫後來改變了。The original plan was afterwards changed.
3. junior
4. early; initial: 初夏蟬鳴。Cicadas chirp in the early summer.

初版(ㄔㄨ ㄅㄢˇ)
the first edition (of a book)

初步(ㄔㄨ ㄅㄨˋ)
①the first or initial step ②a primer, or the rudimentary knowledge of something

初民(ㄔㄨ ㄇㄧㄣˊ)
primitive people

初犯(ㄔㄨ ㄈㄢˋ)
①first offenses ②a first offender

初等(ㄔㄨ ㄉㄥˇ)
primary or elementary (grade)

初等教育(ㄔㄨ ㄉㄥˇ ㄐㄧㄠˋ ㄩˋ)
elementary education; primary education

初度(ㄔㄨ ㄉㄨˋ)
①one's birthday ②the first time

初冬(ㄔㄨ ㄉㄨㄥ)
early winter

初唐(ㄔㄨ ㄊㄤˊ)
(the poetic style of) the early Tang Dynasty

初露鋒芒(ㄔㄨ ㄌㄨˋ ㄈㄥ ㄇㄤˊ)
to display one's ability for the first time

初戀(ㄔㄨ ㄌㄧㄢˋ)
first love

初稿(ㄔㄨ ㄍㄠˇ)
the first draft (of a poem, play, novel, etc.)

初會(ㄔㄨ ㄏㄨㄟˋ)
the first meeting (between people who are previously strangers)

初婚(ㄔㄨ ㄏㄨㄣ)
the first marriage (of a person who has remarried)

初級(ㄔㄨ ㄐㄧˊ)
elementary; primary

初級小學(ㄔㄨ ㄐㄧˊ ㄒㄧㄠˇ ㄒㄩㄝˊ)or
初小(ㄔㄨ ㄒㄧㄠˇ)
formerly, a primary school which comprises only the first four grades

初級中學(ㄔㄨ ㄐㄧˊ ㄓㄨㄥ ㄒㄩㄝˊ)or
初中(ㄔㄨ ㄓㄨㄥ)
junior middle school (corresponding to the seventh through the ninth grades)

初階(ㄔㄨ ㄐㄧㄝ)
a primer, or the rudimentary knowledge of something

初交(ㄔㄨ ㄐㄧㄠ)
a new friendship; a nodding acquaintance

初更(ㄔㄨ ㄍㄥ)
the first watch (between 7 and 9 p.m.)

初經期(ㄔㄨ ㄐㄧㄥ ㄑㄧ)
menarche

初期(ㄔㄨ ㄑㄧˊ)
the first or initial stage; the early or earlier stages

初秋(ㄔㄨ ㄑㄧㄡ)
early autumn; early fall; the first of the autumn months (i.e., the seventh moon)

初夏(ㄔㄨ ㄒㄧㄚˋ)
early summer; the first o the summer months (i.e., the fourth moon)

初學(ㄔㄨ ㄒㄩㄝˊ)
①in the beginning stage or an effort to learn (a subject) ②a beginner

初選(ㄔㄨ ㄒㄩㄢˇ)
a primary election

初旬(ㄔㄨ ㄒㄩㄣˊ)
the first ten days of a month

初志(ㄔㄨ ㄓˋ)
the original ambition (of a youth)

初診(ㄔㄨ ㄓㄣˇ)
①the first visit to a doctor ②to visit a patient for the first time

初衷(ㄔㄨ ㄓㄨㄥ)
the original longing, aspiration, or intention

初產婦(ㄔㄨ ㄔㄢˇ ㄈㄨˋ)
a primiparous woman

初出茅廬(ㄔㄨ ㄔㄨ ㄇㄠˊ ㄌㄨˊ)
still inexperienced

初春(ㄔㄨ ㄔㄨㄣ)
early spring; the first of the spring months (i.e., the first moon)

初創(ㄔㄨ ㄔㄨㄤˋ)
newly founded

初蝕(ㄔㄨ ㄕˊ)or 初虧(ㄔㄨ ㄎㄨㄟ)
(astronomy) the first contact

初試(ㄔㄨ ㄕˋ)
①to try or attempt for the first time; the first trial or attempt ②to make a debut ③a preliminary examination or test

初審(ㄔㄨ ㄕㄣˇ)
①a first hearing (of a case in court) ②a preliminary screening (of applications, entries in a contest, etc.)

初生之犢不畏虎(ㄔㄨ ㄕㄥ ㄓ ㄉㄨˊ ㄅㄨˋ ㄨㄟˋ ㄏㄨˇ)
(literally) A newborn calf doesn't fear the tiger. Young men fresh from school are uncompromising despite difficulties of pressure from above.

初日(ㄔㄨ ㄖˋ)
the rising sun

初祖(ㄔㄨ ㄗㄨˇ)

the founder of a sect

初次(ㄔㄨㄘ)
the first time or occasion

初賽(ㄔㄨㄙㄞ)
a preliminary competition

初葉(ㄔㄨㄧㄝˋ)
the early years (of a century): 十八世紀初葉 the early years in the eighteenth century

初夜權(ㄔㄨㄧㄝˋㄑㄩㄢˊ)
jus primae noctis (the right of a feudal lord to the virginity of a maiden on her wedding night in medieval Europe)

初願(ㄔㄨㄩㄢˋ)
one's initial wish

【刪】370 ㄕㄢ shan shān
to delete; to take out; to erase

刪補(ㄕㄢㄅㄨˇ)
to rid superfluities and fill inadequacies (in a writing); to revise

刪繁就簡(ㄕㄢㄈㄢˊㄐㄧㄡˋㄐㄧㄢˇ)
to simplify something by deleting the superfluous

刪訂(ㄕㄢㄉㄧㄥˋ)
to revise (an edition)

刪改(ㄕㄢㄍㄞˇ)
to remove superfluities and correct errors (in a writing); to revise

刪節(ㄕㄢㄐㄧㄝˊ)or刪減(ㄕㄢㄐㄧㄢˇ)
to abridge or condense (a writing)

刪節號(ㄕㄢㄐㄧㄝˊㄏㄠˋ)
ellipsis (a punctuation mark)

刪削(ㄕㄢㄒㄩㄝ)
to delete, expunge, strike out, erase, or remove (superfluities from a writing)

刪除(ㄕㄢㄔㄨˊ)
to delete; to strike out

刪潤(ㄕㄢㄖㄨㄣˋ)
to revise and polish (a writing)

【判】371 ㄆㄢˋ pann pàn
to judge; to conclude

判別(ㄆㄢˋㄅㄧㄝˊ)
to distinguish; to tell apart

判袂(ㄆㄢˋㄇㄟˋ)
(said of friends) to separate; to part

rate; to part

判明(ㄆㄢˋㄇㄧㄥˊ)
to distinguish

判定(ㄆㄢˋㄉㄧㄥˋ)
to judge; to decide

判斷(ㄆㄢˋㄉㄨㄢˋ)
① to judge; to decide; to conclude ② judgment, decision or conclusion

判例(ㄆㄢˋㄌㄧˋ)
(said of court decisions) a precedent

判官(ㄆㄢˋㄍㄨㄢ)
a fierce-looking judge in the afterlife court of law

判決(ㄆㄢˋㄐㄩㄝˊ)
a verdict; a sentence

判決書(ㄆㄢˋㄐㄩㄝˊㄕㄨ)
a verdict or sentence in writing

判處(ㄆㄢˋㄔㄨˇ)
to sentence; to condemn

判若兩人(ㄆㄢˋㄖㄨㄛˋㄌㄧㄤˇㄖㄣˊ)
to become a completely different person; to become completely unrecognizable

判罪(ㄆㄢˋㄗㄨㄟˋ)
to declare guilty

【別】372 ㄅㄧㄝˊ bye bié
1. to part
2. to distinguish; to differentiate
3. other; another; different
4. (in imperative expressions) do not: 現在別走。Don't go yet.

別本(ㄅㄧㄝˊㄅㄣˇ)
a separate copy; a replica

別忙(ㄅㄧㄝˊㄇㄤˊ)
Don't hurry. 或Don't busy yourself. 或Take your time.

別苗頭(ㄅㄧㄝˊㄇㄧㄠˊㄊㄡˊ)
(informal) to match wits; to rival in competition

別名(ㄅㄧㄝˊㄇㄧㄥˊ)or別號(ㄅㄧㄝˊㄏㄠˋ)
an alias; a second name

別的(ㄅㄧㄝˊㄉㄜˋ)
other; different

別提(ㄅㄧㄝˊㄊㄧˊ)
We needn't mention it.或It's not necessary to say.

別體(ㄅㄧㄝˊㄊㄧˇ)
a different calligraphic style

別來(ㄅㄧㄝˊㄌㄞˊ)
① since parting ② do not

別離(ㄅㄧㄝˊㄌㄧˊ)
parting; separation

別管(ㄅㄧㄝˊㄍㄨㄢˇ)
no matter (who, what, etc.)

別館(ㄅㄧㄝˊㄍㄨㄢˇ)
a villa

別開生面(ㄅㄧㄝˊㄎㄞㄕㄥㄇㄧㄢˋ)
to introduce a novelty or novel feature

別集(ㄅㄧㄝˊㄐㄧˊ)
a separate collection or anthology (of literary works published individually)

別解(ㄅㄧㄝˊㄐㄧㄝˇ)
a new interpretation; an opinion from a different standpoint

別具隻眼(ㄅㄧㄝˊㄐㄩˋㄓㄓㄢˇ)
to have an original view or opinion

別具一格(ㄅㄧㄝˊㄐㄩˋㄧㄍㄜˊ)
having a unique (or distinctive) style

別緒(ㄅㄧㄝˊㄒㄩˋ)
the sorrow of parting

別致(ㄅㄧㄝˊㄓˋ)or別緻
original; fresh; new; novel

別針(ㄅㄧㄝˊㄓㄣ)or別針兒(ㄅㄧㄝˊㄓㄣㄦ)
a safety pin; a pin; a brooch

別稱(ㄅㄧㄝˊㄔㄥ)
another name; an alternative name

別出心裁(ㄅㄧㄝˊㄔㄨㄒㄧㄣㄘㄞˊ)
(said of art or literary works, craftsmanship, etc.) ingenious; original

別史(ㄅㄧㄝˊㄕˇ)
a history compiled privately by someone, as distinguish from an official history

別室(ㄅㄧㄝˊㄕˋ)
①a concubine ②another room

別生枝節(ㄅㄧㄝˊㄕㄥㄓㄐㄧㄝˊ)
to have new complications

別墅(ㄅㄧㄝˊㄕㄨˋ)
a villa; a country house

別樹一幟(ㄅㄧㄝˊㄕㄨˋㄧˋㄓˋ)
①to become independent; to become one's own master ② to start a business or style of one's own

別人(ㄅㄧㄝˊㄖㄣˊ)
other people; others

刀部

〔刀部〕

別字(ㄅㄧㄝˊ ㄗˋ)
①a word which is not correctly written or pronounced
②an alias

別有風味(ㄅㄧㄝˊ ㄧㄡˇ ㄈㄥ ㄨㄟˋ)
to have a unique flavor

別有天地(ㄅㄧㄝˊ ㄧㄡˇ ㄊㄧㄢ ㄉㄧˋ)
a different world (of delight)

別有所本(ㄅㄧㄝˊ ㄧㄡˇ ㄙㄨㄛˇ ㄅㄣˇ)
to be based on another source

別有所指(ㄅㄧㄝˊ ㄧㄡˇ ㄙㄨㄛˇ ㄓˇ)
to imply another thing

別有用心(ㄅㄧㄝˊ ㄧㄡˇ ㄩㄥˋ ㄒㄧㄣ)
to have a hidden purpose (in so doing or saying)

別樣(ㄅㄧㄝˊ ㄧㄤˋ)
of a different kind, sort, type, or fashion

別無所有(ㄅㄧㄝˊ ㄨˊ ㄙㄨㄛˇ ㄧㄡˇ)
to have no other possessions

【刨】 373
ㄆㄠˊ paur pāo
to dig; to excavate

刨地(ㄆㄠˊ ㄉㄧˋ)
to dig the ground

刨根兒(ㄆㄠˊ ㄍㄣ ㄦ)
to dig out the truth

刨坑(ㄆㄠˊ ㄎㄥ)
to dig a pit or hole

刨挖(ㄆㄠˊ ㄨㄚ)
to dig; to excavate

【利】 374
ㄌㄧˋ lih lì
1. profit; benefit; advantage; gain: 這項買賣有利可圖。 There are profits to be made in this transaction.
2. sharp: 這女人伶牙利齒。 This woman is sharp-tongued.
3. to benefit; to serve: 新鐵路將有利於該地區。 The new railway will benefit the district.

利比亞(ㄌㄧˋ ㄅㄧˇ ㄧㄚˋ)
Libya

利弊(ㄌㄧˋ ㄅㄧˋ)or利病(ㄌㄧˋ ㄅㄧㄥˋ)
advantages and disadvantages

利便(ㄌㄧˋ ㄅㄧㄢˋ)
convenient; handy

利馬竇(ㄌㄧˋ ㄇㄚˇ ㄉㄡˋ)
Matteo Ricci, 1552-1610, Italian Jesuit missionary, who was the first one to introduce Western science to China

利鈍(ㄌㄧˋ ㄉㄨㄣˋ)
①smoothness and ruggedness ②fortune and misfortune; prosperity and adversity

利他主義(ㄌㄧˋ ㄊㄚ ㄓㄨˇ ㄧˋ)
altruism

利尿(ㄌㄧˋ ㄋㄧㄠˋ)
diuresis

利令智昏(ㄌㄧˋ ㄌㄧㄥˋ ㄓˋ ㄏㄨㄣ)
blinded or dulled by greed

利祿(ㄌㄧˋ ㄌㄨˋ)
wealth and position

利落(ㄌㄧˋ ㄌㄨㄛˋ)
neat; orderly 亦作「俐落」

利率(ㄌㄧˋ ㄌㄩˋ)
the interest rate

利國利民(ㄌㄧˋ ㄍㄨㄛˊ ㄌㄧˋ ㄇㄧㄣˊ)
to benefit the nation and the people

利害
①(ㄌㄧˋ ㄏㄞˋ) interest and disinterest; good and harm; advantages and disadvantages
②(ㄌㄧˋ ㄏㄞ) sharp; shrewd

利害關係人(ㄌㄧˋ ㄏㄞˋ ㄍㄨㄢ ㄒㄧˋ ㄖㄣˊ)
the interested party

利己主義(ㄌㄧˋ ㄐㄧˇ ㄓㄨˇ ㄧˋ)
egoism

利器(ㄌㄧˋ ㄑㄧˋ)
①cutting instruments; cutlery ②a very useful and effective tool

利權外溢(ㄌㄧˋ ㄑㄩㄢˊ ㄨㄞˋ ㄧˋ)
the loss of economic rights (especially to foreigners)

利息(ㄌㄧˋ ㄒㄧˊ)
interest 亦作「利錢」

利支敦士登(ㄌㄧˋ ㄓ ㄉㄨㄣ ㄕˋ ㄉㄥ)
Liechtenstein, a small principality in central Europe

利之所在(ㄌㄧˋ ㄓ ㄙㄨㄛˇ ㄗㄞˋ)
something that offers a person the chance to enrich himself

利市三倍(ㄌㄧˋ ㄕˋ ㄙㄢ ㄅㄟˋ)or利市百倍(ㄌㄧˋ ㄕˋ ㄅㄞˇ ㄅㄟˋ)
to make an enormous profit (in trade)

利上滾利(ㄌㄧˋ ㄕㄤˋ ㄍㄨㄣˇ ㄌㄧˋ)or利上加利(ㄌㄧˋ ㄕㄤˋ ㄐㄧㄚ ㄌㄧˋ)
the yield of interest by interest; the yield of compound interest

利刃(ㄌㄧˋ ㄖㄣˋ)
a sharp blade; sharp-edged cutlery

利潤(ㄌㄧˋ ㄖㄨㄣˋ)
profit; gain; net profit

利益(ㄌㄧˋ ㄧˋ)
benefit; profit; advantage; good; gain

利益團體(ㄌㄧˋ ㄧˋ ㄊㄨㄢˊ ㄊㄧˇ)
an interest group

利益均霑(ㄌㄧˋ ㄧˋ ㄐㄩㄣ ㄓㄢ)
to let everybody have his hands on the pie

利誘(ㄌㄧˋ ㄧㄡˋ)
to tempt with money or material gain

利物浦(ㄌㄧˋ ㄨˋ ㄆㄨˇ)
Liverpool, a British seaport

利慾(ㄌㄧˋ ㄩˋ)
cupidity

利慾薰心(ㄌㄧˋ ㄩˋ ㄒㄩㄣ ㄒㄧㄣ)
blinded or dulled by greed; lured by profits

利源(ㄌㄧˋ ㄩㄢˊ)
the source of profit

利用(ㄌㄧˋ ㄩㄥˋ)
to utilize; to make use of; to take advantage of; to avail oneself of

利用厚生(ㄌㄧˋ ㄩㄥˋ ㄏㄡˋ ㄕㄥ)
to serve the requirements and to enrich the lives of the people

六畫

【刮】 375
ㄍㄨㄚ gua guā
to pare; to shave; to scrape

刮破(ㄍㄨㄚ ㄆㄛˋ)
to cut or hurt (the face, etc.) in shaving

刮平(ㄍㄨㄚ ㄆㄧㄥˊ)
to pare (so as to make the surface smooth)

刮摩(ㄍㄨㄚ ㄇㄛˊ)
to rub or scrape out

刮目相待(ㄍㄨㄚ ㄇㄨˋ ㄒㄧㄤ ㄉㄞˋ)or刮目相看(ㄍㄨㄚ ㄇㄨˋ ㄒㄧㄤ ㄎㄢˋ)
to marvel at someone's progress or improvement

刮刀(ㄍㄨㄚ ㄉㄠ)
a scraping cutter; a scraper

刮地皮(ㄍㄨㄚ ㄉㄧˋ ㄆㄧˊ)
(said of corrupt local officials) to exact money from the people

刮臉(ㄍㄨㄚ ㄌㄧㄢˇ)
to shave (the face)

刮刮叫(ㄍㄨㄚ ㄍㄨㄚ ㄐㄧㄠˋ)
splendid; wonderful; tops;
very good

刮鬍子(ㄍㄨㄚ ㄏㄨˊ˙ㄗ)
① to shave oneself; to shave
② (colloquial) to meet rejection; to be scolded

刮痧(ㄍㄨㄚ ㄕㄚ)
a popular medical treatment
for sunstroke by scraping
the patient's neck, chest or
back with the fingers or a
coin

【券】376
ㄑㄩㄢˋ chiuann quàn
1. a ticket
2. a certificate
3. a bond

【到】377
ㄉㄠˋ daw dào
1. to reach; to arrive: 火車何時
到達此地? When does the
train reach here?
2. a Chinese family name

到達(ㄉㄠˋ ㄉㄚˊ)
to reach; to arrive

到底(ㄉㄠˋ ㄉㄧˇ)
① after all; in the long run;
at length; in the end; finally
② to reach the extremity

到頂(ㄉㄠˋ ㄉㄧㄥˇ)
① to reach the summit ②
cannot be improved

到頭(ㄉㄠˋ ㄊㄡˊ)
to the end; at an end

到頭來(ㄉㄠˋ ㄊㄡˊ ㄌㄞˊ)
after all; in the long run; in
the end

到來(ㄉㄠˋ ㄌㄞˊ)
arrival; coming; the advent

到會(ㄉㄠˋ ㄏㄨㄟˋ)
to be present at a meeting;
to attend a meeting

到家(ㄉㄠˋ ㄐㄧㄚ)
① to get home ② to become
proficient, or extremely well-
versed; thorough

到齊(ㄉㄠˋ ㄑㄧˊ)
Everybody (who is supposed
to be here) has come.

到期(ㄉㄠˋ ㄑㄧˊ)
(said of payment, a con-
tract, etc.) to reach the
deadline or date of termination; to expire

到職(ㄉㄠˋ ㄓˊ)
to arrive for a new assignment

到差(ㄉㄠˋ ㄔㄚ)
to arrive for a (junior official) post

到場(ㄉㄠˋ ㄔㄤˇ)or(ㄉㄠˋ ㄔㄤˊ)
to show up; to be present

到處(ㄉㄠˋ ㄔㄨˋ)
everywhere; on all sides; far
and wide; all about

到處為家(ㄉㄠˋ ㄔㄨˋ ㄨㄟˊ ㄐㄧㄚ)
Everywhere may be one's
home.

到時(ㄉㄠˋ ㄕˊ)
by that time; when that time
comes; by then

到手(ㄉㄠˋ ㄕㄡˇ)
to come into one's hands or
possession

到任(ㄉㄠˋ ㄖㄣˋ)
to assume a (high official)
post

到案(ㄉㄠˋ ㄢˋ)
to appear in court; to
answer a court summons

【刳】378
ㄎㄨ ku kū
1. to cut apart; to carve apart
2. to gouge; to scoop; to hollow

【刹】379
(刹)ㄔㄚˋ chah chà
a (Buddhist) temple, shrine,
monastery or abbey

刹那(ㄔㄚˋ ㄋㄚˋ)or(ㄔㄚˋ ㄋㄚˊ)
a moment; an instant; a split
second; (in) the twinkling of
an eye

【剁】380
ㄉㄨㄛˋ duoh duò
to chop; to mince; to hash

剁肉(ㄉㄨㄛˋ ㄖㄡˋ)
to mince or hash meat

剁碎(ㄉㄨㄛˋ ㄙㄨㄟˋ)
to mince; to hash

【制】381
ㄓˋ jyh zhì
1. to establish; to institute; to
set up
2. to prevail; to overpower; to
control
3. a system: 學制 the educational system
4. used before the signature in
letter writing to indicate the
writer is in mourning
5. a Chinese family name

制伏(ㄓˋ ㄈㄨˊ)
to subdue; to subjugate; to
prevail over; to overcome;
to surmount; to overpower;
to put down; to quell

制服(ㄓˋ ㄈㄨˊ)
① a uniform ② formerly,
dress of mourning for one's
parents

制敵機先(ㄓˋ ㄉㄧˊ ㄐㄧ ㄒㄧㄢ)
to gain an advantage over
the enemy by taking steps
to forestall him

制定(ㄓˋ ㄉㄧㄥˋ)
to institute; to establish; to
set up; to introduce; to initiate; to draw up; to formulate; to work out

制度(ㄓˋ ㄉㄨˋ)
a system; an institution

制動機(ㄓˋ ㄉㄨㄥˋ ㄐㄧ)or 制動器(ㄓˋ
ㄉㄨㄥˋ ㄑㄧˋ)
a brake

制禮作樂(ㄓˋ ㄌㄧˇ ㄗㄨㄛˋ ㄩㄝˋ)
to establish rules for ceremonies and to compose
appropriate music for different occasions

制空權(ㄓˋ ㄎㄨㄥ ㄑㄩㄢˊ)
air supremacy; air domina-
tion

制海權(ㄓˋ ㄏㄞˇ ㄑㄩㄢˊ)
naval supremacy; command
of the sea

制衡(ㄓˋ ㄏㄥˊ)
to check and balance

制錢(ㄓˋ ㄑㄧㄢˊ)
coins officially designated
for circulation

制限(ㄓˋ ㄒㄧㄢˋ)
① to restrict; to limit; to
confine ② a bound; a limit;
confines

制憲(ㄓˋ ㄒㄧㄢˋ)
to draw up a national constitution

制止(ㄓˋ ㄓˇ)
to stop by force; to stop; to
prevent

制勝(ㄓˋ ㄕㄥˋ)
to be victorious; to prevail;
to triumph; to win

制作(ㄓˋ ㄗㄨㄛˋ)
to formulate

制策(ㄓˋ ㄘㄜˋ)
an examination on political
topics given by the emperor

〔刀
部〕

in old China

制裁 (业 ㄘㄞ)
to restrain, suppress, or hold back by punitive measures; to chasten; to chastise; to sanction

制壓 (业 ㄧㄚ)
①to overpower; to overwhelm; to suppress ②to neutralize (enemy fire)

制約 (业 ㄩㄝ)
to restrict; to condition: 兩者互相制約。The two condition each other.

【刷】 382
1. ㄕㄨㄚ shua shuā
1. to brush; to scrub; to clean; to daub
2. a brush: 牙刷 a toothbrush
3. to eliminate

刷馬 (ㄕㄨㄚ ㄇㄚˇ)
to curry a horse

刷清 (ㄕㄨㄚ ㄑㄧㄥ)
to clear (oneself) of a charge

刷洗 (ㄕㄨㄚ ㄒㄧˇ)
to scrub: 他將地板刷洗乾淨。He scrubs the floor clean.

刷新 (ㄕㄨㄚ ㄒㄧㄣ)
①to make like new (by cleaning, repainting, etc.); to renovate ②to make (a new sports record); to break the records

刷恥 (ㄕㄨㄚ ㄔˇ)
to wipe away disgrace

刷子 (ㄕㄨㄚ ·ㄗ)
a brush

刷牙 (ㄕㄨㄚ ㄧㄚ)
to brush the teeth

刷印 (ㄕㄨㄚ ㄧㄣ)
to print

【刷】 382
2. ㄕㄨㄚˋ shuah shuà
參看「刷白」、「刷選」

刷白 (ㄕㄨㄚˋ ㄅㄞ)
(said of face) pale

刷選 (ㄕㄨㄚˋ ㄒㄩㄢ)
to choose; to pick; to select

【刺】 383
1. ㄘˋ tsyh cì
1. to pierce; to stab; to prick
2. to irritate; to stimulate
3. a thorn; a splinter; small fishbones; a sting
4. to assassinate
5. a name card

刺鼻 (ㄘˋ ㄅㄧ)
to irritate the nose

刺目 (ㄘˋ ㄇㄨ)or 刺眼 (ㄘˋ ㄧㄢˇ)
irritating to the eye; dazzling

刺刀 (ㄘˋ ㄉㄠ)
a bayonet: 上刺刀 to fix bayonets

刺探 (ㄘˋ ㄊㄢˋ)
to spy; to find out secretly

刺桐 (ㄘˋ ㄊㄨㄥˊ)
Erythrina variegata orientalis

刺股 (ㄘˋ ㄍㄨˇ)
to pierce one's thigh with an awl to prevent oneself from falling asleep, an allusion to Su Chin (蘇秦) — (figuratively) extremely diligent in studying

刺股讀書 (ㄘˋ ㄍㄨˇ ㄉㄨˊ ㄕㄨ)
to study hard in defiance of hardships

刺骨 (ㄘˋ ㄍㄨˇ)
① (said of cold) bone-chilling ② (said of hatred) bitter or deep

刺客 (ㄘˋ ㄎㄜˋ)
an assassin

刺激 (ㄘˋ ㄐㄧ)
to stimulate; to provoke; to excite; to irritate; to upset; a stimulus

刺激品 (ㄘˋ ㄐㄧ ㄆㄧㄣˇ)or 刺激物 (ㄘˋ ㄐㄧ ㄨˋ)
a stimulant; a stimulus

刺激性 (ㄘˋ ㄐㄧ ㄒㄧㄥˋ)
stimulativeness; stimulancy; stimulability

刺激作用 (ㄘˋ ㄐㄧ ㄗㄨㄛˋ ㄩㄥˋ)
stimulation

刺青 (ㄘˋ ㄑㄧㄥ)
to tattoo; a tattoo

刺繡 (ㄘˋ ㄒㄧㄡˋ)
to embroider; embroidery

刺史 (ㄘˋ ㄕˇ)
(formerly) a provincial governor; a prefectural governor; a district magistrate

刺殺 (ㄘˋ ㄕㄚ)
①to assassinate ②(baseball) to put out (a base runner)

刺字 (ㄘˋ ㄗˋ)
to tattoo or brand a convict on the face or the arm (usually as a punishment)

刺刺不休 (ㄘˋ ㄘˋ ㄅㄨˋ ㄒㄧㄡ)
to chatter without stop; to gabble on and on

刺兒 (ㄘˋ ㄦ)
a thorn

刺耳 (ㄘˋ ㄦˇ)
unpleasant to the ear; noisy; harsh; screechy; grating; ear-piercing

刺蝟 (ㄘˋ ㄨㄟˋ)
a hedgehog

【刻】 384
1. ㄎㄜˋ keh cè
1. to carve; to engrave; to cut
2. a quarter (of an hour): 三點一刻 a quarter past three
3. cruel; heartless; unfeeling; cutting; harshly; acrimonious; biting
4. moment

刻薄 (ㄎㄜˋ ㄅㄛˊ)
cold-hearted; unfeeling; unkind; acrimonious; mean; caustic

刻薄寡恩 (ㄎㄜˋ ㄅㄛˊ ㄍㄨㄚˇ ㄣ)
to treat harshly and to give rare generosity

刻板 (ㄎㄜˋ ㄅㄢˇ)
①to engrave (for printing) ②monotonous; dull; stereotyped; stiff; mechanical; inflexible

刻本 (ㄎㄜˋ ㄅㄣˇ)
a printed copy (printed from engraved blocks)

刻不容緩 (ㄎㄜˋ ㄅㄨˋ ㄖㄨㄥˊ ㄏㄨㄢˇ)
most urgent; to brook no delay 或 Not a moment is to be lost.

刻刀 (ㄎㄜˋ ㄉㄠ)
a knife used in carving; a burin; a graver

刻毒 (ㄎㄜˋ ㄉㄨˊ)
wicked; fiendish; devilish; cruel; venomous; spiteful

刻度 (ㄎㄜˋ ㄉㄨˋ)
graduations (on a vessel or an instrument)

刻漏 (ㄎㄜˋ ㄌㄡˋ)
a clepsydra; an ancient water clock with hour markings

刻骨 (ㄎㄜˋ ㄍㄨˇ)
deeply ingrained

刻骨銘心 (ㄎㄜˋ ㄍㄨˇ ㄇㄧㄥˊ ㄒㄧㄣ)
to permanently imprint (another's favor, etc.) on the mind; to remember with

gratitude constantly and for-ever

刻苦 (ㄎㄜ ㄎㄨ)
①assiduous; hardworking: 他刻苦研讀。He studies assiduously. ②simple and frugal

刻苦耐勞 (ㄎㄜ ㄎㄨ ㄋㄞ ㄌㄠ)
to endure hardship; to work hard without complaint

刻苦成家 (ㄎㄜ ㄎㄨ ㄔㄥ ㄐㄧㄚ)
to build up a family by hard work and frugality

刻畫 (ㄎㄜ ㄏㄨㄚ)
to depict; to portray

刻畫入微 (ㄎㄜ ㄏㄨㄚ ㄖㄨˋ ㄨㄟ)
vivid portrayal of details; realistic portrayal of a character

刻己 (ㄎㄜ ㄐㄧˇ) 刻苦 self-sacrificing; self-denial in service to others

刻期 (ㄎㄜ ㄑㄧ)
punctually on a fixed date

刻峭 (ㄎㄜ ㄑㄧㄠ)
①(said of terrain features) rugged ②cruel; relentless; ruthless ③(said of writings) pungency or incisiveness

刻舟求劍 (ㄎㄜ ㄓㄡ ㄑㄧㄡˊ ㄐㄧㄢˋ)
to carve a mark on the side of one's boat to indicate the place where one's sword has dropped into the water — (figuratively) ridiculous stupidity; to be stubbornly unimaginative; a very stupid way of doing things

刻石 (ㄎㄜ ㄕˊ)
to engrave (writings) on stone

刻書 (ㄎㄜ ㄕㄨ)
(in ancient China) to carve the words of a book on wood blocks for printing — to publish a book

刻日 (ㄎㄜ ㄖˋ)
this very date; a fixed day

刻字 (ㄎㄜ ㄗˋ)
to engrave words (on stone, blocks, etc.)

刻意 (ㄎㄜ ㄧˋ)
to do something with intensive attention (in order to achieve perfection or great success); painstakingly

刻意求工 (ㄎㄜ ㄧˋ ㄑㄧㄡˊ ㄍㄨㄥ)
to strive sedulously for per-fection

【刻】 384　ㄎㄜ ke kē
to carve; to engrave

刻印 (ㄎㄜ ㄧㄣˋ)or 刻圖章 (ㄎㄜ ㄊㄨˊ ㄓㄤ)
to make a chop by carving; seal engraving

七畫

【則】 385　ㄗㄜˊ tzer zé
1. a law; a rule; a regulation; a standard; a norm; a criterion
2. a particle indicating consequence (usually used after a supposition) or a reason
3. a numerary particle used before news reports, advertisements, etc.: 那是則有趣的報導。It is an interesting piece of news.
4. but; however: 人皆好名利，我則不然。Others may be fond of fame and wealth, but I am not.
5. to imitate; to follow

則聲 (ㄗㄜˊ ㄕㄥ)
to make a sound; to utter a word: 她不敢則聲。She dare not utter a word.

【剃】 386　ㄊㄧˋ tih tì
to shave: 我把我的鬍子剃掉了。I have shaved my beard.

剃髮修行 (ㄊㄧˋ ㄈㄚˇ ㄒㄧㄡ ㄒㄧㄥˊ)
(Buddhism) to cut off one's hair and be a monk or nun

剃刀 (ㄊㄧˋ ㄉㄠ)
a razor

剃度 (ㄊㄧˋ ㄉㄨˋ)
to cut off hair and join a monastery; to tonsure

剃頭 (ㄊㄧˋ ㄊㄡˊ)
to shave the head

剃頭店 (ㄊㄧˋ ㄊㄡˊ ㄉㄧㄢˋ)or 剃頭舖 (ㄊㄧˋ ㄊㄡˊ ㄆㄨˋ)
a barbershop

【剄】 387　ㄐㄧㄥˇ jiing jǐng
to cut the throat: 自剄 to commit suicide by cutting the throat

【剉】 388　ㄘㄨㄛˋ tsuoh cuò
1. a steel file
2. to file; to smooth (as with a file); to cut; to chop up into fine pieces

剉平 (ㄘㄨㄛˋ ㄆㄧㄥˊ)
to smoothen even

剉光 (ㄘㄨㄛˋ ㄍㄨㄤ)
to polish fine

剉子 (ㄘㄨㄛˋ ˙ㄗ)
a file

【削】 389　ㄒㄩㄝˊ shiueh xuē (語音 ㄒㄧㄠ shiau xiāo)
1. to cut; to pare; to shave; to whittle
2. to deprive

削壁 (ㄒㄩㄝˊ ㄅㄧˋ)
a precipice; a cliff

削平 (ㄒㄩㄝˊ ㄆㄧㄥˊ)
①to pare; to smooth (with a knife) ②to conquer; to put down; to suppress (a rebellion)

削木為兵 (ㄒㄩㄝˊ ㄇㄨˋ ㄨㄟˊ ㄅㄧㄥ)
(said of a plebeian uprising) to pare wooden poles and use them as weapons

削髮 (ㄒㄩㄝˊ ㄈㄚˇ)
to shave the head (so as to become a Buddhist nun or monk)

削奪 (ㄒㄩㄝˊ ㄉㄨㄛˊ)
to deprive (someone) of (power, rank, land, etc.); to take by force

削籍 (ㄒㄩㄝˊ ㄐㄧˊ)
to dismiss an official from a government post

削價 (ㄒㄩㄝˊ ㄐㄧㄚˋ)
to cut price to or below the cost level

削減 (ㄒㄩㄝˊ ㄐㄧㄢˇ)
to curtail; to cut down; to slash

削職 (ㄒㄩㄝˊ ㄓˊ)
to deprive a person of a position

削趾適履 (ㄒㄩㄝˊ ㄓˇ ㄕˋ ㄌㄩˇ)
(literally) to cut the feet to fit the shoes — an impractical solution of a problem 亦作「削足適履」

削除 (ㄒㄩㄝˊ ㄔㄨˊ)
to strike out; to take out; to omit

削弱 (ㄒㄩㄝˊ ㄖㄨㄛˋ)
to enfeeble; to weaken; to sap; to devitalize

〔刀部〕

〔刀部〕

剗蒠（ㄒㄩㄢ ㄘㄨㄥ）
slender fingers of a lady

【剋】 390
（ㄎㄜ keh ke）
1. to overcome
2. to cut down
3. to limit
4. to engrave; to imprint
5. can; to be able to

剋夫（ㄎㄜ ㄈㄨ）
to be fated to mourn one's husband's death

剋扣（ㄎㄜ ㄎㄡ）
to withhold (military supplies, etc.) for personal gain

剋妻（ㄎㄜ ㄑㄧ）
to be fated to mourn one's wife's death

剋期（ㄎㄜ ㄑㄧ）or 剋日（ㄎㄜ ㄖ）
① to set a time limit ② on a set date

剋星（ㄎㄜ ㄒㄧㄥ）
(literally) a malignant star—a person who always bars another from success; an unbeatable rival; a jinx

【剌】 391
（ㄌㄚˋ lah la）
to go against; to contradict; perverse; disagreeable; rebellious

剌子（ㄌㄚˋ ˙ㄗ）
① a person hard-hearted by nature ② a ruby

【剌】 391
（ㄌㄚˊ la la）
to slash open

剌破（ㄌㄚˊ ㄆㄛˋ）
to cut

剌開（ㄌㄚˊ ㄎㄞ）
to slash open

【前】 392
（ㄑㄧㄢˊ chyan qián）
1. front; forward; before
2. previous; former; preceding; past; of earlier times: 前任總統 the former president
3. future: 他是一位很有前途的年輕人。He is a young man with a future.
4. to advance; to proceed; to progress; to precede

前輩（ㄑㄧㄢˊ ㄅㄟˋ）
a senior (in age, standing, length of service, etc.)

前半天（ㄑㄧㄢˊ ㄅㄢˋ ㄊㄧㄢ）
forenoon; morning

前半夜（ㄑㄧㄢˊ ㄅㄢˋ ㄧㄝˋ）
the first half of the night (from nightfall to midnight)

前邊（ㄑㄧㄢˊ ㄅㄧㄢ）or 前邊兒（ㄑㄧㄢˊ ㄅㄧㄚㄦ）
① the front; the front side; the fore part ② ahead; in front; preceding

前怕狼，後怕虎（ㄑㄧㄢˊ ㄆㄚˋ ㄌㄤˊ，ㄏㄡˋ ㄆㄚˋ ㄏㄨˇ）
to fear wolves ahead and tigers behind—to be full of fears

前排（ㄑㄧㄢˊ ㄆㄞˊ）
the front row

前仆後繼（ㄑㄧㄢˊ ㄆㄨ ㄏㄡˋ ㄐㄧˋ）
(usually said of bravery of soldiers in battle) Behind the fallen is an endless column of successors.

前茅（ㄑㄧㄢˊ ㄇㄠˊ）
① a (military) patrol ② the top of the list (of successful candidates in an examination)

前門（ㄑㄧㄢˊ ㄇㄣˊ）or 前門兒（ㄑㄧㄢˊ ㄇㄣㄦ）
the front door or gate: 請打開前門。Please open the front door.

前門拒虎，後門進狼（ㄑㄧㄢˊ ㄇㄣˊ ㄐㄩˋ ㄏㄨˇ，ㄏㄡˋ ㄇㄣˊ ㄐㄧㄣˋ ㄌㄤˊ）
to drive the tiger out of the front door and let a wolf in at the back—to fend off one danger only to fall a prey to another

前面（ㄑㄧㄢˊ ㄇㄧㄢˋ）
① the front; the front side ② ahead; in front; preceding: 公園就在前面。The park is right ahead.

前番（ㄑㄧㄢˊ ㄈㄢ）
the last time

前方（ㄑㄧㄢˊ ㄈㄤ）
① the front (in war): 我們必須盡力支援前方。We must do our best to support the front. ② the forward direction

前鋒（ㄑㄧㄢˊ ㄈㄥ）
the vanguard; the van

前夫（ㄑㄧㄢˊ ㄈㄨ）
the former husband (of a woman who has remarried)

前俯後仰（ㄑㄧㄢˊ ㄈㄨˇ ㄏㄡˋ ㄧㄤˇ）
to bend forwards and backwards

前導（ㄑㄧㄢˊ ㄉㄠˇ）or（ㄑㄧㄢˊ ㄉㄠˋ）
the guide or motorcade (of an official party on the road)

前定（ㄑㄧㄢˊ ㄉㄧㄥˋ）
predestined; decided beforehand

前度劉郎（ㄑㄧㄢˊ ㄉㄨˋ ㄌㄧㄡˊ ㄌㄤˊ）
a person who returns to a place he once abandoned

前臺（ㄑㄧㄢˊ ㄊㄞˊ）
the stage; the proscenium

前頭（ㄑㄧㄢˊ ㄊㄡ）
① in front; ahead ② before

前膛鎗（ㄑㄧㄢˊ ㄊㄤˊ ㄑㄧㄤ）
a muzzle-loading gun

前提（ㄑㄧㄢˊ ㄊㄧˊ）
① a (logical) premise; 小前提 the minor premise 大前提 the major premise ② the primary consideration; a prerequisite

前天（ㄑㄧㄢˊ ㄊㄧㄢ）
the day before yesterday

前廳（ㄑㄧㄢˊ ㄊㄧㄥ）
an antechamber

前途（ㄑㄧㄢˊ ㄊㄨˊ）
the prospect; promise (in the sense of an indication of a successful prospect or future): 他的事業前途樂觀。He has good prospects in business.

前途茫茫（ㄑㄧㄢˊ ㄊㄨˊ ㄇㄤˊ ㄇㄤˊ）
One's future is indefinite.

前途無量（ㄑㄧㄢˊ ㄊㄨˊ ㄨˊ ㄌㄧㄤˋ）
to have boundless prospects

前腦（ㄑㄧㄢˊ ㄋㄠˇ）
(anatomy) the forebrain

前年（ㄑㄧㄢˊ ㄋㄧㄢˊ）
the year before last

前例（ㄑㄧㄢˊ ㄌㄧˋ）
a precedent: 此事違反所有前例。It is against all precedents.

前列（ㄑㄧㄢˊ ㄌㄧㄝˋ）
the front row; the forefront; the van

前輪（ㄑㄧㄢˊ ㄌㄨㄣˊ）
① (vehicle) the front wheel ② (airplane) the nosewheel

前滾翻（ㄑㄧㄢˊ ㄍㄨㄣˇ ㄈㄢ）
(sports) a forward roll

前功盡棄（ㄑㄧㄢˊ ㄍㄨㄥ ㄐㄧㄣˋ ㄑㄧˋ）
to nullify all the previous efforts; to turn all the previ-

前功盡棄 ous labor to nothing 或 All one's previous efforts are wasted.

前科(ㄑㄧㄢ ㄎㄜ)
a previous criminal record; a record of previous crime

前科犯(ㄑㄧㄢ ㄎㄜ ㄈㄢ)
an ex-convict

前款(ㄑㄧㄢ ㄎㄨㄢ)
(used in legal documents or code of law) the aforesaid clause or item

前後(ㄑㄧㄢ ㄏㄡ)
① the front and the rear; before and after: 我軍前後受敵。Our troops were attacked by the enemy from front and rear. ② (indicating time) around; about: 中秋節前後 around the Moon Festival ③ from beginning to end; altogether: 這項工程從動工到完成，前後只花了一年。The entire task, from beginning to end, took only one year.

前後矛盾(ㄑㄧㄢ ㄏㄡ ㄇㄠ ㄉㄨㄣ)
inconsistent; contradictory: 他對於發生事件的敘述前後矛盾。His account of what happened was inconsistent.

前後左右(ㄑㄧㄢ ㄏㄡ ㄗㄨㄛ ㄧㄡ)
on all sides; all around

前漢(ㄑㄧㄢ ㄏㄢ)or 西漢(ㄒㄧ ㄏㄢ)
the Former Han Dynasty (206 B.C.—8 A.D.)

前呼後擁(ㄑㄧㄢ ㄏㄨ ㄏㄡ ㄩㄥ)
(said of VIPs) with a large retinue; with many attendants crowding round

前回(ㄑㄧㄢ ㄏㄨㄟ)
① last time ② the last chapter (of a novel)

前街後巷(ㄑㄧㄢ ㄐㄧㄝ ㄏㄡ ㄒㄧㄤ)
front streets and back lanes —everywhere

前腳(ㄑㄧㄢ ㄐㄧㄠ)
the forward foot in a step

前進(ㄑㄧㄢ ㄐㄧㄣ)
to advance; to proceed; to go forward; to progress: 人群向車站前進。The crowd advanced towards the station.

前經(ㄑㄧㄢ ㄐㄧㄥ)or 前已(ㄑㄧㄢ ㄧ)
(indicating time) already; before

前景(ㄑㄧㄢ ㄐㄧㄥ)
① a foreground ② the foreground of a painting ③ prospects; vistas; perspectives: 她在繪畫方面有美好的前景。She has good prospects in painting.

前車之鑒(ㄑㄧㄢ ㄔㄜ ㄓ ㄐㄧㄢ)or 前車之覆，後車之鑒(ㄑㄧㄢ ㄔㄜ ㄓ ㄈㄨ，ㄏㄡ ㄔㄜ ㄓ ㄐㄧㄢ)
warning taken from the overturned cart ahead—a lesson from the failure of one's predecessor

前倨後恭(ㄑㄧㄢ ㄐㄩ ㄏㄡ ㄍㄨㄥ)
proud at first but humble afterwards; to change from arrogance to humility — (figuratively) to change one's attitude snobbishly

前妻(ㄑㄧㄢ ㄑㄧ)
the former wife (of a man who has remarried)

前愆(ㄑㄧㄢ ㄑㄧㄢ)
past errors or faults

前前後後(ㄑㄧㄢ ㄑㄧㄢ ㄏㄡ ㄏㄡ)
the whole story; the ins and outs

前情(ㄑㄧㄢ ㄑㄧㄥ)
① a relevant past event; past affairs ② the past relevant cause

前驅(ㄑㄧㄢ ㄑㄩ)
the forerunner; the vanguard; the van; the precursor; the harbinger; the prelude

前夕(ㄑㄧㄢ ㄒㄧ)
the eve (of an event)

前賢(ㄑㄧㄢ ㄒㄧㄢ)or 前哲(ㄑㄧㄢ ㄓㄜ)or 前脩(ㄑㄧㄢ ㄒㄧㄡ)
the wise men of the past

前嫌(ㄑㄧㄢ ㄒㄧㄢ)
a past grudge

前線(ㄑㄧㄢ ㄒㄧㄢ)
the front line (in war); the front

前項(ㄑㄧㄢ ㄒㄧㄤ)
the aforesaid or the above-mentioned item; the preceding article or clause (used in legal documents)

前置詞(ㄑㄧㄢ ㄓ ㄘ)
a preposition 亦作「介系詞」

前者(ㄑㄧㄢ ㄓㄜ)
the former

前兆(ㄑㄧㄢ ㄓㄠ)
an omen; forewarning; a premonition; an augury; a forerunner; a harbinger: 這是成功的前兆。This is an omen of success.

前站(ㄑㄧㄢ ㄓㄢ)
the next stop or railway station

前塵(ㄑㄧㄢ ㄔㄣ)
① (Buddhism) previous impure conditions, influencing the succeeding stage or stages ② what has happened in the past

前程(ㄑㄧㄢ ㄔㄥ)
① a future; prospects ② a career: 恐怕他前程保不住了。I am afraid his career is finished.

前程似錦(ㄑㄧㄢ ㄔㄥ ㄙ ㄐㄧㄣ)
to have brilliant prospects

前程萬里(ㄑㄧㄢ ㄔㄥ ㄨㄢ ㄌㄧ)
to have the prospect of a very successful career

前世(ㄑㄧㄢ ㄕ)
① the previous generation ② the previous life (by the concept of life and death as a cycle)

前事不忘，後事之師(ㄑㄧㄢ ㄕ ㄅㄨ ㄨㄤ，ㄏㄡ ㄕ ㄓ ㄕ)
To remember past errors insures one against repetition of the same errors. 或 If one doesn't forget past experience, it will be a guide for one's future.

前哨(ㄑㄧㄢ ㄕㄠ)
(military) a sentry; an outpost; an advance guard

前身(ㄑㄧㄢ ㄕㄣ)
the forerunner (of a school, organization, etc.)

前生(ㄑㄧㄢ ㄕㄥ)
the former life or lives; the previous incarnation

前日(ㄑㄧㄢ ㄖ)
the day before yesterday

前人(ㄑㄧㄢ ㄖㄣ)
people of former times; forefathers; predecessors; people of the past

前人種樹，後人乘涼(ㄑㄧㄢ ㄖㄣ ㄓㄨㄥ ㄕㄨ，ㄏㄡ ㄖㄣ ㄔㄥ ㄌㄧㄤ)
One generation plants the trees under whose shade another generation rests.—

刀

部

to profit from the labor of one's forefathers

前任〈くﾉㄢ ㄖㄣ〉
a predecessor

前奏〈くﾉㄢ ㄗㄡ〉
a prelude; a harbinger

前此〈くﾉㄢ ㄘ〉
prior to that or this; before that or this

前次〈くﾉㄢ ㄘ〉
the previous occasion; last time

前思後想〈くﾉㄢ ㄙ ㄏㄡ ㄒﾉㄤ〉
to turn over (a problem) in one's mind; to ponder; to think over again and again

前所未見〈くﾉㄢ ㄙㄨㄛ ㄨㄟ ㄐﾉㄢ〉
to have never seen before

前所未聞〈くﾉㄢ ㄙㄨㄛ ㄨㄟ ㄨㄣ〉
hitherto unknown; unprecedented

前所未聞〈くﾉㄢ ㄙㄨㄛ ㄨㄟ ㄨㄣ〉
to have never heard of before

前額〈くﾉㄢ ㄜ〉
the forehead

前夜〈くﾉㄢ ㄧㄝ〉
the night before last

前言〈くﾉㄢ ﾉㄢ〉
①previous remarks ②the words of past thinkers ③a foreword; a preface; an introduction

前言不對後語〈くﾉㄢ ﾉㄢ ㄅㄨ ㄉㄨㄟ ㄏㄡ ㄩˇ〉
self-contradictory; to talk incoherently

前因〈くﾉㄢ ﾉㄣ〉
an antecedent; a cause

前因後果〈くﾉㄢ ﾉㄣ ㄏㄡ ㄍㄨㄛ〉
cause and effect; the whole story; the ins and outs: 告訴我這件事的前因後果。Let me know the ins and outs of this incident.

前仰後合〈くﾉㄢ ﾉㄤˇ ㄏㄡ ㄏㄜ〉
to shake one's sides with laughter; to split one's sides; to stagger forward and back

前無古人〈くﾉㄢ ㄨ ㄍㄨˇ ㄖㄣ〉
(said of accomplishments) peerless; to have no predecessors; unprecedented

前衛〈くﾉㄢ ㄨㄟ〉
①front line troops ②a forward (in basketball, football, etc.) ③vanguard;

avant-garde

前晚〈くﾉㄢ ㄨㄢˇ〉
the evening before last

前往〈くﾉㄢ ㄨㄤˇ〉
to go to (a place); to visit; to leave for

前月〈くﾉㄢ ㄩㄝ〉
ultimo; in or of the month preceding the current one

前緣〈くﾉㄢ ㄩㄢ〉
predestined ties; predestination (for lovers or enemies)

前院〈くﾉㄢ ㄩㄢ〉
the front courtyard

八畫

【剔】 ³⁹³ 〈ㄊㄧ〉 ti tī
1. to separate bones from meat; to scrape meat off bones
2. to pick out inferior materials; to scrape off
3. a rising stroke in Chinese characters

剔刀〈ㄊㄧ ㄉㄠ〉
a scraping knife

剔透〈ㄊㄧ ㄊㄡ〉
①(said of writings) well-expressed ②(said of persons) keen and perceptive

剔出去〈ㄊㄧ ㄔㄨ ㄑㄩ〉
to pick out; to eliminate

剔除〈ㄊㄧ ㄔㄨ〉
to eliminate (undesirable things); to reject

剔牙〈ㄊㄧ ﾉㄚ〉
to pick the teeth

【剖】 ³⁹⁴ 〈ㄆㄡˇ〉 poou pou
1. to cut, rip or tear open
2. to explain; to analyze; to dissect

剖白〈ㄆㄡˇ ㄅㄞ〉
to dispel suspicion by explanation; to explain oneself; to vindicate oneself; to lay one's heart open

剖辯〈ㄆㄡˇ ㄅﾉㄢ〉
to defend oneself (from a charge) by explanation

剖判〈ㄆㄡˇ ㄆㄢ〉
to give judgment in a case

剖面〈ㄆㄡˇ ㄇﾉㄢ〉
a section (of something cut through at a given plane)

剖分〈ㄆㄡˇ ㄈㄣ〉
to cut apart at the middle

剖腹〈ㄆㄡˇ ㄈㄨ〉
①to cut the belly open ②to tell one's feelings frankly

剖腹取子手術〈ㄆㄡˇ ㄈㄨ ㄑㄩˇ ㄗˇ ㄕㄡ ㄕㄨ〉
a Caesarian operation; a Caesarian section 亦作「剖腹產術」

剖腹自殺〈ㄆㄡˇ ㄈㄨ ㄗˋ ㄕㄚ〉
(to commit) hara-kiri

剖腹藏珠〈ㄆㄡˇ ㄈㄨ ㄘㄤ ㄓㄨ〉
to get killed because of greediness; to sacrifice one's life to gain

剖斷如流〈ㄆㄡˇ ㄉㄨㄢ ㄖㄨ ㄌﾉㄡ〉
(said of a judge) quick in deciding lawsuits

剖肝泣血〈ㄆㄡˇ ㄍㄢ ㄑㄧ ㄒﾉㄝ〉
extremely sad

剖開〈ㄆㄡˇ ㄎㄞ〉
to cut or rip open

剖解〈ㄆㄡˇ ㄐﾉㄝ〉or 剖析〈ㄆㄡˇ ㄒㄧ〉
①to dissect; to anatomize ②to analyze

剖心〈ㄆㄡˇ ㄒㄧㄣ〉
to bare one's heart sincerely

剖字〈ㄆㄡˇ ㄗˋ〉
to tell fortune from the component parts of written characters 亦作「拆字」或「測字」

剖驗〈ㄆㄡˇ ﾉㄢ〉
to hold an inquest 亦作「驗屍」

【剚】 ³⁹⁵ 〈ㄗˋ〉 tzyh zì
to plant on the ground

【剛】 ³⁹⁶ 〈ㄍㄤ〉 gang gāng
1. tough; unyielding; inflexible; hard; firm; strong; indomitable: 她的個性柔中有剛。Her character is strong as well as graceful.
2. just now: 她剛走。She has just gone.
3. just; exactly: 這套衣服大小剛好。This dress is just the right size.
4. barely; only

剛復自用〈ㄍㄤ ㄈㄨ ㄗˋ ㄩㄥ〉
stubborn; obstinate; not yielding to reason or advice

剛烈〈ㄍㄤ ㄌﾉㄝ〉
tough and vehement; violent

剛剛〈ㄍㄤ ㄍㄤ〉

① just now; just a moment ago: 貨剛剛到. The goods came just now. ② just; only

剛果《《尤 《メビ》
① the Congo (Kinshasa) ② the Congo (Leopoldville)

剛果人《《尤 《メビ ㄖㄣ》
a Congolese

剛果語《《尤 《メビ ㄩ》
Congolese

剛…就…《《尤…ㄐㄧㄡ…》
as soon as; no sooner... than; immediately

剛健《《尤 ㄐㄧㄢˋ》
vigorous; energetic; robust

剛勁《《尤 ㄐㄧㄥˋ》
bold; vigorous; sturdy

剛巧《《尤 ㄑㄧㄠˇ》or 剛好《《尤 ㄏㄠˇ》
① exactly; precisely; just: 那剛好是我想說的. That's exactly what I want to say. ② to happen to; it so happened that: 我剛好在公車上碰見她. I happened to meet her in the bus.

剛強《《尤 ㄑㄧㄤˊ》
tough and strong; indomitable; fortitudinous; firm; staunch

剛直《《尤 ㄓˊ》
tough and honest; upright

剛正不阿《《尤 ㄓㄥˋ ㄅㄨˋ ㄜ》
upright and never stooping to flattery

剛柔相濟《《尤 ㄖㄡˊ ㄒㄧㄤ ㄐㄧˋ》
to properly combine toughness and gentleness (in dealing with people)

剛才《《尤 ㄘㄞˊ》
just a moment ago; a very short while ago: 他剛才還在這兒. He was here only a moment ago.

剛毅《《尤 ㄧˋ》
tough and determined; resolute; firm; unwavering

剛毅木訥《《尤 ㄧˋ ㄇㄨˋ ㄋㄜˋ》
resolute and not eloquent

【剜】 397
ㄨㄢ uan wan
to scoop out; to gouge out; to carve out

剜刀《ㄨㄢ ㄉㄠ》
a reamer

剜空《ㄨㄢ ㄎㄨㄥ》
to gouge hollow

剜空心思《ㄨㄢ ㄎㄨㄥ ㄒㄧㄣ ㄙ》

---

to exhaust one's wits or ingenuity

剜肉補瘡《ㄨㄢ ㄖㄡˋ ㄅㄨˇ ㄔㄨㄤ》
(literally) to cut out a piece of flesh to patch up a sore —to make do by temporary improvisation without attempting a permanent solution

【剝】 398
1. ㄅㄛ bo bō
to strip; to skin; to make bare; to peel; to peel off; to shell

剝皮《ㄅㄛ ㄆㄧˊ》
to skin; to peel off the skin; to flay

剝膚之痛《ㄅㄛ ㄈㄨ ㄓ ㄊㄨㄥˋ》
the pain of being skinned —what hurts closely

剝得精光《ㄅㄛ ㄉㄜˊ ㄐㄧㄥ ㄍㄨㄤ》
stripped naked

剝奪《ㄅㄛ ㄉㄨㄛˊ》
to deprive or strip one of (rights, property, etc.)

剝離《ㄅㄛ ㄌㄧˊ》
(said of tissue, skin, covering, etc.) to come off; to be stripped

剝落《ㄅㄛ ㄌㄨㄛˋ》
to come off (as a result of erosion); to be peeled off

剝極必復《ㄅㄛ ㄐㄧˊ ㄅㄧˋ ㄈㄨˋ》
When things are at their worst, they will surely mend.

剝蕉抽繭《ㄅㄛ ㄐㄧㄠ ㄔㄡ ㄐㄧㄢˇ》
peeling a banana plant or unwinding a cocoon—to press an inquiry step by step; to investigate deeper and deeper 亦作「抽絲剝繭」

剝削《ㄅㄛ ㄒㄩㄝˋ》
to exploit (people)

剝製《ㄅㄛ ㄓˋ》
to make (an animal specimen by removing the meat and entrails from the carcass and stuffing it with something else)

剝啄聲《ㄅㄛ ㄓㄨㄛˊ ㄕㄥ》
a knocking sound; a tap

剝蝕《ㄅㄛ ㄕˊ》
to disintegrate (from erosion or weathering); to decay; to corrode; to ravage

---

【剝】 398
2. ㄅㄠ bau bāo
to strip

剝開《ㄅㄠ ㄎㄞ》
to strip the covering off

九畫

【副】 399
ㄈㄨˋ fuh fù
1. to assist
2. secondary; auxiliary; subsidiary
3. deputy; assistant; vice-
4. a set

副本《ㄈㄨˋ ㄅㄣˇ》or 副張《ㄈㄨˋ ㄓㄤ》
a duplicate copy; a copy

副標題《ㄈㄨˋ ㄅㄧㄠ ㄊㄧˊ》
a subheading; a subtitle

副末《ㄈㄨˋ ㄇㄛˋ》
(Peking opera) a clown

副代表《ㄈㄨˋ ㄉㄞˋ ㄅㄧㄠˇ》
a deputy representative

副廳長《ㄈㄨˋ ㄊㄧㄥ ㄓㄤˇ》
a deputy commissioner (of a department in a provincial government)

副領事《ㄈㄨˋ ㄌㄧㄥˇ ㄕˋ》
a vice-consul

副官《ㄈㄨˋ 《ㄍㄨㄢ》
an adjutant; an aide-de-camp

副刊《ㄈㄨˋ ㄎㄢ》
a supplement; a supplementary issue

副會長《ㄈㄨˋ ㄏㄨㄟˋ ㄓㄤˇ》
a vice-president (of an association)

副甲狀腺《ㄈㄨˋ ㄐㄧㄚˇ ㄓㄨㄤˋ ㄒㄧㄢˋ》
the parathyroid

副甲狀腺素《ㄈㄨˋ ㄐㄧㄚˇ ㄓㄨㄤˋ ㄒㄧㄢˋ ㄙㄨˋ》
parathyroid hormone

副駕駛《ㄈㄨˋ ㄐㄧㄚˋ ㄕˇ》
a copilot

副交感神經《ㄈㄨˋ ㄐㄧㄠ 《ㄍㄢˇ ㄕㄣˊ ㄐㄧㄥ》
the parasympathetic nerve

副教授《ㄈㄨˋ ㄐㄧㄠˋ ㄕㄡˋ》
an associate professor

副啟《ㄈㄨˋ ㄑㄧˇ》
a postscript

副校長《ㄈㄨˋ ㄒㄧㄠˋ ㄓㄤˇ》
a provost (of a university)

副職《ㄈㄨˋ ㄓˊ》
the position of a deputy to the chief of an office, a department, etc.

〔刀
部〕

副州長(ㄈㄨ ㄓㄡ ㄓㄤˇ)
a lieutenant governor

副主席(ㄈㄨ ㄓㄨˇ ㄒㄧˊ)
a vice-chairman

副產品(ㄈㄨ ㄔㄢˇ ㄆㄧㄣˇ)
a by-product

副食(ㄈㄨ ㄕˊ)
foods other than the staple
food; nonstaple foods

副室(ㄈㄨ ㄕˋ)
a concubine

副社長(ㄈㄨ ㄕㄜˋ ㄓㄤˇ)
a vice-president or deputy
director (of a newspaper,
news agency, etc.)

副手(ㄈㄨ ㄕㄡˇ)
an assistant; a helper

副傷寒(ㄈㄨ ㄕㄤ ㄏㄢˊ)
paratyphoid fever

副署(ㄈㄨ ㄕㄨˇ)
to countersign

副熱帶高壓(ㄈㄨ ㄖㄜˋ ㄉㄞˋ ㄍㄠ ㄧㄚ)
subtropical anticyclone

副作用(ㄈㄨ ㄗㄨㄛˋ ㄩㄥˋ)
(medicine) side effects; by-
effects

副總統(ㄈㄨ ㄗㄨㄥˇ ㄊㄨㄥˇ)
a vice-president (of a
nation)

副總裁(ㄈㄨ ㄗㄨㄥˇ ㄘㄞˊ)
①a vice director general
(of a political party) ②a
vice-governor (of a bank)

副總司令(ㄈㄨ ㄗㄨㄥˇ ㄙ ㄌㄧㄥˋ)
a deputy commander-in-chief

副詞(ㄈㄨ ㄘˊ)
an adverb that modifies an
adjective, a verb or another
adverb

副議長(ㄈㄨ ㄧˋ ㄓㄤˇ)
a vice-chairman or deputy
speaker (of an assembly,
council, etc.)

副業(ㄈㄨ ㄧㄝˋ)
a side job; on the side

副研究員(ㄈㄨ ㄧㄢˊ ㄐㄧㄡˋ ㄩㄢˊ)
an associate research fellow

【剪】400
(騗) ㄐㄧㄢˇ jean jiǎn
1. to cut or clip with scissors;
to shear; to trim: 修剪草坪。
Cut the lawn.
2. to annihilate; to destroy
completely
3. scissors; shears; clippers

剪報(ㄐㄧㄢˇ ㄅㄠˋ)
a newspaper cutting (or
clipping)

剪票(ㄐㄧㄢˇ ㄆㄧㄠˋ)
to punch a ticket

剪毛(ㄐㄧㄢˇ ㄇㄠˊ)
(animal husbandry) shear-
ing; clipping

剪毛機(ㄐㄧㄢˇ ㄇㄠˊ ㄐㄧ)
a shearing machine

剪滅(ㄐㄧㄢˇ ㄇㄧㄝˋ)
to cut away; to cut off; to
cut down; to eliminate; to
remove; to exterminate

剪伐(ㄐㄧㄢˇ ㄈㄚˊ)
to prune, cut or lop off
(branches)

剪髮(ㄐㄧㄢˇ ㄈㄚˇ)
to cut hair

剪刀(ㄐㄧㄢˇ ㄉㄠ)
scissors; shears; clippers
亦作[剪子]

剪貼(ㄐㄧㄢˇ ㄊㄧㄝ)
①to clip and paste (some-
thing out of a newspaper,
etc.) in a scrapbook or on
cards ②cutting out (as a
schoolchildren's activity)

剪貼簿(ㄐㄧㄢˇ ㄊㄧㄝ ㄅㄨˋ)
a scrapbook

剪輯(ㄐㄧㄢˇ ㄐㄧˊ)
①(movie) montage; film
editing ②editing and re-
arrangement

剪接(ㄐㄧㄢˇ ㄐㄧㄝ)
to edit or cut a film; film
editing

剪徑(ㄐㄧㄢˇ ㄐㄧㄥˋ)
highway robbery; to waylay
travelers in order to rob
them

剪紙(ㄐㄧㄢˇ ㄓˇ)
(art and crafts) paper-cut;
scissor-cut

剪指甲(ㄐㄧㄢˇ ㄓˇ ㄐㄧㄚˇ)
to trim one's nails

剪燭(ㄐㄧㄢˇ ㄓㄨˊ)
to snuff a candle

剪除(ㄐㄧㄢˇ ㄔㄨˊ)
to remove; to exterminate;
to cut off

剪裁(ㄐㄧㄢˇ ㄘㄞˊ)
①to tailor clothing mate-
rials for a dress ②to brush
up or improve a writing by
making additions or dele-
tions; to prune

剪綵(ㄐㄧㄢˇ ㄘㄞˇ)
to cut the ribbon (to inaugurate a building, the opening
of an exhibition, etc.)

剪草(ㄐㄧㄢˇ ㄘㄠˇ)
to mow or cut grass

剪草機(ㄐㄧㄢˇ ㄘㄠˇ ㄐㄧ)
a lawn mower

剪草除根(ㄐㄧㄢˇ ㄘㄠˇ ㄔㄨˊ ㄍㄣ)
(literally) to cut the grass
and remove the root—to ex
terminate completely

剪羊毛(ㄐㄧㄢˇ ㄧㄤˊ ㄇㄠˊ)
to shear wool

剪影(ㄐㄧㄢˇ ㄧㄥˇ)
①to cut out a silhouette; ②
to outline; to sketch; a sil
houette; an outline

十畫

【剩】401
ㄕㄥˋ shenq shèng
to remain; to be left over; in
excess; residues; remainder
surplus; remains: 還剩多少?
How much is left (over)?

剩飯(ㄕㄥˋ ㄈㄢˋ)
leftovers from a meal; left
over rice

剩貨(ㄕㄥˋ ㄏㄨㄛˋ)
leftover goods; leftovers

剩錢(ㄕㄥˋ ㄑㄧㄢˊ)
to have money left; money
left (in one's possession);
the balance

剩下(ㄕㄥˋ ㄒㄧㄚˋ)
to be left over; the remainder

剩餘(ㄕㄥˋ ㄩˊ)
the excess; the surplus; the
balance; the remainder

剩餘價值(ㄕㄥˋ ㄩˊ ㄐㄧㄚˋ ㄓˊ)
(economics) residual value;
(sociology) surplus value

剩餘物資(ㄕㄥˋ ㄩˊ ㄨˋ ㄗ)
surplus materials

【割】402
《ㄜ ge gē
to cut; to sever; to divide

割包皮(《ㄜ ㄅㄠ ㄆㄧˊ)
to shorten prepuce by surgical operation; to circumcise

割刀(《ㄜ ㄉㄠ)
a cutter

割地賠款(《ㄜ ㄉㄧˋ ㄆㄟˊ ㄎㄨㄢˇ)
to cede territory and pay
indemnities (to the victor of

a war)

割斷(《ㄜ ㄉㄨㄢˋ)
to cut off; to sever by cutting; apart from

割裂(《ㄜ ㄌㄧㄝˋ)
to split; to slash or rip open (by means of a knife); to cut apart; to separate

割股療親(《ㄜ ㄍㄨˇ ㄌㄧㄠˊ ㄑㄧㄣ)
to try to cure the illness of one's parent by mixing with medicine a slice of flesh cut from one's own thigh

割開(《ㄜ ㄎㄞ)
to cut open

割雞焉用牛刀(《ㄜ ㄐㄧ ㄧㄢ ㄩㄥˋ ㄋㄧㄡˊ ㄉㄠ)
(literally) It's unnecessary to use a butcher's knife to kill a chicken. —A man of less ability can do the job.

割據(《ㄜ ㄐㄩˋ)
to exercise sovereign powers in each of the regions of a nation under the control of contending warlords; to set up a separate regime by force of arms

割席(《ㄜ ㄒㄧˊ)
to sever friendship

割線(《ㄜ ㄒㄧㄢˋ)
(mathematics) a secant

割除(《ㄜ ㄔㄨˊ)
to cut off; to cut out; to excise

割勢(《ㄜ ㄕˋ)
to castrate

割捨(《ㄜ ㄕㄜˇ)
to part with; to give away: 他割捨不下他的雙親。He found it hard to part with his parents.

割禾機(《ㄜ ㄏㄜˊ ㄐㄧ)
(agriculture) a swather; a windrower

割讓(《ㄜ ㄖㄤˋ)
to cede (land or territory); cession

割草(《ㄜ ㄘㄠˇ)
to cut grass; to mow grass

割草機(《ㄜ ㄘㄠˇ ㄐㄧ)
a mower

割愛(《ㄜ ㄞˋ)
to give up what one treasures; to give up something reluctantly

割與(《ㄜ ㄩˇ)
to cede to

【剴】 403　ㄎㄞˊ kae kǎi
1. a sickle
2. thoroughly; clearly

剴切(ㄎㄞˇ ㄑㄧㄝˋ)
(said of statements) clearly; true and pertinent; earnest and sincere

【創】 404　1. ㄔㄨㄤ chuang chuāng
1. to start; to begin; to initiate; to create; to establish; to found
2. original; unprecedented

創辦(ㄔㄨㄤˋ ㄅㄢˋ)
to start (a business, publication, etc.); to found (a school, club, etc.); to set up; to establish: 哈佛大學創辦於 1636 年。 Harvard University was founded in 1636.

創立(ㄔㄨㄤˋ ㄌㄧˋ)
to start, found or establish (an organization)

創刊(ㄔㄨㄤˋ ㄎㄢ)
to put out the first issue (of a periodical); to start publication

創刊號(ㄔㄨㄤˋ ㄎㄢ ㄏㄠˋ)
the first issue (of a periodical)

創獲(ㄔㄨㄤˋ ㄏㄨㄛˋ)
an original finding; a new discovery

創紀錄(ㄔㄨㄤˋ ㄐㄧˋ ㄌㄨˋ)
to set a record; to make a record

創見(ㄔㄨㄤˋ ㄐㄧㄢˋ)
① an original opinion or view; a new idea: 他是有創見的思想家。 He is an original thinker. ② an unprecedented thing

創建(ㄔㄨㄤˋ ㄐㄧㄢˋ)
to found; to establish

創舉(ㄔㄨㄤˋ ㄐㄩˇ)
an unprecedented undertaking; pioneering work: 這是了不起的創舉。 This is great pioneering work.

創新(ㄔㄨㄤˋ ㄒㄧㄣ)
to bring forth new ideas; to blaze new trails

創制權(ㄔㄨㄤˋ ㄓˋ ㄑㄩㄢˊ)
the right to initiate laws; the initiative

創始(ㄔㄨㄤˋ ㄕˇ)
to start; to begin; to commence

創始人(ㄔㄨㄤˋ ㄕˇ ㄖㄣˊ)
a pioneer or founder

創世紀(ㄔㄨㄤˋ ㄕˋ ㄐㄧˋ)
(Bible) Genesis

創設(ㄔㄨㄤˋ ㄕㄜˋ)
to start or set up (an office, agency, etc.)

創造(ㄔㄨㄤˋ ㄗㄠˋ)
to create; to produce: 神創造了天地。 God created the heaven and the earth.

創造力(ㄔㄨㄤˋ ㄗㄠˋ ㄌㄧˋ)
originality; creative ability; the talent to create

創作(ㄔㄨㄤˋ ㄗㄨㄛˋ)
① to write (original works of literature) ② an original work of literature or art

創業(ㄔㄨㄤˋ ㄧㄝˋ)
to be the founder of a business; to start a business

【創】 404　2. ㄔㄨㄤˋ chuang chuàng
1. a wound
2. same as 瘡—a sore; a boil; an ulcer

創口(ㄔㄨㄤˋ ㄎㄡˇ)
a wound; a cut

創痕(ㄔㄨㄤˋ ㄏㄣˊ)
a scar

創鉅痛深(ㄔㄨㄤˋ ㄐㄩˋ ㄊㄨㄥˋ ㄕㄣ)
The damage is heavy.

創傷(ㄔㄨㄤˋ ㄕㄤ)
a wound; a cut; a scar

創痍(ㄔㄨㄤˋ ㄧˊ)
① a wound (with opening lips showing) ② the suffering of the people

創痍滿目(ㄔㄨㄤˋ ㄧˊ ㄇㄢˇ ㄇㄨˋ)
nothing but ruins and debris (in the wake of a devastating war or a disaster)

十一畫

【剿】 405　(勦) ㄐㄧㄠˇ jeau jiǎo
to exterminate; to stamp out; to destroy; to put down

剿平(ㄐㄧㄠˇ ㄆㄧㄥˊ)
to succeed in suppressing or to put down (a rebellion)

剿滅(ㄐㄧㄠˇ ㄇㄧㄝˋ)

〔刀部〕

to exterminate or destroy (bandits or rebels)

剿匪 (ㄐㄧㄠˇ ㄈㄟˇ)
to launch attacks against the bandits

剿撫兼施 (ㄐㄧㄠˇ ㄈㄨˇ ㄐㄧㄢ ㄕ)
(to try to suppress a rebellion) by military operations as well as inducements to surrender

【剷】 406. ㄔㄢˇ chaan chǎn
1. a shovel
2. to shovel; to level off; to raze to the ground

剷平 (ㄔㄢˇ ㄆㄧㄥˊ)
to level to the ground; to level; to be razed to the ground

剷除 (ㄔㄢˇ ㄔㄨˊ)
to root out; to eradicate

【剽】 407. ㄆㄧㄠ piau piāo
1. to plunder; to rob; to steal
2. agile; fast

剽掠 (ㄆㄧㄠ ㄌㄩㄝˋ)or剽劫 (ㄆㄧㄠ ㄐㄧㄝˊ)
to plunder; to rob

剽悍 (ㄆㄧㄠ ㄏㄢˋ)
agile and fierce; warlike

剽悍善戰 (ㄆㄧㄠ ㄏㄢˋ ㄕㄢˋ ㄓㄢˋ)
swift, daring and skillful at fighting

剽竊 (ㄆㄧㄠ ㄑㄧㄝˋ)
①to steal; to purloin ②to plagiarize

十二畫

【箚】 408. ㄓㄚˊ jar zhá
1. a letter; a brief note
2. a directive (in former times) ; an official communication from a superior to an inferior

箚記 (ㄓㄚˊ ㄐㄧˋ)
①to take notes in reading ②notes taken in reading; reading notes

箚子 (ㄓㄚˊ ㄗˇ)
a directive (in former times) ; a communication to an official subordinate 參看「札」

【劃】 409. ㄏㄨㄚˊ huah huá
1. to unify

2. to lay boundaries
3. to draw a line; to mark; to delineate
4. to plan or design
5. to set aside; to divide
6. a stroke (of a Chinese character)

劃撥 (ㄏㄨㄚˊ ㄅㄛ)
to deposit money under the account of a seller in payment of goods purchased; to transfer funds

劃分 (ㄏㄨㄚˊ ㄈㄣ)
to divide and delimit; to differentiate

劃定 (ㄏㄨㄚˊ ㄉㄧㄥˋ)
to delimit; to define the boundary of; to mark out

劃歸 (ㄏㄨㄚˊ 《ㄨㄟ)or劃入 (ㄏㄨㄚˊ ㄖㄨˋ)
to allot (some revenue, an area, etc.) to a government or an organization); to incorporate into

劃界 (ㄏㄨㄚˊ ㄐㄧㄝˋ)
to fix boundaries; to define limits; to delimit a boundary

劃清 (ㄏㄨㄚˊ ㄑㄧㄥ)
to draw a clear line of demarcation; to make a clear distinction: 我要跟他劃清界線。I want to make a clean break with him.

劃時代 (ㄏㄨㄚˊ ㄕˊ ㄉㄞˋ)
epoch-making; epochal: 此舉具有劃時代的意義。The measure has an epoch-making significance.

劃一 (ㄏㄨㄚˊ ㄧ)
to make uniform; to give uniformity to something

劃一不二 (ㄏㄨㄚˊ ㄧ ㄅㄨˋ ㄦˋ)
uniform (prices), no bargaining or haggling; fixed; unalterable; rigid; hard and fast

【劃】 409. 2. ㄏㄨㄚˋ hua huà
to cut

劃開 (ㄏㄨㄚˋ ㄎㄞ)
to cut open; to slash open

十三畫

【劇】 410. ㄐㄩˋ jiuh jù
1. a drama; a theatrical work;

a play
2. intense; strenuous; acute; severe
3. to play
4. a Chinese family name

劇本 (ㄐㄩˋ ㄅㄣˇ)
a play; a scenario; a script; a libretto

劇評 (ㄐㄩˋ ㄆㄧㄥˊ)
a review of a play or an opera; dramatic criticism

劇目 (ㄐㄩˋ ㄇㄨˋ)
a list of plays or operas; a repertoire

劇坊 (ㄐㄩˋ ㄈㄤ)
a theater workshop

劇盜 (ㄐㄩˋ ㄉㄠˋ)
a notorious bandit

劇毒 (ㄐㄩˋ ㄉㄨˊ)
deadly poison

劇談 (ㄐㄩˋ ㄊㄢˊ)
①to converse enthusiastically ②comments about drama and the theater

劇團 (ㄐㄩˋ ㄊㄨㄢˊ)
a theatrical company; an opera troupe; a troupe

劇烈 (ㄐㄩˋ ㄌㄧㄝˋ)
strenuous; intense; hard; fierce

劇情 (ㄐㄩˋ ㄑㄧㄥˊ)
the plot

劇照 (ㄐㄩˋ ㄓㄠˋ)
a stage photo; a still

劇終 (ㄐㄩˋ ㄓㄨㄥ)
the end; a curtainfall

劇中人 (ㄐㄩˋ ㄓㄨㄥ ㄖㄣˊ)
characters in a play or opera; dramatis personae

劇場 (ㄐㄩˋ ㄔㄤˇ)or(ㄐㄩˋ ㄔㄤˊ)or劇院 (ㄐㄩˋ ㄩㄢˋ)
a theater

劇作家 (ㄐㄩˋ ㄗㄨㄛˋ ㄐㄧㄚ)
a playwright; a dramatist

劇藥 (ㄐㄩˋ ㄧㄠˋ)
strong medicine

劇飲 (ㄐㄩˋ ㄧㄣˇ)
to drink with abandon; to carouse

劇務 (ㄐㄩˋ ㄨˋ)
①stage management ②a stage manager

【劈】 411. 1. ㄆㄧ pi pī
1. to cleave; to split; to rive; to rend
2. a wedge

劈刀(ㄆ丨 ㄉㄠ)
①a chopper ②(military)
saber fighting

劈頭(ㄆ丨 ㄊㄡ)
①straight on the head; right
in the face: 我劈頭就給了他一
拳。I hit him straight on the
head. ②at the very start: 她
一進門劈頭就問:「準備好了
嗎?」The moment she entered
the room she asked, "Are
you ready?"

劈哩啪啦(ㄆ丨 ㄌ丨 ㄆㄚ ㄌㄚ)
(onomatopoeia) a descrip-
tive sound of firecrackers,
guns, etc.: 鞭炮劈哩啪啦地響。
The firecrackers were crackling and spluttering.

劈臉(ㄆ丨 ㄌ丨ㄢˇ)
right in the face

劈開(ㄆ丨 ㄎㄞ)
①to split open ②do not
say the fact that... ③(mining) cleavage

劈胸(ㄆ丨 ㄒㄩㄥ)
right against the chest

劈柴(ㄆ丨 ㄔㄞˊ)
to split or chop firewood

劈手(ㄆ丨 ㄕㄡˇ)
to thrust forth the hand
—(figuratively) in a flash;
instantly

劈山(ㄆ丨 ㄕㄢ)
to level off hilltops; to blast
cliffs

劈刺(ㄆ丨 ㄘ)
(military) saber or bayonet
fighting

【劈】411
2. ㄆ丨ˇ pii, pǐ
to split; to chop

劈柴(ㄆ丨 ㄔㄞˊ)
to split or chop firewood

【劉】412
ㄌ丨ㄡˊ liou, liú
1. a Chinese family name
2. to kill

劉邦(ㄌ丨ㄡˊ ㄅㄤ)
Liu Pang, the founder of the
Han Dynasty, whose reign
lasted from 206 to 194 B.C.

劉海兒(ㄌ丨ㄡˊ ㄏㄞˇ ㄦ)
bangs; a fringe

劉宋(ㄌ丨ㄡˊ ㄙㄨㄥˋ)
the Sung Dynasty under the
house of Liu between 420
and 477 (as distinct from

the Sung Dynasty under the
house of Chao)

【劊】413
ㄍㄨㄟˋ guey, guì
(又讀 ㄎㄨㄞˋ kuay, kuài)
to amputate; to cut off

劊子手(ㄍㄨㄟˋ ㄗˇ ㄕㄡˇ)
①an executioner ②a hatch-
etman; a slaughterman; a
butcher

【劍】414
ㄐ丨ㄢˋ jiann, jiàn
a sword; a dagger; a saber

劍拔弩張(ㄐ丨ㄢˋ ㄅㄚˊ ㄋㄨˇ ㄓㄤ)
(literally) with swords unsheathed and bows drawn
—ready to fight; ready to
destroy each other; becoming dangerously explosive

劍眉(ㄐ丨ㄢˋ ㄇㄟˊ)
straight eyebrows slanting
upwards and outwards

劍蘭(ㄐ丨ㄢˋ ㄌㄢˊ)
(botany) a gladiolus; a
sword lily

劍客(ㄐ丨ㄢˋ ㄎㄜˋ)
a swordsman; a fencing master

劍及履及(ㄐ丨ㄢˋ ㄐ丨ˊ ㄌㄩˇ ㄐ丨ˊ)
to perform a task with full
vigor and urgency

劍橋(ㄐ丨ㄢˋ ㄑ丨ㄠˊ)
Cambridge, England

劍俠(ㄐ丨ㄢˋ ㄒ丨ㄚˊ)
a wandering swordsman in
search of adventures)

劍術(ㄐ丨ㄢˋ ㄕㄨˋ)
swordsmanship; fencing: 他
擅長劍術。He is good at fenc-
ing.

十四畫

【劑】415
ㄐ丨ˋ jih, jì
1. a dose (of medicine)
2. prepared medicines or drugs
3. to prepare (medicines and
drugs)

劑量(ㄐ丨ˋ ㄌ丨ㄤˋ)
(pharmaceutics) a dosage; a
dose

【劓】416
丨ˋ yih, yì
to cut off the nose (as a
form of punishment in

ancient China)

力 部
ㄌ丨ˋ lih, lì

〔力部〕

【力】417
ㄌ丨ˋ lih, lì
1. strength
2. force; power
3. ability
4. vigor
5. vigorously; earnestly
6. to do one's best: 他辦事不力。
He did not do his best in his
work.

力臂(ㄌ丨ˋ ㄅ丨ˋ)
(physics) the lever arm, or
the arm of force

力不勝任(ㄌ丨ˋ ㄅㄨˋ ㄕㄥ ㄖㄣˋ)
to be unequal to one's task

力不從心(ㄌ丨ˋ ㄅㄨˋ ㄘㄨㄥˊ ㄒㄧㄣ)
to have too little power or
too few resources to do as
much as one wishes; lacking
the ability to do what one
wishes

力排衆議(ㄌ丨ˋ ㄆㄞˊ ㄓㄨㄥˋ 丨ˋ)
to refute the consensus and
present a new plan or idea;
to prevail over all dissent

力大無比(ㄌ丨ˋ ㄉㄚˋ ㄨˊ ㄅ丨ˇ)
without a match in physical
prowess

力敵萬夫(ㄌ丨ˋ ㄉ丨ˊ ㄨㄢˋ ㄈㄨ)
able to fight off ten thousand men—(figuratively)
very brave

力點(ㄌ丨ˋ ㄉ丨ㄢˇ)
a point of force (on a lever)

力透紙背(ㄌ丨ˋ ㄊㄡˋ ㄓˇ ㄅㄟˋ)
(calligraphy) So forceful
are the strokes that the
force seems to penetrate the
paper.

力田(ㄌ丨ˋ ㄊ丨ㄢˊ)
to do farming diligently

力圖(ㄌ丨ˋ ㄊㄨˊ)
to try hard; to strive to

力量(ㄌ丨ˋ ㄌ丨ㄤˋ)
strength; force; power

力可拔山(ㄌ丨ˋ ㄎㄜˇ ㄅㄚˊ ㄕㄢ)
so strong as to be able to
lift a mountain

力疾奔走(ㄌ丨ˋ ㄐ丨ˊ ㄅㄣ ㄗㄡˇ)

〔力部〕

to busy oneself in running about (usually doing official duties) despite illness

力疾從公（ㄌㄧˋ ㄐㄧˊ ㄘㄨㄥˊ ㄍㄨㄥ）
to perform official duties in disregard of ailments; to attend to one's duties in spite of illness

力竭聲嘶（ㄌㄧˋ ㄐㄧㄝˊ ㄕㄥ ㄙ）
exhausted and hoarse (as a result of haranguing, crying, etc.)

力薦（ㄌㄧˋ ㄐㄧㄢˋ）
to recommend (someone) strongly

力氣（ㄌㄧˋ ˙ㄑㄧ）
① physical strength or power ② an effort

力求（ㄌㄧˋ ㄑㄧㄡˊ）
to make strenuous efforts to; to do one's best to; to strive to

力求上進（ㄌㄧˋ ㄑㄧㄡˊ ㄕㄤˋ ㄐㄧㄣˋ）
to strive vigorously to improve oneself

力請（ㄌㄧˋ ㄑㄧㄥˇ）
to entreat earnestly; to ask with zeal or eagerness

力行（ㄌㄧˋ ㄒㄧㄥˊ）
to practice or perform energetically; to act with might

力行不怠（ㄌㄧˋ ㄒㄧㄥˊ ㄅㄨˋ ㄉㄞˋ）
to do something persistently without a cessation

力學（ㄌㄧˋ ㄒㄩㄝˊ）
① to study with diligence or industry; to study hard ② (physics) mechanics

力戰（ㄌㄧˋ ㄓㄢˋ）
to fight with might or vigor; to fight hard (usually against great odds)

力爭（ㄌㄧˋ ㄓㄥ）
① to struggle hard; to strive with might; to do all one's best ② to argue strongly; to contend vigorously

力爭上流（ㄌㄧˋ ㄓㄥ ㄕㄤˋ ㄌㄧㄡˊ）or 力爭上游（ㄌㄧˋ ㄓㄥ ㄕㄤˋ ㄧㄡˊ）
to try to excel by strenuous efforts; to strive for progress

力士（ㄌㄧˋ ㄕˋ）
a muscleman; a person of great physical strength

力所能及（ㄌㄧˋ ㄙㄨㄛˇ ㄋㄥˊ ㄐㄧˊ）
within one's power

力役（ㄌㄧˋ ㄧˋ）
the exactions of personal service

力挽狂瀾（ㄌㄧˋ ㄨㄢˇ ㄎㄨㄤˊ ㄌㄢˊ）
to make vigorous efforts to turn the tide—(figuratively) to do one's best to reverse the course of events

力與願違（ㄌㄧˋ ㄩˋ ㄩㄢˋ ㄨㄟˊ）
to be unable to do what one wishes

三畫

【功】 418
《ㄍㄨㄥ gong gong》

1. a merit; an achievement; an accomplishment; an exploit
2. usefulness; effectiveness
3. a function
4. (physics) work: 機械功 mechanical work

功敗垂成（ㄍㄨㄥ ㄅㄞˋ ㄔㄨㄟˊ ㄔㄥˊ）
to fail within reach of success; to meet with failure when victory is within one's grasp

功不補過（ㄍㄨㄥ ㄅㄨˋ ㄅㄨˇ ㄍㄨㄛˋ）
Demerits outweigh merits.

功不可沒（ㄍㄨㄥ ㄅㄨˋ ㄎㄜˇ ㄇㄛˋ）
The contribution (to success) cannot be left unrecognized.

功名（ㄍㄨㄥ ㄇㄧㄥˊ）
① laurels; glory; distinction; honor ② an official rank or an academic title (in former times)

功夫（ㄍㄨㄥ ˙ㄈㄨ）
① time (to do something) ② efforts (devoted to a task) ③ accomplishments ④ skill

功德（ㄍㄨㄥ ㄉㄜˊ）
① merits and virtues ② (Buddhism) charitable and pious deeds; beneficence

功德無量（ㄍㄨㄥ ㄉㄜˊ ㄨˊ ㄌㄧㄤˋ）
(His, your, etc.) kindness knows no bounds; boundless beneficence

功到自然成（ㄍㄨㄥ ㄉㄠˋ ㄗˋ ㄖㄢˊ ㄔㄥˊ）
Constant effort yields sure success.

功能（ㄍㄨㄥ ㄋㄥˊ）
a function: 心臟有很重要的功能。 The heart has a very important function.

功勞（ㄍㄨㄥ ㄌㄠˊ）
merits; credit; meritorious deeds; contribution

功力（ㄍㄨㄥ ㄌㄧˋ）
efficacy; effectiveness; potency

功利（ㄍㄨㄥ ㄌㄧˋ）
utility; material gain

功利主義（ㄍㄨㄥ ㄌㄧˋ ㄓㄨˇ ㄧˋ）
utilitarianism

功令（ㄍㄨㄥ ㄌㄧㄥˋ）
orders; decrees; school regulations

功高震主（ㄍㄨㄥ ㄍㄠ ㄓㄣˋ ㄓㄨˇ）
So great is one's achievements as to make one's boss feel uneasy or insecure.

功過（ㄍㄨㄥ ㄍㄨㄛˋ）
merits and demerits

功過相抵（ㄍㄨㄥ ㄍㄨㄛˋ ㄒㄧㄤ ㄉㄧˇ）
One's mistakes or offenses cancel his contributions.

功課（ㄍㄨㄥ ㄎㄜˋ）
schoolwork; homework

功課表（ㄍㄨㄥ ㄎㄜˋ ㄅㄧㄠˇ）
a class schedule (at school)

功虧一簣（ㄍㄨㄥ ㄎㄨㄟ ㄧ ㄎㄨㄟˋ）
failure to achieve success or perfection by a very narrow margin

功績（ㄍㄨㄥ ㄐㄧ）
meritorious records; achievements; a contribution

功效（ㄍㄨㄥ ㄒㄧㄠˋ）
effectiveness; efficacy; useful results

功勳（ㄍㄨㄥ ㄒㄩㄣ）
distinctive achievements; an eminent contribution; meritorious services; feats

功臣（ㄍㄨㄥ ㄔㄣˊ）
(in old China) a vassal or subject who distinguished himself by meritorious services; (in a modern sense) one who has made a significant contribution to a specific task; a person who has rendered outstanding services

功成名就（ㄍㄨㄥ ㄔㄥˊ ㄇㄧㄥˊ ㄐㄧㄡˋ）or 功成名遂（ㄍㄨㄥ ㄔㄥˊ ㄇㄧㄥˊ ㄙㄨㄟˋ）
to achieve success and acquire fame; to be successful and famous

功成弗居（ㄍㄨㄥ ㄔㄥˊ ㄈㄨˊ ㄐㄩ）
to achieve success but do

not take credit

功成身退(《ㄍㄨㄥ ㄔㄥ ㄕㄣ ㄊㄨㄟ》)or
功成身退(《ㄍㄨㄥ ㄔㄥ ㄕㄣ ㄊㄨㄟ》)
to retire after achieving success; to leave the top post to
others after playing the
leading role in a successful
revolution, movement, etc.

功用(《ㄍㄨㄥ ㄩㄥ》)
use; effect; a function

【加】 419 ㄐㄧㄚ jiā jiá

1. plus; to add: 二加三等於五。
Two plus three makes five.
2. to increase; to augment
3. to append: 他在箱子上加標
籤。He appended a label to
that trunk.

加倍(ㄐㄧㄚ ㄅㄟ)
to double; to make twice as
much; to redouble: 他加倍努
力完成他的工作。He redoubled
his efforts to finish his
work.

加班(ㄐㄧㄚ ㄅㄢ)
to work overtime; to work
an extra shift

加鞭(ㄐㄧㄚ ㄅㄧㄢ)
to whip; to apply the whip

加彭(ㄐㄧㄚ ㄆㄥ)
Gabon

加盟(ㄐㄧㄚ ㄇㄥˊ)
to join an alliance, a fraternity or a secret society

加冕(ㄐㄧㄚ ㄇㄧㄢˇ)
to crown; to coronate

加勉(ㄐㄧㄚ ㄇㄧㄢˇ)
to make greater exertions

加法(ㄐㄧㄚ ㄈㄚˇ)
(arithmetic) addition

加封(ㄐㄧㄚ ㄈㄥ)
①to bestow a title ②to
seal with additional tape

加俸(ㄐㄧㄚ ㄈㄥˋ)
to raise one's pay

加添物(ㄐㄧㄚ ㄊㄧㄢ ㄨˋ)or加添劑
(ㄐㄧㄚ ㄊㄧㄢ ㄐㄧˋ)
an additive

加拿大(ㄐㄧㄚ ㄋㄚˊ ㄉㄚˋ)
Canada

加農砲(ㄐㄧㄚ ㄋㄨㄥˊ ㄆㄠˋ)
a cannon

加勒比海(ㄐㄧㄚ ㄌㄜˋ ㄅㄧˇ ㄏㄞˇ)
the Caribbean Sea

加禮(ㄐㄧㄚ ㄌㄧˇ)
to show more than ordinary
civility; to be particularly
warm (to a guest)

加里波的(ㄐㄧㄚ ㄌㄧˇ ㄅㄛ ㄉㄜ˙)
Giuseppe Garibaldi, 1807–
1882, one of the founders of
modern Italy

加利福尼亞(ㄐㄧㄚ ㄌㄧˋ ㄈㄨˊ ㄋㄧˊ ㄧㄚˇ)
the state of California,
U.S.A.

加料(ㄐㄧㄚ ㄌㄧㄠˋ)
①to feed raw material into
(a container, etc.) ②particu-
lar things made of excellent
materials

加侖(ㄐㄧㄚ ㄌㄨㄣˊ)
a gallon (a unit of liquid
measurement)

加冠(ㄐㄧㄚ ㄍㄨㄢ)
to cap a boy as a symbol of
his coming of age (at 20)

加官(ㄐㄧㄚ ㄍㄨㄢ)
①to hold a concurrent post
②(formerly) to be promot-
ed to a higher position

加官晉爵(ㄐㄧㄚ ㄍㄨㄢ ㄐㄧㄣˋ ㄐㄩㄝˊ)
to advance in rank and position; promotion

加工(ㄐㄧㄚ ㄍㄨㄥ)
to process (goods)

加工出口區(ㄐㄧㄚ ㄍㄨㄥ ㄔㄨ ㄎㄡˇ ㄑㄩ)
an export processing zone

加快(ㄐㄧㄚ ㄎㄨㄞˋ)
to speed up; to accelerate

加寬(ㄐㄧㄚ ㄎㄨㄢ)
to broaden; to widen

加害(ㄐㄧㄚ ㄏㄞˋ)
to inflict injury; to do somebody harm

加號(ㄐㄧㄚ ㄏㄠˋ)
the plus symbol (+); a sign
of addition

加護(ㄐㄧㄚ ㄏㄨˋ)
①(said of gods) to protect
or bless ②to take special
care of

加護病房(ㄐㄧㄚ ㄏㄨˋ ㄅㄧㄥˋ ㄈㄤˊ)
an intensive care unit (ICU)

加價(ㄐㄧㄚ ㄐㄧㄚˋ)
to raise or hike the price

加減乘除(ㄐㄧㄚ ㄐㄧㄢˇ ㄔㄥˊ ㄔㄨˊ)
addition, subtraction, multiplication and division

加緊(ㄐㄧㄚ ㄐㄧㄣˇ)
to intensify; to step up

加勁(ㄐㄧㄚ ㄐㄧㄥˋ)
to put more energy into; to

make a greater effort

加劇(ㄐㄧㄚ ㄐㄩˋ)
to aggravate; to sharpen; to
cause to become worse or
more severe

加強(ㄐㄧㄚ ㄑㄧㄤˊ)
to strengthen; to reinforce;
to invigorate; to enhance

加權指數(ㄐㄧㄚ ㄑㄩㄢˊ ㄓˇ ㄕㄨˋ)
(stock trading) the weighted
index number

加薪(ㄐㄧㄚ ㄒㄧㄣ)
to give a pay raise

加值稅(ㄐㄧㄚ ㄓˊ ㄕㄨㄟˋ)
value-added tax

加重(ㄐㄧㄚ ㄓㄨㄥˋ)
to make heavier; to increase
burdens, work loads, etc.

加深(ㄐㄧㄚ ㄕㄣ)
①to deepen: 這條河需要加深
河道。The river needed to
be deepened the channel. ②
to cause to become worse
or more severe

加數(ㄐㄧㄚ ㄕㄨˋ)
an addend

加熱(ㄐㄧㄚ ㄖㄜˋ)
to heat; to warm

加入(ㄐㄧㄚ ㄖㄨˋ)
①to join (a group); to
accede to ②to add into

加菜(ㄐㄧㄚ ㄘㄞˋ)
to have additional and better foods than the usual fare

加餐(ㄐㄧㄚ ㄘㄢ)
to eat more at meals—to
show one's concern

加薩走廊(ㄐㄧㄚ ㄙㄚˋ ㄗㄡˇ ㄌㄤˊ)
the Gaza Strip on the Sinai
Peninsula

加速(ㄐㄧㄚ ㄙㄨˋ)
to step up; to quicken the
tempo; to accelerate: 他們業
已加速開發工業。They have
speeded up industrial development.

加速度(ㄐㄧㄚ ㄙㄨˋ ㄉㄨˋ)
acceleration

加爾各答(ㄐㄧㄚ ㄦˇ ㄍㄜˋ ㄉㄚˊ)
Calcutta

加一(ㄐㄧㄚ ㄧ)
to add one tenth (of the
original number or quan-
tity)

加意(ㄐㄧㄚ ㄧˋ)
to pay special attention; to
make an additional effort

力部

〔力部〕

加油（ㄐㄧㄚ ㄧㄡ）
① to oil: 這部機器要加油了。
This machine needs oiling.
② to refuel: 飛機要在東京降落加油。 The plane will land in Tokyo for refueling. ③ to step up effort; to cheer (an athlete in the midst of a sport competition with a view to goading him on for victory): 男孩子們大聲爲他們的足球除加油。 The boys cheered their football team loudly.

加油添醬（ㄐㄧㄚ ㄧㄡ ㄊㄧㄢ ㄐㄧㄤ）
to exaggerate or give embellishment to a story

加油站（ㄐㄧㄚ ㄧㄡ ㄓㄢ）
a gas station, or filling station

四畫

【劣】 420
　　　　ㄌㄧㄝˋ lieh liè
inferior; mean; bad; of low quality

劣品（ㄌㄧㄝˋ ㄆㄧㄣˇ）
inferior quality

劣馬（ㄌㄧㄝˋ ㄇㄚˇ）
① an inferior horse; an emaciated nag ② a vicious horse

劣等（ㄌㄧㄝˋ ㄉㄥˇ）
of inferior quality; low-grade; poor

劣等貨（ㄌㄧㄝˋ ㄉㄥˇ ㄏㄨㄛˋ）
goods of inferior quality

劣等生（ㄌㄧㄝˋ ㄉㄥˇ ㄕㄥ）
a dull student

劣點（ㄌㄧㄝˋ ㄉㄧㄢˇ）
a defect; a demerit

劣根性（ㄌㄧㄝˋ ㄍㄣ ㄒㄧㄥˋ）
degraded character; a depravity; meanness; innate wickedness; deep-rooted bad habits

劣貨（ㄌㄧㄝˋ ㄏㄨㄛˋ）
goods of poor quality; substandard goods

劣跡（ㄌㄧㄝˋ ㄐㄧ）
the unsavory records (of a person, especially those of a public official); misdeeds; evil-doing

劣質（ㄌㄧㄝˋ ㄓˊ）
of poor (or low) quality; inferior

劣種（ㄌㄧㄝˋ ㄓㄨㄥˇ）
inferior breeds; inferior stock

劣勢（ㄌㄧㄝˋ ㄕˋ）
inferior strength or position

劣紳（ㄌㄧㄝˋ ㄕㄣ）
evil gentry; an unethical intellectual who bullies the less well-educated in the local community

五畫

【助】 421
　　　　ㄓㄨˋ juh zhù
to help; to aid; to assist; help; assistance: 天助自助者。 God helps those who help themselves.

助跑（ㄓㄨˋ ㄆㄠˇ）
a run-up; an approach

助動詞（ㄓㄨˋ ㄉㄨㄥˋ ㄘˊ）
an auxiliary verb; a helping verb

助聽器（ㄓㄨˋ ㄊㄧㄥ ㄑㄧˋ）
a hearing aid; an audiphone

助理（ㄓㄨˋ ㄌㄧˇ）
① an assistant ② to assist help; assistance

助力（ㄓㄨˋ ㄌㄧˋ）
help; assistance

助攻（ㄓㄨˋ ㄍㄨㄥ）
(military) a holding (or secondary) attack

助桀爲虐（ㄓㄨˋ ㄐㄧㄝˊ ㄨㄟˊ ㄋㄩㄝˋ）
或助紂爲虐（ㄓㄨˋ ㄓㄡˋ ㄨㄟˊ ㄋㄩㄝˋ）
to help the wicked perpetrate wicked deeds; to help a tyrant to do evil

助敎（ㄓㄨˋ ㄐㄧㄠˋ）
a teaching assistant; a TA

助興（ㄓㄨˋ ㄒㄧㄥˋ）
to liven things up; to add to the amusement

助學金（ㄓㄨˋ ㄒㄩㄝˊ ㄐㄧㄣ）
a stipend; a grant-in-aid; a scholarship

助陣（ㄓㄨˋ ㄓㄣˋ）
to cheer or root for (a contestant)

助長（ㄓㄨˋ ㄓㄤˇ）
to encourage (a tendency); to promote the development of; to foster; to nurture

助產士（ㄓㄨˋ ㄔㄢˇ ㄕˋ）
a midwife

助手（ㄓㄨˋ ㄕㄡˇ）
an assistant; a helper; an aide

助人爲快樂之本（ㄓㄨˋ ㄖㄣˊ ㄨㄟˊ ㄎㄨㄞˋ ㄌㄜˋ ㄓ ㄅㄣˇ）
Happiness lies in rendering help to others. 或 Service begets happiness.

助詞（ㄓㄨˋ ㄘˊ）
(grammar) an expletive

助威（ㄓㄨˋ ㄨㄟ）or 助勢（ㄓㄨˋ ㄕˋ）
to encourage (often an evil-doer); to goad on; to boost the morale of; to cheer

【努】 422
　　　　ㄋㄨˇ nuu nǔ
1. to exert oneself; to make an effort
2. to protrude

努力（ㄋㄨˇ ㄌㄧˋ）
to make efforts; to strive; to endeavor; to work hard: 她努力學好外語。 She makes efforts to master a foreign language.

努嘴（ㄋㄨˇ ㄗㄨㄟˇ）or 努嘴兒（ㄋㄨˇ ㄗㄨㄟˇ）
① to move lips (in silent communication); to pout ② to purse up one's lips (to show displeasure)

努爾哈赤（ㄋㄨˇ ㄦˇ ㄏㄚ ㄔˋ）
Nurhachu, 1559-1629, the founder of the Manchu nation and grandfather of Emperor Shunchih (順治), the first monarch of the Ching Dynasty

【劫】 423
　　　　(刧) ㄐㄧㄝˊ jye jié
1. to rob; to plunder; to take by force
2. sufferings; disasters; misfortunes

劫道（ㄐㄧㄝˊ ㄉㄠˋ）
to rob travelers on a road

劫盜（ㄐㄧㄝˊ ㄉㄠˋ）
① robbery ② a robber; a bandit

劫奪（ㄐㄧㄝˊ ㄉㄨㄛˊ）
to plunder; to rob; to pillage

劫難（ㄐㄧㄝˊ ㄋㄢˋ）
a destined calamity

劫牢（ㄐㄧㄝˊ ㄌㄠˊ）
① to free prisoners by force
② jail delivery

劫糧（ㄐㄧㄝˊ ㄌㄧㄤˊ）

to forage; to strip of supplies

力掠 (ㄌㄧ ㄌㄩㄝ)
to plunder; to rob; to pillage

力後餘生 (ㄌㄧ ㄏㄡˋ ㄩˊ ㄕㄥ)
life after surviving a disaster

力機 (ㄌㄧ ㄐㄧ)
to skyjack; to hijack a plane

力寨 (ㄌㄧ ㄓㄞˋ)
to raid the bandits' mountain fortress

力持 (ㄌㄧ ㄔˊ)
① to threaten; to menace ② to hijack: 三impo暴徒昨天劫持一架客機。Three mobs hijacked an airliner yesterday.

力數 (ㄌㄧ ㄕㄨˋ)or 劫運 (ㄌㄧ ㄩㄣˋ)
ill luck; ill fortune; fatal calamity

力案 (ㄌㄧ ㄢˋ)
a case of robbery

力餘 (ㄌㄧ ㄩˊ)
in the wake of a disaster; following a disaster

【劬】 424 (ㄑㄩˊ chyu qú)
labor; toil; diligent; to labor incessantly

劬勞 (ㄑㄩˊ ㄌㄠˊ)
travail; toil (especially said of one's own mother); to labor arduously (as parents for children)

【劭】 425 (ㄕㄠˋ shaw shào)
1. to encourage; to urge
2. graceful; excellent; admirable; respectable: 年高德劭 of venerable age and respectable character

六畫

【劾】 426 (ㄏㄜˊ her hé)
to accuse; to charge; to impeach

劾狀 (ㄏㄜˊ ㄓㄨㄤˋ)
① archives of charges (against a public official)②
to expose someone's crime

劾奏 (ㄏㄜˊ ㄗㄡˋ)
to impeach an official of his crime in a memorandum to the emperor

七畫

【勁】 427 1. (ㄐㄧㄥˋ jinq jìng)
strong; tough; powerful; sturdy

勁風 (ㄐㄧㄥˋ ㄈㄥ)
a gale; a blast

勁敵 (ㄐㄧㄥˋ ㄉㄧˊ)
a powerful enemy; a strong adversary

勁旅 (ㄐㄧㄥˋ ㄌㄩˇ)
a powerful army; crack troops

勁直 (ㄐㄧㄥˋ ㄓˊ)
tough and honest; upright

勁草 (ㄐㄧㄥˋ ㄘㄠˇ)
① tough grass ② an indomitable person

【勁】 427 2. (ㄐㄧㄣˋ jinn jìn)
1. vigor; energy; strength: 這個小孩似乎有用不完的勁。The child seems to have inexhaustible energy.
2. spirit
3. an air; manner

勁兒 (ㄐㄧㄣˋ ㄦ)or 勁頭 (ㄐㄧㄣˋ ㄊㄡˊ)
① vigor; drive: 他工作有勁頭。He is full of drive in his work. ② energy; strength ③ manner; expression: 瞧他那股傻勁兒。See how stupid he looks. ④ enthusiasm

【勃】 428 (ㄅㄛˊ bor bó)
sudden(ly); quick(ly)

勃勃 (ㄅㄛˊ ㄅㄛˊ)
flourishing; vigorous; zestful: 生氣勃勃 full of vitality; spirited

勃發 (ㄅㄛˊ ㄈㄚ)
① to break out; to begin suddenly ② to thrive; to prosper

勃怒 (ㄅㄛˊ ㄋㄨˋ)or 勃然大怒 (ㄅㄛˊ ㄖㄢˊ ㄉㄚˋ ㄋㄨˋ)
to lose one's temper suddenly; to break into a rage

勃起 (ㄅㄛˊ ㄑㄧˇ)
to have an erection; erection

勃谿 (ㄅㄛˊ ㄒㄧ)
to fall to quarreling; a quarrel

勃然變色 (ㄅㄛˊ ㄖㄢˊ ㄅㄧㄢˋ ㄙㄜˋ)
to show displeasure or bewilderment all of a sudden

【勅】 429 (ㄔˋ chyh chì)
1. an imperial decree
2. orders given to demons and spirits by Taoist priests when they exercise magic powers

勅令 (ㄔˋ ㄌㄧㄥˋ)
an imperial decree, edict, command, or ordinance

勅書 (ㄔˋ ㄕㄨ)
an imperial message or letter 亦作「勅諭」

【勇】 430 (ㄩㄥˇ yeong yǒng)
1. brave; courageous; bold; valiant; intrepid; fearless
2. a soldier; a conscript
3. bravery; courage: 他是一個智勇雙全的人。He is a man of wisdom and courage.

勇猛 (ㄩㄥˇ ㄇㄥˇ)
brave and fierce: 他勇猛如獅。He is as brave as a lion.

勇退 (ㄩㄥˇ ㄊㄨㄟˋ)
to withdraw or retire courageously

勇敢 (ㄩㄥˇ ㄍㄢˇ)
brave; courageous: 他們勇敢善戰。They are courageous and skillful in battle.

勇敢善戰 (ㄩㄥˇ ㄍㄢˇ ㄕㄢˋ ㄓㄢˋ)
brave and resourceful in battle

勇冠三軍 (ㄩㄥˇ ㄍㄨㄢˋ ㄙㄢ ㄐㄩㄣ)
(said of soldiers in combat) peerless or matchless in bravery or valor

勇悍 (ㄩㄥˇ ㄏㄢˋ)
brave and fierce

勇將 (ㄩㄥˇ ㄐㄧㄤˋ)
a fearless general

勇決 (ㄩㄥˇ ㄐㄩㄝˊ)
brave and resolute

勇氣 (ㄩㄥˇ ㄑㄧˋ)
courage; bravery; valor; prowess; intrepidity; gallantry; heroism; fearlessness: 他們鼓起最大勇氣。They mustered up all their courage.

勇者不懼 (ㄩㄥˇ ㄓㄜˇ ㄅㄨˋ ㄐㄩˋ)
Bravery admits no fear.

勇士 (ㄩㄥˇ ㄕˋ)
one who knows no fear; a brave fighter; a warrior

勇武 (ㄩㄥˇ ㄨˇ)

brave; daring; valiant; intrepid; courageous

勇往直前(ㄩㄥ ㄨㄤˇ ㄓˊ ㄑㄧㄢˊ)
to march fearlessly onward; to go straight ahead

勇敢(ㄩㄥˇ ㄍㄢˇ)
to be brave in; to have the boldness to; to have the courage to

【力部】

【勉】431 ㄇㄧㄢˇ mean miǎn

1. to urge; to encourage: 他們互勉。 They encourage each other.

2. to strive; to make efforts; to exert oneself to

勉勵(ㄇㄧㄢˇ ㄌㄧˋ)
to encourage; to urge; to rouse to action

勉力(ㄇㄧㄢˇ ㄌㄧˋ)
to make efforts; to try hard

勉力為之(ㄇㄧㄢˇ ㄌㄧˋ ㄨㄟˊ ㄓ)
to do it as best as one can

勉強(ㄇㄧㄢˇ ㄑㄧㄤˇ)or 勉勉強強(ㄇㄧㄢˇ ㄇㄧㄢˇ ㄑㄧㄤˇ ㄑㄧㄤˇ)
①without spontaneity; in a forced manner; involuntarily; reluctantly ② barely (enough, acceptable, etc.) ③ to force ④ unconvincing

勉為其難(ㄇㄧㄢˇ ㄨㄟˊ ㄑㄧˊ ㄋㄢˊ)
to force oneself to do a hard task; to take on some difficult job reluctantly

九畫

【勒】432 1. ㄌㄜˋ leh lè

1. to force; to compel
2. to reign or rule; to control; to command
3. to engrave; to carve
4. a bridle
5. (calligraphy) a horizontal stroke

勒逼(ㄌㄜˋ ㄅㄧ)
to force; to compel; to coerce

勒兵(ㄌㄜˋ ㄅㄧㄥ)
①to halt the troops on the march ②to command troops

勒派(ㄌㄜˋ ㄆㄞˋ)
to force somebody to pay levies or do corvée

勒馬(ㄌㄜˋ ㄇㄚˇ)
to stop the horse from going ahead

勒令(ㄌㄜˋ ㄌㄧㄥˋ)
to compel by an order or injunction; to order

勒令退學(ㄌㄜˋ ㄌㄧㄥˋ ㄊㄨㄟˋ ㄒㄩㄝˊ)
suspended indefinitely

勒借(ㄌㄜˋ ㄐㄧㄝˋ)
to borrow by threats or coercion

勒戒所(ㄌㄜˋ ㄐㄧㄝˋ ㄙㄨㄛˇ)
a clinic where addicts are treated and made to kick the habit

勒交(ㄌㄜˋ ㄐㄧㄠ)
to order the surrender of; to force someone to hand over something

勒捐(ㄌㄜˋ ㄐㄩㄢ)
to order contributions

勒限(ㄌㄜˋ ㄒㄧㄢˋ)
to give a time limit to

勒詐(ㄌㄜˋ ㄓㄚˋ)
to defraud

勒住(ㄌㄜˋ ㄓㄨˋ)
to halt by pulling in reins

勒石(ㄌㄜˋ ㄕˊ)or勒碑(ㄌㄜˋ ㄅㄟ)
to record one's achievements by engraving them on a stone tablet (for posterity)

勒贖(ㄌㄜˋ ㄕㄨˊ)
to kidnap a person for ransom

勒索(ㄌㄜˋ ㄙㄨㄛˇ)
to blackmail; to extort: 他勒索以前的老板。 He extorted money from his former employer.

【勒】432 2. ㄌㄟ lhei lēi
to tighten

勒斃(ㄌㄟ ㄅㄧˋ)
to strangle; to throttle

勒緊褲帶(ㄌㄟ ㄐㄧㄣˇ ㄎㄨˋ ㄉㄞˋ)or 勒緊腰帶(ㄌㄟ ㄐㄧㄣˇ ㄧㄠ ㄉㄞˋ)
to tighten one's belt — to practice parsimony

勒死(ㄌㄟ ㄙˇ)
to strangle; to throttle

【動】433 ㄉㄨㄥˋ dong dòng

1. to move; to stir: 別動。 Don't move.
2. to change; to alter
3. to act
4. to touch (one's heart); to arouse; to excite; to move: 她不為甜言蜜語所動。 She can-

not be moved by fine word

5. to take up: 動筷子 to tal up chopsticks; to begin ea ing

6. to use: 動點腦筋吧! Us your head!

7. to eat or drink: 和尚不動 腥。 Monks never touch mea or fish.

8. movement; action: 他的一 一動都很怪異。 His ever movement is very strang

動筆(ㄉㄨㄥˋ ㄅㄧˇ)
to start writing: 他已動筆寫 自傳。 He has started writin autobiography.

動兵(ㄉㄨㄥˋ ㄅㄧㄥ)
to send out troops to fight

動不動(ㄉㄨㄥˋ ㄅㄨˋ ㄉㄨㄥˋ)
frequently; susceptible t (certain emotional manife tation such as crying, laugh ing, etc.); apt (to take cer tain action); easily: 他動不 就發脾氣。 He is apt to los his temper.

動脈(ㄉㄨㄥˋ ㄇㄞˋ)
an artery

動脈瘤(ㄉㄨㄥˋ ㄇㄞˋ ㄌㄧㄡˊ)
aneurysm

動脈硬化症(ㄉㄨㄥˋ ㄇㄞˋ ㄧㄥˋ ㄏㄨㄚˋ ㄓㄥˋ)
arteriosclerosis

動名詞(ㄉㄨㄥˋ ㄇㄧㄥˊ ㄘˊ)
(grammar) a gerund

動刀動槍(ㄉㄨㄥˋ ㄉㄠ ㄉㄨㄥˋ ㄑㄧㄤ)
to start war

動盪(ㄉㄨㄥˋ ㄉㄤˋ)
uneasy; unstable; turbulence unrest: 這個國家局勢動盪 安。 The situation of this country is turbulent.

動電(ㄉㄨㄥˋ ㄉㄧㄢˋ)
dynamic electricity

動態(ㄉㄨㄥˋ ㄊㄞˋ)
①development(s) (of a event or a situation) ②the movement (in a certai sphere of human activity)

動彈(ㄉㄨㄥˋ ㄊㄢˊ)
to budge; to move; to stir

動聽(ㄉㄨㄥˋ ㄊㄧㄥ)
appealing to the ear; fasci nating to listen to: 這首歌很 動聽。 The song sounds fasci nating.

動土(ㄉㄨㄥˋ ㄊㄨˇ)

to break ground (for a building project); to start construction work; to start building

動腦筋(ㄉㄨㄥˋ ㄋㄠˇ ㄐㄧㄣ)
① to think ② to secretly plan to get some coveted thing ③ to try to obtain the affection of a beautiful woman

動能(ㄉㄨㄥˋ ㄋㄥˊ)
(physics) kinetic energy

動怒(ㄉㄨㄥˋ ㄋㄨˋ)
to lose one's temper; to get angry

動力(ㄉㄨㄥˋ ㄌㄧˋ)
① (physics) power; dynamic force ② driving force; impetus

動量(ㄉㄨㄥˋ ㄌㄧㄤˋ)
(physics) momentum

動亂(ㄉㄨㄥˋ ㄌㄨㄢˋ)
disturbance; disorder; commotion; agitation; unrest; turmoil; upheaval; turbulence: 暴民製造社會動亂。 Mobs arouse a social upheaval.

動干戈(ㄉㄨㄥˋ ㄍㄢ ㄍㄜ)
to take up arms

動工(ㄉㄨㄥˋ ㄍㄨㄥ)
to start (construction) work; to begin construction: 這棟房子是去年動工的。 They started building the house last year.

動口不動手(ㄉㄨㄥˋ ㄎㄡˇ ㄅㄨˋ ㄉㄨㄥˋ ㄕㄡˇ)
to argue without coming to blows

動滑輪(ㄉㄨㄥˋ ㄏㄨㄚˊ ㄌㄨㄣˊ)
a movable pulley

動火(ㄉㄨㄥˋ ㄏㄨㄛˇ)
to lose one's temper; to get angry; to flare up

動機(ㄉㄨㄥˋ ㄐㄧ)
motives; intentions: 他的動機很明顯。 His intentions are clear.

動靜(ㄉㄨㄥˋ ㄐㄧㄥˋ)
① signs of action (being taken) ② in motion or at rest ③ the sound of something astir

動氣(ㄉㄨㄥˋ ㄑㄧˋ)
to take offense; to get angry: 不要動氣，聽我解釋。

Don't get angry. Let me explain.

動情(ㄉㄨㄥˋ ㄑㄧㄥˊ)
to have more than a fleeting interest in a woman; to have one's (sexual) passions aroused; to be enamored of

動心(ㄉㄨㄥˋ ㄒㄧㄣ)
① to be moved or perturbed mentally ② to show interest

動向(ㄉㄨㄥˋ ㄒㄧㄤˋ)
trends; general directions or tendencies

動刑(ㄉㄨㄥˋ ㄒㄧㄥˊ)
to apply torture; to torture

動輒(ㄉㄨㄥˋ ㄓㄜˊ)
easily; frequently: 他動輒發怒。 He easily flew into a rage.

動輒得咎(ㄉㄨㄥˋ ㄓㄜˊ ㄉㄜˊ ㄐㄧㄡˋ)
to draw criticisms at every move

動產(ㄉㄨㄥˋ ㄔㄢˇ)
movable property; movables; personal property 參看「不動產」

動手(ㄉㄨㄥˋ ㄕㄡˇ)
① to start work: 那作家動手寫新作品。 The writer started on a new work. ② to use hands; to touch; to handle: 請勿動手, No touch, please. ③ to raise a hand to strike: 他先動手打人。 He struck the first blow.

動手動腳(ㄉㄨㄥˋ ㄕㄡˇ ㄉㄨㄥˋ ㄐㄧㄠˇ)
① to be unrestrained or unreserved (with women); to take liberties (with women) ② to make motions to start a fight

動手術(ㄉㄨㄥˋ ㄕㄡˇ ㄕㄨˋ)
① to operate on a patient; to perform a surgical operation ② to have an operation

動身(ㄉㄨㄥˋ ㄕㄣ)
to set out (on a trip); to depart: 他們在清晨動身。 They set out at dawn.

動人(ㄉㄨㄥˋ ㄖㄣˊ)
① moving; touching; pathetic ② (said of the beauty of a woman) to arouse interest or passion

動容(ㄉㄨㄥˋ ㄖㄨㄥˊ)
to change one's facial expression when one is

moved

動作(ㄉㄨㄥˋ ㄗㄨㄛˋ)
motions; movements; actions; gestures: 她的動作敏捷。 She is quick in her movement.

動詞(ㄉㄨㄥˋ ㄘˊ)
a verb

動粗(ㄉㄨㄥˋ ㄘㄨ)
to resort to violence

動議(ㄉㄨㄥˋ ㄧˋ)
a motion (at an assembly or a meeting); a proposal: 提出動議 to put forward a motion

動搖(ㄉㄨㄥˋ ㄧㄠˊ)
to waver; to shake

動武(ㄉㄨㄥˋ ㄨˇ)
to resort to violence; to use force; to start a fight

動物(ㄉㄨㄥˋ ㄨˋ)
an animal; a creature

動物界(ㄉㄨㄥˋ ㄨˋ ㄐㄧㄝˋ)
the animal kingdom

動物學(ㄉㄨㄥˋ ㄨˋ ㄒㄩㄝˊ)
zoology

動物誌(ㄉㄨㄥˋ ㄨˋ ㄓˋ)
a fauna—a treatise on the animals of any geographical area or geological period

動物生態學(ㄉㄨㄥˋ ㄨˋ ㄕㄥ ㄊㄞˋ ㄒㄩㄝˊ)
animal-ecology

動物園(ㄉㄨㄥˋ ㄨˋ ㄩㄢˊ)
a zoo; a zoological garden

動問(ㄉㄨㄥˋ ㄨㄣˋ)
to offer a question

動員(ㄉㄨㄥˋ ㄩㄢˊ)
to mobilize; mobilization

動員令(ㄉㄨㄥˋ ㄩㄢˊ ㄌㄧㄥˋ)
a mobilization order

動用(ㄉㄨㄥˋ ㄩㄥˋ)
to use or employ

動用公款(ㄉㄨㄥˋ ㄩㄥˋ ㄍㄨㄥ ㄎㄨㄢˇ)
to use public funds

【勗】434
(勖) ㄒㄩˋ shiuh syù
to encourage; to stimulate

勗勉(ㄒㄩˋ ㄇㄧㄢˇ)
to encourage; to prompt: 總統勗勉國人更加努力。 The president encouraged his countrymen to work harder.

【勘】435
ㄎㄢ kann kàn
(又讀) ㄎㄢˋ kan kàn
1. to investigate; to explore; to examine; to check

〔力部〕

【力部】

2. to collate; to compare critically

勘探(ㄎㄢ ㄊㄢˊ)
exploration; prospecting: 地震勘探 seismic prospecting

勘察(ㄎㄢ ㄔㄚˊ)
to investigate; to inspect; to examine

勘災(ㄎㄢ ㄗㄞ)
to inspect a disaster area

勘測(ㄎㄢ ㄘㄜˋ)
to survey

勘驗(ㄎㄢ ㄧㄢˋ)
to examine; to check

勘誤(ㄎㄢ ㄨˋ)
to collate; to correct errors

勘誤表(ㄎㄢ ㄨˋ ㄅㄧㄠˇ)
corrigenda; errata

【務】 436
ㄨˋ wuh wù

1. to attend to; to strive after; to be engaged in: 他不務正業。He does not attend to his proper duties.
2. duty; business; affairs: 公務 official business
3. must; necessary
4. a Chinese family name

務本(ㄨˋ ㄅㄣˇ)
to attend to fundamentals: 君子務本。A man of virtue attends to fundamentals.

務必(ㄨˋ ㄅㄧˋ)or 務須(ㄨˋ ㄒㄩ)
to be sure; must; by all means

務農(ㄨˋ ㄋㄨㄥˊ)
to be engaged in farming

務求(ㄨˋ ㄑㄧㄡˊ)
to strive for

務希(ㄨˋ ㄒㄧ)
Please be sure to...

務實(ㄨˋ ㄕˊ)
① to strive for thoroughness
② pragmatism; pragmatic

務使(ㄨˋ ㄕˇ)
to make sure; to ensure

十畫

【勝】 437
1. ㄕㄥ shenq shèng

1. to win; to excel; to triumph; to surpass; to get the better of: 你一定會得勝。You are sure to win.
2. victory; success: 他勝不驕，敗不餒。He is not elated by

success, nor discouraged by failure.
3. (sports) a win
4. a scenic view; a place of natural beauty: 尋幽覽勝 to visit places of scenic beauty
5. excellent; distinctive; wonderful

勝負(ㄕㄥ ㄈㄨˋ)or 勝敗(ㄕㄥ ㄅㄞˋ)
victory and defeat; the outcome (of a contest); success or failure: 勝負未定。Victory hangs in the balance.

勝地(ㄕㄥ ㄉㄧˋ)
a scenic spot; a vacationland; a place of natural beauty

勝利(ㄕㄥ ㄌㄧˋ)
① victory; triumph: 他們充滿了勝利的信心。They are fully confident of success. ② successfully; triumphantly: 我軍勝利歸來。Our troops triumphantly came back.

勝過(ㄕㄥ ㄍㄨㄛˋ)
to be superior to; to excel; to surpass; to prevail over

勝會(ㄕㄥ ㄏㄨㄟˋ)
a great, festive occasion

勝迹(ㄕㄥ ㄐㄧ)
historical relics

勝家(ㄕㄥ ㄐㄧㄚ)
① the winner (in gambling) ② Singer (a manufacturer of sewing machines)

勝景(ㄕㄥ ㄐㄧㄥˇ)
scenic beauty

勝之不武(ㄕㄥ ㄓ ㄅㄨˋ ㄨˇ)
It brings no honor to the victor in an unequal contest.

勝仗(ㄕㄥ ㄓㄤˋ)
a victorious battle; a victory

勝朝(ㄕㄥ ㄔㄠˊ)
the preceding dynasty

勝訴(ㄕㄥ ㄙㄨˋ)
to win a lawsuit

勝算(ㄕㄥ ㄙㄨㄢˋ)
to be sure of success; odds or advantages (in a contest): 我們穩操勝算。We are sure of success.

勝友(ㄕㄥ ㄧㄡˇ)
well-known friends

勝於(ㄕㄥ ㄩˊ)
better than: 他勝於常人。He is better than the average

persons.

【勝】 437
2. ㄕㄥ sheng shēng
to be competent enough (for a task)

勝冠(ㄕㄥ ㄍㄨㄢˋ)
(said of boys) at the age of 20

勝任(ㄕㄥ ㄖㄣˋ)
competent; qualified; equal to: 她能勝任教職的工作。She is competent for teaching.

勝任愉快(ㄕㄥ ㄖㄣˋ ㄩˊ ㄎㄨㄞˋ)
to be adequate for and happy with a job

【勞】 438
1. ㄌㄠˊ lau láo

1. to labor; to take the toil; to work
2. to trouble; to worry; to bother
3. meritorious deeds; services: 汗馬之勞 distinguished services in battle; war exploits
4. a Chinese family name

勞保(ㄌㄠˊ ㄅㄠˇ)
labor insurance 參看「勞工保險」

勞民傷財(ㄌㄠˊ ㄇㄧㄣˊ ㄕㄤ ㄘㄞˊ)
to tire the people and waste the resources (said of big construction projects of questionable economic value)

勞乏(ㄌㄠˊ ㄈㄚˊ)
fatigued; exhausted

勞費(ㄌㄠˊ ㄈㄟˋ)
to cost much effort and expenditure

勞煩(ㄌㄠˊ ㄈㄢˊ)
(courtesy) to trouble (someone to do something)

勞方(ㄌㄠˊ ㄈㄤ)
labor

勞頓(ㄌㄠˊ ㄉㄨㄣˋ)
fatigue; exhaustion

勞動(ㄌㄠˊ ㄉㄨㄥˋ)
① (ㄌㄠˊ ㄉㄨㄥˋ) to labor (physically); to toil; to sweat
② (ㄌㄠˊ ˙ㄉㄨㄥ) to trouble (a person with a request)

勞動法(ㄌㄠˊ ㄉㄨㄥˋ ㄈㄚˇ)
labor law; labor legislation

勞動力(ㄌㄠˊ ㄉㄨㄥˋ ㄌㄧˋ)
① labor force; work force; manpower ② capacity or ability for physical labor

勞動量(ㄌㄠˊ ㄉㄨㄥˋ ㄌㄧㄤˋ)

the amount of labor

動改造(ㄉㄨㄥˋ ㄍㄞˇ ㄗㄠˋ)
to reform through forced
labor (a Chinese Communist
practice as a form of punishment)

動階級(ㄉㄨㄥˋ ㄐㄧㄝ ㄐㄧˊ)
the working class

念日(ㄋㄧㄢˋ ㄖˋ)or 勞工紀
Labor Day

動者(ㄉㄨㄥˋ ㄓㄜˇ)
a laborer; a workman

動日(ㄉㄨㄥˋ ㄖˋ)
a workday 亦作「工作日」

累(ㄌㄟˋ)
to fatigue, tire or exhaust (a
person)

力(ㄌㄧˋ)
①(physical) labor; labor
force ②to labor physically

力士手錶(ㄌㄧˋ ㄕˋ ㄕㄡˇ ㄅㄧㄠˇ)
a Rolex watch

碌(ㄌㄨˋ)
to work hard; to toil and
moil; to drudge; to busy oneself with drudgery

碌命(ㄌㄨˋ ㄇㄧㄥˋ)
a born laborer

改(ㄍㄞˇ)
(said of criminals) to
reform through forced labor
參看「勞動改造」

工(ㄍㄨㄥ)
laborers; workers

工保險(ㄍㄨㄥ ㄅㄠˇ ㄒㄧㄢˇ)
labor insurance 亦作「勞保」

苦(ㄎㄨˇ)
①to work hard; to labor; to
toil ②toil; labor; pains: 他將
不辭勞苦地幫你。He will
spare no pains to help you.

苦功高(ㄎㄨˇ ㄍㄨㄥ ㄍㄠ)
to work hard and make a
great contribution (a eulogy
for meritorious service)

績(ㄐㄧˋ)
the fruits of hard work;
accomplishment; merits

駕(ㄐㄧㄚˋ)
to be sorry to have to trouble someone to do some-
thing

心(ㄒㄧㄣ)
①to labor mentally; to
work with one's mind or

brains ②to be worried; to
be anxious

勞形(ㄌㄠˊ ㄒㄧㄥˊ)
physically fatiguing; tired
out

勞師(ㄌㄠˊ ㄕ)
to tire troops

勞師動眾(ㄌㄠˊ ㄕ ㄉㄨㄥˋ ㄓㄨㄥˋ)
①to tire too many troops
and people(for unimportant
things)—to waste manpower
②to involve too many peo-
ple

勞神(ㄌㄠˊ ㄕㄣˊ)
①to bother; to trouble ②to
be worried; to be concerned

勞人草草(ㄌㄠˊ ㄖㄣˊ ㄘㄠˇ ㄘㄠˇ)
Those who toil physically
often have to worry men-
tally.

勞資(ㄌㄠˊ ㄗ)
labor versus management;
labor and management;
labor and capital

勞資關係(ㄌㄠˊ ㄗ ㄍㄨㄢ ㄒㄧˋ)
labor-capital relations

勞資爭議(ㄌㄠˊ ㄗ ㄓㄥ ㄧˋ)
labor dispute

勞作(ㄌㄠˊ ㄗㄨㄛˋ)
①manual work or training
(at school) ②manual labor

勞損(ㄌㄠˊ ㄙㄨㄣˇ)
(medicine) strain

勞而無功(ㄌㄠˊ ㄦˊ ㄨˊ ㄍㄨㄥ)
to labor to no purpose; to
make futile efforts; to plow
the sand; to beat the air

勞役(ㄌㄠˊ ㄧˋ)
hard labor (as punishment);
forced labor

勞逸不均(ㄌㄠˊ ㄧˋ ㄅㄨˋ ㄐㄩㄣ)
unequal distribution of work
with some doing too much
while others doing too little

勞燕分飛(ㄌㄠˊ ㄧㄢˋ ㄈㄣ ㄈㄟ)
(said of people)to separate
or part(like birds flying in
different directions)

勞務(ㄌㄠˊ ㄨˋ)
service

【勞】 438
2. ㄌㄠˋ lào
to comfort or entertain (the
tired)

勞民(ㄌㄠˋ ㄇㄧㄣˊ)
to conciliate the people

勞軍(ㄌㄠˋ ㄐㄩㄣ)

to cheer or entertain troops

十一畫

【勢】 439
ㄕˋ shyh shì

1. power; force; influence: 颱風
來勢甚猛。The typhoon came
with tremendous force.

2. a tendency: 少年犯罪有增加
的趨勢。Juvenile delinquency
shows a tendency to
increase.

3. the natural features: 山勢
the lie of a mountain

4. a situation; circumstances:
乘勢to take advantage of a
situation

5. signs; gestures: 他做了手勢叫
我進去。He gave me a sign to
come in.

6. male genitals: 去勢to castrate; castration

勢必(ㄕˋ ㄅㄧˋ)
certainly; to be bound to;
undoubtedly: 飲酒過度, 勢必
影響健康。Excessive drinking
will certainly affect one's
health.

勢不兩立(ㄕˋ ㄅㄨˋ ㄌㄧㄤˇ ㄌㄧˋ)
unable to coexist; unable to
live peacefully together; incompatible

勢不可當(ㄕˋ ㄅㄨˋ ㄎㄜˇ ㄉㄤ)
irresistible: 民主的潮流洶湧澎
湃, 勢不可當。The democracy
is surging forward irresist-
ibly.

勢頭(ㄕˋ ㄊㄡˊ)
①impetus; momentum ②a
tendency; a situation; a state
of affairs

勢頭不對(ㄕˋ ㄊㄡˊ ㄅㄨˋ ㄉㄨㄟˋ)
The situation is unfavor-
able.

勢難兼顧(ㄕˋ ㄋㄢˊ ㄐㄧㄢ ㄍㄨˋ)
The situation is hard for
one to look after both sides
simultaneously.

勢難從命(ㄕˋ ㄋㄢˊ ㄘㄨㄥˊ ㄇㄧㄥˋ)
Circumstances make it difficult for me to comply with
(or obey) your request.

勢力(ㄕˋ ㄌㄧˋ)
force; power; influence

勢力範圍(ㄕˋ ㄌㄧˋ ㄈㄢˋ ㄨㄟˊ)
the sphere of influence

勢利(ㄕˋ ㄌㄧˋ)

〔力部〕

snobbish

勢利眼(ㄕ ㄌㄧˋ ㄧㄢˇ)
①a snob ②a snobbish attitude; snobbishness; snobbery ③to judge people by wealth and power

〔力部〕

勢均力敵(ㄕ ㄐㄩㄣ ㄌㄧˋ ㄉㄧˊ)
evenly matched; well matched; 雙方勢均力敵。The two sides are well matched.

勢窮力竭(ㄕ ㄑㄩㄥˊ ㄌㄧˋ ㄐㄧㄝˊ)
in a terrible plight and powerless

勢如破竹(ㄕ ㄖㄨˊ ㄆㄛˋ ㄓㄨˊ)
(said of a victorious army) to advance with irresistible force; to push onward with overwhelming momentum

勢在必行(ㄕ ㄗㄞˋ ㄅㄧˋ ㄒㄧㄥˊ)
to be imperative, urgent, or essential(under the circumstances)

勢所必然(ㄕ ㄙㄨㄛˇ ㄅㄧˋ ㄖㄢˊ)
(It is) a matter of necessity, a matter of course, a necessary result of the situation, an inevitable outcome, etc.

勢要(ㄕ ㄧㄠˋ)
the influential and the mighty

勢燄薰天(ㄕ ㄧㄢˋ ㄒㄩㄣ ㄊㄧㄢ)
very influential and powerful

【募】 440　ㄇㄨˋ muh mù
1. to recruit or enlist (personnel); 徵募男子入伍 to enlist men for the army
2. to raise (funds); to collect

募兵(ㄇㄨˋ ㄅㄧㄥ)
to recruit or enlist soldiers; to raise troops

募兵制(ㄇㄨˋ ㄅㄧㄥ ㄓˋ)
a voluntary military service system

募款(ㄇㄨˋ ㄎㄨㄢˇ)
to raise funds

募化(ㄇㄨˋ ㄏㄨㄚˋ)
(said of Buddhist monks or Taoist priests) to beg for alms 亦作「化緣」

募集(ㄇㄨˋ ㄐㄧˊ)
to recruit; to raise; to collect

募捐(ㄇㄨˋ ㄐㄩㄢ)
to solicit or collect contributions; to collect donations

【勤】 441　ㄑㄧㄣˊ chyn qín
1. diligent; industrious; sedulous; hardworking
2. frequently; regularly

勤樸(ㄑㄧㄣˊ ㄆㄨˊ)
industrious and frugal

勤勉(ㄑㄧㄣˊ ㄇㄧㄢˇ)
industrious; diligent; hardworking; sedulous; 勤勉好學 sedulous and eager to learn

勤奮(ㄑㄧㄣˊ ㄈㄣˋ)
diligent; assiduous; industrious: 他工作勤奮。He is diligent in his work.

勤惰(ㄑㄧㄣˊ ㄉㄨㄛˋ)
diligence and negligence; activity and inactivity

勤能補拙(ㄑㄧㄣˊ ㄋㄥˊ ㄅㄨˇ ㄓㄨㄛ)
Stupidity can be remedied by diligence.

勤勞(ㄑㄧㄣˊ ㄌㄠˊ)
to toil or labor sedulously; diligent; industrious; hardworking

勤苦(ㄑㄧㄣˊ ㄎㄨˇ)
to work sedulously in defiance of hardships

勤快(ㄑㄧㄣˊ ㄎㄨㄞˋ)
(colloquial) diligent; industrious

勤儉(ㄑㄧㄣˊ ㄐㄧㄢˇ)
hardworking and thrifty; diligent and frugal

勤儉建國(ㄑㄧㄣˊ ㄐㄧㄢˇ ㄐㄧㄢˋ ㄍㄨㄛˊ)
to establish a country through thrift and hard work

勤儉持家(ㄑㄧㄣˊ ㄐㄧㄢˇ ㄔˊ ㄐㄧㄚ)
to be diligent and frugal in managing a household

勤慎(ㄑㄧㄣˊ ㄕㄣˋ)
diligent and prudent

勤學(ㄑㄧㄣˊ ㄒㄩㄝˊ)
to study diligently

勤有功嬉無益(ㄑㄧㄣˊ ㄧㄡˇ ㄍㄨㄥ ㄒㄧ ㄨˊ ㄧˋ)
Reward lies ahead of diligence, but nothing is gained by indolence.

勤務(ㄑㄧㄣˊ ㄨˋ)
①logistic duties (in the armed forces) ②daily duties (of policemen)

勤務兵(ㄑㄧㄣˊ ㄨˋ ㄅㄧㄥ)
an orderly

勤務員(ㄑㄧㄣˊ ㄨˋ ㄩㄢˊ)

①an odd-job man ②a servant

勤王(ㄑㄧㄣˊ ㄨㄤˊ)
to save the throne (by rushing troops to the monarch's rescue in time of crisis)

【勠】 442　ㄌㄨˋ luh lù
1. to unite or join (forces)
2. to kill; to slay

勠力(ㄌㄨˋ ㄌㄧˋ)
to join forces; to unite efforts; to cooperate

勠力同心(ㄌㄨˋ ㄌㄧˋ ㄊㄨㄥˊ ㄒㄧㄣ)
to work together with the same objective in mind

十三畫

【勰】 443　ㄒㄧㄝˊ shye xié
harmonious

十四畫

【勳】 444　ㄒㄩㄣ shiun xūn
merits; honors; meritorious services; achievements

勳勞(ㄒㄩㄣ ㄌㄠˊ)
meritorious contributions; merits

勳貴(ㄒㄩㄣ ㄍㄨㄟˋ)
the nobility and ministers with close connections with the emperor

勳功(ㄒㄩㄣ ㄍㄨㄥ)
meritorious services 亦作「功勳」

勳績(ㄒㄩㄣ ㄐㄧ)
meritorious services; outstanding achievements

勳爵(ㄒㄩㄣ ㄐㄩㄝˊ)
a rank conferred in recognition of merits

勳章(ㄒㄩㄣ ㄓㄤ)
a medal of honor; a decoration

勳臣(ㄒㄩㄣ ㄔㄣˊ)
an official with a record of meritorious services to the country

勳業(ㄒㄩㄣ ㄧㄝˋ)
meritorious achievements or contribution

十五畫

勵 445 (ㄌㄧˋ lih lì)

to incite; to encourage; to rouse (to action); to exert oneself

精圖治(ㄐㄧㄥ ㄊㄨˊ ㄓˋ)
(said of a government or a national leader) to pursue the task of a national build-up with determination and dedication

行(ㄌㄧˋ ㄒㄧㄥˊ)
to enforce or practice with determination

志(ㄌㄧˋ ㄓˋ)
to pursue a goal with determination

志社(ㄌㄧˋ ㄓˋ ㄕㄜˋ)
the OMEA, which stands for the Officer's Moral Endeavor Association, a semi-official organization in China created in the early 1930's

十七畫

【勸】 446 (ㄑㄩㄢˋ chiuann quàn)

to exhort; to urge; to advise; to persuade: 勸他休息一下。Urge him to take a rest.

勉(ㄑㄩㄢˋ ㄇㄧㄢˇ)
to exhort to great effort; to encourage; to urge

募(ㄑㄩㄢˋ ㄇㄨˋ)
to ask for contributions

導(ㄑㄩㄢˋ ㄉㄠˇ)
to admonish; to exhort and guide

告(ㄑㄩㄢˋ ㄍㄠˋ)
to advise; to counsel; to exhort; advice: 醫生勸告我要好好休息。The doctor advised me to have a good rest.

和(ㄑㄩㄢˋ ㄏㄜˊ)
to reconcile a dispute or quarrel

化(ㄑㄩㄢˋ ㄏㄨㄚˋ)
① to exhort to conversion; to convert ②(said of monks or nuns) to beg for alms

誨(ㄑㄩㄢˋ ㄏㄨㄟˋ)
to advise; to exhort

架(ㄑㄩㄢˋ ㄐㄧㄚˋ)
to mediate a quarrel

駕(ㄑㄩㄢˋ ㄐㄧㄚˋ)
to urge someone to do something

解(ㄑㄩㄢˋ ㄐㄧㄝˇ)
to mediate; to exhort to peace

戒(ㄑㄩㄢˋ ㄐㄧㄝˋ)
to admonish; to dissuade; to expostulate

酒(ㄑㄩㄢˋ ㄐㄧㄡˇ)
to offer a drink (of wine or liquor)

諫(ㄑㄩㄢˋ ㄐㄧㄢˋ)
to remonstrate (with a superior); to plead for rectification

進(ㄑㄩㄢˋ ㄐㄧㄣˋ)
(said of sycophants) to persuade (a hypocritical warlord) to ascend to the throne

降(ㄑㄩㄢˋ ㄒㄧㄤˊ)
to induce to surrender

學(ㄑㄩㄢˋ ㄒㄩㄝˊ)
to urge someone to study hard

世(ㄑㄩㄢˋ ㄕˋ)
to give people a sermon; to admonish

善規過(ㄑㄩㄢˋ ㄕㄢˋ ㄍㄨㄟ ㄍㄨㄛˋ)
to exhort to reformation and to urge to virtue

說(ㄑㄩㄢˋ ㄕㄨㄛ)
to persuade; to advise

勸人為善(ㄑㄩㄢˋ ㄖㄣˊ ㄨㄟˊ ㄕㄢˋ)or 勸善(ㄑㄩㄢˋ ㄕㄢˋ)
to exhort people to do good

阻(ㄑㄩㄢˋ ㄗㄨˇ)or 勸止(ㄑㄩㄢˋ ㄓˇ)
to dissuade someone from; to advise someone against something

誘(ㄑㄩㄢˋ ㄧㄡˋ)
to induce; to prevail upon

慰(ㄑㄩㄢˋ ㄨㄟˋ)
to console; to soothe

勹 部

勹幺 bau bāo

一畫

【勺】 447 ㄕㄠˊ shaur sháo

a ladle; a spoon; a scoop: 飯勺 a ladle for taking rice into bowls

勺子(ㄕㄠˊ ˙ㄗ)
a ladle; a spoon; a scoop; a dipper

二畫

【勻】 448 ㄩㄣˊ yun yún

uniform; even

勻分(ㄩㄣˊ ㄈㄣ)
to divide equally; to share and share alike

勻調(ㄩㄣˊ ㄊㄧㄠˊ)or 勻停(ㄩㄣˊ ˙ㄊㄧㄥ)
even; balanced

勻臉(ㄩㄣˊ ㄌㄧㄢˇ)
to powder and paint one's face evenly

勻整(ㄩㄣˊ ㄓㄥˇ)
neat; even and orderly

勻稱(ㄩㄣˊ ㄔㄣˋ)
symmetrical; balanced; even; harmonious

勻出(ㄩㄣˊ ㄔㄨ)
to spare or share something

勻圓(ㄩㄣˊ ㄩㄢˊ)
evenly round

【勾】 449 1. ㄍㄡ gou gōu

1. to mark; to put a check; to mark on
2. to cancel; to cross out (or off)
3. to hook
4. to join; to connect
5. to evoke
6. to entice; to seduce
7. a hook

勾搭(ㄍㄡ ˙ㄉㄚ)
①to have illegitimate relations (with one of the other sex) ②to conspire with; to gang up ③to seduce; to entice

勾通(ㄍㄡ ㄊㄨㄥ)
to cooperate secretly; to collaborate or collude

勾勒(ㄍㄡ ㄌㄜˋ)
to draw the outline of; to sketch or delineate the contours of; to give a brief account of; to sketch; to outline

〔勹部〕

勾欄(ㄍㄡ ㄌㄢˊ)or勾欄院(ㄍㄡ ㄌㄢˊ ㄩㄢˋ)
a brothel

勾留(ㄍㄡ ㄌㄧㄡˊ)
to be detained (by business); to stay; to stop over

勾連(ㄍㄡ ㄌㄧㄢˊ)
to join; to unite; to connect

勾臉(ㄍㄡ ㄌㄧㄢˇ)
to paint the face (in Peking opera)

勾畫(ㄍㄡ ㄏㄨㄚˋ)
to draw the outline of; to delineate; to sketch

勾魂(ㄍㄡ ㄏㄨㄣˊ)
to bewitch; to enchant; to fascinate

勾結(ㄍㄡ ㄐㄧㄝˊ)
to collude or collaborate; collusion or collaboration; to gang up; 你們全部勾結起來對付我一個。You have all ganged up on me.

勾芡(ㄍㄡ ㄑㄧㄢˋ)
to thicken (soup, etc.) by means of starch

勾情(ㄍㄡ ㄑㄧㄥˊ)
to flirt (with someone)

勾消 or 勾銷(ㄍㄡ ㄒㄧㄠ)
to liquidate; to strike out; to cancel; to nullify; to write off

勾心鬥角(ㄍㄡ ㄒㄧㄣ ㄉㄡˋ ㄐㄧㄠˇ)
to intrigue against each other 參看「鉤心鬥角」

勾除(ㄍㄡ ㄔㄨˊ)
to eliminate; to cancel; to delete

勾串(ㄍㄡ ㄔㄨㄢˋ)
to conspire with; to gang up

勾引(ㄍㄡ ㄧㄣˇ)
to entice; to seduce; to tempt; to inveigle; 她勾引他加入另一黨。She seduced him to the other party.

【勾】 449
2. 《ㄡ gow gòu
1. to manage
2. business; affairs

勾當(ㄍㄡ ㄉㄤ)
an underhand job; a dirty business; a plot; an intrigue; hush-hush activities

【勿】 450
ㄨˋ wuh wù
do not; not; never; a negative word used in formal

speech: 勿急。Don't rush. 請勿吸煙。No Smoking.

勿念(ㄨˋ ㄋㄧㄢˋ)
Do not worry.

勿論(ㄨˋ ㄌㄨㄣˋ)
regardless of; to let alone

勿失(ㄨˋ ㄕ)
Do not let (a chance, etc.) slip away.

勿藥(ㄨˋ ㄧㄠˋ)
to recover from illness

三畫

【包】 451
ㄅㄠ bau bāo
1. to wrap; 用紙把書包起來。Wrap (up) a book in a piece of paper.
2. to include; to contain: 他將小費包括在費用的估計中。He included a sum for tips in his estimate of expenses.
3. to surround
4. to guarantee
5. a parcel; a package; a bundle: 郵包 a postal parcel

包辦(ㄅㄠ ㄅㄢˋ)
to assume full responsibility for; to undertake completely: 這事由他包辦。He will be fully responsible for it.

包庇(ㄅㄠ ㄅㄧˋ)
to harbor; to shelter; to shield; to defend someone who does not deserve defense: 他撒謊以包庇他的弟弟。He told a lie to shield his younger brother.

包賠(ㄅㄠ ㄆㄟˊ)
to guarantee to compensate (for loss, injury, etc.)

包皮(ㄅㄠ ㄆㄧˊ)
① a wrapper; a covering ② the prepuce

包票(ㄅㄠ ㄆㄧㄠˋ)
a guaranty; a certificate of guarantee

包飯(ㄅㄠ ㄈㄢˋ)or包伙(ㄅㄠ ㄏㄨㄛˇ)
to eat meals regularly (at a small restaurant) on a monthly payment basis; to board

包袱(ㄅㄠ ㄈㄨˊ)
① a cloth wrapper ② a bundle in a cloth wrapper ③ a burden; a liability

包賭(ㄅㄠ ㄉㄨˇ)
to protect illegal gambli casinos

包退包換(ㄅㄠ ㄊㄨㄟˋ ㄅㄠ ㄏㄨㄢˋ)
to refund or change for better one (if the mercha dise is defective) 或 Me chandise will be exchange if found unsatisfactory.

包攬(ㄅㄠ ㄌㄢˇ)
to monopolize; to undertal the whole thing; to take everything

包攬訟事(ㄅㄠ ㄌㄢˇ ㄙㄨㄥˋ ㄕˋ)or 攬詞訟(ㄌㄢˇ ㄘˊ ㄙㄨㄥˋ)
(said of unethical lawyer to encourage or instigate l igations with a view to ge ting the fee; to act a shyster; to engage i pettifoggery
to include; to cover: 音樂類包羅甚廣。Music covers wide range.

包羅萬象(ㄅㄠ ㄌㄨㄛˊ ㄨㄢˋ ㄒㄧㄤˋ)
inclusive of everything; al inclusive; to cover and co tain everything

包穀(ㄅㄠ ㄍㄨˇ)
corn

包裹(ㄅㄠ ㄍㄨㄛˇ)
① to wrap up ② a parcel; bundle; a package

包管(ㄅㄠ ㄍㄨㄢˇ)
to guarantee or assure: 包管沒問題。I guarantee it's a right.

包工(ㄅㄠ ㄍㄨㄥ)
① a job or project awarde to a contractor ② a job fo which payment is calculate on the amount of work don (instead of on an hourly o daily basis) 亦作「包活」③ contractor

包公(ㄅㄠ ㄍㄨㄥ)or包拯(ㄅㄠ ㄓㄥˇ)
Pao Cheng, 999-1062, a upright official known fo his stressing the dignity o law

包括(ㄅㄠ ㄎㄨㄛˋ)or(ㄅㄠ ㄍㄨㄚˋ)
to include; to comprise

包含(ㄅㄠ ㄏㄢˊ)
to contain; to comprise; t include: 較大者包含較小者。The greater includes the

lesser.

換(ㄏㄨㄢˋ)
to guarantee replacement (of unsatisfactory goods with satisfactory ones)

機(ㄐㄧ)
a chartered airplane

銷(ㄒㄧㄠ)
to assume the responsibility for the sale (of a certain commodity); to be the sole agent for a production unit or a firm

修(ㄒㄧㄡ)
to guarantee the repair of something

心菜(ㄒㄧㄣ ㄘㄞˋ)
a cabbage

廂(ㄒㄧㄤ)
a box (in a theater, stadium, etc.)

治(ㄓˋ)or 包醫(ㄅㄠ ㄧ)
to guarantee a cure; not to receive fees till the patient is cured

治百病(ㄓˋ ㄅㄞˇ ㄅㄧㄥˋ)
to guarantee to cure all diseases

賺(ㄅㄠ ㄓㄨㄢˋ)
to guarantee profits; profits assured

准(ㄅㄠ ㄓㄨㄣˇ)
to guarantee (that something is sure to happen, etc.)

裝(ㄅㄠ ㄓㄨㄤ)
to pack; packing: 這些書容易包裝。These books pack easily.

車(ㄅㄠ ㄔㄜ)
a chartered bus

抄(ㄔㄠ)
(military) to outflank

娼(ㄔㄤ)
to harbor or protect call girl centers

場(ㄔㄤˇ)
to reserve a whole theater or cinema

商(ㄕㄤ)
a concessionaire (in business); a contractor

容(ㄅㄠ ㄖㄨㄥˊ)
①to tolerate; to forgive: 他不太能包容批評。He is not very tolerant of criticism. ②to contain; to hold

子(ㄗ˙)

a steamed pie; a steamed stuffed bun

包紮(ㄗㄚ)
to wrap; to bandage; to pack; to tie up; to bind up

包租(ㄗㄨ)
①to rent a room or a house for subletting ②a fixed farmland rent one must pay no matter how bad the harvest might be

包藏(ㄘㄤ)
to contain; to conceal

包藏禍心(ㄘㄤ ㄏㄨㄛˋ ㄒㄧㄣ)
to harbor evil intentions or malicious intent

包贏(ㄧㄥˊ)
to guarantee winning in gambling or in a sports match

包圍(ㄨㄟˊ)
to surround; to besiege; to encircle: 一道牆包圍了整個花園。A wall surrounds the garden.

包運(ㄩㄣˋ)
to transport; transportation

包用(ㄩㄥˋ)
to guarantee serviceability (of an article)

四畫

【匈】452
ㄒㄩㄥ shiong xiōng
1. the breast; the bosom; the thorax
2. to clamor

匈奴(ㄒㄩㄥ ㄋㄨˊ)
the Huns, an ancient nationality in China

匈牙利(ㄒㄩㄥ ㄧㄚˊ ㄌㄧˋ)
Hungary

匈牙利人(ㄒㄩㄥ ㄧㄚˊ ㄌㄧˋ ㄖㄣˊ)
a Hungarian

匈牙利語(ㄒㄩㄥ ㄧㄚˊ ㄌㄧˋ ㄩˇ)
Hungarian

七畫

【匍】453
ㄆㄨˊ pwu pú
1. to crawl; to creep
2. to lie prostrate; to prostrate

匍匐 or 匍伏(ㄆㄨˊ ㄈㄨˊ)
①to crawl; to creep ②to prostrate

九畫

【匏】454
ㄆㄠˊ paur páo
1. a gourd; a bottle gourd; a calabash
2. a kind of wind instrument originally made of a gourd

匏瓜(ㄆㄠˊ ㄍㄨㄚ)
a gourd; a bottle gourd; a calabash

匏樽(ㄆㄠˊ ㄗㄨㄣ)
a gourd shell as a wine cup

【匐】455
ㄈㄨˊ fwu fú
1. to lie prostrate; to prostrate
2. to crawl; to creep

匕 部
ㄅㄧˇ bii bǐ

【匕】456
ㄅㄧˇ bii bǐ
1. a ladle; a spoon
2. an arrowhead
3. a dagger

匕首(ㄅㄧˇ ㄕㄡˇ)
a dagger; a short sword

二畫

【化】457
ㄏㄨㄚˋ huah huà
1. to change; to convert; to transform; to influence: 冰在熱天很快化爲水。Ice changes into water rapidly on a hot day.
2. short for "chemistry"

化名(ㄏㄨㄚˋ ㄇㄧㄥˊ)
to assume a pseudonym; a pseudonym

化肥(ㄏㄨㄚˋ ㄈㄟˊ)
chemical fertilizer

化繁爲簡(ㄏㄨㄚˋ ㄈㄢˊ ㄨㄟˊ ㄐㄧㄢˇ)
to simplify what is complicated

化糞池(ㄏㄨㄚˋ ㄈㄣˋ ㄔˊ)
a cesspool or cesspit; a septic tank

化腐朽爲神奇(ㄏㄨㄚˋ ㄈㄨˇ ㄒㄧㄡˇ ㄨㄟˊ ㄕㄣˊ ㄑㄧˊ)

ㄏㄚˋ ㄑˊ
to make the ugly things beautiful; to make use of discarded things; to transform the corruptible into a mysterious life

化敵爲友(ㄏㄨㄚˋ ㄉㄧˊ ㄨㄟˊ ㄧㄡˇ)
to convert an enemy into a friend

化痰止咳(ㄏㄨㄚˋ ㄊㄢˊ ㄓˇ ㄎㄜˊ)
capable of preventing phlegm from forming and stopping coughing (a promotional phrase for medicine)

化膿(ㄏㄨㄚˋ ㄋㄨㄥˊ)
to suppurate; to maturate; to fester

化零爲整(ㄏㄨㄚˋ ㄌㄧㄥˊ ㄨㄟˊ ㄓㄥˇ)
(guerrilla warfare) to concentrate all the forces available in order to deliver a crushing blow to a relatively weak enemy force

化干戈爲玉帛(ㄏㄨㄚˋ ㄍㄢ ㄍㄜ ㄨㄟˊ ㄩˋ ㄅㄛˊ)
to bury the hatchets and work for peace

化工(ㄏㄨㄚˋ ㄍㄨㄥ)
① Nature's work; operations of Nature ② chemical engineering

化開(ㄏㄨㄚˋ ㄎㄞ)
to spread out after being diluted or melted

化合(ㄏㄨㄚˋ ㄏㄜˊ)
to combine (chemically); combination

化合量(ㄏㄨㄚˋ ㄏㄜˊ ㄌㄧㄤˋ)
(chemistry) combining weight

化合物(ㄏㄨㄚˋ ㄏㄜˊ ㄨˋ)
a (chemical) compound

化解(ㄏㄨㄚˋ ㄐㄧㄝˇ)
to bring reconciliation to; to settle (disputes)

化境(ㄏㄨㄚˋ ㄐㄧㄥˋ)
a transcendent or unearthly atmosphere (especially of a work of art); sublimity; perfection

化險爲夷(ㄏㄨㄚˋ ㄒㄧㄢˇ ㄨㄟˊ ㄧˊ)
to turn peril into safety; to head off a disaster

化學(ㄏㄨㄚˋ ㄒㄩㄝˊ)
chemistry

化學變化(ㄏㄨㄚˋ ㄒㄩㄝˊ ㄅㄧㄢˋ ㄏㄨㄚˋ)
chemical change

化學平衡(ㄏㄨㄚˋ ㄒㄩㄝˊ ㄆㄧㄥˊ ㄏㄥˊ)
chemical equilibrium

化學反應(ㄏㄨㄚˋ ㄒㄩㄝˊ ㄈㄢˇ ㄧㄥˋ)
chemical reaction

化學分解(ㄏㄨㄚˋ ㄒㄩㄝˊ ㄈㄣ ㄐㄧㄝˇ)
chemical decomposition

化學分析(ㄏㄨㄚˋ ㄒㄩㄝˊ ㄈㄣ ㄒㄧ)
chemical analysis

化學方程式(ㄏㄨㄚˋ ㄒㄩㄝˊ ㄈㄤ ㄔㄥˊ ㄕˋ)
a chemical equation; a chemical formula

化學工業(ㄏㄨㄚˋ ㄒㄩㄝˊ ㄍㄨㄥ ㄧㄝˋ)
the chemical industry

化學纖維(ㄏㄨㄚˋ ㄒㄩㄝˊ ㄒㄧㄢ ㄨㄟˊ)
synthetic fiber; chemical fiber

化學戰(ㄏㄨㄚˋ ㄒㄩㄝˊ ㄓㄢˋ)
chemical warfare

化學作用(ㄏㄨㄚˋ ㄒㄩㄝˊ ㄗㄨㄛˋ ㄩㄥˋ)
chemical action

化學武器(ㄏㄨㄚˋ ㄒㄩㄝˊ ㄨˇ ㄑㄧˋ)
chemical weapons

化整爲零(ㄏㄨㄚˋ ㄓㄥˇ ㄨㄟˊ ㄌㄧㄥˊ)
(guerrilla warfare) to break up large troops into scattered groups so as to avoid annihilation by a powerful enemy force

化妝(ㄏㄨㄚˋ ㄓㄨㄤ)
to make up; to apply cosmetics

化妝品(ㄏㄨㄚˋ ㄓㄨㄤ ㄆㄧㄣˇ)
cosmetics

化裝(ㄏㄨㄚˋ ㄓㄨㄤ)
to disguise oneself; to masquerade

化裝舞會(ㄏㄨㄚˋ ㄓㄨㄤ ㄨˇ ㄏㄨㄟˋ)
a masquerade

化除(ㄏㄨㄚˋ ㄔㄨˊ)
to dissolve to nothing; to dispel; to remove; to abolish

化除畛域(ㄏㄨㄚˋ ㄔㄨˊ ㄓㄣˇ ㄩˋ)
to eliminate regionalism

化石(ㄏㄨㄚˋ ㄕˊ)
a fossil

化石學(ㄏㄨㄚˋ ㄕˊ ㄒㄩㄝˊ)
petrifactology, or paleontology

化身(ㄏㄨㄚˋ ㄕㄣ)
an incarnation; an embodiment

化生放射戰爭(ㄏㄨㄚˋ ㄕㄥ ㄈㄤˋ ㄕㄜˋ ㄓㄢˋ ㄓㄥ)
chemical, biological and nuclear warfare

化俗(ㄏㄨㄚˋ ㄙㄨˊ)
to improve customs; to civilize

化暗爲明(ㄏㄨㄚˋ ㄢˋ ㄨㄟˊ ㄇㄧㄥˊ)
to legalize what is illegal

化油器(ㄏㄨㄚˋ ㄧㄡˊ ㄑㄧˋ)
a carburetor

化驗(ㄏㄨㄚˋ ㄧㄢˋ)
to subject to chemical analysis; to put to laboratory examination or test

化室(ㄏㄨㄚˋ ㄧ ㄕˋ)
a laboratory

化外(ㄏㄨㄚˋ ㄨㄞˋ)
outer fringes of civilization; outside the pale of Chinese civilization

化外之民(ㄏㄨㄚˋ ㄨㄞˋ ㄓ ㄇㄧㄣˊ)
uncivilized people; barbarians

化爲烏有(ㄏㄨㄚˋ ㄨㄟˊ ㄨ ㄧㄡˇ)
to disappear completely; vanish completely; to come to naught; to vanish in thin air

化雨(ㄏㄨㄚˋ ㄩˇ)
the pervading good influence (of an educator)

化育(ㄏㄨㄚˋ ㄩˋ)
Nature's nourishing

化緣(ㄏㄨㄚˋ ㄩㄢˊ)
to solicit alms (as a means for favorable karma)

三畫

【北】
458
ㄅㄟˇ beei běi
(讀音 ㄅㄛˋ boh bò)

1. north; northern; northerly
2. northward
3. defeated

北半球(ㄅㄟˇ ㄅㄢˋ ㄑㄧㄡˊ)
the Northern Hemisphere

北邊(ㄅㄟˇ ㄅㄧㄢ)or **北邊兒**(ㄅㄟˇ ㄅㄧㄢˊ)
the north; the northern part

北冰洋(ㄅㄟˇ ㄅㄧㄥ ㄧㄤˊ)or **北極海**(ㄅㄟˇ ㄐㄧˊ ㄏㄞˇ)
the Arctic Ocean

北平(ㄅㄟˇ ㄆㄧㄥˊ)
Peiping 亦作「北京」

北美洲(ㄅㄟˇ ㄇㄟˇ ㄓㄡ)
North America

北面(ㄅㄟˇ ㄇㄧㄢˋ)
①in the north; the northern part ② to have an audience (with the emperor); to pay homage to

北伐(ㄅㄟˇ ㄈㄚˊ)or **北伐**(ㄅㄟˇ ㄈㄚˊ)

①the Northward Expedition (the history of the Republic of China) ②to fight north

非
North Africa; North African

方
①the northern region ②the north

方人(ㄅㄟˇ ㄈㄤㄖㄣˊ)
a northerner

達科塔(ㄅㄟˇ ㄉㄚˊ ㄎㄜ ㄊㄚˇ)
the state of North Dakota, U.S.A.

大荒(ㄅㄟˇ ㄉㄚˋ ㄏㄨㄤ)
the Great Northern Wilderness in northeast China

大西洋公約組織(ㄅㄟˇ ㄒㄧ ㄧㄤˊ ㄍㄨㄥ ㄩㄝ ㄗㄨˇ ㄓ)
North Atlantic Treaty Organization (NATO)

大西洋航線(ㄅㄟˇ ㄉㄚˋ ㄒㄧ ㄧㄤˊ ㄏㄤˊ ㄒㄧㄢˋ)
North Atlantic Line

斗星(ㄅㄟˇ ㄉㄡˇ ㄒㄧㄥ)or 北斗七星(ㄅㄟˇ ㄉㄡˇ ㄑㄧ ㄒㄧㄥ)
the Plough; the Big Dipper; the Plow

瓜(ㄅㄟˇ ㄍㄨㄚ)
a bottle gourd

卡羅來納州(ㄅㄟˇ ㄎㄚˇ ㄌㄨㄛˊ ㄌㄞˊ ㄋㄚˋ ㄓㄡ)
the state of North Carolina, U.S.A.

海(ㄅㄟˇ ㄏㄞˇ)
the North Sea

海道(ㄅㄟˇ ㄏㄞˇ ㄉㄠˋ)
Hokkaido, Japan's northernmost island

韓(ㄅㄟˇ ㄏㄢˊ)
North Korea

寒帶(ㄅㄟˇ ㄏㄢˊ ㄉㄞˋ)
the North Frigid Zone

回歸線(ㄅㄟˇ ㄏㄨㄟˊ ㄍㄨㄟ ㄒㄧㄢˋ)
the Tropic of Cancer

極(ㄅㄟˇ ㄐㄧˊ)
① the North Pole; the Arctic Pole ②the north magnetic pole

極光(ㄅㄟˇ ㄐㄧˊ ㄍㄨㄤ)
aurora borealis

極圈(ㄅㄟˇ ㄐㄧˊ ㄑㄩㄢ)
the Arctic Circle

極熊(ㄅㄟˇ ㄐㄧˊ ㄒㄩㄥˊ)
a polar bear

極星(ㄅㄟˇ ㄐㄧˊ ㄒㄧㄥ)
Polaris; the North Star; the

polestar

北京(ㄅㄟˇ ㄐㄧㄥ)
Peking

北京狗(ㄅㄟˇ ㄐㄧㄥ ㄍㄡˇ)
a pekingese

北京人(ㄅㄟˇ ㄐㄧㄥ ㄖㄣˊ)
(archaeology) Sinanthropus; the Peking Man

北軍(ㄅㄟˇ ㄐㄩㄣ)
the Union soldiers, or the Union troops (in the American Civil War)

北上(ㄅㄟˇ ㄕㄤˋ)
to proceed northward; to go north

北宋(ㄅㄟˇ ㄙㄨㄥˋ)
the Northern Sung or Earlier Sung Dynasty, 960-1128

北歐(ㄅㄟˇ ㄡ)
northern Europe; northern European

北洋軍閥(ㄅㄟˇ ㄧㄤˊ ㄐㄩㄣ ㄈㄚˊ)
the northern warlords (in the early years of the Republic of China)

北緯(ㄅㄟˇ ㄨㄟˇ)
north latitude; northern latitude

北溫帶(ㄅㄟˇ ㄨㄣ ㄉㄞˋ)
the North Temperate Zone

北嶽(ㄅㄟˇ ㄩㄝˋ)
another name of Mountain Heng (恆山) in Hopeh Province, one of the Five Sacred Mountains

九畫

【匙】 459
1. ㄔ chyr chí
a spoon 參看「湯匙」or「茶匙」

【匙】 459
2. ㄕ ˙shy shi
a key 參看「鑰匙」

匸 部
匸尢 fang fāng

三畫

【匝】 460
ㄗㄚ tza zā
to make a revolution round;

to encompass; to circle

匝地(ㄗㄚ ㄉㄧˋ)
all over the ground; here, there, and everywhere

匝月(ㄗㄚ ㄩㄝˋ)
a whole month

【匜】 461
ㄧˊ yi yí
a washbasin (of former times)

四畫

【匠】 462
ㄐㄧㄤˋ jiang jiòng
a craftsman; an artisan; a skilled workman; 木匠 a carpenter; 石匠 a mason; a stoneman; 鐵匠 a blacksmith

匠氣(ㄐㄧㄤˋ ㄑㄧˋ)
commonplaceness or triteness in artistic work

匠心(ㄐㄧㄤˋ ㄒㄧㄣ)or 匠意(ㄐㄧㄤˋ ㄧˋ)
inventiveness; ingenuity; originality; craftsmanship; 這位畫家獨具匠心。 This painter has great originality.

匠心經營(ㄐㄧㄤˋ ㄒㄧㄣ ㄐㄧㄥ ㄧㄥˊ)
the original thought in any creation

匠人(ㄐㄧㄤˋ ㄖㄣˊ)
an artisan; a craftsman; a carpenter; a mason; a bricklayer

【匡】 463
ㄎㄨㄤ kuang kuāng
1. to rectify; to correct
2. to deliver from

匡復(ㄎㄨㄤ ㄈㄨˋ)
to restore national prestige or prosperity

匡濟(ㄎㄨㄤ ㄐㄧˋ)
to relieve distress; to help over a difficulty

匡救(ㄎㄨㄤ ㄐㄧㄡˋ)
to deliver from danger or sin; to rescue from disaster or errors

匡正(ㄎㄨㄤ ㄓㄥˋ)
to rectify; to correct; to reform

匡助(ㄎㄨㄤ ㄓㄨˋ)
to assist; to lend a helping hand

匡時(ㄎㄨㄤ ㄕˊ)
to remedy evils of the times; to do things for the good of

society

五畫

匚
部

【匣】 464
ㄒㄧㄚˊ shya shiá
1. a case; a small box
2. a cage 亦作「柙」
匣子(ㄒㄧㄚˊ ㄗ˙)or 匣兒(ㄒㄧㄚˊ ㄦ˙)
　a small box; a casket

八畫

【匪】 465
ㄈㄟˇ feei feǐ
1. bandits; rebels; insurgents
2. not
匪幫(ㄈㄟˇ ㄅㄤ)
　a gang of bandits or rebels;
　a band of robbers
匪徒(ㄈㄟˇ ㄊㄨˊ)
　bandits; brigands; robbers;
　gangsters
匪類(ㄈㄟˇ ㄌㄟˋ)
　bandits; brigands; robbers;
　criminals
匪患(ㄈㄟˇ ㄏㄨㄢˋ)
　the evil of bandits; banditry
匪懈(ㄈㄟˇ ㄒㄧㄝˋ)
　do not idle or relax; to be
　diligent
匪巢(ㄈㄟˇ ㄔㄠˊ)
　a bandits' lair
匪首(ㄈㄟˇ ㄕㄡˇ)
　a bandit chieftain
匪人(ㄈㄟˇ ㄖㄣˊ)
　a bandit; a bad person
匪夷所思(ㄈㄟˇ ㄧˊ ㄙㄨㄛˇ ㄙ)
　unthinkable; outrageous
　ideas; bizarre thoughts;
　unimaginably queer; fantas-
　tic

九畫

【匭】 466
ㄍㄨㄟˇ goei guǐ
　a box; a casket; a chest: 票
匭 a ballot box

十一畫

【匯】 467
ㄏㄨㄟˊ huey huí
1. to remit money: 他每月給父
親匯錢。He remits money to

his father every month.
2. to converge
3. to flow into
匯撥(ㄏㄨㄟˊ ㄅㄛ)
　to transfer a sum of money
匯票(ㄏㄨㄟˊ ㄆㄧㄠˋ)
　a money order; a draft; a
　bill of exchange
匯費(ㄏㄨㄟˊ ㄈㄟˋ)or 匯水(ㄏㄨㄟˊ
ㄕㄨㄟˇ)
　the remitting charge or fee
匯豐銀行(ㄏㄨㄟˊ ㄈㄥ ㄧㄣˊ ㄏㄤˊ)
　Hongkong and Shanghai
　Banking Corporation
匯付(ㄏㄨㄟˊ ㄈㄨˋ)
　to pay to
匯兌(ㄏㄨㄟˊ ㄉㄨㄟˋ)
　(commerce) exchange; the
　transfer of funds; remittance
匯兌銀行(ㄏㄨㄟˊ ㄉㄨㄟˋ ㄧㄣˊ ㄏㄤˊ)
　an exchange bank
匯率(ㄏㄨㄟˊ ㄌㄩˋ)or 匯兌率(ㄏㄨㄟˊ
ㄉㄨㄟˋ ㄌㄩˋ)
　the exchange rate (between
　currencies)
匯款(ㄏㄨㄟˊ ㄎㄨㄢˇ)
　①a remittance ②to remit
　money
匯合(ㄏㄨㄟˊ ㄏㄜˊ)
　to converge; to join: 這兩條
　河在什麼地方匯合? Where do
　the two rivers join?
匯集(ㄏㄨㄟˊ ㄐㄧˊ)or 匯聚(ㄏㄨㄟˊ ㄐㄩˋ)
　to gather in one place; to
　converge; to collect
匯價(ㄏㄨㄟˊ ㄐㄧㄚˋ)
　the exchange rate; the con-
　version rate

十二畫

【匱】 468
ㄎㄨㄟˋ kuey kui
1. to lack; deficient
2. a chest or cabinet
3. exhausted
匱乏(ㄎㄨㄟˋ ㄈㄚˊ)
　lack; want; to lack; to be
　short of: 我的生活不虞匱乏。
　My life is free from want.

十三畫

【奩】 469
(匳) ㄌㄧㄢˊ lian lián
1. a toilet case; a dressing
　case

2. as in the following expres-
　sions: 香奩 a container f
　incense 粧奩 a dowry
奩敬(ㄌㄧㄢˊ ㄐㄧㄥˋ)
　gifts to a bride

匸 部
ㄒㄧ shih xī

二畫

【匹】 470
1. ㄆㄧˇ pi pǐ
　a numerary particle fo
　horses: 他有兩匹馬和一頭
　子。He has two horses and
　mule.
匹馬單槍(ㄆㄧˇ ㄇㄚˇ ㄉㄢ ㄑㄧㄤ)
　single-handed; without hel
　doing something unaccomp
　nied and unaided 亦作「單槍
　匹馬」

【匹】 470
2. ㄆㄧˇ pii pí
1. a bolt (of cloth)
2. to match
3. equal
匹配(ㄆㄧˇ ㄆㄟˋ)
　①to match ②(electricity
　matching
匹夫(ㄆㄧˇ ㄈㄨ)
　①an ordinary man ②even
　man: 國家興亡, 匹夫有責。
　Every man is responsible fo
　the fate of his country. ③a
　ignorant person
匹夫匹婦(ㄆㄧˇ ㄈㄨ ㄆㄧˇ ㄈㄨˋ)
　common people; commoner
匹夫之勇(ㄆㄧˇ ㄈㄨ ㄓ ㄩㄥˇ)
　foolhardiness; reckless cou
　age; mere physical courage
匹敵(ㄆㄧˇ ㄉㄧˊ)
　to match or equal (in a co
　test); to be a match for: 強
　隊實力可匹敵。The two team
　are equally matched.
匹練(ㄆㄧˇ ㄌㄧㄢˋ)
　a waterfall
匹偶(ㄆㄧˇ ㄡˇ)
　①a spouse ②a worthy perso
匹庶(ㄆㄧˇ ㄕㄨˋ)
　common people
匹偶 or 匹耦(ㄆㄧˇ ㄡˇ)

a (married) couple

九畫

【匾】 471
ㄅㄧㄢˇ bean biǎn
a (wooden) tablet

匾額(ㄅㄧㄢˇㄜˊ)
a (wooden) tablet; a horizontal inscribed board

【匿】 472
ㄋㄧˋ nih nì
to hide; to conceal

匿名信(ㄋㄧˋㄇㄧㄥˊㄒㄧㄣˋ)
an anonymous letter

匿伏(ㄋㄧˋㄈㄨˊ)
to lurk; to hide oneself to escape capture

匿迹銷聲(ㄋㄧˋㄐㄧˋㄒㄧㄠㄕㄥ)
to be in complete hiding

匿情(ㄋㄧˋㄑㄧㄥˊ)
to cover up the fact before the law

匿笑(ㄋㄧˋㄒㄧㄠˋ)
to laugh in secret

匿影藏形(ㄋㄧˋㄧㄥˇㄘㄤˊㄒㄧㄥˊ)
to hide from public notice

【區】 473
1. ㄑㄩ chiu qū
to distinguish; to discriminate
2. a district; an area; a zone: 這是純粹的農業區。This is a purely agricultural district.
3. a border
4. little; few

區別(ㄑㄩˊㄅㄧㄝˊ)
① to discriminate; to distinguish; to draw a line (between); to differentiate: 他能區別好書與壞書。He can discriminate good books from poor ones. ② difference; distinction: 兩者之間有區別。There is a distinction between the two.

區分(ㄑㄩㄈㄣ)
to set apart; to consider to be separate or different; to distinguish; to differentiate: 我無法區分這兩種花。I cannot differentiate the two flowers.

區分部(ㄑㄩㄈㄣㄅㄨˋ)
district headquarters of a political party

區公所(ㄑㄩㄍㄨㄥㄙㄨㄛˇ)
a district office

區劃(ㄑㄩㄏㄨㄚˋ)
to divide into districts or areas

區間車(ㄑㄩㄐㄧㄢㄔㄜ)
a bus traveling merely part of its normal route

區區(ㄑㄩㄑㄩ)
① small or unimportant (in quantity, amount or size); trifling: 區區小事，何足掛齒。Such a trifling thing is hardly worth mentioning. ② a polite reference to oneself

區長(ㄑㄩㄓㄤˇ)
a district magistrate

區宇(ㄑㄩ ㄩˇ)
territory

區域(ㄑㄩㄩˋ)
a district; an area; a region; a zone: 本區域已劃為工業發展之用。This area has been zoned for industrial development.

區域代表制(ㄑㄩㄩˋㄉㄞˋㄅㄧㄠˇㄓˋ)
(elections) the regional representation system

區域規劃(ㄑㄩㄩˋㄍㄨㄟㄏㄨㄚˋ)
regional planning

區域性(ㄑㄩㄩˋㄒㄧㄥˋ)
regional: 那是一場區域性戰爭。That was a regional war.

十 部
ㄕˊ shyr shí

【十】 474
ㄕˊ shyr shí
1. ten; the tenth: 他十點鐘來。He will come at ten. 他比你強十倍。He is ten times the man you are. 今天是八月十日。Today's the tenth of August.
2. complete; completely; perfect; perfectly; extremely

十八般武藝(ㄕˊㄅㄚㄅㄢㄨˇㄧˋ)
(literally) eighteen weapons and their uses—allegedly devised by Sun Pin (孫臏) and Wu Chi (吳起) in the Epoch of Warring States—(figuratively, said of a person) all skill and knowledge about one's trade, profes-

sion, etc.; versatility

十八羅漢(ㄕˊㄅㄚㄌㄨㄛˊㄏㄢˋ)
(Buddhism) the eighteen saints, including 16 disciples of Buddha

十八重地獄(ㄕˊㄅㄚㄔㄨㄥˊㄉㄧˋㄩˋ)or 十八層地獄(ㄕˊㄅㄚㄘㄥˊㄉㄧˋㄩˋ)
(Buddhism) the eighteen hells where the souls of evil persons are tortured

十邊形(ㄕˊㄅㄧㄢㄒㄧㄥˊ)or 十角形(ㄕˊㄐㄧㄠˇㄒㄧㄥˊ)
a decagon

十面體(ㄕˊㄇㄧㄢˋㄊㄧˇ)
a decahedron

十目所視，十手所指(ㄕˊㄇㄨˋㄙㄨㄛˇㄕˋ，ㄕˊㄕㄡˇㄙㄨㄛˇㄓˇ)
(literally) to be looked at by ten eyes and pointed at by ten fingers—under the glare of the public

十分(ㄕˊㄈㄣ)
① complete; completely: 他十分滿意。He was completely satisfied. ② very: 他歌唱得十分好。He sings very well. ③ 10 points

十方(ㄕˊㄈㄤ)
(Buddhism) the ten directions—north, south, east, west, northeast, northwest, southeast, southwest, above and below

十拿九穩(ㄕˊㄋㄚˊㄐㄧㄡˇㄨㄣˇ)
to be very sure of (success, etc.); almost certain; 90 per cent sure: 此事我是十拿九穩。I am very sure of success in this matter.

十年九不遇(ㄕˊㄋㄧㄢˊㄐㄧㄡˇㄅㄨˋㄩˋ)
hardly occur once in ten years—to be very rare

十年樹木，百年樹人(ㄕˊㄋㄧㄢˊㄕㄨˋㄇㄨˋ，ㄅㄞˇㄋㄧㄢˊㄕㄨˋㄖㄣˊ)
It takes 10 years to grow a tree, while a sound education program may require 10 times as long before it takes root.

十六開(ㄕˊㄌㄧㄡˋㄎㄞ)
sixteenmo

〔十
部〕

〔十部〕

十戒 (ㄕ ㄐㄧㄝ)
(Buddhism) the Ten Prohibitions

十誡 (ㄕ ㄐㄧㄝ)
the Ten Commandments (in the Bible)

十錦 (ㄕ ㄐㄧㄣ)
multiple ingredients (for a dish)

十進法 (ㄕ ㄐㄧㄣˋ ㄈㄚˇ)
the denary scale

十全十美 (ㄕ ㄑㄩㄢˊ ㄕ ㄇㄟˇ)
perfect; complete

十項運動 (ㄕ ㄒㄧㄤˋ ㄩㄣˋ ㄉㄨㄥˋ)
decathlon 亦作「十項全能運動」

十項運動員 (ㄕ ㄒㄧㄤˋ ㄩㄣˋ ㄉㄨㄥˋ ㄩㄢˊ)
a decathlonist

十之八九 (ㄕ ㄓ ㄅㄚ ㄐㄧㄡˇ)
eight or nine cases out of ten; most likely

十成 (ㄕ ㄔㄥˊ)or **十成兒** (ㄕ ㄔㄥˊ ㄦ)
very sure; one hundred per cent

十室九空 (ㄕ ㄕˋ ㄐㄧㄡˇ ㄎㄨㄥ)
(literally) nine out of ten houses are vacant—almost all the villages or cities are deserted, as a result of wars, natural disasters, etc.

十姊妹 (ㄕ ㄗˇ ㄇㄟˋ)or **十姐妹** (ㄕ ㄐㄧㄝˇ ㄇㄟˋ)
① *Uroloncha domestica* (a kind of sparrow-size bird with a variety of feather colors) ② *Rosa multiflora* (a kind of plant) ③ ten girls who swear not to get married and stick together (an old fad in Kwangtung)

十字路口 (ㄕ ㄗˋ ㄌㄨˋ ㄎㄡˇ)
① the junction of cross-roads ② a moment or point of decision

十字鎬 (ㄕ ㄗˋ ㄍㄠˇ)
a pick; a mattock

十字架 (ㄕ ㄗˋ ㄐㄧㄚˋ)
① the Cross ② a yoke one has to take

十字街頭 (ㄕ ㄗˋ ㄐㄧㄝ ㄊㄡˊ)
① a road intersection ② a point of decision

十字軍 (ㄕ ㄗˋ ㄐㄩㄣ)
the Crusaders

十字軍東征 (ㄕ ㄗˋ ㄐㄩㄣ ㄉㄨㄥ ㄓㄥ)
the Crusade

十字兒 (ㄕ ㄗˋ ㄦ)
anything shaped like a cross

十足 (ㄕ ㄗㄨˊ)
extremely; completely; perfect; perfectly; one hundred per cent; pure (gold); out-and-out; downright

十族 (ㄕ ㄗㄨˊ)
the ten relations of a person

十四行詩 (ㄕ ㄙˋ ㄏㄤˊ ㄕ)
(Western poetry) the sonnet

十三點 (ㄕ ㄙㄢ ㄉㄧㄢˇ)
(slang) silly; acting in a stupid manner which invokes mirth rather than disgust (particularly said of women)

十三太保 (ㄕ ㄙㄢ ㄊㄞˋ ㄅㄠˇ)
① a gang of 13 juvenile gangsters ② anything that is made up of 13 distinguished members

十三陵 (ㄕ ㄙㄢ ㄌㄧㄥˊ)
the Ming Tombs (in Peking)

十三經 (ㄕ ㄙㄢ ㄐㄧㄥ)
the Thirteen Classics of Chinese philosophy and literature—易經, 詩經, 尚書, 禮記, 周禮, 儀禮, 左傳, 公羊傳, 穀梁傳, 論語, 孝經, 爾雅, 孟子 (*Book of Changes, Book of Odes, Historical Records, Book of Rites, Rites of Chou, Book of Etiquettes, Spring and Autumn with Commentary by Tso Chiu-ming, Spring and Autumn with Commentary by Kung-Yang Kao, Spring and Autumn with Commentary by Ku-Liang Chih, Analects of Confucius, Filial Classic, Ancient Dictionary, Works of Mencius*)

十惡不赦 (ㄕ ㄜˋ ㄅㄨˋ ㄕㄜˋ)
guilty of unpardonable evil

十二碼球 (ㄕ ㄦˋ ㄇㄚˇ ㄑㄧㄡˊ)
(soccer) a penalty kick

十二分 (ㄕ ㄦˋ ㄈㄣ)
more than 100 per cent; extremely

十二宮 (ㄕ ㄦˋ ㄍㄨㄥ)
the twelve constellations of the zodiac

十二肖 (ㄕ ㄦˋ ㄒㄧㄠˋ)or **十二屬** (ㄕ ㄦˋ ㄕㄨˇ)
the twelve animals corresponding to the Twelve Ter-

restrial Branches (地支 —子鼠, 丑牛, 寅虎, 卯兔, 辰龍, 巳蛇, 午馬, 未羊, 申猴, 酉鷄, 戌狗, 亥豬 (Rat, Ox Tiger, Hare, Dragon, Serpent, Horse, Sheep, Monkey Cock, Dog and Pig)

十二指腸 (ㄕ ㄦˋ ㄓˇ ㄔㄤˊ)
a duodenum

十二指腸潰瘍 (ㄕ ㄦˋ ㄓˇ ㄔㄤˊ ㄎㄨㄟˋ ㄧㄤˊ)
a duodenal ulcer

十二月 (ㄕ ㄦˋ ㄩㄝˋ)
① December ② the twelfth month of the lunar calendar ③ twelve months

十一月 (ㄕ ㄧ ㄩㄝˋ)
① November ② the eleventh month of the lunar calendar ③ eleven months

十有八九 (ㄕ ㄧㄡˇ ㄅㄚ ㄐㄧㄡˇ)or **十之八九** (ㄕ ㄓ ㄅㄚ ㄐㄧㄡˇ)
eight or nine chances out of ten; most probably; very likely: 十有八九他不會來。 Nine out of ten he won't come.

十羊九牧 (ㄕ ㄧㄤˊ ㄐㄧㄡˇ ㄇㄨˋ)
(literally) There are nine shepherds tending only ten sheep.—too many government officials; bureaucracy

十位 (ㄕ ㄨㄟˋ)
(arithmetic) the tens place

十萬八千里 (ㄕ ㄨㄢˋ ㄅㄚ ㄑㄧㄢ ㄌㄧˇ)
a distance of one hundred and eight thousand *li*—to be poles apart

十萬火急 (ㄕ ㄨㄢˋ ㄏㄨㄛˇ ㄐㄧˊ)
① to be in posthaste ② Most Urgent (as a mark on dispatches)

十月 (ㄕ ㄩㄝˋ)
① October ② the tenth month of the lunar calendar ③ ten months

十月革命 (ㄕ ㄩㄝˋ ㄍㄜˊ ㄇㄧㄥˋ)
the Russian Revolution of 1917

十月十日 (ㄕ ㄩㄝˋ ㄕ ㄖˋ)
October 10 or the Double Tenth, National Day of the Republic of China

一畫

〔千〕 475 く１ㄢ chian qiān

．thousand
：many; numerous
：a Chinese family name

千變萬化(く１ㄢ ㄅ１ㄢ ㄨㄢ ㄏㄨㄚˋ)
countless changes or variations; ever-changing

千不該萬不該(く１ㄢ ㄅㄨˋ ㄍㄞ ㄨㄢ ㄅㄨˋ ㄍㄞ)
really should not; most emphatically not; a thousand no (usually used in the subjunctive mood to indicate one's regret for having done something); deeply (a thousand times) regret

千篇一律(く１ㄢ ㄆ１ㄢ ｜ ㄌㄩˋ)
to harp on a single theme; without changes; dull; monotonous; stereotyped: 這些作品千篇一律，沒什麼創意。The works repeat each other and lack for originality.

千門萬戶(く１ㄢ ㄇㄣˊ ㄨㄢ ㄏㄨˋ)
①descriptive of the numerous buildings of a palace ②numerous households

千米(く１ㄢ ㄇｌˇ)
a kilometer (km)

千佛洞(く１ㄢ ㄈㄛˊ ㄉㄨㄥˋ)
the Tunhuang Caves in Kansu Province, where were found in the 1900's countless Buddha statues, Buddhist scriptures and frescoes of the Tang Dynasty

千方百計(く１ㄢ ㄈㄤ ㄅㄞˇ ㄐｌˋ)
a thousand schemes—by hook or by crook; by all means at one's command; to use all sorts of wiles and methods

千夫所指(く１ㄢ ㄈㄨ ㄙㄨㄛˇ ㄓˇ)
to be pointed at by one thousand accusing fingers—to be universally condemned

千刀萬剮(く１ㄢ ㄉㄠ ㄨㄢ ㄍㄨㄚˇ)
to hack someone to pieces

千島群島(く１ㄢ ㄉㄠˇ くㄩㄣˊ ㄉㄠˇ)
the Kuril Islands

千叮嚀萬囑咐(く１ㄢ ㄉｌㄥ ㄋｌㄥˊ ㄨㄢ ㄓㄨˋ ㄈㄨˋ)
to exhort or enjoin repeatedly

(said of a problem or task) very complicated or confused

千難萬難(く１ㄢ ㄋㄢˊ ㄨㄢ ㄋㄢˊ)
extremely difficult

千年(く１ㄢ ㄋｌㄢˊ)
a thousand years

千里(く１ㄢ ㄌｌˇ)
a thousand li—a long distance: 失之毫釐，差之千里。One false step will make a great difference.

千里馬(く１ㄢ ㄌｌˇ ㄇㄚˇ)
a horse with enormous speed and staying power; a winged steed

千里達一托貝哥(く１ㄢ ㄌｌˇ ㄉㄚˊ ｜ ㄊㄨㄛ ㄅㄟˋ ㄍㄜ)
Trinidad and Tobago, an independent republic in the West Indies

千里迢迢(く１ㄢ ㄌｌˇ ㄊｌㄠˊ ㄊｌㄠˊ)
thousands of li away—from afar

千里駒(く１ㄢ ㄌｌˇ ㄐㄩ)
①a horse with enormous speed and staying power ②(figuratively) a young talent

千里之堤，潰于蟻穴(く１ㄢ ㄌｌˇ ㄓ ㄉｌ ㄎㄨㄟˋ ㄩˊ ｜ˇ ㄒㄩㄝˋ)
One ant-hole may lead to the collapse of a thousand-li dike.—Slight negligence may result in great disaster.

千里之行，始於足下(く１ㄢ ㄌｌˇ ㄓ ㄒｌㄥˊ ㄕˇ ㄩˊ ㄗㄨˊ ㄒｌㄚˋ)
The journey of a thousand li starts with the first step.

千里送鵝毛(く１ㄢ ㄌｌˇ ㄙㄨㄥˋ ㄜˊ ㄇㄠˊ)
a small gift sent from afar with deep affection: 千里送鵝毛，禮輕情意重。The gift sent from afar may be light in itself, but it conveys deep affection.

千里眼(く１ㄢ ㄌｌˇ ｜ㄢˇ)
①farsightedness ②(mythology) name of a god whose eyesight that can reach the heaven ③another name for telescope or binoculars; field glasses

千慮一得(く１ㄢ ㄌㄩˋ ｜ ㄉㄜˊ)
One always gets something by thinking constantly. 愚者千慮，必有一得。Even a fool may sometimes have a good

idea.

千慮一失(く１ㄢ ㄌㄩˋ ｜ ㄕ)
Despite careful planning, there will be a slip here and there. 智者千慮，必有一失。Even a wise man sometimes makes a mistake.

千古(く１ㄢ ㄍㄨˇ)
①a long, long time; through all ages; for all time ②(used in mourning) in eternity

千古奇聞(く１ㄢ ㄍㄨˇ くｌˊ ㄨㄣˊ)
a fantastic story; a forever strange tale

千克(く１ㄢ ㄎㄜˋ)
kilogram (kg)

千赫(く１ㄢ ㄏㄜˋ)
kilohertz (kHz)

千迴百折(く１ㄢ ㄏㄨㄟˊ ㄅㄞˇ ㄓㄜˊ)or
千迴百轉(く１ㄢ ㄏㄨㄟˊ ㄅㄞˇ ㄓㄨㄢˇ)
(said of the plot of a novel or scenery of a resort) a thousand twists and a hundred turns; innumerable twists and turns

千家詩(く１ㄢ ㄐｌㄚ ㄕ)
a collection of poems of the Tang and Sung Dynasties first edited by Liu Kechuang (劉克莊) of the Sung Dynasty as an introduction to poetry, usually for youngsters

千嬌百媚(く１ㄢ ㄐｌㄠ ㄅㄞˇ ㄇㄟˋ)
the beauty of beauties; the pinnacle of beauty and charms

千斤頂(く１ㄢ ㄐｌㄣ ㄉｌㄥˇ)
a jack

千金(く１ㄢ ㄐｌㄣ)
①a courteous expression referring to another's daughter ②a thousand pieces of gold

千金小姐(く１ㄢ ㄐｌㄣ ㄒｌㄠˇ ㄐｌㄝˇ)
a young lady of a wealthy family

千金市骨(く１ㄢ ㄐｌㄣ ㄕˋ ㄍㄨˇ)
very eager and sincere in recruiting talented men

千金一笑(く１ㄢ ㄐｌㄣ ｜ ㄒｌㄠˋ)
A smile of a beautiful lady is worth a thousand taels of gold. 或 A beauty's smile is very valuable.

千金一擲(く１ㄢ ㄐｌㄣ ｜ ㄓˊ)
to spend money in a big

千部

way 亦作「一擲千金」

千鈞一髮 (ㄑㄧㄢ ㄐㄩㄣ ㄧ ㄈㄚˇ)
A thing which weighs one thousand *chiun* (鈞) hangs on a hair.—extremely delicate situation; very precarious (One *chiun* equals to 30 catties.) 亦作「一髮千鈞」

千軍萬馬 (ㄑㄧㄢ ㄐㄩㄣ ㄨㄢˋ ㄇㄚˇ)
a large number of mounted and foot soldiers; a large military force; a powerful, a mighty force

千奇百怪 (ㄑㄧㄢ ㄑㄧˊ ㄅㄞˇ ㄍㄨㄞˋ)
numerous strange forms; grotesque or weird shapes

千秋 (ㄑㄧㄢ ㄑㄧㄡ)
①a thousand years; centuries ②(polite expression) a kind of birthday congratulations (other than one's own)

千秋萬歲 (ㄑㄧㄢ ㄑㄧㄡ ㄨㄢˋ ㄙㄨㄟˋ)
a long, long time; throughout the ages

千辛萬苦 (ㄑㄧㄢ ㄒㄧㄣ ㄨㄢˋ ㄎㄨˇ)
to suffer or undergo all conceivable hardships (to accomplish something)

千真萬確 (ㄑㄧㄢ ㄓㄣ ㄨㄢˋ ㄑㄩㄝˋ)
very real; absolutely true

千差別 (ㄑㄧㄢ ㄔㄚ ㄨㄢˋ ㄅㄧㄝˊ)
to be very different

千錘百鍊 (ㄑㄧㄢ ㄔㄨㄟˊ ㄅㄞˇ ㄌㄧㄢˋ)
①(to undergo) severe training and hammering; stringent coaching; to be thoroughly tempered ②(to write) with the utmost care —with countless changes and corrections; to be revised and rewritten many times

千山萬水 (ㄑㄧㄢ ㄕㄢ ㄨㄢˋ ㄕㄨㄟˇ)
a thousand mountains and rivers—(places, etc.); (a journey from) afar; a long and arduous journey

千日紅 (ㄑㄧㄢ ㄖˋ ㄏㄨㄥˊ)
Gomphrena globosa (a small plant which blossoms in fall with spheric flowers of red, purple and white); globe amaranth

千字文 (ㄑㄧㄢ ㄗˋ ㄨㄣˊ)
The Thousand-Character Classic, a primer for children authored by Chou Hsing-

szu (周興嗣) of the Liang Dynasty

千載一時 (ㄑㄧㄢ ㄗㄞˇ ㄧ ㄕˊ)or 千載難逢 (ㄑㄧㄢ ㄗㄞˇ ㄋㄢˊ ㄈㄥˊ)
once in a thousand years —once in a lifetime; a very rare chance; a golden chance

千絲萬縷 (ㄑㄧㄢ ㄙ ㄨㄢˋ ㄌㄩˇ)
①(usually said of the heart of a person in love) a million thoughts — a heart crammed with thoughts and remembrance ② many ramifications—very complicated

千思萬想 (ㄑㄧㄢ ㄙ ㄨㄢˋ ㄒㄧㄤˇ)
a million thoughts—to think over and over again

千歲 (ㄑㄧㄢ ㄙㄨㄟˋ)
①a thousand years ② Your (His or Her) Highness (when referring to the prince, the princess, the queen, the emperor's brother, etc.)

千恩萬謝 (ㄑㄧㄢ ㄣ ㄨㄢˋ ㄒㄧㄝˋ)
a thousand thanks—many thanks

千億 (ㄑㄧㄢ ㄧˋ)
(literally) 100,000,000,000 (one hundred thousand million)—myriads

千言萬語 (ㄑㄧㄢ ㄧㄢˊ ㄨㄢˋ ㄩˇ)
many, many words in one's heart (but one doesn't know where to begin)

千瓦 (ㄑㄧㄢ ㄨㄚˇ)
a kilowatt (kW)

千萬 (ㄑㄧㄢ ㄨㄢˋ)
①a huge amount ②an expression used to emphasize an injunction or advice: 千萬要記得。Please do remember.

二畫

【升】 476
ㄕㄥ   sheng shēng
1. to rise; to raise; to ascend
2. to advance; to promote
3. a unit of volume measurement (especially for grain)
4. a Chinese family name

升班 (ㄕㄥ ㄅㄢ)
(school) to be promoted; to advance to a higher grade

升平 or 昇平 (ㄕㄥ ㄆㄧㄥˊ)

peace and prosperity

升斗小民 (ㄕㄥ ㄉㄡˇ ㄒㄧㄠˇ ㄇㄧㄣˊ)
those who live from hand to mouth

升等考試 (ㄕㄥ ㄉㄥˇ ㄎㄠˇ ㄕˋ)
an examination held to test government employees to determine whether they are qualified for promotion

升堂 (ㄕㄥ ㄊㄤˊ)
①to appear in court to conduct a trial ②to ascend to the hall

升堂入室 (ㄕㄥ ㄊㄤˊ ㄖㄨˋ ㄕˋ)
(said of scholastic pursuit) to attain mastery

升騰 (ㄕㄥ ㄊㄥˊ)
①(ㄕㄥ ㄊㄥˊ) to fly up; to leap up; to rise: 熱氣升騰。The hot vapor leapt up.
②(ㄕㄥ ·ㄊㄥ) to make good progress; to flourish in business

升天 (ㄕㄥ ㄊㄧㄢ)
①to ascend to heaven—to die ②(Christianity) the Ascension

升格 (ㄕㄥ ㄍㄜˊ)
to promote; to upgrade; to elevate

升官發財 (ㄕㄥ ㄍㄨㄢ ㄈㄚ ㄘㄞˊ)
to attain high ranks and acquire great wealth; to be successful in both politics and business

升火待發 (ㄕㄥ ㄏㄨㄛˇ ㄉㄞˋ ㄈㄚ)
(said of steamers, trains, etc.) ready to start the journey

升級 (ㄕㄥ ㄐㄧˊ)
①(said of an official) to be promoted: 他升級為上校。He was promoted to the rank of colonel. ②(school) to advance to a higher grade

升降 (ㄕㄥ ㄐㄧㄤˋ)
to hoist and lower; to rise and fall

升降機 (ㄕㄥ ㄐㄧㄤˋ ㄐㄧ)
an elevator; a lift

升旗 (ㄕㄥ ㄑㄧˊ)
to hoist a flag

升遷 (ㄕㄥ ㄑㄧㄢ)
to get transferred to a higher position; promotion

升學 (ㄕㄥ ㄒㄩㄝˊ)
to enter a higher school; to

advance to a higher school

升學率 (アㄥ ㄒㄩㄝ ㄌㄩˋ)
the proportion of students entering schools of a higher grade

升學考試 (アㄥ ㄒㄩㄝ ㄎㄠˇ ㄕˋ)
an entrance examination for a higher school

升學主義 (アㄥ ㄒㄩㄝ ㄓㄨˇ ㄧˋ)
the attitude of thinking nothing but entering a higher school, paying no attention to the real purpose of education

升值 (アㄥ ㄓˊ)
(economics) ① to revalue ② to appreciate

升沉 (アㄥ ㄔㄣˊ)
the rise and fall of a public official

【午】 XˇV wuu wǔ
1. noon; high noon
2. (in old Chinese time measurement) 11 a.m. to 1 p.m.
3. the seventh of the Twelve Terrestrial Branches (地支)
4. a Chinese family name

午砲 (Xˇ ㄆㄠˋ)
the gun fired at noon

午飯 (Xˇ ㄈㄢˋ)
lunch; a midday meal

午後 (Xˇ ㄏㄡˋ)
afternoon

午前 (Xˇ ㄑㄧㄢˊ)
before noon; the forenoon

午休 (Xˇ ㄒㄧㄡ)
a noon break; a noontime rest; lunch hour

午時 (Xˇ ㄕˊ) or 午牌 (Xˇ ㄆㄞˊ)
the period of the day from 11 a.m. to 1 p.m.

午睡 (Xˇ ㄕㄨㄟˋ)
an afternoon nap; a siesta; to take a nap after lunch

午日 (Xˇ ㄖˋ)
the fifth day of the fifth moon; the Dragon Boat Festival

午夜 (Xˇ ㄧㄝˋ)
midnight

午月 (Xˇ ㄩㄝˋ)
the fifth moon of the lunar calendar

【卅】 ㄙㄚˋ sah sà　478
thirty; 30th (of a month)

三畫

【半】 ㄅㄢˋ bann bàn　479
1. half: 一天半 one and a half days 半小時 half an hour; a half hour
2. very little
3. in the middle
4. partly; about half: 大門半開著。 The gate was left half open.

半百 (ㄅㄢˋ ㄅㄞˇ)
fifty; half a hundred: 王先生年近半百。 Mr. Wang's getting on for fifty.

半輩子 (ㄅㄢˋ ㄅㄟˋ ˙ㄗ)
half a lifetime

半壁江山 (ㄅㄢˋ ㄅㄧˋ ㄐㄧㄤ ㄕㄢ)
half of the national territory

半邊 (ㄅㄢˋ ㄅㄧㄢ)
half of something; one side of something

半票 (ㄅㄢˋ ㄆㄧㄠˋ)
a half-fare ticket; a half-price ticket

半瓶醋 (ㄅㄢˋ ㄆㄧㄥˊ ㄘㄨˋ)
(literally) a half bottle of vinegar—a half-educated person; a shallow person

半賣半送 (ㄅㄢˋ ㄇㄞˋ ㄅㄢˋ ㄙㄨㄥˋ)
(used by shop owners as a sales gimmick) to sell goods at rock-bottom prices

半明半暗 (ㄅㄢˋ ㄇㄧㄥˊ ㄅㄢˋ ㄢˋ)
half-bright and half-shadowy; not very bright

半明不滅 (ㄅㄢˋ ㄇㄧㄥˊ ㄅㄨˋ ㄇㄧㄝˋ)
(said of lamps, candlelight, etc.) not very bright

半打 (ㄅㄢˋ ㄉㄚˇ)
half a dozen; six

半島 (ㄅㄢˋ ㄉㄠˇ)
a peninsula

半導體 (ㄅㄢˋ ㄉㄠˇ ㄊㄧˇ)
a semiconductor

半道兒 (ㄅㄢˋ ㄉㄠˋ ㄦˊ)
midway; halfway

半吊子 (ㄅㄢˋ ㄉㄧㄠˋ ˙ㄗ)
① a shallow person; a jack of all trades; a dabbler; a smatterer ② a rash person

半點 (ㄅㄢˋ ㄉㄧㄢˇ)
the least bit: 職責所在半點也不能輕忽。 One should never neglect his own duty.

半透明體 (ㄅㄢˋ ㄊㄡˋ ㄇㄧㄥˊ ㄊㄧˇ)
a translucent or subtransparent body

半天 (ㄅㄢˋ ㄊㄧㄢ)
① midair; in the air ② half-day; half a day ③ quite a while; a long time: 他已經等了半天。 He has already waited for a long time.

半天空 (ㄅㄢˋ ㄊㄧㄢ ㄎㄨㄥ)
half of the sky; (in) midair

半途 (ㄅㄢˋ ㄊㄨˊ)
halfway; midway: 他們半途拆伙了。 They parted company halfway.

半途而廢 (ㄅㄢˋ ㄊㄨˊ ㄦˊ ㄈㄟˋ)
to stop (a task) halfway; to give up halfway; to leave something unfinished

半推半就 (ㄅㄢˋ ㄊㄨㄟ ㄅㄢˋ ㄐㄧㄡˋ)
to be half willing (at heart) and half unwilling (in appearance)—to yield with a show of reluctance, often referring to price haggling or girls being seduced

半吞半吐 (ㄅㄢˋ ㄊㄨㄣ ㄅㄢˋ ㄊㄨˇ)
to hum and haw

半通不通 (ㄅㄢˋ ㄊㄨㄥ ㄅㄨˋ ㄊㄨㄥ)
to know or understand a little

半路 (ㄅㄢˋ ㄌㄨˋ)
halfway; midway; on the way: 我們走到半路，天就下雨了。 We had got only halfway when it began to rain.

半路出家 (ㄅㄢˋ ㄌㄨˋ ㄔㄨ ㄐㄧㄚ)
to switch to a new profession one knows little about; to change one's profession when one is no longer young; to start midway

半官方 (ㄅㄢˋ ㄍㄨㄢ ㄈㄤ)
semi-official: 據半官方人士表示物價將會上漲。 According to semi-official sources, prices will go up.

半工半讀 (ㄅㄢˋ ㄍㄨㄥ ㄅㄢˋ ㄉㄨˊ)
part work, and part study; to work while studying at school

半公開 (ㄅㄢˋ ㄍㄨㄥ ㄎㄞ)
semi-overt; more or less open

半開化 (ㄅㄢˋ ㄎㄞ ㄏㄨㄚˋ)
semi-civilized (people)

半開眼兒 (ㄅㄢˋ ㄎㄞ ㄧㄢˇ ㄦˊ)

pseudo-professional

半空中(ㄅㄢ ㄎㄨㄥ ㄓㄨㄥ)
in midair; in the air: 飛機在
半空中互撞了。The airplanes
collided in midair.

半飢半飽(ㄅㄢ ㄐㄧ ㄅㄢ ㄅㄠˇ)
underfed

半價(ㄅㄢ ㄐㄧㄚˋ)
half-price; 50 per cent discount

半截(ㄅㄢ ㄐㄧㄝˊ)or 半截兒
(ㄅㄢ ㄐㄧㄝˊ)
half of a body; a half part;
half (a section): 他把話只說
了半截兒。He finished only
half of what he wanted to
say.

半斤八兩(ㄅㄢ ㄐㄧㄣ ㄅㄚ ㄌㄧㄤˇ)
six of one and half a dozen
of the other; tweedledum
and tweedledee

半徑(ㄅㄢ ㄐㄧㄥˋ)
a radius

半旗(ㄅㄢ ㄑㄧˊ)
half-mast: 國王下葬之日，一律
下半旗。Flags were at half-
mast on the day of the
king's funeral.

半球(ㄅㄢ ㄑㄧㄡˊ)
a hemisphere

半仙(ㄅㄢ ㄒㄧㄢ)
half an immortal—fortune-
tellers or medical quacks
(who claim the ability to
work wonders as immortals
are supposed to)

半新不舊(ㄅㄢ ㄒㄧㄣ ㄅㄨˋ ㄐㄧㄡˋ)
①half new; used (articles)
②neither modern nor obso-
lete

半信半疑(ㄅㄢ ㄒㄧㄣˋ ㄅㄢ ㄧˊ)
between believing and suspicion; half-believing and
half-doubting; not quite
convinced: 我對他所說的話半
信半疑。I was not quite
convinced of his words.

半醒半睡(ㄅㄢ ㄒㄧㄥˇ ㄅㄢ ㄕㄨㄟˋ)
half awake and half asleep;
slumberous

半殖民地(ㄅㄢ ㄓˊ ㄇㄧㄣˊ ㄉㄧˋ)
a country nominally in-
dependent (whose sover-
eignty is often infringed
upon by a great power or
powers); a semi-colony

半真半假(ㄅㄢ ㄓㄣ ㄅㄢ ㄐㄧㄚˇ)

partly true, partly false: 半
真半假的話不見得比說謊好。A
half truth is often no better
than a lie.

半中腰(ㄅㄢ ㄓㄨㄥ ㄧㄠ)or 半中間
(ㄅㄢ ㄓㄨㄥ ㄐㄧㄢ)
(colloquial) middle; halfway; midway: 她的講演講到
半中間就突然間斷了。She
broke off in the middle of
her speech.

半嗔半喜(ㄅㄢ ㄔㄣ ㄅㄢ ㄒㄧˇ)
half-annoyed, half-pleased

半場(ㄅㄢ ㄔㄤˇ)
①a half of a game or con-
test ②half-court

半場緊迫釘人(ㄅㄢ ㄔㄤˇ ㄐㄧㄣˇ
ㄆㄛˋ ㄉㄧㄥ ㄖㄣˊ)
(basketball) half-court press

半成品(ㄅㄢ ㄔㄥˊ ㄆㄧㄣˇ)
semifinished products or
articles; half-finished products or goods

半世(ㄅㄢ ㄕˋ)
half of a person's life span;
(at) middle age

半身不遂(ㄅㄢ ㄕㄣ ㄅㄨˋ ㄙㄨㄟˊ)
hemiplegia—paralysis of
half of one's body; half
paralyzed

半身像(ㄅㄢ ㄕㄣ ㄒㄧㄤˋ)
①a half-length photo or
portrait ②a bust

半晌(ㄅㄢ ㄕㄤˇ)
(for) quite some time; a
long time

半生(ㄅㄢ ㄕㄥ)
①half of one's life span ②
half-baked; half-raw; not
well cooked

半生不熟(ㄅㄢ ㄕㄥ ㄅㄨˋ ㄕㄡˊ)
①half-raw; half-cooked; not
well cooked ②casual ac-
quaintance

半數(ㄅㄢ ㄕㄨˋ)
half the number; half

半日(ㄅㄢ ㄖˋ)
①half a day ②half-day

半子(ㄅㄢ ㄗˇ)
a son-in-law

半自動(ㄅㄢ ㄗˋ ㄉㄨㄥˋ)
semiautomatic

半死不活(ㄅㄢ ㄙˇ ㄅㄨˋ ㄏㄨㄛˊ)
①dying; on the verge of
death ②listless; lethargic ③
half dead; more dead than
alive

半夜(ㄅㄢ ㄧㄝˋ)
①half a night ②midnight:
他工作到半夜。He worked
until midnight.

半夜三更(ㄅㄢ ㄧㄝˋ ㄙㄢ ㄍㄥ)
in the depth of night; late at
night

半音階(ㄅㄢ ㄧㄣ ㄐㄧㄝ)
the chromatic scale (in
music)

半月刊(ㄅㄢ ㄩㄝˋ ㄎㄢ)
a semimonthly; a fortnightly

半圓(ㄅㄢ ㄩㄢˊ)
a semicircle

【卌】ㄒㄧˋ shih xì
forty; fortieth

四畫

【卉】481
(ㄏㄨㄟˋ) ㄏㄨㄟˋ huèy huì
1. a general term for grasses:
這些是奇花異卉。These are
rare flowers and grasses.
2. myriads of

六畫

【卑】482
ㄅㄟ bei bēi
1. low
2. debased; depraved; vile
3. inferior
4. a modest expression referring to oneself 參看「卑職」

卑薄(ㄅㄟ ㄅㄛˊ)
(said of land)poor and barren

卑鄙(ㄅㄟ ㄅㄧˇ)
①(said of a person's character) mean; depraved; crooked; base ②(said of a per-
son's social position) low;
inferior

卑鄙手段(ㄅㄟ ㄅㄧˇ ㄕㄡˇ ㄉㄨㄢˋ)
dirty tricks

卑不足道(ㄅㄟ ㄅㄨˋ ㄗㄨˊ ㄉㄠˋ)or 卑
卑不足道(ㄅㄟ ㄅㄟ ㄅㄨˋ ㄗㄨˊ ㄉㄠˋ)
too inferior (or contemptible) to be worth mentioning; too insignificant to be
worth mentioning

卑陋(ㄅㄟ ㄌㄡˋ)
low; crude; vulgar; inferior

卑劣(ㄅㄟ ㄌㄧㄝˋ)
mean; depraved

卑躬屈節 (ㄅㄟ ㄍㄨㄥ ㄑㄩ ㄐㄧㄝ) or 卑躬曲膝 (ㄅㄟ ㄍㄨㄥ ㄑㄩ ㄒㄧ)
obsequious; servile; fawning; to humiliate oneself in serving master

卑賤 (ㄅㄟ ㄐㄧㄢ)
low; inferior; mean; humble; 他出身卑賤 He is a man of mean birth.

卑親屬 (ㄅㄟ ㄑㄧㄣ ㄕㄨ)
relatives who are junior to oneself either in age or in generation

卑怯 (ㄅㄟ ㄑㄧㄝ)
mean and cowardly 參看「卑躬屈膝」

卑下 (ㄅㄟ ㄒㄧㄚ)
base; mean; humble

卑職 (ㄅㄟ ㄓ)
①(self-reference) your humble servant ②a low or humble position

卑濕 (ㄅㄟ ㄕ)
dampness of low-lying land

卑讓 (ㄅㄟ ㄖㄤ)
to defer; to yield with courtesy or respect

卑辭厚禮 (ㄅㄟ ㄘ ㄏㄡ ㄌㄧ)
sweet words and lavish gifts; humble words and generous (or handsome) gifts

卑污 (ㄅㄟ ㄨ)
despicable and filthy

卑微 (ㄅㄟ ㄨㄟ)
lowly; humble: 他出身卑微。He is a man of humble birth.

【卒】 483 1. ㄗㄨ tzwu zú
1. a servant; an underling; a lackey
2. a soldier: 士卒 soldiers
3. a unit of one hundred soldiers
4. at last; after all; at long last: 我卒償素願。I had my wishes fulfilled at long last.
5. to complete; to finish: 卒其事 to finish one's job
6. dead; to die
7. a community of 300 families
8. a pawn in Chinese chess

卒子 (ㄗㄨ ㄗ)
①a soldier; a private ②a pawn

卒業 (ㄗㄨ ㄧㄝ)
to graduate; to complete

study (at an institution, etc.); to finish a course of study

【卒】 483 2. ㄘㄨ tsuh cù
suddenly; abruptly; hurriedly

卒乍 (ㄘㄨ ㄓㄚ)
suddenly; unexpectedly

卒然 (ㄘㄨ ㄖㄢ)
hurriedly

【卓】 484 ㄓㄨㄛ jwo zhuó
1. lofty; high
2. brilliant; eminent
3. (to stand) upright; erect
4. a Chinese family name

卓立 (ㄓㄨㄛ ㄌㄧ)
to stand alone; to stand out; to stand upright

卓犖 or 卓躒 (ㄓㄨㄛ ㄌㄨㄛ)
excellent; unsurpassed; eminent

卓見 (ㄓㄨㄛ ㄐㄧㄢ)
a brilliant idea or view; an excellent or distinguished opinion 亦作「卓見」

卓絕 (ㄓㄨㄛ ㄐㄩㄝ)
①outstanding; eminent; peerless; prominent; brilliant; unsurpassed ②extreme: 艱苦卓絕 extreme hardships and difficulties

卓絕千古 (ㄓㄨㄛ ㄐㄩㄝ ㄑㄧㄢ ㄍㄨ)
unmatched past or present

卓著 (ㄓㄨㄛ ㄓㄨ)
prominent; eminent; distinguished; outstanding; well-known

卓卓 (ㄓㄨㄛ ㄓㄨㄛ)
outstanding; distinguished

卓識 (ㄓㄨㄛ ㄕ)
brilliant ideas or views; superior insight or judgment

卓然 (ㄓㄨㄛ ㄖㄢ)
outstanding; distinguished; eminent

卓裁 (ㄓㄨㄛ ㄘㄞ)
(your) esteemed decision; brilliant decision (often used in correspondence)

卓爾 (ㄓㄨㄛ ㄦ)
outstanding; eminent

卓異 (ㄓㄨㄛ ㄧ)
outstanding; towering

卓有成效 (ㄓㄨㄛ ㄧㄡ ㄔㄥ ㄒㄧㄠ)
fruitful; highly effective

卓文君 (ㄓㄨㄛ ㄨㄣ ㄐㄩㄣ)
Cho Wen-chün, a famous

widow who eloped with Ssu-Ma Hsiang-ju (司馬相如) of the Han Dynasty (The elopement has been one of the most celebrated romances among the Chinese literati.)

卓越 (ㄓㄨㄛ ㄩㄝ)
excellent; remarkable; outstanding; foremost; brilliant: 楊先生是位卓越的科學家, Mr. Yang is an outstanding scientist.

【協】 485 ㄒㄧㄝ shye xié
1. to agree; an agreement
2. to be united; to bring into harmony; to coordinate
3. to assist; to aid; to help

協防 (ㄒㄧㄝ ㄈㄤ)
to help defend (a place)

協定 (ㄒㄧㄝ ㄉㄧㄥ)
an agreement (usually between nations)

協調 (ㄒㄧㄝ ㄊㄧㄠ)
to coordinate; coordination; harmony; to bring to harmony; to adjust; to bring about full coordination

協同 (ㄒㄧㄝ ㄊㄨㄥ)
to work in coordination with; to cooperate with; to work with (others); to join others in (accomplishing an undertaking, etc.)

協理 (ㄒㄧㄝ ㄌㄧ)
①an official rank in the Ching Dynasty ②an assistant manager

協力 (ㄒㄧㄝ ㄌㄧ)
to work in concert; to exert together; in cooperation with: 我們和他協力工作。We worked in cooperation with him.

協和 (ㄒㄧㄝ ㄏㄜ)
harmony; to harmonize

協和醫學院 (ㄒㄧㄝ ㄏㄜ ㄧ ㄒㄩㄝ ㄩㄢ)
the Union Medical College in Peking (簡稱 PUMC)

協會 (ㄒㄧㄝ ㄏㄨㄟ)
an association; a society

協助 (ㄒㄧㄝ ㄓㄨ)
to assist; to help mutually

協商 (ㄒㄧㄝ ㄕㄤ)
to negotiate; to discuss; to consult with each other: 我與他們協商此事。I consulted

十部

with them about the matter.

協奏曲(ㄒㄧㄝˋ ㄗㄡˋ ㄑㄩˇ)
(music) a concerto

協議(ㄒㄧㄝˋ ㄧˋ)
①an agreement; a draft agreement ②to discuss; to negotiate

協約(ㄒㄧㄝˋ ㄩㄝ)
an alliance; an agreement

協約國(ㄒㄧㄝˋ ㄩㄝ ㄍㄨㄛˊ)
the Allies (during World War I)

協韻(ㄒㄧㄝˋ ㄩㄣˋ)
to have the same rhyme

十部

七畫

【南】 486
1. ㄋㄚ nā
參看「南無」、「南無阿彌陀佛」

南無(ㄋㄚˊ ㄇㄛˊ)
(Sanskrit) Namo, to be converted to (the Buddha, the dharma or the sangha)

南無阿彌陀佛(ㄋㄚˊ ㄇㄛˊ ㄜ ㄇㄧˊ ㄊㄨㄛˊ ㄈㄛˊ)
(Buddhism) Namo Amitabha (Homage to Amitabha Buddha.)

【南】 486
2. ㄋㄢˊ nán
1. south; southward: 暖和的風從南方吹來。A warm wind was blowing from the south.
2. a type of ancient music played in the south of China
3. a Chinese family name

南北(ㄋㄢˊ ㄅㄟˇ)
①north and south ②from north to south ③(in ancient China) a man

南北貨(ㄋㄢˊ ㄅㄟˇ ㄏㄨㄛˋ)
sundry goods

南北戰爭(ㄋㄢˊ ㄅㄟˇ ㄓㄢˋ ㄓㄥ)
the American Civil War of 1861-65

南北朝(ㄋㄢˊ ㄅㄟˇ ㄔㄠˊ)
(literally) the South and North Dynasties—after the Eastern Tsin, China was divided into the Han-ruled south and the barbarian north (420-589 A.D.)

南北史(ㄋㄢˊ ㄅㄟˇ ㄕˇ)
the history of the South and North Dynasties

南半球(ㄋㄢˊ ㄅㄢˋ ㄑㄧㄡˊ)
the Southern Hemisphere

南邊(ㄋㄢˊ ㄅㄧㄢ)or 南邊兒(ㄋㄢˊ ㄅㄧㄚˉㄦ)
①the south; the southern side ②the southern provinces of China

南冰洋(ㄋㄢˊ ㄅㄧㄥ ㄧㄤˊ)
the Antarctic Ocean

南部(ㄋㄢˊ ㄅㄨˋ)
southern part; south: 高雄在台灣的南部。Kaohsiung is in the south of Taiwan.

南美洲(ㄋㄢˊ ㄇㄟˇ ㄓㄡ)
South America; Latin America 亦作「拉丁美洲」

南蠻鴃舌(ㄋㄢˊ ㄇㄢˊ ㄐㄩㄝˊ ㄕㄜˊ)
(originally) a sarcastic remark by Mencius about Hsü Hsing (許行), a southerner who spoke a tongue different from others'—a strange language

南面(ㄋㄢˊ ㄇㄧㄢˋ)
①the south 亦作「南面兒」 ②the throne facing south—the monarch

南非(ㄋㄢˊ ㄈㄟ)
South Africa

南非共和國(ㄋㄢˊ ㄈㄟ ㄍㄨㄥˋ ㄏㄜˊ ㄍㄨㄛˊ)
the Republic of South Africa

南方(ㄋㄢˊ ㄈㄤ)
the south; the South: 他住在南方。He lives in the South.

南方大港(ㄋㄢˊ ㄈㄤ ㄉㄚˋ ㄍㄤˇ)
the biggest south China port which Dr. Sun Yat-sen proposed to build at Whampoa near Canton

南方話(ㄋㄢˊ ㄈㄤ ㄏㄨㄚˋ)
the southern dialect

南方人(ㄋㄢˊ ㄈㄤ ㄖㄣˊ)
a southerner

南風(ㄋㄢˊ ㄈㄥ)
①the wind blowing from the south ②a form of ancient Chinese musical composition

南達科他(ㄋㄢˊ ㄉㄚˊ ㄎㄜ ㄊㄚ)
South Dakota, U.S.A.

南丁格爾(ㄋㄢˊ ㄉㄧㄥ ㄍㄜˊ ㄦˇ)
Florence Nightingale, 1820-1910, the founder of modern nursing

南唐(ㄋㄢˊ ㄊㄤˊ)
one of the ten states during the Five Dynasties (lasting from 937 to 975 A.D., and

occupying parts of today's Kiangsu, Anhwei, Fukien and Kiangsi Provinces

南來北往(ㄋㄢˊ ㄌㄞˊ ㄅㄟˇ ㄨㄤˇ)
①(people) going south and north—descriptive of heavy traffic, a busy place or a hub of communication ②to hurry along here and there to be always on the move

南瓜(ㄋㄢˊ ㄍㄨㄚ)
a pumpkin; a cushaw

南國(ㄋㄢˊ ㄍㄨㄛˊ)
the southern part of the country; the South

南卡羅來納州(ㄋㄢˊ ㄎㄚˇ ㄌㄨㄛˊ ㄌㄞˊ ㄋㄚˋ ㄓㄡ)
South Carolina, U.S.A.

南柯一夢(ㄋㄢˊ ㄎㄜ ㄧ ㄇㄥˋ)
a dream; dreaming; an empty dream (originally, the dream of a person who thought he was made governor of Nanko, a place which did not exist)

南開大學(ㄋㄢˊ ㄎㄞ ㄉㄚˋ ㄒㄩㄝˊ)
The Nankai University at Tientsin

南海(ㄋㄢˊ ㄏㄞˇ)
①name of a county in Kwangtung Province ②the South China Sea, stretching from the Taiwan Straits to Kwangtung ③(in ancient China) a term for faraway places in the south

南寒帶(ㄋㄢˊ ㄏㄢˊ ㄉㄞˋ)
the Antarctic Zone; the South Frigid Zone

南胡(ㄋㄢˊ ㄏㄨˊ)
the two-stringed Chinese viola 亦作「二胡」

南貨(ㄋㄢˊ ㄏㄨㄛˋ)
①delicacies or products from south China (such as dried bamboo shoots, etc.) ②any native product, foodstuff, ham, etc.

南回歸線(ㄋㄢˊ ㄏㄨㄟˊ ㄍㄨㄟ ㄒㄧㄢˋ)
the Tropic of Capricorn

南箕北斗(ㄋㄢˊ ㄐㄧ ㄅㄟˇ ㄉㄡˇ)
something which enjoys an empty name but serves no practical purposes

南極(ㄋㄢˊ ㄐㄧˊ)
the South Pole; the Antarctic Pole

南極光(ㄋㄢ ㄐㄧˊ《ㄨㄤ)
the aurora australis; the southern lights

南極圈(ㄋㄢ ㄐㄧˊ ㄑㄩㄢ)
the Antarctic Circle

南極洲(ㄋㄢ ㄐㄧˊ ㄓㄡ)
Antarctica; the Antarctic Continent

南京(ㄋㄢ ㄐㄧㄥ)
Nanking, capital of the Republic of China

南軍(ㄋㄢ ㄐㄩㄣ)
the Confederate soldiers, or the Confederate troops (in the American Civil War)

南腔北調(ㄋㄢ ㄑㄧㄤ ㄅㄟˇ ㄉㄧㄠˋ)
a tongue which combines accents of the various spoken dialects in China—to speak with a mixed accent

南曲(ㄋㄢ ㄑㄩˇ)
one of the two forms of operas in the Yüan Dynasty

南下(ㄋㄢ ㄒㄧㄚˋ)
to go down south

南針(ㄋㄢ ㄓㄣ)
① a compass ② a guide or guidance

南征北戰(ㄋㄢ ㄓㄥ ㄅㄟˇ ㄓㄢˋ)
to fight up and down the country; to participate in battles everywhere; to fight north and south on many fronts

南朝(ㄋㄢ ㄔㄠˊ)
the Southern Dynasties during the South and North Dynasties (420-589 A.D.), the Sung Dynasty (宋), the Chi Dynasty (齊), the Liang Dynasty (梁), the Chen Dynasty (陳)

南昌(ㄋㄢ ㄔㄤ)
Nanchang, capital of Kiangsi Province

南沙群島(ㄋㄢ ㄕㄚ ㄑㄩㄣˊ ㄉㄠˇ)
Nansha Chuntao; the Spratly Islands

南山(ㄋㄢ ㄕㄢ)
① the Chung-Nan Mountain ② the Chilien Mountain ③ name of a county in Fukien Province

南山壽(ㄋㄢ ㄕㄢ ㄕㄡˋ)
(literally) as long-lived as Nan Mountain— many, many happy returns of the day

亦作「壽比南山」

南人(ㄋㄢ ㄖㄣˊ)
southerners

南斯拉夫(ㄋㄢ ㄙ ㄌㄚ ㄈㄨ)
Yugoslavia

南宋(ㄋㄢ ㄙㄨㄥˋ)
the domain of the Sung Dynasty after Emperor Kao Tzung (高宗) withdrew to the south of the Yangtze (1127-1279)

南亞(ㄋㄢ ㄧㄚˇ)
South Asia

南洋(ㄋㄢ ㄧㄤˊ)
① the area which covers Southeast Asia and Indonesia ② the Chinese coastal region south of Shantung ③ the South Seas

南緯(ㄋㄢ ㄨㄟˇ)
latitudes south of the equator

南溫帶(ㄋㄢ ㄨㄣ ㄉㄞˋ)
the South Temperate Zone

南嶽(ㄋㄢ ㄩㄝˋ)
another name for the Heng Mountain (衡山) in Hunan Province, one of the Five Sacred Mountains

南轅北轍(ㄋㄢ ㄩㄢˊ ㄅㄟˇ ㄔㄜˋ)
to try to go south by driving the chariot north—to act in a way that defeats one's purpose; practice diametrically opposed to preaching; to be diametrically opposite

十畫

【博】 487
ㄅㄛˊ bor bó

1. wide; extensive
2. abundant; ample; rich
3. broadly knowledgeable; well-read; learned; erudite
4. to barter for; to exchange
5. to gamble; to play games
6. to win; to gain
7. a Chinese family name

博大精深(ㄅㄛˊ ㄉㄚˋ ㄐㄧㄥ ㄕㄣ)
broad and profound; extensive and profound (knowledge, study, etc.)

博得(ㄅㄛˊ ㄉㄜˊ)or 博取(ㄅㄛˊ ㄑㄩˇ)
to win; to obtain

博徒(ㄅㄛˊ ㄊㄨˊ)
a gambler

博通(ㄅㄛˊ ㄊㄨㄥ)or 博達(ㄅㄛˊ ㄉㄚˊ)
having a broad knowledge of; to possess extensive knowledge of; to be erudite

博覽(ㄅㄛˊ ㄌㄢˇ)
to read extensively; to be well-read

博覽會(ㄅㄛˊ ㄌㄢˇ ㄏㄨㄟˋ)
a trade fair; an exhibition or exposition

博古通今(ㄅㄛˊ 《ㄨˇ ㄊㄨㄥ ㄐㄧㄣ)
to be acquainted with things ancient and modern; to be well-informed in things past and present; to be well-versed in (or conversant with) ancient and modern learning—erudite and informed

博貫(ㄅㄛˊ 《ㄨㄢˋ)
to have profound and transcending knowledge of; erudite

博局(ㄅㄛˊ ㄐㄩˊ)
① a gambling session ② a gambling place

博學(ㄅㄛˊ ㄒㄩㄝˊ)
well-read; erudite; well-versed in a wide range of studies or learning; excessively study: 他是位博學的學者。 He is a well-read scholar.

博學鴻儒(ㄅㄛˊ ㄒㄩㄝˊ ㄏㄨㄥˊ ㄖㄨˊ)
a rank for great scholars in the reign of Emperor Kang Hsi (康熙)

博施濟眾(ㄅㄛˊ ㄕ ㄐㄧˋ ㄓㄨㄥˋ)
to provide liberal relief to the masses; to relieve the people with liberal aid (especially material); to be interested in charities

博士(ㄅㄛˊ ㄕˋ)
① a doctorate; a doctoral degree ② an official rank, initiated in the Chin Dynasty and conferred upon scholars of profound learning

博斯普魯斯海峽(ㄅㄛˊ ㄙ ㄆㄨˇ ㄌㄨ ㄙ ㄏㄞˇ ㄒㄧㄚˊ)
the Bosporus Strait

博愛(ㄅㄛˊ ㄞˋ)
indiscriminate love; fraternity; universal love; love for all

博弈(ㄅㄛˊ ㄧˋ)
playing a game of "go"

chess

博雅(ㄅㄛˊ ㄧㄚˇ)
①learned and accomplished; well-informed and refined ② erudition

博雅之士(ㄅㄛˊ ㄧㄚˇ ㄓ ㄕˋ)
a scholar of a profound knowledge

博物(ㄅㄛˊ ㄨˋ)
①broadly knowledgeable; well-read ② natural sciences; nature studies

博物館(ㄅㄛˊ ㄨˋ ㄍㄨㄢˇ)or 博物院
(ㄅㄛˊ ㄨˋ ㄩㄢˋ)
a museum

博物學(ㄅㄛˊ ㄨˋ ㄒㄩㄝˊ)
natural history

博聞強記(ㄅㄛˊ ㄨㄣˊ ㄑㄧㄤˊ ㄐㄧˋ)
wide learning and a powerful memory; having an encyclopaedic knowledge

---

卜 部
ㄅㄨˇ buu bǔ

【卜】488 ㄅㄨˇ buu bǔ
1. to divine; to consult the oracle
2. to foretell; to predict: 勝負難卜。It's difficult to foretell who will win.
3. to choose; to select
4. a Chinese family name

卜鄰(ㄅㄨˇ ㄌㄧㄣˊ)
to choose neighbors

卜卦(ㄅㄨˇ ㄍㄨㄚˋ)
to divine by the Eight Diagrams

卜居(ㄅㄨˇ ㄐㄩ)
to choose a residence; to choose a place for one's home

卜宅(ㄅㄨˇ ㄓㄞˊ)
①to choose a residence ②to choose a tomb site

卜晝卜夜(ㄅㄨˇ ㄓㄡˋ ㄅㄨˇ ㄧㄝˋ)
day and night; around the clock

卜筮(ㄅㄨˇ ㄕˋ)
divination; to divine by the tortoise and by the milfoil

卜辭(ㄅㄨˇ ㄘˊ)

---

the writings inscribed on oracle bones; oracle inscriptions of the Shang Dynasty on tortoise shells or animal bones

二畫

【卞】489 ㄅㄧㄢˋ biann biàn
1. hurriedly; rash; impetuous
2. excitable
3. a Chinese family name

卞急(ㄅㄧㄢˋ ㄐㄧˊ)
testy; irascible

三畫

【占】490 1. ㄓㄢ jan zhān
1. to divine
2. to observe
3. a Chinese family name

占卜(ㄓㄢ ㄅㄨˇ)
to divine; to practice divination

占夢(ㄓㄢ ㄇㄥˋ)
to divine by interpreting dreams

占斷吉凶(ㄓㄢ ㄉㄨㄢˋ ㄐㄧˊ ㄒㄩㄥ)
to find out good or bad luck by divination

占卦(ㄓㄢ ㄍㄨㄚˋ)
to divine by the Eight Diagrams (八卦)

占星(ㄓㄢ ㄒㄧㄥ)
to divine by astrology; to cast a horoscope

占星術(ㄓㄢ ㄒㄧㄥ ㄕㄨˋ)
astrology

占驗(ㄓㄢ ㄧㄢˋ)
the confirmation of an oracle

【占】490 2. (佔) ㄓㄢˋ jann zhàn
to occupy

占領(ㄓㄢˋ ㄌㄧㄥˇ)
to occupy

占據(ㄓㄢˋ ㄐㄩˋ)
to occupy illegally or by force

占先(ㄓㄢˋ ㄒㄧㄢ)
to occupy before others; to preempt

占有(ㄓㄢˋ ㄧㄡˇ)
to take possession of

【卡】491 1. ㄎㄚˇ kaa kǎ
1. a card, as a visiting card; cardboard
2. an abbreviated form for "calorie"
3. a guardhouse
4. a customs barrier; a roadblock; a checkpoint
5. to block; to check

卡賓槍(ㄎㄚˇ ㄅㄧㄣ ㄑㄧㄤ)
a carbine

卡片(ㄎㄚˇ ㄆㄧㄢˋ)
a card; a calling card

卡達(ㄎㄚˇ ㄉㄚˊ)
Qatar or Katar

卡達人(ㄎㄚˇ ㄉㄚˊ ㄖㄣˊ)
a Qatari

卡帶(ㄎㄚˇ ㄉㄞˋ)
a cassette tape

卡通(ㄎㄚˇ ㄊㄨㄥ)
a cartoon (especially a cartoon movie)

卡內基(ㄎㄚˇ ㄋㄟˋ ㄐㄧ)
Andrew Carnegie, 1835-1919, an American steel tycoon

卡農(ㄎㄚˇ ㄋㄨㄥˊ)
(music) canon

卡路里(ㄎㄚˇ ㄌㄨˋ ㄌㄧˇ)
a calorie

卡介苗(ㄎㄚˇ ㄐㄧㄝˋ ㄇㄧㄠˊ)
BCG (Bacillus Calmette-Guerin), a TB vaccine

卡其布(ㄎㄚˇ ㄑㄧˊ ㄅㄨˋ)
khaki

卡車(ㄎㄚˇ ㄔㄜ)
a truck; a lorry

卡式(ㄎㄚˇ ㄕˋ)
cassette

卡氏帶(ㄎㄚˇ ㄕˋ ㄉㄞˋ)
a casparian strip

卡薩布蘭加(ㄎㄚˇ ㄙㄚˋ ㄅㄨˋ ㄌㄢˊ ㄐㄧㄚ)
Casablanca, a seaport in north Africa

【卡】491 2. ㄑㄧㄚˇ chya qiǎ
to be squeezed in between; to be sandwiched

【卡】491 3. ㄑㄧㄚˋ chea qià
to choke; to be choked

卡子(ㄑㄧㄚˇ ㄗˇ)
①a customs office; a toll-collecting station ②a checkpost; a checkpoint: 下卡子 or 撤卡子 to set checkposts ③a tool for gripping things (as

a pair of pincers, a clip, a fastener, etc.)

卡鑽(ㄎㄧㄚˇ ㄗㄨㄢ)
the jamming of a drilling tool; the sticking of tools

五畫

【卣】 492 ㄧㄡˇ yeou yǒu
(in ancient China) a container or vessel for wine; a Chinese chalice

六畫

【卦】 493 《ㄨㄚˋ guah guà
one of the Eight Diagrams of the *Book of Changes*

卦攤兒(《ㄨㄚˋ ㄊㄢ)
a fortune-teller's stall

卩 部
ㄐㄧㄝˊ jye jié

三畫

【卮】 494 ㄓ jy zhī
a container for holding wine; a goblet with handles

【卯】 495 ㄇㄠˇ mao mǎo
1. the fourth of the 12 Terrestrial Branches
2. the period from 5 to 7 a.m.
3. a roll call
4. a Chinese family name

卯勁兒(ㄇㄠˇ ㄐㄧㄥ)
to make a sudden all-out effort

卯時(ㄇㄠˇ ㄕ)
the period of the day from 5 a.m. to 7 a.m.

四畫

【印】 496 ㄧㄣˋ yinn yìn
1. a seal; a stamp; a chop
2. to print; to stamp; to imprint
3. an imprint; a mark

4. a Chinese family name

印本(ㄧㄣˋ ㄅㄣˇ)
a printed copy

印譜(ㄧㄣˋ ㄆㄨˇ)
a collection of imprints of seals or chops by famous engravers, ancient and contemporary—appearing first toward the end of the Sung Dynasty

印發(ㄧㄣˋ ㄈㄚ)
to print and distribute

印第安納(ㄧㄣˋ ㄉㄧˋ ㄢ ㄋㄚˋ)
Indiana, U.S.A.

印第安人(ㄧㄣˋ ㄉㄧˋ ㄢ ㄖㄣˊ)
the American Indians

印度(ㄧㄣˋ ㄉㄨˋ)
India

印度半島(ㄧㄣˋ ㄉㄨˋ ㄅㄢˋ ㄉㄠˇ)
the subcontinent of India

印度河(ㄧㄣˋ ㄉㄨˋ ㄏㄜˊ)
the Indus

印度河文化(ㄧㄣˋ ㄉㄨˋ ㄏㄜˊ ㄨㄣˊ ㄏㄨㄚˋ)
Indus culture (3000B.C. — 1500B.C.)

印度教(ㄧㄣˋ ㄉㄨˋ ㄐㄧㄠˋ)
Hinduism

印度支那(ㄧㄣˋ ㄉㄨˋ ㄓ ㄋㄚˋ)
Indochina

印度洋(ㄧㄣˋ ㄉㄨˋ ㄧㄤˊ)
the Indian Ocean

印台(ㄧㄣˋ ㄊㄞˊ)
an ink pad; a stamp pad

印堂(ㄧㄣˋ ㄊㄤˊ)
(physiognomy) the space between the eyebrows

印尼(ㄧㄣˋ ㄋㄧˊ)or 印度尼西亞(ㄧㄣˋ ㄉㄨˋ ㄋㄧˊ ㄒㄧ ㄧㄚˋ)
Indonesia

印泥(ㄧㄣˋ ㄋㄧˊ)or 印色(ㄧㄣˋ ㄙㄜˋ)
ink (usually red) for imprinting of seals

印盒(ㄧㄣˋ ㄏㄜˊ)
a seal box

印花(ㄧㄣˋ ㄏㄨㄚ)
a revenue stamp

印花布(ㄧㄣˋ ㄏㄨㄚ ㄅㄨˋ)
printed cloth; calico

印花稅(ㄧㄣˋ ㄏㄨㄚ ㄕㄨㄟˋ)
stamp tax—a tax imposed on certain legal documents

印加人(ㄧㄣˋ ㄐㄧㄚ ㄖㄣˊ)
an Inca

印鑑(ㄧㄣˋ ㄐㄧㄢˋ)
an imprint or impression of one's chop filed with

agencies concerned (especially banks, etc.) for checking purposes

印信(ㄧㄣˋ ㄒㄧㄣˋ)
official seals

印象(ㄧㄣˋ ㄒㄧㄤˋ)
an impression; a mental image

印象派(ㄧㄣˋ ㄒㄧㄤˋ ㄆㄞˋ)
the impressionist school (of the fine arts)

印象主義(ㄧㄣˋ ㄒㄧㄤˋ ㄓㄨˇ ㄧˋ)
impressionism

印行(ㄧㄣˋ ㄒㄧㄥˊ)
to publish

印章(ㄧㄣˋ ㄓㄤ)
a general name for seals, stamps and chops

印證(ㄧㄣˋ ㄓㄥˋ)
to prove; mutual proof

印刷(ㄧㄣˋ ㄕㄨㄚ)
to print

印刷品(ㄧㄣˋ ㄕㄨㄚ ㄆㄧㄣˇ)
printed matter

印刷機(ㄧㄣˋ ㄕㄨㄚ ㄐㄧ)
a printing machine

印刷廠(ㄧㄣˋ ㄕㄨㄚ ㄔㄤˇ)
a printing plant

印染(ㄧㄣˋ ㄖㄢˇ)
printing and dyeing (of textiles)

印子(ㄧㄣˋ ˙ㄗ)
a trace; a print

印歐語系(ㄧㄣˋ ㄡ ㄩˇ ㄒㄧˋ)
Indo-European

【危】 497 ㄨㄟˊ wei wéi
1. danger; dangerous; precarious; perilous
2. restless
3. to fear; to be upset or afraid
4. lofty; high
5. just; honest; straightforward
6. a Chinese family name

危殆(ㄨㄟˊ ㄉㄞˋ)
in great danger; in jeopardy; in a critical condition

危篤(ㄨㄟˊ ㄉㄨˊ)
(said of a patient's condition) critical; dying

危難(ㄨㄟˊ ㄋㄢˋ)
(in) danger, peril, trouble, disaster or distress

危害(ㄨㄟˊ ㄏㄞˋ)
to endanger; to harm; to injure; to jeopardize

〔卩部〕

危害治安(ㄨㄟ ㄏㄞ ㄓ ㄢ)
to jeopardize public security

危機(ㄨㄟ ㄐㄧ)
a crisis; a danger point; a critical point; a precarious moment

危機重重(ㄨㄟ ㄐㄧ ㄓㄨㄥ ㄓㄨㄥ)
to bog down in crises; crisis-ridden

危急(ㄨㄟ ㄐㄧ)
(connoting risk and danger) urgent; pressing; hazardous; (in) a state of emergency; in a desperate situation

危急存亡之秋(ㄨㄟ ㄐㄧ ㄘㄨㄣ ㄨㄤ ㄓ ㄑㄧㄡ)
(said of a nation) at the moment of survival and downfall; at the moment of crisis

危局(ㄨㄟ ㄐㄩ)
a dangerous, critical or desperate situation: 他們已陷危局。 They have been in a dangerous situation.

危險(ㄨㄟ ㄒㄧㄢ)
danger; dangerous; unsafe

危險份子(ㄨㄟ ㄒㄧㄢ ㄈㄣ ㄗ)
dangerous elements; undesirable elements

危險物(ㄨㄟ ㄒㄧㄢ ㄨ)
dangerous goods (as poisons, explosives or highly inflammable materials)

危如累卵(ㄨㄟ ㄖㄨ ㄌㄟ ㄌㄨㄢ)
(literally) as precarious as a pile of eggs—extremely dangerous

危在旦夕(ㄨㄟ ㄗㄞ ㄉㄢ ㄒㄧ)
①(said of a city under enemy attack) may fall at any moment ②(said of a patient critically ill) may die soon; dying

危坐(ㄨㄟ ㄗㄨㄛ)
to sit rigidly (as on ceremonious occasions or in the presence of superiors)

危言聳聽(ㄨㄟ ㄧㄢ ㄙㄨㄥ ㄊㄧㄥ)
to stir up others with sensational statements; to resort to sensationalism (as news headlines, reporting, etc.)

危亡(ㄨㄟ ㄨㄤ)
in great danger; in danger of elimination; in peril

五畫

【卵】 498
ㄌㄨㄢ loan luǎn
1. an egg; an ovum
2. fish roe
3. the testicles

卵白(ㄌㄨㄢ ㄅㄞ)
albumen; egg white

卵胎生(ㄌㄨㄢ ㄊㄞ ㄕㄥ)
(zoology) ovoviviparity

卵黃(ㄌㄨㄢ ㄏㄨㄤ)
yolk

卵球(ㄌㄨㄢ ㄑㄧㄡ)
the egg cell of a plant

卵細胞(ㄌㄨㄢ ㄒㄧ ㄅㄠ)
an ovum; ova

卵形(ㄌㄨㄢ ㄒㄧㄥ)
ovoid; oval

卵巢(ㄌㄨㄢ ㄔㄠ)
ovaries

卵石(ㄌㄨㄢ ㄕ)
cobbles; pebbles

卵生(ㄌㄨㄢ ㄕㄥ)
oviparous

卵子
①(ㄌㄨㄢ ㄗ) an ovum
②(ㄌㄢ ˙ㄗ) testes; testicles

卵翼(ㄌㄨㄢ ㄧ)
protection; shelter

六畫

【卷】 499
1. ㄐㄩㄢ jiuann juàn
1. painting which can be easily folded or rolled up
2. a book: 開卷有益。 One will be benefited whenever one opens a book.
3. a division of a book; a volume
4. a test paper
5. filed documents; files

卷紙(ㄐㄩㄢ ㄓ)
paper for use in examinations

卷帙(ㄐㄩㄢ ㄓ)
a book; books: 圖書館卷帙繁浩。 The library has a great number of books.

卷軸(ㄐㄩㄢ ㄓㄡ)
a book; books

卷子(ㄐㄩㄢ ˙ㄗ)
a test paper; an examination paper

卷宗(ㄐㄩㄢ ㄗㄨㄥ)
filed documents, especially in public offices; files; dossiers

【卷】 499
2. (捲) ㄐㄩㄢ jeuan juǎn
to roll up

卷土重來(ㄐㄩㄢ ㄊㄨ ㄓㄨㄥ ㄌㄞ)
to come back again after defeat; to make another try after failure

【卷】 499
3. ㄑㄩㄢ chyuan quán
curly; to curl

卷髮(ㄑㄩㄢ ㄈㄚ)
①curly hair; hair curling up
②to curl hair

卷曲(ㄑㄩㄢ ㄑㄩ)
to curl up

【卸】 500
ㄒㄧㄝ shieh xiè
1. to get rid of; to remove
2. to unload (cargoes, etc.)
3. to resign; to retire from office

卸磨殺驢(ㄒㄧㄝ ㄇㄛ ㄕㄚ ㄌㄩ)
to kill the donkey the moment it leaves the millstone—to get rid of someone as soon as he has finished his work

卸貨(ㄒㄧㄝ ㄏㄨㄛ)
to unload (or discharge) cargoes: 這船正在卸貨。 The ship is unloading.

卸肩(ㄒㄧㄝ ㄐㄧㄢ)
to lay down responsibilities

卸妝(ㄒㄧㄝ ㄓㄨㄤ)
to remove make-up and ornaments

卸除(ㄒㄧㄝ ㄔㄨ)
to remove; to get rid of

卸任(ㄒㄧㄝ ㄖㄣ)
to quit a public office

卸責(ㄒㄧㄝ ㄗㄜ)
①to lay down one's responsibilities ② to shirk one's responsibility

卸載(ㄒㄧㄝ ㄗㄞ)
to unload cargoes (from a boat or car)

【卹】 501
ㄒㄩ shiuh xù
1. pity; to pity; sympathy; to sympathize
2. to give relief

卹金(ㄒㄩ ㄐㄧㄣ)

compensation; a pension; an indemnity (especially paid by the government for loss of life on a job, etc.)

卹養 (ㄒㄩˋ一ㄤˇ)
to raise (orphans, etc.); to aid in the sustenance (of the sick, old, etc.)

【卺】 [502] ㄐㄧㄣˇ jiin jǐn
nuptial winecups (made from a gourd split in two)

七畫

【卻】 [503] (卻) ㄑㄩㄝˋ chiueh què
1. still; but; yet
2. to refuse to accept
3. to retreat; to withdraw

卻病 (ㄑㄩㄝˋㄅㄧㄥˋ)
to prevent or cure a disease

卻步 (ㄑㄩㄝˋㄅㄨˋ)
to retreat or withdraw (in fear or in disgust); to shrink back

卻來 (ㄑㄩㄝˋㄌㄞˊ)
① yet ② in reality

卻立 (ㄑㄩㄝˋㄌㄧˋ)
to stand back

卻之不恭 (ㄑㄩㄝˋㄓㄅㄨˋㄍㄨㄥ)
It's not polite to refuse (an offer, present, etc.)—a modest expression implying that one does not deserve what is offered: 卻之不恭, 受之有愧。To refuse would be impolite, but to accept is embarrassing.

卻是 (ㄑㄩㄝˋㄕˋ)
nevertheless; in fact; the fact is…

卻說 (ㄑㄩㄝˋㄕㄨㄛ)
Let's resume our story. 或 Now, let's proceed to (tell our story).

卻走 (ㄑㄩㄝˋㄗㄡˇ)
to run backward; to turn away

卻要 (ㄑㄩㄝˋㄧㄠˋ)
to want or to want to… (contrary to what others expected)

卻又 (ㄑㄩㄝˋㄧㄡˋ)
① but again (emphatic "again") ② then…later

【即】 [504] (即) ㄐㄧˊ jyi jí

1. promptly; immediately; now
2. then; accordingly
3. even if—indicating supposition or sequence

即便 (ㄐㄧˊㄅㄧㄢˋ)
① at this moment; forthwith ② although; even if; even though

即令 (ㄐㄧˊㄌㄧㄥˋ)
① even if; even though ② to order immediately

即刻 (ㄐㄧˊㄎㄜˋ)
immediately; promptly; now; 即刻來這裏。Come here now.

即或 (ㄐㄧˊㄏㄨㄛˋ)
even if; even though

即今 (ㄐㄧˊㄐㄧㄣ)
right now; at this very moment

即將 (ㄐㄧˊㄐㄧㄤ)
to be about to; to be on the point of: 典禮即將開始。The ceremony is about to begin.

即景 (ㄐㄧˊㄐㄧㄥˇ)
to compose poems with the scenery one is looking at as the theme

即景生情 (ㄐㄧˊㄐㄧㄥˇㄕㄥㄑㄧㄥˊ)
the scene arouses a sense (of joy, sorrow, etc.); the scene touches a chord in one's heart

即席 (ㄐㄧˊㄒㄧˊ)
on the spot; at once; extempore; impromptu; off the cuff: 我們請他即席演講。We asked him to speak extempore.

即興 (ㄐㄧˊㄒㄧㄥˋ)
impromptu; extemporaneous

即興之作 (ㄐㄧˊㄒㄧㄥˋㄓㄗㄨㄛˋ)
an improvisation

即時 (ㄐㄧˊㄕˊ)
immediately; at once

即使 (ㄐㄧˊㄕˇ)
even if

即事 (ㄐㄧˊㄕˋ)
① the present affairs ② to do something

即世 (ㄐㄧˊㄕˋ)
to leave the world; to die

即日 (ㄐㄧˊㄖˋ)
on the very day; immediately; as soon as possible; at once

即如 (ㄐㄧˊㄖㄨˊ)
as if

即速 (ㄐㄧˊㄙㄨˋ)
instantly; immediately; soon

即夜 (ㄐㄧˊㄧㄝˋ)
on the very night; within the night; immediately

即位 (ㄐㄧˊㄨㄟˋ)
to ascend the throne

十畫

【卿】 [505] ㄑㄧㄥ ching qing
1. (in ancient China) a salutation of an emperor to his ministers
2. used in addressing one's wife—Honey, Darling, Dear, etc.
3. (in ancient China) a nobleman; a high official rank
4. a Chinese family name

卿卿我我 (ㄑㄧㄥ ㄑㄧㄥ ㄨㄛˇ ㄨㄛˇ)
to be very much in love

卿雲 (ㄑㄧㄥ ㄩㄣˊ)
propitious clouds bringing well-being to all

厂 部
ㄏㄢˇ haan hǎn

二畫

【厄】 [506] ㄜˋ eh è
1. difficulty; adversity; distress; hardship
2. impeded; cramped

厄難 (ㄜˋㄋㄢˊ)
distress; difficulty; hardship

厄瓜多爾 (ㄜˋㄍㄨㄚㄉㄨㄛㄦˇ)
Ecuador

厄瓜多爾人 (ㄜˋㄍㄨㄚㄉㄨㄛㄦˇㄖㄣˊ)
an Ecuadorian

厄爾巴 (ㄜˋㄦˇㄅㄚ)
Elba Island in the Mediterranean

厄運 (ㄜˋㄩㄣˋ)
bad luck; adversity

七畫

厂部

【厖】 507 ㄆㄤ parng póng (又讀 ㄇㄤ máng mǎng)

1. bulky; huge
2. confused; disorderly

厖然大物(ㄆㄤ ㄖㄢˊ ㄉㄚˋ ㄨˋ)
something which is huge in size

厖雜(ㄆㄤ ㄗㄚˊ)
disorderly; messy

【厚】 508 ㄏㄡˋ how hòu

1. thick; thickness
2. deep friendship
3. to treat kindly; generous
4. substantial
5. kind; considerate; virtuous

厚薄(ㄏㄡˋ ㄅㄛˊ)
① thickness and thinness ② munificence and parsimony

厚彼薄此(ㄏㄡˋ ㄅㄧˇ ㄅㄛˊ ㄘˇ)or厚此薄彼(ㄏㄡˋ ㄘˇ ㄅㄛˊ ㄅㄧˇ)
to favor one more than another; to play favoritism; to treat with partiality

厚貌深情(ㄏㄡˋ ㄇㄠˋ ㄕㄣ ㄑㄧㄥˊ)
kindly in appearance but unfathomable at heart

厚德載福(ㄏㄡˋ ㄉㄜˊ ㄗㄞˋ ㄈㄨˊ)
(used as a eulogy) Great virtue carries happiness with it.

厚待(ㄏㄡˋ ㄉㄞˋ)
to treat kindly and generously

厚道(ㄏㄡˋ ㄉㄠˋ)
kind; virtuous; sincere; considerate; generous

厚度(ㄏㄡˋ ㄉㄨˋ)
thickness

厚禮(ㄏㄡˋ ㄌㄧˇ)
lavish gifts; liberal presents

厚利(ㄏㄡˋ ㄌㄧˋ)
substantial profit

厚臉(ㄏㄡˋ ㄌㄧㄢˇ)or厚顏(ㄏㄡˋ ㄧㄢˊ)
brazen-faced; shameless

厚祿(ㄏㄡˋ ㄌㄨˋ)
high government pay

厚古薄今(ㄏㄡˋ ㄍㄨˇ ㄅㄛˊ ㄐㄧㄣ)
to emphasize the past, but slight the present

厚今薄古(ㄏㄡˋ ㄐㄧㄣ ㄅㄛˊ ㄍㄨˇ)
to emphasize the present, but slight the past

厚重(ㄏㄡˋ ㄓㄨㄥˋ)
(said of manner) dignified;
stately; graceful

厚酬(ㄏㄡˋ ㄔㄡˊ)
handsome reward or remuneration

厚實(ㄏㄡˋ ㄕˊ)
thick

厚生(ㄏㄡˋ ㄕㄥ)
to improve people's living conditions

厚澤(ㄏㄡˋ ㄗㄜˊ)
great kindness

厚葬(ㄏㄡˋ ㄗㄤˋ)
an elaborate funeral

厚賜(ㄏㄡˋ ㄙˋ)
to reward generously; generous gifts

厚愛(ㄏㄡˋ ㄞˋ)
great kindness; to treat very kindly and generously

厚意(ㄏㄡˋ ㄧˋ)
great indebtedness

厚意(ㄏㄡˋ ㄧˋ)
good intention; goodwill

厚誼(ㄏㄡˋ ㄧˋ)
deep friendship or hospitality

厚望(ㄏㄡˋ ㄨㄤˋ)
high hopes; high expectations; great expectations

八畫

【原】 509 ㄩㄢˊ yuan yuán

1. the source; the origin; the beginning
2. original; primary: 原來的計畫後來改變了。The original plan was afterward changed.
3. a steppe; a vast plain; a field: 他曾遊覽過加拿大的廣大平原。He has toured the vast plains of Canada.
4. a graveyard
5. to excuse; to pardon
6. a Chinese family name

原版(ㄩㄢˊ ㄅㄢˇ)
the original print; the original edition; the first print or edition; the edition printed by the original publisher

原本(ㄩㄢˊ ㄅㄣˇ)
① the causes of an incident; the ins and outs of an incident ② the origin of something ③ the author's manuscript; the original draft

原配(ㄩㄢˊ ㄆㄟˋ)
one's first wife 亦作「元配」

原木(ㄩㄢˊ ㄇㄨˋ)
a log

原封不動(ㄩㄢˊ ㄈㄥ ㄅㄨˋ ㄉㄨㄥˋ)
(in) original form; (kept or left) intact or unopened

原底子(ㄩㄢˊ ㄉㄧˇ ˙ㄗ)
① the first script (of a writing); the original script; a manuscript ② originally

原點(ㄩㄢˊ ㄉㄧㄢˇ)
(mathematics) origin; the point of origin

原動力(ㄩㄢˊ ㄉㄨㄥˋ ㄌㄧˋ)
① (mechanics) power ② (physics) action

原動機(ㄩㄢˊ ㄉㄨㄥˋ ㄐㄧ)
(mechanics) a prime mover

原來(ㄩㄢˊ ㄌㄞˊ)
originally or formerly

原來如此(ㄩㄢˊ ㄌㄞˊ ㄖㄨˊ ㄘˇ)
① I see. 或 Now I understand what you mean. 或 So, that is what it is! 或 It was as it is now. 或 No change has been made.

原理(ㄩㄢˊ ㄌㄧˇ)
principles: 這些機器按照相同的原理運轉。These machines work on the same principles.

原料(ㄩㄢˊ ㄌㄧㄠˋ)
raw materials

原諒(ㄩㄢˊ ㄌㄧㄤˋ)or原宥(ㄩㄢˊ ㄧㄡˋ)
forgiveness; to forgive; to pardon: 請原諒我這麼說。Please pardon me for saying so.

原稿(ㄩㄢˊ ㄍㄠˇ)
a manuscript: 原稿將於下月初付印。The manuscript will go to press early next month.

原告(ㄩㄢˊ ㄍㄠˋ)
the plaintiff; the appellant; the prosecutor

原故(ㄩㄢˊ ㄍㄨˋ)
a reason; a cause: 告訴我你做這事的原故。Give me the reasons for doing it.

原籍(ㄩㄢˊ ㄐㄧˊ)
hailing from; a native of; originally of (a place); the original domicile: 他 原籍上海。He is a native of Shanghai

原價(ㄩㄢˊ ㄐㄧㄚˋ)

① the original price ② the production cost (of an article, etc.) ③ the price of an article paid by the retailer to the manufacturer or wholesaler

原舊(兒)(ㄩㄢ ㄐㄧㄡˋ(ㄦ))
original

原起(ㄩㄢˊ ㄑㄧˇ)
① the origin (of some event) ② originally

原器(ㄩㄢˊ ㄑㄧˋ)
(in the standard of measurements) the prototype

原隰(ㄩㄢˊ ㄒㄧˊ)
plateaus and low, marshy land

原先(ㄩㄢˊ ㄒㄧㄢ)
in the beginning; originally; in the very beginning: 讓我們照原先的計畫進行。Let us proceed according to our original plan.

原型(ㄩㄢˊ ㄒㄧㄥˊ)
(machinery) the prototype

原形(ㄩㄢˊ ㄒㄧㄥˊ)
① the original form or shape ② one's true colors; the real face or form

原形畢露(ㄩㄢˊ ㄒㄧㄥˊ ㄅㄧˋ ㄌㄨˋ)
completely unmasked or exposed; to reveal the true nature or colors (of a person) completely

原形質(ㄩㄢˊ ㄒㄧㄥˊ ㄓˊ)
(biology) protoplasm

原址(ㄩㄢˊ ㄓˇ)
the former address

原主(ㄩㄢˊ ㄓㄨˇ)
the legal owner; the original owner

原著民(ㄩㄢˊ ㄓㄨˋ ㄇㄧㄣˊ)
an aborigine

原裝(ㄩㄢˊ ㄓㄨㄤ)
made or manufactured by a foreign manufacture

原裝貨(ㄩㄢˊ ㄓㄨㄤ ㄏㄨㄛˋ)
products imported intact (as distinct from those locally assembled or packed)

原狀(ㄩㄢˊ ㄓㄨㄤˋ)
① the original condition: 一切維持原狀。Everything is in its original condition. ② the status quo

原成岩(ㄩㄢˊ ㄔㄥˊ ㄧㄢˊ)
(geology) primary rocks

原處(ㄩㄢˊ ㄔㄨˋ)
the old place; the original place

原始(ㄩㄢˊ ㄕˇ)
① a source; an origin ② primitive; backward

原始分數(ㄩㄢˊ ㄕˇ ㄈㄣ ㄕㄨˋ)
a raw score

原始記錄(ㄩㄢˊ ㄕˇ ㄐㄧˋ ㄌㄨˋ)
original entries

原始價值(ㄩㄢˊ ㄕˇ ㄐㄧㄚˋ ㄓˊ)
original value

原始時代(ㄩㄢˊ ㄕˇ ㄕˊ ㄉㄞˋ)
primeval times or ages

原始社會(ㄩㄢˊ ㄕˇ ㄕㄜˋ ㄏㄨㄟˋ)
a primitive society

原始人(ㄩㄢˊ ㄕˇ ㄖㄣˊ)
a primitive

原始資料(ㄩㄢˊ ㄕˇ ㄗ ㄌㄧㄠˋ)
raw data; firsthand data

原始森林(ㄩㄢˊ ㄕˇ ㄙㄣ ㄌㄧㄣˊ)
a virgin forest

原審(ㄩㄢˊ ㄕㄣˇ)
(law) the first trial

原生動物(ㄩㄢˊ ㄕㄥ ㄉㄨㄥˋ ㄨˋ)
(zoology) a protozoon

原生植物(ㄩㄢˊ ㄕㄥ ㄓˊ ㄨˋ)
a protophyte

原人(ㄩㄢˊ ㄖㄣˊ)
Homo-prigenius (in anthropology)

原任(ㄩㄢˊ ㄖㄣˋ)
① the predecessor ② formerly held the post of...

原子(ㄩㄢˊ ㄗˇ)
an atom

原子筆(ㄩㄢˊ ㄗˇ ㄅㄧˇ)
a ball-point pen

原子炮(ㄩㄢˊ ㄗˇ ㄆㄠˋ)
a cannon firing atomic-tipped shells

原子分裂(ㄩㄢˊ ㄗˇ ㄈㄣ ㄌㄧㄝˋ)
atomic fission

原子彈(ㄩㄢˊ ㄗˇ ㄉㄢˋ)
an atomic bomb

原子能(ㄩㄢˊ ㄗˇ ㄋㄥˊ)
atomic energy

原子量(ㄩㄢˊ ㄗˇ ㄌㄧㄤˋ)
the atomic weight

原子爐(ㄩㄢˊ ㄗˇ ㄌㄨˊ)
an atomic reactor

原子核(ㄩㄢˊ ㄗˇ ㄏㄜˊ)
an atomic nucleus

原子價(ㄩㄢˊ ㄗˇ ㄐㄧㄚˋ)
(chemistry) valences

原子戰爭(ㄩㄢˊ ㄗˇ ㄓㄢˋ ㄓㄥ)
atomic warfare

原子塵(ㄩㄢˊ ㄗˇ ㄔㄣˊ)
atomic fallout

原子時代(ㄩㄢˊ ㄗˇ ㄕˊ ㄉㄞˋ)
the atomic age

原則(ㄩㄢˊ ㄗㄜˊ)
a principle (of handling or doing something)

原作(ㄩㄢˊ ㄗㄨㄛˋ)
the original work; the original

原罪(ㄩㄢˊ ㄗㄨㄟˋ)
(Bible) the original sin

原色(ㄩㄢˊ ㄙㄜˋ)
primary colors

原素(ㄩㄢˊ ㄙㄨˋ)
(chemistry) elements 亦作「元素」

原案(ㄩㄢˊ ㄢˋ)
the original bill; the original documents pertaining to a case at hand; the original records documented

原意(ㄩㄢˊ ㄧˋ)
① original intentions ② original meaning

原議(ㄩㄢˊ ㄧˋ)
the original agreement, resolution, etc.

原野(ㄩㄢˊ ㄧㄝˇ)
the field; a plain

原由(ㄩㄢˊ ㄧㄡˊ)
causes; reasons

原油(ㄩㄢˊ ㄧㄡˊ)
crude oil; crude petroleum

原有(ㄩㄢˊ ㄧㄡˇ)
to possess originally; (what) one had before; (what) was here or there originally

原鹽(ㄩㄢˊ ㄧㄢˊ)
solar salt

原因(ㄩㄢˊ ㄧㄣ)
causes; reasons: 潮汐的原因為何？What are the causes of the tides?

原物(ㄩㄢˊ ㄨˋ)
①(law) things (as money, land, etc.) from which interest is borne or production of other items is effected ② the very original thing; the very same thing

原委(ㄩㄢˊ ㄨㄟˇ)
the reason why a thing happened; the whole story;

厂部

all the details; the ins and outs (of a case, story, etc.)

原文(ㄩㄢˊ ㄨㄣˊ)
the original text

原原本本(ㄩㄢˊ ㄩㄢˊ ㄅㄣˇ ㄅㄣˇ)
the whole (story or thing); in detail

【厝】 510 ㄘㄨㄛˋ tsuoh cuò
1. to place
2. to place a coffin in a temporary shelter pending burial
3. a gravestone
4. to cut or engrave

厝火積薪(ㄘㄨㄛˋ ㄏㄨㄛˇ ㄐㄧ ㄒㄧㄣ)
(literally) to place fire near piles of fagots—in imminent danger

十畫

【厥】 511 ㄐㄩㄝˊ jyue jué
1. to faint
2. same as 撅—to dig
3. a personal and possessive pronoun

厥功甚偉(ㄐㄩㄝˊ ㄍㄨㄥ ㄕㄣˋ ㄨㄟˇ)
to have made great contribution to the successful conclusion of a task

厥後(ㄐㄩㄝˊ ㄏㄡˋ)
after this; afterwards

十二畫

【厭】 512 ㄧㄢˋ yann yàn
1. to dislike; to detest; to hate
2. to get tired of
3. satiated; surfeited

厭煩(ㄧㄢˋ ㄈㄢˊ)
bored; wearied; to dislike; to be vexed; to be fed up with

厭故喜新(ㄧㄢˋ ㄍㄨˋ ㄒㄧ ㄒㄧㄣ)
to dislike the old and to be fond of the new (often said of love affairs)

厭恨(ㄧㄢˋ ㄏㄣˋ)
to loathe; to hate

厭倦(ㄧㄢˋ ㄐㄩㄢˋ)
to be tired of; to be weary of

厭棄(ㄧㄢˋ ㄑㄧˋ)
to reject; to loathe; to give up; to get rid of: 現代的人厭棄戰爭。 Modern people reject war.

厭戰(ㄧㄢˋ ㄓㄢˋ)
to be tired of war; war-weariness; demoralized by war

厭色(ㄧㄢˋ ㄕˊ)
lack of appetite

厭世(ㄧㄢˋ ㄕˋ)
① to be disgusted with the world ② to die ③ misanthropy

厭世主義(ㄧㄢˋ ㄕˋ ㄓㄨˇ ㄧˋ)
pessimism; cynicism

厭惡(ㄧㄢˋ ㄨˋ)
to loathe; to dislike; to detest; to abhor; to abominate; to be disgusted with

十三畫

【厲】 513 ㄌㄧˋ lih lì
1. a coarse whetstone
2. harsh; violent; severe; stern; serious
3. to persuade; to urge; to encourage
4. bad; evil
5. a Chinese family name
6. an epidemic
7. to oppress; oppressive; cruel

厲兵秣馬(ㄌㄧˋ ㄅㄧㄥ ㄇㄛˋ ㄇㄚˇ)
to make military preparations; to maintain combat readiness; to remain alert militarily

厲鬼(ㄌㄧˋ ㄍㄨㄟˇ)
a fierce ghost; a malicious spirit

厲害(ㄌㄧˋ ㄏㄞˋ)
① fierceness; ferociousness ② very (ill, etc.); serious (damage, destruction, etc.)

厲階(ㄌㄧˋ ㄐㄧㄝ)
a steppingstone to disorder—(figuratively) disaster; the cause of trouble; a pestilence

厲禁(ㄌㄧˋ ㄐㄧㄣˋ)
strictly prohibited; to ban strictly

厲行(ㄌㄧˋ ㄒㄧㄥˊ)
to enforce; rigorous enforcement; to practice under strong persuasion or discipline

厲聲(ㄌㄧˋ ㄕㄥ)
to talk harshly; to shout

angrily

厲色(ㄌㄧˋ ㄙㄜˋ)
to look angry; angry-looking

ㄙ 部
ㄙ sy sī

三畫

【去】 514 ㄑㄩˋ chiuh qù
1. to go away; to depart: 我明天就要離去了。 I am going away tomorrow.
2. to get rid of; to remove: 脫去你的帽子。 Remove your hat.
3. to be…apart: 兩地相去十英里。 The two places are ten miles apart.
4. past; gone: 我們的困難過去了。 Our troubles are past.
5. an auxiliary verb: 他早已死去。 He died long ago.
6. the fourth of the four tones in Chinese phonetics
7. (Peking opera) to play the part of

去不成(ㄑㄩˋ ㄅㄨˋ ㄔㄥˊ)
unable to go; can not go

去不得(ㄑㄩˋ ㄅㄨˋ ㄉㄜˊ)
① should not go ② should not get rid of (it)

去不了(ㄑㄩˋ ㄅㄨˋ ㄌㄧㄠˇ)
cannot go; unable to go; unable to attend

去不去(ㄑㄩˋ ㄅㄨˋ ㄑㄩˋ)
Are you (or they) going? or Is he (or she) going? 或 Will you go?

去得了(ㄑㄩˋ ㄉㄜˊ ㄌㄧㄠˇ)or 去得成(ㄑㄩˋ ㄉㄜˊ ㄔㄥˊ)
able to go; able to attend

去泰去甚(ㄑㄩˋ ㄊㄞˋ ㄑㄩˋ ㄕㄣˋ)
to shun the extremes and to maintain the middle course

去你的(ㄑㄩˋ ㄋㄧˇ ㄉㄜ)
Nonsense! 或 Shut up your big mouth!

去年(ㄑㄩˋ ㄋㄧㄢˊ)
last year; the year past

去了(ㄑㄩˋ ㄌㄜ)
① already gone ② already

removed

去留(ㄑㄩ ㄌㄧㄡˊ)
to go or to stay

去路(ㄑㄩ ㄌㄨˋ)
the way along which one is going

去國(ㄑㄩ ㄍㄨㄛˊ)
to leave one's country; to leave one's fatherland

去就(ㄑㄩ ㄐㄧㄡˋ)
to quit or to stay (on a job)

去取之間(ㄑㄩ ㄑㄩ ㄓ ㄐㄧㄢ)
between taking and leaving (it); take it or leave it; undecided; a moment of indecision

去向(ㄑㄩ ㄒㄧㄤˋ)
the direction one is going; whereabouts

去職(ㄑㄩ ㄓˊ)
to be removed from office; resign from office

去處(ㄑㄩ ㄔㄨˋ)
①whereabouts ②the place one is heading for ③a place; a site

去世(ㄑㄩ ㄕˋ)
to die; to leave the world

去勢(ㄑㄩ ㄕˋ)
to castrate; castration; to emasculate

去聲(ㄑㄩ ㄕㄥ)
the falling tone—the fourth tone in Chinese phonetics

去任(ㄑㄩ ㄖㄣˋ)
to resign from a post; to leave a post

去粗取精(ㄑㄩ ㄘㄨ ㄑㄩˇ ㄐㄧㄥ)
to discard the dross and select the essential

去惡從善(ㄑㄩ ㄜˋ ㄘㄨㄥˊ ㄕㄢˋ)
(said of personal conduct) to reform; to shun the evil and follow the good

去蕪存菁(ㄑㄩ ㄨˊ ㄘㄨㄣˊ ㄐㄧㄥ)
(said of editing or compilation work) to keep the good and get rid of the bad

去偽存真(ㄑㄩ ㄨㄟˋ ㄘㄨㄣˊ ㄓㄣ)
to remove the false and retain the true

九畫

【參】 515
1. ㄘㄢ tsan cān
1. to take part in; to get

involved in
2. to visit; to interview; to call on
3. to impeach; to censure
4. to recommend
5. to counsel; to consult together
6. to consider; to collate; to compare

參拜(ㄘㄢ ㄅㄞˋ)
formally call on; to pay a courtesy call

參半(ㄘㄢ ㄅㄢˋ)
half; half-and-half: 他毀譽參半。He got both praise and blame. 或 He was as much praised as blamed.

參謀(ㄘㄢ ㄇㄡˊ)
(military) the staff; a staff officer; a counselor or advisor

參訂(ㄘㄢ ㄉㄧㄥˋ)
to revise (a book, etc.) according to one's own ideas or plans

參透(ㄘㄢ ㄊㄡˋ)
①to understand thoroughly; ②to see through something; to think out ②(Buddhism) to meditate and come to realization

參天(ㄘㄢ ㄊㄧㄢ)
①(usually said of trees, etc.) to reach the sky ② (said of one's scholastic or moral achievements) superb and peerless; profound

參觀(ㄘㄢ ㄍㄨㄢ)
to make a tour; to visit, inspect or tour (a place, a plant, etc.); to watch or witness (military exercises, etc.)

參考(ㄘㄢ ㄎㄠˇ)
①to consult; to collate; to examine and compare②reference: 這些書籍僅供參考。These books are for reference only.

參考書(ㄘㄢ ㄎㄠˇ ㄕㄨ)
a reference book

參看(ㄘㄢ ㄎㄢˋ)
(please) refer to: 請參看第八頁註解。Please refer to the footnotes on page eight.

參劾(ㄘㄢ ㄏㄜˊ)
to impeach (a person)

參互(ㄘㄢ ㄏㄨˋ)

mixed and confused

參加(ㄘㄢ ㄐㄧㄚ)
①to attend; to participate in; to join; participation ② to give (advice, one's viewpoint, etc.)

參見(ㄘㄢ ㄐㄧㄢˋ)
to call on or to visit (a superior); an audience

參軍(ㄘㄢ ㄐㄩㄣ)
①a military staff officer ② to join the army

參軍長(ㄘㄢ ㄐㄩㄣ ㄓㄤˇ)
a presidential chief military aide

參照(ㄘㄢ ㄓㄠˋ)
please refer to; to consult; in accordance with; with reference to: 他參照規則行事。He acts in accordance with the rules.

參戰(ㄘㄢ ㄓㄢˋ)
to participate in a war; to enter a war

參戰國(ㄘㄢ ㄓㄢˋ ㄍㄨㄛˊ)
a belligerent state

參政(ㄘㄢ ㄓㄥˋ)
to take part in politics or the government

參政權(ㄘㄢ ㄓㄥˋ ㄑㄩㄢˊ)
the right to participate in public affairs

參酌(ㄘㄢ ㄓㄨㄛˊ)
to consult and deliberate

參禪(ㄘㄢ ㄔㄢˊ)
(said of Buddhist monks or nuns) to search for the truth by meditation

參事(ㄘㄢ ㄕˋ)
a councilor

參雜(ㄘㄢ ㄗㄚˊ)
to mix; to add something of the different nature, quality, color, etc.

參劃(ㄘㄢ ㄏㄨㄚˋ)
①to participate in planning; to serve as an advisor ②an attache; a councilor

參議(ㄘㄢ ㄧˋ)
①to participate in planning; to counsel; to advise; counsel; advice ②a counselor

參議會(ㄘㄢ ㄧˋ ㄏㄨㄟˋ)
the local legislature

參議員(ㄘㄢ ㄧˋ ㄩㄢˊ)
members of the local legislature; a senator

〔ㄙ 部〕

參議院(ㄘㄢ ㄧˋ ㄩㄢˋ)
the upper house of a parliament; the senate

參謁(ㄘㄢ ㄧㄝˋ)
to visit an official of high rank

參驗(ㄘㄢ ㄧㄢˋ)
to verify (the truth) by personal experience; to inspect personally

參伍錯綜(ㄘㄢ ㄨˇ ㄘㄨㄛˋ ㄗㄨㄥˋ)
to mix up; confused; shuffled; variegated

參悟(ㄘㄢ ㄨˋ)
(Zen Buddhism) to get the meaning of (mystery) from meditation; to perceive the truth with one's mind

參預(ㄘㄢ ㄩˋ)
to play a part (in some decision or task)

參與(ㄘㄢ ㄩˋ)
to take part in; to participate in: 我將要參與那個比賽。 I will take part in that contest.

參閱(ㄘㄢ ㄩㄝˋ)
to see; to consult; to examine and compare

【參】 515
2. ㄕㄣ shen shēn
1. name of a star
2. a ginseng

參商(ㄕㄣ ㄕ)
①animosity between two brothers ②the morning and evening stars—(figuratively) separated

【參】 515
3. ㄘㄣ tsen cēn
參差(ㄘㄣ ㄘ)
of irregular, different or varied sizes; uneven

【參】 515
4. ㄙㄢ san sān
a formal form of the Chinese character "三" —three, used in accounting to prevent fraud

又 部
|ㄡˋ yow yòu

【又】 516
|ㄡˋ yow yòu
1. also; again; in addition to; and
2. moreover; furthermore
3. and (used in a mixed fraction such as one and three fourths)

又打又罵(|ㄡˋ ㄉㄚˇ |ㄡˋ ㄇㄚˋ)
to beat and curse at the same time

又來了(|ㄡˋ ㄌㄞˊ ·ㄌㄜ)
①to have come again ②being repeated again

又聾又啞(|ㄡˋ ㄌㄨㄥˊ |ㄡˋ |ㄚˇ)
deaf-and-dumb; deaf-mute

又哭又笑(|ㄡˋ ㄎㄨ |ㄡˋ ㄒ|ㄠˋ)
to cry and laugh at the same time

又快又好(|ㄡˋ ㄎㄨㄞˋ |ㄡˋ ㄏㄠˇ)
(to do something) very fast with excellent results; efficient; efficiently

又紅又專(|ㄡˋ ㄏㄨㄥˊ |ㄡˋ ㄓㄨㄢ)
(used in mainland China) to be ideologically pure and possess expertise at the same time

又飢又渴(|ㄡˋ ㄐ| |ㄡˋ ㄎㄜˇ)
both hungry and thirsty

又及(|ㄡˋ ㄐ|ˊ)
P.S. (a postscript)

又驚又喜(|ㄡˋ ㄐ|ㄥ |ㄡˋ ㄒ|ˇ)
alarmed and happy at the same time

又稱(|ㄡˋ ㄔㄥ)
①also called; also known as: 北平又稱北京。 Peiping is also called Peking. ②to say also that…; to say further that…

又是(|ㄡˋ ㄕˋ)
①again ②also ③still another ④the same as

又是他(|ㄡˋ ㄕˋ ㄊㄚ)
It's him again. (implying unwelcomeness, surprise, etc.)

又是老調(|ㄡˋ ㄕˋ ㄌㄠˇ ㄉ|ㄠˋ)
(said of cliches, corny statements, etc.) It's the same old tune again.

又是一個(|ㄡˋ ㄕˋ |ˊ ·ㄍㄜ)
still another one

又要(|ㄡˋ |ㄠˋ)
①to want to do something which has been done before

---

②to make additional demands

又問(|ㄡˋ ㄨㄣˋ)
to ask again

一畫

【叉】 517
1. ㄔㄚ cha chā
1. to interlace fingers; to cross arms
2. to thrust; to pierce; to stab
3. a prong; a fork (used in catching fish, etc.)
4. to push another's neck with one's hand

叉路(ㄔㄚ ㄌㄨˋ)
the fork of a road: 他們在叉路處離別。 They parted at the fork of the road.

叉枝(ㄔㄚ ㄓ)
a forked branch

叉手(ㄔㄚ ㄕㄡˇ)
to fold hands in salute

叉子(ㄔㄚ ·ㄗ)
a fork

叉腰(ㄔㄚ |ㄠ)
to stand with arms akimbo (to show defiance, self-satisfaction, etc.); to rest the arms on the hips

【叉】 517
2. ㄔˇ chaa chǒ
叉劈(ㄔˇ ㄆ|ˋ)
(said of the road) divergent

二畫

【及】 518
ㄐ|ˊ jyi jí
1. to reach; to attain; to come up to
2. and; as well as; with
3. just at the moment; when
4. as long as; up to; until
5. to continue; to proceed
6. to extend

及門弟子(ㄐ|ˊ ㄇㄣˊ ㄉ|ˋ ㄗˇ)
a disciple or student who has taken lessons directly from a master (as distinct from 私淑弟子)

及鋒而試(ㄐ|ˊ ㄈㄥ ㄦˊ ㄕˋ)
to seize an opportunity by the forelock

及第(ㄐ|ˊ ㄉ|ˋ)
(in ancient China) to pass

the civil examinations

及齡(ㄐㄧˊㄌㄧㄥˊ)
to reach a required age

及格(ㄐㄧˊㄍㄜˊ)
to pass an examination (especially in school, etc.); to be qualified

及冠之年(ㄐㄧˊㄍㄨㄢ ㄓㄋㄧㄢˊ)
(said of a young man) to reach the age of 20

及笄之年(ㄐㄧˊㄐㄧ ㄓㄋㄧㄢˊ)
(said of a girl) 15 years of age—marriageable age

及肩(ㄐㄧˊㄐㄧㄢ)
to come up to the shoulder

及期(ㄐㄧˊㄑㄧˊ)
to reach the time limit; (said of a bond, etc.) to mature

及至(ㄐㄧˊㄓˋ)
until; up to a given point

及長(ㄐㄧˊㄓㄤˇ)
(when he or she) grew up; in (his or her) adulthood

及時(ㄐㄧˊㄕˊ)
① in time; at the right time or opportune moment; seasonable: 我及時趕上汽船, I was just in time for the steamer. ② promptly; without delay: 我們必須及時糾正錯誤, We must correct a mistake promptly.

及早(ㄐㄧˊㄗㄠˇ)
at an early date; as soon as possible; before it is too late

及早回頭(ㄐㄧˊㄗㄠˇㄏㄨㄟˊㄊㄡˊ)
to repent before it is too late; to mend one's ways without delay; to turn back as soon as possible; to extricate oneself (from evil ways) as soon as possible

及物動詞(ㄐㄧˊㄨˋㄉㄨㄥˋㄘˊ)
a transitive verb

【友】 519
[ㄧㄡˇ yeou *you*]
1. a friend; friendly; friendship
2. fraternity; fraternal love
3. to befriend

友邦(ㄧㄡˇㄅㄤ)
friendly nations; allies

友朋(ㄧㄡˇㄆㄥˊ)
friends; companions

友黨(ㄧㄡˇㄉㄤˇ)
political parties in coalition; a friendly party; parties sharing the same political aspirations

友悌(ㄧㄡˇㄊㄧˋ)
brotherly bonds

友好(ㄧㄡˇㄏㄠˇ)
friendly; friendship; amity (treaty, etc.)

友軍(ㄧㄡˇㄐㄩㄣ)
friendly forces

友情(ㄧㄡˇㄑㄧㄥˊ)
fraternal love; friendship

友善(ㄧㄡˇㄕㄢˋ)
friendly

友人(ㄧㄡˇㄖㄣˊ)
friends

友愛(ㄧㄡˇㄞˋ)
friendship; fraternal love

友誼(ㄧㄡˇㄧˋ)
friendship

友于之愛(ㄧㄡˇㄩˊㄓㄞˋ)
brotherly love

【反】 520
[ㄈㄢˇ faan *fan*]
1. reverse; opposite; contrary
2. to return (something); to turn back; to retreat
3. to introspect; to retrospect
4. to rebel; rebellion; to revolt
5. to infer

反駁(ㄈㄢˇㄅㄛˊ)
to refute; to retort

反敗為勝(ㄈㄢˇㄅㄞˋㄨㄟˊㄕㄥˋ)
to turn defeat into victory

反本(ㄈㄢˇㄅㄣˇ)
to search the original meaning of a thing

反比(ㄈㄢˇㄅㄧˇ)
(mathematics) inverse ratio

反比例(ㄈㄢˇㄅㄧˇㄌㄧˋ)
(mathematics) inverse proportion

反辯(ㄈㄢˇㄅㄧㄢˋ)
to refute; a rebuttal

反哺(ㄈㄢˇㄅㄨˇ)
to repay one's parents when they get old; to show filial piety to one's parents

反派(ㄈㄢˇㄆㄞˋ)
a villain (in drama, etc.); a negative character

反叛(ㄈㄢˇㄆㄢˋ)
to rebel; to revolt; rebellion; treason

反撲(ㄈㄢˇㄆㄨ)
① to pounce on somebody again after being beaten off

② a counterattack

反璞歸眞(ㄈㄢˇㄆㄨˊㄍㄨㄟㄓㄣ)
to return to one's original self and regain truth

反面(ㄈㄢˇㄇㄧㄢˋ)or 反面兒(ㄈㄢˇㄇㄧㄢˋㄦ)
① the reverse side ② the back side; the other side ③ to turn away from; to be cold towards

反面無情(ㄈㄢˇㄇㄧㄢˋㄨˊㄑㄧㄥˊ)
Old friendship is completely forgotten with the sudden change of facial expression.

反目(ㄈㄢˇㄇㄨˋ)
(said of a quarrel between a married couple, etc.) to fight; to squabble

反復 or 反覆(ㄈㄢˇㄈㄨˋ)
① (to study or research) carefully ② not dependable ③ to relapse ④ repeatedly; again and again

反覆思量(ㄈㄢˇㄈㄨˋㄙㄌㄧㄤˊ)
to think over and over again

反覆無常(ㄈㄢˇㄈㄨˋㄨˊㄔㄤˊ)
not dependable; always changing; fickle; capricious

反例(ㄈㄢˇㄌㄧˋ)
on the contrary; instead

反定理(ㄈㄢˇㄉㄧㄥˋㄌㄧˇ)
the inverse theorem

反對(ㄈㄢˇㄉㄨㄟˋ)
to oppose; to object; to be against; to disagree

反對黨(ㄈㄢˇㄉㄨㄟˋㄉㄤˇ)
the opposition party

反對者(ㄈㄢˇㄉㄨㄟˋㄓㄜˇ)
a dissenter

反動(ㄈㄢˇㄉㄨㄥˋ)
reaction; reactionary

反動份子(ㄈㄢˇㄉㄨㄥˋㄈㄣˋㄗˇ)
reactionaries; reactionary elements

反動力(ㄈㄢˇㄉㄨㄥˋㄌㄧˋ)
reaction; the reaction force

反貪汙(ㄈㄢˇㄊㄢㄨ)
anti-corruption

反逆(ㄈㄢˇㄋㄧˋ)
to rebel against (law, order, or government, etc.)

反老還童(ㄈㄢˇㄌㄠˇㄏㄨㄢˊㄊㄨㄥˊ)
to rejuvenate; rejuvenation; to act like a child when one gets old; to get younger with each passing day

又部

反臉(ㄈㄢˇ ㄌㄧㄢˇ)
to fall out; to turn hostile
suddenly 亦作「翻臉」

反亂(ㄈㄢˇ ㄌㄨㄢˋ)
rebellion; revolt; sedition

反戈(ㄈㄢˇ ㄍㄜ)
to revolt; to rebel

反戈一擊(ㄈㄢˇ ㄍㄜ ㄧ ㄐㄧ)
to turn one's weapon around
and strike

反革命(ㄈㄢˇ ㄍㄜˊ ㄇㄧㄥˋ)
counterrevolution

反感(ㄈㄢˇ ㄍㄢˇ)
antipathy

反顧(ㄈㄢˇ ㄍㄨˋ)
to look back; to review; to
cast a look behind

反過來(ㄈㄢˇ ㄍㄨㄛˋ ㄌㄞˊ)
① to turn over; to invert ②
(to look at something from)
the opposite side; (to state
something) in another way;
contrarily; on the other hand

反光(ㄈㄢˇ ㄍㄨㄤ)
reflection; reflected light

反光鏡(ㄈㄢˇ ㄍㄨㄤ ㄐㄧㄥˋ)
a reflector

反攻(ㄈㄢˇ ㄍㄨㄥ)
to counterattack; a counterattack; a counteroffensive

反躬自問(ㄈㄢˇ ㄍㄨㄥ ㄗˋ ㄨㄣˋ)
to introspect; introspection;
to search one's own soul for
answers; self-examination

反共(ㄈㄢˇ ㄍㄨㄥˋ)
anticommunism

反客為主(ㄈㄢˇ ㄎㄜˋ ㄨㄟˊ ㄓㄨˇ)
to exchange the positions of
the host and the guest

反抗(ㄈㄢˇ ㄎㄤˋ)
to counter; to rise up
against; to resist; to rebel

反話(ㄈㄢˇ ㄏㄨㄚˋ)
statements that are contrary
to what the speaker really
believes or thinks to be true

反悔(ㄈㄢˇ ㄏㄨㄟˇ)
to renege (on a promise)

反擊(ㄈㄢˇ ㄐㄧ)
to fight back; to strike back:
他打我，因此我反擊他。He hit
me, so I struck back.

反詰(ㄈㄢˇ ㄐㄧㄝˊ)
to rebut; to refute; a rebuttal

反剪(ㄈㄢˇ ㄐㄧㄢˇ)
① with one's hands behind
one's back ② with one's
hands tied behind one's back

反間(ㄈㄢˇ ㄐㄧㄢ)
to alienate the enemy coalition or alliance; to drive a
wedge in the enemy camp

反切(ㄈㄢˇ ㄑㄧㄝ)
(old Chinese phonetics) to
indicate the pronunciation of
a character by quick enunciation of two other characters

反求諸己(ㄈㄢˇ ㄑㄧㄡˊ ㄓㄨ ㄐㄧˇ)
to make self-examination; to
search one's own soul

反侵略(ㄈㄢˇ ㄑㄧㄣ ㄌㄩㄝˋ)
antiaggression

反情報(ㄈㄢˇ ㄑㄧㄥˊ ㄅㄠˋ)
counterintelligence

反響(ㄈㄢˇ ㄒㄧㄤˇ)
① a counteraction ② an
echo

反向(ㄈㄢˇ ㄒㄧㄤˋ)
the opposite direction; the
reverse

反省(ㄈㄢˇ ㄒㄧㄥˇ)
reflection; self-examination;
to make soul-searching or
self-examination: 我需要時間
反省。I want time for reflection.

反宣傳(ㄈㄢˇ ㄒㄩㄢ ㄔㄨㄢˊ)
① counterpropaganda ② a
slander campaign

反之(ㄈㄢˇ ㄓ)
on the other hand

反照(ㄈㄢˇ ㄓㄠˋ)
(said of light) to reflect;
reflection

反戰者(ㄈㄢˇ ㄓㄢˋ ㄓㄜˇ)
a peacenik

反掌(ㄈㄢˇ ㄓㄤˇ)
a turn of one's hand—an
easy task

反正(ㄈㄢˇ ㄓㄥˋ)
① to shift one's loyalty to
the side of righteousness; to
return to rectitude; to
change one's side to the
right cause ② in any case;
anyway

反證(ㄈㄢˇ ㄓㄥˋ)
the contrary evidence that
nullifies the evidence
presented by the other party
in court; the counter-

evidence

反轉(ㄈㄢˇ ㄓㄨㄢˇ)
① to turn inside out ② to
return

反襯(ㄈㄢˇ ㄔㄣˋ)
to set off by contrast; to
serve as a foil to

反常(ㄈㄢˇ ㄔㄤˊ)
abnormal; not normal; out-
of-the-ordinary; against common practice; abnormality

反芻(ㄈㄢˇ ㄔㄨˊ)
to ruminate; to chew the cud

反芻動物(ㄈㄢˇ ㄔㄨˊ ㄉㄨㄥˋ ㄨˋ)
a ruminant

反串(ㄈㄢˇ ㄔㄨㄢˋ)
① (Peking opera) to play a
role other than one's specialty ② to play the role of
the opposite sex (in a movie
or a drama)

反脣相稽(ㄈㄢˇ ㄔㄨㄣˊ ㄒㄧㄤ ㄐㄧ)
to rebut or rebuke with sarcastic remarks

反時鐘方向(ㄈㄢˇ ㄕˊ ㄓㄨㄥ ㄈㄤ ㄒㄧㄤˋ)
counterclockwise

反噬(ㄈㄢˇ ㄕˋ)
① to implicate others falsely
in a criminal act ② to
accuse one's benefactor
falsely

反舌(ㄈㄢˇ ㄕㄜˊ)
① the mockingbird ② the
name of a barbarian state in
ancient China

反射(ㄈㄢˇ ㄕㄜˋ)
to reflect; reflection; deflection of light or sound waves:
鏡子反射出光線。A mirror
reflects light.

反射角(ㄈㄢˇ ㄕㄜˋ ㄐㄧㄠˇ)
an angle of reflection

反射行為(ㄈㄢˇ ㄕㄜˋ ㄒㄧㄥˊ ㄨㄟˊ)
reflex action

反射運動(ㄈㄢˇ ㄕㄜˋ ㄩㄣˋ ㄉㄨㄥˋ)
reflex movement

反手(ㄈㄢˇ ㄕㄡˇ)
(sports) backhand

反坐(ㄈㄢˇ ㄗㄨㄛˋ)
the punishment meted out to
one who makes a false accusation against others in
court

反作用(ㄈㄢˇ ㄗㄨㄛˋ ㄩㄥˋ)
① undesirable reactions or
results; results contrary to
what were expected or

hoped for ②(physics) reaction

叉側(ㄔㄚ ㄘㄜ)
①to turn over and over; restless ②disloyal; treacherous

叉訴(ㄔㄚ ㄙㄨ)
to file a charge against the plaintiff; a countercharge; a crossaction; a counterclaim

叉而(ㄔㄚ ㄦ)
unexpectedly; contrarily

叉義字(ㄔㄚ ㄧ ㄗ)
an antonym

叉咬一口(ㄔㄚ ㄧㄠˇ ㄧ ㄎㄡˇ)
to fabricate a countercharge against one's accuser; to make a false countercharge

叉游擊戰(ㄔㄚ ㄧㄡˊ ㄐㄧ ㄓㄢˋ)
counter-guerrilla warfare

叉顏相向(ㄔㄚ ㄧㄢˊ ㄒㄧㄤ ㄒㄧㄤˋ)
to become hostile (to a friend)

叉映(ㄔㄚ ㄧㄥˋ)
to reflect (the confusion of the epoch, inner feelings, etc.); a reflection (of one's personality, performance, etc.)

叉應(應)(ㄔㄚ ㄧㄥˋ)
①response: 我向她求情，她沒有反應。My appeal to her pity met with no response. ②chemical reaction

叉應爐(ㄔㄚ ㄧㄥˋ ㄌㄨˊ)
(physics) a reactor

叉胃(ㄔㄚ ㄨㄟˋ)
to upset the stomach; nauseating

叉問(ㄔㄚ ㄨㄣˋ)
to rebut

叉語(ㄔㄚ ㄩˇ)
irony

六畫

【叔】521
ㄕㄨ shwu shú
1. younger brothers of one's father; paternal uncles
2. younger brothers of one's husband
3. a general designation for members of one's father's generation who are younger than one's father
4. declining

5. a Chinese family name

叔伯(ㄕㄨ ㄅㄜˊ)
①paternal uncles ②a relationship among cousins born of the same grandfather

叔本華(ㄕㄨ ㄅㄣˇ ㄏㄨㄚˊ)
Arthur Schopenhauer, 1788-1860, German philosopher

叔婆(ㄕㄨ ㄆㄛˊ)
the wife of one's grandfather's younger brother

叔母(ㄕㄨ ㄇㄨˇ)
the wife of one's father's younger brother

叔父(ㄕㄨ ㄈㄨˋ)
①a younger brother of one's father ②(in ancient China) a term used by the king to address feudal lords bearing his surname

叔公(ㄕㄨ ㄍㄨㄥ)
①a granduncle ②a polite term of a woman addressing to her husband's uncle

叔舅(ㄕㄨ ㄐㄧㄡˋ)
one's mother's younger brother

叔姪(ㄕㄨ ㄓˊ)
uncles and nephews

叔世(ㄕㄨ ㄕˋ)or叔季之世(ㄕㄨ ㄐㄧˋ ㄓ ㄕˋ)
(said of a nation) an age of decline

叔嫂(ㄕㄨ ㄙㄠˇ)
an aunt; the wife of a junior uncle

叔叔(ㄕㄨ •ㄕㄨ)
①a younger brother of one's father ②a younger brother of one's husband

叔子(ㄕㄨ •ㄗ)
one's husband's younger brother 亦作「小叔子」

叔祖(ㄕㄨ ㄗㄨˇ)
one's grandfather's younger brother; granduncle

【取】522
ㄑㄩˇ cheu qǔ
1. to take; to receive; to fetch; to obtain; to take hold of: 他已取得他所要的東西。He has obtained what he wants.
2. to select; to choose
3. to summon; to recall
4. to marry; to take a wife

取保(ㄑㄩˇ ㄅㄠˇ)
to get a guarantor

取便(ㄑㄩˇ ㄅㄧㄢˋ)
①to do as one pleases without restraint ②to promote; to facilitate

取不上(ㄑㄩˇ •ㄅㄨ ㄕㄤˋ)
to fail (in an examination, etc.); to be below the standard (set by the selecting board, etc.); unable to get selected

取譬(ㄑㄩˇ ㄆㄧˋ)
to give examples; to cite analogies

取名(ㄑㄩˇ ㄇㄧㄥˊ)
to name; to christen

取法乎上(ㄑㄩˇ ㄈㄚˇ ㄏㄨ ㄕㄤˋ)
to pattern after the first-rate (scholar, performer, etc.) —implying that one would end up a second fiddler

取得(ㄑㄩˇ ㄉㄜˊ)
to gain; to acquire; to obtain

取代(ㄑㄩˇ ㄉㄞˋ)
to replace; to substitute

取道(ㄑㄩˇ ㄉㄠˋ)
to take a route; to go by way of (some place): 他取道香港到台灣。He came to Taiwan by way of Hong Kong.

取締(ㄑㄩˇ ㄉㄧˋ)
to prohibit; to punish the violator (of a police regulation, etc.); to ban

取閙(ㄑㄩˇ ㄋㄠˋ)
to raise hell; to be unreasonable

取暖(ㄑㄩˇ ㄋㄨㄢˇ)
to warm oneself (by a fire, etc.): 她在爐火旁取暖。She warmed herself by the fire.

取樂(ㄑㄩˇ ㄌㄜˋ)
to make merry; to have a good time: 他們正在舞廳中取樂。They were making merry in the ballroom.

取快一時(ㄑㄩˇ ㄎㄨㄞˋ ㄧ ㄕˊ)
to get joy of the moment; to get temporary pleasure (caring little about adverse consequences afterwards)

取款(ㄑㄩˇ ㄎㄨㄢˇ)
to take money or draw money (from a bank, etc.)

取給(ㄑㄩˇ ㄐㄧˇ)
to rely on (someone or something) for supply

取經(ㄑㄩˇ ㄐㄧㄥ)

【又
部】

①to go on pilgrimage for Buddhist scriptures ②(used in mainland China) to learn or borrow the experience from others

取景(ㄑㄩˇ ㄐㄧㄥˇ)
to find a view (to photograph, paint, etc.)

取決(ㄑㄩˇ ㄐㄩㄝˊ)
It's up to (someone else to make the decision). 是否去買東西，由你取決。It is up to you whether we go shopping or not.

取齊(ㄑㄩˇ ㄑㄧˊ)
①to make even; to even up: 先把兩張紙取齊了再裁。Even up the edges of the two pieces of paper before you cut them. ②to assemble; to meet each other

取巧(ㄑㄩˇ ㄑㄧㄠˇ)
to take a snap course; to use finesse

取消(ㄑㄩˇ ㄒㄧㄠ)
to cancel; to nullify

取笑(ㄑㄩˇ ㄒㄧㄠˋ)
to laugh at; to make fun of

取信於人(ㄑㄩˇ ㄒㄧㄣˋ ㄩˊ ㄖㄣˊ)
to establish credibility among others

取向(ㄑㄩˇ ㄒㄧㄤˋ)
orientation

取之不盡(ㄑㄩˇ ㄓ ㄅㄨˋ ㄐㄧㄣˋ)
The supply is inexhaustible.

取長補短(ㄑㄩˇ ㄔㄤˊ ㄅㄨˇ ㄉㄨㄢˇ)
to learn from others' strong points to make up for one's weaknesses

取士(ㄑㄩˇ ㄕˋ)
to select talented persons for government service

取捨(ㄑㄩˇ ㄕㄜˇ)
to accept or refuse; to make a choice; to choose; to select

取勝(ㄑㄩˇ ㄕㄥˋ)
to win a victory; to score a success

取材(ㄑㄩˇ ㄘㄞˊ)
to select material (for a book, an article, etc.)

取而代之(ㄑㄩˇ ㄦˊ ㄉㄞˋ ㄓ)
to usurp another's (usually higher, and better) position

取義(ㄑㄩˇ ㄧˋ)
to die for the cause of justice and righteousness

取樣(ㄑㄩˇ ㄧㄤˋ)
sampling

取悅(ㄑㄩˇ ㄩㄝˋ)
to please

【受】 523
ㄕㄡˋ show shòu
1. to receive; to accept; to get: 他受過良好教育。He has received a good education.
2. to take; to stand; to suffer; to tolerate; to endure
3. to be pleasant to (the ears, etc.)
4. preceding a verb to form a passive voice

受窘(ㄕㄡˋ ㄐㄩㄥˇ)
to be embarrassed; to be discomfited

受不了(ㄕㄡˋ ㄅㄨˋ ㄌㄧㄠˇ)
①cannot stand it; cannot take it ②very much; too much

受騙(ㄕㄡˋ ㄆㄧㄢˋ)
to be cheated or swindled; to be fooled; to be tricked

受聘(ㄕㄡˋ ㄆㄧㄣˋ)
to accept a job offer

受命(ㄕㄡˋ ㄇㄧㄥˋ)
to accept an order; on the order of; to receive instructions; ·to receive appointment

受罰(ㄕㄡˋ ㄈㄚˊ)
to be punished or penalized; to be fined

受粉(ㄕㄡˋ ㄈㄣˇ)
(botany) pollination

受封(ㄕㄡˋ ㄈㄥ)
to be appointed with a title

受胎(ㄕㄡˋ ㄊㄞ)or 受孕(ㄕㄡˋ ㄩㄣˋ)
to be impregnated; to conceive; fertilization

受託(ㄕㄡˋ ㄊㄨㄛ)
to be entrusted with: 他受託看房子。He is entrusted with the care of a house.

受難(ㄕㄡˋ ㄋㄢˋ)
to suffer calamities or disasters; to be in distress

受累(ㄕㄡˋ ㄌㄟˋ)
to be involved; to get involved in a trouble (often implying innocence); to be put to much trouble: 讓你受累了。Sorry to have given you so much trouble.

受理(ㄕㄡˋ ㄌㄧˇ)
(said of a legal case) to b accepted by a court fo prosecution; to accept (petition, complaint, etc.)

受禮(ㄕㄡˋ ㄌㄧˇ)
①to receive a salutation (to receive a gift

受涼(ㄕㄡˋ ㄌㄧㄤˊ)
to catch cold: 我受涼了。 caught cold.

受凌辱(ㄕㄡˋ ㄌㄧㄥˊ ㄖㄨˇ)
to be insulted; to suffe humiliation

受格(ㄕㄡˋ ㄍㄜˊ)
the objective case

受苦(ㄕㄡˋ ㄎㄨˇ)
to suffer (hardships); t have a rough time

受盡苦難(ㄕㄡˋ ㄐㄧㄣˋ ㄎㄨˇ ㄋㄢˋ)
to suffer all the hardshi there is

受害(ㄕㄡˋ ㄏㄞˋ)
to be victimized; to suffe losses or injuries; to be damaged

受害不淺(ㄕㄡˋ ㄏㄞˋ ㄅㄨˋ ㄑㄧㄢˇ)
badly misguided or ill advised

受害人(ㄕㄡˋ ㄏㄞˋ ㄖㄣˊ)
the victim; the victimizee party

受寒(ㄕㄡˋ ㄏㄢˊ)
to catch cold; to suffer from a cold

受話器(ㄕㄡˋ ㄏㄨㄚˋ ㄑㄧˋ)
a telephone receiver 亦作「聽 筒」

受惠(ㄕㄡˋ ㄏㄨㄟˋ)
to be benefited; to receive benefit

受賄(ㄕㄡˋ ㄏㄨㄟˋ)
to be bribed; to receive bribes

受戒(ㄕㄡˋ ㄐㄧㄝˋ)
(Buddhism) to receive or dainment; to be initiated into priesthood; to do pen ance

受教(ㄕㄡˋ ㄐㄧㄠˋ)
①to receive education ②to receive instructions or guid ance; to be benefited by advice

受盡(ㄕㄡˋ ㄐㄧㄣˋ)
to suffer enough from; to suffer all kinds of; to have

one's fill of: 他們受盡帝國主義的壓迫。They have suffered enough from imperialist oppression.

受獎(ㄕㄡ ㄐㄧㄤˇ)
①to be cited ②to get a prize; to be rewarded: 立功者受獎。Those who accomplish deeds of merit shall be rewarded.

受驚(ㄕㄡ ㄐㄧㄥ)
to be frightened

受精(ㄕㄡ ㄐㄧㄥ)
to be fertilized; fertilization

受精卵(ㄕㄡ ㄐㄧㄥ ㄌㄨㄢˇ)
a zygote

受窘(ㄕㄡ ㄐㄩㄥˇ)
to be embarrassed

受欺侮(ㄕㄡ ㄑㄧ ㄨˇ)
to be bullied or maltreated

受氣(ㄕㄡ ㄑㄧˋ)
to become an object of another's anger; to be a punching bag; to suffer indignities

受屈(ㄕㄡ ㄑㄩ)
to be wronged; to suffer a grievance or indignity

受洗(ㄕㄡ ㄒㄧˇ)
to be baptized

受降(ㄕㄡ ㄒㄧㄤˊ)
to accept the surrender (of the vanquished enemy)

受刑(ㄕㄡ ㄒㄧㄥˊ)
to be tortured; to be punished (by law)

受訓(ㄕㄡ ㄒㄩㄣˋ)
to receive training: 他在軍中受訓。He receives training in the army.

受審(ㄕㄡ ㄕㄣˇ)
to face trial in court

受知(ㄕㄡ ㄓ)
to be appreciated and well-treated by a superior

受之無愧(ㄕㄡ ㄓ ㄨˊ ㄎㄨㄟˋ)
to deserve (a reward, gift, etc.)

受潮(ㄕㄡ ㄔㄠˊ)
to be damaged by moisture or humidity; to be affected with damp

受寵若驚(ㄕㄡ ㄔㄨㄥˇ ㄖㄨㄛˋ ㄐㄧㄥ)
to receive much more favor than one expected; to be agreeably surprised by the great favor one gets

---

受審(ㄕㄡ ㄕㄣˇ)
to stand trial; to be tried; to be on trial

受傷(ㄕㄡ ㄕㄤ)
to be injured; to get hurt; to be wounded

受賞(ㄕㄡ ㄕㄤˇ)
to be awarded; to get a reward

受熱(ㄕㄡ ㄖㄜˋ)
to be heated: 物體受熱則膨脹。When matter is heated, it expands.

受人擺佈(ㄕㄡ ㄖㄣˊ ㄅㄞˇ ㄅㄨˋ)
to be in leading strings

受人之託(ㄕㄡ ㄖㄣˊ ㄓ ㄊㄨㄛ)
to be entrusted by someone to do a job

受辱(ㄕㄡ ㄖㄨˇ)
to be humiliated

受災(ㄕㄡ ㄗㄞ)
to be hit by a natural adversity

受罪(ㄕㄡ ㄗㄨㄟˋ)
to suffer hardships; to have a bad time

受祠(ㄕㄡ ㄘˊ)
an object

受挫(ㄕㄡ ㄘㄨㄛˋ)
to be defeated; to be baffled; to be frustrated; to suffer a setback

受益(ㄕㄡ ㄧˋ)
to benefit from; to benefit by

受益費(ㄕㄡ ㄧˋ ㄈㄟˋ)
money paid to the government for the benefit derived from public construction projects

受益人(ㄕㄡ ㄧˋ ㄖㄣˊ)or 受惠者(ㄕㄡ ㄏㄨㄟˋ ㄓㄜˇ)
a beneficiary

受壓迫(ㄕㄡ ㄧㄚ ㄆㄛˋ)
to suffer oppression

受業(ㄕㄡ ㄧㄝˋ)
①to learn from a master ②your student (used in a letter addressed to a teacher)

受委屈(ㄕㄡ ㄨㄟˇ ㄑㄩ)
①to suffer a wrong or humiliation ②to be troubled or inconvenienced

受愚(ㄕㄡ ㄩˊ)
to be fooled, duped, tricked, etc.

受援(ㄕㄡ ㄩㄢˊ)
to receive aid

受孕(ㄕㄡ ㄩㄣˋ)
to become pregnant; to be impregnated

受用
①(ㄕㄡ ㄩㄥˋ)to enjoy; enjoyable ②(ㄕㄡ ㄩㄥˊ)⑧ to get the benefit ⑧ comfortable; to feel good

受用不盡(ㄕㄡ ㄩㄥˋ ㄅㄨˋ ㄐㄧㄣˋ)
to enjoy a benefit forever

七畫

【叛】 524
　ㄆㄢˋ　pann pàn
to rebel; to revolt

叛變(ㄆㄢˋ ㄅㄧㄢˋ)
a mutiny; an uprising; an insurgence; to revolt; to mutiny

叛兵(ㄆㄢˋ ㄅㄧㄥ)
soldiers in mutiny

叛徒(ㄆㄢˋ ㄊㄨˊ)
a rebel; an insurgent; a turncoat

叛逆(ㄆㄢˋ ㄋㄧˋ)
①to revolt; sedition; a rebellion ② one who rebels against his country or superiors

叛離(ㄆㄢˋ ㄌㄧˊ)
to betray; to desert

叛亂(ㄆㄢˋ ㄌㄨㄢˋ)
a rebellion; revolt; sedition

叛國(ㄆㄢˋ ㄍㄨㄛˊ)
to commit high treason; sedition

叛將(ㄆㄢˋ ㄐㄧㄤˋ)
a turncoat general; a general who mutinies

叛軍(ㄆㄢˋ ㄐㄩㄣ)
the rebellious army; the rebels; the rebellious troops

八畫

【叟】 525
　ㄙㄡˇ　soou sǒu
an elder; a senior; an old man; the old; venerable sir

十六畫

【叢】 526
　ㄘㄨㄥˊ　tsorng cóng

〔口部〕

1. to crowd together; to meet in large numbers
2. a shrub (plant); a thicket
3. a hideout or den (for robbers, etc.)
4. a Chinese family name

叢莽(ㄘㄨㄥ ㄇㄤˇ)
shrubbery

叢木(ㄘㄨㄥ ㄇㄨˋ)
underbrush

叢林(ㄘㄨㄥ ㄌㄧㄣˊ)
①a dense wood; a jungle; a forest ②a Buddhist monastery

叢刊(ㄘㄨㄥ ㄎㄢ)
a series of books; a collection

叢集(ㄘㄨㄥ ㄐㄧˊ)
①to crowd together ②to well up: 百感叢集 all sorts of feelings welling up

叢生(ㄘㄨㄥ ㄕㄥ)
①lush growth; dense growth ②full of (shortcomings)

叢書(ㄘㄨㄥ ㄕㄨ)
a collection of books by an author or on a subject; a library series

叢雜(ㄘㄨㄥ ㄗㄚˊ)
motley

口 部
ㄎㄡˇ koou ˇkou

【口】 527
ㄎㄡˇ koou ˇkou
1. the mouth
2. a person
3. a certain article (as a cistern, a big jar, etc.)
4. the edge or blade of a knife
5. an opening
6. a gate (especially in the Great Wall or city walls)
7. a crack

口碑(ㄎㄡˇ ㄅㄟ)
public praise

口碑載道(ㄎㄡˇ ㄅㄟ ㄗㄞˋ ㄉㄠˋ)
(said of good deeds, expertise, etc.) known widely, known universally, etc.

without considering the consequences of what one says

口蜜腹劍(ㄎㄡˇ ㄇㄧˋ ㄈㄨˋ ㄐㄧㄢˋ)
sweet words but a wicked heart; to flatter another while ready to plant a sword in his back; honey-mouthed and dagger-hearted

口伐(ㄎㄡˇ ㄈㄚˊ)
to attack verbally; to launch verbal attacks

口風(ㄎㄡˇ ㄈㄥ)
one's intention or view as revealed in what one says

口服(ㄎㄡˇ ㄈㄨˊ)
①to profess to be convinced: 口服心不服 to pretend to be convinced ②to take orally

口服避孕藥(ㄎㄡˇ ㄈㄨˊ ㄅㄧˋ ㄩㄣˋ ㄧㄠˋ)
an oral contraceptive; the pill

口服疫苗(ㄎㄡˇ ㄈㄨˊ ㄧˋ ㄇㄧㄠˊ)
oral vaccine

口福(ㄎㄡˇ ㄈㄨˊ)
enjoyment of the palate; luck in having good food

口腹(ㄎㄡˇ ㄈㄨˋ)
appetite (for food); indulgence in good food

口德(ㄎㄡˇ ㄉㄜˊ)
propriety in one's remarks; proper restraints in one's utterances

口袋(ㄎㄡˇ ㄉㄞˋ)
a pocket

口頭(ㄎㄡˇ ㄊㄡˊ)
verbally; orally; oral (communication)

口頭禪(ㄎㄡˇ ㄊㄡˊ ㄔㄢˊ)
platitudes; pet phrases; a meaningless phrase which one uses repetitiously

口頭聲明(ㄎㄡˇ ㄊㄡˊ ㄕㄥ ㄇㄧㄥˊ)
an oral statement

口頭語(ㄎㄡˇ ㄊㄡˊ ㄩˇ)
an expression which one uses regularly or constantly

口糧(ㄎㄡˇ ㄌㄧㄤˊ)
food rations; grain rations

口令(ㄎㄡˇ ㄌㄧㄥˋ)
①a military password ②a verbal instruction; word of command

口蓋(ㄎㄡˇ ㄍㄞˋ)
the palate

口供(ㄎㄡˇ ㄍㄨㄥ)
a confession; a thing confessed; a verbal report in court or police station (by suspect, witness, etc.)

口渴(ㄎㄡˇ ㄎㄜˇ)or口乾(ㄎㄡˇ ㄍㄢ)
thirsty

口快(ㄎㄡˇ ㄎㄨㄞˋ)
①to speak rashly; quick and thoughtless in speech ②to speak frankly or honestly

口號(ㄎㄡˇ ㄏㄠˋ)
①a slogan ②(military) an oral command

口惠(ㄎㄡˇ ㄏㄨㄟˋ)
lip service; empty promises

口紅(ㄎㄡˇ ㄏㄨㄥˊ)
a lipstick 亦作「唇膏」

口吃(ㄎㄡˇ ㄐㄧˊ)
to stammer; to stutter; a stutter: 他說話有點口吃。He speaks with a slight stutter.

口技(ㄎㄡˇ ㄐㄧˋ)
vocal imitation; oral stunts (i.e. the ability to imitate various sounds with the mouth)

口角春風(ㄎㄡˇ ㄐㄧㄠˇ ㄔㄨㄣ ㄈㄥ)
to say good words about others

口講指畫(ㄎㄡˇ ㄐㄧㄤˇ ㄓˇ ㄏㄨㄚˋ)
to gesticulate

口徑(ㄎㄡˇ ㄐㄧㄥˋ)
①the caliber (of a gun etc.) ②the diameter (of a round object)

口訣(ㄎㄡˇ ㄐㄩㄝˊ)
a pithy formula (often in rhyme); tables which should be committed to memory for ready use, as the multiplication table, etc.

口氣(ㄎㄡˇ ㄑㄧˋ)
①the meaning (usually hidden) of words said ②the way of speaking

]琴(ㄎㄡ ㄑㄧㄣ)
a harmonica

]腔(ㄎㄡ ㄑㄧㄤ)
the cavity of the mouth

]腔衛生(ㄎㄡ ㄑㄧㄤ ㄨㄟ ㄕㄥ)
oral hygiene

]血未乾(ㄎㄡ ㄒㄧㄝˇ ㄨㄟˋ ㄍㄢ)
A promise has scarcely been made (before it is broken).

]涎(ㄎㄡ ㄒㄧㄢˊ)
saliva

]信(ㄎㄡ ㄒㄧㄣˋ)
a verbal message

]香糖(ㄎㄡ ㄒㄧㄤ ㄊㄤˊ)
chewing gum: 小孩喜歡口香糖。Kids like chewing gum.

]直心快(ㄎㄡ ㄓˊ ㄒㄧㄣ ㄎㄨㄞˋ)
to talk bluntly; to be frank

]罩(ㄎㄡ ㄓㄠˋ)
a gauze mask (worn over the nose and the mouth); a mouth-muffle (to prevent infections, etc.)

]占(ㄎㄡ ㄓㄢˋ)
to improvise: 他口占一詩。He improvises a poem.

]誅筆伐(ㄎㄡ ㄓㄨ ㄅㄧˇ ㄈㄚ)
to attack both by speech and in writing; to condemn (a wrongdoer) by the public

]拙(ㄎㄡ ㄓㄨㄛˊ)
not good at speaking

]齒留香(ㄎㄡ ㄔˇ ㄌㄧㄡˊ ㄒㄧㄤ)
very delicious; delightful to the taste bud

]齒伶俐(ㄎㄡ ㄔˇ ㄌㄧㄥˊ ㄌㄧˋ)
glib and suave

]齒清晰(ㄎㄡ ㄔˇ ㄑㄧㄥ ㄒㄧ)or 口齒清楚(ㄎㄡ ㄔˇ ㄑㄧㄥ ㄔㄨˇ)
to talk distinctly; clear enunciation

]臭(ㄎㄡ ㄔㄡˋ)
halitosis; bad breath

]稱(ㄎㄡ ㄔㄥ)
to say; to claim

]傳(ㄎㄡ ㄔㄨㄢˊ)
① hearsay ② to teach orally

]傳心授(ㄎㄡ ㄔㄨㄢˊ ㄒㄧㄣ ㄕㄡˋ)
oral teaching that inspires true understanding within

]瘡(ㄎㄡ ㄔㄨㄤ)
an aphtha

]實(ㄎㄡ ㄕˊ)
① an excuse, a pretext ② something which makes one to be ridiculed or criticized by others

]試(ㄎㄡ ㄕˋ)
an oral test

]是心非(ㄎㄡ ㄕˋ ㄒㄧㄣ ㄈㄟ)
to say one thing and mean another; to mean contrary to what is spoken

]舌(ㄎㄡ ㄕㄜˊ)
quarrels, bickerings, squabbles, dispute, argument, etc.

]哨(ㄎㄡ ㄕㄠˋ)
a whistle

]授(ㄎㄡ ㄕㄡˋ)
① to teach orally; oral instruction ② dictate

]述(ㄎㄡ ㄕㄨˋ)
to narrate; to make an oral report of something; to dictate: 他口述自己的冒險。He narrated his adventure.

]說無憑(ㄎㄡ ㄕㄨㄛ ㄨˊ ㄆㄧㄥˊ)
An oral agreement cannot serve as evidence. 或An oral promise is not binding.

]水(ㄎㄡ ㄕㄨㄟˇ)
saliva

]若懸河(ㄎㄡ ㄖㄨㄛˋ ㄒㄩㄢˊ ㄏㄜˊ)
words flowing out like a cataract—glib; eloquent

]子(ㄎㄡ ㄗˇ)
an opening; a hole; a cut

]燥脣乾(ㄎㄡ ㄗㄠˋ ㄔㄨㄣˊ ㄍㄢ)
① very thirsty ② to talk (or to persuade another) until one's mouth is rock-dry

]才(ㄎㄡ ㄘㄞˊ)
eloquence; eloquent: 他很有口才。He is an eloquent speaker.

]岸(ㄎㄡ ㄢˋ)
a harbor; a river port; a trading port

]耳相傳(ㄎㄡ ㄦˇ ㄒㄧㄤ ㄔㄨㄢˊ)
to teach orally

]譯(ㄎㄡ ㄧˋ)
to interpret; to translate orally; oral interpretation

]音(ㄎㄡ ㄧㄣ)
an accent (in speaking a peculiar language or dialect)

]味(ㄎㄡ ㄨㄟˋ)
① a person's taste: 各人口味不同。Tastes differ. ② the flavor or taste of food

]吻(ㄎㄡ ㄨㄣˇ)
a tone; the connotation of what is being said 亦作「語

氣」

]語(ㄎㄡ ㄩˇ)
① plain, spoken language ② to slander

]約(ㄎㄡ ㄩㄝ)
to make an appointment orally; an oral appointment: 我和他有口約。I had an oral appointment with him.

二畫

【叨】528
1. ㄉㄠ dau dāo
talkative; garrulous; fond of talking

叨叨(ㄉㄠ ˙ㄉㄠ)
garrulous; a chatterbox; to talk too much

叨叨念念(ㄉㄠ ㄉㄠ ㄋㄧㄢˋ ㄋㄧㄢˋ)
to mutter and grumble

叨念着(ㄉㄠ ㄋㄧㄢˋ ˙ㄓㄜ)
to chatter incessantly; to nag

叨嘮(ㄉㄠ ˙ㄌㄠ)
① talkative; garrulous; to nag; to chatter ② to complain

【叨】528
2. ㄊㄠ tau tāo
to be favored with; to get the benefit of

叨陪末座(ㄊㄠ ㄆㄟˊ ㄇㄛˋ ㄗㄨㄛˋ)
to be honored with a seat (usually in a distinguished gathering)

叨光(ㄊㄠ ㄍㄨㄤ)
thanks (for a favor done); to have the honor

叨教(ㄊㄠ ㄐㄧㄠˋ)
to trouble you by requesting your instructions 或 Thank you for favoring (us) with your instructions or advice.

叨擾(ㄊㄠ ㄖㄠˇ)
Thanks for the wonderful entertainment (which has put you to great trouble).

叨在知己(ㄊㄠ ㄗㄞˋ ㄓ ㄐㄧˇ)
Since you are my good friend, (I do not have to look for proper words to express my deep appreciation for the great favor you have done me.)

【叼】529
ㄉㄧㄠ diau diāo
to hold in the mouth: 貓叼著

一隻老鼠。The cat held a mouse in its mouth.

[口部]

【古】530
《ㄍㄨ guu gǔ》
1. ancient; antiquated; old; antiquity
2. not following current customs or practices
3. a Chinese family name

古巴《ㄍㄨ ㄅㄚ》
Cuba

古巴人《ㄍㄨ ㄅㄚ ㄖㄣˊ》
a Cuban

古板《ㄍㄨ ㄅㄢˇ》
① inactive; dumb ② anachronistic; out of date; old-fashioned; square 亦作「保守」: 他很古板。He was real square.

古本《ㄍㄨ ㄅㄣˇ》
books of ancient printing

古樸《ㄍㄨ ㄆㄨˊ》
kind and simple; simple and unsophisticated

古法《ㄍㄨ ㄈㄚˇ》
time-honored methods

古方《ㄍㄨ ㄈㄤ》
an ancient medical prescription (believed to be very effective)

古風《ㄍㄨ ㄈㄥ》
① ancient practices—usually connoting honesty and simplicity ② ancient-style poetry

古代《ㄍㄨ ㄉㄞˋ》
ancient times

古道《ㄍㄨ ㄉㄠˋ》
① ancient ways—usually connoting honesty and simplicity ② time-worn roads; ancient paths

古道熱腸《ㄍㄨ ㄉㄠˋ ㄖㄜˋ ㄔㄤˊ》
honest and upright, and willing to help

古調《ㄍㄨ ㄉㄧㄠˋ》
an ancient tune—anachronistic; outdated

古典《ㄍㄨ ㄉㄧㄢˇ》
classics; classical

古典音樂《ㄍㄨ ㄉㄧㄢˇ ㄧㄣ ㄩㄝˋ》
classical music

古典文學《ㄍㄨ ㄉㄧㄢˇ ㄨㄣˊ ㄒㄩㄝˊ》
classical literature

古都《ㄍㄨ ㄉㄨ》
an ancient capital

古董《ㄍㄨ ㄉㄨㄥˇ》
antiques; curios: 他是古董鑑賞家。He is a connoisseur of curios.

古體詩《ㄍㄨ ㄊㄧˇ ㄕ》
ancient-style poetry

古銅色《ㄍㄨ ㄊㄨㄥˊ ㄙㄜˋ》
the color of bronze; brown and healthy

古來《ㄍㄨ ㄌㄞˊ》
since ancient times

古老《ㄍㄨ ㄌㄠˇ》
old; antiquated; ancient

古怪《ㄍㄨ ㄍㄨㄞˋ》
① strange; queer; eccentric; odd ② anachronistic

古柯鹼《ㄍㄨ ㄎㄜ ㄐㄧㄢˇ》
cocaine

古話《ㄍㄨ ㄏㄨㄚˋ》
an old saying: 古話說, 有志者事竟成。As the old saying goes, "Where there's a will, there's a way."

古畫《ㄍㄨ ㄏㄨㄚˋ》
ancient paintings

古跡《ㄍㄨ ㄐㄧ》
relics; ancient remains

古籍《ㄍㄨ ㄐㄧˊ》
ancient books

古今《ㄍㄨ ㄐㄧㄣ》
in ancient and modern times

古今中外《ㄍㄨ ㄐㄧㄣ ㄓㄨㄥ ㄨㄞˋ》
everywhere and all times; ancient and modern, Chinese and foreign

古今一轍《ㄍㄨ ㄐㄧㄣ ㄧ ㄔㄜˋ》
(said of principles, reasoning, etc.) to apply in both ancient and modern times; true in all times

古井不波《ㄍㄨ ㄐㄧㄥˇ ㄅㄨˋ ㄅㄛ》
impervious to desires and passions

古錢《ㄍㄨ ㄑㄧㄢˊ》
ancient money; ancient currency; ancient coins: 他搜集古錢。He collects ancient coins.

古稀《ㄍㄨ ㄒㄧ》
70 years of age

古昔《ㄍㄨ ㄒㄧˊ》
the time long ago; ancient times

古訓《ㄍㄨ ㄒㄩㄣˋ》
① ancient teachings; the lessons of antiquity ② books and works left by a late emperor

古裝 or 古妝《ㄍㄨ ㄓㄨㄤ》
ancient costumes

古塚《ㄍㄨ ㄓㄨㄥˇ》
ancient graves; ancient mounds

古剎《ㄍㄨ ㄔㄚˋ》
an ancient temple

古城《ㄍㄨ ㄔㄥˊ》
an ancient city

古詩《ㄍㄨ ㄕ》
① ancient-style poetry ② poems composed by ancient scholars

古時候《ㄍㄨ ㄕˊ ㄏㄡˋ》
in ancient times; in the olden days

古史《ㄍㄨ ㄕˇ》
ancient history: 他研究古史。He studied ancient history.

古事《ㄍㄨ ㄕˋ》
an old story; a legend

古生代《ㄍㄨ ㄕㄥ ㄉㄞˋ》
(geology) the Paleozoic Era

古生物《ㄍㄨ ㄕㄥ ㄨˋ》
ancient, extinct life

古書《ㄍㄨ ㄕㄨ》
ancient books: 古書十分珍貴。The ancient books are very precious.

古人《ㄍㄨ ㄖㄣˊ》
ancient people

古瓷《ㄍㄨ ㄘˊ》
ancient porcelain

古色古香《ㄍㄨ ㄙㄜˋ ㄍㄨ ㄒㄧㄤ》
(usually said of decor, furniture, etc.) in graceful ancient style

古雅《ㄍㄨ ㄧㄚˇ》
(said of buildings, works of art, etc.) graceful and refined

古諺《ㄍㄨ ㄧㄢˋ》
ancient proverbs or quotations

古音《ㄍㄨ ㄧㄣ》
① the pronunciation of characters in ancient times ② rhyme according to such pronunciation

古物《ㄍㄨ ㄨˋ》
antiques; curios; relics; things that are ancient

古玩《ㄍㄨ ㄨㄢˊ》
curios; antiques

古文《ㄍㄨ ㄨㄣˊ》

① ancient written language
② an old Chinese literary style

文字《ㄨㄣˊㄗˋ》
ancient writing

往今來《ㄨㄤˇㄐㄧㄣㄌㄞˊ》
since time immemorial; from ancient times till today; of all ages; through the ages

語《ㄍㄨˇㄩˇ》
① an archaism ② an old saying

樂《ㄍㄨˇㄩㄝˋ》
ancient music; Chinese classical music; a piece of refined music

【句】 531
1. ㄐㄧㄩˋ jiuh jù
a sentence

法《ㄐㄩˋㄈㄚˇ》
sentence structure; syntax

讀《ㄐㄩˋㄉㄡˋ》
sentences and phrases

號《ㄐㄩˋㄏㄠˋ》
a full stop or period

句實話《ㄐㄩˋㄐㄩˋㄕˊㄏㄨㄚˋ》
Every word said is true.

句有理《ㄐㄩˋㄐㄩˋㄧㄡˇㄌㄧˇ》
Every word sounds reasonable.

型《ㄐㄩˋㄒㄧㄥˊ》
a sentence pattern

子《ㄐㄩˋㄗˇ》
a sentence

【句】 531
2. (勾)《ㄍㄡ gou gōu》
a Chinese family name

踐《ㄍㄡㄐㄧㄢˋ》
Kou Chien—the king of Yüeh during the Epoch of Warring States

【另】 532
ㄌㄧㄥˋ linq lìng
1. another; extra; in addition; besides
2. to separate; separation (as of a couple); to divide

開蹊徑《ㄌㄧㄥˋㄎㄞㄒㄧㄐㄧㄥˋ》
to open or find a new path or snap course

另行《ㄌㄧㄥˋㄒㄧㄥˊ》
to order or arrange (something) separately

函《ㄌㄧㄥˋㄏㄢˊ》
a separate letter; to write another letter

就《ㄌㄧㄥˋㄐㄧㄡˋ》

to leave for a new job; a new position

另起爐灶《ㄌㄧㄥˋㄑㄧˇㄌㄨˊㄗㄠˋ》
① to start a new trade or line of business ② to start all over again; to begin anew

另請高明《ㄌㄧㄥˋㄑㄧㄥˇㄍㄠㄇㄧㄥˊ》
to find someone better qualified (than myself)

另想辦法《ㄌㄧㄥˋㄒㄧㄤˇㄅㄢˋㄈㄚˇ》
to think of some other way or solution

另行安排《ㄌㄧㄥˋㄒㄧㄥˊㄢㄆㄞˊ》
to make separate arrangements

另案辦理《ㄌㄧㄥˋㄢˋㄅㄢˋㄌㄧˇ》
to be handled as a separate case

另議《ㄌㄧㄥˋㄧˋ》
to be discussed or negotiated separately

另有他故《ㄌㄧㄥˋㄧㄡˇㄊㄚㄍㄨˋ》
There must be other reasons.

另有高就《ㄌㄧㄥˋㄧㄡˇㄍㄠㄐㄧㄡˋ》
to have found better employment elsewhere (referring to others)

另有企圖《ㄌㄧㄥˋㄧㄡˇㄑㄧˇㄊㄨˊ》
to have other intentions, plans, or ulterior designs

另有事情《ㄌㄧㄥˋㄧㄡˇㄕˋㄑㄧㄥˊ》
to have other fish to fry

另眼看待《ㄌㄧㄥˋㄧㄢˇㄎㄢˋㄉㄞˋ》
to be offered special treatment; to give favored treatment

另外《ㄌㄧㄥˋㄨㄞˋ》
besides; another; other; in addition; additionally: 那完全是另外一回事。 That's quite another matter.

【叩】 533
ㄎㄡˋ kow kòu
1. to knock; to hit
2. to ask
3. to kotow

叩門《ㄎㄡˋㄇㄣˊ》
to knock at a door

叩頭《ㄎㄡˋㄊㄡˊ》or **叩首**《ㄎㄡˋㄕㄡˇ》
to kotow—to kneel and touch the ground with the forehead to show great deference, practiced in old China as the highest form of salutation

叩見《ㄎㄡˋㄐㄧㄢˋ》or **叩謁**《ㄎㄡˋㄧㄝˋ》
to call on; to interview or visit a superior

叩謝《ㄎㄡˋㄒㄧㄝˋ》
to thank politely

叩安《ㄎㄡˋㄢ》
to send greetings

叩問《ㄎㄡˋㄨㄣˋ》
to ask; to make inquiries

【只】 534
ㄓˇ jyy zhǐ
1. only; merely
2. but; yet

只不過《ㄓˇㄅㄨˊㄍㄨㄛˋ》
only; just; merely

只怕《ㄓˇㄆㄚˋ》
to be afraid of only one thing; to be afraid of no one (or nothing) except…

只得《ㄓˇㄉㄜˊ》
to have to; there is no alternative; to be obliged to

只顧《ㄓˇㄍㄨˋ》
① to care about only (the present, etc.); to be absorbed in—implying shortsightedness ② please don't hesitate to…

只管《ㄓˇㄍㄨㄢˇ》
① (do anything) as you wish; please don't hesitate to… ② to be responsible for…only

只可《ㄓˇㄎㄜˇ》
to be permitted to do this or that only; can only

只好《ㄓˇㄏㄠˇ》
the only alternative is to…; the next best thing to do is to…; to have to

只見《ㄓˇㄐㄧㄢˋ》
① to see only ② to behold

只消《ㄓˇㄒㄧㄠ》
to have only to; to need only (a few minutes, etc.); only; just

只許官放火，不許百姓點燈
《ㄓˇㄒㄩˇㄍㄨㄢㄈㄤˋㄏㄨㄛˇ，ㄅㄨˋㄒㄩˇㄅㄞˇㄒㄧㄥˋㄉㄧㄢˇㄉㄥ》
(literally) The magistrates are free to burn down houses, while the common people are forbidden even to light lamps. —(figuratively) Under tyranny, people can not do anything right while officials are free to do everything wrong.

（口部）

只是（ㄓㄧㄕ）
①but; yet ②merely; only; just

只此一家（ㄓㄧㄘㄧㄐㄧㄚ）
This is the only shop of its kind.—There is no branch.

只要（ㄓㄧㄠ）
①to want only… ②all one has to do is to…

只要功夫深，鐵杵磨成針（ㄓㄧㄠㄍㄨㄥㄈㄨㄕㄣ，ㄊㄧㄝㄔㄨˇㄇㄛˊㄔㄥˊㄓㄣ）
Constant grinding can turn an iron rod into a needle.—Perseverance and diligence make a person successful.

只有（ㄓㄧㄡˇ）
①to have…only; only; alone ②to have to (do or be)

只因（ㄓㄧㄣ）
only because; for the simple reason that…

【叫】 535 （ㄐㄧㄠ jiao jiào）
1. to be called or known as: 這花叫什麼名字？ What is this flower called?
2. to cry; to shout; to scream; a shout or scream: 有人向那男孩吼叫。 Somebody shouted at the boy.
3. to call; to summon
4. to cause: 他真叫母親擔心。 He really caused a lot of anxiety to his mother.

叫不醒（ㄐㄧㄠㄅㄨˋㄒㄧㄥˇ）
cannot wake someone up

叫罵（ㄐㄧㄠㄇㄚˋ）
to scream and use foul language like a fishwife; to shout curses

叫賣（ㄐㄧㄠㄇㄞˋ）
to peddle goods in the streets by chanting; to hawk

叫門（ㄐㄧㄠㄇㄣˊ）
to knock at the door; to call someone from inside

叫姑娘（ㄐㄧㄠㄍㄨㄋㄧㄤ）
to summon a prostitute

叫苦（ㄐㄧㄠㄎㄨˇ）
to complain of hardship or suffering

叫苦連天（ㄐㄧㄠㄎㄨˇㄌㄧㄢˊㄊㄧㄢ）
to be full of complaints; to mouth complaints about hardships

叫好兒（ㄐㄧㄠㄏㄠˇㄦ）
to cheer; to applaud (Peking opera actors); to utter a bravo 亦作「叫采」

叫喊（ㄐㄧㄠㄏㄢˇ）
to shout; to yell; to scream; to cry; to call loudly: 不要對我叫喊！ Don't shout at me!

叫化子（ㄐㄧㄠㄏㄨㄚˋㄗ）
a beggar 亦作「乞丐」

叫貨（ㄐㄧㄠㄏㄨㄛˋ）
to order goods

叫喚（ㄐㄧㄠㄏㄨㄢ）
①to call; to summon ②to shout

叫街的（ㄐㄧㄠㄐㄧㄝㄉㄜ）
a beggar wandering along the streets and crying for pity

叫屈（ㄐㄧㄠㄑㄩ）
to cry out for justice; to protest against injustice; to complain of unfair treatment

叫囂（ㄐㄧㄠㄒㄧㄠ）
to shout and yell; vociferation; clamor

叫醒（ㄐㄧㄠㄒㄧㄥˇ）
to waken; to wake up: 請在明天早晨七點叫醒我。 Please wake me up at 7 tomorrow morning.

叫陣（ㄐㄧㄠㄓㄣˋ）
(in ancient China) to challenge a general of the opposite camp to battle; to challenge the enemy to battle

叫嚷（ㄐㄧㄠㄖㄤˇ）
to shout; to howl; to clamor

叫子（ㄐㄧㄠ˙ㄗ）
a whistle

叫座（兒）（ㄐㄧㄠㄗㄨㄛˋㄦ）
(said of performing artists, plays, dramas, etc.) to have appeal to the audience; good box office: 這音樂會並不叫座。 This concert is not good box office.

叫做（ㄐㄧㄠㄗㄨㄛˋ）
to be called; to be known as: 這種機器叫做起重機。 This machine is called a crane.

叫菜（ㄐㄧㄠㄘㄞˋ）
to order food (in a restaurant); to order dishes: 請替我叫菜。 Please order for me.

【召】 536 （ㄓㄠˋ jaw zhào）
1. to summon; to call up
2. to cause; to invite 參看「召禍」

召募（ㄓㄠˋㄇㄨˋ）
to enlist or recruit (soldiers) 亦作「徵募」

召開（ㄓㄠˋㄎㄞ）
to convene; to convoke

召禍（ㄓㄠˋㄏㄨㄛˋ）
(literary language) to court disaster; to invite disaster

召回（ㄓㄠˋㄏㄨㄟˊ）
to recall (a diplomat from abroad)

召喚（ㄓㄠˋㄏㄨㄢˋ）
to call; to summon

召集（ㄓㄠˋㄐㄧˊ）
①to convene (a meeting, etc.); to summon (a council) ②to call to arms

召見（ㄓㄠˋㄐㄧㄢˋ）
to summon a subordinate; to be summoned by a superior

召之即來（ㄓㄠˋㄓㄐㄧˊㄌㄞˊ）
to come as soon as called

召租（ㄓㄠˋㄗㄨ）
for rent 亦作「招租」

【叭】 537 （ㄅㄚ ba bà）
a trumpet

【叮】 538 （ㄉㄧㄥ ding dīng）
1. the chimes of a bell
2. to exhort or enjoin repeatedly
3. to sting, as a mosquito, etc

叮噹（ㄉㄧㄥㄉㄤ）
dingdong (used for the sound of bells): 我們聽到鐘叮噹地響。 We heard the bell dingdonging.

叮嚀 or 丁寧（ㄉㄧㄥㄋㄧㄥˊ）
to exhort repeatedly

叮囑（ㄉㄧㄥㄓㄨˇ）
to enjoin and urge repeatedly

【可】 539 1. （ㄎㄜˇ kee kě）
1. may; can; to be able to
2. around; estimated at
3. an auxiliary
4. but; however
5. a Chinese family name

可悲（ㄎㄜˇㄅㄟ）
sad; lamentable

可鄙（ㄎㄜˇㄅㄧˇ）

contemptible; despicable; mean

可變(ㄎㄜ ㄅㄧㄢ)
variable

了不得了(ㄌㄜ ㄅㄨ˙ㄉㄜ ㄌㄧㄠˇ)
What a mess! 或 How disastrous!

了不可以(ㄌㄜ ㄅㄨ˙ㄎㄜ ㄧˇ)
can; may (used at the beginning of a question): 我可不可以把它交給你? May I leave this with you?

了不是(ㄌㄜ ㄅㄨㄕˋ)or 可不是嗎(ㄌㄜ ㄅㄨˋ ㄕ ㄇㄚ˙)
really; sure enough

可怕(ㄎㄜ ㄆㄚˋ)
dreadful; frightening; fearsome; terrible: 那次地震是可怕的災難。The earthquake was a dreadful disaster.

可佩(ㄎㄜ ㄆㄟˋ)
admirable: 他的行為可佩。His behavior is admirable.

可免(ㄎㄜ ㄇㄧㄢˇ)
avoidable; may be exempted from; may avoid; may escape

可否(ㄎㄜ ㄈㄡˇ)
①can; may (used at the beginning of a question): 可否一同去呢? Can I go with you? ②an affirmative or negative comment

可分性(ㄎㄜ ㄈㄣ ㄒㄧㄥˋ)
(mathematics) divisibility

可風(ㄎㄜ ㄈㄥ)
exemplary; worthy to be followed: 他廉潔可風。His honesty is worthy to be followed.

可達(ㄎㄜ ㄉㄚˊ)
attainable; accessible; within reach

可大可小(ㄎㄜ ㄉㄚˋ ㄎㄜ ㄒㄧㄠˇ)
(literally) The size is changeable.—elastic

可多可少(ㄎㄜ ㄉㄨㄛ ㄎㄜ ㄕㄠˇ)
The amount (or quantity) doesn't matter.

可鍛性(ㄎㄜ ㄉㄨㄢˋ ㄒㄧㄥˋ)
(metallurgy) malleability; forgeability

可歎(ㄎㄜ ㄊㄢˋ)
Alas! 或 What a pity! 可歎! 他被敵人殺死了。Alas! He was killed by the enemy.

可惱(ㄎㄜ ㄋㄠˇ)
irritable; provoking

可能(ㄎㄜ ㄋㄥˊ)
probable; possible: 儘可能早來。Come as early as possible.

可能性(ㄎㄜ ㄋㄥˊ ㄒㄧㄥˋ)
possibility; probability

可念(ㄎㄜ ㄋㄧㄢˋ)
① worthy of remembering ② to be pitied

可蘭經(ㄎㄜ ㄌㄢˊ ㄐㄧㄥ)
the Koran

可了不得(ㄎㄜ ㄌㄧㄠˇ ㄅㄨˋ ㄉㄜ)
How wonderful! 或 How marvelous!

可留就留(ㄎㄜ ㄌㄧㄡˊ ㄐㄧㄡˋ ㄌㄧㄡˊ)
If you think you can stay on, then stay on. (Otherwise, you may quit as you please.)

可憐(ㄎㄜ ㄌㄧㄢˊ)
pitiful; pitiable; poor; miserable; to have pity on; to be merciful to (a person): 他的處境很可憐。He was in a pitiable condition.

可憐蟲(ㄎㄜ ㄌㄧㄢˊ ㄔㄨㄥˊ)
a poor creature; a poor thing; a poor guy; a guy in trouble

可倫坡(ㄎㄜ ㄌㄨㄣˊ ㄆㄛ)
Colombo, capital of Sri Lanka

可慮(ㄎㄜ ㄌㄩˋ)
worrisome; to be worried

可歌可泣(ㄎㄜ ㄍㄜ ㄎㄜ ㄑㄧˋ)
(said of bravery or fortitude in serving the nation) very moving; very touching

可耕地(ㄎㄜ ㄍㄥ ㄉㄧˋ)
arable land; cultivable land

可怪(ㄎㄜ ㄍㄨㄞˋ)
to be strange

可貴(ㄎㄜ ㄍㄨㄟˋ)
valuable; praiseworthy; commendable: 這種熱情是很可貴的。Such enthusiasm is highly commendable.

可觀(ㄎㄜ ㄍㄨㄢ)
①to be worth seeing ②considerable (sum of money, losses, etc.): 他的收入相當可觀。He has a considerable income.

可攻可守(ㄎㄜ ㄍㄨㄥ ㄎㄜ ㄕㄡˇ)
equally valuable as a steppingstone for offense or a strong point for defense

可可(ㄎㄜ ㄎㄜ)
cocoa

可靠(ㄎㄜ ㄎㄠˋ)
trustworthy; dependable; reliable (sources, etc.): 該班選出一可靠的男孩做財務股長。The class chose a trustworthy boy for treasurer.

可口(ㄎㄜ ㄎㄡˇ)
tasty; pleasant to the palate: 道道菜很可口。This dish is very tasty.

可口可樂(ㄎㄜ ㄎㄡˇ ㄎㄜ ㄌㄜˋ)
Coca Cola or Coke

可恨(ㄎㄜ ㄏㄣˋ)
hateful; detestable; abominable

可嘉(ㄎㄜ ㄐㄧㄚ)
commendable; laudable

可加(ㄎㄜ ㄐㄧㄚ)
(botany) coca—a South American tree whose dried leaves are used to make cocaine and other alkaloids 亦作「古柯」

可見(ㄎㄜ ㄐㄧㄢˋ)
①that can be seen ②to be perceived: 可見他不能達到目的。It is perceived that he can not achieve his goal.

可見度(ㄎㄜ ㄐㄧㄢˋ ㄉㄨˋ)
visibility 亦作「能見度」: 在霧中可見度很低。In a fog the visibility is very poor.

可進可退(ㄎㄜ ㄐㄧㄣˋ ㄎㄜ ㄊㄨㄟˋ)
(where) one can either advance or withdraw—an advantageous position

可驚(ㄎㄜ ㄐㄧㄥ)
surprising; startling

可敬(ㄎㄜ ㄐㄧㄥˋ)
respectable; admirable: 他是可敬的人。He is a respectable man.

可欺(ㄎㄜ ㄑㄧ)
can be imposed upon; can be bullied with impunity

可期(ㄎㄜ ㄑㄧ)
can be expected; one may look forward to

可氣(ㄎㄜ ㄑㄧˋ)
irritable; disgusting; annoying

可巧(ㄎㄜ ㄑㄧㄠˇ)
by a coincidence; coincidently; as luck would have it; luckily: 我們大家正念著她，可

〔口 部〕

〔口部〕

巧她來了。We were just talking about her when she coincidently turned up.

可親(ㄎㄜˇ ㄑㄧㄣ)
kindly; friendly; amiable

可取(ㄎㄜˇ ㄑㄩˇ)
worth having; recommendable; desirable: 這個方案有可取之處。This plan has something recommendable.

可圈可點(ㄎㄜˇ ㄑㄩㄢ ㄎㄜˇ ㄉㄧㄢˇ)
①(said of a writing) very good ②(said of the manner in doing something) very laudable

可惜(ㄎㄜˇ ㄒㄧˊ)
It's a pity that.... 可惜他不能來。It's a pity that he can not come.

可喜可賀(ㄎㄜˇ ㄒㄧˇ ㄎㄜˇ ㄏㄜˋ)
Congratulations! 或 worth cheering and rejoicing

可笑(ㄎㄜˇ ㄒㄧㄠˋ)
laughable; ridiculous: 你穿這種衣服看起來真可笑。You look ridiculous in such a dress.

可信度(ㄎㄜˇ ㄒㄧㄣˋ ㄉㄨˋ)
(sociology) the confidence level

可想而知(ㄎㄜˇ ㄒㄧㄤˇ ㄦˊ ㄓ)
to be obvious; one can well imagine

可行(ㄎㄜˇ ㄒㄧㄥˊ)
feasible; can be carried out: 是否可行, 請斟酌。Please consider if this is feasible.

可行性(ㄎㄜˇ ㄒㄧㄥˊ ㄒㄧㄥˋ)
feasibility

可知(ㄎㄜˇ ㄓ)
①naturally; obviously; evidently: 他的大衣還在這兒。可知他還沒走。His overcoat is still here; evidently he has not gone yet. ②Don't you know? ③imaginable

可恥(ㄎㄜˇ ㄔˇ)
shameful: 以勤勞為光榮, 以懶惰為可恥。It's praiseworthy to work hard, and shameful to idle.

可拆(ㄎㄜˇ ㄔㄞ)
removable; detachable

可長可短(ㄎㄜˇ ㄔㄤˊ ㄎㄜˇ ㄉㄨㄢˇ)
The length is changeable (i.e. collapsible or elastic).

可乘之機(ㄎㄜˇ ㄔㄥˊ ㄓ ㄐㄧ)
an opportunity that can be exploited to somebody's advantage: 我們不給敵人以可乘之機。We give the enemy no opportunity.

可是(ㄎㄜˇ ㄕˋ)
①to be (in a more emphatic sense); will really be ②but; however: 我們工作了一整天, 雖然很累, 可是都很愉快。Having worked all the day, we are tired out but we feel happy. ③Is it that…?

可恃(ㄎㄜˇ ㄕˋ)
①to be reliable ②to have the means or resources

可燃性(ㄎㄜˇ ㄖㄢˊ ㄒㄧㄥˋ)
(chemistry) combustibility

可燃物(ㄎㄜˇ ㄖㄢˊ ㄨˋ)
combustible substance

可人(ㄎㄜˇ ㄖㄣˊ)
①enjoyable; lovable; likable ②a person with many admirable qualities; a charming character

可容(ㄎㄜˇ ㄖㄨㄥˊ)
capable of accommodating or holding…: 這旅館可容兩百位客人住宿。This hotel is capable of accommodating 200 guests.

可溶性(ㄎㄜˇ ㄖㄨㄥˊ ㄒㄧㄥˋ)
(chemistry) solubility

可憎(ㄎㄜˇ ㄗㄥ)or 可厭(ㄎㄜˇ ㄧㄢˋ)
abominable; detestable; disgusting or revolting

可操左券(ㄎㄜˇ ㄘㄠ ㄗㄨㄛˇ ㄑㄩㄢˋ)
to have a winning hand; to have an overwhelming chance to win

可塑性(ㄎㄜˇ ㄙㄨˋ ㄒㄧㄥˋ)
plasticity: 兒童的可塑性很高。The plasticity of children is very high.

可哀(ㄎㄜˇ ㄞ)
(it's) a pity that; sorrowful

可愛(ㄎㄜˇ ㄞˋ)
lovable; likable; lovely: 他是個可愛的孩子。He is a lovable child.

可疑(ㄎㄜˇ ㄧˊ)
①suspicious: 這外國人看起來可疑。The foreigner looked suspicious. ②debatable; questionable; doubtful

可以(ㄎㄜˇ ㄧˇ)
①can; may: 你可以這樣說。You may say so. ②Yes, you

can. 或 Yes, you may. 或 Okay. That will do.

可以意會, 不可以言傳(ㄎㄜˇ ㄧˇ ㄧˋ ㄏㄨㄟˋ, ㄅㄨˋ ㄎㄜˇ ㄧˇ ㄧㄢˊ ㄔㄨㄢˊ)
can be understood but can not be described

可有可無(ㄎㄜˇ ㄧㄡˇ ㄎㄜˇ ㄨˊ)
dispensable; not essential

可惡(ㄎㄜˇ ㄨˋ)
detestable; hateful: 那些人(?) 可惡! How detestable those people are!

可畏(ㄎㄜˇ ㄨㄟˋ)
awful; awe-inspiring; dreadful; horrible

可謂(ㄎㄜˇ ㄨㄟˋ)
one may well say; it may be said; it may be called

可望而不可卽(ㄎㄜˇ ㄨㄤˋ ㄦˊ ㄅㄨˋ ㄎㄜˇ ㄐㄧˊ)
can be looked at but not touched; can be gazed but not approached; will-o'-the wisp

可遇而不可求(ㄎㄜˇ ㄩˋ ㄦˊ ㄅㄨˋ ㄎㄜˇ ㄑㄧㄡˊ)
(something) considered to be uncertain

可用(ㄎㄜˇ ㄩㄥˋ)
①serviceable; in working order: 牙刷是可用的器具。A toothbrush is a serviceable instrument. ②employable; worth employing

【可】 539
　　2. ㄎㄜˋ keh kè
參看「可汗」

可汗(ㄎㄜˋ ㄏㄢˊ)
a khan

【台】 540
　　ㄊㄞˊ tair tái
1. a raised platform 亦作「臺」
2. a polite expression of addressing 參看「台端」

台風(ㄊㄞˊ ㄈㄥ)
stage manners

台甫(ㄊㄞˊ ㄈㄨˇ)
(used in formal speech) your name: 請問台甫? What is your name?

台端(ㄊㄞˊ ㄉㄨㄢ)
you (an honorific in addressing one's equal)

台光(ㄊㄞˊ ㄍㄨㄤ)
your presence (an honorific used in requesting another's presence at a party); 敬請台

光。Your presence is requested.

台駕(ㄊㄞ ㄐㄧㄚˋ)
Your Excellency; you (honorific usage)

台階(ㄊㄞ ㄐㄧㄝ)
① steps leading up to a building ② a chance to extricate oneself from an awkward position

台教(ㄊㄞ ㄐㄧㄠˋ)
your advice

台鑒(ㄊㄞ ㄐㄧㄢ)or 台照(ㄊㄞ ㄓㄠˋ)
a form used after the name in the salutation of a business letter

台啓(ㄊㄞ ㄑㄧˇ)
a term used after the name of the addressee on an envelope

台衙(ㄊㄞ ㄒㄧ)
(formal speech) your title

台柱(ㄊㄞ ㄓㄨˋ)
① an important actor in a troupe or cast ② an important person in an organization

台秤(ㄊㄞ ㄔㄥˋ)
a platform scale

台詞(ㄊㄞ ㄘˊ)
a stage dialogue; the actor's lines

台灣 or 臺灣(ㄊㄞ ㄨㄢ)
Taiwan or Formosa; 台灣是個島嶼。Taiwan is an island.

【叱】541　ㄔ chyh chìh
to scold; to revile

叱罵(ㄔ ㄇㄚˋ)
to scold; to revile; to rail at

叱名請安(ㄔ ㄇㄧㄥˊ ㄑㄧㄥˇ ㄢ)
Please give (your elders, parents, etc.) my compliments.

叱令(ㄔ ㄌㄧㄥˋ)
to shout an order

叱喝(ㄔ ㄏㄜˋ)
to shout or bawl angrily; to yell at

叱咤風雲(ㄔ ㄓㄚˋ ㄈㄥ ㄩㄣˊ)
(said of a dictator, conqueror, etc.) to lord it over the world

叱責(ㄔ ㄗㄜˊ)
to reproach; to scold; to censure; to blame

【史】542　ㄕˇ shyy shǐ
1. history; chronicles; annals
2. a Chinese family name

史筆(ㄕˇ ㄅㄧˇ)
① the writing brush of a historiographer ② what a historiographer recorded in history ③ the way in which a historiographer faithfully recorded facts in history

史部(ㄕˇ ㄅㄨˋ)
the second section of the *Four Collections of Books*

史不絕書(ㄕˇ ㄅㄨˋ ㄐㄩㄝˊ ㄕㄨ)
History abounds in examples of this.

史評(ㄕˇ ㄆㄧㄥˊ)
criticism on historical events, characters, etc.

史達林(ㄕˇ ㄉㄚˊ ㄌㄧㄣˊ)
Joseph V. Stalin, 1879-1953, Russian dictator

史達林格勒(ㄕˇ ㄉㄚˊ ㄌㄧㄣˊ ㄍㄜˊ ㄌㄜˋ)
Stalingrad (now renamed Volgograd), a city in the Soviet Union in Europe, on the Volga River

史料(ㄕˇ ㄌㄧㄠˋ)
historical data 參看「史話」

史官(ㄕˇ ㄍㄨㄢ)
a historiographer

史可法(ㄕˇ ㄎㄜˇ ㄈㄚˋ)
Shih Ko-fa, a general of the late Ming Dynasty during the Manchu invasion

史話(ㄕˇ ㄏㄨㄚˋ)
a historical story

史蹟 or 史跡(ㄕˇ ㄐㄧ)
① historic events ② historic relics

史記(ㄕˇ ㄐㄧˋ)
the *Historical Records*, by Ssu-Ma Chien(司馬遷)

史家(ㄕˇ ㄐㄧㄚ)
a historian

史前時代(ㄕˇ ㄑㄧㄢˊ ㄕˊ ㄉㄞˋ)
the prehistoric age

史學(ㄕˇ ㄒㄩㄝˊ)
history (as a science)

史詩(ㄕˇ ㄕ)
an epic

史實(ㄕˇ ㄕˊ)
historical facts

史書(ㄕˇ ㄕㄨ)or 史籍(ㄕˇ ㄐㄧˊ)
a book of history; an annal

史册(ㄕˇ ㄘㄜˋ)or 史乘(ㄕˇ ㄕㄥˋ)
a book of history

史無前例(ㄕˇ ㄨˊ ㄑㄧㄢˊ ㄌㄧˋ)
unprecedented in history; without precedent in history

史瓦濟蘭(ㄕˇ ㄨㄚˋ ㄐㄧˋ ㄌㄢˊ)
Swaziland

【右】543　ㄧㄡˋ yow yòu
1. right (as opposed to left)
2. west
3. to assist; to aid
4. to emphasize

右臂(ㄧㄡˋ ㄅㄧˋ)
① the right arm ② the right-hand man; an important helper 亦作「得力助手」

右邊(ㄧㄡˋ ㄅㄧㄢ)
the right-hand side

右派(ㄧㄡˋ ㄆㄞˋ)
① the right wing ② the rightists; the right-wingers; the conservatives

右面(ㄧㄡˋ ㄇㄧㄢˋ)
the right side; the right-hand side

右舵(ㄧㄡˋ ㄉㄨㄛˋ)
the right standard rudder; the right rudder

右軍(ㄧㄡˋ ㄐㄩㄣ)
① one of the emperor's three armies, i.e. the right army (右軍), the central army (中軍), and the left army (左軍) ② another name of Wang Hsi-chih(王羲之), the most famous calligrapher in Chinese history

右傾(ㄧㄡˋ ㄑㄧㄥ)
right-leaning; conservative

右舷(ㄧㄡˋ ㄒㄧㄢˊ)
the starboard

右心室(ㄧㄡˋ ㄒㄧㄣ ㄕˋ)
the right ventricle

右心耳(ㄧㄡˋ ㄒㄧㄣ ㄦˇ)
the right auricle

右行(ㄧㄡˋ ㄒㄧㄥˊ)
(said of Chinese calligraphy) written from right to left

右職(ㄧㄡˋ ㄓˊ)
an important position

右手(ㄧㄡˋ ㄕㄡˇ)
① the right hand ② the right-hand side

右首(ㄧㄡˋ ㄕㄡˇ)
the right-hand side; the right

右翼(ㄧㄡˋ ㄧˋ)
①the right wing ②the rightists; the right-wingers; the conservatives ③ the right flank or wing (of an army)

右翼份子(ㄧㄡˋ ㄧˋ ㄈㄣˋ ㄗˇ)
a right-winger; a member of the Right

右武(ㄧㄡˋ ㄨˇ)
giving emphasis to military affairs

右文(ㄧㄡˋ ㄨㄣˊ)
giving emphasis to civil affairs

【回】544 ㄏㄨㄟˊ poo pò
unable; improbable

回耐 or 回奈(ㄏㄨㄟˊ ㄋㄞˋ)
It is an unfortunate fact that....

回信(ㄏㄨㄟˊ ㄒㄧㄣˋ)
unreliable; not trustworthy

回測(ㄏㄨㄟˊ ㄘㄜˋ)
unfathomable; unpredictable

【叶】545 ㄒㄧㄝˊ shye xié
the ancient form of 協

叶韻(ㄒㄧㄝˊ ㄩㄣˋ)
to rime; to put into rime

【司】546 ㄙ sy sī
1. to have charge of; to preside over: 各司其事, Each presides over his own business.
2. a (government) department

司必簧(ㄙ ㄅㄧˋ ㄏㄨㄤˊ)
(machinery) a spring 亦作「發條」

司馬(ㄙ ㄇㄚˇ)
①(in ancient China) the minister of war ②a Chinese family name

司馬光(ㄙ ㄇㄚˇ ㄍㄨㄤ)
Ssu-Ma Kuang, a conservative writer of the Sung Dynasty

司馬遷(ㄙ ㄇㄚˇ ㄑㄧㄢ)
Ssu-Ma Chien, a famous historian of the Han Dynasty

司馬昭之心,路人皆知(ㄙ ㄇㄚˇ ㄓㄠ ㄓ ㄒㄧㄣ, ㄌㄨˋ ㄖㄣˊ ㄐㄧㄝ ㄓ)
Ssu-Ma Chao's ill intent is known to all.—The villain's design is evident.

司牧(ㄙ ㄇㄨˋ)
the ruler; a king or a local

magistrate

司法(ㄙ ㄈㄚˇ)
judicature; judiciary

司法官(ㄙ ㄈㄚˇ ㄍㄨㄢ)
a legal officer; a judge: 司法官必須公正。A judge must be just.

司法機關(ㄙ ㄈㄚˇ ㄐㄧ ㄍㄨㄢ)
judicial organs

司法節(ㄙ ㄈㄚˇ ㄐㄧㄝˊ)
Judicial Day on January 11

司法警察(ㄙ ㄈㄚˇ ㄐㄧㄥˇ ㄔㄚˊ)
judicial police; a judicial policeman

司法行政部(ㄙ ㄈㄚˇ ㄒㄧㄥˊ ㄓㄥˋ ㄅㄨˋ)
the Ministry of Justice

司法院(ㄙ ㄈㄚˇ ㄩㄢˋ)
the Judicial Yuan

司鐸(ㄙ ㄉㄨㄛˊ)
a Roman Catholic priest

司徒(ㄙ ㄊㄨˊ)
①(in ancient China) the minister of education and cultural affairs ②a Chinese family name

司農(ㄙ ㄋㄨㄥˊ)
(in ancient China) the minister of revenue

司令(ㄙ ㄌㄧㄥˋ)or 司令官(ㄙ ㄌㄧㄥˋ ㄍㄨㄢ)
a commander; a commanding officer: 他是遠征隊的司令。He is the commander of an expedition.

司令部(ㄙ ㄌㄧㄥˋ ㄅㄨˋ)
headquarters: 陸軍司令部在那兒呢? Where is the army headquarters?

司令臺(ㄙ ㄌㄧㄥˋ ㄊㄞˊ)
a review stand

司寇(ㄙ ㄎㄡˋ)
(in ancient China) the minister of justice

司空(ㄙ ㄎㄨㄥ)
①(in ancient China) the minister of public works ②a Chinese family name

司空見慣(ㄙ ㄎㄨㄥ ㄐㄧㄢˋ ㄍㄨㄢˋ)
something quite usual; a thing of frequent occurrence; a common thing: 交通事故是司空見慣。Traffic accidents are of everyday occurrence.

司閽(ㄙ ㄏㄨㄣ)
a doorkeeper; a janitor

司機(ㄙ ㄐㄧ)
a driver; a chauffeur: 那機車子開太快了。The driver drives too fast.

司長(ㄙ ㄓㄤˇ)
a director of a department under a ministry

司事(ㄙ ㄕˋ)
a clerk performing miscellaneous duties

司儀(ㄙ ㄧˊ)
a master of ceremonies; an M.C.; an emcee

三畫

【合】547 ㄏㄜˊ her hé
1. to combine; to unite; to gather; to collect: 合眾存, 分則亡. United, we stand; divided, we fall.
2. to close; to shut: 請把書合起來。Shut your books, please.
3. to suit

合抱(ㄏㄜˊ ㄅㄠˋ)
two or more persons with linked arms to encircle (the trunk of a huge tree)

合板(ㄏㄜˊ ㄅㄢˇ)
plywood

合辦(ㄏㄜˊ ㄅㄢˋ)
to operate, manage, or run jointly

合璧(ㄏㄜˊ ㄅㄧˋ)
two well-matched objects being put side by side

合併(ㄏㄜˊ ㄅㄧㄥˋ)
to combine; to unite; to conjoin; to consolidate; to merge; to put together

合不來(ㄏㄜˊ ㄅㄨˋ ㄌㄞˊ)
cannot get along with (somebody): 他與辦公室任何人都合不來。He doesn't get along with anybody in the office.

合浦珠還(ㄏㄜˊ ㄆㄨˇ ㄓㄨ ㄏㄨㄢˊ)
Things lost are regained.

合謀(ㄏㄜˊ ㄇㄡˊ)
to conspire together: 他的敵人合謀毀滅他。His enemies conspired together to ruin him.

合法(ㄏㄜˊ ㄈㄚˇ)
lawful; legal; legitimate

合得來(ㄏㄜˊ ㄉㄜˊ ㄌㄞˊ)
to get along well; to be con

genial: 他跟老闆合得來。He gets along well with his boss.

當(ㄏㄜ ㄉㄤ)
should 亦作「該當」

合訂本(ㄏㄜ ㄉㄧㄥ ㄅㄣˇ)
a bound volume

合度(ㄏㄜ ㄉㄨˋ)
of proper length or size

合同(ㄏㄜ ㄊㄨㄥˊ)
a contract; an agreement: 他們簽合同。They signed a contract.

合理(ㄏㄜ ㄌㄧˇ)
reasonable; logical; rational: 我們要的是合理的解釋。What we want is a rational explanation.

合力(ㄏㄜ ㄌㄧˋ)
①to cooperate; to collaborate; to unite efforts; to join forces ② (physics) a resultant (of more than one force)

合流(ㄏㄜ ㄌㄧㄡˊ)
①to flow together; to merge ②confluence

合攏(ㄏㄜ ㄌㄨㄥˇ)
to close up

合格(ㄏㄜ ㄍㄜˊ)
qualified; up to the standard: 他是位合格醫生。He is a qualified doctor.

合該(ㄏㄜ ㄍㄞ)
to be fated; to be determined by Heaven

合股(ㄏㄜ ㄍㄨˇ)
to pool capital; to enter into partnership

合口(ㄏㄜ ㄎㄡˇ)
①palatable; delicious; tasty; savory ②to quarrel; to wrangle; to squabble

合刊(ㄏㄜ ㄎㄢ)
a combined issue (of a periodical)

合乎(ㄏㄜ ㄏㄨ)
to measure up to; to qualify; to tally with 亦作「符合」: 你的帳目合乎我的帳目。Your account tallies with mine.

合乎情理(ㄏㄜ ㄏㄨ ㄑㄧㄥˊ ㄌㄧˇ)
reasonable

合夥(ㄏㄜ ㄏㄨㄛˇ)
to enter into partnership

合夥經營(ㄏㄜ ㄏㄨㄛˇ ㄐㄧㄥ ㄧㄥˊ)
to run a business in partner-

ship

合夥人(ㄏㄜ ㄏㄨㄛˇ ㄖㄣˊ)
(accounting) partners

合會(ㄏㄜ ㄏㄨㄟˋ)
a mutual help loan association

合歡(ㄏㄜ ㄏㄨㄢ)
①to meet and enjoy together ②a silk tree

合婚(ㄏㄜ ㄏㄨㄣ)
to be united in wedlock

合擊(ㄏㄜ ㄐㄧˊ)
to make a joint attack on

合計(ㄏㄜ ㄐㄧˋ)
a total; to add up to: 合計二十元。It totals up to 20 dollars.

合家(ㄏㄜ ㄐㄧㄚ)
the whole family

合家歡(ㄏㄜ ㄐㄧㄚ ㄏㄨㄢ)
a family reunion

合金(ㄏㄜ ㄐㄧㄣ)
an alloy: 黃銅是銅和鋅的合金。Brass is an alloy of copper and zinc.

合卺(ㄏㄜ ㄐㄧㄣˇ)
the wine drunk by bridegroom and bride on the wedding night to signify mutual devotion

合鏡重圓(ㄏㄜ ㄐㄧㄥˋ ㄔㄨㄥˊ ㄩㄢˊ)
(said of husband and wife) to reunite after separation

合情合理(ㄏㄜ ㄑㄧㄥˊ ㄏㄜ ㄌㄧˇ)
fair and reasonable; fair and sensible: 那個計畫合情合理。The plan is fair and reasonable.

合羣(ㄏㄜ ㄑㄩㄣˊ)
①to be gregarious ②to get on well with others: 他們不能合羣相處。They don't get on well with each other.

合著(ㄏㄜ ㄓㄨˋ)
to write in collaboration with; to coauthor

合衆國(ㄏㄜ ㄓㄨㄥˋ ㄍㄨㄛˊ)
①the United States (of America) ②a union of states; a confederacy

合衆國際社(ㄏㄜ ㄓㄨㄥˋ ㄍㄨㄛˊ ㄐㄧˋ ㄕㄜˋ)
the United Press International or UPI

合唱(ㄏㄜ ㄔㄤˋ)
to sing in chorus

合唱團(ㄏㄜ ㄔㄤˋ ㄊㄨㄢˊ)

a chorus; a choir: 那男孩是合唱團指揮。The boy is a chorus master.

合成(ㄏㄜ ㄔㄥˊ)
(chemistry) synthesis

合成木材(ㄏㄜ ㄔㄥˊ ㄇㄨˋ ㄘㄞˊ)
synthetic wood

合成洗滌劑(ㄏㄜ ㄔㄥˊ ㄒㄧˇ ㄉㄧˊ ㄐㄧˋ)
synthetic detergent

合成纖維(ㄏㄜ ㄔㄥˊ ㄒㄧㄢ ㄨㄟˊ)
synthetic fibers

合成樹脂(ㄏㄜ ㄔㄥˊ ㄕㄨˋ ㄓ)
synthetic resin

合十(ㄏㄜ ㄕˊ)or合掌(ㄏㄜ ㄓㄤˇ)
(said of Buddhist monks or nuns) to clasp both hands in salutation

合時(ㄏㄜ ㄕˊ)
timely; opportune; seasonable

合式 or 合適(ㄏㄜ ㄕˋ)
suitable; fitting; proper; appropriate

合身(ㄏㄜ ㄕㄣ)
to fit: 這件襯衫很合身。This shirt fits very well.

合資經營(ㄏㄜ ㄗ ㄐㄧㄥ ㄧㄥˊ)
to pool capital for a business

合則留不合則去(ㄏㄜ ㄗㄜˊ ㄌㄧㄡˊ ㄅㄨˋ ㄏㄜ ㄗㄜˊ ㄑㄩˋ)
to stay if the condition is agreeable and to leave if it's otherwise

合奏(ㄏㄜ ㄗㄡˋ)
(music) a united performance of the full number of players

合葬(ㄏㄜ ㄗㄤˋ)
to bury (husband and wife) in one grave

合作(ㄏㄜ ㄗㄨㄛˋ)
to cooperate; to collaborate; cooperation: 兩位作家合作寫那本書。Two authors collaborated on that book.

合作農場(ㄏㄜ ㄗㄨㄛˋ ㄋㄨㄥˊ ㄔㄤˇ)
a cooperative farm

合作金庫(ㄏㄜ ㄗㄨㄛˋ ㄐㄧㄣ ㄎㄨˋ)
(Taiwan) Cooperative Bank

合作社(ㄏㄜ ㄗㄨㄛˋ ㄕㄜˋ)
a cooperative store or society; a co-op: 他在一家合作社工作。He works in a cooperative society.

合縱(ㄏㄜ ㄗㄨㄥˋ)

【口部】

the alliance of six states (against the state of Chin during the Epoch of Warring States)

合算(ㄏㄜ ㄙㄨㄢ)
①to reckon up ②worthwhile; profitable

合一(ㄏㄜ ㄧ)
to unite; to become one: 英格蘭和蘇格蘭在1706年合一。England and Scotland were united in 1706.

合宜(ㄏㄜ ㄧ)
fitting; suitable; proper

合意(ㄏㄜ ㄧ)
(said of a thing) to suit one's fancy; to be agreeable; to be to one's liking (or taste); 他沒發現完全合意的領帶。He found no ties completely to his liking.

合議制(ㄏㄜ ㄧ ㄓ)
a joint consultation (as distinct from dictatorship)

合眼(ㄏㄜ ㄧㄢ)
to close the eyes

合音(ㄏㄜ ㄧㄣ)
(music) combination tone

合夥(ㄏㄜ ㄏㄨㄛ)
to run (a business) in partnership

合影留念(ㄏㄜ ㄧㄥ ㄌㄧㄡ ㄋㄧㄢ)
to have a group photo taken to mark the occasion

合圍(ㄏㄜ ㄨㄟ)
to encircle; encirclement

合胃口(ㄏㄜ ㄨㄟ ㄎㄡ)
to suit one's taste; to be to one's taste

合約(ㄏㄜ ㄩㄝ)
a contract; an agreement

【吁】548 ㄒㄩ shiu xu
a sigh

吁吁(ㄒㄩ ㄒㄩ)
the sound of panting

【吃】549
1. (喫) ㄔ chy chī
1. to eat
2. to sustain: 吃得苦中苦, 方為人上人。Hardship increases stature. 或 No pains, no gains.

吃白相飯(ㄔ ㄅㄞ ㄒㄧㄤ ㄈㄢ)
to loaf; to do no work

吃飽(ㄔ ㄅㄠ ㄎㄜ)
to have had enough food; to

be stuffed with food

吃不得(ㄔ ㄅㄨㄎㄜ)
not good to eat; not edible

吃不來(ㄔ ㄅㄨ ㄌㄞ)
not fond of eating (something); unaccustomed to (such food)

吃不了(ㄔ ㄅㄨㄎㄧㄠ)or吃不完(ㄔ ㄅㄨ ㄨㄢ)
cannot finish (so much food)

吃不了兜着走(ㄔ ㄅㄨ ㄎㄧㄠ ㄉㄡ ㄓㄜ ㄗㄡ)
to land oneself in serious trouble

吃不開(ㄔ ㄅㄨ ㄎㄞ)
to be unpopular: 這種人到那兒都吃不開。Such a person is unpopular anywhere.

吃不下去(ㄔ ㄅㄨ ㄒㄧㄚ ㄑㄩ)
cannot eat due to loss of appetite

吃不消(ㄔ ㄅㄨ ㄒㄧㄠ)
cannot stand or bear; too much to take or endure

吃不住(ㄔ ㄅㄨ ㄓㄨ)
①to be unable to control ②to be unable to support

吃飯(ㄔ ㄈㄢ)
to eat, take, or have a meal

吃飯難(ㄔ ㄈㄢ ㄋㄢ)
It's difficult to make a living.

吃得來(ㄔ ㄉㄜ ㄌㄞ)
to be able to eat; not mind eating

吃得開(ㄔ ㄉㄜ ㄎㄞ)
to be popular; to be much sought after

吃得下(ㄔ ㄉㄜ ㄒㄧㄚ)
to be able to eat

吃得消(ㄔ ㄉㄜ ㄒㄧㄠ)
to be able to stand (exertion, fatigue, etc.)

吃得住(ㄔ ㄉㄜ ㄓㄨ)
①to be able to support: 再重的卡車, 這座橋也能吃得住。This bridge can support the weight of the heaviest truck. ②to be able to control: 這些工人能吃得住。He is able to control these workers.

吃豆腐(ㄔ ㄉㄡ ㄈㄨ)
(slang) to make advances to a woman without serious intentions

吃奶(ㄔ ㄋㄞ)

to suck the breast: 他只是個吃奶的孩子。He is only a sucking child.

吃老本(ㄔ ㄌㄠ ㄅㄣ)
to live off one's savings

吃裏扒外(ㄔ ㄌㄧ ㄆㄚ ㄨㄞ)
to work for the interests of an opposing group at the expense of one's own

吃力(ㄔ ㄌㄧ)
tired; exhausted; tiring or exhausting (work)

吃力不討好(ㄔ ㄌㄧ ㄅㄨ ㄊㄠ ㄏㄠ)
to work laboriously only to earn criticisms; a thankless task

吃利錢(ㄔ ㄌㄧ ㄑㄧㄢ)
to live on interest

吃糧(ㄔ ㄌㄧㄤ)
to be a soldier

吃零食(ㄔ ㄌㄧㄥ ㄕ)
to eat snacks in small amounts between meals

吃官司(ㄔ ㄍㄨㄢ ㄙ)
to be sued (in a court of law)

吃館子(ㄔ ㄍㄨㄢ ㄗ)
to eat at a restaurant

吃光(ㄔ ㄍㄨㄤ)
to eat up; to finish (all the food): 把它吃光吧。Eat it up.

吃苦(ㄔ ㄎㄨ)
to suffer hardship; to endure hardship; to bear hardship: 我們應該先吃苦, 後享樂。We should be the first to bear hardship and the last to enjoy comfort.

吃苦頭(ㄔ ㄎㄨ ㄊㄡ)
to suffer: 我要給他們吃苦頭。I'll make them suffer.

吃苦耐勞(ㄔ ㄎㄨ ㄋㄞ ㄌㄠ)
diligent; hardworking; untiring

吃虧(ㄔ ㄎㄨㄟ)
to be at a disadvantage; to suffer a loss; to take a beating; to be wronged

吃空缺(ㄔ ㄎㄨㄥ ㄑㄩㄝ)
to pad the payroll

吃喝嫖賭(ㄔ ㄏㄜ ㄆㄧㄠ ㄉㄨ)
a dissipated or dissolute life

吃喝玩樂(ㄔ ㄏㄜ ㄨㄢ ㄌㄜ)
to eat, drink and make merry—to idle away one's time in seeking pleasure

吃花酒(ㄔ ㄏㄨㄚ ㄐㄧㄡ)

〔口
部〕

to drink and eat at a girlie restaurant

乞葷 (ㄑㄧ ㄏㄨㄣ)
to eat meat and other food produced by fowls or animals (such as eggs and milk)

吃角子老虎 (ㄔ ㄐㄧㄠˇ ·ㄗㄌㄠˇ·ㄏㄨˇ)
a slot machine

吃緊 (ㄔ ㄐㄧㄣˇ)
(usually said of a military situation) hard pressed, critical, or tense: 現在前方情勢吃緊。 Now the situation at the front is critical.

吃勁 (ㄔ ㄐㄧㄣˋ)
to take much effort to do; to take a lot of strength to do

吃驚 (ㄔ ㄐㄧㄥ)
surprised, frightened, startled, or astonished

吃錢 (ㄔ ㄑㄧㄢˊ)
①to take a bribe ②to embezzle

吃閒飯 (ㄔ ㄒㄧㄢˊㄈㄢˋ)
to live like a parasite

吃現成飯 (ㄔ ㄒㄧㄢˋ ㄔㄥˊ ㄈㄢˋ)
to enjoy the fruit of somebody else's labor

吃香 (ㄔ ㄒㄧㄤ)
to be welcome or valued everywhere; popular; in great demand: 棒球在台灣是很吃香的運動。 Baseball is a popular sport in Taiwan.

吃齋 (ㄔ ㄗㄞ)or吃素 (ㄔ ㄙㄨˋ)
to practice vegetarianism

吃重 (ㄔ ㄓㄨㄥˋ)
to play an important role; to shoulder a heavy responsibility

吃喝喝 (ㄔ ㄏㄜ ㄏㄜ)
interested only in eating and drinking

吃茶 (ㄔ ㄔㄚˊ)
①to drink tea ②(said of a girl) to become engaged

吃穿 (ㄔ ㄔㄨㄢ)
food and clothing

吃水 (ㄔ ㄕㄨㄟˇ)
①to drink water ②to absorb water ③to draw water (as a ship); draft or draught (of a ship)

吃軟不吃硬 (ㄔ ㄖㄨㄢˇㄅㄨˋ ㄔ ㄧㄥˋ)
yielding to soft approaches but rejecting force, high-

handedness, etc.

吃歡飯 (ㄔ ㄖㄨㄢˇ ㄈㄢˋ)
to live on the earnings of a prostitute

吃人 (ㄔ ㄖㄣˊ)
①man-eating (animals) ②usurious (interest rate)

吃醋 (ㄔ ㄘㄨˋ)
to be jealous

吃啞吧虧 (ㄔ ㄧㄚˇ ·ㄅㄚ ㄎㄨㄟ)
to be cheated or suffer a loss but unable to talk about it for one reason or another

吃藥 (ㄔ ㄧㄠˋ)
to take medicine: 他吃藥吃太多了。 He took too much medicine.

吃硬不吃軟 (ㄔ ㄧㄥˋ ㄅㄨˋ ㄔ ㄖㄨㄢˇ)
yielding to force but rejecting soft approaches

吃用 (ㄔ ㄩㄥˋ)
daily needs or spendings (of a household or an individual)

【吃】 549
2. ㄐㄧ jyi jí
to stammer; to stutter

吃吃 (ㄐㄧ ㄐㄧ)
the sound of giggling—

【各】 550
《ㄍㄜˋ geh gè
1. each; every: 從各方面看, 這個都比那個好。 This is in every way better than that.

2. all

各半 (《ㄍㄜˋ ㄅㄢˋ)
half-and-half; fifty-fifty

各奔前程 (《ㄍㄜˋ ㄅㄣˋ ㄑㄧㄢˊ ㄔㄥˊ)
Each pursues his own goal (without caring about others' affairs)

各別 (《ㄍㄜˋ ㄅㄧㄝˊ)
individual; isolated (case); separate; separately; individually

各不相謀 (《ㄍㄜˋ ㄅㄨˋ ㄒㄧㄤ ㄇㄡˊ)
to proceed without consulting with one another

各得其所 (《ㄍㄜˋ ㄉㄜˊ ㄑㄧˊ ㄙㄨㄛˇ)
Each person gets his proper position. 或 Each thing finds its proper place.

各地 (《ㄍㄜˋ ㄉㄧˋ)
various places or localities; everywhere: 他們到各地看看。 They visited everywhere.

各條 (《ㄍㄜˋ ㄊㄧㄠˊ)
various items or clauses

各類 (《ㄍㄜˋ ㄌㄟˋ)
each or every sort, kind, class, species, or order: 他們賣各類的書。 They sell every kind of books.

各個擊破 (《ㄍㄜˋ ㄍㄜˋ ㄐㄧˊ ㄆㄛˋ)
to knock out one adversary after another; to defeat enemies by taking on one of them at a time

各個解決 (《ㄍㄜˋ ㄍㄜˋ ㄐㄧㄝˇ ㄐㄩㄝˊ)
a piecemeal solution

各幹各的 (《ㄍㄜˋ ㄍㄢˋ 《ㄍㄜˋ ·ㄉㄜ)
Let each one get on with his job.

各國 (《ㄍㄜˋ 《ㄨㄛˊ)
each and every nation (or country); various nations

各管各的 (《ㄍㄜˋ 《ㄨㄢˇ 《ㄍㄜˋ ·ㄉㄜ)
①Everyone minds his own business. ②lacking in coordination

各款 (《ㄍㄜˋ ㄎㄨㄢˇ)
each and every article (of a document); all the articles; various articles

各行 (《ㄍㄜˋ ㄏㄤˊ)or各業 (《ㄍㄜˋ ㄧㄝˋ)
each and every trade; all professions or various callings

各級 (《ㄍㄜˋ ㄐㄧˊ)
all or different levels

各界 (《ㄍㄜˋ ㄐㄧㄝˋ)
all walks of life; all circles; 這本書受到各界的稱讚。 The book is praised in all circles.

各就各位 (《ㄍㄜˋ ㄐㄧㄡˋ 《ㄍㄜˋ ㄨㄟˋ)
①(military) Man your posts! ②(athletics) On your marks!

各盡所能 (《ㄍㄜˋ ㄐㄧㄣˋ ㄙㄨㄛˇ ㄋㄥˊ)
Each does his best. 或 from each according to his ability

各取所需 (《ㄍㄜˋ ㄑㄩˇ ㄙㄨㄛˇ ㄒㄩ)
Each takes what he wants. 或 to each according to his needs

各顯神通 (《ㄍㄜˋ ㄒㄧㄢˇ ㄕㄣˊ ㄊㄨㄥ)
Each has his own way. 或 Each plays his long suit.

各項 (《ㄍㄜˋ ㄒㄧㄤˋ)
the various items; each and every item; all the items

各行其是 (《ㄍㄜˋ ㄒㄧㄥˊ ㄑㄧˊ ㄕˋ)
Each behaves in the ways which he thinks are right. 或

〔口部〕

Each goes his own way.

各執一詞《ㄍㄜ ㄓ丨ㄘ》
Each (of the disputants) tells a different story.

各種《ㄍㄜ ㄓㄨㄥˇ》
various kinds, species, categories, etc.: 我們談論各種題目。 We talked about various subjects.

各持己見《ㄍㄜ ㄔˊ ㄐ丨ˇ ㄐ丨ㄢˋ》
Each sticks to his own view.

各處《ㄍㄜ ㄔㄨˋ》
everywhere; various places; all the places: 各處似乎都很安靜。 It seemed to be quiet everywhere.

各式各樣《ㄍㄜ ㄕˋ ㄍㄜ 丨ㄤˋ》or 各色各樣《ㄍㄜ ㄙㄜˋ ㄍㄜ 丨ㄤˋ》
all sorts, kinds, or varieties; various

各抒己見《ㄍㄜ ㄕㄨ ㄐ丨ˇ ㄐ丨ㄢˋ》
Each airs his own views.

各人《ㄍㄜ ㄖㄣˊ》
everybody

各人自掃門前雪，莫管他人瓦上霜《ㄍㄜ ㄖㄣˊ ㄗˋ ㄙㄠˇ ㄇㄣˊ ㄑ丨ㄢˊ ㄒㄩㄝˇ, ㄇㄛˋ ㄍㄨㄢˇ ㄊㄚ ㄖㄣˊ ㄨㄚˇ ㄕㄤ ㄕㄨㄤ》
(literally) Each one sweeps the snow from his own doorstep and doesn't bother about the frost on his neighbor's roof.—(figuratively) Everybody minds his own business only.

各自《ㄍㄜ ㄗˋ》
each; respective: 放學後，學生各自回家。 After school, students go home respectively.

各自為政《ㄍㄜ ㄗˋ ㄨㄟˊ ㄓㄥˋ》
Each (office) administers its affairs in its own way without coordination with others.

各色俱全《ㄍㄜ ㄙㄜˋ ㄐㄩˋ ㄑㄩㄢˊ》or 《ㄍㄜ ㄙㄜˋ ㄐㄩˋ ㄑㄩㄢˊ》
Nothing is lacking. 或 complete with everything; of all kinds

各有各的道理《ㄍㄜ 丨ㄡˇ ㄍㄜ ˙ㄉㄜ ㄉㄠˋ ㄌ丨ˇ》
Everybody has a point (in his statement). 或 Each (of the disputants) has given a plausible reason.

各有千秋《ㄍㄜ 丨ㄡˇ ㄑ丨ㄢ ㄑ丨ㄡ》
Each shows a unique quality. 或 Each has a unique style.

各有所好《ㄍㄜ 丨ㄡˇ ㄙㄨㄛˇ ㄏㄠˋ》
Each has his likes and dislikes. 或 Each has his own taste.

各有所長《ㄍㄜ 丨ㄡˇ ㄙㄨㄛˇ ㄔㄤˊ》
Each has a unique merit.

各位《ㄍㄜ ㄨㄟˋ》
ladies and gentlemen; gentlemen or ladies (used in addressing a gathering); everybody: 各位請注意！ Attention please, everybody.

【吉】 551 ㄐ丨ˊ jyi jí
good; lucky; auspicious; propitious; favorable; fortunate

吉卜賽《ㄐ丨ˊ ㄅㄨˇ ㄙㄞˋ》or 吉普賽《ㄐ丨ˊ ㄆㄨˇ ㄙㄞˋ》
the Gipsies or the Gypsies

吉普車《ㄐ丨ˊ ㄆㄨˇ ㄔㄜ》
a jeep

吉房招租《ㄐ丨ˊ ㄈㄤˊ ㄓㄠ ㄗㄨ》or 吉屋招租《ㄐ丨ˊ ㄨ ㄓㄠ ㄗㄨ》
a house for rent; a house to let

吉他《ㄐ丨ˊ ㄊㄚ》
a guitar

吉利《ㄐ丨ˊ ㄌ丨ˋ》
good luck; propitiousness

吉林《ㄐ丨ˊ ㄌ丨ㄣˊ》
①Kirin, a province in northeast China ②name of Kirin's provincial capital

吉隆坡《ㄐ丨ˊ ㄌㄨㄥˊ ㄆㄛ》
Kuala Lumpur

吉光片羽《ㄐ丨ˊ ㄍㄨㄤ ㄆ丨ㄢˋ 丨ㄩˇ》
remnants or broken relics (of ancient art works)

吉期《ㄐ丨ˊ ㄑ丨ˊ》
the wedding day

吉慶《ㄐ丨ˊ ㄑ丨ㄥˋ》
a happy event; an auspicious occasion

吉祥《ㄐ丨ˊ ㄒ丨ㄤˊ》
favorable; propitious; auspicious

吉星高照《ㄐ丨ˊ ㄒ丨ㄥ ㄍㄠ ㄓㄠˋ》
The lucky star shines bright.

吉凶《ㄐ丨ˊ ㄒㄩㄥ》
good or bad luck

吉凶未卜《ㄐ丨ˊ ㄒㄩㄥ ㄨㄟˋ ㄅㄨˇ》
No one knows how it will turn out.

吉兆《ㄐ丨ˊ ㄓㄠˋ》or 吉徵《ㄐ丨ˊ ㄓㄥ》
a good omen: 這被視爲吉兆。 This is taken as a good omen.

吉事《ㄐ丨ˊ ㄕˋ》
ceremonial rites

吉日《ㄐ丨ˊ ㄖˋ》or 吉日良辰《ㄐ丨ˊ ㄖˋ ㄌ丨ㄤˊ ㄔㄣˊ》
①an auspicious day; a lucky day: 今天是吉日。 Today is a lucky day. ②the first day of a lunar month

吉人《ㄐ丨ˊ ㄖㄣˊ》or 吉士《ㄐ丨ˊ ㄕˋ》
a good and virtuous man

吉人天相《ㄐ丨ˊ ㄖㄣˊ ㄊ丨ㄢ ㄒ丨ㄤˋ》
Heaven helps a good man.

【吋】 552 ㄘㄨㄣˋ tsuenn cùn
inch—a unit of length

【同】 553 ㄊㄨㄥˊ torng tóng
1. same; equal; identical; similar; common
2. to share; to agree
3. together

同輩《ㄊㄨㄥˊ ㄅㄟˋ》
one's equal (in seniority); of the same generation; a peer

同胞《ㄊㄨㄥˊ ㄅㄠ》
a compatriot; a fellow countryman

同班《ㄊㄨㄥˊ ㄅㄢ》
a classmate: 他上學期和我同班。 He and I were classmates last term.

同伴《ㄊㄨㄥˊ ㄅㄢˋ》
a companion: 我們是好同伴。 We are good companions.

同榜《ㄊㄨㄥˊ ㄅㄤˇ》or 同科《ㄊㄨㄥˊ ㄎㄜ》
successful candidates whose names were announced on the same list under the old civil service examination system

同病相憐《ㄊㄨㄥˊ ㄅ丨ㄥˋ ㄒ丨ㄤ ㄌ丨ㄢˊ》
Fellow sufferers have mutual sympathy.

同步《ㄊㄨㄥˊ ㄅㄨˋ》
synchronism; to synchronize; synchronous

同袍《ㄊㄨㄥˊ ㄆㄠˊ》
①comrades in arms ②to share the same robes with

同謀《ㄊㄨㄥˊ ㄇㄡˊ》
to conspire

同門《ㄊㄨㄥˊ ㄇㄣˊ》
a fellow disciple

同門異戶《ㄊㄨㄥˊ ㄇㄣˊ 丨ˋ ㄏㄨˋ》
to be alike except for slight

differences

同盟(ㄊㄨㄥˊ ㄇㄥˊ)
an alliance; a league; a confederacy

同盟國(ㄊㄨㄥˊ ㄇㄥˊ ㄍㄨㄜˊ)
① in World War Ⅰ, the Central Powers against the Allies ② in World War Ⅱ, the Allies against the Axis ③ allied nations; an ally

同盟會(ㄊㄨㄥˊ ㄇㄥˊ ㄏㄨㄟˋ)
Tung Meng Hui (an antecedent of Kuomintang)

同名(ㄊㄨㄥˊ ㄇㄧㄥˊ)
a namesake; having the same given name

同名同姓(ㄊㄨㄥˊ ㄇㄧㄥˊ ㄊㄨㄥˊ ㄒㄧㄥˋ)
having the same given name and family name

同命(ㄊㄨㄥˊ ㄇㄧㄥˋ)
to share the same destiny; to be under the influence of the same stars

同房(ㄊㄨㄥˊ ㄈㄤˊ)
to share the same room: 姊妹同房住。The sisters share the same room.

同父異母(ㄊㄨㄥˊ ㄈㄨˋ ㄧˋ ㄇㄨˇ)
having the same father but different mothers

同道(ㄊㄨㄥˊ ㄉㄠˋ)
the people engaged in the same pursuit; the people with the same ideals

同等(ㄊㄨㄥˊ ㄉㄥˇ)
of the same rank or class; the same (in importance, responsibility, etc.)

同等學力(ㄊㄨㄥˊ ㄉㄥˇ ㄒㄩㄝˊ ㄌㄧˋ)
(said of persons without a diploma in comparison with those who have it) with the same intellectual capacity and scholastic achievements; to have the same educational level

同堂兄弟(ㄊㄨㄥˊ ㄊㄤˊ ㄒㄩㄥ ㄉㄧˋ)
male cousins with the same paternal grandfather

同年(ㄊㄨㄥˊ ㄋㄧㄢˊ)
① of the same age: 他們同年。They are of the same age. ② (in former times) having passed the civil service examination in the same year

同樂晚會(ㄊㄨㄥˊ ㄌㄜˋ ㄨㄢˇ ㄏㄨㄟˋ)
an evening party (held within an organization, school, etc.)

同類(ㄊㄨㄥˊ ㄌㄟˋ)
the same kind, class, species, or family

同類相殘(ㄊㄨㄥˊ ㄌㄟˋ ㄒㄧㄤ ㄘㄢˊ)
(literally) self-extermination by animals of the same species—an intramural fight

同僚(ㄊㄨㄥˊ ㄌㄧㄠˊ) or 同事(ㄊㄨㄥˊ ㄕˋ)
colleagues; a coworker; an associate

同流合污(ㄊㄨㄥˊ ㄌㄧㄡˊ ㄏㄜˊ ㄨ)
to follow the bad example of others: 別與他同流合污。Don't follow the bad example of him.

同量(ㄊㄨㄥˊ ㄌㄧㄤˋ)
the same amount or quantity

同路人(ㄊㄨㄥˊ ㄌㄨˋ ㄖㄣˊ)
a fellow traveler

同甘共苦(ㄊㄨㄥˊ ㄍㄢ ㄍㄨㄥˋ ㄎㄨˇ)
to stick together through thick and thin; to share bliss and adversity together; on shares

同感(ㄊㄨㄥˊ ㄍㄢˇ)
to have the same feeling

同庚(ㄊㄨㄥˊ ㄍㄥ)
of the same age: 他們夫妻同庚。He is of the same age as his wife.

同歸於盡(ㄊㄨㄥˊ ㄍㄨㄟ ㄩˊ ㄐㄧㄣˋ)
to end in death or ruin of both combatants; to die together; to end in common ruin

同工同酬(ㄊㄨㄥˊ ㄍㄨㄥ ㄊㄨㄥˊ ㄔㄡˊ)
to reward the same work with the same pay; to pay employees strictly on the basis of their work; equal pay for equal work

同好(ㄊㄨㄥˊ ㄏㄠˋ)
people with the same hobby

同行
① (ㄊㄨㄥˊ ㄏㄤˊ) in the same trade, line, occupation, or profession
② (ㄊㄨㄥˊ ㄒㄧㄥˊ) to go together

同行相妒(ㄊㄨㄥˊ ㄏㄤˊ ㄒㄧㄤ ㄉㄨˋ)
People in the same profession or line of business are apt to be jealous of one another.

同化(ㄊㄨㄥˊ ㄏㄨㄚˋ)
to assimilate; assimilation

同夥(ㄊㄨㄥˊ ㄏㄨㄛˇ)
a fellow worker in the same company; a member of the same group or gang

同機(ㄊㄨㄥˊ ㄐㄧ)
aboard the same plane

同濟會(ㄊㄨㄥˊ ㄐㄧˋ ㄏㄨㄟˋ)
Kiwanis Club

同進退(ㄊㄨㄥˊ ㄐㄧㄣˋ ㄊㄨㄟˋ)
(said of colleagues taking the same stand over an issue) to advance or withdraw together; to stay on or quit together

同居(ㄊㄨㄥˊ ㄐㄩ)
to cohabit (usually said of an unmarried couple); cohabitation

同氣連枝(ㄊㄨㄥˊ ㄑㄧˋ ㄌㄧㄢˊ ㄓ)
brotherly ties

同氣相求(ㄊㄨㄥˊ ㄑㄧˋ ㄒㄧㄤ ㄑㄧㄡˊ)
People with the same ideals have an affinity for one another.

同衾共枕(ㄊㄨㄥˊ ㄑㄧㄣ ㄍㄨㄥˋ ㄓㄣˇ)
(usually said of a married couple) to share the same comforter and the same pillow

同情(ㄊㄨㄥˊ ㄑㄧㄥˊ)
to sympathize; to be in sympathy with; to have sympathy for

同情心(ㄊㄨㄥˊ ㄑㄧㄥˊ ㄒㄧㄣ)
sympathies; compassion; pity; fellow feeling

同慶(ㄊㄨㄥˊ ㄑㄧㄥˋ)
to celebrate together; universal celebration

同席(ㄊㄨㄥˊ ㄒㄧˊ)
to be seated at the same dining table: 他們同席。They seat themselves at the same table.

同心(ㄊㄨㄥˊ ㄒㄧㄣ)
united at heart or in common purpose

同心同德(ㄊㄨㄥˊ ㄒㄧㄣ ㄊㄨㄥˊ ㄉㄜˊ)
to be of one mind: 我們同心同德。We are all of one mind.

同心協力(ㄊㄨㄥˊ ㄒㄧㄣ ㄒㄧㄝˊ ㄌㄧˋ)
to work in cooperation; to make concerted efforts: 讓我們與朋友同心協力。Let's

〔口部〕

work in close cooperation with our friends.

同心圓(ㄊㄨㄥ ㄒㄧㄣ ㄩㄢ)
concentric circles

〔口部〕

同鄉(ㄊㄨㄥ ㄒㄧㄤ)
the people from the same province, county, town, etc.

同鄉會(ㄊㄨㄥ ㄒㄧㄤ ㄏㄨㄟˋ)
a club or association formed by people from the same province, county, city, etc.

同姓(ㄊㄨㄥ ㄒㄧㄥˋ)
members of the same clan

同性(ㄊㄨㄥ ㄒㄧㄥˋ)
of the same sex

同性戀(ㄊㄨㄥ ㄒㄧㄥˋ ㄌㄧㄢˋ)or 同性愛(ㄊㄨㄥ ㄒㄧㄥˋ ㄞˋ)
homosexuality; homosexual love

同性戀者(ㄊㄨㄥ ㄒㄧㄥˋ ㄌㄧㄢˋ ㄓㄜˇ)
a gay; a homosexual

同學(ㄊㄨㄥ ㄒㄩㄝˊ)
a fellow student; a schoolmate 參看「同碩」

同學會(ㄊㄨㄥ ㄒㄩㄝˊ ㄏㄨㄟˋ)
an alumni association

同志(ㄊㄨㄥ ㄓˋ)
a comrade

同舟共濟(ㄊㄨㄥ ㄓㄡ ㄍㄨㄥˋ ㄐㄧˋ)
to show the mutual concern of the people in the same boat

同種(ㄊㄨㄥ ㄓㄨㄥˇ)
(people) of the same race

同車(ㄊㄨㄥ ㄔㄜ)
to ride on the same train or bus: 他們同車。They rode on the same bus.

同儕(ㄊㄨㄥ ㄔㄞˊ)
fellows of the same generation; contemporaries

同仇敵愾(ㄊㄨㄥ ㄔㄡˊ ㄉㄧˊ ㄎㄞˋ)
to share the same hatred and fight against a common enemy

同窗(ㄊㄨㄥ ㄔㄨㄤ)
a classmate or schoolmate

同牀異夢(ㄊㄨㄥ ㄔㄨㄤˊ ㄧˋ ㄇㄥˋ)
①to hide different intentions behind the semblance of accord ②to have different dreams in the same bed (said of a troubled marriage)

同時(ㄊㄨㄥ ㄕˊ)
at the same time; simultaneously

同事(ㄊㄨㄥ ㄕˋ)
①a colleague ②to serve the same (king, etc.) ③to marry the same (man)

同室操戈(ㄊㄨㄥ ㄕˋ ㄘㄠ ㄍㄜ)
(especially said of brothers) to engage in internal strife

同聲相應(ㄊㄨㄥ ㄕㄥ ㄒㄧㄤ ㄧㄥˋ)
to act in unison: 士兵同聲相應。The soldiers act in unison.

同聲一哭(ㄊㄨㄥ ㄕㄥ ㄧ ㄎㄨ)
to share the same feeling of loss or grief (over the death of a national hero, a great tragedy, etc.)

同日而語(ㄊㄨㄥ ㄖˋ ㄦˊ ㄩˇ)
to mention in equal terms

同仁 or 同人(ㄊㄨㄥ ㄖㄣˊ)
a colleague; a fellow member (of an organization)

同族(ㄊㄨㄥ ㄗㄨˊ)
of the same tribe or clan

同宗(ㄊㄨㄥ ㄗㄨㄥ)
of the same clan; having a common ancestor: 我們同宗。We are of the same clan.

同異(ㄊㄨㄥ ㄧˋ)
similarities and differences

同意(ㄊㄨㄥ ㄧˋ)
to agree; to consent; to concur; agreement; consent; approval: 她同意嫁給他。She consented to marry him.

同意權(ㄊㄨㄥ ㄧˋ ㄑㄩㄢˊ)
the right of consent or endorsement

同意書(ㄊㄨㄥ ㄧˋ ㄕㄨ)
a written consent; a letter of authorization; a letter of agreement

同義語(ㄊㄨㄥ ㄧˋ ㄩˇ)
a synonym: 悲傷與悲哀是同義語。"Sad" and "unhappy" are synonyms.

同業(ㄊㄨㄥ ㄧㄝˋ)
the people of the same trade, calling, or occupation

同業公會(ㄊㄨㄥ ㄧㄝˋ ㄍㄨㄥ ㄏㄨㄟˋ)
a guild; a trade union

同硯(ㄊㄨㄥ ㄧㄢˋ)
schoolmates or classmates

同寅(ㄊㄨㄥ ㄧㄣˊ)
(said of government officials in old times) colleagues

同樣(ㄊㄨㄥ ㄧㄤˋ)
①in the same way, manner or fashion; similarly; likewise ②the same; similar

同位角(ㄊㄨㄥ ㄨㄟˋ ㄐㄧㄠˇ)
(mathematics) corresponding angles

同位素(ㄊㄨㄥ ㄨㄟˋ ㄙㄨˋ)
an isotope

同位語(ㄊㄨㄥ ㄨㄟˋ ㄩˇ)
(English grammar) an appositive

同溫層(ㄊㄨㄥ ㄨㄣ ㄘㄥˊ)
the stratosphere

同文同種(ㄊㄨㄥ ㄨㄣˊ ㄊㄨㄥ ㄓㄨㄥˇ)
of the same language and the same race

同源(ㄊㄨㄥ ㄩㄢˊ)
homologous

【吆】554
ㄧㄠ iau yōo
to shout; to cry

吆喝(ㄧㄠ ˙ㄏㄜ)
①to shout; to cry ②to hawk

【吒】555
ㄓㄚˋ jah zhà
1. to shout with anger
2. to smack in eating

【名】556
ㄇㄧㄥˊ míng ming
1. a name; a designation; a title; rank
2. position; honor; fame; renown; reputation
3. famous; noted; distinguished; renowned; valuable; precious; noble; rare; great
4. to name; to describe

名不副實(ㄇㄧㄥˊ ㄅㄨˋ ㄈㄨˋ ㄕˊ)
The reputation is not supported by fact.

名不虛傳(ㄇㄧㄥˊ ㄅㄨˋ ㄒㄩ ㄔㄨㄢˊ)
The reputation is well supported by fact.

名不正言不順(ㄇㄧㄥˊ ㄅㄨˋ ㄓㄥˋ ㄧㄢˊ ㄅㄨˋ ㄕㄨㄣˋ)
There is no justification to do something without some convincing reason.

名牌(ㄇㄧㄥˊ ㄆㄞˊ)
①a famous brand ②a nameplate

名片(ㄇㄧㄥˊ ㄆㄧㄢˋ)or 名刺(ㄇㄧㄥˊ ㄘˋ) or 名帖(ㄇㄧㄥˊ ㄊㄧㄝˇ)

a calling card; a visiting card

名馬(ㄇㄧㄥ ㄇㄚˇ)or 名駒(ㄇㄧㄥ ㄐㄩ)
a champion horse; a thoroughbred horse

名滿天下(ㄇㄧㄥ ㄇㄢˇ ㄊㄧㄢ ㄒㄧㄚˋ)
to enjoy world-wide fame; to be world-famous

名門(ㄇㄧㄥ ㄇㄣˊ)
a distinguished family: 她出自名門。 She comes from an eminent family.

名門閨秀(ㄇㄧㄥ ㄇㄣˊ ㄍㄨㄟ ㄒㄧㄡˋ)
a daughter of an illustrious family

名目(ㄇㄧㄥ ㄇㄨˋ)
a name; a designation

名目繁多(ㄇㄧㄥ ㄇㄨˋ ㄈㄢˊ ㄉㄨㄛ)
a multitude of names (or items)

名閥(ㄇㄧㄥ ㄈㄚˊ)
an illustrious family of many generations

名分(ㄇㄧㄥ ㄈㄣˋ)
a role or duties proper to one's title

名副其實(ㄇㄧㄥ ㄈㄨˋ ㄑㄧˊ ㄕˊ)
to be worthy of the name or reputation

名單(ㄇㄧㄥ ㄉㄢ)
a name list; a roster; a roll

名堂(ㄇㄧㄥ ·ㄊㄤ)
①a dignified name or designation ②a result that is worth mentioning; a worthwhile result

名女人(ㄇㄧㄥ ㄋㄩˇ ㄖㄣˊ)
the women with eminent (or notorious) reputation

名利(ㄇㄧㄥ ㄌㄧˋ)
fame and gain; fame and wealth

名利雙收(ㄇㄧㄥ ㄌㄧˋ ㄕㄨㄤ ㄕㄡ)
to achieve both fame and wealth

名列前茅(ㄇㄧㄥ ㄌㄧㄝˋ ㄑㄧㄢˊ ㄇㄠˊ)
to head the list of successful candidates

名流(ㄇㄧㄥ ㄌㄧㄡˊ)
a celebrity; a distinguished personage

名伶(ㄇㄧㄥ ㄌㄧㄥˊ)
a renowned actor or actress

名落孫山(ㄇㄧㄥ ㄌㄨㄛˋ ㄙㄨㄣ ㄕㄢ)
to fail in an examination

名歌(ㄇㄧㄥ ㄍㄜ)
a great or famous song; 「快樂頌」是首名歌。 "Song of Joy" is a famous song.

名古屋(ㄇㄧㄥ ㄍㄨˇ ㄨ)
Nagoya, a Japanese city

名過其實(ㄇㄧㄥ ㄍㄨㄛˋ ㄑㄧˊ ㄕˊ)
to have an exaggerated reputation

名貴(ㄇㄧㄥ ㄍㄨㄟˋ)
valuable; precious; rare

名花有主(ㄇㄧㄥ ㄏㄨㄚ ㄧㄡˇ ㄓㄨˇ)
The beauty has already been won by somebody.

名宦(ㄇㄧㄥ ㄏㄨㄢˋ)
a distinguished official

名家(ㄇㄧㄥ ㄐㄧㄚ)
①a master (in a branch of art) ②the Nominalist school of philosophy ③an illustrious family

名節(ㄇㄧㄥ ㄐㄧㄝˊ)
honor and integrity

名教(ㄇㄧㄥ ㄐㄧㄠˋ)
①the body of teachings on morality and ethics ②Confucianism, the body of teachings on social relationships

名酒(ㄇㄧㄥ ㄐㄧㄡˇ)
excellent wine or liquor with a famous brand name

名韁利鎖(ㄇㄧㄥ ㄐㄧㄤ ㄌㄧˋ ㄙㄨㄛˇ)
to be a slave of fame and wealth

名將(ㄇㄧㄥ ㄐㄧㄤˋ)
a great general or admiral

名句(ㄇㄧㄥ ㄐㄩˋ)
a famous line or phrase; a well-known phrase; a quotable quote

名脚兒 or 名角兒(ㄇㄧㄥ ㄐㄩㄝˊ ㄦ)
a famed actor or actress

名氣(ㄇㄧㄥ ㄑㄧˋ)
fame; reputation; renown

名器(ㄇㄧㄥ ㄑㄧˋ)
(in ancient China) ranks and proper equipages

名曲(ㄇㄧㄥ ㄑㄩˇ)
a great musical composition; a masterpiece in music

名下(ㄇㄧㄥ ㄒㄧㄚˋ)
①under (one's) account ②to (one's) account

名正言順(ㄇㄧㄥ ㄓㄥˋ ㄧㄢˊ ㄕㄨㄣˋ)
valid in name and in reasoning; to have good reason; to deserve; justified

名著(ㄇㄧㄥ ㄓㄨˋ)
a great book; a literary masterpiece: 伊利亞德是本名著, Iliad is a great book.

名產(ㄇㄧㄥ ㄔㄢˇ)
a noted product or special product (of a place)

名稱(ㄇㄧㄥ ㄔㄥ)
the name or designation (of a thing)

名垂青史(ㄇㄧㄥ ㄔㄨㄟˊ ㄑㄧㄥ ㄕˇ)
to go down in history; to be crowned with eternal glory

名師(ㄇㄧㄥ ㄕ)
a great teacher; a master

名師出高徒(ㄇㄧㄥ ㄕ ㄔㄨ ㄍㄠ ㄊㄨˊ)
An accomplished disciple owes his accomplishments to his great teacher.

名實(ㄇㄧㄥ ㄕˊ)
name and substance

名實相符(ㄇㄧㄥ ㄕˊ ㄒㄧㄤ ㄈㄨˊ)
in deed as well as in name

名氏(ㄇㄧㄥ ㄕˋ)
one's name and family name

名世(ㄇㄧㄥ ㄕˋ)
to become famous

名士(ㄇㄧㄥ ㄕˋ)
a celebrated scholar

名士派(ㄇㄧㄥ ㄕˋ ㄆㄞˋ)
a bohemian; an unconventional scholar

名手(ㄇㄧㄥ ㄕㄡˇ)
a great player (of a game); a master (in a branch of art)

名山大川(ㄇㄧㄥ ㄕㄢ ㄉㄚˋ ㄔㄨㄢ)
famous mountains and mighty streams

名山事業(ㄇㄧㄥ ㄕㄢ ㄕˋ ㄧㄝˋ)
writing as a pursuit or occupation

名聲(ㄇㄧㄥ ㄕㄥ)
fame; renown; reputation; repute; glory: 他是個名聲很好的人。 He is a man of good reputation.

名勝(ㄇㄧㄥ ㄕㄥˋ)
a scenic spot; a resort or vacationland

名勝古跡(ㄇㄧㄥ ㄕㄥˋ ㄍㄨˇ ㄐㄧ)
places of historic interest and scenic beauty

名數(ㄇㄧㄥ ㄕㄨˋ)
(mathematics) a concrete number, or denominate num-

〔口部〕

ber

名人(ㄇㄧㄥˊ ㄖㄣˊ)
①a notable; a celebrity; a famous person; a man of note ② one of the most coveted titles among professional go players in Japan

名人錄(ㄇㄧㄥˊ ㄖㄣˊ ㄌㄨˋ)
Who's Who; 他的大名在名人錄上出現。 His name appeared in Who's Who.

名儒(ㄇㄧㄥˊ ㄖㄨˊ)
a great (Confucian) scholar: 朱熹是位名儒, Chu Hsi was a great scholar.

名字(ㄇㄧㄥˊ ㄗˋ)
the name (of a person, etc.)

名課一時(ㄇㄧㄥˊ ㄗˋ ㄧˋ ㄕˊ)
(said of artists, writers, etc.) very famous at one time

名作(ㄇㄧㄥˊ ㄗㄨㄛˋ)
a masterpiece: 紅字是霍桑的名作。 The Scarlet Letter is Nathaniel Hawthorne's masterpiece.

名詞(ㄇㄧㄥˊ ㄘˊ)
①a noun: 鳥是個名詞。"Bird" is a noun. ② a term

名次(ㄇㄧㄥˊ ㄘˋ)
one's position or standing (as compared with others in a contest, a competitive examination, etc.)

名冊(ㄇㄧㄥˊ ㄘㄜˋ)
a roster; a roll; a record of names

名存實亡(ㄇㄧㄥˊ ㄘㄨㄣˊ ㄕˊ ㄨㄤˊ)
(said of established institutions) to exist in name only

名額(ㄇㄧㄥˊ ㄜˊ)
the number of openings, or quota (for employees, students, etc.)

名醫(ㄇㄧㄥˊ ㄧ)
a great physician; a famous doctor

名醫束手(ㄇㄧㄥˊ ㄧ ㄕㄨˋ ㄕㄡˇ)
Famed physicians are powerless. (said of grave illnesses or strange ailments)

名義(ㄇㄧㄥˊ ㄧˋ)
①the name (as opposed to the reality or substance) ② the outward reason (for doing something) ③ nominally

名言(ㄇㄧㄥˊ ㄧㄢˊ)
a maxim; an adage: 「不浪費，不窮困」是句名言。 "Waste not, want not" is a maxim.

名揚四海(ㄇㄧㄥˊ ㄧㄤˊ ㄙˋ ㄏㄞˇ)
to become famous all over the world

名位(ㄇㄧㄥˊ ㄨㄟˋ)
position and title; official rank

名望(ㄇㄧㄥˊ ㄨㄤˋ)
fame; reputation; repute; renown; popularity

名譽(ㄇㄧㄥˊ ㄩˋ)
①honor; repute; reputation: 他是一位名譽很好的醫生。 He is a doctor of high reputation. ② honorary

名譽博士(ㄇㄧㄥˊ ㄩˋ ㄅㄛˊ ㄕˋ)
an honorary doctorate

名譽董事長(ㄇㄧㄥˊ ㄩˋ ㄉㄨㄥˇ ㄕˋ ㄓㄤˇ)
the honorary board chairman (of an institution, etc.)

名譽會長(ㄇㄧㄥˊ ㄩˋ ㄏㄨㄟˋ ㄓㄤˇ)
the honorary president or chairman (of an association)

名媛(ㄇㄧㄥˊ ㄩㄢˊ)
a young lady of note

【后】557 ㄏㄡˋ how hòu
1. an empress
2. the god of the earth
3. after; behind 亦作「後」

后妃(ㄏㄡˋ ㄈㄟ)
the empress and imperial concubines

后土(ㄏㄡˋ ㄊㄨˇ)
the earth; the god of the earth

后冠(ㄏㄡˋ ㄍㄨㄢ)
a tiara

后稷(ㄏㄡˋ ㄐㄧˋ)
the minister of agriculture under Emperor Shun (舜)

【吐】558 1. ㄊㄨˇ tuu tǔ
to spit; to utter

吐蕃(ㄊㄨˇ ㄈㄢ)
the Tibetan regime in ancient China

吐痰(ㄊㄨˇ ㄊㄢˊ)
to spit phlegm; to spit

吐露(ㄊㄨˇ ㄌㄨˋ)
to confess; to disclose

吐露真情(ㄊㄨˇ ㄌㄨˋ ㄓㄣ ㄑㄧㄥˊ)
to unbosom oneself; to tell

the truth

吐剛茹柔(ㄊㄨˇ ㄍㄤ ㄖㄨˊ ㄖㄨˊ)
to bow to the mighty and powerful but act like a bully toward the weak; to avoid the strong and bully the weak

吐故納新(ㄊㄨˇ ㄍㄨˋ ㄋㄚˋ ㄒㄧㄣ)
①a Taoist art to achieve a long life by breathing out the useless air and breathing in the fresh air ② to get rid of the stale and take in the fresh

吐氣(ㄊㄨˇ ㄑㄧˋ)
to give vent to pent-up feelings

吐棄(ㄊㄨˇ ㄑㄧˋ)
to spurn; to cast aside; to reject

吐出(ㄊㄨˇ ㄔㄨ)
to spit out; to utter

【吐】558 2. ㄊㄨˋ tuh tù
to vomit; to throw up; to spew

吐沫(ㄊㄨˋ ·ㄇㄛ)
saliva

吐劑(ㄊㄨˋ ㄐㄧˋ)
an emetic

吐血(ㄊㄨˋ ㄒㄧㄝˇ)
to vomit blood; hematemesis; hemoptysis

吐瀉(ㄊㄨˋ ㄒㄧㄝˋ)
vomiting and purging

【向】559 ㄒㄧㄤˋ shiang xiàng
1. to turn; to face: 這棟建築物向西。 This building faces west.
2. a direction; a trend
3. until now
4. a Chinese family name

向背(ㄒㄧㄤˋ ㄅㄟˋ)
the support or opposition (of the people)

向壁虛造(ㄒㄧㄤˋ ㄅㄧˋ ㄒㄩ ㄗㄠˋ)
a gross fabrication; to fabricate

向明(ㄒㄧㄤˋ ㄇㄧㄥˊ)
①toward daybreak ② the bright side of a house

向來(ㄒㄧㄤˋ ㄌㄞˊ)
hitherto; heretofore; until now; always: 向來都是他出主意。 He always makes the decisions.

向例(ㄒㄧㄤ ㄌㄧˋ)
according to custom; customarily

向光性(ㄒㄧㄤ ㄍㄨㄤ ㄒㄧㄥˋ)
(biology) phototropism

向後(ㄒㄧㄤ ㄏㄡˋ)
①in the future ②to turn around

向前(ㄒㄧㄤ ㄑㄧㄢˊ)
to go forward: 讓我們向前。
Let's go forward.

向下(ㄒㄧㄤ ㄒㄧㄚˋ)
downward; down: 這條馬路向下傾斜。The road runs downward.

向心力(ㄒㄧㄤ ㄒㄧㄣ ㄌㄧˋ)
centripetal force

向學(ㄒㄧㄤ ㄒㄩㄝˊ)
to determine or to be inclined to study: 他努力向學。He determined to study hard.

向着(ㄒㄧㄤ ·ㄓㄜ)
toward (an object or direction); to face

向上(ㄒㄧㄤ ㄕㄤˋ)
①to turn upward ② to strive upward; to try to improve oneself

向日葵(ㄒㄧㄤ ㄖˋ ㄎㄨㄟˊ)
the sunflower: 向日葵向著太陽。Sunflowers turn towards the sun.

向榮(ㄒㄧㄤ ㄖㄨㄥˊ)
on the road to prosperity; making progress

向左(ㄒㄧㄤ ㄗㄨㄛˇ)
towards the left

向右(ㄒㄧㄤ ㄧㄡˋ)
towards the right

向陽(ㄒㄧㄤ ㄧㄤˊ)
(said of a house) facing south, or the sunny side: 這屋子向陽。The house faces south.

向無此例(ㄒㄧㄤ ㄨˊ ㄘˇ ㄌㄧˋ)
There's no precedent for this.

向外(ㄒㄧㄤ ㄨㄞˋ)
①to turn outside ② upwards of, or more (used after a number)

向晚(ㄒㄧㄤ ㄨㄢˇ)
toward the evening

向往／嚮往(ㄒㄧㄤ ㄨㄤˇ)
to admire and try to imitate (a great person, etc.)

向隅(ㄒㄧㄤ ㄩˊ)
to miss the opportunity (of seeing a great show, getting a handsome gift, buying a new product, etc.)

【吏】 560 ㄌㄧˋ lih lì
a civil officer

吏部(ㄌㄧˋ ㄅㄨˋ)
(in ancient China) the Ministry of Civil Personnel

吏治(ㄌㄧˋ ㄓˋ)
(said of officials) the achievements of an administration

吏員(ㄌㄧˋ ㄩㄢˊ)
a minor official

四畫

【君】 561 ㄐㄩㄣ jiun jūn
1. a sovereign; a monarch; a king; a lord
2. you (used in addressing a male in formal speech)

君臨萬邦(ㄐㄩㄣ ㄌㄧㄣˊ ㄨㄢˋ ㄅㄤ)
to become an emperor of a vast empire

君權(ㄐㄩㄣ ㄑㄩㄢˊ)
sovereign power; monarchical authority; the royal prerogative

君權神授(說)(ㄐㄩㄣ ㄑㄩㄢˊ ㄕㄣˊ ㄕㄡˋ)
(the theory of) the divine right of kings

君主(ㄐㄩㄣ ㄓㄨˇ)
a sovereign; a monarch; a ruler

君主立憲(ㄐㄩㄣ ㄓㄨˇ ㄌㄧˋ ㄒㄧㄢˋ)
constitutional or limited monarchy

君主國(ㄐㄩㄣ ㄓㄨˇ ㄍㄨㄛˊ)
a monarchy

君主專制(ㄐㄩㄣ ㄓㄨˇ ㄓㄨㄢ ㄓˋ)
absolute or despotic monarchy

君士坦丁堡(ㄐㄩㄣ ㄕˋ ㄊㄢˇ ㄉㄧㄥ ㄅㄠˇ)
Constantinople, the old capital of Turkey

君子(ㄐㄩㄣ ㄗˇ)
①a perfect or true gentleman; a man of virtue: 君子成人之美。A gentleman is always ready to assist others in achieving their objectives. ②a superior

君子國(ㄐㄩㄣ ㄗˇ ㄍㄨㄛˊ)
the (imaginary) land of the virtuous

君子協定(ㄐㄩㄣ ㄗˇ ㄒㄧㄝˊ ㄉㄧㄥˋ)
a gentlemen's agreement: 我與他達成君子協定。I made a gentlemen's agreement with him.

君子之交淡如水(ㄐㄩㄣ ㄗˇ ㄓ ㄐㄧㄠ ㄉㄢˋ ㄖㄨˊ ㄕㄨㄟˇ)
The friendship between gentlemen appears indifferent but is pure like water.

君無戲言(ㄐㄩㄣ ㄨˊ ㄒㄧˋ ㄧㄢˊ)
The king's words are to be taken seriously. 或 A monarch or ruler is expected to honor all his promises.

君王(ㄐㄩㄣ ㄨㄤˊ)
a sovereign; a monarch; a ruler

【吝】 562 ㄌㄧㄣˋ linn lìn
stingy; niggardly; parsimonious

吝惜(ㄌㄧㄣˋ ㄒㄧ)
to hold stingily on to; to be stingy about; to stint

吝嗇(ㄌㄧㄣˋ ㄙㄜˋ)
stingy; miserly; niggardly; parsimonious

【吞】 563 ㄊㄨㄣ tuen tūn
to swallow; to engulf; to gulp

吞併(ㄊㄨㄣ ㄅㄧㄥˋ)
to annex (a foreign territory); to take possession of (another's property)

吞沒(ㄊㄨㄣ ㄇㄛˋ)
①to take possession of (another's property); to appropriate ②to engulf

吞滅(ㄊㄨㄣ ㄇㄧㄝˋ)
to conquer and annex (a country)

吞服(ㄊㄨㄣ ㄈㄨˊ)
to swallow or take (medicine)

吞吐(ㄊㄨㄣ ㄊㄨˇ)
①to swallow and spit ②to take in and send out in large quantities

吞吐量(ㄊㄨㄣ ㄊㄨˇ ㄌㄧㄤˋ)
the volume of goods handled at a seaport

吞吞吐吐(ㄊㄨㄣ ㄊㄨㄣ ㄊㄨˇ ㄊㄨˇ)

trying to hide something
while speaking; to hum and
haw

吞公款 (ㄊㄨㄣ ㄍㄨㄥ ㄎㄨㄢˇ)
to embezzle public funds

吞佔 (ㄊㄨㄣ ㄓㄢˋ)
to take possession of land
illegally

吞食 (ㄊㄨㄣ ㄕˊ)
to swallow; to devour

吞噬 (ㄊㄨㄣ ㄕˋ)
①(said of beasts) to swallow or devour (the prey) ②
(said of fire, etc.) to devour;
to engulf

吞聲 (ㄊㄨㄣ ㄕㄥ)
①to suppress complaints or
grudges ② to sob

吞雲吐霧 (ㄊㄨㄣ ㄩㄣˊ ㄊㄨˇ ㄨˋ)
to puff; to take puffs; to
smoke

【吟】 564
ㄧㄣˊ yn yín
1. to chant; to intone; to sing;
to recite
2. to moan; to sigh

吟風弄月 (ㄧㄣˊ ㄈㄥ ㄌㄨㄥˋ ㄩㄝˋ)
to sing of the wind and toy
with the moon (referring to
the leisurely abandon of a
poet)

吟壇 (ㄧㄣˊ ㄊㄢˊ)
the poetic circles: 他在吟壇享
有盛名。He was famous in
the poetic circles.

吟嘯 (ㄧㄣˊ ㄒㄧㄠˋ)
① to sing in freedom; to
whistle or shout in freedom
② to lament; to sigh

吟誦 (ㄧㄣˊ ㄙㄨㄥˋ)
to recite (a verse); to chant
or intone (a verse); 她吟誦李
白的詩。She recited Li Po's
poems.

吟哦 (ㄧㄣˊ ㄜˊ)
to chant or intone (a verse)

吟遊詩人 (ㄧㄣˊ ㄧㄡˊ ㄕ ㄖㄣˊ)
a troubadour; a minstrel

吟味 (ㄧㄣˊ ㄨㄟˋ)
to enjoy or appreciate (a
poem, etc.): 他吟味詩篇。He
appreciated a poem.

吟詠 (ㄧㄣˊ ㄩㄥˇ)
to chant or intone (a verse)

【吠】 565
ㄈㄟˋ fey fèi
(said of a dog) to bark: 狗

對著他吠叫。The dog barks
at him.

吠影吠聲 (ㄈㄟˋ ㄧㄥˇ ㄈㄟˋ ㄕㄥ)
① to bark at shadows and
sounds ② to raise an uproar
over an unconfirmed rumor

【否】 566
ㄈㄡˇ foou fǒu
1. no; not
2. negative

否定 (ㄈㄡˇ ㄉㄧㄥˋ)
① to deny; to negate; to
refute: 事實否定他的推論。
Facts have refuted his inference. ② denial; negation

否決 (ㄈㄡˇ ㄐㄩㄝˊ)
to veto; a veto; to vote
down

否決權 (ㄈㄡˇ ㄐㄩㄝˊ ㄑㄩㄢˊ)
veto power

否認 (ㄈㄡˇ ㄖㄣˋ)
① to deny; to reject; to repudiate; to disown; to disclaim;
to gainsay ②denial; rejection; repudiation; disavowal

否則 (ㄈㄡˇ ㄗㄜˊ)
otherwise; or else; if not,
then…

【否】 566
ㄆㄧˇ pii pǐ
evil; bad

否極泰來 (ㄆㄧˇ ㄐㄧˊ ㄊㄞˋ ㄌㄞˊ)
Adversity, after reaching its
extremity, is followed by
felicity. 或After extreme
bad luck comes good luck.

【吩】 567
ㄈㄣ fen fēn
to instruct or direct (someone to do something)

吩咐 (ㄈㄣ ㄈㄨˋ)
to instruct or direct (someone to do something);
instructions or directions (to
do something)

【含】 568
ㄏㄢˊ harn hán
1. to hold in the mouth
2. to contain; to include
3. to bear

含悲 (ㄏㄢˊ ㄅㄟ)
to exercise restraint over
grief

含苞待放 (ㄏㄢˊ ㄅㄠ ㄉㄞˋ ㄈㄤˋ)
①(said of flowers) in a budding condition; in bud ②
(said of girls in early teens)
in the bud

含怒 (ㄏㄢˊ ㄋㄨˋ)
in anger

含淚 (ㄏㄢˊ ㄌㄟˋ)
with tears in the eyes

含量 (ㄏㄢˊ ㄌㄧㄤˋ)
content

含垢忍辱 (ㄏㄢˊ ㄍㄡˋ ㄖㄣˇ ㄖㄨˋ)
to bear shame and indignity
to endure disgrace and
humiliations (with a nobl
purpose in mind)

含恨 (ㄏㄢˊ ㄏㄣˋ)
to cherish resentment, disap
pointment, etc.

含糊 (ㄏㄢˊ ㄏㄨˊ)or 含混糊糊
ㄏㄢˊ ㄏㄨˊ ㄏㄨˊ)or 含混 (ㄏㄢˊ ㄏㄨㄣˋ)
(said of a statement, man
ners, etc.) vague; ambigu
ous; confusing; befuddling o
uncertain

含糊了事 (ㄏㄢˊ ㄏㄨˊ ㄌㄧㄠˇ ㄕˋ)
to settle the case carelessly

含糊其詞 (ㄏㄢˊ ㄏㄨˊ ㄑㄧˊ ㄘˊ)
to talk ambiguously

含情脈脈 (ㄏㄢˊ ㄑㄧㄥˊ ㄇㄛˋ ㄇㄛˋ)
full of tenderness (in silen
communication of affectio
or love, especially said o
young girls)

含笑 (ㄏㄢˊ ㄒㄧㄠˋ)
①(botany) Michelia figo
to smile; to grin; with a
smile; smilingly

含笑九泉 (ㄏㄢˊ ㄒㄧㄠˋ ㄐㄧㄡˇ ㄑㄩㄢˊ)
含笑地下 (ㄏㄢˊ ㄒㄧㄠˋ ㄉㄧˋ ㄒㄧㄚˋ)
to be able to smile in Hades
—to die with satisfaction

含羞 (ㄏㄢˊ ㄒㄧㄡ)
to wear a bashful expres
sion; to blush

含羞草 (ㄏㄢˊ ㄒㄧㄡ ㄘㄠˇ)
(botany) mimosa; the sensi
tive plant

含辛茹苦 (ㄏㄢˊ ㄒㄧㄣ ㄖㄨˊ ㄎㄨˇ)
(said of women, especially
widows, raising children) to
undergo all sorts of hard
ships and deprivations

含蓄 (ㄏㄢˊ ㄒㄩˋ)
with concealed or implied
deep meanings

含血噴人 (ㄏㄢˊ ㄒㄩㄝˋ ㄆㄣ ㄖㄣˊ)
to bring false accusations
against others

含沙射影 (ㄏㄢˊ ㄕㄚ ㄕㄜˋ ㄧㄥˇ)
to hurt others maliciously

【口
部】

含詬(ㄏㄢ ㄍㄡˋ)
to bear shame

含飴弄孫(ㄏㄢ ㄧˊ ㄋㄨㄥˋ ㄙㄨㄣ)
(literally) to eat sweets and play with grandchildren—to lead a carefree life in one's old age

含義(ㄏㄢˊ ㄧˋ)
a meaning; an implication

含英咀華(ㄏㄢˊ ㄧㄥ ㄐㄩˇ ㄏㄨㄚˊ)
to enjoy the beauty of words

含味(ㄏㄢˊ ㄨㄟˋ)
to fully enjoy (food, pleasure, etc.)

含冤(ㄏㄢˊ ㄩㄢ)
to be the victim of an unjust charge

含冤莫白(ㄏㄢˊ ㄩㄢ ㄇㄛˋ ㄅㄞˊ)
unable to clear oneself of a false accusation

含怨(ㄏㄢˊ ㄩㄢˋ)
to bear a grudge

【吮】 569
　　ㄕㄨㄣˇ **shoen shǔn**
to suck; to lick: 這個小男孩吮拇指。The little boy sucked his thumb.

吮墨(ㄕㄨㄣˇ ㄇㄛˋ)
to be deep in thought while writing

吮癰舐痔(ㄕㄨㄣˇ ㄩㄥ ㄕˋ ㄓˋ)
to practice sycophancy or servile flattery

【呈】 570
　　ㄔㄥˊ **cherng chéng**
1. to submit, present, or hand in (to a superior)
2. to show, manifest, expose, display, disclose, exhibit, etc.
3. a petition or appeal

呈報(ㄔㄥˊ ㄅㄠˋ)
to present or submit a report; to report (to a superior)

呈明(ㄔㄥˊ ㄇㄧㄥˊ)
to state (a case) clearly (to a superior)

呈露(ㄔㄥˊ ㄌㄨˋ)or 呈現(ㄔㄥˊ ㄒㄧㄢˋ)
to expose, disclose, display, exhibit, manifest, or show (something that has been hidden or unobvious); (said of something that has been hidden or unobvious) to become exposed; to come out to the surface

呈核(ㄔㄥˊ ㄏㄜˊ)
to submit (to higher authorities) for review

呈遞(ㄔㄥˊ ㄉㄧˋ)
to handle or submit (to higher authorities)

呈請(ㄔㄥˊ ㄑㄧㄥˇ)
(a phrase used in official communications to introduce a request) It is requested that....

呈現(ㄔㄥˊ ㄒㄧㄢˋ)
to present (a certain appearance); to appear; to emerge

呈獻(ㄔㄥˊ ㄒㄧㄢˋ)or 呈上(ㄔㄥˊ ㄕㄤˋ)
to present (to a superior)

呈祥(ㄔㄥˊ ㄒㄧㄤˊ)
(the appearance of something or phenomenon which is interpreted as) a sign of auspices

呈正 or 呈政(ㄔㄥˊ ㄓㄥˋ)
to present for correction

呈准(ㄔㄥˊ ㄓㄨㄣˇ)
presented (to a higher agency) for review and approval

呈送(ㄔㄥˊ ㄙㄨㄥˋ)
to forward or send (to a higher agency)

呈文(ㄔㄥˊ ㄨㄣˊ)
an official letter to a higher agency (from a lower agency or from the people); a petition; an appeal

呈閱(ㄔㄥˊ ㄩㄝˋ)
to submit (to a superior or higher agency) for perusal

【吳】 571
　　ㄨˊ **wu wú**
1. the name of a state in the Epoch of the Three Kingdoms
2. the name of a state in the Warring States period
3. a Chinese family name

吳鳳(ㄨˊ ㄈㄥˋ)
Wu Feng, (an official who, when head hunting was still common among the aborigines of Taiwan, ended the practice at the cost of his own life in 1768)

吳牛喘月(ㄨˊ ㄋㄧㄡˊ ㄔㄨㄢˇ ㄩㄝˋ) The ox of Wu gasps from heat when it

mistakes the moon for the sun.—to have an excess fear of something

吳儂軟語(ㄨˊ ㄋㄨㄥˊ ㄖㄨㄢˇ ㄩˇ)
the soft speech spoken by the people in the Shanghai-Soochow area (referring to the soft impression one gets from the Wu dialect)

吳郭魚(ㄨˊ ㄍㄨㄛ ㄩˊ)
a mouth breeder

吳國(ㄨˊ ㄍㄨㄛˊ)
the state of Wu in the Epoch of the Three Kingdoms or the one in the Epoch of Warring States

吳下阿蒙(ㄨˊ ㄒㄧㄚˋ ㄚ ㄇㄥˊ)
an ignorant person: 他已非昔日吳下阿蒙矣。He is no more an ignorant person.

吳語(ㄨˊ ㄩˇ)
the Wu dialect (of which the main representative is the Shanghai dialect)

吳越同舟(ㄨˊ ㄩㄝˋ ㄊㄨㄥˊ ㄓㄡ)
Even mortal enemies should help each other in the face of common danger.

【吵】 572
　　ㄔㄠˇ **chao chǎo**
1. to quarrel; to wrangle; to dispute; to row
2. to disturb; to annoy

吵開(ㄔㄠˇ ㄖㄤˊ)or 吵吵鬧鬧(ㄔㄠˇ ㄔㄠˇ ㄋㄠˋ ㄋㄠˋ)
to quarrel noisily; to brawl; noisy

吵架(ㄔㄠˇ ㄐㄧㄚˋ)
to quarrel; to brawl; to argue; to wrangle; to row

吵人(ㄔㄠˇ ㄖㄣˊ)
to disturb others (by noise)

吵嚷(ㄔㄠˇ ㄖㄤˇ)
to quarrel; to dispute; to brawl; to wrangle; to argue; to row

吵嘴(ㄔㄠˇ ㄗㄨㄟˇ)
to dispute; to have a verbal exchange (or quarrel); to wrangle

【吶】 573
　　ㄋㄚˋ **nah nà**
1. to shout
2. to speak hesitatingly

吶吶(ㄋㄚˋ ㄋㄚˋ)
to speak haltingly

吶喊(ㄋㄚˋ ㄏㄢˇ)

〔口部〕

【口部】

to give a whoop, or to shout (in a battle, etc.)

呐喊助威 (ㄋㄚˋ ㄏㄢˇ ㄓㄨˋ ㄨㄟ)
to shout encouragement; to cheer

【吸】 574
(ㄒㄧ) shi xī
to absorb; to imbibe; to suck in; to attract; to draw; to inhale

吸盤 (ㄒㄧ ㄆㄢˊ)
(zoology) sucking disks

吸墨紙 (ㄒㄧ ㄇㄛˋ ㄓˇ)
blotting paper

吸附 (ㄒㄧ ㄈㄨˋ)
(chemistry) adsorption

吸毒 (ㄒㄧ ㄉㄨˊ)
to smoke opium; to become addicted to narcotics

吸毒者 (ㄒㄧ ㄉㄨˊ ㄓㄜˇ)
a drug addict

吸鐵石 (ㄒㄧ ㄊㄧㄝˇ ㄕˊ)
a loadstone (or lodestone)

吸力 (ㄒㄧ ㄌㄧˋ) or吸引力 (ㄒㄧ ㄧㄣˇ ㄌㄧ)
①attraction ②(physics) gravitation

吸管 (ㄒㄧ ㄍㄨㄢˇ)
①a pipette ②a straw

吸氣 (ㄒㄧ ㄑㄧˋ)
to inhale

吸取 (ㄒㄧ ㄑㄩˇ)
①to absorb (knowledge) ②to suck (liquids)

吸取教訓 (ㄒㄧ ㄑㄩˇ ㄐㄧㄠˋ ㄒㄩㄣˋ)
to draw a lesson

吸血鬼 (ㄒㄧ ㄒㄩㄝˋ ㄍㄨㄟˇ)
a vampire

吸塵器 (ㄒㄧ ㄔㄣˊ ㄑㄧˋ)
a vacuum cleaner

吸食 (ㄒㄧ ㄕˊ)
to suck; to take in

吸收 (ㄒㄧ ㄕㄡ)
①to absorb; to take in ②to recruit or attract

吸收游資 (ㄒㄧ ㄕㄡ ㄧㄡˊ ㄗ)
to absorb idle funds

吸吮 (ㄒㄧ ㄕㄨㄣˇ)
to suck; to absorb

吸熱 (ㄒㄧ ㄖㄜˋ)
absorption of heat

吸二手菸 (ㄒㄧ ㄦˋ ㄕㄡˇ ㄧㄢ)
passive smoking

吸煙 (ㄒㄧ ㄧㄢ)
to smoke; smoking

吸煙區 (ㄒㄧ ㄧㄢ ㄑㄩ)
a smoking area

吸煙室 (ㄒㄧ ㄧㄢ ㄕˋ)
a smoking room

吸音 (ㄒㄧ ㄧㄣ)
sound-absorbent

吸引 (ㄒㄧ ㄧㄣˇ)
to attract; to draw: 磁石吸引鋼鐵。A magnet attracts steel.

吸蠅紙 (ㄒㄧ ㄧㄥˊ ㄓˇ)
flypaper

【吹】 575
ㄔㄨㄟ chuei chuī
1. to blow; to puff
2. to brag or boast; to praise in exaggerated words
3. to break up

吹拍 (ㄔㄨㄟ ㄆㄞ) or吹捧 (ㄔㄨㄟ ㄆㄥˇ)
to boast (before equals or inferiors) and to flatter (superiors)

吹毛求疵 (ㄔㄨㄟ ㄇㄠˊ ㄑㄧㄡˊ ㄘ)
(literally) to blow apart the hair to find defects—to go out of the way to discover another's weak points; to engage in faultfinding

吹法螺 (ㄔㄨㄟ ㄈㄚˇ ㄌㄨㄛˊ)
to brag; to boast

吹風 (ㄔㄨㄟ ㄈㄥ)
①to be in a draught; to catch a chill ②to dry (hair, etc.) with a blower

吹風機 (ㄔㄨㄟ ㄈㄥ ㄐㄧ)
a blower; a drier

吹拂 (ㄔㄨㄟ ㄈㄨˊ)
(said of winds, etc.) to move or wave (grass, branches, etc.); to sway

吹打 (ㄔㄨㄟ ㄉㄚˇ) or吹吹打打 (ㄔㄨㄟ ㄔㄨㄟ ㄉㄚˇ ㄉㄚˇ)
to make music by blowing and beating; to play music

吹笛 (ㄔㄨㄟ ㄉㄧˊ)
to play the flute

吹彈 (ㄔㄨㄟ ㄊㄢˊ)
to make music by blowing wind instruments and plucking at string instruments; to play music

吹牛 (ㄔㄨㄟ ㄋㄧㄡˊ)
to brag; to boast

吹牛拍馬 (ㄔㄨㄟ ㄋㄧㄡˊ ㄆㄞ ㄇㄚˇ)
to boast and flatter

吹喇叭 (ㄔㄨㄟ ㄌㄚˇ ㄅㄚ˙)
to blow the trumpet

busted; to have failed; to have ended in a flop

吹鼓手 (ㄔㄨㄟ ㄍㄨˇ ㄕㄡˇ)
①the trumpeters and drummers (of a band) ②musicians (of small bands of low rating)

吹管 (ㄔㄨㄟ ㄍㄨㄢˇ)
a blowpipe

吹口哨 (ㄔㄨㄟ ㄎㄡˇ ㄕㄠˋ)
to whistle: 不要在教堂裏吹口哨。Don't whistle in the church.

吹號 (ㄔㄨㄟ ㄏㄠˋ)
to blow the bugle: 他很會吹號。He blows his bugle well

吹呼 (ㄔㄨㄟ ㄏㄨ)
to bawl at; to give a scolding

吹鬍子瞪眼 (ㄔㄨㄟ ㄏㄨˊ ˙ㄗ ㄉㄥˋ ㄧㄢˇ)
to foam at the mouth and glare with rage

吹灰之力 (ㄔㄨㄟ ㄏㄨㄟ ㄓ ㄌㄧˋ)
strength as little as that needed for blowing dust away

吹簫 (ㄔㄨㄟ ㄒㄧㄠ)
①to play the vertical flute ②to go begging

吹噓 (ㄔㄨㄟ ㄒㄩ)
to recommend or praise (a person) in exaggerated words

吹哨子 (ㄔㄨㄟ ㄕㄠˋ ˙ㄗ)
to blow the whistle: 裁判吹哨子。The referee blew his whistle.

吹奏 (ㄔㄨㄟ ㄗㄡˋ)
to play (wind instruments)

【吻】 576
ㄨㄣˇ woen wěn
1. the lip
2. the tone of one's speech
3. to kiss; a kiss

吻別 (ㄨㄣˇ ㄅㄧㄝˊ)
to kiss someone good-bye

吻合 (ㄨㄣˇ ㄏㄜˊ)
(said of two things) to agree, correspond, match, or tally with: 他所說的和事實吻合。His account tallies with the fact.

【吼】 577
ㄏㄡˇ hoou hòu
(said of beasts) to roar or howl

【吱】 578
ㄗ tzy zī

squeaky cries of an animal

支喳(ㄓ ㄔㄚ)
chatter (made by birds or animals)

支吱(ㄓ)
(to cry) in a squeak; squeaking sounds (made by insects)

【吾】⁵⁷⁹ ㄨ wu wú
1. I, me, we, or us (in literary usage)
2. my; our

吾黨(ㄨ ㄌㄤ)
my fellows

吾弟(ㄨ ㄉㄧ)
my younger brother

吾兄(ㄨ ㄒㄩㄥ)
① my elder brother ② (courteous among friends) you

吾儕(ㄨ ㄔㄞ)or 吾曹(ㄨ ㄘㄠ)or 吾輩(ㄨ ㄅㄟ)or 吾等(ㄨ ㄉㄥ)
we; us

吾人(ㄨ ㄖㄣ)
we

吾子(ㄨ ㄗ)
① you; sir ② my son

吾愛(ㄨ ㄞ)
my love; my darling

吾友(ㄨ ㄧㄡ)
my friend

【告】⁵⁸⁰ ㄍㄠ gaw gào
1. to tell; to inform; to report: 我把我的名字告訴他。 I told him my name.
2. to accuse

告白(ㄍㄠ ㄅㄞ)
a notice; an announcement

告別(ㄍㄠ ㄅㄧㄝ)
to bid farewell; to say good-bye; to take leave; to announce one's departure

告窆(ㄍㄠ ㄅㄧㄢ)
a written announcement of a burial

告奮(ㄍㄠ ㄅㄧㄥ)
to file a petition; to request from a superior

告病(ㄍㄠ ㄅㄧㄥ)
to resign because of illness; to ask for extended sick leave

告密(ㄍㄠ ㄇㄧ)
to give a tip, or a piece of secret information (to some authorities); to tip off; to

inform against somebody

告廟(ㄍㄠ ㄇㄧㄠ)
(said of an emperor) to report major state decisions or great events at the imperial ancestral temple

告發(ㄍㄠ ㄈㄚ)
to accuse or charge (someone) in a (written or verbal) report to the authorities; to inform against

告乏(ㄍㄠ ㄈㄚ)
to run out of supply

告貸(ㄍㄠ ㄉㄞ)
to ask for a loan

告貸無門(ㄍㄠ ㄉㄞ ㄨ ㄇㄣ)
to have no one to turn to for a loan

告退(ㄍㄠ ㄊㄨㄟ)
① to resign ② to withdraw; to leave the scene

告老還鄉(ㄍㄠ ㄌㄠ ㄏㄨㄢ ㄒㄧㄤ)
to retire on account of old age and return to one's native place

告歸(ㄍㄠ ㄍㄨㄟ)
to go home on leave; to ask for leave to go home

告急(ㄍㄠ ㄐㄧ)
in urgent need of help; in a state of emergency; critical; in danger

告假(ㄍㄠ ㄐㄧㄚ)
to ask for leave of absence

告訐(ㄍㄠ ㄐㄧㄝ)
to expose (other's secrets)

告捷(ㄍㄠ ㄐㄧㄝ)
to emerge victorious; to triumph; to win a victory: 他們首戰告捷。 They won a victory in the first battle.

告解(ㄍㄠ ㄐㄧㄝ)
(Catholicism) to confess; confession

告誡(ㄍㄠ ㄐㄧㄝ)
to admonish; to warn; to caution; to exhort

告警(ㄍㄠ ㄐㄧㄥ)
to alert; to issue a distress call

告竣(ㄍㄠ ㄐㄩㄣ)
to be completed; to be ready for inauguration (as a building)

告罄(ㄍㄠ ㄑㄧㄥ)
(said of a supply) to run out or become exhausted: 瓦

斯告罄。 Gas has run out.

告知(ㄍㄠ ㄓ)
to let know; to notify; to inform

告狀(ㄍㄠ ㄓㄨㄤ)
① to file a lawsuit ② (colloquial) to say something bad against a colleague, fellow student, etc. before a superior; to speak ill of

告終(ㄍㄠ ㄓㄨㄥ)
to come to an end or a close; to end

告成(ㄍㄠ ㄔㄥ)
to be completed or accomplished

告吹(ㄍㄠ ㄔㄨㄟ)
to fizzle out; to fail

告示(ㄍㄠ ㄕ)
① (ㄍㄠ ㄕ) to make known; to announce; to proclaim; to give notice
② (ㄍㄠ ‧ㄕ) an official notice, announcement, or proclamation

告饒(ㄍㄠ ㄖㄠ)
to seek pardon; to apologize

告擾(ㄍㄠ ㄖㄠ)
to thank the host for hospitality (after a party, etc.)

告罪(ㄍㄠ ㄗㄨㄟ)
① to admit a mistake; to apologize for a mistake ② to announce the crimes (of the accused)

告辭(ㄍㄠ ㄘ)
to take leave; to say good-bye; to bid farewell: 他向朋友們告辭。 He took leave of his friends.

告喪(ㄍㄠ ㄙㄤ)
to announce a bereavement

告訴(ㄍㄠ ㄙㄨ)
① (ㄍㄠ ㄙㄨ) to file a lawsuit, or a legal complaint
② (ㄍㄠ ‧ㄙㄨ) to tell (a person); to let know

告訴乃論(ㄍㄠ ㄙㄨ ㄋㄞ ㄌㄨㄣ)
Prosecution for an offense may be instituted only upon complaint.

告一段落(ㄍㄠ ㄧ ㄉㄨㄢ ㄌㄨㄛ)
to draw a conclusion (often referring to a temporary conclusion)

告諭(ㄍㄠ ㄩ)
to counsel; to advise; to

〔口部〕

exhort

【呀】 581
ㄧ丫 ia yā
a creaking sound

呀然一聲(ㄧ丫 ㄖㄢˊ ㄧ ㄕㄥ)
(said of a door) to fling
open with a creaking sound

〔口 **【呀】** 2. ·ㄧ丫 ·ia ya
部〕 1. a particle used after a
phrase for emphasis, expressing surprise, etc.: 她是誰呀?
Who is she?
2. to gape (as in surprise):
呀! 毛病在此。Ah! That is
the trouble.

【呃】 582
ㄜˋ eh è
to hiccup or hiccough

【呂】 583
ㄌㄩˇ leu lǚ
a Chinese family name

呂宋(ㄌㄩˇ ㄙㄨㄥˋ)
Luzon (the chief island of
the Philippines)

【呆】 584
ㄉㄞ dai dāi
(又讀 ㄞˊ air ái)
1. dull; dull-witted; stupid;
unintelligent
2. blank; wooden

呆板(ㄉㄞ ㄅㄢˇ)
①boring; dull; monotonous;
unvarying ②stiff

呆笨(ㄉㄞ ㄅㄣˋ)or(ㄅㄣˋ)
stupid; dull witted; dull;
unintelligent

呆頭呆腦(ㄉㄞ ㄊㄡˊ ㄉㄞ ㄋㄠˇ)
stupid; idiot-like

呆滯(ㄉㄞ ㄓˋ)
dull

呆賬 or 呆帳(ㄉㄞ ㄓㄤˋ)
irrecoverable loans or
credits; a bad debt

呆若木雞(ㄉㄞ ㄖㄨㄛˋ ㄇㄨˋ ㄐㄧ)
(literally) as dull as a
wooden chicken—very dull
or stupid; dumbstruck; trans-
fixed (with fear or amazement); standing like a log

呆子(ㄉㄞ ·ㄗ)or 呆人(ㄉㄞ ㄖㄣˊ)
an idiot; a dullard; a mentally retarded person

【呎】 585
ㄔ chyy cyǐ
the foot (a unit of length in
English measure)

呎磅(ㄔ ㄅㄤˋ)
a foot-pound

【吧】 586
1. ·ㄅㄚ ·ba ba
a particle used after an
imperative sentence: 我們去
吧。Let's go. 不會吧! I don't
think it could be that.

【吧】 586
2. ㄅㄚ ba bā
參看「吧吧」

吧吧(ㄅㄚˋ ㄅㄚˋ)
loquacious

吧嗒(ㄅㄚˋ ·ㄉㄚ)
①to smack one's lips (in
surprise, alarm, etc.) ②(dialect) to pull at (a pipe, etc.)

吧孃(ㄅㄚˋ ㄋㄧㄤˊ)
a bar girl

五畫

【呢】 587
1. ㄋㄧˊ ni ní
1. a woolen fabric
2. a murmur

呢帽(ㄋㄧˊ ㄇㄠˋ)
a woolen hat

呢喃(ㄋㄧˊ ㄋㄢˊ)
①the chirps of the swallows
②to murmur; to twitter

呢料子(ㄋㄧˊ ㄌㄧㄠˋ ·ㄗ)
woolen materials; woolen
cloth

呢絨(ㄋㄧˊ ㄖㄨㄥˊ)
a general term for woolen
materials; a wool fabric;
woolen goods

【呢】 587
2. ·ㄋㄜ ·ne ne
an interrogative or emphatic
particle used after a sentence: 他錯在那兒呢? What
has he done wrong? 那人究竟
是誰呢? Who in the world is
that fellow?

【周】 588
ㄓㄡ jou zhōu
1. the Chou Dynasty
2. a circumference; a circuit:
運動員繞場一周。The
athletes made a circuit of the
arena.
3. complete
4. all around; everywhere
5. to aid; to provide for
6. a Chinese family name

周報(ㄓㄡ ㄅㄠˋ)or 周刊(ㄓㄡ ㄎㄢ)
a weekly

周邊(ㄓㄡ ㄅㄧㄢ)
a periphery

周週(ㄓㄡ ㄅㄧㄢ)
all round; all over

周末(ㄓㄡ ㄇㄛˋ)
the weekend

周密(ㄓㄡ ㄇㄧˋ)
careful and thorough; attentive to every detail

周到(ㄓㄡ ㄉㄠˋ)or 周至(ㄓㄡ ㄓˋ)
thorough; considerate
thoughtful: 你把他也請去,
是顧慮周到。You were consid-
erate to invite him too.

周年(ㄓㄡ ㄋㄧㄢˊ)
an anniversary; a full year

周率(ㄓㄡ ㄌㄩˋ)
①(radio) a frequency ②
(electricity) a cycle

周公(ㄓㄡ ㄍㄨㄥ)
the Duke of Chou (the
brother of King Wu, first
ruler of the Chou Dynasty)

周濟 or 賙濟(ㄓㄡ ㄐㄧˋ)
to help the poor with
money: 他必須周濟貧困的親
戚。He has to help his relatives, who are very poor.

周期(ㄓㄡ ㄑㄧˊ)
a period; a cycle

周期性(ㄓㄡ ㄑㄧˊ ㄒㄧㄥˋ)
periodicity; cyclicity

周全(ㄓㄡ ㄑㄩㄢˊ)
①to aid; to help ②complete
with all that is desired

周詳(ㄓㄡ ㄒㄧㄤˊ)
complete and detailed; every
detail taken care of or considered

周旋(ㄓㄡ ㄒㄩㄢˊ)
①to attend to guests or
friends ②to deal with; to
contend with; to fight

周旋到底(ㄓㄡ ㄒㄩㄢˊ ㄉㄠˋ ㄉㄧˇ)
(said of litigation, quarrels,
etc.) to fight to the end

周知(ㄓㄡ ㄓ)
generally known; public
knowledge: 他是索所周知的人
物。He is known to every-
body.

周折(ㄓㄡ ㄓㄜˊ)
a complicated or trouble-
some course of development;
trouble; complication: 這事恐
怕要費一番周折。I'm afraid
this business will cause us a

good deal of trouble.

周章(ㄓㄡ ㄓㄤ)
①to lose composure; to be confused; to show bewilderment ②trouble: 此事煞費周章。This matter takes a lot of trouble.

周轉不靈(ㄓㄡ ㄓㄨㄢ ㄅㄨ ㄌㄧㄥ)
(said of business firms) to be in financial straits; cash to be not available: 他周轉不靈。He doesn't have enough cash to answer needs.

周長(ㄓㄡ ㄔㄤ)
the girth; the circumference; the perimeter

周身(ㄓㄡ ㄕㄣ)
all over the body

周匝(ㄓㄡ ㄗㄚ)
in one round

周遭(ㄓㄡ ㄗㄠ)
around

周歲(ㄓㄡ ㄙㄨㄟ)or 周年(ㄓㄡ ㄋㄧㄢ)
one full year of life; the first anniversary of a child

周而復始(ㄓㄡ ㄦ ㄈㄨ ㄕ)
to repeat the process again and again

周易(ㄓㄡ ㄧ)
the Book of Changes, one of the Five Classics

周遊(ㄓㄡ ㄧㄡ)
to make a tour in search of adventures, enjoyments, etc.

周遊列國(ㄓㄡ ㄧㄡ ㄌㄧㄝ ㄍㄨㄛ)
to tour the various states (especially referring to the tour of Confucius)

周圍(ㄓㄡ ㄨㄟ)
①surroundings; environment ②the circumference (of a round object): 這棵樹周圍有六英尺。This tree has a circumference of six feet.

【咒】 589
ㄓㄡ jow zhòu
1. to curse; to swear: 你在咒什麼？What are you swearing at?
2. words used as charms by Buddhist monks or Taoist priests to exorcize ghosts

咒罵(ㄓㄡ ㄇㄚ)
to swear at; to curse; to call (a person) names

咒詛(ㄓㄡ ㄗㄨ)
to curse; to swear at

咒語(ㄓㄡ ㄩ)
①curses; imprecations ②exorcism; incantation ③hocus-pocus

【咎】 590
ㄐㄧㄡ jiow jiù
1. a disaster; a calamity
2. a fault; a mistake
3. to blame; to punish; to censure: 別歸咎他人。Don't lay the blame on anybody else.

咎責(ㄐㄧㄡ ㄗㄜ)
to be blamed for one's own faults

咎由自取(ㄐㄧㄡ ㄧㄡ ㄗ ㄑㄩ)
a trouble of one's own making

咎有應得(ㄐㄧㄡ ㄧㄡ ㄧㄥ ㄉㄜ)
The punishment is well deserved.

【呱】 591
ㄍㄨㄚ gu gū
(語音 ㄨㄚ ua wa)
1. the cries of an infant
2. to wail

呱呱墜地(ㄍㄨㄚ ㄍㄨㄚ ㄓㄨㄟ ㄉㄧ)
(said of a baby) to come into this world; to raise the first cry of life: 嬰兒呱呱墜地。The baby came into the world with a cry.

呱呱叫(ㄍㄨㄚ ㄍㄨㄚ ㄐㄧㄠ)or(ㄍㄨㄚ ㄍㄨㄚ ㄐㄧㄠ)
tiptop; topnotch

【味】 592
ㄨㄟ wey wèi
1. a taste; a flavor
2. a smell; an odor
3. a delicacy; a dainty

味道(ㄨㄟ ㄉㄠ)or 味兒(ㄨㄟㄦ)
①a taste; a flavor: 我不喜歡這肉的味道。I don't like the taste of this meat. ②a smell ③a feeling: 我心裡有一股說不出的味道。I have an indescribable feeling.

味同嚼蠟(ㄨㄟ ㄊㄨㄥ ㄐㄩㄝ ㄌㄚ)
to taste as chewing wax—to be insipid

味蕾(ㄨㄟ ㄌㄟ)
a taste bud

味精(ㄨㄟ ㄐㄧㄥ)
flavor essence; gourmet powder; monosodium glutamate

味覺(ㄨㄟ ㄐㄩㄝ)
the sense of taste; gustation: 他有敏銳的味覺。He has a keen sense of taste.

【呵】 593
1. ㄏㄜ he hē
1. to scold in a loud voice
2. to yawn

呵呵大笑(ㄏㄜ ㄏㄜ ㄉㄚ ㄒㄧㄠ)
to roar with laughter; to guffaw; to laugh loudly; to cackle: 每講完一個笑話，老人家就呵呵大笑。The old man cackled after each joke.

呵欠(ㄏㄜ ㄑㄧㄢ)
to yawn and to stretch

呵斥 or 呵叱(ㄏㄜ ㄔ)or 呵責(ㄏㄜ ㄗㄜ)
to scold in a loud voice; to thunder against; to berate

呵手(ㄏㄜ ㄕㄡ)
to breathe on one's hands (to warm them)

呵一口氣(ㄏㄜ ㄧ ㄎㄡ ㄑㄧ)
to give a puff

【呵】 593
2. ㄛ．ㄛ 0 0
a particle used after a phrase to express surprise: 這小伙子真棒呵！Oh, what a fine young boy!

【咕】 594
ㄍㄨ gu gū
1. to murmur
2. (said of hens) a cluck; (said of turtledoves, etc.) a coo

咕嘟着嘴(ㄍㄨ ㄉㄨ ㄓㄜ ㄗㄨㄟ)
to keep the mouth firmly closed in anger

咕咚(ㄍㄨ ㄉㄨㄥ)
the sound of impact caused by a falling object; a thumping sound: 他咕咚一聲掉到水裡去了。He fell into the water with a thumping sound.

咕噥(ㄍㄨ ㄋㄨㄥ)
to murmur; to mutter; to whisper

咕嚕(ㄍㄨ ㄌㄨ)
①a mumbled sound or an indistinct utterance ②the rumbling sound in the belly

咕隆(ㄍㄨ ㄌㄨㄥ)
to rumble; to rattle; to roll: 卡車在公路上咕隆咕隆地跑着。The truck rattled along the highway.

咕唧(ㄍㄨ ㄐㄧ)
①(ㄍㄨ ㄐㄧ) to squelch: 農人在稻田裡咕唧地走。The farmer squelched up and down the paddy fields.

〔口部〕

〔口部〕

②《ㄨ‧ㄐㄧ》to murmur; to whisper: 他們兩人一直在咕啾著。They whispered to each other all the while.

【哂】 595　ㄗㄚ tza zā

to take in food with the tongue; to suck; to sip: 那老人正在哂酒。The old man was sipping at the wine.

哂乾（ㄗㄚㄍㄢ）
to suck dry

哂嘴（ㄗㄚ ㄗㄨㄟˇ）or 哂嘴兒（ㄗㄚ ㄗㄨㄟˇㄦ）
to click the tongue (to express admiration or envy)

【咚】 596　ㄉㄨㄥ dong dōng

1. the sound of impact caused by a falling object
2. rub-a-dub
3. rat-tat; rat-a-tat

【呻】 597　ㄕㄣ shen shēn

to groan; to moan

呻吟（ㄕㄣ ㄧㄣˊ）
to groan; to moan: 你們為什麼無病呻吟? Why do you moan and groan without being ill?

【呼】 598　ㄏㄨ hu hū

1. to call; to cry
2. to exhale: 夜裡植物呼出二氧化碳。At night plants exhale carbon dioxide.

呼朋引類（ㄏㄨ ㄆㄥˊㄧㄣˇ ㄌㄟˋ）
to call friends and fellows together (used in a deprecatory sense to indicate bad company)

呼風喚雨（ㄏㄨ ㄈㄥ ㄏㄨㄢˋ ㄩˇ）
①(of immortals with divine power) to summon wind and rain ②to stir up trouble

呼天搶地（ㄏㄨ ㄊㄧㄢ ㄑㄧㄤˇㄉㄧˋ）
to cry bitterly and loudly in excessive grief

呼痛（ㄏㄨ ㄊㄨㄥˋ）
to cry out in pain

呼盧喝雉（ㄏㄨ ㄌㄨˊㄏㄜˋ ㄓˋ）
(in gambling) to shout for the top number to come up

呼口號（ㄏㄨ ㄎㄡˇ ㄏㄠˋ）
to shout slogans

呼號
①（ㄏㄨ ㄏㄠˊ）to cry; to wail: 風在呼號。The wind wails.
②（ㄏㄨ ㄏㄠˋ）to call the sign (of a message sent by radio)

呼喊（ㄏㄨ ㄏㄢˇ）
to yell; to shout: 他們異口同聲地呼喊。They shouted as with one voice.

呼呼（ㄏㄨ ㄏㄨ）
①the howling of winds ②the regular breathing sound of a heavy sleeper: 他呼呼大睡。He sleeps sound.

呼喚（ㄏㄨ ㄏㄨㄢˋ）
to call; to shout; to cry out: 迷途小孩的母親在呼喚他。The boy was called by his mother.

呼叫（ㄏㄨ ㄐㄧㄠˋ）
to shout; to cry out; to yell

呼叫器（ㄏㄨ ㄐㄧㄠˋㄑㄧˋ）
a pager; a beeper

呼救（ㄏㄨ ㄐㄧㄡˋ）
to cry for help; to call for help; to send out a distress signal: 我聽到呼救聲。I heard a call for help.

呼氣（ㄏㄨ ㄑㄧˋ）
exhalation; expiration; to expire; to exhale

呼吸（ㄏㄨ ㄒㄧ）
①to breathe; to inhale and exhale ②breathing; inhalation and exhalation; breath: 他呼吸急促。He was short of breath.

呼吸道（ㄏㄨ ㄒㄧ ㄉㄠˋ）
the respiratory tract

呼吸器官（ㄏㄨ ㄒㄧ ㄑㄧˋ《ㄨㄢ》）
the respiratory organs

呼吸系統（ㄏㄨ ㄒㄧ ㄒㄧˋㄊㄨㄥˇ）
the respiratory system

呼嘯（ㄏㄨ ㄒㄧㄠˋ）
to roar or howl (like a beast); to whistle; to whiz: 汽車從我們身旁呼嘯而過。The car whizzed past us.

呼之欲出（ㄏㄨ ㄓ ㄩˋㄔㄨ）
①obvious; almost certain (said of the identity of a person who remains behind the scene or a criminal suspect against whom no evidence has yet been found)
②(said of lifelike figures in pictures or characters in novels) to seem ready to come out at one's call—to be vividly portrayed

呼叱（ㄏㄨ ㄔˋ）

to shout at (someone): 不要對我呼叱。Don't shout at me

呼聲（ㄏㄨ ㄕㄥ）
loud cries

呼聲甚高（ㄏㄨ ㄕㄥ ㄕㄣˋㄍㄠ《》）
There are wide speculation (about political candidates government appointments etc.)

呼么喝六（ㄏㄨ ㄧㄠ ㄏㄜˋㄌㄧㄡˋ）
the noisy shouting in a dice game

呼應（ㄏㄨ ㄧㄥˋ）
to act in coordination with each other; to echo: 他們遙相呼應。They echo each other over a distance.

呼籲（ㄏㄨ ㄩˋ）
to call (formally) for (action, efforts, etc.); to appeal to petition

【命】 599　ㄇㄧㄥˋ ming mìng

1. life: 醫生救了他的性命。The doctor saved his life.
2. a fate; destiny; a lot
3. the ordinances of Heaven
4. orders; a command

命薄如花（ㄇㄧㄥˋ ㄅㄛˊㄖㄨˊㄏㄨㄚ）
(said of a woman) to have lived a life as short of blessings as that of an evanescent flower

命不該絕（ㄇㄧㄥˋ ㄅㄨˋ《ㄞ ㄐㄩㄝˊ）
(said of one who has had a narrow escape from death) not destined to die

命脈（ㄇㄧㄥˋ ㄇㄞˋ）
(literally) life and artery—(figuratively) a lifeline; lifeblood; a matter of great importance: 外貿是台灣的命脈。Foreign trade is the lifeline of Taiwan.

命名（ㄇㄧㄥˋ ㄇㄧㄥˊ）
to give a name to; to name, christen, baptize, or dub

命婦（ㄇㄧㄥˋ ㄈㄨˋ）
a woman in ancient China who was given a title or rank by the emperor

命定（ㄇㄧㄥˋ ㄉㄧㄥˋ）
predestined; destined: 他命定客死異國。He was predestined to die in a foreign country.

命題（ㄇㄧㄥˋ ㄊㄧˊ）
①a proposition (in logic)
②to prepare examination

questions ③ to name a topic or subject on which the students are asked to write a composition

命途多舛 (ㄇㄧㄥˋ ㄊㄨˊ ㄉㄨㄛ ㄔㄨㄢˇ)
Life is full of frustrations.

命令 (ㄇㄧㄥˋ ㄌㄧㄥˋ)
a command; orders; an injunction; directions; a directive; to order; to command; to direct; to instruct: 哨兵命令他止步。 The sentry commanded him to halt.

命令句 (ㄇㄧㄥˋ ㄌㄧㄥˋ ㄐㄩˋ)
an imperative sentence

命該如此 (ㄇㄧㄥˋ 《ㄞ ㄖㄨˊ ㄘˇ)
It's predestined. (an expression of resignation)

命根 (ㄇㄧㄥˋ 《ㄣ)
① the stem (of a plant) ② lifeblood; a life-giver ③ one's most beloved (usually child of a favorite child)

命苦 (ㄇㄧㄥˋ ㄎㄨˇ)
to suffer from a hard lot; destined to suffer: 他命苦。 His lot has been a hard one.

命中註定 (ㄇㄧㄥˋ ㄓㄨㄥˋ ㄓㄨˋ ㄉㄧㄥˋ)
(said of individuals) predestined

命中 (ㄇㄧㄥˋ ㄓㄨㄥˋ)
to hit the target

命世之才 (ㄇㄧㄥˋ ㄕˋ ㄓ ㄘㄞˊ)
a person whose ability is superior to his contemporaries

命在旦夕 (ㄇㄧㄥˋ ㄗㄞˋ ㄉㄢˋ ㄒㄧˋ)
Death may come (to a person) any minute.

命案 (ㄇㄧㄥˋ ㄢˋ)
a case of murder or homicide

命運 (ㄇㄧㄥˋ ㄩㄣˋ)
a fate; destiny; a lot; fortune: 命運操之於己。 Every man is the architect of his own fortune.

【咀】 600
ㄐㄩˇ jeu jǔ
to chew; to masticate

咀嚼 (ㄐㄩˇ ㄐㄩㄝˊ)
① to chew; to masticate: 你必須在吞嚥前細細咀嚼。 You have to chew thoroughly before swallowing. ② to dwell on (a word, sentence, passage, etc.) in order to

---

fully appreciate or understand its meaning

【咄】 601
ㄉㄨㄛˋ duoh duō
1. an angry cry
2. to scold in a loud voice

咄咄逼人 (ㄉㄨㄛˋ ㄉㄨㄛˋ ㄅㄧ ㄖㄣˊ)
① to overwhelm with awe or fear; to browbeat ② overbearing

咄咄怪事 (ㄉㄨㄛˋ ㄉㄨㄛˋ ㄍㄨㄞˋ ㄕˋ)
What a queer story! 或 What a strange phenomenon!

【咆】 602
ㄆㄠˊ paur páo
to roar

咆哮 (ㄆㄠˊ ㄒㄧㄠˋ)
① (said of a lion, tiger, etc.) to roar ② (said of winds, waves, etc.) to bluster ③ (said of a person) to rage

【咋】 603
ㄓㄚˋ jah zhà
all of a sudden; suddenly

【咋】 603
ㄗㄜˊ tzer zé
1. to bite; to gnaw
2. a loud noise

咋舌 (ㄗㄜˊ ㄕㄜˊ)
to bite the tongue—to show one's surprise or regret

【和】 604
ㄏㄜˊ her hé
1. harmony; harmonious
2. peace; peaceful
3. to be affable
4. the sum or aggregate
5. of Japan
6. and (語音 ㄏㄢˋ): 他和我是好友。 He and I are good friends.

和盤托出 (ㄏㄜˊ ㄆㄢˊ ㄊㄨㄛ ㄔㄨ)
to reveal the whole truth; to disclose the entire fact: 我打算把事實真相和盤托出。 I intend to reveal the whole truth.

和平 (ㄏㄜˊ ㄆㄧㄥˊ)
① peace ② peaceful; mild (such as the weather, etc.)

和平條約 (ㄏㄜˊ ㄆㄧㄥˊ ㄊㄧㄠˊ ㄩㄝ)
the treaty of peace

和平攻勢 (ㄏㄜˊ ㄆㄧㄥˊ ㄍㄨㄥ ㄕˋ)
a peace offensive

和平共存 (ㄏㄜˊ ㄆㄧㄥˊ ㄍㄨㄥˋ ㄘㄨㄣˊ)
peaceful coexistence; to co-exist peacefully

和平會議 (ㄏㄜˊ ㄆㄧㄥˊ ㄏㄨㄟˋ ㄧˋ)
a peace conference

和平主義 (ㄏㄜˊ ㄆㄧㄥˊ ㄓㄨˇ ㄧˋ)
pacifism

和鳴 (ㄏㄜˊ ㄇㄧㄥˊ)
to sound in harmony

和睦 (ㄏㄜˊ ㄇㄨˋ)
to have friendly ties; to be on friendly terms; to be at peace

和風 (ㄏㄜˊ ㄈㄥ)
a gentle breeze

和服 (ㄏㄜˊ ㄈㄨˊ)
a (Japanese) kimono

和談 (ㄏㄜˊ ㄊㄢˊ)
peace talks

和暖 (ㄏㄜˊ ㄋㄨㄢˇ)
(said of the weather or climate) mild and warm

和好 (ㄏㄜˊ ㄏㄠˇ)
① to be on friendly terms; to maintain friendly relations ② to make up: 他們於爭吵後握手和好。 After their quarrel, they shook hands and made it up.

和會 (ㄏㄜˊ ㄏㄨㄟˋ)
a peace conference

和解 (ㄏㄜˊ ㄐㄧㄝˇ)
to be reconciled; to settle differences; to reach an amiable settlement; reconciliation; a friendly or amicable settlement

和解政策 (ㄏㄜˊ ㄐㄧㄝˇ ㄓㄥˋ ㄘㄜˋ)
détente policy

和姦 (ㄏㄜˊ ㄐㄧㄢ)
fornication

和同 (ㄏㄜˊ ㄊㄨㄥˊ)
(said of a contest) a tie or a draw

和棋 (ㄏㄜˊ ㄑㄧˊ)
a chess game that ends in a tie or draw

和氣 (ㄏㄜˊ ㄑㄧˋ) or 和和氣氣 (ㄏㄜˊ ㄏㄜˊ ㄑㄧˋ ㄑㄧˋ)
gentle; affable; agreeable; friendly; cordial; good-natured

和氣致祥 (ㄏㄜˊ ㄑㄧˋ ㄓˋ ㄒㄧㄤˊ)
Good-naturedness leads to propitiousness.

和氣生財 (ㄏㄜˊ ㄑㄧˋ ㄕㄥ ㄘㄞˊ)
(literally) Good-naturedness is a source of wealth.—A good-natured person has good chances to get rich.

和洽 (ㄏㄜˊ ㄑㄧㄚˋ)

congenial; harmonious

和親(ㄏㄜ ㄑㄧㄣ)
①to be friendly and intimate with each other ②to make peace by a marriage between the royal families of two opposing states

和協(ㄏㄜ ㄒㄧㄝ)
to act in concert; to cooperate harmoniously

和諧(ㄏㄜ ㄒㄧㄝ)
harmonious; in harmony; harmony

和弦(ㄏㄜ ㄒㄧㄢ)
(music) a chord

和煦(ㄏㄜ ㄒㄩ)
mild and warm; 天氣和煦。It is mild and warm.

和衷共濟(ㄏㄜ ㄓㄨㄥ ㄍㄨㄥ ㄐㄧ)
to be united and to work in concert

和暢(ㄏㄜ ㄔㄤ)
agreeable; pleasant; cheery

和事老(ㄏㄜ ㄕ ㄌㄠ)
a mediator; a peacemaker

和善(ㄏㄜ ㄕㄢ)
kind and gentle; genial

和尚(ㄏㄜ ㄕㄤ)
a Buddhist monk

和聲(ㄏㄜ ㄕㄥ)
(music) harmony

和聲學(ㄏㄜ ㄕㄥ ㄒㄩㄝ)
harmonics

和聲樂器(ㄏㄜ ㄕㄥ ㄩㄝ ㄑㄧ)
a harmonic instrument

和數(ㄏㄜ ㄕㄨ)
the sum or aggregate (of an addition in arithmetic)

和順(ㄏㄜ ㄕㄨㄣ)
civil and obliging; amiable; complaisant; compliant

和菜(ㄏㄜ ㄘㄞ)
a fixed menu in a restaurant

和藹可親(ㄏㄜ ㄞ ㄎㄜ ㄑㄧㄣ)
gentle and affable; amiable; benign

和衣而臥(ㄏㄜ ㄧ ㄦ ㄨㄛ)
to sleep with clothes on

和議(ㄏㄜ ㄧ)
a peace accord or agreement (between two states)

和顏悅色(ㄏㄜ ㄧㄢ ㄩㄝ ㄙㄜ)
a peaceful and happy look; a kind and pleasant countenance; a smiling face

和約(ㄏㄜ ㄩㄝ)
a peace treaty

【和】 604
2. ㄏㄜ heh hé
1. to match; to harmonize
2. to write a poem in reply: 我奉和一首。I wrote a poem in reply to yours.

和詩(ㄏㄜ ㄕ)
to compose verses to match those by others (as a literary exercise)

和韻(ㄏㄜ ㄩㄣ)
to adapt rhymes to match those of another poem

【和】 604
3. ㄏㄨㄛ huoh huò
to knead (dough, clay, etc.); to mix: 我要在豆沙裡和點兒糖。I'll mix a little sugar into the bean paste.

和麵(ㄏㄨㄛ ㄇㄧㄢ)
to knead flour

和弄(ㄏㄨㄛ ㄋㄨㄥ)
①to mix evenly by stirring
②to cause disputes

【咖】 605
1. ㄎㄚ ka kā
a character used in transliterating

咖啡(ㄎㄚ ㄈㄟ)
coffee

咖啡館(ㄎㄚ ㄈㄟ ㄍㄨㄢ)or 咖啡館
(ㄎㄚ ㄈㄟ ㄍㄨㄢ)
a café; a coffee house; a coffee shop; a coffee bar

咖啡精(ㄎㄚ ㄈㄟ ㄐㄧㄥ)
instant coffee

咖啡因(ㄎㄚ ㄈㄟ ㄧㄣ)
caffeine 亦作「咖啡鹼」

【咖】 605
2. ㄍㄚ ga gā
a character used in transliterating

咖哩(ㄍㄚ ㄌㄧ)
curry

咖哩飯(ㄍㄚ ㄌㄧ ㄈㄢ)
curry and rice

咖哩牛肉(ㄍㄚ ㄌㄧ ㄋㄧㄡ ㄖㄡ)
curried beef

【咐】 606
ㄈㄨ fuh fù
to tell, bid, or instruct (someone to do something): 爸爸吩咐我好好照看小馬。My father told me to take good care of the foal. 他囑咐我們預備去旅行。He bade us prepare for the journey.

六畫

【咧】 607
1. ㄌㄧㄝ liee lie
to stretch (the mouth) horizontally

咧着嘴(ㄌㄧㄝ ㄓㄜ ㄗㄨㄟ)
to grin: 他痛得直咧着嘴。He was grinning with pain.

【咧】 607
2. ㄌㄧㄝ lie liě
參看「咧咧」

咧咧
①(ㄌㄧㄝ ㄌㄧㄝ) to babble
②(ㄌㄧㄝ ㄌㄧㄝ) a baby's crying sound

【咤】 608
ㄓㄚ jah zhà
to shout with anger

【咦】 609
ㄧ yi yí
(an interjection of surprise) well; why; hey: 咦，那是怎麼回事? Hey, what's all that about?

【咨】 610
ㄗ tzy zī
1. to inquire; to consult
2. a very formal official communication between offices of equal rank

咨嗟(ㄗ ㄐㄧㄝ)
to sigh

咨詢(ㄗ ㄒㄩㄣ)
to inquire; to consult

咨政(ㄗ ㄓㄥ)
a political advisor (to the Chinese presidency)

咨文(ㄗ ㄨㄣ)
a very formal official communication between offices of equal rank

【咪】 611
ㄇㄧ mhi mi
1. a meow (meou, miaow, miaou)
2. smiling: 他笑咪咪的。His face was wreathed in smiles. 或 He was all smiles.

咪咪叫(ㄇㄧ ㄇㄧ ㄐㄧㄠ)
to meow (meou, miaow, miaou)

【咫】 612
ㄓ jyy zhǐ
1. the foot measure of the Chou Dynasty (divided into eight inches)
2. near

咫尺(业ˇ 彳ˇ)
very close: 他近在咫尺。She was close at hand.

咫尺天涯(业ˇ 彳ˇ ㄊㄧㄢ ㄧㄚ)
so near and yet so far

【咬】 ㄧㄠ yeau yǎo 613.
to bite; to gnaw: 狗咬了他的手。The dog bit his hand.

咬破(ㄧㄠ ㄆㄛ)
①to break by the teeth; to bite through ②to make a revealing remark about something

咬定(ㄧㄠ ㄉㄧㄥ)
to insist (that someone did such and such a thing)

咬緊牙關(ㄧㄠ ㄐㄧㄣ ㄧㄚ ㄍㄨㄢ)
(literally) to set the teeth firmly—to endure pain or hardships with determination; to persevere

咬住(ㄧㄠ ㄓㄨ)
①to bite into; to grip with one's teeth ②to grip; to take firm hold of; to refuse to let go of: 追擊部隊咬住敵人不放。The pursuing troops refused to let go of the enemy.

咬扯(ㄧㄠ ㄔㄜ)
to give vent by angry talking

咬舌(ㄧㄠ ㄕㄜ)
to speak imperfectly; to lisp; to have a lisp; to speak with a lisp

咬字(ㄧㄠ ㄗ)
to sing or speak in an elaborate pronunciation (in Chinese opera)

咬耳朵(ㄧㄠ ㄦˇ ㄉㄨ˙)
to whisper into another's ear

咬牙(ㄧㄠ ㄧㄚ)
①to grit (or set, clench, gnash) one's teeth: 他恨得直咬牙。He gnashed his teeth in hatred. ②to grind one's teeth (in sleep)

咬牙切齒(ㄧㄠ ㄧㄚ ㄑㄧㄝ ㄔˇ)
to gnash the teeth (in anger or hatred)

咬文嚼字(ㄧㄠ ㄨㄣˊ ㄐㄧㄠˊ ㄗ)
to be overcareful or pedantic about the use of each word; to pay excessive attention to wording

【咯】 ㄎㄜ luoh luò 614.
to cough; a cough

咯血(ㄎㄜ ㄒㄧㄝ)
to cough up blood

【咯】 ·ㄌㄜ lo lo 614. 2.
a phrase-final particle

【咯】 ㄍㄜ ge gē 614.
參看「咯吱」

咯吱(ㄍㄜ ㄓ)
to creak

【咯】 ㄍㄜˇ ger gě 614.
參看「咯噔」、「咯咯」

咯噔(ㄍㄜˇ ㄉㄥ)
to click

咯咯(ㄍㄜˇ ㄍㄜˇ)
①a low, guttural sound made by a hen when brooding or calling her chicks ②(laughter) a chuckle; a titter

【咱】 ㄗㄢˊ tzarn zán 615.
I, me (in North China dialect)

咱們(ㄗㄢˊ ㄇㄣ˙)
(inclusive) we; you and I: 咱們是國家的主人翁。We are masters of our country.

【咳】 ㄎㄜˊ ker ké 616.
to cough

咳嗽(ㄎㄜˊ ㄙㄡˋ)
to cough; a cough: 他咳嗽得很厲害。He coughs badly.

咳嗽糖漿(ㄎㄜˊ ㄙㄡˋ ㄊㄤˊ ㄐㄧㄤ)
cough syrup

【咳】 ㄎㄚˇ kaa kǎ 616. 2.
to cough up

咳痰(ㄎㄚˇ ㄊㄢˊ)
to cough up phlegm

咳血(ㄎㄚˇ ㄒㄧㄝˇ)
to cough up blood; to spit blood; hemoptysis

【咳】 ㄏㄞ hay hāi 616. 3.
an interjection of regret or remorse

【咸】 ㄒㄧㄢˊ shyan xián 617.
all; completely; fully; wholly

咸信(ㄒㄧㄢˊ ㄒㄧㄣˋ)
generally believed that: 我們咸信他已離開此城。We generally believed that he had left the city.

咸認為(ㄒㄧㄢˊ ㄖㄣˋ ㄨㄟˊ)
generally regarded; generally thought

咸陽(ㄒㄧㄢˊ ㄧㄤˊ)
Hsienyang, the capital of the Chin Dynasty, in northwest Shensi Province

【咽】 ㄧㄢ ian yān 618.
the throat; the larynx; the pharynx; the gullet

咽頭(ㄧㄢ ㄊㄡˊ)
the pharynx; the throat

咽喉(ㄧㄢ ㄏㄡˊ)
①the larynx; the throat ②a narrow, throat-like passage of strategic importance

【咽】 ㄧㄢˋ yann yàn 618. 2.
to swallow; to gulp

咽下去(ㄧㄢˋ ㄒㄧㄚˋ ㄑㄩ)
to swallow; to gulp down

【咽】 ㄧㄝˋ yeh yè 618. 3.
to be choked; to weep or speak in a choked voice; to sob

【咿】 ㄧ i yī 619.
a form used to represent a sound

咿呀(ㄧ ㄧㄚ)
①the prattle of a baby ②the creaking sound made by oars

咿呀學語(ㄧ ㄧㄚ ㄒㄩㄝ ㄩˇ)
(said of a baby) to begin to babble, prattle, or lisp

【哀】 ㄞ ai āi 620.
1. to grieve; to mourn; to lament
2. to pity; to sympathize; to commiserate; compassion
3. sad; sorrowful; lamentable
4. sadness; sorrow; grief: 哀莫大於心死。There is no grief so great as that for a dead heart.

哀兵必勝(ㄞ ㄅㄧㄥ ㄅㄧˋ ㄕㄥˋ)
An army filled with righteous indignation is bound to win.

哀愍(ㄞ ㄇㄧㄣˇ)
to pity; to commiserate

哀鳴(ㄞ ㄇㄧㄥˊ)
to give mournful cries; to

[口部]

［口部］

wail

哀悼（ㄞ ㄉㄠ）
to mourn over, or lament (someone's death); condolence

哀的美頓書（ㄞ ㄉㄧ ㄇㄟ ㄉㄨㄣ ㄕㄨ）
an ultimatum

哀嘆（ㄞ ㄊㄢ）
to lament; to bewail; to bemoan

哀痛（ㄞ ㄊㄨㄥ）
to feel the anguish of sorrow; to feel the pain of grief

哀樂
①（ㄞ ㄌㄜ）grief and joy
②（ㄞ ㄩㄝ）funeral music; the music of lament

哀憐（ㄞ ㄌㄧㄢ）
to pity; to commiserate; to have sympathy or compassion for

哀歌（ㄞ ㄍㄜ）
a lament; an elegy; a dirge: 樂隊在哀訴的演奏哀歌。The band was wailing a lament.

哀告（ㄞ ㄍㄠ）
to speak about one's grievances (in appealing for help)

哀懇（ㄞ ㄎㄣ）
to implore, entreat, or beg (for mercy, help, etc.)

哀號（ㄞ ㄏㄠ）
to wail: 風在哀號。The wind wails.

哀毀骨立（ㄞ ㄏㄨㄟ ㄍㄨ ㄌㄧ）
to be consumed away with grief (until nothing but bones and skins are left); to be emaciated by grief

哀鴻遍野（ㄞ ㄏㄨㄥ ㄅㄧㄢ ㄧㄝ）
The wilderness is filled with suffering people. 或 Throngs of famished and homeless people are roaming the country.

哀戚（ㄞ ㄑㄧ）
sorrow; grief; woe; sadness: 他因哀戚而幾至瘋狂。He was nearly driven mad by grief.

哀泣（ㄞ ㄑㄧ）
to weep with sorrow

哀求（ㄞ ㄑㄧㄡ）
to entreat, implore, beg or appeal pathetically

哀愁（ㄞ ㄔㄡ）
sad; sorrowful

哀傷（ㄞ ㄕㄤ）
to feel sorrow or grief; to grieve; to mourn; to be sad

哀榮（ㄞ ㄖㄨㄥ）
posthumous honors

哀子（ㄞ ㄗ）
a male bereaved of his mother (used in obituary)

哀哉（ㄞ ㄗㄞ）
alas

哀詞 或 哀辭（ㄞ ㄘ）
a kind of ancient writing such as a poem that expresses grief over someone's death

哀思（ㄞ ㄙ）
sad feeling about the deceased

哀豔（ㄞ ㄧㄢ）
(said of love stories) sadly touching

【品】 ⁶²¹ ㄆㄧㄣ pǐn pín

1. personality; character: 他是個品性良好的人。He's a man of fine character.
2. an article; a commodity
3. a rank or grade in the government service in former times: 一品 the highest rank in officialdom in an ancient Chinese court
4. to appraise; to rate
5. to find out

品評（ㄆㄧㄣ ㄆㄧㄥ）
to determine the quality or worth of; to appraise; to rate: 他以品評的眼光看這幅畫。He looked at the picture appraisingly.

品貌（ㄆㄧㄣ ㄇㄠ）
one's personality and appearance

品茗（ㄆㄧㄣ ㄇㄧㄥ）or品茶（ㄆㄧㄣ ㄔㄚ）
to drink tea (with critical appreciation of its taste and quality)

品德（ㄆㄧㄣ ㄉㄜ）
personal character

品第（ㄆㄧㄣ ㄉㄧ）
①to appraise or rate; to grade ②a rank (as a result of rating); a grade

品頭論足（ㄆㄧㄣ ㄊㄡ ㄌㄨㄣ ㄗㄨ）
to make critical remarks about a person's physical appearance: 他對女人品頭論

足。He made critical remarks about a woman's appearance.

品題（ㄆㄧㄣ ㄊㄧ）
to make an appraisal or critical comment (on a person or thing); to rate

品脫（ㄆㄧㄣ ㄊㄨㄛ）
a pint

品類（ㄆㄧㄣ ㄌㄟ）
①to classify ②a class (to which an article belongs)

品格（ㄆㄧㄣ ㄍㄜ）
one's moral character: 他品格高雅。He has high character.

品管（ㄆㄧㄣ ㄍㄨㄢ）
Q.C. (quality control)

品級（ㄆㄧㄣ ㄐㄧ）
①a grade or rank (in the nine-grade system for government officials in former times) ②the grade of an article (in terms of quality)

品酒（ㄆㄧㄣ ㄐㄧㄡ）
to taste wine

品鑑（ㄆㄧㄣ ㄐㄧㄢ）
to criticize; to judge

品行（ㄆㄧㄣ ㄒㄧㄥ）
one's moral character and performance; behavior: 他的品行端正。He has good behavior.

品性（ㄆㄧㄣ ㄒㄧㄥ）
one's moral character

品學兼優（ㄆㄧㄣ ㄒㄩㄝ ㄐㄧㄢ ㄧㄡ）
to excel in morals as well as academic performances; excellent not only morally but also academically; good both in morality and learning: 他真是一位品學兼優的學生。He is really a good student in morality and in learning.

品質（ㄆㄧㄣ ㄓ）
quality (of a commodity, etc.)

品種（ㄆㄧㄣ ㄓㄨㄥ）
a species or variety (of flora or fauna)

品嚐（ㄆㄧㄣ ㄔㄤ）
to taste (food) in order to appraise, rate or grade its worth

品味（ㄆㄧㄣ ㄨㄟ）
taste; a savor

〔口

部〕

【哂】 622
ㄕㄣˇ sheen shěn
to give a sneering smile
哂納(ㄕㄣˇ ㄋㄚˋ)or 哂收(ㄕㄣˇ ㄕㄡ)
Please accept (my small gift).
哂笑(ㄕㄣˇ ㄒㄧㄠˋ)
to laugh at (with contempt)

【哄】 623
1. ㄏㄨㄥ hong hōng
(said of a group of people)
to make a roaring noise
哄動(ㄏㄨㄥ ㄉㄨㄥˋ)
to create a sensation; to excite (the public)
哄堂(ㄏㄨㄥ ㄊㄤˊ)
(said of a group of people gathered together) to fill the room or house with laughter; to bring down the house (as a result of witty remarks, clownish acts, etc.)
哄堂大笑(ㄏㄨㄥ ㄊㄤˊ ㄉㄚˋ ㄒㄧㄠˋ)
The whole room rocks with laughter.
哄然(ㄏㄨㄥ ㄖㄢˊ)
boisterous; uproarious

【哄】 623
2. ㄏㄨㄥˇ hoong hǒng
to beguile; to cheat; to defraud
哄騙(ㄏㄨㄥˇ ㄆㄧㄢˋ)
to defraud; to cheat; to swindle; to take in; to humbug; to hoodwink
哄擡物價(ㄏㄨㄥˇ ㄊㄞˊ ㄨˋ ㄐㄧㄚˋ)
to rig prices; price rigging
哄孩子(ㄏㄨㄥˇ ㄏㄞˊ ˙ㄗ)
to coax a child: 她很會哄孩子。She knows how to coax children.

【哆】 624
ㄉㄨㄛ duo duō
哆嗦(ㄉㄨㄛ ˙ㄙㄨㄛ)
to shiver with cold or tremble with fear: 她冷得打哆嗦。She shivered with cold.

【哇】 625
1. ㄨㄚ ua wā
to vomit
the sound of crying by a child: 那小孩哇的一聲哭起來。The child burst out crying.
哇哇大哭(ㄨㄚ ㄨㄚ ㄉㄚˋ ㄎㄨ)
to cry very loudly: 那小男孩

痛得哇哇大哭。The little boy could not help crying loudly with pain.

【哇】 625
2. ˙ㄨㄚ ·ua wa
a phrase-final particle: 你好哇? Well, how are you?

【哈】 626
1. ㄏㄚ ha hā
1. a form used in transliteration
2. a sound of hearty laughter: 哈哈，我猜着了。Aha, I've guessed it.
哈密瓜(ㄏㄚ ㄇㄧˋ ㄍㄨㄚ)
a honey dew melon; a sweet melon grown in Hami, Sinkiang Province
哈佛大學(ㄏㄚ ㄈㄛˊ ㄉㄚˋ ㄒㄩㄝˊ)
Harvard University
哈得孫河(ㄏㄚ ㄉㄜˊ ㄙㄨㄣ ㄏㄜˊ)
the Hudson River
哈雷彗星(ㄏㄚ ㄌㄟˊ ㄏㄨㄟˋ ㄒㄧㄥ)
(astronomy) Halley's Comet; the Halley Comet
哈哈大笑(ㄏㄚ ㄏㄚ ㄉㄚˋ ㄒㄧㄠˋ)
to roar with laughter; to laugh heartily
哈哈鏡(ㄏㄚ ㄏㄚ ㄐㄧㄥˋ)
a magic mirror (which reflects the distorted image of a person or thing)
哈氣(ㄏㄚ ㄑㄧˋ)
to moisten the surface of an object by exhaling: 眼鏡要哈氣後再擦。Exhale on your glasses before wiping them.
哈欠(ㄏㄚ ㄑㄧㄢ)
a yawn: 那枯燥的演講令人連打哈欠。It was a dull speech greeted with yawns.
哈薩克(ㄏㄚ ㄙㄚˋ ㄎㄜˋ)
Kazakh; Kazakhstan
哈爾濱(ㄏㄚ ㄦˇ ㄅㄧㄣ)
Harbin, a city in Northeast China
哈腰(ㄏㄚ ㄧㄠ)
①to bend the body ②to bow (in salutation)
哈瓦那(ㄏㄚ ㄨㄚˋ ㄋㄚˋ)
Havana

【哈】 626
2. ㄏㄚˇ haa hǎ
看看「哈巴狗」
哈巴狗(ㄏㄚ ㄅㄚ ㄍㄡˇ)
①a Pekingese or Pekinese (dog) ②toady; sycophant

【哉】 627
ㄗㄞ tzai zāi
a phrase-final particle expressing surprise, admiration, grief, doubt, etc. (a literary form): 嗚呼! 哀哉! Alas! 或 What a pity! Alas!

【哎】 628
ㄞ ai āi
an interjection of surprise mixed with regret: 哎呀! 我把鑰匙弄丟了。Damn, I've lost the key!
哎呀(ㄞ ˙ㄧㄚ)
an interjection of surprise: 哎呀! 好大的雨呀! My God! It is pouring!
哎喲(ㄞ ㄧㄠ)
an interjection of surprise or grief: 哎喲, 真辣! Ouch! It's hot!

七畫

【員】 629
ㄩㄢˊ yuan yuán
1. a member (of an organization, etc.)
2. a person engaged in some field of activity
3. outer limits (of land, space, etc.)
員工(ㄩㄢˊ ㄍㄨㄥ)
employees (collectively): 這公司擁有二百位員工。The firm has 200 employees.
員額(ㄩㄢˊ ㄜˊ)
the authorized size of a staff; the number of employees
員外(ㄩㄢˊ ㄨㄞˋ)
①a salutation for a rich man in ancient China ② an official title in ancient China

【哥】 630
ㄍㄜ ge gē
an elder brother: 我有三個哥哥和一個妹妹。I have three elder brothers and one younger sister.
哥白尼(ㄍㄜ ㄅㄞˊ ㄋㄧˊ)
Nicolaus Copernicus, 1473-1543, Polish astronomer who promulgated the now accepted theory that the earth and the other planets move around the sun
哥本哈根(ㄍㄜ ㄅㄣˇ ㄏㄚ ㄍㄣ)

[口部]

Copenhagen, capital of Denmark

哥德 ((ㄍㄜ ㄉㄜˊ))
Johann Wolfgang von Goethe, 1749-1832, a German poet

哥德式 ((ㄍㄜ ㄉㄜˊ ㄕˋ))
Gothic—a style of architecture of which the characteristics are pointed arches, etc.

哥倫比亞 ((ㄍㄜ ㄌㄨㄣˊ ㄅㄧˇ ㄧㄚˋ))
① Columbia, an American city ② the Republic of Colombia

哥倫布 ((ㄍㄜ ㄌㄨㄣˊ ㄅㄨˋ))
Christopher Columbus, 1451-1506, discoverer of America: 哥倫布於1492年發現新大陸。 Columbus discovered America in 1492.

哥哥 ((ㄍㄜ ㄍㄜˊ))
an elder brother

哥斯達黎加 ((ㄍㄜ ㄙ ㄉㄚˊ ㄌㄧˊ ㄐㄧㄚ))
Costa Rica

哥薩克 ((ㄍㄜ ㄙㄚˋ ㄎㄜˋ))
the Cossacks

哥兒們 ((ㄍㄜ ㄦ ㄇㄣ˙))
① brothers ② buddies; pals

哥兒倆 ((ㄍㄜ ㄦ ㄌㄧㄤˇ))
two brothers: 他們哥兒倆長得眞像。 The two brothers look alike.

【哦】 631
1. ㄜˊ or ㄛˊ
(an interjection) oh; ah: 哦，多麼令人驚奇啊! Oh, what a surprise!

【哦】 631
2. ㄜˊ or ㄜˊ
to recite (verses, etc.): 他能憑記憶哈哦那首詩。 He can recite that poem from memory.

【哨】 632
ㄕㄠˋ　shaw shǎo
1. a whistle: 他大聲吹口哨。 He gave a loud whistle.
2. to patrol
3. an outpost; a guard station

哨兵 ((ㄕㄠˋ ㄅㄧㄥ))
a sentinel or sentry: 那哨兵擔任警戒。 The sentry is on guard.

哨船 ((ㄕㄠˋ ㄔㄨㄢˊ))
a patrol boat

哨子 ((ㄕㄠˋ ㄗ˙)) or 哨兒 ((ㄕㄠˋ ㄦ))

a whistle

哨所 ((ㄕㄠˋ ㄙㄨㄛˇ))
a sentry post; a post: 前沿哨所 a forward post; an outpost

【哩】 633
1. ㄌㄧ　lhi lī
to speak indistinctly

哩哩啦啦 ((ㄌㄧ · ㄌㄧ ㄌㄚ · ㄌㄚ))
① sporadic; off and on ② to straggle along

哩哩囉囉 ((ㄌㄧ · ㄌㄧ ㄌㄨㄛ · ㄌㄨㄛ))
to speak indistinctly; to utter inarticulate words; verbose and unclear in speech; rambling and indistinct

【哩】 633
2. ㄌㄧˇ　liii lǐ
a mile: 我們的學校離海有二哩。 Our school is two miles from the sea.

【哭】 634
ㄎㄨ　ku kū
to weep; to cry; to sob; to wail; to whimper: 她為失去的孩子在哭泣。 She was wailing for her lost child.

哭哭啼啼 ((ㄎㄨ ㄎㄨ ㄊㄧˊ ㄊㄧˊ))
to whimper; to blubber; to snivel

哭喊 ((ㄎㄨ ㄏㄢˇ))
to cry and shout; crying and shouting

哭泣 ((ㄎㄨ ㄑㄧˋ))
to sob; to weep: 那可憐的男孩哭泣到入睡。 The poor boy sobbed himself to sleep.

哭牆 ((ㄎㄨ ㄑㄧㄤˊ))
the Wailing Wall in Jerusalem

哭窮 ((ㄎㄨ ㄑㄩㄥˊ))
to tell others how badly one needs money; to complain of one's poverty

哭笑不得 ((ㄎㄨ ㄒㄧㄠˋ ㄅㄨˋ ㄉㄜˊ))
to be at a loss whether to cry or to laugh; to find oneself in a very embarrassing situation; to be faced with something at once troublesome and ludicrous: 她那的玩笑使他哭笑不得。 Her joke made him not know whether to laugh or to cry.

哭喪 ((ㄎㄨ ㄙㄤ))
to cry aloud at a funeral

哭喪著臉 ((ㄎㄨ · ㄙㄤ · ㄓㄜ ㄌㄧㄢˇ))
to wear a woeful look; to

look sad or mournful: 他整哭喪著臉。 He looks mournf all the day.

哭訴 ((ㄎㄨ ㄙㄨˋ))
to complain tearfully

【哮】 635
1. ㄒㄧㄠˋ　shiaw xiào
to cry out in a loud voice

【哮】 635
1. ㄒㄧㄠˋ　shiau xiào
1. to pant; to wheeze; to gas to breathe with difficulty
2. a roar; a howl

哮喘 ((ㄒㄧㄠˋ ㄔㄨㄢˇ))
① asthma ② to wheeze

【哲】 636
ㄓㄜˊ　jer zhé
1. a sage; a thinker; a philospher
2. wise; wisdom; sagacity: 我要他明哲保身。 demanded that he be wis and keep out of harm.

哲理 ((ㄓㄜˊ ㄌㄧˇ))
a philosophical principle; philosophical doctrine; ph losophy

哲學 ((ㄓㄜˊ ㄒㄩㄝˊ))
philosophy (as a field o intellectual pursuit)

哲學家 ((ㄓㄜˊ ㄒㄩㄝˊ ㄐㄧㄚ))
a philosopher; a thinker

哲人 ((ㄓㄜˊ ㄖㄣˊ))
a sage; a philosopher: 孔子被視為中國古代最偉大的哲人 Confucius is considered th greatest of the ancien Chinese sages.

哲人其萎 ((ㄓㄜˊ ㄖㄣˊ ㄑㄧˊ ㄨㄟ))
The wise man is dead (use as a eulogy for the dead at funeral service).

哲嗣 ((ㄓㄜˊ ㄙˋ))
a polite reference to other' son

【哺】 637
ㄅㄨˇ　buu bǔ
1. to chew (before swallow ing)
2. to feed (a baby, etc.)

哺乳 ((ㄅㄨˇ ㄖㄨˇ))
to give suck to; to nurse

哺乳類 ((ㄅㄨˇ ㄖㄨˇ ㄌㄟˋ)) or 哺乳動物 ((ㄅㄨˇ ㄖㄨˇ ㄉㄨㄥˋ ㄨˋ))
mammals; Mammalia

哺養 ((ㄅㄨˇ ㄧㄤˇ))
to feed; to rear

哺育 ((ㄅㄨˇ ㄩˋ))

① to feed ② to nurture; to foster

【哼】 638 ㄏㄥ heng hēng

a. to croon; to hum (a melody): 母親哼着歌哄孩子睡覺。The mother crooned the baby to sleep.

b. to groan; to moan: 他痛得直哼哼。He groaned with pain.

c. the grunt of disapproval or contempt: 她輕蔑地哼了一聲。She gave a snort of contempt.

哼哈(ㄏㄥ ㄏㄚ)
to hum and haw

哼哈二將(ㄏㄥ ㄏㄚ ㄦˋ ㄐㄧㄤˋ)
the two sculptured fierce-looking gods usually guarding a temple gate

哼哼(ㄏㄥ ㄏㄥ)
to groan continually

哼哼唧唧(ㄏㄥ ㄏㄥ ㄐㄧ ㄐㄧ)
to groan and moan

哼聲(ㄏㄥ ㄕㄥ)
(electricity) hums

【哽】 639 《ㄥˇ geeng gěng

to choke; to feel a lump in one's throat

哽塞(《ㄥˇ ㄙㄜ)
to choke

哽咽(《ㄥˇ ㄧㄝˋ)
to be choked with sobs; to sob (with catches and breaks in the voice)

【唁】 640 ㄧㄢˋ yann yàn

to condole with or express sympathy for (the bereaved): 謹致唁慰之忱。Please accept my sincere condolences.

唁電(ㄧㄢˋ ㄉㄧㄢˋ)
a condolatory telegram

唁函(ㄧㄢˋ ㄏㄢˊ)
a letter (or message) of condolence 參看「唁信」

唁信(ㄧㄢˋ ㄒㄧㄣˋ)
a condolatory letter

【唆】 641 ㄙㄨㄛ suo suō

to instigate; to incite

使唆(ㄕˇ ㄙㄨㄛ)
to instigate; to incite

【唉】 642 ㄞˊ ai āi

(an interjection of regret or disgust) alas; oh; well: 唉，誰想到啊! Well, who'd have thought of that? 唉，真可惜! What a pity!

唉聲歎氣(ㄞˊ ㄕㄥ ㄊㄢˋ ㄑㄧˋ)
to give deploring interjections and sighs; to moan and groan

【唏】 643 ㄒㄧ shi xī

to weep or sob with sorrow; to grieve

唏噓(ㄒㄧ ㄒㄩ)
to sob

【唐】 644 ㄊㄤˊ tarng táng

1. the Tang Dynasty
2. a Chinese family name
3. abrupt; rude; preposterous; impertinent

唐代(ㄊㄤˊ ㄉㄞˋ)or 唐朝(ㄊㄤˊ ㄔㄠˊ)
the Tang Dynasty (618-907 A.D.)

唐太宗(ㄊㄤˊ ㄊㄞˋ ㄗㄨㄥ)
Emperor Tai Tsung, the second emperor of the Tang Dynasty, who laid the groundwork of later prosperity during his reign (627-649 A. D.)

唐國大國 or 堂皇大國(ㄊㄤˊ ㄊㄤˊ ㄏㄨㄤˊ ㄉㄚˋ ㄍㄨㄛˊ)
a great, powerful nation

唐突(ㄊㄤˊ ㄊㄨˊ)
abrupt; rude; brusque; blunt, to be rude or impertinent: 這個小像伙出言唐突。This little rascal made a blunt remark.

唐努烏梁海(ㄊㄤˊ ㄋㄨˇ ㄨ ㄌㄧㄤˊ ㄏㄞˇ)
Tannu Tuva, in Mongolia

唐璜(ㄊㄤˊ ㄏㄨㄤˊ)
Don Juan, an unfinished epic satire by Byron

唐吉訶德(ㄊㄤˊ ㄐㄧˊ ㄏㄜ ㄉㄜˊ)
Don Quixote

唐玄宗(ㄊㄤˊ ㄒㄩㄢˊ ㄗㄨㄥ)
Emperor Hsüan Tsung, whose preoccupation with the concubine Lady Yang (楊貴妃) in his reign (712-755 A. D.) marked the beginning of the fall of the Tang Dynasty

唐裝(ㄊㄤˊ ㄓㄨㄤ)
① a Chinese dress or garment ② the dresses of the Tang Dynasty

唐詩(ㄊㄤˊ ㄕ)
the poetry of the Tang Dynasty

唐人(ㄊㄤˊ ㄖㄣˊ)
① a Chinese (a term common among the overseas Chinese) ② the people of the Tang Dynasty

唐人街(ㄊㄤˊ ㄖㄣˊ ㄐㄧㄝ)
the Chinatown (of San Francisco, New York, etc.)

唐塞 or 搪塞(ㄊㄤˊ ㄙㄜ)
to do things perfunctorily; to reply questions with evasive answers

唐三藏(ㄊㄤˊ ㄙㄢ ㄗㄤˋ)
a high Buddhist priest, known also as Hsüan Tzang (玄奘), who traveled to and back from India to acquire valued Buddhist scriptures for China

唐三彩(ㄊㄤˊ ㄙㄢ ㄘㄞˇ)
(archeology) the tri-colored glazed pottery of the Tang Dynasty

唐宋八大家(ㄊㄤˊ ㄙㄨㄥˋ ㄅㄚ ㄉㄚˋ ㄐㄧㄚ)
the Eight Great Men of Letters of the Tang (Han Yü, Liu Tzung-yüan) and Sung (Ou-Yang Hsiu, Su Hsün, Su Shih, Su Che, Wang An-shih, Tseng Kung) dynasties

唐堯(ㄊㄤˊ ㄧㄠˊ)
Tang Yao, a sage king of over 4,000 years ago who gave the throne to the capable and virtuous minister Shun (舜) instead of his own son

唐虞之世(ㄊㄤˊ ㄩˊ ㄓ ㄕˋ)
the halcyon days of Emperors Yao (堯) and Shun (舜)

【哪】 645 (那)1. ㄋㄚˇ naa nǎ

(an interrogative particle) where; how; what; which: 你講哪一國的話？What foreign language do you speak?

哪怕(ㄋㄚˇ ㄆㄚˋ)
even if

哪門子(ㄋㄚˇ ㄇㄣˊ ˙ㄗ)
what on earth...; what the devil...: 你說的是哪門子話呀! What the devil are you talking about?

哪能(ㄋㄚˇ ㄋㄥˊ)
how is it possible that...;

〔口部〕

how could it be that...

哪兒(ㄋㄚˇ·ㄌ丨) or 哪兒(ㄋㄚˇ丨)
①(interrogative) where: 你到哪裏去? Where are you going? ② wherever; where

哪個(ㄋㄚˇ·ㄍㄜ)
① Which one? ② Who is it?

哪些(ㄋㄚˇ ㄒㄧㄝ)
which; who; what: 哪些書是你的? Which books are yours?

哪知(ㄋㄚˇ ㄓ)
who would have foreseen that...

哪樣(ㄋㄚˇ 丨ㄤˋ)
what kind of

【哪】645
2.·ㄋㄚ ·na na
a phrase-final particle: 我的天哪! My God! 或 O God!

【哞】646
ㄇ丨ㄝ mhie miē
the cries of sheep; to baa; to bleat: 一隻羊,哞哞叫。A sheep is baaing.

八畫

【售】647
ㄕㄡˋ show shòu
to sell

售票(ㄕㄡˋ ㄆ丨ㄠˋ)
to sell tickets

售票口(ㄕㄡˋ ㄆ丨ㄠˋ ㄎㄡˇ)
a wicket

售票處(ㄕㄡˋ ㄆ丨ㄠˋ ㄔㄨˋ)
a ticket office; a box office

售賣(ㄕㄡˋ ㄇㄞˋ)
to sell

售後服務(ㄕㄡˋ ㄏㄡˋ ㄈㄨˊ ㄨˋ)
after service

售貨店(ㄕㄡˋ ㄏㄨㄛˋ ㄉㄧㄢˋ)
a retail store 亦作「零售店」

售貨機(ㄕㄡˋ ㄏㄨㄛˋ ㄐㄧ)
a vending machine 亦作「自動販賣機」

售貨員(ㄕㄡˋ ㄏㄨㄛˋ ㄩㄢˊ)
a shop clerk; a salesclerk; a salesman; a salesgirl

售價(ㄕㄡˋ 丨ㄚˋ)
the (retail) price (of a commodity): 日用品的售價漸漲上漲。The prices of commodities are going up.

售罄(ㄕㄡˋ ㄑㄧㄥˋ)
completely sold out; to sell out: 我們小號的貨品已售罄。

We are sold out of small sizes.

售出(ㄕㄡˋ ㄔㄨ)
to sell; to succeed in selling (a car, a house, etc.)

【唯】648
1. (唯) ㄨㄟˊ wei wéi
only: 唯有他一人留下來。Only he remained.

唯美主義(ㄨㄟˊ ㄇㄟˇ ㄓㄨˇ 丨ˋ)
aestheticism

唯名論(ㄨㄟˊ ㄇㄧㄥˊ ㄌㄨㄣˋ)
(philosophy) nominalism

唯命是從(ㄨㄟˊ ㄇㄧㄥˋ ㄕˋ ㄘㄨㄥˊ) or 唯命是聽(ㄨㄟˊ ㄇㄧㄥˋ ㄕˋ ㄊㄧㄥ)
obsequious; unconditionally obedient; to do whatever is told

唯獨(ㄨㄟˊ ㄉㄨˊ)
only or alone; an exception: 唯獨他一人留下來。Only he remained.

唯利是圖(ㄨㄟˊ ㄌㄧˋ ㄕˋ ㄊㄨˊ)
to be bent solely on profit; to be intent on nothing but profit

唯恐(ㄨㄟˊ ㄎㄨㄥˇ)
for fear that; for fear of: 他唯恐失敗而努力工作。He's working hard for fear that he should fail.

唯恐天下不亂(ㄨㄟˊ ㄎㄨㄥˇ ㄊㄧㄢ ㄒㄧㄚˋ ㄅㄨˋ ㄌㄨㄢˋ)
to be a troublemaker or warmonger; to sow discord to serve private ends

唯心論(ㄨㄟˊ ㄒㄧㄣ ㄌㄨㄣˋ) or 唯心主義(ㄨㄟˊ ㄒㄧㄣ ㄓㄨˇ 丨ˋ)
idealism

唯心史觀(ㄨㄟˊ ㄒㄧㄣ ㄕˇ ㄍㄨㄢ)
the idealistic conception of history

唯一(ㄨㄟˊ 丨)
the only one, the only kind, etc.

唯一論(ㄨㄟˊ 丨 ㄌㄨㄣˋ)
unitarianism

唯有(ㄨㄟˊ 丨ㄡˇ)
only: 唯有白的了。There are white ones only.

唯物辯證法(ㄨㄟˊ ㄨˋ ㄅ丨ㄢˋ ㄓㄥˋ ㄈㄚˇ)
materialist dialectics

唯物論(ㄨㄟˊ ㄨˋ ㄌㄨㄣˋ) or 唯物主義(ㄨㄟˊ ㄨˋ ㄓㄨˇ 丨ˋ)
materialism

唯物史觀(ㄨㄟˊ ㄨˋ ㄕˇ ㄍㄨㄢ)

the materialistic conception of history

唯我獨尊(ㄨㄟˊ ㄨㄛˇ ㄉㄨˊ ㄗㄨㄣ)
egoistic; autocratic; bossy

唯我論(ㄨㄟˊ ㄨㄛˇ ㄌㄨㄣˋ) or 唯我主義(ㄨㄟˊ ㄨㄛˇ ㄓㄨˇ 丨ˋ)
solipsism

【唯】648
2. ㄨㄟˇ woai wěi
yes or no; the words or answers

唯唯否否(ㄨㄟˇ ㄨㄟˇ ㄈㄡˇ ㄈㄡˇ)
yes or no; to have no independent opinion; to echo others

唯唯諾諾(ㄨㄟˇ ㄨㄟˇ ㄋㄨㄛˋ ㄋㄨㄛˋ)
to say yes to a superior's suggestion; to be a yes man

【唱】649
ㄔㄤˋ chang chàng
1. to sing; to chant: 他喜歡唱歌。He is fond of singing.

2. to crow; to cry: 雞唱三遍
The cock has crowed for the third time.

3. a song or a singing part of a Chinese opera

唱本(ㄔㄤˋ ㄅㄣˇ) or 唱本兒(ㄔㄤˋ ㄅㄣˇ丨)
a song book

唱盤(ㄔㄤˋ ㄆㄢˊ)
the turntable of a phonograph

唱票(ㄔㄤˋ ㄆ丨ㄠˋ)
to count votes aloud

唱片(ㄔㄤˋ ㄆ丨ㄢˋ) or 唱片兒(ㄔㄤˋ ㄆ丨ㄢˋ丨)
a (phonograph) record or a disc

唱名(ㄔㄤˋ ㄇㄧㄥˊ)
to call the roll loudly

唱反調(ㄔㄤˋ ㄈㄢˇ ㄉㄧㄠˋ)
to air an opposing view

唱導(ㄔㄤˋ ㄉㄠˇ)
to lead; to advocate

唱對台戲(ㄔㄤˋ ㄉㄨㄟˋ ㄊㄞˊ ㄒㄧˋ)
to put on a rival show; to enter into rivalry

唱歌(ㄔㄤˋ ㄍㄜ)
to sing songs; to sing: 她很會唱歌。She is a good singer.

唱高調(ㄔㄤˋ ㄍㄠ ㄉㄧㄠˋ)
to make high-sounding statements; to make magnificent but impractical suggestions; to affect a high moral tone

唱工(ㄔㄤˋ ㄍㄨㄥ)

(said of a Peking opera) the
art or skill of singing

唱和(ㄔㄤˋㄏㄜˋ)
to write verses on the same
theme, usually after the
same rhyme pattern, as a
means of social intercourse;
to write and reply in poems
between friends

唱機(ㄔㄤˋㄐㄧ)
a record player or phono-
graph

唱腔(ㄔㄤˋㄑㄧㄤ)
the music for voices in a
Chinese opera

唱戲(ㄔㄤˋㄒㄧˋ)or 唱京戲(ㄔㄤˋㄐㄧㄥ
ㄒㄧˋ)or 唱平劇(ㄔㄤˋㄆㄧㄥˊㄐㄩˋ)
to sing a Peking opera; to
stage a Peking opera show;
to play in a theater

唱針(ㄔㄤˋㄓㄣ)
a phonograph needle; a stylus

唱籌量沙(ㄔㄤˋㄔㄡˊㄌㄧㄤˋㄕㄚ)
to put up a front in order to
fool others

唱詩班(ㄔㄤˋㄕㄅㄢ)
a choir

唱雙簧(ㄔㄤˋㄕㄨㄤㄏㄨㄤˊ)
①to give a two-man comic
show, in which one person
acts according to what the
other hiding behind him
speaks or sings ②to collaborate with each other

唱詞(ㄔㄤˋㄘˊ)
a libretto; the words of a
song, ballad, etc.

唱隨之樂(ㄔㄤˋㄙㄨㄟˊㄓㄌㄜˋ)
marital bliss

唱遊(ㄔㄤˋㄧㄡˊ)
a recreation class in primary schools during which
the children sing and play
under the supervision of the
teacher

唳 650
ㄌㄧˋ lih lì
the cry of a crane, wild
goose, etc.: 風聲鶴唳 the
whistling of winds and the
crying of cranes—a nervous
atmosphere of war and turmoil; a fleeing army's suspicion of danger at the slightest sound

唾 651
ㄊㄨㄛˋ tuoh tuò
1. saliva
2. to spit: 請不要在公共汽車內
唾吐。Please don't spit in
the bus.

唾罵(ㄊㄨㄛˋㄇㄚˋ)
to spit out; to revile

唾沫(ㄊㄨㄛˋˍㄇㄜ)
saliva; spittle

唾沫星子(ㄊㄨㄛˋㄇㄜㄒㄧㄥ‧ㄗ)
particles of saliva

唾面自乾(ㄊㄨㄛˋㄇㄧㄢˋㄗˋㄍㄢ)
(literally) to let the saliva
spit in the face dry by itself
—to show great forbearance
in putting up with an insult;
extreme obsequiousness

唾壺(ㄊㄨㄛˋㄏㄨˊ)
a spittoon

唾棄(ㄊㄨㄛˋㄑㄧˋ)
to spit on or at in contempt;
to show contempt for; to
throw away in disgust; to
cast aside; to spurn

唾腺(ㄊㄨㄛˋㄒㄧㄢˋ)
(biology) a salivary gland

唾手可得(ㄊㄨㄛˋㄕㄡˇㄎㄜˇㄉㄜˊ)
very easily obtainable; (to
accomplish) with extreme
ease 說作「垂手可得」

唾液(ㄊㄨㄛˋㄧㄝˋ)
saliva

啡 652
ㄈㄟ fei fēi
a form used in transliterating 參看「咖啡」or「嗎啡」

啁 653
ㄓㄡ jou zhōu
the twittering or chirping of
a bird

啁啾(ㄓㄡㄐㄧㄡ)
to twitter; to chirp: 小鳥在林
間啁啾地叫。Birds twittered
in the trees.

啄 654
ㄓㄨㄛˊ jwo zhuó
(said of a bird) to peck: 小
雞啄米。The chicks are peck-
ing at the rice.

啄木鳥(ㄓㄨㄛˊㄇㄨˋㄋㄧㄠˇ)
a woodpecker: 啄木鳥把樹啄
了一個洞。The woodpecker
pecked a hole in the tree.

啄啄(ㄓㄨㄛˊㄓㄨㄛˊ)
①the cackling of hens ②
the sound of tapping at a
door

啄食(ㄓㄨㄛˊㄕˊ)
to eat by pecking; to peck:
母雞啄食穀粒。The hen
pecked the corn.

商 655
ㄕㄤ shang shāng
1. commerce; trade; business.
他離校後要去經商。He will go
to business when he leaves
school.
2. a merchant; a trader; a
businessman
3. to discuss; to exchange
views; to confer: 我有要事相
商。I have important matters
to discuss with you.
4. (arithmetic) the quotient
5. the Shang Dynasty (c. 1800-
1100 B.C.)

商標(ㄕㄤㄅㄧㄠ)
a trademark

商標註冊(ㄕㄤㄅㄧㄠㄓㄨˋㄘㄜˋ)
trademark registration

商埠(ㄕㄤㄅㄨˋ)or 商港(ㄕㄤㄍㄤˇ)
a commercial port; a trading
port

商品(ㄕㄤㄆㄧㄣˇ)
commodities; wares; mer-
chandise; goods

商品展覽會(ㄕㄤㄆㄧㄣˇㄓㄢˇㄌㄢˇ
ㄏㄨㄟˋ)or 商展(ㄕㄤㄓㄢˇ)
a trade fair; a trade exposition

商品陳列所(ㄕㄤㄆㄧㄣˇㄔㄣˊㄌㄧㄝˋㄙㄨㄛˇ)
a commercial museum

商民(ㄕㄤㄇㄧㄣˊ)
tradesmen

商法(ㄕㄤㄈㄚˇ)
laws governing all kinds of
business activities

商店(ㄕㄤㄉㄧㄢˋ)
a store; a shop

商定(ㄕㄤㄉㄧㄥˋ)
to decide or settle through
discussions; to come to a
decision as a result of discussions: 他們已商定拆除這棟
古老的建築。They had decid-
ed to pull down the old
building after discussions.

商隊(ㄕㄤㄉㄨㄟˋ)
a caravan

商討(ㄕㄤㄊㄠˇ)
a discussion; to discuss

商談(ㄕㄤㄊㄢˊ)
to exchange views; to con-

（口
部）

fer; to discuss; to negotiate:
你該和律師商談這件事。You
should confer with the
lawyer about this.

【口部】

商團(ㄕㄤ ㄊㄨㄢˊ)
a group or society of
businessmen

商量(ㄕㄤ ㄌㄧㄤ˙)or 商酌(ㄕㄤ ㄓㄨㄛˊ)
to exchange opinions or
views; to hold a discussion;
to confer; to put heads
together; to go into a huddle: 這事好商量。This can be
settled through discussion.

商路(ㄕㄤ ㄌㄨˋ)
a trade route

商旅(ㄕㄤ ㄌㄩˇ)
a traveling merchant

商略(ㄕㄤ ㄌㄩㄝˋ)
to discuss

商港(ㄕㄤ ㄍㄤˇ)
a commercial port; a sea-
port; a trading port

商股(ㄕㄤ ㄍㄨˇ)
privately owned shares or
stock (of a business com-
pany, as opposed to state-
owned shares or stock)

商賈(ㄕㄤ ㄍㄨˇ)
businessmen

商科(ㄕㄤ ㄎㄜ)
a department of commerce
(in a college or university)

商號(ㄕㄤ ㄏㄠˋ)or 商行(ㄕㄤ ㄒㄧㄥˊ)
① name of a shop or firm ②
a business firm; a trading
company; a commercial firm

商會(ㄕㄤ ㄏㄨㄟˋ)
a chamber of commerce

商家(ㄕㄤ ㄐㄧㄚ)
a business firm

商界(ㄕㄤ ㄐㄧㄝˋ)
the business world, or business circles: 這本書受到商界
的稱讚。The book is praised
in business circles.

商榷(ㄕㄤ ㄑㄩㄝˋ)
to discuss and consider; to
deliberate over

商洽(ㄕㄤ ㄑㄧㄚˋ)
to arrange with somebody;
to take up (a matter) with
somebody

商情(ㄕㄤ ㄑㄧㄥˊ)
business or market information: 他供給我許多有用的商
情。He gave me a lot of use-

ful business information.

商學院(ㄕㄤ ㄒㄩㄝˊ ㄩㄢˋ)
the college of commerce

商戰(ㄕㄤ ㄓㄢˋ)
a trade war

商酌(ㄕㄤ ㄓㄨㄛˊ)
to discuss and consider; to
deliberate over: 這個問題尚待
商酌。This matter needs fur-
ther discussion and consideration.

商場(ㄕㄤ ㄔㄤˇ)or 商行(ㄕㄤ ㄒㄧㄥˊ)
a market place; a depart-
ment store; a bazaar

商船(ㄕㄤ ㄔㄨㄢˊ)
a merchantman; a merchant
ship

商事(ㄕㄤ ㄕˋ)
commercial affairs

商事會計(ㄕㄤ ㄕˋ ㄏㄨㄟˋ ㄐㄧˋ)
business accountancy

商數(ㄕㄤ ㄕㄨˋ)
(arithmetic) the quotient: 在
26÷2=13中，13是商數。In
26÷2=13, 13 is the quotient.

商人(ㄕㄤ ㄖㄣˊ)
a merchant; a businessman;
a trader

商議(ㄕㄤ ㄧˋ)
to discuss and debate

商業(ㄕㄤ ㄧㄝˋ)
commerce; profit-seeking
business

商業道德(ㄕㄤ ㄧㄝˋ ㄉㄠˋ ㄉㄜˊ)
business ethics

商業利益(ㄕㄤ ㄧㄝˋ ㄌㄧˋ ㄧˋ)
commercial profit

商業機關(ㄕㄤ ㄧㄝˋ ㄐㄧ ㄍㄨㄢ)
a commercial organization

商業學校(ㄕㄤ ㄧㄝˋ ㄒㄩㄝˊ ㄒㄧㄠˋ)
a vocational school of commerce; a commercial school

商業設計(ㄕㄤ ㄧㄝˋ ㄕㄜˋ ㄐㄧˋ)
commercial design

商業銀行(ㄕㄤ ㄧㄝˋ ㄧㄣˊ ㄏㄤˊ)
a commercial bank

商務(ㄕㄤ ㄨˋ)
commercial affairs; business
affairs

商務代表(ㄕㄤ ㄨˋ ㄉㄞˋ ㄅㄧㄠˇ)
a commercial representative;
a trade representative

商務代表處(ㄕㄤ ㄨˋ ㄉㄞˋ ㄅㄧㄠˇ ㄔㄨˋ)
a trade representative's
office

商務參事(ㄕㄤ ㄨˋ ㄘㄢ ㄕˋ)or 商務專

員(ㄕㄤ ㄨˋ ㄓㄨㄢ ㄩㄢˊ)
a commercial attache;
commercial councilor

商約(ㄕㄤ ㄩㄝ)
a business contract; a commercial treaty

【問】 ㄨㄣˊ wèn wèn

1. to ask; to inquire: 他們問農
人這裡離城有多遠。They ask
the farmer how far it is
from the city.

2. to interrogate; to examine:
他被法官審問。He was
examined by the judge.

3. to ask after; to inquire
after: 她常在信裡問起你。She
frequently asks after you in
her letters.

4. to hold responsible: 出了事
你是問。You'll be held
responsible if anything goes
wrong.

問卜(ㄨㄣˋ ㄅㄨˇ)
to consult fortune-tellers (in
making a decision); to seek
guidance from divination

問明(ㄨㄣˋ ㄇㄧㄥˊ)
to ask for explicit answers;
to find out the details

問答(ㄨㄣˋ ㄉㄚˊ)
questions and answers;
dialogue; a conversation

問道於盲(ㄨㄣˋ ㄉㄠˋ ㄩˊ ㄇㄤˊ)
(literally) to ask the blind
to show the way—to seek
advice from an ignorant person

問鼎(ㄨㄣˋ ㄉㄧㄥˇ)
to inquire about the bronze
tripod (which is the symbol
of imperial power)—(figuratively) to covet the throne

問鼎(ㄨㄣˋ ㄉㄧㄥˇ ㄓㄨㄤ ㄒㄧㄣˋ ㄓㄥˋ)
to aspire after the throne; to
have an ambition for the
throne

問題(ㄨㄣˋ ㄊㄧˊ)
① a problem; a question; an
issue: 我可以問個問題嗎？
May I ask a question? ②
trouble; mishap: 我車子的引
擎有問題。My car has engine
trouble.

問題行為(ㄨㄣˋ ㄊㄧˊ ㄒㄧㄥˊ ㄨㄟˊ)
problem behavior

問題少年(ㄨㄣˋ ㄊㄧˊ ㄕㄠˋ ㄋㄧㄢˊ)
a problem youth; a juvenile

delinquent

問題兒童(ㄨㄣˊ ㄊㄧˊ ㄦˊ ㄊㄨㄥˊ)
a problem child

問難(ㄨㄣˊ ㄋㄢˊ)
to ask difficult questions in a debate

問卦(ㄨㄣˊ ㄍㄨㄚˋ)
to consult oracles

問供(ㄨㄣˊ ㄍㄨㄥ)
to interrogate a criminal suspect; to examine and take an affidavit

問好(ㄨㄣˊ ㄏㄠˇ)or問候(ㄨㄣˊ ㄏㄡˋ)
to ask about a person's health or welfare; to inquire after; to ask after; to send one's regards: 請代我向你雙親問好。Please give my regards to your parents.

問號(ㄨㄣˊ ㄏㄠˋ)
①an interrogation mark; a question mark ② an unknown factor; an unsolved problem

問寒問暖(ㄨㄣˊ ㄏㄢˊ ㄨㄣˊ ㄋㄨㄢˇ)
to be solicitous for somebody's health; to show a kind concern for another's comfort

問話(ㄨㄣˊ ㄏㄨㄚˋ)
to ask questions

問疾(ㄨㄣˊ ㄐㄧˊ)
to visit and console a patient

問津(ㄨㄣˊ ㄐㄧㄣ)
①to show interest (in something for sale or intended to arouse public interest) ②to ask for guidance in a new field of endeavor ③to ask in which direction to go

問卷(ㄨㄣˊ ㄐㄩㄢˋ)
a questionnaire

問心有愧(ㄨㄣˊ ㄒㄧㄣ ㄧㄡˇ ㄎㄨㄟˋ)
to feel a twinge of conscience

問心無愧(ㄨㄣˊ ㄒㄧㄣ ㄨˊ ㄎㄨㄟˋ)
to examine oneself and find nothing to be ashamed of; with a clear conscience; to have a clear conscience; to feel no qualms upon self-examination: 我已盡力而爲，因此問心無愧。I had done my best, so I felt no qualms upon self-examination.

問訊(ㄨㄣˊ ㄒㄩㄣˋ)

①to inquire after a person ②to ask; to inquire ③(said of Buddhist monks or nuns) to press the palms together as a salute

問斬(ㄨㄣˊ ㄓㄢˇ)
to execute a prisoner by beheading him

問診(ㄨㄣˊ ㄓㄣˇ)
interrogation, one of the four methods of diagnosis in Chinese medicine

問住(ㄨㄣˊ ㄓㄨˋ)or問倒(ㄨㄣˊ ㄉㄠˇ)
to be unable to answer a question asked: 他被問住了。He was unable to answer the difficult question.

問長問短(ㄨㄣˊ ㄔㄤˊ ㄨㄣˊ ㄉㄨㄢˇ)
to ask many questions about other people's affairs; to be inquisitive

問世(ㄨㄣˊ ㄕˋ)
①(said of a new book) to come out: 他的第一部小說將在下個月問世。His first novel will come out next month. ②to participate in public affairs actively

問罪(ㄨㄣˊ ㄗㄨㄟˋ)
to call a person to account; to reprimand; to reprove; to rebuke; to condemn; to denounce

問安(ㄨㄣˊ ㄢ)
(usually to elders) to wish somebody good health; to send greetings

問案(ㄨㄣˊ ㄢˋ)
to try (or hear) a case; to hold court

【啊】 657
1. ㄚ ā
an exclamatory particle: 啊! 樹長得真好哇! Oh, what a wonderful tree! 啊 我 們 終於到了。Well, here we are at last.

啊哈(ㄚˊ ㄏㄚ)
"aha" (an exclamation to show irony or mockery)

啊呀(ㄚ ˙ㄧㄚ)
"aya" (an exclamation to show surprise)

啊唷(ㄚ ˙ㄧㄛ)
"ayo" (the sound uttered when suddenly get hurt)

【啊】 657
2. ˙ㄚ ・a a

a phrase-final particle: 她 唱得多麼好聽啊! How well she sings! 務必珍重啊! Do take care of yourself.

【啤】 658
ㄆㄧˊ pyi pí
a character used in transliterating

啤酒(ㄆㄧˊ ㄐㄧㄡˇ)
beer

啤酒花(ㄆㄧˊ ㄐㄧㄡˇ ㄏㄨㄚ)
hops

【啐】 659
1. ㄘㄨㄟˋ tsuey cuì
1. to taste; to sip
2. to spit: I啐他一口. I spat upon him.

啐一口痰(ㄘㄨㄟˋ ㄧˋ ㄎㄡˇ ㄊㄢˊ)
to spit phlegm

【啐】 659
2. ・ㄑ(ㄧ) ・ch(i) q(i)
Fie! (an interjection expressing contempt): 啐! 不要臉。Fie, for shame!

【啓】 660
(啟) ㄑㄧˇ chii qǐ
1. to open
2. to begin; to start
3. to explain
4. to inform; to state
5. a letter

啓報(ㄑㄧˇ ㄅㄠˋ)
to report to one's superior and ask for instructions

啓蒙(ㄑㄧˇ ㄇㄥˊ)
①to enlighten ②a primer

啓蒙老師(ㄑㄧˇ ㄇㄥˊ ㄌㄠˇ ㄕ)
a child's first tutor or teacher

啓蒙運動(ㄑㄧˇ ㄇㄥˊ ㄩㄣˋ ㄉㄨㄥˋ)
the Enlightenment

啓發(ㄑㄧˇ ㄈㄚ)or啓迪(ㄑㄧˇ ㄉㄧˊ)
to prompt mental development (of another); to inspire; to teach; to instruct

啓封(ㄑㄧˇ ㄈㄥ)
①to open an envelope ②to remove the labels on impounded goods or property before returning them to the owner

啓動(ㄑㄧˇ ㄉㄨㄥˋ)
to start (a machine, etc.); to switch on

啓開(ㄑㄧˇ ㄎㄞ)
to open

啓航(ㄑㄧˇ ㄏㄤˊ)
to set sail; to weigh anchor

【口部】

啓行（くゝ ㄒㄧㄥ）or 啓程（くㄧˇ ㄔㄥˊ）
to start on a journey; to set out

啓齒（くㄧˇ）
to open the mouth to say something: 他難以啓齒。He felt difficult to say it.

啓事（くㄧˇ）
a notice; an announcement (in writing)

啓示（くㄧˇ）
revelation; enlightenment; inspiration: 很多詩人和藝術家從大自然中獲得許多啓示。 Many poets and artists have drawn a good deal of inspiration from nature.

啓示錄（くㄧˇ ㄌㄨˋ）
the Revelation (of the New Testament)

啓用（くㄧˇ ㄩㄥˋ）
to start using

【啖】 661　（啗）ㄉㄢˋ dann dàn
1. (a literary expression) to eat
2. to feed

【啣】 662　ㄒㄧㄢˊ shyan xián
the vulgar form of 銜
1. a bridle
2. to hold in the mouth
3. to harbor

【唷】 663　ㄧㄛ io yō
an exclamation expressing surprise or pain: 唷! 好痛! Ouch, it hurts.

【啦】 664　・ㄌㄚ ・la la
a phrase-final particle: 天已不早, 你該走啦! You'd better go now; it's getting late. 他早就來啦! Why, he's been here a long time!

啦啦隊（ㄌㄚ ㄌㄚ ㄉㄨㄟˋ）
a cheer squad

啦啦隊長（ㄌㄚ ㄌㄚ ㄉㄨㄟˋ ㄓㄤˇ）
a cheerleader

【啞】 665　ㄧㄚˇ yea yǎ
1. dumb; mute: 他生來即啞。He has been dumb from birth.
2. hoarse; husky
3. a phrase-final particle

啞巴 or 啞吧（ㄧㄚˇ ・ㄅㄚ）
(a) deaf-mute (person)

啞巴虧（ㄧㄚˇ ・ㄅㄚ ㄎㄨㄟ）
one's grievances which are unable to speak out

啞巴吃黃連（ㄧㄚˇ ・ㄅㄚ ㄔ ㄏㄨㄤˊ ㄌㄧㄢˊ）
to be unable to complain after one suffers a loss, or is unjustly blamed, etc.

啞謎（ㄧㄚˇ ㄇㄧˊ）
a riddle; a puzzling remark; an enigma

啞鈴（ㄧㄚˇ ㄌㄧㄥˊ）
a dumbbell

啞口無言（ㄧㄚˇ ㄎㄡˇ ㄨˊ ㄧㄢˊ）
to be speechless (when a criminal suspect is brought face to face with evidence against him, or when one's argument is completely demolished by the opponent); to be rendered speechless

啞劇（ㄧㄚˇ ㄐㄩˋ）
a pantomime; a dumb show

啞然失笑（ㄧㄚˇ ㄖㄢˊ ㄕ ㄒㄧㄠˋ）
to laugh involuntarily (upon seeing an embarrassing but funny situation); to guffaw

啞然無聲（ㄧㄚˇ ㄖㄢˊ ㄨˊ ㄕㄥ）
Silence reigns.

啞嗓子（ㄧㄚˇ ㄙㄤˇ ・ㄗ）
a hoarse voice

【啃】 666　ㄎㄣˇ keen kěn
to bite; to gnaw; to nibble: 他啃不動甘蔗。He can't bite the sugar cane.

啃骨頭（ㄎㄣˇ ㄍㄨˇ ・ㄊㄡ）
to pick out the residual meat on the bones after teeth

啃書本（ㄎㄣˇ ㄕㄨ ㄅㄣˇ）
to study very hard; to delve into books

【唬】 667　ㄏㄨˇ huu hǔ
1. to intimidate; to scare: 她沒被唬住。She wasn't intimidated.
2. the roar of a tiger

唬人（ㄏㄨˇ ㄖㄣˊ）
to intimidate people; to assume an intimidating air; to bluff: 你別唬人。Quit bluffing.

【唪】 668　ㄈㄥˇ feeng fěng
to chant; to recite

唪經（ㄈㄥˇ ㄐㄧㄥ）
to chant Buddist scriptures

【唸】 669　（念）ㄋㄧㄢˋ niann niàn
to read; to chant; to recite

唸唸有詞（ㄋㄧㄢˋ ㄋㄧㄢˋ ㄧㄡˇ ㄘˊ）
to mumble to oneself

【啥】 670　ㄕㄚˊ shar shá
what: 那有啥關係? What does it matter?

啥事體（ㄕㄚˊ ㄕˋ ㄊㄧˇ）
(Shanghai dialect) What the matter?

啥人（ㄕㄚˊ ㄖㄣˊ）
(Shanghai dialect) Who are you? 或 Who is it? 或 Who is there?

【啜】 671　ㄔㄨㄛˋ chuoh chuò
1. to drink; to sip
2. to cry in a subdued manner; to sob

啜茗（ㄔㄨㄛˋ ㄇㄧㄥˊ）
to drink tea; to sip tea: 那老人喜歡啜茗。The old man likes to sip tea.

啜泣（ㄔㄨㄛˋ ㄑㄧˋ）
to sob

啜汁（ㄔㄨㄛˋ ㄓ）
to take credit

啜蜜（ㄔㄨㄛˋ ㄇㄧˋ）
to make honey promises; to pay lip service

啜菽飲水（ㄔㄨㄛˋ ㄕㄨˊ ㄧㄣˇ ㄕㄨㄟˇ）
One can be a dutiful son to his parents even in poverty.

九畫

【啻】 672　ㄔ chyh chì
1. only; merely
2. as in 不啻—tantamount to

【啼】 673　ㄊㄧˊ tyi tí
(especially said of birds) to crow; to cry: 雞啼狗叫。Cock crow and dogs bark.

啼哭（ㄊㄧˊ ㄎㄨ）
to cry; to weep and wail

啼飢號寒（ㄊㄧˊ ㄐㄧ ㄏㄠˊ ㄏㄢˊ）
to wail with hunger and cold

啼叫（ㄊㄧˊ ㄐㄧㄠˋ）
to scream; to screech; to wail

啼泣（ㄊㄧˊ ㄑㄧˋ）

【口部】

to wail; to sob

哭笑皆非(ㄎㄨ ㄒㄧㄠˋ ㄐㄧㄝ ㄈㄟ)
between tears and laughter; unable to cry or laugh; the farce made us not know whether to laugh or cry.

【啾】 674 ㄐㄧㄡ jiou jiū
1. the chirps of birds or insects
2. the wailing of infants

秋啾(ㄐㄧㄡ ㄐㄧㄡ)
the chirps of insects

【喀】 675 ㄎㄚ kah kǎ
a character used for transliterating

喀麥隆(ㄎㄚ ㄇㄞˋ ㄌㄨㄥˊ)
Cameroon

喀拉蚩(ㄎㄚ ㄌㄚ ㄔ)
Karachi, a port city of Pakistan

喀嚓(ㄎㄚ ㄔㄚ)
to crack; to snap

喀什米爾(ㄎㄚ ㄕˊ ㄇㄧˇ ㄦˇ)
Kashmir

【喁】 676 ㄩㄥˊ yong yóng
1. harmony or unison of sounds
2. the state of a fish putting its mouth above the water surface

喁喁(ㄩˊ ㄩˊ)
①the state of people showing unanimous respect for their leader ②(to talk) in whispers: 她們喁喁私語。They talked in whispers.

【喂】 677 ㄨㄟˋ wey wèi
(an interjection for calling another's attention) hallo; please; if you please; I say; hey; hullo: 喂! 止步! Hey! stop!

【喃】 678 ㄋㄢˊ nan nán
1. the cries of a swallow
2. to murmur; to mumble; to mutter

喃喃自語(ㄋㄢˊ ㄋㄢˊ ㄗˋ ㄩˇ)
to murmur to oneself; to mutter to oneself; to mumble to oneself: 那老人喃喃自語。The old man was mumbling to himself.

【善】 679 ㄕㄢˋ shann shàn
1. good; virtuous; goodness; virtue; good deeds; benevolent actions
2. to be good at; to be skilled in
3. to perfect; to make a success of 工欲善其事，必先利其器。A workman must sharpen his tools if he is to do his work well.
4. to remedy; to relieve
5. properly

善罷甘休(ㄕㄢˋ ㄅㄚˋ ㄍㄢ ㄒㄧㄡ)
to stop quarreling, fighting, etc. with others; to leave the matter at that; to let it go at that

善報(ㄕㄢˋ ㄅㄠˋ)
the reward for kindness

善本書(ㄕㄢˋ ㄅㄣˇ ㄕㄨ)
a rare book

善變(ㄕㄢˋ ㄅㄧㄢˋ)
changeable; fickle; capricious

善門難開(ㄕㄢˋ ㄇㄣˊ ㄋㄢˊ ㄎㄞ)
It is difficult to start charity (as it cannot be stopped halfway).

善謀(ㄕㄢˋ ㄇㄡˊ)
①a good scheme ②good at thinking out schemes; quick-minded

善待(ㄕㄢˋ ㄉㄞˋ)
to treat (a person) well; to accord (a person) good treatment

善刀而藏(ㄕㄢˋ ㄉㄠ ㄦˊ ㄘㄤˊ)
do not push one's advantage too far

善男信女(ㄕㄢˋ ㄋㄢˊ ㄒㄧㄣˋ ㄋㄩˇ)
devotees of Buddha; the faithful

善類(ㄕㄢˋ ㄌㄟˋ)
good people

善鄰(ㄕㄢˋ ㄌㄧㄣˊ)
to maintain good relations with neighboring countries

善良(ㄕㄢˋ ㄌㄧㄤˊ)
(said of a person) good; kindhearted; gentle; well-disposed: 她天性很善良。She is very kind at nature.

善果(ㄕㄢˋ ㄍㄨㄛˇ)
the reward of good deeds

善觀風色(ㄕㄢˋ ㄍㄨㄢ ㄈㄥ ㄙㄜˋ)
quick to see which way the wind blows—very shrewd

善後(ㄕㄢˋ ㄏㄡˋ)
rehabilitation (after a disaster, a tragedy, etc.); to make good arrangements for the aftermath

善後救濟(ㄕㄢˋ ㄏㄡˋ ㄐㄧㄡˋ ㄐㄧˋ)
relief measures for rehabilitation

善舉(ㄕㄢˋ ㄐㄩˇ)or**善行**(ㄕㄢˋ ㄒㄧㄥˊ)
a good deed; a benevolent action

善心(ㄕㄢˋ ㄒㄧㄣ)
kindness; a compassionate heart

善行足式(ㄕㄢˋ ㄒㄧㄥˊ ㄗㄨˊ ㄕˋ)
a kind deed worthy of emulating

善戰(ㄕㄢˋ ㄓㄢˋ)
brave and skillful in fighting

善終(ㄕㄢˋ ㄓㄨㄥ)
to die a natural death

善始善終(ㄕㄢˋ ㄕˇ ㄕㄢˋ ㄓㄨㄥ)
to begin well and end well; to do something from the beginning to the end

善士(ㄕㄢˋ ㄕˋ)
a benevolent person; a good man; a philanthropist

善舉(ㄕㄢˋ ㄐㄩˇ)
good deeds; philanthropic acts; charitable work

善人(ㄕㄢˋ ㄖㄣˊ)
a good Samaritan; a kindhearted and benevolent fellow

善自為謀(ㄕㄢˋ ㄗˋ ㄨㄟˊ ㄇㄡˊ)
versed in planning or working for one's own interests

善惡(ㄕㄢˋ ㄜˋ)
good and evil; virtue and vice

善惡不分(ㄕㄢˋ ㄜˋ ㄅㄨˋ ㄈㄣ)
to be unable to tell good from evil

善以為寶(ㄕㄢˋ ㄧˇ ㄨㄟˊ ㄅㄠˇ)
to value virtue as a treasure

善意(ㄕㄢˋ ㄧˋ)
①good or kindly intentions ②well-meaning; sincere criticisms; constructive criticisms

善游者溺(ㄕㄢˋ ㄧㄡˊ ㄓㄜˇ ㄋㄧˋ)
(literally) A good swimmer often gets drowned.—Over-confidence in one's skill may

bring him disaster.

善有善報 (ㄕㄢˋ ㄧㄡˇ ㄕㄢˋ ㄅㄠˋ)
Kind deeds pay rich dividends to the doer. 善有善報，惡有惡報。 Good will be rewarded with good, and evil with evil.

善言 (ㄕㄢˋ ㄧㄢˊ)
well-intentioned advice

善忘 (ㄕㄢˋ ㄨㄤˋ)
forgetful; weak of memory; to be prone to forget

善於 (ㄕㄢˋ ㄩˊ)
good at; skilled in: 她善於歌舞。 She is good at singing and dancing.

善緣 (ㄕㄢˋ ㄩㄢˊ)
①(Buddhism) the favorable ties resulting from contributions to a temple ②a lucky meeting of good friends

【嗖】 680
ㄙㄡ sou sōu
1. the laughing expression
2. the sound one makes to drive away birds
3. to whiz

嗖嗖 (ㄙㄡ ㄙㄡ)
with laughter; laughingly

【喇】 681
1. ㄌㄚˇ laa lǎ
1. a horn; a trumpet; a bugle
2. a lama
3. a character used in transliteration

喇叭 (ㄌㄚˇ ·ㄅㄚ)
①a horn; a trumpet; a bugle ②a loudspeaker

喇叭褲 (ㄌㄚˇ ·ㄅㄚ ㄎㄨˋ)
bell-shaped pants; flared trousers; bell-bottom pants

喇叭花 (ㄌㄚˇ ·ㄅㄚ ㄏㄨㄚ)or牽牛花 (ㄑㄧㄢ ㄋㄧㄡˊ ㄏㄨㄚ)
(botany) morning glory

喇嘛 (ㄌㄚˇ ·ㄇㄚ)
a lama (a priest of Lamaism)

喇嘛教 (ㄌㄚˇ ·ㄇㄚ ㄐㄧㄠˋ)
Lamaism

【喇】 681
2. ㄌㄚˊ lha lá
a character used for its sound

【喈】 682
ㄐㄧㄝ jie jiē
harmonious sounds

【喉】 683
ㄏㄡˊ hour hóu

the throat; the gullet; guttural: 我喉嚨痛。 I have a sore throat.

喉頭 (ㄏㄡˊ ㄊㄡˊ)
the larynx

喉頭炎 (ㄏㄡˊ ㄊㄡˊ ㄧㄢˊ)
laryngitis; laryngeal catarrh

喉痛 (ㄏㄡˊ ㄊㄨㄥˋ)
a sore throat

喉嚨 (ㄏㄡˊ ㄌㄨㄥˊ)
the throat; the gullet

喉管 (ㄏㄡˊ ㄍㄨㄢˇ)
bronchia

喉科 (ㄏㄡˊ ㄎㄜ)
laryngology (usually together with otology and rhinology, known as otorhinolaryngology)

喉急 (ㄏㄡˊ ㄐㄧˊ)
desperately anxious

喉結 (ㄏㄡˊ ㄐㄧㄝˊ)
Adam's apple

喉舌 (ㄏㄡˊ ㄕㄜˊ)
①that which functions as the mechanics of talking ②the mouthpiece or organ of a party, government, etc.

喉音 (ㄏㄡˊ ㄧㄣ)
(phonetics) guttural sounds

【喊】 684
ㄏㄢˇ haan hǎn
1. to shout; to scream; to cry; a loud call or cry; a shout or scream: 他把嗓子喊啞了。 He shouted himself hoarse.
2. to call (a person): 他從樓上喊我。 He called to me from upstairs.

喊打 (ㄏㄢˇ ㄉㄚˇ)
to shout "Beat him (her or them)!"

喊痛 (ㄏㄢˇ ㄊㄨㄥˋ)
to yell out of pain; to yelp in pain

喊苦 (ㄏㄢˇ ㄎㄨˇ)
to complain about hardships loudly; to cry out one's grievances; to bawl out pain or suffering

喊好 (ㄏㄢˇ ㄏㄠˇ)
to cheer and applaud (a performer, etc.); to yell "Bravo!"

喊話 (ㄏㄢˇ ㄏㄨㄚˋ)
(psychological warfare) to talk to the enemy at close range over a loudspeaker,

asking him to surrender etc.; propaganda directed to the enemy at the front line; to talk to a cornered criminal to effect the same

喊叫 (ㄏㄢˇ ㄐㄧㄠˋ)
to shout, scream, or cry loudly; a loud cry, shout scream, etc.

喊救 (ㄏㄢˇ ㄐㄧㄡˋ)
to call for help; to cry for help

喊殺連天 (ㄏㄢˇ ㄕㄚ ㄌㄧㄢˊ ㄊㄧㄢ)
The air is filled with shouts of "Kill! Kill!"

喊殺之聲 (ㄏㄢˇ ㄕㄚ ㄓ ㄕㄥ)
the voices of soldiers yelling "Sha! Sha!"—"Kill! Kill!" (in close-range combat)

喊聲 (ㄏㄢˇ ㄕㄥ)
shouts and screams

喊冤 (ㄏㄢˇ ㄩㄢ)
to shout out one's grievance in the streets (when a high official is passing) or in court; to demand justice loudly

【喋】 685
ㄉㄧㄝˊ dye dié
to nag; to chatter; to prattle; to babble; to be very talkative; to rattle

喋喋 (ㄉㄧㄝˊ ㄉㄧㄝˊ)
talkative; to nag or chatter; to rattle

喋喋不休 (ㄉㄧㄝˊ ㄉㄧㄝˊ ㄅㄨˋ ㄒㄧㄡ)
to keep talking; to chatter without stopping; to cackle

喋囁 (ㄉㄧㄝˊ ㄋㄧㄝˋ)
to whisper; to converse in a low voice

喋血 (ㄉㄧㄝˊ ㄒㄩㄝˋ)
blood flowing; bloodshed; to bleed

【喏】 686
1. ㄖㄜˇ ree rě
an address or greeting of respect when meeting a superior, etc.

【喏】 686
2. ㄋㄨㄛˋ nuoh nuò
a word used to attract other's attention

【喑】 687
ㄧㄣ in yin
1. to lose one's voice—dumb or mute
2. to keep silent—to say nothing—

ing

音瘖(ㄧㄣ ㄍㄨㄥ)
①deaf-and-mute ②a deaf-mute

音啞(ㄧㄣ ㄧㄚˇ)
dumb; unable to talk; mute

【喔】 688
1. ㄨㄛ woh wò
the crowing of a cock; the cackling of fowls

喔蹴 or **醒戯**(ㄨㄛ ㄨㄛ)
in a hurry; in haste; hastily

喔喔(ㄨㄛ ㄨㄛ)
the crowing of a cock; the cackling of fowls

【喔】 688
2. ㄜ o o̊
an exclamation: 喔, 原來是你! Oh, so it's you!

喔唷(ㄜ·ㄧㄛ)
an exclamation to indicate understanding, surprise, or grief: 喔唷, 好痛! Ouch, it hurts!

【喘】 689
ㄔㄨㄢˇ choan chuǎn
1. to pant; to gasp; to breathe hard
2. (pathology) asthma

喘氣(ㄔㄨㄢˇ ㄑㄧˋ)
①to pant; to gasp; to breathe hard ②to take a breather; to take a break

喘息(ㄔㄨㄢˇ ㄒㄧˊ)
①to take breath, or a rest (after strenuous exercise) ②to pant; to gasp for breath

喘息機會(ㄔㄨㄢˇ ㄒㄧˊ ㄐㄧ ㄏㄨㄟˋ)
a breathing spell; a respite

喘噓噓 or **喘吁吁**(ㄔㄨㄢˇ ㄒㄩ ㄒㄩ)
breathing very hard; panting; to puff and blow

【喙】 690
ㄏㄨㄟˋ huey huì
1. a beak; a bill; a snout
2. a mouth

喙長三尺(ㄏㄨㄟˋ ㄔㄤˊㄙㄢ ㄔˇ)
(literally) to have a beak three feet long—fond of exposing other people's secrets; fond of faultfinding

【喚】 691
ㄏㄨㄢˋ huann huàn
1. to call
2. to summon
3. to arouse

喚起(ㄏㄨㄢˋ ㄑㄧˇ)
①to arouse to action ②to

call; to evoke

喚醒(ㄏㄨㄢˋ ㄒㄧㄥˇ)
to arouse; to awaken; to call up: 早晨喚醒我. Call me in the morning.

【喜】 692
ㄒㄧˇ shii xǐ
1. a joyful thing; a happy event
2. joy: 他充滿歡喜. He was filled with joy.
3. to like; to love; to be fond of
4. joyful; happy; delightful; pleasant; auspicious

喜不自勝(ㄒㄧˇ ㄅㄨˋ ㄗˋ ㄕㄥ)
unable to contain oneself for joy; to be delighted beyond measure

喜馬拉雅山(ㄒㄧˇ ㄇㄚˇ ㄌㄚ ㄧㄚˇ ㄕㄢ)
the Himalayas

喜房(ㄒㄧˇ ㄈㄤˊ)
a bridal chamber

喜堂(ㄒㄧˇ ㄊㄤˊ)
a wedding hall

喜帖(ㄒㄧˇ ㄊㄧㄝˇ)
a wedding invitation: 謝謝你的喜帖. Thank you for your wedding invitation.

喜怒不形於色(ㄒㄧˇ ㄋㄨˋ ㄅㄨˋ ㄒㄧㄥˊ ㄩˊ ㄙㄜˋ)
poker-faced; expressionless; to show no emotion; with a deadpan face

喜怒哀樂(ㄒㄧˇ ㄋㄨˋ ㄞ ㄌㄜˋ)
the feelings of joy, anger, sorrow and delight; different emotions

喜怒無常(ㄒㄧˇ ㄋㄨˋ ㄨˊ ㄔㄤˊ)
having an unpredictable temper

喜樂(ㄒㄧˇ ㄌㄜˋ)
①joy; gladness; great pleasure ②to give a zest to one's joy

喜好(ㄒㄧˇ ㄏㄠˇ)
to be fond of; to delight in; to like; to love: 他喜好運動. He likes sports.

喜歡(ㄒㄧˇ ㄏㄨㄢ)
①to like; to be fond of; to love; to be pleased with: 他很喜歡釣魚. He loves to go fishing. ②happy; joyful; delightful

喜酒(ㄒㄧˇ ㄐㄧㄡˇ)
①a wedding feast ②wine

drunk at a wedding feast

喜劇(ㄒㄧˇ ㄐㄩˋ)
a comedy

喜氣洋洋(ㄒㄧˇ ㄑㄧˋ ㄧㄤˊ ㄧㄤˊ)
①a joyful atmosphere; a festival mood ②a cheerful look or expression

喜慶(ㄒㄧˇ ㄑㄧㄥˋ)
auspicious or happy occasions (such as wedding, birth, promotion, etc.)

喜鵲(ㄒㄧˇ ㄑㄩㄝˋ)
the magpie

喜笑顏開(ㄒㄧˇ ㄒㄧㄠˋ ㄧㄢˊ ㄎㄞ)
cheerful; brimming with smiles; an ear-to-ear grin

喜新厭舊(ㄒㄧˇ ㄒㄧㄣ ㄧㄢˋ ㄐㄧㄡˋ)
to like the new and dislike the old (often referring to love affairs)

喜信(ㄒㄧˇ ㄒㄧㄣˋ)
good news; happy tidings

喜形於色(ㄒㄧˇ ㄒㄧㄥˊ ㄩˊ ㄙㄜˋ)
to look pleased; to have an expression of delight: 他喜形於色. He looked visibly pleased. 或 His face lighted up with pleasure.

喜訊(ㄒㄧˇ ㄒㄩㄣˋ)
happy news; good news; glad tidings

喜幛 or **喜帳**(ㄒㄧˇ ㄓㄤˋ)
a silk hanging gilded with words of blessing, presented as a wedding gift

喜出望外(ㄒㄧˇ ㄔㄨ ㄨㄤˋ ㄨㄞˋ)
joy over unexpected good luck; unexpected joy

喜事(ㄒㄧˇ ㄕˋ)
an occasion for joy (especially a wedding)

喜孜孜 or **喜滋滋**(ㄒㄧˇ ㄗ ㄗ)
joyful; looking pleased

喜色(ㄒㄧˇ ㄙㄜˋ)
a joyful expression; a pleased look

喜愛(ㄒㄧˇ ㄞˋ)
to like; to love; to be fond of; to be keen on: 我們喜愛戶外活動. We are keen on outdoor activities.

喜洋洋(ㄒㄧˇ ㄧㄤˊ ㄧㄤˊ)
beaming with joy; radiant

喜雨(ㄒㄧˇ ㄩˇ)
a timely rainfall; seasonable rain

喜悅(ㄒㄧˇ ㄩㄝˋ)

〔口部〕

joy; delight; gratification: 她的臉上洋溢著喜悅。Her face is radiant with joy.

〔口部〕

【喝】 693
1. ㄏㄜ he hē
to drink

喝墨水兒 (ㄏㄜ ㄇㄛ ㄕㄨㄟˇㄦ)
(literally) to drink ink—to study: 他喝過洋墨水。He has studied abroad.

喝酒 (ㄏㄜ ㄐㄧㄡˇ)
to drink (alcoholic beverages)

喝西北風 (ㄏㄜ ㄒㄧ ㄅㄟˇㄈㄥ)
(literally) to drink the northwest wind—to have nothing to eat; to go hungry; to suffer from hunger

喝醉 (ㄏㄜ ㄗㄨㄟˋ)
to get drunk; to become intoxicated

【喝】 693
2. ㄏㄜˋ heh hè
to shout; to call out aloud

喝道 (ㄏㄜˋ ㄉㄠˋ)
in imperial China when a ranking official was on tour, the advance party of his retinue would loudly announce his arrival so as to clear a passage and to enable the people to have time to show proper respect

喝倒彩 (ㄏㄜˋ ㄉㄠˋ ㄘㄞˇ)
to make catcalls; to hoot; to hiss

喝六呼么 (ㄏㄜˋ ㄌㄧㄡˋㄏㄨ ㄧㄠ)
to gamble at dice game

喝令 (ㄏㄜˋ ㄌㄧㄥˋ)
to shout an order

喝彩 (ㄏㄜˋ ㄘㄞˇ)
to shout "Bravo!"; to applaud; to bring down the house; to acclaim; to cheer: 我們齊聲喝彩。All of us cheer in chorus.

【唧】 694
(喞) ㄐㄧˊ jyi jí
(又讀 ㄐㄧ ji jī)
1. a pump
2. the buzzing sound
3. to squirt: 水從管中噴了出來。The water squirted through a tube.

唧筒 (ㄐㄧˊ ㄊㄨㄥˇ)
a pump

唧咕 (ㄐㄧ ㄍㄨ)
to murmur; to whisper; to

mutter

唧唧喳喳 (ㄐㄧ ㄐㄧ ㄓㄚ ㄓㄚ)
to chirp

唧唧 (ㄐㄧ ㄐㄧ)
to chirp; the buzz (as of cicadas)

【喟】 695
ㄎㄨㄟˋ kuey kuì
to sigh heavily

喟嘆 (ㄎㄨㄟˋ ㄊㄢˋ)
to sigh with deep feeling

喟然長嘆 (ㄎㄨㄟˋ ㄖㄢˊ ㄔㄤˊ ㄊㄢˋ)
to sigh deeply

【喧】 696
1. to talk noisily; to clamor
2. noise; hubbub; uproar; noisy

喧賓奪主 (ㄒㄩㄢ ㄅㄧㄣ ㄉㄨㄛˊ ㄓㄨˇ)
(literally) a talkative guest usurping the place of the host—to act like a boss where one does not belong; to dominate the show on an occasion when one is supposed to be only a spectator

喧騰 (ㄒㄩㄢ ㄊㄥˊ)
noise and excitement; hubbub: 老師進來時，班上一片喧騰。The class was in a hubbub when the teacher came in.

喧天 (ㄒㄩㄢ ㄊㄧㄢ)
to fill the air with noise

喧鬧 (ㄒㄩㄢ ㄋㄠˋ)
noise from a crowd; hubbub; noisy

喧聒 (ㄒㄩㄢ ㄍㄨㄚ)
noisy

喧嘩 (ㄒㄩㄢ ㄏㄨㄚˊ)
noise (especially from a brawling crowd); uproar; turmoil: 不要喧嘩。Don't make such a loud noise.

喧囂 (ㄒㄩㄢ ㄒㄧㄠ)
noise; din; uproar

喧擾 (ㄒㄩㄢ ㄖㄠˇ)
to disturb by noisy talk

喧嚷 (ㄒㄩㄢ ㄖㄤˇ)
clamor; hubbub; din; racket

【喨】 697
ㄌㄧㄤˋ liang liàng
a clear, resonant sound

【喻】 698
ㄩˋ yuh yù
1. to liken; to compare; to use a figure of speech; an illustration; a parable
2. to know; to be acquainted

with: 他是個家喻戶曉的演員。The actor is known widely.
3. to explain; to make clear; to tell the meaning of; to instruct
4. a Chinese family name

【喪】 699
1. ㄙㄤ sang sāng
1. death; dying
2. to mourn
3. funeral

喪服 (ㄙㄤ ㄈㄨˊ)
mourning dress or costume

喪禮 (ㄙㄤ ㄌㄧˇ)
funeral rites

喪亂 (ㄙㄤ ㄌㄨㄢˋ)
death and disorder

喪祭 (ㄙㄤ ㄐㄧˋ)
a funeral service: 我們下星期日要去參加喪祭。We will attend a funeral service next Sunday.

喪家 (ㄙㄤ ㄐㄧㄚ)
the bereaved family

喪居 (ㄙㄤ ㄐㄩ)
to live in mourning

喪期 (ㄙㄤ ㄑㄧ)
a mourning period

喪主 (ㄙㄤ ㄓㄨˇ)
the eldest son taking charge of a parent's funeral or the eldest grandson in the absence of the eldest son

喪鐘 (ㄙㄤ ㄓㄨㄥ)
① a knell; a death knell ② death knell—an action or event presaging death or destruction

喪事 (ㄙㄤ ㄕˋ)
funeral affairs

喪葬 (ㄙㄤ ㄗㄤˋ)
funeral service and burial

【喪】 699
2. ㄙㄤˋ sang sàng
1. to lose; to be deprived of
2. to be defeated
3. to decline; to go down

喪敗 (ㄙㄤˋ ㄅㄞˋ)
to suffer a downfall; to decline and fall

喪明之痛 (ㄙㄤˋ ㄇㄧㄥˊ ㄓ ㄊㄨㄥˋ)
(literally) the pain of losing one's eyesight—the death of one's son

喪命 (ㄙㄤˋ ㄇㄧㄥˋ)
to lose one's life; to die

喪夫 (ㄙㄤˋ ㄈㄨ)

to be deprived of one's husband

喪膽 (ㄙㄤ ㄉㄢˇ)
to be much afraid; to be terror-
stricken; to lose nerve; to be
disheartened

喪國 (ㄙㄤ ㄍㄨㄛˊ)
to lose one's country to the
conqueror

喪家之狗 (ㄙㄤ ㄐㄧㄚ ㄓ ㄍㄡˇ)or 喪家
之犬 (ㄙㄤ ㄐㄧㄚ ㄓ ㄑㄩㄢˇ)
(literally) a homeless dog; a
stray cur—an outcast: 他惶
惶如喪家之犬。He felt as
frightened as a stray cur.

喪盡天良 (ㄙㄤ ㄐㄧㄣˋ ㄊㄧㄢ ㄌㄧㄤˊ)
to have no conscience; impervious to the sense of justice; utterly devoid of conscience; conscienceless;
heartless

喪妻 (ㄙㄤ ㄑㄧ)
to be deprived of one's wife

喪氣 (ㄙㄤ ㄑㄧˋ)
①dejected; despondent; in
low spirits; discouraged ②
bad luck; to be unlucky; to
be out of luck; to have bad
luck

喪權辱國 (ㄙㄤ ㄑㄩㄢˊ ㄖㄨˇ ㄍㄨㄛˊ)
to humiliate the nation and
forfeit its sovereignty; to
surrender a nation's sovereign rights under humiliating terms

喪心病狂 (ㄙㄤ ㄒㄧㄣ ㄅㄧㄥˋ ㄎㄨㄤˊ)
out of one's right mind; to
act as if one were crazy;
seized with crazy ideas; losing the balance of judgment

喪志 (ㄙㄤ ㄓˋ)
to lose one's determination
or ambition; to destroy the
mind

喪失 (ㄙㄤ ㄕ)
to lose; to be deprived of; to
be stripped of

喪師 (ㄙㄤ ㄕ)
to be defeated in battle; to
suffer defeat in battle

喪身 (ㄙㄤ ㄕㄣ)
to lose one's life

喪偶 (ㄙㄤ ㄡˇ)
to be deprived of one's
spouse, especially one's wife

【喬】 700
ㄑㄧㄠˊ chyau qiáo

1. tall
2. to disguise; to pretend
3. a Chinese family name

喬麥 (ㄑㄧㄠˊ ㄇㄞˋ)
buckwheat 亦作「蕎麥」

喬木 (ㄑㄧㄠˊ ㄇㄨˋ)
a tall tree; a large tree

喬遷 (ㄑㄧㄠˊ ㄑㄧㄢ)
to move into a new and better house

喬遷之喜 (ㄑㄧㄠˊ ㄑㄧㄢ ㄓ ㄒㄧˇ)
(an expression used in congratulation) Best wishes for
your new home.

喬治 (ㄑㄧㄠˊ ㄓˋ)
a Chinese transliteration for
George

喬治亞 (ㄑㄧㄠˊ ㄓˋ ㄧㄚˇ)
Georgia, U.S.A.

喬裝 (ㄑㄧㄠˊ ㄓㄨㄤ)
to disguise oneself: 他喬裝成
耶誕老人。He disguised him-
self as Santa Claus.

喬梓 (ㄑㄧㄠˊ ㄗˇ)
father and son 亦作「橋梓」

喬松 (ㄑㄧㄠˊ ㄙㄨㄥ)
the lofty pine

【單】 701
1. ㄉㄢ dan dān

1. single; individual: 房間中有
兩張單人床。There are two
single beds in the room.
2. alone; only
3. simple: 這個解釋十分簡單易
懂。The explanation was
quite simple.
4. of an odd number
5. a slip of paper
6. a list

單薄 (ㄉㄢ ㄅㄛˊ)
weak; feeble; flimsy

單幫 (ㄉㄢ ㄅㄤ)
a traveling work-
ing on his own: 他常跑單幫。
He often makes business
trip on his own account.

單邊 (ㄉㄢ ㄅㄧㄢ)
unilateral

單門獨戶 (ㄉㄢ ㄇㄣˊ ㄉㄨˊ ㄏㄨˋ)
a single isolated house

單名 (ㄉㄢ ㄇㄧㄥˊ)
one-character given name
(instead of the standard
two-character name)

單飛 (ㄉㄢ ㄈㄟ)
a solo flight

單方 (ㄉㄢ ㄈㄤ)

①one-sided ② a prescrip-
tion or formula; a folk prescription; a home remedy

單方面 (ㄉㄢ ㄈㄤ ㄇㄧㄢˋ)
one-sided; unilateral: 他們單
方面撕毀協定。They unilater-
ally tore up an agreement.

單方面行動 (ㄉㄢ ㄈㄤ ㄇㄧㄢˋ ㄒㄧㄥˊ ㄉㄨㄥˋ)
a unilateral action

單打 (ㄉㄢ ㄉㄚˇ)
(sports) singles: 他只參加單
打。He's only playing in the
singles.

單刀 (ㄉㄢ ㄉㄠ)
①a short-hilted broadsword
②(said of martial arts) a
single-broadsword event

單刀直入 (ㄉㄢ ㄉㄠ ㄓˊ ㄖㄨˋ)
(said of action, statement,
etc.) straightforward; direct;
right to the point

單單 (ㄉㄢ ㄉㄢ)
alone; only: 別人都來了! 單單
她沒來。She is the only one
absent. Everybody else is
here.

單調 (ㄉㄢ ㄉㄧㄠˋ)
dull; monotonous; dry; boring: 這是個單調的工作。This
is a monotonous job.

單獨 (ㄉㄢ ㄉㄨˊ)
independent; alone; solely;
singly; individually: 他單獨一
個人在家。He was alone in
the house.

單獨事件 (ㄉㄢ ㄉㄨˊ ㄕˋ ㄐㄧㄢˋ)
isolated incidents

單糖 (ㄉㄢ ㄊㄤˊ)
(chemistry) simple sugar;
monosaccharide

單利 (ㄉㄢ ㄌㄧˋ)
simple interest (as opposed
to compound interest)

單戀 (ㄉㄢ ㄌㄧㄢˋ)
one-sided love; unrequited
love

單個兒 (ㄉㄢ ㄍㄜˇ)
①individually; alone ② an
odd one

單槓 (ㄉㄢ ㄍㄤˋ)
(sports) a horizontal bar

單掛號 (ㄉㄢ ㄍㄨㄚˋ ㄏㄠˋ)
registered mail which does
not require the post office to
deliver the recipient's
acknowledgment of receipt

【口部】

單軌(ㄉㄢ ㄍㄨㄟˇ)
single-track (railroad)

單軌鐵路(ㄉㄢ ㄍㄨㄟˇ ㄊㄧˇ ㄌㄨˋ)
①a monorail ②a single-track railroad

單軌火車(ㄉㄢ ㄍㄨㄟˇ ㄏㄨㄛˇ ㄔㄜ)
a monorail (train)

單號(ㄉㄢ ㄏㄠˋ)
odd numbers (of tickets, seats, etc.)

單記投票(ㄉㄢ ㄐㄧˋ ㄊㄡˊ ㄆㄧㄠˋ)
in an election the votes carrying only the candidate's name

單間兒(ㄉㄢ ㄐㄧㄢ)
a separate room; a single room (in a hotel, restaurant, etc.) 亦作「單人房」

單價(ㄉㄢ ㄐㄧㄚˋ)
a unit price

單句(ㄉㄢ ㄐㄩˋ)
a simple sentence

單據(ㄉㄢ ㄐㄩˋ)
a receipt; documentary evidence; a voucher; a bill; an invoice: 請給我一張關於此款的單據。Please send me a receipt for the money.

單槍匹馬(ㄉㄢ ㄑㄧㄤ ㄆㄧˇ ㄇㄚˇ)
to take on the enemy alone; to do something unaided; single-handed; all by oneself

單細胞(ㄉㄢ ㄒㄧˋ ㄅㄠ)
unicellular

單線(ㄉㄢ ㄒㄧㄢˋ)
①a single line ②one-way (contact); single-line (links) ③a single track: 單線鐵路 single-track railway

單相思(ㄉㄢ ㄒㄧㄤ ㄙ)
unrequited love; one-sided love

單相電流(ㄉㄢ ㄒㄧㄤˋ ㄉㄧㄢˋ ㄌㄧㄡˊ)
a one-phase, or single-face current

單向(ㄉㄢ ㄒㄧㄤˋ)
one-way; unidirectional

單項(ㄉㄢ ㄒㄧㄤˋ)
(sports) an individual event

單行本(ㄉㄢ ㄒㄧㄥˊ ㄅㄣˇ)
a separate volume (e.g. a novel, etc., originally published in series)

單行法(ㄉㄢ ㄒㄧㄥˊ ㄈㄚˇ)
①laws and regulations that are applicable only in cer-tain districts or regions ② laws each dealing with a single matter

單行道(ㄉㄢ ㄒㄧㄥˊ ㄉㄠˋ)
a one-way street, or a one-way path

單行線(ㄉㄢ ㄒㄧㄥˊ ㄒㄧㄢˋ)
a one-way road

單性花(ㄉㄢ ㄒㄧㄥˋ ㄏㄨㄚ)
a unisexual flower

單循環制(ㄉㄢ ㄒㄩㄣˊ ㄏㄨㄢˊ ㄓˋ)
(sports) a single robin (as distinct from 雙循環制, a round robin)

單張兒(ㄉㄢ ㄓㄤ)
individual sheets

單車(ㄉㄢ ㄔㄜ)
bicycles

單產(ㄉㄢ ㄔㄢˇ)
a per unit area yield

單純(ㄉㄢ ㄔㄨㄣˊ)
①simple; plain: 問題絕不像我們想像的那麼單純。The problem is by no means as simple as we think. ②artless; unpretending; unembellished

單式(ㄉㄢ ㄕˋ)
(bookkeeping) a single entry

單式教學(ㄉㄢ ㄕˋ ㄐㄧㄠˋ ㄒㄩㄝˊ)
single-class teaching (with each class consisting of pupils of the same grade)

單身(ㄉㄢ ㄕㄣ)
①alone; unaccompanied: 他單身在外。He lives alone away from home. ②unmarried; single

單身貴族(ㄉㄢ ㄕㄣ ㄍㄨㄟˋ ㄗㄨˊ)
(colloquial) unmarried gentlemen or ladies

單身漢(ㄉㄢ ㄕㄣ ㄏㄢˋ)
a bachelor: 他還是一個單身漢。He is still a bachelor.

單身宿舍(ㄉㄢ ㄕㄣ ㄙㄨˋ ㄕㄜˋ)
quarters for single men or women

單數(ㄉㄢ ㄕㄨˋ)
①an odd number ②(grammar) singular

單日(ㄉㄢ ㄖˋ)
odd-numbered days (of the month)

單人房(ㄉㄢ ㄖㄣˊ ㄈㄤˊ)
a single-bed room (in a hotel)

單人牀(ㄉㄢ ㄖㄣˊ ㄔㄨㄤˊ)
a single bed

單子
①(ㄉㄢ ˙ㄗ)ⓐ(philosophy) monad—any basic metaphysical entity, especially having an autonomous life ⓑ the only son of a family ②(ㄉㄢ ˙ㄗ)ⓐ pieces of paper with written words on; a list; a bill; a form: 你開個單子。You make out a list. ⓑ a bed sheet

單字(ㄉㄢ ㄗˋ)
a single character or word; an individual character

單詞(ㄉㄢ ㄘˊ)
①an individual word; a word; a singular term ② a single-morpheme word

單色(ㄉㄢ ㄙㄜˋ)
monochromatic

單衣(ㄉㄢ ㄧ)
the clothes that have no lining (usually for summer wear)

單(ㄉㄢ ㄧ)
single; unitary

單眼(ㄉㄢ ㄧㄢˇ)
(zoology) single eye

單眼皮(ㄉㄢ ㄧㄢˇ ㄆㄧˊ)
eyelids that do not have a distinct fold along the edges, a typical feature of most Orientals

單音節(ㄉㄢ ㄧㄣ ㄐㄧㄝˊ)
monosyllabic

單音字(ㄉㄢ ㄧㄣ ㄗˋ)
monosyllabic words

單音詞(ㄉㄢ ㄧㄣ ㄘˊ)
monosyllabic words; mono-syllables

單位(ㄉㄢ ㄨㄟˋ)
①a unit (in measurement): 呎是長度的單位; 磅是重量的單位。A foot is a unit of length; a pound is a unit of weight. ②a military unit or organization

單元(ㄉㄢ ㄩㄢˊ)
a unit; a complete entity; a whole

單元劇(ㄉㄢ ㄩㄢˊ ㄐㄩˋ)
a single-episode drama

【單】 701
2. ㄕㄢˋ shann shàn
a Chinese family name

【單】 701
3. ㄔㄢˊ charn chán
the chief of the Huns (a common term during the Han Dynasty)

單于(ㄔㄢˊ ㄩˊ)
the chieftain of the Huns (a common term during the Han Dynasty)

【喳】 702
ㄔㄚ cha chá
the sound of chattering

喳喳
① a chattering sound; jabber
② to whisper

十畫

【嗄】 703
1. ㄕㄚˋ shah shà
(said of voice) hoarse

【嗄】 703
2. ㄚˊ ar á
(interjection) What! 嗄！你又遲到了？What! Are you late again?

【嗅】 704
ㄒㄧㄡˋ shiow xiù
to smell; to scent; to sniff: 狗會靠其嗅覺而找到賊。The dog can smell out a thief.

嗅覺(ㄒㄧㄡˋ ㄐㄩㄝˊ)
the sense of smell; olfactories; scent: 獵犬嗅覺敏銳。Bloodhounds have a keen scent.

嗅鹽(ㄒㄧㄡˋ ㄧㄢˊ)
smelling salts

【嗆】 705
1. ㄑㄧㄤ chiang qiāng
1. to peck
2. stupid; foolish

嗆呼(ㄑㄧㄤ ㄏㄨ)
stupid

【嗆】 705
2. ㄑㄧㄤˋ chiang qiàng
1. to cough because of a temporary blockade of the nasal passage which sometimes happens during eating or drinking water
2. (said of smoke, smell, etc.) to irritate the throat or nose; to suffocate

【嗇】 706
ㄙㄜˋ seh sè
stingy; parsimonious; miserly

嗇己奉公(ㄙㄜˋ ㄐㄧˇ ㄈㄥˋ ㄍㄨㄥ)
to save money for public welfare by being parsimonious in one's personal spending

【嗉】 707
ㄙㄨˋ suh sù
the crop (of a bird)

嗉囊(ㄙㄨˋ ㄋㄤˊ)
the crop (of a bird)

【嗩】 708
ㄙㄨㄛˇ suoo suǒ
a trumpet-like wind instrument

嗩吶(ㄙㄨㄛˇ ㄋㄚˋ)
a trumpet-like wind instrument

【嗎】 709
1. ㄇㄚˇ maa mǎ
a character used in transliterating

嗎啡(ㄇㄚˇ ㄈㄟ)
morphine

嗎啡針(ㄇㄚˇ ㄈㄟ ㄓㄣ)
a morphine shot or injection

嗎啡中毒(ㄇㄚˇ ㄈㄟ ㄓㄨㄥ ㄉㄨˊ)
morphine intoxication

【嗎】 709
2. ㄇㄚ ·ma ma
a phrase-final particle used in questions: 你找他有事嗎？Is there something you want to see him about?

【嗒】 710
ㄊㄚˋ tah tà
depressed; dejected; despondent; in low spirits

嗒然(ㄊㄚˋ ㄖㄢˊ)
looking dejected or despondent

嗒喪(ㄊㄚˋ ㄙㄤˋ)
in low spirits; depressed; dejected; despondent

【嗓】 711
ㄙㄤˇ saang sǎng
1. the throat (as the source of one's voice)
2. one's voice: 她的嗓子啞了。She has lost her voice.

嗓門兒(ㄙㄤˇ ㄇㄣˊ ㄦ)
① one's voice: 他的嗓門兒大。He has a loud voice. ② the vocal organs

嗓子(ㄙㄤˇ ·ㄗ)
① the throat: 我的嗓子痛。I have a sore throat. ② one's voice

嗓音(ㄙㄤˇ ㄧㄣ)
one's voice

【嗔】 712
ㄔㄣ chen chēn
1. to be angry; to take offense; to fly into a temper
2. to be annoyed with

嗔怒(ㄔㄣ ㄋㄨˋ)
to get angry; to be enraged; to be offended; to get or fly into a temper

嗔怪(ㄔㄣ ㄍㄨㄞˋ)
to rebuke; to scold; to reproach; to blame

嗔色(ㄔㄣ ㄙㄜˋ)
angry or sullen looks

【嗚】 713
ㄨ u wū
1. to weep; to sob
2. to toot; to hoot; to zoom
3. Alas!

嗚呼(ㄨ ㄏㄨ)
① Alas! ② to die: 他一命嗚呼。He died.

嗚呼哀哉(ㄨ ㄏㄨ ㄞ ㄗㄞ)
(usually used in lamenting someone's death) What a tragedy! 或What a tragic loss! 或All is lost.

嗚咽(ㄨ ㄧㄝˋ)
sobs; to sob; to weep; to whimper: 他們使他們身體抽動。Sobs shook their bodies.

嗚嗚(ㄨ ㄨ)
(descriptive of the sound of trains, whistles, distant horns, etc.) to hoot

【嗜】 714
ㄕˋ shyh shì
to delight in; to be fond of; to relish; to like; to addict: 他嗜好抽煙。He is addicted to smoking.

嗜癖(ㄕˋ ㄆㄧˇ)
a hobby; a special liking for drink, food, etc.

嗜好(ㄕˋ ㄏㄠˋ)
one's liking, hobby, or weakness for something

嗜痂之癖(ㄕˋ ㄐㄧㄚ ㄓ ㄆㄧˇ)
an eccentric taste

嗜酒(ㄕˋ ㄐㄧㄡˇ)
to be addicted to drinking

嗜血(ㄕˋ ㄒㄩㄝˋ)
bloodthirsty; bloodsucking

嗜殺(ㄕˋ ㄕㄚ)
bloodthirsty; fond of killing

嗜慾(ㄕˋ ㄩˋ)
sensual desires

〔口部〕

【嗝】715
《さ ger gé
to hiccup or hiccough; a belch

嗝兒《さル》
a hiccup or hiccough; a belch: 他打嗝兒。He has the hiccups.

【嗯】716
ㄣˊ ern én
the nasal sound used to express doubt: 嗯! 你說什麼? What? What did you say?

【嗯】716
ㄣˇ een ěn
the nasal sound used when one is surprised or indifferent: 嗯! 你怎還沒去? What! Haven't you started yet?

【嗯】716
ㄣˋ enn èn
the nasal sound used when one makes a response or promise: 他嗯了一聲, 就走了。He merely said, "H'm", and went away.

【嗟】717
ㄐㄧㄝ jie jiē
an exclamation expressing grief or regret

嗟歎（ㄐㄧㄝ ㄊㄢˋ）
to sigh with grief or regret; to lament; to deplore

嗟來之食（ㄐㄧㄝ ㄌㄞˊ ㄓ ㄕˊ）
①a meal offered with pity mixed with contempt ②(figuratively) a favor done without courtesy

嗟悔無及（ㄐㄧㄝ ㄏㄨㄟˇ ㄨˊ ㄐㄧˊ）
too late for regrets and lamentations

【嗣】718
ㄙˋ syh sì
1. to inherit; to succeed to
2. a descendant
3. to continue; to follow

嗣立（ㄙˋ ㄌㄧˋ）
to appoint or to be appointed as heir

嗣後（ㄙˋ ㄏㄡˋ）
thereafter; thenceforth; from that time on; after that; afterward

嗣繼（ㄙˋ ㄐㄧˋ）
to inherit; to succeed to

嗣產（ㄙˋ ㄔㄢˇ）

to inherit a fortune

嗣承（ㄙˋ ㄔㄥˊ）
to inherit; to succeed to

嗣子（ㄙˋ ㄗˇ）
①an heir ②an adopted son

嗣歲（ㄙˋ ㄙㄨㄟˋ）
the coming year

嗣業（ㄙˋ ㄧㄝˋ）
to inherit a business or a fortune; to inherit the family estate and continue to carry on one's father's work

嗣位（ㄙˋ ㄨㄟˋ）
to succeed to the throne

【嗤】719
ㄔ chy chī
to laugh or chuckle sneeringly

嗤鄙（ㄔ ㄅㄧˇ）
to sneer at with contempt

嗤笑（ㄔ ㄒㄧㄠˋ）
to laugh or chuckle sneeringly

嗤之以鼻（ㄔ ㄓ ㄧˇ ㄅㄧˊ）
to pooh-pooh; to give a snicker: 他對那個意見嗤之以鼻。He pooh-poohed the idea.

【嗡】720
ㄨㄥ ueng wēng
the hum or buzz of insects

嗡嗡叫（ㄨㄥ ㄨㄥ ㄐㄧㄠˋ）
(said of insects) to hum; to buzz: 蜜蜂在花園裏嗡嗡叫。The bees were humming in the garden.

【嗑】721
ㄎㄜˋ keh kè
to crack something between the teeth

嗑瓜子兒（ㄎㄜˋ ㄍㄨㄚ ㄗˇㄦ）
to crack melon seeds: 他嗑瓜子兒。He cracked melon seeds between his teeth.

十一畫

【嗷】722
(謷) ㄠˊ aur áo
a cry of hunger

嗷嗷待哺（ㄠˊ ㄠˊ ㄉㄞˋ ㄅㄨˇ）
crying with hunger; waiting to be fed with cries of hunger; to cry piteously for food

【嗶】723
ㄅㄧˋ bih bì
a character used in trans-

literating

嗶嘰（ㄅㄧˋ ㄐㄧ）
serge (a fabric)

【嗽】724
ㄙㄡˋ sow sòu
to cough; to clear the throat: 他咳嗽得很厲害。He coughs badly.

【嗾】725
ㄙㄡˇ soou sǒu
1. to give vocal signals to a dog
2. to instigate

嗾使（ㄙㄡˇ ㄕˇ）
to instigate; to incite; to spur on; to urge on; to abet

【嘅】726
(慨) ㄎㄞˇ kae kǎi
the sound of sighing

【嘈】727
ㄘㄠˊ tsaur cáo
noisy; clamorous

嘈雜（ㄘㄠˊ ㄗㄚˊ）
noisy and confused; full of confused noises; clamorous: 嘈雜之聲將他驚醒。The clamorous noises woke him up.

【嘉】728
ㄐㄧㄚ jia jiā
1. to praise; to commend; to admire
2. good; fine; excellent

嘉賓（ㄐㄧㄚ ㄅㄧㄣ）
an honored guest; a respected guest

嘉勉（ㄐㄧㄚ ㄇㄧㄢˇ）
to praise and encourage

嘉南大圳（ㄐㄧㄚ ㄋㄢˊ ㄉㄚˋ ㄗㄨㄣˋ）
the Chia Nan Canal System (a huge irrigation network in southern Taiwan)

嘉年華會（ㄐㄧㄚ ㄋㄧㄢˊ ㄏㄨㄚˊ ㄏㄨㄟˋ）
a carnival

嘉釀（ㄐㄧㄚ ㄧㄤˋ）
quality wine

嘉禮（ㄐㄧㄚ ㄌㄧˇ）
a wedding

嘉陵江（ㄐㄧㄚ ㄌㄧㄥˊ ㄐㄧㄤ）
the Chialing River, which flows from Shensi to Szechwan via Kansu

嘉惠（ㄐㄧㄚ ㄏㄨㄟˋ）
to benefit

嘉惠後學（ㄐㄧㄚ ㄏㄨㄟˋ ㄏㄡˋ ㄒㄩㄝˊ）
to benefit the students of the younger generation

嘉獎（ㄐㄧㄚ ㄐㄧㄤˇ）
to commend or praise (as

an encouragement); to cite

嘉肴(ㄐㄧㄚ ㄧㄠˊ)or 嘉餚(ㄐㄧㄚ
ㄧㄠˊ)
delicacies

嘉許(ㄐㄧㄚ ㄒㄩˇ)
to approve of; to praise: 每
個人皆嘉許他的觀點。Every-
one approved of his idea.

嘉耦 or 嘉偶(ㄐㄧㄚ ㄡˇ)
an ideal couple; a devoted
couple

嘉耦天成(ㄐㄧㄚ ㄡˇ ㄊㄧㄢ ㄔㄥˊ)
an ideal marriage divinely
arranged

嘉言懿行(ㄐㄧㄚ ㄧㄢˊ ㄧˋ ㄒㄧㄥˊ)
fine words and deeds (worthy of imitation)

嘉裕關(ㄐㄧㄚ ㄩˋ ㄍㄨㄢ)
The Chiayü Fortress in
Kansu, which marks the
western end of the Great
Wall

【嘍】 729
1. ㄌㄡ lou lóu
a bandit's lackey or follower

嘍囉(ㄌㄡ ㄌㄨㄛˊ)
① a bandit's lackey or follower; the rank and file of
a band of outlaws ② noisy
hubbub

【嘍】 729
2. ·ㄌㄡ ·lou lou
a phrase-final particle: 好嘍。
It's ready. 起床嘍。Look, it's
time to get up.

【嘏】 730
《ㄨ guu gǔ
felicity; blessings; happiness;
prosperity

【嘔】 731
1. ㄡˇ oou ǒu
to vomit; to throw up

嘔吐(ㄡˇ ㄊㄨˋ)
to vomit; to throw up; to
disgorge

嘔心瀝血(ㄡˇ ㄒㄧㄣ ㄌㄧˋ ㄒㄧㄝˇ)
to take infinite pains; to
work one's heart out

嘔血(ㄡˇ ㄒㄧㄝˇ)
haematemesis; spitting blood

【嘔】 731
2. ㄡˋ ow òu
to annoy on purpose

嘔氣(ㄡˋ ㄑㄧˋ)
to be angry but refrain from
showing it; to feel annoyed
or irritated; to feel enraged

【嘖】 732
ㄗㄜˊ tzer zé
1. an interjection of approval
or admiration
2. to argue; to dispute

嘖嘖(ㄗㄜˊ ㄗㄜˊ)
① used for the sound to indicate approval or admiration
② the cries of a bird

嘖有煩言(ㄗㄜˊ ㄧㄡˇ ㄈㄢˊ ㄧㄢˊ)
① There are noisy argu-
ments among the people. ②
There are complaints from
everybody.

【嘗】 733
ㄔㄤˊ charng cháng
1. to taste
2. to try
3. to experience

嘗新(ㄔㄤˊ ㄒㄧㄣ)
to taste a new delicacy

嘗嘗(ㄔㄤˊ·ㄔㄤ)or 嘗一嘗(ㄔㄤˊ ㄧ
·ㄔㄤ)
to taste; to have a taste

嘗試(ㄔㄤˊ ㄕˋ)
to try; a try

十二畫

【嘩】 734
1. ㄏㄨㄚ hua huā
an onomatopoeia, such gur-
gle, clang, crack, etc.: 河水嘩
啦啦地地流。The river went
gurgling on.

嘩啦(ㄏㄨㄚ ㄌㄚ)
an onomatopoeia, such as
crash, rustle, etc.

嘩啦一聲(ㄏㄨㄚ ㄌㄚ ㄧ ㄕㄥ)
with a thunderous noise: 這
房子嘩啦一聲。The house
has crashed down with a
thunderous noise.

【嘩】 734
2. ㄏㄨㄚˊ hwa huá
same as 譁—tumult; hubbub;
clamor; uproar

嘩眾取寵(ㄏㄨㄚˊ ㄓㄨㄥˋ ㄑㄩˇ ㄔㄨㄥˇ)
to try to please the public
with claptrap

嘩然(ㄏㄨㄚˊ ㄖㄢˊ)
in an uproar; an outcry: 觀眾
嘩然。The spectators burst
into an uproar.

【噓】 735
ㄒㄩ shiu xū
1. to warm with exhaled air
2. to speak well of (another)

3. a deep sigh
4. to hiss; to boo: 球迷們噓裁判。
The fans hissed the umpire.

噓寒問暖(ㄒㄩ ㄏㄢˊ ㄨㄣˋ ㄋㄨㄢˇ)
to show a kind concern for
another's comfort; to inquire
after somebody's well-being

噓氣(ㄒㄩ ㄑㄧˋ)
to send out breath from the
mouth; to blow

噓唏(ㄒㄩ ㄒㄧ)
to sob

噓聲(ㄒㄩ ㄕㄥ)
a hissing or booing sound
uttered to show hatred or
disapproval; catcalls: 他發噓
聲把狗趕出花園。He drove the
dog out of the garden by
saying "boo!".

噓聲四起(ㄒㄩ ㄕㄥ ㄙˋ ㄑㄧˇ)
to resound with catcalls: 當
他演說時觀眾噓聲四起。When
he delivered a speech, spectators resound with catcalls.

【嘮】 736
ㄌㄠˊ lau láo
loquacious; garrulous; voluble

嘮叨(ㄌㄠˊ ·ㄉㄠ)or 嘮叨叨叨(ㄌㄠˊ
ㄉㄠ ㄉㄠ ㄉㄠ)
to nag; to din; to chatter
incessantly

【嘯】 737
ㄒㄧㄠˋ shiaw xiào
1. to whistle
2. to howl; to cry or shout in
a sustained voice; to roar

嘯聚(ㄒㄧㄠˋ ㄐㄩˋ)
to band together; to gang up

嘯聚山林(ㄒㄧㄠˋ ㄐㄩˋ ㄕㄢ ㄌㄧㄣˊ)
(said of bandits) to gather
in woods or mountains in
response to whistles or
shouts; to go to the greenwood

嘯傲(ㄒㄧㄠˋ ㄠˋ)
to talk and behave freely
without regard for decorum

【嘰】 738
ㄐㄧ ji ji
1. to talk indistinctly in a low
voice
2. to chirp: 小鳥嘰嘰叫。Little
birds chirp.

嘰哩咕嚕(ㄐㄧ ㄌㄧ ㄍㄨ ㄌㄨ)
① to talk in an indistinct
manner; to gabble ②(said of
bowels) to give forth a roll-

〔口部〕

ing sound

嘟咕（ㄐㄩ ·ㄍㄨ）
①to grumble; to mumble or mutter complaints ②to gabble; to jabber

嘤嘤嘤嘤（ㄐㄧ ㄐㄧ ㄓㄚ ㄓㄚ）
①to chirp; to twitter ②to jabber

【嘲】739 ㄔㄠ chaur cháo
to ridicule; to jeer; to sneer; to scoff; to mock; to deride: 他被人嘲弄。He was held up to ridicule.

嘲罵（ㄔㄠ ㄇㄚˋ）
to jeer and abuse

嘲風咏月（ㄔㄠ ㄈㄥ ㄩㄥˇ ㄩㄝˋ）
(said of poets in former times) to sport with the wind and sing of the moon

嘲諷（ㄔㄠ ㄈㄥˋ）
to sneer at; to taunt: 他們諷刺男孩膽怯法。They taunted the boy with cowardice.

嘲弄（ㄔㄠ ㄋㄨㄥˋ）
to mock; to make fun of; to poke fun at

嘲謔（ㄔㄠ ㄒㄩㄝˋ）
to make fun of; to poke fun at

嘲戲（ㄔㄠ ㄒㄧˋ）
to poke fun at

嘲笑（ㄔㄠ ㄒㄧㄠˋ）
to laugh at; to jeer at; to sneer at; to deride; to ridicule; to scoff; to gibe

嘲訕（ㄔㄠ ㄕㄢˋ）
to deride; to sneer at; to mock; to scoff: 人人都嘲訕那老人。Everyone sneered at the old man.

【嘴】740 ㄗㄨㄟˇ tzoei zuǐ
1. the mouth; the bill or beak (of a bird); the snout (of a pig, etc.)
2. a nozzle

嘴巴（ㄗㄨㄟˇ ·ㄅㄚ）
①the mouth: 請張開嘴巴。Open your mouth, please. ②(colloquial) the cheeks

嘴巴不饒人（ㄗㄨㄟˇ ㄅㄚ ㄅㄨˋ ㄖㄠˊ ㄖㄣˊ）
fond of making sarcastic remarks; sharp-tongued

嘴笨（ㄗㄨㄟˇ ㄅㄣˋ）
not skilled in talking; in-

articulate

嘴皮子（ㄗㄨㄟˇ ㄆㄧˊ ·ㄗ）
the lips (of a glib talker)—a ready tongue

嘴貧 or 嘴頻（ㄗㄨㄟˇ ㄆㄧㄣˊ）
talkative; chatty

嘴甜心苦（ㄗㄨㄟˇ ㄊㄧㄢˊ ㄒㄧㄣ ㄎㄨˇ）
to talk sweetly while harboring evil thoughts

嘴懶（ㄗㄨㄟˇ ㄌㄢˇ）
not inclined to talk much; taciturn; reticence

嘴臉（ㄗㄨㄟˇ ㄌㄧㄢˇ）
the face (usually connoting disgust)

嘴甜（ㄗㄨㄟˇ ·ㄉㄨㄥ）
given to sweet talking; soft-spoken

嘴快（ㄗㄨㄟˇ ㄎㄨㄞˋ）
rash in speech; incapable of keeping secrets

嘴角（ㄗㄨㄟˇ ㄐㄧˇ）
corners of the mouth

嘴尖舌巧（ㄗㄨㄟˇ ㄐㄧㄢ ㄕㄜˊ ㄑㄧㄠˇ）
to be sharp-tongued; to have a capable tongue; to be gifted with a quick and sharp tongue

嘴緊（ㄗㄨㄟˇ ㄐㄧㄣˇ）
tight-lipped; closemouthed; secretive

嘴強（ㄗㄨㄟˇ ㄑㄧㄤˊ）
①inclined to argue (especially with a superior) ②to talk toughly

嘴直（ㄗㄨㄟˇ ㄓˊ）
to speak frankly; to speak out without reservation

嘴饞（ㄗㄨㄟˇ ㄔㄢˊ）
inclined to eat greedily; gluttonous; fond of good food: 他真嘴饞。He was really fond of good food.

嘴唇（ㄗㄨㄟˇ ㄔㄨㄣˊ）
the lips

嘴上無毛，做事不牢（ㄗㄨㄟˇ ㄕㄤˋ ㄨˊ ㄇㄠˊ，ㄗㄨㄛˋ ㄕˋ ㄅㄨˋ ㄌㄠˊ）
Young people cannot be trusted with important tasks because they lack experience.

嘴碎（ㄗㄨㄟˇ ㄙㄨㄟˋ）
talkative; loquacious; garrulous: 他嘴碎。He is garrulous.

嘴嚴（ㄗㄨㄟˇ ㄧㄢˊ）
cautious about speech; capable of keeping secrets

嘴硬（ㄗㄨㄟˇ ㄧㄥˋ）
①to talk toughly ②to refuse to admit a mistake

【嘶】741 ㄙ sy sī
1. the neighing of a horse: 人馬嘶。Men shout and horses neigh.
2. (said of voice) hoarse: 他聲嘶力竭。He shouted himself hoarse and felt exhausted.

嘶啞（ㄙ ㄧㄚˇ）
hoarse-voiced; hoarse

【嗥】742 ㄏㄠˊ haur háo
to howl; to yelp; the frantic barks or howls of dogs or wolves: 我們聽見遠處狼嗥。We heard wolves howling in the distance.

【嘹】743 ㄌㄧㄠ liau liáo
(said of voice) resonant

嘹喨（ㄌㄧㄠˊ ㄌㄧㄤˋ）
loud and clear; resonant: 她的歌聲嘹喨。Her singing loud and clear.

【嘻】744 ㄒㄧ shi xī
1. (in literary text) an interjection of grief or surprise
2. laughing happily

嘻皮笑臉（ㄒㄧ ㄆㄧˊ ㄒㄧㄠˋ ㄌㄧㄢˇ）
laughing in a frolicsome manner; showing a frolic some expression

嘻嘻（ㄒㄧ ㄒㄧ）
laughing happily

嘻嘻哈哈（ㄒㄧ ㄒㄧ ㄏㄚ ㄏㄚ）
laughing and talking happily

嘻笑（ㄒㄧ ㄒㄧㄠˋ）
to giggle; to titter

【嘸】745 ㄨ wuu wú
1. an expletive
2. (in Soochow and Shanghai dialect) same as 無

嘸啥稀奇（ㄨ ㄕㄚˊ ㄒㄧ ㄑㄧˊ）
nothing strange; nothing to be proud of

【噎】746 ㄧㄝ ie yē
1. to be choked with food
2. to choke off

噎住（ㄧㄝ ·ㄓㄨ）
to be choked with food

【嘿】747 1. ㄏㄟ hei hēi

an interjection: 嘿！快走吧！
Hey, hurry up!

【嘿】747
2. (默) ㄇㄜˋ moh mò
speechless; silent
quiet; still

【嚼】748
ㄐㄧㄠˊ jiaw jiáo
to chew; to munch; to nibble
類(ㄐㄧㄠ ㄍㄢ)
living persons

【噭】748
ㄐㄧㄠˋ jiaw jiào
(said of voice)high and unpleasant

【噍】748
3.ㄐㄧㄡˋ jiou jiù
(said of birds) chirping

【嚼】
(ㄐㄧㄣ ㄐㄧㄡ)
(said of birds) chirping

【嘬】749
ㄔㄨㄞˋ chuay chuài
(語音 ㄗㄨㄛˊ tzuo zuó)
to bite
to gobble up

十三畫

【噤】750
ㄐㄧㄣˋ jinn jìn
to keep the mouth shut; to shut up
若寒蟬(ㄐㄧㄣ ㄖㄨˋㄏㄢˊ)
(literally) as silent as a winter cicada—to say or reveal nothing (especially out of fear)

【器】751
ㄑㄧˋ chih qì
an instrument; an implement; a utensil; a tool; a piece of apparatus
magnanimity
晚成. A great talent takes time to mature.
to think highly of (a person)
皿(ㄑㄧˋ ㄇㄧㄥˇ)
food containers (such as plates, dishes, bowls, etc.); household utensils
量(ㄑㄧˋ ㄌㄧㄤˋ)
the capacity for magnanimity; tolerance
官(ㄑㄧˋ ㄍㄨㄢ)
the apparatus; the organs

(in animals or plants)
局(ㄑㄧˋ ㄐㄩˊ)
one's intellectual and moral capacity
具(ㄑㄧˋ ㄐㄩˋ)
tools; instruments; apparatus; implements; utensils
械(ㄑㄧˋ ㄒㄧㄝˋ)
a machine; machinery; an apparatus; an appliance
重(ㄑㄧˋ ㄓㄨㄥˋ)
to have a high opinion of (a person); to think highly of; to regard highly
識(ㄑㄧˋ ㄕˋ)
one's magnanimity and intellectual outlook
材(ㄑㄧˋ ㄘㄞˊ)
supplies; implements and materials (for a certain purpose); equipment
物(ㄑㄧˋ ㄨˋ)
an implement; a tool; an instrument; a utensil
宇(ㄑㄧˋ ㄩˇ)
one's physical appearance (usually connoting his moral and intellectual capacity)
宇軒昂(ㄑㄧˋ ㄩˇ ㄒㄩㄢ ㄤˊ)
of dignified bearing
樂(ㄑㄧˋ ㄩㄝˋ)
instrumental music (as opposed to vocal music)

【噩】752
ㄜˋ eh è
1. startling; awesome; dreadful; alarming
2. grave; serious
夢(ㄜˋ ㄇㄥˋ)
a nightmare: 我昨夜做了一個噩夢. I had a nightmare last night.
耗(ㄜˋ ㄏㄠˋ)
shocking news (usually news of a person's death)

【噪】753
ㄗㄠˋ tzaw zào
1. to be noisy
2. (said of birds, insects, etc.) to chirp
聒(ㄗㄠˋ ㄍㄨㄚ)
noisy; to make loud, confused noise
音(ㄗㄠˋ ㄧㄣ)
unpleasant noise; din: 我不喜歡噪音. I don't like noise.
音污染(ㄗㄠˋ ㄧㄣ ㄨ ㄖㄢˇ)

noise pollution

【噫】754
ㄧ yi yī
an interjection of sorrow or regret (in literary texts); alas

【噬】755
ㄕˋ shyh shì
to bite; to snap at; to gnaw
臍何及(ㄕˋ ㄑㄧˊ ㄏㄜˊ ㄐㄧˊ)or 噬臍莫及(ㄕˋ ㄑㄧˊ ㄇㄛˋ ㄐㄧˊ)
(literally) It is too late for a captured musk deer to bite its own navel.—(figuratively) It is too late for one to regret.

【噱】756
1.ㄐㄩㄝˊ jyue jué
loud laughter

【噱】
2.ㄒㄩㄝˊ shiue xué
參看「嘘頭」
嘘頭(ㄒㄩㄝˊ ㄊㄡˊ)
(Shanghai dialect) a promotional gimmick; a trick: 這個小丑嘘頭真多. The clown is full of amusing tricks.

【噸】757
ㄉㄨㄣˋ duenn dùn
ton (a unit of weight): 這部卡車運了五噸的煤炭. This truck carries 5 tons of coal.
位(ㄉㄨㄣˋ ㄨㄟˋ)
tonnage (of a ship)

【嗯】758
ㄏㄣ hm hm
(an interjection) H'm!

【噯】759
1. ㄞˋ ay ài
an interjection: 噯，你錯了。Oh! You are mistaken.

【噯】759
2. ㄞˇ ae ǎi
參看「噯氣」
噯氣(ㄞˇ ㄑㄧˋ)
(medicine) belch; eructation

【噹】760
ㄉㄤ dang dāng
a loud, resonant metallic sound
啷(ㄉㄤ ㄌㄤ)
clanking sound

【噴】761
1.ㄆㄣ pen pēn
to spurt; to gush: 石油從井口噴了出來. Oil gushed from the well.
2. to spray; to sprinkle: 給蔬菜

【口部】

噴點水。Sprinkle some water on the vegetables.

噴門 (ㄆㄣ ㄇㄣˊ)
(physiology) cardia

噴飯 (ㄆㄣ ㄈㄢˋ)
to spurt food out of the mouth when laughing—(figuratively) to burst out laughing; to split one's sides with laughter

噴嚏 (ㄆㄣ ·ㄊㄧ)
sneezing; a sneeze

噴口 (ㄆㄣ ㄎㄡˇ)
the crater of a volcano

噴壺 (ㄆㄣ ㄏㄨˊ)
a watering can

噴火山 (ㄆㄣ ㄏㄨㄛˇ ㄕㄢ)
a volcano

噴漆 (ㄆㄣ ㄑㄧ)
to spray paint; to spray lacquer

噴泉 (ㄆㄣ ㄑㄩㄢˊ)
a fountain

噴香 (ㄆㄣ ㄒㄧㄤ)
fragrant; delicious: 飯菜噴香。 The dishes smell delicious.

噴射 (ㄆㄣ ㄕㄜˋ)
(said of gas or liquid) to shoot out; to jet

噴射機 (ㄆㄣ ㄕㄜˋ ㄐㄧ) or 噴氣機 (ㄆㄣ ㄑㄧˋ ㄐㄧ)
a jet airplane

噴水池 (ㄆㄣ ㄕㄨㄟˇ ㄔˊ)
a fountain

噴 (ㄆㄣ)
to spray; to sprinkle

噴霧器 (ㄆㄣ ㄨˋ ㄑㄧˋ)
a spray gun; an atomizer

噴雲吐霧 (ㄆㄣ ㄩㄣˊ ㄊㄨˇ ㄨˋ)
to smoke (a pipe, cigarette, etc.)

【噴】 761-2 ㄈㄣˋ fèn
參看「噴噴」

十四畫

【嚎】 762 ㄏㄠˊ haur hǎo
to cry loudly; to howl; to wail

嚎啕大哭 (ㄏㄠˊ ㄊㄠˊ ㄉㄚˋ ㄎㄨ)
to cry loudly with abandon

【嚅】 763 ㄖㄨˊ ru rú
to talk indistinctly and falteringly

嚅嚅 (ㄖㄨˊ ㄋㄧ)
to falter in one's speech; to mumble in a low voice (as if out of fear)

【嚆】 764 ㄏㄠ hau hāo
to cry; to yell

嚆矢 (ㄏㄠ ㄕˇ)
① an arrow flying with a hum ② a harbinger; a prelude; a herald

【嚀】 765 ㄋㄧㄥˊ ning níng
to enjoin; to instruct

【嚇】 766 ㄏㄜˋ heh hè
1. to intimidate; to threaten
2. the sound of laughter

嚇嚇 (ㄏㄜˋ ㄏㄜˋ)
ha, ha (sound of laughter)

嚇詐 (ㄏㄜˋ ㄓㄚ)
to take (money, etc.) by threat and deceit

嚇阻 (ㄏㄜˋ ㄗㄨˇ)
to stop (someone) by threat

【嚇】 766-2 ㄒㄧㄚˋ shiah xià
1. to frighten; to startle; to scare; to intimidate: 那種困難嚇不倒我們。 Difficulties like that don't scare us.

嚇唬 (ㄒㄧㄚˋ ·ㄏㄨ)
to scare; to frighten; to intimidate

嚇人 (ㄒㄧㄚˋ ㄖㄣˊ)
① to frighten people ② frightening; terrible; horrible: 那是個嚇人的景象。 That was a horrible sight.

【嚔】 767 ㄊㄧˋ tih tì
sneezing; a sneeze

嚔噴 (ㄊㄧˋ ·ㄆㄣ)
sneezing; a sneeze

十五畫

【嚕】 768 ㄌㄨˊ lhu lū
1. verbose; wordy
2. an indistinct speech sound

嚕嗦 (ㄌㄨˊ ㄙㄨㄛ) or 嚕哩嚕嗦 (ㄌㄨˊ ㄌㄧ ㄌㄨˊ ㄙㄨㄛ)
to talk incessantly and tediously; verbosity 亦作「嚕唆」

十六畫

【嚮】 769 ㄒㄧㄤˋ shiang xiàng
1. to guide; to direct; to lead
2. to lean toward; to be inclined toward

嚮壁虛造 (ㄒㄧㄤˋ ㄅㄧˋ ㄒㄩ ㄗㄠˋ)
to fabricate out of nothing: 他的冒險故事是嚮壁虛造的。 His account of adventures is fabricated.

嚮導 (ㄒㄧㄤˋ ㄉㄠˇ) or (ㄒㄧㄤˋ ㄉㄠˋ)
a guide: 嚮導帶領我們逛這個城市。 A guide led us around the city.

嚮邇 (ㄒㄧㄤˋ ㄦˇ)
to approach

嚮往 (ㄒㄧㄤˋ ㄨㄤˇ)
to aspire; to long; to look forward to: 人人嚮往幸福的生活。 Everyone looks forward to a happy life.

【嚥】 770 ㄧㄢˋ yann yàn
to swallow: 我們吃東西時要細嚼慢嚥。 We must chew carefully and swallow slowly when we eat.

嚥唾沫 (ㄧㄢˋ ㄊㄨㄛˋ ·ㄇㄛ)
(literally) to swallow saliva—to have an appetite for something; to crave; to covet

嚥氣 (ㄧㄢˋ ㄑㄧˋ)
to breathe one's last; to die

【嚨】 771 ㄌㄨㄥˊ long lóng
the throat

十七畫

【嚴】 772 ㄧㄢˊ yan yán
1. stern; strict; severe; grim; inclement; inexorable; relentless; rigorous; rigid; grave; solemn: 嚴是愛，鬆是害。Strictness helps, and indulgence spoils.
2. reverence
3. tight: 他的嘴很嚴。 He is tight-mouthed.
4. father: 家嚴 my father; my deceased father
5. a Chinese family name

嚴辦 (ㄧㄢˊ ㄅㄢˋ)
to deal with severely; to take a severe disciplinary measure against

嚴禁 (ㄧㄢˊ ㄐㄧㄣˋ)

rigid; rigorous; strict; exact; accurate; precise; tight; close

嚴明(1ㄢ ㄇ1ㄥˊ)
(said of discipline) strict and impartial

嚴命(1ㄢ ㄇ1ㄥˋ)
① a strict order ② an order from one's father

嚴防(1ㄢ ㄈㄤˊ)
to guard carefully; to remain vigilant; to take strict precautions against: 我們必須嚴防敵人破壞。We must take strict precautions against sabotage by the enemy.

嚴父(1ㄢ ㄈㄨˋ)
① a stern father ② my father

嚴父慈母(1ㄢ ㄈㄨˋ ㄘˊ ㄇㄨˇ)
stern father and kind mother—pattern of parental love

嚴冬(1ㄢ ㄉㄨㄥ)
severe winter; very cold winter

嚴冷(1ㄢ ㄌㄥˇ)or 嚴寒(1ㄢ ㄏㄢˊ)
severe cold

嚴厲(1ㄢ ㄌ1ˋ)
strict; stern; stringent; severe; ruthless

嚴令(1ㄢ ㄌ1ㄥˋ)
a strict order; to order strictly

嚴格(1ㄢ ㄍㄜˊ)
strict; stringent; rigid; rigorous: 他們嚴格履行協定條款。They accomplish strictly the terms of the agreement.

嚴苛(1ㄢ ㄎㄜ)
harsh (administration of law)

嚴酷(1ㄢ ㄎㄨˋ)
inclement; severe; caustic; ruthless: 嚴酷的評語 caustic remarks

嚴加管束(1ㄢ ㄐ1ㄚ ㄍㄨㄢˇ ㄕㄨˋ)
to exercise strict discipline over (juniors or subordinates)

嚴謹(1ㄢ ㄐ1ㄣˇ)
careful; cautious; not given to rashness or perfunctoriness; well-knit: 這篇文章結構嚴謹。The essay is well-knit.

嚴緊(1ㄢ ㄐ1ㄣˇ)
(said of regulations, require-

ments, etc.) strict; rigorous; tight: 我們的敵人防守嚴密。Our enemy guarded carefully.

嚴禁(1ㄢ ㄐ1ㄣˋ)
to prohibit or forbid strictly: 我們學校嚴禁體罰。Our school strictly forbids corporal punishment.

嚴峻(1ㄢ ㄐㄩㄣˋ)
stern; severe; rigorous; grim: 嚴峻的態度 a stern (or an uncompromising) attitude

嚴刑拷打(1ㄢ ㄒ1ㄥˊ ㄎㄠˇ ㄉㄚˇ)
to torture cruelly; to beat up cruelly

嚴刑峻法(1ㄢ ㄒ1ㄥˊ ㄐㄩㄣˋ ㄈㄚˇ)
severe punishments under strict laws

嚴陣以待(1ㄢ ㄓㄣˋ 1ˇ ㄉㄞˋ)
to wait for (an enemy attack) in combat readiness; to be ready in full battle array

嚴整(1ㄢ ㄓㄥˇ)
well-disciplined; in neat formation: 軍容嚴整。The troops are well-disciplined.

嚴正(1ㄢ ㄓㄥˋ)
strictly correct or just; rigorous; solemn: 昨天外交部發表一嚴正聲明。The Foreign Ministry issued a solemn statement yesterday.

嚴裝(1ㄢ ㄓㄨㄤ)
to dress neatly and properly

嚴重(1ㄢ ㄓㄨㄥˋ)
(said of illness, situation, etc.) serious; severe; grave: 事態嚴重。The situation is grave.

嚴懲(1ㄢ ㄔㄥˊ)
to punish severely: 我們將嚴懲入侵之敵。We will punish the invaders severely.

嚴師(1ㄢ ㄕ)
a stern or strict teacher

嚴守中立(1ㄢ ㄕㄡˇ ㄓㄨㄥ ㄌ1ˋ)
to observe strict neutrality; to remain a neutral strictly

嚴霜(1ㄢ ㄕㄨㄤ)
severe frost—symbolic of severe temperament

嚴詞(1ㄢ ㄘˊ)
stern words; strong terms

嚴詞譴責(1ㄢ ㄘˊ ㄑ1ㄢˇ ㄗㄜˊ)
to denounce in strong terms;

to condemn sternly

嚴慈(1ㄢ ㄘˊ)
father (嚴) and mother (慈)

嚴肅(1ㄢ ㄙㄨˋ)
serious-looking; serious; solemn; austere: 他的面容嚴肅。He looks serious.

嚴以律己，寬以待人(1ㄢ 1ˇ ㄌㄩˋ ㄐ1ˇ，ㄎㄨㄢ 1ˇ ㄉㄞˋ ㄖㄣˊ)
to be strict with oneself and broad-minded towards others

【嚷】 773 1. 日ㄤˇ raang rǎng
to shout; to cry; to call out loudly: 別嚷了! Stop shouting.

嚷叫(ㄖㄤˇ ㄐ1ㄠˋ)
to bellow; to howl

【嚷】 773 2. 日ㄤˊ rhang ráng
參看「嚷嚷」

嚷嚷(ㄖㄤˊ ㄖㄤˊ)
① to shout; to yell: 誰在那兒嚷嚷? Who is shouting there? ② to make widely known: 這件事，你可別瞎嚷。Don't make it widely known.

十八畫

【嚼】 774 ㄐㄩㄝˊ jyue jué
(語音 ㄐ1ㄠ jyau jiáo)
to chew; to masticate; to munch: 細嚼慢嚥 to chew carefully and swallow slowly

嚼蠟(ㄐ1ㄠˊ ㄌㄚˋ)
as tasteless as chewing wax; dry; uninteresting

嚼舌(ㄐ1ㄠˊ ㄕㄜˊ)or 嚼舌根(ㄐ1ㄠˊ ㄕㄜˊ ㄍㄣ)
① to gossip ② to argue meaninglessly: 沒工夫跟你嚼舌。I've got no time to argue with you.

【囀】 775 ㄓㄨㄢˋ joan zhuàn
1. to warble; to twitter; to chirp
2. pleasing to the ear

【囁】 776 ㄋ1ㄝˋ nieh niè
to move the mouth (when speaking); to falter in speech

囁嚅(ㄋ1ㄝˋ ㄖㄨˊ)
to speak haltingly

口部

【囂】⁷⁷⁷ ㄒㄧㄠ shiau xiāo
1. noise; clamor; hubbub
2. to be haughty or proud
囂風(ㄒㄧㄠ ㄈㄥ)
the restlessness of a society
囂浮(ㄒㄧㄠ ㄈㄨˊ)
① frivolous ② the noisy world
囂張(ㄒㄧㄠ ㄓㄤ)
haughty; bossy; rampant; arrogant; aggressive; to push people around: 囂張一時 to run rampant for a time
囂塵(ㄒㄧㄠ ㄔㄣˊ)
① noise and dust ② the noisy, dusty world

十九畫

【囈】⁷⁷⁸ ㄧˋ yih yì
to talk in sleep; somniloquy
囈語(ㄧˇ)
① to talk while asleep; somniloquy: 他常在夢中囈語。He often talks while asleep. ② crazy talk; ravings: 沒人能了解狂人的囈語。Nobody can understand the ravings of a madman.

【囉】1. ㄌㄨㄛˊ lhuo luó
to chatter
囉哩囉唆(ㄌㄨㄛ ㄌㄧ ㄌㄨㄛ ㄙㄨㄛ)or
囉囉唆唆(ㄌㄨㄛ ㄌㄨㄛ ㄙㄨㄛ ㄙㄨㄛ)or 囉唆(ㄌㄨㄛ ㄙㄨㄛ)
vexingly verbose or wordy; long-winded; overelaborate: 他說話太囉唆。He's far too long-winded.

【囉】2. ㄌㄨㄛˊ luo luó
1. noisiness
2. a band of outlaws
3. used as a slightly argumentative final particle: 有的看囉! Wait and see. 或 Something is coming up.

【囊】⁷⁸⁰ ㄋㄤˊ nang nǎng
1. a bag; a sack; a purse: 行囊 a traveling bag
2. to put in a bag
3. a Chinese family name
囊括(ㄋㄤ ㄍㄨㄚ)
to encompass; to include; to

embrace; to comprise; to pocket or win all (the medals in a sports meet)
囊括四海(ㄋㄤ ㄍㄨㄚ ㄙˋ ㄏㄞˇ)
to bring the whole country under imperial rule
囊空如洗(ㄋㄤ ㄎㄨㄥ ㄖㄨˊ ㄒㄧˇ)
to be dead broke; to be penniless
囊中物(ㄋㄤ ㄓㄨㄥ ㄨˋ)
(literally) a thing which is already in one's bag—(figuratively) a thing very easy to get
囊螢讀書(ㄋㄤ ㄧㄥˊ ㄉㄨˊ ㄕㄨ)
(literally) to study by the light of fireflies gathered in a bag—to study under (financial) difficulties

二十一畫

【囑】⁷⁸¹ ㄓㄨˇ juu zhǔ
to ask another to do something; to instruct; to enjoin; to direct; to entrust; to charge
囑咐(ㄓㄨ ㄈㄨˋ)
to exhort; to charge (a person) with a task; to instruct or bid (a person to do something): 醫生囑咐他好好休息。The doctor bade him take a good rest.
囑託(ㄓㄨ ㄊㄨㄛ)
to entrust (a person with a task); to request (a person to do something): 她囑託我辦這件事。She entrusted me with the task.

囗 部
ㄨㄟˊ wei wéi

二畫

【囚】⁷⁸² ㄑㄧㄡˊ chyou qiú
1. a prisoner; a convict: 死囚 a convict sentenced to death
2. to imprison: 他們把我囚禁起來。They imprisoned me.

a prisoner; a convict; a jailbird
囚房(ㄑㄧㄡˊ ㄈㄤˊ)
a prison; a cell
囚牢(ㄑㄧㄡˊ ㄌㄠˊ)
a prison; a jail: 他們因偷錢被送進囚牢。They were taken (or sent) to prison for stealing money.
囚糧(ㄑㄧㄡˊ ㄌㄧㄤˊ)
prison rations; a prisoner's fare
囚籠(ㄑㄧㄡˊ ㄌㄨㄥˊ)
a wooden cage for confinement of prisoners (used in former times to transfer prisoners from one place to another)
囚禁(ㄑㄧㄡˊ ㄐㄧㄣˋ)
to imprison; to jail; to confine; to detain; to shut up in prison
囚車(ㄑㄧㄡˊ ㄔㄜ)
a prison cart; a police van to transport prisoners
囚首垢面(ㄑㄧㄡˊ ㄕㄡˇ ㄍㄡˋ ㄇㄧㄢˋ)
(said of a person) with unkempt hair and a dirty face

【四】⁷⁸³ ㄙˋ syh sì
1. four; fourth: 他四肢並用爬入洞裏。He crept into the cave on all fours.
2. all around
四胞胎(ㄙˋ ㄅㄠ ㄊㄞ)
quadruplets
四壁(ㄙˋ ㄅㄧˋ)
all the walls of a room: 他家徒四壁。He has nothing but all the walls of his room—He is very poor.
四壁蕭條(ㄙˋ ㄅㄧˋ ㄒㄧㄠ ㄊㄧㄠˊ)
(literally) Desolation prevails within four walls of the house—as poor as a church mouse
四表(ㄙˋ ㄅㄧㄠˇ)
all directions; beyond limits of the visible world
四邊(ㄙˋ ㄅㄧㄢ)
all around; four sides
四邊形(ㄙˋ ㄅㄧㄢ ㄒㄧㄥˊ)
a quadrilateral, or tetragon
四不像(ㄙˋ ㄅㄨˋ ㄒㄧㄤˋ)
① name of a wild animal (Elapurus davidianus) ② deviant or deviate (from

any accepted norm, standard, etc.); outlandish; monstrous

四平八穩 (ㄙ ㄆㄧㄥ ㄅㄚ ㄨㄣˇ)
completely stable and safe; dependable: 他辦事四平八穩。 He is dependable in work.

四面 (ㄙ ㄇㄧㄢˋ)
four sides; all sides: 我們四面出擊。 We hit out in all directions.

四面八方 (ㄙ ㄇㄧㄢˋ ㄅㄚ ㄈㄤ)
on every side; on all sides; all directions; all quarters; all around: 敵人從四面八方包圍他們了。 They were surrounded by the enemy on all sides.

四面體 (ㄙ ㄇㄧㄢˋ ㄊㄧˇ)
a tetrahedron

四面玲瓏 (ㄙ ㄇㄧㄢˋ ㄌㄧㄥˊ ㄌㄨㄥˊ)
tactful or diplomatic with all sorts of people

四面楚歌 (ㄙ ㄇㄧㄢˋ ㄔㄨˇ ㄍㄜ)
facing hostility, difficulty, or frustration on all sides

四民 (ㄙ ㄇㄧㄣˊ)
the four classes of people—scholars, farmers, artisans, and merchants

四分五裂 (ㄙ ㄈㄣ ㄨˇ ㄌㄧㄝˋ)
to fall to pieces; to be all split up: 入侵部除內部四分五裂。 The ranks of the invading army are all split up.

四方 (ㄙ ㄈㄤ)
① the four directions (east, west, north, and south) ② every direction; all sides; everywhere: 四方響應。 Response came from all sides. ③ a square

四方步 (ㄙ ㄈㄤ ㄅㄨˋ)
to walk in a pompous manner

四方臉 (ㄙ ㄈㄤ ㄌㄧㄢˇ)
a square face

四大皆空 (ㄙ ㄉㄚˋ ㄐㄧㄝ ㄎㄨㄥ)
(Buddhism) all the four elements (earth, water, fire, and air) are absent from the mind so that one is completely indifferent to worldly temptations

四德 (ㄙ ㄉㄜˊ)
the traditional four fundamentals in girls' education

—behavior (婦德), speech (婦言), appearance (婦容), and needlework and cookery (婦功)

四堵 (ㄙ ㄉㄨˇ)
the four walls

四度空間 (ㄙ ㄉㄨˋ ㄎㄨㄥ ㄐㄧㄢ) or 四次空間 (ㄙ ㄘˋ ㄎㄨㄥ ㄐㄧㄢ)
(physics) four dimensional space; the fourth dimension

四通八達 (ㄙ ㄊㄨㄥ ㄅㄚ ㄉㄚˊ)
(said of a communication network) leading everywhere: 本市公路四通八達。 Highways radiate from the city in all directions.

四楞子 (ㄙ ㄌㄥˊ ˙ㄗ)
① to be rude in speech ② a vulgar fellow

四六 (ㄙ ㄌㄧㄡˋ)
a euphuistic style of parallel sentence structures known especially for pairs of sentences of four and six characters

四鄰 (ㄙ ㄌㄧㄣˊ)
① the neighboring countries ② neighbors

四鄰八舍 (ㄙ ㄌㄧㄣˊ ㄅㄚ ㄕㄜˋ)
all the neighbors; all the neighboring households

四兩撥千金 (ㄙ ㄌㄧㄤˇ ㄅㄛ ㄑㄧㄢ ㄐㄧㄣ)
to accomplish a great task with little effort by clever maneuvers

四顧茫茫 (ㄙ ㄍㄨˋ ㄇㄤˊ ㄇㄤˊ)
to see nothing but emptiness all around

四國 (ㄙ ㄍㄨㄛˊ)
Shikoku, an island of Japan

四開 (ㄙ ㄎㄞ)
quarto

四庫全書 (ㄙ ㄎㄨˋ ㄑㄩㄢˊ ㄕㄨ)
the Four Collections of Books; Encyclopedia Sinica; A Complete Library of the Four Treasures (i.e. classics, history, philosophy and literature)—compiled during the Ching Dynasty

四合院 (ㄙ ㄏㄜˊ ㄩㄢˋ) or 四合房 (ㄙ ㄏㄜˊ ㄈㄤˊ)
a compound with houses around a courtyard

四海 (ㄙ ㄏㄞˇ)
① (ㄙ ㄏㄞˇ) the outer limits of

the China (supposed to be bound by the sea on all sides in former times)—the world: 四海之內皆兄弟也。 All the people of the world are brothers.
② (ㄙ ·ㄏㄞ) (in colloquial speech) loyal to one's friends; straightforward

四海為家 (ㄙ ㄏㄞˇ ㄨㄟˊ ㄐㄧㄚ)
① (said of emperors) to make the country a big family; to achieve perfect unity within the empire ② to lead a wandering life

四胡 (ㄙ ㄏㄨˊ)
a four-stringed Chinese musical instrument

四季 (ㄙ ㄐㄧˋ)
the four seasons: 昆明四季如春。 In Kunming it's like spring all the year round.

四季豆 (ㄙ ㄐㄧˋ ㄉㄡˋ)
string beans; kidney beans

四郊 (ㄙ ㄐㄧㄠ)
the suburbs of a city; outskirts

四腳朝天 (ㄙ ㄐㄧㄠˇ ㄔㄠˊ ㄊㄧㄢ)
to fall on one's back

四腳蛇 (ㄙ ㄐㄧㄠˇ ㄕㄜˊ)
a lizard

四健會 (ㄙ ㄐㄧㄢˋ ㄏㄨㄟˋ)
the 4-H club (4-H—head, heart, hands and health)

四起 (ㄙ ㄑㄧˇ)
to rise everywhere; to rise in every direction

四權 (ㄙ ㄑㄩㄢˊ)
the four rights of the people (election, recall, initiative and referendum) advocated by Dr. Sun Yat-sen

四下 (ㄙ ㄒㄧㄚˋ) or 四下裏 (ㄙ ㄒㄧㄚˋ ·ㄌㄧ)
all around; on all sides

四肢 (ㄙ ㄓ)
the four limbs

四周圍 (ㄙ ㄓㄡ ㄨㄟˊ)
all around; on all sides; on every side: 房子四周圍都是樹林。 Woods lay around the house.

四處 (ㄙ ㄔㄨˋ)
everywhere; all around; in all directions: 我們四處尋找走失的狗。 We looked everywhere for our lost dog.

〔口部〕

口部

四垂 or 四陲(ㄙ ㄔㄨㄟˊ)
the frontiers of a country

四川(ㄙ ㄔㄨㄢ)
Szechwan (province)

四重奏(ㄙ ㄔㄨㄥˊ ㄗㄡˋ)
(instrumental) quartet: 我很喜歡貝多芬晚期的弦樂四重奏。I like Beethoven's late string quartets very much.

四時(ㄙ ㄕˊ)
the four seasons

四史(ㄙ ㄕˇ)
The Four Books of History (the *Historical Records*, the *Book of Han*, the *Book of Later Han*, the *Annals of the Three Kingdoms*)

四捨五入(ㄙ ㄕㄜˇ ㄨˇ ㄖㄨˋ)
(arithmetic) to count five and higher fractions as units and disregard the rest

四聲(ㄙ ㄕㄥ)
①the four tones in ancient Chinese—even, rising, departing and entering tones (平, 上, 去, 入) ② the four tones of Mandarin—first, second, third and fourth tones (陰平, 陽平, 上聲, 去聲)

四書(ㄙ ㄕㄨ)
the *Four Books*—the *Great Learning*, the *Doctrine of the Mean*, the *Analects*, and the *Book of Mencius* (大學, 中庸, 論語, 孟子)

四則(ㄙ ㄗㄜˊ)
(arithmetic) addition, subtraction, multiplication, and division (加, 減, 乘, 除)

四次方程式(ㄙ ㄘˋ ㄈㄤ ㄔㄥˊ ㄕˋ)
a quartic equation, or an equation of the fourth degree

四方形(ㄙ ㄈㄤ ㄒㄧㄥˊ)
having the shape of a real square

四散(ㄙ ㄙㄢˋ)
to disperse everywhere; to disperse or scatter in all directions: 羣眾看到警察而四散。The crowd dispersed at the sight of the police.

四夷(ㄙ ㄧˊ)
the four barbarian tribes on the borders of ancient China

四裔(ㄙ ㄧˋ)
all the farthest corners

四野(ㄙ ㄧㄝˇ)
all the surrounding wildernesses; a vast expanse of the open ground: 四野寂靜無聲。All is quiet on the vast expanse of the open ground.

四言詩(ㄙ ㄧㄢˊ ㄕ)
a type of classical poetry with four characters to a line, popular before the Han Dynasty (206 B.C.-A.D. 220)

四維八德(ㄙ ㄨㄟˊ ㄅㄚ ㄉㄜˊ)
the four ethical principles (禮、義、廉、恥)and eight cardinal virtues (忠、孝、仁、愛、信、義、和、平)

四隅(ㄙ ㄩˊ)
the four corners

四月(ㄙ ㄩㄝˋ)
① April: 四月雨帶來五月花。April showers do bring May flowers. ② the fourth month of the lunar calendar ③ four months

三畫

【回】 784
ㄏㄨㄟˊ hwei huí

1. to return; to go back; to bring back; to turn back
2. to reply; to answer
3. to turn round
4. the number of times: 我來過一回。I have been here once.
5. a kind; a sort: 這完全是兩回事。These are entirely two different kinds of matters.
6. chapters in a novel: 這本小說共一百二十回。This novel has 120 chapters.
7. of Mohammedanism; Moslems

回拜(ㄏㄨㄟˊ ㄅㄞˋ)
to return a visit; to pay a return visit

回報(ㄏㄨㄟˊ ㄅㄠˋ)
①to bring back a report; to return for report ② to repay (a favor or an injury); to reciprocate: 我應回報他的盛情。I must repay him for his hospitality.

回稟(ㄏㄨㄟˊ ㄅㄧㄥˇ)
to report back (to one's superior)

回眸(ㄏㄨㄟˊ ㄇㄡˊ)
(said of a woman) to glance

back

回門(ㄏㄨㄟˊ ㄇㄣˊ)
a bride's first visit to her parents' home

回民(ㄏㄨㄟˊ ㄇㄧㄣˊ)
the Mohammedans; the Moslems (Muslems, Muslims)

回訪(ㄏㄨㄟˊ ㄈㄤˇ)
to pay a return visit: 我將回訪閣下。I'll pay a return visit to you.

回府(ㄏㄨㄟˊ ㄈㄨˇ)
to return home

回覆(ㄏㄨㄟˊ ㄈㄨˋ)
to reply; to answer; a reply; an answer: 他回覆說不願做那事。He replied that he would not do that.

回答(ㄏㄨㄟˊ ㄉㄚˊ)
to reply; to answer; to respond; a reply; an answer; a response: 我無法回答那個問題。I couldn't answer the question.

回單(ㄏㄨㄟˊ ㄉㄢ)
a receipt

回電(ㄏㄨㄟˊ ㄉㄧㄢˋ)
①a cable or telegram sent in reply ②to wire back: 即回電。Wire a reply immediately.

回頭(ㄏㄨㄟˊ ㄊㄡˊ)
①to turn the head around; to turn back ② after a while; later: 回頭再談。We'll talk it over later. ③ to return ④ to repent: 幸好他及早回頭。It was fortunate that he repented before it was too late.

回頭是岸(ㄏㄨㄟˊ ㄊㄡˊ ㄕˋ ㄢˋ)
(literally) Turn the head and there is the shore.—Repent and salvation is at hand. 或 Repentance is salvation.

回條(ㄏㄨㄟˊ ㄊㄧㄠˊ)or 回執(ㄏㄨㄟˊ ㄓˊ)
a brief note in reply; a receipt

回天乏術(ㄏㄨㄟˊ ㄊㄧㄢ ㄈㄚˊ ㄕㄨˋ)
Nothing can be done to revive the dead or to save the dying.

回娘家(ㄏㄨㄟˊ ㄋㄧㄤˊ ㄐㄧㄚ)
(said of a woman) to visit the parental home

回暖(ㄏㄨㄟˊ ㄋㄨㄢˇ)

（said of the weather) to get warm again (after a cold spell)

回來（ㄏㄨㄟˊ ˙ㄌㄞ）
to come back; to return: 他馬上回來。He'll be back in a minute.

回禮（ㄏㄨㄟˊ ㄌㄧˇ）
①to return a salute ②to send a present in return; to present a gift in return

回力球（ㄏㄨㄟˊ ㄌㄧˋ ㄑㄧㄡˊ）
①pelota; jai alai ②the ball used in pelota and jai alai

回祿之災（ㄏㄨㄟˊ ㄌㄨˋ ㄓ ㄗㄞ）
a fire disaster

回籠（ㄏㄨㄟˊ ㄌㄨㄥˊ）
①(said of bank notes, etc.) to return to the bank (which issued the notes) ②to steam again: 把涼包子回回籠。Heat up the cold steamed stuffed buns.

回顧（ㄏㄨㄟˊ ㄍㄨˋ）
to look back; to cast a look behind

回鍋（ㄏㄨㄟˊ ㄍㄨㄛ）
to cook for a second time

回歸（ㄏㄨㄟˊ ㄍㄨㄟ）
①regression ②to regress

回歸線（ㄏㄨㄟˊ ㄍㄨㄟ ㄒㄧㄢˋ）
the tropic: 北回歸線 the tropic of Cancer 南回歸線 the tropic of Capricorn

回歸熱（ㄏㄨㄟˊ ㄍㄨㄟ ㄖㄜˋ）
relapsing fever

回光（ㄏㄨㄟˊ ㄍㄨㄤ）
reflected light

回光返照（ㄏㄨㄟˊ ㄍㄨㄤ ㄈㄢˇ ㄓㄠˋ）
the transient reviving of the dying; a sudden spurt of activity prior to a collapse

回扣（ㄏㄨㄟˊ ㄎㄡˋ）
a commission on sales

回合（ㄏㄨㄟˊ ㄏㄜˊ）
an encounter; a round; a bout

回紇（ㄏㄨㄟˊ ㄏㄜˊ）
the Uigurs

回航（ㄏㄨㄟˊ ㄏㄤˊ）
to sail or fly back

回話（ㄏㄨㄟˊ ㄏㄨㄚˋ）
①to bring back word; to report ②a reply (usually one conveyed by a messenger): 他要我給他帶個回話。He asked me to take him a mes-

sage by way of reply.

回回
①（ㄏㄨㄟˊ ˙ㄏㄨㄟ）an ancient name for all the Moslem nations
②（ㄏㄨㄟˊ ㄏㄨㄟˊ）every time

回擊（ㄏㄨㄟˊ ㄐㄧˊ）
to fight back; to return fire; to counterattack: 他們拚命回擊。They fought back desperately.

回教（ㄏㄨㄟˊ ㄐㄧㄠˋ）
Mohammedanism; Islam

回教徒（ㄏㄨㄟˊ ㄐㄧㄠˋ ㄊㄨˊ）
a Muslim

回教寺（ㄏㄨㄟˊ ㄐㄧㄠˋ ㄙˋ）
a mosque 亦作「清真寺」

回敬（ㄏㄨㄟˊ ㄐㄧㄥˋ）
①to return the salute; to give a gift in return ②tit for tat

回絕（ㄏㄨㄟˊ ㄐㄩㄝˊ）
to decline; to refuse: 他一口回絕我的提議。He flatly refused my proposal.

回請（ㄏㄨㄟˊ ㄑㄧㄥˇ）
to return hospitality; to give a return banquet

回去（ㄏㄨㄟˊ ㄑㄩˋ）
①to go back; to return (home or where one came from) ②to return: 請把這錢退回去給他。Please return the money to him.

回心轉意（ㄏㄨㄟˊ ㄒㄧㄣ ㄓㄨㄢˇ ㄧˋ）
①to decide to return from sin to virtue; to repent ②to change one's mind

回信（ㄏㄨㄟˊ ㄒㄧㄣˋ）
①a letter in reply ②to write back ③a verbal message in a reply; a reply: 我用英文回信給他。I wrote him a reply in English.

回響（ㄏㄨㄟˊ ㄒㄧㄤˇ）
to reverberate; to ring; to echo; to resound; resonance: 雷聲在山谷裏回響。Thunder reverberated in the valley.

回想（ㄏㄨㄟˊ ㄒㄧㄤˇ）
to recollect; to bring back; to recall; to reflect; to look back upon: 這首歌使我回想起小學的生活。The song brought back to my mind our life at the primary school.

回轉（ㄏㄨㄟˊ ㄓㄨㄢˇ）

to turn round

回腸蕩氣 or 迴腸蕩氣（ㄏㄨㄟˊ ㄔㄤˊ ㄉㄤˋ ㄑㄧˋ）
（said of literary works) very touching; soul-stirring; heartrending

回程（ㄏㄨㄟˊ ㄔㄥˊ）
the return trip

回春（ㄏㄨㄟˊ ㄔㄨㄣ）
①the return of spring: 大地回春。Spring returns to the earth. 或 Spring is here again. ②to bring back to life

回收（ㄏㄨㄟˊ ㄕㄡ）
to retrieve; to recover; to reclaim: 紙回收 the reclamation of paper

回手（ㄏㄨㄟˊ ㄕㄡˇ）
①to fight back; to return a blow for a blow ②to turn round and stretch out one's hand

回升（ㄏㄨㄟˊ ㄕㄥ）
to rise again (after a fall); to pick up: 物價又回升。Prices have risen again.

回生（ㄏㄨㄟˊ ㄕㄥ）
①to bring back to life: 醫生能起死回生嗎？Can the doctor bring the dying back to life? ②to forget through lack of practice; to be out of practice; rusty

回聲（ㄏㄨㄟˊ ㄕㄥ）
an echo; reverberation

回族（ㄏㄨㄟˊ ㄗㄨˊ）
the Moslem population (in China)

回嘴（ㄏㄨㄟˊ ㄗㄨㄟˇ）
to talk back; to retort

回溯（ㄏㄨㄟˊ ㄙㄨˋ）
to recall; to look back upon

回憶（ㄏㄨㄟˊ ㄧˋ）or 回首（ㄏㄨㄟˊ ㄕㄡˇ）
to recollect; to recall; to look back upon; recollection; retrospect: 童年的回憶 the recollections of childhood

回憶錄（ㄏㄨㄟˊ ㄧˋ ㄌㄨˋ）
memoirs; recollections

回郵（ㄏㄨㄟˊ ㄧㄡˊ）
return mail

回音（ㄏㄨㄟˊ ㄧㄣ）
①to echo; an echo; reverberation: 當他唱歌時，山谷發出回音。The valley echoed as he sang. ②a reply; an

（口部）

answer; a response: 立候回音
hoping for an immediate
reply

回味 (ㄏㄨㄟˊ ㄨㄟˋ)
to recollect the pleasant flavor of; to ponder over

回文 (ㄏㄨㄟˊ ㄨㄣˊ)
the language of the Moslems
(in China)

【囟】 785
ㄒㄧㄣˋ shinn xìn
the top of the human head;
the skull

【因】 786
ㄧㄣ in yīn
1. cause; reason: 事出有因。
There is good reason for it.
2. for; because of
3. in accordance with; according to; on the basis of; in the
light of
4. to follow (a practice, convention, etc.); to carry on

因病 (ㄧㄣ ㄅㄧㄥˋ)
due to illness; because of illness: 他因病不能到校。He
could not go to school
because of illness.

因病下藥 (ㄧㄣ ㄅㄧㄥˋ ㄒㄧㄚˋ ㄧㄠˋ)
to apply medicine according
to indications

因地制宜 (ㄧㄣ ㄉㄧˋ ㄓˋ ㄧˊ)
to take appropriate meas-
ures in accordance with
local conditions; to take
actions that suit local circumstances

因陋就簡 (ㄧㄣ ㄌㄡˋ ㄐㄧㄡˋ ㄐㄧㄢˇ)
① to do things in the easy,
simple way ② to make do
with whatever is available

因革 (ㄧㄣ ㄍㄜˊ)
the course of change and
development; successive
changes; evolution; vicissitudes or history (of a system, institution, etc.) 亦作「沿
革」

因果 (ㄧㄣ ㄍㄨㄛˇ)
the chain of cause and
effect: 前因後果 antecedents
and consequences

因果報應 (ㄧㄣ ㄍㄨㄛˇ ㄅㄠˋ ㄧㄥˋ)
(Buddhism) the automatic
repayment in one's later life
of whatever one does; retribution for sin

因果律 (ㄧㄣ ㄍㄨㄛˇ ㄌㄩˋ)
the law of causality; the law
of causation

因公出差 (ㄧㄣ ㄍㄨㄥ ㄔㄨ ㄔㄞ)
to take an official trip; to be
absent (from office) on an
official errand

因公死亡 (ㄧㄣ ㄍㄨㄥ ㄙˇ ㄨㄤˊ)
to die while discharging an
official assignment

因禍得福 (ㄧㄣ ㄏㄨㄛˋ ㄉㄜˊ ㄈㄨˊ)
to profit from a misfortune

因習 (ㄧㄣ ㄒㄧˊ)
to follow routines or conventions without change

因襲 (ㄧㄣ ㄒㄧˊ)
to follow conventions and
traditions; conventions; conventional; traditional ways

因小失大 (ㄧㄣ ㄒㄧㄠˇ ㄕ ㄉㄚˋ)
to lose a big opportunity or
large gain because of a trifle consideration; to try to
save a little only to lose a
lot

因循 (ㄧㄣ ㄒㄩㄣˊ)
① to follow (old customs,
etc.); to continue in the
same old rut ② to procrastinate

因循苟且 (ㄧㄣ ㄒㄩㄣˊ ㄍㄡˇ ㄑㄧㄝˇ)
to follow routines without
thinking about improvement;
to be perfunctory and unimaginative in handling things

因時制宜 (ㄧㄣ ㄕˊ ㄓˋ ㄧˊ)
to do what is appropriate
according to the circum-
stances

因勢利導 (ㄧㄣ ㄕˋ ㄌㄧˋ ㄉㄠˇ)
to give judicious guidance
according to circumstances

因人成事 (ㄧㄣ ㄖㄣˊ ㄔㄥˊ ㄕˋ)
to rely on others for success
in work; to do something by
the help of somebody

因人設事 (ㄧㄣ ㄖㄣˊ ㄕㄜˋ ㄕˋ)
to create jobs just to accommodate some people (not
because the jobs are indispensable)

因仍舊慣 (ㄧㄣ ㄖㄥˊ ㄐㄧㄡˋ ㄍㄨㄢˋ)
to follow the old routines

因子 (ㄧㄣ ㄗˇ) or 因數 (ㄧㄣ ㄕㄨˋ)
(mathematics) a factor

因此 (ㄧㄣ ㄘˇ)
therefore; hence; consequently; thus; for this reason;

because of this: 時間已很晚
因此你該去睡覺了。It is ver
late; hence you must go t
bed.

因材施教 (ㄧㄣ ㄘㄞˊ ㄕ ㄐㄧㄠˋ)
to teach according to the
student's ability or aptitude
孔子因材施教。Confucius
taught disciples in accord
ance with their aptitude.

因素 (ㄧㄣ ㄙㄨˋ)
factors; elements

因案革職 (ㄧㄣ ㄢˋ ㄍㄜˊ ㄓˊ)
to get fired because o
involvement in a scandal

因而 (ㄧㄣ ㄦˊ)
therefore; and so; thereupon
我病了，因而不能來。I was ill
and therefore could no
come.

因噎廢食 (ㄧㄣ ㄧㄝ ㄈㄟˋ ㄕˊ)
(literally) to refuse to eat
for fear of choking—to
refuse making renovations
for fear of a little trouble

因應變化 (ㄧㄣ ㄧㄥˋ ㄅㄧㄢˋ ㄏㄨㄚˋ)
to change according to the
circumstances

因為 (ㄧㄣ ㄨㄟˋ)
because; inasmuch as; since;
as: 我因為下雨而沒出門。I did
not go out because it rained.

因緣 (ㄧㄣ ㄩㄢˊ)
(Buddhism) primary and secondary causes; a chance; the
chain of cause and effect

四畫

【困】 787
ㄎㄨㄣˋ kuenn kùn
1. difficult; hard
2. poor
3. tired; weary; fatigued: 你困
了就休息一下吧！Take a rest
if you are tired.
4. to trouble; to worry; to harass; to be stranded; to be
hard pressed

困乏 (ㄎㄨㄣˋ ㄈㄚˊ)
① impoverished ② exhausted;
fatigued; weary; tired

困頓 (ㄎㄨㄣˋ ㄉㄨㄣˋ)
① tired; exhausted; fatigued
② in financial straits

困難 (ㄎㄨㄣˋ ㄋㄢˊ)
difficult; hard; difficulty;
hardship; financial diffi-

culties; straitened circumstances: 情況十分困難。Conditions are very difficult.

困難重重
to be beset with difficulties

困苦 (ㄎㄨㄣˇ ㄎㄨˇ)
in great distress; suffering hardships; poverty-stricken; (live) in privation: 艱難困苦 difficulties and hardships

困惑 (ㄎㄨㄣˇ ㄏㄨㄛˋ)
at a loss; not knowing what to do; perplexed; in perplexity: 他困惑地看着我們。He looked at us in perplexity.

困境 (ㄎㄨㄣˇ ㄐㄧㄥˋ)
a difficult position; a predicament; straits: 我們必須擺脫困境。We must extricate ourselves from a difficult position.

困倦 (ㄎㄨㄣˇ ㄐㄩㄢˋ)
weary; tired

困窘 (ㄎㄨㄣˇ ㄐㄩㄥˇ)
in straitened circumstances; in a difficult position; embarrassment; to embarrass

困窮 (ㄎㄨㄣˇ ㄑㄩㄥˊ)
in great financial difficulties; very poor; impoverished; poverty-stricken: 他生活在極度困窮中。He lives in a state of extreme poverty.

困守 (ㄎㄨㄣˇ ㄕㄡˇ)
to defend against a siege; to stand a siege

困獸之鬪 (ㄎㄨㄣˇ ㄕㄡˋ ㄓ ㄉㄡˋ)
to fight desperately like a cornered wild beast; a desperate fight

困擾 (ㄎㄨㄣˇ ㄖㄠˇ)
to perplex; to puzzle; to confuse: 他為一個難題所困擾。He was puzzled by a difficult question.

困厄 (ㄎㄨㄣˇ ㄜˋ)
dire straits; distress

困阨 (ㄎㄨㄣˇ ㄜˋ)
poverty-stricken

困而學之 (ㄎㄨㄣˇ ㄦˊ ㄒㄩㄝˊ ㄓ)
to learn in consequence of frustration

【囤】 788
ㄊㄨㄣˊ twen tún
to store up; to hoard; to stockpile

囤 (ㄊㄨㄣˋ ㄌㄧㄤˊ)
to store up food for the army

囤貨 (ㄊㄨㄣˋ ㄏㄨㄛˋ)
to store up commodities

囤積 (ㄊㄨㄣˋ ㄐㄧ)
to hoard commodities for speculation; to corner: 囤積小麥 to corner the wheat market

囤積居奇 (ㄊㄨㄣˋ ㄐㄧ ㄐㄩ ㄑㄧˊ)
to store up commodities in the hope of selling them at higher prices later; hoarding and speculation

【囪】 789
ㄘㄨㄥ tsong cōng
a chimney; a flue

【囫】 790
ㄏㄨˊ hwu hú
entire; whole

囫圇 (ㄏㄨˊ ㄌㄨㄣˊ)
whole: 囫圇吞下 to swallow a thing whole

囫圇吞棗 (ㄏㄨˊ ㄌㄨㄣˊ ㄊㄨㄣ ㄗㄠˇ)
(literally) to swallow a date whole—to accept a fact without understanding or analyzing; to read hastily without thinking

五畫

【囷】 791
ㄐㄩㄣ jiun jūn
a granary

【囹】 792
ㄌㄧㄥˊ ling líng
a prison; a jail

囹圄 (ㄌㄧˊ ㄩˇ)
a prison; a jail: 他們因偷錢而身繫囹圄。They were sent to prison for stealing money.

【固】 793
ㄍㄨˋ guh gù
1. stable; firm; sturdy; secure; solid; hard; strong: 這個梯子牢固嗎? Is this ladder secure?
2. obstinate; stubborn; insistent; steadfast: 他像騾子一樣頑固。He is as stubborn as a mule.
3. base; mean; ignorant
4. chronic 參看「固疾」
5. originally; certainly; assuredly; as a matter of course
6. indeed
7. admittedly; no doubt
8. to become solid; to solidify: 果凍冷了就凝固了。Jelly solidifies as it gets cold.
9. to strengthen; to guard; to secure; to consolidate
10. a Chinese family name

固步自封 (ㄍㄨˋ ㄅㄨˋ ㄗˋ ㄈㄥ)
參看「故步自封」

固定 (ㄍㄨˋ ㄉㄧㄥˋ)
①to fix; to make immovable: 我們把火爐固定在適當的地方。We fixed the stove in place. ②fixed; regular; settled: 他沒有固定的工作和住所。He has no regular work and settled abode.

固定格式 (ㄍㄨˋ ㄉㄧㄥˋ ㄍㄜˊ ㄕˋ)
a fixed format

固定匯率 (ㄍㄨˋ ㄉㄧㄥˋ ㄏㄨㄟˋ ㄌㄩˋ)
the fixed exchange rate

固定價格 (ㄍㄨˋ ㄉㄧㄥˋ ㄐㄧㄚˋ ㄍㄜˊ)
the fixed price

固定成本 (ㄍㄨˋ ㄉㄧㄥˋ ㄔㄥˊ ㄅㄣˇ)
fixed cost

固定作用 (ㄍㄨˋ ㄉㄧㄥˋ ㄗㄨㄛˋ ㄩㄥˋ)
fixation

固態 (ㄍㄨˋ ㄊㄞˋ)
(physics) solid state

固體 (ㄍㄨˋ ㄊㄧˇ)
solid (as distinct from liquid or gas)

固陋 (ㄍㄨˋ ㄌㄡˋ)
ill-informed; unenlightened; unlearned; ignorant

固疾 (ㄍㄨˋ ㄐㄧˊ)
a chronic disease 亦作「痼疾」

固結 (ㄍㄨˋ ㄐㄧㄝˊ)
to make or become solid, hard, firm, etc.

固請 (ㄍㄨˋ ㄑㄧㄥˇ)
to invite strongly

固執 (ㄍㄨˋ ㄓˊ)
obstinate; stubborn; opinionated; persistent

固執己見 (ㄍㄨˋ ㄓˊ ㄐㄧˇ ㄐㄧㄢˋ)
to stick to one's opinions

固守 (ㄍㄨˋ ㄕㄡˇ)
to defend or guard firmly; to adhere to; to stick to: 別固守老一套的辦法。Don't stick to the old ways.

固守成規 (ㄍㄨˋ ㄕㄡˇ ㄔㄥˊ ㄍㄨㄟ)
to stick to old rules

固然 (ㄍㄨˋ ㄖㄢˊ)
①of course ②no doubt; true

〔口部〕

〔口部〕

固若金湯(《ㄨ ㄖㄨㄛ ㄐㄧㄣ ㄊㄤ)
(said of a city, military position, etc.) impregnable

固辭(《ㄨˋ ㄘˊ)
to decline firmly

固有(《ㄨˋ ㄧㄡˇ)
intrinsic; inherent; innate: 重量是物質的一種固有特性。Weight is an inherent property of matter.

固有文化(《ㄨˋ ㄧㄡˇ ㄨㄣˊ ㄏㄨㄚˋ)
traditional culture (of a nation)

六畫

【囿】 794 ㄧㄡˋ yow yòu
1. an enclosure for keeping animals; a menagerie; a garden: 園囿 or 苑囿 a pleasure garden; an enclosure for animals
2. to confine; to enclose

囿於見聞(ㄧㄡˋ ㄩˊ ㄐㄧㄢˋ ㄨㄣˊ)
handicapped by lack of knowledge and experience

囿於成見(ㄧㄡˋ ㄩˊ ㄔㄥˊ ㄐㄧㄢˋ)
bound by prejudice; biased

囿於一隅(ㄧㄡˋ ㄩˊ ㄧ ㄩˊ)
confined to a corner; unable to see widely enough

七畫

【圃】 795 ㄆㄨˇ puu pǔ
1. a vegetable garden (or plot); a nursery; an orchard; a plantation: 苗圃 a seed plot 花圃 a flower nursery
2. a planter; a gardener

【圄】 796 ㄧˇ yeu yǔ
a prison; a jail

八畫

【國】 797 《ㄨㄛˊ gwo guó
1. a country; a nation; a kingdom; a state: 全國各地 all over the country 各國 (或 列國) the nations of the world
2. national; governmental
3. Chinese
4. a Chinese family name

國寶(《ㄨㄛˊ ㄅㄠˇ)

① a national treasure: 故宮博物院有很多國寶。The National Palace Museum is full of national treasures. ② national currency

國本(《ㄨㄛˊ ㄅㄣˇ)
① the foundation of a nation ② an heir apparent to a throne

國幣(《ㄨㄛˊ ㄅㄧˋ)
① national currency ② Chinese currency

國賓(《ㄨㄛˊ ㄅㄧㄣ)
a state guest; a government guest

國步艱難(《ㄨㄛˊ ㄅㄨˋ ㄐㄧㄢ ㄋㄢˊ) or 國步方艱(《ㄨㄛˊ ㄅㄨˋ ㄈㄤ ㄐㄧㄢ)
The nation is beset by difficulties. 國步艱難, 大家應有此認識。We all must know that our nation is beset by difficulties.

國破家亡(《ㄨㄛˊ ㄆㄛˋ ㄐㄧㄚ ㄨㄤˊ)
The country is defeated and the home lost.

國門(《ㄨㄛˊ ㄇㄣˊ)
the gateway of a country

國民(《ㄨㄛˊ ㄇㄧㄣˊ)
a citizen; the people

國民兵(《ㄨㄛˊ ㄇㄧㄣˊ ㄅㄧㄥ)
the militia; a militiaman; a citizen soldier; the national guard (of the United States)

國民平均所得(《ㄨㄛˊ ㄇㄧㄣˊ ㄆㄧㄥˊ ㄐㄩㄣ ㄙㄨㄛˇ ㄉㄜˊ)
per capita income

國民福利(《ㄨㄛˊ ㄇㄧㄣˊ ㄈㄨˊ ㄌㄧˋ)
national welfare

國民大會代表(《ㄨㄛˊ ㄇㄧㄣˊ ㄉㄚˋ ㄏㄨㄟˋ ㄉㄞˋ ㄅㄧㄠˇ) or 國大代表(《ㄨㄛˊ ㄉㄚˋ ㄉㄞˋ ㄅㄧㄠˇ)
a member of the National Assembly; a National Assemblyman

國民代表大會(《ㄨㄛˊ ㄇㄧㄣˊ ㄉㄞˋ ㄅㄧㄠˇ ㄉㄚˋ ㄏㄨㄟˋ) or 國民大會(《ㄨㄛˊ ㄇㄧㄣˊ ㄉㄚˋ ㄏㄨㄟˋ)
the National Assembly

國民黨(《ㄨㄛˊ ㄇㄧㄣˊ ㄉㄤˇ)
Kuomintang (founded by Dr. Sun Yat-sen); the Nationalist Party

國民革命軍(《ㄨㄛˊ ㄇㄧㄣˊ ㄍㄜˊ ㄇㄧㄥˋ ㄐㄩㄣ)
the National Revolutionary Army (of the Kuomintang)

國民教育(《ㄨㄛˊ ㄇㄧㄣˊ ㄐㄧㄠˋ ㄩˋ)
compulsory education

國民就業輔導中心(《ㄨㄛˊ ㄇㄧㄣˊ ㄐㄧㄡˋ ㄧㄝˋ ㄈㄨˇ ㄉㄠˇ ㄓㄨㄥ ㄒㄧㄣ)
National Employment Service Center

國民性(《ㄨㄛˊ ㄇㄧㄣˊ ㄒㄧㄥˋ)
national character

國民學校(《ㄨㄛˊ ㄇㄧㄣˊ ㄒㄩㄝˊ ㄒㄧㄠˋ)
a primary school; an elementary school

國民中學(《ㄨㄛˊ ㄇㄧㄣˊ ㄓㄨㄥ ㄒㄩㄝˊ)
a junior high school (from the seventh to ninth grade under the nine-year free education system introduced in China in 1968

國民身分(份)證(《ㄨㄛˊ ㄇㄧㄣˊ ㄕㄣ ㄈㄣˋ ㄓㄥˋ)
a citizen's identification card; an ID card

國民生產毛額(《ㄨㄛˊ ㄇㄧㄣˊ ㄕㄥ ㄔㄢˇ ㄇㄠˊ ㄜˊ)
gross national product, or GNP

國民所得(《ㄨㄛˊ ㄇㄧㄣˊ ㄙㄨㄛˇ ㄉㄜˊ)
national income: 我們的國民所得每年都在增加。Our national income increases every year.

國民外交(《ㄨㄛˊ ㄇㄧㄣˊ ㄨㄞˋ ㄐㄧㄠ)
people-to-people diplomacy

國法(《ㄨㄛˊ ㄈㄚˇ)
the laws of the land, or the laws of the nation

國法不容(《ㄨㄛˊ ㄈㄚˇ ㄅㄨˋ ㄖㄨㄥˊ)
not allowed by laws

國防(《ㄨㄛˊ ㄈㄤˊ)
national defense: 國防建設 the building up of national defense

國防部(《ㄨㄛˊ ㄈㄤˊ ㄅㄨˋ)
the Ministry of National Defense; the Department of Defense (of the United States)

國父(《ㄨㄛˊ ㄈㄨˋ)
① the father of a nation ② Father of the Republic (Dr. Sun Yat-sen): 國父推翻滿清政府。Father of the Republic overthrew the Manchu government.

國定紀念日(《ㄨㄛˊ ㄉㄧㄥˋ ㄐㄧˋ ㄋㄧㄢˋ ㄖˋ)
a national commemoration or memorial day

國定假日(《ㄨㄛˊ ㄉㄧㄥˋ ㄐㄧㄚˇ ㄖˋ)

a national holiday: 我們上學期有很多國定假日。We had many national holidays last semester.

國都《ㄍㄨㄜˊ ㄉㄨ》
the national capital; the capital

國度《ㄍㄨㄜˊ ㄉㄨˋ》
① institutions of a country ② national expenditure

國泰民安《ㄍㄨㄜˊ ㄊㄞˋ ㄇㄧㄣˊ ㄢ》
The country is prosperous and at peace, and the people live in happiness.

國帑《ㄍㄨㄜˊ ㄊㄤˇ》
national funds

國體《ㄍㄨㄜˊ ㄊㄧˇ》
① the political system of a country ② national prestige

國土《ㄍㄨㄜˊ ㄊㄨˇ》
territory of a nation

國內《ㄍㄨㄜˊ ㄋㄟˋ》
inside the country; domestically or internally; domestic or internal

國內貿易《ㄍㄨㄜˊ ㄋㄟˋ ㄇㄠˋ ㄧˋ》
internal trade; domestic trade

國內電話《ㄍㄨㄜˊ ㄋㄟˋ ㄉㄧㄢˋ ㄏㄨㄚˋ》
domestic telephone

國內新聞《ㄍㄨㄜˊ ㄋㄟˋ ㄒㄧㄣ ㄨㄣˊ》
home news

國內市場《ㄍㄨㄜˊ ㄋㄟˋ ㄕˋ ㄔㄤˇ》
a domestic market

國難《ㄍㄨㄜˊ ㄋㄢˊ》
national crises (or calamities): 國難靡止。There is no end to the national crises.

國難方殷《ㄍㄨㄜˊ ㄋㄢˊ ㄈㄤ ㄧㄣ》
The nation is facing great danger (or in the midst of a crisis). 國難方殷，大家都應努力。We all must work hard because our nation is facing great danger.

國力《ㄍㄨㄜˊ ㄌㄧˋ》
national power (usually connoting resources and potentialities); national strength (or might) : 我們的國力雄厚。We have solid national strength.

國立《ㄍㄨㄜˊ ㄌㄧˋ》
(said of an institution) nationally supported or operated; national: 國立大學 a national university

國曆《ㄍㄨㄜˊ ㄌㄧˋ》
the national (i.e., solar) calendar

國聯《ㄍㄨㄜˊ ㄌㄧㄢˊ》
the League of Nations (short for 國際聯盟)

國歌《ㄍㄨㄜˊ ㄍㄜ》
a national anthem. 學生每天早上都要唱國歌。Students must sing the national anthem every morning.

國故《ㄍㄨㄜˊ ㄍㄨˋ》
① a national misfortune (or tragedy) ② the traditional culture and learning of a nation

國光《ㄍㄨㄜˊ ㄍㄨㄤ》
national glory

國庫《ㄍㄨㄜˊ ㄎㄨˋ》
the national coffers; the national treasury; the national exchequer

國庫券《ㄍㄨㄜˊ ㄎㄨˋ ㄑㄩㄢˋ》
an exchequer bond

國號《ㄍㄨㄜˊ ㄏㄠˋ》
① the name of a dynasty ② the official name of a nation

國花《ㄍㄨㄜˊ ㄏㄨㄚ》
the national flower: 梅花是我們的國花。Plum blossom is our national flower.

國畫《ㄍㄨㄜˊ ㄏㄨㄚˋ》
a Chinese painting: 我買了幾張國畫。I've bought several Chinese paintings.

國貨《ㄍㄨㄜˊ ㄏㄨㄛˋ》
native goods; locally manufactured goods; China-made goods; Chinese goods

國徽《ㄍㄨㄜˊ ㄏㄨㄟ》
the national emblem; the national insignia

國會《ㄍㄨㄜˊ ㄏㄨㄟˋ》
Parliament, the Diet, Congress, etc.

國魂《ㄍㄨㄜˊ ㄏㄨㄣˊ》
national spirit; the soul of a nation; the national genius

國籍《ㄍㄨㄜˊ ㄐㄧˊ》
nationality: 在日內瓦有各種不同國籍的人。There were men of nationalities in Geneva.

國計民生《ㄍㄨㄜˊ ㄐㄧˋ ㄇㄧㄣˊ ㄕㄥ》
the fiscal administration and people's livelihood of a nation

international: 聯合國是一國際性的組織。The United Nations is an international organization.

國際貿易《ㄍㄨㄜˊ ㄐㄧˋ ㄇㄠˋ ㄧˋ》
international trade; foreign trade

國際法《ㄍㄨㄜˊ ㄐㄧˋ ㄈㄚˇ》
international law

國際法庭《ㄍㄨㄜˊ ㄐㄧˋ ㄈㄚˇ ㄊㄧㄥˊ》
the International Court of Justice (in The Hague, the Netherlands)

國際婦女節《ㄍㄨㄜˊ ㄐㄧˋ ㄈㄨˋ ㄋㄩˇ ㄐㄧㄝˊ》
(internationally observed) Women's Day

國際地位《ㄍㄨㄜˊ ㄐㄧˋ ㄉㄧˋ ㄨㄟˋ》
international status (or standing)

國際電報《ㄍㄨㄜˊ ㄐㄧˋ ㄉㄧㄢˋ ㄅㄠˋ》
the overseas telegram

國際電話《ㄍㄨㄜˊ ㄐㄧˋ ㄉㄧㄢˋ ㄏㄨㄚˋ》
the overseas telephone

國際童大露營《ㄍㄨㄜˊ ㄐㄧˋ ㄊㄨㄥˊ ㄉㄚˋ ㄌㄨˋ ㄧㄥˊ》
a jamboree

國際勞動節《ㄍㄨㄜˊ ㄐㄧˋ ㄌㄠˊ ㄉㄨㄥˋ ㄐㄧㄝˊ》
(international) Labor Day

國際勞工組織《ㄍㄨㄜˊ ㄐㄧˋ ㄌㄠˊ ㄍㄨㄥ ㄗㄨ ㄓ》
International Labor Organization (ILO)

國際聯盟《ㄍㄨㄜˊ ㄐㄧˋ ㄌㄧㄢˊ ㄇㄥˊ》
the League of Nations (1920-1946)

國際關係《ㄍㄨㄜˊ ㄐㄧˋ ㄍㄨㄢ ㄒㄧˋ》
international relations

國際公法《ㄍㄨㄜˊ ㄐㄧˋ ㄍㄨㄥ ㄈㄚˇ》
public international law

國際共管《ㄍㄨㄜˊ ㄐㄧˋ ㄍㄨㄥˋ ㄍㄨㄢˇ》
joint international administration; condominium

國際航道《ㄍㄨㄜˊ ㄐㄧˋ ㄏㄤˊ ㄉㄠˋ》
an international waterway

國際化《ㄍㄨㄜˊ ㄐㄧˋ ㄏㄨㄚˋ》
internationalization

國際換日線《ㄍㄨㄜˊ ㄐㄧˋ ㄏㄨㄢˋ ㄖˋ ㄒㄧㄢˋ》
International Date Line

國際駕駛執照《ㄍㄨㄜˊ ㄐㄧˋ ㄐㄧㄚˋ ㄕˇ ㄓ ㄓㄠˋ》
international driving permit license

口部

〔口部〕

國際金融中心《ㄍㄨㄛˋ ㄐㄧˋ ㄐㄧㄣ ㄖㄨㄥˊ ㄓㄨㄥ ㄒㄧㄣ》
the international banking center

國際企業《ㄍㄨㄛˋ ㄐㄧˋ ㄑㄧˇ ㄧㄝˋ》
international enterprises

國際形勢《ㄍㄨㄛˋ ㄐㄧˋ ㄒㄧㄥˊ ㄕˋ》
the international (or world) situation

國際傳真電報《ㄍㄨㄛˋ ㄐㄧˋ ㄔㄨㄢˊ ㄓㄣ ㄉㄧㄢˋ ㄅㄠˋ》
the overseas facsimile

國際獅子會《ㄍㄨㄛˋ ㄐㄧˋ ㄕ ㄗˇ ㄏㄨㄟˋ》
International Association of Lions' Club

國際商會《ㄍㄨㄛˋ ㄐㄧˋ ㄕㄤ ㄏㄨㄟˋ》
International Chamber of Commerce (ICC)

國際商展《ㄍㄨㄛˋ ㄐㄧˋ ㄕㄤ ㄓㄢˇ》
international trade fair

國際人權公約《ㄍㄨㄛˋ ㄐㄧˋ ㄖㄣˊ ㄑㄩㄢˊ ㄍㄨㄥ ㄩㄝ》
International Covenants on Human Rights

國際組織《ㄍㄨㄛˋ ㄐㄧˋ ㄗㄨˇ ㄓ》
international organizations

國際私法《ㄍㄨㄛˋ ㄐㄧˋ ㄙ ㄈㄚˇ》
private international law

國際奧林匹克委員會《ㄍㄨㄛˋ ㄐㄧˋ ㄠˋ ㄌㄧㄣˊ ㄆㄧˇ ㄎㄜˋ ㄨㄟˇ ㄩㄢˊ ㄏㄨㄟˋ》
International Olympic Committee (IOC)

國際音標《ㄍㄨㄛˋ ㄐㄧˋ ㄧㄣ ㄅㄧㄠ》
the International Phonetic Alphabet (IPA)亦作「萬國音標」

國際文教組織《ㄍㄨㄛˋ ㄐㄧˋ ㄨㄣˊ ㄐㄧㄠ ㄗㄨˇ ㄓ》
United Nations Educational, Scientific, and Cultural Organization (UNESCO)

國際語音協會《ㄍㄨㄛˋ ㄐㄧˋ ㄩˇ ㄧㄣ ㄒㄧㄝˊ ㄏㄨㄟˋ》
the International Phonetic Association (IPA)亦作「萬國語音協會」

國家《ㄍㄨㄛˋ ㄐㄧㄚ》
a nation; a country

國家公園《ㄍㄨㄛˋ ㄐㄧㄚ ㄍㄨㄥ ㄩㄢˊ》
a national park

國家科學委員會《ㄍㄨㄛˋ ㄐㄧㄚ ㄎㄜ ㄒㄩㄝˊ ㄨㄟˇ ㄩㄢˊ ㄏㄨㄟˋ》
National Science Council

國家機密《ㄍㄨㄛˋ ㄐㄧㄚ ㄐㄧ ㄇㄧˋ》
state secrets: 每一個國民都要保守國家機密。Every citizen has to keep state secrets.

國家興亡，匹夫有責《ㄍㄨㄛˋ ㄐㄧㄚ ㄒㄧㄥ ㄨㄤˊ，ㄆㄧˇ ㄈㄨ ㄧㄡˇ ㄗㄜˊ》
The rise and fall of a nation is the concern of every citizen.

國家至上《ㄍㄨㄛˋ ㄐㄧㄚ ㄓˋ ㄕㄤˋ》
National interest is above everything else.

國家主義《ㄍㄨㄛˋ ㄐㄧㄚ ㄓㄨˇ ㄧˋ》
nationalism

國家安全會議《ㄍㄨㄛˋ ㄐㄧㄚ ㄢ ㄑㄩㄢˊ ㄏㄨㄟˋ ㄧˋ》
National Security Council

國界《ㄍㄨㄛˋ ㄐㄧㄝˋ》
national boundary

國交《ㄍㄨㄛˋ ㄐㄧㄠ》
diplomatic relations between countries

國將不國，何以家爲《ㄍㄨㄛˋ ㄐㄧㄤ ㄅㄨˋ ㄍㄨㄛˊ，ㄏㄜˊ ㄧˇ ㄐㄧㄚ ㄨㄟˊ》
When the nation is in peril, how can one care about home (or marriage)?

國境《ㄍㄨㄛˋ ㄐㄧㄥˋ》
a border; a national boundary: 難民非法偷越國境。The refugees crossed the border illegally.

國劇《ㄍㄨㄛˋ ㄐㄩˋ》
Peking opera: 你喜歡國劇嗎？Do you like Peking opera?

國君《ㄍㄨㄛˋ ㄐㄩㄣ》
a sovereign; a monarch

國軍《ㄍㄨㄛˋ ㄐㄩㄣ》
the armed forces of the Republic of China

國旗《ㄍㄨㄛˋ ㄑㄧˊ》
the national flag

國情《ㄍㄨㄛˋ ㄑㄧㄥˊ》
the condition of a country; national conditions

國情語文《ㄍㄨㄛˋ ㄑㄧㄥˊ ㄩˇ ㄨㄣˊ》
(in the United States) State of the Union message

國慶《ㄍㄨㄛˋ ㄑㄧㄥˋ》or 國慶日《ㄍㄨㄛˋ ㄑㄧㄥˋ ㄖˋ》
the National Day (of a country): 我們的國慶慶祝儀式包括閱兵。Our National Day celebration includes a military parade.

國璽《ㄍㄨㄛˋ ㄒㄧˇ》
①the imperial seal (in old China) ②the official seal of the Central Government

國姓《ㄍㄨㄛˋ ㄒㄧㄥˋ》
the surname of the royal family

國姓爺《ㄍㄨㄛˋ ㄒㄧㄥˋ ㄧㄝˊ》
Koxinga, the name of Chen Cheng-kung as known to Westerners

國學《ㄍㄨㄛˋ ㄒㄩㄝˊ》
the study of the (Chinese) national classics; the Chinese national literature; Chinese studies

國之四維《ㄍㄨㄛˋ ㄓ ㄙˋ ㄨㄟˊ》
the four cardinal principles of the country

國債《ㄍㄨㄛˋ ㄓㄞˋ》
national debt; public debt

國中《ㄍㄨㄛˋ ㄓㄨㄥ》
short for 國民中學

國恥《ㄍㄨㄛˋ ㄔˇ》
national shame (or humiliation)

國產《ㄍㄨㄛˋ ㄔㄢˇ》
(said of products) native or locally manufactured: 這是一輛國產汽車。This is a locally manufactured car.

國史館《ㄍㄨㄛˋ ㄕˇ ㄍㄨㄢˇ》
Academia Historica; the Bureau of National History

國是《ㄍㄨㄛˋ ㄕˋ》
the affairs of a state; national policies

國事《ㄍㄨㄛˋ ㄕˋ》
national (or state) affairs

國勢《ㄍㄨㄛˋ ㄕˋ》
①national strength ②the condition of a country; the situation in a nation: 國勢不振。The condition of the country is failing.

國手《ㄍㄨㄛˋ ㄕㄡˇ》
(said of athletes, etc.) national representatives, who are the national champions in any lines of activities, especially of sports and games

國殤《ㄍㄨㄛˋ ㄕㄤ》
a martyr to the national cause; a national martyr

國書《ㄍㄨㄛˋ ㄕㄨ》
①credentials (of a diplomat) ②documents exchanged between nations

國術《ㄍㄨㄛˋ ㄕㄨˋ》
Chinese martial arts

稅((ㄍㄨㄛˊ ㄕㄨㄟˋ))
taxes collected by the national government

人((ㄍㄨㄛˊ ㄖㄣˊ))
compatriots; people; fellow countrymen

字
Chinese characters

賊((ㄍㄨㄛˊ ㄗㄟˊ))
a traitor of the nation

葬
state funeral

策((ㄍㄨㄛˊ ㄘㄜˋ))
national policies: 我們的國策將永遠不變。We'll never change our national policies.

粹((ㄍㄨㄛˊ ㄘㄨㄟˋ))
unique cultural features of a nation; national legacies

色天香((ㄍㄨㄛˊ ㄙㄜˋ ㄊㄧㄢ ㄒㄧㄤ))
the beauty of a woman or peony

喪((ㄍㄨㄛˊ ㄙㄤ))
national mourning

醫((ㄍㄨㄛˊ ㄧ))
① a Chinese herb doctor ② Chinese herbal medicine

有((ㄍㄨㄛˊ ㄧㄡˇ))
state-owned

有財產局((ㄍㄨㄛˊ ㄧㄡˇ ㄘㄞˊ ㄔㄢˇ ㄐㄩˊ))
The Bureau of National Assets (under the Ministry of Finance)

宴((ㄍㄨㄛˊ ㄧㄢˋ))
state banquet: 總統以國宴款待國賓。The President treated the state guest with state banquet.

音((ㄍㄨㄛˊ ㄧㄣ))
the sound system of the Chinese national language; Mandarin pronunciation

音字母((ㄍㄨㄛˊ ㄧㄣ ㄗˋ ㄇㄨˇ))
the National Phonetic Alphabet (the phonetic alphabet for Mandarin pronunciation)

營((ㄍㄨㄛˊ ㄧㄥˊ))
state-operated; state-run

營事業((ㄍㄨㄛˊ ㄧㄥˊ ㄕˋ ㄧㄝˋ))
a state-owned enterprise; state enterprise

務((ㄍㄨㄛˊ ㄨˋ))
the national affairs; the affairs of a nation

務卿((ㄍㄨㄛˊ ㄨˋ ㄑㄧㄥ))
Secretary of State (of the U. S. Federal Government)

國務總理((ㄍㄨㄛˊ ㄨˋ ㄗㄨㄥˇ ㄌㄧˇ))
the premier (of the early Chinese Republican Government)

國務院((ㄍㄨㄛˊ ㄨˋ ㄩㄢˋ))
①the Department of State (of the U. S. Federal Government) ②the Cabinet of the early Chinese Republican Government) ③State Council (in mainland China)

國外
outside the country; external; abroad; externally; internationally: 他正在國外求學。He is studying abroad.

國外貿易((ㄍㄨㄛˊ ㄨㄞˋ ㄇㄠˋ ㄧˋ))
foreign trade

國外市場((ㄍㄨㄛˊ ㄨㄞˋ ㄕˋ ㄔㄤˇ))
an overseas (or a foreign) market

國文((ㄍㄨㄛˊ ㄨㄣˊ))
①the written national language ②national language and literature ③Chinese literature (a course in Chinese schools)

國王((ㄍㄨㄛˊ ㄨㄤˊ))
a king; a monarch

國亡無日((ㄍㄨㄛˊ ㄨㄤˊ ㄨˊ ㄖˋ))
The nation is in extreme peril.

國語((ㄍㄨㄛˊ ㄩˇ))
the national language; Mandarin: 有些外國人很會講國語。Some foreigners can speak Mandarin very well.

國語羅馬字((ㄍㄨㄛˊ ㄩˇ ㄌㄨㄛˊ ㄇㄚˇ ㄗˋ))
Romanized Chinese characters; Gwoyeu Romatzyh

國語文((ㄍㄨㄛˊ ㄩˇ ㄨㄣˊ))
the vernacular style of written Chinese

國語文學((ㄍㄨㄛˊ ㄩˇ ㄨㄣˊ ㄒㄩㄝˊ))
the vernacular literature

國樂((ㄍㄨㄛˊ ㄩㄝˋ))
① Chinese music ② the music officially approved to be played on great ceremonial occasions

國運((ㄍㄨㄛˊ ㄩㄣˋ))
the destiny of the nation: 祝貴國國運昌隆。May the fortunes of your state prosper.

【圇】 798
ㄌㄨㄣˊ luen lún
entire; whole

【圈】 799
1. ㄑㄩㄢ chiuan quān
1. a circle; a ring
2. with a return to the starting point; round: 我們今天早上環湖走了一圈。We walked right round the lake this morning.
3. to circle: 請圈選正確的答案。Please circle the right answers.
4. a circle—a number of persons bound together by having the same interests: 文化圈 literary circles

圈點((ㄑㄩㄢ ㄉㄧㄢˇ))
to mark (a passage) with circles and dots; to punctuate; to mark a good passage with circles

圈套((ㄑㄩㄢ ㄊㄠˋ))
a snare; a trap; a trick: 他落入敵人圈套。He fell into the enemy's trap.

圈內((ㄑㄩㄢ ㄋㄟˋ))
(literally and figuratively) within a circle

圈圈((ㄑㄩㄢ ㄑㄩㄢ))
①to draw circles ②cliques; circles: 別搞小圈圈。Don't form small cliques.

圈子((ㄑㄩㄢ ·ㄗ))或圈兒((ㄑㄩㄢㄦ))
a circle: 他的生活圈子很小。He moves in a very small circle.

圈外((ㄑㄩㄢ ㄨㄞˋ))
(literally and figuratively) outside a circle

【圈】 799
2. ㄐㄩㄢ jiuan juān
to encircle; to confine

【圈】 799
3. ㄐㄩㄢˋ jiuann juàn
an enclosure or a pen for keeping livestock: 豬圈 a pigpen; a pigsty 牛圈 an enclosure for cows

九畫

【圍】 800
ㄨㄟˊ wei wéi
1. to surround; to enclose; to encircle; to hem in
2. surroundings; environment
3. the circumference of a circle

口部

口
部

formed by a person's arms

圍脖兒(ㄨㄟˊ ㄅㄛˊ) or 圍巾(ㄨㄟˊ ㄐㄧㄣ)
a scarf; a muffler

圍標(ㄨㄟˊ ㄅㄧㄠ)
illegal bidding with the government by a victim (worked out by a government employee and a contractor or manufacturer to make sure that the latter gets the contract while the other bidders are willing collaborators)

圍捕(ㄨㄟˊ ㄅㄨˇ)
to arrest (a criminal) by closing in on him from all sides

圍堵政策(ㄨㄟˊ ㄉㄨˇ ㄓㄥˋ ㄘㄜˋ)
a policy of restricting the territorial growth or ideological influence of a hostile nation

圍獵(ㄨㄟˊ ㄌㄧㄝˋ)
to hunt by encircling the game

圍爐(ㄨㄟˊ ㄌㄨˊ)
to sit and chat around the fireplace

圍攻(ㄨㄟˊ ㄍㄨㄥ)
to attack from all sides; to besiege; to beleaguer: 他遭圍攻。He came under attack from all sides. 或 He was caught in a cross fire.

圍困(ㄨㄟˊ ㄎㄨㄣˋ)
to besiege; to beleaguer; to surround; to pin down: 把敵人困在少數據點中。Pin down the enemy in a few strongholds.

圍剿(ㄨㄟˊ ㄐㄧㄠˇ)
to attack (bandits or rebels) from all sides; to encircle and suppress

圍棋(ㄨㄟˊ ㄑㄧˊ)
the "encirclement chess," known as go in Japan, which was invented by the Chinese at a very early date, played with black and white pieces on a board of 361 crosses

圍牆(ㄨㄟˊ ㄑㄧㄤˊ)
an enclosing wall; a fence

圍裙(ㄨㄟˊ ㄑㄩㄣˊ)
an apron

圍場(ㄨㄟˊ ㄔㄤˊ)

hunting grounds

圍城(ㄨㄟˊ ㄔㄥˊ)
to lay siege to a city; a beleaguered city; a besieged city

圍繞(ㄨㄟˊ ㄖㄠˋ)
to surround; to encircle; to enclose: 一座牆圍繞着這座花園。A wall surrounds the garden.

圍嘴兒(ㄨㄟˊ ㄗㄨㄟˇ ㄦˊ)
a bib

圍腰兒(ㄨㄟˊ ㄧㄠ ㄦˊ)
(formerly) a girdle

十畫

【園】 801
ㄩㄢˊ yuán

1. a piece of ground used for growing flowers, fruit or vegetables; a garden; a plantation

2. a public garden, park or recreation ground

園圃(ㄩㄢˊ ㄆㄨˇ)
a vegetable garden; an orchard; a plantation

園地(ㄩㄢˊ ㄉㄧˋ)
① a garden ②(in a periodical) a space reserved for publishing articles or letters from readers

園丁(ㄩㄢˊ ㄉㄧㄥ)
a gardener: 我們想雇用一位優秀的園丁。We wish to hire a good gardener.

園林(ㄩㄢˊ ㄌㄧㄣˊ)
a park; a garden

園陵(ㄩㄢˊ ㄌㄧㄥˊ)
an emperor's tomb; a mausoleum

園主(ㄩㄢˊ ㄓㄨˇ)
the owner of a park or a garden

園子(ㄩㄢˊ ˙ㄗ)
① a garden ② a theater

園藝(ㄩㄢˊ ㄧˋ)
gardening; horticulture; garden husbandry: 他非常愛好園藝。He is very fond of gardening.

園遊會(ㄩㄢˊ ㄧㄡˊ ㄏㄨㄟˋ)
a garden party

【圓】 802
ㄩㄢˊ yuán

1. round; circular; spherical: 它

既不圓也不方。It is neither round nor square.

2. complete; to complete; to make plausible; to justify

3. satisfactory; tactful

4. a monetary unit

5. a circle

圓盤(ㄩㄢˊ ㄆㄢˊ)
a disc

圓滿(ㄩㄢˊ ㄇㄢˇ)
① satisfactory; satisfactorily: 對此問題他已圓滿地解決了。The problem has been satisfactorily solved by him. ② rounded out ③ complete

圓夢(ㄩㄢˊ ㄇㄥˋ)
to interpret a dream

圓面積(ㄩㄢˊ ㄇㄧㄢˋ ㄐㄧ)
spherical surface

圓明園(ㄩㄢˊ ㄇㄧㄥˊ ㄩㄢˊ)
the Summer Palace (of the Manchu emperors in Peking)

圓房(ㄩㄢˊ ㄈㄤˊ)
to solemnize a marriage (between one's son and the daughter-in-law brought up in the family when the two reach adulthood)

圓頂(ㄩㄢˊ ㄉㄧㄥˇ)
a round top; a dome: 這座教堂有一漂亮的圓頂。The church has a beautiful dome.

圓通(ㄩㄢˊ ㄊㄨㄥ)
capable of adapting oneself to circumstances; accommodating; flexible: 我們老闆很圓通。Our boss is very accommodating.

圓筒(ㄩㄢˊ ㄊㄨㄥˇ)
a cylinder

圓臉(ㄩㄢˊ ㄌㄧㄢˇ)
a round face

圓顱方趾(ㄩㄢˊ ㄌㄨˊ ㄈㄤ ㄓˇ)
round-skulled and square-footed (referring to man) —all human beings are alike

圓規(ㄩㄢˊ ㄍㄨㄟ)
a pair of compasses (an instrument for making circles)

圓弧(ㄩㄢˊ ㄏㄨˊ)
an arc

圓滑(ㄩㄢˊ ㄏㄨㄚˊ)
tactful; diplomatic; slick and sly

圓環(ㄩㄢˊ ㄏㄨㄢˊ)

a rotary; a traffic circle

圜(ㄏㄨㄢˊ)
to straighten out contradictions in a lie and make it plausible

圆寂(ㄐㄧˊ)
to die (said of Buddhist monks or nuns); to pass away

圆徑(ㄐㄧㄥˋ)
a diameter 亦作「直徑」: 圆徑有五公尺。 It is five meters in diameter.

圆球(ㄐㄧㄡˊ)
a ball; a sphere; a globe

圆圈(ㄐㄩㄢˋ)
a circle; a ring: 仙子們圍成一圆圈跳舞。 The fairies danced in a ring.

圆心(ㄐㄧㄣ)
the center of a circle

圆形(ㄐㄧㄥˊ)
round; spherical; circular

圆周(ㄓㄡ)
the circumference of a circle

圆周率(ㄓㄡㄌㄩˋ)
Ludolphian number (π), ratio of the circumference of a circle to its diameter

圆柱(ㄓㄨˋ)
a cylinder

圆柱根(ㄓㄨˋㄍㄣ)
a cylindrical root

圆桌(ㄓㄨㄛ)
a round table

圆桌會議(ㄓㄨㄛㄏㄨㄟˋ)
a round-table conference or discussion

圆錐(ㄓㄨㄟ)
(solid geometry) a cone

圆錐根(ㄓㄨㄟㄍㄣ)
a conic root

圆場
to mediate; to help to effect a compromise: 他是個和事佬喜歡替人打圆場。 As a peacemaker, he likes to mediate a dispute of others.

圆唇元音(ㄔㄨㄣˊㄩㄢ ㄧㄣ)
(phonetics) a round vowel; a rounded vowel

圆熟(ㄕㄡˊ)
skillful; skilled; proficient; dexterous

圆潤(ㄖㄨㄣˋ)
mellow and full: 她天生有一

副圆潤的嗓音。 She is endowed with a sweet, mellow voice.

圆鑿方枘(ㄗㄠˊ ㄈㄤ ㄖㄨㄟˋ)
(literally) a square peg in a round hole—a combination of two things incapable of fitting each other

圆舞曲(ㄨˇ ㄑㄩˇ)
waltz

圆月(ㄩㄝˋ)
①to drink together in the moonlight on Mid-Autumn Festival (中秋節) ②a full moon

十一畫

【圖】 803
ㄊㄨˊ twu tú

1. a picture; a map; a portrait; a chart; a diagram: 你的書上有很多插圖嗎？ Are there many pictures in your book?

2. to seek; to pursue

3. to plan; to scheme; to conspire

4. intention; aim; purpose: 他似乎別有所圖。 He seems to have other aims.

5. a Chinese family name

圖飽私囊(ㄅㄠˇㄙㄋㄤˊ)
to try to enrich oneself (from public services)

圖報恩德(ㄅㄠˋㄣㄉㄜˊ)
to hope or plan to repay kindness or favors

圖表(ㄅㄧㄠˇ)
charts, diagrams and tables —used in statistics

圖片(ㄆㄧㄢˋ)
illustrations in separate sheets; pictures; photographs

圖謀(ㄇㄡˊ)
to plan; to conspire

圖謀不軌(ㄇㄡˊ ㄅㄨˋ ㄍㄨㄟˇ)
to harbor evil intentions; to make dishonest schemes (particularly referring to revolt, revolution or treason)

圖名(ㄇㄧㄥˊ)
to pursue fame; for the sake of prestige

圖釘(ㄉㄧㄥ)
thumbtacks; a drawing pin

圖逃(ㄊㄠˊ)
to attempt to escape

圖騰(ㄊㄥˊ)
①a totem ②(in old China) flags embroidered with the patterns of animals representing the various barbarian tribes

圖賴(ㄌㄞˋ)
to try to deny what one has said or done

圖例(ㄌㄧˋ)
a brief explanation or key to an illustration, map, etc.

圖利(ㄌㄧˋ)
to desire to make money or profit; to plan to make money

圖利他人(ㄌㄧˋㄊㄚ ㄖㄣˊ)
(in lawsuits involving government officials) with the intention to profit others

圖畫(ㄏㄨㄚˋ)
①a drawing; a picture; a painting ②drawing; painting ③to scheme; to plot; to plan

圖籍(ㄐㄧˊ)
land charts and census records

圖記(ㄐㄧˋ)
a seal (of an organization); a stamp

圖解(ㄐㄧㄝˇ)
diagrams and pictures for teaching purposes; illustrations: 我們老師喜歡用圖解說明。 Our teacher likes to explain through diagrams.

圖窮匕見(ㄑㄩㄥˊ ㄅㄧˇ ㄒㄧㄢˋ)
When the map was unrolled, the dagger was revealed. —The real intention is revealed in the end. 或 The plot is exposed.

圖形(ㄒㄧㄥˊ)
a sketch; a contour; an outline; a graph; a figure: 幾何圖形 geometric figures

圖章(ㄓㄤ)
a seal; a chop (usually personal)

圖示(ㄕˋ)
to indicate by a picture; the picture shows...

圖書(ㄕㄨ)
maps, charts and books

圖書目錄(ㄕㄨㄇㄨˋ ㄌㄨˋ)
a catalogue of books; a

口
部

〔土
部〕

library catalogue
圖書館(ㄊㄨˊㄕㄨㄍㄨㄢˇ)
a library: 這個圖書館已經開始
自動化了。The library has
begun to automate.

圖書管理員(ㄊㄨˊㄕㄨㄍㄨㄢˇㄌㄧˇㄩㄢˊ)
a librarian

圖書室(ㄊㄨˊㄕㄨㄕˋ)
a reading room

圖書資料(ㄊㄨˊㄕㄨㄗㄌㄧㄠˋ)
books and reference materials

圖財害命(ㄊㄨˊㄘㄞˊㄏㄞˋㄇㄧㄥˋ)
to murder someone for
money

圖案(ㄊㄨˊㄢˋ)
①(fine arts) patterns: 我喜
歡這壁紙的圖案。I like the
pattern of the wallpaper. ②
(architecture) designs or
drafts

圖樣(ㄊㄨˊㄧㄤˋ)
(architecture) a design; a
blueprint

【團】 804
ㄊㄨㄢˊ twan tuán

1. a sphere; something shaped
like a ball
2. a mass; a lump
3. a group; a party; a mission;
an organization; a society
4. (infantry) a regiment, consisting of three battalions of
foot soldiers
5. to unite

團拜(ㄊㄨㄢˊㄅㄞˋ)
mass greetings (as on New
Year's Day); mass congratulations (on auspicious occasions, etc.)

團隊精神(ㄊㄨㄢˊㄉㄨㄟˋㄐㄧㄥㄕㄣˊ)
team spirit

團體(ㄊㄨㄢˊㄊㄧˇ)
a group, party or mission;
an organization; group
(action, etc.)

團體操(ㄊㄨㄢˊㄊㄧˇㄘㄠ)
callisthenics done by a large
group of people with con-
certed movements under the
command of a physical education instructor

團體賽(ㄊㄨㄢˊㄊㄧˇㄙㄞˋ)
a team competition

團團轉(ㄊㄨㄢˊㄊㄨㄢˊㄓㄨㄢˇ)
to pace about in an agitated
state of mind; to turn round

and round
團團圍住(ㄊㄨㄢˊㄊㄨㄢˊㄨㄟˊㄓㄨˋ)
to be completely surrounded
(by rows of enemy troops)

團練(ㄊㄨㄢˊㄌㄧㄢˋ)
the militia; volunteer home
guards

團管區(ㄊㄨㄢˊㄍㄨㄢˇㄑㄩ)
a regional administration in
charge of conscription and
mobilization (somewhat like
a draft board)

團結(ㄊㄨㄢˊㄐㄧㄝˊ)
union; unity; solidarity; to
unify; to unite: 團結就是力量。
Union is strength.

團聚(ㄊㄨㄢˊㄐㄩˋ)
(said of a family, etc.) to
meet; to congregate; a meeting; a reunion; a gathering

團契(ㄊㄨㄢˊㄑㄧˋ)
fellowship—a Christian association of the youth

團長(ㄊㄨㄢˊㄓㄤˇ)
a regiment commander; a
commanding officer of a
regiment

團扇(ㄊㄨㄢˊㄕㄢˋ)
a circular or moon-shaped
fan

團坐(ㄊㄨㄢˊㄗㄨㄛˋ)
(for many people) to sit
around in circle

團員(ㄊㄨㄢˊㄩㄢˊ)
a member: 他是合唱團的團員。
He is a member of a chorus.

團圓(ㄊㄨㄢˊㄩㄢˊ)
a union or reunion (espe-
cially of a family): 農曆除夕
是全家團圓的日子。Lunar
New Year's Eve is the time
for family reunion.

土 部
ㄊㄨ tuu tǔ

【土】 805
ㄊㄨˇ tuu tǔ

1. earth; soil: 大多數植物在沃土
中長得最好。Most plants
grow best in rich soil.
2. land; territory; domain: 人人
守土有責。Everybody is
responsible for guarding

land from enemy.
3. local; native; indigenous:
是土生土長的德國人。He is
native German.
4. unrefined; unenlightened
5. rustic; countrified
6. opium
7. an abbreviation for Turke

土撥鼠(ㄊㄨˇㄅㄛㄕㄨˇ)
a marmot; a ground hog

土包子(ㄊㄨˇㄅㄠ‧ㄗ)
a rustic or countrified pe
son; a hillbilly; a countr
bumpkin

土辦法(ㄊㄨˇㄅㄢˋㄈㄚˇ)
indigenous methods

土崩瓦解(ㄊㄨˇㄅㄥㄨㄚˇㄐㄧㄝˇ)
in total disintegration;
total disorder or confusion

土布(ㄊㄨˇㄅㄨˋ)
① cotton cloth or piec
goods produced locally (
homewoven or handloome
cloth; homespun cloth

土坯(ㄊㄨˇㄆㄧ)
claybricks (as distinct fror
those treated in a kiln); a
unburnt brick

土黴素(ㄊㄨˇㄇㄟˊㄙㄨˋ)
terramycin; oxytetracycline

土木(ㄊㄨˇㄇㄨˋ)or 土木工程(ㄊㄨˇ
ㄇㄨˋㄍㄨㄥㄔㄥˊ)
civil engineering; construc
tion projects: 他們將大興土木
They will go in for large
scale building or construc
tion.

土木工程師(ㄊㄨˇㄇㄨˋㄍㄨㄥㄔㄥˊㄕ)
a civil engineer

土法(ㄊㄨˇㄈㄚˇ)
an old, local method; a tra
ditional method

土匪(ㄊㄨˇㄈㄟˇ)
bandits; brigands: 這鎮為土匪
所擾。The town is infeste
with bandits.

土番(ㄊㄨˇㄈㄢ)
uncivilized natives; aborig
ines

土方(ㄊㄨˇㄈㄤ)
①a cubic meter of earth ②
a recipe of folk medicine

土房子(ㄊㄨˇㄈㄤˊ‧ㄗ)
a house built with untreated
or unburnt bricks

土風舞(ㄊㄨˇㄈㄥㄨˇ)
folk dance

土茯苓(ㄊㄨˇ ㄈㄨˊ ㄌㄧㄥˊ)
(Chinese herb) China root

土豆(ㄊㄨˇ ㄉㄡˋ)
① peanuts ② potatoes

土地(ㄊㄨˇ ㄉㄧˋ)
① land ② the God of Earth

土地廟(ㄊㄨˇ ㄉㄧˋ ㄇㄧㄠˋ)
the temple of the God of Earth

土地改革(ㄊㄨˇ ㄉㄧˋ《ㄍㄞˇ《ㄜˊ》or 土
改(ㄊㄨˇ ㄍㄞˇ)
land reform; agrarian reform: 新政府實施土地改革。
The new government put through land reform.

土地公(ㄊㄨˇ ㄉㄧˋ《ㄨㄥ)
the God of Earth 亦作「土地爺」「土地神」

土地徵收(ㄊㄨˇ ㄉㄧˋ ㄓㄥ ㄕㄡ)
the requisition of private land holdings (for public use)

土地重劃(ㄊㄨˇ ㄉㄧˋ ㄓㄨㄥˋ ㄏㄨㄚˋ)
land consolidation

土地增值稅(ㄊㄨˇ ㄉㄧˋ ㄗㄥ ㄓˊ ㄕㄨㄟˋ)
the land value increment tax; a tax levied on increment of land value

土堆(ㄊㄨˇ ㄉㄨㄟ)or 土墩(ㄊㄨˇ ㄉㄨㄣ)
a mound

土頭土腦(ㄊㄨˇ ㄊㄡˊ ㄊㄨˇ ㄋㄠˇ)
rustic; hillbilly; unsophisticated

土牛木馬(ㄊㄨˇ ㄋㄧㄡˊ ㄇㄨˋ ㄇㄚˇ)
(literally) an earthen ox and a wooden horse—to exist in form only

土牢(ㄊㄨˇ ㄌㄠˊ)
a dungeon

土老兒(ㄊㄨˇ ㄌㄠˇ ㄦˊ)
①a rustic old man ②a damned fool

土狼(ㄊㄨˇ ㄌㄤˊ)
a hyena

土瀝青(ㄊㄨˇ ㄌㄧˋ ㄑㄧㄥ)
asphalt

土裏土氣(ㄊㄨˇ ㄌㄧˇ ㄊㄨˇ ㄑㄧˋ)
rustic; countrified; hillbilly; uncouth; unsophisticated

土鯪魚(ㄊㄨˇ ㄌㄧㄥˊ ㄩˊ)
a mud carp

土高爐(ㄊㄨˇ ㄍㄠ ㄌㄨˊ)
a small-sized homemade blast furnace

土棍(ㄊㄨˇ ㄍㄨㄣˋ)
a local rascal; a local bully;

a ruffian

土炕(ㄊㄨˇ ㄎㄤˋ)
a heatable adobe sleeping platform; an adobe *kang*; an earthen bed warmed by a fire underneath (in North China)

土豪劣紳(ㄊㄨˇ ㄏㄠˊ ㄌㄧㄝˋ ㄕㄣ)
local ruffians and the oppressive gentry; evil and powerful elements in a community

土話(ㄊㄨˇ ㄏㄨㄚˋ)
local dialects; patois; indigenous languages

土貨(ㄊㄨˇ ㄏㄨㄛˋ)
local products; local produce

土皇帝(ㄊㄨˇ ㄏㄨㄤˊ ㄉㄧˋ)
a local chieftain; a powerful personage in a community; a local despot; a local tyrant

土階茅茨(ㄊㄨˇ ㄐㄧㄝ ㄇㄠˊ ㄘˊ)
earthen steps and thatched roof

土氣(ㄊㄨˇ ㄑㄧˋ)
rustic; uncouth

土星(ㄊㄨˇ ㄒㄧㄥ)
the planet Saturn

土質(ㄊㄨˇ ㄓˊ)
the condition or nature of the soil

土製(ㄊㄨˇ ㄓˋ)
homemade; crudely manufactured

土著(ㄊㄨˇ ㄓㄜˋ)or 土著(ㄊㄨˇ ㄓㄨˋ)
natives; aborigines

土塚(ㄊㄨˇ ㄓㄨㄥˇ)
a burial mound

土產(ㄊㄨˇ ㄔㄢˇ)
local products

土城(ㄊㄨˇ ㄔㄥˊ)
a city wall made of clay

土生土長(ㄊㄨˇ ㄕㄥ ㄊㄨˇ ㄓㄤˇ)
(said of persons who have never traveled outside their native heaths) to be born and to grow up in the local community

土人(ㄊㄨˇ ㄖㄣˊ)
① the natives (usually referring to uncivilized tribes); aborigines: 土人很親切的接待他。The natives received him kindly. ② a mud doll

土壤(ㄊㄨˇ ㄖㄤˇ)
soil: 大多數植物在肥沃的土壤中長得最好。Most plants

grow best in rich soil.

土壤保持(ㄊㄨˇ ㄖㄤˇ ㄅㄠˇ ㄔˊ)
soil conservation

土賊(ㄊㄨˇ ㄗㄟˊ)
bandits

土葬(ㄊㄨˇ ㄗㄤˋ)
a burial in the ground

土司(ㄊㄨˇ ㄙ)
① the chief of a local tribe (especially in the southwestern provinces of China) ② toast: 我吃了兩片烤土司。I ate two slices of toast.

土色(ㄊㄨˇ ㄙㄜˋ)
ashen; pale: 他面如土色。His face turned deadly pale.

土耳其(ㄊㄨˇ ㄦˇ ㄑㄧˊ)
Turkey

土耳其帽(ㄊㄨˇ ㄦˇ ㄑㄧˊ ㄇㄠˋ)
a Turkish cap; a fez

土耳其斯坦(ㄊㄨˇ ㄦˇ ㄑㄧˊ ㄙ ㄊㄢˇ)
Turkistan or Turkestan

土藥(ㄊㄨˇ ㄧㄠˋ)
① native medicine ② domestic opium 參看「洋藥」

土曜日(ㄊㄨˇ ㄧㄠˋ ㄖˋ)
Saturday

土音(ㄊㄨˇ ㄧㄣ)or 土腔(ㄊㄨˇ ㄑㄧㄤ)
local pronunciation; a local accent; a brogue: 他說國語帶有四川土音。He speaks Mandarin with a Szechwan accent.

土語(ㄊㄨˇ ㄩˇ)
local dialects; *patois*

三畫

【在】 ⁸⁰⁶ ㄗㄞˋ tzay zài

1. at; in; on; up to: 你的書在桌子上呢。Your book is on the table.

2. to rest with; to consist in; to depend on: 幸福在於知足。Happiness consists in contentment.

3. to be alive; living; to be present; to exist

4. used to indicate a progressive tense: 她在游泳。She is swimming.

在逃(ㄗㄞˋ ㄊㄠˊ)
(said of a criminal) on the loose or still at large

在堂(ㄗㄞˋ ㄊㄤˊ)
(said of one's parents) still

〔土部〕

alive

在內(ㄗㄞˋ ㄋㄟˋ)
①including; inclusive ②inside

在來米(ㄗㄞˋ ㄌㄞˊ ㄇㄧˇ)
Tsai Lai Rice—a variety of Taiwan paddy

在官言官(ㄗㄞˋ ㄍㄨㄢ ㄧㄢˊ ㄍㄨㄢ)
(literally) When in office, talk like an official.—to speak of one side of a matter only

在公(ㄗㄞˋ ㄍㄨㄥ)
①(to do something) as part of one's duty ② officially; for the sake of the public

在後(ㄗㄞˋ ㄏㄡˋ)
behind; later; as follows

在行(ㄗㄞˋ ㄏㄤˊ)
in the trade; in the know; professional; to be an expert at something: 文學方面我在行。 I'm an expert at literature.

在乎(ㄗㄞˋ ㄏㄨ)
①to care; to mind: 有些士兵一天走五十里路毫不在乎。 Some soldiers think nothing of marching fifty *li* a day. ②to consist in; to depend on (whether…)

在即(ㄗㄞˋ ㄐㄧˊ)
near at hand; imminent; soon: 入學考試在即。 The entrance examination is near at hand.

在家(ㄗㄞˋ ㄐㄧㄚ)
to be at home; to be in: 你媽媽在家嗎? Is your mother in?

在家出家(ㄗㄞˋ ㄐㄧㄚ ㄔㄨ ㄐㄧㄚ)
(said of a layman) to practice abstinence like a Buddhist monk; one who, though retaining family ties, observes all the monastic rules

在家人(ㄗㄞˋ ㄐㄧㄚ ㄖㄣˊ)
a layman (as distinct from a monk)

在假(ㄗㄞˋ ㄐㄧㄚˋ)
on leave

在劫難逃(ㄗㄞˋ ㄐㄧㄝˊ ㄋㄢˊ ㄊㄠˊ)
If one is doomed, one is doomed. 或 There's no escape. 或 Nobody can change his fate.

在昔(ㄗㄞˋ ㄒㄧˊ)
once upon a time; formerly;

in former times

在下(ㄗㄞˋ ㄒㄧㄚˋ)
my humble self; I; your humble servant

在先(ㄗㄞˋ ㄒㄧㄢ)
①before; at that time; formerly; in the past; beforehand ②in front; ahead

在心(ㄗㄞˋ ㄒㄧㄣ)
to keep in mind; to be attentive; to feel concerned

在學(ㄗㄞˋ ㄒㄩㄝˊ)
to be at school

在職(ㄗㄞˋ ㄓˊ)
to hold a position; on the job; to be at one's post

在職訓練(ㄗㄞˋ ㄓˊ ㄒㄩㄣˋ ㄌㄧㄢˋ)
in-service training

在朝(ㄗㄞˋ ㄔㄠˊ)
(said of officials of cabinet rank in old China) to be a ranking official working near the monarch; to hold office at court

在場(ㄗㄞˋ ㄔㄤˇ)or(ㄗㄞˋ ㄔㄤˊ)
to be present (when an incident or accident occurred); to be on the scene; to be on the spot: 當時他不在場。 He wasn't on the scene at the time.

在世(ㄗㄞˋ ㄕˋ)
alive; in this world

在室(ㄗㄞˋ ㄕˋ)
(said of girls) still unmarried

在在(ㄗㄞˋ ㄗㄞˋ)
everywhere

在皆是(ㄗㄞˋ ㄐㄧㄝ ㄕˋ)
to be seen everywhere

在座(ㄗㄞˋ ㄗㄨㄛˋ)
to be present (at a gathering): 在座的還有幾位歸國學人。 Among those present were a few returned overseas scholars.

在此(ㄗㄞˋ ㄘˇ)
here: 你要的東西在此。 Here you are.

在所不免(ㄗㄞˋ ㄙㄨㄛˇ ㄅㄨˋ ㄇㄧㄢˇ)or
在所難免(ㄗㄞˋ ㄙㄨㄛˇ ㄋㄢˊ ㄇㄧㄢˇ)
unavoidable; inevitable; natural

在所不惜(ㄗㄞˋ ㄙㄨㄛˇ ㄅㄨˋ ㄒㄧˊ)
regardless of the cost or sacrifice (The expression is usually preceded by the spe-

cific sacrifice one is prepared to make.)

在所不辭(ㄗㄞˋ ㄙㄨㄛˇ ㄅㄨˋ ㄘˊ)
will not refuse under any circumstances; will not hesitate to

在案(ㄗㄞˋ ㄢˋ)
①on record; written in a document (used only in official documents) ②(said of a person) on the police record

在意(ㄗㄞˋ ㄧˋ)
to mind; to care about; to take notice of: 這些小事我是不會在意的。 I won't take such trifles to heart.

在押(ㄗㄞˋ ㄧㄚ)
under detention; being imprisoned

在野(ㄗㄞˋ ㄧㄝˇ)
①to be out of power; to hold no official position ②(said of politicians) to be in opposition

在野黨(ㄗㄞˋ ㄧㄝˇ ㄉㄤˇ)
the opposition party or parties

在我(ㄗㄞˋ ㄨㄛˇ)
(It is) up to me

在握(ㄗㄞˋ ㄨㄛˋ)
to be within one's grasp; to be under one's control

在外(ㄗㄞˋ ㄨㄞˋ)
①not including; excluding ②outside

在位(ㄗㄞˋ ㄨㄟˋ)
in power; in the position; on the throne

在望(ㄗㄞˋ ㄨㄤˋ)
①to be visible; to be in view: 輪船隱隱在望。 The ship was dimly visible. ②will soon materialize; to be in sight: 和平在望。 Peace is now in sight.

在於(ㄗㄞˋ ㄩˊ)
to lie in; to consist in; to be determined by; to depend on: 挽救之道在於教育。 The cure lies in education.

【坊】 807
ㄨ u wū
1. a trowel used for plastering
2. to plaster

【圭】 808
ㄍㄨㄟ guei guī
a jade tablet with a square base and a pointed top used

in official ceremonies in ancient China

圭
① ritual jades worn by feudal lords in ancient China in a formal meeting or audience ② high virtue and integrity of a person

臬
① ancient timepieces ② a principle for one to look up to: 奉爲圭臬 to look up to as the standard

璋
① a valuable jade ② (said of persons) dignity

亞那
Guiana

a bridge

上老人(ㄕㄤˋ ㄌㄠˇ ㄖㄣˊ)
Huang Shih-kung (黃石公)
—an old man who was supposed to be a teacher of Chang Liang (張良), a great strategist, who helped Liu Pang (劉邦) establish the Han Dynasty

. the earth
. land; soil; ground: 水泥地 concrete floor 耕地 cultivated land
. a region; a territory; a belt; a place; a locality: 他家地處 山區。His house is located in a mountain area.
. a position; a place; a situation: 我們立於危險之地。We are in a dangerous situation.
. an adjunct after a word (usually adjective) to form an adverbial phrase: 偷偷地 stealthily 不聲不響地 silently

地保(ㄉㄧˋ ㄅㄠˇ)
a head of a basic community unit, responsible for law and order in the same neighborhood

地板(ㄉㄧˋ ㄅㄢˇ)
woodplanks used for flooring; wood flooring; a floor

地表(ㄉㄧˋ ㄅㄧㄠˇ)
the surface of the earth

地步(ㄉㄧˋ ㄅㄨˋ)
① a situation; a condition:

局勢到了不可收拾的地步。The situation got out of hand. ② extent: 他興奮到不能入睡的地步。He was so excited that he could not get to sleep. ③ room for action

地盤(ㄉㄧˋ ㄆㄢˊ)
① a place or territory occupied by force; a region under one's sphere of influence; a domain ② the crust of the earth ③ the foundation of a building or house

地皮(ㄉㄧˋ ㄆㄧˊ)
land for building houses; land-estate; real estate

地痞(ㄉㄧˋ ㄆㄧˇ)
ruffians, rascals, bullies, etc.

地痞流氓(ㄉㄧˋ ㄆㄧˇ ㄌㄧㄡˊ ㄇㄤˊ)
local bullies and loafers

地平線(ㄉㄧˋ ㄆㄧㄥˊ ㄒㄧㄢˋ)
the horizon: 太陽沉到地平線下了。The sun sank below the horizon.

地鋪(ㄉㄧˋ ㄆㄨ)
a bed on the floor; a shakedown

地面(ㄉㄧˋ ㄇㄧㄢˋ)
① the surface of the earth ② a region; a territory: 此處已經進入安徽地面。We're now in the Province of Anhwei.

地名(ㄉㄧˋ ㄇㄧㄥˊ)
the name of a place

地方(ㄉㄧˋ ㄈㄤ)
① a locality (in contrast with the central government) ② a place ③ space; room ④ part; respect ⑤ local; locally

地方法院(ㄉㄧˋ ㄈㄤ ㄈㄚˇ ㄩㄢˋ)
a district court: 囚犯被帶到地方法院候審。The prisoner was brought to the district court for trial.

地方分權(ㄉㄧˋ ㄈㄤ ㄈㄣ ㄑㄩㄢˊ)
decentralization; division of powers between local and central governments

地方團體(ㄉㄧˋ ㄈㄤ ㄊㄨㄢˊ ㄊㄧˇ)
local organizations

地方官(ㄉㄧˋ ㄈㄤ ㄍㄨㄢ)
officials of local governments

地方新聞(ㄉㄧˋ ㄈㄤ ㄒㄧㄣ ㄨㄣˊ)
locals; local news: 作爲一個年輕記者，他採訪地方新聞。As a young reporter, he covered the locals.

地方政府(ㄉㄧˋ ㄈㄤ ㄓㄥˋ ㄈㄨˇ)
a local government

地方人士(ㄉㄧˋ ㄈㄤ ㄖㄣˊ ㄕˋ)
distinguished personalities in a locality; local personalities

地方自治(ㄉㄧˋ ㄈㄤ ㄗˋ ㄓˋ)
local self-government

地方色彩(ㄉㄧˋ ㄈㄤ ㄙㄜˋ ㄘㄞˇ)
① local color ② provincialism

地府(ㄉㄧˋ ㄈㄨˇ)
the underworld; Hades

地大物博(ㄉㄧˋ ㄉㄚˋ ㄨˋ ㄅㄛˊ)
vast land and rich natural resources: 中國是個地大物博的國家。China is a big country abounding in natural wealth.

地帶(ㄉㄧˋ ㄉㄞˋ)
a place and its vicinity: 森林地帶 a forest region

地道(ㄉㄧˋ ㄉㄠˋ)
a tunnel

地點(ㄉㄧˋ ㄉㄧㄢˇ)
a site; a location; a place; a spot; a locale: 在這裏建座新公園，地點倒適中。This would be a suitable site for a new park.

地對地飛彈(ㄉㄧˋ ㄉㄨㄟˋ ㄉㄧˋ ㄈㄟ ㄉㄢˋ)
a ground-to-ground missile; a surface-to-surface missile

地對空飛彈(ㄉㄧˋ ㄉㄨㄟˋ ㄎㄨㄥ ㄈㄟ ㄉㄢˋ)
a ground-to-air missile

地段(ㄉㄧˋ ㄉㄨㄢˋ)
the locality of a piece of land (especially referring to the numbered land plots on government file)

地洞(ㄉㄧˋ ㄉㄨㄥˋ)
a hole in the ground; a burrow

地動(ㄉㄧˋ ㄉㄨㄥˋ)
an earthquake

地頭(ㄉㄧˋ ㄊㄡˊ)
a place; a locality: 他地頭熟，聯絡方便。He knows the place well, so he can easily make contact there.

地頭蛇(ㄉㄧˋ ㄊㄡˊ ㄕㄜˊ)

〔土部〕

〔土部〕

an influential gangster in a community; a local villain

地攤(ㄉㄧˋ ㄊㄢ)
a stall with goods displaying on the ground for sale: 他在台北擺地攤。He sells articles displayed on sidewalk floor in Taipei.

地毯(ㄉㄧˋ ㄊㄢˇ)
a carpet or rug: 地板上舖着地毯。The floor is covered with a carpet.

地毯轟炸(ㄉㄧˋ ㄊㄢˇ ㄏㄨㄥ ㄓㄚˋ)
carpet bombing

地圖(ㄉㄧˋ ㄊㄨˊ)
a map

地圖判讀(ㄉㄧˋ ㄊㄨˊ ㄆㄢˋ ㄉㄨˊ)
map reading

地雷(ㄉㄧˋ ㄌㄟˊ)
a land mine: 埋地雷to plant (or lay) mines

地牢(ㄉㄧˋ ㄌㄠˊ)
a dungeon

地老天荒(ㄉㄧˋ ㄌㄠˇ ㄊㄧㄢ ㄏㄨㄤ)
(said of love) to outlast even the heaven and the earth

地理(ㄉㄧˋ ㄌㄧˇ)
① geographical characteristics of a place: 我們熟悉地理民情。We are familiar with the place and its people. ② geography

地理環境(ㄉㄧˋ ㄌㄧˇ ㄏㄨㄢˊ ㄐㄧㄥˋ)
geographical conditions

地理學(ㄉㄧˋ ㄌㄧˇ ㄒㄩㄝˊ)
geography: 我喜歡地理學和歷史學。I like geography and history.

地理位置(ㄉㄧˋ ㄌㄧˇ ㄨㄟˋ ㄓˋ)
a geographical position

地力(ㄉㄧˋ ㄌㄧˋ)
land productivity

地利(ㄉㄧˋ ㄌㄧˋ)
① geographical advantages ② land productivity

地瓜(ㄉㄧˋ ㄍㄨㄚ)
sweet potatoes

地殼(ㄉㄧˋ ㄎㄜˊ)
the crust of the earth

地殼變動(ㄉㄧˋ ㄎㄜˊ ㄅㄧㄢˋ ㄉㄨㄥˋ)
diastrophism

地殼運動(ㄉㄧˋ ㄎㄜˊ ㄩㄣˋ ㄉㄨㄥˋ)
crustal movement

地炕(ㄉㄧˋ ㄎㄤˋ)
a brick bed warmed by a

---

fire underneath (in North China)

地黃(ㄉㄧˋ ㄏㄨㄤˊ)or 地髓(ㄉㄧˋ ㄙㄨㄟˇ)
a foxglove (*Rehmannia glutinosa*)

地基(ㄉㄧˋ ㄐㄧ)
the foundation of a building

地價(ㄉㄧˋ ㄐㄧㄚˋ)
a land price

地價稅(ㄉㄧˋ ㄐㄧㄚˋ ㄕㄨㄟˋ)
land tax

地界(ㄉㄧˋ ㄐㄧㄝˋ)
the border of a piece of land; the borderland

地角天涯(ㄉㄧˋ ㄐㄧㄠˇ ㄊㄧㄢ ㄧㄚˊ)
the farthest end of the earth

地窖(ㄉㄧˋ ㄐㄧㄠˋ)
a cellar; an underground vault: 他把食物貯藏在地窖裡。He stored food in the cellar.

地盡其利(ㄉㄧˋ ㄐㄧㄣˋ ㄑㄧˊ ㄌㄧˋ)
Land should be fully utilized.

地氣(ㄉㄧˋ ㄑㄧˋ)
① a climate ② a subtle essence that supposedly animates the earth

地契(ㄉㄧˋ ㄑㄧˋ)or 地券(ㄉㄧˋ ㄑㄩㄢˋ)
a title deed for landholdings

地球(ㄉㄧˋ ㄑㄧㄡˊ)
the earth; the globe

地球科學(ㄉㄧˋ ㄑㄧㄡˊ ㄎㄜ ㄒㄩㄝˊ)
geoscience

地球儀(ㄉㄧˋ ㄑㄧㄡˊ ㄧˊ)
a terrestrial globe

地球物理學(ㄉㄧˋ ㄑㄧㄡˊ ㄨˋ ㄌㄧˇ ㄒㄩㄝˊ)
geophysics

地錢(ㄉㄧˋ ㄑㄧㄢˊ)
(botany) hepatica

地勤(ㄉㄧˋ ㄑㄧㄣˊ)
(aeronautics) ground service

地區(ㄉㄧˋ ㄑㄩ)
an area; a region; a zone: 熱帶地區最適宜種香蕉。The tropical area is most suitable for growing bananas.

地權(ㄉㄧˋ ㄑㄩㄢˊ)
the right to land; landownership

地峽(ㄉㄧˋ ㄒㄧㄚˊ)
an isthmus

地下(ㄉㄧˋ ㄒㄧㄚˋ)
① underground; subterranean: 礦工們在地下工作。Miners work underground.

---

② in the grave ③ on the ground

地下道(ㄉㄧˋ ㄒㄧㄚˋ ㄉㄠˋ)
a tunnel; a subway

地下鐵(道)(ㄉㄧˋ ㄒㄧㄚˋ ㄊㄧㄝˇ (ㄉㄠˋ))
an underground railroad; the subway: 我們乘地下鐵到住宅區去。We subwayed uptown.

地下工作(ㄉㄧˋ ㄒㄧㄚˋ ㄍㄨㄥ ㄗㄨㄛˋ)
underground activities; cloak-and-dagger operation: 陰謀者從事地下工作。Plotters work underground.

地下街(ㄉㄧˋ ㄒㄧㄚˋ ㄐㄧㄝ)
an underground center

地下莖(ㄉㄧˋ ㄒㄧㄚˋ ㄐㄧㄥ)
(botany) rhizome; rootstock

地下錢莊(ㄉㄧˋ ㄒㄧㄚˋ ㄑㄧㄢˊ ㄓㄨㄤ)
illegal banks; wildcat banking houses

地下室(ㄉㄧˋ ㄒㄧㄚˋ ㄕˋ)
a basement: 地下室很潮濕。is rather damp in the basement.

地下商場(ㄉㄧˋ ㄒㄧㄚˋ ㄕㄤ ㄔㄤˇ)or (ㄉㄧˋ ㄒㄧㄚˋ ㄔㄤˇ ㄔㄤˇ)
a marketplace built below the ground; basement shops

地下水(ㄉㄧˋ ㄒㄧㄚˋ ㄕㄨㄟˇ)
ground water

地下舞廳(ㄉㄧˋ ㄒㄧㄚˋ ㄨˇ ㄊㄧㄥˊ)
unlicensed cabarets

地心(ㄉㄧˋ ㄒㄧㄣ)
the earth core; the center of the earth

地心吸力(ㄉㄧˋ ㄒㄧㄣ ㄒㄧ ㄌㄧˋ)
gravity; the gravitation of the earth

地形(ㄉㄧˋ ㄒㄧㄥˊ)
topography; terrain: 地形佔越the topographical advantages

地形學(ㄉㄧˋ ㄒㄧㄥˊ ㄒㄩㄝˊ)
geomorphology

地支(ㄉㄧˋ ㄓ)
the twelve Terrestrial Branches used in calculation with the Celestial Stems (天干) to designate years, months, days and hours

地質(ㄉㄧˋ ㄓˊ)
geology

地質學(ㄉㄧˋ ㄓˊ ㄒㄩㄝˊ)
geology

地址(ㄉㄧˋ ㄓˇ)
the address of a place; a location: 他已改變地址。He

has changed his address.

志 or 地誌(ㄉㄧ ㄓ)
topography; district history (recording geography and historic sites)

地軸(ㄉㄧ ㄓㄨˊ)
the axis of the earth

地震(ㄉㄧ ㄓㄣˋ)
earthquakes; seism: 臺灣時遭地震危害。Taiwan often suffers from earthquakes.

地震強度(ㄉㄧ ㄓㄣˋ ㄑㄧㄤˊ ㄉㄨˋ)
earthquake intensity

地震區(ㄉㄧ ㄓㄣˋ ㄑㄩ)
a seismic area

地震學(ㄉㄧ ㄓㄣˋ ㄒㄩㄝˊ)
seismology

地震儀(ㄉㄧ ㄓㄣˋ ㄧˊ)
a seismograph or seismometer

地政局(ㄉㄧ ㄓㄥˋ ㄐㄩˊ)
the Bureau of Land Administration

地政學(ㄉㄧ ㄓㄥˋ ㄒㄩㄝˊ)
geopolitics

地主(ㄉㄧ ㄓㄨˇ)
① a host ② a landowner or landlord: 地主極力保護有關土地所有權的利益。The land-owners did their best to protect their landowning interests.

地主國(ㄉㄧ ㄓㄨˇ ㄍㄨㄛˊ)
the host country

地主之誼(ㄉㄧ ㄓㄨˇ ㄓ ㄧˋ)
the friendship or hospitality of a host: 如果你能來，我當盡地主之誼。I'll perform the duties of the host if you can come.

地中海(ㄉㄧ ㄓㄨㄥ ㄏㄞˇ)
the Mediterranean Sea

地產(ㄉㄧ ㄔㄢˇ)
landed property; real estate: 他做地產生意。He is engaged in real estate business.

地沉(ㄉㄧ ㄔㄣˊ)
(geography) ground sinking

地勢(ㄉㄧ ㄕˋ)
topography; terrain: 此處地勢險要。The terrain is strategically situated and difficult of access here.

地上權(ㄉㄧ ㄕㄤˋ ㄑㄩㄢˊ)
(law) the right to use another's land for building or farming purposes

地熱(ㄉㄧ ㄖㄜˋ)
subterranean heat; geothermal energy

地租(ㄉㄧ ㄗㄨ)
land rent; the rent of a piece of land

地層(ㄉㄧ ㄘㄥˊ)
(geology) a stratum of earth; a single layer of sedimentary rock, representing the deposition of a single geological period

地層學(ㄉㄧ ㄘㄥˊ ㄒㄩㄝˊ)
stratigraphy

地位(ㄉㄧ ㄨㄟˋ)
the ranking or position (of a person): 政治地位 political position

地域(ㄉㄧ ㄩˋ)
① boundaries of a piece of land ② a region

地域觀念(ㄉㄧ ㄩˋ ㄍㄨㄢ ㄋㄧㄢˋ)
regionalism

地獄(ㄉㄧ ㄩˋ)
hell; Hades; the inferno

地緣政治學(ㄉㄧ ㄩㄢˊ ㄓㄥˋ ㄓˋ ㄒㄩㄝˊ)
geopolitics

四畫

【坊】 811
ㄈㄤ fang fāng
1. a community; a subdivision of a city; a neighborhood; a city quarter; a street; a lane
2. a workshop of a trade; a mill: 染坊 a dyer's workshop 磨坊 a flour mill
3. an arch-like memorial building: 貞節牌坊 a chastity arch

坊本(ㄈㄤ ㄅㄣˇ)
a block-printed edition issued by a bookshop

坊間(ㄈㄤ ㄐㄧㄢ)
on the market (especially referring to the bookshops); in the streets; city quarters

坊肆(ㄈㄤ ㄙˋ)
shops

【圾】 812
ㄙㄜ seh sè
garbage; refuse; waste: 把那些垃圾丟掉。Throw the waste away.

【址】 813
ㄓˇ jyy zhǐ
1. land on which to build a house; a location; a site: 校址 a school compound; a

campus
2. a foundation

【坂】 814
ㄅㄢˇ baan bǎn
a slope; a hillside 參看「阪」

【均】 815
ㄐㄩㄣ jiun jūn
1. equal; equally; even; level: 他為勞逸不均而埋怨。He complained of the uneven allocation of work.
2. to be fair
3. all; also; too: 一切相關事宜均已就緒。All things concerned have been completed.
4. a potter's wheel
5. an ancient musical instrument

均(ㄐㄩㄣ)
on an average; even

均分(ㄐㄩㄣ ㄈㄣ)
to divide equally; to allot equally

均等(ㄐㄩㄣ ㄉㄥˇ)
equality; equal; impartial; fair: 人的能力並非均等。All men are not equal in ability.

均攤(ㄐㄩㄣ ㄊㄢ)
to share (an expenses etc.) equally: 他們均攤旅行費用。They shared equally the travel expenses.

均可(ㄐㄩㄣ ㄎㄜˇ)
all can; also can; either will do; all permissible or passable

均衡(ㄐㄩㄣ ㄏㄥˊ)
equality; balance (of power, etc.); equilibrium; balanced; proportionate; harmonious

均權(ㄐㄩㄣ ㄑㄩㄢˊ)
the equality of rights

均權制(ㄐㄩㄣ ㄑㄩㄢˊ ㄓˋ)
a political system envisioned by Dr. Sun Yat-sen which underlines the division of powers between the central and local governments

均質(ㄐㄩㄣ ㄓˊ)
homogenized; homogeneous

均沾 or 均霑(ㄐㄩㄣ ㄓㄢ)
to share the benefits, profits, etc. equally

均勢(ㄐㄩㄣ ㄕˋ)
the balance of power; equilibrium

均一(ㄐㄩㄣ ㄧ)
uniform; equal; homogene-

ous

均匀(ㄐㄩㄣ ㄩㄣˊ)
even (blending, etc.); uniform; well-distributed

816

【坍】ㄊㄢ tan tān
sliding of earth (as in a landslide); to fall into ruins; to collapse; to tumble

坍方(ㄊㄢ ㄈㄤ)
a landslide; a landslip; to cave in; to collapse

坍塌(ㄊㄢ ㄊㄚ)
to collapse; to cave in: 大雨使屋頂坍塌。 The heavy rain caused the roof to collapse.

坍臺(ㄊㄢ ㄊㄞˊ)
① to expose one's weakness before the public ② to let someone down

817

【坎】ㄎㄢˇ kaan kǎn
1. a pit; a hole; a depression
2. one of the Eight Diagrams in the *Book of Changes*
3. the sound of percussion
4. a snare; a danger; a crisis

坎培拉(ㄎㄢˇ ㄆㄟˊ ㄌㄚ)
Canberra, the capital of Australia

坎坷(ㄎㄢˇ ㄎㄜˇ)
① unlucky; bad luck ② (said of the road) rough; bumpy; rugged: 這是一條坎坷不平的路。 This is a rough and bumpy road.

坎坷一生(ㄎㄢˇ ㄎㄜˇ ㄧ ㄕㄥ)
a lifetime of frustrations

坎坑(ㄎㄢˇ ㄎㄥ)
a pit in the ground

坎肩兒(ㄎㄢˇ ㄐㄧㄢ ㄦ)
a sleeveless jacket or coat

坎穽 or 坎阱(ㄎㄢˇ ㄐㄧㄥˇ)
a snare; a trap

818

【坐】ㄗㄨㄛˋ tzuoh zuò
1. to sit; a seat: 請坐。 Please sit down.
2. to ride (on a bus, train, etc.): 我常坐飛機到日本。 I often go to Japan by plane.
3. to kneel
4. to reach; to arrive at
5. (said of a building) to have its back toward
6. to get (profit, etc.) without work
7. to keep on; to persist in

8. (said of a building) to fall back from pressure; to sink: 這堵牆往後坐了。 The wall is beginning to give backwards.
9. (said of gun, etc.) to recoil; to kick: 這大砲的後坐力不小。 This cannon kicks badly.
10. to be accused of a crime; to be punished 參看「反坐」
11. owing to; because of

坐標(ㄗㄨㄛˋ ㄅㄧㄠ)
(mathematics) coordinates

坐不下(ㄗㄨㄛˋ ㄅㄨˋ ㄒㄧㄚˋ)
unable to seat oneself—not enough sitting room for the people present

坐不住(ㄗㄨㄛˋ ㄅㄨˋ ㄓㄨˋ)
can not stay long; can not sit still; restless: 聽說英文不及格，他再也坐不住。 When he was told that he failed in English, he could not stay any longer.

坐不穩(ㄗㄨㄛˋ ㄅㄨˋ ㄨㄣˇ)
① cannot sit steady ② (said of a defective chair) unsteady

坐法(ㄗㄨㄛˋ ㄈㄚˇ)
to be sentenced to imprison for breaking the law

坐大(ㄗㄨㄛˋ ㄉㄚˋ)
to emerge big and strong (usually said of an aggressor who could have been stopped when he was weak)

坐等(ㄗㄨㄛˋ ㄉㄥˇ)
to sit back and wait

坐地(ㄗㄨㄛˋ ㄉㄧˋ)
① to sit on the ground ② to do something on the spot; on the spot

坐地分贓(ㄗㄨㄛˋ ㄉㄧˋ ㄈㄣ ㄗㄤ)
to divide the loot on the spot

坐墊(ㄗㄨㄛˋ ㄉㄧㄢˋ)
a seat cushion: 地板上有好幾個坐墊。 There are several cushions on the floor.

坐定(ㄗㄨㄛˋ ㄉㄧㄥˋ)
to be seated

坐牢(ㄗㄨㄛˋ ㄌㄠˊ)
to be jailed or imprisoned; to be shut behind the bars

坐冷板凳(ㄗㄨㄛˋ ㄌㄥˇ ㄅㄢˇ ㄉㄥˋ)
① to hold a position with little or no power ② to be

out in the cold

坐力(ㄗㄨㄛˋ ㄌㄧˋ)
the force of recoil

坐立不安(ㄗㄨㄛˋ ㄌㄧˋ ㄅㄨˋ ㄢ)
fidgety; restless; to feel uneasy whether sitting or standing; to fidget: 什麼事你坐立不安? What's fidgeting you?

坐落(ㄗㄨㄛˋ ㄌㄨㄛˋ)
(said of a house, building, etc.) to be located or situated at: 我們的學校坐落在山腳下。 Our school is located at the foot of a hill.

坐骨神經(ㄗㄨㄛˋ ㄍㄨˇ ㄕㄣˊ ㄐㄧㄥ)
the sciatic nerve

坐骨神經痛(ㄗㄨㄛˋ ㄍㄨˇ ㄕㄣˊ ㄐㄧㄥ ㄊㄨㄥˋ)
sciatica

坐觀成敗(ㄗㄨㄛˋ ㄍㄨㄢ ㄔㄥˊ ㄅㄞˋ)
to watch a struggle with detachment; to look on coldly; to be a mere onlooker

坐困(ㄗㄨㄛˋ ㄎㄨㄣˋ)
to be confined; to be walled in: 這些年來他坐困愁城。 He has been walled in with his own worries all these years.

坐化(ㄗㄨㄛˋ ㄏㄨㄚˋ)
(said of Buddhist monks) to die remaining seated cross-legged

坐懷不亂(ㄗㄨㄛˋ ㄏㄨㄞˊ ㄅㄨˋ ㄌㄨㄢˋ)
(literally) to retain presence of mind even with a beautiful woman sitting on the lap—to be immune from the temptation of feminine charms

坐騎(ㄗㄨㄛˋ ㄐㄧˊ)
one's horse for riding

坐轎(ㄗㄨㄛˋ ㄐㄧㄠˋ)
to travel by sedan chair

坐井觀天(ㄗㄨㄛˋ ㄐㄧㄥˇ ㄍㄨㄢ ㄊㄧㄢ)
(literally) to look at the sky from the bottom of a well—a very limited view, usually implying shortsightedness, ignorance, shallowness, etc.

坐席(ㄗㄨㄛˋ ㄒㄧˊ)
① to take one's seat at a banquet table ② a seat

坐下(ㄗㄨㄛˋ ㄒㄧㄚˋ)
to sit down 或 Sit down. 請坐下。 Sit down, please.

享其成(ㄒㄧㄤˇ ㄑㄧˊ ㄕㄥˊ)
to enjoy the fruit without toil; to enjoy the fruit of toil of others; to reap where one has not sown

—致(ㄓˋ)
to make (profit) without working for it

—鎮(ㄓㄣˋ)
personally take charge of (an operation or mission) —usually referring to an important official or general

—莊(ㄓㄨㄤ)
①(formerly) to be a resident agent for business firms ② to be the banker or dealer in a gambling game

吃山空(ㄔ ㄕㄢ ㄎㄨㄥ)
(literally) Sitting idle, one can consume even a mountain (of food, wealth, etc.). — One cannot live in security without a dependable source of income.

—車(ㄔㄜ)
by bus or train: 我每天坐車上學。 I go to school by bus every day.

—禪(ㄔㄢˊ)
(Buddhism) to sit in deep meditation

—船(ㄔㄨㄢˊ)
by boat or ship

失良機(ㄕ ㄌㄧㄤˊ ㄐㄧ)
to let a golden chance slip by

—視(ㄕˋ)
to keep hands off; to watch (others suffering or getting licked) without extending a helping hand

收漁利(ㄕㄡ ㄩˊ ㄌㄧˋ)
to reap the spoils of war without lifting a finger; to profit from others' conflict 亦作「坐收漁人之利」

山觀虎鬥(ㄕㄢ ㄍㄨㄢ ㄏㄨˇ ㄉㄡˋ)
(literally) to sit on the top of the mountain to watch the tigers fight—to stand by in safety while others fight, then profit at their expense when both sides are exhausted

—褥(ㄖㄨˋ)
a seat cushion

坐蓐(ㄗㄨㄛˋ ㄖㄨˋ)
(said of a woman) in labor

坐罪(ㄗㄨㄛˋ ㄗㄨㄟˋ)
to be punished for crimes committed; to punish or to sentence

坐次(ㄗㄨㄛˋ ㄘˋ)
the order of seats in a meeting or feast

坐以待斃(ㄗㄨㄛˋ ㄧˇ ㄉㄞˋ ㄅㄧˋ)
to do nothing to avert a crisis, peril, etc.; to await one's doom; to resign oneself to death

坐以待旦(ㄗㄨㄛˋ ㄧˇ ㄉㄞˋ ㄉㄢˋ)
to sit and waiting for the morning

坐臥不寧(ㄗㄨㄛˋ ㄨㄛˋ ㄅㄨˋ ㄋㄧㄥˊ)
to feel restless and uneasy; to be on tenterhooks 亦作「坐臥不安」:他坐臥不寧。 He felt restless.

坐位(ㄗㄨㄛˋ ㄨㄟˋ)
a place to sit; a seat: 請留幾個坐位給我們。 Please reserve some seats for us.

坐月子(ㄗㄨㄛˋ ㄩㄝˋ ˙ㄗ)
(said of a woman) to be confined; the month after a woman's childbirth

【坑】 819
ㄎㄥ keng kēng
1. a pit; a hole in the ground: 一個蘿蔔一個坑。 One radish, one hole.—Everyone has his own task.

2. to bury alive: 焚書坑儒 to burn books and bury scholars alive

3. to entrap

坑騙(ㄎㄥ ㄆㄧㄢˋ)
to cheat by tricks

坑道(ㄎㄥ ㄉㄠˋ)
a tunnel; a pit; an underground passage: 坑道工事 tunnel defenses

坑坑窪窪(ㄎㄥ ㄎㄥ ㄨㄚ ㄨㄚ)
(said of a road surface) full of bumps and holes

坑害(ㄎㄥ ㄏㄞˋ)
to lead into a trap; to entrap

坑殺(ㄎㄥ ㄕㄚ)
to bury alive

坑人(ㄎㄥ ㄖㄣˊ)
to entrap, ensnare or harm someone: 奸商坑人。 The profiteers entrapped people.

五畫

【坡】 820
ㄆㄛ po pō
a slope; a bank; a hillside: 陡坡 a steep slope 山坡 a foothill slope

坡地(ㄆㄛ ㄉㄧˋ)
hillside fields; sloping fields; the land on the slopes

坡度(ㄆㄛ ㄉㄨˋ)
the degree of a slope; grade

【坤】 821
ㄎㄨㄣ kuen kūn
1. one of the Eight Diagrams —earth
2. compliance; obedience
3. female; feminine

坤範(ㄎㄨㄣ ㄈㄢˋ)or 坤德(ㄎㄨㄣ ㄉㄜˊ)
① women's virtue ② an exemplary woman

坤伶(ㄎㄨㄣ ㄌㄧㄥˊ)or 坤角兒(ㄎㄨㄣ ㄐㄩㄝˊ ㄦ)
an actress of Peking opera: 坤伶生活 the life of an actress

坤戲(ㄎㄨㄣ ㄒㄧˋ)
a play with an entirely female cast

坤宅(ㄎㄨㄣ ㄓㄞˊ)
the home of the bride

坤輿(ㄎㄨㄣ ㄩˊ)
another name of the earth

【坦】 822
ㄊㄢˇ taan tǎn
1. wide and smooth; level
2. self-possessed; composed; calm; peaceful
3. frank; straightforward
4. a son-in-law
5. a Chinese family name

坦白(ㄊㄢˇ ㄅㄞˊ)
frank; honest; to tell the truth: 坦白對你說 to be frank with you; frankly speaking

坦腹東床(ㄊㄢˇ ㄈㄨˋ ㄉㄨㄥ ㄔㄨㄤˊ)
① an ideal son-in-law ② to lie in bed with a bare belly

坦蕩(ㄊㄢˇ ㄉㄤˋ)
① contented and composed; magnanimous ②(said of a road) broad and level

坦途(ㄊㄢˇ ㄊㄨˊ)
a level road; an easy path; a smooth ride (ahead): 為學之道, 既無捷徑, 亦無坦途。 There

〔土部〕

is neither shortcut nor easy way to the great achievement in learning.

坦干伊喀(ㄊㄢ ㄍㄢ ㄧ ㄎㄚ)
Tanganyika

坦克車(ㄊㄢ ㄎㄜ ㄔㄜ)or 坦克(ㄊㄢ ㄎㄜ)
a tank (an armored vehicle)

坦吉爾(ㄊㄢ ㄐㄧ ㄦ)
Tangier, a seaport in Northwest Africa

坦胸露背(ㄊㄢ ㄒㄩㄥ ㄌㄨ ㄅㄟ)
(said of women wearing plunging neckline dresses) exposing chest and back

坦直(ㄊㄢ ㄓ)
straightforward

坦率(ㄊㄢ ㄕㄨㄞ)
frank; straightforward; blunt; bluntly: 他爲人坦率。He is frank and open.

坦然(ㄊㄢ ㄖㄢ)
self-possessed; calm; peaceful in mind; fearless; fully at ease: 坦然自若 calm and confident

坦桑尼亞(ㄊㄢ ㄙㄤ ㄋㄧ ㄧㄚ)
Tanzania

坦夷(ㄊㄢ ㄧ)
①level and broad ②peaceful and calm

【坷】 823
ㄎㄜ kee kě
1. bad luck; unfortunate
2. rugged, uneven (roads, etc.)

【坼】 824
ㄔㄜ cheh chè
1. to crack
2. to chap; to tear, to rip open

【坳】 825
ㄠ aw ào
a hollow in the ground; a cavity

坳堂(ㄠ ㄊㄤ)
a hollow in the ground

【垂】 826
ㄔㄨㄟ chwei chuí
1. to hang down; to let fall
2. to hand down; to leave a name in history: 他名垂青史。He left his name in history.
3. nearly; almost; approaching
4. to condescend

垂面(ㄔㄨㄟ ㄇㄧㄢ)
a perpendicular plane

垂名(ㄔㄨㄟ ㄇㄧㄥ)
to leave name for future generations

垂暮(ㄔㄨㄟ ㄇㄨ)
dusk; towards sunset

垂暮之年(ㄔㄨㄟ ㄇㄨ ㄓ ㄋㄧㄢ)
in one's old age

垂髮(ㄔㄨㄟ ㄈㄚˇ)or 垂髫(ㄔㄨㄟ ㄊㄧㄠ)
young children; early childhood

垂釣(ㄔㄨㄟ ㄉㄧㄠ)
to fish with a hook and line; to go fishing

垂頭(ㄔㄨㄟ ㄊㄡ)
to hang one's head

垂頭喪氣(ㄔㄨㄟ ㄊㄡ ㄙㄤ ㄑㄧ)
to be crestfallen; to be downcast; to be greatly discouraged or disappointed: 他經常垂頭喪氣。He is always downcast in spirit.

垂念(ㄔㄨㄟ ㄋㄧㄢ)
so gracious as to remember me

垂老(ㄔㄨㄟ ㄌㄠˇ)
to be nearly or almost old; (with) one's old age approaching; (in) declining years

垂柳(ㄔㄨㄟ ㄌㄧㄡˇ)or 垂楊(ㄔㄨㄟ ㄧㄤˊ)
a weeping willow

垂憐(ㄔㄨㄟ ㄌㄧㄢˊ)
to have pity on somebody

垂簾聽政(ㄔㄨㄟ ㄌㄧㄢˊ ㄊㄧㄥ ㄓㄥˋ)
(said of an empress dowager) to administer state affairs behind a bamboo screen; to hold court from behind a screen; power-behind-the-throne

垂青(ㄔㄨㄟ ㄑㄧㄥ)
to give preferential treatment; to bestow favors: 得蒙垂青，不勝感激。I greatly thank you for the favors you bestowed on me.

垂涎(ㄔㄨㄟ ㄒㄧㄢˊ)or 垂涎三尺
(ㄔㄨㄟ ㄒㄧㄢˊ ㄙㄢ ㄔˇ)or 垂涎欲滴
(ㄔㄨㄟ ㄒㄧㄢˊ ㄩˋ ㄉㄧ)
to drool; to yearn for; to covet; to lust for: 千萬不要垂涎財富和權利。Never covet wealth and power.

垂詢(ㄔㄨㄟ ㄒㄩㄣˊ)
to deign to inquire into; to make gracious inquiries

垂直(ㄔㄨㄟ ㄓˊ)
perpendicular; vertical

垂直面(ㄔㄨㄟ ㄓˊ ㄇㄧㄢˋ)
a vertical plane

垂直距離(ㄔㄨㄟ ㄓˊ ㄐㄩˋ ㄌㄧˊ)
a perpendicular distance

垂直線(ㄔㄨㄟ ㄓˊ ㄒㄧㄢˋ)
a vertical line

垂成(ㄔㄨㄟ ㄔㄥˊ)
drawing close to a successful conclusion; to be approaching success or completion

垂手(ㄔㄨㄟ ㄕㄡˇ)
to let the hands hang by the sides: 他垂手站著。He stood with his hands at his sides.

垂手可得(ㄔㄨㄟ ㄕㄡˇ ㄎㄜˇ ㄉㄜˊ)
to get it with hands down—easy to obtain or get 參見【唾手可得】

垂死(ㄔㄨㄟ ㄙˇ)
at the point of death; dying

垂愛(ㄔㄨㄟ ㄞˋ)
to show gracious concern for (me)

垂危(ㄔㄨㄟ ㄨㄟˊ)
(said of an illness or situation) to be in imminent danger or in a precarious state

【垃】 827
ㄌㄜ leh lè
garbage, refuse and waste

垃圾(ㄌㄜ ㄙㄜ)
garbage; refuse

垃圾焚化爐(ㄌㄜ ㄙㄜ ㄈㄣˊ ㄏㄨㄚˋ ㄌㄨˊ)
a refuse incinerator

垃圾堆(ㄌㄜ ㄙㄜ ㄉㄨㄟ)or 垃圾場
(ㄌㄜ ㄙㄜ ㄔㄤˇ)
a rubbish heap; a garbage heap; a refuse dump

垃圾桶(ㄌㄜ ㄙㄜ ㄊㄨㄥˇ)
a dustbin

垃圾箱(ㄌㄜ ㄙㄜ ㄒㄧㄤ)
a garbage container; a garbage can; an ash can

垃圾車(ㄌㄜ ㄙㄜ ㄔㄜ)
a collection truck

【坪】 828
ㄆㄧㄥˊ pyng píng
1. a level piece of ground: 草坪 a lawn 停機坪 an aircraft park
2. (in Japanese measurement) an area of 6 feet square

六畫

【垠】 829
ㄧㄣˊ yn yín

the bank (of a stream)
. a boundary; a limit: 一望無垠 to extend as far as the eye can see

【垓】 830
《ㄞ gai gāi
. far and remote places; wilds beyond the frontier
. a boundary; a limit
. a hundred million

垓下 (ㄍㄞ ㄒㄧㄚˋ)
name of a place, southeast of today's Linpi County (靈璧縣) of Anhwei Province (安徽省), where the first emperor of the Han Dynasty beat Hsiang Yü (項羽) in a decisive battle

【垢】 831
《ㄡ gow gòu
. dirt; filth; stains: 蓬頭垢面 with disheveled hair and a dirty face
. shame; disgrace: 含辱忍垢 to endure disgrace and humiliations; (to be forced) to swallow insults
. (figuratively) evildoers

垢膩 (《ㄡˋ ㄋㄧ) or 垢泥 (《ㄡˋ ㄋㄧˊ)
dirt and grease on human skin; skin excrement and dirt

垢穢 (《ㄡˋ ㄏㄨㄟˋ)
dirty

【型】 832
ㄒㄧㄥˊ shyng xíng
. an earthen mold for casting
. a model; a pattern; a standard: 我買了一艘船的模型給他。I bought him a model of a ship.
. a statute; a law
. a style; a fashion; a type

【垮】 833
ㄎㄨㄚˇ koa kuǎ
. to topple; to collapse: 這堵牆要垮了。The wall is going to collapse.
. to wear down
. to put to rout: 我們決心打垮敵人。We are determined to put the enemy to rout.
. to fall (out of power)

垮臺 (ㄎㄨㄚˇ ㄊㄞˊ)
the fall (of a government, administration, organization, project, person, etc.)；collapse

七畫

【埋】 834
1. ㄇㄞˊ mai mái
1. to bury: 雪把整個山谷埋起來了。The whole valley is buried in snow.
2. to secrete; to lie in wait

埋沒 (ㄇㄞˊ ㄇㄛˋ)
①to conceal from recognition; to bury (one's talents, etc.); to neglect; to stifle: 埋沒人才 to stifle real talents ②to submerge

埋名 (ㄇㄞˊ ㄇㄧㄥˊ)
to conceal one's name; to live incognito

埋伏 (ㄇㄞˊ ㄈㄨˊ)
an ambush; to ambush; to lie in wait: 他們中了埋伏。They fell into an ambush.

埋頭苦幹 (ㄇㄞˊ ㄊㄡˊ ㄎㄨˇ ㄍㄢˋ)
to bury one's head (in studying); to work with all-out effort (while ignoring others' comments)

埋骨 (ㄇㄞˊ ㄍㄨˇ)
①to bury one's remains ②to die: 埋骨沙場 to die on the battlefield

埋葬 (ㄇㄞˊ ㄗㄤˋ)
to bury (a corpse)

埋藏 (ㄇㄞˊ ㄘㄤˊ)
to hide; to conceal; to bury (a treasure, weapons, etc.)

【埋】 834
2. ㄇㄢˊ man mán
參看「埋怨」

埋怨 (ㄇㄢˊ ㄩㄢ)
to blame; to grumble; to complain; complaint: 他的話有埋怨之意。There was a note of complaint in what he said.

【城】 835
ㄔㄥˊ cherng chéng
1. a city; a town: 全城的人都知道這事。The whole town knows of it.
2. the walls of a city; to surround a city with walls

城北徐公 (ㄔㄥˊ ㄅㄟˇ ㄒㄩˊ ㄍㄨㄥ)
a handsome young man

城堡 (ㄔㄥˊ ㄅㄠˇ)
a fort; a castle

城邦 (ㄔㄥˊ ㄅㄤ)
a city-state

城門 (ㄔㄥˊ ㄇㄣˊ)
the gate of a city wall

城門 (ㄔㄥˊ ㄇㄣˊ)
battlements of a city wall; towers over city gates; towers over the wall

城門失火，殃及池魚 (ㄔㄥˊ ㄇㄣˊ ㄕ ㄏㄨㄛˇ，ㄧㄤ ㄐㄧˊ ㄔˊ ㄩˊ)
to suffer from other's disaster; to be a scapegoat

城府很深 (ㄔㄥˊ ㄈㄨˇ ㄏㄣˇ ㄕㄣ)
(said of one's mind) shrewd and deep

城堞 (ㄔㄥˊ ㄉㄧㄝˊ)
battlements

城頭 (ㄔㄥˊ ㄊㄡˊ)
the top of the city wall

城樓 (ㄔㄥˊ ㄌㄡˊ)
a tower on the city wall

城裏人 (ㄔㄥˊ ㄌㄧˇ ㄖㄣˊ)
urbanites; townsfolk; city dwellers

城郭 (ㄔㄥˊ ㄍㄨㄛ)
the inner and outer city walls

城河 (ㄔㄥˊ ㄏㄜˊ) or 城壕 (ㄔㄥˊ ㄏㄠˊ)
the moat of a city; the canal around the city wall

城狐社鼠 (ㄔㄥˊ ㄏㄨˊ ㄕㄜˋ ㄕㄨˇ)
(literally) foxes in the city walls and rats on the altars —evildoers who have some influential people to fall back upon

城隍廟 (ㄔㄥˊ ㄏㄨㄤˊ ㄇㄧㄠˋ)
a temple for the city god

城牆 (ㄔㄥˊ ㄑㄧㄤˊ)
the city wall

城區 (ㄔㄥˊ ㄑㄩ)
the city proper

城闕 (ㄔㄥˊ ㄑㄩㄝˋ)
①the watch towers over city gates ②a palace

城下之盟 (ㄔㄥˊ ㄒㄧㄚˋ ㄓ ㄇㄥˊ)
to sign a humiliating treaty after a crushing defeat or when the military situation has become hopeless

城鎮 (ㄔㄥˊ ㄓㄣˋ)
cities and towns

城池 (ㄔㄥˊ ㄔˊ)
the city wall and moat

城市 (ㄔㄥˊ ㄕˋ)
a city or town

城市規劃 (ㄔㄥˊ ㄕˋ ㄍㄨㄟ ㄏㄨㄚˋ)
city planning 亦作「都市規劃」

（土部）

【埂】 836 《ㄥˇ geeng gěng
1. a pit; a cave
2. an irrigation ditch
3. a low bank of earth between fields: 田埂 footpaths between the fields

【埃】 837 ㄞ ai āi
1. fine dust
2. Egypt
埃及 (ㄞ ㄐㄧˊ)
Egypt
埃及人 (ㄞ ㄐㄧˊ ㄖㄣˊ)
an Egyptian

【埔】 838 ㄅㄨˇ puu pǔ
1. a plain; an arena
2. a port; a mart

八畫

【培】 839 ㄆㄟˊ peir péi
1. to bank up with earth
2. to nourish; to strengthen; to cultivate; to foster: 他正在栽培玫瑰. He is cultivating roses.
培堆 (ㄆㄟˊ ㄎㄞ)
a small hill
培根 (ㄆㄟˊ ㄍㄣ)
① Francis Bacon, 1561-1626, British philosopher ② bacon
培植 (ㄆㄟˊ ㄓˊ)
① to plant; to grow (plants); to bank up with earth ② to educate or train; to foster
培養 (ㄆㄟˊ ㄧㄤˇ)
① to cultivate by banking up; to grow (plants) ② to raise (kids) ③ to cultivate (one's mind); to educate ④ culture: 培養細菌 the culture of bacteria
培養土 (ㄆㄟˊ ㄧㄤˇ ㄊㄨˇ)
specially fertilized earth for pot plants
培養基 (ㄆㄟˊ ㄧㄤˇ ㄐㄧ)
a culture medium (for growing bacteria in a laboratory)
培育 (ㄆㄟˊ ㄩˋ)
to cultivate and grow; to raise; to breed: 他們努力培育稻米新品種. They try hard to breed new varieties of rice.

【域】 840 ㄩˋ yuh yù
1. a frontier; a boundary
2. a region; a country; an area
3. to live; to stay
域外 (ㄩˋ ㄨㄞˋ)
beyond the frontier; a foreign country; outside China

【埠】 841 ㄅㄨˋ buh bù
1. a harbor; a port; a pier: 船在天亮時進埠. The ship entered port at dawn.
2. a mart on the bank of a river or seacoast
埠頭 (ㄅㄨˋ ㄊㄡˊ)
a wharf; a port

【埤】 842 ㄆㄧˊ pyi pí
1. a low wall; a parapet
2. an increase; increasingly; to add to
埤益 (ㄆㄧˊ ㄧˋ)
to increase

【埤】 842 ㄅㄟˋ bei bèi
low-lying
埤污 (ㄆㄧˊ ㄨ)
(said of one's personality) mean

【執】 843 ㄓˊ jyr zhí
1. to hold; to grasp; to seize
2. to detain; to arrest
3. to maintain or uphold (a principle, etc.); to hold on stubbornly to; to stick to; to persist in: 各執己見. Each stuck to his own view.
4. to shut (gossipers, etc.) up
5. a Chinese family name
執筆 (ㄓˊ ㄅㄧˇ)
to write
執鞭 (ㄓˊ ㄅㄧㄢ)
to act as a coach driver for someone
執迷不悟 (ㄓˊ ㄇㄧˊ ㄅㄨˋ ㄨˋ)
to adhere stubbornly to errors; to hold on to wrong beliefs obstinately
執法 (ㄓˊ ㄈㄚˇ)
to enforce (or execute) the law
執法如山 (ㄓˊ ㄈㄚˇ ㄖㄨˊ ㄕㄢ)
to uphold the law strictly; to adhere to legal principles without letup or fear (usually referring to law-

enforcing officers or judges)
執紼 (ㄓˊ ㄈㄨˊ) or 執紼送喪 (ㄓˊ ㄈㄨˊ ㄙㄨㄥˋ ㄙㄤ)
to attend a funeral
執弟子禮 (ㄓˊ ㄉㄧˋ ㄗˇ ㄌㄧˇ)
to regard oneself as a pupil in dealing with somebody; one holds in high esteem
執牛耳 (ㄓˊ ㄋㄧㄡˊ ㄦˇ)
to play the leading role; to be in a dominant position
執禮 (ㄓˊ ㄌㄧˇ)
to stick to etiquette; to observe the formalities (of weddings, master-pupil relationships, etc.)
執兩用中 (ㄓˊ ㄌㄧㄤˇ ㄩㄥˋ ㄓㄨㄥ)
to listen to both sides of opinions and determine from them the course of the Mean
執柯 (ㄓˊ ㄎㄜ)
to be a matchmaker
執箕帚 (ㄓˊ ㄐㄧ ㄓㄡˇ)
to become someone's wife (polite expression)
執教 (ㄓˊ ㄐㄧㄠˋ)
to be a teacher
執經問難 (ㄓˊ ㄐㄧㄥ ㄨㄣˋ ㄋㄢˊ)
to hold the classics and make inquiries
執行 (ㄓˊ ㄒㄧㄥˊ)
to execute (an order); to carry out; to implement
執行秘書 (ㄓˊ ㄒㄧㄥˊ ㄇㄧˋ ㄕㄨ)
an executive secretary
執行死刑 (ㄓˊ ㄒㄧㄥˊ ㄙˇ ㄒㄧㄥˊ)
to carry out a death sentence; to execute a death convict
執行委員 (ㄓˊ ㄒㄧㄥˊ ㄨㄟˇ ㄩㄢˊ)
administrative officers; the persons appointed by a ruling party or an assembly to carry out their decisions; the members of an executive committee
執照 (ㄓˊ ㄓㄠˋ)
a license; a permit: 你得攜帶駕駛執照. You have to carry your driver's license.
執掌 (ㄓˊ ㄓㄤˇ)
to take full charge of; to manage; to superintend; to wield
執政 (ㄓˊ ㄓㄥˋ)
to be in power; to hold the

reins of the government

政執黨(㆞ㄓㄓㄞ)
the party in power; the ruling party

執著(ㄓㄜ)
inflexible; to persist in

執中(ㄓㄨㄥ)
to follow the middle road; to keep to the golden mean; impartial 亦作「允執厥中」

執事(ㄓㄕ)
①an errand man ②a salutation to the other party in correspondence; Sir; you ③(Christianity) a church officer; a deacon

執手(ㄓㄕㄡ)
to hold hands

執拗(ㄓㄋㄧㄡ)
persistent; stubbornly recalcitrant

執意(ㄓㄧ)
to stick to one's own view; to hold on stubbornly to one's own ideas; to insist on

執業(ㄓㄧㄝ)
①to engage in a profession or trade ②a vocation or trade

執友(ㄓㄧㄡ)
a bosom friend; friends of the same circle 亦作「摯友」

執言(ㄓㄧㄢ)
to make positive assertions

【基】 844
ㄐㄧ jī

1. a foundation; a base: 他們正在興建壩基。 They are building the base of a dam.
2. an origin; a basis; a root: 農民是國家的基。 The farmers form the basis of a nation.
3. on the basis of; according to; on the strength of
4. a group; the base of a chemical compound

基本(ㄐㄧㄅㄣ)
①a root, foundation or base ②fundamental; basic; elementary ③basically; on the whole; by and large: 這場音樂會基本上是好的。 This concert is good on the whole.

基本單位(ㄐㄧㄅㄣㄉㄢㄨㄟ)
fundamental units

基本工資(ㄐㄧㄅㄣㄍㄨㄥㄗ)
basic wages

基本結構(ㄐㄧㄅㄣㄐㄧㄝㄍㄡ)
primary structure

基本金(ㄐㄧㄅㄣㄐㄧㄣ)or 基金(ㄐㄧㄐㄧㄣ)
①a fund; an endowment fund ②subscribed capital

基本知識(ㄐㄧㄅㄣㄓㄕ)
elementary knowledge

基本原則(ㄐㄧㄅㄣㄩㄢㄗㄜ)
basic principles

基肥(ㄐㄧㄈㄟ)
main fertilization; fertilizers applied to soil before planting; ground fertilizer

基輔(ㄐㄧㄈㄨ)
Kiev, a Russian city

基地(ㄐㄧㄉㄧ)
a base (of operations): 軍事基地 a military base

基調(ㄐㄧㄉㄧㄠ)
①the central thought; the main theme ②(music) the keynote

基點(ㄐㄧㄉㄧㄢ)
①the basic point; the starting point; the center: 我們的外交政策要放在獨立的基點上。 Our diplomatic policy should rest on the basic point of independency. ②(survey) the base point (BP)

基督(ㄐㄧㄉㄨ)
Jesus Christ

基督徒(ㄐㄧㄉㄨㄊㄨ)
a Christian: 這村子裡有很多基督徒。 There were a lot of Christians in this village.

基督教(ㄐㄧㄉㄨㄐㄧㄠ)
Christianity (particularly referring to the Protestants)

基督教青年會(ㄐㄧㄉㄨㄐㄧㄠㄑㄧㄥㄋㄧㄢㄏㄨㄟ)
the Young Men's Christian Association (Y.M.C.A)

基多(ㄐㄧㄉㄨㄛ)
Quito, the capital of Ecuador

基尼(ㄐㄧㄋㄧ)
a guinea, a British monetary unit

基隆(ㄐㄧㄌㄨㄥ)
Keelung—the northern port city of Taiwan Province

基價(ㄐㄧㄐㄧㄚ)
a basic price

基金(ㄐㄧㄐㄧㄣ)
a reserve fund; a fund for specific use: 許多大學都有作研究用的基金。 Many universities have a reserve fund for research.

基金會(ㄐㄧㄐㄧㄣㄏㄨㄟ)
the board of directors of a fund; foundation

基準(ㄐㄧㄓㄨㄣ)
a pattern; a model; a standard; a rule

基礎(ㄐㄧㄔㄨ)
①the foundation of a building ②the basis or foundation of an argument, etc.: 他的誠實及工作熱誠是他成功的基礎。 His honesty and willingness to work are the foundations of his success.

基礎教育(ㄐㄧㄔㄨㄐㄧㄠㄩ)
elementary education

基石(ㄐㄧㄕ)
a foundation stone; a cornerstone

基數(ㄐㄧㄕㄨ)
cardinal numbers (any of the digits from 1 to 9)

基層(ㄐㄧㄘㄥ)
basic level; a grass-roots unit: 深入基層 to go down to the grass-roots units

基層單位(ㄐㄧㄘㄥㄉㄢㄨㄟ)
a basic unit; a unit at grass-roots level

基層選舉(ㄐㄧㄘㄥㄒㄩㄢㄐㄩ)
elections at basic level

基層組織(ㄐㄧㄘㄥㄗㄨㄓ)
①the basic structure or constitution of an organization ②the low-echelon organizations

基業(ㄐㄧㄧㄝ)
the initial achievements of an empire

基因(ㄐㄧㄧㄣ)
a gene: 顯性基因 a dominant gene

基於(ㄐㄧㄩ)
because of; in view of; on account of: 基於以上理由，我不採納他的意見。 In view of the above-mentioned reasons, I didn't take his opinion.

【堂】 845
ㄊㄤ táng

1. a hall; an office; a reception

〔土部〕

room: 講堂 a lecture room
2. a meeting place; a court of justice: 公堂 the court
3. a salutation for another's mother
4. an open level place on the hill
5. relatives born of the same grandfather
6. venerable; grave; imposing
7. a set: 一堂瓷器 a set of porcelains
8. a team or a group: 一堂鼓手 a team of drummers

堂伯叔(ㄊㄤˊ ㄅㄛˊ ㄕㄨ)
one's father's male first cousins of the same surname

堂堂(ㄊㄤˊ ㄊㄤˊ)
① dignified, venerable (appearances); impressive ② imposing; awe-inspiring; formidable

堂堂大國(ㄊㄤˊ ㄊㄤˊ ㄉㄚˋ ㄍㄨㄛˊ)
a powerful and civilized great country

堂堂正正(ㄊㄤˊ ㄊㄤˊ ㄓㄥˋ ㄓㄥˋ)
dignified and imposing

堂鼓(ㄊㄤˊ ㄍㄨˇ)
a kind of drum used in Peking opera

堂倌(ㄊㄤˊ ㄍㄨㄢ)
a waiter (in restaurants, teahouses, etc.): 堂倌罷工。 Waiters of restaurants went on strike.

堂會(ㄊㄤˊ ㄏㄨㄟˋ)
an entertainment party with hired performers held at home on auspicious occasions

堂皇(ㄊㄤˊ ㄏㄨㄤˊ)
① imposing; impressive; grand; stately; magnificent: 他的房子富麗堂皇。 His house is beautiful and imposing. ② openly and legally

堂姊妹(ㄊㄤˊ ㄗˇ ㄇㄟˋ)
one's female first cousins on the father's side

堂萱(ㄊㄤˊ ㄒㄩㄢ)
one's mother: 堂萱年邁。 My mother is growing old.

堂兄弟(ㄊㄤˊ ㄒㄩㄥ ㄉㄧˋ)
one's male first cousins on the father's side

堂上(ㄊㄤˊ ㄕㄤˋ)
a reference to one's own parents: 堂上健在。 Both par-

ents are in good health.

堂子(ㄊㄤˊ ˙ㄗ)
a brothel

堂奧(ㄊㄤˊ ㄠˋ)
① the advanced stage of learning, a skill, etc.; profundity of thought or knowledge; depths (of teaching) ② deep, hidden recesses

堂屋(ㄊㄤˊ ㄨ)
the central room (of a one-storey Chinese traditional house consisting of several rooms in a row); the main hall of a building

【堅】 846
ㄐㄧㄢ jiān jiān
1. strong and durable: 他有堅決的意志。 He has a strong will.
2. solid; firm
3. to dedicate to; to devote to
4. calm; steady; stable; determined
5. close; intimate
6. armor, etc.
7. the strongest position or point of enemy troops: 攻堅 to storm strongholds
8. firmly; steadfastly; resolutely: 堅拒 to refuse firmly
9. a Chinese family name

堅壁清野(ㄐㄧㄢ ㄅㄧˋ ㄑㄧㄥ ㄧㄝˇ)
to fortify the defense works and to leave nothing usable to the invading enemy

堅不吐實(ㄐㄧㄢ ㄅㄨˋ ㄊㄨˇ ㄕˊ)
to refuse to tell the truth; (said of criminal suspects) obstinately refuse to speak up

堅不可摧(ㄐㄧㄢ ㄅㄨˋ ㄎㄜˇ ㄘㄨㄟ)
invulnerable; impregnable

堅定(ㄐㄧㄢ ㄉㄧㄥˋ)
determined; firm of purpose; steadfast; staunch: 堅定的立場 a firm ground

堅定不移(ㄐㄧㄢ ㄉㄧㄥˋ ㄅㄨˋ ㄧˊ)
unwavering; unswerving; unshakable

堅挺(ㄐㄧㄢ ㄊㄧㄥˇ)
(said of business conditions) thriving; flourishing; (said of prices) strong; rising; (said of stock exchange) bullish

堅牢(ㄐㄧㄢ ㄌㄠˊ)
strong; durable; heavily defended (fortresses)

堅固(ㄐㄧㄢ ㄍㄨˋ)
strong; durable; solid; firm; stable: 這房子造得很堅固。 This house is very solidly built.

堅果(ㄐㄧㄢ ㄍㄨㄛˇ)
nuts

堅苦卓絕(ㄐㄧㄢ ㄎㄨˇ ㄓㄨㄛˊ ㄐㄩㄝˊ)
to endure all the hardships firm; determined; showing the greatest fortitude

堅甲利兵(ㄐㄧㄢ ㄐㄧㄚˇ ㄌㄧˋ ㄅㄧㄥ)
(literally) strong armor and crack troops—ready for combat; combat readiness

堅決(ㄐㄧㄢ ㄐㄩㄝˊ)
firmly (opposed to, etc.); determined; resolute; resolutely: 我們堅決支持你。 We firmly support you.

堅強(ㄐㄧㄢ ㄑㄧㄤˊ)
① strong; firm; unyielding; staunch: 他父親是一個性格堅強的人。 His father is a person of strong character. ② to strengthen

堅信(ㄐㄧㄢ ㄒㄧㄣˋ)
to have absolute faith; to believe firmly

堅貞(ㄐㄧㄢ ㄓㄣ)
chaste; of inflexible virtue

堅持(ㄐㄧㄢ ㄔˊ)or 堅執(ㄐㄧㄢ ㄓˊ)
to insist; to maintain unyieldingly; to persist in: 他堅持他是無辜的。 He insisted on his innocence.

堅持到底(ㄐㄧㄢ ㄔˊ ㄉㄠˋ ㄉㄧˇ)
to stick it out; to go through with it: 我們必須堅持到底，不然就要失敗了。 We must stick it out, or we will fail.

堅持己見(ㄐㄧㄢ ㄔˊ ㄐㄧˇ ㄐㄧㄢˋ)
to be firm in one's view; to hold on to one's own view

堅稱(ㄐㄧㄢ ㄔㄥ)
to insist on saying; to assert positively

堅實(ㄐㄧㄢ ㄕˊ)
solid; strong; durable; substantial: 這條公路堅實平整。 This is a smooth, firmly built highway.

堅守(ㄐㄧㄢ ㄕㄡˇ)
① to firmly stand by (one's promise, principle, etc.): 大家都要堅守崗位。 Everybody should stand fast at his post.

②to defend (a place) resolutely

堅忍(ㄐㄧㄢ ㄖㄣˇ)
fortitude; firmness; dedication; determination

堅忍不拔(ㄐㄧㄢ ㄖㄣˇ ㄅㄨˋ ㄅㄚˊ)
invincible; fortitude; determined; unwavering; indomitable; resolute; unmovable

堅韌(ㄐㄧㄢ ㄖㄣˋ)
great strength or durability; superb resilience; fortitude

堅如鐵石(ㄐㄧㄢ ㄖㄨˊ ㄊㄧㄝˇ ㄕˊ)
(said of one's feelings, sentiments, etc.) as hard as iron and stone; flinty (hearts)

堅毅(ㄐㄧㄢ ㄧˋ)
fortitude; determination; dedication

堅硬(ㄐㄧㄢ ㄧㄥˋ)
hard and solid: 石頭是很堅硬的。Stone is very hard.

【堆】847
ㄉㄨㄟ duei duī
1. to heap up; to pile; to stack: 他的桌上堆滿了書。His desk was piled with books.
2. a heap; a pile; a mass; a crowd: 柴堆 a pile of firewood

堆肥(ㄉㄨㄟ ㄈㄟˊ)
compost—an organic fertilizer

堆高(ㄉㄨㄟ ㄍㄠ)
to pile up to great height

堆垛兒(ㄉㄨㄟ ㄉㄨㄛˇㄦ)
a pile; the things gathered together to form a heap

堆積(ㄉㄨㄟ ㄐㄧ)
to store up; to pile to amass; to heap up

堆金積玉(ㄉㄨㄟ ㄐㄧㄣ ㄐㄧ ㄩˋ)
a vast fortune with piles of gold and jade

堆砌(ㄉㄨㄟ ㄑㄧˋ)
①to lay (bricks, etc.); to pile up ②(composition) allusions, corny expressions, etc. senselessly heaped together

堆棧(ㄉㄨㄟ ㄓㄢˋ)
a warehouse; a storage; a storehouse

九畫

【報】848
ㄅㄠˋ baw bào
1. to repay; to recompense; to requite; to respond; to return: 觀眾報以熱烈的掌聲。The audience responded with warm applause.
2. a reward; a retribution
3. to report; to announce; a report: 我明天提出報告。I'll report tomorrow.
4. a newspaper; a periodical; a journal: 畫報 a pictorial 學報 a college journal 你買什麼報? What newspaper do you take?

報備(ㄅㄠˋ ㄅㄟˋ)
to inform the authorities of what one plans to do (instead of submitting a request for permission)

報表(ㄅㄠˋ ㄅㄧㄠˇ)
forms for reporting statistics, etc.; report forms

報屁股(ㄅㄠˋ ㄆㄧˋ ㄍㄨˇ)
(slang) insignificant spaces on the inside pages of a newspaper where feature articles are printed; supplements of a newspaper

報聘(ㄅㄠˋ ㄆㄧㄣˋ)
to repay a courtesy visit to a friendly nation

報馬(ㄅㄠˋ ㄇㄚˇ)
a courier; a messenger

報名(ㄅㄠˋ ㄇㄧㄥˊ)
to enroll; to enlist; to enter one's name (as in an examination, a competition, etc.)

報明(ㄅㄠˋ ㄇㄧㄥˊ)
to state clearly to the higher authorities

報命(ㄅㄠˋ ㄇㄧㄥˋ)
to report the accomplishment of a mission or an assignment

報幕(ㄅㄠˋ ㄇㄨˋ)
to announce the items on a (theatrical) program

報費(ㄅㄠˋ ㄈㄟˋ)
a newspaper subscription bill

報廢(ㄅㄠˋ ㄈㄟˋ)
①to report (worn-out office equipment, etc.) as unserviceable or useless ②to scrap

報復(ㄅㄠˋ ㄈㄨˋ)
①to avenge; to revenge; to retaliate; vengeance; revenge; retaliation; reprisal: 他向敵人報復。He avenged himself on his enemies. ②to report back (after investigation)

報復關稅(ㄅㄠˋ ㄈㄨˋ ㄍㄨㄢ ㄕㄨㄟˋ)
a retaliatory tariff

報答(ㄅㄠˋ ㄉㄚˊ)
to repay another's kindness: 我如何能報答您的恩惠? How can I ever repay you for your kindness?

報德(ㄅㄠˋ ㄉㄜˊ) or 報恩(ㄅㄠˋ ㄣ)
to repay another's kindness or favors; to show gratitude

報導(ㄅㄠˋ ㄉㄠˇ)
①to report (news); to cover: 記者報導了火災的情況。The reporter covered the fire. ②a news report; a story

報導文學(ㄅㄠˋ ㄉㄠˇ ㄨㄣˊ ㄒㄩㄝˊ)
reportage

報到(ㄅㄠˋ ㄉㄠˋ)
to report one's arrival; to check in; to register: 會員已開始報到。The members have started registering.

報單(ㄅㄠˋ ㄉㄢ)
①an application to pass goods through the customs ②an announcement to friends and relatives of one's success in the civil service examination of former times

報頭(ㄅㄠˋ ㄊㄡˊ)
the masthead of a newspaper

報攤(ㄅㄠˋ ㄊㄢ)
a newsstand; a news stall

報童(ㄅㄠˋ ㄊㄨㄥˊ)
a newspaper delivery boy; a newsboy

報告(ㄅㄠˋ ㄍㄠˋ)
①to report: 他正在報告探險的結果。He's reporting the results of the expedition. ②a report: 氣象報告 a weather report

報告書(ㄅㄠˋ ㄍㄠˋ ㄕㄨ)
a written report

報國(ㄅㄠˋ ㄍㄨㄛˊ)
to devote oneself to the national cause; to dedicate oneself to the service of one's country

報官(ㄅㄠˋ ㄍㄨㄢ)
to notify the local govern-

〔土部〕

ment of a crime, an accident, etc.

報關(ㄅㄠˋ ㄍㄨㄢ)
to declare something at the customs; to apply to the customs: 你們有什麼東西要報關嗎? Have you got anything to declare?

報關行(ㄅㄠˋ ㄍㄨㄢ ㄒㄧㄥˊ)
a customs broker; an agency for clearing customs

報館(ㄅㄠˋ ㄍㄨㄢˇ)
a newspaper office

報功(ㄅㄠˋ ㄍㄨㄥ)
to report an achievement or a victory; to claim credit

報考(ㄅㄠˋ ㄎㄠˇ)
to enter one's name in an examination

報刊(ㄅㄠˋ ㄎㄢ)
newspapers and periodicals

報戶口(ㄅㄠˋ ㄏㄨˋ ㄎㄡˇ)
①to apply for a residence permit ②to register: 別忘了給你的新生嬰兒報戶口。Don't forget to register the birth of your baby.

報佳音(ㄅㄠˋ ㄐㄧㄚ ㄧㄣ)
to carol; caroling

報夾(ㄅㄠˋ ㄐㄧㄚˊ)
a newspaper holder or clip

報價(ㄅㄠˋ ㄐㄧㄚˋ)
(economics) ①a quoted price ②to quote

報架(ㄅㄠˋ ㄐㄧㄚˋ)
a newspaper shelf

報捷(ㄅㄠˋ ㄐㄧㄝˊ)
to announce or report a victory or success

報界(ㄅㄠˋ ㄐㄧㄝˋ)
the press; the news circles; the journalistic circles: 此書獲報界之好評。The book was favorably noticed by the press.

報警(ㄅㄠˋ ㄐㄧㄥˇ)
①to report an alarm or emergency ②to report to the police

報喜(ㄅㄠˋ ㄒㄧˇ)
to announce good news (such as a marriage, etc.)

報喜不報憂(ㄅㄠˋ ㄒㄧˇ ㄅㄨˋ ㄅㄠˋ ㄧㄡ)
to report only what is good while concealing what is unpleasant

報系(ㄅㄠˋ ㄒㄧˋ)
a newspaper chain; a syndicate

報銷(ㄅㄠˋ ㄒㄧㄠ)
①to give a statement on one's expenses (especially for one's trip on business); to apply for reimbursement ②to write off: 他剛報銷了一部車。He has just written off a car.

報曉(ㄅㄠˋ ㄒㄧㄠˇ)
(said of cocks' crowing) to announce the arrival of dawn; to herald the break of day

報效(ㄅㄠˋ ㄒㄧㄠˋ)
①to work for; to repay another's kindness by working hard for him ②to give private means for public use

報信(ㄅㄠˋ ㄒㄧㄣˋ)
to report news; to announce; to pass information; to notify

報紙(ㄅㄠˋ ㄓˇ)
① a newspaper: 他為這報紙寫社論。He writes leading articles for the newspaper. ② newsprint

報章(ㄅㄠˋ ㄓㄤ)
①newspapers ②reply letters; return mail

報賬(ㄅㄠˋ ㄓㄤˋ)
to present a bill of expenses (to the employer or the accountant); to render an account

報仇(ㄅㄠˋ ㄔㄡˊ)
to get one's revenge for (an injury, etc.); to avenge (a grievance, etc.): 他立誓要向敵人報仇。He swore to revenge himself on his enemy.

報仇雪恨(ㄅㄠˋ ㄔㄡˊ ㄒㄩㄝˇ ㄏㄣˋ)
to revenge and wipe out a standing grudge (against somebody)

報酬(ㄅㄠˋ ㄔㄡˊ)
①pay; a salary: 不計報酬 not concerned about pay ②remuneration; reward: 讀書所得的報酬不能以金錢衡量。The rewards of study can't always be measured in money. ③to thank; to show gratitude

報失(ㄅㄠˋ ㄕ)
to report the loss of some-

thing to the authorities concerned

報時(ㄅㄠˋ ㄕˊ)
to give the correct time

報時台(ㄅㄠˋ ㄕˊ ㄊㄞˊ)
(telephone) the time inquiry service

報社(ㄅㄠˋ ㄕㄜˋ)
a newspaper office: 他在一家報社工作。He works in a newspaper office.

報數(ㄅㄠˋ ㄕㄨˋ)
①(drill) to say aloud the number of each one in a row according to the order of the position where he stands, beginning from the one who stands at the head of the row ②(word of command) Count off!

報稅(ㄅㄠˋ ㄕㄨㄟˋ)
to report tax returns; to declare goods for duties

報人(ㄅㄠˋ ㄖㄣˊ)
a newspaperman; a journalist

報災(ㄅㄠˋ ㄗㄞ)
to report a disaster to the authorities

報載(ㄅㄠˋ ㄗㄞˇ)
according to newspaper reports

報喪(ㄅㄠˋ ㄙㄤ)
to announce a death

報案(ㄅㄠˋ ㄢˋ)
to report a case (such as a theft, missing person, murder, etc.) to the police

報恩(ㄅㄠˋ ㄣ)
to pay a debt of gratitude; to repay another's kindness

報業(ㄅㄠˋ ㄧㄝˋ)
the business of the press

報業公會(ㄅㄠˋ ㄧㄝˋ ㄍㄨㄥ ㄏㄨㄟˋ)
a newspaper association; a press union

報應(ㄅㄠˋ ㄧㄥˋ)
retribution (especially in the Buddhist concept that one inevitably reaps what he sows)

報怨(ㄅㄠˋ ㄩㄢˋ)
to avenge a grievance

【堡】 849
ㄅㄠˇ bao ㄅㄠˇ bao
1. a walled village; a town
2. a petty military station; a

fort; a fortress

壘（ㄌㄟˇ ㄌㄟ）
a fortress; a bastion; a stronghold

【堪】 850
ㄎㄢ kan kǎn

1. to sustain; to bear; to stand: 不堪一擊 to be unable to withstand a single blow; to collapse at the first blow

2. fit for; worthy of; adequate for

3. a Chinese family name

堪當重任（ㄎㄢ ㄉㄤ ㄓㄨㄥˋ ㄖㄣˋ）
to be capable of shouldering important tasks; to be able to fill a position of great responsibility

堪察加（ㄎㄢ ㄔㄚˊ ㄐㄧㄚ）
the Kamchatka Peninsula

堪稱佳作（ㄎㄢ ㄔㄥ ㄐㄧㄚ ㄗㄨㄛˋ）
may be rated as an excellent piece of writing or a fine work of art

堪薩斯（ㄎㄢ ㄙㄚˋ ㄙ）
the state of Kansas, U.S.A.

堪虞（ㄎㄢ ㄩˊ）
precarious, distressing, dangerous, etc.

堪輿（ㄎㄢ ㄩˊ）
the science of the influence of a landscape on human destiny; geomancy; the magic art of choosing building or burial sites

堪用（ㄎㄢ ㄩㄥˋ）
good enough for use; usable

【堯】 851
ㄧㄠˊ yau yáo

1. Yao, a legendary sage king in ancient China whose reign is said to have extended from 2357 to 2255 B.C.

2. high; eminent; lofty

3. a Chinese family name

堯天舜日（ㄧㄠˊ ㄊㄧㄢ ㄕㄨㄣˋ ㄖˋ）
an era of blissful peace as in the reigns of Yao and Shun

堯舜（ㄧㄠˊ ㄕㄨㄣˋ）
Yao and Shun, two of the most celebrated sage kings in ancient China

【堰】 852
ㄧㄢˋ yann yàn
a bank of earth; an embankment; a dike; a levee: 在荷蘭

境內到處都是堰。There are dikes everywhere in Holland.

【場】 853
ㄔㄤˊ charng cháng
（又讀 ㄔㄤˇ chaang chǎng）

1. an area of level ground; an open space

2. an act of a play; an act of an opera

3. the stage: 出場 to go on the stage

4. an arena for drill; a playground: 運動場 an athletic field

5. a farm: 養鴨場 a duck farm

6. a site or place for a special purpose, as an examination, a meeting, etc.: 教堂是禮拜的場所。A church is a place of worship.

7. (physics) a field: 電（磁）場 an electric (magnetic) field

場圃（ㄔㄤˊ ㄆㄨˇ）
vegetable gardens

場面（ㄔㄤˊ ㄇㄧㄢˋ）or（ㄔㄤˇ ㄇㄧㄢˋ）
①pageantry; a show of wealth, etc.: 他擺出大場面。He made a great show of his wealth. ②a scene; a spectacle: 熱烈友好的場面 scene of warm friendship ③an appearance; a front: 撐場面 to keep up appearances ④（Chinese opera）the group of accompanying musicians collectively

場地（ㄔㄤˊ ㄉㄧˋ）or（ㄔㄤˇ ㄉㄧˋ）
a playground; a site; a place where a show or game is played, including the space for the audience: 這場是一個理想的露營場地。This is really an ideal camp site.

場合（ㄔㄤˊ ㄏㄜˊ）or（ㄔㄤˇ ㄏㄜˊ）
an occasion; a situation; a condition: 外交場合 a diplomatic occasion

場場客滿（ㄔㄤˊ ㄔㄤˊ ㄎㄜˋ ㄇㄢˇ）or（ㄔㄤˇ ㄔㄤˇ ㄎㄜˋ ㄇㄢˇ）
a houseful of spectators for every show; a capacity audience for every show

場子（ㄔㄤˊ ㄗ˙）
a place or site where people gather for various purposes

場次（ㄔㄤˊ ㄘˋ）
the number of showings of a

film, play, etc.

場所（ㄔㄤˊ ㄙㄨㄛˇ）or（ㄔㄤˇ ㄙㄨㄛˇ）
a location; a place; an arena; a theater; a playground: 投票場所 a balloting place 營業場所 a place of business

場院（ㄔㄤˊ ㄩㄢˋ）or（ㄔㄤˇ ㄩㄢˋ）
an open yard for sunning newly harvested grains

【堵】 854
ㄉㄨˇ duu dǔ

1. to stop; to block up; to shut off: 把老鼠洞堵死。Stop up the mouseholes.

2. a wall

3. a Chinese family name

堵截（ㄉㄨˇ ㄐㄧㄝˊ）
to stop; to intercept; to block up or cut off an approach to

堵牆（ㄉㄨˇ ㄑㄧㄤˊ）
a wall surrounding a house

堵住（ㄉㄨˇ ㄓㄨˋ）
to block up; to stop: 所有的路都為大雪所堵住。All the roads were blocked by the heavy snowfall.

堵嘴（ㄉㄨˇ ㄗㄨㄟˇ）
①to stop talking ②to silence others by bribery

堵塞（ㄉㄨˇ ㄙㄜˋ）
to stop up; to block up; a jam: 交通堵塞 a traffic jam

十畫

【塊】 855
ㄎㄨㄞˋ kuay kuài

1. a lump (or clod) of earth

2. a lump; a piece; a cube: 把肉切成塊兒。Cut the meat into cubes.

3. a piece of (land, bread, etc.)

4. alone; to be all by oneself

塊頭（ㄎㄨㄞˋ ㄊㄡˊ）
stature; build: 他是個大塊頭。He is a man of large stature.

塊壘（ㄎㄨㄞˋ ㄌㄟˇ）
the dejection one feels at heart

塊根（ㄎㄨㄞˋ ㄍㄣ）
root tubers

塊莖（ㄎㄨㄞˋ ㄐㄧㄥ）
a stem tuber

塊肉餘生記（ㄎㄨㄞˋ ㄖㄡˋ ㄩˊ ㄕㄥ ㄐㄧˋ）

〔土部〕

David Copperfield, by Charles Dickens

〔土部〕

【塋】 856.
ㄧㄥˊ yng ying
a grave; a tomb

塋墳(ㄧㄥˊ ㄈㄣˊ)or 塋穴(ㄧㄥˊ ㄒㄩㄝˋ)
a grave; a tomb

塋地(ㄧㄥˊ ㄉㄧˋ) or 塋域(ㄧㄥˊ ㄩˋ)
a graveyard; a cemetery

【塌】 857.
ㄊㄚ ta tā
1. to cave in; to fall in ruins; to collapse: 屋頂塌了。The roof collapsed.
2. to sink; to droop
3. a little house

塌鼻(ㄊㄚ ㄅㄧˊ)
a flat nose; a snub nose

塌臺(ㄊㄚ ㄊㄞˊ)
a business failure; the closing of a shop; a failure; a downfall: 懶惰是他事業塌臺的主要原因。Laziness is the main cause of his downfall in business.

塌下來(ㄊㄚ ㄒㄧㄚˋ ㄌㄞˊ)
to fall down; to cave in; to collapse: 這房子因地震而塌下來。The house collapsed on account of an earthquake.

塌陷(ㄊㄚ ㄒㄧㄢˋ)
to sink; to cave in; to subside: 路基塌陷了。The roadbed has subsided.

【塚】 858.
(冢) ㄓㄨㄥˇ zhong joong
a high tomb; a mound; a grave

【塑】 859.
ㄙㄨˋ suh sù
1. to mold (in clay, etc.); to sculpt
2. a figure; a model: 這是一尊泥塑。It's a clay figure.
3. plastics

塑膠(ㄙㄨˋ ㄐㄧㄠ)
plastics: 現今塑膠被大量用以代替木材和金屬等。Nowadays plastics are widely used instead of wood, metal, etc.

塑膠布(ㄙㄨˋ ㄐㄧㄠ ㄅㄨˋ)
plastic cloth

塑膠皮(ㄙㄨˋ ㄐㄧㄠ ㄆㄧˊ)
plastic leather

塑膠粉(ㄙㄨˋ ㄐㄧㄠ ㄈㄣˇ)
PVC resins

塑膠袋(ㄙㄨˋ ㄐㄧㄠ ㄉㄞˋ)
plastic bags

塑膠粒(ㄙㄨˋ ㄐㄧㄠ ㄌㄧˋ)
a PVC compound

塑膠花(ㄙㄨˋ ㄐㄧㄠ ㄏㄨㄚ)
plastic flowers

塑膠炸彈(ㄙㄨˋ ㄐㄧㄠ ㄓㄚˋ ㄉㄢˋ)
a plastic bomb

塑像(ㄙㄨˋ ㄒㄧㄤˋ)
①to make an idol, image or statue ②a statue; a plastic figure: 自由女神的塑像在紐約港內。The Statue of Liberty is in New York Bay.

塑造(ㄙㄨˋ ㄗㄠˋ)
to mold; to make by molding: 我們用黏土塑造成像。We mold statues out of clay.

【塔】 860.
ㄊㄚˇ taa tǎ
1. a pagoda
2. a tower: 一座白塔立在山頂上。A white tower stands on top of the hill.
3. a lighthouse

塔頂(ㄊㄚˇ ㄉㄧㄥˇ)
the top of a pagoda

塔台(ㄊㄚˇ ㄊㄞˊ)
a control tower

塔里木盆地(ㄊㄚˇ ㄌㄧˇ ㄇㄨˋ ㄆㄣˊ ㄉㄧˋ)
the Tarim Basin

塔虎脫(ㄊㄚˇ ㄏㄨˇ ㄊㄨㄛ)
William Howard Taft, 1857-1930, the 27th president of the United States

塔斯社(ㄊㄚˇ ㄙ ㄕㄜˋ)
Tass, the official Soviet news agency

【塗】 861.
ㄊㄨˊ twu tú
1. to smear; to apply; to spread (ointment on a wound, etc.): 塗點軟膏 to apply some ointment
2. to scribble; to scrawl
3. to erase; to blot out; to efface; to obliterate; to cross out: 塗掉這個字。Cross out this word.
4. mud; mire
5. same as 途—a way; a road

塗抹(ㄊㄨˊ ㄇㄛˇ)
①to erase; to obliterate ②to scribble; to doodle: 那男孩繼續用鉛筆胡亂塗抹。The boy continued to doodle with a pencil.

塗炭(ㄊㄨˊ ㄊㄢˋ)
mud and coals—(said of

people's livelihood) in a distressing plight; in great affliction

塗料(ㄊㄨˊ ㄌㄧㄠˋ)
paint; coating

塗改(ㄊㄨˊ ㄍㄞˇ)
to erase and change the wording of an article; to alter: 本文件塗改無效。The document is invalid if altered.

塗脂抹粉(ㄊㄨˊ ㄓ ㄇㄛˇ ㄈㄣˇ)
①(literally) to apply rouge and face powder—to doll up ②to whitewash

塗飾(ㄊㄨˊ ㄕˋ)
①to cover with paint, lacquer, etc. ②to daub (plaster, etc.) on a wall; to whitewash

塗鴉(ㄊㄨˊ ㄧㄚ)
①poor calligraphy; to write badly; to scribble ②graffiti

【塘】 862.
ㄊㄤˊ tarng tóng
1. an embankment; a bund; a bank; a dike: 河塘 a river embankment
2. a square pool; a pond; a tank: 魚塘 a fish pond 青蛙跳進池塘。A frog jumped into the pond.

【塞】 863.
1. ㄙㄜ seh sè
(語音ㄙㄞˋ sài sai)
1. to block; to stop up; to clog: 樓上的水管塞住了。The water-pipe upstairs is clogged up.
2. to stuff; to squeeze in; to fill
3. a cork or stopper; to cork; to seal

塞門(ㄙㄜ ㄇㄣˊ)
①a screen ②a cock

塞責(ㄙㄜ ㄗㄜˊ)
to perform one's duties perfunctorily; to dabble in one's work: 別敷衍塞責。Don't perform your duty in a perfunctory manner.

塞滿(ㄙㄜ ㄇㄢˇ)
to stuff full; to fill up

塞住(ㄙㄜ ㄓㄨˋ)
to stop up; to block up: 這條街為羣衆所塞住。The street was blocked up with crowds.

塞子(ㄙㄜ ㄗˇ) or 塞兒(ㄙㄜ ㄦˊ)
a cork; a stopper

塞耳不聞(ㄙㄜ ㄦˇ ㄅㄨˋ ㄨㄣˊ)

to turn a deaf ear to

【塞】 863
2. ㄙㄞ say sài

strategic points along the frontiers: 要塞 a fortress

塞班島(ㄙㄞ ㄅㄢ ㄉㄠ)
the Saipan Island

塞浦路斯(ㄙㄞ ㄆㄨ ㄌㄨ ㄙ)
Cyprus

塞得港(ㄙㄞ ㄉㄜˊ ㄍㄤˇ)
Port Said in Egypt

塞納河(ㄙㄞ ㄋㄚˋ ㄏㄜˊ)
the Seine River

塞内加爾(ㄙㄞ ㄋㄟˋ ㄐㄧㄚ)
Senegal

塞爾維亞(ㄙㄞ ㄦˇ ㄨㄟˊ ㄧㄚˋ)
Servia or Serbia, a former kingdom on the Balkans

塞外(ㄙㄞ ㄨㄞˋ)
beyond the borders; beyond the frontiers (especially northern frontiers of China)

塞翁失馬，焉知非福(ㄙㄞ ㄨㄥ ㄕ ㄇㄚˇ, ㄧㄢ ㄓ ㄈㄟ ㄈㄨˊ)
When the old man on the frontier lost his horse, who could have known it was a blessing in disguise?—A loss may turn out to be a gain.

【填】 864
ㄊㄧㄢˊ tyan tián

1. to fill up; to fill in; to stuff: 別填錯地方。Don't fill in the wrong place.
2. the sound of drumbeats

填報(ㄊㄧㄢˊ ㄅㄠˋ)
to fill in a form and submit it to the leadership

填表(ㄊㄧㄢˊ ㄅㄧㄠˇ)
to fill in a blank; to fill out a form

填補(ㄊㄧㄢˊ ㄅㄨˇ)
to fill (vacancies, etc.); to make up a deficiency; to serve as a filler: 牙醫填補蛀牙。A dentist fills decayed teeth.

填坑(ㄊㄧㄢˊ ㄎㄥ)
to fill up the depressions or holes on the ground

填發(ㄊㄧㄢˊ ㄈㄚ)
to fill in and issue (as a certificate, certificate, etc.)

填房(ㄊㄧㄢˊ ㄈㄤˊ)
a second wife one marries after the death of the first

填隘隆(ㄊㄧㄢˊ ㄙㄨ ·ㄌㄨㄥ)

填空(ㄊㄧㄢˊ ㄎㄨㄥˋ)
① to fill a vacant position; to fill a vacancy ②參看「填充」

填海(ㄊㄧㄢˊ ㄏㄞˇ)
to reclaim; reclamation

填寫(ㄊㄧㄢˊ ㄒㄧㄝˇ)
to fill in (a blank, form, etc.): 請在申請表上填寫你的姓名和學歷。Please fill in your name and educational level on the application form.

填胸(ㄊㄧㄢˊ ㄒㄩㄥ)
to fill one's breast or heart (with anger, etc.)

填充(ㄊㄧㄢˊ ㄔㄨㄥ)
① (a form of testing) filling the blanks ② to fill up; to stuff

填字遊戲(ㄊㄧㄢˊ ㄗˋ ㄧㄡˊ ㄒㄧˋ)
a cross-word puzzle

填詞(ㄊㄧㄢˊ ㄘˊ)
to compose tzu (a variation of old-style Chinese poetry with rigid rules)

填塞(ㄊㄧㄢˊ ㄙㄜ)
to fill with; to stuff with 用沙把這洞口填塞起來。Fill the hole with sand.

填鴨(ㄊㄧㄢˊ ㄧㄚ)
① to stuff the duck—a time-honored way of duck feeding by stuffing the ducks to satiation and not letting them to exercise so that their meat will be tender and tasty ② to stuff students with whatever they need to pass an entrance examination to a higher school; to cram

【塢】 865
ㄨˋ wuh wù

1. a low wall around a village for defense; an entrenchment; a fortified building; a castle
2. a structure which slants to a lower center on all sides; a depression; a cove; a recess: 船塢 a dock; a dockyard 花塢 a sunken flower bed

十一畫

【墓】 866
ㄇㄨˋ muh mù

a grave; a tomb; a mausoleum: 陵墓 an emperor's mausoleum 公墓 a public cemetery

墓碑(ㄇㄨˋ ㄅㄟ)or 墓表(ㄇㄨˋ ㄅㄧㄠˇ)
a tombstone; a gravestone

墓門(ㄇㄨˋ ㄇㄣˊ)
the door of a tomb or grave

墓木已拱(ㄇㄨˋ ㄇㄨˋ ㄧˇ ㄍㄨㄥˇ)
(literally) The saplings around the grave have grown into big trees.— A long time has elapsed since one's death.

墓道(ㄇㄨˋ ㄉㄠˋ)
the path before a grave; the tomb passage

墓地(ㄇㄨˋ ㄉㄧˋ)
the site of a grave or tomb; a cemetery

墓穴(ㄇㄨˋ ㄒㄩㄝˋ)
the vault of a tomb; the cave where the deceased is placed

墓誌銘(ㄇㄨˋ ㄓˋ ㄇㄧㄥˊ)
an epitaph

墓園(ㄇㄨˋ ㄩㄢˊ)
a cemetery ground

【塵】 867
ㄔㄣˊ chern chén

1. dust; dirt: 一塵不染 not stained with a particle of dust 他的衣服上佈滿了灰塵。His clothes were covered with dust.
2. trace; trail
3. this world; ways of the world
4. vice; sensual pleasures
5. (Taoism) a lifetime

塵表(ㄔㄣˊ ㄅㄧㄠˇ)
① out-of-the-world; world beyond the material things 亦作「塵外」② excellence; incomparable

塵凡(ㄔㄣˊ ㄈㄢˊ)
this mortal life; ways of the world; this world

塵封(ㄔㄣˊ ㄈㄥ)
to be covered all over by dust—to be laid idle for a long time

塵土(ㄔㄣˊ ㄊㄨˇ)
dust 下雨時塵土變成泥。When it rains, dust turns into mud.

土部

（土部）

塵思(ㄔㄣㄙ|ㄤ)
worldly thoughts

塵累(ㄔㄣㄌㄟ)
duties and obligations of the mortal life

塵露(ㄔㄣㄌㄨ)
dust and dew — (figuratively) ①(said of things) insignificant ②(said of human life) transient

塵慮(ㄔㄣㄌㄩ)
worldly worries or desires

塵垢(ㄔㄣㄍㄡ)
dust and dirt

塵囂(ㄔㄣㄒ|ㄠ)
a place filled with a hubbub and an uproar

塵心(ㄔㄣㄒ|ㄣ)
worldly desires

塵世(ㄔㄣㄕ)
this mortal life; this world

塵俗(ㄔㄣㄙㄨ)
(Buddhism) this mortal life; this world

塵埃(ㄔㄣㄞ)
dust; dirt: 如果你沒有每天打掃房間, 塵埃將積滿。If you do not sweep your room every day, dust will accumulate.

塵務(ㄔㄣㄨ)
worldly affairs; mundane affairs

塵緣(ㄔㄣㄩㄢ)
worldly passions; mundane desires; love affairs

【塹】 868
(ㄑ|ㄢ chiann qiàn)
1. the moat around a city; a chasm; a trench: 天塹 a natural chasm for defense
2. a pit; a hole or cavity in the ground

塹壕(ㄑ|ㄢㄏㄠ)
moats; trenches

【塾】 869
(ㄕㄨ shwu shú)
1. an anteroom or vestibule
2. a family school; a village school; a private primary school: 家塾 a school at home with a private tutor

塾師(ㄕㄨㄕ)
the tutor of a family or village school

【境】 870
(ㄐ|ㄥ jing jìng)
1. a boundary; a frontier; a

border: 強盜逃過邊境。The bandits fled across the border.
2. a place; an area
3. a state; a situation; circumstances: 處境困難 to be in a difficult situation

境地(ㄐ|ㄥㄉ|)
① territory ② a state; a condition; a position; a situation

境內(ㄐ|ㄥㄋㄟ)
within the border; in the country

境況(ㄐ|ㄥㄎㄨㄤ)
a situation; a condition

境界(ㄐ|ㄥㄐ|ㄝ)
① a boundary ② a situation; a condition ③ a state (of mind); a realm: 理想境界 an ideal state

境遇(ㄐ|ㄥㄩ)
① circumstances; condition ② vicissitudes in one's life; what one has encountered in life

境域(ㄐ|ㄥㄩ)
territory; land within the boundary of a nation

【墅】 871
(ㄕㄨ shuh shù)
a villa; a country house: 他在北投有一幢別墅。He has a villa in Peitou.

【墉】 872
(ㄩㄥ iong yōng)
(又讀 ㄩㄥ yong yóng)
a fortified wall; a wall

墉垣(ㄩㄥㄩㄢ)
the city wall

【墊】 873
(ㄉ|ㄢ diann diàn)
1. to advance (money); to pay for another and expect to be paid back
2. a cushion; a pad ; a bed-mat
3. to cushion; to put something under another (to make it level)
4. to sink into
5. to dig

墊被(ㄉ|ㄢㄅㄟ)
a mattress

墊補(ㄉ|ㄢㄅㄨ)
to defray expenses not budgeted

墊平(ㄉ|ㄢㄆ|ㄥ)
to level up 亦作「塡平」: 他們想把運動場墊平。They wish to

level the playground.

墊付(ㄉ|ㄢㄈㄨ)
to pay for another temporarily

墊款(ㄉ|ㄢㄎㄨㄢ)
①to advance money for another on the understanding that he will return it on a future date ② money thus advanced

墊腳石(ㄉ|ㄢㄐ|ㄠㄕ)
a steppingstone

墊肩(ㄉ|ㄢㄐ|ㄢ)
a shoulder pad (or padding)

墊圈(ㄉ|ㄢㄑㄩㄢ)
(machinery) a washer

墊上運動(ㄉ|ㄢㄕㄤㄩㄣㄉㄨㄥ)
gymnastics on mattress

墊子(ㄉ|ㄢ·ㄗ)
cushions; mattresses; mats: 沙發上有好幾個墊子。There are several cushions on the sofa.

十二畫

【墟】 874
(ㄒㄩ shiu xū)
1. a high mound
2. an ancient town; a ghost town: 廢墟 ruins
3. wild, waste land
4. a periodical marketplace where goods are bartered
5. to ruin; to destroy

墟里(ㄒㄩㄌ|)
a small village

墟市(ㄒㄩㄕ)
the fair grounds of a village

【墀】 875
(ㄔ chyr chí)
steps leading up to a palace; palace steps

【墜】 876
(ㄓㄨㄟ juey zhuì)
to fall down; to sink; the fall (of a person, a state, etc.): 飛機墜入海中。The plane crashed into the sea.

墜馬(ㄓㄨㄟㄇㄚ)
to fall off a horse

墜地(ㄓㄨㄟㄉ|)
①to fall ②failure ③to come to this world

墜胎(ㄓㄨㄟㄊㄞ)
abortion; to abort 亦作「墮胎」

墜樓(ㄓㄨㄟㄌㄡ)

to fall from a building; to commit suicide by jumping from a building

墬落(ㄓㄨㄟ ㄌㄨㄛ)
to drop

墬毀(ㄓㄨㄟ ㄏㄨㄟ)
(said of a plane, etc.) to fall and break; to crash: 飛機在山邊墬毀。The airplane crashed on a hillside.

墬結(ㄓㄨㄟ ㄐㄩ)
a failing (business, etc.); a hopeless case

墬子(ㄓㄨㄟ ˙ㄗ)
① earrings; eardrops ② a pendant or pendants attached to a bigger object as ornaments ③ a kind of folk song originated in Honan Province and later spread to other northern provinces

【增】　877
ㄗㄥ tzeng zēng
to add to; to increase; to grow; to enlarge: 他的知識與日俱增。His knowledge is steadily on the increase. 他們的友情日增。Their friendship was growing daily.

增補(ㄗㄥ ㄅㄨ)
to add to; to supplement; to increase and supplement: 本公司人員略有增補。The staff of our company has been slightly augmented.

增訂(ㄗㄥ ㄉㄧㄥ)
(usually said of a book, etc.) to revise and enlarge

增訂本(ㄗㄥ ㄉㄧㄥ ㄅㄣ)
a revised and enlarged edition: 這是最新增訂本。This is the newest revised and enlarged edition.

增多(ㄗㄥ ㄉㄨㄛ)
to add to; to increase: 他家人口增多。His family increased.

增添(ㄗㄥ ㄊㄧㄢ)
to add to; to supplement: 他的病增添家人的困難。His illness added to the family's troubles.

增添項目(ㄗㄥ ㄊㄧㄢ ㄒㄧㄤ ㄇㄨ)
an addition item

增光(ㄗㄥ ㄍㄨㄤ)
to glorify; to do credit to; to add to the prestige of: 他為國增光。He does credit to his country.

增廣(ㄗㄥ ㄍㄨㄤ)
to widen (one's knowledge, etc.); to enlarge; to advance: 增廣知識 to widen one's knowledge

增刊(ㄗㄥ ㄎㄢ)
a supplement—as of newspaper, etc.; (said of newspapers, etc.) an enlarged edition on holidays or Sundays

增加(ㄗㄥ ㄐㄧㄚ)
to add to; to increase; increase: 這件事增加我們的困難。This adds to our difficulties.

增加率(ㄗㄥ ㄐㄧㄚ ㄌㄩ)
the rate of increase

增價(ㄗㄥ ㄐㄧㄚ)
increment

增減(ㄗㄥ ㄐㄧㄢ)
increases and decreases; fluctuations

增進(ㄗㄥ ㄐㄧㄣ)
to advance; to promote (friendship, etc.); to increase (knowledge, etc.)

增強(ㄗㄥ ㄑㄧㄤ)
to strengthen; to heighten; to enhance

增值(ㄗㄥ ㄓ)
to increase the value; value increment; appreciation; increment

增值稅(ㄗㄥ ㄓ ㄕㄨㄟ)
VAT (value-added tax): 土地增值稅 land increment tax

增長(ㄗㄥ ㄓㄤ)
increases and advances; a rise; to grow: 我們國家的人口在迅速增長。The population of our country is growing rapidly.

增產(ㄗㄥ ㄔㄢ)
to increase production; the increase of production

增刪(ㄗㄥ ㄕㄢ)
(usually said of a script, etc.) to emendate; to revise (a book); to add and to delete

增資(ㄗㄥ ㄗ)
to increase capitalization

增損(ㄗㄥ ㄙㄨㄣ)
profits and losses

增益(ㄗㄥ ㄧ)
① to increase; to profit; to

augment ②(electronics) gain

增援(ㄗㄥ ㄩㄢ)
to send reinforcements; to build up troop level

【墨】　878
ㄇㄛ moh mò
1. black; dark
2. a black dye
3. a Chinese inkstick; ink
4. calligraphy; handwriting or painting: 遺墨 writing or paintings left by the deceased
5. literate; letters; learning
6. statutes; institutions
7. greedy; covetous; corrupt
8. to tattoo the face—one of the five punishments in ancient China
9. a Chinese family name

墨寶(ㄇㄛ ㄅㄠ)
treasured calligraphic works

墨斗(ㄇㄛ ㄉㄡ)
an ink cup used by the carpenter to make markings

墨吏(ㄇㄛ ㄌㄧ)
corrupt officials

墨綠(ㄇㄛ ㄌㄩ)
blackish green

墨客(ㄇㄛ ㄎㄜ)
men of letters 參看「騷人墨客」

墨盒(ㄇㄛ ㄏㄜ)
a small case containing Chinese ink held by wet cotton; an ink box

墨海(ㄇㄛ ㄏㄞ)
an ink slab; an inkstone 亦作「墨硯」

墨痕(ㄇㄛ ㄏㄣ)
ink marks

墨迹(ㄇㄛ ㄐㄧ)
the original handwriting of a famous figure; ink marks: 這是中山先生的墨迹。This is Dr. Sun Yat-sen's calligraphy.

墨家(ㄇㄛ ㄐㄧㄚ)
(Chinese philosophy) the school of Mo Ti(墨翟); the Mohists

墨鏡(ㄇㄛ ㄐㄧㄥ)
sunglasses

墨西哥(ㄇㄛ ㄒㄧ ㄍㄜ)
Mexico

墨西哥人(ㄇㄛ ㄒㄧ ㄍㄜ ㄖㄣ)

a Mexican

墨西哥灣(ㄇㄛ ㄒㄧ 《ㄜ ㄨㄢ)
the Gulf of Mexico

墨線(ㄇㄛ ㄒㄧㄢˋ)
a thread used by carpenters
for marking 亦作「繩墨」

墨刑(ㄇㄛ ㄒㄧㄥˊ)
to tattoo the face—an
ancient Chinese punishment

墨汁(ㄇㄛ ㄓ) or 墨水(ㄇㄛ ㄕㄨㄟˇ)
①Chinese dark ink; ink ②
letters; learning: 他肚子裏頭
了不少墨水。He has read a
great many books.

墨竹(ㄇㄛ ㄓㄨˊ)
bamboos painted on paper
with Chinese ink

墨守成規(ㄇㄛ ㄕㄡˇ ㄔㄥˊ ㄍㄨㄟ)
to stick to old rules; conservative: 他墨守成規。He is con-
servative.

墨子(ㄇㄛ ㄗˇ)
Mo Ti (墨翟) or Mocius, one
of the great philosophers
of the Epoch of Warring
States, who preached love
without distinction

墨爾鉢(ㄇㄛ ㄦˇ ㄅㄛ)
Melbourne, an Australian
city

墨魚(ㄇㄛ ㄩˊ)
the squid; the cuttlefish 亦作
「墨斗魚」or「烏賊」

【墩】⁸⁷⁹ ㄉㄨㄣ duen dūn
1. a mound; a heap
2. a block of stone or wood
3. a cluster

【墮】⁸⁸⁰ ㄉㄨㄛˋ duoh duò
1. to fall; to sink; to let fall
2. to indulge in evil ways
3. lazy; idle

墮胎(ㄉㄨㄛˋ ㄊㄞ)
abortion; to abort; to have a
miscarriage

墮落(ㄉㄨㄛˋ ㄌㄨㄛˋ)
①to indulge in evil ways; to
sink in moral standard; to
degenerate; degeneracy: 飲酒
和賭博使他徹底墮落了。Drink-
ing and gambling sank him
completely. ②the fall (of a
nation, family, etc.)

墮入(ㄉㄨㄛˋ ㄖㄨˋ)
to sink or lapse into; to land
oneself in; to fall into: 那隻
熊墮入陷阱裏。The bear fell

into the trap.

十三畫

【墳】⁸⁸¹ ㄈㄣˊ fern fén
1. a mound
2. big; large; great
3. the banks of a river

墳墓(ㄈㄣˊ ㄇㄨˋ)
a grave; a tomb

墳地(ㄈㄣˊ ㄉㄧˋ)or 墳場(ㄈㄣˊ ㄔㄤˇ)or
(ㄈㄣˊ ㄔㄤˊ)
a place of burial; a cemetery; a graveyard

墳典(ㄈㄣˊ ㄉㄧㄢˇ)
ancient books

墳塋(ㄈㄣˊ ㄧㄥˊ)
①a grave; a tomb ②a
graveyard; a cemetery

【壁】⁸⁸² ㄅㄧˋ bih bì
1. a partition wall; the walls
of a room
2. a military breastwork
3. a cliff

壁報(ㄅㄧˋ ㄅㄠˋ)
a wall paper; a wall poster;
a wall newspaper

壁燈(ㄅㄧˋ ㄉㄥ)
lamps hung on a screenwall;
wall lamps; bracket lamps

壁毯(ㄅㄧˋ ㄊㄢˇ)
tapestry (used to hang on
walls)

壁壘分明(ㄅㄧˋ ㄌㄟˇ ㄈㄣ ㄇㄧㄥˊ)
The stands of the opposing
camps are distinctively different. — There is no compromise between the contending factions.

壁壘森嚴(ㄅㄧˋ ㄌㄟˇ ㄙㄣ ㄧㄢˊ)
①an unassailable strong-
hold; strong defense preparations; strongly fortified;
closely guarded ②with a
clear-cut line of demarcation; a strong sense of partisanship; sharply divided

壁立(ㄅㄧˋ ㄌㄧˋ)
①to stand bolt upright ②
poverty-stricken

壁爐(ㄅㄧˋ ㄌㄨˊ)
a fireplace

壁虎(ㄅㄧˋ ㄏㄨˇ)
a house-lizard or gecko

壁虎功(ㄅㄧˋ ㄏㄨˇ ㄍㄨㄥ)

the ability to climb walls
without tools

壁畫(ㄅㄧˋ ㄏㄨㄚˋ)
a mural painting; a fresco

壁櫥(ㄅㄧˋ ㄔㄨˊ)
a closet; a wall chest

壁上觀(ㄅㄧˋ ㄕㄤˋ ㄍㄨㄢ)
to watch a fight or struggle
without helping either party

壁有耳(ㄅㄧˋ ㄧㄡˇ ㄦˇ)
Beware of eavesdropping.

【墾】⁸⁸³ ㄎㄣˇ keen kěn
to open new land for farming, etc.; to reclaim land: 他
開墾過一大片土地。He opened
a large piece of land.

墾丁公園(ㄎㄣˇ ㄉㄧㄥ ㄍㄨㄥ ㄩㄢˊ)
Kengding Park, Pingtung

墾荒(ㄎㄣˇ ㄏㄨㄤ)
to open up barren land for
farming

墾殖(ㄎㄣˇ ㄓˊ)
to reclaim land and cultivate it

【壅】⁸⁸⁴ ㄩㄥ yeong yōng
(又讀 ㄩㄥˋ iong yòng)
1. to stop; to block up
2. to bank up the roots of
plants
3. to obstruct; to impede
(flow, etc.)

壅蔽(ㄩㄥ ㄅㄧˋ)
to conceal; to block up; to
cover 亦作「雍閉」

壅塞(ㄩㄥ ㄙㄜˋ)
to block up; to obstruct or
stop the flow of (a river,
etc.); to dam

壅塞(ㄩㄥ ㄙㄜˋ)
to block up; to obstruct; to
impede; to congeal the flow
of (a sewerage pipe, etc.):
這條街擠滿群眾壅塞不通。The
street was blocked up with
crowds.

【壇】⁸⁸⁵ ㄊㄢˊ tarn tán
1. a platform for sacrificial
rites; an altar: 禮堂裏有一個
供演講人用的講壇。There is a
platform for speakers in the
hall.
2. a hall for important meetings and ceremonies in
ancient China

十四畫

【壓】 886
ㄧㄚ ia yā

1. to press; to oppress; to pressure: 稅金重壓著他。The taxes pressed him.
2. to control; to quell: 我強壓住心頭怒火。I tried hard to control my anger.
3. to crush
4. (said of enemy troops, etc.) to close in; to press near
5. to hold (a document, etc.) without taking action; to pigeonhole; to shelve
6. a way of making a stroke in Chinese calligraphy
7. to excel; to surpass others (in ability, etc.): 他在考試中壓倒群雄。He excelled all the rest in the examination.

壓寶(ㄧㄚ ㄅㄠˇ)
to place one's stake at a Chinese gambling game in which the odds are three to one; a gambling or guessing game, played with dice under a bowl

壓扁(ㄧㄚ ㄅㄧㄢˇ)
to flatten by pressure: 小盒子給上面的重書壓扁了。The small box was flattened by the pressure of the heavy book on it.

壓不住(ㄧㄚ ㄅㄨˋ ㄓㄨˋ)
to be unable to command or exercise control over a group of people due to lack of prestige, personal ability, etc.

壓迫(ㄧㄚ ㄆㄛˋ)
①to press hard; to oppress; to pressure; to force: 好的統治者不會壓迫貧民。A good ruler will not oppress the poor. ②oppression; pressure: 他們是壓迫下的犧牲者。They are victims of oppression.

壓破(ㄧㄚ ㄆㄛˋ)
to break something by applying pressure; broken by high pressure

壓平(ㄧㄚ ㄆㄧㄥˊ)
to press something so as to make it flat and smooth

壓服(ㄧㄚ ㄈㄨˊ)
to subjugate; to force (a nation, person, etc.) to her knees; to coerce

壓得住(ㄧㄚ ˙ㄉㄜ ㄓㄨˋ)
①to have the ability to undertake a task or responsibility ②to keep down (anger, etc.)

壓倒(ㄧㄚ ㄉㄠˇ)
to surpass; to overwhelm; to excel; to win: 困難不能壓倒他們。No difficulty can overwhelm them.

壓倒性勝利(ㄧㄚ ㄉㄠˇ ㄒㄧㄥˋ ㄕㄥˋ ㄌㄧˋ)
an overwhelming victory; a landslide victory

壓隊(ㄧㄚ ㄉㄨㄟˋ)
(literally) to walk behind a team—to supervise, or to oversee

壓臺戲(ㄧㄚ ㄊㄞˊ ㄒㄧˋ)or**壓軸戲**(ㄧㄚ ㄓㄡˊ ㄒㄧˋ)
the best act of a show (which usually comes last in a Chinese operatic performance)

壓條(ㄧㄚ ㄊㄧㄠˊ)or**壓枝**(ㄧㄚ ㄓ)
(agriculture) layering

壓力(ㄧㄚ ㄌㄧˋ)
①(physics) pressure ②overwhelming force; pressure

壓路機(ㄧㄚ ㄌㄨˋ ㄐㄧ)
a roller (for road-surfacing)

壓根兒(ㄧㄚ ㄍㄣ ㄦ)
(used in negative assertions) totally; entirely; or completely: 他壓根兒不會唱歌。He cannot sing at all.

壓克力(ㄧㄚ ㄎㄜˋ ㄌㄧˋ)
(chemistry) acrylic resin

壓克力玻璃(ㄧㄚ ㄎㄜˋ ㄌㄧˋ ㄅㄛ ㄌㄧ)
acrylic-plastic sheets (manufactured in Taiwan under the trademark "Acrypoly")

壓壞(ㄧㄚ ㄏㄨㄞˋ)
damaged by high pressure or a heavy load

壓擠(ㄧㄚ ㄐㄧˇ)
to extrude; extrusion

壓價(ㄧㄚ ㄐㄧㄚˋ)
to force prices down; to demand a lower price

壓緊(ㄧㄚ ㄐㄧㄣˇ)
to make something tight or constrict by applying high pressure; to pack

壓驚(ㄧㄚ ㄐㄧㄥ)
to help someone get over a shock (by entertaining him, etc.); to becalm nerves after a shock

壓境(ㄧㄚ ㄐㄧㄥˋ)
(usually said of enemy troops) to mass on, or approach the border: 敵方大軍壓境。A large enemy force is moving quickly towards the border.

壓卷(ㄧㄚ ㄐㄩㄢˇ)
the composition or writing that excels or surpasses all the others

壓線(ㄧㄚ ㄒㄧㄢˋ)
①(sports) a line ball ②to be kept busy on other's account (like a needle-woman making gold braids for other's wedding dress)

壓制(ㄧㄚ ㄓˋ)
①to suppress (one's anger, etc.); to restrain (usually by force) ②(military) to neutralize (enemy fire by massive bombardment)

壓榨(ㄧㄚ ㄓㄚˋ)or**壓搾**(ㄧㄚ ㄓㄚˋ)
①to oppress; to extort; oppression; extortion ②to extract (liquids) by applying high pressure

壓寨夫人(ㄧㄚ ㄓㄞˋ ㄈㄨ ㄖㄣˊ)
the wife of a brigand chief; the wife of the leader of bandits

壓軸好戲(ㄧㄚ ㄓㄡˊ ㄏㄠˇ ㄒㄧˋ)
the last but best one of a series of performances

壓住(ㄧㄚ ㄓㄨˋ)
to suppress; to put down by force

壓差(ㄧㄚ ㄔㄚ)
pressure difference

壓車(ㄧㄚ ㄔㄜ)
to go with the truck personally as a supervisor 亦作「押車」

壓舌板(ㄧㄚ ㄕㄜˊ ㄅㄢˇ)
(medicine) a tongue depressor

壓死(ㄧㄚ ㄙˇ)
①to crush to death ②to die after being hit by a car

壓縮(ㄧㄚ ㄙㄨㄛ)
to compress; to condense; to

reduce; to cut down: 棉花壓縮成包. Cotton is compressed into bales.

壓縮性(ㄧㄚ ㄙㄨㄛ ㄒㄧㄥ)
compressibility

壓碎(ㄧㄚ ㄙㄨㄟ)
to crush to pieces: 他們壓碎石子以製水泥. They make cement by crushing down stone.

壓歲錢(ㄧㄚ ㄙㄨㄟˋ ㄑㄧㄢˊ)
(red paper bags) containing cash distributed to children by elders on lunar New Year's Eve

壓抑(ㄧㄚ ㄧ)
to curb; to repress; to suppress (one's emotions, etc.); 操心和憂愁壓抑着她. Care and sorrow oppressed her.

壓韻(ㄧㄚ ㄩㄣˋ)
to rhyme 參看「押韻」

【壎】 887
ㄒㄩㄣ shiun xún
an ancient Chinese wind instrument, made of porcelain and shaped like an egg

壎篪(ㄒㄩㄣ ㄔˊ)
two musical instruments played together harmoniously — signifying the love between brothers

【壑】 888
ㄏㄨㄛˋ huoh huò
1. a gully; a channel for water
2. a narrow ravine at the foot of a hill: 林壑之勝 the grandeur of woods and ravines

壑溝(ㄏㄨㄛˋ ㄍㄡ)
a ditch; a narrow strip of water; the moat around a city wall: 死於壑溝 to die in a ditch

【壕】 889
ㄏㄠˊ haur háo
1. the ditch around a city wall; a moat
2. a trench; a dugout

壕溝(ㄏㄠˊ ㄍㄡ)
a trench (in warfare); a ditch

十五畫

【壙】 890
ㄎㄨㄤˋ kuang kuàng
1. a vault; a tomb
2. a field; an open (or wild)

space
3. to leave vacant or idle

壙穴(ㄎㄨㄤˋ ㄒㄩㄝˋ)
the vault of a tomb

【壘】 891
ㄌㄟˇ leei lěi
1. a military wall; a rampart
2. to pile up: 雪愈壘愈高. The snow is piling up.
3. a base (on a baseball diamond): 他在二壘. He is on the second base.
4. a Chinese family name

壘球(ㄌㄟˇ ㄑㄧㄡˊ)
softball: 我喜歡打壘球. I like to play softball.

十六畫

【壟】 892
ㄌㄨㄥˇ loong lǒng
1. a grave; a mound of earth
2. a high place in a field

壟斷(ㄌㄨㄥˇ ㄉㄨㄢˋ)
a monopoly; to monopolize; to corner: 他們壟斷了棉花市場. They cornered the cotton market.

【壞】 893
ㄏㄨㄞˋ huay huài
1. broken down; decaying; rotten; out of order; useless: 肉類比蔬菜更容易腐壞. Meat decays much easier than vegetables.
2. bad; poor (scores, marks, etc.): 有人說吸煙是一種壞習慣. Some people say that smoking is a bad habit.
3. vicious; mean; evil (persons, etc.)

壞坯子(ㄏㄨㄞˋ ㄆㄟ ˙ㄗ)
a bad egg; a lout

壞蛋(ㄏㄨㄞˋ ㄉㄢˋ)
(literally) a rotten egg—a bad fellow; an evil person; a louse; a villain 亦作「壞坯子」

壞東西(ㄏㄨㄞˋ ㄉㄨㄥ ㄒㄧ)
a bad person or thing; an evil fellow

壞透(ㄏㄨㄞˋ ㄊㄡˋ)
bad to the bone; rotten to the core; evil to the very marrow: 這個人的品行壞透了. The man's morals are rotten to the core.

壞良心(ㄏㄨㄞˋ ㄌㄧㄤˊ ㄒㄧㄣ)
heartless; a depraved con-

science

壞話(ㄏㄨㄞˋ ㄏㄨㄚˋ)
slander: 他根本沒有說他們的壞話. He spoke no ill of them.

壞疽(ㄏㄨㄞˋ ㄐㄩ)
gangrene

壞球(ㄏㄨㄞˋ ㄑㄧㄡˊ)
(baseball) ball

壞血病(ㄏㄨㄞˋ ㄒㄧㄝˇ ㄅㄧㄥˋ)
scurvy; scorbutus

壞心眼兒(ㄏㄨㄞˋ ㄒㄧㄣ ㄧㄢˇ)
malicious; ill-intentioned; devious; devilish

壞主意(ㄏㄨㄞˋ ㄓㄨˇ ㄧ)
a wicked or crooked idea; a scheme to trick or trap somebody 亦作「壞念頭」

壞處(ㄏㄨㄞˋ ㄔㄨˋ)
bad points; shortcomings; defects: 從壞處著想, 往好處努力. Prepare for the worst; make an effort for the best.

壞事(ㄏㄨㄞˋ ㄕˋ)
①a bad thing; an evil deed ②to ruin something; to make things worse: 鹵莽只會壞事. Overboldness will only make things worse.

壞人(ㄏㄨㄞˋ ㄖㄣˊ)
a bad guy; an evil person

壞死(ㄏㄨㄞˋ ㄙˇ)
a necrosis: 局部壞死 a local necrosis

十七畫

【壤】 894
ㄖㄤˇ raang rǎng
1. loose soil
2. earth: 他們倆人的個性有天壤之別. They are vastly different from each other in personality as heaven from earth.
3. a region; a place; a land: 他住在窮鄉僻壤. He lives in a remote and backward region.
4. rich; abundant
5. a Chinese family name

壤土(ㄖㄤˇ ㄊㄨˇ)
loam

壤界(ㄖㄤˇ ㄐㄧㄝˋ)
boundary of a piece of land

二十一畫

【壩】 895 ㄅㄚ bah bà

1. an embankment; a dike: 堤壩已築成了。The embankment has been thrown up.
2. a dam: 我們剛完成了一個新的大水壩。We have just completed a new big dam.

壩工 (ㄅㄚ ㄍㄨㄥ)
dam construction works

士 部
ㄕ shyh shì

【士】 896 ㄕ shyh shì

1. a scholar; a man of learning; a gentleman
2. an official rank in ancient China; an officer
3. a noncommissioned officer
4. a person
5. name of a chessman in Chinese chess
6. a Chinese family name

士飽馬騰 (ㄕ ㄅㄠ ㄇㄚˇ ㄊㄥˊ)
(said of troops) well-fed and highly-motivated

士別三日刮目相看 (ㄕ ㄅㄧㄝˊ ㄙㄢ ㄖˋ ㄍㄨㄚ ㄇㄨˋ ㄒㄧㄤ ㄎㄢˋ)
(literally) One should make a reappraisal of a scholar after a separation of three days.—A scholar who constantly makes improvement deserves a new appraisal of his achievements every now and then.

士兵 (ㄕ ㄅㄧㄥ)
soldiers; privates; enlisted men

士敏土 (ㄕ ㄇㄧㄣˇ ㄊㄨˇ)
cement 亦作「水泥」

士大夫 (ㄕ ㄉㄚˋ ㄈㄨ)
① a person with official rank; an official ② a general ③ a person of learning; a scholar

士農工商 (ㄕ ㄋㄨㄥˊ ㄍㄨㄥ ㄕㄤ)
scholars, farmers, workers and merchants—the social castes in ancient China

士林 (ㄕ ㄌㄧㄣˊ)
the intelligentsia; a scholastic community; literary circles

士官 (ㄕ ㄍㄨㄢ)
noncommissioned officers

士官長 (ㄕ ㄍㄨㄢ ㄓㄤˇ)
a master sergeant

士可殺不可辱 (ㄕ ㄎㄜˇ ㄕㄚ ㄅㄨˋ ㄎㄜˇ ㄖㄨˋ)
A gentleman prefers death to humiliation.

士氣 (ㄕ ㄑㄧˋ)
① the morale of a fighting force ② the trends and temperaments of scholars in a given era

士紳 (ㄕ ㄕㄣ)
the gentry

士庶 (ㄕ ㄕㄨˋ)
the common people

士人 (ㄕ ㄖㄣˊ)
a scholar; an educated man

士子 (ㄕ ㄗˇ)
the candidates of the civil service examination in ancient China

士卒 (ㄕ ㄗㄨˊ)
soldiers; enlisted men; army privates: 戰爭中這隊長總是身先士卒。In war the captain always fought at the head of his men.

士族 (ㄕ ㄗㄨˊ)
the gentry (in the South and North Dynasties)

士為知己者死 (ㄕ ㄨㄟˊ ㄓ ㄐㄧˇ ㄓㄜˇ ㄙˇ)
A gentleman is ready to die for his good friends.

一畫

【壬】 897 ㄖㄣˊ ren rén

1. the ninth of the Ten Celestial Stems
2. artful and crafty
3. great
4. pregnant

壬人 (ㄖㄣˊ ㄖㄣˊ)
an artful person; a cunning deceiver

四畫

【壯】 898 ㄓㄨㄤˋ juang zhuàng

1. big; great
2. strong; robust; vigorous; sturdy: 他是個強壯的小伙子。He is a robust young fellow.

3. portly; stout
4. to strengthen; to make better
5. the prime of one's life
6. another name for the eighth moon of the lunar calendar

壯美 (ㄓㄨㄤˋ ㄇㄟˇ)
grandeur and serenity; splendor; sublime

壯大 (ㄓㄨㄤˋ ㄉㄚˋ)
① big and strong; vigorous ② to grow in strength; to expand

壯膽 (ㄓㄨㄤˋ ㄉㄢˇ)
to strengthen one's courage; to embolden

壯丁 (ㄓㄨㄤˋ ㄉㄧㄥ)
① an able-bodied man ② an adult fit for military service

壯舉 (ㄓㄨㄤˋ ㄐㄩˇ)
an ambitious attempt; an attempt at something spectacular

壯年 (ㄓㄨㄤˋ ㄋㄧㄢˊ)
the prime of one's life

壯麗 (ㄓㄨㄤˋ ㄌㄧˋ)
grand and imposing; splendorous

壯烈 (ㄓㄨㄤˋ ㄌㄧㄝˋ)
courageous; on a grand and spectacular scale

壯烈犧牲 (ㄓㄨㄤˋ ㄌㄧㄝˋ ㄒㄧ ㄕㄥ)
to die as a martyr; to die a hero's death; to die for one's country; to heroically give one's life

壯觀 (ㄓㄨㄤˋ ㄍㄨㄢ)
a grand sight; a great sight; a beautiful view; a breathtaking or spectacular view; an impressive sight

壯闊 (ㄓㄨㄤˋ ㄎㄨㄛˋ)
vast; grand; magnificent; grandiose

壯健 (ㄓㄨㄤˋ ㄐㄧㄢˋ)
healthy and strong

壯舉 (ㄓㄨㄤˋ ㄐㄩˇ)
a great achievement; a daring act; a courageous feat; a heroic undertaking: 這是史無前例的壯舉。This is an unprecedented courageous feat.

壯志 (ㄓㄨㄤˋ ㄓˋ)

[夂部]

great aspiration; great ambition

壯志凌雲(ㄓㄨㄤˋㄓˋㄌㄧㄥˊㄩㄣˊ)
a soaring ambition or aspiration; with soaring aspirations

壯志未酬(ㄓㄨㄤˋㄓˋㄨㄟˋㄔㄡˊ)
(usually said of a martyr, a hero, etc.) to die before the fulfillment of his ambition or aspiration

壯實(ㄓㄨㄤˋㄕˊ)
sturdy; robust: 他是一個壯實的小伙子。He's a sturdy young chap.

壯士(ㄓㄨㄤˋㄕˋ)
a brave man; a man of stout heart; a hero; a warrior

壯盛(ㄓㄨㄤˋㄕㄥˋ)
strong and prosperous; healthy

壯遊(ㄓㄨㄤˋㄧㄡˊ)
① a splendid tour; an exciting trip; a great tour or trip ② to take a long trip for an ambitious project; an ambitious trip—as a trip to space by astronauts

九畫

【壻】899 (婿)ㄒㄩˋ shiuh xù
1. one's son-in-law
2. one's husband: 他是我的妹婿。He is my younger sister's husband.

【壹】900 ㄧ yi
an elaborate form of "一" (one) used mostly in accounting and especially in checks to prevent forgery or alterations

【壺】901 ㄏㄨˊ hwu hú
1. a pot; a jug; a winevessel
2. any potbellied container with a small opening
3. a Chinese family name

壺中物(ㄏㄨˊㄓㄨㄥ ㄨˋ)
wine; liquor; drinks

十畫

【壼】902 ㄎㄨㄣˇ koen kǔn
a lane, passageway or corridor in a palace

壼範(ㄎㄨㄣˇ ㄈㄢˋ)
a paragon of feminine virtues

十一畫

【壽】903 ㄕㄡˋ show shòu
1. the life span: 現代醫藥已增加人類的壽命。Modern medicine has increased man's life span.
2. old age; a long life; longevity
3. birthday: 他向張先生祝壽。He congratulated Mr. Chang on his birthday.
4. to die of old age
5. to present another with gold, silk, etc.
6. to toast an elder
7. a Chinese family name

壽比南山(ㄕㄡˋㄅㄧˇㄋㄢˊㄕㄢ)
(a greeting for a person on his birthday) May your life be as lofty as the Southern Mountain Ranges. 或 Many happy returns of the day!

壽屏(ㄕㄡˋㄆㄧㄥˊ)
a long vertical scroll inscribed with writings wishing another a long life

壽麵(ㄕㄡˋㄇㄧㄢˋ)
long noodles eaten on birthday to symbolize a long life; birthday noodles

壽命(ㄕㄡˋㄇㄧㄥˋ)
the life span of a person

壽誕(ㄕㄡˋㄉㄢˋ)
a birthday anniversary

壽桃(ㄕㄡˋㄊㄠˊ)
longevity peaches—made of flour in the shape of a peach and presented to another on his birthday

壽頭壽腦(ㄕㄡˋㄊㄡˊㄕㄡˋㄋㄠˇ)
stupid-looking

壽堂(ㄕㄡˋㄊㄤˊ)
a specially decorated hall where well-wishers come to offer congratulations to a person on his birthday

壽禮(ㄕㄡˋㄌㄧˇ)or 壽儀(ㄕㄡˋㄧˊ)
birthday gifts or presents

壽聯(ㄕㄡˋㄌㄧㄢˊ)
longevity couplets; couplets presented to a person on his birthday wishing him a long life

壽考(ㄕㄡˋㄎㄠˇ)
long life

壽器(ㄕㄡˋㄑㄧˋ)
a coffin prepared when one is alive

壽險(ㄕㄡˋㄒㄧㄢˇ)
life insurance 亦作「人壽保險」

壽星(ㄕㄡˋㄒㄧㄥ)
① the host of a birthday feast or party; a reference to a person on his birthday ② the God of Longevity ③ Canopus

壽序(ㄕㄡˋㄒㄩˋ)
a writing or literary work wishing another longevity on his birthday

壽終正寢(ㄕㄡˋㄓㄨㄥ ㄓㄥˋㄑㄧㄣˇ)
to die of old age; to die a natural death (now used in the obituary)

壽冢(ㄕㄡˋㄓㄨㄥˇ)
a graveyard laid out before one dies

壽辰(ㄕㄡˋㄔㄣˊ)
birthday

壽數(ㄕㄡˋㄕㄨˋ)or 壽算(ㄕㄡˋㄙㄨㄢˋ)
the allotted life span of a person; a person's destined age

壽材(ㄕㄡˋㄘㄞˊ)
① a coffin prepared before one's death ② a coffin

壽衣(ㄕㄡˋㄧ)
clothes prepared by a person during his lifetime to assure that he will be properly dressed after his death

夂 部
ㄙㄨㄟ suei suī

七畫

【夏】904 ㄒㄧㄚˋ shiah xià
1. summer: 我在一九八五年夏天去美國。I went to America in the summer of 1985.
2. big; spacious
3. a big house; a mansion

4. Cathay, the ancient name of China: 華夏 China; Chinese

5. a dynasty in Chinese history (2205-1782 B.C.): 夏朝, 夏代, 夏室 the Hsia Dynasty

6. a Chinese family name

夏布(ㄒㄧㄚˋ ㄅㄨˋ)
Chinese linen cloth for summer wear

夏天(ㄒㄧㄚˋ ㄊㄧㄢ)
summer; summer days

夏曆(ㄒㄧㄚˋ ㄌㄧˋ)
the traditional Chinese calendar; the lunar calendar

夏令(ㄒㄧㄚˋ ㄌㄧㄥˋ)
summer; summer time

夏令時間(ㄒㄧㄚˋ ㄌㄧㄥˋ ㄕˊ ㄐㄧㄢ)
summer time; daylight saving time

夏令營(ㄒㄧㄚˋ ㄌㄧㄥˋ ㄧㄥˊ)
summer camps; summer camping

夏令衛生(ㄒㄧㄚˋ ㄌㄧㄥˋ ㄨㄟˋ ㄕㄥ)
summer sanitation; public health (measures, etc.) in summer months

夏爐冬扇(ㄒㄧㄚˋ ㄌㄨˊ ㄉㄨㄥ ㄕㄢˋ)
(literally) stoves in summer and fans in winter—(figuratively) to do things the wrong way

夏葛冬裘(ㄒㄧㄚˋ ㄍㄜˊ ㄉㄨㄥ ㄑㄧㄡˊ)
(literally) linens for summer and furs for winter—(figuratively) Right things come at the right time.

夏季(ㄒㄧㄚˋ ㄐㄧˋ)
the summer season: 台灣夏季裏有許多不同的水果。 In Taiwan there are many fruits in the summer season.

夏桀(ㄒㄧㄚˋ ㄐㄧㄝˊ)
name of the last emperor of the Hsia Dynasty—a synonym of cruelty and oppression

夏至(ㄒㄧㄚˋ ㄓˋ)
the summer solstice which falls on June 21 or 22 on the Northern Hemisphere

夏至線(ㄒㄧㄚˋ ㄓˋ ㄒㄧㄢˋ)
tropic of Cancer 亦作「北回歸線」

夏裝(ㄒㄧㄚˋ ㄓㄨㄤ)
a summer dress

夏日(ㄒㄧㄚˋ ㄖˋ)
summer days

夏娃(ㄒㄧㄚˋ ㄨㄚˊ)
(the Bible) Eve

夏威夷(ㄒㄧㄚˋ ㄨㄟ ㄧˊ)
Hawaii

夏禹(ㄒㄧㄚˋ ㄩˇ)
Emperor Yü who started the reign of Hsia—a synonym of virtue and enlightened leadership

【夏】 904 2. ㄐㄧㄚˇ jea jiǎ
參看「夏楚」

夏楚(ㄐㄧㄚˇ ㄔㄨˇ)
a ferule; a rod for punishing pupils

十一畫

【夐】 905 ㄒㄩㄥˊ shiong xióng
1. to seek
2. preeminent; superior

夐古(ㄒㄩㄥˊ ㄍㄨˇ)
a long, long time ago; in ancient times

夐絕(ㄒㄩㄥˊ ㄐㄩㄝˊ)
peerless; second to none

十八畫

【夔】 906 ㄎㄨㄟˊ kwei kuí
1. (mythology) a one-legged monster
2. name of a court musician in the reign of Emperor Shun (2255 B.C.)
3. name of a feudal state in the Chou Dynasty
4. a Chinese family name

夔龍(ㄎㄨㄟˊ ㄌㄨㄥˊ)
the figures of two animals (夔 and 龍) in ancient bronzes

夔夔(ㄎㄨㄟˊ ㄎㄨㄟˊ)
awe-struck; in fear

夕 部
ㄒㄧˋ shih xì

【夕】 907 ㄒㄧˋ shih xì
1. dusk; sunset; evening
2. night: 他在一夕之間成名。 He

became famous during the night.
3. slant; oblique
4. to meet in the evening
5. a Chinese family name

夕暉(ㄒㄧˋ ㄏㄨㄟ)
slanting rays of the setting sun; brilliance of the sunset

夕照(ㄒㄧˋ ㄓㄠˋ)
the setting sun; its slanting rays; the reflected light of sunset: 滿目青山夕照明。 All the verdant mountains are bathed in the glorious setting sun.

夕陽(ㄒㄧˋ ㄧㄤˊ)
the setting sun

二畫

【外】 908 ㄨㄞˋ way wài
1. out; outside: 他在門外等著。 He is waiting outside the gates.
2. foreign; alien: 他是個外國學生。 He is a foreign student.
3. diplomatic; diplomacy: 他是位外交關係專家。 He is an expert in diplomatic relations.
4. besides; in addition
5. a term referring to one's husband 參看「外子」
6. a role in Chinese opera for old men
7. to alienate
8. on wife's or mother's side
9. relatives of one's sisters or daughters

外版書(ㄨㄞˋ ㄅㄢˇ ㄕㄨ)
the books not published by the shop selling them

外幣(ㄨㄞˋ ㄅㄧˋ)
foreign currency

外表(ㄨㄞˋ ㄅㄧㄠˇ)
an outward appearance; an exterior: 他喜歡從外表看人。 He likes to judge people by appearances.

外邊(ㄨㄞˋ ㄅㄧㄢ)或 外邊兒(ㄨㄞˋ ㄅㄧㄢ ㄦ)
①out; outside: 我們到外邊走走。 Let's go out for a walk.
②faraway or distant places
③a border region

外賓(ㄨㄞˋ ㄅㄧㄣ)
foreign visitors; foreign

〔夕 部〕

guests

外部(ㄨㄞ ㄅㄨ)
the external of anything; outside: 這房子的外部漆成綠色。The house was painted green outside.

外埠(ㄨㄞ ㄅㄨ)
ports or cities outside of one's own

外婆(ㄨㄞ ㄆㄛ)
one's maternal grandmother

外貌(ㄨㄞ ㄇㄠ)
an outward appearance; external looks

外貿(ㄨㄞ ㄇㄠ)
foreign trade; external trade

外貿協會(ㄨㄞ ㄇㄠ ㄒㄧㄝ ㄏㄨㄟ)
China Export Trade Center (CETDC)

外蒙古(ㄨㄞ ㄇㄥ ㄍㄨ)
Outer Mongolia

外面(ㄨㄞ ㄇㄧㄢ)
①an outward appearance; an exterior; a surface: 那屋子外面是磚砌的。The exterior of the house was of brick. ②outside; out: 車子正在外面等著。The car is waiting outside.

外分泌(ㄨㄞ ㄈㄣ ㄇㄧ)
exocrine; external secretion

外防禦線(ㄨㄞ ㄈㄤ ㄩ ㄒㄧㄢ)or 外圍防禦線(ㄨㄞ ㄨㄟ ㄈㄤ ㄩ ㄒㄧㄢ)
first-line defense; outer defense lines

外放(ㄨㄞ ㄈㄤ)
①to send an official in the capital for a provincial post ②to send an official for an overseas assignment

外數(ㄨㄞ ㄈㄨ)
to apply (ointment, etc.)

外帶(ㄨㄞ ㄉㄞ)
①a tire (cover) ②as well; besides: 這個廠除生產貨車外,也帶修理各種車子。Besides producing trucks, this factory repairs various cars as a sideline.

外敵(ㄨㄞ ㄉㄧ)
a foreign enemy

外地(ㄨㄞ ㄉㄧ)
parts of the country other than where one is

外調(ㄨㄞ ㄉㄧㄠ)
to transfer (materials or personnel) to other places

外電(ㄨㄞ ㄉㄧㄢ)
dispatches from foreign news agencies: 據外電報導,舊金山發生大地震。According to dispatches from foreign news agencies, there was a strong earthquake in San Francisco.

外動詞(ㄨㄞ ㄉㄨㄥ ㄘ)
(grammar) a transitive verb

外太空(ㄨㄞ ㄊㄞ ㄎㄨㄥ)
outer space

外逃(ㄨㄞ ㄊㄠ)
①to flee to some other place ②to flee the country

外套(ㄨㄞ ㄊㄠ)
①an overcoat ②overalls in the Ching Dynasty

外頭(ㄨㄞ ㄊㄡ)
outside: 把車子停在外頭。Park your car outside.

外來(ㄨㄞ ㄌㄞ)
outside; external; foreign: 我們應抵抗外來干涉。We should fight against outside interference.

外來語(ㄨㄞ ㄌㄞ ㄩ)
a term borrowed from a foreign language (such as "kowtow" or "sampan" in English which were borrowed from the Chinese language); foreign terms

外力(ㄨㄞ ㄌㄧ)
foreign influence; external pressure or influence

外流(ㄨㄞ ㄌㄧㄡ)
to flow outward; the outflow (of capital, talents, etc.)

外路(ㄨㄞ ㄌㄨ)
outside; districts, regions, provinces, etc. other than one's own

外路人(ㄨㄞ ㄌㄨ ㄖㄣ)
an outsider; a stranger

外港(ㄨㄞ ㄍㄤ)
an outport

外國(ㄨㄞ ㄍㄨㄛ)
a foreign country: 我有很多外國朋友。I have many foreign friends.

外國貨(ㄨㄞ ㄍㄨㄛ ㄏㄨㄛ)
imported goods; commodities of foreign make

外國人(ㄨㄞ ㄍㄨㄛ ㄖㄣ)
a foreigner; an alien: 此城有多少外國人? How many for-

eigners are there in this town?

外國資本(ㄨㄞ ㄍㄨㄛ ㄗ ㄅㄣ)
foreign capital

外國語(ㄨㄞ ㄍㄨㄛ ㄩ)
a foreign language; a foreign tongue

外觀(ㄨㄞ ㄍㄨㄢ)
an outward appearance external looks: 建築的外觀很吸引人。The external features of the building are very attractive.

外公(ㄨㄞ ㄍㄨㄥ)
one's maternal grandfather

外功(ㄨㄞ ㄍㄨㄥ)
(Chinese boxing) training and exercising of one's physical attributes for speed strength and quick reflex, as opposed to 內功 which involves development of one's internal organs for immense strength and uncanny feats

外科(ㄨㄞ ㄎㄜ)
surgery

外科醫生(ㄨㄞ ㄎㄜ ㄧ ㄕㄥ)or 外科大夫(ㄨㄞ ㄎㄜ ㄉㄞ ㄈㄨ)
a surgeon

外殼(ㄨㄞ ㄎㄜ)
an outer covering; a shell; a case

外客(ㄨㄞ ㄎㄜ)
guests who are not related to oneself by blood or by marriage

外快(ㄨㄞ ㄎㄨㄞ)
extra income; perquisites

外號(ㄨㄞ ㄏㄠ)
a nickname: 他的外號叫「胖仔」。His nickname is "Fatty".

外行(ㄨㄞ ㄏㄤ)
①a raw hand; a greenhorn; one who knows nothing of the trade; an outsider; a layman: 說到法律,我就是個外行。Where the law is concerned, I am only a layman. ②inexperienced; unskilled; amateurish

外行話(ㄨㄞ ㄏㄤ ㄏㄨㄚ)
layman's language

外戶(ㄨㄞ ㄏㄨ)
a door which opens from the outside

外貨(ㄨㄞ ㄏㄨㄛ)

imported goods; foreign goods

外匯(ㄨㄞㄏㄨㄟ)
foreign exchange

外匯兌換率(ㄨㄞㄏㄨㄟㄉㄨㄟㄏㄨㄢㄌㄩ)
the rate of foreign exchange

外匯管理(ㄨㄞㄏㄨㄟㄍㄨㄢㄌㄧ)
foreign exchange control

外匯交易(ㄨㄞㄏㄨㄟㄐㄧㄠㄧ)
foreign exchange transactions

外匯市場(ㄨㄞㄏㄨㄟㄕˋㄔㄤ)
foreign exchange market

外患(ㄨㄞㄏㄨㄢ)
foreign invasion; foreign aggression; foreign intrusion

外籍(ㄨㄞㄐㄧ)
foreign nationality

外籍人士(ㄨㄞㄐㄧㄖㄣˊㄕ)
foreigners; aliens

外加(ㄨㄞㄐㄧㄚ)
plus; in addition (to): 你需要錢和時間，外加勤奮努力。You need money and time. In addition, you need diligence.

外家(ㄨㄞㄐㄧㄚ)
① the parental home of a married woman ② a house to keep "the other woman" ③ a school of Chinese boxing 亦作「外林」

外接(ㄨㄞㄐㄧㄝ)
(mathematics) a circumscribed circle

外界(ㄨㄞㄐㄧㄝ)
① outsiders; those who are not in the know ② the outside: 夢由內心產生，非來自外界。Dreams come from within, not from the outside. ③ one's environment

外交(ㄨㄞㄐㄧㄠ)
diplomacy; diplomatic; foreign relations: 這件事須透過外交途徑解決。This event must be settled through diplomatic channels.

外交部(ㄨㄞㄐㄧㄠㄅㄨ)
Ministry of Foreign Affairs

外交部長(ㄨㄞㄐㄧㄠㄅㄨㄓㄤ)
Minister of Foreign Affairs

外交團(ㄨㄞㄐㄧㄠㄊㄨㄢ)
the diplomatic corps 亦作「使節團」

外交官(ㄨㄞㄐㄧㄠㄍㄨㄢ)
diplomatic officials; diplomats

外交家(ㄨㄞㄐㄧㄠㄐㄧㄚ)
skillful diplomats; experts in diplomacy

外交政策(ㄨㄞㄐㄧㄠㄓㄥˋㄘㄜ)
foreign policy

外交辭令(ㄨㄞㄐㄧㄠㄘˊㄌㄧㄥ)
(literally) diplomatic language—tactful remarks; euphemisms; circumlocutions; subterfuges

外角(ㄨㄞㄐㄩㄝ)
(mathematics) exterior angle

外教(ㄨㄞㄐㄧㄠ)
① a term used by the Buddhists to refer to religions other than Buddhism ② amateurish; green; a greenhorn; a novice

外間(ㄨㄞㄐㄧㄢ)
① the outside ② outsiders; people not in the know

外江人(ㄨㄞㄐㄧㄤㄖㄣˊ)
the southerners' reference to the people along or north of the Yangtze River

外景(ㄨㄞㄐㄧㄥ)
(said of motion picture production) a location; an exterior: 那部電影正在拍外景。The film is on location now.

外戚(ㄨㄞㄑㄧ)
the power group (usually relatives) of an emperor's mother or wife

外僑(ㄨㄞㄑㄧㄠ)
foreign residents

外欠(ㄨㄞㄑㄧㄢ)
debts not included in a statement

外親(ㄨㄞㄑㄧㄣ)
blood relatives of the female members of a family

外勤(ㄨㄞㄑㄧㄣ)
a job which involves activities mostly outside an office building, such as that of a news reporter, policeman, etc.; work done outside the office

外強中乾(ㄨㄞㄑㄧㄤˊㄓㄨㄥㄍㄢ)
a paper tiger; outwardly strong but inwardly weak

外圈(ㄨㄞㄑㄩㄢ)
(sports) an outer lane; an outer circle

外銷(ㄨㄞㄒㄧㄠ)
to export; for export; export: 中國出產的茶及絲到外國。China exported tea and silk to foreign countries.

外縣(ㄨㄞㄒㄧㄢ)
① counties other than one's own ② a provincial capital

外鄉(ㄨㄞㄒㄧㄤ)
another part of the country; some other place: 他操外鄉口音。He speaks with a non-local accent.

外鄉人(ㄨㄞㄒㄧㄤㄖㄣˊ)
strangers; people from other lands

外向(ㄨㄞㄒㄧㄤ)
extrovert; extroversion

外星人(ㄨㄞㄒㄧㄥㄖㄣˊ)
an E. T. (extraterrestrial)

外形(ㄨㄞㄒㄧㄥˊ)
an appearance; an external form; a contour

外姓(ㄨㄞㄒㄧㄥ)
a family name other than one's own

外痔(ㄨㄞㄓ)
external hemorrhoids

外債(ㄨㄞㄓㄞ)
foreign loans; international loans

外長(ㄨㄞㄓㄤ)
Minister of Foreign Affairs

外史(ㄨㄞㄕ)
a narrative of events not recorded in history

外重內輕(ㄨㄞㄓㄨㄥˋㄋㄟˋㄑㄧㄥ)
a political system under which the central government is weak while the local governments enjoy a large degree of autonomy

外城(ㄨㄞㄔㄥˊ)
newly-developed communities outside the old city wall

外出(ㄨㄞㄔㄨ)
to go out; to be out of town; to absent oneself from home or office

外出血(ㄨㄞㄔㄨㄒㄧㄝ)
external hemorrhage

外傳(ㄨㄞㄔㄨㄢˊ)
rumors are circulating...; speculations have it...: 外傳內閣將改組。Rumors have it

〔夕部〕

〔夕部〕

that there will be a change in the Cabinet.

外史(ㄨㄞˋ ㄕˇ)
①an official in ancient China in charge of the collection of legends and narratives ②histories with a more or less fictitious nature

外室(ㄨㄞˋ ㄕˋ)
a mistress living outside one's own home

外商(ㄨㄞˋ ㄕㄤ)
foreign businessmen

外傷(ㄨㄞˋ ㄕㄤ)
external injuries; bruises; injuries that do not affect internal organs

外甥(ㄨㄞˋ ㄕㄥ)
sister's sons; nephews

外甥女(ㄨㄞˋ ㄕㄥ ㄋㄩˇ)
sister's daughters; nieces

外省(ㄨㄞˋ ㄕㄥˇ)
other provinces

外省人(ㄨㄞˋ ㄕㄥˇ ㄖㄣˊ)
persons from another province

外人(ㄨㄞˋ ㄖㄣˊ)
①outsiders; strangers; the people who do not belong to one's own circle or organization: 此事不足爲外人道。 It is not to be mentioned to outsiders. ②foreigners

外資(ㄨㄞˋ ㄗ)
foreign capital

外子(ㄨㄞˋ ㄗˇ)
a reference to one's own husband

外在(ㄨㄞˋ ㄗㄞˋ)
external; extrinsic: 它是外在因素。It's an external factor.

外族(ㄨㄞˋ ㄗㄨˊ)
①families or clans on the maternal side ②foreign or outside clans, tribes or families

外祖(ㄨㄞˋ ㄗㄨˇ)or**外祖父**(ㄨㄞˋ ㄗㄨˇ ㄈㄨˋ)or**外公**(ㄨㄞˋ ㄍㄨㄥ)
one's maternal grandfather

外祖母(ㄨㄞˋ ㄗㄨˇ ㄇㄨˇ)
one's maternal grandmother

外才(ㄨㄞˋ ㄘㄞˊ)
the talents of an extrovert or mixer

外財(ㄨㄞˋ ㄘㄞˊ)

illegal gains; a windfall; riches acquired accidentally

外宿(ㄨㄞˋ ㄙㄨˋ)
to stay outside (one's own home or dormitory) overnight

外孫(ㄨㄞˋ ㄙㄨㄣ)
sons of one's daughters

外孫女(ㄨㄞˋ ㄙㄨㄣ ㄋㄩˇ)
daughters of one's daughters

外耳(ㄨㄞˋ ㄦˇ)
the external ear

外衣(ㄨㄞˋ ㄧ)
a coat; a jacket; outer clothing; an outer garment

外野(ㄨㄞˋ ㄧㄝˇ)
(baseball)outfield

外野手(ㄨㄞˋ ㄧㄝˇ ㄕㄡˇ)
an outfielder

外延(ㄨㄞˋ ㄧㄢˊ)
①(logic) extension ②(mathematics) exterior extent

外因(ㄨㄞˋ ㄧㄣ)
(philosophy)external cause

外洋(ㄨㄞˋ ㄧㄤˊ)
overseas; abroad

外侮(ㄨㄞˋ ㄨˇ)
foreign aggression; insults or humiliations caused by foreign powers: 我們必須抵禦外侮。We have to resist foreign aggression.

外務(ㄨㄞˋ ㄨˋ)
①foreign affairs ②affairs or work which do not really concern one or which one is not obliged to handle

外務部(ㄨㄞˋ ㄨˋ ㄅㄨˋ)
the Ministry of Foreign Affairs of the late Ching Dynasty

外圍(ㄨㄞˋ ㄨㄟˊ)
anything surrounding the central figure or thing; the perimeter

外圍防禦(ㄨㄞˋ ㄨㄟˊ ㄈㄤˊ ㄩˋ)
perimeter defense; peripheral defense

外圍組織(ㄨㄞˋ ㄨㄟˊ ㄗㄨˇ ㄓ)
peripheral organizations; front organizations

外文(ㄨㄞˋ ㄨㄣˊ)
a foreign language

外語(ㄨㄞˋ ㄩˇ)
a foreign language

外域(ㄨㄞˋ ㄩˋ)

foreign lands

外遇(ㄨㄞˋ ㄩˋ)
to have extramarital affairs

外援(ㄨㄞˋ ㄩㄢˊ)
outside help; foreign aid

外緣(ㄨㄞˋ ㄩㄢˊ)
①the outer rim (of an object) ②desires that come from outside temptations

外圓內方(ㄨㄞˋ ㄩㄢˊ ㄋㄟˋ ㄈㄤ)
smooth and easy-going in manners but highly principled in daily life

外用(ㄨㄞˋ ㄩㄥˋ)
external use; external application

三畫

【多】 909
1. ㄉㄨㄛ duo duō

1. many; much; too much: 他有很多朋友。He has a large number of friends.
2. more than; much more over: 十比八多二。Ten is two more than eight.
3. much; greatly; highly; very: 病人好多了。The patient is much better now.
4. to praise
5. only
6. a Chinese family name

多胞胎(ㄉㄨㄛ ㄅㄠ ㄊㄞ)
multiple birth

多半(ㄉㄨㄛ ㄅㄢˋ)or**多半兒**(ㄉㄨㄛ ㄅㄢˋ ㄦ)or**多分**(ㄉㄨㄛ ㄈㄣ)
①most; the greater part: 這支棒球隊的成員多半是學生。Most of the members of this baseball team are students ②most likely; probably: 天空烏雲密佈,多半要下雨了。The sky is darkly clouded; it will probably rain.

多邊(ㄉㄨㄛ ㄅㄧㄢ)
multilateral

多邊協定(ㄉㄨㄛ ㄅㄧㄢ ㄒㄧㄝˊ ㄉㄧㄥˋ)
a multilateral agreement

多邊形(ㄉㄨㄛ ㄅㄧㄢ ㄒㄧㄥˊ)or**多角形**(ㄉㄨㄛ ㄐㄧㄠˇ ㄒㄧㄥˊ)
a polygon

多變(ㄉㄨㄛ ㄅㄧㄢˋ)
changeable; changeful; varied: 你能適應這多變的天氣嗎? Can you be accustomed to the changeable weather?

多病(ㄉㄨㄛ ㄅㄧㄥˋ)
susceptible to diseases;
prone to illness; constantly
ill

多謀善斷(ㄉㄨㄛ ㄇㄡˊ ㄕㄢˋ ㄉㄨㄢˋ)
resourceful and decisive;
sagacious and resolute

多蒙(ㄉㄨㄛ ㄇㄥˊ)
thanks for (your, his, etc.
permission, help, etc.)

多面體(ㄉㄨㄛ ㄇㄧㄢˋ ㄊㄧˇ)
a polyhedron

多明尼加(ㄉㄨㄛ ㄇㄧㄥˊ ㄋㄧˊ ㄐㄧㄚ)
the Dominican Republic

多目標(ㄉㄨㄛ ㄇㄨˋ ㄅㄧㄠ)
(said of construction projects) multipurpose

多方面(ㄉㄨㄛ ㄈㄤ ㄇㄧㄢˋ)
many-sided; in many ways:
此書給大家帶來的好處是多方
面的。The book has proved
useful to us in many ways.

多福多壽(ㄉㄨㄛ ㄈㄨˊ ㄉㄨㄛ ㄕㄡˋ)
happiness and longevity;
amply blessed

多大(ㄉㄨㄛ ㄉㄚˋ)
① How big? ② How old? 他
多大年紀多大? How old is he?

多黨制度(ㄉㄨㄛ ㄉㄤˇ ㄓˋ ㄉㄨˋ)
the multiparty system

多多(ㄉㄨㄛ ㄉㄨㄛ)
a great deal: 請多多幫助這孩
子。Please help the child a
great deal.

多少少(ㄉㄨㄛ ㄕㄠˇ ㄕㄠˇ)
more or less: 她多多少少有點
瘋狂。She is more or less
crazy.

多益善(ㄉㄨㄛ ㄧˋ ㄕㄢˋ)
The more, the better.

多端(ㄉㄨㄛ ㄉㄨㄢ)
① many kinds; a great variety: 他作惡多端，應受嚴懲。He
has done many kinds of misdeeds; therefore, he should
be punished severely. ② in
many ways

多胎孕妊(ㄉㄨㄛ ㄊㄞ ㄩㄣˋ ㄖㄣˋ)
multiple pregnancy

多頭(ㄉㄨㄛ ㄊㄡˊ)
(said of stock exchange) to
buy long; taking a long position

多退少補(ㄉㄨㄛ ㄊㄨㄟˋ ㄕㄠˇ ㄅㄨˇ) 或
多還少補(ㄉㄨㄛ ㄏㄨㄢˊ ㄕㄠˇ ㄅㄨˇ)
to return the overcharge and
demand payment of the

shortage, if any (The
expression is used when
money is paid in advance
for a specific use, the cost
of which is unknown beforehand.)

多瑙河(ㄉㄨㄛ ㄋㄠˇ ㄏㄜˊ)
the Danube River

多難興邦(ㄉㄨㄛ ㄋㄢˋ ㄒㄧㄥ ㄅㄤ)
Foreign aggressions often
awaken a nation from its
slumbers and thus help
make it strong.

多年不見(ㄉㄨㄛ ㄋㄧㄢˊ ㄅㄨˋ ㄐㄧㄢˋ)
to have not met or seen for
many years

多年生植物(ㄉㄨㄛ ㄋㄧㄢˊ ㄕㄥ ㄓˋ ㄨˋ)
perennial plants: 玫瑰是多年
生植物。Roses are perennials.

多禮(ㄉㄨㄛ ㄌㄧˇ)
very polite; overcourteous

多倫多(ㄉㄨㄛ ㄌㄨㄣˊ ㄉㄨㄛ)
Toronto, a Canadian city

多氯聯苯(ㄉㄨㄛ ㄌㄩˋ ㄌㄧㄢˊ ㄅㄣˇ)
(chemistry) polychlorinated
biphenyl

多哥蘭(ㄉㄨㄛ ㄍㄜ ㄌㄢˊ)
Togoland

多哥共和國(ㄉㄨㄛ ㄍㄜ ㄍㄨㄥˋ ㄏㄜˊ
《ㄨㄛˊ)
Republic of Togo

多故(ㄉㄨㄛ ㄍㄨˋ)
many troubles or mishaps:
我們國家多故。There are
many troubles or crises in
our nation.

多寡(ㄉㄨㄛ ㄍㄨㄚˇ)
number; amount: 各省人口多
寡不等。The population in
every province varies in
number.

多寡不拘(ㄉㄨㄛ ㄍㄨㄚˇ ㄅㄨˋ ㄐㄩ)
It doesn't matter how much
or how little (you contribute).

多國企業(ㄉㄨㄛ ㄍㄨㄛˊ ㄑㄧˋ ㄧㄝˋ)
multinational enterprises

多管閒事(ㄉㄨㄛ ㄍㄨㄢˇ ㄒㄧㄢˊ ㄕˋ)
to poke one's nose into
others' business; to be a
busybody: 那個長舌婦總是
喜歡多管閒事。The gossip was
always poking her nose into
other people's business.

多虧(ㄉㄨㄛ ㄎㄨㄟ)
it is fortunate that; we are
lucky to; thanks to…: 多虧他

給我們帶路。We were lucky
to have him leading the
way.

多會兒(ㄉㄨㄛ ㄏㄨㄟˋ ㄦ)
What time…? 或 When…? 或
How much time…? 你要多會
兒才能來? When can you
come?

多角形(ㄉㄨㄛ ㄐㄧㄠˇ ㄒㄧㄥˊ)or 多邊
形(ㄉㄨㄛ ㄅㄧㄢ ㄒㄧㄥˊ)
a polygon; polygonal

多見多聞(ㄉㄨㄛ ㄐㄧㄢˋ ㄉㄨㄛ ㄨㄣˊ)
(literally) to have seen and
heard a lot—to have wide
experience; sophisticated;
well-experienced

多妻制(ㄉㄨㄛ ㄑㄧ ㄓˋ)
polygamy 亦作「一夫多妻」

多歧亡羊(ㄉㄨㄛ ㄑㄧˊ ㄨㄤˊ ㄧㄤˊ)
One will get nowhere if he
lacks single-mindedness and
perseverance.

多情(ㄉㄨㄛ ㄑㄧㄥˊ)
passionate; emotional; sentimental: 她的美麗即刻打動了他
多情的心。Her beauty made
an immediate appeal to his
passionate temperament.

多謝(ㄉㄨㄛ ㄒㄧㄝˋ)
Many thanks. 或 Thank you
very much. 或 Thanks a lot.

多心(ㄉㄨㄛ ㄒㄧㄣ)
① to be very suspicious or
oversensitive; distrustful: 他
總是對別人多心。He is always
distrustful of others. ②
tricky; treacherous

多相電流(ㄉㄨㄛ ㄒㄧㄤˋ ㄉㄧㄢˋ ㄌㄧㄡˊ)
(electricity) a polyphase
current

多行不義必自斃(ㄉㄨㄛ ㄒㄧㄥˊ ㄅㄨˋ
ㄧˋ ㄅㄧˋ ㄗˋ ㄅㄧˋ)
To do evil deeds frequently
will bring ruin to the doer.

多種多樣(ㄉㄨㄛ ㄓㄨㄥˇ ㄉㄨㄛ ㄧㄤˋ)
varied; manifold: 它能滿足人
們多種多樣的需要。It can
meet the manifold needs of
the people.

多種經營(ㄉㄨㄛ ㄓㄨㄥˇ ㄐㄧㄥ ㄧㄥˊ)
a diversified undertaking;
diversification

多愁善感(ㄉㄨㄛ ㄔㄡˊ ㄕㄢˋ ㄍㄢˇ)
sentimental; emotional and
sensitive

多產婦(ㄉㄨㄛ ㄔㄢˇ ㄈㄨˋ)
a multiparous woman

多產作家(ㄉㄨㄛ ㄔㄢ ㄗㄨㄛ ㄐㄧㄚ)
a prolific writer

多重人格(ㄉㄨㄛ ㄔㄨㄥ ㄖㄣ ㄍㄜˊ)
multiple personality

多時(ㄉㄨㄛ ㄕˊ)
a long time: 我們已等候多時。
We have waited a long time.

多事(ㄉㄨㄛ ㄕˋ)
officious; interfering; meddling: 我不想多事。I don't wish to interfere in what others do.

多事之秋(ㄉㄨㄛ ㄕˋ ㄓ ㄑㄧㄡ)
time of national crises; troubled times; a year of many troubles; an eventful year

多少(ㄉㄨㄛ ㄕㄠˇ)
① How much? 或 How many? 或 How long? 多少人在屋子裡? How many people are there in the house? ② more or less; somewhat: 我經過此一長途旅行後，多少有些疲倦了。I am more or less tired after such a long trip.

多神教(ㄉㄨㄛ ㄕㄣˊ ㄐㄧㄠˋ)
polytheism

多數(ㄉㄨㄛ ㄕㄨˋ)
the majority; many: 大多數的人喜愛和平而不要戰爭。The majority of people prefer peace to war.

多子多累(ㄉㄨㄛ ㄗˇ ㄉㄨㄛ ㄌㄟˋ)
The more children one has, the more he toils.

多子多孫(ㄉㄨㄛ ㄗˇ ㄉㄨㄛ ㄙㄨㄣ)
many children and grandchildren (regarded as a blessing among old Chinese)

多災多難(ㄉㄨㄛ ㄗㄞ ㄉㄨㄛ ㄋㄢˋ)
to be plagued by frequent ills; to be dogged by bad luck, misfortune, etc.

多嘴(ㄉㄨㄛ ㄗㄨㄟˇ)
to make statements about things which have nothing to do with oneself; to have a big mouth; to shoot one's mouth off

多此一舉(ㄉㄨㄛ ㄘˇ ㄧ ㄐㄩˇ)
a superfluous or unnecessary action, remark, etc.: 何必多此一舉呢? Why take such an unnecessary action?

多次(ㄉㄨㄛ ㄘˋ)
many times; time and again; repeatedly; on many occa-sions: 這位美國人曾多次訪問中國。This American has visited China many times.

多才多藝(ㄉㄨㄛ ㄘㄞˊ ㄉㄨㄛ ㄧˋ)
versatile; very capable; a master of all trades

多財善賈(ㄉㄨㄛ ㄘㄞˊ ㄕㄢˋ ㄍㄨˇ)
rich and having business acumen

多采多姿 or 多彩多姿(ㄉㄨㄛ ㄘㄞˇ ㄉㄨㄛ ㄗ)
magnificent; colorful; many-faceted

多藏厚亡(ㄉㄨㄛ ㄘㄤˊ ㄏㄡˋ ㄨㄤˊ)
The greater fortune one amasses, the greater loss he will suffer.

多疑(ㄉㄨㄛ ㄧˊ)
suspicious

多義詞(ㄉㄨㄛ ㄧˋ ㄘˊ)
(linguistics) polysemant

多樣化(ㄉㄨㄛ ㄧㄤˋ ㄏㄨㄚˋ)
to diversify; to have varied: 摩天大樓使得天空呈現出多樣化的線條。The skyline is diversified by the sky-scrapers.

多聞闕疑(ㄉㄨㄛ ㄨㄣˊ ㄑㄩㄝˋ ㄧˊ)
Instead of pretending to understand everything, one should listen more to others.

多餘(ㄉㄨㄛ ㄩˊ)
unnecessary; superfluous; superfluity; uncalled-for: 你這話是多餘的。What you say is uncalled-for.

多元論(ㄉㄨㄛ ㄩㄢˊ ㄌㄨㄣˋ)
(philosophy) pluralism

多雲(ㄉㄨㄛ ㄩㄣˊ)
cloudy: 昨天是多雲的天氣。It was cloudy yesterday.

【多】 909
2. ㄉㄨㄛ dwo duó

how, what, etc.—in exclamatory statements: 這小孩多聰明啊! How clever the child is!

多麼(ㄉㄨㄛ ˙ㄇㄜ)
how (good, beautiful, etc.); what: 多麼艷麗的色彩! What bright colors! 多麼美好的一天! What a lovely day!

多美(ㄉㄨㄛ ㄇㄟˇ)
How beautiful! 或 What a beauty! 她長得多美啊! How beautiful she is! 或 What a beauty she is!

多好(ㄉㄨㄛ ㄏㄠˇ)
How nice! 或 How wonderful! 或 How good! 她唱得多好啊! How well she sings!

【夙】 910
ㄙㄨˋ suh sù

1. the early morning
2. old or original (desires, etc.)
3. (Buddhism) inborn; inherited 亦作「宿」

夙慧(ㄙㄨˋ ㄏㄨㄟˋ)
to be born intelligent; inborn intelligence

夙駕(ㄙㄨˋ ㄐㄧㄚˋ)
to start a journey early; to set out early

夙昔(ㄙㄨˋ ㄒㄧˊ)
① past times; in the past ② day and night

夙興夜寐(ㄙㄨˋ ㄒㄧㄥ ㄧㄝˋ ㄇㄟˋ)
to rise early and sleep late—very diligent

夙志(ㄙㄨˋ ㄓˋ)
a long-cherished ambition

夙仇(ㄙㄨˋ ㄔㄡˊ)
an old enemy

夙儒(ㄙㄨˋ ㄖㄨˊ)
a learned scholar

夙素 or 宿素(ㄙㄨˋ ㄙㄨˋ)
a long-cherished ambition

夙夜(ㄙㄨˋ ㄧㄝˋ)
day and night

夙夜匪懈(ㄙㄨˋ ㄧㄝˋ ㄈㄟˇ ㄒㄧㄝˋ)
to work diligently day and night

夙緣(ㄙㄨˋ ㄩㄢˊ)
(Buddhism) a relationship forged in the earlier incarnation 亦作「宿緣」

夙怨(ㄙㄨˋ ㄩㄢˋ)
old grudges 亦作「宿怨」

夙願(ㄙㄨˋ ㄩㄢˋ)
an old wish; a long cherished wish: 這女孩實現了她的夙願。The girl got her long cherished wish.

五畫

【夜】 911
ㄧㄝˋ yeh yè

1. night; dark; darkness: 夜間我不出門。I don't go out after dark. 冬天畫短夜長。In winter the days are short and the nights long.

夜班(ㄧㄝ ㄅㄢ)
night shifts; night work: 大夜班 the graveyard shift 小夜班 the swing shift

夜半(ㄧㄝ ㄅㄢ)
midnight: 他工作至夜半。 He worked until midnight.

夜不閉戶(ㄧㄝ ㄅㄨˋㄅㄧˋㄏㄨˋ)
There's no need to close doors at night. (a description often used to indicate efficient government administration)

夜貓子(ㄧㄝ ㄇㄠ·ㄗ)
①the owl ② a person who enjoys night life

夜盲症(ㄧㄝ ㄇㄤˊㄓㄥˋ)
night blindness; nyctalopia

夜明珠(ㄧㄝ ㄇㄧㄥˊㄓㄨ)
a legendary pearl that shines at night

夜幕(ㄧㄝ ㄇㄨˋ)
a curtain of night; gathering darkness: 夜幕籠罩着大地。 The curtain of darkness covered the earth.

夜大(ㄧㄝ ㄉㄚˋ)or 夜間大學(ㄧㄝ ㄐㄧㄢ ㄉㄚˋㄒㄩㄝˊ)
an evening university

夜度資(ㄧㄝ ㄉㄨˋㄗ)
the money charged by a prostitute for boudoir favors for a night

夜啼(ㄧㄝ ㄊㄧˊ)
the morbid night crying of babies

夜來香(ㄧㄝ ㄌㄞˊㄒㄧㄤ)
(botany) the tuberose

夜闌人靜(ㄧㄝ ㄌㄢˊㄖㄣˊㄐㄧㄥˋ)or 夜深人靜(ㄧㄝ ㄕㄣ ㄖㄣˊㄐㄧㄥˋ)
(in) the quiet of the late night; deep in the night; at the dead of night

夜郎自大(ㄧㄝ ㄌㄤˊㄗˋㄉㄚˋ)
the megalomania of the king of Yehlang (who asked the envoy of Han, "Which was bigger, the Han Empire or the tiny state of Yehlang?") —(figuratively) a braggadocio; ignorant and boastful

夜涼如水(ㄧㄝ ㄌㄧㄤˊㄖㄨˊㄕㄨㄟˇ)
the chilling (autumn) night

夜光杯(ㄧㄝ ㄍㄨㄤ ㄅㄟ)
a cup made of jade that glows in the night

夜光錶(ㄧㄝ ㄍㄨㄤ ㄅㄧㄠˇ)
a watch with luminous markings on the dial

夜工(ㄧㄝ ㄍㄨㄥ)
night work; a night job

夜課(ㄧㄝ ㄎㄜˋ)
night classes

夜合花(ㄧㄝ ㄏㄜˊㄏㄨㄚ)
(botany) *Magnolia coco*

夜壺(ㄧㄝ ㄏㄨˊ)
a chamber pot 亦作「夜淨兒」

夜間(ㄧㄝ ㄐㄧㄢ)or 夜晚(ㄧㄝ ㄒㄧˋ)或 夜裏(ㄧㄝ ㄌㄧˇ)
the night; nighttime; at night: 那不是個夜間可去的地方。 It isn't a place to visit by night.

夜間部(ㄧㄝ ㄐㄧㄢ ㄅㄨˋ)
the night department (of a school, college or university)

夜禁(ㄧㄝ ㄐㄧㄣˋ)
the night curfew

夜驚(ㄧㄝ ㄐㄧㄥ)
nocturnal phobia

夜景(ㄧㄝ ㄐㄧㄥˇ)
night scenes (of a locality)

夜靜(ㄧㄝ ㄐㄧㄥˋ)
the dead of night; the still of the night

夜勤(ㄧㄝ ㄑㄧㄣˊ)
night shift; night work; night duty (especially referring to doctors, policemen, newsmen, etc.)

夜曲(ㄧㄝ ㄑㄩˇ)
(music) a nocturne

夜襲(ㄧㄝ ㄒㄧˊ)
a night attack or raid; to launch an attack under the cover of night

夜戲(ㄧㄝ ㄒㄧˋ)
a night show; an evening performance

夜校(ㄧㄝ ㄒㄧㄠˋ)or 夜學(ㄧㄝ ㄒㄩㄝˊ)
a night school; an evening school

夜行軍(ㄧㄝ ㄒㄧㄥˊㄐㄩㄣ)
the night march

夜行人(ㄧㄝ ㄒㄧㄥˊㄖㄣˊ)
①night travelers ②cavaliers (俠客), thieves, etc. who move about at night

夜叉(ㄧㄝ ㄔㄚ)
①(Chinese mythology) a monstrous-looking devil ②

(Buddhism) a yaksah (a malevolent spirit)

夜車(ㄧㄝ ㄔㄜ)
①a night train ②(figuratively) to study late at night; to burn the midnight oil

夜長夢多(ㄧㄝ ㄔㄤˊㄇㄥˋㄉㄨㄛ)
(literally) The night is long and dreams many.—There'll be twists and obstacles if a problem or an issue is not settled promptly.

夜場(ㄧㄝ ㄔㄤˇ)or 夜市(ㄧㄝ ㄔㄤˇ)
a night show; an evening show

夜市(ㄧㄝ ㄕˋ)
business activities in night hours; markets devoted to nighttime business

夜生活(ㄧㄝ ㄕㄥ ㄏㄨㄛˊ)
night life

夜總會(ㄧㄝ ㄗㄨㄥˇ ㄏㄨㄟˋ)
a nightclub

夜色(ㄧㄝ ㄙㄜˋ)
the dim light of night —moonlight: 他們趁着夜色在花園裏散步。 They walked by moonlight in the garden.

夜色蒼茫(ㄧㄝ ㄙㄜˋㄘㄤ ㄇㄤˊ)
twilight at dusk

夜以繼日(ㄧㄝ ㄧˇㄐㄧˋㄖˋ)
night and day; around the clock; day in and day out: 他夜以繼日地努力工作。 He worked hard night and day.

夜夜(ㄧㄝ ㄧㄝ)
every night; night after night

夜鶯(ㄧㄝ ㄧㄥ)
the nightingale

夜未央(ㄧㄝ ㄨㄟˋㄧㄤ)
It is not dawn yet.

夜晚(ㄧㄝ ㄨㄢˇ)
night; in the night: 那是個滿天星斗的夜晚。 It was a starry night.

八畫

【夠】 912
(够) ㄍㄡˋ gow gòu
1. enough; more than enough; too much; sufficient: 座位夠不夠? Are there enough seats? 五個人就很夠了。 Five men will be quite enough.

【夕 部】

【夕部】

2. fully; quite: 這地區的天然資源真夠豐富。The district is quite abundant in natural resources.

夠本（ㄍㄡˋ ㄅㄣˇ）
enough to cover the cost; to be sufficient to cover the cost; enough to break even with the capital invested; to be worth the effort or money

夠不夠（ㄍㄡˋ ㄅㄨˋ ㄍㄡˋ）
Is it enough?

夠朋友（ㄍㄡˋ ㄆㄥˊ ㄧㄡˇ）
to be such a person whose friendship is worth having; to be true to friends; to be a friend in need

夠忙（ㄍㄡˋ ㄇㄤˊ）
enough work to keep one busy; to have one's hands full

夠面子（ㄍㄡˋ ㄇㄧㄢˋ ˙ㄗ）or 夠體面（ㄍㄡˋ ㄊㄧˇ ㄇㄧㄢˋ）
(said of concessions made by the other side or receptions accorded by others) enough to preserve one's face—to enjoy enough honor

夠你受的（ㄍㄡˋ ㄋㄧˇ ㄕㄡˋ ˙ㄉㄜ）
enough trouble for you

夠格（ㄍㄡˋ ㄍㄜˊ）
to be qualified; to be up to standard: 他很夠格當教師。He's well qualified to be a teacher.

夠勁兒（ㄍㄡˋ ㄐㄧㄥˋㄦ）
①(said of an onerous task) almost too much to cope with②strong or hot (in taste, strength, etc.): 這胡椒真夠勁兒。This pepper is really hot.

夠交情（ㄍㄡˋ ㄐㄧㄠ ˙ㄑㄧㄥ）
the friendship with another person that is deep enough for one to ask a favor of or to do him a favor

夠瞧的（ㄍㄡˋ ㄑㄧㄠˊ˙ㄉㄜ）
(colloquial) ridiculous (sights); considerable (burdens); oppressive (heat); chilling (cold); herculean (tasks); impossible (personality); pitiable (conditions): 天氣熱得真夠瞧的。It's oppressive hot.

夠受（ㄍㄡˋ ㄕㄡˋ）

unbearable; intolerable

夠數（ㄍㄡˋ ㄕㄨˋ）
enough to make up the required number; sufficient in quantity

夠意思（ㄍㄡˋ ㄧˋ˙ㄙ）
①really something; terrific②generous; really kind

夠味兒（ㄍㄡˋ ㄨㄟˋㄦ）
enjoyable; pleasant enough; quite satisfactory

十一畫

【夢】 913 ㄇㄥˋ meng mèng

1. a dream: 他常做怪夢。He often had bad dreams.

2. to dream; to see visions: 你在做夢吧！You are dreaming (or planning something impossible).

3. wishful thinking; wishful

4. a Chinese family name

夢筆生花（ㄇㄥˋ ㄅㄧˇ ㄕㄥ ㄏㄨㄚ）
(literally) to see one's writing brush blooming in a dream—(figuratively) to be capable of writing felicitously

夢寐（ㄇㄥˋ ㄇㄟˋ）
①the state of sleep and dreaming②very eagerly③visionary; vague

夢寐以求（ㄇㄥˋ ㄇㄟˋ ㄧˇ ㄑㄧㄡˊ）
to crave something so that one even dreams about it; to long for something day and night: 世界和平是人們夢寐以求的事。People are longing for world peace day and night.

夢闌（ㄇㄥˋ ㄌㄢˊ）
to become pregnant

夢話（ㄇㄥˋ ㄏㄨㄚˋ）
①an absurd and unthinkable speech②words uttered in one's sleep; somniloquy

夢幻（ㄇㄥˋ ㄏㄨㄢˋ）
illusion; a dream; reverie: 她沉緬於過去的夢幻中。She fell into a reverie about the past.

夢幻泡影（ㄇㄥˋ ㄏㄨㄢˋ ㄆㄠˋ ㄧㄥˇ）
emptiness; nothingness; visionary; illusory

夢魂顛倒（ㄇㄥˋ ㄏㄨㄣˊ ㄉㄧㄢ ㄉㄠˇ）
to be in a trance; bewitched;

to fall head over heels (in love)

夢見（ㄇㄥˋ ㄐㄧㄢˋ）
to dream (of meeting someone or seeing something): 夢見你是個富人。He dreamt that you were a rich man.

夢境（ㄇㄥˋ ㄐㄧㄥˋ）
dreamland; a dream world; a dream: 他覺得好像在夢境裡。He feels as if he were in a dream.

夢鄉（ㄇㄥˋ ㄒㄧㄤ）
asleep; dreamland; sleep; slumber: 他已進入夢鄉了。He has fallen asleep.

夢想（ㄇㄥˋ ㄒㄧㄤˇ）
a daydream; daydreaming; vain hopes; to dream of: 許多人喜歡編織夢想。There are many people who are fond of spinning daydreams.

夢想不到（ㄇㄥˋ ㄒㄧㄤˇ ㄅㄨˋ ㄉㄠˋ）
(said of something very unlikely to happen but actually happened) beyond one's wildest dream

夢熊之喜（ㄇㄥˋ ㄒㄩㄥˊ ㄓ ㄒㄧˇ）
to give birth to a son

夢兆（ㄇㄥˋ ㄓㄠˋ）
a prognostic from a dream

夢中人（ㄇㄥˋ ㄓㄨㄥ ㄖㄣˊ）
a sweetheart

夢遺（ㄇㄥˋ ㄧˊ）
nocturnal emission

夢囈（ㄇㄥˋ ㄧˋ）
①somniloquy②nonsense

夢遊（ㄇㄥˋ ㄧㄡˊ）
to somnambulate; somnambulation; somnambulism

夢魘（ㄇㄥˋ ㄧㄢˇ）
nightmares; bad dreams

【夤】 914 ㄧㄣˊ yín

1. to hang on (power, glory, etc.)

2. to respect

3. a remote place

夤夜（ㄧㄣˊ ㄧㄝˋ）
deep in the night

夤緣（ㄧㄣˊ ㄩㄢˊ）
to rise or climb on somebody's coattails

【夥】 915 ㄏㄨㄛˇ huoǒ

1. many; much; plenty; lots of

2. a partner; a company

a waiter; a clerk

a crowd

大伴 (ㄉㄚ ㄅㄢˋ)
a companion; a partner; a business associate

大同 (ㄉㄚ ㄊㄨㄥˊ)
in league with; to gang up with

大計 (ㄉㄚ ㄐㄧˋ)
① a waiter; a clerk; an employee in a shop 亦作「伙計」 ② buddy

大 部
ㄉㄚ dah dà

【大】 916
1. ㄉㄚ dah dà
1. big; large: 台北是個大城市。Taipei is a big city.
2. great: 貝多芬是個大音樂家。Beethoven was a great musician.
3. much: 無多大希望。There is not much hope.
4. very; highly; extremely; greatly: 他大爲吃驚。He was greatly surprised.
5. (polite expression) your: 大札 your letter
6. the eldest; senior: 他大我五歲。He is eight years senior to me.
7. full-grown; an adult
8. (referring to date only) before; after: 他大前天來過。He came here two days before yesterday.
9. to make large; to make great
10. a Chinese family name

大壩 (ㄉㄚ ㄅㄚˋ)
a dam 參看「水壩」

大波斯菊 (ㄉㄚ ㄅㄛ ㄙ ㄐㄩˊ)
(botany) a cosmos

大伯 (ㄉㄚ ㄅㄛˊ)
① one's father's elder brother; an uncle 亦作「伯父」 ② an uncle (a polite form of address for an elderly man) 亦作「老伯」

大白 (ㄉㄚ ㄅㄛˊ)
① ⓐname of a kind of wine-cup ⓑ(said of truth) to come out to the open; to

be known by all: 真相已經大白。The truth has become known to all.
② (ㄉㄚ ㄅㄞˊ) whiting

大白菜 (ㄉㄚ ㄅㄞˊ ㄘㄞˋ)
a Chinese cabbage

大伯子 (ㄉㄚ ㄅㄛˇ ·ㄗ)
the eldest brother of one's husband

大敗 (ㄉㄚ ㄅㄞˋ)
① to defeat utterly; to put to rout ② to suffer a severe defeat

大悲 (ㄉㄚ ㄅㄟ)
(Buddhism) the great deliverance of Buddha from sufferings and afflictions; the great mercy

大寶 (ㄉㄚ ㄅㄠˇ)
the imperial throne

大班 (ㄉㄚ ㄅㄢ)
① the manager of a foreign firm in China ② the captain (as of taxi dancers) ③ the top class in a kindergarten

大阪 (ㄉㄚ ㄅㄢˇ)
Osaka, a port city of Japan

大半 (ㄉㄚ ㄅㄢˋ)
① the larger half; the greater part; for the most part; mostly: 工作完成了大半。The work is mostly done. ② probably; likely: 他大牛被交通阻塞困住了。He is probably stuck in a traffic jam.

大本營 (ㄉㄚ ㄅㄣˇ ㄧㄥˊ)
headquarters

大筆 (ㄉㄚ ㄅㄧˇ)
① the brush-pen ② your writing; your handwriting

大別 (ㄉㄚ ㄅㄧㄝˊ)
① a rough distinction; roughly classified ② name of a mountain range in Hupeh Province

大變 (ㄉㄚ ㄅㄧㄢˋ)
a tragic incident; a big misfortune

大便 (ㄉㄚ ㄅㄧㄢˋ)
stool; shit; faeces (or feces); excrement; night soil; to empty the bowels; to answer nature's call 參看「大糞」

大便不通 (ㄉㄚ ㄅㄧㄢˋ ㄅㄨˋ ㄊㄨㄥ)
constipation

大兵 (ㄉㄚ ㄅㄧㄥ)
① soldiers; foot soldiers ② a

big battle

大兵團 (ㄉㄚ ㄅㄧㄥ ㄊㄨㄢˊ)
large troop formation

大餅 (ㄉㄚ ㄅㄧㄥˇ)
a kind of large flatbread

大病 (ㄉㄚ ㄅㄧㄥˋ)
a serious illness or ailment: 他患着大病。He is suffering from a serious illness.

大不列顛 (ㄉㄚ ㄅㄨˋ ㄌㄧㄝˋ ㄉㄧㄢ)
Great Britain

大不敬 (ㄉㄚ ㄅㄨˋ ㄐㄧㄥˋ)
① great disrespect (to one's superiors or seniors) ② (in ancient China) a crime—discourtesy to the emperor; lese majesty

大不謂然 (ㄉㄚ ㄅㄨˋ ㄨㄟˋ ㄖㄢˊ)
to hold an entirely different opinion

大不相同 (ㄉㄚ ㄅㄨˋ ㄒㄧㄤ ㄊㄨㄥˊ)
entirely or totally different

大不如前 (ㄉㄚ ㄅㄨˋ ㄖㄨˊ ㄑㄧㄢˊ)
far worse than it was before; to have deteriorated or declined a lot in the interval

大不韙 (ㄉㄚ ㄅㄨˋ ㄨㄟˇ)
a great error; a heinous crime

大不了 (ㄉㄚ ·ㄅㄨˋ ㄌㄧㄠˇ)
① (if the) worst comes to (the) worst; at the worst: 大不了我們也祇損失一萬元。We shall lose at (the) worst only ten thousand dollars. ② serious; frightening: 沒什麼大不了的事情。It's nothing frightening.

大部分 (ㄉㄚ ㄅㄨˋ ㄈㄣˋ)
a great majority; for the most part; a greater part; mainly: 我班上大部分是女學生。The students in my class are mainly girls.

大牌 (ㄉㄚ ㄆㄞˊ)
big-name (actors or actresses); (said of movie stars or other performing artists) leading

大砲 (ㄉㄚ ㄆㄠˋ)
① guns; batteries; howitzers; cannons ② (slang) one who talks big

大鵬 (ㄉㄚ ㄆㄥˊ)
a roc (a legendary bird)

大批 (ㄉㄚ ㄆㄧ)

a large batch of, a good deal of; a horde of

大辟(ㄉㄚˋ ㄅㄧˋ)
　capital punishment or death sentence (in ancient China)

大媽(ㄉㄚˋ ㄇㄚ)
①father's elder brother's wife; an aunt 亦作「伯母」②an aunt (an affectionate or respectful form of address for an elderly woman)

大麻(ㄉㄚˋ ㄇㄚˊ)
①hemp ②marijuana

大麻瘋(ㄉㄚˋ ㄇㄚˊ ㄈㄥ)
①leprosy ②a leper

大馬(ㄉㄚˋ ㄇㄚˇ)
Malaysia

大馬士革(ㄉㄚˋ ㄇㄚˇ ㄕˋ ㄍㄜˊ)
Damascus, capital of Syria

大麥(ㄉㄚˋ ㄇㄞˋ)
barley

大貓熊(ㄉㄚˋ ㄇㄠ ㄒㄩㄥˊ)
a giant panda

大帽子(ㄉㄚˋ ㄇㄠˋ ˙ㄗ)
①(colloquial) the high and mighty person ②a big hat ③an unwarranted charge; a political label

大門(ㄉㄚˋ ㄇㄣˊ)
the main entrance; the main door or gate; the door that faces the street

大夢初醒(ㄉㄚˋ ㄇㄥˋ ㄔㄨ ㄒㄧㄥˇ)
the awakening or realization of past wrongdoings, hopeless pursuits, mistakes, etc.)

大米(ㄉㄚˋ ㄇㄧˇ)
a variety of Chinese rice known to Westerners as "pearl rice"; white rice; rice (as opposed to wheat)

大謬(ㄉㄚˋ ㄇㄧㄡˋ)
a blunder; preposterous; absurd

大謬不然(ㄉㄚˋ ㄇㄧㄡˋ ㄅㄨˋ ㄖㄢˊ)
entirely wrong; greatly mistaken

大名(ㄉㄚˋ ㄇㄧㄥˊ)
①your name (used in formal speech) ②a great name; a reputation ③name of a county in Hopeh Province

大名鼎鼎(ㄉㄚˋ ㄇㄧㄥˊ ㄉㄧㄥˇ ㄉㄧㄥˇ)
the one and only Mr. So-and-so; a big name; very famous; celebrated; well-known. 他是個大名鼎鼎的小說家。He

is a celebrated novelist.

大模大樣(ㄉㄚˋ ㄇㄛˊ ㄉㄚˋ ㄧㄤˋ)
①with full composure ②proudly; haughtily; in an open and showy manner; with a swagger

大拇指(ㄉㄚˋ ㄇㄨˇ ˙ㄓ)
thumb; 他豎起大拇指叫好。He held up his thumb in approval.

大發雷霆(ㄉㄚˋ ㄈㄚ ㄌㄟˊ ㄊㄧㄥˊ)
to be in a fit of anger or wrath; to be furious; to get into a terrible rage; 他昨晚大發雷霆。He flew (or fell) into a rage last night.

大發威風(ㄉㄚˋ ㄈㄚ ㄨㄟ ㄈㄥ)
①(said of a woman) to get very angry; to blow her top ②(said of a woman athlete) to display great prowess

大法(ㄉㄚˋ ㄈㄚˇ)
the fundamental law; the constitution of a nation

大法官(ㄉㄚˋ ㄈㄚˇ ㄍㄨㄢ)
a grand justice

大法官會議(ㄉㄚˋ ㄈㄚˇ ㄍㄨㄢ ㄏㄨㄟˋ ㄧˋ)
the Council of Grand Justices

大費周章(ㄉㄚˋ ㄈㄟˋ ㄓㄡ ㄓㄤ)
to go into great trouble in doing something; to take great pains

大凡(ㄉㄚˋ ㄈㄢˊ)
generally speaking; in most cases; ordinarily

大糞(ㄉㄚˋ ㄈㄣˋ)
feces or faeces; excrement

大方(ㄉㄚˋ ㄈㄤ)
①generous; liberal ②elegant and composed; natural and poised; easy ③experts, connoisseurs

大方向(ㄉㄚˋ ㄈㄤ ㄒㄧㄤˋ)
general orientation

大房(ㄉㄚˋ ㄈㄤˊ)
①the family of the eldest son after the old family breaks up ②name of a mountain in Hopeh Province

大放厥辭(ㄉㄚˋ ㄈㄤˋ ㄐㄩㄝˊ ㄘˊ)
to boast or brag wildly; to talk wildly; to talk absurdities or a lot of nonsense

大放異彩(ㄉㄚˋ ㄈㄤˋ ㄧˋ ㄘㄞˇ)
(said of sports performance, etc.) to yield unusually bril-

liant results

大風(ㄉㄚˋ ㄈㄥ)
a gale; a strong wind

大風大浪(ㄉㄚˋ ㄈㄥ ㄉㄚˋ ㄌㄤˋ)
winds and waves; great storms; 我們的事業是在大風浪中發展起來的。It is amid great storms that our business made progress.

大婦(ㄉㄚˋ ㄈㄨˋ)
the wife (as distinct from concubine)

大副(ㄉㄚˋ ㄈㄨˋ)
the first mate (of a ship)

大腹便便(ㄉㄚˋ ㄈㄨˋ ㄆㄧㄢˊ ㄆㄧㄢˊ)
paunchy; potbellied; big bellied

大腹賈(ㄉㄚˋ ㄈㄨˋ ㄍㄨˇ)
a wealthy but uncultured merchant; a businessman who is only interested in making money

大打出手(ㄉㄚˋ ㄉㄚˇ ㄔㄨ ㄕㄡˇ)
to get into a free-for-all or brawl

大大(ㄉㄚˋ ㄉㄚˋ)
greatly; enormously; 生產率大大提高。Productivity has risen greatly.

大大小小(ㄉㄚˋ ㄉㄚˋ ㄒㄧㄠˇ ㄒㄧㄠˇ)
the big and the small—the whole family

大刀闊斧(ㄉㄚˋ ㄉㄠ ㄎㄨㄛˋ ㄈㄨˇ)
(literally) a big knife and a broad ax—(figuratively) to act decisively and resolutely; to act in a sweeping manner

大刀會(ㄉㄚˋ ㄉㄠ ㄏㄨㄟˋ)
the Society of Big Swords; a quasi-religious secret society in old China

大道(ㄉㄚˋ ㄉㄠˋ)
①a wide road ②the way of virtue and justice

大道理(ㄉㄚˋ ㄉㄠˋ ㄌㄧˇ)
①a persuasive argument; eloquent reasoning; a high-sounding statement ②a major principle; a general principle

大豆(ㄉㄚˋ ㄉㄡˋ)
soybeans

大丹狗(ㄉㄚˋ ㄉㄢ ㄍㄡˇ)
a great Dane

大膽(ㄉㄚˋ ㄉㄢˇ)
bold; boldness; to do things without much forethought

and hesitation: 大膽做它吧!
Do it without hesitation.

大敵當前(ㄉㄚˋ ㄉㄧˊ ㄉㄤ ㄑㄧㄢˊ)
a dangerous enemy ahead;
confronted with a strong
opponent

大抵(ㄉㄚˋ ㄉㄧˇ)
generally speaking; for the
most part; on the whole

大地(ㄉㄚˋ ㄉㄧˋ)
①the earth ②the whole
territory of a nation

大地主(ㄉㄚˋ ㄉㄧˋ ㄓㄨˇ)
a big landowner or landlord

大地春回(ㄉㄚˋ ㄉㄧˋ ㄔㄨㄣ ㄏㄨㄟˊ)
Spring has returned to the
land. 或 Spring is here
again. 亦作「大地回春」

大典(ㄉㄚˋ ㄉㄧㄢˇ)
①a grand ceremony ②a
collection of great classics

大殿(ㄉㄚˋ ㄉㄧㄢˋ)
①the main hall in a palace
②the main hall of a Budd-
hist temple

大都(ㄉㄚˋ ㄉㄨ)
most probably; almost; for
the most part; generally: 兒
童大都喜好遊戲。 Children are
generally fond of play.

大都市(ㄉㄚˋ ㄉㄨ ㄕˋ)
a large city; a metropolis: 紐
約是個繁華的大都市。 New
York is a busy metropolis.

大度(ㄉㄚˋ ㄉㄨˋ)
magnanimity; generosity;
open-mindedness

大肚子(ㄉㄚˋ ㄉㄨˋ·ㄗ)
①pregnant ②a big eater ③
a potbelly

大多(ㄉㄚˋ ㄉㄨㄛ)
for the most part; mostly

大多數(ㄉㄚˋ ㄉㄨㄛ ㄕㄨˋ)
a great majority; the majority; a great many: 大多數的
人喜愛和平而不要戰爭。 The
majority of people prefer
peace to war.

大憝(ㄉㄚˋ ㄉㄨㄟˋ)
①a principal criminal ②a
disgusting fellow

大隊(ㄉㄚˋ ㄉㄨㄟˋ)
①(said of military cadets,
militia, or paramilitary
units) a battalion ②a group
(in air force organization)

大隊人馬(ㄉㄚˋ ㄉㄨㄟˋ ㄖㄣˊ ㄇㄚˇ)
a large number of soldiers
and horses; a large detachment of troops

大端(ㄉㄚˋ ㄉㄨㄢ)
main aspects (or features);
salient points

大動脈(ㄉㄚˋ ㄉㄨㄥˋ ㄇㄞˋ)or (ㄉㄚˋ
ㄉㄨㄥˋ ㄇㄞˋ)
the main artery

大頭針(ㄉㄚˋ ㄊㄡˊ ㄓㄣ)
tacks

大頭菜(ㄉㄚˋ ㄊㄡˊ ㄘㄞˋ)
salted turnips

大提琴(ㄉㄚˋ ㄊㄧˊ ㄑㄧㄣˊ)
a cello

大提琴家(ㄉㄚˋ ㄊㄧˊ ㄑㄧㄣˊ ㄐㄧㄚ)
a cellist

大體(ㄉㄚˋ ㄊㄧˇ)
①generally; on the whole;
for the most part; in the
main: 我大體上還喜歡。On the
whole, I like it. ②the main
principle; the main thing: 我
們要識大體，顧全局。We
should have the cardinal
principles in mind and take
the overall situation into
account.

大廳(ㄉㄚˋ ㄊㄧㄥ)
a big hall; the main hall; the
parlor

大庭廣眾(ㄉㄚˋ ㄊㄧㄥˊ ㄍㄨㄤˇ ㄓㄨㄥˋ)
①public places where the
crowd gather ②in public

大腿(ㄉㄚˋ ㄊㄨㄟˇ)
the thigh

大團圓(ㄉㄚˋ ㄊㄨㄢˊ ㄩㄢˊ)
a happy ending; a happy reunion

大同小異(ㄉㄚˋ ㄊㄨㄥˊ ㄒㄧㄠˇ ㄧˋ)
with slight differences only;
almost the same; generally
similar with differences in
detail only; much of a much-
ness

大同世界(ㄉㄚˋ ㄊㄨㄥˊ ㄕˋ ㄐㄧㄝˋ)
a world where harmony,
equality and justice prevail
—a political utopia

大統(ㄉㄚˋ ㄊㄨㄥˇ)
①the enterprise of unifying
the whole country ②the
throne

大腦(ㄉㄚˋ ㄋㄠˇ)
①the cerebrum ②a sarcas-
tic reference to intellectual
capacity

大難(ㄉㄚˋ ㄋㄢˋ)
a catastrophe; a disaster; a
calamity

大難臨頭(ㄉㄚˋ ㄋㄢˋ ㄌㄧㄣˊ ㄊㄡˊ)
a great calamity just ahead;
an imminent catastrophe or
disaster; to be faced with
great trouble

大逆不道(ㄉㄚˋ ㄋㄧˋ ㄅㄨˋ ㄉㄠˋ)
sedition; treason; traitorous
actions; great crimes—as
patricide, matricide, or regicide

大年初一(ㄉㄚˋ ㄋㄧㄢˊ ㄔㄨ ㄧ)
the first day of the lunar
year; the lunar New Year's
Day

大年夜(ㄉㄚˋ ㄋㄧㄢˊ ㄧㄝˋ)
on the night of the lunar
New Year's Eve

大娘(ㄉㄚˋ ㄋㄧㄤˊ)
①a reference to father's
first wife by children born
of a concubine ②a polite
salutation for an elderly
woman

大牢(ㄉㄚˋ ㄌㄠˊ)
a prison; a jail

大老粗(ㄉㄚˋ ㄌㄠˇ ㄘㄨ)
an uncouth fellow; an uneducated person

大樓(ㄉㄚˋ ㄌㄡˊ)
a multistoried building

大禮(ㄉㄚˋ ㄌㄧˇ)
(in ancient China) the most
solemn of ceremonies—in-
cluding three kneelings and
nine kowtows—performed in
paying respects to a new
master, foster parents, etc.

大禮拜(ㄉㄚˋ ㄌㄧˇ ㄅㄞˋ)
alternate Sunday on which
one has a day off; a fortnightly holiday

大禮服(ㄉㄚˋ ㄌㄧˇ ㄈㄨˊ)
formal dress (worn by diplomats or other dignitaries at
state functions or on other
solemn occasions); ceremonial dress

大禮堂(ㄉㄚˋ ㄌㄧˇ ㄊㄤˊ)
an auditorium

大理石(ㄉㄚˋ ㄌㄧˇ ㄕˊ)
marble: 此碑由大理石刻成。
The monument is carved in
marble.

大理寺(ㄉㄚˋ ㄌㄧˇ ㄙˋ)

〔大部〕

〔大部〕

(in ancient China) the Supreme Court

大理寺卿(ㄉㄚˋ ㄌㄧˇ ㄙˋ ㄑㄩㄥ)
(in ancient China) the president of the Supreme Court

大力(ㄉㄚˋ ㄌㄧˋ)
energetically; vigorously; with a great effort: 此時我們必須大力發展教育事業。We have to devote our major efforts to developing education now.

大力士(ㄉㄚˋ ㄌㄧˋ ㄕˋ)
a hercules; a man of unusual strength

大麗花(ㄉㄚˋ ㄌㄧˋ ㄏㄨㄚ)
(botany) *Dahlia pinnata*

大連(ㄉㄚˋ ㄌㄧㄢˊ)
Tairen—a seaport in Liaoning Province

大殮(ㄉㄚˋ ㄌㄧㄢˋ)
to place the corpse into the coffin; an encoffining ceremony

大量(ㄉㄚˋ ㄌㄧㄤˋ)
①a large quantity; plentiful; abundant; profuse; mass(production, etc.): 今年夏天我們有大量的雨水。We've had great quantities of rain this summer. ②magnanimous; large-minded: 他們是寬宏大量的思想家和政治家。They are large-minded thinkers and statesmen.

大路(ㄉㄚˋ ㄌㄨˋ)
the highroad

大陸(ㄉㄚˋ ㄌㄨˋ)
a continent; the mainland: 歐洲大陸習俗與英國習俗不同。Continental customs differ from those of England.

大陸性氣候(ㄉㄚˋ ㄌㄨˋ ㄒㄧㄥˋ ㄑㄧˋ ㄏㄡˋ)
a continental climate

大露營(ㄉㄚˋ ㄌㄨˋ ㄧㄥˊ)
a jamboree

大亂(ㄉㄚˋ ㄌㄨㄢˋ)
great turmoil; social or political upheaval

大倫(ㄉㄚˋ ㄌㄨㄣˊ)
the important human relations, as parents and children, brothers and sisters, husband and wife, etc.

大略(ㄉㄚˋ ㄌㄩㄝˋ)
①briefly; brief; roughly; generally ②(a man of)

great caliber or talent ③a general outline

大哥(ㄉㄚˋ ㄍㄜ)
①the eldest brother ②elder brother (a polite form of address for a man about one's own age)

大個兒(ㄉㄚˋ ㄍㄜˋㄦ)or 大個子(ㄉㄚˋ ㄍㄜˋ˙ㄗ)
a big man; a giant; a tall guy

大概(ㄉㄚˋ ㄍㄞˋ)
most probably; for the most part; generally; in general

大幹(ㄉㄚˋ ㄍㄢˋ)
to work energetically; to go all out; to make an all-out effort

大綱(ㄉㄚˋ ㄍㄤ)
an outline; a synopsis; a summary: 請告訴我們他授課的內容大綱。Please give us the outline of his lecture.

大姑娘(ㄉㄚˋ ㄍㄨ˙ㄋㄧㄤ)
an unmarried young woman; a maiden; a damsel

大姑子(ㄉㄚˋ ㄍㄨ˙ㄗ)
husband's elder sister; a sister-in-law

大鼓書(ㄉㄚˋ ㄍㄨˇ ㄕㄨ)
(a form of Chinese entertainment) a story told by singing with the accompaniment of drumbeats

大故(ㄉㄚˋ ㄍㄨˋ)
①the death of one's parents ②a big crime

大褂(ㄉㄚˋ ㄍㄨㄚˋ)
the Chinese long gown

大過(ㄉㄚˋ ㄍㄨㄛˋ)
①a big mistake or shortcoming: 他犯了一次大過。He made a serious mistake. ②(said of punishment in school, etc.) a major demerit

大規模(ㄉㄚˋ ㄍㄨㄟ ㄇㄛˊ)
large-scale; on a large scale

大官(ㄉㄚˋ ㄍㄨㄢ)
ranking officials

大觀(ㄉㄚˋ ㄍㄨㄢ)
a grand sight; a magnificent spectacle

大功(ㄉㄚˋ ㄍㄨㄥ)
a great achievement

大功告成(ㄉㄚˋ ㄍㄨㄥ ㄍㄠˋ ㄔㄥˊ)
(said of a big or difficult

task) to have finally come to completion; to have been brought to a successful conclusion

大公無私(ㄉㄚˋ ㄍㄨㄥ ㄨˊ ㄙ)
all for the public without selfish considerations; fair and square; impartial: 法律應該一視同仁，大公無私。Law should be uniform and impartial.

大可不必(ㄉㄚˋ ㄎㄜˇ ㄅㄨˋ ㄅㄧˋ)
It's not at all worth it. It's unnecessary.

大可一試(ㄉㄚˋ ㄎㄜˇ ㄧ ㄕˋ)
really worth a try

大開眼界(ㄉㄚˋ ㄎㄞ ㄧㄢˇ ㄐㄧㄝˋ)
to see something completely new or very strange; to have a wonderful sight or new experience

大楷(ㄉㄚˋ ㄎㄞˇ)
(Chinese calligraphy) large sized characters

大考(ㄉㄚˋ ㄎㄠˇ)
the final or terminal examination in school: 她忙於準備大考。She is busily preparing for the final examination.

大塊頭(ㄉㄚˋ ㄎㄨㄞˋ·ㄊㄡ)
a tall and bulky fellow; a whale of a man

大快人心(ㄉㄚˋ ㄎㄨㄞˋ ㄖㄣˊ ㄒㄧㄣ)
(usually said of a wrong being righted, justice prevailed, etc.) to give all a lift of the heart; to the immense satisfaction of the people

大合唱(ㄉㄚˋ ㄏㄜˊ ㄔㄤˋ)
a chorus sung by a large choir

大海(ㄉㄚˋ ㄏㄞˇ)
①a widemouthed bowl or wine cup ②the ocean

大海撈針(ㄉㄚˋ ㄏㄞˇ ㄌㄠ ㄓㄣ)
(literally) to fish a needle from the sea—to look for a needle in a haystack

大好(ㄉㄚˋ ㄏㄠˇ)
very good; excellent; golden: 這正是個大好時機。It's a golden opportunity.

大好河山(ㄉㄚˋ ㄏㄠˇ ㄏㄜˊ ㄕㄢ)
beautiful rivers and mountains

大好時光(ㄉㄚˋ ㄏㄠˇ ㄕˊ ㄍㄨㄤ)

the golden years; the prime of one's life

大號(ㄉㄚˋ ㄏㄠˋ)
①large-size ②(music) a tuba; a bass horn

大後方(ㄉㄚˋ ㄏㄡˋ ㄈㄤ)
the rear area

大後天(ㄉㄚˋ ㄏㄡˋ ㄊㄧㄢ)
three days from today; two days after tomorrow

大後年(ㄉㄚˋ ㄏㄡˋ ㄋㄧㄢˊ)
three years from the current year; two years after next

大寒(ㄉㄚˋ ㄏㄢˊ)
(literally) Severe cold, one of the 24 Chinese climatic periods, which falls on January 20 or 21

大喊大叫(ㄉㄚˋ ㄏㄢˇ ㄉㄚˋ ㄐㄧㄠˋ)
①to shout at the top of one's voice: 別對我大喊大叫。Don't shout at me. ②to conduct vigorous propaganda

大漢(ㄉㄚˋ ㄏㄢˋ)
①a tall and strong man; a whale of a man: 他是個魁形大漢。He is a tall and strong fellow. ②the great Han Dynasty

大旱雲霓(ㄉㄚˋ ㄏㄢˋ ㄩㄣˊ ㄋㄧˊ)
(literally) clouds in a serious drought—something yielding high hopes

大亨(ㄉㄚˋ ㄏㄥ)
a big shot; a bigwig; a VIP; a tycoon; a magnate

大戶(ㄉㄚˋ ㄏㄨˋ)
a wealthy and influential family

大戶人家(ㄉㄚˋ ㄏㄨˋ ㄖㄣˊ ㄐㄧㄚ)
a wealthy and influential family; a famous family of long standing

大花臉(ㄉㄚˋ ㄏㄨㄚ ㄌㄧㄢˇ)
(Peking opera) a male role of dignified type

大話(ㄉㄚˋ ㄏㄨㄚˋ)
boasts; bragging; big words; big talks: 他愛說大話。He likes to talk big: 或 He is a boaster.

大火(ㄉㄚˋ ㄏㄨㄛˇ)
a big fire; a conflagration

大夥兒(ㄉㄚˋ ㄏㄨㄛˇ ㄦ)
①us; we ②a group of people

大禍(ㄉㄚˋ ㄏㄨㄛˋ)
a calamity; a big disaster: 戰爭是可怕的大禍。War is a frightful calamity.

大惑不解(ㄉㄚˋ ㄏㄨㄛˋ ㄅㄨˋ ㄐㄧㄝˇ)
beyond comprehension; incomprehensible; confused

大會(ㄉㄚˋ ㄏㄨㄟˋ)
a rally; a plenary meeting; a convention; a conference: 這是個全體出席的大會。This is a plenary meeting (or session).

大婚(ㄉㄚˋ ㄏㄨㄣ)
the marriage of the emperor

大黃(ㄉㄚˋ ㄏㄨㄤˊ)
(Chinese medicine) rhubarb

大黃蜂(ㄉㄚˋ ㄏㄨㄤˊ ㄈㄥ)
a hornet

大紅(ㄉㄚˋ ㄏㄨㄥˊ)
crimson; deep red; dark red

大紅大綠(ㄉㄚˋ ㄏㄨㄥˊ ㄉㄚˋ ㄌㄩˋ)
gaudy and showy

大吉大利(ㄉㄚˋ ㄐㄧˊ ㄉㄚˋ ㄌㄧˋ)
(literally) unexcelled luck and great prosperity—very smooth going or operation (often used to offer best wishes to a new store, business, etc.)

大計(ㄉㄚˋ ㄐㄧˋ)
①the policy of a state; national plans or programs ②a matter of fundamental importance: 教育為百年大計。Education is a matter of fundamental importance for generations to come.

大祭司(ㄉㄚˋ ㄐㄧˋ ㄙ)
a high priest

大家(ㄉㄚˋ ㄐㄧㄚ)
①all of us; we ②a rich and influential family of long standing ③a famous expert; a master: 他是位書法大家。He is a great master of calligraphy.

大家庭(ㄉㄚˋ ㄐㄧㄚ ㄊㄧㄥˊ)
①a big family ②a community

大駕(ㄉㄚˋ ㄐㄧㄚˋ)
①to your gracious presence ②the carriage for a sovereign or emperor

大街小巷(ㄉㄚˋ ㄐㄧㄝ ㄒㄧㄠˇ ㄒㄧㄤˋ)
in every street and alley—all over the city

大捷(ㄉㄚˋ ㄐㄧㄝˊ)

a big victory; a smashing victory

大姊 or 大姐(ㄉㄚˋ ㄐㄧㄝˇ)
the eldest sister

大解(ㄉㄚˋ ㄐㄧㄝˇ)
to empty one's bowels; to go to the stool

大教堂(ㄉㄚˋ ㄐㄧㄠˋ ㄊㄤˊ)
a cathedral

大舅子(ㄉㄚˋ ㄐㄧㄡˋ ˙ㄗ)
one's wife's elder brothers

大襟(ㄉㄚˋ ㄐㄧㄣ)
the right forepart of a Chinese gown

大江(ㄉㄚˋ ㄐㄧㄤ)
①a great river ②the Yangtze River

大將(ㄉㄚˋ ㄐㄧㄤ)
①an important general; a capable commander ②a trusted lieutenant; a right-hand man ③a senior general

大將風度(ㄉㄚˋ ㄐㄧㄤ ㄈㄥ ㄉㄨˋ)
the style of a great general or admiral (used as a compliment)

大驚小怪(ㄉㄚˋ ㄐㄧㄥ ㄒㄧㄠˇ ㄍㄨㄞˋ)
to make a fuss; to make much ado about nothing: 不要為小事情大驚小怪。Don't make so much fuss about trifles.

大靜脈(ㄉㄚˋ ㄐㄧㄥˋ ㄇㄞˋ)or(ㄉㄚˋ ㄐㄧㄥˋ ㄇㄛˋ)
the vena cava

大局(ㄉㄚˋ ㄐㄩˊ)
①the situation in general: 我們要顧全大局。We have to take the whole situation into account. ②national interests; the fate of a nation

大舉(ㄉㄚˋ ㄐㄩˇ)
①a large-scale (invasion, etc.); to make a decisive move ②a great undertaking

大軍(ㄉㄚˋ ㄐㄩㄣ)
a great concentration of troops; main forces: 大軍隨後就到。The main forces will be here soon.

大氣(ㄉㄚˋ ㄑㄧˋ)
①the atmosphere; atmospheric ②a grand air or deportment ③heavy breathing ④magnanimity; open-mindedness

〔大部〕

大氣層 (ㄉㄚˋ ㄑㄧˋ ㄘㄥˊ)
the atmospheric boundary layer

大氣壓力 (ㄉㄚˋ ㄑㄧˋ ㄧㄚ ㄌㄧˋ)
atmospheric pressure

大器晚成 (ㄉㄚˋ ㄑㄧˋ ㄨㄢˇ ㄔㄥˊ)
(literally) A great vessel will be long in completion. — A great man will take time to shape and mature.

大千世界 (ㄉㄚˋ ㄑㄧㄢ ㄕˋ ㄐㄧㄝˋ)
①(Buddhism) 1,000,000,000 universes; the boundless universe ②the kaleidoscopic world

大錢 (ㄉㄚˋ ㄑㄧㄢˊ)
①real big money ②an old Chinese coin of a low denomination

大前提 (ㄉㄚˋ ㄑㄧㄢˊ ㄊㄧˊ)
a major premise; a set principle

大前天 (ㄉㄚˋ ㄑㄧㄢˊ ㄊㄧㄢ)
three days ago

大前年 (ㄉㄚˋ ㄑㄧㄢˊ ㄋㄧㄢˊ)
the fourth year counted backward, beginning from the current year; three years ago

大秦 (ㄉㄚˋ ㄑㄧㄣˊ)
an ancient name for the Roman Empire

大清早 (ㄉㄚˋ ㄑㄧㄥ ㄗㄠˇ)
very early in the morning

大情人 (ㄉㄚˋ ㄑㄧㄥˊ ㄖㄣˊ)
a Casanova, or ladies' man; a woman's lover

大慶 (ㄉㄚˋ ㄑㄧㄥˋ)
①an occasion or event deserving a big celebration ②a national festival or holiday ③birthday (in reference to other's birthday)

大去 (ㄉㄚˋ ㄑㄩˋ)
to go away and never to come back—to be dead

大全 (ㄉㄚˋ ㄑㄩㄢˊ)
complete works of; a complete collection of; a complete volume on (civil law, etc.)

大權 (ㄉㄚˋ ㄑㄩㄢˊ)
the authority or power to reign over a state, or office; great power or authority

大權旁落 (ㄉㄚˋ ㄑㄩㄢˊ ㄆㄤˊ ㄌㄨㄛˋ)
Power has fallen into the

hands of others. 或to lose one's power to a subordinate while remaining as a figurehead

大權在握 (ㄉㄚˋ ㄑㄩㄢˊ ㄗㄞˋ ㄨㄛˋ)
to hold power unchallenged; to assume the reins of government or organization

大溪地 (ㄉㄚˋ ㄒㄧ ㄉㄧˋ)
Tahiti

大西洋 (ㄉㄚˋ ㄒㄧ ㄧㄤˊ)
the Atlantic Ocean

大喜 (ㄉㄚˋ ㄒㄧˇ)
great rejoicing

大喜過望 (ㄉㄚˋ ㄒㄧˇ ㄍㄨㄛˋ ㄨㄤˋ)
to be pleased beyond expectations; to be overjoyed

大峽谷 (ㄉㄚˋ ㄒㄧㄚˊ ㄍㄨˇ)
the Grand Canyon in the United States

大廈 (ㄉㄚˋ ㄒㄧㄚˋ)or(ㄉㄚˋ ㄕㄚˋ)
a big building; a mansion

大寫 (ㄉㄚˋ ㄒㄧㄝˇ)
①a capital letter ②the elaborate form of Chinese numerals (used especially in accounting and checks)

大小 (ㄉㄚˋ ㄒㄧㄠˇ)
①adults and children ②one's wife and concubine ③sizes (of dresses, shoes, etc.) ④degree of seniority

大小便 (ㄉㄚˋ ㄒㄧㄠˇ ㄅㄧㄢˋ)
night soil and urine; the act of discharging such

大小不一 (ㄉㄚˋ ㄒㄧㄠˇ ㄅㄨˋ ㄧ)
irregular in size, age, etc.

大小姐 (ㄉㄚˋ ㄒㄧㄠˇ ㄐㄧㄝˇ)
①a maiden; a Miss ②a reference to others' elder or eldest daughters

大笑 (ㄉㄚˋ ㄒㄧㄠˋ)
to laugh heartily; to roar with laughter: 他們都大笑起來。 They all laughed loudly.

大修 (ㄉㄚˋ ㄒㄧㄡ)
major repairs; an overhaul

大顯身手 (ㄉㄚˋ ㄒㄧㄢˇ ㄕㄣ ㄕㄡˇ)
to display one's skill to the full; to give full play to one's abilities; to give a good account of oneself

大顯神通 (ㄉㄚˋ ㄒㄧㄢˇ ㄕㄣˊ ㄊㄨㄥ)
to display one's remarkable skill or abilities to the full

大限 (ㄉㄚˋ ㄒㄧㄢˋ)
the time of one's death

大憲章 (ㄉㄚˋ ㄒㄧㄢˋ ㄓㄤ)
the Magna Charta, or the Magna Carta, signed by King John of England 1215

大相逕庭 (ㄉㄚˋ ㄒㄧㄤ ㄐㄧㄥˋ ㄊㄧㄥˊ)
totally different; entirely contrary; far apart: 他們的見和我的大相逕庭。Their view was diametrically opposed to mine.

大興土木 (ㄉㄚˋ ㄒㄧㄥ ㄊㄨˇ ㄇㄨˋ)
to start a large-scale building project

大興問罪之師 (ㄉㄚˋ ㄒㄧㄥ ㄨㄣˋ ㄗㄨㄟˋ ㄓ ㄕ)
to launch a punitive campaign—to point angrily an accusing finger at someone; to condemn scathingly; to demand an explanation

大刑 (ㄉㄚˋ ㄒㄧㄥˊ)
heavy penalties or stiff sentences

大型 (ㄉㄚˋ ㄒㄧㄥˊ)
(said of machines, etc.) large-sized; large-scale

大行皇帝 (ㄉㄚˋ ㄒㄧㄥˊ ㄏㄨㄤˊ ㄉㄧˋ)
the late emperor

大學 (ㄉㄚˋ ㄒㄩㄝˊ)
①a university or college ②The Great Learning (one of the Four Classics)

大學生 (ㄉㄚˋ ㄒㄩㄝˊ ㄕㄥ)
a college or university student; a collegian

大雪 (ㄉㄚˋ ㄒㄩㄝˇ)
①a heavy snow ②(literally) Heavy snow—one of the 24 climatic periods in China usually falling on the 7th or 8th of December

大選 (ㄉㄚˋ ㄒㄩㄢˇ)
①a presidential election ②general elections for congressmen

大熊座 (ㄉㄚˋ ㄒㄩㄥˊ ㄗㄨㄛˋ)
(astronomy) the Ursa Major

大指 (ㄉㄚˋ ㄓˇ)
the thumb

大志 (ㄉㄚˋ ㄓˋ)
great ambitions; high aims: 他的大志是做一位大政治家。His great ambition is to be a great statesman.

大致 (ㄉㄚˋ ㄓˋ)
①generally; for the most

〔大
部〕

part; as a whole ② more or less; about

智若愚(ㄓ ㄖㄨㄛˋ ㄩ)
The wise man looks dumb (because he never shows off).

札(ㄓㄚˊ)
your letter

展宏圖(ㄓㄢˇ ㄏㄨㄥˊ ㄊㄨˊ)
to realize one's ambition; to ride on the crest of success

張達伐(ㄓㄤ ㄉㄚˊ ㄈㄚˊ)
to let out a broadside; to attack with full force

張旗鼓(ㄓㄤ ㄑㄧˊ ㄍㄨˇ)
① to make a big show; to put up a pageantry ② on a grand scale; in a big way

丈夫(ㄓㄤˋ ㄈㄨ)
a real man; a man of fortitude and courage

主教(ㄓㄨˇ ㄐㄧㄠˋ)
an archbishop

著(ㄓㄨˋ)or 大作(ㄉㄚˋ ㄓㄨㄛˋ)
your work; your script; your book

專學校(ㄓㄨㄢ ㄒㄩㄝˊ ㄒㄧㄠˋ)or 大專院校(ㄉㄚˋ ㄓㄨㄢ ㄩㄢˋ ㄒㄧㄠˋ)
colleges and universities

眾(ㄉㄚˋ ㄓㄨㄥˋ)
the people; the masses; the public

眾媒介(ㄉㄚˋ ㄓㄨㄥˋ ㄇㄟˊ ㄐㄧㄝˋ)
mass media

眾化(ㄉㄚˋ ㄓㄨㄥˋ ㄏㄨㄚˋ)
to popularize; popularized; popularization: 我們必須使科學大眾化。We must popularize science.

眾捷運系統(ㄉㄚˋ ㄓㄨㄥˋ ㄐㄧㄝˊ ㄩㄣˋ ㄒㄧˋ ㄊㄨㄥˇ)
mass rapid transit (MRT)

眾教育(ㄉㄚˋ ㄓㄨㄥˋ ㄐㄧㄠˋ ㄩˋ)
mass education

眾消費(ㄉㄚˋ ㄓㄨㄥˋ ㄒㄧㄠ ㄈㄟˋ)
mass consumption

眾傳播(ㄉㄚˋ ㄓㄨㄥˋ ㄔㄨㄢˊ ㄅㄛˋ)
mass communications

眾傳播媒體(ㄉㄚˋ ㄓㄨㄥˋ ㄔㄨㄢˊ ㄅㄛˋ ㄇㄟˊ ㄊㄧˇ)
mass (communications) media

眾文學(ㄉㄚˋ ㄓㄨㄥˋ ㄨㄣˊ ㄒㄩㄝˊ)
popular literature (as newspapers, magazines, novels, short stories, etc.)

眾娛樂(ㄉㄚˋ ㄓㄨㄥˋ ㄩˊ ㄌㄜˋ)
mass entertainment

大仲馬(ㄉㄚˋ ㄓㄨㄥˋ ㄇㄚˇ)
Alexandre Dumas (Dumas père), 1802-70, French dramatist and novelist

大吃大喝(ㄉㄚˋ ㄔ ㄉㄚˋ ㄏㄜ)
to eat and drink extravagantly

大吃一驚(ㄉㄚˋ ㄔ ㄧ ㄐㄧㄥ)
to be shocked; to be greatly surprised; to be taken aback: 這消息使我們大吃一驚。The news greatly surprised us.

大徹大悟(ㄉㄚˋ ㄔㄜˋ ㄉㄚˋ ㄨˋ)
(usually said of oneself) a profound and complete realization or understanding ② (theology) the great revelation

大臣(ㄉㄚˋ ㄔㄣˊ)
ranking officials; cabinet ministers

大腸(ㄉㄚˋ ㄔㄤˊ)
the large intestine

大腸桿菌(ㄉㄚˋ ㄔㄤˊ ㄍㄢˇ ㄐㄩㄣˋ)
coliform bacillus

大氅(ㄉㄚˋ ㄔㄤˇ)
an overcoat

大成(ㄉㄚˋ ㄔㄥˊ)
great achievement or accomplishment

大成殿(ㄉㄚˋ ㄔㄥˊ ㄉㄧㄢˋ)
the main hall of the Confucius Temple

大成問題(ㄉㄚˋ ㄔㄥˊ ㄨㄣˋ ㄊㄧˊ)
very questionable; very doubtful; in doubt

大出洋相(ㄉㄚˋ ㄔㄨ ㄧㄤˊ ㄒㄧㄤˋ)
to commit a big blunder in public; to have a major contretemps

大處著墨(ㄉㄚˋ ㄔㄨˇ ㄓㄨㄛˊ ㄇㄛˋ)or 大處落墨(ㄉㄚˋ ㄔㄨˇ ㄌㄨㄛˋ ㄇㄛˋ)
to concentrate on the key points

大處著眼，小處著手(ㄉㄚˋ ㄔㄨˇ ㄓㄨㄛˊ ㄧㄢˇ，ㄒㄧㄠˇ ㄔㄨˇ ㄓㄨㄛˊ ㄕㄡˇ)
to make an overall assessment but to start from details 或 Although beginning a task from the bottom, one mustn't forget the ultimate objective.

大吹大擂(ㄉㄚˋ ㄔㄨㄟ ㄉㄚˋ ㄌㄟˊ)
to brag and blare (about one's success, etc.); to talk

big; to give wide publicity; to make a great fanfare; to make a big noise

大醇小疵(ㄉㄚˋ ㄔㄨㄣˊ ㄒㄧㄠˇ ㄘ)
to be sound on the whole though defective in details

大蟲(ㄉㄚˋ ㄔㄨㄥˊ)
a tiger

大師(ㄉㄚˋ ㄕ)
① a master; a maestro ② a reverent title for a Buddhist monk

大師傅(ㄉㄚˋ ㄕ·ㄈㄨ)
① a head cook; a chef ② a salutation for a Buddhist monk

大失所望(ㄉㄚˋ ㄕ ㄙㄨㄛˇ ㄨㄤˋ)
to be greatly disappointed; to be greatly discouraged

大食(ㄉㄚˋ ㄕˊ)
the Moslem empire built by the Arabs

大使(ㄉㄚˋ ㄕˇ)
an ambassador: 他奉派為駐美大使。He was appointed ambassador to the United States.

大使館(ㄉㄚˋ ㄕˇ ㄍㄨㄢˇ)
an embassy

大事(ㄉㄚˋ ㄕˋ)
① important events; significant national events; serious matters: 我們要關心國家大事。We have to concern ourselves with the affairs of our country. ② the death of one's parents

大事鋪張(ㄉㄚˋ ㄕˋ ㄆㄨ ㄓㄤ)
to make lavish preparations; to put up a lavish show (especially of a wedding, etc.)

大事化小，小事化無(ㄉㄚˋ ㄕˋ ㄏㄨㄚˋ ㄒㄧㄠˇ，ㄒㄧㄠˇ ㄕˋ ㄏㄨㄚˋ ㄨˊ)
to turn big problems into small problems and small problems into no problem at all

大事記(ㄉㄚˋ ㄕˋ ㄐㄧˋ)
a record of important events; a chronicle

大事宣傳(ㄉㄚˋ ㄕˋ ㄒㄩㄢ ㄔㄨㄢˊ)
to play up; to ballyhoo

大勢所趨(ㄉㄚˋ ㄕˋ ㄙㄨㄛˇ ㄑㄩ)
general trend indicates...; according to the prevailing tendency

〔大 部〕

大勢已去(ㄉㄚˋ ㄕˋ ㄧˇ ㄑㄩˋ)
The situation is beyond salvation. 或 The situation is irretrievable, hopeless, etc.

大舌頭(ㄉㄚˋ ㄕˊ • ㄊㄡ)
(literally) an oversized tongue—unable to speak clearly

大赦(ㄉㄚˋ ㄕˋ)
an amnesty

大少爺(ㄉㄚˋ ㄕㄠˋ • ㄧㄝ)
①a term used by a servant to address the eldest son of the family ②a dandy; a playboy

大手筆(ㄉㄚˋ ㄕㄡˇ ㄅㄧˇ)
the work or handwriting of a great author or calligrapher

大聲疾呼(ㄉㄚˋ ㄕㄥ ㄐㄧˊ ㄏㄨ)
to urge emphatically; to raise a cry of warning; a clarion call to awaken the public to lurking danger by writings or speeches; to call aloud

大乘(ㄉㄚˋ ㄕㄥˊ)
(Buddhism) the Mahayana or "Great Vehicle" school

大勝(ㄉㄚˋ ㄕㄥˋ)
to win overwhelmingly or decisively; a decisive win; to win a big victory; a major victory

大聖(ㄉㄚˋ ㄕㄥˋ)
an outstanding person; an extraordinary person

大書特書(ㄉㄚˋ ㄕㄨ ㄊㄜˋ ㄕㄨ)
to write repeatedly or elaborately on; to make an issue of something by writing in this manner; to write volumes about—to play up

大暑(ㄉㄚˋ ㄕㄨˇ)
Great heat, one of the 24 Chinese climatic periods, which falls on 23rd or 24th of July

大帥(ㄉㄚˋ ㄕㄨㄞˋ)
①a commander in chief ②a high military officer in the Ching Dynasty

大人(ㄉㄚˋ ㄖㄣˊ)
①(in ancient China) a respectful salutation for one's parents, seniors, etc. ②a grown-up person; an adult; a grown-up

大人物(ㄉㄚˋ ㄖㄣˊ ㄨˋ)
a great personage; a famous or influential person; a VIP; a big shot: 他是個大人物。He is a big shot. 或He is a great personage.

大儒(ㄉㄚˋ ㄖㄨˊ)
a scholar who combines profundity with virtue

大字報(ㄉㄚˋ ㄗˋ ㄅㄠˋ)
a big-character poster

大自然(ㄉㄚˋ ㄗˋ ㄖㄢˊ)
nature; natural phenomena: 人類與大自然競爭。Man is engaged in a constant struggle with nature.

大雜燴(ㄉㄚˋ ㄗㄚˊ ㄏㄨㄟˋ)
a hodgepodge

大雜院(ㄉㄚˋ ㄗㄚˊ ㄩㄢˋ)
(in northern China) a big courtyard shared by many families of the low-income class

大作(ㄉㄚˋ ㄗㄨㄛˋ)
①your work; your script; your book, etc. ②(said of violence, etc.) to erupt; to upheave; eruption; upheaval ③(said of music, etc.) to come out in ensemble and rather suddenly

大宗(ㄉㄚˋ ㄗㄨㄥ)
①a large batch; a large amount; lots of ②staple ③a famous and influential family of long standing

大總統(ㄉㄚˋ ㄗㄨㄥˇ ㄊㄨㄥˇ)
the President—the chief of state of a republic

大慈大悲(ㄉㄚˋ ㄘˊ ㄉㄚˋ ㄅㄟ)
(Buddhism) the great mercy; the great compassion

大才小用(ㄉㄚˋ ㄘㄞˊ ㄒㄧㄠˇ ㄩㄥˋ)
to make little use of great talent; to use talented people for trivial tasks 亦作「大材小用」: 你做這事情是大才小用了。This is a job unworthy of your talents.

大餐(ㄉㄚˋ ㄘㄢ)
①a sumptuous feast or meal ②Western-style foods

大錯特錯(ㄉㄚˋ ㄘㄨㄛˋ ㄊㄜˋ ㄘㄨㄛˋ)
a very serious mistake; to make a gross error; all wet

大錯鑄成(ㄉㄚˋ ㄘㄨㄛˋ ㄓㄨˋ ㄔㄥˊ)
to have committed a big mistake or blunder; to e hopelessly

大蔥(ㄉㄚˋ ㄘㄨㄥ)
(botany) the leek

大肆咆哮(ㄉㄚˋ ㄙˋ ㄆㄠˊ ㄒㄧㄠ)
to complain, threaten, et loudly; to roar with rage

大嫂(ㄉㄚˋ ㄙㄠˇ)
①one's eldest sister-in-la
②a polite name for wome of similar age as oneself

大掃除(ㄉㄚˋ ㄙㄠˇ ㄔㄨˊ)
to make a thorough clean-u (usually before a major fe tival)

大蘇打(ㄉㄚˋ ㄙㄨ ㄉㄚˇ)
the sodium hyposulfite

大蒜(ㄉㄚˋ ㄙㄨㄢˋ)
garlic

大而化之(ㄉㄚˋ ㄦˊ ㄏㄨㄚˋ ㄓ)
careless; carelessly; perfun tory; perfunctorily; slapdas slipshod

大而無當(ㄉㄚˋ ㄦˊ ㄨˊ ㄉㄤˋ)
big but useless; large but ir practical: 它是個大而無當的 畫。It's an ambitious but ir practical plan.

大衣(ㄉㄚˋ ㄧ)
an overcoat

大姨子(ㄉㄚˋ ㄧˊ • ㄗ)
one's wife's elder sisters

大意(ㄉㄚˋ ㄧˋ)
①the general idea; the gis a summary ②careless; neg ligent ③high ambitions

大意失荊州(ㄉㄚˋ ㄧˋ ㄕ ㄐㄧㄥ ㄓㄡ)
to suffer a major setbac due to carelessness

大義滅親(ㄉㄚˋ ㄧˋ ㄇㄧㄝˋ ㄑㄧㄣ)
to uphold justice and righ eousness even at the sacr fice of one's blood relation

大義凜然(ㄉㄚˋ ㄧˋ ㄌㄧˇ ㄖㄢˊ)
to maintain the dignity justice or righteousness

大異其趣(ㄉㄚˋ ㄧˋ ㄑㄧˊ ㄑㄩˋ)
very different; totally differ ent

大牙(ㄉㄚˋ ㄧㄚˊ)
the molar teeth 亦作「白齒」
大爺
①(ㄉㄚˋ ㄧㄝˊ) ⓐ a rich man ⓑ term used by a servant t address his master
②(ㄉㄚˋ • ㄧㄝ) ⓐ an uncle; one father's elder brother ⓑ

大伯 uncle (a respectful form of address for an elderly man)

大業
a big enterprise

大搖大擺(ㄉㄚ ㄧㄠˊ ㄉㄚˋ ㄅㄞˇ)
to swagger; to walk haughtily

大要(ㄉㄚˋ ㄧㄠˋ)
the main points (of a book, article, etc.); a summary; a synopsis; the gist

大有分別(ㄉㄚˋ ㄧㄡˇ ㄈㄣ ㄅㄧㄝˊ)
poles apart or entirely different

大有可觀(ㄉㄚˋ ㄧㄡˇ ㄎㄜˇ ㄍㄨㄢ)
absolutely worth seeing — very considerable

大有可為(ㄉㄚˋ ㄧㄡˇ ㄎㄜˇ ㄨㄟˊ)
very promising (projects, etc.); very hopeful (situation, etc.); to have bright prospects

大有人在(ㄉㄚˋ ㄧㄡˇ ㄖㄣˊ ㄗㄞˋ)
Such people are by no means rare.

大有文章(ㄉㄚˋ ㄧㄡˇ ㄨㄣˊ ㄓㄤ)
There's something behind all this. 或 There's more to it than meets the eye.

大煙 or 大烟(ㄉㄚˋ ㄧㄢ)
opium

大鹽湖(ㄉㄚˋ ㄧㄢˊ ㄏㄨˊ)
the Great Salt Lake

大言不慚(ㄉㄚˋ ㄧㄢˊ ㄅㄨˋ ㄘㄢˊ)
to boast unabashedly or shamelessly; to talk big

大岩桐(ㄉㄚˋ ㄧㄢˊ ㄊㄨㄥˊ)
(botany) gloxinia

大洋(ㄉㄚˋ ㄧㄤˊ)
① a silver dollar ② an ocean

大洋洲(ㄉㄚˋ ㄧㄤˊ ㄓㄡ)
Oceania; Oceanica

大英博物館(ㄉㄚˋ ㄧㄥ ㄅㄛˊ ㄨˋ ㄍㄨㄢˇ)
the British Museum

大無畏(ㄉㄚˋ ㄨˊ ㄨㄟˋ)
dauntless; fearless; dauntlessness; fearlessness

大我(ㄉㄚˋ ㄨㄛˇ)
the big self—the universe, as opposed to the little self —oneself; the public; the state; the nation

大為(ㄉㄚˋ ㄨㄟˊ)
greatly; significantly; markedly

大為震怒(ㄉㄚˋ ㄨㄟˊ ㄓㄣˋ ㄋㄨˋ)
to fly into a rage; to become furious; to blow off the top

大文豪(ㄉㄚˋ ㄨㄣˊ ㄏㄠˊ)
a renowned man of letters; a literary giant

大王(ㄉㄚˋ ㄨㄤˊ)
① Your Majesty; Your Highness ② the chief of brigands

大王椰子(ㄉㄚˋ ㄨㄤˊ ㄧㄝˊ ˙ㄗ)
the palm tree

大魚大肉(ㄉㄚˋ ㄩˊ ㄉㄚˋ ㄖㄡˋ)
(literally) abundant fish and meat—rich food (implying gluttony)

大禹(ㄉㄚˋ ㄩˇ)
Yü the Great, 2276-2177 B. C., founder of the Hsia Dynasty

大雨傾盆(ㄉㄚˋ ㄩˇ ㄑㄧㄥ ㄆㄣˊ)
a pouring rain; to rain cats and dogs: 現在大雨傾盆。It's raining cats and dogs now.

大約(ㄉㄚˋ ㄩㄝ)
about; around; probably; likely: 現在大約是九點鐘。about nine o'clock now.

大月(ㄉㄚˋ ㄩㄝˋ)
① the 31-day months ② the lunar 30-day months

大躍進(ㄉㄚˋ ㄩㄝˋ ㄐㄧㄣˋ)
(Communist terminology) "the great leap forward"

大月氏(ㄉㄚˋ ㄩㄝˋ ㄓ)or(ㄉㄚˋ ㄖㄡˋ ㄓ)
name of an ancient country in southwestern China

大員(ㄉㄚˋ ㄩㄢˊ)
high or ranking officials (usually referring to those of the Central Government)

大元帥(ㄉㄚˋ ㄩㄢˊ ㄕㄨㄞˋ)
a marshal; the commander in chief of the armed forces; a commanding general of a large military force

【大】916
2. ㄉㄞˋ day dài
參看「大夫」

大夫
① (ㄉㄚˋ ㄈㄨ) (in ancient China) high officials of the state
② (ㄉㄞˋ ㄈㄨ) a physician or doctor

一畫

【天】917
ㄊㄧㄢ tian tiān

1. the sky; the heavens; the vault of heavens; the firmament

2. Nature; God; Heaven: 謝天謝地,你終於來了。Thank God, you've come!

3. nature; natural; not artificial: 這風景具有天然美。The scenery has natural beauty.

4. a day: 我每天六點起床。I get up at six every day.

5. seasons; climates; weather: 春天到了。Spring has come.

6. father or husband

7. something indispensable; necessities

天崩地坼(ㄊㄧㄢ ㄅㄥ ㄉㄧˋ ㄔㄜˋ)
deafening sounds—as the falling of heaven and cracking of earth; natural disasters like giant earthquakes and landslides 亦作「天崩地裂」

天邊(ㄊㄧㄢ ㄅㄧㄢ)
the ends of the earth; remotest places

天邊海角(ㄊㄧㄢ ㄅㄧㄢ ㄏㄞˇ ㄐㄧㄠˇ)
the corners of the earth —faraway or distant places

天稟(ㄊㄧㄢ ㄅㄧㄥˇ)
natural endowments; endowed by nature

天不怕地不怕(ㄊㄧㄢ ㄅㄨˋ ㄆㄚˋ ㄉㄧˋ ㄅㄨˋ ㄆㄚˋ)
to fear neither Heaven nor Earth—to fear nothing and no one

天不假年(ㄊㄧㄢ ㄅㄨˋ ㄐㄧㄚˇ ㄋㄧㄢˊ)
(literally) God doesn't give him a life long enough (to accomplish his task, etc.) —usually said of a person who dies on an important job

天棚(ㄊㄧㄢ ㄆㄥˊ)
an awning; a shed; a tent for shading the sun

天平(ㄊㄧㄢ ㄆㄧㄥˊ)or 天秤(ㄊㄧㄢ ㄔㄥˋ)
scales—used in weighing precious stones, gold, etc.

天馬行空(ㄊㄧㄢ ㄇㄚˇ ㄒㄧㄥˊ ㄎㄨㄥ)
(said of calligraphic works or writing) an unrestrained and vigorous style that brims with talent

〔天部〕

〔大部〕

天明(ㄊㄧㄢ ㄇㄧㄥ)
daybreak; dawn: 他天明即起。
He gets up at daybreak.

天命(ㄊㄧㄢ ㄇㄧㄥ)
①a heavenly mandate ②
fate; destiny ③one's life
span

天罰(ㄊㄧㄢ ㄈㄚ)
the punishment meted out by
God; God's punishing hands

天翻地覆(ㄊㄧㄢ ㄈㄢ ㄉㄧ ㄈㄨ)
in total disorder or dis-
arrangement; an extreme upheaval or change, in sheer
pandemonium

天分(ㄊㄧㄢ ㄈㄣ)
natural endowments; talent;
intelligence: 她有音樂天分。
She has a talent for music.

天方夜譚(ㄊㄧㄢ ㄈㄤ ㄧㄝ ㄊㄢ)
*The Arabian Nights' Enter-
tainment*

天府之國(ㄊㄧㄢ ㄈㄨ ㄓ ㄍㄨㄛ)
the land of abundance; a
country with rich natural
resources (usually referring
to Szechwan Province)

天父(ㄊㄧㄢ ㄈㄨ)
(Christianity) Our Heavenly
Father

天賦(ㄊㄧㄢ ㄈㄨ)
①inherent and inborn
(rights, etc.) ②natural
endowments; talent

天賦人權(ㄊㄧㄢ ㄈㄨ ㄖㄣ ㄑㄩㄢ)
inborn human rights; inalien-
able rights

天大的事(ㄊㄧㄢ ㄉㄚ ˙ㄉㄜ ㄕ)
(literally) matters as big as
heavens—important or serious matters; tremendous
events

天道(ㄊㄧㄢ ㄉㄠ)
①the ways of Heaven; natural law ②weather

天底下(ㄊㄧㄢ ㄉㄧ ˙ㄒㄧㄚ)
in this world; under the sun;
on earth: 天底下沒什麼新奇的
事物。There's no new thing
under the sun.

天地(ㄊㄧㄢ ㄉㄧ)
①heaven and earth; the
world; the universe ②a field
of activity; scope of operation ③the upper and lower
margins of a scroll ④a
world of difference

天地良心(ㄊㄧㄢ ㄉㄧ ㄌㄧㄤ ㄒㄧㄣ)
to speak the truth; in fact;
from the bottom of my
heart; in all fairness or justice

天地間(ㄊㄧㄢ ㄉㄧ ㄐㄧㄢ)
in this world; in the universe

天定(ㄊㄧㄢ ㄉㄧㄥ)
preordained; predetermined;
predestined; fixed by Heav-
en

天壇(ㄊㄧㄢ ㄊㄢ)
the Altar of Heaven in Peking; the Temple of Heaven
(in Peking)—where the
emperors used to worship

天堂(ㄊㄧㄢ ㄊㄤ)
heaven; paradise

天堂地獄(ㄊㄧㄢ ㄊㄤ ㄉㄧ ㄩ)
(literally) heaven and hell
— the sharp contrast be-
tween happiness and misery

天體(ㄊㄧㄢ ㄊㄧ)
heavenly bodies; celestial
bodies

天體營(ㄊㄧㄢ ㄊㄧ ㄧㄥ)
a nudist camp

天天(ㄊㄧㄢ ㄊㄧㄢ)
every day: 他天天讀英文。He
studies English every day.

天庭(ㄊㄧㄢ ㄊㄧㄥ)
the forehead

天南地北(ㄊㄧㄢ ㄋㄢ ㄉㄧ ㄅㄟ)
①poles apart ②(to chat or
talk casually about) every
and any subject under the
sun; discursive; rambling

天牛(ㄊㄧㄢ ㄋㄧㄡ)
(entomology) *Apriona rugi-
collis*, a variety of destructive beetles; a longicorn

天年(ㄊㄧㄢ ㄋㄧㄢ)
①the life span alloted by
Heaven; one's natural life
span ②fortune in the cur-
rent year

天怒人怨(ㄊㄧㄢ ㄋㄨ ㄖㄣ ㄩㄢ)
(to incur) the wrath of
Heaven and opposition of
man (usually referring to
outrageous injustice, etc.);
widespread indignation and
discontent

天籟(ㄊㄧㄢ ㄌㄞ)
the sounds of nature (such
as those caused by wind,
water, insects, etc.)

天藍色(ㄊㄧㄢ ㄌㄢ ㄙㄜ)
sky blue

天狼星(ㄊㄧㄢ ㄌㄤ ㄒㄧㄥ)
the Dog Star

天理(ㄊㄧㄢ ㄌㄧ)
natural law; the reason of
Heaven

天理循環(ㄊㄧㄢ ㄌㄧ ㄒㄩㄣ ㄏㄨㄢ)
The guilty are always punished and the kind-hearted
always rewarded under the
law of Heaven. 或The course
of nature goes round.

天理昭彰(ㄊㄧㄢ ㄌㄧ ㄓㄠ ㄓㄤ)
The law of Heaven always
prevails.

天理人情(ㄊㄧㄢ ㄌㄧ ㄖㄣ ㄑㄧㄥ)
(literally) law of nature and
feelings of man--reasonable

天良(ㄊㄧㄢ ㄌㄧㄤ)
one's conscience

天亮(ㄊㄧㄢ ㄌㄧㄤ)
daybreak; daytime: 他們自天
亮工作到天黑。They work
from dawn till dark.

天靈蓋(ㄊㄧㄢ ㄌㄧㄥ ㄍㄞ)
the frontal part of the skull
the crown (of the head)

天路歷程(ㄊㄧㄢ ㄌㄨ ㄌㄧ ㄔㄥ)
Pilgrim's Progress, an allegory by John Bunyan

天羅地網(ㄊㄧㄢ ㄌㄨㄛ ㄉㄧ ㄨㄤ)
the dragnet of justice surrounding on all sides; envel-
opment

天倫之樂(ㄊㄧㄢ ㄌㄨㄣ ㄓ ㄌㄜ)
family love and joy; family
happiness

天各一方(ㄊㄧㄢ ㄍㄜ ㄧ ㄈㄤ)
to be far apart; to live far
apart from each other

天高地厚(ㄊㄧㄢ ㄍㄠ ㄉㄧ ㄏㄡ)
①the immensity of the universe which is beyond the
comprehension of the
human ②immensity (of love,
kindness, etc.)

天高皇帝遠(ㄊㄧㄢ ㄍㄠ ㄏㄨㄤ ㄉㄧ ㄩㄢ)
(literally) The heaven is
high and the emperor is far
away.—① It's difficult to
get justice. ②One may do
whatever one pleases without fear of interference.

天高氣爽(ㄊㄧㄢ ㄍㄠ ㄑㄧ ㄕㄨㄤ)
(usually said of the crisp air

in autumn) The sky is high
and the weather is fine.

天干(ㄊㄧㄢ ㄍㄢ)
the Ten Celestial Stems
—used with the Twelve Terrestrial Branches to form a
cycle of sixty

天國(ㄊㄧㄢ ㄍㄨㄛˊ)
the Kingdom of Heaven

天工(ㄊㄧㄢ ㄍㄨㄥ)
formed by nature; natural; a
work of nature: 巧奪天工. It
rivals nature.

天公不作美(ㄊㄧㄢ ㄍㄨㄥ ㄅㄨˋ ㄗㄨㄛˋ ㄇㄟˇ)
(literally) Heaven is not cooperative.— Weather turns
foul when some activity requiring fine weather is
scheduled to take place.

天空(ㄊㄧㄢ ㄎㄨㄥ)
the sky; the firmament; the
void

天河(ㄊㄧㄢ ㄏㄜˊ)
the Milky Way; the Galaxy

天花(ㄊㄧㄢ ㄏㄨㄚ)
(pathology) the smallpox

天花板(ㄊㄧㄢ ㄏㄨㄚ ㄅㄢˇ)
the ceiling (of a room)

天花亂墜(ㄊㄧㄢ ㄏㄨㄚ ㄌㄨㄢˋ ㄓㄨㄟˋ)
exaggerated description (of
the attractions of a place,
chances of success in a project, etc.)

天火(ㄊㄧㄢ ㄏㄨㄛˇ)
①a fire caused by Heaven,
as by lightning ②a fire
whose cause can not be ascertained

天昏地暗(ㄊㄧㄢ ㄏㄨㄣ ㄉㄧˋ ㄢˋ)
shrouded by gloom; dark
above and below (often
referring to the scene in a
sandstorm, hurricane attack,
etc.)

天荒地老(ㄊㄧㄢ ㄏㄨㄤ ㄉㄧˋ ㄌㄠˇ)
(literally) when the earth
and heaven get old—a long,
long time (often used by
lovers in making vows of
eternal love)

天皇(ㄊㄧㄢ ㄏㄨㄤˊ)
①the emperor of Japan;
mikado ②the king of
heaven

天機(ㄊㄧㄢ ㄐㄧ)
(literally) the secrets of

Heaven; the hidden plans of
Providence—something in-
explicable

天津(ㄊㄧㄢ ㄐㄧㄣ)
Tientsin, a port city in
Hopeh Province

天經地義(ㄊㄧㄢ ㄐㄧㄥ ㄉㄧˋ ㄧˋ)
a matter of course; a universal truth: 他認爲這消息是天經
地義之事. He took the news
as a matter of course.

天井(ㄊㄧㄢ ㄐㄧㄥˇ)
a courtyard; a patio

天氣(ㄊㄧㄢ ㄑㄧˋ)
weather

天氣預報(ㄊㄧㄢ ㄑㄧˋ ㄩˋ ㄅㄠˋ)
a weather forecast

天橋(ㄊㄧㄢ ㄑㄧㄠˊ)
①an overhead bridge or elevated passage, an overline
bridge; a platform bridge ②
name of an amusement cen-
ter in Peiping

天譴(ㄊㄧㄢ ㄑㄧㄢˇ)
the wrath of Heaven; God's
punishment—fire-and-
brimstone

天塹難踰(ㄊㄧㄢ ㄑㄧㄢˋ ㄋㄢˊ ㄩˊ)
The natural barriers (for
defense) are insurmountable.

天下(ㄊㄧㄢ ㄒㄧㄚˋ)
①the world: 它是一支天下無
敵的軍隊. It was an invin-
cible army in the world. ②
(in ancient usage) the whole
country of China

天下洶洶(ㄊㄧㄢ ㄒㄧㄚˋ ㄒㄩㄥ ㄒㄩㄥ)
The whole nation is clamoring, tumultuous, or in upheaval.

天下一家(ㄊㄧㄢ ㄒㄧㄚˋ ㄧ ㄐㄧㄚ)
All people under the sun are
one family. 或 The world is
a big family.

天下烏鴉一般黑(ㄊㄧㄢ ㄒㄧㄚˋ ㄨ
ㄧㄚ ㄧ ㄅㄢ ㄏㄟ)
All crows are black.— Evil
people are bad all over the
world. 或 In every country
dogs bite.

天下爲公(ㄊㄧㄢ ㄒㄧㄚˋ ㄨㄟˊ ㄍㄨㄥ)
The world is for all.

天曉得(ㄊㄧㄢ ㄒㄧㄠˇ ㄉㄜˊ)
God knows! 或 Heaven
knows!

天仙(ㄊㄧㄢ ㄒㄧㄢ)
①a goddess ②a beauty

天仙化人(ㄊㄧㄢ ㄒㄧㄢ ㄏㄨㄚˋ ㄖㄣˊ)
as beautiful as an angel
from heaven; a stunning
beauty

天險(ㄊㄧㄢ ㄒㄧㄢˇ)
impregnable natural barriers
(for defense)

天綫(ㄊㄧㄢ ㄒㄧㄢˋ)
an antenna (for radio, TV,
etc.)

天香國色(ㄊㄧㄢ ㄒㄧㄤ ㄍㄨㄛˊ ㄙㄜˋ)
a woman of great beauty 亦
作「國色天香」

天象(ㄊㄧㄢ ㄒㄧㄤˋ)
celestial phenomena; astronomical phenomena: 他善於
觀測天象. He is expert in
astronomical observation.

天性(ㄊㄧㄢ ㄒㄧㄥˋ)
natural temperaments; natural quality; a natural disposition: 他是個天性和善慷慨的
人. He is by nature a kind,
generous fellow.

天旋地轉(ㄊㄧㄢ ㄒㄩㄢˊ ㄉㄧˋ ㄓㄨㄢˇ)
(to feel as if) the heaven
and the earth were spinning
round; very faint and dizzy

天之驕子(ㄊㄧㄢ ㄓ ㄐㄧㄠ ㄗˇ)
(literally) the apple of God's
eye—to be specially favored
by Heaven; to be extraordinarily blessed

天職(ㄊㄧㄢ ㄓˊ)
bounden duty; natural duty:
遵守法律是國民的天職. Abid-
ing by the law is a citizen's
natural duty.

天眞(ㄊㄧㄢ ㄓㄣ)
naive; naivety; innocent: 他
是個天眞無邪的小孩. He's an
innocent child.

天眞爛漫(ㄊㄧㄢ ㄓㄣ ㄌㄢˋ ㄇㄢˋ)
innocent and carefree—lovely; honest and without affectation—like a child

天誅地滅(ㄊㄧㄢ ㄓㄨ ㄉㄧˋ ㄇㄧㄝˋ)
to be damned by Heaven
and Earth (usually used in
swearing)

天竺(ㄊㄧㄢ ㄓㄨˊ)
the ancient name of India

天竺牡丹(ㄊㄧㄢ ㄓㄨˊ ㄇㄨˇ ㄉㄢ)
dahlia 亦作「大理花」

天竺葵(ㄊㄧㄢ ㄓㄨˊ ㄎㄨㄟˊ)
Pelargonium hortorum, gera-
nium

〔大部〕

天竺鼠(ㄊㄧㄢ ㄓㄨˊ ㄕㄨˇ)
a guinea pig; a cavy

天主(ㄊㄧㄢ ㄓㄨˇ)
(Christianity) God

天主堂(ㄊㄧㄢ ㄓㄨˇ ㄊㄤˊ)
a Catholic church

天主教(ㄊㄧㄢ ㄓㄨˇ ㄐㄧㄠˋ)
Catholicism; the Roman Catholic Church

天助(ㄊㄧㄢ ㄓㄨˋ)
help from Heaven—unexpected help; an uncanny or very lucky break: 天助自助者。God helps those who help themselves.

天差地遠(ㄊㄧㄢ ㄔㄚ ㄉㄧˋ ㄩㄢˇ)
poles apart; far off the beam

天朝(ㄊㄧㄢ ㄔㄠˊ)
a reference to the Chinese imperial court by Chinese envoys or by barbarians who paid tributes to China

天長地久(ㄊㄧㄢ ㄔㄤˊ ㄉㄧˋ ㄐㄧㄡˇ)
(literally) as old as heaven and earth—a very long time

天成(ㄊㄧㄢ ㄔㄥˊ)
natural; springing from nature

天窗(ㄊㄧㄢ ㄔㄨㄤ)
①a skylight; high windows ②as in 打開天窗說亮話—Let's be quite frank.

天師(ㄊㄧㄢ ㄕ)
the title of the head of the Taoists

天時(ㄊㄧㄢ ㄕˊ)
①weather, or climates ②opportunities of time vouchsafed by Heaven

天使(ㄊㄧㄢ ㄕˇ)
①an angel ②an emissary from the emperor

天山(ㄊㄧㄢ ㄕㄢ)
①Mt. Heaven, also known as the Snow Mountain, in Sinkiang Province ②name of a county in Northeast China

天神(ㄊㄧㄢ ㄕㄣˊ)
gods in heaven; deities

天生(ㄊㄧㄢ ㄕㄥ)
natural; to be born with; congenital; inborn: 鴨子會游泳是天生的。It is natural for ducks to swim.

天生尤物(ㄊㄧㄢ ㄕㄥ ㄧㄡˊ ㄨˋ)
a born siren, sexy kitten,

etc.

天書(ㄊㄧㄢ ㄕㄨ)
①(in old China) an imperial order; the emperor's instructions ②(Taoism) a book from Heaven ③a sarcastic reference to a writing difficult to understand or words not easily recognizable

天數(ㄊㄧㄢ ㄕㄨˋ)
a predestined tragedy or disaster

天然(ㄊㄧㄢ ㄖㄢˊ)
natural (as opposed to artificial): 煤與油是天然產物。Coal and oil are natural products.

天然氣(ㄊㄧㄢ ㄖㄢˊ ㄑㄧˋ)
natural gas

天人合一(ㄊㄧㄢ ㄖㄣˊ ㄏㄜˊ ㄧ)
a theory that man is an integral part of nature

天壤之別(ㄊㄧㄢ ㄖㄤˇ ㄓ ㄅㄧㄝˊ)
as far apart as the heaven and earth—vastly different; poles apart

天姿(ㄊㄧㄢ ㄗ)
(a woman's) natural beauty (without the help of make-up)

天資(ㄊㄧㄢ ㄗ)
natural endowments; inborn talent or intellectual capacity

天子(ㄊㄧㄢ ㄗˇ)
(literally) the Son of Heaven—the emperor

天擇(ㄊㄧㄢ ㄗㄜˊ)
the law of natural selection in evolution

天災(ㄊㄧㄢ ㄗㄞ)
a natural disaster; a natural calamity; an act of God: 他們去年遭到天災。They suffered natural disasters last year.

天災人禍(ㄊㄧㄢ ㄗㄞ ㄖㄣˊ ㄏㄨㄛˋ)
natural disasters and man-made calamities; natural disasters and wars

天造地設(ㄊㄧㄢ ㄗㄠˋ ㄉㄧˋ ㄕㄜˋ)
①(said of a couple) matched by Heaven and Earth; a natural match (sometimes, used sarcastically) ②a natural creation; heavenly

天足(ㄊㄧㄢ ㄗㄨˊ)
(women's) natural feet (as distinguished from feet deformed by foot-binding in old China)

天作之合(ㄊㄧㄢ ㄗㄨㄛˋ ㄓ ㄏㄜˊ)
a match by Heaven; a match blessed by God (used in congratulatory messages or greetings to a couple or their wedding)

天縱英明(ㄊㄧㄢ ㄗㄨㄥˋ ㄧㄥ ㄇㄧㄥˊ)
(said of a ruler) born with wisdom and farsightedness

天賜(ㄊㄧㄢ ㄘˋ)
given by Heaven; endowed by Heaven

天才(ㄊㄧㄢ ㄘㄞˊ)
a genius; natural talent: 莎士比亞是個天才。Shakespeare was a genius.

天才兒童(ㄊㄧㄢ ㄘㄞˊ ㄦˊ ㄊㄨㄥˊ)
a child prodigy

天從人願(ㄊㄧㄢ ㄘㄨㄥˊ ㄖㄣˊ ㄩㄢˋ)
(literally) Heaven has complied with man's wishes—What man hoped to happen has come to pass.

天色(ㄊㄧㄢ ㄙㄜˋ)
the color of the sky; the time of the day as shown by the color of the sky; weather

天鵝(ㄊㄧㄢ ㄜˊ)
a swan

天鵝絨(ㄊㄧㄢ ㄜˊ ㄖㄨㄥˊ)
velvet; velvety

天安門(ㄊㄧㄢ ㄢ ㄇㄣˊ)
Tien An Men (the Gate of Heavenly Peace)

天衣無縫(ㄊㄧㄢ ㄧ ㄨˊ ㄈㄥˋ)
without a trace; perfect (jobs); flawless (lies)

天意(ㄊㄧㄢ ㄧˋ)
the will of Heaven; God's will

天涯海角(ㄊㄧㄢ ㄧㄚˊ ㄏㄞˇ ㄐㄧㄠˇ)
the four corners of the earth; the very ends of the earth—faraway, distant or remote places

天有不測風雲，人有旦夕禍福
(ㄊㄧㄢ ㄧㄡˇ ㄅㄨˋ ㄘㄜˋ ㄈㄥ ㄩㄣˊ，ㄖㄣˊ ㄧㄡˇ ㄉㄢˋ ㄒㄧˋ ㄏㄨㄛˋ ㄈㄨˊ)
Human fortunes are as unpredictable as the weather. 或 In nature there are unexpected storms, while in

life there are unpredictable fortune and misfortune.

天演(ㄊㄧㄢ ㄧㄢˇ)
evolution

天演論(ㄊㄧㄢ ㄧㄢˇ ㄌㄨㄣˋ)
the theory of evolution 亦作「進化論」

天無絕人之路(ㄊㄧㄢ ㄨˊ ㄐㄩㄝˊ ㄖㄣˊ ㄓ ㄌㄨˋ)
God will not close all doors. 或 Heaven will always leave a door open.

天無二日(ㄊㄧㄢ ㄨˊ ㄦˋ ㄖˋ)
(literally) There can not be two suns in the sky.—There cannot be two bosses in a country, or two bosses in an office, etc.

天外(ㄊㄧㄢ ㄨㄞˋ)
①unexpected; unexpectedly; a windfall ②far and high

天文(ㄊㄧㄢ ㄨㄣˊ)
heavenly bodies; astronomy

天文地理(ㄊㄧㄢ ㄨㄣˊ ㄉㄧˋ ㄌㄧˇ)
astronomical geography

天文臺(ㄊㄧㄢ ㄨㄣˊ ㄊㄞˊ)
an astronomical observatory; an observatory

天文圖(ㄊㄧㄢ ㄨㄣˊ ㄊㄨˊ)
the star atlas

天文學(ㄊㄧㄢ ㄨㄣˊ ㄒㄩㄝˊ)
astronomy

天文數字(ㄊㄧㄢ ㄨㄣˊ ㄕㄨˋ ㄗˋ)
an astronomical figure; an enormous figure

天文望遠鏡(ㄊㄧㄢ ㄨㄣˊ ㄨㄤˋ ㄩㄢˇ ㄐㄧㄥˋ)
an astronomical telescope

天王星(ㄊㄧㄢ ㄨㄤˊ ㄒㄧㄥ)
the planet Uranus

天網恢恢(ㄊㄧㄢ ㄨㄤˇ ㄏㄨㄟ ㄏㄨㄟ)
The net of Heaven stretches everywhere.—Nobody escapes the judgment of Heaven.

天雨順延(ㄊㄧㄢ ㄩˇ ㄕㄨㄣˋ ㄧㄢˊ)
(said of a ball game, etc.) to be postponed to the following day if it rains on the scheduled date

天淵之別(ㄊㄧㄢ ㄩㄢ ㄓ ㄅㄧㄝˊ)
vastly different; a world of difference

【太】 918
ㄊㄞˋ tay tài
1. very big or large
2. much; too; over; excessively; extremely; very: 天太熱不能

工作. It's too hot to work. 再見您，實在太高興了。 I'm very glad to see you again.
3. a term of respect, used in titles
4. a Chinese family name

太保(ㄊㄞˋ ㄅㄠˇ)
①a very high official in ancient China ②juvenile delinquents

太半(ㄊㄞˋ ㄅㄢˋ)
the greater half 亦作「大半」

太平(ㄊㄞˋ ㄆㄧㄥˊ)
peace; peaceful: 太平無事. All is well. 或 Everything is all right.

太平門(ㄊㄞˋ ㄆㄧㄥˊ ㄇㄣˊ)
(in public buildings, especially in theaters) exits, especially those leading to fire escapes

太平梯(ㄊㄞˋ ㄆㄧㄥˊ ㄊㄧ)
a fire escape; a safety ladder

太平天國(ㄊㄞˋ ㄆㄧㄥˊ ㄊㄧㄢ ㄍㄨㄛˊ)
The Heavenly Kingdom of Peace (1851-1864), founded by Hung Hsiu-chüan (洪秀全) with its capital located in Nanking

太平間(ㄊㄞˋ ㄆㄧㄥˊ ㄐㄧㄢ)
an undertaker's morgue; a mortuary

太平盛世(ㄊㄞˋ ㄆㄧㄥˊ ㄕㄥˋ ㄕˋ)
a reign of peace, order, and prosperity

太平洋(ㄊㄞˋ ㄆㄧㄥˊ ㄧㄤˊ)
the Pacific Ocean

太妹(ㄊㄞˋ ㄇㄟˋ)
a girl delinquent; a wild teenage girl; a tomboy; a bobbysoxer

太廟(ㄊㄞˋ ㄇㄧㄠˋ)
the ancestral shrine of an emperor

太夫人(ㄊㄞˋ ㄈㄨ ㄖㄣˊ)
(in old China) the mother of a nobility; (especially in obituary) mother

太太(ㄊㄞˋ ˙ㄊㄞ)
①a respectful title for women; a madame; Mrs. ②one's wife

太古(ㄊㄞˋ ㄍㄨˇ)
very ancient times; prehistorical times

太公釣魚，願者上鈎(ㄊㄞˋ ㄍㄨㄥ

like Chiang Tai Kung (姜太公) fishing by the Wei River (渭水), the fish willingly rising to his hookless and baitless line—A victim letting himself be caught of his own will.

太空(ㄊㄞˋ ㄎㄨㄥ)
space; the great void: 我們的地球在太空中運行。 Our earth moves through space.

太空被(ㄊㄞˋ ㄎㄨㄥ ㄅㄟˋ)
a nylon comforter

太空船(ㄊㄞˋ ㄎㄨㄥ ㄔㄨㄢˊ)
a spacecraft; a spaceship

太空時代(ㄊㄞˋ ㄎㄨㄥ ㄕˊ ㄉㄞˋ)
the space age

太空人(ㄊㄞˋ ㄎㄨㄥ ㄖㄣˊ)
(in U.S.) astronauts; (in U.S.S.R.) cosmonauts

太空總署(ㄊㄞˋ ㄎㄨㄥ ㄗㄨㄥˇ ㄕㄨˇ)
U.S. National Aeronautics and Space Administration (NASA)

太空艙(ㄊㄞˋ ㄎㄨㄥ ㄘㄤ)
a space capsule

太空梭(ㄊㄞˋ ㄎㄨㄥ ㄙㄨㄛ)
a space shuttle; a shuttle

太空衣(ㄊㄞˋ ㄎㄨㄥ ㄧ)
a space suit

太后(ㄊㄞˋ ㄏㄡˋ)
the mother of an emperor, or the empress dowager

太湖(ㄊㄞˋ ㄏㄨˊ)
the Tai Lake lying across Kiangsu and Chekiang provinces

太極圖(ㄊㄞˋ ㄐㄧˊ ㄊㄨˊ)
the diagram of cosmological scheme

太極拳(ㄊㄞˋ ㄐㄧˊ ㄑㄩㄢˊ)
taichichuan, often referred to as "shadowboxing"

太監(ㄊㄞˋ ㄐㄧㄢˋ)
a eunuch

太息(ㄊㄞˋ ㄒㄧˊ)
to sigh; to lament 亦作「嘆息」: 他為他自己不幸的命運而太息. He sighed over his unhappy fate.

太虛幻境(ㄊㄞˋ ㄒㄩ ㄏㄨㄢˋ ㄐㄧㄥˋ)
an illusory scene; an illusion; a vision

太學(ㄊㄞˋ ㄒㄩㄝˊ)
(in ancient China) an institution of higher learning

〔大部〕

〔大部〕

established by the state; the Imperial College

太學生(ㄊㄞ ㄒㄩㄝ ㄕㄥ)
students in an institution of higher learning or the Imperial College

太初(ㄊㄞ ㄔㄨ)
the beginning of the world

太師(ㄊㄞ ㄕ)
①a very high official in ancient China ②one's teacher's teacher; one's parent's teacher

太師椅(ㄊㄞ ㄕ ㄧˇ)
an armchair with a curved back (usually for persons of senior ranks in old China)

太史公(ㄊㄞ ㄕ ㄍㄨㄥ)
a title for the greatest Chinese historian, Ssu-Ma Chien (司馬遷), and his father Ssu-Ma Tan (司馬談), also a historian ②the title of the chief court historian

太守(ㄊㄞ ㄕㄡˇ)
(in old China) the magistrate of a prefecture

太甚(ㄊㄞ ㄕㄣˋ)
too much: 別欺人太甚. Don't push me too much.

太上(ㄊㄞ ㄕㄤˋ)
①the uppermost; the topmost ②very ancient times; prehistorical times ③the king or emperor

太上皇(ㄊㄞ ㄕㄤˋ ㄏㄨㄤˊ)
①the emperor's father ②(colloquial) a person who exercises supreme powers

太子(ㄊㄞ ㄗˇ)
the crown prince

太祖(ㄊㄞ ㄗㄨˇ)
①the first emperor of a dynasty ②the earliest ancestor of a clan

太座(ㄊㄞ ㄗㄨㄛˋ)
one's wife (a joking expression connoting the dominating position of a wife in the family)

太歲(ㄊㄞ ㄙㄨㄟˋ)
①the planet Jupiter ②a powerful and influential figure in a locality

太歲頭上動土(ㄊㄞ ㄙㄨㄟˋ ㄊㄡˊ ㄕㄤˋ ㄉㄨㄥˋ ㄊㄨˇ)
to offend or provoke the most powerful

太阿倒持(ㄊㄞ ㄜ ㄉㄠˋ ㄔˊ)
to hold the sword by the blade—to yield one's power to another at one's own peril

太醫(ㄊㄞ ㄧ)
the emperor's physician; a court physician

太陰(ㄊㄞ ㄧㄣ)
①the moon ②lunar

太陽(ㄊㄞ ㄧㄤˊ)
the sun: 太陽正照耀著. The sun is shining.

太陽燈(ㄊㄞ ㄧㄤˊ ㄉㄥ)
an ultraviolet lamp; a sun-lamp

太陽能(ㄊㄞ ㄧㄤˊ ㄋㄥˊ)
solar energy

太陽黑點(ㄊㄞ ㄧㄤˊ ㄏㄟ ㄉㄧㄢˇ)or 太陽黑子(ㄊㄞ ㄧㄤˊ ㄏㄟ ㄗˇ)
sunspots

太陽系(ㄊㄞ ㄧㄤˊ ㄒㄧˋ)
the solar system

太陽穴(ㄊㄞ ㄧㄤˊ ㄒㄩㄝˋ)
the temples (of a human being)

太陽神(ㄊㄞ ㄧㄤˊ ㄕㄣˊ)
Apollo

太陽眼鏡(ㄊㄞ ㄧㄤˊ ㄧㄢˇ ㄐㄧㄥˋ)
sunglasses

太原(ㄊㄞ ㄩㄢˊ)
Taiyüan—capital of Shansi Province

【夫】 919
1. ㄈㄨ fu fū
1. a man; a male adult: 一夫當關, 萬夫莫敵. If one man keeps guard over the pass, ten thousand are unable to get through.
2. those eligible for military service
3. a master
4. a husband

夫婦(ㄈㄨ ㄈㄨˋ)
man and wife; husband and wife; a couple: 夫婦偕老. Husband and wife grow old together.

夫家(ㄈㄨ ㄐㄧㄚ)
the husband's family; the husband's side

夫君(ㄈㄨ ㄐㄩㄣ)
①(in old usage) my husband ②(Tang Dynasty) a friend

夫妻(ㄈㄨ ㄑㄧ)

husband and wife; a couple

夫妻反目(ㄈㄨ ㄑㄧ ㄈㄢˇ ㄇㄨˋ)
the disharmony or discord between husband and wife

夫婿(ㄈㄨ ㄒㄩˋ)
a reference to one's own husband

夫唱婦隨(ㄈㄨ ㄔㄤˋ ㄈㄨˋ ㄙㄨㄟˊ)or 夫婦好合(ㄈㄨ ㄈㄨˋ ㄏㄠˇ ㄏㄜˊ)
(literally) The man sings and the wife follows.—domestic harmony; harmony between husband and wife

夫人(ㄈㄨ ㄖㄣˊ)
①the wives of feudal lords in ancient China ②the concubines of an emperor ③the wives of high officials ④the legal wife ⑤ Lady; Madame; Mrs.

夫子(ㄈㄨ ㄗˇ)
①a title of respect for the elders ②a master ③a reference to one's own husband in old China

夫子自道(ㄈㄨ ㄗˇ ㄗˋ ㄉㄠˋ)
One unconsciously exposes one's own defects while criticizing others.

夫役(ㄈㄨ ㄧˋ)
a servant

【夫】 919
2. ㄈㄨˊ fwu fú
1. a demonstrative pronoun—*that* in most cases
2. a final particle; a particle

【夬】 920
《ㄍㄨㄞˋ guay guài
one of the eight diagrams in the *Book of Changes*

【夭】 921
1. ㄧㄠˇ yeau yǎo
1. to die young
2. to suppress; to repress

夭折(ㄧㄠˇ ㄓㄜˊ)
①to die young; an early death ②to come to a premature end: 會議中途夭折. The meeting came to a premature end.

夭壽(ㄧㄠˇ ㄕㄡˋ)
to die young

夭亡(ㄧㄠˇ ㄨㄤˊ)
to die young

【夭】 921
2. ㄧㄠ iau yāo
young; freshlooking; tender

二畫

【失】 922

失 ㄕ shy shī

. to let slip; to neglect; to miss: 不要坐失良機。Don't let this opportunity slip.

. to lose: 他已經失業了。He has lost his job.

. an omission; a mistake

失敗(ㄕㄅㄞ)

to fail; a failure; a defeat: 失敗是成功之母。Failure is the mother of success.

失敗主義(ㄕㄅㄞㄓㄨˇㄧˋ)

defeatism

失敗主義者(ㄕㄅㄞㄓㄨˇㄧˋㄓㄜˇ)

a defeatist

失陪(ㄕㄆㄟˊ)

Please excuse me for not being able to keep you company for the moment.

失迷(ㄕㄇㄧˊ)

to get lost (on the road, etc.) 亦作「迷失」

失眠(ㄕㄇㄧㄢˊ)

to suffer from insomnia; insomnia

失面子(ㄕㄇㄧㄢˋㄗˇ)

to lose face

失民心(ㄕㄇㄧㄣˊㄒㄧㄣ)

to lose the support of the people

失明(ㄕㄇㄧㄥˊ)

to lose one's eyesight; to become blind; blind: 他右眼失明。He is blind in the right eye.

失風(ㄕㄈㄥ)

to be caught stealing; to fail in the act of stealing

失竊(ㄕㄑㄧㄝˋ)

to be robbed or burglarized

失當(ㄕㄉㄤ)

improper; improperly; impropriety: 這個案子處理失當。This case was not properly handled.

失地(ㄕㄉㄧˋ)

the territory occupied by enemy forces; the territory ceded to the victor; to cede land to the victorious enemy

失掉(ㄕㄉㄧㄠˋ)

to lose (a chance, faith, confidence, courage, etc.)

失度(ㄕㄉㄨˋ)

excessive; excessively; immoderate; immoderately

失態(ㄕㄊㄞˋ)

to misbehave; to conduct oneself ludicrously (after drinking, etc.): 他在宴會中失態。He misbehaved himself in the party.

失調(ㄕㄊㄧㄠˊ)

①ⓐ maladjustment; incoordination ⓑ to be careless about one's health, diet, etc.

②(ㄕㄉㄧㄠˋ)to be out of tune

失樂園(ㄕㄌㄜˋㄩㄢˊ)

Paradise Lost: 失樂園是密爾頓的傑作。Paradise Lost is Milton's masterpiece.

失禮(ㄕㄌㄧˇ)

to commit a breach of etiquette; to be impolite; to be rude; impropriety; misbehavior

失利(ㄕㄌㄧˋ)

to suffer a defeat (or setback); to lose

失戀(ㄕㄌㄧㄢˋ)

to be jilted; to lose one's love; to get the "Dear John" letter

失靈(ㄕㄌㄧㄥˊ)

(said of a machine, instrument, etc.) not to work or not to work properly; to be out of order

失落(ㄕㄌㄨㄛˋ)

to lose

失口(ㄕㄎㄡˇ)

a slip of the tongue; to say something improper

失歡(ㄕㄏㄨㄢ)

①to lose money ②lost money

失控(ㄕㄎㄨㄥˋ)

out of control; runaway

失和(ㄕㄏㄜˊ)

to be on bad terms; (said of a couple) to be at loggerheads: 他們失和了。They were on bad terms.

失候(ㄕㄏㄡˋ)

①(said of food) to suffer from faulty timing ②(courteous) to be absent and fail to greet somebody when he calls 亦作「失迎」

失怙(ㄕㄏㄨˋ)

to lose one's father; to be orphaned: 戰爭使他早年失怙。The war orphaned him at an early age.

失火(ㄕㄏㄨㄛˇ)

to catch fire: 昨夜郵局失火。The post office caught fire last night.

失魂落魄(ㄕㄏㄨㄣˊㄌㄨㄛˋㄆㄛˋ)

despondent; listless; despondency; dejection

失計(ㄕㄐㄧˋ)

miscalculation; poor scheming or planning

失節(ㄕㄐㄧㄝˊ)

①(said of a man) to commit a breach of virtue, especially to surrender to the enemy ②(said of a woman) to commit adultery; to lose chastity

失檢(ㄕㄐㄧㄢˇ)

indiscretion; careless in personal conduct or behavior: 他行為失檢。He committed a grave indiscretion.

失禁(ㄕㄐㄧㄣˋ)

incontinence

失敬(ㄕㄐㄧㄥˋ)

Excuse me for being disrespectful, or wanting in regard, propriety, etc. (a polite expression in greeting a guest)

失據(ㄕㄐㄩˋ)

to lose one's guidance

失覺(ㄕㄐㄩㄝˊ)

to fail to perceive; to be negligent

失竊(ㄕㄑㄧㄝˋ)

to be stolen; to be visited by a burglar

失去(ㄕㄑㄩˋ)

to lose: 不要失去你的自信。Don't lose your confidence.

失效(ㄕㄒㄧㄠˋ)

①(law) to lose legal force; to be invalidated; null and void ②(said of medicines, etc.) to lose potency or efficacy (usually owing to a prolonged lapse of time, etc.)

失笑(ㄕㄒㄧㄠˋ)

cannot help laughing

失修(ㄕㄒㄧㄡ)

wanting in repair or proper maintenance; in a dilapi-

〔大部〕

dated state

失陷(ㄕ ㄒㄧㄢ)
(said of cities, territory, etc.) to fall to enemy; to be lost to the enemy

失信(ㄕ ㄒㄧㄣ)
to break one's word or promise: 他常失信。He always breaks his promise.

失學(ㄕ ㄒㄩㄝ)
to lack formal schooling or education; to neglect to learn; not to have learned

失血(ㄕ ㄒㄩㄝ)
to lose blood

失之東隅，收之桑榆(ㄕ ㄓ ㄉㄨㄥ ㄩ，ㄕㄡ ㄓ ㄙㄤ ㄩ)
to suffer a loss in one place but make a gain somewhere else

失之毫釐，差之千里(ㄕ ㄓ ㄏㄠ ㄌㄧ，ㄔㄚ ㄓ ㄑㄧㄢ ㄌㄧ)
A slight mistake will result in a great error in the end.

失之交臂(ㄕ ㄓ ㄐㄧㄠ ㄅㄧ)
to miss (a person or chance) at very close range: 機會難得，切勿失之交臂。Don't let slip such a golden opportunity.

失職(ㄕ ㄓ)
to be delinquent; dereliction of one's duty; to neglect one's duty

失著(ㄕ ㄓㄠ)
to miscalculate; a miscalculation

失眞(ㄕ ㄓㄣ)
(said of photograph, voice, etc.) to be in disagreement with the actual image or sound; not true to life; to lack fidelity

失政(ㄕ ㄓㄥ)
to misrule a nation

失主(ㄕ ㄓㄨ)
(law) the owner of lost property or the victim of a robbery, burglary, etc.

失察(ㄕ ㄔㄚ)
to be neglectful of one's duty of supervision; to neglect to inquire into

失常(ㄕ ㄔㄤ)
off form; to perform below one's normal capacity; odd

失傳(ㄕ ㄔㄨㄢ)

lost (arts, skills, etc.); to lose the record of; to lose the tradition of

失寵(ㄕ ㄔㄨㄥ)
to fall out of imperial favor; to be in disgrace; to lose one's boss's confidence

失時(ㄕ ㄕ)
to miss the opportune moment; to miss the right opportunity

失實(ㄕ ㄕ)
inaccurate

失事(ㄕ ㄕ)
an accident; to meet with an accident

失恃(ㄕ ㄕ)
①to lose one's mother ② to lose somebody or something one used to rely on

失勢(ㄕ ㄕ)
to lose one's position, authority, influence, etc.

失手(ㄕ ㄕㄡ)
to break something or hurt somebody by accident; to slip

失守(ㄕ ㄕㄡ)
①to fail to fulfill one's duty ②(said of a city, territory, etc.) to fall into the hands of the enemy

失閃(ㄕ ㄕㄢ)
accident; accidentally

失身(ㄕ ㄕㄣ)
①(said of women) to lose chastity ②to incur danger

失身分 or 失身份(ㄕ ㄕㄣ ˙ㄈㄣ)
(to do something) beneath one's dignity

失神(ㄕ ㄕㄣ)
inattentive; absent-minded; careless

失愼(ㄕ ㄕㄣ)
①careless; carelessness ②(literary) to cause a fire out of carelessness

失聲(ㄕ ㄕㄥ)
to lose one's voice for crying too much

失足(ㄕ ㄗㄨ)
①to slip; to lose one's footing; a slip ②to commit a mistake; to take a wrong step in life

失蹤(ㄕ ㄗㄨㄥ)
missing

失策(ㄕ ㄘㄜ)
poor tactic or strategy; bad scheming or planning; a mistake; unwise; inexpedient

失措(ㄕ ㄘㄨㄛ)
to lose one's head or presence of mind in fright or panic

失色(ㄕ ㄙㄜ)
to lose color; to turn pale; to become pale because of fear or other sudden emotional changes

失散(ㄕ ㄙㄢ)
lost and scattered (usually referring to the original script of a book, etc.); to be separated from and lose touch with each other

失速(ㄕ ㄙㄨ)
(aviation)to stall

失所(ㄕ ㄙㄨㄛ)
to be homeless

失算(ㄕ ㄙㄨㄢ)
to miscalculate; a miscalculation

失而復得(ㄕ ㄦ ㄈㄨ ㄉㄜ)
to be lost and found again

失意(ㄕ ㄧ)
not doing well; disappointed; very discouraged; frustrated

失業(ㄕ ㄧㄝ)
to lose one's job; jobless; unemployed; unemployment

失言(ㄕ ㄧㄢ)
to make improper utterances; to say what should not be said; an improper pronunciation, remark, etc.

失迎(ㄕ ㄧㄥ)
Excuse me for not having greeted you.

失誤(ㄕ ㄨ)
①an error; a slip; an omission ②(golf) duff; (bowling) miss; error; (tennis) fault; (softball & basketball) error

失物(ㄕ ㄨ)
lost property

失物招領(ㄕ ㄨ ㄓㄠ ㄌㄧㄥ)
lost items or articles (found by others) kept for claimants

失望(ㄕ ㄨㄤ)
to be disappointed or discouraged; disappointment: 我

對他甚感失望。I was disappointed in him.

失約(ㄕ ㄩㄝ)
①to break one's promise: 請別失約。Please don't break your promise. ②to break a date or an appointment

【央】 923 ㄧㄤ iang yāng
1. the center; central; middle
2. the finish or conclusion; to finish: 夜未央。The night has not passed off.
3. to request; to entreat
央記(ㄧㄤ ㄐㄧ)
to request (someone) to do something
央告(ㄧㄤ ㄍㄠ)
to beg; to beseech
央求(ㄧㄤ ㄑㄧㄡ)
to beg; to entreat; to implore; to plead
央請(ㄧㄤ ㄑㄧㄥ)
to make a request

【夯】 924 ㄏㄤ hang hāng
1. to raise with force
2. a heavy load; a burden
3. (levee construction) to fill cracks and leaks with earth

三畫

【夷】 925 ㄧ yi yí
1. (in ancient China) barbarians in the east
2. foreign tribes or foreigners
3. at ease; peaceful
4. to level; to make level, even or smooth
5. safe
6. to eliminate; to exterminate; to kill; to execute
7. injuries; wounds
8. grades; classes
9. common; usual; ordinary
10. great; big
11. a Chinese family name
夷滅(ㄧ ㄇㄧㄝ)
to wipe out (a tribe, family, etc.)
夷狄(ㄧ ㄉㄧ)
the barbarian tribes in the east and north of ancient China
夷戮(ㄧ ㄌㄨ)
to slaughter

夷九族(ㄧ ㄐㄧㄡ ㄗㄨ)
the execution of nine branches of a family (the most severe punishment in ancient China)
夷為平地(ㄧ ㄨㄟ ㄆㄧㄥ ㄉㄧ)
to level (a town, etc.) with the ground: 大火把建築物夷為平地。The fire levelled buildings to the ground.

【夸】 926 ㄎㄨㄚ kua kuā
1. big; large
2. lavish; luxurious
3. good-looking; pleasant
4. to brag; to talk big
5. a Chinese family name
夸誕(ㄎㄨㄚ ㄉㄢ)
boastful; bragging

四畫

【夾】 927 ㄐㄧㄚ jya jiā
(又讀 ㄐㄧㄚ jia jiá)
1. to be wedged between; to be sandwiched
2. to squeeze; to press; to occupy both sides of
3. pincers
4. of two or more layers; lined (garments, etc.)
5. a folder to keep sheets of paper, etc.
6. to carry secretly
7. to mix; to mingle
夾子(ㄐㄧㄚ ˙ㄗ)
folders for keeping documents, papers, pictures, etc.; clips
夾被(ㄐㄧㄚ ㄅㄟ)
a bedcover with a lining
夾板(ㄐㄧㄚ ㄅㄢ)
①boards for supporting or pressing the sides of anything—as a fractured leg ② plywood
夾縫(ㄐㄧㄚ ㄈㄥ)
a crack; a narrow opening; a loophole (in the law)
夾帶(ㄐㄧㄚ ㄉㄞ)
①things brought in secretly such as contraband: 郵寄包裹不能夾帶信件。Don't put letters into a parcel. ②a crib
夾道(ㄐㄧㄚ ㄉㄠ)
a narrow passageway between two walls or rows of trees,

etc.
夾道歡迎(ㄐㄧㄚ ㄉㄠ ㄏㄨㄢ ㄧㄥ)
to line the street to welcome (a state guest, a conquering hero, etc.)
夾攻(ㄐㄧㄚ ㄍㄨㄥ)or 夾擊(ㄐㄧㄚ ㄐㄧ)
to attack from both sides: 我軍被敵人兩面夾攻。Our troops were attacked by the enemies from both sides.
夾七夾八(ㄐㄧㄚ ㄑㄧ ㄐㄧㄚ ㄅㄚ)
mixed and not pure; mixed up; not clear
夾心(ㄐㄧㄚ ㄒㄧㄣ)
with a filling
夾注(ㄐㄧㄚ ㄓㄨ)
(especially in Chinese classics) explanatory notes immediately following the words or sentences to be explained
夾注號(ㄐㄧㄚ ㄓㄨ ㄏㄠ)
parentheses used to mark off explanatory notes
夾持(ㄐㄧㄚ ㄔ)
to hold in between
夾書板(ㄐㄧㄚ ㄕㄨ ㄅㄢ)
a book brace
夾雜(ㄐㄧㄚ ㄗㄚ)
mixed up
夾層(ㄐㄧㄚ ㄘㄥ)
a double layer; a secret compartment; a false bottom (of a trunk, etc.)
夾衣(ㄐㄧㄚ ㄧ)
lined garments without padding
夾尾巴(ㄐㄧㄚ ㄨㄟ ㄅㄚ)
(said of dogs) to put the tail between the legs——(figuratively) to act like a coward

【夾】 927 2. ㄐㄧㄚ jiah jiá
參看「夾竹桃」或「夾生」
夾竹桃(ㄐㄧㄚ ㄓㄨ ㄊㄠ)
an oleander
夾生(ㄐㄧㄚ ˙ㄕㄥ)
(usually said of rice) half-cooked; parboiled

五畫

【奄】 928 1. ㄧㄢ yean yǎn
1. to cover; to surround
2. suddenly; abruptly; rapidly

〔大部〕

3. a Chinese family name

奄忽(ㄧㄢ ㄈㄨˋ)
suddenly; abruptly; rapidly

奄有(ㄧㄢ ㄧㄡˇ)
to put under one's control

【奄】 928
2. ㄧㄢ ian yǎn
1. to soak; to bathe; to drown
2. to remain
3. to castrate; a castrated man

奄留(ㄧㄢ ㄌㄧㄡˊ)
to tarry for a long time

奄奄一息(ㄧㄢ ㄧㄢ ㄧ ㄒㄧ)
dying; barely breathing; at one's last gasp; on the verge of death

【奇】 929
1. ㄑㄧˊ chyi qí
1. strange; uncanny; occult; rare
2. wonderful
3. to feel strange about; to wonder

奇兵(ㄑㄧˊ ㄅㄧㄥ)
(military) to ambush by surprise; to ambush; troops used for such a purpose; a surprise attack, etc.

奇謀(ㄑㄧˊ ㄇㄡˊ)
a very clever strategy or trick; an uncanny scheme

奇妙(ㄑㄧˊ ㄇㄧㄠˋ)
wonderful; rare; too good to be true

奇妙莫測(ㄑㄧˊ ㄇㄧㄠˋ ㄇㄛˋ ㄘㄜˋ)
mysterious and inscrutable

奇特(ㄑㄧˊ ㄊㄜˋ)
unique; outstanding; strange

奇談(ㄑㄧˊ ㄊㄢˊ)
a strange story; an unusual story: 我從來沒聽過這種奇談。I've never heard of such a strange story.

奇男子(ㄑㄧˊ ㄋㄢˊ ㄗˇ)
a remarkable man; a man among men

奇女子(ㄑㄧˊ ㄋㄩˇ ㄗˇ)
a remarkable woman

奇怪(ㄑㄧˊ ㄍㄨㄞˋ)
①strange; unusual; odd; surprising: 多奇怪呵! How odd! ②something of unusual or strange sizes or shapes ③(said of the ways of the world) wonders; kaleidoscopic

奇觀(ㄑㄧˊ ㄍㄨㄢ)
a spectacular or wonderful sight or phenomenon

奇功(ㄑㄧˊ ㄍㄨㄥ)
remarkable achievements; outstanding services

奇花異木(ㄑㄧˊ ㄏㄨㄚ ㄧˋ ㄇㄨˋ)
exotic flowers and unusual trees

奇貨可居(ㄑㄧˊ ㄏㄨㄛˋ ㄎㄜˇ ㄐㄩ)
(literally) rare commodities which can be hoarded for better prices—rare or precious goods

奇蹟(ㄑㄧˊ ㄐㄧ)
miracles; wonders; strange things or happenings

奇技(ㄑㄧˊ ㄐㄧˋ)
an uncanny feat; a stunt; some rare skill

奇景(ㄑㄧˊ ㄐㄧㄥˇ)
wonderful scenes or unusual sights

奇襲(ㄑㄧˊ ㄒㄧˊ)
a surprise attack; to raid; to attack by surprise: 他們決定向敵營奇襲。They decided to attack the enemy's camp by surprise.

奇效(ㄑㄧˊ ㄒㄧㄠˋ)
(said of medicines) with miraculous efficacy

奇形怪狀(ㄑㄧˊ ㄒㄧㄥˊ ㄍㄨㄞˋ ㄓㄨㄤˋ)
of strange, bizarre or grotesque shapes and sizes

奇勛(ㄑㄧˊ ㄒㄩㄣ)
outstanding contribution

奇裝異服(ㄑㄧˊ ㄓㄨㄤ ㄧˋ ㄈㄨˊ)
strange or queer clothing; outlandish dresses

奇恥大辱(ㄑㄧˊ ㄔˇ ㄉㄚˋ ㄖㄨˋ)
①great shame, dishonor or disgrace ②a great insult or humiliation

奇事(ㄑㄧˊ ㄕˋ)
a strange matter; an inexplicable occurrence

奇人(ㄑㄧˊ ㄖㄣˊ)
①a strange or queer person ②a person of unusual ability

奇才(ㄑㄧˊ ㄘㄞˊ)
a rare talent; a genius: 愛因斯坦是個數學奇才。Einstein was a mathematical genius.

奇異(ㄑㄧˊ ㄧˋ)
①strange; unusual; odd; curious ②Chinese transla-tion for GE—General Electric

奇異果(ㄑㄧˊ ㄧˋ ㄍㄨㄛˇ)
kiwi; Chinese gooseberries

奇驗(ㄑㄧˊ ㄧㄢˋ)
①(said of medicines, etc. unusual efficacy ②(said o fortune-telling, etc.)uncann accuracy

奇文(ㄑㄧˊ ㄨㄣˊ)
①a remarkable piece o writing ②queer writing

奇聞(ㄑㄧˊ ㄨㄣˊ)
something unheard-of; a electrifying, fantastic story 這真是千古奇聞。It is really an unheard-of fantastic story.

奇遇(ㄑㄧˊ ㄩˋ)
an unexpected encounter (usually referring to pleas ant encounters)

奇緣(ㄑㄧˊ ㄩㄢˊ)
an unexpected relationship

【奇】 929
2. ㄐㄧ ji jī
odd (numbers); 奇日 on odd days 六十有奇 sixty odd

奇零(ㄐㄧ ㄌㄧㄥˊ)
any number that is not a round figure

奇數(ㄐㄧ ㄕㄨˋ)
an odd number

奇偶(ㄐㄧ ㄡˇ)
odd and even numbers

【奈】 930
ㄋㄞˋ nay nài
1. what; how; but: 其奈我何? What can they do to me?
2. to bear; to endure

奈煩 or 耐煩(ㄋㄞˋ ㄈㄢˊ)
to bear; to endure

奈良(ㄋㄞˋ ㄌㄧㄤˊ)
Nara, ancient Japanese capital

奈何(ㄋㄞˋ ㄏㄜˊ)
①What to do now? 或What can we do now? 或What then? 或Why? ②to cope with; to deal with

奈及利亞(ㄋㄞˋ ㄐㄧˊ ㄌㄧˋ ㄧㄚˇ)
Nigeria

【奉】 931
ㄈㄥˋ fenq fèng
1. to receive with respect
2. an expression of respect
3. to offer; to present
4. to admire; to love and

respect
. pay; salary
. to serve; to wait on
. a Chinese family name

奉派(ㄈㄥ ㄆㄞˋ)
to be assigned to do a job
or to a post

奉陪(ㄈㄥ ㄆㄟˊ)
(a polite expression) to
accompany (you); to keep
(you) company: 恕不奉陪。
I'm sorry to be unable to
keep you company.

奉命(ㄈㄥ ㄇㄧㄥˋ)or 奉令(ㄈㄥ ㄌㄧㄥˋ)
to receive orders from
above; (to do something) as
ordered

奉天(ㄈㄥ ㄊㄧㄢ)
a former name of Mukden,
capital of Liaoning Prov-
ince

奉託(ㄈㄥ ㄊㄨㄛ)
May I request you to (forward the letter, etc.)?

奉告(ㄈㄥ ㄍㄠˋ)
to let somebody know; to
inform: 關於這件事我無可奉
告。I have no comment about
this matter.

奉公守法(ㄈㄥ ㄍㄨㄥ ㄕㄡˇ ㄈㄚˇ)
law-abiding

奉候(ㄈㄥ ㄏㄡˋ)
to offer greetings

奉還(ㄈㄥ ㄏㄨㄢˊ)
respectfully return with
thanks

奉勸(ㄈㄥ ㄑㄩㄢˋ)
May I venture to advise you
to...?

奉獻(ㄈㄥ ㄒㄧㄢˋ)
①to offer (something to a
deity, superior, etc.) ②
(Christianity) to contribute;
contributions to the church

奉行(ㄈㄥ ㄒㄧㄥˊ)
to act or perform something
as ordered

奉行故事(ㄈㄥ ㄒㄧㄥˊ ㄍㄨˋ ㄕˋ)
①to do something perfunc-
torily ②to follow the old
example or traditional practice

奉職(ㄈㄥ ㄓˊ)
to work with; to have a job
at; to get an appointment: 他
奉職於海關。He has a job at
the custom house.

奉旨(ㄈㄥ ㄓˇ)
on the imperial order

奉召(ㄈㄥ ㄓㄠˋ)
to be summoned or recalled
by the emperor or chief of a
state

奉趙(ㄈㄥ ㄓㄠˋ)
to return something with
thanks

奉承(ㄈㄥ ㄔㄥˊ)
①respectfully receive ②to
flatter; to pay court to: 他
在奉承你。He is flattering
you.

奉上(ㄈㄥ ㄕㄤˋ)
May I present...?

奉贈(ㄈㄥ ㄗㄥˋ)
with the compliments of...;
to present with respect

奉此(ㄈㄥ ㄘˇ)
"upon receipt of this..." a
platitude in Chinese documentary writing)

奉祀(ㄈㄥ ㄙˋ)
to offer sacrifices (to the
dead, etc.)

奉祀官(ㄈㄥ ㄙˋ ㄍㄨㄢ)
"a sacrificial official," a
government post held from
generation to generation by
the eldest male descendant
of Confucius and four minor
sages—Mencius, Tzu-szu,
Tseng-tzu and Yen Hui (孟
子, 子思, 曾子, 顏回)

奉送(ㄈㄥ ㄙㄨㄥˋ)
①to present respectfully ②
(shop language) to give
away as a gift

奉安(ㄈㄥ ㄢ)
(in old China) the burial of
the emperor or queen; the
burial of the president or
founder of a nation

奉養(ㄈㄥ ㄧㄤˇ)
to support (one's parents):
子女應該奉養雙親。Children
should support their parents.

奉為典範(ㄈㄥ ㄨㄟˊ ㄉㄧㄢˇ ㄈㄢˋ)
to look upon as a model

奉為圭臬(ㄈㄥ ㄨㄟˊ ㄍㄨㄟ ㄋㄧㄝˋ)
to look up to something as a
model

六畫

【奔】 932 1.(奔) ㄅㄣ ben bēn
1. to move quickly; to run; to
hurry
2. to run for one's life; to
flee
3. to elope

奔波(ㄅㄣ ㄅㄛ)
to be on the run; to work
very hard; to toil; toil

奔跑(ㄅㄣ ㄆㄠˇ)
to run in a great hurry

奔忙(ㄅㄣ ㄇㄤˊ)
to be on the move constantly; to be in a great hurry; to
be busy; to toil

奔命(ㄅㄣ ㄇㄧㄥˋ)
to rush about on errands

奔放(ㄅㄣ ㄈㄤˋ)
①(said of a horse) galloping ②(said of a writing or
emotional manifestation)
expressive and unrestrained;
moving and forceful

奔騰(ㄅㄣ ㄊㄥˊ)
① to gallop ② to surge forward; to roll in surges

奔流(ㄅㄣ ㄌㄧㄡˊ)
a swift flow (of water); a
torrent

奔逐(ㄅㄣ ㄓㄨˊ)
①to run after; to chase ②
(figuratively) to contest or
jockey for position (in politics, etc.)

奔馳(ㄅㄣ ㄔˊ)
to travel quickly; to move
fast; to hasten; to run quickly; to speed on: 火車向前奔
馳。The train sped on.

奔走(ㄅㄣ ㄗㄡˇ)
①to solicit help (in trying
to land a job, get an
appointment, etc.) ②to do a
job on orders; to run
errands: 他替我們所有的鄰居
奔走。He ran errands for
all our neighbors.

奔竄(ㄅㄣ ㄘㄨㄢˋ)
(usually said of bandits, defeated troops, etc.) to flee;
to run in a hurry: 敵人被擊敗
後奔竄。The enemy were
defeated and fled in dis-
order.

奔喪(ㄅㄣ ㄙㄤ)
to hasten home upon the
death of one's parents

〔大
部〕

【奔】 932
2.(奔) ㄅㄣ benn bèn
to go straight forwards; to head for

奔命(ㄅㄣ ㄇㄧㄥˋ)
to be in a desperate hurry

【奎】 933
ㄎㄨㄟˊ kwei kuí
1. between the buttocks; the stride made by a man
2. one of the 28 constellations which ancient Chinese astrologers believed to control the literary trends of the world
3. a Chinese family name

奎寧(ㄎㄨㄟˊ ㄋㄧㄥˊ)
quinine: 奎寧是有效的瘧疾預防藥。Quinine is an effectual preventive for malaria.

奎松市(ㄎㄨㄟˊ ㄙㄨㄥ ㄕˋ)
Quezon City, near Manila

【奏】 934
ㄗㄡˋ tzow zòu
1. to report to the throne
2. to play (music or musical instruments); 他們奏國歌。They played the national anthem. 我女兒在彈奏鋼琴。My daughter is playing the piano.
3. to move; to advance

奏本(ㄗㄡˋ ㄅㄣˇ)
a written report or letter to the king or emperor; a memorial

奏明(ㄗㄡˋ ㄇㄧㄥˊ)
to report or explain to the throne; to memorialize to the emperor

奏鳴曲(ㄗㄡˋ ㄇㄧㄥˊ ㄑㄩˇ)
(music) a sonata: 今晚布蘭德爾演奏貝多芬的「月光奏鳴曲」。Tonight Breudel played Beethoven's "Moonlight Sonata."

奏功(ㄗㄡˋ ㄍㄨㄥ)
to have the intended effect; effective; to achieve success: 他那些治療失業的措施奏功了。His measures to cure unemployment have the intended effect.

奏凱(ㄗㄡˋ ㄎㄞˇ)
(literally) to play the song of triumph—to be victorious

奏捷(ㄗㄡˋ ㄐㄧㄝˊ)
(literally) to report the news of victory (to superiors)—to win; to be victorious: 我們的球隊再度奏捷。Our team has won again.

奏效(ㄗㄡˋ ㄒㄧㄠˋ)
effective; efficacious; to have the intended effect

奏摺(ㄗㄡˋ ㄓㄜˊ)
a written report, statement, or letter to the throne; a memorial

奏章(ㄗㄡˋ ㄓㄤ)
a written report or statement to the emperor; a memorial

奏疏(ㄗㄡˋ ㄕㄨ)
a written report or statement to the throne; a memorial

奏議(ㄗㄡˋ ㄧˋ)
a petition to the emperor; a report or statement to the throne; a memorial

奏樂(ㄗㄡˋ ㄩㄝˋ)
to play music (in solemn ceremonies); 他們開始奏樂。They begin to play music.

【奐】 935
ㄏㄨㄢˋ huann huàn
1. leisurely
2. brilliant; colorful; gay; lively
3. excellent; elegant
4. numerous; many
5. a Chinese family name

【契】 936
1. ㄑㄧˋ chìh qì
1. a contract; an agreement; a bond: 他與邦公司訂一項工作契約。He made a contract with the company for a work.
2. a divining instrument in ancient China
3. to be compatible, harmonious in thought and aspiration
4. to adopt
5. to cut; to carve; to notch

契刀(ㄑㄧˋ ㄉㄠ)
an ancient coin introduced by Wang Mang (王莽) with a round head and a knife-shaped handle

契丹(ㄑㄧˋ ㄉㄢ)
Kitan, a Sinicized ancient country in northern China

契合(ㄑㄧˋ ㄏㄜˊ)
to be in agreement; compatible; harmony: 你所說的與我契合。Your story agrees with mine.

契機(ㄑㄧˋ ㄐㄧ)
①(philosophy) a moment ②a turning point; a critical point of time

契據(ㄑㄧˋ ㄐㄩˋ)
a contract; an agreement; deeds or similar documents

契券(ㄑㄧˋ ㄑㄩㄢˋ)
a written contract or agreement; a bond; a deed

契紙(ㄑㄧˋ ㄓˇ)
a title deed 亦作「所有權狀」

契舟求劍(ㄑㄧˋ ㄓㄡ ㄑㄧㄡˊ ㄐㄧㄢˋ)(ㄑㄧㄝ ㄓㄡ ㄑㄧㄡˊ ㄐㄧㄢˋ)
to carve on a gunwale of a moving boat, marking where a sword was dropped—a foolish undertaking

契友(ㄑㄧˋ ㄧㄡˇ)
an intimate friend; a bosom friend

契文(ㄑㄧˋ ㄨㄣˊ)
①a written agreement ②ancient Chinese characters carved on oracle bones

契約(ㄑㄧˋ ㄩㄝ)
a written contract or agreement

【契】 936
2. ㄑㄧㄝ chieh qiè
1. to carve
2. to be separated from

契闊(ㄑㄧㄝ ㄎㄨㄛˋ)
to be separated from one another

【奕】 937
ㄧˋ yih yì
1. great; grand; abundant
2. gorgeous; elegant; good-looking
3. worried; unsettled; anxious
4. in good order; in sequence

奕奕(ㄧˋ ㄧˋ)
①grand and graceful; gorgeous ②anxious; unsettled

七畫

【奘】 938
ㄗㄤˋ tzang zàng
large; stout; thick; powerful

【套】 939
ㄊㄠˋ taw tào
1. a case; an envelope; a wrap-

per; a sheath

2. a trap; a snare; a noose

3. to wear or slip on (a sweater, etc.)

4. to trap or trick a person (into telling the truth)

5. to harness: 他去套牲口。He went and harnessed the livestock.

6. to pattern or model after; a set pattern

7. convention; a formula: "你好嗎?" 是一句禮貌的客套話。"How do you do?" is a polite formula.

8. a suit (of clothes); a set (of tableware, etc.)

套杯(ㄊㄠˋ ㄅㄟ)
a set of cups, one inside another

套版(ㄊㄠˋ ㄅㄢˇ)
①(printing) registering ②ancient color woodblock printing

套房(ㄊㄠˋ ㄈㄤˊ)
a suite (of rooms)

套筒(ㄊㄠˋ ㄊㄨㄥˇ)
(machinery) a sleeve

套牢(ㄊㄠˋ ㄌㄠˊ)
lockup; to lock up

套利(ㄊㄠˋ ㄌㄧˋ)
arbitrage; to make a profit (usually by money exchanging)

套管(ㄊㄠˋ ㄍㄨㄢˇ)
(petroleum) a casing pipe

套口供(ㄊㄠˋ ㄎㄡˇ ㄍㄨㄥ)
to trap a suspect into admitting his guilt

套褲(ㄊㄠˋ ㄎㄨˋ)
trouser legs worn over one's trousers

套環兒(ㄊㄠˋ ㄏㄨㄢˊ)
①pretzel-like biscuits ②a set of connected rings

套話(ㄊㄠˋ ㄏㄨㄚˋ) or 套語(ㄊㄠˋ ㄩˇ)
①polite, conventional verbal exchanges ②to trap a person into telling the truth

套匯(ㄊㄠˋ ㄏㄨㄟˋ)
illegal remittance of foreign exchange for a profit from the discrepancy between official and black market rates of exchange

套間(ㄊㄠˋ ㄐㄧㄢ)
①a small room opening off

another ②an apartment; a flat

套曲(ㄊㄠˋ ㄑㄩˇ)
a divertimento 亦作「套數」

套鞋(ㄊㄠˋ ㄒㄧㄝˊ)
overshoes; galoshes

套袖(ㄊㄠˋ ㄒㄧㄡˋ)
an oversleeve

套裝(ㄊㄠˋ ㄓㄨㄤ)
an ensemble

套車(ㄊㄠˋ ㄔㄜ)
to harness an animal to a carriage

套衫(ㄊㄠˋ ㄕㄢ)
a pullover

套色(ㄊㄠˋ ㄙㄜˋ)
(printing) chromatography; color process

套色捲筒機(ㄊㄠˋ ㄙㄜˋ ㄐㄩㄢˇ ㄊㄨㄥˇ ㄐㄧ)
a color rotogravure

套衣(ㄊㄠˋ ㄧ)
an outer garment

套印(ㄊㄠˋ ㄧㄣˋ)
multiple-printing (especially in color printing)

套問(ㄊㄠˋ ㄨㄣˋ)
to find out by asking seemingly unexceptional questions; tactfully sound somebody out

套用(ㄊㄠˋ ㄩㄥˋ)
to apply mechanically; to use indiscriminately: 他喜歡套用成語。He likes to use hackneyed formulas.

【畚】 940 ㄅㄣˇ been bēn
a basket or hod for earth

畚斗(ㄅㄣˇ ㄉㄡˇ)
a dustbin

畚箕(ㄅㄣˇ ㄐㄧ)
a hod for collecting household garbage, dust, etc.; a dust basket

【奚】 941 ㄒㄧ shi xī
1. why; how; what; which

2. a servant

3. name of a Tartar tribe in ancient China

4. a Chinese family name

奚落(ㄒㄧ ㄌㄨㄛˋ)
to laugh at; to make a fool of 亦作「嘲笑」: 不要奚落她。Don't laugh at her.

奚取(ㄒㄧ ㄑㄩˇ)

What merits or advantages are there?

奚如(ㄒㄧ ㄖㄨˊ) or 奚若(ㄒㄧ ㄖㄨㄛˋ) or 奚似(ㄒㄧ ㄙˋ)
How about it? 或 Why not (do something else)? 或 Would it be better to...?

奚自(ㄒㄧ ㄗˋ)
Wherefrom?

九畫

【奠】 942 ㄉㄧㄢˋ diann diàn
1. to settle; to lay (foundation, etc.)

2. to secure; to consolidate

3. to offer libations

奠邊府(ㄉㄧㄢˋ ㄅㄧㄢ ㄈㄨˇ)
Dienbienphu, in North Vietnam

奠定(ㄉㄧㄢˋ ㄉㄧㄥˋ)
to lay foundation and consolidate it; to settle

奠都(ㄉㄧㄢˋ ㄉㄨ)
to establish a capital

奠基(ㄉㄧㄢˋ ㄐㄧ)
to lay the foundation of a building

奠祭(ㄉㄧㄢˋ ㄐㄧˋ)
the pouring of wine on the ground in sacrifice

奠酒(ㄉㄧㄢˋ ㄐㄧㄡˇ)
a libation of wine

奠儀(ㄉㄧㄢˋ ㄧˊ) or 奠敬(ㄉㄧㄢˋ ㄐㄧㄥˋ)
the money presented to the bereaved family in place of offerings; a money gift for a funeral

【奢】 943 ㄕㄜ she shē
1. extravagant; wasteful; lavish

2. excess; excessive

3. to exaggerate; to brag

奢靡(ㄕㄜ ㄇㄧˊ)
wasteful; lavish spending (of money)

奢華(ㄕㄜ ㄏㄨㄚˊ)
showy; to be indulgent in luxurious and expensive habits

奢想(ㄕㄜ ㄒㄧㄤˇ)
to think wishfully

奢侈(ㄕㄜ ㄔˇ)
luxury; waste; wasteful; prodigal: 他生活於奢侈環境

[大部]

中。He lived in luxurious surroundings.

奢侈品 (ㄕㄜ ㄔ ㄆㄧㄣˇ)
articles of luxury

奢易儉難 (ㄕㄜ ㄧˋ ㄐㄧㄢˇ ㄋㄢˊ)
Once one is accustomed to luxury, it is hard for him to live a frugal life.

奢望 (ㄕㄜ ㄨㄤˋ)
to entertain hopes beyond one's ability to realize; a wild hope; a fancy; an extravagant wish

奢願 (ㄕㄜ ㄩㄢˋ)
to wish for something which one does not deserve; wishful thinking; a wild wish

十畫

【奧】 944
　ㄠˋ aw ào

1. mysterious; obscure; profound (learning); 科學家探索宇宙的奧妙。Scientists probed into the mysteries of the universe.

2. a secret cabin or corner of a house or palace

3. Austria

奧秘 (ㄠˋ ㄇㄧˋ)
deep, profound and mysterious; subtle; subtlety

奧妙 (ㄠˋ ㄇㄧㄠˋ)
① marvels; wonder; mysterious; marvelous; subtle ② the secret of doing something

奧地利 (ㄠˋ ㄉㄧˋ ㄌㄧˋ)
Austria 簡稱「奧國」

奧地利人 (ㄠˋ ㄉㄧˋ ㄌㄧˋ ㄖㄣˊ)
an Austrian

奧林匹克運動會 (ㄠˋ ㄌㄧㄣˊ ㄆㄧˇ ㄎㄜˋ ㄩㄣˋ ㄉㄨㄥˋ ㄏㄨㄟˋ)
the Olympic Games

奧古斯都大帝 (ㄠˋ ㄍㄨˇ ㄙ ㄉㄨ ㄉㄚˋ ㄉㄧˋ)
Augustus, 63B.C.-14A.D., the first emperor of Rome

奧克拉荷馬 (ㄠˋ ㄎㄜˋ ㄌㄚ ㄏㄜˊ ㄇㄚˇ)
Oklahoma, U.S.A.

奧匈帝國 (ㄠˋ ㄒㄩㄥ ㄉㄧˋ ㄍㄨㄛˊ)
Austria-Hungary (1867-1918)

奧旨 (ㄠˋ ㄓˇ)
the main theme (of writing, etc.): 這篇短篇小說的奧旨是什麼呢? What is the main theme of this short story?

奧斯曼帝國 (ㄠˋ ㄙ ㄇㄢˋ ㄉㄧˋ ㄍㄨㄛˊ)
the Ottoman Empire, founded about 1300 by Osman I 亦作「鄂圖曼帝國」

奧斯陸 (ㄠˋ ㄙ ㄌㄨˋ)
Oslo, capital of Norway

奧義 (ㄠˋ ㄧˋ)
subtle or hidden meaning; deep and profound meaning

十一畫

【奪】 945
　ㄉㄨㄛˊ dwo duó

1. to take by force; to rob: 這場病剝奪了他的體力。This disease had robbed him of his strength.

2. to snatch; to grasp; to carry away (the first prize, etc.)

3. to settle; to decide

奪標 (ㄉㄨㄛˊ ㄅㄧㄠ)
to win the first prize—as in a race or contest: 他在賽跑中奪標。He won the first prize in the race.

奪魄 (ㄉㄨㄛˊ ㄆㄛˋ)
(literally) to be robbed of one's nerves—terrifying; diabolically monstrous

奪門而出 (ㄉㄨㄛˊ ㄇㄣˊ ㄦˊ ㄔㄨ)
to force one's way out; to force a door and rush out

奪目 (ㄉㄨㄛˊ ㄇㄨˋ)
(literally) to dazzle the eyes —eye-catching

奪魁 (ㄉㄨㄛˊ ㄎㄨㄟˊ)
to win a race or tournament; to emerge at the top in a contest or competitive examination

奪眶而出 (ㄉㄨㄛˊ ㄎㄨㄤ ㄦˊ ㄔㄨ)
(said of tears) to break out; cannot be kept back: 他感動得眼淚奪眶而出。He was affected so much that his tears started from his eyes.

奪回 (ㄉㄨㄛˊ ㄏㄨㄟˊ)
to recapture; to retake; to seize back

奪錦標 (ㄉㄨㄛˊ ㄐㄧㄣˇ ㄅㄧㄠ)
to win the first prize—as in a race or game

奪取 (ㄉㄨㄛˊ ㄑㄩˇ)
to take by force; to wrest from

奪權 (ㄉㄨㄛˊ ㄑㄩㄢˊ)

to seize power; to take over power

奪職 (ㄉㄨㄛˊ ㄓˊ)
to be dismissed from office to deprive (somebody) of office

奪志 (ㄉㄨㄛˊ ㄓˋ)
to lose or change one's purpose in life; to change one's belief; to take one's will

奪佔 (ㄉㄨㄛˊ ㄓㄢˋ)
to take possession of (something) illegally

奪寵 (ㄉㄨㄛˊ ㄔㄨㄥˇ)
to supplant someone in the favor of the emperor; to beat a rival in seeking the favor or confidence of a superior

【獎】 946
　ㄐㄧㄤˇ jeang jiǎng

1. to encourage; to exhort

2. to praise; to commend

3. to cite or give a prize or reward (for a merit, etc.)

4. a prize or reward

獎杯 (ㄐㄧㄤˇ ㄅㄟ)
a cup (as a prize)

獎牌 (ㄐㄧㄤˇ ㄆㄞˊ)
a gold, silver or bronze medal given as an award

獎品 (ㄐㄧㄤˇ ㄆㄧㄣˇ)
prizes or rewards

獎勵 (ㄐㄧㄤˇ ㄌㄧˋ)
to encourage by rewards

獎金 (ㄐㄧㄤˇ ㄐㄧㄣ)
prize money; a bounty; a bonus

獎進 (ㄐㄧㄤˇ ㄐㄧㄣˋ)
to encourage to advance further

獎券 (ㄐㄧㄤˇ ㄑㄩㄢˋ)
a lottery ticket or raffle ticket: 他賣獎券。He sold lottery tickets.

獎許 (ㄐㄧㄤˇ ㄒㄩˇ)
to praise; plaudits; to give encouragement to

獎學金 (ㄐㄧㄤˇ ㄒㄩㄝˊ ㄐㄧㄣ)
a scholarship; a fellowship: 他申請一個二千元的獎學金。He applied for a scholarship of two thousand dollars.

獎章 (ㄐㄧㄤˇ ㄓㄤ)
a medal: 他獲得獎章的榮譽。He was honored with a medal.

旌狀 (ㄐㄧㄥ ㄓㄨㄤˋ)
a citation of meritorious services, etc.: 他的老闆以獎狀酬謝他的勞績。His boss rewarded his meritorious services with a citation.

懲 (ㄔㄥˊ)

懲戒 (ㄔㄥˊ ㄐㄧㄝˋ)
rewards and punishments: 獎懲制度對一個團體是很重要的。The system of rewards and penalties is important to a group.

懲飾 (ㄐㄧㄥ ㄕˋ)
to praise

懲是 (ㄐㄧㄥ ㄕˋ)
① rewards in money, etc.
② to reward

懲掖 (ㄐㄧㄥ ㄧㄝˋ)
to encourage and help a young person, the younger generation, etc.)

懲譽 (ㄐㄧㄥ ㄩˋ)
(said of a superior) to give recognition

十二畫

【奭】 947
1. ㄕˋ　shyh shì
1. red
2. a Chinese family name

奭然 (ㄕˋ ㄖㄢˊ)
in a free manner; in utter freedom

【奭】 947
1. ㄏㄜˋ　heh hè
to be angry

十三畫

【奮】 948
ㄈㄣˋ　fenn fèn
1. to rise in force; to arouse; to exert with force
2. (said of a bird) to take wing
3. to advance, promote or invigorate (a cause, etc.)

奮臂 (ㄈㄣˋ ㄅㄧˋ)
to raise one's arms and rise; to get up and act

奮臂一呼 (ㄈㄣˋ ㄅㄧˋ ㄧ ㄏㄨ)
to raise one's hand and issue a rousing call

奮不顧身 (ㄈㄣˋ ㄅㄨˋ ㄍㄨˋ ㄕㄣ)
to do something regardless of personal safety: 他奮不顧身救那小孩。He saved the

child regardless of his own safety.

奮袂 (ㄈㄣˋ ㄇㄟˋ)
to flick one's sleeves (and be ready for action)

奮勉 (ㄈㄣˋ ㄇㄧㄢˇ)
to exert with dedication or determination

奮發 (ㄈㄣˋ ㄈㄚ)
to rouse oneself; to exert oneself

奮發圖強 (ㄈㄣˋ ㄈㄚ ㄊㄨˊ ㄑㄧㄤˊ)
to rejuvenate a nation by dedicated work

奮發有為 (ㄈㄣˋ ㄈㄚ ㄧㄡˇ ㄨㄟˊ)
(often said of a young person) hardworking and promising: 他是個奮發有為的年輕人。He is a hardworking and promising young man.

奮飛 (ㄈㄣˋ ㄈㄟ)
(literally) to spread the wings and fly away—to go far away

奮鬥 (ㄈㄣˋ ㄉㄡˋ)
to struggle; to strive; to fight for: 孫中山先生為革命大業奮鬥終身。Dr. Sun Yat-sen fought all his life for the cause of revolution.

奮力 (ㄈㄣˋ ㄌㄧˋ)
to do one's best; to spare no effort

奮激 (ㄈㄣˋ ㄐㄧ)
to spur oneself to action

奮擊 (ㄈㄣˋ ㄐㄧˊ)
① to strike with force ② to rise up and fight

奮志 (ㄈㄣˋ ㄓˋ)
to rise with dedication or determination

奮戰 (ㄈㄣˋ ㄓㄢˋ)
to fight bravely

奮勇 (ㄈㄣˋ ㄩㄥˇ)
courageously; bravely (especially in fighting enemy troops): 他們奮勇地為正義而戰。They fought bravely on the side of justice.

女 部
ㄋㄩˇ　neu nǚ

【女】 949
ㄋㄩˇ　neu nǚ
1. a daughter; a girl; a maiden; a lady
2. a woman; a female
3. name of one of the 28 constellations

女伴 (ㄋㄩˇ ㄅㄢˋ)
a lady companion; a female companion: 誰是她旅途的女伴? Who are her lady companions on the journey?

女扮男裝 (ㄋㄩˇ ㄅㄢˋ ㄋㄢˊ ㄓㄨㄤ)
a woman in a man's clothes; a woman disguising herself as a man

女儐相 (ㄋㄩˇ ㄅㄧㄣ ㄒㄧㄤˋ)
a bridesmaid

女朋友 (ㄋㄩˇ ㄆㄥˊ ㄧㄡˇ)
a girl friend: 昨晚他帶他女朋友去看電影。He took his girl friend to the movies last night.

女僕 (ㄋㄩˇ ㄆㄨˊ)
a female servant; a maid

女方 (ㄋㄩˇ ㄈㄤ)
on the woman's part (when the other party concerned is a man)

女服務員 (ㄋㄩˇ ㄈㄨˊ ㄨˋ ㄩㄢˊ)
① an air hostess; a stewardess ② a waitress

女大不中留 (ㄋㄩˇ ㄉㄚˋ ㄅㄨˋ ㄓㄨㄥ ㄌㄧㄡˊ)
A grown daughter cannot be kept unmarried for long.

女大當嫁 (ㄋㄩˇ ㄉㄚˋ ㄉㄤ ㄐㄧㄚˋ)
A girl should get married upon reaching womanhood.

女大十八變 (ㄋㄩˇ ㄉㄚˋ ㄕˊ ㄅㄚ ㄅㄧㄢˋ)
A girl changes fast in physical appearance from childhood to adulthood.

女德 (ㄋㄩˇ ㄉㄜˊ)
① feminine virtues; chastity ② feminine beauty ③ a nun

女低音 (ㄋㄩˇ ㄉㄧ ㄧㄣ)
a contralto; an alto

女弟子 (ㄋㄩˇ ㄉㄧˋ ㄗˇ)
one's girl student

女童子軍 (ㄋㄩˇ ㄊㄨㄥˊ ㄗˇ ㄐㄩㄣ)
girl scouts: 她是女童子軍。She is a girl scout.

女奴 (ㄋㄩˇ ㄋㄨˊ)
slave girls

女牢 (ㄋㄩˇ ㄌㄠˊ)

（女部）

（女部）

a prison for women criminals; a penitentiary for women

女郎(ㄋㄩˇ ㄌㄤˊ)
a young girl; a young woman; a maiden

女流(ㄋㄩˇ ㄌㄧㄡˊ)
(collectively) women; the weaker sex

女伶(ㄋㄩˇ ㄌㄧㄥˊ)or 女優(ㄋㄩˇ ㄧㄡ) or 女演員(ㄋㄩˇ ㄧㄢˇ ㄩㄢˊ)
an actress: 他妹妹是個名女伶。His sister is a famous actress.

女高音(ㄋㄩˇ ㄍㄠ ㄧㄣ)
a soprano

女管家(ㄋㄩˇ ㄍㄨㄢˇ ㄐㄧㄚ)
a woman head servant; a housekeeper

女工(ㄋㄩˇ ㄍㄨㄥ)
women labor; a girl working in a plant

女紅(ㄋㄩˇ ㄍㄨㄥ)
needlework

女公子(ㄋㄩˇ ㄍㄨㄥ ㄗˇ)
①a polite reference to others' daughters ②the daughter of a feudal prince

女孩(ㄋㄩˇ ㄏㄞˊ)
a girl

女孩兒(ㄋㄩˇ ㄏㄞˊㄦ)
a female child

女皇(ㄋㄩˇ ㄏㄨㄤˊ)
an empress

女角(ㄋㄩˇ ㄐㄩㄝˊ)
an actress; a movie or theatrical role played by a woman

女眷(ㄋㄩˇ ㄐㄩㄢˋ)
the female members of a family

女強人(ㄋㄩˇ ㄑㄧㄤˊ ㄖㄣˊ)
a successful career woman

女青年會(ㄋㄩˇ ㄑㄧㄥ ㄋㄧㄢˊ ㄏㄨㄟˋ)
YWCA—Young Women's Christian Association

女權(ㄋㄩˇ ㄑㄩㄢˊ)
women's rights

女權主義(ㄋㄩˇ ㄑㄩㄢˊ ㄓㄨˇ ㄧˋ)
feminism

女權運動(ㄋㄩˇ ㄑㄩㄢˊ ㄩㄣˋ ㄉㄨㄥˋ)
feminism; a women's liberation movement

女先生(ㄋㄩˇ ㄒㄧㄢ ㄕㄥ)
women teachers

女性(ㄋㄩˇ ㄒㄧㄥˋ)
female; the fair sex

女性荷爾蒙(ㄋㄩˇ ㄒㄧㄥˋ ㄏㄜˊ ㄦˇ ㄇㄥˊ)
female sex hormone

女性化(ㄋㄩˇ ㄒㄧㄥˋ ㄏㄨㄚˋ)
feminization; to feminize

女性中心社會(ㄋㄩˇ ㄒㄧㄥˋ ㄓㄨㄥ ㄒㄧㄣ ㄕㄜˋ ㄏㄨㄟˋ)
matriarchy

女婿 or 女壻(ㄋㄩˇ ㄒㄩˋ)
a son-in-law

女職員(ㄋㄩˇ ㄓˊ ㄩㄢˊ)
a woman employee

女員(ㄋㄩˇ ㄓㄣ)
Nüchen, or Jurchen, ancestors of the Manchus

女主角(ㄋㄩˇ ㄓㄨˇ ㄐㄩㄝˊ)
a leading lady; a heroine

女主人(ㄋㄩˇ ㄓㄨˇ ㄖㄣˊ)
a hostess

女裝(ㄋㄩˇ ㄓㄨㄤ)
a woman dress

女中丈夫(ㄋㄩˇ ㄓㄨㄥ ㄓㄤˋ ㄈㄨ)or 女中豪傑(ㄋㄩˇ ㄓㄨㄥ ㄏㄠˊ ㄐㄧㄝˊ)
a woman of great capability

女史(ㄋㄩˇ ㄕˇ)
①(formerly) a female official in charge of etiquettes in the palace ②a polite term to address a lady

女士(ㄋㄩˇ ㄕˋ)
Miss...; a lady

女神(ㄋㄩˇ ㄕㄣˊ)
a goddess: 維娜斯是羅馬人所崇拜的女神。Venus was a goddess worshiped by the Roman.

女聲(ㄋㄩˇ ㄕㄥ)
female voice

女生(ㄋㄩˇ ㄕㄥ)
co-eds; girl students

女生宿舍(ㄋㄩˇ ㄕㄥ ㄙㄨˋ ㄕㄜˋ)
a women's dormitory: 她住在女生宿舍。She lived in the women's dormitory.

女生外嚮(ㄋㄩˇ ㄕㄥ ㄨㄞˋ ㄒㄧㄤˋ)
A girl will get married sooner or later and be prone to take the side of her husband (instead of her own family).

女人(ㄋㄩˇ ㄖㄣˊ)
①a woman: 女人善變。Woman changes her mind easily. ②one's wife

女子(ㄋㄩˇ ㄗˇ)
a woman; a girl

女子參政權(ㄋㄩˇ ㄗˇ ㄘㄢ ㄓㄥˋ ㄑㄩㄢˊ)
woman suffrage

女次高音(ㄋㄩˇ ㄘˋ ㄍㄠ ㄧㄣ)or 女中音(ㄋㄩˇ ㄓㄨㄥ ㄧㄣ)
a mezzo-soprano

女廁所(ㄋㄩˇ ㄘˋ ㄙㄨㄛˇ)
a women's lavatory; a ladies' room

女色(ㄋㄩˇ ㄙㄜˋ)
woman's charms

女兒(ㄋㄩˇ ㄦˊ)
①one's daughter ②a girl

女巫(ㄋㄩˇ ㄨ)
a witch 亦作「巫婆」

女為悦己者容(ㄋㄩˇ ㄨㄟˋ ㄩㄝˋ ㄐㄧˇ ㄓㄜˇ ㄖㄨㄥˊ)
A girl will doll herself up for him who loves her.

女王(ㄋㄩˇ ㄨㄤˊ)
a queen regnant

二畫

【奴】 950
ㄋㄨˊ nu, nú

1. a slave; a servant
2. a self-derogatory expression used by a girl to refer to herself in former times
3. a despicable yes-man

奴婢(ㄋㄨˊ ㄅㄧˋ)
slaves; servants

奴僕(ㄋㄨˊ ㄆㄨˊ)
slaves; servants; lackeys

奴隸(ㄋㄨˊ ㄌㄧˋ)
a serf; a slave

奴隸解放(ㄋㄨˊ ㄌㄧˋ ㄐㄧㄝˇ ㄈㄤˋ)
slave emancipation

奴隸制度(ㄋㄨˊ ㄌㄧˋ ㄓˋ ㄉㄨˋ)
slavery: 在某些地方尚有奴隸制度。In certain places slavery is still permitted.

奴隸社會(ㄋㄨˊ ㄌㄧˋ ㄕㄜˋ ㄏㄨㄟˋ)
slave society

奴工(ㄋㄨˊ ㄍㄨㄥ)
slave labor; slave laborers; serfhood

奴工營(ㄋㄨˊ ㄍㄨㄥ ㄧㄥˊ)
a slave labor camp; a concentration camp

奴化(ㄋㄨˊ ㄏㄨㄚˋ)
to enslave; to make a slave of

奴唇婢舌(ㄋㄨˊ ㄔㄨㄣˊ ㄅㄧˋ ㄕㄜˊ)
(said of speech) talkative like a slave or maid

奴家(ㄋㄨˊ ㄐㄧㄚ)

I or me (a self-reference of girls in former times)

性(ㄋㄩㄒㄧㄥ)
servility; slavishness; servile attitude

才(ㄋㄨㄘㄞˊ)
①a slave; a serf; a bond-man ② a good-for-nothing; a useless fellow; a yes-man ③ used by an official referring to himself when addressing the emperor, especially in the Ching Dynasty

役(ㄋㄨㄧˋ)
to enslave

顏婢膝(ㄋㄨˊㄧㄢˊㄅㄧˋㄒㄧ)
servile behavior; fawning; obsequious: 國王喜歡奴顏婢膝的朝臣。The king liked the fawning courtiers.

【奶】 951 ㄋㄞˇ nae nǎi
1. the breasts of a woman
2. milk
3. grandma
4. to feed with milk; to breast-feed: 她每天奶孩子。She feeds the baby with milk every day.
5. a term of respect for married women

奶脖子(ㄋㄞˇㄅㄛ˙ㄗ)
breasts 亦作「奶房」

奶品(ㄋㄞˇㄆㄧㄣˇ)
milk products

奶瓶(ㄋㄞˇㄆㄧㄥˊ)
a milk bottle: 我找不到奶瓶。I can't find the milk bottle.

奶媽(ㄋㄞˇㄇㄚ)or**奶母**(ㄋㄞˇㄇㄨˇ)
a wet nurse 亦作「乳母」

奶名(ㄋㄞˇㄇㄧㄥˊ)
a pet name given to a child by his parents

奶粉(ㄋㄞˇㄈㄣˇ)
milk powder

奶頭(ㄋㄞˇ˙ㄊㄡ)
the nipples

奶奶(ㄋㄞˇ˙ㄋㄞ)
①a term of respect for older women ② grandma

奶牛(ㄋㄞˇㄋㄧㄡˊ)
a milk cow

奶娘(ㄋㄞˇㄋㄧㄤˊ)
a wet nurse

奶酪(ㄋㄞˇㄌㄠˋ)
cheese 亦作「乳酪」

奶糕(ㄋㄞˇㄍㄠ)

rice pastry used as substitute for milk in feeding babies

奶汁(ㄋㄞˇㄓ)
milk (from a woman's breast)

奶罩(ㄋㄞˇㄓㄠˋ)
a brassiere or bra

奶茶(ㄋㄞˇㄔㄚˊ)
tea with milk

奶水(ㄋㄞˇㄕㄨㄟˇ)
milk

奶子(ㄋㄞˇ˙ㄗ)
①the mother's milk ② breasts ③ a wet nurse

奶嘴(ㄋㄞˇㄗㄨㄟˇ)
the nipple (of a nursing bottle)

奶油(ㄋㄞˇㄧㄡˊ)
butter

三畫

【奸】 952 ㄐㄧㄢ jian jiān
1. false
2. selfish
3. disloyal
4. crafty; wicked; villainous; cunning; evil
5. adultery; fornication; licentiousness
6. a traitor; a villain

奸夫(ㄐㄧㄢㄈㄨ)
an adulterer

奸婦(ㄐㄧㄢㄈㄨˋ)
an adulteress

奸黨(ㄐㄧㄢㄉㄤˇ)
a traitorous clique or party

奸佞(ㄐㄧㄢㄋㄧㄥˋ)
①cunning and fawning ② a crafty sycophant

奸滑(ㄐㄧㄢㄏㄨㄚˊ)
crafty and cunning

奸計(ㄐㄧㄢㄐㄧˋ)
a wicked scheme; a cunning trick; a treacherous plot: 他們奸計不得逞。Their wicked scheme failed.

奸細(ㄐㄧㄢㄒㄧˋ)
a spy (from the enemy side); a stool pigeon 亦作「間諜」

奸邪(ㄐㄧㄢㄒㄧㄝˊ)
①crafty and evil; treacherous ② a crafty and evil person

奸笑(ㄐㄧㄢㄒㄧㄠˋ)
a sinister, malicious or villainous smile

奸險(ㄐㄧㄢㄒㄧㄢˇ)
crafty, mean and malicious; treacherous

奸雄(ㄐㄧㄢㄒㄩㄥˊ)
(usually referring to those in high positions) a very capable but crafty person; a very ambitious scoundrel

奸詐(ㄐㄧㄢㄓㄚˋ)
crafty; cunning: 他奸詐如狐狸。He is as cunning as a fox.

奸臣(ㄐㄧㄢㄔㄣˊ)
(formerly) a selfish, disloyal and cunning minister; a traitor

奸商(ㄐㄧㄢㄕㄤ)
unethical merchants; profiteers

奸人(ㄐㄧㄢㄖㄣˊ)
a mean fellow; a villain; a scoundrel

奸賊(ㄐㄧㄢㄗㄟˊ)
a scoundrel; a traitor

奸淫(ㄐㄧㄢㄧㄣˊ)
①illicit sexual relations; adultery ② lustful; lecherous ③ to rape; to seduce

奸淫擄掠(ㄐㄧㄢㄧㄣˊㄌㄨˇㄌㄩㄝˋ)
to rape and loot

【她】 953 ㄊㄚ ta tā
she: 她喜歡古典音樂。She likes classical music.

她們(ㄊㄚ˙ㄇㄣ)
(referring to the feminine) they

【好】 954 ㄏㄠˇ hao hǎo
1. good; nice; fine; excellent: 這是一本好字典。This is a good dictionary.
2. pleasing (looks, taste, etc.); easy (to deal with, etc.)
3. to finish (dressing, eating, etc.): 他離開之前已把工作做好了。He finished off the work before he left.
4. very; much
5. can; so that: 把這個做完好再開始另外一件。Finish this so that you can start another.
6. All right! 或 Wonderful! 或 Bravo!
7. an exclamatory expression

【女部】

8. a friendly meeting
9. fit; suitable; proper

好辦(ㄏㄠˇ ㄅㄢˋ)
easy to manage or arrange: 這件事好辦。The matter can be easily arranged.

好半天(ㄏㄠˇ ㄅㄢˋ ㄊㄧㄢ)
quite a while; a long time

好比(ㄏㄠˇ ㄅㄧˇ)
to be likened to; to be like; to be tantamount to

好不(ㄏㄠˇ ㄅㄨˋ)
very; what; how: 大家見了面，好不歡喜啊! How happy we are to see each other!

好不(ㄏㄠˇ ㄅㄨˋ)
① Is it all right? 或 Okay? ② Won't you...?

好不講理(ㄏㄠˇ ㄅㄨˋ ㄐㄧㄤˇ ㄌㄧˇ)
utterly impervious to reasoning or argument

好不容易(ㄏㄠˇ ㄅㄨˋ ㄖㄨㄥˊ ㄧˋ)
① very difficult ② after all the trouble: 他好不容易才擠上了那輛公車。He had a hard time squeezing through the crowd to get on the bus.

好不要臉(ㄏㄠˇ ㄅㄨˋ ㄧㄠˋ ㄌㄧㄢˇ)
brazen; absolutely without shame

好評(ㄏㄠˇ ㄆㄧㄥˊ)
favorable comment; a high opinion: 老師對他頗有好評。The teacher has a rather high opinion of him.

好大(ㄏㄠˇ ㄉㄚˋ)
① How big? ② what a (bad temper, big house, etc.)

好的(ㄏㄠˇ ㄉㄜ˙)
Good! 或 All right. 或 O.K.

好歹(ㄏㄠˇ ㄉㄞˇ)
① emergency; an accident ② by hook or by crook ③ good and bad ④ anyhow; in any case: 好歹試試看。Let's try, anyhow.

好多(ㄏㄠˇ ㄉㄨㄛ)
① How much or many? ② a good deal; so much; so many

好多了(ㄏㄠˇ ㄉㄨㄛ ㄌㄜ˙)
much better: 她已經好多了。She is much better.

好端端(ㄏㄠˇ ㄉㄨㄢ ㄉㄨㄢ)
in perfectly good state or condition; when everything is all right

好天兒(ㄏㄠˇ ㄊㄧㄢ ㄦ)
a fine day

好聽(ㄏㄠˇ ㄊㄧㄥ)
pleasant to hear: 好聽的話並非人人都愛聽。Not everyone likes sweet words.

好萊塢(ㄏㄠˇ ㄌㄞˊ ㄨ)
Hollywood, California, U.S.A.

好感(ㄏㄠˇ ㄍㄢˇ)
a good opinion; a favorable impression: 我對她有好感。I have a good opinion of her.

好過(ㄏㄠˇ ㄍㄨㄛˋ)
① well-to-do; to be in easy circumstances ② to feel better (after an attack of disease, etc.); to feel fine

好看(ㄏㄠˇ ㄎㄢˋ)
① good-looking; beautiful; nice ② interesting ③ proud ④ in an embarrassing situation; on the spot

好合(ㄏㄠˇ ㄏㄜˊ)
(said of couples) to live in perfect union

好好的(ㄏㄠˇ ㄏㄠˇ ㄉㄜ˙)
① (to do something) in earnest or seriously ② perfectly all right

好好先生(ㄏㄠˇ ㄏㄠˇ ㄒㄧㄢ ˙ㄙㄥ)
a nice guy who bears no grudge against the world and vice versa; a "soft" fellow who never quarrels with the world; an easy-going person

好好兒(ㄏㄠˇ ㄏㄠˇ ㄦ)
① delighted; joyful ② in perfectly good condition; when everything is all right ③ all out; thoroughly ④ carefully; cautiously: 好好地想一想。Think it over carefully.

好漢(ㄏㄠˇ ㄏㄢˋ)
a brave man; a hero: 只有好漢才配得上美人。Only the hero deserve the fair.

好漢不怕出身低(ㄏㄠˇ ㄏㄢˋ ㄅㄨˋ ㄆㄚˋ ㄔㄨ ㄕㄣ ㄉㄧ)
(informal) One's humble origin will not prevent him from achieving success in life.

好漢不吃眼前虧(ㄏㄠˇ ㄏㄢˋ ㄅㄨˋ ㄔ ㄧㄢˇ ㄑㄧㄢˊ ㄎㄨㄟ)
A wise man knows how to avoid being beaten.

好話(ㄏㄠˇ ㄏㄨㄚˋ)
① a good word; a word of praise: 請為我說句好話。Please put in a good word for me. ② fine words

好極了(ㄏㄠˇ ㄐㄧˊ ㄌㄜ˙)
Excellent! 或 Wonderful! 或 Exquisite! 或 Tops! 他的英文好極了! His English is excellent!

好幾天(ㄏㄠˇ ㄐㄧˇ ㄊㄧㄢ)
quite a few days

好幾個(ㄏㄠˇ ㄐㄧˇ ˙ㄍㄜ)
quite a few (people, months etc.): 昨天有好幾個學生缺席。Quite a few students were absent yesterday.

好傢伙(ㄏㄠˇ ㄐㄧㄚ ˙ㄏㄨㄛ)
① The scoundrel! ② Fine thing indeed! ③ What a powerful blow!

好久(ㄏㄠˇ ㄐㄧㄡˇ)
① How long? 做這件工作要好久時間? How long will it take to do the job? ② a long time: 我已經等了好久了。have waited for a long time

好景不長(ㄏㄠˇ ㄐㄧㄥˇ ㄅㄨˋ ㄔㄤˊ)
The good circumstance don't last long. 或 Good fortune won't last forever.

好球(ㄏㄠˇ ㄑㄧㄡˊ)
Bravo! 或 well played; a good shot

好戲(ㄏㄠˇ ㄒㄧˋ)
① good play ② (sarcastic) great fun: 這回有好戲可看了 We're going to see great fun!

好些(ㄏㄠˇ ㄒㄧㄝ)
① a little better ② many (people, etc.)

好些個(ㄏㄠˇ ㄒㄧㄝ ˙ㄍㄜ)
many

好消息(ㄏㄠˇ ㄒㄧㄠ ㄒㄧˊ)
good news: 沒消息便是好消息。No news is good news.

好小子(ㄏㄠˇ ㄒㄧㄠˇ ˙ㄗ)
a smart guy; a wise guy

好笑(ㄏㄠˇ ㄒㄧㄠˋ)
laughable; funny; ridiculous 這個問題有什麼好笑? What is so funny about such a question?

好心(ㄏㄠˇ ㄒㄧㄣ)
well-intentioned; kindness; goodwill; kind-hearted

像(ㄒㄧㄤˋ)
to seem; to look like; to resemble very much: 天好像要下雨的樣子。It looks like rain.

轉(ㄓㄨㄢˇ)
to take a turn for the better; a favorable turn: 情勢好轉。The situation took a favorable turn.

吃(ㄔ)
good to eat; tasty; delicious: 這餐後點心很好吃。The dessert is delicious.

處(ㄔㄨˋ)
① good points; advantages ② profit

使(ㄕˇ)
① easy to operate; convenient for use ② in order to make

事(ㄕˋ)
① good things; wonderful things ② charity; philanthropic acts ③ marriage; wedding ④ a very bad thing (used only in an exclamatory sentence)

好事多磨(ㄏㄠˇ ㄕˋ ㄉㄨㄛ ㄇㄛˊ)
The realization of good things is usually preceded by rough going.

手(ㄕㄡˇ)
an adept; an expert; a professional

受(ㄕㄡˋ)
pleasant; comfortable; much better

聲好氣(ㄕㄥ ㄏㄠˇ ㄑㄧˋ)
in a soft and kindly manner; gently

說(ㄕㄨㄛ)
Thanks for your kind word or compliments

說歹說(ㄕㄨㄛ ㄉㄞˇ ㄕㄨㄛ)
to try every possible way to persuade somebody

說話兒(ㄕㄨㄛ ㄏㄨㄚˋㄦ)
obliging; good-natured; open to persuasion

日子(ㄖˋ ㄗ˙)
① an auspicious day ② a wedding day ③ good days; a happy life: 人人都想要過好日子。Everybody wants to live a happy life.

好人(ㄏㄠˇ ㄖㄣˊ)

① a beauty ② a person of virtue ③ a person who gets along very well with everyone

好人難做(ㄏㄠˇ ㄖㄣˊ ㄋㄢˊ ㄗㄨㄛˋ)
(literally) It's difficult to be a nice guy. — One always gets the blame from somebody no matter how fair and just he is.或 It's difficult to please everybody.

好人好事(ㄏㄠˇ ㄖㄣˊ ㄏㄠˇ ㄕˋ)
good people and exemplary deeds

好人家兒(ㄏㄠˇ ㄖㄣˊ ㄐㄧㄚ˙ㄦ)
a good family

好容易(ㄏㄠˇ ㄖㄨㄥˊ ㄧˋ)
with great difficulty; have a hard time (doing something) 亦作「不好容易」

好自爲之(ㄏㄠˇ ㄗˋ ㄨㄟˊ ㄓ)
to do one's best (to keep a job, run a business, etc.)

好在(ㄏㄠˇ ㄗㄞˋ)
it's fortunate that; thanks to; fortunately; luckily: 好在他來訪時我在家。Luckily, I was at home when he called.

好死(ㄏㄠˇ ㄙˇ)
to die a natural death (as distinct from an accidental death)

好死不如惡活(ㄏㄠˇ ㄙˇ ㄅㄨˋ ㄖㄨˊ ㄜˋ ㄏㄨㄛˊ)
To live even in adversity is better than to die under the most satisfactory circumstances.

好似(ㄏㄠˇ ㄙˋ)
(it) seems; (it) looks like: 這本書好似很有趣。The book seems quite interesting.

好一個(ㄏㄠˇ ㄧ˙ ㄍㄜˋ)
what a: 好一個正人君子！What a just and upright man, indeed!

好意(ㄏㄠˇ ㄧˋ)
to mean well; kindly or benevolently; goodwill; kindness: 謝謝您的好意。Thank you for your kindness

好意相勸(ㄏㄠˇ ㄧˋ ㄒㄧㄤ ㄑㄩㄢˋ)
to give well-intentioned advice

好意思(ㄏㄠˇ ㄧˋ ㄙ˙)
to have the nerve

好玩(ㄏㄠˇ ㄨㄢˊ)

interesting; full of fun

好望角(ㄏㄠˇ ㄨㄤˋ ㄐㄧㄠˇ)
the Cape of Good Hope, in South Africa

【好】954
1. ㄏㄠˋ haw hào
1. to love to; to like to; to be fond of
2. to be addicted to
3. what one likes or prefers

好辯(ㄏㄠˋ ㄅㄧㄢˋ)
argumentative; disputatious

好大喜功(ㄏㄠˋ ㄉㄚˋ ㄒㄧˇ ㄍㄨㄥ)
given to vanity; love to brag and show off

好賭(ㄏㄠˋ ㄉㄨˇ)
fond of gambling

好動(ㄏㄠˋ ㄉㄨㄥˋ)
(said of one's disposition) very active or restless

好高騖遠(ㄏㄠˋ ㄍㄠ ㄨˋ ㄩㄢˇ)
to aim high but care nothing about the fundamental; unrealistic

好客(ㄏㄠˋ ㄎㄜˋ)
to be hospitable: 他是個好客的人。He is a hospitable man.

好靜(ㄏㄠˋ ㄐㄧㄥˋ)
(said of one's disposition) to be fond of tranquility; sedate

好奇(ㄏㄠˋ ㄑㄧˊ)
to be curious; curiosity

好強(ㄏㄠˋ ㄑㄧㄤˊ)
to be eager to do well in everything

好學(ㄏㄠˋ ㄒㄩㄝˊ)
to be fond of studying; to be diligent in the pursuit of knowledge

好戰(ㄏㄠˋ ㄓㄢˋ)
hawkish; warmongering

好整以暇(ㄏㄠˋ ㄓㄥˇ ㄧˇ ㄒㄧㄚˊ)
to remain calm and composed while handling urgent affairs

好吃懶做(ㄏㄠˋ ㄔ ㄌㄢˇ ㄗㄨㄛˋ)
lazy; piggish: 不要這樣好吃懶做。Don't be so lazy.

好事者(ㄏㄠˋ ㄕˋ ㄓㄜˇ)or 好事之徒
(ㄏㄠˋ ㄕˋ ㄓ ㄊㄨˊ)
a meddler; a busybody

好尚(ㄏㄠˋ ㄕㄤˋ)
likes; desires; preferences: 你的好尚是什麼？What is your preference?

好生之德(ㄏㄠˋ ㄕㄥ ㄓ ㄉㄜˊ)

【女部】

【女部】

the virtue in sparing animal life; restraint from killing

好生惡死 (ㄏㄠˋ ㄕㄥ ㄨˋ ㄙˇ)
to be afraid of death; to cling to life

好勝 (ㄏㄠˋ ㄕㄥˋ)
to love to win; to be fond of preeminence; emulative: 他是個好勝的人。He is an emulative person.

好色 (ㄏㄠˋ ㄙㄜˋ)
(said of men) to be fond of pleasures of the flesh; lewd; libidinous; lustful

好色不淫 (ㄏㄠˋ ㄙㄜˋ ㄅㄨˋ ㄧㄣˊ)
to be fond of beautiful women without being lewd

好逸惡勞 (ㄏㄠˋ ㄧˋ ㄨˋ ㄌㄠˊ)
to love ease and hate work; pleasure-seeking

好勇鬥狠 (ㄏㄠˋ ㄩㄥˇ ㄉㄡˋ ㄏㄣˇ)
combative; fond of fighting 亦作「鬥狠」

好惡 (ㄏㄠˋ ㄨˋ)
likes and dislikes

好為人師 (ㄏㄠˋ ㄨㄟˊ ㄖㄣˊ ㄕ)
(literally) to like to be teachers of others—(figuratively) to be fond of giving advice to others despite one's own ignorance

好玩 (ㄏㄠˇ ㄨㄢˊ)
pleasure-seeking

好問 (ㄏㄠˋ ㄨㄣˋ)
inquisitive; to be fond of asking questions

【妁】 955
ㄕㄨㄛˋ shuoh shuō
a matchmaker; a go-between

【如】 956
ㄖㄨˊ rú rú
1. like; as: 一日不見，如三秋兮。(詩經・國風・采葛) A day without seeing him/ Is like three seasons.
2. if; supposing: 假如你希望我幫助你，我願幫忙。If you wish, I will help you.
3. as if
4. as good as; equal to: 我不如她。I'm not as good as she is.
5. to follow (advice); to listen to
6. to go to; to arrive at
7. should; ought to
8. on or in (time)

如夢初醒 (ㄖㄨˊ ㄇㄥˋ ㄔㄨ ㄒㄧㄥˇ)
(literally) as if awakened

from a dream—to come to a sudden realization

如法炮製 (ㄖㄨˊ ㄈㄚˇ ㄆㄠˊ ㄓˋ) or 如法泡製 (ㄖㄨˊ ㄈㄚˇ ㄆㄠˋ ㄓˋ)
to do things according to an approved routine method; to do something exactly as others have done; to follow suit; to follow the same formula

如飛 (ㄖㄨˊ ㄈㄟ)
like flying; quickly; swiftly

如風過耳 (ㄖㄨˊ ㄈㄥ ㄍㄨㄛˋ ㄦˇ)
to turn a deaf ear to (exhortations, etc.)

如夫人 (ㄖㄨˊ ㄈㄨ ㄖㄣˊ)
a concubine

如墮五里霧中 (ㄖㄨˊ ㄉㄨㄛˋ ㄨˇ ㄌㄧˇ ㄨˋ ㄓㄨㄥ)
as if lost in a thick fog, utterly being mystified

如何 (ㄖㄨˊ ㄏㄜˊ)
like (a dream, etc.)

如擬 (ㄖㄨˊ ㄋㄧˇ)
as suggested (an expression used by a superior in approving a written proposal submitted by a subordinate)

如鳥獸散 (ㄖㄨˊ ㄋㄧㄠˇ ㄕㄡˋ ㄙㄢˋ)
to flee helter-skelter

如來 (ㄖㄨˊ ㄌㄞˊ)
(Buddhism) one of the designation of Buddha

如雷貫耳 (ㄖㄨˊ ㄌㄟˊ ㄍㄨㄢˋ ㄦˇ)
(literally) like thunders roaring in one's ears—(one's famous name) has long been known to people: 久仰大名，如雷貫耳。Your name has long resounded in my ears.

如狼似虎 (ㄖㄨˊ ㄌㄤˊ ㄙˋ ㄏㄨˇ)
(literally) like tigers and wolves—(to eat) piggishly; (to treat or loot people) heartlessly and cruelly; (said of appearances) menacing or threatening

如臨大敵 (ㄖㄨˊ ㄌㄧㄣˊ ㄉㄚˋ ㄉㄧˊ)
(literally) like confronting a dangerous enemy—very careful or cautious; to take all possible precautions; to make all preparations; to take undue alarm

如鯁在喉 (ㄖㄨˊ ㄍㄥˇ ㄗㄞˋ ㄏㄡˊ)
to give vent to one's pent-up

feelings

如故 (ㄖㄨˊ ㄍㄨˋ)
①(often said of a new acquaintance) like an old friend: 他們一見如故。They felt like old friends at the first meeting. ② as it has always been; as usual 亦作「如舊」

如果 (ㄖㄨˊ ㄍㄨㄛˇ)
if; supposing: 如果下雨，我們還是要去嗎? Supposing it rains, shall we still go?

如何 (ㄖㄨˊ ㄏㄜˊ)
① How (can we deal with…)?: 我如何處理這種事呢? How can I deal with such case? ② What do you think of it? 或 How about it? What to do now? 或 How it?

如何是好 (ㄖㄨˊ ㄏㄜˊ ㄕˋ ㄏㄠˇ)
What should one do? What is the best way (of doing it)? 她不知如何是好 She doesn't know what she should do.

如虎添翼 (ㄖㄨˊ ㄏㄨˇ ㄊㄧㄢ ㄧˋ)
(literally) like adding wings to a tiger—with added strength; greatly strengthened or reinforced

如花似玉 (ㄖㄨˊ ㄏㄨㄚ ㄙˋ ㄩˋ)
(literally) like flower and jade—(said of a girl) young, beautiful and pure

如火如荼 (ㄖㄨˊ ㄏㄨㄛˇ ㄖㄨˊ ㄊㄨˊ)
(troops) in an imposing array; luxuriant (growth, etc.); like wildfire

如獲至寶 (ㄖㄨˊ ㄏㄨㄛˋ ㄓˋ ㄅㄠˇ)
(literally) like acquiring a rare treasure—to get what one has wished or desired for a long time

如飢似渴 (ㄖㄨˊ ㄐㄧ ㄙˋ ㄎㄜˇ)
like thirsting or hungering for something eagerly

如膠似漆 (ㄖㄨˊ ㄐㄧㄠ ㄙˋ ㄑㄧ)
(literally) like glue and lacquer—very much in love; inseparable

如舊 (ㄖㄨˊ ㄐㄧㄡˋ)
as it has always been; as usual

如箭在弦 (ㄖㄨˊ ㄐㄧㄢˋ ㄗㄞˋ ㄒㄧㄢˊ)
(literally) as an arrow on the strained cord—ready to

go or start; imminent; no turning back; inevitable

如今(ㄖㄨˊ ㄐㄧㄣ)
now; nowadays

如期(ㄖㄨˊ ㄑㄧˊ)
on time; punctually; at the appointed time; as scheduled; on schedule: 貨物已如期運到。The goods arrived at the appointed time.

如下(ㄖㄨˊ ㄒㄧㄚˋ)
as follows; as below: 其結果如下。The results were as follows.

如新(ㄖㄨˊ ㄒㄧㄣ)
brand as if it were new

如須(ㄖㄨˊ ㄒㄩ)
if (you) want to; if (you) have to: 如須去，你可立即去。If you want to go, you may go at once.

如需(ㄖㄨˊ ㄒㄩ)
if (you) need (any information)

如兄如弟(ㄖㄨˊ ㄒㄩㄥ ㄖㄨˊ ㄉㄧˋ)
like brothers; a term used by sworn brothers to address each other

如之奈何(ㄖㄨˊ ㄓ ㄋㄞˋ ㄏㄜˊ)
What can I (or we) do about it?

如常(ㄖㄨˊ ㄔㄤˊ)
as usual

如初(ㄖㄨˊ ㄔㄨ)
as always; as it was before

如出一口(ㄖㄨˊ ㄔㄨ ㄧˋ ㄎㄡˇ)
with one voice; unanimously

如出一轍(ㄖㄨˊ ㄔㄨ ㄧˋ ㄔㄜˋ)
(said of events) very similar; almost the same; to be cut from the same cloth

如實(ㄖㄨˊ ㄕˊ)
strictly according to the facts; as things really are; accurately: 他們如實地說明情況。They stated the situation accurately.

如是我聞(ㄖㄨˊ ㄕˋ ㄨㄛˇ ㄨㄣˊ)
①so I heard ②(Buddhism) the beginning clause of Buddha's quotations as recorded by his disciple, Anan

如釋重負(ㄖㄨˊ ㄕˋ ㄓㄨㄥˋ ㄈㄨˋ)
to feel greatly relieved (after discharging a duty)

如手足(ㄖㄨˊ ㄕㄡˇ ㄗㄨˊ)
like brothers: 陳先生與李先生

兩人如手足。Mr. Chen and Mr. Lee are like brothers.

如上所述(ㄖㄨˊ ㄕㄤˋ ㄙㄨㄛˇ ㄕㄨˋ)
as stated above; as mentioned above

如數家珍(ㄖㄨˊ ㄕㄨˋ ㄐㄧㄚ ㄓㄣ)
(literally) like counting family treasures—to describe distinctly and in good order; very familiar with one's subject

如數(ㄖㄨˊ ㄕㄨˋ)
(to pay, deliver, etc.) according to the amount agreed upon

如數償還(ㄖㄨˊ ㄕㄨˋ ㄔㄤˊ ㄏㄨㄢˊ)
to pay back in full

如日東升(ㄖㄨˊ ㄖˋ ㄉㄨㄥ ㄕㄥ)
(literally) rising like the sun in the eastern sky — (said of careers, prospects, etc.) beginning to prosper

如日中天(ㄖㄨˊ ㄖˋ ㄓㄨㄥ ㄊㄧㄢ)
(literally) like the sun at the zenith—①to ride on the crest of success ②very influential; very powerful

如入無人之境(ㄖㄨˊ ㄖㄨˋ ㄨˊ ㄖㄣˊ ㄓ ㄐㄧㄥˋ)
(usually said of a victorious army) like walking into a no man's land; to encounter little resistance

如坐針氈(ㄖㄨˊ ㄗㄨㄛˋ ㄓㄣ ㄓㄢ)
(literally) like sitting on a rug of needles—very anxious; uncomfortable; in a state of agitation; to sit on thorns

如醉如癡(ㄖㄨˊ ㄗㄨㄟˋ ㄖㄨˊ ㄔ)
to be drunk with; to fall head over heels in love; to be crazy about

如此(ㄖㄨˊ ㄘˇ)
thus; like this

如此這般(ㄖㄨˊ ㄘˇ ㄓㄜˋ ㄅㄢ)
and so on

如此如此(ㄖㄨˊ ㄘˇ ㄖㄨˊ ㄘˇ)
and so on

如此而已(ㄖㄨˊ ㄘˇ ㄦˊ ㄧˇ)
That is what it all amounts to

如廁(ㄖㄨˊ ㄘㄜˋ)
to go to the toilet

如喪考妣(ㄖㄨˊ ㄙㄤ ㄎㄠˇ ㄅㄧˇ)
(literally) as if to have lost one's parents—very sad;

very sorrowful; very worried

如所週知(ㄖㄨˊ ㄙㄨㄛˇ ㄓㄡ ㄓ)
as is well known; as everyone knows: 如所週知，他是一位科學家。As everyone knows, he is a scientist.

如一(ㄖㄨˊ ㄧ)
without change; consistent: 他言行不如一。His actions are not consistent with his words.

如一日(ㄖㄨˊ ㄧ ㄖˋ)
as one day; without any change in a long period; very consistent

如意(ㄖㄨˊ ㄧˋ)
①as one wishes: 祝你萬事如意。May everything turn out as you wish. ②(formerly) a kind of scepter usually made of wood or jade, used as a symbol of Buddha

如意算盤(ㄖㄨˊ ㄧˋ ㄙㄨㄢˋ ㄆㄢˊ)
wishful thinking

如有(ㄖㄨˊ ㄧㄡˇ)
if there be; if anyone has; should it happen that; in case

如影隨形(ㄖㄨˊ ㄧㄥˇ ㄙㄨㄟˊ ㄒㄧㄥˊ)
(said of two persons) to move together always; inseparable; to tag after: 他們倆如影隨形。They two are inseparable.

如晤(ㄖㄨˊ ㄨˋ)
(literally) as face to face —an expression used in letters between brothers, close friends or married couple

如魚得水(ㄖㄨˊ ㄩˊ ㄉㄜˊ ㄕㄨㄟˇ)
(literally) like fish in water —(said of newlyweds, friends, the king and the ministers, etc.) in agreeable circumstances; very satisfied and pleased; to be in one's element

如約(ㄖㄨˊ ㄩㄝ)or如命(ㄖㄨˊ ㄇㄧㄥˋ)
as agreed upon; according to

如願以償(ㄖㄨˊ ㄩㄢˋ ㄧˇ ㄔㄤˊ)
to have one's wish fulfilled: 最後，他終於如願以償。At last, he has his wish fulfilled.

如怨如慕，如泣如訴(ㄖㄨˊ ㄩㄢˋ ㄖㄨˊ ㄇㄨˋ，ㄖㄨˊ ㄑㄧˋ ㄖㄨˊ ㄙㄨˋ)
(usually said of music) very

pathetic and touching

如雲(ㄖㄨˊ ㄩㄣˊ)
(literally) like gathering clouds—many; plenty or plentiful

【女部】

【妃】 957 ㄈㄟ fēi fēi
1. a wife; a spouse
2. the concubine of a king or an emperor
3. the wife or spouse of a crown prince

妃嬪(ㄈㄟ ㄆㄧㄣˊ)
concubines or wives of a king or an emperor

妃子(ㄈㄟ ˙ㄗ)
a king's or an emperor's concubine

【妄】 958 ㄨㄤˋ wàng wàng
1. absurd; untrue; false
2. ignorant; stupid
3. reckless; rash: 切勿妄加評論。 Do not make reckless comments.
4. wild; frantic; frenetic

妄費(ㄨㄤˋ ㄈㄟˋ)
to waste (money, etc.); to lavish; a waste: 眞是妄費精力! What a waste of energy!

妄斷(ㄨㄤˋ ㄉㄨㄢˋ)
to jump to a (or the) conclusion

妄動(ㄨㄤˋ ㄉㄨㄥˋ)
reckless or rash actions; to act recklessly or rashly: 不要輕舉妄動。 Don't take any rash action.

妄圖(ㄨㄤˋ ㄊㄨˊ)
to try (or attempt) boldly: 他妄圖游過河流。 He attempted boldly to swim across the river.

妄念(ㄨㄤˋ ㄋㄧㄢˋ)
an idea or desire one is not supposed to have; a fancy

妄求(ㄨㄤˋ ㄑㄧㄡˊ)
an absurd pursuit or desire; to wish wildly

妄想(ㄨㄤˋ ㄒㄧㄤˇ)
a daydream; an absurd desire, a fancy; to desire wildly: 那不過是你的妄想。 That's only your fancy.

妄人(ㄨㄤˋ ㄖㄣˊ)
a stupid and reckless person; an incorrigible person

妄自菲薄(ㄨㄤˋ ㄗˋ ㄈㄟˇ ㄅㄛˊ)
to underestimate oneself: 別妄自菲薄。 Don't underestimate yourself.

妄自尊大(ㄨㄤˋ ㄗˋ ㄗㄨㄣ ㄉㄚˋ)
self-importance; conceited; self-important

妄言(ㄨㄤˋ ㄧㄢˊ)
to speak recklessly or without forethought; a wild talk; a lie; to rant

妄為(ㄨㄤˋ ㄨㄟˊ)
to act without principle or wildly; untoward behavior; reckless acts

妄語(ㄨㄤˋ ㄩˇ)
a wild talk; a lie: 別信他的妄語。 Don't believe his wild talk.

四畫

【妓】 959 ㄐㄧˋ jìh jì
1. a prostitute; a whore
2. a young woman who sings or dances to amuse her customers, such as 舞妓 (a female dancer), 藝妓 (a geisha)

妓女(ㄐㄧˋ ㄋㄩˇ)
a prostitute; a whore

妓院(ㄐㄧˋ ㄩㄢˋ)
a brothel

【妊】 960 ㄖㄣˋ renn rèn
pregnant; to be expecting

妊婦(ㄖㄣˋ ㄈㄨˋ)
a pregnant woman; an expectant mother

妊娠(ㄖㄣˋ ㄕㄣ)
to be pregnant; pregnancy

【妒】 961 (妬) ㄉㄨˋ duh dù
jealous; envious; jealousy; envy: 相妒 to be jealous of each other

妒恨(ㄉㄨˋ ㄏㄣˋ)
to be very jealous; bitter jealousy; the hate born of jealousy

妒忌(ㄉㄨˋ ㄐㄧˋ)or 妒嫉(ㄉㄨˋ ㄐㄧˊ)
jealousy; envy: 他妒嫉的理由是什麼? What is the reason of his jealousy?

妒心(ㄉㄨˋ ㄒㄧㄣ)
a jealous mind

妒殺(ㄉㄨˋ ㄕㄚ)
homicide caused by jealous

【妖】 962 ㄧㄠ iau yāo
1. weird; unaccountable; monstrous; supernatural
2. an evil; a monster; a goblin a phantom; a ghost
3. (usually said of a woman) bewitching; seductive

妖魔鬼怪(ㄧㄠ ㄇㄛˊ ㄍㄨㄟˇ ㄍㄨㄞˋ)
a general term for evil spirits, goblins, devils demons and monsters

妖媚(ㄧㄠ ㄇㄟˋ)
seductively charming bewitching: 她給他妖媚的笑。 She gave him a bewitching smile.

妖氛(ㄧㄠ ㄈㄣˊ)or 妖氣(ㄧㄠ ㄑㄧˋ)
abnormal conditions such a chaos, moral degeneracy etc.

妖法(ㄧㄠ ㄈㄚˇ)
witchcraft; the black magic

妖孽(ㄧㄠ ㄋㄧㄝˋ)
①unlucky omens ②the monsters who cause great calamities ③a person like a devil

妖女(ㄧㄠ ㄋㄩˇ)
a fairy enchantress

妖裏妖氣(ㄧㄠ ㄌㄧˇ ㄧㄠ ㄑㄧˋ)
seductive and bewitching

妖蠱(ㄧㄠ ㄍㄨˇ)
(said of a woman) to bewitch a man with seductive charms

妖怪(ㄧㄠ ㄍㄨㄞˋ)or 妖精(ㄧㄠ ㄐㄧㄥ)
①a monster or demon ②Circe; a siren ③a spirit transformed from a very old animal or tree, etc.

妖邪(ㄧㄠ ㄒㄧㄝˊ)
weird; strange; wicked; monstrous

妖聲妖氣(ㄧㄠ ㄕㄥ ㄧㄠ ㄑㄧˋ)
(said of a woman) to speak flirtatiously

妖術(ㄧㄠ ㄕㄨˋ)
sorcery; witchcraft: 巫婆施行妖術。 The witch practiced witchcraft.

妖嬈(ㄧㄠ ㄖㄠˊ)
flirtatious; bewitching enchanting; fascinating charming

妖人(ㄧㄠ ㄖㄣˊ)

an evil enchanter

冶(ㄧㄝˇ)or 妖艷(ㄧㄠ ㄧㄢˋ)
seductive charms; seductive;
bewitchingly pretty; (with)
heavy make-up; meretricious

言(ㄧㄢˊ)
heresies; fallacies; absurd
statements

言惑衆(ㄧㄢˊ ㄏㄨㄛˋ ㄓㄨㄥˋ)
to arouse people with wild
talks; to cheat people with
sensational speeches; to
spread fallacies to deceive
people

妞 963
（ㄋㄧㄡ nhiou niū）
a girl; a little girl

兒(ㄋㄧㄡ ㄦˊ)or 妞妞(ㄋㄧㄡ・ㄋㄧㄡ)
a girl

妙 964
（ㄇㄧㄠˋ miaw miào）
wonderful; excellent: 這主意
真妙. That's an wonderful
idea.

intriguing, very interesting
subtle; clever; ingenious: 她
回答得很妙. She made a
clever answer.

不可言(ㄅㄨˋ ㄎㄜˇ ㄧㄢˊ)
too subtle to be described;
ingenious beyond description

品(ㄇㄧㄠˋ ㄆㄧㄣˇ)
excellent articles; a masterpiece: 這雕刻品是件妙品. This
sculpture is a masterpiece.

年(ㄇㄧㄠˋ ㄋㄧㄢˊ)or 妙齡(ㄇㄧㄠˋ
ㄌㄧㄥˊ)
young; in one's youth

論(ㄇㄧㄠˋ ㄌㄨㄣˋ)
an ingenious comment; a
very clever remark: 這真是妙
論. This is really a very
clever remark.

極(ㄇㄧㄠˋ ㄐㄧˊ)
Wonderful! 你的建議妙極了!
Your suggestion is wonder-
ful.

計(ㄇㄧㄠˋ ㄐㄧˋ)
a subtle scheme; a capital
plan; a wonderful idea: 他有
妙計. He has a wonderful
idea.

句(ㄇㄧㄠˋ ㄐㄩˋ)
an exquisite quote: 他引了個
妙句. He quoted an exquisite
quote.

訣(ㄇㄧㄠˋ ㄐㄩㄝˊ)

a clever way; an ingenious
method (of doing something,
etc.); a knack: 這裡面有妙訣.
There's a knack in it.

妙絕古今(ㄇㄧㄠˋ ㄐㄩㄝˊ ㄍㄨˇ ㄐㄧㄣ)
an all-time wonder; un-
matched subtlety

妙趣橫生(ㄇㄧㄠˋ ㄑㄩˋ ㄏㄥˊ ㄕㄥ)
full of wit and humor

妙想天開(ㄇㄧㄠˋ ㄒㄧㄤˇ ㄊㄧㄢ ㄎㄞ)
to have fantastic ideas: 他總
是妙想天開. He always has
some fantastic ideas.

妙手空空(ㄇㄧㄠˋ ㄕㄡˇ ㄎㄨㄥ ㄎㄨㄥ)
① a pickpocket: 當心妙手空
空. Beware of pickpockets.
② a crafty but impecunious
financier who knows his
business; a wheeler-dealer

妙手回春(ㄇㄧㄠˋ ㄕㄡˇ ㄏㄨㄟˊ ㄔㄨㄣ)
the hands that cure—used to
praise a good physician

妙人妙事(ㄇㄧㄠˋ ㄖㄣˊ ㄇㄧㄠˋ ㄕˋ)
an interesting person and
his amusing episodes

妙哉妙哉(ㄇㄧㄠˋ ㄗㄞ ㄇㄧㄠˋ ㄗㄞ)
Wonderful! Bravo!

妙藥(ㄇㄧㄠˋ ㄧㄠˋ)
an efficacious drug; a wonder drug

妙語(ㄇㄧㄠˋ ㄩˇ)
a wisecrack; an intriguing
remark; a witticism

妙語解頤(ㄇㄧㄠˋ ㄩˇ ㄐㄧㄝˇ ㄧˊ)
wisecracks that really tickle

妙語雙關(ㄇㄧㄠˋ ㄩˇ ㄕㄨㄤ ㄍㄨㄢ)
a clever double-entendre; an
exquisite pun; an ingenious
remark which can be interpreted differently and
equally appropriate

妙趣如珠(ㄇㄧㄠˋ ㄑㄩˋ ㄖㄨˊ ㄓㄨ)
sparkling discourse

妙用(ㄇㄧㄠˋ ㄩㄥˋ)
ingenious uses; (serving unexpected) subtle effects

妝 965
（ㄓㄨㄤ juang zhuāng）
1. to doll up; to adorn oneself;
to apply makeup
2. jewels, etc. for adornment
3. to disguise; to pretend

妝扮(ㄓㄨㄤ ㄅㄢˋ)
to doll up

妝點(ㄓㄨㄤ ㄉㄧㄢˇ)
to dress up; to adorn; to
apply makeup

妝臺(ㄓㄨㄤ ㄊㄞˊ)
a lady's dressing table

妝樓(ㄓㄨㄤ ㄌㄡˊ)
a lady's private boudoir

妝奩(ㄓㄨㄤ ㄌㄧㄢˊ)
① a lady's dressing case ②
the bride's trousseau

妝飾(ㄓㄨㄤ ㄕˋ)
to adorn; to dress up; to
deck out; to decorate

妝梳(ㄓㄨㄤ ㄕㄨ)
(said of a woman) to comb
and dress one's hair; hairdressing

【妣】 966
（ㄅㄧˇ bii bǐ）
one's deceased mother

【好】 967
（ㄩˋ yu yù）
an official title 參看「婕妤」

【安】 968
（ㄊㄨㄛ tuoo tuǒ）
1. firm; safe; secure
2. appropriate
3. ready; set; to settle: 這件事
情已辦妥了. The matter has
been settled.

妥當(ㄊㄨㄛ ㄉㄤ)
① appropriate or secure ②
ready

妥貼 or 妥帖(ㄊㄨㄛ ㄊㄧㄝ)
properly (arranged); firmly
(placed); satisfactorily (prepared, etc.); fitting

妥協(ㄊㄨㄛ ㄒㄧㄝˊ)
① amity ② a compromise; a
reconciliation ③ appease-
ment (in international relations)

妥協份子(ㄊㄨㄛ ㄒㄧㄝˊ ㄈㄣˋ ㄗˇ)
an appeaser

妥善(ㄊㄨㄛ ㄕㄢˋ)
proper; appropriate; satisfactory (arrangements, etc.)

妥善安排(ㄊㄨㄛ ㄕㄢˋ ㄢ ㄆㄞˊ)
to make appropriate arrangements

妥善照料(ㄊㄨㄛ ㄕㄢˋ ㄓㄠˋ ㄌㄧㄠˋ)
to take good care

妥為安排(ㄊㄨㄛ ㄨㄟˊ ㄢ ㄆㄞˊ)
to make proper arrange-
ments: 讓我們事先妥為安排.
Let's make proper arrangements beforehand.

【妨】 969
（ㄈㄤ farng fáng）
（又讀 ㄈㄤ fang fāng）
1 to hinder; to impede; to

〔女部〕

妨書(ㄈㄤ ㄕㄨ)
to impair; to be harmful to: 空氣汙染妨害健康。Air pollution is harmful to our health.

妨害兵役(ㄈㄤ ㄏㄞˋ ㄅㄧㄥ ㄧˋ)
to undermine the draft law of a nation

妨害名譽(ㄈㄤ ㄏㄞˋ ㄇㄧㄥˊ ㄩˋ)
to libel; to slander: 那記者被控妨害名譽。The reporter was charged with slandering.

妨害風化(ㄈㄤ ㄏㄞˋ ㄈㄥ ㄏㄨㄚˋ)
to undermine public morality (especially referring to pornographic materials)

妨害家庭(ㄈㄤ ㄏㄞˋ ㄐㄧㄚ ㄊㄧㄥˊ)
to wreck a family (especially said of adultery)

妨害秩序(ㄈㄤ ㄏㄞˋ ㄓˋ ㄒㄩˋ)
an offense against public order

妨害治安(ㄈㄤ ㄏㄞˋ ㄓˋ ㄢ)
an offense against public security

妨害自由(ㄈㄤ ㄏㄞˋ ㄗˋ ㄧㄡˊ)
an offense against personal freedom

妨礙(ㄈㄤ ㄞˋ)
to hinder; to hamper; to impede; to interfere with: 疾病妨礙了他功課上的進步。Illness impeded his progress in study.

妨礙工作(ㄈㄤ ㄞˋ ㄍㄨㄥ ㄗㄨㄛˋ)
to hinder one's work

妨礙交通(ㄈㄤ ㄞˋ ㄐㄧㄠ ㄊㄨㄥ)
to obstruct traffic flow: 倒下的樹妨礙交通。The fallen trees obstruct traffic flow.

五畫

【妲】 970 ㄉㄚˊ dar dá
the concubine of Chou Hsin who was the last ruler of the Shang Dynasty

妲己(ㄉㄚˊ ㄐㄧˇ)
the concubine of Chou Hsin (紂王辛) who was the last ruler of the Shang Dynasty noted for his cruelty and orgies

【妮】 971 ㄋㄧˊ ni ní
1. a maid
2. a little girl; a little darling

妮婢(ㄋㄧˊ ㄅㄧˋ)
a maidservant

妮子(ㄋㄧˊ ㄗˇ)or 妮兒(ㄋㄧˊ ㄦ)
a girl

【妯】 972 ㄓㄡˊ jour zhóu
sisters-in-law 看著「妯娌」

妯娌(ㄓㄡˊ ㄌㄧ)
sisters-in-law (a reference among the wives of one's husband's brothers)

【妹】 973 ㄇㄟˋ mey mèi
a younger sister

妹妹(ㄇㄟˋ ㄇㄟ)or 妹子(ㄇㄟˋ ㄗ)
a younger sister

妹夫(ㄇㄟˋ ㄈㄨ)or 妹婿(ㄇㄟˋ ㄒㄩˋ)or 妹丈(ㄇㄟˋ ㄓㄤˋ)
the husband of one's younger sister; a brother-in-law

【妻】 974 ㄑㄧ chi qī
one's formal or legal wife

妻黨(ㄑㄧ ㄉㄤˇ)
the members and relatives of wife's family

妻孥(ㄑㄧ ㄋㄨˊ)
one's wife and children

妻女(ㄑㄧ ㄋㄩˇ)
one's wife and daughter(s)

妻離子散(ㄑㄧ ㄌㄧˊ ㄗˇ ㄙㄢˋ)
(literally) wife leaving and children dispersing—The family breaks up. 戰爭使他妻離子散。The war makes his family break up

妻妾(ㄑㄧ ㄑㄧㄝˋ)
one's wife and concubine(s)

妻室(ㄑㄧ ㄕˋ)
one's formal or legal wife

妻子(ㄑㄧ ㄗˇ)
①one's wife ②one's wife and children

妻兒老小(ㄑㄧ ㄦˊ ㄌㄠˇ ㄒㄧㄠˇ)
a married man's entire family (parents, wife and children)

【妻】 974 ㄑㄧˋ chìh qì
to marry one's daughter to someone

妻之(ㄑㄧˋ ㄓ)
to get someone marry one daughter, niece, etc.

【妾】 975 ㄑㄧㄝˋ chieh qiè
1. a concubine
2. (in old China) a polite te used by a woman to refer herself when speaking to h husband

妾婦(ㄑㄧㄝˋ ㄈㄨˋ)
①a concubine referring herself ②(derogatory) common person; an infer person

【姆】 976 ㄇㄨˇ muu mǔ
1. (in old China) a governe a woman tutor
2. a matron who looks aft small children

姆媽(ㄇㄨˇ ㄇㄚ)
(Shanghai dialect) a ter for one's mother

【姊】 977 (讀) ㄐㄧㄝˇ jiee ji (讀音 ㄗˇ tzyy zì)
one's elder sister or sisters

姊兒倆(ㄐㄧㄝˇ ㄦ ㄌㄧㄤˇ)
the two sisters

姊妹(ㄐㄧㄝˇ ㄇㄟˋ)or(ㄗˇ ㄇㄟˋ)
sisters

姊妹篇(ㄐㄧㄝˇ ㄇㄟˋ ㄆㄧㄢ)or(ㄗˇ ㄇㄟˋ ㄆㄧㄢ)
twin literary products, us ally by the same autho which run in the same veir

姊妹花(ㄐㄧㄝˇ ㄇㄟˋ ㄏㄨㄚ)or(ㄗˇ ㄇㄟˋ ㄏㄨㄚ)
beautiful sisters

姊妹校(ㄐㄧㄝˇ ㄇㄟˋ ㄒㄧㄠˋ)
sister universities or schoo

姊妹市(ㄐㄧㄝˇ ㄇㄟˋ ㄕˋ)or(ㄗˇ ㄇㄟˋ ㄕˋ)
sister cities

姊們兒(ㄐㄧㄝˇ ㄇㄣˊ ㄦ)
①sisters old and young (sisters ③(colloqual sisters-in-law or intima girl friends collectively

姊夫(ㄐㄧㄝˇ ㄈㄨ)or 姊丈(ㄐㄧㄝˇ ㄓㄤˋ)
the husband of one's elde sister

姊姊(ㄐㄧㄝˇ ㄐㄧㄝ)
elder sisters

【始】 978 ㄕˇ shyy shǐ
1. the beginning; the start; th

first

to start; to begin; to be the first: 火始於廚房。The fire started in the kitchen.

only then

a Chinese family name

末(ㄕˇ)
①from beginning to end —throughout ②the ins and outs (of an incident, story, etc.)

料末及(ㄕˇ ㄌㄧㄠˋㄨㄟˋㄐㄧˊ)
unexpected

濫終棄(ㄕˇ ㄌㄢˋ ㄓㄨㄥ ㄑㄧˋ)
to desert a girl after robbing her of her chastity

基(ㄐㄧ)
beginning and foundation

終(ㄕˇ ㄓㄨㄥ)
from beginning to end; from start to finish, all along; throughout: 比賽始終在友好氣氛中進行。The competition proceeded in a friendly atmosphere from beginning to end.

終不懈(ㄕˇ ㄓㄨㄥ ㄅㄨˋ ㄒㄧㄝˋ)
untiring perseverance; indefatigable: 他工作始終不懈。He works with indefatigable zeal.

終不渝(ㄕˇ ㄓㄨㄥ ㄅㄨˋ ㄩˊ)
unswerving; steadfast; steadfastly

終其事(ㄕˇ ㄓㄨㄥ ㄑㄧˊ)
to manage something from beginning to end; to dedicate oneself to a job from first to last

終如一(ㄕˇ ㄓㄨㄥ ㄖㄨˊ ㄧ)
(literally) the same from beginning to end—consistent; unremitting: 他的努力始終如一。His efforts are unremitting.

創(ㄕˇ ㄔㄨㄤˋ)
to found, initiate, create, or originate: 他們始創一個計劃。They initiated a plan.

祖(ㄕˇ ㄗㄨˇ)
①the founder ②the first ancestor

作俑者(ㄕˇ ㄗㄨㄛˋ ㄩㄥˇ ㄓㄜˇ)
the originator (usually of a bad practice, etc.)

業(ㄕˇ ㄧㄝˋ)
①to establish a business ②

A school opens (after a vacation).

始業式(ㄕˇ ㄧㄝˋ ㄕˋ)
the ceremonies marking the beginning of a school year or semester

始願(ㄕˇ ㄩㄢˋ)
①the first wish; the very first ambition ②only then (is one) willing to...

【姍】 979
ㄕㄢ shan shān
1. to ridicule; to laugh at
2. (said of a woman) to walk slowly

姍笑(ㄕㄢ ㄒㄧㄠˋ)
to ridicule 亦作「訕笑」

姍姍來遲(ㄕㄢ ㄕㄢ ㄌㄞˊ ㄔˊ)
to walk or proceed slowly (and keep others waiting); to be late in reaching the destination

【姐】 980
ㄐㄧㄝˇ jiee jiě
1. one's elder sister or sisters
2. a general term for women, usually young

姐妹(ㄐㄧㄝˇ ㄇㄟˋ)
a sister; sisters: 他有姐妹三人。He has three sisters.

姐夫(ㄐㄧㄝˇ ㄈㄨ)or姐丈(ㄐㄧㄝˇ ㄓㄤˋ)
the husband of one's elder sister; a brother-in-law

姐姐(ㄐㄧㄝˇ ·ㄐㄧㄝ)
one's elder sister

【姑】 981
ㄍㄨ gu gū
1. aunts; the sister of one's father
2. the mother of one's husband
3. the sister of one's husband
4. a general term for unmarried women
5. for the time being; meanwhile; for a while
6. a nun

姑表(ㄍㄨ ㄅㄧㄠˇ)
first cousins when the father of one and the mother of the other are brother and sister

姑婆(ㄍㄨ ㄆㄛˊ)
①the sister of one's grandfather ②the sister of a woman's father-in-law

姑媽(ㄍㄨ ㄇㄚˊ)or姑母(ㄍㄨ ㄇㄨˇ)
the sister of one's father; an aunt

姑父 or 姑夫(ㄍㄨ ·ㄈㄨ)or

the husband of one's father's sister; uncle; a paternal aunt's husband

姑奶奶(ㄍㄨ ㄋㄞˇ·ㄋㄞ)
the sister of one's paternal grandfather; a grandaunt

姑娘(ㄍㄨ ㄋㄧㄤˊ)
①an unmarried girl; a maiden ②a term used to refer to one's own or another's daughter(s) ③a euphemism for a prostitute

姑姑(ㄍㄨ·ㄍㄨ)
one's father's sister; an aunt; a paternal aunt

姑且(ㄍㄨ ㄑㄧㄝˇ)
for the time being; in the meantime; for the time being; to be

姑且不談(ㄍㄨ ㄑㄧㄝˇ ㄅㄨˋ ㄊㄢˊ)
to leave something aside for the moment

姑息(ㄍㄨ ㄒㄧˊ)
to be indulgent; to be over lenient toward; to be easy with; to spoil (a child); to appease: 我們不應該姑息這些小孩的錯誤。We shouldn't be indulgent towards the children's mistakes.

姑息政策(ㄍㄨ ㄒㄧˊ ㄓㄥˋ ㄘㄜˋ)
a policy of appeasement

姑息養奸(ㄍㄨ ㄒㄧˊ ㄧㄤˇ ㄐㄧㄢ)
To tolerate evil is to encourage evil-doers.

姑置不論(ㄍㄨ ㄓˋ ㄅㄨˋ ㄌㄨㄣˋ)
Let's not talk about (this offense, mistake, etc. which is serious enough).—with the implication that there are other mistakes, offenses, etc. which are even more serious

姑准(ㄍㄨ ㄓㄨㄣˇ)
to permit reluctantly; to permit for the time being: 他姑准我們離開。He permits us to leave for the time being.

姑嫂(ㄍㄨ ㄙㄠˇ)
sisters-in-law (the relationship between a man's sisters and his wife)

姑蘇(ㄍㄨ ㄙㄨ)
Soochow, Kiangsu Province

姑爺(ㄍㄨ ㄧㄝˊ)
a son-in-law

姑爺爺(ㄍㄨ ㄧㄝˊ·ㄧㄝ)

〔女部〕

〔女部〕

the husband of one's father's paternal aunt

姑妄聽之(ㄍㄨ ㄨㄤˋ ㄊㄧㄥ ㄓ)
Let's hear (him) out.—implying the listener's skepticism: 我們暫且姑妄聽之。We may as well hear him out.

姑妄言之(ㄍㄨ ㄨㄤˋ ㄧㄢˊ ㄓ)
Please take my words as a gossip. (a polite and modest expression in making suggestions, etc.)

【姒】982
ㄙˋ syh sì
1. the wife of one's husband's elder brother
2. (in ancient China) the elder of the twin sisters
3. a Chinese family name

【姓】983
ㄒㄧㄥˋ shìng xìng
1. surname; one's family name: 他姓楊。He is surnamed Yang.
2. a clan; a family; people

姓名(ㄒㄧㄥˋ ㄇㄧㄥˊ)
the full name of a person

姓氏(ㄒㄧㄥˋ ㄕˋ)
the surname; the family name

【委】984
1. ㄨㄟˇ woei wěi
1. to depute; to deputize
2. to send; to put in charge of; to commission
3. to give up; to abandon
4. to be frustrated, weakened or tired
5. really; truly; indeed
6. a grievance; a wrong
7. to stoop or lower oneself (in order to avoid an open conflict, etc.)
8. a Chinese family name

委派(ㄨㄟˇ ㄆㄞˋ)
to appoint; to send (one) in charge of; to commission: 他被委派爲本市市長。He was appointed (to be) mayor of the city.

委靡(ㄨㄟˇ ㄇㄧˊ)
listless; dispirited; dejected

委靡不振(ㄨㄟˇ ㄇㄧˊ ㄅㄨˋ ㄓㄣˋ)
dispirited and lethargic; in low spirits; dejected and apathetic

委命(ㄨㄟˇ ㄇㄧㄥˋ)
①to leave oneself to fate; to yield to fate ②to commission; to depute ③to serve under someone with dedication

委頓(ㄨㄟˇ ㄉㄨㄣˋ)
worn-out; tired out; wearied; broken down

委託 or 委托(ㄨㄟˇ ㄊㄨㄛ)
to commission; to entrust: 他把財產委託他的朋友看管。He entrusted his friend with the property.

委託商行(ㄨㄟˇ ㄊㄨㄛ ㄕㄤ ㄏㄤˊ)
a commission house

委託書(ㄨㄟˇ ㄊㄨㄛ ㄕㄨ)
a power of attorney 亦作委託狀

委託人(ㄨㄟˇ ㄊㄨㄛ ㄖㄣˊ)
a client

委託所(ㄨㄟˇ ㄊㄨㄛ ㄙㄨㄛˇ)
a consignment store

委內瑞拉(ㄨㄟˇ ㄋㄟˋ ㄖㄨㄟˋ ㄌㄚ)
Venezuela, in South America

委內瑞拉人(ㄨㄟˇ ㄋㄟˋ ㄖㄨㄟˋ ㄌㄚ ㄖㄣˊ)
a Venezuelan

委過(ㄨㄟˇ ㄍㄨㄛˋ)
to shift blame: 他常委過於人。He often shifts the blame to somebody else.

委咎(ㄨㄟˇ ㄐㄧㄡˋ)
to shift blame to others

委決不下(ㄨㄟˇ ㄐㄩㄝˊ ㄅㄨˋ ㄒㄧㄚˋ)
to be indecisive

委棄(ㄨㄟˇ ㄑㄧˋ)
to give up; to abandon; to discard; to throw away

委屈(ㄨㄟˇ ㄑㄩ)
①a grievance; complaints ②to be frustrated or wronged ③to take an office, etc. far below one's ability ④to put someone to inconvenience

委曲(ㄨㄟˇ ㄑㄩ)
① (said of roads, rivers, etc.) winding; tortuous ② the twists of events

委曲求全(ㄨㄟˇ ㄑㄩ ㄑㄧㄡˊ ㄑㄩㄢˊ)
to make great concessions for the purpose of accommodating to a situation

委政(ㄨㄟˇ ㄓㄥˋ)
to deputize a minister to run the government

委實(ㄨㄟˇ ㄕˊ)
really; indeed

委身(ㄨㄟˇ ㄕㄣ)

①to become the wife of... ②to consign oneself to some one or something

委任(ㄨㄟˇ ㄖㄣˋ)
①to appoint; to commission ②the designated appointment rank—the lowest of four major ranks in China's civil service

委任統治(ㄨㄟˇ ㄖㄣˋ ㄊㄨㄥˇ ㄓˋ)
to mandate

委任管理(ㄨㄟˇ ㄖㄣˋ ㄍㄨㄢˇ ㄌㄧˇ)
mandatory adminstration

委任狀(ㄨㄟˇ ㄖㄣˋ ㄓㄨㄤˋ)
a certificate of appointment or deputation

委罪(ㄨㄟˇ ㄗㄨㄟˋ)
to impute; to blame another (for a mistake committed by oneself)

委瑣(ㄨㄟˇ ㄙㄨㄛˇ)
①petty; trifling; details ② of a wretched appearance ③ being a stickler for forms

委以重任(ㄨㄟˇ ㄧˇ ㄓㄨㄥˋ ㄖㄣˋ)
to entrust someone with an important task

委婉(ㄨㄟˇ ㄨㄢˇ)
soft-spoken or ingratiating; suave and moving (statement, etc.); tactful; unobtrusively

委員(ㄨㄟˇ ㄩㄢˊ)
a member of a committee

委員會(ㄨㄟˇ ㄩㄢˊ ㄏㄨㄟˋ)
a committee; a commission; a council; 委員會今天四點開會。The committee meets today at four.

【委】984
2. ㄨㄟ uei wēi
參見「委蛇」

委蛇(ㄨㄟ ㄧˊ)
in a carefree manner; descriptive of ease and self possession

【妳】985
ㄋㄧˇ nǐi
you (the feminine gender)

六畫

【姚】986
ㄧㄠˊ yau yáo
1. handsome; elegant; good looking
2. a Chinese family name

姜】 987 ㄐㄧ�大 jiang jiāng
a Chinese family name
ginger
太公 (ㄊㄞ ㄍㄨㄥ 《ㄨㄥ) or 姜子牙
Chiang Tzu-ya, who helped
King Wu (武王) found the
Chou Dynasty

姝】 988 ㄕㄨ shu shū
a beautiful girl

姣】 989 ㄐㄧㄠ jiau jiāo
handsome; pretty; beautiful
coquettish
童 (ㄊㄨㄥ ㄊㄨㄥˊ)
a handsome boy
好 (ㄐㄧㄠ ㄏㄠˇ)
good-looking; pleasant (looks)

姤】 990 《ㄡˋ gow gòu
to pair off; to copulate
good; excellent
one of the Eight Diagrams in the *Book of Changes*

姥】 991 ㄌㄠ lao lǎo
one's maternal grandmother
an old woman
姥 (ㄌㄠˇ) ① one's maternal grandmother 亦作「外祖母」② a midwife

姦】 992 ㄐㄧㄢ jian jiān
adultery; debauchery; licentiousness
to debauch; to ravish; to attack (a woman) sexually
a crook!
夫 (ㄐㄧㄢ ㄈㄨ)
① an adulterer ② a man who acts criminally
婦 (ㄐㄧㄢ ㄈㄨˋ)
an adulteress
拐 (ㄐㄧㄢ 《ㄨㄞˇ)
to seduce and abduct (especially a girl)
究 (ㄐㄧㄢ 《ㄡ)
thieves and robbers
錢 (ㄐㄧㄢ ㄑㄧㄢˊ)
(in ancient China) coins produced by unauthorized mints
情 (ㄐㄧㄢ ㄑㄧㄥˊ)

the circumstances of adultery; the ins and outs of an affair
細 (ㄐㄧㄢ ㄒㄧˋ)
a spy 亦作「奸細」
邪 (ㄐㄧㄢ ㄒㄧㄝˊ)
wicked; vicious 亦作「姦回」
殺 (ㄐㄧㄢ ㄕㄚ)
to kill a woman after sexually molesting her
淫 (ㄐㄧㄢ ㄧㄣˊ)
fornication; debauchery; adultery; lewdness; to seduce; to rape
淫擄掠 (ㄐㄧㄢ ㄧㄣˊ ㄌㄨˇ ㄌㄩㄝˋ)
rape and rapine (said of atrocities committed by invading troops)
污 (ㄐㄧㄢ ㄨ)
to seduce and rape

姨】 993 ㄧ yi yí
1. the sisters of one's wife
2. the sisters of one's mother
3. a concubine
表 (ㄧ ㄅㄧㄠˇ)
the relatives on one's mother's side
表婚 (ㄧ ㄅㄧㄠˇ ㄏㄨㄣ)
a parallel cousin marriage
婆 (ㄧ ㄆㄛˊ)
a grandaunt
媽 (ㄧ ㄇㄚ) or 姨母 (ㄧ ㄇㄨˇ)
the married sisters of one's mother
妹 (ㄧ ㄇㄟˋ)
the younger sisters of one's wife
父 (ㄧ ㄈㄨˋ) or 姨丈 (ㄧ ㄓㄤˋ) or 姨夫 (ㄧ ㄈㄨ)
the husband of a maternal aunt; an uncle
太太 (ㄧ ㄊㄞˋ ㄊㄞˋ)
a concubine
娘 (ㄧ ㄋㄧㄤˊ)
a concubine of one's father
姊妹 (ㄧ ㄐㄧㄝˇ ㄐㄧㄝˇ ㄇㄟˋ) or 姨姊妹 (ㄧ ㄐㄧㄝˇ ㄇㄟˋ)
the cousin sisters on one's mother's side
兄弟 (ㄧ ㄒㄩㄥ ㄉㄧˋ)
the male cousins on one's mother's side

姪】 994 ㄓ jyr zhí
1. the children of one's brother —nephews or nieces

2. I; me (when speaking to a family friend of one's father's generation)
婦 (ㄓ ㄈㄨˋ)
the wife of one's nephew
女 (ㄓ ㄋㄩˇ)
a niece—a daughter of one's brother
女婿 (ㄓ ㄋㄩˇ ㄒㄩˋ) or 姪婿 (ㄓ ㄒㄩˋ)
the husband of one's niece
兒 (ㄓ ㄦˊ) or 姪子 (ㄓ ㄗˇ)
nephews—the sons of one's brother
兒媳婦 (ㄓ ㄦˊ ㄒㄧˊ ㄈㄨˋ) or 姪媳婦 (ㄓ ㄒㄧˊ ㄈㄨˋ)
the wife of one's nephew

姱】 995 ㄎㄨㄚ kua kuā
pretty; good-looking; fascinating; elegant

妍】 996 (姸) ㄧㄢˊ yan yán
1. beautiful; pretty; good-looking; cute; attractive; charming
2. seductive; coquettish
麗 (ㄧㄢˊ ㄌㄧˋ)
beautiful; attractive; charming; beauty; charms
媸 (ㄧㄢˊ ㄔ) or 妍蚩 (ㄧㄢˊ ㄔ)
the beauty and the ugliness

姹】 997 (奼) ㄔㄚˋ chah chà
1. young (girls)
2. charming; attractive; seductive
3. to boast; to talk big; to lie
紫嫣紅 (ㄔㄚˋ ㄗˇ ㄧㄢ ㄏㄨㄥˊ) or 奼紫嫣紅 (ㄔㄚˋ ㄗˇ ㄧㄢ ㄏㄨㄥˊ)

(said of flowers) beautiful and luxuriant: 花園裡奼紫嫣紅，十分絢麗。With beautiful and luxuriant flowers everywhere, the garden is a blaze of color.

姻】 998 ㄧㄣ in yīn
1. one's husband's family
2. marriage
3. relations or connections through marriage
家 (ㄧㄣ ㄐㄧㄚ)
① the families of the married couple ② the elders of such families
戚 (ㄧㄣ ㄑㄧ)
relatives by marriage
親 (ㄧㄣ ㄑㄧㄣ) or 姻婭 (ㄧㄣ ㄧㄚˋ)

【女部】

relatives by marriage

姻兄弟(ㄧㄣ ㄒㄩㄥ ㄉㄧˋ)or 姻親兄弟(ㄧㄣ ㄑㄧㄣ ㄒㄩㄥ ㄉㄧˋ)
a cousin-in-law

姻緣(ㄧㄣ ㄩㄢˊ)
the invisible bond that makes a man and a woman husband and wife

【姿】 999
ㄗ tzy zī
1. the manner; an air; carriage; bearing
2. looks

姿媚(ㄗ ㄇㄟˋ)
elegant and graceful manners

姿貌(ㄗ ㄇㄠˋ)
a woman's looks

姿態(ㄗ ㄊㄞˋ)
①carriage; deportment; bearing: 她姿態優雅。She has a graceful carriage. ② a gesture; a feigned move

姿質 or 資質(ㄗ ㄓˊ)
quality; natural endowments; talent: 她有音樂的姿質。She has a talent for music.

姿勢(ㄗ ㄕˋ)
①carriage; deportment; bearing ②posture; (in photography) a pose: 好的姿勢幫助你保持健康。Good posture helps you to keep well.

姿容(ㄗ ㄖㄨㄥˊ)
(said of a woman) looks —usually implying good looks: 她姿容秀美。She is good-looking.

姿色(ㄗ ㄙㄜˋ)
looks (of a woman); (female) beauty: 她不久就會失去她的姿色。She will soon lose her looks.

【威】 1000
ㄨㄟ uei wēi
1. dignity; majesty
2. authority; might; power
3. awe; awe-inspiring
4. the mother of one's husband
5. a Chinese family name

威逼(ㄨㄟ ㄅㄧ)
to coerce; to intimidate

威逼利誘(ㄨㄟ ㄅㄧ ㄌㄧˋ ㄧㄡˋ)
to threaten and to bribe

威猛(ㄨㄟ ㄇㄥˇ)
domineering

威名(ㄨㄟ ㄇㄧㄥˊ)

prestige; an awe-inspiring reputation: 那件事將有損我們國家的威名。The incident will damage our national prestige.

威風(ㄨㄟ ㄈㄥ)
①power and prestige ② imposing; awe-inspiring; militant bearing

威風凜凜(ㄨㄟ ㄈㄥ ㄌㄧㄣˇ ㄌㄧㄣˇ)
awe-inspiring; imposing

威風掃地(ㄨㄟ ㄈㄥ ㄙㄠˇ ㄉㄧˋ)
to suffer a drastic fall in one's prestige

威服(ㄨㄟ ㄈㄨˊ)
to overawe; to coerce

威尼斯(ㄨㄟ ㄋㄧˊ ㄙ)
Venice, a city in Italy

威力(ㄨㄟ ㄌㄧˋ)
①the force that inspires awe ②military force ③the destructive force (of a typhoon, earthquake, nuclear device, etc.)

威廉(ㄨㄟ ㄌㄧㄢˊ)
a transliteration of William

威靈頓(ㄨㄟ ㄌㄧㄥˊ ㄉㄨㄣˋ)
①Wellington, capital of New Zealand ② Arthur Wellesley, the Duke of Wellington, 1769-1852

威嚇(ㄨㄟ ㄏㄜˋ)
to awe; to intimidate; to cow

威海衛(ㄨㄟ ㄏㄞˇ ㄨㄟˋ)
Weihaiwei, a naval base on the Shantung Peninsula

威權(ㄨㄟ ㄑㄩㄢˊ)
an authority; power and prestige

威脅(ㄨㄟ ㄒㄧㄝˊ)
to threaten; to intimidate; a threat; intimidation

威信(ㄨㄟ ㄒㄧㄣˋ)
①one's dignity and credit; the prestige built up by keeping good faith: 他威信掃地。His prestige takes a nosedive. ② the name of a county in Yünnan Province

威懾(ㄨㄟ ㄕㄜˋ)
to submit someone to power and threat

威震九州(ㄨㄟ ㄓㄣˋ ㄐㄧㄡˇ ㄓㄡ)
to hold the world in awe; to awe the whole land

威重(ㄨㄟ ㄓㄨㄥˋ)

dignified and awe-inspiring

威勢(ㄨㄟ ㄕˋ)
prestige and influence

威士忌(ㄨㄟ ㄕˋ ㄐㄧˋ)
whisky: 他偶而喝杯威士忌。takes an occasional whisk

威斯康辛(ㄨㄟ ㄙ ㄎㄤ ㄒㄧㄣ)
the state of Wisconsin, U A.

威而不猛(ㄨㄟ ㄦˊ ㄅㄨˋ ㄇㄥˇ)
awe-inspiring but kind heart

威爾遜(ㄨㄟ ㄦˇ ㄒㄩㄣˋ)
(Thomas) Woodrow Wilso 1856-1924, American Pre dent

威爾斯(ㄨㄟ ㄦˇ ㄙ)
Wales, England

威儀(ㄨㄟ ㄧˊ)
majesty; the dignity of d meanor

威嚴(ㄨㄟ ㄧㄢˊ)
①sternness; severity ② awe-inspiring air

威武(ㄨㄟ ㄨˇ)
an awe-inspiring display military force, etc.

威武不屈(ㄨㄟ ㄨˇ ㄅㄨˋ ㄑㄩ)
not to be subdued by forc not to bow to the pressure

威武雄壯(ㄨㄟ ㄨˇ ㄒㄩㄥˊ ㄓㄨㄤˋ)
full of power and grandeur

威望(ㄨㄟ ㄨㄤˋ)
prestige; an imposing reput tion

【娃】 1001
ㄨㄚˊ wa wá
1. a beautiful woman
2. a baby; a child
3. exquisite; fine

娃子(ㄨㄚˊ ㄗˇ)
①a baby; a child ②a new born animal ③ a slav (among the minority nation alities in the Liangsha Mountains)

娃娃(ㄨㄚˊ ㄨㄚˊ)
a baby; a young child

娃娃臉(ㄨㄚˊ ㄨㄚˊ ㄌㄧㄢˇ)
a baby face; baby-faced

娃娃車(ㄨㄚˊ ㄨㄚˊ ㄔㄜ)
a baby car; a baby carriage a baby buggy

娃娃床(ㄨㄚˊ ㄨㄚˊ ㄔㄨㄤˊ)
a crib; a cot

娃娃魚(ㄨㄚˊ ㄨㄚˊ ㄩˊ)
a giant salamander—ㄧ

species of fish in Kwangsi and Kweichow that utters cries like a baby

七畫

【娓】 1002 ㄨㄟˇ woei wěi

complying; subservient

beautiful; attractive; pleasant

diligent and tireless

娓娓 (ㄨㄟˇ ㄨㄟˇ)

(to talk) tirelessly: 她娓娓不倦。 She talks tirelessly.

娓娓動聽 (ㄨㄟˇ ㄨㄟˇ ㄉㄨㄥˋ ㄊㄧㄥ)

persuasive (accounts, narration, etc.); persuasively: 她說得娓娓動聽。 She speaks persuasively.

【娉】 1003 ㄆㄧㄥ ping pīng

good-looking; elegant; graceful; charming

娉婷 (ㄆㄧㄥ ㄊㄧㄥˊ)

slender and elegant; graceful and charming

【娌】 1004 ㄌㄧˇ lii lǐ

sisters-in-law 參看「妯娌」

【姬】 1005 ㄐㄧ ji jī

a beautiful lady; a charming girl

a concubine

a Chinese family name

姬妾 (ㄐㄧ ㄑㄧㄝˋ)

concubines

【娑】 1006 ㄙㄨㄛ suo suō

to dance

【娘】 1007 (孃) ㄋㄧㄤ niang niáng

mother

girls or women

娘胎 (ㄋㄧㄤ ㄊㄞ)

the mother's womb

娘娘 (ㄋㄧㄤ ㄋㄧㄤ)

① the queen ② a goddess

娘娘腔 (ㄋㄧㄤ ㄋㄧㄤ ㄑㄧㄤ)

sissy; womanish

娘家 (ㄋㄧㄤ ㄐㄧㄚ)

one's wife's family

娘舅 (ㄋㄧㄤ ㄐㄧㄡˋ)

a maternal uncle

娘親 (ㄋㄧㄤ ㄑㄧㄣ)

one's mother

娘子 (ㄋㄧㄤ ˙ㄗ)

① a term used for addressing one's wife ② a polite form for addressing a young woman

娘子軍 (ㄋㄧㄤ ˙ㄗ ㄐㄩㄣ)

① an army made up of women ② (used now figuratively) a team or group of women, as a women's basketball team, etc.

娘兒 (ㄋㄧㄤ ㄦ)

① women; girls (a derogatory expression) ② mother and child (or children)

娘倆 (ㄋㄧㄤ ㄌㄧㄚˇ)

mother and son (or daughter)

娘姨 (ㄋㄧㄤ ㄧˊ)

(Shanghai dialect) a maidservant; a woman servant (often married)

【娛】 1008 ㄩ yu yú

to amuse; to give pleasure to; to entertain; amusement; entertainment; pleasure

娛樂 (ㄩ ㄌㄜˋ)

amusement; entertainment; to amuse; to entertain: 我以收集郵票為娛樂。 I find amusement in collecting stamps.

娛樂活動 (ㄩ ㄌㄜˋ ㄏㄨㄛˊ ㄉㄨㄥˋ)

recreational activities

娛樂場所 (ㄩ ㄌㄜˋ ㄔㄤˇ ㄙㄨㄛˇ)

entertainment establishments; public places of entertainment

娛樂稅 (ㄩ ㄌㄜˋ ㄕㄨㄟˋ)

cabaret tax

娛親 (ㄩ ㄑㄧㄣ)

to please one's parents

娛人 (ㄩ ㄖㄣˊ)

① to please somebody ② pleased: 他顯出娛悅的樣子。 He looked pleased.

【娜】 1009 1. ㄋㄨㄛˊ nuoo nuó

tender, slender and graceful

【娜】 1009 2. ㄋㄨㄛˋ nuò nuò

the word used in a female name

【娜】 1009 3. ㄋㄚˋ nah nà

a word used in the transliteration of a western female name

【娟】 1010 ㄐㄩㄢ jiuan juān

pretty; good-looking; graceful; attractive

娟秀 (ㄐㄩㄢ ㄒㄧㄡˋ)

good-looking; pretty; cute; beautiful; graceful: 這女孩很娟秀。 This girl is beautiful.

【娠】 1011 ㄕㄣ shen shēn

pregnant

【娣】 1012 ㄉㄧˋ dih dì

the wife of a younger brother of one's husband

娣婦 (ㄉㄧˋ ㄈㄨˋ)

the wife of a younger brother of one's husband

【娥】 1013 ㄜˊ é é

1. good; beautiful

2. a common name for a girl

3. a Chinese family name

娥眉 (ㄜˊ ㄇㄟˊ)

(literally) beautiful eyebrows—a beautiful girl or woman

【婉】 1014 1. ㄨㄢˇ woan wǎn

complaisant

【娩】 1014 2. ㄇㄧㄢˇ mean miǎn

to give birth to a child

娩痛 (ㄇㄧㄢˇ ㄊㄨㄥˋ)

labor pains

八畫

【婆】 1015 ㄆㄛˊ por pó

1. an old woman

2. the mother of one's husband

3. one's grandmother

婆婆 (ㄆㄛˊ ˙ㄆㄛ)

① the mother of one's husband ② a term of respect for an old lady

婆婆媽媽 (ㄆㄛˊ ˙ㄆㄛ ㄇㄚ ㄇㄚ)

① sissy ② over-sentimental; mawkish; maudlin ③ nagging

婆婆家 (ㄆㄛˊ ˙ㄆㄛ ㄐㄧㄚ) or 婆家 (ㄆㄛˊ ㄐㄧㄚ)

one's husband's family

婆羅門教 (ㄆㄛˊ ㄌㄨㄛˊ ㄇㄣˊ ㄐㄧㄠˋ)

Brahmanism

婆羅洲 (ㄆㄛˊ ㄌㄨㄛˊ ㄓㄡ)

Island of Borneo

〔女部〕

【女部】

【婆媳】(ㄆㄛˊ ㄒㄧˊ)
a woman and her daughter-in-law

【婆心】(ㄆㄛˊ ㄒㄧㄣ)
a kind and compassionate heart

【婆子】(ㄆㄛˊ ˙ㄗ)
(derogatively) an old woman

【婆娑】(ㄆㄛˊ ㄙㄨㄛ)
① to make dancing motions
② hovering

【婆娑起舞】(ㄆㄛˊ ㄙㄨㄛ ㄑㄧˇ ㄨˇ)
to start dancing: 她們婆娑起舞。They start dancing.

【婀】 1016
ㄜ ē
1. graceful; elegant
2. a Chinese family name

【婀娜多姿】(ㄜ ㄋㄨㄛˋ ㄉㄨㄛ ㄗ)
graceful; well-poised: 她婀娜多姿。She is very pretty and well-poised.

【娶】 1017
ㄑㄩˇ cheu qǔ
to take a wife

【娶親】(ㄑㄩˇ ㄑㄧㄣ)or 娶妻(ㄑㄩˇ ㄑㄧ)
(said of a man) to get married; to take a wife

【娶媳婦兒】(ㄑㄩˇ ㄒㄧˊ ˙ㄈㄨㄦ)
① to take a wife ② to get a daughter-in-law

【姘】 1018
(姘) ㄆㄧㄥ pin pīn
to make love without a formal wedding; illicit intercourse

【姘夫】(ㄆㄧㄥ ㄈㄨ)
a man one cohabits with; illegal husband

【姘婦】(ㄆㄧㄥ ㄈㄨˋ)
a woman one cohabits with out of wedlock; a mistress

【姘頭】(ㄆㄧㄥ ˙ㄊㄡ)
a lover; a paramour

【姘居】(ㄆㄧㄥ ㄐㄩ)
to live together without a formal wedding; to cohabit

【婁】 1019
1. ㄌㄡˊ lou lóu
1. one of the 28 constellations
2. a Chinese family name

【婁】 1019
2. ㄌㄩˇ liu lǚ
to trail along; to wear

【婁】 1019
3. ㄌㄡˊ leu lóu
to tether (oxen)

【婉】 1020
ㄨㄢˇ woan wǎn
1. amiable; genial; agreeable; pleasant; gently; genially; amicably
2. good-looking; beautiful

【婉勸】(ㄨㄢˇ ㄑㄩㄢˋ)
to persuade or advise gently; friendly persuasion

【婉謝】(ㄨㄢˇ ㄒㄧㄝˋ)
to decline (an invitation, a present, etc.) with great gentleness and courtesy: 他婉謝邀請。He declined the invitation with thanks.

【婉轉】
(to persuade or state something) mildly, gently, suavely—without hurting another's feelings; tactfully; persuasively

【婉商】(ㄨㄢˇ ㄕㄤ)
to negotiate or discuss with tact and courtesy

【婉順】(ㄨㄢˇ ㄕㄨㄣˋ)
complaisant; obliging

【婉辭】(ㄨㄢˇ ㄘˊ)
① (said of speech) gentle wording; smooth and ingratiating ② to decline with great courtesy

【婉言】(ㄨㄢˇ ㄧㄢˊ)
soft-spoken; (to advise with) gentle and ingratiating words; to speak tenderly

【婉言相勸】(ㄨㄢˇ ㄧㄢˊ ㄒㄧㄤ ㄑㄩㄢˋ)
to persuade gently; to plead tactfully

【婉約】(ㄨㄢˇ ㄩㄝ)
① (said of speech) gentle; smooth and courteous ② (style of poetry) restrained; soft; plaintive

【婕】 1021
ㄐㄧㄝˊ jye jié
the word used in a female name

【婕妤】(ㄐㄧㄝˊ ㄩˊ)
an official title conferred upon an accomplished imperial concubine during the Han Dynasty

【婚】 1022
ㄏㄨㄣ huen hūn
1. to wed; to marry
2. marriage

【婚變】(ㄏㄨㄣ ㄅㄧㄢˋ)
a serious marriage trouble such as legal separation divorce

【婚配】(ㄏㄨㄣ ㄆㄟˋ)
marriage; to get married

【婚禮】(ㄏㄨㄣ ㄌㄧˇ)
a wedding ceremony; a wedding

【婚齡】(ㄏㄨㄣ ㄌㄧㄥˊ)
(legally) marriageable age

【婚媾】(ㄏㄨㄣ ㄍㄡˋ)
marriage 亦作「婚姻」

【婚後】(ㄏㄨㄣ ㄏㄡˋ)
after marriage; after wedding

【婚假】(ㄏㄨㄣ ㄐㄧㄚˋ)
a wedding leave

【婚嫁】(ㄏㄨㄣ ㄐㄧㄚˋ)
to take a wife or marry a man; to wed; marriage

【婚期】(ㄏㄨㄣ ㄑㄧˊ)
the date of a wedding

【婚前】(ㄏㄨㄣ ㄑㄧㄢˊ)
before marriage

【婚事】(ㄏㄨㄣ ㄕˋ)
marriage

【婚生子女】(ㄏㄨㄣ ㄕㄥ ㄗˇ ㄋㄩˇ)
the children born in (lawful) wedlock

【婚書】(ㄏㄨㄣ ㄕㄨ)
a marriage contract or certificate 亦作「結婚證書」

【婚喪喜慶】(ㄏㄨㄣ ㄙㄤ ㄒㄧˇ ㄑㄧㄥˋ)
marriage, funeral, birth, etc.—important occasions of family

【婚筵】(ㄏㄨㄣ ㄧㄢˊ)
a wedding reception; a wedding feast

【婚姻】(ㄏㄨㄣ ㄧㄣ)
marriage: 她的婚姻很美滿。Her marriage is a very happy one.

【婚姻破裂】(ㄏㄨㄣ ㄧㄣ ㄆㄛˋ ㄌㄧㄝˋ)
break down of marriage

【婚姻法】(ㄏㄨㄣ ㄧㄣ ㄈㄚˇ)
marriage law

【婚姻糾紛】(ㄏㄨㄣ ㄧㄣ ㄐㄧㄡ ㄈㄣ)
matrimonial dispute

【婚姻狀況】(ㄏㄨㄣ ㄧㄣ ㄓㄨㄤˋ ㄎㄨㄤˋ)
marital status

【婚姻自由】(ㄏㄨㄣ ㄧㄣ ㄗˋ ㄧㄡˊ)
freedom of marriage

【婚約】(ㄏㄨㄣ ㄩㄝ)
a marriage contract; a trothal

〔女部〕

婢】 1023
ㄅㄧˋ bih bì
a maidservant; a female slave

(in old China) a humble term used by a girl to refer to herself

婢女(ㄅㄧˋ ㄋㄩˇ)
a slave girl; a servant girl; a maidservant

婢學夫人(ㄅㄧˋ ㄒㄩㄝˊ ㄈㄨ ㄖㄣˊ)
(literally) a maidservant trying to imitate the mistress—to mimic awkwardly

婢子(ㄅㄧˋ ㄗˇ)
① a maidservant ② a concubine ③ a humble term used by a woman to refer to herself

婦】 1024
ㄈㄨˋ fuh fù
a woman; a female; a matron
the wife of one's son
a wife
a married woman

婦德(ㄈㄨˋ ㄉㄜˊ)
feminine or female virtues —such as chastity, thrift, obedience, etc.

婦道(ㄈㄨˋ ㄉㄠˋ)
① (ㄈㄨˋ ㄉㄠˋ) proper rules of female behavior; female virtues, especially chastity
② (ㄈㄨˋ ˙ㄉㄠ) womanhood

婦道人家(ㄈㄨˋ ˙ㄉㄠ ㄖㄣˊ ㄐㄧㄚ)
(derogatively) womenfolk

婦女(ㄈㄨˋ ㄋㄩˇ)
women; female; womenfolk; womankind

婦女會(ㄈㄨˋ ㄋㄩˇ ㄏㄨㄟˋ)
a women's association

婦女節(ㄈㄨˋ ㄋㄩˇ ㄐㄧㄝˊ)
Women's Day, on March 8

婦女參政權(ㄈㄨˋ ㄋㄩˇ ㄘㄢ ㄓㄥˋ ㄑㄩㄢˊ)
or 婦女投票權(ㄈㄨˋ ㄋㄩˇ ㄊㄡˊ ㄆㄧㄠˋ ㄑㄩㄢˊ)
female suffrage

婦女運動(ㄈㄨˋ ㄋㄩˇ ㄩㄣˋ ㄉㄨㄥˋ)
a women's movement

婦聯會(ㄈㄨˋ ㄌㄧㄢˊ ㄏㄨㄟˋ)
short for 中華婦女聯合會
(Chinese Women's League)

婦產醫生(ㄈㄨˋ ㄔㄢˇ ㄧ ㄕㄥ)
gynecologist

婦解運動(ㄈㄨˋ ㄐㄧㄝˇ ㄩㄣˋ ㄉㄨㄥˋ)
Women's Liberation; Fem Lib 亦作「女權運動」

婦職(ㄈㄨˋ ㄓˊ)
the duties of a woman or housewife; woman's duty

婦產科(ㄈㄨˋ ㄔㄢˇ ㄎㄜ)
the department of gynecology and obstetrics

婦人(ㄈㄨˋ ㄖㄣˊ)
a woman; a female; a married woman

婦人病(ㄈㄨˋ ㄖㄣˊ ㄅㄧㄥˋ)
women's peculiar diseases

婦人之仁(ㄈㄨˋ ㄖㄣˊ ㄓ ㄖㄣˊ)
womanly kindness

婦孺(ㄈㄨˋ ㄖㄨˊ)
women and children

婦孺皆知(ㄈㄨˋ ㄖㄨˊ ㄐㄧㄝ ㄓ)
(so famous or simple that) it's known even to women and children

婦容(ㄈㄨˋ ㄖㄨㄥˊ)
women's proper deportment and appearance

婦幼(ㄈㄨˋ ㄧㄡˋ)
women and children

婦幼衛生(ㄈㄨˋ ㄧㄡˋ ㄨㄟˋ ㄕㄥ)
hygiene for women and children: 婦幼衛生十分重要。
Hygiene for women and children is very important.

婪】 1025
ㄌㄢˊ lan lán
covetous; greedy; avarice

娼】 1026
(倡) ㄔㄤ chang chāng
a prostitute; a whore

娼門(ㄔㄤ ㄇㄣˊ)
a house of prostitution

娼婦(ㄔㄤ ㄈㄨˋ)
a whore; a prostitute; a slut; a bitch; a harlot

娼寮(ㄔㄤ ㄌㄧㄠˊ)
a brothel

娼妓(ㄔㄤ ㄐㄧˋ)
a prostitute; a streetwalker

娼家(ㄔㄤ ㄐㄧㄚ)
a brothel keeper

婭】 1027
ㄧㄚˋ yah yà
a mutual address between one's sons-in-law

婊】 1028
ㄅㄧㄠˇ beau biǎo
a prostitute

婊子(ㄅㄧㄠˇ ˙ㄗ)
a prostitute; a whore

婊子養的(ㄅㄧㄠˇ ˙ㄗ ㄧㄤˇ ˙ㄉㄜ) or 婊子的兒子(ㄅㄧㄠˇ ˙ㄗ ˙ㄉㄜ ㄦˊ ˙ㄗ) or 婊子孫子(ㄅㄧㄠˇ ˙ㄗ ㄙㄨㄣ ˙ㄗ)
You s.o.b.! 或 Bastard!

嫵】 1029
(嫵) ㄨˇ wuu wǔ
attractive; lovely

嫵媚(ㄨˇ ㄇㄟˋ)
very attractive or lovely: 她是個嫵媚的女孩。 She is a very attractive girl.

九畫

婷】 1030
ㄊㄧㄥˊ tyng tíng
pretty; attractive; graceful

婷婷(ㄊㄧㄥˊ ㄊㄧㄥˊ)
attractive and well poised; graceful

嫇】 1031
ㄨˇ wuh wǔ
beautiful; charming

媒】 1032
ㄇㄟˊ mei méi
1. a marriage go-between; a matchmaker
2. a medium

媒婆(ㄇㄟˊ ㄆㄛˊ)
a professional female matchmaker (sometimes used with a slightly derogative connotation)

媒體(ㄇㄟˊ ㄊㄧˇ)
a medium: 報紙和雜誌為廣告之重要媒體。 Newspapers and magazines are important media for advertising.

媒介(ㄇㄟˊ ㄐㄧㄝˋ)
① a go-between ② a medium: 商業電視是一種廣告媒介。 Commercial television is a medium for advertising.

媒介體(ㄇㄟˊ ㄐㄧㄝˋ ㄊㄧˇ) or 媒介物(ㄇㄟˊ ㄐㄧㄝˋ ㄨˋ)
a medium: 錢是交易的媒介物。 Money is the medium of exchange.

媒妁(ㄇㄟˊ ㄕㄨㄛˋ) or 媒人(ㄇㄟˊ ㄖㄣˊ)
a marriage go-between; a matchmaker

媒妁之言(ㄇㄟˊ ㄕㄨㄛˋ ㄓ ㄧㄢˊ)
(literally) the words of a matchmaker—the marriage arranged by a matchmaker (usually with the consent or approval of one's parents)

〔女部〕

【媚】 1033 ㄇㄟˋ mey mèi

1. to fawn on; to flatter
2. to please
3. to love
4. attractive; fascinating; seductive
5. to coax

媚態(ㄇㄟˋ ㄊㄞˋ)
①seductive appearance or gestures of a girl ②fawning manner; obsequiousness

媚世(ㄇㄟˋ ㄕˋ)
to fawn on others; to flatter others

媚人(ㄇㄟˋ ㄖㄣˊ)
attractive, winsome (appearances, or manners); fascinating; enchanting

媚眼(ㄇㄟˋ ㄧㄢˇ)
a soft glance; an ogle: 王小姐向他抛兩三次媚眼。 Miss Wang gave him two or three ogles.

媚外(ㄇㄟˋ ㄨㄞˋ)
to fawn on a foreign power; to act obsequiously in dealing with foreigners

【媛】 1034 ㄩㄢˊ yuann yuàn
1. a beauty; a beautiful woman
2. (southern dialects) a young lady; a miss

【媧】 1035 ㄨㄚ ua wā
the mythical sister and successor of Fu Hsi (伏羲), the legendary emperor (2852-2738 B.C.).

【媖】 1036 ㄧㄥ ing yīng
a beautiful woman; beautiful

十畫

【嫁】 1037 ㄐㄧㄚˋ jiah jià
1. (said of a woman) to get married; to marry a man
2. to marry off a daughter
3. to impute (blame, a crime, etc.) to another

嫁禍(ㄐㄧㄚˋ ㄏㄨㄛˋ)
to impute blame, a crime, punishment, etc. (to another person)

嫁禍於人(ㄐㄧㄚˋ ㄏㄨㄛˋ ㄩˊ ㄖㄣˊ)
to shift the misfortune onto somebody else; to put the blame on somebody else

嫁雞隨雞，嫁狗隨狗(ㄐㄧㄚˋ ㄐㄧ ㄙㄨㄟˊ ㄐㄧ， ㄐㄧㄚˋ ㄍㄡˇ ㄙㄨㄟˊ ㄍㄡˇ)
A woman shares the fate of the man she married, no matter what he is.

嫁接(ㄐㄧㄚˋ ㄐㄧㄝ)
(botany) to graft

嫁娶(ㄐㄧㄚˋ ㄑㄩˇ)
marriage

嫁妝(ㄐㄧㄚˋ ㄓㄨㄤ)
a bride's trousseau; a dowry

嫁人(ㄐㄧㄚˋ ㄖㄣˊ)
(said of women) to marry

嫁怨(ㄐㄧㄚˋ ㄩㄢˋ)
to impute blame or fault to another: 他嫁怨於我。 He imputed blame to me.

【嫂】 1038 ㄙㄠˇ sao sǎo
the wife of one's elder brother

嫂夫人(ㄙㄠˇ ㄈㄨ ㄖㄣˊ)
(a polite expression to a friend) your wife

嫂子(ㄙㄠˇ ˙ㄗ)or嫂嫂(ㄙㄠˇ ˙ㄙㄠ)
the wife of one's elder brother; a sister-in-law

【媳】 1039 ㄒㄧˊ shyi xí
a daughter-in-law

媳婦(ㄒㄧˊ ㄈㄨˋ)
①a daughter-in-law: 她是個好媳婦。 She is a good daughter-in-law. ②(colloquial) a wife ③a maid-servant

【媵】 1040 ㄧㄥ yinq yìng
1. to escort ladies to the harem of a newly married wife
2. to present as a gift

媵婢(ㄧㄥˋ ㄅㄧˋ)
a maid who accompanies a bride to her new home

【嫦】 1041 ㄔ chy chí
ugly

【媼】 1042 ㄠˇ ao ǎo
1. an old woman
2. (in old China) a general term for older women
3. the goddess of earth

媼婆(ㄠˇ ㄆㄛˊ)
female examiner of corpses

嫏娘(ㄠˇ ㄋㄧㄤˊ)
an old maid

【媽】 1043 ㄇㄚ mha mā
1. one's mother
2. a woman servant

媽媽(ㄇㄚ ㄇㄚ)
①mama; mother: 她是五個子的媽媽。 She is a mother of five. ②a woman servant

媽咪(ㄇㄚ ㄇㄧ)
mummy

媽祖(ㄇㄚ ㄗㄨˇ)
Matsu, Goddess of the Sea, worshiped by most fishermen in Fukien and Taiwan provinces: 台灣很多人信媽祖. In Taiwan, many people believe in Matsu.

媽祖廟(ㄇㄚ ㄗㄨˇ ㄇㄧㄠˋ)
a Matsu temple

【媾】 1044 ㄍㄡˋ gow gòu
1. to marry; to wed
2. to negotiate peace; amity
3. to couple; to copulate

媾合(ㄍㄡˋ ㄏㄜˊ)
to copulate

媾和(ㄍㄡˋ ㄏㄜˊ)
to negotiate (for) peace; to make peace: 他們終於媾和。 They finally negotiated for peace.

【嫉】 1045 ㄐㄧˊ jyi jí
1. jealous; envious; jealousy
2. to hate; to detest

嫉妒(ㄐㄧˊ ㄉㄨˋ)
jealous; envy; jealousy

嫉恨(ㄐㄧˊ ㄏㄣˋ)
to envy and hate; to hate out of jealousy: 他嫉恨她。 He hates her out of jealousy.

嫉賢妒能(ㄐㄧˊ ㄒㄧㄢˊ ㄉㄨˋ ㄋㄥˊ)
to detest the good and to undermine the capable

嫉惡如仇(ㄐㄧˊ ㄜˋ ㄖㄨˊ ㄔㄡˊ)
not to compromise with evil deeds or evil persons; to view good and evil on a black-and-white basis: 他嫉惡如仇。 He never compromises with evil deeds or evil persons.

【嫌】 1046 ㄒㄧㄢˊ shyan xián
1. to detest; to dislike
2. ill will; a grudge: 前嫌盡棄.

All past grudges have been removed.
嫌 to suspect; suspicion
嫌 to complain; to reject; to object
忌(ㄐㄧˋ)
to reject or suspect; to be dissatisfied with what others do
棄(ㄑㄧˋ)
to reject; to give up in disgust; to abandon (one's wife, or lover); to cold-shoulder
隙(ㄒㄧˋ)
the suspicion born out of dislike; an old grudge
憎(ㄗㄥ)
to hate; to dislike
猜(ㄘㄞ)
dislike and suspicion
疑(ㄧˊ)
suspicion; to suspect: 他因嫌疑而被捕。He was arrested on suspicion of theft.
疑犯(ㄧˊ ㄈㄢˋ)
a suspect (of a crime, etc.)
厭(ㄧㄢˋ)
to dislike; to loathe
惡(ㄒㄧㄢˋㄨㄨˋ)
to loathe

十一畫

嫠 1047 ㄌㄧˊ
a widow
婦(ㄈㄨˋ ㄈㄨˊ)
a widow

嫖 1048 ㄆㄧㄠˊ ㄆㄧㄠ
to patronize whorehouses; to visit prostitutes; to go whoring
賭(ㄉㄨˇ ㄉㄨˇ)
to patronize whore houses and gambling houses—to lead a life of debauchery
客(ㄎㄜˋ)
a patron of brothels
妓(ㄐㄧˋ)
to visit prostitutes

嫗 1049 ㄩˋ yuh yù
an old woman

嫚 1050 ㄇㄢˋ mann màn
to slight; to despise; to insult; to affront
2. haughty; arrogant
3. slowly; negligently
嫚罵(ㄇㄢˋ ㄇㄚˋ)
to slight and insult verbally

【嫚】 1050 ㄩㄢˊ iuan yuán
slender; tender

【嫡】 1051 ㄉㄧˊ dyi dí
1. the legal wife as opposed to a concubine
2. the sons born of the legal wife
嫡派(ㄉㄧˊ ㄆㄞˋ)
the legal or official branch of a family tree—the children born of the legal wife of a man
嫡母(ㄉㄧˊ ㄇㄨˇ)
term used by the children of a concubine to address the legal wife of their father
嫡妻(ㄉㄧˊ ㄑㄧ)
a legal wife
嫡親(ㄉㄧˊ ㄑㄧㄣ)
blood relatives
嫡系(ㄉㄧˊ ㄒㄧˋ)
the legal or official branch of the family tree—the children begotten by the legal wife of a man
嫡出(ㄉㄧˊ ㄔㄨ)
children of the legal wife
嫡傳(ㄉㄧˊ ㄔㄨㄢˊ)
(said of a learning, skill, etc.) handed down directly from the master or his official heir
嫡子(ㄉㄧˊ ㄗˇ)
the sons born of the legal wife of a man
嫡嗣(ㄉㄧˊ ㄙˋ)
the eldest son born of the official wife of a man

【媽】 1052 ㄧㄢ ian yān
captivating; charming; lovely; fascinating
媽紅(ㄧㄢ ㄏㄨㄥˊ)
bright deep red; rich crimson
媽然一笑(ㄧㄢ ㄖㄢˊ ㄧˊ ㄒㄧㄠˋ)
a captivating smile; to give a winsome smile: 她對他媽然一笑。She gave him a captivating smile.

【婣】 1053 ㄔㄤ charng cháng
參看「嫦娥」

嫦娥(ㄔㄤˊ ㄜˊ)
(Chinese legend) Chang-o, who ascended the moon after secretly eating her husband's elixir of life

【嫩】 1054 ㄋㄣˋ nenn nèn
1. tender; delicate: 這塊肉很嫩。This meat is very tender. 她的皮膚很嫩嫩。She has very delicate skin.
2. young; immature
3. (of color) light
嫩豆腐(ㄋㄣˋ ㄉㄡˋ ㄈㄨˇ)
tender bean curd
嫩綠(ㄋㄣˋ ㄌㄩˋ)
light green
嫩骨頭(ㄋㄣˋ ㄍㄨˇ ㄊㄡˊ)
① cartilage ②a weak-minded person
嫩寒(ㄋㄣˋ ㄏㄢˊ)
chilly; slightly cold
嫩黃(ㄋㄣˋ ㄏㄨㄤˊ)
light yellow
嫩江(ㄋㄣˋ ㄐㄧㄤ)
Nen River
嫩精(ㄋㄣˋ ㄐㄧㄥ)
a tenderizer: 我們用嫩精使牛肉變軟。We use the tenderizer to tenderize beef.
嫩晴(ㄋㄣˋ ㄑㄧㄥˊ)
fine weather after a long period of rain
嫩枝(ㄋㄣˋ ㄓ)
a sprig
嫩手(ㄋㄣˋ ㄕㄡˇ)
① a raw hand; a new hand ② delicate hands
嫩肉(ㄋㄣˋ ㄖㄡˋ)
tender meat
嫩芽(ㄋㄣˋ ㄧㄚˊ)
a tender shoot
嫩葉(ㄋㄣˋ ㄧㄝˋ)
a young leaf; a tender leaf

十二畫

【嬉】 1055 ㄒㄧ shi xī
to have fun; to sport; to play; to frolic: 業精於勤荒於嬉。The progress of studies comes from hard work and is retarded by frolics.
嬉皮(ㄒㄧ ㄆㄧˊ)
hippies

【女部】

嬉皮笑臉(ㄒㄧ ㄆㄧˊ ㄒㄧㄠˋ ㄌㄧㄢˇ)
grinning cheekily; smiling and grimacing

嬉鬧(ㄒㄧ ㄋㄠˋ)
to romp: 男孩與女孩們彼此嬉鬧。The boys and girls romped together.

嬉戲(ㄒㄧ ㄒㄧˋ)
to frolic; to play; to sport; to have fun; to make merry; to gambol; to romp: 孩子們在海邊嬉戲。Children are sporting on the seashore.

嬉笑(ㄒㄧ ㄒㄧㄠˋ)
to be laughing and playing; a mischievous smile

嬉笑怒罵(ㄒㄧ ㄒㄧㄠˋ ㄋㄨˋ ㄇㄚˋ)
playing, laughing, getting angry and scolding—a stimulating style of writing which makes even merry laughters and angry shoutings delightful reading

嬉遊(ㄒㄧ ㄧㄡˊ)
to play; to sport: 孩子們喜歡嬉遊。Children like to play.

【嫻】 1056
(嫺) ㄒㄧㄢˊ shyan xián
1. refined; gracious
2. skillful; skilled

嫻靜(ㄒㄧㄢˊ ㄐㄧㄥˋ)
quiet and refined (women)

嫻習(ㄒㄧㄢˊ ㄒㄧˊ)
skilled in; adept at: 她嫻習新聞寫作。She is adept at news writing.

嫻熟(ㄒㄧㄢˊ ㄕㄨˊ)
expert; consummate; adept in; skilled in: 他在足球場上表現了嫻熟的技巧。He showed consummate skill at soccer.

嫻雅(ㄒㄧㄢˊ ㄧㄚˇ)
polished; cultured; refined: 她舉止嫻雅。She is refined in manners.

嫻於辭令(ㄒㄧㄢˊ ㄩˊ ㄘˊ ㄌㄧㄥˋ)
skilled in speech; eloquent; to be gifted with a silver tongue: 他是個嫻於辭令的人。He is an eloquent speaker.

【嬋】 1057
ㄔㄢˊ charn chán
graceful; lady-like; attractive; beautiful; pretty

嬋娟(ㄔㄢˊ ㄐㄩㄢ)
①graceful ②the moon; moonlight: 但願人長久，千里共嬋娟。(蘇軾‧水調歌頭)

Though miles apart, could men but live for ever / Dreaming they shared this moonlight endlessly!

【嬌】 1058
ㄐㄧㄠ jiau jiāo
1. tender; delicate; beautiful; lovely
2. spoiled; pampered; coddled

嬌美(ㄐㄧㄠ ㄇㄟˇ)
beautiful and graceful

嬌媚(ㄐㄧㄠ ㄇㄟˋ)
beautiful; handsome

嬌滴滴(ㄐㄧㄠ ㄉㄧ ㄉㄧ)
charming; fascinatingly beautiful

嬌態(ㄐㄧㄠ ㄊㄞˋ)
delicate and beautiful

嬌童(ㄐㄧㄠ ㄊㄨㄥˊ)
a handsome boy

嬌嫩(ㄐㄧㄠ ㄋㄣˋ)
delicate and soft; tender; fragile

嬌娘(ㄐㄧㄠ ㄋㄧㄤˊ)
a beautiful woman

嬌娜(ㄐㄧㄠ ㄋㄨㄛˊ)
winsome; graceful: 她有嬌娜的姿態。She has a winsome manner.

嬌女(ㄐㄧㄠ ㄋㄩˇ)
a beloved daughter: 她是我的嬌女。She is my beloved daughter.

嬌兒(ㄐㄧㄠ ㄦˊ)
an over-pampered child

嬌貴(ㄐㄧㄠ ㄍㄨㄟˋ)
(said of children) spoiled; coddled

嬌慣(ㄐㄧㄠ ㄍㄨㄢˋ)
to pamper; to coddle; to spoil; to dote: 她嬌慣她的孩子。She pampers her child.

嬌客(ㄐㄧㄠ ㄎㄜˋ)
a son-in-law

嬌喉(ㄐㄧㄠ ㄏㄡˊ)
a pleasing singing voice

嬌憨(ㄐㄧㄠ ㄏㄢ)
lovely and innocent

嬌妻(ㄐㄧㄠ ㄑㄧ)
a beloved wife

嬌氣(ㄐㄧㄠ ㄑㄧˋ)
delicate; not very healthy

嬌小(ㄐㄧㄠ ㄒㄧㄠˇ)
dainty and little: 我的老師個子很嬌小。My teacher is very dainty and little.

嬌小玲瓏(ㄐㄧㄠ ㄒㄧㄠˇ ㄌㄧㄥˊ ㄌㄨㄥˊ)

delicate and refined

嬌羞(ㄐㄧㄠ ㄒㄧㄡ)
bashful; modest and retiring: 她有點兒嬌羞。She is rather bashful.

嬌痴(ㄐㄧㄠ ㄔ)
lovely and innocent; guileless

嬌嗔(ㄐㄧㄠ ㄔㄣ)
(said of women) to pretend angry

嬌喘(ㄐㄧㄠ ㄔㄨㄢˇ)
(said of women) to gasp for breath for lack of strength

嬌生慣養(ㄐㄧㄠ ㄕㄥ ㄍㄨㄢˋ ㄧㄤˇ)
to grow up in soft surroundings; to live a sheltered life

嬌聲嬌氣(ㄐㄧㄠ ㄕㄥ ㄐㄧㄠ ㄑㄧˋ)
to speak in a seductive tone: 她說話總是嬌聲嬌氣的。She always speaks in a seductive tone.

嬌媚(ㄐㄧㄠ ㄖㄨㄟˋ)
seductive and charming

嬌柔(ㄐㄧㄠ ㄖㄡˊ)
beautiful and frail

嬌縱(ㄐㄧㄠ ㄗㄨㄥˋ)
to let a child have his own way; to pamper: 他嬌縱他孩子。He lets his child have his own way.

嬌兒(ㄐㄧㄠ ㄗˇ)
a beloved son

嬌艷(ㄐㄧㄠ ㄧㄢˋ)
beautiful; gorgeous; delicate and charming: 嬌艷的杏花開了。The delicate apricot trees in full blossom.

嬌養慣了(ㄐㄧㄠ ㄧㄤˇ ㄍㄨㄢˋ ㄌㄜˋ)
accustomed to a soft and pampered life: 她嬌養慣了。She is accustomed to a soft and pampered life.

嬌娃(ㄐㄧㄠ ㄨㄚˊ)
a beauty: 她是個嬌娃。She is a beauty.

十三畫

【嬖】 1059
ㄅㄧˋ bih bì
1. to enjoy the favor of a powerful person (said of people of mean birth)
2. a minion

【嬖】(ㄅㄧ) or 嬖御 (ㄅㄧ ㄩ)
(said of concubines and sycophants) to be favored by
the ruler

嬖人 (ㄅㄧ ㄖㄣˊ)
a favorite of the ruler

【嬗】 1060
ㄕㄢˋ shann shàn
to change; to be replaced

【嬙】 1061
ㄑㄧㄤˊ chyang qiáng
a court lady

嬙媛 (ㄑㄧ ㄩㄢˊ)
ladies-in-waiting

【嬛】 1062
ㄑㄩㄥˊ chyong qióng
lonely; solitary

【嬛】 1062
ㄒㄩㄢ shiuan xuān
fickle; frivolous

澴薄 (ㄒㄩㄢ ㄅㄛˊ)
frivolous

【媛】 1063
ㄞˇ ay ǎi
the daughter (a complimentary term referring to the daughter of the person one is speaking to)

【嬴】 1064
ㄧㄥˊ yng yíng
1. to win: 他嬴得她的芳心。He won her heart.
2. to have a surplus
3. a Chinese family name

嬴土 (ㄧㄥˊ ㄊㄨˇ)
fertile land; fertile soil

嬴秦 (ㄧㄥˊ ㄑㄧㄣˊ)
the state of Chin during the Warring States period

【嬝】 1065
(嫋) ㄋㄧㄠˇ neau niǎo
delicate; graceful

嬝嬝 (ㄋㄧㄠˇ ㄋㄧㄠˇ)
①(said of a willow) waving gracefully ② (said of a young woman) appealingly slender and graceful ③ (said of smoke, etc.) dying out slowly ④(said of sound) to linger in the air long

嬝娜 (ㄋㄧㄠˇ ㄋㄨㄛˊ)
showing womanly beauty; slender and delicate; willowy

十四畫

【嬰】 1066
ㄧㄥ ing yīng
an infant; a baby; a suckling

嬰孩 (ㄧㄥ ㄏㄞˊ) or 嬰兒 (ㄧㄥ ㄦˊ)
a baby; an infant

嬰兒奶粉 (ㄧㄥ ㄦˊ ㄋㄞˇ ㄈㄣˇ)
soft curd milk

嬰兒死亡率 (ㄧㄥ ㄦˊ ㄙˇ ㄨㄤˊ ㄌㄩˋ)
the infant mortality rate

【嬲】 1067
ㄋㄧㄠˇ neau niǎo
to dally with; to flirt with

【嬪】 1068
ㄆㄧㄣˊ pyn pín
1. a court lady
2. (said of a woman) to be married to

嬪從 (ㄆㄧㄣˊ ㄘㄨㄥˊ)
ladies-in-waiting 亦作「宮女」

十五畫

【嬸】 1069
ㄕㄣˇ sheen shěn
1. an aunt (the wife of one's father's younger brother)
2. a sister-in-law (the wife of one's husband's younger brother)

嬸母 (ㄕㄣˇ ㄇㄨˇ) or 嬸娘 (ㄕㄣˇ ㄋㄧㄤˊ) or 嬸嬸 (ㄕㄣˇ ㄕㄣˇ)
①an aunt (the wife of one's father's younger brother) ② an address for one's aunt

十七畫

【孀】 1070
ㄕㄨㄤ shuang shuāng
a widow

孀婦 (ㄕㄨㄤ ㄈㄨˋ)
a widow

孀閨 (ㄕㄨㄤ ㄍㄨㄟ)
the chamber of a widow

孀居 (ㄕㄨㄤ ㄐㄩ)
to remain in widowhood; to live as a widow: 她孀居數年。She remains in widowhood several years.

【孅】 1071
ㄒㄧㄢ shian xiān
slender; thin; small; fine; delicate

孅介 (ㄒㄧㄢ ㄐㄧㄝˋ)
tiny; a small bit

孅手 (ㄒㄧㄢ ㄕㄡˇ)
delicate hands (of a woman)

孅弱 (ㄒㄧㄢ ㄖㄨㄛˋ)
frail; weak; delicate: 他是個孅弱的孩子。He is a frail child.

孅嗇 (ㄒㄧㄢ ㄙㄜˋ)
miserly; stingy

十九畫

【孌】 1072
ㄌㄩㄢˊ leuan lüán
1. beautiful; handsome
2. obedient; docile

孌童 (ㄌㄩㄢˊ ㄊㄨㄥˊ)
a catamite

子 部
ㄗˇ tzyy zǐ

【子】 1073
ㄗˇ tzyy zǐ
1. a child; a son; an offspring: 你的獨生子很受看重。Your only son is highly considered.
2. a seed; an egg: 瓜子 melon seed
3. the first of the twelve Terrestrial Branches (地支)
4. a rank of the nobility equivalent to a viscount
5. a designation used in speaking or to a man in former times (somewhat similar to 'mister')

子部 (ㄗˇ ㄅㄨˋ)
one of the four categories of ancient Chinese books (經、史、子、集)

子民 (ㄗˇ ㄇㄧㄣˊ)
the people

子母 (ㄗˇ ㄇㄨˇ)
①mother and child ②principal and interest

子母相權 (ㄗˇ ㄇㄨˇ ㄒㄧㄤ ㄑㄩㄢˊ)
heavy and light coins circulated side by side in ancient China

子目 (ㄗˇ ㄇㄨˋ)
a subdivision (of a division in a code, a book, etc.); a subtitle

子房 (ㄗˇ ㄈㄤˊ)
(botany) an ovary

子代(ㄗ ㄉㄞˋ)
a filial generation: 第一子代
the first filial generation

子彈(ㄗ ㄉㄢˋ)
a bullet: 子彈差一英吋就擊中他。The bullet missed him by one inch

子彈箱(ㄗ ㄉㄢˋ ㄒㄧㄤ)
a cartridge box

子弟(ㄗ ㄉㄧˋ)
① young dependents; children ② those who patronize brothels

子弟兵(ㄗ ㄉㄧˋ ㄅㄧㄥ)
an army made up of the sons of the people; our own army

子囊(ㄗ ㄋㄤˊ)
(botany) sporangium

子女(ㄗ ㄋㄩˇ)
sons and daughters; children (as opposed to parents)

子粒(ㄗ ㄌㄧˋ)
seeds; grains; kernels; tiny particles; beans: 子粒飽滿full grains

子路(ㄗ ㄌㄨˋ)
Tzu-lu (a disciple of Confucius)

子規(ㄗ ㄍㄨㄟ)
the cuckoo 亦作「杜鵑」

子宮(ㄗ ㄍㄨㄥ)
the womb; the uterus

子宮癌(ㄗ ㄍㄨㄥ ㄞˊ)
uterine cancer

子宮外孕(ㄗ ㄍㄨㄥ ㄨㄞˋ ㄩㄣˋ)
ectopic (or extrauterine) pregnancy

子金(ㄗ ㄐㄧㄣ)
interest from principal

子薑(ㄗ ㄐㄧㄤ)
young ginger

子句(ㄗ ㄐㄩˋ)
(grammar) a clause

子爵(ㄗ ㄐㄩㄝˊ)
a viscount

子爵夫人(ㄗ ㄐㄩㄝˊ ㄈㄨ ㄖㄣˊ)
a viscountess

子錢(ㄗ ㄑㄧㄢˊ)
① money put out at interest ② interest from money lent

子息(ㄗ ㄒㄧˊ)
① one's children ② interest (in monetary sense)

子系(ㄗ ㄒㄧˋ)
posterity; offspring

子虛(ㄗ ㄒㄩ)
① emptiness; nothingness: 聲音化為子虛 The sound faded into nothingness. ② fiction

子虛烏有(ㄗ ㄒㄩ ㄨ ㄧㄡˇ)
pure imagination

子姪 or 子侄(ㄗ ㄓˊ)
the generation younger than oneself in the family or clan; one's sons, daughters, nephews and nieces

子時(ㄗ ㄕˊ)
the period of the day from 11 p.m. to 1 a.m.

子實(ㄗ ㄕˊ)
seeds; grains; kernels; beans

子書(ㄗ ㄕㄨ)
ancient Chinese books other than the *Six Classics*

子孫孫(ㄗ ㄙㄨㄣ ㄙㄨㄣ)
generation after generation of descendants

子思(ㄗ ㄙ)
Tzu-szu (Confucius' grandson)

子嗣(ㄗ ㄙˋ)
a son; a male offspring: 李先生是他唯一的子嗣。Mr. Li is his only male offspring.

子孫(ㄗ ㄙㄨㄣ)
descendants; posterity

子夜(ㄗ ㄧㄝˋ)
midnight: 他經常工作到子夜。He usually worked until midnight.

子葉(ㄗ ㄧㄝˋ)
a cotyledon

子音(ㄗ ㄧㄣ)
a consonant

子午線(ㄗ ㄨˇ ㄒㄧㄢˋ)
a meridian 亦作「經線」

子曰(ㄗ ㄩㄝ)
Confucius said

【孑】 *1074*
ㄐㄧㄝˊ jye jié
1. the larvae of mosquitoes
2. solitary; unaccompanied; lonely

孑立(ㄐㄧㄝˊ ㄌㄧˋ)
to stand in isolation; to be alone; 他的房子孑立山邊。His house stands alone on the hillside.

孑孑為義(ㄐㄧㄝˊ ㄐㄧㄝˊ ㄨㄟˊ ㄧˋ)
petty favors

孑孓(ㄐㄧㄝˊ ㄐㄩㄝˊ)
the larvae of mosquitoes;

wigglers

孑然一身(ㄐㄧㄝˊ ㄖㄢˊ ㄧ ㄕㄣ)
alone; living without companions: 他至今仍孑然一身。He is still living alone.

孑遺(ㄐㄧㄝˊ ㄧˊ)
the sole survivor

【孒】 *1075*
ㄐㄩㄝˊ jyue jué
the larvae of mosquitoes

一畫

【孔】 *1076*
ㄎㄨㄥˇ koong kǒng
1. a hole; an orifice; an opening; an aperture
2. very; exceedingly
3. of or pertaining to Confucius or Confucianism
4. urgent; badly
5. a Chinese family name

孔門(ㄎㄨㄥˇ ㄇㄣˊ)
the Confucianists

孔孟(ㄎㄨㄥˇ ㄇㄥˋ)
Confucius and Mencius: 孔孟乃中國之聖人也。Confucius and Mencius were sages of China.

孔孟之道(ㄎㄨㄥˇ ㄇㄥˋ ㄓ ㄉㄠˋ)
the doctrines of Confucius and Mencius

孔廟(ㄎㄨㄥˇ ㄇㄧㄠˋ)
a Confucian temple: 他們到孔廟去參觀。They went to visit the Confucian temple.

孔明(ㄎㄨㄥˇ ㄇㄧㄥˊ)
another name of 諸葛亮, prime minister of the state of Shu during the Epoch of the Three Kingdoms

孔方兄(ㄎㄨㄥˇ ㄈㄤ ㄒㄩㄥ)
money, or cash (a colloquial expression derived from the fact that a coin is round and has a square hole in the center)

孔夫子(ㄎㄨㄥˇ ㄈㄨ ㄗˇ)
Confucius: 孔夫子被尊稱為至聖人。Confucius is called Confucius the Sage.

孔父(ㄎㄨㄥˇ ㄈㄨˋ)
Confucius

孔道(ㄎㄨㄥˇ ㄉㄠˋ)
① a key road ② the Confucian teachings

孔誕(ㄎㄨㄥˇ ㄉㄢˋ) or 孔子誕辰紀念

誕(ㄉㄢˋ ㄗㄉㄞ ㄖㄣˋ ㄐㄧ ㄋㄧㄢˋ ㄖˋ)
Confucius' Birthday on September 28: 孔子誕辰紀念日是
假日。Confucius' Birthday is
a holiday.

洞(ㄉㄨㄥˋ)
an opening or a hole

老(ㄌㄠˇ ㄗˇ)
Confucius and Lau-tzu

林(ㄌㄨˊ ㄌㄧㄣˊ)
the tomb of Confucius in
Shangtung

急(ㄐㄧˊ ㄐㄧ)或孔殷(ㄎㄨㄥˇ ㄧㄣ)
urgent; urgently; badly

教(ㄎㄨㄥˇ ㄐㄧㄠˋ)
Confucianism; the Confucian
teachings

殷(ㄎㄨㄥˇ ㄑㄩㄝˋ)
said of the eyes, ears, mouth
and nose of a human

雀(ㄎㄨㄥˇ ㄑㄩㄝˋ)
a peacock: 小孩喜歡孔雀。
Childern like the peacocks.

雀石(ㄎㄨㄥˇ ㄑㄩㄝˋ ㄕˊ)
malachite

隙(ㄎㄨㄥˇ ㄒㄧˋ)
a small opening; a hole

穴(ㄎㄨㄥˇ ㄒㄩㄝˋ)
a hole; an aperture; an opening

聖(ㄎㄨㄥˇ ㄕㄥˋ)
Confucius the Sage

子(ㄎㄨㄥˇ ㄗˇ)
Confucius

武有力(ㄎㄨㄥˇ ㄨˇ ㄧㄡˇ ㄌㄧˋ)
(said of a man) very strong
and brave; herculean: 他是個
孔武有力的戰士。He is a herculean warrior.

二畫

【孕】 1077
ㄩㄣˋ yunn yùn
to be pregnant; to conceive

婦(ㄩㄣˋ ㄈㄨˋ)
a pregnant woman

期(ㄩㄣˋ ㄑㄧˊ)
(medicine) pregnancy; gestation

育(ㄩˋ ㄩˋ)
to let develop (as in the womb); to nourish; to foster; to nurture; to nurse

三畫

【字】 1078
ㄗˋ tzyh zì
1. a word; a character; a letter; a logograph: 這個字是什麼意思? What does this word mean?
2. to betroth a girl: 她尚待字閨中。She is not betrothed yet.
3. (formerly) a name or style taken at the age of 20, by which one was sometimes called

碼(ㄗˋ ㄇㄚˇ)
a form of digits used by old-fashioned businessmen to prevent tampering

模(ㄗˋ ㄇㄛˊ)
(printing) a type matrix

謎(ㄗˋ ㄇㄧˊ)
a riddle, the answer to which is a single word or character

面(ㄗˋ ㄇㄧㄢˋ)
words (as found in some text and interpreted literally)

母(ㄗˋ ㄇㄨˇ)
an alphabet; a letter (of an alphabet): 英文字母有二十六個。There are twenty-six letters in the English alphabet.

幕(ㄗˋ ㄇㄨˋ)
subtitles (in a motion picture); a transcript of singing lines in Peking opera projected on the screen for the benefit of the audience

典(ㄗˋ ㄉㄧㄢˇ)
a dictionary; a lexicon; a thesaurus: 字典是他的常伴。A dictionary is his frequent companion.

體(ㄗˋ ㄊㄧˇ)
(printing) a style of letter or character; a type

帖(ㄗˋ ㄊㄧㄝˋ)
a copybook

條(兒)(ㄗˋ ㄊㄧㄠˊ ㄦ)
a brief note: 他的上司留給他一張字條。His boss left him a brief note.

裏行間(ㄗˋ ㄌㄧˇ ㄏㄤˊ ㄐㄧㄢ)
between the lines; the overtone (of a piece of writing)

根(ㄗˋ ㄍㄣ)
(linguistics) a root; a radical

號(ㄗˋ ㄏㄠˋ)
① a mark made with letters or characters ② the name of a shop or store ③ reputation; fame

號人物(ㄗˋ ㄏㄠˋ ㄖㄣˊ ㄨˋ)
personages and their reputation

畫(ㄗˋ ㄏㄨㄚˋ)
① the strokes in a character ② calligraphy and painting

彙(ㄗˋ ㄏㄨㄟˋ)
① a vocabulary: 他的字彙有限。His vocabulary is limited. ② a glossary

跡(ㄗˋ ㄐㄧˋ)
one's handwriting: 她的字跡很難辨。Her handwriting is difficult to read.

跡模糊(ㄗˋ ㄐㄧˋ ㄇㄛˊ ㄏㄨˊ)
illegible handwriting

跡工整(ㄗˋ ㄐㄧˋ ㄍㄨㄥ ㄓㄥˇ)
neat writing

句(ㄗˋ ㄐㄩˋ)
words and phrases

據(ㄗˋ ㄐㄩˋ)
a written proof; a receipt; a certificate: 請給我一張此款的字據。Please send me a receipt for the money.

形(ㄗˋ ㄒㄧㄥˊ)
the form of a (written or printed) character

紙(ㄗˋ ㄓˇ)
paper with words written or printed upon it

紙簍兒(ㄗˋ ㄓˇ ㄌㄡˇ)
a wastepaper basket; a wastebasket: 字紙簍兒在那裡呢? Where is the wastebasket?

斟句酌(ㄗˋ ㄓㄣ ㄐㄩˋ ㄓㄨㄛˊ)
to choose one's words carefully; to weigh every word: 你必須字斟句酌。You must weigh your words.

首(ㄗˋ ㄕㄡˇ)
a prefix

書(ㄗˋ ㄕㄨ)
a wordbook; a dictionary

人(ㄗˋ ㄖㄣˊ)
(said of a girl) to become engaged

字(ㄗˋ ㄗˋ)
every word

義(ㄗˋ ㄧˋ)
the definition, connotation, or meaning of a word

子 部

字眼(ㄗ ㄧㄢˇ)
a word; a character: 這個字眼什麼意思? What does this word mean?

字眼兒(ㄗ ㄧㄢˇ)
wording; diction; expression

字樣(ㄗ ㄧㄤˋ)
①models of Chinese characters ②words and phrases used in a certain context: 在我們的契約裏並無此等字樣。There are no such words and phrases in our contract.

字尾(ㄗ ㄨㄟˇ)
a suffix

字源(ㄗ ㄩㄢˊ)
the etymology of a word

【存】 1079 (ㄘㄨㄣˊ) tswen cún

1. to live; to exist; to survive; to remain: 父母俱存。Both parents are still living.

2. to keep; to deposit: 我把盛存入銀行。I keep money in a bank.

存歿(ㄘㄨㄣˊ ㄇㄛˋ)
a question of remaining in existence or not

存歿均感(ㄘㄨㄣˊ ㄇㄛˋ ㄐㄩㄣ ㄍㄢˇ)
Both the dead and the living are grateful.

存放(ㄘㄨㄣˊ ㄈㄤˋ)
to deposit (money); to leave (something somewhere) for safekeeping: 我把行李存放在朋友那裡了。I've left my luggage with a friend of mine.

存放處(ㄘㄨㄣˊ ㄈㄤˋ ㄔㄨˋ)
a depository

存單(ㄘㄨㄣˊ ㄉㄢ)
(accounting) a deposit receipt

存檔(ㄘㄨㄣˊ ㄉㄤˋ)
to keep in the archives; to place on file; to file: 把這些信仔細存檔。File these letters carefully.

存底兒(ㄘㄨㄣˊ ㄉㄧˇ ㄦ)
to keep the first draft; to keep a file copy

存念(ㄘㄨㄣˊ ㄋㄧㄢˋ)
to have something as a keepsake or as a memento

存欄(ㄘㄨㄣˊ ㄌㄢˊ)
(animal husbandry) the amount of livestock on hand

存糧(ㄘㄨㄣˊ ㄌㄧㄤˊ)
to store up grain

存錄(ㄘㄨㄣˊ ㄌㄨˋ)
to put on record

存根(ㄘㄨㄣˊ ㄍㄣ)
a counterfoil; a stub

存庫(ㄘㄨㄣˊ ㄎㄨˋ)
a treasury; to keep in a vault

存款(ㄘㄨㄣˊ ㄎㄨㄢˇ)
the money put in a bank; a deposit; to make a deposit

存款簿(ㄘㄨㄣˊ ㄎㄨㄢˇ ㄅㄨˋ)
a deposit book

存款單(ㄘㄨㄣˊ ㄎㄨㄢˇ ㄉㄢ)
a deposit slip

存款利息(ㄘㄨㄣˊ ㄎㄨㄢˇ ㄌㄧˋ ㄒㄧˊ)
interest on deposit

存款人(ㄘㄨㄣˊ ㄎㄨㄢˇ ㄖㄣˊ)
a depositor

存候(ㄘㄨㄣˊ ㄏㄡˋ)
to send regards

存戶(ㄘㄨㄣˊ ㄏㄨˋ)
a depositor (of money in a bank, etc.): 存戶要提款。The depositor wants to withdraw his money.

存活(ㄘㄨㄣˊ ㄏㄨㄛˊ)
to survive; to keep alive

存貨(ㄘㄨㄣˊ ㄏㄨㄛˋ)
remaining (still unsold) goods; inventory: 一位店商減價以減少他的存貨。A storekeeper had a sale to reduce his inventory.

存貨表(ㄘㄨㄣˊ ㄏㄨㄛˋ ㄅㄧㄠˇ)
(accounting) a stock sheet

存貨簿(ㄘㄨㄣˊ ㄏㄨㄛˋ ㄅㄨˋ)
(accounting) a stock book

存貨記錄(ㄘㄨㄣˊ ㄏㄨㄛˋ ㄐㄧˋ ㄌㄨˋ)
(accounting) inventory records

存記(ㄘㄨㄣˊ ㄐㄧˋ)
to register for future reference (as an applicant, etc.)

存取(ㄘㄨㄣˊ ㄑㄩˇ)
(computers) access

存息(ㄘㄨㄣˊ ㄒㄧˊ)
the interest from a deposit

存心(ㄘㄨㄣˊ ㄒㄧㄣ)
intentions; intentional; intentionally; on purpose: 他存心傷害她的感情。He hurt her feelings with intention.

存心回測(ㄘㄨㄣˊ ㄒㄧㄣ ㄏㄨㄟˊ ㄘㄜˋ)
to cherish unscrupulous intentions

存恤(ㄘㄨㄣˊ ㄒㄩˋ)
to give comfort and relief

存續(ㄘㄨㄣˊ ㄒㄩˋ)
to continue to exist; to keep existing

存摺(ㄘㄨㄣˊ ㄓㄜˊ)
a bankbook; a passbook

存查(ㄘㄨㄣˊ ㄔㄚˊ)or存照(ㄘㄨㄣˊ ㄓㄠˋ)
to keep (a business letter, document, etc.) for future reference; to file (papers)

存車處(ㄘㄨㄣˊ ㄔㄜ ㄔㄨˋ)
a parking lot (for bicycles); a bicycle park 亦作「停車處」

存儲(ㄘㄨㄣˊ ㄔㄨˇ)
to hoard; to store up; to stockpile: 松鼠存儲堅果過冬。A squirrel hoards nuts for the winter.

存儲量(ㄘㄨㄣˊ ㄔㄨˇ ㄌㄧㄤˋ)
(computers) storage capacity; memory capacity

存在(ㄘㄨㄣˊ ㄗㄞˋ)
to exist; to be present; existence: 你相信上帝存在嗎? Do you believe that God exists?

存在主義(ㄘㄨㄣˊ ㄗㄞˋ ㄓㄨˇ ㄧˋ)
existentialism: 沙特提倡存在主義。Sartre popularized existentialism.

存案(ㄘㄨㄣˊ ㄢˋ)
to put (a legal document, etc.) on public record; to file

存而不論(ㄘㄨㄣˊ ㄦˊ ㄅㄨˋ ㄌㄨㄣˋ)
to exclude a problem from consideration though aware of its existence; to ignore

存疑(ㄘㄨㄣˊ ㄧˊ)
①an unanswered question; a remaining doubt ②to leave a doubtful point unquestioned

存有(ㄘㄨㄣˊ ㄧㄡˇ)
being: 我們不知這個世界是如何時開始有的。We do not know when this world came into being.

存思(ㄘㄨㄣˊ ㄙ)
to send a messenger to express sympathy for (a person in mourning, distress, etc.)

存問(ㄘㄨㄣˊ ㄨㄣˋ)
to send a messenger to inquire after (a person)

存亡(ㄘㄨㄣˊ ㄨㄤˊ)
to survive or to perish; to live or to die; life-and-death; survival and downfall

子亡關頭(ㄗㄨˊ ㄨㄤ ㄍㄨㄢ ㄊㄡˊ)
at a most critical moment

四畫

【孚】 1080
ㄈㄨ fwu fú
1. confidence; trust
2. a Chinese family name

【孛】 1081
ㄅㄟˋ bey bèi
a comet

孛孛(ㄅㄟˋ ㄅㄟˋ)
radiant

孛星(ㄅㄟˋ ㄒㄧㄥ)
a comet 亦作「彗星」

【孜】 1082
ㄗ tzy zī
never weary; unwearied and
diligent

孜孜(ㄗ ㄗ)
diligent; industrious

孜孜不倦(ㄗ ㄗ ㄅㄨˋ ㄐㄩㄢˋ)
to work with diligence and
without fatigue

【孝】 1083
ㄒㄧㄠˋ shiaw xiào
filial piety; of or having to
do with filial piety

孝服(ㄒㄧㄠˋ ㄈㄨˊ)
mourning dress worn by
bereaved children

孝婦(ㄒㄧㄠˋ ㄈㄨˋ)
①a filial woman ②a
woman in mourning

孝道(ㄒㄧㄠˋ ㄉㄠˋ)
the principle of filial piety

孝悌 or 孝弟(ㄒㄧㄠˋ ㄊㄧˋ)
to be a dutiful son and to be
respectful to one's elder
brothers

孝男(ㄒㄧㄠˋ ㄋㄢˊ)
a bereaved son (used in an
obituary)

孝女(ㄒㄧㄠˋ ㄋㄩˇ)
a bereaved daughter (used
in an obituary)

孝廉(ㄒㄧㄠˋ ㄌㄧㄢˊ)
①a term for 舉人 (in Ming
and Ching dynasties) ②
(Han Dynasty) a person of
virtue recommended by a
country

孝陵(ㄒㄧㄠˋ ㄌㄧㄥˊ) or 孝陵衛(ㄒㄧㄠˋ ㄌㄧㄥˊ ㄨㄟˋ)
the tomb of Chu Yüan-chang
(朱元璋), the founder of the
Ming Dynasty, in Nanking

孝經(ㄒㄧㄠˋ ㄐㄧㄥ)
the Canon of Filial Piety

孝敬(ㄒㄧㄠˋ ㄐㄧㄥˋ)
①to show filial piety and
respect for one's parents: 這
些孩子孝敬他們的父母。The chil-
dren treated their parents
with filial respect。②to
present one's parents (or
superiors) with gifts

孝心(ㄒㄧㄠˋ ㄒㄧㄣ)
filial piety; the love toward
parents

孝行(ㄒㄧㄠˋ ㄒㄧㄥ)
filial conduct

孝順(ㄒㄧㄠˋ ㄕㄨㄣˋ)
to show filial obedience or
devotion for (one's parents)

孝子(ㄒㄧㄠˋ ㄗˇ)
①a devoted child ②a
bereaved son

孝子賢孫(ㄒㄧㄠˋ ㄗˇ ㄒㄧㄢˊ ㄙㄨㄣ)
worthy progeny; a true son

孝慈(ㄒㄧㄠˋ ㄘˊ)
filial piety and parental tenderness

孝思(ㄒㄧㄠˋ ㄙ)
the heart of filial piety

孝義(ㄒㄧㄠˋ ㄧˋ)
devotion to one's parents
and loyalty to one's friends

孝友(ㄒㄧㄠˋ ㄧㄡˇ)
filial piety and brotherly
love

五畫

【孟】 1084
ㄇㄥˋ manq mèng
1. a Chinese family name
2. the eldest of children
3. rude; rough
4. of or having to do with
Mencius
5. the first month of a season

孟婆(ㄇㄥˋ ㄆㄛˊ)
the goddess of wind

孟買(ㄇㄥˋ ㄇㄞˇ)
Bombay, India

孟母(ㄇㄥˋ ㄇㄨˇ)
the mother of Mencius

孟母三遷(ㄇㄥˋ ㄇㄨˇ ㄙㄢ ㄑㄧㄢ)
(literally) The mother of
Mencius changed her abode
three times (to avoid bad
influence on her son)—A

wise mother would do everything for the healthy growth
of her children.

孟德斯鳩(ㄇㄥˋ ㄉㄜˊ ㄙ ㄐㄧㄡ)
Montesquieu (Charles Louis
de Secondat. Baron de la
Brède et de Montesquieu),
1689-1755, French philosophical writer

孟浪(ㄇㄥˋ ㄌㄤˋ)
rude; rough; rash: 不可孟浪行
事。Don't act rashly.

孟浪之言(ㄇㄥˋ ㄌㄤˋ ㄓ ㄧㄢˊ)
reckless talk: 他因孟浪之言而
受責。He was scolded for his
reckless talk.

孟加拉(ㄇㄥˋ ㄐㄧㄚ ㄌㄚ)
Bengal

孟加拉人(ㄇㄥˋ ㄐㄧㄚ ㄌㄚ ㄖㄣˊ)
Bengalese; Bengali

孟加拉灣(ㄇㄥˋ ㄐㄧㄚ ㄌㄚ ㄨㄢ)
the Bay of Bengal

孟姜女(ㄇㄥˋ ㄐㄧㄤ ㄋㄩˇ)
name of a heroine in
Chinese folklore, whose bitter cry over her husband's
death at the Great Wall was
said to have caused a section of the wall to crumble
down

孟春(ㄇㄥˋ ㄔㄨㄣ)
the first month of the spring
season

孟什維克(ㄇㄥˋ ㄕˊ ㄨㄟˊ ㄎㄜˋ)
Menshevik

孟子(ㄇㄥˋ ㄗˇ)
Mencius: 孟子是中國的「亞
聖」。Mencius is China's "Second Sage".

孟宗竹(ㄇㄥˋ ㄗㄨㄥ ㄓㄨˊ)
famous bamboo south of the
Yangtze River

孟月(ㄇㄥˋ ㄩㄝˋ)
the first month of a season
(the first, fourth, seventh,
and tenth moon)

【季】 1085
ㄐㄧˋ jih jì
1. a season; a quarter of a
year
2. the last (month of a season)
3. the youngest (of brothers)
4. a Chinese family name

季票(ㄐㄧˋ ㄆㄧㄠˋ)
a season ticket

季風(ㄐㄧˋ ㄈㄥ)
(meteorology) the monsoon

〔子部〕

〔子部〕

亦作「季候風」

季刊(ㄐㄧ ㄎㄢ)或季報(ㄐㄧ ㄅㄠ)
a quarterly (publication): 紐
約客是月刊，不是季刊。*New Yorker* is a monthly, not a quarterly.

季候風(ㄐㄧ ㄏㄡ ㄈㄥ)
the monsoon, or any other seasonal wind 參看「季風」

季節(ㄐㄧ ㄐㄧㄝ)
a season: 這是多雨的季節。This is the rainy season.

季節性(ㄐㄧ ㄐㄧㄝ ㄒㄧㄥ)
seasonal: 賣聖誕卡是季節性的生意。The selling of Christmas cards is a seasonal trade.

季軍(ㄐㄧ ㄐㄩㄣ)
the second runner-up in a contest; the third prize winner

季常癖(ㄐㄧ ㄔㄤ ㄆㄧ)
henpecked 亦作「懼內症」

季世(ㄐㄧ ㄕ)
the declining years of a dynasty; a period of decadence

季子(ㄐㄧ ㄗ)
the youngest son

季月(ㄐㄧ ㄩㄝ)
the last month of a season (the third, sixth, ninth and twelfth moon)

【孥】1086
ㄋㄨ nú
one's children

【孤】1087
ㄍㄨ gū
1. solitary; lone; lonely; friendless; helpless; unaided
2. fatherless; orphaned: 戰爭使他在早年就變成孤兒。The war orphaned him at an early age.
3. (said of disposition) eccentric
4. negligent in an obligation

孤本(ㄍㄨ ㄅㄣ)
the sole copy (of a book) in existence

孤僻(ㄍㄨ ㄆㄧ)
(said of a person's disposition) eccentric; idiosyncratic: 他是個孤僻的人。He is an eccentric person.

孤貧(ㄍㄨ ㄆㄧㄣ)
lonely and poor

孤墳(ㄍㄨ ㄈㄣ)
an isolated grave

孤憤(ㄍㄨ ㄈㄣ)
cynical of the world and its way

孤芳自賞(ㄍㄨ ㄈㄤ ㄗ ㄕㄤ)
to indulge in self-admiration

孤負 or 辜負(ㄍㄨ ㄈㄨ)
to fail to live up to; to let down

孤島(ㄍㄨ ㄉㄠ)
a solitary island; an isolated island

孤單(ㄍㄨ ㄉㄢ) or 孤另(ㄍㄨ ㄌㄧㄥ)
solitary; single; alone; unaccompanied; friendless: 他孤單一人在家。He was alone in the house.

孤獨(ㄍㄨ ㄉㄨ)
solitary; friendless; solitude: 愛迪生說：「最好的思想是孤獨中想出來的。」Thomas Alva Edison said: "The best thinking has been done in solitude."

孤特(ㄍㄨ ㄊㄜ)
isolated; unaided

孤老(ㄍㄨ ㄌㄠ)
① the childless old people ② a woman's paramour ③ the protector of a singsong girl, maid or prostitute

孤陋寡聞(ㄍㄨ ㄌㄡ ㄍㄨㄚ ㄨㄣ)
having seen very little of the world; ignorant

孤立(ㄍㄨ ㄌㄧ)
isolation; isolated; unaided: 沒有人能孤立地存在著。No man can live in isolation.

孤立主義(ㄍㄨ ㄌㄧ ㄓㄨ ㄧ)
isolationism

孤零(ㄍㄨ ㄌㄧㄥ)
lonely; friendless

孤孀(ㄍㄨ ㄕㄨㄤ)
a widow; a widower

孤寡(ㄍㄨ ㄍㄨㄚ)
① a widow and an orphan ② the humble first-person destination used by the rulers in former times

孤苦伶仃 or 孤苦零丁(ㄍㄨ ㄎㄨ ㄌㄧㄥ ㄉㄧㄥ)
lonely and helpless; poor and friendless

孤魂(ㄍㄨ ㄏㄨㄣ)
① a wandering soul ② one without a family or friends

to depend on

孤寂(ㄍㄨ ㄐㄧ)
lonely; friendless: 她在陌生人群中甚感孤寂。She was lonely when among strangers.

孤家寡人(ㄍㄨ ㄐㄧㄚ ㄍㄨㄚ ㄖㄣ)
alone; a bachelor

孤軍深入(ㄍㄨ ㄐㄩㄣ ㄕㄣ ㄖㄨ)
an isolated force penetrating deep into enemy territory

孤掌難鳴(ㄍㄨ ㄓㄤ ㄋㄢ ㄇㄧㄥ)
(literally) A single hand cannot produce clapping sounds. —to be unable to cope with a situation or accomplish something without help

孤證(ㄍㄨ ㄓㄥ)
solitary (and therefore dubious) evidence

孤注一擲(ㄍㄨ ㄓㄨ ㄧ ㄓ)
(said of a gambler) to stake all on a single throw of the dice

孤臣孽子(ㄍㄨ ㄔㄣ ㄋㄧㄝ ㄗ)
① a person in disfavor with his ruler and parents ② an unaided person

孤子(ㄍㄨ ㄗ)
a male bereaved of his father

孤哀子(ㄍㄨ ㄞ ㄗ)
a male bereaved of both his parents

孤傲(ㄍㄨ ㄠ)
proud and aloof

孤兒(ㄍㄨ ㄦ)
an orphan

孤兒寡婦(ㄍㄨ ㄦ ㄍㄨㄚ ㄈㄨ)
orphans and widows

孤兒院(ㄍㄨ ㄦ ㄩㄢ)
an orphanage

孤雲野鶴(ㄍㄨ ㄩㄣ ㄧㄝ ㄏㄜ)
descriptive of the carefreeness of a hermit's life (literally like a lone cloud or a wild crane)

六畫

【孩】1088
ㄏㄞ hái
1. a child; an infant; a baby
2. young; small

孩提(ㄏㄞ ㄊㄧ) or 孩抱(ㄏㄞ ㄅㄠ)
a child that still has to be carried in arms; an infant; childhood

子部

七畫

【孫】 1089
(ㄙㄨㄣ) suen sun
. a grandchild; a descendant: 曾孫 a great-grandson
. a Chinese family name
孫女 (ㄙㄨㄣ ㄋㄩ)
a granddaughter
孫權 (ㄙㄨㄣ ㄑㄩㄢ)
Sun Chüan, ruler of the state of Wu (吳) during the Epoch of the Three Kingdoms
孫媳 (ㄙㄨㄣ ㄒㄧ)or 孫媳婦 (ㄙㄨㄣ ㄒㄧ ㄈㄨ)
a granddaughter-in-law; a grandson's wife
孫婿 (ㄙㄨㄣ ㄒㄩ)or 孫女婿
a grandson-in-law
孫中山 (ㄙㄨㄣ ㄓㄨㄥ ㄕㄢ)or 孫逸仙 (ㄙㄨㄣ ㄧ ㄒㄧㄢ)or 孫文 (ㄙㄨㄣ ㄨㄣ)
Dr. Sun Yat-sen, father of the Republic of China
孫子 (ㄙㄨㄣ ㄗ)or 孫武
Sun Tzu, a pre-Chin strategist, noted for his book, *The Art of War*
孫子兵法 (ㄙㄨㄣ ㄗ ㄅㄧㄥ ㄈㄚ)
The Art of War by Sun Tzu: 孫子兵法已被譯成英文。 *The Art of War* by Sun Tzu was translated into English.
孫兒 (ㄙㄨㄣ ㄦ)or 孫兒 (ㄙㄨㄣ ㄦ)
① a grandchild ② a grandson

八畫

【孰】 1090
(ㄕㄨ) shwu shú
. (in literary texts) what; which: 是可忍也，孰不可忍也？ If he can bear to do this, what may he not bear to do?
. who; whom
孰是孰非 (ㄕㄨ ㄕ ㄕㄨ ㄈㄟ)

Which is right and which is wrong?
孰勝孰負 (ㄕㄨ ㄕㄥ ㄕㄨ ㄈㄨ)
Who wins and who loses?
孰若 (ㄕㄨ ㄖㄨㄛ)
what is better than; it would be better to

九畫

【孱】 1091
(ㄔㄢ) charn chán
weak; feeble; frail
孱夫 (ㄔㄢ ㄈㄨ)or 孱頭 (ㄔㄢ ㄊㄡ)
a cowardly person; a weakling
孱弱 (ㄔㄢ ㄖㄨㄛ)
feeble; weak; frail: 他是孱弱的老人。 He is a feeble old man.

【孳】 1092
(ㄗ) tzy zī
1. to bear or beget in large numbers
2. to work with sustained diligence
孳息 (ㄗ ㄒㄧ)
① to grow ② interest (from money)
孳生 (ㄗ ㄕㄥ)
to grow and multiply: 園中孳生綠草。 Green grass grows in the garden.
孳乳 (ㄗ ㄖㄨ)
to bear or beget abundantly; to grow and multiply
孳孳 (ㄗ ㄗ)
working with sustained diligence
孳孳為利 (ㄗ ㄗ ㄨㄟ ㄌㄧ)
to work hard from morning till night for money
孳孳為善 (ㄗ ㄗ ㄨㄟ ㄕㄢ)
to persevere in doing good
孳衍 (ㄗ ㄧㄢ)
to grow in number; to multiply

十一畫

【孵】 1093
(ㄈㄨ) fu fū
1. to hatch (eggs); to incubate
2. to emerge from eggs or spawn
孵卵 (ㄈㄨ ㄌㄨㄢ)
to hatch eggs; to incubate

孵卵器 (ㄈㄨ ㄌㄨㄢ ㄑㄧ)
an incubator
孵化 (ㄈㄨ ㄏㄨㄚ)
to emerge from eggs; to spawn

十三畫

【學】 1094
(ㄒㄩㄝ) shyue xué
(舊音 ㄒㄧㄠ) shyau xiáu
1. to learn; to study; to imitate: 活到老學到老。 It's never too late to learn.
2. of or having to do with learning; academic
學報 (ㄒㄩㄝ ㄅㄠ)
an academic journal; a journal: 他訂了幾份學報。 He subscribed some journals.
學步 (ㄒㄩㄝ ㄅㄨ)
(said of a child) to learn to walk
學不像 (ㄒㄩㄝ ㄅㄨ ㄒㄧㄤ)or 學不來 (ㄒㄩㄝ ㄅㄨ ㄌㄞ)
to try to imitate or copy in vain
學不厭 (ㄒㄩㄝ ㄅㄨ ㄧㄢ)
to learn with indefatigable zeal; tireless in learning
學不完 (ㄒㄩㄝ ㄅㄨ ㄨㄢ)
to have an endless amount to learn
學派 (ㄒㄩㄝ ㄆㄞ)
a school (of thought): 他屬於康德學派。 He belongs to the Kantian school.
學名 (ㄒㄩㄝ ㄇㄧㄥ)
① the scientific name (of a plant, an animal, etc.) ② a name given to one on beginning school life
學閥 (ㄒㄩㄝ ㄈㄚ)
an academic clique
學費 (ㄒㄩㄝ ㄈㄟ)
tuition
學分 (ㄒㄩㄝ ㄈㄣ)
units, credits, or semester hours (of course work to meet degree requirements)
學風 (ㄒㄩㄝ ㄈㄥ)
school discipline; school traditions
學府 (ㄒㄩㄝ ㄈㄨ)
a seat of learning; an insti-

〔子部〕

tute of higher learning: 哈佛大學是著名的學府。Harvard University is a famous institute of higher learning.

學得不錯(ㄒㄩㄝˊ·ㄉㄜ ㄅㄨˋ ㄘㄨㄛˋ)or 學得不壞(ㄒㄩㄝˊ·ㄉㄜ ㄅㄨˋ ㄏㄨㄞˋ)
to imitate or copy with creditable result

學得像(ㄒㄩㄝˊ·ㄉㄜ ㄒㄧㄤˋ)
to imitate or copy with marked skill

學到老, 學不了(ㄒㄩㄝˊ ㄉㄠˋ ㄌㄠˇ, ㄒㄩㄝˊ ㄅㄨˋ ㄌㄧㄠˇ)
Learning is an endless process.

學店(ㄒㄩㄝˊ ㄉㄧㄢˋ)
a school that indulges in making money in total disregard of the students' scholastic progress

學堂(ㄒㄩㄝˊ ㄊㄤˊ)
a school

學徒(ㄒㄩㄝˊ ㄊㄨˊ)
① an apprentice ② a student

學徒制(ㄒㄩㄝˊ ㄊㄨˊ ㄓˋ)
apprenticeship

學童(ㄒㄩㄝˊ ㄊㄨㄥˊ)
school children; primary school students

學年(ㄒㄩㄝˊ ㄋㄧㄢˊ)
an academic year; a school year

學理(ㄒㄩㄝˊ ㄌㄧˇ)
a (scientific) theory

學力(ㄒㄩㄝˊ ㄌㄧˋ)
scholastic ability; scholarship

學歷(ㄒㄩㄝˊ ㄌㄧˋ)
educational background; record of formal schooling

學齡(ㄒㄩㄝˊ ㄌㄧㄥˊ)
school age

學齡前兒童(ㄒㄩㄝˊ ㄌㄧㄥˊ ㄑㄧㄢˊ ㄦˊ ㄊㄨㄥˊ)
preschool children; preschoolers

學齡兒童(ㄒㄩㄝˊ ㄌㄧㄥˊ ㄦˊ ㄊㄨㄥˊ)
school-age children

學館 or 學館(ㄒㄩㄝˊ ㄍㄨㄢˇ)
a school (usually a small one for private tutoring)

學科(ㄒㄩㄝˊ ㄎㄜ)
a subject; a course (of study or instruction at school): 你最喜歡那一學科? Which course do you like most?

學海(ㄒㄩㄝˊ ㄏㄞˇ)
the sea of learning

學好(ㄒㄩㄝˊ ㄏㄠˇ)
to learn from good examples; to emulate one's betters

學會(ㄒㄩㄝˊ ㄏㄨㄟˋ)
① a learned society; an institute ② to succeed in learning (a skill): 她學會溜冰。She's learned to skate.

學籍(ㄒㄩㄝˊ ㄐㄧˊ)
one's status as a student of a particular school

學級(ㄒㄩㄝˊ ㄐㄧˊ)
grade or form (division of years in a school curriculum)

學界(ㄒㄩㄝˊ ㄐㄧㄝˋ)
the academic circles

學究(ㄒㄩㄝˊ ㄐㄧㄡˋ)
a pedagogue; a pedant; an egghead

學期(ㄒㄩㄝˊ ㄑㄧˊ)
a (school) term; a semester; a quarter: 一年中有兩個學期。There are two semesters in a year.

學前教育(ㄒㄩㄝˊ ㄑㄧㄢˊ ㄐㄧㄠˋ ㄩˋ)
preschool education; infant school education: 他專習學前教育。He majors in preschool education.

學區(ㄒㄩㄝˊ ㄑㄩ)
a school district

學習(ㄒㄩㄝˊ ㄒㄧˊ)
to learn; to study: 你應當學習如何忍耐。You ought to learn how to be patient.

學校(ㄒㄩㄝˊ ㄒㄧㄠˋ)
a school (for education)

學行(ㄒㄩㄝˊ ㄒㄧㄥˊ)
scholastic and moral performance

學制(ㄒㄩㄝˊ ㄓˋ)
an educational system

學者(ㄒㄩㄝˊ ㄓㄜˇ)
a scholar; a learned person

學長(ㄒㄩㄝˊ ㄓㄤˇ)
① one's senior at school ② the head of a department or division (in a college or university under a now obsolete system)

學潮(ㄒㄩㄝˊ ㄔㄠˊ)
a student strike; a campus commotion

學時髦(ㄒㄩㄝˊ ㄕˊ ㄇㄠˊ)

to follow the fashion: 他這樣做是學時髦。He follows the fashion to do this.

學士(ㄒㄩㄝˊ ㄕˋ)
a holder of the bachelor degree

學士服(ㄒㄩㄝˊ ㄕˋ ㄈㄨˊ)
academicals

學識(ㄒㄩㄝˊ ㄕˋ)
erudition; learning; scholarship; academic attainments 常識比學識更有價值。Common sense is worth more than learning.

學舌(ㄒㄩㄝˊ ㄕㄜˊ)
to mimic; to parrot

學舍(ㄒㄩㄝˊ ㄕㄜˋ)
a school building

學生(ㄒㄩㄝˊ ㄕㄥ)
a student; a pupil

學生會(ㄒㄩㄝˊ ㄕㄥ ㄏㄨㄟˋ)
a student union; a student association

學生證(ㄒㄩㄝˊ ㄕㄥ ㄓㄥˋ)
a student's identity card

學生時代(ㄒㄩㄝˊ ㄕㄥ ㄕˊ ㄉㄞˋ)
school days

學生自治會(ㄒㄩㄝˊ ㄕㄥ ㄗˋ ㄓˋ ㄏㄨㄟˋ)
a student government

學生運動(ㄒㄩㄝˊ ㄕㄥ ㄩㄣˋ ㄉㄨㄥˋ)
a student movement

學術(ㄒㄩㄝˊ ㄕㄨˋ)
learning; science

學術風氣(ㄒㄩㄝˊ ㄕㄨˋ ㄈㄥ ㄑㄧˋ)
academic atmosphere

學術地位(ㄒㄩㄝˊ ㄕㄨˋ ㄉㄧˋ ㄨㄟˋ)
academic position or standing

學術團體(ㄒㄩㄝˊ ㄕㄨˋ ㄊㄨㄢˊ ㄊㄧˇ)
a learned organization; an academic organization

學術論文(ㄒㄩㄝˊ ㄕㄨˋ ㄌㄨㄣˋ ㄨㄣˊ)
a research paper; a thesis

學術界(ㄒㄩㄝˊ ㄕㄨˋ ㄐㄧㄝˋ)
academic circles

學術自由(ㄒㄩㄝˊ ㄕㄨˋ ㄗˋ ㄧㄡˊ)
academic freedom

學術研究(ㄒㄩㄝˊ ㄕㄨˋ ㄧㄢˊ ㄐㄧㄡˋ)
an academic approach

學術演講(ㄒㄩㄝˊ ㄕㄨˋ ㄧㄢˇ ㄐㄧㄤˇ)
an academic lecture

學說(ㄒㄩㄝˊ ㄕㄨㄛ)
a theory

學然後知不足(ㄒㄩㄝˊ ㄖㄢˊ ㄏㄡˋ ㄓ ㄅㄨˋ ㄗㄨˊ)
One discovers his ignorance

only through learning.

學人(ㄒㄩㄝˊ ㄖㄣˊ)
a scholar

學如逆水行舟(ㄒㄩㄝˊ ㄖㄨˊ ㄋㄧˋ ㄕㄨㄟˇ ㄒㄧㄥˊ ㄓㄡ)
(literally) Learning is like sailing a boat upstream. --either to keep progressing or to be washed backward

學子(ㄒㄩㄝˊ ㄗˇ)
a student

學而不厭(ㄒㄩㄝˊ ㄦˊ ㄅㄨˋ ㄧㄢˋ)
to have an insatiable thirst for knowledge

學而優則仕(ㄒㄩㄝˊ ㄦˊ ㄧㄡ ㄗㄜˊ ㄕˋ)
Excellence in scholarship leads to officialdom.

學以致用(ㄒㄩㄝˊ ㄧˇ ㄓˋ ㄩㄥˋ)
to make use of what one has learned

學藝(ㄒㄩㄝˊ ㄧˋ)
①sciences and arts ②to learn a trade

學業(ㄒㄩㄝˊ ㄧㄝˋ)
school work: 她的學業很重。 Her school work is very heavy.

學業成績(ㄒㄩㄝˊ ㄧㄝˋ ㄔㄥˊ ㄐㄧ)
scholastic achievements (or attainments)

學友(ㄒㄩㄝˊ ㄧㄡˇ)
a schoolmate; a fellow student

學有專長(ㄒㄩㄝˊ ㄧㄡˇ ㄓㄨㄢ ㄔㄤˊ)
to have acquired a speciality from study

學樣(ㄒㄩㄝˊ ㄧㄤˋ)
to imitate someone's example

學無止境(ㄒㄩㄝˊ ㄨˊ ㄓˇ ㄐㄧㄥˋ)
There is no limit to knowledge.

學位(ㄒㄩㄝˊ ㄨㄟˋ)
an academic degree

學問(ㄒㄩㄝˊ ㄨㄣˋ)
learning; scholarship; erudition: 他的學問很淵博。 The range of his erudition is wide.

學院(ㄒㄩㄝˊ ㄩㄢˋ)
①a college (in a university) ②an academy

十四畫

【孺】 1095 ㄖㄨˊ ru rú

a young child; an infant

孺慕(ㄖㄨˊ ㄇㄨˋ)
to adore someone as a child adores its parents; to love and respect very much

孺子(ㄖㄨˊ ㄗˇ)
a child; a boy: 孺子可教也。 That boy is teachable!

十七畫

【孽】 1096 (孼) ㄋㄧㄝˋ nieh niè
1. the son of a concubine
2. a monster
3. sin; evil

孽黨(ㄋㄧㄝˋ ㄉㄤˇ)
the members of a traitorous party, band, etc.

孽障(ㄋㄧㄝˋ ㄓㄤˋ)
①(a term of abuse formerly used by the elders of a family cursing their juniors) an evil creature; vile spawn; wicked children ②(Buddhism) karmic obstruction; retribution for the evil one is supposed to have committed

孽種(ㄋㄧㄝˋ ㄓㄨㄥˇ)
①the seeds of misfortune ②a child born of adultery; a bastard

孽子(ㄋㄧㄝˋ ㄗˇ)
①a son born of a concubine ②a sinner

十九畫

【孿】 1097 ㄌㄩㄢˊ liuan lüán
twin

孿生(ㄌㄩㄢˊ ㄕㄥ)or**孿子**(ㄌㄩㄢˊ ㄗˇ)or**孿件兒**(ㄌㄩㄢˊ ㄗˇㄦ)
born as twins; to bear twins

宀 部
ㄇㄧㄢˊ myan mián

二畫

【宄】 1098 ㄍㄨㄟˇ goei guǐ

a treacherous fellow; a traitor; a thief

【它】 1099 ㄊㄚ ta tā
(讀音 ㄊㄨㄛ tuo tuō)
it; that; this: 狗到哪兒去了? Where is the dog? It is in the room.

它們(ㄊㄚ ·ㄇㄣ)
they

【宁】 1100 ㄓㄨ juh zhù
1. to store; to save; to stockpile
2. to stand

【宂】 1101 ㄖㄨㄥˇ roong rǒng
1. redundant; superfluous
2. disorderly

宂筆(ㄖㄨㄥˇ ㄅㄧˇ)
①verbosity in writing ②unnecessary strokes in painting

宂費(ㄖㄨㄥˇ ㄈㄟˋ)
unnecessary expenses

宂長(ㄖㄨㄥˇ ㄓㄤˇ)or(ㄖㄨㄥˇ ㄔㄤˊ)or**宂贅**(ㄖㄨㄥˇ ㄓㄨㄟˋ)
①redundant; superfluous; supernumerary ②(said of writing) redundant; verbose ③tediously long

宂雜(ㄖㄨㄥˇ ㄗㄚˊ)
confused; mixed up; disorderly: 他討厭宂雜的房子。 He disliked a disorderly room.

宂詞(ㄖㄨㄥˇ ㄘˊ)
superfluous words

宂散(ㄖㄨㄥˇ ㄙㄢˇ)
leisurely; relaxed

宂員(ㄖㄨㄥˇ ㄩㄢˊ)
the superfluous members of a staff or organization; supernumerary

三畫

【宅】 1102 ㄓㄞˊ jain zhái
(讀音 ㄓㄜˋ jeh zhè)
a dwelling; a residence; a house

宅門(ㄓㄞˊ ㄇㄣˊ)
①the gate of an old-style big house ②the family living in such a house

宅第(ㄓㄞˊ ㄉㄧˋ)
a mansion

宅眷(业务 ㄐㄩㄢ)
one's dependents

宅心(业务 ㄒㄧㄣ)
intention

宅心仁厚(业务 ㄒㄧㄣ ㄖㄣ ㄏㄡ)
a benevolent and generous nature

宅神(业务 ㄕㄣ)
household deities; the patron gods of a household

宅子(业务 ·ㄗ)
a residence; a house: 我的宅子很小。My house is quite small.

宅院(业务 ㄩㄢ)
a house with a courtyard; a house: 他在鄉下有一座宅院。He has a house in the country.

【宇】 1103
ㄩˇ yeu yǔ

1. a house; a roof
2. look; appearance; countenance
3. space

宇內(ㄩ ㄋㄟ)
in the country; in the world

宇宙(ㄩ 业ㄡ)
the universe: 我們的世界只是宇宙的一小部分。Our world is but a small part of the universe.

宇宙爆(ㄩ 业ㄡ ㄅㄠ)
a cosmic burst

宇宙通訊(ㄩ 业ㄡ ㄊㄨㄥ ㄒㄩㄣ)
cosmic communication

宇宙論(ㄩ 业ㄡ ㄌㄨㄣ)
cosmology

宇宙線(ㄩ 业ㄡ ㄒㄧㄢ)or 宇宙射線(ㄩ 业ㄡ ㄕㄜ ㄒㄧㄢ)
cosmic rays; cosmic radiations

宇宙塵(ㄩ 业ㄡ ㄔㄣ)
(astronomy) meteoroid

宇宙噪音(ㄩ 业ㄡ ㄗㄠ ㄧㄣ)
cosmic noise

宇宙速度(ㄩ 业ㄡ ㄙㄨ ㄉㄨ)
cosmic velocity

宇宙醫學(ㄩ 业ㄡ ㄧ ㄒㄩㄝ)
cosmic or space medicine

宇宙微粒(ㄩ 业ㄡ ㄨㄟ ㄌㄧ)
a cosmic particle

宇宙衛星(ㄩ 业ㄡ ㄨㄟ ㄒㄧㄥ)
a cosmos satellite

【守】 1104
ㄕㄡˇ shoou shǒu

1. to guard; to protect; to

defend; to watch
2. to wait
3. to keep (a secret, etc.)
4. to stick to; to maintain
5. to abide by

守備(ㄕㄡ ㄅㄟ)
to be on garrison duty; garrison: 守備部隊 garrison force

守門(ㄕㄡ ㄇㄣ)
to watch the door against burglars

守門員(ㄕㄡ ㄇㄣ ㄩㄢ)
(football) a goalkeeper

守秘密(ㄕㄡ ㄇㄧ ㄇㄧ)
to keep a secret: 這件事你最好守秘密。You had better keep the matter secret.

守法(ㄕㄡ ㄈㄚ)
to abide by the law

守分(ㄕㄡ ㄈㄣ)
to be content with one's lot; to stick to what one is suited for

守土(ㄕㄡ ㄊㄨ)
① to defend the country ② to take care of a locality (as a local official in former times)

守壘員(ㄕㄡ ㄌㄟ ㄩㄢ)
(baseball) a baseman

守靈(ㄕㄡ ㄌㄧㄥ)
to stand as guards at the bier

守寡(ㄕㄡ ㄍㄨㄚ)
to remain in widowhood

守口如瓶(ㄕㄡ ㄎㄡ ㄖㄨ ㄆㄧㄥ)
to keep one's mouth shut

守候(ㄕㄡ ㄏㄡ)
to wait; to bide one's time

守護(ㄕㄡ ㄏㄨ)
to guard; to protect

守紀律(ㄕㄡ ㄐㄧ ㄌㄩ)
to observe the rules; to behave in accordance with the regulations

守節(ㄕㄡ ㄐㄧㄝ)or 守貞(ㄕㄡ 业ㄣ)
① to remain a widow forever although one is still young ② to stick to principle

守舊(ㄕㄡ ㄐㄧㄡ)
resistant to advances; sticking to old ways; conservative: 老年人通常比青年人更守舊。Old people are usually more conservative than young people.

守將(ㄕㄡ ㄐㄧㄤ)
the commanding general in charge of the defense of a city or strategic point

守更(ㄕㄡ ㄍㄥ)
to keep watch during the night

守軍(ㄕㄡ ㄐㄩㄣ)
defending troops; defenders

守孝(ㄕㄡ ㄒㄧㄠ)
to be in mourning for one's parent

守信(ㄕㄡ ㄒㄧㄣ)or 守信用(ㄕㄡ ㄒㄧㄣ ㄩㄥ)
to keep promises; to honor one's words: 人人都應該守信。Everyone should keep his promises.

守職(ㄕㄡ 业)
to stick to one's duty

守制(ㄕㄡ 业)
to remain in mourning for one's parent

守正不阿(ㄕㄡ 业ㄥ ㄅㄨ ㄜ)
to stick to justice or fairness despite pressure

守株待兔(ㄕㄡ 业ㄨ ㄉㄞ ㄊㄨ)
(originally said of a farmer) to wait by the stump hoping other hares will come by the spot because he once caught a hare there—stupid and unimaginative in doing things

守住(ㄕㄡ 业ㄨ)
to hold (a city or position)

守拙(ㄕㄡ 业ㄨㄛ)
to be content with one's coarseness; to remain free from ambitions

守中立(ㄕㄡ 业ㄨㄥ ㄌㄧ)
to maintain neutrality; to keep away from disputes or conflicts

守車(ㄕㄡ ㄔㄜ)
a caboose (of a freight train)

守成(ㄕㄡ ㄔㄥ)
to keep what one has already accomplished; (usually said of property) to preserve what is handed down by one's ancestors

守成不變(ㄕㄡ ㄔㄥ ㄅㄨ ㄅㄧㄢ)
holding to existing custom; reluctant to accept changes: 他唯一的缺點是守成不變。The

safe hit,

only defect he has is that he is reluctant to accept changes.

守城 (ㄕㄡˇ ㄔㄥˊ)
to defend a city

守時 (ㄕㄡˇ ㄕˊ)
punctual

守身如玉 (ㄕㄡˇ ㄕㄣ ㄖㄨˊ ㄩˋ)
to keep one's integrity intact in adversity

守則 (ㄕㄡˇ ㄗㄜˊ)
rules; regulations; 工作守則 work regulations

守財奴 (ㄕㄡˇ ㄘㄞˊ ㄋㄨˊ)
a miser; a niggard

守喪 (ㄕㄡˇ ㄙㄤ)
to remain in mourning for one's parent

守歲 (ㄕㄡˇ ㄙㄨㄟˋ)
to see the old year out and the new year in by staying up on the Lunar New Year's Eve

守夜 (ㄕㄡˇ ㄧㄝˋ)
to keep night watch

守夜者 (ㄕㄡˇ ㄧㄝˋ ㄓㄜˇ)
a watchman

守衛 (ㄕㄡˇ ㄨㄟˋ)
to guard; a guard

守望 (ㄕㄡˇ ㄨㄤˋ)
to keep watch

守望臺 (ㄕㄡˇ ㄨㄤˋ ㄊㄞˊ)
a watchtower

守望相助 (ㄕㄡˇ ㄨㄤˋ ㄒㄧㄤ ㄓㄨˋ)
(said of neighbors in a community) to help each other in guarding against enemies

守約 (ㄕㄡˇ ㄩㄝ)
to keep a promise; to honor a pledge; 你應該守約。 You should honor your pledge.

【安】 1105
ㄢ ān

1. peaceful; quiet; calm; tranquil
2. to quiet; to stabilize; to pacify; to console
3. to put; to place; to arrange
4. to be content with
5. how; why; 安能袖手旁觀? How can one stand by and do nothing?
6. safe; secure; stable
7. a Chinese family name

安邦定國 (ㄢ ㄅㄤ ㄉㄧㄥˋ ㄍㄨㄛˊ)
(said of a ruler) to give peace and stability to the

country

安步當車 (ㄢ ㄅㄨˋ ㄉㄤˋ ㄐㄩ)
①to be content to go on foot instead of riding in a vehicle ②to be content with a simple life

安排 (ㄢ ㄆㄞˊ)
arrangements; to arrange; to make arrangements for: 在離開之前，他把業務都安排好了。 Before going away, he arranged his business affairs.

安培 (ㄢ ㄆㄟˊ)
an ampere

安培計 (ㄢ ㄆㄟˊ ㄐㄧˋ)
an ammeter

安貧樂道 (ㄢ ㄆㄧㄣˊ ㄌㄜˋ ㄉㄠ)
happy to lead a simple, virtuous life: 他安貧樂道。 He is happy to lead a simple, virtuous life.

安平古堡 (ㄢ ㄆㄧㄥˊ ㄍㄨˇ ㄅㄠˇ)
Fort Zeelandia in Taiwan, built by the Dutch in the 17th century

安眠 (ㄢ ㄇㄧㄢˊ)
to sleep peacefully

安眠藥 (ㄢ ㄇㄧㄢˊ ㄧㄠˋ)
sleeping pills; hypnotics; soporifics

安民 (ㄢ ㄇㄧㄣˊ)
to quiet the people; (after conquering a city) to give peace to the people

安民告示 (ㄢ ㄇㄧㄣˊ ㄍㄠˋ ㄕˋ)
a notice to reassure the public

安命 (ㄢ ㄇㄧㄥˋ)
content with one's lot; to accept one's lot

安非他命 (ㄢ ㄈㄟ ㄊㄚ ㄇㄧㄥˋ)
amphetamine

安分 (ㄢ ㄈㄣˋ)
do not go beyond one's bounds; to be law-abiding

安分守己 (ㄢ ㄈㄣˋ ㄕㄡˇ ㄐㄧˇ)
content or happy to be what one is; law-abiding: 他們是安分守己的良民。 They are law-abiding people.

安放 (ㄢ ㄈㄤˋ)
to put in a proper manner; to lay (a keel, etc.)

安撫 (ㄢ ㄈㄨˇ) or 安慰 (ㄢ ㄈㄨˋ)
to pacify

安富尊榮 (ㄢ ㄈㄨˋ ㄗㄨㄣ ㄖㄨㄥˊ)
to enjoy wealth and honor

安打 (ㄢ ㄉㄚˇ)
(baseball) a safe hit, a safety hit, or a safety: 那是一支很巧妙的安打。 That was a very clever safe hit.

安得 (ㄢ ㄉㄜˊ)
How can it be? 或 How could it be?

安道爾 (ㄢ ㄉㄠˋ ㄦˇ)
Andorra, a small republic hemmed in by France and Spain

安第斯山脈 (ㄢ ㄉㄧˋ ㄙ ㄕㄢ ㄇㄞˋ) or 安廸斯山脈 (ㄢ ㄉㄧˋ ㄙ ㄕㄢ ㄇㄞˋ)
the Andes Mountains in South America

安定 (ㄢ ㄉㄧㄥˋ)
stable; steadfast; unchanging; to stabilize; stability

安定團結 (ㄢ ㄉㄧㄥˋ ㄊㄨㄢˊ ㄐㄧㄝˊ)
stability and unity

安定社會秩序 (ㄢ ㄉㄧㄥˋ ㄕㄜˋ ㄏㄨㄟˋ ㄓˋ ㄒㄩˋ)
to maintain social order

安定人心 (ㄢ ㄉㄧㄥˋ ㄖㄣˊ ㄒㄧㄣ)
to reassure the public

安頓 (ㄢ ㄉㄨㄣˋ)
to put in order; to help settle down; to make proper arrangement (for the family before leaving home for a long period of time)

安東 (ㄢ ㄉㄨㄥ)
①Antung Province ②Antung city

安特衛普 (ㄢ ㄊㄜˋ ㄨㄟˋ ㄆㄨˇ)
Antwerp, a seaport in northern Belgium

安胎藥 (ㄢ ㄊㄞ ㄧㄠˋ)
the medicine given to a pregnant woman to prevent miscarriage

安泰 (ㄢ ㄊㄞˋ)
healthy; in good health

安徒生 (ㄢ ㄊㄨˊ ㄕㄥ)
Hans Christian Andersen, 1805–1875, Danish writer

安土重遷 (ㄢ ㄊㄨˇ ㄓㄨㄥˋ ㄑㄧㄢ)
to be attached to one's native land and unwilling to leave it

安內攘外 (ㄢ ㄋㄟˋ ㄖㄤˇ ㄨㄞˋ)
to maintain internal security and to expel foreign invasion

安南 (ㄢ ㄋㄢˊ)

Annam

安寧(ㄢ ㄋㄧㄥ)
peace; repose; tranquility

安樂(ㄢ ㄌㄜ)
comfort: 她在兒女那裏得到安樂。She finds comfort in her children.

安樂國(ㄢ ㄌㄜ ㄍㄨㄜ)
a Utopia; (Buddhism) Paradise

安樂死(ㄢ ㄌㄜ ㄙ)
euthanasia

安老院(ㄢ ㄌㄠ ㄩㄢ)
a home for the old people

安理會(ㄢㄌㄧㄏㄨㄟ)or 安全理事會(ㄢ ㄑㄩㄢ ㄌㄧ ㄕ ㄏㄨㄟ)
the Security Council (of the United Nations)

安哥拉(ㄢ ㄍㄜ ㄌㄚ)
Angola

安哥拉人(ㄢ ㄍㄜ ㄌㄚ ㄖㄣ)
an Angolan

安固(ㄢ ㄍㄨ)
secure

安卡拉(ㄢ ㄎㄚ ㄌㄚ)
Ankara, capital of Turkey

安康(ㄢ ㄎㄤ)
in a state of peace and good health: 祝您安康. I wish you the best of health.

安好(ㄢ ㄏㄠ)
enjoying peace and good health; well; safe and sound: 全家安好, 請勿掛念。You will be pleased to know that everyone in the family is safe and sound.

安徽(ㄢ ㄏㄨㄟ)
Anhwei Province

安魂曲(ㄢ ㄏㄨㄣ ㄑㄩ)
(music) a requiem

安家(ㄢ ㄐㄧㄚ)
①to insure the welfare of one's family ②to set up a household (by marriage)

安家費(ㄢ ㄐㄧㄚ ㄈㄟ)
allowances for the support of dependents (given to draftees or officials assigned to overseas posts)

安家落戶(ㄢ ㄐㄧㄚ ㄌㄨㄛ ㄏㄨ)
to make one's home in a place; to settle

安靜(ㄢ ㄐㄧㄥ)
quiet; tranquil; still; peaceful: 請保持安靜。Keep quiet.

安居樂業(ㄢ ㄐㄩ ㄌㄜ ㄧㄝ)or 安家樂業(ㄢ ㄐㄧㄚ ㄌㄜ ㄧㄝ)
(said of people under a good government) to live and work in peace and content

安琪兒(ㄢ ㄑㄧ ㄦ)
an angel

安慶(ㄢ ㄑㄧㄥ)
Anching, capital of Anhwei Province

安全(ㄢ ㄑㄩㄢ)
①safe; secure ②safety; security

安全玻璃(ㄢ ㄑㄩㄢ ㄅㄛ ㄌㄧ)
safety glass

安全瓣(ㄢ ㄑㄩㄢ ㄅㄢ)
a safety valve

安全別針(ㄢ ㄑㄩㄢ ㄅㄧㄝ ㄓㄣ)
a safety pin

安全帽(ㄢ ㄑㄩㄢ ㄇㄠ)
a safety helmet

安全門(ㄢ ㄑㄩㄢ ㄇㄣ)
an exit

安全閥(ㄢ ㄑㄩㄢ ㄈㄚ)
a safety valve

安全帶(ㄢ ㄑㄩㄢ ㄉㄞ)
a safety belt (or strap): 請繫上安全帶。Tie your safety belt, please.

安全島(ㄢ ㄑㄩㄢ ㄉㄠ)
a traffic island

安全燈(ㄢ ㄑㄩㄢ ㄉㄥ)
a miner's lamp; a safety lamp

安全地帶(ㄢ ㄑㄩㄢ ㄉㄧ ㄉㄞ)
a safety zone

安全第一(ㄢ ㄑㄩㄢ ㄉㄧ ㄧ)
safety first

安全梯(ㄢ ㄑㄩㄢ ㄊㄧ)
an emergency staircase

安全刮刀(ㄢ ㄑㄩㄢ ㄍㄨㄚ ㄉㄠ)
a safety razor

安全理事會(ㄢ ㄑㄩㄢ ㄌㄧ ㄕ ㄏㄨㄟ)
the Security Council 參看「安理會」

安全感(ㄢ ㄑㄩㄢ ㄍㄢ)
a sense of security

安全開關(ㄢ ㄑㄩㄢ ㄎㄞ ㄍㄨㄢ)
a safety switch

安全火柴(ㄢ ㄑㄩㄢ ㄏㄨㄛ ㄔㄞ)
a safety match

安全期(ㄢ ㄑㄩㄢ ㄑㄧ)
a safe period

安全期避孕法(ㄢ ㄑㄩㄢ ㄑㄧ ㄅㄧ ㄩㄣ ㄈㄚ)

rhythm method

安全系統(ㄢ ㄑㄩㄢ ㄒㄧ ㄊㄨㄥ)
the fail-safe system

安全設施(ㄢ ㄑㄩㄢ ㄕㄜ ㄕ)
safety devices (or equipment, installations)

安全操作(ㄢ ㄑㄩㄢ ㄘㄠ ㄗㄨㄛ)
safe operation

安全措施(ㄢ ㄑㄩㄢ ㄘㄨㄛ ㄕ)
safety measures (or precautions)

安全存量(ㄢ ㄑㄩㄢ ㄘㄨㄣ ㄌㄧㄤ)
safety stock

安全因素(ㄢ ㄑㄩㄢ ㄧㄣ ㄙㄨ)
the factor of security

安息(ㄢ ㄒㄧ)
①to rest ②Parthia, an ancient country in W. Asia

安息年(ㄢ ㄒㄧ ㄋㄧㄢ)
a sabbatical year

安息香(ㄢ ㄒㄧ ㄒㄧㄤ)
benzoin

安息日(ㄢ ㄒㄧ ㄖ)
the Sabbath

安息油(ㄢ ㄒㄧ ㄧㄡ)
benzol

安歇(ㄢ ㄒㄧㄝ)
to retire for the night; to rest; to sleep

安閒(ㄢ ㄒㄧㄢ)
leisure; relaxation

安閒無事(ㄢ ㄒㄧㄢ ㄨ ㄕ)
to have no work or duties

安心(ㄢ ㄒㄧㄣ)
to have peace of mind; to be relieved: 聽到這消息,他就安心了。He was relieved at the news.

安詳(ㄢ ㄒㄧㄤ)or 安舒(ㄢ ㄕㄨ)
(said of one's manner) undisturbed; composed

安知非福(ㄢ ㄓ ㄈㄟ ㄈㄨ)
Who knows it isn't a blessing in disguise?

安置(ㄢ ㄓ)
①to put in a proper place: 請把行李安置好。Please put the luggage in the right place. ②to settle (people in need of employment, refugees, etc.)

安置費(ㄢ ㄓ ㄈㄟ)
settlement allowances

安枕(ㄢ ㄓㄣ)
to sleep in peace

安裝(ㄢ ㄓㄨㄤ)

to install (a device): 電話已
經安裝好了。The telephone
has been installed.

安插 (ㄢ ㄔㄚ)
to plant; to get a position
(for a person) in an organization: 老闆在公司裡安插了黨
探。The boss planted a stool
pigeon in the company.

安插親信 (ㄢ ㄔㄚ ㄑㄧㄣ ㄒㄧㄣ)
to put one's trusted fellows
in key positions

安史之亂 (ㄢ ㄕ ㄓ ㄌㄨㄢ)
the rebellion of An Lu-shan
(安祿山) and Shih Sze-ming
(史思明), 755—763 A.D.,
which shook the foundation
of the Tang Dynasty

安適 (ㄢ ㄕ)
peaceful and comfortable

安身 (ㄢ ㄕㄣ)
to find settled place for life;
to take shelter

安身立命 (ㄢ ㄕㄣ ㄌㄧ ㄇㄧㄥ)
to enjoy peace and stability
both physically and spiritually

安神 (ㄢ ㄕㄣ)
to calm or quiet down the
mind

安睡 (ㄢ ㄕㄨㄟ)
to sleep undisturbedly;
sleep soundly

安然 (ㄢ ㄖㄢ)
① safely ② peacefully

安然無恙 (ㄢ ㄖㄢ ㄨ ㄧㄤ)
completely uninjured; completely free from trouble;
safe and sound

安如磐石 (ㄢ ㄖㄨ ㄆㄢ ㄕ)
as solid as a rock: 這城堡安
如磐石。The castle is as solid
as a rock.

安如泰山 (ㄢ ㄖㄨ ㄊㄞ ㄕㄢ)
(literally) as secure as Mt.
Tai—not in the slightest
danger

安葬 (ㄢ ㄗㄤ)
to bury (the dead); to inter:
他昨天安葬。He was buried
yesterday.

安坐 (ㄢ ㄗㄨㄛ)
to sit idly (without making
any effort)

安詳 (ㄢ ㄒㄧㄤ)
peaceful and serene

安穩穩 (ㄢ ㄨㄣ ㄨㄣ) or 安穩 (ㄢ

ㄨㄣ)
secure and stable

安逸 (ㄢ ㄧ)
ease and comfort

安營 (ㄢ ㄧㄥ)
(said of troops) to bivouac:
士兵在那兒安營至天明。The
soldiers bivouacked there
until morning.

安營紮寨 (ㄢ ㄧㄥ ㄓㄚ ㄓㄞ)
to pitch a camp; to camp

安危 (ㄢ ㄨㄟ)
security and danger

安危與共 (ㄢ ㄨㄟ ㄩ ㄍㄨㄥ)
to stick together in security
as well as in danger

安慰 (ㄢ ㄨㄟ)
to console; to comfort; to
soothe; to show sympathy
for

安穩 (ㄢ ㄨㄣ)
① smoothly: 船走得很安穩。
The boat sailed smoothly. ②
peacefully: 他睡得很安穩。
He slept peacefully.

安於 (ㄢ ㄩ)
to be content with; to be
satisfied with: 我們安於現狀。
We are content with things
as they are.

四畫

【宋】 1106 ㄙㄨㄥ song sòng
1. the Sung Dynasty (960-
1279A.D.); of, or having to
do with the Sung Dynasty
2. a state in the Warring
States period
3. a Chinese family name

宋本 (ㄙㄨㄥ ㄅㄣ)
a copy (of a book) printed
in the Sung Dynasty

宋體字 (ㄙㄨㄥ ㄊㄧ ㄗ)
the form of characters prevalent since the Sung Dynasty
now used for a printing
type

宋學 (ㄙㄨㄥ ㄒㄩㄝ)
the philosophical theories of
the scholars of the Sung
Dynasty, especially those of
Cheng Yi (程頤), Cheng Hao
(程顥) and Chu Hsi (朱熹)

宋朝 (ㄙㄨㄥ ㄔㄠ)
the Sung Dynasty (960-1279
A.D.)

宋史 (ㄙㄨㄥ ㄕ)
the *Annals of the Sung
Dynasty* (one of the *Twenty-
Four Books of History*)

宋儒 (ㄙㄨㄥ ㄖㄨ)
philosophers of the Sung
Dynasty

宋詞 (ㄙㄨㄥ ㄘ)
the poetry of the Sung
Dynasty (characterized by
lines of irregular length)

【完】 1107
ㄨㄢ wan wán
1. to finish; to complete; to
bring to a conclusion
2. to run out; to use up
3. whole; complete; perfect;
intact: 覆巢之下無完卵。When
a bird's nest is overturned,
no egg can remain complete.
4. a Chinese family name

完備 (ㄨㄢ ㄅㄟ)
complete with everything;
having nothing short

完畢 (ㄨㄢ ㄅㄧ)
finished; completed: 第二期工
程已經完畢。The second
phase of the project has
been completed.

完整 (ㄨㄢ ㄓㄥ)
① something undamaged or
intact ② virginity

完璧歸趙 (ㄨㄢ ㄅㄧ ㄍㄨㄟ ㄓㄠ)
to return something intact
to its owner

完美 (ㄨㄢ ㄇㄟ)
perfect

完美主義 (ㄨㄢ ㄇㄟ ㄓㄨ ㄧ)
perfectionism

完滿 (ㄨㄢ ㄇㄢ)
(said of meetings, negotiations, etc.) satisfactory; successful: 這會議完滿結束。The
conference came to a satisfactory close.

完膚 (ㄨㄢ ㄈㄨ)
unhurt skin; unscathed skin

完蛋 (ㄨㄢ ㄉㄢ)
(colloquial) ruined; busted;
done for: 我們看到那爆炸時以
為他完蛋了。When we saw
the explosion, we thought he
was done for.

完了 (ㄨㄢ ·ㄌㄜ)
finished; completed; over:
你已將你的工作做完了嗎?
Have you finished your

【宀部】

work? ② hopeless; doomed

完糧(ㄨㄢˊㄌㄧㄤˊ)
to pay farm tax

完稿(ㄨㄢˊㄍㄠˇ)
to finish a piece of writing;
to complete the manuscript

完工(ㄨㄢˊㄍㄨㄥ)or完竣(ㄨㄢˊㄐㄩㄣˋ)
(said of work, especially of
construction work) finished
or completed

完好(ㄨㄢˊㄏㄠˇ)
flawless; faultless; perfect; in
good condition: 瓷器已到，完
好無損。The porcelain has
arrived in good condition.

完好無缺(ㄨㄢˊㄏㄠˇㄨˊㄑㄩㄝ)
intact; undamaged

完婚(ㄨㄢˊㄏㄨㄣ)or完姻(ㄨㄢˊㄧㄣ)
to get married

完結(ㄨㄢˊㄐㄧㄝˊ)
to come to an end; to end

完聚(ㄨㄢˊㄐㄩˋ)
(said of all members of the
family) to get together

完清(ㄨㄢˊㄑㄧㄥ)
to clear off (accounts)

完全(ㄨㄢˊㄑㄩㄢˊ)or完完全全(ㄨㄢˊㄨㄢˊㄑㄩㄢˊㄑㄩㄢˊ)
complete; entire; perfect;
thorough; completely; entirely; fully; totally; thoroughly: 她完全同意我們的意見。She
fully agrees with us

完全獨佔(ㄨㄢˊㄑㄩㄢˊㄉㄨˊㄓㄢˋ)
complete monopoly

完全燃燒(ㄨㄢˊㄑㄩㄢˊㄖㄢˊㄕㄠ)
complete combustion

完全責任(ㄨㄢˊㄑㄩㄢˊㄗㄜˊㄖㄣˋ)
full liability

完整(ㄨㄢˊㄓㄥˇ)
complete; whole; undamaged;
intact: 許多珍貴的歷史文物完
整地保存下來了。Many pre-
cious historical relics have
been preserved undamaged.

完成(ㄨㄢˊㄔㄥˊ)
to accomplish; to complete;
to fulfill

完成任務(ㄨㄢˊㄔㄥˊㄖㄣˋㄨˋ)
to complete one's mission; to
accomplish a task

完事(ㄨㄢˊㄕˋ)
(of an affair) to be over; to
finish: 他們工作到深夜才完事。
They didn't finish their
work until late at night.

完善(ㄨㄢˊㄕㄢˋ)
perfect; immaculate; untarnished

完數(ㄨㄢˊㄕㄨˋ)
(mathematics) a perfect
number

完稅(ㄨㄢˊㄕㄨㄟˋ)or完納(ㄨㄢˊㄋㄚˋ)
to pay taxes

完稅憑證(ㄨㄢˊㄕㄨㄟˋㄆㄧㄥˊㄓㄥ)
(accounting) duty-paid proof

完稅貨價(ㄨㄢˊㄕㄨㄟˋㄏㄨㄛˋㄐㄧㄚˋ)
(accounting) price duty paid

完人(ㄨㄢˊㄖㄣˊ)
a perfect person; a paragon
of virtue

完案(ㄨㄢˊㄢˋ)
a case closed

【宏】 1108 ㄏㄨㄥˊ horng hóng
1. great; vast; wide; ample
2. a Chinese family name

宏辯(ㄏㄨㄥˊㄅㄧㄢˋ)
a well-supported argument:
他的宏辯獲得與會者的讚賞。
His well-supported argument
wins the applause of the
participants.

宏放(ㄏㄨㄥˊㄈㄤˋ)
broad-minded and unre-
strained

宏富(ㄏㄨㄥˊㄈㄨˋ)
rich; abundant

宏達(ㄏㄨㄥˊㄉㄚˊ)
learned; intelligent; knowledgeable

宏大(ㄏㄨㄥˊㄉㄚˋ)
great; grand; vast; immense

宏都拉斯(ㄏㄨㄥˊㄉㄨㄉㄚㄙ)
Honduras, a republic in NE
Central America

宏圖(ㄏㄨㄥˊㄊㄨˊ)
an ambitious plan

宏亮(ㄏㄨㄥˊㄌㄧㄤˋ)
(said of a voice) loud and
clear; sonorous

宏量(ㄏㄨㄥˊㄌㄧㄤˋ)
great generosity: 他的窮人之
宏量爲人所共知。His great
generosity to the poor is
well-known.

宏構(ㄏㄨㄥˊㄍㄡˋ)
a majestic building, monument, etc.

宏旨(ㄏㄨㄥˊㄓˇ)
the main theme; the leading
idea of an article: 愛國乃該
文之宏旨。Patriotism is the

main theme of the article.

宏儒碩學(ㄏㄨㄥˊㄖㄨˊㄕㄨㄛˋㄒㄩㄝˊ)
a learned person; an erudit
person

宏業(ㄏㄨㄥˊㄧㄝˋ)
a great achievement

宏揚(ㄏㄨㄥˊㄧㄤˊ)
to disseminate

宏偉(ㄏㄨㄥˊㄨㄟˇ)
magnificent; grand

宏願(ㄏㄨㄥˊㄩㄢˋ)
an ambition; an ambitiou
plan: 他的宏願是做一個大政治
家。His ambition is to be
great statesman.

五畫

【宕】 1109 ㄉㄤˋ dang dàng
1. a quarryman
2. to delay; to procrastinate
延宕 to procrastinate; to pu
off 懸宕 to keep unsettled
3. to dissolute

宕戶(ㄉㄤˋㄏㄨˋ)
a quarryman

【宓】 1110 ㄇㄧˋ mih mì
1. quiet; silent; still
2. a Chinese family name

【宗】 1111 ㄗㄨㄥ tzong zōng
1. an ancestor; a clan
2. a sect; a religion
3. to believe in
4. a Chinese family name

宗派(ㄗㄨㄥㄆㄞˋ)
①branches of a clan or a
religion ② schools of philosophy or academic learning

宗派活動(ㄗㄨㄥㄆㄞˋㄏㄨㄛˊㄉㄨㄥˋ)
factional activities

宗派主義(ㄗㄨㄥㄆㄞˋㄓㄨˇㄧˋ)
sectarianism; factionalism

宗派主義者(ㄗㄨㄥㄆㄞˋㄓㄨˇㄧˋㄓㄜˇ)
a sectarian; a factionalist

宗廟(ㄗㄨㄥㄇㄧㄠˋ)or宗祧(ㄗㄨㄥㄊㄧㄠ)
the ancestral temple (of the
ruling family); the imperial
ancestral temple

宗法(ㄗㄨㄥㄈㄚˇ)
the rules within a clan governing order of succession,
marriage, etc.

宗法社會(ㄗㄨㄥㄈㄚˇㄕㄜˋㄏㄨㄟˋ)
a society centered around

宗弟(ㄗㄨㄥ ㄉㄧˋ)
a clansman of one's generation who is younger than oneself

宗老(ㄗㄨㄥ ㄌㄠˇ)
the elders of a clan

宗教(ㄗㄨㄥ ㄐㄧㄠˋ)
religion

宗教派別(ㄗㄨㄥ ㄐㄧㄠˋ ㄆㄞˋ ㄅㄧㄝˊ)
a religious sect

宗教復興(ㄗㄨㄥ ㄐㄧㄠˋ ㄈㄨˋ ㄒㄧㄥ)
religious revival

宗教觀(ㄗㄨㄥ ㄐㄧㄠˋ ㄍㄨㄢ)
religious view of life

宗教界(ㄗㄨㄥ ㄐㄧㄠˋ ㄐㄧㄝˋ)
the religious world

宗教戒律(ㄗㄨㄥ ㄐㄧㄠˋ ㄐㄧㄝˋ ㄌㄩˋ)
religious taboo

宗教教育(ㄗㄨㄥ ㄐㄧㄠˋ ㄐㄧㄠˋ ㄩˋ)
religious education

宗教取向(ㄗㄨㄥ ㄐㄧㄠˋ ㄑㄩˇ ㄒㄧㄤˋ)
religious orientation

宗教信仰(ㄗㄨㄥ ㄐㄧㄠˋ ㄒㄧㄣˋ ㄧㄤˇ)
religious belief

宗教性(ㄗㄨㄥ ㄐㄧㄠˋ ㄒㄧㄥˋ)
religious character

宗教學(ㄗㄨㄥ ㄐㄧㄠˋ ㄒㄩㄝˊ)
the science of religion

宗教制度(ㄗㄨㄥ ㄐㄧㄠˋ ㄓˋ ㄉㄨˋ)
a religious institution

宗教哲學(ㄗㄨㄥ ㄐㄧㄠˋ ㄓㄜˊ ㄒㄩㄝˊ)
philosophy of religion

宗教史(ㄗㄨㄥ ㄐㄧㄠˋ ㄕˇ)
the history of religion

宗教裁判所(ㄗㄨㄥ ㄐㄧㄠˋ ㄘㄞˊ ㄆㄢˋ ㄙㄨㄛˇ)
the Holy Office or tribunal established during the period of Inquisition

宗教儀式(ㄗㄨㄥ ㄐㄧㄠˋ ㄧˊ ㄕˋ)
religious rites; ritual

宗教藝術(ㄗㄨㄥ ㄐㄧㄠˋ ㄧˋ ㄕㄨˋ)
religious art

宗教文化(ㄗㄨㄥ ㄐㄧㄠˋ ㄨㄣˊ ㄏㄨㄚˋ)
religious culture

宗親(ㄗㄨㄥ ㄑㄧㄣ)
① members of the same clan; people of the same ancestry ② brothers by the same mother

宗兄(ㄗㄨㄥ ㄒㄩㄥ)
① a clansman of one's generation who is older than oneself ② a polite designation for a friend with the same surname as oneself

宗校(ㄗㄨㄥ ㄒㄧㄠˋ)
a branch of the same clan

宗旨(ㄗㄨㄥ ㄓˇ)
purport; a purpose; an aim; an objective

宗主(ㄗㄨㄥ ㄓㄨˇ)
① a memorial ancestral tablet in ancestral shrine ② the eldest son begotten by one's legal wife 參看「庶子」

宗主國(ㄗㄨㄥ ㄓㄨˇ ㄍㄨㄛˊ)
a suzerain

宗主權(ㄗㄨㄥ ㄓㄨˇ ㄑㄩㄢˊ)
suzerainty; sovereignty; sovereign rights

宗師(ㄗㄨㄥ ㄕ)
one whose virtue and learning command the respect of others

宗室(ㄗㄨㄥ ㄕˋ)
① the imperial family ② the ancestral shrine of a large clan

宗人(ㄗㄨㄥ ㄖㄣˊ)
people of the same clan

宗子(ㄗㄨㄥ ㄗˇ)
the eldest son of one's legal wife

宗族(ㄗㄨㄥ ㄗㄨˊ)or宗類(ㄗㄨㄥ ㄌㄟˋ)
a clan; a paternal clan

宗祠(ㄗㄨㄥ ㄘˊ)
the ancestral temple or shrine of a clan 亦作「家廟」

宗仰(ㄗㄨㄥ ㄧㄤˇ)
to hold in esteem

【官】 1112

(ㄍㄨㄢ guān guàn)
1. a government official
2. of, or having to do with the government or the state
3. (biology) an organ
4. a Chinese family name

官罷(ㄍㄨㄢ ㄅㄚˋ)
the settlement of people's dispute by official mediation

官報(ㄍㄨㄢ ㄅㄠˋ)
a government journal; an official newspaper; a communiqué

官辦(ㄍㄨㄢ ㄅㄢˋ)
run or operated by the government; government-operated: 這份報紙是官辦的。This newspaper is run by the government.

官逼民反(ㄍㄨㄢ ㄅㄧ ㄇㄧㄣˊ ㄈㄢˇ)
The people are driven to rebellion by tyranny.

官婢(ㄍㄨㄢ ㄅㄧˋ)
the women drafted into lowly service by the government because of offenses

官兵(ㄍㄨㄢ ㄅㄧㄥ)
① officers and men (in the armed forces) ② government troops

官派(ㄍㄨㄢ ㄆㄞˋ)
to be appointed by the government

官賣(ㄍㄨㄢ ㄇㄞˋ)
government monopoly sale

官媒(ㄍㄨㄢ ㄇㄟˊ)
a jail matron

官迷(ㄍㄨㄢ ㄇㄧˊ)
one lured by the splendor of officialdom; an aspirant after government offices

官名(ㄍㄨㄢ ㄇㄧㄥˊ)
the title of a government position

官費(ㄍㄨㄢ ㄈㄟˋ)
the funds from public coffers

官費生(ㄍㄨㄢ ㄈㄟˋ ㄕㄥ)
a government scholarship student

官方(ㄍㄨㄢ ㄈㄤ)
the government (as opposed to private citizens); official (sources, information, etc.)

官方報告(ㄍㄨㄢ ㄈㄤ ㄅㄠˋ ㄍㄠˋ)
an official report

官方統計(ㄍㄨㄢ ㄈㄤ ㄊㄨㄥˇ ㄐㄧˋ)
official statistics

官方消息(ㄍㄨㄢ ㄈㄤ ㄒㄧㄠ ㄒㄧˊ)
news from government sources

官方組織(ㄍㄨㄢ ㄈㄤ ㄗㄨˇ ㄓ)
official organization

官方人士(ㄍㄨㄢ ㄈㄤ ㄖㄣˊ ㄕˋ)
official quarters

官俸(ㄍㄨㄢ ㄈㄥˋ)
the salary drawn from the government

官府(ㄍㄨㄢ ㄈㄨˇ)
① the local authorities ② a feudal official

官倒(ㄍㄨㄢ ㄉㄠˇ)
(in mainland China) an official or a cadre who abuses his power to line his pocket; an official profiteer

官邸(《ㄍㄨㄢ ㄉㄧˇ》)
an official residence

官田(《ㄍㄨㄢ ㄊㄧㄢˊ》)
government-owned farmland

官廳(《ㄍㄨㄢ ㄊㄧㄥ》)
a government office (or agency)

官能(《ㄍㄨㄢ ㄋㄥˊ》)
physical faculties (of a human being); body functions

官能心理學(《ㄍㄨㄢ ㄋㄥˊ ㄒㄧㄣ ㄌㄧˇ ㄒㄩㄝˊ》)
faculty psychology

官能障礙(《ㄍㄨㄢ ㄋㄥˊ ㄓㄤ ㄞˋ》)
functional disorder

官能症(《ㄍㄨㄢ ㄋㄥˊ ㄓㄥˋ》)
(pathology) functional disease

官吏(《ㄍㄨㄢ ㄌㄧˋ》)
a government official

官裏(《ㄍㄨㄢ ㄌㄧˇ》)
①a government office ② the emperor

官僚(《ㄍㄨㄢ ㄌㄧㄠˊ》)
bureaucrats

官僚機構(《ㄍㄨㄢ ㄌㄧㄠˊ ㄐㄧ ㄍㄡˋ》)
a bureaucratic structure

官僚政治(《ㄍㄨㄢ ㄌㄧㄠˊ ㄓㄥˋ ㄓˋ》)
officialism; bureaucracy

官僚主義者(《ㄍㄨㄢ ㄌㄧㄠˊ ㄓㄨˇ ㄧˋ ㄓㄜˇ》)
bureaucrat

官僚資本(《ㄍㄨㄢ ㄌㄧㄠˊ ㄗ ㄅㄣˇ》)
the capital controlled by government officials

官僚作風(《ㄍㄨㄢ ㄌㄧㄠˊ ㄗㄨㄛˋ ㄈㄥ》)
official red tape; a bureaucratic style of work

官股(《ㄍㄨㄢ ㄍㄨˇ》)
government-owned stocks (in an enterprise)

官官相護(《ㄍㄨㄢ ㄍㄨㄢ ㄒㄧㄤ ㄏㄨˋ》)
An official tends to defend another official subjected to criticism. 或 to side with one's associate

官話(《ㄍㄨㄢ ㄏㄨㄚˋ》)
①the language of officialdom ② Mandarin

官宦(《ㄍㄨㄢ ㄏㄨㄢˋ》)
the discipline of government officials

官家(《ㄍㄨㄢ ㄐㄧㄚ》)
①the emperor ② the government authorities

官價(《ㄍㄨㄢ ㄐㄧㄚˋ》)
an official price (as opposed

to a black market price)

官架子(《ㄍㄨㄢ ㄐㄧㄚˋ ˙ㄗ》)
the airs of an official; bureaucratic airs

官階(《ㄍㄨㄢ ㄐㄧㄝ》)
the rank (of a military officer or a civil servant)

官眷(《ㄍㄨㄢ ㄐㄩㄢˋ》)
the dependents of a government official

官軍(《ㄍㄨㄢ ㄐㄩㄣ》)
government troops

官腔(《ㄍㄨㄢ ㄑㄧㄤ》)
a bureaucratic tone; official jargon: 打官腔 to stall with official jargon

官銜(《ㄍㄨㄢ ㄒㄧㄢˊ》)
the formal title (of a government official)

官職(《ㄍㄨㄢ ㄓˊ》)
a government post or position: 他的官職頗高。His government post is rather high.

官制(《ㄍㄨㄢ ㄓˋ》)
the system of civil service

官箴(《ㄍㄨㄢ ㄓㄣ》)
maxims for government officials

官差(《ㄍㄨㄢ ㄔㄞ》)
① official business ② a government messenger

官娼(《ㄍㄨㄢ ㄔㄤ》)
a licensed prostitute

官常(《ㄍㄨㄢ ㄔㄤˊ》)
the duty of government officials

官場(《ㄍㄨㄢ ㄔㄤˇ》)or 官界(《ㄍㄨㄢ ㄐㄧㄝˋ》)
officialdom: 他對官場感到厭倦。He is tired of the officialdom.

官場現形記(《ㄍㄨㄢ ㄔㄤˇ ㄒㄧㄢˋ ㄒㄧㄥˊ ㄐㄧˋ》)
the title of a novel by Li Pao-chia (李寶嘉) of the Ching Dynasty, in which the author made sarcastic descriptions about the practices of officialdom

官事(《ㄍㄨㄢ ㄕˋ》)
①public affairs ②a lawsuit: 他官事纏身。He was involved in a lawsuit.

官式訪問(《ㄍㄨㄢ ㄕˋ ㄈㄤˇ ㄨㄣˋ》)
an official visit or call

官紳(《ㄍㄨㄢ ㄕㄣ》)
officials and the gentry

官聲(《ㄍㄨㄢ ㄕㄥ》)
(honest, or corrupt) reputation of an official

官商合辦(《ㄍㄨㄢ ㄕㄤ ㄏㄜˊ ㄅㄢˋ》)or 官私合營(《ㄍㄨㄢ ㄙ ㄏㄜˊ ㄧㄥˊ》)
jointly run or operated by the government and private citizens: 這個書局是官商合辦的。This bookstore is jointly run by the government and private citizens.

官書(《ㄍㄨㄢ ㄕㄨ》)
①official documents ②government publications

官署(《ㄍㄨㄢ ㄕㄨˇ》)
a government agency

官人(《ㄍㄨㄢ ㄖㄣˊ》)
①a holder of a government office; a government official: 官人把他拿去了。He was arrested by a government official. ②(in ancient China) my husband; your husband

官司(《ㄍㄨㄢ ㄙ》)
a lawsuit

官衙(《ㄍㄨㄢ ㄧㄚˊ》)
a government agency

官窰(《ㄍㄨㄢ ㄧㄠˊ》)
government-operated porcelain kilns of the Sung Dynasty

官癮(《ㄍㄨㄢ ㄧㄣˇ》)
the obsession to hold a government post: 他官癮很重。He has strong obsession to hold a government post.

官印(《ㄍㄨㄢ ㄧㄣˋ》)
an official seal of a government agency

官廕(《ㄍㄨㄢ ㄧㄣˋ》)
government offices conferred upon the offsprings of meritorious officials as a reward

官樣文章(《ㄍㄨㄢ ㄧㄤˋ ㄨㄣˊ ㄓㄤ》)
(literally) stereotyped writing characteristic of official communications, documents, etc.—something done superficially as a mere formality

官員(《ㄍㄨㄢ ㄩㄢˊ》)
an official

官運(《ㄍㄨㄢ ㄩㄣˋ》)
①a person's opportunity of official promotion ②government freight or cargo

官運亨通(《ㄍㄨㄢ ㄩㄣˋ ㄏㄥ ㄊㄨㄥ》)

to have a successful official career; to advance smoothly in officialdom: 郡位市長官運亨通。The mayor has a successful official career.

宙 1113 ㄓㄡ jow zhòu
infinite time; time without beginning or end; eternity

宙合(ㄓㄡ ㄏㄜ)
all embracing, or all encompassing

定 1114 ㄉㄧㄥ dìng dǐng
1. to decide; to fix; to settle
2. definite; sure
3. stable
4. to remain

定本(ㄉㄧㄥ ㄅㄣ)
①a definite foundation or basis ②a finalized version or definite edition (of a book): 四書定本the definite edition of the *Four Books*

定比定律(ㄉㄧㄥ ㄅㄧˇ ㄉㄧㄥ ㄌㄩ)
the law of definite (or constant) proportions

定聘(ㄉㄧㄥ ㄆㄧㄣˋ)
to betroth: 他們已經定聘。They are betrothed.

定評(ㄉㄧㄥ ㄆㄧㄥˊ)
a final judgement (as to the worth of a work, a person, etc.)

定名(ㄉㄧㄥ ㄇㄧㄥˊ)
to give a name; to christen; to dub

定命(ㄉㄧㄥ ㄇㄧㄥˋ)or 定數(ㄉㄧㄥ ㄕㄨˋ)
predestination

定命論(ㄉㄧㄥ ㄇㄧㄥˋ ㄌㄨㄣˋ)
determinism

定命論者(ㄉㄧㄥ ㄇㄧㄥˋ ㄌㄨㄣˋ ㄓㄜˇ)
a determinist

定單(ㄉㄧㄥ ㄉㄢ)
an order (for goods)

定點連續攝影機(ㄉㄧㄥ ㄉㄧㄢˇ ㄌㄧㄢˊ ㄒㄩˋ ㄕㄜˋ ㄧㄥˇ ㄐㄧ)
a slit camera

定都(ㄉㄧㄥ ㄉㄨ)or 定都(ㄉㄧㄥ ㄉㄨ)
to pick a city as capital after uniting the empire

定奪(ㄉㄧㄥ ㄉㄨㄛˊ)
to decide; to settle

定理(ㄉㄧㄥ ㄌㄧˇ)
(mathematics) a theorem

定力(ㄉㄧㄥ ㄌㄧˋ)
(Buddhism) strength of concentration

定例(ㄉㄧㄥ ㄌㄧˋ)
an irrevocable or unchangeable rule

定量(ㄉㄧㄥ ㄌㄧㄤˋ)
fixed amount; fixed quantity; to fix the amount or quantity

定量配給(ㄉㄧㄥ ㄌㄧㄤˋ ㄆㄟˋ ㄐㄧˇ)
rationing

定量分析(ㄉㄧㄥ ㄌㄧㄤˋ ㄈㄣ ㄒㄧ)
(chemistry) quantitative analysis

定論(ㄉㄧㄥ ㄌㄨㄣˋ)
an accepted argument (not questioned any more)

定率(ㄉㄧㄥ ㄌㄩˋ)
a fixed rate; a fixed ratio

定律(ㄉㄧㄥ ㄌㄩˋ)
(science) a law

定稿(ㄉㄧㄥ ㄍㄠˇ)
①to finalize a manuscript, text, etc. ②a final version or text

定購(ㄉㄧㄥ ㄍㄡˋ)
to order (goods, etc.); to place an order for something

定規(ㄉㄧㄥ ㄍㄨㄟ)
①an established rule or practice; a set pattern ②to be bent on; to be determined

定冠詞(ㄉㄧㄥ ㄍㄨㄢˋ ㄘˊ)
definite article "the"

定貨(ㄉㄧㄥ ㄏㄨㄛˋ)
to order goods; to place an order for goods

定貨單(ㄉㄧㄥ ㄏㄨㄛˋ ㄉㄢ)
an order form

定婚(ㄉㄧㄥ ㄏㄨㄣ)
to be betrothed

定計(ㄉㄧㄥ ㄐㄧˋ)
to devise a stratagem

定價(ㄉㄧㄥ ㄐㄧㄚˋ)
①to fix a price ②a fixed price; a list price

定見(ㄉㄧㄥ ㄐㄧㄢˋ)
a definite opinion; a fixed view

定金(ㄉㄧㄥ ㄐㄧㄣ)or 定錢(ㄉㄧㄥ ㄑㄧㄢˊ)
down payment; earnest money

定居(ㄉㄧㄥ ㄐㄩ)
to settle down

定局(ㄉㄧㄥ ㄐㄩˊ)
a foregone conclusion; an irreversible situation

定期(ㄉㄧㄥ ㄑㄧ)
①periodic; regular ②to fix a time or date (for some activity)

定期保險(ㄉㄧㄥ ㄑㄧ ㄅㄠˇ ㄒㄧㄢˇ)
term insurance

定期報表(ㄉㄧㄥ ㄑㄧ ㄅㄠˋ ㄅㄧㄠˇ)
(accounting) periodical statements

定期報告(ㄉㄧㄥ ㄑㄧ ㄅㄠˋ ㄍㄠˋ)
periodical reports

定期放款(ㄉㄧㄥ ㄑㄧ ㄈㄤˋ ㄎㄨㄢˇ)
time loans

定期付款(ㄉㄧㄥ ㄑㄧ ㄈㄨˋ ㄎㄨㄢˇ)
payment on term

定期抵押放款(ㄉㄧㄥ ㄑㄧ ㄉㄧˇ ㄧㄚ ㄈㄤˋ ㄎㄨㄢˇ)
fixed loans secured

定期刊物(ㄉㄧㄥ ㄑㄧ ㄎㄢ ㄨˋ)
a periodical (publication)

定期匯票(ㄉㄧㄥ ㄑㄧ ㄏㄨㄟˋ ㄆㄧㄠˋ)
a dated draft

定期交付(ㄉㄧㄥ ㄑㄧ ㄐㄧㄠ ㄈㄨˋ)
delivery on term

定期信用放款(ㄉㄧㄥ ㄑㄧ ㄒㄧㄣˋ ㄩㄥˋ ㄈㄤˋ ㄎㄨㄢˇ)
fixed loans unsecured

定期車票(ㄉㄧㄥ ㄑㄧ ㄔㄜ ㄆㄧㄠˋ)
a commutation ticket

定期存款(ㄉㄧㄥ ㄑㄧ ㄘㄨㄣˊ ㄎㄨㄢˇ)
a fixed deposit; a time deposit (T/D)

定期維修(ㄉㄧㄥ ㄑㄧ ㄨㄟˊ ㄒㄧㄡ)
periodic maintenance

定親(ㄉㄧㄥ ㄑㄧㄣ)
to betroth

定情(ㄉㄧㄥ ㄑㄧㄥˊ)
①to get married ②to fall in love

定限(ㄉㄧㄥ ㄒㄧㄢˋ)
①a fixed limit ②to set a time limit

定心(ㄉㄧㄥ ㄒㄧㄣ)
free of worries; confident; composed or calm

定心丸(ㄉㄧㄥ ㄒㄧㄣ ㄨㄢˊ)
something capable of setting someone's mind at ease

定向(ㄉㄧㄥ ㄒㄧㄤˋ)
to fix the direction; to orientate

定向儀(ㄉㄧㄥ ㄒㄧㄤˋ ㄧˊ)

〔宀部〕

a direction finder

定型（ㄉㄧㄥˋ ㄒㄧㄥˊ）
to finalize the design; already fixed or hardened (as opposed to formative or pliant)

定省（ㄉㄧㄥˋ ㄒㄧㄥˇ）
inquiry after one's own parents in the morning and evening

定性分析（ㄉㄧㄥˋ ㄒㄧㄥˋ ㄈㄣ ㄒㄧ）
(chemistry) qualitative analysis

定製（ㄉㄧㄥˋ ㄓˋ）
to have something made to order

定章（ㄉㄧㄥˋ ㄓㄤ）
fixed regulations or rules

定準（ㄉㄧㄥˋ ㄓㄨㄣˇ）
a fixed standard

定產（ㄉㄧㄥˋ ㄔㄢˇ）
a system of fixed quotas for grain production

定時（ㄉㄧㄥˋ ㄕˊ）
① to set time ② at fixed time

定時電路（ㄉㄧㄥˋ ㄕˊ ㄉㄧㄢˋ ㄌㄨˋ）
timing circuits

定時開關（ㄉㄧㄥˋ ㄕˊ ㄎㄞ ㄍㄨㄢ）
a time switch

定時控制（ㄉㄧㄥˋ ㄕˊ ㄎㄨㄥˋ ㄓˋ）
timing control

定時訊號（ㄉㄧㄥˋ ㄕˊ ㄒㄩㄣˋ ㄏㄠˋ）
timing signals

定時炸彈（ㄉㄧㄥˋ ㄕˊ ㄓㄚˋ ㄉㄢˋ）
a time bomb

定神（ㄉㄧㄥˋ ㄕㄣˊ）
① to compose oneself; to pull oneself together ② to concentrate one's attention

定然（ㄉㄧㄥˋ ㄖㄢˊ）
certainly; definitely

定則（ㄉㄧㄥˋ ㄗㄜˊ）
(science) a rule

定罪（ㄉㄧㄥˋ ㄗㄨㄟˋ）
to declare someone guilty; to convict someone (of a crime)

定做（ㄉㄧㄥˋ ㄗㄨㄛˋ）or 定製（ㄉㄧㄥˋ ㄓˋ）
to be made to order; to custom-tailor; tailor-made: 這件外套是定做的。This coat was made to order.

定額（ㄉㄧㄥˋ ㄜˊ）
a fixed amount or number

定案（ㄉㄧㄥˋ ㄢˋ）
① to decide on a verdict; to reach a conclusion on a case ② a verdict; a final decision

定義（ㄉㄧㄥˋ ㄧˋ）
a definition

定銀（ㄉㄧㄥˋ ㄧㄣˊ）
deposit money

定影劑（ㄉㄧㄥˋ ㄧㄥˇ ㄐㄧˋ）
(photography) a fixer

定位（ㄉㄧㄥˋ ㄨㄟˋ）
① a fixed position; a location; orientation ② to orientate; to position

定員（ㄉㄧㄥˋ ㄩㄢˊ）
a fixed number of staff members

【宛】 ¹¹¹⁵ ㄨㄢˇ woan wǎn
1. as if; as though
2. crooked; roundabout
3. a Chinese family name

宛轉（ㄨㄢˇ ㄓㄨㄢˇ）
(to persuade, explain, etc.) mildly and indirectly; tactfully

宛然（ㄨㄢˇ ㄖㄢˊ）
as if; as though; like: 這裡山明水秀，宛然江南風景。The scenery here has great charm, as though it were the land south of the Yangtze River.

宛如（ㄨㄢˇ ㄖㄨˊ）or 宛若（ㄨㄢˇ ㄖㄨㄛˋ）
as if; as though; like: 他爬樹宛如一隻貓。He climbed the tree like a cat.

宛若遊龍（ㄨㄢˇ ㄖㄨㄛˋ ㄧㄡˊ ㄌㄨㄥˊ）
(said of a woman's bodily movement) lithesome as a wandering dragon

宛延（ㄨㄢˇ ㄧㄢˊ）
long and winding (roads, lines, etc.); to meander: 一條小溪從山谷中宛延流過。A brook meanders through the valley.

【宜】 ¹¹¹⁶ ㄧˊ yí yí
1. right; fitting; proper; good
2. should; ought to; had better: 不宜操之過急。You should not act in haste.
3. a matter
4. to fit; to suit; to put in order
5. a Chinese family name

宜男（ㄧˊ ㄋㄢˊ）
(said of a woman) prolific

of male children

宜興壺（ㄧˊ ㄒㄧㄥ ㄏㄨˊ）
famous pottery teapot made in Yihsing, Kiangsu

宜室宜家（ㄧˊ ㄕˋ ㄧˊ ㄐㄧㄚ）
to make a harmonious and orderly home (used as congratulatory message on wedding)

宜然（ㄧˊ ㄖㄢˊ）
suitable

宜人（ㄧˊ ㄖㄣˊ）
pleasant; agreeable; delightful: 此地氣候宜人。The weather here is pleasant.

宜於（ㄧˊ ㄩˊ）
to be suitable for

六畫

【客】 ¹¹¹⁷ ㄎㄜˋ keh kè
1. a guest
2. a stranger; an alien; a foreigner: 笑問客從何處來。(賀知章·回鄉偶書) "Where do you come from, stranger?" they ask with a giggle.
3. a customer
4. a spectator; an audience
5. foreign; strange; alien
6. an adventurer
7. a Chinese family name

客票（ㄎㄜˋ ㄆㄧㄠˋ）
a free ticket

客滿（ㄎㄜˋ ㄇㄢˇ）
(said of theater tickets, etc.) sold out; a full house

客飯（ㄎㄜˋ ㄈㄢˋ）
meals sold at a fixed price per customer according to the quality of the dishes served

客房（ㄎㄜˋ ㄈㄤˊ）
a guest room

客地（ㄎㄜˋ ㄉㄧˋ）
a strange or an alien land

客店（ㄎㄜˋ ㄉㄧㄢˋ）or 客館（ㄎㄜˋ ㄍㄨㄢˇ）
an inn; a hotel

客隊（ㄎㄜˋ ㄉㄨㄟˋ）
(sports) the visiting team; the guest team: 客隊輸了。The visiting team lost the game.

客套（ㄎㄜˋ ㄊㄠˋ）
civilities; ceremonious greetings or compliments in ad

dressing one's guest

客堂(ㄎㄜ ㄊㄤ)
a parlor; a sitting room; a living room; a reception room

客題(ㄎㄜ ㄊㄧˊ)
a parlor; a living room

客離主safe(ㄎㄜ ㄌㄧˊ ㄓㄨˇ ㄢ)
The host gets some rest after the guests have left.

客觀(ㄎㄜ ㄍㄨㄢ)
objective (as opposed to subjective); not biased: 科學家必須客觀. A scientist must be objective.

客觀批評(ㄎㄜ ㄍㄨㄢ ㄆㄧ ㄆㄧㄥˊ)
objective criticism

客觀世界(ㄎㄜ ㄍㄨㄢ ㄕˋ ㄐㄧㄝˋ)
the objective world

客觀事物(ㄎㄜ ㄍㄨㄢ ㄕˋ ㄨˋ)
objective things (or reality)

客戶(ㄎㄜ ㄏㄨˋ)
a client

客貨船(ㄎㄜ ㄏㄨㄛˋ ㄔㄨㄢˊ)
a passenger-cargo vessel

客機(ㄎㄜ ㄐㄧ)
a passenger plane; an airliner

客家(ㄎㄜ ㄐㄧㄚ)
(literally) "guest families" which moved from northern to southern China during periods of invasions by the northern tribes in Chinese history—the Hakka people of South China; the Hakkas

客家話(ㄎㄜ ㄐㄧㄚ ㄏㄨㄚˋ)
Hakka

客居異地(ㄎㄜ ㄐㄩ ㄧˋ ㄉㄧˋ)
to be a stranger in a strange land

客氣(ㄎㄜ ˙ㄑㄧ)
sticking to the proprieties; polite; courteous; respectful

客氣話(ㄎㄜ ˙ㄑㄧ ㄏㄨㄚˋ)
polite remarks

客卿(ㄎㄜ ㄑㄧㄥ)
① a foreign-born government official ② one who works for an organization temporarily on guest status

客棧(ㄎㄜ ㄓㄢˋ)
an inn

客車(ㄎㄜ ㄔㄜ)
a passenger train or bus

客船(ㄎㄜ ㄔㄨㄢˊ)

a passenger ship; a liner

客串(ㄎㄜ ㄔㄨㄢˋ)
(said of an amateur actor or actress, etc.) to appear onstage for an impromptu performance; to be a guest performer; (said of an established actor or actress) to play unimportant roles for a promotional purpose

客舍(ㄎㄜ ㄕㄜˋ)
a hotel 參看「客店」

客商(ㄎㄜ ㄕㄤ)
a traveling salesman; a traveling businessman

客人(ㄎㄜ ㄖㄣˊ)
a guest

客座教授(ㄎㄜ ㄗㄨㄛˋ ㄐㄧㄠˋ ㄕㄡˋ)
a visiting professor

客座指揮(ㄎㄜ ㄗㄨㄛˋ ㄓˇ ㄏㄨㄟ)
a guest conductor

客死他鄉(ㄎㄜ ㄙˇ ㄊㄚ ㄒㄧㄤ)
to die away from home; to die abroad

客歲(ㄎㄜ ㄙㄨㄟˋ)
last year

客位(ㄎㄜ ㄨㄟˋ)
the seats reserved for guests

客運(ㄎㄜ ㄩㄣˋ)
passenger service, or passenger transportation

客運列車(ㄎㄜ ㄩㄣˋ ㄌㄧㄝˋ ㄔㄜ)
a passenger train

【宣】 1118
ㄒㄩㄢ shiuan xuān
1. to announce; to declare
2. to propagate; to circulate
3. a Chinese family name

宣佈 or 宣布(ㄒㄩㄢ ㄅㄨˋ)
to announce

宣佈獨立(ㄒㄩㄢ ㄅㄨˋ ㄉㄨˊ ㄌㄧˋ)
to declare independence

宣佈和約(ㄒㄩㄢ ㄅㄨˋ ㄏㄜˊ ㄩㄝˋ)
to announce a peace treaty

宣佈戒嚴(ㄒㄩㄢ ㄅㄨˋ ㄐㄧㄝˋ ㄧㄢˊ)
to declare martial law

宣判(ㄒㄩㄢ ㄆㄢˋ)
to announce the verdict: 陪審團宣判「無罪」. The jury announced a verdict of "not guilty".

宣撫(ㄒㄩㄢ ㄈㄨˇ)
to pacify or mollify (the people) by propaganda

宣導(ㄒㄩㄢ ㄉㄠˇ) or (ㄒㄩㄢ ㄉㄠˋ)
to guide (the people) by

creating a better understanding

宣讀(ㄒㄩㄢ ㄉㄨˊ)
to read out (a declaration, an announcement, etc.) in public

宣統(ㄒㄩㄢ ㄊㄨㄥˇ)
the reigning title of Henry Pu Yi, the last Manchu emperor of the Ching Dynasty

宣勞(ㄒㄩㄢ ㄌㄠˊ)
① (ㄒㄩㄢ ㄌㄠˊ) to comfort (people in distress) by an official message
② (ㄒㄩㄢ ㄌㄠˋ) to contribute one's labor, time and energy, etc. to a public cause

宣告(ㄒㄩㄢ ㄍㄠˋ)
to announce; to declare; to pronounce; an announcement; a declaration

宣告破產(ㄒㄩㄢ ㄍㄠˋ ㄆㄛˋ ㄔㄢˇ)
to declare bankruptcy; to go bankrupt

宣告成立(ㄒㄩㄢ ㄍㄠˋ ㄔㄥˊ ㄌㄧˋ)
to proclaim the founding of (a state, organization, etc.)

宣告死亡(ㄒㄩㄢ ㄍㄠˋ ㄙˇ ㄨㄤˊ)
a declaration of death

宣告無效(ㄒㄩㄢ ㄍㄠˋ ㄨˊ ㄒㄧㄠˋ)
to declare something null and void

宣揚(ㄒㄩㄢ ㄏㄨㄟˋ)
to preach; to deliver a speech; to orate

宣洩(ㄒㄩㄢ ㄒㄧㄝˋ)
① to reveal, disclose, or divulge (a secret) ② to drain (liquid)

宣洩洪水(ㄒㄩㄢ ㄒㄧㄝˋ ㄏㄨㄥˊ ㄕㄨㄟˇ)
to drain off floodwater

宣紙(ㄒㄩㄢ ㄓˇ)
the fine paper from Hsüancheng (宣城縣) in Anhwei Province, used especially for painting or calligraphic works; rice paper

宣召(ㄒㄩㄢ ㄓㄠˋ)
(said of an emperor) to summon a subject, etc. to an imperial audience

宣戰(ㄒㄩㄢ ㄓㄢˋ)
to declare war; a declaration of war

宣戰書(ㄒㄩㄢ ㄓㄢˋ ㄕㄨ)
a declaration of war

一部

宣稱(ㄒㄩㄢ ㄔㄥ)
to claim; to assert

宣傳(ㄒㄩㄢ ㄔㄨㄢ)
to publicize; to promote; (sales) propaganda; (sales) promotion

宣傳品(ㄒㄩㄢ ㄔㄨㄢ ㄆㄧㄣˇ)
propaganda material; promotion material

宣傳費(ㄒㄩㄢ ㄔㄨㄢ ㄈㄟˋ)
publicity expenses

宣傳電影(ㄒㄩㄢ ㄔㄨㄢ ㄉㄧㄢˋ ㄧㄥˇ)
public relations movies

宣傳隊(ㄒㄩㄢ ㄔㄨㄢ ㄉㄨㄟˋ)
a propaganda team

宣傳工具(ㄒㄩㄢ ㄔㄨㄢ ㄍㄨㄥ ㄐㄩˋ)
mass media; the instrument of propaganda or publicity

宣傳畫(ㄒㄩㄢ ㄔㄨㄢ ㄏㄨㄚˋ)
a picture poster

宣傳機構(ㄒㄩㄢ ㄔㄨㄢ ㄐㄧ ㄍㄡˋ)
a propaganda organ

宣傳週(ㄒㄩㄢ ㄔㄨㄢ ㄓㄡ)
the publicity week (for publicizing themes such as traffic safety, environmental sanitation, etc.)

宣傳戰(ㄒㄩㄢ ㄔㄨㄢ ㄓㄢˋ)
a propaganda war

宣傳車(ㄒㄩㄢ ㄔㄨㄢ ㄔㄜ)
a propaganda car

宣傳網(ㄒㄩㄢ ㄔㄨㄢ ㄨㄤˇ)
a propagandary network

宣示(ㄒㄩㄢ ㄕˋ)
to make publicly known; to publish

宣誓(ㄒㄩㄢ ㄕˋ)
to take an oath

宣誓就職(ㄒㄩㄢ ㄕˋ ㄐㄧㄡˋ ㄓˊ)
(said of government officials) to be sworn in

宣誓書(ㄒㄩㄢ ㄕˋ ㄕㄨ)
a written oath

宣言(ㄒㄩㄢ ㄧㄢˊ)
a declaration; a manifesto

宣淫(ㄒㄩㄢ ㄧㄣˊ)
to engage in lascivious activities in public

宣揚(ㄒㄩㄢ ㄧㄤˊ)
to publicize and exalt

【室】 1119
ㄕˋ shyh shì
1. a room; an apartment; a home
2. wife

室內(ㄕˋ ㄋㄟˋ)

indoor

室內溜冰場(ㄕˋ ㄋㄟˋ ㄌㄧㄡ ㄅㄧㄥ ㄔㄤˇ)
an indoor skating rink

室內照明(ㄕˋ ㄋㄟˋ ㄓㄠˋ ㄇㄧㄥˊ)
interior illumination

室內裝璜 or 室內裝潢(ㄕˋ ㄋㄟˋ
ㄓㄨㄤ ㄏㄨㄤˊ)
interior decoration

室內設計(ㄕˋ ㄋㄟˋ ㄕㄜˋ ㄐㄧˋ)
interior design

室內遊戲(ㄕˋ ㄋㄟˋ ㄧㄡˊ ㄒㄧˋ)
indoor games

室內游泳池(ㄕˋ ㄋㄟˋ ㄧㄡˊ ㄩㄥˇ ㄔˊ)
an indoor swimming pool

室內音樂(ㄕˋ ㄋㄟˋ ㄧㄣ ㄩㄝˋ) or 室內
樂(ㄕˋ ㄋㄟˋ ㄩㄝˋ)
chamber music

室內運動(ㄕˋ ㄋㄟˋ ㄩㄣˋ ㄉㄨㄥˋ)
indoor sports

室女(ㄕˋ ㄋㄩˇ)
an unmarried girl; a virgin

室家(ㄕˋ ㄐㄧㄚ)
①a home; a family ②a married couple

家家之樂(ㄕˋ ㄐㄧㄚ ㄓ ㄌㄜˋ)
the connubial bliss

室人(ㄕˋ ㄖㄣˊ)
wife

室如懸磬(ㄕˋ ㄖㄨˊ ㄒㄩㄢˊ ㄑㄧㄥˋ)
(literally) The house is as empty as a hollow musical instrument.—as poor as a church mouse

室外(ㄕˋ ㄨㄞˋ)
outdoor (as opposed to indoor)

室外活動(ㄕˋ ㄨㄞˋ ㄏㄨㄛˊ ㄉㄨㄥˋ)
outdoor activities

室溫(ㄕˋ ㄨㄣ) or 室內溫度(ㄕˋ ㄋㄟˋ
ㄨㄣ ㄉㄨˋ)
room temperature

【宥】 1120
ㄧㄡˋ yow yòu
to forgive; to pardon; to be lenient

宥過(ㄧㄡˋ ㄍㄨㄛˋ)
to excuse a mistake

宥恕(ㄧㄡˋ ㄕㄨˋ)
to forgive; to pardon; to excuse

宥罪(ㄧㄡˋ ㄗㄨㄟˋ)
to forgive an offense; to pardon a crime

【宦】 1121
ㄏㄨㄢˋ huann huàn
1. a government official; the

government service
2. castrated

宦途(ㄏㄨㄢˋ ㄊㄨˊ)
a career as a government official (with its ups an downs)

宦囊(ㄏㄨㄢˋ ㄋㄤˊ)
savings from a career as a government official

宦官(ㄏㄨㄢˋ ㄍㄨㄢ)
a eunuch 亦作「太監」

宦海(ㄏㄨㄢˋ ㄏㄞˇ)
(archaic expression) offi cialdom; official circles

宦海浮沉(ㄏㄨㄢˋ ㄏㄞˇ ㄈㄨˊ ㄔㄣˊ)
the ups and downs in offi cialdom

宦遊(ㄏㄨㄢˋ ㄧㄡˊ)
to leave home and take up government employment

七畫

【宮】 1122
ㄍㄨㄥ gong gōng
1. a palace
2. castration

宮袍(ㄍㄨㄥ ㄆㄠˊ)
court robes

宮門(ㄍㄨㄥ ㄇㄣˊ)
a palace gate

宮燈(ㄍㄨㄥ ㄉㄥ)
a palace lantern (now used for an ornament)

宮殿(ㄍㄨㄥ ㄉㄧㄢˋ)
a palace

宮殿式建築(ㄍㄨㄥ ㄉㄧㄢˋ ㄕˋ ㄐㄧㄢˋ ㄓㄨˊ)
palatial architecture

宮廷(ㄍㄨㄥ ㄊㄧㄥˊ)
the living quarters of a monarch in his palace

宮廷服(ㄍㄨㄥ ㄊㄧㄥˊ ㄈㄨˊ)
court dress

宮廷政變(ㄍㄨㄥ ㄊㄧㄥˊ ㄓㄥˋ ㄅㄧㄢˋ)
a palace coup; a coup

宮廷藝術(ㄍㄨㄥ ㄊㄧㄥˊ ㄧˋ ㄕㄨˋ)
court art

宮廷外交(ㄍㄨㄥ ㄊㄧㄥˊ ㄨㄞˋ ㄐㄧㄠ)
boudoir diplomacy

宮女(ㄍㄨㄥ ㄋㄩˇ)
a court lady; a lady-in-waiting

宮禁(ㄍㄨㄥ ㄐㄧㄣˋ)
①the emperor's living quarters in his palace ②palace

taboos

牆《《ㄑㄧㄤ》
①palace walls ②the house of one's teacher (a term of respect)

闕《《ㄑㄩㄝ》
a palace (as seen from outside)

刑《《ㄒㄧㄥ》
castration as a punishment

城《《ㄔㄥ》
the imperial capital

室《《ㄕ》
a mansion ② wife

人《《ㄖㄣ》
①court ladies ②(in the Chou Dynasty) the official whose responsibility was to bathe the emperor

人草《《ㄖㄣㄘㄠ》
(botany) an amaryllis

娥《《ㄜ》
court ladies; ladies-in-waiting

【宰】 1123 [ㄗㄞˇ] tzae zǎi

to preside; to govern
to slaughter; to butcher
a Chinese family name

輔 [ㄗㄞˇ ㄈㄨˇ] or 宰衡 [ㄗㄞˇ ㄏㄥˊ]
a premier; a prime minister

輔之量 [ㄗㄞˇ ㄈㄨˇ ㄓ ㄌㄧㄤˋ]
the capacity to serve as prime minister

割 [ㄗㄞˇ ㄍㄜ]
①to cut up (meat) ②to partition or dismember (a country) ③to kill; to destroy; to slaughter

相 [ㄗㄞˇ ㄒㄧㄤ] or 宰輔 [ㄗㄞˇ ㄈㄨˇ]
a prime minister (in former times)

相之器 [ㄗㄞˇ ㄒㄧㄤ ㄓ ㄑㄧˋ]
the potentialities to be a prime minister; the talent for statesmanship

殺 [ㄗㄞˇ ㄕㄚ]
to slaughter; to butcher; to kill

肉 [ㄗㄞˇ ㄖㄡˋ]
to cut up meat; to chop meat

予 [ㄗㄞˇ ㄩˊ]
Tsai Yü, a disciple of Confucius, whose afternoon nap evoked severe admonition from the master

【害】 1124 [ㄏㄞˋ] hay hài

1. to injure; to hurt; to damage; to destroy
2. to kill
3. damage; injury; harm; detriment
4. a vital point

害病 [ㄏㄞˋ ㄅㄧㄥˋ]
to get sick; to fall ill; to be taken ill: 他突然害病了。He was suddenly taken ill.

害怕 [ㄏㄞˋ ㄆㄚˋ]
to be afraid of; to be scared of; to fear

害命 [ㄏㄞˋ ㄇㄧㄥˋ]
to commit murder

害鳥 [ㄏㄞˋ ㄋㄧㄠˇ]
injurious birds; vermin

害羣之馬 [ㄏㄞˋ ㄑㄩㄣˊ ㄓ ㄇㄚˇ]
(literally) a horse that troubles the whole herd—a public nuisance; a public enemy; a black sheep: 他是他家的害羣之馬。He was the black sheep of his family.

害喜 [ㄏㄞˋ ㄒㄧˇ]
pregnant

害羞 [ㄏㄞˋ ㄒㄧㄡ]
shy; bashful: 她有點害羞。She is rather bashful.

害處 [ㄏㄞˋ ㄔㄨˋ]
harm; detriment; disadvantages; shortcomings

害蟲 [ㄏㄞˋ ㄔㄨㄥˊ]
injurious or noxious insects

害人 [ㄏㄞˋ ㄖㄣˊ]
to harm or injure others; to inflict injury upon others; to involve others in troubles

害人精 [ㄏㄞˋ ㄖㄣˊ ㄐㄧㄥ]
a mischief-maker

害死人 [ㄏㄞˋ ㄙˇ ㄖㄣˊ]
to bring great trouble to others

害臊 [ㄏㄞˋ ㄙㄠˋ]
bashful; shy: 李先生害臊，不喜歡參加social交際會。Mr. Lee is shy and dislikes parties.

【宴】 1125 [ㄧㄢˋ] yann yàn

1. to entertain; to feast
2. leisurely; comfort; ease

宴客 [ㄧㄢˋ ㄎㄜˋ]
to entertain guests at a banquet

宴會 [ㄧㄢˋ ㄏㄨㄟˋ] or 宴席 [ㄧㄢˋ ㄒㄧˊ]
a banquet; a dinner party; a feast

宴會廳 [ㄧㄢˋ ㄏㄨㄟˋ ㄊㄧㄥ]
a banquet hall

宴集 [ㄧㄢˋ ㄐㄧˊ]
to gather together

宴居 [ㄧㄢˋ ㄐㄩ]
to lead a leisurely life

宴客 [ㄧㄢˋ ㄎㄜˋ]
to entertain (to dinner)

宴饗 [ㄧㄢˋ ㄒㄧㄤˇ]
(said of the emperor) to give a great dinner

宴安 [ㄧㄢˋ ㄢ]
to live in idle comfort; to feel happy, contented, or relaxed

宴安酖毒 [ㄧㄢˋ ㄢ ㄓㄣˋ ㄉㄨˊ]
to live in easy comfort and suffer its poisonous effect

宴爾 [ㄧㄢˋ ㄦˇ] or 宴爾新婚 [ㄧㄢˋ ㄦˇ ㄒㄧㄣ ㄏㄨㄣ]
the bliss of the newlyweds

宴遊 [ㄧㄢˋ ㄧㄡˊ]
a leisurely trip: 他們宴遊杭州。They made a leisurely trip to Hangchow.

宴飲 [ㄧㄢˋ ㄧㄣˇ]
to feast; to dine and wine 亦作「燕飲」

【宵】 1126 [ㄒㄧㄠ] shiau xiāo

night; dark; evening: 通宵 all night; throughout the night

宵禁 [ㄒㄧㄠ ㄐㄧㄣˋ]
a curfew (enforced at night for public order): 宵禁業已解除。The curfew has been lifted.

宵小 [ㄒㄧㄠ ㄒㄧㄠˇ]
thieves; evildoers: 他們捉到宵小沒有? Have they caught the thieves?

宵行 [ㄒㄧㄠ ㄒㄧㄥˊ]
to travel by night

宵征 [ㄒㄧㄠ ㄓㄥ]
a journey at night

宵中 [ㄒㄧㄠ ㄓㄨㄥ]
midnight

宵人 [ㄒㄧㄠ ㄖㄣˊ]
a mean person

宵衣旰食 [ㄒㄧㄠ ㄧ ㄍㄢˋ ㄕˊ]
diligent in discharging official duties

宵夜 [ㄒㄧㄠ ㄧㄝˋ]
a snack before going to bed

a midnight snack: 他睡前吃
宵夜。 He eats a snack before
going to bed.

【家】 1127
ㄐㄧㄚ jiā

1. home; house; household;
family; of a household;
domestic
2. a specialist (in any branch
of art or science): 科學家 a
scientist 政治家 a statesman
畫家 a painter

家破人亡 (ㄐㄧㄚ ㄆㄛ ㄖㄣˊ ㄨㄤˊ)
with one's home in ruins
and family members dead or
scattered (referring to situations resulting from great
disasters)

家貧如洗 (ㄐㄧㄚ ㄆㄧㄣˊ ㄖㄨˊ ㄒㄧˇ)
to be in extreme poverty: 他
們家貧如洗。 They are in
extreme poverty.

家僕 (ㄐㄧㄚ ㄆㄨˊ) or 家丁 (ㄐㄧㄚ ㄉㄧㄥ)
a servant (in a family)

家譜 (ㄐㄧㄚ ㄆㄨˇ)
a family pedigree; a family
genealogy; a family tree

家門 (ㄐㄧㄚ ㄇㄣˊ)
a family (viewed in the light
of its social standing)

家廟 (ㄐㄧㄚ ㄇㄧㄠˋ)
the ancestral temple or
shrine of a family

家母 (ㄐㄧㄚ ㄇㄨˇ)
my mother (used in a polite
conversation)

家法 (ㄐㄧㄚ ㄈㄚˇ)
①the law of the home;
domestic discipline; domestic
regulations ②the thoughts
or teachings of a teacher
passed down through generations of followers

家訪 (ㄐㄧㄚ ㄈㄤˇ) or 家庭訪問 (ㄐㄧㄚ
ㄊㄧㄥˊ ㄈㄤˇ ㄨㄣˋ)
a visit to the parents of
schoolchildren or young
workers

家風 (ㄐㄧㄚ ㄈㄥ)
a family tradition; the customs of a family: 「誠實」是
我們的家風。 "Honesty" is our
family tradition.

家父 (ㄐㄧㄚ ㄈㄨˋ)
my father (used in a polite
conversation)

家道 (ㄐㄧㄚ ㄉㄠˋ)

①financial condition of the
family; a family livelihood
②principle of homemaking

家道小康 (ㄐㄧㄚ ㄉㄠˋ ㄒㄧㄠˇ ㄎㄤ)
to be comfortably off

家道中落 (ㄐㄧㄚ ㄉㄠˋ ㄓㄨㄥ ㄌㄨㄛˋ)
to suffer a fall in one's family fortune

家當 (ㄐㄧㄚ ㄉㄤˋ)
the belongings of a family;
family property

家底 (ㄐㄧㄚ ㄉㄧˇ)
the family property ac-
cumulated over a long time;
resources

家電用品 (ㄐㄧㄚ ㄉㄧㄢˋ ㄩㄥˋ ㄆㄧㄣˇ)
home appliances; electric
appliances

家天下 (ㄐㄧㄚ ㄊㄧㄢ ㄒㄧㄚˋ)
All the world belongs to the
ruling house.—monopoly of
power by members of a
single family

家庭 (ㄐㄧㄚ ㄊㄧㄥˊ)
a home; a household: 我們有
一個舒適的小家庭。 We have a
comfortable little home.

家庭背景 (ㄐㄧㄚ ㄊㄧㄥˊ ㄅㄟˋ ㄐㄧㄥˇ)
family background

家庭負擔 (ㄐㄧㄚ ㄊㄧㄥˊ ㄈㄨˋ ㄉㄢ)
family responsibilities

家庭副業 (ㄐㄧㄚ ㄊㄧㄥˊ ㄈㄨˋ ㄧㄝˋ)
household sideline production

家庭地位 (ㄐㄧㄚ ㄊㄧㄥˊ ㄉㄧˋ ㄨㄟˋ)
family status

家庭觀念 (ㄐㄧㄚ ㄊㄧㄥˊ ㄍㄨㄢ ㄋㄧㄢˋ)
attachment to one's family

家庭工業 (ㄐㄧㄚ ㄊㄧㄥˊ ㄍㄨㄥ ㄧㄝˋ)
household industries: 我們並
不鼓勵家庭工業。 We don't
encourage household industries.

家庭計畫 (ㄐㄧㄚ ㄊㄧㄥˊ ㄐㄧˋ ㄏㄨㄚˋ)
family planning—birth control

家庭教師 (ㄐㄧㄚ ㄊㄧㄥˊ ㄐㄧㄠˋ ㄕ)
a tutor; a private teacher; a
governess

家庭教育 (ㄐㄧㄚ ㄊㄧㄥˊ ㄐㄧㄠˋ ㄩˋ)
home education; training at
home

家庭糾紛 (ㄐㄧㄚ ㄊㄧㄥˊ ㄐㄧㄡ ㄈㄣ)
a family quarrel; domestic
discord

家庭主婦 (ㄐㄧㄚ ㄊㄧㄥˊ ㄓㄨˇ ㄈㄨˋ)

a housewife: 她不善做家庭
婦。 She's a bad housewife

家庭出身 (ㄐㄧㄚ ㄊㄧㄥˊ ㄔㄨ ㄕㄣ)
family origin; the class status of one's family

家庭生活 (ㄐㄧㄚ ㄊㄧㄥˊ ㄕㄥ ㄏㄨㄛˊ)
home life; family life

家庭作業 (ㄐㄧㄚ ㄊㄧㄥˊ ㄗㄨㄛˋ ㄧㄝˋ)
homework

家庭溫暖 (ㄐㄧㄚ ㄊㄧㄥˊ ㄨㄣ ㄋㄨㄢˇ)
family love

家徒壁立 (ㄐㄧㄚ ㄊㄨˊ ㄅㄧˋ ㄌㄧˋ) or
徒四壁 (ㄊㄨˊ ㄙˋ ㄅㄧˋ)
(literally) There stand on
the walls of the house
—extremely poor

家僮 (ㄐㄧㄚ ㄊㄨㄥˊ)
a young male domestic servant

家奴 (ㄐㄧㄚ ㄋㄨˊ)
a domestic servant; a family
slave

家累 (ㄐㄧㄚ ㄌㄟˋ)
the family as a burden;
family burden

家裏 (ㄐㄧㄚ ㄌㄧˇ)
①a home ②my wife

家規 (ㄐㄧㄚ ㄍㄨㄟ)
family rules: 我們家規甚嚴。
Our family rules are very
strict.

家和萬事興 (ㄐㄧㄚ ㄏㄜˊ ㄨㄢˋ ㄕˋ ㄒㄧㄥ)
Harmony in the family is
the basis for success in any
undertaking.

家伙 or 傢伙 (ㄐㄧㄚ ·ㄏㄨㄛ)
(colloquial) ①furniture;
tool; a utensil; a weapon ②
a fellow; a guy

家給人足 (ㄐㄧㄚ ㄐㄧˇ ㄖㄣˊ ㄗㄨˊ)
(descriptive of an affluent
society) Homes have ade-
quate supplies and people
live in contentment.

家計 (ㄐㄧㄚ ㄐㄧˋ)
a family livelihood

家祭 (ㄐㄧㄚ ㄐㄧˋ)
a funeral service attended
by the members of the
bereaved family

家家戶戶 (ㄐㄧㄚ ㄐㄧㄚ ㄏㄨˋ ㄏㄨˋ)
every family and household:
我們要做到家家戶戶有有餘糧。
We want to ensure that
every household has surplus
grain.

家家有本難念的經 (ㄐㄧㄚ ㄐㄧㄚ

家（ㄐㄧㄚ）

Every family has some sort of trouble. 或 Each family has its own hard nut to crack.

家教（ㄐㄧㄚ ㄐㄧㄠ）
①family education ②a private teacher; a tutor

家境（ㄐㄧㄚ ㄐㄧㄥˋ）
the financial condition of a family

家境困難（ㄐㄧㄚ ㄐㄧㄥˋ ㄎㄨㄣˋ ㄋㄢˊ）
with one's family in straitened circumstances

家境好（ㄐㄧㄚ ㄐㄧㄥˋ ㄏㄠˇ）
to come from a well-to-do family

家具 or 家俱（ㄐㄧㄚ ㄐㄩˋ）
furniture

家眷（ㄐㄧㄚ ㄐㄩㄢˋ）
one's family; one's dependents

家雀兒（ㄐㄧㄚ ㄑㄧㄠˇ ㄦ）
a sparrow

家禽（ㄐㄧㄚ ㄑㄧㄣˊ）
domestic fowls; poultry

家慶（ㄐㄧㄚ ㄑㄧㄥˋ）
a happy event of a family

家系（ㄐㄧㄚ ㄒㄧˋ）
lineage

家小（ㄐㄧㄚ ㄒㄧㄠˇ）
my wife and children (used in polite speech)

家信（ㄐㄧㄚ ㄒㄧㄣˋ）or 家書（ㄐㄧㄚ ㄕㄨ）
a letter from home or addressed to a member of the family: 你何時接到家信？ When did you receive the letter from home?

家鄉（ㄐㄧㄚ ㄒㄧㄤ）
one's hometown; one's native heath

家鄉話（ㄐㄧㄚ ㄒㄧㄤ ㄏㄨㄚˋ）
the native dialect

家學淵源（ㄐㄧㄚ ㄒㄩㄝˊ ㄩㄢ ㄩㄢˊ）
(from) a family of scholars

家訓（ㄐㄧㄚ ㄒㄩㄣˋ）
family precepts

家兄（ㄐㄧㄚ ㄒㄩㄥ）
my elder brother (used in polite speech)

家宅（ㄐㄧㄚ ㄓㄞˊ）
a family dwelling

家珍（ㄐㄧㄚ ㄓㄣ）
family treasure or heirlooms

家長（ㄐㄧㄚ ㄓㄤˇ）
the head of a family or household

家政（ㄐㄧㄚ ㄓㄥˋ）
①housekeeping ②home economics: 她主修家政。She is a home economics major.

家政學校（ㄐㄧㄚ ㄓㄥˋ ㄒㄩㄝˊ ㄒㄧㄠˋ）
a school of home economics

家主婆（ㄐㄧㄚ ㄓㄨˇ ㄆㄛˊ）
(Soochow dialect) wife

家主公（ㄐㄧㄚ ㄓㄨˇ ㄍㄨㄥ）
(Soochow dialect) husband

家醜（ㄐㄧㄚ ㄔㄡˇ）
a family scandal; the skeleton in the cupboard (or closet)

家醜不可外揚（ㄐㄧㄚ ㄔㄡˇ ㄅㄨˋ ㄎㄜˇ ㄨㄞˋ ㄧㄤˊ）
Domestic scandals should not be publicized. 或 Don't wash your dirty linen in public.

家產（ㄐㄧㄚ ㄔㄢˇ）
family property

家常（ㄐㄧㄚ ㄔㄤˊ）
the daily life of a family; domestic trivia: 他們常一起話家常。They often talk about domestic trivia together.

家常便飯（ㄐㄧㄚ ㄔㄤˊ ㄅㄧㄢˋ ㄈㄢˋ）
①an ordinary plain meal (such as one normally eats at home); potluck ②a common occurrence; routine

家常話（ㄐㄧㄚ ㄔㄤˊ ㄏㄨㄚˋ）
a conversation about domestic routine; an ordinary conversation

家畜（ㄐㄧㄚ ㄔㄨˋ）
livestock; domestic animals

家傳（ㄐㄧㄚ ㄔㄨㄢˊ）
a family heritage; a family trait

家傳秘方（ㄐㄧㄚ ㄔㄨㄢˊ ㄇㄧˋ ㄈㄤ）
a secret recipe handed down in the family 亦作「祖傳秘方」

家世（ㄐㄧㄚ ㄕˋ）
one's descent or origin, one's family background

家室（ㄐㄧㄚ ㄕˋ）
one's dependents

家事（ㄐㄧㄚ ㄕˋ）
household affairs; housekeeping; housework; domestic chores

家聲（ㄐㄧㄚ ㄕㄥ）

family reputation

家書抵萬金（ㄐㄧㄚ ㄕㄨ ㄉㄧˇ ㄨㄢˋ ㄐㄧㄣ）
A letter from home is worth ten thousand pieces of gold.

家塾（ㄐㄧㄚ ㄕㄨˊ）
a family school

家屬（ㄐㄧㄚ ㄕㄨˇ）
one's family or dependents: 她有十位家屬。She has ten dependents.

家人（ㄐㄧㄚ ㄖㄣˊ）
the members of one's family

家賊（ㄐㄧㄚ ㄗㄟˊ）
a thief working from within

家賊難防（ㄐㄧㄚ ㄗㄟˊ ㄋㄢˊ ㄈㄤˊ）
Thieves within a household are hard to guard against. 或 It's difficult to guard against traitors.

家族（ㄐㄧㄚ ㄗㄨˊ）
a family; a clan

家族公司（ㄐㄧㄚ ㄗㄨˊ ㄍㄨㄥ ㄙ）
a family company

家慈（ㄐㄧㄚ ㄘˊ）
my mother (used in polite speech) 亦作「家母」

家廟（ㄐㄧㄚ ㄇㄧㄠˋ）
an ancestral temple or shrine

家財（ㄐㄧㄚ ㄘㄞˊ）
family property

家私（ㄐㄧㄚ ㄙ）
family property or wealth

家業（ㄐㄧㄚ ㄧㄝˋ）
family property

家嚴（ㄐㄧㄚ ㄧㄢˊ）
my father (used in polite speech) 亦作「家父」

家務（ㄐㄧㄚ ㄨˋ）
domestic chores; household affairs; housework

家喻戶曉（ㄐㄧㄚ ㄩˋ ㄏㄨˋ ㄒㄧㄠˇ）
known to every family and household; well-known; widely known

家園（ㄐㄧㄚ ㄩㄢˊ）
hometown; native heath

家用（ㄐㄧㄚ ㄩㄥˋ）
domestic expenses; family expenses; housekeeping money

家用電腦（ㄐㄧㄚ ㄩㄥˋ ㄉㄧㄢˋ ㄋㄠˇ）
a home computer

【辰】1128
ㄔㄣˊ　chén chén
1. an abode of the emperor

2. a large mansion
宸遊(彳ㄣˊ 一ㄡˊ)
an emperor on tour

【容】 1129
(ㄖㄨㄥˊ rong róng)
1. a face; an expression; a countenance
2. to contain; to hold
3. to allow; to permit
4. to forgive; to pardon
5. to forbear; forbearance

容不下(ㄖㄨㄥˊ ㄅㄨˋ ㄒㄧㄚˋ)
unable to contain, hold, accommodate or take in

容貌(ㄖㄨㄥˊ ㄇㄠˋ)
looks; a countenance; features: 永遠不要以容貌來取人。 Never judge a man by his looks.

容電器(ㄖㄨㄥˊ ㄉㄧㄢˋ ㄑㄧˋ)
a condenser

容圖後報(ㄖㄨㄥˊ ㄊㄨˊ ㄏㄡˋ ㄅㄠˋ)
We (or I) will return your kindness (help, generosity, etc.) at a later date.

容納(ㄖㄨㄥˊ ㄋㄚˋ)
①to contain; to accommodate ②to tolerate; to take in: 他不能容納不同意見。He can not tolerate different opinions.

容量(ㄖㄨㄥˊ ㄌㄧㄤˋ)or 容額(ㄖㄨㄥˊ ㄜˊ)
the capacity (of a container, reservoir, etc.): 這桶的容量有四夸脫。This can has a capacity of four quarts.

容光煥發(ㄖㄨㄥˊ ㄍㄨㄤ ㄏㄨㄢˋ ㄈㄚ)
to have a face radiant with well-being

容或有之(ㄖㄨㄥˊ ㄏㄨㄛˋ 一ㄡˇ ㄓ)
(The story or claim) may not be a pure fabrication. 或 There might be a grain of truth in it.

容積(ㄖㄨㄥˊ ㄐㄧ)
① floor space ② volume; cubic capacity

容器(ㄖㄨㄥˊ ㄑㄧˋ)
a container

容情(ㄖㄨㄥˊ ㄑㄧㄥˊ)
to be forgiving; to spare; to pardon

容膝(ㄖㄨㄥˊ ㄒㄧ)
(said of room) just big enough for the knees—a very small spot; a tiny nook

容限(ㄖㄨㄥˊ ㄒㄧㄢˋ)

(physics) tolerance; allowance

容許(ㄖㄨㄥˊ ㄒㄩˇ)
to allow; to permit: 如果時間容許，我會來看你。I will come and see you if time permits.

容受(ㄖㄨㄥˊ ㄕㄡˋ)
①to be able to contain ②to endure; to put up with; to bear

容身(ㄖㄨㄥˊ ㄕㄣ)
to find living space: 無他容身之地。There is no place for him in society.

容恕(ㄖㄨㄥˊ ㄕㄨˋ)
to forgive; to pardon; to excuse

容人(ㄖㄨㄥˊ ㄖㄣˊ)
to be tolerant or magnanimous

容人之過(ㄖㄨㄥˊ ㄖㄣˊ ㄓ ㄍㄨㄛˋ)
to be tolerant of other people's mistakes (wrongdoing, or weaknesses)

容忍(ㄖㄨㄥˊ ㄖㄣˇ)
to endure; to bear; to tolerate; endurance; tolerance; forbearance

容讓(ㄖㄨㄥˊ ㄖㄤˋ)
to make a concession; to yield; to give in: 我不肯容讓一步。I will not yield one step.

容易(ㄖㄨㄥˊ 一ˋ)
①easy; facile: 來得容易，去得快，Easy come, easy go. ②apt to; liable to

容顏(ㄖㄨㄥˊ 一ㄢˊ)
a facial appearance

八畫

【密】 1130
(ㄇㄧˋ mih mì)
1. dense; tight; thick: 雪下得很密。The snow was falling thick.
2. close; intimate: 他們是親密的朋友。They are intimate friends.
3. secret; confidential; hidden

密報(ㄇㄧˋ ㄅㄠˋ)
to send a secret message (or report); a secret message (or report)

密閉(ㄇㄧˋ ㄅㄧˋ)
airtight; hermetic

密閉管道(ㄇㄧˋ ㄅㄧˋ ㄍㄨㄢˇ ㄉㄠˋ)
a closed conduit

密不透風(ㄇㄧˋ ㄅㄨˋ ㄊㄡˋ ㄈㄥ)
hermetically sealed; tightl shut

密佈 or 密布(ㄇㄧˋ ㄅㄨˋ)
closely or densely spread over; densely covered b (clouds); (with secre agents, guards, etc.) every where

密碼(ㄇㄧˋ ㄇㄚˇ)
a secret code

密碼員(ㄇㄧˋ ㄇㄚˇ ㄩㄢˊ)
a cryptographer

密謀(ㄇㄧˋ ㄇㄡˊ)
to plan secretly; to plot; secret scheme; a plot

密密麻麻(ㄇㄧˋ ㄇㄧˋ ㄇㄚˊ ㄇㄚˊ)
very dense; close and numero ous

密訪(ㄇㄧˋ ㄈㄤˇ)
①to pay a secret visit ②t make investigation b; traveling incognito

密封(ㄇㄧˋ ㄈㄥ)
to seal tightly or securely

密封室(ㄇㄧˋ ㄈㄥ ㄕˋ)
a hermetically sealed cham ber

密封文件(ㄇㄧˋ ㄈㄥ ㄨㄣˊ ㄐㄧㄢˋ)
sealed documents

密電(ㄇㄧˋ ㄉㄧㄢˋ)
a confidential telegram; a coded telegram

密度(ㄇㄧˋ ㄉㄨˋ)
density: 水銀的密度比水大得多。Mercury has a much greater density than water.

密談(ㄇㄧˋ ㄊㄢˊ)
to hold a confidential tal or conference; to have a secret or close conversation to be closeted with; a secre conversation, talk or confer ence; a tête-à-tête

密探(ㄇㄧˋ ㄊㄢˋ)
a secret detective; a secret agent; a spy: 他僱了一名密探。He hired a secret detec tive.

密通聲息(ㄇㄧˋ ㄊㄨㄥ ㄕㄥ ㄒㄧˊ)
to secretly communicate with each other

密令(ㄇㄧˋ ㄌㄧㄥˋ)
a secret or confidential order

告(ㄐㄧㄠˋ《ㄠˋ)... inform (secretly); to tip off: 他密告他的朋友。He ...pped his friend off.

克羅尼西亞(ㄎㄜˋ ㄌㄨㄛˊ ㄋㄧˊ ㄒㄧ ㄧㄚˋ) Micronesia

函(ㄇㄧˋ ㄏㄢˊ) ... secret letter; a confidential letter

集(ㄇㄧˋ ㄐㄧˊ) concentrated; crowded together: 這是一個人口密集的城市。This is a thickly populated city.

集轟炸(ㄇㄧˋ ㄐㄧˊ ㄏㄨㄥ ㄓㄚˋ) mass bombing

集栽植法(ㄇㄧˋ ㄐㄧˊ ㄗㄞ ㄓˊ ㄈㄚˇ) close planting

...o adjoin; to be contiguous to: 這兩幢房屋密接在一起。The two houses adjoin.

件(ㄇㄧˋ ㄐㄧㄢˋ) confidential or secret documents: 他把密件鎖起來。He locked the confidential documents.

切(ㄇㄧˋ ㄑㄧㄝˋ) (said of relations, contact, etc.) close or intimate: 他們必須密切配合。They must act in close coordination.

切注意(ㄇㄧˋ ㄑㄧㄝˋ ㄓㄨˋ ㄧˋ) to pay close attention; to watch closely

西根(ㄇㄧˋ ㄒㄧ ㄍㄣ) Michigan, U.S.A.

西西比(ㄇㄧˋ ㄒㄧ ㄒㄧ ㄅㄧˇ) Mississippi, U.S.A.

西西比河(ㄇㄧˋ ㄒㄧ ㄒㄧ ㄅㄧˇ ㄏㄜˊ) the Mississippi River, U.S.A.

植(ㄇㄧˋ ㄓˊ) close planting; close sowing

室(ㄇㄧˋ ㄕˋ) a secret chamber; a hidden room

商(ㄇㄧˋ ㄕㄤ) to hold private counsel; to hold secret talks

宗(ㄇㄧˋ ㄗㄨㄥ) (Buddhism) the esoteric doctrine

蘇里(ㄇㄧˋ ㄙㄨ ㄌㄧˇ) Missouri, U.S.A.

爾頓(ㄇㄧˋ ㄦˇ ㄉㄨㄣˋ) Milton (1608-1674): 失樂園是約翰·密爾頓的傑作。*Paradise Lost* is John Milton's masterpiece.

密醫(ㄇㄧˋ ㄧ) an unlicensed doctor; a quack

密議(ㄇㄧˋ ㄧˋ) to hold a secret conference; to be closeted with; a secret conference; a confidential talk

密友(ㄇㄧˋ ㄧㄡˇ) a close friend; an intimate: 她是我唯一的密友。She is my only close friend.

密網(ㄇㄧˋ ㄨㄤˇ) a fine net—severe and exacting laws

密約(ㄇㄧˋ ㄩㄝ) a secret engagement or appointment: 他跟朋友有密約。He has a secret appointment with his friend.

密雲(ㄇㄧˋ ㄩㄣˊ) dense clouds

密雲不雨(ㄇㄧˋ ㄩㄣˊ ㄅㄨˋ ㄩˇ) It is extremely cloudy but no rain bursts yet. 或 The storm is still brewing.

【宿】1131　1. ㄙㄨˋ suh sù

1. to stay overnight; to lodge; to sojourn
2. long-harbored; long-cherished
3. of the former life; inborn; innate; destined
4. veteran; old
5. a Chinese family name

宿命(ㄙㄨˋ ㄇㄧㄥˋ) predestination

宿命論(ㄙㄨˋ ㄇㄧㄥˋ ㄌㄨㄣˋ) fatalism

宿頭(ㄙㄨˋ ㄊㄡˊ) an inn (or a place) to stop at for the night

宿老(ㄙㄨˋ ㄌㄠˇ) an old man (usually referring to a respectable old man)

宿根(ㄙㄨˋ ㄍㄣ) ①(Buddhism) the root of one's present lot planted in previous existence ②(botany) perennial roots; biennial roots

宿好 ①(ㄙㄨˋ ㄏㄠˇ) an old friend ②(ㄙㄨˋ ㄏㄠˋ) a predilection: 他對古典音樂有宿好。He has a predilection for classical music.

宿恨(ㄙㄨˋ ㄏㄣˋ) an old grudge; an old feud; long-harbored resentment; deep-rooted rancor

宿慧(ㄙㄨˋ ㄏㄨㄟˋ) innate intelligence

宿疾(ㄙㄨˋ ㄐㄧˊ) a chronic disease; an old complaint: 咳嗽是他的宿疾。Cough is his chronic disease.

宿將(ㄙㄨˋ ㄐㄧㄤˋ) a veteran general

宿昔(ㄙㄨˋ ㄒㄧˊ) ①the past; days gone by: 他心中滿懷宿昔之回憶。Memories of the past filled his mind. ②long-standing

宿志(ㄙㄨˋ ㄓˋ)or宿心(ㄙㄨˋ ㄒㄧㄣ) a long-cherished ambition or desire; one's heart's desire

宿主(ㄙㄨˋ ㄓㄨˇ) the host (of parasites)

宿世(ㄙㄨˋ ㄕˋ) former existence (by the Buddhist concept of life and death as a cycle)

宿舍(ㄙㄨˋ ㄕㄜˋ) a dormitory; living quarters

宿膳(ㄙㄨˋ ㄕㄢ) board and lodging

宿儒(ㄙㄨˋ ㄖㄨˊ) a learned scholar

宿賊(ㄙㄨˋ ㄗㄟˊ) an old experienced thief

宿醉(ㄙㄨˋ ㄗㄨㄟˋ) hangover: 他宿醉未醒。He hasn't recovered from the hangover.

宿業(ㄙㄨˋ ㄧㄝˋ) (Buddhism) karma

宿營(ㄙㄨˋ ㄧㄥˊ) (said of troops) to bivouac for the night

宿緣(ㄙㄨˋ ㄩㄢˊ) (Buddhism) causation or inheritance from previous existence

宿怨(ㄙㄨˋ ㄩㄢˋ) an old grudge; long-harbored resentment; an old feud

〔宀部〕

【宀部】

宿願(ㄙㄨˋ ㄩㄢˋ)
a long-fostered wish; a cherished hope; one's heart's desire: 到巴黎去玩是他的宿願。To take a tour to Paris is his cherished hope.

【宿】 1131
2. ㄒㄧㄡˇ shiow xiu
an ancient term for a constellation; an asterism

【宿】 1131
3. ㄒㄧˋ sheou xiu
night: 我們談了半宿。We chat till midnight.

宿夕(ㄒㄧˋ ㄒㄧˋ)
① a single night ② a short period of time

【寂】 1132
ㄐㄧˊ jyi jí
1. the death of a Buddhist monk or nun
2. quiet; still; serene; peaceful; desolate: 萬籟俱寂。All is quiet and still.

寂寞(ㄐㄧˊ ㄇㄛˋ)
lonely; lonesome

寂滅(ㄐㄧˊ ㄇㄧㄝˋ)
(Buddhism) calmness and extinction; nirvana

寂寥(ㄐㄧˊ ㄌㄧㄠˊ)
lonely; still; desolate; deserted: 他在陌生的人羣中覺寂寥。He was lonely among strangers.

寂寂(ㄐㄧˊ ㄐㄧˊ)
quiet; still

寂靜(ㄐㄧˊ ㄐㄧㄥˋ)
quiet; still

寂然(ㄐㄧˊ ㄖㄢˊ)
quiet; still; silent: 一切寂然。All is silent.

【寄】 1133
ㄐㄧˋ jih jì
1. to send; to transmit; to mail: 我寄給她一封航空信。I sent her a letter by air mail.
2. to entrust; to consign; to commit; to deposit

寄賣(ㄐㄧˋ ㄇㄞˋ)or 寄售(ㄐㄧˋ ㄕㄡˋ)
to consign (goods, etc.) for sale

寄費(ㄐㄧˋ ㄈㄟˋ)
postage: 一本書的寄費要多少呢? What is the postage for a book?

寄放(ㄐㄧˋ ㄈㄤˋ)or 寄存(ㄐㄧˋ ㄘㄨㄣˊ)
to place or leave (a thing) in (another's) custody; to

leave with; to leave in the care of

寄頓(ㄐㄧˋ ㄉㄨㄣˋ)
to place in safekeeping

寄託 or 寄托(ㄐㄧˋ ㄊㄨㄛ)
① to consign or commit (one's soul to God, emotions to writing, etc.) ② to leave with somebody; to entrust to the care of somebody

寄懷(ㄐㄧˋ ㄏㄨㄞˊ)
to express one's feeling (by literary means, etc.) or to consign one's emotions to (writing, etc.)

寄籍(ㄐㄧˋ ㄐㄧˊ)
to have one's home temporarily in another town, country, etc.

寄居人(ㄐㄧˋ ㄐㄩ ㄖㄣˊ)
a sender

寄居(ㄐㄧˋ ㄐㄩ)
to live temporarily (with a family, in a place, etc.)

寄情(ㄐㄧˋ ㄑㄧㄥˊ)
to give expression to one's feelings (through writing, etc.)

寄情詩酒(ㄐㄧˋ ㄑㄧㄥˊ ㄕ ㄐㄧㄡˇ)
to abandon oneself to wine and poetry: 李白寄情詩酒。Li Po abandoned himself to wine and poetry.

寄情山水(ㄐㄧˋ ㄑㄧㄥˊ ㄕㄢ ㄕㄨㄟˇ)
to abandon oneself to nature: 吾友寄情山水。My friend abandons himself to nature.

寄銷(ㄐㄧˋ ㄒㄧㄠ)
(accounting) goods-out on a consignment; shipment outward; consignment; consignment-out (outward); consignment sales

寄銷商店(ㄐㄧˋ ㄒㄧㄠ ㄕㄤ ㄉㄧㄢˋ)
a consignment store; a consignment business

寄信(ㄐㄧˋ ㄒㄧㄣˋ)
to send or mail a letter: 我已寄信給他。I have sent him a letter.

寄信人(ㄐㄧˋ ㄒㄧㄣˋ ㄖㄣˊ)
a sender

寄興(ㄐㄧˋ ㄒㄧㄥˋ)
to give vent to one's interest

寄食(ㄐㄧˋ ㄕˊ)
to live with another at his

expense; to live by eating another's table; to be a pa site

寄寓(ㄐㄧˋ ㄩˋ)
to live or sojourn (abroad etc.) for the time being

寄生(ㄐㄧˋ ㄕㄥ)
parasitism; to be a paras (on); to be parasitic (on)

寄生動物(ㄐㄧˋ ㄕㄥ ㄉㄨㄥˋ ㄨˋ)
a parasitic animal

寄生昆蟲(ㄐㄧˋ ㄕㄥ ㄎㄨㄣ ㄔㄨㄥˊ)
a parasitic insect

寄生植物(ㄐㄧˋ ㄕㄥ ㄓˊ ㄨˋ)
a parasitic plant

寄生蟲(ㄐㄧˋ ㄕㄥ ㄔㄨㄥˊ)
a parasite

寄人籬下(ㄐㄧˋ ㄖㄣˊ ㄌㄧˊ ㄒㄧㄚˋ)
to live in another's ho (either for protection or a dependent)

寄宿(ㄐㄧˋ ㄙㄨˋ)
to lodge (at anothe house); to take up lodgings in; to board: 你现 寄宿在何處? Where are lodging now?

寄宿學校(ㄐㄧˋ ㄙㄨˋ ㄒㄩㄝˊ ㄒㄧㄠ)
a boarding school; a reside tial college

寄宿生(ㄐㄧˋ ㄙㄨˋ ㄕㄥ)
a resident student

寄意(ㄐㄧˋ ㄧˋ)
to send one's regards

寄養(ㄐㄧˋ ㄧㄤˇ)
① to send a child to anoth family for temporary ca ② to depend on others for living

寄予(ㄐㄧˋ ㄩˇ)
① to place (hope, etc,) on to show; to give; to expres

寄語(ㄐㄧˋ ㄩˇ)
to send word; to convey message: 寄語友人報喜訊 Send our dear friends t happy news.

【寅】 1134
ㄧㄣˊ yn yín
1. the third of the twelve Te restrial Branches (地支)
2. a fellow officer; a colleagu
3. a horary term (for th period from 3 to 5 a.m.)

寅支卯糧(ㄧㄣˊ ㄓ ㄇㄠˇ ㄌㄧㄤˊ)or 寅吃 卯糧(ㄧㄣˊ ㄔ ㄇㄠˇ ㄌㄧㄤˊ)
(literally) to have consum

（一
部

n the present year the sup-
lies that belong to the next
-unable to make both ends
neet

寺(ㄕ·ㄣ)or 黃刻(ㄏㄨㄤ ㄎㄜ)
the period of the day from 3
.m. to 5 a.m.

he first month of the lunar
alendar

【寇】 1135
ㄎㄡˋ kow kòu
bandits; enemies; robbers；
to invade; to pillage; to
plunder

a Chinese family name

盜(ㄉㄠˋ ㄎㄡˋ)or 寇讎(ㄎㄡˋ ㄔㄡˊ)
兀 or 寇讎(ㄔㄡˊ ㄨˊ)
an enemy; a foe

九畫

【富】 1136
ㄈㄨˋ fuh fù
rich; wealthy; affluent; abundant; plentiful: 他出身於一個
富裕的家庭。He comes from a
wealthy family.
a Chinese family name

態(ㄈㄨˋ ㄋㄞˋ)
looking gentle and prosperous

農(ㄈㄨˋ ㄋㄨㄥˊ)
a rich farmer: 他是個富農。
He is a rich farmer.

麗堂皇(ㄈㄨˋ ㄌㄧˋ ㄊㄤˊ ㄏㄨㄤˊ)
majestic; grand; splendid;
gorgeous; magnificent; stately: 他住在一所富麗堂皇的房子
裡。He lives in a grand
house.

國強兵(ㄈㄨˋ ㄍㄨㄛˊ ㄑㄧㄤˊ ㄅㄧㄥ)
to make one's country rich
and to build up its military
power

貴(ㄈㄨˋ ㄍㄨㄟˋ)
wealth and high position
① Wealth and honor come
to us only of their own
accord. ② snobbish
貴不能淫(ㄈㄨˋ ㄍㄨㄟˋ ㄅㄨˋ ㄧㄣˊ)
to be impervious to the
temptation of wealth and
high position; utterly incorruptible

富貴利達(ㄈㄨˋ ㄍㄨㄟˋ ㄌㄧˋ ㄉㄚˊ)
rich and powerful

富貴花(ㄈㄨˋ ㄍㄨㄟˋ ㄏㄨㄚ)
a peony

富豪(ㄈㄨˋ ㄏㄠˊ)
a man of wealth and influence

富戶(ㄈㄨˋ ㄏㄨˋ)
a wealthy family

富家子(ㄈㄨˋ ㄐㄧㄚ ㄗˇ)
children of a wealthy family

富家翁(ㄈㄨˋ ㄐㄧㄚ ㄨㄥ)
a man of wealth; a rich man

富甲天下(ㄈㄨˋ ㄐㄧㄚˇ ㄊㄧㄢ ㄒㄧㄚˋ)
the richest in the world

富強(ㄈㄨˋ ㄑㄧㄤˊ)
(said of a state) wealthy
and powerful

富士山(ㄈㄨˋ ㄕˋ ㄕㄢ)
Mt. Fuji, the highest peak in
Japan

富商(ㄈㄨˋ ㄕㄤ)
a wealthy merchant

富庶(ㄈㄨˋ ㄕㄨˋ)
(said of land) plentiful and
populous

富孀(ㄈㄨˋ ㄕㄨㄤ)
a rich widow

富饒(ㄈㄨˋ ㄖㄠˊ)
plentiful; abundant; rich;
plenty; abundance: 這土地礦
產富饒。This land is abun-
dant in minerals.

富足(ㄈㄨˋ ㄗㄨˊ)
well-off; well-to-do: 他出身富
足之家。He came from a
well-to-do family.

富而好禮(ㄈㄨˋ ㄦˊ ㄏㄠˋ ㄌㄧˇ)
wealthy and courteous

富而無驕(ㄈㄨˋ ㄦˊ ㄨˊ ㄐㄧㄠ)
rich but not smug

富爾敦(ㄈㄨˋ ㄦˇ ㄉㄨㄣ)
Robert Fulton, 1765-1815,
inventor of the steamboat

富有(ㄈㄨˋ ㄧㄡˇ)
① to abound in; to team
with ② rich; wealthy

富翁(ㄈㄨˋ ㄨㄥ)
a rich man

富於(ㄈㄨˋ ㄩˊ)
rich in (imagination, creative capacity, etc.): 詩人富於
想像力。Poets are rich in
imagination.

富裕(ㄈㄨˋ ㄩˋ)
rich; wealthy; prosperous

【寐】 1137
ㄇㄟˋ mey mèi
a sound sleep; a deep sleep;
to doze; to drowse; to sleep

【寒】 1138
ㄏㄢˊ harn hán
1. cold; chilly; wintry
2. poor

寒毛(ㄏㄢˊ ㄇㄠˊ)
downy hair (on human
body)

寒門(ㄏㄢˊ ㄇㄣˊ)
① a poor family: 他出身寒
門。He came from a poor
family. ② my poor family (a
self-depreciatory expression)

寒風(ㄏㄢˊ ㄈㄥ)
a cold wind: 寒風自北方吹來。
A cold wind was blowing
from the north.

寒風刺骨(ㄏㄢˊ ㄈㄥ ㄘˋ ㄍㄨˇ)
The cold wind chilled one to
the bone.

寒帶(ㄏㄢˊ ㄉㄞˋ)
the Frigid Zone: 阿拉斯加屬
於寒帶。Alaska belongs to
the Frigid Zone.

寒來暑往(ㄏㄢˊ ㄌㄞˊ ㄕㄨˇ ㄨㄤˇ)
(literally) The cold comes
and the heat departs.—a
change of seasons; a lapse
of time

寒冷(ㄏㄢˊ ㄌㄥˇ)
cold; chilly; chilling: 他怕寒
冷。He is afraid of cold.

寒流(ㄏㄢˊ ㄌㄧㄡˊ)
① a cold current; polar currents ② a scholar of little
means

寒苦(ㄏㄢˊ ㄎㄨˇ)
poor; in financial straits;
destitute

寒劑(ㄏㄢˊ ㄐㄧˋ)
a freezing mixture

寒假(ㄏㄢˊ ㄐㄧㄚˋ)
the winter vacation: 寒假他
到日本去。He left for Japan
during the winter vacation.

寒賤(ㄏㄢˊ ㄐㄧㄢˋ)
of humble origin

寒噤(ㄏㄢˊ ㄐㄧㄣˋ)
a shudder; a shiver; a tremble: 他打了一個寒噤。A shiver
ran over his body.

寒氣(ㄏㄢˊ ㄑㄧˋ)
chilly air; cold air: 寒氣逼人。
There is a nip in the air.

（宀部）

寒心(ㄏㄢ ㄒㄧㄣ)
to feel the blood running cold; afraid; fearful: 他的無情令人寒心。His ruthlessness makes me afraid.

寒暄(ㄏㄢ ㄒㄩㄢ)or 寒溫(ㄏㄢ ㄨㄣ)
to talk about the weather (in a conversation); to exchange a few words of greeting with (somebody)

寒顫(ㄏㄢ ㄓㄢˋ)
to tremble with cold or fear

寒戰(ㄏㄢ ㄓㄢˋ)
a tremble caused by cold; to tremble with cold: 我們因冷而寒戰。We were trembling with cold.

寒窗(ㄏㄢ ㄔㄨㄤ)
the financial difficulties of a scholar

寒食(節)(ㄏㄢ ㄕˊ ㄐㄧㄝˊ)
the 105th to 107th day after the winter solstice, a period set aside in memory of Chieh Tsu-tuei (介子推), during which food is supposed to be eaten cold

寒士(ㄏㄢ ㄕˋ)
a scholar of little means; a poor scholar: 他是位寒士。He is a poor scholar.

寒舍(ㄏㄢ ㄕㄜˋ)
(a self-depreciatory term) my poor house

寒暑表(ㄏㄢ ㄕㄨˇ ㄅㄧㄠˇ)
a thermometer

寒傖(ㄏㄢ ㄔㄤ)
(colloquial) ① ugly; unsightly ② shabby; disgraceful ③ to ridicule

寒酸(ㄏㄢ ㄙㄨㄢ)
① poverty; poverty-stricken condition (especially referring to face-loving intellectuals) ② unpresentable (dress, gifts, etc.)

寒衣(ㄏㄢ ㄧ)
winter clothes

寒意(ㄏㄢ ㄧˋ)
a nip (or chill) in the air: 初春季節仍有寒意。It's spring but there's still a chill in the air.

寒夜(ㄏㄢ ㄧㄝˋ)
a cold night; a chilly night

寒微(ㄏㄢ ㄨㄟ)
of low station; of humble

origin: 他出身寒微。He is a man of humble origin.

【寓】 ㄩ yuh yù   1139
1. to live temporarily; to sojourn; to dwell
2. to consign

寓目(ㄩ ㄇㄨˋ)
to stare; to gaze; to look closely

寓託(ㄩ ㄊㄨㄛ)
to imply (meaning); to show (something) in parables or by indirect means

寓公(ㄩ ㄍㄨㄥ)
① a man of wealth living as an exile ② (formerly) a government official residing away from home

寓禁關稅(ㄩ ㄐㄧㄣˋ ㄍㄨㄢ ㄕㄨㄟˋ)
prohibitive tariff or duties

寓禁於征(ㄩ ㄐㄧㄣˋ ㄩˊ ㄓㄥ)
to try to prohibit a business by taxing it heavily

寓居(ㄩ ㄐㄩ)
to make one's home in (a place other than one's native place): 他晚年寓居美國。He made America his home in his old age.

寓所(ㄩ ㄙㄨㄛˇ)
one's residence or dwelling

寓意(ㄩˋ ㄧˋ)
a moral (of a fable): 這故事含有多種寓意。There is more than one moral to be drawn from this story.

寓意深刻(ㄩˋ ㄧˋ ㄕㄣ ㄎㄜˋ)
to be pregnant with meaning

寓言(ㄩˋ ㄧㄢˊ)
a fable; an allegory

十畫

【寘】 ㄓˋ jyh zhì   1140
1. to put; to place
2. to discard
3. to make or cause
4. full

十一畫

【寞】 ㄇㄛˋ moh mò   1141
still; silent; quiet; lonely

【察】 ㄔㄚˊ char chá   1142

to examine; to observe; investigate; to survey; study; to scrutinize

察辦(ㄔㄚˊ ㄅㄢˋ)
to investigate a case and determine how to handle

察破(ㄔㄚˊ ㄆㄛˋ)
to see through (a plot, trick, etc.)

察訪(ㄔㄚˊ ㄈㄤˇ)
to investigate by visiting sources of information

察看(ㄔㄚˊ ㄎㄢˋ)
to observe; to watch

察勘(ㄔㄚˊ ㄎㄢ)
to survey; to examine: 他勘房間。He examined

察哈爾(ㄔㄚˊ ㄏㄚ ㄦˇ)
Chahar Province

察核(ㄔㄚˊ ㄏㄜˊ)
to investigate a case and then decide what to do

察覺(ㄔㄚˊ ㄐㄩㄝˊ)
to be conscious of; become aware of; to perceive

察言觀色(ㄔㄚˊ ㄧㄢˊ ㄍㄨㄢ ㄙㄜˋ)
to gather another's frame mind through his words and expressions

【寧】 ㄋㄧㄥˊ ning níng   1143
1. peace; repose; serenity; tranquility
2. would rather; had rather
3. could there be

寧波(ㄋㄧㄥˊ ㄅㄛ)
Ningpo, a city in Chekiang Province

寧波幫(ㄋㄧㄥˊ ㄅㄛ ㄅㄤ)
the merchants from Ning (noted for their business acumen)

寧謐(ㄋㄧㄥˊ ㄇㄧˋ)
tranquil

寧非奇事(ㄋㄧㄥˊ ㄈㄟ ㄑㄧˊ ㄕˋ)
Isn't it strange that...?

寧可(ㄋㄧㄥˊ ㄎㄜˇ)or 寧肯(ㄋㄧㄥˊ ㄎㄣˇ)
would rather: 寧可信其有，可信且無。We'd rather believe it to be true than not.

寧靜(ㄋㄧㄥˊ ㄐㄧㄥˋ)
quiet; tranquil; serene; placid; calm

寧靜以致遠(ㄋㄧㄥˊ ㄐㄧㄥˋ ㄧˇ ㄓˋ ㄩㄢˇ)

to accomplish something
asting by leading quiet life
快毋濫（ㄅㄧㄠ ㄍㄨㄥ ㄨ ㄌㄢˋ）
t is better to leave a defi-
iency uncovered than to
ave it covered without dis-
retion.

夏（ㄋㄧㄚ ㄒㄧㄚˋ）
Ningxia Province

嬌兒（ㄋㄧㄚ ㄦˊ）
a lovely child

日（ㄋㄧㄚ ㄖˋ）
peaceful days

甯有內賊，不與家奴（ㄋㄧㄥˊ ㄧㄡˇ
ㄋㄟ ㄗㄟˊ，ㄅㄨˋ ㄩˇ ㄐㄧㄚ ㄋㄨˊ）
said of a dictator or war-
ord) would rather betray
he nation in order to keep
ersonal power than intro-
uce democracy

死（ㄋㄧㄥˊ ㄙˇ）
vould rather die: 他寧死不
屈 He would rather die than
surrender.

死不屈（ㄋㄧㄥˊ ㄙˇ ㄅㄨˋ ㄑㄩ）
vould rather die than sub-
nit (or surrender)

為鷄口，毋為牛後（ㄋㄧㄥˊ ㄨㄟˊ
ㄐㄧ ㄎㄡˇ，ㄨˊ ㄨㄟˊ ㄋㄧㄡˊ ㄏㄡˋ）
vould rather have a low but
ndependent position than
old a high position under
he control of others

為玉碎，不為瓦全（ㄋㄧㄥˊ ㄨㄟˊ
ㄩˋ ㄙㄨㄟˋ，ㄅㄨˋ ㄨㄟˊ ㄨㄚˇ ㄑㄩㄢˊ）
vould rather die for justice
han live in disgrace

願（ㄋㄧㄥˊ ㄩㄢˋ）
vould rather; would sooner

【**寡**】 1144
　　　　ㄍㄨㄚˇ goa guǎ
widowed; surviving the
spouse
lonely; alone; solitary
little; few; scant; rare: 失道
寡助。An unjust cause finds
scant support.

不敵眾（ㄍㄨㄚˇ ㄅㄨˋ ㄉㄧˊ ㄓㄨㄥˋ）
o be overwhelmed by sheer
number; to be overpowered
by the enemy's larger number

夫（ㄍㄨㄚˇ ㄈㄨ）
a widower 亦作「鰥夫」

婦（ㄍㄨㄚˇ ㄈㄨˋ）
a widow

斷（ㄍㄨㄚˇ ㄉㄨㄢˋ）

---

irresolute; indecisive: 他是個
優柔寡斷的領導者。He is an
indecisive leader.

寡頭（ㄍㄨㄚˇ ㄊㄡˊ）
an oligarch

寡頭政治（ㄍㄨㄚˇ ㄊㄡˊ ㄓˋ ㄓ）
oligarchy

寡陋（ㄍㄨㄚˇ ㄌㄡˋ）
ignorant; having seen little
of the world

寡廉鮮恥（ㄍㄨㄚˇ ㄌㄧㄢˊ ㄒㄧㄢˇ ㄔˇ）
shameless; unabashed; having no sense of morality

寡過（ㄍㄨㄚˇ ㄍㄨㄛˋ）
to discipline oneself (so as
to commit fewer and fewer
mistakes daily)

寡合（ㄍㄨㄚˇ ㄏㄜˊ）
having little intercourse
with others

寡歡（ㄍㄨㄚˇ ㄏㄨㄢ）
unhappy: 他獨處時落落寡歡。
He was unhappy when
alone.

寡見少聞（ㄍㄨㄚˇ ㄐㄧㄢˋ ㄕㄠˇ ㄨㄣˊ）
shallow; poorly informed;
ignorance

寡居（ㄍㄨㄚˇ ㄐㄩ）
to live as a widow

寡情（ㄍㄨㄚˇ ㄑㄧㄥˊ）
unfeeling; cold; cold-hearted;
heartless

寡人（ㄍㄨㄚˇ ㄖㄣˊ）
(the royal) we

寡恩（ㄍㄨㄚˇ ㄣ）
showing little favor; unkind

寡言（ㄍㄨㄚˇ ㄧㄢˊ）
taciturn; not given to talk:
他是個沈默寡言的人。He is a
taciturn man.

寡聞（ㄍㄨㄚˇ ㄨㄣˊ）
having little knowledge: 他
因寡聞而孤陋寡聞。Living
alone, he is ill-informed.

寡慾（ㄍㄨㄚˇ ㄩˋ）
having few desires; ascetic

【**寢**】 1145
　　　　ㄑㄧㄣˇ chiin qǐn
1. to sleep; to rest
2. a tomb
3. a residence
4. stop; end

寢兵（ㄑㄧㄣˇ ㄅㄧㄥ）
to stop wars (or fighting)

寢寐（ㄑㄧㄣˇ ㄇㄟˋ）
to sleep

寢寐難安（ㄑㄧㄣˇ ㄇㄟˋ ㄋㄢˊ ㄢ）

---

a restless sleep (from
worries)

寢陋（ㄑㄧㄣˇ ㄌㄡˋ）
ugly

寢戈（ㄑㄧㄣˇ ㄍㄜ）
(descriptive of combat
readiness) to use weapons
as pillows

寢饋其中（ㄑㄧㄣˇ ㄎㄨㄟˋ ㄑㄧˊ ㄓㄨㄥ）
completely absorbed (in a
subject of study)

寢疾（ㄑㄧㄣˇ ㄐㄧˊ）
to be confined to bed by illness

寢具（ㄑㄧㄣˇ ㄐㄩˋ）
bedding

寢其皮而食其肉（ㄑㄧㄣˇ ㄑㄧˊ ㄆㄧˊ ㄦˊ
ㄕˊ ㄑㄧˊ ㄖㄡˋ）
(descriptive of deep hatred)
to sleep on his hide and eat
his flesh

寢處（ㄑㄧㄣˇ ㄔㄨˋ）
①（ㄑㄧㄣˇ ㄔㄨˇ）to sit or to sleep
—to rest
②（ㄑㄧㄣˇ ㄔㄨˋ）a sleeping place

寢食不安（ㄑㄧㄣˇ ㄕˊ ㄅㄨˋ ㄢ）
uneasy when eating and
sleeping; restless due to deep
worries

寢寐難忘（ㄑㄧㄣˇ ㄇㄟˋ ㄋㄢˊ ㄨㄤˋ）
constantly in one's mind

寢食俱廢（ㄑㄧㄣˇ ㄕˊ ㄐㄩˋ ㄈㄟˋ）
wanting neither food nor
sleep because of deep
worries or sorrow

寢室（ㄑㄧㄣˇ ㄕˋ）
a bedroom

【**寤**】 1146
　　　　ㄨˋ wuh wù
to awake from a sound
sleep

寤寐（ㄨˋ ㄇㄟˋ）
between sleep and wakeful-
ness

寤夢（ㄨˋ ㄇㄥˋ）
to see something during the
day and to dream about it
at night

寤生（ㄨˋ ㄕㄥ）
to give birth to a baby
while asleep

【**寥**】 1147
　　　　ㄌㄧㄠˊ liau liáo
1. few; not many
2. deserted; desolate; empty

寥寥（ㄌㄧㄠˊ ㄌㄧㄠˊ）
empty; scarce

宀部

【二
部】

寥寥無幾(ㄌㄧㄠ ㄌㄧㄠ ㄨˊ ㄐㄧˇ)
not many; few; 他的朋友寥寥無幾。He has few friends.

寥落(ㄌㄧㄠˊ ㄌㄨㄛˋ)
sparse

寥闊(ㄌㄧㄠˊ ㄎㄨㄛˋ)
expansive; expanse

寥廓(ㄌㄧㄠˊ ㄎㄨㄛˋ)
vast and empty; boundless

寥若晨星(ㄌㄧㄠˊ ㄖㄨㄛˋ ㄔㄣˊ ㄒㄧㄥ)
as few as morning stars

【實】 ¹¹⁴⁸
ㄕˊ shyr shí

1. real; true; actual; 你所說的不確實。What you say is not true.
2. practically; 實際上，這計畫行不通。Practically, the plan did not work well.
3. honest; faithful; sincere
4. concrete; substantial; solid; tangible
5. fact; reality; truth; actuality
6. fruit; seed

實報實銷(ㄕˊ ㄅㄠˋ ㄕˊ ㄒㄧㄠ)
to report expenses honestly; to be reimbursed for what one spends actually

實繁有徒(ㄕˊ ㄈㄢˊ ㄧㄡˇ ㄊㄨˊ)
Many people are involved.

實彈射擊(ㄕˊ ㄉㄢˋ ㄕㄜˋ ㄐㄧ)
a live ammunition fire practice

實彈演習(ㄕˊ ㄉㄢˋ ㄧㄢˇ ㄒㄧˊ)
to practice with live ammunition

實地調查(ㄕˊ ㄉㄧˋ ㄉㄧㄠˋ ㄔㄚˊ)
an on-the-spot investigation

實體(ㄕˊ ㄊㄧˇ)
substance (as opposed to form)

實力(ㄕˊ ㄌㄧˋ)
strength (often said of collective strength, including resources and potentialities)

實力相當(ㄕˊ ㄌㄧˋ ㄒㄧㄤ ㄉㄤ)
to match each other in strength; to be well-matched in strength

實利(ㄕˊ ㄌㄧˋ)
practical value; tangible benefits

實例(ㄕˊ ㄌㄧˋ)
a living example; an example

實齡(ㄕˊ ㄌㄧㄥˊ)
age at last birthday

實錄(ㄕˊ ㄌㄨˋ)
a faithful record

實感(ㄕˊ ㄍㄢˇ)
the sensation acquired from an actual experience (not from other media)

實幹(ㄕˊ ㄍㄢˋ)
to take real action

實料(ㄕˊ ㄌㄧㄠˋ)
practical courses (as opposed to theoretical courses)

實況(ㄕˊ ㄎㄨㄤˋ)
factual conditions; actual conditions; live (broadcasts or telecasts)

實況錄音(ㄕˊ ㄎㄨㄤˋ ㄌㄨˋ ㄧㄣ)
a live recording; an on-the-spot recording

實況轉播(ㄕˊ ㄎㄨㄤˋ ㄓㄨㄢˇ ㄅㄛˋ)
a live broadcast; a live telecast; 這是實況轉播，不是錄音轉播。It was a live broadcast, not a recording.

實話(ㄕˊ ㄏㄨㄚˋ)
the truth

實話實說(ㄕˊ ㄏㄨㄚˋ ㄕˊ ㄕㄨㄛ)
to tell the truth (without adding or withholding anything)

實惠(ㄕˊ ㄏㄨㄟˋ)
a real benefit; a tangible benefit; beneficial in a tangible way: 我們讓顧客買到經濟實惠的物品。We offer the customers inexpensive but substantial articles.

實績(ㄕˊ ㄐㄧˋ)
actual results; tangible achievements

實際(ㄕˊ ㄐㄧˋ)
①actual; real; concrete ②practical; realistic; 你這種想法不實際。This idea of yours is unrealistic. ③reality; practice: 這是個實際和理論相結合的例子。This example is the unity of practice and theory.

實際工資(ㄕˊ ㄐㄧˋ ㄍㄨㄥ ㄗ)
real wages

實際經驗(ㄕˊ ㄐㄧˋ ㄐㄧㄥ ㄧㄢˋ)
practical experience

實際情況(ㄕˊ ㄐㄧˋ ㄑㄧㄥˊ ㄎㄨㄤˋ)
reality; the actual situation

實際收入(ㄕˊ ㄐㄧˋ ㄕㄡ ㄖㄨˋ)
real income

實際人口(ㄕˊ ㄐㄧˋ ㄖㄣˊ ㄎㄡˇ)
actual population

實價(ㄕˊ ㄐㄧㄚˋ)
an honest price; an actual price

實踐(ㄕˊ ㄐㄧㄢˋ)
to practice (a principle); put in practice: 真知來自實踐。Genuine knowledge comes from practice.

實踐哲學(ㄕˊ ㄐㄧㄢˋ ㄓㄜˊ ㄒㄩㄝˊ)
practical philosophy

實證(ㄕˊ ㄓㄥˋ)
substantial evidence; substantial proof

實情(ㄕˊ ㄑㄧㄥˊ)
the actual situation; the real picture or real story (of a case)

實缺(ㄕˊ ㄑㄩㄝ)
a vacancy or opening; 內閣裡有實缺。There is a vacancy in the Cabinet.

實權(ㄕˊ ㄑㄩㄢˊ)
real power or authority; 首相有實權。The prime minister has real power.

實習(ㄕˊ ㄒㄧˊ)
(said of students or trainees shortly before or immediately after graduation) to practice what one has been taught

實習工廠(ㄕˊ ㄒㄧˊ ㄍㄨㄥ ㄔㄤˇ)
a factory attached to school

實習生(ㄕˊ ㄒㄧˊ ㄕㄥ)
a trainee

實習醫生(ㄕˊ ㄒㄧˊ ㄧ ㄕㄥ)
an intern(e)

實效(ㄕˊ ㄒㄧㄠˋ)
real effect; effect

實現(ㄕˊ ㄒㄧㄢˋ)
to realize (a plan, etc); (said of a dream, etc) to come true: 這計劃不容易實現。This plan is difficult to realize.

實在(ㄕˊ ㄗㄞˋ)
①sincere; honest ②in a serious manner ③solid; distinct from hollow): 這輪胎是實心的。These tires are solid.

實心眼兒(ㄕˊ ㄒㄧㄣ ㄧㄢˇㄦ)
frank; unfeigned; honest; 他很實心眼兒。This man

uite honest.

...(ㄕ ㄌ)
physics) a real image

...(ㄕ ㄒㄧㄥ)
o practice (a principle); to
arry out; to put into prac-
ice

界(ㄕ ㄐㄧㄝ)
earning of genuine value

值(ㄕ ㄓ)
et value; intrinsic value;
eal value

項(ㄕ ㄓ)
ssence; substance

所得(ㄕ ㄙㄨㄛ ㄉㄜ)
real income

至名歸(ㄕ ㄓ ㄇㄧㄥ ㄍㄨㄟ)
Where there is real ability,
here is fame.

戰(ㄕ ㄓㄢ)
actual combat

戰演習(ㄕ ㄓㄢ ㄧㄢ ㄒㄧ)
combat exercises with live
ammunition

證(ㄕ ㄓㄥ)
①(Chinese medicine) a case
of a physically strong patient running a high fever
or suffering from such disorders as stasis of blood,
constipation, etc. ② concrete
evidence

證主義(ㄕ ㄓㄥ ㄓㄨ ㄧ)or 實證論
(ㄕ ㄓㄥ ㄌㄨㄣ)
(philosophy) positivism

施(ㄕ)
to put (regulations, plans,
etc.) into effect; to implement: 新的條款已付諸實施.
The new provisions have
been put into effect.

事求是(ㄕ ㄕ ㄑㄧㄡ ㄕ)
to work conscientiously or
seriously; to make conscientious efforts to do things

收(ㄕ ㄕㄡ)
net receipts

數(ㄕ ㄕㄨ)
(mathematics) a true num-
ber

字(ㄕ ㄗ)
a content word (as opposed
to a function word or particle)

在(ㄕ ㄗㄞ)or 實實在在(ㄕ ㄕ
ㄗㄞ ㄗㄞ)
①really; truly; certainly; in

---

fact ② real; solid; concrete;
tangible ③ well-done: 工作做
得很實在. The work is well-
done.

實足(ㄕ ㄗㄨ)
full; solid: 我實足等了三個鐘
頭. I waited for three solid
hours.

實足年齡(ㄕ ㄗㄨ ㄋㄧㄢ ㄌㄧㄥ)
one's full age (as distinct
from the age by the Chinese
custom of counting the fraction of a year as one full
year)

實業(ㄕ ㄧㄝ)
industry; business

實業家(ㄕ ㄧㄝ ㄐㄧㄚ)
an industrialist; a businessman; an entrepreneur

實業界(ㄕ ㄧㄝ ㄐㄧㄝ)
industry; the business world
or circles; the industrial
world or circles: 實業界與政
府的意見一致嗎? Does indus-
try agree with the government?

實驗(ㄕ ㄧㄢ)
to experiment; to test; an
experiment; a test: 科學家靠
實驗證明理論. Scientists test
out theories by experiment.

實驗法(ㄕ ㄧㄢ ㄈㄚ)
the experimental method

實驗劇場(ㄕ ㄧㄢ ㄐㄩ ㄔㄤ)
an experimental theater

實驗主義(ㄕ ㄧㄢ ㄓㄨ ㄧ)
experimentalism

實驗室(ㄕ ㄧㄢ ㄕ)
a laboratory

實驗員(ㄕ ㄧㄢ ㄩㄢ)
a laboratory technician

實物(ㄕ ㄨ)
goods or produce (as
opposed to money); in kind

實物教學(ㄕ ㄨ ㄐㄧㄠ ㄒㄩㄝ)
object teaching

實用(ㄕ ㄩㄥ)
①practical use ② practical;
useful: 那勸告對我很實用. The
advice was very useful to
me.

實用主義(ㄕ ㄩㄥ ㄓㄨ ㄧ)
pragmatism

【寨】 1149 ㄓㄞ jay zhài
a stockade

寨主(ㄓㄞ ㄓㄨ)

---

a leader (used by bandits in
speaking of their leader)

寨子(ㄓㄞ ˙ㄗ)
a stockaded village

十二畫

【審】 1150 ㄕㄣˇ sheen shén

1. to examine; to review; to
investigate: 他被警察審問. He
was examined by the police.
2. to know; to discern; to
appreciate
3. cautious; judicious; careful
4. really; indeed

審判(ㄕㄣ ㄆㄢ)
①to try (a case or person
in a law court) ② a trial: 他
因謀殺而受審判. He was on
trial for murder.

審判長(ㄕㄣ ㄆㄢ ㄓㄤ)
the chief justice; the presiding judge

審美(ㄕㄣ ㄇㄟ)
to be esthetic or artistic; to
appreciate the beautiful;
estheticism; appreciation of
the beautiful

審美觀念(ㄕㄣ ㄇㄟ ㄍㄨㄢ ㄋㄧㄢ)
esthetic sense (or notions)

審定(ㄕㄣ ㄉㄧㄥ)
to authorize (a publication,
etc.); to examine and ap-
prove: 這建議已由委員會審定.
The proposal has been
examined and approved by
the committee.

審訂(ㄕㄣ ㄉㄧㄥ)
to examine and revise: 教授
們仔細地審訂教材. Professors
carefully revise teaching
materials.

審度(ㄕㄣ ㄉㄨㄛ)
to consider the pros and
cons; to deliberate

審斷(ㄕㄣ ㄉㄨㄢ)
to examine and decide; to
pass a judgement after an
examination

審理(ㄕㄣ ㄌㄧ)
to try; to hear

審核(ㄕㄣ ㄏㄜ)
to examine and consider

審計(ㄕㄣ ㄐㄧ)
an audit; to audit

審計部(ㄕㄣ ㄐㄧ ㄅㄨ)

(ㄕ)部

Ministry of Audit

審查 or 審察(ㄕㄣ ㄔㄚˊ)
to examine; to review; to
investigate; 審查屬實。The
fact was established after
investigation.

審處(ㄕㄣ ㄔㄨˇ)
①法院審處 to hand over to
the local court for trial ②to
deliberate and decide

審慎(ㄕㄣ ㄕㄣˋ)
cautious; careful; 審慎的人不
信沒有證據的事。A cautious
man doesn't believe things
without proof.

審案(ㄕㄣ ㄢˋ)
to hold court trial

審議(ㄕㄣ ㄧˋ)
① consideration; deliberation; discussion; 這議議正在
審議中。The proposal is
under discussion. ② the title
of a civil post

審議會(ㄕㄣ ㄧˋ ㄏㄨㄟˋ)
a deliberative meeting or
session

審音(ㄕㄣ ㄧㄣ)
to discern or distinguish
tones in music or in words

審問(ㄕㄣ ㄨㄣˋ)or 審訊(ㄕㄣ ㄒㄩㄣˋ)
to hold a hearing (on a
legal case); to interrogate a
prisoner

審閱(ㄕㄣ ㄩㄝˋ)
to examine; to review

審閱稿件(ㄕㄣ ㄩㄝˋ ㄍㄠˇ ㄐㄧㄢˋ)
to go over a manuscript

【寫】 1151
1. ㄒㄧㄝˇ shiee xiě
to write; to sketch; to draw;
to represent

寫本(ㄒㄧㄝˇ ㄅㄣˇ)
a handwritten copy (of a
book)

寫稿(ㄒㄧㄝˇ ㄍㄠˇ)
to write for (or contribute
to) a magazine, etc.

寫照(ㄒㄧㄝˇ ㄓㄠˋ)
an image; a representation;
portrayal; a description

寫眞(ㄒㄧㄝˇ ㄓㄣ)
to draw or paint a portrait;
to paint or draw a likeness;
to portray

寫實(ㄒㄧㄝˇ ㄕˊ)
realistic (as distinct from

romantic): 這是一部寫實的小
說。This is a realistic novel.

寫實主義(ㄒㄧㄝˇ ㄕˊ ㄓㄨˇ ㄧˋ)
realism

寫生(ㄒㄧㄝˇ ㄕㄥ)
to draw, or paint, from
nature; to sketch: 畫家寫生。
The artist sketches from
nature.

寫生畫(ㄒㄧㄝˇ ㄕㄥ ㄏㄨㄚˋ)
a sketch

寫字(ㄒㄧㄝˇ ㄗˋ)
to practice penmanship or
calligraphy; to write

寫字檯(ㄒㄧㄝˇ ㄗˋ ㄊㄞˊ)
a desk

寫字間(ㄒㄧㄝˇ ㄗˋ ㄐㄧㄢ)
an office room

寫字員(ㄒㄧㄝˇ ㄗˋ ㄩㄢˊ)
a scribe; a clerk 亦作「書記」
or「抄寫員」

寫作(ㄒㄧㄝˇ ㄗㄨㄛˋ)
writing: 他以寫作為生。He
takes up writing as his
career.

寫意(ㄒㄧㄝˇ ㄧˋ)
(said of painting) to make
an impressionistic portrayal

寫意畫(ㄒㄧㄝˇ ㄧˋ ㄏㄨㄚˋ)
ideal painting

【寫】 1151
2. ㄒㄧㄝ shieh xiè
unrestrained

寫意(兒)(ㄒㄧㄝ ㄧˋ(ㄦ))
free and happy

【寬】 1152
ㄎㄨㄢ kuan kuān
1. broad; wide; spacious; vast:
他眼界寬。He has a broad
outlook.
2. magnanimous; lenient; tolerant; liberal; forgiving; indulgent
3. to loosen; to widen
4. well-off

寬猛相濟(ㄎㄨㄢ ㄇㄥˇ ㄒㄧㄤ ㄐㄧˋ)
to use a proper mixture of
severity and gentleness (in
ruling a country, handling
one's subordinates, etc.)

寬免(ㄎㄨㄢ ㄇㄧㄢˇ)
to be exempt (from a tax,
penalty, etc.)

寬大(ㄎㄨㄢ ㄉㄚˋ)
lenient; magnanimous: 他對
孩子們很寬大。He is lenient
toward (or to) the children.

寬大為懷(ㄎㄨㄢ ㄉㄚˋ ㄨㄟˊ ㄏㄨㄞˊ)
magnanimous; forgiving;
erant; liberal; open-hear
benignant

寬待(ㄎㄨㄢ ㄉㄞˋ)
to treat generously

寬度(ㄎㄨㄢ ㄉㄨˋ)
width; breadth

寬廣(ㄎㄨㄢ ㄍㄨㄤˇ)
vast; broad; spacious; ex
sive; wide: 這是一條寬廣的
道。This is a wide street.

寬闊(ㄎㄨㄢ ㄎㄨㄛˋ)
roomy; wide; spacious: 他
在一棟寬闊的公寓裡。He li
in a roomy apartment.

寬厚(ㄎㄨㄢ ㄏㄡˋ)
tolerant and generous

寬宏大量(ㄎㄨㄢ ㄏㄨㄥˊ ㄉㄚˋ ㄌㄧㄤˋ)
magnanimous; open-hear
broad-minded; benignant

寬假(ㄎㄨㄢ ㄐㄧㄚˇ)
to excuse magnanimously

寬解(ㄎㄨㄢ ㄐㄧㄝˇ)
to ease somebody's anxie
to ease somebody of
trouble

寬限(ㄎㄨㄢ ㄒㄧㄢˋ)
① to extend a time limit ②
moratorium

寬心(ㄎㄨㄢ ㄒㄧㄣ)
to feel at rest; to set or
mind at ease; to feel f
from anxiety

寬窄(ㄎㄨㄢ ㄓㄞˇ)
breadth; width

寬敞(ㄎㄨㄢ ㄔㄤˇ)
spacious; having much roc
roomy; commodious: 這是
間寬敞的房子。It is a comr
dious house.

寬綽(ㄎㄨㄢ ㄔㄨㄛˋ)
① composed; unperturbe
relax; relieved ② with mu
space or room to spare; s
cious ③ well-off

寬弛(ㄎㄨㄢ ㄔˊ)
relaxed; not tense

寬舒(ㄎㄨㄢ ㄕㄨ)
roomy and comfortable

寬恕(ㄎㄨㄢ ㄕㄨˋ)
to forgive; to pardon; f
giveness; pardon

寬容(ㄎㄨㄢ ㄖㄨㄥˊ)
to forgive; to pardon;
excuse; magnanimity; f
giveness; leniency; forbe

ance; tolerance

寬縱(ㄎㄨㄢ ㄗㄨㄥˋ)
① to impose no restrictions; to be indulgent: 不要這麼寬縱自己。Don't be so self-indulgent. ② breadth and depth

寬鬆(ㄎㄨㄢ ㄙㄨㄥ)
loose and comfortable

寬衣(ㄎㄨㄢ ㄧ)
① a loose garment ② to remove the upper coat (for relaxation); 請寬衣。Do take off your coat.

寬衣解帶(ㄎㄨㄢ ㄧ ㄐㄧㄝˇ ㄉㄞˋ)
to undress

寬銀幕(ㄎㄨㄢ ㄧㄣˊ ㄇㄨˋ)
(movie) Cinerama; wide-screen

寬慰(ㄎㄨㄢ ㄨㄟˋ)
to console; to comfort; to soothe: 他遭遇不幸，我們寬慰他。We comforted him for his misfortune.

寬裕(ㄎㄨㄢ ㄩˋ)
well-to-do; well-off; ample: 時間很寬裕。There's plenty of time yet.

【寮】 1153
ㄌㄧㄠˊ liau liáo
1. a fellow officer or official; a colleague
2. a hut; a cottage

寮國(ㄌㄧㄠˊ ㄍㄨㄛˊ)
Laos

寮國人(ㄌㄧㄠˊ ㄍㄨㄛˊ ㄖㄣˊ)
a Laotian

十三畫

【寰】 1154
ㄏㄨㄢˊ hwan huán
1. a large domain; a vast space

寰內(ㄏㄨㄢˊ ㄋㄟˋ)
the domain of the empire

寰區(ㄏㄨㄢˊ ㄑㄩ)
all within the country

寰宇(ㄏㄨㄢˊ ㄩˇ)or 寰球(ㄏㄨㄢˊ ㄑㄧㄡˊ)
the world; the earth

十六畫

【寵】 1155
ㄔㄨㄥˇ choong chǒng
1. a concubine
2. to favor; to dote on; to patronize

3. favor or love (especially of the emperor)

寵嬖(ㄔㄨㄥˇ ㄅㄧˋ)
a court favorite

寵壞(ㄔㄨㄥˇ ㄏㄨㄞˋ)
to spoil (a child): 別把孩子寵壞了。Don't spoil the child.

寵姬(ㄔㄨㄥˇ ㄐㄧ)
the emperor's favorite concubine

寵信(ㄔㄨㄥˇ ㄒㄧㄣˋ)
to favor and trust (a subordinate)

寵幸(ㄔㄨㄥˇ ㄒㄧㄥˋ)
to show special favor to a lady or minister

寵辱不驚(ㄔㄨㄥˇ ㄖㄨˇ ㄅㄨˋ ㄐㄧㄥ)
to remain indifferent whether granted favor or subjected to humiliation

寵愛(ㄔㄨㄥˇ ㄞˋ)
to favor or patronize; to dote on: 她寵愛她的孫女。She doted on her granddaughter.

寵兒(ㄔㄨㄥˇ ㄦˊ)
a favored person; a pet; a favorite; a minion

寵遇(ㄔㄨㄥˇ ㄩˋ)
to treat as a favorite

十七畫

【寶】 1156
(寶) ㄅㄠˇ bao bǎo
1. treasure
2. precious; valuable
3. respectable; honorable

寶貝(ㄅㄠˇ ㄅㄟˋ)
① a cherished thing; a jewel ② darling (a term of endearment) ③ a kind of cowrie (*Cypraea tigris*) ④ a good-for-nothing or queer character: 這人真是個寶貝! What a fellow!

寶寶(ㄅㄠˇ ·ㄅㄠ)
baby (a term of endearment)

寶刀(ㄅㄠˇ ㄉㄠ)
a treasured sword or dagger

寶刀未老(ㄅㄠˇ ㄉㄠ ㄨㄟˋ ㄌㄠˇ)
old but still vigorous in mind and body

寶島(ㄅㄠˇ ㄉㄠˇ)
a treasure island: 臺灣是個寶島。Taiwan is a treasure island.

寶典(ㄅㄠˇ ㄉㄧㄢˇ)
a valuable book; a treasury of knowledge; a thesaurus: 此書為知識之寶典。This book is a treasury of knowledge.

寶鼎勳章(ㄅㄠˇ ㄉㄧㄥˇ ㄒㄩㄣ ㄓㄤ)
the Order of Precious Tripod, a Chinese government decoration

寶塔(ㄅㄠˇ ㄊㄚˇ)
a pagoda

寶貴(ㄅㄠˇ ㄍㄨㄟˋ)
valuable; precious: 故宮博物館收藏許多寶貴文物。The National Palace Museum collected and kept many valuable cultural relics.

寶庫(ㄅㄠˇ ㄎㄨˋ)
a treasury; a treasure house: 海洋是礦物和食物的寶庫。The sea is a treasure house of minerals and food.

寶盒(ㄅㄠˇ ㄏㄜˊ)
a jewel box; a box of treasures

寶號(ㄅㄠˇ ㄏㄠˋ)
(an honorific term) your shop, firm or store

寶劍(ㄅㄠˇ ㄐㄧㄢˋ)
a treasured sword

寶眷(ㄅㄠˇ ㄐㄩㄢˋ)
(an honorific term) your family

寶珠(ㄅㄠˇ ㄓㄨ)
a precious jewel

寶刹(ㄅㄠˇ ㄔㄚˋ)
① your temple (an honorific term used in speaking to a monk or nun) ② the pagoda of a temple

寶鈔(ㄅㄠˇ ㄔㄠ)
paper money

寶石(ㄅㄠˇ ㄕˊ)
a precious stone; a gem; a jewel: 她買了許多寶石。She bought many jewels.

寶山(ㄅㄠˇ ㄕㄢ)
a golconda; a source of great wealth

寶山空回(ㄅㄠˇ ㄕㄢ ㄎㄨㄥ ㄏㄨㄟˊ)
to miss a golden chance; to gain nothing from a rare opportunity

寶藏(ㄅㄠˇ ㄗㄤˋ)
a treasury; a treasure house; a collection of treasures

寶座(ㄅㄠˇ ㄗㄨㄛˋ)

〔宀部〕

the throne

寶物(ㄅㄠˇ ㄨˋ)
a treasure: 那博物館藏有很多寶物。The museum is full of treasures.

寶玉(ㄅㄠˇ ㄩˋ)
a precious stone

寸 部

ㄘㄨㄣˋ tsuenn cùn

【寸】 1157
ㄘㄨㄣˋ tsuenn cùn

1. a measure of length (equal to about 1/10 foot)
2. as small as an inch; small; tiny; little

寸步不離(ㄘㄨㄣˋ ㄅㄨˋ ㄅㄨˋ ㄌㄧˊ)
to tag; to follow closely (without allowing the distance to widen more than an inch)

寸步難移(ㄘㄨㄣˋ ㄅㄨˋ ㄋㄢˊ ㄧˊ)or 寸步難行(ㄘㄨㄣˋ ㄅㄨˋ ㄋㄢˊ ㄒㄧㄥˊ)
hard to walk even an inch; tough going

寸木岑樓(ㄘㄨㄣˋ ㄇㄨˋ ㄘㄣˊ ㄌㄡˊ)
(said of two things in comparison) vastly different in size and weight

寸地(ㄘㄨㄣˋ ㄉㄧˋ)
an inch of land; a tiny piece of land

寸斷(ㄘㄨㄣˋ ㄉㄨㄢˋ)or 寸裂(ㄘㄨㄣˋ ㄌㄧㄝˋ)
(heart) torn to pieces (used to describe extreme grief)

寸鐵(ㄘㄨㄣˋ ㄊㄧㄝˇ)
a dagger (emphasizing its smallness)

寸土必爭(ㄘㄨㄣˋ ㄊㄨˇ ㄅㄧˋ ㄓㄥ)
Even an inch of land has to be fought for.

寸土寸地(ㄘㄨㄣˋ ㄊㄨˇ ㄘㄨㄣˋ ㄉㄧˋ)
a wisp of territory

寸縷無存(ㄘㄨㄣˋ ㄌㄩˇ ㄨˊ ㄘㄨㄣˊ)
There is not even an inch of thread in the house.—descriptive of extreme poverty

寸功(ㄘㄨㄣˋ ㄍㄨㄥ)
a small contribution

寸簡(ㄘㄨㄣˋ ㄐㄧㄢˇ)or 寸札(ㄘㄨㄣˋ ㄓㄚˊ)
a short note: 他留下寸簡。He left me a short note.

寸金難買寸光陰(ㄘㄨㄣˋ ㄐㄧㄣ ㄋㄢˊ ㄇㄞˇ ㄘㄨㄣˋ ㄍㄨㄤ ㄧㄣ)
Money cannot buy time. 或 Time is more precious than gold.

寸進(ㄘㄨㄣˋ ㄐㄧㄣˋ)
①a little progress ②to advance by inches

寸陰難留(ㄘㄨㄣˋ ㄧㄣ ㄋㄢˊ ㄌㄧㄡˊ)
It's impossible to stop time passing away.

寸心(ㄘㄨㄣˋ ㄒㄧㄣ)or 寸衷(ㄘㄨㄣˋ ㄓㄨㄥ)
the heart (with emphasis on its smallness and its being the source of sincerity); feelings

寸腸(ㄘㄨㄣˋ ㄔㄤˊ)
innermost feelings

寸長(ㄘㄨㄣˋ ㄔㄤˊ)
modest ability; mediocre ability

寸草不留(ㄘㄨㄣˋ ㄘㄠˇ ㄅㄨˋ ㄌㄧㄡˊ)
to leave not even a blade of grass; to destroy completely (often used as a threat in calling the enemy to surrender)

寸草春暉(ㄘㄨㄣˋ ㄘㄠˇ ㄔㄨㄣ ㄏㄨㄟ)
A mother's love to a child is like spring light to a blade of grass.—One can never fully repay the love and care he has received from his mother no matter how hard he tries to please her.

寸絲不掛(ㄘㄨㄣˋ ㄙ ㄅㄨˋ ㄍㄨㄚˋ)
①to have not even a thread on; to be stark-naked 亦作「一絲不掛」②to be completely free from worries or care

寸陰(ㄘㄨㄣˋ ㄧㄣ)
a very short time; a few minutes; a brief moment

寸陰尺璧(ㄘㄨㄣˋ ㄧㄣ ㄔˇ ㄅㄧˋ)
(literally) An inch of time is worth a foot of jade.—Time is more precious than money.

寸陰若歲(ㄘㄨㄣˋ ㄧㄣ ㄖㄨㄛˋ ㄙㄨㄟˋ)
A brief moment seems to last a whole year.—(figuratively) one's longing to see a dear one

三畫

【寺】 1158
ㄙˋ syh sì

a temple; a monastery; a shrine; a mosque

寺觀(ㄙˋ ㄍㄨㄢ)
Buddhist temples and Taoist temples

寺舍(ㄙˋ ㄕㄜˋ)
a temple building housing monks or nuns

寺人(ㄙˋ ㄖㄣˊ)
eunuchs

寺院(ㄙˋ ㄩㄢˋ)
temples

寺院法(ㄙˋ ㄩㄢˋ ㄈㄚˇ)
canon law

六畫

【封】 1159
ㄈㄥ feng fēng

1. a numerary adjunct for letters
2. to install as a feudal lord or a nobleman
3. to seal; to block; to close completely: 山路已被大雪封住。The mountain path is already blocked by the heavy snow.
4. a covering; a wrapper; an envelope

封閉(ㄈㄥ ㄅㄧˋ)
to seal; to close completely: 他把閘關閉。He sealed a leak.

封閉機場(ㄈㄥ ㄅㄧˋ ㄐㄧ ㄔㄤˇ)
to close an airport

封皮(ㄈㄥ ㄆㄧˊ)
①a covering; a cover ②a wrapper ③a sealing tape

封門(ㄈㄥ ㄇㄣˊ)
①to seal a door ②to close a business establishment or an organization (as a form of punishment)

封面(ㄈㄥ ㄇㄧㄢˋ)
the cover (of a book): 這本書需要換新的封面。This book needs a new cover.

封面女郎(ㄈㄥ ㄇㄧㄢˋ ㄋㄩˇ ㄌㄤˊ)
a cover girl; a girl whose photo is used as a magazine cover: 她是個很受歡迎的封面女郎。She is a very popular

cover girl.

封底(ㄈㄥ ㄉㄧˇ)
the back cover

封地(ㄈㄥ ㄉㄧˋ)
a fief; a feud; a manor

封臺(ㄈㄥ ㄊㄞˊ)or封箱(ㄈㄥ ㄒㄧㄤ)
(said of theater) stopping performance for the period near New Year

封套(ㄈㄥ ㄊㄠˋ)
an envelope; a wrapper

封條(ㄈㄥ ㄊㄧㄠˊ)
a sealing tape

封泥(ㄈㄥ ㄋㄧˊ)
(metallurgy) lute; luting

封蠟(ㄈㄥ ㄌㄚˋ)
sealing wax

封裡(ㄈㄥ ㄌㄧˇ)
①the inside front cover ②
the inside back cover

封口(ㄈㄥ ㄎㄡˇ)
①to seal (a letter) ②to
block the entrance (to a
passage) ③to heal

封侯(ㄈㄥ ㄏㄡˊ)
to create feudal lords

封建領土(ㄈㄥ ㄐㄧㄢˋ ㄌㄧㄥˇ ㄊㄨˇ)
feudatory

封建割據(ㄈㄥ ㄐㄧㄢˋ ㄍㄜ ㄐㄩˋ)
rule of feudal separationist

封建制度(ㄈㄥ ㄐㄧㄢˋ ㄓˋ ㄉㄨˋ)
feudalism; the feudal system

封建時代(ㄈㄥ ㄐㄧㄢˋ ㄕˊ ㄉㄞˋ)
the feudal age (or times)

封建勢力(ㄈㄥ ㄐㄧㄢˋ ㄕˋ ㄌㄧˋ)
feudalistic influence

封建思想(ㄈㄥ ㄐㄧㄢˋ ㄙ ㄒㄧㄤˇ)
feudalistic ideas; anachronistic thinking

封禁(ㄈㄥ ㄐㄧㄣˋ)
to blockade; to shut up and
prevent access 參看「封鎖」

封疆大吏(ㄈㄥ ㄐㄧㄤ ㄉㄚˋ ㄌㄧˋ)
the governor of a border
province

封爵(ㄈㄥ ㄐㄩㄝˊ)
to confer a degree of nobility on someone

封殺(ㄈㄥ ㄕㄚˋ)
(baseball) to shut out; force
play

封山(ㄈㄥ ㄕㄢ)
to seal a mountain pass: 昨
晚大雪把封山山。Heavy snow has
sealed the mountain passes
last night.

封禪(ㄈㄥ ㄕㄢˋ)
the ancient rite of worshipping Heaven and Earth on a
mountain with the emperor
officiating

封神榜(ㄈㄥ ㄕㄣˊ ㄅㄤˇ)
a classical novel of Chinese
gods and heroes

封賞(ㄈㄥ ㄕㄤˇ)
to give tips

封存(ㄈㄥ ㄘㄨㄣˊ)
to seal and put away

封鎖(ㄈㄥ ㄙㄨㄛˇ)
to blockade (a place or
region); a blockade: 道路被
封鎖。The road was blockaded.

封鎖邊境(ㄈㄥ ㄙㄨㄛˇ ㄅㄧㄢ ㄐㄧㄥˋ)
to close the border

封鎖港口(ㄈㄥ ㄙㄨㄛˇ ㄍㄤˇ ㄎㄡˇ)
to blockade a port

封鎖新聞(ㄈㄥ ㄙㄨㄛˇ ㄒㄧㄣ ㄨㄣˊ)
to suppress news

封邑(ㄈㄥ ㄧˋ)
a manor estate bestowed by
a monarch

封印(ㄈㄥ ㄧㄣˋ)
(postal service) a seal

封網(ㄈㄥ ㄨㄤˇ)
(volleyball) to block

封翁(ㄈㄥ ㄨㄥ)or封君(ㄈㄥ ㄐㄩㄣ)
(in ancient China) a man
whose children was high-ranking officials and was
thus given a title by the
government

七畫

1160
ㄕㄜˋ sheh shè
【射】 (動詞語音ㄕˋ shyr shì)
(音律名ㄧˋ yih yì)
(於「僕射」等ㄧㄝˋ yeh
yè)

1. to shoot: 他射下一隻鳥。He
shot down a bird.
2. to send out (light, heat,
etc.): 太陽射出光與熱。The
sun sends out light and heat.
3. archery (listed by Confucius
as one of six arts required
of a scholar)

射門(ㄕㄜˋ ㄇㄣˊ)
(in soccer, etc.) to shoot or
kick the ball toward the
goal

射彈(ㄕㄜˋ ㄉㄢˋ)
a projectile

射垛(ㄕㄜˋ ㄉㄨㄛˇ)
a rampart used as a target
for practicing shooting
arrows

射獵(ㄕㄜˋ ㄌㄧㄝˋ)
hunting: 他很喜歡射獵。He's
very fond of hunting.

射擊(ㄕㄜˋ ㄐㄧ)
to shoot; shooting

射擊場(ㄕㄜˋ ㄐㄧ ㄔㄤˇ)
a shooting range

射擊術(ㄕㄜˋ ㄐㄧ ㄕㄨˋ)
marksmanship

射界(ㄕㄜˋ ㄐㄧㄝˋ)
the field of fire

射角(ㄕㄜˋ ㄐㄧㄠˇ)
the angle of fire

射箭(ㄕㄜˋ ㄐㄧㄢˋ)
to shoot an arrow; archery

射精(ㄕㄜˋ ㄐㄧㄥ)
(biology) ejection

射球(ㄕㄜˋ ㄑㄧㄡˊ)
to kick or shoot the ball

射線(ㄕㄜˋ ㄒㄧㄢˋ)
(physics) a ray

射中(ㄕㄜˋ ㄓㄨㄥˋ)
to hit (with a shot) the target; to score a hit

射程(ㄕㄜˋ ㄔㄥˊ)
a range (of the projectile):
他在五哩的射程內射擊。He
fires at a range of five
miles.

射石飲羽(ㄕㄜˋ ㄕˊ ㄧㄣˇ ㄩˇ)
to have the strong will
power that can make an
arrow pierce even a stone

射手(ㄕㄜˋ ㄕㄡˇ)
an archer; a shooter; a
marksman; a gunner: 他是個
好射手。He is a good archer.

射影(ㄕㄜˋ ㄧㄥˇ)
projection

八畫

1161
ㄓㄨㄢ juan zhuān
【專】
1. to concentrate; to focus
2. to monopolize
3. to specialize: 許多學生專攻農
業。Many students specialize
in agriculture.
4. exclusive; special: 你修的專
門學科是什麼? What is your

寸
部

special study?

專賣 (ㄓㄨㄢ ㄇㄞˋ)
a monopoly; the exclusive possession of the trade in some commodity

專賣局 (ㄓㄨㄢ ㄇㄞˋ ㄐㄩˊ)
a monopoly bureau

專賣權 (ㄓㄨㄢ ㄇㄞˋ ㄑㄩㄢˊ)or 專利權 (ㄓㄨㄢ ㄌㄧˋ ㄑㄩㄢˊ)
a patent; a monopoly right

專美 (ㄓㄨㄢ ㄇㄟˇ)
to attain distinction alone

專門 (ㄓㄨㄢ ㄇㄣˊ)
① a specialty; a special field
② exclusively; specially

專門知識 (ㄓㄨㄢ ㄇㄣˊ ㄓ ㄕˋ)
expertise; specialized knowledge

專門人材 (ㄓㄨㄢ ㄇㄣˊ ㄖㄣˊ ㄘㄞˊ)
the people with professional skill

專門委員 (ㄓㄨㄢ ㄇㄣˊ ㄨㄟˇ ㄩㄢˊ)
a senior specialist in the government

專名 (ㄓㄨㄢ ㄇㄧㄥˊ)
a proper name; a proper noun

專訪 (ㄓㄨㄢ ㄈㄤˇ)
a report produced by a journalist after having paid a special visit to the person or persons concerned

專電 (ㄓㄨㄢ ㄉㄧㄢˋ)
a news dispatch; a special dispatch (or telegram)

專斷 (ㄓㄨㄢ ㄉㄨㄢˋ)
to make decisions without consulting others; arbitrary

專題 (ㄓㄨㄢ ㄊㄧˊ)
a special subject

專題報導 (ㄓㄨㄢ ㄊㄧˊ ㄅㄠˋ ㄉㄠˇ)
a report on a special topic

專題研究 (ㄓㄨㄢ ㄊㄧˊ ㄧㄢˊ ㄐㄧㄡˋ)
a monographic study

專題演講 (ㄓㄨㄢ ㄊㄧˊ ㄧㄢˇ ㄐㄧㄤˇ)
a lecture on a special topic

專欄 (ㄓㄨㄢ ㄌㄢˊ)
a special column (in a newspaper or magazine)

專欄作家 (ㄓㄨㄢ ㄌㄢˊ ㄗㄨㄛˋ ㄐㄧㄚ)
a columnist

專利 (ㄓㄨㄢ ㄌㄧˋ)
a monopoly; a patent: 他申請到該器具的專利。He got a patent for the gadget.

專利品 (ㄓㄨㄢ ㄌㄧˋ ㄆㄧㄣˇ)

a patent; a patent article

專利連鎖店 (ㄓㄨㄢ ㄌㄧˋ ㄌㄧㄢˊ ㄙㄨㄛˇ ㄉㄧㄢˋ)
a franchise chain

專利權 (ㄓㄨㄢ ㄌㄧˋ ㄑㄩㄢˊ)
a patent; a patent right

專管 (ㄓㄨㄢ ㄍㄨㄢˇ)
to take exclusive charge of (a matter)

專攻 (ㄓㄨㄢ ㄍㄨㄥ)
to study (a subject) exclusively; to specialize in

專科 (ㄓㄨㄢ ㄎㄜ)
a particular course or field of study

專科學校 (ㄓㄨㄢ ㄎㄜ ㄒㄩㄝˊ ㄒㄧㄠˋ)
a junior college

專款 (ㄓㄨㄢ ㄎㄨㄢˇ)
the fund designated for a specific use

專款專用 (ㄓㄨㄢ ㄎㄨㄢˇ ㄓㄨㄢ ㄩㄥˋ)
to earmark a fund for its specified purpose only

專號 (ㄓㄨㄢ ㄏㄠˋ)
a special issue (of a periodical)

專函 (ㄓㄨㄢ ㄏㄢˊ)
a letter written for a specific purpose

專橫 (ㄓㄨㄢ ㄏㄥˊ)
dictatorial; arbitrary; despotic; tyrannical: 我無法忍受他專橫的態度。 I can't stand his dictatorial manner.

專橫跋扈 (ㄓㄨㄢ ㄏㄥˊ ㄅㄚˊ ㄏㄨˋ)
imperious and despotic

專戶 (ㄓㄨㄢ ㄏㄨˋ)
a special bank account

專機 (ㄓㄨㄢ ㄐㄧ)
a plane designated for a special use (such as flying a VIP or some valuable goods); a chartered plane

專家 (ㄓㄨㄢ ㄐㄧㄚ)
a specialist; an expert

專精 (ㄓㄨㄢ ㄐㄧㄥ)
to concentrate one's efforts or energy on

專權 (ㄓㄨㄢ ㄑㄩㄢˊ)
to be in full power; to be dictatorial

專修 (ㄓㄨㄢ ㄒㄧㄡ)
to study (a subject) exclusively

專修科 (ㄓㄨㄢ ㄒㄧㄡ ㄎㄜ)
a two-year program of study

in a four-year college that does not lead to a degree and is consequently equivalent to work in a junior (two-year) college

專線 (ㄓㄨㄢ ㄒㄧㄢˋ)
① a special railway line ② special telephone line

專心一志 (ㄓㄨㄢ ㄒㄧㄣ ㄧ ㄓˋ)
to concentrate or focus one's attention, thoughts, or efforts on

專職 (ㄓㄨㄢ ㄓˊ)
① sole duty; specific duty ② full-time

專制 (ㄓㄨㄢ ㄓˋ)
tyrannical; despotic; autocratic; dictatorial

專制君主 (ㄓㄨㄢ ㄓˋ ㄐㄩㄣ ㄓㄨˇ)
an autocrat

專制政體 (ㄓㄨㄢ ㄓˋ ㄓㄥˋ ㄊㄧˇ)or 專制政治 (ㄓㄨㄢ ㄓˋ ㄓㄥˋ ㄓˋ)
autocracy

專政 (ㄓㄨㄢ ㄓㄥˋ)
dictatorship

專注 (ㄓㄨㄢ ㄓㄨˋ)
to concentrate one's attention on; to be absorbed in; to devote one's mind to: 他專注於研究物理學。He devotes his attention to the study of physics.

專著 (ㄓㄨㄢ ㄓㄨˋ)
a monograph; a treatise

專車 (ㄓㄨㄢ ㄔㄜ)
a train or bus run for a particular purpose

專差 (ㄓㄨㄢ ㄔㄞ)
a special messenger (sent exclusively for a particular errand); a specially sent messenger or emissary

專長 (ㄓㄨㄢ ㄔㄤˊ)
a special skill; a specialty

專程 (ㄓㄨㄢ ㄔㄥˊ)
a special trip

專誠 (ㄓㄨㄢ ㄔㄥˊ)
with the exclusive purpose of

專使 (ㄓㄨㄢ ㄕˇ)
a special envoy

專擅 (ㄓㄨㄢ ㄕㄢˋ)
to act without authorization; to do things without asking for approval

專人 (ㄓㄨㄢ ㄖㄣˊ)
a person specially assigned

for a task

任(ㄓㄨㄢ ㄖㄣˋ)
(of an employee) full time; full-time: 他在那裡專任. He works there full time.

責(ㄓㄨㄢ ㄗㄜˊ)
a specific responsibility

才(ㄓㄨㄢ ㄘㄞˊ)
a specialist; a person specially good at something

案(ㄓㄨㄢ ㄢˋ)
a special case (to be dealt with separately): 這件事應成立專案. This should be made a special case to be dealt with separately.

一(ㄓㄨㄢ ㄧ)
to concentrate one's attention on; single-minded

業(ㄓㄨㄢ ㄧㄝˋ)
①a special field of study; a specialized subject; a specialty ②a specialized trade

業道德(ㄓㄨㄢ ㄧㄝˋ ㄉㄠˋ ㄉㄜˊ)
professional ethics

業課程(ㄓㄨㄢ ㄧㄝˋ ㄎㄜˋ ㄔㄥˊ)
a specialized course

業化(ㄓㄨㄢ ㄧㄝˋ ㄏㄨㄚˋ)
specialization

業精神(ㄓㄨㄢ ㄧㄝˋ ㄐㄧㄥ ㄕㄣˊ)
dedication to a job

業訓練(ㄓㄨㄢ ㄧㄝˋ ㄒㄩㄣˋ ㄌㄧㄢˋ)
training in a specialty

業知識(ㄓㄨㄢ ㄧㄝˋ ㄓ ㄕˋ)
professional knowledge

業人員(ㄓㄨㄢ ㄧㄝˋ ㄖㄣˊ ㄩㄢˊ)
the personnel in a specific field

有名詞(ㄓㄨㄢ ㄧㄡˇ ㄇㄧㄥˊ ㄘˊ)
a proper noun

員(ㄓㄨㄢ ㄩㄢˊ)
a specialist in the government; a commissioner (a prefectual official); a senior official

用(ㄓㄨㄢ ㄩㄥˋ)
to use exclusively; to be used exclusively

用電話(ㄓㄨㄢ ㄩㄥˋ ㄉㄧㄢˋ ㄏㄨㄚˋ)
a telephone for special use

【將】 1162
1. ㄐㄧㄤ jiang jiāng
1. (used with a verb expressing future action) going to; about to
2. used with a noun functioning as a direct object

3. to nourish

將來(ㄐㄧㄤ ㄌㄞˊ)
the future; the days to come: 我希望你有一個幸福的將來. I hope you have a happy future before you.

將功補過(ㄐㄧㄤ ㄍㄨㄥ ㄅㄨˇ ㄍㄨㄛˋ)
to make amends for one's faults by good deeds

將功贖罪(ㄐㄧㄤ ㄍㄨㄥ ㄕㄨˊ ㄗㄨㄟˋ)
to atone for mistakes by meritorious service

將計就計(ㄐㄧㄤ ㄐㄧˋ ㄐㄧㄡˋ ㄐㄧˋ)
to adapt one's scheme to that of the opponent; to deal with an opponent by taking advantage of his scheme

將就(ㄐㄧㄤ ㄐㄧㄡˋ)
to make the best of an unsatisfactory situation; to make do with something not good enough; to manage with something unsatisfactory

將近(ㄐㄧㄤ ㄐㄧㄣˋ)
approximately; close to; nearly; almost

將軍(ㄐㄧㄤ ㄐㄩㄣ)
①a general or admiral ②a call to indicate a checkmate (in Chinese chess) ③ to embarrass; to challenge

將信將疑(ㄐㄧㄤ ㄒㄧㄣˋ ㄐㄧㄤ ㄧˊ)
wavering between doubt and belief; half in doubt; skeptical

將錯就錯(ㄐㄧㄤ ㄘㄨㄛˋ ㄐㄧㄡˋ ㄘㄨㄛˋ)
to accept the consequences of a mistake and try to adapt oneself thereto

將要(ㄐㄧㄤ ㄧㄠˋ)
going to or about to (do something); on the point of (doing something): 此機將要起飛. The plane is about to take off.

將養(ㄐㄧㄤ ㄧㄤˇ)or 將息(ㄐㄧㄤ ㄒㄧˊ)
to rest so as to restore one's strength

【將】 1162
2. ㄐㄧㄤˋ jiang jiàng
1. a general; an admiral; a military leader of high rank: 他是一位偉大的將帥. He is a great general.
2. to lead (soldiers)

將兵(ㄐㄧㄤˋ ㄅㄧㄥ)
to command troops

將門(ㄐㄧㄤˋ ㄇㄣˊ)
the family of a high-ranking military officer

將門虎子(ㄐㄧㄤˋ ㄇㄣˊ ㄏㄨˇ ㄗˇ)
a capable young man from a distinguished family

將領(ㄐㄧㄤˋ ㄌㄧㄥˇ)
high-ranking military officers; a general

將令(ㄐㄧㄤˋ ㄌㄧㄥˋ)
the orders given by a commanding general

將官(ㄐㄧㄤˋ ㄍㄨㄢ)
a general officer

將校(ㄐㄧㄤˋ ㄒㄧㄠˋ)
general officers and field officers

將相(ㄐㄧㄤˋ ㄒㄧㄤˋ)
generals and ministers; military and political leaders

將種(ㄐㄧㄤˋ ㄓㄨㄥˇ)
a person born of military forbears

將士(ㄐㄧㄤˋ ㄕˋ)
officers and men

將士用命(ㄐㄧㄤˋ ㄕˋ ㄩㄥˋ ㄇㄧㄥˋ)
(said of troops in combat) Officers and men perform their assigned duties conscientiously.

將帥(ㄐㄧㄤˋ ㄕㄨㄞˋ)
a general

將才(ㄐㄧㄤˋ ㄘㄞˊ)
the talent as a field commander

【尉】 1163
1. ㄨㄟˋ wey wèi
1. a company-grade military officer
2. (in former times) a grade of military official

尉官(ㄨㄟˋ ㄍㄨㄢ)
a military officer above the rank of warrant officer and below that of major; a junior officer

【尉】 1163
2. ㄩˋ yuh yù
as in 尉遲—a double family name

九畫

【尊】 1164
1. ㄗㄨㄣ tzuen zūn
1. to honor; to respect; to venerate; to revere; to esteem

寸部

〔寸部〕

2.honored; honorable; noble; esteemed; respectable

尊卑（ㄗㄨㄣ ㄅㄟ）
①seniors and juniors ②superiors and inferiors

尊名（ㄗㄨㄣ ㄇㄧㄥ）
(courteously) Your name, Sir?

尊命（ㄗㄨㄣ ㄇㄧㄥ）
(courteously) your order

尊夫人（ㄗㄨㄣ ㄈㄨ ㄖㄣ）
(courteously) your wife

尊府（ㄗㄨㄣ ㄈㄨ）
(courteously) your home

尊大人（ㄗㄨㄣ ㄉㄚ ㄖㄣ）
(courteously) your father; your esteemed father

尊堂（ㄗㄨㄣ ㄊㄤ）
(courteously) your esteemed mother

尊貴（ㄗㄨㄣ ㄍㄨㄟ）
noble; honorable; respectable

尊號（ㄗㄨㄣ ㄏㄠ）
①titular honors offerred to the king, queen or other members of the royal family ②(courteously) your name

尊駕（ㄗㄨㄣ ㄐㄧㄚ）
(courteously) you; your esteemed self

尊教（ㄗㄨㄣ ㄐㄧㄠ）
(courteously) your esteemed teaching or instruction

尊見（ㄗㄨㄣ ㄐㄧㄢ）
(courteously) your opinion or view; your esteemed opinion: 您對那人尊見如何? What is your opinion of that man?

尊敬（ㄗㄨㄣ ㄐㄧㄥ）
to respect; to revere; respect; reverence; 尊敬長者. Show respect to those who are older.

尊君（ㄗㄨㄣ ㄐㄩㄣ）
①(courteously) your esteemed father ②to respect the king

尊前（ㄗㄨㄣ ㄑㄧㄢ）
a conventional term placed after the salutation in letters addressed to one's senior

尊親（ㄗㄨㄣ ㄑㄧㄣ）
(courteously) your parents; your esteemed parents

尊顯（ㄗㄨㄣ ㄒㄧㄢ）
of high position; noble; honorable; respectable; vener-

able: 公爵是尊貴之人. A duke is a man of high position.

尊姓大名（ㄗㄨㄣ ㄒㄧㄥ ㄉㄚ ㄇㄧㄥ）
(courteously) your name: 請問尊姓大名? May I know your name?

尊長（ㄗㄨㄣ ㄓㄤ）
an older person; an elder; a senior

尊重（ㄗㄨㄣ ㄓㄨㄥ）
to venerate; to hold in reverence; to honor; to respect; to esteem; to uphold: 沒有人比我更尊重他的父親. No one esteems your father more than I do.

尊稱（ㄗㄨㄣ ㄔㄥ）
an honorific term; a title of respect; an honorific

尊處（ㄗㄨㄣ ㄔㄨ）
(courteously) your abode; your honorable abode

尊崇（ㄗㄨㄣ ㄔㄨㄥ）
to revere; to venerate; to hold in reverence; to honor; to esteem: 我們尊崇神聖事物. We revere sacred things.

尊師重道（ㄗㄨㄣ ㄕ ㄓㄨㄥ ㄉㄠ）
to respect the teacher and his teachings: 人人需尊師重道. Everyone should respect the teacher and his teachings.

尊容（ㄗㄨㄣ ㄖㄨㄥ）
①(courteously) your face ②(Buddhism) the venerable face of the Buddha ③(colloquial) that disgusting face of yours (his or hers)

尊榮（ㄗㄨㄣ ㄖㄨㄥ）
dignity and honor

尊俎折衝（ㄗㄨㄣ ㄗㄨ ㄓㄜ ㄔㄨㄥ）
to win a war at the conference table 參看「折衝尊俎」

尊嚴（ㄗㄨㄣ ㄧㄢ）
dignity; respectability; honor

尊王攘夷（ㄗㄨㄣ ㄨㄤ ㄖㄤ ㄧ）
to honor the emperor and repel the barbarians (a slogan common in the days before the republic)

尊翁（ㄗㄨㄣ ㄨㄥ）
(courteously) your father

【尋】1165
1. ㄒㄩㄣ　shyun xún
1. a measure of length in former times (roughly equiva-

lent to eight feet)
2. to seek; to search

尋寶（ㄒㄩㄣ ㄅㄠ）
to hunt for treasure; treasure hunt

尋覓（ㄒㄩㄣ ㄇㄧ）
to search for; to look for; seek for

尋芳（ㄒㄩㄣ ㄈㄤ）
①to go on a picnic for viewing flowers ②to seek carnal pleasure

尋芳客（ㄒㄩㄣ ㄈㄤ ㄎㄜ）
a patron of brothels

尋訪（ㄒㄩㄣ ㄈㄤ）
to look for (somebody whose whereabouts is unknown); to try to locate; to make inquiries about

尋短見（ㄒㄩㄣ ㄉㄨㄢ ㄐㄧㄢ）
to end one's own life; to commit suicide: 人不應尋短見. One should not commit suicide.

尋歡（ㄒㄩㄣ ㄏㄨㄢ）or 尋歡作樂（ㄒㄩㄣ ㄏㄨㄢ ㄗㄨㄛ ㄌㄜ）
to seek amusement; to seek pleasure

尋根問底（ㄒㄩㄣ ㄍㄣ ㄨㄣ ㄉㄧ）or 尋根究底（ㄒㄩㄣ ㄍㄣ ㄐㄧㄡ ㄉㄧ）
to make a thorough investigation; to probe deeply

尋開心（ㄒㄩㄣ ㄎㄞ ㄒㄧㄣ）
(dialect) to make fun of; to joke

尋花問柳（ㄒㄩㄣ ㄏㄨㄚ ㄨㄣ ㄌㄧㄡ）
①to enjoy natural beauty in springtime ②to seek carnal pleasure

尋究（ㄒㄩㄣ ㄐㄧㄡ）
to try insistently to find out (cause, origin)

尋求（ㄒㄩㄣ ㄑㄧㄡ）
to seek: 大多數人尋求財富. Most men seek wealth.

尋釁（ㄒㄩㄣ ㄒㄧㄣ）
to pick a quarrel; to provoke

尋找（ㄒㄩㄣ ㄓㄠ）
to look for; to seek for: 你仍然在尋找工作嗎? Are you still looking for a job?

尋章摘句（ㄒㄩㄣ ㄓㄤ ㄓㄞ ㄐㄩ）
to labor over the wording in a pointless manner

尋常（ㄒㄩㄣ ㄔㄤ）
usual; ordinary; common

commonplace; routine: 給侍者小費是尋常的事。It is usual to tip the waiter.

尋事生非(TUム アㄥ ㄈㄟ)
to seek a quarrel; to make trouble

尋人啓事(TUム ㄖㄣ ㄑㄧ ㄕ)
a notice in a missing person column

尋思
to ponder; to consider; to reflect; to meditate: 尋思一下這事該怎麼辦。Think over what to do about it.

尋幽探勝(TUム ㄧㄡ ㄊㄢ ㄕㄥ)
to visit scenic spots

尋味(TUム ㄨㄟ)
to relish or enjoy (a literary work): 他這番話耐人尋味。What he has said affords much meaning for enjoying.

尋 1165
2. Tㄧㄣ shyn xin
to beg; to entreat

尋覓(Tㄧㄣ ㄑㄧ ㄈ·ㄎㄜ)
a beggar

尋死覓活(Tㄧㄣ ㄙ ㄇㄧ ㄏㄨㄛ)
to attempt suicide repeatedly (in order to threaten)

尋 1165
3. Tㄩ世 shyue xue
to look around

尋摸(Tㄩㄝ·ㄇㄜ)
to look around as to seek something

十一畫

對 1166
ㄉㄨㄟˋ duey dui
right; correct; proper: 說謊是不對的。It's not right to tell lies.
parallel; opposing
. a pair; a couple
. to check; ascertain
. to; as to; with regard to
. to be directed at: 我的話不是針對你說的。What I said was not directed at you.

對白(ㄉㄨㄟ ㄅㄞ)
dialogue

對保(ㄉㄨㄟ ㄅㄠ)
to confirm or verify a guaranty

對半(ㄉㄨㄟ ㄅㄢ)
a half; one half

對比(ㄉㄨㄟ ㄅㄧ)

contrast; correlation

對筆跡(ㄉㄨㄟ ㄅㄧ ㄐㄧ)
to analyze a handwriting (in an effort to ascertain its author)

對邊(ㄉㄨㄟ ㄅㄧㄢ)
the opposite side

對簿公庭(ㄉㄨㄟ ㄅㄨ ㄍㄨㄥ ㄊㄧㄥ)
to face or confront each other in court at a trial

對不起(ㄉㄨㄟ ㄅㄨ ㄑㄧ)or 對不住
(ㄉㄨㄟ·ㄅㄨ ㄓㄨˋ)
①to let a person down②I am sorry. 或 I apologize.

對馬海峽(ㄉㄨㄟ ㄇㄚˇ ㄏㄞˇ ㄒㄧㄚˊ)
the Tsushima Strait

對罵(ㄉㄨㄟ ㄇㄚˋ)
to call each other names

對門(ㄉㄨㄟ ㄇㄣˊ)
①the family, or household, right across the front street②(two buildings) opposite to (each other): 工廠與門市是郵局。Opposite to the factory is the post office.

對面(ㄉㄨㄟ ㄇㄧㄢ)
on the opposite side; right in front: 他家就在我家對面。His house is opposite to mine.

對方(ㄉㄨㄟ ㄈㄤ)
the other side; the other party

對付(ㄉㄨㄟ ㄈㄨˋ)
to deal with; to cope with

對答(ㄉㄨㄟ ㄉㄚˊ)
to answer questions

對答如流(ㄉㄨㄟ ㄉㄚˊ ㄖㄨˊ ㄌㄧㄡ)
to give answers fluently

對打(ㄉㄨㄟ ㄉㄚˇ)
to fight each other; to exchange blows

對得起(ㄉㄨㄟ·ㄉㄜ ㄑㄧ)or 對得住
(ㄉㄨㄟ·ㄉㄜ ㄓㄨˋ)
not let somebody down; to treat somebody fairly

對待(ㄉㄨㄟ ㄉㄞ)
to treat (a person kindly, cruelly, etc.): 這公司對待員工一直很好。This firm has always treated its workers well.

對等(ㄉㄨㄟ ㄉㄥˇ)
equal

對敵(ㄉㄨㄟ ㄉㄧˊ)
opponent; to oppose; to antagonize

對調(ㄉㄨㄟ ㄉㄧㄠ)
to exchange positions: 我想與你對調工作。I wish to exchange jobs with you.

對頂角(ㄉㄨㄟ ㄉㄧㄥˇ ㄐㄧㄠˇ)
(mathematics) vertically opposite angles

對子(ㄉㄨㄟ·ㄗ)
to engage in the literary exercise of supplying a sentence that parallels a given one (so as to form an antithesis or couplet)

對臺戲(ㄉㄨㄟ ㄊㄞˊ ㄒㄧ)
a rival show—(figuratively) competition

對頭
①(ㄉㄨㄟ ㄊㄡˊ) right: 這方法對頭。This method is right.②(ㄉㄨㄟ·ㄊㄡ) an opponent; an adversary; a rival: 他在選舉中擊敗了他的對頭。He defeated his opponent in the election.

對內(ㄉㄨㄟ ㄋㄟˋ)
for domestic or internal (consumption, use, etc.)

對牛彈琴(ㄉㄨㄟ ㄋㄧㄡˊ ㄊㄢˊ ㄑㄧㄣˊ)
(literally) to play a lute before an ox—to speak to someone about something completely incomprehensible to him; to cast pearls before swine

對壘(ㄉㄨㄟ ㄌㄟˇ)
to confront each other; to be encamped face to face: 兩軍對壘。Two armies confronted each other.

對立(ㄉㄨㄟ ㄌㄧ)
to be opposed to each other; to be in opposition to each other: 求學與工作不應相互對立。Study and work should not be opposed to each other.

對流(ㄉㄨㄟ ㄌㄧㄡˊ)
(physics) convection

對聯(ㄉㄨㄟ ㄌㄧㄢˊ)
a Chinese couplet (often written and mounted on scrolls to be hung up on the wall)

對路(ㄉㄨㄟ ㄌㄨˋ)or 對路子(ㄉㄨㄟ ㄌㄨˋ·ㄗ)
①to satisfy the need: 這些貨到都市正對路。These goods

（寸部）

【寸部】

will satisfy the needs of the city. ② to be to one's liking; to suit one

對過兒(ㄉㄨㄟˋ《ㄨㄛˋㄦ) or 對過(ㄉㄨㄟˋ《ㄨㄛˋ)
① the family, or household, right in front of one's house ② across the way: 他就住在對過兒。 He lives just across the way.

對光(ㄉㄨㄟˋ《ㄨㄤ)
① (said of spectacles) of the right power; ② (cinematography) to focus

對開(ㄉㄨㄟˋㄎㄞ)
①(said of buses or trains) to head for each other from two stations along the same road ② folio

對口(ㄉㄨㄟˋㄎㄡˇ)
to speak or sing alternately

對口相聲(ㄉㄨㄟˋㄎㄡˇㄒㄧㄤˋㄕㄥ)
the Chinese comic dialogue

對口唱(ㄉㄨㄟˋㄎㄡˇㄔㄤˋ)
antiphonal singing; dialogue in antiphonal singing

對抗(ㄉㄨㄟˋㄎㄤˋ)
to be opposed to each other; to be in opposition to each other; to face each other in opposition

對抗賽(ㄉㄨㄟˋㄎㄤˋㄙㄞˋ)
a duel meet (between opposing teams from two different cities or countries)

對空射擊(ㄉㄨㄟˋㄎㄨㄥㄕㄜˋㄐㄧ)
ground-to-air firing; to fire to the air

對號(ㄉㄨㄟˋㄏㄠˋ)
① to check the number ② to fit; to tally ③ a check mark

對號入座(ㄉㄨㄟˋㄏㄠˋㄖㄨˋㄗㄨㄛˋ)
to seat oneself according to the designated number indicated on the ticket

對話(ㄉㄨㄟˋㄏㄨㄚˋ)
a dialogue; a conversation

對換(ㄉㄨㄟˋㄏㄨㄢˋ)
to exchange; to barter; to swap

對角線(ㄉㄨㄟˋㄐㄧㄠˇㄒㄧㄢˋ)
(mathematics) a diagonal

對襟(ㄉㄨㄟˋㄐㄧㄣ)
the front part of a garment with buttons straight down in the middle

對勁(ㄉㄨㄟˋㄐㄧㄣˋ) or 對勁兒(ㄉㄨㄟˋㄐㄧㄣˋ)
of the right or agreeable nature; in the right or agreeable condition

對獎(ㄉㄨㄟˋㄐㄧㄤˇ)
to check the results of a lottery or raffle to see if one holds the winning ticket

對講機(ㄉㄨㄟˋㄐㄧㄤˇㄐㄧ)
an interphone; an intercom; an intercommunication system

對局(ㄉㄨㄟˋㄐㄩˊ)
to play a game of chess, etc.

對句(ㄉㄨㄟˋㄐㄩˋ)
a Chinese couplet or antithesis

對象(ㄉㄨㄟˋㄒㄧㄤˋ)
the object (of an action); the subject (of consideration)

對質(ㄉㄨㄟˋㄓˊ)
to face each other and exchange questions (in order to find out the truth): 被告與原告對質。 The accused was confronted with his accuser.

對時(ㄉㄨㄟˋㄕˊ)
to face each other; to confront each other: 兩軍對時。 The two armies confronted each other.

對折(ㄉㄨㄟˋㄓㄜˊ)
a 50% discount: 他們以對折賣舊書。 They sold used books at a 50% discount.

對照(ㄉㄨㄟˋㄓㄠˋ)
to compare; to contrast; cross reference: 將這些外國貨與本國貨對照一下。 Contrast these foreign goods with the domestic product.

對照表(ㄉㄨㄟˋㄓㄠˋㄅㄧㄠˇ)
a contrastive or comparative table

對仗(ㄉㄨㄟˋㄓㄤˋ)
verbal parallelism (in classical Chinese poetry)

對證(ㄉㄨㄟˋㄓㄥˋ)
to establish evidence through personal confrontation or signed statement, etc.

對症下藥(ㄉㄨㄟˋㄓㄥˋㄒㄧㄚˋㄧㄠˋ)
(literally) to give the right prescription for an illness — (figuratively) to take the

right remedial steps to correct a shortcoming

對酌(ㄉㄨㄟˋㄓㄨㄛˊ)
to drink, sitting face to face

對準(ㄉㄨㄟˋㄓㄨㄣˇ)
① to adjust (a machine part needing adjustment) to the right or proper position ② to aim at. 遠盜瞄準他。 The bandit aimed at him.

對稱(ㄉㄨㄟˋㄔㄥ)
symmetry; symmetrical

對唱(ㄉㄨㄟˋㄔㄤˋ)
a musical dialogue in antiphonal style; antiphonal singing

對手(ㄉㄨㄟˋㄕㄡˇ)
an opponent; an adversary; a match: 我不是他的對手。 I am no match for him.

對數(ㄉㄨㄟˋㄕㄨˋ)
a logarithm

對數表(ㄉㄨㄟˋㄕㄨˋㄅㄧㄠˇ)
the logarithmic table

對子(ㄉㄨㄟˋ·ㄗ) or 對兒(ㄉㄨㄟˋㄦ)
a Chinese couplet or antithesis

對策(ㄉㄨㄟˋㄘㄜˋ)
a measure (to deal with a problem, etc.); a counter-measure; a counterplot: 我們必須採取正當的對策，否則將失敗。 We must take the right measure, or we shall fail.

對偶(ㄉㄨㄟˋㄡˇ)
① to match; to pair ② verbal parallelism (in poetry)

對岸(ㄉㄨㄟˋㄢˋ)
the opposite shore: 他游到對岸。 He swam to the opposite shore.

對奕(ㄉㄨㄟˋㄧˋ)
to confront each other in chess game

對應(ㄉㄨㄟˋㄧㄥˋ)
corresponding; homologous

對味兒(ㄉㄨㄟˋㄨㄟˋㄦ)
① to one's taste ② to be all right: 你說的話聽起來很對味兒。 What you say sounds all right.

對外(ㄉㄨㄟˋㄨㄞˋ)
① for foreign or overseas (consumption, use, etc.) ② foreign (policies, etc.) ③ to resist a foreign aggression

對外貿易(ㄉㄨㄟˋㄨㄞˋㄇㄠˋㄧˋ)

foreign trade

對於(ㄉㄨㄟˋ ㄩˊ)
to; as to; in relation to; with regard to: 對於其他，我一無所知。I don't know anything as to the others.

十三畫

【導】 1167
(ㄉㄠˇ daw dǎo)
(語音 ㄉㄠˋ dao dào)
to guide; to lead; to instruct; to conduct; to direct

導播(ㄉㄠˇ ㄅㄛ)
(TV)a director

導彈(ㄉㄠˇ ㄉㄢˋ)
a guided missile

導彈基地(ㄉㄠˇ ㄉㄢˋ ㄐㄧ ㄉㄧˋ)
a missile base

導電(ㄉㄠˇ ㄉㄧㄢˋ)
electric conduction

導電體(ㄉㄠˇ ㄉㄧㄢˋ ㄊㄧˇ)or導體(ㄉㄠˇ ㄊㄧˇ)
an electric conductor

導尿(ㄉㄠˇ ㄋㄧㄠˋ)
catheterization

導流(ㄉㄠˇ ㄌㄧㄡˊ)
(irrigation) diversion

導論(ㄉㄠˇ ㄌㄨㄣˋ)or導言(ㄉㄠˇ ㄧㄢˊ)
an introductory remark; an introduction: 他教哲學導論。He taught an introduction to philosophy.

導管(ㄉㄠˇ ㄍㄨㄢˇ)
①(machinery) a conduit; a pipe; a duct ②(biology) a vessel; a duct

導航(ㄉㄠˇ ㄏㄤˊ)
to navigate; navigation

導航系統(ㄉㄠˇ ㄏㄤˊ ㄒㄧˋ ㄊㄨㄥˇ)
a guidance system

導火線(ㄉㄠˇ ㄏㄨㄛˇ ㄒㄧㄢˋ)
①a fuse (for setting off explosives) ②the direct cause (of a development or event)

導火索(ㄉㄠˇ ㄏㄨㄛˇ ㄙㄨㄛˇ)
(military) a (blasting) fuse

導線(ㄉㄠˇ ㄒㄧㄢˋ)
(electricity) a lead; conducting wire

導向飛彈(ㄉㄠˇ ㄒㄧㄤˋ ㄈㄟ ㄉㄢˋ)
guided missiles

導向系統(ㄉㄠˇ ㄒㄧㄤˋ ㄒㄧˋ ㄊㄨㄥˇ)
a guidance system

導致(ㄉㄠˇ ㄓˋ)
to lead to; to cause something to happen: 這將導致無窮的糾紛。This will lead to endless confusion.

導師(ㄉㄠˇ ㄕ)
①a spiritual guide ②a tutor; a teacher charged with the responsibility to provide guidance to a class of students in their conduct or other nonacademic activities

導師制(ㄉㄠˇ ㄕ ㄓˋ)
the tutorial system

導熱(ㄉㄠˇ ㄖㄜˋ)
(physics) heat conduction

導遊(ㄉㄠˇ ㄧㄡˊ)
a tourist guide

導演(ㄉㄠˇ ㄧㄢˇ)
the director (of a dramatic performance)

導引(ㄉㄠˇ ㄧㄣˇ)
Taoist breathing exercises

導源(ㄉㄠˇ ㄩㄢˊ)
①(said of a river) to flow from ②to originate; to come from

小 部
ㄒㄧㄠˇ sheau xiǎo

【小】 1168
ㄒㄧㄠˇ sheau xiǎo
1. small; little; tiny
2. minor: 這是小錯。It is a minor fault.
3. young; junior: 他比我小三歲。He is three years junior to me. 或 He is junior to me by three years.
4. humble; mean; lowly
5. light; slight; unimportant; trivial; petty

小把戲(ㄒㄧㄠˇ ㄅㄚˇ ㄒㄧˋ)
a child (in the Wu dialect)

小白臉(ㄒㄧㄠˇ ㄅㄞˊ ㄌㄧㄢˇ)
a handsome young man with effeminate features

小白菜(ㄒㄧㄠˇ ㄅㄞˊ ㄘㄞˋ)
a variety of Chinese cabbage; a pak-choi

小輩(ㄒㄧㄠˇ ㄅㄟˋ)
the members of the younger

generation in a family or clan; a junior

小報(ㄒㄧㄠˇ ㄅㄠˋ)
a small newspaper

小班(ㄒㄧㄠˇ ㄅㄢ)
①the lowest of the three grades of kindergarten children ②a first-rate brothel (in Peking)

小半(ㄒㄧㄠˇ ㄅㄢˋ)
the smaller half

小本經營(ㄒㄧㄠˇ ㄅㄣˇ ㄐㄧㄥ ㄧㄥˊ)
(business) to run or operate with a small capital

小本生意(ㄒㄧㄠˇ ㄅㄣˇ ㄕㄥ ㄧˋ)
a small business

小辮兒(ㄒㄧㄠˇ ㄅㄧㄢˋ ㄦ)or小辮子(ㄒㄧㄠˇ ㄅㄧㄢˋ ㄗˇ)
a braid: 她扎頭髮梳成小辮子。She wears her hair in braids.

小別(ㄒㄧㄠˇ ㄅㄧㄝˊ)
to part for a short while; a brief separation

小別勝新婚(ㄒㄧㄠˇ ㄅㄧㄝˊ ㄕㄥˋ ㄒㄧㄣ ㄏㄨㄣ)
A brief parting is as sweet as a honeymoon.

小癟三(ㄒㄧㄠˇ ㄅㄧㄝˇ ㄙㄢ)
(dialect) a bum; a trash

小標題(ㄒㄧㄠˇ ㄅㄧㄠ ㄊㄧˊ)
a subheading; a subhead

小便(ㄒㄧㄠˇ ㄅㄧㄢˋ)or小解(ㄒㄧㄠˇ ㄐㄧㄝˇ)
①to urinate; to pass urine; to empty the bladder; to make water ②urine; urination

小步(ㄒㄧㄠˇ ㄅㄨˋ)
to stroll

小部份 or 小部分(ㄒㄧㄠˇ ㄅㄨˋ ㄈㄣˋ)
a small part; a small portion; the minority

小不忍則亂大謀(ㄒㄧㄠˇ ㄅㄨˋ ㄖㄣˇ ㄗㄜˊ ㄌㄨㄢˋ ㄉㄚˋ ㄇㄡˊ)
Lack of forbearance in small matters upsets great plans. 或 He who cannot forbear in small matters spoils great undertakings.

小不點兒(ㄒㄧㄠˇ ㄅㄨˋ ㄉㄧㄢˇ ㄦ)
a very small or tiny thing or person

小朋友(ㄒㄧㄠˇ ㄆㄥˊ ㄧㄡˇ)
children (a term expressing goodwill): 小朋友是國家未來的主人翁。Children are the

【小部】

小便宜(ㄒㄧㄠˇ ㄆㄧㄢ·ㄧ)
a small advantage

小品文(ㄒㄧㄠˇ ㄆㄧㄣˇ ㄨㄣˊ)
an essay

小舖子 or 小鋪子(ㄒㄧㄠˇ ㄆㄨˋ·ㄗ)
a small store: 他開個小舖子。
He runs a small store.

小買賣(ㄒㄧㄠˇ ㄇㄞˇ·ㄇㄞ)
small business

小麥(ㄒㄧㄠˇ ㄇㄞˋ)
wheat: 農夫種小麥。Farmers
plant wheat.

小妹(ㄒㄧㄠˇ ㄇㄟˋ)
①a little sister ②a little
girl ③a young female servant

小貓(ㄒㄧㄠˇ ㄇㄠ)
a kitten

小貓熊(ㄒㄧㄠˇ ㄇㄠ ㄒㄩㄥˊ)
a lesser panda 亦作「小熊貓」

小滿(ㄒㄧㄠˇ ㄇㄢˇ)
Grain fills—one of a year's
24 solar periods, which falls
on May 21 or 22

小門小戶(ㄒㄧㄠˇ ㄇㄣˊ ㄒㄧㄠˇ ㄏㄨˋ)
a poor, humble family

小米(ㄒㄧㄠˇ ㄇㄧˇ)
millet

小民(ㄒㄧㄠˇ ㄇㄧㄣˊ)
a commoner; common peo-
ple 亦作「老百姓」

小名(ㄒㄧㄠˇ ㄇㄧㄥˊ)
one's childhood name

小拇指(ㄒㄧㄠˇ ㄇㄨˇ ㄓˇ)
one's little finger

小費(ㄒㄧㄠˇ ㄈㄟˋ)
a tip (given to a waiter, porter, etc.)

小販(ㄒㄧㄠˇ ㄈㄢˋ)
stall holders; hawkers; peddlers

小腹(ㄒㄧㄠˇ ㄈㄨˋ)
the lower abdomen

小婦(ㄒㄧㄠˇ ㄈㄨˋ)
①a concubine ②a young
woman

小大由之(ㄒㄧㄠˇ ㄉㄚˋ ㄧㄡˊ ㄓ)
to be of either little value or
great use

小的(ㄒㄧㄠˇ·ㄉㄜ)
①(ㄒㄧㄠˇ·ㄉㄜ) the small one: 他
要那小的。He wants the small
one.
②(ㄒㄧㄠˇ·ㄉㄧ) (in ancient
China) a self reference by

servants when speaking to
the master

小刀(ㄒㄧㄠˇ ㄉㄠ)
①a small sword ②a pocket
knife

小島(ㄒㄧㄠˇ ㄉㄠˇ)
an islet: 我們不知道這小島的
名字。We don't know the
name of this islet.

小道消息(ㄒㄧㄠˇ ㄉㄠˋ ㄒㄧㄠ·ㄒㄧ)
hearsay; the grapevine

小旦(ㄒㄧㄠˇ ㄉㄢˋ)
(Chinese opera) a female
role

小登科(ㄒㄧㄠˇ ㄉㄥ ㄎㄜ)
(colloquial) to take a wife

小弟(ㄒㄧㄠˇ ㄉㄧˋ)
①a little brother ②a little
boy ③a young male servant

小調(ㄒㄧㄠˇ ㄉㄧㄠˋ)
folk songs; ballads

小店(ㄒㄧㄠˇ ㄉㄧㄢˋ)
①an inn; a lodging house ②
a small store ③my or our
store (a self-depreciatory
term)

小電影(ㄒㄧㄠˇ ㄉㄧㄢˋ ㄧㄥˇ)
(slang) a porno film; a skin
flick

小隊(ㄒㄧㄠˇ ㄉㄨㄟˋ)
a small contingent or
detachment

小動作(ㄒㄧㄠˇ ㄉㄨㄥˋ ㄗㄨㄛˋ)
petty action; little tricks

小偷(ㄒㄧㄠˇ ㄊㄡ)
a thief; a burglar

小題大做(ㄒㄧㄠˇ ㄊㄧˊ ㄉㄚˋ ㄗㄨㄛˋ)
to make much of a trifle; a
storm in a teacup; to make
a mountain out of a mole-
hill: 這未免小題大做。This is
making a mountain out of a
molehill.

小提琴(ㄒㄧㄠˇ ㄊㄧˊ ㄑㄧㄣˊ)
violin

小蹄子(ㄒㄧㄠˇ ㄊㄧˊ·ㄗ)
an abusive reference to a
maidservant

小天地(ㄒㄧㄠˇ ㄊㄧㄢ ㄉㄧˋ)
small world; limited sphere
of activities

小艇(ㄒㄧㄠˇ ㄊㄧㄥˇ)
a small boat; a skiff

小腿(ㄒㄧㄠˇ ㄊㄨㄟˇ)
the calf (of the leg)

小腦(ㄒㄧㄠˇ ㄋㄠˇ)

the cerebellum

小妮子(ㄒㄧㄠˇ ㄋㄧˊ·ㄗ)
①a girl (expressing endearment) ②a housemaid

小鳥依人(ㄒㄧㄠˇ ㄋㄧㄠˇ ㄧ ㄖㄣˊ)
(said of a child or young
girl) lovely and pliant like a
little bird

小妞兒(ㄒㄧㄠˇ ㄋㄧㄡ ㄦ)
a small girl; a young girl

小牛(ㄒㄧㄠˇ ㄋㄧㄡˊ)
a calf

小牛肉(ㄒㄧㄠˇ ㄋㄧㄡˊ ㄖㄡˋ)
veal

小年夜(ㄒㄧㄠˇ ㄋㄧㄢˊ ㄧㄝˋ)
the night before Lunar New
Year's Eve

小娘兒(ㄒㄧㄠˇ ㄋㄧㄤˊ·ㄦ)
a young girl

小農(ㄒㄧㄠˇ ㄋㄨㄥˊ)
a farmer with small land-
holding

小女(ㄒㄧㄠˇ ㄋㄩˇ)
my daughter (a self-
depreciatory term)

小喇叭(ㄒㄧㄠˇ ㄌㄚˇ·ㄅㄚ)
a trumpet

小老婆(ㄒㄧㄠˇ ㄌㄠˇ·ㄆㄛ)
a concubine

小老頭兒(ㄒㄧㄠˇ ㄌㄠˇ ㄊㄡˊ·ㄦ)
a man who ages prematurely

小嘍囉(ㄒㄧㄠˇ ㄌㄡˊ·ㄌㄨㄛ)
unimportant followers; lackeys; underlings

小笠原群島(ㄒㄧㄠˇ ㄌㄧˋ ㄩㄢˊ ㄑㄩㄣˊ ㄉㄠˇ)
Bonin Islands or Ogasawa-
ra Jima

小絡(ㄒㄧㄠˇ ㄌㄧˋ)or 小李(ㄒㄧㄠˇ ㄌㄧˇ)
a pickpocket

小斂(ㄒㄧㄠˇ ㄌㄧㄢˋ)
to dress up the dead in preparation for the funeral service

小兩口子(ㄒㄧㄠˇ ㄌㄧㄤˇ ㄎㄡˇ·ㄗ)
a young couple

小路(ㄒㄧㄠˇ ㄌㄨˋ)
a path; a trail: 他們在雪中剷
出一條小路。They shovel a
path through the snow.

小呂宋(ㄒㄧㄠˇ ㄌㄩˇ ㄙㄨㄥˋ)
Manila

小歌劇(ㄒㄧㄠˇ ㄍㄜ ㄐㄩˋ)
an operetta

小哥兒們(丁Ⅰㄠ ㄍㄜ ·ㄦ ·ㄇㄣ)
a group of young men

小個子(丁Ⅰㄠ ㄍㄜ ·ㄗ)
a little chap; a small fellow

小狗(丁Ⅰㄠ ㄍㄡ)
a young dog; a puppy

小姑(丁Ⅰㄠ ㄍㄨ)
one's husband's younger sister

小姑獨處(丁Ⅰㄠ ㄍㄨ ㄉㄨ ㄔㄨ)
to remain a spinster: 她仍然
小姑獨處。She remains a spinster.

小姑娘(丁Ⅰㄠ ㄍㄨ ·ㄋㄧㄤ)
a missy; a young girl

小掛子(丁Ⅰㄠ ㄍㄨㄚˋ·ㄗ)
a short outer garment

小過(丁Ⅰㄠ ㄍㄨㄛˋ)
① a minor mistake ② a
minor demerit (recorded for
an employee by the employer
or for a student by the
school authorities)

小鬼(丁Ⅰㄠ ㄍㄨㄟˇ)
① the spirits serving the
ruler of the lower world ② a
mischievous child; an imp

小廣告(丁Ⅰㄠ ㄍㄨㄤˇ ㄍㄠˋ)
a classified ad

小工(丁Ⅰㄠ ㄍㄨㄥ)
an unskilled laborer

小可(丁Ⅰㄠ ㄎㄜˇ)
I, me (a self-depreciatory
expression); 小可在此。I am
here.

小開(丁Ⅰㄠ ㄎㄞ)
(Shanghai dialect) a
businessman's son

小楷(丁Ⅰㄠ ㄎㄞˇ)
the calligraphy in small
characters of the standard
type

小考(丁Ⅰㄠ ㄎㄠˇ)
a quiz or test conducted for
students by the teacher

小口(丁Ⅰㄠ ㄎㄡˇ)
an infant as a minor food
consumer in the family (as
distinct from medium and
major consumers)

小口徑(丁Ⅰㄠ ㄎㄡˇ ㄐㄧㄥˋ)
(said of gun barrels) small-
bore

小看(丁Ⅰㄠ ㄎㄢˋ)
to think little of; to make
light of; to treat lightly; to
slight

小康(丁Ⅰㄠ ㄎㄤ)
① (said of a family) well-
to-do: 她出身小康之家。She
came from a well-to-do family.
② (said of a nation)
fairly prosperous and secure

小河(丁Ⅰㄠ ㄏㄜˊ)
a rivulet: 小河上有座橋。The
rivulet is crossed by a
bridge.

小孩(丁Ⅰㄠ ㄏㄞˊ)or 小孩子(丁Ⅰㄠ
ㄏㄞˊ·ㄗ)or 小孩兒(丁Ⅰㄠ ㄏㄞˊㄦ)
a child

小號(丁Ⅰㄠ ㄏㄠˋ)
① my or our store (a self-
depreciatory term) ② small
size (as distinct from medium and large sizes)

小寒(丁Ⅰㄠ ㄏㄢˊ)
Little cold—one of the 24
solar periods, into which the
year is divided, which falls
on January 6 or 7

小戶人家(丁Ⅰㄠ ㄏㄨˋ ㄖㄣˊ ㄐㄧㄚ)
a poor, humble family

小花臉(丁Ⅰㄠ ㄏㄨㄚ ㄌㄧㄢˇ)
a clown in Chinese opera

小花樣(丁Ⅰㄠ ㄏㄨㄚ ㄧㄤˋ)
a little stunt

小划子(丁Ⅰㄠ ㄏㄨㄚˊ ·ㄗ)
a small rowing boat

小夥子(丁Ⅰㄠ ㄏㄨㄛˇ ·ㄗ)or 小夥兒
(丁Ⅰㄠ ㄏㄨㄛˇㄦ)
a young fellow

小惠(丁Ⅰㄠ ㄏㄨㄟˋ)
small favors

小雞(丁Ⅰㄠ ㄐㄧ)
a chick

小家碧玉(丁Ⅰㄠ ㄐㄧㄚ ㄅㄧˋ ㄩˋ)
a daughter of a humble family

小家庭(丁Ⅰㄠ ㄐㄧㄚ ㄊㄧㄥˊ)
a small family

小家子(丁Ⅰㄠ ㄐㄧㄚ ·ㄗ)
a vulgar, lower-class person

小家子氣(丁Ⅰㄠ ㄐㄧㄚ ·ㄗ ·ㄑㄧ)
showing nervous in public,
characteristic of people of
low birth

小結(丁Ⅰㄠ ㄐㄧㄝˊ)
① a brief summary; an
interim summary ② to summarize briefly

小節(丁Ⅰㄠ ㄐㄧㄝˊ)
① a minor, trivial, or unimportant point; a triviality

② a measure (in music)

小姐(丁Ⅰㄠ ㄐㄧㄝˇ)
a young (unmarried) lady

小腳(丁Ⅰㄠ ㄐㄧㄠˇ)
the small feet deformed by
the practice of foot binding
in old China

小轎車(丁Ⅰㄠ ㄐㄧㄠˋ ㄔㄜ)
a sedan (car)

小舅子(丁Ⅰㄠ ㄐㄧㄡˋ·ㄗ)
a brother-in-law (one's wife's
younger brother)

小襟(丁Ⅰㄠ ㄐㄧㄣ)
the inner piece on the right
side of a Chinese garment
which buttons on the right

小憩(丁Ⅰㄠ ㄑㄧˋ)
to rest for a while

小器 or 小氣(丁Ⅰㄠ ㄑㄧˋ)
① narrow-minded ② niggardly: 他很小氣。He is niggardly of money.

小氣鬼(丁Ⅰㄠ ㄑㄧˋ ㄍㄨㄟˇ)
a niggard

小巧玲瓏(丁Ⅰㄠ ㄑㄧㄠˇ ㄌㄧㄥˊ ㄌㄨㄥˊ)
① (said of a woman) small,
trim, and lovely; petite ②
(said of a decorative item)
small and exquisite

小前提(丁Ⅰㄠ ㄑㄧㄢˊ ㄊㄧˊ)
the minor premise (of a syllogism)

小圈子(丁Ⅰㄠ ㄑㄩㄢ ·ㄗ)
a small circle; an inner circle; a tightly knit clique

小犬(丁Ⅰㄠ ㄑㄩㄢˇ)
① a puppy ② (a self-
depreciatory term) my son:
小犬明日歸來。My son will
come home tomorrow.

小媳婦兒(丁Ⅰㄠ ㄒㄧˊ ·ㄈㄨㄦ)
① a little girl engaged to be
one's daughter-in-law when
grown-up ② a young woman

小寫(丁Ⅰㄠ ㄒㄧㄝˇ)
a lowercase letter (of the
Roman alphabet)

小心(丁Ⅰㄠ ㄒㄧㄣ)
careful; cautious; to pay
attention to

小心火燭(丁Ⅰㄠ ㄒㄧㄣ ㄏㄨㄛˇ ㄓㄨˊ)
Guard against fire!

小心輕放(丁Ⅰㄠ ㄒㄧㄣ ㄑㄧㄥ ㄈㄤˋ)
Handle with care!

小心翼翼(丁Ⅰㄠ ㄒㄧㄣ Ⅰˋ Ⅰˋ)
very timidly; very gingerly;
with the greatest circum-

〔小部〕

〔小
部〕

spection: 他小心翼翼地工作。
He did his work with great
care.

小心眼兒(ㄒㄧㄠˇㄒㄧㄣ ㄧㄢˇ)
narrow-minded; extremely
sensitive: 她很小心眼兒。She
is narrow-minded.

小相公(ㄒㄧㄠˇㄒㄧㄤˋㄍㄨㄥ)
a mah-jong player who, due
to oversight, takes in one
tile less than the required 13
at the beginning of a game
and is thus disqualified to
win that particular game

小星(ㄒㄧㄠˇㄒㄧㄥ)
a concubine

小型(ㄒㄧㄠˇㄒㄧㄥˊ)
small-sized; small; midget;
miniature

小型報紙(ㄒㄧㄠˇㄒㄧㄥˊㄅㄠˋㄓˇ)
a tabloid

小型電腦(ㄒㄧㄠˇㄒㄧㄥˊㄉㄧㄢˋㄋㄠˇ)
a minicomputer

小型企業(ㄒㄧㄠˇㄒㄧㄥˊㄑㄧˇㄧㄝˋ)
a small enterprise

小行星(ㄒㄧㄠˇㄒㄧㄥˊㄒㄧㄥ)
a planetoid; an asteroid

小壻 or 小婿(ㄒㄧㄠˇㄒㄩˋ)
①my son-in-law (a self-
depreciatory term): 小婿擔任
市長職務。My son-in-law
served as mayor. ②I or me
(when addressing one's own
parent-in-law)

小學(ㄒㄧㄠˇㄒㄩㄝˊ)
a primary school; an ele-
mentary school: 小孩在上中
學前先上小學。Children attend
primary school before high
school.

小學生(ㄒㄧㄠˇㄒㄩㄝˊㄕㄥ)
a (primary school) pupil; a
schoolchild; a schoolboy or
schoolgirl

小雪(ㄒㄧㄠˇㄒㄩㄝˇ)
①Little snow—one of the
twenty-four solar periods,
into which the year is
divided, falling either on
November 22 or 23 ②a light
snow

小熊貓(ㄒㄧㄠˇㄒㄩㄥˊㄇㄠ)
a lesser panda 亦作「小貓熊」

小熊座(ㄒㄧㄠˇㄒㄩㄥˊㄗㄨㄛˋ)
(astronomy) Ursa Minor

小指(ㄒㄧㄠˇㄓˇ)
the little finger

小照(ㄒㄧㄠˇㄓㄠˋ)
a portrait

小眼(ㄒㄧㄠˇㄧㄢˇ)or 小費(ㄒㄧㄠˇㄈㄟˋ)
tips for waiters, etc.

小住(ㄒㄧㄠˇㄓㄨˋ)
to live at a place temporarily; to sojourn: 他小住旅館。
He sojourns at an inn.

小註(兒)(ㄒㄧㄠˇㄓㄨˋ(ㄦˋ))
footnotes

小酌(ㄒㄧㄠˇㄓㄨㄛˊ)or 小飲(ㄒㄧㄠˇ
ㄧㄣˇ)
a little drink or a few
drinks (of some alcoholic
beverage)

小傳(ㄒㄧㄠˇㄓㄨㄢˋ)
brief (or short) biography:
他則我寫小傳。He asked
me how to write a brief (or
short) biography.

小篆(ㄒㄧㄠˇㄓㄨㄢˋ)
the "small seal," a style of
characters much in vogue
during the Chin Dynasty
shortly before 200 B.C.

小仲馬(ㄒㄧㄠˇㄓㄨㄥˋㄇㄚˇ)
Dumas fils, the younger
Dumas (Alexandre Dumas,
1824-1895, son of Alexandre
Dumas, 1802-1870)

小吃(ㄒㄧㄠˇㄔ)
①supplementary dishes
(usually cold) at a dinner in
addition to the regular
courses ②a snack

小吃館(ㄒㄧㄠˇㄔㄍㄨㄢˇ)
a small restaurant; an eatery: 他經營一家小吃館。He
runs a small restaurant.

小丑(ㄒㄧㄠˇㄔㄡˇ)
a clown: 小孩子喜歡小丑。
Children like clowns.

小醜跳梁(ㄒㄧㄠˇㄔㄡˇㄊㄧㄠˋㄌㄧㄤˊ)
petty thieves going on the
rampage

小產(ㄒㄧㄠˇㄔㄢˇ)
spontaneous abortion; a miscarriage

小腸(ㄒㄧㄠˇㄔㄤˊ)
the small intestine

小腸氣(ㄒㄧㄠˇㄔㄤˊㄑㄧˋ)
hernia 亦作「疝氣」

小成(ㄒㄧㄠˇㄔㄥˊ)
small achievement; moderate
success

小時(ㄒㄧㄠˇㄕˊ)

an hour: 他在那兒停留三小時。
He stayed there three hours.

小時了了(ㄒㄧㄠˇㄕˊㄌㄧㄠˇㄌㄧㄠˇ)
very intelligent when young

小時候(ㄒㄧㄠˇㄕˊㄏㄡˋ)
as a child; in childhood; during one's childhood: 他們從小
時候就是好朋友。They are
good friends since child-
hood.

小事(ㄒㄧㄠˇㄕˋ)
a trifle; a trivial matter; a
triviality

小試(ㄒㄧㄠˇㄕˋ)
①to make a casual trial ②
the annual prefectural civil
service examination in
ancient times

小試鋒芒(ㄒㄧㄠˇㄕˋㄈㄥㄇㄤˊ)
to make a casual demonstration of one's capability

小市民(ㄒㄧㄠˇㄕˋㄇㄧㄣˊ)
the urban petty bourgeois

小舌(ㄒㄧㄠˇㄕㄜˊ)
①the uvula ②the ligule

小手小腳(ㄒㄧㄠˇㄕㄡˇㄒㄧㄠˇㄐㄧㄠˇ)
①stingy; miserly; mean ②
lacking boldness; timid

小嬸(ㄒㄧㄠˇㄕㄣˇ)
a sister-in-law (the wife of
one's husband's younger
brother)

小聲(ㄒㄧㄠˇㄕㄥ)
to lower one's voice; to
speak low: 請小聲說話。Speak
low, please!

小生(ㄒㄧㄠˇㄕㄥ)
the young man's role (especially in Chinese opera)

小生意(ㄒㄧㄠˇㄕㄥ ㄧˋ)
small business

小乘(ㄒㄧㄠˇㄕㄥˋ)
(Buddhism) the Hinayana
(or "Lesser Vehicle") school

小叔(ㄒㄧㄠˇㄕㄨ)
a brother-in-law (one's husband's younger brother): 她
小叔在經商。Her brother-in-
law is in business.

小暑(ㄒㄧㄠˇㄕㄨˇ)
Slight heat—one of the 24
solar periods, into which the
year is divided, falling on
July 7 or 8

小樹(ㄒㄧㄠˇㄕㄨˋ)
a sapling

小數(ㄒㄧㄠˇㄕㄨˋ)

a decimal fraction; a decimal

小數點(ㄒㄧㄠˇ ㄕㄨˋ ㄉㄧㄢˇ)
the decimal point

小說(ㄒㄧㄠˇ ㄕㄨㄛ)
a novel; fiction

小說家(ㄒㄧㄠˇ ㄕㄨㄛ ㄐㄧㄚ)
a novelist

小人(ㄒㄧㄠˇ ㄖㄣˊ)
① a mean person (as opposed to a real gentleman): 他是小人。He is a mean person. ② a self-depreciatory term used by the common people of ancient times in referring to oneself when speaking to government officials or by servants when speaking to the master or mistress

小人國(ㄒㄧㄠˇ ㄖㄣˊ ㄍㄨㄛˊ)
Lilliput; the Land of Pygmies: 小人國是格列佛遊記中的一個國家。Lilliput is a country in *Gulliver's Travels*.

小人書(ㄒㄧㄠˇ ㄖㄣˊ ㄕㄨ)
(colloquial) a picture-story book

小資產階級(ㄒㄧㄠˇ ㄗ ㄔㄢˇ ㄐㄧㄝ ㄐㄧˊ)
the petty bourgeoisie: 他們屬於小資產階級。They belong to the bourgeoisie.

小子(ㄒㄧㄠˇ ㄗˇ)
① one's children ② a self-depreciatory term used in referring to oneself ③ young fellow (usually with slight contempt)

小字(ㄒㄧㄠˇ ㄗˋ)
① one's childhood name ② the calligraphy in small characters

小組(ㄒㄧㄠˇ ㄗㄨˇ)
a group formed for a specific purpose

小組討論(ㄒㄧㄠˇ ㄗㄨˇ ㄊㄠˇ ㄌㄨㄣˋ)
a group discussion

小組會議(ㄒㄧㄠˇ ㄗㄨˇ ㄏㄨㄟˋ ㄧˋ)
a sectional conference; a sub-committee meeting

小冊子(ㄒㄧㄠˇ ㄘㄜˋ ˙ㄗ)
a pamphlet or brochure

小才大用(ㄒㄧㄠˇ ㄘㄞˊ ㄉㄚˋ ㄩㄥˋ)
to give great responsibility to a man of common ability

小菜(ㄒㄧㄠˇ ㄘㄞˋ)
plain dishes (as distinct from expensive courses)

小聰明(ㄒㄧㄠˇ ㄘㄨㄥ ㄇㄧㄥ)
clever or smart in a small way: 他的兒子有小聰明。His son is clever in a small way.

小廝(ㄒㄧㄠˇ ㄙ)
a servant (especially a mean one); a subaltern; an underling

小蘇打(ㄒㄧㄠˇ ㄙㄨ ㄉㄚˇ)
sodium bicarbonate

小恩小惠(ㄒㄧㄠˇ ㄣ ㄒㄧㄠˇ ㄏㄨㄟˋ)
petty favors; small favors; economic sops; economic bribes

小兒(ㄒㄧㄠˇ ㄦˊ)
① an infant; a child ② my son (a self-depreciatory term)

小兒麻痺症(ㄒㄧㄠˇ ㄦˊ ㄇㄚˊ ㄅㄧˋ ㄓㄥˋ)
poliomyelitis; polio; infantile paralysis

小兒麻痺疫苗(ㄒㄧㄠˇ ㄦˊ ㄇㄚˊ ㄅㄧˋ ㄧˋ ㄇㄧㄠˊ)
polio vaccine

小兒科(ㄒㄧㄠˇ ㄦˊ ㄎㄜ)
① pediatrics ② (slang) parsimonious

小兒子(ㄒㄧㄠˇ ㄦˊ ˙ㄗ)
the youngest son: 他的小兒子從軍為國家作戰。His youngest son joined up to fight for the country.

小耳朵(ㄒㄧㄠˇ ㄦˇ ˙ㄉㄨㄛ)
① (slang) DBS (Direct Broadcasting Satellite)亦作「直播衛星」② a spy

小二(ㄒㄧㄠˇ ㄦˋ)
(formerly) a waiter at a tavern or hotel

小衣(ㄒㄧㄠˇ ㄧ)
a garment covering the lower half of the body; trousers; pants

小姨子(ㄒㄧㄠˇ ㄧˊ ˙ㄗ)
a sister-in-law (one's wife's younger sister)

小意思(ㄒㄧㄠˇ ㄧˋ ˙ㄙ)
① a trifle; a triviality ② a small token of regard (such as a gift)

小鴨(ㄒㄧㄠˇ ㄧㄚ)
a duckling

小丫頭(ㄒㄧㄠˇ ㄧㄚ ˙ㄊㄡ)
① a little girl (expressing

contempt or endearment) ② a young housemaid

小亞細亞(ㄒㄧㄠˇ ㄧㄚˇ ㄒㄧˋ ㄧㄚˇ)
Asia Minor

小夜曲(ㄒㄧㄠˇ ㄧㄝˋ ㄑㄩˇ)
(music) a serenade

小妖精(ㄒㄧㄠˇ ㄧㄠ ㄐㄧㄥ)
a coquettish young girl

小引(ㄒㄧㄠˇ ㄧㄣˇ)
a foreword

小羊(ㄒㄧㄠˇ ㄧㄤˊ)
a lamb: 她像小羊般天真活潑。She is as innocent as a lamb.

小陽春(ㄒㄧㄠˇ ㄧㄤˊ ㄔㄨㄣ)
balmy weather in the tenth month of the lunar calendar

小巫見大巫(ㄒㄧㄠˇ ㄨ ㄐㄧㄢˋ ㄉㄚˋ ㄨ)
① (literally) a giant in the presence of a supergiant—a man with a little learning in the presence of a great scholar ② no comparison between

小娃娃(ㄒㄧㄠˇ ㄨㄚˊ ˙ㄨㄚ)
a small child: 這小娃娃逗人喜愛。This small child is cute.

小我(ㄒㄧㄠˇ ㄨㄛˇ)
the individual; the ego; the self

小玩藝兒(ㄒㄧㄠˇ ㄨㄢˊ ㄧˋ ㄦ)
a small toy or plaything

小魚(ㄒㄧㄠˇ ㄩˊ)
a fry

小雨兒(ㄒㄧㄠˇ ㄩˇ ㄦ)
a light rain; a drizzle: 只不過是一場小雨兒。It's only a drizzle.

小月(ㄒㄧㄠˇ ㄩㄝˋ)
a 30-day month of the Gregorian calendar; a 29-day month of the lunar calendar

一畫

【少】 1169
1. ㄕㄠ shao shǎo
1. small or little (in number, quantity, or duration)
2. missing; absent; wanting; lost: 牛群裡少了幾頭牛。A few bulls have been lost from the herd.
3. cannot do without: 鹽不可少。Salt is something we cannot go without.
4. to stop; to quit: 少給我胡

〔小部〕

謅! Stop talking nonsense!

少不得(ㄕㄠˇ·ㄅㄨˋ·ㄉㄜ)
indispensable; not to be
dispensed with

少不了(ㄕㄠˇ·ㄅㄨˋ ㄌㄧㄠˇ)
①indispensable; not to be
dispensed with; cannot do
without ②unlikely to be
lost ③unlikely to be small
in number or quantity ④to
be bound to; to be unavoidable

少不了有你的(ㄕㄠˇ·ㄅㄨˋ ㄌㄧㄠˇ ㄧㄡˇ ㄋㄧˇ·ㄉㄜ)
You'll get your share.

少陪(ㄕㄠˇ ㄆㄟˊ)
I'm sorry I can't keep you
company any longer.

少待(ㄕㄠˇ ㄉㄞˋ)
to wait for a little while: 請
少待片刻. Please wait for a
little while.

少停(ㄕㄠˇ ㄊㄧㄥˊ)
①to pause for a little while:
我們少停片刻. Let's pause for
a little while. ②Don't pause
too often.

少了(ㄕㄠˇ·ㄌㄜ)
less than the required or
expected amount, quantity,
etc.

少了不賣(ㄕㄠˇ·ㄌㄜ ㄅㄨˋ ㄇㄞˋ)
not to sell for less

少來(ㄕㄠˇ ㄌㄞˊ)
①to refrain from coming ②
to be sparing (in doing
something)

少來道一套(ㄕㄠˇ ㄌㄞˊ ㄉㄠˋ ㄧ ㄊㄠˋ)
(an expression showing one's
displeasure) Let's have no
more of this. 或 Let's quit
that!

少禮(ㄕㄠˇ ㄌㄧˇ)
I'm sorry for my inadequate
regard for propriety. 或
Excuse me for having not
shown you enough polite-
ness.

少量(ㄕㄠˇ ㄌㄧㄤˋ)
a small amount (or quan-
tity); a little; a few: 請給我
少量的水. Please give me a
little water.

少管閒事(ㄕㄠˇ ㄍㄨㄢˇ ㄒㄧㄢˊ ㄕˋ)
Mind your own business.

少刻(ㄕㄠˇ ㄎㄜˋ)
after a little while; a

moment later

少候(ㄕㄠˇ ㄏㄡˋ)
Please wait for a little
while.

少見(ㄕㄠˇ ㄐㄧㄢˋ)
seldom seen; unique; rare

少見多怪(ㄕㄠˇ ㄐㄧㄢˋ ㄉㄨㄛ ㄍㄨㄞˋ)
to wonder much because one
has seen little; to make
much ado about nothing; to
kick up a fuss: 用不着少見多
怪。There's nothing to be
surprised at.

少頃(ㄕㄠˇ ㄑㄧㄥˇ)
a little while; a short while;
a short time

少許(ㄕㄠˇ ㄒㄩˇ)
a little bit; a little; a sprinkling of

少數(ㄕㄠˇ ㄕㄨˋ)
①a few; a small number
(of) ②minority: 少數服從多
數。The minority is subordinate to the majority.

少數民族(ㄕㄠˇ ㄕㄨˋ ㄇㄧㄣˊ ㄗㄨˊ)
a minority ethnic group (in
a multiracial nation)

少數黨(ㄕㄠˇ ㄕㄨˋ ㄉㄤˇ)
a minority political party

少數人(ㄕㄠˇ ㄕㄨˋ ㄖㄣˊ)
the minority

少說廢話(ㄕㄠˇ ㄕㄨㄛ ㄈㄟˋ ㄏㄨㄚˋ)
Stop talking nonsense' 或
Stop chattering!

少算(ㄕㄠˇ ㄙㄨㄢˋ)
to reduce prices (to an old
customer)

少安毋躁(ㄕㄠˇ ㄢ ㄨˊ ㄗㄠˋ)
Be patient! 請少安毋躁!
Please be patient!

少有(ㄕㄠˇ ㄧㄡˇ)
rare; scarce

少問(ㄕㄠˇ ㄨㄣˋ)
to refrain from asking

【少】 1169
2. ㄕㄠˋ shaw shòo
young; youthful; junior; juvenile

少輩兒(ㄕㄠˋ ㄅㄟˋ ㄦ)
the younger generation of a
family

少白頭(ㄕㄠˋ ㄅㄞˊ ㄊㄡˊ)
①to be prematurely gray ②
a youth with graying hair

少不更事(ㄕㄠˋ ㄅㄨˋ ㄍㄥ ㄕˋ)
young and inexperienced: 我
們經理少不更事。Our manager

is young and inexperienced.

少婦(ㄕㄠˋ ㄈㄨˋ)
a young woman

少東(ㄕㄠˋ ㄉㄨㄥ)
(formerly) the son of the
master

少奶奶(ㄕㄠˋ ㄋㄞˇ·ㄋㄞ)
the wife of the young lord
or master

少年(ㄕㄠˋ ㄋㄧㄢˊ)
①a boy; a juvenile; a youth
②young

少年法庭(ㄕㄠˋ ㄋㄧㄢˊ ㄈㄚˇ ㄊㄧㄥˊ)
a juvenile court

少年犯罪(ㄕㄠˋ ㄋㄧㄢˊ ㄈㄢˋ ㄗㄨㄟˋ)
juvenile delinquency; 少年犯
罪問題很嚴重。The problem
of juvenile delinquency is
very serious.

少年讀物(ㄕㄠˋ ㄋㄧㄢˊ ㄉㄨˊ ㄨˋ)
juvenile books; books for
young people

少年老成(ㄕㄠˋ ㄋㄧㄢˊ ㄌㄠˇ ㄔㄥˊ)
young but competent;
accomplished though young

少年人(ㄕㄠˋ ㄋㄧㄢˊ ㄖㄣˊ)
a young person; a youth: 他
喜歡被少年人包圍。He loved
to be surrounded by youths.

少女(ㄕㄠˋ ㄋㄩˇ)
a young girl; a damsel: 我在
花園看見幾個漂亮的少女。I
saw some pretty young girls
in the garden.

少林拳(ㄕㄠˋ ㄌㄧㄣˊ ㄑㄩㄢˊ)
name of a school of boxing
started during the Tang
Dynasty

少林寺(ㄕㄠˋ ㄌㄧㄣˊ ㄙˋ)
name of a Buddhist monas-
tery famous for its pugilist
monks

少將(ㄕㄠˋ ㄐㄧㄤˋ)
major general (in the army,
air force and marine corps);
rear admiral (in the navy):
那少將升做中將。The major
general was promoted lieutenant general.

少校(ㄕㄠˋ ㄒㄧㄠˋ)
major (in the army, air
force and marine corps);
lieutenant commander (in
the navy)

少壯(ㄕㄠˋ ㄓㄨㄤˋ)
young and energetic: 少壯不
努力，老大徒傷悲。One who

〔尤
部〕

doesn't work hard in the prime of life would only grieve in the evening of life. 或 Laziness in youth spells regret in old age.

少壯派(ㄕㄠ ㄓㄨㄤˋ ㄆㄞˋ)
the stalwarts; a young Turk: 少壯派不肯講和。The stalwarts refuse to negotiate for peace.

少艾(ㄕㄠˋ ㄞˋ)
a young beauty

少爺(ㄕㄠˋ ˙ㄧㄝ)
① a young master (of a rich family); a young lord ② your son (an honorific term)

少爺脾氣(ㄕㄠˋ ˙ㄧㄝ ㄆㄧˊ ˙ㄑㄧ)
to do whatever one pleases

少尉(ㄕㄠˋ ㄨㄟˋ)
second lieutenant (in the army, air force or marine corps); ensign (in the navy)

三畫

【尖】 ¹¹⁷⁰ (ㄐㄧㄢ jiān jiān)
sharp; acute; pointed; keen

尖兵(ㄐㄧㄢ ㄅㄧㄥ)
(military) a point

尖端(ㄐㄧㄢ ㄉㄨㄢ)
a pointed end or head

尖端科學(ㄐㄧㄢ ㄉㄨㄢ ㄎㄜ ㄒㄩㄝˊ)
the frontiers of science

尖利(ㄐㄧㄢ ㄌㄧˋ)
① sharp; keen; cutting: 這是一根尖利的針。This is a sharp needle. ② shrill; piercing: 尖利的汽笛聲 a shrill whistle

尖刻(ㄐㄧㄢ ㄎㄜˋ)
relentless; ruthless; unsympathetic; merciless; exacting; acrimonious: 很少人能忍受他尖刻的話。Few can stand his acrimonious words.

尖銳(ㄐㄧㄢ ㄖㄨㄟˋ)
① sharp—pointed ② penetrating; sharp; keen; incisive ③ shrill; piercing ④ intense; acute; sharp

尖嘴薄舌(ㄐㄧㄢ ㄗㄨㄟˇ ㄅㄛˊ ㄕㄜˊ)
to have a caustic (or biting)

and flippant tongue

尖酸(ㄐㄧㄢ ㄙㄨㄢ)
(said of words, speech, etc.) sarcastic; petty; mean

尖酸刻薄(ㄐㄧㄢ ㄙㄨㄢ ㄎㄜˋ ㄅㄛˊ)
unforgiving; unsympathetic; relentless; ruthless; merciless; pitiless; exacting: 他是個尖酸刻薄的主人。He is an exacting master.

五畫

【尚】 ¹¹⁷¹ (ㄕㄤˋ shang shàng)
1. yet; still: 他的工作尚未完成。He has not finished his work yet.
2. to uphold; to honor; to esteem
3. a Chinese family name

尚比亞(ㄕㄤˋ ㄅㄧˇ ㄧㄚˋ)
Zambia

尚可(ㄕㄤˋ ㄎㄜˇ)
① passable; acceptable: 他的提議尚可。His proposal is acceptable. ② still permissible; still possible

尚佳(ㄕㄤˋ ㄐㄧㄚ)
passable; not too bad: 他的法文尚佳。His French is passable.

尚祈(ㄕㄤˋ ㄑㄧˊ) or 尚希(ㄕㄤˋ ㄒㄧ)
I hope.... 或 I pray....

尚且(ㄕㄤˋ ㄑㄧㄝˇ)
① yet; still ② even

尚西巴(ㄕㄤˋ ㄒㄧ ㄅㄚ)
Zanzibar

尚賢(ㄕㄤˋ ㄒㄧㄢˊ)
the exaltation of the virtuous

尚書(ㄕㄤˋ ㄕㄨ)
① an ancient government post in charge of secretarial duties ② another name for Book of History (書經), one of the Thirteen Classics

尚友(ㄕㄤˋ ㄧㄡˇ)
to acquaint oneself with peopie of the past (through reading their books)

尚有可爲(ㄕㄤˋ ㄧㄡˇ ㄎㄜˇ ㄨㄟˊ)
(said of a bad situation) still retrievable

尚無不可(ㄕㄤˋ ㄨˊ ㄅㄨˋ ㄎㄜˇ)
acceptable; passable; permissible

尚武(ㄕㄤˋ ㄨˇ)
militaristic: 斯巴達人尚武，Spartans were militaristic.

尚武精神(ㄕㄤˋ ㄨˇ ㄐㄧㄥ ㄕㄣˊ)
martial spirit: 他是個有尚武精神的青年。He is a youth of martial spirit.

尚勇(ㄕㄤˋ ㄩㄥˇ)
to esteem valor

九畫

【尞】 ¹¹⁷² (ㄌㄧㄠˊ liau liáo)
a Chinese family name

十畫

【尠】 ¹¹⁷³ (陝)(ㄒㄧㄢˇ shean xiǎn)
few; rare 參看「鮮 2.」

尢 部
ㄨㄤ uang wāng

一畫

【尤】 ¹¹⁷⁴ (ㄧㄡˊ you yóu)
1. to feel bitter against; to reproach; to blame
2. a mistake; an error
3. especially or particularly
4. outstanding or special
5. a Chinese family name

尤其(ㄧㄡˊ ㄑㄧˊ)
above all; in particular; particularly; especially: 本書的第一章尤其重要。The first chapter of the book is particularly important.

尤甚(ㄧㄡˊ ㄕㄣˋ)
① more than; worse than ② especially so; particularly so

尤人(ㄧㄡˊ ㄖㄣˊ)
to blame others: 他性喜尤人。He likes to blame others.

尤而效之(ㄧㄡˊ ㄦˊ ㄒㄧㄠˋ ㄓ)
to imitate what one knows to be improper

尤有進者(ㄧㄡˊ ㄧㄡˇ ㄐㄧㄣˋ ㄓㄜˇ)
furthermore; in addition: 尤有進者, 他下令不得打擾他。

Furthermore, he left orders not to be disturbed.

尤物(ㄧㄡ ㄨ)
①an uncommon person; a rare personage ② a woman of extraordinary beauty; a rare beauty

〔尢
部〕

四畫

【尨】 1175
1. ㄇㄤˊ parng páng
1. a shaggy dog
2. blended; variegated

尨大(ㄇㄤˊ ㄉㄚˋ)
giant

尨雜(ㄇㄤˊ ㄗㄚˊ)
mixed; variegated

【尨】 1175
2. ㄇㄥˊ meng méng
disorderly; confused

尨茸(ㄇㄥˊ ㄖㄨㄥˊ)
disorderly; confused

【尬】 1176
《ㄚˋ gah gà
embarrassed; ill at ease

九畫

【就】 1177
ㄐㄧㄡˋ jiow jiù
1. to receive
2. to undergo
3. to assume
4. to follow
5. to come or go to
6. to suit; to fit; to accommodate oneself to: 我反正有空，就你的時間吧! Make it anytime that suits you; I'm always free.
7. forthwith; right away: 我這就去. I'll be going at once.
8. exactly; precisely: 我就要這隻. This is the one I want.
9. namely
10. even if

就便(ㄐㄧㄡˋ ㄅㄧㄢˋ)or就手兒(ㄐㄧㄡˋ ㄕㄡˇ ㄦ)
to do something in the course of doing something else more important (the additional task does not involve too much trouble or divert one's attention from his main work)

就木(ㄐㄧㄡˋ ㄇㄨˋ)
to enter the coffin; about to die

就範(ㄐㄧㄡˋ ㄈㄢˋ)
to come to terms; to give up; to be subdued; to yield: 強盜不肯就範. The robbers refused to yield.

就逮(ㄐㄧㄡˋ ㄉㄞˋ)
to be arrested: 小偷就逮, 被送入獄. The thief was arrested and imprisoned.

就得(ㄐㄧㄡˋ ㄉㄟˇ)
must; should (used in connection with suggestion, advice, etc.): 你要病好就得吃藥. If you want to recover, you've got to take drugs.

就道(ㄐㄧㄡˋ ㄉㄠˋ)
to embark on a journey; to start a trip

就地(ㄐㄧㄡˋ ㄉㄧˋ)
on the spot

就地解決(ㄐㄧㄡˋ ㄉㄧˋ ㄐㄧㄝˇ ㄐㄩㄝˊ)
to settle or solve (a problem) right on the spot: 他們就地解決問題. They settled the problem on the spot.

就地取材(ㄐㄧㄡˋ ㄉㄧˋ ㄑㄩˇ ㄘㄞˊ)
①to acquire necessary material locally ②to employ local talents

就地正法(ㄐㄧㄡˋ ㄉㄧˋ ㄓㄥˋ ㄈㄚˇ)
to execute an offender summarily right on the spot (of his offense)

就裏(ㄐㄧㄡˋ ㄌㄧˇ)
the inside story

就教(ㄐㄧㄡˋ ㄐㄧㄠˋ)
to ask for advice

就近(ㄐㄧㄡˋ ㄐㄧㄣˋ)
from the nearest source; at the nearest convenient place

就寢(ㄐㄧㄡˋ ㄑㄧㄣˇ)
to go to bed; to retire for the night

就緒(ㄐㄧㄡˋ ㄒㄩˋ)
(said of preparations) to be complete; to be all set; to take shape; to be in order; ready: 一切都已就緒. Everything is ready (or in order).

就學(ㄐㄧㄡˋ ㄒㄩㄝˊ)
to go to school; to receive schooling

就職(ㄐㄧㄡˋ ㄓˊ)
to be sworn into office; to be sworn in; to be inaugurated; to assume office

就枕(ㄐㄧㄡˋ ㄓㄣˇ)
to go to bed

就正(ㄐㄧㄡˋ ㄓㄥˋ)
to correct oneself by receiving instruction from men of virtue or learning; to submit writings to somebody for comment and correction

就是(ㄐㄧㄡˋ ㄕˋ)
①exactly: 是的, 就是如此! Yes, exactly so. ② namely; that is ③ even if; even though ④ only; but

就是說(ㄐㄧㄡˋ ㄕˋ ㄕㄨㄛ)
that is to say; in other words; namely

就勢(ㄐㄧㄡˋ ㄕˋ)
to take advantage of a situation; to take the opportunity

就事(ㄐㄧㄡˋ ㄕˋ)
①to take up responsibility ② to take account of something

就事論事(ㄐㄧㄡˋ ㄕˋ ㄌㄨㄣˋ ㄕˋ)
to confine the discussion to the matter at issue

就手(ㄐㄧㄡˋ ㄕㄡˇ)
while you're at it

就任(ㄐㄧㄡˋ ㄖㄣˋ)
to take office

就座(ㄐㄧㄡˋ ㄗㄨㄛˋ)
to take one's seat; to be seated: 同學們依次就座. The students took their seats in due order.

就此(ㄐㄧㄡˋ ㄘˇ)
then; thereupon; thereafter

就算(ㄐㄧㄡˋ ㄙㄨㄢˋ)
(colloquial) even if; even though; granted that

就醫(ㄐㄧㄡˋ ㄧ)
to receive or undergo medical treatment: 他已就醫一週. He has undergone medical treatment for one week.

就義(ㄐㄧㄡˋ ㄧˋ)
to become a martyr to a worthy cause or principle

就業(ㄐㄧㄡˋ ㄧㄝˋ)
to get employment; to get a job: 他已就業當教員. He has got a job as a teacher.

就業輔導(ㄐㄧㄡˋ ㄧㄝˋ ㄈㄨˇ ㄉㄠˇ)
placement or appointment service

就要(ㄐㄧㄡˋ ㄧㄠˋ)

to be about to; to be going to; to be on the point of: 飛機快要起飛了。The plane is about to take off.

養（ㄐㄧㄡˇ）
①to support one's parents
②to live with one's children as dependents

位（ㄐㄧㄡˋ）
to take one's proper or designated position; to take one's seat: 請就位。Take your seat, please.

十四畫

【尷】1178
《ㄢ gan gān
embarrassed; ill at ease

尷尬
embarrassing; embarrassed: 不要問令人尷尬的問題。Don't ask embarrassing questions.

尸 部

尸 shy shī

【尸】1179
尸 shy shī
1. a corpse
2. to preside; to direct

尸（ㄕ ）
a corpse 參看「屍體」

尸諫（ㄕ ㄐㄧㄢˋ）
to admonish (one's master, lord, etc.) at the cost of one's own life 參看「屍諫」

尸祝代庖（ㄕ ㄓㄨˋ ㄉㄞˋ ㄆㄠˊ）
to perform a duty on behalf of another without authorization

尸首（兒）（ㄕ ㄕㄡˇ）
a corpse 參看「屍體」

尸身（ㄕ ㄕㄣ）
a dead body 參看「屍身」

尸位素餐（ㄕ ㄨㄟˋ ㄙㄨˋ ㄘㄢ）
to neglect the duties of an office while taking the pay; redundant: 這些工人中有很多是尸位素餐。Many of these workers are redundant.

一畫

【尺】1180
1. ㄔ chyy chǐ
1. a unit in Chinese linear measurement, equivalent to ⅓ meter
2. a ruler; a rule

尺璧非寶（ㄔ ㄅㄧˋ ㄈㄟ ㄅㄠˇ）
Wealth and treasure is of secondary importance compared with time.

尺布斗粟（ㄔ ㄅㄨˋ ㄉㄡˇ ㄙㄨˋ）
brothers quarrelling between themselves

尺碼（ㄔ ㄇㄚˇ）
①dimensions (of an object)
②measure; size: 你穿多大尺碼的襯衫? What size shirt do you wear?

尺幅千里（ㄔ ㄈㄨˊ ㄑㄧㄢ ㄌㄧˇ）
(of a painting) having a thousand miles of contents in a foot of space

尺地（ㄔ ㄉㄧˋ）
a very small piece of land

尺地寸土（ㄔ ㄉㄧˋ ㄘㄨㄣˋ ㄊㄨˇ）
tiny pieces of land

尺牘（ㄔ ㄉㄨˊ）or尺翰（ㄔ ㄏㄢˋ）
letters; correspondence

尺度（ㄔ ㄉㄨˋ）
measure; a scale; measurements

尺短寸長（ㄔ ㄉㄨㄢˇ ㄘㄨㄣˋ ㄔㄤˊ）or尺有所短，寸有所長（ㄔ ㄧㄡˇ ㄙㄨㄛˇ ㄉㄨㄢˇ ㄘㄨㄣˋ ㄧㄡˇ ㄙㄨㄛˇ ㄔㄤˊ）
(literally) While there are things for which the foot may be too short, there are things for which the inch can be long enough.—Every person has weak points as well as strong points.

尺土（ㄔ ㄊㄨˇ）
a tiny territory

尺土之封（ㄔ ㄊㄨˇ ㄓ ㄈㄥ）
a very small fief under the feudalistic system

尺蠖之屈（ㄔ ㄏㄨㄛˋ ㄓ ㄑㄩ）
a temporary setback or adversity (used as a consolation to those out of luck)

尺簡（ㄔ ㄐㄧㄢˇ）
①slips of bamboo for writing (a letter); a short note

尺書（ㄔ ㄕㄨ）
①letters; correspondence ②books

尺寸（ㄔ ㄘㄨㄣ）

a small quantity 參看「尺（彳）寸」

尺寸之效（ㄔ ㄘㄨㄣ ㄓ ㄒㄧㄠˋ）
a modicum of (desired) effect

尺素（ㄔ ㄙㄨˋ）
letters; correspondence

【尺】1180
2. 彳 chyr chǐ
as in 尺寸—measurements

尺寸（彳 ㄘㄨㄣ）
measurements; dimensions; size 參看「尺（彳）寸」: 這雙鞋子尺寸正好。This shoes is just the right size.

【尺】1180
3. ㄔㄜˇ chee chě
a note in an old Chinese musical scale: 工尺譜 Chinese musical notes

【尹】1181
1. ㄧㄣˇ yiin yǐn
1. to govern; to rule
2. a Chinese family name

二畫

【尻】1182
ㄎㄠ kau kāo
the sacrum

【尼】1183
ㄋㄧˊ ni ní
a nun

尼泊爾（ㄋㄧˊ ㄅㄛˊ ㄦˇ）
Nepal

尼泊爾人（ㄋㄧˊ ㄅㄛˊ ㄦˇ ㄖㄣˊ）
a Nepalese

尼布楚（ㄋㄧˊ ㄅㄨˋ ㄔㄨˇ）
Nertchinsk, a city in Siberia

尼父（ㄋㄧˊ ㄈㄨˇ）
Confucius

尼祿（ㄋㄧˊ ㄌㄨˋ）
Nero (A.D. 37-68), Roman emperor

尼羅河（ㄋㄧˊ ㄌㄨㄛˊ ㄏㄜˊ）
the Nile River 或 the Nile

尼龍（ㄋㄧˊ ㄌㄨㄥˊ）
(textile) nylon

尼龍襪（ㄋㄧˊ ㄌㄨㄥˊ ㄨㄚˋ）
nylon socks

尼姑（ㄋㄧˊ ㄍㄨ）
a nun

尼古丁（ㄋㄧˊ ㄍㄨˇ ㄉㄧㄥ）
nicotine

尼加拉大瀑布（ㄋㄧˊ ㄐㄧㄚ ㄌㄚ ㄉㄚˋ ㄆㄨˋ ㄅㄨˋ）
Niagara Falls

尼加拉瓜(ㄋㄧ ㄐㄧㄚ ㄌㄚ ㄍㄨㄚ)
Nicaragua

尼日(ㄋㄧ ㄖ)
Niger (in Africa)

尼日利亞(ㄋㄧ ㄖ ㄌㄧ ㄧㄚ)
Nigeria

尼采(ㄋㄧ ㄘㄞ)
Friedrich Wilhelm Nietzsche
(1844—1900), German philosopher

尼斯(ㄋㄧ ㄙ)
Nice, a city in France

尼庵(ㄋㄧ ㄢ)or 尼姑庵(ㄋㄧ ㄍㄨ ㄢ)
a nunnery; a convent

四畫

【尾】 1184
ㄨㄟˇ woei wei
1. the tail; the rear; the stern (of a ship); rear; back
2. last; final
3. remaining
4. a Chinese family name

尾巴(ㄨㄟˇ ㆍㄅㄚ)or(ㄨㄟˇ ㆍㄅㄛ)
①a tail ②a follower (in a derogatory sense)

尾大不掉(ㄨㄟˇ ㄉㄚˋ ㄅㄨˋ ㄉㄧㄠˋ)
(literally) to have a tail that is too big to wag—to have subordinates too powerful to control

尾端(ㄨㄟˇ ㄉㄨㄢ)
the tail (of something)

尾款(ㄨㄟˇ ㄎㄨㄢˇ)
the remaining sum to be paid upon the completion of a transaction

尾欠(ㄨㄟˇ ㄑㄧㄢˋ)
the balance owing

尾追(ㄨㄟˇ ㄓㄨㄟ)
to chase after: 狗尾追其後。
The dog chased after him.

尾聲(ㄨㄟˇ ㄕㄥ)
①(music) a coda ②an epilogue: 序幕與尾聲a prologue and an epilogue ③an end: 會議已接近尾聲。The meeting is drawing to an end.

尾生之信(ㄨㄟˇ ㄕㄥ ㄓ ㄒㄧㄣˋ)
to stubbornly stick to an appointment when the other party will not show up

尾數(ㄨㄟˇ ㄕㄨˋ)
①an additional number to a whole mentioned in round numbers; an odd sum; odd

change ②the balance of an account

尾隨(ㄨㄟˇ ㄙㄨㄟˊ)
to follow close behind; to tail; to shadow: 孩子們尾隨遊行隊伍走了好遠。The kids tailed after the parade for quite a distance.

尾翼(ㄨㄟˇ ㄧˋ)
a tail surface; an empennage

尾牙(ㄨㄟˇ ㄧㄚˊ)
a year-end dinner given by a shop owner to entertain his employees on the 16th day of the twelfth moon, during which an employee would know that he will not be hired for the coming year if the head of a cooked chicken is pointed at his seat

【尿】 1185
ㄋㄧㄠˋ niaw niào
urine; to urinate

尿布(ㄋㄧㄠˋ ㄅㄨˋ)
a diaper; a napkin; a nappy

尿盆(ㄋㄧㄠˋ ㄆㄣˊ)
a chamber pot; a urinal

尿頻(ㄋㄧㄠˋ ㄆㄧㄣˊ)
frequent micturition

尿道(ㄋㄧㄠˋ ㄉㄠˋ)
a urethra; a urinary canal

尿道炎(ㄋㄧㄠˋ ㄉㄠˋ ㄧㄢˊ)
urethritis; the inflammation of the urethra

尿毒症(ㄋㄧㄠˋ ㄉㄨˊ ㄓㄥˋ)
urine poisoning; uremia

尿桶(ㄋㄧㄠˋ ㄊㄨㄥˇ)
a urinal; a urinary; a chamber pot

尿管(ㄋㄧㄠˋ ㄍㄨㄢˇ)
①a urinary canal; a urethra ②a ureter

尿壺(ㄋㄧㄠˋ ㄏㄨˊ)
a urinal; a bedpan; a chamber pot

尿器(ㄋㄧㄠˋ ㄑㄧˋ)
a urinal; a urinary

尿血(ㄋㄧㄠˋ ㄒㄧㄝˇ)
hematuria

尿床(ㄋㄧㄠˋ ㄔㄨㄤˊ)or 尿坑(ㄋㄧㄠˋ ㄎㄥ)
(said of a child) to wet the bed: 小孩尿床。The child wet the bed.

尿失禁(ㄋㄧㄠˋ ㄕ ㄐㄧㄣˋ)
urinary incontinence

尿素(ㄋㄧㄠˋ ㄙㄨˋ)
urea

尿酸(ㄋㄧㄠˋ ㄙㄨㄢ)
uric acid

【局】 1186
ㄐㄩˊ jyu jú
1. an office; a bureau: 氣象局告每天天氣狀況。The Weather Bureau makes daily report on weather conditions.
2. a situation; a state of affairs: 政治局勢正在改善中。The political situation is improving.
3. an inning
4. a game

局部(ㄐㄩˊ ㄅㄨˋ)
having to do only with part; partial; local

局部麻醉(ㄐㄩˊ ㄅㄨˋ ㄇㄚˊ ㄗㄨㄟˋ)
local anesthesia

局部地區(ㄐㄩˊ ㄅㄨˋ ㄉㄧˋ ㄑㄩ)
some areas; parts of an area

局部戰爭(ㄐㄩˊ ㄅㄨˋ ㄓㄢˋ ㄓㄥ)
a local war; partial war

局騙(ㄐㄩˊ ㄆㄧㄢˋ)
swindling; to cheat; to swindle: 誠實的商人不局騙顧客。Honest merchants do not swindle their customers.

局面(ㄐㄩˊ ㄇㄧㄢˋ)
an aspect; a situation; a state of affairs: 事情出現了新的局面。Things have taken on a new aspect.

局內(ㄐㄩˊ ㄋㄟˋ)or 局內人(ㄐㄩˊ ㄋㄟˋ ㄖㄣˊ)
an insider: 局內人知道那件事。The insiders knew it.

局量(ㄐㄩˊ ㄌㄧㄤˋ)
one's capacity for forgiveness

局限(ㄐㄩˊ ㄒㄧㄢˋ)
to limit; to confine; limited; confined: 他的活動局限於教育界。He confined his activities in educational circles.

局長(ㄐㄩˊ ㄓㄤˇ)
the head or director of a government office or bureau

局勢(ㄐㄩˊ ㄕˋ)
a situation: 目前的國際局勢很危險。The present international situation is dangerous.

局子(ㄐㄩˊ ㆍㄗ)
①an office ②a place with-

out the shop front ③ a place for the sale or manufacture of goods ④ the game of chess; a chessboard and chessmen

促 (ㄐㄩ ㄘㄨˋ)
① narrow-minded ② nervous; ill at ease ③ narrow; cramped: 這地方太局促，走動不便。This place is too cramped for us to move.

外人 (ㄐㄩ ㄨㄞˋ ㄖㄣˊ)
an outsider

員 (ㄐㄩ ㄩㄢˊ)
the staff of a bureau

屁 1187
ㄆㄧˋ pih pì
. a fart
. the hip

股 (ㄆㄧˋ ㄍㄨˇ)
the hip; the buttocks; the rump; the bottom

滾尿流 (ㄆㄧˋ ㄍㄨㄣˇ ㄋㄧㄠˋ ㄌㄧㄡˊ)
to be frightened out of one's wits

話 (ㄆㄧˋ ㄏㄨㄚˋ)
Baloney!

精 (ㄆㄧˋ ㄐㄧㄥ)
(slang) a catamite

五畫

【居】 1188
ㄐㄩ jiu jū
1. to dwell; to reside; to inhabit; to occupy; an abode; a dwelling: 他居住嗎? He dwells in the country.
2. to stay put; to be at a standstill: 歲月不居。Time marches on.
3. a Chinese family name

居民 (ㄐㄩ ㄇㄧㄣˊ)
residents or inhabitants

居多 (ㄐㄩ ㄉㄨㄛ)
to be the majority; mostly: 我們班上南方人居多。Most of the students in our class are southerners.

居停 (ㄐㄩ ㄊㄧㄥˊ)
① an employer ② the house of somebody else where one lives temporarily

居里 (ㄐㄩ ㄌㄧˇ)
Pierre Curie (1859-1906), French physicist

居里夫人 (ㄐㄩ ㄌㄧˇ ㄈㄨ ㄖㄣˊ)
Marie Sklodowska Curie

(1867-1934), Polish chemist and physicist in France, wife of Pierre Curie; Madame Curie: 居里夫人是位偉大的科學家。Madame Curie was a great scientist.

居留 (ㄐㄩ ㄌㄧㄡˊ)
to reside

居留地 (ㄐㄩ ㄌㄧㄡˊ ㄉㄧˋ)
the place of residence (as distinct from the place of birth)

居留權 (ㄐㄩ ㄌㄧㄡˊ ㄑㄩㄢˊ)
the right of permanent residence (in a foreign country)

居留證 (ㄐㄩ ㄌㄧㄡˊ ㄓㄥˋ)
. a residence permit

居高臨下 (ㄐㄩ ㄍㄠ ㄌㄧㄣˊ ㄒㄧㄚˋ)
① to overlook; to command a view from a high position ② to enjoy a strategic advantage by holding a high ground overlooking the enemy position

居功 (ㄐㄩ ㄍㄨㄥ)
to take credit (for a success, achievement, etc.)

居功自傲 (ㄐㄩ ㄍㄨㄥ ㄗˋ ㄠˋ)
to claim credit for oneself and become arrogant

居官 (ㄐㄩ ㄍㄨㄢ)
to hold a government office

居官守法 (ㄐㄩ ㄍㄨㄢ ㄕㄡˇ ㄈㄚˇ)
to be a law-abiding official

居家 (ㄐㄩ ㄐㄧㄚ)
to lead one's life at home; to spend time at home

居間 (ㄐㄩ ㄐㄧㄢ)
(to mediate) between two parties

居奇 (ㄐㄩ ㄑㄧˊ)
to stockpile goods for sale at higher prices

居心何在 (ㄐㄩ ㄒㄧㄣ ㄏㄜˊ ㄗㄞˋ)
to harbor (evil) intentions; 歹徒居心何在? What are the hoodlums up to?

居心不良 (ㄐㄩ ㄒㄧㄣ ㄅㄨˋ ㄌㄧㄤˊ)
to harbor evil intentions

居心叵測 (ㄐㄩ ㄒㄧㄣ ㄆㄛˇ ㄘㄜˋ)
There is no way of telling his (or her) real intentions. 或 to cherish evil designs

居止 (ㄐㄩ ㄓˇ)
to stay and live: 此地頗堪居止。It's a nice place to reside in.

居住 (ㄐㄩ ㄓㄨˋ)
to reside; to dwell; to inhabit; to live: 他家一直居住在鄉下。His family have always lived in the country.

居中 (ㄐㄩ ㄓㄨㄥ)
situated in the middle; in the middle position: 小標題 · 律居中。Subheads should be placed in the middle of the column.

居中調停 (ㄐㄩ ㄓㄨㄥ ㄊㄧㄠˊ ㄊㄧㄥˊ) or 居中斡旋 (ㄐㄩ ㄓㄨㄥ ㄨㄛˋ ㄒㄩㄢˊ)
to mediate (between two quarreling parties)

居處 (ㄐㄩ ㄔㄨˋ)
① (ㄐㄩ ㄔˇ) to live (in a place); to occupy (a position)
② (ㄐㄩ ㄔˋ) a residence; a dwelling

居士 (ㄐㄩ ㄕˋ)
① a retired scholar; an official out of office ② a secular Buddhist devotee

居室 (ㄐㄩ ㄕˋ)
① a room or house for living in ② to cohabit

居首 (ㄐㄩ ㄕㄡˇ)
to be at the head; to be in the leading position: 她在全班居首。She is at the head of her class.

居孀 (ㄐㄩ ㄕㄨㄤ)
to remain in widowhood

居然 (ㄐㄩ ㄖㄢˊ)
incredibly; to my surprise; to my disbelief; to go so far as to

居喪 (ㄐㄩ ㄙㄤ)
to be in mourning

居所 (ㄐㄩ ㄙㄨㄛˇ)
a residence (usually a temporary one)

居安思危 (ㄐㄩ ㄢ ㄙ ㄨㄟˊ)
to think of the time of peril at the time of peace; to be prepared for possible future perils while enjoying peace

【屆】 1189
ㄐㄧㄝˋ jieh jiè
1. a numeral adjunct for periodic terms or events
2. (said of an appointed date) to arrive
3. (said of a term) to expire

居滿 (ㄐㄧㄝˋ ㄇㄢˇ)

尸部

〔尸部〕

(said of a term) to expire:
他的任期行將屆滿。His term
of office will soon expire.

屆期（ㄐㄧㄝˋ ㄑㄧˊ）
(said of an appointed time)
to arrive

屆時（ㄐㄧㄝˋ ㄕˊ）
at the appointed time (in
the future):屆時請出席。Your
presence is requested for the
occasion.

【屈】 1190
ㄑㄩ chiu qū

1. to bend; to flex; to bow; to
crook
2. to humiliate; to humble; to
sumbit; to subdue: 大丈夫威
武不能屈。A great man will
not submit to force.
3. wrong; injustice
4. in the wrong
5. to be in an inferior or uncomfortable position: 不要屈
居人下。Don't occupy an infe-
rior position.
6. a Chinese family name

屈服（ㄑㄩ ㄈㄨˊ）
to succumb, yield, or submit
(to power, a threat, etc.); to
give in: 我們絕不向暴力屈服。
We should never yield to
force.

屈打成招（ㄑㄩ ㄉㄚˇ ㄔㄥˊ ㄓㄠ）
to confess under torture to a
crime one hasn't committed

屈駕（ㄑㄩ ㄐㄧㄚˋ）
a conventional phrase used
to solicit another's presence
on an occasion

屈節（ㄑㄩ ㄐㄧㄝˊ）
to compromise one's integrity; to depart from principle

屈就（ㄑㄩ ㄐㄧㄡˋ）
to accept a job too humble
for one's position or ability

屈曲（ㄑㄩ ㄑㄩ）
crooked; winding: 我們沿著屈
曲的小溪走去。We went on,
following the winding creek.

屈膝（ㄑㄩ ㄒㄧ）
to fall, drop, or go down, on
one's knees; to kneel down

屈指可數（ㄑㄩ ㄓˇ ㄎㄜˇ ㄕㄨˋ）
can be counted on one's fingers—very few

屈指一算（ㄑㄩ ㄓˇ ㄧ ㄙㄨㄢˋ）
to count on one's fingers

屈折（ㄑㄩ ㄓㄜˊ）
① refraction (of light) ②
bent; to bend

屈伸（ㄑㄩ ㄕㄣ）
to move elastically; to be
easily bent and stretched;
to be flexible; (figuratively)
to submit or rise according to
circumstances

屈辱（ㄑㄩ ㄖㄨˋ）
humiliation; disgrace; to suffer an insult, humiliation, or
disgrace

屈尊（ㄑㄩ ㄗㄨㄣ）
condescension; to conde-
scend

屈從（ㄑㄩ ㄘㄨㄥˊ）
to submit to; to yield to; to
give way to

屈原（ㄑㄩ ㄩㄢˊ）
Chü Yüan (343-290 B.C.), a
patriotic poet remembered
today through the Dragon-
Boat Festival on the fifth
day of the fifth moon

【屄】 1191
ㄅㄧ bī bī
the vagina

六畫

【屋】 1192
ㄨ wū
a house; a room; a shelter

屋頂（ㄨ ㄉㄧㄥˇ）
a roof

屋頂花園（ㄨ ㄉㄧㄥˇ ㄏㄨㄚ ㄩㄢˊ）
a roof garden

屋漏偏遭連夜雨（ㄨ ㄌㄡˋ ㄆㄧㄢ ㄗㄠ
ㄌㄧㄢˊ ㄧㄝˋ ㄩˇ）
(literally) The rain fell
throughout the night with
the roof already leaking.
——an added misfortune

屋脊（ㄨ ㄐㄧˇ）
the ridge of a roof

屋主（ㄨ ㄓㄨˇ）
the owner of a house

屋子（ㄨ ˙ㄗ）
a house; a room

屋簷（ㄨ ㄧㄢˊ）
the eaves

屋烏之愛（ㄨ ㄨ ㄓ ㄞˋ）
to extend one's love or
affection by association; the
love by association

屋宇（ㄨ ㄩˇ）

houses in general

【屍】 1193
ㄕ shy shī
a corpse; a carcass

屍體（ㄕ ㄊㄧˇ）or 屍首（ㄕ ㄕㄡˇ）
a corpse; remains 參看「尸體」

屍骨（ㄕ ㄍㄨˇ）
the skeleton of a corpse 亦作
「尸骸」

屍橫遍野（ㄕ ㄏㄥˊ ㄆㄧㄢˋ ㄧㄝˇ）
a field littered with corpses

屍諫（ㄕ ㄐㄧㄢˋ）
to admonish (usually th
emperor or a superior) at
the cost of one's own life 參
看「尸諫」

屍親（ㄕ ㄑㄧㄣ）
the next of kin to a murde
victim

屍身（ㄕ ㄕㄣ）
a corpse; a dead body
remains 亦作「屍首」

【屎】 1194
ㄕ shy shǐ
excrement: 屎可用作肥料
Excrement can be used a
fertilizer.

屎尿（ㄕ ㄋㄧㄠˋ）
excrement and urine; body
waste

屎坑（ㄕ ㄎㄥ）
a dung pit

七畫

【展】 1195
ㄓㄢˇ jaan zhǎn

1. to open: 景色在我們眼前展開。
The view opened out before
our eyes.
2. to stretch; to extend: 原野中
展到海邊。The field stretches
away to the sea.
3. to unfold; to unroll: 他展開
報紙閱讀。He unfolds a news-
paper and reads it.
4. to expand; to dilate
5. to prolong
6. to visit

展品（ㄓㄢˇ ㄆㄧㄣˇ）
exhibits; items on display

展墓（ㄓㄢˇ ㄇㄨˋ）
to visit a grave

展覽（ㄓㄢˇ ㄌㄢˇ）
to exhibit; to display; to put
on display

展覽會（ㄓㄢˇ ㄌㄢˇ ㄏㄨㄟˋ）

an exhibition or exposition

開(ㄎㄞ ㄎㄞ)
①to spread out; to unfold; to deploy; to dilate ② to start (an activity, task, etc.)

緻(ㄓㄢ ㄏㄨㄢ)
①to postpone or put off ② to extend the deadline or time limit

技(ㄓㄢ ㄐㄧ)
to demonstrate one's ability or skill to the fullest extent

卷(ㄓㄢ ㄐㄩㄢ)
to open a scroll or a book —to apply oneself to study

緩(ㄓㄢ ㄏㄨㄢ)
①to be postponed; to be put off ② to extend the deadline or time limit

現(ㄓㄢ ㄒㄧㄢ)
to present before one's eyes; to develop

限(ㄓㄢ ㄒㄧㄢ)
①to extend the deadline or time limit ②(law) to grant a moratorium

性(ㄓㄢ ㄒㄧㄥ)
(said of metals)malleability

轉(ㄓㄢ ㄓㄨㄢ)
①to turn round and round ② indirectly 亦作「輾轉」

翅(ㄓㄢ ㄔˋ)
to spread the wings; to fly

出(ㄓㄢ ㄔㄨ)
to display or to put on display at an exhibition; 商店怕在展出春裝 The stores are displaying new spring clothes.

示(ㄓㄢ ㄕˋ)
to show; to display; to exhibit

示會(ㄓㄢ ㄕˋ ㄏㄨㄟˋ)
an exhibition; a trade show

望(ㄓㄢ ㄨㄤˋ)
to view or survey (physically or mentally, usually in a general, comprehensive way); a general or comprehensive view regarding the prospects of an undertaking, the future development of an event, etc.

【屐】 1196 ㄐㄧ jī
wooden shoes; clogs; pattens; 現代人很少穿木屐。 Nowadays

people scarcely wear clogs.

展齒(ㄐㄧ ㄔˇ)
the teeth of clogs or pattens

【屑】 1197 ㄒㄧㄝ shieh xiè
1. chips; crumbs; bits; odds and ends; trifles
2. to care; to mind

屑意(ㄒㄧㄝ ㄧ)
to care; to mind

八畫

【屏】 1198 1. ㄆㄧㄥ pyng píng
a shield; a screen; to shield; to screen; to guard

屏障(ㄆㄧㄥ ㄅㄥ)
to shield; to protect

屏門(ㄆㄧㄥ ㄇㄣˊ)
a door separating the outer and inner courts of an old-style Chinese house

屏幕(ㄆㄧㄥ ㄇㄨˋ)
a screen

屏風(ㄆㄧㄥ ㄈㄥ)
a screen

屏東(ㄆㄧㄥ ㄉㄨㄥ)
Pingtung county in Taiwan

屏障(ㄆㄧㄥ ㄓㄤˋ)
a barrier; to shield; to guard; to protect; a protective screen

【屏】 1198 2. ㄅㄧㄥ bǐng bǐng
to reject; to discard; to dismiss; to get rid of; to abandon

屏退(ㄅㄧㄥ ㄊㄨㄟ)
to order (servants, retainers, etc.) to retire

屏跡 or 屏迹(ㄅㄧㄥ ㄐㄧ)
to stay away from; to avoid

屏居(ㄅㄧㄥ ㄐㄩ)
to live in retirement; to be out of public life

屏絕(ㄅㄧㄥ ㄐㄩㄝˊ)
to stop having contact or intercourse with

屏氣(ㄅㄧㄥ ㄑㄧ)or 屏息(ㄅㄧㄥ ㄒㄧ)
to hold one's breath; to bate one's breath; 我們都屏息以聽那聲音再度發生。 We all held our breath as we listened for the noise again.

屏棄(ㄅㄧㄥ ㄑㄧ)
to reject; to discard; to

throw away; to abandon

屏斥(ㄆㄧㄥ ㄔˋ)
to reproach; to rebuke; to reprove; to accuse

屏除(ㄆㄧㄥ ㄔㄨˊ)
to get rid of; to banish; to dismiss; to brush aside; 在讀書時他屏除雜念。 While studying, he dismissed distracting thoughts.

屏黜(ㄆㄧㄥ ㄔㄨˋ)
to dismiss; to banish

【屜】 1199 (屉) ㄊㄧ tih tì
a drawer

屜子(ㄊㄧ ˙ㄗ)
a drawer

【屙】 1200 ㄜ ē
to discharge excrement or urine

屙肚(ㄜ ㄉㄨˋ)
diarrhea

屙屎(ㄜ ㄕˇ)
to move the bowels

【尸部】

九畫

【屠】 1201 ㄊㄨˊ twu tú
1. to slaughter; to butcher; to massacre
2. a Chinese family name

屠門大嚼(ㄊㄨˊ ㄇㄣˊ ㄉㄚˋ ㄐㄩㄝˊ)
(literally) to eat meat vicariously in front of a butcher's shop—to enjoy vicariously something which one cannot have

屠販(ㄊㄨˊ ㄈㄢˋ)
butchers and vendors

屠夫(ㄊㄨˊ ㄈㄨ)
a butcher

屠刀(ㄊㄨˊ ㄉㄠ)
a butcher's knife

屠格涅夫(ㄊㄨˊ ㄍㄜˊ ㄋㄧㄝˋ ㄈㄨ)
Ivan Sergeevich Turgenev, 1818-1883, Russian novelist

屠戶(ㄊㄨˊ ㄏㄨˋ)
a butcher

屠城(ㄊㄨˊ ㄔㄥˊ)
to massacre the inhabitants of a captured city; to annihilate a city

屠殺(ㄊㄨˊ ㄕㄚ)or 屠戮(ㄊㄨˊ ㄌㄨˋ)
to massacre; a wholesale slaughter; a massacre

屠燒(ㄊㄨˊ ㄕㄠ)
to kill and to burn on a conquered land

屠宰(ㄊㄨˊ ㄗㄞˇ)
to slaughter (livestock); to
butcher

屠宰場(ㄊㄨˊ ㄗㄞˇ ㄔㄤˇ)or(ㄊㄨˊ ㄗㄞˇ
ㄔㄤˊ)
a slaughterhouse; an abat-
toir

屠宰稅(ㄊㄨˊ ㄗㄞˇ ㄕㄨㄟˋ)
slaughter tax (levied on
slaughtered animals)

十一畫

【屢】 1202
ㄌㄩˇ leu lǚ
frequently; repeatedly; often;
time after time; time and
again; again and again: 台灣
屢次發生輕微地震。Slight
earthquakes frequently happen in Taiwan.

屢敗屢戰(ㄌㄩˇ ㄅㄞˋ ㄌㄩˇ ㄓㄢˋ)
to fight repeatedly in spite
of repeated setbacks

屢屢(ㄌㄩˇ ㄌㄩˇ)
frequently; repeatedly; again
and again; time and again;
time after time

屢見不鮮(ㄌㄩˇ ㄐㄧㄢˋ ㄅㄨˋ ㄒㄧㄢ)
not rare; of ordinary occurrence or common sight;
nothing new

屢勸不改(ㄌㄩˇ ㄑㄩㄢˋ ㄅㄨˋ ㄍㄞˇ)
to persist in doing wrong
against repeated advice

屢戰屢勝(ㄌㄩˇ ㄓㄢˋ ㄌㄩˇ ㄕㄥˋ)
to fight repeatedly and win
every battle

屢試不爽(ㄌㄩˇ ㄕˋ ㄅㄨˋ ㄕㄨㄤˇ)
to have the same result or
reaction (usually positive
result or reaction) after
each try

屢次(ㄌㄩˇ ㄘˋ)
repeatedly; frequently; time
and again; again and again;
time after time

屢次三番(ㄌㄩˇ ㄘˋ ㄙㄢ ㄈㄢ)
again and again; over and
over again; many times

【屣】 1203
ㄒㄧˇ shii xǐ
shoes; sandals: 他視富貴如敝
屣。He regards wealth and

rank as insignificant as
worn-out shoes.

十二畫

【層】 1204
ㄘㄥˊ tserng céng
a layer; a stratum; a story
(of a building)

層樓(ㄘㄥˊ ㄌㄡˊ)
a pagoda; a tower; a multistoried building

層巒疊嶂(ㄘㄥˊ ㄌㄨㄢˊ ㄉㄧㄝˊ ㄓㄤˋ)
peaks rising one upon
another

層霄(ㄘㄥˊ ㄒㄧㄠ)
the sky; the space above

層狀岩(ㄘㄥˊ ㄓㄨㄤˋ ㄧㄢˊ)
(geology) stratified or bed-
ded rocks

層出不窮(ㄘㄥˊ ㄔㄨ ㄅㄨˋ ㄑㄩㄥˊ)
to be found in layer upon
layer without end; to be
found in endlessly large
numbers; to happen again
and again

層次(ㄘㄥˊ ㄘˋ)
①order (of importance or
priority)②the arrangement
of ideas (in writing or
speech)

層雲(ㄘㄥˊ ㄩㄣˊ)
(meteorology) a stratus

【履】 1205
ㄌㄩˇ leu lǚ
1. shoes
2. to step on; to tread on; to
walk; to follow: 有些老人步
履維艱。Some old people
walk with difficulty.

履冰(ㄌㄩˇ ㄅㄧㄥ)
(literally) to walk on ice—
cautious; to remain vigilant
or alert

履帶(ㄌㄩˇ ㄉㄞˋ)
the track (of a vehicle)

履歷(ㄌㄩˇ ㄌㄧˋ)
one's personal history or
background (usually con-
fined to past working experience

履歷表(ㄌㄩˇ ㄌㄧˋ ㄅㄧㄠˇ)
a biographic sketch (used in
applying for a position);
curriculum vitae

履易交錯(ㄌㄩˇ ㄧˋ ㄐㄧㄠ ㄘㄨㄛˋ)
Shoes lie about in disorder.

(descriptive of a large nu
ber of guests)

履險如夷(ㄌㄩˇ ㄒㄧㄢˇ ㄖㄨˊ ㄧˊ)
to go through danger as
there were no danger at a
to emerge unscathed fro
danger

履新(ㄌㄩˇ ㄒㄧㄣ)or履任(ㄌㄩˇ ㄖㄣˋ)
to take or assume one's ne
office or post

履行(ㄌㄩˇ ㄒㄧㄥˊ)
to fulfill or carry out
promise, pledge, etc.); to di
charge (an obligation,
responsibility, etc.); to per
form (a duty); to observe
treaty): 他應該履行諾言。H
should keep his word.

履約(ㄌㄩˇ ㄩㄝ)
to keep or fulfill an agre
ment; to keep a promise o
pledge; to keep an appoin
ment

十四畫

【屨】 1206
ㄐㄩ jiuh jù
sandals; shoes made o
coarse material

十八畫

【屬】 1207
1. ㄕㄨˇ shuu shǔ
1. a category; a class; a kind
2. to belong to; to be subordi
nate to; to be governed by

屬地(ㄕㄨˇ ㄉㄧˋ)
a territory; a dependen
domain; a colony

屬吏(ㄕㄨˇ ㄌㄧˋ)
subordinate officials

屬僚(ㄕㄨˇ ㄌㄧㄠˊ)
a colleague under one'
direction; a subordinate

屬國(ㄕㄨˇ ㄍㄨㄛˊ)
a dependency; a vassal state

屬下(ㄕㄨˇ ㄒㄧㄚˋ)
one's subordinate: 他很信任
屬下。He trusts his subordi
nates very much.

屬性(ㄕㄨˇ ㄒㄧㄥˋ)
an attribute

屬實(ㄕㄨˇ ㄕˊ)
true: 他的口供屬實。His con
fession was true.

〔尸部〕

望(ㄨㄤˋ)
(said of a person) popular

於(ㄩˊ)
to belong to: 這商店是屬於我
的。This shop belongs to me.

員(ㄩˊ)
a staff member or staffer
(of a government agency,
etc.)

屬 1207
2. ㄓㄨˇ juu zhǔ

to compose (a piece of writing)
. to instruct; to direct

目(ㄓㄨˋ ㄇㄨˋ)
to gaze; to look eagerly

對(ㄓㄨˋ ㄉㄨㄟˋ)
to search for a suitable sentence or poem to match
another (a favorite intellectual exercise among the
intelligentsia in old Chinese)

託(ㄓㄨˋ ㄊㄨㄛ)
to ask or instruct somebody
to do something

令(ㄓㄨˋ ㄌㄧㄥˋ)
to direct; to instruct

草(ㄓㄨˋ ㄘㄠˇ)
to draft (a manuscript, etc.)

意(ㄓㄨˋ ㄧˋ)
to have a preference for

文(ㄓㄨˋ ㄨㄣˊ)
to compose a piece of writing

垣有耳(ㄓㄨˋ ㄩㄢˊ ㄧㄡˇ ㄦˇ)
Beware of eavesdroppers!

屮 部
ㄔㄜˋ cheh chè

一畫

【屯】 1208
ㄊㄨㄣˊ twen tún

1. to station (an army)
2. to stockpile

屯兵(ㄊㄨㄣˊ ㄅㄧㄥ)
to station troops

屯田(ㄊㄨㄣˊ ㄊㄧㄢˊ)
to station an army in the
countryside and make it
engage in farming

糧(ㄊㄨㄣˊ ㄌㄧㄤˊ)

---

to hoard up or stockpile
grains

屯墾(ㄊㄨㄣˊ ㄎㄣˇ)
to develop (a region) by
means of the militia's labor

屯積(ㄊㄨㄣˊ ㄐㄧ)
to hoard up (goods, food
supplies, etc.)

屯聚(ㄊㄨㄣˊ ㄐㄩˋ)
to assemble; to gather
together

屯紮(ㄊㄨㄣˊ ㄓㄚˊ)
to encamp; to be stationed:
軍隊在樹林中屯紮。The troops
encamped in the woods.

山 部
ㄕㄢ shan shān

【山】 1209
ㄕㄢ shan shān
a mountain; a hill

山獺鼠(ㄕㄢ ㄅㄜ ㄕㄨˇ)
a marmot

山崩(ㄕㄢ ㄅㄥ)
a landslide; a landslip

山崩地裂(ㄕㄢ ㄅㄥ ㄉㄧˋ ㄌㄧㄝˋ)
mountains collapsing and
the earth cracking up
(descriptive of sound)

山坡(ㄕㄢ ㄆㄛ)
a mountainside; a hillside; a
mountain slope

山砲(ㄕㄢ ㄆㄠˋ)
a mountain cannon; artillery
pieces used in mountain
warfare

山脈(ㄕㄢ ㄇㄞˋ)or(ㄕㄢ ㄇㄛˋ)
a mountain range; moun-
tains

山貓(ㄕㄢ ㄇㄠ)
a wildcat; a lynx

山門(ㄕㄢ ㄇㄣˊ)
a Buddhist monastery or
temple

山盟海誓(ㄕㄢ ㄇㄥˊ ㄏㄞˇ ㄕˋ)
a vow between lovers that
their mutual love will last
as long as the mountain and
the sea

山鳴谷應(ㄕㄢ ㄇㄧㄥˊ ㄍㄨˇ ㄧㄥˋ)
the echo in mountains; the
mountain echoes

山明水秀(ㄕㄢ ㄇㄧㄥˊ ㄕㄨㄟˇ ㄒㄧㄡˋ)or
山清水秀(ㄕㄢ ㄑㄧㄥ ㄕㄨㄟˇ ㄒㄧㄡˋ)
The mountains are bright
and the waters are fair.
(descriptive of scenic beauty)

山木自寇(ㄕㄢ ㄇㄨˋ ㄗˋ ㄎㄡˋ)
(literally) The trees in the
mountains are felled because
timber is useful. — One's
ability may be his own ruin.

山峯(ㄕㄢ ㄈㄥ)
a mountaintop

山大王(ㄕㄢ ㄉㄚˋ ㄨㄤˊ)
the leader of a group of outlaws operating from a
mountain stronghold

山斗之望(ㄕㄢ ㄉㄡˇ ㄓ ㄨㄤˋ)
(said of one's virtue) respected by all

山地(ㄕㄢ ㄉㄧˋ)
① a mountainous region ②
the reservations for the aboriginal people (in the mountainous regions of Taiwan)

山地同胞(ㄕㄢ ㄉㄧˋ ㄊㄨㄥˊ ㄅㄠ)
aboriginal tribes (of the
Malayan stock in Taiwan),
most of whom live in mountainous regions

山地管制區(ㄕㄢ ㄉㄧˋ ㄍㄨㄢˇ ㄓˋ ㄑㄩ)
the reservations for the
aboriginal people

山巔(ㄕㄢ ㄉㄧㄢ)or 山頂(ㄕㄢ ㄉㄧㄥˇ)
a hilltop; a mountaintop; the
summit of a mountain

山頂洞人(ㄕㄢ ㄉㄧㄥˇ ㄉㄨㄥˋ ㄖㄣˊ)
(archaeology) Upper Cave
Man, a type of primitive
man who lived ten to twenty
thousand years ago and
whose fossil remains were
found in 1933 at Chou-
koutien (周口店) in Hopeh
Province

山東(ㄕㄢ ㄉㄨㄥ)
Shantung Province

山東大鼓(ㄕㄢ ㄉㄨㄥ ㄉㄚˋ ㄍㄨˇ)
a style of storytelling to the
accompaniment of a drum
and two semicircular splices
of metals

山洞(ㄕㄢ ㄉㄨㄥˋ)
a cave; a tunnel; a grotto

山頭(ㄕㄢ ㄊㄡˊ)
a mountaintop; a hilltop

山頹木壞(ㄕㄢ ㄊㄨㄟˊ ㄇㄨˋ ㄏㄨㄞˋ)

(figuratively) the death of a sage

山嵐(ㄕㄢ ㄌㄢˊ)
clouds and mists in the mountains

山裏紅(ㄕㄢ ㄌㄧˇ ㄏㄨㄥˊ)
the hill haw

山林(ㄕㄢ ㄌㄧㄣˊ)
①a mountain forest ②the place where a hermit lives

山林地區(ㄕㄢ ㄌㄧㄣˊ ㄉㄧˋ ㄑㄩ)
mountain and forest regions

山林文學(ㄕㄢ ㄌㄧㄣˊ ㄨㄣˊ ㄒㄩㄝˊ)
the literature of recluses (characterized by exclusive interest in nature)

山梁雌雉(ㄕㄢ ㄌㄧㄤˊ ㄘ ㄓˋ)
a hen-pheasant on the hill bridge —（figuratively）a capable man denied the opportunity to use his abilities

山陵(ㄕㄢ ㄌㄧㄥˊ)
①a plateau ②an imperial tomb

山陵崩(ㄕㄢ ㄌㄧㄥˊ ㄅㄥ)
(a euphemism) the death of the emperor or queen

山嶺(ㄕㄢ ㄌㄧㄥˇ)
the mountain range

山路(ㄕㄢ ㄌㄨˋ)
a mountain path

山麓(ㄕㄢ ㄌㄨˋ)
the foot of a mountain

山巒(ㄕㄢ ㄌㄨㄢˊ)
the chain of mountains with pointed peaks

山歌(ㄕㄢ ㄍㄜ)
a mountaineers' song; a kind of folk songs

山高水低(ㄕㄢ ㄍㄠ ㄕㄨㄟˇ ㄉㄧ)
unexpected misfortune, especially referring to death

山高水長(ㄕㄢ ㄍㄠ ㄕㄨㄟˇ ㄔㄤˊ)
(descriptive of the virtues of a great man) to be like lofty mountains and mighty streams

山高水遠(ㄕㄢ ㄍㄠ ㄕㄨㄟˇ ㄩㄢˇ)
(descriptive of a long distance) high mountains and long rivers

山溝(ㄕㄢ ㄍㄡ)
a gully; a ravine; a valley

山岡(ㄕㄢ ㄍㄤ)
a ridge; a mountain ridge

山谷(ㄕㄢ ㄍㄨˇ)
a valley; a dale; a ravine; a gorge; a glen: 台灣有很多風景壯麗的山谷。Many spectacular valleys can be found in Taiwan.

山河(ㄕㄢ ㄏㄜˊ)
mountains and rivers——(figuratively) the territory of a nation

山海關(ㄕㄢ ㄏㄞˇ ㄍㄨㄢ)
Shanhai Pass (at the eastern end of the Great Wall)

山海經(ㄕㄢ ㄏㄞˇ ㄐㄧㄥ)
The Book of Mountains and Seas—the title of a book dealing with geography as known to the ancient Chinese, author unknown

山貨(ㄕㄢ ㄏㄨㄛˋ)
①mountain products (such as haws and chestnuts)②household utensils made of wood, clay, etc.

山環水抱(ㄕㄢ ㄏㄨㄢˊ ㄕㄨㄟˇ ㄅㄠˋ)
(said of a resort or vacationland) surrounded by mountains and girdled by a river

山洪(ㄕㄢ ㄏㄨㄥˊ)
mountain torrents

山洪暴發(ㄕㄢ ㄏㄨㄥˊ ㄅㄠˋ ㄈㄚ)
A flood is unleashed from the mountains all of a sudden.

山積(ㄕㄢ ㄐㄧ)
so much (or many) as to form a mountain-like heap

山雞(ㄕㄢ ㄐㄧ)
a pheasant

山雞舞鏡(ㄕㄢ ㄐㄧ ㄨˇ ㄐㄧㄥˋ)
(literally) The pheasant dances before a mirror (until it drops dead).—self-appreciation

山脊(ㄕㄢ ㄐㄧˊ)
a mountain ridge; a ridge

山腳(ㄕㄢ ㄐㄧㄠˇ)
the foot of a mountain

山澗(ㄕㄢ ㄐㄧㄢˋ)
mountain creeks

山居(ㄕㄢ ㄐㄩ)
to live away from civilization; to lead the life of a recluse or hermit

山妻(ㄕㄢ ㄑㄧ)
(a self-depreciatory term)

my wife

山丘(ㄕㄢ ㄑㄧㄡ)
mountains and hills

山區(ㄕㄢ ㄑㄩ)
a mountain area

山泉(ㄕㄢ ㄑㄩㄢˊ)
a mountain spring

山窮水盡(ㄕㄢ ㄑㄩㄥˊ ㄕㄨㄟˇ ㄐㄧㄣˋ)
to be at the end of the rope in a desperate situation

山西(ㄕㄢ ㄒㄧ)
Shansi Province

山西梆子(ㄕㄢ ㄒㄧ ㄅㄤ˙ㄗ)
a style of Chinese opera prevalent in Shansi

山楂(ㄕㄢ ㄓㄚ)
a hawthorn 亦作「山查」

山楂糕(ㄕㄢ ㄓㄚ ㄍㄠ)
a sweetened, reddish jelly-like food made from hawthorn

山寨(ㄕㄢ ㄓㄞˋ)
a mountain fortress (especially one built by bands of bandits)

山珍海錯(ㄕㄢ ㄓㄣ ㄏㄞˇ ㄘㄨㄛˋ)or 山珍海味(ㄕㄢ ㄓㄣ ㄏㄞˇ ㄨㄟˋ)
dainties of all lands and seas; a sumptuous repast

山茱萸(ㄕㄢ ㄓㄨ ㄩˊ)
(botany) a dogwood

山莊(ㄕㄢ ㄓㄨㄤ)
a country house, or villa built in the mountains

山中(ㄕㄢ ㄓㄨㄥ)
in the mountains

山茶(ㄕㄢ ㄔㄚˊ)
(botany) a camellia

山城(ㄕㄢ ㄔㄥˊ)
a city in the mountains

山川(ㄕㄢ ㄔㄨㄢ)
mountains and rivers

山川修阻(ㄕㄢ ㄔㄨㄢ ㄒㄧㄡ ㄗㄨˇ)
The place is far beyond the mountains and rivers (and therefore requires a long journey to reach).

山重水複(ㄕㄢ ㄔㄨㄥˊ ㄕㄨㄟˇ ㄈㄨˋ)
(said of a place) surrounded by mountain ranges and girdled by winding rivers (and therefore the topography is much complicated)

山神(ㄕㄢ ㄕㄣˊ)
the mountain deity

山水(ㄕㄢ ㄕㄨㄟˇ)

① mountains and rivers ②
natural scenery; a landscape

水畫 (ㄕㄨㄟ ㄏㄨㄚˋ)
a landscape painting

人 (ㄖㄢˊ ㄖㄣˊ)
a hermit; a recluse

村 (ㄖㄢˊ ㄘㄨㄣ)
a mountain village

阿 (ㄖㄢˊ ㄜ)
a bend in a mountain range

隘 (ㄖㄢˊ ㄞˋ)
a mountain pass

坳 (ㄖㄢˊ ㄠˋ)
a col

野 (ㄖㄢˊ 一ㄝˇ)
mountain villages and the
remote wilderness

崖 (ㄖㄢˊ 一ㄞˊ)
a cliff

腰 (ㄖㄢˊ 一ㄠ) or 山腹 (ㄖㄢˊ ㄈㄨˋ)
the mid-slope of a mountain

藥 (ㄖㄢˊ 一ㄠˋ)
(botany) a yam 亦作「薯蕷」

陰道 (ㄖㄢˊ 一ㄣ ㄉㄠˋ)
① a sightseeing route with
so many scenic wonders that
one is constantly kept busy
② a life in which one is constantly kept receiving
guests

羊 (ㄖㄢˊ 一ㄤˊ)
a goat

隅 (ㄖㄢˊ 一ㄤˊ)
the southern or sunny side
of a mountain

坳 (ㄖㄢˊ ㄠˋ)
a col

峝 (ㄖㄢˊ ㄨㄛˋ)
a place enclosed by moun-
tains

雨欲來風滿樓 (ㄖㄢˊ ㄩˇ ㄩˋ ㄌㄞˊ ㄈㄥ ㄇㄢˇ
ㄌㄡˊ)
The wind sweeping through
the tower indicates a rising
storm in the mountains.
— (figuratively) an omen
indicating that something
will happen

芋 (ㄖㄢˊ ㄩˋ)
sweet potatoes

岳 (ㄖㄢˊ ㄩㄝˋ) or 山嶽 (ㄖㄢˊ ㄩㄝˋ)
mountains

三畫

【屹】 1210
一ˋ yih yì
(said of a mountain, building, etc.) to rise high; to
stand erect or majestical

屹立 (一ˋ ㄌ一ˋ)
to stand erect; to stand magnificent (like a mountain)

屹然 (一ˋ ㄖㄢˊ)
firm and erect (like a mountain): 他站在那裡屹然不動。He
is standing there firm and
erect.

【屺】 1211
ㄑ一ˇ chii qǐ
a bare mountain or hill

四畫

【岔】 1212
ㄔㄚˋ chah chà
1. to branch; to fork; to
diverge
2. a branching point; a fork

岔道 (ㄔㄚˋ ㄉㄠˋ) or 岔路 (ㄔㄚˋ ㄌㄨˋ)
a diverging road

岔開 (ㄔㄚˋ ㄎㄞ)
① to branch off; to diverge
② to diverge to (another
topic); to change (the subject of conversation) ③ to
stagger

岔口 (ㄔㄚˋ ㄎㄡˇ)
a fork (in a road): 他們護送
他到岔口。They escorted him
to a fork in the road.

岔氣 (ㄔㄚˋ ㄑ一ˋ)
sudden discomfort in the
chest

岔子 (ㄔㄚˋ ˙ㄗ) or 岔兒 (ㄔㄚˋ ㄦ)
an accident; a trouble (in
the course of an activity):
你放心吧，沒有人會找你岔子。
Don't worry; nobody will
cause trouble to you.

【岌】 1213
ㄐ一ˊ jyi jí
1. (said of a peak) rising high
above others
2. perilous; hazardous

岌岌可危 (ㄐ一ˊ ㄐ一ˊ ㄎㄜˇ ㄨㄟ)
in a very critical situation;
to hang by a thread: 病人的
病況岌岌可危。The patient's
condition is critical.

【岐】 1214
(歧) ㄑ一ˊ chyi qí
1. Chi, name of a mountain

---

2. to diverge; to branch

岐黃 (ㄑ一ˊ ㄏㄨㄤˊ)
short for 岐伯 and 黃帝,
founders of Chinese medi-
cine—(figuratively) the medical profession

岐黃之術 (ㄑ一ˊ ㄏㄨㄤˊ ㄓ ㄕㄨˋ)
Chinese herbal medical science

岐山 (ㄑ一ˊ ㄕㄢ)
Mt. Chi (There are two: one
is in Shansi and the other in
Shensi).

【岑】 1215
ㄘㄣˊ tsern cén
1. a relatively high, pointed
hill
2. silent; still; quiet

岑樓 (ㄘㄣˊ ㄌㄡˊ)
a mountain-like, lofty and
tapering building

岑寂 (ㄘㄣˊ ㄐ一ˊ)
quiet; still; silent: 槍聲劃破了
夜的岑寂。A shot disturbed
the quiet of the night.

五畫

【岡】 1216
(崗) ㄍㄤ gang gāng
(又讀 ㄍㄤˇ gǎang
gāng)
the ridge (of a hill or mountain)

岡比亞 (ㄍㄤ ㄅ一ˇ 一ㄚˇ)
the Gambia

岡比亞人 (ㄍㄤ ㄅ一ˇ 一ㄚˇ ㄖㄣˊ)
a Gambian 亦作「甘比亞人」

岡陵 (ㄍㄤ ㄌ一ㄥˊ)
a mound

岡巒起伏 (ㄍㄤ ㄌㄨㄢˊ ㄑ一ˇ ㄈㄨˋ)
full of mountain ridges

【岫】 1217
ㄒ一ㄡˋ shiow xiù
1. a cavern; a cave
2. a mountain peak

【岬】 1218
ㄐ一ㄚˇ jea jiǎ
a cape; a promontory; a
headland; a point

岬碣 (ㄐ一ㄚˇ ㄐ一ㄝˊ)
continuous

岬角 (ㄐ一ㄚˇ ㄐ一ㄠˇ)
a cape; a promontory

【岭】 1219
ㄌ一ㄥˇ ling lǐng
(said of mountains) waste
and remote

〔山部〕

【岱】 1220　ㄉㄞˋ day dài
Mt. Tai (in Shantung Province, one of the five Sacred Mountains)
岱宗(ㄉㄞˋ ㄗㄨㄥ)or 岱嶽(ㄉㄞˋ ㄩㄝˋ)
Mt. Tai (泰山 in Shantung, one of the five Sacred Mountains)

【岳】 1221　ㄩㄝˋ yueh yuè
1. a great mountain; a high mountain
2. the parents of one's wife
3. a Chinese family name
岳廟(ㄩㄝˋ ㄇㄧㄠˋ)
the shrine dedicated to General Yüeh Fei (岳飛), a hero of the Sung Dynasty
岳母(ㄩㄝˋ ㄇㄨˇ)
①one's mother-in-law (one's wife's mother)② General Yüeh Fei's mother
岳飛(ㄩㄝˋ ㄈㄟ)
Yüeh Fei (1103-1141), a hero of the Sung Dynasty
岳父(ㄩㄝˋ ㄈㄨˋ)or 岳丈(ㄩㄝˋ ㄓㄤˋ)
one's father-in-law (one's wife's father)
岳家軍(ㄩㄝˋ ㄐㄧㄚ ㄐㄩㄣ)
the invincible troops under the command of Yüeh Fei (岳飛)

【岷】 1222　ㄇㄧㄣˊ min mín
1. the Min River (in Szechwan)
2. Mt. Min (in Szechwan)

【岸】 1223　ㄢˋ ann àn
1. a shore; a bank; a beach; a coast
2. majestic
3. proud
岸巾(ㄢˋ ㄐㄧㄣ)
to wear a head covering in a neglectful manner so as to expose the forehead
岸然(ㄢˋ ㄖㄢˊ)
a solemn and dignified look: 這個老人道貌岸然。The old man looks severe and solemn.

【岩】 1224　ㄧㄢˊ yan yán
1. a large rock
2. a mountain
岩壁(ㄧㄢˊ ㄅㄧˋ)

①(geology) a dyke ② a cliff
岩脈(ㄧㄢˊ ㄇㄞˋ)or岩(ㄧㄢˊ ㄇㄞˋ)
(geology) a rock vein
岩洞(ㄧㄢˊ ㄉㄨㄥˋ)or 岩穴(ㄧㄢˊ ㄒㄩㄝˋ)
a cavern; a cave; a grotto
岩基(ㄧㄢˊ ㄐㄧ)
(geology) batholith
岩漿(ㄧㄢˊ ㄐㄧㄤ)
(geology) magma; lava
岩林(ㄧㄢˊ ㄌㄧㄣˊ)
(geology) an intrusive sheet; a lava bed
岩石(ㄧㄢˊ ㄕˊ)
a rock; a crag
岩石學(ㄧㄢˊ ㄕˊ ㄒㄩㄝˊ)
petrology
岩層(ㄧㄢˊ ㄘㄥˊ)
a rock stratum; a rock formation
岩岸(ㄧㄢˊ ㄢˋ)
(geography) a rocky coast
岩鹽(ㄧㄢˊ ㄧㄢˊ)
rock salt

六畫

【峋】 1225　ㄒㄩㄣˊ shyun xún
irregular stretches of mountains

【峒】 1226　ㄊㄨㄥˊ torng tóng
Mt. Kungtung—name of a mountain in Kansu Province

【峒】 1226　ㄉㄨㄥˋ donq dòng
name of a tribe in Kwangsi and Kweichow
峒蠻(ㄉㄨㄥˋ ㄇㄢˊ)
the Tung tribe (considered as uncivilized)
峒丁(ㄉㄨㄥˋ ㄉㄧㄥ)
the soldiers from the Tung tribe
峒人(ㄉㄨㄥˋ ㄖㄣˊ)
the people of the Tung tribe

【峙】 1227　ㄓˋ jyh zhì
to stand erect like a mountain

七畫

【峨】 1228　ㄜˊ eré é
lofty
峨眉(ㄜˊ ㄇㄟˊ)

Mt. Omei (a Buddhist res in Szechwan)
峨冠博帶(ㄜˊ ㄍㄨㄢ ㄅㄛˊ ㄉㄞˋ)
a high-topped hat and wi waist band (the attire ch acteristic of an official, an intellectual, in form times) — (figuratively) t official class; the intellectu class
峨髻(ㄜˊ ㄐㄧˋ)
a large chignon, or knot hair, worn atop the head
峨然不羣(ㄜˊ ㄖㄢˊ ㄅㄨˋ ㄑㄩㄣˊ)
to stand head and shoulde above others — (figurativ ly) to excel others far; to outstanding
峨峨(ㄜˊ ㄜˊ)
with solemn gravity; looki majestic

【峭】 1229　ㄑㄧㄠˋ chiaw qiào
1. steep; precipitous
2. harsh; sharp; stern; unkin severe
峭拔(ㄑㄧㄠˋ ㄅㄚˊ)
①high and steep ② (said penmanship or calligraph style) vigorous: 他的筆勢 拔。He has a vigorous sty of writing.
峭薄(ㄑㄧㄠˋ ㄅㄛˊ)
strict; unkind; relentless
峭壁(ㄑㄧㄠˋ ㄅㄧˋ)
a precipice; a cliff: 這山的 邊是峭壁。One side of th mountain is a precipitou cliff.
峭厲(ㄑㄧㄠˋ ㄌㄧˋ)
(said of speech, etc.) hars or sharp
峭刻(ㄑㄧㄠˋ ㄎㄜˋ)
exacting; relentless; unkine strict
峭急(ㄑㄧㄠˋ ㄐㄧˊ)
impatient; quick-tempered
峭絕(ㄑㄧㄠˋ ㄐㄩㄝˊ)
precipitous; very steep
峭直(ㄑㄧㄠˋ ㄓˊ)
stern; strict

【峯】 1230　ㄈㄥ feng fēng
1. a peak; a summit
2. a hump: 駱駝象 a camel' hump
峯巒(ㄈㄥ ㄌㄨㄢˊ)

peaks and ridges

【岘】 1231
ㄒㄧㄢˋ shiann xiàn
a mountain in Hupeh Province
a steep hill

巷【ㄒㄧㄤˋ (ㄊ)】
Danang, a seaport in central Vietnam

【岛】 1232
ㄉㄠˇ dao dǎo
an island; an isle

民【ㄇㄧㄣˊ】
an islander

國【ㄍㄨㄛˊ】
an island nation

夷【ㄉㄠˇ ㄧˊ】
savage islanders

嶼【】
islands; islets and islands

【峻】 1233
ㄐㄩㄣˋ jiunn jùn
high; lofty
steep
severe; harsh; rigorous: 她是一位嚴峻的老師。She is a severe teacher.

法【ㄐㄩㄣˋ ㄈㄚˇ】
severe, harsh, or rigorous law: 他們贊成嚴峻法。They uphold severe punishment and harsh law.

嶺【ㄐㄩㄣˋ ㄌㄧㄥˇ】
a lofty range (of mountains)

刻【ㄐㄩㄣˋ ㄎㄜˋ】
stern and exacting

酷【ㄐㄩㄣˋ ㄎㄨˋ】
severe; relentless; ruthless; merciless

急【ㄐㄩㄣˋ ㄐㄧˊ】
intolerant and impatient

節【ㄐㄩㄣˋ ㄐㄧㄝˊ】
noble principle

拒【ㄐㄩㄣˋ ㄐㄩˋ】
to reject or refuse sternly: 他們峻拒我的要求。They sternly refused me permission.

切【ㄐㄩㄣˋ ㄑㄧㄝˋ】
severe and urgent

峭【ㄐㄩㄣˋ ㄑㄧㄠˋ】
①high and steep; precipitous ②severe; strict; unkind

發刑【ㄐㄩㄣˋ ㄒㄧㄥˊ】
severe punishment or penalty

【峽】 1234
ㄒㄧㄚˊ shya xiá
1. a gorge
2. an isthmus
3. straits

峽谷【ㄒㄧㄚˊ ㄍㄨˇ】
(geography) a dale; a gorge; a valley; a canyon

峽灣【ㄒㄧㄚˊ ㄨㄢ】
(geography) a fiord

【峪】 1235
ㄩˋ yuh yù
1. a valley; a ravine
2. Chiayü (嘉峪) in Kansu Province, where the Great Wall terminates

八畫

【崇】 1236
ㄔㄨㄥˊ chorng chóng
1. to honor; to respect; to revere; to adore; to worship; to venerate; to esteem: 她尊崇有學問的人。She always shows respect to those who are learned.
2. high; lofty; noble; dignified; exalted
3. a Chinese family name

崇拜【ㄔㄨㄥˊ ㄅㄞˋ】
to worship; to idolize; to adore; to lionize: 大多數人崇拜英雄。Most people worship heroes.

崇本務實【ㄔㄨㄥˊ ㄅㄣˇ ㄨˋ ㄕˊ】
(said of one's attitude) to do things in a solid manner; practical

崇奉【ㄔㄨㄥˊ ㄈㄥˋ】
to worship

崇論閎議【ㄔㄨㄥˊ ㄌㄨㄣˋ ㄏㄨㄥˊ ㄧˋ】
ringing comments or statements; stirring speeches

崇高【ㄔㄨㄥˊ ㄍㄠ】
lofty; sublime; high

崇敬【ㄔㄨㄥˊ ㄐㄧㄥˋ】
to honor; to revere; to adore; to regard with esteem

崇信【ㄔㄨㄥˊ ㄒㄧㄣˋ】
to worship

崇禎皇帝【ㄔㄨㄥˊ ㄓㄣ ㄏㄨㄤˊ ㄉㄧˋ】
the last emperor of the Ming Dynasty, who reigned during 1628-1644

崇山峻嶺【ㄔㄨㄥˊ ㄕㄢ ㄐㄩㄣˋ ㄌㄧㄥˇ】
lofty and precipitous peaks

崇尚【ㄔㄨㄥˊ ㄕㄤ】
①to uphold; to advocate: 他們崇尚勤儉。They advocate industry and thrift. ②fashion; a trend

崇洋【ㄔㄨㄥˊ ㄧㄤˊ】
to admire everything of foreign (especially western) origin

【崎】 1237
ㄑㄧ chi qī
rugged; uneven; rough

崎嶇【ㄑㄧ ㄑㄩ】
(said of terrain) uneven; rolling; rough; rugged: 這條小徑崎嶇而多泥。This path is rugged and muddy.

【崎】 1237
ㄑㄧˊ chyi qí
the banks of a winding river

【崑】 1238
ㄎㄨㄣ kuen kūn
1. the Kunlun Mountains
2. Kunshan, name of a county and mountain in Kiangsu

崑崙山【ㄎㄨㄣ ㄌㄨㄣˊ ㄕㄢ】
the Kunlun Mountains (between Tibet and Sinkiang extending to Central China, whose highest peak is 25,000 ft.)

崑曲【ㄎㄨㄣ ㄑㄩ】
name of a class of tunes originating in Kunshan, Kiangsu 亦作「崑腔」

崑山【ㄎㄨㄣ ㄕㄢ】
①Kunshan—a county in Kiangsu Province ②Mt. Kung—a mountain in Kiangsu Province

崑玉【ㄎㄨㄣ ㄩˋ】
①the jade produced in the Kunlun Mountains ②a polite term used to address the brothers of other people

【崔】 1239
ㄘㄨㄟ tsuei cuī
1. a Chinese family name
2. high and steep

崔嵬【ㄘㄨㄟ ㄨㄟˊ】
①a rocky height or peak ②high; towering

崔巍【ㄘㄨㄟ ㄨㄟˊ】
(said of mountains) lofty and steep

【崖】 1240
ㄧㄞˊ yai yái
1. a cliff; a precipice
2. the brink; the verge

〔山部〕

〔山部〕

3. precipitous; high and steep; forbidding

崖壁 (lⁿˊ ㄅˋ)
a precipice

崖略 (lⁿˊ ㄌㄩㄝˋ)
an outline

崖谷 (lⁿˊ ㄍㄨˇ)
a valley between precipices

崖岸 (lⁿˊ ㄢˋ)
haughty

崖鹽 (lⁿˊ lⁿˊ)
rock salt 亦作「岩鹽」

〔岡〕 1241
(岡) 《ㄤ gang gāng
(又讀)《ㄤ gaang gāng)

1. the place where a sentry is posted; a post
2. a position

崗警 (《ㄤ ㄐㄧㄥˇ)
a policeman who performs his duties at a fixed post

崗哨 (《ㄤ ㄕㄠˋ)
① a lookout post ② a sentry; a sentinel

崗子 (《ㄤˉ˙ㄗ)
① a mound; a hillock ② a ridge

崗位 (《ㄤ ㄨㄟˋ)
one's post; one's duty: 兵士們各堅守職門崗位。The soliders stood fast at their fighting posts.

〔崙〕 1242
ㄌㄨㄣˊ luen lún
the Kunlun Mountains

〔崛〕 1243
ㄐㄩㄝˊ jyue júe
to rise abruptly

崛崎 (ㄐㄩㄝˊ ㄑㄧˊ)
steep

崛起 (ㄐㄩㄝˊ ㄑㄧˇ)
to rise suddenly

〔崢〕 1244
ㄓㄥ jeng zhēng

1. lofty
2. outstanding; distinguished
3. steep; perilous; dangerous
4. harsh; severe; rigorous

崢嶸 (ㄓㄥ ㄖㄨㄥˊ)
① lofty and steep ② (said of a person) distinguished; outstanding; extraordinary

〔崤〕 1245
ㄧㄠˊ yau yáo
Mt. Yao, name of a mountain in Honan

〔崧〕 1246
ㄙㄨㄥ song sōng

1. a high mountain
2. lofty

〔崩〕 1247
ㄅㄥ beng bēng

1. to collapse; to disintegrate; to fall
2. (said of an emperor) to die

崩坍 (ㄅㄥ ㄊㄢ)
to collapse; to crumble: 道房屋因地震而崩塌。The house collapsed on account of an earthquake.

崩坍 (ㄅㄥ ㄊㄢˉ)
to collapse; to crumble; to go to pieces

崩裂 (ㄅㄥ ㄌㄧㄝˋ)
to crack up: 炸藥使山石崩裂。The dynamite cracked up the mountain rocks.

崩潰 (ㄅㄥ ㄎㄨㄟˋ)
to collapse; to break down; to fall to pieces; to cave in

崩塌 (ㄅㄥ ㄊㄚˉ)
to cave in; to fall in; to collapse; to subside; to sink

〔崍〕 1248
ㄌㄞˊ lai lái
Mt. Lai—name of a mountain in Szechwan

〔崌〕 1249
ㄐㄩ jiu jū

1. Mount Chü in Szechwan
2. Mt. Chülai (崌崍山) in Szechwan

〔嶼〕 1250
ㄏㄢˊ harn hán
name of a checkpoint during the Chin and Han dynasties, located in what is Honan today

〔崦〕 1251
ㄧㄢ ian yān
Mt. Yen— name of a mountain in Kansu

九畫

〔崴〕 1252
ㄨㄟ uei wēi
lofty

〔嵑〕 1253
ㄐㄧㄝˊ jye jié
lofty (mountains)

〔崽〕 1254
ㄗㄞˇ tzae zǎi

1. a son
2. a young animal; a whelp

3. as in 西崽—a Chinese servant of a foreigner (a derogatory term)

崽子 (ㄗㄞˇ ˙ㄗ)
the son of a bitch; s.o.b.

〔嵇〕 1255
ㄐㄧ ji jī

1. a Chinese family name
2. name of a mountain in Honan

嵇康 (ㄐㄧ ㄎㄤ)
Chi Kang, a man of letters of the Wei Dynasty, one the Seven Wise Men of t Bamboo Grove (竹林七賢)

嵇山 (ㄐㄧ ㄕㄢ)
Mt. Chi— name of a mountain in Honan

〔嵋〕 1256
ㄇㄟˊ mei méi
Mount Omei, a Buddhist resort in Szechwan

〔嵌〕 1257
ㄑㄧㄢ chian qiān
to inlay; to set in

嵌工 (ㄑㄧㄢ ㄍㄨㄥ)
the handicraftsmanship di played in a piece of jewel inlaid with gold or stones

嵌金 (ㄑㄧㄢ ㄐㄧㄣ)
to inlay with gold

嵌石 (ㄑㄧㄢ ㄕˊ)
to inlay with precious stone

〔嵐〕 1258
ㄌㄢˊ lan lán
mountain vapor; mist

嵐氣 (ㄌㄢˊ ㄑㄧˋ)
mountain vapor; mist

嵐影湖光 (ㄌㄢˊ ㄧㄥˇ ㄏㄨˊ ㄍㄨㄤ)
the hazy atmosphere of th mountains and the shimme ing light of the lake (description about a sceni spot)

〔嵎〕 1259
ㄩ yu yú
a curved place in the moun tains; a corner of a hill

〔崿〕 1260
ㄜˋ eh è
a cliff; a precipice

十畫

〔嵩〕 1261
(崧) ㄙㄨㄥ song sōng

1. Mountain Sung, the highes and central peak of the Five

〔山部〕

Sacred Mountains, situated in Honan
lofty

嵩(ムメム《メ》)or 嵩山(ムメム アㄢ)
Mt. Sung, the highest and central peak of the Five Sacred Mountains (or Five Peaks), located in Honan

乎
to shout "Long live the Emperor!"

壽
longevity; to live as long as Mountain Sung

【嵬】 1262
　　メヽ wei wéi
(said of a mountain) high and uneven

然(メヽ ロㄢ日)
lofty

嵬 or 嵬巍(メヽ メヽ)
lofty; towering

【乘】 1263
　　アム shenq shèng
name of a mountain in Chekiang
name of a county in Chekiang

【嵯】 1264
　　ㄘㄨㄛˊ tswo cuó
(said of mountains) high and steep; precipitous

我(ㄘㄨㄛˊ ㄜˊ)
(said of mountains) high and steep; precipitous

十一畫

【嶇】 1265
　　ㄑㄩ chiu qū
rugged; uneven; irregular

【嶂】 1266
　　ㄓㄤˋ janq zhàng
precipitous mountain

【嶄】 1267
　　ㄓㄢˇ jaan zhǎn
(said of a mountain) high and steep
towering (above)
novel; new

新(ㄓㄢˇ ㄒㄧㄣ)
brand-new

絕(ㄓㄢˇ ㄐㄩㄝˊ ロㄢ日)
①completely changed ②(said of a mountain) high and steep

十二畫

【嶙】 1268
　　ㄌㄧㄣˊ lin lín
(said of mountains) rugged

嶙峋(ㄌㄧㄣˊ ㄒㄩㄣˊ)
(said of hills) rolling and rugged

嶙峋(ㄌㄧㄣˊ ㄒㄩㄣˊ)
①(said of mountain rocks) rugged; craggy ②(said of a person) upright

【嶒】 1269
　　ㄘㄥˊ tserng céng
steep; lofty

【嶓】 1270
　　ㄅㄛ bo bō
name of a mountain in Shensi

嶓冢(ㄅㄛ ㄓㄨㄥˇ)
name of a mountain in Shensi

【嶝】 1271
　　ㄉㄥˋ denq dèng
a path leading up a mountain

【嶠】 1272
　　ㄐㄧㄠˋ jiaw jiào
(又讀ㄑㄧㄠˊ chyau qiáo)
a high pointed mountain

【嶢】 1273
　　ㄧㄠˊ yau yáo
(said of a mountain) high or tall

【嶔】 1274
　　ㄑㄧㄣ chin qīn
(said of a mountain) lofty

嶔崎磊落(ㄑㄧㄣ ㄑㄧˊ ㄌㄟˇ ㄌㄨㄛˋ)
(said of a person) honest and upright

嶔崟(ㄑㄧㄣ ㄧㄣˊ)
(said of mountains) precipitous

十三畫

【嶧】 1275
　　ㄧˋ yih yì
peaks rising one upon another

【嶮】 1276
　　(險)ㄒㄧㄢˇ shean xiǎn
steep; precipitous; lofty

十四畫

【嶸】 1277
　　ロㄨㄥˊ rong róng
(said of mountains) lofty 參

看「崝嶸」

【嶺】 1278
　　ㄌㄧㄥˇ liing lǐng
1. the ridge of a mountain; a mountain range
2. a mountain

嶺表(ㄌㄧㄥˇ ㄅㄧㄠˇ)
the front, or southern side of the Five Ridges (i.e., Kwangtung)

嶺南(ㄌㄧㄥˇ ㄋㄢˊ)
the area south of the Five Ridges (i.e., Kwangtung)

【嶼】 1279
　　ㄩˇ yeu yǔ
an islet; an island

【嶽】 1280
　　ㄩㄝˋ yueh yuè
a high mountain

嶽峙(ㄩㄝˋ ㄓ)
(said of one's character or bearing) as noble as a lofty peak

十七畫

【巇】 1281
　　ㄒㄧ shi xī
1. a crack
2. (said of a mountain path) hazardous

巇嶮 or 巇嶮(ㄒㄧ ㄒㄧㄢˇ)
①steep and difficult to ascend ②(figuratively) full of danger and hardship 亦作「嶮巇」

【巉】 1282
　　ㄔㄢˊ charn chán
precipitous

巉巖(ㄔㄢˊ ㄧㄢˊ)
a rock; a crag

【巋】 1283
　　ㄎㄨㄟ kuei kuī
1. grand and secure; stately and lasting
2. rows after rows of small hills

巋然(ㄎㄨㄟ ロㄢ日)
towering; lofty

巋然獨存(ㄎㄨㄟ ロㄢ日 ㄉㄨˊ ㄘㄨㄣˊ)
to remain secure majestically while all others have crumbled into decay

十八畫

【巍】 1284
　　メヽ wei wéi

**《《
部》**

towering; lofty; majestic

巍然(ㄨㄟ ㄖㄢˊ)
towering; lofty and massive;
majestic; imposing

巍然聳立(ㄨㄟ ㄖㄢˊ ㄙㄨㄥˇ ㄌㄧˋ) or
巍然矗立(ㄨㄟ ㄖㄢˊ ㄔㄨˋ ㄌㄧˋ)
to stand out majestically

巍峨(ㄨㄟ ㄜˊ)
towering; lofty; majestic

巍巍(ㄨㄟ ㄨㄟ)
towering; lofty; majestic;
imposing

十九畫

【巒】 1285
ㄌㄨㄢˊ luán
a pointed hill

【巔】 1286
ㄉㄧㄢ diān
1. a mountain top; a peak; the
summit of a mountain
2. a treetop

巔峰(ㄉㄧㄢ ㄈㄥ)
the highest point; a summit;
a climax; the zenith; a peak

巔峰狀態(ㄉㄧㄢ ㄈㄥ ㄓㄨㄤˋ ㄊㄞˋ)
(said of athletes, performing
artists, etc.) in peak condition

二十畫

【巖】 1287
(岩) ㄧㄢˊ yán yán
1. a rock; a crag
2. a cave

巖洞(ㄧㄢˊ ㄉㄨㄥˋ)
a mountain cave

巖居穴處(ㄧㄢˊ ㄐㄩ ㄒㄩㄝˊ ㄔㄨˋ)
①(said of primitive people)
to live in mountain caves ②
to live in seclusion or away
from civilization as a recluse or hermit

巖穴(ㄧㄢˊ ㄒㄩㄝˊ)
a cave, or cavern

【巘】 1288
ㄧㄢˇ yǎn yǎn
a peak; a hilltop

《《 部
ㄔㄨㄢ chuan chuān

【川】 1289
ㄔㄨㄢ chuan chuān
1. a river; a stream
2. a flow; a constant flow
3. (cooking) to boil with water
4. Szechwan Province

川北(ㄔㄨㄢ ㄅㄟˇ)
the northern part of Sze-
chwan Province

川貝(ㄔㄨㄢ ㄅㄟˋ)
(Chinese medicine) fritillar-
ia produced in Szechwan
Province

川朴(ㄔㄨㄢ ㄆㄛˋ)
(Chinese medicine) Magnolia
obovata

川東(ㄔㄨㄢ ㄉㄨㄥ)
the eastern part of Sze-
chwan Province

川南(ㄔㄨㄢ ㄋㄢˊ)
the southern part of Sze-
chwan Province

川流不息(ㄔㄨㄢ ㄌㄧㄡˊ ㄅㄨˋ ㄒㄧˊ)
(said of traffic, people, etc.)
a constant flow; an incessant flow; continuous

川漢鐵路(ㄔㄨㄢ ㄏㄢˋ ㄊㄧㄝˇ ㄌㄨˋ)
the railway from Chengtu of
Szechwan to Hankow of
Hupeh

川椒(ㄔㄨㄢ ㄐㄧㄠ)
the pepper produced in Szechwan—used in food seasoning and in Chinese herbal
medicine

川薑(ㄔㄨㄢ ㄐㄧㄤ)
the ginger produced in Szechwan—used especially in
herbal medicine

川芎(ㄔㄨㄢ ㄒㄩㄥ)
(Chinese medicine)
conioselinum

川綢(ㄔㄨㄢ ㄔㄡˊ)
silks from Szechwan

川資(ㄔㄨㄢ ㄗ)
traveling expenses

川澤(ㄔㄨㄢ ㄗㄜˊ)
(literally) rivers and lakes
—marshes; swamps

川菜(ㄔㄨㄢ ㄘㄞˋ)
the Szechwan style of cooking or cuisine featuring liberal use of hot pepper and
strong seasonings

川鹽(ㄔㄨㄢ ㄧㄢˊ)
the mineral salt produced in
Szechwan

三畫

【州】 1290
ㄓㄡ jou zhōu
1. chou, an administrative
trict in ancient China, roughly equivalent to a provir
today
2. (Chou Dynasty) a regi
with 2,500 families
3. (in old China) a county
4. a state (in the USA)
5. a place surrounded
water; an islet; a sand ba
6. a Chinese family name

州伯(ㄓㄡ ㄅㄛˊ)
the governor of a chou(州

州判(ㄓㄡ ㄆㄢˋ)
an official rank in ancie
China roughly equivalent
a deputy governor

州牧(ㄓㄡ ㄇㄨˋ)
a governor or magistrate
ancient China

州里(ㄓㄡ ㄌㄧˇ)
① an administrative unit
ancient China (州 consists
2,500 families; 里 consists
25 families) ② neighborho

州閭(ㄓㄡ ㄌㄩˊ)
a small village; a hamlet
neighborhood

州官(ㄓㄡ ㄍㄨㄢ)
①(in ancient China) o
cials in a chou(州) ②(in
China) the magistrate of
chou(州)

州官放火(ㄓㄡ ㄍㄨㄢ ㄈㄤˋ ㄏㄨㄛˇ)
(literally) The govern
may commit arson w
impunity (while the peo
are not allowed to li
their lamps).—(figurative
Officials in authority
free to indulge in any n
chief while interfering in
personal freedom of the p
ple they govern.

州郡(ㄓㄡ ㄐㄩㄣˋ)
an administrative district
ancient China

州縣(ㄓㄡ ㄒㄧㄢˋ)
a county within a chou(州

州治(ㄓㄡ ㄓˋ)
the capital city of a ch
(州)

州長(ㄓㄡ ㄓㄤˇ)

① the governor of a *chou* (州) ② the governor of a state (in the USA)

城(业又 イム)
a town within a *chou* (州)

四畫

【巡】 1291
(巡) Tロケ shyun xún
to patrol; to inspect; to cruise; to go on circuit: 警察在城裏巡邏。 The policemen patrolled the town.
a round (of drinks)
a policeman; a cop

捕(Tロケ ケメ)
(formerly) a policeman

捕房(Tロケ ケメ ㄷㄜ)
(formerly) a police station, or police precinct office

防(Tロケ ㄷㄤ)
① a patrolman; a watchman
② to patrol (especially in civil defense)

風(Tロケ ㄷㄥ)
a guard who keeps a look-out for the police while a criminal act is being committed 參看「把風」

撫(Tロケ ㄈㄨ)
① (in Ming Dynasty) an imperial inspector ② the governor of a province

丁(Tロケ ㄌㄧㄥ)or 巡役(Tロケ ㄧ) or 巡差(Tロケ ㄔㄞ)
a watchman; a patrolman; a policeman

禮(Tロケ ㄌㄧˇ)
① a pilgrimage to a holyland
② an inspection or sightseeing tour

邏(Tロケ ㄌㄨㄛ)
to patrol; to make the inspection rounds

邏隊(Tロケ ㄌㄨㄛ ㄉㄨㄟ)
a military patrol

邏車(Tロケ ㄌㄨㄛ ㄔㄜ)
a squad car

更(Tロケ ㄍㄥ)
(said of a watchman) to strike a gong during night patrol

官(Tロケ ㄍㄨㄢ)

a police inspector

巡航(Tロケ ㄏㄤ)
to cruise; a cruise

巡迴(Tロケ ㄏㄨㄟ)
to go the rounds; to tour; to make a circuit of: 馬戲團正在全國各地巡迴演出。 The circus is touring the country.

巡迴法庭(Tロケ ㄏㄨㄟ ㄈㄚ ㄊㄧㄥ)
a circuit court

巡迴放映隊(Tロケ ㄏㄨㄟ ㄈㄤ ㄧㄥ ㄉㄨㄟ)
a mobile film projection team

巡迴大使(Tロケ ㄏㄨㄟ ㄉㄚ ㄕ)
an ambassador-at-large; a roving ambassador

巡迴圖書館(Tロケ ㄏㄨㄟ ㄊㄨ ㄕㄨ ㄍㄨㄢ)
a circulating library

巡迴劇團(Tロケ ㄏㄨㄟ ㄐㄩ ㄊㄨㄢ)
an itinerant theatrical troupe

巡迴學校(Tロケ ㄏㄨㄟ ㄒㄩㄝ ㄒㄧㄠ)
a circulating school

巡迴審判(Tロケ ㄏㄨㄟ ㄕㄣ ㄆㄢ)
(until 1971 in England) assizes

巡檢(Tロケ ㄐㄧㄢˇ)
an official in frontier areas vested with the training of the militia and policing authorities in former times

巡警(Tロケ ㄐㄧㄥˇ)
① a policeman; a patrolman
② to inspect; to patrol

巡緝(Tロケ ㄑㄧ)
to patrol to arrest thieves and smugglers

巡行(Tロケ ㄒㄧㄥ)
to make the rounds of inspection

巡幸(Tロケ ㄒㄧㄥ)
(said of an emperor) to make an inspection tour

巡查(Tロケ ㄔㄚˊ)
to patrol and investigate

巡察(Tロケ ㄔㄚˊ)
to make the rounds of inspection

巡視(Tロケ ㄕˋ)
(said of ranking officials) to inspect; to make (or be on) an inspection tour

巡哨(Tロケ ㄕㄠˋ)or 巡邏(Tロケ ㄌㄨㄛˊ)
a military patrol; patrolling

巡守(Tロケ ㄕㄡˇ)or 巡狩(Tロケ ㄕㄡˋ)
an imperial inspection tour in the country; to make an imperial inspection tour in the country

巡按(Tロケ ㄢˋ)
an inspector general in the Ming Dynasty

巡使(Tロケ ㄕˇ)or(Tロケ ㄕˋ)
(in early years of the Chinese Republic) the governor of a province

巡弋飛彈(Tロケ ㄧˋ ㄈㄟ ㄉㄢˋ)
a cruise missile

巡夜(Tロケ ㄧㄝˋ)
to make nightly patrols

巡洋艦(Tロケ ㄧㄤˊ ㄐㄧㄢˋ)
a cruiser

巡閱(Tロケ ㄩㄝˋ)
to make the rounds of inspection; to inspect

巡閱使(Tロケ ㄩㄝˋ ㄕˇ)or(Tロケ ㄩㄝˋ ㄕˋ)
a commanding officer or civil administrative chief of a region, usually quite large, in the early days of the Chinese Republic

〔 巛 部 〕

八畫

【巢】 1292
㔷ㄠ chaur cháo
1. living quarters in the trees
2. a bird's nest: 燕子正在簷下築巢。 The swallows are making a nest under the eaves.
3. a haunt; a hideout (for bandits, etc.)
4. a Chinese family name

巢父(㔷ㄠ ㄈㄨˋ)
a legendary hermit-scholar during the time of Emperor Yao (2356 B.C.), who lived high up in a tree and declined the throne offered by the emperor

巢窟(㔷ㄠ ㄎㄨ)or 巢穴(㔷ㄠ ㄒㄩㄝ)
a den; a lair; a haunt

巢湖(㔷ㄠ ㄏㄨˊ)
Chao Lake—name of a lake in Anhwei Province

巢居(㔷ㄠ ㄐㄩ)
to live in trees (before the house was introduced)

工 部
《ㄍㄨㄥ gōng gōng

〔工部〕

【工】 1293
《ㄍㄨㄥ gong gōng

1. a laborer; a worker
2. a shift; the time used in doing a piece of work
3. work
4. a day's work
5. an engineering or building project
6. a defense work
7. fine; delicate
8. to be skilled in

工本費《ㄍㄨㄥ ㄅㄣ ㄈㄟˋ》
the net cost of a product (the cost of raw materials plus labor)

工筆畫《ㄍㄨㄥ ㄅㄧˇ ㄏㄨㄚˋ》
(Chinese painting) very fine, delicate drawings

工兵《ㄍㄨㄥ ㄅㄧㄥ》
(military) ① engineering corps ② a serviceman in the engineering corps

工部《ㄍㄨㄥ ㄅㄨˋ》
(in old China) the Ministry of Public Works

工部侍郎《ㄍㄨㄥ ㄅㄨˋ ㄕˋ ㄌㄤˊ》
(in old China) a Vice Minister of Public Works

工部尚書《ㄍㄨㄥ ㄅㄨˋ ㄕㄤˋ ㄕㄨ》
(in old China) the Minister of Public Works

工棚《ㄍㄨㄥ ㄆㄥˊ》
① a builders' temporary shed ② a work shed

工蜂《ㄍㄨㄥ ㄈㄥ》
a worker or a working bee

工夫《ㄍㄨㄥ ·ㄈㄨ》
① time; leisure: 我沒有工夫和你閒聊。I have no time to chat with you. ② efforts put into a piece of work; labor ③ skill; workmanship; art: 這位魔術師可真有工夫! The magician's skill is really superb.

工黨《ㄍㄨㄥ ㄉㄤˇ》
① the British Labor Party ② a labor party

工地《ㄍㄨㄥ ㄉㄧˋ》
a building site; a place where an engineering work is under way

工讀《ㄍㄨㄥ ㄉㄨˊ》
to work on a job in order to finance one's study or education

工讀生《ㄍㄨㄥ ㄉㄨˊ ㄕㄥ》
a worker-student; a student who works his way through college

工頭《ㄍㄨㄥ ㄊㄡˊ》
a foreman (of workers)

工農《ㄍㄨㄥ ㄋㄨㄥˊ》
workers and peasants

工力《ㄍㄨㄥ ㄌㄧˋ》
the amount of efforts made; force and skill (especially for calligraphic works and paintings)

工寮《ㄍㄨㄥ ㄌㄧㄠˊ》
a simple hut for workmen at a construction site

工料《ㄍㄨㄥ ㄌㄧㄠˋ》
the cost of labor and materials; labor and raw materials

工棍《ㄍㄨㄥ ㄍㄨㄣˋ》
a labor union official who makes use of his power to promote self-interest instead of the welfare of union members

工科《ㄍㄨㄥ ㄎㄜ》
the engineering department of a college

工會《ㄍㄨㄥ ㄏㄨㄟˋ》
a labor union; a trade union

工價《ㄍㄨㄥ ㄐㄧㄚˋ》
the money paid to a skilled worker (as a goldsmith, jeweler, etc.) for piecework

工匠《ㄍㄨㄥ ㄐㄧㄤˋ》
a skilled worker; a craftsman; an artisan

工具《ㄍㄨㄥ ㄐㄩˋ》
tools; implements: 工匠愛護工具。Artisans take good care of their tools.

工具箱《ㄍㄨㄥ ㄐㄩˋ ㄒㄧㄤ》
a toolbox; a workbox

工具書《ㄍㄨㄥ ㄐㄩˋ ㄕㄨ》
reference books, such as an encyclopedia, dictionary, etc.

工巧《ㄍㄨㄥ ㄑㄧㄠˇ》
① fine and delicate ② a craftsman of unusual artistic skill

工錢《ㄍㄨㄥ ㄑㄧㄢˊ》
pay; wages; the payment ▉ a piece of work

工區《ㄍㄨㄥ ㄑㄩ》
a work area; a work regi▉

工效《ㄍㄨㄥ ㄒㄧㄠˋ》
work efficiency

工學院《ㄍㄨㄥ ㄒㄩㄝˊ ㄩㄢˋ》
a college of engineering

工緻《ㄍㄨㄥ ㄓˋ》
delicate, fine and skill▉ craftsmanship

工整《ㄍㄨㄥ ㄓㄥˇ》
neat (style, calligraph▉ etc.)

工裝《ㄍㄨㄥ ㄓㄨㄤ》
a workman's fatigues; wor▉ ing clothes; overalls

工尺《ㄍㄨㄥ ㄔㄜˇ》
a musical score in old Chi▉

工潮《ㄍㄨㄥ ㄔㄠˊ》
labor unrest or agitation; labor strike; sabotage

工場《ㄍㄨㄥ ㄔㄤˇ》
a workshop; a workplace: 位工程師監督工場。The eng▉ neer supervises the wor▉ place.

工廠《ㄍㄨㄥ ㄔㄤˇ》
a factory; a plant; a wor▉ shop

工廠經濟《ㄍㄨㄥ ㄔㄤˇ ㄐㄧㄥ ㄐㄧˋ》
factory economy

工廠制度《ㄍㄨㄥ ㄔㄤˇ ㄓˋ ㄉㄨˋ》
the factory system

工廠自動化《ㄍㄨㄥ ㄔㄤˇ ㄗˋ ㄉㄨㄥˋ ㄏㄨㄚˋ》
factory automation (F. A.)

工程《ㄍㄨㄥ ㄔㄥˊ》
engineering; an engineerin▉ or building project—(figur▉ tively) a job or task

工程隊《ㄍㄨㄥ ㄔㄥˊ ㄉㄨㄟˋ》
the public works corps

工程力學《ㄍㄨㄥ ㄔㄥˊ ㄌㄧˋ ㄒㄩㄝˊ》
practical dynamics

工程學《ㄍㄨㄥ ㄔㄥˊ ㄒㄩㄝˊ》
engineering

工程處《ㄍㄨㄥ ㄔㄥˊ ㄔㄨˋ》
the department of engineer▉ ing; the engineering depar▉ ment of a huge buildin▉ project

工程師《ㄍㄨㄥ ㄔㄥˊ ㄕ》
an engineer

工程師節《ㄍㄨㄥ ㄔㄥ ㄕ ㄐㄧㄝˊ》
Engineer's Day

工時《ㄍㄨㄥ ㄕˊ》
a man-hour

工事《ㄍㄨㄥ ㄕˋ》
① matters pertaining to civil engineering work ② defense works; military fortifications

工商部《ㄍㄨㄥ ㄕㄤ ㄅㄨˋ》
Ministry of Reconstruction and Commerce

工商界《ㄍㄨㄥ ㄕㄤ ㄐㄧㄝˋ》
the industrial and business circles

工商業《ㄍㄨㄥ ㄕㄤ ㄧㄝˋ》
industry and commerce: 他是工商業大亨。He is a magnate in industrial and commercial enterprises.

工人《ㄍㄨㄥ ㄖㄣˊ》
a laborer; a workman

工人階級《ㄍㄨㄥ ㄖㄣˊ ㄐㄧㄝ ㄐㄧˊ》
the working class; labor class

工資《ㄍㄨㄥ ㄗ》
wages

工作《ㄍㄨㄥ ㄗㄨㄛˋ》
① to work ② a piece of work; one's job or duty

工作母機《ㄍㄨㄥ ㄗㄨㄛˋ ㄇㄨˇ ㄐㄧ》
a machine tool

工作分配《ㄍㄨㄥ ㄗㄨㄛˋ ㄈㄣ ㄆㄟˋ》
work allocation

工作服《ㄍㄨㄥ ㄗㄨㄛˋ ㄈㄨˊ》
working clothes

工作大隊《ㄍㄨㄥ ㄗㄨㄛˋ ㄉㄚˋ ㄉㄨㄟˋ》
a team or group of persons dispatched for a special task

工作天《ㄍㄨㄥ ㄗㄨㄛˋ ㄊㄧㄢ》
a man-day: 那項工程需要二十個工作天。That project will take twenty man-days to complete.

工作者《ㄍㄨㄥ ㄗㄨㄛˋ ㄓㄜˇ》
workers: 教育工作者 educational workers 美術工作者 art workers; artists

工作日《ㄍㄨㄥ ㄗㄨㄛˋ ㄖˋ》
a workday: 通常我們一週有六個工作日。Usually we have six workdays per week.

工作人員《ㄍㄨㄥ ㄗㄨㄛˋ ㄖㄣˊ ㄩㄢˊ》
workers; the workers assigned to do a specific task or job

工作物《ㄍㄨㄥ ㄗㄨㄛˋ ㄨˋ》
(law) a product of labor, such as a house, a bridge, etc.

工蟻《ㄍㄨㄥ ㄧˇ》
a worker (ant)

工役《ㄍㄨㄥ ㄧˋ》
a laborer; a worker

工藝《ㄍㄨㄥ ㄧˋ》
technology; a craft: 手工藝 handicrafts

工藝品《ㄍㄨㄥ ㄧˋ ㄆㄧㄣˇ》
handicrafts; handmade products; items made by artisans

工藝設計《ㄍㄨㄥ ㄧˋ ㄕㄜˋ ㄐㄧˋ》
technological design

工業《ㄍㄨㄥ ㄧㄝˋ》
industry; industrial: 輕工業 the light industry 重工業 the heavy industry

工業廢物《ㄍㄨㄥ ㄧㄝˋ ㄈㄟˋ ㄨˋ》
industrial waste

工業垃圾《ㄍㄨㄥ ㄧㄝˋ ㄌㄜˋ ㄙㄜˋ》
industrial refuse

工業革命《ㄍㄨㄥ ㄧㄝˋ ㄍㄜˊ ㄇㄧㄥˋ》
Industrial Revolution: 工業革命發生於十八世紀及十九世紀初期。The Industrial Revolution took place in the 18th and early 19th centuries.

工業國家《ㄍㄨㄥ ㄧㄝˋ ㄍㄨㄛˊ ㄐㄧㄚ》
industrial nations or powers; developed countries

工業公害《ㄍㄨㄥ ㄧㄝˋ ㄍㄨㄥ ㄏㄞˋ》
industrial public nuisances

工業化《ㄍㄨㄥ ㄧㄝˋ ㄏㄨㄚˋ》
industrialization; industrialized: 高度工業化的經濟 highly industrialized economics

工業化學《ㄍㄨㄥ ㄧㄝˋ ㄏㄨㄚˋ ㄒㄩㄝˊ》
industrial chemistry

工業機器人《ㄍㄨㄥ ㄧㄝˋ ㄐㄧ ㄑㄧˋ ㄖㄣˊ》
an industrial robot

工業酒精《ㄍㄨㄥ ㄧㄝˋ ㄐㄧㄡˇ ㄐㄧㄥ》
industrial alcohol

工業區《ㄍㄨㄥ ㄧㄝˋ ㄑㄩ》
an industrial zone; an industrial park 亦作「工業園」

工業學校《ㄍㄨㄥ ㄧㄝˋ ㄒㄩㄝˊ ㄒㄧㄠˋ》
technical schools; industrial schools

工業城市《ㄍㄨㄥ ㄧㄝˋ ㄔㄥˊ ㄕˋ》
an industrial city

工業時代《ㄍㄨㄥ ㄧㄝˋ ㄕˊ ㄉㄞˋ》
an industrial age

工業設計《ㄍㄨㄥ ㄧㄝˋ ㄕㄜˋ ㄐㄧˋ》
industrial design

工業危害《ㄍㄨㄥ ㄧㄝˋ ㄨㄟˊ ㄏㄞˋ》
industrial hazard

工業電視《ㄍㄨㄥ ㄧㄝˋ ㄉㄧㄢˋ ㄕˋ》
industrial television (ITV)

工業用具《ㄍㄨㄥ ㄧㄝˋ ㄩㄥˋ ㄐㄩˋ》
equipment and tools used in industries

工業用水《ㄍㄨㄥ ㄧㄝˋ ㄩㄥˋ ㄕㄨㄟˇ》
industrial water

工友《ㄍㄨㄥ ㄧㄡˇ》
an office boy; an office errand man

工務局《ㄍㄨㄥ ㄨˋ ㄐㄩˊ》
the (municipal) bureau of public works

工穩《ㄍㄨㄥ ㄨㄣˇ》
(usually said of literary works, calligraphy, wording of documents, etc.) neat and proper; flawless

工於心計《ㄍㄨㄥ ㄩˊ ㄒㄧㄣ ㄐㄧˋ》
scheming; crafty

工欲善其事，必先利其器《ㄍㄨㄥ ㄩˋ ㄕㄢˋ ㄑㄧˊ ㄕˋ，ㄅㄧˋ ㄒㄧㄢ ㄌㄧˋ ㄑㄧˊ ㄑㄧˋ》
Good tools are prerequisite to the successful execution of a job.

〔工部〕

二畫

【左】 1294
ㄗㄨㄛˇ tzuoo zuǒ

1. the left side
2. the east side: 江左 the east side of the river 山左 the east side of the mountain
3. improper
4. supporting (documents, evidence, etc.); to assist
5. to be demoted; to descend
6. inconvenience; inconvenient
7. erroneous; mistaken
8. unduly stubborn
9. a Chinese family name
10. to disobey; to disregard

左臂《ㄗㄨㄛˇ ㄅㄟˋ》
the left arm

左邊《ㄗㄨㄛˇ ㄅㄧㄢ》or 左邊兒《ㄗㄨㄛˇ ㄅㄧㄤ兒》or 左面《ㄗㄨㄛˇ ㄇㄧㄢˋ》
the left side; the left-hand side: 來，坐到我的左邊。Come and sit on my left.

左鞭右引《ㄗㄨㄛˇ ㄅㄧㄢ ㄧㄡˋ ㄌㄚˇ》
to make deceiving moves;

pretending to strike in one direction but actually delivering the blow in another direction

左不過(ㄗㄨㄛˇ·ㄅㄨˋ《ㄨㄛˋ)
certainly; must be; can't be otherwise

左派(ㄗㄨㄛˇ ㄆㄞˋ)
①a radical; a leftist ②a leftist faction: 政黨的左派 the left faction of the party

左脾氣(ㄗㄨㄛˇ ㄆㄧˊ·ㄑㄧ)
a stubbornly peevish temper

左撇子(ㄗㄨㄛˇ ㄆㄧㄝˇ·ㄗ)
a left-handed person; a southpaw; a portsider

左方(ㄗㄨㄛˇ ㄈㄤ)
on the left; to the left

左輔右弼(ㄗㄨㄛˇ ㄈㄨˇ ㄧㄡˋ ㄅㄧˋ)
the emperor's top ministers

左道(ㄗㄨㄛˇ ㄉㄠˋ)
①heresy ②unlawful and tricky ways; evil ways

左袒(ㄗㄨㄛˇ ㄊㄢˇ)
to be biased; to favor one side

左提右挈(ㄗㄨㄛˇ ㄊㄧˊ ㄧㄡˋ ㄑㄧㄝˋ)
to give mutual help or assistance

左圖右史(ㄗㄨㄛˇ ㄊㄨˊ ㄧㄡˋ ㄕˇ)
a large private collection of books; an impressive personal library

左鄰右舍(ㄗㄨㄛˇ ㄌㄧㄣˊ ㄧㄡˋ ㄕㄜˋ)
neighbors

左輪鎗(ㄗㄨㄛˇ ㄌㄨㄣˊ ㄑㄧㄤ)
a revolver; a six-shooter

左改右改(ㄗㄨㄛˇ ㄍㄞˇ ㄧㄡˋ ㄍㄞˇ)
to make changes over and over again

左顧右盼(ㄗㄨㄛˇ ㄍㄨˋ ㄧㄡˋ ㄆㄢˋ)
①to look left and right—inattentive; lack of concentration ②flirtatious ③to cheat in the examination

左近(ㄗㄨㄛˇ ㄐㄧㄣˋ)
in the neighborhood; in the vicinity: 左近有銀行嗎? Is there a bank in the vicinity?

左遷(ㄗㄨㄛˇ ㄑㄧㄢ)or左黜(ㄗㄨㄛˇ ㄔㄨˋ)or左降(ㄗㄨㄛˇ ㄐㄧㄤˋ)
to be demoted

左傾(ㄗㄨㄛˇ ㄑㄧㄥ)
left-leaning: 社會黨員是左傾的。The Socialists are left-leaning.

左券(ㄗㄨㄛˇ ㄑㄩㄢˋ)
a winning hand; full confidence in (winning)

左舷(ㄗㄨㄛˇ ㄒㄧㄢˊ)
the port (of a ship)

左心室(ㄗㄨㄛˇ ㄒㄧㄣ ㄕˋ)
the left ventricle

左心耳(ㄗㄨㄛˇ ㄒㄧㄣ ㄦˇ)or左心房(ㄗㄨㄛˇ ㄒㄧㄣ ㄈㄤˊ)
the left auricle

左行(ㄗㄨㄛˇ ㄒㄧㄥˊ)
①(said of writing) from left to right—Western written languages ②to keep to the left

左性子(ㄗㄨㄛˇ ㄒㄧㄥˋ·ㄗ)
a peevish or very stubborn temper; cantankerous

左支右絀(ㄗㄨㄛˇ ㄓ ㄧㄡˋ ㄔㄨˋ)
not have enough money to cover the expenses; hard-pressed for money; in financial straits; to be in straitened circumstances

左證(ㄗㄨㄛˇ ㄓㄥˋ)
supporting evidence (of one's statement, etc.) 亦作「佐證」

左轉(ㄗㄨㄛˇ ㄓㄨㄢˇ)
to turn left

左傳(ㄗㄨㄛˇ ㄓㄨㄢˋ)or左氏傳(ㄗㄨㄛˇ ㄕˋ ㄓㄨㄢˋ)
Spring and Autumn with Commentary by Tso Chiu-ming — a commentary on the Spring and Autumn Annals（春秋）, authored by Tso Chiu-ming(左丘明)of the Chou Dynasty

左丞相(ㄗㄨㄛˇ ㄔㄥˊ ㄒㄧㄤˋ)
an old official rank, roughly equivalent to vice premiership

左史(ㄗㄨㄛˇ ㄕˇ)
an official historian

左手(ㄗㄨㄛˇ ㄕㄡˇ)
①the left hand ②the left hand side

左首(ㄗㄨㄛˇ ㄕㄡˇ)
the left side

左書(ㄗㄨㄛˇ ㄕㄨ)
①(Chinese calligraphy) the "clerical" style ②characters written by one's left hand

左衽 or 左袵(ㄗㄨㄛˇ ㄖㄣˋ)
①to wear the clothes of a barbarian ②the barbarian

clothes buttoning on the left side

左宗棠(ㄗㄨㄛˇ ㄗㄨㄥ ㄊㄤˊ)
Tso Chung-tang, one of the major figures in the suppression of the Taiping Rebellion

左側(ㄗㄨㄛˇ ㄘㄜˋ)
on the left side

左思右想(ㄗㄨㄛˇ ㄙ ㄧㄡˋ ㄒㄧㄤˇ)
to think over and over; to ponder; to muse

左嗓子(ㄗㄨㄛˇ ㄙㄤˇ·ㄗ)
a high-pitched and unpleasant voice; a voice which is high but not refined

左翼(ㄗㄨㄛˇ ㄧˋ)
①(politics) the left wing or leftist ②(ball games) the left wing ③(military operations) the left flank

左右(ㄗㄨㄛˇ ㄧㄡˋ)
①left and right—nearby; by one's side; at hand: 她的小孩子常在她左右。Her children are always by her side. ②servants; aides ③a term of respect placed after the name when addressing another (usually in correspondence) ④to influence or sway; to be influenced or swayed

左右逢源(ㄗㄨㄛˇ ㄧㄡˋ ㄈㄥˊ ㄩㄢˊ)
to get help from all sides; to have everything going one's way

左右袒(ㄗㄨㄛˇ ㄧㄡˋ ㄊㄢˇ)
to take sides; to be unneutral; to be biased

左右開弓(ㄗㄨㄛˇ ㄧㄡˋ ㄎㄞ ㄍㄨㄥ)
to slap someone's face with both hands

左右手(ㄗㄨㄛˇ ㄧㄡˋ ㄕㄡˇ)
①left and right hands ②able assistants; top aides

左右翼(ㄗㄨㄛˇ ㄧㄡˋ ㄧˋ)
the left and right wings or flanks

左右為難(ㄗㄨㄛˇ ㄧㄡˋ ㄨㄟˊ ㄋㄢˊ)
to know not which side to turn to—to be indecisive; to be in a dilemma

左驗(ㄗㄨㄛˇ ㄧㄢˋ)
a witness

左擁右抱(ㄗㄨㄛˇ ㄩㄥ ㄧㄡˋ ㄅㄠˋ)
(literally) to have a woman

in each arm—(figuratively) to have two or more concubines; to have several mistresses at the same time

【巧】 1295 〈ㄑㄧㄠˇ chǎu qiǎo〉
clever; witty

. ingenious; artful; skillful
a clever feat; a stunt

. pretty; cute
. coincidence; coincidental; coincidentally; opportune

巧辯〈ㄑㄧㄠˇ ㄅㄧㄢˋ〉
a plausible argument; an ingenious argument

巧不可階〈ㄑㄧㄠˇ ㄅㄨˋ ㄎㄜˇ ㄐㄧㄝ〉
unmatched in ingenuity

巧妙〈ㄑㄧㄠˇ ㄇㄧㄠˋ〉
ingenuity; ingenious; skillful; clever. 巧妙的戰術 ingenious tactics 巧妙的回答 a clever answer

巧手段〈ㄑㄧㄠˇ ㄇㄧㄢˋ ㄉㄨㄢˋ〉
an ingenious or clever move

巧婦難為無米之炊〈ㄑㄧㄠˇ ㄈㄨˋ ㄋㄢˊ ㄨㄟˊ ㄨˊ ㄇㄧˇ ㄓ ㄔㄨㄟ〉
(literally) Even the cleverest woman cannot prepare a meal without rice.—(figuratively) Nobody can accomplish anything without the necessary means.

巧得很〈ㄑㄧㄠˇ ㄉㄜˊ ㄏㄣˇ〉
quite by coincidence; as luck would have it; fortunately

巧當兒〈ㄑㄧㄠˇ ㄉㄤ ㄦˊ〉
①(at) the opportune moment ②coincidence

巧奪天工〈ㄑㄧㄠˇ ㄉㄨㄛˊ ㄊㄧㄢ ㄍㄨㄥ〉
(often referring to a work of art) ingenuity that rivals the work of God

巧立名目〈ㄑㄧㄠˇ ㄌㄧˋ ㄇㄧㄥˊ ㄇㄨˋ〉
to fabricate various excuses; to invent all sorts of names

巧固球〈ㄑㄧㄠˇ ㄍㄨˋ ㄑㄧㄡˊ〉
tchouk ball

巧克力糖〈ㄑㄧㄠˇ ㄎㄜˋ ㄌㄧˋ ㄊㄤˊ〉
chocolate

巧合〈ㄑㄧㄠˇ ㄏㄜˊ〉
a coincidence

巧極了〈ㄑㄧㄠˇ ㄐㄧˊ ㄌㄜ˙〉
quite by coincidence; extremely coincidental; extremely fortunate

巧計〈ㄑㄧㄠˇ ㄐㄧˋ〉
an ingenious scheme; a very

clever device; a capital plan

巧妻常伴拙夫眠〈ㄑㄧㄠˇ ㄑㄧ ㄔㄤˊ ㄅㄢˋ ㄓㄨㄛ ㄈㄨ ㄇㄧㄢˊ〉
Smart girls usually have dumb men for husbands.

巧取豪奪〈ㄑㄧㄠˇ ㄑㄩˇ ㄏㄠˊ ㄉㄨㄛˊ〉
to rob others by hook or by crook

巧笑〈ㄑㄧㄠˇ ㄒㄧㄠˋ〉
(said of women) an artful smile; to smile artfully

巧詐〈ㄑㄧㄠˇ ㄓㄚˋ〉
artful; tricky; ingenious fraud: 他是一個巧詐的政客。 He is a tricky politician.

巧事〈ㄑㄧㄠˇ ㄕˋ〉
a coincidence

巧舌如簧〈ㄑㄧㄠˇ ㄕㄜˊ ㄖㄨˊ ㄏㄨㄤˊ〉
a very plausible tongue

巧手〈ㄑㄧㄠˇ ㄕㄡˇ〉
a skillful person; a dab: 她是網球巧手。 she's a dab at tennis.

巧言令色〈ㄑㄧㄠˇ ㄧㄢˊ ㄌㄧㄥˋ ㄙㄜˋ〉
sweet words and insinuating manners (which are seldom associated with virtue)

巧遇〈ㄑㄧㄠˇ ㄩˋ〉
a chance encounter

【巨】 1296 〈ㄐㄩˋ〉 (鉅) ㄐㄩˋ jiùh jù〉
1. great; big: 我們聽見一聲巨響。 We heard a great noise.
2. very
3. a Chinese family name

巨擘〈ㄐㄩˋ ㄅㄛˋ〉
①the thumb ②an outstanding person; the foremost figure (in a field); a magnate: 他是建築業的巨擘。 He is a magnate in the construction business.

巨富〈ㄐㄩˋ ㄈㄨˋ〉
a multimillionaire; a person of immense wealth

巨大〈ㄐㄩˋ ㄉㄚˋ〉
giant (size); mammoth; gargantuan; gigantic

巨盜〈ㄐㄩˋ ㄉㄠˋ〉
a notorious bandit; a monstrous villain or robber

巨惡〈ㄐㄩˋ ㄜˋ〉
an influential criminal; Public Enemy No. One

巨頭〈ㄐㄩˋ ㄊㄡˊ〉
a national leader; a big chief

巨頭會議〈ㄐㄩˋ ㄊㄡˊ ㄏㄨㄟˋ ㄧˋ〉
a summit conference; a meeting of chiefs

巨流〈ㄐㄩˋ ㄌㄧㄡˊ〉
a mighty current: 許多小溪滙成一股巨流。 Many brooks converge into a mighty current.

巨量〈ㄐㄩˋ ㄌㄧㄤˋ〉
a tremendous amount; a great deal

巨輪〈ㄐㄩˋ ㄌㄨㄣˊ〉
①a large wheel ②a large ship

巨構〈ㄐㄩˋ ㄍㄡˋ〉
(of literature, etc.) a great work; (of a movie, etc.) a colossal production

巨賈〈ㄐㄩˋ ㄍㄨˇ〉
a business tycoon; a business magnate

巨工〈ㄐㄩˋ ㄍㄨㄥ〉
a gigantic task; a mammoth project

巨款〈ㄐㄩˋ ㄎㄨㄢˇ〉
a huge sum of money

巨猾〈ㄐㄩˋ ㄏㄨㄚˊ〉
a notorious swindler; a very evil person

巨奸〈ㄐㄩˋ ㄐㄧㄢ〉
a big swindler; a person of many evils; a big crook

巨艦〈ㄐㄩˋ ㄐㄧㄢˋ〉
a large warship

巨匠〈ㄐㄩˋ ㄐㄧㄤˋ〉
a maestro; a master; an expert; a leading figure (in the literary, painting, etc. world)

巨細〈ㄐㄩˋ ㄒㄧˋ〉
(the) big and (the) small

巨細靡遺〈ㄐㄩˋ ㄒㄧˋ ㄇㄧˇ ㄧˊ〉
not to leave out any detail; not to leave out anything, big or small

巨星〈ㄐㄩˋ ㄒㄧㄥ〉
①(astronomy) a giant star ②a giant

巨型〈ㄐㄩˋ ㄒㄧㄥˊ〉
a large model (of cars, etc.)

巨著〈ㄐㄩˋ ㄓㄨˋ〉
a great book; a monumental literary work

巨室〈ㄐㄩˋ ㄕˋ〉
①a powerful or influential family ②a big house or palace

〔工 部〕

〔工部〕

巨人 (ㄐㄩˋ ㄖㄣˊ)
a giant; 他是這個時代的巨人。
He is a giant of the present era.

巨子 (ㄐㄩˋ ㄗˇ)
①a business tycoon ②a master; a maestro

巨額 (ㄐㄩˋ ㄜˊ)
a great deal of; a tremendous amount of; a huge sum of; 建大廈要花一筆巨額的錢。
Building a mansion takes a great amount of money.

巨案 (ㄐㄩˋ ㄢˋ)
a sensational case

巨毋霸 or 巨無霸 (ㄐㄩˋ ㄨˊ ㄅㄚˋ)
① name of a giant during the time of Wang Mang (王莽) ② (figuratively) a giant

巨萬 (ㄐㄩˋ ㄨㄢˋ)
an immense amount (of money, wealth, etc.)

四畫

【巫】 1297
ㄨ wu wū
(語音 ㄨ u wū)
1. a wizard or witch
2. witchcraft; sorcery
3. a Chinese family name

巫婆 (ㄨ ㄆㄛˊ)
a witch

巫蠱 (ㄨ ㄍㄨˇ)
the art of casting a spell over somebody

巫覡 (ㄨ ㄒㄧˊ)
witches and wizards; (collectively) sorcerers

巫峽 (ㄨ ㄒㄧㄚˊ)
Wu Gorge—one of the three gorges of the upper Yangtze River

巫祝 (ㄨ ㄓㄨˋ)
a witch or a wizard

巫師 (ㄨ ㄕ)
a sorcerer; a wizard

巫山 (ㄨ ㄕㄢ)
①Mountain Wu, in the east of Szechwan ② name of a county in Szechwan

巫山雲雨 (ㄨ ㄕㄢ ㄩㄣˊ ㄩˇ)
a rendezvous between two lovers—coitus

巫術 (ㄨ ㄕㄨˋ)
sorcery; black magic; witch-ery

巫醫 (ㄨ ㄧ)
a witch doctor

七畫

【差】 1298
ㄔ cha chā
1. errors; mistakes; 未犯差錯的人，亦未能成一事。One who never made a mistake never made anything.
2. difference; discrepancy; 這沒有什麼差別。It makes no difference.
3. (mathematics) difference; 七與十五之差為八。The difference between seven and fifteen is eight.

差別 (ㄔ ㄅㄧㄝˊ)
discrepancy; difference; distinction

差別關稅 (ㄔ ㄅㄧㄝˊ ㄍㄨㄢ ㄕㄨㄟˋ)
differential duties

差可 (ㄔ ㄎㄜˇ)
barely passable

差號 (ㄔ ㄏㄠˋ)
the "—" sign to show the difference between two figures

差價 (ㄔ ㄐㄧㄚˋ)
price differences; 季節差價
seasonal price differences

差距 (ㄔ ㄐㄩˋ)
gap; disparity; difference; 你的意見和我的差距很大。There is a wide gap between your opinion and mine.

差強人意 (ㄔ ㄑㄧㄤˊ ㄖㄣˊ ㄧˋ)
barely satisfactory; barely passable

差池 or 差泜 (ㄔ ㄔˊ)
①accidents ②errors; mis-calculations; mistakes

差 (mathematics) difference

差錯 (ㄔ ㄘㄨㄛˋ)
①errors; mistakes; miscal-culations ②accidents

差額 (ㄔ ㄜˊ)
the difference between two amounts or figures

差以毫釐謬以千里 (ㄔ ㄧˇ ㄏㄠˊ ㄌㄧˊ, ㄇㄧㄡˋ ㄧˇ ㄑㄧㄢ ㄌㄧˇ)
A slight error in the beginning results in a big mistake in the end. 亦作〔差之毫釐，失之千里〕

差異 (ㄔ ㄧˋ)
discrepancy; difference; variance; variation ② to differ

差誤 (ㄔ ㄨˋ)
errors; blunders; miscalculations

【差】 1298
ㄔㄚˋ chah chà
1. to differ
2. wrong; 此言差矣。You are wrong there.
3. to want; to fall short of; 距約定的時間還差半小時。I wants half an hour to the appointed time.
4. not up to standard; poor; 他的記憶力很差。He has a poor memory.

差不多 (ㄔˋ ㄅㄨˋ ㄉㄨㄛ)
① with little difference almost the same ② almost nearly; approximately ③ just about enough

差得多 (ㄔˋ ㄉㄜˊ ㄉㄨㄛ)
① very different; much dif-ference; poles apart ② far below (the required sum standard, criterion, etc.)

差點兒 (ㄔˋ ㄉㄧㄢˇ ㄦ)
① almost; nearly; 這盤棋他差點兒贏了。He almost won the chess game. ② with a slight difference; nearly the same ③ not good enough

差勁 (ㄔˋ ㄐㄧㄣˋ)
disappointing; poor (work, records, etc.); 她本學期的成績很差勁。She made a poor record this term.

【差】 1298
ㄔㄞ chai chāi
1. a messenger; an errand man; 這青年担任一家公司的信差。This young man serves as a messenger in a company.
2. to dispatch; to send (a person)
3. one's duty or job; one's offi-cial business or assignment
4. an errand; 他被派出差。He was sent on an errand.

差派 (ㄔㄞ ㄆㄞˋ)
to dispatch or appoint (a person to do a job, etc.)

差遣(彳历 く1 弓)or 差使(彳历 ㄕ)
to dispatch or send (a person on an errand, etc.): 他差遣她去買麵包。He dispatched her to buy bread.

差事(彳历 ㄕ)
a job

差人(彳历 ㄖㄣ)or 差役(彳历 ㄧ)or 差使(彳历 ㄕ)
the servants of an official; an official messenger

【差】1298
4. ㄘ tsy cī
uneven; irregular

差等(彳历 ㄉㄥ)
classification; classes

己 部
ㄐㄧˇ jii jǐ

【己】1299
ㄐㄧˇ jii jǐ
1. self; one's own; oneself: 人不應該專為自己而活。One should not live for oneself alone.
2. the sixth of the ten Celestial Stems (天干)

己方(ㄐㄧˇ ㄈㄤ)
one's own side

己飢己溺(ㄐㄧˇ ㄐㄧ ㄐㄧˇ ㄋㄧˋ)
(literally) to feel responsible for the hungry and the drowning of the people —(said of a person in authority) to feel responsible for the welfare of the people

己身(ㄐㄧˇ ㄕㄣ)
oneself; one's own person

己任(ㄐㄧˇ ㄖㄣˋ)
one's duty, responsibility or obligation

己所不欲，勿施於人(ㄐㄧˇ ㄙㄨㄛˇ ㄅㄨˋ ㄩˋ ㄨㄨˋ ㄕ ㄩˊ ㄖㄣˊ)
Do not do to others what you don't want to be done to you.

【已】1300
ㄧˇ yii yǐ
1. to cease; to stop
2. to come to an end; to finish; to complete
3. already: 郵差已經來了。The postman has been here already.

4. used to indicate the past
5. excessive; very; much
6. a final particle to add emphasis: 相信你祇是開玩笑而已。I believe you only joke about this.

已滿(ㄧˇ ㄇㄢˇ)
①already full; already filled up ②(said of a time limit) already expired: 他的任期已滿。His term of office has expired.

已定(ㄧˇ ㄉㄧㄥˋ)
already settled; already fixed; to have come to a final arrangement: 諸事已定。All affairs are already settled.

已故(ㄧˇ ㄍㄨˋ)
already dead; the deceased; the late...: 已故的主席定下這條規則。The late chairman set up this rule.

已過(ㄧˇ ㄍㄨㄛˋ)
already past; to have passed already

已開發國家(ㄧˇ ㄎㄞ ㄈㄚ ㄍㄨㄛˊ ㄐㄧㄚ)
a developed country

已還(ㄧˇ ㄏㄨㄢˊ)
already repaid; already returned

已極(ㄧˇ ㄐㄧˊ)
the utmost; the extreme limit: 目前的情況危險已極。The present situation is in the utmost danger.

已久(ㄧˇ ㄐㄧㄡˇ)
(for) a long time already

已經(ㄧˇ ㄐㄧㄥ)
already; some time ago: 這點我已經說過了。This has been dealt with already.

已決(ㄧˇ ㄐㄩㄝˊ)
to have already decided

已去(ㄧˇ ㄑㄩˋ)
already gone

已知數(ㄧˇ ㄓ ㄕㄨˋ)
(mathematics) a known number, or known quantity

已甚(ㄧˇ ㄕㄣˋ)
excessive; quite enough; to go to extremes

已然(ㄧˇ ㄖㄢˊ)
to be already so; to have already become a fact

已足(ㄧˇ ㄗㄨˊ)
already sufficient: 我們的旅

費已足。Our traveling expenses are already sufficient.

已死(ㄧˇ ㄙˇ)
already dead: 她已死多年。She has been dead for many years.

已而(ㄧˇ ㄦˊ)
①to give up one's vain pursuit ② then; afterward

已矣(ㄧˇ ㄧˇ)
an expression to indicate total disappointment or desperation

已完(ㄧˇ ㄨㄢˊ)
①already finished or completed; to bring to completion ② already hopeless

已往(ㄧˇ ㄨㄤˇ)
before; in the past

【巳】1301
ㄙˋ syh sì
1. the sixth of the twelve Terrestrial Branches (地支)
2. 9 to 11 a.m.
3. a Chinese family name

巳時(ㄙˋ ㄕ)or 巳牌(ㄙˋ ㄆㄞˊ)
the period of the day from 9 a.m. to 11 a.m.

一畫

【巴】1302
ㄅㄚ ba bā
1. name of an ancient state which occupied today's eastern Szechwan
2. a crust formed as a result of heat or dryness
3. to expect; to hope for anxiously
4. used with parts of human body (such as hands, cheeks, chin, etc.)
5. a final particle implying closeness or adhesion
6. to be close to: 前不巴村，後不巴店 to be close neither to a village ahead nor to an inn behind—in a desolate place
7. (physics) a bar: 毫巴 a millibar
8. a Chinese family name

巴巴(ㄅㄚ ㄅㄚ)
①an expression indicating anxiousness or urgency ② especially ③(used for the sound of) slapping

【己部】

巴貝多 (ㄅㄚ ㄅㄟˋ ㄉㄨㄛ)
Barbados

巴比倫 (ㄅㄚ ㄅㄧˇ ㄌㄨㄣˊ)
Babylon

巴不得 (ㄅㄚ ㄅㄨˋ ㄉㄜˊ)
an expression indicating expectancy—can't wait to..; would that; to be only too anxious (to do something)

巴布亞新幾內亞 (ㄅㄚ ㄅㄨˋ ㄧㄚˋ ㄒㄧㄣ ㄐㄧˇ ㄋㄟˋ ㄧㄚˋ)
Papua New Guinea

巴答 (ㄅㄚ ㄉㄚˊ)
the sound of a slap, a stroke, or an object falling

巴達維亞 (ㄅㄚ ㄉㄚˊ ㄨㄟˊ ㄧㄚˇ)
Batavia, or Jakarta, capital of Indonesia

巴得 (ㄅㄚ ㄉㄜˊ)
an expression indicating expectancy—Would it.... 或 May...

巴到 (ㄅㄚ ㄉㄠˋ)
to have waited patiently or anxiously until

巴豆 (ㄅㄚ ㄉㄡˋ)
(botany) a croton

巴頭探腦 (ㄅㄚ ㄊㄡˊ ㄊㄢ ㄋㄠˇ)
to stretch one's head in search or prying

巴拿馬 (ㄅㄚ ㄋㄚˊ ㄇㄚˇ)
Panama

巴拿馬運河 (ㄅㄚ ㄋㄚˊ ㄇㄚˇ ㄩㄣˋ ㄏㄜˊ)
the Panama Canal

巴拉圭 (ㄅㄚ ㄌㄚ ㄍㄨㄟ)
Paraguay

巴拉松 (ㄅㄚ ㄌㄚ ㄙㄨㄥ)
parathion

巴樂 (ㄅㄚ ㄌㄜˋ)
a guava

巴勒斯坦 (ㄅㄚ ㄌㄜˋ ㄙ ㄊㄢˇ)
Palestine

巴攬 (ㄅㄚ ㄌㄢˇ)
something to hold on to; a principle to hold on to

巴黎 (ㄅㄚ ㄌㄧˊ)
Paris

巴黎和會 (ㄅㄚ ㄌㄧˊ ㄏㄜˊ ㄏㄨㄟˋ)
the Paris Peace Conference (held at Versailles), which led to the signing of a peace treaty (1919) between the Allies and Germany following World War I

巴里島 (ㄅㄚ ㄌㄧˇ ㄉㄠˇ)
Bali Island

巴林 (ㄅㄚ ㄌㄧㄣˊ)
Bahrain

巴格達 (ㄅㄚ ㄍㄜˊ ㄉㄚˊ)
Bagdad or Baghdad, capital of Iraq

巴高枝兒 (ㄅㄚ ㄍㄠ ㄓ ㄦ)
(literally) to stretch with effort for a higher branch—to try hard to advance one's social position by any means within one's command

巴高望上 (ㄅㄚ ㄍㄠ ㄨㄤˋ ㄕㄤˋ)
to seek advancement or promotion

巴庫 (ㄅㄚ ㄎㄨˋ)
Baku, a city in Russia

巴哈 (ㄅㄚ ㄏㄚ)
Johann Sebastian Bach (1685-1750), German musician and composer

巴哈馬群島 (ㄅㄚ ㄏㄚ ㄇㄚˇ ㄑㄩㄣˊ ㄉㄠˇ)
the Bahamas

巴基斯坦 (ㄅㄚ ㄐㄧ ㄙ ㄊㄢˇ)
Pakistan

巴基斯坦人 (ㄅㄚ ㄐㄧ ㄙ ㄊㄢˇ ㄖㄣˊ)
a Pakistani; the Pakistanis

巴結 (ㄅㄚ ㄐㄧㄝˊ)
①to curry favor; to toady; to flatter; to try hard to please ② to exert oneself for advancement; to manage to come by

巴西 (ㄅㄚ ㄒㄧ)
Brazil

巴峽 (ㄅㄚ ㄒㄧㄚˊ)
Pa Gorge—one of the three gorges of the upper Yangtze River

巴想 (ㄅㄚ ㄒㄧㄤˇ)
to hope or await anxiously

巴掌 (ㄅㄚ ·ㄓㄤ)
① the palm of the hand ② a slap

巴士 (ㄅㄚ ㄕˋ)
a bus

巴士底獄 (ㄅㄚ ㄕˋ ㄉㄧˇ ㄩˋ)
the Bastille

巴士海峽 (ㄅㄚ ㄕˋ ㄏㄞˇ ㄒㄧㄚˊ)
the Bashi Channel

巴蛇 (ㄅㄚ ㄕㄜˊ)
a big snake; a serpent

巴蜀 (ㄅㄚ ㄕㄨˇ)
two ancient states in modern Szechwan

巴斯脫 (ㄅㄚ ㄙ ㄊㄨㄛ)
Louis Pasteur, 1822-1895 French chemist

巴斯噶 (ㄅㄚ ㄙ 《ㄚˊ)
Blaise Pascal, 1623-1662 French scientist

巴塞隆納 (ㄅㄚ ㄙㄞˋ ㄌㄨㄥˊ ㄋㄚˋ)
Barcelona, a seaport in Northeast Spain

巴爾幹半島 (ㄅㄚ ㄦˇ 《ㄢˋ ㄅㄢˋ ㄉㄠˇ)
the Balkan Peninsula

巴爾札克 (ㄅㄚ ㄦˇ ㄓㄚˊ ㄎㄜˋ)
Honoré de Balzac (1799-1850), French novelist

巴顏喀喇山 (ㄅㄚ ㄧㄢˊ ㄎㄚ ㄌㄚ ㄕㄢ)
Bayan Kara Shan where the Yangtze River and the Yellow River begin

巴望 (ㄅㄚ ㄨㄤˋ)
to hope for anxiously

六畫

【巷】 1303
(ㄒㄧㄤˋ shianq xiàng)
a lane; an alley

巷陌 (ㄒㄧㄤˋ ㄇㄛˋ)
(collectively) streets and lanes

巷道 (ㄒㄧㄤˋ ㄉㄠˋ)
①(mining) a tunnel ② an alley; a lane; a back street

巷口 (ㄒㄧㄤˋ ㄎㄡˇ)
either end of a lane; an entrance to a lane

巷戰 (ㄒㄧㄤˋ ㄓㄢˋ)
street-fighting

巷子 (ㄒㄧㄤˋ ·ㄗ)
a lane; an alley

巷議 (ㄒㄧㄤˋ ㄧˋ)
local rumors or gossips; the comments among the men in the street

巷尾 (ㄒㄧㄤˋ ㄨㄟˇ)
the end of a lane or alley

九畫

【巽】 1304
(ㄒㄩㄣˋ shiunn xùn)
1. subservient; submissive; mild; bland
2. the 5th of the Eight Diagrams
3. a Chinese family name

巽他群島 (ㄒㄩㄣˋ ㄊㄚ ㄑㄩㄣˊ ㄉㄠˇ)
the Sunda Islands including Sumatra, Java, Bali, Lom-

bok, Sumbawa and Flores

巾 部
ㄐㄧㄣ jin jīn

【巾】 1305
ㄐㄧㄣ jin jīn

1. a napkin, kerchief or towel:
她丢了手巾。 She lost her handkerchief.

2. a headgear; articles for dressing the hair

巾帕(ㄐㄧㄣ ㄆㄚˋ)
① a napkin or kerchief ② a headwrapper

巾幗(ㄐㄧㄣ ㄍㄨㄛˊ)
① female; woman; womankind ② articles for decorating a woman's head such as headwrappers, hairpins, etc.

巾幗鬚眉(ㄐㄧㄣ ㄍㄨㄛˊ ㄒㄩ ㄇㄟˊ)
(literally) a man among women—a woman who acts and talks like a man courageously, straightforwardly, frankly, etc.

巾幗英雄(ㄐㄧㄣ ㄍㄨㄛˊ ㄧㄥ ㄒㄩㄥˊ)
a heroine

巾櫛(ㄐㄧㄣ ㄐㄧˊ)
(literally) towel and comb —lowly service a woman renders to a man

巾箱(ㄐㄧㄣ ㄒㄧㄤ)
a small box for keeping napkins or kerchiefs

巾箱本(ㄐㄧㄣ ㄒㄧㄤ ㄅㄣˇ)
a pocket-size book; the condensed version of a book

巾幘(ㄐㄧㄣ ㄗㄜˊ)
a headwrapper; a hairdressing article of linen, silk, etc.

二畫

【市】 1306
ㄕˋ shyh shì

1. a marketplace; a market; a place for bartering goods
2. a city
3. to buy or sell
4. a Chinese family name

市司(ㄕˋ ㄙ)
an office (in old China)

located at seaports functioning like today's customs

市面(ㄕˋ ㄇㄧㄢˋ)or市面兒(ㄕˋ ㄇㄧㄢˋㄦ)
① business situations; market conditions: 台北市面繁榮。 Business in Taipei is flourishing. ② the world of the rich; the sights and splendors in big cities

市民(ㄕˋ ㄇㄧㄣˊ)
the residents of a city; citizens

市民文化(ㄕˋ ㄇㄧㄣˊ ㄨㄣˊ ㄏㄨㄚˋ)
civic culture

市畝(ㄕˋ ㄇㄡˇ)
a unit in Chinese measurement roughly 6,000 square feet in area

市道小人(ㄕˋ ㄉㄠˋ ㄒㄧㄠˇ ㄖㄣˊ)
a small-time trader (who counts only the pennies)

市內(ㄕˋ ㄋㄟˋ)
in the city

市里(ㄕˋ ㄌㄧˇ)
a unit of length equivalent to 500 meters

市立(ㄕˋ ㄌㄧˋ)
established with city government funds; operated by, or under the jurisdiction of a city government; municipal

市棍(ㄕˋ ㄍㄨㄣˋ)
a city shark; rascal of a city or marketplace

市公所(ㄕˋ ㄍㄨㄥ ㄙㄨㄛˇ)
a city or town office

市儈(ㄕˋ ㄎㄨㄞˋ)
① a broker ② a crafty businessman:市儈紙顧賺錢。A crafty businessman knows only how to make money.

市儈氣(ㄕˋ ㄎㄨㄞˋ ㄑㄧˋ)
vulgar and greedy (persons)

市虎(ㄕˋ ㄏㄨˇ)
① automobiles (which maim or kill people like tigers on the loose) ② If repeated often, a lie is accepted as a truth.

市集(ㄕˋ ㄐㄧˊ)
a gathering held regularly at intervals for trading or bartering purposes; a market

市價(ㄕˋ ㄐㄧㄚˋ)
market prices; the current price of a commodity): 這

種貨品的市價是多少? What is the market price of this product?

市郊(ㄕˋ ㄐㄧㄠ)
the suburbs or outskirts of a city; suburbia: 在夏天他們遷居市郊。They moved to the suburbs in summer.

市斤(ㄕˋ ㄐㄧㄣ)
a catty (equaling to 500 grams or half a kilogram)

市井之徒(ㄕˋ ㄐㄧㄥˇ ㄓ ㄊㄨˊ)
vulgar people who place money before anything else in life

市井無賴(ㄕˋ ㄐㄧㄥˇ ㄨˊ ㄌㄞˋ)
the scoundrels of the marketplace

市區(ㄕˋ ㄑㄩ)
① the area within the city limits ② the downtown area: 市區的公車交通極為便利。Bus service in the downtown area is excellent.

市制(ㄕˋ ㄓˋ)or市用制(ㄕˋ ㄩㄥˋ ㄓˋ)
a supplementary system in Chinese measurement

市鎮(ㄕˋ ㄓㄣˋ)
small towns; towns

市鎮公所(ㄕˋ ㄓㄣˋ ㄍㄨㄥ ㄙㄨㄛˇ)
a town office

市長(ㄕˋ ㄓㄤˇ)
the mayor of a city: 他是這城市的市長。He is the mayor of the city.

市政(ㄕˋ ㄓㄥˋ)
municipal administration

市政府(ㄕˋ ㄓㄥˋ ㄈㄨˇ)
a city government

市尺(ㄕˋ ㄔˇ)
a unit of Chinese measurement equivalent to ⅓ of a meter

市朝(ㄕˋ ㄔㄠˊ)
a public place or square (in a city)

市廛(ㄕˋ ㄔㄢˊ)
① a business district ② stores in a market or street

市場(ㄕˋ ㄔㄤˇ)or(ㄕˋ ㄔㄤˊ)
(domestic or world) market; a marketplace: 市場正欣欣向榮。The market is flourishing.

市場調查(ㄕˋ ㄔㄤˇ ㄉㄧㄠˋ ㄔㄚˊ)
a market survey

市場價格(ㄕˋ ㄔㄤˇ ㄐㄧㄚˋ ㄍㄜˊ)

（巾部）

the market price

市聲 (ㄕ ㄕㄥ)
(literally) the voices of the
marketplace—hawkings and
hagglings

市容 (ㄕ ㄖㄨㄥˊ)
the appearance of a city (including buildings, roads,
environmental sanitation,
etc.)

市肆 (ㄕ ㄙˋ)
shops and stores in a market

市恩 (ㄕ ㄣ)
to distribute favors with a
view to gaining popularity

市議會 (ㄕ ㄧˋ ㄏㄨㄟˋ)
a city council

市隱 (ㄕ ㄧㄣˇ)
a hermit in a city

【布】¹³⁰⁷ ㄅㄨˋ buh bù

1. cloth; textiles
2. to declare, announce or proclaim
3. to display; to distribute or
disseminate; to spread out
4. a Chinese family name

布帛 (ㄅㄨˋ ㄅㄛˊ)
(collectively) cloth or textiles

布被之識 (ㄅㄨˋ ㄅㄟˋ ㄓ ㄕˋ)
pretending to be humble or
thrifty

布匹 or 布疋 (ㄅㄨˋ ㄆㄧˇ)
piece goods; dry goods

布票 (ㄅㄨˋ ㄆㄧㄠˋ)
a cloth coupon

布幕 (ㄅㄨˋ ㄇㄨˋ)
the curtain of a stage

布防 (ㄅㄨˋ ㄈㄤˊ)
to deploy troops in anticipation of an enemy attack; to
organize the defence

布達佩斯 (ㄅㄨˋ ㄉㄚˊ ㄆㄟˋ ㄙ)
Budapest, capital of Hun-
gary

布達拉寺 (ㄅㄨˋ ㄉㄚˊ ㄌㄚ ㄙˋ)
Potala, palace of the Dalai
Lama at Lhasa

布袋 (ㄅㄨˋ ㄉㄞˋ)
a sack made of cloth; a calico sack (for grains, etc.)

布袋蓮 (ㄅㄨˋ ㄉㄞˋ ㄌㄧㄢˊ)
a water hyacinth

布袋戲 (ㄅㄨˋ ㄉㄞˋ ㄒㄧˋ)
a kind of puppet show typi-

cal in southeast China featuring figures of tiny sacks
topped with painted heads
manipulated with hands and
fingers

布袋裝 (ㄅㄨˋ ㄉㄞˋ ㄓㄨㄤ)
the sack dress

布道 (ㄅㄨˋ ㄉㄠˋ)
(religion) to preach the
Gospel; to evangelize

布店 (ㄅㄨˋ ㄉㄧㄢˋ)
a drapery store

布丁 (ㄅㄨˋ ㄉㄧㄥ)
a pudding

布頭 (ㄅㄨˋ ㄊㄡˊ)
odd bits of cloth

布農 (ㄅㄨˋ ㄋㄨㄥˊ)
the Bunu tribe among the
aborigines in Taiwan

布拉格 (ㄅㄨˋ ㄌㄚ ㄍㄜˊ)
Prague, the capital of
Czechoslovakia

布雷 (ㄅㄨˋ ㄌㄟˊ)
to lay mines; to mine

布簾 (ㄅㄨˋ ㄌㄧㄢˊ)
a door curtain made of cloth

布魯塞爾 (ㄅㄨˋ ㄌㄨˇ ㄙㄞˋ ㄦˇ)
Brussels, capital of Belgium

布隆迪 (ㄅㄨˋ ㄌㄨㄥˊ ㄉㄧˊ)
Burundi 亦作「蒲隆地」

布告 (ㄅㄨˋ ㄍㄠˋ)
① a public notice: 他在張貼
布告。He is pasting up a
notice. ② to make a public
announcement

布告牌 (ㄅㄨˋ ㄍㄠˋ ㄆㄞˊ)
a notice board; a bulletin
board

布穀 (ㄅㄨˋ ㄍㄨˇ)
① a cuckoo ② to sow seeds
of grain

布穀鳥 (ㄅㄨˋ ㄍㄨˇ ㄋㄧㄠˇ)
a cuckoo

布鼓雷門 (ㄅㄨˋ ㄍㄨˇ ㄌㄟˊ ㄇㄣˊ)
to show off one's limited
knowledge in the presence
of a learned man; to make
oneself a laughingstock

布褐 (ㄅㄨˋ ㄏㄜˊ)
① unbleached cotton clothes
② commoners

布景 (ㄅㄨˋ ㄐㄧㄥˇ)
(in motion picture production or stage shows) sets; a
setting 亦作「佈景」

① overall arrangement; lay
out; distribution: 台北新市區
的布局自可。The layout o[f]
new urban districts in
Taipei is acceptable. ② the
composition (of a picture, a
piece of writing, etc.) ③ the
position (of pieces on a
chessboard)

布置 (ㄅㄨˋ ㄓˋ)
to fix up; to decorate: 他們正
在布置會場。They are fixing
up a place for a meeting.

布政使 (ㄅㄨˋ ㄓㄥˋ ㄕˇ)or(ㄅㄨˋ ㄓㄥˋ ㄕˋ)
(Ching Dynasty) a provin-
cial official in charge of
civil and financial administration

布施 (ㄅㄨˋ ㄕ)
(Buddhism) almsgiving;
donation: 不要懇求別人布施。
Don't beg others for alms.

布商 (ㄅㄨˋ ㄕㄤ)
dry goods dealers; clothiers

布爾喬亞 (ㄅㄨˋ ㄦˇ ㄑㄧㄠˊ ㄧㄚ)
the bourgeois 亦作「中產階級」

布爾希維克 (ㄅㄨˋ ㄦˇ ㄒㄧ ㄨㄟˊ ㄎㄜˋ)
Bolshevik, a member of the
Russian Communist Party

布衣 (ㄅㄨˋ ㄧ)
① dresses made of common
cloth ② commoners

布衣之交 (ㄅㄨˋ ㄧ ㄓ ㄐㄧㄠ)
a friend one made when one
was a commoner or in hum-
ble circumstances

布宜諾斯艾利斯 (ㄅㄨˋ ㄧˊ ㄋㄨㄛˋ ㄙ ㄞˋ ㄌㄧˋ ㄙ)
Buenos Aires, capital of Argentina

三畫

【帆】¹³⁰⁸ 1.(帆) ㄈㄢˊ farn fán

1. a sail (of a boat): 我們的
船將所有的帆都張開了。Our
ship had all sail spread.
2. a boat

帆蓬 (ㄈㄢˊ ㄆㄥˊ)
a sail

帆檣 (ㄈㄢˊ ㄑㄧㄤˊ)
the mast of a ship

帆柱 (ㄈㄢˊ ㄓㄨˋ)
a mast

帆船 (ㄈㄢˊ ㄔㄨㄢˊ)
a sailboat

帆影(ㄈㄢ ㄧㄥˇ)
(literally) the shadows of
sails—boats in water

【帆】 1308
2. (帆) ㄈㄢ fan fān
canvas; sailcloth; sailcloth: 船起滿帆疾
駛。The ship flew all its
canvas.

帆布(ㄈㄢ ㄅㄨˋ)
canvas

帆布鞋(ㄈㄢ ㄅㄨˋ ㄒㄧㄝˊ)
canvas shoes

四畫

【希】 1309
ㄒㄧ shī xī
1. rare; uncommon; precious: 那博
物館中藏有很多希世之寶。The
museum is full of rare treasures.
2. to hope; to expect; to wish;
to desire; to long: 我希望明天
不會下雨。I hope it will not
rain tomorrow.
3. to come to a stop gradually
4. to become silent
5. very; much
6. a Chinese family name

希伯來人(ㄒㄧ ㄅㄛˊ ㄌㄞˊ ㄖㄣˊ)
Hebrew (the race)

希伯來文(ㄒㄧ ㄅㄛˊ ㄌㄞˊ ㄨㄣˊ)
Hebrew (the language)

希慕(ㄒㄧ ㄇㄨˋ)
to long for; to be desirous
of: 這位女伶希慕成名。This
actress longs for fame.

希特勒(ㄒㄧ ㄊㄜˋ ㄌㄜˋ)
Adolf Hitler (1889-1945),
German dictator

希圖(ㄒㄧ ㄊㄨˊ)
to hope and scheme for

希臘(ㄒㄧ ㄌㄚˋ)
Greece; Greek

希臘教會(ㄒㄧ ㄌㄚˋ ㄐㄧㄠˋ ㄏㄨㄟˋ)or
希臘正教(ㄒㄧ ㄌㄚˋ ㄓㄥˋ ㄐㄧㄠˋ)
Greek Orthodox Church, or
Orthodox Eastern Church

希臘主義(ㄒㄧ ㄌㄚˋ ㄓㄨˇ ㄧˋ)
Grecism; Hellenism

希臘人(ㄒㄧ ㄌㄚˋ ㄖㄣˊ)
a Greek

希臘字母(ㄒㄧ ㄌㄚˋ ㄗˋ ㄇㄨˇ)
the Greek alphabet

希臘文化(ㄒㄧ ㄌㄚˋ ㄨㄣˊ ㄏㄨㄚˋ)
Greek culture

希罕(ㄒㄧ ㄏㄢˇ)

① rare; uncommon ② to
care; to value; to hold pre-
ciously

希冀(ㄒㄧ ㄐㄧˋ)
to desire; to wish for: 我們都
希冀獲得快樂和健康。We all
desire happiness and health.

希奇(ㄒㄧ ㄑㄧˊ)
① strange; rare; uncommon
② to value; to attach importance; to appreciate

希企(ㄒㄧ ㄑㄧˇ)or 希求(ㄒㄧ ㄑㄧˊ)
to hope for; to hope to

希寵(ㄒㄧ ㄔㄨㄥˇ)
to curry favor (especially
from a superior)

希世之珍(ㄒㄧ ㄕˋ ㄓ ㄓㄣ)
a very rare treasure; an invaluable gem; a timeless
treasure

希榮(ㄒㄧ ㄖㄨㄥˊ)
to aspire for the glory of
high office

希有(ㄒㄧ ㄧㄡˇ)
very rare

希有之事(ㄒㄧ ㄧㄡˇ ㄓ ㄕˋ)
a rarity; an uncommon
occurrence

希微(ㄒㄧ ㄨㄟˊ)
extremely little (amount);
very little

希望(ㄒㄧ ㄨㄤˋ)
a hope; a wish; expectations;
to hope; to wish; to desire;
to look forward to: 希望全落
空了。All hope is gone.

五畫

【帔】 1310
ㄆㄟˋ pey pèi
a cape (usually worn by a
woman)

【帑】 1311
ㄊㄤˇ taang tǎng
1. a treasury
2. public funds or money

帑藏(ㄊㄤˇ ㄗㄤˋ)
a treasury

【帕】 1312
ㄆㄚˋ pah pà
1. a turban
2. to wrap and bind
3. a handkerchief
4. a veil
5. a curtain made of cloth

帕米爾(ㄆㄚˋ ㄇㄧˇ ㄦˇ)

the Pamirs, known as the
"roof of the world"
a turban; a headdress

帕頭(ㄆㄚˋ ㄊㄡˊ)
a kerchief used for carrying
a package

【帖】 1313
1. ㄊㄧㄝ tie tiē
1. submissive or obedient
2. proper

帖伏(ㄊㄧㄝ ㄈㄨˊ)or 帖服(ㄊㄧㄝ ㄈㄨˊ)
submissive and subservient

帖耳(ㄊㄧㄝ ㄦˇ)
(literally) to droop one's
ears like a dog—submissive

【帖】 1313
2. ㄊㄧㄝˇ tie tiě
1. an invitation card: 市長發出
宴客請帖。The mayor sent
out invitation cards to a dinner party.
2. a label; a placard; a document
3. a copybook (of calligraphy)
4. a medical prescription

帖子(ㄊㄧㄝˇ ㄗ)or 帖兒(ㄊㄧㄝˇ ㄦ)
① an invitation card or letter ② a money order

【帖】 1313
3. ㄊㄧㄝˋ tie tiè
1. to write on silk
2. to engrave characters of
famous calligraphers on
stone
3. test papers (in the dynasties
of Tang, Sung and Yüan)

帖木兒(ㄊㄧㄝˋ ㄇㄨˋ ㄦ)
Timur, a Mongolian con-
queror who founded the
Timur Empire, 1369-1502, in
the greater part of the Middle East and parts of India

帖括(ㄊㄧㄝˋ ㄍㄨㄚˋ)
(formerly) a style of formal
writing adopted by candi-
dates during civil service
examinations

【帗】 1314
ㄈㄨˊ fwu fú
(in ancient China) a multicolored prop used in dancing rituals

【帘】 1315
ㄌㄧㄢˊ lian lián
1. a flag sign of a winehouse
or tavern
2. a door or window screen

【巾部】

帝子(ヵ│ ˙ヤ) or 帝兒(ヵ│ル)
a screen for a door or a window

【峡】 1316 ㄓ jyh zhí
a book wrapper or casing:
書桌上有一峡公文。There is a casing of documents on the desk.

【帚】 1317 ㄓㄡˇ joou zhǒu
a broom; a besom

帚星(ㄓㄡ ㄒ│ㄥ)
① a comet ② a jinx

【帛】 1318 ㄅㄛˊ bor bó
1. (collectively) silk fabrics
2. a Chinese family name

帛帶(ㄅㄛˊ ㄉㄞˋ)
a silk waist band worn by officials or wealthy men in old China

帛書(ㄅㄛˊ ㄕㄨ)
a letter, a book or a document written on silk (before paper was invented)

六畫

【帥】 1319 ㄕㄨㄞˋ shuay shuài
　　　 (又讀 ㄕㄨㄛˋ shuoh shuò)
1. the commanding general; commander-in-chief: 誰是陸軍統帥? Who's the commanding general of the army?
2. to command; to lead
3. to follow an order (with instruction or orders)
4. (slang) dashing; smart-looking: 他長得真帥。He is very smart-looking.
5. a Chinese family name

帥領(ㄕㄨㄞˋ ㄌ│ㄥˇ)
to command: 誰領陸軍? Who commands the army?

帥令(ㄕㄨㄞˋ ㄌ│ㄥˋ)
the orders of the commander-in-chief

帥旗(ㄕㄨㄞˋ ㄑ│ˊ)
the flag of the commander-in-chief

帥字旗(ㄕㄨㄞˋ ㄗˋ ㄑ│ˊ)
a flag on which the character "帥" is embroidered; the flag of the commander-in-chief

帥印(ㄕㄨㄞˋ │ㄣˋ)
the seal of the commander-in-chief

【帝】 1320 ㄉ│ˋ dih dì
1. the emperor; a ruler
2. Heaven (as a divine being)
3. Heaven (as a divine being)
4. imperial

帝都(ㄉ│ˋ ㄉㄨ)
the imperial capital

帝庭(ㄉ│ˋ ㄊ│ㄥˊ)
the Heavenly court

帝國(ㄉ│ˋ ㄍㄨㄛˊ)
an empire; a monarchy

帝國大學(ㄉ│ˋ ㄍㄨㄛˊ ㄉㄚˋ ㄒㄩㄝˊ)
Imperial University (of Tokyo)

帝國主義(ㄉ│ˋ ㄍㄨㄛˊ ㄓㄨˇ │ˋ)
imperialism

帝嚳(ㄉ│ˋ ㄎㄨˋ)
name of an ancient emperor (accession, c. 2435 B.C.)

帝號(ㄉ│ˋ ㄏㄠˋ)
the appellation of an emperor

帝畿(ㄉ│ˋ ㄐ│)
the imperial capital and its environs

帝京(ㄉ│ˋ ㄐ│ㄥ)
the imperial capital

帝居(ㄉ│ˋ ㄐㄩ)
the imperial capital 參看 「帝畿」

帝闕(ㄉ│ˋ ㄑㄩㄝˋ)
the gate of the emperor's palace

帝鄉(ㄉ│ˋ ㄒ│ㄤ)
① the hometown of the emperor ② the palace of the King of Heaven; heavenly abodes

帝制(ㄉ│ˋ ㄓˋ)
the institutions of an empire; monarchy

帝雉(ㄉ│ˋ ㄓˋ)
(fowl) a mikado pheasant

帝嚳(ㄉ│ˋ ㄎㄨˋ)
name of an ancient emperor (accession, c. 2365 B.C.)

帝室(ㄉ│ˋ ㄕˋ)
the royal family

帝舜(ㄉ│ˋ ㄕㄨㄣˋ)
Emperor Shun (accession, c. 2255 B.C.), one of China's sage kings

帝祚(ㄉ│ˋ ㄗㄨㄛˋ)
the imperial throne

帝俄(ㄉ│ˋ ㄜˊ)
tsarist Russia

帝業(ㄉ│ˋ │ㄝˋ)
the reign of an emperor; an empire

帝堯(ㄉ│ˋ │ㄠˊ)
Emperor Yao (accession, c. 2356 B.C.), one of China's sage kings

帝位(ㄉ│ˋ ㄨㄟˋ)
the emperor's throne

帝王(ㄉ│ˋ ㄨㄤˊ)
the emperor; the king; the throne

七畫

【帨】 1321 ㄕㄨㄟˋ shuey shuì
a kerchief; a handkerchief

【師】 1322 ㄕ shy shī
1. a division in the Chinese army
2. an army
3. a model; an example
4. a master; a teacher; a tutor
5. to teach
6. to pattern or model after another
7. a specialist (especially of medicine, painting, music, divining, etc.)
8. a local administrative chief
9. a Chinese family name

師保萬民(ㄕ ㄅㄠˇ ㄨㄢˋ ㄇ│ㄣˊ)
to act as teacher and guardian of the myriad people

師表(ㄕ ㄅ│ㄠˇ)
a paragon or model worthy of emulation: 她不愧是爲人師表。She is worthy of the name of teacher.

師部(ㄕ ㄅㄨˋ)
a division headquarters

師妹(ㄕ ㄇㄟˋ)
① a younger female fellow student under the same master or teacher ② a polite salutation for the teacher's daughter younger than oneself

師門(ㄕ ㄇㄣˊ)
a school or sect founded by a master

師母(ㄕ ㄇㄨˇ)or 師娘(ㄕ ㄋ一ㄤˊ)
① the wife of one's tutor, teacher or master ② a polite reference to the wife of one's senior

師法(ㄕ ㄈㄚˇ)
① to pattern after; to imitate; to emulate ② methods taught by one's teacher

師範(ㄕ ㄈㄢˋ)
① worthy of being patterned after ② a master, tutor or teacher ③ to imitate; to emulate ④ short for normal schools

師範大學(ㄕ ㄈㄢˋ ㄉㄚˋ ㄒㄩㄝˊ)
a normal university: 師範大學的目的是培訓師資. A normal university aims at training teachers.

師範教育(ㄕ ㄈㄢˋ ㄐ一ㄠˋ ㄩˋ)
normal education

師範學校(ㄕ ㄈㄢˋ ㄒㄩㄝˊ ㄒ一ㄠˋ)
a normal school

師範學院(ㄕ ㄈㄢˋ ㄒㄩㄝˊ ㄩㄢˋ)
a normal (or teachers) college

師範專科學校(ㄕ ㄈㄢˋ ㄓㄨㄢ ㄎㄜ ㄒㄩㄝˊ ㄒ一ㄠˋ)
a junior teachers college

師範生(ㄕ ㄈㄢˋ ㄕㄥ)
the students of a normal school or university

師傅(ㄕ ㄈㄨˋ)
① (collectively) teachers; masters; tutors ② the tutors of a king or an emperor ③ a polite term of address for an artisan as a carpenter, cook, etc.

師父(ㄕ ㄈㄨˋ)
① tutors; masters; teachers ② a respectful term of address for monks, nuns, etc.

師道(ㄕ ㄉㄠˋ)
the teacher's status and teachings: 我們應當尊崇師道. We should respect the teacher's status and teachings.

師弟(ㄕ ㄉ一ˋ)
① a younger male fellow student or apprentice under the same tutor ② a polite salutation for the teacher's son younger than oneself

師徒(ㄕ ㄊㄨˊ)
the master and his student(s) or apprentice(s)

師團(ㄕ ㄊㄨㄢˊ)
(in Japanese military system) a division of approximately 10,000 men which can be expanded to 20,000 in wartime

師老無功(ㄕ ㄌㄠˇ ㄨˊ ㄍㄨㄥ)
troops fighting for a long time without success; bogged down in a war

師旅(ㄕ ㄌㄩˇ)
divisions and brigades — troops in general

師姑(ㄕ ㄍㄨ)
a polite salutation for a Buddhist nun

師古(ㄕ ㄍㄨˇ)
to pattern after the ancient or old (ways, methods, etc.)

師姊(ㄕ ㄐ一ˇ)
① an elder female fellow student under the same master or teacher ② a polite salutation for the teacher's daughter elder than oneself

師其故智(ㄕ ㄑ一ˊ ㄍㄨˋ ㄓˋ)
to copy an old plan or method

師心自用(ㄕ ㄒ一ㄣ ㄗˋ ㄩㄥˋ)
conceited; opinionated: 他這個人師心自用. He is an opinionated person.

師兄(ㄕ ㄒㄩㄥ)
① an elder male fellow student under the same master or tutor ② a polite salutation for the teacher's son elder than oneself

師直爲壯(ㄕ ㄓˊ ㄨㄟˊ ㄓㄨㄤˋ)
The morale of troops will be high if they fight for a just cause.

師長(ㄕ ㄓㄤˇ)
① one's teachers; faculty members ② a division commander

師丈(ㄕ ㄓㄤˋ)
the husband of one's teacher

師承(ㄕ ㄔㄥˊ)
to have learned under (especially referring to a particular school of learning)

師出無名(ㄕ ㄔㄨ ㄨˊ ㄇ一ㄥˊ)
to fight a war without a just cause

師事(ㄕ ㄕˋ)
to serve and respect (another) as one's teacher

師生(ㄕ ㄕㄥ)
teachers and students

師資(ㄕ ㄗ)
① the qualifications of a teacher ② teachers

師恩如海(ㄕ ㄣ ㄖㄨˊ ㄏㄞˇ)
The bequeathal of a good teacher is as deep as the sea. 或 The benefits one gets from his teacher are immeasurable.

師爺(ㄕ 一ㄝˊ)
① one's teacher's father ② one's teacher's teacher ③ (in ancient China) a confidential secretary who knows all the tricks of officialdom and the loopholes of the law

師友(ㄕ 一ㄡˇ)
① a friend from whom one can seek advice ② (in ancient China) an official post in charge of the princes' education

師嚴道尊(ㄕ 一ㄢˊ ㄉㄠˋ ㄗㄨㄣ)
The teacher is strict in teaching; therefore, what he teaches will be respected.

【席】 *1323*
ㄒ一ˊ shyi xí

1. a mat
2. a feast
3. a seat; to take a seat
4. to rely on
5. (rarely) a sail
6. a Chinese family name

席不暇暖(ㄒ一ˊ ㄅㄨˋ ㄒ一ㄚˊ ㄋㄨㄢˇ)
(literally) cannot sit long enough to warm the seat — very busy

席夢思床(ㄒ一ˊ ㄇㄥˊ ㄙ ㄔㄨㄤˊ)
a Simmons bed

席豐履厚(ㄒ一ˊ ㄈㄥ ㄌㄩˇ ㄏㄡˋ)
(usually said of large inherited wealth) very well-to-do

席地而坐(ㄒ一ˊ ㄉ一ˋ ㄦˊ ㄗㄨㄛˋ)
to sit on the ground

席卷 or 席捲(ㄒ一ˊ ㄐㄩㄢˇ)
① to roll up like a mat — to take away everything ② to sweep across

席卷天下 or 席捲天下(ㄒ一ˊ ㄐㄩㄢˇ ㄊ一ㄢ ㄒ一ㄚˋ)

（巿部）

(literally) to roll the world up like a mat—to take all of it; to conquer the world

席捲而去（ㄒㄧˊ ㄐㄩㄢˇ ㄦˊ ㄑㄩˋ）
to leave nothing behind; to take everything away

席珍待聘（ㄒㄧˊ ㄓㄣ ㄉㄞˋ ㄆㄧㄣˋ）
a man of capability awaiting employment

席上（ㄒㄧˊ ㄕㄤˋ）
①scholars; the learned ②on the dining table

席上之珍（ㄒㄧˊ ㄕㄤˋ ㄓ ㄓㄣ）
(literally) the dainties for a feast—the virtues of a person

席次（ㄒㄧˊ ㄘˋ）
the order of seats; seating arrangement

席位（ㄒㄧˊ ㄨㄟˋ）
a seat (at a conference, in a legislative assembly, etc.)

八畫

【帳】 1324
ㄓㄤˋ janq zhàng
1. a canopy above the bed
2. a tent
3. a curtain or screen; a mosquito net
4. a scroll (sent as a gift for a wedding, birthday party, funeral, etc.)
5. same as 賬

帳簿（ㄓㄤˋ ㄅㄨˋ）
an account book; books of accounts 亦作「賬簿」

帳棚（ㄓㄤˋ ㄆㄥˊ）
a tent

帳篷（ㄓㄤˋ ㄆㄥˊ）
a tent; a mat-shed

帳幔（ㄓㄤˋ ㄇㄢˋ）
a tent

帳目（ㄓㄤˋ ㄇㄨˋ）
accounts; itemized bills 亦作「賬目」

帳幕（ㄓㄤˋ ㄇㄨˋ）
a tent 參看「帳棚」

帳房（ㄓㄤˋ ㄈㄤˊ）
①a cashier; a bursar ②a cashier's office 亦作「賬房」

帳單（ㄓㄤˋ ㄉㄢ）
a bill; a check 亦作「賬單」

帳額（ㄓㄤˋ ㄜˊ）
the top of a mosquito net

帳簷（ㄓㄤˋ ㄌㄧㄢˊ）

screens or curtains for doors or windows

帳鉤（ㄓㄤˋ 《ㄡ）
hooks for holding open a mosquito net; curtain-hooks

帳款（ㄓㄤˋ ㄎㄨㄢˇ）
funds on account; credit

帳戶（ㄓㄤˋ ㄏㄨˋ）
a bank account: 我想在銀行開立帳戶。 I want to open an account in this bank.

帳戶名稱（ㄓㄤˋ ㄏㄨˋ ㄇㄧㄥˊ ㄔㄥ）
name of an account; title of an account

帳子（ㄓㄤˋ ˙ㄗ）
a mosquito net

帳簷（ㄓㄤˋ ㄧㄢˊ）
the flaps along the edge of a tent roof

帳務（ㄓㄤˋ ㄨˋ）
accounts in general 亦作「賬務」

【帶】 1325
ㄉㄞˋ day dài
1. a girdle; a sash; a belt; a band; a ribbon; a string; a tie
2. to wear (a smile, sword, etc.)
3. to bear; to take or bring along: 請帶這封信給他。 Please bring this letter to him.
4. to lead (the way, troops, etc.); to head (an army, etc.)
5. a climatic zone: 臺灣位在亞熱帶。 Taiwan is in the subtropical zone.

帶兵（ㄉㄞˋ ㄅㄧㄥ）
①to lead troops ②to carry arms

帶兵官（ㄉㄞˋ ㄅㄧㄥ ㄍㄨㄢ）
an officer who has a field command (as distinct from a staff officer doing office work)

帶病工作（ㄉㄞˋ ㄅㄧㄥˋ ㄍㄨㄥ ㄗㄨㄛˋ）
to keep on working in spite of one's illness: 她帶病繼續工作。 She went on working in spite of her illness.

帶髮修行（ㄉㄞˋ ㄈㄚˇ ㄒㄧㄡ ㄒㄧㄥˊ）
to submit to Buddhist discipline while still wearing one's hair (A Buddhist monk or nun is supposed to have his or her head shaved.)

帶分數（ㄉㄞˋ ㄈㄣ ㄕㄨˋ）
(mathematics) a mixed fraction

帶電（ㄉㄞˋ ㄉㄧㄢˋ）
electrification

帶電體（ㄉㄞˋ ㄉㄧㄢˋ ㄊㄧˇ）
an electrified body

帶隊（ㄉㄞˋ ㄉㄨㄟˋ）
①to lead a group ②the leader of a group, party or mission

帶動（ㄉㄞˋ ㄉㄨㄥˋ）
to drive; to spur on; to bring along: 這機器是由蒸汽所帶動的。 This machinery is driven by steam.

帶頭（ㄉㄞˋ ㄊㄡˊ）
to pioneer; to initiate; to lead; to do trailblazing work

帶頭作用（ㄉㄞˋ ㄊㄡˊ ㄗㄨㄛˋ ㄩㄥˋ）
the example set by someone in pioneering work

帶徒弟（ㄉㄞˋ ㄊㄨˊ ㄉㄧˋ）
to train apprentices

帶牛佩犢（ㄉㄞˋ ㄋㄧㄡˊ ㄆㄟˋ ㄉㄨˊ）
to take to farming after discarding the arms

帶來（ㄉㄞˋ ㄌㄞˊ）
to bring here

帶累（ㄉㄞˋ ㄌㄟˇ）
to compromise oneself; to get others involved in (trouble, etc.)

帶礪山河（ㄉㄞˋ ㄌㄧˋ ㄕㄢ ㄏㄜˊ）
(a congratulatory greeting to a feudal lord on his inauguration) May the land bestowed on you remain forever in your family!

帶領（ㄉㄞˋ ㄌㄧㄥˇ）
to lead (an army, a party, etc.): 這探險隊係由我叔父帶領。 The expedition was led by my uncle.

帶路（ㄉㄞˋ ㄌㄨˋ）or 帶道（ㄉㄞˋ ㄉㄠˋ）
to lead the way

帶壞（ㄉㄞˋ ㄏㄨㄞˋ）
to lead astray: 這小孩被不良的同伴帶壞了。 The boy was led astray by bad companions.

帶回（ㄉㄞˋ ㄏㄨㄟˊ）
to bring back: 士兵們帶回十個俘虜。 The soldiers came back bringing ten prisoners with them.

帶甲（ㄉㄞˋ ㄐㄧㄚˇ）

armored (fighters or soldiers)

帶勁(ㄉㄞ ㄐㄧㄥ)
①energetic; forceful: 他做事可真帶勁。He works energetically. ②interesting; exciting; wonderful; terrific: 這場網球比賽真帶勁。This tennis tournament is really terrific.

帶菌者(ㄉㄞ ㄐㄩㄣ ㄓㄜ)
(medicine) a carrier

帶球走(ㄉㄞ ㄑㄧㄡ ㄗㄡ)
(basketball) traveling; running with the ball

帶去(ㄉㄞ ·ㄑㄩ)
to bring away; to take along: 你不能把這些報紙帶去。You cannot bring away these newspapers with you.

帶小數(ㄉㄞ ㄒㄧㄠ ㄕㄨ)
a whole number with a decimal

帶孝(ㄉㄞ ㄒㄧㄠ)
to wear mourning

帶笑(ㄉㄞ ㄒㄧㄠ)
smilingly; wearing a smile

帶羞(ㄉㄞ ㄒㄧㄡ)
to look shy or bashful

帶信(ㄉㄞ ㄒㄧㄣ)or 帶信兒(ㄉㄞ ㄒㄧㄦ)
to take or bring a message; to bear a message

帶徵(ㄉㄞ ㄓㄥ)
a system of taxation in which the government can postpone levying taxes for famine, flood, etc. but people must pay a portion of the postponed taxes in each of the following years

帶手兒(ㄉㄞ ㄕㄡㄦ)
to do something at one's convenience

帶傷(ㄉㄞ ㄕㄤ)
to get wounded or injured

帶上(ㄉㄞ ·ㄕㄤ)
①to present to you ②to bring out (the prisoner, etc.) ③to send or attach as incidental; in addition to

帶子(ㄉㄞ ㄗ)
a piece of string; a ribbon; laces (of shoes, boots, etc.)

帶彩(ㄉㄞ ㄘㄞ)
(Peking opera) to play the act of bleeding from wound or injury

帶魚(ㄉㄞ ㄩ)
ribbonfish; hairtail

【帷】 1326
ㄨㄟ wéi wéi
a curtain; a screen; a tent

帷薄不修(ㄨㄟ ㄅㄛ ㄅㄨ ㄒㄧㄡ)
(literally) The curtains are not fixed.—lewdness or debauchery of the females of one's family

帷幔(ㄨㄟ ㄇㄢ)
screens; cloth partitions

帷幕(ㄨㄟ ㄇㄨ)
①a tent ②參看「帷幄」

帷房(ㄨㄟ ㄈㄤ)
(literally) a curtained room—a woman's bedchamber

帷蓋(ㄨㄟ ㄍㄞ)
(literally) the curtain and cover of a cart—a repayment for services rendered

帷幄(ㄨㄟ ㄨㄛ)
a military tent 亦作「帷幕」：司令官運籌帷幄。The commander devises strategies within the command tent.

【常】 1327
ㄔㄤ cháng cháng
1. common; ordinary; normal: 這個字常用嗎？Is this word in common use?
2. long; lasting; permanent (jobs, etc.); eternal: 人生無常。Nothing is permanent in life.
3. often; frequent; frequently; regular; regularly: 她常去看電影。She goes to the movies quite often.
4. ordinarily; usually; on ordinary occasions
5. a rule; a principle
6. a Chinese family name

常備兵(ㄔㄤ ㄅㄟ ㄅㄧㄥ)
regulars (as distinct from reservists)

常備軍(ㄔㄤ ㄅㄟ ㄐㄩㄣ)
the standing army

常步走(ㄔㄤ ㄅㄨ ㄗㄡ)
(military drill) to march in measured steps but in a less rigid manner than goose step

常法(ㄔㄤ ㄈㄚ)
a law, practice, or principle that lasts

常服(ㄔㄤ ㄈㄨ)
ordinary or everyday clothes (as distinguished from formal dress)

常儀(ㄔㄤ ㄧ)
usual rites; regular ceremony

常度(ㄔㄤ ㄉㄨ)
①a normal manner ②ordinary rules

常態(ㄔㄤ ㄊㄞ)
a normal carriage or manner; a normal state

常談(ㄔㄤ ㄊㄢ)
commonplace talks or remarks; platitudes

常年(ㄔㄤ ㄋㄧㄢ)
throughout the year; all the year round

常年費(ㄔㄤ ㄋㄧㄢ ㄈㄟ)
regular annual fees

常年大會(ㄔㄤ ㄋㄧㄢ ㄉㄚ ㄏㄨㄟ)
annual meetings or conventions

常禮(ㄔㄤ ㄌㄧ)
common or everyday courtesy

常禮服(ㄔㄤ ㄌㄧ ㄈㄨ)
ordinary formal clothes as distinguished from full formal dress

常理(ㄔㄤ ㄌㄧ)
convention; general consent

常例(ㄔㄤ ㄌㄧ)
regular order or procedures; usual or common practices; an ordinary way

常綠植物(ㄔㄤ ㄌㄩ ㄓ ㄨ)
an evergreen plant

常綠樹(ㄔㄤ ㄌㄩ ㄕㄨ)
evergreen trees: 松、柏和針樅是常綠樹。The pine, cedar and spruce are evergreen trees.

常規(ㄔㄤ ㄍㄨㄟ)
ordinary rules or practices

常軌(ㄔㄤ ㄍㄨㄟ)
the ordinary course of events

常客(ㄔㄤ ㄎㄜ)
a frequent guest; a frequenter (of bars, theaters, etc.)

常會(ㄔㄤ ㄏㄨㄟ)
①regular meetings or conventions ②to be apt to; to happen often

常久(ㄔㄤ ㄐㄧㄡ)
for a long time: 你常久沒來

〔巾部〕

了。You have not been here for a long time.

常見(彳ㄤ ㄐㄧㄢ)
to see or to be seen frequently: 我們常見他去公園。We often see him go to the park.

常青(彳ㄤ ㄑㄧㄥ)or 常綠(彳ㄤ ㄌㄩ)
evergreen

常情(彳ㄤ ㄑㄧㄥ)
man's natural action or reaction under certain circumstances

常去(彳ㄤ ㄑㄩ)
to go often: 在夏天他常去游泳。In summer he often goes swimming.

常州(彳ㄤ ㄓㄡ)
Changchow, a city in Kiangsu along the Shanghai-Nanking Railway

常住(彳ㄤ ㄓㄨ)
①(Buddhism) changeless; permanent ② a permanent lodger—a monk or a nun ③ a Buddhist ritual apparatus ④ a temple

常駐(彳ㄤ ㄓㄨ)
① standing (members, etc.) ②(said of a taxcollector, policeman, etc.) to be stationed (at a school, factory, locality, etc.) ③ durable (beauty, charm or youthfulness)

常產(彳ㄤ ㄔㄢ)
immovable property; real estate

常常(彳ㄤ ㄔㄤ)
often; frequently: 她常常讀書到深夜。She often studies deep into the night.

常川(彳ㄤ ㄔㄨㄢ)
incessantly; constantly; regularly

常春藤(彳ㄤ ㄔㄨㄣ ㄊㄥ)
ivy; bindwood

常事(彳ㄤ ㄕ)
① an oft-repeated incident or event; routine ② a commonplace happening

常識(彳ㄤ ㄕ)
① general knowledge (as distinct from expertise) ② common sense ③ a subject in primary school curricula which includes the ABCs of

natural and social sciences

常設(彳ㄤ ㄕㄜ)
standing; permanent

常勝軍(彳ㄤ ㄕㄥ ㄐㄩㄣ)
① the "Ever Triumphant Army", a term referring to the rifle troops which quelled the Taiping Rebellion in the Ching Dynasty ② an invincible army

常數(彳ㄤ ㄕㄨ)
(mathematics) a constant

常人(彳ㄤ ㄖㄣ)
ordinary people; an ordinary man; a normal person

常任(彳ㄤ ㄖㄣ)
standing (members of a committee, government organ, etc.)

常有(彳ㄤ ㄧㄡ)
usually; often; more often than not

常言(彳ㄤ ㄧㄢ)
a popular saying; a proverb: 常言道: 「健康勝於財富」。As the saying goes, "Health is above wealth."

常務委員(彳ㄤ ㄨ ㄨㄟ ㄩㄢ)or 常委(彳ㄤ ㄨㄟ)
the standing members of a committee

常溫(彳ㄤ ㄨㄣ)
① normal atmospheric temperature (between 15° and 25°C) ② homoiothermy

常用(彳ㄤ ㄩㄥ)
to use often; used often

九畫

【幅】 1328
ㄈㄨ fwu fú
1. the breadth of cloth or paper; a width (of cloth)
2. a border
3. a numerary adjunct for pictures, scrolls, etc.: 她畫了一幅母親的肖像。She painted a portrait of her mother.

幅度(ㄈㄨ ㄉㄨ)
①(said of stocks, commodity prices, etc.) the rate of rise or fall ② a range; an extent

幅寬(ㄈㄨ ㄎㄨㄢ)
the breadth (of a piece of cloth, etc.)

幅員(ㄈㄨ ㄩㄢ)
(literally) breadth and circumference—the territory (of a country)

幅員遼闊(ㄈㄨ ㄩㄢ ㄌㄧㄠ ㄎㄨㄛ)
(said of a country) very large: 中國是幅員遼闊的國家。China is a country with a vast territory.

【帽】 1329
ㄇㄠ maw mào
1. a hat; a headwear
2. a cap (of a fountain pen, screw, etc.)

帽澤(ㄇㄠ ㄗㄜ)
a hatband

帽鋪(ㄇㄠ ㄆㄨ)or 帽店(ㄇㄠ ㄉㄧㄢ)
a hat shop

帽帶(ㄇㄠ ㄉㄞ)
hat strings

帽花(ㄇㄠ ㄏㄨㄚ)
ornaments at the front of a hat (usually of jewels, etc.)

帽徽(ㄇㄠ ㄏㄨㄟ)
insignia on a cap

帽架(ㄇㄠ ㄐㄧㄚ)
a hatrack or stand; a hat tree

帽匠(ㄇㄠ ㄐㄧㄤ)
a hatter

帽針(ㄇㄠ ㄓㄣ)
a hatpin

帽章(ㄇㄠ ㄓㄤ)
a hat badge; a badge for a cap

帽舌(ㄇㄠ ㄕㄜ)
a visor

帽筒(ㄇㄠ ㄊㄨㄥ)
a milliner; a hatter

帽子(ㄇㄠ ㄗ)
① a hat; a headgear; a cap ② a label; a brand; a tag

帽簷(ㄇㄠ ㄧㄢ)
the brim of a hat

帽纓(ㄇㄠ ㄧㄥ)
a hat ribbon to hold the hat

【幀】 1330
ㄓㄥ jenq zhèng
1. a numerary adjunct (for paintings, pictures, photos, etc.)
2. one of a pair—as of scrolls

【幃】 1331
ㄨㄟ wei wéi
1. a curtain
2. a perfume bag

幃幄 or 帷幄(ㄨㄟ ㄨㄛ)

【幌】 1332
ㄨㄛ woh wò
a big tent: 士兵常居於帷幄中。
Soldiers usually live in big tents.

十畫

【幌】 1333
ㄏㄨㄤ hoang huǎng
a curtain; a cloth screen; a strip of cloth

幌子(ㄏㄨㄤ·ㄗ)
①a flag-sign for a wine-shop or a store②a front (especially a gaudy front)③something to dazzle or cheat another with. as boasts or swashbuckling ways; a facade

十一畫

【幔】 1334
ㄇㄢ mann màn
1. a curtain; a screen
2. a tent

幔帳(ㄇㄢ ㄓㄤˋ)
a tent pavilion

幔帳(ㄇㄢ ㄓㄤ)
a curtain; a screen; a canopy

幔室(ㄇㄢ ㄕˋ)
a tent chamber

幔子(ㄇㄢ·ㄗ)
a curtain; a cloth screen

【幕】 1335
ㄇㄨ muh mù
1. a screen; a curtain
2. a tent
3. an advisor; staffs; private secretaries
4. an act: 那是一齣三幕五景的話劇。It is a play in three acts and five scenes.
5. to cover

幕賓(ㄇㄨ ㄅㄧㄣ)or 幕友(ㄇㄨ ㄧㄡˋ) or 幕客(ㄇㄨ ㄎㄜˋ)
staffs

幕府(ㄇㄨ ㄈㄨˇ)
①the office of the commanding officer②a secretary or secretaries in such an office③(in Japan) shogunate (government by a shogun or shoguns)

幕天席地(ㄇㄨ ㄊㄧㄢ ㄒㄧˊ ㄉㄧˋ)
(literally) to have the sky for canopy and the earth for

mat—ambitious and broad-minded

幕僚(ㄇㄨ ㄌㄧㄠˊ)
staffs; secretaries; advisors

幕後(ㄇㄨ ㄏㄡˋ)
behind the scenes; backstage

幕後交易(ㄇㄨ ㄏㄡˋ ㄐㄧㄠ ㄧˋ)
behind-the-scenes deals

幕後新聞(ㄇㄨ ㄏㄡˋ ㄒㄧㄣ ㄨㄣˊ)
behind-the-scenes news; inside story

幕後人物(ㄇㄨ ㄏㄡˋ ㄖㄣˊ ㄨˋ)
behind-the-scenes personalities; string-pullers

幕後操縱(ㄇㄨ ㄏㄡˋ ㄘㄠ ㄗㄨㄥˋ)
to pull strings behind the scenes

幕燕(ㄇㄨ ㄧㄢˋ)
(literally) swallows that nest in a tent—being unaware of one's precarious situation

【幗】 1336
《ㄨㄛˊ gwo guó
a woman's headdress

【幘】 1337
ㄗㄜˊ tzer zé
a turban; a headdress

【幛】 1338
ㄓㄤˋ janq zhàng
a scroll of silk or cloth mounted or embroidered with appropriate wording sent as a gift for a wedding, funeral, etc.

幛子(ㄓㄤˋ·ㄗ)
same as 幛

十二畫

【幟】 1339
ㄓ jyh zhì
1. a flag; a pennant; a pennon
2. a mark; a sign

【幞】 1340
ㄆㄨˊ pwu pú
a turban; a headdress; a scarf

幞頭(ㄆㄨˊ ㄊㄡˊ)
a turban; a headdress; a scarf

【幡】 1341
ㄈㄢ fan fān
1. a flag; a pennant; a pennon; a streamer
2. sudden; suddenly: 那浪子幡然改塗。That vagabond suddenly repents and changes his

course.

幡兒(ㄅㄧㄦ)
a streamer-like object held by the sons of the deceased at a funeral

幡信(ㄈㄢ ㄒㄧㄣˋ)
(in ancient China) a flag marked with the title of a high official

幡幟(ㄈㄢ ㄓˋ)
flags; pennants; streamers

幡幢(ㄈㄢ ㄔㄨㄤˊ)
flags; pennants; streamers; pendant streamers of silk hung before a shrine

幡然(ㄈㄢ ㄖㄢˊ)
suddenly; to come to a sudden realization

【幢】 1342
ㄔㄨㄤˊ chwang chuáng
1. a curtain for a carriage
2. a numeracy adjunct for buildings of more than one story
3. flags, pennants, streamers, etc.
4. flickering; waving

幢隊(ㄔㄨㄤˊ ㄉㄨㄟˋ)
a squad of soldiers holding pennants to lead marching troops

幢節(ㄔㄨㄤˊ ㄐㄧㄝˊ)
a kind of tally broken in two pieces to prove the identity of the holders

幢幢(ㄔㄨㄤˊ ㄔㄨㄤˊ)
wavering; flapping in the wind: 屋子裏人影幢幢。The shadows of people are moving about in the house.

【幣】 1343
ㄅㄧˋ bih bì
1. currency; money; a legal tender: 外幣 foreign currency 紙幣 paper currency
2. a present; an offering

幣帛(ㄅㄧˋ ㄅㄛˊ)
gifts (in money and silks)

幣貢(ㄅㄧˋ 《ㄨㄥˋ)
(in ancient China) tributes offered by the feudal princes

幣值(ㄅㄧˋ ㄓˊ)
the purchasing power of a currency

幣制(ㄅㄧˋ ㄓˋ)
a currency system

幣制改革(ㄅㄧˋ ㄓˋ 《ㄞˇ 《ㄜˊ)
currency reform

幣制局（ㄅㄧˋ ㄓˋ ㄐㄩˊ）
a government agency in charge of the minting of coins, issuance of banknotes and other related matters in the early republican years

十四畫

【幬】 1344
1. ㄔㄡˊ chour chóu
a curtain; a canopy

【幬】 1344
2. ㄉㄠˋ daw dào
to cover

【幫】 1345
（帮）ㄅㄤ bang bāng
1. to help; to assist: 我幫他找到他的手錶。I helped him (to) find his watch.
2. a gang; a group; a class; a fleet
3. the sides of a shoe or gutter

幫辦（ㄅㄤ ㄅㄢˋ）
①to assist in managing ② the deputy director of a department under a cabinet ministry ③an assistant manager

幫派（ㄅㄤ ㄆㄞˋ）
a faction

幫浦（ㄅㄤ ㄆㄨˇ）
a pump

幫忙（ㄅㄤ ㄇㄤˊ）
help; assistance; to help or assist

幫倒忙（ㄅㄤ ㄉㄠˋ ㄇㄤˊ）
to cause trouble while trying to help

幫工（ㄅㄤ ㄍㄨㄥ）
an assistant of a skilled worker

幫夥（ㄅㄤ ㄏㄨㄛˇ）
assistants in a shop

幫會（ㄅㄤ ㄏㄨㄟˋ）
① secret societies ② an underworld gang

幫錢（ㄅㄤ ㄑㄧㄢˊ）
to help with money

幫腔（ㄅㄤ ㄑㄧㄤ）
①to give verbal support to a person (usually one of higher position) ②to follow another in singing

幫閒（ㄅㄤ ㄒㄧㄢˊ）
parasitism; to be a parasite

幫兇（ㄅㄤ ㄒㄩㄥ）
an accomplice in a crime or a condemnable act

幫助（ㄅㄤ ㄓㄨˋ）
to help; to assist; help or assistance: 他幫助我學日文。He helped me to learn Japanese.

幫襯（ㄅㄤ ㄔㄣˋ）
help; aid; assistance

幫手（ㄅㄤ ㄕㄡˇ）
a helper; an assistant; a helpmate: 你是我的有力幫手。You were a great helper to me.

幫嘴（ㄅㄤ ㄗㄨㄟˇ）
to help in an altercation; to speak for another

【幪】 1346
ㄇㄥˊ meng méng
a cover; a screen; cover

幪幪（ㄇㄥˊ ㄇㄥˊ）
lush or luxuriant (growth of vegetation)

十五畫

【幮】 1347
ㄔㄨˊ chwu chú
a bed-screen or mosquito net that looks like a small cabinet

干 部
《ㄢ gan gān

【干】 1348
《ㄢ gan gān
1. to offend; to oppose; to invade
2. to jam (radiobroadcasts, etc.); to interfere; to intervene
3. to concern; to involve
4. to seek; to beseech
5. the bank (of a river, etc.)
6. (how) many or much; a group
7. a shield
8. a stem; the Celestial Stems
9. a Chinese family name

干貝（《ㄢ ㄅㄟˋ）
a dried scallop

干冒（《ㄢ ㄇㄠˋ）
to transgress; to offend intentionally

干名采譽（《ㄢ ㄇㄧㄥˊ ㄘㄞˇ ㄩˋ）
to seek publicity

干犯（《ㄢ ㄈㄢˋ）
①to offend ②to invade

干瀆 or 干讀（《ㄢ ㄉㄨˊ）
(a polite expression) to offend by beseeching

干擾（《ㄢ ㄖㄠˇ）
①to interfere; to harass: 請不要干擾我的工作。Please don't interfere with my work. ②(said of radiobroadcasts) to jam

干你屁事（《ㄢ ㄋㄧˇ ㄆㄧˋ ㄕˋ）
(abusive) None of your business. 或What has that got to do with you?!

干連（《ㄢ ㄌㄧㄢˊ）
to involve; to implicate; involvement; implication

干祿（《ㄢ ㄌㄨˋ）
①to seek an official post ② official emolument

干戈（《ㄢ ㄍㄜ）
(literally) shields and spears —warfare; armed conflicts

干戈相見（《ㄢ ㄍㄜ ㄒㄧㄤ ㄐㄧㄢˋ）
to declare war on each other

干戈擾攘（《ㄢ ㄍㄜ ㄖㄠˇ ㄖㄤˇ）
incessant wars and the resultant unrest

干己（《ㄢ ㄐㄧˇ）
to concern oneself

干進（《ㄢ ㄐㄧㄣˋ）
to seek official promotion or a higher office in the government

干將（《ㄢ ㄐㄧㄤˋ）
name of a famous sword, made by a master ironsmith of that name in the Epoch of Spring and Autumn

干求（《ㄢ ㄑㄧㄡˊ）
to request; to beseech; to importune

干卿底事（《ㄢ ㄑㄧㄥ ㄉㄧˇ ㄕˋ）
What has that got to do with you? 或None of your business!

干係（《ㄢ ㄒㄧˋ）
involvement; concern; implication

干休（《ㄢ ㄒㄧㄡ）
to give up; to bring to an end

干支（《ㄢ ㄓ

the system of Celestial Stems and Terrestrial Branches which makes the 60-year cycle

干政(ㄍㄢ ㄓㄥˋ)
to interfere in politics

干證
the witnesses involved in a lawsuit

干城
defenders; protectors; champions

干城之選(ㄍㄢ ㄔㄥˊ ㄓ ㄒㄩㄢˇ)
a capable general who can be trusted with the defense of the nation

干時
to suit the occasion; to seek to keep up with the times

干世
to seek to conform with the world

干涉(ㄍㄢ ㄕㄜˋ)
to interfere; interference; intervention

干擾(ㄍㄢ ㄖㄠˇ)or 干擾(ㄍㄢ ㄖㄠˇ)
①to disturb; to interfere ②(physics) interference; to jam

干謁
to seek an audience with someone in power, hoping for a position

干預 or 干與(ㄍㄢ ㄩˋ)
to intervene; to interfere; intervention

干譽(ㄍㄢ ㄩˋ)
to seek for higher reputation

干雲蔽日(ㄍㄢ ㄩㄣˊ ㄅㄧˋ ㄖˋ)
(said of tall and luxuriant trees) towering into the clouds and covering up the sun

二畫

〔平〕 ¹³⁴⁹
ㄆㄧㄥˊ pyng píng

1. level; even: 桌面不平。The table is not level.
2. equal; equity; equality
3. peaceful; amity
4. to conquer; to quell (a revolt); to calm down
5. to control; to regulate
6. (said of prices) to go back to normal after sharp rises:

最近物價平落。Recently prices have dropped to normal.
7. (sports) to make the same score; to tie; to draw; a draw: 這場棒球賽最後打平了。The baseball game ended in a draw.
8. to pacify; to bring peace to: 治國平天下 to rule a country and unify the world in peace
9. short for Peiping: 她喜愛平劇。She is fond of Peiping opera.
10. a Chinese family name

平白(ㄆㄧㄥˊ ㄅㄞˊ) or 平白無故(ㄆㄧㄥˊ ㄅㄞˊ ㄨˊ ㄍㄨˋ)
without reason or cause; without provocation: 他平白挨一頓罵。He got a scolding without reason.

平輩
of the same generation

平版(ㄆㄧㄥˊ ㄅㄢˇ)
(printing) a lithographic plate

平板(ㄆㄧㄥˊ ㄅㄢˇ)
dull and stereotyped; flat

平板玻璃(ㄆㄧㄥˊ ㄅㄢˇ ㄅㄛ ㄌㄧˊ)
plate glass

平步青雲(ㄆㄧㄥˊ ㄅㄨˋ ㄑㄧㄥ ㄩㄣˊ)
(said of a career or social position) a meteoric rise

平平(ㄆㄧㄥˊ ㄆㄧㄥˊ)
average; common; usual; ordinary; so-so

平平安安(ㄆㄧㄥˊ ㄆㄧㄥˊ ㄢ ㄢ)
peaceful(ly); without any accident. 我們希望你平平安安的回家。We hope you return home peacefully

平平穩穩(ㄆㄧㄥˊ ㄆㄧㄥˊ ㄨㄣˇ ㄨㄣˇ)
sure and steady; peaceful and without mishaps

平鋪直敍(ㄆㄧㄥˊ ㄆㄨ ㄓˊ ㄒㄩˋ)
factual description; straight reporting; (said of a narration) without turns or twists

平脈(ㄆㄧㄥˊ ㄇㄞˋ)
(medicine) a normal pulse; the pulse of a healthy person

平面(ㄆㄧㄥˊ ㄇㄧㄢˋ)
a plane, or plane surface

平面圖(ㄆㄧㄥˊ ㄇㄧㄢˋ ㄊㄨˊ)
a plane (of a building or machine)

平面幾何(ㄆㄧㄥˊ ㄇㄧㄢˋ ㄐㄧˇ ㄏㄜˊ)
plane geometry

平面鏡(ㄆㄧㄥˊ ㄇㄧㄢˋ ㄐㄧㄥˋ)
a plane mirror

平面三角(ㄆㄧㄥˊ ㄇㄧㄢˋ ㄙㄢ ㄐㄧㄠˇ)
plane trigonometry

平民(ㄆㄧㄥˊ ㄇㄧㄣˊ)
a commoner; a civilian

平民教育(ㄆㄧㄥˊ ㄇㄧㄣˊ ㄐㄧㄠˋ ㄩˋ)
education of the masses; adult education 亦作「民眾教育」

平民政治(ㄆㄧㄥˊ ㄇㄧㄣˊ ㄓㄥˋ ㄓˋ)
popular government; democracy

平明
at dawn or daybreak: 他平明即起。He gets up at daybreak.

平反
to reverse or redress a miscarriage of justice

平凡(ㄆㄧㄥˊ ㄈㄢˊ)
common; ordinary; usual; not outstanding or remarkable

平分(ㄆㄧㄥˊ ㄈㄣ)
to divide into equal shares; to divide equally

平分秋色(ㄆㄧㄥˊ ㄈㄣ ㄑㄧㄡ ㄙㄜˋ)
(said of two sides) to share (top honors, fame, etc.); to equal each other in (achievements, scores, etc.)

平方(ㄆㄧㄥˊ ㄈㄤ)
(mathematics) a square

平方根(ㄆㄧㄥˊ ㄈㄤ ㄍㄣ)
a square root

平房(ㄆㄧㄥˊ ㄈㄤˊ)
a one-storied house; a bungalow

平服(ㄆㄧㄥˊ ㄈㄨˊ)
to stabilize; stable; steadfast

平復(ㄆㄧㄥˊ ㄈㄨˋ)
①(said of situations, social order, etc.) to return to normal; to calm down; to subside ②to recover from an illness, etc.

平旦(ㄆㄧㄥˊ ㄉㄢˋ)
dawn; daybreak

平淡(ㄆㄧㄥˊ ㄉㄢˋ)
ordinary; commonplace; insipid; nothing particular or remarkable: 那是一個平淡的故事。That is an insipid story.

平淡無奇(ㄆㄧㄥˊ ㄉㄢˋ ㄨˊ ㄑㄧˊ)

（〔干部〕）

nothing extraordinary or remarkable; insipid or dull

平淡無味 (ㄆㄧㄥˊ ㄉㄢˋ ㄨˊ ㄨㄟˋ)
insipid; without flavor; tasteless

平等 (ㄆㄧㄥˊ ㄉㄥˇ)
①equality; equal ②name of a county in Honan Province

平等待遇 (ㄆㄧㄥˊ ㄉㄥˇ ㄉㄞˋ ㄩˋ)
equal treatment

平等互利 (ㄆㄧㄥˊ ㄉㄥˇ ㄏㄨˋ ㄌㄧˋ)
equality and mutual benefit

平糴 (ㄆㄧㄥˊ ㄉㄧˊ)
In ancient China, the government bought grain during bumper harvests in order to sell it at a low price in the time of scarcity.

平底船 (ㄆㄧㄥˊ ㄉㄧˇ ㄔㄨㄢˊ)
a flat-bottom boat

平地 (ㄆㄧㄥˊ ㄉㄧˋ)
①the plain; a piece of level ground ②suddenly

平地風波 (ㄆㄧㄥˊ ㄉㄧˋ ㄈㄥ ㄅㄛ)
an unexpected turn of event; troubles that arise all of a sudden

平地登天 (ㄆㄧㄥˊ ㄉㄧˋ ㄉㄥ ㄊㄧㄢ)
a sudden rise (to fame, success, etc.): 求學問不能希望平地登天, In the pursuit of knowledge, one cannot expect a sudden rise.

平地一聲雷 (ㄆㄧㄥˊ ㄉㄧˋ ㄧ ㄕㄥ ㄌㄟˊ)
(literally) a bolt from the blue—a sudden shot to fame

平定 (ㄆㄧㄥˊ ㄉㄧㄥˋ)
①(often said of situations, etc.) settled: 這裡情勢已平定下來. The situation here is settled. ②to quell (rebellions, etc.)

平臺 (ㄆㄧㄥˊ ㄊㄞˊ)
①a flat-top building ②a stadium-like building ③balcony, open porch or portico

平頭 (ㄆㄧㄥˊ ㄊㄡˊ)
①block—having no indentation in addresses, headings, etc. ②a crew cut; closely cropped hair: 他留着平頭. He has closely cropped hair. ③common; ordinary

平頭正臉 (ㄆㄧㄥˊ ㄊㄡˊ ㄓㄥˋ ㄌㄧㄢˇ)
a neat appearance (of a person)

平坦 (ㄆㄧㄥˊ ㄊㄢˇ)

level, even and smooth (roads, going, etc.): 這條公路的路面寬闊平坦。This highway has a broad and smooth surface.

平糶 (ㄆㄧㄥˊ ㄊㄧㄠˋ)
In ancient China, the government sold grain at a low price in the time of scarcity, when the market price was high.

平添 (ㄆㄧㄥˊ ㄊㄧㄢ)
to add or acquire something unexpectedly

平年 (ㄆㄧㄥˊ ㄋㄧㄢˊ)
an ordinary year (as distinct from a leap year)

平列 (ㄆㄧㄥˊ ㄌㄧㄝˋ)
of equal rank

平林 (ㄆㄧㄥˊ ㄌㄧㄣˊ)
wood groves on level ground

平亂 (ㄆㄧㄥˊ ㄌㄨㄢˋ)
to suppress a rebellion or revolt

平光 (ㄆㄧㄥˊ ㄍㄨㄤ)
(said of eyeglasses) ordinary lenses which are neither concave nor convex

平康 (ㄆㄧㄥˊ ㄎㄤ)
a brothel

平曠 (ㄆㄧㄥˊ ㄎㄨㄤˋ)
open and flat (fields, land, etc.)

平空 (ㄆㄧㄥˊ ㄎㄨㄥ)
to occur without any reason or cause; to fabricate or invent

平和 (ㄆㄧㄥˊ ㄏㄜˊ)
①mildly; mild: 他的性情平和. He is of a mild disposition. ②name of a county in Fukien Province

平漢鐵路 (ㄆㄧㄥˊ ㄏㄢˋ ㄊㄧㄝˇ ㄌㄨˋ)
the Peiping-Hankow Railway

平衡 (ㄆㄧㄥˊ ㄏㄥˊ)
equilibrium; balance; (muscular) coordination

平衡力 (ㄆㄧㄥˊ ㄏㄥˊ ㄌㄧˋ)
equilibrant

平衡稅 (ㄆㄧㄥˊ ㄏㄥˊ ㄕㄨㄟˋ)
(international trade) countervailing duties

平穩 (ㄆㄧㄥˊ ㄨㄣˇ)
even and smooth

平話 or 評話 (ㄆㄧㄥˊ ㄏㄨㄚˋ)

storytelling (using the style of language of the professional storytellers in Sung Dynasty somewhere between the spoken and the written languages)

平緩 (ㄆㄧㄥˊ ㄏㄨㄢˇ)
①gently: 這條河水流平緩. The river flows gently. ②mild; gentle: 他說話語調平緩. He speaks in a mild tone.

平假名 (ㄆㄧㄥˊ ㄐㄧㄚˇ ㄇㄧㄥˊ)
a form of Japanese phonetic signs which are often used in place of the Chinese characters

平價 (ㄆㄧㄥˊ ㄐㄧㄚˋ)
①a fair price: 他以平價出售了他的房子. He has sold his house at a fair price. ②lower prices

平交道 (ㄆㄧㄥˊ ㄐㄧㄠ ㄉㄠˋ)
a level crossing; the intersection between a railroad and a roadway

平肩 (ㄆㄧㄥˊ ㄐㄧㄢ)
①shoulder-to-shoulder ②of equal footing or rank

平津 (ㄆㄧㄥˊ ㄐㄧㄣ)
Peiping and Tientsin; the Peiping and Tientsin area

平靖 (ㄆㄧㄥˊ ㄐㄧㄥˋ)
peace and order; settled

平靜 (ㄆㄧㄥˊ ㄐㄧㄥˋ)
quiet; calm: 沒有風，一切都是平靜的。There was no wind and everything was calm.

平居 (ㄆㄧㄥˊ ㄐㄩ)
(literally) on usual days—ordinarily

平局 (ㄆㄧㄥˊ ㄐㄩˊ)
a draw; a tie: 這場網球比賽最後打成平局. The tennis game finally ended in a draw.

平劇 (ㄆㄧㄥˊ ㄐㄩˋ)
Peiping opera; Peking opera; Chinese opera

平均 (ㄆㄧㄥˊ ㄐㄩㄣ)
the average; even (distribution, etc.)

平均地權 (ㄆㄧㄥˊ ㄐㄩㄣ ㄉㄧˋ ㄑㄩㄢˊ)
the equalization of land rights (envisaged by Dr. Sun Yat-sen, with a three-fold measure—the purchase of private land at the values declared, the levy of land

（干部）

tax at the land value assessed and the government takeover of increment of land value)

平均年齡(ㄆㄧㄥ ㄐㄩㄣ ㄋㄧㄢ ㄌㄧㄥ)
composite life

平均利潤(ㄆㄧㄥ ㄐㄩㄣ ㄌㄧ ㄖㄨㄣˋ)
the average of profit

平均計算(ㄆㄧㄥ ㄐㄩㄣ ㄐㄧˋ ㄙㄨㄢˋ)
a general average; on the average

平均價(ㄆㄧㄥ ㄐㄩㄣ ㄐㄧㄚˋ)
average price

平均成本(ㄆㄧㄥ ㄐㄩㄣ ㄔㄥˊ ㄅㄣˇ)
average cost

平均壽命(ㄆㄧㄥ ㄐㄩㄣ ㄕㄡˋ ㄇㄧㄥˋ)
mean life

平均數(ㄆㄧㄥ ㄐㄩㄣ ㄕㄨˋ)
a mean; an average

平均速度(ㄆㄧㄥ ㄐㄩㄣ ㄙㄨˋ ㄉㄨˋ)
average speed; mean velocity

平均溫度(ㄆㄧㄥ ㄐㄩㄣ ㄨㄣ ㄉㄨˋ)
the mean temperature

平起平坐(ㄆㄧㄥ ㄑㄧˇ ㄆㄧㄥˊ ㄗㄨㄛˋ)
① to treat another as one's equal ② to show no deference

平情而論(ㄆㄧㄥ ㄑㄧㄥˊ ㄦˊ ㄌㄨㄣˋ)
objectively speaking

平權(ㄆㄧㄥ ㄑㄩㄢˊ)
equal rights

平昔(ㄆㄧㄥ ㄒㄧˊ)
in the past; in the past days

平息(ㄆㄧㄥ ㄒㄧˊ)
(said of an uprising or waves, etc.) to come to an end; to subside; to cause to stop; to quell: 海嘯平息了。The tidal waves subsided.

平心靜氣(ㄆㄧㄥ ㄒㄧㄣ ㄐㄧㄥˋ ㄑㄧˋ)
to be calm and fair (in resolving a dispute, etc.); to think calmly in detachment

平心而論(ㄆㄧㄥ ㄒㄧㄣ ㄦˊ ㄌㄨㄣˋ)
to discuss something fairly; to be fair: 平心而論，他是個勤勉的學生。To be fair to him, he is a diligent student.

平信(ㄆㄧㄥ ㄒㄧㄣˋ)
ordinary mail: 她寄了一封平信給他。She sent a letter to him by ordinary mail.

平行(ㄆㄧㄥ ㄒㄧㄥˊ)
① parallel: 這條街和那條街平行。This street is parallel to

that one. ② of equal rank; on the same footing

平行線(ㄆㄧㄥ ㄒㄧㄥˊ ㄒㄧㄢˋ)
parallel lines

平行四邊形(ㄆㄧㄥ ㄒㄧㄥˊ ㄙˋ ㄅㄧㄢ ㄒㄧㄥˊ)
a parallelogram

平直(ㄆㄧㄥ ㄓˊ)
fair and frank

平治(ㄆㄧㄥ ㄓˋ)
peace; tranquillity and good order

平展(ㄆㄧㄥ ㄓㄢˇ)
(said of land, plain, etc.) open and flat

平章(ㄆㄧㄥ ㄓㄤ)
① to make comments (on literary works) ② an official post in ancient China

平整(ㄆㄧㄥ ㄓㄥˇ)
① to level: 他們平整了一塊土地。They leveled a plot of land. ② neat; smooth

平正(ㄆㄧㄥ ㄓㄥˋ)
fair and just; without trickery or chicanery

平裝本(ㄆㄧㄥ ㄓㄨㄤ ㄅㄣˇ)
paperback (books); a paper-bound edition

平常(ㄆㄧㄥ ㄔㄤˊ)
① normal; natural ② usual; as usual ③ ordinary; common; so-so: 這種現象很平常。This sort of thing is quite a common occurrence. ④ usually; ordinarily: 她平常於星期六晚上出去。She usually goes out on Saturday nights.

平時(ㄆㄧㄥ ㄕˊ)
ordinarily; in normal times; in time of peace: 他平時在十點鐘睡覺。Ordinarily he goes to bed at ten o'clock.

平時不燒香，臨時抱佛腳(ㄆㄧㄥ ㄕˊ ㄅㄨˋ ㄕㄠ ㄒㄧㄤ，ㄌㄧㄣˊ ㄕˊ ㄅㄠˋ ㄈㄛˊ ㄐㄧㄠˇ)
(literally) One embraced the feet of Buddha in supplication but neglected burning incense to him when one did not need his help.— Last-minute efforts are useless if

no preparatory work has been done beforehand.

平視(ㄆㄧㄥ ㄕˋ)
to look at something with the line of sight parallel to the ground

平射砲(ㄆㄧㄥ ㄕㄜˋ ㄆㄠˋ)
a cannon which fires along a flat trajectory (as distinct from a howitzer)

平手(ㄆㄧㄥ ㄕㄡˇ)
(in a competition, etc.) to draw; to tie another; to come out with even scores as one's opponent: 這些隊賽成平手。The teams drew.

平身(ㄆㄧㄥ ㄕㄣ)
Stand up. or At ease. (the emperor's command to his minister after the latter had kowtowed to him)

平上去入(ㄆㄧㄥ ㄕㄤˋ ㄑㄩˋ ㄖㄨˋ)
level tone, falling-rising tone, falling tone, and entering tone—the four tones in classical Chinese phonetics

平生(ㄆㄧㄥ ㄕㄥ)
in all one's life; throughout one's life: 這是他平生的志願。This is his lifelong wish.

平聲(ㄆㄧㄥ ㄕㄥ)
level tone—the first tone in classical Chinese phonetics

平順(ㄆㄧㄥ ㄕㄨㄣˋ)
① smooth and orderly ② the name of a county in Shansi Province

平日(ㄆㄧㄥ ㄖˋ)
on usual days; ordinarily; on usual occasions: 她平日喜歡運動。Ordinarily she likes sports.

平壤(ㄆㄧㄥ ㄖㄤˇ)
Pyongyang, capital of Communist North Korea

平仄(ㄆㄧㄥ ㄗㄜˋ)
level and oblique tones—the four tones in classical Chinese phonetics (the first tone belongs to 平 while the remaining three tones belong to 仄)

平色(ㄆㄧㄥ ㄙㄜˋ)
the weight (or contents) and quality of silver

平素(ㄆㄧㄥ ㄙㄨˋ)
usually; ordinarily: 這女孩平

素不愛說話。This girl is usually very quiet.

平綏鐵路(ㄆㄧㄥˊ ㄙㄨㄟ ㄊㄧㄝˇ ㄌㄨˋ)
the Peiping-Kweisui Railway

〔干部〕

平安(ㄆㄧㄥˊ ㄢ)
safe and sound; free from danger; peace: 全家平安。The whole family is safe and sound.

平安醮(ㄆㄧㄥˊ ㄢ ㄐㄧㄠˋ)
a religious service held in an area after an epidemic

平安無事(ㄆㄧㄥˊ ㄢ ㄨˊ ㄕˋ)
All is well. 或safe and without any mishaps; safe and sound; in good order

平一宇內(ㄆㄧㄥˊ ㄧ ㄩˇ ㄋㄟˋ)
the unification of a nation after quelling rebellions

平議(ㄆㄧㄥˊ ㄧˋ)
a fair and just discussion; a fair commentary that takes care of both sides of an argument

平易近人(ㄆㄧㄥˊ ㄧˋ ㄐㄧㄣˋ ㄖㄣˊ)
(said of one's personality) easy to approach; easy to get along with: 我的鄰居們都平易近人。My neighbors are easy to get along with.

平野(ㄆㄧㄥˊ ㄧㄝˇ)
an open field

平穩(ㄆㄧㄥˊ ㄨㄣˇ)
steady and smooth (bus rides, driving, etc.); stable: 這次飛行很平穩。The flight was smooth.

平原(ㄆㄧㄥˊ ㄩㄢˊ)
a plain; a steppe

平原君(ㄆㄧㄥˊ ㄩㄢˊ ㄐㄩㄣ)
a famous official of Chao (趙) in the Epoch of Warring States, who had many protégés with various talents

平允(ㄆㄧㄥˊ ㄩㄣˇ)
fair and proper; just and appropriate

平庸(ㄆㄧㄥˊ ㄩㄥ)
commonplace; dull (persons, etc.); without talent: 這學生資質平庸，但很努力。Though without talent, this student works hard.

三畫

【年】 1350
ㄋㄧㄢˊ nian nián

1. a year: 我到此地恰恰一年了。It is just a year since I arrived here.

2. one's age: 他們的年齡是四歲、七歲、九歲。Their ages are 4, 7 and 9.

3. a Chinese family name

年伯(ㄋㄧㄢˊ ㄅㄛˊ)
a term used to address the 同年 of one's father參看「同年②」

年輩(ㄋㄧㄢˊ ㄅㄟˋ)
age and generation

年表(ㄋㄧㄢˊ ㄅㄧㄠˇ)
a chronicle

年譜(ㄋㄧㄢˊ ㄆㄨˇ)
a biography arranged in chronological order

年邁(ㄋㄧㄢˊ ㄇㄞˋ)or年老(ㄋㄧㄢˊ ㄌㄠˇ)
to get old; aged

年貌(ㄋㄧㄢˊ ㄇㄠˋ)
the age and appearance of a person (recorded for identification before the invention of photography)

年飯(ㄋㄧㄢˊ ㄈㄢˋ)or年夜飯(ㄋㄧㄢˊ ㄧㄝˋ ㄈㄢˋ)
the dinner for the whole family on the eve of the Lunar New Year

年分 or 年份(ㄋㄧㄢˊ ㄈㄣˋ)
age; time; a particular year: 這件古董的年分比那件久。This piece of antique is older than that one.

年方二八(ㄋㄧㄢˊ ㄈㄤ ㄦˋ ㄅㄚ)
(said of girls) only 16 years of age

年俸(ㄋㄧㄢˊ ㄈㄥˋ)or年薪(ㄋㄧㄢˊ ㄒㄧㄣ)
an annual salary; annual pay

年富力強(ㄋㄧㄢˊ ㄈㄨˋ ㄌㄧˋ ㄑㄧㄤˊ)
the prime of one's life: 青年時期年富力強。Youthhood is the prime of one's life.

年代(ㄋㄧㄢˊ ㄉㄞˋ)
①an age, era, generation, etc. ②years in a decade

年底(ㄋㄧㄢˊ ㄉㄧˇ)
the end of a year

年度(ㄋㄧㄢˊ ㄉㄨˋ)
a year fixed arbitrarily for convenience, a better administrative purpose, etc., as a

fiscal year, a school year, etc.

年度計畫(ㄋㄧㄢˊ ㄉㄨˋ ㄐㄧˋ ㄏㄨㄚˋ)
an annual plan

年度決算(ㄋㄧㄢˊ ㄉㄨˋ ㄐㄩㄝˊ ㄙㄨㄢˋ)
(accounting) annual closing

年度總報告(ㄋㄧㄢˊ ㄉㄨˋ ㄗㄨㄥˇ ㄅㄠˋ ㄍㄠˋ)
general annual reports

年頭(ㄋㄧㄢˊ ㄊㄡˊ)
①times: 年頭好。Times are good. ②the beginning of year ③a year ④a harvest: 今年年頭真好。This year's harvest is rich indeed.

年頭年尾(ㄋㄧㄢˊ ㄊㄡˊ ㄋㄧㄢˊ ㄨㄟˇ)
the beginning and the end of a year

年內(ㄋㄧㄢˊ ㄋㄟˋ)
within the year: 他將在年內回來。He will be back within the year.

年年(ㄋㄧㄢˊ ㄋㄧㄢˊ)
every year; year after year

年來(ㄋㄧㄢˊ ㄌㄞˊ)
①in recent years ②during the year past

年禮(ㄋㄧㄢˊ ㄌㄧˇ)
New Year's presents

年利(ㄋㄧㄢˊ ㄌㄧˋ)or年息(ㄋㄧㄢˊ ㄒㄧˊ)
annual interest (rate)

年例(ㄋㄧㄢˊ ㄌㄧˋ)
customs or routines handed down year after year

年曆(ㄋㄧㄢˊ ㄌㄧˋ)
a calendar with the whole year printed on one sheet

年力就衰(ㄋㄧㄢˊ ㄌㄧˋ ㄐㄧㄡˋ ㄕㄨㄞ)
aging and feeble

年齡(ㄋㄧㄢˊ ㄌㄧㄥˊ)
age: 他們同年齡。They are of the same age.

年齡結構(ㄋㄧㄢˊ ㄌㄧㄥˊ ㄐㄧㄝˊ ㄍㄡˋ)
age structure

年輪(ㄋㄧㄢˊ ㄌㄨㄣˊ)
annual rings (indicating the age of a tree)

年糕(ㄋㄧㄢˊ ㄍㄠ)
New Year's cake; glutinous rice cake eaten during the Lunar New Year's holidays

年高德劭(ㄋㄧㄢˊ ㄍㄠ ㄉㄜˊ ㄕㄠˋ)
advanced in years and virtue

年庚八字(ㄋㄧㄢˊ ㄍㄥ ㄅㄚ ㄗˋ)
the hour, day, month and

year of a person's birth
—used by fortunetellers to
tell a person's fortune or
whether a couple are well-
matched

藥堯(ㄋㄧㄢˊㄥˋㄧㄠˊ)
Nien Keng-yao, a general in
the early Ching Dynasty

穀(ㄋㄧㄢˊㄍㄨˇ)
an annual harvest or crop;
the total amount of grain
harvested in a year

關(ㄋㄧㄢˊㄍㄨㄢ)
(literally) the crisis of a
year — the end of a year
when all accounts and debts
must be settled: 年關近了。
The end of the year is coming near.

光荏苒(ㄋㄧㄢˊㄍㄨㄤ ㄖㄣˇ ㄖㄢˇ)
(said of time) to elapse
gradually and imperceptibly

功(ㄋㄧㄢˊㄍㄨㄥ)
the merits one earns during
his years of service—a reference used in consideration
of promotion or granting of
pension, etc.

號(ㄋㄧㄢˊㄏㄠˋ)
the title of an emperor's
reign

華(ㄋㄧㄢˊㄏㄨㄚˊ)
time; years; age: 李小姐年華
雙十。Miss Lee is twenty
years of age.

華虛度(ㄋㄧㄢˊㄏㄨㄚˊ ㄒㄩ ㄉㄨˋ)
to have spent one's best
years without any achievements; to have wasted the
best years of one's life

畫兒(ㄋㄧㄢˊㄏㄨㄚˋㄦ)
drawings or pictures sold at
Lunar New Year, usually on
the subject of good luck

貨(ㄋㄧㄢˊㄏㄨㄛˋ)
food items and other con-
sumer goods that a house-
hold must keep in store for
the Lunar New Year's
holidays when shops are
closed

會(ㄋㄧㄢˊㄏㄨㄟˋ)
an annual meeting or con-
vention: 這家公司在下週一舉
行年會。This company will
hold an annual meeting next
Monday.

級(ㄋㄧㄢˊㄐㄧˊ)
(in school) a grade: 美國的
小學有八個年級。An elemen-
tary school in America has
eight grades.

年紀(ㄋㄧㄢˊㄐㄧˋ)
years; age: 她的年紀多大？
How (many years) old is
she?

年假(ㄋㄧㄢˊㄐㄧㄚˋ)
New Year's holidays or
vacation

年節(ㄋㄧㄢˊㄐㄧㄝˊ)
the three major festivals of
the year—the Dragon Boat,
the Mid-Autumn and the
Lunar New Year festivals

年久失修(ㄋㄧㄢˊㄐㄧㄡˇㄕ ㄒㄧㄡ)
in a dilapidated condition;
worn down by the years
without repair

年間(ㄋㄧㄢˊㄐㄧㄢ)
a certain period of time,
such as the reign of an
emperor, etc.

年鑑(ㄋㄧㄢˊㄐㄧㄢˋ)
an almanac; a yearbook

年金(ㄋㄧㄢˊㄐㄧㄣ)
an annuity

年近歲迫(ㄋㄧㄢˊㄐㄧㄣˋㄙㄨㄟˋ ㄆㄛˋ)
The Lunar New Year is ap-
proaching fast.

年景(ㄋㄧㄢˊㄐㄧㄥˇ)
① New Year's scenes ② a
harvest

年前(ㄋㄧㄢˊㄑㄧㄢˊ)
before the turn of the year

年歉(ㄋㄧㄢˊㄑㄧㄢˋ)
a year of poor harvest

年輕(ㄋㄧㄢˊㄑㄧㄥ)
young; youthful; youth

年輕銳美(ㄋㄧㄢˊㄑㄧㄥ ㄖㄨㄟˋ ㄇㄟˇ)
young and pretty

年禧(ㄋㄧㄢˊㄒㄧ)
New Year's greetings

年下(ㄋㄧㄢˊ•ㄒㄧㄚ)
during the New Year's
holidays

年限(ㄋㄧㄢˊㄒㄧㄢˋ)
the number of years set as a
time limit within which a
job must be completed; a
service life

年兄(ㄋㄧㄢˊㄒㄩㄥ)
(in old China) a mutual reference among those who
passed the same imperial
civil service examination

年紙(ㄋㄧㄢˊㄓˇ)
paper items made for the
New Year Festival—door
couplets, paper horses, etc.

年長(ㄋㄧㄢˊㄓㄤˇ)
old or aged; older: 我較他年
長。I am older than he.

年終(ㄋㄧㄢˊㄓㄨㄥ)
the close or end of the year

年終考績(ㄋㄧㄢˊㄓㄨㄥ ㄎㄠˇ ㄐㄧ)
the grading of an employee's
performance at the end of
the year

年齒(ㄋㄧㄢˊㄔˇ)
the age of a person

年成(ㄋㄧㄢˊ•ㄔㄥ)
the harvests of the year

年初(ㄋㄧㄢˊㄔㄨ)
the beginning of the year: 去
年年初我曾見過他。I saw him
at the beginning of last
year.

年事(ㄋㄧㄢˊㄕˋ)
the age of a person

年少(ㄋㄧㄢˊㄕㄠˋ)
young

年數(ㄋㄧㄢˊㄕㄨˋ)
the age of a person; the
length of a person's life
span

年深日久(ㄋㄧㄢˊㄕㄣ ㄖˋㄐㄧㄡˇ)
after a long lapse of time;
as the years go by

年賞(ㄋㄧㄢˊㄕㄤˇ)
a year-end award; a year-
end bonus

年入(ㄋㄧㄢˊㄖㄨˋ)
annual income

年資(ㄋㄧㄢˊㄗ)
① the years one spends in
an endeavor or job ② seniority

年租(ㄋㄧㄢˊㄗㄨ)
an annual rental (of a piece
of land, a house, etc.)

年柞(ㄋㄧㄢˊㄗㄨˋ)
one's life span

年菜(ㄋㄧㄢˊㄘㄞˋ)
food and dishes prepared for
the Lunar New Year

年歲(ㄋㄧㄢˊㄙㄨㄟˋ)
① the age of a person ②
years; an age ③ harvests

年誼(ㄋㄧㄢˊㄧˋ)
the friendship among those
who passed the same impe-

（干部）

〔年部〕

rial civil service examination in old China

年夜(ㄋㄧㄢˊ ㄧㄝˋ)
New Year's Eve: 每年年夜我們都有家庭團圓。We have a family reunion every New Year's Eve.

年幼無知(ㄋㄧㄢˊ ㄧㄡˋ ㄨˊ ㄓ)
ignorance for being young of age (often used in court verdict or petition pleading leniency for a young offender)

年湮代遠(ㄋㄧㄢˊ ㄧㄢ ㄉㄞˋ ㄩㄢˇ)
① time immemorial ② oblivion resulting from the passing of the years

年尾(ㄋㄧㄢˊ ㄨㄟˇ)
the end of the year

年逾不惑(ㄋㄧㄢˊ ㄩˊ ㄅㄨˋ ㄏㄨㄛˋ)
to have passed 40: 我們的老師年逾不惑。Our teacher has passed the age of forty.

年月(ㄋㄧㄢˊ ㄩㄝˋ)
① times; an age ② the exact time when a given event occurred

五畫

【并】 1351 1.(併) ㄅㄧㄥˋ bing bing
1. on a level with; even; equal
2. and; also; or; at the same time, together with 參看「並」

并日而食(ㄅㄧㄥˋ ㄖˋ ㄦˊ ㄕˊ)
to eat on alternate days—to live a poor life

【并】 1351 2.ㄅㄧㄥ bing bing
Pingchou, one of the ancient Chinese administrative divisions, consisting of parts of today's Hopeh, Shansi, etc.

并州快剪(ㄅㄧㄥ ㄓㄡ ㄎㄨㄞˋ ㄐㄧㄢˇ)
scissors made in Pingchou—famous for sharp blades (now used figuratively to depict a person with a quick and witty tongue or crisp writing)

【幸】 1352 ㄒㄧㄥˋ shinq xing
1. well-being and happiness: 他們都有幸福愉快之感。They all have a sense of well-being and happiness.

2. fortunately; luckily; thanks to: 我們幸而及時趕到那裏。We fortunately got there in time.
3. to feel happy about; to favor
4. an imperial tour or progress
5. a Chinese family name

幸免於難(ㄒㄧㄥˋ ㄇㄧㄢˇ ㄩˊ ㄋㄢˋ)
to have a narrow escape from（death, etc.); to have luckily survived an accident or incident

幸福(ㄒㄧㄥˋ ㄈㄨˊ)
happiness and well-being; bliss

幸福主義(ㄒㄧㄥˋ ㄈㄨˊ ㄓㄨˇ ㄧˋ)
eudemonism

幸得(ㄒㄧㄥˋ ㄉㄜˊ)
fortunately; thanks to

幸虧(ㄒㄧㄥˋ ㄎㄨㄟ)or 幸好(ㄒㄧㄥˋ ㄏㄠˇ)or 幸喜(ㄒㄧㄥˋ ㄒㄧˇ)
luckily; fortunately; thanks to

幸臣(ㄒㄧㄥˋ ㄔㄣˊ)
a favorite courtier

幸事(ㄒㄧㄥˋ ㄕˋ)
① something that happened out of sheer luck ② something pleasant

幸甚(ㄒㄧㄥˋ ㄕㄣˋ)
① very much hoped for ② very much blessed

幸災樂禍(ㄒㄧㄥˋ ㄗㄞ ㄌㄜˋ ㄏㄨㄛˋ)
to rejoice in the calamity of others, to take pleasure in others' misfortune; to gloat over others' misfortune

幸蘇涸轍(ㄒㄧㄥˋ ㄙㄨ ㄏㄜˊ ㄓㄜˊ)
(literally) to pump water into a dried pond to save the fish—to give financial help to those in need

幸而(ㄒㄧㄥˋ ㄦˊ)
luckily; fortunately; thanks to

幸有(ㄒㄧㄥˋ ㄧㄡˇ)
to be fortunate to have

幸勿推卻(ㄒㄧㄥˋ ㄨˋ ㄊㄨㄟ ㄑㄩㄝˋ)
(We're) hopeful that you won't refuse or reject; please do not refuse (our offer, request, etc.)

幸未(ㄒㄧㄥˋ ㄨㄟˋ)
Fortunately, it's not,...

幸運(ㄒㄧㄥˋ ㄩㄣˋ)
① good fortune; good luck

② lucky

幸運之神(ㄒㄧㄥˋ ㄩㄣˋ ㄓ ㄕㄣˊ)
Lady Luck; the goddess fortune

幸運兒(ㄒㄧㄥˋ ㄩㄣˋ ㄦ)
a person who always g good breaks; a lucky guy

十畫

【幹】 1353 《ㄍㄢˋ gann gàn
1. the trunk (of a tree or of human body): 樹幹支持著枝。The trunk supports t branches.
2. the main part of anything
3. capabilities; talents; capab skillful: 他是一位能幹的教 He is a capable instructor
4. to do; to attend to busine to manage: 這件事沒甚麼好 的。This matter is not wor doing.
5. (slang) to kill

幹部(《ㄍㄢˋ ㄅㄨˋ)
a cadre; a hardcore memb of any organization

幹不來(《ㄍㄢˋ ㄅㄨˋ ㄌㄞˊ)
cannot be done; cannot managed

幹不了(《ㄍㄢˋ ㄅㄨˋ ㄌㄧㄠˇ)
cannot be done or manage (because of incompetence)

幹不幹(《ㄍㄢˋ ㄅㄨˋ ㄍㄢˋ)
Will you do it?

幹不出(《ㄍㄢˋ ㄅㄨˋ ㄔㄨ)
cannot do (such a cruel unethical thing)

幹麼(《ㄍㄢˋ ㄇㄜ˙)
① Why? or Why (are you doing this? 他幹麼不走？Wh didn't he leave? ② What (c you do)? 你在幹麼？What a you doing?

幹得來(《ㄍㄢˋ ㄉㄜˊ ㄌㄞˊ)
can be done or managed

幹得了(《ㄍㄢˋ ㄉㄜˊ ㄌㄧㄠˇ)
can be done or manage (denoting competence)

幹的好事(《ㄍㄢˋ ㄉㄜˊ ㄏㄠˇ ㄕˋ)
① See what you have don ② How did you dare d such a thing!?

幹得出(《ㄍㄢˋ ㄉㄜˊ ㄔㄨ)
capable of, or not abov doing (a sordid or mea

act)

幹道((ㄍㄢ ㄉㄠ)or幹線((ㄍㄢ ㄒㄧㄢ)
or幹路((ㄍㄢ ㄌㄨ)
a trunk line; a main line

幹掉((ㄍㄢ ㄉㄧㄠ)
to kill or eliminate (a person)

幹頭兒((ㄍㄢ ㄊㄡ ㄦ)
worth the effort: 那事沒什麼
幹頭兒 That is not worth
the effort.

幹吏((ㄍㄢ ㄌㄧ)
a capable official!

幹練((ㄍㄢ ㄌㄧㄢ)
capable and experienced: 李
先生是一個幹練的人。Mr. Lee
is a capable and experienced
person.

幹略((ㄍㄢ ㄌㄩㄝ)
capable and full of ideas

幹活兒((ㄍㄢ ㄏㄨㄛ ㄦ)
to work; to do a job: 幹活兒
去吧! Let's get to work.

幹勁兒((ㄍㄢ ㄐㄧㄥ ㄦ)
enthusiasm; eagerness in
doing things; drive; vigor

幹器((ㄍㄢ ㄑㄧ)
capability

幹事((ㄍㄢ ㄕ)
①to manage business or
affairs; to do a job ②a
clerk; a member of an executive
committee

幹甚麼((ㄍㄢ ㄕㄜ ˙ㄇㄜ)
① What are you doing? ②
What do you want? ③ Why
(do you…)? 你幹甚麼不走?
Why don't you leave?

幹才((ㄍㄢ ㄘㄞ)
①a very capable person; a
person gifted with managing
talent ②capability

幹員((ㄍㄢ ㄩㄢ)
a very capable officer or
official

幺 部
ㄧㄠ iau yāo

【幺】 1354
(幺) ㄧㄠ iau yāo
.tiny; small; insignificant
. the youngest son or daughter of a family: 他是我們的幺

弟。He is our youngest
brother.
3. one on dice; one
4. lone; alone
5. a Chinese family name

幺麼((ㄧㄠ ㄇㄛ)
tiny; diminutive; minute

幺麼小醜((ㄧㄠ ㄇㄛ ㄒㄧㄠ ㄔㄡ)
a petty skunk; a despicable
wretch

幺妹((ㄧㄠ ㄇㄟ)
the youngest sister

幺豚((ㄧㄠ ㄊㄨㄣ)
a little pig

幺小((ㄧㄠ ㄒㄧㄠ)
diminutive; puny; minute

幺兒((ㄧㄠ ㄦ)
the youngest son

幺二三((ㄧㄠ ㄦ ㄙㄢ)
one, two, three—the lowest
combination in dice

一畫

【幻】 1355
ㄏㄨㄢ huann huàn
1.illusion; hallucination; magic;
fantasy: 別把幻想當作現實。
Don't regard illusions as
reality.
2. illusory; unreal; deceptive;
changeable

幻夢((ㄏㄨㄢ ㄇㄥ)
a daydream; a fantasy; a
fantasm: 她生活在幻夢的世界
中。She lives in a world of
fantasy.

幻滅((ㄏㄨㄢ ㄇㄧㄝ)
disillusionment

幻燈((ㄏㄨㄢ ㄉㄥ)
a magic lantern

幻燈片((ㄏㄨㄢ ㄉㄥ ㄆㄧㄢ)
a slide

幻燈機((ㄏㄨㄢ ㄉㄥ ㄐㄧ)
a slide projector

幻化((ㄏㄨㄢ ㄏㄨㄚ)
① magical change; metamorphosis
② death

幻景((ㄏㄨㄢ ㄐㄧㄥ)
a mirage; fata morgana

幻境((ㄏㄨㄢ ㄐㄧㄥ)
①a dreamland ②(said of a
Buddhist concept) the illusory
world of the mortals

幻覺((ㄏㄨㄢ ㄐㄩㄝ)
hallucination; illusion; a
fantasm; a phantasm

幻想((ㄏㄨㄢ ㄒㄧㄤ)
to daydream; to be lost in
reverie; a daydream; reverie;
a fantasy; illusion; a vision:
她沈湎於舊日的幻想中。She
fell into a reverie about the
past.

幻想曲((ㄏㄨㄢ ㄒㄧㄤ ㄑㄩ)
a fantasia or fantasy (a
form of musical composition)

幻象((ㄏㄨㄢ ㄒㄧㄤ)
a mental image; a vision; an
illusion; a phantasm or
fantasm

幻塵((ㄏㄨㄢ ㄔㄣ)
(said of a Buddhist concept)
the illusory world of the
mortals 亦作「幻境②」

幻世((ㄏㄨㄢ ㄕ)
(said of a Buddhist concept)
the illusory world of the
mortals 亦作「幻塵」

幻術((ㄏㄨㄢ ㄕㄨ)
magic; sorcery; theurgy;
thaumaturgy

幻影((ㄏㄨㄢ ㄧㄥ)
an unreal and visionary
image

二畫

【幼】 1356
ㄧㄡ yow yòu
1. young; delicate; tender; immature
2. to take care of the young

幼苗((ㄧㄡ ㄇㄧㄠ)
a tender seedling

幼發拉底河((ㄧㄡ ㄈㄚ ㄌㄚ ㄉㄧ ㄏㄜ)
the Euphrates (River)

幼童((ㄧㄡ ㄊㄨㄥ)
a young child

幼童軍((ㄧㄡ ㄊㄨㄥ ㄐㄩㄣ)
a cub scout

幼嫩((ㄧㄡ ㄋㄣ)
young and tender; delicate

幼年((ㄧㄡ ㄋㄧㄢ)
childhood: 他們從幼年開始即
爲好友。They are good
friends since childhood.

幼女((ㄧㄡ ㄋㄩ)
a young girl

幼女軍((ㄧㄡ ㄋㄩ ㄐㄩㄣ)
a brownie

幼根((ㄧㄡ ㄍㄣ)
(botany) a radicle

幼小(ㄧㄡˋ ㄒㄧㄠˇ)
young and small

幼稚 or 幼穉(ㄧㄡˋ ㄓˋ)
immature; naïve; unsophisticated

幼稚可笑(ㄧㄡˋ ㄓˋ ㄎㄜˇ ㄒㄧㄠˋ)
ridiculously childish

幼稚教育(ㄧㄡˋ ㄓˋ ㄐㄧㄠˋ ㄩˋ)
preschool education

幼稚園(ㄧㄡˋ ㄓˋ ㄩㄢˊ)
a kindergarten

幼主(ㄧㄡˋ ㄓㄨˇ)
a youthful monarch; a monarch who is crowned in childhood

幼蟲(ㄧㄡˋ ㄔㄨㄥˊ)
a larva: 蝌蚪是青蛙的幼蟲。 The tadpole is the larva of the frog.

幼弱(ㄧㄡˋ ㄖㄨㄛˋ)
young and delicate

幼子(ㄧㄡˋ ㄗˇ)
a young son

幼兒(ㄧㄡˋ ㄦˊ)
an infant; a baby

幼兒期(ㄧㄡˋ ㄦˊ ㄑㄧˊ)
infancy

幼芽(ㄧㄡˋ ㄧㄚˊ)
young buds; plumules: 樹木在生長幼芽。 The trees are unfolding their buds.

六畫

【幽】 1357
(ㄧ ㄧㄡ yōu)
1. dark; gloomy; obscure
2. lonely; solitary; secluded
3. quiet; tranquil
4. deep; profound
5. hidden; secret
6. to imprison; to confine

幽閉(ㄧㄡ ㄅㄧˋ)
①to keep in confinement; to confine ②formerly, to sterilize a woman (as punishment)

幽閉恐懼症(ㄧㄡ ㄅㄧˋ ㄎㄨㄥˇ ㄐㄩˋ ㄓㄥˋ)
claustrophobia

幽默(ㄧㄡ ㄇㄛˋ)
humorous; humor

幽默文學(ㄧㄡ ㄇㄛˋ ㄨㄣˊ ㄒㄩㄝˊ)
humorous literature

幽美(ㄧㄡ ㄇㄟˇ)
pathetically beautiful; showing melancholy beauty

幽門(ㄧㄡ ㄇㄣˊ)
(anatomy) the pylorus

幽眇(ㄧㄡ ㄇㄧㄠˇ)
①distant; remote ②exquisite and delicate

幽冥(ㄧㄡ ㄇㄧㄥˊ)
①dark; gloomy; somber; obscure ②(Buddhism) hell; the lower world

幽明異路(ㄧㄡ ㄇㄧㄥˊ ㄧˋ ㄌㄨˋ)
The dead and the living do not mix.

幽憤(ㄧㄡ ㄈㄣˋ)
the sulks; resentment; to be sulky; to sulk; to resent

幽房(ㄧㄡ ㄈㄤˊ)
a secluded inner room

幽浮(ㄧㄡ ㄈㄨˊ)
UFO (unidentified flying object)

幽獨(ㄧㄡ ㄉㄨˊ)
solitary; lonely

幽蘭(ㄧㄡ ㄌㄢˊ)
(botany) an orchid

幽流(ㄧㄡ ㄌㄧㄡˊ)
subterranean flow of water

幽囚(ㄧㄡ ㄌㄧㄡˊ)
to keep in confinement; to confine

幽靈(ㄧㄡ ㄌㄧㄥˊ)
the disembodied spirit of a dead person; a ghost: 你喜歡幽靈故事嗎? Do you like ghost stories?

幽谷(ㄧㄡ ㄍㄨˇ)
a deep valley

幽會(ㄧㄡ ㄏㄨㄟˋ)
a tryst, or secret meeting (between a couple in love)

幽婚(ㄧㄡ ㄏㄨㄣ)
the marriage between a living person and a dead person

幽魂(ㄧㄡ ㄏㄨㄣˊ)
the spirit of a dead person; a ghost

幽界(ㄧㄡ ㄐㄧㄝˋ)
the lower world; Hades

幽禁(ㄧㄡ ㄐㄧㄣˋ)
to confine; to imprison

幽靜(ㄧㄡ ㄐㄧㄥˋ)
tranquil; placid; serene

幽居(ㄧㄡ ㄐㄩ)
to live in retirement; to live away from society

幽棲(ㄧㄡ ㄑㄧ)
to live away from society

幽期(ㄧㄡ ㄑㄧˊ)
①contemplated time for retirement ②an appointment for a secret meeting (especially between a couple in love) 亦作「幽會」

幽囚(ㄧㄡ ㄑㄧㄡˊ)
to confine; to imprison; to shut up 亦作「幽禁」

幽情(ㄧㄡ ㄑㄧㄥˊ)
a pensive mood; the musing state of mind

幽閒(ㄧㄡ ㄒㄧㄢˊ)
①(said of a woman) gentle and graceful ②leisurely and carefree

幽香(ㄧㄡ ㄒㄧㄤ)
a delicate, faint fragrance

幽深(ㄧㄡ ㄕㄣ)
deep and dark

幽人(ㄧㄡ ㄖㄣˊ)
a recluse; a hermit

幽壤(ㄧㄡ ㄖㄤˇ)
the lower world; Hades

幽思(ㄧㄡ ㄙ)
sober musing; melancholy contemplation

幽邃(ㄧㄡ ㄙㄨㄟˋ)
profound; unfathomable

幽暗(ㄧㄡ ㄢˋ)
dim; gloomy

幽雅(ㄧㄡ ㄧㄚˇ)
chaste and elegant

幽咽(ㄧㄡ ㄧㄝ)
the sobs, or murmurs, of flowing water: 山間有幽咽的泉水。 There are murmuring springs in the mountain areas.

幽幽(ㄧㄡ ㄧㄡ)
①deep; profound; unfathomable ②dim

幽微(ㄧㄡ ㄨㄟ)
(said of sound, smell, etc.) obscure; weak

幽怨(ㄧㄡ ㄩㄢˋ)
hidden bitterness (of a lady frustrated in love)

九畫

【幾】 1358
1. (ㄐㄧˇ jǐ jī)
1. how many; how much
2. a few; several; some: 我已經讀過好幾遍了。 I have read it several times.

which; when

番風雨(ㄐㄧˇ ㄈㄥ ㄩˇ)
(the devastation of) a few
storms and gusts

分(ㄐㄧ ㄈㄣ)
a bit; somewhat; rather: 他有
幾分醉意。 He is a bit tipsy.

分姿色(ㄐㄧ ㄈㄣ ㄗ ㄙㄜˋ)
rather charming looks (of a
woman)

度(ㄐㄧ ㄉㄨˋ)
① several times ② how
many times ③ how many
degrees ④ several degrees

多(ㄐㄧ ㄉㄨㄛ)
how many; how much

天(ㄐㄧ ㄊㄧㄢ)
① several days: 過幾天我便回
來。 I'll be back in several
days. ② how many days

年(ㄐㄧ ㄋㄧㄢˊ)
① several years ② how many
years

何(ㄐㄧ ㄏㄜˊ)
① how much ② geometry

何畫(ㄐㄧ ㄏㄜˊ ㄏㄨㄚˋ)
a geometric pattern

何級數(ㄐㄧ ㄏㄜˊ ㄐㄧˊ ㄕㄨˋ)
a geometric progression

何學(ㄐㄧ ㄏㄜˊ ㄒㄩㄝˊ)
geometry

回(ㄐㄧ ㄏㄨㄟˊ)or幾次(ㄐㄧ ㄘˋ)
① several times; on several
occasions: 我曾見過他幾回。 I
have met him on several
occasions. ② how many
times

許(ㄐㄧ ㄒㄩˇ)
how many; how much: 不知
幾許。 No one can tell how
much.

十(ㄐㄧ ㄕˊ)
① (a few or several) dozens
of; (a few or several) scores
of ② how many tens

時(ㄐㄧ ㄕˊ)
what time; when: 你幾時能
來? When can you come?

曾(ㄐㄧ ㄗㄥˊ)
Was it ever so? 或 Has it
ever happened?

兒(ㄐㄧ ㄦ)
what time; what day; when

樣(ㄐㄧ ㄧㄤˋ)
several kinds; several
sorts; a few kinds; a few

sorts: 她買了幾樣甜點。 She
bought several kinds of desserts. ② how many kinds;
how many sorts

【幾】 1358
　ㄐㄧ ji jǐ
1. small; minute; tiny; slight
2. nearly; almost: 這兩者相去幾
希。 The two are very nearly
the same.
3. an omen; a portent

幾殆(ㄐㄧ ㄉㄞˋ)
in great danger

幾納樹(ㄐㄧ ㄋㄚˋ ㄕㄨˋ)
(botany) the cinchona

幾納霜(ㄐㄧ ㄋㄚˋ ㄕㄨㄤ)
(medicine) quinine 亦作「金雞
納霜」

幾內亞(ㄐㄧ ㄋㄟˋ ㄧㄚ)
Guinea

幾乎(ㄐㄧ ㄏㄨ)
almost; nearly: 幾乎沒有一個
人相信這消息。 Almost no one
believed the news.

幾幾乎(ㄐㄧ ㄐㄧ ㄏㄨ)
almost; nearly 參看「幾乎」

幾希(ㄐㄧ ㄒㄧ)
(said of the degree of difference) slight; little; not much

幾兆(ㄐㄧ ㄓㄠˋ)
an omen; a portent; an
augury

幾事(ㄐㄧ ㄕˋ)
details

幾微(ㄐㄧ ㄨㄟˊ)
an omen; a portent; an
augury: 他能洞察幾微。 He can
know much from the omens.

广 部
ㄧㄢˇ yean yǎn

二畫

【庀】 1359
　ㄆㄧˇ pii pǐ
to prepare; to provide; to
arrange

三畫

【庄】 1360
（莊）ㄓㄨㄤ juang
　　　zhuāng
1. a farmhouse
2. a marketplace
3. a banker (in gambling
games)
4 a cottage

四畫

【庇】 1361
　ㄅㄧˋ bih bì
to hide; to conceal; to harbor; to protect

庇冒(ㄅㄧˋ ㄇㄠˋ)
to conceal (or shield) a
defect

庇護(ㄅㄧˋ ㄏㄨˋ)
① to give protection to; to
harbor ② asylum; refuge: 他
將尋求政治庇護。 He will seek
political asylum. ③ Chinese
transliteration for Pius

庇護所(ㄅㄧˋ ㄏㄨˋ ㄙㄨㄛˇ)
a sanctuary or asylum

庇祐(ㄅㄧˋ ㄧㄡˋ)
(said of a god) to give
divine assistance to a mortal

庇廕(ㄅㄧˋ ㄧㄣˋ)
to shelter; to harbor

【庋】 1362
　ㄐㄧˇ jii jǐ
1. a cupboard; a closet
2. to put into a cupboard or
closet; to put into the proper
place; to put away; to store
up

庋置(ㄐㄧˇ ㄓˋ)
to put into the proper place;
to put away

庋藏(ㄐㄧˇ ㄘㄤˊ)
to put away for safekeeping

【序】 1363
　ㄒㄩˋ shiuh xù
1. a preface; a foreword; an
introduction
2. the sequence of things;
order: 井然有序 in perfect
order

序跋(ㄒㄩˋ ㄅㄚˊ)
the style or composition of
prefaces and postscripts

序幕(ㄒㄩˋ ㄇㄨˋ)
the prologue; the prelude;
the curtain raiser

序列(ㄒㄩˋ ㄌㄧㄝˋ)
a rank; order

【广部】

序論(ㄒㄩˋ ㄌㄨㄣˊ)
an introduction (in a piece of writing)

序曲(ㄒㄩˋ ㄑㄩˇ)
a prelude

序齒(ㄒㄩˋ ㄔˇ)
the order of seniority (in age)

序數(ㄒㄩˋ ㄕㄨˋ)
an ordinal number

序次(ㄒㄩˋ ㄘˋ)
the sequence of things; order

序言(ㄒㄩˋ ㄧㄢˊ)or序文(ㄒㄩˋ ㄨㄣˊ)
a preface; a foreword

五畫

【底】 1364
ㄉㄧˇ dii dǐ
①underside; base; bottom; basis; foundation ②the end; the last part

底版(ㄉㄧˇ ㄅㄢˇ)
a photographic plate; a negative

底本(ㄉㄧˇ ㄅㄣˇ)
①(said of a book) the master copy; the original manuscript copy ②capital (in business)

底邊(ㄉㄧˇ ㄅㄧㄢ)
the base (of a triangle, etc.)

底牌(ㄉㄧˇ ㄆㄞˊ)
cards in one's hand: 亮底牌 to show the cards in one's hand—to show one's last power or strength

底盤(ㄉㄧˇ ㄆㄢˊ)
a chassis (of an automobile, a car, a radio, etc.)

底片(ㄉㄧˇ ㄆㄧㄢˋ)
(photography) a negative

底面(ㄉㄧˇ ㄇㄧㄢˋ)
the base (of a cone, etc.)

底定(ㄉㄧˇ ㄉㄧㄥˋ)
①to establish peace in a region after an insurgence is put down ②to settle, still (disturbed waters)

底特律(ㄉㄧˇ ㄊㄜˋ ㄌㄩˋ)
Detroit, in Michigan

底裏(ㄉㄧˇ ㄌㄧˇ)
the invisible side; the inside

底格里斯河(ㄉㄧˇ ㄍㄜˊ ㄌㄧˇ ㄙ ㄏㄜˊ)
the Tigris (River)

底稿(ㄉㄧˇ ㄍㄠˇ)

a manuscript; MS. or ms.

底極(ㄉㄧˇ ㄐㄧˊ)
the ultimate point; extremity

底架(ㄉㄧˇ ㄐㄧㄚˋ)
a chassis (of an automobile, a car, a radio, etc.)

底價(ㄉㄧˇ ㄐㄧㄚˋ)
the floor or minimum price

底角(ㄉㄧˇ ㄐㄧㄠˇ)
a base angle (of a triangle, etc.)

底漆(ㄉㄧˇ ㄑㄧ)
priming (of paint); primer 亦稱「底層漆」

底缺(ㄉㄧˇ ㄑㄩㄝ)
an authorized vacancy or opening (for personnel) in a government agency

底細(ㄉㄧˇ ㄒㄧˋ)
①the unapparent details (of a matter); ins and outs ②the unknown background (of a person)

底下(ㄒㄧㄚˋ)
①(ㄉㄧˇ ㄒㄧ ㄚˋ) the underside; the downward position
②(ㄉㄧˇ ㄒㄧ ㄚˋ) mean; depraved

底下人(ㄉㄧˇ ㄒㄧ ㄚˋ ㄖㄣˊ)
servants; underlings

底線(ㄉㄧˇ ㄒㄧㄢˋ)
the base line; the bottom line

底薪(ㄉㄧˇ ㄒㄧㄣ)
base pay

底止(ㄉㄧˇ ㄓˇ)
an end; termination; a limit: 他的忍耐已達底止。He was at the end of his patience.

底滯(ㄉㄧˇ ㄓˋ)
to clog; to obstruct; to hamper; to hinder

底數(ㄉㄧˇ ㄕㄨˋ)
a base (for a logarithm)

底子(ㄉㄧˇ ˙ㄗ)or底兒(ㄉㄧˇ ㄦ)
①foundation; basis; groundwork: 他的作文底子好。He has a good basis in composition. ②a manuscript; a rough draft or sketch ③a shoe sole

底座(ㄉㄧˇ ㄗㄨㄛˋ)
a support; a base; a stand; a pedestal

底冊(ㄉㄧˇ ㄘㄜˋ)
the original copy (in bound form)

底層(ㄉㄧˇ ㄘㄥˊ)
①the bottom layer ②the ground floor

底樣(ㄉㄧˇ ㄧㄤˋ)
the original pattern (to be copied); a sample; a pattern

底蘊(ㄉㄧˇ ㄩㄣˋ)
the reality beneath the surface; inside information; the inner secret

【庖】 1365
ㄆㄠˊ paur páo
the kitchen; the cuisine

庖代(ㄆㄠˊ ㄉㄞˋ)
to act for another

庖丁(ㄆㄠˊ ㄉㄧㄥ)
a cook; a cook named Ding

庖犧(ㄆㄠˊ ㄒㄧ)or伏犧(ㄈㄨˊ ㄒㄧ)
Fu-hsi, a legendary emperor of ancient China

庖廚(ㄆㄠˊ ㄔㄨˊ)
a kitchen

【店】 1366
ㄉㄧㄢˋ diann diàn
1. a commercial establishment; a shop; a store: 他的父親開一家小店鋪。His father keeps small shop.

2. an inn; a hotel: 他住在此店中。He is stopping in this inn.

店鋪(ㄉㄧㄢˋ ㄆㄨˋ)
a store; a shop

店面(ㄉㄧㄢˋ ㄇㄧㄢˋ)
a shop front

店底(ㄉㄧㄢˋ ㄉㄧˇ)
the stock in trade

店東(ㄉㄧㄢˋ ㄉㄨㄥ)
a proprietor (of a store)

店櫃(ㄉㄧㄢˋ ㄍㄨㄟˋ)
a shop counter

店客(ㄉㄧㄢˋ ㄎㄜˋ)
a customer

店夥(ㄉㄧㄢˋ ㄏㄨㄛˇ)
a shop clerk

店家(ㄉㄧㄢˋ ㄐㄧㄚ)
a manager (of an inn, shop etc.): 店家對顧客慇勤招待。The manager of the shop serves the customer enthusiastically.

店錢(ㄉㄧㄢˋ ㄑㄧㄢˊ)
inn expenses; the cost of lodging; a hotel bill

店小二(ㄉㄧㄢˋ ㄒㄧㄠˇ ㄦ)
a waiter (in an inn or tavern)

与主(ㄐㄩˇ ㄓㄨˇ)
a proprietor (of a store or shop)亦作「店東」

与肆(ㄐㄩˇ ㄙˋ)
a shop; a store; a firm

与務(ㄐㄩˇ ㄨˋ)
routine work in a store or shop

与員(ㄐㄩˇ ㄩㄢˊ)
a shop clerk; a shopman; a salesman or saleswoman: 他是那百貨公司的店員。He is a clerk of that department store.

【庚】 1367
《ㄥ geng gēng
1. the seventh of the Ten Celestial Stems (天干)
2. the age (of a person): 請問貴庚? May I know your age?

庚帖(ㄍㄥ ㄊㄧㄝˇ)
a card containing the horoscopes of a betrothed couple

庚子賠款(ㄍㄥ ㄗˇ ㄆㄟˊ ㄎㄨㄢˇ)
the indemnities for the Boxer Uprising; Boxer Indemnity

庚子之役(ㄍㄥ ㄗˇ ㄓ ㄧˋ)
the Boxer Uprising or Rebellion (against foreign aggressors in 1900, as a result of which, China was forced to make economic and territorial concessions)

【府】 1368
ㄈㄨˇ fuu fǔ
1. a mansion
2. a government agency; a government office
3. an administrative district in former times; a prefecture
4. your home
5. a treasury; archives

府邸(ㄈㄨˇ ㄉㄧˇ)
a mansion

府第(ㄈㄨˇ ㄉㄧˋ)
a mansion 亦作「府邸」

府帑(ㄈㄨˇ ㄊㄤˇ)
the money in the treasury

府庫(ㄈㄨˇ ㄎㄨˋ)
a treasury for public funds

府君(ㄈㄨˇ ㄐㄩㄣ)
①(formerly) the magistrate of a prefecture ②a reference to one's ancestors

府學(ㄈㄨˇ ㄒㄩㄝˊ)
a prefectural school (in former times)

府治(ㄈㄨˇ ㄓˋ)
the seat of a prefectural government during the Ming and Ching dynasties

府綢(ㄈㄨˇ ㄔㄡˊ)
a kind of stiff silk fabric produced in Shantung Province; poplin; pongee

府試(ㄈㄨˇ ㄕˋ)
a prefectural examination under the former system of civil service examinations

府上(ㄈㄨˇ ㄕㄤˋ)
①your native place ②your home ③your family.

六畫

【度】 1369
1. ㄉㄨˋ duh dù
1. an instrument for measuring length
2. a kilowatt-hour
3. a unit of measurement for angles, temperature, etc.; a degree: 直角為九十度。A right angle is an angle of 90 degrees.
4. (number of) times: 他曾數度前往巴黎。He has been to Paris several times.
5. a system: 該公司制度健全。This company has a sound system.
6. a manner; bearing: 這青年風度翩翩。This youth has a charming manner.
7. to pass: 他將在何處度暑假? Where will he pass the summer holidays?
8. consideration; careful thought: 我把生死置之度外。I have given no thought to personal safety.

度命(ㄉㄨˋ ㄇㄧㄥˋ)
to make a living

度牒(ㄉㄨˋ ㄉㄧㄝˊ)
the certificate issued to a Buddhist monk or nun at the time of ordainment

度量(ㄉㄨˋ ㄌㄧㄤˋ)
①an instrument for measuring ②the capacity for forgiveness; the degree of magnanimity

度量衡(ㄉㄨˋ ㄌㄧㄤˋ ㄏㄥˊ)
weights and measures

度假(ㄉㄨˋ ㄐㄧㄚˋ)

---

to spend one's holidays (or vacation); to go vacationing

度曲(ㄉㄨˋ ㄑㄩˇ)
①to sing in accordance with the score ②to compose tunes

度支(ㄉㄨˋ ㄓ)
an official in charge of the nation's finance

度世(ㄉㄨˋ ㄕˋ)
to transcend the worldly life (as a Buddhist way of salvation)

度數(ㄉㄨˋ ㄕㄨˋ)
a reading (of a barometer, thermometer, water meter, etc.)

度日(ㄉㄨˋ ㄖˋ)
to make a living (usually said of poorly-paid jobs)

度日如年(ㄉㄨˋ ㄖˋ ㄖㄨˊ ㄋㄧㄢˊ)
to pass days as if they were years (because of deep anxiety, worries, or misery)

度外(ㄉㄨˋ ㄨㄞˋ)
outside one's consideration

度越(ㄉㄨˋ ㄩㄝˋ)
to transcend; to surpass; to exceed

【度】 1369
2. ㄉㄨㄛˊ duoh duó
to consider; to measure; to infer

度德量力(ㄉㄨㄛˊ ㄉㄜˊ ㄌㄧㄤˋ ㄌㄧˋ)
to act with due consideration of one's own abilities

【庠】 1370
ㄒㄧㄤˊ shyang xiáng
a school during the Chou Dynasty

庠序(ㄒㄧㄤˊ ㄒㄩˋ)
schools

庠生(ㄒㄧㄤˊ ㄕㄥ)
a student of a prefectural or county school in former times

【庥】 1371
ㄒㄧㄡ shiou xiū
to shelter; to protect

七畫

【座】 1372
ㄗㄨㄛˋ tzuoh zuò
a seat; a stand: 請入座。Please take your seat.

座標 or 坐標(ㄗㄨㄛˋ ㄅㄧㄠ)

〔广部〕

（广部）

(mathematics) coordinates

座談(ㄗㄨㄛˋ ㄊㄢˊ)
to have an informal discussion

座談會(ㄗㄨㄛˋ ㄊㄢˊ ㄏㄨㄟˋ)
a discussion meeting; a symposium; a panel discussion

座落(ㄗㄨㄛˋ ㄌㄨㄛˋ)
to be situated or located at; a site or locality 亦作「坐落」

座前(ㄗㄨㄛˋ ㄑㄧㄢˊ)
a conventional phrase placed after the salutation in a letter addressed to one's senior

座像(ㄗㄨㄛˋ ㄒㄧㄤˋ)
a seated portrait or statue

座上客(ㄗㄨㄛˋ ㄕㄤˋ ㄎㄜˋ)
a guest of honor

座次(ㄗㄨㄛˋ ㄘˋ)
seating order

座兒(ㄗㄨㄛˋ ㄦ)
a seat

座右銘(ㄗㄨㄛˋ ㄧㄡˋ ㄇㄧㄥˊ)
a motto: 「天助自助」是一句很好的座右銘。"God helps those who help themselves" is a good motto.

座無虛席(ㄗㄨㄛˋ ㄨˊ ㄒㄩ ㄒㄧˊ)
There is standing room only.

座位(ㄗㄨㄛˋ ㄨㄟˋ)
a seat

【庫】 1373
ㄎㄨˋ kuh kù
1. a storeroom; a storehouse; a warehouse; a granary: 我們的貨物已經入庫。Our goods are already in the granary.
2. a treasury: 海洋是礦物和食物的寶庫。The sea is a treasury of minerals and food.

庫兵(ㄎㄨˋ ㄅㄧㄥ)
the troops guarding the national treasury (in the Ching Dynasty)

庫部(ㄎㄨˋ ㄅㄨˋ)
(in ancient China) a department under the Defense Ministry, in charge of arms and supplies

庫平(ㄎㄨˋ ㄆㄧㄥˊ)
(in ancient China) a scale used by the national treasury as a standard in taxation

庫房(ㄎㄨˋ ㄈㄤˊ)
a storeroom; a storehouse; a warehouse

庫倫(ㄎㄨˋ ㄌㄨㄣˊ)
Kulun, or Ulan Bator, or Ulan Bator Khoto, in Mongolia

庫券(ㄎㄨˋ ㄑㄩㄢˋ)
government reserve notes (as distinct from banknotes issued by a commercial bank); treasury notes

庫收(ㄎㄨˋ ㄕㄡ)
the receipts of the treasury

庫容(ㄎㄨˋ ㄖㄨㄥˊ)
storage capacity

庫藏(ㄎㄨˋ ㄘㄤˊ)
the contents of a storeroom

庫存(ㄎㄨˋ ㄘㄨㄣˊ)
a stock; reserve: 這家公司有大量庫存貨物。This company has a large stock of commodities.

庫頁島(ㄎㄨˋ ㄧㄝˋ ㄉㄠˇ)
Sakhalin

庫銀(ㄎㄨˋ ㄧㄣˊ)
the silver money minted by the government

【庭】 1374
ㄊㄧㄥˊ tyng tíng
1. a hall
2. a yard
3. the imperial court
4. a court of justice: 這件案子將在庭外和解。The case will be settled out of court.

庭決(ㄊㄧㄥˊ ㄐㄩㄝˊ)
to hand down a sentence summarily

庭訓(ㄊㄧㄥˊ ㄒㄩㄣˋ)
exhortation or admonition from one's father

庭長(ㄊㄧㄥˊ ㄓㄤˇ)
a chief justice; a presiding judge; the president of a law court

庭中(ㄊㄧㄥˊ ㄓㄨㄥ)
in the yard

庭除(ㄊㄧㄥˊ ㄔㄨˊ)
the ground before the steps leading to the hall of a house

庭舍(ㄊㄧㄥˊ ㄕㄜˋ)
a house

庭上(ㄊㄧㄥˊ ㄕㄤˋ)
① in court, (of justice) ② at (imperial) court

庭議(ㄊㄧㄥˊ ㄧˋ)

a court meeting

庭闈(ㄊㄧㄥˊ ㄨㄟˊ)
① parents' abode ② parents

庭園(ㄊㄧㄥˊ ㄩㄢˊ)
a garden

庭院(ㄊㄧㄥˊ ㄩㄢˋ)
a courtyard; a garden

八畫

【庵】 1375
ㄢ an ān
1. a hut; a cottage
2. a nunnery

庵堂(ㄢ ㄊㄤˊ)
a nunnery; a convent

庵主(ㄢ ㄓㄨˇ)
the superior (of a convent or nunnery)

庵寺(ㄢ ㄙˋ)
① a nunnery ② a temple

【庶】 1376
ㄕㄨˋ shuh shù
1. born of a concubine
2. numerous; various; populous
3. general; common
4. the common people; the commoners
5. almost; nearly

庶民(ㄕㄨˋ ㄇㄧㄣˊ) or 庶眾(ㄕㄨˋ ㄓㄨㄥˋ) or 庶人(ㄕㄨˋ ㄖㄣˊ)
the common people; the commoners; the multitude; the populace; the masses

庶母(ㄕㄨˋ ㄇㄨˇ)
one's father's concubine

庶婦(ㄕㄨˋ ㄈㄨˋ)
the wives of a concubine's children

庶孽(ㄕㄨˋ ㄋㄧㄝˋ)
the son of a concubine

庶女(ㄕㄨˋ ㄋㄩˇ)
a commoner's daughter

庶類(ㄕㄨˋ ㄌㄟˋ)
a multitude of things or beings

庶黎(ㄕㄨˋ ㄌㄧˊ)
the common people; the multitude; the masses

庶官(ㄕㄨˋ ㄍㄨㄢ)
officials of all ranks

庶乎(ㄕㄨˋ ㄏㄨ)
① almost; nearly ② probably; maybe

庶幾(ㄕㄨˋ ㄐㄧ)
① almost; nearly ② probably; maybe ③ the capable

and the virtuous

吉士 (ㄐㄧˊ ㄕˋ)
one of the official titles conferred on those who have passed the annual civil service examination with high grades during the Ming and Ching dynasties

羞 (ㄒㄧㄡ)
the various kinds of delicacies

長 (ㄔㄤˊ ㄓㄤˇ)
①the eldest son of a concubine ②an official title during the Chin and Han dynasties

政 (ㄓㄥˋ)
the numerous affairs of the state

出 (ㄔㄨ)
the offspring of a concubine

事 (ㄕˋ)
general affairs

子 (ㄗˇ)
①the son of a concubine ②an ancient official title

孫 (ㄙㄨㄣ)
the grandson of a concubine

務 (ㄨˋ)
general affairs

務員 (ㄨˋ ㄩㄢˊ)
a general affairs clerk

【康】 1377
ㄎㄤ kang kāng

1. healthy: 孩子們看來很健康. The children look very healthy.
2. peaceful
3. abundant
4. level, even and smooth (road, etc.)
5. a Chinese family name

康復 (ㄎㄤ ㄈㄨˋ)
recovery (from illness): 祝你早日康復. I wish you a speedy recovery.

康德 (ㄎㄤ ㄉㄜˊ)
Immanuel Kant (1724-1804), German philosopher

康定 (ㄎㄤ ㄉㄧㄥˋ)
Kangting, capital of Sikang Province

康泰 (ㄎㄤ ㄊㄞˋ)
healthy and free from trouble

康涅狄克 (ㄎㄤ ㄋㄧㄝˋ ㄉㄧˊ ㄎㄜˋ)
the state of Connecticut,

U.S.A.

康年 (ㄎㄤ ㄋㄧㄢˊ)
an abundant year; a plentiful year

康寧 (ㄎㄤ ㄋㄧㄥˊ)
healthy and undisturbed

康樂 (ㄎㄤ ㄌㄜˋ)
①(wholesome) recreation ②peace and happiness: 敬祝康樂. I wish you peace and happiness.

康健 (ㄎㄤ ㄐㄧㄢˋ)
in good health; healthy

康強 (ㄎㄤ ㄑㄧㄤˊ)
healthy and strong

康衢 (ㄎㄤ ㄑㄩˊ)
a level and easy highway

康熙字典 (ㄎㄤ ㄒㄧ ㄗˋ ㄉㄧㄢˇ)
Kang Hsi Tzu Tien (a 42-volume dictionary compiled during the reign of Kang Hsi in the Ching Dynasty)

康莊大道 (ㄎㄤ ㄓㄨㄤ ㄉㄚˋ ㄉㄠˋ)
a level and easy thoroughfare leading to many places

康有為 (ㄎㄤ ㄧㄡˇ ㄨㄟˊ)
Kang Yu-wei, a scholar who advocated political reform during the reign of Emperor Kwang Hsü (光緒) of the Ching Dynasty

【庸】 1378
ㄩㄥ iong yōng
(又讀 ㄩㄥ yong yōng)

1. mediocre; common
2. stupid
3. a hired laborer
4. to require; need
5. to reward
6. an interrogative (as how, etc.)

庸民 (ㄩㄥ ㄇㄧㄣˊ)
the common people; the masses

庸夫愚婦 (ㄩㄥ ㄈㄨ ㄩˊ ㄈㄨˋ)
simple, ignorant people

庸碌 (ㄩㄥ ㄌㄨˋ)or庸庸碌碌 (ㄩㄥ ㄩㄥ ㄌㄨˋ ㄌㄨˋ)
mediocre; common

庸詎 (ㄩㄥ ㄐㄩˋ)or庸孰 (ㄩㄥ ㄕㄨˊ)
an interrogative in formal text—how; is it not

庸行 (ㄩㄥ ㄒㄧㄥˊ)
a regular course of action

庸虛 (ㄩㄥ ㄒㄩ)
mediocre and incapable

(usually said of oneself in self-depreciation)

庸中佼佼 (ㄩㄥ ㄓㄨㄥ ㄐㄧㄠˇ ㄐㄧㄠˇ)
a giant among many dwarfs—outstanding

庸豎 (ㄩㄥ ㄕㄨˋ)
a mediocre person

庸人 (ㄩㄥ ㄖㄣˊ)
a mediocre person

庸人自擾 (ㄩㄥ ㄖㄣˊ ㄗˋ ㄖㄠˇ)
(literally) Stupid people create trouble for themselves.

庸才 (ㄩㄥ ㄘㄞˊ)
a man of mediocre ability

庸俗 (ㄩㄥ ㄙㄨˊ)
vulgar; unrefined

庸闇 (ㄩㄥ ㄢˋ)
stupidity; ignorance; ignorant

庸醫 (ㄩㄥ ㄧ)
①a quack doctor; a quack; a charlatan ②a term used to scold a doctor who makes mistakes in treatment

庸醫殺人 (ㄩㄥ ㄧ ㄕㄚ ㄖㄣˊ)
homicide by quackery

庸言庸行 (ㄩㄥ ㄧㄢˊ ㄩㄥ ㄒㄧㄥˊ)
commonplace words and deeds

【庹】 1379
ㄊㄨㄛˇ tuoo tuǒ
the distance between one's two middle fingertips when one outstretches one's arms

九畫

【庾】 1380
ㄩˇ yeu yǔ

1. an enclosed place for storing grain
2. a unit of an ancient measure of capacity, equivalent to 16 decaliters
3. a Chinese family name

庾信 (ㄩˇ ㄒㄧㄣˋ)
Yü Hsin (513-581 A.D.), a man of letters in the Epoch of Division Between North and South

【廁】 1381
1. ㄘㄜˋ tseh cè
a toilet, lavatory or latrine

廁所 (ㄘㄜˋ ㄙㄨㄛˇ)
a water closet; a toilet; a lavatory; a rest room; a latrine; a men's room;

〔广部〕

【广
部】

women's room

【厠】 1381
2. ㄘ tsyh cì
to mingle with; to be a member of

厠身社會(ㄔㄣ ㄕㄣ ㄕㄜˋ ㄏㄨㄟˋ)
to be a member of society

厠足其間(ㄔㄗㄨˊ ㄑㄧˊ ㄐㄧㄢ)
to participate in; to be directly concerned

【厠】 1381
3. ㄙ syh sì
used only in 茅厠—a latrine, lavatory, etc.

【厢】 1382
ㄒㄧㄤ shiang xiāng
1. the wing (of a building); a side room
2. a box in the theater
3. the vicinity or outskirts of a city

厢兵(ㄒㄧㄤ ㄅㄧㄥ)or 厢軍(ㄒㄧㄤ ㄐㄩㄣ)
the garrison troops of the Tang and Sung dynasties

厢房(ㄒㄧㄤ ㄈㄤˊ)or 厢屋(ㄒㄧㄤ ㄨ)
a side room

十　畫

【廈】 1383
ㄒㄧㄚˋ shiah xià
(語音 ㄕㄚˋ shà)
a tall building; an edifice

廈門(ㄒㄧㄚˊ ㄇㄣˊ)
Amoy, a port city in Fukien Province

【廉】 1384
ㄌㄧㄢˊ lian lián
1. incorrupt; incorruptible; honest; upright
2. inexpensive; cheap
3. to examine; to inspect
4. a Chinese family name

廉白(ㄌㄧㄢˊ ㄅㄞˊ)
immaculate

廉頗(ㄌㄧㄢˊ ㄆㄛ)
Lien Po, a general of the state of Chao during the Warring States period

廉明(ㄌㄧㄢˊ ㄇㄧㄥˊ)
(said of officials) incorruptible and intelligent; clean-handed and clearheaded

廉俸(ㄌㄧㄢˊ ㄈㄥˋ)
extra allowances paid to government officials in addition to regular salaries during the Ching Dynasty

廉得其情(ㄌㄧㄢˊ ㄉㄜˊ ㄑㄧˊ ㄑㄧㄥˊ)
to learn the truth after investigation

廉吏(ㄌㄧㄢˊ ㄌㄧˋ)
an incorrupt official

廉價(ㄌㄧㄢˊ ㄐㄧㄚˋ)
a low price

廉價物(ㄌㄧㄢˊ ㄐㄧㄚˋ ㄨˋ)or 廉價貨物(ㄌㄧㄢˊ ㄐㄧㄚˋ ㄏㄨㄛˋ ㄨˋ)
cheap goods; a bargain

廉節(ㄌㄧㄢˊ ㄐㄧㄝˊ)
frugal; thrifty

廉潔(ㄌㄧㄢˊ ㄐㄧㄝˊ)
incorrupt; incorruptible; honest; disinterestedness and purity

廉介(ㄌㄧㄢˊ ㄐㄧㄝˋ)
incorrupt and uncompromising

廉直(ㄌㄧㄢˊ ㄓˊ)
honest and upright

廉恥(ㄌㄧㄢˊ ㄔˇ)
the integrity of character and a sense of honor

廉察(ㄌㄧㄢˊ ㄔㄚˊ)
to inspect; to investigate; to examine

廉士(ㄌㄧㄢˊ ㄕˋ)
a man of principle: 廉吏必為廉士。An incorrupt official must be a man of principle.

廉售(ㄌㄧㄢˊ ㄕㄡˋ)
to sell at a low price

廉讓(ㄌㄧㄢˊ ㄖㄤˋ)
to sell (property) at a low price: 他廉讓他的車子。He sold his car at a low price.

廉隅(ㄌㄧㄢˊ ㄩˊ)
punctilious; scrupulous

廉遠堂高(ㄌㄧㄢˊ ㄩㄢˇ ㄊㄤˊ ㄍㄠ)
(said of a monarch) dignified

【廊】 1385
ㄌㄤˊ lang láng
a portico; a corridor; a hallway: 她站在走廊上。She stood in the corridor.

廊廟(ㄌㄤˊ ㄇㄧㄠˋ)
the court (of a monarch)

廊廟器(ㄌㄤˊ ㄇㄧㄠˋ ㄑㄧˋ)
capacity for administering the affairs of state

廊廟之志(ㄌㄤˊ ㄇㄧㄠˋ ㄓ ㄓˋ)
political aspiration or ambition

廊房(ㄌㄤˊ ㄈㄤˊ)
houses built by the government near the city towers in Peiping and leased to the people during the Ming Dynasty

廊下(ㄌㄤˊ ㄒㄧㄚˋ)
a corridor; a portico; a hallway

廊子(ㄌㄤˊ ˙ㄗ)
a corridor; a portico; a hallway

廊腰(ㄌㄤˊ ㄧㄠ)
the corner of a corridor

廊簷(ㄌㄤˊ ㄧㄢˊ)
a portico

【廋】 1386
ㄙㄡ sou sōu
1. to conceal; to hide
2. to search

廋疏(ㄙㄡ ㄕㄨ)
to search

廋辭(ㄙㄡ ㄘˊ)
a riddle; a puzzle; an enigma

廋語(ㄙㄡ ㄩˇ)
a riddle; a puzzle; an enigma

十一畫

【廄】 1387
ㄐㄧㄡˋ jiow jiù
a stable

廄肥(ㄐㄧㄡˋ ㄈㄟˊ)
the animal refuse used as fertilizer

廄卒(ㄐㄧㄡˋ ㄗㄨˊ)
a groom

【廖】 1388
ㄌㄧㄠˋ liaw liào
a Chinese family name

【廑】 1389
ㄐㄧㄣˇ jiin jǐn
1. a hut; a cottage
2. eager

廑心(ㄐㄧㄣˇ ㄒㄧㄣ)
eager attention or concern

廑注(ㄐㄧㄣˇ ㄓㄨˋ)
eager attention or concern

【廓】 1390
ㄎㄨㄛˋ kuoh kuò
1. open; wide
2. empty

廓土(ㄎㄨㄛˋ ㄊㄨˇ)
an open ground

廓落(ㄎㄨㄛˋ ㄌㄨㄛˋ)
wide; open

廓清(ㄌㄨˋ ㄑㄧㄥ)
to liquidate; to clean up; to wipe out

廓然(ㄌㄨˋ ㄖㄢˊ)
① spacious ② vast; boundless ③ unprejudiced; unbiased

廓爾喀(ㄌㄨˋㄦˇㄎㄚ)
① the Gurkha people of Nepal ② old name of Nepal

廕 1391
ㄧㄣˋ yinn yin
to shelter; to harbor; to protect

廕庇(ㄧㄣˋㄅㄧˋ)
to protect; to shelter; to harbor; protection; shelter

廕監(ㄧㄣˋㄐㄧㄢ)
(Ching Dynasty) the system in which the offspring of distinguished officials admitted to the Imperial Academy in recognition of the latter's contribution

廕生(ㄧㄣˋㄕㄥ)
(Ching Dynasty) the offspring of distinguished officials admitted to the Imperial Academy in recognition of the latter's contribution

十二畫

廚 1392
ㄔㄨˊ chwu chú
a kitchen; a cookroom

a closet; a chest; a wardrobe; a cupboard

廚房(ㄔㄨˊㄈㄤˊ)
a kitchen

廚夫(ㄔㄨˊㄈㄨ)or廚子(ㄔㄨˊ˙ㄗ)
a chef; a cook

廚娘(ㄔㄨˊㄋㄧㄤˊ)
a female cook; a kitchen-maid

廚櫃(ㄔㄨˊㄍㄨㄟˋ)
a closet; a chest; a cupboard

廚具(ㄔㄨˊㄐㄩˋ)
kitchen utensils

廚師傅(ㄔㄨˊㄕ˙ㄈㄨ)or廚司務(ㄔㄨˊㄙㄨˋ)
a chef; a cook

廛 1393
ㄔㄢˊ charn chán
a living space for one family in ancient times

a store; a shop

廛肆(ㄔㄢˊㄙˋ)
a store; a shop

廝 1394
ㄙ sy sī
1. a servant; a person who performs mean labor
2. a fellow; a guy
3. each other; together

廝伴(ㄙㄅㄢˋ)
to keep (a person) company

廝併(ㄙㄅㄧㄥˋ)
to fight desperately

廝打(ㄙㄉㄚˇ)
to have a melee; to fight

廝徒(ㄙㄊㄨˊ)or廝僕(ㄙㄆㄨˊ)or廝隸(ㄙㄌㄧˋ)or廝役(ㄙㄧˋ)or廝養(ㄙㄧㄤˋ)
the servants performing mean duties

廝鬧(ㄙㄋㄠˋ)
to have a spree

廝濫(ㄙㄌㄢˋ)
meanness; baseness

廝共(ㄙㄍㄨㄥˋ)
in company with each other; together

廝會(ㄙㄏㄨㄟˋ)
to meet each other

廝混(ㄙㄏㄨㄣˋ)
① to mix with each other; to mingle ② to fool around together ③ to make trouble

廝見(ㄙㄐㄧㄢˋ)
to see each other

廝下(ㄙㄒㄧㄚˋ)
a mean or lowly position

廝纏(ㄙㄔㄢˊ)
to tangle with each other

廝殺(ㄙㄕㄚ)
to slaughter one another (as in a battle); to fight at close quarters (with weapons)

廝舍(ㄙㄕㄜˋ)
the living quarters of people who perform mean labor

廝守(ㄙㄕㄡˇ)
to wait upon each other; to take care of each other

廝認(ㄙㄖㄣˋ)
to recognize each other

廟 1395
ㄇㄧㄠˋ miaw miào
a temple; a shrine: 廟是奉祀神的地方。A temple is a building used for offering sacrifices to a god or gods.

廟堂(ㄇㄧㄠˋㄊㄤˊ)
① the ancestral temple of the royal family ② the court (of a monarch)

廟堂文學(ㄇㄧㄠˋㄊㄤˊㄨㄣˊㄒㄩㄝˊ)
court literature

廟廊(ㄇㄧㄠˋㄌㄤˊ)
the imperial court

廟算(ㄇㄧㄠˋㄙㄨㄢˋ)or廟算(ㄇㄧㄠˋㄙㄨㄢˋ)
decision made at court (of the monarch)

廟號(ㄇㄧㄠˋㄏㄠˋ)
the posthumous title of an emperor

廟會(ㄇㄧㄠˋㄏㄨㄟˋ)
a fair held at the site of a temple when the faithful converge to worship the deity: 他們去趕廟會了。They went to the temple fair.

廟諱(ㄇㄧㄠˋㄏㄨㄟˋ)
name of a deceased emperor

廟寢(ㄇㄧㄠˋㄑㄧㄣˇ)
the imperial ancestral temple

廟主(ㄇㄧㄠˋㄓㄨˇ)
the head priest of a temple

廟祝(ㄇㄧㄠˋㄓㄨˋ)
a person whose duty is to keep incense burning at a temple; a temple attendant

廟策(ㄇㄧㄠˋㄘㄜˋ)
the planning made at the imperial court

廟議(ㄇㄧㄠˋㄧˋ)
deliberation at (imperial) court

廟宇(ㄇㄧㄠˋㄩˇ)
a temple; a shrine

廠 1396
ㄔㄤˇ chaang chǎng
a factory; a plant; a workshop

廠棚(ㄔㄤˇㄆㄥˊ)
a crude plant or factory building

廠房(ㄔㄤˇㄈㄤˊ)
a factory building

廠房設計(ㄔㄤˇㄈㄤˊㄕㄜˋㄐㄧˋ)
a plant designing

廠條(ㄔㄤˇㄊㄧㄠˊ)
the silver ingots minted by the government mint in the early republican days, each worth 1,000 silver coins; gold ingots

（广部）

【广
部】

廠址(彳ㄤ ㄓˇ)
a factory address; a factory site or location

廠長(彳ㄤ ㄓㄤˇ)
a factory manager; a plant superintendent

廠主(彳ㄤ ㄓㄨˇ)
a factory owner; a mill owner

廠房設備(彳ㄤ ㄈㄤˊ ㄕㄜˋ ㄅㄟˋ)
plant equipment

廠商(彳ㄤ ㄕㄤ)
manufacturers

廠營(彳ㄤ ㄧㄥˊ)
the temporary barracks for troops

【廡】 1397
ㄨˇ wuǔ wǔ
1. small rooms around a main building
2. (said of vegetation) dense or luxuriant

【廢】 1398
ㄈㄟˋ fey fèi
1. to give up; to abandon; to discontinue; to abolish: 做事不要半途而廢。Don't give up halfway in doing anything.
2. to reject: 不以人廢言。Do not reject an opinion because of the speaker.
3. useless; disused: 我家門前有一口廢井。In front of my house there is a disused well.
4. disabled

廢票(ㄈㄟˋ ㄆㄧㄠˋ)
①an invalidated ballot ②a used ticket

廢品(ㄈㄟˋ ㄆㄧㄣˇ)
①a waste product ②scrap; waste

廢品回收(ㄈㄟˋ ㄆㄧㄣˇ ㄏㄨㄟˊ ㄕㄡ)
waste recovery

廢帝(ㄈㄟˋ ㄉㄧˋ)
a dethroned emperor

廢掉(ㄈㄟˋ ㄉㄧㄠˋ)
to abolish; to abrogate

廢鐵(ㄈㄟˋ ㄊㄧㄝˇ)
scrap iron

廢料(ㄈㄟˋ ㄌㄧㄠˋ)
useless materials; scrap materials; waste materials 參看「廢品」

廢后(ㄈㄟˋ ㄏㄡˋ)
a dethroned queen; a queen divorced by the monarch; an ex-empress or ex-queen

廢話(ㄈㄟˋ ㄏㄨㄚˋ)
a superfluous statement; a meaningless remark; rubbish; nonsense: 少廢話! No more nonsense!

廢疾(ㄈㄟˋ ㄐㄧˊ)
①an incapacitating disease; an incurable disease ②a disabled person

廢氣(ㄈㄟˋ ㄑㄧˋ)
waste gas; exhaust

廢棄(ㄈㄟˋ ㄑㄧˋ)
to abandon as useless; to scrap; to discard

廢寢忘餐(ㄈㄟˋ ㄑㄧㄣˇ ㄨㄤˋ ㄘㄢ)
so absorbed (in a pursuit) as to neglect sleep and meals

廢墟(ㄈㄟˋ ㄒㄩ)
ruins (of a city, castle, etc.)

廢學(ㄈㄟˋ ㄒㄩㄝˊ)
to discontinue one's education

廢止(ㄈㄟˋ ㄓˇ)
to abolish; to cancel; to abrogate; to annul; to repeal; to rescind; to discontinue

廢紙(ㄈㄟˋ ㄓˇ)
wastepaper; a scrap of paper

廢置不用(ㄈㄟˋ ㄓˋ ㄅㄨˋ ㄩㄥˋ)
to shelve or put aside as useless

廢除(ㄈㄟˋ ㄔㄨˊ)
to abolish; to cancel; to annul; to abrogate; to repeal; to rescind; to discontinue: 不平等條約應該被廢除。All unequal treaties should be abrogated.

廢弛(ㄈㄟˋ ㄔˊ)or(ㄈㄟˋ ㄕˊ)
to neglect

廢水(ㄈㄟˋ ㄕㄨㄟˇ)
waste water; liquid waste

廢水處理(ㄈㄟˋ ㄕㄨㄟˇ ㄔㄨˇ ㄌㄧˇ)
waste water treatment

廢人(ㄈㄟˋ ㄖㄣˊ)
a disabled person

廢業(ㄈㄟˋ ㄧㄝˋ)
to give up a business; to neglect one's work

廢物(ㄈㄟˋ ㄨˋ)
①waste material; rubbish; scrap; ②a good-for-nothing

廢物利用(ㄈㄟˋ ㄨˋ ㄌㄧˋ ㄩㄥˋ)
the utilization of waste material

【廣】 1399
《ㄨㄤˇ goang guǎng
1. wide; broad; spacious; extensive
2. to stretch; to extend
3. Kwangtung or Kwangsi

廣播(《ㄨㄤˇ ㄅㄛ)or(《ㄨㄤˇ ㄅㄛˋ)
①to broadcast; to telecast ②a broadcast

廣播電臺(《ㄨㄤˇ ㄅㄛ ㄉㄧㄢˋ ㄊㄞˊ)
a broadcasting station; radio station

廣播公司(《ㄨㄤˇ ㄅㄛ 《ㄨㄥ ㄙ)
a broadcasting company

廣播節(《ㄨㄤˇ ㄅㄛ ㄐㄧㄝˊ)
Broadcasting Day (falling on March 26 annually)

廣播節目(《ㄨㄤˇ ㄅㄛ ㄐㄧㄝˊ ㄇㄨˋ)
①a radio program; a broadcast: 你喜歡那一項廣播節目? What is your favorite radio program? ②a television program; a telecast

廣播劇(《ㄨㄤˇ ㄅㄛ ㄐㄩˋ)
a radio drama; a radio play

廣播網(《ㄨㄤˇ ㄅㄛ ㄨㄤˇ)
a broadcasting network

廣播員(《ㄨㄤˇ ㄅㄛ ㄩㄢˊ)
a radio announcer; a broadcaster

廣博(《ㄨㄤˇ ㄅㄛˊ)
wide; extensive: 他對這主題有廣博的知識。His knowledge of this subject is extensive.

廣被(《ㄨㄤˇ ㄅㄟˋ)
far-reaching (love or benefit)

廣漠(《ㄨㄤˇ ㄇㄛˋ)
boundless; vast

廣袤(《ㄨㄤˇ ㄇㄠˋ)
length and breadth (of land); area

廣泛(《ㄨㄤˇ ㄈㄢˋ)
extensive; comprehensive; widespread

廣方言館(《ㄨㄤˇ ㄈㄤ ㄧㄢˊ 《ㄨㄢˇ)
a school for training translators, set up in Shanghai by Li Hung-chang (李鴻章) during the Ching Dynasty

廣大(《ㄨㄤˇ ㄉㄚˋ)
vast

廣大無邊(《ㄨㄤˇ ㄉㄚˋ ㄨˊ ㄅㄧㄢ)
boundless: 廣大無邊的海洋 boundless ocean

廣島(《ㄨㄤ ㄉㄠˇ)
Hiroshima, Japan

廣度(《ㄨㄤ ㄉㄨˋ)
scope; range

廣東(《ㄨㄤ ㄉㄨㄥ)
Kwangtung Province

廣庭(《ㄨㄤ ㄊㄧㄥˊ)
①a large yard or garden ②
a public place

廣土衆民(《ㄨㄤ ㄊㄨˇ ㄓㄨㄥˋ ㄇㄧㄣˊ)
(said of a country) having a
large territory and a large
population

廣內(《ㄨㄤ ㄋㄟˋ)
the royal library in the Han
Dynasty

廣陵散(《ㄨㄤ ㄌㄧㄥˊ ㄙㄢˇ)
(originally) name of a piece
of Chinese harp music—any
ancient learning or skill
that has not been handed
down to posterity; a lost
art

廣告(《ㄨㄤ ㄍㄠˋ)
advertisement

廣告部(《ㄨㄤ ㄍㄠˋ ㄅㄨˋ)
the advertising department
(of a commercial firm)

廣告牌(《ㄨㄤ ㄍㄠˋ ㄆㄞˊ)
a billboard

廣告片(《ㄨㄤ ㄍㄠˋ ㄆㄧㄢˋ)
an advertising film

廣告費(《ㄨㄤ ㄍㄠˋ ㄈㄟˋ)
advertising rates

廣告欄(《ㄨㄤ ㄍㄠˋ ㄌㄢˊ)
the ad column (in a newspaper)

廣告公司(《ㄨㄤ ㄍㄠˋ ㄍㄨㄥ ㄙ)
an advertising agency

廣告客戶(《ㄨㄤ ㄍㄠˋ ㄎㄜˋ ㄏㄨˋ)
an advertiser

廣告業(《ㄨㄤ ㄍㄠˋ ㄧㄝˋ)
advertising

廣開才路(《ㄨㄤ ㄎㄞ ㄘㄞˊ ㄌㄨˋ)
to open all avenues for people of talent

廣開言路(《ㄨㄤ ㄎㄞ ㄧㄢˊ ㄌㄨˋ)
to encourage freedom of
speech: 民主的政府廣開言路。
A democratic government
encourages freedom of
speech.

廣闊(《ㄨㄤ ㄎㄨㄛˋ)
wide; extensive; vast; spacious; broad: 河在愈近海處愈
廣闊。The river grows

broader as it nears the sea.

廣寒宮(《ㄨㄤ ㄏㄢˊ ㄍㄨㄥ)
a mythological palace on
the moon

廣貨(《ㄨㄤ ㄏㄨㄛˋ)
a Kwangtung product

廣結善緣(《ㄨㄤ ㄐㄧㄝˊ ㄕㄢˋ ㄩㄢˊ)
to make friends all around

廣交(《ㄨㄤ ㄐㄧㄠ)
to make friends extensively;
to have a large number of
friends: 他喜交朋友。He has a
large number of friends.

廣角鏡頭(《ㄨㄤ ㄐㄧㄠˇ ㄐㄧㄥˋ ㄊㄡˊ)
a wide-angle lens

廣九鐵路(《ㄨㄤ ㄐㄧㄡˇ ㄊㄧㄝˇ ㄌㄨˋ)
the Canton-Kowloon Railway

廣錢通神(《ㄨㄤ ㄑㄧㄢˊ ㄊㄨㄥ ㄕㄣˊ)
Money is all-powerful.

廣西(《ㄨㄤ ㄒㄧ)
Kwangsi Province

廣廈萬間(《ㄨㄤ ㄒㄧㄚˋ ㄨㄢˋ ㄐㄧㄢ)
(literally) ten thousand spacious buildings to house the
homeless—the help that benefits large numbers of people

廣行善事(《ㄨㄤ ㄒㄧㄥˊ ㄕㄢˋ ㄕˋ)
to perform good deeds extensively; to be philanthropic

廣州(《ㄨㄤ ㄓㄡ)
Canton, or Kwangchow, capital of Kwangtung Province

廣州灣(《ㄨㄤ ㄓㄡ ㄨㄢ)
Kwangchow Bay (the southwestern coast of Kwangtung
Province)

廣衆(《ㄨㄤ ㄓㄨㄥˋ)
the multitude of people

廣長舌(《ㄨㄤ ㄔㄤˊ ㄕㄜˊ)
eloquence

廣場(《ㄨㄤ ㄔㄤˇ or ㄨㄤ ㄔㄤˊ)
a square (in a city); a plaza:
他們聆聽廣場上樂隊的演奏。
They are listening to the
band playing in the square.

廣瘡(《ㄨㄤ ㄔㄨㄤ)
syphilis

廣嗣(《ㄨㄤ ㄙˋ)
to have many children

廣而言之(《ㄨㄤ ㄦˊ ㄧㄢˊ ㄓ)
generally speaking; in a general sense

廣益(《ㄨㄤ ㄧˋ)
to solicit good advice

廣義(《ㄨㄤ ㄧˋ)
the wider sense (of a term);
the broad definition

廣韻(《ㄨㄤ ㄩㄣˋ)
Kwang Yun, a riming dictionary, authorized during
the Sung Dynasty

广
部

十三畫

【廨】¹⁴⁰⁰
ㄒㄧㄝˋ shieh xiè
a public office; a government building

廨宇(ㄒㄧㄝˋ ㄩˇ)
a government office building

【廩】¹⁴⁰¹
ㄌㄧㄣˇ liin lǐn
1. a granary
2. to supply (foodstuffs)
3. to stockpile

廩餼(ㄌㄧㄣˇ ㄒㄧˋ)
government-supplied foodstuffs

廩食(ㄌㄧㄣˇ ㄕˊ)
government-supplied foodstuffs

廩膳(ㄌㄧㄣˇ ㄕㄢˋ)
government-supplied meals

廩生(ㄌㄧㄣˇ ㄕㄥ)
the scholars who lived on
government grants during
the Ming and Ching
dynasties

廩人(ㄌㄧㄣˇ ㄖㄣˊ)
an official in charge of government granaries

廩倉(ㄌㄧㄣˇ ㄘㄤ)
a public granary

廩粟(ㄌㄧㄣˇ ㄙㄨˋ)
government-supplied millet

十六畫

【廬】¹⁴⁰²
ㄌㄨˊ lu lú
1. a thatched cottage
2. Mt. Lu (in Kiangsi)

廬墓(ㄌㄨˊ ㄇㄨˋ)
①to mourn for one's deceased parent by dwelling
in a hut built by the grave;
to tend the grave ②the
grave and hut for those
tending it

廬帳(ㄌㄨˊ ㄓㄤˋ)
a tent used as a dwelling

廬舍(ㄌㄨˊ ㄕㄜˋ)

a cottage; a hut; 沿着湖邊有
幾間蘆舍. Along the bank of
the lake there are a few
huts.

蘆山
(ㄌㄨ ㄕㄢ)
Mt. Lu, a famous summer
resort (in Kiangsi)

蘆山眞面目 (ㄌㄨ ㄕㄢ ㄓㄣ ㄇㄧㄢ ㄇㄨ)
(literally) the real appearance of Mt. Lu (which is
often shrouded in fog)—the
real appearance (of a thing
or person in disguise)

【龐】 1403
ㄆㄤˊ parng pang
1. disorderly; confused; numerous and jumbled
2. huge; enormous
3. a face
4. a Chinese family name

龐貝
Pompeii, an ancient city in
SW Italy, near Naples

龐培
Gnaeus Pompeius Magnus,
106-48 B.C., Roman gener-
al

龐眉皓髮 (ㄆㄤˊ ㄇㄟˊ ㄏㄠˋ ㄈㄚˇ)
bushy brows and white hair
(of an aged man)

龐大 (ㄆㄤˊ ㄉㄚˋ)
immense; huge; enormous

龐然大物 (ㄆㄤˊ ㄖㄢˊ ㄉㄚˋ ㄨˋ)
①a huge object ②a mam-
moth animal

龐雜 (ㄆㄤˊ ㄗㄚˊ)
disorderly; confused

龐錯 (ㄆㄤˊ ㄘㄨㄛˋ)
disorderly; confused

十八畫

【龐】 1404
ㄩㄥˊ iong yǒng
1. harmonious
2. an imperial university or
academy

龐龐 (ㄩㄥˊ ㄩㄥˊ)
(said of sound) harmonious

二十二畫

【廳】 1405
ㄊㄧㄥ ting tīng
1. a central or main room of a
house
2. a hall
3. a government agency

廳房 (ㄊㄧ ㄈㄤˊ)
a central room open to a
number of other rooms; a
hall

廳堂 (ㄊㄧ ㄊㄤˊ)
the central room of a house;
a hall

廳長 (ㄊㄧ ㄔㄤˊ)
the director of a department
under a provincial government

廳事 (ㄊㄧ ㄕˋ)
an office 亦作「聽事」

廴 部
ㄧㄣˇ yiin yǐn

四畫

【延】 1406
ㄧㄢˊ yan yán
1. to extend; to spread; to
lengthen
2. to delay; to defer; to postpone: 這會議將延後. The
meeting will be postponed.
3. to prolong
4. to invite
5. to procrastinate: 他以各種藉口拖延歸期. He procrastinated his return on various pre-
texts.

延聘 (ㄧㄢˊ ㄆㄧㄣˋ)
to invite the service of

延蔓 (ㄧㄢˊ ㄇㄢˋ)
to spread like a vine

延宕 (ㄧㄢˊ ㄉㄤˋ)
to procrastinate; slow in
taking action

延眺 (ㄧㄢˊ ㄊㄧㄠˋ)
to crane the neck to look

延納 (ㄧㄢˊ ㄋㄚˋ)
to employ (talents)

延年益壽 (ㄧㄢˊ ㄋㄧㄢˊ ㄧˋ ㄕㄡˋ)
to lengthen one's life

延攬 (ㄧㄢˊ ㄌㄢˇ)
to recruit the service of (talented men)

延擱 (ㄧㄢˊ ㄍㄜ)
①to procrastinate ② to neglect

延宕 (ㄧㄢˊ ㄍㄨㄛ)
to put off a meeting

延緩 (ㄧㄢˊ ㄏㄨㄢˇ)
to postpone; to put off; to
defer

延接 (ㄧㄢˊ ㄐㄧㄝ)
to receive (guests)

延見 (ㄧㄢˊ ㄐㄧㄢˋ)
to grant an interview with
someone; to give an audi-
ence to someone: 經理延見
他. The manager gave him
an interview.

延頸舉踵 (ㄧㄢˊ ㄐㄧㄥˇ ㄐㄩˇ ㄓㄨㄥˇ)
延頸企足 (ㄧㄢˊ ㄐㄧㄥˇ ㄑㄧˋ ㄗㄨˊ)
延企 (ㄧㄢˊ ㄑㄧˋ)
(literally) with a craned
neck and on tiptoe—to
expect or look forward anxiously

延期 (ㄧㄢˊ ㄑㄧˊ)
①to be postponed; to be put
off: 這會議延期到下禮拜. The
meeting has been put off
until next week. ②to
extend: 我希望我的簽證能延
期. I hope that my visa can
be extended.

延請 (ㄧㄢˊ ㄑㄧㄥˇ)
to invite (talented people to
provide assistance); to
extend an invitation to

延釐 (ㄧㄢˊ ㄒㄧ)
a term written on the wall
facing the gate, used for
inviting luck

延性 (ㄧㄢˊ ㄒㄧㄥˋ)or延展性 (ㄧㄢˊ ㄓㄢˇ
ㄒㄧㄥˋ)
(physics) ductility

延續 (ㄧㄢˊ ㄒㄩˋ)
to continue; to be continued:
不能讓這種情況延續下去. This
situation must not be al-
lowed to continue.

延遲 (ㄧㄢˊ ㄔˊ)
to delay; to be delayed

延長 (ㄧㄢˊ ㄔㄤˊ)
to lengthen; to extend; to
prolong: 會議延長四天. The
conference will be prolonged
for four more days.

延長記號 (ㄧㄢˊ ㄔㄤˊ ㄐㄧˋ ㄏㄠˋ)
(music) a pause

延長線 (ㄧㄢˊ ㄔㄤˊ ㄒㄧㄢˋ)
an extension line; an extension

延時炸彈 (ㄧㄢˊ ㄕˊ ㄓㄚˋ ㄉㄢˋ)
a delayed-action bomb

延燒 (ㄧㄢˊ ㄕㄠ)

(said of fire) to spread

壽(ㄕㄡ ㄕㄥ)
to prolong one's life

伸(ㄕㄣ)
to extend; to stretch; to elongate: 這條公路一直延伸到海邊。This highway stretches right to the coast.

入(ㄖㄨˋ)
to invite to enter

髓(ㄒㄧㄢˊ ㄙㄨㄟˇ)or 延髓(ㄧㄢˊ ㄕㄨㄟˇ)
medulla oblongata; the afterbrain

安
Yenan, a county in Shensi Province

誤(ㄨˋ)
to fail because of procrastination

譽(ㄩˋ)
to make someone's good name widely known

廷 [1407] ㄊㄧㄥ tyng tíng
the imperial court; the court

對(ㄉㄨㄟˋ)
to respond to the emperor's queries at court

魁(ㄎㄨㄟˊ)
the top successful candidate in the imperial examination

杖(ㄓㄤˋ)
to beat a courtier with cane at court in the presence of other courtiers; caning a courtier at court in the presence of other courtiers as a punishment

爭(ㄓㄥ)
to debate at court in the emperor's presence

試(ㄕˋ)
the imperial examination (the last step in the periodic civil service examinations in former times)

議(ㄧˋ)
a discussion at imperial court; a court discussion; a court meeting

六畫

【建】 [1408] ㄐㄧㄢˋ jiann jiàn
1. to establish; to build; to construct: 我們必須重建家園。We

have to rebuild our homeland.

2. to bring up; to propose; to suggest: 他建議更改計畫。He proposed a change of plan.

建白(ㄅㄞˊ)
to state one's opinion on public affairs

建坪(ㄆㄧㄥˊ)
the floor space of a building in *ping* (equivalent to 36 square feet)

建黨(ㄉㄤˇ)
to found a political party

建都(ㄉㄨ)
to select a city as the capital (of the empire)

建立(ㄌㄧˋ)
to establish; to set up; to build; to found

建國(ㄍㄨㄛˊ)
① to found (or to establish) a state ② to build up a country

建國方略(ㄍㄨㄛˊ ㄈㄤ ㄌㄩㄝˋ)
Plans for National Reconstruction, by Dr. Sun Yat-sen

建國大綱(ㄍㄨㄛˊ ㄉㄚˋ ㄍㄤ)
Fundamentals of National Reconstruction, by Dr. Sun Yat-sen

建功立業(ㄍㄨㄥ ㄌㄧˋ ㄧㄝˋ)
to make a great contribution and accomplish great tasks

建基(ㄐㄧ)
to lay the foundations

建交(ㄐㄧㄠ)
to establish diplomatic relations

建教合作(ㄐㄧㄠˋ ㄏㄜˊ ㄗㄨㄛˋ)
cooperation between a school or university and a business establishment or factory whereby the students get practical experience by working for the latter while the latter get free manpower or research contracts

建艦(ㄐㄧㄢˋ)
to build a warship

建軍(ㄐㄩㄣ)
to build a fighting force

建制(ㄓˋ)
organization of a government agency or military unit

建築(ㄐㄧㄢˋ ㄓㄨˊ)
① to build; to construct ② a building or structure

建築學(ㄐㄧㄢˋ ㄓㄨˊ ㄒㄩㄝˊ)
architecture

建築師(ㄐㄧㄢˋ ㄓㄨˊ ㄕ)
an architect

建築物(ㄐㄧㄢˋ ㄓㄨˊ ㄨˋ)
a building; a structure: 這是一幢優美的建築物。This is a fine building.

建朝(ㄐㄧㄢˋ ㄔㄠˊ)
to found a dynasty

建設(ㄐㄧㄢˋ ㄕㄜˋ)
to construct; to build; construction: 他們正在努力建設他們的家鄉。They are trying hard to construct their hometown.

建設廳(ㄐㄧㄢˋ ㄕㄜˋ ㄊㄧㄥ)
Department of Reconstruction (of a provincial government)

建設性(ㄐㄧㄢˋ ㄕㄜˋ ㄒㄧㄥˋ)
constructive: 我們需要建設性的批評。We need constructive criticism.

建樹(ㄐㄧㄢˋ ㄕㄨˋ)
an achievement; contribution

建造(ㄐㄧㄢˋ ㄗㄠˋ)
to build; to construct; to frame: 他們正在建造房屋。They are building a house.

建安七子(ㄐㄧㄢˋ ㄢ ㄑㄧ ㄗˇ)
the seven leading writers during the Chien An Period at the end of the Han Dynasty—孔融、陳琳、王粲、徐幹、阮瑀、應瑒、劉楨

建安文學(ㄐㄧㄢˋ ㄢ ㄨㄣˊ ㄒㄩㄝˊ)
literature of the Chien An Period, noted both for excellence and abundance

建議(ㄐㄧㄢˋ ㄧˋ)
to propose; to suggest; proposal; suggestion: 我們建議休會。We propose that the meeting be adjourned.

建議案(ㄐㄧㄢˋ ㄧˋ ㄢˋ)
a (parliamentary) motion; a proposal: 這項建議案已在會議中通過了。The motion was adopted at the meeting.

廷部

〔廾部〕

廾 部
《ㄍㄨㄥ goong gǒng

一畫

【廿】 1409
ㄋㄧㄢ niann niàn
twenty

廿四史（ㄋㄧㄢㄙ ㄙˇ）
the *Twenty-Four Books of History*, or the *Twenty-Four Dynastic Histories* (up to the Ming Dynasty, authorized during the Ching Dynasty)

二畫

【弁】 1410
ㄅㄧㄢ biann biàn
1. a conical cap worn on ceremonious occasions in ancient times
2. in the Ching Dynasty low-ranking military officers
3. a Chinese family name

弁髦（ㄅㄧㄢ ㄇㄠ）
① useless things ② to slight; to underestimate; to despise

弁冕（ㄅㄧㄢ ㄇㄧㄢˇ）
an ancient cap worn on ceremonious occasions

弁目（ㄅㄧㄢ ㄇㄨˋ）
a squad leader (in the infantry units of the Ching Dynasty)

弁經（ㄅㄧㄢ ㄐㄧㄥ）
a patch of coarse linen worn on the mourning cap during a funeral service

弁言（ㄅㄧㄢ ㄧㄢˊ）
a preface; a foreword; an prefatory remark

四畫

【弄】 1411
ㄌㄨㄥˋ nonq nòng
（讀音 ㄌㄨㄥˋ long）

1. to play with; to sport with: 孩子們喜歡玩弄泥沙。Children like to play with sand.
2. to make fun of; to mock

---

3. to handle; to do; to perform: 你要把事情弄好。You should do a good job.

弄筆（ㄌㄨㄥˋ ㄅㄧˇ）
to distort facts or exaggerate in writing

弄兵（ㄌㄨㄥˋ ㄅㄧㄥ）
to start a war or a rebellion recklessly

弄飯（ㄌㄨㄥˋ ㄈㄢˋ）
to prepare a meal

弄通（ㄌㄨㄥˋ ㄊㄨㄥ）
to get a good grasp of

弄鬼（ㄌㄨㄥˋ ㄍㄨㄟˇ）
to hatch plots; to play tricks behind the scenes

弄口（ㄌㄨㄥˋ ㄎㄡˇ）
to sow discord by making false statements

弄好（ㄌㄨㄥˋ ㄏㄠˇ）
① to get or put into (good) shape ② to finish doing something ③ to do well

弄糊塗（ㄌㄨㄥˋ ㄏㄨˊ ㄊㄨˊ）
to puzzle; to confuse

弄壞（ㄌㄨㄥˋ ㄏㄨㄞˋ）
to bungle; to spoil: 他把事情弄壞了。He bungled the job.

弄假成真（ㄌㄨㄥˋ ㄐㄧㄚˇ ㄔㄥˊ ㄓㄣ）
to turn simulation into reality unintentionally

弄僵（ㄌㄨㄥˋ ㄐㄧㄤ）
to bring to a deadlock

弄巧成拙（ㄌㄨㄥˋ ㄑㄧㄠˇ ㄔㄥˊ ㄓㄨㄛ）
to bungle an ingenious scheme; to suffer a setback in trying to take advantage of a situation

弄錢（ㄌㄨㄥˋ ㄑㄧㄢˊ）
to raise money

弄清（ㄌㄨㄥˋ ㄑㄧㄥ）
to make clear; to clarify; to gain a clear idea of; to understand fully: 我們必須弄清事實。We have to understand the facts fully.

弄權（ㄌㄨㄥˋ ㄑㄩㄢˊ）
to abuse one's power

弄小（ㄌㄨㄥˋ ㄒㄧㄠˇ）
to keep a concubine

弄璋（ㄌㄨㄥˋ ㄓㄤ）
to give birth to a son

弄潮兒（ㄌㄨㄥˋ ㄔㄠˊ ㄦ）
① a seaman ② a beach swimmer

弄臣（ㄌㄨㄥˋ ㄔㄣˊ）

---

an emperor's minion; a court jester

弄出事來（ㄌㄨㄥˋ ㄔㄨ ㄕˋ ㄌㄞˊ）
to get into trouble as a result of doing something

弄蛇（ㄌㄨㄥˋ ㄕㄜˊ）
to handle snakes

弄姿（ㄌㄨㄥˋ ㄗ）
(said of women) to assume a charming pose; to act coquettishly

弄糟（ㄌㄨㄥˋ ㄗㄠ）
to make a mess of; to mess up; to bungle; to spoil

弄髒（ㄌㄨㄥˋ ㄗㄤ）
to stain; to soil; to pollute; to smudge; to smear

弄嘴弄舌（ㄌㄨㄥˋ ㄗㄨㄟˇ ㄌㄨㄥˋ ㄕㄜˊ）
to talk idly

弄錯（ㄌㄨㄥˋ ㄘㄨㄛˋ）
to make a mistake; to commit an error: 你弄錯了時間。You made a mistake about the time.

弄死（ㄌㄨㄥˋ ㄙˇ）
to kill; to do away with

弄孫（ㄌㄨㄥˋ ㄙㄨㄣ）
to amuse oneself by playing with grandchildren

弄瓦（ㄌㄨㄥˋ ㄨㄚˇ）
to give birth to a daughter

弄月（ㄌㄨㄥˋ ㄩㄝˋ）
to enjoy the moonlight; to admire the moon

六畫

【龕】 1412
ㄧㄢ yean yān
1. a narrow-necked container
2. to cover
3. profound

【弈】 1413
ㄧˋ yih yì
the "go" game

弈徒（ㄧˋ ㄊㄨˊ）
a "go" player; a "go" fan

弈具（ㄧˋ ㄐㄩˋ）
the black and white stones and the chessboard for the "go" game

弈棋（ㄧˋ ㄑㄧˊ）
the "go" game

弈聖（ㄧˋ ㄕㄥˋ）
a "go" wizard, usually referring to Huang Lung-shih (黃龍士) during the reign of

Kang Hsi in the Ching Dynasty

十二畫

【弊】 1414
（ㄅㄧˋ bih bì）
1. bad; undesirable
2. dishonesty; fraud
3. exhausted; tired; worn-out
4. disadvantages; harm: 這樣做有利有弊。 There are both advantages and disadvantages to work in such a way.

弊病（ㄅㄧˋ ㄅㄧㄥˋ）or 弊竇（ㄅㄧˋ ㄉㄡˋ）or 弊端（ㄅㄧˋ ㄉㄨㄢ）
corrupt practices; drawbacks: 每件事都有其弊病。 Everything has its drawback.

弊害（ㄅㄧˋ ㄏㄞˋ）
harm; damage: 那樣做並無弊害。 There is no harm in doing that.

弊壞（ㄅㄧˋ ㄏㄨㄞˋ）
worn and damaged

弊車駑馬（ㄅㄧˋ ㄔㄜ ㄋㄨˊ ㄇㄚˇ）
(descriptive of incorruptible officials) a decrepit cart drawn by a lean horse

弊絕風清（ㄅㄧˋ ㄐㄩㄝˊ ㄈㄥ ㄑㄧㄥ）
姬茵(said of a clean government) absolutely free from corruption

弊帚自珍（ㄅㄧˋ ㄓㄡˋ ㄗˋ ㄓㄣ）or 弊帚千金（ㄅㄧˋ ㄓㄡˋ ㄑㄧㄢ ㄐㄧㄣ）
One loves some thing of little value simply because it is his own.

弊政（ㄅㄧˋ ㄓㄥˋ）
misrule; maladministration

弋 部
（ㄧˋ yih yì）

【弋】 1415
（ㄧˋ yih yì）
1. to catch; take take
2. to shoot with arrow and bow

弋繳（ㄧˋ ㄐㄧㄠˊ）

to hunt

弋獲（ㄧˋ ㄏㄨㄛˋ）
to catch (game in hunting, a thief, etc.)

弋取（ㄧˋ ㄑㄩˇ）
to catch

弋腔（ㄧˋ ㄑㄧㄤ）
a singing style in Chinese opera 亦作「高腔」

三畫

【式】 1416
（ㄕˋ shyh shì）
1. fashion; style; form; a mode: 她穿著最新款式的外衣。 She wears a coat of the latest style.
2. a pattern; a type; a model; an example
3. a system: 這是教授英國的一種良好方式。 This is a good system of teaching English.
4. a ceremony

式子（ㄕˋ ㄗˇ）
(mathematics) a formula or equation

式樣（ㄕˋ ㄧㄤˋ）
a type; a model; a mode; a style

式微（ㄕˋ ㄨㄟ）
the decline (of a nation, a dynasty, a family, etc.)

十畫

【弒】 1417
（ㄕˋ shyh shì）
to kill or murder one's superior, senior, etc.

弒母（ㄕˋ ㄇㄨˇ）
matricide; to commit matricide

弒父（ㄕˋ ㄈㄨˋ）
patricide; to commit patricide

弒逆者（ㄕˋ ㄋㄧˋ ㄓㄜˇ）
one who commits patricide or regicide

弒君（ㄕˋ ㄐㄩㄣ）
regicide; to commit regicide

弒兄（ㄕˋ ㄒㄩㄥ）
fratricide (murder of one's own elder brother)

弓 部
《ㄨㄥ gong gōng

【弓】 1418
《ㄨㄥ gong gōng
1. a bow: 小提琴是用弓拉奏的。 A violin is played with a bow.
2. bent; arching; arched: 彩虹在天上成弓形。 A bright rainbow arched above.
3. a measure of length (equal to five Chinese feet)

弓背《ㄨㄥ ㄅㄟˋ）
to bend the back like a bow; a back arched like a bow

弓袋（《ㄨㄥ ㄉㄞˋ）
a bow case 參看「弓韇」

弓弩手（《ㄨㄥ ㄋㄨˇ ㄕㄡˇ）or 弓箭手（《ㄨㄥ ㄐㄧㄢˋ ㄕㄡˇ）or 弓手（《ㄨㄥ ㄕㄡˇ）
an archer: 他是一個優良的弓箭手。 He is a good archer.

弓韇（《ㄨㄥ ㄉㄨˊ）
a bow case

弓箭（《ㄨㄥ ㄐㄧㄢˋ）or 弓矢（《ㄨㄥ ㄕˇ）
bow and arrow

弓匠（《ㄨㄥ ㄐㄧㄤˋ）
a bowyer

弓鞋（《ㄨㄥ ㄒㄧㄝˊ）
the shoes with upturned and worn by women with bound feet in former times

弓弦（《ㄨㄥ ㄒㄧㄢˊ）
a bowstring: 他的情緒緊張得有如弓弦。 His nerves are as taut as a bowstring.

弓形（《ㄨㄥ ㄒㄧㄥˊ）
(mathematics) a segment of a circle

弓人（《ㄨㄥ ㄖㄣˊ）
an ancient official whose duty was to make bows

弓腰（《ㄨㄥ ㄧㄠ）
to curve one's body backward like an arch

弓影（《ㄨㄥ ㄧㄥˇ）or 弓蛇（《ㄨㄥ ㄕㄜˊ）
(literally) the reflection of a bow in a wine cup mistaken for a snake—a false alarm

一畫

【引】 1419 (ㄧㄣˇ yǐn yǐn)

〔弓部〕

1. to pull; to attract: 抛磚引玉 to cast a brick to attract jade; to throw out a minnow to catch a whale
2. to guide: 盲人有時由狗引路. A blind man is sometimes guided by a dog.
3. to introduce
4. to quote: 傳教士引用聖經. The minister quoted from the Bible.
5. to retire
6. a unit of length (=33⅓ metres)
7. to cause; to make

引避 (ㄧㄣˇ ㄅㄧˋ)
①to yield one's place ②to avoid

引滿 (ㄧㄣˇ ㄇㄢˇ)
①to draw a bow to the full ②to fill the cup to the brim

引發 (ㄧㄣˇ ㄈㄚ)
(chemistry) initiation

引風吹火 (ㄧㄣˇ ㄈㄥ ㄔㄨㄟ ㄏㄨㄛˇ)
①to fan the flame ②to excite or stir up trouble

引得 (ㄧㄣˇ ㄉㄜˊ)
an index (a transliteration of the English word)

引導 (ㄧㄣˇ ㄉㄠˇ) or (ㄧㄣˇ ㄉㄠˇ)
to guide; to lead

引逗 (ㄧㄣˇ ㄉㄡˋ)
to entice

引渡 (ㄧㄣˇ ㄉㄨˋ)
to extradite; extradition

引對 (ㄧㄣˇ ㄉㄨㄟˋ)
to summon for an imperial court interview

引愆 (ㄧㄣˇ ㄑㄧㄢ)
to assume blame

引退 (ㄧㄣˇ ㄊㄨㄟˋ)
to retire; to resign: 他已從校刊編輯的職務引退. He has resigned from the editorship of the school paper.

引狼入室 (ㄧㄣˇ ㄌㄤˊ ㄖㄨˋ ㄕˋ)
(literally) to usher the wolf into the house—to bring in a troublemaker

引力 (ㄧㄣˇ ㄌㄧˋ)
attracting force; attraction; gravitation: 萬有引力 universal gravitation

引領 (ㄧㄣˇ ㄌㄧㄥˇ)
to stretch the neck in order to have a better look

引領而望 (ㄧㄣˇ ㄌㄧㄥˇ ㄦˊ ㄨㄤˋ)
to long for; to expect eagerly

引路 (ㄧㄣˇ ㄌㄨˋ)
to lead the way

引港 (ㄧㄣˇ ㄍㄤˇ)
to act as a pilot in a harbor

引弓 (ㄧㄣˇ ㄍㄨㄥ)
to draw the bow

引號 (ㄧㄣˇ ㄏㄠˋ)
a quotation mark; a quote

引航 (ㄧㄣˇ ㄏㄤˊ)
pilotage

引吭高歌 (ㄧㄣˇ ㄏㄤˊ ㄍㄠ ㄍㄜ)
to sing aloud

引火 (ㄧㄣˇ ㄏㄨㄛˇ)
to ignite; to light; to kindle a fire: 他們擦火柴引火. They kindled a fire by scratching a match.

引火焚身 (ㄧㄣˇ ㄏㄨㄛˇ ㄈㄣˊ ㄕㄣ)
to get oneself into trouble

引火點 (ㄧㄣˇ ㄏㄨㄛˇ ㄉㄧㄢˇ)
the ignition point; the flashing point

引接 (ㄧㄣˇ ㄐㄧㄝ)
to receive (guests)

引咎 (ㄧㄣˇ ㄐㄧㄡˋ)
to take the blame on oneself: 他對這事件引咎. He takes the blame on himself in this matter.

引咎辭職 (ㄧㄣˇ ㄐㄧㄡˋ ㄘˊ ㄓˊ)
to resign from office as a gesture to show self-reproach

引見 (ㄧㄣˇ ㄐㄧㄢˋ)
to present a person to the emperor, a high official, etc.

引薦 (ㄧㄣˇ ㄐㄧㄢˋ)
to recommend

引進 (ㄧㄣˇ ㄐㄧㄣˋ)
①to recommend ②to introduce from elsewhere: 我們必須引進新的技術與裝備. We have to import new technology and equipment.

引經據典 (ㄧㄣˇ ㄐㄧㄥ ㄐㄩˋ ㄉㄧㄢˇ)
①to quote from classics ②pedantic

引頸 (ㄧㄣˇ ㄐㄧㄥˇ)
to crane one's neck to look forward

引頸就戮 (ㄧㄣˇ ㄐㄧㄥˇ ㄐㄧㄡˋ ㄌㄨˋ)
to stretch the neck to be beheaded

引決 (ㄧㄣˇ ㄐㄩㄝˊ)
to commit suicide

引起 (ㄧㄣˇ ㄑㄧˇ)
to cause; to give rise to; to trigger: 切勿引起公憤. Never arouse public indignation.

引擎 (ㄧㄣˇ ㄑㄧㄥˊ)
an engine: 他發動了汽車的引擎. He started the engine of his car.

引嫌 (ㄧㄣˇ ㄒㄧㄢˊ)
to step away from a delicate case in order to avoid others' suspicion

引線 (ㄧㄣˇ ㄒㄧㄢˋ)
①a sewing needle ②a go-between ③a fuse

引信 (ㄧㄣˇ ㄒㄧㄣˋ)
a fuse

引證 (ㄧㄣˇ ㄓㄥˋ)
to cite supporting facts, proofs, or evidence

引錐刺股 (ㄧㄣˇ ㄓㄨㄟ ㄘˋ ㄍㄨˇ)
(literally) to prick one's own thigh with a drill to keep oneself from falling asleep—to goad oneself to hard work

引出 (ㄧㄣˇ ㄔㄨ)
to draw forth; to lead: 我們的討論可引出正確的結論. Our discussion can draw a correct conclusion.

引伸 or 引申 (ㄧㄣˇ ㄕㄣ)
to extend in meaning; to expound

引商刻羽 (ㄧㄣˇ ㄕㄤ ㄎㄜˋ ㄩˇ)
highbrow music

引書為證 (ㄧㄣˇ ㄕㄨ ㄨㄟˊ ㄓㄥˋ)
to cite proofs from books

引水 (ㄧㄣˇ ㄕㄨㄟˇ)
①to pilot a ship into a harbor ②to draw water ③(irrigation) diversion

引水工程 (ㄧㄣˇ ㄕㄨㄟˇ ㄍㄨㄥ ㄔㄥˊ)
diversion works

引水人 (ㄧㄣˇ ㄕㄨㄟˇ ㄖㄣˊ)
a harbor pilot 亦作「領航員」

引水隧道 (ㄧㄣˇ ㄕㄨㄟˇ ㄙㄨㄟˋ ㄉㄠˋ)
a diversion tunnel

引稅 (ㄧㄣˇ ㄕㄨㄟˋ)
salt tax 亦作「鹽稅」

引人注目 (ㄧㄣˇ ㄖㄣˊ ㄓㄨˋ ㄇㄨˋ)
noticeable; conspicuous

引人入勝(lㄧㄣ ㄖㄨˊ ㄖㄨˋ ㄕㄥˋ)
①to lead one into wonder-land ②(of books) absorbing

引入(lㄧㄣˇ ㄖㄨˋ)
to lead into; to draw into

引入歧途(lㄧㄣˇ ㄖㄨˋ ㄑㄧˊ ㄊㄨˊ)
to lead (somebody) astray;
別把小孩們引入歧途。Don't
lead the children astray.

引子(lㄧㄣˇ ˙ㄗ)
①a prologue; a prelude; a
preface; an introduction ②a
supplementary dose (in
Chinese herb medicine)

引以為戒(lㄧㄣˇ ㄧˇ ㄨㄟˊ ㄐㄧㄝˋ)
to learn a lesson (from a
previous error)

引藥(lㄧㄣˇ ㄧㄠˋ)
a supplementary dose (in
Chinese medicine) which
leads the principal drug to
the seat of the disease

引誘(lㄧㄣˇ ㄧㄡˋ)
to induce; to lure; to attract; to entice; to tempt;
to seduce

引言(lㄧㄣˇ ㄧㄢˊ)
a preface; a foreword

引文(lㄧㄣˇ ㄨㄣˊ)
a quoted passage; a quotation

引用(lㄧㄣˇ ㄩㄥˋ)
to quote. 讓我引用莎士比亞的
話給你。Let me quote you the
words of Shakespeare.

【弔】 1420
(吊) ㄉㄧㄠˋ diaw diào
1. to condole; to console
2. to mourn
3. to hang; to suspend; suspend

弔膀子(ㄉㄧㄠˋ ㄅㄤˇ ˙ㄗ)
to lure the other sex by
casting coquettish glances,
making indecent remarks,
etc.

弔臂(ㄉㄧㄠˋ ㄅㄧˋ)
the arm of a crane

弔民伐罪(ㄉㄧㄠˋ ㄇㄧㄣˊ ㄈㄚˊ ㄗㄨㄟˋ)
to console the people by
punishing the wicked (often
used by revolutionaries as a
slogan in overthrowing the
monarch)

弔帶(ㄉㄧㄠˋ ㄉㄞˋ)
suspenders; garters

弔燈(ㄉㄧㄠˋ ㄉㄥ)

a low-hanging ceiling lamp,
such as a chandelier.

弔桶(ㄉㄧㄠˋ ㄊㄨㄥˇ)
a well bucket

弔鈎(ㄉㄧㄠˋ ㄍㄡ)
(machinery) a hook

弔桿(ㄉㄧㄠˋ ㄍㄢˇ)
a suspended pole

弔古(ㄉㄧㄠˋ ㄍㄨˇ)
to think of the ancients or
ancient events

弔詭(ㄉㄧㄠˋ ㄍㄨㄟˇ)
bizarre

弔客(ㄉㄧㄠˋ ㄎㄜˋ)
one who attends a funeral
service as a friend of the
deceased or of the bereaved
family

弔環(ㄉㄧㄠˋ ㄏㄨㄢˊ)
(gymnastics) flying rings

弔祭(ㄉㄧㄠˋ ㄐㄧˋ)
to mourn over (somebody's
death)

弔架(ㄉㄧㄠˋ ㄐㄧㄚˋ)
a suspended frame or stand

弔起(ㄉㄧㄠˋ ㄑㄧˇ)
①to hang ②to lift by crane

弔橋(ㄉㄧㄠˋ ㄑㄧㄠˊ)
①a suspension bridge ②a
drawbridge over the moat

弔銷(ㄉㄧㄠˋ ㄒㄧㄠ)
to revoke; to withdraw: 政府
弔銷他的護照。The govern-
ment withdrew his passport.

弔孝(ㄉㄧㄠˋ ㄒㄧㄠˋ)
to condole with a bereaved
son

弔鐘花(ㄉㄧㄠˋ ㄓㄨㄥ ㄏㄨㄚ)
a bellflower 亦作「風鈴草」

弔車(ㄉㄧㄠˋ ㄔㄜ)
①a wrecker (a truck crane)
②a cable car

弔林(ㄉㄧㄠˋ ㄌㄧㄣˊ)
a hammock: 他在花園中的弔
床上小睡。He takes a nap in
a hammock in his garden.

弔扇(ㄉㄧㄠˋ ㄕㄢˋ)
a ceiling fan

弔死(ㄉㄧㄠˋ ㄙˇ)
to hang (a criminal); to die
by hanging

弔死鬼(ㄉㄧㄠˋ ㄙˇ ㄍㄨㄟˇ)
the ghost of one who has
committed suicide by hanging

弔喪(ㄉㄧㄠˋ ㄙㄤ)

to attend a memorial ser-
vice; to condole

弔嗓子(ㄉㄧㄠˋ ㄙㄤˇ ˙ㄗ)
(Chinese opera) to sing
aloud off stage as a vocal
training and practice

弔索(ㄉㄧㄠˋ ㄙㄨㄛˇ)
a sling: 鋼絲弔索 a wire sling
繩弔索 a rope sling

弔兒郎當(ㄉㄧㄠˋ ㄦˊ ㄌㄤˊ ㄉㄤ)
to act or behave irreverent-
ly; to do things perfunctorily; to regard nothing as serious

弔唁(ㄉㄧㄠˋ ㄧㄢˋ)
to mourn in sympathy; to
condole

弔唁函電(ㄉㄧㄠˋ ㄧㄢˋ ㄏㄢˊ ㄉㄧㄢˋ)
messages of condolence

弔影(ㄉㄧㄠˋ ㄧㄥˇ)
(literally) to have sympathetic communication with
no one but one's own
shadow——to be completely
alone

弔慰(ㄉㄧㄠˋ ㄨㄟˋ)
to condole with

弔胃口(ㄉㄧㄠˋ ㄨㄟˋ ㄎㄡˇ)
to tantalize

弔文(ㄉㄧㄠˋ ㄨㄣˊ)
a message of condolence;
words of condolence; a
funeral oration; a memorial
address

二畫

【弗】 1421
ㄈㄨˊ fwu fú
not

弗蘭克林(ㄈㄨˊ ㄌㄢˊ ㄎㄜˋ ㄌㄧㄣˊ)
Benjamin Franklin, 1706-
1790, American statesman
and philosopher

弗克(ㄈㄨˊ ㄎㄜˋ)
unable

弗齒(ㄈㄨˊ ㄔˇ)
not held in esteem

弗成(ㄈㄨˊ ㄔㄥˊ)
not satisfactory; not good

弗如(ㄈㄨˊ ㄖㄨˊ)
not as good as; not equal to;
worse than: 他對那位學者自
愧弗如: He felt ashamed that
he is not as good as that
scholar.

弗豫(ㄈㄨˊ ㄩˋ)

【弓 部】

not well; not in good health

【弘】 ㄏㄨㄥˊ horng hóng　1422

1. great; magnanimous; capacious
2. to enlarge; to broaden

弘大（ㄏㄨㄥˊ ㄉㄚˋ）
　great; immense

弘量（ㄏㄨㄥˊ ㄌㄧㄤˋ）
　magnanimous; liberal; generous; large capacity for forgiveness; magnanimity

弘毅（ㄏㄨㄥˊ ㄧˋ）
　having a broad and strong mind

弘揚（ㄏㄨㄥˊ ㄧㄤˊ）
　to propagate; to promote; to develop: 他的志願是弘揚文化。 His ambition is to promote and develop the culture.

弘遠（ㄏㄨㄥˊ ㄩㄢˇ）
　far and wide

弘願（ㄏㄨㄥˊ ㄩㄢˋ）
　great ambition

三畫

【弛】 ㄕˇ shyy shǐ　1423
（又讀 ㄔˊ chyr chí）

to unstring; to relax; to neglect: 不要鬆弛警戒。 Don't relax your vigilance.

弛廢（ㄕˇ ㄈㄟˋ）
　to neglect; negligence

弛緩（ㄕˇ ㄏㄨㄢˇ）
　to relax

弛禁（ㄕˇ ㄐㄧㄣˋ）
　to rescind a prohibition; to lift or remove a restriction

弛張（ㄕˇ ㄓㄤ）
　tension and relaxation

四畫

【弟】 1. ㄉㄧˋ dìh dì　1424
1. a younger brother
2. a junior

弟妹（ㄉㄧˋ ㄇㄟˋ）
　younger brothers and sisters

弟婦（ㄉㄧˋ ㄈㄨˋ）or 弟媳（ㄉㄧˋ ㄒㄧˊ）
　a sister-in-law (younger brother's wife)

弟弟（ㄉㄧˋ ·ㄉㄧ）
　a younger brother

弟兄（ㄉㄧˋ ㄒㄩㄥ）

① brothers: 我們是親弟兄。 We are blood brothers. ② soldiers

弟子（ㄉㄧˋ ㄗˇ）
　① a disciple; a pupil; a student ② a youngster; a youth

【弟】 2. (佛) ㄊㄧˋ tìh tì　1424
to show brotherly love

五畫

【弦】 1425
1. strings (of bows, musical instruments, etc.): 一條弦斷了。 One of the strings broke.
2. the chord of an arc
3. the first or last quarter of a lunar month

弦歌（ㄒㄧㄢˊ ㄍㄜ）
　① to sing with stringed accompaniment ② the means of education

弦歌不輟（ㄒㄧㄢˊ ㄍㄜ ㄅㄨˋ ㄔㄨㄛˋ）
　The schooling goes on without interruption.

弦琴（ㄒㄧㄢˊ ㄑㄧㄣˊ）
　a stringed instrument with a number of strings

弦線（ㄒㄧㄢˊ ㄒㄧㄢˋ）
　strings (of a musical instrument)

弦柱（ㄒㄧㄢˊ ㄓㄨˋ）
　the neck (of a stringed instrument)

弦索（ㄒㄧㄢˊ ㄙㄨㄛˇ）
　the strings of instruments

弦誦（ㄒㄧㄢˊ ㄙㄨㄥˋ）
　to chant (music or passages from classics)

弦音（ㄒㄧㄢˊ ㄧㄣ）
　the music (from a stringed instrument)

弦外之音（ㄒㄧㄢˊ ㄨㄞˋ ㄓ ㄧㄣ）
　overtones; implied meaning; connotations: 他的話有弦外之音。 There are overtones in his remarks.

弦月（ㄒㄧㄢˊ ㄩㄝˋ）
　a crescent moon

弦樂隊（ㄒㄧㄢˊ ㄩㄝˋ ㄉㄨㄟˋ）
　string orchestra (or band)

弦樂器（ㄒㄧㄢˊ ㄩㄝˋ ㄑㄧˋ）
　a stringed instrument

【弧】 ㄏㄨˊ hwu hú　1426

1. a wooden bow
2. a segment of a circle

弧度（ㄏㄨˊ ㄉㄨˋ）
　circular measure

弧光燈（ㄏㄨˊ ㄍㄨㄤ ㄉㄥ）
　an arc light; an arc lamp

弧角（ㄏㄨˊ ㄐㄧㄠˇ）
　a spherical angle

弧形（ㄏㄨˊ ㄒㄧㄥˊ）
　an arc; a curve

弧矢形（ㄏㄨˊ ㄕˇ ㄒㄧㄥˊ）
　a segment of a circle

【弨】 ㄔㄠ chau chāo　1427
　a bow

【弩】 ㄋㄨˇ nuu nǔ　1428
　a crossbow

弩砲（ㄋㄨˇ ㄆㄠˋ）
　a sling shot; a catapult

弩末（ㄋㄨˇ ㄇㄛˋ）
　powerless because of exhaustion; weakened; exhausted; spent

弩弓（ㄋㄨˇ ㄍㄨㄥ）
　a crossbow

弩箭離弦（ㄋㄨˇ ㄐㄧㄢˋ ㄌㄧˊ ㄒㄧㄢˊ）
　as fast as the arrow flies off the string

弩張劍拔（ㄋㄨˇ ㄓㄤ ㄐㄧㄢˋ ㄅㄚˊ）
　(literally) with bows drawn and swords unsheathed —War is likely to start at any moment.

弩手（ㄋㄨˇ ㄕㄡˇ）
　an archer; a crossbowman 亦作「射手」: 他是國內最佳的弩手。 He is the best archer in our country.

弩牙（ㄋㄨˇ ㄧㄚˊ）
　the trigger of a crossbow

六畫

【弭】 ㄇㄧˇ mii mǐ　1429
1. to stop; to end: 將位將軍出兵弭亂。 The general led the army to stop the rebellion.
2. the ends of a bow

弭謗（ㄇㄧˇ ㄅㄤˋ）
　to stop slanders

弭兵（ㄇㄧˇ ㄅㄧㄥ）
　to stop war; to have a truce; to cease hostilities

弭亂（ㄇㄧˇ ㄌㄨㄢˋ）
　to stop disturbance of a

civil war
洱患(ㄦ ㄏㄨㄢˋ)
to eliminate trouble
洱赋(ㄦ ㄔˊ)
to travel very fast
洱灾(ㄦ ㄗㄞ)
to end disaster

【叁】 1430
ㄑㄩㄢˊ chiuan quán
a bowstring

七畫

【弴】 1431
ㄕㄠˋ shau shǎo
the ends of a bow

【弱】 1432
ㄖㄨㄛˋ ruoh ruò
1. weak; fragile; feeble; tender; delicate; infirm: 他病後覺得很虛弱。He felt very weak after illness.
2. inferior: 她的能力並不比別人弱。She's not inferior to others in capability.
3. young
4. a little less than: 三分之一弱 a little less than one-third

弱不好弄(ㄖㄨㄛˋ ㄅㄨˋ ㄏㄠˋ ㄋㄨㄥˋ)
not fond of playing in childhood

弱不禁風(ㄖㄨㄛˋ ㄅㄨˋ ㄐㄧㄣ ㄈㄥ)
so weak as to have inadequate strength to withstand the wind

弱不勝衣(ㄖㄨㄛˋ ㄅㄨˋ ㄕㄥ ㄧ)
(said of a woman) so fragile as to lack even the strength to bear the weight of clothing

弱風(ㄖㄨㄛˋ ㄈㄥ)
southeast wind

弱弟(ㄖㄨㄛˋ ㄉㄧˋ)
a young brother

弱點(ㄖㄨㄛˋ ㄉㄧㄢˇ)
a weak point; a weakness

弱女(ㄖㄨㄛˋ ㄋㄩˇ)
a young girl

弱柳(ㄖㄨㄛˋ ㄌㄧㄡˇ)
①a pliant willow tree ②a prostitute

弱國(ㄖㄨㄛˋ ㄍㄨㄛˊ)
a weak nation

弱冠(ㄖㄨㄛˋ ㄍㄨㄢˋ)
a twenty-year-old man (who has just undergone the capping ceremony); a youth

弱息(ㄖㄨㄛˋ ㄒㄧˊ)
my child

弱小(ㄖㄨㄛˋ ㄒㄧㄠˇ)
small and weak

弱小民族(ㄖㄨㄛˋ ㄒㄧㄠˇ ㄇㄧㄣˊ ㄗㄨˊ)
a small nation

弱質(ㄖㄨㄛˋ ㄓˋ)
feeble constitution; infirm

弱者(ㄖㄨㄛˋ ㄓㄜˇ)
the weak and the timid

弱視(ㄖㄨㄛˋ ㄕˋ)
amblyopia

弱勢團體(ㄖㄨㄛˋ ㄕˋ ㄊㄨㄢˊ ㄊㄧˇ)
an underprivileged group; a social group that has little or no influence in public affairs

弱水三千(ㄖㄨㄛˋ ㄕㄨㄟˇ ㄙㄢ ㄑㄧㄢ)
the river Jo (also known as 張掖河) with a supposed course of 3000 *li*

弱肉強食(ㄖㄨㄛˋ ㄖㄡˋ ㄑㄧㄤˊ ㄕˊ)
the stronger preying upon the weaker; the weak falling victim to the strong—the law of the jungle

弱卒(ㄖㄨㄛˋ ㄗㄨˊ)
weak soldiers; soldiers having no fighting capability: 弱卒會在戰爭中被淘汰。Weak soldiers will be eliminated in the war.

弱歲(ㄖㄨㄛˋ ㄙㄨㄟˋ)
a youth

八畫

【張】 1433
ㄓㄤ jang zhāng
1. to open; to stretch; to extend: 張開你的手。Open your hands.
2. to display
3. a sheet (of paper); a leaf (of a book): 請拿一張紙給我。Bring me a sheet of paper, please.
4. a Chinese family name

張伯倫(ㄓㄤ ㄅㄛˊ ㄌㄨㄣˊ)
Arthur Neville Chamberlain, 1869-1940, British prime minister

張本(ㄓㄤ ㄅㄣˇ)
①advance preparations or arrangements ②(in writing or storytelling) an advance hint of what to follow

張目(ㄓㄤ ㄇㄨˋ)
①to help publicize an unworthy cause ②to open one's eyes wide

張飛(ㄓㄤ ㄈㄟ)
Chang Fei, a general of the state of Shu (蜀) during the period of the Three Kingdoms

張大其辭(ㄓㄤ ㄉㄚˋ ㄑㄧˊ ㄘˊ)
to make exaggerated statements

張道陵(ㄓㄤ ㄉㄠˋ ㄌㄧㄥˊ)
Chang Tao-lin, a Taoist in the Han Dynasty, named as the first head priest of the Taoist sect 五斗米教

張燈結彩(ㄓㄤ ㄉㄥ ㄐㄧㄝˊ ㄘㄞˇ)
decorated with lanterns and colored hangings (for a joyous occasion)

張貼(ㄓㄤ ㄊㄧㄝ)
to paste up (labels, posters, etc.): 此處禁止張貼。Post no bills here.

張天師(ㄓㄤ ㄊㄧㄢ ㄕ)
the title of the head priest of the Taoist sect created during the Later Han Dynasty, conferred on the descendants of Chang Tao-lin (張道陵), and abolished in the republican time

張力(ㄓㄤ ㄌㄧˋ)
tensile strength; tension

張力計(ㄓㄤ ㄌㄧˋ ㄐㄧˋ)
(physics) a tensimeter

張良(ㄓㄤ ㄌㄧㄤˊ)
Chang Liang, the tactician who helped Liu Pang (劉邦) found the Han Dynasty

張羅(ㄓㄤ ㄌㄨㄛˊ)
①to raise funds ②to set a snare for birds ③to serve guests ④to take care of; to get busy about

張掛(ㄓㄤ ㄍㄨㄚˋ)
to hang up

張冠李戴(ㄓㄤ ㄍㄨㄢ ㄌㄧˇ ㄉㄞˋ)
(literally) Chang's hat on Li's head—wrong attribution; a mistake in identification; misappropriation

張開(ㄓㄤ ㄎㄞ)
to stretch open; to open

張口結舌(ㄓㄤ ㄎㄡˇ ㄐㄧㄝˊ ㄕㄜˊ)
agape and tongue-tied: 所有

〔弓部〕

〔弓部〕

的孩子們對他的大膽都吃驚得
張口結舌。All the children
were agape and tongue-tied
at his daring.

張狂 (坐尢 丂ㄨㄤ)
to abandon oneself to pleasure; to dissipate without
inhibition

張皇失措 or 張惶失措 (坐尢 ㄏㄨㄤˊ ㄕ ㄘㄨㄛˋ)
to lose composure; panicky

張家口 (坐尢 ㄐㄧㄚ ㄎㄡˇ)
Kalgan, or Changchiakou
(in Inner Mongolia)

張家長、李家短 (坐尢 ㄐㄧㄚ ㄓㄤˇ ㄌㄧˇ ㄐㄧㄚ ㄉㄨㄢˇ)
(literally) The Changs are
long and the Lis are short.
—typical subject matter of a
gossip

張騫 (坐尢 ㄑㄧㄢ)
Chang Chien, a soldier of
fortune of the Han Dynasty,
whose exploits helped China
pacify the tribes to the west

張獻忠 (坐尢 ㄒㄧㄢˋ ㄓㄨㄥ)
Chang Hsien-chung, one of
the rebels who contributed
to the fall of the Ming
Dynasty

張巡 (坐尢 ㄒㄩㄣˊ)
Chang Hsun (709-757), a
hero who died in the rebellion of An Lu-shan (安祿山)
during the Tang Dynasty

張之洞 (坐尢 ㄓ ㄉㄨㄥˋ)
Chang Chih-tung, a war minister and governor of several provinces in the Ching
Dynasty, who advocated
modernization of China during the late 19th century

張敞畫眉 (坐尢 ㄔㄤˇ ㄏㄨㄚˋ ㄇㄟˊ)
marital bliss (張敞 an able
and straightforward official
of the Han Dynasty, chiefly
known for his painting his
wife's eyebrows)

張弛 (坐尢 ㄔˊ)
tension and relaxation; fast
and loose

張設 (坐尢 ㄕㄜˋ)
to set up curtains, decorations, etc. for a ceremony

張手 (坐尢 ㄕㄡˇ)
to open one's hands

張作霖 (坐尢 ㄗㄨㄛˋ ㄌㄧㄣˊ)

Chang Tso-lin, a warlord in
Manchuria in the 1920's

張嘴 (坐尢 ㄗㄨㄟˇ)
① to open the mouth ② to
ask for a loan or a favor

張三李四 (坐尢 ㄙㄢ ㄌㄧˇ ㄙˋ)
anybody; (every) Tom, Dick,
and Harry

張儀 (坐尢 ㄧˊ)
Chang Yi, a strategist during the Warring States
Epoch, who advocated alliance with the state of Chin

張牙舞爪 (坐尢 ㄧㄚˊ ㄨˇ ㄓㄠˇ)
(said of wild beasts) to
frighten people by showing
the fangs and flourishing the
paws

張揚 (坐尢 ㄧㄤˊ)
to publicize; to make widely
known (usually said of a
scandal, secret, etc.); 這事還
未決定,不可張揚開來。This
matter is not yet decided;
don't make it widely known.

張望 (坐尢 ㄨㄤˋ)
to look around; to look
about

【強】 1434
1. (強、彊) ㄑㄧㄤˊ
 chyang qiáng
1. strong; powerful; vigorous:
他比他的弟弟強壯。He is
stronger than his younger
brother.
2. better: 勝利強於失敗。It is
better to win than to lose.
3. violent: 那次地震很強烈。The
earthquake was very violent.

強暴 (ㄑㄧㄤˊ ㄅㄠˋ)
① violent; fierce; ferocious;
atrocious ② rape

強迫進食 (ㄑㄧㄤˊ ㄆㄛˋ ㄐㄧㄣˋ ㄕˊ)
to force-feed; force-feeding

強風 (ㄑㄧㄤˊ ㄈㄥ)
(meteorology) strong breeze

強打者 (ㄑㄧㄤˊ ㄉㄚˇ ㄓㄜˇ)
a slugger

強大 (ㄑㄧㄤˊ ㄉㄚˋ)
powerful and strong

強得多 (ㄑㄧㄤˊ ㄉㄜˊ ㄉㄨㄛ)
① much better than ② much
stronger than

強盜 (ㄑㄧㄤˊ ㄉㄠˋ)
a robber; a bandit

強敵 (ㄑㄧㄤˊ ㄉㄧˊ)
a formidable foe or enemy
a powerful foe or enemy

強調 (ㄑㄧㄤˊ ㄉㄧㄠˋ)
to emphasize; to stress

強度 (ㄑㄧㄤˊ ㄉㄨˋ)
intensity (of light, magnetic
force, etc.)

強挺 (ㄑㄧㄤˊ ㄉㄧㄥˇ)
unyielding; indomitable

強弩之末 (ㄑㄧㄤˊ ㄋㄨˇ ㄓ ㄇㄛˋ)
(literally) at the end of an
arrow's flight—weakened;
spent; exhausted; powerless

強力膠 (ㄑㄧㄤˊ ㄌㄧˋ ㄐㄧㄠ)
glue

強烈 (ㄑㄧㄤˊ ㄌㄧㄝˋ)
violent; strong; intense;
severe; acute; keen: 他有強烈
的政治信仰。He has intense
political convictions.

強梁 (ㄑㄧㄤˊ ㄌㄧㄤˊ)
a bully; a ruffian

強幹 (ㄑㄧㄤˊ ㄍㄢˋ)
competent; capable; able

強梗 (ㄑㄧㄤˊ ㄍㄥˇ)
to obstruct like a bully

強固 (ㄑㄧㄤˊ ㄍㄨˋ)
strong; solid

強國 (ㄑㄧㄤˊ ㄍㄨㄛˊ)
a powerful country; a power

強攻 (ㄑㄧㄤˊ ㄍㄨㄥ)
to take by storm; to storm

強悍 (ㄑㄧㄤˊ ㄏㄢˋ)
fierce; truculent

強橫 (ㄑㄧㄤˊ ㄏㄥˋ)
high-handed; tyrannical; despotic; dictatorial

強化 (ㄑㄧㄤˊ ㄏㄨㄚˋ)
to strengthen; to intensify;
to consolidate

強記 (ㄑㄧㄤˊ ㄐㄧˋ)
having a good memory; strong
in memory

強加 (ㄑㄧㄤˊ ㄐㄧㄚ)
to impose; to force: 不要把你
的觀點強加於別人。Don't force
your viewpoint on others.

強姦 (ㄑㄧㄤˊ ㄐㄧㄢ)
to rape; to violate; to assault or attack sexually

強健 (ㄑㄧㄤˊ ㄐㄧㄢˋ)
strong and healthy: 她雖然年
老但很強健。Though she is
old, she remains very strong
and healthy.

諫(ㄐㄧㄢˋ)
to admonish vigorously

將手下無弱兵(ㄐㄧㄤ ㄕㄡˇ ㄒㄧㄚˋ ㄨˊ ㄖㄨㄛˋ ㄅㄧㄥ)
There are no weak troops under a strong general.

勁(ㄐㄧㄥˋ)
powerful; forceful; strong:
沿岸有強勁的海風。Along the coast there was a strong wind blowing from the sea.

權(ㄑㄩㄢˊ)
brute force; might

即公理(ㄑㄧㄤˊ ㄐㄧˊ ㄍㄨㄥ ㄌㄧˇ)
Might is right.

心劑(ㄑㄧㄤˊ ㄒㄧㄣ ㄐㄧˋ)
a heart stimulant

心針(ㄑㄧㄤˊ ㄒㄧㄣ ㄓㄣ)
a cardinala ampoule

行(ㄑㄧㄤˊ ㄒㄧㄥˊ)
to force: 那名醉漢強行闖入別人的屋子。That drunkard forced his way into another person's house.

震(ㄑㄧㄤˊ ㄓㄣˋ)
(geology) a strong shock

壯(ㄑㄧㄤˊ ㄓㄨㄤˋ)
strong; vigorous; virile; robust; energetic

壯劑(ㄑㄧㄤˊ ㄓㄨㄤˋ ㄐㄧˋ)
a tonic; an invigorant

中自有強中手(ㄑㄧㄤˊ ㄓㄨㄥ ㄗˋ ㄧㄡˇ ㄑㄧㄤˊ ㄓㄨㄥ ㄕㄡˇ)
No matter how strong you are, there's always someone stronger.

身(ㄑㄧㄤˊ ㄕㄣ)
to strengthen the body; to be conducive to health

盛(ㄑㄧㄤˊ ㄕㄥˋ)
(said of a nation, dynasty, etc.) strong and prosperous:
和平使國家強盛。Peace makes a nation strong and prosperous.

人(ㄑㄧㄤˊ ㄖㄣˊ)
①robbers; highwaymen ②a powerful person; a strong-man

韌(ㄑㄧㄤˊ ㄖㄣˋ)
strong; tough; tenacious; resilient

似(ㄑㄧㄤˊ ㄙˋ)
to be better than; to be superior to

硬(ㄑㄧㄤˊ ㄧㄥˋ)
①hard; strong; tough; stiff:
措詞強硬的聲明 a strongly worded statement ②defiant; truculent

【強】 1434 2. (强,彊) ㄑㄧㄤˇ
cheang qiǎng

1. to force
2. to make an effort; to strive:
他強作鎮靜。He made an effort to appear composed.

迫(ㄑㄧㄤˇ ㄆㄛˋ)or強迫(ㄑㄧㄤˊ ㄆㄛˋ)
to force (one to do something); to make (one take some action) by force or coercion: 我強迫他作此事。I forced him to do this.

辯(ㄑㄧㄤˇ ㄅㄧㄢˋ)
to obstinately stick to false reasoning or a lame excuse

迫教育(ㄑㄧㄤˇ ㄆㄛˋ ㄐㄧㄠˋ ㄩˋ)
compulsory or mandatory education

迫降落(ㄑㄧㄤˇ ㄆㄛˋ ㄐㄧㄤˋ ㄌㄨㄛˋ)
forced landing

迫遷移(ㄑㄧㄤˇ ㄆㄛˋ ㄑㄧㄢ ㄧˊ)
forced migration

派(ㄑㄧㄤˇ ㄆㄞˋ)
to force one to contribute or buy something

買強賣(ㄑㄧㄤˇ ㄇㄞˇ ㄑㄧㄤˇ ㄇㄞˋ)
to buy or sell under coercion

聒不舍(ㄑㄧㄤˇ ㄍㄨㄚ ㄅㄨˋ ㄕㄜˇ)
to preach tirelessly

記(ㄑㄧㄤˇ ㄐㄧˋ)
to force oneself to memorize

借(ㄑㄧㄤˇ ㄐㄧㄝˋ)
to borrow forcibly

求(ㄑㄧㄤˇ ㄑㄧㄡˊ)
to demand; to extort; to exact; to impose

取(ㄑㄧㄤˇ ㄑㄩˇ)
to take by force: 他強取了我的筆。He took my pen by force.

制(ㄑㄧㄤˇ ㄓˋ)
forcible; compulsory; to compel; to force

制執行(ㄑㄧㄤˇ ㄓˋ ㄓˊ ㄒㄧㄥˊ)
to execute forcibly; forcible execution

to subject to a forcible measure

佔(ㄑㄧㄤˇ ㄓㄢˋ)
to occupy forcibly; to take (property, one's wife, etc.) by force

使(ㄑㄧㄤˇ ㄕˇ)
to force; to compel: 他強使別人服從。He compelled obedience.

人(ㄑㄧㄤˇ ㄖㄣˊ ㄙㄨㄛˇ ㄋㄢˊ)
to impose a difficult task on someone; to force someone to do something against his will

詞奪理(ㄑㄧㄤˊ ㄘˊ ㄉㄨㄛˊ ㄌㄧˇ)
to argue irrationally

顏歡笑(ㄑㄧㄤˇ ㄧㄢˊ ㄏㄨㄢ ㄒㄧㄠˋ)
to force a smile; to assume a joyous mood reluctantly

【強】 1434 3. (强,彊) ㄐㄧㄤˋ
jiang jiàng

inflexible; obstinate; stubborn: 他像騾子般的倔強。He is as stubborn as a mule.

脾氣(ㄐㄧㄤˋ ㄆㄧˊ ㄑㄧˋ)
an obstinate disposition

九畫

【弼】 1435 ㄅㄧˋ bih bì
1. a device for regulating bows; a bow regulator
2. to correct
3. to assist; to aid: 國王有良臣輔弼。The king has good ministers to assist him.

教(ㄅㄧˋ ㄐㄧㄠˋ)
to assist in education

十畫

【彀】 1436 ㄍㄡˋ gow gòu
1. to draw a bow to the full
2. a trap; a snare
3. sufficient: 她有足彀的東西了。She has quite sufficient.

十二畫

【彈】 1437 1. ㄉㄢˋ dann dàn
a pellet; a bullet; a bomb: 他被流彈擊中。He was hit by a stray bullet.

弓部

〔弓部〕

彈片 (ㄉㄢˋ ㄆㄧㄢˋ)
a shell fragment; shrapnel

彈道 (ㄉㄢˋ ㄉㄠˋ)
a trajectory

彈道飛彈 (ㄉㄢˋ ㄉㄠˋ ㄈㄟ ㄉㄢˋ)
a ballistic missile

彈道學 (ㄉㄢˋ ㄉㄠˋ ㄒㄩㄝˊ)
ballistics

彈頭 (ㄉㄢˋ ㄊㄡˊ)
a projectile nose; a warhead

彈膛 (ㄉㄢˋ ㄊㄤˊ)
a chamber

彈弓 (ㄉㄢˋ ㄍㄨㄥ)
a slingshot; a catapult

彈殼 (ㄉㄢˋ ㄎㄜˊ)
an empty cartridge case

彈痕 (ㄉㄢˋ ㄏㄣˊ)
a bullet mark

彈夾 (ㄉㄢˋ ㄐㄧㄚˊ)
a magazine (of an automatic firearm)

彈盡援絕 (ㄉㄢˋ ㄐㄧㄣˋ ㄩㄢˊ ㄐㄩㄝˊ)
The ammunition is gone, and reinforcements are nowhere in sight.

彈匣 (ㄉㄢˋ ㄒㄧㄚˊ)
(military) a magazine

彈著點 (ㄉㄢˋ ㄓㄨㄛˊ ㄉㄧㄢˇ)
the point of impact

彈子 (戲) (ㄉㄢˋ ㄗˇ ㄒㄧˋ)
billiards; marbles

彈子房 (ㄉㄢˋ ㄗˇ ㄈㄤˊ)
a billiard room; a billiard saloon; a poolroom

彈子檯 (ㄉㄢˋ ㄗˇ ㄊㄞˊ)
a billiard table

彈藥 (ㄉㄢˋ ㄧㄠˋ)
ammunition

彈藥庫 (ㄉㄢˋ ㄧㄠˋ ㄎㄨˋ)
an ammunition depot; a magazine

彈丸 (ㄉㄢˋ ㄨㄢˊ)
a pellet

彈丸小國 (ㄉㄢˋ ㄨㄢˊ ㄒㄧㄠˇ ㄍㄨㄛˊ)
a tiny country

彈丸之地 (ㄉㄢˋ ㄨㄢˊ ㄓ ㄉㄧˋ)
a very small piece of land

彈雨 (ㄉㄢˋ ㄩˇ)
a hail of bullets

【彈】 1437
2. ㄊㄢˊ tarn tán
1. to rebound
2. to play (a stringed instrument sounded by snapping action): 她正在彈鋼琴。She is playing the piano.
3. to impeach: 法官被彈劾受賄。The judge was impeached

for taking a bribe.

彈墨線 (ㄊㄢˊ ㄇㄛˋ ㄒㄧㄢˋ)
to strike a line with an inky string (as a carpenter does)

彈腿 (ㄊㄢˊ ㄊㄨㄟˇ)
a leg action in Chinese boxing

彈力 (ㄊㄢˊ ㄌㄧˋ)
elasticity; elastic force

彈冠 (ㄊㄢˊ ㄍㄨㄢ)
to flip one's cap (so as to remove dust in preparation for an official career)

彈冠相慶 (ㄊㄢˊ ㄍㄨㄢ ㄒㄧㄤ ㄑㄧㄥˋ)
(said of people) to rejoice over the downfall of the guilty or the rise of the virtuous and capable

彈劾 (ㄊㄢˊ ㄏㄜˊ)
to impeach

彈劾權 (ㄊㄢˊ ㄏㄜˊ ㄑㄩㄢˊ)
the power to impeach; impeachment power

彈簧 (ㄊㄢˊ ㄏㄨㄤˊ)
a spring (for absorbing shock, etc.)

彈簧刀 (ㄊㄢˊ ㄏㄨㄤˊ ㄉㄠ)
a switchblade

彈簧墊 (ㄊㄢˊ ㄏㄨㄤˊ ㄉㄧㄢˋ)
a trampoline

彈簧秤 (ㄊㄢˊ ㄏㄨㄤˊ ㄔㄥˋ)
a spring balance

彈琴 (ㄊㄢˊ ㄑㄧㄣˊ)
to play (stringed instruments); to play the piano or an organ

彈性 (ㄊㄢˊ ㄒㄧㄥˋ)
elasticity; resilience: 橡皮有很大的彈性。Rubber has great elasticity.

彈性疲乏 (ㄊㄢˊ ㄒㄧㄥˋ ㄆㄧˊ ㄈㄚˊ)
elastic fatigue

彈性橡皮 (ㄊㄢˊ ㄒㄧㄥˋ ㄒㄧㄤˋ ㄆㄧˊ)
India rubber; caoutchouc

彈指之間 (ㄊㄢˊ ㄓˇ ㄓ ㄐㄧㄢ)
in a snap of the fingers —(figuratively) a very brief space of time

彈唱 (ㄊㄢˊ ㄔㄤˋ)
to sing and play (the piano, guitar, etc.) at the same time

彈奏 (ㄊㄢˊ ㄗㄡˋ)
to play (a stringed musical instrument)

彈詞 (ㄊㄢˊ ㄘˊ)

stories put into rhyme for chanting with accompaniment of musical instruments

彈壓 (ㄊㄢˊ ㄧㄚ)
to put down or suppress (a riot, uprising, etc.)

【彆】 1438
ㄅㄧㄝˋ bieh biè
awkward

彆扭 (ㄅㄧㄝˋ ㄋㄧㄡˇ)
① awkward; refractory; uncomfortable; difficult: 那個人真彆扭。That chap is really refractory. ② an awkward situation

彆氣 (ㄅㄧㄝˋ ㄑㄧˋ)
silently resentful

十四畫

【彌】 1439
ㄇㄧˊ mi mí
1. to fill; to complete: 煙彌漫了那房間。Smoke filled the room.
2. more

彌補 (ㄇㄧˊ ㄅㄨˇ)
to stop or fill up (a gap); to make up for or offset (a loss, shortcoming, etc.); to supplement

彌滿 (ㄇㄧˊ ㄇㄢˇ)
to be full

彌漫 (ㄇㄧˊ ㄇㄢˋ)
to be present all over; to fill the air; 煙霧彌漫 heavy with smoke; smoke-laden

彌封 (ㄇㄧˊ ㄈㄥ)
to seal the examinee's name on an examination paper

彌縫 (ㄇㄧˊ ㄈㄥˊ)
① to fill cracks ② to cover up mistakes

彌天大謊 (ㄇㄧˊ ㄊㄧㄢ ㄉㄚˋ ㄏㄨㄤˇ)
a monstrous lie

彌天大罪 (ㄇㄧˊ ㄊㄧㄢ ㄉㄚˋ ㄗㄨㄟˋ)
a great crime (so great as to fill the universe)

彌陀 (ㄇㄧˊ ㄊㄨㄛˊ)
Amida; Amitabha

彌年 (ㄇㄧˊ ㄋㄧㄢˊ)
the completion of one whole year

彌勒 (ㄇㄧˊ ㄌㄜˋ)
Maitreya, the Buddhist Messiah or next Buddha, whose potbellied statue at a Bud-

dhist temple always carries a
ear-to-ear grin

歸留 (ㄍㄨㄟ ㄌㄧㄡˊ)
on the point of death from a
serious disease

歸合 (ㄍㄨㄟ ㄏㄜˊ)
to close; to bridge

歸撒 (ㄍㄨㄟ ㄙㄚ)
(Catholic) a Mass

歸賽亞 (ㄍㄨㄟ ㄙㄞˋ ㄧㄚˋ)
the Messiah

歸望 (ㄍㄨㄟ ㄨㄤˋ)
as far as the eye can see

歸月 (ㄍㄨㄟ ㄩㄝˋ)
the completion of the first
month after birth of a child

十九畫

【彎】 1440
ㄨㄢ uan wān

to bend; to curve: 他把一鐵線
彎成圓圈。 He bends a wire
into a loop.

彎路 (ㄨㄢ ㄌㄨˋ)
①a crooked road; a tortu-
ous path ② a roundabout
way; a detour: 開車時少走彎
路。When you are driving,
you should avoid detours.

彎弓 (ㄨㄢ ㄍㄨㄥ)
①a drawn bow ② ready to
shoot the arrow ③ an arch

彎接管 (ㄨㄢ ㄐㄧㄝ ㄍㄨㄢˇ)
a bend (to connect two
pipes)

彎曲 (ㄨㄢ ㄑㄩ)
bent; curved: 這是一張彎曲的
弓。This is a bent bow.

彎子 (ㄨㄢ ㄗˇ)or 彎兒(ㄨㄢ ㄦ)
a curve; a bend

彎腰曲背 (ㄨㄢ ㄧㄠ ㄑㄩ ㄅㄟˋ)
(said of a standing posture)
not straight or erect

彎彎曲曲 (ㄨㄢ ㄨㄢ ㄑㄩ ㄑㄩ)
having many bends or
curves; winding; twisting;
snaky: 這條小河彎彎曲曲。
This stream has many
bends.

彐 部
ㄐㄧ jih jì

五畫

【彔】 1441
ㄌㄨ luh lù

1. to carve wood
2. an abbreviated form of 祿

彔彔 (ㄌㄨ ㄌㄨ)
very distinct or clear

六畫

【彖】 1442
ㄊㄨㄢˋ tuann tuàn

1. a chapter of generalization
on divination in the Book of
Changes; a work expounding
the Book of Changes
2. a hog; a hedgehog; a porcupine

彖辭 (ㄊㄨㄢˋ ㄘˊ)
a chapter of generalization
on divination in the Book of
Changes, which was sup-
posedly authored by King
Wen (文王) of the Chou Dy-
nasty

八畫

【彗】 1443
ㄏㄨㄟˋ huey huì

1. a broom
2. a comet
3. to expose to sunlight

彗星 (ㄏㄨㄟˋ ㄒㄧㄥ)
a comet

彗掃 (ㄏㄨㄟˋ ㄙㄠˇ)
to sweep with a broom

彗雲 (ㄏㄨㄟˋ ㄩㄣˊ)
clouds that look like dust
swept by a broom

九畫

【彘】 1444
ㄓˋ jyh zhì

a hog; a pig; a swine

彘肩 (ㄓˋ ㄐㄧㄢ)
the shoulder of a hog

十畫

【彙】 1445
ㄏㄨㄟˋ huey huì

1. a category; a class; a series
2. to categorize; to classify
3. to collect (materials, data,

etc.)

彙報 (ㄏㄨㄟˋ ㄅㄠˋ)
to collect (all information)
and report; to make a collective report

彙編 (ㄏㄨㄟˋ ㄅㄧㄢ)
to edit (assembled reports,
data, etc.)

彙篇 (ㄏㄨㄟˋ ㄆㄧㄢ)
a collection of articles of
similar nature; a publication
of articles by an organization

彙核 (ㄏㄨㄟˋ ㄏㄜˊ)
to examine collectively

彙集 (ㄏㄨㄟˋ ㄐㄧˊ)
to collect (materials, data,
etc.)

彙解 (ㄏㄨㄟˋ ㄐㄧㄝˇ)
a collection of opinions, for
expounding a book, etc.

彙注 (ㄏㄨㄟˋ ㄓㄨˋ)
a collection of footnotes,
remarks, etc., for expounding a book, etc.

彙纂 (ㄏㄨㄟˋ ㄗㄨㄢˇ)
to classify; to categorize; to
edit*

彙冊 (ㄏㄨㄟˋ ㄘㄜˋ)
to collect, categorize and
arrange (materials, data,
reports, etc.) into a volume
for review, inspection, etc.

彙萃 (ㄏㄨㄟˋ ㄘㄨㄟˋ)
to collect (materials, data,
reports, etc.)

十五畫

【彝】 1446
(彝) ㄧˊ yi yí

1. a vessel for wine; a goblet
2. laws or regulations
3. normal nature
4. regular; constant
5. the vessels or items used in
ceremonies at temples, etc.,
such as bells, tripods, chal-
ices, etc.

彝器 (ㄧˊ ㄑㄧˋ)
the vessels or items used in
ceremonies at temples, etc.

彝憲 (ㄧˊ ㄒㄧㄢˋ)
laws; regulations; rules

彝訓 (ㄧˊ ㄒㄩㄣˋ)
regular exhortations

三 部
ㄕㄢ shan **shān**

四畫

【彤】 1447　ㄊㄨㄥˊ torng **tóng**

1. red; vermilion
2. name of an ancient state

彤管 (ㄊㄨㄥˊ ㄍㄨㄢˇ)
(literally) a red tube—a red-tube writing brush, used in ancient China by lady historians

彤弓 (ㄊㄨㄥˊ ㄍㄨㄥ)
a crimson bow 參看「彤矢」

彤矢 (ㄊㄨㄥˊ ㄕˇ)
a crimson arrow, which was bestowed with the crimson bow to noblemen of merits by emperors in ancient China

彤史 (ㄊㄨㄥˊ ㄕˇ)
court-appointed lady historians during the Tang and Ming dynasties

彤闈 (ㄊㄨㄥˊ ㄨㄟˊ)
an imperial palace

彤雲 (ㄊㄨㄥˊ ㄩㄣˊ)
red clouds

【形】 1448　(彤) ㄒㄧㄥˊ shyng **xíng**

1. a form; a shape; an appearance; a figure: 她的外形修長而優雅。 She has a tall graceful form.
2. a complexion
3. a terrain; a contour
4. expression; description; to describe: 這風景美得難以形容。 The scenery is beautiful beyond description.
5. in comparison
6. to show; to manifest

形便 (ㄒㄧㄥˊ ㄅㄧㄢˋ)
advantages offered by terrain

形貌 (ㄒㄧㄥˊ ㄇㄠˋ)
the appearance of a person; a countenance

形單影隻 (ㄒㄧㄥˊ ㄉㄢ ㄧㄥˇ ㄓ)
only me and my shadow—to be all alone

形態 (ㄒㄧㄥˊ ㄊㄞˋ)
an appearance; a form; a state

形態學 (ㄒㄧㄥˊ ㄊㄞˋ ㄒㄩㄝˊ)
morphology

形體 (ㄒㄧㄥˊ ㄊㄧˇ)
the human body which has a form or shape (as contrasted to the spirit which is invisible)

形同虛設 (ㄒㄧㄥˊ ㄊㄨㄥˊ ㄒㄩ ㄕㄜˋ)
to exist in name only

形格勢禁 (ㄒㄧㄥˊ ㄍㄜˊ ㄕˋ ㄐㄧㄣˋ)
unable to act freely; to have one's hands tied

形骸 (ㄒㄧㄥˊ ㄏㄞˊ)
one's body or skeleton

形穢 (ㄒㄧㄥˊ ㄏㄨㄟˋ)
a vulgar appearance

形跡 or 形迹 (ㄒㄧㄥˊ ㄐㄧ)
① one's appearance and manner ② one's behavior or conduct

形跡可疑 (ㄒㄧㄥˊ ㄐㄧ ㄎㄜˇ ㄧˊ)
behavior or a manner that arouses suspicion

形解 (ㄒㄧㄥˊ ㄐㄧㄝˇ)
postmortem; dismemberment of a body

形銷骨立 (ㄒㄧㄥˊ ㄒㄧㄠ ㄍㄨˇ ㄌㄧˋ)
thin and bony; emaciated

形相 (ㄒㄧㄥˊ ㄒㄧㄤ)
① a form; an appearance: 他有高尚的形相。 He is a man of noble appearance. ② to look somebody up and down

形象 (ㄒㄧㄥˊ ㄒㄧㄤˋ)
① a form; an appearance; the physical description of a person; an image ② (fine arts) form as contrasted to substance

形形色色 (ㄒㄧㄥˊ ㄒㄧㄥˊ ㄙㄜˋ ㄙㄜˋ)
of all shapes and colors; a great variety and diversity: 這家商店有形形色色的玩具。 This shop has a variety of toys.

形質 (ㄒㄧㄥˊ ㄓˊ)
form and substance

形制 (ㄒㄧㄥˊ ㄓˋ)
① the design of a manufactured object ② to command a situation by holding a strategic position

形狀 (ㄒㄧㄥˊ ㄓㄨㄤˋ)
the appearance, form or shape of a thing

形成 (ㄒㄧㄥˊ ㄔㄥˊ)
formation; to form; to take shape; to produce as result: 熱使水形成水蒸氣。 Heat causes the formation of steam from water.

形成組織 (ㄒㄧㄥˊ ㄔㄥˊ ㄗㄨˇ ㄓ)
(botany) cambium

形式 (ㄒㄧㄥˊ ㄕˋ)
① form; outward appearance; shape ② formality; for appearance's sake ③ style

形式邏輯 (ㄒㄧㄥˊ ㄕˋ ㄌㄨㄛˊ ㄐㄧˊ)
formalistic logic; formal science

形式主義 (ㄒㄧㄥˊ ㄕˋ ㄓㄨˇ ㄧˋ)
formalism

形式上 (ㄒㄧㄥˊ ㄕˋ ˙ㄕㄤ)
nominally; for formality's sake

形勢 (ㄒㄧㄥˊ ㄕˋ)
① a situation; condition ② a terrain or contour: 這地區形勢險要。 This district is a strategically important terrain.

形聲 (ㄒㄧㄥˊ ㄕㄥ)
determinative-phonetics—one of the six groups into which the Chinese characters are classified (This group of characters is formed by a radical—the determinative—and a phonetic, with the former element indicating the category within which the meaning of the word is to be sought while the latter indicating the pronunciation.)

形勝之地 (ㄒㄧㄥˊ ㄕㄥˋ ㄓ ㄉㄧˋ)
① an advantageous terrain; vantage ground ② a scenic spot

形如槁木 (ㄒㄧㄥˊ ㄖㄨˊ ㄍㄠˇ ㄇㄨˋ)
as lean as a rake; thin and emaciated

形容 (ㄒㄧㄥˊ ㄖㄨㄥˊ)
① to describe ② appearance; form; shape

形容枯槁 (ㄒㄧㄥˊ ㄖㄨㄥˊ ㄎㄨ ㄍㄠˇ)
a thin, bony, or emaciated appearance

形容盡致 (ㄒㄧㄥˊ ㄖㄨㄥˊ ㄐㄧㄣˋ ㄓˋ)

彭 (ㄒㄧㄥ ㄖㄨˋ ㄌㄧ)

an accurate and detailed description

彭容詞 (ㄒㄧㄥ ㄖㄨㄥˊ ㄘˊ)
an adjective

彭蹤 (ㄒㄧㄥˊ ㄗㄨㄥ)
① the traces or tracks of a person; the whereabouts of a person ② the behavior or conduct of a person

彭蹤不定 (ㄒㄧㄥˊ ㄗㄨㄥ ㄅㄨˋ ㄉㄧㄥˋ)
to have no fixed residence; to wander here and there unpredictably

彭蹤詭秘 (ㄒㄧㄥˊ ㄗㄨㄥ ㄍㄨㄟˇ ㄇㄧˋ)
(said of a person) of dubious background, or of many secrets of doubtful character; secretive movements

彭似 (ㄒㄧㄥˊ ㄙˋ)
to resemble; to look like; shaped like

彭色倉皇 (ㄒㄧㄥˊ ㄙㄜˋ ㄘㄤ ㄏㄨㄤˊ)
to look anxious and tense; to appear in a big hurry—as a fugitive

彭而下學 (ㄒㄧㄥˊ ㄦˊ ㄒㄧㄚˋ ㄒㄩㄝˊ)
concrete science

彭而上學 (ㄒㄧㄥˊ ㄦˊ ㄕㄤˋ ㄒㄩㄝˊ)
metaphysics

彭影不離 (ㄒㄧㄥˊ ㄧㄥˇ ㄅㄨˋ ㄌㄧˊ)
(usually said of lovers and devoted couples) inseparable, like a person and his shadow

彭相弔 (ㄒㄧㄥˊ ㄒㄧㄤ ㄉㄧㄠˋ)
(literally) body and shadow comforting each other—solitary; lonely

彭影相隨 (ㄒㄧㄥˊ ㄧㄥˇ ㄒㄧㄤ ㄙㄨㄟˊ)
to follow somebody like his shadow—inseparable; very intimate

六畫

【彥】 1449 (ㄧㄢˋ yann yàn)
a man of ability and virtue; an erudite scholar

彥會 (ㄧㄢˋ ㄏㄨㄟˋ)
a gathering of distinguished personalities

彥士 (ㄧㄢˋ ㄕˋ)
a refined and accomplished scholar

七畫

【彧】 1450 (ㄩˋ yuh yù)
refined, learned and accomplished; abundant

八畫

【彫】 1451 (雕) (ㄉㄧㄠ diau diāo)
1. to tattoo; to carve; to paint; to engrave
2. to wither; emaciated: 花彫謝了。 The flowers withered.
3. to adorn or decorate

彫弓 (ㄉㄧㄠ ㄍㄨㄥ)
to decorate or hide (one's defects, etc.); to beautify

彫弓 (ㄉㄧㄠ ㄍㄨㄥ)
an ornamental bow

彫牆 (ㄉㄧㄠ ㄑㄧㄤˊ)
a wall decorated with a painting or drawing

彫喪 (ㄉㄧㄠ ㄙㄤ)
to look depressed or dejected

【彩】 1452 (ㄘㄞˇ tsae cǎi)
1. colors; variegated colors
2. makeup in various Chinese operas
3. special feats or stunts in Chinese operas
4. ornamental; brilliant; gay
5. stakes in a gambling game; prize money

彩筆 (ㄘㄞˇ ㄅㄧˇ)
① the pen that produces masterpieces ② color crayons

彩排 (ㄘㄞˇ ㄆㄞˊ)
a dress rehearsal: 這些演員們今天有一場彩排。The actors have a dress rehearsal today.

彩票 (ㄘㄞˇ ㄆㄧㄠˋ)
a lottery ticket; a raffle ticket: 他以賣彩票爲生。He makes a living by selling lottery tickets.

彩屏 (ㄘㄞˇ ㄆㄧㄥˊ)
ornamental screens; multicolored screens

彩鳳隨鴉 (ㄘㄞˇ ㄈㄥˋ ㄙㄨㄟˊ ㄧㄚ)
(literally) a beautiful phoenix mated to a crow—a perfect woman married to a worthless man

彩帶 (ㄘㄞˇ ㄉㄞˋ)
a colored ribbon (or streamer)

彩旦 (ㄘㄞˇ ㄉㄢˋ)
(Chinese opera) the clown who plays the role of a female, usually of the vicious type

彩蛋 (ㄘㄞˇ ㄉㄢˋ)
(arts and crafts) a painted eggshell; a painting on an eggshell

彩陶文化 (ㄘㄞˇ ㄊㄠˊ ㄨㄣˊ ㄏㄨㄚˋ)
(archaeology) Painted-Pottery Culture

彩頭 (ㄘㄞˇ ㄊㄡˊ)
good luck; lucky

彩禮 (ㄘㄞˇ ㄌㄧˇ)
the presents for the bride's family

彩繪 (ㄘㄞˇ ㄏㄨㄟˋ)
a colored drawing or pattern

彩虹 (ㄘㄞˇ ㄏㄨㄥˊ)
a rainbow

彩轎 (ㄘㄞˇ ㄐㄧㄠˋ)
a bridal sedan chair

彩氣 (ㄘㄞˇ ㄑㄧˋ)
good luck or fortune

彩球 (ㄘㄞˇ ㄑㄧㄡˊ)
① a ball-shaped bundle of colored silk ribbons for decoration ② the corona around the sun during an eclipse

彩錢 (ㄘㄞˇ ㄑㄧㄢˊ)
(Chinese opera) money given to an actor who plays the act of being wounded

彩霞 (ㄘㄞˇ ㄒㄧㄚˊ)
rosy clouds in the morning or evening

彩車 (ㄘㄞˇ ㄔㄜ)
a float (in a parade)

彩綢 (ㄘㄞˇ ㄔㄡˊ)
silk of various colors

彩飾 (ㄘㄞˇ ㄕˋ)
to adorn; to ornament; ornaments; adornments

彩色 (ㄘㄞˇ ㄙㄜˋ)
color (film, pictures, photography, etc.)

彩色版 (ㄘㄞˇ ㄙㄜˋ ㄅㄢˇ)
chromolithograph printing

彩色電視 (ㄘㄞˇ ㄙㄜˋ ㄉㄧㄢˋ ㄕˋ)
color television

〔彡 部〕

彡部

彩色軟片(ちㄞ ㄙㄜ ㄖㄨㄢ ㄆㄧㄢˋ)
color film

彩色印刷(ちㄞˇ ㄙㄜ ㄧㄣˋ ㄕㄨㄚ)
chromolithograph; color
lithography

彩葉芋(ちㄞˇ ㄧㄝˋ ㄩˋ)
galadium

彩釉(ちㄞˇ ㄧㄡˋ)
color ceramic glaze

彩雲(ちㄞˇ ㄩㄣˊ)
clouds of many hues: 天空佈
滿了彩雲。There are clouds
of many hues in the sky.

彩暈(ちㄞˇ ㄩㄣˋ)
halos of many colors

【彬】 1453
　　 ㄅㄧㄣ bin bīn

1. intelligent, refined and gentle: 他是一個文質彬彬的人。He
is an intelligent and refined
gentleman.

2. a Chinese family name

彬彬(ㄅㄧㄣ ㄅㄧㄣ)
refined, gentle and elegant

彬彬君子(ㄅㄧㄣ ㄅㄧㄣ ㄐㄩㄣ ㄗˇ)
a refined gentleman

彬彬有禮(ㄅㄧㄣ ㄅㄧㄣ ㄧㄡˇ ㄌㄧˇ)
refined and courteous; suave

彬蔚(ㄅㄧㄣ ㄨㄟˋ)
extremely erudite and
refined

【彪】 1454
　　 ㄅㄧㄠ biau biāo

1. a tiger cub

2. stripes or streaks on the
skin of a tiger

3. tall and big; shining and
brilliant; outstanding

4. a Chinese family name

彪炳(ㄅㄧㄠ ㄅㄧㄥˇ)
brilliant and shining; splendid (achievements, exam-
ples, etc.)

彪煥(ㄅㄧㄠ ㄏㄨㄢˋ)
brilliant and shining; outstanding and elegant

彪休(ㄅㄧㄠ ㄒㄧㄡ)
angry; wrathful

彪形(ㄅㄧㄠ ㄒㄧㄥˊ)
tall and big

彪形大漢(ㄅㄧㄠ ㄒㄧㄥˊ ㄉㄚˋ ㄏㄢˋ)
a whale of a man

九畫

【彭】 1455
　　 ㄆㄥˊ perng péng

1. a Chinese family name

2. big

3. longevity

4. proud

彭彭(ㄆㄥˊ ㄆㄥˊ)
① to be numerous ②
descriptive of a team of
horses advancing without
stopping

彭公案(ㄆㄥˊ ㄍㄨㄥ ㄢˋ)
a famous Chinese novel (a
forerunner of modern detective stories), authored by 貪
夢道人 of the Ching Dynasty

彭亨(ㄆㄥˊ ㄏㄥ)
① potbellied ② proud and
smug

彭殤(ㄆㄥˊ ㄕㄤ)
longevity and early death

彭祖(ㄆㄥˊ ㄗㄨˇ)
name of a legendary offi-
cial in the reign of Em-
peror Yao (2356 B.C.), who
was said to have lived 800
years

十一畫

【彰】 1456
　　 ㄓㄤ jang zhāng

1. ornamental; colorful

2. evident; obvious; clear

3. to manifest; to make known;
to display

彰明(ㄓㄤ ㄇㄧㄥˊ)
① to manifest; to clarify; to
expound ② name of a county
in Szechwan

彰明較著(ㄓㄤ ㄇㄧㄥˊ ㄐㄧㄠˋ ㄓㄨˋ)
extremely obvious and
ostensible

彰化(ㄓㄤ ㄏㄨㄚˋ)
Changhua, a county in central Taiwan

彰顯(ㄓㄤ ㄒㄧㄢˇ)
to manifest; to show forth;
obvious

彰彰(ㄓㄤ ㄓㄤ)
famous; well-known; evident:
她的德行彰彰在人耳目。Her
virtues are evident to everybody.

彰善癉惡(ㄓㄤ ㄕㄢˋ ㄉㄢˋ ㄜˋ)
to publicize and encourage
the good and detest the evil

彰往察來(ㄓㄤ ㄨㄤˇ ㄔㄚˊ ㄌㄞˊ)
to evidence the past and

scrutinize the future

十二畫

【影】 1457
　　 ㄧㄥˇ yíng yǐng

1. a shadow; an image; a reflection

2. a trace; a vague impression:
我早就忘得沒影兒。I haven't
the vaguest impression of it.

3. to copy and imitate

4. to hide; to conceal

5. a sundial

影本(ㄧㄥˇ ㄅㄣˇ)
a facsimile edition; a rubbing

影壁(ㄧㄥˇ ㄅㄧˋ)
a protecting wall immediately inside or outside the front
door of a house

影片(ㄧㄥˇ ㄆㄧㄢˋ)
a motion picture; movies;
the film of a motion picture

影評(ㄧㄥˇ ㄆㄧㄥˊ)
brief comments on motion
pictures; film criticism or
evaluation

影評人(ㄧㄥˇ ㄆㄧㄥˊ ㄖㄣˊ)
a movie critic

影迷(ㄧㄥˇ ㄇㄧˊ)
a movie fan: 這位電影明星有
很多影迷。This movie star
has a great number of fans.

影碟片(ㄧㄥˇ ㄉㄧㄝˊ ㄆㄧㄢˋ)
a videodisk

影碟機(ㄧㄥˇ ㄉㄧㄝˊ ㄐㄧ)
a videodisk player

影壇(ㄧㄥˇ ㄊㄢˊ)
the movie circles; moviedom

影集(ㄧㄥˇ ㄐㄧˊ)
a miniseries (or a mini
series)

影劇界(ㄧㄥˇ ㄐㄩˋ ㄐㄧㄝˋ)
the entertainment world;
movie and drama circles

影戲(ㄧㄥˇ ㄒㄧˋ)
① a motion picture ② a kind
of shadowgraph perfor-
mance

影響(ㄧㄥˇ ㄒㄧㄤˇ)
influence; impact; effect; to
affect; to influence

影像(ㄧㄥˇ ㄒㄧㄤˋ)
an image; a portrait: 她看見
鏡中她的影像。She saw her
image in the mirror.

影星(ㄧㄥ ㄒㄧㄥ)
a movie star

影展(ㄧㄥ ㄓㄢˇ)
a photographic exhibition; a film festival

影鈔(ㄧㄥ ㄔㄠ)
to make a true-to-life copy (of old books of great value, etc.)

影事(ㄧㄥ ㄕˋ)
(Buddhism) a theory that everything in this world is made up of shadows and visions which will vanish in no time

影射(ㄧㄥ ㄕㄜˋ)
① to counterfeit (trademarks, etc.); to delude; to humbug ② to hint by suggestive remarks or association

影子(ㄧㄥ ˙ㄗ)or影兒(ㄧㄥˇ)
① a shadow ② (figuratively) a trace; a sign; a vague impression

影子內閣(ㄧㄥ ˙ㄗ ㄋㄟˋ ㄍㄜˊ)
a shadow cabinet

影從(ㄧㄥ ㄘㄨㄥ)
to follow like a shadow

影印(ㄧㄥ ㄧㄣ)
① photogravure ② xerography; to xerox

影印本(ㄧㄥ ㄧㄣ ㄅㄣˇ)
a photolithographic edition; a photostatic copy

影印中心(ㄧㄥ ㄧㄣ ㄓㄨㄥ ㄒㄧㄣ)
a copy center

影影綽綽(ㄧㄥ ㄧㄥ ㄔㄨㄜˋ ㄔㄨㄜˋ)
shadowy; vague outlines (of somebody, etc.)

影院(ㄧㄥ ㄩㄢˋ)
a movie theater

彳 部

彳 chyh chì

【彳】 1458
彳 chyh chì
1. short steps or paces
2. a step taken with the left foot
3. a phonetic sign for "ch"
彳亍(ㄔˋ ㄔㄨˋ)
to walk (with left and right

feet)

四畫

【彷】 1459
1. ㄆㄤ parng páng
hesitating; unsettled
彷徨(ㄆㄤˊ ㄏㄨㄤˊ)
to hesitate; undecided: 他曾在歧路彷徨過。He hesitated at the crossroads.
彷徉(ㄆㄤˊ ㄧㄤˊ)
① unsettled; doubtful ② to roam about

【彷】 1459
2. ㄈㄤˇ faang fǎng
like; similar to; to resemble: 它們的形狀相彷彿。They resemble each other in shape.
彷彿(ㄈㄤˇ ㄈㄨˊ)
① to seem; as if ② to be more or less the same; to be alike

【役】 1460
役 ㄧˋ yih yì
1. military service
2. to guard the frontier
3. to dispatch
4. to employ as a servant
5. to serve; a servant
6. to do; to undertake
役夫(ㄧˋ ㄈㄨ)
a laborer; a servant
役男(ㄧˋ ㄋㄢˊ)
the male citizens between 18 and 45 who are eligible for military service
役齡(ㄧˋ ㄌㄧㄥˊ)
enlistment age
役志(ㄧˋ ㄓˋ)
to bring one's into submission
役種(ㄧˋ ㄓㄨㄥˇ)
the classification of military service status such as militia, reserve, standing, etc.
役使(ㄧˋ ㄕˇ)
to employ as a servant; to make (someone) work
役使動物(ㄧˋ ㄕˇ ㄉㄨㄥˋ ㄨˋ)
beasts of burden; draft animals
役屬(ㄧˋ ㄕㄨˇ)
to control; to master
役人(ㄧˋ ㄖㄣˊ)
① (in old China) underlings

in a magistrate's office; an attendant ② to order other people to do work; to be served by others
役卒(ㄧˋ ㄗㄨˊ)
lictors; runners
役於人(ㄧˋ ㄩˊ ㄖㄣˊ)
to serve others
役於外物(ㄧˋ ㄩˊ ㄨㄞˋ ㄨˋ)
to crave for worldly goods; to be a slave to material comfort

五畫

【彼】 1461
彼 ㄅㄧˇ bii bǐ
1. that; those: 彼書遠較此書爲佳。That book is much better than this one.
2. the other; another: 他們彼此感情融洽。They are friendly to one another.
3. there: 我將迅達於達彼處。I shall soon be there.
彼輩(ㄅㄧˇ ㄅㄟˋ)
those people; that gang
彼方(ㄅㄧˇ ㄈㄤ)
the other party; the other side ●
彼得大帝(ㄅㄧˇ ㄉㄜˊ ㄉㄚˋ ㄉㄧˋ)
Peter the Great (1672-1725), Russian emperor
彼等(ㄅㄧˇ ㄉㄥˇ)
those people
彼此(ㄅㄧˇ ㄘˇ)
you and me; both parties; that and this; each other: 他們每天彼此見面。They saw each other every day.
彼此彼此(ㄅㄧˇ ㄘˇ ㄅㄧˇ ㄘˇ)
We are alike. 或 We are in similar position.或 The feeling is mutual.
彼此之間(ㄅㄧˇ ㄘˇ ㄓ ㄐㄧㄢ)
between you, between them; between you and me; between two persons or parties
彼蒼(ㄅㄧˇ ㄘㄤ)
the heavens
彼岸(ㄅㄧˇ ㄢˋ)
① the other side (of the river, ocean, etc.) ② (Buddhism) paradise
彼一時此一時(ㄅㄧˇ ㄧ ㄕˊ ㄘˇ ㄧ ㄕˊ)
Time makes all the differ-

〔彳部〕

ence. 或 Different times call
for different actions.

【往】 1462 1. ㄨㄤˇ woang wáng

1. to go toward; to depart; to
be bound for: The train is
bound for Keelung.
2. formerly; past; bygone;
gone: 既往不咎。 Let bygones
be bygones.

往返(ㄨㄤˇ ㄈㄢˇ)
to come and go; to arrive
and depart; to make a round
trip; to and fro: 往返要多少時
間? How long does it take
to go there and back?

往復(ㄨㄤˇ ㄈㄨˋ)
① continuous ② comings
and goings between friends,
etc.

往年(ㄨㄤˇ ㄋㄧㄢˊ)
in the years past; in bygone
years

往來(ㄨㄤˇ ㄌㄞˊ)
① to go and return ② per-
sonal contact between two
persons or parties, etc.: 他們
倆往來密切。 The two of them
are in close contact.

往來銀行(ㄨㄤˇ ㄌㄞˊ ㄧㄣˊ ㄏㄤˊ)
a bank with whom the
credits opened

往來無阻(ㄨㄤˇ ㄌㄞˊ ㄨˊ ㄗㄨˇ)
freedom of movements; coming and going without hindrance

往古來今(ㄨㄤˇ ㄍㄨˇ ㄌㄞˊ ㄐㄧㄣ)
from ancient time until now;
since time immemorial

往後(ㄨㄤˇ ㄏㄡˋ)
① backward; going back ②
hereafter; in the future; from
now on: 往後我們要更加用功。
From now on we'll study
more diligently.

往還(ㄨㄤˇ ㄏㄨㄢˊ)
① coming and going ② con-
tact between two people or
parties: 他們兩家常有往還。
Their two families always
keep in contact with each
other.

往教(ㄨㄤˇ ㄐㄧㄠˋ)
to ask the teacher to come
to the pupil's place to teach
(an act considered disrespectful to the teacher)

往昔(ㄨㄤˇ ㄒㄧˊ)
in the past; in ancient times:
我們不知道他往昔的生活情形。
We know nothing of his life
in the past.

往哲(ㄨㄤˇ ㄓㄜˊ)
ancient saints and sages

往者已矣(ㄨㄤˇ ㄓㄜˇ ㄧˇ)
What's gone is gone.

往常(ㄨㄤˇ ㄔㄤˊ)
usually; heretofore; in the
past; used to

往時(ㄨㄤˇ ㄕˊ)
formerly; in the past

往事(ㄨㄤˇ ㄕˋ)
things that have come to
pass

往事休提(ㄨㄤˇ ㄕˋ ㄒㄧㄡ ㄊㄧˊ)
Let bygones be bygones.

往聖(ㄨㄤˇ ㄕㄥˋ)
ancient sages

往日(ㄨㄤˇ ㄖˋ)
in the olden days; in the
past; in bygone days

往往(ㄨㄤˇ ㄨㄤˇ)
usually; often; frequently;
more often than not: 他禮拜天
往往待在家裏。 He usually
stays at home on Sundays.

往往如此(ㄨㄤˇ ㄨㄤˇ ㄖㄨˊ ㄘˇ)
It happens frequently that...;
usually like that

【往】 1462 2. ㄨㄤˋ wang wàng

an adverb indicating time or
direction: 水性低處流。 Water
naturally flows downhill.

往好處想(ㄨㄤˋ ㄏㄠˇ ㄔㄨˋ ㄒㄧㄤˇ)
to think of the better possibilities of a situation, etc.

往回走(ㄨㄤˋ ㄏㄨㄟˊ ㄗㄡˇ)
to turn back and proceed

往壞處想(ㄨㄤˋ ㄏㄨㄞˋ ㄔㄨˋ ㄒㄧㄤˇ)
to think of the unfavorable
possibilities of a situation,
etc.

往前看(ㄨㄤˋ ㄑㄧㄢˊ ㄎㄢˋ)
to look forward

往下說(ㄨㄤˋ ㄒㄧㄚˋ ㄕㄨㄛ)
to talk on 或 Go ahead. 或
Please continue.

往上跑(ㄨㄤˋ ㄕㄤˋ ㄆㄠˇ)
to run up; to go uphill

往左拐(ㄨㄤˋ ㄗㄨㄛˇ ㄍㄨㄞˇ)
to turn left: 這條路是往左拐
的。 The road is turning off
to the left.

往右轉(ㄨㄤˋ ㄧㄡˋ ㄓㄨㄢˇ)
to turn right

【征】 1463 ㄓㄥ jeng zhēng

1. to journey far away
2. to attack; to reduce to submission; to conquer; to take
3. to levy taxes; to collec
taxes
4. to take; to snatch
5. a Chinese family name

征旂(ㄓㄥ ㄕ)
(in old China) military
standards for troops marching to war

征馬(ㄓㄥ ㄇㄚˇ)
① a war horse; a charger ②
a traveler's horse

征伐(ㄓㄥ ㄈㄚˊ)
to battle; to be on the war
path; a punitive military
action

征帆(ㄓㄥ ㄈㄢˊ)
the boat that makes long
voyages

征夫(ㄓㄥ ㄈㄨ)或征人(ㄓㄥ ㄖㄣˊ)
① a traveler who has jour-
neyed far ② a warrior or
soldier

征服(ㄓㄥ ㄈㄨˊ)
to conquer; conquest: 他們用
武力征服了敵人。 They con-
quered the enemy by force
of arms.

征服者(ㄓㄥ ㄈㄨˊ ㄓㄜˇ)
a conqueror

征服自然(ㄓㄥ ㄈㄨˊ ㄗˋ ㄖㄢˊ)
to conquer nature; the conquest of nature: 科學家企圖征
服自然。 Scientists attempt to
conquer nature.

征討(ㄓㄥ ㄊㄠˇ)
to quell (an uprising, rebellion, etc.); to subjugate

征途(ㄓㄥ ㄊㄨˊ)
the journey of a traveler; a
traveler's progress

征稅(ㄓㄥ ㄕㄨㄟˋ)
to levy and collect taxes

征客(ㄓㄥ ㄎㄜˋ)
the person who has jour-
neyed a long way; a traveler

征戰(ㄓㄥ ㄓㄢˋ)
to fight in battle

征塵(ㄓㄥ ㄔㄣˊ)
the dust on the route by
which a traveler comes from

afar; the dust on the traveler's clothing

征收(ㄓㄥ ㄕㄡ)
to levy and collect (taxes); to impose: 政府每年征收稅金。 The government levies and collects taxes every year.

征夫(ㄓㄥ ㄈㄨ)
dependents of conscripts; dependents of servicemen fighting at the front

征戍(ㄓㄥ ㄕㄨ)
to garrison on the frontiers

征衣(ㄓㄥ ㄧ)
① traveling clothes ② warrior's costume

【徂】 1464
ㄘㄨ tswu cú
1. to go to; to go ahead; to advance
2. the preposition "to"
3. to die
4. past

徂落(ㄘㄨ ㄌㄨㄛ)
to pass away; to die

徂謝(ㄘㄨ ㄒㄧㄝ)
① to wither; to fade ② to die

徂暑(ㄘㄨ ㄕㄨ)
the hottest days of summer

徂歲(ㄘㄨ ㄙㄨㄟ)
the past year; last year

【佛】 1465
ㄈㄨ fwu fú
like; similar to; as if

六畫

【待】 1466
1. ㄉㄞ day dài
1. to treat; to entertain: 這位老師待人誠懇。 This teacher treats people sincerely.
2. to await; to wait for
3. need
4. until
5. a Chinese family name

待除(ㄉㄞ ㄔㄨ)
yet to be taken care of

待斃(ㄉㄞ ㄅㄧ)
to await death; to be a sitting duck

待哺(ㄉㄞ ㄅㄨ)
to wait for feeding (as babies)

待補(ㄉㄞ ㄅㄨ)
① (said of an alternate candidate, etc.) to await a vacancy for him to fill ② a pending further supplement, or addition

待聘(ㄉㄞ ㄆㄧㄣ)
to wait for employment

待命(ㄉㄞ ㄇㄧㄥ)
to await orders

待發(ㄉㄞ ㄈㄚ)
ready to depart: 他們整裝待發。 They have packed up and are ready to depart.

待得(ㄉㄞ ㄉㄜ)
to wait for; to wait until (one gets old, etc.)

待旦(ㄉㄞ ㄉㄢ)
to wait for the morning (usually said of soldiers on night watch, or people working hard through the night)

待敵(ㄉㄞ ㄉㄧ)
to wait for the enemy; to lie in ambush

待漏(ㄉㄞ ㄌㄡ)
(said of courtiers) to wait for the emperor to appear at court at an early hour in the morning

待理不理(ㄉㄞ ㄌㄧ ㄅㄨ ㄌㄧ)
a lukewarm reception; to give the cold shoulder to another

待領(ㄉㄞ ㄌㄧㄥ)
(said of money, articles) to wait for a claimant

待客(ㄉㄞ ㄎㄜ)
to receive guests; to entertain guests

待考(ㄉㄞ ㄎㄠ)
(said of a report, theory, statement, etc.) remaining to be confirmed or substantiated

待機(ㄉㄞ ㄐㄧ)
to await the opportune moment (for action)

待價而沽(ㄉㄞ ㄐㄧㄚ ㄦ ㄍㄨ)
to wait for the right (favorable) price to sell

待見(ㄉㄞ ㄐㄧㄢ)
① to like; to be fond of ② to wait to be received (by the host, etc.)

待舉(ㄉㄞ ㄐㄩ)
to be ready for action

待宵草(ㄉㄞ ㄒㄧㄠ ㄘㄠ)
an evening primrose

待續(ㄉㄞ ㄒㄩ)
to be continued

待制(ㄉㄞ ㄓ)
(in ancient China) an advisor; a staff officer

待詔(ㄉㄞ ㄓㄠ)
① an official rank in the Ming and Ching dynasties ② a barber ③ a shop clerk

待茶(ㄉㄞ ㄔㄚ)
to entertain guests with tea

待查(ㄉㄞ ㄔㄚ)
yet to be investigated: 此事是否屬實待查。 Whether it is true or not is yet to be investigated.

待時(ㄉㄞ ㄕ)
to bide one's time

待人接物(ㄉㄞ ㄖㄣ ㄐㄧㄝ ㄨ) or 待物(ㄉㄞ ㄨ)
the way one treats people: 她待人接物和藹可親。 She treats people kindly.

待如己出(ㄉㄞ ㄖㄨ ㄐㄧ ㄔㄨ)
to treat a child as if he were one's own

待字閨中(ㄉㄞ ㄗ ㄍㄨㄟ ㄓㄨㄥ)
(said of a young woman) not betrothed yet

待罪(ㄉㄞ ㄗㄨㄟ)
① to wait for punishment ② (in old China) a term referring to oneself when addressing a superior

待業(ㄉㄞ ㄧㄝ)
(in mainland China) out of employment

待要(ㄉㄞ ㄧㄠ)
to be about to

待遇(ㄉㄞ ㄩ)
① pay, salary, or remuneration ② the manner of treating people

待月西廂(ㄉㄞ ㄩㄝ ㄒㄧ ㄒㄧㄤ)
(literally) to wait under the moon at the West Chamber —to wait for one's lover in the night; to have a nocturnal rendezvous with one's lover

【待】 1466
2. ㄉㄞ dai dāi
1. to stay: 他在台北待了三週。 He stayed in Taipei for three weeks.
2. later

待不住(ㄉㄞ ㄅㄨ ㄓㄨ)
can't or won't stay long

【彳部】

〔彳部〕

待到(ㄉㄞˋ ㄉㄠˋ)
to wait until

待了(ㄉㄞˋ ·ㄌㄜ ㄔㄨㄥ ㄊㄞˊ)
to have stayed for a long while

待兩天(ㄉㄞˋ ㄌㄧㄤˇ ㄊㄧㄢ)
to wait for a few days; two days later; to have stayed for a few days

待一會兒(ㄉㄞˋ ㄧˋ ㄏㄨㄟˋㄦ)
moments later; just a little while

待在家裏(ㄉㄞˋ ㄗㄞˋ ㄐㄧㄚ ·ㄌㄧ)
to stay at home; to stay in

【徇】 1467 1. (徇) ㄒㄩㄣˋ xiunn

1. to show; to display
2. to issue orders in the army
3. to follow; to comply with
4. quick
5. to die for a cause

徇死(ㄒㄩㄣˋ ㄙˇ)
to die for a just cause or for one's country

徇行(ㄒㄩㄣˋ ㄒㄧㄥˊ)
to make rounds of inspection

徇首(ㄒㄩㄣˋ ㄕㄡˇ)
to show the head (of a decapitated offender) to people, troops, etc. to warn against repetition of the offense

徇義(ㄒㄩㄣˋ ㄧˋ)
to follow the cause of righteousness even at the expense of one's life; to die a martyr's death

【徇】 1467 2. ㄒㄩㄣˊ shyun xún

1. pervading
2. to profit

徇情(ㄒㄩㄣˊ ㄑㄧㄥˊ)
favoritism; to let personal feelings influence one's decision

徇私(ㄒㄩㄣˊ ㄙ)
to profit oneself; favoritism; nepotism

徇私舞弊(ㄒㄩㄣˊ ㄙ ㄨˇ ㄅㄧˋ)
to play favoritism and commit irregularities

【很】 1468 ㄏㄣˇ heen hěn

1. very; quite: 你的話很有道理。 What you said was very reasonable.

2. fierce; cruel; truculent
3. disobedient; intractable; quarrelsome
4. dispute; quarrel

【徉】 1469 ㄧㄤˊ yang yáng

1. to stray; to roam: 他常在林間徜徉。 He often roams about the forest.
2. hesitating; unsettled

【徊】 1470 ㄏㄨㄞˊ hwai huái
(又讀 ㄏㄨㄟˊ hwei huí)

1. hesitating; irresolute; indecisive
2. to move to and fro; to walk around

【律】 1471 ㄌㄩˋ liuh lǜ

1. a law; a rule; a regulation; a statute
2. to bind by law; to control or restrain; to discipline
3. a series of standard bamboo tuning pitch pipes used in ancient music
4. a form in Chinese poetry— a stanza of eight lines

律賦(ㄌㄩˋ ㄈㄨˋ)
a form of literary style, called fu (賦), with couplets of an identical number of characters neatly paired off word for word

律度(ㄌㄩˋ ㄉㄨˋ)
laws and institutions

律例(ㄌㄩˋ ㄌㄧˋ)
laws or statutes and precedents

律令(ㄌㄩˋ ㄌㄧㄥˋ)
① laws and regulations; orders given according to law ② a Taoist incantation

律呂(ㄌㄩˋ ㄌㄩˇ)
a series of 12 standard bamboo tuning pitch pipes used in ancient Chinese music

律己(ㄌㄩˋ ㄐㄧˇ)
to discipline oneself; self-restraint; to be strict with oneself: 律己以嚴，待人以寬。 One should be strict with oneself but liberal toward others.

律詩(ㄌㄩˋ ㄕ)
a poem of eight lines with five or seven characters each and with certain rules about rhymes, tones, and antitheses, popular since the Tang Dynasty

律師(ㄌㄩˋ ㄕ)
① a lawyer; a barrister ② a polite expression for Buddhist monks

律師公會(ㄌㄩˋ ㄕ ㄍㄨㄥ ㄏㄨㄟˋ)
a bar association

律師事務所(ㄌㄩˋ ㄕ ㄕˋ ㄨˋ ㄙㄨㄛˇ)
a lawyer's office

【後】 1472 ㄏㄡˋ how hòu

1. behind; at the back of
2. afterwards; to come after
3. descendants; posterity
4. an auxiliary to indicate "then" or "afterwards"
5. a Chinese family name

後輩(ㄏㄡˋ ㄅㄟˋ)
① juniors; inferiors ② descendants; posterity

後備軍(ㄏㄡˋ ㄅㄟˋ ㄐㄩㄣ)
reserve forces

後備軍人(ㄏㄡˋ ㄅㄟˋ ㄐㄩㄣ ㄖㄣˊ)
military reservists

後半部(ㄏㄡˋ ㄅㄢˋ ㄅㄨˋ)
the latter portion of a book or movie

後半天(ㄏㄡˋ ㄅㄢˋ ㄊㄧㄢ)
the latter half of a day

後半晌兒(ㄏㄡˋ ㄅㄢˋ ㄕㄤˇㄦ)
the late afternoon or evening

後半生(ㄏㄡˋ ㄅㄢˋ ㄕㄥ)
the latter half of one's life

後半夜(ㄏㄡˋ ㄅㄢˋ ㄧㄝˋ)
after midnight; in the wee hours

後邊兒(ㄏㄡˋ ㄅㄧㄢㄦ)
behind; at the back of

後補(ㄏㄡˋ ㄅㄨˇ)
① to make amends ② to replenish

後部(ㄏㄡˋ ㄅㄨˋ)
behind; the back of

後排(ㄏㄡˋ ㄆㄞˊ)
a back row: 後排座位 back row seats

後門(ㄏㄡˋ ㄇㄣˊ)
① the back door; the rear gate (of a city wall) ② backdoor influence: 走後門 to get something done through pull

後面(ㄏㄡˋ ㄇㄧㄢˋ)
① behind; at the back: 這房子後面有一花園。 There is a

garden at the back of the house. ② afterwards; what is to follow: 這個問題我後面還要講。I'll come back to this question later.

後命(ㄏㄡˋ ㄇㄧㄥˋ)
further orders or instructions

後母(ㄏㄡˋ ㄇㄨˇ)
one's stepmother 亦作「繼母」

後方(ㄏㄡˋ ㄈㄤ)
the rear (as contrasted to the war front)

後方勤務(ㄏㄡˋ ㄈㄤ ㄑㄧㄣˊ ㄨˋ)
logistics

後房(ㄏㄡˋ ㄈㄤˊ)
① the living quarters for one's concubines ② the rear of a house

後夫(ㄏㄡˋ ㄈㄨ)
one's second husband (after the divorce or death of the first)

後福(ㄏㄡˋ ㄈㄨˊ)
the blessings to follow; the good days to come (in a person's life); luck in one's later life

後代(ㄏㄡˋ ㄉㄞˋ)
descendants or posterity; future generations: 他們是孔子的後代。They are the descendants of Confucius.

後凋(ㄏㄡˋ ㄉㄧㄠ)
(literally) the last (among plants) to wither—the perseverance of a person in his virtuous ways

後殿(ㄏㄡˋ ㄉㄧㄢˋ)
the rear court rooms in a palace

後段(ㄏㄡˋ ㄉㄨㄢˋ)
① the latter part of a piece of writing or a musical composition, etc. ② the back rows in a theater, etc.

後盾(ㄏㄡˋ ㄉㄨㄣˋ)
a support or supporter; a prop to lean back; a backing

後臺(ㄏㄡˋ ㄊㄞˊ)
① a backstage ② (usually in politics) one's backing or backers; good connections: 他的後臺很硬。He has very strong backing.

後臺老板(ㄏㄡˋ ㄊㄞˊ ㄌㄠˇ ㄅㄢˇ)
(powerful and influential)

backers; the string-puller behind the scenes; backstage bosses

後頭骨(ㄏㄡˋ ㄊㄡˊ ㄍㄨˇ)
(anatomy) the parietal bone

後頭(ㄏㄡˋ ㄊㄡˊ)
① behind; at the back of (a person) ② in the future; days to come

後唐(ㄏㄡˋ ㄊㄤˊ)
the Posterior Tang Dynasty (923-936 A.D.)

後膛鎗(ㄏㄡˋ ㄊㄤˊ ㄑㄧㄤ)
a breechloading gun; a rifle; a breechloader

後天(ㄏㄡˋ ㄊㄧㄢ)
① the day after tomorrow: 我後天將去學校。I will go to school the day after tomorrow. ② acquired; postnatal

後天性免疫不全症候群(ㄏㄡˋ ㄊㄧㄢ ㄒㄧㄥˋ ㄇㄧㄢˇ ㄧˋ ㄅㄨˋ ㄑㄩㄢˊ ㄓㄥˋ ㄏㄡˋ ㄑㄩㄣˊ)
AIDS (Acquired Immune Deficiency Syndrome) 亦作「愛滋病」

後庭(ㄏㄡˋ ㄊㄧㄥˊ)
imperial harems or seraglios

後圖(ㄏㄡˋ ㄊㄨˊ)
to plan later; future planning

後腿兒(ㄏㄡˋ ㄊㄨㄟˇ ㄦ)
the hind legs of an animal

後退(ㄏㄡˋ ㄊㄨㄟˋ)
to retreat; to withdraw; retreat; withdrawal

後腦(ㄏㄡˋ ㄋㄠˇ)
the hindbrain, consisting of the cerebellum and medulla oblongata

後腦杓子(ㄏㄡˋ ㄋㄠˇ ㄕㄠˊ˙ㄗ)
the back side of one's head

後年(ㄏㄡˋ ㄋㄧㄢˊ)
the year after next

後娘(ㄏㄡˋ ㄋㄧㄤˊ)
one's stepmother

後來(ㄏㄡˋ ㄌㄞˊ)
① then; afterwards: 後來的情況是怎麼樣? What happened afterwards? ② latecomers; to come afterward

後來居上(ㄏㄡˋ ㄌㄞˊ ㄐㄩ ㄕㄤˋ)
The latecomer (or newcomer) ends up in front. 他因年輕力壯,所以後來居上。As he was young and energetic, he ended up in front.

後力不繼(ㄏㄡˋ ㄌㄧˋ ㄅㄨˋ ㄐㄧˋ)
to lack the strength to continue

後梁(ㄏㄡˋ ㄌㄧㄤˊ)
① the Posterior Liang Dynasty (907-923 A.D.) ② the Later Liang Dynasty (555-587 A.D.)

後路(ㄏㄡˋ ㄌㄨˋ)
① the rear of an army; the route of retreat ② room for a manoeuver; a road for retreat: 聰明人預先留下後路。A wise man leaves room for a manoeuver.

後感(ㄏㄡˋ ㄍㄢˇ)
① an afterthought; a reflection after an event; feelings incurred after an event has taken place ② a review

後跟(ㄏㄡˋ ㄍㄣ)or 後跟兒(ㄏㄡˋ ㄍㄣ ㄦ)
the heel

後顧(ㄏㄡˋ ㄍㄨˋ)
① to look back (to the past): 後顧不如前瞻。It is better to look ahead into the future than to look back to the past. ② to think of the future; to plan for the future

後顧之憂(ㄏㄡˋ ㄍㄨˋ ㄓ ㄧㄡ)
the worries behind; trouble back at home—as the wife and children left behind by a fighting man on the front

後果(ㄏㄡˋ ㄍㄨㄛˇ)
consequences

後宮(ㄏㄡˋ ㄍㄨㄥ)
① the inner courts of the ancient Chinese emperor; imperial harems or seraglios ② the concubines of a monarch

後漢(ㄏㄡˋ ㄏㄢˋ)
① the Later Han Dynasty, also known as Eastern Han (25-220 A.D.) ② the Posterior Han Dynasty (947-950 A.D.) during the Epoch of Five Dynasties

後漢書(ㄏㄡˋ ㄏㄢˋ ㄕㄨ)
The History of Later Han, a 120-volume work, compiled and authored by Fan Yeh (范曄) of the Sung Dynasty

後花園(ㄏㄡˋ ㄏㄨㄚ ㄩㄢˊ)
a backyard; a garden at the back of a house

〔ㄔ 部〕

【彳部】

後悔(ㄏㄡˋ ㄏㄨㄟˇ)
to regret; to repent; remorse:
我毫不後悔.I have no regrets.

後悔不及(ㄏㄡˋ ㄏㄨㄟˇ ㄅㄨˋ ㄐㄧˊ)
to be overcome with regret

後悔無及(ㄏㄡˋ ㄏㄨㄟˇ ㄨˊ ㄐㄧˊ)or 後悔莫及(ㄏㄡˋ ㄏㄨㄟˇ ㄇㄛˋ ㄐㄧˊ)
It will be too late to regret. 或 It's useless crying over spilled milk.

後會有期(ㄏㄡˋ ㄏㄨㄟˋ ㄧㄡˇ ㄑㄧ)
See you again. 曲終人散,後會有期. The meeting is over; see you again.

後患(ㄏㄡˋ ㄏㄨㄢˋ)
the lurking dangers which will become manifest afterward (usually said of a vanquished enemy permitted to retain potentials for a comeback)

後患無窮(ㄏㄡˋ ㄏㄨㄢˋ ㄨˊ ㄑㄩㄥˊ)
an endless flow of disastrous aftermath (because no preventive measures are taken)

後脊樑(ㄏㄡˋ ㄐㄧˇ ㄌㄧㄤˊ)
the spinal column; the spine; the backbone

後記(ㄏㄡˋ ㄐㄧˋ)
a postscript

後繼無人(ㄏㄡˋ ㄐㄧˋ ㄨˊ ㄖㄣˊ)
There is no successor (capable of continuing the task).

後甲板(ㄏㄡˋ ㄐㄧㄚˇ ㄅㄢˇ)
the quarterdeck of a ship

後街(ㄏㄡˋ ㄐㄧㄝ)
the back street; the street at the back of one's house

後腳(ㄏㄡˋ ㄐㄧㄠˇ)
① the rear foot (in walking) ② immediately after (used with 前腳)

後勁(ㄏㄡˋ ㄐㄧㄥˋ) ⓐ (said of liquor, etc.) aftereffects ⓑ staying power (of a person, horse, etc.); the strength one reserves for a final thrust ② (ㄏㄡˋ ㄐㄧㄥ) crack troops in the rear

後進(ㄏㄡˋ ㄐㄧㄣˋ)
juniors; the rising generation

後晉(ㄏㄡˋ ㄐㄧㄣˋ)
the Posterior Tsin Dynasty (936-946 A.D.), a reign during the Epoch of the Five Dynasties

後妻(ㄏㄡˋ ㄑㄧ)
one's second wife (after the divorce or death of the first)

後期(ㄏㄡˋ ㄑㄧ)
① to be behind schedule; to take place after. the time fixed ② the latter part of an era

後起之秀(ㄏㄡˋ ㄑㄧˇ ㄓ ㄒㄧㄡˋ)
a standout among the rising generation; a remarkable young person

後勤(ㄏㄡˋ ㄑㄧㄣˊ)
logistic service in the rear

後衛(ㄏㄡˋ ㄨㄟˋ)
a rear guard

後效(ㄏㄡˋ ㄒㄧㄠˋ)
future performance

後先輝映(ㄏㄡˋ ㄒㄧㄢ ㄏㄨㄟ ㄧㄥˋ)
(said of masterpieces, shining personalities, etc. of different generations) to add brilliance or greatness to each other

後現代主義(ㄏㄡˋ ㄒㄧㄢˋ ㄉㄞˋ ㄓㄨˇ ㄧˋ)
postmodernism

後序 or 後敘(ㄏㄡˋ ㄒㄩˋ)
an epilogue

後續部隊(ㄏㄡˋ ㄒㄩˋ ㄅㄨˋ ㄉㄨㄟˋ)
follow-up units

後學(ㄏㄡˋ ㄒㄩㄝˊ)
① students of the younger generation ② a polite expression referring to oneself when addressing an elder, superior, etc.

後知後覺(ㄏㄡˋ ㄓ ㄏㄡˋ ㄐㄩㄝˊ)
to know afterwards

後肢(ㄏㄡˋ ㄓ)
hind legs

後者(ㄏㄡˋ ㄓㄜˇ)
the latter (as opposed to the former)

後周(ㄏㄡˋ ㄓㄡ)
① the Posterior Chou Dynasty (951-960 A.D.) ② the Later Chou Dynasty (557-588 A.D.), also known as the Northern Chou

後主(ㄏㄡˋ ㄓㄨˇ)
the last emperor of a dynasty

後車(ㄏㄡˋ ㄔㄜ)
the carriage(s) occupied by one's entourage

後塵(ㄏㄡˋ ㄔㄣˊ)
(literally) dust kicked up by someone walking in front—(to follow in another's) footsteps

後世(ㄏㄡˋ ㄕˋ)
descendants; future generations; posterity: 我們為後世利益而種桶。We plant trees for the benefit of posterity.

後市(ㄏㄡˋ ㄕˋ)
the afternoon market

後事(ㄏㄡˋ ㄕˋ)
① matters calling for immediate attention after a person's death—as funerals, etc. ② (usually used at the end of a chapter in old novels) what happened afterward (would be told in the next chapter)

後視鏡(ㄏㄡˋ ㄕˋ ㄐㄧㄥˋ)
a rearview (or rear-vision) mirror

後手(ㄏㄡˋ ㄕㄡˇ)
① preparations made to meet contingencies ② (in chess) a passive or defensive move

後身(ㄏㄡˋ ㄕㄣ)
① one's next or future life; the next incarnation ② the back of a dress or garment

後生可畏(ㄏㄡˋ ㄕㄥ ㄎㄜˇ ㄨㄟˋ)
The young hold potentials for greatness. 或 There is no limit to the youngsters' promise.

後生小子(ㄏㄡˋ ㄕㄥ ㄒㄧㄠˇ ㄗ)
young greenhorns; naive youths

後述(ㄏㄡˋ ㄕㄨˋ)
as follows; as stated below

後燃器(ㄏㄡˋ ㄖㄢˊ ㄑㄧˋ)
an afterburner

後人(ㄏㄡˋ ㄖㄣˊ)
① people of future generations; one's descendants or posterity ② to be behind others (in doing good things, charity work, etc.)

後任(ㄏㄡˋ ㄖㄣˋ)
the successor to an office after the incumbent quits

後奏曲(ㄏㄡˋ ㄗㄡˋ ㄑㄩˇ)
(music) an epilogue; a postlude

夎坐力(ㄗㄨㄛˋ ㄌㄧˋ)
recoil

夎此(ㄘˇ)
after this

夎死(ㄙˇ)
a survivor

夎嗣(ㄙˋ)
descendants; posterity

夎遺症(ㄧˊ ㄓㄥˋ)
(pathology) sequela; after-effect

夎裔(ㄧˋ)
descendants

夎尾兒(ㄨㄟˇ ㄦˊ)
① the end ② after; behind

夎腰(ㄧㄠ)
the back of one's waist

夎言(ㄧㄢˊ)
① gossips or slanders behind one's back ② an account of happenings which occurred later than the event being told

夎影兒(ㄧㄥˇ ㄦˊ)
the outline of someone's back

夎五代(ㄨˇ ㄉㄞˋ)
a period of 53 years between A.D. 907 and 960, during which five dynastic changes (梁,唐,晉,漢,周) took place before the reunification of China under the Sung Dynasty founded by the House of Chao

夎魏(ㄨㄟˋ)
the Later Wei Dynasty (386-534 A.D.)

夎衛(ㄨㄟˋ)
① the rear guard (in military operations) ② the fullback (in football); the guard (in basketball)

夎衛陣地(ㄨㄟˋ ㄓㄣˋ ㄉㄧˋ)
the position of the rear guard which provides cover for the withdrawal of the main force

夎援(ㄩㄢˊ)
reinforcement from the rear; support: 後部隊已到達前線。The supporting troops have reached the front.

夎院(ㄩㄢˋ)
a backyard: 他到後院去整修籬笆。He went out into the backyard to fix the fence.

七畫

【徐】 1473 ㄒㄩˊ shyu xú

1. slow; calm; composed; gently: 早晨清風徐來。A refreshing breeze is blowing gently in the morning.
2. Hsü—a state in ancient China occupying part of today's Anhwei Province
3. a Chinese family name

徐步
to walk slowly; to walk in a leisurely manner

徐圖發展(ㄒㄩˊ ㄊㄨˊ ㄈㄚ ㄓㄢˇ)
gradually plan for future development, expansion, etc.

徐娘半老(ㄒㄩˊ ㄋㄧˊ ㄅㄢˋ ㄌㄠˇ)
(originally) Lady Hsü, a concubine of Emperor Yüan of the Liang Dynasty, who carried on amorous affairs even when she was getting old — a flirtatious middle-aged woman who still retains traces of her erstwhile beauty

徐光啓(ㄒㄩˊ ㄍㄨㄤ ㄑㄧˇ)
Hsü Kuang-chi (1562-1633), a high official in the Ming Dynasty, who was famed for his translation of Western books dealing with astronomy and geometry

徐緩(ㄒㄩˊ ㄏㄨㄢˇ)
slowly; unhurriedly: 她徐緩地走進房間。She walked slowly into the room.

徐徐(ㄒㄩˊ ㄒㄩˊ)
① steady; calm; relaxed and dignified ② slow; slowly: 國旗徐徐升起。The national flag slowly went up the pole.

徐徐而來(ㄒㄩˊ ㄒㄩˊ ㄦˊ ㄌㄞˊ)
to come with relaxed and dignified steps: 那老人徐徐而來。The old man came with relaxed and dignified steps.

徐州(ㄒㄩˊ ㄓㄡ)
① Hsüchow, a city in Kiangsu Province, famous for its strategic position ② one of the nine ancient Chinese political divisions

---

【徑】 1474 ㄐㄧㄥˋ jing jìng

1. a narrow path; a byway; a shortcut: 求學無捷徑。There is no shortcut to knowledge.
2. a diameter
3. to decide and proceed (to do something, etc.) without getting orders, etc.; direct; straight: 你可逕行辦理。You may deal with the matter straightaway.
4. already—implying a sense of surprise

徑庭(ㄐㄧㄥˋ ㄊㄧㄥˊ)
quite different; poles apart: 他們對此議論大相徑庭。They are poles apart on this argument.

徑路(ㄐㄧㄥˋ ㄌㄨˋ)
a byway; a narrow path

徑情(ㄐㄧㄥˋ ㄑㄧㄥˊ)
at will; unrestrained

徑行(ㄐㄧㄥˋ ㄒㄧㄥˊ)
to proceed on (a task, etc.) or make (a decision, etc.) at one's own discretion or without authorization

徑直(ㄐㄧㄥˋ ㄓˊ)
straight; directly; straightaway: 飛機將徑直飛往洛杉磯。The plane will fly nonstop to Los Angeles.

徑尺(ㄐㄧㄥˋ ㄔˇ)
a caliber ruler

徑自(ㄐㄧㄥˋ ㄗˋ)
without leave; without consulting anyone: 他悶聲不吭地徑自走了。He left abruptly without saying a word.

徑寸(ㄐㄧㄥˋ ㄘㄨㄣˋ)
a circle or sphere with a diameter of one inch

徑賽(ㄐㄧㄥˋ ㄙㄞˋ)
(sports) track events

徑一周三(ㄐㄧㄥˋ ㄧ ㄓㄡ ㄙㄢ)
The ratio between the diameter and the circumference is roughly 1 : 3 according to an ancient Chinese calculation.

徑庭(ㄐㄧㄥˋ ㄊㄧㄥˊ)
to proceed on other than regular course; to trespass

【徒】 1475 ㄊㄨˊ twu tú

1. disciples; followers; pupils; apprentices

〔彳〕部

2. a crowd; a gang; a group of people

3. to go on foot: 徒步旅行比坐車要花費較長的時間。It takes longer to travel on foot than by car.

4. a punishment

5. only; merely; in vain: 不徒無益，反而有害。It is not only useless but harmful.

6. empty, as empty-handed; barehanded: 男孩們徒手拳鬥。These boys were fighting with bare hands.

7. foot soldiers; infantry

徒搏(ㄊㄨˊ ㄅㄛˊ)
hand-to-hand combat

徒兵(ㄊㄨˊ ㄅㄧㄥ)
foot soldiers; infantry

徒步(ㄊㄨˊ ㄅㄨˋ)
to go on foot

徒法不行(ㄊㄨˊ ㄈㄚˇ ㄅㄨˋ ㄒㄧㄥˊ)
Good laws without enforcement are useless.

徒費口舌(ㄊㄨˊ ㄈㄟˋ ㄎㄡˇ ㄕㄜˊ)
(literally) to use one's tongue in vain—to waste one's breath (in persuading another, etc.)

徒黨(ㄊㄨˊ ㄉㄤˇ)
a clique; a faction; a band; followers (used derogatively)

徒弟(ㄊㄨˊ ㄉㄧˋ)
an apprentice; a disciple; a pupil

徒讀父書(ㄊㄨˊ ㄉㄨˊ ㄈㄨˋ ㄕㄨ)
unable to profit from what one has read

徒託空言(ㄊㄨˊ ㄊㄨㄛ ㄎㄨㄥ ㄧㄢˊ)
to boast; to jaw but do nothing; to render lip service

徒勞(ㄊㄨˊ ㄌㄠˊ)
futile effort; fruitless labor: 他徒勞往返。He made a futile round trip. 或 He hurried to and fro for nothing.

徒勞無功(ㄊㄨˊ ㄌㄠˊ ㄨˊ ㄍㄨㄥ)
to labor in vain; to work without achieving anything; to avail (someone) nothing

徒隸(ㄊㄨˊ ㄌㄧˋ)
a prisoner undergoing labor service as a form of punishment

徒歌(ㄊㄨˊ ㄍㄜ)
to sing without accompani-

---

ment of any musical instrument

徒呼負負(ㄊㄨˊ ㄏㄨ ㄈㄨˋ ㄈㄨˋ)
to exclaim in disappointment for having achieved nothing

徒驥(ㄊㄨˊ ㄐㄧˋ)
foot and horse; infantry and cavalry

徒楊(ㄊㄨˊ ㄒㄧˊ)
barefooted and barebreasted

徒跣(ㄊㄨˊ ㄒㄧㄢˇ)
to move on one's bare feet

徒行(ㄊㄨˊ ㄒㄧㄥˊ)
to go on foot; to walk; to hike

徒刑(ㄊㄨˊ ㄒㄧㄥˊ)
a prison term; imprisonment

徒眾(ㄊㄨˊ ㄓㄨㄥˋ)
a gang; a crowd; a group of followers

徒餉(ㄊㄨˊ ㄓ)
foot soldiers; infantry

徒涉(ㄊㄨˊ ㄕㄜˋ)
to wade across (a stream, etc.)

徒首(ㄊㄨˊ ㄕㄡˇ)
bareheaded (after the helmet is lost in battle)

徒手(ㄊㄨˊ ㄕㄡˇ)
empty-handed; barehanded; unarmed

徒手體操(ㄊㄨˊ ㄕㄡˇ ㄊㄧˇ ㄘㄠ)
calisthenics

徒手致富(ㄊㄨˊ ㄕㄡˇ ㄓˋ ㄈㄨˋ)
to start out empty-handed and become rich later; from rags to riches

徒善(ㄊㄨˊ ㄕㄢˋ)
① a well-intentioned plan which is not feasible ② kind-hearted but taking no action

徒屬(ㄊㄨˊ ㄕㄨˇ)
followers; disciples

徒然(ㄊㄨˊ ㄖㄢˊ)
in vain; useless; meaningless; ineffectual

徒子徒孫(ㄊㄨˊ ㄗˇ ㄊㄨˊ ㄙㄨㄣ)
(mostly used comically or abusively) followers

徒增(ㄊㄨˊ ㄗㄥ)
to increase (cost, trouble, age, etc.) without gaining advantage of any kind

徒卒(ㄊㄨˊ ㄗㄨˊ)
foot soldiers; infantry

徒坐(ㄊㄨˊ ㄗㄨㄛˋ)
to sit in leisure; to sit without doing anything

徒饗(ㄊㄨˊ)
only to .. (without serving a useful purpose)

徒擁虛名(ㄊㄨˊ ㄩㄥˇ ㄒㄩ ㄇㄧㄥˊ)
to have an undeserved reputation; a reputation not backed by facts

八畫

【得】 1476
1. ㄉㄜˊ der de

1. to get; to obtain; to acquire; to gain; to attain; to effect; to win: 今天的富裕生活得來不易。The rich life we have today was not easily won.

2. complacent

3. agreement; harmony

4. can; may; to be able to

5. All right! 或 That's enough! 得，就這麼辦。All right! Just go ahead.

得罷且罷(ㄉㄜˊ ㄅㄚˋ ㄑㄧㄝˇ ㄅㄚˋ)
It's better to forget about it

得標(ㄉㄜˊ ㄅㄧㄠ)
(in an open tender) to win the contract; to be awarded the contract

得便(ㄉㄜˊ ㄅㄧㄢˋ)
at (your) convenience

得病(ㄉㄜˊ ㄅㄧㄥˋ)
to get sick or ill; to fall sick

得不到(ㄉㄜˊ ㄅㄨˋ ㄉㄠˋ) or 得不著(ㄉㄜˊ ㄅㄨˋ ㄓㄠˊ)
cannot get

得不償失(ㄉㄜˊ ㄅㄨˋ ㄔㄤˊ ㄕ)
(literally) What one gains cannot offset the losses —not worth the effort

得票(ㄉㄜˊ ㄆㄧㄠˋ)
to gain votes; the votes one obtained in an election

得民(ㄉㄜˊ ㄇㄧㄣˊ)
to get popular support; to win the people's heart

得法(ㄉㄜˊ ㄈㄚˇ)
to do something in the right way: 他解釋得不甚得法。He did not explain in the right way.

得非(ㄉㄜˊ ㄈㄟ)
Can it be...?

得分(ㄉㄜˊ ㄈㄣ)

〔彳部〕

得(ㄉㄜ ㄉㄞ)
①(descriptive of walking) leisurely ② specially; on purpose

得到(ㄉㄜ ㄉㄠ)
to succeed in getting or obtaining

得道(ㄉㄜ ㄉㄠ)
to attain perfection in Taoism or Buddhism; to enter Nirvana; to attain enlightment

得道多助(ㄉㄜ ㄉㄠ ㄉㄨㄛ ㄓㄨ)
Those who uphold justice shall not be alone.

得當(ㄉㄜ ㄉㄤ)
proper; appropriate (ways, measures, arrangements, etc.)

得體(ㄉㄜ ㄊㄧˇ)
proper (deportment, behavior, conduct, etc.)

得天獨厚(ㄉㄜ ㄊㄧㄢ ㄉㄨˊ ㄏㄡˋ)
(said of a land rich in natural resources or a gifted person) to be particularly favored by nature; to be endowed by nature

得天下(ㄉㄜ ㄊㄧㄢ ㄒㄧㄚˋ)
to unite the country and ascend the throne

得年(ㄉㄜ ㄋㄧㄢˊ)
to die at an age below 60: 李君得年五十有八。Mr. Lee died at the age of 58.

得了(ㄉㄜ ·ㄌㄜ)
①Stop it! 或 Hold it! 或 Well! ② finished; completed

得力(ㄉㄜ ㄌㄧˋ)
① capable (assistants, etc.); competent; very useful ② thanks to ③ to benefit from; to get help from; to profit from

得隴望蜀(ㄉㄜ ㄌㄨㄥˇ ㄨㄤˋ ㄕㄨˇ)
greedy; avarice; cupidity; to have insatiable desires

得過且過(ㄉㄜ ㄍㄨㄛˋ ㄑㄧㄝˇ ㄍㄨㄛˋ)
to harbor no ambition of achievement; easygoing; to make do; to be satisfied with whatever lot one has; resigned; to muddle on or along; to drift along

得空兒(ㄉㄜ ㄎㄨㄥˋㄦ)
to have spare time or leisure; in (one's) spare time; at leisure

得計(ㄉㄜ ㄐㄧˋ)
to have a winning hand; to succeed

得濟(ㄉㄜ ㄐㄧˋ)
①(said of an old person) to get financial support from one's offspring ②(said of a plan, scheme, arrangement, etc.) useful; satisfactory

得救(ㄉㄜ ㄐㄧㄡˋ)
(especially in Christianity) to obtain salvation; to be saved

得間(ㄉㄜ ㄐㄧㄢˋ)
to get a chance to start doing something

得勁(ㄉㄜ ㄐㄧㄥˋ)
①easy and comfortable going ②fit for use; handy

得獎(ㄉㄜ ㄐㄧㄤˇ)
to win (or be awarded) a prize: 得獎人 a prizewinner 得獎單位 a prizewinning unit

得君(ㄉㄜ ㄐㄩㄣ)
to win imperial favor or confidence

得其所哉(ㄉㄜ ㄑㄧˊ ㄙㄨㄛˇ ㄗㄞ)
to be in one's element (like fish in water); to have a satisfactory position or circumstance; very much satisfied

得竅(ㄉㄜ ㄑㄧㄠˋ)
to get the knack of (doing something, etc.)

得悉(ㄉㄜ ㄒㄧ)
(usually used in correspondence, etc.) to have learned that...; to hear of

得暇(ㄉㄜ ㄒㄧㄚˊ)
to get spare time or leisure; to have the leisure or time to (undertake a task, etc.); in one's spare time; at leisure

得匣還珠(ㄉㄜ ㄒㄧㄚˊ ㄏㄨㄢˊ ㄓㄨ)
to place emphasis on the wrong thing; misdirected attention

得閒(ㄉㄜ ㄒㄧㄢˊ)
to get leisure or find leisure for; (usually used in letters) at (your) leisure

得新厭舊(ㄉㄜ ㄒㄧㄣ ㄧㄢˋ ㄐㄧㄡˋ)
to disdain the old when one

gets the new—(figuratively) to favor a concubine and treat the legal wife with disdain

得心應手(ㄉㄜ ㄒㄧㄣ ㄧㄥˋ ㄕㄡˇ)
(literally) The hand moves as the mind wishes.—very smooth operation or going; to show facility

得幸(ㄉㄜ ㄒㄧㄥˋ)
to have won the favor of the throne

得知(ㄉㄜ ㄓ)
to have learned; to have become acquainted with

得職(ㄉㄜ ㄓˊ)
①to get an official post ② to hold one's occupation in content

得志(ㄉㄜ ㄓˋ)
to have one's ambition fulfilled; to be successful in one's career: 他少年得志。He enjoys success when young.

得中(ㄉㄜ ㄓㄨㄥˋ)
to pass the imperial examination

得逞(ㄉㄜ ㄔㄥˇ)
to succeed

得寵(ㄉㄜ ㄔㄨㄥˇ)
to be favored; to win the favor of (used in connection with concubines, courtiers, etc.)

得失(ㄉㄜ ㄕ)
gain and loss; success and failure; merits and faults (of a plan, measure, etc.); advantages and disadvantages

得失榮枯(ㄉㄜ ㄕ ㄖㄨㄥˊ ㄎㄨ)
gain and loss; ups and downs—the vicissitudes of life

得失參半(ㄉㄜ ㄕ ㄘㄢ ㄅㄢˋ)
to have both merits and demerits, advantages and disadvantages, or gain and loss, etc.

得時(ㄉㄜ ㄕˊ)
to be in luck; riding with Lady Luck

得實(ㄉㄜ ㄕˊ)
to find out the truth from a prisoner

得勢(ㄉㄜ ㄕˋ)
to be in a powerful position; to become influential; to be

〔彳
部〕

at the helm; to have the advantage of

得手(ㄉㄜˊ ㄕㄡˇ)
to succeed (in performing a task, usually a criminal act)

得神(ㄉㄜˊ ㄕㄣˊ)
lifelike; vivid (impersonation, etc.)

得勝(ㄉㄜˊ ㄕㄥˋ)
to win; to triumph over an enemy or opponent

得數(ㄉㄜˊ ㄕㄨˋ)
the solution of a problem in arithmetic

得人(ㄉㄜˊ ㄖㄣˊ)
to have got the right man (for a job)

得人心(ㄉㄜˊ ㄖㄣˊ ㄒㄧㄣ)
to be popular; to have won the favor of the people

得子(ㄉㄜˊ ㄗˇ)
to get a son; give birth to a boy

得罪(ㄉㄜˊ ㄗㄨㄟˋ)
① to offend: 我們不怕得罪人。 We are not afraid of giving offence. ② to violate the law

得策(ㄉㄜˊ ㄘㄜˋ)
the best policy; advisability

得寸進尺(ㄉㄜˊ ㄘㄨㄣˋ ㄐㄧㄣˋ ㄔˇ)
The more one gets, the more one wants. 或Small concessions lead to greater demands.

得色(ㄉㄜˊ ㄙㄜˋ)
an air of complacency; smug

得所(ㄉㄜˊ ㄙㄨㄛˇ)
to be rightly placed; to be in an ideal position or place

得一望十(ㄉㄜˊ ㄧ ㄨㄤˋ ㄕˊ)
to have an insatiable desire to acquire more

得宜(ㄉㄜˊ ㄧˊ)
proper; appropriate; suitable

得以(ㄉㄜˊ ㄧˇ)
to be able to

得益(ㄉㄜˊ ㄧˋ)
to benefit from

得意(ㄉㄜˊ ㄧˋ)
to be complacent; to be very satisfied; (said of a person in business or politics) very successful

得意揚揚(ㄉㄜˊ ㄧˋ ㄧㄤˊ ㄧㄤˊ)
an air of complacency; an appearance of extreme satisfaction; proudly

得意忘形(ㄉㄜˊ ㄧˋ ㄨㄤˋ ㄒㄧㄥˊ)
to have one's head turned by success; to be too complacent; to watch one's manners; to be carried away by one's success; to get dizzy with success

得意忘言(ㄉㄜˊ ㄧˋ ㄨㄤˋ ㄧㄢˊ)
a tacit understanding; an understanding without words; a meeting of minds

得一枝棲(ㄉㄜˊ ㄧ ㄓ ㄑㄧ)
to get a job (not a very good one) after a long period of unemployment

得未曾有(ㄉㄜˊ ㄨㄟˋ ㄘㄥˊ ㄧㄡˇ)
to have never happened

得魚忘筌(ㄉㄜˊ ㄩˊ ㄨㄤˋ ㄑㄩㄢˊ)
(literally) to get the fish but forget the fish trap—ungrateful

得用(ㄉㄜˊ ㄩㄥˋ)
to be suitable for use; to be useful

【得】 1476
2. ㄉㄞˇ deei děi
1. must; should; ought to
2. to need; to take

得負責任(ㄉㄜˇ ㄈㄨˋ ㄓㄜˊ ㄖㄣˋ)
should be responsible for; must shoulder the responsibility

得用功(ㄉㄜˇ ㄩㄥˋ ㄍㄨㄥ)
must be more studious; should put in more time studying

【得】 1476
3. ˙ㄉㄜ ˙de de
an adverbial expletive: 那辦得到。 That can be done. 我凍得發抖。 I trembled with cold.

【徘】 1477
ㄆㄞˊ pair pái
1. hesitating; irresolute; indecisive
2. to walk to and fro; to move around; to linger around; to pace up and down

徘徊(ㄆㄞˊ ㄏㄨㄞˊ)
① to linger; to walk to and fro; to move around without purpose ② hesitating; irresolute ③ to fluctuate

徘徊流連(ㄆㄞˊ ㄏㄨㄞˊ ㄌㄧㄡˊ ㄌㄧㄢˊ)
to walk to and fro hesitatingly with reluctance to leave

徘徊觀望(ㄆㄞˊ ㄏㄨㄞˊ ㄍㄨㄢ ㄨㄤˋ)

to take an observer's seat to see but cannot make up one's mind; to wait and see; to wait for the dust to settle

徘徊歧途(ㄆㄞˊ ㄏㄨㄞˊ ㄑㄧˊ ㄊㄨˊ)
to linger towards the wrong (or evil) path; to hesitate at the crossroads

【徜】 1478
ㄔㄤˊ charng cháng
going to and fro; lingering; loitering

徜徉(ㄔㄤˊ ㄧㄤˊ)
lingering or loitering

【徙】 1479
ㄒㄧˇ shii xǐ
1. to move one's abode; to migrate; to shift
2. to be exiled

徙邊(ㄒㄧˇ ㄅㄧㄢ)
to move or banish prisoners to the border areas

徙貫(ㄒㄧˇ ㄍㄨㄢˋ)
to move one's residence to another place

徙居(ㄒㄧˇ ㄐㄩ)
to change one's residence; to move; to migrate

徙宅忘妻(ㄒㄧˇ ㄓㄞˊ ㄨㄤˋ ㄑㄧ)
(said of one's absurdity or preposterousness) to move one's living place but forget (to take along) one's wife

徙善(ㄒㄧˇ ㄕㄢˋ)
to change for the better; to reform

徙任(ㄒㄧˇ ㄖㄣˋ)
to be transferred to another post

徙移(ㄒㄧˇ ㄧˊ)
to move; (said of birds, fish etc.) to migrate: 有些鳥類隨季節徙移。 Some birds migrate.

徙倚(ㄒㄧˇ ㄧˇ)
irresolution; indecision; to linger in hesitation

徙義(ㄒㄧˇ ㄧˋ)
to change one's course toward what is right

【從】 1480
1. (从) ㄘㄨㄥˊ tsorng cóng
1. from; by; whence; through: 我們從國外買來這些貨物。 We get these goods from foreign countries.
2. to undertake; to manage; to

dedicate oneself to; to attend to; to engage in: 他從事多項冒險事業。He engages in risky undertakings.

從 to follow; to yield to; to listen to; to comply with; to obey: 我們應當遵從醫生的要求。We should comply with the doctor's request.

從 a follower; an attendant

從便(ㄘㄨㄥ ㄅㄧㄢˋ) whenever convenient

從不(ㄘㄨㄥ ㄅㄨˋ) never; to have never (done a thing): 他上學從不遲到。He has never been late for school.

從旁(ㄘㄨㄥ ㄆㄤˊ) (to help, to encourage, etc.) from the side: 你可從旁觀看。You may see it from the side.

從風(ㄘㄨㄥ ㄈㄥ) to follow the trend; to submit (to a powerful nation) quickly; to comply with a leader's call, etc.

從豐(ㄘㄨㄥ ㄈㄥ)or 從優(ㄘㄨㄥ ㄧㄡ) liberally (as of payment); (to pay) according to a higher scale

從頭至尾(ㄘㄨㄥ ㄊㄡˊ ㄓˋ ㄨㄟˇ) from beginning to end; throughout: 這本旅遊的書從頭至尾都很有趣。The book of travels was interesting from beginning to end.

從天而降(ㄘㄨㄥ ㄊㄧㄢ ㄦˊ ㄐㄧㄤˋ) (literally) to descend from heaven—very unexpectedly

從來(ㄘㄨㄥ ㄌㄞˊ) from the beginning (used only in a negative expression)

從流(ㄘㄨㄥ ㄌㄧㄡˊ) to yield to one's environment; to follow the prevailing fashion

從良(ㄘㄨㄥ ㄌㄧㄤˊ) (said of a prostitute) to get married; to become a decent woman again; to come back to normal civic life

從龍(ㄘㄨㄥ ㄌㄨㄥˊ) (literally) to follow the dragon—to follow the new emperor and start a new reign

從略(ㄘㄨㄥ ㄌㄩㄝˋ) to forego (mentioning it since it's of no consequence); to omit: 此處原文從略。The text is omitted here.

從公(ㄘㄨㄥ ㄍㄨㄥ) to manage or dedicate to official affairs

從寬(ㄘㄨㄥ ㄎㄨㄢ) to be lenient (usually said of meting out punishment)

從緩(ㄘㄨㄥ ㄏㄨㄢˇ) to bide one's time; to postpone; to put off

從簡(ㄘㄨㄥ ㄐㄧㄢˇ) (said of ceremonies) to be simple; to forgo pageantry

從諫如流(ㄘㄨㄥ ㄐㄧㄢˋ ㄖㄨˊ ㄌㄧㄡˊ) to listen to or follow good advice as water flows downward

從今以後(ㄘㄨㄥ ㄐㄧㄣ ㄧˇ ㄏㄡˋ) from now on; from this day on

從井救人(ㄘㄨㄥ ㄐㄧㄥˇ ㄐㄧㄡˋ ㄖㄣˊ) to risk one's life or to compromise one's own interest without doing others any good

從軍(ㄘㄨㄥ ㄐㄩㄣ) to enlist oneself in military service; to become a soldier

從其所好(ㄘㄨㄥ ㄑㄧˊ ㄙㄨㄛˇ ㄏㄠˋ) to cater to one's wishes

從前(ㄘㄨㄥ ㄑㄧㄢˊ) once upon a time; a long time ago; some time ago; formerly; in the past; before: 我從前看過那部影片。I've seen that film before.

從輕發落(ㄘㄨㄥ ㄑㄧㄥ ㄈㄚ ㄌㄨㄛˋ) to use leniency in meting out punishment

從權(ㄘㄨㄥ ㄑㄩㄢˊ) to be flexible; to handle something without rigid application of rules

從小(ㄘㄨㄥ ㄒㄧㄠˇ) from one's childhood; since one was very young: 他們從小即是好友。They are good friends since childhood.

從新做人(ㄘㄨㄥ ㄒㄧㄣ ㄗㄨㄛˋ ㄖㄣˊ) (said of a criminal, etc.) to start one's life anew

從心所欲(ㄘㄨㄥ ㄒㄧㄣ ㄙㄨㄛˇ ㄩˋ)

to do as one wishes (connoting an absence of opposition or objection); as one pleases: 他從心所欲。He does as he pleases.

從公(ㄘㄨㄥ ㄍㄨㄥ) on active military service

從政(ㄘㄨㄥ ㄓㄥˋ) to enter politics; to become a government official

從政黨員(ㄘㄨㄥ ㄓㄥˋ ㄉㄤˇ ㄩㄢˊ) a member of a political party who holds a government post

從中(ㄘㄨㄥ ㄓㄨㄥ) ①in the process (of doing something): 有人從中漁利。Someone profits from it. ②from the inside (of something) ③in the middle

從眾(ㄘㄨㄥ ㄓㄨㄥˋ) to follow the others; to comply with public opinion; to do as others do

從長計議(ㄘㄨㄥ ㄔㄤˊ ㄐㄧˋ ㄧˋ) to take time to make careful deliberations

從事(ㄘㄨㄥ ㄕˋ) to be engaged in (a task); to devote oneself to (a career, task, job, etc.)

從善如登(ㄘㄨㄥ ㄕㄢˋ ㄖㄨˊ ㄉㄥ) To follow what is right is like walking uphill (or climbing a hill).

從善如流(ㄘㄨㄥ ㄕㄢˋ ㄖㄨˊ ㄌㄧㄡˊ) to forge ahead in doing what is right

從屬(ㄘㄨㄥ ㄕㄨˇ) subordinate

從人(ㄘㄨㄥ ㄖㄣˊ) entourage; attendants; servants

從戎(ㄘㄨㄥ ㄖㄨㄥˊ) to join the armed service; to enlist in the armed service

從早到晚(ㄘㄨㄥ ㄗㄠˇ ㄉㄠˋ ㄨㄢˇ) from morning till night

從此以後(ㄘㄨㄥ ㄘˇ ㄧˇ ㄏㄡˋ) from now on; from this moment on; henceforth

從俗(ㄘㄨㄥ ㄙㄨˊ) to follow local customs; to follow traditions; to conform to conventions

從速辦理(ㄘㄨㄥ ㄙㄨˋ ㄅㄢˋ ㄌㄧˇ) to expedite the execution

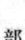

〔彳部〕

彳部

(of an official instruction, etc.); to do something with dispatch

從而 (ㄘㄨㄥˊ ㄦˊ)
and thereupon; thus; as a result; then; so then

從一而終 (ㄘㄨㄥˊ ㄧ ㄦˊ ㄓㄨㄥ)
to be faithful to one husband all her life (even after she is divorced or in widowhood)

從嚴 (ㄘㄨㄥˊ ㄧㄢˊ)
severely; strictly

從違 (ㄘㄨㄥˊ ㄨㄟˊ)
to follow or object (an order, etc.); to obey or reject

從未 (ㄘㄨㄥˊ ㄨㄟˋ)
to have never (happened, etc.)

【從】 1480
2. (以) ㄗㄨㄥˋ tzong
    zòng

1. entourage; an attendant; a servant: 牧師是上帝之僕從。 A priest is a servant of God.
2. secondary; the relation other than one's direct blood relatives
3. an accessory: 他是這謀殺案的從犯。 He is an accessory to the murder.
4. vice or deputy

從伯 (ㄗㄨㄥˋ ㄅㄛˊ)
one's father's paternal male cousins who are older than him

從妹 (ㄗㄨㄥˋ ㄇㄟˋ)
a younger female cousin

從母 (ㄗㄨㄥˋ ㄇㄨˇ)
maternal aunts; one's mother's sisters

從犯 (ㄗㄨㄥˋ ㄈㄢˋ)
an accessory

從父 (ㄗㄨㄥˋ ㄈㄨˋ)
one's father's brothers; paternal uncles

從弟 (ㄗㄨㄥˋ ㄉㄧˋ)
sons of one's paternal uncles, who are younger than oneself; male cousins

從女 (ㄗㄨㄥˋ ㄋㄩˇ)
a niece

從吏 (ㄗㄨㄥˋ ㄌㄧˋ)
a subordinate to an official

從官 (ㄗㄨㄥˋ ㄍㄨㄢ)
an official aide; an official

whose duties are to attend to the personal affairs of the chief

從刑 (ㄗㄨㄥˋ ㄒㄧㄥˊ)
accessory punishment—as deprivation of rights, confiscation of property, etc.

從兄 (ㄗㄨㄥˋ ㄒㄩㄥ)
sons of one's paternal uncles, who are older than oneself; male cousins

從者 (ㄗㄨㄥˋ ㄓㄜˇ)
attendants; servants

從叔 (ㄗㄨㄥˋ ㄕㄨˊ)
one's father's paternal male cousins who are younger than him

從子 (ㄗㄨㄥˋ ㄗˇ)
a nephew

從孫 (ㄗㄨㄥˋ ㄙㄨㄣ)
grandsons of one's brothers

【從】 1480
3. ㄘㄨㄥ tsong
    cōng

1. lax; easy
2. plentiful; abundant
3. to urge; to persuade strongly

從容 (ㄘㄨㄥ ㄖㄨㄥˊ)
①unhurried; naturally; calm; composed; unflinchingly ② plentiful; plenty of

從容不迫 (ㄘㄨㄥ ㄖㄨㄥˊ ㄅㄨˋ ㄆㄛˋ)
in an unhurried or leisurely manner

【從】 1480
4. (縱) ㄗㄨㄥˋ tzong
    zòng

from north to south

從橫 or 從衡 (ㄗㄨㄥˋ ㄏㄥˊ)
vertical and horizontal: 合從連橫 the opposite theories of the vertical alliance of six states against Chin (秦) and the horizontal alliance of the states with Chin (秦) during the Warring States Period

【徠】 1481
ㄌㄞˊ lai lói

the ancient version of 來—to come; to induce (customers) to come; to solicit (customers or business); to encourage (customers) to come to buy

【御】 1482
ㄩˋ yuh yù

1. to drive a chariot or carriage
2. a driver; an attendant
3. to resist; to keep out
4. to control; to manage; to superintend; to tame (a shrew); to harness
5. imperial
6. to wait on; to set before, as food; to offer or present to
7. a Chinese family name

御寶 (ㄩˋ ㄅㄠˇ)
the imperial seal; the seal of the emperor

御筆 (ㄩˋ ㄅㄧˇ)
the handwriting or painting of the emperor

御批 (ㄩˋ ㄆㄧ)
the comments made by an emperor

御風 (ㄩˋ ㄈㄥ)
to fly; to ride the winds

御夫有術 (ㄩˋ ㄈㄨ ㄧㄡˇ ㄕㄨˋ)
very skilful in keeping one's husband on leash or under harness

御女 (ㄩˋ ㄋㄩˇ)
①court women; court ladies ②to have sexual intercourse with a woman

御覽 (ㄩˋ ㄌㄢˇ)
①to have been read by the emperor ②books provided for the emperor's reading

御林軍 (ㄩˋ ㄌㄧㄣˊ ㄐㄩㄣ)
imperial guards; troops assigned for the protection of the emperor

御溝 (ㄩˋ ㄍㄡ)
a ditch which flows through the imperial garden

御河 (ㄩˋ ㄏㄜˊ)
①a river used exclusively by the emperor ②a small stream running through the Forbidden City ③name of a river in Shansi (山西)

御花園 (ㄩˋ ㄏㄨㄚ ㄩㄢˊ)
an imperial garden; the emperor's garden

御駕 (ㄩˋ ㄐㄧㄚˋ)
①the imperial carriage ②the emperor

御駕親征 (ㄩˋ ㄐㄧㄚˋ ㄑㄧㄣ ㄓㄥ)
The emperor personally led his soldiers in a military operation.

御街(ㄩ ㄐㄧㄝ)
the streets in the capital

御妻(ㄩ ㄑㄧ)
to control one's wife

御前(ㄩ ㄑㄧㄢ)
in the presence of the emperor

御前會議(ㄩ ㄑㄧㄢ ㄏㄨㄟˋ ㄧˋ)
a conference in which the emperor takes part

御前試(ㄩ ㄑㄧㄢ ㄕˋ)
the Imperial Examination in old China for selecting high officials with the emperor's officiating

御旨(ㄩ ㄓˇ)
an imperial decree

御製(ㄩ ㄓˋ)
① poems and writings authored by the emperor ② vessels produced in the imperial kiln

御札(ㄩ ㄓㄚˊ)
instructions or orders issued by the emperor

御者(ㄩ ㄓㄜˇ)
① the driver of a carriage or chariot ② an attendant

御仗(ㄩ ㄓㄤˋ)
the imperial guard

御醫(ㄩ ㄧ)
a court physician; the emperor's physician

御食(ㄩ ㄕˊ)
① the food for the emperor ② to attend on the senior at the table

御史(ㄩ ㄕˇ)
an official rank in ancient China with varied duties in the various dynasties, the prominent ones being those of censoring and impeachment; a censor

御史大夫(ㄩ ㄕˇ ㄉㄚˋ ㄈㄨ)
an imperial censor, whose duty is to censure and impeach the officials

御膳(ㄩ ㄕㄢˋ)
the imperial cuisine

御膳房(ㄩ ㄕㄢˋ ㄈㄤˊ)
the imperial kitchen

御書(ㄩ ㄕㄨ)
① books offered to the emperor for reading ② writings authored by the emperor

御人(ㄩ ㄖㄣˊ)
① a driver ② a maid ③ a woman ④ to control others

御容(ㄩ ㄖㄨㄥˊ)
a portrait of the emperor

御賜(ㄩ ㄘˋ)
bestowed by the emperor

御醫(ㄩ ㄧˋ)
the emperor's physician

御宴(ㄩ ㄧㄢˋ)
a royal feast

御宇(ㄩ ㄩˇ)
the reign of an emperor over the nation

御苑(ㄩ ㄩㄢˋ)
an imperial park

御用(ㄩ ㄩㄥˋ)
(said of articles, etc.) used by the emperor; for the use of the emperor

九畫

【徧】 1483
ㄅㄧㄢˋ biann biàn
(舊音 ㄆㄧㄢˋ piann piàn)

1. everywhere; all over: 他遊徧天下。He has traveled all over the world.
2. the whole (world, etc.)

徧佈 or 徧布(ㄅㄧㄢˋ ㄅㄨˋ)
all over; everywhere

徧地(ㄅㄧㄢˋ ㄉㄧˋ)
everywhere; all places

徧體鱗傷(ㄅㄧㄢˋ ㄊㄧˇ ㄌㄧㄣˊ ㄕㄤ)
to suffer injuries all over one's body; the whole body covered with wounds

徧歷(ㄅㄧㄢˋ ㄌㄧˋ)
① to have experienced (every hardship, danger, etc.) ② to have traveled or reached (all corners of the world, all places, etc.)

徧告(ㄅㄧㄢˋ ㄍㄠˋ)
to inform all people or everybody; to pass the word around

徧觀(ㄅㄧㄢˋ ㄍㄨㄢ)
to see them all; to have observed everything

徧及(ㄅㄧㄢˋ ㄐㄧˊ)
all over; to have reached everywhere

徧照(ㄅㄧㄢˋ ㄓㄠˋ)
to shine upon all, as the sun

徧身(ㄅㄧㄢˋ ㄕㄣ)
all over one's body; the whole body

徧搜(ㄅㄧㄢˋ ㄙㄡ)
to search everywhere

【徨】 1484
ㄏㄨㄤˊ hwang huáng

1. agitated, alarmed
2. irresolute

徨徨(ㄏㄨㄤˊ ㄏㄨㄤˊ)
alarmed and anxious; agitated and indecisive

【復】 1485
ㄈㄨˋ fuh fù

1. to return; to come back
2. to answer; to reply
3. to repeat; again; repeatedly
4. to recover; a recovery: 祝早日康復。Best wishes for a quick recovery.
5. to return to a normal or original state
6. A Chinese family name

復辟(ㄈㄨˋ ㄅㄧˋ)
① (said of a monarch) to return to the throne after being deposed ② the restoration of monarchy (after revolution ushers in a republican government)

復命(ㄈㄨˋ ㄇㄧㄥˋ)
to report to a superior or elder after completing an assigned mission

復發(ㄈㄨˋ ㄈㄚ)
(said of illness) a relapse; to relapse

復返(ㄈㄨˋ ㄈㄢˇ)
to return

復旦(ㄈㄨˋ ㄉㄢˋ)
the dawning of light after darkness

復電(ㄈㄨˋ ㄉㄧㄢˋ)
a cable reply; to cable a reply: 我復電慶賀她。I cabled congratulations to her.

復古(ㄈㄨˋ ㄍㄨˇ)
to revive old customs, traditions, etc.

復工(ㄈㄨˋ ㄍㄨㄥ)
(said of workers on strike, etc.) to go back to work; (said of a plant after work stoppage) to start operations again

復課(ㄈㄨˋ ㄎㄜˋ)
to resume classes

復刊(ㄈㄨˋ ㄎㄢ)

〔彳部〕

to resume publication

復合(ㄈㄨˋㄏㄜˊ)
to reunite

復核(ㄈㄨˋㄏㄜˊ)
to reexamine; to review

〔彳部〕

復函(ㄈㄨˋㄏㄢˊ)
① to write a letter in reply
② a letter in reply

復活(ㄈㄨˋㄏㄨㄛˊ)
resurrection; to revive

復活節(ㄈㄨˋㄏㄨㄛˊㄐㄧㄝˊ)
the Easter holiday

復籍(ㄈㄨˋㄐㄧˊ)
to regain one's nationality

復交(ㄈㄨˋㄐㄧㄠ)
to reestablish diplomatic
relations; to resume friendship

復舊(ㄈㄨˋㄐㄧㄡˋ)
to return to the original condition

復健(ㄈㄨˋㄐㄧㄢˋ)
rehabilitation

復健中心(ㄈㄨˋㄐㄧㄢˋㄓㄨㄥㄒㄧㄣ)
a rehabilitation center

復權(ㄈㄨˋㄑㄩㄢˊ)
to restore one's lost right

復習(ㄈㄨˋㄒㄧˊ)
to review lessons learned 亦
作「複習」

復校(ㄈㄨˋㄒㄧㄠˋ)
to reactivate a school; re-
activation of a school

復現(ㄈㄨˋㄒㄧㄢˋ)
to reappear; reappearance

復新(ㄈㄨˋㄒㄧㄣ)
to make new; to make
(something) look new

復興(ㄈㄨˋㄒㄧㄥ)
a revival; a return to prosperity renaissance; to revive;
to restore (a nation's power
and glory)

復行視事(ㄈㄨˋㄒㄧㄥˊㄕˋㄕˋ)
to resume office after stepping down from a public
post

復醒(ㄈㄨˋㄒㄧㄥˇ)
to wake up again

復姓(ㄈㄨˋㄒㄧㄥˋ)
to resume the original family name

復學(ㄈㄨˋㄒㄩㄝˊ)
to go back to school (after a
prolonged absence for health
or other reasons); to resume

one's interrupted studies

復職(ㄈㄨˋㄓˊ)
to reinstate an official to his
former position; reinstate-
ment

復診(ㄈㄨˋㄓㄣˇ)
visits to a doctor, hospital,
etc. after the first visit for
the treatment of the same
disease

復政(ㄈㄨˋㄓㄥˋ)
(said of a monarch) to
regain power

復轉(ㄈㄨˋㄓㄨㄢˇ)
to repay; to return

復燃(ㄈㄨˋㄖㄢˊ)
to flare up again; to become
rampant again

復查(ㄈㄨˋㄔㄚˊ)
to check; to reexamine

復仇, or 復讎(ㄈㄨˋㄔㄡˊ)
① to take one's revenge;
to avenge ② a reprisal;
revenge; vengeance

復出(ㄈㄨˋㄔㄨ)
to come out of retirement
again; to come out again

復審(ㄈㄨˋㄕㄣˇ)
① to reexamine ② (law) to
review a case

復生(ㄈㄨˋㄕㄥ)
to become alive again

復任(ㄈㄨˋㄖㄣˋ)
to return to one's former
office; to take up a position
one held formerly

復次(ㄈㄨˋㄘˋ)
to repeat over and over—in
detail (used mostly in Bud-
hist Scriptures)

復甦 or 復蘇 or 復穌(ㄈㄨˋㄙㄨ)
(said of vegetation) to come
to life again; to revive;
recovery: 花在水中復甦.
Flowers revive in water.

復議(ㄈㄨˋㄧˋ)
to discuss a proposal or project which had been rejected
or discarded previously

復業(ㄈㄨˋㄧㄝˋ)
to resume or return to business again

復位(ㄈㄨˋㄨㄟˋ)
to be restored to the throne

復元(ㄈㄨˋㄩㄢˊ)
(said of a patient, store,
etc.) to have recovered; to

be as good as new

復原(ㄈㄨˋㄩㄢˊ)
to return to the original
state or condition; to restore

復員(ㄈㄨˋㄩㄢˊ)
to demobilize; demobilization

復員令(ㄈㄨˋㄩㄢˊㄌㄧㄥˋ)
demobilization orders

【循】 1486 (ㄒㄩㄣˊ) shyun xún
1. to follow; to comply with
2. to postpone; to procrastinate
3. in orderly fashion
4. (obsolete) to touch
5. to inspect

循便(ㄒㄩㄣˊㄅㄧㄢˋ)
to take advantage of expediency; to be guided by expediency in performing tasks,
etc.

循名責實(ㄒㄩㄣˊㄇㄧㄥˊㄗㄜˊㄕˊ)
① to do things in a prag-
matic manner ② to do
rather than preach; to stress
results instead of rhetoric ③
to expect the reality to correspond to the name

循分(ㄒㄩㄣˊㄈㄣˋ)
to act according to one's
duty; to fulfill one's obligations

循理(ㄒㄩㄣˊㄌㄧˇ)
in accordance with reason,
rules, or common practices:
他未循理行事. He did not act
in accordance with reason.

循吏(ㄒㄩㄣˊㄌㄧˋ)
a square and benevolent
official

循例(ㄒㄩㄣˊㄌㄧˋ)
in accordance with prece-
dents, common practices, or
former examples; according
to rules

循良(ㄒㄩㄣˊㄌㄧㄤˊ)
(usually said of officials)
properly discharge duties
with meritorious records

循規蹈矩(ㄒㄩㄣˊㄍㄨㄟ ㄉㄠˇㄐㄩˇ)
to observe all rules and regulations; to toe the line in
all sincerity; law-abiding; to
obey the rules and regulations

循環(ㄒㄩㄣˊㄏㄨㄢˊ)
to move in a cycle; to come

round in order; to circulate; circulation

循環法(ㄒㄩㄣㄏㄨㄢㄈㄚˇ)
a method of teaching in which the teaching materials become progressively complicated as the grades go up although the subjects remain the same

循環器(ㄒㄩㄣㄏㄨㄢㄑㄧˋ)
organs of circulation

循環系統(ㄒㄩㄣㄏㄨㄢㄒㄧㄊㄨㄥˇ)
the circulatory system

循環小數(ㄒㄩㄣㄏㄨㄢㄒㄧㄠˇㄕㄨˋ)
recurring decimals

循環賽(ㄒㄩㄣㄏㄨㄢㄙㄞˋ)
a round robin

循階(ㄒㄩㄣㄐㄧㄝ)
to advance step by step; to get promoted in good order, according to one's seniority, merits, service records, etc.

循序(ㄒㄩㄣㄒㄩˋ)
to follow in proper sequence; to proceed in good order, or step by step

循序漸進(ㄒㄩㄣㄒㄩˋㄐㄧㄢㄐㄧㄣˋ)
to follow in proper sequence and make gradual progress; to follow in order and advance step by step; to proceed in an orderly way and step by step

循循善誘(ㄒㄩㄣㄒㄩㄣㄕㄢˋㄧㄡˋ)
(said of a good teacher, etc.) to lead students gradually and patiently on the right path (of learning, etc.)

循資(ㄒㄩㄣㄗ)
to get promotion according to seniority

循俗(ㄒㄩㄣㄙㄨˊ)
to follow customs and traditions

十畫

【徬】 ㄆㄤˊ　parng páng 1487
anxious, agitated and indecisive

徬徨(ㄆㄤˊㄏㄨㄤˊ)
to be anxious, agitated and not knowing what to do

【徭】 ㄧㄠˊ　yau yáo 1488
compulsory labor service;

conscript labor

徭賦(ㄧㄠˊㄈㄨˋ)
compulsory labor and land tax

徭糧(ㄧㄠˊㄌㄧㄤˊ)
food provisions for forced laborers

徭戍(ㄧㄠˊㄕㄨˋ)
compulsory labor service on the frontier

徭役(ㄧㄠˊㄧˋ)
compulsory labor service; corvée

【徯】 ㄒㄧ　shì xǐ 1489
1. to wait for; to expect
2. a narrow path; a shortcut

徯待(ㄒㄧㄉㄞˋ)
to expect; to look forward to

徯徑(ㄒㄧㄐㄧㄥˋ)
a narrow path; a shortcut; a snap course: 求學無徯徑。There is no shortcut to knowledge.

【微】 ㄨㄟ　wei wéi 1490
(又讀 ㄨㄟˊ　uei wěi)
1. small; minute; diminutive; trifling; little; slight: 相差甚微。The difference is slight.
2. low; mean; humble: 他出身微賤。He is a man of mean birth.
3. a polite expression for "I, my, me"
4. weak; sickly; feeble: 她以微弱的聲音說話。She spoke in a weak voice.
5. subtle
6. obscure
7. hidden; concealed
8. to spy
9. if not; but for
10. a Chinese family name

微波(ㄨㄟˊㄅㄛ)
microwaves

微波爐(ㄨㄟˊㄅㄛㄌㄨˊ)
a microwave oven

微薄(ㄨㄟˊㄅㄛˊ)
low; mean; trifling; thin; little

微辭(ㄨㄟˊㄘˊ)
to hint by sarcastic remarks

微不足道(ㄨㄟˊㄅㄨˋㄗㄨˊㄉㄠˋ)
(literally) too small to be worth mentioning—too trifling to be of any conse-

quence; insignificant

微汇(ㄨㄟˊㄏㄨㄟ)
obscure; unclear; uncertain

微妙(ㄨㄟˊㄇㄧㄠˋ)
small; trifling; very slight

微妙(ㄨㄟˊㄇㄧㄠˋ)
subtle (positions); delicate (relations); obscure and mysterious (meanings, etc.): 現在國際情勢甚爲微妙。The international situation is very delicate at present.

微分學(ㄨㄟˊㄈㄣㄒㄩㄝˊ)
differential calculus

微風(ㄨㄟˊㄈㄥ)
a breeze

微服出遊(ㄨㄟˊㄈㄨˊㄔㄨㄧㄡˊ)
to make a tour in mufti; to make a tour in disguise

微電腦(ㄨㄟˊㄉㄧㄢˋㄋㄠˇ)
a microcomputer

微調(ㄨㄟˊㄊㄧㄠˊ)
fine tuning; trimming

微粒子(ㄨㄟˊㄌㄧˋㄗˇ)
① corpuscles or particles ② Nosema bombycis

微量(ㄨㄟˊㄌㄧㄤˋ)
trace; micro

微觀(ㄨㄟˊㄍㄨㄢ)
microscopic

微管現象(ㄨㄟˊㄍㄨㄢˇㄒㄧㄢˋㄒㄧㄤˋ)or
微管引力(ㄨㄟˊㄍㄨㄢˇㄧㄣˇㄌㄧˋ)
capillary phenomena, or capillarity

微乎其微(ㄨㄟˊㄏㄨㄑㄧˊㄨㄟˊ)
extremely trifling or minute; an iota; very little: 他一個人的力量是微乎其微的。On his own he can do very little.

微積分(ㄨㄟˊㄐㄧㄈㄣˋ)
calculus

微賤(ㄨㄟˊㄐㄧㄢˋ)
low and mean; inferior; humble

微晶(ㄨㄟˊㄐㄧㄥ)
microlite

微情(ㄨㄟˊㄑㄧㄥˊ)
a subtle affair; a delicate affair

微息(ㄨㄟˊㄒㄧˊ)
weak and feeble

微細(ㄨㄟˊㄒㄧˋ)
very small; minute

微血管(ㄨㄟˊㄒㄧㄝˋㄍㄨㄢˇ)
(anatomy) capillaries

微小(ㄨㄟˊㄒㄧㄠˇ)

〔彳部〕

①diminutive; very small; minute ②very low (voices, sounds, etc.)

微笑(ㄨㄟ ㄒㄧㄠˋ)
to smile; a smile: 她露出奇怪的微笑。She smiled a strange smile.

微嫌(ㄨㄟ ㄒㄧㄢˊ)
slight animosity: 他們之間存有微嫌。There exist slight animosities between them.

微行(ㄨㄟ ㄒㄧㄥˊ)
①to go out in mufti or disguise; to travel incognito ②a narrow path

微醺(ㄨㄟ ㄒㄩㄣ)
slightly drunk

微旨(ㄨㄟ ㄓˇ)
a deep or abstruse meaning or idea

微震(ㄨㄟ ㄓㄣˋ)
an earthquake of low intensity; microseism; a slight shock: 昨夜有微震。A slight shock occurred last night.

微衷(ㄨㄟ ㄓㄨㄥ)
my true feelings, or innermost sentiments (used in polite conversation or correspondence, particularly with superiors)

微忱(ㄨㄟ ㄔㄣˊ)
a slight token of my regard

微塵(ㄨㄟ ㄔㄣˊ)
①fine dust ② (Buddhism) very minute

微時(ㄨㄟ ㄕˊ)
when one was poor and low

微傷(ㄨㄟ ㄕㄤ)
slightly injured

微生蟲(ㄨㄟ ㄕㄥ ㄔㄨㄥˊ)
microbes; bacteria; germs

微生物(ㄨㄟ ㄕㄥ ㄨˋ)
microbes; microorganisms

微生物學(ㄨㄟ ㄕㄥ ㄨˋ ㄒㄩㄝˊ)
microbiology

微弱(ㄨㄟ ㄖㄨㄛˋ)
weak or feeble (voices, strength, etc.): 她以微弱的聲音歌唱。She sang in a feeble voice.

微子(ㄨㄟ ㄗˇ)
①an adopted son ②name of the stepbrother of Emperor Chou of the Shang Dynasty

微瑕不舉(ㄨㄟ ㄒㄧㄚˊ ㄅㄨˋ ㄐㄩˇ)
to forgive minor offenses

微辭 or 微詞(ㄨㄟ ㄘˊ)
a hint or circumlocution (to point out another's mistake, fault, etc.); veiled criticism

微意(ㄨㄟ ㄧˋ)
a token of sincerity, gratitude, etc. (an expression used in presenting someone with a gift)

微言大義(ㄨㄟ ㄧㄢˊ ㄉㄚˋ ㄧˋ)
to expound the "great way" with subtle and profound language; sublime words with deep meaning

微驗(ㄨㄟ ㄧㄢˋ)
to spy on another; to secretly observe another's intention, etc.

微恙(ㄨㄟ ㄧㄤˋ)
a slight indisposition

微微(ㄨㄟ ㄨㄟ)
small; minute; diminutive

微微的(ㄨㄟ ㄨㄟ˙ㄉㄜ)
slightly; gently

微雨(ㄨㄟ ㄩˇ)
a light rain; a drizzle

十二畫

【徵】 1491
1. ㄓ jeng zhēng

1. to summon
2. to levy or raise (taxes): 政府向人民徵稅。The government levied taxes on people.
3. to call to arms
4. to ask; to inquire
5. to request; to seek for
6. to prove; to evidence
7. signs: 病人已有好轉的徵候。The patient has shown signs of a turn for the better.
8. a Chinese family name

徵辟(ㄓ ㄅㄧˋ)
to use or draft commoners as officials; to appoint commoners to public offices

徵兵(ㄓ ㄅㄧㄥ)
to draft able-bodied male citizens for military service

徵兵制(ㄓ ㄅㄧㄥ ㄓˋ)
the conscription system (as distinct from the volunteer system)

徵聘(ㄓ ㄆㄧㄣˊ)
to solicit a competent person for a vacancy

徵募(ㄓ ㄇㄨˋ)
to enlist and hire

徵發(ㄓ ㄈㄚ)
to requisition supplies and labor service from the people for public use

徵答(ㄓ ㄉㄚˊ)
to solicit answers to questions or problems

徵調(ㄓ ㄉㄧㄠˋ)
to issue orders to conscript men and make military deployment

徵歌(ㄓ ㄍㄜ)
to summon singers or musicians to perform

徵歌選色(ㄓ ㄍㄜ ㄒㄩㄢˇ ㄙㄜˋ)
to pursue sensory pleasure

徵候(ㄓ ㄏㄡˋ)
symptoms, signs, or indications

徵候群(ㄓ ㄏㄡˋ ㄑㄩㄣˊ)
a symptom group 亦作「併合症狀」or「綜合病徵」

徵集(ㄓ ㄐㄧˊ)
to collect or requisition; to levy: 戰時徵集隊伍。Troops are levied in time of war.

徵求(ㄓ ㄑㄧㄡˊ)
to seek; to solicit (answers, etc.); to want (an office clerk, etc.)

徵求會員(ㄓ ㄑㄧㄡˊ ㄏㄨㄟˋ ㄩㄢˊ)
to recruit or enlist members; to canvass for members

徵求意見(ㄓ ㄑㄧㄡˊ ㄧˋ ㄐㄧㄢˋ)
to ask for opinions; to solicit others' views; to seek the opinion of: 我們徵求專家對教學的意見。We ask for experts' opinions on teaching.

徵信錄(ㄓ ㄒㄧㄣˋ ㄌㄨˋ)
a financial report or statement of income and expenditure of a foundation, charity organization, etc.

徵信所(ㄓ ㄒㄧㄣˋ ㄙㄨㄛˇ)
a credit information office

徵象(ㄓ ㄒㄧㄤˋ)
a symptom; indication; a sign

徵詢(ㄓ ㄒㄩㄣˊ)
to solicit opinions, consent, etc.

徵召(ㄓ ㄓㄠˋ)
to draft the capable and vir-

tuous for public service

徵兆 (ㄓㄥˊ ㄓㄠˋ)
a symptom; an omen; symptomatic

徵逐 (ㄓㄥˊ ㄓㄨˊ)
exchanges of visits, etc. between friends

徵詩 (ㄓㄥˊ ㄕ)
to ask another for a poem

徵實 (ㄓㄥˊ ㄕˊ)
to verify, verification

徵收 (ㄓㄥˊ ㄕㄡ)
to collect (taxes, duty, etc.); to levy and collect

徵收稅 (ㄓㄥˊ ㄕㄡˋ)
to levy and collect taxes: 政府為了國家的消費而徵收。The government levies taxes for national expenses.

徵驗 (ㄓㄥˊ ㄧㄢˋ)
to verify; verification; to examine whether the results have come up to expectations

徵引 (ㄓㄥˊ ㄧㄣˇ)
①to recommend a person (for a job, a new position, etc.) ②to evidence; to prove

徵文 (ㄓㄥˊ ㄨㄣˊ)
to solicit writings publicly (as in a contest, etc.)

徵用 (ㄓㄥˊ ㄩㄥˋ)
to requisition; requisition; to conscript; to take over for use; to commandeer

【徵】 1491
2. ㄓˇ jyy zhǐ
one of the five musical notes in Chinese scale

【徹】 1492
ㄔㄜˋ cheh chè
1. penetrating; discerning
2. to remove
3. a tax in tithe
4. to manage; to cultivate (farms)
5. to destroy
6. to deprive; to take away

徹底 (ㄔㄜˋ ㄉㄧˇ)
①(said of a stream, etc.) to be able to see the bottom ②to get to the bottom of; thorough; exhaustive

徹底澄清 (ㄔㄜˋ ㄉㄧˇ ㄔㄥˊ ㄑㄧㄥ)
to clarify a matter thoroughly; to make a thorough investigation of (a case, etc.): 他發表聲明徹底澄清他的情

勢。He issued a statement to clarify the situation thoroughly.

徹頭徹尾 (ㄔㄜˋ ㄊㄡˊ ㄔㄜˋ ㄨㄟˇ)
thoroughly; thorough; (to understand something, etc.) from beginning to end; through and through

徹骨 (ㄔㄜˋ ㄍㄨˇ)
penetrating the bone; to the bone: 寒風徹骨。The bitter wind chills one to the bone.

徹上徹下 (ㄔㄜˋ ㄕㄤˋ ㄔㄜˋ ㄒㄧㄚˋ)
from top to bottom; thoroughly; up and down everywhere

徹夜 (ㄔㄜˋ ㄧㄝˋ)
all through the night; from dusk to dawn; all night: 他徹夜不眠。He lay awake all night.

徹悟 (ㄔㄜˋ ㄨˋ)
to understand thoroughly

【德】 1493
ㄉㄜˊ der dé
1. morality; decency; virtues
2. favor; kindness
3. behavior; conduct
4. to feel grateful
5. Germany; German

德薄能鮮 (ㄉㄜˊ ㄅㄛˊ ㄋㄥˊ ㄒㄧㄢˇ)
(a self-derogatory expression used in polite exchanges) I'm lacking in both virtues and abilities.

德便 (ㄉㄜˊ ㄅㄧㄢˋ)
convenience; proper and convenient

德配 (ㄉㄜˊ ㄆㄟˋ)
(a polite expression) a virtuous wife

德配天地 (ㄉㄜˊ ㄆㄟˋ ㄊㄧㄢ ㄉㄧˋ)
a paragon of virtue; very virtuous

德謨克拉西 (ㄉㄜˊ ㄇㄛˊ ㄎㄜˋ ㄌㄚ ㄒㄧ)
a transliteration of "democracy"

德門 (ㄉㄜˊ ㄇㄣˊ)
a family of high moral standing

德拉瓦 (ㄉㄜˊ ㄌㄚ ㄨㄚˇ)
the state of Delaware, U.S.A.

德高望重 (ㄉㄜˊ ㄍㄠ ㄨㄤˋ ㄓㄨㄥˋ)
(said of a person) of virtue and prestige; of good moral standing and reputation; to

enjoy high prestige and command universal respect

德國 (ㄉㄜˊ ㄍㄨㄛˊ)
Germany

德國麻疹 (ㄉㄜˊ ㄍㄨㄛˊ ㄇㄚˊ ㄓㄣˇ)
German measles

德克薩斯 (ㄉㄜˊ ㄎㄜˋ ㄙㄚˋ ㄙ) or 德州 (ㄓㄡ)
the state of Texas, U.S.A.

德黑蘭 (ㄉㄜˊ ㄏㄟ ㄌㄢˊ)
Teheran, the capital of Iran

德行 (ㄉㄜˊ ㄒㄧㄥˊ)
①morality and conduct: 他的德行永遠令人欽佩。His morality and conduct are always admirable. ②(colloquial) manners or appearances; mannerisms

德政 (ㄉㄜˊ ㄓㄥˋ)
benevolent administration or government

德澤 (ㄉㄜˊ ㄗㄜˊ)
the kindness and charity extended to the people

德才兼備 (ㄉㄜˊ ㄘㄞˊ ㄐㄧㄢ ㄅㄟˋ)
to have both ability and virtue

德操 (ㄉㄜˊ ㄘㄠ)
morality and conduct; virtuous behavior

德意志 (ㄉㄜˊ ㄧˋ ㄓˋ)
Deutschland; Germany

德音 (ㄉㄜˊ ㄧㄣ)
①virtuous utterances ②(I'm eagerly awaiting) your kind reply ③excellent fame

德文 (ㄉㄜˊ ㄨㄣˊ)
the German language; German: 我不會講德文。I cannot speak German.

德望 (ㄉㄜˊ ㄨㄤˋ)
virtuous conduct and high prestige: 他德望兼具。He is a man of virtuous conduct and high prestige.

德育 (ㄉㄜˊ ㄩˋ)
moral education; ethical training: 德育是一件重要的事情。Moral education is an important thing.

十三畫

【徼】 1494
1. ㄐㄧㄠ jiaw jiāo
1. frontiers or boundaries
2. to take an inspection trip

徽外(ㄐㄧㄠ ㄨㄞˋ)
beyond the frontiers; land out of borders

【徼】 1494
2. (僥) ㄐㄧㄠˇ jeau
jiao
to be lucky; fortunate

徼幸(ㄐㄧㄠˇ ㄒㄧㄥˋ)
lucky; (said of happy events) beyond one's expectations

【徼】 1494
3. ㄧㄠ iau yāo
1. to pray for
2. to shade; to hide

徼福(ㄧㄠ ㄈㄨˊ)
to pray for blessings

十四畫

【徽】 1495 ㄏㄨㄟ huei huī
1. good and beautiful; honorable
2. stops on a lute
3. a streamer, flag, pennant, etc.; a flag-sign
4. an emblem; a badge; insignia
5. Anhwei or Huichow

徽墨(ㄏㄨㄟ ㄇㄛˋ)
the inkstick produced at Huichow of Anhwei Province, considered the best of its kind

徽號(ㄏㄨㄟ ㄏㄠˋ)
①a flag with an emblem ② a high-sounding title

徽州(ㄏㄨㄟ ㄓㄡ)
Huichow, a district in Anhwei Province, famous for producing inksticks

徽章(ㄏㄨㄟ ㄓㄤ)
a badge

徽宗(ㄏㄨㄟ ㄗㄨㄥ)
Emperor Hui Tsung of the Sung Dynasty, whose reign extended from 1101 to 1125 A.D., noted for his accomplishments as an artist

心 部
ㄒㄧㄣ shin xīn

【心】 1496
ㄒㄧㄣ shin xīn
1. the heart
2. the mind
3. conscience; moral nature
4. intention; idea; ambition; design
5. the core; the middle, center or inside
6. one of the 28 constellations

心搏(ㄒㄧㄣ ㄅㄛˊ)
(physiology) heartbeat

心版(ㄒㄧㄣ ㄅㄢˇ)
the mind

心病(ㄒㄧㄣ ㄅㄧㄥˋ)
①mental disorder; the illness caused by deep worries ② worries which one cannot share with another

心不在焉(ㄒㄧㄣ ㄅㄨˋ ㄗㄞˋ ㄧㄢ)
absent-minded; absence of mind: 他上課總是心不在焉。He is always absent-minded in classes.

心不由主(ㄒㄧㄣ ㄅㄨˋ ㄧㄡˊ ㄓㄨˇ)
cannot control one's mind or emotion; cannot help but...

心平氣和(ㄒㄧㄣ ㄆㄧㄥˊ ㄑㄧˋ ㄏㄜˊ)
①to be perfectly calm; calmly: 我們心平氣和地討論問題。We discussed the question calmly. ② to be very fair, without involving one's personal feelings

心滿意足(ㄒㄧㄣ ㄇㄢˇ ㄧˋ ㄗㄨˊ)
to be fully contented; complacent

心迷(ㄒㄧㄣ ㄇㄧˊ)
to be confused of mind; to be puzzled

心明如鏡(ㄒㄧㄣ ㄇㄧㄥˊ ㄖㄨˊ ㄐㄧㄥˋ)
(literally) The mind is as clear as a mirror.—devoid of personal emotions, feelings or sense of gain and loss

心明眼亮(ㄒㄧㄣ ㄇㄧㄥˊ ㄧㄢˇ ㄌㄧㄤˋ)
(to talk) without hiding anything; to/ lay all one's cards on the table; to be frank

心目中(ㄒㄧㄣ ㄇㄨˋ ㄓㄨㄥ)
①in one's heart or mind; in one's mental view ② in one's memory: 他仍活在我們的心目中。He still lives in our memories.

心慕手追(ㄒㄧㄣ ㄇㄨˋ ㄕㄡˇ ㄓㄨㄟ)
(literally) What one's heart admires the hands follow. —trying one's best to emulate someone whom he admires

心法(ㄒㄧㄣ ㄈㄚˇ)
①(Buddhism) teaching without scriptures—through persuasion and a meeting of minds ②(a way of teaching) by sharing the tutor's thoughts with his pupils

心非(ㄒㄧㄣ ㄈㄟ)
The mind disagrees (with what the lips utter). 他一向口是心非。His mind always disagrees with what he says.

心扉(ㄒㄧㄣ ㄈㄟ)
(figuratively) the door of one's heart

心煩(ㄒㄧㄣ ㄈㄢˊ)
piqued; annoyed; fretful

心煩意亂(ㄒㄧㄣ ㄈㄢˊ ㄧˋ ㄌㄨㄢˋ)
fretful and confused; to be upset

心房(ㄒㄧㄣ ㄈㄤˊ)
①(anatomy) auricles ② the seat of one's inmost thoughts and secret feelings; soul; mind

心房擴大(ㄒㄧㄣ ㄈㄤˊ ㄎㄨㄛˋ ㄉㄚˋ)
dilation of heart

心浮(ㄒㄧㄣ ㄈㄨˊ)
frivolous; restless; impatient; flighty

心浮氣躁(ㄒㄧㄣ ㄈㄨˊ ㄑㄧˋ ㄗㄠˋ)
to be unsettled and short-tempered; to be restless and fretful

心服(ㄒㄧㄣ ㄈㄨˊ)
to have one's heart won; to submit, admire, etc. sincerely and willingly

心服口服(ㄒㄧㄣ ㄈㄨˊ ㄎㄡˇ ㄈㄨˊ)
to admit somebody's superiority, etc. with sincerity; fully convinced

心腹(ㄒㄧㄣ ㄈㄨˋ)
①faith; loyalty ②(military) a region of great strategic importance ③ a confidant; a trusted subordinate

心腹話(ㄒㄧㄣ ㄈㄨˋ ㄏㄨㄚˋ)
a confidential talk: 他向我說心腹話。He told me something in strict confidence.

心腹之患(ㄒㄧㄣㄈㄨˋㄓㄏㄨㄢˋ)
the threat from within (the organization, nation, etc.); serious hidden trouble or danger; a festering wound: 貪污腐化是該國的心腹之患。 Corruption in that country is a festering wound.

心腹事(ㄒㄧㄣㄈㄨˋㄕ)
one's innermost secrets

心得(ㄒㄧㄣㄉㄜˊ)
what one gains from intense study, meditation or long practice

心到(ㄒㄧㄣㄉㄠˋ)
the sincerity of one's heart (as distinct from the formality or mere show of piety)

心膽俱裂(ㄒㄧㄣㄉㄢˇㄐㄩㄌㄧㄝˋ)
to be frightened out of one's wits; to be terror-stricken

心蕩神馳(ㄒㄧㄣㄉㄤˋㄕㄣˊㄔˊ)
to be infatuated (with a stunning beauty, etc.); to lose control of one's mind and will; to fall head over heels for

心地(ㄒㄧㄣㄉㄧˋ)
conscience; intentions; the true nature of a person; a person's mind; character; moral nature: 她是個心地單純的女孩。She is a simple-minded girl.

心地光明(ㄒㄧㄣㄉㄧˋㄍㄨㄤㄇㄧㄥˊ)
clear conscience; upright

心地善良(ㄒㄧㄣㄉㄧˋㄕㄢˋㄌㄧㄤˊ)
good-natured; kind-hearted

心電圖(ㄒㄧㄣㄉㄧㄢˋㄊㄨˊ)
an electrocardiogram

心電感應(ㄒㄧㄣㄉㄧㄢˋㄍㄢˇㄧㄥˋ)
telepathy

心毒手辣(ㄒㄧㄣㄉㄨˊㄕㄡˇㄌㄚˋ)
callous and cruel; cold-blooded; merciless at heart and in deeds

心多(ㄒㄧㄣㄉㄨㄛ)
over-suspicious

心動(ㄒㄧㄣㄉㄨㄥˋ)
① palpitation or fluttering of the heart ② to become interested in something (usually as a result of persuasion)

心態(ㄒㄧㄣㄊㄞˋ)
mentality

心頭(ㄒㄧㄣㄊㄡˊ)
① the heart; the mind; intentions ② the hearts of animals

心頭火起(ㄒㄧㄣㄊㄡˊㄏㄨㄛˇㄑㄧˇ)
to be angry; to be infuriated

心頭肉(ㄒㄧㄣㄊㄡˊㄖㄡˋ)
the apple of one's eye; something or someone dear to the heart

心投意合(ㄒㄧㄣㄊㄡˊㄧˋㄏㄜˊ)
(usually said of intimate friends or lovers, etc.) to be in perfect agreement; to be in rapport: 他與女朋友心投意合。He is in rapport with his girlfriend.

心疼(ㄒㄧㄣㄊㄥˊ)
①(literally) heartache; the heart bleeds (over financial loss, the suffering of a beloved one, etc.): 我為她心疼。My heart bleeds for her. ② to love dearly

心跳(ㄒㄧㄣㄊㄧㄠˋ)
① heartbeat ② palpitation of the heart caused by fear or anxiety

心跳口跳(ㄒㄧㄣㄊㄧㄠˋㄎㄡˇㄊㄧㄠˋ)
to be in an extreme hurry which causes confusion and trepidation

心田(ㄒㄧㄣㄊㄧㄢˊ)
① one's heart: 我將你的恩惠記在心田。I have your best favor at heart. ② one's disposition or intentions

心痛(ㄒㄧㄣㄊㄨㄥˋ)
to feel the pangs of heart

心勞日拙(ㄒㄧㄣㄌㄠˊㄖˋㄓㄨㄛˊ)
to make laborious pretensions without contributing anything; to make thing and useless pretensions

心理(ㄒㄧㄣㄌㄧˇ)
① mentality; psychology ② thought and ideas ③ mental; psychogenic

心理病態(ㄒㄧㄣㄌㄧˇㄅㄧㄥˋㄊㄞˋ)
a morbid state of mind; mental abnormality

心理分析(ㄒㄧㄣㄌㄧˇㄈㄣㄒㄧ)
psychoanalysis

心理輔導(ㄒㄧㄣㄌㄧˇㄈㄨˇㄉㄠˇ)
psychological counseling

心理健康(ㄒㄧㄣㄌㄧˇㄐㄧㄢˋㄎㄤ)
mental health

心理建設(ㄒㄧㄣㄌㄧˇㄐㄧㄢˋㄕㄜˋ)

psychological fortification; mental readjustment

心理現象(ㄒㄧㄣㄌㄧˇㄒㄧㄢˋㄒㄧㄤˋ)
mental phenomena

心理學(ㄒㄧㄣㄌㄧˇㄒㄩㄝˊ)
psychology; mental management

心理戰(ㄒㄧㄣㄌㄧˇㄓㄢˋ)
psychological warfare, or pywsar

心理作用(ㄒㄧㄣㄌㄧˇㄗㄨㄛˋㄩㄥˋ)
imaginary perception; mental reaction

心理測驗(ㄒㄧㄣㄌㄧˇㄘㄜˋㄧㄢˋ)
a mental test

心理因素(ㄒㄧㄣㄌㄧˇㄧㄣㄙㄨˋ)
a psychological factor

心理衛生(ㄒㄧㄣㄌㄧˇㄨㄟˋㄕㄥ)
mental hygiene

心力(ㄒㄧㄣㄌㄧˋ)
the exercise of one's mental capabilities; mental power; the vigor of the mind

心力交瘁(ㄒㄧㄣㄌㄧˋㄐㄧㄠㄘㄨㄟˋ)
to feel exhausted both mentally and physically

心裏(ㄒㄧㄣ·ㄌㄧ)
① the region of the human body around the chest ② in one's heart; in one's mind; mentally

心裏話(ㄒㄧㄣ·ㄌㄧㄏㄨㄚˋ)
one's innermost thoughts and feelings: 他說出群眾的心裏話。He gave voice to the innermost feelings of the crowd.

心裏有數(ㄒㄧㄣ·ㄌㄧㄧㄡˇㄕㄨˋ)
aware of something without speaking out

心連心(ㄒㄧㄣㄌㄧㄢˊㄒㄧㄣ)
heart linked to heart: 父母與子女心心連心。The hearts of parents and their children are linked to each other.

心靈(ㄒㄧㄣㄌㄧㄥˊ)
mind; spirit; spiritual; mental

心靈手巧(ㄒㄧㄣㄌㄧㄥˊㄕㄡˇㄑㄧㄠˇ)
The mind is clever as the hands are nimble. 或clever and deft: 她心靈手巧。She is clever and deft.

心領(ㄒㄧㄣㄌㄧㄥˇ)
① to understand without verbal exchange ② to appreciate (the offer of service or

〔心 部〕

a gift while declining it): 你的好意我心領了。I appreciate your kindness but must decline your offer.

心領神會 (ㄒㄧㄣ ㄌㄧㄥˇ ㄕㄣˊ ㄏㄨㄟˋ)
to know or understand without being told

心亂 (ㄒㄧㄣ ㄌㄨㄢˋ)
confused and perturbed

心亂如麻 (ㄒㄧㄣ ㄌㄨㄢˋ ㄖㄨˊ ㄇㄚˊ)
extremely confused and disturbed; to have one's mind as confused as a tangled skein

心律 (ㄒㄧㄣ ㄌㄩˋ)
(medicine) the rhythm of the heart

心略 (ㄒㄧㄣ ㄌㄩㄝˋ)
scheming; schemes; artful

心高氣傲 (ㄒㄧㄣ ㄍㄠ ㄑㄧˋ ㄠˋ)
proud and arrogant

心肝 (ㄒㄧㄣ ㄍㄢ)
① a darling; a honey; a sweetheart ② conscience

心甘情願 (ㄒㄧㄣ ㄍㄢ ㄑㄧㄥˊ ㄩㄢˋ)
to be totally willing; willingly

心廣體胖 (ㄒㄧㄣ ㄍㄨㄤˇ ㄊㄧˇ ㄆㄢˊ)
A clear conscience (or absence of worries) contributes to physical well-being. 或 fit and happy: 他心廣體胖。He feels fit and happy.

心開 (ㄒㄧㄣ ㄎㄞ)
to have one's mind opened; to be tremendously benefited intellectually

心口 (ㄒㄧㄣ ㄎㄡˇ)
① the region of the human body between the ribs; the bosom ② one's utterance and what he really thinks

心口如一 (ㄒㄧㄣ ㄎㄡˇ ㄖㄨˊ ㄧ)
(literally) The mouth agrees with the mind.—to speak one's mind frankly; to say what one thinks; to be frank and unreserved; to practice what one preaches

心坎 (ㄒㄧㄣ ㄎㄢˇ) or 心坎兒 (ㄒㄧㄣ ㄎㄢˇ ㄦˊ)
① the heart's chord ② dear to the heart; bosom ③ the center of the heart; the bottom of one's heart

心肯 (ㄒㄧㄣ ㄎㄣˇ)
an acceptance in the heart;

inner approval or assent

心虧 (ㄒㄧㄣ ㄎㄨㄟ)
a guilty conscience

心寬 (ㄒㄧㄣ ㄎㄨㄢ)
open-minded; carefree; optimistic; feeling at peace with the world

心曠神怡 (ㄒㄧㄣ ㄎㄨㄤˋ ㄕㄣˊ ㄧˊ)
to feel way above par; the spiritual uplift which one often experiences when he enjoys the beauty of nature; to feel on top of the world

心孔 (ㄒㄧㄣ ㄎㄨㄥˇ)
intellectual capacity

心寒膽怯 (ㄒㄧㄣ ㄏㄢˊ ㄉㄢˇ ㄑㄧㄝˋ)
shuddering and fearful; extreme apprehension; trepidation

心狠 (ㄒㄧㄣ ㄏㄣˇ)
heartless; hardhearted; flinty; unfeeling; callous

心花怒放 (ㄒㄧㄣ ㄏㄨㄚ ㄋㄨˋ ㄈㄤˋ)
to be brimming with joy; to feel exuberantly happy; to be elated: 他因成功而心花怒放。He is highly elated over the success.

心火 (ㄒㄧㄣ ㄏㄨㄛˇ)
① (Chinese medicine) the "inner temperature" of a patient ② (literally) the fire of the heart—the fidgets ③ one of the 28 constellations

心懷 (ㄒㄧㄣ ㄏㄨㄞˊ)
to entertain; to cherish; to harbor: 他心懷叵測。He cherishes evil designs.

心灰意懶 (ㄒㄧㄣ ㄏㄨㄟ ㄧˋ ㄌㄢˇ)
to be downcast and disappointed; extremely discouraged; to be disheartened: 不要因一次失敗而心灰意懶。Don't be disheartened by a single failure.

心灰意冷 (ㄒㄧㄣ ㄏㄨㄟ ㄧˋ ㄌㄥˇ)
pessimistic and dejected due to repeated failures and frustrations; to feel discouraged and hopeless

心回意轉 (ㄒㄧㄣ ㄏㄨㄟˊ ㄧˋ ㄓㄨㄢˇ)
to change one's mind; to give up one's old (evil) ways; to repent; to start a new life

心慌 (ㄒㄧㄣ ㄏㄨㄤ)
to be greatly shaken and

perturbed; panicky

心慌意亂 (ㄒㄧㄣ ㄏㄨㄤ ㄧˋ ㄌㄨㄢˋ)
to lose one's wits totally; to be shaken and perturbed; extremely nervous: 面臨危機別心慌意亂。Don't lose your wits in the face of a crisis.

心肌 (ㄒㄧㄣ ㄐㄧ)
(anatomy) cardiac muscle; myocardium

心機 (ㄒㄧㄣ ㄐㄧ)
schemes, devices or designs; craftiness

心跡 or 心迹 (ㄒㄧㄣ ㄐㄧ)
real intentions; innermost feelings

心疾 (ㄒㄧㄣ ㄐㄧˊ)
① illness caused by deep worries ② a mental ailment

心急 (ㄒㄧㄣ ㄐㄧˊ)
impatient: 不要如此心急!Don't be so impatient!

心急腿慢 (ㄒㄧㄣ ㄐㄧˊ ㄊㄨㄟˇ ㄇㄢˋ)
the more impatient the slower the movement

心計 (ㄒㄧㄣ ㄐㄧˋ)
devices, schemes or designs of the mind; scheming; calculating: 這商人工於心計。The businessman is adept at scheming.

心悸 (ㄒㄧㄣ ㄐㄧˋ)
palpitation of the heart—a symptom of psychoneurosis

心交 (ㄒㄧㄣ ㄐㄧㄠ)
a close or intimate friend

心焦 (ㄒㄧㄣ ㄐㄧㄠ)
anxious; impatient; very eager; worried; vexed: 他們對她的延遲甚感心焦。They became anxious at her delay.

心堅石穿 (ㄒㄧㄣ ㄐㄧㄢ ㄕˊ ㄔㄨㄢ)
With a strong will power, nothing is impossible.

心匠 (ㄒㄧㄣ ㄐㄧㄤˋ)
a welding of ideas into plans

心旌 (ㄒㄧㄣ ㄐㄧㄥ)
wavering; an unsettled state of mind

心經 (ㄒㄧㄣ ㄐㄧㄥ)
the Buddhist sutra of the heart of prajna

心驚膽戰 (ㄒㄧㄣ ㄐㄧㄥ ㄉㄢˇ ㄓㄢˋ)
shuddering and terrified; to tremble with fear; to shake with fear: 這景象使他心驚膽

戰。The sight makes him shake with fear.

驚肉跳(ㄐㄧㄥ ㄖㄡˋ ㄊㄧㄠˋ)
trembling with fear; to make one's flesh creep; trepidation

境(ㄒㄧㄣ ㄐㄧㄥˋ)
a mood; a humor: 她心境非常愉快。She is in a very happy mood.

鏡(ㄒㄧㄣ ㄐㄧㄥˋ)
(literally) the mirror of the heart—the cleanliness of one's mind

淨 or 心靜(ㄒㄧㄣ ㄐㄧㄥˋ)
a mind free of worries and cares; calm

淨地自滾(ㄒㄧㄣ ㄐㄧㄥˋ ㄉㄧˋ ㄗˋ ㄎㄨㄞˋ)
When the mind is free of worries and cares, one will feel cooler (in hot weather).

期(ㄒㄧㄣ ㄑㄧˊ)
① what one secretly aspires ② mutual approval or admiration

契(ㄒㄧㄣ ㄑㄧˋ)
① (literally) a meeting of minds—a bosom friend; a very close friend ② teamwork

怯(ㄒㄧㄣ ㄑㄧㄝˋ)
timid; timorous; shy

竅(ㄒㄧㄣ ㄑㄧㄠˋ)
the pores of one's mind—the source of one's intellectual capacity; the capacity for clear thinking; the intellect 亦作「心孔」: 他財迷心竅。He was obsessed by a lust for gold.

情(ㄒㄧㄣ ㄑㄧㄥˊ)
a mood; the frame (or state) of one's mind

曲(ㄒㄧㄣ ㄑㄩ)
(literally) ① the innermost being, the corner of one's heart; the hidden feelings; the mind ② something weighing on one's mind; one's secret concern

細(ㄒㄧㄣ ㄒㄧˋ)
cautious; careful; carefulness: 他辦心心細。He is both courageous and cautious.

邪形穢(ㄒㄧㄝˊ ㄒㄧㄥˊ ㄒㄧˋ ㄏㄨㄞˋ)
When the mind is filthy, the appearance will not look

any better.

弦(ㄒㄧㄣ ㄒㄧㄢˊ)
the heart's cord; heartstrings: 她的歌聲動人心弦。Her singing played upon our heartstrings.

險(ㄒㄧㄣ ㄒㄧㄢˇ)
crafty and evil-minded

心念念(ㄒㄧㄣ ㄒㄧㄣ ㄋㄧㄢˋ ㄋㄧㄢˋ)
to remember always; to keep in mind always

心相印(ㄒㄧㄣ ㄒㄧㄣ ㄒㄧㄤ ㄧㄣˋ)
a complete meeting of minds; in complete rapport; all of one mind: 我倆心心相印。Both of us are all of one mind.

香(ㄒㄧㄣ ㄒㄧㄤ)
sincerity; devotion; piety

想(ㄒㄧㄣ ㄒㄧㄤˇ)
to think; to expect; to figure

性(ㄒㄧㄣ ㄒㄧㄥˋ)
temperament; tempers; constitution of the mind

虛(ㄒㄧㄣ ㄒㄩ)
apprehension caused by one's feeling of guilt; a guilty conscience: 他做賊心虛。He had a guilty conscience.

許(ㄒㄧㄣ ㄒㄩˇ)
a tacit acceptance or approval; acclaim without words

許目成(ㄒㄧㄣ ㄒㄩˇ ㄇㄨˋ ㄔㄥˊ)
to convey love by exchanging longing glances

緒(ㄒㄧㄣ ㄒㄩˋ)
a mood; the state of mind: 他心緒不寧。He is in a disturbed state of mind.

血(ㄒㄧㄣ ㄒㄩㄝˋ)
energy; painstaking care (or efforts): 我們在這計畫上費盡心血。We expended all our energies on this project.

血來潮(ㄒㄧㄣ ㄒㄩㄝˋ ㄌㄞˊ ㄔㄠˊ)
to hit upon a sudden idea; to have a brainstorm; in an impulsive moment; a whim: 他心血來潮忘乎所以。He forgot himself in an impulsive moment.

懸兩地(ㄒㄧㄣ ㄒㄩㄢˊ ㄌㄧㄤˇ ㄉㄧˋ)
(literally) a mind concerned with two places—divided attention; to have worries at two places at the same time

胸(ㄒㄧㄣ ㄒㄩㄥ)

① will; ambition ② capacity for tolerance; breadth of mind: 我們心胸開闊。We are broad-minded.

織筆耕(ㄒㄧㄣ ㄓ ㄅㄧˇ ㄍㄥ)
(said of a writing career) The pen labors on the ideas of the mind.

心直口快(ㄒㄧㄣ ㄓˊ ㄎㄡˇ ㄎㄨㄞˋ)
honest and outspoken: 年輕人心直口快。The young man is honest and outspoken.

志(ㄒㄧㄣ ㄓˋ)
will power; fortitude: 心志可以克服習慣。Will power can conquer habit.

智(ㄒㄧㄣ ㄓˋ)
mentality; the abilities and powers of the mind

折(ㄒㄧㄣ ㄓㄜˊ)
to have one's heart won; to admire without reservations

窄(ㄒㄧㄣ ㄓㄞˇ)
narrow-minded

照不宣(ㄒㄧㄣ ㄓㄠˋ ㄅㄨˋ ㄒㄩㄢ)
a tacit understanding or agreement: 我們心照不宣。We have a tacit understanding.

證(ㄒㄧㄣ ㄓㄥˋ)
① (Buddhism) the accord between mind and truth ② (law) to pass a judgment according to the judge's conviction after listening to the arguments of both parties

中(ㄒㄧㄣ ㄓㄨㄥ)
in one's heart or mind

中有數(ㄒㄧㄣ ㄓㄨㄥ ㄧㄡˇ ㄕㄨˋ)
to have a pretty good idea of; to know fairly well; to know at heart: 我對工作進行情況心中有數。I have a pretty clear idea of how the work is progressing.

潮(ㄒㄧㄣ ㄔㄠˊ)
emotions which churn inside like the flow and ebb of the tide; surging thoughts and emotions: 他感到心潮澎湃。He felt an upsurge of emotion.

腸(ㄒㄧㄣ ㄔㄤˊ)
① heart: 他是一個心腸仁慈的人。He is a man with a kind heart. ② affections; sympathies ③ conscience ④ a natural bent of the mind

【心
部】

心傳(ㄒㄧㄣ ㄔㄨㄢˊ)
①to teach ②the secret of teaching

心室(ㄒㄧㄣ ㄕˋ)
ventricles

心事(ㄒㄧㄣ ㄕˋ)
①secrets in one's mind ②something weighing on one's mind: 她最近有些心事煩擾她。She's had something weighing on her mind recently.

心手相應(ㄒㄧㄣ ㄕㄡˇ ㄒㄧㄤ ㄧㄥˋ)
(usually said of calligraphy or writing) As the mind wills, the hand responds.

心善(ㄒㄧㄣ ㄕㄢˋ)
kind-hearted; a kind heart

心神(ㄒㄧㄣ ㄕㄣˊ)
①a mood; the state of mind ②attention

心神不定(ㄒㄧㄣ ㄕㄣˊ ㄅㄨˋ ㄉㄧㄥˋ)
a restless or unstable mood; a confused state of mind; to have no peace of mind; to be distracted

心神不安(ㄒㄧㄣ ㄕㄣˊ ㄅㄨˋ ㄢ)
to feel uneasy or perturbed

心上(ㄒㄧㄣ ㄕㄤˋ)
in one's mind; in one's heart

心上人(ㄒㄧㄣ ㄕㄤˋ ㄖㄣˊ)
a sweetheart; a lover

心聲(ㄒㄧㄣ ㄕㄥ)
①spoken language ②the heart's desire; intentions; thoughts

心術(ㄒㄧㄣ ㄕㄨˋ)
designs; schemes; intentions: 他的心術不正。He harbors evil intentions.

心如刀割(ㄒㄧㄣ ㄖㄨˊ ㄉㄠ ㄍㄜ)
(literally) a heart being cut by a knife—heartbroken; heart-stricken; to stab somebody to the heart

心如止水(ㄒㄧㄣ ㄖㄨˊ ㄓˇ ㄕㄨㄟˇ)
(literally) The heart is like still water.—a mind without worries, cares, ambitions or worldly desires

心如死灰(ㄒㄧㄣ ㄖㄨˊ ㄙˇ ㄏㄨㄟ)
One's heart is like dead ashes.

心軟(ㄒㄧㄣ ㄖㄨㄢˇ)
soft-hearted; kind-hearted; tender-hearted

心臟(ㄒㄧㄣ ㄗㄤˋ)
the heart (as an organ)

心臟病(ㄒㄧㄣ ㄗㄤˋ ㄅㄧㄥˋ)
heart disease

心臟病發作(ㄒㄧㄣ ㄗㄤˋ ㄅㄧㄥˋ ㄈㄚ ㄗㄨㄛˋ)
a heart attack

心臟痙攣(ㄒㄧㄣ ㄗㄤˋ ㄐㄧㄥˋ ㄌㄩㄢˊ)
stenocardia

心臟移植(ㄒㄧㄣ ㄗㄤˋ ㄧˊ ㄓˊ)
heart transplantation

心臟炎(ㄒㄧㄣ ㄗㄤˋ ㄧㄢˊ)
carditis

心醉(ㄒㄧㄣ ㄗㄨㄟˋ)
①to admire without reserve ②to be captivated or held spellbound; to be in ecstasies over; to be charmed; to be fascinated: 他對音樂心醉神迷。He was in ecstasies over music.

心慈面軟(ㄒㄧㄣ ㄘˊ ㄇㄧㄢˋ ㄖㄨㄢˇ)
tender-hearted and unable to turn down others' requests

心裁(ㄒㄧㄣ ㄘㄞˊ)
(usually said of objects of art or handicrafts) design; style

心粗(ㄒㄧㄣ ㄘㄨ)
thoughtless; careless: 心粗的孩子常常犯錯誤。Thoughtless boys often make blunders.

心存魏闕(ㄒㄧㄣ ㄘㄨㄣˊ ㄨㄟˋ ㄑㄩㄝˋ)
undying loyalty to one's own country while living on a strange land

心思(ㄒㄧㄣ ㄙ)
①ideas; thoughts; intelligence ②intentions ③a state of mind; a mood: 我沒有心思去看電影。I was not in the mood to see a movie.

心死(ㄒㄧㄣ ㄙˇ)
heartless; abandoned; in a state of stupor

心碎(ㄒㄧㄣ ㄙㄨㄟˋ)
heartbreak; heartbroken: 她的死命他心碎。Her death left him broken-hearted.

心酸(ㄒㄧㄣ ㄙㄨㄢ)
heartsick; heartsore; grief-stricken; to sadden; to feel sad

心算(ㄒㄧㄣ ㄙㄨㄢˋ)
mental arithmetic

心愛(ㄒㄧㄣ ㄞˋ)
to be extremely fond of; (things or persons) dear to one's heart

心安(ㄒㄧㄣ ㄢ)
heartsease; peace of mind; calmness of emotion; care free

心安理得(ㄒㄧㄣ ㄢ ㄌㄧˇ ㄉㄜˊ)
to have achieved a perfect peace of mind; to feel no qualm; to feel at ease and justified

心耳(ㄒㄧㄣ ㄦˇ)
(anatomy) the auricles

心儀(ㄒㄧㄣ ㄧˊ)
admiration in one's mind for another; to look upon someone as a model due to admiration: 我心儀其人。I admire that person.

心意(ㄒㄧㄣ ㄧˋ)
①ideas; intentions; opinions; decisions: 我們不了解他的心意。We don't understand his intention. ②regard: 這物是我們大家的一點心意。This is a token of our regard.

心藥(ㄒㄧㄣ ㄧㄠˋ)
(literally) the medicine for the heart—anything which removes one's worries and anxieties, or satisfies one's secret longings or desires

心有餘悸(ㄒㄧㄣ ㄧㄡˇ ㄩˊ ㄐㄧˋ)
one's heart still fluttering with fear; to have a lingering fear

心有餘而力不足(ㄒㄧㄣ ㄧㄡˇ ㄩˊ ㄦˊ ㄌㄧˋ ㄅㄨˋ ㄗㄨˊ)
ability or resources at one's command inadequate to achieve what is desired, or to do what one wishes: 我們感到心有餘而力不足。We feel unable to do what we want very much to do.

心眼(兒)(ㄒㄧㄣ ㄧㄢˇ (ㄦ))
①one's intention; conscience ②mind (especially used in "a narrow mind" or "narrow-minded"); overattention to details ③cleverness or wits

心癢(ㄒㄧㄣ ㄧㄤˇ)
an itching heart—an intense desire (to make a try, etc.)

心漾(ㄒㄧㄣ ㄧㄤˋ)
one's heart aroused by desires (usually carnal)

心營目注(ㄒㄧㄣ ㄧㄥˊ ㄇㄨˋ ㄓㄨˋ)

to watch closely while making plans at heart

影(ㄒ一ㄥˇ)
impression; mental image

無旁騖(ㄒㄧㄥ ㄨ ㄆㄤˊ ㄨˋ)
single-minded; without distraction

無二用(ㄒㄧㄥ ㄦˋ ㄩㄥˋ)
One's attention cannot be divided by two undertakings simultaneously. 或 To succeed in an undertaking, one needs single-mindedness or concentration.

窩(ㄒㄧㄥ ㄨㄛ)
① in one's heart ② the region between the ribs

爲之動(ㄒㄧㄥ ㄨㄟˋ ㄓ ㄉㄨㄥˋ)
to be tempted

悅誠服(ㄒㄧㄥ ㄩㄝˋ ㄔㄥˊ ㄈㄨˊ)
to concede or submit willingly; to be completely convinced: 他對你的批評心悅誠服。He conceded willingly your criticism.

猿意馬(ㄒㄧㄥ ㄩㄢˊ ㄧˋ ㄇㄚˇ)
① cannot make up one's mind; indecision ② restless and whimsical; fanciful and fickle; capricious

願(ㄒㄧㄥ ㄩㄢˋ)
① a wish (usually a long-cherished one); aspiration; a dream ② a promise to a god

一畫

【必】 1497
ㄅㄧˋ bih bì
. most certainly; must; necessarily
. an emphatic particle

敗(ㄅㄧˋ ㄅㄞˋ)
will certainly be defeated; will certainly fail: 驕兵必敗。An army puffed up with pride will certainly be defeated.

備條件(ㄅㄧˋ ㄅㄟˋ ㄊㄧㄠˊ ㄐㄧㄢˋ)
the requisitions (for)

必剝剝(ㄅㄧˋ ㄅㄧˋ ㄅㄛ ㄅㄛ)
"pi pi po po"—the crackling sounds of a burning log, etc.

不可免(ㄅㄧˋ ㄅㄨˋ ㄎㄜˇ ㄇㄧㄢˇ)
unavoidable; inevitable

不可少(ㄅㄧˋ ㄅㄨˋ ㄎㄜˇ ㄕㄠˇ)
absolutely necessary

必非(ㄅㄧˋ ㄈㄟ)
certainly not

必得
①(ㄅㄧˋ ㄉㄟˇ) must; to have to: 我必得立刻去做遺件事。I must do it at once.
②(ㄅㄧˋ ㄉㄜˊ) determined to possess something, to have to obtain something by every possible means

必定(ㄅㄧˋ ㄉㄧㄥˋ)
most certainly; must; to be sure to

必讀(ㄅㄧˋ ㄉㄨˊ)
a must for reading

必恭必敬(ㄅㄧˋ ㄍㄨㄥ ㄅㄧˋ ㄐㄧㄥˋ)
displaying full courtesy; showing great politeness; showing great respect

必修科(ㄅㄧˋ ㄒㄧㄡ ㄎㄜ)
a required course in the college curriculum; an obligatory course

必需(ㄅㄧˋ ㄒㄩ)
what is essential or indispensable; necessary incidentals or outlays: 食物與空氣是生命所必需的。Food and air are indispensable to life.

必須(ㄅㄧˋ ㄒㄩ)
must; to have to: 人必須吃東西才能活。Man must eat to live.

必需品(ㄅㄧˋ ㄒㄩ ㄆㄧㄣˇ)
daily necessities; consumer goods; necessaries; necessary wants; requisites

必傳之作(ㄅㄧˋ ㄔㄨㄢˊ ㄓ ㄗㄨㄛˋ)
(literally) a work that will certainly go down to posterity—a masterpiece

必勝(ㄅㄧˋ ㄕㄥˋ)
will most certainly win; can not fail or be defeated

必然(ㄅㄧˋ ㄖㄢˊ)
to have to be (like this); inevitable

必然之勢(ㄅㄧˋ ㄖㄢˊ ㄓ ㄕˋ)
a natural trend; a certainty

必死(ㄅㄧˋ ㄙˇ)
will certainly die or get killed

必死之心(ㄅㄧˋ ㄙˇ ㄓ ㄒㄧㄣ)
with one's back to the wall; determination arising from a desperate situation

必要(ㄅㄧˋ ㄧㄠˋ)

necessary; necessity; need; requisite: 沒有必要再討論了。There's no need to discuss it any more.

必要條件(ㄅㄧˋ ㄧㄠˋ ㄊㄧㄠˊ ㄐㄧㄢˋ)
a necessary condition

二畫

【忉】 1498
ㄉㄠ dau dāo
grieved; distressed

忉怛(ㄉㄠ ㄉㄚˊ)
grieved; distressed; sad; worried

忉忉(ㄉㄠ ㄉㄠ)
distressed; worried

三畫

【忌】 1499
ㄐㄧˋ jih jì
1. jealous; to envy: 他妒忌的理由是什麼? What is the reason for his jealousy?
2. to fear; a fear (usually superstitious)
3. to shun
4. to prohibit or proscribe (usually for superstitious purposes); taboo: 百無禁忌。Nothing is taboo.
5. death anniversaries of one's parents or grandparents

忌憚(ㄐㄧˋ ㄉㄢˋ)
fears that keep a person from committing irregularities; to dread; dread; scruple

忌賭(ㄐㄧˋ ㄉㄨˇ)
to quit gambling

忌妒(ㄐㄧˋ ㄉㄨˋ)
to be jealous of; envy

忌刻(ㄐㄧˋ ㄎㄜˋ)
jealous and acrid

忌口(ㄐㄧˋ ㄎㄡˇ)or忌嘴(ㄐㄧˋ ㄗㄨㄟˇ)
to be on a diet (because of ailment, etc.); to avoid certain foods

忌恨(ㄐㄧˋ ㄏㄣˋ)or忌心(ㄐㄧˋ ㄒㄧㄣ)
jealousy; to envy and hate

忌諱(ㄐㄧˋ ㄏㄨㄟˋ)
① things which one does not like others to do or say; things which one avoids saying or doing; a taboo ② to avoid as taboo ③ to avoid

〔心部〕

【心 部】

as harmful ④ vinegar

忌酒(ㄐㄧ ㄐㄧㄡˇ)or **戒酒**(ㄐㄧㄝˋ ㄐㄧㄡˇ)
to quit drinking; to give up alcohol; to abstain from wine

忌妻(ㄐㄧˋ ㄑㄧ)
a jealous wife

忌辰(ㄐㄧˋ ㄔㄣˊ)or **忌日**(ㄐㄧˋ ㄖˋ)
death anniversaries of one's parents, etc.: (in ancient China) the death anniversary of the emperor or empress of the reigning dynasty

忌煙(ㄐㄧˋ ㄧㄢ)
to quit smoking 亦作「戒煙」：他已忌煙。He has quit smoking.

【忍】 1500
ㄖㄣˇ reen rén
1. to endure; to bear; to tolerate; to put up with; to suffer; to stand: 我再也不能忍耐那噪音。I couldn't put up with the noise any longer.
2. merciless; truculence
3. to forbear; to repress

忍不住(ㄖㄣˇ ·ㄅㄨ ㄓㄨˋ)
①cannot stand it any more; unable to resist ②can not help (laughing, etc.)

忍冬(ㄖㄣˇ ㄉㄨㄥ)
(botany) honeysuckle

忍淚(ㄖㄣˇ ㄌㄟˋ)
to hold back one's tears

忍痛(ㄖㄣˇ ㄊㄨㄥˋ)
to bear or suffer pain with dignity (to give up or sell something) reluctantly: 我們忍痛割愛。We parted reluctantly with what we treasured.

忍耐(ㄖㄣˇ ㄋㄞˋ)
patience; forbearance; to persevere; patient

忍淚(ㄖㄣˇ ㄌㄟˋ)
to hold back one's tears

忍垢(ㄖㄣˇ ㄍㄡˋ)
to live in shame or disgrace

忍飢挨餓(ㄖㄣˇ ㄐㄧ ㄞˊ ㄜˋ)
to suffer hunger

忍俊不禁(ㄖㄣˇ ㄐㄩㄣˋ ㄅㄨˋ ㄐㄧㄣ)
cannot help smiling or laughing; cannot repress one's smile

to restrain one's temper and say nothing; to keep quiet and swallow the insults

忍笑(ㄖㄣˇ ㄒㄧㄠˋ)
to hold back laughter; to stifle a laugh

忍心(ㄖㄣˇ ㄒㄧㄣ)
unfeeling; merciless; hardhearted; to steel one's heart; to have the heart to

忍心害理(ㄖㄣˇ ㄒㄧㄣ ㄏㄞˋ ㄌㄧˇ)
to do a cruel thing or commit a crime in cold blood

忍性(ㄖㄣˇ ㄒㄧㄥˋ)
to forcibly restrain one's temper

忍住(ㄖㄣˇ ㄓㄨˋ)
to restrain or hold back the manifestation of feelings by the force of will: 她不能忍住她的好奇心。She could not restrain her curiosity.

忍受(ㄖㄣˇ ㄕㄡˋ)
to endure; to bear; to suffer; to stand: 我們忍受艱難困苦。We endured hardships.

忍讓(ㄖㄣˇ ㄖㄤˋ)
to forbear; to be forbearing and conciliatory

忍辱(ㄖㄣˇ ㄖㄨˋ)
to bear disgrace and insults while discharging one's duties conscientiously

忍辱負重(ㄖㄣˇ ㄖㄨˋ ㄈㄨˋ ㄓㄨㄥˋ)
to endure or suffer all disgrace and insults in order to accomplish a task

忍死(ㄖㄣˇ ㄙˇ)
to live when one would rather die (for the sake of a noble cause, etc.)

忍尤含垢(ㄖㄣˇ ㄧㄡˊ ㄏㄢˊ ㄍㄡˋ)
to be able to endure all disgrace and hardships; to swallow insults

忍無可忍(ㄖㄣˇ ㄨˊ ㄎㄜˇ ㄖㄣˇ)
beyond one's endurance; to have one's patience or forbearance tested too far, can not stand (insults or provocation) any longer; to come to the end of one's patience

【忒】 1501
1. ㄊㄜ te. tè
a word descriptive of sound

【忒】 1501
2. ㄊㄜˋ teh tè
1. excessive; too; very: 坡忒陡。

The slope is very steep.
2. to change
3. to err

忒煞(ㄊㄜˋ ㄕㄚˋ)or **忒煞**(ㄊㄜˋ ㄕㄚˋ)
excessive; too much

忒甚(ㄊㄜˋ ㄕㄣˋ)
much; too much

【忐】 1502
ㄊㄢˇ taan tǎn
1. timid; apprehensive
2. indecisive; vacillating

忐忑(ㄊㄢˇ ㄊㄜˋ)
①indecisive, vacillating ③ apprehensive ③ a fidget; t fidget ④honesty

【忑】 1503
ㄊㄜˋ teh tè
1. nervous; apprehensive
2. indecisive

【志】 1504
ㄓˋ jyh zhì
1. to make up one's mind t pursue some object; to b bent on doing something
2. will; purpose; determination 有志者事竟成。Where there a will, there's a way.
3. an ideal; a desire; ambitio interest; wish: 他有志於此。I takes a deep interest in this
4. annals; records

志不在此(ㄓˋ ㄅㄨˋ ㄗㄞˋ ㄘˇ)
to have an ambition fo things beyond what is pres ently available or obtainabl

志大才疏(ㄓˋ ㄉㄚˋ ㄘㄞˊ ㄕㄨ)
to have high aspirations bu little ability

志得意滿(ㄓˋ ㄉㄜˊ ㄧˋ ㄇㄢˇ)
fully satisfied or contented complacent

志同道合(ㄓˋ ㄊㄨㄥˊ ㄉㄠˋ ㄏㄜˊ)
(said of a group of people t share the same ambitio and purpose; of one mind: 我 們志同道合。We share th same ambition and purpose

志略(ㄓˋ ㄌㄩㄝˋ)
①ambition and talent ②t record the general outline ③t a sketch; a synopsis; annals

志怪(ㄓˋ ㄍㄨㄞˋ)
to record the weird, occul and mysterious; a collectio of such

志節(ㄓˋ ㄐㄧㄝˊ)
one's ambition and mora fortitude

志氣(业 くì)
ambition; will; the determination and courage to get ahead

志趣(业 くù)
purpose and interest; inclination; a bent: 他的志趣是音樂。He has a bent for music.

志趣相投(业 くù Tーた ㄊㄡ)
(friends) of similar purpose and interest

志向(业 Tーた)
purpose; ambition; aspiration: 我們應有遠大的志向。We should have lofty aspirations.

志行(业 Tーㄥ)
purpose and behavior; principle and conduct

志學(业 ㄩㄝ)
to dedicate oneself to the pursuit of learning

志士(业 ㄕ)
① a man of purpose and virtue ② a man of high ambitions

志士仁人(业 ㄕ ㄖㄣ ㄖㄣ)
people of purpose and virtues; people with lofty ideals

志書(业 ㄕㄨ)
a record of geographical names, people, products, customs, relics, histories, etc. of various localities

志在必得(业 ㄗㄞ ㄅì ㄉㄜ)
to get it at any cost; determined to have

志在千里(业 ㄗㄞ くーㄢ ㄌì)
cherishing a great ambition

志操(业 ㄘㄠ)
ambition and moral fortitude

志願(业 ㄩㄢ)
① to volunteer; voluntary; free choice ② aspiration; ambition; an ideal: 他的志願是做一個大政治家。His ambition is to be a great statesman.

志願兵(业 ㄩㄢ ㄅㄧㄥ)
volunteers

志願軍(业 ㄩㄢ ㄐㄩㄣ)
an army made up of volunteers

志願書(业 ㄩㄢ ㄕㄨ)
a pledge in writing; an application form

---

1. to forget: 別忘了給我打電話。Don't forget to phone me. 飲水不忘掘井人。When we drink the water, think of those who dug the well.
2. to omit; to miss (a line, etc.)
3. to neglect; to overlook

忘本(ㄨㄤ ㄅㄣ)
① ungrateful; to bite the hand that feeds one ② to forget one's past suffering

忘不了(ㄨㄤ ㄅㄨ ㄌㄧㄠ)
will not or cannot forget

忘操(ㄨㄤ ㄘㄠ)
to forget; to let slip from one's mind: 你應該把這件不愉快的事忘掉。You should forget the unpleasantness.

忘年交(ㄨㄤ ㄋㄧㄢ ㄐㄧㄠ)
a friendship in which the difference in age between the friends is forgotten

忘了(ㄨㄤ ㄌㄜ)
to forget; to have forgotten; to be oblivious of: 我忘了你將要來此。I forgot (that) you were coming.

忘懷(ㄨㄤ ㄏㄨㄞ)
unmindful; to forget; forgetful; to dismiss from one's mind: 他們忘懷得失。They are unmindful of their gains and losses.

忘機(ㄨㄤ ㄐㄧ)
without a single scheme or design in one's mind; to be at peace with the world; a carefree state of mind

忘記(ㄨㄤ ㄐㄧ)
① to fail to remember; to forget; to have forgotten; obliviscence: 我忘記帶我的樂譜。I forgot to bring my music book. ② to neglect: 我們不能忘記自己的職責。We must not neglect our duties.

忘舊(ㄨㄤ ㄐㄧㄡ)
to forget the old (friends, folks, etc.); snobbish

忘其所以(ㄨㄤ くㄧ ㄙㄨㄛ ㄧ)
to be carried away; to be beside oneself with enthusiasm, joy, etc.

忘情(ㄨㄤ くㄧㄥ)
to be unmindful of all emo-

---

tions and the ups and downs of life; to be unmoved

忘卻(ㄨㄤ くㄩㄝ)
to forget: 有些事情是難忘卻的。Some things are hard to forget.

忘形(ㄨㄤ Tㄧㄥ)
to get carried away; to be beside oneself with joy, etc.: 你忘形了！You are beside yourself with joy!

忘形之交(ㄨㄤ Tㄧㄥ 业 ㄐㄧㄠ)
a friendship in which all rules of good manners or etiquette can be ignored

忘性(ㄨㄤ Tㄧㄥ)
absent-mindedness; forgetfulness

忘食(ㄨㄤ ㄕ)
so busy or concentrated as to forget mealtime: 他發憤忘食。He was roused to such diligence as to forget his meals.

忘身忘家(ㄨㄤ ㄕㄣ ㄨㄤ ㄐㄧㄚ)
(literally) to forget one's family and oneself—complete dedication

忘餐(ㄨㄤ ㄘㄢ)
(literally) to forget one's meals—dedication; devotion; deep absorption

忘憂(ㄨㄤ ㄧㄡ)
to forget cares and worries

忘憂草(ㄨㄤ ㄧㄡ ㄘㄠ)
day lily—*Hemerocallis fulva*

忘我(ㄨㄤ ㄨㄛ)
oblivious of self-existence; selfless: 他忘我地工作。He worked selflessly.

忘八(ㄨㄤ ㄅㄚ)
① a tortoise ② a cuckold 參看「王八」

1. busy; short of time; fully occupied: 你在忙什麼？What are you busy at？ 他忙於準備考試。He is busy in preparing for the examination.
2. hurried; in haste; to make

---

haste; hurry: 不要忙，時間還多着呢。Don't hurry. There's plenty of time.

忙不迭(ㄇㄤ·ㄅㄨㄉㄧㄝˊ)
to hasten to do something; to do something with eagerness; to do something with alacrity

忙不過來(ㄇㄤ·ㄅㄨㄍㄨㄛˋ·ㄌㄞ)
to have more work than one can handle properly; very busy

忙迫(ㄇㄤ ㄆㄛˋ)
pressed with work

忙得碌碌(ㄇㄤ ㄉㄜˊㄌㄨˋㄌㄨˋ)or 忙碌(ㄇㄤ ㄌㄨˋ)
① busy; fully occupied ② hurriedly; in great haste

忙得不可開交(ㄇㄤ·ㄉㄜ ㄅㄨˋㄎㄜˇ ㄎㄞ ㄐㄧㄠ)
as busy as one can possibly be; to have one's hands full (of work)

忙得很(ㄇㄤ·ㄉㄜ ㄏㄣˇ)
very busy

忙裏偷閒(ㄇㄤ·ㄌㄧˇㄊㄡ ㄒㄧㄢˊ)
to steal a moment of leisure under the pressure of heavy workload: 我常忙裏偷閒。I often steal a moment of leisure in the midst of pressing affairs.

忙亂(ㄇㄤ ㄌㄨㄢˋ)
busy and flurried; to be in a rush and a muddle

忙工(ㄇㄤ ㄍㄨㄥ)
a hired temporary farm hand during the sowing or harvest seasons

忙中有錯(ㄇㄤ ㄓㄨㄥ ㄧㄡˇ ㄘㄨㄛˋ)
Haste makes waste. 或 Errors are likely to occur in haste.

忙甚麼(ㄇㄤ ㄕㄜˊ·ㄇㄜ)
What (are you) busy about? 或 Why the rush?

忙人(ㄇㄤ ㄖㄣˊ)
a busy person

忙於(ㄇㄤ ㄩˊ)
busy doing something

忙月(ㄇㄤ ㄩㄝˋ)
(originally) the busy months in farming (120 days after the approach of summer); the busy months in every trade

【忖】 1507 ㄘㄨㄣˇ tsoen cǔn

to surmise; to consider; to presume; to suppose

忖度(ㄘㄨㄣˇ ㄉㄨㄛˋ)or 忖摸(ㄘㄨㄣˇ·ㄇㄜ)
to suppose; to consider; to gauge what's on another's mind; to presume; to surmise: 我們忖度這遲延是由某種意外所致。We surmised that the delay was caused by some accident.

忖量(ㄘㄨㄣˇㄌㄧㄤˊ)
① to consider; to reflect ② to suppose; to gauge what's on another's mind; to conjecture

忖思(ㄘㄨㄣˇ ㄙ)
to imagine 亦作「忖想」

四畫

【忡】 1508 ㄔㄨㄥ chong chōng

worried; anxious; uneasy; sad

忡征(ㄔㄨㄥ ㄓㄥ)
feeling anxious and unsettled

忡忡(ㄔㄨㄥ ㄔㄨㄥ)
worried and sad; laden with anxiety: 他憂心忡忡。He felt laden with anxiety.

【忤】 1509 ㄨˇ wuu wǔ

1. recalcitrant; stubbornly defiant; disobedient; uncongenial: 我與人無忤。I am not uncongenial to anyone else.
2. a blunder; a mistake; wrong

忤逆(ㄨˇ ㄋㄧˋ)
① recalcitrant; stubborn defiance ② disobedient to one's parents (a crime in former times)

忤視(ㄨˇ ㄕˋ)
to look at with a jaundiced eye; to look defiantly at

忤耳(ㄨˇ ㄦˇ)
(said of words, utterances, etc.) to grate on the ear

忤物(ㄨˇ ㄨˋ)
to disagree with others; to be at odds with others; can not get along with people

【快】 1510 ㄎㄨㄞˋ kuay kuài

1. quickly; fast; hasty; soon; prompt; rapid: 他做得很快。He did it quickly. 她進步得快。She has made rapid progress.
2. nearly; near: 暑假快到了。The summer vacation is drawing near.
3. to hurry up; to make haste: 快上車吧! Hurry up and get on the bus!
4. quick-witted; ingenious: 你腦子快。You're quick-witted.
5. sharp (blades, etc.); keen
6. pleasant; happy; to make happy; pleasurable: 他心中不快。He feels unhappy.
7. (in old China) as in 捕快 —the criminal police; a constable; a sheriff deputy
8. honest; straightforward

快報(ㄎㄨㄞˋㄅㄠˋ)
a dispatch; a bulletin

快班(ㄎㄨㄞˋ ㄅㄢ)
a jailor; a policeman 亦作「捕快」

快板(ㄎㄨㄞˋ ㄅㄢˇ)or 快板兒(ㄎㄨㄞˋ ㄅㄢˇ ㄦ)
(Chinese opera) quick tempo

快步(ㄎㄨㄞˋ ㄅㄨˋ)
(military) a half step; a trot

快跑(ㄎㄨㄞˋ ㄆㄠˇ)
to run fast; Go quick! On the double!

快馬加鞭(ㄎㄨㄞˋ ㄇㄚˇ ㄐㄧㄚ ㄅㄧㄢ)
(literally) to use the whip on a fast horse—to proceed as quickly as possible; posthaste

快慢(ㄎㄨㄞˋ ㄇㄢˋ)
speed

快門(ㄎㄨㄞˋ ㄇㄣˊ)
a camera shutter

快刀斬亂麻(ㄎㄨㄞˋ ㄉㄠ ㄓㄢˇ ㄌㄨㄢˋ ㄇㄚˊ)
(literally) to chop a bunch of tangled hemp with a sharp knife—to straighten up a complicated or messy situation by taking drastic steps and with dispatch; to cut the Gordian knot

快當(ㄎㄨㄞˋ ㄉㄤ·)
quickly; with expedition; prompt; quick: 她是個既細心又快當的祕書。She is a careful and prompt secretary.

快遞(ㄎㄨㄞˋ ㄉㄧˋ)

express delivery; special delivery

夬點兒(ㄎㄨㄞ ㄉㄧㄢˇ)
Make it snappy. 或 Be quick!

快電(ㄎㄨㄞ ㄉㄧㄢˋ)
an urgent cable

快讀(ㄎㄨㄞ ㄉㄨˊ)
fast reading; speed-reading

快艇(ㄎㄨㄞ ㄊㄧㄥˇ)
a speedboat; a motorboat

夬樂(ㄎㄨㄞ ㄌㄜˋ)or **快活**(ㄎㄨㄞˋ ·ㄏㄨㄛˊ)
happy; joy; joyful; cheerful: 他因升遷而顯得快樂。He showed joy at being promoted.

夬樂主義(ㄎㄨㄞˋ ㄌㄜˋ ㄓㄨˇ ㄧˋ)
hedonism

快來(ㄎㄨㄞˋ ㄌㄞˊ)
Come quick! 或 to come or arrive very soon

快覽(ㄎㄨㄞ ㄌㄢˇ)
a collection of categorized daily information for reference; a directory

快乾(ㄎㄨㄞ ㄍㄢ)
quick-drying

快感(ㄎㄨㄞ ㄍㄢˇ)
a pleasant feeling

快幹(ㄎㄨㄞ ㄍㄢˋ)
Do it promptly! 或 to do quickly

快鍋(ㄎㄨㄞ ㄍㄨㄛ)
a digester; a pressure cooker

快攻(ㄎㄨㄞ ㄍㄨㄥ)
a quick attack (in ball games)

快快兒的(ㄎㄨㄞˋ ㄎㄨㄞㄦ ·ㄉㄜ)
quickly; promptly

快捷(ㄎㄨㄞ ㄐㄧㄝˊ)
speedy; fast; nimble

快進(ㄎㄨㄞˋ ·ㄐㄧㄣˋ)
Hurry! 或faster than; quicker than: 快些! 你要遲到了。Hurry up! You'll be late.

快心(ㄎㄨㄞ ㄒㄧㄣ)
to be pleased; to feel happy

快信(ㄎㄨㄞ ㄒㄧㄣˋ)
an express letter

快婿(ㄎㄨㄞˋ ㄒㄩˋ)
an intelligent and promising son-in-law; an attractive son-in-law

快照(ㄎㄨㄞ ㄓㄠˋ)
a snapshot

快車(ㄎㄨㄞ ㄔㄜ)
an express train: 我沒趕上這班快車。I missed the express train.

快車道(ㄎㄨㄞ ㄔㄜ ㄉㄠˋ)
a fast-traffic lane on a street; a speedway

快事(ㄎㄨㄞ ㄕˋ)
happenings that make the heart throb with joy; something done with overwhelming public approval; a delightful experience

快適(ㄎㄨㄞ ㄕˋ)
happy and contented; pleased and satisfied: 他顯出快適的樣子。He looked pleased and satisfied.

快手快腳(ㄎㄨㄞ ㄕㄡˇ ㄎㄨㄞ ㄐㄧㄠˇ)
(literally) nimble of hands and fast of feet—to do things quickly; to perform a task with expedition

快書(ㄎㄨㄞ ㄕㄨ)
quick patter (rhythmic storytelling accompanied by bamboo or copper clappers)

快說(ㄎㄨㄞ ㄕㄨㄛ)
Speak up! 或 Be quick! 或 Speak quickly. 儘量快說。Speak as quick as you can.

快人快事(ㄎㄨㄞ ㄖㄣˊ ㄎㄨㄞ ㄕˋ)
a heroic deed performed by a straightforward person

快人快語(ㄎㄨㄞ ㄖㄣˊ ㄎㄨㄞ ㄩˇ)
the straight talk of a straightforward person

快哉(ㄎㄨㄞ ㄗㄞ)
How pleasant!

快走(ㄎㄨㄞ ㄗㄡˇ)
Hurry, let's go. 或 Beat it!

快嘴快舌(ㄎㄨㄞ ㄗㄨㄟˇ ㄎㄨㄞ ㄕㄜˊ)
quick of tongue; prone to talk rashly

快餐(ㄎㄨㄞ ㄘㄢ)
a simple meal consisting of a couple of dishes which are served promptly in small restaurants; a quick meal; a snack

快速(ㄎㄨㄞ ㄙㄨˋ)
fast; quick; prompt: 不要說得這樣快速。Don't speak so fast.

快意(ㄎㄨㄞ ㄧˋ)
pleasing; satisfying

快郵代電(ㄎㄨㄞ ㄧㄡˊ ㄉㄞˋ ㄉㄧㄢˋ)or

代電(ㄉㄞˋ ㄉㄧㄢˋ)
official correspondence between government agencies having no direct superior-subordinate relationship

快我朵頤(ㄎㄨㄞˋ ㄨㄛˇ ㄉㄨㄛˇ)
to please my palate (the expression is often seen on the walls of Chinese restaurants as a sort of ad boasting the chef's skill)

快慰(ㄎㄨㄞ ㄨㄟˋ)
happy; satisfying; to be pleased

快完(ㄎㄨㄞ ㄨㄢˊ)
nearly completed or finished; almost set

【忮】 ㄓ jhih zhì
jealous; jealousy; to dislike

忮求(ㄓ ㄑㄧㄡˊ)
jealous and greedy

忮心(ㄓ ㄒㄧㄣ)
jealousy

【忭】 1512
ㄅㄧㄢˋ biann biàn
overjoyed; pleased; delighted: 聽到你的成功我大為忭忭。I was overjoyed at your success.

忭賀(ㄅㄧㄢˋ ㄏㄜˋ)
to congratulate with joy; to celebrate

忭懽(ㄅㄧㄢˋ ㄏㄨㄢ)
pleased and delighted

忭頌(ㄅㄧㄢˋ ㄙㄨㄥˋ)
to be pleased to offer best wishes

忭躍(ㄅㄧㄢˋ ㄩㄝˋ)
great joy; tremendous pleasure; to leap with joy: 他舞興忭躍。He danced for great joy.

【忱】 1513
ㄔㄣˊ chern chén
1. sincere; sincerity
2. to rely on

忱悃(ㄔㄣˊ ㄎㄨㄣˇ)
genuine feelings; sincere sentiments

忱辭(ㄔㄣˊ ㄘˊ)
words uttered in all sincerity; words from the bottom of one's heart

【忸】 1514
ㄋㄧㄡˇ neou niǔ
(讀音 ㄋㄩˇ niuh nǜ)
1. to be accustomed to; to be

inclined to (evils, etc.)
2. bashful; ashamed

忸怩(ㄋㄧㄡˇ ㄋㄧˊ)
blush; ashamed; bashful; coyly

忸怕(ㄋㄧㄡˇ ㄆㄚˋ)
to be accustomed to

【忻】 1515
(欣) ㄒㄧㄣ shin xīn
happy; joy; delight

忻忭(ㄒㄧㄣ ㄅㄧㄢˋ)
great joy; overjoyed

【忪】 1516
1. ㄓㄨㄥ jong
    zhōng
1. agitated
2. frightened

【忪】 1516
2. ㄙㄨㄥ song
    sōng
參見「惺忪」

【忠】 1517
ㄓㄨㄥ jong zhōng
1. faithful; loyal; sincere; patriotic; constant; loyalty; sincerity: 他忠於國家。He is loyal to his country.
2. devoted; honest (advice, etc.)

忠烈(ㄓㄨㄥ ㄌㄧㄝˋ)
to be loyal till death; patriotism; martyrdom

忠烈祠(ㄓㄨㄥ ㄌㄧㄝˋ ㄘˊ)
a martyr's shrine

忠良(ㄓㄨㄥ ㄌㄧㄤˊ)
①faithful and honest ②virtuous persons

忠告(ㄓㄨㄥ ㄍㄠˋ)or(ㄓㄨㄥ ㄍㄨˋ)
honest or sincere advice; sincere counsel

忠肝義膽(ㄓㄨㄥ ㄍㄢ ㄧˋ ㄉㄢˇ)
having good faith, virtue and patriotism

忠告善道(ㄓㄨㄥ ㄍㄨˋ ㄕㄢˋ ㄉㄠˋ)
to offer advice with sincerity and tact

忠厚(ㄓㄨㄥ ㄏㄡˋ)
honest and tolerant; kind and big-hearted

忠君愛國(ㄓㄨㄥ ㄐㄩㄣ ㄞˋ ㄍㄨㄛˊ)
patriotic and loyal to the throne

忠孝兩全(ㄓㄨㄥ ㄒㄧㄠˋ ㄌㄧㄤˇ ㄑㄩㄢˊ)
both loyal to one's country and filial to one's parents; to be perfect both as a national hero and as a dutiful son

忠心(ㄓㄨㄥ ㄒㄧㄣ)
loyalty; faithfulness; sincerity

忠心耿耿(ㄓㄨㄥ ㄒㄧㄣ ㄍㄥˇ ㄍㄥˇ)
loyal, faithful and true: 他們是忠心耿耿的愛國者。They are loyal and constant patriots.

忠信(ㄓㄨㄥ ㄒㄧㄣˋ)
faithful and honest

忠直(ㄓㄨㄥ ㄓˊ)
straightforward; faithful and upright

忠貞(ㄓㄨㄥ ㄓㄣ)
loyal (subjects, etc.); patriotic (citizens, elements, etc.); faithful and true: 他忠貞不渝。He is unswerving in his loyalty.

忠貞不貳(ㄓㄨㄥ ㄓㄣ ㄅㄨˋ ㄦˋ)
the loyalty that can stand all tests and trials

忠臣不事二主(ㄓㄨㄥ ㄔㄣˊ ㄅㄨˋ ㄕˋ ㄦˋ ㄓㄨˇ)
A loyal subject (or official) never serves two kings (or masters).

忠誠(ㄓㄨㄥ ㄔㄥˊ)
loyal; faithful; staunch

忠實(ㄓㄨㄥ ㄕˊ)
①loyal and faithful: 他擴忠實地守信約。He kept his promise faithfully. ②reliable or truthful (reports, etc.)

忠恕(ㄓㄨㄥ ㄕㄨˋ)
magnanimity—a summation of Confucian teaching: "to be true to one's principles and benevolent in their application towards others"

忠義(ㄓㄨㄥ ㄧˋ)
①faithful and virtuous ②people of loyalty and virtue

忠言(ㄓㄨㄥ ㄧㄢˊ)
sincere advice

忠言逆耳(ㄓㄨㄥ ㄧㄢˊ ㄋㄧˋ ㄦˇ)
Honest advice is often grating on the ear. 或 Truth seldom sounds pleasant.

忠於國家(ㄓㄨㄥ ㄩˊ ㄍㄨㄛˊ ㄐㄧㄚ)
to be faithful to one's fatherland

忠勇(ㄓㄨㄥ ㄩㄥˇ)
loyal and courageous

【念】 1518
ㄋㄧㄢˋ niann niàn
1. to think of; to miss; to

remember (someone): 他們念着你。They miss you very much.
2. to read out aloud; to chant; to intone; to mumble: 把它念給我聽。Read it to me.
3. to study; to attend school: 他念過中學。He attended middle school.
4. twenty
5. a Chinese family name

念白(ㄋㄧㄢˋ ㄅㄞˊ)
the spoken part in Chinese opera

念佛(ㄋㄧㄢˋ ㄈㄛˊ)
to call out Buddha's name aloud as an expression of devotion; to call out "Amitabha" aloud to show devotion; to pray to Buddha

念法(ㄋㄧㄢˋ ㄈㄚˇ)
①pronunciation ②a method of studying

念叨(ㄋㄧㄢˋ ㄉㄠ)
①to mention in what one says; to be always talking about; to remember ②to nag; to be garrulous ③to talk over

念頭(ㄋㄧㄢˋ ㄊㄡˊ)
an idea; a thought; intention: 不知她有什麼念頭。I don't know what her intentions are.

念念不忘(ㄋㄧㄢˋ ㄋㄧㄢˋ ㄅㄨˋ ㄨㄤˋ)
lasting memory of; to have (somebody or something) always in one's mind; to bear in mind constantly

念念有詞(ㄋㄧㄢˋ ㄋㄧㄢˋ ㄧㄡˇ ㄘˊ)
to mumble; to mutter: 那老人口中念念有詞。The old man was mumbling (away) to himself.

念舊(ㄋㄧㄢˋ ㄐㄧㄡˋ)
to remember old friends; to cherish old friendship: 他非常念舊。He cherishes old friendship very much.

念經(ㄋㄧㄢˋ ㄐㄧㄥ)
to chant or intone (Buddhist) scriptures

念咒(ㄋㄧㄢˋ ㄓㄡˋ)
to chant or intone charms

念珠(ㄋㄧㄢˋ ㄓㄨ)
a Buddhist rosary (with 108 beads)

念熟(ㄋㄧㄢˋ ㄕㄡˊ)or(ㄋㄧㄢˋ ㄕˊ)

to learn by heart; to read over and over until one can memorize what is being read

念書(ㄋㄧㄢ ㄕㄨ)
① to read a book aloud ② to study ③ to receive an education

念茲在茲(ㄋㄧㄢ ㄗ ㄗㄞ ㄗ)
to bear in mind always; to have (somebody or something) constantly in one's mind

念誦(ㄋㄧㄢ ·ㄙㄨㄥ)
① to recite; to intone; to read out ② to remember (somebody) in speaking to another

【忽】 1519 ㄏㄨ hu hū
1. suddenly; abruptly; unexpectedly: 我忽發奇想。I suddenly hit upon a wild idea.
2. to disregard; to be careless or indifferent; to neglect
3. to forget
4. one millionth of a tael
5. a Chinese family name

忽必烈(ㄏㄨ ㄅㄧ ㄌㄧㄝ)
Kublai, the fifth emperor of the Yüan (Mongol) Dynasty, who reigned from 1260 to 1294

忽明忽滅(ㄏㄨ ㄇㄧㄥ ㄏㄨ ㄇㄧㄝ)
flickering; appearing and disappearing, as a distant star, a blinking light, etc.

忽發奇想(ㄏㄨ ㄈㄚ ㄑㄧ ㄒㄧㄤ)
to suddenly hit upon a wild idea; to suddenly harbor a dream; to suddenly come upon a strange notion

忽地(ㄏㄨ ㄉㄧ)
suddenly; abruptly; unexpectedly

忽冷忽熱(ㄏㄨ ㄌㄥ ㄏㄨ ㄖㄜ)
① now hot, now cold — abrupt changes of temperature ② sudden changes in one's affection, attitude, enthusiasm, etc.

忽略(ㄏㄨ ㄌㄩㄝ)
to overlook; to neglect; an oversight

忽忽(ㄏㄨ ㄏㄨ)
① fast; quickly ② restless; dejected; to look lost or absent-minded: 他忽忽若有所

失。He looks absent-minded.

忽忽不樂(ㄏㄨ ㄏㄨ ㄅㄨ ㄌㄜ)
to be discouraged and unhappy

忽忽一年(ㄏㄨ ㄏㄨ ㄧ ㄋㄧㄢ)
another year slipping away imperceptibly 或 Suddenly, another year has come to an end.

忽見(ㄏㄨ ㄐㄧㄢ)
to see suddenly; to behold all of a sudden

忽起忽落(ㄏㄨ ㄑㄧ ㄏㄨ ㄌㄨㄛ)
① sudden rise and sudden fall, as a flying object or a darting bird ② the erratic fluctuation of market prices, etc. ③ sudden changes (of mood); now···, now···

忽親(ㄏㄨ ㄑㄧㄣ)
(said of men) to get married while in mourning for parents

忽視(ㄏㄨ ㄕ)
to disregard; to overlook; to neglect; to treat with indifference; to give a cold shoulder: 我們不應忽視我們的弱點。We should not overlook our weaknesses.

忽哨(ㄏㄨ ㄕㄠ)
to whistle; a whistle (usually used as a signal to start a collective action by a band of people, as bandits, etc.)

忽然(ㄏㄨ ㄖㄢ) or 忽然間(ㄏㄨ ㄖㄢ ㄐㄧㄢ)
suddenly; unexpectedly

忽作忽止(ㄏㄨ ㄗㄨㄛ ㄏㄨ ㄓ)
by fits and starts

忽而(ㄏㄨ ㄦ)
suddenly; unexpectedly; now ···, now···: 她忽而哭，忽而笑。She cried and laughed unexpectedly.

忽有感觸(ㄏㄨ ㄧㄡ ㄍㄢ ㄔㄨ)
to be seized by a sudden feeling; to be unexpectedly moved or touched

忽微(ㄏㄨ ㄨㄟ)
an extremely fine particle; something of infinitesimal quantity or weight

忽聞(ㄏㄨ ㄨㄣ)
to hear suddenly; to learn of something unexpectedly

【忿】 1520 ㄈㄣ fenn fèn
1. anger; indignation; fury: 他的餘忿未平。His anger has not yet appeased.
2. complaining; hatred; a grudge

忿懑(ㄈㄣ ㄇㄣ)
anger; a grudge; animus; indignation: 他對我有忿懑。He bears me a grudge.

忿悶(ㄈㄣ ㄇㄣ)
angry and complaining; bitter

忿忿不平(ㄈㄣ ㄈㄣ ㄅㄨ ㄆㄧㄥ)
resentful and complaining; bitter; indignant and disturbed

忿怒(ㄈㄣ ㄋㄨ)
indignation; wrath; fury; angry; furious; indignant

忿戾(ㄈㄣ ㄌㄧ)
angry and perverseness

忿厲粗暴(ㄈㄣ ㄌㄧ ㄘㄨ ㄅㄠ)
angry, fierce and rough

忿恨(ㄈㄣ ㄏㄣ)
wrath; fury; indignation; animosity; resentment; angry; hateful

忿火(ㄈㄣ ㄏㄨㄛ)
the flames of anger; fury or furies

忿恚(ㄈㄣ ㄏㄨㄟ)
hate and anger

忿懷(ㄈㄣ ㄏㄨㄞ)
anger; wrath; fury

忿爭(ㄈㄣ ㄓㄥ)
to argue or fight in anger; to wrangle; wrangling

忿躁(ㄈㄣ ㄗㄠ)
irascible

忿言(ㄈㄣ ㄧㄢ)
angry words or utterances

忿怨(ㄈㄣ ㄩㄢ)
to harbor a grudge; animus: 他對我忿怨。He has a grudge against me.

【忞】 1521 ㄇㄧㄣ min mín
to strive for improvement or progress

【忝】 1522 ㄊㄧㄢ tean tiǎn
1. ashamed; to disgrace: 他有忝家族聲名。He disgraced his family's name.
2. a depreciatory expression

（心部）

【心部】

referring to oneself

3. to be unworthy of the honor

忝不知恥(ㄊㄧㄢˇ ㄅㄨˋ ㄓ ㄔˇ) or 忝不知羞(ㄊㄧㄢˇ ㄅㄨˋ ㄓ ㄒㄧㄡ)
shameless; brazen-faced

忝附葭莩(ㄊㄧㄢˇ ㄈㄨˋ ㄐㄧㄚ ㄈㄨˊ)
I'm honored to be related to you (by marriage)

忝列門牆(ㄊㄧㄢˇ ㄌㄧㄝˋ ㄇㄣˊ ㄑㄧㄤˊ)
to have served and learned under a master; to have the honor to be accepted as your disciple 或 I've learned under you.

忝居(ㄊㄧㄢˇ ㄐㄩ)
(a self-depreciatory expression) I've shamefully occupied (a position which I don't deserve)

忝眷(ㄊㄧㄢˇ ㄐㄩㄢˋ)
a self-reference used by the father of a bride or groom at the wedding

忝竊(ㄊㄧㄢˇ ㄑㄧㄝˋ)
(a self-depreciatory expression) to usurp

忝任(ㄊㄧㄢˇ ㄖㄣˋ)
to have served (in an office); I have served as…

忝辱家門(ㄊㄧㄢˇ ㄖㄨˋ ㄐㄧㄚ ㄇㄣˊ)
to disgrace one's family

忝為知己(ㄊㄧㄢˇ ㄨㄟˊ ㄓ ㄐㄧˇ)
As an intimate friend of yours, I…; (I'm sure you'll forgive me) since we have been good friends

五畫

【怍】1523 ㄗㄨㄛˋ tzuoh zuò
1. shame
2. to change color; to blush

怍色(ㄗㄨㄛˋ ㄙㄜˋ)
ashamed; to blush; to color

怍意(ㄗㄨㄛˋ ㄧˋ)
to feel ashamed; to be ashamed

【怏】1524 ㄧㄤˋ yang yàng
discontented; disheartened; dispirited

怏然(ㄧㄤˋ ㄖㄢˊ)
unhappy; discontent

怏悒(ㄧㄤˋ ㄧˋ)
discontent; melancholy; sad

快快(ㄧㄤˋ ㄧㄤˋ)
discontented; dispirited; sad

怏鬱(ㄧㄤˋ ㄩˋ)
the depression of feelings; pensiveness; gloom; melancholy

【怖】1525 ㄅㄨˋ buh bù
1. terrified; frightened
2. to frighten; to threaten

怖慄(ㄅㄨˋ ㄌㄧˋ)
trembling with fear

怖駭(ㄅㄨˋ ㄏㄞˋ)
frightened; scared; alarmed

怖禍(ㄅㄨˋ ㄏㄨㄛˋ)
a terrifying danger or calamity

怖懼(ㄅㄨˋ ㄐㄩˋ)
a scare; fear; dread: 懷疑和焦慮變成怖懼。Doubt and anxiety changed into dread.

怖懾(ㄅㄨˋ ㄓㄜˋ)
scared and faint-hearted

怖畏(ㄅㄨˋ ㄨㄟˋ)
to dread; to be scared; to be afraid

【怕】1526 ㄆㄚˋ pah pà
1. to fear; to dread; afraid; scared or frightened; apprehensive: 此次地震你駭得怕嗎? Were you frightened by the earthquake?
2. maybe; perhaps; I am afraid …; I suppose…: 我怕無法幫助你。I am afraid I can't help you.
3. a Chinese family name

怕不怕(ㄆㄚˋ ㄅㄨˋ ㄆㄚˋ)
Are you afraid? 或 Are you scared?

怕得罪人(ㄆㄚˋ ㄉㄜˊ ㄗㄨㄟˋ ㄖㄣˊ)
afraid of offending others (by speaking frankly, etc.)

怕得很(ㄆㄚˋ ㄉㄜˊ ㄏㄣˇ)
very much scared; in great fear

怕的是(ㄆㄚˋ ㄉㄜˊ ㄕˋ)
What I am afraid of is that…

怕他不來(ㄆㄚˋ ㄊㄚ ㄅㄨˋ ㄌㄞˊ)
① afraid that he won't come ② He will come, because he has to!

怕他不成(ㄆㄚˋ ㄊㄚ ㄅㄨˋ ㄔㄥˊ)
(an expression of defiance) What? We are afraid of him!

怕他什麼(ㄆㄚˋ ㄊㄚ ㄕㄜˊ ㄇㄜ˙)
① What is there to be afraid of him? ② Don't be afraid of him!

怕老婆(ㄆㄚˋ ㄌㄠˇ ㄆㄛ˙) or 怕太太(ㄆㄚˋ ㄊㄞˋ ㄊㄞ˙)
henpecked

怕冷(ㄆㄚˋ ㄌㄥˇ)
to dread cold (weather etc.); to dislike the cold

怕前怕後(ㄆㄚˋ ㄑㄧㄢˊ ㄆㄚˋ ㄏㄡˋ)
timid and apprehensive of everything

怕羞(ㄆㄚˋ ㄒㄧㄡ)
shy; bashful: 她有點怕羞。She is rather bashful.

怕甚麼(ㄆㄚˋ ㄕㄜˊ ㄇㄜ˙)
(an expression of encouragement) What is there to be afraid of? 或 What are you afraid of?

怕事(ㄆㄚˋ ㄕˋ)
to be timid and overcautious: 他膽小怕事。He was timid and overcautious.

怕是(ㄆㄚˋ ㄕˋ)
(I'm) afraid that…; maybe; perhaps (referring to some unpleasant fact or consequence)

怕生(ㄆㄚˋ ㄕㄥ)
(said of a child) to be shy with strangers

怕熱(ㄆㄚˋ ㄖㄜˋ)
to dislike heat; to feel discomfortable in hot weather

怕人(ㄆㄚˋ ㄖㄣˊ)
① terrifying; frightening; horrible ② (said of wild beasts and birds) to shun human beings

怕死(ㄆㄚˋ ㄙˇ)
afraid of death; very nervous and scared

怕臊(ㄆㄚˋ ㄙㄠˋ)
shy; bashful

怕癢(ㄆㄚˋ ㄧㄤˇ)
to be afraid of tickling

【怙】1527 ㄏㄨˋ huh hù
1. to rely on; to presume on
2. one's father; things or persons that one relies on: 他自幼失怙。He has had nobody to rely on since childhood.

怙富(ㄏㄨˋ ㄈㄨˋ)
to presume on one's wealth

過(ㄍㄨㄛˋ)
showing no regret for one's faults or errors; showing no repentance for one's wrong-doings

終不改(ㄓㄨㄥㄅㄨˋㄍㄞˇ)
to persist in one's (wrong-ful) ways: 頑抗的學生怙終不改. The recalcitrant students persist in their ways.

寵(ㄔㄨㄥˇ)
to be proud and arrogant for having won the favor of a powerful or influential person

恃(ㄕˋ)
①those one relies on (as troops, gangsters, an influen-tial person, etc.) ②one's parents—father (恬) and mother (恃)

勢(ㄕˋ)
to presume on one's power, position or influence

惡不悛(ㄜˋㄅㄨˋㄑㄩㄢ)
incorrigible (criminals); obdurate and irreclaimable; to be steeped in evil and refuse to repent

惡凌人(ㄜˋㄌㄧㄥˊㄖㄣˊ)
to intimidate and oppress others

恬(ㄍㄨˋㄧ)
things or persons that one relies on

【怛】 1528
ㄍㄚ´ dar do
1. grieved; distressed
2. surprised; shocked; alarmed
3. (obsolete) striving and toil-ing

怛怛(ㄍㄚˊㄍㄚˊ)
toiling; grieved

怛化(ㄍㄚˊ ㄏㄨㄚˋ)
①(said of mankind) dead; to die; to pass away ②the process of change—(figura-tively) a dying person

怛傷(ㄍㄚˊ ㄕㄤ)
distressed; grieved

【怦】 1529
ㄆㄥ peng pēng
1. eager; anxious; impulsive

怦怦(ㄆㄥ ㄆㄥ)
①eager and anxious (to do something) ②faithful and upright ③with quick beat-ing; pit-a-pat: 我的心怦怦地

跳。My heart went pit-a-pat.

怦然(ㄆㄥ ㄖㄢˊ)
with a sudden shock; palpi-tating (with excitement): 她怦然心動。She was palpi-tating with excitement.

【怡】 1530
ㄧˊ yí
1. harmony; on good terms
2. pleasure; joy; jubilation
3. a Chinese family name

怡蕩(ㄧˊㄉㄤˋ)
to find pleasure in wanton ways

怡樂(ㄧˊㄌㄜˋ)
pleasures

怡和(ㄧˊㄏㄜˊ)
delightful harmony; on very pleasant terms (with each other)

怡情養性(ㄧˊㄑㄧㄥˊㄧㄤˇㄒㄧㄥˋ)
(said of things or environs) to contribute to one's peace of mind or inner tranquility

怡情悅性(ㄧˊㄑㄧㄥˊㄩㄝˋㄒㄧㄥˋ)
to please one's mind and delight one's spirit

怡神(ㄧˊㄕㄣˊ)
to inspire peace and har-mony in one's mind

怡聲(ㄧˊㄕㄥ)
a soft and tender voice that is pleasing

怡怡(ㄧˊㄖㄢˊ)
pleasant and contented; satisfied and happy

怡然自得(ㄧˊㄖㄢˊㄗˋㄉㄜˊ)
happy and contented; to have found one's inner peace

怡色(ㄧˊㄙㄜˋ)
a pleasant look; to look pleased or cheerful

怡怡(ㄧˊㄧˊ)
harmony; harmonious—as brothers

怡顏(ㄧˊㄧㄢˊ)
a pleasant look; smiling

怡養(ㄧˊㄧㄤˇ)
to enjoy good health and live a happy life

怡悅(ㄧˊㄩㄝˋ)
to find joy in; to take delight in

【性】 1531
ㄒㄧㄥˋ shìng xìng
1. nature; natural property; disposition; temper

2. a quality or property
3. sex

性暴(ㄒㄧㄥˋㄅㄠˋ)
hot-tempered; irascible

性本善(ㄒㄧㄥˋㄅㄣˇㄕㄢˋ)or 性善
(ㄒㄧㄥˋㄕㄢˋ)
the theory of Mencius that men are born good

性別(ㄒㄧㄥˋㄅㄧㄝˊ)
the sex of a person—male or female

性別檢查(ㄒㄧㄥˋㄅㄧㄝˊㄐㄧㄢˇㄔㄚˊ)
a sex check

性變態(ㄒㄧㄥˋㄅㄧㄢˋㄊㄞˋ)
sex perversion

性病(ㄒㄧㄥˋㄅㄧㄥˋ)
venereal diseases—VD

性病醫院(ㄒㄧㄥˋㄅㄧㄥˋㄧㄩㄢˋ)
a VD hospital

性癖(ㄒㄧㄥˋㄆㄧˇ)
idiosyncrasy; one's hobbies, peculiar likes and dislikes, etc.

性命(ㄒㄧㄥˋㄇㄧㄥˋ)
a person's life: 醫生救了他的性命。The doctor saved his life.

性命干連(ㄒㄧㄥˋㄇㄧㄥˋㄍㄢㄌㄧㄢˊ)
It's a serious matter involv-ing a person's life.

性命交關(ㄒㄧㄥˋㄇㄧㄥˋㄐㄧㄠ ㄍㄨㄢ)
a matter of life and death

性發(ㄒㄧㄥˋㄈㄚ)
tempers flaring; to get mad

性犯罪(ㄒㄧㄥˋㄈㄢˋㄗㄨㄟˋ)
sexual offence

性分(ㄒㄧㄥˋㄈㄣˋ)
the natural property, dispo-sition and endowments of a person

性地(ㄒㄧㄥˋㄉㄧˋ)
one's natural qualities of mind and character 亦作「心地」

性能(ㄒㄧㄥˋㄋㄥˊ)
①natural ability ②qualities and capabilities of machin-ery

性冷感症(ㄒㄧㄥˋㄌㄥˇㄍㄢˇㄓㄥˋ)
frigidity

性烈(ㄒㄧㄥˋㄌㄧㄝˋ)
fierce tempered; fiery tem-pered; a fiery disposition

性靈(ㄒㄧㄥˋㄌㄧㄥˊ)
natural disposition and intel-ligence

〔心部〕

〔心 部〕

性格(ㄒㄧㄥㄍㄜˊ)
disposition; personality; character: 他的性格開朗。He has a bright and cheerful disposition.

性格分析(ㄒㄧㄥㄍㄜˊㄈㄣㄒㄧ)
(sociology) character analysis

性感(ㄒㄧㄥㄍㄢˇ)
sex appeal; sexy

性感明星(ㄒㄧㄥㄍㄢˇㄇㄧㄥㄒㄧㄥ)
(in motion pictures) sex sirens; sex-pots; sexy stars

性荷爾蒙(ㄒㄧㄥㄏㄜˊㄦˇㄇㄥˊ)
(physiology) sex hormone

性急(ㄒㄧㄥㄐㄧˊ)
impetuous; impulsive; impatient: 這個人性急得很。This man is very impatient.

性交(ㄒㄧㄥㄐㄧㄠ)
sexual intercourse

性教育(ㄒㄧㄥㄐㄧㄠˋㄩˋ)
sex education

性靜情逸(ㄒㄧㄥㄐㄧㄥˋㄑㄧㄥˊㄧˋ)
a quiet and easy disposition

性器(ㄒㄧㄥㄑㄧˋ)or 性器官(ㄒㄧㄥㄑㄧˋㄍㄨㄢ)
sexual organs; genitals; reproductive organs

性情(ㄒㄧㄥㄑㄧㄥˊ)
disposition; temperament: 她的性情溫柔。She has a gentle disposition.

性細胞(ㄒㄧㄥㄒㄧˋㄅㄠ)
germ cell

性向(ㄒㄧㄥㄒㄧㄤˋ)
disposition

性向測驗(ㄒㄧㄥㄒㄧㄤˋㄘㄜˋㄧㄢˋ)
aptitude test

性行為(ㄒㄧㄥㄒㄧㄥˊㄨㄟˊ)
sexual behavior

性知識(ㄒㄧㄥㄓㄕˋ)
sex knowledge; information regarding human sexual behaviors, organs, etc.

性質(ㄒㄧㄥㄓˊ)
property; characteristics; nature: 我們應弄清產品的性質。We should ascertain the property of the product.

性週期(ㄒㄧㄥㄓㄡㄑㄧ)
sexual cycle

性眞(ㄒㄧㄥㄓㄣ)
(Buddhism) the real self; the natural quality or property of a person

性徵(ㄒㄧㄥㄓㄥ)
(biology) sexual character

性子(ㄒㄧㄥ˙ㄗ)
① a temper; a disposition: 她在使性子。She got into a temper. ② strength; potency

性色(ㄒㄧㄥㄙㄜˋ)
colors indicative of different sexes of animals, especially insects

性騷擾(ㄒㄧㄥㄙㄠㄖㄠˇ)
sexual harassment

性惡(ㄒㄧㄥㄜˋ)
the theory advocated by Hsün Tzu (荀子) that men are born evil

性愛(ㄒㄧㄥˋㄞˋ)
sexual love

性無能(ㄒㄧㄥㄨˊㄋㄥˊ)
impotence; impotent

性慾(ㄒㄧㄥㄩˋ)
sexual desire or urge

性慾衝動(ㄒㄧㄥㄩˋㄔㄨㄥㄉㄨㄥˋ)
sexual impulse

【怩】 1532
ㄋㄧˊ ní ní
1. shy and bashful; coyly: 她忸怩作態。She behaves coyly.
2. to blush; to look embarrassed

【怫】 1533
1. ㄈㄨˊ fwu fú
depressed and discontented

怫鬱(ㄈㄨˊㄩˋ)
depressed and discontented

【怫】 1533
2. ㄈㄟˋ fey fèi
angry; annoyed; indignant

怫悲(ㄈㄟˋㄨˋ)
angry; indignant

怫然作色(ㄈㄟˋㄖㄢˊㄗㄨㄛˋㄙㄜˋ)
to color with anger; to get mad

【怯】 1534
ㄑㄧㄝˋ chieh qiè
(語音 ㄑㄩㄝˋ chiueh què)
1. lacking in courage; cowardly: 她是一個膽怯的人。She is a coward.
2. nervous; socially timid; fright; fear; afraid

怯夫(ㄑㄧㄝˋㄈㄨ)
a coward

怯頭怯腦(ㄑㄧㄝˋㄊㄡˊㄑㄧㄝˋㄋㄠˇ)
(usually used by city people to ridicule country folks)

nervous and clumsy, tim and unsophisticated

怯懦(ㄑㄧㄝˋㄋㄨㄛˋ)
cowardice

怯官(ㄑㄧㄝˋㄍㄨㄢ)
official fright—a fear o meeting government officia or policemen

怯懼(ㄑㄧㄝˋㄐㄩˋ)
to fear; to be nervous out o fear

怯陣(ㄑㄧㄝˋㄓㄣˋ)
① to feel nervous when go ing into battle ② to have stage fright

怯症(ㄑㄧㄝˋㄓㄥˋ)
① impotent; impotency ② the fear and nervousness cause by poor health

怯場(ㄑㄧㄝˋㄔㄤˇ)or(ㄑㄧㄝˋㄔㄤˇ)
stage fright: 大多數的新手有怯場。Most of the tyros have stage fright.

怯上(ㄑㄧㄝˋㄕㄤˋ)
superior fright—a fear of facing one's superiors

怯生(ㄑㄧㄝˋㄕㄥ)
(dialect) shy with strangers

怯弱(ㄑㄧㄝˋㄖㄨㄛˋ)
timid, weak and cowardly cowardice

怯疑(ㄑㄧㄝˋㄧˊ)
timid and vacillating

【怪】 1535
ㄍㄨㄞˋ guay guài
1. strange; queer; monstrous odd; peculiar: 你說怪不怪？Isn't this strange? 多麼奇怪！How strange!
2. to be surprised at: 那有什麼可怪的? Is that anything to be surprised at?
3. a ghost; a goblin; an apparition; a monster; an evil spirit
4. uncanny; weird: 他們被一聲奇怪的尖叫所驚醒。They were awakened by a weird shriek.
5. rather; very (interesting, tired, etc.): 這行李怪沉的。The baggage is rather heavy.
6. to blame: 不能怪你們。You are not to blame. 或 It's not your fault.

怪病(ㄍㄨㄞˋㄅㄧㄥˋ)
a strange or rare disease or ailment; an ailment that can

not be diagnosed

怪不得 (ㄍㄨㄞˋ ㄅㄨˋ ㄉㄜˊ)
①No wonder! 或 it explains why… ② cannot put the blame on: 這事怪不得他. We cannot put the blame on him.

怪癖 (ㄍㄨㄞˋ ㄆㄧˇ)
strange hobbies; eccentric behavior; eccentricities

怪僻 (ㄍㄨㄞˋ ㄆㄧˋ)
peculiar; eccentric; queer

怪模怪樣 (ㄍㄨㄞˋ ㄇㄛˊ ㄍㄨㄞˋ 一ㄤˋ)
queer appearance and manner; acting in a strange manner (usually said of beatniks or hippies)

怪誕不經 (ㄍㄨㄞˋ ㄉㄢˋ ㄅㄨˋ ㄐㄧㄥ)
weird, wild, uncanny, or absurd (stories, accounts, etc.)

怪道 (ㄍㄨㄞˋ ㄉㄠˋ)
no wonder that…; small wonder that…: 怪道他沒來. No wonder (that) he did not come.

怪特 (ㄍㄨㄞˋ ㄊㄜˋ)
strange and peculiar; extraordinary

怪態 (ㄍㄨㄞˋ ㄊㄞˋ)
affected and disgusting manners; revolting mannerisms

怪談 (ㄍㄨㄞˋ ㄊㄢˊ)
weird talks; accounts of something uncanny

怪力亂神 (ㄍㄨㄞˋ ㄌㄧˋ ㄌㄨㄢˋ ㄕㄣˊ)
extraordinary things, feats of strength, disorder, and spiritual beings (which Confucius avoided touching in his conversations)

怪裡怪氣 (ㄍㄨㄞˋ 一ˇ ㄍㄨㄞˋ ㄑㄧˋ)
eccentric; strange; queer

怪談 (ㄍㄨㄞˋ ㄊㄢˊ)
absurd talks; wild talks; strange statements

怪可憐的 (ㄍㄨㄞˋ ㄎㄜˇ ㄌㄧㄢˊ ㄉㄜ˙)
very pitiable

怪傑 (ㄍㄨㄞˋ ㄐㄧㄝˊ)
an extraordinary person; an outstanding person; a man among men

怪笑 (ㄍㄨㄞˋ ㄒㄧㄠˋ)
to laugh without cause; a laugh that grates on the ear; sardonic laughter

怪現象 (ㄍㄨㄞˋ ㄒㄧㄢˋ ㄒㄧㄤˋ)
strange phenomena (of a society, nature, etc.)

怪石 (ㄍㄨㄞˋ ㄕˊ)
rocks of grotesque shapes

怪石嶙峋 (ㄍㄨㄞˋ ㄕˊ ㄌㄧㄣˊ ㄒㄩㄣˊ)
weird-looking rocks presenting a sight of rugged beauty

怪事 (ㄍㄨㄞˋ ㄕˋ)
How strange! 或 strange happenings or things: 怪事年年有. Wonders will never cease.

怪手 (ㄍㄨㄞˋ ㄕㄡˇ)
.an excavator

怪獸 (ㄍㄨㄞˋ ㄕㄡˋ)
a rare animal (especially a large-sized one); a legendary animal

怪聲怪氣 (ㄍㄨㄞˋ ㄕㄥ ㄍㄨㄞˋ ㄑㄧˋ)
to speak in an unpleasant falsetto: 他說話怪聲怪氣. He spoke in an unpleasant falsetto.

怪人 (ㄍㄨㄞˋ ㄖㄣˊ)
a peculiar person

怪哉 (ㄍㄨㄞˋ ㄗㄞ)
Strange! 或 How strange! 或 What a strange thing!

怪異 (ㄍㄨㄞˋ 一ˋ)
strange; wild (talks, account, etc.); weird; uncanny

怪物 (ㄍㄨㄞˋ ㄨˋ)
① a monster; a strange creature ② an eccentric fellow: 他是一個怪物. He is an eccentric fellow.

怪偉 (ㄍㄨㄞˋ ㄨㄟˇ)
great and grotesque (in size and shape)

【悅】 1536 (悅) ㄏㄨㄤ huang
huang
1. despondent; dejected
2. wild; mad; flurried

悅惚 (ㄏㄨㄤ ㄏㄨ)
① a state of daze, stupor or trance ② (descriptive of something) vague

【怔】 1537 ㄓㄥ jeng zhēng
terrified; stunned; scared

怔忪 (ㄓㄥ ㄓㄨㄥ)
scared and nervous; fearful; frightened

怔仲 (ㄓㄥ ㄔㄨㄥˋ)
(Chinese medicine) a disease resembling neurosis

with such common symptoms as palpitation of the heart, melancholia and aptness to get tired; severe palpitation

怔營 (ㄓㄥ 一ㄥˊ)
scared and nervous

（心
部）

【伶】 1. (伶) ㄌㄧㄥˊ ling
ling
(often said of a child, young girl, etc.) agile, nimble, or pleasing; cute and pleasing

伶俐 or 伶俐 (ㄌㄧㄥˊ ㄌㄧˋ)
agile; nimble; bright and pleasing; cute. 她十分伶俐. She has a nimble mind

伶牙俐齒 (ㄌㄧㄥˊ 一ㄚˊ ㄌㄧˋ ㄔˇ)
to have the gift of the gab; to have a glib tongue

【伶】 2. ㄌㄧㄢˊ lian lián
an abbreviated form of 憐— to pity; pity

【恞】 1539 ㄋㄠˊ nau nǎo
confusion; confused; wild

恞恞 (ㄋㄠˊ ㄋㄠˊ)
to be prone to talk ceaselessly and unintelligently; to babble

【怗】 1540 ㄊㄧㄝ tie tiē
1. observant; submissive; subservient; compliant
2. peaceful; quiet

怗服 (ㄊㄧㄝ ㄈㄨˊ)
submissive; compliant; resigned

怗靜 (ㄊㄧㄝ ㄐㄧㄥˋ)
peaceful and quiet

【怵】 1541 ㄔㄨˋ chuh chù
1. scared; afraid; timorous; frightened
2. to entice; to induce

怵迫之徒 (ㄔㄨˋ ㄆㄛˋ ㄓ ㄊㄨˊ)
a person who is tempted and coerced; a person under duress

怵目驚心 (ㄔㄨˋ ㄇㄨˋ ㄐㄧㄥ ㄒㄧㄣ)
frightening; shocking

怵惕 (ㄔㄨˋ ㄊㄧˋ)
scared and cautious; fear; fearful and conscious

怵場 (ㄔㄨˋ ㄔㄤˇ) or (ㄔㄨˋ ㄔㄤˊ)
stage fright; the fear of facing a large crowd

心

部

忧然(ㄒㄩ ㄖㄢˊ)
scared; to look frightened

【怎】 1542
1. ㄗㄣˇ tzeen zěn
why; how; what: 事情是怎樣
發生的呢? How did it hap-
pen? 她怎不早說呢? Why didn't
she say so earlier?
怎的 or 怎地(ㄗㄣˇ ·ㄉㄜ)
how; in what way; what
怎奈(ㄗㄣˇ ㄋㄞˋ)
but alas; except that; unfortunately: 怎奈我那時不在家.
Unfortunately, I was not at
home then.
怎能(ㄗㄣˇ ㄋㄥˊ)
how can (he do this to me)?
或 how could (you...)?
怎敢(ㄗㄣˇ ㄍㄢˇ)
How can one dare? 或 don't
dare: 我怎敢和他談話. I don't
dare to speak to him.
怎見得(ㄗㄣˇ ㄐㄧㄢˋ ·ㄉㄜ)
How? 或Why? 或How come?
怎生(ㄗㄣˇ ㄕㄥ)
How? 或 In what way?
怎樣(ㄗㄣˇ ㄧㄤˋ)
How? 或 In what way? 這件
事你怎樣解釋? How do you
explain it?
怎樣好(ㄗㄣˇ ·ㄧ ㄏㄠˇ)
Which is the better way? 或
What (can we, I, etc.) do
now?

【怎】 1542
2. ㄗㄜˇ tzee zě
Why? 或How? 或What?
怎麼(ㄗㄜˇ ·ㄇㄜ)or 怎麼着
(ㄗㄜˇ ·ㄇㄜ ·ㄓㄜ) or 怎麼樣 (ㄗㄜˇ ·ㄇㄜ ·ㄧㄤˋ)
or 怎樣(ㄗㄣˇ ·ㄧ ㄤˋ)
Why? 或 How? 或 What? 這是
怎麼回事? What's all this
about? 坐公車去怎麼樣? How
about going by bus?
怎麼辦(ㄗㄜˇ ·ㄇㄜ ㄅㄢˋ)
How (or what) to do now?
或 What should (I, etc.) do?
怎麼得了(ㄗㄜˇ ·ㄇㄜ ㄉㄜ ㄌㄧㄠˇ)
There is no telling the serious consequences.
怎麼搞的(ㄗㄜˇ ·ㄇㄜ ㄍㄠˇ ·ㄉㄜ)
How did it happen? 或 How
did you mess it up? 或 Look
at what you've done!
怎麼好(ㄗㄜˇ ·ㄇㄜ ㄏㄠˇ)
Which is better? 或 don't
know what to do now: 我不

知道怎麼好. I don't know what
to do.
怎麼可能(ㄗㄜˇ ·ㄇㄜ ㄎㄜˇ ㄋㄥˊ)
How could this be possible?
或 How could it be like this?
或 How could it happen?
怎麼行(ㄗㄜˇ ·ㄇㄜ ㄒㄧㄥˊ)
How could it be possible?
(with the implied answer
"It's impossible.")
怎麼着(ㄗㄜˇ ·ㄇㄜ ·ㄓㄜ)
① what about ② whatever
happens
怎麼成(ㄗㄜˇ ·ㄇㄜ ㄔㄥˊ)
How could this be done? 或
How could this be possible?
(with the implied answer
"It's impossible." 或 "It can
not be done.")
怎麼說(ㄗㄜˇ ·ㄇㄜ ㄕㄨㄛ)
What do you say? 或What
(did he, etc.) say?

【怒】 1543
ㄋㄨˋ nuh nù
1. temper; anger; rage; angry;
furious: 他惱羞成怒. He lost
his temper from embarrassment. 他勃然大怒. He flew
into a rage.
2. to put forth with vigor (as
plants, etc.); to sprout; to
spring up
3. forceful and vigorous
怒臂(ㄋㄨˋ ㄅㄧˋ)
to raise one's arms in anger
怒不可遏(ㄋㄨˋ ㄅㄨˋ ㄎㄜˇ ㄜˋ)
(literally) The anger cannot
be suppressed.—furious; to
be beside oneself with anger:
他怒不可遏. He was beside
himself with anger.
怒馬(ㄋㄨˋ ㄇㄚˇ)
a sturdy and powerful horse
怒罵(ㄋㄨˋ ㄇㄚˋ)
to curse in rage
怒目切齒(ㄋㄨˋ ㄇㄨˋ ㄑㄧㄝˋ ㄔˇ)
(literally) to cast an angry
look while grinding one's
teeth—intense hatred or fury
怒目相視(ㄋㄨˋ ㄇㄨˋ ㄒㄧㄤ ㄕˋ)
to look black at each other;
to look daggers at each
other: 他們怒目相視. They
looked daggers at each
other.
怒目而視(ㄋㄨˋ ㄇㄨˋ ㄦˊ ㄕˋ)
to look at angrily
怒髮衝冠(ㄋㄨˋ ㄈㄚˇ ㄔㄨㄥ ㄍㄨㄢ)

(literally) so angry that th
hair stands up and tips o
the hat—intense anger; t
bristle with anger
怒放(ㄋㄨˋ ㄈㄤˋ)
① in full bloom: 玫瑰花怒放
The roses are in full bloom
② (figuratively) wild wit
joy: 她心花怒放. She wa
wild with joy.
怒濤(ㄋㄨˋ ㄊㄠˊ)
furious billows; roarin
waves; turbulent waters
怒猊渴驥(ㄋㄨˋ ㄋㄧˊ ㄎㄜˋ ㄐㄧˋ)
(said of Chinese calligra
phy) forceful and vigorou
(style)
怒號(ㄋㄨˋ ㄏㄠˊ)
(said of winds) howling
roaring: 狂風怒號. A violen
wind is howling.
怒吼(ㄋㄨˋ ㄏㄡˇ)
to roar; roars; stentoria
calls (also used figurative
ly)
怒恨(ㄋㄨˋ ㄏㄣˋ)
raging animosity or hatred
full of anger and spite
怒火(ㄋㄨˋ ㄏㄨㄛˇ)
flames of fury; fury: 他滿腔
怒火.He was filled with fury
怒轟轟 or 怒哄哄 or 怒烘烘
(ㄋㄨˋ ㄏㄨㄥ ㄏㄨㄥ)
roaring fury; very angry
furiously
怒江(ㄋㄨˋ ㄐㄧㄤ)
the Salween River
怒氣(ㄋㄨˋ ㄑㄧˋ)
anger; wrath; rage; fury
怒氣填胸(ㄋㄨˋ ㄑㄧˋ ㄊㄧㄢˊ ㄒㄩㄥ)
(literally) a breast filled
with anger—brimming with
fury
怒氣沖沖(ㄋㄨˋ ㄑㄧˋ ㄔㄨㄥ ㄔㄨㄥ)
furious; angry; in a great
rage: 他怒氣沖沖. He was in
a great rage.
怒吼(ㄋㄨˋ ㄔˋ)
to shout in rage; angry
shouts
怒潮(ㄋㄨˋ ㄔㄠˊ)
an angry tide; an over-
whelming aspiration
怒視(ㄋㄨˋ ㄕˋ)
an angry look; to look at
someone angrily
怒容滿面(ㄋㄨˋ ㄖㄨㄥˊ ㄇㄢˇ ㄇㄧㄢˋ)

（心 部）

flushed with rage; to look furious: 他氣容滿面。His face was flushed with rage.

色(ㄙㄜˋ)
an angry air or look: 他面帶怒色。He wore an angry look.

憗(ㄙㄜˋ)
wrath and spite

意(ㄙㄜˋ)
anger; wrath; (an action, utterance, expression, etc.) indicative of anger

思 1544
ㄙ sy sī
. to think; to contemplate; to consider: 你應該三思而後行。You should think twice before doing that.
. memory; remembrance; to remember; to recall; to think of
. to mourn; to grieve
. to admire
. to pine for
. a final particle to sound off an expression

思辨(ㄙ ㄅㄧㄢˋ)
① speculation; to speculate ② (usually sarcastically) armchair thinking ③ to analyze mentally

思辨哲學(ㄙ ㄅㄧㄢˋ ㄓㄜˊ ㄒㄩㄝˊ)
speculative philosophy

思不出位(ㄙ ㄅㄨˋ ㄔㄨ ㄨㄟˋ)
(literally) not to think of things outside one's position —without ambition; do not entertain high aspirations

思慕(ㄙ ㄇㄨˋ)
① to admire (a girl, etc.) ② to remember (old days, etc.)

思凡(ㄙ ㄈㄢˊ)
(said of monks, nuns, angels, etc.) to think of worldly pleasures

思婦(ㄙ ㄈㄨˋ)
① a woman who bosoms sad thoughts or memories ② the name of a legendary bird

思念(ㄙ ㄋㄧㄢˋ)
to remember (old days, friends, etc.); to recall

思慕(ㄙ ㄇㄨˋ)
to cherish the memory of

思量(ㄙ ㄌㄧㄤˊ)
to think; to consider; to turn over; to contemplate;

consideration; contemplation: 一個人應慎重思量後才決定。One must consider the matter well before deciding.

思路(ㄙ ㄌㄨˋ)
(literally) the paths or ramifications of one's thought —the clarity of thinking, or the lack of it (usually said of writing): 他打斷我的思路。He interrupted my train of thought.

思慮(ㄙ ㄌㄩˋ)
consideration; contemplation; to think carefully; to turn over and over in the mind

思過(ㄙ ㄍㄨㄛˋ)
to ponder or ruminate upon one's faults; to repent

思過半矣(ㄙ ㄍㄨㄛˋ ㄅㄢˋ ㄧˇ)
(literally) to have thought more than half—to have already understood or realized a lot

思歸鳥(ㄙ ㄍㄨㄟ ㄋㄧㄠˇ)
the goatsucker 亦作「子規」or「蚊母鳥」

思考(ㄙ ㄎㄠˇ)
to ponder; to contemplate; to think; rumination; contemplation: 人是能思考的動物。Man is a thinking animal.

思考力(ㄙ ㄎㄠˇ ㄌㄧˋ)
the power to think, analyze and speculate

思舊(ㄙ ㄐㄧㄡˋ)
to remember old times, friends, etc.

思齊(ㄙ ㄑㄧˊ)
to wish to equal (a sage, etc.); to want to emulate: 見賢思齊 to see the virtuous and think of equaling or emulating them

思前想後(ㄙ ㄑㄧㄢˊ ㄒㄧㄤˇ ㄏㄡˋ)
to ponder over (a matter, problem, situation, etc.)

思親(ㄙ ㄑㄧㄣ)
to think of one's relatives, especially parents

思鄉(ㄙ ㄒㄧㄤ)or 思家(ㄙ ㄐㄧㄚ)
to think of one's home; homesick

思鄉病(ㄙ ㄒㄧㄤ ㄅㄧㄥˋ)
homesickness; nostalgia

思想(ㄙ ㄒㄧㄤˇ)

① to think of; to remember, to recall ② thought; ideas; mentality; ideological inclination; ideology

思想落伍(ㄙ ㄒㄧㄤˇ ㄌㄨㄛˋ ㄨˇ)
old-fashioned in thinking; outdated ideas

思想家(ㄙ ㄒㄧㄤˇ ㄐㄧㄚ)
a thinker

思想戰(ㄙ ㄒㄧㄤˇ ㄓㄢˋ)
ideological warfare; the battle over people's minds

思想自由(ㄙ ㄒㄧㄤˇ ㄗˋ ㄧㄡˊ)
freedom of thought

思想幼稚(ㄙ ㄒㄧㄤˇ ㄧㄡˋ ㄓˋ)
childish thinking; naïve

思省(ㄙ ㄒㄧㄥˇ)
① to think of ② to inspect

思緒(ㄙ ㄒㄩˋ)
a train of thought; the paths of one's thought; myriad ramifications of one's thought: 他思緒紛亂。He was in a confused state of mind.

思致(ㄙ ㄓˋ)
the power of thinking

思潮(ㄙ ㄔㄠˊ)
① the prevailing trend of thought; popular ideas: 民主政治是一種國際思潮。Democracy is an international trend. ② the changing tides of one's thought: 他的思潮起伏不定。His disquieting thoughts surged in his mind.

思春(ㄙ ㄔㄨㄣ)
(usually said of girls) to pine for the opposite sex

思深慮遠(ㄙ ㄕㄣ ㄌㄩˋ ㄩㄢˇ)or 思深憂遠(ㄙ ㄕㄣ ㄧㄡ ㄩㄢˇ)
to think deep and far ahead

思惹情牽(ㄙ ㄖㄜˇ ㄑㄧㄥˊ ㄑㄧㄢ)
to be a prisoner of love; to admire (a girl, etc.) deeply

思如泉湧(ㄙ ㄖㄨˊ ㄑㄩㄢˊ ㄩㄥˇ)
(literally) ideas coming like a swelling spring—brimming with ideas and thoughts

思存(ㄙ ㄘㄨㄣˊ)
to show concern or interest; to favor in heart (a choice, candidate, etc.)

思忖(ㄙ ㄘㄨㄣˇ)
to think; to consider; to ponder; to contemplate: 我們思忖了許多事情。We pondered many things.

【心部】

思索 (ㄙㄨㄛˇ)
(literally) to search one's mind for an answer—to study; to ponder over: 我用心思索了一夜。I did some hard thinking all night.

思憶 (ㄧˋ)
to think of and remember (old times, friends, etc.); to recall; to cherish the memory of

思議 (ㄧˋ)
thinkable; imaginable

思維 or 思惟 (ㄨㄟˊ)
thought; thinking; pondering over

【怠】 1545
ㄉㄞˋ day dài
1. idle; remiss; lax; negligent
2. to treat coldly

怠慢 (ㄉㄞˋ ㄇㄢˋ)
① to neglect a visitor or guest (often used as a polite expression); 不要怠慢了來客。See that none of the visitors are neglected. ② lax and crude; idle and remiss

怠廢 (ㄉㄞˋ ㄈㄟˋ)
idle

怠惰 (ㄉㄞˋ ㄉㄨㄛˋ)
idle and lazy

怠工 (ㄉㄞˋ ㄍㄨㄥ) or 怠業 (ㄧㄝˋ)
① a slowdown ② to goof off

怠忽 (ㄉㄞˋ ㄏㄨ)
to be remiss; to neglect: 他怠忽職守。He was remiss in his duties.

怠緩 (ㄉㄞˋ ㄏㄨㄢˇ)
idle and lax; procrastinating

怠荒 (ㄉㄞˋ ㄏㄨㄤ)
to idle and waste (time, etc.)

怠倦 (ㄉㄞˋ ㄐㄩㄢˋ)
tired of work; lax and tired

怠情養性 (ㄉㄞˋ ㄑㄧㄥˊ ㄧㄤˇ ㄒㄧㄥˋ)
to renounce aggressiveness and practice relaxation

怠息 (ㄉㄞˋ ㄒㄧˊ)
to idle and rest

怠隙 (ㄉㄞˋ ㄒㄧˋ)
an opportunity—as when the enemy relaxes his vigilance; an opportune moment for one to take advantage of

怠散 (ㄉㄞˋ ㄙㄢˇ)
remiss, lax and negligent

【急】 1546
ㄐㄧˊ jyi jí
1. quick; quickly; with expedition: 他急急開門。He quickly opened the door.
2. urgent; hurried; hasty: 她急忙走了。She left in a hurry.
3. anxious; very eager; worried

急巴巴 (ㄐㄧˊ ㄅㄚ ㄅㄚ)
very anxious; very anxiously

急奔 (ㄐㄧˊ ㄅㄣ) or 急步 (ㄅㄨˋ)
to walk hurriedly

急變 (ㄐㄧˊ ㄅㄧㄢˋ)
a quick turn of events; an emergency; a crisis; a presto change

急病 (ㄐㄧˊ ㄅㄧㄥˋ)
a sudden illness; an emergency medical case

急不可待 (ㄐㄧˊ ㄅㄨˋ ㄎㄜˇ ㄉㄞˋ)
so urgent that there is no time for waiting; extremely anxious

急不暇擇 (ㄐㄧˊ ㄅㄨˋ ㄒㄧㄚˊ ㄗㄜˊ)
too urgent to make a wise or careful choice

急迫 (ㄐㄧˊ ㄆㄛˋ)
urgent; pressing: 這件事很急迫。The matter is pressing.

急拍 (ㄐㄧˊ ㄆㄞ)
(music) allegro or presto

急脈緩受 (ㄐㄧˊ ㄇㄞˋ ㄏㄨㄢˇ ㄕㄡˋ)
to counter fierce and sudden thrust with slow but steady measures

急忙 (ㄐㄧˊ ㄇㄤˊ)
urgently; hastily; hurriedly; quickly; in a hurry

急風暴雨 (ㄐㄧˊ ㄈㄥ ㄅㄠˋ ㄩˇ)
a violent storm; a hurricane; a tempest

急電 (ㄐㄧˊ ㄉㄧㄢˋ)
① an urgent cable ② to call urgently: 我們急電回答。We answered urgently, calling in reply.

急圖 (ㄐㄧˊ ㄊㄨˊ)
① urgent business or tasks ② to make quick plans (to cope with a crisis, an emergency, etc.); to counter quickly

急湍 (ㄐㄧˊ ㄊㄨㄢ)
a swift flow of water; angry torrents

急難 (ㄐㄧˊ ㄋㄢˊ)
① a critical time; a crisis; an emergency; a disaster ② to offer help in an emergency

急淚 (ㄐㄧˊ ㄌㄟˋ)
sudden tears

急來抱佛腳 (ㄐㄧˊ ㄌㄞˊ ㄅㄠˋ ㄈㄛˊ ㄐㄧㄠˇ)
to seek help in time of emergency (implying lack of preparation when one has plenty of time)

急流 (ㄐㄧˊ ㄌㄧㄡˊ)
swift currents; rapids

急流勇退 (ㄐㄧˊ ㄌㄧㄡˊ ㄩㄥˇ ㄊㄨㄟˋ)
to retire when one has ridden the crest of success

急公好義 (ㄐㄧˊ ㄍㄨㄥ ㄏㄠˋ ㄧˋ)
to be enthusiastic about charity work; zealous for public welfare or interests: 那老人急公好義。The old man was zealous for the public welfare.

急功近利 (ㄐㄧˊ ㄍㄨㄥ ㄐㄧㄣˋ ㄌㄧˋ)
so eager to be successful that one sees only the immediate advantages: 他急功近利。He was eager for quick success and instant benefit.

急客 (ㄐㄧˊ ㄎㄜˋ)
an unexpected visitor; a self-invited guest

急口令 (ㄐㄧˊ ㄎㄡˇ ㄌㄧㄥˋ)
a tongue twister 亦作「繞口令」

急壞 (ㄐㄧˊ ㄏㄨㄞˋ)
to feel extremely worried but helpless; anxious but powerless

急激 (ㄐㄧˊ ㄐㄧ)
radical; vehement

急急忙忙 (ㄐㄧˊ ㄐㄧˊ ㄇㄤˊ ㄇㄤˊ)
in great haste; in a great hurry

急救 (ㄐㄧˊ ㄐㄧㄡˋ)
first-aid; first aid: 我們買了些急救藥品。We bought a lot of first-aid medicine

急救法 (ㄐㄧˊ ㄐㄧㄡˋ ㄈㄚˇ)
first-aid methods or techniques

急救方 (ㄐㄧˊ ㄐㄧㄡˋ ㄈㄤ)
a prescription for an emergency case

急救箱 (ㄐㄧˊ ㄐㄧㄡˋ ㄒㄧㄤ)
a first-aid kit

急就 (ㄐㄧˊ ㄐㄧㄡˋ)

hurriedly made, composed, etc.; improvised; to complete rapidly

急就章(ㄐㄧˊㄐㄧㄡˋㄓㄤ)
hurriedly composed writing; an article written or a task performed under tremendous pressure of time or at short notice; an improvisation

急件(ㄐㄧˊㄐㄧㄢˋ)
an urgent document; a dispatch

急進(ㄐㄧˊㄐㄧㄣˋ)
to forge ahead vigorously

急進份子(ㄐㄧˊㄐㄧㄣˋㄈㄣˋㄗˇ)
a radical

急進派(ㄐㄧˊㄐㄧㄣˋㄆㄞˋ)
a radical or an extremist faction

急進主義(ㄐㄧˊㄐㄧㄣˋㄓㄨˇㄧˋ)
radicalism; extremism

急降(ㄐㄧˊㄐㄧㄤˋ)
to dive sharply; to drop sharply

急驚風(ㄐㄧˊㄐㄧㄥㄈㄥ)
(Chinese medicine) a disease among children, especially of infants, symptomized by involuntary, incessant twitchings of the limbs and tightly shut mouth; infantile eclampsia; acute infantile convulsions; sudden onset of infantile convulsion

急驚風偏遇慢郎中(ㄐㄧˊㄐㄧㄥㄈㄥㄆㄧㄢㄩˋㄇㄢˋㄌㄤˊㄓㄨㄥ)
① One is impatient while the other takes it easy. ② One sees no need to hurry while something requires one's immediate attention.

急景凋年(ㄐㄧˊㄐㄧㄥˇㄉㄧㄠㄋㄧㄢˊ)
Time slips away fast, and the year is approaching its end.

急遽(ㄐㄧˊㄐㄩˋ)
quick (falls, rises, advances, etc.); urgent; hasty: 急遽的變化 a rapid change

急起直追(ㄐㄧˊㄑㄧˇㄓˊㄓㄨㄟ)
to rise and make a hot chase; to make amends as quickly as possible; to try to catch up in great haste

急切(ㄐㄧˊㄑㄧㄝ)
① urgent; eager; anxiously (awaiting, etc.) ② in a

hurry; in haste

急先鋒(ㄐㄧˊㄒㄧㄢㄈㄥ)
① a brave vanguard ② a most aggressive, daring henchman

急相(ㄐㄧˊㄒㄧㄤˋ)
an anxious expression or manner

急行(ㄐㄧˊㄒㄧㄥˊ)
① to walk hurriedly ② to start doing something immediately

急行軍(ㄐㄧˊㄒㄧㄥˊㄐㄩㄣ)
a forced march; a rapid march

急性(ㄐㄧˊㄒㄧㄥˋ)
(medicine) an acute case

急性闌尾炎(ㄐㄧˊㄒㄧㄥˋㄌㄢˊㄨㄟˇㄧㄢˊ)
acute appendicitis 亦作「急性盲腸炎」

急性子(ㄐㄧˊㄒㄧㄥˋ˙ㄗ)
quick-tempered; prone to do things quickly; rash; impatient; impetuous 亦作「急性兒」

急性胃炎(ㄐㄧˊㄒㄧㄥˋㄨㄟˋㄧㄢˊ)
acute gastritis

急需(ㄐㄧˊㄒㄩ)
to need urgently: 我急需幫助。I was in need of immediate help.

急智(ㄐㄧˊㄓˋ)
quick-witted; a calm and quickly responsive mind, especially in a crisis; a mind capable of making quick and intelligent decisions, especially in time of crisis or danger; wit

急診(ㄐㄧˊㄓㄣˇ)
(medicine) an emergency case; emergency treatment

急症(ㄐㄧˊㄓㄥˋ)
(medicine) an emergency case

急轉直下(ㄐㄧˊㄓㄨㄢˇㄓˊㄒㄧㄚˋ)
a quick and decisive turn of events for the worse; rapid deterioration of a situation; to take a sudden turn and then develop rapidly

急轉彎(ㄐㄧˊㄓㄨㄢˇㄨㄢ)
① to make a sharp turn ② a hairpin turn

急中生智(ㄐㄧˊㄓㄨㄥㄕㄥㄓˋ)
suddenly hit upon a way out of a predicament; driven by

circumstances to find a way out; a bright idea that hits one in an emergency

急事(ㄐㄧˊㄕˋ)
an urgent matter

急煞(ㄐㄧˊㄕㄚˋ)
to be very worried or anxious but powerless to do anything about it

急煞車(ㄐㄧˊㄕㄚˋㄔㄜ)
① to brake a car abruptly; to brake a car to a screeching stop: 他來個急煞車。He braked his car abruptly. ② to bring to a halt

急甚麼(ㄐㄧˊㄕㄣˋ˙ㄇㄜ)
What's the hurry? 或 No need to hurry. (There is plenty of time.)

急如星火(ㄐㄧˊㄖㄨˊㄒㄧㄥㄏㄨㄛˇ)
(literally) as urgent as sparks that may start a conflagration—extremely urgent: 災民需要醫藥急如星火。Medical aid must be sent to the victims posthaste.

急則生變(ㄐㄧˊㄗㄜˊㄕㄥㄅㄧㄢˋ)
Hastiness upsets carefully laid out plans. 或 Rashness spoils chances of success.

急躁(ㄐㄧˊㄗㄠˋ)
rash and impatient; peevish; impetuous; irritable

急促(ㄐㄧˊㄘㄨˋ)
① urgently; hastily; hurriedly ②(said of time) short: 時間很急促，我們必須對那件事下決心。Time is running short. We must make up our mind about it.

急色鬼(ㄐㄧˊㄙㄜˋㄍㄨㄟˇ)or **急色兒**(ㄐㄧˊㄙㄜˋㄦ)
a prurient male in constant heat; a woman-grabber

急速(ㄐㄧˊㄙㄨˋ)
hurriedly; hastily: 事情急速變化。The matter changed quickly

急務(ㄐㄧˊㄨˋ)
pressing and urgent business: 我有急務在身。I have some urgent task on hand.

急彎(ㄐㄧˊㄨㄢ)
a sharp turn: 車子拐了個急彎。The car made a sharp turn.

急於(ㄐㄧˊㄩˊ)

（心部）

to be in a hurry or anxious to (finish the task, conclude the war, etc.); eager: 他急於完成任務。He is eager to fulfill a task.

急雨 (ㄐㄧˊ ㄩˇ)
a heavy downpour; a driving rain

急用 (ㄐㄧˊ ㄩㄥˋ)
(for) urgent use or need: 我們應節約儲蓄, 以備急用。We should practice economy and save money against a rainy day.

【怨】 1547
ㄩㄢˋ yuann yuàn

1. ill will; hatred; enmity; animus; resentment; to resent: 他怨恨批評。He resents criticism.

2. to complain; to blame (others); to impute: 她總是在抱怨。She is always complaining.

怨不得 (ㄩㄢˋ ˙ㄅㄨˊ ˙ㄉㄜ)
no wonder; cannot blame

怨命 (ㄩㄢˋ ㄇㄧㄥˋ)
to blame one's fate (for all misfortunes encountered)

怨誹 (ㄩㄢˋ ㄈㄟˇ)
blames or curses; to blame; to murmur against

怨恨 (ㄩㄢˋ ㄏㄣˋ)
animus; bitterness; a grudge; ill will

怨毒 (ㄩㄢˋ ㄉㄨˊ)
malice; hatred; venom; enmity

怨懟 (ㄩㄢˋ ㄉㄨㄟˋ)
ill will; hatred; a grudge

怨歎 (ㄩㄢˋ ㄊㄢˋ)
to sigh with bitterness

怨天尤人 (ㄩㄢˋ ㄊㄧㄢ ㄧㄡˊ ㄖㄣˊ)
(literally) to murmur against Heaven and blame others (for one's misfortune) -- (figuratively) to impute all faults and wrongs to others; to be neurotically dissatisfied: 他不怨天尤人。He didn't blame God or man.

怨女 (ㄩㄢˋ ㄋㄩˇ)
an old maid or spinster

怨女曠夫 (ㄩㄢˋ ㄋㄩˇ ㄎㄨㄤˋ ㄈㄨ)
unmarried women and men (who could be easily persuaded to marry to mutual satisfaction)

怨骨 (ㄩㄢˋ ㄍㄨˇ)
those who died with grudges or complaints

怨鬼 (ㄩㄢˋ ㄍㄨㄟˇ)
the ghost of a wronged man --as a man executed by mistake, etc.

怨恨 (ㄩㄢˋ ㄏㄣˋ)
ill will; enmity; animus; grudges: 他對我有怨恨。He bears me a grudge

怨結 (ㄩㄢˋ ㄐㄧㄝˊ)
a pent-up hatred or grudge

怨氣 (ㄩㄢˋ ㄑㄧˋ)
spite; resentment; complaints; strong dissatisfaction: 我一肚子怨氣。I was full of complaints.

怨仇 (ㄩㄢˋ ㄔㄡˊ)
an old enemy

怨聲載道 (ㄩㄢˋ ㄕㄥ ㄗㄞˋ ㄉㄠˋ)
(said of bad administration, etc.) Complaints can be heard everywhere. or Cries of discontent rise all round.

怨入骨髓 (ㄩㄢˋ ㄖㄨˋ ㄍㄨˇ ㄙㄨㄟˇ)
to hate to the very marrow

怨容 (ㄩㄢˋ ㄖㄨㄥˊ)
to repine; to grumble

怨色 (ㄩㄢˋ ㄙㄜˋ)
a resentful look

怨艾 (ㄩㄢˋ ㄞˋ)
(literally) resentment; a grudge

怨偶 or 怨耦 (ㄩㄢˋ ㄡˇ)
a couple who love each other no more; an unharmonious couple; a couple at loggerheads

怨尤 (ㄩㄢˋ ㄧㄡˊ)
spite; complaining; a grudge; a grumble; bitterness

怨言 (ㄩㄢˋ ㄧㄢˊ)
complaints; spiteful remarks; grumbles: 他從未發過一句怨言。He has never uttered a word of complaint.

怨望 (ㄩㄢˋ ㄨㄤˋ)
ill will; hatred; animus

【他】 1548
ㄊㄢ tan tān
a polite version of 他

【怱】 1549
(悤,匆) ㄘㄨㄥ tsong cōng
hasty; hastily; hurriedly

怱忙 (ㄘㄨㄥ ㄇㄤˊ)

haste; in haste; hastily; hurriedly: 我怱忙作出決定。made a hasty decision.

怱促 (ㄘㄨㄥ ㄘㄨˋ) or 怱遽 (ㄘㄨㄥ ㄐㄩˋ)
haste; hastily: 他怱促離去。He left in haste.

怱怱 (ㄘㄨㄥ ㄘㄨㄥ)
hurriedly; suddenly and imperceptibly (said of the passage of time): 他怱怱吃了一餐飯。He took a hurried meal.

六畫

【恂】 1550
ㄒㄩㄣˊ shyun xún

1. to trust; to have faith in
2. sincere
3. suddenly
4. afraid; scared

恂達 (ㄒㄩㄣˊ ㄉㄚˊ)
intelligent

恂慄 (ㄒㄩㄣˊ ㄌㄧˋ)
scared; severe-looking; awe-inspiring

恂恂 (ㄒㄩㄣˊ ㄒㄩㄣˊ)
① faithfully; trustingly; simple and sincere ② courteously

恂直 (ㄒㄩㄣˊ ㄓˊ)
frank and sincere

恂實 (ㄒㄩㄣˊ ㄕˊ)
sincerely honest

恂然 (ㄒㄩㄣˊ ㄖㄢˊ)
sincerely

【恆】 1551
(恒) ㄏㄥˊ herng héng

1. constant; regular; persevering: 我們讀書要持之以恆。We persevere in our studies.

2. lasting; continual; continually

3. a Chinese family name

恆民 (ㄏㄥˊ ㄇㄧㄣˊ)
common people; ordinary people

恆風 (ㄏㄥˊ ㄈㄥ)
a permanent wind

恆等 (ㄏㄥˊ ㄉㄥˇ)
(mathematics) identically equal; identical

恆例 (ㄏㄥˊ ㄌㄧˋ)
common practices

恆河 (ㄏㄥˊ ㄏㄜˊ)
the Ganges River, in north-

ern India

恆河沙數(ㄏㄥˊㄏㄜˊㄕㄚ ㄕㄨˋ)
(literally) the sands of the Ganges; too many to be counted—innumerable; countless

恆久(ㄏㄥˊㄐㄧㄡˇ)
constancy; constant; lasting; forever; enduring

恆情(ㄏㄥˊㄑㄧㄥˊ)
general propensities; common practices

恆心(ㄏㄥˊㄒㄧㄣ)
perseverance: 我們要是沒有恆心可學不好。Unless we persevere with a subject, we can't hope to master it.

恆星(ㄏㄥˊㄒㄧㄥ)
fixed stars

恆星年(ㄏㄥˊㄒㄧㄥ ㄋㄧㄢˊ)
a sidereal year

恆星系(ㄏㄥˊㄒㄧㄥ ㄒㄧˋ)
a stellar system; a galaxy

恆星時(ㄏㄥˊㄒㄧㄥ ㄕˊ)
sidereal time

恆星日(ㄏㄥˊㄒㄧㄥ ㄖˋ)
a sidereal day

恆星月(ㄏㄥˊㄒㄧㄥ ㄩㄝˋ)
a sidereal month

恆齒(ㄏㄥˊㄔˇ)
(anatomy) permanent teeth

恆產(ㄏㄥˊㄔㄢˇ)
immovable property—real estate

恆(ㄏㄥˊㄔㄤˊ)
①permanent; enduring; constant ②regular; common (practices), etc.

恆春(ㄏㄥˊㄔㄨㄣ)
Hengchun, a town on the southernmost end of Taiwan

恆山(ㄏㄥˊㄕㄢ)
Mountain Heng, also known as the Northern Mountain, located between Hopeh and Shansi Provinces

恆言(ㄏㄥˊㄧㄢˊ)
a common saying; a proverb

恆溫器(ㄏㄥˊㄨㄣ ㄑㄧˋ)
a thermostat

恆溫層(ㄏㄥˊㄨㄣ ㄘㄥˊ)
a stratum of invariable temperature; the stratosphere

【恃】 1552
ㄕˋ shyh shì
to rely on; to depend on; to presume upon: 他有恃無恐.

He feels secure in the knowledge that he has strong backing.

恃習(ㄕˋㄒㄧˊ)or 恃橫(ㄏㄥˊ)
to rely on crooked ways and violence

恃力(ㄕˋㄌㄧˋ)or 恃強(ㄕˋㄑㄧㄤˊ)
to rely on one's power; to rely on force

恃論平允(ㄕˋㄌㄨㄣˊㄆㄧㄥˊㄩㄣˇ)
to pass a fair opinion

恃貴(ㄕˋㄍㄨㄟˋ)
to presume on one's high position or blue blood

恃強凌弱(ㄕˋㄑㄧㄤˊㄌㄧㄥˊㄖㄨㄛˋ)
to use one's strength (or power) to bully the weak: 他恃強凌弱。He uses his strength to bully the weak.

恃衆(ㄕˋㄓㄨㄥˋ)
to presume on numbers; to take advantage of superiority in numbers (to commit an act of violence)

恃寵(ㄕˋㄔㄨㄥˇ)
to presume on being a favorite (of a high-placed personality): 他恃寵而驕。His haughtiness relies on his master's (or superior's) love and indulgence

恃勢(ㄕˋㄕˋ)
to presume on one's position or influence

恃才傲物(ㄕˋㄘㄞˊㄠˋㄨˋ)
to be arrogant because of one's talents or ability: 他恃才傲物。He is inordinately proud of his ability.

恃愛(ㄕˋㄞˋ)
(usually used in polite correspondence) to presume on your kindness and affection

【恌】 1553
ㄊㄧㄠ tiau tiǎo
1. flippant; playful; sportive; frivolous

【恓】 1554
ㄒㄧ shi xī
frightened and worried

恓惶(ㄒㄧㄏㄨㄤˊ)
frightened and worried; vexed

【恍】 1555
ㄏㄨㄤˇ hoang huǎng
1. absent-minded; unconscious
2. all of a sudden; suddenly
3. seem; as if

恍惚(ㄏㄨㄤˇㄏㄨ)or 恍恍惚惚(ㄏㄨㄤˇㄏㄨㄤˇㄏㄨㄏㄨ)
①in a trance; absent-minded; unconscious: 他精神恍惚。He was in a trance. ②dimly; faintly

恍然大悟(ㄏㄨㄤˇㄖㄢˊㄉㄚˋㄨˋ)
to come to understand suddenly

恍然若失(ㄏㄨㄤˇㄖㄢˊㄖㄨㄛˋㄕ)
to feel as if one had lost his bearings

恍如隔世(ㄏㄨㄤˇㄖㄨˊㄍㄜˊㄕˋ)
so different that it is as if a generation had passed

恍如一場大夢(ㄏㄨㄤˇㄖㄨˊㄧ ㄔㄤˊㄉㄚˋㄇㄥˋ)
It seems as if it were a dream.

恍若(ㄏㄨㄤˇㄖㄨㄛˋ)or 恍如(ㄏㄨㄤˇㄖㄨˊ)
as if; as though; rather like

【恟】 1556
ㄒㄩㄥ shiong xiōng
1. afraid; frightened
2. noisy

恟懼(ㄒㄩㄥㄐㄩˋ)
afraid; frightened

恟恟(ㄒㄩㄥㄒㄩㄥ)
tumultuous

【恢】 1557
ㄏㄨㄟ huei huī
1. great; immense; enormous; vast; extensive
2. to recover; to restore; to regain: 他很快地恢復健康。He regained his health quickly.

恢復(ㄏㄨㄟˊㄈㄨˋ)
to restore; to regain; to recover: 恢復知覺 to recover consciousness

恢復健康(ㄏㄨㄟˊㄈㄨˋㄐㄧㄢˋㄎㄤ)
to restore one's health; to recover from illness

恢復青春(ㄏㄨㄟˊㄈㄨˋㄑㄧㄥㄔㄨㄣ)
to be rejuvenated; to regain youth

恢復秩序(ㄏㄨㄟˊㄈㄨˋㄓˋㄒㄩˋ)
to restore order

恢復自由(ㄏㄨㄟˊㄈㄨˋㄗˋㄧㄡˊ)
to regain freedom; restoration of freedom

恢復元氣(ㄏㄨㄟˊㄈㄨˋㄩㄢˊㄑㄧˋ)
to recover energy or strength (after a calamity, illness, etc.)

恢復原狀(ㄏㄨㄟˊㄈㄨˋㄩㄢˊㄓㄨㄤˋ)
to restore the original condi-

（心部）

（心部）

tion; to be restored to the original condition

恢誕（ㄏㄨㄟ ㄉㄢ）
exaggerated

恢廓（ㄏㄨㄟ ㄎㄨㄛ）
broad-minded

恢恢（ㄏㄨㄟ ㄏㄨㄟ）
spacious; extensive; vast: 天網恢恢，疏而不漏。Nobody escapes the judgement of Heaven.

恢恢有餘（ㄏㄨㄟ ㄏㄨㄟ ㄧㄡˇ ㄩˊ）
to have plenty of space; very spacious; very roomy

恢宏 or 恢弘（ㄏㄨㄟ ㄏㄨㄥˊ）
extensive; broad; magnanimous

恢張（ㄏㄨㄟ ㄓㄤ）
to extend

恢偉（ㄏㄨㄟ ㄨㄟˇ）
great

【恨】 ㄏㄣˋ henn hèn 1558

1. to resent; to hate; hatred; hate: 她懷恨在心。She nursed hatred in her heart.

2. to regret

恨不相逢未嫁時（ㄏㄣˋ ㄅㄨˋ ㄒㄧㄤ ㄈㄥˊ ㄨㄟˇ ㄐㄧㄚˋ ㄕˊ）
to regret meeting one's lover only after marriage (to another man)

恨不得（ㄏㄣˋ ·ㄅㄨ ㄉㄜˊ）
to wish that one could (do something which is not proper to do); to itch to: 我恨不得馬上投入戰場。I itched to plunge into the battlefield.

恨不能（ㄏㄣˋ ·ㄅㄨ ㄋㄥˊ）
to wish that one could (do something impossible or beyond one's means to do)

恨透了（ㄏㄣˋ ㄊㄡˋ ·ㄌㄜ）
to hate to the utmost degree; to detest

恨鐵不成鋼（ㄏㄣˋ ㄊㄧㄝˇ ㄅㄨˋ ㄔㄥˊ ㄍㄤ）
to be exasperated at a son's failure to make good

恨海（ㄏㄣˋ ㄏㄞˇ）
deep hatred

恨事（ㄏㄣˋ ㄕˋ）
a regrettable thing; something lamented; a matter for regret

恨人（ㄏㄣˋ ㄖㄣˊ）
①a misanthrope or misanthropist ②a sentimental person ③a frustrated man given to regrets

恨入骨髓（ㄏㄣˋ ㄖㄨˋ ㄍㄨˇ ㄙㄨㄟˇ）
to hate to the marrow; to hate with one's soul

恨晚（ㄏㄣˋ ㄨㄢˇ）
to regret that something happened too late 參看「相見恨晚」

恨惡（ㄏㄣˋ ㄨˋ）
to loathe

【恤】 ㄒㄩˋ shiuh xù 1559
(卹) 1. to relieve; to help

2. to sympathize; to be considerate: 我甚體恤他。I understand and sympathize with him.

恤病（ㄒㄩˋ ㄅㄧㄥˋ）
to show sympathy for the sick

恤貧（ㄒㄩˋ ㄆㄧㄣˊ）
to give relief to the poor

恤民（ㄒㄩˋ ㄇㄧㄣˊ）
to be mindful of the people's hardships

恤老（ㄒㄩˋ ㄌㄠˇ）
to relieve the aged

恤嫠（ㄒㄩˋ ㄌㄧˊ）
to relieve widows

恤孤（ㄒㄩˋ ㄍㄨ）
to relieve orphans

恤金（ㄒㄩˋ ㄐㄧㄣ）
relief payment; compensation

恤刑（ㄒㄩˋ ㄒㄧㄥˊ）
very careful in meting out punishment

恤政（ㄒㄩˋ ㄓㄥˋ）
benevolent government

恤然（ㄒㄩˋ ㄖㄢˊ）
startled; astonished

恤養金（ㄒㄩˋ ㄧㄤˇ ㄐㄧㄣ）
a pension

【恪】 ㄎㄜˋ keh kè 1560
(又讀 ㄑㄩㄝˋ chiueh què)
respectful; reverent; to respect; respectfully

恪勤（ㄎㄜˋ ㄑㄧㄣˊ）
cautious and industrious

恪守（ㄎㄜˋ ㄕㄡˇ）
to observe (rules) strictly; scrupulously abide by (a treaty, promise, etc.); carefully obey (laws, orders, tradition)

恪慎（ㄎㄜˋ ㄕㄣˋ）
respectful and cautious; careful; reverent

恪遵（ㄎㄜˋ ㄗㄨㄣ）
to obey or follow (orders, rules, etc.) with respect

【恫】 1. ㄊㄨㄥ tong tōng 1561
pain

恫瘝 or 恫矜（ㄊㄨㄥ ㄍㄨㄢ）
hardship; illness

恫瘝在抱（ㄊㄨㄥ ㄍㄨㄢ ㄗㄞˋ ㄅㄠˋ）
to show intimate concern over the people's hardships

【恫】 2. ㄉㄨㄥˋ donq dòng 1561
to threaten, intimidate, or scare loudly

恫嚇（ㄉㄨㄥˋ ㄏㄜˋ）
to threaten; to intimidate; to scare

恫喝（ㄉㄨㄥˋ ㄏㄜˋ）
to threaten, intimidate, or scare loudly; to browbeat; to bully

恫疑虛喝（ㄉㄨㄥˋ ㄧˊ ㄒㄩ ㄏㄜˋ）
to threaten loudly; to bully; to browbeat

【恇】 ㄎㄨㄤ kuang kuāng 1562
afraid; timid; timorous; fearful

恇懼（ㄎㄨㄤ ㄐㄩˋ）
afraid; fearful; timorous

恇怯（ㄎㄨㄤ ㄑㄧㄝˋ）
timid

【恬】 ㄊㄧㄢˊ tyan tián 1563
quiet; peaceful; undisturbed

恬波（ㄊㄧㄢˊ ㄅㄛ）
calm waters

恬不知恥（ㄊㄧㄢˊ ㄅㄨˋ ㄓ ㄔˇ）
brazen-faced; to be totally devoid of sense of shame; not feel ashamed; to have no sense of shame; to be shameless: 他恬不知恥。He has no sense of shame.

恬不為怪（ㄊㄧㄢˊ ㄅㄨˋ ㄨㄟˊ ㄍㄨㄞˋ）
not surprised at all

恬謐（ㄊㄧㄢˊ ㄇㄧˋ）
tranquil; peaceful; quiet

恬澹 or 恬淡（ㄊㄧㄢˊ ㄉㄢˋ）
indifferent to worldly gain; contented: 他過恬淡生活。He

leads a tranquil life without worldly desires.

退(ㄊㄧˋ ㄊㄨㄟˋ)
contented and reserved; uninterested in wealth and glory

和(ㄊㄧˊ ㄏㄜˊ)
quiet and gentle

靜
undisturbed; having peace of mind; tranquil

然
easygoing; undisturbed; unhurried; unperturbed; calm; nonchalant: 我處之恬然。I remain undisturbed.

逸
free from worry or disturbance; peaceful and leisurely

【恰】 1564
くㄧㄚˋ chiah qià
proper; appropriate; suitable

待(くㄧㄚˋ ㄉㄞ)
just on the point of (doing something)

到好處(くㄧㄚˋ ㄉㄠˋ ㄏㄠˇ ㄔㄨˋ)
neither too much nor too little; just right: 此事恰到好處。The matter is just right.

當(くㄧㄚˋ ㄉㄤˋ)
appropriate; fitting; apt; apposite: 作禮貌上的拜訪是恰當的。It is fitting to make courtesy calls.

好(くㄧㄚˋ ㄏㄠˇ)
①just; exactly: 那恰好是我所要的。That's exactly what I want. ②by coincidence

恰(くㄧㄚˋ くㄧㄚˋ)
①by coincidence ②the chirping of birds ③just; exactly: 它恰恰相反。It is just the opposite. 或 It is exactly the reverse.

巧(くㄧㄚˋ ㄏㄠˇ)
coinciding luckily; by coincidence; by chance; as chance would have it: 昨天恰巧他也在那裡。He happened to be there yesterday, too.

值(くㄧㄚˋ ㄓˊ)
just at the time of

正(くㄧㄚˋ ㄓㄥˋ)
just when

如(くㄧㄚˋ ㄖㄨˊ) or 恰似(くㄧㄚˋ ㄙˋ)
just like; just as if; just as though

恰如其分(くㄧㄚˋ ㄖㄨˊ くㄧˊ ㄈㄣˋ)
just suited or becoming to one's importance; appropriate

恰遇(くㄧㄚˋ ㄩˋ)
to chance upon.

【協】 1565
ㄒㄧㄝˊ shye xié
1. to intimidate
2. fearful and timid
3. same as 脅

【恁】 1566
ㄖㄣˊ renn rèn
1. this; such; so; that
2. how; what; 他恁的大膽! How bold he is!

恁般(ㄖㄣˊ ㄅㄢ)
to such an extent

恁麼(ㄖㄣˊ ˙ㄇㄜ)
①in this way; like this ②what; which

恁的(ㄖㄣˊ ˙ㄉㄜ)
①in this way; to such an extent ②why; how 參看「恁地」

恁地(ㄖㄣˊ ㄉㄧˋ)
①in this way; to such an extent ②how; why: 恁地道他們不是人? Why do you say that they are brutes?

恁時(ㄖㄣˊ ㄕˊ)
when that happens; then

恁時節(ㄖㄣˊ ㄕˊ ㄐㄧㄝˊ)
when that time comes; at that time

【恐】 1567
ㄎㄨㄥˇ koong kǒng
1. to fear; to dread
2. I am afraid.: 消息恐不可靠。I am afraid the news is not reliable.

恐怖(ㄎㄨㄥˇ ㄅㄨˋ)
terror; horror; fear

恐怖病(ㄎㄨㄥˇ ㄅㄨˋ ㄅㄧㄥˋ)
phobia

恐怖分子(ㄎㄨㄥˇ ㄅㄨˋ ㄈㄣ˙ㄗ)
terrorists

恐怖主義(ㄎㄨㄥˇ ㄅㄨˋ ㄓㄨˇ ㄧˋ)
terrorism

恐怖時代(ㄎㄨㄥˇ ㄅㄨˋ ㄕˊ ㄉㄞˋ)
①an age of terror ②the Reign of Terror

恐怕(ㄎㄨㄥˇ ㄆㄚˋ)
(with reference to an unpleasant fact) probably; perhaps; I think; maybe 或 I am afraid that.... 我恐怕不能來。I

am afraid that I cannot come.

恐龍(ㄎㄨㄥˇ ㄌㄨㄥˊ)
a dinosaur

恐嚇 or 恐喝(ㄎㄨㄥˇ ㄏㄜˋ)
to intimidate; to scare; to threaten; to menace; to blackmail

恐嚇罪(ㄎㄨㄥˇ ㄏㄜˋ ㄗㄨㄟˋ)
an offense of blackmail or intimidation

恐慌(ㄎㄨㄥˇ ㄏㄨㄤ)
①panic; panicky ②(economic) depression or crises

恐懼(ㄎㄨㄥˇ ㄐㄩˋ)
fear; dread; fright

恐其(ㄎㄨㄥˇ くㄧˊ)
possibly or probably (with reference to a fearful fact)

【恕】 1568
ㄕㄨˋ shuh shù
1. to forgive; to excuse: 我們寬恕他。We forgave him.
2. Excuse me. 恕難從命。I regret that I cannot comply with your wishes.
3. benevolence

恕不奉陪(ㄕㄨˋ ㄅㄨˋ ㄈㄥˋ ㄆㄟˊ)
I am sorry but I cannot keep you company. 或 Excuse my inability to keep you company.

恕不一一(ㄕㄨˋ ㄅㄨˋ ㄧ ㄧ)
I am sorry I cannot go into details. (a phrase common in correspondence)

恕不遠送(ㄕㄨˋ ㄅㄨˋ ㄩㄢˇ ㄙㄨㄥˋ)
I am sorry I cannot escort you farther. 或 Excuse my inability to escort you farther.

恕道(ㄕㄨˋ ㄉㄠˋ)
the principle of forgiveness; magnanimity; the principle of reciprocity

恕過(ㄕㄨˋ ㄍㄨㄛˋ)
to pardon the mistake; to forgive a fault

恕罪(ㄕㄨˋ ㄗㄨㄟˋ)
to forgive a fault; to pardon an offense; to forgive a sin: 請恕罪。Please forgive my fault.

恕邀(ㄕㄨˋ ㄧㄠ)
Excuse my, or our, informality in requesting your presence. (a conventional phrase

(心 部)

〔心部〕

on an invitation card)

恕宥（ㄕㄨˋ ㄧㄡˋ）
to forgive; to excuse

【恚】 1569
ㄏㄨㄟˋ huey huì
to rage; to anger: 他既愧且恚。He was shamed and angered.

恚憤（ㄏㄨㄟˋ ㄈㄣˋ）
to be enraged; to be indignant

恚怒（ㄏㄨㄟˋ ㄋㄨˋ）
to be enraged; to be indignant; to be furious

恚恨（ㄏㄨㄟˋ ㄏㄣˋ）
to hate vehemently

恚怨（ㄏㄨㄟˋ ㄩㄢˋ）
to resent bitterly

【恝】 1570
ㄐㄧㄚˊ jya jiá
indifferent; unworried; unconcerned

恝置（ㄐㄧㄚˊ ㄓˋ）
to disregard; to neglect; to ignore

【恙】 1571
ㄧㄤˋ yang yàng
1. disease: 我偶感微恙。I felt slightly indisposed.
2. worry

恙蟲（ㄧㄤˋ ㄔㄨㄥˊ）
a chigger or jigger; a redbug

【恣】 1572
1. ㄗˋ tzyh zì
to throw off restraint; to dissipate; to debauch

恣情（ㄗˋ ㄑㄧㄥˊ）
to abandon oneself to passion; to give rein to passion

恣行無忌（ㄗˋ ㄒㄧㄥˊ ㄨˊ ㄐㄧˋ）
to throw off all restraint; to act without the least regard for accepted rules or standards

恣性（ㄗˋ ㄒㄧㄥˋ）
unrestrained behavior

恣縱（ㄗˋ ㄗㄨㄥˋ）
①having no regard for rules; heedless of restraint ②licentious; morally unrestrained; dissolute; libertine

恣肆（ㄗˋ ㄙˋ）
licentious; willful; heedless of restraint

恣睢（ㄗˋ ㄙㄨㄟ）
unscrupulous; unbridled; willful

恣意妄為（ㄗˋ ㄧˋ ㄨㄤˋ ㄨㄟˊ）
to act willfully; to act as one pleases; to act without regard for any authority; to behave unscrupulously

【�006】 1572
2. ㄘˊ tsy cí
參看「恣睢」

恣睢（ㄗˋ ㄙㄨㄟ）
①carefree; unbridled ②extremely conceited

【恩】 1573
ㄣ en ēn
favor; grace; gratitude; kindness; benevolence; mercy; charity: 我向他販恩。I paid a debt of gratitude to him.

恩俸（ㄣ ㄈㄥˋ）
a pension

恩撫金（ㄣ ㄈㄨˇ ㄐㄧㄣ）
the pensions given to the families of those who were killed in action

恩德（ㄣ ㄉㄜˊ）
benevolence; benignity; charity; generosity; kindness; bounty; favor; grace

恩惠在民（ㄣ ㄉㄜˊ ㄗㄞˋ ㄇㄧㄣˊ）
(said of government officials) with benevolence felt by the people

恩典（ㄣ ㄉㄧㄢˇ）
①(in old China) an imperial favor ②a favor

恩同再造（ㄣ ㄊㄨㄥˊ ㄗㄞˋ ㄗㄠˋ）
unusual favor or help rendered to someone in bad luck, which enables him to stand on his own feet again

恩禮（ㄣ ㄌㄧˇ）
gifts and kindness; gracious courtesy

恩禮有加（ㄣ ㄌㄧˇ ㄧㄡˇ ㄐㄧㄚ）
(said of persons in high position) to shower someone with favors and courtesy

恩格爾（ㄣ ㄍㄜˊ ㄦˇ）
Friedrich Engels, 1820-1895, German socialist

恩公（ㄣ ㄍㄨㄥ）
a benefactor

恩科（ㄣ ㄎㄜ）
civil service examinations held on auspicious occasions of the nation such as an imperial wedding, coronation, etc. (as distinct from

regular civil service examinations which were held between fixed intervals)

恩化（ㄣ ㄏㄨㄚˋ）
to reform, influence, or convert (people) by benevolence

恩惠（ㄣ ㄏㄨㄟˋ）
a kind act; kindness; charity; bounty

恩給（ㄣ ㄐㄧˇ）
a pension

恩舊（ㄣ ㄐㄧㄡˋ）
the friends bound by ties lasting through generations

恩將仇報（ㄣ ㄐㄧㄤ ㄔㄡˊ ㄅㄠˋ）
to return evil for good; ungrateful; to return kindness with hatred; to requite kindness with enmity

恩眷（ㄣ ㄐㄩㄢˋ）
imperial favor

恩情（ㄣ ㄑㄧㄥˊ）
loving-kindness; devotion (between friends, teacher and student, husband and wife, etc.); kindness and affection: 父母的恩情說不完。We can never say enough about our parents' devotion for us.

恩幸（ㄣ ㄒㄧㄥˋ）
imperial favor

恩詔（ㄣ ㄓㄠˋ）
an edict proclaiming an imperial act of grace

恩准（ㄣ ㄓㄨㄣˇ）
to grant graciously

恩仇分明（ㄣ ㄔㄡˊ ㄈㄣ ㄇㄧㄥˊ）
to make a clear distinction between kindnesses and wrongs done by others

恩寵（ㄣ ㄔㄨㄥˇ）
the emperor's affection or favor

恩師（ㄣ ㄕ）
a teacher to whom one is greatly indebted; one's beloved or respected teacher

恩赦（ㄣ ㄕㄜˋ）
gracious pardon; amnesty

恩深義重（ㄣ ㄕㄣ ㄧˋ ㄓㄨㄥˋ）
The spiritual debt is deep and great.

恩賞（ㄣ ㄕㄤˇ）
the emperor's reward

恩人（ㄣ ㄖㄣˊ）or 恩主（ㄣ ㄓㄨˇ）
a benefactor; a benefactress

榮(ㄖㄨㄥˊ)
honor granted by the emperor

榮宴(ㄖㄨㄥˊ ㄧㄢˋ)
an imperial banquet in honor of those who have lately passed the Imperial Examination

澤(ㄗㄜˊ)
the pervading benevolence (of the ruler)

賜(ㄙˋ)
① a gift of grace from the emperor ②to bestow (favors)

愛(ㄞˋ)
(said of a married couple) mutual affection; loving; love between husband and wife

愛夫妻(ㄞˋ ㄈㄨ ㄑㄧ)
loving husband and wife; a devoted couple; an affectionate couple

義(ㄧˋ)
spiritual debt; gratitude

廕(ㄧㄣˋ)
the conferment of an official rank on a minister's son as a special favor

威並用(ㄅㄨ ㄨㄟ ㄅㄧㄥˋ ㄩㄥˋ)
to make proper use of both kindness and sternness in dealing with subordinates, subjugated people, etc.; to apply the carrot and stick judiciously

遇(ㄩˋ)
① to treat someone with grace or kindness ② special recognition of the ruler or the superior

怨(ㄩㄢˋ)
① gratitude and grudges ② resentment; grievance: 我不計較個人恩怨。I don't allow myself to be swayed by personal resentment.

恩(ㄋㄩˊ) ¹⁵⁷⁴
ㄋㄩˊ niuh nǚ
ashamed

恩縮(ㄋㄩˊ ㄙㄨㄛˋ)
to recoil on account of shame

息 ¹⁵⁷⁵
ㄒㄧˊ shyi xí
1. a breath
2. news; tidings
3. to stop; to end: 風止雨息。

The wind has ceased and the rain stopped.
4. interest (on money): 我們請求無息貸款。We asked for an interest-free loan.
5. a son
6. to rest: 我們按時作息。We work and rest according to the timetable.

息謗(ㄒㄧˊ ㄅㄤˋ)
to silence slanders

息兵(ㄒㄧˊ ㄅㄧㄥ)or 息戰(ㄒㄧˊ ㄓㄢˋ)
to stop fighting; to end hostilities

息婦 or 媳婦(ㄒㄧˊ ㄈㄨˋ)
① a daughter-in-law ② wife

息燈 or 熄燈(ㄒㄧˊ ㄉㄥ)
to put out the light; to turn off the light

息念頭(ㄒㄧˊ ㄋㄧㄢˋ ㄊㄡˊ)
to give up the idea

息怒(ㄒㄧˊ ㄋㄨˋ)
to let one's anger cool off: 請息怒。Please let your anger cool off. 或 Please calm your anger.

息干戈(ㄒㄧˊ ㄍㄢ ㄍㄜ)
to end hostilities; to stop fighting: 兩國互息干戈。Two nations ended hostilities

息款(ㄒㄧˊ ㄎㄨㄢˇ)or 息金(ㄒㄧˊ ㄐㄧㄣ) or 息錢(ㄒㄧˊ ㄑㄧㄢˊ)
interest (on money)

息火 or 熄火(ㄒㄧˊ ㄏㄨㄛˇ)
to put out a fire

息跡(ㄒㄧˊ ㄐㄧ)or 息影(ㄒㄧˊ ㄧㄥˇ)
to live in retirement

息交絕遊(ㄒㄧˊ ㄐㄧㄠ ㄐㄩㄝˊ ㄧㄡˊ)
to break off intercourse with the world; to go into seclusion

息肩(ㄒㄧˊ ㄐㄧㄢ)
to put down one's burden; to be relieved of a responsibility

息息相關(ㄒㄧˊ ㄒㄧˊ ㄒㄧㄤ ㄍㄨㄢ)
related as closely as each breath is to the next; to be closely bound up

息心(ㄒㄧˊ ㄒㄧㄣ)
to set one's heart at rest

息燭 or 熄燭(ㄒㄧˊ ㄓㄨˊ)
to blow out the candle

息事(ㄒㄧˊ ㄕˋ)
to settle a matter

息事寧人(ㄒㄧˊ ㄕˋ ㄋㄧㄥˊ ㄖㄣˊ)
to settle disputes and bring about peace: 我們應息事寧人。We should settle our disputes and bring about peace among us.

息災延命(ㄒㄧˊ ㄗㄞ ㄧㄢˊ ㄇㄧㄥˋ)
to end disasters and prolong lives

息訟(ㄒㄧˊ ㄙㄨㄥˋ)
to terminate a lawsuit

息業(ㄒㄧˊ ㄧㄝˋ)
to stop one's trade or business

恭 ¹⁵⁷⁶
《ㄨㄥ gong gōng
respectful; reverent; deferential: 他對年齡較大的人總是恭敬。He is always respectful to older people.

恭奉(《ㄨㄥ ㄈㄥˋ)
to accept with respect

恭讀(《ㄨㄥ ㄉㄨˊ)
to read respectfully

恭賀(《ㄨㄥ ㄏㄜˋ)
I, or we, congratulate you upon; to congratulate; congratulation: 請接受我的恭賀。Please accept my congratulations.

恭賀新禧(《ㄨㄥ ㄏㄜˋ ㄒㄧㄣ ㄒㄧˇ)
Best wishes for a Happy New Year. 或 Happy New Year.

恭候(《ㄨㄥ ㄏㄡˋ)
to await respectfully

恭謹(《ㄨㄥ ㄐㄧㄣˇ)
respectfully serious

恭敬(《ㄨㄥ ㄐㄧㄥˋ)or 恭敬敬敬(《ㄨㄥ 《ㄨㄥ ㄐㄧㄥˋ)
respectful; reverent; deferential (also used adverbially): 我們恭恭敬敬地向老師學習。We learned respectfully from our teachers.

恭敬不如從命(《ㄨㄥ ㄐㄧㄥˋ ㄅㄨˋ ㄖㄨˊ ㄘㄨㄥˊ ㄇㄧㄥˋ)
Obedience is a better way of showing respect than outward reverence.

恭讓(《ㄨㄥ ㄖㄤˋ)
respect and modesty

恭請(《ㄨㄥ ㄑㄧㄥˇ)
to invite respectfully; to invite with respect

恭喜(《ㄨㄥ ㄒㄧˇ)
①Congratulations! ②to work: 你在那裡恭喜? Where are you

〔心

部〕

【心部】

working?

恭喜發財（《ㄨㄥ ㄒㄧ ㄈㄚ ㄘㄞ）
(a familiar Lunar New Year's greeting) Congratulations and be prosperous.

恭祝（《ㄨㄥ ㄓㄨˋ）
I, or we, congratulate you upon

恭順（《ㄨㄥ ㄕㄨㄣˋ）
obedient; docile; submissive; allegiance

恭謁（《ㄨㄥ ㄧㄝˋ）
to pay a call with respect

恭迎（《ㄨㄥ ㄧㄥˊ）
to welcome respectfully

恭維 or 恭惟（《ㄨㄥ ㄨㄟˊ）
to pay compliments; to praise; to flatter: 他們非常恭維他。They paid him a high compliment.

【恥】 1577
　（ㄔˇ chyy chǐ
shame; disgrace; humiliation; to feel ashamed: 他恥為人師。He is ashamed to be called a teacher.

恥骨（ㄔˇ ㄍㄨˇ）
(anatomy) the pubic bone; a pubis

恥笑（ㄔˇ ㄒㄧㄠˋ）
to laugh at; to ridicule; to sneer at; to mock; to scoff at

恥辱（ㄔˇ ㄖㄨˋ）
shame; disgrace; humiliation

恥與為伍（ㄔˇ ㄩˇ ㄨㄟˊ ㄨˇ）
to feel ashamed to be in (their, his) company

【恉】 1578
　ㄓ jyy zhǐ
same as 旨—purport; meaning; intention

七畫

【悃】 1579
　ㄎㄨㄣˇ koen kǔn
honest; sincere

悃愊無華（ㄎㄨㄣˇ ㄅㄧˋ ㄨˊ ㄏㄨㄚˊ）
honest and simple

悃款（ㄎㄨㄣˇ ㄎㄨㄢˇ）
① single-minded ② sincere

悃誠（ㄎㄨㄣˇ ㄔㄥˊ）
sincere

【悁】 1580
1. ㄐㄩㄢ jiuann
juān

impatient; irritable

悁急（ㄐㄩㄢ ㄐㄧˊ）
impatient; irritable; anxious; fretful; restless

【悁】 1580
2. ㄐㄩㄢˋ jiuan
juàn

indignant; angry

悁忿（ㄐㄩㄢˋ ㄈㄣˋ）
angry; enraged; indignant

悁悁（ㄐㄩㄢˋ ㄐㄩㄢˋ）
① sad; unhappy; worried; fretting ② angry; irritable

【悄】 1581
　（ㄑㄧㄠˇ cheau qiǎo
quiet

悄悄地（ㄑㄧㄠˇ ㄑㄧㄠˇ·ㄉㄜ）
stealthily; secretly; in a clandestine way; quietly: 我悄悄地走過去。I walked over quietly.

悄聲（ㄑㄧㄠˇ ㄕㄥ）
quietly; in a low voice

悄然（ㄑㄧㄠˇ ㄖㄢˊ）
① quietly: 他悄然離去。He left quietly. ② sorrowfully: 她悄然淚下。She shed tears sorrowfully.

悄語（ㄑㄧㄠˇ ㄩˇ）
to talk in a low voice; to speak softly; to whisper

【悅】 1582
　ㄩㄝˋ yueh yuè
to delight; to gratify; to please; contented; pleased; gratified; happy; happily; glad; gladly: 他取悅於人。He tried to please others.

悅目（ㄩㄝˋ ㄇㄨˋ）
pleasant to the eye; having a pleasant appearance

悅服（ㄩㄝˋ ㄈㄨˊ）
to concede or submit willingly

悅口（ㄩㄝˋ ㄎㄡˇ）
tasty; savory; palatable

悅心（ㄩㄝˋ ㄒㄧㄣ）
to gladden; to cheer

悅人（ㄩㄝˋ ㄖㄣˊ）
pleasant; pleasing; delightful

悅澤（ㄩㄝˋ ㄗㄜˊ）
pleasantly bright; gorgeous

悅從（ㄩㄝˋ ㄘㄨㄥˊ）
to follow or submit willingly

悅色（ㄩㄝˋ ㄙㄜˋ）
a happy look or expression

悅耳（ㄩㄝˋ ㄦˇ）
pleasant to the ear; musica 她的歌聲悅耳。Her singing pleasant.

悅意（ㄩㄝˋ ㄧˋ）
① pleasantness; agreeable ness ② an expression of ha piness

悅懌（ㄩㄝˋ ㄧˋ）
delighted; pleased; happy

【悌】 1583
　ㄊㄧˋ tih tì
to show brotherly love; lov and respect for one's elde brother

悌睦（ㄊㄧˋ ㄇㄨˋ）
to live at peace as brothers

悌友（ㄊㄧˋ ㄧㄡˇ）
to be kind to friends; to show brotherly love fo friends

【悔】 1584
　ㄏㄨㄟˇ hoei huǐ
to regret; to repent; remors

悔不當初（ㄏㄨㄟˇ ㄅㄨˋ ㄉㄤ ㄔㄨ）
to regret a previous mistak

悔改（ㄏㄨㄟˇ ㄍㄞˇ）
to repent of '(a sin); to b repentant of; to repent an mend one's ways

悔過（ㄏㄨㄟˇ ㄍㄨㄛˋ）
to show penitence; to b penitent; to be repentant: 悔過自新。He repented an turned over a new leaf.

悔過書（ㄏㄨㄟˇ ㄍㄨㄛˋ ㄕㄨ）
a written statement o repentance pledging not t commit the same offens again (a form of punish ment)

悔恨（ㄏㄨㄟˇ ㄏㄣˋ）
to feel remorse for; to re gret; remorse

悔禍（ㄏㄨㄟˇ ㄏㄨㄛˋ）
to wish the disaster woul not be repeated

悔氣（ㄏㄨㄟˇ ㄑㄧˋ）
bad luck

悔心（ㄏㄨㄟˇ ㄒㄧㄣ）
penitence

悔之已晚（ㄏㄨㄟˇ ㄓ ㄧˇ ㄨㄢˇ）
It is too late to repent o regret.

悔之晚矣（ㄏㄨㄟˇ ㄓ ㄨㄢˇ ㄧˇ）
It will be too late to regret (often used in warning o

dissuading somebody from doing something)

悔罪 (ㄏㄨㄟ ㄗㄨㄟˋ)
to repent of a sin; to show repentance; to show penitence

尤 (ㄏㄨㄟ ㄧㄡˊ)
a cause for self-reproach

悔悟 (ㄏㄨㄟ ㄨˋ)
to awake from sin; to repent: 他悔悟他的罪過。He repented of his sin.

【悒】 1585
ㄧ yih yì
troubled in the mind; unhappy

悒悶 (ㄧ ㄇㄣˋ)
depressed; low-spirited

悒憤 (ㄧ ㄈㄣˋ)
unhappy with anger; to resent

悒悒 (ㄧ ㄧˋ)
sad; grieved; worried; depressed; unhappy: 他悒悒不樂。He felt depressed.

悒怏 (ㄧ ㄧㄤ)
sad; grieved; unhappy; dejected; depressed

悒鬱 (ㄧ ㄩˋ)
melancholy; disconsolate; unhappy

【悍】 1586
ㄏㄢˋ hann hàn
1. violent; fierce; cruel
2. brave; audacious: 他短小精悍。He is short but brave.
3. stubborn

悍婦 (ㄏㄢˋ ㄈㄨˋ)
a shrew; a virago; a termagant

悍戾 (ㄏㄢˋ ㄌㄧˋ)
cruel; atrocious

悍梗 (ㄏㄢˋ ㄍㄥˇ)
stubbornly defiant; recalcitrant

悍將 (ㄏㄢˋ ㄐㄧㄤ)
① a brave general ② a recalcitrant general

悍妻 (ㄏㄢˋ ㄑㄧ)
a shrewish wife

悍戆 (ㄏㄢˋ ㄓㄨㄤˋ)
fierce and simple-minded

悍室 (ㄏㄢˋ ㄕˋ)
a shrewish wife

悍然 (ㄏㄢˋ ㄖㄢˊ)
outrageously; rudely; unreasonably

悍然不顧 (ㄏㄢˋ ㄖㄢˊ ㄅㄨˋ ㄍㄨˋ)
to ignore (advice) stubbornly

悍藥 (ㄏㄢˋ ㄧㄠˋ)
a violent medicine; a drastic remedy

【悚】 1587
ㄙㄨㄥˇ soong sǒng
fearful; terrified; frightened

悚惕 (ㄙㄨㄥˇ ㄊㄧˋ)
fearful

悚慄 (ㄙㄨㄥˇ ㄌㄧˋ)or悚惶 (ㄙㄨㄥˇ ㄏㄨㄤˊ)or悚懼 (ㄙㄨㄥˇ ㄐㄩˋ)
to tremble with fear; frightened; terrified

悚然 (ㄙㄨㄥˇ ㄖㄢˊ)
in terror; terror-stricken: 毛骨悚然 to be in terror with one's hair standing on end

【悛】 1588
ㄑㄩㄢ chiuan quān
to repent; to reform: 他怙惡不悛。He was incorrigible and refused to repent.

悛改 (ㄑㄩㄢ ㄍㄞˇ)
to reform oneself; to repent of one's sin

悛悔 (ㄑㄩㄢ ㄏㄨㄟˇ)
to reform oneself; to repent of one's sin

【悖】 1589
ㄅㄟˋ bey bèi
to go against; to go counter to; to revolt against; contrary to

悖叛 (ㄅㄟˋ ㄆㄢˋ)
to revolt; to rebel

悖謾 (ㄅㄟˋ ㄇㄢˊ)
arrogantly impolite; disrespectful; to show irreverence

悖謬 (ㄅㄟˋ ㄇㄧㄡˋ)
absurd; irrational; unreasonable; preposterous

悖德 (ㄅㄟˋ ㄉㄜˊ)
to be immoral

悖逆 (ㄅㄟˋ ㄋㄧˋ)
to revolt; to rebel: 他悖逆不道。He revolted against established values.

悖理 (ㄅㄟˋ ㄌㄧˇ)
absurd; unreasonable; irrational; contrary to reason

悖禮 (ㄅㄟˋ ㄌㄧˇ)
uncivil; impolite; contrary to etiquette: 他的行為悖禮。His behavior was uncivil.

悖戾 (ㄅㄟˋ ㄌㄧˋ)
to deviate from accepted rules or standards; to be perverse

悖亂 (ㄅㄟˋ ㄌㄨㄢˋ)
revolt; rebellion; sedition

悖棄 (ㄅㄟˋ ㄑㄧˋ)
to turn away from something in revolt

悖入悖出 (ㄅㄟˋ ㄖㄨˋ ㄅㄟˋ ㄔㄨ)
Things ill-gotten are ill-spent. 或 Evil begets evil.

【悟】 1590
ㄨˋ wuh wù
to become aware of; to realize; to awake to; to comprehend

悟道 (ㄨˋ ㄉㄠˋ)
(Buddhism) to awake to Truth

悟空 (ㄨˋ ㄎㄨㄥ)
① (Buddhism) to awake to the nihility of life ② name of a fictitious monkey with supernatural powers

悟性 (ㄨˋ ㄒㄧㄥˋ)
the capacity for understanding; understanding; the power of understanding; the power of insight

悟禪 (ㄨˋ ㄔㄢˊ)
to come to understand the principle of Zen (禪)

【悝】 1591
1. ㄌㄧˇ lii lǐ
sad; grieved; worried

【悝】 1591
2. ㄎㄨㄟ kuei kuī
to ridicule

【悠】 1592
ㄧㄡ iou yōu
1. far; long; vast; extensive
2. sad; pensive; meditative
3. gentle; slow; soft
4. to swing

悠邈 (ㄧㄡ ㄇㄧㄠˋ)
far or distant (in space or time)

悠緬 (ㄧㄡ ㄇㄧㄢˇ)
far or distant (in space or time)

悠忽 (ㄧㄡ ㄏㄨ)
to idle away the time; lazy and idle

悠長 (ㄧㄡ ㄔㄤˊ)or悠長 (ㄧㄡ ㄓㄤˇ)
long in time

悠閒 (ㄧㄡ ㄒㄧㄢˊ)

（心部）

（心

部）

leisurely; unrestrained; unhurried: 他悠閒地工作。He worked leisurely.

悠悠
①to refrain from excesses ②(dialect) to take things easy

悠然
unhurriedly; in a leisurely manner; naturally

悠哉悠哉
①anxiously ②free from restraint; carefree

悠悠
①leisurely; unhurried; slow: 他悠悠自得。He was leisurely and content. ②far or vast (in space or time) ③meditative; pensive; sad ④long; distant; remote

悠悠蕩蕩
drifting gently

悠悠忽忽
①spending time idly ②to be in a trance

悠悠蒼天
O thou vast and azure Heaven！

悠揚
①flowing gently sometimes high, sometimes low (as sound); melodious ②extending far (as scenery)

悠颺
(said of wind) rising gently

悠遠
distant; far (in time or space): 他聆聽那些悠遠的往事。He listened to those events of the distant past.

【悉】 1593 ㄒㄧ shi ㄒㄧ
1. to know
2. all; whole; total; entire: 此悉爲我所有。This was all taken by me.

悉力
with all one's strength; with might and main

悉皆
altogether; entirely; without exception

悉心
with one's whole heart; with concentrated effort; to take the utmost care

悉數
all; the entire sum (of money): 我們將悉數奉還。We will return all that has been borrowed.

悉索敝賦
to mobilize all military forces for a punitive war

【患】 1594 ㄏㄨㄢˋ huann huàn
1. suffering; adversity; disaster; peril: 我們應當防患於未然。We ought to take preventive measures of disaster.
2. trouble; worry: 何患之有。There is no need to worry.
3. to be troubled by; to be worried about

患病
to get sick; to fall ill

患部
(said of wounds or skin diseases) the infected part

患得患失
to worry about worldly gain and loss: 他患得患失的。He was swayed by considerations of gain and loss.

患難
suffering; distress; adversity; trouble: 他是一個可以共患難的人。He is a man who can be trusted in times of trouble.

患難之交
the friendship cemented in adversity

患寡患貧
to be concerned over the nation's dwindling population and increasing poverty

患苦
distress; adversity; suffering

患者
a patient (at a hospital): 那醫生有許多位患者。The doctor has a large number of patients.

患處
the infected part; the wounded part

【悤】 1595 (匆) ㄘㄨㄥ tsong cōng
excited; hurried; agitated

悤忙 or 悤卒 or 悤遽
hurried; hasty; flurried

悤悤
①hurriedly; hastily; in haste ②obviously; apparently

【您】 1596 ㄋㄧㄣˊ nin nín
a deferential form of "你"

八畫

【悱】 1597 ㄈㄟ feei fěi
1. inarticulate; unable to give vent to one's emotion; unable to explain one's self; to be at a loss for words
2. sorrowful

悱�француз's
sadness kept to oneself; peeved; infuriated; vexed

悱惻
affected by sorrow; sad at heart; sorrowful 參看「纏綿悱惻」

【悵】 1598 ㄔㄤˋ chang chàng
disappointed; frustrated; dissatisfied; sorry

悵恨
bitterness from disappointment

悵悵
unhappy because of disappointment

悵然
disappointed: 我悵然若失。I felt disappointed.

悵恨
to regret (the failure of a hope) sorrowfully

悵惘
depressed; in low spirits; distracted

悵望
to long pensively or wistfully

【悸】 1599 ㄐㄧˋ jih jì
1. palpitation of the heart
2. fear: 我心有餘悸。I had a lingering fear.

悸動
to palpitate with terror

【悻】 1600 ㄒㄧㄥˇ shing xǐng
angry; indignant; enraged

悻悻然 or 悻悻
angry; enraged; huffish; anger; huff: 他悻悻而去。He

went away angry.

直直 (ㄒㄧㄥ ㄓˊ)
blunt; bluff; brusque

【悴】 1601 ㄘㄨㄟˋ tsuey cuì

1. haggard; worn-out; tired
out: 他滿面憔悴之容。He has
a haggard face.

2. worried; sad

悴 (ㄘㄨㄟˊ ㄖㄨㄛˋ)
weakened; enfeebled; impoverished

悴暧 (ㄘㄨㄟˋ ㄒㄧㄚ)
needy and lowly

悴族 (ㄘㄨㄟˋ ㄗㄨˊ)
a family or clan that has
seen better days

【悼】 1602 ㄉㄠˋ daw dào
to mourn (for or over); to
lament; to regret; to grieve:
我們哀悼死者。We mourned
for the dead.

悼痛 (ㄉㄠˋ ㄊㄨㄥˋ)
to mourn in anguish

悼念 (ㄉㄠˋ ㄋㄧㄢˋ)
to mourn; to grieve over

悼歌 (ㄉㄠˋ ㄍㄜ)
a funeral hymn; a dirge

悼惜 (ㄉㄠˋ ㄒㄧˊ)
to deplore or lament (one's
death): 他悼惜摯友。He de-
plored the loss of his dear
friend.

悼傷 (ㄉㄠˋ ㄕㄤ)
to remember (the deceased)
with sorrow

悼詞 (ㄉㄠˋ ㄘˊ)
a memorial speech

悼亡 (ㄉㄠˋ ㄨㄤˊ)
to be bereaved of one's wife

【悾】 1603 ㄎㄨㄥ kong kōng
sincere; candid

悾悾 (ㄎㄨㄥ ㄎㄨㄥ)
①sincere; candid ②simple-
minded

【悽】 1604 ㄑㄧ chi qī

1. grieved; sorrowful; afflicted

2. tragic; pathetic; pitiful;
grievous

悽涼 (ㄑㄧ ㄌㄧㄤˊ)
dreary; desolate: 戰爭帶來滿
目悽涼。The war brought des-
olation all round.

悽苦 (ㄑㄧ ㄎㄨˇ)
suffering tragically

悽惶 (ㄑㄧ ㄏㄨㄤˊ)
①sorrowful and apprehen-
sive ②in a hurry

悽戚 (ㄑㄧ ㄑㄧ)
tragically unhappy

悽悽 (ㄑㄧ ㄑㄧ)
pathetic; pitiful; grievous

悽惶惶 (ㄑㄧ ㄏㄨㄤˊ ㄏㄨㄤˊ)
hurriedly; hastily

悽切 (ㄑㄧ ㄑㄧㄝ)
pathetic; pitiful; saddening;
grievous

悽楚 (ㄑㄧ ㄔㄨˇ)
pathetic; pitiful; saddening;
grievous: 那是一種悽楚的景
象。It is a pitiful sight.

悽愴 (ㄑㄧ ㄔㄨㄤˋ)
①pathetic; pitiful; saddening ②cold; dreary; desolate

悽傷 (ㄑㄧ ㄕㄤ)
sad; sorrowful

悽然 (ㄑㄧ ㄖㄢˊ)
sad; sorrowful: 他悽然淚下。
He shed tears in sadness.

悽惻 (ㄑㄧ ㄘㄜˋ)
sad; sorrowful

悽慘 (ㄑㄧ ㄘㄢˇ)
tragic; heartrending

悽婉 (ㄑㄧ ㄨㄢˇ)
pathetic or pitiful (said
especially of sounds); plaintive

悽惘 (ㄑㄧ ㄨㄤˇ)
sad and dejected

【惆】 1605 ㄔㄡˊ chour chóu

1. regretful; rueful; disconsolate; melancholy

2. disappointed; frustrated

惆悵 (ㄔㄡˊ ㄔㄤˋ)
rueful; regretful; to be saddened

惆然 (ㄔㄡˊ ㄖㄢˊ)
regretful; wistful; disappointed; downcast; heavy-
hearted

惆怳 (ㄔㄡˊ ㄨㄤˇ)
regretful; wistful

【情】 1606 ㄑㄧㄥˊ chyng qíng

1. feelings; emotions; sentiments: 天理人情 law of
nature and feelings of a man

2. fact; detail; situation; condition

3. love; affection; passion: 父母
親情深似海。Parents' affec-

tion for their children is as
deep as the ocean.

4. nature; reason

情報 (ㄑㄧㄥˊ ㄅㄠˋ)
information; intelligence;
reports: 這陌生人刺探情報。
The stranger pried for information.

情報司 (ㄑㄧㄥˊ ㄅㄠˋ ㄙ)
Department of Information,
Ministry of Foreign Affairs

情報網 (ㄑㄧㄥˊ ㄅㄠˋ ㄨㄤˇ)
an intelligent network

情報員 (ㄑㄧㄥˊ ㄅㄠˋ ㄩㄢˊ)
a secret agent; an intelligence agent

情弊 (ㄑㄧㄥˊ ㄅㄧˋ)
dishonest practices; irregularities

情不自禁 (ㄑㄧㄥˊ ㄅㄨˋ ㄗˋ ㄐㄧㄣ)
to be seized with an
impulse; to feel an irresistible impulse

情貌 (ㄑㄧㄥˊ ㄇㄠˋ)
internal and external reverence or loyalty

情面 (ㄑㄧㄥˊ ㄇㄧㄢˋ)
①friendship; regard for
others ②face (self-respect,
good name, reputation); feelings; sensibilities: 請給我留情
面。Please spare my feelings.

情難卻 (ㄑㄧㄥˊ ㄋㄢˊ ㄑㄩㄝˋ)
hard to refuse or decline for
the sake of friendship or
face

情分 (ㄑㄧㄥˊ ㄈㄣˋ)
①friendship ②good inten-
tions; good will; solicitude

情夫 (ㄑㄧㄥˊ ㄈㄨ)
the paramour of a married
woman

情婦 (ㄑㄧㄥˊ ㄈㄨˋ)
a mistress; the other woman

情竇初開 (ㄑㄧㄥˊ ㄉㄡˋ ㄔㄨ ㄎㄞ)
(said of girls) to reach
puberty; the time when a
girl becomes sex-conscious;
first awaking of love

情敵 (ㄑㄧㄥˊ ㄉㄧˊ)
a rival in a love affair

情調 (ㄑㄧㄥˊ ㄉㄧㄠˋ)
①a mood; taste; an atmos-
phere ②（psychology）af-
fective feeling tone

情態 (ㄑㄧㄥˊ ㄊㄞˋ)
①a situation; a condition ②

【心
部】

（心
部）

情投意合（ㄑㄧㄥ ㄊㄡ ㄧˋ ㄏㄜˊ）
to be congenial; to agree in
tastes and temperament: 我
們倆情投意合。We both found
each other congenial.

情天恨海（ㄑㄧㄥ ㄊㄧㄢ ㄏㄣˋ ㄏㄞˇ）
the deep love or regret
between men and women

情同手足（ㄑㄧㄥ ㄊㄨㄥˊ ㄕㄡˇ ㄗㄨˊ）
to be attached to each other
like brothers; with brotherly
love for each other

情濃（ㄑㄧㄥ ㄋㄨㄥˊ）
strong affection

情累（ㄑㄧㄥ ㄌㄟˇ）
the burden of love

情郎（ㄑㄧㄥ ㄌㄤˊ）
a girl's lover

情理（ㄑㄧㄥ ㄌㄧˇ）
reason; common sense

情理難容（ㄑㄧㄥ ㄌㄧˇ ㄋㄢˊ ㄖㄨㄥˊ）
contrary to reason or common sense; preposterous;
absurd

情侶（ㄑㄧㄥ ㄌㄩˇ）
lovers

情歌（ㄑㄧㄥ ㄍㄜ）
a love song

情甘（ㄑㄧㄥ ㄍㄢ）
willing; voluntary: 我情甘等
待。I am willing to wait.

情感（ㄑㄧㄥ ㄍㄢˇ）
emotions; feelings; frame of
mind; affection; sentiments;
friendship between two persons

情感衝動（ㄑㄧㄥ ㄍㄢˇ ㄔㄨㄥ ㄉㄨㄥˋ）
an emotional impulse; an
outburst of emotion

情況（ㄑㄧㄥ ㄎㄨㄤˋ）
① a situation; state of
affairs; circumstances: 他們
的情況如何？How do matters
stand with them? ② military
situation

情況不明（ㄑㄧㄥ ㄎㄨㄤˋ ㄅㄨˋ ㄇㄧㄥˊ）
the situation unknown

情海（ㄑㄧㄥ ㄏㄞˇ）
deep love; the vast, tumultuous sea of love between men
and women

情好（ㄑㄧㄥ ㄏㄠˇ）
an attachment; friendship

情話（ㄑㄧㄥ ㄏㄨㄚˋ）
① whispers of love; sweet
nothings; lovers' prattle ②

intimate talks or words;
hearty talks

情話綿綿（ㄑㄧㄥ ㄏㄨㄚˋ ㄇㄧㄢˊ ㄇㄧㄢˊ）
occupied with endless whispers of love

情火（ㄑㄧㄥ ㄏㄨㄛˇ）or 情焰（ㄑㄧㄥ
ㄧㄢˋ）
the flames of love

情懷（ㄑㄧㄥ ㄏㄨㄞˊ）
a mood; feelings

情急智生（ㄑㄧㄥ ㄐㄧˊ ㄓˋ ㄕㄥ）
Good ideas come in time of
crisis.

情節（ㄑㄧㄥ ㄐㄧㄝˊ）
① a plot (of a play, novel,
etc.) ② details (of an affair
or event); circumstances

情景（ㄑㄧㄥ ㄐㄧㄥˇ）
a scene; a sight: 有一場感人
的情景。There is a moving
sight.

情境（ㄑㄧㄥ ㄐㄧㄥˋ）
circumstances; a situation

情趣（ㄑㄧㄥ ㄑㄩˋ）
① quiet appeal to the emotions; sentiment; interest: 這
首詩寫得很有情趣。This poem
is full of interest. ② temperament and interest: 他們情趣
相投。They are temperamen-
tally compatible.

情見乎辭（ㄑㄧㄥ ㄐㄧㄢˋ ㄏㄨ ㄘˊ）
The feeling or sincerity is
alive in the words.

情性（ㄑㄧㄥ ㄒㄧㄥˋ）
temperament — the real nature or character

情形（ㄑㄧㄥ ㄒㄧㄥˊ）
a situation; circumstances;
state of affairs; conditions

情緒（ㄑㄧㄥ ㄒㄩˋ）
① emotions; feelings; spirits;
a mood: 他們情緒低落。They
are in low spirits. ② depression; the sulks

情知（ㄑㄧㄥ ㄓ）
to know for sure (said of
something going on secretly
or before it takes place)

情致（ㄑㄧㄥ ㄓˋ）
effect on the emotions;
appeal

情意纏綿（ㄑㄧㄥ ㄧˋ ㄔㄢˊ ㄇㄧㄢˊ）
(said of a poem, story, etc.)
to have a delicate lasting
effect on the emotions

情至義盡（ㄑㄧㄥ ㄓˋ ㄧˋ ㄐㄧㄣˋ）

with entire sincerity

情狀（ㄑㄧㄥ ㄓㄨㄤˋ）
a situation: 他發現自己處於危
險的情狀。He found himself
in a dangerous situation.

情場（ㄑㄧㄥ ㄔㄤˇ）
the arena of love

情場老手（ㄑㄧㄥ ㄔㄤˇ ㄌㄠˇ ㄕㄡˇ）
a skirt chaser

情場失意（ㄑㄧㄥ ㄔㄤˇ ㄕ ㄧˋ）
frustrated in love; jilted: 他
最近在情場失意。Recently he
was frustrated in love.

情腸（ㄑㄧㄥ ㄔㄤˊ）
a loving heart

情長紙短（ㄑㄧㄥ ㄔㄤˊ ㄓˇ ㄉㄨㄢˇ）
(a cliché in correspon-
dence) The paper is too
short to contain what I have
to say.

情詩（ㄑㄧㄥ ㄕ）
amatory poems; love poems

情實（ㄑㄧㄥ ㄕˊ）
① facts of an affair or case
② The crime has been con-
firmed.

情史（ㄑㄧㄥ ㄕˇ）
a love story

情事（ㄑㄧㄥ ㄕˋ）
the facts

情勢（ㄑㄧㄥ ㄕˋ）
a situation; the state of
affairs: 情勢危急。This situa-
tion is dangerous.

情殺（ㄑㄧㄥ ㄕㄚ）
murder caused by love
entanglement

情深似海（ㄑㄧㄥ ㄕㄣ ㄙˋ ㄏㄞˇ）
(usually said of parental
love) Love is as deep as
the sea.

情商（ㄑㄧㄥ ㄕㄤ）
to ask for a favor as a
friend

情書（ㄑㄧㄥ ㄕㄨ）
a love letter; a billet-doux

情人（ㄑㄧㄥ ㄖㄣˊ）
a paramour, sweetheart or
lover

情人節（ㄑㄧㄥ ㄖㄣˊ ㄐㄧㄝˊ）
St. Valentine's Day

情人眼裏出西施（ㄑㄧㄥ ㄖㄣˊ ㄧㄢˇ
ㄌㄧˇ ㄔㄨ ㄒㄧ ㄕ）
Love makes one blind to all
imperfections. 或 Beauty is
in the eye of the beholder.

情操(ㄑㄧㄥ ㄘㄠ)
①sentiment (connoting high-brow and complicated sentiment) ②noble thoughts and feelings

情絲不斷(ㄑㄧㄥ ㄙ ㄅㄨ ㄉㄨㄢ)
The ties of love remain unbroken.

情死(ㄑㄧㄥ ㄙ)
martyrdom to love; to commit suicide for the sake of love

情愫 or 情素(ㄑㄧㄥ ㄙㄨ)
innermost feelings

情愛(ㄑㄧㄥ ㄞ)
love (between men and women)

情誼(ㄑㄧㄥ ㄧ)
friendly relations; friendship; amity

情感(ㄑㄧㄥ ㄍㄢ)
feeling; sentiment; affection

情意綿綿(ㄑㄧㄥ ㄧ ㄇㄧㄢ ㄇㄧㄢ)
long-lasting love expressing itself in a subdued but sweet form

情由(ㄑㄧㄥ ㄧㄡ)
reason; cause

情有可原(ㄑㄧㄥ ㄧㄡ ㄎㄜˇ ㄩㄢˊ)
pardonable; excusable; under extenuating circumstances

情有所鍾(ㄑㄧㄥ ㄧㄡˇ ㄙㄨㄛˇ ㄓㄨㄥ)
to have already had a lover in one's heart

情文並茂(ㄑㄧㄥ ㄨㄣˊ ㄅㄧㄥ ㄇㄠˋ)
(said of a composition) rich in feelings and eloquent in expression

情網(ㄑㄧㄥ ㄨㄤˇ)
the cobweb of love; the snare of love; 她陷入情網。
She fell into the cobweb of love.

情慾 or 情欲(ㄑㄧㄥ ㄩ)
passion; sensual or carnal desire; lust; eroticism

情願(ㄑㄧㄥ ㄩㄢˋ)
①to be willing ②would rather

【惇】 1607
ㄉㄨㄣ duen dūn
sincere; kind; generous

惇惇(ㄉㄨㄣ ㄉㄨㄣ)
kind; generous; sincere

惇惠(ㄉㄨㄣ ㄏㄨㄟˋ)
benign; benignant

惇誨(ㄉㄨㄣ ㄏㄨㄟ`)

to teach kindly

【惋】 1608
ㄨㄢˇ wann wǎn
1. to regret
2. to be alarmed

惋歎(ㄨㄢˇ ㄊㄢˋ)
to regret; to deplore

惋慟(ㄨㄢˇ ㄊㄨㄥˋ)
to deplore; to lament

惋惜(ㄨㄢˇ ㄒㄧ)
to feel sorry for (a loss, etc.); to regret

惋傷(ㄨㄢˇ ㄕㄤ)
to regret sorrowfully

惋愕(ㄨㄢˇ ㄜˋ)
to be alarmed; to be astonished

【惕】 1609
ㄊㄧˋ tih tì
1. cautious; careful; prudent; watchout; to be on the alert
2. afraid
3. anxious

惕惕(ㄊㄧˋ ㄊㄧˋ)
apprehensive; fearful

惕厲(ㄊㄧˋ ㄌㄧˋ)
to exercise caution and discipline

惕息(ㄊㄧˋ ㄒㄧˊ)
to pant from fear or anxiety

【惓】 1610
ㄑㄩㄢˊ chyuan quán
sincere; candid

惓惓(ㄑㄩㄢˊ ㄑㄩㄢˊ)
sincere; candid

惓惓於懷(ㄑㄩㄢˊ ㄑㄩㄢˊ ㄩˊ ㄏㄨㄞˊ)
to remember something or somebody at heart constantly

【惘】 1611
ㄨㄤˇ woang wǎng
dejected; frustrated; discouraged

惘然(ㄨㄤˇ ㄖㄢˊ)
in a daze; at a loss; stupefied

【惚】 1612
ㄏㄨ hu hū
absent-minded; entranced

【惙】 1613
ㄔㄨㄛˋ chuoh chuò
melancholy; doleful; mournful; gloomy

惙怛(ㄔㄨㄛˋ ㄉㄚˊ)
mournful; doleful; rueful

惙惙(ㄔㄨㄛˋ ㄔㄨㄛˋ)
melancholy; gloomy

【惛】 1614
ㄏㄨㄣ huen hūn
1. confused
2. senile

惛憒(ㄏㄨㄣ ㄎㄨㄟˋ)
muddleheaded

惛眊(ㄏㄨㄣ ㄇㄠˋ)
senile; senility

惛懵(ㄏㄨㄣ ㄇㄥˊ)
dim-eyed

惛惛(ㄏㄨㄣ ㄏㄨㄣ)
①confused in mind ②absorbed; carried away; entranced

【惝】 1615
ㄔㄤˇ taang tǎng
(又讀 ㄔㄤ chaang chǎng)
dispirited; disheartened; discouraged

惝悅(ㄔㄤˇ ㄏㄨㄟˋ)
dispirited; dejected; disheartened; despondent; discouraged

惝恍無定(ㄔㄤˇ ㄏㄨㄤˇ ㄨˊ ㄉㄧㄥˋ)
dispirited and distracted

惝然(ㄔㄤˇ ㄖㄢˊ)
crestfallen; dispirited; discouraged; disheartened; dejected

【惦】 1616
ㄉㄧㄢˋ diann diàn
to remember; to bear in mind; to miss; to be concerned about; to keep thinking about

惦念(ㄉㄧㄢˋ ㄋㄧㄢˋ)
to worry about; to feel or regret the absence or loss of; to miss (a friend or beloved one): 一切均妥請勿惦念。 Everything is fine. Don't worry about me.

惦懷(ㄉㄧㄢˋ ㄏㄨㄞˊ)
to remember nostalgically; to be nostalgic about

惦記(ㄉㄧㄢˋ ㄐㄧˋ) or惦掛(ㄉㄧㄢˋ ㄍㄨㄚˋ)
to keep thinking about; to feel concern about someone far away

【惜】 1617
ㄒㄧ shyi xí
1. to pity; to sympathize; to regret; to feel sorry for somebody: 我為他感到惋惜。I felt sorry for him.
2. to value highly; to have a

〔心部〕

心
部

high opinion of (something);
to show love or fondness for
3. to spare; to grudge

惜別 (ㄒㄧˊ ㄅㄧㄝˊ)
reluctant to part company;
to say good-bye

惜墨如金 (ㄒㄧˊ ㄇㄛˋ ㄖㄨˊ ㄐㄧㄣ)
(said of a calligrapher or a
painter) to grudge ink as if
it were gold—reluctant to
write or paint

惜福 (ㄒㄧˊ ㄈㄨˊ)
to refrain from leading an
excessively comfortable life;
to make sparing use of one's
wealth

惜老憐貧 (ㄒㄧˊ ㄌㄠˇ ㄌㄧㄢˊ ㄆㄧㄣˊ)
to pity the aged and the
poor

惜力 (ㄒㄧˊ ㄌㄧˋ)
to contribute one's labor
very reluctantly; to be sparing of one's energy

惜乎 (ㄒㄧˊ ㄏㄨ)
It is a pity that.... 或 What
a pity!

惜指失掌 (ㄒㄧˊ ㄓˇ ㄕ ㄓㄤˇ)
(literally) to lose the hand
in trying to save the fingers
—to be penny-wise and
pound-foolish

惜字紙 (ㄒㄧˊ ㄗˋ ㄓˇ)
to treat written or printed
paper with respect

惜寸陰 (ㄒㄧˊ ㄘㄨㄣˋ ㄧㄣ) or 惜分陰
(ㄒㄧˊ ㄈㄣ ㄧㄣ)
to be careful not to waste
even a moment; to harness
one's time

惜玉憐香 (ㄒㄧˊ ㄩˋ ㄌㄧㄢˊ ㄒㄧㄤ)
to be tender to the fair sex;
to be tender toward pretty
girls

【惟】 1618
(惟) ㄨㄟˊ wei wéi
1. to think; to meditate
2. only; alone
3. but; however

惟妙惟肖 (ㄨㄟˊ ㄇㄧㄠˋ ㄨㄟˊ ㄒㄧㄠˋ)
so skillfully imitated as to
be indistinguishable from
the original

惟命是聽 (ㄨㄟˊ ㄇㄧㄥˋ ㄕˋ ㄊㄧㄥ) 惟
命是從 (ㄨㄟˊ ㄇㄧㄥˋ ㄕˋ ㄘㄨㄥˊ)
always do as one is told; to
be slavishly obedient

惟獨 (ㄨㄟˊ ㄉㄨˊ)

only; alone: 別人都回家了, 惟
獨我還在工作. Only I kept on
working when all the others
had gone home.

惟利是圖 (ㄨㄟˊ ㄌㄧˋ ㄕˋ ㄊㄨˊ)
interested only in material
gain

惟恐 (ㄨㄟˊ ㄎㄨㄥˇ)
for fear that; lest; afraid of
nothing but; The only fear
is that...: 他努力讀書惟恐落
後. He strives to study for
fear that he should fall
behind.

惟恐天下不亂 (ㄨㄟˊ ㄎㄨㄥˇ ㄊㄧㄢ ㄒㄧㄚˋ
ㄅㄨˋ ㄌㄨㄢˋ)
to be displeased to see the
prospect of peace in the
world; anxious to see trouble

惟心 (ㄨㄟˊ ㄒㄧㄣ)
spiritualistic

惟心論 (ㄨㄟˊ ㄒㄧㄣ ㄌㄨㄣˋ)
spiritualism; idealism

惟我獨尊 (ㄨㄟˊ ㄨㄛˇ ㄉㄨˊ ㄗㄨㄣ)
(literally) No one is noble
but me.—egoistic; arrogant

惟我論 (ㄨㄟˊ ㄨㄛˇ ㄌㄨㄣˋ)
solipsism; egoism

惟一 (ㄨㄟˊ ㄧ)
the only one; the only thing
of its kind

惟有 (ㄨㄟˊ ㄧㄡˇ)
only

惟物 (ㄨㄟˊ ㄨˋ)
materialistic

惟物論 (ㄨㄟˊ ㄨˋ ㄌㄨㄣˋ)
materialism

惟物史觀 (ㄨㄟˊ ㄨˋ ㄕˇ ㄍㄨㄢ)
materialistic view of history;
historical materialism

【悶】 1619
1. ㄇㄣˋ menn mèn
melancholy; depressed;
bored; in low spirits

悶悶不樂 (ㄇㄣˋ ㄇㄣˋ ㄅㄨˋ ㄌㄜˋ)
sulky; unhappy; depressed:
他悶悶不樂. He felt depressed
and unhappy.

悶得慌 (ㄇㄣˋ ㄉㄜˊ ㄏㄨㄤ) or 悶得很
(ㄇㄣˋ ㄉㄜˊ ㄏㄣˇ)
bored; to feel restless
(because there is nothing
interesting to occupy one's
time)

悶雷 (ㄇㄣˋ ㄌㄟˊ)
①a thunderbolt; a thunder-

clap ②an unpleasant sur-
prise; shock

悶葫蘆 (ㄇㄣˋ ㄏㄨˊ ㄌㄨˊ)
something difficult to understand; a riddle or puzzle

悶酒 (ㄇㄣˋ ㄐㄧㄡˇ)
alcoholic drinks for drowning one's cares, sorrows, etc.
(usually said of drinking
alone)

悶氣 (ㄇㄣˋ ㄑㄧˋ)
the sulks; pent-up sorrow or
resentment: 他在生悶氣. He
was sulky. 或 He was in the
sulks.

悶香 (ㄇㄣˋ ㄒㄧㄤ)
incense with a choking smell

悶沈沈 (ㄇㄣˋ ㄔㄣˊ ㄔㄣˊ)
depressed; heavy-hearted;
melancholy

悶躁 (ㄇㄣˋ ㄗㄠˋ)
melancholy and irritable

【悶】 1619
2. ㄇㄣ mben mēn
1. (said of weather, rooms,
etc.) oppressive or suffocat-
ing; stuffy
2. (said of a sound) muffled
3. to shut oneself or somebody
indoors
4. to cover the tea pot for a
while when one makes tea
with boiling water

悶得慌 (ㄇㄣ ㄉㄜ ㄏㄨㄤ) or 悶得很
(ㄇㄣ ㄉㄜ ㄏㄣˇ)
very stuffy

悶頭兒 (ㄇㄣ ㄊㄡ ㄦ)
(to do something) diligently
but quietly; silently

悶氣 (ㄇㄣ ㄑㄧ)
oppressive air (due to poor
ventilation)

悶著 (ㄇㄣ ㄓㄜ)
①to refrain from speaking
out ②stewing or being
stewed

悶聲不響 (ㄇㄣ ㄕㄥ ㄅㄨˋ ㄒㄧㄤˇ)
to keep one's mouth shut; to
remain quiet; to remain
silent

悶熱 (ㄇㄣ ㄖㄜˋ)
sticky; oppressive; humid;
sultry; sweltering

悶死 (ㄇㄣ ㄙˇ)
to die of suffocation; to die
of asphyxiation; to be suffocated

【怒】 1620
ろ | nih nì
pensive; worried

【惑】 1621
ㄏㄨㄛˋ huoh huò
1. to confuse; to perplex; to delude; to beguile; to mislead; to misguide; to puzzle: 他大惑不解。 He was greatly puzzled.
2. to doubt; to suspect
惑溺（ㄏㄨㄛˋ ㄋ丨ˋ)
to indulge in
惑弄（ㄏㄨㄛˋ ㄋㄨㄥˋ)
to delude; to befool; to beguile
惑亂（ㄏㄨㄛˋ ㄌㄨㄢˋ)
to delude or confuse
惑志（ㄏㄨㄛˋ ㄓˋ)
suspicion; doubt
惑衆（ㄏㄨㄛˋ ㄓㄨㄥˋ)
to mislead; to delude or confuse the people: 他們造惑衆。 They fabricated rumors to mislead people.
惑術（ㄏㄨㄛˋ ㄕㄨˋ)
deceitful tricks; guile; ruses

【悲】 1622
ㄅㄟ bei bēi
1. sad; sorrowful; mournful; woeful; rueful; doleful
2. to lament; to deplore; to mourn; to pity; to sympathize
悲悲切切（ㄅㄟ ㄅㄟ ㄑ丨ㄝ ㄑ丨ㄝ)
full of grief
悲不自勝（ㄅㄟ ㄅㄨˋ ㄗˋ ㄕㄥ)
to abandon oneself to grief; unable to restrain one's grief; to be overcome with grief
悲憫（ㄅㄟ ㄇ丨ㄣˇ)
to pity; to have sympathy for; to have compassion for
悲鳴（ㄅㄟ ㄇ丨ㄥˊ)
to cry mournfully; to bemoan
悲憤（ㄅㄟ ㄈㄣˋ)
① to lament and resent (an injustice) ② grief and indignation: 他悲憤填膺。 He is filled with grief and indignation.
悲風（ㄅㄟ ㄈㄥ)
the baleful sound of wind; a moaning wind
悲夫（ㄅㄟ ㄈㄨˊ)
Alas! 或 What a pity! 或 How sad it is!

悲悼（ㄅㄟ ㄉㄠˋ）
to mourn (for or over)
悲調（ㄅㄟ ㄉ丨ㄠˋ)
a mournful tune
悲歎（ㄅㄟ ㄊㄢˋ)
to lament; to deplore; to sigh over
悲啼（ㄅㄟ ㄊ丨ˊ)
to cry mournfully
悲天憫人（ㄅㄟ ㄊ丨ㄢ ㄇ丨ㄣˇ ㄖㄣˊ)
to be concerned over the destiny of mankind; the feeling for the universal compassion and cosmic pity; to bemoan the state of the universe and to pity the fate of mankind
悲痛（ㄅㄟ ㄊㄨㄥˋ)
grieved; deep sorrow; painfully sad: 我們感到深切的悲痛。 We are deeply grieved.
悲慟（ㄅㄟ ㄊㄨㄥˋ)
to weep loudly for sorrow
悲憐（ㄅㄟ ㄌ丨ㄢˊ)
to take pity on (a person)
悲涼（ㄅㄟ ㄌ丨ㄤˊ)
sad and dreary; somber; dismal
悲歌（ㄅㄟ ㄍㄜ)
a song of lament; an elegy
悲觀（ㄅㄟ ㄍㄨㄢ)
pessimistic
悲觀主義（ㄅㄟ ㄍㄨㄢ ㄓㄨˇ丨ˋ)
pessimism
悲懷（ㄅㄟ ㄏㄨㄞˊ)
sad feelings; a sorrowful mood
悲歡離合（ㄅㄟ ㄏㄨㄢ ㄌ丨ˊ ㄏㄜˊ)
the sorrow of parting and the joy of union in life; weal and woe, parting and meeting—the vicissitudes of life
悲笳（ㄅㄟ ㄐ丨ㄚ)
a mournful tune from a military flageolet
悲劇（ㄅㄟ ㄐㄩˋ)
a tragedy type: 哈姆雷特是一齣悲劇。 Hamlet is a tragedy.
悲戚（ㄅㄟ ㄑ丨)
rueful; doleful; mournful
悲泣（ㄅㄟ ㄑ丨ˋ)
to sob, or weep sorrowfully
悲切（ㄅㄟ ㄑ丨ㄝ)
mournful
悲秋（ㄅㄟ ㄑ丨ㄡ)
to feel sad with the coming

of autumn
悲喜交集（ㄅㄟ ㄒ丨ˇ ㄐ丨ㄠ ㄐ丨ˊ)
intermingling of sorrow and joy; mixed feelings of grief and joy
悲喜劇（ㄅㄟ ㄒ丨ˇ ㄐㄩˋ)
a tragicomedy
悲壯（ㄅㄟ ㄓㄨㄤˋ)
tragically heroic; heroically tragic
悲愁（ㄅㄟ ㄔㄡˊ)
melancholy; sad; grievous; pensive
悲傷（ㄅㄟ ㄕㄤ）
sad; sorrowful
悲聲（ㄅㄟ ㄕㄥ)
plaintive cries; sad voice
悲哉（ㄅㄟ ㄗㄞ)
Alas! 或 How sad it is! 或 How lamentable! 或 What a pity!
悲惻（ㄅㄟ ㄘㄜˋ)
sad; sorrowful; woeful
悲慘（ㄅㄟ ㄘㄢˇ)
tragic; tragical; pathetic; miserable
悲從中來（ㄅㄟ ㄘㄨㄥˊ ㄓㄨㄥ ㄌㄞˊ)
to feel sadness welling up
悲酸（ㄅㄟ ㄙㄨㄢ)
sad and bitter
悲哀（ㄅㄟ ㄞ)
mournful; woeful

【惠】 1623
ㄏㄨㄟˋ huey huì
1. to benefit; benefit; to profit; profit; to favor; a favor
2. kind; benevolent; gracious
3. gentle and yielding
惠風（ㄏㄨㄟˋ ㄈㄥ)
a gentle wind; a breeze
惠特曼（ㄏㄨㄟˋ ㄊㄜˋ ㄇㄢˋ)
Walt Whitman, 1819-1892, American poet
惠臨（ㄏㄨㄟˋ ㄌ丨ㄣˊ)
(honorific expression) to favor with one's presence: 敬請惠臨。 Your presence is requested.
惠顧（ㄏㄨㄟˋ ㄍㄨˋ)
① to be my customer; to patronize (my business establishment) ② your kindness, favor or patronage
惠鑒（ㄏㄨㄟˋ ㄐ丨ㄢˋ)
for your gracious perusal (a conventional phrase placed after the salutation in a letter)

【心部】

（心部）

惠恤(ㄏㄨㄟ ㄒㄩˋ)
to give relief to (the poor or victims of a disaster)

惠政(ㄏㄨㄟ ㄓㄥˋ)
benevolent rule or administration

惠示(ㄏㄨㄟ ㄕˋ)
(honorific expression) to condescend to show or instruct

惠聲(ㄏㄨㄟ ㄕㄥ)
the prestige of humanitarian rule

惠然肯來(ㄏㄨㄟ ㄖㄢˊ ㄎㄣˇ ㄌㄞˊ)
to be so kind as to come; to honor me with your presence

惠澤(ㄏㄨㄟ ㄗㄜˊ)
kindness; benevolence; favor

惠存(ㄏㄨㄟ ㄘㄨㄣˊ)
to be so kind as to keep (my gift); to condescend to accept; to keep as a souvenir: 敬請惠存。Please keep (this photograph, book, etc. as a souvenir).

惠賜(ㄏㄨㄟ ㄘˋ)
to be kind enough to give (me something); to bestow graciously

惠而不費(ㄏㄨㄟ ㄦˊ ㄅㄨˋ ㄈㄟˋ)
kindness that costs one nothing; a kind act which does not cost much

惠音(ㄏㄨㄟ ㄧㄣ)
your esteemed letter; your kind letter

【惡】 1624
1. bad; evil; wicked; vice; wickedness: 他無惡不作。He stops at nothing in doing evil.
2. fierce; ferocious

惡霸(ㄜˋ ㄅㄚˋ)
a powerful bully; a local bandit leader; a local tyrant; a local despot

惡報(ㄜˋ ㄅㄠˋ)
deserved punishment for evil done; retribution; evil recompense

惡病(ㄜˋ ㄅㄧㄥˋ)
①a malignant disease; disgusting disease ②a euphemism for venereal diseases

惡癖(ㄜˋ ㄆㄧˇ)
a bad habit

惡罵(ㄜˋ ㄇㄚˋ)
abuse; vilification; vicious abuse

惡魔(ㄜˋ ㄇㄛˊ)or 惡鬼(ㄜˋ ㄍㄨㄟˇ)
an evil spirit; a demon; a fiend; the devil; Satan

惡眉惡眼(ㄜˋ ㄇㄟˊ ㄜˋ ㄧㄢˇ)
a fierce or ferocious look

惡夢(ㄜˋ ㄇㄥˋ)
a nightmare: 我昨夜做了個惡夢。I had a nightmare last night.

惡名(ㄜˋ ㄇㄧㄥˊ)
a bad reputation; ill fame; a bad name; infamy; notoriety

惡模惡樣(ㄜˋ ㄇㄨˊ ㄜˋ ㄧㄤˋ)
a fierce or ferocious appearance

惡木(ㄜˋ ㄇㄨˋ)
wood of inferior quality

惡風(ㄜˋ ㄈㄥ)
a bad custom; evil ways

惡德(ㄜˋ ㄉㄜˊ)
vice; corruption; immorality

惡毒(ㄜˋ ㄉㄨˊ)
venomous; malicious; vicious: 他們惡毒地攻擊我們。They viciously attack us.

惡徒(ㄜˋ ㄊㄨˊ)
a scoundrel; a rascal; a villain; a rogue; a knave

惡逆(ㄜˋ ㄋㄧˋ)
(old criminal law) a crime as beating or killing one's parents

惡念(ㄜˋ ㄋㄧㄢˋ)
evil intentions

惡辣(ㄜˋ ㄌㄚˋ)
villainous; knavish

惡例(ㄜˋ ㄌㄧˋ)
a bad precedent; a bad example

惡劣(ㄜˋ ㄌㄧㄝˋ)
①of very poor quality, very inferior ②rude; revolting; distasteful ③vile; satanic

惡劣環境(ㄜˋ ㄌㄧㄝˋ ㄏㄨㄢˊ ㄐㄧㄥˋ)
adverse circumstances

惡劣氣候(ㄜˋ ㄌㄧㄝˋ ㄑㄧˋ ㄏㄡˋ)
vile weather

惡劣行徑(ㄜˋ ㄌㄧㄝˋ ㄒㄧㄥˊ ㄐㄧㄥˋ)
disgusting conduct

惡劣手段(ㄜˋ ㄌㄧㄝˋ ㄕㄡˇ ㄉㄨㄢˋ)
mean tricks

惡劣作風(ㄜˋ ㄌㄧㄝˋ ㄗㄨㄛˋ ㄈㄥ)
abominable behavior

惡感(ㄜˋ ㄍㄢˇ)
unfriendly feeling; ill will; enmity; dislike; hate; malice

惡果(ㄜˋ ㄍㄨㄛˇ)
undesirable consequences; disastrous effect; evil results of evildoing

惡鬼(ㄜˋ ㄍㄨㄟˇ)
a bad spirit; a fiend; a demon

惡貫滿盈(ㄜˋ ㄍㄨㄢˋ ㄇㄢˇ ㄧㄥˊ)
to reach the limit of crimes (tolerated by Heaven); to come to the end of a criminal career

惡棍(ㄜˋ ㄍㄨㄣˋ)
a villain; a rascal; a scoundrel; a hoodlum; a hooligan; a ruffian

惡客(ㄜˋ ㄎㄜˋ)
an ill-meaning guest

惡口(ㄜˋ ㄎㄡˇ)
an abusive tongue; bad language: 他惡口傷人。He uses bad language to insult people.

惡耗(ㄜˋ ㄏㄠˋ)
news of death or disaster

惡漢(ㄜˋ ㄏㄢˋ)
a rascal; a scoundrel; a villain; a knave; a ruffian

惡狠狠(ㄜˋ ㄏㄣˇ ㄏㄣˇ)
ferocious

惡化(ㄜˋ ㄏㄨㄚˋ)
to get worse; to deteriorate; to degenerate; to worsen; to be aggravated; to go from bad to worse: 雙方關係不斷惡化。The relations between the both sides have steadily deteriorated.

惡疾(ㄜˋ ㄐㄧˊ)
a malignant disease

惡計(ㄜˋ ㄐㄧˋ)
a vicious scheme; a cruel design; an evil plan

惡氣(ㄜˋ ㄑㄧˋ)
noxious air; offensive gas

惡錢(ㄜˋ ㄑㄧㄢˊ)
counterfeit coin

惡犬(ㄜˋ ㄑㄩㄢˇ)
a fierce dog

惡習(ㄜˋ ㄒㄧˊ)
a bad habit: 他染上惡習。He contracted a bad habit.

惡戲(ㄜˋ ㄒㄧˋ)

a practical joke; mischief

相(さ Tↀせ)
a fierce or ferocious look

行(さ Tↀゝ)
an evil deed; a wicked act; a misdeed; evildoing; evil conduct; vice

性(さ Tↀゝ)
malignant; virulent; vicious; unsound

性補習(さ Tↀゝ ㄒㄩˊ Tↀ)
unhealthy cram sessions (at schools)

性倒閉(さ Tↀゝ ㄉㄠˇ ㄅㄧˋ)
fraudulent insolvency; fraudulent closedown

性循環(さ Tↀゝ Tㄩㄣˊㄏㄨㄢˊ)
a vicious circle

性腫瘤(さ Tↀゝ ㄓㄨㄥˇ ㄌㄧㄡˊ)
a malignant tumor

戰(さ ㄓㄢˋ)
hard fighting

濁(さ ㄓㄨㄛˊ)
foul; filthy; dirty

臭(さ ㄔㄡˋ)
an offensive odor; a bad smell; an unpleasant smell; a stink; a stench

瘡(さ ㄔㄨㄤ)
a foul ulcer

食(さ ㄕˊ)
bad food; poor food; coarse food

勢力(さ ㄕˋ ㄌㄧˋ)
vicious power; pressure groups; evil force

事傳千里(さ ㄕˋ ㄔㄨㄢˊ くㄧㄢ ㄌㄧˇ)
An evil deed will become known a thousand miles off. 或 Scandal travels fast.

少(さ ㄕㄠˋ)
a young hoodlum; a hooligan; a juvenile delinquent

衊(さ ㄇㄧㄝˋ)
to slander; to libel

聲(さ ㄕㄥ)
① abusive language ② an inauspicious sound

人(さ ㄖㄣˊ)
a bad man; a wicked person; a scoundrel; a villain

作劇(さ ㄗㄨㄛˋ ㄐㄩˋ)
mischief; a practical joke

俗(さ ㄙㄨˊ)
a bad custom or practice

葳(さ ㄙㄨㄟˋ)

---

a bad year; a year of poor harvest

惡衣惡食(さ ㄧ さ ㄕˊ)
① to be clothed poorly and eat poorly ② poor clothing and poor food

惡意(さ ㄧˋ)
① malicious; spiteful ② malice; evil intentions; sinister motives

惡有惡報(さ ㄧㄡˇ さ ㄅㄠˋ)
Evil will be recompensed with evil.

惡言(さ ㄧㄢˊ)
abusing language; abusive language; 勿口出惡言。Don't use abusing language.

惡因(さ ㄧㄣ)
the cause of evil or disaster

惡語(さ ㄩˇ)
bad language; abusive language

惡語中傷(さ ㄩˇ ㄓㄨㄥ Tↀㄤ)
viciously slander; to calumniate

惡運(さ ㄩㄣˋ)
bad luck; ill luck

【惡】 1624
2. さ ee ě
to disgust; to sicken; to scorn

惡心(さ Tↀㄣ)
① nauseated; disgusted: 我感到惡心。I felt nauseated. ② disgusting; disgust; sickening

【惡】 1624
3. ㄨ wuh wù
to hate; to detest; to dislike; to abhor; to loathe

惡嫌(ㄨ Tↀㄢ)
to hate; to detest; to abhor; to loathe

惡(ㄨ)
to hate evil

【惡】 1624
4. ㄨ u wū
1. how; where
2. O; oh; ah

九畫

【惰】 1625
ㄉㄨㄛˋ duoh duò
lazy; idle; indolent: 懶惰為萬惡之源。Idleness is the parent of all vice.

惰民(ㄉㄨㄛˋ ㄇㄧㄣˊ)

---

a caste of people in Chekiang-Kiangsu area formerly barred from officialdom and believed to be descendants of prisoners under the Sung Dynasty

惰力(ㄉㄨㄛˋ ㄌㄧˋ)
inertia; momentum

惰懈(ㄉㄨㄛˋ Tↀㄝ)
to be negligent or neglectful

惰性(ㄉㄨㄛˋ Tↀゝ)
inertia; sloth; laziness

【惱】 1626
ㄋㄠˇ nao nǎo
1. to anger; to exasperate; to annoy; to irritate; to vex; to trouble
2. angered; offended; vexed; annoyed

惱巴巴(ㄋㄠˇ ㄅㄚ ㄅㄚ)
angry; cross; annoyed

惱悶(ㄋㄠˇ ㄇㄣˋ)
troubled in the mind; grieved and sad

惱犯(ㄋㄠˇ ㄈㄢˋ)
to anger; to annoy; to enrage; to infuriate

惱忿忿地(ㄋㄠˇ ㄈㄣˋ ㄈㄣˋ ㄉㄧˋ)
indignantly; angrily

惱怒(ㄋㄠˇ ㄋㄨˋ)
① angry; indignant; irritated ② anger; indignation; rage

惱了(ㄋㄠˇ ·ㄌㄜ)
angered; enraged; infuriated; offended

惱亂(ㄋㄠˇ ㄌㄨㄢˋ)
to disturb to trouble

惱恨(ㄋㄠˇ ㄏㄣˋ)
to be angry at; to be offended by; to be vexed at; to resent

惱火(ㄋㄠˇ ㄏㄨㄛˇ)
to become irritated; annoyed; to see red

惱氣(ㄋㄠˇ くㄧˋ)
anger; rage; indignation; irritation

惱羞成怒(ㄋㄠˇ Tↀㄡ ㄔㄥˊ ㄋㄨˋ)
to be moved to anger by the feeling of shame; to fly into a rage from shame

惱心(ㄋㄠˇ Tↀㄣ)
irritated state of mind

惱人(ㄋㄠˇ ㄖㄣˊ)
to disturb peace of mind; irritating

惱人春色(ㄋㄠˇ ㄖㄣˊ ㄔㄨㄣ ㄙㄜˋ)

（心

部）

suffering from love in spring

惛意（ㄅㄨˋ ㄧˋ）
the feeling of anger

【惴】 1627
　　ㄓㄨㄟˋ juey zhuì
worried; afraid; anxious;
apprehensive

惴慄（ㄓㄨㄟˋ ㄌㄧˋ）
to tremble with fear; to
shudder

惴恐（ㄓㄨㄟˋ ㄎㄨㄥˇ）
to fear; to dread

惴惴（ㄓㄨㄟˋ ㄓㄨㄟˋ）
anxious and worried; in fear
and trembling

惴悒（ㄓㄨㄟˋ ㄓㄨㄟˋ）
timorous; afraid; fearful; apprehensive; to feel uneasy or
apprehensive

【惵】 1628
　　ㄉㄧㄝˊ dye dié
afraid; fearful; terrified

惵慄（ㄉㄧㄝˊ ㄌㄧˋ）
terrified; fearful; timorous;
afraid

惵息（ㄉㄧㄝˊ ㄒㄧˊ）
holding breath from fear

【惲】 1629
　　ㄩㄣˇ yunn yǔn
1. to plan; to consider; to
deliberate
2. a Chinese family name

惲謀（ㄩㄣˇ ㄇㄡˊ）
to scheme; to plan

惲議（ㄩㄣˇ ㄧˋ）
to discuss; to deliberate

【惶】 1630
　　ㄏㄨㄤˊ hwang
　　　　　huáng
1. afraid; fearful; apprehensive
2. anxious; uneasy
3. flurried; hurried

惶恐（ㄏㄨㄤˊ ㄎㄨㄥˇ）
apprehensive; fearful; afraid

惶汗（ㄏㄨㄤˊ ㄏㄢˋ）
to perspire from fear or
apprehension

惶惑（ㄏㄨㄤˊ ㄏㄨㄛˋ）
anxious and perplexed; uneasy and confused; suspi-
cious and fearful

惶惶（ㄏㄨㄤˊ ㄏㄨㄤˊ）
① anxious; uneasy; appre-
hensive; perturbed; in a
state of anxiety ② hurried;
hasty

惶遽（ㄏㄨㄤˊ ㄐㄩˋ）

to lose one's head; to lose
self-possession; scared: 他的
神色惶遽。He looked scared.

惶擾（ㄏㄨㄤˊ ㄖㄠˇ）
to agitate; to perturb

【愒】 1631
　　ㄎㄞˋ kay kài
to idle away (time)

愒時（ㄎㄞˋ ㄕˊ）
to idle away the time

愒日（ㄎㄞˋ ㄖˋ）
to idle away the days

【愐】 1632
　　ㄇㄧㄢˇ mean miǎn
1. to remember; to give
thought to
2. shy

愐愧（ㄇㄧㄢˇ ㄎㄨㄟˋ）
bashful; shy; modest: 她有點
愐愧。She is rather bashful.

愐懷（ㄇㄧㄢˇ ㄏㄨㄞˊ）
to think of; to remember

【愕】 1633
　　ㄜˋ eh è
startled; astonished; amazed

愕眙（ㄜˋ ㄔˋ）
to look in amazement

愕眙（ㄜˋ ㄔˋ）
to stare in amazement

愕然（ㄜˋ ㄖㄢˊ）
astonished; flabbergasted;
dumbfounded; stunned: 他環
然四顧。He looked around in
astonishment.

愕愣（ㄜˋ ㄌㄥˋ）
startled; astonished; amazed;
stunned; astounded

【愣】 1634
　　ㄌㄥˋ leng lèng
1. dumbfounded; agape with
horror; stupefied
2. reckless; irresponsible; rash;
rude
3. outspoken

愣頭愣腦（ㄌㄥˋ ㄊㄡˊ ㄌㄥˋ ㄋㄠˇ）
① rash; reckless ② stupid-
looking; stupid; in a stupor

愣頭愣腦（ㄌㄥˋ ㄊㄡˊ ㄋㄥ˙ ㄋㄠˇ）
① stupid ② rash

愣小子（ㄌㄥˋ ㄒㄧㄠˇ ˙ㄗ）
a little fool; a rash young
fellow; a young hothead

愣住了（ㄌㄥˋ ㄓㄨˋ ˙ㄌㄜ）
to become speechless or
stunned because of astonishment, an unexpected ques-
tion, etc.; to be taken aback

愣葱（ㄌㄥˋ ㄘㄨㄥ）
a rash fellow

【惸】 1635
　　ㄑㄩㄥˊ chyong
　　　　　qióng
1. worried; distressed
2. brotherless; friendless

惸獨（ㄑㄩㄥˊ ㄉㄨˊ）
brotherless and childless;
helpless and lonely; friendless

惸嫠（ㄑㄩㄥˊ ㄌㄧˊ）
a friendless widow

惸惸（ㄑㄩㄥˊ ㄑㄩㄥˊ）
worried; distressed; anxious

【惺】 1636
　　1. ㄒㄧㄥ shing xīng
1. clever; intelligent; wise
2. wavering; indecisive

惺惺（ㄒㄧㄥ ㄒㄧㄥ）
① intelligent; clever ②
wakeful; alert 參看「假惺惺」

惺惺惜惺惺（ㄒㄧㄥ ㄒㄧㄥ ㄒㄧˊ ㄒㄧㄥ
ㄒㄧㄥ）
Clever people like clever
people. 或 The wise people
appreciate one another.

惺惺作態（ㄒㄧㄥ ㄒㄧㄥ ㄗㄨㄛˋ ㄊㄞˋ）
to be affected; to simulate
(friendship, innocence, etc.)

惺忪（ㄒㄧㄥ ㄙㄨㄥ）
① wavering; indecisive ②
(said of eyes) not yet full
open on waking up: 她睡眼惺
忪。She has a drowsy look.

惺憶（ㄒㄧㄥ ㄙㄨㄥ）
① intelligent; wise ② a man
of intelligence

【惺】 1636
　　2. ㄒㄧㄥˇ shiing xǐng
to become aware of; to
awake from ignorance

惺悟（ㄒㄧㄥˇ ㄨˋ）
to awake to (the truth); to
realize

【愀】 1637
　　ㄑㄧㄠˇ cheau qiǎo
1. anxious-looking
2. to show a sudden change of
expression

愀愴（ㄑㄧㄠˇ ㄔㄨㄤˋ）
rueful; doleful; sad; sorrowful

愀然（ㄑㄧㄠˇ ㄖㄢˊ）
① showing a sudden change
of expression; turning pale
or red suddenly ② anxious;
sorrowful

【惻】 1638 ㄘㄜˋ tseh cè
to feel anguish

惻怛(ㄘㄜˋ ㄉㄚˊ)
sad and worried

惻愴(ㄘㄜˋ ㄔㄨㄤˋ)
sad; mournful; grieved

惻然
sadly; sorrowful

惻恻(ㄘㄜˋ ㄘㄜˋ)
in anguish; sad; sorrowful

惻隱之心(ㄘㄜˋ ㄧㄣˇ ㄓ ㄒㄧㄣ)
natural compassion; innate
mercy; a sense of pity; the
sense of mercy

【愎】 1639 ㄅㄧˋ bih bì
perverse; self-willed; obstinate; stubborn

愎諫(ㄅㄧˋ ㄐㄧㄢˋ)
deaf to remonstrances

【愉】 1640 ㄩˊ yu yú
happy; contented; pleased: 他
面有不愉之色。 He wore an
unhappy expression.

愉樂(ㄩˊ ㄌㄜˋ)
pleasant and joyful

愉快(ㄩˊ ㄎㄨㄞˋ)
cheerful; happy; pleased;
delighted: 她心情愉快。 She
was in a cheerful frame of
mind.

愉色(ㄩˊ ㄙㄜˋ)
a pleased look; a cheerful
expression

愉逸(ㄩˊ ㄧˋ)
happy and leisurely

愉悅(ㄩˊ ㄩㄝˋ)
joyful; glad; happy

【愔】 1641 ㄧㄣ in yīn
peaceful; composed; serene

愔愔(ㄧㄣ ㄧㄣ)
peaceful; composed; serene

【愊】 1642 ㄅㄧˋ bih bì
. sincere; honest
. melancholy; depressed

【愜】 1643 ㄑㄧㄝˋ chieh qiè
cheerful; satisfied; contented

愜當(ㄑㄧㄝˋ ㄉㄤˋ)
proper; appropriate: 這是愜
當之論。 This is a proper
remark.

愜懷(ㄑㄧㄝˋ ㄏㄨㄞˊ)
satisfied; contented

愜情(ㄑㄧㄝˋ ㄑㄧㄥˊ)
satisfied; contented

愜心(ㄑㄧㄝˋ ㄒㄧㄣ)
satisfied; contented

愜意(ㄑㄧㄝˋ ㄧˋ)
satisfied; contented: 結果令人
愜意。 The result was satis-
factory.

【想】 1644 ㄒㄧㄤˇ sheang
xiǎng

1. to think; to consider; to suppose: 讓我想一想。 Let me
think it over.
2. to hope; to expect
3. to plan
4. to remember with longing;
to miss
5. to want; would like to: 他也
想試一試。 He'd also like to
have a try.

想必(ㄒㄧㄤˇ ㄅㄧˋ) or 想必是(ㄒㄧㄤ
ˇ ㄅㄧˋ 戶)
presumably; probably; most
likely: 這事想必他知道。 He
most probably knows this.

想不到(ㄒㄧㄤˇ ㄅㄨˋ ㄉㄠˋ)
to one's surprise; unexpectedly: 那真是想不到的事!
That is something quite unexpected!

想不通(ㄒㄧㄤˇ ㄅㄨˋ ㄊㄨㄥ)
can't figure it out; incomprehensible; beyond comprehension

想不開(ㄒㄧㄤˇ ㄅㄨˋ ㄎㄞ)
unable to take a resigned
attitude; to take some misfortune too seriously; to
take things too hard: 你們太
想不開。 You take things too
hard.

想不起來(ㄒㄧㄤˇ ㄅㄨˋ ㄑㄧˇ ㄌㄞˊ)
unable to call to mind; can
not remember

想法子(ㄒㄧㄤˇ ㄈㄚˇ 戶)
to devise means; to think of
a scheme

想法(ㄒㄧㄤˇ ㄈㄚˇ)
the way of looking at something; an idea; an opinion; a
view: 這想法不錯。 This is a
good idea.

想得到(ㄒㄧㄤˇ ㄉㄜˊ ㄉㄠˋ)
to think; to imagine; to
expect

想得開(ㄒㄧㄤˇ ㄉㄜˊ ㄎㄞ)
not to take to heart; to take
philosophically; to try to
look on the bright side of
things

想得要命(ㄒㄧㄤˇ ㄉㄜˊ ㄧㄠˋ ㄇㄧㄥˋ)
to want to do or get something very badly

想到(ㄒㄧㄤˇ ㄉㄠˋ)
to think of; to remember; to
hit upon (an idea): 我忽然想
到一件重要的事情。 I suddenly
think of something impor-
tant.

想當然(ㄒㄧㄤˇ ㄉㄤ ㄖㄢˊ)
as may be taken for granted; presumably; to assume
something as a matter of
course

想法(ㄒㄧㄤˇ ㄈㄚˇ)
① a notion; thought; an idea:
他有個想頭。 He's got an idea.
②expectation; hope: 沒什麼
想頭了。 There's no hope now.
③ thinking

想通(ㄒㄧㄤˇ ㄊㄨㄥ)
to straighten out one's thinking; to become convinced: 你
要是仍無法想通。 可以問問其他
人。 Ask the others if you're
still not convinced.

想念(ㄒㄧㄤˇ ㄋㄧㄢˋ)
to give thought to (a person); to miss (something or
someone): 我們都很想念你。
We all miss you very much.

想來(ㄒㄧㄤˇ ㄌㄞˊ)
in my conjecture; in my
guess; it may be assumed
that; presumably; to sup-
pose; to think of: 想來真是後
悔。 When I come to think of
it, I really feel sorry.

想來想去(ㄒㄧㄤˇ ㄌㄞˊ ㄒㄧㄤˇ ㄑㄩˋ)
to turn (a matter) over and
over in one's mind; to ponder

想開了(ㄒㄧㄤˇ ㄎㄞ ㄌㄜˋ)
to have succeeded in getting
over a loss or misfortune; to
stop worrying: 我們想開了。
We stop worrying now.

想家(ㄒㄧㄤˇ ㄐㄧㄚ)
homesick; nostalgic

想見(ㄒㄧㄤˇ ㄐㄧㄢˋ)
to infer; to gather; to imagine; to visualize: 我想見其為
人。 I imagine what he was

like.

想起(ㄒㄧㄤˇ ㄑㄧˇ)
to think of; to remember; to occur

想想看(ㄒㄧㄤˇ ㄒㄧㄤˇ ㄎㄢˋ)
to think about it

想像(ㄒㄧㄤˇ ㄒㄧㄤˋ)
to imagine; to fancy: 她想像自己是詩人。She imagines herself to be a poet.

想像力(ㄒㄧㄤˇ ㄒㄧㄤˋ ㄌㄧˋ)
imagination; imaginative power or faculty: 他有很強的想像力。He has a very strong imagination.

想著(ㄒㄧㄤˇ ·ㄓㄜ)
to keep in mind

想入非非(ㄒㄧㄤˇ ㄖㄨˋ ㄈㄟ ㄈㄟ)
to let one's imagination run wild; to indulge in wishful thinking; to build castles in the air

想死(ㄒㄧㄤˇ ㄙˇ)
① to long for death; to get tired of life ② to long very much for; dying for

想一想(ㄒㄧㄤˇ ㄧ· ㄒㄧㄤˇ)
to pause to think

想要(ㄒㄧㄤˇ ㄧㄠˋ)
to want to; to feel like: 我想要回家。I want to go home.

想望(ㄒㄧㄤˇ ㄨㄤˋ)
① to hope; to expect; to desire; to long for ② to admire

【惹】 1645
ㄖㄜˇ ree rě
to provoke; to rouse; to induce; to attract; to cause; to bring upon oneself; to offend; to incur: 我可沒惹她呀! I did nothing to provoke her.

惹不起(ㄖㄜˇ ㄅㄨˋ ㄑㄧˇ)
① not daring to provoke or offend ② too powerful or vicious to be provoked or offended

惹麻煩(ㄖㄜˇ ㄇㄚˊ ㄈㄢˊ)
to excite trouble; to invite trouble

惹起(ㄖㄜˇ ㄑㄧˇ)
to have provoked or aroused; to have been provoked or aroused

惹得起(ㄖㄜˇ ·ㄉㄜ ㄑㄧˇ)
to dare to provoke

惹亂子(ㄖㄜˇ ㄌㄨㄢˋ ·ㄗ)
to bring trouble

惹火燒身(ㄖㄜˇ ㄏㄨㄛˇ ㄕㄠ ㄕㄣ)
to bring trouble upon oneself; to ask for trouble

惹禍(ㄖㄜˇ ㄏㄨㄛˋ)
to bring disaster or misfortune; to stir up trouble; to bring calamity on oneself: 這都是他惹的禍。It was he who stirred up the trouble.

惹起(ㄖㄜˇ ㄑㄧˇ)
to incite; to provoke; to incur

惹氣(ㄖㄜˇ ㄑㄧˋ)
to provoke one to anger; to incur wrath

惹嫌(ㄖㄜˇ ㄒㄧㄢˊ)
to incur hatred; to provoke dislike

惹事(ㄖㄜˇ ㄕˋ)
to create trouble

惹是非(ㄖㄜˇ ㄕˋ ㄈㄟ) or 惹是生非(ㄖㄜˇ ㄕˋ ㄕㄥ ㄈㄟ)
to incur unnecessary trouble; to stir up ill will; to provoke a dispute; to stir up trouble

惹人討厭(ㄖㄜˇ ㄖㄣˊ ㄊㄠˇ ㄧㄢˋ)
to make a nuisance of oneself

惹人注目(ㄖㄜˇ ㄖㄣˊ ㄓㄨˋ ㄇㄨˋ)
to attract attention (particularly undesirable attention)

惹草沾花(ㄖㄜˇ ㄘㄠˇ ㄓㄢ ㄏㄨㄚ)
(said of men) to have one love affair after another; to have promiscuous relations with women

惹厭(ㄖㄜˇ ㄧㄢˋ)
to incur dislike

【愁】 1646
ㄔㄡˊ chour chóu
1. sad; distressed; worried; unhappy; melancholy
2. depressing; saddening; gloomy
3. to worry about; to be anxious about
4. sorrow; woe

愁眉(ㄔㄡˊ ㄇㄟˊ)
knitted brows; a distressed look

愁眉不展(ㄔㄡˊ ㄇㄟˊ ㄅㄨˋ ㄓㄢˇ)
to wear a sad or distressed expression

愁眉苦臉(ㄔㄡˊ ㄇㄟˊ ㄎㄨˇ ㄌㄧㄢˇ)
a sad or worried look; a dis-

tressed expression

愁悶(ㄔㄡˊ ㄇㄣˋ)
unhappy; distressed; distressful; worried; to feel gloomy

愁歎(ㄔㄡˊ ㄊㄢˋ)
to give sighs of distress

愁苦(ㄔㄡˊ ㄎㄨˇ)
distress; misery

愁海(ㄔㄡˊ ㄏㄞˇ)
a very great amount of worries; a sea of worries

愁懷(ㄔㄡˊ ㄏㄨㄞˊ)
sad feelings; sadness

愁緒(ㄔㄡˊ ㄒㄩˋ)
a sad mood; a gloomy mood

愁吃愁穿(ㄔㄡˊ ㄔ ㄔㄡˊ ㄔㄨㄢ)
to have to worry about food and clothing; to suffer from poverty

愁腸(ㄔㄡˊ ㄔㄤˊ)
a tangled feeling of grief

愁腸百結(ㄔㄡˊ ㄔㄤˊ ㄅㄞˇ ㄐㄧㄝˊ)
It is as if the worries were tied in knots to one another

愁腸寸斷(ㄔㄡˊ ㄔㄤˊ ㄘㄨㄣˋ ㄉㄨㄢˋ)
The sorrow is so deep that it seems to have cut the bowels to pieces.

愁城(ㄔㄡˊ ㄔㄥˊ)
the realm of sorrow

愁容滿面(ㄔㄡˊ ㄖㄨㄥˊ ㄇㄢˇ ㄇㄧㄢˋ)
to wear a sad look; to look distressed: 他愁容滿面。He looked distressed.

愁滋味(ㄔㄡˊ ㄗ ㄨㄟˋ)
the taste of sorrow: 少年不知愁滋味。The taste of sorrow was unknown to a youth.

愁坐(ㄔㄡˊ ㄗㄨㄛˋ)
to sit quietly in sorrow or distress

愁思(ㄔㄡˊ ㄙ)
sorrowful thoughts

愁意(ㄔㄡˊ ㄧˋ)
an expression of sorrow; a touch of sorrow

愁顏(ㄔㄡˊ ㄧㄢˊ)
a distressed or sad look

愁霧(ㄔㄡˊ ㄨˋ)
a depressing fog or mist (often used figuratively)

愁雲(ㄔㄡˊ ㄩㄣˊ)
depressing clouds; heavy clouds (often used figuratively)

心
部

【憫】 1647
ㄇㄧㄣˇ miin miǎn
to pity; to commiserate

憫惻(ㄇㄧㄣˇ ㄘㄜˋ)
to pity (for)

憫恤(ㄇㄧㄣˇ ㄒㄩˋ)
to feel pity; to show kindness (toward people)

【愆】 1648
ㄑㄧㄢ chiān qiān
1. a fault; a mistake; a misdemeanor
2. to lose
3. a malignant disease

愆咎(ㄑㄧㄢ ㄐㄧㄡˋ)
a fault; a mistake

愆期(ㄑㄧㄢ ㄑㄧˊ)
to fail to meet a deadline; to be behind time; to fall behind schedule; to pass the appointed time

愆滯(ㄑㄧㄢ ㄓˋ)
behind time or schedule

愆尤(ㄑㄧㄢ ㄧㄡˊ) or 愆過(ㄑㄧㄢ ㄍㄨㄛˋ)
a fault; an offense; a mistake

【愈】 1649
ㄩˋ yù yù
1. to recover (from illness); to heal 亦作「癒」: 他病愈。He recovers from an illness.
2. to a greater degree; even more

愈多愈好(ㄩˋ ㄉㄨㄛ ㄩˋ ㄏㄠˇ)
The more, the better.

愈合(ㄩˋ ㄏㄜˊ)
(medicine) to heal 亦作「癒合」

愈加(ㄩˋ ㄐㄧㄚ)
increasingly; more and more

愈甚(ㄩˋ ㄕㄣˋ)
intenser; to become intense

愈益(ㄩˋ ㄧˋ)
increasingly; more and more

愈恋(ㄩˋ ㄉㄚˋ)
to wax more and more; to become greater

【意】 1650
ㄧˋ yìh yì
1. a thought; an idea; sentiments
2. intention; inclination
3. expectations
4. meaning: 詞不達意。The words fail to express the meaning.
5. a hint; suggestion: 天氣頗有

秋意。The weather makes us feel that autumn has set in.

意表(ㄧˋ ㄅㄧㄠˇ)
expectations: 此事出人意表。The matter is beyond our expectations.

意馬心猿(ㄧˋ ㄇㄚˇ ㄒㄧㄣ ㄩㄢˊ)
indecisive; wavering

意大利(ㄧˋ ㄉㄚˋ ㄌㄧˋ)
Italy

意大利人(ㄧˋ ㄉㄚˋ ㄌㄧˋ ㄖㄣˊ)
an Italian

意到筆隨(ㄧˋ ㄉㄠˋ ㄅㄧˇ ㄙㄨㄟˊ)
(literally) The pen follows where the mind reaches.—to write with ease

意態(ㄧˋ ㄊㄞˋ)
an air; bearing; a manner; an appearance

意圖(ㄧˋ ㄊㄨˊ)
intention; intent; design; to intend to do something

意念(ㄧˋ ㄋㄧㄢˋ)
an idea

意懶心灰(ㄧˋ ㄌㄢˇ ㄒㄧㄣ ㄏㄨㄟ)
greatly discouraged

意裏意思(ㄧˋ ㄇㄧˇ ㄧˋ ㄙ)
to speak hesitatingly and indistinctly

意料(ㄧˋ ㄌㄧㄠˋ)
expectations: 這結果出乎意料。The result was unexpected.

意會(ㄧˋ ㄏㄨㄟˋ)
to sense; to perceive spontaneously (not through explanations): 只可意會,不可言傳。It can be sensed, but not explained in words.

意見(ㄧˋ ㄐㄧㄢˋ)
① an opinion; a suggestion; a view; an idea; a proposal: 我們交換意見。We exchanged ideas. ② objection; complaint: 他們對你意見很多。They have a lot of complaints about you.

意見簿(ㄧˋ ㄐㄧㄢˋ ㄅㄨˋ)
a visitors' book

意見溝通(ㄧˋ ㄐㄧㄢˋ ㄍㄡ ㄊㄨㄥ)
communication

意見箱(ㄧˋ ㄐㄧㄢˋ ㄒㄧㄤ)
a suggestion box

意見書(ㄧˋ ㄐㄧㄢˋ ㄕㄨ)
written opinions; proposals submitted in written form

意匠(ㄧˋ ㄐㄧㄤˋ)

① creativity; ingenuity ② novel design; artistic conception

意匠慘淡(ㄧˋ ㄐㄧㄤˋ ㄘㄢˇ ㄉㄢˋ)
an ingenious composition and color scheme (said of painting)

意境(ㄧˋ ㄐㄧㄥˋ)
a frame of mind; a mood; conception

意氣(ㄧˋ ㄑㄧˋ)
spirits; heart; emotion

意氣風發(ㄧˋ ㄑㄧˋ ㄈㄥ ㄈㄚ)
high-spirited and vigorous

意氣沮喪(ㄧˋ ㄑㄧˋ ㄐㄩˇ ㄙㄤˋ)
in low spirits; crestfallen; dispirited; disheartened; depressed

意氣相投(ㄧˋ ㄑㄧˋ ㄒㄧㄤ ㄊㄡˊ)
congenial; to share the same aspirations and have the same temperament: 他們意氣相投。They are alike in temperament.

意氣之爭(ㄧˋ ㄑㄧˋ ㄓ ㄓㄥ)
to quarrel over a matter of emotion (rather than reason)

意氣衝天(ㄧˋ ㄑㄧˋ ㄔㄨㄥ ㄊㄧㄢ)
high-spirited

意氣自得(ㄧˋ ㄑㄧˋ ㄗˋ ㄉㄜˊ) or 意氣自如(ㄧˋ ㄑㄧˋ ㄗˋ ㄖㄨˊ) or 意氣自若(ㄧˋ ㄑㄧˋ ㄗˋ ㄖㄨㄛˋ)
easy and dignified

意氣揚揚(ㄧˋ ㄑㄧˋ ㄧㄤˊ ㄧㄤˊ)
triumphant; in high spirits; elated

意氣用事(ㄧˋ ㄑㄧˋ ㄩㄥˋ ㄕˋ)
to act on impulse; to be influenced by sentiments or emotions (rather than the mind) in handling things: 他們意氣用事。They acted on impulse.

意趣(ㄧˋ ㄑㄩˋ)
intent; implication

意下(ㄧˋ ㄒㄧㄚˋ)
① in one's heart or mind ② an opinion; an idea

意下如何(ㄧˋ ㄒㄧㄚˋ ㄖㄨˊ ㄏㄜˊ)
How about it? 或 What do you think?

意想不到(ㄧˋ ㄒㄧㄤˇ ㄅㄨˋ ㄉㄠˋ)
unexpected; unexpectedly; beyond expectation; never thought of

意向(ㄧˋ ㄒㄧㄤˋ)

intentions; inclinations: 敵軍
意向不明。The enemy's incli-
nations are not clear.

意象(ㄧ ㄒㄧㄤ)
an image; imagery; an idea;
a concept

意興(ㄧ ㄒㄧㄥ)
interest; enthusiasm: 意興索
然 to have not the least
interest

意興闌珊(ㄧ ㄒㄧㄥ ㄌㄢ ㄕㄢ)
to feel dispirited

意緒(ㄧ ㄒㄩˋ)
①threads of thoughts ②a
mood; a state of mind

意旨(ㄧ ㄓˇ)
intent; intention; meaning;
wish; will

意志(ㄧ ㄓˋ)
volition; will; will power: 我
們鍛鍊意志。We discipline
our will power.

意志消沉(ㄧ ㄓˋ ㄒㄧㄠ ㄔㄣˊ)
pessimistic; depressed; dejected; low-spirited; despondent

意轉心回(ㄧ ㄓㄨㄢˇ ㄒㄧㄣ ㄏㄨㄟˊ)
to change one's mind

意中(ㄧ ㄓㄨㄥ)
expected; anticipated

意中人(ㄧ ㄓㄨㄥ ㄖㄣˊ)
the man, or lady, of one's
heart; the person with whom
one is in love; the person
one is in love with; the person of one's heart

意識(ㄧ ㄕˋ)
consciousness

意識到(ㄧ ㄕˋ ㄉㄠˋ)
to be conscious of; to realize: 他意識到自己的責任重大。
He was conscious of his
great responsibilities.

意識流(ㄧ ㄕˋ ㄌㄧㄡˊ)
(psychology) stream of consciousness

意識形態(ㄧ ㄕˋ ㄒㄧㄥˊ ㄊㄞˋ)
ideology

意在筆先(ㄧ ㄗㄞˋ ㄅㄧˇ ㄒㄧㄢ)or意在
筆前(ㄧ ㄗㄞˋ ㄅㄧˇ ㄑㄧㄢˊ)
The idea seems to run
ahead of the brush. (said of
painting or calligraphy)

意在言外(ㄧ ㄗㄞˋ ㄧㄢˊ ㄨㄞˋ)
The real meaning is not expressed but implied.

意思(ㄧ ˙ㄙ)

①meaning: 他不明白我的意
思。He doesn't understand
what I mean. ②intention;
wish; desire: 你是不是有意思
跟我妹妹見面？Do you wish
to meet my sister? ③inter-
est; interesting; fun: 打籃球很
有意思。Basketball is a lot of
fun.

意思意思(ㄧ ˙ㄙ ㄧ ˙ㄙ)
to serve as a token

意色(ㄧ ㄙㄜˋ)
mental condition and facial
expression

意義(ㄧ ㄧˋ)
meaning; significance: 我不懂
他話中的意義。I could not
understand the significance
of his words.

意譯(ㄧ ㄧˋ)
free translation; paraphrase

意有未盡(ㄧ ㄧㄡˇ ㄨㄟˋ ㄐㄧㄣˋ)
to wish to continue doing
something one has done for
a long time

意淫(ㄧ ㄧㄣˊ)
to get satisfaction by
imagining a sexual act; mental adultery

意外(ㄧ ㄨㄞˋ)
①unexpected; unforeseen;
accidental; surprising ②a
surprise; an accident: 我有一
項出你意外的消息奉告。I have
a surprise for you.

意外保險(ㄧ ㄨㄞˋ ㄅㄠˇ ㄒㄧㄢˇ)
accident insurance

意外風波(ㄧ ㄨㄞˋ ㄈㄥ ㄅㄛ)
unforeseen trouble

意外事件(ㄧ ㄨㄞˋ ㄕˋ ㄐㄧㄢˋ)
an accident

意味(ㄧ ㄨㄟˋ)
①an impression; a touch; a
flavor ②to portend

意味著(ㄧ ㄨㄟˋ ˙ㄓㄜ)
to signify; to mean

意味深長(ㄧ ㄨㄟˋ ㄕㄣ ㄔㄤˊ)
profound in meaning; meaningful: 他帶著意味深長的微
笑。He wore a meaningful
smile.

意欲(ㄧ ㄩˋ)
volition; desire; to want to
do something

意願(ㄧ ㄩㄢˋ)
inclination; wish; volition

【愚】 1651 (ㄩˊ yú yù)

1. stupid; foolish; silly; unwise
unintelligent
2. to fool; to cheat; to deceive
3. (courteous self-reference) I
me

愚笨(ㄩˊ ㄅㄣˋ)
stupid; foolish

愚不可及(ㄩˊ ㄅㄨˋ ㄎㄜˇ ㄐㄧˊ)
most foolish: 他愚不可及。He
couldn't be more foolish.

愚昧(ㄩˊ ㄇㄟˋ)
benighted; stupid; ignorant
他愚昧無知。He is a benight-
ed man.

愚蒙(ㄩˊ ㄇㄥˊ)
ignorant; stupid

愚民(ㄩˊ ㄇㄧㄣˊ)
①the ignorant masses ②to
prevent people from know-
ing the truth; to keep people
in ignorance

愚民政策(ㄩˊ ㄇㄧㄣˊ ㄓㄥˋ ㄘㄜˋ)
the policy to keep the people in ignorance under a dictatorship; obscurantism; the
policy to misguide and
cheat people

愚夫愚婦(ㄩˊ ㄈㄨ ㄩˊ ㄈㄨˋ)
①the masses ②the ignorant
multitude; the uneducated
public

愚魯(ㄩˊ ㄌㄨˇ)
blockheaded; dull; slow to
learn; unintelligent

愚弟(ㄩˊ ㄉㄧˋ)
a self-depreciatory reference
to oneself in addressing a
colleague of similar age
(usually used in corre-
spondence)

愚鈍(ㄩˊ ㄉㄨㄣˋ)
(in mind) dull; dull-witted;
stupid

愚懦(ㄩˊ ㄋㄨㄛˋ)
stupid and cowardly

愚弄(ㄩˊ ㄋㄨㄥˋ)
to make a fool of somebody

愚陋(ㄩˊ ㄌㄡˋ)
stupid and vulgar

愚魯(ㄩˊ ㄌㄨˇ)
stupid; dull

愚公移山(ㄩˊ ㄍㄨㄥ ㄧˊ ㄕㄢ)
A determined effort can
move a mountain. 或 Where
there is a will, there is a

way.

愚見(ㄩˊ ㄐㄧㄢˋ)
(self-depreciatory term) my humble opinion

愚孝(ㄩˊ ㄒㄧㄠˋ)
blind devotion to one's parents

愚兄(ㄩˊ ㄒㄩㄥ)
a self-depreciatory reference to oneself when addressing a colleague or friend less advanced in age (usually used in correspondence)

愚直(ㄩˊ ㄓˊ) or 愚戇(ㄩˊ ㄓㄨㄤˋ)
stupidly honest

愚者千慮，必有一得(ㄩˊ ㄓㄜˇ ㄑㄧㄢ ㄌㄩˋ，ㄅㄧˋ ㄧㄡˇ ㄧ ㄉㄜˊ)
Even a fool may hits on a good idea.

愚者一得(ㄩˊ ㄓㄜˇ ㄧ ㄉㄜˊ)
a lucky hit by a fool (an expression often used to show one's modesty when praised for some clever act); a fluke

愚拙(ㄩˊ ㄓㄨㄛˊ)
stupid and clumsy

愚忠(ㄩˊ ㄓㄨㄥ)
blind devotion to one's lord

愚蠢(ㄩˊ ㄔㄨㄣˇ)
stupid; dull

愚人(ㄩˊ ㄖㄣˊ)
a fool; a simpleton

愚人節(ㄩˊ ㄖㄣˊ ㄐㄧㄝˊ)
All Fools' Day

愚騃(ㄩˊ ㄞˊ)
ignorant and stupid

愚而好自用(ㄩˊ ㄦˊ ㄏㄠˋ ㄗˋ ㄩㄥˋ)
stupid but willful

愚意(ㄩˊ ㄧˋ)
my humble opinion

愚頑(ㄩˊ ㄨㄢˊ)
stupid and obstinate

愚妄(ㄩˊ ㄨㄤˋ)
stupid and rash; ignorant but self-important; stupid but conceited

【感】 1652 (ㄍㄢˇ gaan gǎn)

1. to find; to feel; to sense; to perceive; to respond to: 我感到自己錯了。I sensed that I myself was wrong.

2. to affect, move, or touch

3. feeling; sensation; emotion

4. to be grateful

感佩(ㄍㄢˇ ㄆㄟˋ)
to show one's appreciation for the help received

感冒(ㄍㄢˇ ㄇㄠˋ)
① a cold ② to catch a cold

感銘(ㄍㄢˇ ㄇㄧㄥˊ)
very grateful; to always remember a favor one has received

感慕(ㄍㄢˇ ㄇㄨˋ)
to feel gratitude and adoration for; to thank and adore

感憤(ㄍㄢˇ ㄈㄣˋ)
to be indignant

感奮(ㄍㄢˇ ㄈㄣˋ)
to be moved to action

感奮激勵(ㄍㄢˇ ㄈㄣˋ ㄐㄧ ㄌㄧˋ)
encouragement and stimulation

感激(ㄍㄢˇ ㄐㄧ)
to be grateful for a kindness

感戴(ㄍㄢˇ ㄉㄞˋ)
to feel gratitude and respect for

感到(ㄍㄢˇ ㄉㄠˋ)
to feel; to sense

感電(ㄍㄢˇ ㄉㄧㄢˋ)
electric induction; electrification

感動(ㄍㄢˇ ㄉㄨㄥˋ)
(mentally) to move, affect, or touch: 她的演說令人感動得流淚。Her speech moved people to tears.

感歎(ㄍㄢˇ ㄊㄢˋ)
to exclaim

感歎號(ㄍㄢˇ ㄊㄢˋ ㄏㄠˋ)
the exclamation mark; the exclamation point

感同身受(ㄍㄢˇ ㄊㄨㄥˊ ㄕㄣ ㄕㄡˋ)
to feel deeply moved by a kindness (shown to somebody else) as if one were actually the object thereof (an expression used often in letters asking favors on behalf of someone else)

感念(ㄍㄢˇ ㄋㄧㄢˋ)
to remember with gratitude

感念五中(ㄍㄢˇ ㄋㄧㄢˋ ㄨˇ ㄓㄨㄥ)
to feel deep gratitude

感官(ㄍㄢˇ ㄍㄨㄢ)
① the senses ② a sensory organ

感光(ㄍㄢˇ ㄍㄨㄤ)
to be exposed to light

感光劑(ㄍㄢˇ ㄍㄨㄤ ㄐㄧˋ)
sensitizer

感光紙(ㄍㄢˇ ㄍㄨㄤ ㄓˇ)
sensitized or sensitive paper

感慨(ㄍㄢˇ ㄎㄞˇ)
emotional excitement; regrets; painful recollections: 他感慨萬千。He was filled with regrets.

感慨系之(ㄍㄢˇ ㄎㄞˇ ㄒㄧˋ ㄓ)
to feel deeply touched about something

感喟(ㄍㄢˇ ㄎㄨㄟˋ)
to feel moved and sigh

感愧交集(ㄍㄢˇ ㄎㄨㄟˋ ㄐㄧㄠ ㄐㄧˊ)
moved and ashamed simultaneously

感荷(ㄍㄢˇ ㄏㄜˋ)
gratitude

感化(ㄍㄢˇ ㄏㄨㄚˋ)
to reform (a person); to influence (a person) by personal examples of moral uprightness: 我們想要感化犯人。We try to reform the prisoners.

感化教育(ㄍㄢˇ ㄏㄨㄚˋ ㄐㄧㄠˋ ㄩˋ)
reformatory education (for juvenile delinquents)

感化院(ㄍㄢˇ ㄏㄨㄚˋ ㄩㄢˋ)
a reformatory

感懷(ㄍㄢˇ ㄏㄨㄞˊ)
① stirred or aroused emotions (often used in titles of old-style poems) ② to recall with emotion

感激(ㄍㄢˇ ㄐㄧ)
① to feel grateful: 他對你的一切幫助甚表感激。He felt grateful for all you did. ② to be moved, touched, or affected

感激涕零(ㄍㄢˇ ㄐㄧ ㄊㄧˋ ㄌㄧㄥˊ)
moved to tears (by kindness, generosity, etc.)

感舊(ㄍㄢˇ ㄐㄧㄡˋ)
① to remember the deceased with emotion ② to remember the bygone days with emotion

感覺(ㄍㄢˇ ㄐㄩㄝˊ)
① sense; perception; feeling; sensation: 我對顏色有敏銳的感覺。I have a keen perception of color. ② to feel; to sense; to become aware of: 你感覺怎麼樣？How do you feel now?

（心部）

感覺器官(《ㄢ ㄐㄩㄝ ㄑㄧ ㄍㄨㄢ)
sensory organs

感覺神經(《ㄢ ㄐㄩㄝ ㄕㄣ ㄐㄧㄥ)
sensory nerves

感情(《ㄢ ㄑㄧㄥ)
feelings; affection; emotions;
devotion (between friends,
relatives, etc.): 他是個凡事訴
諸感情而少用理智的人。He is a
man who feels but seldom
thinks.

感情破裂(《ㄢ ㄑㄧㄥ ㄆㄛ ㄌㄧㄝ)
(said of friends, married
couples, etc.) to fall out

感情主義(《ㄢ ㄑㄧㄥ ㄓㄨ ㄧ)
emotionalism

感情衝動(《ㄢ ㄑㄧㄥ ㄔㄨㄥ ㄉㄨㄥ)
an impulse (to do some-
thing); impulsiveness; to act
on momentary impulse

感情作用(《ㄢ ㄑㄧㄥ ㄗㄨㄛ ㄩㄥ)
action of the emotions

感情用事(《ㄢ ㄑㄧㄥ ㄩㄥ ㄕ)
to appeal to emotions; to
give free rein to emotions;
swayed by one's feelings

感謝(《ㄢ ㄒㄧㄝ)
to thank; gratitude: 我表示衷
心的感謝。I express heartfelt
thanks.

感想(《ㄢ ㄒㄧㄤ)
mental reaction; an impression; an opinion: 請你談談你
對這電視節目的感想。Please
tell us your impressions of
the T.V. program.

感性(《ㄢ ㄒㄧㄥ)
perceptual

感性文化(《ㄢ ㄒㄧㄥ ㄨㄣ ㄏㄨㄚ)
sensate culture

感召(《ㄢ ㄓㄠ)
the inspiration (to do a
noble or brave deed) given
by religious teachings, great
leaders, etc.

感觸(《ㄢ ㄔㄨ)
effect on the mind; feeling;
mental reaction: 他很感觸地
說:「我老了!」He said with
deep feeling, "I'm old!"

感受(《ㄢ ㄕㄡ)
to perceive; to feel; to be
affected by: 我們感受到我們
的拜訪不受歡迎。We per-
ceived that our visit were
unwelcome.

感傷(《ㄢ ㄕㄤ)

sentimental; sentimentality:
這是一個感傷的故事。This is a
sentimental story.

感傷主義(《ㄢ ㄕㄤ ㄓㄨ ㄧ)
sentimentalism

感染(《ㄢ ㄖㄢ)
to be infected with; to tinge;
to affect; to contract (a disease): 作家的激情感染了每個
讀者。The author's passion
affected all his readers.

感恩(《ㄢ ㄣ)
to be grateful; to feel thankful

感恩圖報(《ㄢ ㄣ ㄊㄨ ㄅㄠ)
to feel grateful for a kind
act and plan to repay it

感恩節(《ㄢ ㄣ ㄐㄧㄝ)
Thanksgiving Day

感應(《ㄢ ㄧㄥ)
① to feel and respond ②
(physics) induction

感應電(《ㄢ ㄧㄥ ㄉㄧㄢ)
induced electricity

感應器(《ㄢ ㄧㄥ ㄑㄧ)
an induction machine

感應圈(《ㄢ ㄧㄥ ㄑㄩㄢ)
an induction coil

感悟(《ㄢ ㄨ)
to realize; to become aware
of

【愛】 1653
ㄞ ay ài

1. to love; to like; to be fond
of; to be kind to: 我愛上她
了。I've fallen in love with
her.

2. love; affection; kindness;
benevolence; likes: 他極愛冒
險。He has a strong love of
adventure.

3. to be apt to: 她愛發脾氣。She
is apt to lose her temper.

愛不忍釋(ㄞ ㄅㄨ ㄖㄣ ㄕ)or 愛不釋
手(ㄞ ㄅㄨ ㄕ ㄕㄡ)
loving something too much
to part with it; to fondle
admiringly

愛漂亮(ㄞ ㄆㄧㄠ ㄌㄧㄤ)
to like to look pretty or
attractive

愛莫能助(ㄞ ㄇㄛ ㄋㄥ ㄓㄨ)
desirous but unable to help;
willing to help but unable to
do so

愛默生(ㄞ ㄇㄛ ㄕㄥ)
Ralph Waldo Emerson,

1803-1882, American poet
and philosopher

愛美(ㄞ ㄇㄟ)
① to love beauty ② to be
fond of making up

愛美感(ㄞ ㄇㄟ ㄍㄢ)
esthetic sense

愛面子(ㄞ ㄇㄧㄢ ‧ㄗ)
to be concerned about face-
saving; to be sensitive about
one's reputation

愛民如子(ㄞ ㄇㄧㄣ ㄖㄨ ㄗ)
(said of a ruler or an official) to love the subjects as
if they were his own children

愛慕(ㄞ ㄇㄨ)
to adore; adoration: 我們相互
愛慕。We adore each other.

愛撫(ㄞ ㄈㄨ)
to show tender care for; to
caress

愛達荷(ㄞ ㄉㄚ ㄏㄜ)
the state of Idaho, U. S. A.

愛德華(ㄞ ㄉㄜ ㄏㄨㄚ)
a transliteration of Edward

愛的結晶(ㄞ ‧ㄉㄜ ㄐㄧㄝ ㄐㄧㄥ)
(literally) the crystallization
of love—the child of a couple in love

愛戴(ㄞ ㄉㄞ)
to love and support (a political leader, etc.); to enjoy
popular support

愛迪生(ㄞ ㄉㄧ ㄕㄥ)
Thomas Alva Edison, 1847-
1931, American inventor

愛丁堡(ㄞ ㄉㄧㄥ ㄅㄠ)
Edinburgh, Scotland

愛他主義(ㄞ ㄊㄚ ㄓㄨ ㄧ)
altruism

愛女(ㄞ ㄋㄩ)
a beloved daughter; a favorite daughter

愛理不理的(ㄞ ㄌㄧ ㄅㄨ ㄌㄧ ‧ㄉㄜ)
① (listening to another person) in an unenthusiastic
manner, or with little interest ② cold and indifferent:
她老是一副愛理不理的樣子。
She always looked cold and
indifferent.

愛憐(ㄞ ㄌㄧㄢ)
to show love or fondness for

愛戀(ㄞ ㄌㄧㄢ)
to be in love with; to feel

心部

deeply attached to

愛顧(ㄞ ㄍㄨ)
① to take loving care of ② (customers') kind patronization of a store

愛國(ㄞ ㄍㄨㄛ)
patriotic

愛國公債(ㄞ ㄍㄨㄛ ㄍㄨㄥ ㄓㄞ)
government bonds

愛國心(ㄞ ㄍㄨㄛ ㄒㄧㄣ)
patriotism

愛國主義(ㄞ ㄍㄨㄛ ㄓㄨ ㄧ)
patriotism

愛國運動(ㄞ ㄍㄨㄛ ㄩㄣ ㄉㄨㄥ)
a patriotic movement

愛克司光(ㄞ ㄎㄜˋ ㄙ ㄍㄨㄤ)
X ray; Roentgen rays

愛克司光照相(ㄞ ㄎㄜˋ ㄙ ㄍㄨㄤ ㄓㄠˋ ㄒㄧㄤ)
a roentgenogram

愛河永浴(ㄞ ㄏㄜˊ ㄩㄥˇ ㄩ)
to bathe forever in the river of love (a conventional phrase in congratulatory messages on the occasion of a wedding)

愛好(ㄞ ㄏㄠˋ)
to be interested in, or to love (sport, art, etc.): 我們愛好和平。We love peace. 或 We are peace-loving.

愛好者(ㄞ ㄏㄠˋ ㄓㄜˇ)
a lover (of art, sports, etc.); an amateur; an enthusiast; a fan: 音樂愛好者 a music-lover

愛護(ㄞ ㄏㄨˋ)
to give kind protection to; to take kind care of

愛火(ㄞ ㄏㄨㄛˇ)or 愛慾(ㄞ ㄩˋ)
(Buddhism) passion; sexual drive

愛妾(ㄞ ㄑㄧㄝˋ)
a beloved concubine

愛琴海(ㄞ ㄑㄧㄣˊ ㄏㄞˇ)
Aegean Sea, an arm of the Mediterranean Sea between Greece and Turkey

愛卿(ㄞ ㄑㄧㄥ)
my darling (a form of address found in older novels); my beloved wife

愛情(ㄞ ㄑㄧㄥˊ)
love (between man and woman)

愛情不專(ㄞ ㄑㄧㄥˊ ㄅㄨˋ ㄓㄨㄢ)
changeable or unstable in

love; fickle

愛情專一(ㄞ ㄑㄧㄥˊ ㄓㄨㄢ ㄧ)
steadfast in love

愛犬(ㄞ ㄑㄩㄢˇ)
a beloved dog

愛羣(ㄞ ㄑㄩㄣˊ)
① to love company; gregarious ② to love the multitude

愛惜(ㄞ ㄒㄧˊ)
① to prize; to cherish; to value: 我們愛惜我們團體的榮譽。We cherish the good name of our group. ② stingy; niggardly; miserly

愛心(ㄞ ㄒㄧㄣ)
compassion; kindness

愛新覺羅(ㄞ ㄒㄧㄣ ㄐㄩㄝˊ ㄌㄨㄛˊ)
Aisin Gioro, the family name of the Manchu rulers during the Ching Dynasty

愛虛榮(ㄞ ㄒㄩ ㄖㄨㄥˊ)
vainglorious

愛寵(ㄞ ㄔㄨㄥˇ)
① to love (one lower in position); to favor: 他獲得他雙親的愛寵。He won his parents' favor. ② one's beloved person

愛沙尼亞(ㄞ ㄕㄚ ㄋㄧˊ ㄧㄚˇ)
Estonia

愛神(ㄞ ㄕㄣˊ)
Cupid

愛人(ㄞ ㄖㄣˊ)
① a sweetheart; a lover ② to love others

愛人如己(ㄞ ㄖㄣˊ ㄖㄨˊ ㄐㄧˇ)
to love others as one loves oneself

愛滋病毒(ㄞ ㄗ ㄅㄧㄥˋ ㄉㄨˊ)
AIDS virus

愛子(ㄞ ㄗˇ)
a beloved son; a favorite son

愛憎(ㄞ ㄗㄥ)
love and hate: 他愛憎分明。He is clear about what to love and what to hate.

愛才若命(ㄞ ㄘㄞˊ ㄖㄨㄛˋ ㄇㄧㄥˋ)或愛才若渴(ㄞ ㄘㄞˊ ㄖㄨㄛˋ ㄎㄜˇ)
very fond of talented people

愛財若命(ㄞ ㄘㄞˊ ㄖㄨㄛˋ ㄇㄧㄥˋ)
to love wealth as much as life; very stingy; miserly

愛斯基摩(ㄞ ㄙ ㄐㄧ ㄇㄛˊ)
the Eskimos

愛死症(ㄞ ㄙˇ ㄓㄥˋ)or 愛死病(ㄞ ㄙˇ

ㄅㄧㄥˋ)or 愛滋病(ㄞ ㄗ ㄅㄧㄥˋ)
AIDS (acquired immune deficiency syndrome)

愛阿華(ㄞ ㄚ ㄏㄨㄚˊ)
the state of Iowa, U. S. A.

愛爾蘭(ㄞ ㄦˇ ㄌㄢˊ)
Ireland

愛爾蘭人(ㄞ ㄦˇ ㄌㄢˊ ㄖㄣˊ)
an Irish

愛因斯坦(ㄞ ㄧㄣ ㄙ ㄊㄢˇ)
Albert Einstein, 1879-1955, Jewish physicist and mathematician known for his theory of relativity

愛屋及烏(ㄞ ㄨ ㄐㄧˊ ㄨ)
(literally) When one loves a house, one tends to love even the crows perching on it.—to extend love to someone who is close or dear to one's direct object of love 或 Love me, love my dog.

愛物(ㄞ ㄨˋ)
① a cherished object ② to love all creatures

愛用(ㄞ ㄩㄥˋ)
to love to use; to prefer to use

十畫

【愧】 1654
(愧) ㄎㄨㄟˋ kuey
kuì
ashamed; shameful; abashed; conscience-stricken; to have something on one's conscience: 我問心無愧。I have a clear conscience.

愧不敢當(ㄎㄨㄟˋ ㄅㄨˋ ㄍㄢˇ ㄉㄤ)
(an expression used to show humbleness and politeness) ashamed to accept (an honor); do not deserve (a gift, compliment, etc.)

愧服(ㄎㄨㄟˋ ㄈㄨˊ)
to admire (another) with a feeling of shame about one's own inferiority

愧天怍人(ㄎㄨㄟˋ ㄊㄧㄢ ㄗㄨㄛˋ ㄖㄣˊ)
to feel shame before Heaven and fellow human beings

愧覿見人(ㄎㄨㄟˋ ㄉㄧˇ ㄐㄧㄢˋ ㄖㄣˊ)
ashamed to be seen in public

愧赧(ㄎㄨㄟˋ ㄋㄢˇ)
to redden from shame

愧恧(ㄎㄨㄟˋ ㄋㄩˋ)

to feel shame; ashamed

愧汗（ㄎㄨㄟˋㄏㄢˋ）
perspiration of shame

愧（ㄎㄨㄟˋㄏㄨㄟˋ）
remorseful; to feel mortification as well as resentment: 我內心深自愧恨。I feel bitterly remorseful.

愧悔（ㄎㄨㄟˋㄏㄨㄟˇ）
to feel mortified and regretful

愧疚（ㄎㄨㄟˋㄐㄧㄡˋ）
to feel the discomfort of shame; to feel a sense of guilt; to suffer a guilty conscience

愧心（ㄎㄨㄟˋㄒㄧㄣ）
a feeling of shame: 他感到愧心。He feels ashamed at heart.

愧煞（ㄎㄨㄟˋㄕㄚˋ）
to feel very much ashamed

愧怍（ㄎㄨㄟˋㄗㄨㄛˋ）
to feel shame; ashamed

愧色（ㄎㄨㄟˋㄙㄜˋ）
an expression of shame: 他毫無愧色。He looks unashamed.

愧無以報（ㄎㄨㄟˋㄨˊㄧˇㄅㄠˋ）
ashamed of one's inability to repay a favor

【愴】 1655
ㄔㄨㄤˋ chuang
chuàng
broken-hearted; sad; sorrowful

愴恨（ㄔㄨㄤˋㄏㄣˋ）
sad; sorrowful

愴怳（ㄔㄨㄤˋㄏㄨㄤˇ）
disheartened; depressed; discouraged

愴愴（ㄔㄨㄤˋㄔㄨㄤˋ）
in anguish of sorrow; broken-hearted; anguished

愴然（ㄔㄨㄤˋㄖㄢˊ）
broken-hearted; sick at heart; in anguish of sorrow: 她愴然淚下。She burst into sorrowful tears.

愴惻（ㄔㄨㄤˋㄘㄜˋ）
sad; grieved; sorrowful

【愫】 1656
ㄙㄨˋ suh sù
sincerity; honesty

【慍】 1657
ㄩㄣˋ yunn yùn
angry; indignant; displeased; irritated; vexed: 他面有慍色。

He looked irritated.

慍懟（ㄩㄣˋㄉㄨㄟˋ）
to resent

慍怒（ㄩㄣˋㄋㄨˋ）
angry; irritated; displeased; chagrin

慍恨（ㄩㄣˋㄏㄣˋ）
indignation; resentment; rancor

慍恚（ㄩㄣˋㄏㄨㄟˋ）
to feel resentment; rancorous

慍容（ㄩㄣˋㄖㄨㄥˊ）
a displeased look; an angry appearance; a face of resentment

慍色（ㄩㄣˋㄙㄜˋ）
a displeased look; an angry appearance

【愷】 1658
（凱）ㄎㄞˇ kae kǎi
joyful; good; kind; gentle

愷悌（ㄎㄞˇㄊㄧˋ）
happy and easygoing; friendly; amiable

愷歌 or 凱歌（ㄎㄞˇㄍㄜ）
the song of triumph

愷切（ㄎㄞˇㄑㄧㄝˋ）
gently and sincerely

愷撒（ㄎㄞˇㄙㄚ）
Julius Caesar, 100-44 B.C., Roman general, statesman, and historian

愷樂（ㄎㄞˇㄩㄝˋ）
the tune or music in celebration of victory

【愾】 1659
ㄎㄞˋ kay kài
enmity; hatred; anger; wrath: 我們同仇敵愾。We share a bitter hatred of the enemy.

愾憤（ㄎㄞˋㄈㄣˋ）
angry; to show wrath

【慄】 1660
ㄌㄧˋ lih lì
to shudder; to tremble

慄慄（ㄌㄧˋㄌㄧˋ）
①timorous; fearful; terrified; frightful ②cold; chilly

慄冽（ㄌㄧˋㄌㄧㄝˋ）
piercingly cold; bone-chilling; chilly

慄斯（ㄌㄧˋㄙ）
to act in an obsequious manner in order to please somebody

【慎】 1661
ㄕㄣˋ shenn shèn
cautious; careful; scrupulous; prudent

慎默（ㄕㄣˋㄇㄛˋ）
cautious and reticent

慎密（ㄕㄣˋㄇㄧˋ）
meticulous

慎獨（ㄕㄣˋㄉㄨˊ）
to exercise caution about one's personal life; to be cautious when one is alone

慎刑（ㄕㄣˋㄒㄧㄥˊ）
to mete out penalties very carefully

慎終追遠（ㄕㄣˋㄓㄨㄥ ㄓㄨㄟ ㄩㄢˇ）
thoroughgoing about the funeral rites for parents and the worship of ancestors

慎重（ㄕㄣˋㄓㄨㄥˋ）
cautious; careful; prudent; discreet: 處理這個問題必須慎重。The problem has to be handled with great care.

慎重其事（ㄕㄣˋㄓㄨㄥˋㄑㄧˊㄕˋ）
to take careful precautions; to do something in a serious manner

慎始（ㄕㄣˋㄕˇ）
careful or cautious about the beginning (of an activity)

慎思明辨（ㄕㄣˋㄙㄇㄧㄥˊㄅㄧㄢˋ）
to think carefully and clearly

慎言慎行（ㄕㄣˋㄧㄢˊㄕㄣˋㄒㄧㄥˊ）
to exercise caution in speech and conduct: 我勸告他慎言慎行。I advised him to exercise caution in speech and conduct.

慎微（ㄕㄣˋㄨㄟˊ）
careful about minute details

【慊】 1662
1. ㄑㄧㄢˋ chiann qiàn
to resent

慊慊（ㄑㄧㄢˋㄑㄧㄢˋ）
resentful and discontented

【慊】 1662
2. ㄑㄧㄝˋ chieh qiè
contented; gratified; pleased; satisfied

【慌】 1663
ㄏㄨㄤ huang huāng
to lose self-possession; to lose one's head; panic; confused: 我心慌意亂。I lose my

head totally.

荒忙 (ㄏㄨㄤ ㄇㄤ)
hurried and flustered; hurry-scurry; in a great rush: 我們慌忙趕到現場。We went to the spot in a great rush.

荒了神兒 (ㄏㄨㄤ·ㄌㄜ ㄕㄣˊㄦ)
to lose one's head; to lose self-possession

慌亂 (ㄏㄨㄤ ㄌㄨㄢˋ)
in a hurry and confusion

慌張 (ㄏㄨㄤ ㄓㄤ) or 慌慌張張 (ㄏㄨㄤ ㄏㄨㄤ ㄓㄤ ㄓㄤ) or 慌裏慌張 (ㄏㄨㄤ·ㄌㄧ ㄏㄨㄤ ㄓㄤ)
lacking self-possession; nervous and confused; flustered

【惝】 1664
ㄔㄤˇ tau tǎo
1. fleeting
2. for an extended period; long
3. delighted; happy
4. suspicious; doubtful
5. to cover up; to hide

惝恍 (ㄔㄤˇ ㄊㄤˇ)
for an extended period; long

惝怳 (ㄔㄤˇ ㄏㄨㄤˇ)
excessive neglect (of duties, serious pursuits, etc.); to live a licentious life

【慉】 1665
ㄒㄩˋ shiuh xù
to bring up; to raise

慉結 (ㄒㄩˋ ㄐㄧㄝˊ)
melancholy; depressed

【慈】 1666
ㄘˊ tsyr cí
1. kind; benevolent; benignant; charitable; merciful; loving; fond: 父慈子孝。The father is loving and his son is filial.
2. of one's mother; maternal

慈悲 (ㄘˊ ㄅㄟ)
benevolence; pity; mercy; clemency

慈眉善目 (ㄘˊ ㄇㄟˊ ㄕㄢˋ ㄇㄨˋ)
a benign face; a benignant look

慈命 (ㄘˊ ㄇㄧㄥˋ)
the commands of one's mother; one's mother's command

慈母 (ㄘˊ ㄇㄨˇ)
①a loving mother; a fond mother; a kind mother ②a reference to one's father's concubine who raised one as if one were her own child

慈母敗子 (ㄘˊ ㄇㄨˇ ㄅㄞˋ ㄗˇ)
A fond mother spoils the son.

慈父 (ㄘˊ ㄈㄨˋ)
an affectionate father; a kind father

慈姑 (ㄘˊ ㄍㄨ)
①(ㄍㄨ) a kind mother-in-law; one's husband's mother ②·(ㄍㄨ) (botany) arrowhead 亦作「茨菰」

慈和 (ㄘˊ ㄏㄜˊ)
friendly and kind to each other or one another

慈航普渡 (ㄘˊ ㄏㄤˊ ㄆㄨˇ ㄉㄨˋ)
(literally) The "barge of mercy" ferries all the miserable people to the world of bliss.—(Buddhism) the salvation through charity to others (particularly referring to the Goddess of Mercy or *Avalokitesvara Bodhisattva*)

慈誨 (ㄘˊ ㄏㄨㄟˋ)
the teachings of one's mother; maternal instructions

慈禧太后 (ㄘˊ ㄒㄧˇ ㄊㄞˋ ㄏㄡˋ)
Empress Dowager Tzu Hsi, 1835-1908, who dominated the Manchu court for 47 years toward the end of the Ching Dynasty

慈祥 (ㄘˊ ㄒㄧㄤˊ)
(said of elderly persons) benevolent; kind; benign; benignant

慈訓 (ㄘˊ ㄒㄩㄣˋ)
the teachings of one's mother

慈善 (ㄘˊ ㄕㄢˋ)
benevolence; charity; philanthropy; humanitarianism

慈善機構 (ㄘˊ ㄕㄢˋ ㄐㄧ ㄍㄡˋ)
a charity organization

慈善家 (ㄘˊ ㄕㄢˋ ㄐㄧㄚ)
a philanthropist; a man of charity

慈善事業 (ㄘˊ ㄕㄢˋ ㄕˋ ㄧㄝˋ)
a charitable enterprise; a philanthropic undertaking

慈愛 (ㄘˊ ㄞˋ)
(said of elderly persons) benevolence; affection; love; kindness: 我母親對我非常慈愛。My mother's love for me

was very great.

慈幼 (ㄘˊ ㄧㄡˋ)
to love the young

慈顏 (ㄘˊ ㄧㄢˊ)
①your kindly face (a term of respectful address to elders or parents) ②the face of one's mother

慈烏反哺 (ㄘˊ ㄨ ㄈㄢˇ ㄅㄨˇ)
(literally) the feeding of its mother by a crow—filial piety

慈幛 or 慈闈 (ㄘˊ ㄨㄟˊ)
a reference to one's mother

慈雲 (ㄘˊ ㄩㄣˊ)
(Buddhism) the Buddha heart—immeasurable kindness and mercy

【慂】 1667
ㄩㄥˇ yeong yǒng
to persuade; to urge

【態】 1668
ㄊㄞˋ tay tài
1. an attitude; a position
2. a manner; carriage; bearing; deportment
3. a situation; a condition; circumstances
4. (physics) state of matter

態度 (ㄊㄞˋ ㄉㄨˋ)
①an attitude; a position: 我們必須採取堅定的態度。We must take a firm attitude. ②a manner: 我喜歡他坦率的態度。I like his frank manner.

態度和平 (ㄊㄞˋ ㄉㄨˋ ㄏㄜˊ ㄆㄧㄥˊ)
friendly; a peaceful attitude

態度好 (ㄊㄞˋ ㄉㄨˋ ㄏㄠˇ)
well-mannered; courteous; well-behaved; elegant

態度壞 (ㄊㄞˋ ㄉㄨˋ ㄏㄨㄞˋ)
ill-mannered; impolite; discourteous; impertinent

態度嫻雅 (ㄊㄞˋ ㄉㄨˋ ㄒㄧㄢˊ ㄧㄚˇ)
to have refined manners

態勢 (ㄊㄞˋ ㄕˋ)
①(military) a situation ②a posture

【慇】 1669
ㄧㄣ in yīn
1. mournful; sorrowful
2. regardful; respectful

慇懃 (ㄧㄣ ㄑㄧㄣˊ)
polite; courteous; civil; attentions; attentive: 他向他的老板慇懃慇懃。He was attentive to his boss.

慇憂 (ㄧㄣ ㄧㄡ)

〔心部〕

deep grief; distress; sorrow

愍愍(ㄇㄧㄣˊㄇㄧㄣˊ)
mournful; sorrowful; sad;
melancholy

【愳】(愳) ㄏㄨㄣˊ huenn 1670
   hùn

1. to disturb; to distress; to upset
2. to disgrace
3. to worry

【愬】(訴) ㄙㄨˋ suh sù 1671

1. to tell; to complain
2. scared, frightened

【愿】 ㄩㄢˋ yuann yuàn 1672

sincere; honest; faithful; virtuous

十一畫

【慘】 ㄘㄢˇ tsaan cǎn 1673

1. sorrowful; sad; miserable;
tragic: 他慘遭不幸。He died a
tragic death.
2. cruel; merciless; brutal
3. dark; gloomy; dull
4. disastrously

慘白(ㄘㄢˇㄅㄞˊ)
dreadfully pale; pale

慘敗(ㄘㄢˇㄅㄞˋ)
to suffer a crushing or ignominious defeat; crushing
defeat

慘變(ㄘㄢˇㄅㄧㄢˋ)
a tragic change; a tragedy

慘不忍睹(ㄘㄢˇㄅㄨˋㄖㄣˇㄉㄨˇ)
so tragic that one cannot
bear to look at it

慘怛(ㄘㄢˇㄉㄚˊ)
heavy-hearted; sad; grieved

慘澹 or 慘淡(ㄘㄢˇㄉㄢˋ)
①lacking brightness; dull;
gloomy; dismal; dim: 天色慘
淡。It was dismal weather. ②
laborious; arduous; with
strenuous effort

慘澹經營 or 慘淡經營(ㄘㄢˇㄉㄢˋ
ㄐㄧㄥㄧㄥˊ)
to manage with great pains;
to build up a business from
scratch; to keep an enterprise going by painstaking
effort; to take great pains to
carry on one's work under
difficult circumstances

慘痛(ㄘㄢˇㄊㄨㄥˋ)
bitter; very painful; agonizing: 我們獲得慘痛的教訓。We
learned a bitter lesson.

慘虐(ㄘㄢˇㄋㄩㄝˋ)
extreme cruelty

慘慄(ㄘㄢˇㄌㄧˋ)
bitterly cold

慘烈(ㄘㄢˇㄌㄧㄝˋ)
(said of weather, etc.) very
severe

慘綠少年(ㄘㄢˇㄌㄩˋㄕㄠˋㄋㄧㄢˊ)
(literally) a young man in
dark green—a handsome
young man

慘酷(ㄘㄢˇㄎㄨˋ)
cruel and sadistic; ruthless;
merciless; pitiless

慘禍(ㄘㄢˇㄏㄨㄛˋ)
a terrible disaster; a frightful calamity

慘急(ㄘㄢˇㄐㄧˊ)
to enforce the law in a
harsh manner

慘叫(ㄘㄢˇㄐㄧㄠˋ)
to give a bloodcurdling
scream or shriek

慘劇(ㄘㄢˇㄐㄩˋ)
a tragic event; a tragedy; a
calamity

慘絕人寰(ㄘㄢˇㄐㄩㄝˊㄖㄣˊㄏㄨㄢˊ)
a rare tragedy on earth;
bloodcurdling (atrocities)

慘切(ㄘㄢˇㄑㄧㄝˋ)
tragic; heartbreaking; sad;
pathetic

慘号号的(ㄘㄢˇㄒㄧㄠˊ·ㄌㄜ)
sad-looking

慘相(ㄘㄢˇㄒㄧㄤˋ)
a woebegone look; a crestfallen look; a pitiable condition

慘狀(ㄘㄢˇㄓㄨㄤˋ)
a tragic sight; a sad sight; a
miserable condition; a pitiful
sight

慘重(ㄘㄢˇㄓㄨㄥˋ)
heavy; grievous; disastrous

慘悽(ㄘㄢˇㄑㄧ)
anguished; grieved

慘殺(ㄘㄢˇㄕㄚ)
to kill by cruel or violent
means; to slaughter

慘然(ㄘㄢˇㄖㄢˊ)
sad; saddened; grieved

慘遭橫禍(ㄘㄢˇㄗㄠㄏㄥˋㄏㄨㄛˋ)
to meet a tragic accident

慘惻(ㄘㄢˇㄊㄜˋ)
anguished; grieved

慘死(ㄘㄢˇㄙˇ)
to meet a violent or tragic
death

慘案(ㄘㄢˇㄢˋ)
a cruel murder case; a case
of cold-blooded massacre

慘無天日(ㄘㄢˇㄨˊㄊㄧㄢㄖˋ)
(said of the life under a
tyrannical government) so
dark, or full of suffering,
that it is as if the sun were
not in the sky

慘無人道(ㄘㄢˇㄨˊㄖㄣˊㄉㄠˋ)
inhuman; inhumane; brutal;
cold-blooded; very cruel

慘獄(ㄘㄢˇㄩˋ)
a case that involves a mass
execution

【慢】 ㄇㄢˋ mann màn 1674

1. slow; sluggish: 這條河流得很
慢。The stream is very sluggish.
2. negligent
3. haughty; rude; disrespectful;
arrogant; supercilious
4. to postpone; to defer: 且慢!
Hold on a moment. 或 Just a
moment!

慢板(ㄇㄢˋㄅㄢˇ)
①(Peking opera) a slow
movement or passage ②
(music) adagio

慢步(ㄇㄢˋㄅㄨˋ)
to walk slowly; to slow-poke

慢跑(ㄇㄢˋㄆㄠˇ)
to jog; jogging

慢慢(ㄇㄢˋㄇㄢˋ) or 慢慢兒(ㄇㄢˋ
ㄇㄢˊ)
①leisurely; slowly; unhurriedly; to take one's time ②
by and by; gradually; little
by little

慢慢來(ㄇㄢˋ·ㄇㄢㄌㄞˊ) or 慢來(ㄇㄢˋ
ㄌㄞˊ)
①Don't rush! Take your
time. ②to come or occur
slowly or gradually

慢打法器(ㄇㄢˋㄉㄚˇㄈㄚˇㄑㄧˋ)
(literally) to refrain from
beating the gong for Bud-
dhist services—to refrain
from giving publicity to
something

心部

待(ㄏㄢ ㄌㄞ)
(often used in a polite conversation) to treat (a guest) rudely or discourteously; to treat haughtily or discourteously

到(ㄏㄢ ㄌㄞ)
to arrive late

點兒(ㄏㄢ ㄉㄧㄢ)
Be slower! 或 to slow down a bit; 告訴司機開慢點兒。 Tell the driver to go slower.

調(ㄇㄢ ㄉㄧㄠ)
a slow movement (in music)

動作(ㄇㄢ ㄉㄨㄥ ㄗㄨㄛ)
slow motion

騰騰(ㄇㄢ ㄊㄥ·ㄊㄥ)
at a leisurely pace; unhurriedly; sluggishly

條斯理(ㄇㄢ ㄊㄧㄠ ㄙ ㄌㄧ)
unhurried; unhurriedly; without haste; leisurely; very slowly and imperturbably: 她說話做事總是慢條斯理的。 She always speaks slowly and acts unhurriedly.

吞吞(ㄇㄢ ㄊㄨㄣ ㄊㄨㄣ)
irritatingly slow; exasperatingly slow: 他們慢吞吞地來回於河上。 They slow-poked up and down the river.

工出巧匠(ㄇㄢ ㄍㄨㄥ ㄔㄨ ㄑㄧㄠ ㄐㄧㄤ)or 慢工出細活(ㄇㄢ ㄍㄨㄥ ㄔㄨ ㄒㄧ ㄏㄨㄛ)
Fine products come from slow work. 或 Slow work means careful work. 參看「欲速不達」

曼客(ㄇㄢ ㄎㄜ)
to treat a guest impolitely or rudely; to give a cold reception to a guest

慢火(ㄇㄢ ㄏㄨㄛ)
a slow fire (in cooking)

慢驚風(ㄇㄢ ㄐㄧㄥ ㄈㄥ)
(pathology) eclampsia

慢鏡頭(ㄇㄢ ㄐㄧㄥ ㄊㄡ)
slow motion in the movies

慢些(ㄇㄢ ㄒㄧㄝ)
slower than; to slow down a bit; not so fast

慢行(ㄇㄢ ㄒㄧㄥ)
to walk slowly: 經過村莊時慢行。 Go slow through the village.

慢性病(ㄇㄢ ㄒㄧㄥ ㄅㄧㄥ)
a chronic disease

慢性子(ㄇㄢ ㄒㄧㄥ·ㄗ)
①a sluggish disposition; a phlegmatic disposition ②a slowpoke; a slow coach ③not active in doing things

慢著(ㄇㄢ·ㄓㄜ)
Go slow! 或 Wait a minute!

慢車(ㄇㄢ ㄔㄜ)
a way train; a stopping train; a local train; a slow train

慢車道(ㄇㄢ ㄔㄜ ㄉㄠ)
slow-traffic lanes

慢世(ㄇㄢ ㄕ)
to disregard social conventions and common practices; cynical

慢手慢腳(ㄇㄢ ㄕㄡ ㄇㄢ ㄐㄧㄠ)
slow in doing things; slow-moving; sluggish

慢說(ㄇㄢ ㄕㄨㄛ)
①to speak slowly ②not to speak now ③let alone; to say nothing of

慢走(ㄇㄢ ㄗㄡ)
①Don't go yet! 或 Halt! 或 Wait a minute! ②(polite formula) Good-bye! 或 Take care.

慢藏誨盜(ㄇㄢ ㄘㄤ ㄏㄨㄟ ㄉㄠ)
Slackness in putting things away is tantamount to teaching others to steal. 或 To be careless of jewels is to invite thieves.

慢悠悠地(ㄇㄢ ㄧㄡ ㄧㄡ·ㄉㄜ)
unhurriedly; without haste; in a leisurely manner

【慣】 1675
(ㄍㄨㄢ guann guàn)
1. habitual; customary; usual; accustomed
2. to spoil (a child)
3. to be accustomed to; to be used to

慣例(ㄍㄨㄢ ㄌㄧ)
usual practice; established practice; custom

慣壞(ㄍㄨㄢ ㄏㄨㄞ)
to spoil (a child): 別把孫子慣壞了。 Don't spoil the grandson.

慣技(ㄍㄨㄢ ㄐㄧ)
a customary trick; the usual gimmick

慣竊(ㄍㄨㄢ ㄑㄧㄝ)
a habitual thief; an incorri-

gible thief

慣行犯(ㄍㄨㄢ ㄒㄧㄥ ㄈㄢ)
a habitual criminal; a confirmed criminal; a hardened offender

慣性(ㄍㄨㄢ ㄒㄧㄥ)
(physics) inertia: 慣性使火車滑過了車站。 Inertia carried the train past the station.

慣常(ㄍㄨㄢ ㄔㄤ)
customary; usual

慣賊(ㄍㄨㄢ ㄗㄟ)
a habitual thief

慣養(ㄍㄨㄢ ㄧㄤ)
to let (a child) grow up in comfort; to spoil: 他嬌生慣養的。 He was brought up by indulgent parents.

慣於(ㄍㄨㄢ ㄩ)
accustomed to; used to

慣用(ㄍㄨㄢ ㄩㄥ)
in common use; commonly used

慣用伎倆(ㄍㄨㄢ ㄩㄥ ㄐㄧ ㄌㄧㄤ)
customary tactics; old tricks

慣用手法(ㄍㄨㄢ ㄩㄥ ㄕㄡ ㄈㄚ)
a habitual practice

【慥】 1676
(ㄗㄠ tzaw zào)
(又讀 ㄘㄠ tsaw cào)
sincere; kindhearted

慥慥(ㄗㄠ ㄗㄠ)
sincere and honest; earnestly; wholeheartedly

【慟】 1677
(ㄊㄨㄥ tonq tòng)
extreme grief

慟哭(ㄊㄨㄥ ㄎㄨ)
to weep bitterly

【慨】 1678
(ㄎㄞ kae kǎi)
(又讀 ㄎㄞ kay kǎi)
1. to sigh emotionally
2. generous; magnanimous

慨憤(ㄎㄞ ㄈㄣ)
indignant; angry

慨歎(ㄎㄞ ㄊㄢ)
to deplore or lament with sighs

慨諾(ㄎㄞ ㄋㄨㄛ)or 慨允(ㄎㄞ ㄩㄣ)
to consent generously or readily

慨慷(ㄎㄞ ㄎㄤ)
indignant; angry

慨乎言之(ㄎㄞ ㄏㄨ ㄧㄢ ㄓ)
to say it with a sigh (in-

【心部】

dicating the speaker's nostalgia, sense of regret or loss, etc.)

慨想（ㄎㄞˋ ㄒㄧㄤˇ）
to think of or remember with emotion

慨然（ㄎㄞˋ ㄖㄢˊ）
①to sigh with deep feelings
②generous; kind; magnanimous

1679
【慷】 ㄎㄤ kang kāng
（又讀 ㄎㄤˇ kǎang kǎng）

1. ardent; impassioned
2. generous; liberal; magnanimous; unselfish

慷他人之慨（ㄎㄤ ㄊㄚ ㄖㄣˊ ㄓ ㄎㄞˋ）
to show generosity or unselfishness by another's wealth; to be generous at the expense of others

慷慨（ㄎㄤ ㄎㄞˋ）
①generous; unselfish; liberal ②(usually said of a hero) vehement; fervent; ardent

慷慨悲憤（ㄎㄤ ㄎㄞˋ ㄅㄟ ㄈㄣˋ）
impassioned by lamentation and indignation

慷慨悲歌（ㄎㄤ ㄎㄞˋ ㄅㄟ ㄍㄜ）
to chant in a heroic but mournful tone

慷慨激昂（ㄎㄤ ㄎㄞˋ ㄐㄧ ㄤˊ）
(said of speech or conduct) impassioned; arousing

慷慨解囊（ㄎㄤ ㄎㄞˋ ㄐㄧㄝˇ ㄋㄤˊ）
to make generous contributions (of funds)

慷慨就義（ㄎㄤ ㄎㄞˋ ㄐㄧㄡˋ ㄧˋ）
to sacrifice one's life heroically for a cause, belief, or principle

慷慨成仁（ㄎㄤ ㄎㄞˋ ㄔㄥˊ ㄖㄣˊ）or 慷慨捐軀（ㄎㄤ ㄎㄞˋ ㄐㄩㄢ ㄑㄩ）
to sacrifice one's life heroically for justice; to die heroically in battle

1680
【慳】 ㄑㄧㄢ chian qiān

1. stingy; niggardly; parsimonious; close
2. deficient

慳囊（ㄑㄧㄢ ㄋㄤˊ）
(literally) a moneybag which is closed after money is put in—(figuratively) a miser; a niggard

慳吝（ㄑㄧㄢ ㄌㄧㄣˋ）
stingy; niggardly; miserly

1681
【慵】 ㄩㄥ iong yōng
（又讀 ㄩㄥˊ yong yóng）

indolent; lazy; idle

慵惰（ㄩㄥ ㄉㄨㄛˋ）or 慵懶（ㄩㄥ ㄌㄢˇ）
lazy; indolent; idle; inactive

慵困（ㄩㄥ ㄎㄨㄣˋ）
tired and indolent

1682
【慴】 ㄓㄜˊ jer zhé
fearful; terrified; frightened

慴伏（ㄓㄜˊ ㄈㄨˊ）
to submit out of fear

1583
【慪】 ㄡˋ ow òu

1. same as 嘔—to irritate, to exasperate
2. to be stingy about something

慪氣（ㄡˋ ㄑㄧˋ）
to become exasperated; to be difficult and sulky

慪人（ㄡˋ ㄖㄣˊ）
exasperating; disgusting

1684
【憭】 ㄌㄧㄠˊ liau liáo

1. to rely; to depend
2. disappointed; sad; forlorn
3. clear; easy to understand
4. for the time being

憭亮（ㄌㄧㄠˊ ㄌㄧㄤˋ）
loud and clear

1685
【慝】 ㄊㄜˋ teh tè
an evil idea; evil; vice; iniquity

1686
【愨】 ㄑㄩㄝˋ chiueh què
honest; prudent

1687
【慫】 ㄙㄨㄥˇ soong sǒng
to instigate; to incite

慫動（ㄙㄨㄥˇ ㄉㄨㄥˋ）
to instigate; to incite

慫恿 or 慫慂（ㄙㄨㄥˇ ㄩㄥˇ）
to instigate; to incite; to egg on

1688
【慚】 （慙）ㄘㄢˊ tsarn cán
ashamed; mortified; humiliated: 他 大言不慚. He was shamelessly boastful.

慚覺人企羨（ㄘㄢˊ ㄐㄩㄝˋ ㄖㄣˊ ㄑㄧˋ ㄒㄧㄢˋ）
ashamed of one's inadequacy while envying another's competence

慚德（ㄘㄢˊ ㄉㄜˊ）
ashamed of being defective in morality

慚赧（ㄘㄢˊ ㄋㄢˇ）
to redden from shame

慚恶（ㄘㄢˊ ㄜˋ）
to feel shame; ashamed

慚愧（ㄘㄢˊ ㄎㄨㄟˋ）
ashamed

慚恨（ㄘㄢˊ ㄏㄣˋ）
mortified; humiliated; to feel hurt

慚惶（ㄘㄢˊ ㄏㄨㄤˊ）
ashamed and bewildered; embarrassed

慚沮（ㄘㄢˊ ㄐㄩˇ）
ashamed and depressed

慚怍（ㄘㄢˊ ㄗㄨㄛˋ）
to feel ashamed; to feel shame

慚色（ㄘㄢˊ ㄙㄜˋ）
a shamefaced look

慚悚（ㄘㄢˊ ㄙㄨㄥˇ）
affected with shame and fear

1689
【慧】 ㄏㄨㄟˋ huey huì
intelligent; bright; wise

慧門法海（ㄏㄨㄟˋ ㄇㄣˊ ㄈㄚˇ ㄏㄞˇ）
(literally) the gate of intelligence and the sea of truth —the Buddhistic faith

慧目（ㄏㄨㄟˋ ㄇㄨˋ）
(Buddhism) discerning eyes

慧能（ㄏㄨㄟˋ ㄋㄥˊ）
Hui Neng, a noted Buddhist monk in the Tang Dynasty, the sixth patriarch of the Zen (禪) sect

慧力（ㄏㄨㄟˋ ㄌㄧˋ）
(Buddhism) the power of intelligence

慧根（ㄏㄨㄟˋ ㄍㄣ）
(Buddhism) the root of wisdom that can lead one to truth

慧光（ㄏㄨㄟˋ ㄍㄨㄤ）
(Buddhism) the wisdom which, like the light, pierces darkness

慧劍（ㄏㄨㄟˋ ㄐㄧㄢˋ）
(Buddhism) the sword of wisdom which cuts away illusion

慧劍斬情絲（ㄏㄨㄟˋ ㄐㄧㄢˋ ㄓㄢˇ ㄑㄧㄥˊ ㄙ）

to cut the thread of carnal love with the sword of wisdom

點(ㄉㄧㄢˇ)
(literary language) clever and artful; shrewd; astute

心明(ㄒㄧㄣ ㄇㄧㄥˊ)
(Buddhism) a bright mind; a clear, alert mind; intelligence; the enlightened mind

星(ㄒㄧㄥ)
a comet

性(ㄒㄧㄥˋ)
intelligence

中(ㄓㄨㄥ)
intelligent inside (usually used together with the expression "beautiful outside" in describing a woman)

日(ㄖˋ)
the wisdom of Buddha

眼(ㄧㄢˇ)
① discerning eyes; insight; one's penetrating insight ② (Buddhism) the eye of religious insight

眼識英雄(ㄧㄢˇ ㄕˋ ㄧㄥ ㄒㄩㄥˊ)
Discerning eyes can tell greatness from mediocrity.

【慰】 1690
ㄨㄟˋ wey wèi
to console; to comfort; to soothe; to assuage; to relieve: 鄰居們安慰這個受傷孩子的母親。 Neighbors comforted the mother of the wounded child.

慰勞(ㄨㄟˋ ㄌㄠ)
to entertain and cheer (sometimes by means of material gifts)

慰留(ㄨㄟˋ ㄌㄧㄡˊ)
to try to retain (a person intending to resign) in office

慰解(ㄨㄟˋ ㄐㄧㄝˇ)
to console by relieving one's pain or depression

慰藉(ㄨㄟˋ ㄐㄧㄝˋ)
to console; to comfort; to soothe; to give solace

慰情勝無(ㄨㄟˋ ㄑㄧㄥˊ ㄕㄥˋ ㄨˊ)
Though it gives nothing but a little comfort, it is better than nothing.

慰存(ㄨㄟˋ ㄘㄨㄣˊ)
to show sympathy; to comfort

慰安(ㄨㄟˋ ㄢ)
to soothe; to comfort

慰唁(ㄨㄟˋ ㄧㄢˋ)
to condole with (the bereaved)

慰問(ㄨㄟˋ ㄨㄣˋ)
to show sympathy by making inquiries; to express sympathy and solicitude: 請向他們轉達我真誠的慰問。 Please convey to them my sincere solicitude.

慰問團(ㄨㄟˋ ㄨㄣˋ ㄊㄨㄢˊ)
a group sent to convey greetings and appreciation

慰問金(ㄨㄟˋ ㄨㄣˋ ㄐㄧㄣ)
money sent to express one's gratitude or sympathy

【慼】 1691
(慽) ㄑㄧ chí qí
1. mournful; woeful
2. ashamed

慼貌(ㄑㄧ ㄇㄠˋ)
an appearance of sorrow

慼慼(ㄑㄧ ㄑㄧ)
sorrowful; sad; rueful

慼容(ㄑㄧ ㄖㄨㄥˊ)
a sad look; a sorrowful expression

慼憂(ㄑㄧ ㄧㄡ)
sad and depressed

【慾】 1692
ㄩˋ yuh yù
desire; appetite; passion; lust; greed: 她食慾不振。 She is suffering from lack of appetite.

慾念(ㄩˋ ㄋㄧㄢˋ)
desire; a longing; a craving

慾令智昏(ㄩˋ ㄌㄧㄥˋ ㄓˋ ㄏㄨㄣ)
Greed can benumb reason.

慾海無邊(ㄩˋ ㄏㄞˇ ㄨˊ ㄅㄧㄢ)
Greed knows no bounds.

慾火(ㄩˋ ㄏㄨㄛˇ)
passion; the fire of lust

慾火焚身(ㄩˋ ㄏㄨㄛˇ ㄈㄣˊ ㄕㄣ)
The fire of lust is so hot that it consumes the body.

慾壑難填(ㄩˋ ㄏㄜˋ ㄋㄢˊ ㄊㄧㄢˊ)
The gulf of greed is hard to fill. 或 Greed is hard to satisfy.

慾障(ㄩˋ ㄓㄤˋ)
(Buddhism) desire as a barrier to salvation

慾望(ㄩˋ ㄨㄤˋ)
desire; a longing; aspira-

tions; a craving; an urge: 他有做電影明星的慾望。 He has an urge to become a cinema star.

【慕】 1693
ㄇㄨˋ muh mù
1. to yearn for; to long for
2. to adore; to admire: 我仰慕你已久。 I have long looked up to you with admiration.

慕名(ㄇㄨˋ ㄇㄧㄥˊ)
① eager for fame ② to admire another's reputation

慕名而來(ㄇㄨˋ ㄇㄧㄥˊ ㄦˊ ㄌㄞˊ)
① to be attracted to a place by its reputation as a scenic spot, etc. ② to visit a stranger far away because of his or her reputation as a hero, great beauty, etc.

慕尼黑(ㄇㄨˋ ㄋㄧˊ ㄏㄟ)
① Munich, Germany ② (figuratively) international appeasement

慕化(ㄇㄨˋ ㄏㄨㄚˋ)
(said of barbarians) to be drawn to and assimilated by civilization

慕效(ㄇㄨˋ ㄒㄧㄠˋ)
to imitate in admiration

慕勢(ㄇㄨˋ ㄕˋ)
to try to cling to one in power

慕容(ㄇㄨˋ ㄖㄨㄥˊ)
a family name of the Hsien-pei (鮮卑) tribe, which founded three of the sixteen small states in China during the Tsin (晉) Dynasty

慕義(ㄇㄨˋ ㄧˋ)
to admire righteousness; to emulate a good action

慕悅(ㄇㄨˋ ㄩㄝˋ)
mutual liking

【憂】 1694
ㄧㄡ iou yōu
1. sad; pensive; mournful; grieved
2. anxiety: 她無憂無慮。 She is free from anxieties.
3. to worry about; concerned about; anxious; apprehensive

憂悶(ㄧㄡ ㄇㄣˋ)
to suffer mental agonies; worried; grieved; depressed; low-spirited

憂憤(ㄧㄡ ㄈㄣˋ)
grieved and indignant

憂天憫人(一ㄡ ㄊㄧㄢ ㄇㄧㄣ ㄖㄣˊ)
to worry about the destiny of mankind

憂樂相關(一ㄡ ㄌㄜˋ ㄒㄧㄤ ㄍㄨㄢ)
to share worries and blessings

憂勞成疾(一ㄡ ㄌㄠˊ ㄔㄥˊ ㄐㄧˊ)
to lose one's health because of care

憂慮(一ㄡ ㄌㄩˋ)
worried; anxious; apprehensive; to worry; worries; anxiety: 我甚感憂慮。I felt extremely anxious.

憂國憂民(一ㄡ ㄍㄨㄛˊ 一ㄡ ㄇㄧㄣˊ)
to be concerned about the fate of the nation

憂患(一ㄡ ㄏㄨㄢˋ)
suffering; hardship; misery; distress; trouble; worry: 他飽經憂患。He has gone through a good deal of hardship.

憂患餘生(一ㄡ ㄏㄨㄢˋ ㄩˊ ㄕㄥ)
to survive countless worries and distresses

憂煎(一ㄡ ㄐㄧㄢ)
in agonies of worry

憂懼(一ㄡ ㄐㄩˋ)
anxious and fearful; worried and apprehensive

憂懼萬狀(一ㄡ ㄐㄩˋ ㄨㄢˋ ㄓㄨㄤˋ)
extremely anxious and fearful

憂感(一ㄡ ㄑㄧˋ)
sad and worried

憂心(一ㄡ ㄒㄧㄣ)
a sad heart

憂心忡忡(一ㄡ ㄒㄧㄣ ㄔㄨㄥ ㄔㄨㄥ)
care-ridden; to have a heart loaded with worry

憂心如焚(一ㄡ ㄒㄧㄣ ㄖㄨˊ ㄈㄣˊ)
very anxious; deeply worried

憂形於色(一ㄡ ㄒㄧㄥˊ ㄩˊ ㄙㄜˋ)
to wear a sad or worried expression

憂愁(一ㄡ ㄔㄡˊ)
melancholy; grief; grievous; mournful; sad

憂傷(一ㄡ ㄕㄤ)
worried and grieved

憂容(一ㄡ ㄖㄨㄥˊ)or憂色(一ㄡ ㄙㄜˋ)
a sad or worried look

憂思(一ㄡ ㄙ)
pensive

憂悒(一ㄡ 一ˋ)

melancholy; depressed; cheerless; dispirited; dejected

憂鬱(一ㄡ ㄩˋ)
melancholy; depressed; dejected; cheerless; despondent: 他非常憂鬱地走開。He went away in great dejection.

憂鬱症(一ㄡ ㄩˋ ㄓㄥˋ)
melancholia; hypochondria

【慮】 1695
ㄌㄩˋ liuh lŭ
1. to consider; to take into account: 一個人應慎重考慮後，才做決定。One must consider the matter well before deciding.
2. to worry about; anxious about: 此事不足為慮。This matter gives no cause for anxiety.

慮患(ㄌㄩˋ ㄏㄨㄢˋ)
apprehensive of trouble

慮及(ㄌㄩˋ ㄐㄧˊ)
to have anticipated; to have taken into account: 他早慮及會有麻煩。He had anticipated trouble.

慮事(ㄌㄩˋ ㄕˋ)
① to make plans for a matter ② to have misgivings about a matter

慮遠(ㄌㄩˋ ㄩㄢˇ)
to think far ahead; to plan for the distant future

【慶】 1696
ㄑㄧㄥˋ chinq qìng
1. festivity; blessing; felicity; joy
2. to celebrate; to congratulate; to rejoice

慶弔(ㄑㄧㄥˋ ㄉㄧㄠˋ)
congratulations on happy occasions and condolences on bereavements

慶典(ㄑㄧㄥˋ ㄉㄧㄢˇ)
national festivities and celebration ceremonies

慶功論賞(ㄑㄧㄥˋ ㄍㄨㄥ ㄌㄨㄣˋ ㄕㄤˇ)
to confer honors according to merits in service while celebrating a success or victory

慶功宴(ㄑㄧㄥˋ ㄍㄨㄥ 一ㄢˋ)
a dinner party in celebration of triumph; a celebration party

慶賀(ㄑㄧㄥˋ ㄏㄜˋ)
to celebrate; to rejoice over; to offer congratulations: 的成功值得慶賀。His success deserves congratulation.

慶幸(ㄑㄧㄥˋ ㄒㄧㄥˋ)
to congratulate or rejoice oneself

慶祝(ㄑㄧㄥˋ ㄓㄨˋ)
to celebrate; celebration: 他們慶祝豐收。They celebrated a bumper harvest.

慶壽(ㄑㄧㄥˋ ㄕㄡˋ)
to celebrate the birthday (of an old person)

慶賞(ㄑㄧㄥˋ ㄕㄤˇ)
to celebrate and reward

慶生會(ㄑㄧㄥˋ ㄕㄥ ㄏㄨㄟˋ)
a birthday party

十二畫

【憍】 1697
ㄐㄧㄠ jiau jiāo
self-conceited; arrogant

【憐】 1698
ㄌㄧㄢˊ lian lián
1. to sympathize; to pity; to commiserate: 同病相憐。Fellow sufferers have mutual sympathy.
2. to feel tender regard for
3. touching

憐貧(ㄌㄧㄢˊ ㄆㄧㄣˊ)
to pity or commiserate the poor

憐憫 or 憐閔 or 憐愍(ㄌㄧㄢˊ ㄇㄧㄣˇ)
to pity; to take compassion on; to commiserate

憐惜(ㄌㄧㄢˊ ㄒㄧˊ)
to feel tender regard for: 我們憐惜孩子。We feel tender regard for our children.

憐下(ㄌㄧㄢˊ ㄒㄧㄚˋ)
to have tender regard for one's subordinates; kind to one's inferiors

憐香惜玉(ㄌㄧㄢˊ ㄒㄧㄤ ㄒㄧˊ ㄩˋ)
to have a tender heart for the fair sex

憐恤(ㄌㄧㄢˊ ㄒㄩˋ)
to help or relieve out of compassion: 我們憐恤那些無助的孤兒。We help those helpless orphans out of compassion.

憐才(ㄌㄧㄢˊ ㄘㄞˊ)

to have sympathy for talented persons

愛(ㄞˊ ㄞˇ)
to have tender regard for; to feel pity and love for

憎 ㄗㄥ tzeng zeng   1699
to hate; to loathe; to abhor; to abominate; to detest: 他愛憎分明。 He is clear about what to love and what to hate.

妬(ㄗㄥ ㄉㄨˋ)
to bear a jealous hatred for

恨(ㄗㄥ ㄏㄣˋ)
to hate; to hold a grudge against

嫉(ㄗㄥ ㄐㄧˊ)
to feel a jealous hatred for

厭(ㄗㄥ ㄧㄢˋ)
to hate; to dislike

惡
①(ㄗㄥ ㄨˋ)to hate; to loathe; to abominate; to detest; to abhor
②(ㄗㄥ ㄜˋ)to hate evil

怨(ㄗㄥ ㄩㄢˋ)
to bear a grudge against; to feel bitterness for

憔 ㄑㄧㄠˊ chyau qiáo   1700
emaciated; haggard; worn

慮(ㄑㄧㄠˊ ㄌㄩˋ)
impatient and anxious

悴(ㄑㄧㄠˊ ㄘㄨㄟˋ)
①to have a worn look; to look haggard ②to suffer distress, worries, etc. ③(said of plants) withered

憚 ㄉㄢˋ dann dàn   1701
to fear; to shirk; to dread

煩(ㄉㄢˋ ㄈㄢˊ)
afraid of trouble; to dislike taking trouble

服(ㄉㄢˋ ㄈㄨˊ)
to submit from awe

勞(ㄉㄢˋ ㄌㄠˊ)
to avoid trouble; to shrink from toils

改(ㄉㄢˋ ㄍㄞˇ)
reluctant to correct for fear of difficulty or trouble; afraid to reform: 過則勿憚改。 Don't be afraid to correct errors.

憧 ㄔㄨㄥ chong chóng   1702
1. indecisive; irresolute
2. to yearn; to aspire

憬(ㄔㄨㄥ ㄐㄧㄥˇ)
to imagine something or a place with yearning or longing

憧憧(ㄔㄨㄥ ㄔㄨㄥ)
indecisive; irresolute

憬 ㄐㄧㄥˇ jiing jǐng   1703
to realize; to come to understand; to awake

然(ㄐㄧㄥˇ ㄖㄢˊ)
aware; knowing

悟(ㄐㄧㄥˇ ㄨˋ)
to become aware of; to realize; to come to understand; to come to see the truth: 我憬悟了。 I came to see the truth.

憒 ㄎㄨㄟˋ kuey kuì   1704
muddleheaded; confused in one's mind

眊(ㄎㄨㄟˋ ㄇㄠˋ)
muddleheaded; dull-witted

亂(ㄎㄨㄟˋ ㄌㄨㄢˋ)
confused in one's mind; at a loss; dazed

憒憒(ㄎㄨㄟˋ ㄎㄨㄟˋ)
confused; muddleheaded

憫 ㄇㄧㄣˇ miin mǐn   1705
1. to pity; to commiserate; to feel concerned over: 其情可憫。 His case deserves sympathy.
2. to sorrow;to grieve

惜(ㄇㄧㄣˇ ㄒㄧˊ)
to pity; to have compassion on

恤(ㄇㄧㄣˇ ㄒㄩˋ)
to pity and help

惻(ㄇㄧㄣˇ ㄘㄜˋ)
to pity

憮 ㄨˋ wuu wù   1706
regretful; disappointed

然(ㄨˋ ㄖㄢˊ)
regretfully; disappointedly: 他憮然興嘆。 He gave a sigh of disappointment.

憭 ㄌㄧㄠˊ liau liáo   1707
1. severe; inclement

慄(ㄌㄧㄠˊ ㄌㄧˋ)

cold; inclement; severe; dreary; dismal

憭 2.ㄌㄧㄠˇ leau liǎo   1707
clear; intelligible

懊 ㄠˋ law làо   1708
to regret; to feel remorse

憯 ㄘㄢˇ tsaan cǎn   1709
sad; sorrowful; grieved

憑 ㄆㄧㄥˊ pyng píng   1710
1. to rely on
2. to lean on
3. to be based on; to go by; to base on; to take as a basis
4. a basis; proof; evidence: 口說無憑。 Oral agreement can not serve as evidence.
5. no matter (what, how, etc.)

本事(ㄆㄧㄥˊ ㄅㄣˇ ㄕˋ)
by virtue of sheer competence or talent (as distinct from pure luck or chance)

票(ㄆㄧㄥˊ ㄆㄧㄠˋ)
by showing tickets

票入座(ㄆㄧㄥˊ ㄆㄧㄠˋ ㄖㄨˋ ㄗㄨㄛˋ)
to gain admission by showing tickets; admission by ticket

單(ㄆㄧㄥˊ ㄉㄢ)
a certificate; a receipt

弔(ㄆㄧㄥˊ ㄉㄧㄠˋ)
①to pay homage to (the deceased) ②to contemplate (a ruin, relics, etc.) with emotion

眺(ㄆㄧㄥˊ ㄊㄧㄠˋ)
to look far from an eminence

欄(ㄆㄧㄥˊ ㄌㄢˊ)
to lean upon a balustrade or a railing

良心(ㄆㄧㄥˊ ㄌㄧㄤˊ ㄒㄧㄣ)
as one's conscience dictates

口說(ㄆㄧㄥˊ ㄎㄡˇ ㄕㄨㄛ)
to make an unfounded assertion; mere talk

空(ㄆㄧㄥˊ ㄎㄨㄥ)
without substantial support or proof; without foundation or good reason

几(ㄆㄧㄥˊ ㄐㄧ)
to lean on a desk

藉(ㄆㄧㄥˊ ㄐㄧㄝˋ)
①by means of, on the

〔心

部〕

520 1711—1718

【心部】

憑藉(ㄆㄧㄥˊ ㄐㄧㄝˋ)
strength of ② to rely on: 我憑藉自己的力量。I relied on my own strength. ③ something on which one relies

憑據(ㄆㄧㄥˊ ㄐㄩˋ)
a basis (for belief or supposition); grounds; reasons; proof; evidence

憑信(ㄆㄧㄥˊ ㄒㄧㄣˋ)
to rely upon, or accept, as well-founded

憑虛公子(ㄆㄧㄥˊ ㄒㄩ ㄍㄨㄥ ㄗˇ)
(literally) a nonexistent gentleman—existing in name only

憑虛御風(ㄆㄧㄥˊ ㄒㄩ ㄩˋ ㄈㄥ)
to ride winds; to sail about in the void

憑摺(ㄆㄧㄥˊ ㄓㄜˊ)
a passbook

憑照(ㄆㄧㄥˊ ㄓㄠˋ)
certificates and licenses

憑仗(ㄆㄧㄥˊ ㄓㄤˋ)
to rely upon; to depend upon; by dint of

憑證(ㄆㄧㄥˊ ㄓㄥˋ)
a voucher; proof; evidence

憑準(ㄆㄧㄥˊ ㄓㄨㄣˇ)
a standard; a criterion

憑中(ㄆㄧㄥˊ ㄓㄨㄥ)
① in the presence of a witness ② a witness to a legal document

憑仗(ㄆㄧㄥˊ ㄓㄤˋ)
to rely upon; to depend upon; to lean upon

憑軾結轍(ㄆㄧㄥˊ ㄕˋ ㄐㄧㄝˊ ㄓㄜˊ)
to travel fast on a chariot or cart

憑甚麼(ㄆㄧㄥˊ ㄕㄣˊ ˙ㄇㄜ)
on what basis; why; on what ground: 你憑什麼說這話？What is your basis for saying so?

憑依(ㄆㄧㄥˊ ㄧ)
to rely upon; to depend upon; to be based on; to lean upon

【憋】 1711
ㄅㄧㄝ bie bie
1. to suppress inner feelings with efforts: 我憋了一肚子火。I was filled with pent-up anger.
2. to feel oppressed: 教室裡太悶，憋得人透不過氣來。The classroom was so stuffy; I

could hardly breathe.

憋不住(ㄅㄧㄝ ˙ㄅㄨ ㄓㄨˋ)
cannot suppress (feelings, emotions, etc.); cannot help (speaking out something)

憋悶(ㄅㄧㄝ ㄇㄣˋ)
melancholy; depressed

憋得慌(ㄅㄧㄝ ˙ㄉㄜ ㄏㄨㄤ)
to feel oppressed: 我心裡憋得慌。I feel very much oppressed.

憋扭(ㄅㄧㄝ ㄋㄧㄡˇ)
① to be of contrary opinion ② (said of performance, writing, etc.) clumsy; not smooth

憋氣(ㄅㄧㄝ ㄑㄧˋ)
① to suffer breathing obstruction ② to suppress resentment, grudge, etc.

【憊】 1712
ㄅㄟˋ bey bei
tired; exhausted; weary

憊乏(ㄅㄟˋ ㄈㄚˊ)
tired; weary; exhausted

憊懶(ㄅㄟˋ ㄌㄢˇ)
tired and indolent

憊色(ㄅㄟˋ ㄙㄜˋ)
a tired look; an expression of fatigue: 她面有憊色。She had a tired look.

憊(ㄅㄟˋ ㄩㄢˋ)
tired; exhausted; weary; fatigued: 我太憊倦了以致於站不住。I am too tired to stand.

【憩】
(憩) ㄑㄧˋ chih qi
to rest; to repose

憩息(ㄑㄧˋ ㄒㄧˊ)or憩歇(ㄑㄧˋ ㄒㄧㄝ)
to pause for rest; to rest; to take a rest

【憙】 1714
ㄒㄧˇ shii xi
happy; glad; delighted; pleased; joyful

【憝】 1715
ㄉㄨㄟˋ duey dui
1. wicked or vicious persons
2. to hate

【憖】 1716
ㄧㄣˋ yinn yin
1. willing
2. cautious

【憨】 1717
ㄏㄢ han hān
1. silly; stupid; foolish
2. naive; straightforward

憨態(ㄏㄢ ㄊㄞˋ)

① naive; straightforward: 憨態可掬。She is charming naive. ② a silly appearance

憨頭憨腦(ㄏㄢ ㄊㄡˊ ㄏㄢ ㄋㄠˇ)
stupid; silly; idiotic

憨厚(ㄏㄢ ㄏㄡˋ)
simple and honest

憨睡(ㄏㄢ ㄕㄨㄟˋ)
to sleep soundly

憨笑(ㄏㄢ ㄒㄧㄠˋ)
to giggle; to titter; to smi foolishly

憨直(ㄏㄢ ㄓˊ)
honest and straightforward

憨(ㄏㄢ)
idiotic; silly; stupid

憨子(ㄏㄢ ˙ㄗ)
a nincompoop; an idiot

【憲】 1718
ㄒㄧㄢˋ shiann xian
1. law; a code; a statute; a ordinance; a constitution
2. intelligent
3. a reference to superiors

憲兵(ㄒㄧㄢˋ ㄅㄧㄥ)
military police; gendarmes: 憲兵奉命維持治安。The mili tary police were ordered t keep public security.

憲法(ㄒㄧㄢˋ ㄈㄚˇ)
constitution (of a nationa government): 美國有成文的憲法。The United States has written constitution.

憲法條文(ㄒㄧㄢˋ ㄈㄚˇ ㄊㄧㄠˊ ㄨㄣˊ)
constitutional provisions

憲法草案(ㄒㄧㄢˋ ㄈㄚˇ ㄘㄠˇ ㄢˋ)
a draft constitution

憲典(ㄒㄧㄢˋ ㄉㄧㄢˇ)
a body of laws; a code

憲台(ㄒㄧㄢˋ ㄊㄞˊ)
Your Excellency (a saluta tion for one's superior)

憲天(ㄒㄧㄢˋ ㄊㄧㄢ)
the highest authorities

憲令(ㄒㄧㄢˋ ㄌㄧㄥˋ)
laws and ordinances

憲綱(ㄒㄧㄢˋ ㄍㄤ)
legal provisions

憲章(ㄒㄧㄢˋ ㄓㄤ)
a charter

憲政(ㄒㄧㄢˋ ㄓㄥˋ)
constitutional government; constitutional rule

憲政時期(ㄒㄧㄢˋ ㄓㄥˋ ㄕˊ ㄑㄧ)
the Constitutional Period

(the final of the three stages of the political growth of the Republic of China envisaged by Dr. Sun Yat-sen)

則
laws and institutions

十三畫

憤 1719 ㄈㄣˋ fenn fèn
to resent; indignant; indignation; angry: 別引起公憤。Don't rouse public indignation.

憤不欲生(ㄈㄣˋ ㄅㄨˋ ㄩˋ ㄕㄥ)
to tire of life at the extremity of indignation

憤憤(ㄈㄣˋ ㄈㄣˋ)
① indignant; resentful ② depressed and discontented

憤不平(ㄈㄣˋ ㄅㄨˋ ㄆㄧㄥˊ)
resentful or indignant because of injustice

憤怒(ㄈㄣˋ ㄋㄨˋ)
anger; wrath; indignation; rage: 他甚憤怒。He was in a rage.

憤慨(ㄈㄣˋ ㄎㄞˇ)
anger (especially at injustice); indignation: 他表示憤慨。He expressed his indignation.

憤恨(ㄈㄣˋ ㄏㄣˋ)
resentment; bitterness; rancor: 他心中對你並無憤恨。He has no rancor at heart against you.

憤激(ㄈㄣˋ ㄐㄧ)
vehemence; excitement; fury

憤切(ㄈㄣˋ ㄑㄧㄝˋ)
to grind the teeth with anger

憤世嫉俗(ㄈㄣˋ ㄕˋ ㄐㄧˊ ㄙㄨˊ)or 憤嫉(ㄈㄣˋ ㄐㄧˊ)
resentful of the world; misanthropic; cynical

憤然(ㄈㄣˋ ㄖㄢˊ)
angrily: 她憤然離去。She left angrily.

憤惋(ㄈㄣˋ ㄨㄢˇ)
resentful and regretful

憶 1720 ㄧˋ yih yì
to remember; to bear in mind; to recall; to recollect

憶念(ㄧˋ ㄋㄧㄢˋ)

nostalgic memory; recollection

憶苦思甜(ㄧˋ ㄎㄨˇ ㄙ ㄊㄧㄢˊ)
to recall one's past misfortune and think over one's present happiness

憶及(ㄧˋ ㄐㄧˊ)
to call to mind; to remember; to recollect

憶舊(ㄧˋ ㄐㄧㄡˋ)
to recall the bygone days with nostalgia; to recollect the past

憶起(ㄧˋ ㄑㄧˇ)
to call to mind; to remember; to recall: 他憶起童年時代的日子。He recollected his childhood days.

憶昔(ㄧˋ ㄒㄧˊ)
to recall the bygone days with nostalgia; to recollect the past

憾 1721 ㄏㄢˋ hann hàn
regret; remorse; dissatisfaction

憾恨(ㄏㄢˋ ㄏㄣˋ)
chagrin

憾事(ㄏㄢˋ ㄕˋ)
a regrettable thing; a matter for regret

憾怨(ㄏㄢˋ ㄩㄢˋ)
chagrin

憺 1722 ㄉㄢˋ dann dàn
1. content and stable
2. to fear

憺然(ㄉㄢˋ ㄖㄢˊ)
content; satisfied

懂 1723 ㄉㄨㄥˇ doong dǒng
to understand; to comprehend; to know: 我不懂英語。I don't know English.

懂不懂(ㄉㄨㄥˇ ㄅㄨˋ ㄉㄨㄥˇ)
Do you understand?

懂得(ㄉㄨㄥˇ ㄉㄜˊ)
to understand; to comprehend; to know: 他什麼也不懂得。He knows nothing.

懂道理(ㄉㄨㄥˇ ㄉㄠˋ ㄌㄧˇ)
to be reasonable; to be considerate

懂理(ㄉㄨㄥˇ ㄌㄧˇ)
reasonable and understanding

懂事(ㄉㄨㄥˇ ㄕˋ)

(said of the young) familiar with human affairs; sensible: 她是一個懂事的孩子。She is a sensible child.

懂人情(ㄉㄨㄥˇ ㄖㄣˊ ㄑㄧㄥˊ)
to understand human nature; to understand how to behave

懂人意(ㄉㄨㄥˇ ㄖㄣˊ ㄧˋ)
to understand the ideas of man

懆 1724 ㄘㄠˇ tsao cǎo
anxious; uneasy; apprehensive

懆懆(ㄘㄠˇ ㄘㄠˇ)
uneasy; anxious; apprehensive

懈 1725 ㄒㄧㄝˋ shieh xiè
negligent; remiss; relaxed; inattentive: 我們要努力不懈。We must strive without cease.

懈怠(ㄒㄧㄝˋ ㄉㄞˋ)
neglectful; negligent

懈意(ㄒㄧㄝˋ ㄌㄢˋ)
to neglect; to goldbrick; slack; negligent; to slack; to relax: 工作不可懈怠。Don't get slack at your work.

懈弛(ㄒㄧㄝˋ ㄔˊ)
to relax

懈惰(ㄒㄧㄝˋ ㄉㄨㄛˋ)
indolence; inactivity

懊 1726 ㄠˋ aw ào
to regret; to resent; regretful; remorseful; resentful: 做過的事已經做過了，懊惱無益。What is done is done and regret is of no use.

懊悶(ㄠˋ ㄇㄣˋ)
to eat one's heart out; to pine away

懊恨(ㄠˋ ㄏㄣˋ)
to feel remorseful and angry; upset

懊恨(ㄠˋ ㄏㄣˋ)
resentful

懊悔(ㄠˋ ㄏㄨㄟˇ)
to regret; regretful; remorseful: 我懊悔不該錯怪了他。I regretted having blamed him unjustly.

懊喪(ㄠˋ ㄙㄤˋ)
depressed; dejected; despondent: 她為什麼神情如此懊喪?

心部

Why is she looking so dejected?

【懍】 1727
ㄌㄧㄣˇ liin lǐn
1. filled with awe; awe-struck
2. inspiring awe; awful

懍懍(ㄌㄧˇㄌㄧˇ)
trembling with awe; fearful

懍懍(ㄌㄧˇㄌㄧˇ)
① awe-struck; awe-stricken
② inspiring awe; dignified

懍慄(ㄌㄧˇㄌㄧˋ)
① awe-struck; awe-stricken;
filled with awe ② inspiring
fear

【懌】 1728
ㄧˋ yih yì
delighted; pleased; happy;
glad

懌悅(ㄧˋㄩㄝˋ)
delighted; pleased; happy;
glad

【應】 1729
1. ㄧㄥ ing yīng
should; ought to; need: 你應
該趁熱把咖啡喝掉。You should
drink your coffee while it
is hot.

應辦(ㄧㄥㄅㄢˋ)
(said of tasks, business,
etc.) that should be handled

應否(ㄧㄥㄈㄡˇ)
should or should not

應付費用(ㄧㄥㄈㄨˋㄈㄟˋㄩㄥˋ)
expenses payable

應付利息(ㄧㄥㄈㄨˋㄌㄧˋㄒㄧˊ)
interest payable

應付借款(ㄧㄥㄈㄨˋㄐㄧㄝˋㄎㄨㄢˇ)
loans payable

應付項目(ㄧㄥㄈㄨˋㄒㄧㄤˋㄇㄨˋ)
payables

應付帳款(ㄧㄥㄈㄨˋㄓㄤˋㄎㄨㄢˇ)
accounts payable

應負之責(ㄧㄥㄈㄨˋㄓㄗㄜˊ)
inescapable responsibility

應得(ㄧㄥㄉㄜˊ)
that one deserves to receive;
deserved; due: 你應有應得。
You deserve your punishment.

應當(ㄧㄥㄉㄤ)
duty-bound; should; ought
to: 咱們是同學，應當互相幫助。
As classmates we ought to
help each other.

應該(ㄧㄥㄍㄞ)
ought to; should: 他不應該作

邪惡事情。He should not do
things like that. 兒童應該
服從他們的父母。Children
should obey their parents.

應計工資(ㄧㄥㄐㄧˋㄍㄨㄥㄗ)
accrued wages

應計薪工(ㄧㄥㄐㄧˋㄒㄧㄣㄍㄨㄥ)
accrued payroll

應計項目(ㄧㄥㄐㄧˋㄒㄧㄤˋㄇㄨˋ)
accrued items

應屆畢業生(ㄧㄥㄐㄩˋㄅㄧˋㄧㄝˋㄕㄥ)
graduating students or pupils; this year's graduates

應興應革(ㄧㄥㄒㄧㄥㄧㄥㄍㄜˊ)
what should be started and
what should be abolished;
necessary innovation and
abolishment

應行事項(ㄧㄥㄒㄧㄥˊㄕˋㄒㄧㄤˋ)
things that should be done

應須(ㄧㄥㄒㄩ)
should; ought to; duty-bound

應收票據(ㄧㄥㄕㄡㄆㄧㄠˋㄐㄩˋ)
(accounting) bills receivable; notes receivable

應收利息(ㄧㄥㄕㄡㄌㄧˋㄒㄧˊ)
interest accrued

應收股利(ㄧㄥㄕㄡㄍㄨˇㄌㄧˋ)
(accounting) dividends receivable

應收項目(ㄧㄥㄕㄡㄒㄧㄤˋㄇㄨˋ)
(accounting) receivables

應收帳款(ㄧㄥㄕㄡㄓㄤˋㄎㄨㄢˇ)
(accounting) account receivable

應有(ㄧㄥㄧㄡˇ)
due; proper; deserved: 他做出
應有的貢獻。He made a due
contribution.

應有盡有(ㄧㄥㄧㄡˇㄐㄧㄣˋㄧㄡˇ)
Everything that has to be
available is available. 或
Nothing is wanting.

【應】 1729
2. ㄧㄥˋ ying yìng
1. to respond to; to answer; to
echo; to react to: 我喊他，他
不應。I called him, but he
didn't answer.
2. to comply with; to grant: 菩
薩是有求必應。Buddha grants
whatever is requested.
3. to deal with; to cope with:
這事是你接下來的，由你應付
吧。You're the one who took
on the job, so you deal with
it.

4. to assent to
5. a Chinese family name

應變(ㄧㄥˋㄅㄧㄢˋ)
① to adapt oneself to change
② to prepare oneself for
change ③ (physics) strain

應變措施(ㄧㄥˋㄅㄧㄢˋㄘㄨㄛˋㄕ)
an emergency measure

應聘(ㄧㄥˋㄆㄧㄣˋ)
to accept an offer of employment

應卯(ㄧㄥˋㄇㄠˇ)
(said of officials in former
times) to answer the morning roll call

應門(ㄧㄥˋㄇㄣˊ)
① to keep the gate; to be
gatekeeper ② to answer the
door: 我應門。I answered the
door.

應募(ㄧㄥˋㄇㄨˋ)
① to subscribe (to shares)
② to answer a draft call: 他
兒子應募入伍。His son responded to a call for recruits.

應付(ㄧㄥˋㄈㄨˋ)
① to deal with; to cope with;
to handle: 他應付自如。He
handles a situation with
ease. ② to do something perfunctorily: 他採取應付的態度。
He took a perfunctory attitude. ③ to make do with: 我
這些長靴，今年多天還可以應付
過去。I'll make do with these
boots for this winter.

應答(ㄧㄥˋㄉㄚˊ)
to reply; to answer: 我應答如
流。I reply readily and fluently.

應電荷(ㄧㄥˋㄉㄧㄢˋㄏㄜˊ)
(physics) induced charge

應對(ㄧㄥˋㄉㄨㄟˋ)
① to answer questions ②
repartee: 他擅長應對。He is
accomplished in repartee.

應對如流(ㄧㄥˋㄉㄨㄟˋㄖㄨˊㄌㄧㄡˊ)
to answer questions fluently

應天順人(ㄧㄥˋㄊㄧㄢㄕㄨㄣˋㄖㄣˊ)
(said of monarchs) in harmony with Heaven and men

應諾(ㄧㄥˋㄋㄨㄛˋ)
to assent; to consent; to
promise; to undertake: 他應
諾五點鐘到這裡來。He undertook to be here at five

o'clock.

應力(一ㄥ ㄌㄧˋ)
(physics): stress: 正應力
direct stress 內應力 internal
stress

應考(一ㄥ ㄎㄠˇ)or 應試(一ㄥ ㄕˋ)
to participate in an examination; to sit for an examination: 去年應考的人很多。
Many sat for the examina-
tion last year.

應機立斷(一ㄥ ㄐㄧ ㄌㄧˋ ㄉㄨㄢˋ)
to make quick decisions
when an opportunity offers
itself: 老板要應機立斷。The
boss must make quick decisions as situation demands.

應急(一ㄥ ㄐㄧˊ)
to meet an emergency; for
use in time of emergency

應急措施(一ㄥ ㄐㄧˊ ㄘㄨㄛˋ ㄕ)
an emergency measure

應接(一ㄥ ㄐㄧㄝ)
to receive (visitors or customers)

應接不暇(一ㄥ ㄐㄧㄝ ㄅㄨˋ ㄒㄧㄚˊ)
too busy to make proper
response to

應景詩(一ㄥ ㄐㄧㄥˇ ㄕ)
occasional verses

應景兒(一ㄥ ㄐㄧㄥˇ ㄦ)
to do something appropriate
on the occasion

應試(一ㄥ ㄕˋ)
to become a candidate in
the imperial civil service
examination

應許(一ㄥ ㄒㄩˇ)
to assent; to promise: 他們應
許援助。They promised help.

應選(一ㄥ ㄒㄩㄢˇ)
to be a candidate in an election; to run for an elective
post

應詔(一ㄥ ㄓㄠˋ)
to respond to an imperial
decree

應召(一ㄥ ㄓㄠˋ)
to respond to a call or summons

應召女郎(一ㄥ ㄓㄠˋ ㄋㄩˇ ㄌㄤˊ)
a call girl

應召站(一ㄥ ㄓㄠˋ ㄓㄢˋ)
a call girl center

應召入伍(一ㄥ ㄓㄠˋ ㄖㄨˋ ㄨˇ)
to be drafted (for military
service)

應戰(一ㄥ ㄓㄢˋ)
to accept a challenge; to
meet the enemy on the
battlefield: 我們沉着應戰。We
met the attack calmly.

應診(一ㄥ ㄓㄣˇ)
(said of a doctor) to see
patients

應徵(一ㄥ ㄓㄥ)
① to respond to a want ad
② to be recruited: 他應徵入
伍。He was recruited into the
army.

應徵稿件(一ㄥ ㄓㄥ ㄍㄠˇ ㄐㄧㄢˋ)
contributions to a magazine,
etc. at the editor's public
invitation

應酬(一ㄥ ㄔㄡˊ)
① social appointments ② to
treat with courtesy: 我們應酬
幾句。We exchange a few
polite words.

應承(一ㄥ ㄔㄥˊ)
① to assent; to consent. 這件
事她一口應承下來了。She
agreed to do it without hesitation. ② to pledge

應時(一ㄥ ㄕˊ)
① to adapt oneself to the
times ② to meet the current
requirements; seasonable:
葡萄應時。Grapes are in sea-
son. ③ at the appointed time
④ at once; immediately

應時大果(一ㄥ ㄕˊ ㄉㄚˋ ㄍㄨㄛˇ)
the fruits of the season

應時貨品(一ㄥ ㄕˊ ㄏㄨㄛˋ ㄆㄧㄣˇ)
seasonable merchandise

應市(一ㄥ ㄕˋ)
to go on the market; to be
put on the market; to be offered for sale

應試(一ㄥ ㄕˋ)
to take examinations; to sit
for examinations

應手(一ㄥ ㄕㄡˇ)
smoothly; without a hitch

應聲(一ㄥ ㄕㄥ)
① an echo ② to happen
right at the sound of something

應聲蟲(一ㄥ ㄕㄥ ㄔㄨㄥˊ)
a yes-man; a servile sycophant

應聲而倒(一ㄥ ㄕㄥ ㄦˊ ㄉㄠˇ)
to fall as soon as the bang
(of the gun) was heard

at somebody's invitation; on
invitation

應驗(一ㄥ ㄧㄢˋ)
(said of prophecies, expectations, etc.) to come true,
or to be fulfilled: 她的話應
驗了。What she said has
come true.

應毋庸議(一ㄥ ㄨˊ ㄩㄥ ㄧˋ)
The matter should not be
considered. (a cliché to say
"no" to a request or sug-
gestion in official correspondence)

應援(一ㄥ ㄩㄢˊ)
to render assistance at
another's request

應允(一ㄥ ㄩㄣˇ)
to assent; to consent; an
assent: 他們獲得我的應允。
They had my assent.

應運而生(一ㄥ ㄩㄣˋ ㄦˊ ㄕㄥ)
to come with the tide of
fashion; to rise because of a
demand, opportunity, etc.; to
arise at the historic moment

應用(一ㄥ ㄩㄥˋ)
① to utilize; to make use of
② for practical application;
applied: 我們把理論應用於實
踐。We apply theory to practice.

應用品(一ㄥ ㄩㄥˋ ㄆㄧㄣˇ)
necessities; consumer goods

應用科學(一ㄥ ㄩㄥˋ ㄎㄜ ㄒㄩㄝˊ)
applied science: 他決定研究應
用科學。He decided to study
applied science.

應用心理學(一ㄥ ㄩㄥˋ ㄒㄧㄣ ㄌㄧˇ
ㄒㄩㄝˊ)
applied psychology

應用數學(一ㄥ ㄩㄥˋ ㄕㄨˋ ㄒㄩㄝˊ)
applied mathematics

應用文(一ㄥ ㄩㄥˋ ㄨㄣˊ)
business writing; practical
writing

【懃】 1730
ㄑㄧㄣˊ chyn qín
cordial; hearty

懃懇懇(ㄑㄧㄣˊ ㄑㄧㄣˊ ㄎㄣˇ ㄎㄣˇ)
cordial and sincere

【懇】 1731
ㄎㄣˇ keen kěn
cordial; sincere; earnest: 他
說話很誠懇。He is sincere in
his statement.

【心部】

懇談(ㄎㄣˇ ㄊㄢˊ)
to have a sincere talk; to talk in a sincere manner

懇託(ㄎㄣˇ ㄊㄨㄛ)
to make a sincere request; to ask or request earnestly

懇留(ㄎㄣˇ ㄌㄧㄡˊ)
to make a sincere or earnest attempt to make a person stay

懇諫(ㄎㄣˇ ㄐㄧㄢˋ)
to admonish with sincerity; to admonish earnestly

懇乞(ㄎㄣˇ ㄑㄧˇ)
to entreat

懇切(ㄎㄣˇ ㄑㄧㄝˋ)
very sincere; earnest: 他的言詞懇切。He spoke in an earnest tone.

懇求(ㄎㄣˇ ㄑㄧㄡˊ)
to entreat; to beseech; to implore; to plead: 他懇求幫忙。He entreats a favor of me.

懇親會(ㄎㄣˇ ㄑㄧㄣ ㄏㄨㄟˋ)
PTA (parent-teacher association or meeting)

懇請(ㄎㄣˇ ㄑㄧㄥˇ)
to ask earnestly; to implore; to entreat; to beseech; to plead: 懇請協助。Your assistance is earnestly requested.

懇摯(ㄎㄣˇ ㄓˋ)
sincere; earnest; eager: 他的情意懇摯。He showed his sincere feelings.

懇准(ㄎㄣˇ ㄓㄨㄣˇ)
to beg your kind permission

懇商(ㄎㄣˇ ㄕㄤ)
to ask for a favor earnestly; to seek consent sincerely

懇辭(ㄎㄣˇ ㄘˊ)
to decline (an offer) earnestly

【懋】 1732   ㄇㄠˋ maw mào
1. grand; majestic; great
2. trade
3. to encourage

懋典(ㄇㄠˋ ㄉㄧㄢˇ)
a grand occasion

懋功(ㄇㄠˋ ㄍㄨㄥ)
great achievements

懋績(ㄇㄠˋ ㄐㄧ)
great achievements or contribution

懋遷(ㄇㄠˋ ㄑㄧㄢ)
trade; commerce

懋勳(ㄇㄠˋ ㄒㄩㄣ)
great exploits or contribution

懋賞(ㄇㄠˋ ㄕㄤˇ)
to reward in order to encourage

十四畫

【懥】 1733   ㄓˋ jyh zhì
enraged; indignant; angry; resentful

【懦】 1734   ㄋㄨㄛˋ nuoh nuò
timid; cowardly; weak: 那個人怯懦如兔。That fellow is as timid as a rabbit.

懦夫(ㄋㄨㄛˋ ㄈㄨ)
a coward: 他是懦夫。He is a coward.

懦鈍(ㄋㄨㄛˋ ㄉㄨㄣˋ)
weak and dull

懦怯(ㄋㄨㄛˋ ㄑㄧㄝˋ)
coward; timid

懦弱(ㄋㄨㄛˋ ㄖㄨㄛˋ)
weak; cowardly

【懨】 1735   (懕) ㄧㄢ ian yān
1. sickly; in poor health
2. peaceful; tranquil

懨懨(ㄧㄢ ㄧㄢ)
①sickly; in poor health ②peaceful; content

【懣】 1736   ㄇㄣˋ menn mèn
resentful; sullen; sulky

【懟】 1737   ㄉㄨㄟˋ duey duì
to resent; to resent; rancor: 他心中對你並無怨懟。He has no rancor at heart against you.

十五畫

【懲】 1738   ㄔㄥˊ cherng chéng
(又讀 ㄔㄥˇ cheeng chěng)
1. to punish; to chastise; to reprimand; to reprove; to warn
2. to stop

懲辦(ㄔㄥˊ ㄅㄢˋ)
to take disciplinary action against

懲罰(ㄔㄥˊ ㄈㄚˊ)
to punish; to chastise; to penalize; a penalty: 他受到一次嚴厲的懲罰。He paid a severe penalty.

懲忿窒欲(ㄔㄥˊ ㄈㄣˋ ㄓˋ ㄩˋ)
to curb one's temper and desire

懲戒(ㄔㄥˊ ㄐㄧㄝˋ)
to reprimand; to discipline; to punish

懲戒處分(ㄔㄥˊ ㄐㄧㄝˋ ㄔㄨˋ ㄈㄣˋ)
disciplinary action (against government officials) ranging from reprimand to dismissal

懲前毖後(ㄔㄥˊ ㄑㄧㄢˊ ㄅㄧˋ ㄏㄡˋ)or 懲毖(ㄔㄥˊ ㄅㄧˋ)
to act cautiously in consequence of the penalty received for a previous offense

懲治(ㄔㄥˊ ㄓˋ)
to remedy by punishment

懲處(ㄔㄥˊ ㄔㄨˋ)
to penalize; to punish: 他依法懲處犯人。He punished the criminals in accordance with the law.

懲惡勸善(ㄔㄥˊ ㄜˋ ㄑㄩㄢˋ ㄕㄢˋ)
to punish wickedness and encourage virtue

懲一警百(ㄔㄥˊ ㄧ ㄐㄧㄥˇ ㄅㄞˇ)
to punish one person as a warning to a hundred others

懲役(ㄔㄥˊ ㄧˋ)
hard labor as a form of punishment

十六畫

【懷】 1739   ㄏㄨㄞˊ hwai huái
1. bosom; breast
2. to hold; to harbor: 他不懷好意。He harbored evil designs.
3. to think of; to recollect
4. to conceive (a child): 她懷了孩子。She became pregnant.
5. mind: 他的胸懷坦白。He is frank and open-minded.
6. as in 開懷暢飲(to drink to one's heart's content)
7. a Chinese family name

懷寶迷邦(ㄏㄨㄞˊ ㄅㄠˇ ㄇㄧˊ ㄅㄤ)
to possess great talent but to live as a recluse

懷抱(ㄏㄨㄞˊ ㄅㄠˋ)
①an embrace; a hug; to

embrace; to hug ②the ideas one entertains; ambition ③to cherish: 我們懷抱遠大的理想。We cherish lofty ideals.

懷璧其罪(ㄏㄨㄞˊ ㄅㄧˋ ㄑㄧˊ ㄗㄨㄟˋ)
(literally) The precious stone lands its innocent possessor in jail.—An innocent man gets into trouble because of his wealth.

懷錶(ㄏㄨㄞˊ ㄅㄧㄠˇ)
a pocket watch

懷服(ㄏㄨㄞˊ ㄈㄨˊ)
to yield; to submit; to give in

懷胎(ㄏㄨㄞˊ ㄊㄞ) or 懷孕(ㄏㄨㄞˊ ㄩㄣˋ) or 懷孕(ㄏㄨㄞˊ ㄖㄣˊ)
to become pregnant; to conceive: 她懷孕五個月了。She is five months pregnant.

懷土(ㄏㄨㄞˊ ㄊㄨˇ)
homesick; to yearn for home

懷念(ㄏㄨㄞˊ ㄋㄧㄢˋ)
to have a sweet memory of, to remember with longing or nostalgia; to think of; to long for; to miss: 我懷念遠方的友人。I thought of an absent friend who was far away.

懷祿(ㄏㄨㄞˊ ㄌㄨˋ)
to yearn for a high official position

懷古(ㄏㄨㄞˊ ㄍㄨˇ)
to look back upon the past; to think of the past with emotion

懷鬼胎(ㄏㄨㄞˊ ㄍㄨㄟˇ ㄊㄞ)
to harbor an evil scheme; to conceive mischief

懷恨(ㄏㄨㄞˊ ㄏㄣˋ) or 懷仇(ㄏㄨㄞˊ ㄔㄡˊ)
to bear a grudge; to nurse hatred; to harbor resentment

懷舊(ㄏㄨㄞˊ ㄐㄧㄡˋ)
①to recollect the good old days; to think of the bygone days with yearning; to yearn for the past ②to think of old friends

懷瑾握瑜(ㄏㄨㄞˊ ㄐㄧㄣˇ ㄨㄛˋ ㄩˊ)
(literally) to hold gems in one's bosom and grasp jades in one's hand—to be in possession of learning and virtue

懷奇(ㄏㄨㄞˊ ㄑㄧˊ)
to possess a rare talent or ability

懷鉛提槧(ㄏㄨㄞˊ ㄑㄧㄢ ㄊㄧˊ ㄑㄧㄢˋ)
to have writing instruments constantly with oneself; to be ready to write down anything encountered

懷惡(ㄏㄨㄞˊ ㄜˋ)
to harbor evil

懷挾(ㄏㄨㄞˊ ㄒㄧㄚˊ)
to secretly carry notes or books into an examination room

懷鄉(ㄏㄨㄞˊ ㄒㄧㄤ)
homesick

懷想(ㄏㄨㄞˊ ㄒㄧㄤˇ)
to think of with yearning; to remember with fondness; to yearn for

懷中(ㄏㄨㄞˊ ㄓㄨㄥ)
①in the arms ②in the mind

懷春(ㄏㄨㄞˊ ㄔㄨㄣ)
(usually said of young girls) to begin to think of love, or become sexually awakened

懷柔(ㄏㄨㄞˊ ㄖㄡˊ)
to conciliate; to appease; to pacify

懷柔政策(ㄏㄨㄞˊ ㄖㄡˊ ㄓㄥˋ ㄘㄜˋ)
conciliationism; a conciliatory policy (adopted by a powerful country in dealing with a weak nation or subjugated people)

懷才不遇(ㄏㄨㄞˊ ㄘㄞˊ ㄅㄨˋ ㄩˋ)
to have talent but no opportunity to use it

懷藏(ㄏㄨㄞˊ ㄘㄤˊ)
to conceal (weapons, jewels, etc.)

懷俄明(ㄏㄨㄞˊ ㄜˊ ㄇㄧㄥˊ)
the state of Wyoming, U.S.A.

懷貳(ㄏㄨㄞˊ ㄦˋ)
to harbor a treasonous intention, idea, or design

懷疑(ㄏㄨㄞˊ ㄧˊ)
to doubt; to suspect; to question; suspicious; doubt: 我懷疑故事的真實性。I doubt the truth of this story.

懷憂(ㄏㄨㄞˊ ㄧㄡ)
to be concerned or worried

【懶】 1740
ㄌㄢˇ laan lǎn
lazy; indolent; idle; inactive; listless; reluctant; disinclined: 他是一個懶人。He's a

lazy fellow.

懶得(ㄌㄢˇ ㄉㄜ˙)
not to feel like (doing something); not disposed or too tired to do anything; not to be in the mood to; to be disinclined to 亦作「懶待」: 我懶得出去。I don't feel like going out.

懶得動(ㄌㄢˇ ㄉㄜ˙ ㄉㄨㄥˋ)
lethargic; disinclined to move

懶得要命(ㄌㄢˇ ㄉㄜ˙ ㄧㄠˋ ㄇㄧㄥˋ)
very lazy

懶惰(ㄌㄢˇ ㄉㄨㄛˋ) or 懶惰(ㄌㄢˇ ㄉㄨㄛˋ)
lazy; idle; indolent; slothful; inactive: 不要這樣懶惰。Don't be so lazy.

懶惰成性(ㄌㄢˇ ㄉㄨㄛˋ ㄔㄥˊ ㄒㄧㄥˋ)
to be habitually lazy; to have laziness as one's second nature

懶骨頭(ㄌㄢˇ ㄍㄨˇ ㄊㄡˊ)
lazybones; a lazy person

懶慣了(ㄌㄢˇ ㄍㄨㄢˋ ㄌㄜ˙)
accustomed to being lazy

懶漢(ㄌㄢˇ ㄏㄢˋ)
a lazy fellow

懶蟲(ㄌㄢˇ ㄔㄨㄥˊ)
(abusive) a lazy person; lazybones

懶散(ㄌㄢˇ ㄙㄢˇ)
indolent; inactive; sluggish: 不要這樣懶散，振作起來。Do not be so sluggish. Pull yourself together.

懶洋洋(ㄌㄢˇ ㄧㄤ ㄧㄤ)
indolent; sluggish

懶於(ㄌㄢˇ ㄩˊ)
too lazy to do something; not enthusiastic about something: 他懶於做功課。He is too lazy to do his homework.

【懜】 1741
ㄇㄥˊ meng
meng
ignorant

懜懜無知(ㄇㄥˊ ㄇㄥˊ ㄨˊ ㄓ)
quite ignorant

懜然(ㄇㄥˊ ㄖㄢˊ)
ignorant

【懵】 1741
ㄇㄥˇ meeng měng
muddleheaded; confused

懵懂(ㄇㄥˇ ㄉㄨㄥˇ)
①to have a confused mind;

〔心部〕

〔心部〕

muddleheaded ② dull-witted; ignorant

【懸】 1742
ㄒㄩㄢˊ shyuan xuán
1. to hang or be hanged or hung; to suspend or be suspended
2. to be in suspension; to be in suspense; unsettled; unsolved: 這筆賬懸了數年了。 This account has remained unsettled for many years.
3. unfounded; without a basis; unsupported
4. far apart
5. to be concerned for

懸瀑(ㄒㄩㄢˊ ㄆㄨˋ)
a cascade; a waterfall

懸門(ㄒㄩㄢˊ ㄇㄣˊ)
a suspended gate which could be dropped

懸法(ㄒㄩㄢˊ ㄈㄚˇ)
to display written laws on some hangings

懸浮(ㄒㄩㄢˊ ㄈㄨˊ)
(physics) suspension

懸膽(ㄒㄩㄢˊ ㄉㄢˇ)
a drooping nose like a suspended gall

懸燈結綵(ㄒㄩㄢˊ ㄉㄥ ㄐㄧㄝˊ ㄘㄞˇ)
to celebrate an occasion by hanging lanterns and festoons

懸擬(ㄒㄩㄢˊ ㄋㄧˇ)
to make conjectures

懸念(ㄒㄩㄢˊ ㄋㄧㄢˋ)
worry and concern for a friend or close family member far away: 他突然失蹤促我們大為懸念。 His sudden disappearance causes us considerable concern.

懸梁自盡(ㄒㄩㄢˊ ㄌㄧㄤˊ ㄗˋ ㄐㄧㄣˋ)
to hang oneself; to commit suicide by hanging

懸隔(ㄒㄩㄢˊ ㄍㄜˊ)
① remote; inaccessible ② to be separated by a great distance

懸鉤子(ㄒㄩㄢˊ ㄍㄡ ㄗ)
blackberry 亦作「山莓」

懸谷(ㄒㄩㄢˊ ㄍㄨˇ)
(geography) hanging valley

懸掛(ㄒㄩㄢˊ ㄍㄨㄚˋ)
to hang (decorations); to suspend: 此畫懸掛在牆上。 The picture was hanging on the wall.

懸空(ㄒㄩㄢˊ ㄎㄨㄥ)
to be suspended (or hung) in the air

懸河(ㄒㄩㄢˊ ㄏㄜˊ)
① to pour continually ② to speak eloquently or glibly: 她口若懸河地表達自己的意思。 She expressed herself in a flow of words.

懸壺(ㄒㄩㄢˊ ㄏㄨˊ)
to show (laws, etc.) as a public standard

懸壺濟世(ㄒㄩㄢˊ ㄏㄨˊ ㄐㄧˋ ㄕˋ)
to practice medicine or pharmacy

懸記(ㄒㄩㄢˊ ㄐㄧˋ)
prophecy; a prediction; forecast

懸絕(ㄒㄩㄢˊ ㄐㄩㄝˊ)
completely different

懸旗(ㄒㄩㄢˊ ㄑㄧˊ)
to hoist a flag; to hang a flag

懸缺(ㄒㄩㄢˊ ㄑㄩㄝ)
an unfilled vacancy or opening (in a government agency): 我們公司尚有懸缺。 There is an unfilled vacancy in our company.

懸心(ㄒㄩㄢˊ ㄒㄧㄣ)
concerned about someone or something

懸心吊膽(ㄒㄩㄢˊ ㄒㄧㄣ ㄉㄧㄠˋ ㄉㄢˇ)
on tenterhooks; to be filled with anxiety or fear

懸想(ㄒㄩㄢˊ ㄒㄧㄤˇ)
to speculate; to conjecture; to imagine

懸慮(ㄒㄩㄢˊ ㄒㄩ)
hard to believe; unbelievable; incredible

懸針(ㄒㄩㄢˊ ㄓㄣ)
① a tadpole ② the hanging-needle stroke; an upright stroke in calligraphy seen in the character for ten (十)

懸腸掛肚(ㄒㄩㄢˊ ㄔㄤˊ ㄍㄨㄚˋ ㄉㄨˋ)
to harbor deep concern for something, as if it were suspended on one's bowels

懸揣(ㄒㄩㄢˊ ㄔㄨㄞˇ)
to speculate or conjecture

懸首(ㄒㄩㄢˊ ㄕㄡˇ)
to hang the head of a decapitated criminal in the market or over the city gate

懸賞(ㄒㄩㄢˊ ㄕㄤˇ)
to offer a prize, or reward (for the capture of a criminal, etc.): 警方懸賞緝拿該逃犯。 The police offered a reward for the capture of the runaway criminal.

懸殊(ㄒㄩㄢˊ ㄕㄨ)
to differ by a wide margin; very different; a great disparity; a wide gap: 那個國家貧富懸殊。 There is a wide gap between the rich and the poor in that country.

懸在空中(ㄒㄩㄢˊ ㄗㄞˋ ㄎㄨㄥ ㄓㄨㄥ)
to suspend or be suspended in midair

懸索橋(ㄒㄩㄢˊ ㄙㄨㄛˇ ㄑㄧㄠˊ)
a suspension bridge 亦作「吊橋」

懸案(ㄒㄩㄢˊ ㄢˋ)
an unsettled case; an outstanding issue (between nations)

懸而未決(ㄒㄩㄢˊ ㄦˊ ㄨㄟˋ ㄐㄩㄝˊ)
suspense; in suspense: 歷經數日，事情仍是懸而未決。 For some days matters hung in suspense.

懸疑(ㄒㄩㄢˊ ㄧˊ)
suspense

懸崖(ㄒㄩㄢˊ ㄧㄞˊ)
a precipice

懸崖勒馬(ㄒㄩㄢˊ ㄧㄞˊ ㄌㄜˋ ㄇㄚˇ)
(literally) to rein in the horse at the edge of a precipice—to stop just before committing a serious blunder; to stop before it is too late

懸崖峭壁(ㄒㄩㄢˊ ㄧㄞˊ ㄑㄧㄠˋ ㄅㄧˋ)
overhanging precipices and steep cliffs

懸腕(ㄒㄩㄢˊ ㄨㄢˋ)or 懸肘(ㄒㄩㄢˊ ㄓㄡˇ)
to keep the arm off the desk (when writing characters in order to gain forcefulness in the strokes)

懸望(ㄒㄩㄢˊ ㄨㄤˋ)
to hope with misgivings

十七畫

【懺】 1743
ㄔㄢˋ chann chàn
to confess one's sin; to repent

【懺禮(ㄔㄢˋㄌㄧˇ)】
a ritual for penance; a ceremony of penitence

【懺悔(ㄔㄢˋㄏㄨㄟˇ)】
to repent of one's sin; to feel or show repentance: 他懺悔自己的罪過。He repented of his sin.

【懺悔錄(ㄔㄢˋㄏㄨㄟˇㄌㄨˋ)】
confessions

【懺悔自新(ㄔㄢˋㄏㄨㄟˇㄗˋㄒㄧㄣ)】
to repent and turn over a new leaf

十八畫

【懼】 1744
ㄐㄩˋ jiuh jù
1. to fear; to dread; to be afraid of; in fear of: 人們恐懼生病。People dread falling ill (or to fall ill).
2. to frighten

【懼怕(ㄐㄩˋㄆㄚˋ)】
to fear; to dread; to be afraid of

【懼內(ㄐㄩˋㄋㄟˋ)】
henpecked

【懼高症(ㄐㄩˋㄍㄠㄓㄥˋ)】
acrophobia

【懼怯(ㄐㄩˋㄑㄧㄝˋ)】
timid; afraid

【懼者不死(ㄐㄩˋㄓㄜˇㄅㄨˋㄙˇ)】
He who has come is no coward. 亦作「來者不懼」

【懼水症(ㄐㄩˋㄕㄨㄟˇㄓㄥˋ)】
hydrophobia 亦作「恐水症」

【懼色】
a look of fear

【懾】 1745
ㄓㄜˋ jer zhé
fearful; awe-struck: 他懾於淫威之下。He is terrorized by tyrannical methods.

【懾服】
to yield from fear; to submit because of fear

【懾慴】
to lose one's courage in fear

【懿】 1746
ㄧˋ yih yì
1. virtuous; fine; good; exemplary
2. having to do with womanly virtue; modest; chaste

【懿範(ㄧˋㄈㄢˋ)】
a fine example or model of womanly virtue; exemplary character

【懿德(ㄧˋㄉㄜˊ)】
①fine virtue ②woman's worthy or meritorious character

【懿戚(ㄧˋㄑㄧ)】
the emperor's relatives by marriage

【懿親(ㄧˋㄑㄧㄣ)】
close relatives

【懿行(ㄧˋㄒㄧㄥˊ)】
①a virtuous deed ②women's virtuous conduct

【懿旨(ㄧˋㄓˇ)】
a decree by the empress; a command or wish of the empress or empress dowager

【懿言(ㄧˋㄧㄢˊ)】
fine words

【懿望(ㄧˋㄨㄤˋ)】
good reputation

【懽】 1747
(歡) ㄏㄨㄢ huan
huān
happy; glad; joyous

十九畫

【戀】 1748
ㄌㄧㄢˋ liann liàn
1. to love (one of the other sex); to be in love: 他們在戀愛中。They are in love with each other.
2. to feel a persistent attachment (for a thing)

【戀母情結(ㄌㄧㄢˋㄇㄨˇㄑㄧㄥˊㄐㄧㄝˊ)】
Oedipus complex

【戀慕(ㄌㄧㄢˋㄇㄨˋ)】
to have a tender feeling towards; to lose one's heart to; to pine for; to love at a distance or silently

【戀父情結(ㄌㄧㄢˋㄈㄨˋㄑㄧㄥˊㄐㄧㄝˊ)】
Electra complex

【戀戀不捨(ㄌㄧㄢˋㄌㄧㄢˋㄅㄨˋㄕㄜˇ)】
to feel a persistent attachment (for a thing or a person); to feel reluctant to part company with (a person or thing)

【戀歌(ㄌㄧㄢˋㄍㄜ)】
a love song

【戀家(ㄌㄧㄢˋㄐㄧㄚ)】
to be reluctant to leave home; to prefer to stay at home; to long for home; to be reluctant to be away from home

【戀舊(ㄌㄧㄢˋㄐㄧㄡˋ)】
①to yearn for the past; to long for the good old days ②to yearn for old friends, or for a place one visited before

【戀奸情熱(ㄌㄧㄢˋㄐㄧㄢㄑㄧㄥˊㄖㄜˋ)】
to have an illicit and passionate love affair

【戀情(ㄌㄧㄢˋㄑㄧㄥˊ)】
love between man and woman

【戀棧(ㄌㄧㄢˋㄓㄢˋ)】
reluctant to give up a position (particularly a public post) one is holding; to cling to an official post when one should leave

【戀主(ㄌㄧㄢˋㄓㄨˇ)】
to feel an attachment for one's master

【戀人(ㄌㄧㄢˋㄖㄣˊ)】
a sweetheart; a lover

【戀愛(ㄌㄧㄢˋㄞˋ)】
tender passions; a romantic attachment

二十畫

【戄】 1749
ㄐㄩㄝˊ jyue jué
1. respectful
2. awe-struck

【戄然(ㄐㄩㄝˊㄖㄢˊ)】
awe-struck; surprisingly

二十四畫

【戇】 1750
ㄓㄨㄤˋ juang
zhuàng
simple-minded

【戇直(ㄓㄨㄤˋㄓˊ)】
simple and upright; simple and honest; blunt and tactless: 他爲人戇直。He is simple and honest.

戈 部
ㄍㄜ ge gē

【戈】 1751
ㄍㄜ ge gē

〔戈部〕

1. a spear; a lance; a javelin
2. a Chinese family name

戈比 (ㄍㄜ ㄅㄧˇ)
(a coin of the U.S.S.R.)
kopek, kopeck, or copeck

戈壁 (ㄍㄜ ㄅㄧˋ)
Mongolian for "desert"

戈壁大沙漠 (ㄍㄜ ㄅㄧˋ ㄉㄚˋ ㄕㄚ ㄇㄛˋ)
the Gobi Desert

戈矛 (ㄍㄜ ㄇㄠˊ)
spears and lances: 戰士們攜帶戈矛。 The warriors carried spears and lances.

戈登 (ㄍㄜ ㄉㄥ)
Charles George Gordon, 1833-1885, a British general who helped put down the Taiping Rebellion

戈戟 (ㄍㄜ ㄐㄧˇ)
spears; lances

一畫

【戊】 ¹⁷⁵²
ㄨ wuh wù
the fifth of the Ten Celestial Stems

戊戌政變 (ㄨˋ ㄒㄩ ㄓㄥˋ ㄅㄧㄢˋ)
the Coup of Wu Hsü Year (1898), in which Kang Yu-wei (康有為) and other progressives tried in vain to introduce political reforms in China

戊夜 (ㄨˋ ㄧㄝˋ)
the predawn hours

【戉】 ¹⁷⁵³
ㄩㄝˋ yueh yuè
a large ax 亦作「鉞」

二畫

【戌】 ¹⁷⁵⁴
ㄒㄩ shiu xū
the eleventh of the Twelve Terrestrial Branches

戌時 (ㄒㄩ ㄕˊ)
7-9 p.m.

戌月 (ㄒㄩ ㄩㄝˋ)
the ninth month of the lunar year

【戍】 ¹⁷⁵⁵
ㄕㄨˋ shuh shù
to guard; to defend: 英勇戰士戍衛邊疆抵禦敵人。 The brave soldiers defended the frontier regions against enemies.

戍邊 (ㄕㄨˋ ㄅㄧㄢ)
to guard the border or the frontier; to garrison the frontier

戍樓 (ㄕㄨˋ ㄌㄡˊ)
a garrison watchtower

戍鼓 (ㄕㄨˋ ㄍㄨˇ)
the drums of garrison troops

戍守 (ㄕㄨˋ ㄕㄡˇ) or 戍戌 (ㄕㄡˇ ㄨˋ)
to be stationed as garrison troops at (a fortified place, the border, etc.); to set up the frontier garrison: 軍隊被派在邊區戍守。 The troops were stationed at the border.

戍人 (ㄕㄨˋ ㄖㄣˊ) or 戍卒 (ㄕㄨˋ ㄗㄨˊ)
garrison soldiers; a frontier guard

戍役 (ㄕㄨˋ ㄧˋ)
garrison duty or military service as a punishment in former times

【戎】 ¹⁷⁵⁶
ㄖㄨㄥˊ rong róng
1. war; fighting
2. arms; the apparatus of war
3. military affairs; army: 許多青年投筆從戎。 Many young people cast aside the pen to join the army.
4. barbarians to the west
5. great
6. you
7. to help

戎馬 (ㄖㄨㄥˊ ㄇㄚˇ)
war-horses; army horses

戎馬倥傯 (ㄖㄨㄥˊ ㄇㄚˇ ㄎㄨㄥ ㄗㄨㄥˇ)
to lead a hectic life with war horses; to have a hectic military career (usually said of ranking commanders)

戎馬之間 (ㄖㄨㄥˊ ㄇㄚˇ ㄓ ㄐㄧㄢ)
among war-horses; on the fighting line

戎馬生涯 (ㄖㄨㄥˊ ㄇㄚˇ ㄕㄥ ㄧㄚˊ)
an army life; a military career

戎幕 (ㄖㄨㄥˊ ㄇㄨˋ)
a military camp

戎服 (ㄖㄨㄥˊ ㄈㄨˊ)
military dress

戎狄 (ㄖㄨㄥˊ ㄉㄧˊ)
barbarians to the west and the north of ancient China

戎旅 (ㄖㄨㄥˊ ㄌㄩˇ)
the army

戎略 (ㄖㄨㄥˊ ㄌㄩㄝˋ)
war plans; strategy

戎行 (ㄖㄨㄥˊ ㄏㄤˊ)
the army; the armed forces the ranks

戎機 (ㄖㄨㄥˊ ㄐㄧ)
military secrets (or strategy)

戎車 (ㄖㄨㄥˊ ㄐㄩ)
a war vehicle; a chariot

戎器 (ㄖㄨㄥˊ ㄑㄧˋ)
arms; weapons

戎裝 (ㄖㄨㄥˊ ㄓㄨㄤ) or 戎衣
military dress; military uniform

戎事 (ㄖㄨㄥˊ ㄕˋ)
military affairs

戎首 (ㄖㄨㄥˊ ㄕㄡˇ)
the one who starts a war the top war criminal

戎衣 (ㄖㄨㄥˊ ㄧ)
armor

戎伍 (ㄖㄨㄥˊ ㄨˇ)
the ranks; the army; the armed forces

三畫

【成】 ¹⁷⁵⁷
ㄔㄥˊ cherng chéng
1. completed; accomplished finished; fixed; settled; to accomplish; to succeed; to complete: 他完成了他的工作。 He completed his work.
2. to achieve
3. to become: 他已成為很著名的人。 He has become quite a famous man.
4. acceptable; all right: 成! 我在十點時和你見面。 All right, I'll meet you at ten.
5. able; capable
6. one tenth
7. a Chinese family name

成敗 (ㄔㄥˊ ㄅㄞˋ)
success or failure: 成敗全憑此舉。 Success or failure depends on this one action.

成敗利鈍 (ㄔㄥˊ ㄅㄞˋ ㄌㄧˋ ㄉㄨㄣˋ)
successes and failures advantages and disadvantages: 成敗利鈍尚難逆料。 Whether it will be successful or not is still difficult to predict.

成本 (ㄔㄥˊ ㄅㄣˇ)
(commerce) cost

成本分析 (ㄔㄥˊ ㄅㄣˇ ㄈㄣ ㄒㄧ)

成本會計(ㄔㄥ ㄅㄣ ㄎㄨㄞ ㄐㄧˋ)
cost accounting

成本計算(ㄔㄥ ㄅㄣ ㄐㄧˋ ㄙㄨㄢˋ)
(accounting) costing; cost-finding

成本價格(ㄔㄥ ㄅㄣ ㄐㄧㄚˋ ㄍㄜˊ)
(accounting) the cost price

成病(ㄔㄥ ㄅㄧㄥˋ)
to fall ill; to become sick

成不了氣候(ㄔㄥ ㄅㄨˋ ㄌㄧㄠˇ ㄑㄧˋ ㄏㄡˋ)
(informal) unable to become formidable

成批(ㄔㄥ ㄆㄧ)
group by group; in batches

成品(ㄔㄥ ㄆㄧㄣˇ)
finished products

成眠(ㄔㄥ ㄇㄧㄢˊ)
(literary language) to fall asleep; to go to sleep: 他整夜不能成眠。He couldn't fall asleep all night.

成名(ㄔㄥ ㄇㄧㄥˊ)
to achieve fame; to become famous

成命(ㄔㄥ ㄇㄧㄥˋ)
① already issued orders ② the determinate appointment

成法(ㄔㄥ ㄈㄚˇ)
① promulgated laws; existing laws ② to become a law

成佛(ㄔㄥ ㄈㄛˊ)
to become a Buddha

成分(ㄔㄥ ㄈㄣˋ)
① an ingredient; a component; composition ② a factor ③ personal background

成方兒(ㄔㄥ ㄈㄤ ㄦ)
patent medicine; apothecary's formulas; physician's prescriptions

成風(ㄔㄥ ㄈㄥ)
to become a common practice; to become the order of the day: 現下勤儉成風。Diligence and frugality are now the order of the day.

成服(ㄔㄥ ㄈㄨˊ)
to put on mourning dress after the remains of the deceased is laid in the coffin for funeral service

成副兒(ㄔㄥ ㄈㄨˋ ㄦ)
to form an acceptable set (said of pieces or cards held in one's hand in mah-jong or a card game)

成丁(ㄔㄥ ㄉㄧㄥ)
(said of a male) to come of age

成都(ㄔㄥ ㄉㄨ)
Chengtu, capital city of Szechwan Province

成堆(ㄔㄥ ㄉㄨㄟ)
to pile up; to make into a pile; to be in heaps: 我的家庭作業成堆未做。My homework has piled up.

成對(ㄔㄥ ㄉㄨㄟˋ)
to match; to form a pair

成套(ㄔㄥ ㄊㄠˋ)
① to form a complete set: 這些器具是成套的。These instruments form a complete set. ② a whole set

成湯(ㄔㄥ ㄊㄤ)
Prince Tang, who overthrew the tyrant Chieh of Hsia (夏桀) and established the Shang Dynasty in 1766 B.C.

成天(ㄔㄥ ㄊㄧㄢ)
all day long; the whole day: 他成天無所事事。He has been doing nothing all day long.

成年(ㄔㄥ ㄋㄧㄢˊ)
① to come of age; to reach adulthood: 他三個月後就成年了。He will reach adulthood in three months. ② adult: 他是成年人。He is an adult. ③ the whole year long; through out the whole year

成年累月(ㄔㄥ ㄋㄧㄢˊ ㄌㄟˇ ㄩㄝˋ)
year after year and month after month; year in, year out

成年期(ㄔㄥ ㄋㄧㄢˊ ㄑㄧ)
adulthood

成了(ㄔㄥ ㄌㄜˋ)
acceptable; all right; okay; O.K.; enough; accomplished

成禮(ㄔㄥ ㄌㄧˇ)
to complete the ceremonies; to solemnize

成立(ㄔㄥ ㄌㄧˋ)
① to establish; to found; to come into existence; to set up: 他最近成立一家新店舖。He has set up a new store recently. ② (said of a relation, theory, etc.) to hold good or to be recognized as irrefutable; to hold water

成立大會(ㄔㄥ ㄌㄧˋ ㄉㄚˋ ㄏㄨㄟˋ)

the inaugural meeting (of an organization): 他們開過成立大會。They held an inaugural meeting.

成例(ㄔㄥ ㄌㄧˋ)
an established precedent

成殮(ㄔㄥ ㄌㄧㄢˋ)
to have the deceased properly dressed and put into coffin

成個兒(ㄔㄥ ㄍㄜˋ ㄦ)
① to grow to a good size ② to be in the proper form ③ the whole piece

成果(ㄔㄥ ㄍㄨㄛˇ)
results achieved; achievements; the fruits (of efforts): 他的成功是努力工作的成果。His success was the result of hard work.

成規(ㄔㄥ ㄍㄨㄟ)
an established practice, rule or regulation; a rut: 別墨守成規。Don't stick to conventions.

成功(ㄔㄥ ㄍㄨㄥ)
① to complete one's work ② success: 他終於獲得成功。He finally achieved success.

成何體統(ㄔㄥ ㄏㄜˊ ㄊㄧˇ ㄊㄨㄥˇ)
What a scandal!!

成歡(ㄔㄥ ㄏㄨㄢ)
① to enjoy oneself to one's heart's content ② to have sexual relation

成婚(ㄔㄥ ㄏㄨㄣ)
to get married

成績(ㄔㄥ ㄐㄧ)
records established or set; results; showing

成績單(ㄔㄥ ㄐㄧ ㄉㄢ)
a report card; a transcript of a student's scholastic record in school

成吉思汗(ㄔㄥ ㄐㄧˊ ㄙ ㄏㄢˊ)
Genghis Khan or Jenghiz Khan, 1162-1227, Mongolian conqueror

成家(ㄔㄥ ㄐㄧㄚ)
(said of men reaching adulthood) to have a family; to get married

成家立業(ㄔㄥ ㄐㄧㄚ ㄌㄧˋ ㄧㄝˋ)
(said of men reaching adulthood) to get married and start a career

成交(ㄔㄥ ㄐㄧㄠ)

〔戈部〕

to get accepted by both parties, or to go through a business deal; the consummation of a business transaction; to strike (or close) a bargain: 我們終於和他成交了。We finally closed a bargain with him.

成就(イㄥˊ ㄐㄧㄡˋ)
an achievement; an accomplishment: 實現這個計畫真是件偉大的成就。It was a great accomplishment to carry out the plan.

成就感(イㄥˊ ㄐㄧㄡˋ ㄍㄢˇ)
a sense of fulfillment; the feeling of having accomplished something important

成姦(イㄥˊ ㄐㄧㄢ)
to have illicit sexual relations

成見(イㄥˊ ㄐㄧㄢˋ)
a prejudice; a preconception; a bias: 他對此計畫有成見。He has a bias towards (or against) the plan.

成精作怪(イㄥˊ ㄐㄧㄥ ㄗㄨㄛˋ《ㄨㄞˋ)
(said of animals or plants in the mind of the superstitious) to turn into a mischievous spirit

成局(イㄥˊ ㄐㄩˊ)
① an irrevocable situation ② to become fixed or irrevocable

成器(イㄥˊ ㄑㄧˋ)
to become a useful person

成千累萬(イㄥˊ ㄑㄧㄢ ㄌㄟˇ ㄨㄢˋ)or 成千成萬(イㄥˊ ㄑㄧㄢ イㄥˊ ㄨㄢˋ)
hundreds upon thousands; tens of thousands; countless; numerous

成親(イㄥˊ ㄑㄧㄣ)
to get married

成擒(イㄥˊ ㄑㄧㄣˊ)
to get captured

成全(イㄥˊ ㄑㄩㄢˊ)
to help (others) accomplish something

成群(イㄥˊ ㄑㄩㄣˊ)
in groups; in large numbers; in hordes; swarms: 成群的牛羊 herds of cattle and sheep

成群打野(イㄥˊ ㄑㄩㄣˊ ㄌㄚˇ ㄧㄝˇ)
to band together; to gather in groups; to form into groups

成群結隊(イㄥˊ ㄑㄩㄣˊ ㄐㄧㄝˊ ㄉㄨㄟˋ)
to band together; to gather in groups; in crowds (or throngs)

成效(イㄥˊ ㄒㄧㄠˋ)
result; effect; efficacy; effectiveness: 這藥對那種病無成效。The medicine has no efficacy in that disease.

成效卓著(イㄥˊ ㄒㄧㄠˋ ㄓㄨㄛˊ ㄓㄨˋ)
The achievement is outstanding.

成憲(イㄥˊ ㄒㄧㄢˋ)
existing laws

成心(イㄥˊ ㄒㄧㄣ)
① intentionally; on purpose; with deliberate intent: 他成心跟我們作對。He purposely antagonized us. ② a preconceived notion

成行(イㄥˊ ㄒㄧㄥˊ)
to embark on a journey

成形(イㄥˊ ㄒㄧㄥˊ)
to take shape: 我們的新圖書館計畫開始成形了。Our plans of a new library are beginning to take shape.

成性(イㄥˊ ㄒㄧㄥˋ)
to become habitual; to become second nature: 這個傢伙竊取成性。Stealing has become that villain's second nature.

成長(イㄥˊ ㄓㄤˇ)
to grow up; growth: 她成長得多麼快啊! How quickly she is growing!

成竹在胸(イㄥˊ ㄓㄨˊ ㄗㄞˋ ㄒㄩㄥ)
to know what one is doing; to have already made careful planning for what one is doing 亦作「胸有成竹」

成仇(イㄥˊ ㄔㄡˊ)
to become enemies; to be at feud with

成蟲(イㄥˊ ㄔㄨㄥˊ)
(zoology) an imago

成事(イㄥˊ ㄕˋ)
① bygones ② to succeed in doing something ③ things done

成事不足，敗事有餘(イㄥˊ ㄕˋ ㄅㄨˋ ㄗㄨˊ, ㄅㄞˋ ㄕˋ ㄧㄡˇ ㄩˊ)
(literally) to have a capacity not enough for success yet more than enough for disaster—apt to bungle; to

be unable to accomplish anything but liable to spoil things

成事在天(イㄥˊ ㄕˋ ㄗㄞˋ ㄊㄧㄢ)
(Man proposes but) God disposes. 或 Heaven makes the final decision as to how things shall end up.

成熟(イㄥˊ ㄕㄡˊ)
to mature; to ripen: 葡萄成熟了。The grapes are ripe.

成數(イㄥˊ ㄕㄨˋ)
① whole numbers ② percentage

成說(イㄥˊ ㄕㄨㄛ)
① an accepted theory or formulation ② to pledge one's word

成雙(イㄥˊ ㄕㄨㄤ)
to form a pair; to match

成日(イㄥˊ ㄖˋ)
the whole day; all day: 他成日遊手好閒無所事事。He has been loitering about and doing nothing all day.

成人(イㄥˊ ㄖㄣˊ)
an adult; a grownup

成人教育(イㄥˊ ㄖㄣˊ ㄐㄧㄠˋ ㄩˋ)
adult education

成人之美(イㄥˊ ㄖㄣˊ ㄓ ㄇㄟˇ)
to help fulfill another's cherished hopes; to assist others in achieving an objective

成仁取義(イㄥˊ ㄖㄣˊ ㄑㄩˇ ㄧˋ)
to die to preserve one's principle intact; to be a martyr to one's principle

成則王侯，敗則寇賊(イㄥˊ ㄗㄜˊ ㄨㄤˊ ㄏㄡˊ, ㄅㄞˋ ㄗㄜˊ ㄎㄡˋ ㄗㄟˊ)
(literally) The victors are declared kings and marquises, while the vanquished are branded thieves and traitors.—Might is right.

成災(イㄥˊ ㄗㄞ)
to cause disaster: 豪雨成災。The downpour caused disastrous flood.

成總兒(イㄥˊ ㄗㄨㄥˇㄦ)
① to put together a round sum ② in whole batches

成材(イㄥˊ ㄘㄞˊ)
to become a useful person

成色(イㄥˊ ㄙㄜˋ)
① the percentage of pure metal in an alloy ② worth; stuff; quality: 我們看成色定

錢。We fix the prices according to the quality.

戈俗(ㄍㄜˊㄙㄨˊ)
①an established social custom ②to become a social custom

戈訟(ㄍㄜˊㄙㄨㄥˋ)
to become a legal case well; to take a matter into court

戈誦(ㄍㄜˊㄙㄨㄥˋ)
to have learned a passage so well as to be able to recite it

戈案(ㄍㄜˊㄢˋ)
a legal precedent

戈衣(ㄍㄜˊㄧ)
ready-made clothes; garments: 那是件戈衣。It's a ready-made suit

戈衣鋪(ㄍㄜˊㄧㄆㄨˋ)
a tailor shop

戈議(ㄍㄜˊㄧˋ)
an already adopted resolution or agreement; to come to an agreement

戈窰(ㄍㄜˊㄧㄠˊ)
name of a kiln in the Ming Dynasty, which produced the finest porcelain ware of the period

戈藥(ㄍㄜˊㄧㄠˋ)
patent medicine; medicine already prepared by a pharmacy

戈因(ㄍㄜˊㄧㄣ)
the cause of formation; a contributing factor

戈樣(ㄍㄜˊㄧㄤˋ)
an established model (of manufactured goods); to perpetuate as a model

戈爲(ㄍㄜˊㄨㄟˊ)
to become; to turn into: 她已經成爲一個出色的作家。She's become an excellent writer.

戈爲泡影(ㄍㄜˊㄨㄟˊㄆㄠˋㄧㄥˇ)
to end in naught; to come to nothing: 他的計劃已成爲泡影。His plan has come to nothing.

戈文(ㄍㄜˊㄨㄣˊ)
①existing writings: 不可抄襲戈文。Don't copy existing writings. ②presentable 亦作「成樣兒」

戈文法(ㄍㄜˊㄨㄣˊㄈㄚˇ)
written or statute law; a statute; lex scripta

成問題(ㄔㄥˊㄨㄣˋㄊㄧˊ)
to be a problem; to be open to question, doubt, or objection

成語(ㄔㄥˊㄩˇ)
an idiom; a phrase

成員(ㄔㄥˊㄩㄢˊ)
a member; 他是這小組的成員。He is a member of the group.

【戒】 1758 ㄐㄧㄝˋ jieh jiè

1. to warn; to admonish; to caution
2. to abstain from; to refrain from; to give up
3. to guard against; to avoid
4. a commandment; Buddhist monastic discipline

戒備(ㄐㄧㄝˋㄅㄟˋ)
on guard (against enemy attacks, natural disasters, etc.); on the alert

戒備森嚴(ㄐㄧㄝˋㄅㄟˋㄙㄣㄧㄢˊ)
to be heavily guarded

戒不掉(ㄐㄧㄝˋㄅㄨˋㄉㄧㄠˋ)
to try in vain to abstain (from a bad habit)

戒刀(ㄐㄧㄝˋㄉㄠ)
the knife of interdiction (used by Buddhists)

戒牒(ㄐㄧㄝˋㄉㄧㄝˊ)
the certificate of the Buddhist vow

戒掉(ㄐㄧㄝˋㄉㄧㄠˋ)
to abstain or give up (a bad habit)

戒定慧(ㄐㄧㄝˋㄉㄧㄥˋㄏㄨㄟˋ)
(Buddhism) discipline, meditation, wisdom—Discipline wards off bodily evil, meditation calms mental disturbance, and wisdom gets rid of delusion and proves truth.

戒賭(ㄐㄧㄝˋㄉㄨˇ)
to abstain from gambling; to give up gambling: 這賭徒決心戒賭了。The gambler determined to give up gambling.

戒壇(ㄐㄧㄝˋㄊㄢˊ)
a place for taking the Buddhist vow

戒條(ㄐㄧㄝˋㄊㄧㄠˊ)or 戒律(ㄐㄧㄝˋㄌㄩˋ)
commandments; don'ts; (Buddhism) the rules

戒塗 or 戒途(ㄐㄧㄝˋㄊㄨˊ)

---

to prepare for a trip

戒臘(ㄐㄧㄝˋㄌㄚˋ)
the number of years a Buddhist monk has been ordained

戒葷(ㄐㄧㄝˋㄏㄨㄣ)
to go on a vegetarian diet

戒酒(ㄐㄧㄝˋㄐㄧㄡˇ)
to abstain from alcohol: 醫生勸他戒酒。The doctor ordered him to abstain from wine.

戒懼(ㄐㄧㄝˋㄐㄩˋ)
to be afraid and watchful

戒絕(ㄐㄧㄝˋㄐㄩㄝˊ)
to get rid of (a bad habit, drug addiction, etc.) completely

戒心(ㄐㄧㄝˋㄒㄧㄣ)
watchfulness; vigilance; on one's guard; wariness

戒指(ㄐㄧㄝˋㄓˇ)
a ring (on a finger)

戒尺(ㄐㄧㄝˋㄔˇ)
a ferule; a teacher's ruler for beating pupils

戒除(ㄐㄧㄝˋㄔㄨˊ)
to abstain from; to give up: 他戒除了一項惡習。He gave up a bad habit.

戒奢崇儉(ㄐㄧㄝˋㄕㄜㄔㄨㄥˊㄐㄧㄢˇ)
to refrain from luxury and uphold frugality

戒色(ㄐㄧㄝˋㄙㄜˋ)or 戒淫(ㄐㄧㄝˋㄧㄣˊ)
to abstain from carnal pleasure

戒煙(ㄐㄧㄝˋㄧㄢ)
to give up smoking; to abstain from smoking; to refrain from smoking: 他已戒煙了。He has given up smoking.

戒嚴(ㄐㄧㄝˋㄧㄢˊ)
to proclaim martial law; to impose a curfew

戒嚴令(ㄐㄧㄝˋㄧㄢˊㄌㄧㄥˋ)
martial law

戒嚴時期(ㄐㄧㄝˋㄧㄢˊㄕˊㄑㄧ)
the period during which martial law is in force

【我】 1759 ㄨㄛˇ woo wǒ (讀音ㄜˋ ee è)

1. I; me; my
2. we; our; us: 我軍爲自由而戰。Our army battled for freedom.
3. self: 我敬重他忘我的獻身精

神。I admire his selfless
devotion.

我輩(ㄨㄛˇ ㄅㄟˋ)
we; us

我慢(ㄨㄛˇ ㄇㄢˋ)
(Buddhism) egotism; exalting
self and depreciating others;
self-intoxication

〔戈
部〕

我們(ㄨㄛˇ ·ㄇㄣ)or 我等(ㄨㄛˇ ㄉㄥˇ)
我曹(ㄨㄛˇ ㄘㄠˊ)
we; us

我們的(ㄨㄛˇ ·ㄇㄣ ·ㄉㄜ)
our; ours

我方(ㄨㄛˇ ㄈㄤ)
our side; we

我國(ㄨㄛˇ ㄍㄨㄛˊ)
our country

我家(ㄨㄛˇ ㄐㄧㄚ)
my home; my house

我見猶憐(ㄨㄛˇ ㄐㄧㄢˋ ㄧㄡˊ ㄌㄧㄢˊ)
Even I, a woman, cannot
help loving her upon seeing
her. (The statement is
attributed to the wife of
Huan Wen (桓溫) when she
saw the concubine he had
taken. The expression is
now used by both sexes to
describe a very beautiful
woman.)

我軍(ㄨㄛˇ ㄐㄩㄣ)
our troops; our military
forces; our army

我行我素(ㄨㄛˇ ㄒㄧㄥˊ ㄨㄛˇ ㄙㄨˋ)
to act according to one's
will regardless of others'
opinions; to stick to one's
old way of doing things

我執(ㄨㄛˇ ㄓˊ)
(Buddhism) ātma-graha;
holding to the concept of the
ego

我儕(ㄨㄛˇ ㄔㄞˊ)
we; us

我朝(ㄨㄛˇ ㄔㄠˊ)
our dynasty

我人(ㄨㄛˇ ㄖㄣˊ)
we; us

我自己(ㄨㄛˇ ㄗˋ ㄐㄧˇ)
I myself

我武維揚(ㄨㄛˇ ㄨˇ ㄨㄟˊ ㄧㄤˊ)
Our national influence has
been spreading. 或 My military prowess is displayed.

四畫

【或】 1760 ㄏㄨㄛˋ huò huo
1. a certain; some
2. perhaps; probably; maybe:
他明晨或可抵達。He may
arrive tomorrow morning.
3. or: 你可離去或留下。You can
go or stay.

或明或暗(ㄏㄨㄛˋ ㄇㄧㄥˊ ㄏㄨㄛˋ ㄢˋ)
either overt or covert

或大或小(ㄏㄨㄛˋ ㄉㄚˋ ㄏㄨㄛˋ ㄒㄧㄠˇ)
either large or small; big or
little; irregular in size

或多或少(ㄏㄨㄛˋ ㄉㄨㄛ ㄏㄨㄛˋ ㄕㄠˇ)
more or less

或體(ㄏㄨㄛˋ ㄊㄧˇ)
an alternative style of
Chinese characters

或來或往(ㄏㄨㄛˋ ㄌㄞˊ ㄏㄨㄛˋ ㄨㄤˇ)
either coming or going; back
and forth; to and fro

或可(ㄏㄨㄛˋ ㄎㄜˇ)
may be possible; probably
can: 我或可儘早前來。I will
come as soon as I possibly
can.

或許(ㄏㄨㄛˋ ㄒㄩˇ)
perhaps; probably; maybe:
或許我能做此事。Probably I
can do it.

或者(ㄏㄨㄛˋ ㄓㄜˇ)
or; perhaps: 請把這本書交給
張先生或者李先生。Please
give this book to either Mr.
Chang or Mr. Lee.

或是(ㄏㄨㄛˋ ㄕˋ)
①perhaps; may be. 或是如此。Per-
haps so. ②or: 它是黑的或是
白的? Is it black or white?

或然率(ㄏㄨㄛˋ ㄖㄢˊ ㄌㄩˋ)or 或然性
(ㄏㄨㄛˋ ㄖㄢˊ ㄒㄧㄥˋ)
(mathematics) probability

或人(ㄏㄨㄛˋ ㄖㄣˊ)
someone

或早或晚(ㄏㄨㄛˋ ㄗㄠˇ ㄏㄨㄛˋ ㄨㄢˇ)
sooner or later 亦作「或遲或
早」

或此或彼(ㄏㄨㄛˋ ㄘˇ ㄏㄨㄛˋ ㄅㄧˇ)
either this or that; here and
there; hither and thither

或謂(ㄏㄨㄛˋ ㄨㄟˋ)or 或曰(ㄏㄨㄛˋ ㄩㄝ)
or 或云(ㄏㄨㄛˋ ㄩㄣˊ)
some people say that...

或問(ㄏㄨㄛˋ ㄨㄣˋ)
someone may ask

【戕】 1761 ㄑㄧㄤ chyang qiáng
1. to slay; to kill; to destroy
自戕 to commit suicide; t
kill oneself
2. to be injurious

戕害(ㄑㄧㄤ ㄏㄞˋ)
to slay

戕賊(ㄑㄧㄤ ㄗㄜˊ)
to injure; to destroy; to ruir
to do violence to

【戔】 1762 ㄐㄧㄢ jiān
small; little; tiny

戔戔(ㄐㄧㄢ ㄐㄧㄢ)
tiny; small

戔戔之數(ㄐㄧㄢ ㄐㄧㄢ ㄓ ㄕㄨˋ)
an insignificant amount (
money)

七畫

【戚】 1763 ㄑㄧ chi qī
1. relatives by marriage: 皇稱
國戚 relatives of an emperor
2. sad; mournful; woeful; sor
row; woe: 我們休戚相關。W
share joys and sorrows.
3. a battle-ax
4. a Chinese family name

戚里(ㄑㄧ ㄌㄧˇ)
an exclusive village fo
imperial relatives by mar
riage

戚繼光(ㄑㄧ ㄐㄧˋ ㄍㄨㄤ)
Chi Chi-kuang, a general o
the Ming Dynasty, credite
with repelling the invasion
of Japanese pirates

戚舊(ㄑㄧ ㄐㄧㄡˋ)
relatives and old friends: 戚
舊星散。Relatives and old
friends scattered like stars.

戚戚(ㄑㄧ ㄑㄧ)
①woeful; mournful ②
moved; affected; touched

戚然(ㄑㄧ ㄖㄢˊ)
melancholy; distressed
depressed; dejected: 戚然動
to change countenance fo
being distressed

戚容(ㄑㄧ ㄖㄨㄥˊ)
a sad look; a sorrowfu
expression

戚誼(ㄑㄧ ㄧˊ)
the ties between relatives

【戛】 1764 (戛) ㄐㄧㄚˊ jya jiá
. a lance
. natural principles
. to tap; to strike

戛夏 (ㄐㄧㄚˊ)
difficult

戛戛獨造 (ㄐㄧㄚˊ ㄐㄧㄚˊ ㄉㄨˊ ㄗㄠˋ)
to go one's unique and independent way; creative; original; out of the common run

戛乎其難哉 (ㄐㄧㄚˊ ㄏㄨ ㄐㄧˊ ㄋㄢˊ ㄗㄞ)
How unmanageably difficult it is! or How formidable or impossible the task is!

戛然長鳴 (ㄐㄧㄚˊ ㄖㄢˊ ㄔㄤˊ ㄇㄧㄥˊ)
long and loud cries

戛然而止 (ㄐㄧㄚˊ ㄖㄢˊ ㄦˊ ㄓˇ)
(said of a sound) to stop abruptly

八畫

【戟】 1765 (戟) ㄐㄧˇ jii jǐ
a two-pronged spear or lance; a halberd

戟門 (ㄐㄧˇ ㄇㄣˊ)
the door of a noble family

戟手 (ㄐㄧˇ ㄕㄡˇ) or 戟指 (ㄐㄧˇ ㄓˇ)
to point at another and scold him

九畫

【戡】 1766 ㄎㄢ kan kān
. to subdue; to suppress; to put down
. to kill; to slay

戡定 (ㄎㄢ ㄉㄧㄥˋ)
to put down or suppress (a rebellion); to subdue (barbarian tribes)

戡亂 (ㄎㄢ ㄌㄨㄢˋ)
to suppress a rebellion: 他戡亂有功。 He was meritorious for suppressing a rebellion.

戡夷 (ㄎㄢ ㄧˊ)
to subdue barbarian tribes

【戢】 1767 ㄐㄧˊ jyi jí
. to put away or store up
. to fold; to cease; to restrain; to become placated

戢暴鋤強 (ㄐㄧˊ ㄅㄠˋ ㄔㄨˊ ㄑㄧㄤˊ)
to run down the tyrants

戢兵 (ㄐㄧˊ ㄅㄧㄥ)
to cease hostilities

戢鱗 (ㄐㄧˊ ㄌㄧㄣˊ)
to await opportunity in seclusion

戢翼 (ㄐㄧˊ ㄧˋ)
①(said of a bird) to fold the wings: 戢翼而棲 to fold the wings and roost② (figuratively) to retire

戢影 (ㄐㄧˊ ㄧㄥˇ)
to retire (from active life)

【戥】 1768 ㄉㄥˇ deeng děng
a small steelyard for weighing gold, jewels, etc.

戥子 (ㄉㄥˇ ㄗˇ)
the weighing scale of a small steelyard

戥盒 (ㄉㄥˇ ㄏㄜˊ)
a case for keeping a small steelyard

戥星 (ㄉㄥˇ ㄒㄧㄥ)
the sliding weight of a small steelyard

戥秤 (ㄉㄥˇ ㄔㄥˋ) or 戥子 (ㄉㄥˇ ·ㄗ)
a small steelyard for weighing gold, jewels, etc.

十畫

【戩】 1769 ㄐㄧㄢˇ jean jiǎn
1. to exterminate
2. blessing
3. full; complete; entirely

【截】 1770 ㄐㄧㄝˊ jye jié
1. to cut; to section; to truncate: 截成兩段 to cut in two
2. a slice; a division; a section; a segment; a chunk
3. to detain; to withhold
4. to keep; to set in order
5. to stop; to close; to end; to intercept

截面 (ㄐㄧㄝˊ ㄇㄧㄢˋ)
a section (of a solid body cut straight through): 橫截面 a cross section

截斷 (ㄐㄧㄝˊ ㄉㄨㄢˋ)
to disrupt; to interrupt; to cut off: 我們截斷了敵人的後路。We cut off the enemy's retreat.

截斷交通 (ㄐㄧㄝˊ ㄉㄨㄢˋ ㄐㄧㄠ ㄊㄨㄥ)
to disrupt communication

截留 (ㄐㄧㄝˊ ㄌㄧㄡˊ)
to withhold goods that ought to be issued or delivered

截稿 (ㄐㄧㄝˊ ㄍㄠˇ)
the deadline for the editor of a newspaper to send the last news copy to the composition room

截開 (ㄐㄧㄝˊ ㄎㄞ)
to cut apart

截獲 (ㄐㄧㄝˊ ㄏㄨㄛˋ)
to capture by interception

截擊 (ㄐㄧㄝˊ ㄐㄧ)
to intercept (a marching army, a convoy, etc.)

截角 (ㄐㄧㄝˊ ㄐㄧㄠˇ)
to cut off or tear off a corner (of an envelope, a ticket, etc.); to truncate; truncated

截句 (ㄐㄧㄝˊ ㄐㄩˋ)
a poem of 4 lines, with 5 or 7 characters in each line, and the third line blank 亦作「絕句」

截去一段 (ㄐㄧㄝˊ ㄑㄩˋ ㄧ ㄉㄨㄢˋ)
to cut off a portion

截線 (ㄐㄧㄝˊ ㄒㄧㄢˋ)
(mathematics) a transversal

截肢 (ㄐㄧㄝˊ ㄓ)
amputation

截止 (ㄐㄧㄝˊ ㄓˇ)
to close (application, registration, etc.) upon reaching the deadline; to come to an end: 報名登記已經截止了。The registration has come to an end.

截趾適履 (ㄐㄧㄝˊ ㄓˇ ㄕˋ ㄌㄩˇ)
(literally) to trim the foot to suit the shoe—to do something very foolishly or in an impractical manner 亦作「削足適履」

截至 (ㄐㄧㄝˊ ㄓˋ)
by (a specified time); up to

截住 (ㄐㄧㄝˊ ㄓㄨˋ)
to stop; to interrupt; to obstruct; to hinder; to intercept: 他說到這裏突然截住。He suddenly stopped short at this point.

截長補短 (ㄐㄧㄝˊ ㄔㄤˊ ㄅㄨˇ ㄉㄨㄢˇ)
(literally) to cut what is too long to supplement what is

〔戈 部〕

too short—to even up scarcity and superabundance

截然(ㄐ一ㄝ ㄖㄢˊ)
distinctly; markedly; sharply; completely; entirely: 這兩兄弟的性格截然不同。The two brothers were completely different in personality.

截人歸路(ㄐ一ㄝˊ ㄖㄣˊ ㄍㄨㄟ ㄌㄨˋ)
to cut someone's route of retreat

截(ㄐ一ㄝˊ)
a slice; a section; a division; a part

【戕】1771 ㄑ一ㄤ chiang qiāng
1. to be broken off; to clash
2. against; in an opposite direction

【戕】1771 ㄑ一ㄤ chiang qiāng
to support; to prop up; to shore up

戕柱(ㄑ一ㄤ ㄐ一ㄣ)
gold jewelries; to sprinkle gold (on furniture, etc.)

戕柱(ㄑ一ㄤ ㄓㄨˋ)
a side support (for a falling house, etc.)

戕銀(ㄑ一ㄤ 一ㄣˊ)
silver jewelries

十一畫

【戮】1772 ㄌㄨˋ luh lù
1. to slay; to massacre, to slaughter
2. to unite or join

戮民(ㄌㄨˋ ㄇㄧㄣˊ)
people who are serving their terms of imprisonment

戮力(ㄌㄨˋ ㄌㄧˋ)
to join forces; to cooperate; to join hands

戮力同心(ㄌㄨˋ ㄌㄧˋ ㄊㄨㄥˊ ㄒㄧㄣ)
to join forces and work for a common cause

戮誅(ㄌㄨˋ ㄓㄨ)or 戮殺(ㄌㄨˋ ㄕㄚ)
to slay

戮屍(ㄌㄨˋ ㄕ)
to chop up a corpse (for punishment)

戮尸梟示(ㄌㄨˋ ㄕ ㄒㄧㄠ ㄕˋ)
to execute a criminal and exhibit his head as a warning to potential lawbreakers

十二畫

【戰】1773 ㄓㄢˋ jann zhàn
1. war; warfare; fighting; battle
2. to contest; to fight; to contend: 他們為了維護獨立而戰。They were fighting to preserve their independence
3. to shudder; to shiver; to tremble: 他冷得打（寒）戰。He shivered with cold.
4. a Chinese family name

戰敗(ㄓㄢˋ ㄅㄞˋ)
to suffer (a) defeat; to be defeated

戰敗國(ㄓㄢˋ ㄅㄞˋ ㄍㄨㄛˊ)
a defeated nation; the vanquished country

戰備(ㄓㄢˋ ㄅㄟˋ)
war preparations; combat readiness: 我們應加強戰備。We should step up combat readiness.

戰報(ㄓㄢˋ ㄅㄠˋ)
war bulletins; the reports from the battle front

戰袍(ㄓㄢˋ ㄆㄠˊ)
battle dress (in former times); combat uniform

戰馬(ㄓㄢˋ ㄇㄚˇ)
a war-horse; a battle steed

戰歿(ㄓㄢˋ ㄇㄛˋ)
to die in battle; to be killed in action

戰法(ㄓㄢˋ ㄈㄚˇ)
tactics

戰犯(ㄓㄢˋ ㄈㄢˋ)
a war criminal

戰俘(ㄓㄢˋ ㄈㄨˊ)
prisoners of war

戰抖(ㄓㄢˋ ㄉㄡˇ)
to shudder; to shiver; to tremble 亦作「顫抖」

戰鬥(ㄓㄢˋ ㄉㄡˋ)
①to fight; to combat; to engage in a battle: 我們在戰鬥中把敵人打敗了。We defeated the enemy in the battle. ②action (in military sense): 兵士們在戰鬥。The soldiers are in action.

戰鬥力(ㄓㄢˋ ㄉㄡˋ ㄌㄧˋ)
fighting capability; combat strength

戰鬥轟炸機(ㄓㄢˋ ㄉㄡˋ ㄏㄨㄥ ㄓㄚˋ ㄐㄧ)
a fighter-bomber

戰鬥機(ㄓㄢˋ ㄉㄡˋ ㄐㄧ)
a fighter plane; a fighter

戰艦(ㄓㄢˋ ㄐㄧㄢˋ)
a battleship

戰鬥巡洋艦(ㄓㄢˋ ㄉㄡˋ ㄒㄩㄣˊ 一ㄤˊ ㄐㄧㄢˋ)
a battle cruiser

戰鬥任務(ㄓㄢˋ ㄉㄡˋ ㄖㄣˋ ㄨˋ)
a combat mission

戰鬥演習(ㄓㄢˋ ㄉㄡˋ 一ㄢˇ ㄒㄧˊ)
military maneuvers or exercises; a war game

戰鬥員(ㄓㄢˋ ㄉㄡˋ ㄩㄢˊ)
a combatant

戰地(ㄓㄢˋ ㄉㄧˋ)
a battlefield

戰地記者(ㄓㄢˋ ㄉㄧˋ ㄐㄧˋ ㄓㄜˇ)
a war correspondent (for mass communication media)

戰地政務(ㄓㄢˋ ㄉㄧˋ ㄓㄥˋ ㄨˋ)
the civil administration in a war zone or theater of war

戰慄(ㄓㄢˋ ㄌㄧˋ)
to shiver; to shudder; to tremble: 他嚇得全身戰慄。He trembled all over with fear.

戰利品(ㄓㄢˋ ㄌㄧˋ ㄆㄧㄣˇ)
a war trophy; a trophy booty; a prize; spoils of war; loot

戰亂(ㄓㄢˋ ㄌㄨㄢˋ)
chaos and social upheaval brought about by war

戰略(ㄓㄢˋ ㄌㄩㄝˋ)
strategy

戰略核子武器(ㄓㄢˋ ㄌㄩㄝˋ ㄏㄜˊ ㄗˇ ㄨˇ ㄑㄧˋ)
strategic nuclear weapons

戰略轟炸機(ㄓㄢˋ ㄌㄩㄝˋ ㄏㄨㄥ ㄓㄚˋ ㄐㄧ)
a strategic bomber; a long range bomber

戰略計劃(ㄓㄢˋ ㄌㄩㄝˋ ㄐㄧˋ ㄏㄨㄚˋ)
a strategic plan

戰鼓(ㄓㄢˋ ㄍㄨˇ)
battle drums

戰國七雄(ㄓㄢˋ ㄍㄨㄛˊ ㄑㄧ ㄒㄩㄥˊ)
the seven states (秦、楚、齊、韓、魏、趙、燕) in the Epoch of Warring States 參看「戰國時代」

戰國時代(ㄓㄢˋ ㄍㄨㄛˊ ㄕˊ ㄉㄞˋ)
the Epoch of Warring States (403-221B.C.) during which

seven states (秦、楚、齊、韓、趙、魏、燕) contended for hegemony until Chin (秦) emerged victorious to become the unchallenged ruler of the empire under the First Emperor (始皇帝)

戰國策(ㄓㄢˋ ㄍㄨㄛˊ ㄘㄜˋ)
Record of the Warring States, compiled in the Former Han Dynasty

戰果(ㄓㄢˋ ㄍㄨㄛˇ)
military achievements; war results: 他們取得輝煌的戰果。 They achieved splendid results on the battlefield.

戰功(ㄓㄢˋ ㄍㄨㄥ)或戰庸(ㄓㄢˋ ㄩㄥ)
military exploits; distinguished services in war

戰況(ㄓㄢˋ ㄎㄨㄤˋ)
the war situation; the progress of a battle: 目前戰況不明。 The war situation is unknown to us.

戰壕(ㄓㄢˋ ㄏㄠˊ)
a trench

戰後(ㄓㄢˋ ㄏㄡˋ)
postwar; after the war: 戰後問題 postwar problems

戰火(ㄓㄢˋ ㄏㄨㄛˇ)
flames of war

戰禍(ㄓㄢˋ ㄏㄨㄛˋ)
the calamities (or disasters) of war

戰績(ㄓㄢˋ ㄐㄧ)
military successes (or exploits, feats); battle achievements

戰績輝煌(ㄓㄢˋ ㄐㄧ ㄏㄨㄟ ㄏㄨㄤˊ)
brilliant combat performances; extraordinary battle achievements

戰機(ㄓㄢˋ ㄐㄧ)
① an opportunity for combat: 他們喪失了致勝的戰機。 They missed the opportunity to win a battle. ② a fighter

戰艦(ㄓㄢˋ ㄐㄧㄢˋ)
a warship; a battleship

戰局(ㄓㄢˋ ㄐㄩˊ)
the war situation; the tide of the war

戰前(ㄓㄢˋ ㄑㄧㄢˊ)
prewar; before the war

戰區(ㄓㄢˋ ㄑㄩ)
a theater of war; a war zone or area

戰線(ㄓㄢˋ ㄒㄧㄢˋ)
a battle line, a battle front; the action front

戰戰兢兢(ㄓㄢˋ ㄓㄢˋ ㄐㄧㄥ ㄐㄧㄥ)
trembling with fear; very cautious; with fear and trepidation

戰陣(ㄓㄢˋ ㄓㄣˋ)
the deployment of troops; order of battle

戰爭(ㄓㄢˋ ㄓㄥ)
war

戰爭保險(ㄓㄢˋ ㄓㄥ ㄅㄠˇ ㄒㄧㄢˇ)
war risk insurance

戰爭販子(ㄓㄢˋ ㄓㄥ ㄈㄢˋ ˙ㄗ)
a warmonger

戰爭狀態(ㄓㄢˋ ㄓㄥ ㄓㄨㄤˋ ㄊㄞˋ)
a state of war; a state of hostilities

戰爭與和平(ㄓㄢˋ ㄓㄥ ㄩˇ ㄏㄜˊ ㄆㄧㄥˊ)
① war and peace ② *War and Peace*, by Leo Tolstoy (1828-1910)

戰車(ㄓㄢˋ ㄔㄜ)
① a tank (an armored vehicle) ② a chariot

戰場(ㄓㄢˋ ㄔㄤˇ)
a battlefield; a war field; a battleground

戰船(ㄓㄢˋ ㄔㄨㄢˊ)
a war vessel; a man-of-war; a warship

戰時(ㄓㄢˋ ㄕˊ)
wartime

戰時國際公法(ㄓㄢˋ ㄕˊ ㄍㄨㄛˊ ㄐㄧˋ ㄍㄨㄥ ㄈㄚˇ)
wartime international law

戰史(ㄓㄢˋ ㄕˇ)
war history; military history

戰士(ㄓㄢˋ ㄕˋ)
a warrior; a fighting man; an enlisted man: 他曾是位英勇的戰士。 He was a brave warrior.

戰事(ㄓㄢˋ ㄕˋ)
war; hostilities; fighting; clashes: 戰事已停止了嗎？ Has the fighting stopped yet?

戰守(ㄓㄢˋ ㄕㄡˇ)
offense and defense

戰勝(ㄓㄢˋ ㄕㄥˋ)
to conquer; to win a victory; to emerge victorious; to be victorious; to be the victor: 他戰勝了對手。 He was victori-

ous over his rival.

戰勝國(ㄓㄢˋ ㄕㄥˋ ㄍㄨㄛˊ)
a victorious nation

戰勝攻取(ㄓㄢˋ ㄕㄥˋ ㄍㄨㄥ ㄑㄩˇ)
to triumph in every battle and succeed in every invasion

戰書(ㄓㄢˋ ㄕㄨ)
a written declaration of war

戰術(ㄓㄢˋ ㄕㄨˋ)
tactics; the art of war

戰術轟炸機(ㄓㄢˋ ㄕㄨˋ ㄏㄨㄥ ㄓㄚˋ ㄐㄧ)
a tactical bomber; a short-range bomber

戰死(ㄓㄢˋ ㄙˇ)
to die in battle; to be killed in action: 他戰死在沙場。 He died on the battlefield.

戰役(ㄓㄢˋ ㄧˋ)
a (military) campaign; a battle: 諾曼第登陸是一場英勇的戰役。 The Normandy landing was a daring battle.

戰友(ㄓㄢˋ ㄧㄡˇ)
a comrade in arms

戰無不勝，攻無不克(ㄓㄢˋ ㄨˊ ㄅㄨˋ ㄕㄥˋ，ㄍㄨㄥ ㄨˊ ㄅㄨˋ ㄎㄜˋ)
to triumph in every battle and succeed in every invasion; to go undefeated

戰雲彌漫(ㄓㄢˋ ㄩㄣˊ ㄇㄧˊ ㄇㄢˋ)
The clouds of war hang low. 或 War is imminent.

十三畫

【戲】 1774 1. (戲) ㄒㄧˋ shih ㄒㄧˋ xì

1. to play; to toy; to sport: 小羊在田裡嬉戲。 Lambs sport in the fields.
2. to jest; to have fun; to make fun
3. a drama; a play; a show: 我們去看戲吧！ Let's go to the play.
4. a game

戲班(ㄒㄧˋ ㄅㄢ)
a dramatic troupe

戲本子(ㄒㄧˋ ㄅㄣˇ ˙ㄗ)
a script (of a play); a text for a play or an opera

戲票(ㄒㄧˋ ㄆㄧㄠˋ)
an admission ticket for a play

戲碼(ㄒㄧˋ ㄇㄚˇ)

〔戈部〕

a repertoire (particularly that of Peking opera)

戲迷 (ㄒㄧˋ ㄇㄧˊ)
a drama fan

戲目 (ㄒㄧˋ ㄇㄨˋ)
a theatrical program

戲法(兒) (ㄒㄧˋ ㄈㄚˇ (ㄦ))
jugglery; a trick; sleight of hand; magic

戲單子 (ㄒㄧˋ ㄉㄢ ˙ㄗ)
the program of a play; a playbill

戲臺 (ㄒㄧˋ ㄊㄞˊ)
a stage (for plays)

戲弄 (ㄒㄧˋ ㄋㄨㄥˋ) or 戲耍 (ㄒㄧˋ ㄕㄨㄚˇ)
to play a trick on; to tease

戲謔 (ㄒㄧˋ ㄒㄩㄝˋ)
a joke; a witticism; a pleasantry; a jest; fun

戲館子 (ㄒㄧˋ ㄍㄨㄢˇ ˙ㄗ)
a playhouse; a theater

戲考 (ㄒㄧˋ ㄎㄠˇ)
A Collection of Plays

戲具 (ㄒㄧˋ ㄐㄩˋ)
theatrical appurtenances; stage properties 亦作「道具」

戲劇 (ㄒㄧˋ ㄐㄩˊ)
drama; the theater; a play: 他是研究戲劇的人。 He is a student of drama.

戲劇團 (ㄒㄧˋ ㄐㄩˊ ㄊㄨㄢˊ)
a dramatic troupe

戲劇化 (ㄒㄧˋ ㄐㄩˊ ㄏㄨㄚˋ)
to dramatize; dramatic; to playact; theatrical: 戲劇化的悲哀表現 a theatrical display of grief

戲劇家 (ㄒㄧˋ ㄐㄩˊ ㄐㄧㄚ)
a playwright; a dramatist

戲劇節 (ㄒㄧˋ ㄐㄩˊ ㄐㄧㄝˊ)
Drama Day (falling on February 15)

戲劇界 (ㄒㄧˋ ㄐㄩˊ ㄐㄧㄝˋ)
the dramatic circles; the theatrical circles

戲曲 (ㄒㄧˋ ㄑㄩˇ)
a drama; a play; a theatrical composition; a traditional opera: 地方戲曲 local operas

戲嬉 (ㄒㄧˋ ㄒㄧ)
to play; merrymaking

戲箱 (ㄒㄧˋ ㄒㄧㄤ)
boxes for keeping theatrical properties and garments

戲照 (ㄒㄧˋ ㄓㄠˋ)
a photo of a person in stage costume

戲裝 (ㄒㄧˋ ㄓㄨㄤ)
theatrical (or stage) costume

戲水 (ㄒㄧˋ ㄕㄨㄟˇ)
to play with water; to play in water

戲子 (ㄒㄧˋ ˙ㄗ)
a dramatic player; an actor or actress (a derogatory reference to show biz personalities who used to occupy the lowest social stratum in ancient China)

戲詞 (ㄒㄧˋ ㄘˊ)
the words of an actor's part; an actor's lines 亦作「臺詞」

戲言 (ㄒㄧˋ ㄧㄢˊ)
a joke; a witticism; a jest: 戲言中常含眞理。 Many a true word is spoken in jest.

戲文 (ㄒㄧˋ ㄨㄣˊ)
theatrical writing; drama

戲園子 (ㄒㄧˋ ㄩㄢˊ ˙ㄗ) or 戲場 (ㄒㄧˋ ㄔㄤˇ) or 戲樓 (ㄒㄧˋ ㄌㄡˊ)
a playhouse; a theater

戲院 (ㄒㄧˋ ㄩㄢˋ)
a theater; a movie house

【戲】 1774
2. ㄏㄨ hu hū
alas; oh; o; ah

十四畫

【戴】 1775
ㄉㄞˋ day dài
1. to wear on the head, the nose, the ear, or the hand; to put on
2. to support; to sustain; to bear
3. a Chinese family name
4. to respect; to honor: 我們十分愛戴他。 We love and respect him very much.

戴不上 (ㄉㄞˋ ㄅㄨˋ ㄕㄤˋ)
incapable of wearing (or being worn) on the head

戴盆望天 (ㄉㄞˋ ㄆㄣˊ ㄨㄤˋ ㄊㄧㄢ)
(literally) to try to view the sky with a tray on the head —to take an action cuntrary to one's objective

戴帽子 (ㄉㄞˋ ㄇㄠˋ ˙ㄗ)
①to wear a hat or a cap ②(said of a business broker) to demand payment in addition to what is due ③to

falsely accuse someone of a crime (usually political in nature)

戴綠頭巾 (ㄉㄞˋ ㄌㄩˋ ㄊㄡˊ ㄐㄧㄣ)
to be a cuckold 亦作「戴綠帽」

戴高帽 (ㄉㄞˋ ㄍㄠ ㄇㄠˋ)
to receive a flattery or compliment; to flatter

戴孝 (ㄉㄞˋ ㄒㄧㄠˋ)
to go into mourning (for a parent, relative, etc.); to be in mourning: 他爲母親戴孝。 He is in mourning for his mother.

戴星 (ㄉㄞˋ ㄒㄧㄥ)
to leave home at dawn and return in the evening 參看「戴月披星」

戴罪立功 (ㄉㄞˋ ㄗㄨㄟˋ ㄌㄧˋ ㄍㄨㄥ)
to atone for a mistake or failure by meritorious services; to redeem oneself by good services

戴眼鏡 (ㄉㄞˋ ㄧㄢˇ ㄐㄧㄥˋ)
to wear glasses or spectacles

戴月披星 (ㄉㄞˋ ㄩㄝˋ ㄆㄧ ㄒㄧㄥ)
to be outdoors when there are the moon and the stars in the sky; to travel, work, or play outdoors at night

戴圓履方 (ㄉㄞˋ ㄩㄢˊ ㄌㄩˇ ㄈㄤ)
to stand between Heaven and Earth

【戳】 1776
ㄔㄨㄛ chuo chuō
1. to jab; to poke; to pierce: 他在今天的報紙上戳一個洞。 He poked a hole in today's newspaper.
2. a chop; a stamp; a seal: 橡皮戳 a rubber stamp

戳記 (ㄔㄨㄛ ㄐㄧˋ)
a stamp; a seal; a business stamp

戳穿 (ㄔㄨㄛ ㄔㄨㄢ)
to puncture; to lay bare; to expose; to uncover: 我們戳穿了他的謊言和詭辯。 We laid bare his lies and sophistry.

戳子 (ㄔㄨㄛ ˙ㄗ) or 戳兒 (ㄔㄨㄛ ㄦ)
a stamp; a seal; a chop: 他在文件上蓋戳子。 He put a seal on the document.

戳印 (ㄔㄨㄛ ㄧㄣˋ)
to stamp; a stamp

戶 部
ㄏㄨ huh hù

【戶】 1777
ㄏㄨ huh hù
1. a door: 戶外很冷。It is rather cold out of doors.
2. a household; a family: 他的名字喻戶曉。His name became a household word.
3. a Chinese family name
戶部(ㄏㄨ ㄅㄨ)
(in ancient times) Ministry of Finance
戶頭(ㄏㄨ ㄊㄡ)or 戶名(ㄏㄨ ㄇㄧㄥ)
① a depositor (in banking); a bank account: 他在銀行開戶頭。He opened an account in the bank. ② the family head; the householder
戶庭(ㄏㄨ ㄊㄧㄥ)
the entrance hall (of a house)
戶內(ㄏㄨ ㄋㄟ)
indoor, indoors
戶內運動(ㄏㄨ ㄋㄟ ㄩㄣ ㄉㄨㄥ)
indoor games
戶口(ㄏㄨ ㄎㄡ)
households; registered permanent residence
戶口普查(ㄏㄨ ㄎㄡ ㄆㄨ ㄔㄚˊ)
census taking; a census
戶口米(ㄏㄨ ㄎㄡ ㄇㄧ)
rice rationed for family consumption; rationed rice
戶口名簿(ㄏㄨ ㄎㄡ ㄇㄧㄥˊ ㄅㄨ)
a household identification book
戶口謄本(ㄏㄨ ㄎㄡ ㄊㄥˊ ㄅㄣ)or 戶口抄本(ㄏㄨ ㄎㄡ ㄔㄠ ㄅㄣ)
a transcript of one's household register; a census register; a family register
戶戶(ㄏㄨ ㄏㄨ)
every household
戶籍(ㄏㄨ ㄐㄧˊ)
a domicile; household registration
戶籍簿(ㄏㄨ ㄐㄧˊ ㄅㄨ)
a domiciliary register
戶籍法(ㄏㄨ ㄐㄧˊ ㄈㄚˇ)
census law; household regis-

tration law
戶限(ㄏㄨ ㄒㄧㄢ)
a threshold; a doorsill
戶限爲穿(ㄏㄨ ㄒㄧㄢ ㄨㄟˊ ㄔㄨㄢ)
There are so many visitors that the doorsill has worn through under their feet.
戶長(ㄏㄨ ㄓㄤˇ)
the household head; the family head
戶政(ㄏㄨ ㄓㄥˋ)
the administration with regard to residents and residence
戶樞(ㄏㄨ ㄕㄨ)
a door pivot; a door hinge; a door axis
戶樞不蠹(ㄏㄨ ㄕㄨ ㄅㄨˋ ㄉㄨˋ)
(literally) The door pivot will not become worm-eaten. —Human faculties should be constantly used to prevent them from getting rusty.
戶稅(ㄏㄨ ㄕㄨㄟˋ)
household tax: 你繳納多少戶稅? How much household tax do you pay?
戶牖(ㄏㄨ ㄧㄡˇ)
① doors and windows ② (academic or philosophic) schools or sects
戶外(ㄏㄨ ㄨㄞˋ)
outdoor: 你喜歡戶外活動嗎? Do you like outdoor activities?
戶外運動(ㄏㄨ ㄨㄞˋ ㄩㄣˋ ㄉㄨㄥˋ)
outdoor games

一畫

【厄】 1778
(阨) ㄜˋ eh ò
narrow; strait; straits; difficult

四畫

【戾】 1779
ㄌㄧˋ lih lì
1. perverse; recalcitrant; irregular; abnormal
2. atrocity; atrocious; violence; violent
3. to come to ; up to
戾氣(ㄌㄧˋ ㄑㄧˋ)
perversity; disharmony; irregularity

戾怒(ㄌㄧˋ ㄋㄨˋ)
sin; crime; guilt

【戽】 1780
ㄏㄨˋ huh hù
a pail; a bucket
戽斗(ㄏㄨˋ ㄉㄡˇ)
a device operated by manual labor to draw water for irrigation of the farms
戽水(ㄏㄨˋ ㄕㄨㄟˇ)
to draw water for farm irrigation by the above device

【房】 1781
ㄈㄤˊ farng fáng
1. a house; a building: 他的房子在沿街第三家。His house is three doors down the street.
2. a room; a chamber: 他們正在佈置新房。They are arranging their bridal chamber.
3. a compartmentalized structure
4. a wife; a concubine
5. a Chinese family name
房門(ㄈㄤˊ ㄇㄣˊ)
a door to a room
房地產(ㄈㄤˊ ㄉㄧˋ ㄔㄢˇ)
real estates
房地產經紀人(ㄈㄤˊ ㄉㄧˋ ㄔㄢˇ ㄐㄧㄥ ㄐㄧˋ ㄖㄣˊ)
a realtor
房頂(ㄈㄤˊ ㄉㄧㄥˇ)
the roof of a house 亦作「屋頂」
房東(ㄈㄤˊ ㄉㄨㄥ)
the landlord or landlady (of a house)
房東太太(ㄈㄤˊ ㄉㄨㄥ ㄊㄞˋ ·ㄊㄞ)
a landlady
房柁(ㄈㄤˊ ㄊㄨㄛˊ)
a ridgepole; a ridgepiece
房樑(ㄈㄤˊ ㄌㄧㄤˊ)
a house beam 亦作「房梁」
房梁(ㄈㄤˊ ㄌㄧㄤˊ)
a house beam
房客(ㄈㄤˊ ㄎㄜˋ)
the tenant (of a house); a guest (at a hotel, etc.)
房脊(ㄈㄤˊ ㄐㄧˇ)
the ridge of the roof
房間(ㄈㄤˊ ㄐㄧㄢ)
a room; a chamber: 這所房屋有多少房間? How many rooms are there in this house?
房捐(ㄈㄤˊ ㄐㄩㄢ)
house tax 亦作「房屋稅」

房契(ㄈㄤˊ ㄑㄧˋ)
　a house ownership certificate

房錢(ㄈㄤˊ ㄑㄧㄢˊ)
　house rentals 參看「房租」

房玄齡(ㄈㄤˊ ㄒㄩㄢ ㄌㄧㄥˊ)
　Fang Hsüan-ling, 578-648, a statesman who helped Emperor Tai Tsung of the Tang Dynasty to bring about one of the most prosperous eras in Chinese history

房主(ㄈㄤˊ ㄓㄨˇ)
　a house proprietor or owner

房中術(ㄈㄤˊ ㄓㄨㄥ ㄕㄨˋ)
　the art of lovemaking

房產(ㄈㄤˊ ㄔㄢˇ)
　property in the form of a house or houses

房事(ㄈㄤˊ ㄕˋ)
　sexual activity; lovemaking

房舍(ㄈㄤˊ ㄕㄜˋ)
　a house

房子(ㄈㄤˊ ˙ㄗ)
　a house; a building

房租(ㄈㄤˊ ㄗㄨ)
　a house rental

房簷(ㄈㄤˊ ㄧㄢˊ)
　eaves

房屋(ㄈㄤˊ ㄨ)
　a house; a building

房屋稅(ㄈㄤˊ ㄨ ㄕㄨㄟˋ)
　the building tax

【所】 1782
ㄙㄨㄛˇ　suǒ　suò

1. a place; a location; a position: 這就是意外事件發生的所在地。This is the place where the accident happened.

2. a building; an office: 他在律師事務所做事。He works in a lawyer's office.

3. that which

所費不貲(ㄙㄨㄛˇ ㄈㄟˋ ㄅㄨˋ ㄗ)
　to have spent a fortune; to incur a considerable or great expense

所答非所問(ㄙㄨㄛˇ ㄉㄚˊ ㄈㄟ ㄙㄨㄛˇ ㄨㄣˋ)
　to give an irrelevant answer

所得(ㄙㄨㄛˇ ㄉㄜˊ)
　①income ②what one gets or receives: 所得不償所失。What one gets cannot make up for what one loses.

所得稅(ㄙㄨㄛˇ ㄉㄜˊ ㄕㄨㄟˋ)
　income tax

所到之處(ㄙㄨㄛˇ ㄉㄠˋ ㄓ ㄔㄨˋ)
　wherever one goes

所天(ㄙㄨㄛˇ ㄊㄧㄢ)
　①one's sovereign ②one's father ③one's husband

所羅門(ㄙㄨㄛˇ ㄌㄨㄛˊ ㄇㄣˊ)
　Solomon, 993-953 B.C., king of Israel (son of David)

所感(ㄙㄨㄛˇ ㄍㄢˇ)
　one's impression about something

所好(ㄙㄨㄛˇ ㄏㄠˋ)
　one's hobbies or likes: 我對他的所好與所惡一無所知。I know nothing of his likes and dislikes.

所懷(ㄙㄨㄛˇ ㄏㄨㄞˊ)
　the ideas in one's mind; thoughts

所歡(ㄙㄨㄛˇ ㄏㄨㄢ)
　a sweetheart; a lover

所見所聞(ㄙㄨㄛˇ ㄐㄧㄢˋ ㄙㄨㄛˇ ㄨㄣˊ)
　what one has seen and heard

所期(ㄙㄨㄛˇ ㄑㄧ)
　one's expectations from someone or something

所欽(ㄙㄨㄛˇ ㄑㄧㄣ)
　①a respected friend ②a brother

所向披靡(ㄙㄨㄛˇ ㄒㄧㄤˋ ㄆㄧ ㄇㄧˇ)
　(said of an invincible army) victorious wherever it goes

所向無敵(ㄙㄨㄛˇ ㄒㄧㄤˋ ㄨˊ ㄉㄧˊ)
　to encounter no significant opponent on the way; undefeatable; invincible

所需(ㄙㄨㄛˇ ㄒㄩ)
　needs or requirements (in doing something); 耐心是教學所需的要件。Patience is a requirement in teaching.

所學(ㄙㄨㄛˇ ㄒㄩㄝˊ)
　one's specialty; what one has majored in

所知(ㄙㄨㄛˇ ㄓ)
　①what one knows ②an acquaintance

所致(ㄙㄨㄛˇ ㄓˋ)
　as a result of; to result from: 這損害由火災所致。The damage resulted from the fire.

所長(ㄙㄨㄛˇ ㄓㄤˇ)
　①(ㄙㄨㄛˇ ㄓㄤˇ) the head or director of an office

②(ㄙㄨㄛˇ ㄔㄤˊ) one's specialty; what one excels in

所識(ㄙㄨㄛˇ ㄕˋ)
　acquaintances: 他所識甚多。He has a large circle of acquaintances.

所事(ㄙㄨㄛˇ ㄕˋ)
　everything

所事非人(ㄙㄨㄛˇ ㄕˋ ㄈㄟ ㄖㄣˊ)
　①to serve under the wrong leader ②to have married a bad man

所生(ㄙㄨㄛˇ ㄕㄥ)
　parents

所屬(ㄙㄨㄛˇ ㄕㄨˇ)
　①subordinates; subordinate agencies ②the authority to which an agency belongs

所自(ㄙㄨㄛˇ ㄗˋ)或所從(ㄙㄨㄛˇ ㄘㄨㄥˊ)
　cause; origin; source

所載(ㄙㄨㄛˇ ㄗㄞˋ)
　what is printed, published or reported in a publication

所在(ㄙㄨㄛˇ ㄗㄞˋ)
　①where one dwells ②a place; a location; a position: 這就是肇事的所在。This is the place where the accident happened.

所在地(ㄙㄨㄛˇ ㄗㄞˋ ㄉㄧˋ)
　the place where an institution or organization is located; a seat: 大學是求學研究的所在地。A university is a seat of learning.

所作所為(ㄙㄨㄛˇ ㄗㄨㄛˋ ㄙㄨㄛˇ ㄨㄟˊ)
　actions; behavior; conduct; what one does and how he behaves

所藏(ㄙㄨㄛˇ ㄘㄤˊ)
　one's collection (of rare books, masterpieces, etc.)

所司(ㄙㄨㄛˇ ㄙ)
　what a person or an agency is in charge of; a function

所思(ㄙㄨㄛˇ ㄙ)
　①one's thoughts: 他看起來若有所思。He looked as if he were absorbed in thought. ②the person one is in love with

所以(ㄙㄨㄛˇ ㄧˇ)
　therefore; so; consequently: 我病了，所以不能來。I was ill, and therefore could not come.

所以然(ㄙㄨㄛˇ ㄧˇ ㄖㄢˊ)

reason; cause: 我們只知其然
却不知其所以然。We only
know it is so, but do not
know (the reason) why it is
so.

所由(ㄙㄨㄛˇ 丨ㄡˊ)
①a cause ②a local magis-
trate

所有(ㄙㄨㄛˇ 丨ㄡˇ)
①what one owns; belong-
ings; possessions ②to own:
這房子為誰所有? Who owns
this house? ③all; every: 我把
所有的錢都給了他。I gave him
all the money I had.

所有權(ㄙㄨㄛˇ 丨ㄡˊ ㄑㄩㄢˊ)
ownership; proprietary
rights

所有權狀(ㄙㄨㄛˇ 丨ㄡˇ ㄑㄩㄢˊ ㄓㄨㄤˋ)
an ownership certificate

所有者(ㄙㄨㄛˇ 丨ㄡˇ ㄓㄜˇ)
an owner; a proprietor: 他是
該旅館的所有者。He is the
proprietor of the hotel.

所有人(ㄙㄨㄛˇ 丨ㄡˇ ㄖㄣˊ)
an owner; a proprietor: 他將
錶歸還所有人。He returned
the watch to the owner.

所有物(ㄙㄨㄛˇ 丨ㄡˇ ㄨˋ)
belongings; possessions

所為何來(ㄙㄨㄛˇ ㄨㄟˊ ㄏㄜˊ ㄌㄞˊ)
What for? 或What are you
here for?

所謂(ㄙㄨㄛˇ ㄨㄟˋ)
①so-called: 他是個所謂的君
子。He is a so-called gentleman. ②what is called

所餘(ㄙㄨㄛˇ ㄩˊ)
what remains; what is left; a
remnant; leftovers: 你可把所
餘全都拿去。You may have
all those that remain.

所願(ㄙㄨㄛˇ ㄩㄢˋ)
one's wishes: 這女孩之所願已
實現。The girl has got her
wish.

五畫

【匾】 1783
1. ㄅㄧㄢˇ bean biǎn
1. flat: 這箱子被壓扁了。The
box was crushed flat.
2. a tablet
3. an ancient surname

匾柏(ㄅㄧㄢˇ ㄅㄞˊ)
Japanese cypress

扁平(ㄅㄧㄢˇ ㄆㄧㄥˊ)
thin and flat

扁豆(ㄅㄧㄢˇ ㄉㄡˋ)
lentil

扁擔(ㄅㄧㄢˇ ˙ㄉㄢ)
a flat carrying pole or
shouldering pole

扁塌鼻(ㄅㄧㄢˇ ㄊㄚˋ ㄅㄧˊ)
a snub nose

扁桃腺(ㄅㄧㄢˇ ㄊㄠˊ ㄒㄧㄢˋ)
the tonsils

扁桃腺腫大(ㄅㄧㄢˇ ㄊㄠˊ ㄒㄧㄢˋ ㄓㄨㄥˇ ㄉㄚˋ)
hypertrophy of tonsils

扁桃腺炎(ㄅㄧㄢˇ ㄊㄠˊ ㄒㄧㄢˋ 丨ㄢˊ)
tonsillitis; quinsy

扁球面(ㄅㄧㄢˇ ㄑㄧㄡˊ ㄇㄧㄢˋ)
(mathematics) an oblate
spheroid

扁鵲(ㄅㄧㄢˇ ㄑㄩㄝˋ)
Pien Chüeh, a famed physician of the Epoch of War-
ring States

扁食(ㄅㄧㄢˇ ㄕˊ)
dumpling or ravioli

扁額(ㄅㄧㄢˇ ㄜˊ)
a large plaque hanging over
a door or in the living room
亦作「匾額」

【扁】 1783
2. ㄆㄧㄢ pian piān
small

扁舟(ㄆㄧㄢ ㄓㄡ)
a small boat; a skiff

【扃】 1784
1. ㄐㄩㄥ jiong jiōng
a bolt; to bolt (doors); to
shut a door

扃門(ㄐㄩㄥ ㄇㄣˊ)
to bolt the doors

扃門謝客(ㄐㄩㄥ ㄇㄣˊ ㄒㄧㄝˋ ㄎㄜˋ)
to shut the door and decline
visitors

扃關(ㄐㄩㄥ ㄍㄨㄢ)
a bolt or bar (for doors)

扃鐍(ㄐㄩㄥ ㄐㄩㄝˊ)
①to lock ②a door bolt

【扃】 1784
2. ㄐㄩㄥ jeong
jiōng
perceiving; discerning

扃扃(ㄐㄩㄥ ㄐㄩㄥ)
perceiving; discerning; dis-
criminating

六畫

【扆】 1785
丨ˇ yiǐ yǐ
a screen decorated with a
design in hatchets placed
behind the emperor in the
imperial audience chamber

【扇】 1786
1. ㄕㄢˋ shann
shàn
1. a fan
2. a numeracy auxiliary for
door or gate leaves: 他打破
了一扇窗戶。He broke a win-
dow.

扇骨子(ㄕㄢˋ ㄍㄨˇ ˙ㄗ)
the framework of a fan; the
ribs of a fan

扇形(ㄕㄢˋ ㄒㄧㄥˊ)
fan-shaped; a sector (of a
circle)

扇墜兒(ㄕㄢˋ ㄓㄨㄟˋ ㄦ)
a pendant attached to a fan

扇子(ㄕㄢˋ ˙ㄗ)
a fan

扇舞(ㄕㄢˋ ㄨˇ)
fan dance

【扇】 1786
2. (搧) ㄕㄢ shan
shān
to fan; to instigate; to incite

扇風(ㄕㄢ ㄈㄥ)
to fan the air

扇風點火(ㄕㄢ ㄈㄥ ㄉㄧㄢˇ ㄏㄨㄛˇ)
to fan a fire—to inflame and
agitate people; to stir up
trouble or chaos

扇動(ㄕㄢ ㄉㄨㄥˋ)
to incite; to instigate: 他扇動
兩家吵架。He instigated a
quarrel between the two
families.

扇惑(ㄕㄢ ㄏㄨㄛˋ)
to instigate and mislead; to
agitate; to lead astray by
incitement: 他的謊言扇惑了
我。His lies misled me.

扇枕溫被(ㄕㄢ ㄓㄣˇ ㄨㄣ ㄅㄟˋ)
to cool the pillow and warm
the bedding (for one's parents); to be a model of filial
piety 亦作「扇枕溫席」

扇揚(ㄕㄢ 丨ㄤˊ)
to glorify; to uphold; to
exalt; to spread out: 這消息
很快就扇揚開了。The news
soon spread out.

【戶部】

七畫

【屭】 1787
ㄏㄨ huh hǔ

1. to follow as escort or retinue
2. insolent; impertinent
3. a Chinese family name

屭驆(ㄏㄨㄅㄧˋ)
to escort the emperor in travel

屭輦(ㄏㄨㄋㄧㄢˇ) or 屭駕(ㄏㄨㄐㄧㄚˋ)
to escort the emperor in travel

屭從(ㄏㄨㄗㄨㄥˊ)
the escort or retinue of the emperor when he travels

八畫

【扉】 1788
ㄈㄟ fei fēi
a door leaf

扉葉(ㄈㄟˋㄧㄝˋ) or 扉頁(ㄈㄟˋㄧㄝˋ)
a flyleaf; a title page

手部
ㄕㄡˇ shoou shǒu

【手】 1789
ㄕㄡˇ shoou shǒu

1. hand; of the hand; having to do with the hand: 他们手牵手地走開了。They walked away hand in hand. 那是件手編的毛衣。It is a hand- knitted woolen sweater.
2. to have in one's hand; to hold: 他陷入敵人手中。He fell into the enemy's hands.
3. a skilled person; a person
4. action
5. personally

手把(ㄕㄡˇㄅㄚˇ)
a handle

手搏(ㄕㄡˇㄅㄛˊ)
to fight with bare hands

手拜(ㄕㄡˇㄅㄞˋ)
to worship or pay homage by kowtowing

手背(ㄕㄡˇㄅㄟˋ)
① the back of the hand ② (gambling) having bad luck

手背朝下(ㄕㄡˇㄅㄟˋㄔㄠˊㄒㄧㄚˋ)
to hold out one's hand with the open palm—to beg for money or help

手臂(ㄕㄡˇㄅㄧˋ)or(ㄕㄡˇㄅㄟˋ)
the arm from the wrist up

手版 or 手板(ㄕㄡˇㄅㄢˇ)or 手本(ㄕㄡˇㄅㄣˇ)
① (in former times) an official calling card presented when requesting an interview with one's superior ② (Ching Dynasty) a memo presented by a successful candidate in a formal visit to the examiner

手板子(ㄕㄡˇㄅㄢˇ‧ㄗ)
a ferule

手筆(ㄕㄡˇㄅㄧˇ)
① a literary work or handwriting (by a famed person): 那篇名家的作品表現出名家手筆。The artist's work showed a master's hand. ② the courage of spending money on a grand scale: 他自小手筆就闊。He has been liberal with money since his childhood.

手錶(ㄕㄡˇㄅㄧㄠˇ)
a wrist watch

手邊(ㄕㄡˇㄅㄧㄢ)
at hand; handy; 他寫字時總放本字典在手邊。When he writes, he always keeps a dictionary at hand.

手不釋卷(ㄕㄡˇㄅㄨˋㄕˋㄐㄩㄢˋ)
to hold a book in hand all the time; to be studying constantly; to read avariciously

手不停揮(ㄕㄡˇㄅㄨˋㄊㄧㄥˊㄏㄨㄟ)
to write without rest; to be assiduously engaged in writing

手不老實(ㄕㄡˇㄅㄨˋㄌㄠˇ‧ㄕ)
light-fingered; given to pilfering; thievish

手不穩(ㄕㄡˇㄅㄨˋㄨㄣˇ)
light-fingered; thievish

手帕(ㄕㄡˇㄆㄚˋ)
a handkerchief

手模(ㄕㄡˇㄇㄛˊ)
an impression of the thumb in place of a signature; a fingerprint

手慢(ㄕㄡˇㄇㄢˋ)
slow in action; slow-moving

手忙脚亂(ㄕㄡˇㄇㄤˊㄐㄧㄠˇㄌㄨㄢˋ)
to be in a flurry; to be flustered; to be very busy: 他一陣手忙脚亂。He is all in a fluster.

手面闊綽(ㄕㄡˇㄇㄧㄢˋㄎㄨㄛˋㄔㄨㄛˋ)
extravagantly generous or liberal; lavish

手民(ㄕㄡˇㄇㄧㄣˊ)
① an engraver of printing blocks; a compositor ② a carpenter

手民誤植(ㄕㄡˇㄇㄧㄣˊㄨˋㄓˊ)
a typographic mistake or error; a misprint

手法(ㄕㄡˇㄈㄚˇ)
workmanship; artistry; skill; technique

手風琴(ㄕㄡˇㄈㄥㄑㄧㄣˊ)
an accordion

手縫(ㄕㄡˇㄈㄥˊ)
① (ㄕㄡˇㄈㄥˊ) ⓐ to tailor or make dress personally ⓑ to sew by hand ② (ㄕㄡˇㄈㄥˋ) the spaces between the fingers

手到病除(ㄕㄡˇㄉㄠˋㄅㄧㄥˋㄔㄨˊ)
to cure a patient by a mere touch

手到擒來(ㄕㄡˇㄉㄠˋㄑㄧㄣˊㄌㄞˊ)
to capture an enemy easily

手底下(ㄕㄡˇㄉㄧˇㄒㄧㄚˋ)
① one's subordinates: 他從不信任手底下。He never trusts his subordinates. ② ways of doing things

手電筒(ㄕㄡˇㄉㄧㄢˋㄊㄨㄥˇ)
a flashlight; an electric torch

手段(ㄕㄡˇㄉㄨㄢˋ)
① the means (as opposed to the end) ② a devious way of dealing with people

手動機器(ㄕㄡˇㄉㄨㄥˋㄐㄧㄑㄧˋ)
a hand-operated machine; a manually operated machine

手套(ㄕㄡˇㄊㄠˋ)
gloves; gauntlets; mittens: 他昨天買了一副手套。He bought a pair of gloves yesterday.

手頭(ㄕㄡˇㄊㄡˊ)
① on hand; at hand; in hand: 我手頭還有些錢。I still have some money in hand. ② financial conditions 參看「手頭緊」or「手頭鬆」③ personal experience

手頭好(ㄕㄡˇ ㄊㄡˊ ㄏㄠˇ)
dexterous; deft

手頭緊(ㄕㄡˇ ㄊㄡˊ ㄐㄧㄣˇ)
①short of cash (or money)
②closefisted

手頭巧(ㄕㄡˇ ㄊㄡˊ ㄑㄧㄠˇ)
skillful in the use of the
hands; dexterous; deft

手頭字(ㄕㄡˇ ㄊㄡˊ ㄗˋ)
words in everyday use;
everyday words

手頭鬆(ㄕㄡˇ ㄊㄡˊ ㄙㄨㄥ)or 手頭寬
(ㄕㄡˇ ㄊㄡˊ ㄎㄨㄢ)
liberal in spending; to be
quite well off at the
moment; to be in easy circumstances

手談(ㄕㄡˇ ㄊㄢˊ)
to play a "go" game

手提(ㄕㄡˇ ㄊㄧˊ)
portable; to carry with a
hand; 他有一台手提打字機。He
has a portable typewriter.

手提袋(ㄕㄡˇ ㄊㄧˊ ㄉㄞˋ)
a valise; a Boston bag; a
handbag

手提箱(ㄕㄡˇ ㄊㄧˊ ㄒㄧㄤ)
a portmanteau; an attaché
case; a suitcase

手推車(ㄕㄡˇ ㄊㄨㄟ ㄔㄜ)or 手車
(ㄕㄡˇ ㄔㄜ)
a handcart; a wheelbarrow

手拿(ㄕㄡˇ ㄋㄚˊ)
to hold in hand; to take by
hand

手拉手(ㄕㄡˇ ㄌㄚ ㄕㄡˇ)
hand in hand

手辣(ㄕㄡˇ ㄌㄚˋ)
ruthless: 那是一種心狠手辣的
行為。That was an act of
savage, ruthless ferocity.

手翰(ㄕㄡˇ ㄏㄢˋ)
①a personally handwritten
article ②a personal letter
亦作「手書」

手榴彈(ㄕㄡˇ ㄌㄧㄡˊ ㄉㄢˋ)
a hand grenade

手令(ㄕㄡˇ ㄌㄧㄥˋ)
a personally handwritten
order (by a man at the top)

手爐(ㄕㄡˇ ㄌㄨˊ)
a portable charcoal stove
(used as a hand warmer)

手稿(ㄕㄡˇ ㄍㄠˇ)
manuscript

手骨(ㄕㄡˇ ㄍㄨˇ)
bones of the human fore-

limbs

手工(ㄕㄡˇ ㄍㄨㄥ)
①handwork; handiwork ②
by hand: 這是手工做的嗎?
Was this made by hand?

手工藝(ㄕㄡˇ ㄍㄨㄥ ㄧˋ)
handicrafts; handiwork

手工藝品(ㄕㄡˇ ㄍㄨㄥ ㄧˋ ㄆㄧㄣˇ)
handicraft articles; fancy
works

手工業(ㄕㄡˇ ㄍㄨㄥ ㄧㄝˋ)
a manual trade

手銬(ㄕㄡˇ ㄎㄠˋ)
handcuffs: 犯人都帶上手銬。
The prisoners were all put
on handcuffs.

手快(ㄕㄡˇ ㄎㄨㄞˋ)
quick in action; nimble: 他眼
明手快。He's sharp of sight
and quick of hand.

手翰(ㄕㄡˇ ㄏㄢˋ)
a personally handwritten letter

手虎口(ㄕㄡˇ ㄏㄨˇ ㄎㄡˇ)
the space between the thumb
and the index finger

手滑(ㄕㄡˇ ㄏㄨㄚˊ)
to do something at will

手揮目送(ㄕㄡˇ ㄏㄨㄟ ㄇㄨˋ ㄙㄨㄥˋ)
conveyance of a double
meaning

手迹(ㄕㄡˇ ㄐㄧ)
one's handwriting (or painting)

手機關鎗(ㄕㄡˇ ㄐㄧ ㄍㄨㄢ ㄑㄧㄤ)
a Lewis machine gun; a
Lewis gun; a Lewis auto-
matic rifle; a Thompson sub-
machine gun; a Tommy gun

手急眼快(ㄕㄡˇ ㄐㄧˊ ㄧㄢˇ ㄎㄨㄞˋ)
moving or acting quickly;
nimble: to be quick of eye
and deft of hand

手技(ㄕㄡˇ ㄐㄧˋ)
①manual skill ②jugglery;
sleight of hand

手脚(ㄕㄡˇ ㄐㄧㄠˇ)
①hand and foot ②motion;
action ③tricks; juggles: 我懷
疑有人從中動過手脚。I suspect
that someone must have juggled things.

手脚不乾淨(ㄕㄡˇ ㄐㄧㄠˇ ㄅㄨˋ ㄍㄢ
ㄐㄧㄥˋ)
(slang) to be in the habit
of stealing

手脚利落(ㄕㄡˇ ㄐㄧㄠˇ ㄌㄧˋ ㄌㄨㄛˋ)

nimble; agile

手簡(ㄕㄡˇ ㄐㄧㄢˇ)
a letter

手巾(ㄕㄡˇ ㄐㄧㄣ)
a towel

手緊(ㄕㄡˇ ㄐㄧㄣˇ)
①short of cash ②thrifty;
reluctant to spend money

手絹兒(ㄕㄡˇ ㄐㄩㄢˋ ㄦ)
a handkerchief

手卷(ㄕㄡˇ ㄐㄩㄢˇ)
a scroll

手啓(ㄕㄡˇ ㄑㄧˇ)
handwritten by (a conven-
tional phrase for ending a
letter)

手氣(ㄕㄡˇ ㄑㄧˋ)
(gambling) luck

手巧(ㄕㄡˇ ㄑㄧㄠˇ)
dexterous; skillful

手球(ㄕㄡˇ ㄑㄧㄡˊ)
(sports) handball

手鎗(ㄕㄡˇ ㄑㄧㄤ)
a pistol; a revolver; a gun

手輕(ㄕㄡˇ ㄑㄧㄥ)
light-handed

手下(ㄕㄡˇ ㄒㄧㄚˋ)
①subordinates ②under the
leadership of: 我們在他手下工
作。We work under him.

手下敗將(ㄕㄡˇ ㄒㄧㄚˋ ㄅㄞˋ ㄐㄧㄤˋ)
one who has suffered defeat
at (my, your, etc.) hands

手下留情(ㄕㄡˇ ㄒㄧㄚˋ ㄌㄧㄡˊ ㄑㄧㄥˊ)
to show leniency or mercy

手心(ㄕㄡˇ ㄒㄧㄣ)
the center of the palm—(figuratively) control

手相(ㄕㄡˇ ㄒㄧㄤˋ)
the lines of the palm by
which fortunetellers tell
one's fortune: 看手相 to read
one's palm

手相家(ㄕㄡˇ ㄒㄧㄤˋ ㄐㄧㄚ)
a palmist

手相術(ㄕㄡˇ ㄒㄧㄤˋ ㄕㄨˋ)
palmistry

手續(ㄕㄡˇ ㄒㄩˋ)
procedures; red tape; formalities

手續費(ㄕㄡˇ ㄒㄩˋ ㄈㄟˋ)
service charges

手植(ㄕㄡˇ ㄓˊ)
(said of a tree) personally
planted (by a dignitary, etc.)

手指(ㄕㄡˇ ㄓˇ·ㄊㄡˇ)

① fingertips ② fingers

手指(ㄕㄡ ㄓ)
① a finger ② to point at something with the index finger: 他手指著什麼？What is he pointing at?

手紙(ㄕㄡ ㄓ)
toilet paper

手札(ㄕㄡ ㄓㄚˊ)
a personally handwritten letter

手摺(ㄕㄡ ㄓㄜ)
① (in former times) paper for making appeals to a superior official ② an account book (of a merchant)

手詔(ㄕㄡ ㄓㄠ)
a personally handwritten imperial decree or edict

手掌(ㄕㄡ ㄓㄤˇ)
the palm (of the hand)

手杖(ㄕㄡ ㄓㄤ)
a cane; a walking stick

手鐲(ㄕㄡ ㄓㄨㄛˊ)
a bracelet

手重(ㄕㄡ ㄓㄨㄥ)
heavy-handed; with too much force

手車(ㄕㄡ ㄔㄜ)
a wheelbarrow; a pushcart; a handcart 參看「手推車」

手抄(ㄕㄡ ㄔㄠ)
to copy by hand; to make a handwritten copy

手抄本(ㄕㄡ ㄔㄠ ㄅㄣˇ)
a hand-copied book; a handwritten copy

手示(ㄕㄡ ㄕ)
personally handwritten instructions or directions

手勢(ㄕㄡ ㄕ)
a gesture; a sign; to sign: 他做友善的手勢。He made a friendly gesture.

手煞車(ㄕㄡ ㄕㄚ ㄔㄜ)
a hand brake

手上(ㄕㄡ ㄕㄤ·)
in one's hands

手書(ㄕㄡ ㄕㄨ)
a personally handwritten message or article; a personal letter

手術(ㄕㄡ ㄕㄨ)
a surgical operation; surgery

手術刀(ㄕㄡ ㄕㄨ ㄉㄠ)
a scalpel

手術台(ㄕㄡ ㄕㄨ ㄊㄞˊ)
an operation table

手術室(ㄕㄡ ㄕㄨ ㄕ)
an operation room

手刃(ㄕㄡ ㄖㄣˋ)
to kill someone personally with a sword

手軟(ㄕㄡ ㄖㄨㄢˇ)
to hesitate to inflict punishment from pity; the pity toward an intended victim

手澤(ㄕㄡ ㄗㄜˊ)
personal implements and handwritings left behind by one's immediate ancestors

手足(ㄕㄡ ㄗㄨˊ)
brothers

手足情深(ㄕㄡ ㄗㄨˊ ㄑㄧㄥˊ ㄕㄣ)
The love between brothers is deep. 或 Blood is thicker than water.

手足之情(ㄕㄡ ㄗㄨˊ ㄓ ㄑㄧㄥˊ)
brotherly affection

手足重繭(ㄕㄡ ㄗㄨˊ ㄔㄨㄥ ㄐㄧㄢˇ)
with hands and feet covered with thick calluses as a result of hard work

手足無措(ㄕㄡ ㄗㄨˊ ㄨˊ ㄘㄨㄛ)
to be at a loss what to do

手刺(ㄕㄡ ㄘˋ)
a visiting card (of an official)

手冊(ㄕㄡ ㄘㄜ)
a handbook; a manual: 英文文法手冊 a handbook of English grammar

手策(ㄕㄡ ㄘㄜ)
the means (as opposed to the end)

手廟(ㄕㄡ ㄙㄨㄛ)
personally handwritten by (a conventional phrase at the end of a letter)

手鬆(ㄕㄡ ㄙㄨㄥ)
spending money freely or lavishly; spendthrift; liberal; generous; freehanded; open-handed

手兒(ㄕㄡ ㄦ)
① the hand ② skill; workmanship; craft ③ a trick; means ④ handiwork

手藝(ㄕㄡ ㄧ)
handicraft; skill to enable one to earn a living; a trade

a craftsman; an artisan

手眼快(ㄕㄡ ㄧㄢˇ ㄎㄨㄞ)
quick in action; nimble

手淫(ㄕㄡ ㄧㄣˊ)
masturbation; self-abuse

手印(ㄕㄡ ㄧㄣ)
an impression of the thumb as a signature

手癢(ㄕㄡ ㄧㄤˇ)
① an itch on one's hands ② to have an itch to do something

手無縛鷄之力(ㄕㄡ ㄨˊ ㄈㄨˊ ㄐㄧ ㄓ ㄌㄧ)
to lack the strength to truss up a chicken

手無寸鐵(ㄕㄡ ㄨˊ ㄘㄨㄣ ㄊㄧㄝˇ)
(literally) to carry not even an inch of iron—totally unarmed

手舞足蹈(ㄕㄡ ㄨˇ ㄗㄨˊ ㄉㄠˋ)
to wave the arms and stamp the feet for joy; to caper beyond oneself with joy

手腕(ㄕㄡ ㄨㄢ)
① the wrist ② ability; tricks; skill; tact: 外交手腕 diplomacy; diplomatic skill

手腕子(ㄕㄡ ㄨㄢ·ㄗ)
the wrist

手紋(ㄕㄡ ㄨㄣˊ)
the lines on the palm

手語(ㄕㄡ ㄩˇ)
① dactylology; sign language ② to play string instruments

手諭(ㄕㄡ ㄩ)
a personally written order

【才】　1790
ㄘㄞˊ　tsair　cái

1. natural abilities; a gift; talent; a mental faculty: 她有音樂的天才。She is a talent for music.

2. a gifted person; a talented person; a brilliant man; a talent: 她是位才藝出衆的演員。She is a talented performer.

3. people of a certain type: 奴才 a flunky; a flunkey

4. certainly; indeed: 我才不怕他呢! I'm certainly not afraid of him.

5. just; just now: 節目才剛開始。The program has just started.

才筆(ㄘㄞˊ ㄅㄧˇ)

a literary talent

才貌 (ㄘㄞˊ ㄇㄠˋ)
talent and appearance

才貌雙全 (ㄘㄞˊ ㄇㄠˋ ㄕㄨㄤ ㄑㄩㄢˊ)
(said of women) talented and good-looking; impressive both in talent and appearance; brilliant and pretty

才名 (ㄘㄞˊ ㄇㄧㄥˊ)
a reputation for talent or brilliance

才分 (ㄘㄞˊ ㄈㄣˋ)
natural abilities, gifts or talent; brilliance of mind

才大心細 (ㄘㄞˊ ㄉㄚˋ ㄒㄧㄣ ㄒㄧˋ)
to have a great talent and an attentive mind; gifted and careful

才德兼備 (ㄘㄞˊ ㄉㄜˊ ㄐㄧㄢ ㄅㄟˋ) or 才德兼備 (ㄘㄞˊ ㄉㄜˊ ㄐㄧㄢ ㄅㄟˋ)
to have both talent and virtue; talented and virtuous

才童 (ㄘㄞˊ ㄊㄨㄥˊ)
a talented child; a whiz kid; a child prodigy

才難 (ㄘㄞˊ ㄋㄢˊ)
Talents are hard to find. 或 Really able men are difficult to come by.

才能 (ㄘㄞˊ ㄋㄥˊ) or 才力 (ㄘㄞˊ ㄌㄧˋ)
ability; abilities; a gift: 他是位極有才能的人。He is a man of great talent.

才女 (ㄘㄞˊ ㄋㄩˇ)
a talented woman: 她是位才女。She is a talented woman.

才郎 (ㄘㄞˊ ㄌㄤˊ)
my talented husband

才略 (ㄘㄞˊ ㄌㄩㄝˋ)
talent for scheming

才高意廣 (ㄘㄞˊ ㄍㄠ ㄧˋ ㄍㄨㄤˇ)
to have a brilliant mind and a broad vision

才幹 (ㄘㄞˊ ㄍㄢˋ)
talent or ability to get things done; competence: 他具有做將軍的才幹。He had great ability as a general.

才華 (ㄘㄞˊ ㄏㄨㄚˊ)
brilliance (of mind); a gift; a talent

才華出眾 (ㄘㄞˊ ㄏㄨㄚˊ ㄔㄨ ㄓㄨㄥˋ)
of uncommon brilliance: 王先生才華出眾。Mr. Wang is a person of uncommon brilliance.

才兼文武 (ㄘㄞˊ ㄐㄧㄢ ㄨㄣˊ ㄨˇ)
talented both mentally and physically; having both military and literary gifts

才盡 (ㄘㄞˊ ㄐㄧㄣˋ)
to have exhausted one's talent

才具 (ㄘㄞˊ ㄐㄩˋ)
natural capacity or abilities

才氣 (ㄘㄞˊ ㄑㄧˋ)
talent; brilliance; keen intelligence

才氣洋溢 (ㄘㄞˊ ㄑㄧˋ ㄧㄤˊ ㄧˋ)
a brilliant mind; brilliant intelligence

才情 (ㄘㄞˊ ㄑㄧㄥˊ)
brilliant expression of emotions (in a writing)

才學 (ㄘㄞˊ ㄒㄩㄝˊ)
intelligence and scholarship

才智 (ㄘㄞˊ ㄓˋ)
intelligence; brilliance; wisdom and ability

才儲八斗 (ㄘㄞˊ ㄔㄨˇ ㄅㄚ ㄉㄡˇ)
exceedingly talented or brilliant 亦作「才高八斗」

才士 (ㄘㄞˊ ㄕˋ)
a man of ability or talent; a brilliant man

才識 (ㄘㄞˊ ㄕˋ)
ability and insight: 他識過過人。He is gifted with talent and insight far beyond the average person.

才疏學淺 (ㄘㄞˊ ㄕㄨ ㄒㄩㄝˊ ㄑㄧㄢˇ)
untalented and unlearned; to have little talent and less learning (a polite expression referring to oneself)

才人 (ㄘㄞˊ ㄖㄣˊ)
①a talented person; a man of talent; a brilliant man ②a rank of ladies-in-waiting during the Tsin, Tang and Sung dynasties

才子 (ㄘㄞˊ ㄗˇ)
a talented person, a man of talent; a brilliant man; a genius

才子佳人 (ㄘㄞˊ ㄗˇ ㄐㄧㄚ ㄖㄣˊ)
marriage between the brilliant man and the beautiful woman; an ideal couple; gifted scholars and beautiful ladies

才子書 (ㄘㄞˊ ㄗˇ ㄕㄨ)
(literally) books by brilliant

writers—specifically referring to 莊子、離騷、史記、杜詩、水滸傳、西廂記

才思 (ㄘㄞˊ ㄙ)
brilliant thoughts (as reflected in a writing)

才思敏捷 (ㄘㄞˊ ㄙ ㄇㄧㄣˇ ㄐㄧㄝˊ)
to have an agile imagination

才藝卓絕 (ㄘㄞˊ ㄧˋ ㄓㄨㄛˊ ㄐㄩㄝˊ)
to stand out in talent and skill

才媛 (ㄘㄞˊ ㄩㄢˊ)
a talented woman; a gifted maiden

一畫

【扎】 1791
1. ㄓㄚ ja zhā
to pierce; to prick: 他的手指上扎了一根刺。He pricked his finger on a thorn.

扎蓬棵 (ㄓㄚ ㄆㄥˊ ㄎㄜ)
uncombed hair 亦稱「蓬髮」

扎猛子 (ㄓㄚ ㄇㄥˇ ㄗ)
to plunge headlong into the water

扎根 (ㄓㄚ ㄍㄣ)
to take root

扎花兒 (ㄓㄚ ㄏㄨㄚ ㄦ)
to embroider a design

扎心 (ㄓㄚ ㄒㄧㄣ)
heartbreaking

扎針 (ㄓㄚ ㄓㄣ)
to perform an acupuncture; to acupuncture; to have acupuncture treatment

扎實 (ㄓㄚ ˙ㄕ)
solid; firm: 他的事業很扎實。He had a solid business.

扎手 (ㄓㄚ ㄕㄡˇ)
①to prick the hand: 小心扎手。Mind you don't prick your hands. ②difficult to handle; thorny: 他這個人可真扎手。He is really difficult to handle.

扎手舞腳 (ㄓㄚ ㄕㄡˇ ㄨˇ ㄐㄧㄠˇ)
to make exaggerated gestures

扎耳朵 (ㄓㄚ ㄦˇ ˙ㄉㄨㄛ)
unpleasant to the ear; to grate

扎耳朵眼兒 (ㄓㄚ ㄦˇ ˙ㄉㄨㄛ ㄧㄢˇ)
to pierce the earlobe in order to wear an earring

扎眼 (ㄓㄚ ㄧㄢˇ)

〖手部〗

①dazzling; offending to the eye; loud; garish: 陽光太扎眼了。The sunshine is too dazzling. ②offensively conspicuous

【扎】 1791
1. 业丫 jar zhā
to struggle; to strive

扎掙(业丫·业ㄥ)
to struggle; to strive 亦作「挣扎」

扎掙不住(业丫·业ㄣㄅㄨ·业ㄨ)
to struggle or strive in vain; cannot keep up or maintain

扎營(业丫 1ㄥ)
to pitch a tent; to encamp

二畫

【扑】 1792
ㄆㄨ pu pū
to beat; to strike

扑笪(ㄆㄨ ㄉㄚˊ)
flogging or whipping as a punishment; a scourge

扑撻(ㄆㄨ ㄊㄚˋ)
to whip; to lash; to flog

扑擊(ㄆㄨ ㄐ一ˊ)
to hit; to strike

扑作教刑(ㄆㄨ ㄗㄨㄛˋ ㄐㄧㄠ ㄒㄧㄥˊ)
to use the rod to teach and punish

【扒】 1793
1. ㄅㄚ ba bā
1. to claw; to strip
2. to rake; to rake earth
3. to climb; to scale

扒皮(ㄅㄚ ㄆㄧˊ)
to peel off the skin

扒得高跌得重(ㄅㄚ ·ㄉㄜ ㄍㄠ ㄉㄧㄝ
·ㄉㄜ ㄓㄨㄥˋ)
The higher one climbs, the harder he falls.

扒住(ㄅㄚ ·业ㄨ)
to hold on to; to cling to

【扒】 1793
2. ㄆㄚˊ par pá
1. to gather up; to rake up: 她把落葉扒在一起。She raked the fallen leaves together.
2. to stew; to braise
3. to scratch; to claw

扒灰(ㄆㄚˊ ㄏㄨㄟ)
(literally) to scoop up ashes —to commit incest with a daughter-in-law

扒竊(ㄆㄚˊ ㄑㄧㄝ`)
to pick pockets and steal; pickpockets and burglars: 我

被扒竊了。I had my pocket picked.

扒手(ㄆㄚˊ ㄕㄡˇ)
a pickpocket: 當心扒手! Beware of pickpockets!

扒山虎(ㄆㄚˊ ㄕㄢ ㄏㄨˇ)
①a sedan chair for transportation in mountains ②a kind of ivy

【打】 1794
1. ㄉㄚˇ daa dǎ
1. to strike; to beat
2. to attack; to fight: 他們打了一場硬仗。They fought a hard battle.
3. to smash: 盤子打破在地上。The dish smashed on the floor.
4. to make, do, get, fetch, play, buy, etc. (depending on the object):我們來打網球吧。Let's play tennis.
5. from; to; toward: 你打那兒來? Where did you come from?

打靶(ㄉㄚˇ ㄅㄚˇ)
target practice

打靶場(ㄉㄚˇ ㄅㄚˇ ㄔㄤˇ)
a target range; a shooting gallery

打把式(ㄉㄚˇ ㄅㄚˇ ㄕ)
to demonstrate pugilistic skills

打擺子(ㄉㄚˇ ㄅㄞˇ ·ㄗ)
malaria; to suffer from malaria

打敗(ㄉㄚˇ ㄅㄞˋ)
①to defeat; to beat; to worst ②to suffer a defeat; to be defeated

打敗仗(ㄉㄚˇ ㄅㄞˋ 业ㄤˋ)
to suffer a defeat; to be defeated in battle

打包(ㄉㄚˇ ㄅㄠ)
①to pack ②the bundle carried on the back by a traveling Buddhist monk

打包票(ㄉㄚˇ ㄅㄠ ㄆㄧㄠ)
to vouch for; to guarantee: 我敢打包票,禮物一定準時送到。I guarantee that the gifts will be delivered on time.

打飽嗝兒(ㄉㄚˇ ㄅㄠˇ ㄍㄜˊㄦ)
to belch after a solid meal

打抱不平(ㄉㄚˇ ㄅㄠˋ ㄅㄨˋ ㄆㄧㄥˊ)
to help the victims of injustice; to try to redress an injustice to the weak; to come

out against the powerful on behalf of the downtrodden

打扮(ㄉㄚˇ ㄅㄢ)
①(said of a woman, an actor or actress)to make up ②to dress up; dressed like to dress: 孩子們打扮得像春天的花朵一樣。The dressed children looked like spring flowers.

打邊鼓(ㄉㄚˇ ㄅㄧㄢ ㄍㄨˇ)
to incite; to instigate; to drum up

打辮子(ㄉㄚˇ ㄅㄧㄢˋ ·ㄗ)
to wear a pigtail, or a pair of pigtails; to knit a pigtail

打補釘(ㄉㄚˇ ㄅㄨˇ ·ㄉㄧㄥ)
to put a patch (on a shoe sole, a garment, etc.)

打不破(ㄉㄚˇ ·ㄅㄨ ㄆㄛˋ)
①unbreakable: 這是隻打不破的碗。It's an unbreakable bowl. ②to try in vain to break

打不得(ㄉㄚˇ ·ㄅㄨ ㄉㄜˊ)
cannot be beaten with impunity; cannot beat and get away with it

打不倒(ㄉㄚˇ ·ㄅㄨ ㄉㄠˇ)
①unconquerable; that cannot be knocked down ②to try in vain to knock down

打不到(ㄉㄚˇ ·ㄅㄨ ㄉㄠˋ)
①to try in vain to hit ②that cannot be hit

打不過(ㄉㄚˇ ·ㄅㄨ ㄍㄨㄛˋ)
to be no fighting match for

打不開(ㄉㄚˇ ·ㄅㄨ ㄎㄞ)
①that cannot be opened: 門打不開。The door cannot be opened. ②to try in vain to open

打不還手(ㄉㄚˇ ·ㄅㄨ ㄏㄨㄢˊ ㄕㄡˇ)
not to strike back when attacked

打不死(ㄉㄚˇ ·ㄅㄨ ㄙˇ)
①still alive after a hard beating ②to try in vain to beat to death

打不碎(ㄉㄚˇ ·ㄅㄨ ㄙㄨㄟˋ)
①that cannot be broken to pieces; unbreakable: 那是張打不碎的唱片。It's an unbreakable record. ②to try in vain to break to pieces

打破(ㄉㄚˇ ㄆㄛˋ)
to smash to pieces; to break: 玻璃窗被打破了。The window

pane is broken.

破紀錄(カY タと ㄐㄧ ㄌㄨ)
to break the record; to set a new record; to rewrite the record

破前例(カY くㄧㄢ ㄌㄧ)
to depart from precedents

破砂鍋問到底(カY タと ㄕㄚ ㄍㄨㄜ ㄨㄣ ㄉㄠ ㄉㄧ)
to interrogate persistently; to fire one question after another; to raise an endless stream of questions (a pun on 問 and 璺)

打拍子(カY タㄞ ˙ㄗ)
to beat time (for a singer, dancer, etc.)

打牌(カY タㄞ)
to play a card game, mahjong, etc.: 他喜歡打牌。He likes to play cards.

打砲(カY タㄠ)
① to fire shells; to fire artillery pieces ② (slang) to visit a brothel

打屁股(カY ㄆㄧ ˙ㄍㄨ)
spanking; to flog the buttocks as a form of punishment: 他打這頑皮小孩的屁股。He spanked the naughty child.

打票(カY タㄠ)
to buy tickets

打鋪蓋(カY ㄆㄨ ˙ㄍㄞ)
to set up a bed

打撲克(カY ㄆㄨ ㄎㄜ)
to play poker

打麻將(カY ㄇㄚ ㄐㄧㄤ)
to play mah-jong

打馬虎眼(カY ㄇㄚ ˙ㄏㄨ ㄧㄢ)
to exploit other's carelessness; to pretend to be ignorant of something in order to gloss it over; to act dumb

打罵(カY ㄇㄚ)
to beat and scold; maltreatment (to a child, orphan)

打磨(カY ˙ㄇㄛ)
to polish; to burnish

打麥(カY ㄇㄞ)
to thresh wheat or barley

打毛線衣(カY ㄇㄠ ㄒㄧㄢ ㄧ)
to knit a woolen sweater

打門(カY ㄇㄣ)
to knock at a door

打悶棍(カY ㄇㄣ ㄍㄨㄣ)
to rob a victim after beating

him unconscious with a club

打鳴兒(カY ㄇㄧㄥㄦ)
(said of a rooster) to crow

打明兒起(カY ㄇㄧㄥ ㄑㄧ)
to begin from tomorrow: 打明兒起，要更努力用功啦。You have to study harder from tomorrow on.

打發(カY ˙ㄈㄚ)
① to dispatch; to send away: 他把客人打發走了。He sent the guests away. ② to fire; to dismiss: 老板將那位員工打發了。The boss dismissed the worker from his job. ③ to spend (time)

打翻(カY ㄈㄢ)
to overturn; to tip over; to knock over: 誰把瓶子打翻了？Who knocked that bottle over?

打分數(カY ㄈㄣ ㄕㄨ)
to grade (students' papers); to grade (a performance): 老師在試卷上打分數。The teacher graded the papers.

打粉底(カY ㄈㄣ ㄉㄧ)
to apply grease paint in makeup

打鬧鬧(カY ˙ㄋㄠ ㄊㄠ ㄋㄠ)
to fight in jest or for fun; boisterous

打打談談(カY ㄉㄚ ㄊㄢ ㄊㄢ)
to fight and talk alternately (without reaching a real settlement); to fight, then talk, then fight again, and then talk again

打得好(カY ˙ㄉㄜ ㄏㄠ)
① to deserve the beating or spanking ② an excellent performance (said of ball players, knitting women, etc.)

打得火熱(カY ˙ㄉㄜ ㄏㄨㄛ ㄖㄜ)
① to be in the middle of a white-hot battle ② to be passionately in love with each other

打倒(カY ㄉㄠ)
to knock down; to overthrow; (slogans) down with...: 他打倒他的敵人。He knocked his enemy down.

打稻(カY ㄉㄠ)
to thrash rice

打鬥(カY ㄉㄡ)
a fight; a skirmish; to fight

打蛋(カY ㄉㄢ)
to beat, stir or whip eggs

打蛋機(カY ㄉㄢ ㄐㄧ)
an egg beater

打彈子(カY ㄉㄢ ˙ㄗ)
to play billiards

打燈籠(カY ㄉㄥ ˙ㄌㄨㄥ)
to hold a lighted lantern (when traveling by night)

打底(カY ㄉㄧ)
(textile and dyeing) bottoming

打底稿(カY ㄉㄧ ㄍㄠ)
to prepare a draft

打底子(カY ㄉㄧ ˙ㄗ)
① to sketch (a plan, picture, etc.) ② to lay a foundation

打地舖(カY ㄉㄧ ㄆㄨ)
to make a bed on the floor or the ground

打疊(カY ㄉㄧㄝ)
① to pile up one atop the other ② to arrange

打掉(カY ㄉㄧㄠ)
to destroy; to knock out; to wipe out: 他們把那棟建築物打掉。They destroyed the building.

打點(カY ㄉㄧㄢ)
① to examine and put in order; to pack up (luggage): 你的東西打點好沒有? Have you packed (up) your things? ② to bribe

打點滴(カY ㄉㄧㄢ ㄉㄧ)
to administer intravenous drip

打電報(カY ㄉㄧㄢ ㄅㄠ)
to send a telegram or cable; to telegraph a message; to telegraph; to cable a message

打電話(カY ㄉㄧㄢ ㄏㄨㄚ)
to make a telephone call; to telephone a message; to telephone

打賭(カY ㄉㄨ)
to make a bet; to wager; to bet: 我打賭她今晚準會來。I bet she'll come tonight.

打哆嗦(カY ㄉㄨㄛ ˙ㄙㄨㄛ)
to tremble; to shiver (especially in cold weather): 她冷得直打哆嗦。She shivered with cold.

打盹兒(カY ㄉㄨㄣㄦ)
to doze; to take a nap: 他在

〔手部〕

椅子上打盹。He napped in the chair.

打對臺 (ㄉㄚˇ ㄉㄨㄟˋ ㄊㄞˊ)
to compete in business

打斷 (ㄉㄚˇ ㄉㄨㄢˋ)
① to break ② to interrupt; to cut short; to punctuate

打斷念頭 (ㄉㄚˇ ㄉㄨㄢˋ ㄋㄧㄢˋ ㄊㄡˊ)
to give up an idea

打斷說話 (ㄉㄚˇ ㄉㄨㄢˋ ㄕㄨㄛ ㄏㄨㄚˋ)
to interrupt a person while he is speaking

打動 (ㄉㄚˇ ㄉㄨㄥˋ)
to move (a person mentally); to make someone interested in something; to succeed in persuading someone to do something: 他的話深深地打動了我的心。I was deeply moved by his words.

打胎 (ㄉㄚˇ ㄊㄞ)
to have an abortion on purpose

打頭陣 (ㄉㄚˇ ㄊㄡˊ ㄓㄣˋ)
to lead the attack; to be at the foremost front in an attack

打頭兒 (ㄉㄚˇ ㄊㄡˊㄦ)
from the beginning; from the start: 咱們再打頭兒來好嗎? Let's do it from the start, shall we?

打探 (ㄉㄚˇ ㄊㄢˋ)
to find out

打探子 (ㄉㄚˇ ㄊㄢˋ ˙ㄗ)
to dispatch spies or detectives

打噴嚏 (ㄉㄚˇ ㄆㄣ ·ㄊㄧ) or 打噴嚏 (ㄉㄚˇ ㄆㄣ ㄊㄧˋ)
to sneeze; to make a sneeze

打鐵的 (ㄉㄚˇ ㄊㄧㄝˇ ·ㄉㄜ)
a blacksmith

打鐵趁熱 (ㄉㄚˇ ㄊㄧㄝˇ ㄔㄣˋ ㄖㄜˋ)
Strike while the iron is hot. 或 To do a job while the favorable condition exists.

打聽 (ㄉㄚˇ ㄊㄧㄥ)
to inquire; to find out through inquiries; to make inquiries: 他設法打聽那件事。He tries to make inquiries about that thing.

打退 (ㄉㄚˇ ㄊㄨㄟˋ)
to beat back (or off); to repulse: 他們打退敵人的進攻。They repulsed an enemy attack.

打退堂鼓 (ㄉㄚˇ ㄊㄨㄟˋ ㄊㄤˊ ㄍㄨˇ)
to give up a pursuit without attaining the goal; to give up halfway; to back out: 我們不能遇到困難就打退堂鼓了。We can't back out the moment we run up against a little difficulty.

打通 (ㄉㄚˇ ㄊㄨㄥ)
to open a connecting road; to establish a connection; to remove the block in a passage; to get through

打通關 (ㄉㄚˇ ㄊㄨㄥ ㄍㄨㄢ)
to take on everyone else at the table in turn in the finger-guessing game while drinking

打鬧 (ㄉㄚˇ ㄋㄠˋ)
to quarrel and fight noisily

打蠟 (ㄉㄚˇ ㄌㄚˋ)
to rub, or treat with wax; to wax

打來回 (ㄉㄚˇ ㄌㄞˊ ㄏㄨㄟˊ)
to make a round trip; to make a return trip

打雷 (ㄉㄚˇ ㄌㄟˊ)
to thunder

打擂臺 (ㄉㄚˇ ㄌㄟˋ ㄊㄞˊ)
(said of Chinese pugilists) to join a contest in feats of prowess on stage

打撈 (ㄉㄚˇ ㄌㄠ)
to salvage sunken ships; to drag sunken things out of water: 我們打撈到一具屍體。We retrieved a corpse from the water.

打冷戰 (ㄉㄚˇ ㄌㄥˇ ㄓㄢˋ)
① to shudder ② to fight a cold war

打獵 (ㄉㄚˇ ㄌㄧㄝˋ)
to go hunting; to go on a hunting expedition: 他很喜歡打獵。He's very fond of hunting.

打量 (ㄉㄚˇ ㄌㄧㄤˊ)
① to size up; to look someone up and down: 她上下打量著那個陌生人。She looked the stranger up and down. ② to think; to suppose; to conjecture

打領帶 (ㄉㄚˇ ㄌㄧㄥˇ ㄉㄞˋ)
to tie a necktie

打門牙和血吊 (ㄉㄚˇ ㄇㄣˊ ㄧㄚˊ ㄏㄜˊ ㄒㄩㄝˋ ㄊㄧㄠˋ)

to suffer great loss or pain with fortitude

打落水狗 (ㄉㄚˇ ㄌㄨㄛˋ ㄕㄨㄟˇ ㄍㄡˇ)
(literally) to beat a drowning dog—to attack someone already down in his luck

打歌 (ㄉㄚˇ ㄍㄜ)
to promote a new song by singing it frequently in public appearance

打呃兒 (ㄉㄚˇ ㄜˋㄦ)
to hiccough; to hiccup; to have the hiccups

打個照面 (ㄉㄚˇ ㄍㄜˋ ㄓㄠˋ ㄇㄧㄢˋ)
to meet face to face

打個招呼 (ㄉㄚˇ ·ㄍㄜ ㄓㄠ ㄏㄨ)
to let someone know; to give someone a notice

打高空 (ㄉㄚˇ ㄍㄠ ㄎㄨㄥ)
to make grandiose but impractical plans; to talk persuasively without substance; to embellish narrative or rumors

打狗看主人 (ㄉㄚˇ ㄍㄡˇ ㄎㄢˋ ㄓㄨˇ ㄖㄣˊ)
(literally) to consider who its master is before beating a dog—to use discretion as to the possibility of reprisal when bullying people with powerful connections

打狗欺主 (ㄉㄚˇ ㄍㄡˇ ㄑㄧ ㄓㄨˇ)
(literally) To beat a dog is to insult its master.—To humiliate the protected is to humiliate the protector.

打箍 (ㄉㄚˇ ㄍㄨ)
to hoop; to put a hoop around something

打鼓 (ㄉㄚˇ ㄍㄨˇ)
① to beat a drum ② to feel uncertain or nervous: 他的心裏直在打鼓。He felt extremely nervous.

打穀 (ㄉㄚˇ ㄍㄨˇ)
to thresh grain

打滾兒 (ㄉㄚˇ ㄍㄨㄣˇㄦ)
to roll about

打官話 (ㄉㄚˇ ㄍㄨㄢ ㄏㄨㄚˋ)
to talk in the formal language of officialdom

打官腔 (ㄉㄚˇ ㄍㄨㄢ ㄑㄧㄤ)
bureaucratic jargon

打官司 (ㄉㄚˇ ㄍㄨㄢ ·ㄙ)
to have a lawsuit; to go to law: 我要和你打官司。I'll go to law with you.

打光棍(カˇ «ㄨㄤ «ㄨㄣˇ)
(said of a man) to remain a
bachelor; to stay a single
man

打工(カˇ «ㄨㄥ)
to do odd jobs as distinct
from a regular employment

打躬(カˇ «ㄨㄥ)
to make a deep bow

打拱作揖(カˇ «ㄨㄥ ㄗㄨㄛˋ) or 打
躬作揖(カˇ «ㄨㄥ ㄗㄨㄛˋ)
to salute with folded hands
again and again; to fold the
hands and make deep bows
—to beg humbly

打卡(カˇ ㄎㄚˇ)
to record the time of one's
presence or departure by
punching a time clock

打卡機(カˇ ㄎㄚˇ ㄐㄧ)
a key punch machine

打卡鐘(カˇ ㄎㄚˇ ㄓㄨㄥ)
a time clock

打瞌睡(カˇ ㄎㄜ ㄕㄨㄟˋ)
to doze: 他看書時打瞌睡。He
dozed over a book.

打開(カˇ ㄎㄞ)
① to open: 請把門打開。
Please open the door. ② to
turn on: 請打開收音機。Turn
on the radio, please.

打開天窗說亮話(カˇ ㄎㄞ ㄊㄧㄢ
ㄔㄨㄤ ㄕㄨㄛ ㄌㄧㄤˋ ㄏㄨㄚˋ)
to speak frankly; frankly
speaking 或 Let's not mince
matters.

打開僵局(カˇ ㄎㄞ ㄐㄧㄤ ㄐㄩˊ)
to break the impasse; to find
the solution to a problem; to
get out of a difficult situation: 我們終於打開僵局了。We
finally found the solution to
the problem.

打開眼界(カˇ ㄎㄞ ㄧㄢˇ ㄐㄧㄝˋ)
to widen one's horizons

打坑(カˇ ㄎㄥ)
to dig or excavate a pit

打垮(カˇ ㄎㄨㄚˇ)
to strike down; to defeat; to
beat

打孔(カˇ ㄎㄨㄥˇ)
to drill a hole; to punch a
hole; to perforate

打孔機(カˇ ㄎㄨㄥˇ ㄐㄧ)
a perforator; a puncher

打哈哈(カˇ ㄏㄚ ·ㄏㄚ)
① to roar with laughter ②
to have fun; to frolic; to
make merry: 快別拿他打哈
哈。Don't make fun of him.
③ to talk irrelevantly in an
apparent effort to avoid
touching the real issue

打哈欠(カˇ ㄏㄚ ·ㄑㄧㄢ)or 打哈息
(カˇ ㄏㄚ ·ㄒㄧ)
to yawn

打鼾(カˇ ㄏㄢ)
to snore

打寒噤(カˇ ㄏㄢˊ ㄐㄧㄣˋ)
to tremble or shudder
because of cold

打呼嚕(カˇ ㄏㄨ ·ㄌㄨ)
to snore

打火機(カˇ ㄏㄨㄛˇ ㄐㄧ)
a (cigarette) lighter

打火石(カˇ ㄏㄨㄛˇ ㄕˊ)
a flint

打火印(カˇ ㄏㄨㄛˇ ㄧㄣˋ)or 打烙印
(カˇ ㄌㄠˋ ㄧㄣˋ)
to brand (cattle)

打諢(カˇ ㄏㄨㄣˋ)
to crack jokes; to joke; to
jest; to mock in fun

打基礎(カˇ ㄐㄧ ㄔㄨˇ)
to do spadework; to lay the
foundations; to prepare oneself for bigger tasks ahead

打擊(カˇ ㄐㄧˊ)
to deal a blow upon; to give
a blow to; to strike a blow
against: 打擊不良風氣,人人有
責。It's everyone's duty to
strike a blow against un-
healthy tendencies.

打擊率(カˇ ㄐㄧˊ ㄌㄩˋ)
a batting average

打擊手(カˇ ㄐㄧˊ ㄕㄡˇ)
a batter

打擊樂器(カˇ ㄐㄧˊ ㄩㄝˋ ㄑㄧˋ)
a percussion instrument

打家劫舍(カˇ ㄐㄧㄚ ㄐㄧㄝˊ ㄕㄜˋ)
to raid homes and plunder
houses; to rob

打架(カˇ ㄐㄧㄚˋ)
to have a brawl, a blow, a
row or a fight: 他們吵嚷後就
打起架來。After words they
came to blows.

打劫(カˇ ㄐㄧㄝˊ)
to commit robbery or pil-
lage; to plunder; to loot

打結子(カˇ ㄐㄧㄝˊ ·ㄗ)
to tie a knot; to make a
knot

打交道(カˇ ㄐㄧㄠ ㄉㄠˋ)
to have intercourse; to associate with; to have dealings
with: 他和各式各樣的朋友打交
道。He associated with all
kinds of people.

打攪(カˇ ㄐㄧㄠˇ)
to bother; to disturb; to trouble: 不要打攪他。Don't disturb
him.

打醮(カˇ ㄐㄧㄠˋ)
to hold services for pacify-
ing ghosts (usually on the
Ghost Festival, on the 15th
day of the seventh moon)

打酒(カˇ ㄐㄧㄡˇ)
to buy wine or liquor (by
quantity, not by bottles)

打尖(カˇ ㄐㄧㄢ)
to make a brief stopover; to
lodge temporarily

打緊(カˇ ㄐㄧㄣˇ)
serious; important: 不打緊。It
does not matter. 或 It is of
no importance.

打更(カˇ ㄐㄧㄥ)
to beat the night watches

打旗語(カˇ ㄑㄧˊ ㄩˇ)
to signal with a flag; to use
semaphore

打起精神(カˇ ㄑㄧˇ ㄐㄧㄥ ㄕㄣˊ)
to cheer up; to pluck up
spirits; to keep one's chin up

打氣(カˇ ㄑㄧˋ)
① to fill a tire, balloon, etc.
with air or gas; to inflate
② (figuratively) to invigorate or encourage; to pep up

打氣筒(カˇ ㄑㄧˋ ㄊㄨㄥˇ)
an air pump

打橋牌(カˇ ㄑㄧㄠˊ ㄆㄞˊ)
to play a bridge game

打秋風(カˇ ㄑㄧㄡ ㄈㄥ)or 打抽豐
(カˇ ㄔㄡ ㄈㄥ)
to seek gratuitous financial
help

打鞦韆(カˇ ㄑㄧㄡ ㄑㄧㄢ)
to sit in a swing; to swing

打球(カˇ ㄑㄧㄡˊ)
to play a ball game

打千(カˇ ㄑㄧㄢ)
to salute by falling on one
knee

打搶(カˇ ㄑㄧㄤˇ)

〔手部〕

〔手部〕

to loot; to rob by force

打情罵俏(ㄉㄚ ㄑㄧㄥ ㄇㄚ ㄑㄧㄠ)
to tease one's lover by showing false displeasure

打趣(ㄉㄚ ㄑㄩ)
to make fun of another; to tease; to poke fun

打圈子(ㄉㄚ ㄑㄩㄢ ˙ㄗ)
①to circle. The kite circled in the sky. ②(figuratively) to bog down: 不要在瑣事上打圈子。 Don't get bogged down in trifles.

打拳(ㄉㄚ ㄑㄩㄢ)
to practice boxing

打群架(ㄉㄚ ㄑㄩㄣ ㄐㄧㄚ)
to engage in a gang fight

打消(ㄉㄚ ㄒㄧㄠ)
to give up (an intention, etc.): 他打消了創業的念頭。 He gave up the idea of starting a business.

打小報告(ㄉㄚ ㄒㄧㄠ ㄅㄠ ㄍㄠ)
to inform secretly on a colleague, etc.

打小算盤(ㄉㄚ ㄒㄧㄠ ㄙㄨㄢ ㄆㄢ)
to show petty shrewdness

打先鋒(ㄉㄚ ㄒㄧㄢ ㄈㄥ)
to fight in the van; to be a pioneer

打信號(ㄉㄚ ㄒㄧㄣ ㄏㄠ)
to signal; to communicate by signals

打響(ㄉㄚ ㄒㄧㄤ)
①to start shooting; to begin to exchange fire ②to win initial success

打雪仗(ㄉㄚ ㄒㄩㄝ ㄓㄤ)
to have a snowball fight

打知名度(ㄉㄚ ㄓ ㄇㄧㄥ ㄉㄨ)
to seek publicity

打摺(ㄉㄚ ㄓㄜ)
to fold

打折扣(ㄉㄚ ㄓㄜ ㄎㄡ)
①to allow a discount; at a discount: 這家商店打折扣出售商品。 This shop sells goods at a discount. ② to detract (from some desirable quality)

打招呼(ㄉㄚ ㄓㄠ ㄏㄨ)
①to say hello; to greet a person: 他朗聲「早安」向親友打招呼。 He greeted a friend by saying "Good morning." ②to use one's influence in

other's behalf

打照面(ㄉㄚ ㄓㄠ ㄇㄧㄢ)
to meet face to face; to have an encounter with someone

打戰 or 打顫(ㄉㄚ ㄓㄢ)or 打冷顫
(ㄉㄚ ㄌㄥ ㄓㄢ)
to shudder: 她一看到蛇便直打顫。 She shuddered at the sight of a snake.

打針(ㄉㄚ ㄓㄣ)
to give or receive an injection; to give or receive a shot

打仗(ㄉㄚ ㄓㄤ)
to engage in a battle; to fight; to wage war: 他們準備好去打仗。 They were ready to fight in the war.

打主意(ㄉㄚ ㄓㄨ ㄧ)
①to devise a course of action; to decide what to do ②to scheme for something to which one has no claim; to try to obtain ③to try to win the affection of a young woman

打住(ㄉㄚ ㄓㄨ)
Hold! 或 Stop it! 或 Halt!

打轉兒(ㄉㄚ ㄓㄨㄢㄦ)
①to move in a circle; to spin; to revolve: 陀螺在地上打轉兒。 The top was spinning on the ground. ②to go round

打樁(ㄉㄚ ㄓㄨㄤ)
to hammer in piles or stakes; to impale; piling

打樁機(ㄉㄚ ㄓㄨㄤ ㄐㄧ)
a pile driver; a pile engine

打腫臉充胖子(ㄉㄚ ㄓㄨㄥ ㄌㄧㄢ
ㄔㄨㄥ ㄆㄤ ˙ㄗ)
(literally) to feign obesity by slapping one's own face until it becomes swollen —(figuratively) to try to satisfy one's own vanity at any cost

打中(ㄉㄚ ㄓㄨㄥ)
to hit the mark

打中要害(ㄉㄚ ㄓㄨㄥ ㄧㄠ ㄏㄞ)
to hit the vital spot

打赤膊(ㄉㄚ ㄔ ㄅㄛ)
to bare the upper body

打赤腳(ㄉㄚ ㄔ ㄐㄧㄠ)
to go barefoot(barefooted)

打喳喳(ㄉㄚ ㄔㄚ ㄔㄚ)
to whisper; to speak very

softly and low

打茶圍(ㄉㄚ ㄔㄚ ㄨㄟ)
to hold a merrymaking tea party at a brothel

打岔(ㄉㄚ ㄔㄚ)
to interrupt another's speech; to break into a conversation: 當別人談話時, 打岔是不禮貌的。 It is not polite to interrupt when someone is talking.

打柴(ㄉㄚ ㄔㄞ)
to collect firewood

打吵子(ㄉㄚ ㄔㄠ ˙ㄗ)
to be noisy; to brawl

打成平手(ㄉㄚ ㄔㄥ ㄆㄧㄥ ㄕㄡ)
to fight to a standoff; to fight to a draw: 這場賽結果打成平手。 The game ended in a draw.

打成一片(ㄉㄚ ㄔㄥ ㄧ ㄆㄧㄢ)
to combine into a whole; to be united so as to form a single body

打蟲(ㄉㄚ ㄔㄨㄥ)
to get rid of intestinal parasites by means of drugs

打手巾把子(ㄉㄚ ㄕㄡ ㄐㄧㄣ ㄅㄚ ˙ㄗ)
(said of waiters or waitresses) to hand out hot towels on a train, at a theater, etc.

打手心(ㄉㄚ ㄕㄡ ㄒㄧㄣ)
to beat the palm (of a child as a punishment)

打手銃(ㄉㄚ ㄕㄡ ㄔㄨㄥ)
(slang) masturbation

打手勢(ㄉㄚ ㄕㄡ ㄕ)
to gesticulate: 他沒有說話, 只打手勢要我跟他走。 He did not speak, but with a gesture told me to follow him.

打手印(ㄉㄚ ㄕㄡ ㄧㄣ)
to make an impression of the hand as a signature

打手(ㄉㄚ ㄕㄡ)
thugs hired by men of wealth or power; bouncers

打閃(ㄉㄚ ㄕㄢ)
(said of lightning) to flash

打傷(ㄉㄚ ㄕㄤ)
to wound or injure by beating

打勝仗(ㄉㄚ ㄕㄥ ㄓㄤ)
to be victorious; to win a war

打水(ㄉㄚ ㄕㄨㄟ)

to draw water (from a well, a spring, etc.)

打水漂兒 (ㄉㄚˇ ㄕㄨㄟˇ ㄆㄧㄠ兒)
to make ducks and drakes

打擾 (ㄉㄚˇ ㄖㄠˇ)
to disturb; to bother; to trouble: 我們抱歉打擾你。I am sorry to disturb you.

打如意算盤 (ㄉㄚˇ ㄖㄨˊ ㄧˋ ㄙㄨㄢˋ ㄆㄢˊ)
to expect things to turn out as one wishes

打入 (ㄉㄚˇ ㄖㄨˋ)
①to work one's way into (a secret organization, a tight-knit group, etc.) ② to enter by attacking ③ to throw into; to banish… to

打入冷宮 (ㄉㄚˇ ㄖㄨˋ ㄌㄥˇ ㄍㄨㄥ)
to put (the queen or an imperial concubine) under confinement (after she has lost the emperor's favor)

打字 (ㄉㄚˇ ㄗˋ)
to do typing work; to type-write; to type

打字機 (ㄉㄚˇ ㄗˋ ㄐㄧ)
a typewriter

打字員 (ㄉㄚˇ ㄗˋ ㄩㄢˊ)
a typist

打雜兒 (ㄉㄚˇ ㄗㄚˊ兒)
to drudge; to do a handy-man's work; to do odds and ends

打坐 (ㄉㄚˇ ㄗㄨㄛˋ)
(said of a Buddhist) to sit in meditation

打嘴巴 (ㄉㄚˇ ㄗㄨㄟˇ ·ㄅㄚ)
to slap someone on the face or cheek

打草稿 (ㄉㄚˇ ㄘㄠˇ ㄍㄠˇ)
to prepare a draft

打草驚蛇 (ㄉㄚˇ ㄘㄠˇ ㄐㄧㄥ ㄕㄜˊ)
(literally) to beat the grass and startle the snakes—to cause undesired agitation; to alert unintentionally a criminal in hiding as a result of clumsy police moves

打從 (ㄉㄚˇ ㄘㄨㄥˊ)
from; since

打死 (ㄉㄚˇ ㄙˇ)
to beat to death; to shoot to death

打掃 (ㄉㄚˇ ㄙㄠˇ)
to clean (a room, house, etc.): 她在打掃房間。She is cleaning up her room.

打傘 (ㄉㄚˇ ㄙㄢˇ)
to use an umbrella

打散 (ㄉㄚˇ ㄙㄢˇ)
to break up; to scatter: 那聲巨響把鳥群打散了。The loud noise scattered the birds.

打碎 (ㄉㄚˇ ㄙㄨㄟˋ)
to smash to pieces; to break to pieces: 誰把那瓶子打碎了? Who broke that bottle to pieces?

打算 (ㄉㄚˇ ㄙㄨㄢˋ)
①to plan; to intend; to prepare: 我打算當工程師。I intend to become an engineer. ② a plan; intention: 你有打算到那裡去嗎? Have you any intention of going there?

打算盤 (ㄉㄚˇ ㄙㄨㄢˋ ㄆㄢˊ)
①to use an abacus; to work an abacus ② to reckon ③ calculating; shrewd

打暗號 (ㄉㄚˇ ㄢˋ ㄏㄠˋ)
to give a prearranged signal; to hint; to give a cue

打耳光 (ㄉㄚˇ ㄦˇ ㄍㄨㄤ)
to slap somebody in the face; to box a person's ears; to give someone a box on the ear

打牙祭 (ㄉㄚˇ ㄧㄚˊ ㄐㄧˋ)
to have a rare sumptuous meal; to have something special to eat

打嗝 (ㄉㄚˇ ㄍㄜˊ)
to belch; to hiccup

打野雞 (ㄉㄚˇ ㄧㄝˇ ㄐㄧ)
to visit a brothel

打野外 (ㄉㄚˇ ㄧㄝˇ ㄨㄞˋ)
to receive field training in combat techniques

打藥 (ㄉㄚˇ ㄧㄠˋ)
a laxative; a cathartic; a purgative

打游擊 (ㄉㄚˇ ㄧㄡˊ ㄐㄧˊ)
①to engage in guerrilla warfare ②(humorously) to use, borrow or take another's belongings without permission; to board or lodge at one place after another without payment

打油詩 (ㄉㄚˇ ㄧㄡˊ ㄕ)
doggerel; ragged verse

打眼 (ㄉㄚˇ ㄧㄢˇ)
①to drill a hole; to punch a

hole; to perforate ② to pay more than a thing is worth

打印 (ㄉㄚˇ ㄧㄣˋ)
to affix a stamp to something

打印子 (ㄉㄚˇ ㄧㄣˋ ·ㄗ)
a high-interest loan paid back in installments, each of which is certified by placing a chop when it is paid

打烊 (ㄉㄚˇ ㄧㄤˋ)
to close the store for the night: 這家店昨天晚上九點打烊。The store closes at 9 last night.

打樣 (ㄉㄚˇ ㄧㄤˋ)
①to draw a design; to prepare drawings (for a building, a machine, etc.) ②(printing) to make a proof; to print a galley proof

打魚 (ㄉㄚˇ ㄩˊ)
to catch fish with nets

打樂器 (ㄉㄚˇ ㄩㄝˋ ㄑㄧˋ)
(said of an orchestra) percussion instruments

打圓場 (ㄉㄚˇ ㄩㄢˊ ㄔㄤˇ)
to mediate a dispute; to smooth things over

【打】 1794
2. ㄉㄚˊ dar dá
a dozen: 他買了一打原子筆。He bought a dozen ball pens.

【扔】 1795
ㄖㄥ rheng reng
1.to throw; to hurl: 把那本書扔給我。Throw me that book.

2. to abandon; to discard

扔掉 (ㄖㄥ ㄉㄧㄠˋ)
to throw away; to cast away: 不要扔掉那些雜誌。Don't throw away those magazines.

扔過去 (ㄖㄥ ㄍㄨㄛˋ ·ㄑㄩ)
to throw or hurl over (to the other side)

扔開 (ㄖㄥ ㄎㄞ)
to dismiss from consideration

扔棄 (ㄖㄥ ㄑㄧˋ)
to throw away; to discard; to get rid of

扔下 (ㄖㄥ ㄒㄧㄚˋ)
to throw down; to leave behind; to put aside: 她扔下手邊的工作，逛街去了。She put

aside her work and went shopping.

三畫

〔手部〕

【扞】 1796 厂弓 hann hàn

1. to resist; to oppose; to obstruct
2. to defend; to guard; to withstand

扞蔽 (厂弓 ケ一)
a protective barrier

扞格 (厂弓 《さ)
to conflict; incompatible

扞格不入 (厂弓 《さ ㄅㄨ ㄖㄨ)
incompatible; to disagree; to contradict; to conflict; do not mesh: 他所說的話與事實扞格不入。His statement contradicts with the facts.

扞拒 (厂弓 ㄐㄩ)
to withstand; to resist; to oppose: 她的父母扞拒這門親事。Her parents are opposed to the match.

扞衛 (厂弓 ㄨㄟ)
to defend; to guard: 軍人的職責是扞衛這個國家。The duty of a soldier is to defend his country.

扞票 (厂弓 ㄠ)
to guard against; to keep back

【扣】 1797 ㄎㄡ kow kòu

1. to tap; to strike; to rap; to pull
2. to fasten; to button; to buckle
3. to detain; to confine
4. to deduct
5. a button; a hook; a buckle
6. to impound; to withhold
7. to cover on top

扣扳機 (ㄎㄡ ㄅㄢ ㄐㄧ)
to pull the trigger

扣槃捫燭 (ㄎㄡ ㄆㄢ ㄇㄣ ㄓㄨ)
to understand a fact superficially or erroneously (as a certain blind man did when, mistaking the sun for a sound and sunlight did when, shape, he tried to know what they were like by tapping a tray and feeling a candle which, he had been told, resembled the sun and sunlight respectively)

扣馬而諫 (ㄎㄡ ㄇㄚ ㄦ ㄐㄧㄢ)
(literally) to stop the horse and admonish the rider—to admonish a person just before he makes a reckless move

扣帽子 (ㄎㄡ ㄇㄠ ㄗ)
to put a label on someone

扣門 (ㄎㄡ ㄇㄣ)
to knock at a door: 誰在扣門? Who is knocking at the door?

扣抵 (ㄎㄡ ㄉㄧ)
to withhold money or goods from a debtor as payment of his debt

扣牢 (ㄎㄡ ㄌㄠ)
to tie securely

扣籃 (ㄎㄡ ㄌㄢ)
(basketball) to dunk; dunking

扣留 (ㄎㄡ ㄌㄧㄡ)
①to keep in custody; to detain; to confine: 警察扣留那人以便進一步偵訊。The police detained that man to make further inquiries. ②to suspend; to impound: 警察扣留他的行車執照。The policeman suspended his driving license.

扣繳額 (ㄎㄡ ㄐㄧㄠˊ)
a deductible amount (as distinct from a taxable amount); a tax write-off

扣減 (ㄎㄡ ㄐㄧㄢ)
to deduct

扣緊 (ㄎㄡ ㄐㄧㄣ)
to button tightly; to fasten tightly

扣來 (ㄎㄡ ㄐㄩ ㄌㄞ)
①to button up (one's coat, etc.) ②to take (a person) into custody

扣薪 (ㄎㄡ ㄒㄧㄣ)
to deduct a certain amount from an employee's pay (as a punishment, or compensation for damaged public property, etc.)

扣住 (ㄎㄡ ㄓㄨ)
held or fastened (by a button, hook, etc.); to hook

扣除 (ㄎㄡ ㄔㄨ)
to deduct: 會計員從他的薪水中扣除稅金。The accountant deducted taxes from his salary.

扣肉 (ㄎㄡ ㄖㄡ)
a Chinese dish of richly seasoned steamed pork

扣人心絃 (ㄎㄡ ㄖㄣ ㄒㄧㄣ ㄒㄧㄢˊ)
(said of music, writing, etc.) very touching

扣子 (ㄎㄡ ㄗ)
a button; a buckle; a hook

扣押 (ㄎㄡ ㄧㄚ)
to detain; to confine; to keep in custody; to seize: 如果你不還債, 你的財產將被扣押。If you don't pay your debt, your property will be seized.

扣壓 (ㄎㄡ ㄧㄚ)
to withhold; to pigeonhole: 扣壓公文 to withhold a public document

扣問 (ㄎㄡ ㄨㄣ)
to stop and ask

【扛】 1798 ㄎㄤ karng káng

to lift (especially when only a single person is involved); to shoulder: 每位軍人都扛著槍。Each soldier shoulders a gun.

扛夫 (ㄎㄤ ㄈㄨ)
a porter; a worker employed to carry loads on his shoulders

扛鼎 (ㄎㄤ ㄉㄧㄥ)
to lift a tripod (as a feat of strength)

扛在肩上 (ㄎㄤ ㄗㄞ ㄐㄧㄢ ㄕㄤ)
to carry on the shoulder; to shoulder

【托】 1799 ㄊㄨㄛ tuo tuō

1. to hold or lift, on the palm: 他用手托住頭。He held his head in his hands.
2. to entrust; to charge; to consign; to rely; to ask: 我把這封信交託給你。I entrust this letter to you.
3. a tray; a pad

托跋氏 (ㄊㄨㄛ ㄅㄚˊ ㄕ)
the House of Toba, the ruling family of the Northern Wei Dynasty (386-534 A.D.)

托鉢 (ㄊㄨㄛ ㄅㄛ)
(Buddhism) to beg for alms

托病 (ㄊㄨㄛ ㄅㄧㄥ)
on the pretext of sickness; to use sickness as an excuse:

他托病不見客。He refused to see visitors on the pretext of sickness.

托盤(ㄊㄨㄛ ㄆㄢˊ)
a tray

托墨(ㄊㄨㄛ ㄛˋ)
(said of writing paper) properly absorbent of ink

托夢(ㄊㄨㄛ ㄇㄥˋ)
(said of a spirit or deity) to convey a message to a mortal through his dream

托名(ㄊㄨㄛ ㄇㄧㄥˊ)
to do something in the name of someone else

托福(ㄊㄨㄛ ㄈㄨˊ)
Thanks. (used in reply to others' congratulations on a success, a narrow escape, etc.)

托福測驗(ㄊㄨㄛ ㄈㄨˊ ㄘㄜˋ ㄧㄢˋ)
Test of English as a Foreign Language (TOEFL)

托付(ㄊㄨㄛ ㄈㄨˋ)
to entrust; to charge; to consign: 他把財產托付給他的朋友看管。He entrusted his friend with the property.

托辣斯(ㄊㄨㄛ ㄌㄚˋ ㄙ)
a trust (a combination of corporations under a board of trustees)

托賴(ㄊㄨㄛ ㄌㄞˋ)
to rely upon, or be indebted to (a phrase usually used to show one's modesty)

托領(ㄊㄨㄛ ㄌㄧㄥˇ)
the base of the collar (on a garment)

托洛斯基(ㄊㄨㄛ ㄌㄨㄛˋ ㄙ ㄐㄧ)
Leon Trotsky (or Trotski), 1879-1940, Russian Communist leader murdered on the order of Stalin

托孤(ㄊㄨㄛ ㄍㄨ)
to entrust to another's care the children one is about to leave behind as orphans

托故(ㄊㄨㄛ ㄍㄨˋ)
to rely on a pretext; to use an excuse: 她托故不來。She failed to come on some pretext.

托管(ㄊㄨㄛ ㄍㄨㄢˇ)
trusteeship; mandate

托管地(ㄊㄨㄛ ㄍㄨㄢˇ ㄉㄧˋ)
a trust territory

托身(ㄊㄨㄛ ㄕㄣ)
to have a place to live in or work in

托人情(ㄊㄨㄛ ㄖㄣˊ ㄑㄧㄥˊ)
to ask an influential person to help arrange something; to gain one's end through pull

托丁(ㄊㄨㄛ ㄉㄧㄥ)or **托盤**(ㄊㄨㄛ ㄆㄢˊ)
①a pad (underneath an object) ②a tray; a salver ③ a base; a support

托足(ㄊㄨㄛ ㄗㄨˊ)
to have a foothold; to have a place to live in

托辭(ㄊㄨㄛ ㄘˊ)
①to put forth a false reason or motive; to make excuses ②a pretext; an excuse

托兒所(ㄊㄨㄛ ㄦˊ ㄙㄨㄛˇ)
a nursery school

托爾斯泰(ㄊㄨㄛ ㄦˊ ㄙ ㄊㄞˋ)
Leo (or Lev) Nikolaevich Tolstoy, 1828-1910, Russian writer

托運(ㄊㄨㄛ ㄩㄣˋ)
to consign for shipment; to check

托運人(ㄊㄨㄛ ㄩㄣˋ ㄖㄣˊ)
a consignor

托運物(ㄊㄨㄛ ㄩㄣˋ ㄨˋ)
a consignment

【托】 1800

ㄑㄧㄢ chian qiān
1. to pierce; to penetrate; to pick
2. a pick: 牙托 a toothpick

扦腳(ㄑㄧㄢ ㄐㄧㄠˇ)
to trim toenails; pedicure

扦手(ㄑㄧㄢ ㄕㄡˇ)
a customs examiner or searcher

【扠】 1801

ㄔㄚ cha chā
a harpoon

扠腰(ㄔㄚ ㄧㄠ)
akimbo: 他兩手扠腰而立。He stood with arms akimbo.

四畫

【扭】 1802

ㄋㄧㄡˇ neou niǔ
1. to wrench; to twist; to turn; to wring: 他扭到足踝。He turned his ankle.

---

2. to seize; to grasp: 他將小偷扭送警方。He seized the thief and handed him over to the police.

扭打(ㄋㄧㄡˇ ㄉㄚˇ)
to have a grapple or to grapple with somebody

扭搭扭搭(ㄋㄧㄡˇ·ㄉㄚ ㄋㄧㄡˇ·ㄉㄚ)
turning or swiveling from side to side

扭斷(ㄋㄧㄡˇ ㄉㄨㄢˋ)
to dislocate (the bones) by twisting or wrenching; to twist and break (something)

扭捏(ㄋㄧㄡˇ ㄋㄧㄝ)
①to twist the waist from side to side when walking (as a woman does); to mince ②to do things in an unmanly way

扭扭捏捏(ㄋㄧㄡˇ ㄋㄧㄡˇ ㄋㄧㄝ ㄋㄧㄝ)
①twisting the waist from side to side (like a woman); mincingly ②unmanly in handling business; to be affectively bashful

扭扭舞(ㄋㄧㄡˇ ㄋㄧㄡˇ ㄨˇ)
the twist

扭了脖子(ㄋㄧㄡˇ·ㄌㄜ ㄅㄛˊ·ㄗ)
to have a sprained the neck

扭力(ㄋㄧㄡˇ ㄌㄧˋ)
(physics) torsion

扭乾(ㄋㄧㄡˇ ㄍㄢ)
to wring (a towel, clothes, etc.) dry

扭筋(ㄋㄧㄡˇ ㄐㄧㄣ)
a sprain

扭曲(ㄋㄧㄡˇ ㄑㄩ)
to twist: 他的面容因痛苦而扭曲。His face was twisted with pain.

扭曲作直(ㄋㄧㄡˇ ㄑㄩ ㄗㄨㄛˋ ㄓˊ)
to distort the fact

扭轉(ㄋㄧㄡˇ ㄓㄨㄢˇ)
①to wring; to wrench; to twist ②to turn (the tide of a war or contest) for the better ③to turn round

扭轉乾坤(ㄋㄧㄡˇ ㄓㄨㄢˇ ㄑㄧㄢˊ ㄎㄨㄣ)
to retrieve a hopeless situation; to tip the scale when a situation appears hopeless

扭傷(ㄋㄧㄡˇ ㄕㄤ)
a sprain; a wrench; to wrench: 他扭傷手腕了。He sprained his wrist.

扭送(ㄋㄧㄡˇ ㄙㄨㄥˋ)

〔手部〕

to seize and hand over (to the authorities)

扭殿（ㄋㄧㄡˇ ㄉㄧㄢˋ）
to have a grapple or to grapple with somebody

扭一扭（ㄋㄧㄡˇ‧ㄧ‧ㄋㄧㄡˇ）
to give a twist

扭腰（ㄋㄧㄡˇ ㄧㄠ）
①to twist the hip or the waist ②to sprain one's back

【扮】 1803
ㄅㄢˋ bann bàn
to dress up; to disguise; to play

扮鬼臉（ㄅㄢˋ ㄍㄨㄟˇ ㄌㄧㄢˇ）
to make faces

扮戲（ㄅㄢˋ ㄒㄧˋ）
to perform on stage; to play a role in a play

扮相（ㄅㄢˋ ㄒㄧㄤˋ）
the stage appearance or makeup (of an actor or actress)

扮裝（ㄅㄢˋ ㄓㄨㄤ）
to disguise; to make up

扮作（ㄅㄢˋ ㄗㄨㄛˋ）
to dress up as; to disguise as: 那警察扮作一個商人。The policeman disguised himself as a merchant.

扮演（ㄅㄢˋ ㄧㄢˇ）
to play or act (a part or role): 他扮演哈姆雷特。He played Hamlet.

【扶】 1804
ㄈㄨˊ fwu fú
1. to support; to prop up; to aid; to help; to shield; to shelter; to harbor; to protect: 請扶這位老人進來。Help this old man in, please.
2. to lean upon

扶病（ㄈㄨˊ ㄅㄧㄥˋ）or 扶疾（ㄈㄨˊ ㄐㄧˊ）
to brave sickness; to work while in ill health: 他扶病出席。He was present in spite of illness.

扶不起的阿斗（ㄈㄨˊ ㄅㄨˋ ㄑㄧˇ‧ㄉㄜ ㄚ ㄉㄡˇ）
one who is so incompetent that no amount of help can make him successful

扶梯（ㄈㄨˊ ㄊㄧ）
a flight of stairs with a handrail or balustrade; a staircase

①to help the aged along and lead the young by the hand ②to go or appear with one's whole family regardless of age

扶靈（ㄈㄨˊ ㄌㄧㄥˊ）or 扶柩（ㄈㄨˊ ㄐㄧㄡˋ）or 扶櫬（ㄈㄨˊ ㄔㄣˋ）
to escort a casket or coffin; to serve as a pallbearer

扶鸞（ㄈㄨˊ ㄌㄨㄢˊ）or 扶乩（ㄈㄨˊ ㄐㄧ）or 扶箕（ㄈㄨˊ ㄐㄧ）
a form of planchette; the superstitious practice of providing a sand table on which an invoked spirit is supposed to spell out a message

扶輪社（ㄈㄨˊ ㄌㄨㄣˊ ㄕㄜˋ）
Rotary Club

扶植（ㄈㄨˊ ㄓˊ）
to help grow or develop; to patronize a junior employee

扶著（ㄈㄨˊ‧ㄓㄜ）
to support or prop: 他被扶著回家。He was supported home.

扶杖（ㄈㄨˊ ㄓㄤˋ）or 扶筇（ㄈㄨˊ ㄑㄩㄥˊ）
to lean on a staff or stick

扶正（ㄈㄨˊ ㄓㄥˋ）
to give a concubine the status of a legitimate wife

扶助（ㄈㄨˊ ㄓㄨˋ）
to aid; to help; to assist; to support: 我們應扶助老弱。We should help the old and the weak.

扶持（ㄈㄨˊ ㄔˊ）or 扶挾（ㄈㄨˊ ㄒㄧㄝˊ）
to back up; to support: 隊友們扶持著那受傷的球員。Teammates supported the injured player.

扶手（ㄈㄨˊ ㄕㄡˇ）
a handrail (of a staircase) or any support to be held by the hand

扶疏（ㄈㄨˊ ㄕㄨ）
(said of a plant) branching out with a thick foliage; luxuriant; lush: 枝葉扶疏。The branches and leaves are luxuriant.

扶桑（ㄈㄨˊ ㄙㄤ）
①(botany) hibiscus ②where the sun rises ③（archaic or poetic）Japan

扶蘇（ㄈㄨˊ ㄙㄨ）
the elder son of the First

Emperor of Chin (秦始皇帝) who was murdered immed ately after his father's deat

扶翼（ㄈㄨˊ ㄧˋ）
to support; to shelter; to pro tect

扶掖（ㄈㄨˊ ㄧㄝˋ）
to shelter; to protect; to sup port; to harbor

扶搖直上（ㄈㄨˊ ㄧㄠˊ ㄓˊ ㄕㄤˋ）
①to rise (in a career) ver fast as if to be lifted by a cyclone; to be promotee quickly ②(said of prices etc.) to rise rapidly; to sky rocket: 物價扶搖直上。 prices are skyrocketing.

扶養（ㄈㄨˊ ㄧㄤˇ）
to provide with means o livelihood; to provide subsist ence or sustenance for; tc support

扶危定傾（ㄈㄨˊ ㄨㄟˊ ㄉㄧㄥˋ ㄑㄧㄥ）
to deliver the country fron distress

扶危濟困（ㄈㄨˊ ㄨㄟˊ ㄐㄧˋ ㄎㄨㄣˋ）
to help those in danger and relieve those in distress

扶擁（ㄈㄨˊ ㄩㄥ）
to raise high; to uphold

【扯】 1805
ㄔㄜˇ chee chě
1. to tear
2. to pull; to drag; to haul; to strain
3. to lump
4. to talk nonsense; to lie; to prevaricate; to digress

扯不動（ㄔㄜˇ ㄅㄨˋ ㄉㄨㄥˋ）
cannot tear or be torn

扯破（ㄔㄜˇ ㄆㄛˋ）or 扯碎（ㄔㄜˇ ㄙㄨㄟˋ）
to tear to pieces or shreds: 我扯破了衣服。I've torn my coat.

扯篷拉縴（ㄔㄜˇ ㄆㄥˊ ㄌㄚ ㄑㄧㄢˋ）
(literally) to hoist the sail and pull the towline—①to render assistance ②to make double effort

扯票（ㄔㄜˇ ㄆㄧㄠˋ）
①to kill the hostage held for ransom ②to destroy (a ballot, ticket, etc.)

扯倒（ㄔㄜˇ ㄉㄠˇ）
to give up a plan or pursuit

扯淡（ㄔㄜˇ ㄉㄢˋ）
to talk nonsense: 不要扯淡

了! Don't talk nonsense!

上脫(ㄕㄜ ㄊㄨㄛˊ)
to break loose

止拉(ㄕㄜ ㄌㄚ)
①to make baseless reference to another person in a nonsensical talk ②to pull about 亦作「拉扯」

止開嗓子(ㄕㄜ ㄎㄞ ㄙㄤˇ·ㄗ)
to shout at the top of one's voice; to strain the vocal cords by shouting

止後腿(ㄕㄜ ㄏㄡˋ ㄊㄨㄟˇ)
to hinder someone from action

止謊(ㄕㄜ ㄏㄨㄤˇ)
to tell a lie; to lie: 不要扯謊啦! Don't lie to me!

止旗(ㄕㄜ ㄑㄧˊ)
to raise or hoist a flag (so as to display it)

止脖子(ㄕㄜ·ㄅㄛ ㄗ·ㄗ)
to strain the neck in shouting

止住(ㄕㄜ ㄓㄨˋ)
to grasp firmly

止腺(ㄕㄜ ㄙㄠ)
to talk nonsense shamelessly

【扳】 1806
ㄅㄢ ban bān
1. to pull
2. to count (on one's fingers)

扳倒(ㄅㄢ ㄉㄠˇ)
to pull down

扳開(ㄅㄢ ㄎㄞ)
to pull open

扳機(ㄅㄢ ㄐㄧ)
a trigger

扳轉(ㄅㄢ ㄓㄨㄢˇ)
①to turn around (an object) ②to tip the scale; to turn the tide

扳手(ㄅㄢ ㄕㄡˇ)
①a spanner; a wrench ②a lever (of a machine)

【扱】 1807
1. ㄒㄧ shí xī
1. to gather; to collect
2. to kneel and bow with both hands touching the ground or the floor

扱地(ㄒㄧ ㄉㄧˋ)
to kneel and bow with both hands touching the ground

扱引高賢(ㄒㄧ ㄧㄣˇ ㄍㄠ ㄒㄧㄢˊ)
to gather men of wisdom

【扱】 1807
2. ㄔㄚ cha chā
to insert

扱祂(ㄔㄚ ㄌㄚ)
to tuck the skirts of a garment into the girdle

【批】 1808
ㄆㄧ pī pì
1. to comment; to judge; to criticize: 他批評時事。He commented on current events.
2. a whole batch (of things or people); a large quantity or number; wholesale: 他大批地發出申請函。He sent out application letters wholesale.
3. to slap

批八字兒(ㄆㄧ ㄅㄚˊ ㄗㄦ)
to tell fortune from the year, month, day and hour of one's birth; to make an astrologer's comment

批駁(ㄆㄧ ㄅㄛˊ)
to turn down (an appeal or request) or reverse (a decision by a subordinate), usually by writing on the paper carrying the message; to reject (an official request); to refute: 主任批駁了她的建議。The director rejected her suggestion.

批辦(ㄆㄧ ㄅㄢˋ)
to handle (business) by writing instructions on the paper carrying messages

批判(ㄆㄧ ㄆㄢˋ)or批斷(ㄆㄧ ㄉㄨㄢˋ)
to appraise; to judge

批評(ㄆㄧ ㄆㄧㄥˊ)
to criticize; criticism; comment: 他對這問題未作批評。He made no comment on the subject.

批評家(ㄆㄧ ㄆㄧㄥˊ ㄐㄧㄚ)
a critic: 他是位文學批評家。He's a literary critic.

批發(ㄆㄧ ㄈㄚ)
wholesale: 以批發售出的日用品 a commodity sold by wholesale

批發價(ㄆㄧ ㄈㄚ ㄐㄧㄚˋ)
a wholesale price

批發商(ㄆㄧ ㄈㄚ ㄕㄤ)
a wholesale dealer; a wholesaler; a wholesale merchant

批覆(ㄆㄧ ㄈㄨˋ)or批答(ㄆㄧ ㄉㄚˊ)
to reply (to a message from

---

a subordinate), usually by writing on the paper carrying the message

批門(ㄆㄧ ㄇㄣˊ)
to criticize and denounce someone

批點(ㄆㄧ ㄉㄧㄢˇ)
to punctuate and annotate (a text)

批逆鱗(ㄆㄧ ㄋㄧˋ ㄌㄧㄣˊ)
to offend the emperor or a powerful person

批令(ㄆㄧ ㄌㄧㄥˋ)
instructions (usually given in reply to inquiries)

批改(ㄆㄧ ㄍㄞˇ)
to correct (students' papers)

批購(ㄆㄧ ㄍㄡˋ)
to buy wholesale: 我們批購貨物。We buy goods wholesale.

批亢搗虛(ㄆㄧ ㄎㄤˋ ㄉㄠˇ ㄒㄩ)
to attack vital and unguarded points of an enemy

批回(ㄆㄧ ㄏㄨㄟˊ)
to reply (to a message from a subordinate), usually by writing on the paper carrying the message

批紅判白(ㄆㄧ ㄏㄨㄥˊ ㄆㄢˋ ㄅㄞˊ)
to graft plants of various colors in order to produce new varieties

批頰(ㄆㄧ ㄐㄧㄚˊ)or批面(ㄆㄧ ㄇㄧㄢˋ)
to slap one in the face; to box one's ear

批導轄繁(ㄆㄧ ㄒㄧ ㄉㄠˇ ㄈㄢˊ)
to manage or handle business properly

批行(ㄆㄧ ㄒㄧㄥˊ)
to endorse a proposal submitted by a subordinate in written form

批正(ㄆㄧ ㄓㄥˋ)or批削(ㄆㄧ ㄒㄩㄝ)
to improve (a copy written by another)

批註(ㄆㄧ ㄓㄨˋ)
to write commentaries; to annotate with comments; annotations and commentaries: 有些人一面讀書一面做批註。Some people annotate as they read.

批准(ㄆㄧ ㄓㄨㄣˇ)
to give official approval or permission for; to approve; to ratify; ratification: 還條約已被批准。The treaty has

〔手部〕

〔手部〕

been ratified.

批示 (ㄆㄧ ㄕˋ)
to instruct or direct (usually by writing on the paper carrying a message from a subordinate)

批首 (ㄆㄧ ㄕㄡˇ)
(in annual civil service examinations of former times) the head of the successful candidates

批語 (ㄆㄧ ㄩˇ)
comments; a commentary (usually referring to a teacher's comments written at the end of a student's composition)

批諭 (ㄆㄧ ㄩˋ)
imperial rescripts or directions

批閱 (ㄆㄧ ㄩㄝˋ)
to read (a message from a subordinate) and write down comments or instructions

批月抹風 (ㄆㄧ ㄩㄝˋ ㄇㄛˇ ㄈㄥ)
(said of a poet) to sing in praise of the beauty of nature

【找】 1809
ㄓㄠˇ jao zhǎo
1. to seek; to look for; to search for; to find: 其理由不難找到。The reason is not far to seek.
2. to return (change): 這是找給你的錢。Here's your change.

找偏 or 找遍 (ㄓㄠˇ ㄅㄧㄢˋ)
to have searched or looked everywhere

找補 (ㄓㄠˇ ˙ㄅㄨ)
to pay or return what is owed (either by the buyer or by the seller); to make up a deficiency

找不著 (ㄓㄠˇ ㄅㄨˋ ㄓㄠˊ) or 找不到 (ㄓㄠˇ ㄅㄨˋ ㄉㄠˋ)
to search or look in vain

找麻煩 (ㄓㄠˇ ㄇㄚˊ ˙ㄈㄢ)
①to ask for trouble; to ask for it ②to pick on somebody; to find fault ③to give somebody trouble

找門路 (ㄓㄠˇ ㄇㄣˊ ㄌㄨˋ)
to look for employment by seeking help from the right connections

找面子 (ㄓㄠˇ ㄇㄧㄢˋ ˙ㄗ)
to try to recover lost face or honor; to try to save face

找到 (ㄓㄠˇ ㄉㄠˋ ˙ㄌㄜ) or 找著了 (ㄓㄠˇ ˙ㄓㄜ)
to have succeeded in finding

找對頭 (ㄓㄠˇ ㄉㄨㄟˋ ˙ㄊㄡ)
to look for the real adversary

找對象 (ㄓㄠˇ ㄉㄨㄟˋ ㄒㄧㄤˋ)
to look for a partner in marriage

找換 (ㄓㄠˇ ㄏㄨㄢˋ)
to give change for money of larger denominations

找齊 (ㄓㄠˇ ㄑㄧˊ)
①to make equal; to even up ②to make up a deficiency

找錢 (ㄓㄠˇ ㄑㄧㄢˊ)
to give change

找尋 (ㄓㄠˇ ㄒㄩㄣˊ)
to search for; to look for: 他正在找尋他的弟弟。He's looking for his younger brother.

找碴兒 (ㄓㄠˇ ㄔㄚˊ ㄦ) or 找錯兒 (ㄓㄠˇ ㄘㄨㄛˋ ㄦ)
to look for excuse or occasion for a quarrel or fight; to pick (up) quarrels

找事 (ㄓㄠˇ ㄕˋ)
①to look for jobs; to seek employment: 他整天忙著找事。He spent all day looking for a job. ②to look for trouble

找人 (ㄓㄠˇ ㄖㄣˊ)
to look for someone: 我在找人。I'm looking for someone

找死 (ㄓㄠˇ ㄙˇ)
to invite death; to seek death

【拚】 1810
ㄅㄧㄢˋ biann biàn
to clap hands; to cheer

拚掌 (ㄅㄧㄢˋ ㄓㄤˇ)
to clap hands; to applaud

拚難 (ㄅㄧㄢˋ ㄋㄢˊ)
to cheer and dance; to make merry; to dance for joy

拚悅 (ㄅㄧㄢˋ ㄩㄝˋ)
to clap hands for joy; to cheer

拚踴 (ㄅㄧㄢˋ ㄩㄥˇ)
to cheer and dance

【技】 1811
ㄐㄧ jih jì
skill; ingenuity; dexterity; special ability; tricks

技不如人 (ㄐㄧ ㄅㄨˋ ㄖㄨˊ ㄖㄣˊ)
to be inferior to others i skills

技能 (ㄐㄧ ㄋㄥˊ)
skill; technical ability

技工 (ㄐㄧ ㄍㄨㄥ)
a skilled worker

技擊 (ㄐㄧ ㄐㄧˊ)
martial arts

技巧 (ㄐㄧ ㄑㄧㄠˇ)
ingenuity; dexterity; adroitness; skill: 技巧必經由練習獲得。Technique must be gained by practice.

技正 (ㄐㄧ ㄓㄥˋ)
the title of a senior specialist (an official rank in some organizations)

技師 (ㄐㄧ ㄕ)
an engineer or a technician

技士 (ㄐㄧ ㄕˋ)
the title of a specialist (an official rank below 技正 in some organizations)

技術 (ㄐㄧ ㄕㄨˋ)
techniques; technology; skill: 修理鐘需要技術。It takes skill to repair a clock.

技術犯規 (ㄐㄧ ㄕㄨˋ ㄈㄢˋ ㄍㄨㄟ)
a technical foul

技術高超 (ㄐㄧ ㄕㄨˋ ㄍㄠ ㄔㄠ)
in possession of superb skills or superb techniques

技術官僚 (ㄐㄧ ㄕㄨˋ ㄍㄨㄢ ㄌㄧㄠˊ)
a technocrat

技術工人 (ㄐㄧ ㄕㄨˋ ㄍㄨㄥ ㄖㄣˊ)
a skilled worker

技術性 (ㄐㄧ ㄕㄨˋ ㄒㄧㄥˋ)
technical; of a technical nature: 這是技術性的工作。This is a technical job.

技術學校 (ㄐㄧ ㄕㄨˋ ㄒㄩㄝˊ ㄒㄧㄠˋ)
a technical school

技術指導 (ㄐㄧ ㄕㄨˋ ㄓˇ ㄉㄠˇ)
①technological guidance; technical guidance ②a technical adviser

技術水準 (ㄐㄧ ㄕㄨˋ ㄕㄨㄟˇ ㄓㄨㄣˇ)
technological standards

技術(人)員 (ㄐㄧ ㄕㄨˋ ㄖㄣˊ ㄩㄢˊ)
technical personnel; technicians

技佐 (ㄐㄧ ㄗㄨㄛˇ)
the title of a junior specialist (an official rank below 技士 in some organiza-

tions)

支(ㄓㄧˋ)
skill; art; craft

支撐(ㄓㄧˋ)
anxious or itching to demonstrate some skill; to itch for a chance to display one's skill

【抄】 1812
ㄔㄠ chau chāo
1. to copy; to transcribe; transcription; to plagiarize: 這是抄寫之誤。It's a mistake in transcription.
2. to confiscate
3. to seize; to take: 他抄起一把鐵鍬就幹起活來了。He took up a spade and plunged into the job.

抄本(ㄔㄠ ㄅㄣˇ)
a handwritten copy; a transcript

抄附(ㄔㄠ ㄈㄨˋ)
to append a copy of...

抄道(ㄔㄠ ㄉㄠˋ)
to take a shortcut; (colloquial) a shortcut

抄賭(ㄔㄠ ㄉㄨˇ)
to search a place for gamblers

抄謄(ㄔㄠ ㄊㄥˊ)
to transcribe; to make a copy of; to make a transcript of

抄拿(ㄔㄠ ㄋㄚˊ)
to seize; to grab

抄錄(ㄔㄠ ㄌㄨˋ)or 抄寫(ㄔㄠ ㄒㄧㄝˇ)or 抄緒(ㄔㄠ ㄒㄩˋ)
to copy by hand; to make a copy of

抄襲(ㄔㄠ ㄒㄧˊ)
to plagiarize

抄稿(ㄔㄠ ㄍㄠˇ)
to make a neat copy (of a draft)

抄後路(ㄔㄠ ㄏㄡˋ ㄌㄨˋ)
to outflank the enemy and attack them from the rear

抄獲(ㄔㄠ ㄏㄨㄛˋ)
to discover by searching; to ferret out

抄集(ㄔㄠ ㄐㄧˊ)
to collect by copying

抄家(ㄔㄠ ㄐㄧㄚ)or 抄沒(ㄔㄠ ㄇㄛˋ)
to confiscate the property of an offender

抄家滅門(ㄔㄠ ㄐㄧㄚ ㄇㄧㄝˋ ㄇㄣˊ)
to confiscate the property and exterminate the family (of an offender)

抄近路(ㄔㄠ ㄐㄧㄣˋ ㄌㄨˋ)
to take a shortcut; to cut corners: 他抄近路去。He took a shortcut.

抄襲(ㄔㄠ ㄒㄧˊ)
①to plagiarize; to copy off: 他常抄襲別人文字。He often plagiarized. ②to attack the flank of

抄下來(ㄔㄠ ㄒㄧㄚˋ •ㄌㄞ)
to take down (words from the blackboard, a book, etc.)

抄呈(ㄔㄠ ㄔㄥˊ)
to submit a copy of...

抄手(ㄔㄠ ㄕㄡˇ)
①a copyist ②(Szechwan dialect) same as 餛飩

抄書(ㄔㄠ ㄕㄨ)
to plagiarize a book (in school composition, etc.)

抄錯(ㄔㄠ ㄘㄨㄛˋ)
to make inadvertent mistakes in copying or plagiarizing

抄送(ㄔㄠ ㄙㄨㄥˋ)
to send a copy of...; to make a copy for

【抉】 1813
ㄐㄩㄝ jyue jué
1. to choose; to pick; to select
2. to gouge; to dig

抉目(ㄐㄩㄝ ㄇㄨˋ)
to gouge out an eye or eyes

抉剔(ㄐㄩㄝ ㄊㄧ)
to pick out; to choose; to select

抉弦(ㄐㄩㄝ ㄒㄧㄢˊ)
to draw a bow

抉摘(ㄐㄩㄝ ㄓㄞ)
to choose; to select; to pick out

抉拾(ㄐㄩㄝ ㄕˊ)
devices used by archers to facilitate efforts to draw a bow

抉首(ㄐㄩㄝ ㄕㄡˇ)
to decapitate; to behead

抉擇(ㄐㄩㄝ ㄗㄜˊ)
choice; to choose

【抆】 1814
ㄨㄣˇ wenn wèn
to wipe

抆淚(ㄨㄣˇ ㄌㄟˋ)
to wipe one's tears away

抆拭(ㄨㄣˇ ㄕˋ)
to wipe away

【抒】 1815
ㄕㄨ shu shū
1. to give expression to; to express: 讓我們各抒己見吧。Let's freely express our own views.
2. to relieve; to ease; to lighten; to unburden: 他對我抒發他的隱衷 (心事)。He unburdened himself of his feelings to me.

抒發(ㄕㄨ ㄈㄚ)
to express; to voice; to give expression to: 這首歌抒發了他的愛國熱情。The song expresses his patriotic fervor.

抒難 or 紓難(ㄕㄨ ㄋㄢˊ)
to relieve, ease, or lighten distress

抒念(ㄕㄨ ㄋㄧㄢˋ)
to be relieved of thoughts or emotions burdening one's mind

抒懷(ㄕㄨ ㄏㄨㄞˊ)
to relieve the heart of emotions

抒情(ㄕㄨ ㄑㄧㄥˊ)
to express one's feelings

抒情詩(ㄕㄨ ㄑㄧㄥˊ ㄕ)
a lyric; a lyric poem; lyric poetry

抒情文(ㄕㄨ ㄑㄧㄥˊ ㄨㄣˊ)
lyrical writing

抒寫(ㄕㄨ ㄒㄧㄝˇ)
to express; to describe

抒意(ㄕㄨ ㄧˋ)
to express one's ideas

【抓】 1816
ㄓㄨㄚ jua zhuā
1. to scratch: 貓抓了我。The cat scratched me.
2. to grasp; to seize; to take; to snatch; to make a snatch at; to clutch; to catch: 他抓住我的手，熱誠地與我握手。He caught my hand and shook it heartily.
3. to arrest: 警察抓住這小偷並送進獄中。The police arrested the thief and put him in prison.

抓辮子(ㄓㄨㄚ ㄅㄧㄢˋ •ㄗ)
to seize on someone's mistake; to capitalize on someone's vulnerable spot

抓不起來(ㄓㄨㄚ ㄅㄨˋ ㄑㄧˇ •ㄌㄞ)

【手部】

incapable of taking, or being taken, by clutching or grasping

抓破(ㄓㄨㄚ ㄆㄛ)
to injure skin by scratching; to damage tissue by scratching

抓破臉(ㄓㄨㄚ ㄆㄛ ㄌㄧㄢ)
① to hurt the face by scratching ② to break off friendly relations ③ (said of a flower) white with red spots

抓賭(ㄓㄨㄚ ㄉㄨ)
(said of the police or other law enforcement agencies) to raid unlicensed gambling houses; to break up a gambling party

抓頭(ㄓㄨㄚ ㄊㄡ)
to scratch the head (often indicating puzzlement)

抓功夫兒(ㄓㄨㄚ ㄍㄨㄥ·ㄈㄨㄦ)
to find leisure out of a busy life; to steal time for idling

抓空(ㄓㄨㄚ ㄎㄨㄥ)
to use leisure moments

抓會(ㄓㄨㄚ ㄏㄨㄟ)
to bid for a loan from a private monetary cooperative in competition with other members

抓尖兒(ㄓㄨㄚ ㄐㄧㄢㄦ)
to come off first; to get the best portion

抓鬮兒(ㄓㄨㄚ ㄐㄧㄡㄦ)
to draw lots

抓緊(ㄓㄨㄚ ㄐㄧㄣ)
to grasp firmly; to pay close attention to; to hold...tight; to seize: 我們要抓緊好時機。Let's seize a good opportunity.

抓局(ㄓㄨㄚ ㄐㄩ)
to raid a gambling den

抓舉(ㄓㄨㄚ ㄐㄩ)
(weightlifting) a snatch

抓取(ㄓㄨㄚ ㄑㄩ)
to take by grasping

抓權(ㄓㄨㄚ ㄑㄩㄢ)
to grab power

抓瞎(ㄓㄨㄚ ㄒㄧㄚ)
to lose one's head; to lose composure

抓住(ㄓㄨㄚ ㄓㄨ)
① to grasp; to grip; to clutch: 他抓住一根繩子。He

grasped a rope. ② to keep from going away; to hold ③ to grip somebody's attention

抓壯丁(ㄓㄨㄚ ㄓㄨㄤ ㄉㄧㄥ)
to impress young men into military service

抓碴兒(ㄓㄨㄚ ㄔㄚㄦ)
to seek excuses for quarrels; to pick (up) quarrels

抓差(ㄓㄨㄚ ㄔㄞ)
to draft someone for a particular task; to force someone into service

抓人(ㄓㄨㄚ ㄖㄣ)
① to dragoon people (for military service, slavery, etc.) ② to arrest

抓賊(ㄓㄨㄚ ㄗㄟ)
to catch a thief

抓彩(ㄓㄨㄚ ㄘㄞ)
to draw lots for a lottery; to raffle

抓耳撓腮(ㄓㄨㄚ ㄦ ㄋㄠ ㄙㄞ)
① to tweak one's ears and scratch one's cheeks ② impatient; uneasy ③ flurried; agitated ④ depressed; anguished

抓一把(ㄓㄨㄚ ㄧ ㄅㄚ)
to take a handful

抓藥(ㄓㄨㄚ ㄧㄠ)
to buy (Chinese herbal) medicine according to a doctor's prescription

抓癢(ㄓㄨㄚ ㄧㄤ)
to scratch an itchy part

【抔】1817
ㄆㄡ pour póu
to scoop up with both hands

抔土(ㄆㄡ ㄊㄨ)
① a double handful of earth ② a grave

抔土未乾(ㄆㄡ ㄊㄨ ㄨㄟ ㄍㄢ)
(literally) The grave is still fresh.—It is not long since his, or her, death.

抔錢濟貧(ㄆㄡ ㄑㄧㄢ ㄐㄧ ㄆㄧㄣ)
(literally) to give money in double handfuls to relieve the poor—to give generously to help the poor

抔飲(ㄆㄡ ㄧㄣ)
to drink out of the hands

【把】1818
1. ㄅㄚ baa bǎ
1. a handle; a hold
2. to take: 他把著小孩的手教他

怎麼做。He took his child by the hand and taught him how to do it.
3. to hold: 她在給孩子把尿。She is holding her baby out to let it urinate.
4. to guard; to watch over; to keep under surveillance
5. a bundle; a grasp; a handful: 一把泥土 a handful of clay
6. around; about; approximately; more or less: 我花了個把月。It took me about a month.
7. sworn
8. (now rarely) to give
9. (colloquial) used before a direct object, followed by a transitive verb: 他把故事講完了。He finished telling the story.

把臂(ㄅㄚ ㄅㄧ)
(literally) arm in arm—very intimate: 他們是把臂之交。They are intimate friends.

把柄(ㄅㄚ ㄅㄧㄥ) or 把鼻(ㄅㄚ ㄅㄧ)
a hold (on somebody); an utterance that yields a bar gaining advantage to the other party; a handle

把袂(ㄅㄚ ㄇㄟ)
(said of two persons) to catch hold of each other's sleeves — (figuratively) to be very friendly to each other

把門(ㄅㄚ ㄇㄣ)
to stand watch at a door or gate; to guard a door

把風(ㄅㄚ ㄈㄥ)
a person posted as a lookout, especially in a robbery or other criminal acts

把舵(ㄅㄚ ㄉㄨㄛ)
① to steer the rudder ② a helmsman

把頭(ㄅㄚ ㄊㄡ)
a labor contractor

把尿(ㄅㄚ ㄋㄧㄠ)
to help a small child urinate by holding his legs apart

把來(ㄅㄚ ㄌㄞ)
to use something to blame, threaten, cheat, please, etc.

把牢(ㄅㄚ ㄌㄠ)
strong; dependable

把攬(ㄅㄚ ·ㄌㄢ)
to use undue influence to

monopolize (a piece of business, etc.); to arrange to do a catchall job

把關(ㄅㄚˇ ㄍㄨㄢ)
①to guard a pass ②to check on

把口兒(ㄅㄚˇ ㄎㄡˇ ㄦ)
exactly at the intersection of roads; right at the road corner

把家(ㄅㄚˇ ㄐㄧㄚ)
to guard family belongings jealously

把酒(ㄅㄚˇ ㄐㄧㄡˇ)
to hold a wineglass—to drink

把卷(ㄅㄚˇ ㄐㄩㄢˋ)
to hold a book in one's hand; to read

巴戲(ㄅㄚˇ ㄒㄧˋ)
①acrobatic performances as juggling, etc.: 他用球耍把戲。He juggled with balls. ②a trick or scheme: 他愛耍鬼把戲。He likes to play dirty tricks. ③a child; a toddler

把兄弟(ㄅㄚˇ ㄒㄩㄥ ㄉㄧˋ)
sworn brothers: 他們是把兄弟。They are sworn brothers.

把盞(ㄅㄚˇ ㄓㄢˇ)
to hold winecups; to drink

把捉(ㄅㄚˇ ㄓㄨㄛ)
①to grasp ②to assess: 把握不定。It's difficult to assess.

把持(ㄅㄚˇ ㄔˊ)
to monopolize; to dominate or control: 他想把持一切。He wants to monopolize everything.

把持不定(ㄅㄚˇ ㄔˊ ㄅㄨˋ ㄉㄧㄥˋ)
vacillating; undecided

把勢(ㄅㄚˇ ㄕˋ)
vain gestures

把式(ㄅㄚˇ ㄕˋ)
①movements in Chinese boxing ②a skilled laborer ③a skill

把守(ㄅㄚˇ ㄕㄡˇ)
to watch over; to guard or defend (a city, etc.): 他們英勇地把守城門。They bravely guarded the city gate.

把手(ㄅㄚˇ ㄕㄡˇ)
①to hold hands: 他們把手言歡。They hold hands and converse cheerfully. ②a handle: 我們握住把手提桶。We

carry a bucket by the handle.

把子(ㄅㄚˇ ˙ㄗ)
①a group of (bandits, soldiers, etc.) ②a group of sworn brothers ③a posture held by a warrior in Chinese opera; poise

把總(ㄅㄚˇ ㄗㄨㄥˇ)
(formerly) a company grade officer

把兒(ㄅㄚˇ ㄦ)
a bundle; a grasp; a handful

把晤(ㄅㄚˇ ㄨˋ)
to meet; to see each other

把握(ㄅㄚˇ ㄨㄛˋ)
①something one holds in hand②confident; sure; to have absolute confidence ③to have a firm grasp of the situation: 我們應把握時機。We should seize the opportunity.

把玩(ㄅㄚˇ ㄨㄢˊ)
to keep at hand for appreciation; to fondle

把穩(ㄅㄚˇ ㄨㄣˇ)
firm; stable; steady; dependable; trustworthy

【把】 1818
2. ㄅㄚˋ bah bà
a handle

把子(ㄅㄚˋ ˙ㄗ)
a handle

把兒(ㄅㄚˋ ㄦ)or把手(ㄅㄚˋ ㄕㄡˇ)
a handle: 槍把兒 a rifle butt

把兒鏡子(ㄅㄚˋ ㄦ ㄐㄧㄥˋ ˙ㄗ)
a mirror with a handle

【投】 1819
ㄊㄡˊ tour tóu
1. to throw; to pitch; to toss: 他向我們投石。He threw a stone at us.
2. to present as a gift
3. to lodge; to stay: 你現在投宿在何處? Where are you lodging now?
4. to head (west, etc.)
5. agreeable; congenial; harmonious; to fit in with; to cater to
6. to join; to submit to: 他已經投軍了。He has already joined the army.
7. to project; to cast: 樹投影於草地上。The tree projects a shadow on the grass.
8. to deliver (mail, etc.); to send (letters, scripts, etc.)

投保(ㄊㄡˊ ㄅㄠˇ)
to take out an insurance policy

投保人(ㄊㄡˊ ㄅㄠˇ ㄖㄣˊ)
a policyholder

投報(ㄊㄡˊ ㄅㄠˋ)
to give and return love tokens, etc.

投奔(ㄊㄡˊ ㄅㄣˋ)
①to flee (to freedom): 他們投奔自由了。They escaped to freedom. ②to seek employment or protection from somebody

投筆從戎(ㄊㄡˊ ㄅㄧˇ ㄘㄨㄥˊ ㄖㄨㄥˊ)
to throw away one's pen and get into a military uniform; (said of a student or intellectual) to join the army voluntarily

投標(ㄊㄡˊ ㄅㄧㄠ)
to bid in a public tender

投鞭斷流(ㄊㄡˊ ㄅㄧㄢ ㄉㄨㄢˋ ㄌㄧㄡˊ)
a quotation from Fu Chien (苻 堅): "If each of my mounted troops throws in his whip, the flow of the river will be stopped." (used boastfully by an invading army to intimidate the defenders)

投票(ㄊㄡˊ ㄆㄧㄠˋ)
to cast a vote; to ballot; a vote; poll: 我投票給張先生。I gave my vote to Mr. Chang.

投票表決(ㄊㄡˊ ㄆㄧㄠˋ ㄅㄧㄠˇ ㄐㄩㄝˊ)
to decide by voting

投票法(ㄊㄡˊ ㄆㄧㄠˋ ㄈㄚˇ)
laws and regulations governing balloting

投票權(ㄊㄡˊ ㄆㄧㄠˋ ㄑㄩㄢˊ)
the ballot; the right to vote

投票箱(ㄊㄡˊ ㄆㄧㄠˋ ㄒㄧㄤ)or投票匭(ㄊㄡˊ ㄆㄧㄠˋ ㄍㄨㄟˇ)
a ballotbox

投票選舉(ㄊㄡˊ ㄆㄧㄠˋ ㄒㄩㄢˇ ㄐㄩˇ)
to elect by ballot; elections

投票人(ㄊㄡˊ ㄆㄧㄠˋ ㄖㄣˊ)
a voter

投票所(ㄊㄡˊ ㄆㄧㄠˋ ㄙㄨㄛˇ)
a polling place; a place where voters cast their ballots; polls

投袂而起(ㄊㄡˊ ㄇㄟˋ ㄦˊ ㄑㄧˇ)
(literally) to throw up one's sleeves and rise—to rise up suddenly (indicating deter-

〔手
部〕

mination or indignation)

投門路(ㄊㄡ ㄇㄣˊ ﹒ㄌㄨ)
to seek a job by looking for the right connections

投明(ㄊㄡ ㄇㄧㄥˊ)
(literally) to head oneself in the direction of light—to shift one's allegiance to the cause of justice and righteousness

投命(ㄊㄡ ㄇㄧㄥˋ)
to die for (a cause, etc.); to give one's life to

投暮(ㄊㄡ ㄇㄨˋ)
to get dark; dusk

投分(ㄊㄡ ㄈㄣˋ)
to have a meeting of minds; on very friendly terms

投放(ㄊㄡ ㄈㄤˋ)
①to throw in ②to put (money) into circulation; to put (goods) on the market

投附(ㄊㄡ ㄈㄨˋ)
to offer one's services to (a leader, cause, etc.)

投彈(ㄊㄡ ㄉㄢˋ)
①to drop a bomb ②to throw a hand grenade

投敵(ㄊㄡ ㄉㄧˊ)
to defect (or desert) to the enemy

投遞(ㄊㄡ ㄉㄧˋ)
to send or deliver (letters, etc.); delivery

投店(ㄊㄡ ㄉㄧㄢˋ)
to seek lodging in a tavern; to put up at an inn

投胎(ㄊㄡ ㄊㄞ)
to get into the cycle of reincarnation

投桃報李(ㄊㄡ ㄊㄠˊ ㄅㄠˋ ㄌㄧˇ)
to return a favor with a favor

投體(ㄊㄡ ㄊㄧˇ)
to worship; to kowtow; to admire tremendously

投托(ㄊㄡ ㄊㄨㄛ)
to place in the care of another

投籃(ㄊㄡ ㄌㄢˊ)
(basketball) to shoot; to try for the basket: 他跳起投籃。 He jumped and shot.

投戈(ㄊㄡ ㄍㄜ)
(literally) to throw away weapons—to effect a cease-fire or truce

投戈講藝(ㄊㄡ ㄍㄜ ㄐㄧㄤˇ ㄧˋ)
(literally) to lay aside weapons (for a while) so as to pursue learning—Even in war, one should not forget about learning.

投稿(ㄊㄡ ㄍㄠˇ)
a contributed article; to contribute an article; to submit a piece of writing for publication

投稿者(ㄊㄡ ㄍㄠˇ ㄓㄜˇ)
one who contributes articles (especially unsolicited) for publication by a newspaper or magazine

投竿(ㄊㄡ ㄍㄢ)
to fish with a hook and line

投考(ㄊㄡ ㄎㄠˇ)
to take an entrance examination of a school; to go in for an examination

投靠(ㄊㄡ ㄎㄠˋ)
to go and seek refuge with somebody; to join and serve (a new leader, master, etc.); to seek the patronage of the high and mighty

投河(ㄊㄡ ㄏㄜˊ)
to commit suicide by throwing oneself into the river; to drown oneself

投合(ㄊㄡ ㄏㄜˊ)
to see eye to eye; in rapport; to agree with; to cater to

投壺(ㄊㄡ ㄏㄨˊ)
(in ancient China) a game during a feast in which the winner was decided by the number of arrows thrown into a distant pot

投火(ㄊㄡ ㄏㄨㄛˇ)
to jump into the fire; to commit suicide in this manner; to throw into the fire

投懷送抱(ㄊㄡ ㄏㄨㄞˊ ㄙㄨㄥˋ ㄅㄠˋ)
(said of a woman) overtly aggressive in love affairs; acting like a man-chaser

投繯(ㄊㄡ ㄏㄨㄢˊ)
to commit suicide by hanging

投荒(ㄊㄡ ㄏㄨㄤ)
to head for or flee to distant places

投機(ㄊㄡ ㄐㄧ)
①to speculate; speculation

(as in stocks, houses, land etc.): 他投機股票買賣。He speculated in stocks. ②t see eye to eye; the meetin of minds; agreeable; congenial: 他們談得投機。The talked very congenially.

投機分子(ㄊㄡ ㄐㄧ ㄈㄣ﹒ㄗ)
an opportunist; a speculato a soldier of fortune: 他是個 投機分子。He is an opportu

投機取巧(ㄊㄡ ㄐㄧ ㄑㄩˇ ㄑㄧㄠˇ)
to speculate and take advar tage of an opportunity; to use every trick in shortcut and finesse; to cut corners the ways of an opportunist

投機事業(ㄊㄡ ㄐㄧ ㄕˋ ㄧㄝˋ)
speculative business

投寄(ㄊㄡ ㄐㄧˋ)
to send a letter to: 我已投寄 給他好幾封信。I have sen him several letters.

投交(ㄊㄡ ㄐㄧㄠ)
friendly intercourse; friend ship

投進去(ㄊㄡ ㄐㄧㄣˋ ㄑㄩˋ)
to throw in (or into)

投井(ㄊㄡ ㄐㄧㄥˇ)
to drown oneself in a well

投井下石(ㄊㄡ ㄐㄧㄥˇ ㄒㄧㄚˋ ㄕˊ)
to attack someone who has already fallen from power to kick a man when he is down

投軍(ㄊㄡ ㄐㄩㄣ)
to enlist oneself; to join the army; to become a service man: 今年許多學生投軍了。 Many students enlisted in the army this year.

投其所好(ㄊㄡ ㄑㄧˊ ㄙㄨㄛˇ ㄏㄠˋ)
to cater to another's pleasure; to please someone by doing what he wishes to be done without being told; to suit one's fancy

投契(ㄊㄡ ㄑㄧˋ)
meeting of minds (between friends); to get along well; to be congenial: 他們相處得 很投契。They get along well together.

投棄(ㄊㄡ ㄑㄧˋ)
to abandon or give up (sinful ways, old methods, etc.)

投親(ㄊㄡˊㄑㄧㄣ)
(said of an orphan, etc.) to go and live with one's relatives; to seek refuge with one's relatives

投下(ㄊㄡˊㄒㄧㄚˋ)
①to throw down; to drop ②to invest (capital): 他在書籍上投下大筆金錢。He invested large sums in books.

投效(ㄊㄡˊㄒㄧㄠˋ)
to offer one's services to

投閒置散(ㄊㄡˊㄒㄧㄢˊㄓˋㄙㄢˋ)
to stay idle; to occupy an insignificant position (especially said of people of talent)

投降(ㄊㄡˊㄒㄧㄤˊ)
to surrender; surrender; to capitulate: 我們決不向敵人投降。We shall never surrender to the enemy.

投擲(ㄊㄡˊㄓˊ)
to throw (a discus, etc.); to throw away: 他使勁地投擲標槍。He threw the javelin vigorously.

投止或投訖(ㄊㄡˊㄓˇ)
to stay at or with

投炸彈(ㄊㄡˊㄓㄚˋㄉㄢˋ)
to drop bombs from a plane; to throw bombs

投杼之疑(ㄊㄡˊㄓㄨˋㄓㄧˊ)
When slanderers are many, a lie will become believable. 或A lie, if repeated often enough, becomes a truth to the listener.

投誠(ㄊㄡˊㄔㄥˊ)
(said of enemy troops, bandits, etc.) to voluntarily surrender to the government forces; to return to allegiance

投師(ㄊㄡˊㄕ)
to seek instruction from a master

投石打狗(ㄊㄡˊㄕˊㄉㄚˇㄍㄡˇ)
to throw a stone at a dog

投石問路(ㄊㄡˊㄕˊㄨㄣˋㄌㄨˋ)
(said of burglars) to throw a stone into a house to find out if the occupants are awake

投射(ㄊㄡˊㄕㄜˋ)
①to project; to shoot: 金色陽光投射到平靜的湖面上。

The sun cast its golden rays on the calm lake. ②to harvest profit from speculation

投射點(ㄊㄡˊㄕㄜˋㄉㄧㄢˇ)
(physics) an incident point

投射角(ㄊㄡˊㄕㄜˋㄐㄧㄠˇ)
(physics) an angle of incidence

投射器(ㄊㄡˊㄕㄜˋㄑㄧˋ)
a projector

投射線(ㄊㄡˊㄕㄜˋㄒㄧㄢˋ)
(physics) an incident ray

投射物(ㄊㄡˊㄕㄜˋㄨˋ)
a projectile

投首(ㄊㄡˊㄕㄡˇ)
①to confess to a criminal act ②to give oneself up to the authorities

投手(ㄊㄡˊㄕㄡˇ)
(baseball) a pitcher

投身(ㄊㄡˊㄕㄣ)
①to give oneself to (the revolutionary cause, a military career, etc.); to throw oneself into ②to find employment or shelter

投生(ㄊㄡˊㄕㄥ)
to get reincarnated

投書(ㄊㄡˊㄕㄨ)or投函(ㄊㄡˊㄏㄢˊ)
to send a letter to (a newspaper editor, etc.)

投鼠忌器(ㄊㄡˊㄕㄨˇㄐㄧˋㄑㄧˋ)
a quotation from Chia Yi (賈誼), "afraid to kill the rat for fear of damaging the vase in which it's hiding" —① One is afraid to impeach a corrupt official for fear of incriminating the emperor. ② to have scruples in doing something; to fear the repercussions of a certain action

投水(ㄊㄡˊㄕㄨㄟˇ)
①to jump into the water ②to commit suicide in this manner

投稅(ㄊㄡˊㄕㄨㄟˋ)
to pay taxes

投入(ㄊㄡˊㄖㄨˋ)
①to throw in: 他投入戰鬥之中。He threw himself into the battle. ②to join (the army, revolutionaries, etc.): 他已投入民主黨。He has joined himself to the Democratic Party.

投入資本(ㄊㄡˊㄖㄨˋㄗ ㄅㄣˇ)
invested capital; vested proprietorship (capital)

投資(ㄊㄡˊㄗ)
to invest; investment: 他把錢投資在股票上。He invested his money in stocks.

投資公司(ㄊㄡˊㄗㄍㄨㄥㄙ)
an investment company

投資市場(ㄊㄡˊㄗㄕˋㄔㄤˇ)
an investment market

投子(ㄊㄡˊㄗˇ)
dice 亦作「骰子」; 他賭投子輸得一文不名。He diced away all his money.

投閒(ㄊㄡˊㄗㄞˋ)
to give up one's official position

投刺(ㄊㄡˊㄘˋ)
①to present one's visiting card; to pay a call on ②to retire from public life

投死(ㄊㄡˊㄙˇ)
to be faithful till one breathes his last

投宿(ㄊㄡˊㄙㄨˋ)
to stay or check in (at a hotel, etc.) for the night; to put up for the night

投梭(ㄊㄡˊㄙㄨㄛ)
①to put up strong resistance against a rapist; to reject harshly when being seduced ②fast and agile

投案(ㄊㄡˊㄢˋ)
to appear before court in answer to summons; to surrender oneself to justice or the police: 他已向警方投案。He has surrendered himself to the police.

投郵(ㄊㄡˊㄧㄡˊ)
to mail; to send a letter or package by mail

投影(ㄊㄡˊㄧㄥˇ)
①(mathematics) projection ②(art) cast shadow ③to project: 樹投影於草上。The tree projects a shadow on the grass.

投影畫(ㄊㄡˊㄧㄥˇㄏㄨㄚˋ)or投影圖(ㄊㄡˊㄧㄥˇㄊㄨˊ)
a projective drawing

投網(ㄊㄡˊㄨㄤˇ)
(literally) to get caught by the net—(usually said of a criminal at large) to get

〔手部〕

〔手部〕

caught; to get trapped or snared

投獄(ㄊㄡ ㄩˋ)
to jail; to imprison

投緣(ㄊㄡ ㄩㄢˊ)
to be on intimate terms at once; to have a meeting of minds

【抗】 1820 ㄎㄤˋ kang kàng

1. to resist; to oppose: 他們抵抗攻擊。They resisted the attack.

2. to reject; to refute; to rebuke; to defy

3. high and virtuous

4. to raise; to set up

5. to hide; to conceal; to screen; to secrete

6. a Chinese family name

抗暴(ㄎㄤˋ ㄅㄠˋ)
to oppose tyranny

抗辯(ㄎㄤˋ ㄅㄧㄢˋ)
to speak out in one's own defense; to refute; to rebut or retort

抗病(ㄎㄤˋ ㄅㄧㄥˋ)
(agriculture) disease-resistant

抗捕(ㄎㄤˋ ㄅㄨˇ)
to resist arrest

抗邁(ㄎㄤˋ ㄇㄞˋ)
elegant and outstanding; smart and remarkable

抗命(ㄎㄤˋ ㄇㄧㄥˋ)
to disobey orders

抗敵(ㄎㄤˋ ㄉㄧˊ)
① to resist or fight enemy troops ② to treat as equals; to equal or match: 她的聰明伶俐可以與他抗敵。She equals him in cleverness.

抗毒素(ㄎㄤˋ ㄉㄨˊ ㄙㄨˋ)
an antitoxin

抗體(ㄎㄤˋ ㄊㄧˇ)
an antibody

抗禮(ㄎㄤˋ ㄌㄧˇ)
to equal, to treat each other as equals without regard to etiquette or formalities

抗力(ㄎㄤˋ ㄌㄧˋ)
(physics) resistance or resistance strength

抗糧(ㄎㄤˋ ㄌㄧㄤˊ)
to refuse to pay farm tax in kind

抗論(ㄎㄤˋ ㄌㄨㄣˋ)

① a straightforward statement ② to retort; to argue against

抗告(ㄎㄤˋ ㄍㄠˋ)
(law) interlocutory appeal

抗旱(ㄎㄤˋ ㄏㄢˋ)
drought-resistant; drought-resistance: 這種植物能抗旱。This plant is drought-resistant.

抗衡(ㄎㄤˋ ㄏㄥˊ)
to contend; to compete; to match: 在辯論上無人可以與他抗衡。No one can match him in argument.

抗節不附(ㄎㄤˋ ㄐㄧㄝˊ ㄅㄨˋ ㄈㄨˋ)
to uphold one's high principles without submitting to threats, bribery, etc.

抗拒(ㄎㄤˋ ㄐㄩˋ)
to resist; to oppose

抗心希古(ㄎㄤˋ ㄒㄧㄣ ㄒㄧ ㄍㄨˇ)
a heart of gold that rivals those of the ancients

抗行(ㄎㄤˋ ㄒㄧㄥˊ)
① (ㄎㄤˋ ㄒㄧㄥˊ) virtuous conduct or behavior
② (ㄎㄤˋ ㄒㄧㄥˊ) to match each other; to be able to rival with

抗直(ㄎㄤˋ ㄓˊ)
straightforward and upright

抗志不屈(ㄎㄤˋ ㄓˋ ㄅㄨˋ ㄑㄩ)
to adhere to high purposes and not to submit to threats, etc.

抗戰(ㄎㄤˋ ㄓㄢˋ)
① a war of resistance; to fight the invading army ② the War of Resistance against Japan (1937-1945)

抗戰到底(ㄎㄤˋ ㄓㄢˋ ㄉㄠˋ ㄉㄧˇ)
to fight an invading enemy to the last man

抗戰時期(ㄎㄤˋ ㄓㄢˋ ㄕˊ ㄑㄧˊ)
the period of the War of Resistance (especially the one against the Japanese 1937-1945)

抗震(ㄎㄤˋ ㄓㄣˋ)
anti-seismic

抗爭(ㄎㄤˋ ㄓㄥ)
to contend; to oppose; to resist

抗塵走俗(ㄎㄤˋ ㄔㄣˊ ㄗㄡˇ ㄙㄨˊ)
to be on constant run for worldly pursuit

抗傳(ㄎㄤˋ ㄔㄨㄢˊ)
to refuse to answer a cou summons

抗手(ㄎㄤˋ ㄕㄡˇ)
to raise one's hand (as salute)

抗聲(ㄎㄤˋ ㄕㄥ)
to raise one's voice

抗生素(ㄎㄤˋ ㄕㄥ ㄙㄨˋ)
antibiotics

抗疏(ㄎㄤˋ ㄕㄨ)
a straight and frank repo to the emperor

抗水性(ㄎㄤˋ ㄕㄨㄟˇ ㄒㄧㄥˋ)
water-resistance; a wate resisting property

抗稅(ㄎㄤˋ ㄕㄨㄟˋ)
to refuse to pay taxes

抗日戰爭(ㄎㄤˋ ㄖˋ ㄓㄢˋ ㄓㄥ)
the War of Resistance Against Japanese Aggre sion; the Sino-Japanese Wa (1937-1945)

抗熱(ㄎㄤˋ ㄖㄜˋ)
heat-resistant

抗熱板(ㄎㄤˋ ㄖㄜˋ ㄅㄢˇ)
the heat shield

抗熱材料(ㄎㄤˋ ㄖㄜˋ ㄘㄞˊ ㄌㄧㄠˋ)
heat-resistant material

抗議(ㄎㄤˋ ㄧˋ)
to protest; a protest; to rai one's voice against: 他對判ˋ 提出抗議。He made a prote against the verdict.

抗議書(ㄎㄤˋ ㄧˋ ㄕㄨ)
a form of protest; a writte protest

抗議遊行(ㄎㄤˋ ㄧˋ ㄧㄡˊ ㄒㄧㄥˊ)
a protest march

抗藥性(ㄎㄤˋ ㄧㄠˋ ㄒㄧㄥˋ)
resistance to the action of drug

抗顏(ㄎㄤˋ ㄧㄢˊ)
to be calm and fearless face of threats, etc.

抗氧化劑(ㄎㄤˋ ㄧㄤˇ ㄏㄨㄚˋ ㄐㄧˋ)
antioxidant

抗違(ㄎㄤˋ ㄨㄟˊ)
to oppose; to disobe (orders, etc.): 你曾抗違父命嗎? Did you ever disob your parents?

抗原(ㄎㄤˋ ㄩㄢˊ)
(medicine) an antigen

【抖】 1821 ㄉㄡˇ doou dǒu

1. to shiver; to tremble: 他的聲音因憤怒而顫抖。His voice trembled with anger.

2. to shake; to jerk: 她把衣服上的雪抖掉。She shook the snow off her clothes.

3. to rouse

4. (colloquial) to make good; to become well-to-do

抖翻
to turn up; to expose; to dig up old stories to discredit somebody: 他抖翻了他們的秘密。He exposed their secrets.

抖動
to shake; to tremble; to vibrate: 樹葉在風中抖動。The leaves tremble in the wind.

抖擻(カさˇ·ムメˇ)
① to exhaust one's means; to waste; to squander ② to expose another's secrets ③ to catch cold ④ to shake off

抖攬(カさˇ カㄢˇ)
to solicit 亦作「兜攬」

抖亂(カさˇ カㄨㄢˋ)
a shallow, gaudy, small-time house (usually young)

抖起來了(カさˇ くㄧˇ カㄞˊ·カㄜ)
to become ostensibly successful and prosperous; to make good

抖出來(カさˇ ㄔㄨ ·カㄞˊ)
to spill out

抖擻精神(カさˇ ㄙㄨˇ ㄐㄧㄥ ㄕㄣˊ)
to pull oneself together or to muster one's energies (for an important task ahead)

抖威風(カさˇ ㄨㄟ ㄈㄥ)
to throw one's weight around

【折】 *1822*
1. ㄓㄜˊ jer *zhé*

1. to break; to snap 別把樹枝折斷了。Don't break the branches.

2. to bend; to humble; to bow: 悲哀挫折了他的銳氣。Sorrow has bowed his spirit.

3. to decide a course; to judge

4. to sell, barter or exchange: 她將英鎊折換成美元。She exchanged pounds for dollars.

5. a discount in the price

6. to fold: 他把紙對折，然後放到一邊。He folded the paper in half and put it away.

7. to tear into halves; to destroy

8. to submit to; to be willing

9. a Chinese family name

折半
to reduce by half; to reduce to half; to sell at half price: 本書按原價折半出售。This book sells at half price.

折變(ㄓㄜˊ ㄅㄧㄢˋ)
① to substitute one thing for another of equal value or price ② to auction one's property to repay debts

折磨(ㄓㄜˊ ·ㄇㄛ)
to submit to an ordeal; trials and afflictions; grillings; torment: 她遭受牙痛的折磨。She suffered torment from an aching tooth.

折賣(ㄓㄜˊ ㄇㄞˋ)
to sell or auction one's property (to repay debts, etc.)

折服(ㄓㄜˊ ㄈㄨˊ)
① to acknowledge the superiority of others ② to submit; to bring into submission: 他不肯折服。He would not submit.

折福(ㄓㄜˊ ㄈㄨˊ)
to reduce blessings in one's later life because of excessive easy living (sometimes used as a polite expression in response to great favors bestowed upon oneself)

折抵(ㄓㄜˊ ㄉㄧˇ)
to set off against

折疊(ㄓㄜˊ ㄉㄧㄝˊ)
to fold: 請把報紙折疊好。Fold up the newspaper,please.

折疊床(ㄓㄜˊ ㄉㄧㄝˊ ㄔㄨㄤˊ)
a folding bed

折疊椅(ㄓㄜˊ ㄉㄧㄝˊ ㄧˇ)
a folding chair

折兌(ㄓㄜˊ ㄉㄨㄟˋ)
to exchange (gold or silver) for money; to convert

折斷(ㄓㄜˊ ㄉㄨㄢˋ)
to snap; to break: 槳咖喳一聲折斷了。The oar broke with a snap.

折扣(ㄓㄜˊ·ㄓㄡˋ)
a discount rate

折柳(ㄓㄜˊ ㄌㄧㄡˇ)
(literally) to break a willow branch—to send off a friend

折桂(ㄓㄜˊ ㄍㄨㄟˋ)
to pass the imperial civil

service examination, particularly one held in autumn

折光(ㄓㄜˊ ㄍㄨㄤ)
refracted light; to refract light

折肱(ㄓㄜˊ ㄍㄨㄥ)
experienced

折扣(ㄓㄜˊ ㄎㄡˋ)
abatement; a discount in the price; a discount rate; a rebate: 那是打過折扣的價錢。That is the discounted price.

折扣率(ㄓㄜˊ ㄎㄡˋ ㄌㄩˋ)
the discount rate

折合(ㄓㄜˊ ㄏㄜˊ)
(said of two currencies, etc.) equivalent to

折回(ㄓㄜˊ ㄏㄨㄟˊ)
to turn back (half way): 難民到邊界時被折回。The refugees were turned back at the frontier.

折戟(ㄓㄜˊ ㄐㄧˇ)
to break the spear—as a token of peace or truce

折價(ㄓㄜˊ ㄐㄧㄚˋ)
(said of an article used in repaying a debt, etc.) equivalent to

折節(ㄓㄜˊ ㄐㄧㄝˊ)
① to act obsequiously ② to change the habit or way of living

折節讀書(ㄓㄜˊ ㄐㄧㄝˊ ㄉㄨˊ ㄕㄨ)
to take a sudden liking to studying

折交(ㄓㄜˊ ㄐㄧㄠ)
to pay proportionately

折舊(ㄓㄜˊ ㄐㄧㄡˋ)
depreciation (especially said of machinery in use)

折舊率(ㄓㄜˊ ㄐㄧㄡˋ ㄌㄩˋ)
the depreciation rate

折箭為盟(ㄓㄜˊ ㄐㄧㄢˋ ㄨㄟˊ ㄇㄥˊ)
to break an arrow as a vow or pledge to keep one's promise

折券(ㄓㄜˊ ㄑㄩㄢˋ)
to destroy a debtor's IOU—to renounce the right of asking for repayment; to destroy a deed without asking for money

折現(ㄓㄜˊ ㄒㄧㄢˋ)
to convert into cash

折線(ㄓㄜˊ ㄒㄧㄢˋ)
(mathematics) a broken line

（手部）

折枝（业ㄜ 业）
①to massage ②to snap a twig ③a style of flower painting with one or two stems minus the root

折賬 or 折帳（业ㄜ 业ㄤ）
to repay a creditor in kind

折中 or 折衷（业ㄜ 业ㄨㄥ）
to compromise; a compromise: 這是個折中的辦法。It's a compromise.

折衝（业ㄜ ㄔㄨㄥ）
to ward off the enemy; to repulse the enemy

折衝尊俎（业ㄜ ㄔㄨㄥ ㄗㄨㄣ ㄗㄨˇ）
(literally) to fight off the enemy over cups of wine—to subdue an enemy by diplomacy; to win a war at the conference table

折煞 or 折殺（业ㄜ ·ㄕㄚ）
to break one's luck

折射（业ㄜ ㄕㄜˋ）
refraction; to refract: 水可使光折射。Water refracts light.

折射角（业ㄜ ㄕㄜˋ ㄐㄧㄠˇ）
a refraction angle; an angle of refraction

折射線（业ㄜ ㄕㄜˋ ㄒㄧㄢˋ）
a refractor ray

折壽（业ㄜ ㄕㄡˋ）
(said of excessive happiness, blessings, etc.) that will cut one's natural allotment of life expectancy

折扇（业ㄜ ㄕㄢ）
a folding fan 亦作「摺扇」

折入（业ㄜ ㄖㄨˋ）
①to turn into another street ②capital recovered after suffering losses in business

折辱（业ㄜ ㄖㄨˇ）
to humiliate; to insult

折子（业ㄜ ·ㄗ）
a folding notebook

折足覆餗（业ㄜ ㄗㄨˊ ㄈㄨˋ ㄙㄨˋ）
not equal to the task

折算（业ㄜ ㄙㄨㄢˋ）
calculated at; equivalent to (said of the value of property, possessions, etc.)

折損（业ㄜ ㄙㄨㄣˇ）
to damage; damage (in property, reputation, etc.): 因火災使得那房子受到相當的折損。The fire did considerable damage to the building.

折頁（业ㄜ ㄧㄝˋ）
(printing) folding

折腰（业ㄜ ㄧㄠ）
to bow; to humble oneself

折獄（业ㄜ ㄩˋ）
to decide a lawsuit

【折】 1822
2. ㄕㄜˊ　sher shé
1. to lose money; to fail in business
2. to break; to snap: 釣魚竿折了。The fishing pole broke.

折本（业ㄜ ㄅㄣˇ）
to lose money; to get into the red: 那是折本生意。That's a losing business.

折了（业ㄜ ·ㄌㄜ）
broken

折耗（业ㄜ ㄏㄠˋ）
to lose money

【折】 1822
3. 业ㄜ　je zhē
1. to turn upside down; to fall head over heels; to somersault; a somersault: 他折了個跟斗。He turned a somersault.
2. to pour all out

折騰（业ㄜ ·ㄊㄥ）
①to turn upside down ②to squander; to waste; to spend (money) extravagantly; to exhaust all reserves ③to toss about

折跟頭（业ㄜ ㄍㄣ ·ㄊㄡ）
to somersault; to fall head over heels

【抑】 1823
ㄧˋ　yih yì
1. to press down; to repress: 他的創作天才被壓抑太久了。His creative talents had been repressed for too long.
2. to restrain; to force to (do, perform, etc.): 你不可抑制他們的自由。You must not restrain them of their liberty.
3. to bend or lower (one's head)
4. or; or if; still; else; either; then
5. but; an opening particle of an expression
6. an exclamatory, roughly equivalent to "oh," or "alas"
7. to stop

抑勒（ㄧˋ ㄌㄜˋ）
to repress and restrain (one's anger, etc.)

抑且（ㄧˋ ㄑㄧㄝˇ）or 抑或（ㄧˋ ㄏㄨㄛˋ）
besides; moreover; or

抑強扶弱（ㄧˋ ㄑㄧㄤˊ ㄈㄨˊ ㄖㄨㄛˋ）
to restrain the strong and help the weak; to curb the violent and assist the weak

抑止（ㄧˋ 业ˇ）
to restrain; to check; to stop; to suppress: 老師抑止孩子們惡作劇。The teacher restrained children from doing mischief.

抑制（ㄧˋ 业ˋ）
to repress; to restrain; to control: 她不能抑制她的好奇心。She could not restrain her curiosity.

抑首（ㄧˋ ㄕㄡˇ）
to bend or lower one's head

抑挫（ㄧˋ ㄘㄨㄛˋ）
to curb

抑塞（ㄧˋ ㄙㄜˋ）
①to give no chance to; to reject ②despondency; dejection

抑遏（ㄧˋ ㄜˋ）
to curb; to restrain; to suppress; to coerce: 她無法抑遏佳她的憤怒。She could not restrain her anger.

抑壓（ㄧˋ ㄧㄚ）
to coerce; to curb; to restrain

抑揚（ㄧˋ ㄧㄤˊ）
①rising and falling in cadence ②the flow of sentiments in a writing ③to praise and to censure ④the rise and fall (of one's career, etc.)

抑揚頓挫（ㄧˋ ㄧㄤˊ ㄉㄨㄣˋ ㄘㄨㄛˋ）
melodious; rich in melody; cadence; modulation in tone

抑鬱（ㄧˋ ㄩˋ）
despondency; sad and melancholy: 他對自己的健康不佳感到抑鬱不安。He was despondent about his poor health.

【扼】 1824
(搤) ㄜˋ　eh è
1. to repress; to restrain; to control
2. to clutch; to grasp; to grip
3. to hold and defend (a city, etc.)

扼喉撫背(さ ㄏㄡ ㄈㄨ ㄅㄟ)
to hold the best strategic positions (which will render the enemy helpless)

扼吭(さ ㄏㄤ)
to choke; to throttle

扼虎(さ ㄏㄨˇ)
to choke a tiger to death —very powerful; with enormous strength

扼據(さ ㄐㄩ)
to occupy and hold (key positions, etc.)

扼險(さ ㄒㄧㄢˇ)
to hold the most strategic position (in military operations)

扼制(さ ㄓˋ)
to repress; to keep under control by force

扼殺(さ ㄕㄚ)
to strangle; to smother; to throttle

扼守(さ ㄕㄡˇ)
to hold and defend (a strategic position): 我軍勇敢地扼守堡壘. Our soldiers held the fort bravely.

扼阻要塞(さ ㄗㄨˇ ㄧㄠˋ ㄙㄞ)
(military) a stronghold which will jeopardize military operations of the enemy

扼死(さ ㄙˇ)
to strangle; to throttle

扼要(さ ㄧㄠˋ)
①to hold a strategic position ② main points of a statement or article; in summary: 請扼要說明, Please tell us the key points.

扼腕(さ ㄨㄢˇ)
(literally) to seize one's wrist — ① disappointment; regret ② anger ③ excitement

【承】 1825
ㄔㄥˊ chéng

1. to receive; to inherit; to succeed (another in a task,etc.): 他沒有兒子繼承他. He had no son to succeed him.

2. to undertake; to make it one's responsibility

3. by (order of)

4. to continue; to carry on, as a theme

5. to hold; to contain; to support: 我無法再承受他

的無禮. I can support his insolence no longer.

6. to confess: 他坦承自己不懂. He confessed (that) he did not understand it.

7. obliged; with thanks: 承您幫助, 十分感激. We are very much obliged to you for your help.

8. to please; to flatter: 他在奉承你. He is flattering you.

承包(ㄔㄥˊ ㄅㄠ)
to undertake to do a job; to undertake a construction job under contract; to contract

承包商(ㄔㄥˊ ㄅㄠ ㄕㄤ)
a contractor

承保(ㄔㄥˊ ㄅㄠˇ)
to accept insurance; to act as a guarantor

承辦(ㄔㄥˊ ㄅㄢˋ)
to handle (a case); to be responsible for (a task); to undertake: 該律師免費承辦那宗案件. The lawyer undertook that case without a fee.

承辦人員(ㄔㄥˊ ㄅㄢˋ ㄖㄣˊ ㄩㄢˊ)
officials concerned (in a task); officials in charge of a specific task

承敝 or 承弊(ㄔㄥˊ ㄅㄧˋ)
in the wake of a declining period

承平(ㄔㄥˊ ㄆㄧㄥˊ)
successive peaceful reigns

承蒙(ㄔㄥˊ ㄇㄥˊ)
to be obliged to; much indebted to...: 承蒙您的好意, 心裏非常感激. I am greatly indebted to you for your kindness.

承命(ㄔㄥˊ ㄇㄧㄥˋ)
to accept instructions

承乏(ㄔㄥˊ ㄈㄚˊ)
a conventional expression used by an incumbent referring to himself

承奉(ㄔㄥˊ ㄈㄥˋ)
by order of; in compliance with an order: 軍隊承奉指揮官的命令前進. The army advanced by order of the commander.

承擔(ㄔㄥˊ ㄉㄢ) or 承當(ㄔㄥˊ ㄉㄤ)
to shoulder or to take (the responsibility, task, etc.): 我對這行動承擔全責. (take full

responsibility for this action.

承兌(ㄔㄥˊ ㄉㄨㄟˋ)
to accept; acceptance

承祧(ㄔㄥˊ ㄊㄧㄠ)
to adopt as an heir

承諾(ㄔㄥˊ ㄋㄨㄛˋ)
a promise; to promise; to agree to; to undertake: 我不能作承諾. I can not promise.

承攬(ㄔㄥˊ ㄌㄢˇ)
to take full charge or responsibility (usually under contract); to manage or undertake a task, project, etc.

承露盤(ㄔㄥˊ ㄌㄨˋ ㄆㄢˊ)
a plate for collecting dewdrops which Chinese emperors used to pray to gods

承購(ㄔㄥˊ ㄍㄡˋ)
to act as a purchasing agent

承管(ㄔㄥˊ ㄍㄨㄢˇ)
to take full charge and responsibility (of)

承歡(ㄔㄥˊ ㄏㄨㄢ)
①to please parents ②to cater to (superiors)

承歡膝下(ㄔㄥˊ ㄏㄨㄢ ㄒㄧ ㄒㄧㄚˋ)
to please one's parents by living with them

承繼(ㄔㄥˊ ㄐㄧˋ)
①to inherit ②to continue an unfinished task left by a predecessor

承繼權(ㄔㄥˊ ㄐㄧˋ ㄑㄩㄢˊ)
the right of inheritance

承繼人(ㄔㄥˊ ㄐㄧˋ ㄖㄣˊ)
an heir or heiress

承接(ㄔㄥˊ ㄐㄧㄝ)
to receive and carry on; to continue; to succeed to

承教(ㄔㄥˊ ㄐㄧㄠˋ)
much obliged for your instructions, advice, etc.

承情(ㄔㄥˊ ㄑㄧㄥˊ)
much obliged for your kindness

承襲(ㄔㄥˊ ㄒㄧˊ)
to inherit (a title, etc.): 他承襲了父親的爵位. He inherited his father's title.

承銷(ㄔㄥˊ ㄒㄧㄠ)
consignment-in (or inward); goods-in on consignments; shipment inward

承銷人(ㄔㄥˊ ㄒㄧㄠ ㄖㄣˊ)
a consignee

〔手部〕

〔手部〕

承先啟後(ㄔㄥ ㄒㄧㄢ ㄑㄧˇ ㄏㄡˋ)
to be heir to ancient sages and the teacher of posterity (usually said of a person of profound learning)

承輯(ㄔㄥ ㄓㄨㄢˇ)
to forward (a document to the next level above or below)

承重(ㄔㄥ ㄓㄨㄥˋ)
bearing; load-bearing

承重孫(ㄔㄥ ㄓㄨㄥˋ ㄙㄨㄣ)
eldest grandson whose deceased father was heir to the grandparents—a term referring to oneself in the death announcement of either of one's grandparents

承寵(ㄔㄥ ㄔㄨㄥˇ)
Thank you for your kindness and favors.

承受(ㄔㄥ ㄕㄡˋ)
to take; to receive; to accept; to bear: 他承受不了那噪鬧聲。He can't bear the noise.

承上啟下(ㄔㄥ ㄕㄤˋ ㄑㄧˇ ㄒㄧㄚˋ)
to carry on; to continue (a statement, an account, etc.); to pass on (learning, etc.)

承認(ㄔㄥ ㄖㄣˋ)
①to confess; to admit: 他承認偷了錢。He confessed to having stolen money. ②to recognize (a nation, a new regime, etc): 他們承認他是合法繼承人。They recognized him as the lawful heir.

承載(ㄔㄥ ㄗㄞˋ)
to bear the weight of

承造(ㄔㄥ ㄗㄠˋ)
to manufacture or build something for someone else

承租(ㄔㄥ ㄗㄨ)
to rent

承恩(ㄔㄥ ㄣ)
to receive grace (from the emperor, etc.)

承顏(ㄔㄥ ㄧㄢˊ)
①to be pleased to meet ②to carry favor by fawning

承問(ㄔㄥ ㄨㄣˋ)
Thank you for inquiring.

承望(ㄔㄥ ㄨㄤˋ)
to think of; to expect

承允(ㄔㄥ ㄩㄣˇ)
to agree; to promise

承運(ㄔㄥ ㄩㄣˋ)
(said of the throne) to be ordained by Heaven; to have received the heavenly mandate

五畫

【抱】 1826
ㄅㄠˋ baw bào

1. to embrace; to enfold; to hold in the arms: 他擁抱著她。He embraced her in his arms.
2. to harbor; to cherish; to bosom
3. to adopt
4. aspirations; ambition: 她的抱負是成爲一位爲醫生。Her ambition is to become a doctor.
5. a Chinese family name

抱悲觀(ㄅㄠˋ ㄅㄟ ㄍㄨㄢ)
to feel pessimistic; to be pessimistic

抱病(ㄅㄠˋ ㄅㄧㄥˋ)or抱恙(ㄅㄠˋ ㄧㄤˋ)
indisposed; sick or ill: 她抱病工作。She went on working in spite of ill health.

抱不平(ㄅㄠˋ ㄅㄨˋ ㄆㄧㄥˊ)
indignant at injustice; to feel the injustice done to another and wish to help: 他替她打抱不平。He defended her against an injustice.

抱璞(ㄅㄠˋ ㄆㄨˊ)
to harbor no ambitions and be content with what one already has; free from passions and desires

抱璞(ㄅㄠˋ ㄆㄨˊ)
to possess talent which is not recognized

抱佛脚(ㄅㄠˋ ㄈㄛˊ ㄐㄧㄠˇ)
(literally) to clasp Buddha's feet—a last-minute rush

抱負(ㄅㄠˋ ㄈㄨˋ)
aspirations; ambition

抱負不凡(ㄅㄠˋ ㄈㄨˋ ㄅㄨˋ ㄈㄢˊ)
to entertain high aspirations; very ambitious

抱定決心(ㄅㄠˋ ㄉㄧㄥˋ ㄐㄩㄝˊ ㄒㄧㄣ)
determined; to hold on to one's determination

抱獨身主義(ㄅㄠˋ ㄉㄨˊ ㄕㄣ ㄓㄨˇ ㄧˋ)
to decide to live as a bachelor or spinster

抱頭痛哭(ㄅㄠˋ ㄊㄡˊ ㄊㄨㄥˋ ㄎㄨ)
to bury one's head in one's arms and cry bitterly

抱頭鼠竄(ㄅㄠˋ ㄊㄡˊ ㄕㄨˇ ㄘㄨㄢˋ)
to flee ignominiously; to run helter-skelter

抱樂觀(ㄅㄠˋ ㄌㄜˋ ㄍㄨㄢ)
to feel optimistic; to be optimistic

抱關擊柝(ㄅㄠˋ ㄍㄨㄢ ㄐㄧ ㄊㄨㄛˋ)
(literally) doorkeepers and night watchmen—humblest government employees

抱愧(ㄅㄠˋ ㄎㄨㄟˋ)
to feel ashamed

抱空窩(ㄅㄠˋ ㄎㄨㄥ ㄨㄛ)
(literally) to guard an empty nest—to cherish no ambitions; unsuccessful but resigned

抱憾(ㄅㄠˋ ㄏㄢˋ)
to deplore; to regret; to be sorry about

抱恨終身(ㄅㄠˋ ㄏㄣˋ ㄓㄨㄥ ㄕㄣ)or恨終天(ㄅㄠˋ ㄏㄣˋ ㄓㄨㄥ ㄊㄧㄢ)
to feel remorse for the rest of one's life; to regret something to the end of one's days

抱節君(ㄅㄠˋ ㄐㄧㄝˊ ㄐㄩㄣ)
bamboo

抱緊(ㄅㄠˋ ㄐㄧㄣˇ)
to hold tightly in one's arms

抱歉(ㄅㄠˋ ㄑㄧㄢˋ)
to feel sorry about; to regret: 抱歉給你添麻煩。I am sorry to trouble you.

抱屈(ㄅㄠˋ ㄑㄩ)
to bear a grudge; to harbor resentment

抱屈含冤(ㄅㄠˋ ㄑㄩ ㄏㄢˊ ㄩㄢ)
to be wronged and aggrieved; to bear a deep grudge

抱薪救火(ㄅㄠˋ ㄒㄧㄣ ㄐㄧㄡˋ ㄏㄨㄛˇ)
to add fuel to the fire—to make the situation even worse

抱着(ㄅㄠˋ ˙ㄓㄜ)
to hold in one's arms; to embrace

抱住(ㄅㄠˋ ㄓㄨˋ)
to hold in one's arms; to hold on to

抱柱(ㄅㄠˋ ㄓㄨˋ)
to keep one's promise faithfully

抱罪(ㄅㄠˋ ㄗㄨㄟˋ)

to be conscious of guilt; to be ashamed

抱殘守缺 (ㄅㄠ ㄘㄢ ㄕㄡ ㄑㄩㄝ)
(literally) to cherish broken and worn-out things—extremely conservative; sticking to old ways

抱粗腿 (ㄅㄠ ㄘㄨ ㄊㄨㄟ)
to have strong support or backing of an influential person

抱一 (ㄅㄠ ㄧ)
to stick to one principle

抱慘 (ㄅㄠ ㄘㄢ)
to assist; to help; to lend support to

抱養 (ㄅㄠ ㄧㄤ)
to adopt and raise: 他們抱養那小孩為後嗣。They adopted the child as their heir.

抱窩 (ㄅㄠ ㄨㄛ) or 抱蛋 (ㄅㄠ ㄉㄢ)
(said of hens, etc.) to hatch eggs; to brood

抱甕灌園 (ㄅㄠ ㄨㄥ ㄍㄨㄢ ㄩㄢ)
(literally) to water the vegetable garden with an urn in one's arms—to do things in an unimaginative or inefficient way; to make a lot of efforts but get poor result

抱怨 (ㄅㄠ ㄩㄢ)
to complain; to grumble; to blame (another)

【抨】 1827
ㄆㄥ peng pēng
to impeach; to censure; to attack or to assail by words

抨劾 (ㄆㄥ ㄏㄜ) or 抨彈 (ㄆㄥ ㄊㄢ)
to impeach; to censure

抨擊 (ㄆㄥ ㄐㄧ)
to attack or assail by words; to criticize; to lash

【披】 1828
ㄆㄧ pi pī
(又讀 ㄆㄟ pei pēi)

1. to open (a book, scroll, etc.); to unroll
2. to spread out; to disperse
3. to thumb through or read casually
4. to throw on (a garment, etc.); to wear untidily

披蔴帶孝 (ㄆㄧ ㄇㄚˊ ㄉㄞˋ ㄒㄧㄠˋ)
to put on mourning apparel (especially said of sons or daughters of the deceased)

①(said of grass, etc.) blown about by the wind ②(said of an army) beaten and scattered; routed; to put to rout; to flee

披髮 (ㄆㄧ ㄈㄚˇ)
disheveled hair

披風 (ㄆㄧ ㄈㄥ)
a cape

披拂 (ㄆㄧ ㄈㄨˊ)
windblown

披讀 (ㄆㄧ ㄉㄨˊ)
to read; to open and read

披頭 (ㄆㄧ ㄊㄡˊ)
the Beatles—a British vocal group popular in the mid-1960's

披頭散髮 (ㄆㄧ ㄊㄡˊ ㄙㄢˋ ㄈㄚˇ)
disheveled hair (often referring to an untidy woman); with hair in disarray

披覽 (ㄆㄧ ㄌㄢˇ)
to peruse; to open and read: 他披覽群書。He perused books of all sorts.

披離 (ㄆㄧ ㄌㄧˊ)
blown about, as leaves; scattered

披歷 (ㄆㄧ ㄌㄧˋ) or 披肝瀝膽 (ㄆㄧˋ ㄍㄢ ㄌㄧˋ ㄉㄢˇ)
to open one's heart and talk; to have a heart-to-heart talk; to talk without reserve; to be perfectly frank

披露 (ㄆㄧ ㄌㄨˋ)
to reveal; to make known; to publish

披露心曲 (ㄆㄧ ㄌㄨˋ ㄒㄧㄣ ㄑㄩˇ)
to tell one's innermost thoughts

披掛 (ㄆㄧ ㄍㄨㄚˋ)
to wear full battle dress; to saddle up

披掛上陣 (ㄆㄧ ㄍㄨㄚˋ ㄕㄤˋ ㄓㄣˋ)
to wear full battle dress and go into battle

披豁 (ㄆㄧ ㄏㄨㄛˋ)
to open one's heart in perfect frankness; to talk without reserve

披懷 (ㄆㄧ ㄏㄨㄞˊ)
to be very frank; to open one's heart; to harbor no secret

披紅 (ㄆㄧ ㄏㄨㄥˊ)
to drape a person with red silk—to congratulate or cel-

ebrate his success, exploits, etc.

披枷帶鎖 (ㄆㄧ ㄐㄧㄚ ㄉㄞˋ ㄙㄨㄛˇ)
(said of criminals) manacled and cangued

披甲 (ㄆㄧ ㄐㄧㄚˇ)
to wear armor

披肩 (ㄆㄧ ㄐㄧㄢ)
a shawl

披堅執銳 (ㄆㄧ ㄐㄧㄢ ㄓˊ ㄖㄨㄟˋ)
to wear armor and hold weapons—in full combat-readiness

披襟 (ㄆㄧ ㄐㄧㄣ)
①to open the front of one's garment ②to be honest and sincere

披荊斬棘 (ㄆㄧ ㄐㄧㄥ ㄓㄢˇ ㄐㄧˊ)
①to cultivate land as a pioneer ②to travel through thick bushes and dense jungles ③to fight an uphill battle: 他披荊斬棘以獲成功。He fought an uphill battle to win success.

披卷 (ㄆㄧ ㄐㄩㄢˇ)
to open a volume and read

披心 (ㄆㄧ ㄒㄧㄣ)
①to open and show one's heart—perfectly honest and sincere ②extremely attentive and careful

披星戴月 (ㄆㄧ ㄒㄧㄥ ㄉㄞˋ ㄩㄝˋ)
①to travel by night: 他披星戴月趕回家。He went home by night.②to toil night and day

披猖揚屬 (ㄆㄧ ㄔㄤ ㄧㄤˊ ㄕㄨˇ)
(said of gangsters) to treat law and order with contempt

披沙揀金 (ㄆㄧ ㄕㄚ ㄐㄧㄢˇ ㄐㄧㄣ)
(literally) to spread the sand and pick the gold—to be extremely careful in making selection; to get essentials from a large mass of material

披緇 (ㄆㄧ ㄗ)
to become a monk or nun

披散著頭 (ㄆㄧ ㄙㄢˋ ˙ㄓㄜ ㄊㄡˊ)
with disheveled hair

披索 (ㄆㄧ ㄙㄨㄛˇ)
(monetary) peso

披衣 (ㄆㄧ ㄧ)
to throw on clothes: 她披衣而起。She threw on a gown

〔手部〕

and rose.

披阅(ㄆㄧ ㄩㄝˋ)
to read and appreciate

披阅(ㄆㄧ ㄩㄝˋ)
to read

披云雾见青天(ㄆㄧ ㄩㄣˊ ㄨˋ ㄐㄧㄢˋ ㄑㄧㄥ ㄊㄧㄢ)
(literally) to open the clouds and see the blue skies —to see the truth after the dust settles

【抵】 1829
ㄉㄧˇ dǐi dǐ

1. to resist; to oppose: 他们勇敢地抵抗敌人。They resisted the enemy bravely.

2. to prop; to sustain

3. to offset; to balance: 收支相抵。The accounts are balanced.

4. to substitute; to give as an equivalent

5. to offer as collateral

6. to arrive at; to reach (a place): 我们已平安抵达。We have arrived safely.

7. to go against; to offend against (the law and regulations)

抵埠(ㄉㄧˇ ㄅㄨˋ)
to reach port; to arrive in port

抵不住(ㄉㄧˇ ㄅㄨˋ ㄓㄨˋ)
①unable to resist or hold out ②(said of a collateral) inadequate or insufficient

抵冒(ㄉㄧˇ ㄇㄠˋ)
to offend

抵命(ㄉㄧˇ ㄇㄧㄥˋ)
a life for a life

抵法(ㄉㄧˇ ㄈㄚˇ)
to be punished by law

抵达(ㄉㄧˇ ㄉㄚˊ)
to arrive at or reach (a place)

抵挡(ㄉㄧˇ ㄉㄤˇ)
to resist; to sustain; to ward off: 他们抵挡敌人的攻击。They ward off the enemy's attack.

抵当(ㄉㄧˇ ㄉㄤ)
to offer as a collateral; to give as an equivalent

抵敌(ㄉㄧˇ ㄉㄧˊ)
to resist the enemy

抵赖(ㄉㄧˇ ㄌㄞˋ)
to deny mistakes or crimes one has committed, or to

renege a promise one has given: 你的过错是不容抵赖的。Your fault cannot be denied.

抵扣(ㄉㄧˇ ㄎㄡˋ)
to deduct from

抵抗(ㄉㄧˇ ㄎㄤˋ)
to resist; to oppose; to fight against (an enemy, etc.); to withstand; to hold out against; resistance: 他们正在抵抗敌人的攻击。They are withstanding the enemy's attack.

抵抗力(ㄉㄧˇ ㄎㄤˋ ㄌㄧˋ)
the force or power of resistance

抵抗器(ㄉㄧˇ ㄎㄤˋ ㄑㄧˋ)
(electricity) a rheostat 亦作「變阻器」

抵抗圈(ㄉㄧˇ ㄎㄤˋ ㄑㄩㄢ)
(electricity) a resistance coil

抵抗性(ㄉㄧˇ ㄎㄤˋ ㄒㄧㄥˋ)
resistibility

抵换(ㄉㄧˇ ㄏㄨㄢˋ)
to substitute (one thing for another)

抵借(ㄉㄧˇ ㄐㄧㄝˋ)
to pledge against a loan

抵蹈瑕隙(ㄉㄧˇ ㄒㄧㄚˊ ㄒㄧˋ)
to exploit the shortcomings of another

抵销(ㄉㄧˇ ㄒㄧㄠ)
to offset; to counteract; to neutralize; to nullify

抵销关税(ㄉㄧˇ ㄒㄧㄠ ㄍㄨㄢ ㄕㄨㄟˋ)
countervailing duties

抵制(ㄉㄧˇ ㄓˋ)
①to resist ②to boycott: 他们抵制日货。They boycotted Japanese goods.

抵制外货(ㄉㄧˇ ㄓˋ ㄨㄞˋ ㄏㄨㄛˋ)
to boycott foreign goods

抵债(ㄉㄧˇ ㄓㄞˋ)
to pay a debt with goods or by labor

抵掌而谈(ㄉㄧˇ ㄓㄤˇ ㄦˊ ㄊㄢˊ)
to talk pleasantly or intimately; to have a pleasant conversation

抵账 or 抵帐(ㄉㄧˇ ㄓㄤˋ)
to repay a debt with goods or articles of equivalent value

抵住(ㄉㄧˇ ㄓㄨˋ)
to resist; to hold out

抵偿(ㄉㄧˇ ㄔㄤˊ)
to compensate; to atone for: 没有什麽可以抵偿一个人健康的损失。Nothing can compensate for the loss of one's health.

抵触(ㄉㄧˇ ㄔㄨˋ)
in contravention of (the law or regulations); to contravene: 這是與法律相抵触的举动。It is an act in contravention of the law.

抵充(ㄉㄧˇ ㄔㄨㄥ)
to use something as a substitute

抵数(ㄉㄧˇ ㄕㄨˋ)
to balance an account

抵足而眠(ㄉㄧˇ ㄗㄨˊ ㄦˊ ㄇㄧㄢˊ)
(said of very good friends) to share the same bed

抵罪(ㄉㄧˇ ㄗㄨㄟˋ)
to mete out appropriate punishment for a crime committed

抵死(ㄉㄧˇ ㄙˇ)
①to persist; to insist; persistently: 我们抵死不降。We persistently refuse to surrender. ②excessive

抵押(ㄉㄧˇ ㄧㄚ)
to mortgage; to collateralize

抵押品(ㄉㄧˇ ㄧㄚ ㄆㄧㄣˇ)
collateral; security; pledges: 她拿他的錶當抵押品。She held his watch as a pledge.

抵押权(ㄉㄧˇ ㄧㄚ ㄑㄩㄢˊ)
(law) the right of the creditor to receive payment on priority basis upon the selling of the property offered him as security by the debtor; mortgage

抵押书(ㄉㄧˇ ㄧㄚ ㄕㄨ)
a letter of hypothecation

抵押人(ㄉㄧˇ ㄧㄚ ㄖㄣˊ)
a mortgagor

抵悟(ㄉㄧˇ ㄨˋ)
to conflict with; to go against

抵禦(ㄉㄧˇ ㄩˋ)
to resist; to withstand

抵禦外侮(ㄉㄧˇ ㄩˋ ㄨㄞˋ ㄨˇ)
to resist foreign aggression

【抹】 1830
ㄇㄛˇ moo mǒ

1. to wipe; to rub; to mop

2. to smear; to apply to: 他替手抹上油。He smeared his

hands with grease.

3. to obliterate; to blot out: 好幾個字都被塗抹掉了。Several words have been blotted out.

抹脖子(ㄇㄛ ㄅㄛ ˙ㄗ)or 抹頸(ㄇㄛ ㄐㄧㄥ)
to commit suicide by slicing one's throat

抹布(ㄇㄛ ㄅㄨ)
a dish cloth; a mopper; a cleaning rag

抹片(ㄇㄛ ㄆㄧㄢ)
a smear (a small quantity of something spread thinly on a slide for microscopic examination)

抹了良心(ㄇㄛ ˙ㄌㄜ ㄌㄧㄤ ㄒㄧㄣ)
to blot out all the moral sense; unconscionable; devoid of conscience

抹淚(ㄇㄛ ㄌㄟ)
to wipe away one's tears

抹乾(ㄇㄛ ㄍㄢ)
to wipe dry

抹乾淨(ㄇㄛ ㄍㄢ ㄐㄧㄥ)
to wipe clean

抹黑(ㄇㄛ ㄏㄟ)
(informal) to blacken someone's name; to throw mud at; to bring shame on; to discredit; mudslinging 亦作「中傷」

抹去(ㄇㄛ ㄑㄩ)or 抹掉(ㄇㄛ ㄉㄧㄠ)
to wipe up; to obliterate; to blot out; to cross out; to erase: 這男孩抹去了所有鉛筆的筆跡。The boy erased all pencil marks.

抹稀泥(ㄇㄛ ㄒㄧ ㄋㄧ)
to calm an angry person with soft and gentle words

抹下臉來(ㄇㄛ ㄒㄧㄚ ㄌㄧㄢ ㄌㄞ)
to show anger or displeasure suddenly

抹香鯨(ㄇㄛ ㄒㄧㄤ ㄐㄧㄥ)
sperm whale, so named on account of the ambergris (龍涎香)

抹桌子(ㄇㄛ ㄓㄨㄛ ˙ㄗ)
to wipe a table

抹殺(ㄇㄛ ㄕㄚ)or 抹煞(ㄇㄛ ㄕㄚ)
purposely fail to mention (one's merits, achievements, etc.); to withhold recognition for; do not give credit to: 他們抹殺了某些事實。They purposely failed to mention

certain facts.

抹子(ㄇㄛ ˙ㄗ)
a trowel for plastering; a mason's spade for applying mortar

抹一鼻子灰(ㄇㄛ ㄧ ㄅㄧ ˙ㄗ ㄏㄨㄟ)
to get rebuffed when trying to please; to get an awkward rebuff; to suffer a snub

【抹】 1830
2. ㄇㄛ moh mò
1. to plaster: 他 在 抹牆。He's plastering a wall.
2. a tight undergarment
3. to turn: 他們剛抹過轉角。They just turned the corner of the road.

抹灰(ㄇㄛ ㄏㄨㄟ)
(construction) plastering

抹胸(ㄇㄛ ㄒㄩㄥ)
a tight undergarment for women worn across the breasts; a stomacher

抹額(ㄇㄛ ㄜ)
a sort of scarf worn across the forehead; a kind of turban

【抽】 1831
ㄔㄡ chou chōu
1. to draw out; to pull out or open; to take out: 他從書架上抽出一本書。He took a book out of his bookshelf.
2. to sprout; to put forth shoots; to bud: 樹在春天開始抽出嫩芽。Trees begin to bud in the spring.
3. to rid; to take away
4. to whip; to lash: 他正在抽陀螺。He is whipping a top.
5. to smoke (cigarettes, etc.): 他抽煙斗。He was smoking a pipe.
6. to shrink: 這件襯衫一洗就抽。This shirt shrinks in the wash.

抽鼻兒(ㄔㄡ ㄅㄧˊㄦ)
to take a deep breath by the nose so as to halt it from running for a while in a bad cold

抽風(ㄔㄡ ㄈㄥ)
(medicine) convulsions

抽風機(ㄔㄡ ㄈㄥ ㄐㄧ)
an exhaust fan

抽搭(ㄔㄡ ㄉㄚ)
the sound of irregular and heavy breathing after a good

cry; to sob in the wake of a bitter cry

抽打(ㄔㄡ ㄉㄚˇ)
to lash; to whip: 他用鞭子抽打馬背。He lashed his horse across the back with a whip.

抽刀(ㄔㄡ ㄉㄠ)
to draw a knife or blade

抽調(ㄔㄡ ㄉㄧㄠˋ)
to transfer (personnel or material)

抽丁(ㄔㄡ ㄉㄧㄥ)
to draft able-bodied men for military service; to press-gang

抽動(ㄔㄡ ㄉㄨㄥˋ)
to twitch; to spasm; a spasmodic jerk: 這小孩抽動著嘴唇像是要哭。The child's mouth twitched as if she were about to cry.

抽頭聚賭(ㄔㄡ ㄊㄡˊ ㄐㄩˋ ㄉㄨˇ)
to operate an unlicensed gambling joint

抽頭兒(ㄔㄡ ㄊㄡˊㄦ)
(said of a gambling house, etc.) to collect from the gamblers a certain percentage of their wins

抽屜(ㄔㄡ ˙ㄊㄧ)
a drawer: 他封住抽屜, 使人無法打開He sealed up a drawer so that it couldn't be opened.

抽工夫兒(ㄔㄡ ㄍㄨㄥ ˙ㄈㄨㄦ)
to spare some time; at one's spare time; to find time (for a task, etc.): 他抽不出工夫兒做那件事。He is unable to find time to do it.

抽考(ㄔㄡ ㄎㄠˇ)
①to select at random a few students from a class for a test ② an unannounced quiz or test

抽空兒(ㄔㄡ ㄎㄨㄥˋㄦ)or 抽閒(ㄔㄡ ㄒㄧㄢˊ)
to find time (to do something); at one's spare time: 出國之前請抽空去探望她。Try and find time to visit her before going abroad.

抽換(ㄔㄡ ㄏㄨㄢˋ)
①to change by rotation as of railroad ties or parts of machinery ② to change the contents of a package with-

〔手部〕

【手部】

抽筋 (イヌ リ lㄣ)
to be seized by spasms or cramps: 他的腿抽筋了。He had a cramp in the leg.

抽筋拔骨 (イヌ リlㄣ ㄅㄚˊ 《ㄨˇ)
very reluctantly; with great difficulty

抽獎 (イヌ リlㄤ)
to draw a lottery or raffle: 抽獎機 a lottery wheel

抽泣 (イヌ くlˋ)
to sob: 她抽泣著述說她的悲慘故事。She sobbed out her sad story.

抽球 (イヌ くlㄡˊ)
(sports) to drive

抽籤 (イヌ くlㄢ)
to draw (or cast) lots: 我們抽籤決定誰當隊長。We draw lots to decide who should be captain.

抽取 (イヌ くㄩˇ)
① to charge or collect a certain percentage of a sum ② to take at random from a batch of samples, etc.

抽薪止沸 (イヌ エlㄣ ㄓˇ ㄈㄟˋ)
(literally) to stop the boiling by taking out the fire — to stop or prevent trouble by removing the cause

抽象 (イヌ エlㄤˋ)
abstract (as opposed to concrete): 請勿如此抽象地談問題。Please don't speak in such abstract terms.

抽象名詞 (イヌ エlㄤˋ ㄇlㄥˊ ㄘˊ)
abstract nouns

抽象概念 (イヌ エlㄤˋ 《ㄞˋ ㄋlㄢˋ)
abstract concepts or ideas

抽象畫 (イヌ エlㄤˋ ㄏㄨㄚˋ)
abstract painting

抽選 (イヌ エㄩㄢˇ)
to select from a lot

抽壯丁 (イヌ ㄓㄨㄤˋ ㄉlㄥ)
to draft able-bodied men for military service; to press-gang

抽查 (イヌ イㄚˊ)
to investigate, survey or test a part of a group

抽出 (イヌ イㄨ)
to draw out; to pull out; to take out: 他把手從口袋抽出。He drew his hand from his pocket.

抽紗 (イヌ ㄕㄚ)
drawnwork

抽身 (イヌ ㄕㄣ)
to get away (while one is fully occupied): 希望於下星期一開始我能抽身去度一星期的假。I hope to get away next Monday for a week.

抽水 (イヌ ㄕㄨㄟˇ)
to pump water: 他們從河裏抽水。They pumped water from the river.

抽水馬桶 (イヌ ㄕㄨㄟˇ ㄇㄚˇ ㄊㄨㄥˇ)
a flush toilet

抽水機 (イヌ ㄕㄨㄟˇ リl)
a water pump: 村裏的抽水機供應全村的用水。A village pump is one that supplies the whole village with water.

抽稅 (イヌ ㄕㄨㄟˋ)
to levy taxes

抽簪 (イヌ ㄗㄢ)
(literally) to pull out the pins of one's official cap—to renounce one's office

抽絲 (イヌ ㄙ)
① to reel silk ② to do things slowly

抽絲剝繭 (イヌ ㄙ ㄅㄛ リlㄢˇ)
to make a painstaking investigation or examination

抽穗 (イヌ ㄙㄨㄟˋ)
heading; earing: 玉蜀黍正在抽穗。The corn is in the ear.

抽鴉片 (イヌ lㄚ ㄆlㄢˋ)
to smoke opium

抽芽 (イヌ lㄚˊ)
to sprout; to put forth shoots; to bud

抽噎 (イヌ lㄝ)
to sob; sobs; spasms of muscles around the throat, as during or after a cry

抽油煙機 (イヌ lㄡˊ lㄢ リl)
a suction fan installed above a kitchen range to remove oily smoke from the kitchen

抽烟 or 抽煙 (イヌ lㄢ)
to smoke (a pipe, cigars, cigarets, etc.): 這部車內不可抽煙。You must not smoke in this carriage.

抽印 (イヌ lㄣˋ)
to offprint: 抽印本 an offprint

抽樣 (イヌ lㄤˋ)
a sample; sampling

抽樣調查 (イヌ lㄤˋ ㄊlㄠˋ イㄚˊ)
sampling

【押】 1832 (lㄚ ia yā)

1. to mortgage; to pawn; to pledge; to obtain loans against securities: 他以車子作押。He left his car as security.

2. to detain or imprison (temporarily): to keep under detention

3. to escort: 他們把小偷押到警所去。They escorted the thief to the police station.

4. a signature: 畫押 to mark (a document) in lieu of signature (for the illiterate); to sign

押寶 (lㄚ ㄅㄠˇ)
a gambling game, played with dice under a bowl

押票 (lㄚ ㄆlㄠˋ)
a warrant for arrest

押封 (lㄚ ㄈㄥ)
to seal and attach (property)

押當 (lㄚ ㄉㄤ)
① to pawn: 我押當了手錶。I pawned my watch. ② a pawnshop

押定 (lㄚ ㄉlㄥˋ)
to sign an agreement

押頭 (lㄚ ˙ㄊㄡ)
collateral; goods offered as security

押款 (lㄚ ㄎㄨㄢˇ)
to obtain loans against security; to mortgage

押貨 (lㄚ ㄏㄨㄛˋ)
① to mortgage goods ② to escort a shipment of goods from one place to another

押匯 (lㄚ ㄏㄨㄟˋ)
documentary draft negotiation

押解 (lㄚ リlㄝˋ)
to transfer or deport (suspects, prisoners, goods, etc.) from one place to another under escort or guard: 這個間諜被押解出境。The spy was deported under escort.

押金 (lㄚ リlㄣ)
a cash pledge; a deposit

押陣 (lㄚ ㄓㄣˋ)
(formerly) crack troops, etc.

which were supposed to secure the whole position in a battle

押賬 or 押帳 (丨ㄚ ㄓㄤ)
goods, etc. offered as security for a loan

押租 (丨ㄚ ㄗㄨ)
key money advanced by the lodger as a guarantee of his compliance with the terms of the renting agreement; a rent deposit; deposit money

押歲錢 (丨ㄚ ㄙㄨㄟˋ ㄑ丨ㄢˊ)
money given to children by elders on the Lunar New Year's Eve

押送 (丨ㄚ ㄙㄨㄥˋ)
to send (goods or criminals) to another place under escort or guard

押尾 (丨ㄚ ㄨㄟˇ) or 押字 (丨ㄚ ㄗ)
to sign one's name at the end of a legal document

押運 (丨ㄚ ㄩㄣˋ)
to supervise and escort the transportation of goods, etc.

押韻 (丨ㄚ ㄩㄣˋ)
to rhyme: 使一字與另一字押韻 to rhyme one word with another

【拄】 1833 ㄓㄨˇ juu zhǔ
1. a post; a prop
2. to lean on (a stick, etc.): 他拄著拐杖走路。He walked with (the help of) a stick.
3. to ridicule; to make sarcastic remarks

拄笏看山 (ㄓㄨˇ ㄏㄨˋ ㄎㄢˋ ㄕㄢ)
to have a deep liking for natural charms even when occupying a high position; to retain refined taste despite the corruptive influence of officialdom

拄杖 (ㄓㄨˇ ㄓㄤˋ) or 拄拐 (ㄓㄨˇ ㄍㄨㄞˇ) or 拄棍 (ㄓㄨˇ ㄍㄨㄣˋ)
a crutch, staff or stick: 他們拄杖而行。They went on crutches.

【拂】 1834 1. ㄈㄨˊ fwu fú
1. to brush; to shake; to whisk: 她拂去桌子上的碎屑。She whisked the crumbs from the table.
2. to dust; a duster: 請小心拂拭。Please dust carefully.

3. to oppose; to disobey: 他不忍拂其雙親意。He does not have the heart to disobey his parents' wishes.
4. to expel; to drive away

拂面 (ㄈㄨˊ ㄇㄧㄢˋ)
(said of breezes, leaves, etc.) to brush or caress the face lightly or gently: 春風拂面。The spring wind caresses the cheeks.

拂拂 (ㄈㄨˊ ㄈㄨˊ)
the soft blowing of breezes

拂逆 (ㄈㄨˊ ㄋㄧˋ) or 拂戾 (ㄈㄨˊ ㄌㄧˋ)
① disagreeable ② disastrous

拂慮 (ㄈㄨˊ ㄌㄩˋ)
to drive away cares and worries; to be carefree

拂曉 (ㄈㄨˊ ㄒㄧㄠˇ) or 拂曙 (ㄈㄨˊ ㄕㄨˋ)
daybreak; dawn

拂袖 (ㄈㄨˊ ㄒㄧㄡˋ)
to shake one's sleeve—an expression of displeasure or anger

拂袖而去 (ㄈㄨˊ ㄒㄧㄡˋ ㄦˊ ㄑㄩˋ)
to leave in displeasure or anger

拂晨 (ㄈㄨˊ ㄔㄣˊ)
daybreak; dawn

拂塵 (ㄈㄨˊ ㄔㄣˊ)
① to shake off dust; to whisk the dust off ② a duster made of long animal hairs

拂除 (ㄈㄨˊ ㄔㄨˊ)
to wipe off; to brush off (dust, etc.): 我不能將這塊泥土拂除。I can't brush the dirt off.

拂拭 (ㄈㄨˊ ㄕˋ)
to wipe and clean (a piece of furniture, etc.): 將桌子拂拭乾淨。Wipe the table clean.

拂暑 (ㄈㄨˊ ㄕㄨˇ)
to expel the heat (of summer)

拂人性 (ㄈㄨˊ ㄖㄣˊ ㄒㄧㄥˋ)
to go against human nature

拂耳 (ㄈㄨˊ ㄦˇ)
(said of words, etc.) that grate on the ear

拂衣 (ㄈㄨˊ 丨)
① to tidy up one's dress upon leaving ② to resign and retire

拂意 (ㄈㄨˊ 丨ˋ)
to run counter to one's ideas; to feel thwarted

【拂】 1834 2. (粵) ㄅㄧˋ bih bì
1. to aid; to assist
2. to make correct or right

拂士 (ㄅㄧˋ ㄕˋ)
a wise counselor; a straight-forward adviser

【拇】 1835 ㄇㄨˇ muu mǔ
1. the thumb
2. the big toe

拇指 (ㄇㄨˇ ㄓˇ)
the thumb

拇趾 (ㄇㄨˇ ㄓˇ)
the big toe

拇戰 (ㄇㄨˇ ㄓㄢˋ)
a finger guessing game (played at drinking parties)

拇印 (ㄇㄨˇ 丨ㄣˋ)
a thumbprint—used in lieu of a chop in an agreement, etc.

【拈】 1836 ㄋㄧㄢˊ nian niān
1. to take or hold with fingers; to pick up: 那些書是信手拈來的。Those books were picked up at random.
2. to draw (lots)

拈筆 (ㄋㄧㄢˊ ㄅㄧˇ)
to take a pen; to pick up a pen to write; to write

拈提 (ㄋㄧㄢˊ ㄊㄧˊ)
to point out; to refer to

拈題 (ㄋㄧㄢˊ ㄊㄧˊ)
to select a topic or theme for a piece of writing

拈弄 (ㄋㄧㄢˊ ㄋㄨㄥˋ)
to finger and play; to fondle: 這女孩在拈弄着洋娃娃。The girl is fondling her doll.

拈花惹草 (ㄋㄧㄢˊ ㄏㄨㄚ ㄖㄜˇ ㄘㄠˇ)
to fool around with women; to play Casanova; lewd and prurient; to have many love affairs

拈花微笑 (ㄋㄧㄢˊ ㄏㄨㄚ ㄨㄟˊ ㄒㄧㄠˋ)
to gain a thorough understanding of esoteric Buddhist teachings

拈鬮 (ㄋㄧㄢˊ ㄐㄧㄡ)
to draw lots

拈香 (ㄋㄧㄢˊ ㄒㄧㄤ)
to offer incense; to burn joss sticks: 她去廟裡拈香。She went to the temple to offer incense.

拈鬚 (ㄋㄧㄢˊ ㄒㄩ)

〔手部〕

〔手部〕

to finger one's beard; to stroke one's beard

拈酸(ㄋㄧㄢ ㄙㄨㄢ)or 拈酸吃醋
(ㄋㄧㄢ ㄙㄨㄢ ㄔ ㄘㄨ)
to be jealous

1837

【拆】(ㄔㄞ chai chāi)(讀音 ㄔㄜ cheh che)

1. to split; to break; to rip open: 他 拆開一封信。He ripped open a letter.

2. to take down; to tear down (a house, etc.); to destroy; to dismantle; to take apart: 他把機器拆了。He took the machine apart.

3. to analyze; to scrutinize

拆字(ㄔㄞ ㄗˋ)
to take apart characters and recombine them for fortune-telling「測字」

拆字格(ㄔㄞ ㄗˋ ㄍㄜ˙)
a kind of poem-writing by dissecting and combining characters in a poem

拆白(ㄔㄞ ㄅㄞˊ)
to swindle

拆白黨(ㄔㄞ ㄅㄞˊ ㄉㄤˇ)
swindlers

拆房屋(ㄔㄞ ㄈㄤˊ ㄨ)
to tear or pull down a house

拆封(ㄔㄞ ㄈㄥ)
to break up a seal; to open a sealed envelope

拆東牆補西牆(ㄔㄞ ㄉㄨㄥ ㄑㄧㄤˊ ㄅㄨˇ ㄒㄧ ㄑㄧㄤˊ)
(literally) to mend the west wall by tearing down the east wall—to try very hard to make ends meet

拆臺(ㄔㄞ ㄊㄞˊ)
(literally) to pull down the stage—to split up; to pull away a prop; to render an organization, operation, measure, etc. ineffective; to obstruct; to counteract: 別拆我的臺。Don't undermine what I am doing.

拆爛汙(ㄔㄞ ㄌㄢˋ ㄨ)
①to do a slipshod piece of work with damaging result; to do slovenly work; to be irresponsible ②to fail to keep a promise or an appointment

拆股(ㄔㄞ ㄍㄨˇ)

to dissolve a partnership

拆開(ㄔㄞ ㄎㄞ)
to take apart; to dismantle (a machine, etc.); to pull apart; to part from each other; to open (a package, letter, etc.); to separate

拆夥(ㄔㄞ ㄏㄨㄛˇ)
to break up partnership; to part company

拆壞(ㄔㄞ ㄏㄨㄞˋ)
to damage; to destroy

拆毀(ㄔㄞ ㄏㄨㄟˇ)
to damage; to destroy; to demolish

拆息(ㄔㄞ ㄒㄧˊ)
short-term interest

拆洗(ㄔㄞ ㄒㄧˇ)
to unpick (a cover, bedspread, etc.) and wash; to take apart (a machine, etc.) for cleaning

拆卸(ㄔㄞ ㄒㄧㄝˋ)
to take apart a large cargo (usually a large piece of machinery, etc.) for unloading purposes; to dismantle

拆線(ㄔㄞ ㄒㄧㄢˋ)
(medicine) to take out stitches

拆信(ㄔㄞ ㄒㄧㄣˋ)
to open a letter

拆除(ㄔㄞ ㄔㄨˊ)
to dismantle and get rid of; to pull down (an old house); to remove; to demolish: 工人們 拆除了那建築物。The workers pulled the building down.

拆穿(ㄔㄞ ㄔㄨㄢ)
to expose (a secret, scheme, etc.); to see through (a mystery, secret arrangement, etc.): 他拆穿了他們的陰謀。He exposed their plot.

拆穿西洋鏡(ㄔㄞ ㄔㄨㄢ ㄒㄧ ㄧㄤˊ ㄐㄧㄥˋ)
to expose a secret arrangement, device, scheme, etc.

拆船(ㄔㄞ ㄔㄨㄢˊ)
to break up or scrap a ship; shipbreaking

拆散(ㄔㄞ ㄙㄢˋ)
to break up or split apart a family, a married couple, etc.); to dismantle

拆散鴛鴦(ㄔㄞ ㄙㄢˋ ㄩㄢ ㄧㄤ)

(said of some happenings or incidents) to separate lovers or break up a married couple

拆閱(ㄔㄞ ㄩㄝˋ)
to open (a letter, document, etc.) and read

1838

【拉】 1. (ㄌㄚ lha lā)

1. to pull; to drag; to hold; to seize; to draw: 把你的椅子拉近桌子。Draw your chair nearer to the table.

2. to discharge (especially stool, urine, etc.)

3. to lengthen; to elongate: 薄暮時影子拉得長長的。The shadows lengthened at dusk.

4. to play: 他在早晨拉提琴。He plays the violin in the morning.

拉巴脫(ㄌㄚ ㄅㄚ ㄊㄨㄛ)
Rabat, capital of Morocco

拉巴拉他(ㄌㄚ ㄅㄚ ㄌㄚ ㄊㄚ)
①La Plata, a seaport in eastern Argentina ②Río de la Plata, capital of Buenos Aires Province

拉巴斯(ㄌㄚ ㄅㄚ ㄙ)
①La Paz, former capital of Bolivia in South America ②La Paz, a seaport of Mexico, on the Gulf of California

拉拔(ㄌㄚˇ ㄅㄚˊ)
to help (a protégé) advance

拉不斷扯不斷(ㄌㄚ ㄅㄨˋ ㄉㄨㄢˋ ㄔㄜˇ ㄅㄨˋ ㄉㄨㄢˋ)
long, drawn-out nagging; loquacious; talkative

拉不動(ㄌㄚ ㄅㄨˋ ㄉㄨㄥˋ)
unable to make it move by pulling

拉不開(ㄌㄚ ㄅㄨˋ ㄎㄞ)
cannot pull it open (as a drawer, window, etc.)

拉不下臉來(ㄌㄚ ㄅㄨˋ ㄒㄧㄚˋ ㄌㄧㄢˇ ㄌㄞˊ)
cannot do something for fear of hurting another person's feelings

拉不出來(ㄌㄚ ㄅㄨˋ ㄔㄨ ㄌㄞˊ)
①cannot pull out ②constipated

拉篷(ㄌㄚ ㄆㄥˊ)
to haul up the sail; to set sail

拉皮條(ㄌㄚ ㄆㄧˊ ㄊㄧㄠˊ)

to act as a procurer; to act as a pimp

拉票(カY ㄆㄧㄠ)
to solicit votes; to canvass

拉平(カY ㄆㄧㄥ)
to even up; to end up in a draw; to draw: 兩隊的比分拉平。The game ended in a draw.

拉買賣(カY ㄇㄞˇ·ㄇㄞ)
to act as a broker; to solicit business

拉麵 or **拉麪**(カY ㄇㄧㄢˋ)
noodles made by pulling the dough instead of cutting it by knife

拉斐爾(カY ㄈㄟˇ ㄦˇ)
Sanzio Raphael, 1483-1520, Italian painter

拉夫(カY ㄈㄨ)
to impress civilians for military service or as coolies in war

拉倒(カY ㄉㄠˇ)
① Never mind. 或 Let's forget it. 這件事我看還是拉倒吧!! Let's forget it! ② to pull down

拉丁(カY ㄉㄧㄥ)
Latin

拉丁美洲(カY ㄉㄧㄥ ㄇㄟˇ ㄓㄡ)
Latin America

拉丁化(カY ㄉㄧㄥ ㄏㄨㄚˋ)
Latinized

拉丁教會(カY ㄉㄧㄥ ㄐㄧㄠˋ ㄏㄨㄟˋ)
the Latin Church

拉丁文(カY ㄉㄧㄥ ㄨㄣˊ)
Latin (language)

拉肚子(カY ㄉㄨˋ·ㄗ)
to suffer from diarrhea; to have loose bowels

拉替身兒(カY ㄊㄧˋ·ㄕㄦ)
①(in Chinese folklore) The ghost of a person who died because of injustice has to cause the death of another person in order to achieve his own reincarnation. ② to look for someone to be the scapegoat for oneself

拉脫維亞(カY ㄊㄨㄛ ㄨㄟˊ ㄧㄚˇ)
Latvia

拉尿(カY ㄋㄧㄠˋ)
to urinate

拉弄(カY ·ㄋㄨㄥ)
①to pull apart ② wear and tear

拉扯(カY カㄜˇ ㄔㄜ·ㄔㄜ)
① to pull and drag a person, asking him to do something against his will ② to digress (in speaking)

拉拉雜雜(カY カY ㄗㄚˊ ㄗㄚˊ)or 拉雜(カY ㄗㄚˊ)
(said of writing, narration, etc.) not well organized and without a central theme

拉力(カY カㄧˋ)
(physics) pulling force

拉力試驗(カY カㄧˋ ㄕˋ ㄧㄢˋ)
(machinery) a pull test; a tension test

拉鍊(カY カㄧㄢˋ)
a zipper; a zip fastener

拉攏(カY ·カㄨㄥˇ)
① to befriend another person with a view to winning him over; to draw someone over to one's side; to draw persons with different views together: 不要受敵人拉攏。Don't get roped in by the enemy. ② to make two persons or parties become friends

拉哥斯(カY ·ㄍㄜ ㄙ)
Lagos, capital of Nigeria

拉過來(カY ㄍㄨㄛˋ ·カㄞ)
to drag here

拉關係(カY ㄍㄨㄢ ㄒㄧˋ)
to seek special favor or help from somebody by elaborating on one's relationship (usually remote and indirect) with him; to try to cement ties or establish connections with an ulterior motive

拉廣告(カY ㄍㄨㄤˇ ㄍㄠˋ)
to solicit advertisements from business firms

拉弓(カY ㄍㄨㄥ)
to draw a bow

拉客(カY ㄎㄜˋ)
(said of a prostitute, etc.) to solicit patrons forcibly

拉開(カY ㄎㄞ)
①to pull apart (two persons fighting); to pull open (wrapping paper, drawers, etc.); to draw aside: 把門拉開。Pull the door open. ② to increase the distance between: 兩隊比分已拉開了。The

gap between the scores has widened.

拉後腿(カY ㄏㄡˋ ㄊㄨㄟˇ)
to hold someone back; to be a drag on someone

拉胡琴兒(カY ㄏㄨˊ ㄑㄧㄣˊ·ㄦ)
to play the Chinese violin (a two-string instrument)

拉壞了(カY ㄏㄨㄞˋ·ㄌㄜ)
①damaged because of pulling ② weakened by diarrhea

拉回(カY ㄏㄨㄟˊ)
to pull back

拉家帶口(カY ㄐㄧㄚ ㄉㄞˋ ㄎㄡˇ)
to have a family burden

拉架(カY ㄐㄧㄚˋ)
to mediate in a street fight; to stop a brawl by separating the disputants

拉交情(カY ㄐㄧㄠ ㄑㄧㄥˊ)
to show friendship to someone (usually with a selfish motive or having an ax to grind); to try to seek the friendship of influential persons

拉角(カY ㄐㄧㄠˇ)
to hire employees, actors, actresses, etc. from a rivaling company by offering them high pay, high positions or other incentives

拉緊(カY ㄐㄧㄣˇ)
①to draw or pull tight ② to hang on firmly

拉近(カY ㄐㄧㄣˋ)
to draw close or near

拉鋸(カY ㄐㄩˋ)
①to cut with a saw ② to be locked in a seesaw struggle

拉鋸戰(カY ㄐㄩˋ ㄓㄢˋ)
a seesaw battle; stalemate

拉倒(カY ㄎㄜˇ ㄑㄧˇ)
to pull up; to draw back

拉縴(カY ㄑㄧㄢˋ)
①to tow a boat against the current in a swift stream from the bank ② to act as a go-between

拉稀(カY ㄒㄧ)
to suffer from diarrhea; to have loose bowels

拉下臉來(カY ㄒㄧㄚˋ カㄧㄢˇ·カㄞ)
to make a long face; to look mean

拉下水(カY ㄒㄧㄚˋ ㄕㄨㄟˇ)
to drag someone into the

〔**手部**〕

〔手部〕

mire; to make an accomplice of someone; to corrupt someone

拉賬(ㄌㄚ ㄓㄤ˙)
to run into debt

拉主顧(ㄌㄚ ㄓㄨˇ·ㄍㄨ)
to attract or solicit customers

拉住(ㄌㄚ ㄓㄨˋ)
to hold on firmly: 我們過街時要拉住我的手。Hold on to my hand tightly while we cross the street.

拉持(ㄌㄚ ·ㄔ)
(dialect) to bring someone up

拉車(ㄌㄚ ㄔㄜ)
to pull or haul a cart (or ricksha)

拉車的(ㄌㄚ ㄔㄜ ·ㄉㄜ)
a ricksha puller

拉扯(ㄌㄚ ㄔㄜˇ)
①to pull and drag ②to implicate or involve ③to talk a lot outside of one's topic; to indulge in aimless talks

拉長(ㄌㄚ ㄔㄤˊ)
①to prolong (business, voice, etc.) ②to draw

拉出去(ㄌㄚ ㄔㄨ·ㄑㄩ)
to pull out; to drag out

拉屎(ㄌㄚ ㄕˇ)
to go to stool; to empty the bowels; to move one's bowels

拉舌頭(ㄌㄚ ㄕㄜˊ·ㄊㄡ)
to gossip; to slander

拉手(ㄌㄚ ㄕㄡˇ)
①to hold another's hands ②to pull by the hand ③to join hands; to work together ④a knob

拉手兒(ㄌㄚ ㄕㄡˇㄦ)
①to hold hands; to shake hands ②to collaborate in a scheme, conspiracy, etc.

拉伸(ㄌㄚ ㄕㄣ)
(textile) drawing; stretch

拉上補下(ㄌㄚ ㄕㄤˋㄅㄨˇㄒㄧㄚˋ)
to even things up

拉生意(ㄌㄚ ㄕㄥ·ㄧ)
to solicit business; to tout

拉雜(ㄌㄚ ㄗㄚˊ)
①rambling; jumbled; ill-organized: 那篇文章寫得太拉雜。That article is very bad-

ly organized. ②(said of a room, etc.) untidy; confused

拉絲(ㄌㄚ ㄙ)
①(metallurgy) wiredrawing: 拉絲機a wiredrawing machine ②(said of action) to hesitate ③(said of speech) long-winded

拉斯維加斯(ㄌㄚ ㄙ ㄨㄟˊ ㄐㄧㄚ ㄙ)
Las Vegas, a gambling resort in New Mexico, U.S.A.

拉撒(ㄌㄚ ㄙㄚ)or 拉颯(ㄌㄚ ㄙㄚˋ)
refuse; garbage 亦作「垃圾」

拉薩(ㄌㄚ ㄙㄚˋ)
Lhasa, capital of Tibet

拉曳(ㄌㄚ ㄧ)
to pull; to drag

拉洋片(ㄌㄚ ㄧㄤˊ ㄆㄧㄢˋ)
①a show of still pictures (through a magnifying glass, the viewer looks at pictures which are changed at regular intervals by pulling a rope) ②to talk big

拉網(ㄌㄚ ㄨㄤˇ)
to pull a net

拉運(ㄌㄚ ㄩㄣˋ)
to pull a cart; to transport

【拉】 1838
2.ㄍㄚˇ la lá
參看「拉遢」

拉遢(ㄌㄚ ·ㄊㄚ)
dirty; untidy

【拊】 1839
ㄈㄨˇ fuu fǔ
1. to touch with hand lightly or tenderly; to pat
2. to indulge
3. to slap; to tap
4. the handle of a vessel or utensil

拊背扼喉(ㄈㄨˇ ㄅㄟˋ ㄜˋ ㄏㄡˊ)
to occupy a strategic or advantageous position

拊髀(ㄈㄨˇ ㄅㄧˋ)
to slap one's own buttocks in excitement or despair

拊髀興嘆(ㄈㄨˇ ㄅㄧˋ ㄒㄧㄥ ㄊㄢˋ)
to lament one's own inability to resume work

拊心(ㄈㄨˇ ㄒㄧㄣ)or 拊膺(ㄈㄨˇ ㄧㄥ)
to slap one's chest—an expression of distress or indignation

拊循(ㄈㄨˇ ㄒㄩㄣˊ)
to comfort; to soothe

拊掌(ㄈㄨˇ ㄓㄤˇ)or 拊手(ㄈㄨˇ ㄕㄡˇ)

to clap hands: 他們拊掌大笑。They clapped hands and laughed.

【拋】 1840
(拋) ㄆㄠ pau pāo
1. to throw; to cast; to hurl; to throw away: 他把球拋給我。He threw the ball to me.
2. to abandon; to reject; to give up
3. to cast aside; to leave behind

拋盤(ㄆㄠ ㄆㄢˊ)
(stock market) to buy or sell futures

拋撇(ㄆㄠ ㄆㄧㄝ)
to abandon; to throw away

拋錨(ㄆㄠ ㄇㄠˊ)
①to cast anchor ②(said of a car) to develop engine trouble and become stuck midway; to break down

拋頭露面(ㄆㄠ ㄊㄡˊ ㄌㄨˋ ㄇㄧㄢˋ)
(said of women in old China) to go out and be seen in public; to hold a job which involves a lot of exposure to the public (considered unbecoming to a decent woman)

拋體運動(ㄆㄠ ㄊㄧˇ ㄩㄣˋ ㄉㄨㄥˋ)
projectile movement

拋戈棄甲(ㄆㄠ ㄍㄜ ㄑㄧˋ ㄐㄧㄚˇ)
to throw away weapons and armor—to be routed

拋空(ㄆㄠ ㄎㄨㄥ)
(stock market) to sell short

拋荒(ㄆㄠ ㄏㄨㄤ)
to lay idle; to become rusty because of lack of practice

拋棄(ㄆㄠ ㄑㄧˋ)or 拋捨(ㄆㄠ ㄕㄜˇ)
to abandon; to throw away; to give up: 我們決不拋棄真正的朋友。We shall never give up our true friends.

拋繡球(ㄆㄠ ㄒㄧㄡˋ ㄑㄧㄡˊ)or 拋綵球(ㄆㄠ ㄘㄞˇ ㄑㄧㄡˊ)
to throw an embroidered ball—to choose a husband

拋擲(ㄆㄠ ㄓˋ)
①to cast; to throw; to hurl: 獵人向一野獸拋擲標槍。The hunter hurled a spear at a wild animal. ②to throw away; to abandon

拋磚引玉(ㄆㄠ ㄓㄨㄢ ㄧㄣˇ ㄩˋ)
(literally) to throw a brick

and to get a piece of jade in return—a polite term in requesting an exchange of literary works or in making a donation to a worthy cause in the hope others may follow suit

抛出（ㄠ ㄔㄨ）
①to throw out; to cast away ②(especially in the stock market) to sell short; to sell

抛射（ㄠ ㄕㄜˋ）
to project

抛售（ㄠ ㄕㄡˋ）
to dump large stocks of merchandise in the market in order to force down prices and relieve shortage of supply

抛梭（ㄠ ㄙㄨㄛ）
to throw the shuttle

抛物線（ㄠ ㄨˋ ㄒㄧㄢˋ）
a parabola

【拌】 1841
1. ㄅㄢˋ bann bàn
to mix: 你會拌沙拉嗎? Can you mix salad?

拌麵（ㄅㄢˋ ㄇㄧㄢˋ）
noodles served with soy sauce, sesame butter, etc.

拌和（ㄅㄢˋ ㄏㄨㄜˋ）
to mix properly; to blend: 油和水不能摻和在一起。Oil and water do not blend.

拌和車（ㄅㄢˋ ㄏㄨㄜˋ ㄔㄜ）
a truck mixer 亦作「混凝土拌和車」

拌嘴（ㄅㄢˋ ㄗㄨㄟˇ）
to wrangle; to quarrel; to bicker

拌匀（ㄅㄢˋ ㄩㄣˊ）
to mix evenly or properly

【拌】 1841
2. ㄆㄢˋ pann pàn
to throw away; to abandon

拌命（ㄆㄢˋ ㄇㄧㄥˋ）
to risk one's life

拌石（ㄆㄢˋ ㄕˊ）
to throw a stone

【拐】 1842
《ㄍㄨㄞˇ goai guǎi
1. to kidnap; to abduct: 這孩子昨天被拐走了。The child was abducted yesterday.
2. to turn or change direction (in walking, driving, etc.):

路在此處拐向北邊。The road turns to the north here.
3. to swindle
4. same as 枴—a staff for an old person; a cane

拐脖兒（ㄍㄨㄞˇ ㄅㄛˊ ㄦ）
an elbow (of a stovepipe)

拐騙（ㄍㄨㄞˇ ㄆㄧㄢˋ）or 拐誘《ㄍㄨㄞˇ ㄧㄡˋ》
①to abduct; to kidnap ②to swindle

拐賣（ㄍㄨㄞˇ ㄇㄞˋ）
to abduct or kidnap and sell; to engage in white slavery

拐販（ㄍㄨㄞˇ ㄈㄢˋ）
to deal in white slavery

拐帶（ㄍㄨㄞˇ ㄉㄞˋ）
to abduct; to kidnap

拐逃（ㄍㄨㄞˇ ㄊㄠˊ）
to abscond with money or valuables, or both

拐過去（ㄍㄨㄞˇ ㄍㄨㄛˋ ˙ㄑㄩ）
to make a turn; to turn the corner

拐孩子（ㄍㄨㄞˇ ㄏㄞˊ ˙ㄗ）
to kidnap a child

拐回來（ㄍㄨㄞˇ ㄏㄨㄟˊ ˙ㄌㄞ）
①to turn back ②to take back things in confusion illegally (as in a busy store, etc.); to filch ③to give something to another and then take it back

拐彎(兒)（ㄍㄨㄞˇ ㄨㄢ ㄦ）
①to turn the corner ②at the corner: 這房屋在大街的拐角上。The building is located at the corner of the main street.

拐肘（ㄍㄨㄞˇ ㄓㄡˇ）
the elbow

拐杖（ㄍㄨㄞˇ ㄓㄤˋ）
a staff, a stick; crutches: 他拿著拐杖走路。He walks with the help of a stick.

拐子（ㄍㄨㄞˇ ˙ㄗ）
a kidnapper; a swindler; an abductor

拐馬（ㄍㄨㄞˇ ㄇㄚˇ）
(Sung Dynasty) a tactical horse-formation used by a famous barbarian general, Chin Wu-chu (金兀朮), who linked three horses together in a row in mounting a charge on the battlefield

拐彎兒（ㄍㄨㄞˇ ㄨㄢ ㄦ）
①to turn the corner: 拐彎兒時要慢行。Slow down when turning a corner. ②at the corner: 請在大街拐彎兒處與我碰面。Meet me at the corner of the street.

拐彎抹角兒（ㄍㄨㄞˇ ㄨㄢ ㄇㄛˋ ㄐㄧㄠˇ ㄦ）
①to proceed along a zigzag road ②a roundabout way of talking; circumlocution; to beat around the bush: 說話要直截了當，不要拐彎抹角兒。Get to the point. Don't beat about the bush.

【拑】 1843
ㄑㄧㄢˊ chyan qián
to hold; to grasp

拑釘子（ㄑㄧㄢˊ ㄉㄧㄥ ˙ㄗ）
to pull out a nail

拑口（ㄑㄧㄢˊ ㄎㄡˇ）
to hold the tongue

拑住他（ㄑㄧㄢˊ ㄓㄨˋ ㄊㄚ）
Hold him tight!

【拍】 1844
ㄆㄞ pai pāi
（讀音 ㄆㄛˋ poh pò）
1. to strike with the hand; to slap; to clap; to pat; to swat: 他拍著他的肩膀。He clapped her on the shoulder.
2. the time or beat of a piece of music: 這首歌是幾拍的? What time is the song in?
3. to fawn; to flatter: 他是在拍你的馬屁。He is flattering you.

拍巴掌（ㄆㄞ ㄅㄚ ˙ㄓㄤ）or 拍掌（ㄆㄞ ㄓㄤˇ）
to clap hands

拍板（ㄆㄞ ㄅㄢˇ）
①to beat time ②castanets

拍髀（ㄆㄞ ㄅㄧˋ）
①to pat the thigh ②a sword worn at one's waist

拍片（ㄆㄞ ㄆㄧㄢˋ）
to shoot a film

拍馬屁（ㄆㄞ ㄇㄚˇ ㄆㄧˋ）or 拍馬（ㄆㄞ ㄇㄚˇ）
to flatter; to soft-soap; to claw (or curry) favor

拍賣（ㄆㄞ ㄇㄞˋ）
to auction off; an auction

拍賣者（ㄆㄞ ㄇㄞˋ ㄓㄜˇ）
an auctioneer

拍門（ㄆㄞ ㄇㄣˊ）
to knock or strike at the

（手部）

door

拍打(ㄆㄞˇ·ㄉㄚ)
to pat; to slap or tap lightly: 他拍打身上的雪。He patted the snow off his clothes.

拍電(ㄆㄞˇ ㄉㄧㄢˋ)or 拍發電報(ㄆㄞˇ ㄈㄚ ㄉㄧㄢˋ ㄅㄠˋ)
to cable; to send a telegram

拍電影(ㄆㄞˇ ㄉㄧㄢˋ ㄧㄥˇ)
to shoot a film; to photograph with a movie camera

拍擊(ㄆㄞˇ ㄐㄧ)
to strike; to slap: 他以手拍擊膝蓋。He struck his knee with his hand.

拍肩膀(ㄆㄞˇ ㄐㄧㄢ ㄅㄤˇ)
to pat on the shoulder

拍球(ㄆㄞˇ ㄑㄧㄡˊ)
to bounce a ball; to pat a ball

拍胸脯(ㄆㄞˇ ㄒㄩㄥ ㄆㄨˊ)
to pat one's chest (to show confidence, defiance, acceptance of a challenge or responsibility, etc.)

拍紙簿(ㄆㄞˇ ㄓˇ ㄅㄨˋ)
a writing pad

拍照(ㄆㄞˇ ㄓㄠˋ)
to take a picture or photo: 我們把它拍照下來。Let's take a picture of it.

拍桌子(ㄆㄞˇ ㄓㄨㄛ·ㄗ)
to pound the table—a gesture of anger, surprise or admiration

拍攝(ㄆㄞˇ ㄕㄜˋ)
to take (a picture); to shoot: 他在拍攝一張照片。He is taking a photo.

拍手(ㄆㄞˇ ㄕㄡˇ)
to clap hands

拍手喝采(ㄆㄞˇ ㄕㄡˇ ㄏㄜˋ ㄘㄞˇ)
to clap hands and shout "Bravo!"

拍子(ㄆㄞˇ·ㄗ)
①(music) time; rhythm; a beat: 打拍子 to beat time ② a fly swatter ③a bat; a racket: 網球拍子 a tennis racket

拍子記號(ㄆㄞˇ ㄗ ㄐㄧˋ ㄏㄠˋ)
(music) a time signature 亦作「拍號」

拍蒼蠅(ㄆㄞˇ ㄘㄤ ㄧㄥˊ)
to swat a fly

拍案(ㄆㄞˇ ㄢˋ)
to pound the table—a gesture of anger or surprise

拍案叫絕(ㄆㄞˇ ㄢˋ ㄐㄧㄠˋ ㄐㄩㄝˊ)
to show extreme surprise or admiration by pounding the table

拍案驚奇(ㄆㄞˇ ㄢˋ ㄐㄧㄥ ㄑㄧˊ)
name of a collection of short stories edited in the Ming Dynasty

拍外景(ㄆㄞˇ ㄨㄞˋ ㄐㄧㄥˇ)
(cinema) to be on location

【拎】 1845　ㄌㄧㄥ lhing ling
to haul; to take; to carry; to lift: 她拎著菜籃上市場。She carried a basket in her hand to the market.

拎他一把(ㄌㄧㄥ ㄊㄚ ㄧ ㄅㄚˇ)
to lend him a helping hand 或 Give him a hand.

拎起一桶水(ㄌㄧㄥ ㄑㄧˇ ㄊㄜ ㄊㄨㄥˇ ㄕㄨㄟˇ)
to haul a bucket of water; to draw a bucket of water

【拒】 1846　ㄐㄩˋ jiuh jù
1. to defend; to ward off; to resist: 他們抵拒敵人的攻擊。They warded off the enemy's attack.
2. to refuse; to reject: 他拒絕同我一起去。He refused to go with me.

拒捕(ㄐㄩˋ ㄅㄨˇ)
to resist arrest; to resist being arrested

拒馬(ㄐㄩˋ ㄇㄚˇ)
an abatis

拒付(ㄐㄩˋ ㄈㄨˋ)
to refuse to pay; to dishonor (a check)

拒敵(ㄐㄩˋ ㄉㄧˊ)
to resist the enemy; to keep the enemy at bay; to ward off or defend against the enemy

拒繳(ㄐㄩˋ ㄐㄧㄠˇ)
to refuse to pay (taxes or money one is obliged to pay)

拒諫飾非(ㄐㄩˋ ㄐㄧㄢˋ ㄕˋ ㄈㄟ)
to refuse to listen to counsels and cover up one's faults

拒絕(ㄐㄩˋ ㄐㄩㄝˊ)or 拒卻(ㄐㄩˋ ㄑㄩㄝˋ)
to refuse; to reject; to turn down; a refusal: 他拒絕我的幫助。He refused my offer of help.

拒絕來往(ㄐㄩˋ ㄐㄩㄝˊ ㄌㄞˊ ㄨㄤˇ)
to sever communications, intercourse or relations

拒絕往來戶(ㄐㄩˋ ㄐㄩㄝˊ ㄨㄤˇ ㄌㄞˊ ㄏㄨˋ)
a client with very poor credit standing and thus denied the banking service; a dishonored account

拒性(ㄐㄩˋ ㄒㄧㄥˋ)
(physics) impenetrability

拒守(ㄐㄩˋ ㄕㄡˇ)
to guard; to defend (a position, territory, etc.)

拒霜(ㄐㄩˋ ㄕㄨㄤ)
(botany) a hibiscus 亦作「芙蓉」

拒人於千里之外(ㄐㄩˋ ㄖㄣˊ ㄩˊ ㄑㄧㄢ ㄌㄧˇ ㄓ ㄨㄞˋ)
(literally) to keep people a thousand miles away — extremely indifferent and cool

【拓】 1847　①ㄊㄨㄛˋ tuoh tuo
1. to expand; to aggrandize; to open up (new frontiers, etc.); to develop: 我們應開拓邊遠地區。We should open up the frontier regions.
2. to push with hands

拓拔(ㄊㄨㄛˋ ㄅㄚˊ)
the Toba family which founded the Northern Wei Dynasty in the 4th century

拓邊(ㄊㄨㄛˋ ㄅㄧㄢ)or 拓境(ㄊㄨㄛˋ ㄐㄧㄥˋ)
to open up borderlands; to open up new frontiers

拓地(ㄊㄨㄛˋ ㄉㄧˋ)or 拓土(ㄊㄨㄛˋ ㄊㄨˇ)
to expand the territory (of a nation); territorial expansion

拓提(ㄊㄨㄛˋ ㄊㄧˊ)
a temple or monastery

拓落(ㄊㄨㄛˋ ㄌㄨㄛˋ)
①mortified and alone ② spacious

拓荒(ㄊㄨㄛˋ ㄏㄨㄤ)
to open up virgin soil; to reclaim a barren tract of land

拓殖(ㄊㄨㄛˋ ㄓˊ)
to open up new land for settlement

拓展(ㄊㄨㄛˋ ㄓㄢˇ)

to expand (business, etc.); to realize (great ambitions, etc.); to expand and develop: 他正努力拓展業務。He is trying to expand his business.

【拓】 ¹⁸⁴⁷
2. (搨) ㄊㄚˋ tah tò

to copy characters from an ancient tablet or tomb by rubbing over a paper placed on its surface; to make rubbings of inscriptions: 這幅碑帖拓得甚好。This rubbing of inscription is well made.

拓本(ㄊㄚˋ ㄅㄣˇ)
a stone rubbing, especially of the ancient inscription; a book of rubbing

【拔】 ¹⁸⁴⁸
ㄅㄚˊ bar bá

1. to pull out; to uproot: 風將一些樹連根拔起。The wind uprooted some trees.

2. to promote (another to a higher position, etc.); 拔擢俊才 to select and promote the talents

3. to stand out; outstanding; remarkable

4. to attack and take (a city); to capture

5. as in 海拔—elevation; above sea level: 海拔五千英尺 5,000 feet above sea level

拔本塞原(ㄅㄚˊ ㄅㄣˇ ㄙㄜˋ ㄩㄢˊ)
to despise the source; to abandon the origin

拔步(ㄅㄚˊ ㄅㄨˋ)or拔脚(ㄅㄚˊ ㄐㄧㄠˇ)
to walk with big and quick strides; to take to one's heels

拔不出腿來(ㄅㄚˊ ㄅㄨˋ ㄔㄨ ㄊㄨㄟˇ ㄌㄞˊ)
cannot get away (from something); cannot get rid of (something); can not get off from pressing duties

拔毛(ㄅㄚˊ ㄇㄠˊ)
to pluck out hairs

拔茅連茹(ㄅㄚˊ ㄇㄠˊ ㄌㄧㄢˊ ㄖㄨˊ)
(originally) from the *Book of Changes:* "The good will attract people of their own kind."—(figuratively) Once a capable man is recruited by the emperor for a high office, his talented friends will flock to the imperial

court without being invited.

拔苗助長(ㄅㄚˊ ㄇㄧㄠˊ ㄓㄨˋ ㄓㄤˇ)
to try to help the seedlings grow by pulling them upward—(figuratively) to spoil things by excessive enthusiasm 亦作「揠苗助長」

拔得頭籌(ㄅㄚˊ ㄉㄜˊ ㄊㄡˊ ㄔㄡˊ)
to become the first to do something

拔刀相助(ㄅㄚˊ ㄉㄠ ㄒㄧㄤ ㄓㄨˋ)
to help another (usually a stranger) for the sake of justice

拔地擎天(ㄅㄚˊ ㄉㄧˋ ㄑㄧㄥˊ ㄊㄧㄢ)
remarkable and outstanding (heroes, etc.)

拔釘鎚(ㄅㄚˊ ㄉㄧㄥ ㄔㄨㄟˊ)
a claw hammer

拔都(ㄅㄚˊ ㄉㄨ)
①(Mongolian) bravery; courage ②name of a general in the Yüan (Mongol) Dynasty

拔腿(ㄅㄚˊ ㄊㄨㄟˇ)
to take to one's heels

拔根(ㄅㄚˊ ㄍㄣ)
to uproot

拔罐子(ㄅㄚˊ ㄍㄨㄢˋ・ㄗ)
(Chinese medicine) cupping

拔貢(ㄅㄚˊ ㄍㄨㄥˋ)
(Ching Dynasty) outstanding young scholars selected to the capital for a civil service examination once every 12 years with the top ones kept for government assignment

拔河(ㄅㄚˊ ㄏㄜˊ)
a tug of war

拔虎鬚(ㄅㄚˊ ㄏㄨˇ ㄒㄩ)
(literally) to pluck the tiger's hair—too rash or ignorant to realize the danger of offending a powerful personage

拔尖兒(ㄅㄚˊ ㄐㄧㄢ ㄦ)
top-notch; to come off first; to get the best position 亦作「抓尖兒」: 他的成績是拔尖兒的。He's a top-notch student.

拔劍(ㄅㄚˊ ㄐㄧㄢˋ)
to draw a sword; to whip out a sword

拔薦(ㄅㄚˊ ㄐㄧㄢˋ)
to recommend for a post

拔取(ㄅㄚˊ ㄑㄩˇ)

to take or capture (a city, etc.)

拔去眼中釘(ㄅㄚˊ ㄑㄩˋ ㄧㄢˇ ㄓㄨㄥ ㄉㄧㄥ)
(literally) to pull out the sting in one's eye—(figuratively) to remove a person one hates most

拔萃(ㄅㄚˊ ㄘㄨㄟˋ)或 拔萃(ㄅㄚˊ ㄘㄨㄟˋ)
(said of persons) to stand out; outstanding: 他表現得出類拔萃。He stands out among his fellows.

拔薙(ㄅㄚˊ ㄊㄧˋ)
to eliminate bullies

拔幟易幟(ㄅㄚˊ ㄓˋ ㄧˋ ㄓˋ)
to occupy the enemy camp or position; to triumph by force of arms

拔著短籌(ㄅㄚˊ ・ㄓㄜ ㄉㄨㄢˇ ㄔㄡˊ)
to die young

拔寨(ㄅㄚˊ ㄓㄞˋ)or拔營(ㄅㄚˊ ㄧㄥˊ)
to break up a camp

拔擢(ㄅㄚˊ ㄓㄨㄛˊ)
to promote; to raise: 拔擢某人爲經理 to raise a man to manager

拔城(ㄅㄚˊ ㄔㄥˊ)
to take or capture a city

拔出來(ㄅㄚˊ ㄔㄨ ㄌㄞˊ)
to pull out; to draw out; to extract

拔除(ㄅㄚˊ ㄔㄨˊ)
to uproot; to eradicate; to remove; to pluck; to wipe out: 他拔除園中野草。He is plucking up weeds from the garden.

拔十得五(ㄅㄚˊ ㄕˊ ㄉㄜˊ ㄨˇ)
to get only half of what one asked for

拔舌地獄(ㄅㄚˊ ㄕㄜˊ ㄉㄧˋ ㄩˋ)
(Buddhism) the hell where the tongue is pulled out, as a punishment for an oral sin

拔身(ㄅㄚˊ ㄕㄣ)
to get away (from pressing duties); to escape

拔樹尋根(ㄅㄚˊ ㄕㄨˋ ㄒㄩㄣˊ ㄍㄣ)
to go to the very source of something

拔草(ㄅㄚˊ ㄘㄠˇ)
to weed: 他們正在園裡拔草。They are weeding the garden.

拔俗(ㄅㄚˊ ㄙㄨˊ)
to rise far above the com-

（手部）

mon lot; outstanding and unique

拔牙(ㄅㄚˊ ㄧㄚˊ)
to extract a tooth

拔尤(ㄅㄚˊ ㄧㄡˊ)
to promote men of outstanding ability

拔營(ㄅㄚˊ ㄧㄥˊ)
to pull up stakes and roll up tents (at the end of a camporee, bivouac, etc.); to strike camp

【拗】 1849
1. ㄠˋ ao ǎo
to bend or twist so as to break

拗折(ㄠˋ ㄓㄜˊ)or 拗斷(ㄠˋ ㄉㄨㄢˋ)
to break by twisting

【拗】 1849
2. ㄠˋ aw ào
(又讀) ㄠˋ yaw yào
(翻音) ㄋㄧㄡˋ niow niù)

1. obstinate; stubborn; unmanageable; recalcitrant
2. hard to pronounce; awkward-sounding

拗不過(ㄋㄧㄡˋ ㄅㄨˋ ㄍㄨㄛˋ)
to be unable to dissuade; to fail to talk someone out of doing something

拗性(ㄠˋ ㄒㄧㄥˋ)
obstinacy; stubbornness; recalcitrance 亦作「執拗」

拗犄(ㄠˋ ㄑㄧˊ)
recalcitrant; stubbornly defiant; obstinate

拗體詩(ㄠˋ ㄊㄧˇ ㄕ)
poems that do not conform to the rule of conventional versification

拗強(ㄠˋ ㄐㄧㄤˋ)
obstinate and pigheaded; recalcitrant

拗相公(ㄠˋ ㄒㄧㄤˋ ㄍㄨㄥ)
"The Obstinate Lord", a sobriquet given to Wang An-shih (王安石)

拗口(ㄠˋ ㄎㄡˇ)
to twist the tongue; tongue-twisting

拗口令(ㄠˋ ㄎㄡˇ ㄌㄧㄥˋ)
a tongue twister 亦作「繞口令」

【拗】 1849
3. ㄩˋ yuh yù
to restrain; to repress; to curb; to suppress

【拖】 1850
(拕) ㄊㄨㄛ tuo tuō

1. to drag along, after or out: 他拖着我陪他去看電影。He dragged me along with him to a movie.
2. to procrastinate; to drag out; to delay: 時候已晚，不要拖了。It's getting late; don't delay.
3. to involve; to implicate

拖把(ㄊㄨㄛ ㄅㄚˇ)
a mop

拖帶(ㄊㄨㄛ ㄉㄞˋ)
① to drag along ② to involve; to implicate (a whole family, etc.)

拖刀計(ㄊㄨㄛ ㄉㄠ ㄐㄧˋ)
a delaying tactic

拖宕(ㄊㄨㄛ ㄉㄤˋ)
to procrastinate; to delay

拖沓(ㄊㄨㄛ ㄊㄚˋ)
to do things in a muddled manner; confused, indecisive and sloppy

拖泥帶水(ㄊㄨㄛ ㄋㄧˊ ㄉㄞˋ ㄕㄨㄟˇ)
(literally) to drag through mud and water—confused, sloppy and muddled (style of writing or acting); not snappy or clean-cut; unable to make a decision

拖拉(ㄊㄨㄛ ㄌㄚ)
①dilatory: 他辦事總是拖拉。He is always dilatory in doing things. ②to put off: 他工作從不拖拉。He never puts off his work.

拖累(ㄊㄨㄛ ㄌㄟˋ)
①to involve or implicate; to suffer because of another's fault ② a drag; a burden: 子女過多對父母是個拖累。Too many children are a burden to their parents.

拖露(ㄊㄨㄛ ㄌㄡˋ)
to hang down

拖輪(ㄊㄨㄛ ㄌㄨㄣˊ)
a tugboat; a tug; a towboat

拖垮(ㄊㄨㄛ ㄎㄨㄚˇ)
to be worn down; to be bled white or weakened

拖後腿(ㄊㄨㄛ ㄏㄡˋ ㄊㄨㄟˇ)
to hold back or hinder; to obstruct

拖家帶眷(ㄊㄨㄛ ㄐㄧㄚ ㄉㄞˋ ㄐㄩㄢˋ)
to have a family burden

拖欠(ㄊㄨㄛ ㄑㄧㄢˋ)
to owe and delay payment for a long time; arrears

拖鞋(ㄊㄨㄛ ㄒㄧㄝˊ)
slippers: 他買了一雙新拖鞋。He bought a new pair of slippers.

拖車(ㄊㄨㄛ ㄔㄜ)
a trailer

拖長(ㄊㄨㄛ ㄔㄤˊ)
① to lengthen ② to drag on (or out): 他以長篇演講拖長了開會時間。He dragged out a meeting with long speeches.

拖船(ㄊㄨㄛ ㄔㄨㄢˊ)
a tugboat

拖牀(ㄊㄨㄛ ㄔㄨㄤˊ)
to procrastinate in getting up; reluctant to get up

拖尾(ㄊㄨㄛ ㄨㄟˇ)
to "toss"—a joke played upon new students in English and American colleges and schools

拖時間(ㄊㄨㄛ ㄕˊ ㄐㄧㄢ)
to stall for time; to delay

拖人下水(ㄊㄨㄛ ㄖㄣˊ ㄒㄧㄚˋ ㄕㄨㄟˇ)
to implicate another intentionally; to involve others in an illegal or unethical undertaking

拖曳(ㄊㄨㄛ ㄧˋ)
to drag; to pull; to tow: 這車容易拖曳。The wagon draws easily. 那遊艇是用拖船拖曳。The barge was tugged by a tugboat.

拖拉機(ㄊㄨㄛ ㄌㄚ ㄐㄧ)
a tractor

拖油瓶(ㄊㄨㄛ ㄧㄡˊ ㄆㄧㄥˊ)
a woman's children by previous marriage

拖延(ㄊㄨㄛ ㄧㄢˊ)
to procrastinate; to delay; to postpone; to drag on: 他拖延歸期。He procrastinated his return.

拖網(ㄊㄨㄛ ㄨㄤˇ)
a trawl; a dragnet; a trawl net

【拙】 1851
ㄓㄨㄛ jwo zhuó

1. stupid; crude; poor (works, etc.); slow and clumsy: 他拙於言詞。He is clumsy in expressing himself.

2. a conventional term referring to oneself

拙笨 (ㄓㄨㄛˊ ㄅㄣˋ)
stupid; clumsy: 他是個拙笨的工人。 He is a clumsy workman.

拙筆 (ㄓㄨㄛˊ ㄅㄧˇ)
my poor writing; my clumsy pen (used in polite conversation)

拙夫 (ㄓㄨㄛˊ ㄈㄨ)
a clumsy husband; my clumsy husband (used in polite conversation)

拙劣 (ㄓㄨㄛˊ ㄌㄧㄝˋ)
clumsy and inferior: 他們賣手工拙劣的貨品。 They sell goods of inferior workmanship.

拙稿 (ㄓㄨㄛˊ ㄍㄠˇ)
my poor manuscript, article, or writing (used in polite conversation)

拙工 (ㄓㄨㄛˊ ㄍㄨㄥ)
a poor craftsman; an incompetent worker

拙宦 (ㄓㄨㄛˊ ㄏㄨㄢˋ)
an official who does not know how to exert his influence to make extra money

拙計 (ㄓㄨㄛˊ ㄐㄧˋ)
a foolish scheme; my stupid plan (used in polite conversation)

拙見 (ㄓㄨㄛˊ ㄐㄧㄢˋ)
my humble idea or view (used in polite conversation): 依拙見, 他不日可癒。 In my opinion, he will recover soon.

拙荊 (ㄓㄨㄛˊ ㄐㄧㄥ) or 拙妻 (ㄓㄨㄛˊ ㄑㄧ)
my stupid wife (used in polite conversation)

拙性 (ㄓㄨㄛˊ ㄒㄧㄥˋ)
stupidity; slow-witted; clumsy

拙著 (ㄓㄨㄛˊ ㄓㄨˋ) or 拙作 (ㄓㄨㄛˊ ㄗㄨㄛˋ)
my (poor) writing; my clumsy work (used in polite conversation)

拙實 (ㄓㄨㄛˊ ㄕˊ)
raw and sturdy; big and strong; solidly built

拙嘴笨腮 (ㄓㄨㄛˊ ㄗㄨㄟˇ ㄅㄣˋ ㄙㄞ) or 拙嘴笨舌 (ㄓㄨㄛˊ ㄗㄨㄟˇ ㄅㄣˋ ㄕㄜˊ)

slow of tongue and clumsy in utterance

【拘】 1852
(ㄐㄩ jiu ju)
1. to apprehend; to detain; to arrest
2. inflexible; to adhere rigidly to (conventions, etc.)
3. confined; restricted; not free; restrained: 他是無拘無束的。 He was unrestrained.

拘捕 (ㄐㄩ ㄅㄨˇ)
to detain or arrest (a suspect); to take in: 他因偷竊而被拘捕。 He was arrested for theft.

拘票 (ㄐㄩ ㄆㄧㄠˋ)
a warrant for arrest

拘泥 (ㄐㄩ ㄋㄧˋ)
to feel restricted; to have one's hands tied; straitjacketed

拘提 (ㄐㄩ ㄊㄧˊ)
(law) to summon a defendant by forcible means for a court trial

拘拿 (ㄐㄩ ㄋㄚˊ)
to arrest: 警察正要拘拿那個兇手。 The police are going to arrest the murderer.

拘泥 (ㄐㄩ ㄋㄧˋ) or 拘板 (ㄐㄩ ㄅㄢˇ)
to be tied down by conventions; to adhere to laws and rules, etc.; to the very letter; to go strictly by the book

拘泥不通 (ㄐㄩ ㄋㄧˋ ㄅㄨˋ ㄊㄨㄥ)
slow-witted, stubborn and stupid

拘泥小節 (ㄐㄩ ㄋㄧˋ ㄒㄧㄠˇ ㄐㄧㄝˊ)
to be tied down by trifles or petty conventions; to be punctilious

拘女 (ㄐㄩ ㄋㄩˇ)
girls who were employed by the imperial household and were not allowed to marry

拘禮 (ㄐㄩ ㄌㄧˇ)
strict adherence to social etiquette

拘留 (ㄐㄩ ㄌㄧㄡˊ) or 拘絷 (ㄐㄩ ㄌㄧˋ)
to detain; detention: 他已遭拘留。 He is under arrest.

拘留所 (ㄐㄩ ㄌㄧㄡˊ ㄙㄨㄛˇ)
a detention house to keep criminal suspects pending a court decision

拘攣 (ㄐㄩ ㄌㄨㄢˊ)

① involuntary twitchings of the limbs; cramps; spasms ② restrained and restricted

拘忌 (ㄐㄩ ㄐㄧˋ)
to be restricted by cares and worries; restrained by superstitions

拘介 (ㄐㄩ ㄐㄧㄝˋ)
(said of the conduct of a person) clean and virtuous

拘檢 (ㄐㄩ ㄐㄧㄢˇ)
restricted and restrained

拘謹 (ㄐㄩ ㄐㄧㄣˇ)
restrained and cautious—implying social timidity

拘禁 (ㄐㄩ ㄐㄧㄣˋ) or 拘押 (ㄐㄩ ㄧㄚ)
or 拘管 (ㄐㄩ ㄍㄨㄢˇ)
to detain; to imprison: 警察將他拘押在派出所裏。 The police held him at the station house.

拘拘 (ㄐㄩ ㄐㄩ)
① sticking to forms; formalistic ② hunchbacked

拘局縮 (ㄐㄩ ㄐㄩˊ ㄙㄨㄛˋ)
restricted and shrinking; shy and timid; uneasy and awkward (manner)

拘囚 (ㄐㄩ ㄑㄧㄡˊ)
to imprison; to put behind bars

拘牽 (ㄐㄩ ㄑㄧㄢ)
to restrict; to restrain

拘盧 (ㄐㄩ ㄌㄨ)
provincial; shortsighted and narrow-minded

拘執 (ㄐㄩ ㄓˊ)
① to detain or imprison ② to be tied down by conventions

拘住 (ㄐㄩ ㄓㄨˋ)
to seize; to restrain

拘守 (ㄐㄩ ㄕㄡˇ)
holding fast to (conventions, traditions, etc.)

拘束 (ㄐㄩ ㄕㄨˋ)
① to tie (someone) down; to restrain; restrained ② timid and awkward; not feeling at home

拘儒 (ㄐㄩ ㄖㄨˊ)
a narrow-minded scholar; a pedant

拘役 (ㄐㄩ ㄧˋ)
(law) forced labor service under detention imposed on an offender for not more

〔手部〕

【手部】

than 60 days

拘押(ㄐㄩ ㄧㄚ)
to take into custody; to put under arrest

拘文(ㄐㄩ ㄨㄣˊ)
adherence to the letter of rules, etc.

【拚】 1853
ㄅㄢˋ pann pàn

1. to go all out; to try very hard to: 他拚命做生意。He goes all out to do his business.
2. at the risk of; to disregard
3. to reject; to abandon; to discard

拚命(ㄅㄢˋ ㄇㄧㄥˋ)or 拚死(ㄅㄢˋ ㄙˇ)
to go all out (for a cause) even at the risk of one's life; to risk one's life: 他拚命去拯救他人。He risked his life to save another.

拚棄(ㄅㄢˋ ㄑㄧˋ)or 拚除(ㄅㄢˋ ㄔㄨˊ)
or 拚去(ㄅㄢˋ ㄑㄩˋ)
to reject; to abandon

拚財(ㄅㄢˋ ㄘㄞˊ)
to make rash speculations

【抿】 1854
ㄇㄧㄣˇ miin mǐn

1. to smooth (hair); to stroke; to caress
2. to purse up (lips); to contract; to tuck: 她抿着嘴唇。She pursed up her lips.
3. to sip; a sip: 她抿一口茶。She sipped her tea.

抿頭(ㄇㄧㄣˇ ㄊㄡˊ)
(especially said of women) to smooth one's hair

抿子(ㄇㄧㄣˇ ㄗˇ)
a small brush for smoothing the hair; a small hairbrush

抿嘴笑(ㄇㄧㄣˇ ㄗㄨㄟˇ ㄒㄧㄠˋ)
to smile with mouth closed; to pucker in smile: 她抿着嘴笑。She smiled with closed lips.

【招】 1855
ㄓㄠ jau zhāo

1. to beckon with one's hand; to summon: 招之即來，揮之即去 to be at one's beck and call
2. to raise (an army, capital, etc.); to recruit
3. to confess; to admit: 他不打自招。He confessed without being pressed.

4. a poster; a notice; a sign-board
5. to cause; to effect; to incite; to incur; to invite: 這樣的談論會招來非議。Such talk will invite criticism.
6. to entice; to induce: 她在招生意。She is inducing customers.
7. to welcome; to receive
8. to infect; to be infectious
9. (now rarely) a target; a bull's-eye
10. a move, a trick; a device: 這一招可謂厲害。This was a beautiful move.
11. a Chinese family name

招標(ㄓㄠ ㄅㄧㄠ)
to invite to a tender (or bids, or public bidding); invitation to bid at a tender

招兵(ㄓㄠ ㄅㄧㄥ)
to recruit soldiers; to raise troops

招兵買馬(ㄓㄠ ㄅㄧㄥ ㄇㄞˇ ㄇㄚˇ)
to raise an army (usually in preparation for an insurrection); to prepare for war; to expand a fighting force

招兵聚將(ㄓㄠ ㄅㄧㄥ ㄐㄩˋ ㄐㄧㄤˋ)
to summon troops

招牌(ㄓㄠ ㄆㄞˊ)
① the signboard of a store or any other business concern ② the reputation of a large business firm or a quality product

招盤(ㄓㄠ ㄆㄢˊ)
(said of a shop) to solicit a buyer who will take over the whole business

招聘(ㄓㄠ ㄆㄧㄣˋ)
to advertise for office vacancies: 他們招聘技術工人。They advertised for skilled workers.

招門納婿(ㄓㄠ ㄇㄣˊ ㄋㄚˋ ㄒㄩˋ)
(a Chinese custom) to take a husband (Children thus born will bear the wife's family name.)

招募(ㄓㄠ ㄇㄨˋ)
① to enlist troops (usually mercenaries) ② to solicit (investment, capital, etc.)

招風(ㄓㄠ ㄈㄥ)
to catch the wind — (figuratively) to attract too much

attention and invite trouble

招風耳(ㄓㄠ ㄈㄥ ㄦˇ)
protruding ears

招蜂引蝶(ㄓㄠ ㄈㄥ ㄧㄣˇ ㄉㄧㄝˊ)
(said of a woman) to act like a habitual flirt; to make passes to men without discrimination

招福(ㄓㄠ ㄈㄨˊ)
to welcome and invite blessings

招撫(ㄓㄠ ㄈㄨˇ)
to call to surrender; to pacify

招撫使(ㄓㄠ ㄈㄨˇ ㄕˇ)or(ㄓㄠ ㄈㄨˇ ㄕˋ)
formerly, High Commissioner for Pacification

招附(ㄓㄠ ㄈㄨˋ)
to call the enemy to join one's own side

招待(ㄓㄠ ㄉㄞˋ)
① to receive; to welcome; to serve; to entertain: 他招待他的朋友吃飯。He entertained his friends at dinner. ② reception: 謝謝您的熱誠招待。Thank you for your kind hospitality. ③ a receptionist

招待會(ㄓㄠ ㄉㄞˋ ㄏㄨㄟˋ)
a reception

招待券(ㄓㄠ ㄉㄞˋ ㄑㄩㄢˋ)
a free ticket; a complimentary ticket

招待室(ㄓㄠ ㄉㄞˋ ㄕˋ)
a reception room

招待所(ㄓㄠ ㄉㄞˋ ㄙㄨㄛˇ)
a guest house; a hostel

招待員(ㄓㄠ ㄉㄞˋ ㄩㄢˊ)
a receptionist; a touring guide; a steward; an usher; one appointed to receive visitors

招瞪(ㄓㄠ ㄉㄥˋ)
(literally) to invite a stare — to incur resentment or disgust

招討(ㄓㄠ ㄊㄠˇ)
to call for surrender and quell rebellion

招討使(ㄓㄠ ㄊㄠˇ ㄕˇ)or(ㄓㄠ ㄊㄠˇ ㄕˋ)
an officer responsible for calling for surrender and quelling uprisings

招提(ㄓㄠ ㄊㄧˊ)
(Sanskrit) a temple

招貼(ㄓㄠ ㄊㄧㄝ)
① posters; notices; placards

②to placard

招女壻 (ㄓㄠ ㄋㄩˇ ㄒㄩ˙)

(said of a family without a male heir) to marry the daughter to a man who live with her family and bear her family name 亦作「招贅」

招徕 (ㄓㄠ ㄌㄞˊ)

to induce customers to purchase; to solicit customers; to canvass: 推銷員走遍全城招徠顧主訂貨。Salesmen canvassed the whole city for subscriptions.

招攬 (ㄓㄠ ㄌㄢˇ)

①to collect; to gather together ②(commerce) to canvass; to solicit customers

招攬訟事 (ㄓㄠ ㄌㄢˇ ㄙㄨㄥˋ ㄕˋ)

to incite or instigate litigation for personal gain

招冷 (ㄓㄠ ㄌㄥˇ)

to catch cold

招領 (ㄓㄠ ㄌㄧㄥˇ)

to advertise for the claimant or legal owner of a lost article; a public request to call for lost-and-found

招股 (ㄓㄠ ㄍㄨˇ)

to solicit shareholders; to call for capital

招供 (ㄓㄠ ㄍㄨㄥ)

①to confess (to a crime, etc.) ②a confession (by a criminal)

招考 (ㄓㄠ ㄎㄠˇ)

to advertise for employees or students through competitive examinations

招呼 (ㄓㄠ ㄏㄨ)

①to beckon; to call; to accost: 他向我打招呼。He beckoned (to) me. ②to receive; to take care of: 請招呼一下老年人。Please take care of old people. ③to engage in a fight ④to watch out; to take care; to mind

招呼站 (ㄓㄠ ㄏㄨ ㄓㄢˋ)

a designated bus or taxi stop

招花惹草 (ㄓㄠ ㄏㄨㄚ ㄖㄜˇ ㄘㄠˇ)

(usually said of a man) lascivious; to play Don Juan or Casanova 亦作「拈花惹草」

招禍 (ㄓㄠ ㄏㄨㄛˋ)

to invite troubles; to invite disasters

招麾 (ㄓㄠ ㄏㄨㄟ)

to command

招魂 (ㄓㄠ ㄏㄨㄣˊ)

(an ancient rite) to call home the soul of the dead

招集 (ㄓㄠ ㄐㄧˊ)

to gather together

招嫉 (ㄓㄠ ㄐㄧˊ)

to invite jealousy; to bring upon oneself envy or jealousy

招架 (ㄓㄠ ㄐㄧㄚˋ)

to resist; to defend; to ward off blows; to hold one's own

招架不住 (ㄓㄠ ㄐㄧㄚˋ ㄅㄨˋ ㄓㄨˋ)

to be unable to hold on or unable to hold off; to be no match (for someone)

招咎 (ㄓㄠ ㄐㄧㄡˋ)

to invite troubles

招親 (ㄓㄠ ㄑㄧㄣ)

to take a husband; to get married at the bride's home

招權納賄 (ㄓㄠ ㄑㄩㄢˊ ㄋㄚˋ ㄏㄨㄟˋ)

(said of government officials) to abuse one's powers and take bribes

招笑兒 (ㄓㄠ ㄒㄧㄠˋ ㄦˊ)

to incite laughter; hilarious; funny; to incur ridicule; to be laughable (or funny)

招賢 (ㄓㄠ ㄒㄧㄢˊ)

(said of a ruler) to solicit the service of the virtuous and capable

招賢館 (ㄓㄠ ㄒㄧㄢˊ ㄍㄨㄢˇ)

a reception center for the accommodation of those answering the ruler's call for public service

招降 (ㄓㄠ ㄒㄧㄤˊ)

to call for surrender (of the enemy, etc.)

招致 (ㄓㄠ ㄓˋ)

to bring about; to incur; to result in; to invite; to induce: 此信招致許多問題。This letter invited many problems.

招展 (ㄓㄠ ㄓㄢˇ)

(said of a banner, etc.) to sway; to flutter; to wave

招承 (ㄓㄠ ㄔㄥˊ)

to confess; a confession

招式 (ㄓㄠ ㄕˋ)

a stance or posture in Chinese martial art

招收 (ㄓㄠ ㄕㄡ)

to advertise for students, apprentices, etc.

招手兒 (ㄓㄠ ㄕㄡˇ ㄦˊ)

to beckon with the hand; to wave a hand: 他向我們招手致意。He waved his greetings to us.

招商局 (ㄓㄠ ㄕㄤ ㄐㄩˊ)

The China Merchants' Steam Navigation Company, a steamship company established in the late 19th century and nationalized in 1927 under the Ministry of Communications

招生 (ㄓㄠ ㄕㄥ)

to advertise for students; to enrol students

招生簡章 (ㄓㄠ ㄕㄥ ㄐㄧㄢˇ ㄓㄤ)

a brochure listing the essential points a student needs to know before taking the entrance examination of a school, which is sent upon request

招生委員會 (ㄓㄠ ㄕㄥ ㄨㄟˇ ㄩㄢˊ ㄏㄨㄟˋ)

a commission set up by a school for handling admission of students

招數 (ㄓㄠ ㄕㄨˋ)

①a scheme; a trick; a device ②one move in Chinese martial arts

招惹 (ㄓㄠ ㄖㄜˇ)

to incur, to bring upon oneself; to cause (trouble, etc.); to provoke: 疏忽招惹禍事。Carelessness invites accidents.

招認 (ㄓㄠ ㄖㄣˋ)

①confession ②to confess (to a certain crime, etc.)

招災 (ㄓㄠ ㄗㄞ) or 招非 (ㄓㄠ ㄈㄟ)

to invite disasters; to bring disasters upon oneself

招災惹禍 (ㄓㄠ ㄗㄞ ㄖㄜˇ ㄏㄨㄛˋ)

to court disasters; to invite troubles

招租 (ㄓㄠ ㄗㄨ)

(said of a house) for rent; to advertise for tenants

招罪 (ㄓㄠ ㄗㄨㄟˋ)

(said of excesses, etc.) to invite curses from Heaven

〔手部〕

②to bring something bad upon oneself

招財進寶 (业幺 专两 ㄐㄧㄣ ㄅㄠˇ)
to bring in wealth and riches (a self-congratulatory idiom written on a piece of red paper put up in a store to bring good luck)

招安 (业幺 ㄢ)
to grant amnesty and enlistment to bandits, etc.

招兒 (业幺 儿)
①a trick or strike in Chinese martial arts ②(now also used figuratively) a trick; a scheme ③a poster; a signboard

招邀 or 招要 (业幺 ㄧㄠ)
to invite; to request somebody to come

招搖 (业幺 ㄧㄠˊ)
to swagger with full pomp; to attract undue publicity; to act ostentatiously

招搖過市 (业幺 ㄧㄠˊ ㄍㄨㄛˋ ㄕˋ)
to swagger around town; to swagger down the streets

招搖撞騙 (业幺 ㄧㄠˊ 业ㄨㄤˋ ㄆㄧㄢˋ)
to swindle or cheat by posing as a VIP or claiming to be related to a VIP

招延 (业幺 ㄧㄢˊ)
to recruit (the capable and virtuous)

招引 (业幺 ㄧㄣˇ)
to invite (troubles, etc.); to incur; to cause; to attract; to induce: 亮光招引飛蛾。 Bright lights attract moths.

招隱 (业幺 ㄧㄣˇ)
①to recruit people in retirement for government service ②to invite or persuade to rusticate or live in anonymity in an out-of-the-way place

招物議 (业幺 ㄨˋ ㄧˋ)
to incur criticisms: 他的話已招物議。 What he said has incurred criticisms.

招怨 (业幺 ㄩㄢˋ)
to incur animosity or grudges; to inspire hatred

招怨樹敵 (业幺 ㄩㄢˋ ㄕㄨˋ ㄉㄧˊ)
to inspire animosity and make enemy

【拜】 1856
ㄅㄞˋ bay bài

1. to do obeisance; to salute; to pay respects to
2. to appoint (as a government official); an appointment
3. to visit; to pay a visit to; to call on or at: 他拜訪一位朋友。 He made a call on a friend of his.
4. a Chinese family name

拜把子 (ㄅㄞˋ ㄅㄚˇ ·ㄗ)
to become sworn brothers by going through the ritual of making vows of eternal friendship

拜拜 (ㄅㄞˋ ·ㄅㄞˋ)
①to bring hands together and take a bow—as women and children did in old China ②a worshipping festival in Taiwan

拜別 (ㄅㄞˋ ㄅㄧㄝˊ)
to say good-bye or farewell; to take leave

拜表 (ㄅㄞˋ ㄅㄧㄠˇ)
to present a report, petition, etc. to the emperor; to memorialize the emperor

拜門 (ㄅㄞˋ ㄇㄣˊ)
①to call on another and offer thanks ②to become a pupil or apprentice to a master

拜盟 (ㄅㄞˋ ㄇㄥˊ)
to become sworn brothers

拜廟 (ㄅㄞˋ ㄇㄧㄠˋ)
to worship at a temple

拜命 (ㄅㄞˋ ㄇㄧㄥˋ)
①to receive an order ②to express thanks for an assignment

拜墓 (ㄅㄞˋ ㄇㄨˋ)or 拜墳 (ㄅㄞˋ ㄈㄣˊ)
to worship at the tomb

拜佛 (ㄅㄞˋ ㄈㄛˊ)
to worship Buddha

拜訪 (ㄅㄞˋ ㄈㄤˇ)
to pay a visit; to visit; to call on: 我明天要到他家拜訪。 I shall call at his house tomorrow.

拜服 (ㄅㄞˋ ㄈㄨˊ)
to admire (another's erudition, courage, moral strength, etc.); to be won heart and soul

拜覆 (ㄅㄞˋ ㄈㄨˋ)
a term of respect in a replying letter

拜禱 (ㄅㄞˋ ㄉㄠˇ)
to pray

拜倒 (ㄅㄞˋ ㄉㄠˇ)
to prostrate oneself; to fall on one's knees; to grovel

拜倒石榴裙下 (ㄅㄞˋ ㄉㄠˇ ㄕˊ ㄌㄧㄡˊ ㄑㄩㄣˊ ㄒㄧㄚˋ)
to fall head over heels for a woman

拜墊 (ㄅㄞˋ ㄉㄧㄢˋ)
a cushion for the kneeling rite

拜讀 (ㄅㄞˋ ㄉㄨˊ)
(a polite expression) to read with respect: 來函已拜讀。 I've read your letter.

拜堂 (ㄅㄞˋ ㄊㄤˊ)
(in old China) the wedding ceremony in which the bride and her bridegroom underwent the kneeling rituals in the ceremonial hall

拜帖 (ㄅㄞˋ ㄊㄧㄝˇ)
a visiting card

拜天地 (ㄅㄞˋ ㄊㄧㄢ ㄉㄧˋ)
(in old China) the wedding ceremony in which the bride and bridegroom must kowtow to Heaven and Earth

拜託 (ㄅㄞˋ ㄊㄨㄛ)
a polite expression in asking another to do something for oneself

拜年 (ㄅㄞˋ ㄋㄧㄢˊ)
to call on another and offer New Year's greetings

拜老師 (ㄅㄞˋ ㄌㄠˇ ㄕ)or 拜師 (ㄅㄞˋ ㄕ)
to become a pupil or apprentice to a master in a solemn ceremony

拜禮 (ㄅㄞˋ ㄌㄧˇ)or 拜見禮 (ㄅㄞˋ ㄐㄧㄢˋ ㄌㄧˇ)
gifts that one gives to those who pay respects to oneself

拜領 (ㄅㄞˋ ㄌㄧㄥˇ)
to accept with thanks

拜跪 (ㄅㄞˋ ㄍㄨㄟˋ)
to kneel and kowtow—the most respectful form of salute to an elder or a superior

拜官 (ㄅㄞˋ ㄍㄨㄢ)
to be appointed to a public office

拜客 (ㄅㄞˋ ㄎㄜˋ)

（手部）

to visit; to call on

拜懇（ㄅㄞ ㄎㄣˇ）
to beg humbly; to implore; to request

拜賀（ㄅㄞ ㄏㄜˋ）
to congratulate; to offer congratulations

拜候（ㄅㄞ ㄏㄡˋ）
to visit; to call on

拜火敎（ㄅㄞ ㄏㄨㄛˇ ㄐㄧㄠˋ）
Zoroastrianism 亦作「祆敎」

拜會（ㄅㄞ ㄏㄨㄟˋ）or 拜望（ㄅㄞ ㄨㄤˋ）
to visit; to call on

拜嘉（ㄅㄞ ㄐㄧㄚ）
to receive with pleasure your favor, gifts, advice, etc.

拜節（ㄅㄞ ㄐㄧㄝˊ）
to offer greetings on festivals; to pay respects on festivals

拜敎（ㄅㄞ ㄐㄧㄠˋ）
to submit to another's exhortations

拜見（ㄅㄞ ㄐㄧㄢˋ）
to visit, or call on (an elder or superior)

拜金主義（ㄅㄞ ㄐㄧㄣ ㄓㄨˇ ㄧˋ）
mammonism

拜金主義者（ㄅㄞ ㄐㄧㄣ ㄓㄨˇ ㄧˋ ㄓㄜˇ）
a mammonist

拜爵（ㄅㄞ ㄐㄩㄝˊ）
to be knighted

拜匣（ㄅㄞ ㄒㄧㄚˊ）
a wooden box in which a visitor places his calling card, gift, etc.

拜謝（ㄅㄞ ㄒㄧㄝˋ）
to express one's thanks

拜相（ㄅㄞ ㄒㄧㄤˋ）
to be appointed prime minister

拜占庭（ㄅㄞ ㄓㄢ ㄊㄧㄥˊ）
Byzantium, the ancient name of Istanbul, Turkey; Byzantine

拜占庭帝國（ㄅㄞ ㄓㄢ ㄊㄧㄥˊ ㄉㄧˋ ㄍㄨㄛˊ）
the Byzantine Empire (395-1453)

拜手（ㄅㄞ ㄕㄡˇ）
an old form of obeisance by placing the hands palms down on the ground and then placing the head on the hands

拜壽（ㄅㄞ ㄕㄡˋ）
to congratulate one on his birthday; to come to offer birthday greetings

拜神（ㄅㄞ ㄕㄣˊ）
to worship gods

拜疏（ㄅㄞ ㄕㄨ）
to present reports, petitions, etc. to the emperor; to memorialize the emperor

拜在門下（ㄅㄞ ㄗㄞˋ ㄇㄣˊ ㄒㄧㄚˋ）
to become a pupil or apprentice to someone

拜祖（ㄅㄞ ㄗㄨˇ）
ancestor worship

拜辭（ㄅㄞ ㄘˊ）
to take leave; to say good-bye: 她依依不捨地跟他拜辭。 She took an affectionate leave of him.

拜掃（ㄅㄞ ㄙㄠˇ）
to pay respects or worship at the tomb (of one's ancestors, etc.)

拜偶像（ㄅㄞ ㄡˇ ㄒㄧㄤˋ）
idol-worshipping

拜謁（ㄅㄞ ㄧㄝˋ）
to pay a courtesy call; to wait on (or upon); to pay one's respects to somebody: 我拿著一封介紹信去拜謁他。 I waited upon him with a letter of introduction.

拜印（ㄅㄞ ㄧㄣˋ）
to be appointed to a public office

拜物敎（ㄅㄞ ㄨˋ ㄐㄧㄠˋ）
fetishism, or fetichism

拜違（ㄅㄞ ㄨㄟˊ）
to say good-bye

六畫

【拭】 1857
ㄕˋ　shyh　shì

1. to wipe; to rub (eyes, etc.): 將淚跡拭去。 Wipe out the stain.

2. to dust; to clean: 她拭去椅子上的灰塵。 She dusted the chairs.

拭目以待（ㄕˋ ㄇㄨˋ ㄧˇ ㄉㄞˋ）
to wipe or rub the eyes and take a good look at what is going to happen—to wait for the result anxiously (or to wait and see)

to wipe, dust and clean

拭淚（ㄕˋ ㄌㄟˋ）
to wipe tears

拭淨（ㄕˋ ㄐㄧㄥˋ）
to wipe and clean

【拮】 1858
ㄐㄧㄝˊ　jye　jié
laboring hard; occupied

拮据（ㄐㄧㄝˊ ㄐㄩ）
①troubles or difficulties ②in financial straits ③to seize and grasp with the claws

【拯】 1859
ㄓㄥˇ　jeeng　zhěng

1. to save; to deliver
2. to raise; to lift up

拯民於水火之中（ㄓㄥˇ ㄇㄧㄣˊ ㄩˊ ㄕㄨㄟˇ ㄏㄨㄛˇ ㄓ ㄓㄨㄥ）
to deliver the people from extreme sufferings

拯焚救溺（ㄓㄥˇ ㄈㄣˊ ㄐㄧㄡˋ ㄋㄧˋ）
(literally) to save people from fire and drowning—to deliver the people from extreme misery

拯救（ㄓㄥˇ ㄐㄧㄡˋ）
①deliverance ②to save; to rescue; to deliver: 把我們從邪惡中拯救出來吧! Deliver us from evil!

拯恤（ㄓㄥˇ ㄒㄩˋ）
to save and help (the refugees, the poor, etc.)

【括】 1860
ㄎㄨㄛˋ　kuoh　kuò
（又讀《ㄨㄚ　gua　guà）

1. to include; to embrace; to enclose; to sum up; to comprise: 總括言之, 她是一個可愛的女孩。 To sum up, she is a nice girl.

2. to seek; to search for; to ransack: 土匪搜括了鎭上的糧食。 The bandits ransacked the town of food.

3. to come; to arrive
4. to bound; to tie
5. to restrain

括號（ㄎㄨㄛˋ ㄏㄠˋ）
(mathematics) the sign of aggregation

括弧（ㄎㄨㄛˋ ㄏㄨˊ）
parentheses; braces; brackets 一（ ）；｛ ｝；〔 〕

括線（ㄎㄨㄛˋ ㄒㄧㄢˋ）
a vinculum—a straight line over figures

（手部）

括約肌(ㄍㄨㄚ ㄩㄝ ㄐㄧ)
(anatomy) a constrictor; a sphincter

【拱】 1861 ㄍㄨㄥ goong gǒng

1. to fold hands before the breast when making a bow; to salute
2. to encircle with the hands
3. to surround: 眾星拱月。A myriad of stars surround the moon.
4. (architecture) arched (doors, windows, etc.)
5. to raise up (in the middle); to hump up; to arch: 新出的芽兒把土壤拱起來了。The young shoots have raised up the soil.

拱把(ㄍㄨㄥ ㄅㄚˇ)
the circumference of something which is the same as the circle formed by two hands

拱壩(ㄍㄨㄥ ㄅㄚˋ)
an arch dam

拱北(ㄍㄨㄥ ㄅㄟˇ)or 拱辰(ㄍㄨㄥ ㄔㄣˊ)
All the border tribes pay homage to the country, like stars encircling Polaris.

拱抱(ㄍㄨㄥ ㄅㄠˋ)
to encircle with two arms; to surround: 絕壁拱抱著小海灣。The cove was surrounded by cliffs.

拱璧(ㄍㄨㄥ ㄅㄧˋ)
a large piece of jade

拱別(ㄍㄨㄥ ㄅㄧㄝˊ)
to bid farewell by holding one's hands together in an up-and-down motion

拱默(ㄍㄨㄥ ㄇㄛˋ)
to salute in silence

拱門(ㄍㄨㄥ ㄇㄣˊ)
an arched door or doorway

拱木(ㄍㄨㄥ ㄇㄨˋ)
a large tree whose trunk can be encircled only with two arms

拱道(ㄍㄨㄥ ㄉㄠˋ)
an archway

拱頂(ㄍㄨㄥ ㄉㄧㄥˇ)
a dome; a vault

拱廊(ㄍㄨㄥ ㄌㄤˊ)
a cloister

拱立(ㄍㄨㄥ ㄌㄧˋ)
to stand in a reverent posture

拱肩縮背(ㄍㄨㄥ ㄐㄧㄢ ㄙㄨㄛ ㄅㄟˋ)
to shrink one's shoulders and bow one's back—as in cold weather, or an expression of obsequiousness

拱橋(ㄍㄨㄥ ㄑㄧㄠˊ)
an arch bridge

拱手(ㄍㄨㄥ ㄕㄡˇ)
to fold one's hands in a bow (usually in greeting or saying farewell)

拱手讓人(ㄍㄨㄥ ㄕㄡˇ ㄖㄤˋ ㄖㄣˊ)
to give up something to others without putting up a fight

拱瓦(ㄍㄨㄥ ㄨㄚˇ)
curved tiles which are slightly raised in the middle

拱衛(ㄍㄨㄥ ㄨㄟˋ)
to guard; to stand in circular positions and defend

【拴】 1862 ㄕㄨㄢ shuan shuān

1. to tie up; to fasten: 請將馬拴在樹上。Tie the horse to the tree, please.
2. to drive a wedge between two parties

拴兒(ㄕㄨㄢ ㄦ)
①a wooden peg for joining two objects together ②a cork

拴不住心(ㄕㄨㄢ ㄅㄨˋ ㄓㄨˋ ㄒㄧㄣ)
①(said of a woman) unable to hold a man's heart ②unable to keep one's mind fixed

拴馬(ㄕㄨㄢ ㄇㄚˇ)
to tie up a horse

拴馬樁(ㄕㄨㄢ ㄇㄚˇ ㄓㄨㄤ)
a post for fastening a horse

拴縛(ㄕㄨㄢ ㄈㄨˋ)
to tie up (with a rope or chain, etc.): 他們將他的雙手拴綁起來。They tied his hands together

拴扣兒(ㄕㄨㄢ ㄎㄡˋ ㄦ)
①to make a knot ②to alienate two parties; to drive a wedge between two persons

拴捆(ㄕㄨㄢ ㄎㄨㄣˇ)
to bind; to tie up

拴著(ㄕㄨㄢ ㄓㄜ)
tied up; fastened

拴住(ㄕㄨㄢ ㄓㄨˋ)

①to hold (one's attention, heart, etc.) ②to tie up; to make fast: 把船拴住。Make the boat fast.

拴上(ㄕㄨㄢ ㄕㄤˋ)
to fasten (the door, window, etc.): 他把門拴上了。He fastened the door.

拴繩(ㄕㄨㄢ ㄕㄥˊ ㄗ)
to tie or fasten with a rope

拴束(ㄕㄨㄢ ㄕㄨˋ)
①to pack (one's baggage, etc.); to tie up ②to restrain (one's heart)

拴娃娃(ㄕㄨㄢ ㄨㄚˊ ㄨㄚ)
(an old Chinese superstition) to tie a string around a clay baby at a temple or take it home, hoping to beget a child

【拶】 1863 ㄗㄢˇ tzaan zǎn (又讀 ㄗㄚˊ 'tzar zá)

a torture device in old China consisting of several contractible wooden sticks, in between which the fingers of a suspect were placed and pressed to extort confessions

拶指(ㄗㄢˇ ㄓˇ)
to press the fingers with the device described above

拶子(ㄗㄢˇ ㄗ)
an old Chinese torture device 看看「拶」

【拾】 1864 1. ㄕˊ shyr shí

1. to pick up; to collect
2. to put away: 請把你的書收拾整齊。Please put your books away.
3. a formal form of the figure "ten" used to prevent fraud in a document or check
4. an armlet used by archers

拾得(ㄕˊ ㄉㄜˊ)
to find; to pick up

拾得者(ㄕˊ ㄉㄜˊ ㄓㄜˇ)
the founder; one who picks up something lost by another person

拾掇(ㄕˊ ㄉㄨㄛˊ)or(ㄕ·ㄉㄨㄛ)
①to tidy up; to arrange in order ②(colloquial) to punish; to discipline ③to repair; to fix

拾漏子(ㄕ ㄌㄡˋ·ㄗ)or 拾漏兒(ㄕ

カスル
to take advantage of a loop-hole, etc.

拾荒(ㄕ ㄏㄨㄤ)
①to collect bits (which others have discarded) ②a collection of interesting tid-bits or anecdotes, etc.

拾芥(ㄕ ㄐㄧㄝ)
to glean and scraps (to eke out an existence)

拾芥(ㄕ ㄐㄧㄝ)
just for the picking or tak-ing—very easily gotten

拾金不昧(ㄕ ㄐㄧㄣ ㄅㄨ ㄇㄟ)
to pick up a piece of lost gold and return it to the owner

拾起(ㄕ ㄑㄧ)
to pick up

拾取(ㄕ ㄑㄩ)or 拾掇(ㄕ ㄓㄨ)
to collect; to pick up

拾人涕唾(ㄕ ㄖㄣ ㄊㄧ ㄊㄨㄛ)
to repeat what others have said or written; to plagia-rize; to practise me-tooism

拾人牙慧(ㄕ ㄖㄣ ㄧㄚ ㄏㄨㄟ)
to pick up what others have said or written and take it as one's own idea—to plagiarize 亦作「拾人唾餘」

拾翠踏青(ㄕ ㄘㄨㄟ ㄊㄚ ㄑㄧㄥ)
to go to scenic spots; to en-joy natural charms

拾穗(ㄕ ㄙㄨㄟ)
to glean

拾穗人(ㄕ ㄙㄨㄟ ㄖㄣ)
the gleaner

拾遺(ㄕ ㄧ)
①to pick up what others have lost and keep it as one's own: 路不拾遺。No one pockets anything found on the road. ②a collection of anecdotes which have not been recorded by other historians ③an official post in the Tang Dynasty with the responsibility of counseling on the conduct of the emperor

【拾】 1864
2. ㄕㄜ sheh shè
to go up; to ascend

拾級而上(ㄕㄜ ㄐㄧ ㄦ ㄕㄤ)or 拾級而登(ㄕㄜ ㄐㄧ ㄦ ㄉㄥ)
to ascend by stairs; to go up

by a flight of steps; to mount up a flight of steps

【拾】 1864
2. ㄕ shy shí
拾翻(ㄕ ㄈㄢ)
to turn upside down

【持】 1865
ㄔ chyr chí

1. to hold; to grasp: 他手中持著一本書。He is holding a book in his hands.

2. to maintain; to support; to keep; to uphold: 要小心保持你的名譽。Be careful to main-tain your reputation.

3. to manage; to preside

4. a tie or stalemate

持筆(ㄔ ㄅㄧ)
to hold the pen—to write

持票人(ㄔ ㄆㄧㄠ ㄖㄣ)
a check holder; the bearer of a check or bill

持平(ㄔ ㄆㄧㄥ)
fair and unbiased

持滿(ㄔ ㄇㄢ)
①brimming and in danger of spilling out (implying over-confidence, complacen-cy, etc.) ②to draw a bowful ly and be ready to shoot

持法(ㄔ ㄈㄚ)
to maintain or enforce law or discipline

持法森嚴(ㄔ ㄈㄚ ㄙㄣ ㄧㄢ)
to administer sharp justice

持服(ㄔ ㄈㄨ)
three years of mourning for one's parents

持刀(ㄔ ㄉㄠ)
to hold a knife

持橐簪筆(ㄔ ㄊㄨㄛ ㄗㄢ ㄅㄧ)
to serve as a counselor or adviser

持兩端(ㄔ ㄌㄧㄤ ㄉㄨㄢ)
hesitating as to which of two opposing groups to sup-port

持祿(ㄔ ㄌㄨ)
to hold an office without achieving anything

持論(ㄔ ㄌㄨㄣ)
to present an argument; to put a case; to express a view

持論公允(ㄔ ㄌㄨㄣ ㄍㄨㄥ ㄩㄣ)
to hold an unbiased view; to make impartial comments or

statements

持衡(ㄔ ㄏㄥ)
①to observe and measure the capability of a person ②to weigh the advantages and disadvantages

持戟(ㄔ ㄐㄧ)
①a soldier ②an aide

持家(ㄔ ㄐㄧㄚ)
①to run one's home; to manage the household ②to keep the family estates

持節(ㄔ ㄐㄧㄝ)
to serve as a diplomatic envoy

持戒(ㄔ ㄐㄧㄝ)
(said of a Buddhist monk or nun) to observe the com-mandments

持械搶劫(ㄔ ㄐㄧㄝ ㄑㄧㄤ ㄐㄧㄝ)
armed robbery; to commit robbery with firearms

持久(ㄔ ㄐㄧㄡ)
to hold out; to last for a long time; lasting; durable: 我們必須建立持久的和平。We must make a durable peace.

持久戰(ㄔ ㄐㄧㄡ ㄓㄢ)
a military strategy adopted by the weaker of the bellig-erents to avoid decisive bat-tles so that the war will become protracted and the other side worn down by attrition; a long-drawn-out war; a war of attrition

持槍(ㄔ ㄑㄧㄤ)
①to hold a gun ②(mili-tary) to port arms

持續(ㄔ ㄒㄩ)
①continuous; incessant; un-interrupted: 雨已經持續下了一禮拜了。We've had a week of incessant rain. ②to hold; to go on: 天氣持續暖和。The weather held warm.

持之以恆(ㄔ ㄓ ㄧ ㄏㄥ)
to persevere: 他讀書持之以恆。He persevered in his studies.

持之有故(ㄔ ㄓ ㄧㄡ ㄍㄨ)
a view or opinion which finds its source in ancient sayings; a well-founded view or opinion

持齋(ㄔ ㄓㄞ)
(said of Buddhists) to stick

〔手部〕

to a vegetarian diet

持正 (彳 ㄓㄥˋ)
fair and just; to uphold justice and propriety

持重 (彳 ㄓㄨㄥˋ)
①to observe rules of justice and propriety ②to act cautiously and carefully: 他老成持重。 He acts cautiously and carefully. ③dignified

持身 (彳 ㄕㄣ)
to conduct oneself (properly)

持身涉世 (彳 ㄕㄣ ㄕㄜˋ ㄕˋ)
to exercise proper restraints in dealing with the world

持勝 (彳 ㄕㄥˋ)
to maintain one's superiority or advantage

持贈 (彳 ㄗㄥˋ)
to carry and present to; to present (a gift) to

持喪 (彳 ㄙㄤ)
to be in mourning

持異議 (彳 ㄧˋ ㄧˋ)
to maintain a different or opposite view: 他們各持異議。 They are divided in their opinions.

持有 (彳 ㄧㄡˇ)
to hold: 他持有美國護照。 He holds an American passport.

持養 (彳 ㄧㄤˇ)
①to preserve (one's energy, vitality, etc.) by sticking to a regimen ②to comply with or respect (one's idea, view, etc.)

持盈保泰 (彳 ㄧㄥˊ ㄅㄠˇ ㄊㄞˋ)
(said of the high and mighty) to remain modest and humble and thus to be rewarded with security on his position; to maintain good luck by restraint

持危扶傾 (彳 ㄨㄟˊ ㄈㄨˊ ㄑㄧㄥ)
to act as a champion of justice; to uphold justice; to come to the aid of the weak and the unfortunate

【按】 1866 ㄢˋ àn àn
1. to place the hand on; to press, control, etc. with one's hand: 按鈕使鈴響。 Press the button to ring the bell.
2. to examine
3. to stop; to halt; to repress;

---

to leave aside: 他按捺不住心頭怒火。 He is unable to repress his anger.
4. to impeach; to censure
5. according to; in (good order); as: 我將按你的建議去做。 I'll do as you advise.
6. to follow (a map, river, etc.)
7. a note; a comment: 編者按 the editor's note (or comment)

按兵不動 (ㄢˋ ㄅㄧㄥ ㄅㄨˋ ㄉㄨㄥˋ)
①to refuse to send troops to relieve friendly forces in distress; to keep back army from battle ②to bide one's time; to take no action; to remain motionless

按部就班 (ㄢˋ ㄅㄨˋ ㄐㄧㄡˋ ㄅㄢ)
(to do things) in good order or according to logical order 或 First things first. 訛作「按步就班」

按轡 (ㄢˋ ㄆㄟˋ)
to rein in the horse (to keep it from galloping)

按摩 (ㄢˋ ㄇㄛˊ)
①massage ②to massage

按摩女 (ㄢˋ ㄇㄛˊ ㄋㄩˇ)
a masseuse

按摩師 (ㄢˋ ㄇㄛˊ ㄕ)
a masseur

按脈 (ㄢˋ ㄇㄞˋ)
(said of a Chinese herb doctor) to feel the patient's pulse; to take the pulse

按名次 (ㄢˋ ㄇㄧㄥˊ ㄘˋ)
according to the order of names listed on a roster

按法嚴懲 (ㄢˋ ㄈㄚˇ ㄧㄢˊ ㄔㄥˊ)
to mete out severe punishment according to law

按討 (ㄢˋ ㄊㄠˇ)
to investigate a rebellion and put it down; to quell an uprising

按圖索驥 (ㄢˋ ㄊㄨˊ ㄙㄨㄛˇ ㄐㄧˋ)
①(literally) to find a horse according to a drawing —using a hackneyed method; lacking originality, initiative or imagination in doing a job; to try to locate something by following up a clue ②to use something as a starting point for further exploration or study

---

按捺 (ㄢˋ ㄋㄚˋ)
to restrain, repress or hold back (one's anger, etc.): 他按捺不住激動的心情。 He was unable to hold back his excitement.

按鈕 (ㄢˋ ㄋㄧㄡˇ)
①a push button ②to push the button

按年 (ㄢˋ ㄋㄧㄢˊ)
yearly; annually

按理 (ㄢˋ ㄌㄧˇ)
according to common practice or simple reasoning; normally

按例 (ㄢˋ ㄌㄧˋ)
according to precedents

按鈴 (ㄢˋ ㄌㄧㄥˊ)
to press the button of a buzzer; to ring the bell

按劍 (ㄢˋ ㄐㄧㄢˋ)
to place one's hand on one's sword; to grasp one's sword

按期 (ㄢˋ ㄑㄧˊ)
according to the dates, periods, etc. agreed upon or specified; on time; on schedule: 這份雜誌將按期出版。 The magazine will come out on time.

按下不表 (ㄢˋ ㄒㄧㄚˋ ㄅㄨˋ ㄅㄧㄠˇ)
(literally) Let's suspend the narration for a while (and talk about....) —(in old novels) Let's now turn to....

按下去 (ㄢˋ ㄒㄧㄚˋ ㄑㄩˋ)
to press down

按序 (ㄢˋ ㄒㄩˋ)
according to the order of sequence; in (regular) sequence

按址 (ㄢˋ ㄓˇ)
(to find a place) according to the address

按捺 (ㄢˋ ㄓˋ)
①according to ②to repress or restrain (one's anger, etc.)

按照 (ㄢˋ ㄓㄠˋ)
according to; in accordance with; in conformity with: 他未按照命令行事。 He did not act in accordance with the orders.

按住 (ㄢˋ ㄓㄨˋ)
to repress or restrain; to press down and not to let go

按察(ㄢ ㄔㄚˊ)
to investigate; to examine

按察使(ㄢ ㄔㄚˊ ㄕˇ)or(ㄢ ㄔㄚˊ ㄕ)
a provincial official in old China roughly equivalent to today's chief prosecutor of a high court

按成兒(ㄢ ㄔㄥˊ)
according to the percentage; proportionately

按時(ㄢ ㄕˊ)
①according to the time specified or agreed upon ② on time: 他昨晚按時抵達。He arrived on time last night. ③regularly

按手(ㄢ ㄕㄡˇ)
(Christianity) to place the hand on the head of the ordained in an ordination ceremony

按數(ㄢ ㄕㄨˋ)or 按額(ㄢ ㄜˊ)
according to the number; proportionately

按說(ㄢ ㄕㄨㄛ)
according to common sense, common practice, etc.; ordinarily; normally: 按說這時該下雨了。Ordinarily it should be raining at this time of the year.

按日(ㄢ ㄖˋ)
daily; every day

按次(ㄢ ㄘˋ)
according to order

按壓(ㄢ ㄧㄚ)
(said of bureaucracy) to shelve an official business without justification

按問(ㄢ ㄨㄣˋ)
to investigate, examine and question

按據(ㄢ ㄐㄩˋ)
according to (investigation, surveys, references, data, etc.)

按月(ㄢ ㄩㄝˋ)
monthly; by the month: 他按月來此一次。He comes here monthly.

【指】 1867
1. ㄓ jyy zhǐ
1. the finger: 她用手指指我。She was pointing her finger at me.
2. to point; to direct: 他指出了我的錯誤。He pointed out my

mistake.
3. to indicate; to refer to; to mean
4. the number of people
5. intentions
6. the main theme
7. to hope
8. to depend on: 我們就指望這點錢度日。We depended on this money for expenses.

指標(ㄓ ㄅㄧㄠ)
①(mathematics) characteristic ②an index sign; a target: 他們完成計畫的指標。They attained the targets set in the plan.

指不勝屈(ㄓ ㄅㄨˋ ㄕㄥ ㄑㄩ)
too many to be counted; countless

指派(ㄓ ㄆㄞˋ)
to appoint; to assign: 他們指派了一位新秘書。They appointed a new secretary.

指摹 or 指模(ㄓ ㄇㄛˊ)
a fingerprint

指迷(ㄓ ㄇㄧˊ)
to direct another out of a maze; to show or indicate the way; to give advice or guidance

指明(ㄓ ㄇㄧㄥˊ)
to indicate clearly; to point out; to single out: 把你喜歡的那些指明給我看。Point me out the ones you would like

指名(ㄓ ㄇㄧㄥˊ)
to mention by name; to single out by name

指名道姓(ㄓ ㄇㄧㄥˊ ㄉㄠˋ ㄒㄧㄥˋ)
to mention someone's name; to name names

指法(ㄓ ㄈㄚˇ)
①fingering ②a book or manual explaining how fingers are used or applied in a certain kind of work or art, such as playing string instruments, typing, etc.

指腹為婚(ㄓ ㄈㄨˋ ㄨㄟˊ ㄏㄨㄣ)
(in old China) a prenatal betrothal

指導(ㄓ ㄉㄠˇ)or(ㄓ ㄉㄠˋ)
①direction or guidance: 我的課業需要些指導。I need some guidance with my studies. ②to instruct; to direct; to guide; to supervise: 老師指導學生的課業。The

teacher directs the work of his students.

指導委員會(ㄓ ㄉㄠˇ ㄨㄟˋ ㄩㄢˊ ㄏㄨㄟˋ)
a steering committee

指導員(ㄓ ㄉㄠˇ ㄩㄢˊ)or(ㄓ ㄉㄠˋ ㄩㄢˊ)
a supervisor

指點(ㄓ ㄉㄧㄢˇ)
to give directions or pointers; to teach; to advise; to instruct: 教練耐心地指點他的球員。The coach patiently instructs his players.

指頂花(ㄓ ㄉㄧㄥˇ ㄏㄨㄚ)
a foxglove

指定(ㄓ ㄉㄧㄥˋ)
①to appoint; to assign: 指定開會的時間為八點。The time appointed for the meeting was eight o'clock. ②to indicate clearly and with certainty: 我指定這幢房子給我的兒子。I mean this house for my son. ③to allot; to set aside (a sum of money for a certain purpose, etc.)

指東話西(ㄓ ㄉㄨㄥ ㄏㄨㄚˋ ㄒㄧ)
(literally) to point to the east and talk the west—irrelevant; to mislead with talk; to talk nonsense; to try to avoid the main theme by talking about something else 亦作「指東說西」

指天畫地(ㄓ ㄊㄧㄢ ㄏㄨㄚˋ ㄉㄧˋ)
①to talk straight and frankly ②to talk wildly; to behave without regard to decorum

指天誓日(ㄓ ㄊㄧㄢ ㄕˋ ㄖˋ)
to swear by Heaven and the sun—to swear by all the gods

指禿說瞎(ㄓ ㄊㄨ ㄕㄨㄛ ㄒㄧㄚ)
(literally) to point to the bald and talk of the blind —to talk circuitously

指南(ㄓ ㄋㄢˊ)
to indicate a definite direction; a directory; a guidebook; a primer

指南針(ㄓ ㄋㄢˊ ㄓㄣ)
a compass

指南車(ㄓ ㄋㄢˊ ㄔㄜ)
a chariot which showed correct directions, said to have been invented by the legendary Huangti (黃帝)

〔手部〕

指令(坐ㄌㄧㄥˋ)
a directive; an order; instructions from a higher office: 他發出一連串的命令。He issued a stream of directives.

指路碑(坐ㄌㄨˋ ㄅㄟ)
roadside tablets showing direction

指路標(坐ㄌㄨˋ ㄅㄧㄠ)
a signpost; a finger post; a guidepost 亦作「指路牌」

指鹿為馬(坐ㄌㄨˋ ㄨㄟˊ ㄇㄚˇ)
(literally) to call a stag a horse—to confound right and wrong

指骨(坐ㄍㄨˇ)
phalanges of fingers

指間(坐ㄐㄧㄢ)
in a short while

指顧間事(坐ㄍㄨˋ ㄐㄧㄢ ㄕˋ)
in no time at all; to happen very soon; in a matter of moments

指歸(坐ㄍㄨㄟ)
a concourse where all points meet; a main theme or tenet

指靠(坐ㄎㄠˋ)
to depend on (for one's livelihood); to look to (for help); to count on: 這件事我們就指靠你了。We'll depend on you for this.

指控(坐ㄎㄨㄥˋ)
to accuse; to charge; accusation; a charge: 他們指控他受賄。They accused him of taking bribes.

指痕(坐ㄏㄣˊ)
fingermarks; marks made by fingernails

指畫(坐ㄏㄨㄚˋ)
①finger painting; to paint by using finger paints ②a finger painting

指揮 or 指麾(坐ㄏㄨㄟ)
to conduct or direct (an orchestra, etc.); to command (an army, etc.): 這兒誰負責指揮? Who commands here?

指揮棒(坐ㄏㄨㄟ ㄅㄤˋ)
the baton (for a conductor)

指揮部(坐ㄏㄨㄟ ㄅㄨˋ)
the command post; headquarters

指揮刀(坐ㄏㄨㄟ ㄉㄠ)
the saber of a commanding officer

指揮官(坐ㄏㄨㄟ ㄍㄨㄢ)
the commanding officer; the commander

指揮若定(坐ㄏㄨㄟ ㄖㄨㄛˋ ㄉㄧㄥˋ)
to retain full composure even in command of a big operation (especially said of those given a major assignment for the first time); to direct (work, etc.) with perfect ease; to give highly competent leadership

指環(坐ㄏㄨㄢˊ)
a ring: 他送她一個指環。He presented her a ring.

指婚(坐ㄏㄨㄣ)
(Ching Dynasty) marriages of members of the royal family with their mates picked by the emperor

指雞罵狗(坐ㄐㄧ ㄇㄚˋ ㄍㄡˇ)
(literally) to point at a chicken and revile the dog—to scold indirectly or in circumlocution

指教(坐ㄐㄧㄠˋ)
①direction and guidance ②(a polite expression) your advice or counsel: 請你多多指教。Kindly give us your advice.

指向(坐ㄒㄧㄤˋ)
to point to; to direct to: 指標牌指向北邊。The signboard points north.

指指點點(坐ˇ 坐ˇ ㄉㄧㄢˇ ㄉㄧㄢˇ)
①gesticulating ②to point; to point out; to indicate

指摘(坐ㄓㄞ)
to point out the faults of another; to blame; to criticize

指針(坐ㄓㄣ)
①a guide; a manual ②an index; an indication needle in a measuring instrument

指掌(坐ㄓㄤˇ)
①pointing at one's palm: 易如指掌 to be as easy as pointing at one's palm ②fingers and palms: 瞭如指掌 to be as clear as one were looking at one's own fingers and palms

指正(坐ㄓㄥˋ)
①to correct ②(a polite expression) to present here with for your correction: 請惠予指正。Please oblige me with your valuable comments.

指證(坐ㄓㄥˋ)
to produce evidence (in court, etc.); to prove

指斥(坐ㄔˋ)
to refute; to rebuke; to accuse: 他嚴厲指斥她的疏忽。He rebuked her strongly for her negligence.

指使(坐ㄕˇ)
to hire or entice another to do a task for oneself; to instigate or incite behind the scenes: 不要受別人指使。Don't act at the instigation of others.

指事(坐ㄕˋ)
"pointing to situations", or "indirect symbols"—one of six categories under which Chinese characters are roughly grouped, which is formed by various kinds of substitutions, such as making parts stand for wholes, attributes for things, effects for causes, instruments for activities, gestures for actions, etc. in a metaphorical way

指示(坐ㄕˋ)
①instruction; indication ②to direct; to instruct; to show; to indicate: 你能指示我去郵局的方向嗎? Can you direct me to the post office?

指示代名詞(坐ㄕˋ ㄉㄞˋ ㄇㄧㄥˊ ㄘˊ)
demonstrative pronouns

指示劑(坐ㄕˋ ㄐㄧˋ)
(chemistry) an indicator

指示器(坐ㄕˋ ㄑㄧˋ)
an indicator

指示形容詞(坐ㄕˋ ㄒㄧㄥˊ ㄖㄨㄥˊ ㄘˊ)
demonstrative adjectives

指手畫腳(坐ㄕㄡˇ ㄏㄨㄚˋ ㄐㄧㄠˇ)
to gesticulate profusely

指書(坐ㄕㄨ)
to write with one's finger instead of a pen

指數(坐ㄕㄨˋ)
index; exponent; index number

〔手部〕

旦 (ㄓㄡˋ ㄖˋ)
in a matter of days; in a few days

旦高陞 (ㄓㄡˋ ㄖˋ ㄍㄠ ㄕㄥ)
to get promoted soon (a well-wishing expression)

旦可下 (ㄓㄡˋ ㄖˋ ㄎㄜˇ ㄒㄧㄚˋ)
to capture (an enemy-held city, strategic position, etc.) very soon

旦可待 (ㄓㄡˋ ㄖˋ ㄎㄜˇ ㄉㄞˋ)
can be expected very shortly or soon: 我們的勝利是指日可待的。Our victory can be expected very shortly.

認 (ㄓㄡˋ ㄖˋ)
to identify (a suspect, a lost item, etc.) from a group

責 (ㄓㄡˋ ㄖˋ)
to accuse; to censure; to charge; to disparage: 他受到輿論的指責。He was subjected to the censure of public opinion.

桑罵槐 (ㄓㄨˊ ㄙㄤ ㄇㄚˋ ㄏㄨㄞˊ)
(literally) to point to the mulberry and revile the locust tree—to scold somebody indirectly

要 (ㄓㄡˋ ㄧㄠˋ)
the theme; the essential points

引 (ㄓㄡˋ ㄧㄣˇ)
to direct; to guide; guidance: 我在他的指引之下完成了論文。I wrote my dissertation under his guidance.

紋 (ㄓㄡˋ ㄨㄣˊ) or 指印 (ㄓㄡˋ ㄧㄣˋ)
a fingerprint; a dactylogram

紋學 (ㄓㄡˋ ㄨㄣˊ ㄒㄩㄝˊ)
dactylography

望 (ㄓㄡˋ ㄨㄤˋ)
to hope for; to expect; expectations; to look forward to: 我們指望最好的一面。We're hoping for the best.

指 *1867*
2. ㄓˇ jy **zhǐ**

頭 (ㄓˇ ㄊㄡˊ)
fingers

頭畫 (ㄓˇ ㄊㄡˊ ㄏㄨㄚˋ)
paintings with fingers; finger painting

頭尖兒 (ㄓˇ ㄊㄡˊ ㄐㄧㄢ ㄦ)
the tip of the finger; a fingertip

指 *1867*
3. ㄓˋ jy **zhì**

指甲 (ㄓˋ ㄐㄧㄚˇ)
a fingernail

指甲刀 (ㄓˋ ㄐㄧㄚˇ ㄉㄠ)
nailclippers

指甲蓋兒 (ㄓˋ ㄐㄧㄚˇ ㄍㄞˋ ㄦ)
a fingernail

指甲心兒 (ㄓˋ ㄐㄧㄚˇ ㄒㄧㄣ ㄦ)
where the fingernail joins the flesh

指甲草 (ㄓˋ ㄐㄧㄚˇ ㄘㄠˇ)
balsamine

指甲油 (ㄓˋ ㄐㄧㄚˇ ㄧㄡˊ)
fingernail polish

挑 *1868*
1. ㄊㄧㄠ tiau **tiāo**

1. to carry things with a pole on one's shoulder; to shoulder: 他挑起生產的重擔。He shouldered heavy loads in production.

2. to select; to choose; to pick: 挑最好的。Pick the best one.

3. to pick by pitchfork

挑不動 (ㄊㄧㄠ ㄅㄨˋ ㄉㄨㄥˋ) or 挑不起 (ㄊㄧㄠ ㄅㄨˋ ㄑㄧˇ)
too heavy to carry

挑肥揀瘦 (ㄊㄧㄠ ㄈㄟˊ ㄐㄧㄢˇ ㄕㄡˋ)
to be very particular in one's selection (of a mate or things); to be fastidious

挑夫 (ㄊㄧㄠ ㄈㄨ)
a coolie; a bearer; a porter

挑大梁 (ㄊㄧㄠ ㄉㄚˋ ㄌㄧㄤˊ)
to play the leading role; to shoulder the main responsibility

挑擔 (ㄊㄧㄠ ㄉㄢˋ)
to carry a load with a carrying pole

挑剔 (ㄊㄧㄠ ㄊㄧ)
① to be very particular in making selection; to be over-punctilious in making a choice: 他對食物很挑剔。He is particular about his food. ② to find fault with somebody or something; to nitpick

挑開 (ㄊㄧㄠ ㄎㄞ)
to brush aside with a poker or stick

挑好的 (ㄊㄧㄠ ㄏㄠˇ ㄉㄜ)
to choose or select the better ones; to pick the good ones

挑花 (ㄊㄧㄠ ㄏㄨㄚ)

---

to embroider; a kind of embroidery

挑揀 (ㄊㄧㄠ ㄐㄧㄢˇ)
to pick; to select or choose

挑精揀肥 (ㄊㄧㄠ ㄐㄧㄥ ㄐㄧㄢˇ ㄈㄟˊ)
to pick the best; to be very choosy

挑取 (ㄊㄧㄠ ㄑㄩˇ)
to pick; to choose; to select

挑選 (ㄊㄧㄠ ㄒㄩㄢˇ)
to select; to choose; to pick; to take one's pick of: 他挑選了一套新衣服。He picked out a new suit.

挑飭 (ㄊㄧㄠ ㄒㄧ)
to make punctilious demands; to pick on another; to find fault

挑水的 (ㄊㄧㄠ ㄕㄨㄟˇ ㄉㄜ)
a water bearer

挑字眼兒 (ㄊㄧㄠ ㄗˋ ㄧㄢˇ ㄦ)
to pick on someone for negligible faults or flaws

挑子 (ㄊㄧㄠ ㄗˇ) or 挑兒 (ㄊㄧㄠ ㄦ)
loads, things, stock-in-trade, etc. carried by means of a carrying pole

挑刺兒 (ㄊㄧㄠ ㄘˋ ㄦ)
to find fault; to be captious

挑錯 (ㄊㄧㄠ ㄘㄨㄛˋ)
to find fault; to pick flaws

挑三揀四 (ㄊㄧㄠ ㄙㄢ ㄐㄧㄢˇ ㄙˋ)
to pick and choose; to be choosy: 購物的顧客越來越喜歡挑三揀四。The shopping public is getting more choosy.

挑么挑六 (ㄊㄧㄠ ㄇㄜ ㄊㄧㄠ ㄌㄧㄡˋ)
to indulge in faultfinding; to pick flaws

挑眼 (ㄊㄧㄠ ㄧㄢˇ) or 挑眼兒 (ㄊㄧㄠ ㄧㄢˇ ㄦ)
to pick flaws; to find fault; to be fastidious (about formalities, etc.)

挑挖 (ㄊㄧㄠ ㄨㄚ)
to dredge; to clear (a waterway, etc.)

挑運費 (ㄊㄧㄠ ㄩㄣˋ ㄈㄟˋ)
porterage

挑 *1868*
2. ㄊㄧㄠˇ teau **tiǎo**

1. to stir; to provoke; to arouse

2. to dally; to make a pass at; to seduce

挑撥 (ㄊㄧㄠˇ ㄅㄛ)
to provoke or arouse; to

〔手部〕

instigate; to cause disputes; to cause the alienation; to sow discord. 她在朋友之間挑撥是非。She causes the alienation between friends by spreading rumors.

挑撥離間(ㄊㄧㄠ ㄅㄛ ㄌㄧ ㄐㄧㄢ)
to stir up ill will or bad feelings; to sow discord

挑逗 or 挑鬥(ㄊㄧㄠ ㄉㄡ)
to seduce; to arouse amorous desires

挑燈(ㄊㄧㄠ ㄉㄥ)
to stir the wick of a lamp so that it will put forth more light

挑撥夜戰(ㄊㄧㄠ ㄅㄛ ㄧㄝˋ ㄓㄢ)
to continue working by lamplight

挑動(ㄊㄧㄠ ㄉㄨㄥˋ)
①to arouse; to seduce ②to instigate; to incite

挑弄(ㄊㄧㄠ ㄋㄨㄥˋ)
to tease; to play a joke on

挑弄是非(ㄊㄧㄠ ㄋㄨㄥˋ ㄕ ㄈㄟ)
to arouse ill will between two parties; to stir up one side against the other

挑起(ㄊㄧㄠ ㄑㄧˇ)
to provoke; to stir up; to instigate

挑情(ㄊㄧㄠ ㄑㄧㄥˊ)
to make amorous advances; to arouse one of the other sex in love making 參看「調情」

挑戰(ㄊㄧㄠ ㄓㄢˋ)
to make a pass at a woman with amorous intentions 亦作「調戲」

挑釁(ㄊㄧㄠ ㄒㄧㄣˋ)
to provoke

挑戰(ㄊㄧㄠ ㄓㄢˋ)
to challenge to a duel; a challenge; to provoke or pick up a fight

挑戰行為(ㄊㄧㄠ ㄓㄢˋ ㄒㄧㄥˊ ㄨㄟˊ)
provocative actions

挑戰書(ㄊㄧㄠ ㄓㄢˋ ㄕㄨ)
a cartel; a written challenge

挑事(ㄊㄧㄠ ㄕˋ)
to stir up trouble; to sow discord

挑唆(ㄊㄧㄠ ㄙㄨㄛ)
to stir up something with mischievous intentions; to alienate people by arousing

ill will among them: 別在背後挑撥。Don't stir up trouble behind the scenes.

【挑】1868 ㄊㄧㄠ tau tiáo
light and frivolous

挑達(ㄊㄧㄠˊ ㄉㄚˊ)
to walk to and fro in a free manner

【拽】1869 1. ㄓㄨㄞ juai
zhuāi
to fling; to hurl

【拽】1869 2. ㄓㄨㄞˇ juay
zhuǎi
to pull; to drag; to catch: 他一把拽住它不放。He caught hold of it and would not let it go.

【拽】1869 3. 讠ㄝ yeh yè
(又讀)ㄧ yih yì
1. to trail; to drag after: 她的衣服在地上拽拖著。Her dress trailed on the ground.
2. to pull or drag

【挖】1870 ㄨㄚ ua wā
1. to scoop out; to dig out: 他們在挖防空洞。They were digging an air-raid shelter.
2. to engrave with a knife; to cut or gouge

挖補(ㄨㄚ ㄅㄨˇ)
①to gouge and mend (a surfaced road, etc.) ②cutting and mending (of writings, etc.)

挖煤(ㄨㄚ ㄇㄟˊ)
to mine for coal

挖墊(ㄨㄚ ㄉㄧㄢˋ)
a kind of needle work in old China done by cutting off various forms on a piece of cloth and mounting them on another piece of cloth of different color so as to make a picture or design

挖洞(ㄨㄚ ㄉㄨㄥˋ)or挖窟窿(ㄨㄚ ㄎㄨ ㄌㄨㄥ)
to make a hole or cave; to dig out a hole; to scoop (out) a hole

挖泥(ㄨㄚ ㄋㄧˊ)
to dredge (up) mud

挖泥機(ㄨㄚ ㄋㄧˊ ㄐㄧ)
a dredger

挖泥船(ㄨㄚ ㄋㄧˊ ㄔㄨㄢˊ)

a suction dredger (a boat)

挖改(ㄨㄚ ㄍㄞˇ)
(said of a piece of writing etc.) to cut and make changes

挖根(ㄨㄚ ㄍㄣ)
to uproot

挖苦(ㄨㄚ ㄎㄨˇ)
①to ridicule; to make caustic remarks ②a dig: 這是挖苦他的。This was a dig at him.

挖空(ㄨㄚ ㄎㄨㄥ)
to hollow

挖空心思(ㄨㄚ ㄎㄨㄥ ㄒㄧㄣ ㄙ)
to cudgel (or rack) one's brains: 他挖空心思找適當的字句。He dredged into himself for words.

挖角(ㄨㄚ ㄐㄧㄠˇ)
to lure away the employee of another company or organization by making attractive offers

挖井(ㄨㄚ ㄐㄧㄥˇ)
to dig a well

挖掘(ㄨㄚ ㄐㄩㄝˊ)
to dig; to excavate; to unearth: 他在挖掘地下寶藏。He's unearthing buried treasure.

挖掘機(ㄨㄚ ㄐㄩㄝˊ ㄐㄧ)
an excavator; a navvy 亦作「挖土機」or「怪手」

挖牆腳(ㄨㄚ ㄑㄧㄤˊ ㄐㄧㄠˇ)
to undermine the foundation

挖塚(ㄨㄚ ㄓㄨㄥˇ)
to dig a grave; grave-digging

挖出來(ㄨㄚ ㄔㄨ ㄌㄞˊ)
to dig out; to gouge out; to excavate

挖肉補瘡(ㄨㄚ ㄖㄡˋ ㄅㄨˇ ㄔㄨㄤ)
(literally) to cut a piece of flesh to mend a wound—to make up for a deficit by raising loans

挖耳朵(ㄨㄚ ㄦˇ ㄉㄨㄛ)
to pick ears

挖眼睛(ㄨㄚ ㄧㄢˇ ㄐㄧㄥ)
to gouge out eyes

【拷】1871 ㄎㄠˇ kao kǎo
to flog, whip, torture, etc.(in order to get a confession etc.)

拷貝(ㄎㄠˇ ㄅㄟˋ)
a copy

拷打(ㄎㄠˇ ㄉㄚˇ)

to flog or whip; to torture:
土匪將他嚴刑拷打。The bandit
subjected him to severe torture.

間(ㄐㄧㄢ ㄒㄩㄣ)拷訊(ㄎㄠ ㄒㄩㄣ)
to extort information, confessions, etc. by means of
torture: 他受拷問。He is sub-
jected to torture.

挓 1872
ㄓㄚ ja zha

參看「挓抒」

抄(ㄓㄨ˙ ㄗˊ)
widespread; open 亦作「扎挓」

拳 1873
ㄑㄩㄢˊ chyuan quán
a fist: 我給了他一拳。I gave
him a blow with the fist;
sparring feats; various
forms of boxing: 他們彼此以
拳。They boxed with each
other.

拳棒(ㄑㄩㄢˊ ㄅㄤˋ)
fighting feats

拳匪(ㄑㄩㄢˊ ㄈㄟˇ)
(contemptuous) the Boxers of
the late 19th century, whose
slogan was "supporting the
Ching Dynasty and wiping
out the foreign devils"

拳打(ㄑㄩㄢˊ ㄉㄚˇ)or 拳擊(ㄑㄩㄢˊ ㄐㄧ)
to strike with fists

拳打腳踢(ㄑㄩㄢˊ ㄉㄚˇ ㄐㄧㄠˇ ㄊㄧ)
to cuff and kick; to beat up;
to strike and kick

拳頭(ㄑㄩㄢˊ ㄊㄡ˙)
a fist: 他用拳頭打我。He
struck me with his fist.

拳來腳去(ㄑㄩㄢˊ ㄌㄞˊ ㄐㄧㄠˇ ㄑㄩˋ)
to give tit for tat; to
exchange blows

拳擊(ㄑㄩㄢˊ ㄐㄧ)
boxing; the boxing art; to
strike with fist: 你喜歡拳擊
嗎? Do you like boxing?

拳擊手(ㄑㄩㄢˊ ㄐㄧ ㄕㄡˇ)
a boxer; a pugilist

拳擊手套(ㄑㄩㄢˊ ㄐㄧ ㄕㄡˇ ㄊㄠˋ)
boxing gloves

拳腳(ㄑㄩㄢˊ ㄐㄧㄠˇ)
Chinese boxing (which uses
both the fists and the feet)

拳腳交加(ㄑㄩㄢˊ ㄐㄧㄠˇ ㄐㄧㄠ ㄐㄧㄚ)
or 拳足交加(ㄑㄩㄢˊ ㄗㄨˊ ㄐㄧㄠ
ㄐㄧㄚ)
to beat up with fists and

kicks; a violent beating

拳跼 or 拳局(ㄑㄩㄢˊ ㄐㄩˊ)
to be confined or restrained
to a small place

拳曲(ㄑㄩㄢˊ ㄑㄩ)
① to bend oneself as a fist
② to be gnarled and twisted

拳拳服膺(ㄑㄩㄢˊ ㄑㄩㄢˊ ㄈㄨˊ ㄧㄥ)
to adhere to faithfully; to
have a sincere belief in

拳師(ㄑㄩㄢˊ ㄕ)
an expert in the art of boxing; a boxing master; a
boxer: 他是一個好拳師。He is
a good boxer.

拳師狗(ㄑㄩㄢˊ ㄕ ㄍㄡˇ)
a boxer (dog)

拳術(ㄑㄩㄢˊ ㄕㄨˋ)or 拳法(ㄑㄩㄢˊ ㄈㄚˇ)
the boxing art; the pugilistic
art

拳賽(ㄑㄩㄢˊ ㄙㄞˋ)
a boxing match

拳握(ㄑㄩㄢˊ ㄨㄛˋ)
to hold in the fist

拳王(ㄑㄩㄢˊ ㄨㄤˊ)
a boxing champion

拳勇(ㄑㄩㄢˊ ㄩㄥˇ)
a tough and powerful boxer;
a good boxer

【拿】 1874
(拏) ㄋㄚˊ na ná
1. to hold in one's hand; to
grasp; to take: 誰拿了我的筆?
Who has taken my pen?
2. to arrest; to apprehend; to
capture: 將他拿下! Arrest
him!
3. to use; to employ (a
method, device, etc.)
4. with; in: 請拿事實來證明。
Please prove with facts.
5. (now rarely) to be confined
or restrained

拿班做勢(ㄋㄚˊ ㄅㄢ ㄗㄨㄛˋ ㄕˋ)
to act affectedly; affectations 亦作「裝腔作勢」

拿捏(ㄋㄚˊ ㄋㄧㄝ)
to embarrass or make it difficult for another intentionally

拿不定主意(ㄋㄚˊ ㄅㄨˋ ㄉㄧㄥˋ ㄓㄨˇ ㄧˋ)
cannot make up one's mind:
他永遠拿不定主意。He would
never make up his mind.

拿不動(ㄋㄚˊ ㄅㄨˋ ㄉㄨㄥˋ)
cannot take or hold it—too
heavy

拿不了(ㄋㄚˊ ㄅㄨˋ ㄌㄧㄠˇ)
① cannot take or hold it
—too heavy ② cannot take
them all—too many

拿不起來(ㄋㄚˊ ㄅㄨˋ ㄑㄧˇ ㄌㄞˊ)
① cannot raise it—too heavy
② cannot control

拿不著(ㄋㄚˊ ㄅㄨˋ ㄓㄠˊ)
① can't reach it—too far out
② cannot get (the first
prize, award, etc.)

拿不住(ㄋㄚˊ ㄅㄨˋ ㄓㄨˋ)
① cannot be grasped—too
slippery; cannot keep in possession ② cannot hold it
—too heavy ③ cannot seize
or arrest ④ cannot control

拿不出手(ㄋㄚˊ ㄅㄨˋ ㄔㄨ ㄕㄡˇ)
not be presentable

拿不穩(ㄋㄚˊ ㄅㄨˋ ㄨㄣˇ)
cannot hold it steadily; unable to get a firm grasp;
cannot be sure

拿破崙(ㄋㄚˊ ㄆㄛˋ ㄌㄨㄣˊ)
Napoleon Bonaparte (1769-
1821), a famous French military strategist and emperor

拿大頂(ㄋㄚˊ ㄉㄚˋ ㄉㄧㄥˇ)
to stand on one's hands

拿得動(ㄋㄚˊ ㄉㄜˊ ㄉㄨㄥˋ)
able to hold or take it—not
too heavy

拿得了(ㄋㄚˊ ㄉㄜˊ ㄌㄧㄠˇ)
able to take or hold them
—not too many

拿得起(ㄋㄚˊ ㄉㄜˊ ㄑㄧˇ)
able to afford it

拿得起，放得下(ㄋㄚˊ ㄉㄜˊ ㄑㄧˇ,
ㄈㄤˋ ㄉㄜˊ ㄒㄧㄚˋ)
able to advance or retreat,
to attack or withdraw, etc.
as the occasion demands;
flexible; adaptable

拿得來(ㄋㄚˊ ㄉㄜˊ ㄌㄞˊ)
① able to afford it ② able
to raise it—not too heavy ③
(a person) of decision and
determination ④ (said of a
person) competent

拿得住(ㄋㄚˊ ㄉㄜˊ ㄓㄨˋ)
① able to hold it steadily ②
able to have a firm grasp on
③ able to restrain (a prisoner, etc.)

拿刀動杖(ㄋㄚˊ ㄉㄠ ㄉㄨㄥˋ ㄓㄤˋ)
to use force

拿定方針(ㄋㄚˊ ㄉㄧㄥˋ ㄈㄤ ㄓㄣ)

〔手部〕

to decide on a way, measure, or policy without backing down

拿定主意 (ㄋㄚˊ ㄉㄧㄥˋ ㄓㄨˇ ㄧˋ)
to make up one's mind; to be determined: 她拿定主意了。 Her mind is made up.

拿捏 (ㄋㄚˊ ㄋㄧㄝ)
① deliberately make things difficult for others ② to pretend to observe rules of propriety

拿過來 (ㄋㄚˊ ㄍㄨㄛˋ ㄌㄞˊ) or 拿來 (ㄋㄚˊ ㄌㄞˊ)
Bring it here. 或 Take it here.

拿開 (ㄋㄚˊ ㄎㄞ)
Take it away! 或 to take away

拿獲 (ㄋㄚˊ ㄏㄨㄛˋ)
to apprehend or arrest (a criminal)

拿架子 (ㄋㄚˊ ㄐㄧㄚˋ ˙ㄗ)
to play the VIP; to put on airs; haughty; arrogant

拿究 (ㄋㄚˊ ㄐㄧㄡˋ)
to arrest and prosecute

拿緝 (ㄋㄚˊ ㄑㄧ)
to search and arrest

拿去 (ㄋㄚˊ ˙ㄑㄩ)
Take it away. 或 to take away

拿主意 (ㄋㄚˊ ㄓㄨˇ ㄧˋ)
to make a decision; to make up one's mind; to decide

拿住 (ㄋㄚˊ ㄓㄨˋ)
① to apprehend; to put under arrest or custody ② to hold firmly

拿出 (ㄋㄚˊ ㄔㄨ)
to take out; to produce: 他拿出一本書。 He took a book out.

拿手 (ㄋㄚˊ ㄕㄡˇ)
to be particularly good or dexterous at; one's special skill or ability: 我對剪紙很拿手。 I am good at making paper-cuts.

拿手好戲 (ㄋㄚˊ ㄕㄡˇ ㄏㄠˇ ㄒㄧˋ)
one's specialty; a part in which one feels particularly at home or competent; what one most excels in

拿人 (ㄋㄚˊ ㄖㄣˊ)
to arrest a criminal

拿三搬四 (ㄋㄚˊ ㄙㄢ ㄅㄢ ㄙˋ)

to resist orders and disobey instructions

拿送 (ㄋㄚˊ ㄙㄨㄥˋ)
to arrest and turn over to court

拿穩 (ㄋㄚˊ ㄨㄣˇ)
① to hold steadily ② to predict with confidence: 這件事他們拿穩嗎? Are they sure of it?

拿問 (ㄋㄚˊ ㄨㄣˋ)
to detain for questioning

【挈】 1875
ㄑㄧㄝˋ chieh ch'ieh
1. to lead: 挈出紅塵 to lead a person away from the mundane world
2. to rise above; to raise

挈領 (ㄑㄧㄝˋ ㄌㄧㄥˇ)
to present the main points; to make a summary or a synopsis

挈眷 (ㄑㄧㄝˋ ㄐㄩㄢˋ)
to travel with one's dependents

七畫

【挨】 1876
ㄞ ai ái
(又讀 ㄞˊ air ái)
1. (to stay) near, next to, close to; to lean to: 他挨著窗子坐著。 He is sitting by the window.
2. to suffer (from cold, hunger, etc.): 他在挨餓。 He is suffering from hunger.
3. to wait; to delay; to put off: 我們再挨三天。 Let's wait another three days.
4. according to order; in good order: 還沒挨到她吧? It isn't her turn yet, is it?
5. (now rarely) to rub; to scratch

挨罵 (ㄞˊ ㄇㄚˋ)
to be blamed; to take the blame; to suffer revilement; to be scolded

挨磨 (ㄞˊ ㄇㄛˊ)
to delay; to procrastinate

挨門兒 (ㄞˊ ㄇㄣˊ)
from door to door

挨門逐戶 (ㄞˊ ㄇㄣˊ ㄓㄨˊ ㄏㄨˋ)
to go from door to door: 他挨門挨戶給他們禮物。 He went from door to door to give

them presents.

挨佛勒斯峰 (ㄞˊ ㄈㄛˊ ㄌㄜˋ ㄙ ㄈㄥ)
Mount Everest

挨打 (ㄞˊ ㄉㄚˇ)
to come under attack; to suffer a beating; to deserve beating: 這小孩應該挨打。 The child deserves a beating.

挨延 (ㄞˊ ㄧㄢˊ)
to delay, procrastinate and shirk (one's responsibility, etc.)

挨冷受凍 (ㄞˊ ㄌㄥˇ ㄕㄡˋ ㄉㄨㄥˋ)
to suffer from cold

挨個兒 (ㄞˊ ˙ㄍㄜ)
one by one; in turn: 我們挨個兒上車吧。 Let's get on the bus one by one.

挨靠 (ㄞˊ ㄎㄠˋ)
① to lean on; to depend on ② to rely on ② to be near to

挨擠 (ㄞˊ ㄐㄧˇ)
to be pushed here and there in a large crowd

挨肩擦膀 (ㄞˊ ㄐㄧㄢ ㄘㄚ ㄅㄤˇ)
to rub shoulders; to be near and intimate 亦作「挨肩兒」

挨近 (ㄞˊ ㄐㄧㄣˋ)
near to; to be close to: 他挨近火車站。 His house is close to the railway station.

挨牆靠壁兒 (ㄞˊ ㄑㄧㄤˊ ㄎㄠˋ ㄅㄧˋ)
(literally) to lean on the wall—to place things in a safe place so that they won't get kicked over

挨著 (ㄞˊ ˙ㄓㄜ)
① next to: 他挨著她坐。 He sits next to her. ② one by one: 他們一個挨著一個過去。 They passed one by one.

挨著大樹有柴燒 (ㄞˊ ˙ㄓㄜ ㄉㄚˋ ㄕㄨˋ ㄧㄡˇ ㄔㄞˊ ㄕㄠ)
(literally) When you live close to big trees, there'll be enough firewood.—One's livelihood or career is assured if he has powerful friends.

挨揍 (ㄞˊ ㄗㄡˋ)
to take a beating

挨次 (ㄞˊ ㄘˋ)
in order; according to order; one after another: 乘客們挨次上車。 The passengers go on the bus one after another.

挨餓 (ㄞˊ ㄜˋ)

to suffer from hunger or starvation

挨躋躋(ㄞ ㄐㄧ ㄐㄧ)
very crowded

挪 1877
(ㄋㄨㄛˊ nuo nuó)
to move; to shift; to transfer: 請把椅子挪到那兒。Move the chair over there, please.

挪不動(ㄋㄨㄛˊ ㄅㄨˋ ㄉㄨㄥˋ)
cannot move it

挪不開(ㄋㄨㄛˊ ㄅㄨˋ ㄎㄞ)
cannot move away

挪墊(ㄋㄨㄛˊ ㄉㄧㄢˋ)
to borrow from public fund for private use

挪東補西(ㄋㄨㄛˊ ㄉㄨㄥ ㄅㄨˇ ㄒㄧ)
to make up deficiency at one place by drawing upon the surplus at another

挪動(ㄋㄨㄛˊ ㄉㄨㄥˋ)
to move: 請往前挪動幾步。Move a few steps forward, please.

挪款(ㄋㄨㄛˊ ㄎㄨㄢˇ)
to transfer money or an account

挪借(ㄋㄨㄛˊ ㄐㄧㄝˋ)
to borrow from the public funds; to get a short-term loan

挪移(ㄋㄨㄛˊ ㄧˊ)
①to move ②to borrow from the public funds

挪威(ㄋㄨㄛˊ ㄨㄟ)
Norway

挪威人(ㄋㄨㄛˊ ㄨㄟ ㄖㄣˊ)
a Norwegian

挪用(ㄋㄨㄛˊ ㄩㄥˋ)
to use money for a purpose not originally intended; to embezzle; to misappropriate

挪用公款(ㄋㄨㄛˊ ㄩㄥˋ ㄍㄨㄥ ㄎㄨㄢˇ)
to embezzle public money; misappropriation of public funds

抄 1878
(ㄙㄨㄛ suo suǒ)
(ㄕㄚ sha shǎ)
to touch; to feel with hands

挫 1879
(ㄘㄨㄛˋ tsuoh cuò)
to defeat; to frustrate: 他想做那件事而遭受挫折。He was frustrated in an attempt to do it.

to damp: 沒什麼東西可以使他

興致挫滅。Nothing could damp his spirits.

3. to humiliate; to treat harshly

挫敗(ㄘㄨㄛˋ ㄅㄞˋ)
a setback; a defeat; failure

挫磨(ㄘㄨㄛˋ ㄇㄛˊ)
to ill-use; to ill-treat; ill-treatment

挫敵(ㄘㄨㄛˋ ㄉㄧˊ)
to defeat the enemy; to give the enemy a bloody nose

挫折(ㄘㄨㄛˋ ㄓㄜˊ)
①a setback; defeat; failure: 他應遭挫折。He often suffered setbacks. ②to frustrate

挫辱(ㄘㄨㄛˋ ㄖㄨˋ)
to humiliate; to put to shame

挫銳(ㄘㄨㄛˋ ㄖㄨㄟˋ)
to damp the morale (of the enemy); to demoralize

【振】 1880
1. ㄓㄣˋ jenn zhèn
1. to arouse to action; to raise; to rise: 他的精神振奮起來。His spirits rose.
2. to pull up; to relieve: 振作起精神, 正視人生。Pull yourself together and face up to life.
3. to shake; to flap as wings: 大將軍威震天下。The great general's power shook the world.
4. to restore order

振筆直書(ㄓㄣˋ ㄅㄧˇ ㄓˊ ㄕㄨ)
to write rapidly; to wield the pen furiously

振臂(ㄓㄣˋ ㄅㄧˋ)
to raise one's arm

振臂一呼(ㄓㄣˋ ㄅㄧˋ ㄧ ㄏㄨ)
to raise one's arm and issue a clarion call; to arouse to action

振兵(ㄓㄣˋ ㄅㄧㄥ)
to rally the troops

振怖(ㄓㄣˋ ㄅㄨˋ)
to alarm

振靡(ㄓㄣˋ ㄇㄧˇ)
to awaken the weak and enervated

振奮(ㄓㄣˋ ㄈㄣˋ)
①to arouse to action; to arouse; to stimulate; to excite ②heartening; encouraging; exciting

振幅(ㄓㄣˋ ㄈㄨˊ)
(physics) amplitude

振盪(ㄓㄣˋ ㄉㄤˋ)
①(physics) vibration ②(electricity) oscillation

振動(ㄓㄣˋ ㄉㄨㄥˋ)
(physics) vibration; to vibrate: 火車經過時房屋往振動。The house vibrates when a train passes.

振鈴(ㄓㄣˋ ㄌㄧㄥˊ)
to ring a bell

振聾發聵(ㄓㄣˋ ㄌㄨㄥˊ ㄈㄚ ㄍㄨㄟˋ)
(said of ringing statements) to awaken the laggard and to arouse the phlegmatic

振旅(ㄓㄣˋ ㄌㄩˇ)
the neat formation of a triumphant army; the orderly return of a victorious army

振古(ㄓㄣˋ ㄍㄨˇ)
from ancient times

振翮(ㄓㄣˋ ㄏㄜˊ)or 振翼(ㄓㄣˋ ㄧˋ)
to spread the wings; to flap; ready to take off: 鳥正振翼飛翔。The bird is flapping its wings.

振起(ㄓㄣˋ ㄑㄧˇ)
to stir up; to get aroused; to rise and meet a challenge: 你應該振起精神來。You should put forth fresh energy.

振興(ㄓㄣˋ ㄒㄧㄥ)
to promote or develop (industrial endeavor, etc.); to prosper

振振有詞(ㄓㄣˋ ㄓㄣˋ ㄧㄡˇ ㄘˊ)
to talk fluently and loudly (as if one has all the reasons on his side); never short of words in defending oneself against a charge, criticism, etc.

振翅(ㄓㄣˋ ㄔˋ)
to flap (wings); to flutter: 鳥在樹林中振翅 (鼓翼)。The birds fluttered in the trees.

振刷(ㄓㄣˋ ㄕㄨㄚ)
to rise; to arouse (oneself)

振作(ㄓㄣˋ ㄗㄨㄛˋ)
to arouse (oneself); to bestir (oneself); to brace up: 喂！振作起精神來。Come, bestir yourself! 或 Brace up!

振衣(ㄓㄣˋ ㄧ)
to shake one's clothing

振縷(ㄓㄣˋ ㄌㄩˇ)

〔手部〕

to rise to officialdom; to become an official

振威(ㄓㄣ ㄨㄟ)
to inspire awe; to extend one's imposing prestige

【振】 1880
2. ㄓㄣ jen zhēn
benevolent and generous

振振(ㄓㄣ ㄓㄣ)
benevolent and generous; noble

【挼】 1881
ㄖㄨㄛˊ nuo nuó
(醫音曰ㄖㄨㄛˋ ruo ruó)

1. to rub; to stroke
2. to crumple (paper into a ball, etc.)

挼搓(ㄖㄨㄛˊ ㄘㄨㄛ)
to roll up

【挹】 1882
ㄧˋ yìh yì

1. to decant liquids, especially wine
2. to retreat

挹彼注此(ㄧˇ ㄅㄧˇ ㄓㄨˋ ㄘˇ)
(literally) to pour from one vessel to another—to make up the deficiency of one by drawing upon the surplus of another

挹掬(ㄧˋ ㄐㄩˊ)
to scoop up water with hands

挹注(ㄧ ㄓㄨ)
to supplement; to draw from one to make up the deficits in another

挹酌(ㄧ ㄓㄨㄛˊ)
to pour out wine

【挽】 1883
ㄨㄢˇ woan wǎn

1. to draw (a bow, etc.); to pull: 他挽著弓。He drew a bow.
2. to restore
3. to seize
4. to roll up (sleeves, etc.): 他們挽起袖子。They rolled up their sleeves.

挽留(ㄨㄢˇ ㄌㄧㄡˊ)
to request to stay; to urge to stay

挽弓當挽強(ㄨㄢˇ ㄍㄨㄥ ㄉㄤ ㄨㄢˇ ㄑㄧㄤˊ)
(literally) If you want to draw a bow, take the most powerful. —to try the toughest so as to get the most

far-reaching result

挽回(ㄨㄢˇ ㄏㄨㄟˊ)
to try with effort to turn back an adverse tide; to retrieve; to redeem: 他挽回了名譽。He redeemed his honor.

挽回大局(ㄨㄢˇ ㄏㄨㄟˊ ㄉㄚˋ ㄐㄩˊ)
to save the general situation from worsening; to restore the general situation

挽髻(ㄨㄢˇ ㄐㄧˋ)
to tie the hair into a knot

挽救(ㄨㄢˇ ㄐㄧㄡˋ)
to save (a situation, a failing concern, etc.): 醫生挽救了病人的生命。The doctor saved the patient's life.

挽袖(ㄨㄢˇ ㄒㄧㄡˋ)
to roll up sleeves

挽住(ㄨㄢˇ ㄓㄨˋ)
to hold back; to hold another (from going away, etc.)

挽車(ㄨㄢˇ ㄔㄜ)
to pull a cart

挽手(ㄨㄢˇ ㄕㄡˇ)
to hold hands; arm in arm; hand in hand: 他們挽手離去。They walked away hand in hand.

挽引(ㄨㄢˇ ㄧㄣˇ)
to pull with force

【挺】 1884
ㄊㄧㄥˇ tǐing tǐng

1. to stand straight (or upright); to square; to straighten; rigid: 他挺起胸膛。He squared his shoulders.
2. to pull up
3. unyielding; unbending; tough
4. outstanding; remarkable; eminent; prominent
5. to thrust forward (as one's breast)
6. to sustain; to endure; to pull through; to stand; to hold out: 她挺得住嗎? Can she stand it?
7. very; pretty
8. the number of machine guns: 一百多挺機槍 over one hundred machine guns

挺拔(ㄊㄧㄥˇ ㄅㄚˊ)
independent, outstanding and eminent

挺不住(ㄊㄧㄥˇ ㄅㄨˋ ㄓㄨˋ)
cannot stand it; cannot take it any more—too heavy, dif-

ficult, etc: 她挺不住這種寒了。She cannot stand th cold any longer.

挺挺(ㄊㄧㄥˇ ㄊㄧㄥˇ)
straightforward; unyielding or unbending; stiff: 他直挺地躺著。He lied stiff.

挺立(ㄊㄧㄥˇ ㄌㄧˋ)
to stand upright; to star erect; to stand up straight

挺好(ㄊㄧㄥˇ ㄏㄠˇ)
very good; quite good: 那主意挺好。That idea is ve good.

挺節(ㄊㄧㄥˇ ㄐㄧㄝˊ)
to hold fast to one's princ ple; virtuous

挺緊(ㄊㄧㄥˇ ㄐㄧㄣˇ)
to pull tight; very tight

挺進(ㄊㄧㄥˇ ㄐㄧㄣˋ)
(said of troops) to drive c boldly; to push forward

挺進隊(ㄊㄧㄥˇ ㄐㄧㄣˋ ㄉㄨㄟˋ)or挺進軍(ㄊㄧㄥˇ ㄐㄧㄣˋ ㄐㄩㄣ)
tough vanguard units

挺舉(ㄊㄧㄥˇ ㄐㄩˇ)
(weightlifting) clean ar jerk

挺秀(ㄊㄧㄥˇ ㄒㄧㄡˋ)
(looking) elegant and prom inent

挺胸(ㄊㄧㄥˇ ㄒㄩㄥ)
to thrust out one's chest

挺直(ㄊㄧㄥˇ ㄓˊ)
straight and upright; erec 他挺直身子站著。He stoo erect.

挺尸(ㄊㄧㄥˇ ㄕ)
a stiff corpse—(now com cally) to sleep in this man ner

挺腰(ㄊㄧㄥˇ ㄧㄠ)
to straighten one's back

挺身而出(ㄊㄧㄥˇ ㄕㄣ ㄦˊ ㄔㄨ)
to thrust oneself out to fac a challenge; to stand up an volunteer to help

挺升(ㄊㄧㄥˇ ㄕㄥ)
(said of prices) to ris steeply

挺然不羣(ㄊㄧㄥˇ ㄖㄢˊ ㄅㄨˋ ㄑㄩㄣˊ)
towering above others; out standing; to be distinguishe from others

挺而走險(ㄊㄧㄥˇ ㄦˊ ㄗㄡˇ ㄒㄧㄢˇ)
① to risk danger in despera tion; to make a reckles

move ②to be forced to break the law 亦作「鋌而走險」

【硬】ㄧㄥˋ
very hard; stiff and stubborn; unyielding and tough

【捃】 1885 ㄐㄩㄣˋ juinn jùn
to pick up; to gather; to collect

捃華（ㄐㄩㄣˋ ㄏㄨㄚˊ）
to gather the most important or significant points or parts; a collection of such; to select the most essential points

捃摭（ㄐㄩㄣˋ）
to collect (samples, specimens, etc.)

捃拾（ㄐㄩㄣˋ）
to collect; to gather; to pick up

【捆】 1886 ㄎㄨㄣˇ koen kǔn
1. to bind; to tie up: 他在捆包裏。He is tying up his parcel.
2. a bundle: 一捆乾草 a bundle of hay

捆綁（ㄎㄨㄣˇ ㄅㄤˇ）
to bind: 他們把他的手腳捆綁起來。They bound him hand and foot.

捆紮（ㄎㄨㄣˇ ㄗㄚ）
to bind; to tie up; bound

捆起來（ㄎㄨㄣˇ ㄑㄧˇ ㄌㄞˊ）
to tie up (a prisoner, etc.): 我會把你的東西用手帕捆起來。I'll tie up your things in a handkerchief.

捆住（ㄎㄨㄣˇ ㄓㄨˋ）
to tie up; to bind up

捆上（ㄎㄨㄣˇ ㄕㄤˋ）
to bind up

捆子（ㄎㄨㄣˇ ˙ㄗ）or 捆兒（ㄎㄨㄣˇ ㄦ）
a bundle

捆鎖（ㄎㄨㄣˇ ㄙㄨㄛˇ）
to chain or fetter; anything that serves as such

捆押（ㄎㄨㄣˇ ㄧㄚ）
to put under restraint; to tie up and escort (a criminal)

【捋】 1887 ㄌㄜˋ leh lè
to pluck; to gather in the fingers

捋虎鬚（ㄌㄜˋ ㄏㄨˇ ㄒㄩ）
(literally) to pluck the tiger's whiskers--to offend the powerful

【捋】 1887 ㄌㄩˇ leu lǚ
to stroke (one's beard, etc.): to smooth out with fingers: 他把紙抹平。He smoothed out a piece of paper.

捋鬍鬚（ㄌㄩˇ ㄏㄨˊ ㄒㄩ）
to stroke one's beard

【捼】 1887 ㄋㄨㄛˊ thuo luó
1. to rub one's palm along (something long)
2. to squeeze with hands

捼奶（ㄋㄨㄛˊ ㄋㄞˇ）
to milk (a cow, goat, etc.)

捼胳膊（ㄋㄨㄛˊ ㄍㄜ ˙ㄅㄛ）
to pull up one's sleeves and show the arms

捼汗（ㄋㄨㄛˊ ㄏㄢˋ）
to be very much embarrassed

【捉】 1888 ㄓㄨㄛ juo zhuō
1. to seize; to grasp; to catch; to hold: 他捉住小偷不放。He seized hold of the thief and would not let him go.
2. to apprehend; to arrest: 他們在捕捉竊賊。They were apprehending a thief.

捉摸不定（ㄓㄨㄛ ㄇㄛ ㄅㄨˋ ㄉㄧㄥˋ）
unfathomable; unpredictable; difficult to ascertain; elusive: 那個意思叫我捉摸不定。The meaning is elusive to me.

捉脈（ㄓㄨㄛ ㄇㄛˋ）
(said of Chinese herb doctors) to feel the patient's pulse

捉迷藏（ㄓㄨㄛ ㄇㄧˊ ㄘㄤˊ）
①to play hide-and-seek; hide-and-seek ②to beat about the bush

捉刀（ㄓㄨㄛ ㄉㄠ）
to ghostwrite; to have something written by a ghost-writer

捉拿（ㄓㄨㄛ ㄋㄚˊ）or 捉搦（ㄓㄨㄛ ㄋㄨㄛˋ）
to apprehend; to arrest: 警方捉拿逃犯。The police arrested an escaped prisoner.

捉弄（ㄓㄨㄛ ㄋㄨㄥˋ）
to play a joke (or trick) on (somebody); to make fun of;

to harass

捉虎容易放虎難（ㄓㄨㄛ ㄏㄨˇ ㄖㄨㄥˊ ㄧˋ ㄈㄤˋ ㄏㄨˇ ㄋㄢˊ）
(literally) It's easier to catch a tiger than to set it free.--It's easier to start something than to conclude it satisfactorily.

捉姦（ㄓㄨㄛ ㄐㄧㄢ）
to catch a person in the act of adultery (usually by the wronged husband or wife)

捉襟見肘（ㄓㄨㄛ ㄐㄧㄣ ㄐㄧㄢˋ ㄓㄡˇ）
hard-pressed for money; in financial straits

捉狹（ㄓㄨㄛ ㄒㄧㄚˊ）
mischievous

捉狹鬼（ㄓㄨㄛ ㄒㄧㄚˊ ㄍㄨㄟˇ）
one who likes to play jokes; a mischievous fellow

捉住（ㄓㄨㄛ ㄓㄨˋ）
to catch; to seize

捉賊（ㄓㄨㄛ ㄗㄟˊ）
to catch thieves: 作賊喊著捉賊。The thief was crying "Stop the thief!"

捉妖（ㄓㄨㄛ ㄧㄠ）
(Taoism) to catch the evil spirit; to exorcise

【挾】 1889 ㄒㄧㄝˊ shye xié （又讀）ㄒㄧㄚˊ shya xiá）
1. to clasp or hold under the arm: 他挾着一個書包。He carried a satchel under the arm.
2. to embrace; to bosom
3. to presume upon (one's influence, advantage, etc.)
4. to extort; to blackmail; to hold (a crown prince, etc.) as a hostage

挾帶（ㄒㄧㄝˊ ㄉㄞˋ）
①（ㄒㄧㄝˊ ㄉㄞˋ）to carry under arms
②（ㄐㄧㄚ ㄉㄞˋ）ⓐ to smuggle ⓑ things smuggled (into a country or an examination room, etc.)

挾泰山以超北海（ㄒㄧㄝˊ ㄊㄞˋ ㄕㄢ ㄧˇ ㄔㄠ ㄅㄟˇ ㄏㄞˇ）
(literally) to clasp Mt. Tai under the arm and cross the North Sea--an impossible task

挾天子以令諸侯（ㄒㄧㄝˊ ㄊㄧㄢ ㄗˇ ㄧˇ ㄌㄧㄥˋ ㄓㄨ ㄏㄡˊ）

〔手部〕

〔手部〕

to usurp power by holding the emperor as a hostage and acting in his name

挾貴 (ㄒㄧㄚˊ ㄍㄨㄟˋ)
to presume upon one's blue blood or high position

挾貴自重 (ㄒㄧㄚˊ ㄍㄨㄟˋ ㄗˋ ㄓㄨㄥˋ)
to be proud of one's high position

挾恨 (ㄒㄧㄚˊ ㄏㄣˋ) or 挾仇 (ㄒㄧㄚˊ ㄔㄡˊ) or 挾怨 (ㄒㄧㄚˊ ㄩㄢˋ)
to bear a grudge

挾嫌 (ㄒㄧㄚˊ ㄒㄧㄢˊ)
to bear a grudge; to harbor resentment

挾制 (ㄒㄧㄚˊ ㄓˋ)
to force someone into submission by taking advantage of his weaknesses or threatening to expose his secrets

挾持 (ㄒㄧㄚˊ ㄔˊ)
① to grasp someone on both sides by the arms ② to hold someone under duress

挾勢 (ㄒㄧㄚˊ ㄕˋ)
to presume upon one's influence or high position

【捍】 1890
ㄏㄢˋ hann hàn
to defend; to guard; to ward off: 他們捍衛這城以禦敵。 They defended the city against the enemy.

捍海塘 (ㄏㄢˋ ㄏㄞˇ ㄊㄤˊ)
① name of a dike built in the first decades of the 10th century by Chien Liu (錢鏐) at today's Hangchow ② name of a dike along the sea coast of Kiangsu and Chekiang built during the Tang Dynasty

捍衛 (ㄏㄢˋ ㄨㄟˋ)
to defend (a nation's territory, etc.); to protect: 捍衛國家是軍人的責任。 The duty of a soldier is to defend his country.

捍禦 (ㄏㄢˋ ㄩˋ)
to ward off; to guard against

【捌】 1891
ㄅㄚ ba bā
1. an elaborate form of eight (八)— used in checks or accounts to prevent fraud
2. to pull apart; to break 亦作「扒」

【捕】 1892
ㄅㄨˇ buu bǔ
1. to arrest; to apprehend; to catch; to seize: 他已被捕。 He is under arrest. 或 He is arrested.
2. (formerly) a policeman

捕票 (ㄅㄨˇ ㄆㄧㄠˋ)
a warrant for arrest; an arrest warrant

捕房 (ㄅㄨˇ ㄈㄤˊ)
(formerly) a police station or precinct in the foreign settlements or concessions

捕風捉影 (ㄅㄨˇ ㄈㄥ ㄓㄨㄛ ㄧㄥˇ)
(literally) to chase the wind and catch the shadow—talks that are not substantiated by any evidence or proof

捕頭 (ㄅㄨˇ ㄊㄡˊ)
(formerly) a head constable

捕拿 (ㄅㄨˇ ㄋㄚˊ)
to arrest; to apprehend; to capture; to catch

捕撈 (ㄅㄨˇ ㄌㄠ)
to fish for (aquatic animals and plants); to catch: 他們在捕撈龍蝦。 They're catching lobsters.

捕撈能力 (ㄅㄨˇ ㄌㄠ ㄋㄥˊ ㄌㄧˋ)
fishing capacity

捕快 (ㄅㄨˇ ㄎㄨㄞˋ)
(formerly) constables or policemen

捕獲 (ㄅㄨˇ ㄏㄨㄛˋ)
to arrest; to catch; to capture: 有五名敵人被捕獲。 Five of the enemy were captured.

捕鯨船 (ㄅㄨˇ ㄐㄧㄥ ㄔㄨㄢˊ)
a whaleboat; a whaleship; a whaler

捕捉 (ㄅㄨˇ ㄓㄨㄛ)
to chase or hunt down; to seize; to arrest; to capture: 他在捕捉昆蟲。 He was catching insects.

捕蟲燈 (ㄅㄨˇ ㄔㄨㄥˊ ㄉㄥ)
a lamp installed on farms to catch insects in night hours

捕蟲葉 (ㄅㄨˇ ㄔㄨㄥˊ ㄧㄝˋ)
an insect-catching leaf

捕蟲網 (ㄅㄨˇ ㄔㄨㄥˊ ㄨㄤˇ)
an insect-catching net

捕食 (ㄅㄨˇ ㄕˊ)
to catch and feed on; to prey on: 貓捕食老鼠。 Cats prey upon mice.

捕殺 (ㄅㄨˇ ㄕㄚ)
to catch and kill (wild unlicensed dogs, etc.)

捕手 (ㄅㄨˇ ㄕㄡˇ)
(baseball) a catcher: 他是好捕手。 He is a good catcher.

捕鼠器 (ㄅㄨˇ ㄕㄨˇ ㄑㄧˋ)
a mousetrap

捕役 (ㄅㄨˇ ㄧˋ) or 捕差 (ㄅㄨˇ ㄔㄞ)
(formerly) constables or policemen

捕蠅器 (ㄅㄨˇ ㄧㄥˊ ㄑㄧˋ)
a flytrap

捕蠅紙 (ㄅㄨˇ ㄧㄥˊ ㄓˇ)
a flypaper

捕蠅草 (ㄅㄨˇ ㄧㄥˊ ㄘㄠˇ)
a flycatcher; a flytrap

捕魚 (ㄅㄨˇ ㄩˊ)
to catch fish; to fish: 他們在海上捕魚。 They fished in the sea.

【捐】 1893
ㄐㄩㄢ jiuan juān
1. tax; duty; charge; dues: 稅捐 taxes and surtaxes
2. to donate; to contribute; to subscribe: 他捐了一大筆錢給那所孤兒院。 He donated a large sum of money to that orphanage.
3. to buy or purchase (an official rank)
4. to give up (one's life for a cause, etc.)
5. to remove

捐背 (ㄐㄩㄢ ㄅㄟˋ)
to desert; to walk out on somebody

捐命 (ㄐㄩㄢ ㄇㄧㄥˋ)
to die

捐納 (ㄐㄩㄢ ㄋㄚˋ)
to buy a government appointment with grain or money

捐官 (ㄐㄩㄢ ㄍㄨㄢ)
to purchase an official rank or a title (especially in the Ching Dynasty)

捐款 (ㄐㄩㄢ ㄎㄨㄢˇ)
① to donate money ② donations

捐款收入 (ㄐㄩㄢ ㄎㄨㄢˇ ㄕㄡ ㄖㄨˋ)
contribution receipts

捐棄 (ㄐㄩㄢ ㄑㄧˋ)
to renounce; to reject; to relinquish; to give up

捐棄成見 (ㄐㄩㄢ ㄑㄧˋ ㄔㄥˊ ㄐㄧㄢˋ)

to cast away all prejudices; to divest prejudices from one's mind

捐錢(ㄐㄩㄢ ㄑㄧㄢˊ)
to donate money; donations

捐軀(ㄐㄩㄢ ㄑㄩ)
to die for one's country or duty

捐軀赴義(ㄐㄩㄢ ㄑㄩ ㄈㄨˋ ㄧˋ)
to die for the cause of justice and righteousness

捐血(ㄐㄩㄢ ㄒㄩㄝˋ)
① to donate blood ② blood donation

捐獻(ㄐㄩㄢ ㄒㄧㄢˋ)
to contribute; contributions; donations: 請惠予捐獻。Contributions are requested.

捐助(ㄐㄩㄢ ㄓㄨˋ)
to contribute; to donate to help the poor, relief work, etc.: 他們經常捐助紅十字會。They often contributed to the Red Cross.

捐輸(ㄐㄩㄢ ㄕㄨ)
to donate; to contribute; to make financial contributions to the government

捐稅(ㄐㄩㄢ ㄕㄨㄟˋ)
taxes and surcharges

捐資 or 捐資(ㄐㄩㄢ ㄗ)
to donate one's property

捐贈(ㄐㄩㄢ ㄗㄥˋ)
① (said of a newspaper, radio or TV station, etc.) to allot free space, time, services, etc. for a worthy cause ② to donate or contribute: 林先生把這批藏書捐贈給我們學校。Mr. Lin has donated this library to our school.

捐冊(ㄐㄩㄢ ㄘㄜˋ) or 捐簿(ㄐㄩㄢ ㄅㄨˋ)
a book recording names of the donators and the amounts donated

【捎】 1894
ㄕㄠ shau shāo
1. to carry; to take or bring along at one's convenience: 請捎個口信給他。Please take a message to him.
2. to brush over lightly
3. to wipe out

捎帶(ㄕㄠ ㄉㄞˋ)
to carry; to take along at one's convenience

【捎】 1894
2. ㄕㄠˋ shaw shào
1. (said of colors, etc.) to fade; to discolor
2. to sprinkle water
3. to watch secretly; to spy on; to glance at

捎色(ㄕㄠˋ ㄙㄜˋ)
to discolor; to fade

【捏】 1895
(捏) ㄋㄧㄝ nhie niē
1. to knead; to pinch; to squeeze or press with fingers: 麵包師正在捏揉麵團。The baker was kneading dough.
2. to mold (mud, etc.): 他用黏土捏成一座半身雕塑像。He molded clay into a bust.
3. to fabricate; to trump up; to make up

捏報(ㄋㄧㄝ ㄅㄠˋ) or 捏告(ㄋㄧㄝ ㄍㄠˋ)
to present a false report or charge; to fabricate a report or charge; to fake a report

捏弄(ㄋㄧㄝ ㄋㄨㄥˋ)
① to fabricate; to trump up ② to bring together (two people, a couple, etc.)

捏控(ㄋㄧㄝ ㄎㄨㄥˋ) or 捏稱(ㄋㄧㄝ ㄔㄥ)
to fabricate a charge or an accusation

捏合(ㄋㄧㄝ ㄏㄜˊ)
to bring a couple together; to try to make a pair get into a union

捏陷(ㄋㄧㄝ ㄒㄧㄢˋ)
to incriminate another by fabricated charges

捏著(ㄋㄧㄝ ˙ㄓㄜ)
to squeeze or hold with fingers

捏著鼻子(ㄋㄧㄝ ˙ㄓㄜ ㄅㄧˊ ˙ㄗ)
① to hold one's nose (as a protection against obnoxious odors) ② to get ready for an unpleasant experience ahead

捏手捏脚(ㄋㄧㄝ ㄕㄡˇ ㄋㄧㄝ ㄐㄧㄠˇ)
stealthily; to move around lightly; to pussyfoot

捏神捏鬼(ㄋㄧㄝ ㄕㄣˊ ㄋㄧㄝ ㄍㄨㄟˇ)
to do or negotiate stealthily

捏造(ㄋㄧㄝ ㄗㄠˋ)
to fabricate (evidence, etc.); to trump up (charges); to fake; to make up: 他們捏

造口實。They trumped up an excuse.

捏造罪名(ㄋㄧㄝ ㄗㄠˋ ㄗㄨㄟˋ ㄇㄧㄥˊ)
to fabricate an accusation

捏造謠言(ㄋㄧㄝ ㄗㄠˋ ㄧㄠˊ ㄧㄢˊ)
to fabricate and spread rumors; to invent slanders: 他捏造謠言。He fabricated a story.

捏詞(ㄋㄧㄝ ㄘˊ)
lies; slanders

捏塑(ㄋㄧㄝ ㄙㄨˋ)
to mold (mud) into a statue, etc.: 我們用黏土捏塑出塑像。We mold statues out of clay.

捏酸(ㄋㄧㄝ ㄙㄨㄢ)
to feign gentleness and erudition; to pretend to be a scholar

捏一把汗(ㄋㄧㄝ ㄧ ㄅㄚˇ ㄏㄢˋ)
to break out into cold perspiration (before, during or immediately after a very dangerous situation, narrow escape, etc.); to be breathless with anxiety; to be seized with fear or deep concern

【捄】 1896
ㄐㄩ jyu jú
a receptacle for earth

八畫

【捨】 1897
(舍) ㄕㄜˇ shee shě
1. to reject; to give up; to abandon; to relinquish; to renounce; to part with; to forsake; to let go: 捨棄所有的爛蘋果。Reject all spotted apples.
2. to give alms; to give to charity: 施捨給窮人 to give alms to the poor

捨本逐末(ㄕㄜˇ ㄅㄣˇ ㄓㄨˊ ㄇㄛˋ)
to concentrate on details but forget the main purpose or objective; to attend to trifles to the extent of neglecting essentials

捨不得(ㄕㄜˇ ㄅㄨˋ ˙ㄉㄜ) or 捨不了(ㄕㄜˇ ㄅㄨˋ ㄌㄧㄠˇ)
reluctant to give up, let go, etc. (because of emotional attachment or high value of the object to be given up); to hate to part with: 她捨不

〔手部〕

〔手部〕

得亂花一分錢。She hates to waste a single cent.

捨命 (アさ ㄇㄧㄥˋ)
in disregard of one's safety or life; to give up one's life; to risk one's life

捨得 (アさ ㄉㄜˊ)
to be willing to part with (a person, thing, etc.); not to grudge: 他很捨得付出你所要的價錢。He is quite willing to pay the price you asked.

捨短取長 (アさ ㄉㄨㄢˇ ㄑㄩˇ ㄔㄤˊ)
to disregard shortcomings and adopt good points

捨己從人 (アさ ㄐㄧˇ ㄘㄨㄥˊ ㄖㄣˊ)
to give up one's views and follow those of another person

捨己為人 (アさ ㄐㄧˇ ㄨㄟˋ ㄖㄣˊ)
to give up one's own interests for the sake of others

捨近求遠 (アさ ㄐㄧㄣˋ ㄑㄧㄡˊ ㄩㄢˇ)
to reject what is near at hand and seek for what is far away 亦作「捨近取遠」

捨棄 (アさ ㄑㄧˋ)
to give up or renounce; to abandon; to relinquish: 我永遠不捨棄我的朋友。I would never abandon my friends.

捨身 (アさ アㄣ)
to give up one's life (for a cause, principle, etc.): 他捨身救了那男孩。He gave his life to rescue the boy.

捨生取義 (アさ アㄥ ㄑㄩˇ ㄧˋ)
to give up one's life for righteousness; to sacrifice oneself for righteousness; to prefer honor to life; to lay down one's life for a just cause

捨死忘生 (アさ ㄙˇ ㄨㄤˋ アㄥ)
to disregard one's safety or life—full devotion or dedication

【捧】 1898
ㄆㄥˇ peeng pěng
1. to hold something in both hands; to scoop up something with one's hands: 他雙手捧著一些蘋果。He held some apples in his hands.
2. to boost; to flatter; to treat as a VIP: 她把他捧得太高了。She praised him too highly.
3. to support, cheer or render

assistance by one's presence

捧腹 (ㄆㄥˇ ㄈㄨˊ) or 捧腹大笑 (ㄆㄥˇ ㄈㄨˊ ㄉㄚˋ Tㄧㄠˋ) or 捧腹絕倒 (ㄆㄥˇ ㄈㄨˊ ㄐㄩㄝˊ ㄉㄠˇ)
to hold one's sides with laughter: 他的笑話令我們捧腹。His joke made us burst out laughing.

捧讀 (ㄆㄥˇ ㄉㄨˊ)
to have the privilege of reading your (book, letter, etc.); to read carefully 亦作「捧誦」

捧角 (ㄆㄥˇ ㄐㄩㄝˊ)
to cheer one's favorite actor or actress with constant presence, applause, cash reward, gifts, etc.

捧心 (ㄆㄥˇ Tㄧㄣ)
(said of homely women) to ape the mannerism of a beautiful woman

捧著雞毛當令箭 (ㄆㄥˇ ㄓㄜ˙ ㄐㄧ ㄇㄠˊ ㄉㄤ ㄌㄧㄥˋ ㄐㄧㄢˋ)
to make a fuss about a casual remark of the boss

捧住 (ㄆㄥˇ ㄓㄨˋ)
to hold firmly and securely

捧臭腳 (ㄆㄥˇ ㄔㄡˋ ㄐㄧㄠˇ)
(literally) to hold with respect an odorous foot — to act obsequiously

捧場 (ㄆㄥˇ ㄔㄤˇ) or (ㄆㄥˇ ㄔㄤˊ)
to render support or assistance by one's presence, endorsement, etc.

捧上天 (ㄆㄥˇ アㄤˋ ㄊㄧㄢ)
to overpraise someone: 他們把他捧上天。They praised him to the skies.

捧日 (ㄆㄥˇ ㄖˋ)
to support (a king, leader, etc.)

【捩】 1899
ㄌㄧㄝˋ lieh liè
1. to twist with hands
2. to rip or tear apart

【掰】 1900
ㄅㄞ bae bāi
1. to open; to spread out
2. to strike with both hands

掰開縱橫 (ㄅㄞ ㄎㄞ ㄗㄨㄥˋ ㄏㄥˊ)
suave and ingenious persuasion 亦作「縱橫捭闔」

【摸】 1901
ㄇㄣˊ men mén
1. to feel or touch with hands;

to hold
2. to search (in one's pocket, etc.)

捫心自問 (ㄇㄣˊ Tㄧㄣ ㄗˋ ㄨㄣˋ)
to examine oneself; introspection

捫心無愧 (ㄇㄣˊ Tㄧㄣ ㄨˊ ㄎㄨㄟˋ)
to examine oneself and find nothing to be ashamed of

捫蝨而談 (ㄇㄣˊ アˋ ㄦˊ ㄊㄢˊ)
to talk freely without being awed in the presence of the high and mighty

捫舌 (ㄇㄣˊ アㄜˊ)
to hold the tongue with fingers so that one cannot talk; to hold one's tongue

【据】 1902
1. ㄐㄩ jiū jū
as in 拮据—stiff joints in the hand, used most often to describe financial stringency or short of money

【据】 1902
2. ㄐㄩˋ jiuh jù
1. same as 捧—according to
2. same as 倨—arrogant; haughty

【捱】 1903
ㄞˊ air ái
1. to suffer; to endure
2. to procrastinate; to put off
3. to rub (shoulders)
4. to draw near; to come close to

捱不住 (ㄞˊ ㄅㄨˋ ㄓㄨˋ)
cannot endure any more

捱過 (ㄞˊ ㄍㄨㄛˋ)
to weather, or to survive (a crisis, an ordeal, etc.): 這船平安捱過風暴。The ship weathered the storm.

捱苦 (ㄞˊ ㄎㄨˇ)
to endure hardships

捱肩擦背 (ㄞˊ ㄐㄧㄢ ㄘㄚ ㄅㄟˋ)
to rub shoulders and backs in a large crowd

捱一會 (ㄞˊ ㄧ ㄏㄨㄟˋ)
to delay a moment; to endure a moment

【搋】 1904
ㄔㄣ chen chēn
1. to stretch; to lengthen (as in making noodles, etc.)
2. to drag out; to draw out: 把它搋出來。Draw it out.

搋麵 (ㄔㄣ ㄇㄧㄢˋ)
to make noodles by length-

ening dough

捵練(ㄔㄣ ㄌㄧㄢˋ)
to embarrass someone by making him solve a difficult problem or answer a tough question

捵長(ㄔㄣ ㄔㄤˊ)
to lengthen

【捺】 1905
ㄋㄚˋ nah nà

1. to press hard with hands; to press down
2. a downstroke slanting toward the right in Chinese calligraphy
3. to repress; to restrain: 他無法按捺住他的好奇心。He could not restrain his curiosity.
4. to stitch

捺後(ㄋㄚˋ ㄏㄡˋ)
to delay something intentionally

捺印(ㄋㄚˋ ㄧㄣˋ)
①to press one's thumbprint on a document, etc., in place of a signature or chop ②a seal or chop

【捽】 1906
ㄗㄨˊ tzwu zú
(語音 ㄗㄨㄛˊ tzwo zuó)

1. to hold with hands; to seize; to grasp
2. to pull up
3. to go against; to contradict; to be in conflict with

捽頸(ㄗㄨˊ ㄐㄧㄥˇ)
to seize by the throat

捽住頭髮(ㄗㄨˊ ㄓㄨˋ ㄊㄡˊ ㄈㄚˇ)
to grasp by the hair 亦作「捽髮」

【捲】 1907
ㄐㄩㄢˇ jeuan juǎn

1. to roll up; a roll: 她把毛線捲成球。She rolled the wool into a ball.
2. to curl (hair, etc.); curly (hair): 她的頭髮捲成一束。Her hair curled into a lock.
3. to sweep off: 一個巨浪把獨木舟捲走了。A huge wave swept the canoe away.

捲伴兒(ㄐㄩㄢˇ ㄅㄢˋ)
to abduct a woman

捲包兒(ㄐㄩㄢˇ ㄅㄠ)
to clear up everything and escape; to abscond with money and property

捲盤(ㄐㄩㄢˇ ㄆㄢˊ)
a reel

捲鋪蓋(ㄐㄩㄢˇ ㄆㄨˋ ·《ㄞ)
(literally) to roll up one's bedclothes—to quit a job for good

捲髮(ㄐㄩㄢˇ ㄈㄚˇ)
①to curl hair (at a hairdresser's, etc.); to keep the hair in curl ②curly hair

捲地皮(ㄐㄩㄢˇ ㄉㄧˋ ㄆㄧˊ)
(said of public officials) to practice graft and corruption

捲逃(ㄐㄩㄢˇ ㄊㄠˊ)
(especially said of a married woman or an employee) to clear up everything and run away; to abscond

捲土重來(ㄐㄩㄢˇ ㄊㄨˇ ㄔㄨㄥˊ ㄌㄞˊ)
to stage a comeback; resurgence

捲筒(ㄐㄩㄢˇ ㄊㄨㄥˇ)
a reel

捲筒機(ㄐㄩㄢˇ ㄊㄨㄥˇ ㄐㄧ)
a rotary printing machine; a web press 亦作「捲筒印刷機」

捲筒紙(ㄐㄩㄢˇ ㄊㄨㄥˇ ㄓˇ)
a web

捲簾(ㄐㄩㄢˇ ㄌㄧㄢˊ)
to roll up a screen or curtain

捲甲(ㄐㄩㄢˇ ㄐㄧㄚˇ)
to gather the armors—to stop fighting

捲起(ㄐㄩㄢˇ ㄑㄧˇ)
① to roll up (sleeves, screens, etc.): 他捲起了袖子。He rolled up his sleeves. ② to cause (an incident, trouble) ③ to sweep off

捲席(ㄐㄩㄢˇ ㄒㄧˊ)
to roll up the mat—to go away; to travel

捲袖(ㄐㄩㄢˇ ㄒㄧㄡˋ)
to roll up the sleeves; to curl up one's sleeves

捲心菜(ㄐㄩㄢˇ ㄒㄧㄣ ㄘㄞˋ)
a cabbage 亦作「甘藍」

捲尺(ㄐㄩㄢˇ ㄔˇ)
a tape measure or tapeline

捲舌音(ㄐㄩㄢˇ ㄕㄜˊ ㄧㄣ)
the pronunciation of a Chinese character which requires the tongue to roll up

捲繞(ㄐㄩㄢˇ ㄖㄠˋ)

to wind

捲入(ㄐㄩㄢˇ ㄖㄨˋ)
to be drawn into; to be involved in; to become embroiled in: 他捲入一場糾紛。He was involved in a dispute.

捲入漩渦(ㄐㄩㄢˇ ㄖㄨˋ ㄒㄩㄢˊ ㄨㄛ)
to be drawn into a whirlpool—to get involved in a conflict, trouble, etc.

捲子(ㄐㄩㄢˇ ·ㄗ)or 捲兒(ㄐㄩㄢˇ)
rolls; small cakes of bread

捲煙(ㄐㄩㄢˇ ㄧㄢ)
cigarettes

捲雲(ㄐㄩㄢˇ ㄩㄣˊ)
(meteorology) cirrus

【捻】 1908
1. ㄋㄧㄢˇ nean niǎn

1. to nip with fingers
2. the "Nien Bandits"
3. to twist: 這條繩是由許多線捻成的。This rope is twisted from many threads.
4. to follow up
5. something made by twisting: 紙捻兒 a twist of paper

捻匪(ㄋㄧㄢˇ ㄈㄟˇ)
the "Nien Bandits", who collaborated with the Taiping rebels (太平軍) during the mid-nineteenth century 亦作「捻子」

捻燈(ㄋㄧㄢˇ ㄉㄥ)
to turn up the wick of a lamp

捻子(ㄋㄧㄢˇ ·ㄗ)or 捻兒(ㄋㄧㄢˇ)
①something twisted into the shape of a piece of thread ②the "Nien Bandits"

【捻】 1908
2. ㄋㄧㄝ nhie niè
to pinch or knead with the fingers

捻花(ㄋㄧㄝ ㄏㄨㄚ)
to pluck flowers

捻手捻腳(ㄋㄧㄝ ㄕㄡˇ ㄋㄧㄝ ㄐㄧㄠˇ)
stealthily or clandestinely; to pussyfoot

【捷】 1909
(簡) ㄐㄧㄝˊ jye jié

1. to win; to triumph; the prizes of a victory: 我軍首戰告捷。Our army won the first battle.
2. swift; quick; rapid; agile; fast; alert: 他是個工作敏捷的

人。He is a rapid worker.

3. a Chinese family name

捷報(ㄐㄧㄝˊㄅㄠˋ)
　a report of success in an examination; a war bulletin announcing a victory: 捷報頻頻傳來。Reports of victory keep pouring in.

捷克人(ㄐㄧㄝˊㄎㄜˋㄖㄣˊ)
　a Czechoslovak; a Czechoslovakian

捷克斯拉夫(ㄐㄧㄝˊㄎㄜˋㄙㄌㄚㄈㄨ)
　or 捷克(ㄐㄧㄝˊㄎㄜˋ)
　Czechoslovakia

捷口(ㄐㄧㄝˊㄎㄡˇ)
　a sharp tongue; swift in verbal response

捷徑(ㄐㄧㄝˊㄐㄧㄥˋ)
　a shortcut; a snap course: 求學無捷徑。There is no shortcut to knowledge.

捷黠(ㄐㄧㄝˊㄒㄧㄚˊ)
　shrewd; cunning; crafty

捷書(ㄐㄧㄝˊㄕㄨ)
　a report of victory

捷足先得(ㄐㄧㄝˊㄗㄨˊㄒㄧㄢㄉㄜˊ)or
捷足先登(ㄐㄧㄝˊㄗㄨˊㄒㄧㄢㄉㄥ)
　The first prize will go to the nimblest. 或 The early bird catches the worm. 或 to beat others to a goal or an objective: 他們捷足先登，把最好的工作搶走了。They grabbed the best work before the others had a chance to.

捷速(ㄐㄧㄝˊㄙㄨˋ)
　rapidly; quickly

捷運(ㄐㄧㄝˊㄩㄣˋ)
　rapid transit

捷運系統(ㄐㄧㄝˊㄩㄣˋㄒㄧˋㄊㄨㄥˇ)
　a system for rapid transit

【掂】 1910
　ㄉㄧㄢ dian diān
　to estimate the weight of something by weighing it with hands: 請掂掂這有多重。Weigh this in your hand, please.

掂對(ㄉㄧㄢㄉㄨㄟˋ)
　to weigh and consider (situations, alternatives, etc.)

掂斤播兩(ㄉㄧㄢㄐㄧㄣㄅㄛˋㄌㄧㄤˇ)
　to concentrate on details; to make a fuss over trifles

掂算(ㄉㄧㄢㄙㄨㄢˋ)
　to consider; to ponder; to estimate; to weigh

【掀】 1911
　ㄒㄧㄢ shian xiān
1. to lift with the hands; to raise: 進房前請掀門簾。Lift the door curtain before you enter the room.
2. to stir; to stir up; to cause; to rise; to expose; to reveal: 我不喜歡掀人罪狀。I don't like to expose others' crime.

掀被(ㄒㄧㄢㄅㄟˋ)
　to throw off a coverlet

掀不動(ㄒㄧㄢㄅㄨˋㄉㄨㄥˋ)
　unable to move it or lift it

掀不起(ㄒㄧㄢㄅㄨˋㄑㄧˇ)
　cannot lift (a lid, a cover, etc.)

掀房頂(ㄒㄧㄢㄈㄤˊㄉㄧㄥˇ)
　to lift the roof off a house

掀風播浪(ㄒㄧㄢㄈㄥㄅㄛˋㄌㄤˋ)
　to stir up a turmoil or an upheaval; to cause unrest; to stir up trouble 亦作「興風作浪」

掀動(ㄒㄧㄢㄉㄨㄥˋ)
　to raise; to stir up; to instigate; to lift

掀騰(ㄒㄧㄢㄊㄥˊ)
　to stir; to overturn

掀天(ㄒㄧㄢㄊㄧㄢ)
　①(said of a billow) to rise to the sky: 海浪掀天。Waves rise to the sky. ②(said of sound, noise, etc.)to reach the heaven

掀天揭地(ㄒㄧㄢㄊㄧㄢㄐㄧㄝㄉㄧˋ)或
掀天動地(ㄒㄧㄢㄊㄧㄢㄉㄨㄥˋㄉㄧˋ)
　(said of an extraordinary achievement, ability, etc.) to stir the heavens and shake the earth; overwhelming (force)

掀天事業(ㄒㄧㄢㄊㄧㄢㄕˋㄧㄝˋ)
　an awe-inspiring achievement or endeavor

掀簾子(ㄒㄧㄢㄌㄧㄢˊㄗˇ)
　to pull aside a screen or curtain

掀開(ㄒㄧㄢㄎㄞ)
　to cause; to open; to uncover or unveil (a secret, etc.); to expose: 他們掀開了他的陰謀。They exposed his plot.

掀起(ㄒㄧㄢㄑㄧˇ)
　to stir up (a movement, etc.); to surge: 大海掀起了巨浪。Large waves surged on the sea.

掀腫(ㄒㄧㄢㄓㄨㄥˇ)
　a swelling

掀唇(ㄒㄧㄢㄔㄨㄣˊ)
　to open the mouth; to speak

掀髯(ㄒㄧㄢㄖㄢˊ)
　the rising of the beard when laughing or smiling

掀舞(ㄒㄧㄢㄨˇ)
　(said of waves) churning and pounding

【掃】 1912
　1. (掃)ㄙㄠˇ sao
　　　　　　sào
1. to sweep with a broom; to clear away; to clean
2. to wipe out; to weed out; to exterminate; to mop up
3. sweepingly; totally
4. to paint (the eyebrows, etc.)
5. to pass over to examine; to sweep: 他向教室掃了一眼。He swept his eyes over the classroom.

掃平(ㄙㄠˇㄆㄧㄥˊ)or 掃清(ㄙㄠˇㄑㄧㄥ)
　to put down; to crush; to suppress; to quell an uprising, etc.

掃眉(ㄙㄠˇㄇㄟˊ)
　to paint eyebrows

掃眉才子(ㄙㄠˇㄇㄟˊㄘㄞˊㄗˇ)
　a female scholar

掃描(ㄙㄠˇㄇㄧㄠˊ)
　(electricity) scanning

掃墓(ㄙㄠˇㄇㄨˋ)or 掃墳(ㄙㄠˇㄈㄣˊ)
　(literally) to sweep the tomb—to pay respects to one's ancestor at his grave

掃房(ㄙㄠˇㄈㄤˊ)or 掃舍(ㄙㄠˇㄕㄜˋ)
　to sweep a house—in preparation for the new year, etc.

掃蕩(ㄙㄠˇㄉㄤˋ)
　to make a clean sweep of (enemy troops, rebels, etc.); a mop-up operation

掃地(ㄙㄠˇㄉㄧˋ)
　①to sweep the floor ②(said of reputation) to soil: 他威信掃地。He is shorn of his prestige.

掃地出門(ㄙㄠˇㄉㄧˋㄔㄨㄇㄣˊ)
　to force a family to leave their home without taking anything with them (as the Chinese Communists did to landlords and wealthy families in the mainland China)

掃斷(ㄙㄠ ㄉㄨㄢ)
totally eliminated

掃榻(ㄙㄠ ㄊㄚˋ)
to sweep the mat—to welcome a visitor

掃榻以待(ㄙㄠ ㄊㄚˋ ㄧˇ ㄉㄞˋ)
to tidy the bedding and await (your) coming; to welcome (your) visit

掃堂腿(ㄙㄠ ㄊㄤˊ ㄊㄨㄟˇ)
(Chinese boxing) a feat in which the boxer squats with one leg extended while managing a quick spin to fell his adversary

掃田刮地(ㄙㄠ ㄊㄧㄢˊ ㄍㄨㄚ ㄉㄧˋ)
to engage in manual labor; to toil; to do menial work

掃雷艇(ㄙㄠ ㄌㄟˊ ㄊㄧㄥˇ)or 掃雷艦
(ㄙㄠ ㄌㄟˊ ㄐㄧㄢˋ)
a minesweeper

掃臉(ㄙㄠ ㄌㄧㄢˇ)
to lose face

掃除乾淨(ㄙㄠ ㄔㄨˊ ㄐㄧㄥˋ)
to sweep clean: 在冬天，街上的雪必須掃乾淨。In winter, the streets have to be cleared of snow.

掃黑(ㄙㄠ ㄏㄟ)
to crack down on crime

掃黃(ㄙㄠ ㄏㄨㄤˊ)
to crack down on pornography

掃興(ㄙㄠ ㄒㄧㄥˋ)
①to throw cold water on; to spoil pleasure ② to feel disappointed or discouraged: 眞掃興！How disappointing!

掃塵(ㄙㄠ ㄔㄣˊ)
①to sweep clean ② to quell rebellions

掃蕩(ㄙㄠ ㄉㄤˋ)
①to sweep up; to clean ② to eliminate (bad habits, undesirable elements, rebels, etc.); to wipe out; to remove: 讓我們掃除一切疑惑。Let's remove all doubts.

掃除天地(ㄙㄠ ㄔㄨˊ ㄊㄧㄢ ㄉㄧˋ)
to rid the world of bad elements; to bring peace and justice to the world

掃除文盲(ㄙㄠ ㄔㄨˊ ㄨㄣˊ ㄇㄤˊ)
to eliminate illiteracy

掃射(ㄙㄠ ㄕㄜˋ)
①to strafe (with machine-gun fire) ② to look around:

他用目光掃射房間一遍。His glance swept around the room.

掃數(ㄙㄠ ㄕㄨˋ)
totally; completely

1912
【掃】 2. (掃) ㄙㄠ saw
sao
a broom

掃帚(ㄙㄠ ˙ㄓㄡ)or 掃把
a broom: 沒掃帚我無法打掃。
I can't sweep without a broom.

掃帚星(ㄙㄠ ˙ㄓㄡ ㄒㄧㄥ)
①(astronomy) a comet ② any person who brings bad luck; a jinx

1913
【授】 ㄕㄡˋ show shòu
1. to give; to hand over to; to confer (a degree, prize, etc.)
2. to teach; to tutor: 函授to teach by correspondence
3. to give up (one's life, etc.)

授兵(ㄕㄡˋ ㄅㄧㄥ)
(in ancient China) to hand over arms to soldiers at the outbreak of war

授命(ㄕㄡˋ ㄇㄧㄥˋ)
to sacrifice one's life; to give up one's life

授粉(ㄕㄡˋ ㄈㄣˇ)
(botany) to pollinate; pollination

授田(ㄕㄡˋ ㄊㄧㄢˊ)
to allot public land to a person for the farming purpose

授徒(ㄕㄡˋ ㄊㄨˊ)
to teach students or pupils

授課(ㄕㄡˋ ㄎㄜˋ)
to teach; to tutor: 他每週必須授課十小時。He has to teach ten hours every week.

授記(ㄕㄡˋ ㄐㄧˋ)
(Buddhism) to prophesy; prophecy

授戒(ㄕㄡˋ ㄐㄧㄝˋ)
to give rules for a monk or nun to observe in the initiation ceremony

授獎(ㄕㄡˋ ㄐㄧㄤˇ)
to award a prize

授精(ㄕㄡˋ ㄐㄧㄥ)
to inseminate; insemination: 人工授精artificial insemination

授爵(ㄕㄡˋ ㄐㄩㄝˊ)

to elevate to the peerage

授旗(ㄕㄡˋ ㄑㄧˊ)
to give the national flag to a sports team leaving for competitions abroad, etc.

授槍(ㄕㄡˋ ㄑㄧㄤ)
to issue rifles to new recruits

授權(ㄕㄡˋ ㄑㄩㄢˊ)
①to authorize; to delegate powers ② to license

授勳(ㄕㄡˋ ㄒㄩㄣ)
to confer orders; to award a decoration

授職(ㄕㄡˋ ㄓˊ)
to confer a rank; to give an official job to

授時(ㄕㄡˋ ㄕˊ)
(in ancient China) to teach people the knowledge of calendar to insure timely cultivation of the land

授室(ㄕㄡˋ ㄕˋ)
to accept a daughter-in-law in a formal ceremony

授首(ㄕㄡˋ ㄕㄡˇ)
to get killed; to be beheaded

授受(ㄕㄡˋ ㄕㄡˋ)
to give and receive; to give and accept; to grant and receive: 公務人員不得私相授受。Public servants should not give and accept privately.

授受不親(ㄕㄡˋ ㄕㄡˋ ㄅㄨˋ ㄑㄧㄣ)
(formerly) no physical contact between a man and a woman except man and wife

授人以柄(ㄕㄡˋ ㄖㄣˊ ㄧˇ ㄅㄧㄥˇ)
to give others something to talk about oneself; to offer another a hold on oneself

授餐(ㄕㄡˋ ㄘㄢ)
to give someone food

授意(ㄕㄡˋ ㄧˋ)
to intimate; to inspire; to make someone do something by giving a hint or suggestion

授業(ㄕㄡˋ ㄧㄝˋ)
to teach; to tutor

授與(ㄕㄡˋ ㄩˇ)
to confer; to give

1914
【掇】 ㄉㄨㄛ dwo duó
1. to collect; to gather
2. to plagiarize; to pirate

〔手部〕

【手部】

3. to select; to pluck

撥弄(カメɛ ㄈㄨㄥ)
①to stir up (conflicts, etc.)
②to handle a matter; to deal with something

撥拾(カメɛ ㄕ)
to collect; to select

撥探(カメɛ)
to gather; to select; to pluck

【掄】 1915
1. ㄌㄨㄣ luen lún
to select; to choose

掄魁(ㄌㄨㄣ ㄎㄨㄟ)
to head the list of successful candidates in the imperial civil service examination

掄選(ㄌㄨㄣ ㄒㄩㄢ)or 掄擇(ㄗㄜ)
to select (competent persons, adequate materials, etc.)

掄才(ㄌㄨㄣ ㄘㄞ)
to select men of ability

掄元(ㄌㄨㄣ ㄩㄢ)
to come out first in examinations

【掄】 1915
2. ㄌㄨㄣ lhuen lún
1. to turn or spin with hands or arms; to swing
2. to brandish; to wave
3. to squander

掄刀(ㄌㄨㄣ ㄉㄠ)
to swing a knife (at somebody)

掄棍(ㄍㄨㄣ)
to swing a stick

掄拳(ㄑㄩㄢ)
to swing a fist

【掎】 1916
ㄐㄧ jii jǐ
to draw aside; to drag; to pull

掎角(ㄐㄧ ㄐㄩㄝ)
(literally) to seize the horns and tie up the feet—to defeat (the enemy)

掎摭(ㄓ)
①to find fault with ②to gather

【掏】 1917
ㄊㄠ tau táo
1. to take out; to pull out: 他從口袋裏掏出鑰匙。He took a key out of his pocket.
2. to dig; to scoop out: 他在牆上掏個洞。He dug a hole in the wall.

3. to steal from somebody's pocket: 她的錢被扒手掏走了。She had her money stolen by a pickpocket.

掏摸(ㄇㄛ)
①to search and feel (in the pocket, etc.) ②to steal ③to be given (money, etc.) after begging, etc.

掏溝(ㄍㄡ)
to dredge a gutter or ditch

掏井(ㄐㄧㄥ)
to dredge a well

掏錢(ㄑㄧㄢ)
to take out money; to spend money

掏出來(ㄔㄨ ㄌㄞ)
to pull out or draw out

掏耳朵(ㄦ ㄉㄨㄛ)
to pick or clean ears

掏腰包(ㄧㄠ ㄅㄠ)
(colloquial) to spend one's own money; to shell out

【掐】 1918
ㄑㄧㄚ chia qiā
1. to dig the nail into
2. to cut with fingernails; to nip; to pinch; to give a pinch
3. to hold; to grasp; to clutch; to gather with the hand

掐斷(ㄑㄧㄚ ㄉㄨㄢ)
to break; to nip

掐頭去尾(ㄑㄧㄚ ㄊㄡ ㄑㄩ ㄨㄟ)
to do away with unnecessary parts or details at both ends: 引用報紙的話你不能掐頭去尾。If you quote passages from newspapers, you should quote them in full.

掐嗓(ㄑㄧㄚ ㄙㄤ)
to seize by the throat; to choke

掐花兒(ㄑㄧㄚ ㄏㄨㄚㄦ)
to pluck flowers with fingernails

掐尖兒(ㄑㄧㄚ ㄐㄧㄢㄦ)
①to cut off branches of plants so as to hasten growth ②to practice irregularities, etc. in a deal in order to get profits, kickbacks, etc.

掐指一算(ㄑㄧㄚ ㄓ ㄧ ㄙㄨㄢ)or 掐算(ㄑㄧㄚ ㄙㄨㄢ)
to count; to calculate

掐佳(ㄑㄧㄚ ㄓㄚ)

to seize; to grasp; to hold: 在恐懼中她抓住他的臂。In fright she seized his arm.

掐死(ㄑㄧㄚ ㄙ)
to choke to death by strangling with hands

【掊】 1919
1. ㄆㄡ poou pǒu
to strike; to cut; to cudgel; to attack

掊斗折衡(ㄆㄡ ㄉㄡ ㄓㄜ ㄏㄥ)
to break the measure and destroy the scales so as to prevent wrangling (a political philosophy advocated by 莊子)

掊擊(ㄐㄧ)
to strike; to break

【掊】 1919
2. ㄆㄡ pour póu
to exact; to collect (taxes)

掊克(ㄆㄡ ㄎㄜ)or 掊斂(ㄆㄡ ㄌㄧㄢ)
to exact high taxes from people; to levy heavy taxes from people

【掉】 1920
1. ㄉㄧㄠ diaw diào
1. to turn: 請把椅子掉過來。Please turn the chair round.
2. to fall; to shed: 她掉下幾滴眼淚。She shed a few tears.
3. to lose; to be missing: 我掉了手錶。I've lost my watch.
4. to fall behind; to lag behind
5. to change; to substitute
6. to move; to shake; to wag
7. used as an adverbial particle after verbs expressing conditions of fulfillment: 吃掉 to eat off 擦掉 to wipe off

掉背臉(ㄉㄧㄠ ㄅㄟ ㄌㄧㄢ)
to turn one's face

掉包兒(ㄉㄧㄠ ㄅㄠㄦ)
to substitute in secret an object with something else identical in appearance but different in quality or contents; to substitute stealthily one thing for another

掉臂不顧(ㄉㄧㄠ ㄅㄧ ㄅㄨ ㄍㄨ)or 掉臂而去(ㄉㄧㄠ ㄅㄧ ㄦ ㄑㄩ)
to walk out on (somebody)

掉皮(ㄉㄧㄠ ㄆㄧ)
to peel off

掉隊(ㄉㄧㄠ ㄉㄨㄟ)
to drop out; to fall behind

掉動(ㄉㄧㄠ ㄉㄨㄥ)

①to move; to stir ②to change; to exchange

掉胎(カ|ㄠ ㄊㄞ)
to abort; abortion; to miscarry; a miscarriage

掉頭(カ|ㄠ ㄊㄡ)
①to turn one's head (and walk away) ②to shake one's head ③to turn back; to turn round; to turn about ④to get killed; to get beheaded

掉頭就走(カ|ㄠ ㄊㄡ ㄐ|ㄡ ㄗㄡ)or 掉頭不顧(カ|ㄠ ㄊㄡ ㄅㄨ ㄍㄨ)
to turn one's head and walk away; to turn away and leave

掉腦袋(カ|ㄠ ㄋㄠ ·ㄉㄞ)
to get beheaded

掉淚(カ|ㄠ ㄌㄟ)
to come to tears; tears falling

掉過來(カ|ㄠ ㄍㄨㄛ ·ㄌㄞ)
①to turn around ②on the other hand

掉花槍(カ|ㄠ ㄏㄨㄚ ㄑ|ㄤ)
to play tricks; to divert another's attention by words or action (in order to gain some time, etc.)

掉換(カ|ㄠ ㄏㄨㄢ)
to change; to exchange; to invert; to substitute: 我們掉換一下座位吧! Let's change seats.

掉魂(カ|ㄠ ㄏㄨㄣ)
to lose one's wits; terrified; very scared

掉價(カ|ㄠ ㄐ|ㄚ)
to fall the price

掉下來(カ|ㄠ ㄒ|ㄚ ·ㄌㄞ)
to fall down

掉轉(カ|ㄠ ㄓㄨㄢ)
to turn back; to turn round

掉舌(カ|ㄠ ㄕㄜ)
①eloquent; to speak eloquently and persuasively ②to chatter ③to stir up ill will between others by loose gossip

掉書袋(カ|ㄠ ㄕㄨ ㄉㄞ)
excessive fondness of making literary quotations and historical allusions; to parade learning

掉色(カ|ㄠ ㄙㄜ)or 掉色兒(カ|ㄠ ㄕㄞ ㄦ)
to discolor; to fade: 這種質料

不掉色。This material won't fade.

掉以輕心(カ|ㄠ |ˇ ㄑ|ㄥ ㄒ|ㄣ)
to lower one's guard; to treat something lightly

掉尾(カ|ㄠ ㄨㄟˇ)
to wag the tail

【排】 *1921*
ㄆㄞˊ pair pói

1. a row; a line; a rank
2. to arrange; to put in order; to fall in line: 把椅子排好。 Put the chairs in order.
3. (military) a platoon
4. to clear out; to drain away; to discharge: 水不久就會排出去了。 The water will soon drain away.
5. to reject; to expel; to exclude
6. to rehearse
7. a raft: 竹排 a bamboo raft
8. to push

排八卦(ㄆㄞˊ ㄅㄚ ㄍㄨㄚ)
to arrange the Eight Diagrams

排班(ㄆㄞˊ ㄅㄢ)
①to fall in line (according to order, ranks, etc.) ②to arrange turns of work

排版(ㄆㄞˊ ㄅㄢˇ)
(printing) to set type ; composing; typesetting

排筆(ㄆㄞˊ ㄅ|ˇ)
a row of brushes (used by house painters)

排比(ㄆㄞˊ ㄅ|ˇ)
①to arrange in order ②(linguistics) parallelism

排便(ㄆㄞˊ ㄅ|ㄢ)
defecation; the evacuation of the bowels; a bowel movement

排排坐(ㄆㄞˊ ㄆㄞˊ ㄗㄨㄛˋ)
to sit in rows

排砲(ㄆㄞˊ ㄆㄠˋ)
(military) a volley of artillery fire; a salvo; a broadside

排門兒(ㄆㄞˊ ㄇㄣ ㄦ)
from door to door; door-to-door

排悶(ㄆㄞˊ ㄇㄣˋ)
to kill time; to dispel boredom: 你如何排悶? How did you kill time?

排名(ㄆㄞˊ ㄇ|ㄥˊ)

to list names according to the order of seniority or position

排檔(ㄆㄞˊ ㄉㄤˋ)
a gear (in an automobile engine)

排隊(ㄆㄞˊ ㄉㄨㄟˋ)
to fall in line or formation; to line up; to stand in a queue: 請排隊上車。Please queue up for a bus.

排他性(ㄆㄞˊ ㄊㄚ ㄒ|ㄥˋ)
exclusiveness; impenetrability

排闥直入(ㄆㄞˊ ㄊㄚˋ ㄓˊ ㄖㄨˋ)
to push the door open and walk straight into a house; to barge in; to walk straight in without knocking

排頭(ㄆㄞˊ ㄊㄡˊ)
to stand first in the line; a file leader

排難解紛(ㄆㄞˊ ㄋㄢˋ ㄐ|ㄝˇ ㄈㄣ)
to mediate disputes; to offer good offices to the parties in dispute

排尿(ㄆㄞˊ ㄋ|ㄠˋ)
to urinate; to micturate

排列(ㄆㄞˊ ㄌ|ㄝˋ)
①to arrange in series, rows, etc.: 請排好我書架上的書排列好。 Please arrange my books on the shelf in order. ②(mathematics) permutation or arrangement

排練(ㄆㄞˊ ㄌ|ㄢˋ)
to rehearse for a show; rehearsal: 這齣戲需要多排練。 This play will need a lot of rehearsal.

排卵(ㄆㄞˊ ㄌㄨㄢˇ)
(biology) to ovulate

排律(ㄆㄞˊ ㄌㄩˋ)
a verse form, made up of an indefinite number of rhymed couplets with five or seven characters in each line

排骨(ㄆㄞˊ ·ㄍㄨ)
①ribs of animals; spareribs ②(slang) a skinny person

排課(ㄆㄞˊ ㄎㄜˋ)
to work out a teaching schedule (at a school)

排開(ㄆㄞˊ ㄎㄞ)
to spread out

排行(ㄆㄞˊ ㄏㄤˊ)
one's seniority among

〔手部〕

brothers and sisters: 他排行老大。He's the first child of the family.

排華(ㄆㄞˊ ㄏㄨㄚˊ)
anti-Chinese

排擠(ㄆㄞˊ ㄐㄧˇ)
①to expel somebody out of an inner circle or clique, etc. ②to push aside; to elbow out: 他們互相排擠。They try to squeeze the others out.

排解(ㄆㄞˊ ㄐㄧㄝˇ)
to resolve (disputes); to mediate; to make peace; to reconcile

排解糾紛(ㄆㄞˊ ㄐㄧㄝˇ ㄐㄧㄡ ㄈㄣ)
to mediate a quarrel; to reconcile a dispute

排氣管(ㄆㄞˊ ㄑㄧˋ ㄍㄨㄢˇ)
an exhaust pipe

排球(ㄆㄞˊ ㄑㄧㄡˊ)
volleyball

排遣(ㄆㄞˊ ㄑㄧㄢˇ)
(said of a disappointed person) to find comfort in; to divert oneself from loneliness

排戲(ㄆㄞˊ ㄒㄧˋ)
to rehearse for a show

排洩(ㄆㄞˊ ㄒㄧㄝˋ)
to excrete; to discharge; excretion

排洩器(ㄆㄞˊ ㄒㄧㄝˋ ㄑㄧˋ)or排泄器官(ㄆㄞˊ ㄒㄧㄝˋ ㄑㄧˋ ㄍㄨㄢ)
excretory organs

排泄物(ㄆㄞˊ ㄒㄧㄝˋ ㄨˋ)
excreta; excrement

排簫(ㄆㄞˊ ㄒㄧㄠ)
a kind of ancient musical instrument consisting of a cluster of bamboo pipes ranging from 16 to 20 in number

排陣(ㄆㄞˊ ㄓㄣˋ)
to deploy troops: 軍隊排陣備戰。The army is arranged for battle.

排長(ㄆㄞˊ ㄓㄤˇ)
a platoon leader

排斥(ㄆㄞˊ ㄔˋ)
to expel; to repel; to discriminate against

排場(ㄆㄞˊ ㄔㄤˇ)or(ㄆㄞˊ ㄔㄤˊ)
①ostentation and extravagance: 他喜歡講排場。He goes in for ostentation and extravagance. ②a person's

social position

排除(ㄆㄞˊ ㄔㄨˊ)
to get rid of; to remove; to eliminate: 我們必須排除任何可能導致意外的因素。We have to eliminate any possible causes of accidents.

排除障礙(ㄆㄞˊ ㄔㄨˊ ㄓㄤˋ ㄞˋ)
to remove an obstacle

排除異己(ㄆㄞˊ ㄔㄨˊ ㄧˋ ㄐㄧˇ)or排斥異己(ㄆㄞˊ ㄔˋ ㄧˋ ㄐㄧˇ)
to get rid of those who hold a view different from one's own or who do not conform to one's ideas; to eliminate those not belonging to one's clique, etc.; to expel "outsiders"

排除萬難(ㄆㄞˊ ㄔㄨˊ ㄨㄢˋ ㄋㄢˊ)
to overcome all difficulties

排沙揀金 or 排沙簡金(ㄆㄞˊ ㄕㄚ ㄐㄧㄢˇ ㄐㄧㄣ)
①to sift sand for gold ②to be expert at selecting (the right person or thing) for a job, etc.

排山倒海(ㄆㄞˊ ㄕㄢ ㄉㄠˇ ㄏㄞˇ)
overwhelming or sweeping

排水(ㄆㄞˊ ㄕㄨㄟˇ)
to drain water; drainage

排水量(ㄆㄞˊ ㄕㄨㄟˇ ㄌㄧㄤˋ)
①the volume of water displacement ②displacement (of a ship)

排水溝(ㄆㄞˊ ㄕㄨㄟˇ ㄍㄡ)
a discharge ditch; a drainage ditch

排水溝渠(ㄆㄞˊ ㄕㄨㄟˇ ㄍㄡ ㄑㄩ)
escape canals

排水管(ㄆㄞˊ ㄕㄨㄟˇ ㄍㄨㄢˇ)
a drainpipe

排水工程(ㄆㄞˊ ㄕㄨㄟˇ ㄍㄨㄥ ㄔㄥˊ)
drainage works

排水口(ㄆㄞˊ ㄕㄨㄟˇ ㄎㄡˇ)
a drainage outlet

排水系統(ㄆㄞˊ ㄕㄨㄟˇ ㄒㄧˋ ㄊㄨㄥˇ)
a drainage system

排字(ㄆㄞˊ ㄗˋ)
①to set types; typesetting; composition ②to form words or figures with colored cardboards held in the hands of persons seated or standing in rows

排字房(ㄆㄞˊ ㄗˋ ㄈㄤˊ)
a composition room (in a printing shop)

排字機(ㄆㄞˊ ㄗˋ ㄐㄧ)
a linotype

排演(ㄆㄞˊ ㄧㄢˇ)
to rehearse for a show: 他們正在排演一齣歌劇。They are rehearsing an opera.

排印(ㄆㄞˊ ㄧㄣˋ)
to set type and print; typesetting and printing

排外(ㄆㄞˊ ㄨㄞˋ)
antiforeign; chauvinistic; ultranationalistic: 他是個盲目排外的人。He had blind opposition to everything foreign.

排外主義(ㄆㄞˊ ㄨㄞˋ ㄓㄨˇ ㄧˋ)
exclusivism

排灣(ㄆㄞˊ ㄨㄢ)
the Paiwans, an aboriginal tribe in Taiwan

【掘】 1922
ㄐㄩㄝˊ jyue jué
to dig; to excavate; to make a hole or cave

掘地(ㄐㄩㄝˊ ㄉㄧˋ)
to dig the earth

掘洞(ㄐㄩㄝˊ ㄉㄨㄥˋ)
to dig a hole; to make a hole or cave

掘土機(ㄐㄩㄝˊ ㄊㄨˇ ㄐㄧ)
an excavator 亦作「挖土機」

掘開(ㄐㄩㄝˊ ㄎㄞ)
to dig (a closed cave, etc.)

坑(ㄎㄥ)
to dig or make a pit

掘壕(ㄐㄩㄝˊ ㄏㄠˊ)
to entrench; to dig in

掘金(ㄐㄩㄝˊ ㄐㄧㄣ)
to dig for gold; gold digging: 礦工們在掘金。The miners were digging for gold.

掘金者(ㄐㄩㄝˊ ㄐㄧㄣ ㄓㄜˇ)
①a gold digger ②an opportunist or adventurist

掘強 or 倔強(ㄐㄩㄝˊ ㄐㄧㄤˋ)
intransigent; stubborn; obstinate

掘井(ㄐㄩㄝˊ ㄐㄧㄥˇ)
to dig a well

掘壙(ㄐㄩㄝˊ ㄎㄨㄤˋ)
to prepare a tomb; to dig a grave

掘穿(ㄐㄩㄝˊ ㄔㄨㄢ)
to dig through

掘鑿(ㄐㄩㄝˊ ㄗㄠˊ)
excavation

掘藏(ㄐㄩㄝˊ ㄗㄤˋ)

to sack a tomb for its hidden treasure

掘足類（ㄐㄩㄝ ㄗㄨˊ ㄌㄟˋ）
(zoology) scaphopoda

1923

【掖】①ㄧˋ yih yih（語音ㄧㄝˋ yeh ye）

1. to support another; to extend a helping hand; to promote
2. armpits
3. side; by the side
4. side apartments in the palace

掖門（ㄧˋ ㄇㄣˊ）
a small side door of the palace

掖庭（ㄧˋ ㄊㄧㄥˊ）
side apartments or quarters of a palace

掖垣（ㄧˋ ㄩㄢˊ）
sidewalls of a palace

1923

【掖】②ㄧㄝˋ ie ye

1. to conceal; to tuck away; to hide
2. to fold; to roll up (part of one's clothing)

掖掖蓋蓋（ㄧㄝˋ ㄧㄝˋ ㄍㄞˋ ㄍㄞˋ）
stealthily; clandestinely

1924

【拼】（拚）ㄆㄧㄣ pin pin

1. to join together; to incorporate; to put together; to make a whole
2. to spell (a word)
3. to risk

拼版（ㄆㄧㄣ ㄅㄢˇ）
(printing) a makeup

拼盤（ㄆㄧㄣ ㄆㄢˊ）
assorted cold dishes; hors d'oeuvres

拼命（ㄆㄧㄣ ㄇㄧㄥˋ）①to risk one's life ②exerting the utmost strength; with all one's might: 他用拼命讀書。He studies very hard.

拼法（ㄆㄧㄣ ㄈㄚˇ）
spelling

拼到底（ㄆㄧㄣ ㄉㄠˋ ㄉㄧˇ）
to fight to the bitter end

拼湊（ㄆㄧㄣ ㄘㄡˋ）
①to put bits together to make a whole ②(machinery) to cannibalize ③to raise money here and there

拼死（ㄆㄧㄣ ㄙˇ）
to risk one's life; to fight

desperately

拼音（ㄆㄧㄣ ㄧㄣ）
to spell phonetically; to pronounce a word by enunciating the phonetic signs

拼音字母（ㄆㄧㄣ ㄧㄣ ㄗˋ ㄇㄨˇ）
the phonetic alphabet

1925

【掙】①ㄓㄥ jeng zheng

1. to make efforts; to strive
2. to get free from

掙脫（ㄓㄥ ㄊㄨㄛ）
to break away with force; to shake off

掙開（ㄓㄥ ㄎㄞ）
to get free with effort

掙扎（ㄓㄥ ㄓㄚ）
to struggle; a struggle; to strive

1925

【掙】②ㄓㄥˋ jenq zheng

1. to struggle (for one's life, etc.)
2. to earn (money, etc.)

掙命（ㄓㄥˋ ㄇㄧㄥˋ）
to fight or struggle for one's life

掙飯吃（ㄓㄥˋ ㄈㄢˋ ㄔ）
to earn a living

掙家立業（ㄓㄥˋ ㄐㄧㄚ ㄌㄧˋ ㄧㄝˋ）
to establish a home and make achievements

掙錢（ㄓㄥˋ ㄑㄧㄢˊ）
to earn money

1926

【掞】ㄕㄢˋ shann shàn
easy; smooth; suave; comfortable

掞張（ㄕㄢˋ ㄓㄤ）
suave but exaggerating (in one's statement, etc.); smooth but untruthful

掞藻（ㄕㄢˋ ㄗㄠˇ）
the smooth, flowery literary style

1927

【掠】ㄌㄩㄝˋ liueh lüe

1. to take by force; to rob; to plunder; to pillage
2. to brush; to pass lightly on the side; to sweep past; to skim over: 輕風掠面。A gentle breeze brushed my face.
3. to whip; to flog
4. a long stroke to the left in Chinese calligraphy

掠美（ㄌㄩㄝˋ ㄇㄟˇ）
to take credit for what has

been done by somebody else

掠地（ㄌㄩㄝˋ ㄉㄧˋ）
(said of troops) to conquer land; to seize land; to plunder the land conquered

掠奪（ㄌㄩㄝˋ ㄉㄨㄛˊ）
to seize or rob by force; to plunder; to pillage

掠過（ㄌㄩㄝˋ ㄍㄨㄛˋ）
to skim over; to flicker across: 她母親的嘴角上掠過一絲微笑。A faint smile flickered across my mother's lips.

掠取（ㄌㄩㄝˋ ㄑㄩˇ）
to take by force; to rob

掠食（ㄌㄩㄝˋ ㄕˊ）
to hunt for food

掠影浮光（ㄌㄩㄝˋ ㄧㄥˇ ㄈㄨˊ ㄍㄨㄤ）
superficial

1928

【掛】ㄍㄨㄚˋ guah guà

1. to hang up; to suspend: 夜空中掛著一輪明月。A bright moon hung in the night sky.
2. to ring off: 他已經把電話掛斷了。He's hung up.
3. to worry; to think of; anxious: 他非常掛念他母親的病。He's much worried about his mother's illness.
4. with one's name registered or listed; recorded; to register: 我要掛牙科。I want to register for dental surgery.
5. to hitch; to get caught: 她的毛衣給釘子掛住了。Her sweater got caught on a nail.

掛不下（ㄍㄨㄚˋ ㄅㄨˋ ㄒㄧㄚˋ）
There's no room to hang it.

掛不住（ㄍㄨㄚˋ ㄅㄨˋ ㄓㄨˋ）
①cannot be hung securely ②to feel ashamed

掛牌（ㄍㄨㄚˋ ㄆㄞˊ）
①to go into practice (said of lawyers, doctors, etc.) ②(said of banks) to hang out a bulletin board listing the current exchange rates

掛麵（ㄍㄨㄚˋ ㄇㄧㄢˋ）
thin, string-like dried noodles; vermicelli

掛名（ㄍㄨㄚˋ ㄇㄧㄥˊ）
in name only; nominally; titular: 他是掛名的總經理。He is the general manager only in

〔手部〕

〔手部〕

name.

掛單《ㄍㄨㄚˋ ㄉㄢ》or **掛褡**《ㄍㄨㄚˋ ㄉㄚ》
(said of a traveling Buddhist monk) to lodge in a temple for the night

掛燈《ㄍㄨㄚˋ ㄉㄥ》
a low-hanging ceiling lamp

掛頭牌《ㄍㄨㄚˋ ㄊㄡˊ ㄆㄞˊ》
to play the leading role (especially in show business)

掛圖《ㄍㄨㄚˋ ㄊㄨˊ》
a wall chart or map

掛念《ㄍㄨㄚˋ ㄋㄧㄢˋ》or **掛心**《ㄍㄨㄚˋ ㄒㄧㄣ》
to think of; to be anxious about; to worry about; to be on one's mind: 我如晚回，請勿掛念。Don't be anxious if I am late.

掛累《ㄍㄨㄚˋ ㄌㄟˋ》
to involve (another) in

掛零《ㄍㄨㄚˋ ㄌㄧㄥˊ》
odd (as, 50-odd); more than

掛慮《ㄍㄨㄚˋ ㄌㄩˋ》
to be worried or anxious about

掛鈎《ㄍㄨㄚˋ ㄍㄡ》
①a hook for hanging clothes, etc. (usually nailed to the wall) ②(said of railway cars) the coupling links ③to establish contact with

掛冠《ㄍㄨㄚˋ ㄍㄨㄢ》
(literally) to hang up one's official cap—to quit or resign: 他掛冠而去。He resigned and went home.

掛號《ㄍㄨㄚˋ ㄏㄠˋ》
①registered (mail, etc.); to register a mail: 請把此信掛號。Please register this letter. ②to register (at the outpatient department of a hospital): 請排隊掛號。Please line up to register.

掛號信《ㄍㄨㄚˋ ㄏㄠˋ ㄒㄧㄣˋ》
a registered letter

掛號處《ㄍㄨㄚˋ ㄏㄠˋ ㄔㄨˋ》
a register office (of a hospital)

掛紅《ㄍㄨㄚˋ ㄏㄨㄥˊ》
①to hang red silk for congratulations on the opening of a new shop ②a sign of repentance by the perpetrator of an offense by hanging

a piece of red silk or cloth at the door of his victim

掛劍《ㄍㄨㄚˋ ㄐㄧㄢˋ》
to hang the precious sword on its admirer's grave—a last gift to show one's memory of the deceased

掛欠《ㄍㄨㄚˋ ㄑㄧㄢˋ》or **掛賬**《ㄍㄨㄚˋ ㄓㄤˋ》
(to buy) on credit; to owe

掛孝《ㄍㄨㄚˋ ㄒㄧㄠˋ》
to wear mourning

掛鐘《ㄍㄨㄚˋ ㄓㄨㄥ》
a wall clock

掛齒《ㄍㄨㄚˋ ㄔˇ》
to mention: 這點小事，何足掛齒。Such a trifling thing is not worth mentioning.

掛車《ㄍㄨㄚˋ ㄔㄜ》
(said of a locomotive) to hook up with the train

掛失《ㄍㄨㄚˋ ㄕ》
to report the loss (of a check, etc.) to the bank to prevent the bearer from cashing it

掛上《ㄍㄨㄚˋ ㄕㄤˋ》
①to hang up ②to enter into the book (of one's debts, etc.)

掛帥《ㄍㄨㄚˋ ㄕㄨㄞˋ》
①to be appointed commander-in-chief; to assume command; to assume leadership ②to dominate; to be the most important

掛彩《ㄍㄨㄚˋ ㄘㄞˇ》
①to hang colored silk in celebration of happy occasions ②to get wounded in action; (now comically) to get injured in a brawl or fight, etc.

掛礙《ㄍㄨㄚˋ ㄞˋ》
to meet many obstacles and obstructions

掛一漏萬《ㄍㄨㄚˋ ㄧ ㄌㄡˋ ㄨㄢˋ》or **掛漏**
(literally) to list one item while missing 10,000 others—totally incomplete or inadequate (a polite expression often used by an editor or compiler in the preface of a book)

掛衣鈎《ㄍㄨㄚˋ ㄧ ㄍㄡ》
a clothes hook

掛意《ㄍㄨㄚˋ ㄧˋ》
to mind: 不管你做什麼我都不掛意。I don't mind what you do.

掛羊頭賣狗肉《ㄍㄨㄚˋ ㄧㄤˊ ㄊㄡˊ ㄇㄞˋ ㄍㄡˇ ㄖㄡˋ》
(literally) to sell dog meat while hanging a sheep's head outside the shop as advertisement—to cheat

【採】《ㄘㄞˇ》 tsae cǎi
1. to pluck (flowers, etc.); to gather; to collect; to extract; to pick: 請爲我採一些花。Please gather me some flowers.
2. to select; to adopt: 經理採用他的意見。The manager adopted his idea.
3. (now rarely) to drag
4. (now rarely) to beckon; to take notice of

採辦《ㄘㄞˇ ㄅㄢˋ》
to purchase; to procure

採購《ㄘㄞˇ ㄍㄡˋ》or **採買**《ㄘㄞˇ ㄇㄞˇ》
to pick and buy; to purchase; procurement

採煤《ㄘㄞˇ ㄇㄟˊ》
coal mining; coal cutting

採伐《ㄘㄞˇ ㄈㄚˊ》
to fell (trees); to open up (a mine)

採訪《ㄘㄞˇ ㄈㄤˇ》
to cover (a news item or story); to interview

採訪部《ㄘㄞˇ ㄈㄤˇ ㄅㄨˋ》
the city desk

採訪記者《ㄘㄞˇ ㄈㄤˇ ㄐㄧˋ ㄓㄜˇ》
a news reporter

採訪新聞《ㄘㄞˇ ㄈㄤˇ ㄒㄧㄣ ㄨㄣˊ》
to cover a news item

採訪主任《ㄘㄞˇ ㄈㄤˇ ㄓㄨˇ ㄖㄣˋ》
a city editor

採風《ㄘㄞˇ ㄈㄥ》
to collect folk songs

採風問俗《ㄘㄞˇ ㄈㄥ ㄨㄣˋ ㄙㄨˊ》
to learn local practices and customs

採納《ㄘㄞˇ ㄋㄚˋ》
to accept or adopt (an idea, opinion, proposal, etc.); 他不肯採納我的建議。He won't accept my proposal.

採納良言《ㄘㄞˇ ㄋㄚˋ ㄌㄧㄤˊ ㄧㄢˊ》
to accept good counsel

採運《ㄘㄞˇ ㄩㄣˋ》

採錄(ㄘㄞ ㄌㄨ)
to collect and record

採購(ㄘㄞ ㄍㄡ)
to make purchases for an organization; to purchase

採購團(ㄘㄞ ㄍㄡ ㄊㄨㄢ)
a purchase mission

採光(ㄘㄞ ㄍㄨㄤ)
①lighting ②to pick or pluck until none is left

採礦(ㄘㄞ ㄎㄨㄤ)
to mine (for minerals): 露天採礦 opencut mining

採花(ㄘㄞ ㄏㄨㄚ)
①to pluck flowers ②(said of bandits, etc.) to force into a house in the night and commit rape

採花賊(ㄘㄞ ㄏㄨㄚ ㄗㄟ)
a rapist

採集(ㄘㄞ ㄐㄧ)
to gather (samples, etc.); to collect (materials, etc.): 他喜歡採集標本。He likes to collect specimens.

採擷(ㄘㄞ ㄒㄧㄝ)
to quote from; to take selections (from a book, article, etc.)

採取(ㄘㄞ ㄑㄩ)
to take or adopt (an attitude, a measure, etc.)

採取主動(ㄘㄞ ㄑㄩ ㄓㄨ ㄉㄨㄥ)
to take the initiative

採薪(ㄘㄞ ㄒㄧㄣ)
to gather firewood

採薪之憂(ㄘㄞ ㄒㄧㄣ ㄓ ㄧㄡ)
ill or sick; illness or sickness

採信(ㄘㄞ ㄒㄧㄣ)
to believe; to accept as true: 部份人講的話不足採信。We cannot believe what that man says.

採選(ㄘㄞ ㄒㄩㄢ)
to select; to pick (for use or purchase)

採摘(ㄘㄞ ㄓㄞ)
①to select and pick (tea leaves, etc.) ②to quote from; to translate in part or select from (a book, article, etc.)

採珠(ㄘㄞ ㄓㄨ)
to dive for pearls

採茶(ㄘㄞ ㄔㄚ)
to pick the cupules of lotus

to pick tea leaves

採場(ㄘㄞ ㄔㄤ)or 採鑛場(ㄘㄞ ㄎㄨㄤ ㄔㄤ)
(mining) a stope

探石場(ㄘㄞ ㄕ ㄔㄤ)or(ㄘㄞ ㄕ ㄔㄤ)
(mining) a stone pit; a quarry

採生折割(ㄘㄞ ㄕㄥ ㄓㄜ ㄍㄜ)
a witchcraft that resembled voodoo

採擇(ㄘㄞ ㄗㄜ)
to pick or select: 他提出幾種辦法供你採擇。He has proposed several measures for you to choose from.

採桑(ㄘㄞ ㄙㄤ)
to gather mulberry leaves

採藥(ㄘㄞ ㄧㄠ)
①to gather herbs of medicinal value ②to become a hermit

採油(ㄘㄞ ㄧㄡ)
(petroleum) oil extraction; oil recovery

採用(ㄘㄞ ㄩㄥ)
to adopt (a suggestion, new technique, etc.)

【探】 1930
I. ㄊㄢ tann tàn

1. to find; to search; to locate; to prospect; to feel (in a pocket or bag)
2. to watch; to spy; a spy; a detective; to investigate; a secret agent
3. to try; to venture; to tempt
4. to stick out: 行車時不要探身車窗外。Don't stick out of the window while the train is in motion.
5. to explore
6. to visit; to inquire about: 他常常在假日探視朋友。He often visits his relatives and friends on holidays.

探病(ㄊㄢ ㄅㄧㄥ)
to visit the sick

探馬(ㄊㄢ ㄇㄚ)
a mounted scout

探明(ㄊㄢ ㄇㄧㄥ)
to find out by inquiry; to prove

探訪(ㄊㄢ ㄈㄤ)
①to investigate; to make inquiries; to seek out by inquiry or search: 探訪民間傳奇 to seek out the folklore

②to pay a visit to; to visit

探討(ㄊㄢ ㄊㄠ)
to investigate; to study; to explore (possibilities, etc.); to approach (a problem, etc.); to discuss (causes or effects, etc.)

探頭探腦(ㄊㄢ ㄊㄡ ㄊㄢ ㄋㄠ)
to act stealthily

探聽(ㄊㄢ ㄊㄧㄥ)
to investigate secretly; to spy; to pry into; to try to find out: 不要探聽別人的私事。Don't pry into other people's private affairs.

探聽虛實(ㄊㄢ ㄊㄧㄥ ㄒㄩ ㄕ)
to try to find out about an opponent or adversary; to try to ascertain the strength of the enemy

探囊取物(ㄊㄢ ㄋㄤ ㄑㄩ ㄨ)
as easy as taking things out of one's own pocket

探驪得珠(ㄊㄢ ㄌㄧ ㄉㄜ ㄓㄨ)
(said of a writing) to the point; relevant or pertinent

探戈(ㄊㄢ ㄍㄜ)
(dancing) tango

探口氣(ㄊㄢ ㄎㄡ ㄑㄧ)
to sound out another person's views (by making seemingly irrelevant remarks or indirect references)

探勘(ㄊㄢ ㄎㄢ)
to prospect: 在一地區探勘銀鑛 to prospect a region for silver

探鑛(ㄊㄢ ㄎㄨㄤ)
to prospect mineral deposits

探空火箭(ㄊㄢ ㄎㄨㄥ ㄏㄨㄛ ㄐㄧㄢ)
a sounding rocket

探花(ㄊㄢ ㄏㄨㄚ)
(formerly) one who finished third in the imperial examination

探騎(ㄊㄢ ㄐㄧ)
a mounted spy or scout

探究(ㄊㄢ ㄐㄧㄡ)
to investigate; to probe: 科學家探究自然現象。Scientists investigate natural phenomena.

探監(ㄊㄢ ㄐㄧㄢ)
to visit a prisoner

探求(ㄊㄢ ㄑㄧㄡ)
to seek; to search for; to study; to find out; to look

【手部】

into

探親(ㄊㄢ ㄑㄧㄣ)
to visit one's relatives

探取(ㄊㄢ ㄑㄩ)
to draw money in advance

探悉(ㄊㄢ ㄒㄧ)
to learn after investigating, spying, or obtaining information from some (usually indirect) sources: 他從有關當局探悉此事。He learned the matter from the authorities concerned.

探險(ㄊㄢ ㄒㄧㄢˇ)
to undertake an exploratory trip; exploration: 他到北極地區探險。He went to explore the Arctic regions.

探險隊(ㄊㄢ ㄒㄧㄢˇ ㄉㄨㄟˋ)
an expedition team; an exploration party

探險家(ㄊㄢ ㄒㄧㄢˇ ㄐㄧㄚ)
an explorer

探信(ㄊㄢ ㄒㄧㄣˋ)or探詢(ㄊㄢ ㄒㄩㄣˊ)
to make inquiries

探照燈(ㄊㄢ ㄓㄠˋ ㄉㄥ)
a searchlight

探春(ㄊㄢ ㄔㄨㄣ)
a spring outing; an excursion to the countryside in early spring

探視(ㄊㄢ ㄕˋ)
to visit (a patient , etc.); 醫生探視他的病人。A doctor visits his patients.

探身子(ㄊㄢ ㄕㄣ ˙ㄗ)
to bend forward (for a better look)

探子(ㄊㄢ ˙ㄗ)
a scout; a spy; a detective

探測(ㄊㄢ ㄘㄜˋ)
to survey; to sound; to probe: 他們將探測基隆港口的水深。They will sound the entrance to the harbor of Keelung.

探喪(ㄊㄢ ㄙㄤ)
to condole with someone on his bereavement

探索(ㄊㄢ ㄙㄨㄛˇ)
to probe; to search for; to look into; to seek; to find out; to study; to explore: 他喜歡探索宇宙的奧秘。He likes to explore the secrets of the universe.

探案(ㄊㄢ ㄢˋ)
detective stories; adventures of a detective

探幽尋勝(ㄊㄢ ㄧㄡ ㄒㄩㄣˊ ㄕㄥ)
to visit scenic spots: 很多人喜歡在春天探幽尋勝。Many people like to visit scenic spots in spring.

探友(ㄊㄢ ㄧㄡˇ)
to visit friends

探問(ㄊㄢ ㄨㄣˋ)
to inquire about or after

探望(ㄊㄢ ㄨㄤˋ)
①to visit: 他們回國探望親友。They returned to their home country to visit relatives and friends. ②to look about

探原 or 探源(ㄊㄢ ㄩㄢˊ)
to make an exhaustive investigation or study in order to find out the root cause or source of something

【探】 1930
2. ㄊㄢ tan tān
to try; to tempt; to test

探湯(ㄊㄢ ㄊㄤ)
(literally) to test boiling water with one's hand and get scalded——(figuratively) A burnt child dreads the fire.

【控】 1931
ㄎㄨㄥˋ kong kòng
1. to accuse; to charge; to sue: 司機被控超速。The driver is charged with speeding.
2. to control; control: 遙控 remote control
3. to draw (a bow)
4. (now rarely) to throw; to hit

控馬(ㄎㄨㄥˋ ㄇㄚˇ)
to rein in a horse

控告(ㄎㄨㄥˋ ㄍㄠˋ)
to sue somebody in court; to accuse

控弦(ㄎㄨㄥˋ ㄒㄧㄢˊ)
to draw a bow

控制(ㄎㄨㄥˋ ㄓˋ)
to control; control; to dominate: 飛機如失去控制, 必定撞毀。If an airplane is out of control, it will certainly be smashed.

控詞(ㄎㄨㄥˋ ㄘˊ)
a charge; a complaint

控訴(ㄎㄨㄥˋ ㄙㄨˋ)
①to appeal to a higher court ②to accuse before an authority

控訴狀(ㄎㄨㄥˋ ㄙㄨˋ ㄓㄨㄤˋ)
a written appeal

控訴人(ㄎㄨㄥˋ ㄙㄨˋ ㄖㄣˊ)
the appellant

【接】 1932
ㄐㄧㄝ jie jiē
1. to receive; to accept; to take with the hand: 我昨天接到你的來信。I received your letter yesterday.
2. to welcome; to meet: 我會到車站接你。I'll go to the station to meet you.
3. to join; to connect: 起來發問的人一個接著一個。 People got up to ask questions one after another.
4. to graft
5. to come close to; to make contact with
6. to succeed to

接駁(ㄐㄧㄝ ㄅㄛˊ)
to ferry train passengers by bus across a gap between two sections of a railroad

接班(ㄐㄧㄝ ㄅㄢ)
to relieve another in work

接辦(ㄐㄧㄝ ㄅㄢˋ)
to succeed another in managing a task; to carry on the work left unfinished by another

接棒(ㄐㄧㄝ ㄅㄤˋ)
(originally) to receive the stick or pin from the preceding runner in a relay race——(figuratively) to continue the work left unfinished by a leading scholar, thinker, etc.

接不住(ㄐㄧㄝ ㄅㄨˊ ㄓㄨˋ)
cannot catch it—the object being too fast or out of the way, etc.

接不上(ㄐㄧㄝ ㄅㄨˊ ㄕㄤˋ)
①cannot be connected ②disruption in continuity

接片機(ㄐㄧㄝ ㄆㄧㄢˋ ㄐㄧ)
a splicer

接木法(ㄐㄧㄝ ㄇㄨˋ ㄈㄚˇ)
(botany) graft method

接防(ㄐㄧㄝ ㄈㄤˊ)
(said of military troops) to relieve friendly forces from their duties by taking over their assignment

接防部隊(ㄐㄧㄝ ㄈㄤˊ ㄅㄨˋ ㄉㄨㄟˋ)

a relieving unit

接風(ㄐㄧㄝ ㄈㄥ)
a welcome party in honor of a distinguished visitor or someone who returns after a long period of absence from home

接風酒(ㄐㄧㄝ ㄈㄥ ㄐㄧㄡˇ)
a welcome feast 參看「接風」

接待(ㄐㄧㄝ ㄉㄞˋ)
to receive (a guest); reception: 受到親切接待 to be accorded a cordial reception

接待單位(ㄐㄧㄝ ㄉㄞˋ ㄉㄢ ㄨㄟˋ)
a host organization

接待室(ㄐㄧㄝ ㄉㄞˋ ㄕˋ)
a reception room

接待人員(ㄐㄧㄝ ㄉㄞˋ ㄖㄣˊ ㄩㄢˊ)
reception personnel

接待外賓(ㄐㄧㄝ ㄉㄞˋ ㄨㄞˋ ㄅㄧㄣ)
to receive foreign guests

接待員(ㄐㄧㄝ ㄉㄞˋ ㄩㄢˊ)
a receptionist

接到(ㄐㄧㄝ ㄉㄠˋ)
to receive

接地線(ㄐㄧㄝ ㄉㄧˋ ㄒㄧㄢˋ)
(electricity) a ground wire; an earth lead

接頭(ㄐㄧㄝ ㄊㄡˊ)
①to have a firm grasp of the situation so that one can manage a matter by oneself; to know ②to get in touch with; to make contact with (the responsible person) ③a joint

接替(ㄐㄧㄝ ㄊㄧˋ)
to relieve; to succeed (a predecessor); to take over; to substitute for

接通(ㄐㄧㄝ ㄊㄨㄥ)
to put through: 請幫我接通經理。Please put me through to the Manager.

接納(ㄐㄧㄝ ㄋㄚˋ)
to accept (a proposal, advice, etc.)

接力(ㄐㄧㄝ ㄌㄧˋ)
a relay: 八百公尺接力 a 800-meter relay

接力棒(ㄐㄧㄝ ㄌㄧˋ ㄅㄤˋ)
a relay baton

接力賽跑(ㄐㄧㄝ ㄌㄧˋ ㄙㄞˋ ㄆㄠˇ)
a relay race

接連(ㄐㄧㄝ ㄌㄧㄢˊ)
repeatedly; continuously; to

continue; on end; one after another

接連不斷(ㄐㄧㄝ ㄌㄧㄢˊ ㄅㄨˋ ㄉㄨㄢˋ)
continuously; incessantly; in succession

接骨(ㄐㄧㄝ ㄍㄨˇ)
to unite a fractured bone; to set broken bones

接骨眼兒(ㄐㄧㄝ ㄍㄨˇ ㄧㄢˇㄦ)
the critical moment; the right time; an opportune moment 亦作「節骨眼兒」

接過來(ㄐㄧㄝ ㄍㄨㄛˋ ㄌㄞˊ)
to receive; to take over

接管(ㄐㄧㄝ ㄍㄨㄢˇ)
to take over (the management of)

接客(ㄐㄧㄝ ㄎㄜˋ)
①(said of a hotel, etc.) to receive lodgers or guests ②(said of prostitutes) to receive patrons in boudoirs

接合(ㄐㄧㄝ ㄏㄜˊ)
to connect; to assemble

接合面(ㄐㄧㄝ ㄏㄜˊ ㄇㄧㄢˋ)
(mineralogy) a composition face or plane

接濟(ㄐㄧㄝ ㄐㄧˋ)
to give financial or material assistance to

接駕(ㄐㄧㄝ ㄐㄧㄚˋ)
(originally) to welcome or receive the king; (figuratively) to welcome or receive someone

接界(ㄐㄧㄝ ㄐㄧㄝˋ)or接境(ㄐㄧㄝ ㄐㄧㄥˋ)
to border on; to share a common border; adjacent

接交(ㄐㄧㄝ ㄐㄧㄠ)
to make friends with

接角(ㄐㄧㄝ ㄐㄧㄠˇ)
an adjacent angle

接見(ㄐㄧㄝ ㄐㄧㄢˋ)
to grant an audience to; to receive (a visitor, etc.): 總統每年都要接見許多外賓。The President has to receive many foreign guests every year.

接近(ㄐㄧㄝ ㄐㄧㄣˋ)
to draw near; to come close; to approach; near to; approaching: 我們的科技正接近國際水平。Our technology is approaching the international level.

接頸交臂(ㄐㄧㄝ ㄐㄧㄥˇ ㄐㄧㄠ ㄅㄧˋ)
to neck; to be very intimate with; to make love with

接球(ㄐㄧㄝ ㄑㄧㄡˊ)
to catch the ball; to return a served ball

接戲(ㄐㄧㄝ ㄒㄧˋ)
(said of an actor or actress) to sign a contract for a role in a new movie

接洽(ㄐㄧㄝ ㄒㄧㄚˋ)
to contact, discuss or negotiate; to take up a matter with; to arrange (business, etc.) with; to consult with: 我將同有關部門接洽。I will take up the matter with the department concerned.

接線(ㄐㄧㄝ ㄒㄧㄢˋ)
①to connect (telephone) lines; to make a telephone connection ②to wire

接線生(ㄐㄧㄝ ㄒㄧㄢˋ ㄕㄥ)
a switchboard operator

接續(ㄐㄧㄝ ㄒㄩˋ)
continuously; to continue; to connect

接續香烟(ㄐㄧㄝ ㄒㄩˋ ㄒㄧㄤ ㄧㄢ)
to continue the family line

接續詞(ㄐㄧㄝ ㄒㄩˋ ㄘˊ)
a conjunction 亦作「連接詞」

接枝(ㄐㄧㄝ ㄓ)
(botany) to graft; a graft

接著(ㄐㄧㄝ ·ㄓㄜ)
①then; shortly afterwards; thereupon: 春天先來, 接著就是夏天。First comes spring, then summer. ②to follow; to add: 你先走, 我接著就來。You go first and I'll follow. ③to catch: 給你一個梨, 接著！Here's a pear for you. Catch!

接戰(ㄐㄧㄝ ㄓㄢˋ)
to meet in battle

接住(ㄐㄧㄝ ㄓㄨˋ)
to catch (a flying object): 你能接住他的球嗎？Can you catch his ball?

接篆(ㄐㄧㄝ ㄓㄨㄢˋ)or接印(ㄐㄧㄝ ㄧㄣˋ)
to take over the seal of office—to take over a public post

接踵(ㄐㄧㄝ ㄓㄨㄥˇ)
one on the heels of another—to come in close succes-

〔手部〕

〔手部〕

sion

接踵而至 (ㄐㄧㄝ ㄓㄨㄥˇ ㄦˊ ㄓˋ)
to come in quick succession; to follow at the heels of

接觸 (ㄐㄧㄝ ㄔㄨˋ)
①(said of nations) to wage war against each other ②to make contact with; to come in contact with; contact: 促進兩國文化的接觸 to promote cultural contacts between two countries

接觸不良 (ㄐㄧㄝ ㄔㄨˋ ㄅㄨˋ ㄌㄧㄤˊ)
loose or poor contact

接觸劑 (ㄐㄧㄝ ㄔㄨˋ ㄐㄧˋ)
a catalyst

接充 (ㄐㄧㄝ ㄔㄨㄥ)
to replace (someone)

接拿 (ㄐㄧㄝ ㄋㄚˊ)
to take over an office or official duties: 新校長昨天接事。 The new chancellor took over yesterday.

接煞 (ㄐㄧㄝ ㄕㄚ)
(folklore) to receive the soul of the deceased within 10 to 18 days after his death

接收 (ㄐㄧㄝ ㄕㄡ)
to take over; to receive

接收天線 (ㄐㄧㄝ ㄕㄡ ㄊㄧㄢ ㄒㄧㄢˋ)
a receiving antenna

接收儀式 (ㄐㄧㄝ ㄕㄡ ㄧˊ ㄕˋ)
a takeover ceremony

接手 (ㄐㄧㄝ ㄕㄡˇ)
①to carry on the task of the predecessor: 他將接手他父親的事業。He will carry on his father's business. ②assistants or aides

接受 (ㄐㄧㄝ ㄕㄡˋ)
to accept (an invitation, an assignment, etc.); to take: 你最好接受我的意見。 You had better take my advice.

接受教訓 (ㄐㄧㄝ ㄕㄡˋ ㄐㄧㄠˋ ㄒㄩㄣˋ)
to learn a lesson

接上帶下 (ㄐㄧㄝ ㄕㄤˋ ㄉㄞˋ ㄒㄧㄚˋ)
to link what precedes with what follows

接生 (ㄐㄧㄝ ㄕㄥ)
to assist in childbirth; to practice midwifery

接生婆 (ㄐㄧㄝ ㄕㄥ ㄆㄛˊ)
a midwife 亦作「助產士」

接任 (ㄐㄧㄝ ㄖㄣˋ)
to take over an office; to succeed: 他的職務已由他人接

任。 His job has been taken over by another.

接壤 (ㄐㄧㄝ ㄖㄤˇ)
adjoining boundary; adjacency; adjacent to; contiguous to

接壤地區 (ㄐㄧㄝ ㄖㄤˇ ㄉㄧˋ ㄑㄩ)
contiguous areas

接財神 (ㄐㄧㄝ ㄘㄞˊ ㄕㄣˊ)
to welcome back the "God of Wealth" (a Chinese custom during the Lunar New Year)

接送 (ㄐㄧㄝ ㄙㄨㄥˋ)
①to receive and send off (guests or visitors) ②transportation to and from a certain place

接二連三 (ㄐㄧㄝ ㄦˋ ㄌㄧㄢˊ ㄙㄢ)
one after another; continuously; repeatedly: 他們接二連三地跑來. They came running one after another.

接引 (ㄐㄧㄝ ㄧㄣˇ)
to guide; to receive

接應 (ㄐㄧㄝ ㄧㄥˋ)
to stand ready for assistance; to come to somebody's aid; to coordinate with; to supply: 誰來接應我? Who will come to my aid?

接物待人 (ㄐㄧㄝ ㄨˋ ㄉㄞˋ ㄖㄣˊ)
to attend a matter and to receive a person

接尾詞 (ㄐㄧㄝ ㄨㄟˇ ㄘˊ) or 接尾語
(ㄐㄧㄝ ㄨㄟˇ ㄩˇ)
a suffix

接吻 (ㄐㄧㄝ ㄨㄣˇ)
to kiss; a kiss

接吻魚 (ㄐㄧㄝ ㄨㄣˇ ㄩˊ)
kissing gourami

【推】 1933 ㄊㄨㄟ tuei tuī

1. to push; to shove: 他把門推開。He pushed the door open.
2. to look into; to find out; to ponder; to infer; to deduce
3. to shirk; to shift (responsibility, etc.); to refuse: 別想把責任推給我。Don't try to shift the responsibility onto me.
4. to elect; to recommend; to praise; to esteem: 我們推他擔任主席。We elect him as chairman.
5. to move along; to change in succession (as seasons)
6. to extend; to enlarge

推波助瀾 (ㄊㄨㄟ ㄅㄛ ㄓㄨˋ ㄌㄢˊ)
to add fuel to the fire; to egg on; to instigate; to incite

推背圖 (ㄊㄨㄟ ㄅㄟˋ ㄊㄨˊ)
a book of prophecy, allegedly written by Li Chun-feng (李淳風) and Yüan Tien-kang (袁天綱) of the Tang Dynasty

推鉋 (ㄊㄨㄟ ㄅㄠˋ)
a plane (for leveling wood)

推本溯源 (ㄊㄨㄟ ㄅㄣˇ ㄙㄨˋ ㄩㄢˊ)
to go into the source of a matter; to trace the origins

推病 (ㄊㄨㄟ ㄅㄧㄥˋ)
to feign sickness; to excuse oneself on the pretext of illness: 他推病不上學。He feigned that he was sick and did not go to school.

推不開 (ㄊㄨㄟ ㄅㄨˋ ㄎㄞ)
unable to push away; unable to get out of (an involvement, etc.); unable to shirk (responsibility, etc.)

推不出 (ㄊㄨㄟ ㄅㄨˋ ㄔㄨ)
①unable to decline ②unable to push out

推牌九 (ㄊㄨㄟ ㄆㄞˊ ㄐㄧㄡˇ)
to play a gambling game of pai chiu (a kind of domino)

推派代表 (ㄊㄨㄟ ㄆㄞˋ ㄉㄞˋ ㄅㄧㄠˇ)
to elect representatives (to present a petition, to a negotiation, etc.)

推磨 (ㄊㄨㄟ ㄇㄛˋ)
to turn a mill manually

推翻 (ㄊㄨㄟ ㄈㄢ)
①to overthrow (a government, etc.); to topple ②to stultify (a theory, principle, etc.); to repudiate (an agreement); to cancel: 他們推翻原定計畫。They cancel their original plan.

推戴 (ㄊㄨㄟ ㄉㄞˋ)
to support (a leader, etc.)

推倒 (ㄊㄨㄟ ㄉㄠˇ)
①to overturn; to topple ②to shove: 他把她推倒在地。He shoved her to the ground.

推擋 (ㄊㄨㄟ ㄉㄤˇ)
(table tennis) half volley

推宕 (ㄊㄨㄟ ㄉㄤˋ) or 推延 (ㄊㄨㄟ ㄧㄢˊ)
to delay; to procrastinate

推定 (ㄊㄨㄟ ㄉㄧㄥˋ)
to infer; to deduce

推度(ㄊㄨㄟ ㄉㄨㄛˋ)
to infer; to conclude; to speculate

推斷(ㄊㄨㄟ ㄉㄨㄢˋ)
to infer; to predict by means of inference; inference

推動(ㄊㄨㄟ ㄉㄨㄥˋ)
to push (a sales project, etc.); to lend impetus to (a movement, etc.); to propel; to expedite

推頭(ㄊㄨㄟ ㄊㄡˊ)
to cut hair with clippers

推土機(ㄊㄨㄟ ㄊㄨˇ ㄐㄧ)
a bulldozer

推託(ㄊㄨㄟ ㄊㄨㄛ)
to make excuses; to shirk; to plead: 推託責任 to evade or shift responsibility

推拏 or 推拿(ㄊㄨㄟ ㄋㄚˊ)
①to massage ②to fix a dislocated bone by massage

推來推去(ㄊㄨㄟ ㄌㄞˊ ㄊㄨㄟ ㄑㄩˋ)
①to pass the buck ②to refuse to accept a present, assignment, etc.) by pushing it back and forth

推類(ㄊㄨㄟ ㄌㄟˋ)
to reason by analogy

推理(ㄊㄨㄟ ㄌㄧˇ)
to reason (out); reasoning; to infer

推理小說(ㄊㄨㄟ ㄌㄧˇ ㄒㄧㄠˇ ㄕㄨㄛ)
detective stories

推論(ㄊㄨㄟ ㄌㄨㄣˋ)
①inference; to infer. 人類曾用各種方法作觀察及推論 Men have observed and inferred in all sorts of ways. ② (mathematics) corollary

推聾裝啞(ㄊㄨㄟ ㄌㄨㄥˊ ㄓㄨㄤ ㄧˇ)
to pretend to be deaf and mute—to avoid getting involved in something by pretending ignorance

推乾淨兒(ㄊㄨㄟ ㄍㄢ ㄐㄧㄥˋㄦ)
to shirk all one's responsibilities; to pass the buck

推薦(ㄊㄨㄟ ㄐㄧㄢ)
①to recommend (men of abilities) ②to help people achieve something

推故(ㄊㄨㄟ ㄍㄨˋ)
to make excuses: 他推故不來. He excused himself from coming.

推廣(ㄊㄨㄟ ㄍㄨㄤˇ)
to propagate; to extend; to popularize; to spread: 推廣國語 to popularize Mandarin

推廣教育(ㄊㄨㄟ ㄍㄨㄤˇ ㄐㄧㄠˋ ㄩˋ)
extension education

推開(ㄊㄨㄟ ㄎㄞ)
①to push away ②to get away from (social activities, etc.)

推己及人(ㄊㄨㄟ ㄐㄧˇ ㄐㄧˊ ㄖㄣˊ)
to put oneself in another's position; to be considerate

推究(ㄊㄨㄟ ㄐㄧㄡˋ)
to study; to reason out; to investigate

推薦(ㄊㄨㄟ ㄐㄧㄢ)
to recommend (somebody for a job, etc.): 他們推薦我擔任這項工作. They recommended me for the job.

推薦書(ㄊㄨㄟ ㄐㄧㄢ ㄕㄨ)or 推薦信(ㄊㄨㄟ ㄐㄧㄢ ㄒㄧㄣˋ)
a letter of recommendation: 請寫給我一封推薦信. Please write me a recommendation.

推襟送抱(ㄊㄨㄟ ㄐㄧㄣ ㄙㄨㄥˋ ㄅㄠˋ)
to be sincere in dealing with others

推進(ㄊㄨㄟ ㄐㄧㄣˋ)
to push forward; to move ahead; to advance

推進機(ㄊㄨㄟ ㄐㄧㄣˋ ㄐㄧ)or 推進器(ㄊㄨㄟ ㄐㄧㄣˋ ㄑㄧˋ)
the propeller (of a ship, plane, etc.)

推獎(ㄊㄨㄟ ㄐㄧㄤˇ)
to praise

推舉(ㄊㄨㄟ ㄐㄩˇ)
①to elect (to an office, etc.); to recommend for a post ②(weightlifting) to press

推敲(ㄊㄨㄟ ㄑㄧㄠ)
①to weigh or consider words in writing ②to investigate or examine carefully

推敲詞句(ㄊㄨㄟ ㄑㄧㄠ ㄘˊ ㄐㄩˋ)
to weigh one's words

推求(ㄊㄨㄟ ㄑㄧㄡˊ)
to ascertain; to analyze and study (for a solution, answer, etc.)

推遷(ㄊㄨㄟ ㄑㄧㄢ)
to make excuses and delay; to procrastinate

推鉛球(ㄊㄨㄟ ㄑㄧㄢ ㄑㄧㄡˊ)
(track and field) ①shot put ②to throw or put the shot

推卻(ㄊㄨㄟ ㄑㄩㄝˋ)
to decline (an invitation, offer, etc.): 我推卻他的聚餐邀約. I declined his invitation to dinner.

推卸(ㄊㄨㄟ ㄒㄧㄝˋ)
to be irresponsible; to shirk (responsibility): 他因爲推卸工作而失去職業. He lost his job because he shirked his work.

推卸責任(ㄊㄨㄟ ㄒㄧㄝˋ ㄗㄜˊ ㄖㄣˋ)
to shirk one's responsibility

推銷(ㄊㄨㄟ ㄒㄧㄠ)
to promote sales; to sell

推銷員(ㄊㄨㄟ ㄒㄧㄠ ㄩㄢˊ)
a salesman or saleswoman

推心置腹(ㄊㄨㄟ ㄒㄧㄣ ㄓˋ ㄈㄨˋ)
to treat others with the utmost sincerity; to put every trust in

推想(ㄊㄨㄟ ㄒㄧㄤˇ)
to infer; to deduce

推行(ㄊㄨㄟ ㄒㄧㄥˊ)
to promote (a cause, movement, etc.); to implement (a policy)

推許(ㄊㄨㄟ ㄒㄩˇ)
to praise; to approve (a performance): 教練對球隊的良好表現備加推許. The coach praised the team for its fine playing.

推選(ㄊㄨㄟ ㄒㄩㄢˇ)
to elect

推重(ㄊㄨㄟ ㄓㄨㄥˋ)
to hold in high esteem; to admire; admiration: 他是大家所推重的人. He is the admiration of everyone.

推陳出新(ㄊㄨㄟ ㄔㄣˊ ㄔㄨ ㄒㄧㄣ)
to find new ways of doing things from old theories; to find something new in what is old

推誠(ㄊㄨㄟ ㄔㄥˊ)
to place confidence in; to act in sincerity

推誠相見(ㄊㄨㄟ ㄔㄥˊ ㄒㄧㄤ ㄐㄧㄢˋ)
to deal with or treat somebody with sincerity

推出(ㄊㄨㄟ ㄔㄨ)
①to push out ②to present (a picture, a show, etc.)

推崇(ㄊㄨㄟ ㄔㄨㄥˊ)

〔手部〕

〔手部〕

to hold in high esteem; to respect; to praise highly: 他們對這位科學家推崇備至。They have the greatest esteem for the scientist.

推食解衣 (ㄊㄨㄟ ㄕ ㄐㄧㄝˇ ㄧ)
to do anything one possibly can to help (as a friend in need)

推事 (ㄊㄨㄟ ㄕˋ)
(court) a judge

推讓 (ㄊㄨㄟ ㄖㄤˋ)
to yield to someone as a token of deference to the other party; to decline (a position, favor, etc. out of modesty)

推讓之風 (ㄊㄨㄟ ㄖㄤˋ ㄓ ㄈㄥ)
the practice of yielding or showing deference

推子 (ㄊㄨㄟ˙ ㄗ)
a hair clipper

推燥居溼 (ㄊㄨㄟ ㄗㄠˋ ㄐㄩ ㄕ)
to give the best to the young

推尊 (ㄊㄨㄟ ㄗㄨㄣ)
to admire and respect

推辭 (ㄊㄨㄟ ㄘˊ)
to decline (an offer, invitation, etc.); to reject

推測 (ㄊㄨㄟ ㄘㄜˋ)
①to infer; to deduce; to predict; to conjecture: 我推測他會贏。I predict that he will win. ②to conjecture: 謠言引起很多推測。The rumor raised much conjecture.

推三阻四 (ㄊㄨㄟ ㄙㄢ ㄗㄨˇ ㄙˋ)
to make numerous excuses; to decline with all sorts of excuses

推算 (ㄊㄨㄟ ㄙㄨㄢˋ)
to calculate; calculation; to reckon

推恩 (ㄊㄨㄟ ㄣ)
to extend benevolence to others (especially said of a ruler)

推移 (ㄊㄨㄟ ㄧˊ)
①changes; vicissitudes ②to follow others ③ to transpose

推壓 (ㄊㄨㄟ ㄧㄚ)
(said of bureaucrats in handling official business) to delay and procrastinate

推延 (ㄊㄨㄟ ㄧㄢˊ)
to delay; to procrastinate; to

---

put off

推諉 (ㄊㄨㄟ ㄨㄟˇ)
to shirk (responsibility, etc.); to make excuses: 他們都有推諉之詞。They all had excuses to offer.

推輓 or 推挽 (ㄊㄨㄟ ㄨㄢˇ)
①(literally) to push and pull—to recommend a young man for a job ②(electricity) push-pull

推問 (ㄊㄨㄟ ㄨㄣˋ)
to examine and investigate; to interrogate (in court)

推原 (ㄊㄨㄟ ㄩㄢˊ)
to trace the cause (of an incident, etc.)

【措】 1934
ㄘㄨㄛˋ tsuoh cuò
1. to place
2. to collect; to arrange; to manage; to handle
3. to abandon; to renounce
4. to make preparation for an undertaking; to make plans

措大 (ㄘㄨㄛˋ ㄉㄚˋ)
①a scholar; a pedant ② a penniless fellow 亦作「窮措大」

措置 (ㄘㄨㄛˋ ㄓˋ)
to execute; to arrange; to manage

措置失當 (ㄘㄨㄛˋ ㄓˋ ㄕ ㄉㄤˋ)
to mismanage; mismanagement

措施 (ㄘㄨㄛˋ ㄕ)
a (political, financial, etc.) measure; a step

措手不及 (ㄘㄨㄛˋ ㄕㄡˇ ㄅㄨˋ ㄐㄧˊ)
to be caught unawares or unprepared; to be taken by surprise: 我們打他個措手不及。Let's make a surprise attack on them.

措辭 (ㄘㄨㄛˋ ㄘˊ)
wording (of a letter, diplomatic note, etc.); diction

措意 (ㄘㄨㄛˋ ㄧˋ)
to pay attention to; to mind

【掩】 1935
ㄧㄢˇ yean yǎn
1. to cover; to hide; to conceal; to cover up: 他敏於掩飾他的無知。He was clever at covering up his ignorance.
2. to shut; to close: 別關門，讓它半掩著。Don't close the door, let it half shut.
3. to mount a surprise attack;

---

to take or catch by surprise

掩鼻而過 (ㄧㄢˇ ㄅㄧˇ ㄦˊ ㄍㄨㄛˋ)
to cover the nose and hurry away (from a stench)

掩蔽 (ㄧㄢˇ ㄅㄧˋ)
to cover; to conceal; to take cover; to shelter; cover: 黑夜掩蔽了他的惡行。The night covered his evil deed.

掩不住 (ㄧㄢˇ ㄅㄨˋ ㄓㄨˋ)
unable to cover or hide; can not shut out

掩埋 (ㄧㄢˇ ㄇㄞˊ)
to bury: 海盜將財寶掩埋在土裡。Pirates buried treasure in the ground.

掩門 (ㄧㄢˇ ㄇㄣˊ)
to close the door; to shut the door

掩面而泣 (ㄧㄢˇ ㄇㄧㄢˋ ㄦˊ ㄑㄧˋ)
to cover one's face and weep

掩目捕雀 (ㄧㄢˇ ㄇㄨˋ ㄅㄨˇ ㄑㄩㄝˋ)
(literally) to cover the eyes and try to catch the bird—to fool oneself; self-deception

掩體 (ㄧㄢˇ ㄊㄧˇ)
a rampart or emplacement (for a crew-served weapon); a bunker

掩蓋 (ㄧㄢˇ ㄍㄞˋ)
to cover up; to conceal: 他企圖掩蓋事實。He tried to cover up (or conceal) the facts.

掩口 (ㄧㄢˇ ㄎㄡˇ)
to cover one's mouth with one's hand

掩口而笑 (ㄧㄢˇ ㄎㄡˇ ㄦˊ ㄒㄧㄠˋ)
to laugh in secret; to hide one's smile

掩護 (ㄧㄢˇ ㄏㄨˋ)
①to cover (friendly troops on a special assignment) ②camouflage; to camouflage

掩襟 (ㄧㄢˇ ㄐㄧㄣ)
to throw on a garment without buttoning up

掩卷 (ㄧㄢˇ ㄐㄩㄢˇ)
to close books; to stop reading: 掩卷而睡 to close the book and fall asleep

掩旗息鼓 (ㄧㄢˇ ㄑㄧˊ ㄒㄧˊ ㄍㄨˇ)
to stop clamoring; to stay quiet; to keep silent 亦作「偃旗息鼓」

掩泣 (ㄧㄢˇ ㄑㄧˋ)
to cover one's face and

weep; to weep silently

掩襲(ㄧㄢ ㄒㄧˊ)
to mount a surprise attack

掩飾(ㄧㄢ ㄕˋ)
to cover; to conceal; to paper over; to gloss over: 不要試圖掩飾你的錯誤。Don't try to gloss over your mistakes.

掩殺(ㄧㄢ ㄕㄚ)
to attack by surprise

掩上(ㄧㄢ˙ㄕㄤˋ)
to shut (the door, window, etc.)

掩人耳目(ㄧㄢ ㄖㄣˊ ㄦˇ ㄇㄨˋ)
to deceive others; to hood-wink people

掩藏(ㄧㄢ ㄘㄤˊ)
to hide; to conceal

掩耳不聞(ㄧㄢ ㄦˇ ㄅㄨˋ ㄨㄣˊ)
to turn a deaf ear: 他對我的一切解釋掩耳不聞。He was deaf to all my excuses.

掩耳盜鈴(ㄧㄢ ㄦˇ ㄉㄠˋ ㄌㄧㄥˊ)
(literally) to cover one's ears when he steals a bell—to deceive oneself

掩映(ㄧㄢ ㄧㄥˋ)
① the mingling, or contrast, of light and shadow (usually said of enchanting scenery) ② to set off (one another): 紅瓦綠竹相掩映。The red tiles and green bamboos set each other off.

【掮】 1936
ㄑㄧㄢˊ chyan qián
to bear a load on the shoulder

掮客(ㄑㄧㄢˊ ㄎㄜˋ)
a broker: 他是個政治掮客。He is a political broker.

【掬】 1937
ㄐㄩˊ jyu jú
1. to hold in both hands
2. (classifier) a double handful of

掬水(ㄐㄩˊ ㄕㄨㄟˇ)
to scoop up water with the hands

【捶】 1938
ㄔㄨㄟˊ chwei chuí
1. to beat; to thrash; to pound
2. a stick for beating: 鼓捶 a drumstick

捶平(ㄔㄨㄟˊ ㄆㄧㄥˊ)
to flatten by pounding

捶扑(ㄔㄨㄟˊ ㄆㄨˋ)
to beat up a criminal

捶打(ㄔㄨㄟˊ ㄉㄚˇ)
to beat; to thump: 他捶打桌子。He thumped the table.

捶鍊(ㄔㄨㄟˊ ㄌㄧㄢˋ)
to submit to strict discipli-nary training

捶鼓(ㄔㄨㄟˊ ㄍㄨˇ)
to beat a drum 亦作「搥鼓」

捶胸頓足(ㄔㄨㄟˊ ㄒㄩㄥ ㄉㄨㄣˋ ㄗㄨˊ)
to beat one's breast and stamp one's feet—in deep grief

捶楚(ㄔㄨㄟˊ ㄔㄨˇ)
(an ancient form of punish-ment) flogging

【掫】 1939
ㄗㄡ tzou zōu
to be on the night watch

【掌】 1940
ㄓㄤˇ jaang zhǎng
1. the palm of the hand; the sole of the foot; paws of an animal
2. to slap with one's hand; to smack
3. to have charge of; to super-vise; to control
4. to stand; to bear
5. a Chinese family name

掌兵權(ㄓㄤˇ ㄅㄧㄥ ㄑㄩㄢˊ)
to wield military power; to command the armed forces

掌燈(ㄓㄤˇ ㄉㄥ)
to light the lantern or lamp (at nightfall)

掌舵(ㄓㄤˇ ㄉㄨㄛˋ)
① to steer a ship; the steers-man; the helmsman ② the man in charge

掌理(ㄓㄤˇ ㄌㄧˇ)
to supervise, manage or take charge of: 他掌理一家大百貨公司的業務。He manages the business of a large department store.

掌骨(ㄓㄤˇ ㄍㄨˇ)
the metacarpal bones

掌故(ㄓㄤˇ ㄍㄨˋ)
① historical anecdotes or records; national legends ② national institutions

掌櫃(ㄓㄤˇ ㄍㄨㄟˋ)
a shopkeeper

掌櫃的(ㄓㄤˇ ㄍㄨㄟˋ˙ㄉㄜ)
① a manager; a shopkeeper; a superintendent ② a refer-ence to one's husband ③ a

respectful term of address

掌管(ㄓㄤˇ ㄍㄨㄢˇ)
to take charge of; to super-vise; to manage: 他掌管這裏的一切。He takes care of everything here.

掌頰(ㄓㄤˇ ㄐㄧˊ)
to slap someone's face

掌權(ㄓㄤˇ ㄑㄩㄢˊ)
to be in power or authority

掌心(ㄓㄤˇ ㄒㄧㄣ)
the center of the palm

掌政(ㄓㄤˇ ㄓㄥˋ)
to head a government

掌狀脈(ㄓㄤˇ ㄓㄨㄤˋ ㄇㄞˋ)
palmate veins

掌中戲(ㄓㄤˇ ㄓㄨㄥ ㄒㄧˋ)
a kind of puppet show in Taiwan

掌上明珠(ㄓㄤˇ ㄕㄤˋ ㄇㄧㄥˊ ㄓㄨ)or掌珠(ㄓㄤˇ ㄓㄨ)
a beloved daughter; the apple of one's eye

掌聲(ㄓㄤˇ ㄕㄥ)
clapping; applause: 他博得熱烈的掌聲。He received warm applause.

掌聲如雷(ㄓㄤˇ ㄕㄥ ㄖㄨˊ ㄌㄟˊ)
thunderous applause

掌印(ㄓㄤˇ ㄧㄣˋ)
to have charge of the offi-cial seal—the man in charge

掌握(ㄓㄤˇ ㄨㄛˋ)
① in one's grasp; within one's power; at the mercy of: 他們正在我們的掌握中。They are at our mercy now. ② to con-trol; to take into one's own hands ③ to master; to have a good command of: 掌握現代科學知識 to master modern scientific knowledge

掌紋(ㄓㄤˇ ㄨㄣˊ)
hand lines (in palmistry)

【掣】 1941
ㄔㄜˋ cheh chè
1. to pull; to drag; to draw
2. to hinder
3. to snatch away

掣電(ㄔㄜˋ ㄉㄧㄢˋ)
in the twinkle of an eye; as fast as lightning

掣後腿(ㄔㄜˋ ㄏㄡˋ ㄊㄨㄟˇ)
(literally) to pull the leg from behind—to hinder

掣肘(ㄔㄜˋ ㄓㄡˇ)
to impede another from

doing work; a handicap

掣收據(彳さ ㄕㄡ ㄐㄩ)
to make or take a receipt

掣曳(彳さ 一ˋ)
to pull

手
部

【掰】 1942
ㄅㄞ bāi
to pull apart with hands

掰開(ㄅㄞ ㄎㄞ)
to pull apart with hands

掰交情(ㄅㄞ ㄐ一ㄠ ㄑ一ㄥ)
to break friendship; to sever relations

【掔】 1943
(牽) ㄑ一ㄢ chian qiān
1. thick; firm; substantial
2. to drag along; to pull
3. to lead

九畫

【揀】 1944
ㄐ一ㄢ jean jiǎn
1. to select; to choose; to pick: 謹慎揀擇你的朋友。Choose your friends carefully.
2. to pick up (something another has left behind, etc.)

揀別(ㄐ一ㄢ ㄅ一ㄝ)
to distinguish; to tell one thing from another: 揀別是非 to distinguish between right and wrong

揀破爛的(ㄐ一ㄢ ㄆㄛˋ ㄌㄢˋ ㄉ˙)
a ragpicker; a ragman

揀佛燒香(ㄐ一ㄢ ㄈㄛˊ ㄕㄠ ㄒ一ㄤ)
(literally) to offer incense to the right deity—to curry favor with the right person

揀肥挑瘦(ㄐ一ㄢ ㄈㄟˊ ㄊ一ㄠ ㄕㄡ)
to be very particular or choosy

揀到便宜(ㄐ一ㄢ ㄉㄠˋ ㄆ一ㄢˊ 一)
to get the better (of a bargain, etc.)

揀選(ㄐ一ㄢ ㄒㄩㄢˇ)
to choose; to select; to pick

揀柴(ㄐ一ㄢ ㄔㄞˊ)
to gather firewood

揀擇(ㄐ一ㄢ ㄗㄜˊ)
to select; to choose

【揄】 1945
ㄩ yu yú
1. to draw out; to scoop out (grain from a mortar)
2. to praise; to show the merits of
3. to hang

揄袂(ㄩ ㄇㄟˋ)
to walk with hands swinging in one's sleeves

揄揚(ㄩ 一ㄤˊ)
to praise; to recommend: 揄揚友人 to recommend one's friend

【揆】 1946
ㄎㄨㄟˊ kwei kuí
1. to survey and weigh; to consider; to investigate; to estimate
2. a premier; a prime minister
3. important affairs; events
4. principles; reasons

揆度(ㄎㄨㄟˊ ㄉㄨㄛˋ)
to investigate and consider; to observe and estimate

揆情度理(ㄎㄨㄟˊ ㄑ一ㄥˊ ㄉㄨㄛˋ ㄌ一ˇ)
measured or weighed by reason and common practice

揆席(ㄎㄨㄟˊ ㄒ一ˊ)
a prime minister or premier

揆測(ㄎㄨㄟˊ ㄘㄜˋ)
to calculate or guess; to estimate

【掾】 1947
ㄩㄢˋ yuann yuàn
a general term referring to public officials in ancient China

掾史(ㄩㄢˋ ㄕˇ)
secretaries in ancient Chinese public offices

掾屬(ㄩㄢˋ ㄕㄨˇ)
aides and subordinates of an official

掾佐(ㄩㄢˋ ㄗㄨㄛˇ)
assistants or subordinates of an official

【揉】 1948
ㄖㄡˊ rou róu
1. to rub; to knead: 她用雙手揉眼睛。She rubbed her eyes with her hands.
2. to crumple by hand: 他把信揉成一團。He crumpled up the letter into a ball.
3. to massage
4. to subdue; to make smooth or peaceful
5. mixed-up; confused

揉輪(ㄖㄡˊ ㄌㄨㄣˊ)
to bend trees to make wheels

揉合(ㄖㄡˊ ㄏㄜˊ)
to combine; to blend; to merge; to incorporate: 他的

論文揉合了理論與實際。His thesis combines theory with practice.

揉雜(ㄖㄡˊ ㄗㄚˊ)
mixed-up

揉搓(ㄖㄡˊ ㄘㄨㄛ)
① to rub; to massage ② to tease or play jokes on

揉碎(ㄖㄡˊ ㄙㄨㄟˋ)
to crumble to pieces: 小女孩將麵包揉碎。The little girl crumbled her bread.

揉眼睛(ㄖㄡˊ 一ㄢˇ ㄐ一ㄥ)
to rub eyes

【描】 1949
ㄇ一ㄠˊ miau miáo
1. to trace; to draw; to sketch; to retouch: 這張照片應予修描。The photograph should be retouched.
2. to describe; to depict

描摹(ㄇ一ㄠˊ ㄇㄛˊ)
to imitate (an old painting, etc.); to copy

描摹盡致(ㄇ一ㄠˊ ㄇㄛˊ ㄐ一ㄣˋ ㄓˋ)
to imitate or describe (a person's manner, etc.) to the very last detail

描圖(ㄇ一ㄠˊ ㄊㄨˊ)
tracing

描花(ㄇ一ㄠˊ ㄏㄨㄚ)
to make a flower design

描畫(ㄇ一ㄠˊ ㄏㄨㄚˋ)
to draw; to paint; to depict; to describe: 此景之美非筆墨所能描畫。Words can't describe the beauty of the scene.

描繪(ㄇ一ㄠˊ ㄏㄨㄟˋ)
to paint; to sketch; to depict; to describe

描紅(ㄇ一ㄠˊ ㄏㄨㄥˊ)
(said of children) to learn to write by tracing in black ink over the characters printed in red

描金(ㄇ一ㄠˊ ㄐ一ㄣ)
to paint in gold (usually on lacquerware, etc.); to gild

描寫(ㄇ一ㄠˊ ㄒ一ㄝˇ)
to describe; to depict; to portray; description

描出(ㄇ一ㄠˊ ㄔㄨ)
to portray; to depict vividly

描述(ㄇ一ㄠˊ ㄕㄨˋ)
to describe

描字(ㄇ一ㄠˊ ㄗˋ)
to trace writing; to paint

characters

【揍】 1950 　ㄗㄡ tzow zòu
1. to beat; to slug (somebody); to hit hard: 揍他一頓。Beat him up.
2. to break (a glass, etc.); to smash

揍人 (ㄗㄡ ㄖㄣˊ)
to slug a person

揍一頓 (ㄗㄡ ㄧ ㄉㄨㄣˋ)
to give a sound beating; to beat

【提】 1951 　1、ㄊㄧˊ tyi tí
1. to lift by hand; to pull up; to raise; to arouse; to carry: 他手裏提着個皮包。He carried a satchel in his hand.
2. to cause to rise or happen
3. to mention; to bring forward; to suggest; to propose (a motion, etc.): 我提議早些動身。I propose to start early.
4. to obtain; to make delivery; to draw out
5. to manage; to control
6. a rising stroke (in Chinese calligraphy)
7. a Chinese family name

提拔 (ㄊㄧˊ ㄅㄚˊ)
to promote (a person); to elevate; to give (somebody) a pull; 提拔英才 to elevate a talent

提包 (ㄊㄧˊ ㄅㄠ)
a handbag; a bag; a valise

提筆 (ㄊㄧˊ ㄅㄧˇ)
to lift one's pen—to write

提不起來 (ㄊㄧˊ ㄅㄨˋ ㄑㄧˇ ㄌㄞˊ)
①unable to lift ②to have sunk too deep for rescue (said of a dissipated person)

提不起精神 (ㄊㄧˊ ㄅㄨˋ ㄑㄧˇ ㄐㄧㄥ ㄕㄣˊ)
unable to pull oneself together (for a task ahead, etc.); to feel tired and spiritless

提票 (ㄊㄧˊ ㄆㄧㄠˋ)
a summons which orders a person to appear in court

提名 (ㄊㄧˊ ㄇㄧㄥˊ)
to nominate; nomination: 他被提名為候選人。He was nominated for election.

提防 (ㄊㄧˊ ㄈㄤˊ)
to be cautious or watchful;

to be on the alert; to guard against

提袋 (ㄊㄧˊ ㄉㄞˋ)
a handbag

提到 (ㄊㄧˊ ㄉㄠˋ)
①to mention: 他提到一本有用的書。He mentioned a useful book. ②to have summoned (prisoners) to court

提單 (ㄊㄧˊ ㄉㄢ)
a bill of lading (B/L) 參看「提貨單」

提燈會 (ㄊㄧˊ ㄉㄥ ㄏㄨㄟˋ)
a lantern parade or procession

提調 (ㄊㄧˊ ㄉㄧㄠˋ)
an official post in ancient China equivalent to a subordinate executive or business manager of an office

提督 (ㄊㄧˊ ㄉㄨ)
(in ancient China) a provincial commander in chief

提臺 (ㄊㄧˊ ㄊㄞˊ)
(in ancient China) a polite term of address for a provincial commander in chief

提頭兒 (ㄊㄧˊ ㄊㄡˊ ㄦ)
something worth mentioning

提條件 (ㄊㄧˊ ㄊㄧㄠˊ ㄐㄧㄢˋ)
to specify the terms (of a deal)

提桶 (ㄊㄧˊ ㄊㄨㄥˇ)
a pail

提籃 (ㄊㄧˊ ㄌㄢˊ)
a handbasket

提煉 (ㄊㄧˊ ㄌㄧㄢˋ)
to refine (crude oil, etc.); to extract: 從礦砂中提鍊金屬 to extract metal from ore

提梁 (ㄊㄧˊ ㄌㄧㄤˊ)
the handles of handbags, baskets, vessels, etc.

提高 (ㄊㄧˊ ㄍㄠ)
to lift (morale, etc.); to raise (prices, etc.); to heighten (vigilance, etc.); to put to a higher position; to enhance; to increase; to improve: 提高嗓子 to raise one's voice

提高警覺 (ㄊㄧˊ ㄍㄠ ㄐㄧㄥˇ ㄐㄩㄝˊ)
to be on the ball; to heighten one's vigilance; to keep a watchful eye on

提綱 (ㄊㄧˊ ㄍㄤ)
an outline: 他熬夜寫演講提

綱。He sat up late making the outline for the speech.

提綱挈領 (ㄊㄧˊ ㄍㄤ ㄑㄧㄝˋ ㄌㄧㄥˇ)
to mention the main points; to bring out the essentials: 我將提綱挈領地談一談。I'll just touch briefly on the essentials.

提供 (ㄊㄧˊ ㄍㄨㄥ)
①to offer (proposals, opinions, etc.); to provide (assistance, etc.): 提供貸款 to offer a loan ②to sponsor (a TV or radio program, etc.)

提款 (ㄊㄧˊ ㄎㄨㄢˇ)
to draw money from a bank

提壺 (ㄊㄧˊ ㄏㄨˊ)
①to take a wine vessel (to buy wine) ②the name of a bird

提貨 (ㄊㄧˊ ㄏㄨㄛˋ)
to make delivery of goods or cargo; to pick up goods: 我們將到港口提貨。We'll pick up the goods at the port.

提貨單 (ㄊㄧˊ ㄏㄨㄛˋ ㄉㄢ)
a bill of lading (B/L)

提及 (ㄊㄧˊ ㄐㄧˊ)
to mention

提交 (ㄊㄧˊ ㄐㄧㄠ)
①to hand over to the custody of ②to submit to another body for discussion

提拔 (ㄊㄧˊ ㄅㄚˊ)
to promote someone

提起 (ㄊㄧˊ ㄑㄧˇ)
①to lift up; to arouse (oneself to action, etc.) ②to mention; to speak of: 他每天都提起你。He spoke of (or mentioned) you every day.

提起公訴 (ㄊㄧˊ ㄑㄧˇ ㄍㄨㄥ ㄙㄨˋ)
to indict; to arraign; to accuse

提起精神 (ㄊㄧˊ ㄑㄧˇ ㄐㄧㄥ ㄕㄣˊ)
to cheer up; to raise one's spirit; to brace oneself up

提挈 (ㄊㄧˊ ㄑㄧㄝˋ)
①to help; assistance; recommendation for a job ②to carry

提名同黨 (ㄊㄧˊ ㄇㄧㄥˊ ㄊㄨㄥˊ ㄉㄤˇ)
to recommend party members

提前 (ㄊㄧˊ ㄑㄧㄢˊ)
①to give precedence or priority to ②(to complete a

〔手部〕

task, etc.) ahead of schedule; to advance to an earlier date: 會議日期提前了。 The date of the meeting has been moved up.

提前考試(ㄊㄧˊㄑㄧㄢˊㄎㄠˇㄕˋ)
to take an examination ahead of schedule

提親(ㄊㄧˊㄑㄧㄣ)
a matchmaking; to talk about the marriage of a young man or woman

提琴(ㄊㄧˊㄑㄧㄣˊ)
a violin

提請(ㄊㄧˊㄑㄧㄥˇ)
to make a proposal and request for discussion or approval; to submit something (for approval, etc.)

提取(ㄊㄧˊㄑㄩˇ)
①to draw (deposits from the bank) ②to pick up; to make delivery of goods (from a warehouse, etc.) ③to extract; to abstract; to recover

提攜(ㄊㄧˊㄒㄧ)or(ㄊㄧˊㄒㄧˊ)
help; assistance; to help; to aid

提心弔膽(ㄊㄧˊㄒㄧㄣㄉㄧㄠˋㄉㄢˇ)
to be scared; cautious and anxious; in constant fear; jittery

提箱(ㄊㄧˊㄒㄧㄤ)
a suitcase

提醒(ㄊㄧˊㄒㄧㄥˇ)
to remind; to call attention to: 請你提醒我回覆那封信。 Please remind me to answer that letter.

提訊(ㄊㄧˊㄒㄩㄣˋ)
to arraign 參看「提審」

提倡(ㄊㄧˊㄔㄤˋ)
to promote (a cause, etc.); to advocate; to encourage; to recommend; recommendation: 動儉建國的觀念值得提倡。 The idea of building our country through diligence and thrift deserves recommendation.

提倡新說(ㄊㄧˊㄔㄤˋㄒㄧㄣㄕㄨㄛ)
to set forth a new doctrine

提成(ㄊㄧˊㄔㄥˊ)
to take a certain percentage of a sum; to deduct a percentage (from a sum of

money)

提出(ㄊㄧˊㄔㄨ)
to raise (a question, etc.); to propose (a bill, motion, etc.); to put forth; to lodge; to put forward: 請提出建議。 Please put forward your proposal.

提示(ㄊㄧˊㄕˋ)
①to hint; a hint ②(teaching) presentation (of new ideas as related to what a pupil already knows); to brief ③(drama) to prompt; to give a cue: 如果我忘了台詞，請給我提示一下。 Prompt me if I forget my lines.

提示機宜(ㄊㄧˊㄕˋㄐㄧㄧˊ)
to indicate a policy

提手躡腳(ㄊㄧˊㄕㄡˇㄋㄧㄝˋㄐㄧㄠˇ)
to walk on tiptoe

提神(ㄊㄧˊㄕㄣˊ)
①to be cautious or vigilant; to watch out ②to arouse; to stimulate; to elate; to refresh: 喝杯茶或咖啡提神吧! Refresh yourself with a cup of tea or coffee.

提審(ㄊㄧˊㄕㄣˇ)
to bring forward for trial

提升(ㄊㄧˊㄕㄥ)
to promote (an officer, etc.); to elevate: 提升他當總經理。 Promote him to be general manager.

提早(ㄊㄧˊㄗㄠˇ)
to advance to an earlier hour or date; ahead of schedule; in advance: 請提早通知一聲。 Please notify in advance.

提訴(ㄊㄧˊㄙㄨˋ)
to prosecute; a prosecution

提案(ㄊㄧˊㄢˋ)
a motion; a proposal; a draft resolution

提案人(ㄊㄧˊㄢˋㄖㄣˊ)
one who makes a motion or proposal

提議(ㄊㄧˊㄧˋ)
to propose; to put forth suggestions; a proposal, suggestion, motion, etc.: 他的提議被否決了。 His proposal was rejected.

提議人(ㄊㄧˊㄧˋㄖㄣˊ)
one who makes a proposal

or suggestion

提掖(ㄊㄧˊㄧㄝ)
to recommend for promotion; to lead and support (a person); to give assistance and help: 他們經常提掖後輩。 They often lead and support the juniors.

提要(ㄊㄧˊㄧㄠˋ)
①to bring forth the main points ②the main points; a synopsis; a resume; a summary: 你能告訴我本課內容提要嗎? Could you tell me the capsule summary of the lesson?

提腕(ㄊㄧˊㄨㄢˋ)
(calligraphy) to write without the wrist touching the desk

【提】　1951
2. ㄉㄧ dī
to hold or take in hand

提溜(ㄉㄧ·ㄌㄧㄡ)
to hold or take in hand

提溜著(ㄉㄧ·ㄌㄧㄡ·ㄓㄜ ㄒㄧㄣ)
to be anxious, worried or nervous

【撜】　1952
ㄓㄣ jenn zhēn
to strike; to stab; to thrust

【揖】　1953
ㄧ ī
1. to bow with hands folding in front
2. to yield politely; to defer to

揖拜(ㄧㄅㄞˋ)
to make a bow with the hands folding in front (usually during greeting or parting)

揖別(ㄧㄅㄧㄝˊ)
to bid adieu

揖客(ㄧㄎㄜˋ)
to greet a guest; to salute a visitor by folding hands in front

揖謝(ㄧㄒㄧㄝˋ)
to bow in thanks

揖讓(ㄖㄤˋ)
①courtesy between the host and his guests ②to abdicate; to give up a position for a better man

揖讓再三(ㄖㄤˋㄗㄞˋㄙㄢ)
to bow complaisantly and give way again and again 亦作「再三揖讓」

【插】 1954
(捶) ㄔㄚ chā chā
. to insert; to put in; to stick
into: 他把双手插在口袋裏。He
put his hands in his pockets.
. to interpose; to get a word
in edgeways
. to plant
. to take part in
插播廣告 (ㄔㄚ ㄅㄛ ㄍㄨㄤ ㄍㄠ)
a spot announcement
插播新聞 (ㄔㄚ ㄅㄛ ㄒㄧㄣ ㄨㄣ)
spot news
插班 (ㄔㄚ ㄅㄢ)
to place a student from
another school according to
his grade; to enter another
school according to one's
grade
插班生 (ㄔㄚ ㄅㄢ ㄕㄥ)
a student who enters another
school according to his grade
插屏 (ㄔㄚ ㄆㄧㄥ)
①a miniature screen for
ornamental purpose ②framed
paintings or calligraphy
hanging on the wall
插隊 (ㄔㄚ ㄉㄨㄟ)
to cut in; to push in
插頭 (ㄔㄚ ㄊㄡ)
a plug: 三(脚)插頭 a three-
pin plug
插天 (ㄔㄚ ㄊㄧㄢ)
(said of high peaks) to soar
into the sky
插圖 (ㄔㄚ ㄊㄨ)
illustrations or plates (in a
book, magazine, etc.): 這本書
有幾幅彩色插圖。The book
has several color plates.
插柳成蔭 (ㄔㄚ ㄌㄧㄡ ㄔㄥ ㄧㄣ)
to do something which
brings results easily
插關兒 (ㄔㄚ ㄍㄨㄢ ㄦ)
a kind of door bolt
插科打諢 (ㄔㄚ ㄎㄜ ㄉㄚˇ ㄏㄨㄣˋ)
(said of clowns in a show)
to ad-lib; buffooneries; jesting
插花 (ㄔㄚ ㄏㄨㄚ)
①to arrange flowers; flower
arrangement ②(in old China)
the top candidates of the
imperial examinations who
wore flowers to show dis-
tinction
插話 (ㄔㄚ ㄏㄨㄚˋ)or 插言(ㄔㄚ ㄧㄢˊ)

①to break into a conversation ②an irrelevant episode;
digression
插畫 (ㄔㄚ ㄏㄨㄚˋ)
illustrations (in a book,
magazine, etc.) 參看「插圖」
插架 (ㄔㄚ ㄐㄧㄚˋ)
a bamboo shelf suspended
on the wall
插脚 (ㄔㄚ ㄐㄧㄠˇ)or 插足(ㄔㄚ ㄗㄨˊ)
to have a foothold in (an
organization, activity, etc.);
to participate in; to gain a
place
插句 (ㄔㄚ ㄐㄩˋ)
a parenthesis 亦作「插入語」
插曲 (ㄔㄚ ㄑㄩˇ)
①a musical interlude ②
songs and tunes used in
motion picture dubbing ③an
episode
插圈弄套 (ㄔㄚ ㄑㄩㄢ ㄋㄨㄥˋ ㄊㄠˋ)or
插圈弄計 (ㄔㄚ ㄓㄨㄥ ㄋㄨㄥˋ ㄐㄧˋ)
to trap or snare others with
tricks
插敍 (ㄔㄚ ㄒㄩˋ)
narration interspersed with
flashbacks
插枝 (ㄔㄚ ㄓ)
(botany) a cutting; to plant
by sticking branches in soil
插燭 (ㄔㄚ ㄓㄨˊ)
to put a candle onto a candlestick
插翅難飛 (ㄔㄚ ㄔˋ ㄋㄢˊ ㄈㄟ)
(literally) Even if you were
given wings, you couldn't fly
away.—completely surrounded
插手 (ㄔㄚ ㄕㄡˇ)
to take part in; to meddle:
他插手別人的事情。He med-
dles in other people's affairs.
插身 (ㄔㄚ ㄕㄣ)
to take part in; to join in; to
edge in; to involve in: 這裏很
難插身。It's difficult to take
part in here.
插入 (ㄔㄚ ㄖㄨˋ)
to stick into; to insert; to
plug in: 他把硬幣插入投幣口。
He inserted a coin into the
slot.
插座 (ㄔㄚ ㄗㄨㄛˋ)
a receptacle; a socket; an
outlet
插嘴 (ㄔㄚ ㄗㄨㄟˇ)or 插口 (ㄔㄚ ㄎㄡˇ)

to interrupt a narration, conversation, etc.; to put a
word in; to chip in: 他無法插
嘴。He could not get a word
in edgeways.
插草標 (ㄔㄚ ㄘㄠˇ ㄅㄧㄠ)
(an old custom) to put up a
wisp of straw to indicate
that an item is for sale
插秧 (ㄔㄚ ㄧㄤ)
to transplant rice seedlings

【揚】 1955
ㄧㄤˊ yang yáng
1. to raise: 他揚起左手。He
raised his left hand.
2. (said of flames) blazing
3. to wave; to flutter
4. to praise; to acclaim: 人人讚
揚他是個偉大的演員。Every-
body acclaimed him as a
great actor.
5. to display; to expose; to
make evident; to make known
6. high or raised (voice, cry,
etc.)
7. to scatter; to spread: 消息很
快就傳揚整個城市。The news
quickly spread all over
town.
8. to stir; to get excited
9. a Chinese family name
揚波 (ㄧㄤˊ ㄅㄛ)
the swelling of waves
揚鑣 (ㄧㄤˊ ㄅㄧㄠ)
to raise the bridle—to part
from a friend
揚鞭 (ㄧㄤˊ ㄅㄧㄢ)
to raise the whip—to leave
揚眉吐氣 (ㄧㄤˊ ㄇㄟˊ ㄊㄨˇ ㄑㄧˋ)
to feel proud and elated
after one suddenly comes to
fame, wealth or good luck
揚名 (ㄧㄤˊ ㄇㄧㄥˊ)
to become famous: 他以一個
鋼琴家而揚名。He was famous
as a pianist.
揚名天下 (ㄧㄤˊ ㄇㄧㄥˊ ㄊㄧㄢ ㄒㄧㄚˋ)
to be known throughout the
land; to have one's name
spread far and wide; to
become world-famous
揚帆 (ㄧㄤˊ ㄈㄢˊ)
to set sail
揚湯止沸 (ㄧㄤˊ ㄊㄤ ㄓˇ ㄈㄟˋ)
(literally) to try to stop
water from boiling by stirring it (without removing
the fire underneath the pot)

〔手部〕

—①a stupid way of solving a problem ②to provide temporary relief to the suffering people

揚花(ㄧㄤˊ ㄏㄨㄚ)
flowering (of cereal crops)

揚棄(ㄧㄤˊ ㄑㄧˋ)
①to discard; to renounce: 我們不可揚棄老朋友。We should not discard our old friends. ②(philosophy) to sublate

揚琴(ㄧㄤˊ ㄑㄧㄣˊ)
a dulcimer

揚清激濁(ㄧㄤˊ ㄑㄧㄥ ㄐㄧ ㄓㄨㄛˊ)
to publicize the good deeds of good people in the hope that others will emulate them

揚雄(ㄧㄤˊ ㄒㄩㄥˊ)
Yang Hsiung (53 B.C.—18 A.D.), alias 子雲, a scholar-writer in the Han Dynasty

揚州(ㄧㄤˊ ㄓㄡ)
①Yangchow, one of nine administrative divisions in ancient China ②Yangchow, a city on the northern shore of the lower Yangtze River

揚州八怪(ㄧㄤˊ ㄓㄡ ㄅㄚ ㄍㄨㄞˋ)
the eight artists of Yangchow in the Ching Dynasty, famous for their eccentricities and originality (金農、羅聘、鄭燮、李方膺、汪士慎、高翔、黃慎、李鱓)

揚塵(ㄧㄤˊ ㄔㄣˊ)
to raise dust

揚長而去(ㄧㄤˊ ㄔㄤˊ ㄦˊ ㄑㄩˋ)
to stride away without looking back; to take leave rudely; to hold one's head proudly high while walking away with big strides; to stalk off; to swagger off

揚善(ㄧㄤˊ ㄕㄢˋ)
to spread or make known others' good deeds

揚聲(ㄧㄤˊ ㄕㄥ)
①to raise one's voice ②to boast prestige

揚子江(ㄧㄤˊ ㄗˇ ㄐㄧㄤ)
the Yangtze River

揚言(ㄧㄤˊ ㄧㄢˊ)
to spread words; to pass the word that; to exaggerate; to declare in public. 他揚言要報

復。He spread words to retaliate.

揚揚(ㄧㄤˊ ㄧㄤˊ)
triumphantly; complacently

揚揚自得(ㄧㄤˊ ㄧㄤˊ ㄗˋ ㄉㄜˊ)
to be very pleased with oneself; to be complacent

揚揚得意(ㄧㄤˊ ㄧㄤˊ ㄉㄜˊ ㄧˋ)
to be smug and complacent

揚威(ㄧㄤˊ ㄨㄟ)
to show one's great authority, superiority, power, etc. to attain eminence (in a certain field, etc.)

【捬】 1956
(捬) (ㄈㄨˇ) yean yǎn
1. to rob; to take by force
2. to cover up; to conceal
3. to shut

【揠】 1957
(ㄧㄚˋ) yah yà
to pull up or out

揠苗助長(ㄧㄚˋ ㄇㄧㄠˊ ㄓㄨˋ ㄓㄤˇ)
(literally) to pull up the seedling hoping to make it grow faster—a stupid and self-defeating effort; to spoil things by excessive enthusiasm

【換】 1958
(ㄏㄨㄢˋ) huann huàn
to exchange; to change; to alter; to substitute; 請你幫我換十元的零錢好嗎? Can you change a ten-dollar bill for me?

換班(ㄏㄨㄢˋ ㄅㄢ)
(said of factory workers) to change a shift; to relieve (guard, or sentry duties)

換邊(ㄏㄨㄢˋ ㄅㄧㄢ)
(sports) to change sides

換毛(ㄏㄨㄢˋ ㄇㄠˊ)to molt: 小鳥正在換毛。The bird's feathers are molting.

換檔(ㄏㄨㄢˋ ㄉㄤˇ)
to shift gears

換調(ㄏㄨㄢˋ ㄉㄧㄠˋ)
transition 亦作「調換」

換湯不換藥(ㄏㄨㄢˋ ㄊㄤ ㄅㄨˋ ㄏㄨㄢˋ ㄧㄠˋ)
a change in form but not in content

換替(ㄏㄨㄢˋ ㄊㄧˋ)
①by turns; alternately: 他們通常換替著開車。They usually drive by turns. ②to replace

亦作「替換」

換帖(ㄏㄨㄢˋ ㄊㄧㄝˇ)
to exchange cards containing all personal details and thus become sworn brothers

換流機(ㄏㄨㄢˋ ㄌㄧㄡˊ ㄐㄧ)or換頻機(ㄏㄨㄢˋ ㄆㄧㄣˊ ㄐㄧ)
an inverted converter; an inverted frequency converter

換崗(ㄏㄨㄢˋ ㄍㄤˇ)
to relieve a guard or sentry; the changing of the guards 中午會有人來換崗。You will be relieved at noon.

換骨(ㄏㄨㄢˋ ㄍㄨˇ)
①(Taoism) to change mortal into immortal bones ②to effect basic or fundamental change

換貨(ㄏㄨㄢˋ ㄏㄨㄛˋ)
to exchange goods; to barter

換口味(ㄏㄨㄢˋ ㄎㄡˇ ㄨㄟˋ)
to have a change in diet environment, etc.

換季(ㄏㄨㄢˋ ㄐㄧˋ)
①the change of seasons ②to change clothing or uniforms according to the season

換氣(ㄏㄨㄢˋ ㄑㄧˋ)
to breathe; to take breath (in swimming); 我將頭伸出水面換氣。I got my head above the water to take breath.

換錢(ㄏㄨㄢˋ ㄑㄧㄢˊ)
①to change money (into small change) ②to convert one currency to another ③to barter goods for money

換取(ㄏㄨㄢˋ ㄑㄩˇ)
to change; to exchange

換血(ㄏㄨㄢˋ ㄒㄧㄝˇ)
blood exchange transfusion

換新(ㄏㄨㄢˋ ㄒㄧㄣ)
to change something for a new one

換主(ㄏㄨㄢˋ ㄓㄨˇ)
to change the owner; to change ownership

換車(ㄏㄨㄢˋ ㄔㄜ)
to change buses, trains, etc.: 我們必須在台中換車。We have to change trains at Taichung.

換上(ㄏㄨㄢˋ ㄕㄤˋ)
to make changes; to substitute

換入(ㄏㄨㄢ ㄖㄨˋ)
　substitution (of players)

換算(ㄏㄨㄢ ㄙㄨㄢˋ)
　to convert (one system of
　measurement into another)

換算表(ㄏㄨㄢ ㄙㄨㄢˋ ㄅㄧㄠˇ)
　a conversion table

換衣(ㄏㄨㄢ ㄧ)or換衣服(ㄏㄨㄢ ㄧ
　˙ㄈㄨ)
　to change a dress

換牙(ㄏㄨㄢ ㄧㄚˊ)
　(said of a child) to grow
　permanent teeth

換藥(ㄏㄨㄢ ㄧㄠˋ)
　①to change a medical pre-
　scription ②to change a
　fresh dressing for a wound

換言之(ㄏㄨㄢ ㄧㄢˊ ㄓ)or換句話說
　(ㄏㄨㄢ ㄐㄩˋ ㄏㄨㄚˋ ㄕㄨㄛ)
　in other words: 換句話說, 她
　不會來。In other words, she
　will not come.

換樣兒(ㄏㄨㄢ ㄧㄤˋ ㄦ)
　to change in appearance; to
　change fashion

換文(ㄏㄨㄢ ㄨㄣˊ)
　an exchange of diplomatic
　notes

換約(ㄏㄨㄢ ㄩㄝ)
　to exchange the instruments
　of ratification of a treaty

換韻(ㄏㄨㄢ ㄩㄣˋ)
　to shift to another rhyme

【握】 1959
ㄨㄛˋ woh wò
1. to hold fast; to grasp; to
　grip: 她因害怕而握住我的手。
　She gripped my hand in
　fear.
2. a handful

握筆(ㄨㄛˋ ㄅㄧˇ)
　to hold a pen

握晉(ㄨㄛˋ ㄅㄧˋ)
　to grasp the arm (of an old
　friend)—to meet an old
　friend

握別(ㄨㄛˋ ㄅㄧㄝˊ)
　to part; to shake hands at
　parting; to say good-bye: 握
　別以來, 已逾三月。It is more
　than three months since we
　parted.

握髮(ㄨㄛˋ ㄈㄚˇ)
　(said of a leader) to be anx-
　ious to meet men of ability

握符(ㄨㄛˋ ㄈㄨˊ)
　to be in command (of an

army, etc.)

握力(ㄨㄛˋ ㄌㄧˋ)
　the power of gripping; a
　grip

握力計(ㄨㄛˋ ㄌㄧˋ ㄐㄧˋ)
　a hand dynamometer

握管(ㄨㄛˋ ㄍㄨㄢˇ)
　to hold a pen—to write or
　paint

握翰(ㄨㄛˋ ㄏㄢˋ)
　to hold a pen—to write or
　paint 參看「握筆」or「握管」

握緊(ㄨㄛˋ ㄐㄧㄣˇ)
　to hold fast; to grasp firmly

握卷(ㄨㄛˋ ㄐㄩㄢˋ)
　to hold a book—to read

握權(ㄨㄛˋ ㄑㄩㄢˊ)
　to be in power or authority;
　to be in command; to hold
　the rein (of government,
　etc.)

握拳(ㄨㄛˋ ㄑㄩㄢˊ)
　to make a fist; to clench
　one's fist

握拳透爪(ㄨㄛˋ ㄑㄩㄢˊ ㄊㄡˋ ㄓㄠˇ)
　to harbor a deep hatred for

握手(ㄨㄛˋ ㄕㄡˇ)
　to shake hands: 這兩人握手。
　The two men shook hands.

握手言歡(ㄨㄛˋ ㄕㄡˇ ㄧㄢˊ ㄏㄨㄢ)
　to hold hands and converse
　cheerfully

【揣】 1960
ㄔㄨㄞ chuai chuǎi
1. to measure; to weigh; to
　estimate; to calculate; to
　reckon
2. to try; to probe (for pos-
　sibilities); to put out a feeler

揣摩(ㄔㄨㄞ ㄇㄛˊ)
　①to study; to learn; to pon-
　der; to examine ②to
　assume; to speculate; to
　guess

揣度(ㄔㄨㄞ ㄉㄨㄛˋ)
　to speculate; to conjecture;
　to appraise; to make an
　intelligent guess

揣摩(ㄔㄨㄞ ㄇㄛˊ)
　to study and imitate (a good
　author, etc.)

揣骨(ㄔㄨㄞ ㄍㄨˇ)
　a branch of physiognomy in
　which a fortuneteller feels
　the bones (especially facial)
　of a person to tell his or
　her fortune

揣想(ㄔㄨㄞ ㄒㄧㄤˇ)
　to imagine; to conjecture; to
　make an intelligent guess

揣測(ㄔㄨㄞ ㄘㄜˋ)
　to conjecture; to fathom; to
　speculate; to make an intelli-
　gent guess

揣測之詞(ㄔㄨㄞ ㄘㄜˋ ㄓ ㄘˊ)
　a mere speculation or con-
　jecture

〔手
部〕

【揩】 1961
ㄎㄞ kai kāi
　to wipe; to scrub; to rub; to
　dust; to clean

揩背(ㄎㄞ ㄅㄟˋ)
　to scrub a customer's back
　for a fee at an old-fashioned
　public bath

揩面(ㄎㄞ ㄇㄧㄢˋ)
　to wipe the face

揩乾淨(ㄎㄞ ㄍㄢ ㄐㄧㄥˋ)
　to wipe clean: 把地板揩乾淨。
　Wipe the floor clean.

揩油(ㄎㄞ ㄧㄡˊ)or(ㄎㄞ ㄧㄡˊ)
　①to make some (usually
　small) outside gains not in-
　cluded in a deal; to report a
　purchase at a blown-up
　price (so that one gets the
　difference) ②(said of a
　male) to caress or touch a
　woman without her knowl-
　edge or when she is unable
　or it is inconvenient for her
　to offer resistance

揩眼淚(ㄎㄞ ㄧㄢˇ ㄌㄟˋ)
　to wipe away tears

【揪】 1962
(舊) ㄐㄧㄡ jiou jiū
1. to clutch; to grasp with
　one's hand; to grab; to hold
　fast; to seize
2. to pull; to drag: 把他從床上
　揪起來。Drag him from his
　bed.
3. to pick on

揪辮子(ㄐㄧㄡ ㄅㄧㄢˋ ˙ㄗ)
　to seize somebody's queue
　—to seize upon somebody's
　mistakes or shortcomings

揪扭(ㄐㄧㄡ ㄋㄧㄡˇ)
　to seize by hand; to grapple

揪心(ㄐㄧㄡ ㄒㄧㄣ)
　①anxious; nervous; worried
　②heartrending; agonizing;
　gnawing

揪心錢(ㄐㄧㄡ ㄒㄧㄣ ㄑㄧㄢˊ)
　(said of a miser) money

〔手部〕

spent with a bleeding heart

揪住（ㄐㄧㄡ ㄓㄨˋ）
to seize or grasp (somebody) with force

揪（ㄐㄧㄡ ㄔㄨ）
to uncover; to ferret out

揪耳朵（ㄐㄧㄡ ㄦˇ ㄉㄨㄛ）
to hold (another) by the ear; to seize another's ear

【揮】 1963 （ㄏㄨㄟ huī）
1. to wield (a sword, pen, etc.); to move; to shake; to wave; to brandish; to make a light or rapid stroke
2. to conduct; to direct (troop movements, a concert, a course of action, etc.)
3. to wipe away (sweat, tears, etc.)
4. to scatter; to sprinkle
5. to squander (money, etc.)
6. to swing (fists)

揮鞭（ㄏㄨㄟ ㄅㄧㄢ）
to wave a whip; to swish a whip

揮兵（ㄏㄨㄟ ㄅㄧㄥ）
to march troops to war

揮發（ㄏㄨㄟ ㄈㄚ）
to volatilize; volatilization; to evaporate

揮發油（ㄏㄨㄟ ㄈㄚ ㄧㄡˊ）
gasoline, naphtha, or other volatile oils; benzine

揮刀（ㄏㄨㄟ ㄉㄠ）
to wield a sword; to brandish a sword

揮動（ㄏㄨㄟ ㄉㄨㄥˋ）
to wield (a sword, etc.); to swing (fists, etc.)

揮淚（ㄏㄨㄟ ㄌㄟˋ）
to shed tears

揮戈（ㄏㄨㄟ ㄍㄜ）
① to brandish one's weapons ② to lead troops to battle

揮毫（ㄏㄨㄟ ㄏㄠˊ）
(said of calligraphers) to wield the writing brush——to write

揮翰（ㄏㄨㄟ ㄏㄢˋ）
to write

揮汗成雨（ㄏㄨㄟ ㄏㄢˋ ㄔㄥˊ ㄩˇ）
① drops of perspiration falling down like a shower ② a considerable amount of people; a squeeze of people

to spend freely; to squander

揮霍無度（ㄏㄨㄟ ㄏㄨㄛˋ ㄨˊ ㄉㄨˋ）
to squander money

揮劍（ㄏㄨㄟ ㄐㄧㄢˋ）
to brandish a sword; to whip out a sword

揮金如土（ㄏㄨㄟ ㄐㄧㄣ ㄖㄨˊ ㄊㄨˇ）
to squander money like dirt

揮軍（ㄏㄨㄟ ㄐㄩㄣ）
to march troops to war: 那位將軍揮軍上陣。The general marched his troops to war.

揮拳（ㄏㄨㄟ ㄑㄩㄢˊ）
to swing fists—to strike somebody

揮塵（ㄏㄨㄟ ㄓㄣˋ）or揮犀（ㄏㄨㄟ ㄒㄧ）
to wave a long-haired duster —to engage in a leisurely conversation on unworldly subjects

揮手（ㄏㄨㄟ ㄕㄡˇ）
to wave one's hand (in greeting or bidding farewell): 他向我揮手致意。He waved greetings to me.

揮觴（ㄏㄨㄟ ㄕㄤ）
to raise a cup—to drink

揮灑（ㄏㄨㄟ ㄙㄚˇ）
to write or paint freely

揮舞（ㄏㄨㄟ ㄨˇ）
to wave; to wield; to brandish

【揭】 1964 （ㄐㄧㄝ jiē）
1. to lift up or off; to raise high
2. to unveil, uncover or unearth; to expose; to tear off; to take off: 把盒蓋揭開。Take that cover off this box.
3. to announce; to publicize
4. a Chinese family name

揭榜（ㄐㄧㄝ ㄅㄤˇ）
to publish or make public a list of successful candidates; to announce the results of an examination

揭破（ㄐㄧㄝ ㄆㄛˋ）
to expose or uncover (a secret, conspiracy, etc.)

揭幕（ㄐㄧㄝ ㄇㄨˋ）
to raise or lift the curtain (of a meeting, exhibition, etc.); to unveil—to inaugurate

揭幕禮（ㄐㄧㄝ ㄇㄨˋ ㄌㄧˇ）
an opening ceremony: 新戲院

舉行揭幕禮。The new theatre held an unveiling ceremony

揭發（ㄐㄧㄝ ㄈㄚ）
to expose (a plot, scandal, etc.)

揭封（ㄐㄧㄝ ㄈㄥ）
to tear off the seal

揭底（ㄐㄧㄝ ㄉㄧˇ）
to reveal the inside story

揭短（ㄐㄧㄝ ㄉㄨㄢˇ）
to expose the blemishes (or faults) of others

揭貼（ㄐㄧㄝ ㄊㄧㄝ）or揭帖（ㄐㄧㄝ ㄊㄧㄝˇ）
① libelous posters, pamphlets, or anonymous letters ② to put up a poster, bulletin, etc.

揭露（ㄐㄧㄝ ㄌㄨˋ）
to uncover or expose (another's secret, etc.); to unmask: 警方揭發了罪犯的陰謀。The police exposed the criminal's plot.

揭蓋兒（ㄐㄧㄝ ㄍㄞˋ）
(literally) to lift up the lid —to uncover or unveil (the inside story)

揭竿而起（ㄐㄧㄝ ㄍㄢ ㄦˊ ㄑㄧˇ）
to raise the standard of revolt with poles—to start a revolution or an uprising 亦作「揭竿起義」

揭開（ㄐㄧㄝ ㄎㄞ）
① to pull apart or separate ② to uncover; to unmask; to reveal: 天文學揭開了宇宙的奧秘。Astronomy reveals the secrets of the universe.

揭曉（ㄐㄧㄝ ㄒㄧㄠˇ）
to make public; to publish; to announce

揭櫫（ㄐㄧㄝ ㄓㄨ）
to announce (goals, objectives, etc. of a movement, cause, etc.); to proclaim; to publish

揭穿（ㄐㄧㄝ ㄔㄨㄢ）
to expose (a conspiracy, trick, etc.); to belie; to lay bare: 我們要揭穿這個偽君子的陰謀。We want to expose this hypocrite's conspiracy.

揭瘡疤（ㄐㄧㄝ ㄔㄨㄤ ㄅㄚ）
to reopen old wounds (in order to put someone to shame)

揭(丩ㄧㄝˊㄕ)
①to make public; to put up a public notice; to announce
②to reveal; to bring to light
③(figuratively) to delineate (the inner world of the characters in a novel)

揭示板(丩ㄧㄝˊㄕㄅㄢˇ)
a bulletin board

揭人陰私(丩ㄧㄝˊㄖㄣˊㄧㄣㄙ)
to expose another person's secrets

【援】 1965
　　ㄩㄢˊ yuan yuán
1. to lead
2. to take hold of; to pull by hand
3. to aid; to help; to reinforce; to rescue: 我們必須增援前線之部隊。We must reinforce the troops at the front.
4. to invoke (a law, precedent, etc.): 有例可援。There's a precedent to invoke.

援筆(ㄩㄢˊㄅㄧˇ)
to take up a pen to write

援兵(ㄩㄢˊㄅㄧㄥ)
reinforcements

援例(ㄩㄢˊㄌㄧˋ)or 援以爲例(ㄩㄢˊㄧˇㄨㄟˊㄌㄧˋ)
to follow a precedent; to invoke a precedent: 他擅引出去，我也援例行事。He sneaked out, and I followed suit.

援救(ㄩㄢˊㄐㄧㄡˋ)
to rescue; to come to the aid of

援據(ㄩㄢˊㄐㄩˋ)
to adduce or cite as proof

援軍(ㄩㄢˊㄐㄩㄣ)
(military) reinforcements; relief troops

援照(ㄩㄢˊㄓㄠˋ)
according to; to adduce; to cite (as an example, reason, etc.)

援助(ㄩㄢˊㄓㄨˋ)
to aid; aid; to help: 紅十字會援助水災難民。The Red Cross aids flood victims.

援手(ㄩㄢˊㄕㄡˇ)
①to extend a helping hand
②a helper

援案(ㄩㄢˊㄢˋ)
to quote a precedent; in accordance with a precedent

援引(ㄩㄢˊㄧㄣˇ)
to cite (a precedent) as proof, etc.

援用(ㄩㄢˊㄩㄥˋ)
to invoke or quote (a precedent, provisions of laws, etc.)

【揲】 1966
　　ㄕㄜˊ sher shé
to sort out divining stalks

【揸】 1967
　　ㄓㄚ ja zhā
to pick up with fingers; to grasp by hand

【揶】 1968
　　ㄧㄝˊ ye yé
to jeer at; to ridicule; to play a joke on

揶揄(ㄧㄝˊㄩˊ)
to ridicule; to jeer at; to play a joke on; to tease; to taunt; teasing: 不要揶揄別人的錯誤或不幸。Do not jeer at the mistakes or misfortunes of others.

【攢】 1969
　　(攢) ㄗㄨㄢˇ tzuann zuǎn
to hold or seize with the hand; to grip; to clench; to grasp

【攢】 1969
　　2.(攢) ㄗㄢˇ tzaan zǎn
to save (money); to hoard

揝錢(ㄗㄢˇㄑㄧㄢˊ)
to save money; to save up

【揹】 1970
　　(揹) ㄅㄟ bei bēi
to carry on the back; to shoulder (a load, responsibility, etc.)

揹黑袱(ㄅㄟ ㄈㄨˊ·ㄈㄨ)
①to carry a fardel on the back; to carry a burden ②to have a weight on one's mind; to take on a mental burden: 你不要因此揹包袱。Don't let it weigh on your mind.

揹黑鍋(ㄅㄟㄏㄟ《ㄨㄛ)
to be made the scapegoat for somebody; to take blame for someone: 他替他的兄弟揹黑鍋。He takes blame for his brother.

【揎】 1971
　　ㄒㄩㄢ shiuan xuān
1. to pull up the sleeves and show the arms

2. to fight with bare hands

捩拳攞袖(ㄒㄩㄢ ㄑㄩㄢˊㄌㄨㄛ ㄒㄧㄡˋ)
to pull up the sleeves—to get ready to work or fight

【推】 1972
　　ㄑㄩㄝ chiueh què
1. to knock; to strike
2. to discuss; to negotiate; to consult

推商(ㄑㄩㄝ ㄕㄤ)
to consult; to discuss; consultation; discussion 亦作「酌推」

【搊】 1973
　　ㄔㄡ chou chōu
1. to pluck stringed instruments with fingers
2. to tighten
3. to hold and support

【搋】 1974
　　ㄔㄨㄞ chuai chuāi
1. to conceal something in the bosom
2. to knead (dough); to rub

搋麵(ㄔㄨㄞㄇㄧㄢˋ)
to knead dough

搋手兒(ㄔㄨㄞㄕㄡˇㄦ)
to put each hand in the other sleeve (in order to keep both hands warm)

搋在懷裏(ㄔㄨㄞ ㄗㄞˋㄏㄨㄞˊ·ㄌㄧ)
to carry or hold in the bosom

【損】 1975
　　ㄙㄨㄣˇ soen sǔn
1. to detract; to damage; to injure; to destroy; harm; damage: 吸煙對你有損無益。Smoking does you more harm than good.
2. to lose; loss
3. to reduce; to decrease
4. weak; emaciated
5. to ridicule; to jeer at
6. wicked and mean; cruel: 這話真損透了。It is really mean to say so.
7. (Chinese medicine) long-term emaciation

損德(ㄙㄨㄣˇㄉㄜˊ)
to cause damage to one's virtue (for too many wrong-doings)

損到家(ㄙㄨㄣˇㄉㄠˋㄐㄧㄚ)
①to reduce (prices) to cost level ②(said of utterances, actions) very mean; cruel

〔手部〕

and heartless

損年 (ㄙㄨㄣ ㄋㄧㄢˊ)
to shorten one's life span; to die young

損害 (ㄙㄨㄣˇ ㄏㄞˋ)
to impair; to cause damage or loss; to injure; damages or losses: 抽菸會損害健康。 Smoking will impair one's health.

損害賠償 (ㄙㄨㄣˇ ㄏㄞˋ ㄆㄟˊ ㄔㄤˊ)
schadenersatz; indemnity; compensation

損耗 (ㄙㄨㄣˇ ㄏㄠˋ)
to deplete; to exhaust (supply); to weaken (strength); loss

損壞 (ㄙㄨㄣˇ ㄏㄨㄞˋ)
to damage; damage; spoilage: 損壞公物要賠償。One should pay for public property he damaged.

損失 (ㄙㄨㄣˇ ㄕ)
losses; casualties: 四十鎊的損失對我而言是很大的, A loss of £40 is great to me.

損失不貲 (ㄙㄨㄣˇ ㄕ ㄅㄨˋ ㄗ)
to suffer no small amount of damage

損失總數 (ㄙㄨㄣˇ ㄕ ㄗㄨㄥˇ ㄕㄨˋ)
total loss

損壽 (ㄙㄨㄣˇ ㄕㄡˋ)
to shorten one's life (because of overindulgence, etc.)

損傷 (ㄙㄨㄣˇ ㄕㄤ)
losses; casualties; to hurt (another's feelings, etc.)

損元氣 (ㄙㄨㄣˇ ㄩㄢˊ ㄑㄧˋ)
to suffer tremendous loss in strength or resources

損人 (ㄙㄨㄣˇ ㄖㄣˊ)
①to ridicule others; to make caustic remarks; to injure another with mean words: 他老是愛損人。He always delights in making caustic remarks. ②to cause material damage to others

損人利己 (ㄙㄨㄣˇ ㄖㄣˊ ㄌㄧˋ ㄐㄧˇ)
to profit oneself at the expense of others

損益 (ㄙㄨㄣˇ ㄧˋ)
profit and loss; increase and decrease: 損益相抵。The gains offset the losses.

損益表 (ㄙㄨㄣˇ ㄧˋ ㄅㄧㄠˇ)
a statement of profit and

loss; an income statement

損友 (ㄙㄨㄣˇ ㄧㄡˇ)
an injurious friend; bad company

損陰壞德 (ㄙㄨㄣˇ ㄧㄣ ㄏㄨㄞˋ ㄉㄜˊ)or 損陰騭 (ㄙㄨㄣˇ ㄧㄣ ㄓˋ)
to indulge in evildoings; to harm by underhand means

〔搆〕《ㄍㄡ gow gòu
1. to pull; to drag
2. to reach
3. to implicate
4. to make (war, peace, etc.); to bring (a disaster, a grudge, etc.); to incur (animosity, etc.)
5. to compose

搆不著 (ㄍㄡ ‧ㄅㄨ ㄓㄠˊ)
unable to reach it

搆兵 (ㄍㄡ ㄅㄧㄥ)
to be at war or on the warpath: 這兩個國家為了爭霸權而搆兵。The two states were on the warpath for supremacy.

搆和 (ㄍㄡ ㄏㄜˊ)
to make or negotiate for peace

搆禍 (ㄍㄡ ㄏㄨㄛˋ)
to bring disaster upon oneself; to incur misfortune

搆陷 (ㄍㄡ ㄒㄧㄢˋ)
to set a trap to incriminate someone; to frame up a charge against someone

搆訟 (ㄍㄡ ㄙㄨㄥˋ)
to go to law; to enter a lawsuit: 他們已搆訟多年。They had proceeded in a lawsuit for years.

搆怨 (ㄍㄡ ㄩㄢˋ)
to incur an animosity or a grudge

〔搏〕　1977　ㄅㄛˊ bor bó
1. to pounce on (or at); to spring upon
2. to grasp; to catch; to arrest; to seize
3. to strike; to box; to engage in a hand-to-hand combat

搏拊 (ㄅㄛˊ ㄈㄨˇ)
to keep the beat (of a song, tune, etc.) by slapping one's hip

搏鬥 (ㄅㄛˊ ㄉㄡˋ)
to battle; to wrestle; to fight; to struggle: 他們與暴風

雨搏鬥。They battled against the storm.

搏虎 (ㄅㄛˊ ㄏㄨˇ)
to fight a tiger with one's bare hands

搏擊 (ㄅㄛˊ ㄐㄧˊ)
to strike; to fight with hands

搏香弄粉 (ㄅㄛˊ ㄒㄧㄤ ㄋㄨㄥˋ ㄈㄣˇ)
to doll up oneself; to apply a lot of make-up

搏鬥 (ㄅㄛˊ ㄉㄡˋ)
to combat; to box; to engage in hand-to-hand combat 參看「搏鬥」

搏殺 (ㄅㄛˊ ㄕㄚ)
to fight and kill

搏手 (ㄅㄛˊ ㄕㄡˇ)
at the end of one's wits

搏影 (ㄅㄛˊ ㄧㄥˇ)
to fight the shadow (descriptive of a regular army fighting an elusive guerrilla force)

〔搔〕　1978　ㄙㄠ sau sāo
1. to scratch lightly
2. to irritate; to annoy

搔背 (ㄙㄠ ㄅㄟˋ)
to scratch the back

搔爬 (ㄙㄠ ㄆㄚˊ)
to scratch lightly

搔動 (ㄙㄠ ㄉㄨㄥˋ)
disturbance; commotion; to become restless 亦作「騷動」

搔頭 (ㄙㄠ ㄊㄡˊ)or 搔首 (ㄙㄠ ㄕㄡˇ)
to scratch one's head (in perplexity, etc.); to rub gently

搔頭摸耳 (ㄙㄠ ㄊㄡˊ ㄇㄛ ㄦˇ)
hesitating; undecided

搔頭弄虎鬚 (ㄙㄠ ㄊㄡˊ ㄋㄨㄥˋ ㄏㄨˇ ㄒㄩ)
to offend the mighty and powerful

搔著癢處 (ㄙㄠ ‧ㄓㄜ ㄧㄤˇ ㄔㄨˋ)
①to touch somebody to the quick ②to say something exactly to the point: 你的話正好搔著癢處。What you said was just to the point.

搔首弄姿 (ㄙㄠ ㄕㄡˇ ㄋㄨㄥˋ ㄗ)
(said of women) to act coquettishly to attract men's attention; to flirt

搔首踟躕 (ㄙㄠ ㄕㄡˇ ㄔˊ ㄔㄨˊ)
to be at a loss as to what to do; to be in perplexity; to

hesitate; to be undecided

搔擾 (ㄙㄠ ㄖㄠˊ)
to annoy; to harass; to cause disturbances 亦作「騷擾」

搔癢 (ㄙㄠ ㄧㄤˇ)
to scratch the itching place

【搾】 1979
ㅤㄓㄚˋ jah zhà
to press (for juice or oil); to extract; to squeeze; to wring: 貪官搾取人民的金錢。Corrupt officials squeeze people's money by pressure.

搾甘蔗 (ㄓㄚˋ ㄍㄢ ㄓㄜˋ)
to press sugar cane (for juice)

搾果機 (ㄓㄚˋ ㄍㄨㄛˇ ㄐㄧ) or 搾汁機 (ㄓㄚˋ ㄓ ㄐㄧ)
a juicer

搾果汁 (ㄓㄚˋ ㄍㄨㄛˇ ㄓ)
to press or squeeze fruit for juice

搾取 (ㄓㄚˋ ㄑㄩˇ)
①to extract; to press for juice or oil ②to extort; to exploit; to rob

搾菜 (ㄓㄚˋ ㄘㄞˋ)
a kind of salted vegetable root; the hot pickled mustard tuber

搾油 (ㄓㄚˋ ㄧㄡˊ)
to press (soybeans, peanuts, etc.) for oil; to extract oil

【搓】 1980
ㄘㄨㄛ tsuo cuō
1. to rub hands; to rub between the hands
2. to scrub
3. to twist (a thread, etc.) between the hands

搓板 (ㄘㄨㄛ ㄅㄢˇ)
a washboard

搓麻將 (ㄘㄨㄛ ㄇㄚˊ ㄐㄧㄤˋ)
to play mah-jong

搓麻繩 (ㄘㄨㄛ ㄇㄚˊ ㄕㄥˊ)
to make cord by twisting hemp fibers between the palms

搓弄 (ㄘㄨㄛ ㄋㄨㄥˋ)
to rub

搓線 (ㄘㄨㄛ ㄒㄧㄢˋ)
to twist a thread between the hands

搓手 (ㄘㄨㄛ ㄕㄡˇ)
to rub one's hands together

搓手頓腳 (ㄘㄨㄛ ㄕㄡˇ ㄉㄨㄣˋ ㄐㄧㄠˇ)
to wring one's hands and

stamp one's feet—to be anxious and impatient

搓繩子 (ㄘㄨㄛ ㄕㄥˊ ·ㄗ)
to make a rope by twisting the strands together

搓揉 (ㄘㄨㄛ ㄖㄡˊ)
to rub; to massage (a swelling, sore spot, etc.): 護士搓揉我扭傷的背。The nurse rubbed my lame back.

搓澡 (ㄘㄨㄛ ㄗㄠˇ)
to scrub and wash—a special service in a Chinese bath-house

搓作一團 (ㄘㄨㄛ ㄗㄨㄛˋ ㄧˋ ㄊㄨㄢˊ)
to roll or crumble (a sheet of paper, etc.) into a ball

搓碎 (ㄘㄨㄛ ㄙㄨㄟˋ)
to rub into powder or bits

搓衣裳 (ㄘㄨㄛ ㄧ ·ㄕㄤ)
to clean garments by rubbing

【搽】 1981
ㄔㄚˊ char chá
to rub on (ointment, etc.); to smear; to anoint; to paint

搽粉 (ㄔㄚˊ ㄈㄣˇ)
to powder (the face, etc.): 她在鼻子上搽粉。She powdered her nose.

搽脂抹粉 (ㄔㄚˊ ㄓ ㄇㄛˇ ㄈㄣˇ)
to apply powder and rouge; to doll up

搽藥 (ㄔㄚˊ ㄧㄠˋ)
to rub on some external medicine, ointment, etc.

【搗】 1982
ㄉㄠˇ dao dǎo
1. to thresh (grains); to hull or unhusk
2. to beat; to pound
3. to drive; to attack
4. to sabotage

搗米 (ㄉㄠˇ ㄇㄧˇ)
to hull rice with a pestle and a mortar

搗蛋 (ㄉㄠˇ ㄉㄢˋ)
to make trouble; to be mischievous; to cause a disturbance; to sabotage; to raise hell; heckling: 他是個調皮搗蛋的孩子。He is a mischievous boy.

搗爛 (ㄉㄠˇ ㄌㄢˋ)
to pound something until it becomes pulp

搗亂 (ㄉㄠˇ ㄌㄨㄢˋ)

to cause disturbance; to sabotage; to make trouble: 我正忙，你別搗亂。I am busy. Do not disturb me.

搗亂份子 (ㄉㄠˇ ㄌㄨㄢˋ ㄈㄣˋ ㄗ)
troublemakers; the "bad elements"; saboteurs

搗鬼 (ㄉㄠˇ ㄍㄨㄟˇ)
to play tricks; to gossip and cause trouble; to sow discord

搗毀 (ㄉㄠˇ ㄏㄨㄟˇ)
to smash; to sabotage; to damage or destroy: 我軍已搗毀敵人基地。Our army had destroyed the enemy base.

搗碎 (ㄉㄠˇ ㄙㄨㄟˋ)
to pound to pieces

搗藥 (ㄉㄠˇ ㄧㄠˋ)
to pound medicine in a mortar

【搖】 1983
ㄧㄠˊ yau yáo
1. to wag; to wave; to rock: 使用前搖一搖。Shake before using.
2. (said of one's confidence, determination, etc.) to sway, wobble, shake: 他的信心未為旁人的話所動搖。His determination was not shaken by anything people said.
3. to scull; to row (a boat, etc.): 你會搖船嗎? Can you row a boat?
4. to agitate; to incite; to annoy

搖擺 (ㄧㄠˊ ㄅㄞˇ)
to swing to and fro; to oscillate; oscillation; to vacillate; vacillation: 樹枝在風中搖擺。The branches of the trees swayed in the wind.

搖筆即來 (ㄧㄠˊ ㄅㄧˇ ㄐㄧˊ ㄌㄞˊ)
(said of a writer) to be brimming with ideas; to be gifted with the ability of writing quickly

搖盪 (ㄧㄠˊ ㄉㄤˋ)
to sway; to swing; to wobble; unstable (situations, etc.)

搖動 (ㄧㄠˊ ㄉㄨㄥˋ)
to shake; to rock; to wave; to sway: 服藥前先搖動瓶子。Shake the bottle before taking the medicine.

搖頭 (ㄧㄠˊ ㄊㄡˊ) or 搖首 (ㄧㄠˊ ㄕㄡˇ)

〔手部〕

〔手部〕

to shake one's head—in disapproval or out of sympathy

搖頭擺尾 (ㄧㄠˊ ㄊㄡˊ ㄅㄞˇ ㄨㄟˇ)
(literally) to shake the head and wag the tail (like a dog hoping to please the master)—to act obsequiously; to assume an air of complacency

搖頭晃腦 (ㄧㄠˊ ㄊㄡˊ ㄏㄨㄤˋ ㄋㄠˇ)
the funny manner of a half-witted scholar in reading a book—to look pleased with oneself; to assume an air of self-approbation or self-conceit

搖來搖去 (ㄧㄠˊ ㄌㄞˊ ㄧㄠˊ ㄑㄩˋ)
① to swagger along ② to swing to and fro

搖籃 (ㄧㄠˊ ㄌㄢˊ) or 搖籃兒 (ㄧㄠˊ ㄌㄢˊㄦ)
a cradle—(figuratively) the place of origin: 黃河是中國古代文化的搖籃. The Yellow River was the cradle of ancient Chinese culture.

搖籃曲 (ㄧㄠˊ ㄌㄢˊ ㄑㄩˇ)
a cradle song; a lullaby; a nursery song

搖鈴 (ㄧㄠˊ ㄌㄧㄥˊ)
to ring the bell

搖鈴的 (ㄧㄠˊ ㄌㄧㄥˊ˙ㄉㄜ)
a peddler who announces his presence by ringing a hand-bell

搖滾樂 (ㄧㄠˊ ㄍㄨㄣˇ ㄩㄝˋ)
rock'n'roll; rock music 亦作「搖擺樂」

搖鼓兒 (ㄧㄠˊ ㄍㄨˇㄦ)
a small drum with a handle and two suspending beads, one on each side, which beat the drum when the handle is twisted

搖撼 (ㄧㄠˊ ㄏㄢˋ)
to shake violently

搖會 (ㄧㄠˊ ㄏㄨㄟˋ)
to throw the dice to determine who should get the loan at the periodic meeting of a small loan association

搖晃 (ㄧㄠˊ ㄏㄨㄤˋ)
to shake (a bottle, etc.); to swing to and fro; shaky; unsteady

搖旗吶喊 (ㄧㄠˊ ㄑㄧˊ ㄋㄚˋ ㄏㄢˇ)
(literally) to wave flags and shout—to cheer or encour-age

搖錢樹 (ㄧㄠˊ ㄑㄧㄢˊ ㄕㄨˋ)
(literally) a money tree—a hen that lays golden eggs; anything or anyone one depends on as a steady dollar-earner

搖船 (ㄧㄠˊ ㄔㄨㄢˊ)
to row a boat

搖臂鼓舌 (ㄧㄠˊ ㄅㄟˋ ㄍㄨˇ ㄕㄜˊ)
to instigate by talking; to persuade someone (to do evil things) by sweet talk

搖手 (ㄧㄠˊ ㄕㄡˇ)
to wave one's hand (to indicate disapproval, admonition, etc.)

搖身一變 (ㄧㄠˊ ㄕㄣ ㄧ ㄅㄧㄢˋ)
① (often said of an upstart, turncoat, etc.) to transform into another person all of a sudden ② (in fairy tales) to change to another form in the twinkle of the eye

搖椅 (ㄧㄠˊ ㄧˇ)
a rocking chair; a swinging chair

搖曳 (ㄧㄠˊ ㄧˋ)
① wavering gently; shaking: 樹在風中搖曳. The trees were shaking in the wind. ② (said of light) flickering: 燭光在微風中搖曳. The candlelight flickered in the breeze. ③ (said of a girl's hips) to sway enticingly

搖搖擺擺 (ㄧㄠˊ ㄧㄠˊ ㄅㄞˇ ㄅㄞˇ)
to swagger; to swing

搖搖晃晃 (ㄧㄠˊ ㄧㄠˊ ㄏㄨㄤˋ ㄏㄨㄤˋ)
faltering; tottering; shaky

搖搖欲跌 (ㄧㄠˊ ㄧㄠˊ ㄩˋ ㄉㄧㄝˊ)
tottering; shaky (economy, regimes, etc.)

搖搖欲墜 (ㄧㄠˊ ㄧㄠˊ ㄩˋ ㄓㄨㄟˋ)
shaky; wobbling; on the verge of collapse; very unstable (regimes, authority, etc.): 這棟建築物搖搖欲墜. The building is shaky.

搖尾乞憐 (ㄧㄠˊ ㄨㄟˇ ㄑㄧˇ ㄌㄧㄢˊ)
(literally) to wag the tail and court favor—to fawn and be obsequious: 小狗向牠的主人搖尾乞憐. The puppy was fawning on its master.

【搢】 1984
ㄐㄧㄣˋ jinn jìn
1. to stick into
2. to shake

搢笏 (ㄐㄧㄣˋ ㄏㄨˋ)
to stick the official tablet into the girdle

搢紳 (ㄐㄧㄣˋ ㄕㄣ)
the gentry; the official class; the officialdom

【搘】 1985
ㄓ jy zhī
to support; to prop up

搘拄 (ㄓ ㄓㄨˇ)
a prop; a support

【搥】 1986
ㄔㄨㄟˊ chwei chuí
to pound; to beat; to strike with a stick or fist: 誰在用拳搥門? Who is pounding (on) the door with fists?

搥背 (ㄔㄨㄟˊ ㄅㄟˋ)
to massage the back by pounding with fists

搥打 (ㄔㄨㄟˊ ㄉㄚˇ)
to pound with fists; to beat

搥檯拍凳 (ㄔㄨㄟˊ ㄊㄞˊ ㄆㄞ ㄉㄥˋ)
(literally) to pound the table and slap the chair—in great rage

搥鼓 (ㄔㄨㄟˊ ㄍㄨˇ)
to beat a drum

搥胸頓足 (ㄔㄨㄟˊ ㄒㄩㄥ ㄉㄨㄣˋ ㄗㄨˊ)
to beat the breast and stamp the feet—in deep grief

搥腰 (ㄔㄨㄟˊ ㄧㄠ)
to massage the waist by light pounding

【搜】 1987
ㄙㄡ sou sōu
1. to search; to seek
2. to inquire into; to investigate

搜捕 (ㄙㄡ ㄅㄨˇ)
to hunt for (a fugitive); to search and arrest: 警察在樹林裡搜捕逃犯. The police hunted the woods for a fugitive.

搜狀 (ㄙㄡ ㄓㄨㄤˋ)
a search warrant

搜討 (ㄙㄡ ㄊㄠˇ)
to study carefully; to scrutinize and investigate

搜剔 (ㄙㄡ ㄊㄧ)
select; choosy; faultfinding; to pick; to weed out (textual errors)

搜尋 (ㄙㄡ ㄒㄩㄣˊ)
to hunt for (a fugitive)

搜羅 (ㄙㄡ ㄌㄨㄛˊ)

① to seek and invite (men of ability, specialists, etc.) ② to collect (rare stamps, antiques, etc.) ③ to scratch the bottom (for money, materials, etc.)

搜購(ㄙㄡ ㄍㄡ)
to collect or select for purchase

搜根剔齒(ㄙㄡ ㄍㄣ ㄊㄧ ㄔˇ)
to be very choosy; very particular about one's choice

搜括(ㄙㄡ ㄍㄨㄚ)
① to search ② to extort; to loot; to plunder

搜看(ㄙㄡ ㄎㄢˋ) or 搜閱(ㄙㄡ ㄩㄝˋ)
to search (a room, or building)

搜集(ㄙㄡ ㄐㄧˊ)
to seek and gather; to collect (rare stamps, books, data, evidence against a suspect, etc.) 他喜歡搜集昆蟲標本。He likes to collect insect specimens.

搜救(ㄙㄡ ㄐㄧㄡˋ)
to search for and rescue

搜檢(ㄙㄡ ㄐㄧㄢˇ)
to search and investigate

搜緝(ㄙㄡ ㄑㄧ)
to search for (a criminal, etc.); to hunt down (an escaped prisoner, etc.)

搜求(ㄙㄡ ㄑㄧㄡˊ)
to seek; to find; to look for

搜尋(ㄙㄡ ㄒㄩㄣˊ)
to search for; to seek and find

搜尋時間(ㄙㄡ ㄒㄩㄣˊ ㄕˊ ㄐㄧㄢ)
(computers) search time

搜章摘句(ㄙㄡ ㄓㄤ ㄓㄞ ㄐㄩˋ)
to search for chapters and pick sentences

搜查(ㄙㄡ ㄔㄚˊ)
to search (a house, a person, etc.)

搜出來(ㄙㄡ ㄔㄨ ·ㄌㄞ)
to search out; to find; to recover (stolen goods, evidence of crime, etc.)

搜身(ㄙㄡ ㄕㄣ)
to frisk

搜索(ㄙㄡ ㄙㄨㄛˇ)
to search; to reconnoiter

搜索枯腸(ㄙㄡ ㄙㄨㄛˇ ㄎㄨ ㄔㄤˊ)
to cudgel (or rack) one's brains (for new ideas, etc.)

搜索前進(ㄙㄡ ㄙㄨㄛˇ ㄑㄧㄢˊ ㄐㄧㄣˋ)
to advance and reconnoiter

搜索狀(ㄙㄡ ㄙㄨㄛˇ ㄓㄨㄤˋ)
a search warrant

【搭】 1988
ㄉㄚ **da dā**
1. to attach to; to join together; to add to: 張弓搭箭 to attach an arrow to the bow
2. to hang over: 把衣服搭在竹竿上。Hang the laundry on the bamboo pole.
3. to raise; to build (a shed, etc.); to put up; to pitch (a tent, etc.): 他們正在搭帳篷。They are pitching a tent.
4. to travel by; to take (a passage on a bus, train, boat, etc.): 他搭便車到車站。He hitched a ride to the station.
5. to help; to rescue
6. a short garment
7. a cover; to cover

搭把手(ㄉㄚ ㄅㄚˇ ㄕㄡˇ)
to give a helping hand: 您願意搭把手兒, 幫我一下嗎? Will you give me a hand?

搭伴兒(ㄉㄚ ㄅㄢˋㄦ)
to keep company; to go together

搭幫(ㄉㄚ ㄅㄤ)
(to travel, etc.) in company or together

搭配(ㄉㄚ ㄆㄟˋ)
① to match (colors, etc.) ② to select (items as a present to a person, or dishes for a feast, etc.) ③ to mate; to arrange in pairs or groups ④ (said of words) to go together: 這兩個片語搭配不當。These two phrases do not go together.

搭棚(ㄉㄚ ㄆㄥˊ)
to put up a shed or a makeshift shelter

搭姘頭(ㄉㄚ ㄆㄧㄣ ·ㄊㄡ)
to cohabit with somebody without being married

搭擋(ㄉㄚ ·ㄉㄤ)
a partner; to cooperate; to work together: 我們倆是老搭擋。We two are old partners.

搭談(ㄉㄚ ㄊㄢˊ)
to talk to; to have conversation with

搭客(ㄉㄚ ㄎㄜˋ)
① the passengers (of a bus, train, boat, plane, etc.) ② to take passengers

搭話(ㄉㄚ ㄏㄨㄚˋ)
to strike up a conversation with somebody

搭伙(ㄉㄚ ㄏㄨㄛˇ)
to eat regularly in (a mess, etc.)

搭夥(ㄉㄚ ㄏㄨㄛˇ)
to go into partnership; to join

搭機(ㄉㄚ ㄐㄧ)
to board an airplane

搭架子(ㄉㄚ ㄐㄧㄚˋ ·ㄗ)
① to put up a scaffold ② to put on airs; to look down a social nose upon

搭街坊(ㄉㄚ ㄐㄧㄝ ·ㄈㄤ)
to be neighbors

搭截題(ㄉㄚ ㄐㄧㄝˊ ㄊㄧˊ)
(in the Ching Dynasty civil service examinations) the designated composition title that consists of a combination of disconnected quotations from the classics, often ridiculous or meaningless, for the purpose of preventing speculation in advance on the part of the participants

搭腳(ㄉㄚ ㄐㄧㄠˇ)
to get a foothold

搭救(ㄉㄚ ㄐㄧㄡˋ)
to rescue; to help; to go to the rescue of: 警察從盜匪手裏搭救一人。The police rescued a man from bandits.

搭箭(ㄉㄚ ㄐㄧㄢˋ)
to get ready to shoot an arrow

搭橋(ㄉㄚ ㄑㄧㄠˊ)
to build a bridge: 工程師在河上搭橋。The engineers built a bridge over the river.

搭腔(ㄉㄚ ㄑㄧㄤ)
① to answer; to respond ② to talk to each other

搭線(ㄉㄚ ㄒㄧㄢˋ)
① to make contact ② to act as a go-between or matchmaker

搭住(ㄉㄚ ㄓㄨˋ)
to take up one's lodgings

搭車(ㄉㄚ ㄔㄜ)

〔手部〕

〔手部〕

to take a car, bus or train: 我們搭(火)車到那裏去。We took a train to go there.

搭乘(ㄉㄚ ㄔㄥ)
to travel by (air, ship, bus, etc.): 我搭乘火車上班。I go to work by train.

搭船(ㄉㄚ ㄔㄨㄢˊ)
to board a ship

搭訕(ㄉㄚ ㄕㄢˋ)
to converse heedlessly, or absent-mindedly

搭上(ㄉㄚ ㄕㄤˋ)
①to take (a bus, ship, plane, etc.): 你昨天搭上公車了嗎? Did you take the bus yesterday? ②to add to ③to make contact or liaison with

搭載(ㄉㄚ ㄗㄞˋ)
to carry (passengers): 這輛公車可搭載五十名乘客。The bus will carry fifty passengers.

【搶】 1989 1. ㄑㄧㄤˇ cheang　qiǎng
1. to take by force; to snatch; to rob; to loot: 他把信搶了過去。He snatched away the letter.
2. to do something in haste, as in an emergency; to rush
3. to oppose
4. to try to beat others in a performance; to vie for; to scramble for a ball, position, etc: 搶球to scramble for the ball

搶白(ㄑㄧㄤˇ ㄅㄞˊ)
to reprimand or to refute someone to his face: 我被他搶白了一頓。I was refuted by him rudely.

搶跑(ㄑㄧㄤˇ ㄆㄠˇ)or **搶走**(ㄑㄧㄤˇ ㄗㄡˇ)
to take away by force

搶渡(ㄑㄧㄤˇ ㄉㄨˋ)
to cross (a river) speedily

搶奪(ㄑㄧㄤˇ ㄉㄨㄛˊ)or **搶掠**(ㄑㄧㄤˇ ㄌㄩㄝˋ)
to rob; to loot; to plunder; robbery; looting: 士兵們搶掠屠殺了三天。The soldiers looted and massacred for three days.

搶灘(ㄑㄧㄤˇ ㄊㄢ)
to make a beach landing in face of enemy resistance; to make a forced beach land-

ing

搶購(ㄑㄧㄤˇ ㄍㄡˋ)
to try to beat others in making purchases (as in time of war, etc.); a shopping rush; panic buying

搶光(ㄑㄧㄤˇ ㄍㄨㄤ)
to take away by force everything that is movable

搶婚(ㄑㄧㄤˇ ㄏㄨㄣ)
to carry away a woman and marry her by force

搶劫(ㄑㄧㄤˇ ㄐㄧㄝˊ)
to rob; robbery; to take by force

搶劫一空(ㄑㄧㄤˇ ㄐㄧㄝˊ ㄧ ㄎㄨㄥ)
to loot or rob to the last pin

搶救(ㄑㄧㄤˇ ㄐㄧㄡˋ)
to make emergency rescue; to take urgent steps to save (precious articles, etc. from destruction): 醫生搶救病人。The doctors gave emergency treatment to the patient.

搶鏡頭(ㄑㄧㄤˇ ㄐㄧㄥˋ ㄊㄡˊ)
①to steal the show; to outshine others ②(said of cameramen) to fight for a vantage point in taking news pictures

搶親(ㄑㄧㄤˇ ㄑㄧㄣ)
to take a woman for marriage by force

搶修(ㄑㄧㄤˇ ㄒㄧㄡ)
to race against time in making a repair job: 工人搶修河堤。The workers rushed to repair dykes.

搶先(ㄑㄧㄤˇ ㄒㄧㄢ)
to rush ahead; to try to be the first; to try to beat others in performing something

搶出風頭(ㄑㄧㄤˇ ㄔㄨ ㄈㄥ ㄊㄡˊ)
to try to outshine others

搶收(ㄑㄧㄤˇ ㄕㄡ)
to rush in the harvest; to get the harvest in quickly

搶手貨(ㄑㄧㄤˇ ㄕㄡˇ ㄏㄨㄛˋ)
a commodity in great demand

搶上風(ㄑㄧㄤˇ ㄕㄤˋ ㄈㄥ)
to jockey for (an advantageous) position

搶嘴(ㄑㄧㄤˇ ㄗㄨㄟˇ)
①to try to beat others in being the first to talk ②

argumentative; assertive

搶案(ㄑㄧㄤˇ ㄢˋ)
(law) a case of robbery

搶運(ㄑㄧㄤˇ ㄩㄣˋ)
to rush delivery (of goods); to race against time in sending out or transporting (materials, cargoes, etc.)

【搶】 1989 2. ㄑㄧㄤ chiang　qiāng
1. head (winds); adverse
2. to strike; to hit; to knock

搶風(ㄑㄧㄤ ㄈㄥ)
head winds

【搦】 1990 ㄋㄨㄛˋ nuoh nuò
1. to hold; to seize
2. to challenge
3. to incite
4. to suppress; to restrain

搦管(ㄋㄨㄛˋ ㄍㄨㄢˇ)
to hold a pen—to write

搦戰(ㄋㄨㄛˋ ㄓㄢˋ)
to challenge to battle

【搧】 1991 (扇) ㄕㄢ shan　shān
1. to fan
2. to stir up; to incite
3. to slap on the face

搧風(ㄕㄢ ㄈㄥ)
to fan

搧動(ㄕㄢ ㄉㄨㄥˋ)
to stir up; to incite; to agitate

搧火(ㄕㄢ ㄏㄨㄛˇ)
to fan a fire

搧扇(ㄕㄢ ㄕㄢˋ)
to fan with a fan

搧耳光(ㄕㄢ ㄦˇ ㄍㄨㄤ)
to box the ear

【搨】 1992 (拓) ㄊㄚˋ tah tà
1. to take a rubbing of an inscription on stone, etc.
2. to make an exact copy with paper and a writing brush

搨碑(ㄊㄚˋ ㄅㄟ)
to take a rubbing of an inscription on a stone tablet

搨本(ㄊㄚˋ ㄅㄣˇ)or **搨片**(ㄊㄚˋ ㄆㄧㄢˋ)
a rubbing from a stone tablet or bronze vessel

【搬】 1993 ㄅㄢ ban bān
1. to move; to transport: 他們搬到鄉下了。They moved to

the country.

2. to present

搬東西 (ㄅㄢ ㄉㄨㄥ ˙ㄒㄧ)
to move things

搬動 (ㄅㄢ ㄉㄨㄥˋ)
to move; to shift: 不要搬動我桌上的東西。Don't move the things on my table.

搬弄 (ㄅㄢ ㄋㄨㄥˋ)
① to move something about ② to fiddle with ③ to show off; to display

搬弄是非 (ㄅㄢ ㄋㄨㄥˋ ㄕˋ ㄈㄟ)
to stir up or incite trouble between people; to say bad things about one person in the presence of another; to sow discord

搬來搬去 (ㄅㄢ ㄌㄞˊ ㄅㄢ ㄑㄩˋ)
to carry or move here and there

搬家 (ㄅㄢ ㄐㄧㄚ)
to move from one dwelling to another; to change one's residence: 我們下個月搬家。We're moving next month.

搬救兵 (ㄅㄢ ㄐㄧㄡˋ ㄅㄧㄥ)
to call in reinforcements; to ask for help

搬磚砸腳 (ㄅㄢ ㄓㄨㄢ ㄗㄚˊ ㄐㄧㄠˇ)
to hurt oneself by one's own doing; to boomerang

搬移 (ㄅㄢ ㄧˊ) or 搬遷 (ㄅㄢ ㄑㄧㄢ)
to move

搬運 (ㄅㄢ ㄩㄣˋ)
to move; to transport; to carry

搬運費 (ㄅㄢ ㄩㄣˋ ㄈㄟˋ)
carriage; freight: 這筆搬運費我付不起。The freight was more than I could pay.

搬運公司 (ㄅㄢ ㄩㄣˋ ㄍㄨㄥ ㄙ)
a moving company, or a transportation company

【搪】 1994 ㄊㄤˊ tarng tóng

1. to ward off rain; to keep out: 這棚子搪不住風雨。The shed cannot keep out wind and rain.

2. to parry

搪突 (ㄊㄤˊ ㄊㄨˊ)
abrupt; rude 參看「唐突」: 她說這話太搪突了。It's rude of her to say so.

搪饑 (ㄊㄤˊ ㄐㄧ)
to ward off hunger by eating whatever is available

搪眼 (ㄊㄤˊ ㄧㄢˇ)
to evade paying of debts 亦作「搪眼」

搪差使 (ㄊㄤˊ ㄔㄞ ˙ㄕ) or 搪差事 (ㄊㄤˊ ㄔㄞ ˙ㄕ)
to do something for appearance's sake; to perform a task perfunctorily; to gold-brick

搪瓷 (ㄊㄤˊ ㄘˊ)
enamel

搪塞 (ㄊㄤˊ ㄙㄜˋ)
to parry something; to stall something off; to perform a task perfunctorily or for form's sake: 搪塞他幾句。Stall him off with a vague answer.

【搐】 1995 ㄔㄨˋ chuh chù

spasm; cramp; convulsions; to shake involuntarily; to twitch

【掏】 1996 ㄊㄠ tau tāo

(掏)
to pull out; to take out (money, cigarettes, etc.): 他掏出槍來。He took out a gun.

【摁】 1997 ㄣˋ enn èn

1. to press (a doorbell, etc.)
2. to delay or hold

摁電鈴 (ㄣˋ ㄉㄧㄢˋ ㄌㄧㄥˊ)
to press an electric bell

【搵】 1998 ㄨㄣˋ wenn wèn

1. to wipe off (tears) 參看「拭淚」: 搵英雄淚 to wipe off a hero's tears
2. to press with fingers

【搠】 1999 ㄕㄨㄛ shuoh shuò

1. to thrust (at one's enemy)
2. to smear; to daub

【搗】 2000 ㄨˇ wuu wǔ

1. to cover; to conceal; to hide
2. to put into an airtight container (in cooking)

搗不住 (ㄨˇ ㄅㄨˋ ㄓㄨˋ)
cannot be covered or concealed: 這種事情是搗不住的。Such things cannot be covered.

搗蓋 (ㄨˇ ㄍㄞˋ)
① to cover up; to hide (the

truth); to keep secret ② to disguise; to masquerade

搗起來 (ㄨˇ ㄓ˙ ㄌㄞˊ)
① to imprison ② (cooking) to put food in airtight container (for steaming, etc.)

搗著耳朵 (ㄨˇ ㄓㄜ ㄦˇ ˙ㄉㄨㄛ)
to cover one's ears

搗上眼睛 (ㄨˇ ㄕㄤˋ ㄧㄢˇ ㄐㄧㄥ)
to cover up one's eyes

搗搗蓋蓋 (ㄨˇ ㄨˇ ㄍㄞˋ ㄍㄞˋ)
secretive; hiding and concealing

【搌】 2001 ㄓㄢˇ jaan zhǎn

1. to bind
2. to wipe; to mop

搌布 (ㄓㄢˇ ㄅㄨˋ)
a mopping cloth; a dishcloth: 用搌布將玻璃擦乾淨。Clean the glass with a mopping cloth.

【搴】 2002 ㄑㄧㄢ chian qiān

to pull or pluck up

搴旗斬將 (ㄑㄧㄢ ㄑㄧˊ ㄓㄢˇ ㄐㄧㄤˋ) or 搴旗取將 (ㄑㄧㄢ ㄑㄧˊ ㄑㄩˇ ㄐㄧㄤˋ)
(literally) to pull up the enemy flag and kill the opposing general—to defeat the enemy decisively

【搞】 2003 ㄍㄠˇ gao gǎo

1. to stir up; to cause trouble; to make a mess of; to mix up: 你把事情搞糟了。You have made a mess of things.
2. to do; to carry on; to be engaged in: 他是搞建築的。He is engaged in building.
3. to get; to secure: 幫我們搞點吃的來。Go and get us something to eat.
4. to set up; to start; to organize: 我們打算在學校搞個合唱團。We are planning to set up a chorus in our school.

搞把戲 (ㄍㄠˇ ㄅㄚˇ ㄒㄧˋ)
to play tricks

搞鬼 (ㄍㄠˇ ㄍㄨㄟˇ)
(said of a person) to cause trouble or pull legs in secret

搞垮 (ㄍㄠˇ ㄎㄨㄚˇ)
to overthrow; to cause to fail

搞好 (ㄍㄠˇ ㄏㄠˇ)
to make a good job of; to do well

【手部】

搞花樣（《ㄍㄠ ㄏㄨㄚ｜ㄤˋ）
to play tricks; to cheat; to deceive

搞七搞八（《ㄍㄠ ㄑ｜ 《ㄍㄠ ㄅㄚ）
to annoy; to cause mischief; to cause delay by doing a lot of useless things

搞錢（《ㄍㄠ ㄑ｜ㄢˊ）
to make money (by illegal means)

搞清楚（《ㄍㄠ ㄑ｜ㄥ ˙ㄔㄨ）
to make clear; to clarify (a matter, etc.)

搞政治（《ㄍㄠ ㄓㄥˋ ㄓˋ）
to play politics

搞運動（《ㄍㄠ ㄩㄣˋ ㄉㄨㄥˋ）
to carry on a movement (or campaign)

十一畫

【摘】 2004 ㄓㄞ jai zhāi （讀音 ㄓㄜˊ jer zhé）
1. to take off (one's hat, etc.); to pluck; to pick
2. to choose; to select
3. to jot down (notes)
4. to expose; to unveil (a conspiracy, etc.)

摘發（ㄓㄞ ㄈㄚ）
to make charges (of crimes)

摘奸發伏（ㄓㄞ ㄐ｜ㄢ ㄈㄚ ㄈㄨˊ）
to expose or reveal conspiracies and secrets

摘帽子（ㄓㄞ ㄇㄠˋ ˙ㄗ）
to take off one's hat

摘東補西（ㄓㄞ ㄉㄨㄥ ㄅㄨˇ ㄒ｜）
(literally) to pluck from the east to repair the west—to try very hard to make both ends meet

摘錄（ㄓㄞ ㄌㄨˋ）
an excerpt; to make an extract of a report, article, document, etc.

摘花（ㄓㄞ ㄏㄨㄚ）
to pluck flowers

摘記（ㄓㄞ ㄐ｜ˋ）
notes or observations (by an author); to jot down: 我摘記了要點。I jotted down the important points.

摘句（ㄓㄞ ㄐㄩˋ）
quotations; quotes; to make quotations: 這本書包括一些無

名作者的摘句。The book contained quotations from obscure authors.

摘取（ㄓㄞ ㄑㄩˇ）
to select; to pick; to take

摘下（ㄓㄞ ㄒ｜ㄚˋ）
to pick off (flowers, etc.); to take off: 他把眼鏡摘下來。He takes off his glasses.

摘除（ㄓㄞ ㄔㄨˊ）
to excise

摘要（ㄓㄞ ｜ㄠˋ）
① to summarize; to make an epitome ② an epitome; an abstract

摘由（ㄓㄞ ｜ㄡˊ）
to excerpt the most important points of an official document for filing purpose); excerpts (of an official document)

【摑】 2005 ㄍㄨㄛˊ gwo guó
to slap another on his face; to smack; to box: 她摑了她兒子耳光。She boxed her son on his ear.

【摜】 2006 ㄍㄨㄢˋ guann guàn
1. to throw to the ground
2. to be accustomed or used to

摜砲（ㄍㄨㄢˋ ㄆㄠˋ）
a type of firecracker which explodes when thrown to the ground with force

摜交（ㄍㄨㄢˋ ㄐ｜ㄠ）
to wrestle; wrestling

摜出（ㄍㄨㄢˋ ㄔㄨ）
to throw off

摜紗帽（ㄍㄨㄢˋ ㄕㄚ ㄇㄠˋ）
to resign a government post in anger; to quit one's job

【摟】 2007 1. ㄌㄡˇ lou lǒu
to drag; to pull; to drag away

【摟】 2007 2. ㄌㄡ lhou lōu
1. to hold up; to tuck up: 她摟起衣裳裝花。She held up the lower part of her long gown to put flowers.
2. to squeeze or extort (money, etc.)
3. to gather up; to collect; to rake together: 一位老婦人正在摟柴火。An old woman is raking up twigs and dead

leaves (for fuel)

摟攬（ㄌㄡ ㄌㄢˇ）
to monopolize (a project, business, etc.); to contract to do certain services

摟錢（ㄌㄡ ㄑ｜ㄢˊ）
to exact money (often said of dishonest officials, etc.)

摟算（ㄌㄡ ㄙㄨㄢˋ）
to calculate; to audit; to check an account

摟衣裳（ㄌㄡˇ ｜ ㄕㄤ˙）
to hold up the lower part of one's gown

【摟】 2007 3. ㄌㄡ loou lōu
to hold in the arms; to embrace; to hug

摟抱（ㄌㄡˇ ㄅㄠˋ）
to hold in the arms; to embrace

摟著（ㄌㄡˇ ˙ㄓㄜ）
to embrace; to press to one's chest: 母親摟著女兒。The mother embraced her daughter.

摟住（ㄌㄡˇ ㄓㄨˋ）
to hold in the arms; to embrace

【摒】 2008 ㄅ｜ㄥˋ binq bìng
1. to get rid of; to expel; to remove; to dismiss; to brush aside
2. to arrange in order

摒擋（ㄅ｜ㄥˋ ㄉㄤˇ）
to arrange in order; to pack up for traveling: 摒擋一切 to get everything ready

摒絕（ㄅ｜ㄥˋ ㄐㄩㄝˊ）
to cut loose entirely

摒棄（ㄅ｜ㄥˋ ㄑ｜ˋ）
to abandon; to get rid of: 我永遠不會摒棄我的朋友。I would never abandon my friends.

摒除（ㄅ｜ㄥˋ ㄔㄨˊ）
to get rid of; to remove (bad habits, evil thoughts, etc.): 他已摒除一切壞習慣。He has got rid of all his bad habits.

【摛】 2009 ㄔ chy chī
1. (said of fame, news, etc.) to spread
2. to brandish (a pen)
3. to be known widely

摛(彳 ㄔ)
to write a composition; to brandish a pen

摛藻(彳 ㄗㄠˇ)or 摛詞(彳 ㄘˊ)
to write in a flowery style; to use poetic diction; to weave an ornate passage

【摔】 2010 ㄕㄨㄞ shuāi shuǎi
1. to throw to the ground; to fling; to break: 我 把 腿 摔 斷 了。 I had a fall and broke my leg.
2. to get rid of; to shake off (a tail, etc.)
3. to fall down; to tumble; to lose one's balance: 他 從 馬 背 上 摔 下 來。 He fell off his horse.

摔破(ㄕㄨㄞ ㄆㄛˋ)
①to suffer bruises or injuries in a fall ②to break something by dashing it on the ground; to become broken after falling to the ground

摔牌(ㄕㄨㄞ ㄆㄞˊ)
(literally) to dash one's reputation to the ground—to smear one's reputation

摔倒(ㄕㄨㄞ ㄉㄠˇ)
①(said of a person) to fall down ②(in wrestling, etc.) to fell the opponent or to throw the opponent to the ground

摔掉(ㄕㄨㄞ ㄉㄧㄠˋ)
①to throw away; to dash down; to cast off: 不要把舊書 摔掉。Don't throw away used books. ②to shake off (a tail, annoying companion, etc.)

摔跟頭(ㄕㄨㄞ ㄍㄣ·ㄊㄡ)
①to fall flat②to fail ignominiously in an endeavor; to blunder

摔跤(ㄕㄨㄞ ㄐㄧㄠ)
to fall down; to suffer a fall: 他因摔 跤 而 受 傷。He was hurt by a fall.

摔角(ㄕㄨㄞ ㄐㄧㄠˇ)
to wrestle; wrestling

摔折(ㄕㄨㄞ ㄓㄜˊ)
to break (a bone, stick, etc.) after falling to the ground

摔傷(ㄕㄨㄞ ㄕㄤ)
to get hurt in a fall: 他滑雪 時摔傷了。 He got hurt in a

fall when he was skiing.

摔死(ㄕㄨㄞ ㄙˇ)
to fall to death; to be dashed to death

摔碎(ㄕㄨㄞ ㄙㄨㄟˋ)
to break into pieces after falling or being dashed to the ground; to shatter; to smash: 我 斟 茶 時，不 小 心 摔 碎 一個杯子。I shattered a cup when I tried to have a cup of tea.

【摭】 2011 ㄓˊ jyr zhí
to pick up from the ground; to take up; to collect

摭取(ㄓˊ ㄑㄩˇ)
①to pick up; to take; to collect ②to plagiarize

摭拾(ㄓˊ ㄕˊ)
to pick; to collect (samples, gossip, phrases)

摭拾遺文(ㄓˊ ㄕˊ ㄧˊ ㄨㄣˊ)
to make random quotes from obsolete writings

摭採(ㄓˊ ㄘㄞˇ)
to collect

【摧】 2012 ㄘㄨㄟ tsuei cuī
1. to break; to smash; to destroy; to injure; to harm: 我 們 的 軍 隊 無 堅 不 摧。Our army is capable of destroying any stronghold.
2. to damp
3. to cause to cease; to extinguish
4. to be sad and sorrowful; to grieve

摧敗(ㄘㄨㄟ ㄅㄞˋ)
①to beat the enemy ②to grieve

摧鋒陷陣(ㄘㄨㄟ ㄈㄥ ㄒㄧㄢˋ ㄓㄣˋ)
to mow down enemy troops and take their position

摧頹(ㄘㄨㄟ ㄊㄨㄟˊ)
①dilapidated; in ruins ②to idle about

摧枯拉朽(ㄘㄨㄟ ㄎㄨ ㄌㄚ ㄒㄧㄡˇ)
(literally) to destroy or pull apart something already in a state of ruin or decay —easily accomplished

摧壞(ㄘㄨㄟ ㄏㄨㄞˋ)
to destroy

摧毀(ㄘㄨㄟ ㄏㄨㄟˇ)
to destroy (enemy positions, heavy weapons, etc.)

摧堅折銳(ㄘㄨㄟ ㄐㄧㄢ ㄓㄜˊ ㄖㄨㄟˋ)
to defeat the enemy's crack troops and break their main force

摧陷(ㄘㄨㄟ ㄒㄧㄢˋ)
to smash enemy resistance and break their position

摧廓廓清(ㄘㄨㄟ ㄒㄧㄚˋ ㄏㄨㄛˋ ㄑㄧㄥ)
to defeat and completely wipe out (the forces of evil, etc.)

摧折(ㄘㄨㄟ ㄓㄜˊ)
to break; to destroy; to smash

摧殘(ㄘㄨㄟ ㄘㄢˊ)
①to destroy; to ruin: 切勿摧 殘你的健康。Never ruin your health. ②to humiliate

【摶】 2013 ㄊㄨㄢˊ twan tuán
1. to roll round with the hand; to knead
2. to rely on
3. to take or follow (a trail, etc.)

摶飯(ㄊㄨㄢˊ ㄈㄢˋ)
to roll rice balls

摶風(ㄊㄨㄢˊ ㄈㄥ)
(literally) to ride on the wind—to rise very quickly

摶土作人(ㄊㄨㄢˊ ㄊㄨˇ ㄗㄨㄛˋ ㄖㄣˊ)
to mold the mud and create man (according to the Chinese version of Genesis, man was created in this manner by Nü Wa (女媧), the mythical sister and successor of Fu-hsi (伏羲))

摶沙(ㄊㄨㄢˊ ㄕㄚ)
(literally) a ball of sand —lacking cohesion and unity of purpose

【摳】 2014 ㄎㄡ kou kōu
1. to raise
2. to grope for
3. to inquire into; to delve into
4. to dig with fingers (or something pointed): 他 在 地 上 摳 個 洞。He dug a hole in the ground.
5. to be stingy

摳破(ㄎㄡ ㄆㄛˋ)
to damage or injure by scratching

摳破除(ㄎㄡ ㄆㄛˋ ㄌㄧㄢˊ)
(to take action, measures, etc.) in disregard of the

「手部」

"face" of the other party

摳門兒(ㄎㄡ ㄇㄣˊㄦ)
stingy; miserly; niggardly

摳得緊(ㄎㄡˊㄉㄜˊㄐㄧㄣˇ)
to be very stingy

摳字眼兒(ㄎㄡˊㄗˋㄧㄢˇㄦ)
to pay too much attention to the different meanings of words; to find fault with diction

【摎】 2015 ㄐㄧㄡ jiou jiū
entwined—as branches of a tree

【摺】 2016 ㄓㄜˊ jer zhé
1. to fold (paper, etc.); to plait
2. a folder; a folded brochure
3. curved and winding
4. to pull and break

摺門(ㄓㄜˊㄇㄣˊ)
folding doors

摺刀(ㄓㄜˊㄉㄠ)
a folding knife; a pocket knife

摺疊(ㄓㄜˊㄉㄧㄝˊ)
to fold up (clothing, etc.); to plait together: 把信摺疊好放入信封。Fold the letter and put it in an envelope.

摺痕(ㄓㄜˊㄏㄣˊ)
a crease; a fold; a line made by folding

摺角(ㄓㄜˊㄐㄧㄠˇ)
to make a dog-ear; to dog-ear

摺裙(ㄓㄜˊㄑㄩㄣˊ)
a plaited skirt 亦作「百褶裙」:她喜歡穿摺裙。She likes to wear plaited skirts.

摺紙工(ㄓㄜˊㄓˇㄍㄨㄥ)
(in primary school) paper folding as a kind of manual training

摺尺(ㄓㄜˊㄔˇ)
a folding ruler

摺床(ㄓㄜˊㄔㄨㄤˊ)
a folding bed

摺扇(ㄓㄜˊㄕㄢˋ)or摺疊扇(ㄓㄜˊㄉㄧㄝˊㄕㄢˋ)
a folding fan

摺子(ㄓㄜˊㄗ)
a piece of paper folded into pages

摺奏(ㄓㄜˊㄗㄡˋ)
a memorial submitted to the emperor 亦作「奏摺」

【摸】 2017 ㄇㄛ mho mō (又讀 ㄇㄠ mhau māo)
1. to feel or touch lightly with fingers; to caress
2. to grope: 我們摸著走過黑暗的街道。We groped our way through the dark streets.
3. to try to find out; to feel out: 我摸透了這裡的情況。I have found out the situation here.
4. to seek after; to try to get at

摸不清(ㄇㄛˊㄅㄨˋㄑㄧㄥ)
do not understand; not quite sure

摸不著邊兒(ㄇㄛˊㄅㄨˋㄓㄜˊㄅㄧㄢㄦ)
(literally) unable to touch the edge—cannot understand at all

摸不著門兒(ㄇㄛˊㄅㄨˋㄓㄜˊㄇㄣˊㄦ)
(literally) cannot find the door—do not have the slightest idea; do not understand at all; cannot find the proper approach

摸不著頭腦(ㄇㄛˊㄅㄨˋㄓㄜˊㄊㄡˊㄋㄠˇ)
to be at a loss; cannot make head or tail of it: 我當時摸不著頭腦,不知如何說好。I was then at a loss for words.

摸摸(ㄇㄛˊㄇㄛ)
to feel; to touch: 讓我摸摸看。Let me have a feel.

摸骨相(ㄇㄛˊㄍㄨˇㄒㄧㄤˋ)
a kind of physiognomy practiced by blind fortunetellers who tell the fortune of clients by feeling their bones, especially facial bones

摸黑兒(ㄇㄛˊㄏㄟㄦ)
to do something in the dark: 他常常摸黑兒趕路。He often gropes his way on dark nights.

摸瞎(ㄇㄛˊㄒㄧㄚ)
to move around in the dark

摸彩(ㄇㄛˊㄘㄞˇ)
to draw lots to determine the prize winners in a raffle or lottery

摸索(ㄇㄛˊㄙㄨㄛˇ)
①to feel about; to feel (in one's pocket, etc.); to grope (in the dark, the meaning of, etc.): 我們在黑暗的走廊上

摸索著走。We groped our way along the dark corridor. ②to do things slowly

摸魚(ㄇㄛˊㄩˊ)摸灰(ㄇㄛˊㄏㄨㄟ)
to idle; to loaf on a job

【摽】 2018 ㄅㄧㄠ biau biāo
1. to motion (somebody) to go out
2. to strike
3. high; lofty
4. sometimes used in place of 標—to glorify, etc.
5. the razor of a sword
6. to throw away; to give up; to abandon

摽牌(ㄅㄧㄠ ㄆㄞˊ)
a rattan shield (used in ancient warfare)

摽末(ㄅㄧㄠ ㄇㄛˋ)
the edge of a sword

【摽】 2018 ㄆㄧㄠˋ peau piào
1. to fall; falling
2. to lock together: 這兩個男孩摽着胳膊走。These two boys walk locked arm in arm.

摽梅(ㄆㄧㄠˋㄇㄟˊ)
the fruit of a plum tree that are ripe and about to fall—(said of girls) marriageable age

【撬】 2019 (扦) ㄑㄧㄢ chian qiān
1. to stick into
2. a rod with a sharp point used by a tidewaiter to examine goods; anything of the similar shape
3. to trim feet (a special Chinese bathhouse service)

【摴】 2020 ㄕㄨ shu shū
1. comfortable; easy
2. an ancient Chinese gambling game roughly resembling today's dice game

摴蒲(ㄕㄨ ㄆㄨˊ)
an ancient Chinese gambling game roughly resembling today's dice game

【撂】 2021 ㄌㄧㄠˋ liaw liào
1. to put down; to lay down
2. to leave behind

撂跤(ㄌㄧㄠˋㄐㄧㄠ)
a form of wrestling

撂下(ㄌㄧㄠˋㄒㄧㄚˋ)

①to put down; to lay down
②to leave behind: 母親死了，撇下二個小孩。 The mother died, leaving two children behind.

撒手(ㄆㄧㄝ ㄕㄡˇ)
to pocket one's hands; to have nothing to do with it; to give up: 你不應該撒手不管。 You should not wash your hands of the matter.

【摩】 2022 (ㄇㄛ mo mó)
1. to chafe; to scour; to rub; to scrape: 岐嶺摩天。 The high mountains seem to scrape the sky.
2. friction
3. to feel with the hand
4. (now rarely) to work and encourage each other (especially in study)
5. to learn from long and constant study

摩門教(ㄇㄛ ㄇㄣˊ ㄐㄧㄠˋ)
Mormon Church, or Church of Jesus Christ of Latter-day Saints

摩登(ㄇㄛ ㄉㄥ)
modern; fashionable: 她穿上一襲摩登的服裝。 She is in a fashionable dress.

摩登女郎(ㄇㄛ ㄉㄥ ㄋㄩˇ ㄌㄤˊ)
a modern girl

摩頂(ㄇㄛ ㄉㄧㄥˇ)
the ordainment of a Buddhist monk

摩頂放踵(ㄇㄛ ㄉㄧㄥˇ ㄈㄤˋ ㄓㄨㄥˇ)
to scrape one's whole body from crown to heel—(figuratively) to dedicate oneself completely to the welfare of mankind

摩天樓(ㄇㄛ ㄊㄧㄢ ㄌㄡˊ)or 摩天樓(ㄇㄛ ㄊㄧㄢ ㄌㄡˊ)
skyscrapers

摩托(ㄇㄛ ㄊㄨㄛ)
a motor

摩托卡(ㄇㄛ ㄊㄨㄛ ㄎㄚˇ)
a motorcar, or automobile

摩托化(ㄇㄛ ㄊㄨㄛ ㄏㄨㄚˋ)
motorization

摩托車(ㄇㄛ ㄊㄨㄛ ㄔㄜ)
a motorcycle: 他昨天買了一輛嶄新的摩托車。 He bought a brand-new motorcycle yesterday.

摩納哥(ㄇㄛ ㄋㄚˋ ㄍㄜ)
Monaco

摩尼教(ㄇㄛ ㄋㄧˊ ㄐㄧㄠˋ)
Manicheism

摩羯宮(ㄇㄛ ㄐㄧㄝˊ ㄍㄨㄥ)or 摩羯座
(ㄇㄛ ㄐㄧㄝˊ ㄗㄨㄛˋ)
(astronomy)Capricornus

摩肩接踵(ㄇㄛ ㄐㄧㄢ ㄐㄧㄝ ㄓㄨㄥˇ)
to rub shoulders and follow one another in close succession—as in a crowd; to jostle one another in a crowd

摩拳擦掌(ㄇㄛ ㄑㄩㄢˊ ㄘㄚ ㄓㄤˇ)
①to get ready for a fight ②to be eager to start on a task

摩西(ㄇㄛ ㄒㄧ)
Moses, the Hebrew prophet who led the Israelites out of Egypt and delivered the Law during their years of wandering in the wilderness

摩擦(ㄇㄛ ㄘㄚ)
①to chafe; to scour ②friction; conflict and disagreement

摩擦力(ㄇㄛ ㄘㄚ ㄌㄧˋ)
frictional force

摩擦音(ㄇㄛ ㄘㄚ ㄧㄣ)
(phonetics) fricatives

摩擦生熱(ㄇㄛ ㄘㄚ ㄕㄥ ㄖㄜˋ)
Friction generates heat.

摩抄or 摩掌
①(ㄇㄚ ˙ㄙㄚ) to caress, touch, rub, etc. with the hand
②(ㄇㄚ ˙ㄙㄚ) to smooth out creases with the hand

摩爾人(ㄇㄛ ㄦˇ ㄖㄣˊ)
the Moors

【摹】 2023 (ㄇㄛ mo mó)
1. to copy; to make an exact copy
2. to model or pattern after; to imitate

摹本(ㄇㄛ ㄅㄣˇ)
①an exact copy of the original; a facsimile ②(now rarely) a kind of embroidered satin

摹仿(ㄇㄛ ㄈㄤˇ)
to copy; to model or pattern after; to imitate; to ape 亦作「模仿」

摹擬(ㄇㄛ ㄋㄧˇ)
to model or pattern after; to simulate

摹臨(ㄇㄛ ㄌㄧㄣˊ)
(art and calligraphy) to copy or imitate the works of ancient masters 亦作「臨摹」

摹古(ㄇㄛ ㄍㄨˇ)
to model or pattern after ancient (styles, customs, etc.)

摹刻(ㄇㄛ ㄎㄜˋ)
①to carve a replica ②a carved reproduction of an inscription

摹寫(ㄇㄛ ㄒㄧㄝˇ)
①to trace the original (writing, calligraphy, etc.) ②to describe; to depict

摹印(ㄇㄛ ㄧㄣˋ)
one of the eight calligraphic styles in the Chin Dynasty, usually used in today's seals

【摯】 2024 (ㄓˋ jyh zhì)
1. sincere; cordial
2. a Chinese family name

摯友(ㄓˋ ㄧㄡˇ)
a bosom friend: 他是我的摯友。 He is my bosom (or intimate) friend.

【研】 2025 (ㄧㄢˊ yán yún)
1. to grind; to powder
2. to study thoroughly

研經(ㄧㄢˊ ㄐㄧㄥ)
to study the classics

十二畫

【撅】 2026 (ㄐㄩㄝ jiue juē)
1. to break; to snap: 他把樹枝撅成兩段。 He broke the twig in two.
2. to stick up; to protrude

撅嘴小人(ㄐㄩㄝ ㄗㄨˇ ㄒㄧㄠˇ ㄖㄣˊ)
a mean fellow

撅嘴(ㄐㄩㄝ ㄗㄨㄟˇ)
to protrude the lips (in displeasure); to pout 亦作「噘嘴」

【撐】 2027 (撑) (ㄔㄥ cheng chēng)
1. to prop; to support: 她用兩手撐著下巴。 She held her chin in her hands.
2. to stretch tight; to burst: 他撐病了。 He is sick with bursting pressure.
3. to pole or punt (a raft or a

【手部】

boat)
4. to maintain; to keep up; to go on with
5. to open

撐不住 (イㄥ·ㄅㄨ ㄓㄨˋ)
too weak to prop up or support

撐破 (イㄥ ㄆㄛˋ)
to burst: 群衆把門撐破了。The crowd burst open the door.

撐得慌 (イㄥ·ㄉㄜ ㄏㄨㄤ)
having an excessively full stomach

撐得住 (イㄥ·ㄉㄜ ㄓㄨˋ)
strong enough to prop up or support: 木橋的力量撐得住一列火車嗎？Is a wooden bridge strong enough to support a railway train?

撐天柱地 (イㄥ ㄊㄧㄢ ㄓㄨˋ ㄉㄧˋ)
(literally) to support the heaven and pillar the earth —to assume an important responsibility in the nation

撐竿跳 (イㄥ ㄍㄢ ㄊㄧㄠˋ)
the pole vault

撐開 (イㄥ ㄎㄞ)
to prop open: 請你把麻袋撐開。Please hold open the gunny bag.

撐拒 (イㄥ ㄐㄩˋ)
to resist desperately

撐起 (イㄥ ㄑㄧˇ ·ㄌㄞ)
to prop up

撐住 (イㄥ ㄓㄨˋ)
to prop with a pole; to prop from under

撐持 (イㄥ ㄔˊ)
to prop up; to shore up; to sustain: 他們努力著撐持局面。They tried hard to shore up a shaky situation.

撐腸拄肚 (イㄥ ㄔㄤˊ ㄓㄨˇ ㄉㄨˋ)
to fill the stomach

撐場面 (イㄥ ㄔㄤˇ ㄇㄧㄢˋ) or (イㄥ ㄔㄤˇ ㄇㄧㄢˋ)
to maintain an outward show of prosperity; to keep up appearances

撐船 (イㄥ ㄔㄨㄢˊ) or 撐舟 (イㄥ ㄓㄡ)
to pole (or punt) a boat

撐傘 (イㄥ ㄙㄢˇ)
to prop open an umbrella

撐腰 (イㄥ ㄧㄠ)
to support, or to give backing to someone; to stand by someone

---

【撈】 2028 ㄌㄠ lāu
(讀音 ㄌㄠˊ lau láo)

1. to pull or drag out of the water
2. to fish up; to get by improper means: 他喜歡混水撈魚。He is fond of fishing in troubled waters.

撈本 (ㄌㄠ ㄅㄣˇ)
①to win back money (lost in gambling) ②to recover invested capital

撈摸 (ㄌㄠ ㄇㄛ)
to search underwater for; to feel about in water

撈起 (ㄌㄠ ㄑㄧˇ)
to recover from water, the riverbed, the sea bottom, etc.

撈取 (ㄌㄠ ㄑㄩˇ)
to fish for; to gain

撈屍 (ㄌㄠ ㄕ)
to recover the body of a drowned person

撈一票 (ㄌㄠ ㄧ ㄆㄧㄠˋ)
to make money, legally or otherwise: 走，咱們也撈一票去。Go, let's make money at it, too.

撈一把 (ㄌㄠ ㄧ ㄅㄚˇ)
to reap some profit; to profiteer

撈魚 (ㄌㄠ ㄩˊ)
to catch fish by a net, a bucket, etc.

撈什子 (ㄌㄠ ㄕㄜˊ·ㄗ)
a disgusting thing; an eyesore

【撒】 2029 1. ㄙㄚ sa sā

1. to relax; to ease
2. to loosen; to unleash
3. to exhibit; to display; to show

撒潑 (ㄙㄚ ㄆㄛ)
to behave rudely; to be in a tantrum; to be unreasonable and make a scene: 她又在撒潑了。She is in one of her tantrums again.

撒潑打滾 (ㄙㄚ ㄆㄛ ㄉㄚˇ ㄍㄨㄣˇ)
to fly into a tantrum (as a peevish child)

撒馬 (ㄙㄚ ㄇㄚˇ)
to give free rein to a horse

撒糞 (ㄙㄚ ㄈㄣˋ)
①to defecate; to empty the

---

bowels ②to talk rubbish

撒放 (ㄙㄚ ㄈㄤˋ)
to release; to unleash

撒放撒癡 (ㄙㄚ ㄈㄥˊㄙㄚ ㄔ)
headlong; reckless

撒旦 (ㄙㄚ ㄉㄢˋ)
Satan

撒地尼亞 (ㄙㄚ ㄉㄧˋ ㄋㄧˊ ㄧㄚˇ)
Sardinia 亦作「薩丁尼亞」

撒腿 (ㄙㄚ ㄊㄨㄟˇ) or 撒鴨子 (ㄙㄚ ㄧㄚ·ㄗ)
to take to one's heels; to run

撒溺 (ㄙㄚ ㄋㄧㄠˋ) or 撒尿 (ㄙㄚ ㄋㄧㄠˋ)
to urinate; to pass urine; to piss; to pee

撒賴 (ㄙㄚ ㄌㄞˋ)
to behave like a rascal; to show villainy; to make a scene; to act shamelessly

撒科打諢 (ㄙㄚ ㄎㄜ ㄉㄚˇ ㄏㄨㄣˋ)
to introduce comic remarks in dialogue

撒開 (ㄙㄚ ㄎㄞ)
①to get away ②to part ③to release; to let go

撒哈拉沙漠 (ㄙㄚ ㄏㄚ ㄌㄚˊ ㄕㄚ ㄇㄛˋ)
the Sahara Desert

撒歡兒 (ㄙㄚ ㄏㄨㄢ ㄦˊ)
to gambol; to frolic; to romp about (as a cat)

撒謊 (ㄙㄚ ㄏㄨㄤˇ)
to tell a lie; to lie: 不要對我撒謊。Don't lie to me.

撒嬌 (ㄙㄚ ㄐㄧㄠ)
①to show pettishness, as a spoilt child ②(said of a woman) to pretend to be angry or displeased

撒腳 (ㄙㄚ ㄐㄧㄠˇ)
to take to one's heels

撒酒風兒 (ㄙㄚ ㄐㄧㄡˇ ㄈㄥ ㄦ)
to show drunkenness

撒氣 (ㄙㄚ ㄑㄧˋ)
①to vent anger: 你別拿我撒氣嘛。Don't vent your anger on me. ②to let air out (from a ball, tire, etc.): 前輪撒氣了。The front tire is flat.

撒線 (ㄙㄚ ㄒㄧㄢˋ)
to let out the string (of a kite)

撒手 (ㄙㄚ ㄕㄡˇ)
①to relax the hold or grasp ②to neglect a responsibility: 這件事你不能撒手不管。You cannot neglect the

responsibility of the business.

撒手鐧 (ㄙㄚ ㄕㄡ ㄐㄧㄢ)
an unexpected thrust with the mace—(figuratively) the climaxing act; one's specialty

撒手西歸 (ㄙㄚ ㄕㄡ ㄒㄧ ㄍㄨㄟ)
to die

撒手塵寰 (ㄙㄚ ㄕㄡ ㄔㄣ ㄏㄨㄢ)
to pass away

撒嘴 (ㄙㄚ ㄗㄨㄟˇ)
to relax the bite

撒村 (ㄙㄚ ㄘㄨㄣ)
to use vulgar or profane language; to curse; to swear

撒野 (ㄙㄚ ㄧㄝˇ)
to act boorishly; to act wildly; to behave atrociously

撒網 (ㄙㄚ ㄨㄤˇ)
①to cast a net; to spread a net ②to invite relatives and friends on an occasion with the intention of collecting presents

【撒】 2029
2. ㄙㄚ saa sǎ
to scatter; to sprinkle; to disperse; to spread; to spill: 她在食物上撒鹽。She sprinkled food with salt.

撒播 (ㄙㄚ ㄅㄛ)
①broadcast sowing ②to sow

撒豆成兵 (ㄙㄚ ㄉㄡ ㄔㄥ ㄅㄧㄥ)
(literally) to turn sprinkled beans into soldiers—to work miracles

撒種 (ㄙㄚ ㄓㄨㄥˇ)
to sow seeds: 如何撒種，如何收穫。As a man sows, so shall he reap.

撒施 (ㄙㄚ ㄕ)
to spread fertilizer over fields; to broadcast (fertilizer)

撒水 (ㄙㄚ ㄕㄨㄟˇ)
to sprinkle or spray water

撒水車 (ㄙㄚ ㄕㄨㄟˇ ㄔㄜ)
a truck sprayer; a street sprinkler: 撒水車在街上撒水。A truck sprayer sprinkles the street with water.

撒散 (ㄙㄚ ㄙㄢˇ)
to spread; to scatter about; to strew; to sprinkle: 秋葉撒散在草地上。Autumn leaves strewed the lawn.

撒鹽 (ㄙㄚ ㄧㄢˊ)
①to sprinkle salt ②to snow

【撤】 2030
ㄔㄜˋ cheh chè
to remove; to withdraw; to take back; to withdraw; to evacuate

撤保 (ㄔㄜˋ ㄅㄠˇ)
to withdraw a guaranty

撤辦 (ㄔㄜˋ ㄅㄢˋ)
to fire a delinquent official and subject him to disciplinary action

撤兵 (ㄔㄜˋ ㄅㄧㄥ)
to withdraw troops: 敵人不得不自邊境撤兵。The enemy had to withdraw from the border.

撤廢 (ㄔㄜˋ ㄈㄟˋ)
to abolish; to rescind; to revoke

撤防 (ㄔㄜˋ ㄈㄤˊ)
to withdraw a garrison; to withdraw from a defended position

撤退 (ㄔㄜˋ ㄊㄨㄟˋ)
(said of troops) to move back or withdraw: 軍隊撤退。The troops withdrew.

撤離 (ㄔㄜˋ ㄌㄧˊ)
(said of troops) to move away or withdraw; to evacuate: 軍隊撤離碉堡。The soldiers evacuated the fort.

撤簾 (ㄔㄜˋ ㄌㄧㄢˊ)
(said of an empress dowager) to turn over the reign of government to the young monarch when he comes of age

撤回 (ㄔㄜˋ ㄏㄨㄟˊ)
to take back or withdraw: 原告已撤回起訴。The plaintiff has withdrawn charges.

撤去 (ㄔㄜˋ ㄑㄩˋ) or 撤退 (ㄔㄜˋ ㄔㄨˋ)
to remove; to withdraw; to pull out

撤席 (ㄔㄜˋ ㄒㄧˊ)
to remove a dinner table (after a feast is over)

撤銷 (ㄔㄜˋ ㄒㄧㄠ)
to abolish; to do away with

撤職 (ㄔㄜˋ ㄓˊ)
to remove from office: 那位警官必須撤職。That police officer must be removed from his position.

撤差 (ㄔㄜˋ ㄔㄚ)
to dismiss from a position; to fire: 你再遲到就要被撤差了。If you're late again, you will be dismissed (from your job).

撤懲 (ㄔㄜˋ ㄔㄥˊ)
to remove from office and subject to disciplinary action

撤出 (ㄔㄜˋ ㄔㄨ)
(said of troops) to withdraw or pull out

撤除 (ㄔㄜˋ ㄔㄨˊ)
to abolish; to do away with; to remove; to dismantle

撤守 (ㄔㄜˋ ㄕㄡˇ)
(said of a garrison) to withdraw or move back

撤任 (ㄔㄜˋ ㄖㄣˋ)
to remove from office

【撥】 2031
ㄅㄛ bo bō
1. to dispel; to remove
2. to move; to transfer
3. to poke
4. to distribute; to issue
5. to set aside; to set apart; to appropriate; to allocate: 撥幾個房間給新生。Set aside a few rooms for the new students.

撥付 (ㄅㄛ ㄈㄨˋ)
to make payment; to appropriate

撥電話號碼 (ㄅㄛ ㄉㄧㄢˋ ㄏㄨㄚˋ ㄏㄠˋ ㄇㄚˇ)
to dial a telephone number

撥動 (ㄅㄛ ㄉㄨㄥˋ)
①to move (the minute hand, etc.) by finger ②to turn (a switch)

撥剌 (ㄅㄛ ㄌㄚˋ)
①the sound of fish jumping out of water or a sound similar to that ②not in the proper position ③to draw the bow

撥浪鼓 (ㄅㄛ ㄌㄤˋ ㄍㄨˇ)
a kind of rattle for children; a rattle drum

撥亂反正 (ㄅㄛ ㄌㄨㄢˋ ㄈㄢˇ ㄓㄥˋ)
to put down rebellions and restore order; to bring order out of chaos

〔手部〕

撥弄(ㄅㄛ ㄋㄨㄥˋ)
① to toy with ② to move to and fro; to pluck (a stringed instrument); to fiddle with: 這個小女孩正在撥弄其琴弦。The little girl is plucking the strings of a fiddle. ③ to stir up (disputes)

撥弄是非(ㄅㄛ ㄋㄨㄥˋ ㄕˋ ㄈㄟ)
to stir up (disputes): 撥弄是非的人終將自取其辱。Those who like to stir up disputes will finally invite humiliation.

撥給(ㄅㄛ ㄍㄟˇ)
to appropriate (supplies, funds, etc.): 前房撥給你的朋友用。The front room is appropriated to your friend.

撥開(ㄅㄛ ㄎㄞ)
to push aside

撥款(ㄅㄛ ㄎㄨㄢˇ)
to issue or appropriate funds; an appropriation. 已撥款一千萬高建築新校舍之用。Ten million dollars has been appropriated for the new school buildings.

撥火棍(ㄅㄛ ㄏㄨㄛˇ ㄍㄨㄣˋ)
a poker (for stirring fire)

撥交(ㄅㄛ ㄐㄧㄠ)
to issue (supplies) to; to appropriate (funds) to

撥正(ㄅㄛ ㄓㄥˋ)
to set correct

撥準(ㄅㄛ ㄓㄨㄣˇ)
to set (a clock) correct

撥充(ㄅㄛ ㄔㄨㄥ)
to appropriate something for (a specific use)

撥冗(ㄅㄛ ㄖㄨㄥˇ)
to set aside a little time (for a special purpose) out of a tight schedule

撥雲見日(ㄅㄛ ㄩㄣˊ ㄐㄧㄢˋ ㄖˋ)
(literally) to dispel the clouds and see the sun—to give up sin in favor of virtue

撥用(ㄅㄛ ㄩㄥˋ)
to set apart for a specific use; to appropriate

【撳】 2032
ㄑㄧㄣˋ chinn qin
to press with the hand

撳鈕戰(ㄑㄧㄣˋ ㄋㄧㄡˇ ㄓㄢˋ)
push-button warfare

撳鈴(ㄑㄧㄣˋ ㄌㄧㄥˊ)
to push a bell

撳壓(ㄑㄧㄣˋ ㄧㄚ)
to press down; to push down

【捋】 2033
ㄒㄩㄣ shyun xun
to take; to pick; to pluck

捋得 or 捋是(ㄒㄩㄣˊ ㄉㄜ˙)
to pick here and there

【撇】 2034
ㄆㄧㄝ pie piē
1. to cast away; to throw away; to abandon; to neglect: 他撇下妻兒女。He abandoned his wife and children.
2. to skim

撇掉(ㄆㄧㄝ ㄉㄧㄠˋ)
to throw away; to cast away; to discard; to abandon: 不要把舊書撇掉。Don't throw away used books.

撇開(ㄆㄧㄝ ㄎㄞ)
to dismiss or exclude (from discussion or consideration); to set aside. 我們撇開這個問題不談。We'll dismiss this issue and not talk about it.

撇棄(ㄆㄧㄝ ㄑㄧˋ)
to cast away; to abandon; to give up; to discard

撇清(ㄆㄧㄝ ㄑㄧㄥ)
to pretend innocence

撇下不管(ㄆㄧㄝ ㄒㄧㄚˋ ㄅㄨˋ ㄍㄨㄢˇ)
① to disregard (one's responsibility): 工作暫且撇下不管。The work is disregarded temporarily. ② to desert (wife, children, etc.): 你不能撇妻兒撇下不管。You should not desert your wife and children.

【撇】 2034
ㄆㄧㄝˇ pie piě
1. (calligraphy) a stroke made in the lower left direction
2. to purse the mouth (in contempt or to resist an impulse to cry)

撇闌(ㄆㄧㄝˇ ㄌㄢˊ)
to raise money (for a drinking party, etc.) by drawing lots

撇嘴(ㄆㄧㄝˇ ㄗㄨㄟˇ)
to purse the mouth (in contempt, or to resist an impulse to cry)

【撓】 2035
ㄋㄠˊ nau náo
1. to bend; to daunt; to subjugate; to yield; to submit to superior force
2. to hinder; to obstruct: 罷工阻撓了工廠作業。A strike obstructed the work of the factory.
3. to scratch; to rub

撓敗(ㄋㄠˊ ㄅㄞˋ)or撓北(ㄋㄠˊ ㄅㄟˇ)
to suffer defeat

撓頭(ㄋㄠˊ ㄊㄡˊ)
to scratch one's head (when one faces a difficult problem)—(figuratively) difficult to tackle; knotty; full of difficulty: 這是撓頭的事。This is a knotty problem.

撓鈎(ㄋㄠˊ ㄍㄡ)
① a hook with a long handle used in fire fighting ② name of an ancient weapon

撓屈(ㄋㄠˊ ㄑㄩ)
to yield; to submit; to give way

撓性(ㄋㄠˊ ㄒㄧㄥˋ)
pliant; flexibility

撓折(ㄋㄠˊ ㄓㄜˊ)
to bend and break

撓癢處(ㄋㄠˊ ㄧㄤˇ ㄔㄨˋ)
to scratch an itchy part

【撙】 2036
ㄗㄨㄣˇ tzoen zŭn
1. to comply with
2. to economize; to save: 她每個月都撙下一些錢。She saved some money every month.

撙節(ㄗㄨㄣˇ ㄐㄧㄝˊ)
① to follow rule and order; to restrain; to exercise self-restraint ② to economize

撙節開支(ㄗㄨㄣˇ ㄐㄧㄝˊ ㄎㄞ ㄓ)
to economize expenses; to retrench

撙省(ㄗㄨㄣˇ ㄕㄥˇ)
to economize: 我們必須撙省燈光和燃料。We must economize on light and fuel.

【撚】 2037
ㄋㄧㄢˇ nean niǎn
to twist with fingers; to toy with

撚虎鬚(ㄋㄧㄢˇ ㄏㄨˇ ㄒㄩ)
to twist a tiger's whiskers—recklessly bold

撚錢(ㄋㄧㄢˇ ㄑㄧㄢˊ)
to spin a coin (for amusement, etc.)

撚香(ㄋㄧㄢˇㄒㄧㄤ)
to burn joss sticks in worship

撚鬚(ㄋㄧㄢˇㄒㄩ)
to toy with or stroke one's beard

撚指間(ㄋㄧㄢˇㄓˇㄐㄧㄢ)
at the snap of one's fingers—in an instant; in a jiffy

撚酸(ㄋㄧㄢˇㄙㄨㄢ)
to be jealous

【撕】 ㄙ sy sī 2038
to tear; to rip: 他將那封信撕得粉碎。He tore the letter into tiny pieces.

撕破(ㄙㄆㄛˋ)
to tear; to rip: 紙很容易撕破。Paper tears easily

撕票(ㄙㄆㄧㄠˋ)
to kill a hostage

撕打(ㄙㄉㄚˇ)
to beat up; to maul

撕掉(ㄙㄉㄧㄠˋ)
to tear up; to tear off: 誰撕掉佈告? Who has torn the notice down from the notice board?

撕爛(ㄙㄌㄢˋ)
to tear to shreds; to rip to pieces

撕開(ㄙㄎㄞ)
to tear open; to rip open: 他撕開信封。He tore the envelope open.

撕毀(ㄙㄏㄨㄟˇ)
to destroy by tearing; to tear; to rip

撕去(ㄙㄑㄩˋ)or撕走(ㄙㄗㄡˇ)
to tear off; to tear away

撕下(來)(ㄙㄒㄧㄚˋ(˙ㄌㄞ))
to tear off (a leaf from a book, calendar, etc.): 撕下他的假面具。Tear off his mask.

撕碎(ㄙㄙㄨㄟˋ)
to tear or rip to pieces: 他將窗帘撕碎。He ripped the curtains to pieces.

【撞】 ㄓㄨㄤˋ juang zhuàng 2039

1. to bump; to run into; to collide; to dash
2. to meet by chance

撞壁(ㄓㄨㄤˋㄅㄧˋ)
to be up against a blank wall—to be faced with difficulties

撞破(ㄓㄨㄤˋㄆㄛˋ)
①to hurt or damage by bumping ②to surprise somebody in an illegal act or awkward situation

撞騙(ㄓㄨㄤˋㄆㄧㄢˋ)
to swindle: 誠實的人不會撞騙。An honest man does not swindle.

撞大運(ㄓㄨㄤˋㄉㄚˋㄩㄣˋ)
to try one's luck

撞倒(ㄓㄨㄤˋㄉㄠˇ)
to knock down by bumping: 牆被卡車撞倒了。The wall was knocked down by a truck.

撞個滿懷(ㄓㄨㄤˋ˙ㄍㄜ(ㄇㄢˇㄏㄨㄞˊ)
to bump into somebody

撞鬼(ㄓㄨㄤˋㄍㄨㄟˇ)
①to encounter a ghost ②to run around in distraction

撞開(ㄓㄨㄤˋㄎㄞ)
to knock away by bumping; to burst open

撞壞(ㄓㄨㄤˋㄏㄨㄞˋ)
to damage by bumping: 一輛公車撞壞了他的汽車。A bus ran into his car and damaged it.

撞擊(ㄓㄨㄤˋㄐㄧ)
to ram; to dash; to strike: 波浪撞擊岩石。The waves dashed on the rocks.

撞見(ㄓㄨㄤˋㄐㄧㄢˋ)
to meet unexpectedly; to run into; to bump into

撞球(ㄓㄨㄤˋㄑㄧㄡˊ)
①billiards ②billiard balls

撞球場(ㄓㄨㄤˋㄑㄧㄡˊㄔㄤˇ)or撞球間(ㄓㄨㄤˋㄑㄧㄡˊㄐㄧㄢ)
a billiard room; a billiard saloon; a billiard parlor; a poolroom

撞針(ㄓㄨㄤˋㄓㄣ)
the firing pin (in a firearm)

撞傷(ㄓㄨㄤˋㄕㄤ)
to injure by bumping (as in car accidents)

撞入(ㄓㄨㄤˋㄖㄨˋ)or撞進(ㄓㄨㄤˋㄐㄧㄣˋ)
to thrust into; to break into: 他撞入房間。He burst into the room.

撞死(ㄓㄨㄤˋㄙˇ)
to kill by bumping (as in car accidents)

【撟】 1.(矯)ㄐㄧㄠˇ jeau jiǎo 2040
to put right; to set right

撟捷(ㄐㄧㄠˇㄐㄧㄝˊ)
nimble; agile 亦作「矯捷」

【撟】 2.ㄐㄧㄠ jiau jiāo 2040
to raise; to lift up

撟舌(ㄐㄧㄠㄕㄜˊ)
to raise the tongue in a futile effort to speak; to become speechless (as a result of extreme fear or surprise); tongue-tied

【撦】 (扯)ㄔㄜˇ chee chě 2041
to tear

撦破(ㄔㄜˇㄆㄛˋ)
to tear open 亦作「扯破」

【撫】 ㄈㄨˇ fuu fǔ 2042

1. to stroke; to touch
2. to soothe; to comfort; to console; to relieve
3. to bring up; to rear; to nurture; to foster

撫嘆興歎(ㄈㄨˇㄊㄢˋㄒㄧㄥㄊㄢˋ)
to sigh in disappointment (said of one living in retirement but still burning with ambition)

撫摸(ㄈㄨˇㄇㄛ)or撫摩(ㄈㄨˇㄇㄛˊ)
to pass one's hand over; to feel; to stroke

撫臺(ㄈㄨˇㄊㄞˊ)
a provincial governor (during the Ching Dynasty)

撫弄(ㄈㄨˇㄋㄨㄥˋ)
to stroke; to fondle

撫孤(ㄈㄨˇㄍㄨ)
to bring up orphans

撫棺痛哭(ㄈㄨˇㄍㄨㄢㄊㄨㄥˋㄎㄨ)
to mourn loudly over a coffin

撫躬自問(ㄈㄨˇㄍㄨㄥㄗˋㄨㄣˋ)
to perform self-examination

撫劍(ㄈㄨˇㄐㄧㄢˋ)
①to place the left hand on the sword one wears ②to hold a sword

撫今追昔(ㄈㄨˇㄐㄧㄣㄓㄨㄟㄒㄧˊ)
to contemplate the present and recall the past with emotion

撫軍(ㄈㄨˇㄐㄩㄣ)
①a provincial governor

〔手部〕

(during the Ching Dynasty)
②a military title in ancient
China

撫琴(ㄈㄨ ㄑㄧㄣˊ)
to strum a stringed instrument

撫恤(ㄈㄨ ㄒㄩˋ)
to relieve; to comfort and
compensate a bereaved family

撫恤金(ㄈㄨ ㄒㄩˋ ㄐㄧㄣ)
a pension: 他靠撫恤金過日子。
He lives on a pension.

撫掌(ㄈㄨ ㄓㄤˇ)
to clap hands (to show happiness)

撫順(ㄈㄨ ㄕㄨㄣˋ)
Fushun (a city in Liaoning
Province)

撫字(ㄈㄨ ㄗˋ)
①to love children ②(said
of government officials in
old China) to treat the people kindly

撫存(ㄈㄨ ㄘㄨㄣˊ)
to comfort and relieve

撫綏(ㄈㄨ ㄙㄨㄟ)
to soothe the people

撫愛(ㄈㄨ ㄞˋ)
to caress; to fondle

撫養(ㄈㄨ ㄧㄤˇ)
to bring up; to rear; to nurture: 是他祖母把他撫養大的。It
was his grandmother that
brought him up.

撫慰(ㄈㄨ ㄨㄟˋ)
to soothe; to comfort; to
console: 母親用手撫慰孩子。
The child was caressed by
his mother with her hand.

撫育(ㄈㄨ ㄩˋ)
to bring up; to rear: 她獨力
撫育子女。She reared all her
children alone.

【播】 2043
ㄅㄛ boh bō
(舊音 ㄅㄛ bò bòˇ)

1. to sow; to seed: 尚不到播種
的時候。It's not yet time to
sow.

2. to spread; to propagate: 這
消息很快傳播開了。The news
soon spread.

3. to move

4. to cast away; to abandon

播報(ㄅㄛ ㄅㄠˋ)
to broadcast

播放(ㄅㄛ ㄈㄤˋ)
to broadcast (news, etc.) on
the air: 這家電台正在播放晚間
新聞。The station is broadcasting the evening news.

播湯(ㄅㄛ ㄊㄤ)
to live in vagrancy; to be
homeless

播弄(ㄅㄛ ㄋㄨㄥˋ)
①to stir up disputes on purpose ②to make a mess (of
something)

播棄(ㄅㄛ ㄑㄧˋ)
to throw away; to cast
away; to abandon; to discard

播遷(ㄅㄛ ㄑㄧㄢ)
to live a wandering life

播種(ㄅㄛ ㄓㄨㄥˇ)
to sow seed; to sow; to seed

播種機(ㄅㄛ ㄓㄨㄥˇ ㄐㄧ)
a sowing machine; a seeder;
a drill (for row seeding)

播散(ㄅㄛ ㄙㄢˋ)
to disseminate

播送(ㄅㄛ ㄙㄨㄥˋ)
to broadcast (messages, programs, etc.); to transmit by
radio

播音(ㄅㄛ ㄧㄣ)
to make broadcasts; to
transmit; transmission

播音員(ㄅㄛ ㄧㄣ ㄩㄢˊ)
a broadcaster; an announcer

播揚(ㄅㄛ ㄧㄤˊ)
to propagate and uphold

【撩】 2044
1. ㄌㄧㄠ liāo liáo

1. to provoke; to excite; to stir
up; to tease; to tantalize
2. disorderly; confused

撩撥(ㄌㄧㄠ ㄅㄛ)
to provoke; to entice

撩蜂剔蠍(ㄌㄧㄠˊ ㄈㄥ ㄊㄧ ㄒㄧㄝ)
(literally) to provoke the
bees and vex the scorpions
—to provoke a wicked being
and bring trouble upon oneself

撩逗(ㄌㄧㄠ ㄉㄡˋ)
to provoke; to entice

撩動肝火(ㄌㄧㄠ ㄉㄨㄥˋ ㄍㄢ ㄏㄨㄛˇ)
to stir up anger

撩慄(ㄌㄧㄠ ㄌㄧˋ)
dreary; dismal 亦作「憭慄」

撩亂(ㄌㄧㄠ ㄌㄨㄢˋ)
confused; disorderly

撩情(ㄌㄧㄠ ㄑㄧㄥˊ)
to flirt

撩人(ㄌㄧㄠ ㄖㄣˊ)
to make one excited

【撩】 2044
2. ㄌㄧㄠˇ lhiau liǎo

1. to raise; to hold up
2. to sprinkle

撩起(ㄌㄧㄠˇ ㄑㄧˇ)
to raise or lift up (a curtain,
screen, etc.)

撩水(ㄌㄧㄠˇ ㄕㄨㄟˇ)
to scoop water with the
hands to sprinkle it

撩衣(ㄌㄧㄠˇ ㄧ)
to hold up the lower part of
a garment

【撬】 2045
1. ㄑㄧㄠˋ chiaw qiào
to pry; to prize

撬不動(ㄑㄧㄠˋ ㄅㄨˋ ㄉㄨㄥˋ)
incapable of prying or being
pried

撬不開(ㄑㄧㄠˋ ㄅㄨˋ ㄎㄞ)
incapable of prying open or
being pried open

撬門(ㄑㄧㄠˋ ㄇㄣˊ)
to pry a door open

撬開(ㄑㄧㄠˋ ㄎㄞ)
to open by prying

撬孔(ㄑㄧㄠˋ ㄎㄨㄥˇ)
to make a hole by prying

【撬】 2045
2. ㄑㄧㄠ chiau qiāo
to raise; to lift

【撲】 2046
ㄆㄨ pu pū

1. to beat; to strike; to pound
2. to dash; to smash
3. to throw oneself on; to
spring at
4. to flap; to flutter

撲鼻(ㄆㄨ ㄅㄧˊ)
to come suddenly into one's
nostrils (as a strong smell):
香氣撲鼻。A sweet smell
greeted us.

撲(ㄆㄨ ㄊㄨㄥ)
throbs (of the heart, etc.); to
throb: 他的心因興奮而撲撲地
跳。His heart was throbbing
with excitement.

撲滿(ㄆㄨ ㄇㄢˇ)
a savings box; a piggy bank

撲滅(ㄆㄨ ㄇㄧㄝˋ)
to exterminate (vermins); to
extinguish (a fire)

Left column (entries partially cut off at margin)

……(ㄨㄚ ㄇㄧㄥˊ)
o brush the face (as a gust f wind): 和風摸面而來。The ght breeze brushes my ace.

……刑
logging; corporal punishment

……分
① to powder (one's face) ② alcum powder; face powder

……(ㄨㄚˊ)
o beat; to pat; to swat

……蛾(ㄨㄚ ㄌ ㄜˊ)
a night butterfly

……也(ㄨㄚˇ)
① all over the ground ② to ie on the ground ③ the ound of an object dropping nto the water, etc. ④ suddenly

……跌(ㄊㄨㄚ ㄌㄧㄝˊ)
umping and falling (in restling, etc.)

……鼕(ㄊㄨㄚ ·ㄌ)
The sound of jumping; a hump ② to dance awkwardy ③ to be extravagant in pending ④ to make a big plash

……(ㄊㄨㄚ ㄊㄨㄛ)
a plop; a splash; a thump

……翅(ㄊㄨㄚ ㄔˋ)
whiz; the sound of a bird lapping its wings

……落(ㄊㄨㄚ ㄌㄨㄛˋ)
cattered about

……來(ㄊㄨㄚ 《ㄨㄞ ㄌㄞˊ)
o come in a dash

……克(ㄊㄨㄚ ·ㄎㄜ)
oker (a gambling game)

……牌
laying cards

……空(ㄊㄨㄚ ㄎㄨㄥ)
① to fail to meet a person ne intended to meet ② to o a thing in vain

……救(ㄊㄨㄚ ㄐㄧˋ)
o fight (a fire)

……(ㄊㄨㄚ ㄏㄨㄚ)
① a chuckle ② a splash

……(ㄊㄨㄚ ㄕˊ)
o seize for prey

撲殺(ㄆㄨ ㄕㄚ)
to kill

撲朔迷離(ㄆㄨ ㄕㄨㄛ ㄇㄧˊ ㄌㄧˊ)
①(said of a person) to look both like a man and a woman ② vague or ambiguous; complicated and confusing

撲簌簌(ㄆㄨ ㄙㄨˋ ㄙㄨˋ)
① dropping; trickling down ② rolling

撲兒(ㄆㄨㄦ)
a powder puff 亦作「粉撲兒」

【撰】 2047　ㄓㄨㄢˋ juann zhuan
to write; to compose: 他常為報紙撰稿。He often writes articles for newspapers.

撰擬(ㄓㄨㄢˋ ㄋㄧˊ)
to draw up or compose (a document)

撰錄(ㄓㄨㄢˋ ㄌㄨˋ)
to make a selection

撰稿(ㄓㄨㄢˋ ㄍㄠˇ)
to prepare manuscripts; to write

撰稿人(ㄓㄨㄢˋ ㄍㄠˇ ㄖㄣˊ)
a copywriter; a writer

撰寫(ㄓㄨㄢˋ ㄒㄧㄝˇ)
to write or compose (usually light works)

撰著(ㄓㄨㄢˋ ㄓㄨˋ)
to write or author (usually imposing works)

撰述(ㄓㄨㄢˋ ㄕˋ)
to write an account of (facts, happenings, etc.); to narrate

撰文(ㄓㄨㄢˋ ㄨㄣˊ)
to compose; to write

【撮】 2048
1. ㄘㄨㄛ tsuo cuo
(又讀 ㄘㄨㄛˊ tsuoh cuo)
1. to take with fingers
2. to gather
3. to extract; to summarize
4. a pinch of: 一小撮鹽 a pinch of salt

撮土(ㄘㄨㄛ ㄊㄨˇ)
① to take earth with fingers ② a pinch of earth

撮牛奶(ㄘㄨㄛ ㄋㄧㄡˊ ㄋㄞˇ)
to milk a cow

撮弄(ㄘㄨㄛ ㄋㄨㄥˋ)
① to juggle ② to instigate; to incite ③ to make fun of;

to kid; to make a fool of

撮口呼(ㄘㄨㄛ ㄎㄡˇ ㄏㄨ)or(ㄔㄨㄛ ㄎㄡˇ ㄏㄨ)
(traditional Chinese phonetics) rhymes containing a rounded front vowel as in 魚 (yü)、圓 (yüan)、虛 (hsü), etc.

撮合(ㄘㄨㄛ ㄏㄜˊ)
to bring (two persons or parties) together; to make a match

撮合山(ㄘㄨㄛ ㄏㄜˊ ㄕㄢ)
a matchmaker

撮箕(ㄘㄨㄛ ㄐㄧ)
a dustpan

撮壤(ㄘㄨㄛ ㄖㄤˇ)
a pinch of soil

撮要(ㄘㄨㄛ ㄧㄠˋ)
to select what is important; to make extracts; a synopsis; an abstract; an extract

撮影(ㄘㄨㄛ ㄧㄥˇ)
photography

【撮】 2048
2. ㄗㄨㄛˇ tzuoo zuo
a tuft (of hair, grass, etc.)

撮子(ㄗㄨㄛˇ ·ㄗ)
a tuft (of hair)

【撝】 2049　ㄏㄨㄟ huei hui
1. to wave; to brandish
2. modest; humble

撝謙(ㄏㄨㄟ ㄑㄧㄢ)
modest; humble

撝損(ㄏㄨㄟ ㄙㄨㄣˇ)
to humble 亦作「撝遜」

撝挹(ㄏㄨㄟ ㄧˋ)
to be extremely modest or polite

【撣】 2050　(撢) ㄉㄢˇ daan dan
1. to dust; to brush lightly; to whisk
2. a duster

撣灰(ㄉㄢˇ ㄏㄨㄟ)
to brush off dust; to dust: 請更加小心地撣灰。Please dust more carefully.

撣子(ㄉㄢˇ ·ㄗ)
a duster: 雞毛撣子 a feather duster

十三畫

【撻】 2051　ㄊㄚˋ tah ta
to strike; to chastise; to flog;

〔手部〕

to whip

撻伐 (ㄊㄚˋ ㄷㄚˊ)
to send troops to punish; to launch a punitive expedition: 大張撻伐 to declare war on a country to punish its iniquities

撻罰 (ㄊㄚˋ ㄈㄚˊ)
flogging; corporal punishment; to flog

撻市 (ㄊㄚˋ ㄕˋ)
to disgrace somebody in public

撻辱 (ㄊㄚˋ ㄖㄨˋ)
to beat and disgrace

【撼】 2052
ㄏㄢˋ hann hàn
to shake; to rock; to jolt; to joggle

撼頓 (ㄏㄢˋ ㄉㄨㄣˋ)
to shake; to stagger; to totter

撼動 (ㄏㄢˋ ㄉㄨㄥˋ)
to shake; to rock

撼天動地 (ㄏㄢˋ ㄊㄧㄢ ㄉㄨㄥˋ ㄉㄧˋ)
to shake both the heaven and the earth—to cause a great sensation

撼落 (ㄏㄢˋ ㄌㄨㄛˋ)
to shake and drop; to shake down

撼山岳，泣鬼神 (ㄏㄢˋ ㄕㄢ ㄩㄝˋ，ㄑㄧˋ ㄍㄨㄟˇ ㄕㄣˊ)
so moving or affecting as to shake the mountains and wring tears from the spirits

撼樹 (ㄏㄢˋ ㄕㄨˋ)
to shake a tree

撼搖 (ㄏㄢˋ ㄧㄠˊ)
to shake; to rock; to jolt; to joggle

【撾】 2053
ㄓㄨㄚ jua zhuā
to beat; to strike

撾鼓 (ㄓㄨㄚ ㄍㄨˇ)
to beat a drum

【擂】 2054
1. ㄌㄟˊ lei léi
1. to grind; to pestle
2. to beat; to hit: 我擂了他一下。 I give him a punch.

擂鉢 (ㄌㄟˊ ㄅㄛ)
a mortar (for grinding)

擂鼓 (ㄌㄟˊ ㄍㄨˇ)
to beat a drum

擂鼓鳴鑼 (ㄌㄟˊ ㄍㄨˇ ㄇㄧㄥˊ ㄌㄨㄛˊ)
to beat the drum and strike the gong—to have fanfare

【擂】 2054
2. ㄌㄟˋ ley lèi
see「擂臺」

擂臺 (ㄌㄟˊ ㄊㄞˊ)
a platform for contests in martial arts; a ring (for martial contests); an arena

【擄】 2055
ㄌㄨˇ luu lǔ
(又讀 ㄌㄨㄛˊ luó luo)
to capture; to take captive

擄掠 (ㄌㄨˇ ㄌㄩㄝˋ)
to plunder; to rob; to pillage

擄獲 (ㄌㄨˇ ㄏㄨㄛˋ)
to capture; to take captive

擄劫 (ㄌㄨˇ ㄐㄧㄝˊ)
to plunder; to rob

擄人勒贖 (ㄌㄨˇ ㄖㄣˊ ㄌㄜˋ ㄕㄨˊ)
to kidnap a person for ransom

【擁】 2056
ㄩㄥ yeong yōng
(又讀 ㄩㄥ iong yōng)
1. to hug; to embrace; to hold
2. to have; to possess
3. to crowd; to throng; to swarm
4. to follow; to support

擁被而臥 (ㄩㄥ ㄅㄟˋ ㄦˊ ㄨㄛˋ)
to lie down and cover oneself with a quilt

擁抱 (ㄩㄥ ㄅㄠˋ)
to embrace; to hug; to hold in one's arms: 他熱烈地擁抱她。 He held her to him in a warm embrace.

擁鼻 (ㄩㄥ ㄅㄧˊ)
to hold one's nose

擁兵自重 (ㄩㄥ ㄅㄧㄥ ㄗˋ ㄓㄨㄥˋ)
(said of warlords) to maintain an army and defy orders from the central government

擁兵自衛 (ㄩㄥ ㄅㄧㄥ ㄗˋ ㄨㄟˋ)
to maintain an army for personal safety

擁戴 (ㄩㄥ ㄉㄞˋ)
to support a leader or ruler; support

擁立 (ㄩㄥ ㄌㄧˋ)
to set up a ruler or leader and declare allegiance to him

擁爐賞雪 (ㄩㄥ ㄌㄨˊ ㄕㄤˇ ㄒㄩㄝˇ)
to enjoy the view of snow by the fireplace (a typical idle enjoyment of the Chinese intelligentsia)

擁護 (ㄩㄥ ㄏㄨˋ)
to advocate; to endorse; support; to back

擁擠 (ㄩㄥ ㄐㄧˇ)
crowded; packed: 假日時車特別擁擠。 The vehicles are especially crowded on holiday.

擁擠不堪 (ㄩㄥ ㄐㄧˇ ㄅㄨˋ ㄎㄢ)
intolerably crowded: 這個房間擁擠不堪。 The room was intolerably crowded.

擁經問疾 (ㄩㄥ ㄐㄧㄥ ㄨㄣˋ ㄐㄧˊ)
(said of a person in power) to treat a former teacher with respect

擁衾 (ㄩㄥ ㄑㄧㄣˊ)
to go to bed

擁腫 (ㄩㄥ ㄓㄨㄥˇ)
①(said of rock) rugged; gnarled ②morbidly swollen; unusually corpulent ③stupid and ignorant 亦用「臃腫」

擁上來 (ㄩㄥ ㄕㄤˋ ﹒ㄌㄞ)
to come in a swarm

擁上心來 (ㄩㄥ ㄕㄤˋ ㄒㄧㄣ ﹒ㄌㄞ)
(said of memories, emotions etc.) to well up

擁書 (ㄩㄥ ㄕㄨ)
to possess a large collection of books

擁入 (ㄩㄥ ㄖㄨˋ)
to crowd into

擁塞 (ㄩㄥ ㄙㄜˋ)
to clog or be clogged; block up or be blocked up; jam

擁遏 (ㄩㄥ ㄜˋ)
to obstruct; to block

擁有 (ㄩㄥ ㄧㄡˇ)
to have; to possess; to own 中國擁有豐富的礦藏。 China has rich mineral resources.

【擅】 2057
ㄕㄢˋ shann shàn
1. unauthorized; unilateral; arbitrary
2. to monopolize; to take exclusive possession
3. to be good at; to be expert in

擅便 (ㄕㄢˋ ㄅㄧㄢˋ)
to consult one's own convenience

nience only

兵(ㄅㄧㄥ ㄅㄧㄥˋ)
to maintain an army without authorization

美(ㄅㄧㄥ ㄇㄟˇ)
to get all (the) credit: 我不敢擅美。I dare not claim all credit to myself.

命(ㄅㄧㄥ ㄇㄧㄥˋ)
to defy restrictions or orders; to arrogate power to oneself

離職守(ㄅㄧㄥ ㄓˊ ㄕㄡˇ)
to be absent without leave; to leave one's post without permission

利(ㄅㄧㄥ ㄌㄧˋ)
to enjoy monopoly

改(ㄅㄧㄥ ㄍㄞˇ)
to change or revise without authorization: 請不要擅改我的稿子。Please do not change or revise my manuscript.

國(ㄅㄧㄥ ㄍㄨㄛˊ)
to assume the reins of government; to usurp the powers of the throne

取(ㄅㄧㄥ ㄑㄩˇ)
to take without authorization (or permission)

權(ㄅㄧㄥ ㄑㄩㄢˊ)
to assume dictatorial powers

長(ㄅㄧㄥ ㄔㄤˊ)
to excel in; to be good at: 他擅長數學。He excels in mathematics.

場(ㄅㄧㄥ ㄔㄤˇ)or(ㄅㄧㄥ ㄔㄤˇ)
to dominate the scene

自(ㄅㄧㄥ ㄗˋ)
to do something without authorization

自作主(ㄅㄧㄥ ㄗˋ ㄗㄨㄛˋ ㄓㄨˇ)
to take an unauthorized action; to make a decision without authorization

作主張(ㄅㄧㄥ ㄗㄨㄛˋ ㄓㄨˇ ㄓㄤ)
to make an unilateral or arbitrary decision

作威福(ㄅㄧㄥ ㄗㄨㄛˋ ㄨㄟ ㄈㄨˊ)
to punish or reward according to one's whim

違(ㄅㄧㄥ ㄨㄟˊ)
to disobey; to violate (regulations)

用(ㄅㄧㄥ ㄩㄥˋ)
to use without permission

【操】 2058　ㄘㄠ tsau cāo

1. to handle; to manage
2. to hold; to grasp
3. to exercise; to drill
4. to speak
5. a Chinese family name

操法(ㄘㄠ ㄈㄚˇ)
method or procedure of military drill, physical exercises, etc.

操刀(ㄘㄠ ㄉㄠ)
to hold a knife or sword

操刀必割(ㄘㄠ ㄉㄠ ㄅㄧˋ ㄍㄜ)
to be sure to take advantage of a chance when it comes

操刀傷錦(ㄘㄠ ㄉㄠ ㄕㄤ ㄐㄧㄣˇ)
to do something beyond one's capability and end in failure

操典(ㄘㄠ ㄉㄧㄢˇ)
a drill manual; drill regulations

操勞(ㄘㄠ ㄌㄠˊ)
① to be under the weight of cares; to be loaded with cares; to work hard ② to take care; to look after

操勞過度(ㄘㄠ ㄌㄠˊ ㄍㄨㄛˋ ㄉㄨˋ)
to be excessively loaded with cares; to overwork (or strain) oneself; to burn the candle at both ends: 他因操勞過度而生病。He got ill by (or through) overwork.

操練(ㄘㄠ ㄌㄧㄢˋ)
to drill (in the military sense); to practice

操戈(ㄘㄠ ㄍㄜ)
to take up arms: 同室操戈 an internecine fight

操觚(ㄘㄠ ㄍㄨ)
① to engage in writing ② to practice a profession or craft

操奇計贏(ㄘㄠ ㄑㄧˊ ㄐㄧˋ ㄧㄥˊ)
(said of businessmen) shrewd and canny

操切(ㄘㄠ ㄑㄧㄝ)
hasty; hurried; rash

操琴(ㄘㄠ ㄑㄧㄣˊ)
to accompany a singer with a fiddle, etc. (especially in Chinese opera)

操槍(ㄘㄠ ㄑㄧㄤ)
rifle drill: 學生們到兵營操槍。The students went to the barracks for rifle drill.

操權(ㄘㄠ ㄑㄩㄢˊ)
to wield power

操券(ㄘㄠ ㄑㄩㄢˋ)
to be sure of success

操心(ㄘㄠ ㄒㄧㄣ)
① to worry about; to trouble about; to take pains: 請不要操心。Please don't worry about it. ② to rack one's brains

操行(ㄘㄠ ㄒㄧㄥˊ)
conduct (in the moral sense); behavior or conduct of a student

操之過急(ㄘㄠ ㄓ ㄍㄨㄛˋ ㄐㄧˊ)
to be too eager for success

操舟(ㄘㄠ ㄓㄡ)
to steer a boat

操持(ㄘㄠ ㄔˊ)
to manage; to handle: 她终日操持家務。She managed household affairs all day long.

操場(ㄘㄠ ㄔㄤˇ)or(ㄘㄠ ㄔㄤˇ)
an athletic ground; a drill ground; a playground: 他們在操場上玩足球。They are playing football in the playground.

操手(ㄘㄠ ㄕㄡˇ)
(said of boxers) to spar as a practice

操守(ㄘㄠ ㄕㄡˇ)
discretion (in conduct); attention to moral principles; moral fortitude; integrity

操神(ㄘㄠ ㄕㄣˊ)
to worry; to tax the mind or energy

操作(ㄘㄠ ㄗㄨㄛˋ)
to manipulate or operate (a machine); operation: 操作方法 the method of operation

操縱(ㄘㄠ ㄗㄨㄥˋ)
to manage, control, manipulate or operate (activities, machines, people, etc.)

操演(ㄘㄠ ㄧㄢˇ)
to drill; to exercise

【擔】 2059　1. (担) ㄉㄢ dan　ㄉㄢˋ dàn

to shoulder; to take upon oneself; to undertake; to suffer; to endure

擔保(ㄉㄢ ㄅㄠˇ)
to guarantee; to pledge; a

（right margin）〔手部〕

〔手部〕

guaranty or guarantee; a pledge: 你能拿出什麼做擔保? What guarantee can you offer?

擔保人(ㄉㄢ ㄅㄠ ㄖㄣˊ)
a guarantor (or guarantee)

擔不是(ㄉㄢ ㄅㄨˋ ㄕ)
to bear the blame; to take the blame

擔不起(ㄉㄢ ㄅㄨˋ ㄑㄧˇ)
incapable of shouldering (a responsibility); do not dare to assume a responsibility

擔風險(ㄉㄢ ㄈㄥ ㄒㄧㄢˇ)
to run a risk

擔負(ㄉㄢ ㄈㄨˋ)
①a burden; responsibility ②to assume a responsibility; to undertake; to shoulder; to bear: 他不願擔負責任。He was not willing to shoulder responsibility.

擔待(ㄉㄢ ㄉㄞˋ)
to be lenient; to be magnanimous

擔戴(ㄉㄢ ㄉㄞˋ)
to assume responsibility for; to take upon oneself

擔當(ㄉㄢ ㄉㄤ)
to take (responsibility) upon oneself, or undertake (a task): 我懷疑他能否擔當重任。I wonder if he can take on heavy responsibilities.

擱擱(ㄉㄢ ㄍㄜ)
to delay; delay: 疾病擱擱了他學業的進步。Illness delayed his progress of study.

擔荷(ㄉㄢ ㄏㄜˋ)
to shoulder a burden; to assume a responsibility

擔架(ㄉㄢ ㄐㄧㄚˋ)
a stretcher (for carrying the sick and injured)

擔架兵(ㄉㄢ ㄐㄧㄚˋ ㄅㄧㄥ)
a stretcher-bearer

擔驚受怕(ㄉㄢ ㄐㄧㄥ ㄕㄡˋ ㄆㄚˋ)
to remain in a state of apprehension; to feel alarmed; to be in a state of anxiety

擔險(ㄉㄢ ㄒㄧㄢˇ)
to run a risk

擔心(ㄉㄢ ㄒㄧㄣ)
to worry; to feel anxious: 每週寫信給你母親, 免得她擔心。Write to your mother every

week lest she might feel anxious.

擔承(ㄉㄢ ㄔㄥˊ)
to undertake, or assume the responsibility for (a task): 爲了家計, 他擔承額外工作。For the sake of the family's livelihood, he takes on extra work.

擔水(ㄉㄢ ㄕㄨㄟˇ)
to carry water with a carrying pole

擔任(ㄉㄢ ㄖㄣˋ)
to take charge of (a task); to work in the capacity of; to hold the post of

擔錯(ㄉㄢ ㄘㄨㄛˋ)
to take the blame for others

擔憂(ㄉㄢ ㄧㄡ)
to be anxious; to be apprehensive; to worry: 不用爲她的安全擔憂。Don't be anxious about her safety.

【擔】 2059
2. ㄉㄢˋ dann dàn
1. a load; a burden: 一擔菜 (米) a load of vegetables (rice)
2. as in 扁擔—a carrying pole
3. a unit of weight or capacity

擔麵(ㄉㄢˋ ㄇㄧㄢˋ)
cooked noodles with liberal use of seasoning—a specialty in Szechwan cookery

擔子(ㄉㄢˋ ㄗ)
a load or burden upon the shoulder or the back

【擇】 2060
ㄗㄜˊ tzer zé
(又讀) ㄓㄞˊ jair zhái
to select; to choose; to pick out: 二者任擇其一。Choose either of the two.

擇配(ㄗㄜˊ ㄆㄟˋ)
to choose a spouse

擇木(ㄗㄜˊ ㄇㄨˋ)
(literally) to choose a perch —to choose a master: 良禽擇木而棲。Good birds select trees on which they roost.

擇肥而噬(ㄗㄜˊ ㄈㄟˊ ㄦˊ ㄕˋ)
(literally) to select the fat ones and eat them—to select the rich for extortion

擇地(ㄗㄜˊ ㄉㄧˋ)
to choose a site (for a conference, building, etc.)

擇對(ㄗㄜˊ ㄉㄨㄟˋ)
to select a spouse or a mate

擇鄰(ㄗㄜˊ ㄌㄧㄣˊ)
to select neighbors

擇吉(ㄗㄜˊ ㄐㄧˊ)
to select an auspicious d (for a wedding, the open of a store, etc.)

擇吉開張(ㄗㄜˊ ㄐㄧˊ ㄎㄞ ㄓㄤ)
to choose an auspicious d to start a business

擇交(ㄗㄜˊ ㄐㄧㄠ)
to select friends

擇期(ㄗㄜˊ ㄑㄧˊ)
to select a good time or d (for an undertaking, a w ding, etc.)

擇親(ㄗㄜˊ ㄑㄧㄣ)
to make marriage arran ments for one's children

擇婿(ㄗㄜˊ ㄒㄩˋ)
to choose a good husba for one's daughter

擇選(ㄗㄜˊ ㄒㄩㄢˇ)
to select; to choose 亦作「擇」

擇食(ㄗㄜˊ ㄕˊ)
to select one's food: 飢不 食。When one is starving, food is delicious to him.

擇善固執(ㄗㄜˊ ㄕㄢˋ ㄍㄨˋ ㄓˊ)
to choose what is good a stick to it

擇善而從(ㄗㄜˊ ㄕㄢˋ ㄦˊ ㄘㄨㄥˊ)
to choose what is good a follow it

擇日(ㄗㄜˊ ㄖˋ)
to choose a good day f an undertaking or ce mony)

擇人而事(ㄗㄜˊ ㄖㄣˊ ㄦˊ ㄕˋ)
①to choose the virtuous serve ②to find the ri man to marry

擇偶(ㄗㄜˊ ㄡˇ)
to select a spouse or a ma

擇業(ㄗㄜˊ ㄧㄝˋ)
to choose an occupation

擇友(ㄗㄜˊ ㄧㄡˇ)
to choose friends 參看「擇

【擋】 2061
1. ㄉㄤ dang dāng
used in the combination
擤擋—to arrange in order
to pack up for traveling

【擋】 2061
2. ㄉㄤˋ daang dàn
1. to obstruct; to impede; stop; to resist; to ward o

to block; to get in the way
of: 防波堤無法擋住海浪的力
量。The sea wall cannot
resist the force of the
waves.
a fender; a blind

a gear: 前進(後退)擋 for-
ward (reverse) gear 低速擋
low (bottom) gear

不住(ㄌㄚ‧ㄅㄨ ㄓㄨ)
incapable of blocking, hin-
dering, impeding, stopping
or shutting out

風(ㄌㄚ ㄈㄥ)
to keep the wind away; to
keep off the wind

風玻璃(ㄌㄚ ㄈㄥ ㄅㄛ ‧ㄌㄧ)
a windshield

(ㄌㄚ)
to fight as a vanguard

土牆(ㄌㄚ ㄊㄨˇ ㄑㄧㄤˊ)
(construction) a retaining
wall

泥板(ㄌㄚ ㄋㄧˊ ㄅㄢˇ)
a mudguard, or a fender

路(ㄌㄚ ㄌㄨˋ)
to be in the way; to obstruct
traffic: 落石擋路。The roads
were obstructed by falls of
rock.

橫兒(ㄌㄚ ㄏㄥˊㄦ)
to guard someone from violence

駕(ㄌㄚ ㄐㄧㄚˋ)
to decline to receive visitors;
to stop visitors from entering a place or calling on
somebody

箭牌(ㄌㄚ ㄐㄧㄢˋ ㄆㄞˊ)
①a shield ②(figuratively)
anyone or anything which is
used as a protective shield;
an excuse; a pretext

住(ㄌㄚ ㄓㄨˋ)
to block; to impede; to hinder; to obstruct: 濃霧擋住了
司機的視線。The thick mist
obstructed the driver's view.

眼(ㄌㄚ ㄧㄢˇ)
to obstruct one's view

雨(ㄌㄚ ㄩˇ)
to keep off the rain; to shelter one from the rain: 她撐著
傘擋雨。She held an umbrella
to shelter herself from the
rain.

【擒】 2062
ㄑㄧㄣˊ chyn qín
to arrest; to capture; to
seize: 罪犯已就擒。The crimi-
nal has submitted to arrest.

擒捕(ㄑㄧㄣˊ ㄅㄨˇ)
to arrest; to capture

擒拿(ㄑㄧㄣˊ ㄋㄚˊ)
to arrest; to capture

擒拿法(ㄑㄧㄣˊ ㄋㄚˊ ㄈㄚˇ)or擒拿術
(ㄑㄧㄣˊ ㄋㄚˊ ㄕㄨˋ)
arrest technique

擒獲(ㄑㄧㄣˊ ㄏㄨㄛˋ)
to capture

擒斬(ㄑㄧㄣˊ ㄓㄢˇ)
to capture and behead

擒住(ㄑㄧㄣˊ ㄓㄨˋ)
to succeed in capturing

擒捉(ㄑㄧㄣˊ ㄓㄨㄛ)
to arrest; to capture

擒賊先擒王(ㄑㄧㄣˊ ㄗㄟˊ ㄒㄧㄢ ㄑㄧㄣˊ
ㄨㄤˊ)
(literally) If you want to
capture a group of bandits,
capture the ringleader first.
—to assign priority properly; to stress what should be
done first

擒縱(ㄑㄧㄣˊ ㄗㄨㄥˋ)
arresting and releasing;
alternate measures of severity and mercy

【據】 2063
(据) ㄐㄩˋ jiuh jù
1. according to; on the basis
of; on the grounds of
2. to depend on
3. to occupy; to take possession of; to seize
4. proof; evidence
5. a Chinese family name

據報(ㄐㄩˋ ㄅㄠˋ)or據報導(ㄐㄩˋ ㄅㄠˋ
ㄉㄠˇ)
according to reports

據點(ㄐㄩˋ ㄉㄧㄢˇ)
a base (for operations or
activities); a fortified point;
a stronghold

據理力爭(ㄐㄩˋ ㄌㄧˇ ㄌㄧˋ ㄓㄥ)
to argue vigorously on the
basis of sound reason or justice

據情(ㄐㄩˋ ㄑㄧㄥˊ)
according to circumstances

據悉(ㄐㄩˋ ㄒㄧ)
It is reported that....

據險(ㄐㄩˋ ㄒㄧㄢˇ)

to hold strategic positions

據稱(ㄐㄩˋ ㄔㄥ)
according to reports, claims,
or assertions

據傳(ㄐㄩˋ ㄔㄨㄢˊ)
a story is going around that;
the story goes that; rumour
has it that; it is rumoured
that

據實(ㄐㄩˋ ㄕˊ)
according to the fact

據守(ㄐㄩˋ ㄕㄡˇ)
to hold a position against
attack; to make a stand; to
stand one's ground

據說(ㄐㄩˋ ㄕㄨㄛ)
It is said that.... 或 according to hearsay

據此(ㄐㄩˋ ㄘˇ)
(a conventional phrase in
official correspondence) on
these grounds

據有(ㄐㄩˋ ㄧㄡˇ)
to take possession of; to
appropriate

據我看(來)(ㄐㄩˋ ㄨㄛˇ ㄎㄢˋ (ㄌㄞˊ))
as I see it; in my opinion: 據
我看來,你錯了。In my opin-
ion, you're wrong.

據我所知(ㄐㄩˋ ㄨㄛˇ ㄙㄨㄛˇ ㄓ)
as far as I know

據als己有(ㄐㄩˋ ㄨㄟˊ ㄐㄧˇ ㄧㄡˇ)
to take possession (of what
does not belong to oneself)

據云(ㄐㄩˋ ㄩㄣˊ)
according to report; it is
said that…

【擗】 2064
ㄆㄧˇ pih pǐ
to beat the breast

擗踊(ㄆㄧˇ ㄩㄥˇ)
to beat the breast and stamp
the feet in great grief

【擀】 2065
ㄍㄢˇ gaan gǎn
1. to stretch out with a rolling
pin: 擀餃子皮to roll out
dumpling wrappers
2. to polish; to shine

擀麵(ㄍㄢˇ ㄇㄧㄢˋ)
to roll dough

擀麵杖(ㄍㄢˇ ㄇㄧㄢˋ ㄓㄤˋ)
a rolling pin

【擐】 2066
ㄏㄨㄢˋ huann huàn
to put on; to wear

擐甲執兵(ㄏㄨㄢˋ ㄐㄧㄚˊ ㄓˊ ㄅㄧㄥ)

〔手部〕

to put on one's armor and take up arms

【撿】 2067 ㄐㄧㄢˇ jean jiǎn
to pick up; to collect; to gather: 我昨天撿到一個錢包。I picked up a purse yesterday.

撿破爛的 (ㄐㄧㄢˇ ㄆㄛˋ ㄌㄢˊ)
to collect scrap

撿破爛的 (ㄐㄧㄢˇ ㄆㄛˋ ㄌㄢˊ ㄉㄜ˙)
a rag picker; a junk collector

撿起來 (ㄐㄧㄢˇ ㄑㄧˇ ㄌㄞˊ)
to pick up (from the ground or floor): 將地上的紙片撿起來。Pick up the scraps of paper on the floor.

撿柴 (ㄐㄧㄢˇ ㄔㄞˊ)
to collect firewood

【摑】 2068 ㄎㄨㄞˇ koai kuǎi
1. to scratch (lightly)
2. to carry on the arm

摑破 (ㄎㄨㄞˇ ㄆㄛˋ)
to break by scratching

摑籃子 (ㄎㄨㄞˇ ㄌㄢˊ ㄗ˙)
to carry a basket on the arm

摑癢癢兒 (ㄎㄨㄞˇ ㄧㄤˇ ˙ㄧㄤㄦ)
to scratch an itchy spot

【擊】 2069 ㄐㄧ jyi jī
to beat; to strike; to attack; to hit; to bump into: 聲東擊西 to make a feint attack on the east but strike on the west

擊敗 (ㄐㄧ ㄅㄞˋ)
to defeat; to beat; to conquer: 被擊敗的敵人很快就投降了。The beaten enemy soon surrendered.

擊斃 (ㄐㄧ ㄅㄧˋ)
to beat to death; to shoot to death

擊破 (ㄐㄧ ㄆㄛˋ)
to smash or defeat (an enemy force); to crush (enemy defense); to destroy one by one: 各個擊破 to destroy one by one

擊缶 (ㄐㄧ ㄈㄡˇ)
to beat time with a percussion instrument made of clay

擊倒 (ㄐㄧ ㄉㄠˇ)
to knock down; to floor

擊柝 (ㄐㄧ ㄊㄨㄛˋ)

to beat the watches

擊退 (ㄐㄧ ㄊㄨㄟˋ)
to beat back; to drive back; to repel; to repulse: 敵人慘遭擊退。The enemy was badly beaten back.

擊落 (ㄐㄧ ㄌㄨㄛˋ)
to shoot down (aircraft); to down: 他們擊落一些鴨子。They shot down several ducks.

擊鼓鳴冤 (ㄐㄧ ㄍㄨˇ ㄇㄧㄥˊ ㄩㄢ)
(in old China) to beat the drum at the magistrate's door to bring a grievance to his attention

擊潰 (ㄐㄧ ㄎㄨㄟˋ)
① to knock to pieces ② to defeat; to rout (the enemy troops)

擊毀 (ㄐㄧ ㄏㄨㄟˇ)
to smash; to wreck; to shatter; to destroy

擊楫中流 (ㄐㄧ ㄐㄧˊ ㄓㄨㄥ ㄌㄧㄡˊ)
to vow to annihilate the rebels—referring to Tsu Ti (祖逖), a general who made such a vow while crossing a river

擊節稱賞 (ㄐㄧ ㄐㄧㄝˊ ㄔㄥ ㄕㄤˇ)
to applaud; to admire greatly; to show appreciation (of a poem or a piece of music) by beating time

擊劍 (ㄐㄧ ㄐㄧㄢˋ)
fencing: 我哥哥是擊劍教師。My elder brother is a fencing master.

擊球 (ㄐㄧ ㄑㄧㄡˊ)
(baseball) batting

擊掌 (ㄐㄧ ㄓㄤˇ)
to clap hands

擊筑 (ㄐㄧ ㄓㄨˊ)
to strike a stringed instrument which resembles 箏 but is played with a bamboo rod

擊沉 (ㄐㄧ ㄔㄣˊ)
to sink (vessels by bombarding, bombing, or torpedoing)

擊傷 (ㄐㄧ ㄕㄤ)
to wound (with bullets); to damage (a vessel, airplane, tank, etc.) by shelling, bombing, etc.

擊賞 (ㄐㄧ ㄕㄤˇ)
to show appreciation by clapping hands

擊壤 (ㄐㄧ ㄖㄤˇ)
(literally) to play pushy —to live in peace and comfort

擊刺 (ㄐㄧ ㄘˋ)
to stab: 他由背後擊刺敵人。stabbed his enemy in the back.

擊碎 (ㄐㄧ ㄙㄨㄟˋ)
to knock to pieces; to smash to pieces: 石頭擊碎窗戶。The rock smashed the window.

【擎】 2070 ㄑㄧㄥˊ chyng qíng
to lift; to support; to prop up: 眾擎易舉。It is much easier for many people to lift a load.

擎天柱 (ㄑㄧㄥˊ ㄊㄧㄢ ㄓㄨˋ)
a mythological pillar supporting the heaven—person who is the mainstay of a nation or a family

擎天神 (ㄑㄧㄥˊ ㄊㄧㄢ ㄕㄣˊ)
Atlas (a Titan, son of Iapetus)

擎起 (ㄑㄧㄥˊ ㄑㄧˇ)
to lift up

擎手 (ㄑㄧㄥˊ ㄕㄡˇ)
to raise one's hands—to start doing a thing

【擘】 2071 ㄅㄛˋ boh bò
1. the thumb
2. an outstanding person; an authority in a certain field
3. to split; to tear apart; to break: 擘紙 to tear paper

擘裂 (ㄅㄛˋ ㄌㄧㄝˋ)
to hew apart; to rend apart

擘窠 (ㄅㄛˋ ㄎㄜ)
to cleave; to split

the technique of writing characters of gigantic size

擘開 (ㄅㄛˋ ㄎㄞ)
to open (hard-rinded fruit); to break open; to break off

擘篌箜 (ㄅㄛˋ ㄎㄨㄥ ㄏㄡˊ)
name of an ancient musical instrument

擘畫 (ㄅㄛˋ ㄏㄨㄚˋ)
to plan; to scheme; to make arrangements for: 此事尚待擘畫。This has yet to be planned.

擘肌分理 (ㄅㄛˋ ㄐㄧ ㄈㄣ ㄌㄧˇ)
to make a very detailed

---

analysis
根 (ㄍㄣ ㄓㄥ)
o draw (a bow)

十四畫

【擠】 2072 ㄐㄧ jii jí
o push; to jostle 別擠。Do
not push. 或 Stop pushing.
to wring; to squeeze; to
twist; to press: 把水擠掉
squeeze the water out; to
wring out water
to make room; to throng; to
cram; to pack: 不要統統擠在
一塊。Don't all crowd
together.

不動(ㄐㄧ·ㄅㄨ ㄉㄨㄥ)
unable to budge because of
crowdedness

眉弄眼(ㄐㄧ ㄇㄟ ㄋㄨㄥ ㄧㄢˇ)
to make eyes; to wink

滿(ㄐㄧ ㄇㄢˇ)
to pack (a place, car, etc.)
to capacity: 這房間擠滿了客
人。The room was crowded
with guests.

兌(ㄐㄧ ㄉㄨㄟˋ)
a run on a bank

奶(ㄐㄧ ㄋㄞˇ)or 擠乳(ㄐㄧ ㄖㄨˇ)
to draw or press milk; to
milk a cow

來擠去(ㄐㄧ ㄌㄞˊ ㄐㄧˇ ㄑㄩˋ)
to push about; to jostle

眨眼(ㄐㄧˇ ㄓㄚˇ ㄧㄢˇ)
to wink

擠捱捱(ㄐㄧ ㄐㄧ ㄔㄚˊ ㄔㄚˊ)
crowded

進擠出(ㄐㄧ ㄐㄧㄣ ㄐㄧˇ ㄔㄨ)
to squeeze in and out (of a
crowded place)

陷(ㄐㄧ ㄒㄧㄢ)
to do harm intentionally

上去(ㄐㄧˇ ㄕㄤˋ·ㄑㄩ)
to force oneself up (onto a
crowded bus, etc.)

擠軋(ㄐㄧˇ ㄧㄚˋ)or 擠壓(ㄐㄧˇ ㄧㄚ)
to keep another down or out

壓(ㄐㄧˇ ㄧㄚ)
extruding

牙膏(ㄐㄧ ㄧㄚˊ ㄍㄠ)
to squeeze toothpaste from
the tube

【擡】 2073 (抬) ㄊㄞˊ tair tái
to lift; to raise; to carry: 他

起右手。He raised his right
hand.

不動(ㄊㄞˊ·ㄅㄨ ㄉㄨㄥˋ)
incapable of lifting or being
lifted

擡頭(ㄊㄞˊ ㄊㄡˊ)
① to raise one's head ②
(said of the price) an upsurge; (said of fortune) a
turn for the better ③ a
bank's salutation for a client

擡頭挺胸(ㄊㄞˊ ㄊㄡˊ ㄊㄧㄥˇ ㄒㄩㄥ)
(literally) chin up and chest
out—full of confidence or
pride

擡頭見喜(ㄊㄞˊ ㄊㄡˊ ㄐㄧㄢˋ ㄒㄧˇ)
to raise one's head and see
bliss (a self-congratulatory
expression written on a slip
of red paper pasted up at a
prominent place in a house
to greet the Chinese Lunar
New Year)

擡高身價(ㄊㄞˊ ㄍㄠ ㄕㄣ ㄐㄧㄚˋ)
to raise oneself in others'
esteem (by means of stratagems instead of real accomplishments)

擡高物價(ㄊㄞˊ ㄍㄠ ㄨˋ ㄐㄧㄚˋ)
to raise commodity prices;
to effect a price hike

擡槓(ㄊㄞˊ ㄍㄤˋ)
to argue for the sake of arguing; to wrangle; to quarrel; to bicker: 他們倆已擡槓
幾個小時了。Those two have
been bickering for hours.

擡轎的(ㄊㄞˊ ㄐㄧㄠˋ ·ㄉㄜ)
① a sedan-chair bearer ②
supporters; followers

擡轎子(ㄊㄞˊ ㄐㄧㄠˋ ·ㄗ)
① to carry a sedan chair ②
to gang up in cheating someone in gambling ③ to sup-
port or help someone

擡舉(ㄊㄞˊ ㄐㄩˇ)
to do a good turn or favor;
a good turn or favor

擡手動脚(ㄊㄞˊ ㄕㄡˇ ㄉㄨㄥˋ ㄐㄧㄠˇ)
personal behavior or bearing; manner

【擢】 2074 ㄓㄨㄛˊ jwo zhuó
1. to take out; to pull out; to
extract; to pick out; to
select
2. to promote; to raise (in
rank)

擢髮難數(ㄓㄨㄛˊ ㄈㄚˇ ㄋㄢˊ ㄕㄨˇ)
① guilty of faults as in-
numerable as one's hair ②
to be too numerous to count

擢第(ㄓㄨㄛˊ ㄉㄧˋ)
to get chosen by passing an
examination

擢秀(ㄓㄨㄛˊ ㄒㄧㄡˋ)
①(said of vegetation) luxuriant ②(said of a person)
talented, or gifted

擢升 or 擢昇(ㄓㄨㄛˊ ㄕㄥ)
to promote (an official,
etc.); to advance (to a
higher position or rank)

擢引(ㄓㄨㄛˊ ㄧㄣˇ)
to pick and promote (promising employees or subordinates)

擢用(ㄓㄨㄛˊ ㄩㄥˋ)
to pick and promote (promising employees or subordinates)

【搗】 2075 (擣) ㄉㄠˇ dao dǎo
1. to pound; to beat
2. to attack
3. to harass; to disturb

搗米(ㄉㄠˇ ㄇㄧˇ)
to hull rice in a mortar

搗爛(ㄉㄠˇ ㄌㄢˋ)
to pound into a pulp

搗練(ㄉㄠˇ ㄌㄧㄢˋ)
to mix or knead by pound-
ing

搗亂(ㄉㄠˇ ㄌㄨㄢˋ)
to make trouble

搗鬼(ㄉㄠˇ ㄍㄨㄟˇ)
to do mischief

搗虛(ㄉㄠˇ ㄒㄩ)
to launch a surprise attack

搗衣(ㄉㄠˇ ㄧ)
to wash clothes by pounding
them with a wooden pound-
er

搗藥(ㄉㄠˇ ㄧㄠˋ)
to mix drugs by pounding in
a mortar

【擬】 2076 ㄋㄧˇ nii nǐ
1. to plan; to intend; to decide;
to determine
2. to draft; to draw up; to
design
3. to imitate

擬辦(ㄋㄧˇ ㄅㄢˋ)
to intend to execute or man-

〔手部〕

age (a cliché in official documents)

擬定(ㄋㄧˇㄉㄧㄥˋ)
to draw up or map out (a plan); to draft

擬態
mimicry (of insects); imitation

擬妥(ㄋㄧˇㄊㄨㄛˇ)
to have drawn up (a plan, a draft, etc.)

擬稿(ㄋㄧˇㄍㄠˇ)
to prepare manuscripts or write copies (for publication)

擬古(ㄋㄧˇㄍㄨˇ)
to imitate classical models

擬規畫圓(ㄋㄧˇㄍㄨㄟㄏㄨㄚˋㄩㄢˊ)
(literally) to draw circles with a compass— to stick to convention unimaginatively

擬就(ㄋㄧˇㄐㄧㄡˋ)
to have completed formulation or preparation (of a plan, a draft, etc.)

擬具(ㄋㄧˇㄐㄩˋ)
to draw up (a proposal, a plan, etc.)

擬請(ㄋㄧˇㄑㄧㄥˇ)
to intend to ask or request

擬人法(ㄋㄧˇㄖㄣˊㄈㄚˇ)
(rhetoric) personification 亦作「擬人化」

擬作(ㄋㄧˇㄗㄨㄛˋ)
an imitation

擬議(ㄋㄧˇㄧˋ)
① a tentative decision reached after discussion ② a proposal for deliberation: 他的擬議不會被採用的。His recommendations won't be adopted.

【擯】2077
ㄅㄧㄣˋ binn bìn
1. to expel; to reject; to oust; to get rid of; to discard
2. same as 儐—an usher

擯落(ㄅㄧㄣˋㄌㄨㄛˋ)
to suffer rejection and downfall

擯介(ㄅㄧㄣˋㄐㄧㄝˋ)
a person serving to bridge the gap between the host and the guest

擯棄(ㄅㄧㄣˋㄑㄧˋ)
to cast away; to set aside; to discard; to desert

擯相(ㄅㄧㄣˋㄒㄧㄤ)
① the master of ceremonies ② the best man or bridesmaid 亦作作儐相): 誰當你的女擯相? Who will be your bridesmaid?

擯斥(ㄅㄧㄣˋㄔˋ)
to reject; to expel; to repudiate: 他們將他擯斥於圈外。They expelled him from their circle.

擯除(ㄅㄧㄣˋㄔㄨˊ)
to expel; to oust; to eliminate; to dispense with

擯黜(ㄅㄧㄣˋㄔㄨˋ)
to banish; to exile

【擦】2078
ㄘㄚ tsa cā
1. to wipe; to mop; to scrub; to polish
2. to spread on; to put on
3. to rub; to graze; to scratch
4. to brush; to shaved

擦玻璃(ㄘㄚㄅㄛˉㄌㄧ)
to wipe glass; to wipe window panes

擦布(ㄘㄚㄅㄨˋ)
wiping rags

擦皮鞋(ㄘㄚㄆㄧˊㄒㄧㄝˊ)
to shine shoes

擦抹(ㄘㄚㄇㄛˇ)
to wipe

擦地板(ㄘㄚㄉㄧˋㄅㄢˇ)
to scrub the floor; to mop the floor

擦銅油(ㄘㄚㄊㄨㄥˊㄧㄡˊ)
brass polish

擦臉(ㄘㄚㄌㄧㄢˇ)
to wipe one's face

擦亮(ㄘㄚㄌㄧㄤˋ)
to shine (shoes, utensils, etc.): 好好擦亮靴子。Put a good shine on the boots.

擦亮眼睛(ㄘㄚㄌㄧㄤˋㄧㄢˇㄐㄧㄥ)
① to remove the scales from one's eyes ② to be watchful

擦乾(ㄘㄚㄍㄢ)
to swab up; to wipe dry

擦乾淨(ㄘㄚㄍㄢㄐㄧㄥˋ)
to wipe clean; to clean by wiping: 將濺出的牛奶擦乾淨。Wipe up the spilt milk.

擦黑兒(ㄘㄚㄏㄟˊㄦ)
approaching evening; dusk

擦汗(ㄘㄚㄏㄢˋ)
to wipe off sweat or perspiration: 運動之後要記得擦汗。

Remember to wipe off sw after exercise.

擦槍(ㄘㄚㄑㄧㄤ)
to swab rifles

擦去(ㄘㄚㄑㄩˋ)
to wipe off: 他擦去臉上的 He wiped the sweat fr his face.

擦洗(ㄘㄚㄒㄧˇ)
to scrub: 這地板需要好好擦一番。The floor needs a go scrub.

擦鞋童(ㄘㄚㄒㄧㄝˊㄊㄨㄥˊ)
a shoeshine boy; a shoebla

擦鞋油(ㄘㄚㄒㄧㄝˊㄧㄡˊ)
shoe polish

擦車(ㄘㄚㄔㄜ)
to wax a car, bicycle, etc.

擦拭(ㄘㄚㄕˋ)
to clean; to cleanse

擦身而過(ㄘㄚㄕㄣㄦˊㄍㄨㄛˋ)
肩而過(ㄘㄚㄐㄧㄢㄦˊㄍㄨㄛˋ)
to pass each other so clo that they almost rub ea other; to brush past son body

擦傷(ㄘㄚㄕㄤ)
a scratch; to suffer scratch: 他擦傷了膝蓋。 rubbed the skin off his kne

擦子(ㄘㄚㄗˇ)
a rubber; an eraser

擦擦(ㄘㄚㄘㄚ)
the sound of footsteps

擦油(ㄘㄚㄧㄡˊ)
to coat with oil; to app pomade; to oil; to varnish grease

【擱】2079
ㄍㄜ ge gē
1. to lay; to leave; to put: 他手揣在口袋中。He put h hands in his pockets.
2. to file: 把這些信件仔細擱來。File these letters car fully.
3. to delay; to put aside

擱筆(ㄍㄜㄅㄧˇ)
to lay down the pen—t stop writing: 我已擱筆十幾了。I've stopped writing fo ten years.

擱下(ㄍㄜˉㄒㄧㄚˋ)
unable to lay down or asid (work); unable to forget: 擱不下那些瑣事。She is unabl to forget those trifles.

攔不住(《ㄢ ·ㄅㄨ ㄓㄨ)
① not fit to be kept long ②
cannot stand

攔得下(《ㄢ ·ㄉㄜ ㄒㄧㄚ)
capable of putting down or
aside: 我怎麼攔得下這麼重要
的事呢? How can I put aside
such an important matter?

攔得住(《ㄢ ·ㄉㄜ ㄓㄨ)
fit to be kept long

攔遲(《ㄢ ·ㄔ)
to delay; to hold up

攔淺(《ㄢ ㄑㄧㄢ)
① to be held up by some
obstacle; to run aground; to
get stranded: 船攔淺了。The
ship got stranded (or ran
aground). ②(said of negotiations) to come to a dead-
lock: 會議完全攔淺了。The
meeting has totally reached
a deadlock.

攔開(《ㄢ ·ㄎㄞ)
to put aside or lay down
(work): 他把工作攔開了。He
put aside his work.

攔置(《ㄢ ·ㄓ)
to shelve or pigeonhole (a
plan, proposal, etc.): 我們攔
置了一項動議。We have
shelved a motion.

【攫】2080 ㄏㄨㄛˊ huoh huó
1. a trap; a snare
2. to catch; to seize

【擤】2081 ㄒㄧㄥˇ shing xíng
to blow (the nose)
擤鼻涕(ㄒㄧㄥˇ ㄅㄧˊ ·ㄊㄧ)or擤鼻子
(ㄒㄧㄥˇ ㄅㄧˊ ·ㄗ)
to blow the nose

【擰】2082
1. ㄋㄧㄥˊ ning níng
to twist; to pinch; to wring:
把溼毛巾擰乾。Wring out the
wet towel.
擰眉瞪眼(ㄋㄧㄥˊ ㄇㄟˊ ㄉㄥ` ㄧㄢˇ)
to look angry
擰眉立目(ㄋㄧㄥˊ ㄇㄟˊ ㄌㄧ` ㄇㄨˋ)
to look angry

【擰】2082
2. ㄋㄧㄥˇ niing nǐng
1. to wrench; to twist; to
screw: 請把瓶蓋擰開。Screw
(or Twist) the cap off the
bottle, please.
2. wrong; mistaken
3. to differ; to disagree

擰了(ㄋㄧㄥˇ ·ㄌㄜ)
to fail: 我們的計畫全擰了。All
our plans failed.

擰開(ㄋㄧㄥˇ ㄎㄞ)
to wrench apart: 他擰開門鎖。
He wrenched the locked
door open.

【擰】2082
2. ㄋㄧㄥˋ ning nìng
determined; dogged; stub-
born

擰性(ㄋㄧㄥˋ ·ㄒㄧㄥ)
doggedness; stubbornness

擰種(ㄋㄧㄥˋ ㄓㄨㄥˇ)
a stubborn fellow

【擪】2083
1 ㄧㄝ` yeh yè
to press with a finger

十五畫

【擲】2084
ㄓ` jyr zhí
to throw; to cast

擲標槍(ㄓ` ㄅㄧㄠ ㄑㄧㄤ)
(sports) ① javelin throw ②
to throw the javelin

擲瓶(ㄓ` ㄆㄧㄥˊ)
to throw the bottle (in
launching a ship)

擲彈筒(ㄓ` ㄉㄢˋ ㄊㄨㄥˇ)
a grenade launcher

擲地(ㄓ` ㄉㄧ`)
to throw to the ground

擲地金聲(ㄓ` ㄉㄧ` ㄐㄧㄣ ㄕㄥ)or擲地
有聲(ㄓ` ㄉㄧ` ㄧㄡˇ ㄕㄥ)
(said of literary works) extremely elegant and valu-
able: 他的文章真是擲地有聲。
His articles are indeed
extremely valuable.

擲鐵餅(ㄓ` ㄊㄧㄝˇ ㄅㄧㄥˇ)
(sports) discus throw

擲鉛球(ㄓ` ㄑㄧㄢ ㄑㄧㄡˊ)or擲鉛球
(ㄓ` ㄑㄧㄢ ㄑㄧㄡˊ)
(sports) shot put

擲還(ㄓ` ㄏㄨㄢˊ)
to return (something)to me
或 Please return(something)
to me.

擲交(ㄓ` ㄐㄧㄠ)
to hand over; please hand
to me

擲下(ㄓ` ㄒㄧㄚ`)
please hand···to me

擲骰子 or 擲色子(ㄓ` ㄕㄞˇ ·ㄗ)
to cast dice; to throw dice

擲梭(ㄓ` ㄙㄨㄛ)
(said of time) to pass as
quickly as a shuttle

【擷】2085
ㄒㄧㄝˊ shye xié
(又讀 ㄐㄧㄝˊ jye jié)
to pick; to collect; to gather

擷芳(ㄒㄧㄝˊ ㄈㄤ)
to pick flowers

擷取菁華(ㄒㄧㄝˊ ㄑㄩ ㄐㄧㄥ ㄏㄨㄚˊ)
to pick the best

擷采(ㄒㄧㄝˊ ㄘㄞˇ)
to cull; to pick; to gather

【擴】2086
ㄎㄨㄛ` kuoh kuò
to enlarge; to magnify; to
expand; to extend

擴大(ㄎㄨㄛ` ㄉㄚˋ)
① to enlarge; to expand; to
magnify; to widen; to
broaden: 擴大眼界 to widen
one's outlook; to broaden
one's horizons ② to swell; to
distend; to dilate

擴建(ㄎㄨㄛ` ㄐㄧㄢˋ)
to extend (a factory, mine,
etc.)

擴軍(ㄎㄨㄛ` ㄐㄩㄣ)
a military buildup; arma-
ment expansion; to enlarge
military forces

擴展(ㄎㄨㄛ` ㄓㄢˇ)
to stretch; to expand; to
extend; to spread: 日本的貿
易很快地擴展至世界各地。
Japanese trade expanded
rapidly in all parts of the
world.

擴張(ㄎㄨㄛ` ㄓㄤ)
① to stretch; to expand; to
spread; to expand ② to
dilate; dilation: 血管擴張
blood vessel dilation

擴充(ㄎㄨㄛ` ㄔㄨㄥ)
to expand; to enlarge;
expansion; extension

擴散(ㄎㄨㄛ` ㄙㄢ`)
① (physics) to diffuse; diffusion ② to scatter about

擴音器(ㄎㄨㄛ` ㄧㄣ ㄑㄧ`)
a megaphone; a microphone

【擺】2087
ㄅㄞˇ bae bǎi
1. to arrange; to display; to
place; to put: 把這本書擺到架
子上。Put the book on the
shelf.
2. to wave; to swing; to oscil-

〔手
部〕

(手部)

late; to wag: 這隻狗的尾巴來回地擺動著。The dog's tail waves to and fro.
3. a pendulum
4. to assume; to put on

擺撥 (ㄅㄞˇ ㄅㄛ)
to dismiss from attention; to put aside

擺佈 (ㄅㄞˇ ㄅㄨˋ)
①to manage or handle (a person): 我絕不任人擺佈。I'll never allow myself to be ordered about. ②to arrange

擺不開 (ㄅㄞˇ·ㄅㄨ ㄎㄞ) or 擺不下 (ㄅㄞˇ·ㄅㄨ ㄒㄧㄚˋ)
①There is no room to place it. ②The business in hand cannot be shaken off.

擺平 (ㄅㄞˇ ㄆㄧㄥˊ)
①(slang) to make satisfied
②to put down something securely

擺譜兒 (ㄅㄞˇ ㄆㄨˇㄦˊ)
to take pains to show off; to try to appear rich and elegant

擺門面 (ㄅㄞˇ ㄇㄣˊㄇㄧㄢˋ) or 擺場面 (ㄅㄞˇ ㄔㄤˇ ㄇㄧㄢˋ)
to keep up appearances

擺飯 (ㄅㄞˇ ㄈㄢˋ)
to lay the table for a meal

擺渡 (ㄅㄞˇ ㄉㄨˋ)
to cross a river on a ferry; to ferry

擺動 (ㄅㄞˇ ㄉㄨㄥˋ)
to sway; to flicker; to swing; to oscillate

擺動角 (ㄅㄞˇ ㄉㄨㄥˋ ㄐㄧㄠˇ)
an angle of oscillation

擺攤兒 (ㄅㄞˇ ㄊㄢ ㄦˊ)
to set up a (vending) stand

擺頭 (ㄅㄞˇ ㄊㄡˊ)
to shake one's head (to show disapproval)

擺脫 (ㄅㄞˇ ㄊㄨㄛ)
to free oneself from; to cast off; to get away from; to shake off (a tailer)

擺弄 (ㄅㄞˇ ㄋㄨㄥˋ)
①to toy with; to play with ②to make fun of; to trick

擺擂臺 (ㄅㄞˇ ㄌㄟˊ ㄊㄞˊ)
to give an open challenge

擺列 (ㄅㄞˇ ㄌㄧㄝˋ)
to display in neat rows; to place in order

擺龍門陣 (ㄅㄞˇ ㄌㄨㄥˊ ㄇㄣˊ ㄓㄣˋ)
to get together and gossip; to make leisurely conversation

擺供 (ㄅㄞˇ ㄍㄨㄥˋ)
to offer sacrifices

擺開 (ㄅㄞˇ ㄎㄞ)
to arrange; to place for display

擺闊 (ㄅㄞˇ ㄎㄨㄛˋ)
to show off one's wealth

擺空架子 (ㄅㄞˇ ㄎㄨㄥ ㄐㄧㄚˋ·ㄗ)
to affect superiority

擺好 (ㄅㄞˇ ㄏㄠˇ)
to place or set properly

擺架子 (ㄅㄞˇ ㄐㄧㄚˋ·ㄗ)
to be arrogant; to be snobbish; to put on airs

擺酒 (ㄅㄞˇ ㄐㄧㄡˇ)
to give a banquet

擺局 (ㄅㄞˇ ㄐㄩˊ)
to arrange a ruse

擺齊 (ㄅㄞˇ ㄑㄧˊ)
to place in neat order: 把架子上的東西全擺齊。Place everything on the shelf in neat order.

擺下 (ㄅㄞˇ ㄒㄧㄚˋ)
①to put down ②to arrange

擺針 (ㄅㄞˇ ㄓㄣ)
an oscillating needle (on a meter, etc.)

擺陣 (ㄅㄞˇ ㄓㄣˋ)
to deploy troops

擺桌子 (ㄅㄞˇ ㄓㄨㄛ·ㄗ)
to set the table

擺出(來) (ㄅㄞˇ ㄔㄨ ·ㄌㄞ/·ㄌㄞˊ)
①to take out for display ②to assume; to put on: 他擺出一副無辜的樣子。He assumed a look of innocence.

擺錘 (ㄅㄞˇ ㄔㄨㄟˊ)
a pendulum

擺時 (ㄅㄞˇ ㄕˊ)
the period of oscillation

擺設 (ㄅㄞˇ ㄕㄜˋ)
to furnish and decorate (a room): 屋裏擺設得很好。The house is well furnished.

擺設兒 (ㄅㄞˇ ㄕㄜˋ ㄦˊ)
articles for interior decoration: 這間屋子有很多小擺設兒。There are a lot of knick-knacks in this room.

擺手 (ㄅㄞˇ ㄕㄡˇ)
to swing one's arms: 他擺手

向我告別。He waved goodbye to me.

擺上 (ㄅㄞˇ ㄕㄤˋ)
to put up (for display)

擺子 (ㄅㄞˇ·ㄗ)
malaria 亦作「瘧疾」

擺夷 (ㄅㄞˇ ㄧˊ)
a small ethnic group living in Szechwan and Yünnan

擺樣子 (ㄅㄞˇ ㄧㄤˋ·ㄗ)
to put on for appearance's sake

擺烏龍 (ㄅㄞˇ ㄨ ㄌㄨㄥˊ)
to talk irresponsibly; to speak with exaggeration

擺尾 (ㄅㄞˇ ㄨㄟˇ)
to wag the tail

【擾】 2088   ㄖㄠˇ rao rǎo
1. to disturb; to agitate; to harass; to trouble
2. to trespass on somebody's hospitality: 叨擾, 叨擾。Thank you for your hospitality.
3. disorder

擾民 (ㄖㄠˇ ㄇㄧㄣˊ)
to harass the people (by tyrannical policies, etc.)

擾動 (ㄖㄠˇ ㄉㄨㄥˋ)
to disturb; to agitate

擾亂 (ㄖㄠˇ ㄌㄨㄢˋ)
to disturb; to agitate; to harass (enemy troops); to create confusion: 別擾亂我的視線。Don't interfere with my view.

擾亂治安 (ㄖㄠˇ ㄌㄨㄢˋ ㄓˋ ㄢ)
to disturb peace and order

擾害 (ㄖㄠˇ ㄏㄞˋ)
to harass and injure

擾攘 (ㄖㄠˇ ㄖㄤˇ)
disturbance; tumult; hustle and bustle

【擿】 2089   ㄊㄧ tih tì
1. to instigate; to incite
2. to expose

擿伏 (ㄊㄧ ㄈㄨˊ)
to bring a secret to light; to expose evil

擿問 (ㄊㄧˋ ㄨㄣˋ)
to interrogate

【擻】 2090   ㄙㄡˇ sǒu sou
to shake; to quake; to tremble; to flutter

擻抖抖 (ㄙㄡˇ ㄉㄡˇ ㄉㄡˇ)

trembling; shivering

【攄】 2091　ㄕㄨ shu shū
to make known; to vent

攄憤 (ㄕㄨ ㄈㄣˋ)
to vent one's indignation

攄懷 (ㄕㄨ ㄏㄨㄞˊ)
to give vent to one's emotion

攄陳 (ㄕㄨ ㄔㄣˊ)
to present (a proposal, an opinion, etc.)

攄誠 (ㄕㄨ ㄔㄥˊ)
to be frank

攄意 (ㄕㄨ ㄧˋ)
to give expression to one's feelings

【攆】 2092　ㄋㄧㄢˇ nean niǎn
1. to expel; to oust; to drive
2. to catch up

攆不開 (ㄋㄧㄢˇㄅㄨˋㄎㄞ)
to try in vain to drive (a person) away; impossible to drive (a person) away

攆跑了 (ㄋㄧㄢˇㄆㄠˇ·ㄌㄜ)
to have driven (someone) away

攆逐 (ㄋㄧㄢˇ ㄓㄨˊ)
to drive (someone) away; to throw (someone) out; to expel; to oust

攆出去 (ㄋㄧㄢˇㄔㄨ·ㄑㄩ)
to throw (someone) out; to drive away; 你不該把他攆出去的。You shouldn't have thrown him out.

攆走 (ㄋㄧㄢˇㄗㄡˇ)
to drive (someone) away; to dismiss; 他攆走一個做事拖延的工人。He dismissed a dilatory worker.

【攀】 2093　ㄆㄢ pan pān
1. to hold to; to climb; to hang on; to clamber
2. to involve

攀附 (ㄆㄢ ㄈㄨˋ)
to hang on to or to attach oneself to (power, glory, etc.)

攀登 (ㄆㄢ ㄉㄥ)
to climb; to scale

攀談 (ㄆㄢ ㄊㄢˊ)
to strike up a conversation; to drag another into conversation; 他們用英語攀談。They struck up a conversation in

English.

攀留 (ㄆㄢ ㄌㄧㄡˊ)
to detain (a guest)

攀連 (ㄆㄢ ㄌㄧㄢˊ)
to involve; to implicate

攀戀 (ㄆㄢ ㄌㄧㄢˋ)
to regret the resignation of (a popular superior, official, etc.)

攀鱗 (ㄆㄢ ㄌㄧㄣˊ)
to ride on the coattails of a brilliant master

攀龍附鳳 (ㄆㄢ ㄌㄨㄥˊㄈㄨˋㄈㄥˋ)
(literally) to hang on a dragon and to stick to a phoenix—to establish oneself by riding on the coattails of a brilliant master; to put oneself under the patronage of a bigwig

攀龍附驥 (ㄆㄢ ㄌㄨㄥˊㄈㄨˋㄐㄧˋ)
(literally) to ride on a dragon and a steed—to achieve success by riding on the coattails of a brilliant master

攀桂 (ㄆㄢ ㄍㄨㄟˋ)
(in old China) to pass the civil service examination

攀供 (ㄆㄢ ㄍㄨㄥ)
to offer a false testimony to implicate someone

攀花折柳 (ㄆㄢ ㄏㄨㄚ ㄓㄜˊ ㄌㄧㄡˇ)
(literally) to injure flowers and willows—to lead a life of debauchery

攀親 (ㄆㄢ ㄑㄧㄣ)
①to seek marriage ②to remind others (particularly the influential and wealthy) of the relationship one has with them

攀親道故 (ㄆㄢ ㄑㄧㄣ ㄉㄠˋㄍㄨˋ)
to claim the ties of blood or friendship

攀折 (ㄆㄢ ㄓㄜˊ)
to injure (a plant) by picking or breaking

攀扯 (ㄆㄢ ㄔㄜˇ)
to drag into an affair; to implicate; 他被攀扯於一件罪案中。He is implicated in a crime.

攀纏 (ㄆㄢ ㄔㄢˊ)
to hang on persistently; to keep annoying by inappropriate talks or requests

攀鞍上馬 (ㄆㄢ ㄢ ㄕㄤˋㄇㄚˇ)
to mount a horse

攀援 (ㄆㄢ ㄩㄢˊ)
to hang on to an influential person

攀緣 (ㄆㄢ ㄩㄢˊ)
①(Buddhism) to be affected by one's environment ②to climb; to clamber

攀緣莖 (ㄆㄢ ㄩㄢˊㄐㄧㄥ)
(botany) clinging stem

攀轅扣馬 (ㄆㄢ ㄩㄢˊㄎㄡˋㄇㄚˇ)
(said of people in old China) to try to stop the departure of a popular official by stopping his carriage from leaving

攀轅臥轍 (ㄆㄢ ㄩㄢˊㄨㄛˋㄔㄜˋ)
(said of people in old China) to try to stop the departure of a popular official by grasping the shafts of his carriage and lying down in the wheel ruts

十六畫

【攏】 2094　1. ㄌㄨㄥˇ loong lǒng
1. to gather; to collect; to tie: 把乾草攏住。Tie the hay in a bundle.
2. to lean
3. to come alongside; to approach; to reach
4. to add up; to sum up
5. to comb (hair)

攏頭 (ㄌㄨㄥˇㄊㄡˊ)
to comb hair

攏共 (ㄌㄨㄥˇㄍㄨㄥˋ)
altogether; in total

攏總 (ㄌㄨㄥˇㄗㄨㄥˇ)
altogether; in total

攏岸 (ㄌㄨㄥˇㄢˋ)
(said of a ship) to approach the shore

【攏】 2094　2. ㄌㄨㄥˊ iong lóng
a special fingering in playing the lute

十七畫

【攔】 2095　ㄌㄢˊ lan lán
to impede; to obstruct; to hinder; to block; to bar; to hold back

〔手部〕

攔不住（カラ・ㄅㄨㄓㄨˋ）
incapable of impeding or being impeded; cannot stop or be stopped

攔擋（カラ ㄉㄤˇ）
to impede; to obstruct; to hinder; to block: 球員想攔擋他的對手。The player tried to block his opponent.

攔路（カラ ㄌㄨˋ）or 攔道（カラ ㄉㄠˋ）
to block the way: 攔路搶劫 to waylay; to hold up

攔河壩（カラ ㄏㄜˊ ㄅㄚˋ）
a dam (across a river)

攔擊（カラ ㄐㄧˊ）
to intercept and attack; to volley

攔街虎（カラ ㄐㄧㄝ ㄏㄨˇ）
a street robber

攔劫（カラ ㄐㄧㄝˊ）
to intercept and rob

攔截（カラ ㄐㄧㄝˊ）
to intercept; to attack or stop on the way

攔住（カラ ㄓㄨˋ）
to obstruct; to block; to hinder; to stop

攔車（カラ ㄔㄜ）
to interrupt the course of a vehicle; to stop a vehicle

攔沙壩（カラ ㄕㄚ ㄅㄚˋ）
a check dam

攔水閘（カラ ㄕㄨㄟˇ ㄓㄚˊ）
a dam lock; a dam gate

攔阻（カラ ㄗㄨˇ）
to impede; to obstruct; to hinder; to block; to stop: 倒下的樹木攔阻道路。The fallen trees obstruct the road.

攔腰（カラ ㄧㄠ）
①by the waist: 他把我攔腰抱住。He held me by the waist. ② to cut across in the middle

【攖】 ㄧㄥ ing yīng 2096
1. to offend; to irritate
2. to disturb; to stir up

攖其鋒（ㄧㄥ ㄑㄧˊ ㄈㄥ）
to blunt the thrust (of an attacking force)

攖人心（ㄧㄥ ㄖㄣˊ ㄒㄧㄣ）
to disturb peace of mind

【攘】 1. 日尤 raang rǎng 2097
confused; disorderly

in a state of confusion: 街上人潮熙熙攘攘。Streams of people busily come and go on the street.

【攘】 2. 日尤 rang rǎng 2097
1. to take by force
2. to eliminate; to repel; to resist
3. to shake

攘辟（日尤 ㄆㄧˋ）
to stand off; to make way

攘臂（日尤 ㄅㄧˋ）
to bare one's hands—to rise to action with a determined shake of the arms

攘臂高呼（日尤 ㄅㄧˋ《ㄠ ㄏㄨ）
to raise one's hands and shout

攘袂（日尤 ㄇㄟˋ）
to push up one's sleeves and bare one's arms—to rise to action with a determined shake of the arms

攘奪（日尤 ㄉㄨㄛˊ）
to take by force

攘詬（日尤 《ㄡˋ）
to clear oneself of a dishonor; to cleanse oneself of dishonor

攘竊（日尤 ㄑㄧㄝˋ）
to steal; to pilfer; to filch

攘袖（日尤 ㄒㄧㄡˋ）
to roll up sleeves

攘場（日尤 ㄔㄤˊ）or（日尤 ㄔㄤˊ）
to spread harvested grain over an area

攘除（日尤 ㄔㄨˊ）
to rid; to eliminate; to dispel

攘善（日尤 ㄕㄢˋ）
to appropriate other's credit or honor to be his own

攘災（日尤 ㄗㄞ）
to ward off calamities; to avoid disaster

攘夷（日尤 ㄧˊ）
to repel the barbarians

【攙】 ㄔㄢ chan chān 2098
1. to lead (a person) by the hand; to support or assist somebody while standing or walking
2. to mix; to blend

攙扶（ㄔㄢ ㄈㄨ）
to lead (a person) by the hand

攙合（ㄔㄢ ㄏㄜˊ）or 攙和（ㄔㄢ ㄏㄜˊ）
to mix; to blend; to mingle

攙話接舌（ㄔㄢ ㄏㄨㄚˋ ㄐㄧㄝ ㄕㄜˊ）
to slander others

攙雜（ㄔㄢ ㄗㄚˊ）
to mix up; to jumble together

攙假（ㄔㄢ ㄐㄧㄚˇ）
to add impurities; to adulterate: 攙假的食物有害健康。Adulterated food is bad for the health.

攙起（ㄔㄢ ㄑㄧˇ）
to help someone stand up by giving him a hand

攙親（ㄔㄢ ㄑㄧㄣ）
to help the bride out of her sedan chair (a rite performed usually by a relatively well-to-do matron among her new relatives)

攙雜（ㄔㄢ ㄗㄚˊ）
to make impure; to add imitation goods or inferior products to a shipment of merchandise in violation of business ethics: 別把糖和鹽攙雜在一起。Don't mix up the sugar with the salt.

攙嘴（ㄔㄢ ㄗㄨㄟˇ）
to interrupt

十八畫

【攛】 ㄘㄨㄢ tsuan cuān 2099
1. to throw; to fling
2. to urge; to persuade
3. to do in a hurry

攛掇（ㄘㄨㄢ ㄉㄨㄛˊ）
to urge; to persuade; to induce; to egg on: 他們攛掇我們一同去。They urged us to go with them.

攛弄（ㄘㄨㄢ ㄋㄨㄥˋ）
to urge; to persuade; to induce

【攜】（攜、携、擕）ㄒㄧㄝˊ shye xié（讀音ㄒㄧˋ shi xī） 2100
1. to take; to carry
2. to help; to lead

攜抱（ㄒㄧㄝˊ ㄅㄠˋ）
to carry in one's arms

攜帶（ㄒㄧㄝˊ ㄉㄞˋ）
to carry with oneself; to

take along

攜 (ㄒㄧㄝˊ ㄊㄨㄥˊ)
to bring along

攜眷 (ㄒㄧㄝˊ ㄐㄩㄢˋ)
to take one's family along:
如果我出國讀書，我想攜眷同
行。If I study abroad, I want
to travel with my family.

攜手 (ㄒㄧㄝˊ ㄕㄡˇ)
① to hold each other's hand:
讓我們攜手並進。Let's join
hands and advance together.
② to cooperate

攜貳 (ㄒㄧㄝˊ ㄦˋ)
to cherish treachery

攜幼 (ㄒㄧㄝˊ ㄧㄡˋ)
to take one's young children
along

【攝】 2101
ㄕㄜˋ sheh shè
1. to take in; to absorb; to
attract
2. to take a photograph (or a
shot) of
3. to regulate
4. to represent

攝理 (ㄕㄜˋ ㄌㄧˇ)
to manage in place of an-
other; to hold (an office) in
an acting capacity

攝力 (ㄕㄜˋ ㄌㄧˋ)
(physics) attraction

攝錄放映機 (ㄕㄜˋ ㄌㄨˋ ㄈㄤˋ ㄧㄥˋ ㄐㄧ)
(television) a camcorder

攝護腺 (ㄕㄜˋ ㄏㄨˋ ㄒㄧㄢˋ)
the prostate; the prostate
gland

攝魂 (ㄕㄜˋ ㄏㄨㄣˊ)
to summon souls of the dead

攝魂奪魄 (ㄕㄜˋ ㄏㄨㄣˊ ㄉㄨㄛˊ ㄆㄛˋ)
to hold spellbound; spell-
binding

攝取 (ㄕㄜˋ ㄑㄩˇ)
① to take in; to absorb; to
assimilate ② to take a photograph of; to shoot

攝行 (ㄕㄜˋ ㄒㄧㄥˊ)
to act for another

攝製 (ㄕㄜˋ ㄓˋ)
(said of a movie or docu-
mentary) produced by; to
produce

攝政 (ㄕㄜˋ ㄓㄥˋ)or 攝主 (ㄕㄜˋ ㄓㄨˇ)
to serve as regent; the
Prince Regent

攝政王 (ㄕㄜˋ ㄓㄥˋ ㄨㄤˊ)
the Prince Regent

攝篆 (ㄕㄜˋ ㄓㄨㄢˋ)
to act as a deputy

攝持 (ㄕㄜˋ ㄔˊ)
to take proper care of one's
life

攝氏寒暑表 (ㄕㄜˋ ㄕˋ ㄏㄢˊ ㄕㄨˇ ㄅㄧㄠˇ)
or 攝氏溫度計 (ㄕㄜˋ ㄕˋ ㄨㄣ ㄉㄨˋ ㄐㄧˋ)
a centigrade thermometer; a
Celsius thermometer

攝生 (ㄕㄜˋ ㄕㄥ)
to pay attention to health;
to keep fit; hygiene: 你應該學
習攝生之道。You should learn
how to keep fit.

攝影 (ㄕㄜˋ ㄧㄥˇ)
photography; to take a photograph of: 我們畢業時攝影
留念。We took a souvenir
photograph at graduation.

攝影棚 (ㄕㄜˋ ㄧㄥˇ ㄆㄥˊ)
a sound stage; a (movie)
studio

攝影機 (ㄕㄜˋ ㄧㄥˇ ㄐㄧ)
a camera

攝位 (ㄕㄜˋ ㄨㄟˋ)
to assume the throne in
place of the legitimate ruler

攝衛 (ㄕㄜˋ ㄨㄟˋ)
to take care of one's health

十九畫

【攢】 2102
1. ㄗㄢˇ tzaan zǎn
to hoard; to save; to accumulate

攢錢 (ㄗㄢˇ ㄑㄧㄢˊ)
to hoard money: 這對夫婦正
攢錢買別墅。The couple are
saving money to buy a villa.

【攢】 2102
2. ㄘㄨㄢˊ tswan
cuán
to bring together; to gather;
to assemble; to collect

攢盤兒 (ㄘㄨㄢˊ ㄆㄢˊ ㄦˊ)
a sundry dish

攢眉蹙額 (ㄘㄨㄢˊ ㄇㄟˊ ㄘㄨˋ ㄜˊ)
to knit the brows: 她攢眉蹙
額，似乎感到不快。She knitted
her brows and looked dis-
pleased.

攢蹄 (ㄘㄨㄢˊ ㄊㄧˊ)
(said of horses) to gallop

攢盒 (ㄘㄨㄢˊ ㄏㄜˊ)
a container for holding vari-

ous foods simultaneously

攢聚 (ㄘㄨㄢˊ ㄐㄩˋ)
to huddle together; to crowd
together: 孩子們攢聚在一起取
暖。The children huddled
together for warmth.

攢錢 (ㄘㄨㄢˊ ㄑㄧㄢˊ)
to put money together (for
some purpose)

攢簇 (ㄘㄨㄢˊ ㄘㄨˋ)
to crowd together

攢攢 (ㄘㄨㄢˊ ㄘㄨㄢˊ)
to gather together and beat
(a person)

【攤】 2103
ㄊㄢ tan tōn
1. to spread; to open: 把棉被攤
開曬一曬。Spread the quilt to
dry in the sun.
2. to divide equally; to apportion: 分攤責任 to distribute
responsibility
3. a booth; a stand; a stall: 水
果攤 a fruit stall
4. a collection of liquid; a pool
of (water, mud, blood, etc.):
我的車子陷入一攤泥中。My
car stuck in a pool of mud
of the road.

攤牌 (ㄊㄢ ㄆㄞˊ)
a showdown; to have a showdown

攤派 (ㄊㄢ ㄆㄞˋ)
to apportion

攤販 (ㄊㄢ ㄈㄢˋ)
a vender or stallkeeper; a
seller on the sidewalk

攤開 (ㄊㄢ ㄎㄞ)
to spread out; to unfold

攤錢 (ㄊㄢ ㄑㄧㄢˊ)or 攤款 (ㄊㄢ ㄎㄨㄢˇ)
to share the burden of a
payment: 每人攤款一百元。
Each will share one hundred
dollars.

攤還 (ㄊㄢ ㄏㄨㄢˊ)
to repay in installments; to
amortize

攤認 (ㄊㄢ ㄖㄣˋ)
① to share (a financial burden) ② to subscribe (to
charitable projects, funds,
etc.)

攤子 (ㄊㄢ ˙ㄗ)or 攤兒 (ㄊㄢ ㄦˊ)
a stand; a booth; a stall

攤位 (ㄊㄢ ㄨㄟˋ)
a stall or booth (especially
a fixed one in a market)

【攞】 2104
ㄌㄨㄛ lhuo luó
to tuck; to pull

攞起衣服(ㄌㄨㄛ ㄑㄧˇ ㄧ ㄈㄨˊ)
to tuck up the skirt of a garment

【擷】 2105
ㄉㄧㄢ dian diǎn
to stumble; to fall

【攣】 2106
ㄌㄩㄢ liuan luán
1. tangled; entwined
2. crooked
3. contraction: 痙攣 spasm; convulsions

攣手足(ㄌㄩㄢ ㄕㄡˇ ㄗㄨˊ)
hands and feet crooked

攣弱(ㄌㄩㄢ ㄖㄨㄛˋ)
crooked and weak

攣縮(ㄌㄩㄢ ㄙㄨㄛˋ)
a spasm; a twitch; contraction

攣腕(ㄌㄩㄢ ㄨㄢˋ)
a sort of arthropathy

二十畫

【攩】 2107
ㄉㄤˇ daang dǎng
1. to impede; to obstruct; to hinder; to block 亦作「擋」
2. a party; a faction; a clique; an association 亦作「黨」

【攪】 2108
1. ㄐㄧㄠˇ jeau jiǎo
1. to stir; to mix
2. to agitate; to disturb; to annoy

攪拌(ㄐㄧㄠˇ ㄅㄢˋ)
to stir or churn; to mix: 你無法將油與水攪拌在一塊兒。You can't mix oil with water.

攪拌器(ㄐㄧㄠˇ ㄅㄢˋ ㄑㄧˋ)
a mixer; an agitator

攪動(ㄐㄧㄠˇ ㄉㄨㄥˋ)
to mix; to churn; to stir: 船的推進器攪動水產生泡沫。The ship's propeller churned the waves to foam.

攪亂(ㄐㄧㄠˇ ㄌㄨㄢˋ)
to disturb; to ruffle; to disarrange

攪和(ㄐㄧㄠˇ ㄏㄜ˙)
①to mix evenly by stirring; to mingle ②to mix up; to confuse: 別把這兩碼事攪和在一起。Don't mix up these two different matters.

攪混(ㄐㄧㄠˇ ㄏㄨㄣˇ)
to mix by stirring; to blend; to mingle

攪局(ㄐㄧㄠˇ ㄐㄩˊ)
to spoil; to disturb

攪擾(ㄐㄧㄠˇ ㄖㄠˇ)
to disturb; to stir

攪勻(ㄐㄧㄠˇ ㄩㄣˊ)
to make even by stirring; to mix

【攪】 2108
2. (攪) 《ㄍㄠ gao
gāo
to do; to manage; to handle; 胡攪 to make a mess of

攪鬼(ㄍㄠ ㄍㄨㄟˇ)
to play underhand tricks

【攫】 2109
ㄐㄩㄝˊ jyue jué
to seize; to take hold of; to snatch; to catch

攫搏(ㄐㄩㄝˊ ㄅㄛˊ)
to snatch with the claw or the paw

攫奪(ㄐㄩㄝˊ ㄉㄨㄛˊ)
to seize; to snatch; to grab

攫攫(ㄐㄩㄝˊ ㄘㄞˊ)
to scramble for

攫取(ㄐㄩㄝˊ ㄑㄩˇ)
to take by force; to seize

【攥】 2110
(攥) ㄗㄨㄢˋ tzuan
zuàn
to grasp; to grip; to clutch: 他一把攥住我的手。He caught hold of my hand.

二十一畫

【攬】 2111
(攬) ㄌㄢˇ laan lǎn
1. to be in full possession of: 總攬權綱 to hold the reins of government; to get hold of the power in the state
2. to take into one's arms: 她把兒子摟在懷裡。She clasped her son to her bosom.
3. to make a selective collection of
4. to take on; to undertake
5. to grasp; to monopolize: 包攬 to monopolize; to undertake the whole thing
6. to round up: 延攬人才 to round up talents

攬筆(ㄌㄢˇ ㄅㄧˇ)
to take the pen—to write

攬轡(ㄌㄢˇ ㄆㄟˋ)
to hold the reins

攬轡澄清(ㄌㄢˇ ㄆㄟˋ ㄔㄥˊ ㄑㄧㄥ)
to aspire to bring perfect order to the nation when one enters upon a political career

攬貨(ㄌㄢˇ ㄏㄨㄛˋ)
to monopolize the distribution or delivery of certain goods

攬鏡自照(ㄌㄢˇ ㄐㄧㄥˋ ㄗˋ ㄓㄠˋ)
to hold a mirror to watch one's own reflection

攬取(ㄌㄢˇ ㄑㄩˇ)
to get hold of

攬權(ㄌㄢˇ ㄑㄩㄢˊ)
to grasp full authority; to arrogate power to oneself

攬勝(ㄌㄢˇ ㄕㄥˋ)
to enjoy scenery; to see scenic sights

二十二畫

【攮】 2112
ㄋㄤˇ naang nǎng
to thrust; to stab: 他的手臂被攮了一刀。He was stabbed in the arm.

攮子(ㄋㄤˇ ˙ㄗ)
a dagger or bodkin

支部
ㄓ jy zhī

【支】 2113
ㄓ jy zhī
1. to pay; to disburse; to defray
2. to support; to sustain; to bear
3. to prop up; to put up
4. to prick up; to raise: 她支起耳朵聽。She pricked up her ears.
5. to send away; to put somebody off: 她把推銷員給支走了。She sent the salesman away.
6. a branch; a subdivision; an offshoot: 我們住在一家郵政支局附近。We lived near a branch post office.

7. a term for indicating amount or number: 一支蠟燭 one candle 一支筆 one pen

8. (textile) count: 六十支紗 60-count yarn

9. as in 地支, the Terrestrial Branches used in calculation with the Celestial Stems (天干)

支撥 (ㄓ ㄅㄛ)
to make (funds) available

支部 (ㄓ ㄅㄨ)
① branch headquarters (of a political party) ② the radical (支)

支派 (ㄓ ㄆㄞ)
① a subdivision; a branch (of a school of thought) ② to order; to send; to appoint

支配 (ㄓ ㄆㄟ)
① to control; to dominate: 人受環境的支配。Man is governed by circumstances. ② to manage; to administer; to allocate; to arrange: 他善於支配自己的金錢。He is good at budgeting his money.

支票 (ㄓ ㄆㄧㄠ)
a cheque or check: 空頭支票 a bad (or rubber) check 旅行支票 a traveler's check

支票簿 (ㄓ ㄆㄧㄠ ㄅㄨ)
a checkbook

支脈 (ㄓ ㄇㄞ)
a branch (of a mountain range); an offshoot: 這座山是天山的支脈。The mountain is an offshoot of the Tienshan Mountains.

支費 (ㄓ ㄈㄟ)
expenses; payment

支付 (ㄓ ㄈㄨ)
to pay (what is owed); to defray

支付憑證 (ㄓ ㄈㄨ ㄆㄧㄥ ㄓㄥ)
(accounting) payment vouchers

支點 (ㄓ ㄉㄧㄢ)
a point of support; a fulcrum

支店 (ㄓ ㄉㄧㄢ)
a branch store: 我們在這個城市有許多支店。We have many branch stores in the city.

支隊 (ㄓ ㄉㄨㄟ)
a military detachment or contingent: 游擊支隊 a guer-

rilla detachment

支 (ㄓˊ)
China (a term used in the Buddhist scriptures and formerly used by the Japanese)

支那通 (ㄓˋ ㄋㄚˋ ㄊㄨㄥ)
a China expert or Sinologue (a term formerly used by the Japanese)

支那語 (ㄓˋ ㄋㄚˋ ㄩˇ)
the Chinese language (a term formerly used by the Japanese)

支孽 (ㄓ ㄋㄧㄝ)or 支庶 (ㄓ ㄕ)
the son of a concubine

支離 (ㄓ ㄌㄧ)
① to disintegrate; to disunite ② incoherent; disjointed; fragmented; broken

支離破碎 (ㄓ ㄌㄧ ㄆㄛ ㄙㄨㄟ)
completely disintegrated; torn to pieces; fragmented: 我只能聽到他們支離破碎的談話。I could hear only fragments of their conversation.

支流 (ㄓ ㄌㄧㄡ)
① a tributary (of a river): 漢水是揚子江的支流之一。The Han River is one of the tributaries of the Yangtze River. ② minor aspects; non-essentials

支領 (ㄓ ㄌㄧㄥ)
to draw money

支路 (ㄓ ㄌㄨ)
a branch way

支根 (ㄓ ㄍㄣ)
(botany) a lateral root

支款 (ㄓ ㄎㄨㄢ)
to withdraw money

支行 (ㄓ ㄒㄧㄥ)
a subbranch (of a bank)

支架 (ㄓ ㄐㄧㄚ)
a support; a stand; a trestle

支節 (ㄓ ㄐㄧㄝ)
a joint (of bones, etc.)
to dismember

支氣管 (ㄓ ㄑㄧ ㄍㄨㄢ)
bronchi

支氣管氣喘 (ㄓ ㄑㄧ ㄍㄨㄢ ㄑㄧ ㄔㄨㄢ)
bronchial asthma

支氣管炎 (ㄓ ㄑㄧ ㄍㄨㄢ ㄧㄢ)
bronchitis

支取 (ㄓ ㄑㄩ)
to draw (money): 我想到銀行

支取一筆款子。I want to go to the bank and draw some money.

支線 (ㄓ ㄒㄧㄢ)
a branch line; a feeder (line): 鐵路(公路)支線 a feeder railway (highway)

支柱 (ㄓ ㄓㄨ)
a prop; a support; a stay

支持 (ㄓ ㄔ)
to support; to sustain; to bear; support; backing

支持不住 (ㄓ ㄔ ㄅㄨ ㄓㄨ)
unable to keep up efforts; unable to hold out: 我凍得支持不住了。I am so cold that I cannot bear any longer.

支撐 (ㄓ ㄔㄥ)
to prop up; to support; to sustain

支撐危局 (ㄓ ㄔㄥ ㄨㄟ ㄐㄩ)
to play a leading role during a national crisis

支出 (ㄓ ㄔㄨ)
expense; expenditure; outlay; disbursement; to spend; to expend

支絀 (ㄓ ㄔㄨ)
short of money; hard up; needy

支使 (ㄓ ㄕ)
① to engage the services or labor of; to order about ② to send away

支子 (ㄓ ㄗ)
the son of a concubine

支移 (ㄓ ㄧ)
to make up a deficit by drawing upon the surplus

支頤 (ㄓ ㄧ)
to support the chin with the hand

支應 (ㄓ ㄧㄥ)
① to take charge of cash receipts and payments ② to look after; to attend to; to take care of; to deal with

支吾 (ㄓ ㄨ)
① to speak haltingly; to falter; to hem and haw: 她支吾地說了一個藉口。She faltered out an excuse. ② to deal with (a person) just for the occasion

支吾其詞 (ㄓ ㄨ ㄑㄧ ㄘ)
to speak haltingly or ambiguously (with a view to hid-

〔支部〕

ing the truth); to hem and haw; to speak evasively

支援(ㄓ ㄩㄢˋ)
to aid; to support; to assist; to help

支援部隊(ㄓ ㄩㄢˋ ㄅㄨˋ ㄉㄨㄟˋ)
a support unit

支用(ㄓ ㄩㄥˋ)
to disburse

八畫

【攲】 2114 　ㄑㄧ　chī qī
to incline; to lean; to slant

攲倒(ㄑㄧ ㄉㄠˇ)
to slant and fall

攲傾(ㄑㄧ ㄑㄧㄥ)
to slant; to incline

攲斜(ㄑㄧ ㄒㄧㄝˊ)
to slant; to incline; to lurch

攲側(ㄑㄧ ㄘㄜˋ)
to incline; to lean; to lurch

攲臥(ㄑㄧ ㄨㄛˋ)
to lie in a reclined position

攲危(ㄑㄧ ㄨㄟˊ)
tottering

支 部
ㄆㄨ pu pū

二畫

【收】 2115 　ㄕㄡ shou shōu
1. to draw together; to gather; to collect
2. to contain: 這本字典收字一萬五千。The dictionary contains 15,000 entries.
3. to receive; to accept; to take: 她收到他的禮物，但沒接受。She received a gift from him, but did not accept it.
4. to end; to come to a close
5. to retrieve; to take back; to put away

收報機(ㄕㄡ ㄅㄠˋ ㄐㄧ)
a telegraph receiver

收編(ㄕㄡ ㄅㄧㄢ)
to reorganize and incorporate (rebel troops, bandits, etc.) into government forces

收兵(ㄕㄡ ㄅㄧㄥ)
to recall troops; to end hostilities; to call off a battle

收捕(ㄕㄡ ㄅㄨˇ)
to arrest

收不回來(ㄕㄡ ㄅㄨˋ ㄏㄨㄟˊ ㄌㄞˊ)
impossible to get back, regain, or recover

收不住腳(ㄕㄡ ㄅㄨˋ ㄓㄨˋ ㄐㄧㄠˇ)
① unable to put an end to a pursuit ② unable to come to a quick stop (such as during a foot race)

收盤(ㄕㄡ ㄆㄢˊ)
the closing quotation (of a stock or commodity) for the day

收票員(ㄕㄡ ㄆㄧㄠˋ ㄩㄢˊ)
a ticket collector

收捕(ㄕㄡ ㄅㄨˇ)
to confiscate 亦作「沒收」

收埋(ㄕㄡ ㄇㄞˊ)
to collect and bury (dead bodies)

收買(ㄕㄡ ㄇㄞˇ)
① to bribe: 他們用貴重的禮物收買他。They bribed him with costly presents. ② to buy up; to win (support, people's hearts, etc. by less than honorable means): 議員想收買人心。The legislator tried to win popular support.

收發(ㄕㄡ ㄈㄚ)
① to receive and send out (official papers, documents, etc.) ② an office clerk who takes care of the receiving and sending out of official correspondence

收發報機(ㄕㄡ ㄈㄚ ㄅㄠˋ ㄐㄧ)
a transmitter-receiver; a transceiver

收發處(ㄕㄡ ㄈㄚ ㄔㄨˋ)
an office through which official correspondence of an organization is received or sent out

收費(ㄕㄡ ㄈㄟˋ)
to collect fees; to charge

收費站(ㄕㄡ ㄈㄟˋ ㄓㄢˋ)
a toll station

收服(ㄕㄡ ㄈㄨˊ)
to subdue and win the allegiance of (someone)

收復(ㄕㄡ ㄈㄨˋ)
to recover (lost territory): 將軍已收復失陷的城鎮。The general has recovered a conquered town.

收復河山(ㄕㄡ ㄈㄨˋ ㄏㄜˊ ㄕㄢ)
to recover lost territory

收到(ㄕㄡ ㄉㄠˋ)
to receive; to obtain; to achieve: 我這個月收到很多請帖。I have received many invitations this month.

收攤(ㄕㄡ ㄊㄢ)
to pack up the stall or booth (after a day's business is over)

收條(ㄕㄡ ㄊㄧㄠˊ)
(informal) a receipt 亦作「收據」

收聽(ㄕㄡ ㄊㄧㄥ)
to tune in ; to listen to (the radio): 我每天早上都收聽他的節目。I listen to your program every morning.

收納(ㄕㄡ ㄋㄚˋ)
to accept

收孥(ㄕㄡ ㄋㄨˊ)
to try an offender's family along with him

收淚(ㄕㄡ ㄌㄟˋ)
to stop crying

收攬(ㄕㄡ ㄌㄢˇ)
① to collect extensively ② to win (the people's hearts)

收禮(ㄕㄡ ㄌㄧˇ)
to accept a present or gift

收留(ㄕㄡ ㄌㄧㄡˊ)
to give shelter to; to take somebody in

收殮(ㄕㄡ ㄌㄧㄢˋ)
to prepare a corpse for burial

收斂(ㄕㄡ ㄌㄧㄢˇ)
① to collect (taxes, grains, etc.) ② to draw together; to contract ③ to weaken or disappear ④ to pull in one's horns; to become less flagrant in behavior

收斂劑(ㄕㄡ ㄌㄧㄢˇ ㄐㄧˋ)
(medicine) astringents

收錄(ㄕㄡ ㄌㄨˋ)
① to employ; to enter; to enroll; to recruit ② to include (in a list, etc.): 這篇文章已收錄在我編的讀本裏。The article is included in the reader I edited. ③ to

record: 我從不收錄新聞廣播。I never make a recording of the news broadcast.

收羅(ㄕㄡ ㄌㄨㄛˊ)
①to collect; to gather ②to enlist

收羅人才(ㄕㄡ ㄌㄨㄛˊ ㄖㄣˊ ㄘㄞˊ)
to recruit qualified personnel

收攏(ㄕㄡ ㄌㄨㄥˇ)
to draw something in

收割(ㄕㄡ ㄍㄜ)or 收刈(ㄕㄡ ㄧˋ)
to reap; to harvest

收割機(ㄕㄡ ㄍㄜ ㄐㄧ)
a reaping machine; a harvester

收購(ㄕㄡ ㄍㄡˋ)
to buy up; to purchase: 他們購收所有的玩具。He bought up all the toys they had.

收歸國有(ㄕㄡ ㄍㄨㄟ ㄍㄨㄛˊ ㄧㄡˇ)
to nationalize (enterprises)

收工(ㄕㄡ ㄍㄨㄥ)
to end the day's work; to knock off: 該收工了。It's time to knock off.

收口(兒)(ㄕㄡ ㄎㄡˇ ㄦ)
the closure of a wound (as a result of healing)

收看(ㄕㄡ ㄎㄢˋ)
to watch (television)

收款人(ㄕㄡ ㄎㄨㄢˇ ㄖㄣˊ)
a recipient (of remittance); a payee

收款員(ㄕㄡ ㄎㄨㄢˇ ㄩㄢˊ)
a receiving teller

收貨(ㄕㄡ ㄏㄨㄛˋ)
to receive delivered goods

收貨人(ㄕㄡ ㄏㄨㄛˋ ㄖㄣˊ)
a consignee 亦作「受貨人」

收穫(ㄕㄡ ㄏㄨㄛˋ)
①harvest; fruit (of efforts); gains ②to reap; to reward: 這是一次很有收穫的旅行。This is a most rewarding trip.

收回(ㄕㄡ ㄏㄨㄟˊ)
to recover; to recall; to retrieve; to recoup; repossession: 他收回發出的文件。He recalled the documents which had been issued.

收回成命(ㄕㄡ ㄏㄨㄟˊ ㄔㄥˊ ㄇㄧㄥˋ)
to withdraw an order; to revoke a command

收賄(ㄕㄡ ㄏㄨㄟˋ)
to accept bribes; bribery: 公

務員收賄是重罪。Bribery of a public official is a felony.

收集(ㄕㄡ ㄐㄧˊ)
collection; to collect; to gather: 這些畫的收集花費了他畢生之力。The collection of these paintings took him a lifetime.

收繳(ㄕㄡ ㄐㄧㄠˇ)
to take over; to capture

收監(ㄕㄡ ㄐㄧㄢ)
to imprison; to commit to jail; to take into custody

收件人(ㄕㄡ ㄐㄧㄢˋ ㄖㄣˊ)
an addressee; a consignee

收驚(ㄕㄡ ㄐㄧㄥ)
to quiet the soul of a terrified child by a charm; to stop a child's crying by charms

收據(ㄕㄡ ㄐㄩ)
a receipt: 請給我此款的收據。Please send me a receipt for the money.

收齊(ㄕㄡ ㄑㄧˊ)
to get into a collection everything that must go therein

收起(ㄕㄡ ㄑㄧˇ)
to pack up; to cut out; to stop: 你還是收起你的空談泛論吧。You'd better stop this worthless talk.

收訖(ㄕㄡ ㄑㄧˋ)
received

收錢(ㄕㄡ ㄑㄧㄢˊ)
to collect payments

收禁(ㄕㄡ ㄐㄧㄣˋ)
to keep in confinement

收下(ㄕㄡ ˙ㄒㄧㄚˋ)
to accept; to receive: 他收下了朋友的禮物。He accepted a present from his friend.

收效(ㄕㄡ ㄒㄧㄠˋ)
to get the desired result or effect; to prove effective

收心(ㄕㄡ ㄒㄧㄣ)
to bring the mind back from distraction; to concentrate attention

收支(ㄕㄡ ㄓ)
income and expenditure; revenue and expenditure; earnings and expenses; receipts and disbursements

收支表(ㄕㄡ ㄓ ㄅㄧㄠˇ)
the accounts of receipts and

payments; the statement of income and expenditure; the statement of receipts and disbursements

收支平衡(ㄕㄡ ㄓ ㄆㄧㄥˊ ㄏㄥˊ)
The accounts are balanced. 或 Income and expenditure are balanced.

收支員(ㄕㄡ ㄓ ㄩㄢˊ)
a cashier

收執(ㄕㄡ ㄓˊ)
①to receive and keep (a receipt, etc.) ②a receipt

收債(ㄕㄡ ㄓㄞˋ)
to collect debts

收帳 or **收賬**(ㄕㄡ ㄓㄤˋ)
to collect payments of bills

收帳人(ㄕㄡ ㄓㄤˋ ㄖㄣˊ)
a collector; a bill collector

收場(ㄕㄡ ㄔㄤˇ)or 收場(ㄕㄡ ㄔㄤˇ)
①the end of an affair or a story; conclusion; denouement; ending: 這小說有圓滿的收場。This novel had a happy ending. ②to wind up; to end up: 他做事總是草草收場。He winds up everything hastily.

收成(ㄕㄡ ㄔㄥˊ)
harvest: 去年收成不好。We had poor harvests last year.

收拾(ㄕㄡ ˙ㄕ)
①to put (things) in order; to clear away; to tidy: 你現在可以收拾碗筷了。You can clear the table now. ②to manage ③to torture; to punish: 他們早晚要收拾那個壞蛋。They will punish the rascal one of these days.

收拾停當(ㄕㄡ ˙ㄕ ㄊㄧㄥˊ ㄉㄤˋ)
to put in good order

收拾殘局(ㄕㄡ ˙ㄕ ㄘㄢˊ ㄐㄩˊ)
to clear up a messy situation

收受(ㄕㄡ ㄕㄡˋ)
to receive; to accept

收生婆(ㄕㄡ ㄕㄥ ㄆㄛˊ)
a midwife

收束(ㄕㄡ ㄕㄨˋ)
①to bring together; to collect ②to bring to a close; to wind up: 寫到這裡，我的信也該收束了。It's time for me to wind up my letter.

收稅(ㄕㄡ ㄕㄨㄟˋ)
to collect taxes: 政府的歲入

靠收税。The government obtains revenue from taxes.

收税單 (ㄕㄡ ㄕㄨㄟˋ ㄉㄢ)
a tax form

收入 (ㄕㄡ ㄖㄨˋ)
①to take in; to include ②income; earnings; revenue; receipts: 低收入家庭需要政府幫忙。Low-income families need government help.

收入表 (ㄕㄡ ㄖㄨˋ ㄅㄧㄠˇ)
the account of receipts; an income statement

收容 (ㄕㄡ ㄖㄨㄥˊ)
to give shelter to; to accommodate

收容所 (ㄕㄡ ㄖㄨㄥˊ ㄙㄨㄛˇ)
a camp, temporary home or reception center (for refugees); an asylum

收贓 (ㄕㄡ ㄗㄤ)
to receive stolen property

收租 (ㄕㄡ ㄗㄨ)
to collect rents or rentals

收藏 (ㄕㄡ ㄘㄤˊ)
to collect and keep

收藏家 (ㄕㄡ ㄘㄤˊ ㄐㄧㄚ)
a collector: 他是古董收藏家。He is an antique collector.

收存 (ㄕㄡ ㄘㄨㄣˊ)
to receive for keeps; to receive for custody

收縮 (ㄕㄡ ㄙㄨㄛ)
①to shrink; to contract; to deflate: 這種布下水後會收縮。This kind of cloth shrinks in the wash. ②systole

收縮壓 (ㄕㄡ ㄙㄨㄛ ㄧㄚ)
systolic pressure

收益 (ㄕㄡ ㄧˋ)
to get benefit; to benefit; to profit; earnings; returns; income

收益稅 (ㄕㄡ ㄧˋ ㄕㄨㄟˋ)
revenue tax

收押 (ㄕㄡ ㄧㄚ)
to take (a criminal suspect) into custody; to detain

收音機 (ㄕㄡ ㄧㄣ ㄐㄧ)
a radio receiving set; a radio

收銀機 (ㄕㄡ ㄧㄣˊ ㄐㄧ)
a cash register

收養 (ㄕㄡ ㄧㄤˇ)
to adopt (a child); (child) adoption

收尾 (ㄕㄡ ㄨㄟˇ)
①to come to a conclusion; to wind up ②a concluding passage, movement, etc.

三畫

【攸】2116 (ㄧㄡ iou yōu)
1. far; distant
2. fast; fleeting
3. same as 所 — the place where
4. to concern
5. a Chinese family name

攸關 (ㄧㄡ ㄍㄨㄢ)
to concern (reputation, life, etc.); a matter of (reputation, life and death, etc.)

攸然 (ㄧㄡ ㄖㄢˊ)
joyfully; leisurely

攸攸 (ㄧㄡ ㄧㄡ)
①far; distant ②deep

【改】2117 (ㄍㄞˇ gae gǎi)
1. to change; to transform; to convert; to alter; to modify
2. to correct
3. to revise
4. to switch over to: 今年大部分農民改種蔬菜。Most of the farmers switch over to growing vegetables this year.

改版 (ㄍㄞˇ ㄅㄢˇ)
to make a revision (of a book); to change the format (of a newspaper)

改編 (ㄍㄞˇ ㄅㄧㄢ)
①to make a revision (of a book) ②to reorganize (a military unit, etc.) ③(said of a movie, stage play, etc.) adapted from or based on (a book, novel, etc.): 這部電影是由小說改編的。The movie was adapted from a novel.

改變 (ㄍㄞˇ ㄅㄧㄢˋ)
to change; to alter; to modify; to transform; to convert

改變主意 (ㄍㄞˇ ㄅㄧㄢˋ ㄓㄨˇ ㄧˋ)
to change one's mind

改不了 (ㄍㄞˇ ㄅㄨˋ ㄌㄧㄠˇ)
cannot change; cannot be changed 亦作「改不過來」: 人性是改不了的。Human nature cannot be changed.

改判 (ㄍㄞˇ ㄆㄢˋ)
to change a sentence (meted out by a lower court); to amend a judgement; to commute

改脾氣 (ㄍㄞˇ ㄆㄧˊ ㄑㄧˋ)
to change one's disposition

改名換姓 (ㄍㄞˇ ㄇㄧㄥˊ ㄏㄨㄢˋ ㄒㄧㄥˋ)
to change one's whole name

改道 (ㄍㄞˇ ㄉㄠˋ)
①to change the course (of a river): 黃河曾多次改道。The Yellow River has changed its course many times. ②to change one's route

改掉 (ㄍㄞˇ ㄉㄧㄠˋ)
to give up; to drop

改訂 (ㄍㄞˇ ㄉㄧㄥˋ)
①to revise (a book); to reformulate ②to choose a new date (for a scheduled event)

改動 (ㄍㄞˇ ㄉㄨㄥˋ)
to change; to modify: 我在文字上做少許改動。I made a few changes in wording.

改頭換面 (ㄍㄞˇ ㄊㄡˊ ㄏㄨㄢˋ ㄇㄧㄢˋ)
to change only the appearance; to change the outward look without changing the substance

改天 (ㄍㄞˇ ㄊㄧㄢ)
some other day

改途 or 改途 (ㄍㄞˇ ㄊㄨˊ)
to take a new road; to use a new approach or method

改圖 (ㄍㄞˇ ㄊㄨˊ)
to change the plan

改土歸流 (ㄍㄞˇ ㄊㄨˇ ㄍㄨㄟ ㄌㄧㄡˊ)
to replace hereditary local chieftains with nonhereditary appointees from the central government (a practice adopted during the Ming and Ching dynasties in dealing with the southwest aboriginal tribes)

改良 (ㄍㄞˇ ㄌㄧㄤˊ)
to ameliorate; to improve; to better

改良主義 (ㄍㄞˇ ㄌㄧㄤˊ ㄓㄨˇ ㄧˋ)
reformism

改良種 (ㄍㄞˇ ㄌㄧㄤˊ ㄓㄨㄥˇ)
the improved variety or species (created by cross-breeding)

改革 (ㄍㄞˇ ㄍㄜˊ)
to reform; a reform: 新政府

實施多項必要改革。The new government put through many needed reforms.

改過《ㄍㄞ ㄍㄨㄛˋ》
to mend one's ways; to correct one's mistakes

改過遷善《ㄍㄞ ㄍㄨㄛˋ ㄑㄧㄢ ㄕㄢˋ》
to repent and be good

改過自新《ㄍㄞ ㄍㄨㄛˋ ㄗˋ ㄒㄧㄣ》
to turn over a new leaf; to correct one's errors and make a fresh start; to reform

改觀《ㄍㄞ ㄍㄨㄢ》
to assume a new look; to change the appearance of

改口《ㄍㄞ ㄎㄡˇ》or**改嘴**《ㄍㄞ ㄗㄨㄟˇ》
to say something different from what one is expected to say or has been saying; to eat one's words; to correct oneself

改行《ㄍㄞ ㄏㄤˊ》
to change one's trade, profession or career

改悔《ㄍㄞ ㄏㄨㄟˇ》
to repent 亦作「悔改」：那傢伙毫無改悔之意。That guy shows not the least sign of repentance.

改換《ㄍㄞ ㄏㄨㄢˋ》
to replace; to change: 他已改換一套新的做法。He has changed over to new ways.

改嫁《ㄍㄞ ㄐㄧㄚˋ》or**改醮**《ㄍㄞ ㄐㄧㄠˋ》
(said of a woman) to re-marry

改節《ㄍㄞ ㄐㄧㄝˊ》
to change one's principles; to turn renegade; to switch loyalty (to a new ruler)

改建《ㄍㄞ ㄐㄧㄢˋ》
to remodel; to rebuild: 他去年改建老房子。He remodeled an old house last year.

改進《ㄍㄞ ㄐㄧㄣˋ》
to improve; to better: 尚有改進餘地。There is room for improvement.

改期《ㄍㄞ ㄑㄧˊ》
to postpone a scheduled event: 期中考已改期。The midterm examination has been postponed.

改邪歸正《ㄍㄞ ㄒㄧㄝˊ ㄍㄨㄟ ㄓㄥˋ》
to give up evil and return to virtue; to turn over a new

leaf

改寫《ㄍㄞ ㄒㄧㄝˇ》
to rewrite; to adapt: 這個故事是為電影而改寫的。The story was adapted for the movies.

改弦更張《ㄍㄞ ㄒㄧㄢˊ ㄍㄥ ㄓㄤ》
to start a thorough reform; to make a complete change; to make a fresh start

改弦易轍《ㄍㄞ ㄒㄧㄢˊ ㄧˋ ㄔㄜˋ》
to change rules and systems; to effect a thorough reform; to change one's course; to strike out on a new path

改憲《ㄍㄞ ㄒㄧㄢˋ》
to amend the constitution

改削《ㄍㄞ ㄒㄩㄝ》
to correct errors and delete superfluities (in a draft)

改選《ㄍㄞ ㄒㄩㄢˇ》
to hold a new election; to reelect: 班長每年改選一次。A new class leader is elected every year.

改制《ㄍㄞ ㄓˋ》
to change a system

改轍《ㄍㄞ ㄓㄜˋ》
(literally) to get the vehicle out of the old ruts—to take a new course

改正《ㄍㄞ ㄓㄥˋ》
to correct; to rectify; to reform; to amend

改鑄《ㄍㄞ ㄓㄨˋ》
to recast; to mint again

改錐《ㄍㄞ ㄓㄨㄟ》
a screwdriver

改裝《ㄍㄞ ㄓㄨㄤ》
①to change dress ②to convert (a machine, vehicle, etc.) for a new use; to refit; to reequip

改朝換代《ㄍㄞ ㄔㄠˊ ㄏㄨㄢˋ ㄉㄞˋ》
the change of regime

改常《ㄍㄞ ㄔㄤˊ》
to change the usual attitude

改善《ㄍㄞ ㄕㄢˋ》
to improve; to ameliorate; improvement: 這些國家間的關係已略有改善。The relations among these countries have shown some improvement.

改日《ㄍㄞ ㄖˋ》
some other time; later on

改造《ㄍㄞ ㄗㄠˋ》
to remodel; to remold; to re-

build; to convert; to reconstruct; to reform: 要對一個人思想改造是不容易的。It's not easy to remold one's ideology.

改葬《ㄍㄞ ㄗㄤˋ》
to reinter

改組《ㄍㄞ ㄗㄨˇ》
to reshuffle (an organization); to reorganize

改作文《ㄍㄞ ㄗㄨㄛˋ ㄨㄣˊ》
to correct compositions (for students)

改次《ㄍㄞ ㄘˋ》
some other time; on some other occasion

改錯《ㄍㄞ ㄘㄨㄛˋ》
to correct mistakes

改竄《ㄍㄞ ㄘㄨㄢˋ》
to emend

改歲《ㄍㄞ ㄙㄨㄟˋ》
to enter a new year; to begin a new year

改惡從善《ㄍㄞ ㄜˋ ㄘㄨㄥˊ ㄕㄢˋ》
to turn over a new leaf; to improve one's behavior

改易《ㄍㄞ ㄧˋ》
to change; to transform

改樣《ㄍㄞ ㄧㄤˋ》or**改式**《ㄍㄞ ㄕˋ》
to alter the style of

改物《ㄍㄞ ㄨˋ》
to change systems and institutions (of previous reigns)

改元《ㄍㄞ ㄩㄢˊ》
to change the reigning title (after a new emperor ascends the throne); to change the title of a reign

【攻】 2118
《ㄍㄨㄥ》 gong gōng
1. to attack; to raid; to assault
2. to accuse; to charge; to assail; to criticize; to rebuke
3. to work at; to apply oneself to; to study

攻拔《ㄍㄨㄥ ㄅㄚˊ》
to storm and capture

攻砭《ㄍㄨㄥ ㄅㄧㄢ》
to acupuncture

攻破《ㄍㄨㄥ ㄆㄛˋ》
to attack and conquer; to make a breakthrough; to breach

攻伐《ㄍㄨㄥ ㄈㄚˊ》or《ㄍㄨㄥ ㄈㄚˊ》
to send troops against (bandits, rebels, etc.)

攻防《ㄍㄨㄥ ㄈㄤˊ》

〔支部〕

〔支部〕

offense and defense

攻打《ㄍㄨㄥ ㄉㄚˇ》
to attack; to raid; to invade

攻讀《ㄍㄨㄥ ㄉㄨˊ》or 攻書《ㄍㄨㄥ ㄕㄨ》
to apply oneself diligently to study: 他正在攻讀博士學位。
He is working for a doctorate.

攻克《ㄍㄨㄥ ㄎㄜˋ》
to attack and conquer; to take

攻乎異端《ㄍㄨㄥ ㄏㄨ ㄧˋ ㄉㄨㄢ》
to apply oneself to heretical doctrines or thoughts

攻擊《ㄍㄨㄥ ㄐㄧ》
① to attack; to assault; to launch an offensive ② to accuse; to charge (or attack verbally); to vilify

攻擊點《ㄍㄨㄥ ㄐㄧ ㄉㄧㄢˇ》
the point of attack

攻擊出發線《ㄍㄨㄥ ㄐㄧ ㄔㄨ ㄈㄚ ㄒㄧㄢˋ》
(military) the line of departure

攻訐《ㄍㄨㄥ ㄐㄧㄝˊ》
to accuse; to charge; to rake up somebody's past and attack him; to censure; to flay

攻堅《ㄍㄨㄥ ㄐㄧㄢ》
to attack the enemy's strongest fortifications; to assault fortified positions; to storm strongholds

攻進《ㄍㄨㄥ ㄐㄧㄣˋ》
to breach enemy defense and enter (a position, city, etc.)

攻其無備《ㄍㄨㄥ ㄑㄧˊ ㄨˊ ㄅㄟˋ》
to attack when the enemy is unprepared; to take somebody by surprise

攻取《ㄍㄨㄥ ㄑㄩˇ》
to attack and capture

攻下《ㄍㄨㄥ ㄒㄧㄚˋ》
① to succeed in capturing (a city, a fort, etc.) by attack ② to overcome

攻陷《ㄍㄨㄥ ㄒㄧㄢˋ》
to succeed in capturing (a city, a fort, etc.) by attack

攻心《ㄍㄨㄥ ㄒㄧㄣ》
to launch a psychological offense

攻心爲上《ㄍㄨㄥ ㄒㄧㄣ ㄨㄟˊ ㄕㄤˋ》
Psychological offense is the best of tactics.

攻佔《ㄍㄨㄥ ㄓㄢˋ》
to attack and occupy: 敵人攻佔我們的堡壘。The enemy occupied our fort.

攻城砲《ㄍㄨㄥ ㄔㄥˊ ㄆㄠˋ》
a siege gun

攻城略地《ㄍㄨㄥ ㄔㄥˊ ㄌㄩㄝˋ ㄉㄧˋ》
to attack cities and invade territories

攻勢《ㄍㄨㄥ ㄕˋ》
the offensive: 軍隊採取攻勢。The army took the offensive.

攻殺《ㄍㄨㄥ ㄕㄚ》
to attack and massacre

攻守《ㄍㄨㄥ ㄕㄡˇ》
offense and defense

攻守同盟《ㄍㄨㄥ ㄕㄡˇ ㄊㄨㄥˊ ㄇㄥˊ》
an alliance for offense and defense; a military alliance for mutual defense

攻人之短《ㄍㄨㄥ ㄖㄣˊ ㄓ ㄉㄨㄢˇ》
to criticize the faults of others

攻錯《ㄍㄨㄥ ㄘㄨㄛˋ》or 攻玉《ㄍㄨㄥ ㄩˋ》
to mend one's own faults by observing the virtues of others

攻無不克《ㄍㄨㄥ ㄨˊ ㄅㄨˋ ㄎㄜˋ》
all-conquering; invincible

四畫

【放】 2119
《ㄈㄤˋ》 fang fàng
1. to let go; to release; to free; to liberate; to loosen; to relax: 她不放我走。She won't let me go.
2. to put; to place
3. to put in; to add: 菜裏多放點鹽。Put a bit more salt in the dish.
4. to dissipate; to debauch; to indulge

放爆竹《ㄈㄤˋ ㄅㄠˋ ㄓㄨˊ》
to set off firecrackers

放榜《ㄈㄤˋ ㄅㄤˇ》
to announce or publish the result of a competitive examination

放不下心《ㄈㄤˋ ㄅㄨˋ ㄒㄧㄚˋ ㄒㄧㄣ》
cannot stop worrying

放不下手《ㄈㄤˋ ㄅㄨˋ ㄒㄧㄚˋ ㄕㄡˇ》
cannot stop doing something

放砲《ㄈㄤˋ ㄆㄠˋ》
① to fire an artillery piece;

blasting ② to shoot off one's mouth

放盤 (stock) the opening quotation 參看「開盤」

放屁《ㄈㄤˋ ㄆㄧˋ》
① to let out gas; to break wind ② Nonsense! 或 Shit What a crap! 別放屁。Don't talk nonsense.

放馬後砲《ㄈㄤˋ ㄇㄚˇ ㄏㄡˋ ㄆㄠˋ》
to criticize or make comments on something after it is already over; to second-guess

放免《ㄈㄤˋ ㄇㄧㄢˇ》
to acquit (a suspect)

放牧《ㄈㄤˋ ㄇㄨˋ》
to put out to pasture; to graze; to herd

放牧地《ㄈㄤˋ ㄇㄨˋ ㄉㄧˋ》
a pasture

放風箏《ㄈㄤˋ ㄈㄥ ㄓㄥ》
to fly a kite

放大《ㄈㄤˋ ㄉㄚˋ》
to magnify; to enlarge; to amplify: 我想把這照片放大。I want to have the photograph enlarged.

放大鏡《ㄈㄤˋ ㄉㄚˋ ㄐㄧㄥˋ》
a magnifying glass

放膽《ㄈㄤˋ ㄉㄢˇ》
to get bold; to act boldly and with confidence

放誕《ㄈㄤˋ ㄉㄢˋ》
rash or reckless (in conduct or speech)

放蕩《ㄈㄤˋ ㄉㄤˋ》
dissolute; debauched; dissipated; unconventional: 他的行爲總是放蕩不羈。His behavior is always unconventional and unbridled.

放刁《ㄈㄤˋ ㄉㄧㄠ》
to show villainy; to act in a rascally manner 亦作「要無賴」

放電《ㄈㄤˋ ㄉㄧㄢˋ》
electric discharge

放毒《ㄈㄤˋ ㄉㄨˊ》
to put poison in food, water, etc.; to poison

放牛《ㄈㄤˋ ㄋㄧㄡˊ》
to graze cattle; to pasture cattle

放浪《ㄈㄤˋ ㄌㄤˋ》
to debauch; to dissipate

放浪形骸(ㄈㄤ ㄌㄤ ㄒㄧㄥ ㄏㄞˊ)
to abandon oneself to Bohemianism

放冷箭(ㄈㄤ ㄌㄥˇ ㄐㄧㄢˋ)
to injure others secretly

放利(ㄈㄤ ㄌㄧˋ)
to lend money for interest

放糧(ㄈㄤ ㄌㄧㄤˊ)
to distribute relief grains in a disaster-stricken area

放量(ㄈㄤ ㄌㄧㄤˋ)
(to drink) to full capacity

放領(ㄈㄤ ㄌㄧㄥˇ)
to lease (public land)

放龍入海(ㄈㄤ ㄌㄨㄥˊ ㄖㄨˋ ㄏㄞˇ)
(literally) to release a dragon into the sea—to give a man the chance to make the best of his abilities

放歌(ㄈㄤ ㄍㄜ)
to sing with uninhibited loudness

放高利貸(ㄈㄤ ㄍㄠ ㄌㄧˋ ㄉㄞˋ)
to lend money at high interest; to practice usury

放過(ㄈㄤ ㄍㄨㄛˋ)
to let go; to let slip away; to overlook

放光(ㄈㄤ ㄍㄨㄤ)
to emit light; to shine; to gleam; to glisten; to glitter

放工(ㄈㄤ ㄍㄨㄥ)
①to close work (for lunch, for the night, etc.); to quit work; to knock off ②to give workers a holiday

放開(ㄈㄤ ㄎㄞ)
to relax or loosen (a grasp, etc.); to let go

放寬(ㄈㄤ ㄎㄨㄢ)
to ease or relax (restrictions, etc.); to liberalize

放寬期限(ㄈㄤ ㄎㄨㄢ ㄑㄧˊ ㄒㄧㄢˋ)
to extend a time limit

放款(ㄈㄤ ㄎㄨㄢˇ)
a loan; loaning; to loan

放空氣(ㄈㄤ ㄎㄨㄥ ㄑㄧˋ)
to put out feelers; to send out trial balloons; to create an impression: 他放空氣說他要辭職。He created the impression that he would resign.

放虎歸山(ㄈㄤ ㄏㄨˇ ㄍㄨㄟ ㄕㄢ)
to let a tiger back to mountains—to sow the seeds of calamity 亦作「縱虎歸山」

放花(ㄈㄤ ㄏㄨㄚ)or 放花炮(ㄈㄤ ㄏㄨㄚ ㄆㄠˋ)
to set off fireworks

放火(ㄈㄤ ㄏㄨㄛˇ)
to set fire; to commit arson

放懷(ㄈㄤ ㄏㄨㄞˊ)
①to be uninhibited; to one's heart's content ②to be free from anxiety; to stop worrying

放假(ㄈㄤ ㄐㄧㄚˋ)
to have or give a holiday or vacation

放棄(ㄈㄤ ㄑㄧˋ)
①to give up; to abandon; to renounce; to discard; to relinquish ②(law) to waive; waiver

放槍(ㄈㄤ ㄑㄧㄤ)
to fire a gun

放晴(ㄈㄤ ㄑㄧㄥˊ)
(said of the weather) to clear up: 天一放晴，我們就攻擊。We'll attack as soon as it clears up.

放下(ㄈㄤ ㄒㄧㄚˋ)
to put down; to lay down: 我無法放下手頭的工作。I cannot put aside the work on hand.

放下屠刀(ㄈㄤ ㄒㄧㄚˋ ㄊㄨˊ ㄉㄠ)
(literally) to lay down the butcher knife—to repent and reform

放下屠刀，立地成佛(ㄈㄤ ㄒㄧㄚˋ ㄊㄨˊ ㄉㄠ，ㄌㄧˋ ㄉㄧˋ ㄔㄥˊ ㄈㄛˊ)
A butcher becomes a Buddha the moment he drops his cleaver.—A wrongdoer may become a man of virtue once he does good.

放心(ㄈㄤ ㄒㄧㄣ)
to stop worrying; to be free from anxiety; to rest assured

放心不下(ㄈㄤ ㄒㄧㄣ ㄅㄨˋ ㄒㄧㄚˋ)
to be kept in suspense

放鞭炮(ㄈㄤ ㄅㄧㄢ ㄆㄠˋ)
to set off firecrackers

放行(ㄈㄤ ㄒㄧㄥˊ)
to let go; to let pass: 請放行。Please let us pass.

放學(ㄈㄤ ㄒㄩㄝˊ)
to return home from school at the end of the day's classes: 學校下午四時半放學。The school closes at 4:30 p.m.

放置(ㄈㄤ ㄓˋ)
to place; to put down

放債(ㄈㄤ ㄓㄞˋ)
to make loans; to extend loans; to lend money for interest

放粥(ㄈㄤ ㄓㄡ)
to distribute free meals for the starving; to operate a soup kitchen

放賑(ㄈㄤ ㄓㄣˋ)
to distribute relief materials to the poor; to give alms

放賬(ㄈㄤ ㄓㄤˋ)
to make loans

放諸四海而皆準(ㄈㄤ ㄓㄨ ㄙˋ ㄏㄞˇ ㄦˊ ㄐㄧㄝ ㄓㄨㄣˇ)or 放之四海而皆準(ㄈㄤ ㄓ ㄙˋ ㄏㄞˇ ㄦˊ ㄐㄧㄝ ㄓㄨㄣˇ)
(said of a principle, theory, etc.) to be applicable everywhere

放逐(ㄈㄤ ㄓㄨˊ)
to exile; to banish

放長線釣大魚(ㄈㄤ ㄔㄤˊ ㄒㄧㄢˋ ㄉㄧㄠˋ ㄉㄚˋ ㄩˊ)
(literally) To catch a big fish, one must cast a long line.—to make a bigger investment with a view to gaining a bigger reward

放唱片(ㄈㄤ ㄔㄤˋ ㄆㄧㄢˋ)
to play a phonograph

放出(ㄈㄤ ㄔㄨ)
to give forth; to send out; to emit: 太陽放出光和熱。The sun emits light and heat.

放逐(ㄈㄤ ㄔㄨˊ)
to exile; to banish

放銃(ㄈㄤ ㄔㄨㄥˋ)
(mah-jong game) to release a tile that enables any one of the other three players to complete his winning pattern

放射(ㄈㄤ ㄕㄜˋ)
to emit; to radiate; to send out; to emanate

放射線(ㄈㄤ ㄕㄜˋ ㄒㄧㄢˋ)
radioactive rays

放射性(ㄈㄤ ㄕㄜˋ ㄒㄧㄥˋ)
radioactivity

放射性同位素(ㄈㄤ ㄕㄜˋ ㄒㄧㄥˋ ㄊㄨㄥˊ ㄨㄟˋ ㄙㄨˋ)
a radioisotope

放哨(ㄈㄤ ㄕㄠˋ)
to go on patrol duty; to

〔支
部〕

【支部】

放手 (ㄈㄤ ㄕㄡˇ)
①to loosen the grasp or hold; to let go: 抓緊, 不要放手。Hold it tight and don't let go. ②to give up ③to have a free hand

放手去做 (ㄈㄤ ㄕㄡˇ ㄑㄩˋ ㄗㄨㄛˋ)
to act without considering consequences or difficulties

放生 (ㄈㄤ ㄕㄥ)
to free or release a captured animal (out of pity)

放生池 (ㄈㄤ ㄕㄥ ㄔˊ)
a pond where fishes are released

放聲大哭 (ㄈㄤ ㄕㄥ ㄉㄚˋ ㄎㄨ)
to cry loudly

放水 (ㄈㄤ ㄕㄨㄟˇ)
①to let water out; to draw off ②to let the other side win (a game, contest, etc.) purposely; to throw a game

放熱 (ㄈㄤ ㄖㄜˋ)
exothermic

放任 (ㄈㄤ ㄖㄣˋ)
to leave alone; to let (a person) do as he pleases; to let (a matter) take its own course

放任政策 (ㄈㄤ ㄖㄣˋ ㄓㄥˋ ㄘㄜˋ) or
任主義 (ㄈㄤ ㄖㄣˋ ㄓㄨˇ ㄧˋ)
laissez faire or laisser faire

放恣 (ㄈㄤ ㄗˋ)
to disregard all restrictions; to be licentious

放在心裏 (ㄈㄤ ㄗㄞˋ ㄒㄧㄣ·ㄌㄧ)
to keep in mind; to bear in mind

放走 (ㄈㄤ ㄗㄡˇ)
to release; to set free; to let go; 你照我的話做, 我就放她走。Do as I tell you, and I'll set her free.

放縱 (ㄈㄤ ㄗㄨㄥˋ)
①to debauch; to dissipate; to indulge ②to break rules of conduct

放肆 (ㄈㄤ ㄙˋ)
to take liberties; unruly; unbridled: 他的行為很放肆。His behavior is unbridled.

放散 (ㄈㄤ ㄙㄢˋ)
(said of smoke, scent, etc.) to diffuse; to spread

放鬆 (ㄈㄤ ㄙㄨㄥ)
to relax; to ease; to loosen;

放送 (ㄈㄤ ㄙㄨㄥˋ)
to broadcast; to send out (over a loudspeaker, etc.)

放言高論 (ㄈㄤ ㄧㄢˊ ㄍㄠ ㄌㄨㄣˋ)
to speak or write in an outspoken manner; high-flown talk

放閻王賬 (ㄈㄤ ㄧㄢˊ ㄨㄤˊ ㄓㄤˋ)
to practice usury

放眼 (ㄈㄤ ㄧㄢˇ)
to take a broad view; to scan widely

放燄口 (ㄈㄤ ㄧㄢˋ ㄎㄡˇ)
a Buddhist ritual wherein the monks chant sutra for the dead and give food to hungry ghosts

放焰火 (ㄈㄤ ㄧㄢˋ ㄏㄨㄛˇ)
to set off fireworks

放洋 (ㄈㄤ ㄧㄤˊ)
①to spend some time abroad ②(said of a ship) to put out to sea

放養 (ㄈㄤ ㄧㄤˇ)
to put (fish, etc.) in a suitable place to breed: 水池裏放養了許多種魚。Various kinds of fish are being bred in the pond.

放映 (ㄈㄤ ㄧㄥˋ)
to project (on the screen); to show: 環球電影院今晚放映什麼片子? What will show at Universal Cinema this evening?

放映機 (ㄈㄤ ㄧㄥˋ ㄐㄧ)
a projector

放映室 (ㄈㄤ ㄧㄥˋ ㄕˋ)
a projection room

放穩重些 (ㄈㄤ ㄨㄣˇ ㄓㄨㄥˋ·ㄒㄧㄝ)
Be gentlemanlike!

【攽】 2120
ㄅㄧㄣ bin bin
1. to divide
2. to reduce

五畫

【政】 2121
ㄓㄥˋ jeng zheng
1. government
2. administration; management
3. politics; political affairs

政變 (ㄓㄥˋ ㄅㄧㄢˋ)
a coup d'état; a coup: 有些謀叛者試圖要發動政變。Some

---

conspirators tried to stage a coup d'état.

政柄 (ㄓㄥˋ ㄅㄧㄥˇ)
reins of government

政府 (ㄓㄥˋ ㄈㄨˇ)
a government

政府機關 (ㄓㄥˋ ㄈㄨˇ ㄐㄧ ㄍㄨㄢ)
a government agency; a government organization

政黨 (ㄓㄥˋ ㄉㄤˇ)
a political party

政黨政治 (ㄓㄥˋ ㄉㄤˇ ㄓㄥˋ ㄓˋ)
a form of democracy wherein the majority party forms the cabinet with the opposition acting as watchdog

政敵 (ㄓㄥˋ ㄉㄧˊ)
a political rival; a political enemy

政體 (ㄓㄥˋ ㄊㄧˇ)
the form of government; a political system; a polity

政通人和 (ㄓㄥˋ ㄊㄨㄥ ㄖㄣˊ ㄏㄜˊ)
The government functions well, and the people enjoy peace.

政令 (ㄓㄥˋ ㄌㄧㄥˋ)
a government order (or decree)

政論 (ㄓㄥˋ ㄌㄨㄣˋ)
articles, statements or comments about politics

政論家 (ㄓㄥˋ ㄌㄨㄣˋ ㄐㄧㄚ)
a political commentator; a publicist

政略 (ㄓㄥˋ ㄌㄩㄝˋ)
a government policy

政綱 (ㄓㄥˋ ㄍㄤ)
the platform (of a political party)

政綱不振 (ㄓㄥˋ ㄍㄤ ㄅㄨˋ ㄓㄣˋ)
The political platform does not rouse.

政工 (ㄓㄥˋ ㄍㄨㄥ)
(military) political work

政工幹校 (ㄓㄥˋ ㄍㄨㄥ ㄍㄢˋ ㄒㄧㄠˋ)
Political Staff College (operated by the Ministry of National Defense)

政工人員 (ㄓㄥˋ ㄍㄨㄥ ㄖㄣˊ ㄩㄢˊ)
(military) political staff officers

政躬康泰 (ㄓㄥˋ ㄍㄨㄥ ㄎㄤ ㄊㄞˋ)
(an expression used in addressing a high government official) May you be healthy and strong.

政客(ㄓㄥˋㄎㄜˋ)
a politician who places personal gain above public interests: 他不過是個小政客。He is only a petty politician.

政況(ㄓㄥˋㄎㄨㄤˋ)
political situations

政績(ㄓㄥˋㄐㄧ)
administrative achievements (of a government, ruler, or magistrate)

政績斐然(ㄓㄥˋㄐㄧㄈㄟˇㄖㄢˊ)
One's achievement in politics is distinguished.

政界(ㄓㄥˋㄐㄧㄝˋ)
political circles; officialdom; the political arena: 他在一九八六年退出政界。He withdrew from political circles in 1986.

政教(ㄓㄥˋㄐㄧㄠˋ)
the state and the church

政教分離(ㄓㄥˋㄐㄧㄠˋㄈㄣㄌㄧˊ)
the separation of the church from the state

政教合一(ㄓㄥˋㄐㄧㄠˋㄏㄜˊㄧ)
the unification of the state and the church

政見(ㄓㄥˋㄐㄧㄢˋ)
political views; politics; platform

政局(ㄓㄥˋㄐㄩˊ)
the political situation or scene

政權(ㄓㄥˋㄑㄩㄢˊ)
① reins of government; regime; political power

政修年豐(ㄓㄥˋㄒㄧㄡㄋㄧㄢˊㄈㄥ)
The people enjoy good government and good crops.

政制(ㄓㄥˋㄓˋ)
a political system; a government hierarchy

政治(ㄓㄥˋㄓˋ)
① politics; political affairs
② government administration

政治庇護(ㄓㄥˋㄓˋㄅㄧˋㄏㄨˋ)
political asylum

政治犯(ㄓㄥˋㄓˋㄈㄢˋ)
a political offender; a political prisoner; a political criminal

政治地理(ㄓㄥˋㄓˋㄉㄧˋㄌㄧˇ)
political geography

政治活動(ㄓㄥˋㄓˋㄏㄨㄛˊㄉㄨㄥˋ)
political activities

政治家(ㄓㄥˋㄓˋㄐㄧㄚ)
a statesman

政治局(ㄓㄥˋㄓˋㄐㄩˊ)
Political Bureau; Politburo (of Communist parties)

政治學(ㄓㄥˋㄓˋㄒㄩㄝˊ)
political science; politics

政治史(ㄓㄥˋㄓˋㄕˇ)
political history

政治生涯(ㄓㄥˋㄓˋㄕㄥㄧㄚˊ)
one's political life

政爭(ㄓㄥˋㄓㄥ)
political strife

政潮(ㄓㄥˋㄔㄠˊ)
a political upheaval or crisis

政事(ㄓㄥˋㄕˋ)
affairs of the government; the principles and business of government

政聲(ㄓㄥˋㄕㄥ)
one's reputation as a statesman or magistrate; reputation of an official

政策(ㄓㄥˋㄘㄜˋ)
a policy

政要(ㄓㄥˋㄧㄠˋ)
government VIPs; ranking officials of the government or political parties; high-ranking government officials

政務(ㄓㄥˋㄨˋ)
affairs of the government

政務官(ㄓㄥˋㄨˋㄍㄨㄢ)
high-ranking government officials in charge of administrative affairs (as distinct from 事務官, who are executive officers)

政務委員(ㄓㄥˋㄨˋㄨㄟˇㄩㄢˊ)
a minister without portfolio

【故】2122
(ㄍㄨˋ guh gù)
1. former; past; earlier; previous; old; antique; ancient
2. intentional; willful; on purpose; knowingly: 他明知故犯。He committed the offense willfully.
3. cause; reason: 他不知何故失蹤。The reason for his disappearance remains unknown.
4. to die: 王先生昨晚病故。Mr. Wang died of illness last night.
5. an incident; an event; a matter; a happening
6. consequently; hence; there-

fore
7. a friend; an acquaintance: 他跟我非親非故。He is neither my relative nor my friend.

故步自封(ㄍㄨˋㄅㄨˋㄗˋㄈㄥ)
to confine oneself to the old method or traditional way; very conservative 訛作「固步自封」

故犯(ㄍㄨˋㄈㄢˋ)
to offend knowingly or willfully: 我不會原諒明知故犯的人。I'll not forgive those who offend knowingly.

故夫(ㄍㄨˋㄈㄨ)
(my) late husband

故道(ㄍㄨˋㄉㄠˋ)
① the old road; the old way
② the old method

故蹈前轍(ㄍㄨˋㄉㄠˋㄑㄧㄢˊㄔㄜˋ)
to continue to tread on the former ruts

故地(ㄍㄨˋㄉㄧˋ)
an old haunt

故都(ㄍㄨˋㄉㄨ)
a former capital

故態(ㄍㄨˋㄊㄞˋ)
① one's former attitude ② one's usual attitude

故態復萌(ㄍㄨˋㄊㄞˋㄈㄨˋㄇㄥˊ)
The old (bad) attitude is back.

故土(ㄍㄨˋㄊㄨˇ)
one's homeland; one's native land

故土難移(ㄍㄨˋㄊㄨˇㄋㄢˊㄧˊ)
It is hard to leave one's homeland.

故弄玄虛(ㄍㄨˋㄋㄨㄥˋㄒㄩㄢˊㄒㄩ)
to puzzle people intentionally; to mystify deliberately

故老(ㄍㄨˋㄌㄠˇ)
respectable old people

故里(ㄍㄨˋㄌㄧˇ)
one's home village; one's hometown; one's native heath

故吏(ㄍㄨˋㄌㄧˋ)
a former subordinate

故國(ㄍㄨˋㄍㄨㄛˊ)
① one's fatherland; one's mother country ② an old country ③ one's hometown

故國喬木(ㄍㄨˋㄍㄨㄛˊㄑㄧㄠˊㄇㄨˋ)
(figuratively) an ancient and famous family

故國之思(ㄍㄨˋㄍㄨㄛˊㄓㄙ)

nostalgic memories of one's mother country

故宮《ㄍㄨˋ ㄍㄨㄥ》
a former palace

故宮博物院《ㄍㄨˋ ㄍㄨㄥ ㄅㄛˊ ㄨˋ ㄩㄢˋ》
National Palace Museum (housing China's art treasures)

故伎《ㄍㄨˋ ㄐㄧˋ》
a stock trick; old tactics: 他再次重施故伎。He played the same old trick again.

故家《ㄍㄨˋ ㄐㄧㄚ》
a family with illustrious ancestors

故交《ㄍㄨˋ ㄐㄧㄠ》or 故知《ㄍㄨˋ ㄓ》or 故友《ㄍㄨˋ ㄧㄡˇ》
an old friend

故舊《ㄍㄨˋ ㄐㄧㄡˋ》
old friends

故劍之思《ㄍㄨˋ ㄐㄧㄢˋ ㄓ ㄙ》
to remember a former wife with tender feelings

故居《ㄍㄨˋ ㄐㄩ》
one's former residence

故去《ㄍㄨˋ ㄑㄩˋ》
to die; to pass away: 他的一位朋友在上個月故去。One of his friends passed away last month.

故鄉《ㄍㄨˋ ㄒㄧㄤ》
one's native place, land, or province; one's hometown or village; one's homeland; one's birthplace

故墟《ㄍㄨˋ ㄒㄩ》
historic remains; ruins

故址《ㄍㄨˋ ㄓˇ》
an ancient landmark; a historic spot; a place of historic interest

故紙堆《ㄍㄨˋ ㄓˇ ㄉㄨㄟ》
old books (used in a derogatory sense)

故智《ㄍㄨˋ ㄓˋ》
an old scheme; a repeatedly used trick

故障《ㄍㄨˋ ㄓㄤˋ》
a bug or breakdown (of a machine); a stoppage; trouble: 我車子的引擎發生了故障。My car had engine trouble.

故主《ㄍㄨˋ ㄓㄨˇ》
the late king or master; the former king or master

故轍《ㄍㄨˋ ㄓㄜˋ》
(literally) an old rut—an

old method or system

故常《ㄍㄨˋ ㄔㄤˊ》
constant

故城《ㄍㄨˋ ㄔㄥˊ》
an old city

故失《ㄍㄨˋ ㄕ》
an improper verdict; miscarriage of justice

故實《ㄍㄨˋ ㄕˊ》
a past fact; an incident in former times

故事《ㄍㄨˋ ㄕˋ》
a story; a narrative; a tale: 請你講個故事給我們聽。Please tell us a story.

故殺《ㄍㄨˋ ㄕㄚ》
premeditated murder

故書《ㄍㄨˋ ㄕㄨ》
an antique book

故人《ㄍㄨˋ ㄖㄣˊ》
①an old friend ②one's former wife

故入故出《ㄍㄨˋ ㄖㄨˋ ㄍㄨˋ ㄔㄨ》
(law) to mete out penalties not commensurate with the offenses committed

故入人罪《ㄍㄨˋ ㄖㄨˋ ㄖㄣˊ ㄗㄨㄟˋ》
to accuse someone of a crime falsely

故作不知《ㄍㄨˋ ㄗㄨㄛˋ ㄅㄨˋ ㄓ》
to play dumb; to pretend ignorance

故縱《ㄍㄨˋ ㄗㄨㄥˋ》
to go beyond restrictions intentionally

故此《ㄍㄨˋ ㄘˇ》
on this account; for this reason; therefore

故所《ㄍㄨˋ ㄙㄨㄛˇ》
an old place

故而《ㄍㄨˋ ㄦˊ》or 故爾《ㄍㄨˋ ㄦˇ》
therefore; on this account; for this reason

故意《ㄍㄨˋ ㄧˋ》
intentional; on purpose; willfully; deliberately; intentionally; purposedly

故吾《ㄍㄨˋ ㄨˊ》or 故我《ㄍㄨˋ ㄨㄛˇ》
my former self

故違《ㄍㄨˋ ㄨㄟˊ》
to disobey; to violate knowingly

故宇《ㄍㄨˋ ㄩˇ》
one's former residence

故園《ㄍㄨˋ ㄩㄢˊ》
one's hometown and the

countryside around it

六畫

【效】 (効)《ㄒㄧㄠˋ shiaw / xiào》 *2123*

1. to imitate; to mimic; to follow
2. effect; effectiveness; efficacy
3. to devote
4. to offer

效顰《ㄒㄧㄠˋ ㄆㄧㄣˊ》
to blindly imitate with ludicrous effect

效命《ㄒㄧㄠˋ ㄇㄧㄥˋ》
①to obey orders ②to pursue an end at the cost of one's life

效法《ㄒㄧㄠˋ ㄈㄚˇ》
to take as a model; to imitate

效能《ㄒㄧㄠˋ ㄋㄥˊ》
effect

效勞《ㄒㄧㄠˋ ㄌㄠˊ》
to render service; to work for

效力《ㄒㄧㄠˋ ㄌㄧˋ》
①effect; efficacy: 這殺蟲劑很有效力。The insecticide is efficacious. ②to render service: 我願為國效力。I will serve my country.

效率《ㄒㄧㄠˋ ㄌㄩˋ》
efficiency

效果《ㄒㄧㄠˋ ㄍㄨㄛˇ》
effect; result: 懲罰似乎對他沒什麼效果。Punishment does not seem to have much effect on him.

效忠《ㄒㄧㄠˋ ㄓㄨㄥ》
to be loyal to; to pledge allegiance to; allegiance

效誠《ㄒㄧㄠˋ ㄔㄥˊ》
to be faithful; to be sincere

效死《ㄒㄧㄠˋ ㄙˇ》
to render service at the cost of one's life

效益《ㄒㄧㄠˋ ㄧˋ》
beneficial result; benefit

效尤《ㄒㄧㄠˋ ㄧㄡˊ》
to imitate vice knowingly

效驗《ㄒㄧㄠˋ ㄧㄢˋ》
actual proof of efficacy; desired effect

效應《ㄒㄧㄠˋ ㄧㄥˋ》
(physics) effect

效用(ㄒㄧㄠˋ ㄩㄥˋ)
usefulness; use; utility computer

效用遞減律(ㄒㄧㄠˋ ㄩㄥˋ ㄉㄧˋ ㄐㄧㄢˇ ㄌㄩˋ)
the law of diminishing returns

效用論(ㄒㄧㄠˋ ㄩㄥˋ ㄌㄨㄣˊ)
utility theory

【敉】 2124
ㄇㄧˇ mii mǐ
to stabilize; to quiet; to pacify; to soothe

敉平(ㄇㄧˇ ㄆㄧㄥˊ)
to succeed in putting down a revolt or rebellion; to subjugate

敉寧(ㄇㄧˇ ㄋㄧㄥˊ)
to give peace; to pacify

七畫

【敍】 2125
(敍、叙) ㄒㄩˋ shiuh xù

1. to tell; to narrate; to describe; to express
2. to talk; to chat: 若得閒請來一敍。Please come over for a chat if you are free.
3. to arrange in order
4. to rate or evaluate (as a basis for reward, appointment, etc.); to assess

敍別(ㄒㄩˋ ㄅㄧㄝˊ)
to get together for talk before a separation; to say good-bye to each other; to have a farewell talk

敍談(ㄒㄩˋ ㄊㄢˊ)
to get together and chat; to chitchat

敍利亞(ㄒㄩˋ ㄌㄧˋ ㄧㄚˇ)
Syria

敍錄(ㄒㄩˋ ㄌㄨˋ)
commentaries

敍功(ㄒㄩˋ ㄍㄨㄥ)
to rate and reward merits or contributions

敍功行賞(ㄒㄩˋ ㄍㄨㄥ ㄒㄧㄥˊ ㄕㄤˇ)
to go over the records and decide on awards

敍寒溫(ㄒㄩˋ ㄏㄢˊ ㄨㄣ)or敍寒暄(ㄒㄩˋ ㄏㄢˊ ㄒㄩㄢ)
to make mutual inquiries after a long separation

敍家常(ㄒㄩˋ ㄐㄧㄚ ㄔㄤˊ)
to talk about daily life

敍舊(ㄒㄩˋ ㄐㄧㄡˋ)
to talk about the old days

敍情(ㄒㄩˋ ㄑㄧㄥˊ)
to bare one's heart (in conversation, writing, etc.)

敍勳(ㄒㄩˋ ㄒㄩㄣˊ)
to rate and reward merits or contributions

敍傳(ㄒㄩˋ ㄓㄨㄢˋ)
to write a preface for a book

敍事詩(ㄒㄩˋ ㄕˋ ㄕ)
a narrative poem

敍事文(ㄒㄩˋ ㄕˋ ㄨㄣˊ)
a narration

敍述(ㄒㄩˋ ㄕㄨˋ)
to narrate; to recount; to relate

敍說(ㄒㄩˋ ㄕㄨㄛ)
to tell; to narrate

敍言(ㄒㄩˋ ㄧㄢˊ)or敍文(ㄒㄩˋ ㄨㄣˊ)
a preface; a foreword 亦作「序言」或「序文」

敍用(ㄒㄩˋ ㄩㄥˋ)
to employ (as government officials); to appoint

【教】 2126
1. ㄐㄧㄠ jiaw jiāo
1. a religion: 他不信基督教。He does not believe in the Christian religion.
2. an order; a directive
3. to educate
4. to incite; to urge; to bid; to instigate
5. to instruct; instruction(s); to advise; advice: 請不吝賜教。Please advise me graciously.
6. to have; to make; to let: 誰教你進那屋子的? Who let you into the building?

教本(ㄐㄧㄠˋ ㄅㄣˇ)
a textbook

教鞭(ㄐㄧㄠˋ ㄅㄧㄢ)
①a pointer or rod (used by a teacher) ②a teaching career

教不倦(ㄐㄧㄠˋ ㄅㄨˋ ㄐㄩㄢˋ)
diligent or untiring in teaching

教派(ㄐㄧㄠˋ ㄆㄞˋ)
religious sects or denominations

教門(ㄐㄧㄠˋ ㄇㄣˊ)
①the door to Buddhism ②Islam

教名(ㄐㄧㄠˋ ㄇㄧㄥˊ)
one's Christian name or forename

教母(ㄐㄧㄠˋ ㄇㄨˇ)
godmother

教法(ㄐㄧㄠˋ ㄈㄚˇ)
teaching methods; pedagogy

教坊(ㄐㄧㄠˋ ㄈㄤ)
an institution for the training of musicians and song-stresses (in former times)

教父(ㄐㄧㄠˋ ㄈㄨˋ)
godfather

教導(ㄐㄧㄠˋ ㄉㄠˇ)or(ㄐㄧㄠˋ ㄉㄠˋ)
①to teach and guide; to instruct ②guidance

教導主任(ㄐㄧㄠˋ ㄉㄠˇ ㄓㄨˇ ㄖㄣˋ)or(ㄐㄧㄠˋ ㄉㄠˋ ㄓㄨˇ ㄖㄣˋ)
the head teacher or assistant principal (in a primary school)

教導有方(ㄐㄧㄠˋ ㄉㄠˇ ㄧㄡˇ ㄈㄤ)or(ㄐㄧㄠˋ ㄉㄠˋ ㄧㄡˇ ㄈㄤ)
skillful in teaching and providing guidance (The expression is often used in citations for outstanding teachers and schools.)

教督(ㄐㄧㄠˋ ㄉㄨ)
to teach and supervise

教頭(ㄐㄧㄠˋ ㄊㄡˊ)
the head instructor (of martial arts); chief trainer

教堂(ㄐㄧㄠˋ ㄊㄤˊ)
a church; a mosque; a cathedral; a chapel; a tabernacle; a temple; a shrine

教條(ㄐㄧㄠˋ ㄊㄧㄠˊ)
a doctrine; a dogma; a creed; a tenet

教條主義(ㄐㄧㄠˋ ㄊㄧㄠˊ ㄓㄨˇ ㄧˋ)
doctrinairism; dogmatism

教廷(ㄐㄧㄠˋ ㄊㄧㄥˊ)
the Holy See; the Vatican

教廷大使(ㄐㄧㄠˋ ㄊㄧㄥˊ ㄉㄚˋ ㄕˇ)
an apostolic nuncio

教廷公使(ㄐㄧㄠˋ ㄊㄧㄥˊ ㄍㄨㄥ ㄕˇ)
an apostolic internuncio

教徒(ㄐㄧㄠˋ ㄊㄨˊ)
a (religious) believer or follower

教猱升木(ㄐㄧㄠˋ ㄋㄠˊ ㄕㄥ ㄇㄨˋ)
(literally) to teach monkeys to climb a tree—to encourage wicked people to do wicked things

教練(ㄐㄧㄠ ㄌㄧㄢˋ)
①a coach (of athletes); an instructor ②to train; to drill; to coach

教練機(ㄐㄧㄠ ㄌㄧㄢˋ ㄐㄧ)
a trainer

教練車(ㄐㄧㄠ ㄌㄧㄢˋ ㄔㄜ)
a learner-driven vehicle

教令(ㄐㄧㄠ ㄌㄧㄥˋ)
①the commands, or orders, of a ruler (as distinct from the law) ②a religious decree or proclamation

教規(ㄐㄧㄠ ㄍㄨㄟ)
rules of a religion; canons

教官(ㄐㄧㄠ ㄍㄨㄢ)
a military instructor; a drill-master

教科書(ㄐㄧㄠ ㄎㄜ ㄕㄨ)
the textbook

教化(ㄐㄧㄠ ㄏㄨㄚˋ)
①culture ②to bring enlightenment to the people by education; to civilize the masses by education

教會(ㄐㄧㄠ ㄏㄨㄟˋ)
the church: 天主教會 the Catholic Church

教會學校(ㄐㄧㄠ ㄏㄨㄟˋ ㄒㄩㄝˊ ㄒㄧㄠˋ)
a missionary school; a church school

教誨(ㄐㄧㄠ ㄏㄨㄟˋ)
to teach and admonish; teachings and admonitions

教皇(ㄐㄧㄠ ㄏㄨㄤˊ)
the Pope; the Pontiff

教誡(ㄐㄧㄠ ㄐㄧㄝˋ)
prohibitions of a religion or religious sect

教具(ㄐㄧㄠ ㄐㄩˋ)
teaching aids (such as charts, samples, etc.)

教區(ㄐㄧㄠ ㄑㄩ)
a diocese; a parish

教習(ㄐㄧㄠ ㄒㄧˊ)
to teach; to instruct

教學(ㄐㄧㄠ ㄒㄩㄝˊ)
①instruction; teaching ②to teach and to learn; teaching and learning

教學法(ㄐㄧㄠ ㄒㄩㄝˊ ㄈㄚˇ)
pedagogy; teaching methods 參看「教授法」

教學相長(ㄐㄧㄠ ㄒㄩㄝˊ ㄒㄧㄤ ㄓㄤˇ)
The teacher and the student can profit from each other.

教訓(ㄐㄧㄠ ㄒㄩㄣˋ)or(ㄐㄧㄠˋ·ㄒㄩㄣ)
①a moral; a lesson: 那件車禍給了他一個教訓。The car accident taught him a lesson. ②to admonish; admonitions; teachings; a scolding: 我狠狠地教訓他一頓。I gave him a good scolding.

教訓詩(ㄐㄧㄠ ㄒㄩㄣˋ ㄕ)
didactic poetry

教職(ㄐㄧㄠ ㄓˊ)
the occupation of teaching: 他擔任教職已四十年。He has been teaching for forty years.

教職員(ㄐㄧㄠ ㄓˊ ㄩㄢˊ)
the teaching and administrative staff of a school

教戰(ㄐㄧㄠ ㄓㄢˋ)
to teach martial arts

教長(ㄐㄧㄠ ㄓㄤˇ)
a mullah or mulla; an imam

教主(ㄐㄧㄠ ㄓㄨˇ)
the founder of a religion; a religious leader

教場(ㄐㄧㄠ ㄔㄤˇ)or(ㄐㄧㄠ ㄔㄤˊ)
a military drill ground

教師(ㄐㄧㄠ ㄕ)
a teacher; a school teacher; a pedagogue: 經驗是最好的教師。Experience is the best teacher.

教師節(ㄐㄧㄠ ㄕ ㄐㄧㄝˊ)
Teacher's Day (falling on September 28 and corresponding to Confucius' birthday)

教士(ㄐㄧㄠ ㄕˋ)
an evangelist; a preacher; a missionary; a priest; a clergyman

教室(ㄐㄧㄠ ㄕˋ)
a classroom: 你的教室裏有多少桌子？How many desks are there in your classroom?

教社(ㄐㄧㄠ ㄕㄜˋ)
(Catholicism) an order

教授(ㄐㄧㄠ ㄕㄡˋ)
a professor: 他是心理學副教授。He is an associate professor of psychology.

教授法(ㄐㄧㄠ ㄕㄡˋ ㄈㄚˇ)or 教學法 (ㄐㄧㄠ ㄒㄩㄝˊ ㄈㄚˇ)
teaching methods; the method of instruction; pedagogy

教授得法(ㄐㄧㄠ ㄕㄡˋ ㄉㄜˊ ㄈㄚˇ)
to have tact in teaching

教澤(ㄐㄧㄠ ㄗㄜˊ)
cultural influence

教宗(ㄐㄧㄠ ㄗㄨㄥ)
the Pope; the Pontiff

教材(ㄐㄧㄠ ㄘㄞˊ)
teaching materials

教唆(ㄐㄧㄠ ㄙㄨㄛ)
to instigate; to incite; to abet; to suborn: 她教唆他做壞事。She abetted him in his folly.

教唆犯(ㄐㄧㄠ ㄙㄨㄛ ㄈㄢˋ)
an abettor

教唆罪(ㄐㄧㄠ ㄙㄨㄛ ㄗㄨㄟˋ)
the offense of instigation or subornation; the guilt of instigation

教案(ㄐㄧㄠ ㄢˋ)
a teaching plan (prepared by a teacher before class time)

教益(ㄐㄧㄠ ㄧˋ)
a useful lesson; enlightenment

教義(ㄐㄧㄠ ㄧˋ)
the doctrine of a religion; creed

教友(ㄐㄧㄠ ㄧㄡˇ)
a fellow believer (of a religion); a member of a church

教友派(ㄐㄧㄠ ㄧㄡˇ ㄆㄞˋ)or教友會 (ㄐㄧㄠ ㄧㄡˇ ㄏㄨㄟˋ)
Society of Friends, founded in 1650 by George Fox in England (also called Quakers)

教養(ㄐㄧㄠ ㄧㄤˇ)
to bring up; to rear; upbringing: 他很有教養。He was well brought up.

教務(ㄐㄧㄠ ㄨˋ)
instructional affairs (as distinct from administrative affairs in a school)

教務長(ㄐㄧㄠ ㄨˋ ㄓㄤˇ)
the dean of studies (of a college or university)

教務主任(ㄐㄧㄠ ㄨˋ ㄓㄨˇ ㄖㄣˋ)
the dean of studies (of a primary or secondary school)

教務處(ㄐㄧㄠ ㄨˋ ㄔㄨˋ)
the office of the dean of studies

教諭(ㄐㄧㄠ ㄩˋ)
an official instructor (in a public school in former times)

教育(ㄐㄧㄠ ㄩˋ)
①to educate ②education

教育部(ㄐㄧㄠ ㄩˋ ㄅㄨˋ)
Ministry of Education

教育部長(ㄐㄧㄠ ㄩˋ ㄅㄨˋ ㄓㄤˇ)
a minister of education; an education minister

教育費(ㄐㄧㄠ ㄩˋ ㄈㄟˋ)
the cost of education; an education bill

教育方針(ㄐㄧㄠ ㄩˋ ㄈㄤ ㄓㄣ)
a policy for education; an educational policy

教育廳(ㄐㄧㄠ ㄩˋ ㄊㄧㄥ)
Department of Education (under a provincial government)

教育廳長(ㄐㄧㄠ ㄩˋ ㄊㄧㄥ ㄓㄤˇ)
the commissioner of education or education commissioner (under a provincial government)

教育科(ㄐㄧㄠ ㄩˋ ㄎㄜ)
an education section (under a county or city government)

教育科長(ㄐㄧㄠ ㄩˋ ㄎㄜ ㄓㄤˇ)
the chief of the education section (under a city or county government)

教育會(ㄐㄧㄠ ㄩˋ ㄏㄨㄟˋ)
an educational association

教育基金(ㄐㄧㄠ ㄩˋ ㄐㄧ ㄐㄧㄣ)
educational funds

教育基金會(ㄐㄧㄠ ㄩˋ ㄐㄧ ㄐㄧㄣ ㄏㄨㄟˋ)
an educational foundation

教育家(ㄐㄧㄠ ㄩˋ ㄐㄧㄚ)
an educator or educationist

教育界(ㄐㄧㄠ ㄩˋ ㄐㄧㄝˋ)
educational circles

教育局(ㄐㄧㄠ ㄩˋ ㄐㄩˊ)
the bureau of education (under a special municipal government)

教育局長(ㄐㄧㄠ ㄩˋ ㄐㄩˊ ㄓㄤˇ)
the director of the bureau of education (under a special municipal government)

教育系(ㄐㄧㄠ ㄩˋ ㄒㄧˋ)
the department of education (in a university)

教育心理學(ㄐㄧㄠ ㄩˋ ㄒㄧㄣ ㄌㄧˇ ㄒㄩㄝˊ)
educational psychology

教育行政(ㄐㄧㄠ ㄩˋ ㄒㄧㄥˊ ㄓㄥˋ)
educational administration

教育學(ㄐㄧㄠ ㄩˋ ㄒㄩㄝˊ)
pedagogy; pedagogics

教育制度(ㄐㄧㄠ ㄩˋ ㄓˋ ㄉㄨˋ)
the educational system

教育程度(ㄐㄧㄠ ㄩˋ ㄔㄥˊ ㄉㄨˋ)
the level of education; educational attainment

教育總長(ㄐㄧㄠ ㄩˋ ㄗㄨㄥˇ ㄓㄤˇ)
Director-General of Education (a title used in the early republican years which was equivalent to the Education Minister)

教員(ㄐㄧㄠ ㄩㄢˊ)
a member of the teaching profession; a teacher

教員休息室(ㄐㄧㄠ ㄩㄢˊ ㄒㄧㄡ ㄒㄧˊ ㄕˋ)
a staff room; a common room

【教】 2126
2. ㄐㄧㄠ jiau jiāo
to teach; to guide: 他教我們做實驗。He taught us how to conduct experiments.

教法(ㄐㄧㄠ ㄈㄚˇ)
teaching methods

教給(ㄐㄧㄠ ㄍㄟˇ)
to impart (knowledge or skill) to someone

教壞(ㄐㄧㄠ ㄏㄨㄞˋ)
to misguide; to lead astray

教書(ㄐㄧㄠ ㄕㄨ)
to teach (usually for a living): 我哥哥在小學教書。My brother teaches in a primary school.

教書匠(ㄐㄧㄠ ㄕㄨ ㄐㄧㄤˋ)
a teacher (used in a derogatory sense): 我當了十年的教書匠。I have been a teacher for ten years.

【敏】 2127
ㄇㄧㄣˇ miin mǐn
1.quick; agile; speedy; clever; smart; nimble; sensitive: 這孩子很聰敏。The child is very clever.

2. diligent; industrious; earnest; eager

敏力(ㄇㄧㄣˇ ㄌㄧˋ)
to apply oneself diligently

敏感(ㄇㄧㄣˇ ㄍㄢˇ)
①sensitive; susceptible ② (medicine) allergic

敏慧(ㄇㄧㄣˇ ㄏㄨㄟˋ)
clever; sharp-witted; keen;

quick in understanding

敏捷(ㄇㄧㄣˇ ㄐㄧㄝˊ)
agile; adroit; quick; nimble: 他的頭腦敏捷。He is quick in mind.

敏求(ㄇㄧㄣˇ ㄑㄧㄡˊ)
to pursue diligently or earnestly

敏銳(ㄇㄧㄣˇ ㄖㄨㄟˋ)
keen; sharp; sharp-witted; acute: 他的目光敏銳。He has sharp eyes.

敏悟(ㄇㄧㄣˇ ㄨˋ)
quick to understand: 他學習語言的敏悟力很強。He is quick at learning languages.

敏於事而慎於言(ㄇㄧㄣˇ ㄩˊ ㄕˋ ㄦˊ ㄕㄣˋ ㄩˊ ㄧㄢˊ)
speedy as a worker and cautious as a speaker; quick in work and cautious in speech

【救】 2128
ㄐㄧㄡˋ jiow jiù
to save; to relieve; to rescue; to deliver; to aid; to help

救兵(ㄐㄧㄡˋ ㄅㄧㄥ)
relieving troops; reinforcements

救兵如救火(ㄐㄧㄡˋ ㄅㄧㄥ ㄖㄨˊ ㄐㄧㄡˋ ㄏㄨㄛˇ)
The urgency to despatch relieving troops or reinforcements is similar to that of firefighting—the sooner the better.

救民(ㄐㄧㄡˋ ㄇㄧㄣˊ)
to save the people

救命(ㄐㄧㄡˋ ㄇㄧㄥˋ)
①to save one's life ②Help!

救命恩人(ㄐㄧㄡˋ ㄇㄧㄥˋ ㄣ ㄖㄣˊ)
the savior of one's life

救溺(ㄐㄧㄡˋ ㄋㄧˋ)
to save the life of a drowning person

救國(ㄐㄧㄡˋ ㄍㄨㄛˊ)
to save one's country

救國救民(ㄐㄧㄡˋ ㄍㄨㄛˊ ㄐㄧㄡˋ ㄇㄧㄣˊ)
to save the country and people from an impending danger

救苦救難(ㄐㄧㄡˋ ㄎㄨˇ ㄐㄧㄡˋ ㄋㄢˋ)
to relieve the suffering and the distressed

救護(ㄐㄧㄡˋ ㄏㄨˋ)

〔支部〕

【支部】

to relieve and nurse (the wounded, etc.); to rescue

救護法(ㄐㄧㄡ ㄏㄨˋ ㄈㄚˇ)
techniques of first aid

救護站(ㄐㄧㄡ ㄏㄨˋ ㄓㄢˋ)
an aid station

救護車(ㄐㄧㄡ ㄏㄨˋ ㄔㄜ)
an ambulance (a vehicle for carrying people who are ill, wounded in war or hurt in accidents)

救活(ㄐㄧㄡ ㄏㄨㄛˊ)
to resuscitate; to revive

救火(ㄐㄧㄡ ㄏㄨㄛˇ)
①to fight a fire; to try to extinguish a fire ②fire-fighting

救火隊(ㄐㄧㄡ ㄏㄨㄛˇ ㄉㄨㄟˋ)
a fire brigade

救火機(ㄐㄧㄡ ㄏㄨㄛˇ ㄐㄧ)
a fire extinguisher

救火車(ㄐㄧㄡ ㄏㄨㄛˇ ㄔㄜ)
a fire engine

救火揚沸(ㄐㄧㄡ ㄏㄨㄛˇ ㄧㄤˊ ㄈㄟˋ)
(literally) to try to stop water boiling by stirring it instead of removing the fire underneath—to try to solve a problem without removing the root cause

救火員(ㄐㄧㄡ ㄏㄨㄛˇ ㄩㄢˊ)
a fireman

救飢(ㄐㄧㄡ ㄐㄧ)
to relieve the starving

救急(ㄐㄧㄡ ㄐㄧˊ)
①to give help in emergency; to help meet an urgent need ②to apply first aid

救急不救窮(ㄐㄧㄡ ㄐㄧˊ ㄅㄨˋ ㄐㄧㄡ ㄑㄩㄥˊ)
One may give financial aid to others in an emergency but should not do so if they are perennially in need of money.

救濟(ㄐㄧㄡ ㄐㄧˋ)
to relieve (the suffering, the poor, etc.); to succor

救濟金(ㄐㄧㄡ ㄐㄧˋ ㄐㄧㄣ)
relief funds

救濟權(ㄐㄧㄡ ㄐㄧˋ ㄑㄩㄢˊ)
(law) secondary right

救濟院(ㄐㄧㄡ ㄐㄧˋ ㄩㄢˋ)
an institution for the poor; a poorhouse; a workhouse

to come to the rescue of the emperor; to come to the aid of the monarch

救窮(ㄐㄧㄡ ㄑㄩㄥˊ)
to relieve the poor

救星(ㄐㄧㄡ ㄒㄧㄥ)
a savior

救治(ㄐㄧㄡ ㄓˋ)
to treat and cure (the sick); to remedy: 這種藥可救治你的頭痛。This medicine will cure your headache.

救主(ㄐㄧㄡ ㄓㄨˇ)
the Savior; the Messiah

救助(ㄐㄧㄡ ㄓㄨˋ)
to relieve or help (persons)

救時(ㄐㄧㄡ ㄕˊ)
to save the age (from degeneration)

救世(ㄐㄧㄡ ㄕˋ)
to save mankind; to save the world

救世軍(ㄐㄧㄡ ㄕˋ ㄐㄩㄣ)
the Salvation Army

救世主(ㄐㄧㄡ ㄕˋ ㄓㄨˇ)
①the Savior; the Messiah ②*Messiah*, an oratorio (1742) by George Frideric Handel

救生(ㄐㄧㄡ ㄕㄥ)
①to save the dying; to save one's life ②lifesaving

救生帶(ㄐㄧㄡ ㄕㄥ ㄉㄞˋ)
a life belt

救生艇(ㄐㄧㄡ ㄕㄥ ㄊㄧㄥˇ)
a lifeboat

救生圈(ㄐㄧㄡ ㄕㄥ ㄑㄩㄢ)
a life ring; a life buoy

救生船(ㄐㄧㄡ ㄕㄥ ㄔㄨㄢˊ)
a lifeboat

救生衣(ㄐㄧㄡ ㄕㄥ ㄧ)
a life jacket

救生員(ㄐㄧㄡ ㄕㄥ ㄩㄢˊ)
a lifeguard; a lifesaver

救人一命，勝造七級浮屠(ㄐㄧㄡ ㄖㄣˊ ㄧˊ ㄇㄧㄥˋ，ㄕㄥˋ ㄗㄠˋ ㄑㄧ ㄐㄧˊ ㄈㄨˊ ㄊㄨˊ)
Better save one life than build a seven-story pagoda.

救災(ㄐㄧㄡ ㄗㄞ)
to relieve victims of a disaster

救藥(ㄐㄧㄡ ㄧㄠˋ)
to remedy; to cure—to save the situation; to rectify abuses; to redress

救亡圖存(ㄐㄧㄡ ㄨㄤˊ ㄊㄨˊ ㄘㄨㄣˊ)
to save one's country so that it may survive

救援(ㄐㄧㄡ ㄩㄢˊ)
to help or aid (the distressed)

救援投手(ㄐㄧㄡ ㄩㄢˊ ㄊㄡˊ ㄕㄡˇ)
(baseball) a relief pitcher

【敕】 2129 (動) ㄔˋ chyh chi
1. an imperial order or decree
2. cautious
3. to warn; to caution

敕(ㄔˋ)
an imperial order to confer a title or rank on an official

敕封(ㄔˋ ㄈㄥ)
the imperial appointment or bestowal of titles of nobility

敕勒(ㄔˋ ㄌㄜˋ)
an imperial order

敕勒(ㄔˋ ㄌㄜˋ)
one of the ethnic tribes in the west

敕令(ㄔˋ ㄌㄧㄥˋ)
a rescript

敕授(ㄔˋ ㄕㄡˋ)
the imperial appointment or bestowal of titles of nobility

敕身(ㄔˋ ㄕㄣ)
to discipline oneself; to be prudent in conduct

敕書(ㄔˋ ㄕㄨ)
an imperial letter

敕葬(ㄔˋ ㄗㄤˋ)
to bury with a funeral organized by an imperial order

敕贈(ㄔˋ ㄗㄥˋ)
the imperial appointment or bestowal of titles of nobility

【敖】 2130 1. ㄠˊ aur áo
leisurely; idle

敖民(ㄠˊ ㄇㄧㄣˊ)
loafers; idlers

敖得薩(ㄠˊ ㄉㄜˊ ㄙㄚˋ)
Odessa, a Russian port city

敖放(ㄠˊ ㄈㄤˋ)
to loaf about; to frisk or play about; to idle away one's time

敖戲(ㄠˊ ㄒㄧˋ)
to play; to frolic

敖敖(ㄠˊ ㄠˊ)
tall; long

敖遊(ㄠˊ ㄧㄡˊ)

to travel or wander idly

【敖】 2130
2.(傲) ㄠ aw āo
1. proud; haughty
2. to make fun of

敖弄(ㄠ ㄋㄨㄥˋ)
to make fun of; to poke fun at

【敗】 ㄅㄞˋ bay bài
1. to defeat or be defeated; to thwart or be thwarted; to go down; to fail; to lose
2. to decline; to decay; to wither
3. to spoil or be spoiled; to corrupt or be corrupted

敗北(ㄅㄞˋ ㄅㄛˇ)
to suffer defeat; a defeat; to lose a battle

敗筆(ㄅㄞˋ ㄅㄧˇ)
① a worn-out writing brush; a spoiled pen ② poor calligraphy; a flaw in the making of a stroke — a faulty expression in writing

敗門風(ㄅㄞˋ ㄇㄣˊ ㄈㄥ)
to tarnish the good name of one's family; to disgrace one's family

敗盟(ㄅㄞˋ ㄇㄥˊ)
to break a covenant

敗名(ㄅㄞˋ ㄇㄧㄥˊ)
to tarnish one's reputation; to disgrace oneself

敗德(ㄅㄞˋ ㄉㄜˊ)
evil conduct; licentious behaviors

敗敵(ㄅㄞˋ ㄉㄧˊ)
to crush the enemy; to defeat the enemy

敗退(ㄅㄞˋ ㄊㄨㄟˋ)
to retreat after defeat

敗類(ㄅㄞˋ ㄌㄟˋ)
① to ruin or corrupt one's fellows ② corrupt people; the dregs of society; the scum of a community; a degenerate

敗柳殘花(ㄅㄞˋ ㄌㄧㄡˇ ㄘㄢˊ ㄏㄨㄚ)
prostitutes; immoral women

敗露(ㄅㄞˋ ㄌㄨˋ)
(said of a crime, plot, etc.) to fail and be exposed

敗落(ㄅㄞˋ ㄌㄨㄛˋ)
to fall into a decline; to go down: 這部電影反映人性的敗落. The movie reflects the decline of human nature.

敗火(ㄅㄞˋ ㄏㄨㄛˇ)
to alleviate fever; to relieve inflammation or internal heat

敗壞(ㄅㄞˋ ㄏㄨㄞˋ)
to corrupt or be corrupted; to ruin or be ruined: 賭博敗壞社會風氣. Gambling corrupts the morals of society.

敗壞門楣(ㄅㄞˋ ㄏㄨㄞˋ ㄇㄣˊ ㄇㄟˊ)
to disgrace one's family

敗績(ㄅㄞˋ ㄐㄧ)
a defeat

敗家子(ㄅㄞˋ ㄐㄧㄚ ㄗˇ)or 敗子(ㄅㄞˋ ㄗˇ)
a prodigal; a spendthrift; a wastrel

敗將(ㄅㄞˋ ㄐㄧㄤˋ)
① a defeated enemy general ② one who is defeated in a contest: 他是我的手下敗將. He is the one who has suffered defeat at my hands.

敗軍(ㄅㄞˋ ㄐㄩㄣ)
a defeated army

敗軍之將不足言勇(ㄅㄞˋ ㄐㄩㄣ ㄓ ㄐㄧㄤˋ ㄅㄨˋ ㄗㄨˊ ㄧㄢˊ ㄩㄥˇ)
The general of a defeated army is in no position to claim bravery.

敗血(ㄅㄞˋ ㄒㄧㄝˇ)or(ㄅㄞˋ ㄒㄩㄝˋ)
poisonous blood

敗血病(ㄅㄞˋ ㄒㄧㄝˇ ㄅㄧㄥˋ)or 敗血症(ㄅㄞˋ ㄒㄧㄝˇ ㄓㄥˋ)
septicemia

敗血膿毒症(ㄅㄞˋ ㄒㄧㄝˇ ㄋㄨㄥˊ ㄉㄨˊ ㄓㄥˋ)
septicopyemia

敗興而歸(ㄅㄞˋ ㄒㄧㄥˋ ㄦˊ ㄍㄨㄟ)
to come back disappointed: 我興興而去, 敗興而歸. I went with great enthusiasm and came back disappointed.

敗絮(ㄅㄞˋ ㄒㄩˋ)
waste cotton—a dry and useless thing

敗陣(ㄅㄞˋ ㄓㄣˋ)
a defeat

敗伏(ㄅㄞˋ ㄓㄜˊ)
a defeat

敗事(ㄅㄞˋ ㄕˋ)
to spoil or bungle a matter

敗肉(ㄅㄞˋ ㄖㄡˋ)
spoiled meat

敗走(ㄅㄞˋ ㄗㄡˇ)

to flee after defeat

敗挫(ㄅㄞˋ ㄘㄨㄛˋ)
to defeat; to frustrate; to thwart

敗訴(ㄅㄞˋ ㄙㄨˋ)
to lose a lawsuit: 他因敗訴而破產. Losing the lawsuit bankrupted him.

敗葉(ㄅㄞˋ ㄧㄝˋ)
shriveled leaves; fallen leaves

敗亡(ㄅㄞˋ ㄨㄤˊ)
to be defeated and overthrown

【敔】 ㄩˇ yeu yǔ
an ancient musical instrument

八畫

【敝】 2133 ㄅㄧˋ bih bì
1. worn-out; broken; tattered
2. exhausted; tired
3. (a self-depreciatory term) my, or our: 歡迎蒞臨敝公司. Welcome to our firm.

敝店(ㄅㄧˋ ㄉㄧㄢˋ)
my humble store: 敝店供應各種參考書. My humble store offers all kinds of reference books.

敝屣(ㄅㄧˋ ㄒㄧˇ)
worn-out shoes

敝國(ㄅㄧˋ ㄍㄨㄛˊ)
(a self-depreciatory term) my or our country

敝屣(ㄅㄧˋ ㄒㄧˇ)
worn-out shoes—useless things

敝校(ㄅㄧˋ ㄒㄧㄠˋ)
(a self-depreciatory term) my or our school: 敝校創立於一九四八年. Our school was founded in 1948.

敝鄉(ㄅㄧˋ ㄒㄧㄤ)
(a self-depreciatory term) my or our hometown or village

敝姓(ㄅㄧˋ ㄒㄧㄥˋ)
(a self-depreciatory term) my family name

敝帚千金(ㄅㄧˋ ㄓㄡˇ ㄑㄧㄢ ㄐㄧㄣ)
(literally) My worn-out broom is worth a thousand crowns.—Everyone values

〔支部〕

things of his own.

敝帚自珍 (ㄅㄧˋ ㄓㄡˇ ㄗˋ ㄓㄣ)
(literally) My worn-out broom is a treasure to me. --Everyone values things of his own.

敝處 (ㄅㄧˋ ㄔㄨˋ)
(a self-depreciatory term) my place

敝舍 (ㄅㄧˋ ㄕㄜˋ)
(a self-depreciatory term) my house: 請駕臨敝舍一談。 Please come to my house and have a talk.

敝衣惡食 (ㄅㄧˋ ㄧ ㄜˋ ㄕˊ)
meanly clothed and poorly fed — having a very low standard of living

敝邑 (ㄅㄧˋ ㄧˋ)
(a self-depreciatory term) my kingdom

敝友 (ㄅㄧˋ ㄧㄡˇ)
(a self-depreciatory term) my friend

敝寓 (ㄅㄧˋ ㄩˋ)
(a self-depreciatory term) my residence

【敞】 2134
ㄔㄤˇ chaang chǎng
1. open; uncovered
2. spacious; broad

敞篷(兒)車 (ㄔㄤˇ ㄆㄥˊ (ㄦ) ㄔㄜ)
an open coach; an open car

敞地兒 (ㄔㄤˇ ㄉㄧˋ ㄦ)
open ground; unsheltered ground

敞廳 (ㄔㄤˇ ㄊㄧㄥ)
a spacious hall; a large hall

敞亮 (ㄔㄤˇ ㄌㄧㄤˋ)
spacious and light: 你的房子很敞亮。 Your house is light and spacious.

敞開 (ㄔㄤˇ ㄎㄞ)
to open; to unfold: 請把門敞開。 Open the door wide, please.

敞伏 (ㄔㄤˇ ㄈㄨˊ)
straightforward and broad-minded

敞胸露懷 (ㄔㄤˇ ㄒㄩㄥ ㄌㄨˋ ㄏㄨㄞˊ)
敞胸 (ㄔㄤˇ ㄒㄩㄥ) or 敞著懷 (ㄔㄤˇ
·ㄓㄜ ㄏㄨㄞˊ)
to bare the breast; décolleté

敞著 (ㄔㄤˇ ·ㄓㄜ)
open

敞車 (ㄔㄤˇ ㄔㄜ)
an open carriage; an open

wagon; an open freight car

【敠】 2135
ㄉㄨㄛ dwo duó
1. to weigh (a thing) in the hand
2. to weigh and consider (a matter)

【敢】 2136
ㄍㄢˇ gaan gǎn
1. to dare: 我不敢去。 I dare not go.
2. to have the confidence to; to be sure; to be certain
3. bold; courageous; daring
4. to make bold; to venture

敢當 (ㄍㄢˇ ㄉㄤ)
to dare to accept (a compliment, responsibility, etc.)

敢怒而不敢言 (ㄍㄢˇ ㄋㄨˋ ㄦˊ ㄅㄨˋ ㄍㄢˇ
ㄧㄢˊ)
angry but not daring to speak out; to choke with silent fury; to suppress one's rage

敢請 (ㄍㄢˇ ㄑㄧㄥˇ)
I venture to request....

敢情 (ㄍㄢˇ ·ㄑㄧㄥ)
①naturally; of course; as might be expected ②at the start; originally ③perhaps; maybe

敢是 (ㄍㄢˇ ㄕˋ)
perhaps; maybe

敢作敢當 (ㄍㄢˇ ㄗㄨㄛˋ ㄍㄢˇ ㄉㄤ)
to have the courage to accept the consequences of one's doing; to shoulder responsibility bravely

敢作敢為 (ㄍㄢˇ ㄗㄨㄛˋ ㄍㄢˇ ㄨㄟˊ)
to have the courage to do what one believes should be done

敢死 (ㄍㄢˇ ㄙˇ)
to dare to die; to defy death

敢死隊 (ㄍㄢˇ ㄙˇ ㄉㄨㄟˋ)
a suicide squad; a death band; a dare-to-die corps; a commando unit given a very dangerous mission

敢言 (ㄍㄢˇ ㄧㄢˊ)
courageous enough to express one's beliefs

敢問 (ㄍㄢˇ ㄨㄣˋ)
I venture to ask....

敢於 (ㄍㄢˇ ㄩˊ)
to dare to; to be bold in; to have the courage to

【散】 2137
ㄙㄢˋ sann sàn
1. to scatter; to disperse: 烏雲散了。 Dark clouds dispersed.
2. to end; to be over; to stop: 戲散了。 The play has ended.
3. to disseminate; to give out

散播 (ㄙㄢˋ ㄅㄛˋ)
to disseminate; to spread: 不要散播謠言, Don't spread rumors.

散佈 or 散布 (ㄙㄢˋ ㄅㄨˋ)
①to scatter; to sprinkle; to strew ②to spread; to disseminate: 她喜歡散布流言蜚語。 She likes to spread slanderous rumors.

散步 (ㄙㄢˋ ㄅㄨˋ)
to take a walk, a stroll, or a ramble: 我們在鄉間散步很開心。 We had a pleasant walk in the country.

散漫 (ㄙㄢˋ ㄇㄢˋ)
incompact; loose; disorganized

散悶 (ㄙㄢˋ ㄇㄣˋ)
to dissipate care or worries; to kill time

散發 (ㄙㄢˋ ㄈㄚ)
①to send out; to emit: 這朵花散發著香味。 The flower is sending forth a sweet smell. ②to distribute; to issue; to give out

散髮 (ㄙㄢˋ ㄈㄚˇ)
disheveled hair; unkempt hair

散隊 (ㄙㄢˋ ㄉㄨㄟˋ)
to break up a formation

散攤子 (ㄙㄢˋ ㄊㄢ ·ㄗ)
(said of a group) to break up

散落 (ㄙㄢˋ ㄌㄨㄛˋ)
to fall here and there; to be strewn or scattered

散亂 (ㄙㄢˋ ㄌㄨㄢˋ)
confused; in disorder

散館 (ㄙㄢˋ ㄍㄨㄢˇ)
(said of students of private schools in former times) to end the day's sessions

散光 (ㄙㄢˋ ㄍㄨㄤ)
astigmatism; astigmatic

散光眼鏡 (ㄙㄢˋ ㄍㄨㄤ ㄧㄢˇ ㄐㄧㄥˋ) or
(ㄙㄢˋ ㄍㄨㄤ ㄐㄧㄠˇ ㄐㄧㄥˋ)
astigmatic lenses

散工 (ㄙㄢˋ ㄍㄨㄥ)

to leave the factory after the day's work is over

散開(ㄙㄢ ㄎㄞ)
to disperse; to scatter

散布(ㄙㄢ ㄅㄨˋ)
to strew flowers as offering; to display textile flowers in a Buddhist ceremony

散夥(ㄙㄢ ㄏㄨㄛˇ)
(said of a group) to break up; to dissolve; to disband

散會(ㄙㄢ ㄏㄨㄟˋ)
to dissolve a meeting; (said of a meeting) to be over: 主席宣布散會. The chairman declared the meeting over.

散見(ㄙㄢ ㄐㄧㄢˋ)
to be seen at scattered places (especially in books)

散心(ㄙㄢ ㄒㄧㄣ)
to have some recreation; to drive away one's cares; to relieve boredom

散場(ㄙㄢ ㄔㄤˇ)
(said of a show, a meeting, etc.) to be over

散失(ㄙㄢ ㄕ)
to get scattered and lost; missing

散熱(ㄙㄢ ㄖㄜˋ)
to dissipate heat

散熱器(ㄙㄢ ㄖㄜˋ ㄑㄧˋ)
a radiator

散財(ㄙㄢ ㄘㄞˊ)
to give away money generously for charitable projects

【散】 2137
2. ㄙㄢˇ　saan　sǎn
1. loose; loosened
2. idle; leisurely
3. powdered medicine

散兵(ㄙㄢˇ ㄅㄧㄥ)
①soldiers in combat formation; skirmishers ②stragglers

散兵坑(ㄙㄢˇ ㄅㄧㄥ ㄎㄥ)
(military) a foxhole

散兵線(ㄙㄢˇ ㄅㄧㄥ ㄒㄧㄢˋ)
(military) an open skirmish line

散兵遊勇(ㄙㄢˇ ㄅㄧㄥ ㄧㄡˊ ㄩㄥˇ)
straggling troops

散木(ㄙㄢˇ ㄇㄨˋ)
odd pieces of wood; useless timber

散夫(ㄙㄢˇ ㄈㄨ)
an unskilled worker

散彈(ㄙㄢˇ ㄉㄢˋ)
a grapeshot; a pellet

散淡(ㄙㄢˇ ㄉㄢˋ)
to lead an idle life; to relax

散蕩(ㄙㄢˇ ㄉㄤˋ)
to play idly; to loaf about

散官(ㄙㄢˇ ㄍㄨㄢ)
one who holds a sinecure post in a government agency

散逛(ㄙㄢˇ ㄍㄨㄤˋ)
to loaf about

散工(ㄙㄢˇ ㄍㄨㄥ)
odd jobs: 他靠做散工生活. He makes a living by doing odd jobs.

散記(ㄙㄢˇ ㄐㄧˋ)
random notes

散居(ㄙㄢˇ ㄐㄩ)
to live in scattered places: 游擊隊員散居在山區. The guerrillas lived scattered in the mountains.

散曲(ㄙㄢˇ ㄑㄩˇ)
(Chinese opera) a piece with neither action nor dialogue; a type of verse popular in the Yüan Dynasty, with tonal patterns modeled on tunes drawn from folk music

散職(ㄙㄢˇ ㄓˊ)
a featherbedding or sinecure post

散軼(ㄙㄢˇ ㄓˋ)
to open a book

散裝(ㄙㄢˇ ㄓㄨㄤ)
loose; not in a package; bulk; in bulk

散沙(ㄙㄢˇ ㄕㄚ)
loose sand—(figuratively) lack of the spirit of cooperation

散人(ㄙㄢˇ ㄖㄣˊ)
an idle man; a person not harnessed with duties

散儒(ㄙㄢˇ ㄖㄨˊ)or散才(ㄙㄢˇ ㄘㄞˊ)
a scholar who disdains social conventions

散文(ㄙㄢˇ ㄨㄣˊ)
prose: 這故事是用散文寫的. The story is in prose.

散文詩(ㄙㄢˇ ㄨㄣˊ ㄕ)
a prose poem

【敦】 2138
1. ㄉㄨㄣ　duen　dūn
1. honest; candid
2. to deepen or strengthen

(relations, etc.)
3. to urge; to press

敦品力學(ㄉㄨㄣ ㄆㄧㄣˇ ㄌㄧˋ ㄒㄩㄝˊ)
upright in character and diligent in the pursuit of knowledge

敦聘(ㄉㄨㄣ ㄆㄧㄣˋ)
to cordially invite (to render some service)

敦樸(ㄉㄨㄣ ㄆㄨˊ)
honest; sincere; upright

敦勉(ㄉㄨㄣ ㄇㄧㄢˇ)
honest and diligent

敦睦(ㄉㄨㄣ ㄇㄨˋ)
to have cordial and friendly ties; to promote friendly relations

敦實(ㄉㄨㄣ ㄕˊ)
honest; cordial; upright; sincere

敦倫(ㄉㄨㄣ ㄌㄨㄣˊ)
①sexual act between husband and wife②to strengthen moral ties between humans

敦厚(ㄉㄨㄣ ㄏㄡˋ)or敦篤(ㄉㄨㄣ ㄉㄨˇ)
honest; sincere

敦煌(ㄉㄨㄣ ㄏㄨㄤˊ)
Tunhwang, Kansu Province

敦煌石室(ㄉㄨㄣ ㄏㄨㄤˊ ㄕˊ ㄕˋ)or敦煌石窟(ㄉㄨㄣ ㄏㄨㄤˊ ㄕˊ ㄎㄨ)
the Caves of Tunhwang, a treasure house of Buddhist scriptures, paintings and statues

敦親睦族(ㄉㄨㄣ ㄑㄧㄣ ㄇㄨˋ ㄗㄨˊ)
to strengthen the relations among kinsfolk and among different clans

敦請(ㄉㄨㄣ ㄑㄧㄥˇ)
to extend a cordial invitation to; to invite cordially

敦促(ㄉㄨㄣ ㄘㄨˋ)
to urge or press earnestly: 父親敦促我早日起程. Father urged me to start on my journey early.

【敦】 2138
2. ㄉㄨㄟˋ　duey　duì
a sort of container

九畫

【敬】 2139
1. ㄐㄧㄥˋ　jinq　jìng
1. to respect; to revere; to honor; to esteem; respect; respectfully: 我很尊敬她. I

（支部）

have great respect for her.
2. to present; to offer
3. a Chinese family name

敬稟者(ㄐㄧㄥ ㄅㄧㄣˇ ㄓㄜˇ)
a conventional phrase referring to oneself used at the beginning of a letter addressed to an elder or superior

敬陪末坐(ㄐㄧㄥ ㄆㄟˊ ㄇㄛˋ ㄗㄨㄛˋ)
to sit below the salt; to sit at an inconspicuous seat

敬佩(ㄐㄧㄥ ㄆㄟˋ)
to admire; to respect; to esteem; to think highly of: 我們敬佩那女孩的勇氣。We admired the girl for her courage.

敬慕(ㄐㄧㄥ ㄇㄨˋ)
to respect and admire

敬奉(ㄐㄧㄥ ㄈㄥˋ)
①to receive respectfully ②to present (or offer) respectfully

敬服(ㄐㄧㄥ ㄈㄨˊ)
to respect, esteem or admire unreservedly

敬覆者(ㄐㄧㄥ ㄈㄨˋ ㄓㄜˇ)
a conventional phrase referring to oneself at the beginning of a letter in reply

敬老(ㄐㄧㄥ ㄌㄠˇ)
to respect the old

敬老尊賢(ㄐㄧㄥ ㄌㄠˇ ㄗㄨㄣ ㄒㄧㄢˊ)
to revere the aged and honor the wise

敬禮(ㄐㄧㄥ ㄌㄧˇ)
to salute; to extend one's greetings

敬領(ㄐㄧㄥ ㄌㄧㄥˇ)
to accept with respect

敬告(ㄐㄧㄥ ㄍㄠˋ)
to tell respectfully

敬鬼神而遠之(ㄐㄧㄥ ㄍㄨㄟˇ ㄕㄣˊ ㄦˊ ㄩㄢˇ ㄓ)or(ㄐㄧㄥ ㄍㄨㄟˇ ㄕㄣˊ ㄦˊ ㄩㄢˇ ㄓ)
to keep at a respectable distance; to avoid someone (or something) as if he (or it) were plague

敬賀(ㄐㄧㄥ ㄏㄜˋ)
to congratulate with respect

敬候(ㄐㄧㄥ ㄏㄡˋ)
①to inquire after respectfully ②to await respectfully

敬酒(ㄐㄧㄥ ㄐㄧㄡˇ)
to drink a toast; to toast: 我們向新娘新郎敬酒。We drank

a toast to the bride and bridegroom.

敬酒不吃吃罰酒(ㄐㄧㄥ ㄐㄧㄡˇ ㄅㄨˋ ㄔ ㄔ ㄈㄚˊ ㄐㄧㄡˇ)
to refuse a toast only to drink a penalty—(figuratively) to yield to somebody's pressure after first turning down his request; to be constrained to do what one at first refused

敬謹(ㄐㄧㄥ ㄐㄧㄣˇ)
respectfully; deferentially

敬軍(ㄐㄧㄥ ㄐㄩㄣ)
to honor the armed forces

敬啓(ㄐㄧㄥ ㄑㄧˇ)
to state with respect (a conventional phrase in correspondence)

敬啓者(ㄐㄧㄥ ㄑㄧˇ ㄓㄜˇ)
a conventional phrase referring to the letter-writer placed at the beginning of the letter

敬虔(ㄐㄧㄥ ㄑㄧㄢˊ)
pious; devout

敬請(ㄐㄧㄥ ㄑㄧㄥˇ)
to invite respectfully

敬請指教(ㄐㄧㄥ ㄑㄧㄥˇ ㄓˇ ㄐㄧㄠˋ)
I humbly request your advice.

敬惜字紙(ㄐㄧㄥ ㄒㄧ ㄗˋ ㄓˇ)
to cherish paper bearing written or printed words

敬謝(ㄐㄧㄥ ㄒㄧㄝˋ)
to thank respectfully

敬謝不敏(ㄐㄧㄥ ㄒㄧㄝˋ ㄅㄨˋ ㄇㄧㄣˇ)
to decline a request politely

敬獻(ㄐㄧㄥ ㄒㄧㄢˋ)
to offer (a present) to a superior or an elder

敬香(ㄐㄧㄥ ㄒㄧㄤ)
to offer incense (to ancestors or deities)

敬祝(ㄐㄧㄥ ㄓㄨˋ)
to wish respectfully (a conventional phrase used at the end of a letter)

敬重(ㄐㄧㄥ ㄓㄨㄥˋ)
to respect; to esteem; to revere; to have high regard for

敬茶(ㄐㄧㄥ ㄔㄚˊ)
to serve tea to guests

敬陳(ㄐㄧㄥ ㄔㄣˊ)
to state respectfully

敬稱(ㄐㄧㄥ ㄔㄥ)

an honorific appellation; an honorific

敬呈(ㄐㄧㄥ ㄔㄥˊ)
to present with respect

敬師(ㄐㄧㄥ ㄕ)
to respect teachers: 學生應該敬師。Students should respect teachers.

敬事(ㄐㄧㄥ ㄕˋ)
to handle business with respectful attention

敬神(ㄐㄧㄥ ㄕㄣˊ)
to revere the gods: 有些原始社會的人非常敬神。Some primitive societies pay great reverence to gods.

敬贈(ㄐㄧㄥ ㄗㄥˋ)
to present respectfully

敬遵(ㄐㄧㄥ ㄗㄨㄣ)
to obey respectfully

敬頌(ㄐㄧㄥ ㄙㄨㄥˋ)
(a conventional phrase used at the end of a letter) to wish with respect

敬愛(ㄐㄧㄥ ㄞˋ)
to respect and love: 他是我們敬愛的教授。He is our esteemed and beloved professor.

敬而遠之(ㄐㄧㄥ ㄦˊ ㄩㄢˇ ㄓ)or(ㄐㄧㄥ ㄦˊ ㄩㄢˇ ㄓ)
to keep a person or a thing at a respectful distance; to keep a person or a thing at arm's length 參看「敬鬼神而遠之」

respects; regards: 我要向你表示由衷的敬意。I want to extend my heartfelt respects to you.

敬業樂羣(ㄐㄧㄥ ㄧㄝˋ ㄌㄜˋ ㄑㄩㄣˊ)
to respect work and enjoy company

敬煙(ㄐㄧㄥ ㄧㄢ)
to offer cigarettes

敬仰(ㄐㄧㄥ ㄧㄤˇ)
to admire; to esteem; to respect

敬長(ㄐㄧㄥ ㄓㄤˇ)
to hold in awe; to stand in awe of; to revere; to venerate

十畫

【敲】 ㄑㄧㄠ chiau qiāo　2140

1. to rap; to strike; to tap; to beat; to knock
2. as in 敲扑—a truncheon
3. to extort; to blackmail; to overcharge

敲梆(ㄑㄧㄠ ㄅㄤ)or 敲更(ㄑㄧㄠ ㄍㄥ)
　to beat the watches; to sound night watch with a clapper

敲邊鼓(ㄑㄧㄠ ㄅㄧㄢ ㄍㄨ)
　to speak for someone in order to help him

敲破(ㄑㄧㄠ ㄆㄛ)
　to smash; to shatter

敲枰(ㄑㄧㄠ ㄆㄧㄥ)
　to play a "go" game

敲門(ㄑㄧㄠ ㄇㄣ)
　to knock at (or on)the door: 你聽見敲門聲嗎? Did you hear someone knock?

敲門磚(ㄑㄧㄠ ㄇㄣ ㄓㄨㄢ)
　(literally) a brickbat used to knock at a door and thrown away after the door is open—learning used merely as a means for achieving success; a steppingstone to success

敲木魚(ㄑㄧㄠ ㄇㄨˋ ㄩˊ)
　to beat the wooden drum (when chanting a Buddhist sutra)

敲打(ㄑㄧㄠ ㄉㄚˇ)
　to tap; to rap; to knock; to beat

敲鐘(ㄑㄧㄠ ㄓㄨㄥ)
　to beat a gong

敲鼓(ㄑㄧㄠ ㄍㄨˇ)
　to beat drums

敲骨吸髓(ㄑㄧㄠ ㄍㄨˇ ㄒㄧ ㄙㄨㄟˇ)
　(literally) to crush the bone and suck the marrow—① to read an article carefully in order to profit thereby; ② cruel, bloodsucking exploitation; to suck the lifeblood

敲擊(ㄑㄧㄠ ㄐㄧ)
　to beat; to knock

敲經念佛(ㄑㄧㄠ ㄐㄧㄥ ㄋㄧㄢˋ ㄈㄛˊ)
　to beat time and chant a prayer

敲起警鐘(ㄑㄧㄠ ㄑㄧˇ ㄐㄧㄥˇ ㄓㄨㄥ)
　to sound the alarm bell

敲鑼打鼓(ㄑㄧㄠ ㄌㄨㄛˊ ㄉㄚˇ ㄍㄨˇ)
　to beat drums, gongs, etc.

continually

敲詐(ㄑㄧㄠ ㄓㄚˋ)
　to blackmail; to extort; to racketeer

敲竹槓(ㄑㄧㄠ ㄓㄨˊ ㄍㄤˋ)
　to squeeze a person for money; to extort money; to fleece; to sponge a person

敲鐘(ㄑㄧㄠ ㄓㄨㄥ)
　to toll a bell

敲詩(ㄑㄧㄠ ㄕ)
　a riddle in verse form

敲碎(ㄑㄧㄠ ㄙㄨㄟˋ)
　to knock or beat to pieces

十一畫

【敵】 ㄉㄧˊ dyi dí　2141

1. an enemy; a foe; a rival: 他是我的情敵。He is my rival in love.
2. to oppose; to resist
3. to match; to rival; to equal: 在這方面無人能與他匹敵。No one could rival him in this respect.

敵兵(ㄉㄧˊ ㄅㄧㄥ)
　an enemy soldier; the hostile troops

敵不住(ㄉㄧˊ ㄅㄨˋ ㄓㄨˋ)or 敵不過
　(ㄉㄧˊ ㄅㄨˋ ㄍㄨㄛˋ)
　to be no match for

敵黨(ㄉㄧˊ ㄉㄤˇ)
　a hostile group or party

敵對(ㄉㄧˊ ㄉㄨㄟˋ)
　to turn against; to be hostile to; to oppose: 愛與恨是敵對的。Love is opposed to hate.

敵對行為(ㄉㄧˊ ㄉㄨㄟˋ ㄒㄧㄥˊ ㄨㄟˊ)
　a hostile act

敵體(ㄉㄧˊ ㄊㄧˇ)
　equal standing or status

敵國(ㄉㄧˊ ㄍㄨㄛˊ)
　①a hostile country; a hostile power ②a foreign country equal to one's own in terms of strength ③(said of personal wealth) capable of matching the national treasury

敵愾(ㄉㄧˊ ㄎㄞˋ)
　enmity; hostility; hatred toward the enemy

敵愾同仇(ㄉㄧˊ ㄎㄞˋ ㄊㄨㄥˊ ㄔㄡˊ)
　to hate a common enemy and fight against him to-

gether

敵寇(ㄉㄧˊ ㄎㄡˋ)
　an enemy

敵後(ㄉㄧˊ ㄏㄡˋ)
　behind enemy lines; the enemy's rear area: 敵人員深入敵後。The agents penetrated into the enemy's rear area.

敵機(ㄉㄧˊ ㄐㄧ)
　an enemy plane; a hostile plane

敵騎(ㄉㄧˊ ㄐㄧˊ)
　enemy cavalry units

敵艦(ㄉㄧˊ ㄐㄧㄢˋ)
　an enemy warship; a hostile ship: 我們的飛機轟炸敵艦。Our planes bombed the enemy's ship.

敵軍(ㄉㄧˊ ㄐㄩㄣ)
　enemy troops; hostile forces: 敵軍被迫撤退。The enemy were forced to retreat.

敵前登陸(ㄉㄧˊ ㄑㄧㄢˊ ㄉㄥ ㄌㄨˋ)
　to make a landing in face of enemy resistance

敵情(ㄉㄧˊ ㄑㄧㄥˊ)
　the enemy's situation: 他派出飛機偵察敵情。He sent planes to make a reconnaissance of the enemy's situation.

敵住(ㄉㄧˊ ㄓㄨˋ)
　to hold the enemy at bay

敵眾我寡(ㄉㄧˊ ㄓㄨㄥˋ ㄨㄛˇ ㄍㄨㄚˇ)
　We are outnumbered by the enemy.

敵屍遍野(ㄉㄧˊ ㄕ ㄅㄧㄢˋ ㄧㄝˇ)
　The battlefield is littered with killed enemy soldiers.

敵視(ㄉㄧˊ ㄕˋ)
　to regard with hostility

敵勢(ㄉㄧˊ ㄕˋ)
　the strength (or morale) of the enemy

敵手(ㄉㄧˊ ㄕㄡˇ)
　an opponent, a match, a rival, an antagonist, an adversary, or an enemy of equal strength: 我看你不是他的敵手。I think you are no match for him.

敵人(ㄉㄧˊ ㄖㄣˊ)
　an enemy; a foe: 疾病是人類的敵人。Disease is an enemy of mankind.

敵意(ㄉㄧˊ ㄧˋ)

（支部）

enmity; hostility; antagonism: 他們懷着敵意的面孔顯示他不受歡迎。Their hostile looks showed that he was unwelcome.

敵營(ㄉㄧˊㄧㄥˊ)
an enemy camp: 我機成功地突襲敵營。Our planes made a raid upon the enemy camp successfully.

【敷】 2142
ㄈㄨ fu fū
1. to apply or spread over (a surface); to paint
2. to suffice; to be enough
3. to state; to explain; to expound

敷粉(ㄈㄨㄈㄣˇ)
to powder: 她在鼻子上敷粉。She powdered her nose.

敷化(ㄈㄨㄏㄨㄚˋ)
to teach and convert (heathens or barbarians)

敷教(ㄈㄨㄐㄧㄠˋ)
to spread a religion or a culture

敷政(ㄈㄨㄓㄥˋ)
to execute administration

敷陳(ㄈㄨㄔㄣˊ)
to state in detail

敷陳其事(ㄈㄨㄔㄣˊㄑㄧˊㄕˋ)
to set forth the fact

敷設(ㄈㄨㄕㄜˋ)
to install; to arrange; to lay; to fix: 工人正忙着敷設鐵軌。The workers are busy laying a railway track.

敷榮(ㄈㄨㄖㄨㄥˊ)
to blossom; to sprout

敷藥(ㄈㄨㄧㄠˋ)
to salve; to apply a salve

敷衍(ㄈㄨㄧㄢˇ)
①to act in a perfunctory manner: 他辦事認真，從不敷衍。He is very conscientious and never does his work perfunctorily. ②to deal with a person insincerely: 那女孩敷衍的答了幾句就走了。The girl made a few casual answers and left.

敷衍了事(ㄈㄨㄧㄢˇㄌㄧㄠˇㄕˋ)
to carry out a task in a perfunctory manner

敷衍塞責(ㄈㄨㄧㄢˇㄙㄜˋㄗㄜˊ)
to discharge a responsibility in a perfunctory manner

敷文(ㄈㄨ ㄨㄣˊ)
to write literary compositions

【數】 2143
1. ㄕㄨˋ shuh shù
1. number; quantity; sum; amount: 圖書館遺失的書籍爲數甚多。The number of books missing from the library is large.
2. (mathematics) numbers:複名數 compound numbers
3. several; a few
4. a plan; an idea: 她心中有數。She has a good idea of how things stand.
5. fate; destiny: 凡事皆有定數。Everything is destined.
6. art

數倍(ㄕㄨˋㄅㄟˋ)
several times; manifold

數碼(兒)(ㄕㄨˋㄇㄚˇ)
①number; amount ②a numeral: 阿拉伯數碼 Arabic numerals

數目(ㄕㄨˋㄇㄨˋ)
number; sum

數目字(ㄕㄨˋㄇㄨˋㄗˋ)
numerals; numbers; digits

數滴(ㄕㄨˋㄉㄧ)
several drops; a few drops

數天(ㄕㄨˋㄊㄧㄢ)
several days; a few days: 他每隔數天來看我們。He came to see us every few days.

數年(ㄕㄨˋㄋㄧㄢˊ)
several years; a few years: 我學英文已有數年了。I have studied English for several years.

數年如一日(ㄕㄨˋㄋㄧㄢˊㄖㄨˊㄧˋㄖˋ)
with perseverance and consistency

數量(ㄕㄨˋㄌㄧㄤˋ)
quantity; amount: 只有數量方面的差別。There is only quantitative difference.

數口之家(ㄕㄨˋㄎㄡˇㄓ ㄐㄧㄚ)
a family of several members; a small family

數盡(ㄕㄨˋㄐㄧㄣˋ)
running out of life; days numbered

數據(ㄕㄨˋㄐㄩˋ)
data: 這些數據已列於諸表中。These data are listed in tables.

數學(ㄕㄨˋㄒㄩㄝˊ)
mathematics

數學家(ㄕㄨˋㄒㄩㄝˊㄐㄧㄚ)
a mathematician

數值(ㄕㄨˋㄓˊ)
numerical value

數日(ㄕㄨˋㄖˋ)
several days; a few days: 我要在那裏停留數日。I'm going to stay there for a few days.

數字(ㄕㄨˋㄗˋ)
①a numeral; a figure; a digit: 那個是天文數字。An astronomical figure. ②quantity: 不要只追求數字。Don't just go after quantity.

數罪併罰(ㄕㄨˋㄗㄨㄟˋㄅㄧㄥˋㄈㄚˊ)
combined punishment for several offences

數次(ㄕㄨˋㄘˋ)
several times; a few times: 我已經這樣說過數次了。I have said so several times.

數額(ㄕㄨˋㄜˊ)
amount; sum: 我做的還不足規定數額。What I have done falls short of the amount required.

數兒(ㄕㄨˋㄦ)
①numbers ②plans; calculations; reckonings

數以萬計(ㄕㄨˋㄧˇㄨㄢˋㄐㄧˋ)
by tens of thousands; numerous

數易寒暑(ㄕㄨˋㄧˋㄏㄢˊㄕㄨˇ)
to go through many changes of seasons

數位(ㄕㄨˋㄨㄟˋ)
digital

數月(ㄕㄨˋㄩㄝˋ)
several months; a few months: 我們已數月未見。We haven't seen each other for several months.

【數】 2143
2. ㄕㄨˇ shuu shǔ
1. to count; to enumerate
2. to count (as best, etc.); to be reckoned as exceptionally (good, bad, etc.): 這裏數我最小。I am the youngest here.

數不過來(ㄕㄨˇㄅㄨˋㄍㄨㄛˋㄌㄞˊ)
too many to be counted; innumerable; countless

數不清(ㄕㄨˇㄅㄨˋㄑㄧㄥ)
innumerable; countless: 太多

了，我數不清。There were so many that I couldn't keep count of them.

數米而炊(ㄕㄨˇ ㄇㄧˇ ㄦˊ ㄔㄨㄟ)
(literally) to count the grains of rice before cooking it—to be contemptibly parsimonious or overcareful

數得著(ㄕㄨˋ ㄉㄜ˙ ㄓㄠˊ)
can be accounted among (the best, most notorious, etc.): 他是班上數得著的好學生。He is one of the outstanding students in the class.

數典忘祖(ㄕㄨˇ ㄉㄧㄢˇ ㄨㄤˋ ㄗㄨˇ)
(literally) to enumerate past records but ignore one's ancestry—to forget one's origin; ungrateful

數來寶(ㄕㄨˇ ㄌㄞˊ ㄅㄠˇ)
a beggar that begs by beating time and chanting rhymed words in flattery

數落(ㄕㄨˇ ㄌㄨㄛˋ)
to scold somebody by enumerating his wrongdoings; to blame; to reprove: 老師把她數落一頓。The teacher gave her a good scolding.

數黑論黃(ㄕㄨˇ ㄏㄟ ㄌㄨㄣˊ ㄏㄨㄤˊ)
to talk wildly; to make unfounded or exaggerated statements

數錢(ㄕㄨˇ ㄑㄧㄢˊ)
to count money: 這守財奴每晚都在數錢。The miser counted his money every night.

數數兒(ㄕㄨˇ ㄕㄨˋ ㄦ)
to name numbers; to count

數數看(ㄕㄨˇ ㄕㄨˋ ㄎㄢˋ)
to count and see (how many there are): 數數班上有多少學生。Count and see how many students in the class.

數說(ㄕㄨˇ ㄕㄨㄛ)
① to accuse; to reproach ② to enumerate

數一數二(ㄕㄨˇ ㄧ ㄕㄨˇ ㄦ)
either the best or second only to the best; one of the best: 他是本國數一數二的翻譯高手。He is one of the best translators in this country.

數一數(ㄕㄨˇ ㄧ˙ ㄕㄨˇ)
to count

數往知來(ㄕㄨˋ ㄨㄤˇ ㄓ ㄌㄞˊ)
to deduce what is likely to happen in the future by reviewing what has taken place in the past

【數】 2143
3. ㄕㄨㄛˋ shuoh shuò
often; frequently

數見不鮮(ㄕㄨㄛˋ ㄐㄧㄢˋ ㄅㄨˋ ㄒㄧㄢ)
not uncommon; found not infrequently; nothing new: 這種事情數見不鮮。Such occurrences are not uncommon.

數數(ㄕㄨㄛˋ ㄕㄨㄛˋ)
frequently; often

數四(ㄕㄨㄛˋ ㄙˋ)
over and over again; repeatedly

【毆】 2144
1. (毆) ㄑㄧㄡ chiu ㄑㄧㄡ
to drive away; to expel

【毆】 2144
2. (毆) ㄡˇ ou ㄡˇ
to beat; to assault physically

十二畫

【整】 2145
ㄓㄥˇ jeeng zhěng
1. orderly; systematic; neat; tidy: 椅子一排排的很整齊。The chairs are in orderly rows.
2. sharp: 現在是七點整。It's seven o'clock sharp.
3. whole; complete; entire; intact: 請整句唸出來。Read the whole sentence, please.
4. to tidy; to set in order; to adjust; to arrange; to repair; to make ready

整備(ㄓㄥˇ ㄅㄟˋ)
to make ready

整編(ㄓㄥˇ ㄅㄧㄢ)
to reorganize troops: 軍隊明年要整編。The army will be reorganized next year.

整裝(ㄓㄥˇ ㄓㄨㄤ)
to set out; to begin a journey

整批(ㄓㄥˇ ㄆㄧ)
batch

整風運動(ㄓㄥˇ ㄈㄥ ㄩㄣˋ ㄉㄨㄥˋ)
rectification movement

整黨(ㄓㄥˇ ㄉㄤˇ)
to consolidate a party organization

整隊(ㄓㄥˇ ㄉㄨㄟˋ)
① (said of troops, etc.) to form neat lines; to file ② the whole unit, band, column, etc.

整頓(ㄓㄥˇ ㄉㄨㄣˋ)
to put in order, or to put to right a poorly managed organization, firm, etc.: 他們的棒球隊需要好好整頓一下。Their baseball team needs a good shake-up.

整套(ㄓㄥˇ ㄊㄠˋ)
the whole set: 整套設備都是新的。The complete set of equipment is brand-new.

整體(ㄓㄥˇ ㄊㄧˇ)
the whole

整體規劃(ㄓㄥˇ ㄊㄧˇ ㄍㄨㄟ ㄏㄨㄚˋ)
corporate planning

整天(ㄓㄥˇ ㄊㄧㄢ)
the whole day; all day long

整年(ㄓㄥˇ ㄋㄧㄢˊ)
the whole year; all the year round; throughout the year

整理(ㄓㄥˇ ㄌㄧˇ)
to arrange; to put in order; to adjust; to regulate; to straighten up; to repair: 我整理自己的房間整理好。I put my room in order.

整列(ㄓㄥˇ ㄌㄧㄝˋ)
① (said of a group of people) to form neat lines ② the whole row or column

整流器(ㄓㄥˇ ㄌㄧㄡˊ ㄑㄧˋ)
(physics) ① a rectifier ② a commutator

整個(兒)(ㄓㄥˇ ㄍㄜˋ(ㄦ))
wholly; entirely; whole; entire: 整個教室響起熱烈的掌聲。The whole classroom resounded with warm applause.

整塊(ㄓㄥˇ ㄎㄨㄞˋ)
the whole piece: 他把整塊蛋糕吃掉了。He has eaten the whole cake.

整合(ㄓㄥˇ ㄏㄜˊ)
(geology) conformity

整行(ㄓㄥˇ ㄏㄤˊ)
the whole line

整潔(ㄓㄥˇ ㄐㄧㄝˊ)
neat and clean: 她將房間收拾得很整潔。She kept her room clean and tidy.

整舊如新(ㄓㄥˇ ㄐㄧㄡˋ ㄖㄨˊ ㄒㄧㄣ)
to repair something and make it brand-new

整軍經武(ㄓㄥˇ ㄐㄩㄣ ㄐㄧㄥ ㄨˇ)

to strengthen armaments; to beef up national defense

整齊 (ㄓㄥ ㄑㄧˊ)
① neat; orderly; tidy; well-arranged ② even; well-balance

整齊花 (ㄓㄥ ㄑㄧˊ ㄏㄨㄚ)
(botany) regular flower

整齊劃一 (ㄓㄥ ㄑㄧˊ ㄏㄨㄚˋ ㄧ)
neat and uniform

整修 (ㄓㄥ ㄒㄧㄡ)
to rebuild; to renovate; recondition; to touch up

整形 (ㄓㄥ ㄒㄧㄥˊ)
orthopedics

整形手術 (ㄓㄥ ㄒㄧㄥˊ ㄕㄡˇ ㄕㄨˋ)
plastic operation

整治 (ㄓㄥ ㄓˋ)
① to set in order; to adjust and repair; to fix ② to dredge (a river): 市政府計畫整治河道. The municipal government plans to dredge waterways. ③ to punish: 這男孩發需整治一下. The boy needs to be punished.

整裝 (ㄓㄥ ㄓㄨㄤ)
to dress up

整裝待發 (ㄓㄥ ㄓㄨㄤ ㄉㄞˋ ㄈㄚ)
(usually said of troops on an expedition) to pack up and be ready to go

整莊 (ㄓㄥ ㄓㄨㄤ)
whole; intact; entire

整飭 (ㄓㄥ ㄔˋ)
① orderly; systematic ② to set to order; to subject to orderly control

整除 (ㄓㄥ ㄔㄨˊ)
to be divided with no remainder; to divide exactly

整數 (ㄓㄥ ㄕㄨˋ)
a whole number; an integer; an integral number; a round number; a round sum

整日 (ㄓㄥ ㄖˋ) or 整日價 (ㄓㄥ ㄖˋ ㄐㄧㄚˋ)
the whole day; all day long

整日整夜 (ㄓㄥ ㄖˋ ㄓㄥ ㄧㄝˋ)
whole day and night

整人 (ㄓㄥ ㄖㄣˊ)
(slang) to give someone a hard time; to fix somebody

整容 (ㄓㄥ ㄖㄨㄥˊ)
① to improve one's looks by plastic surgery ② to tidy one's appearance (by shaving, a haircut, etc.); face-

lifting

整容醫生 (ㄓㄥ ㄖㄨㄥˊ ㄧ ㄕㄥ)
a plastic surgeon

整存零付 (ㄓㄥ ㄘㄨㄣˊ ㄌㄧㄥˊ ㄈㄨˋ)
to deposit a whole sum and withdraw the interest in monthly installments

整存整付 (ㄓㄥ ㄘㄨㄣˊ ㄓㄥ ㄈㄨˋ)
to deposit a sum and withdraw the principal and interest in a lump sum at the expiration of the deposit period

整廳 (ㄓㄥ ㄙㄨˋ)
① strict; rigid; stern ② to purge (a government or political leader) ③ to rectify

整衣 (ㄓㄥ ㄧ)
to adjust one's clothes

整夜 (ㄓㄥ ㄧㄝˋ)
all night; the whole night; throughout the night: 我們整夜看守. We watched all night.

十三畫

【斁】 2146
1. ㄧˋ yih yì
to dislike; to be tired; to be weary of

【斁】 2146
2. ㄉㄨˊ duh dú
to corrupt; to spoil

【斂】 2147
ㄌㄧㄢˋ liann liàn
1. to draw together; to contract
2. to hold back; to restrain
3. to collect; to gather

斂步 (ㄌㄧㄢˋ ㄅㄨˋ)
to slow down one's steps—to hesitate to advance further

斂法 (ㄌㄧㄢˋ ㄈㄚˇ)
tax law

斂迹 or 斂跡 (ㄌㄧㄢˋ ㄐㄧ)
to abstain from vice; (said of undesirable elements) to be subdued

斂局 (ㄌㄧㄢˋ ㄐㄩˊ)
to gather people together for gambling

斂錢 (ㄌㄧㄢˋ ㄑㄧㄢˊ)
to collect money illegally or immorally

斂手 (ㄌㄧㄢˋ ㄕㄡˇ)
to refrain or abstain from

doing something

斂然 (ㄌㄧㄢˋ ㄖㄢˊ)
gathered; assembled

斂衽 (ㄌㄧㄢˋ ㄖㄣˋ)
to pull the lapels of one's garment together respectfully in saluting

斂容 (ㄌㄧㄢˋ ㄖㄨㄥˊ)
to assume a serious expression; to put on a sober face

斂足 (ㄌㄧㄢˋ ㄗㄨˊ)
to slow down one's steps—to hesitate to advance further

斂財 (ㄌㄧㄢˋ ㄘㄞˊ)
to collect wealth illegally or immorally

斂翼 (ㄌㄧㄢˋ ㄧˋ)
to fold the wings—to flinch

斂怨 (ㄌㄧㄢˋ ㄩㄢˋ)
to accumulate hatred

十四畫

【斃】 2148
ㄅㄧˋ bih bì
1. to come to a bad end; decline; destruction
2. to fall; to prostrate
3. dead; to come to the end of life
4. (colloquial) to kill or execute by shooting; to shoot

斃命 (ㄅㄧˋ ㄇㄧㄥˋ)
to meet violent death; to get killed

斃敵 (ㄅㄧˋ ㄉㄧˊ)
to kill enemy troops (usually followed by the number of enemy soldiers killed)

十六畫

【斅】 2149
ㄒㄧㄠˋ shiaw xiào
1. to teach
2. to be awakened; to realize

文 部
ㄨㄣˊ　wen　wén

【文】 2150
1. ㄨㄣˊ wen wén
1. a composition; an article: 他寫了一篇談交通的文章. He

wrote an article on traffic.

2. language: 他會說英文。He can speak the English language.

3. literature; culture; education

4. elegant; cultured; polished; suave; civil; polite; urbane; mild

5. civilian or civil (as opposed to military): 文職 civilian posts

6. a former monetary unit

7. as in 一文不名 (to own nothing): 他一文不名。He owns nothing.

8. a Chinese family name

文筆 (ㄨㄣˊ ㄅㄧˇ)
the pen; literary talent: 文筆勝於刀劍。The pen is mightier than the sword.

文柄 (ㄨㄣˊ ㄅㄧㄥˇ)
the duties of a chief secretary in handling the correspondence for a government agency or high official

文不對題 (ㄨㄣˊ ㄅㄨˋ ㄉㄨㄟˋ ㄊㄧˊ)
The content of the writing is inconsistent with the title. 你說的都是文不對題的話。All you are saying is beside the mark.

文不加點 (ㄨㄣˊ ㄅㄨˋ ㄐㄧㄚ ㄉㄧㄢˇ)
to write with facility

文憑 (ㄨㄣˊ ㄆㄧㄥˊ)
a diploma: 她拿到工程文憑。She has got a diploma in engineering.

文墨 (ㄨㄣˊ ㄇㄛˋ)
① writing as an occupation ② writing ③ cultured; elegant

文墨人兒 (ㄨㄣˊ ㄇㄛˋ ㄖㄣˊ ㄦˊ)
an intellectual; a scholarly person

文貌 (ㄨㄣˊ ㄇㄠˋ)
courtesy; politeness; civility

文盲 (ㄨㄣˊ ㄇㄤˊ)
an illiterate: 政府努力掃除文盲。The government tried hard to wipe out illiteracy.

文廟 (ㄨㄣˊ ㄇㄧㄠˋ)
a Confucian temple

文面 (ㄨㄣˊ ㄇㄧㄢˋ)
to tattoo the face (as punishment)

文名 (ㄨㄣˊ ㄇㄧㄥˊ)
literary fame: 他熱衷追求文名。He is eager to pursue literary fame.

文明 (ㄨㄣˊ ㄇㄧㄥˊ)
civilized; civilization: 中國是文明古國。China is a country with an ancient civilization.

文明結婚 (ㄨㄣˊ ㄇㄧㄥˊ ㄐㄧㄝˊ ㄏㄨㄣ)
a Western-style wedding

文明戲 (ㄨㄣˊ ㄇㄧㄥˊ ㄒㄧˋ)
a crude stage play

文法 (ㄨㄣˊ ㄈㄚˇ)
grammar: 我發現德文文法很難。I find German grammar very difficult.

文房 (ㄨㄣˊ ㄈㄤˊ)
a study; a library

文房四寶 (ㄨㄣˊ ㄈㄤˊ ㄙˋ ㄅㄠˇ)
the four treasures in the study—the writing brush, the ink stick, the writing paper and the inkstone

文風 (ㄨㄣˊ ㄈㄥ)
① literary style ② popular interest in learning

文風不動 (ㄨㄣˊ ㄈㄥ ㄅㄨˋ ㄉㄨㄥˋ)
① calm; quiet; not given to excitement ② no change from origin

文德 (ㄨㄣˊ ㄉㄜˊ)
the refining influence of learning and art

文旦 (ㄨㄣˊ ㄉㄢˋ)
a shaddock; a pomelo

文定 (ㄨㄣˊ ㄉㄧㄥˋ)
to become betrothed; a betrothal

文牘 (ㄨㄣˊ ㄉㄨˊ)
① business correspondence; documents ② a secretary

文壇 (ㄨㄣˊ ㄊㄢˊ)
the literary circles, world, or arena

文壇耆宿 (ㄨㄣˊ ㄊㄢˊ ㄑㄧˊ ㄙㄨˋ)
an elder scholar commanding wide respect in the literary world

文體 (ㄨㄣˊ ㄊㄧˇ)
literary style: 兒童讀物要有明晰流暢的文體。Books for children should have a clear, easy style.

文天祥 (ㄨㄣˊ ㄊㄧㄢ ㄒㄧㄤˊ)
Wen Tien-hsiang, 1236 1283, last prime minister of the Sung Dynasty, who was executed by the Mongols after a three-year imprisonment

文鳥 (ㄨㄣˊ ㄋㄧㄠˇ)
the Java sparrow (*Padda oryzivora*)

文理 (ㄨㄣˊ ㄌㄧˇ)
the reasoning and arrangement of a literary composition; the sequence of thought; literary form and literary ideas

文例 (ㄨㄣˊ ㄌㄧˋ)
illustrative articles or passages

文林 (ㄨㄣˊ ㄌㄧㄣˊ)
a writers' resort

文稿 (ㄨㄣˊ ㄍㄠˇ)
a manuscript

文告 (ㄨㄣˊ ㄍㄠˋ)
a public notice; an announcement in writing; a manifesto; a message from the president issued on an important occasion

文過其實 (ㄨㄣˊ ㄍㄨㄛˋ ㄑㄧˊ ㄕˊ)
(said of a writing) beautiful in words but poor in contents

文官 (ㄨㄣˊ ㄍㄨㄢ)
a civil servant

文官考試 (ㄨㄣˊ ㄍㄨㄢ ㄎㄠˇ ㄕˋ)
a civil service examination

文科 (ㄨㄣˊ ㄎㄜ)
the liberal arts

文庫 (ㄨㄣˊ ㄎㄨˋ)
a collection of literary works; a library

文豪 (ㄨㄣˊ ㄏㄠˊ)
a literary lion; a great writer

文翰 (ㄨㄣˊ ㄏㄢˋ)
① literary writings ② a pheasant-like bird

文虎 (ㄨㄣˊ ㄏㄨˇ)
lantern riddles, or lantern puzzles

文化 (ㄨㄣˊ ㄏㄨㄚˋ)
culture; civilization: 中國文化注重道德。Chinese culture emphasizes morality.

文化復興 (ㄨㄣˊ ㄏㄨㄚˋ ㄈㄨˋ ㄒㄧㄥ)
cultural revitalization

文化大革命 (ㄨㄣˊ ㄏㄨㄚˋ ㄉㄚˋ ㄍㄜˊ ㄇㄧㄥˋ)
the Great Cultural Revolution

文化流氓 (ㄨㄣˊ ㄏㄨㄚˋ ㄌㄧㄡˊ ㄇㄤˊ)
a cultural villain

〔文部〕

文化界(ㄨㄣ ㄏㄨㄚˋ ㄐㄧㄝˋ)
參看「文化圈」

文化交流(ㄨㄣ ㄏㄨㄚˋ ㄐㄧㄠ ㄌㄧㄡˊ)
cultural exchange

文化圈(ㄨㄣ ㄏㄨㄚˋ ㄑㄩㄢ)
the intellectual or literary
circles

文化史(ㄨㄣ ㄏㄨㄚˋ ㄕˇ)
cultural history

文化事業(ㄨㄣ ㄏㄨㄚˋ ㄕˋ ㄧㄝˋ)
cultural enterprises

文化水準(ㄨㄣ ㄏㄨㄚˋ ㄕㄨㄟˇ ㄓㄨㄣˇ)
the cultural standing or
level

文化人(ㄨㄣ ㄏㄨㄚˋ ㄖㄣˊ)
cultured people

文火(ㄨㄣ ㄏㄨㄛˇ)
a slow fire (in cooking)

文會(ㄨㄣ ㄏㄨㄟˋ)
a literary society

文集(ㄨㄣ ㄐㄧˊ)
a collection of prose works

文籍(ㄨㄣ ㄐㄧˊ)
books

文教(ㄨㄣ ㄐㄧㄠˋ)
culture and education

文件(ㄨㄣ ㄐㄧㄢˋ)
documents; legal papers: 他
的一些重要文件被竊了。Some
of his important papers
were stolen.

文景之治(ㄨㄣ ㄐㄧㄥˇ ㄓ ㄓˋ)
the enlightened administration during the reign of
Emperors Wen and Ching
(179-143 B.C.) of the Han
Dynasty

文靜(ㄨㄣ ㄐㄧㄥˋ)
gracefully quiet: 她是一位個
性文靜的女人。She's a woman
of gracefully quiet character.

文具(ㄨㄣ ㄐㄩˋ)
writing tools; stationery

文卷(ㄨㄣ ㄐㄩㄢˋ)
documents; papers: 我們已將
這些文卷歸檔了。We have
placed the documents on our
files.

文君新寡(ㄨㄣ ㄐㄩㄣ ㄒㄧㄣ ㄍㄨㄚˇ)
a newly widowed woman

文起八代之衰(ㄨㄣ ㄑㄧˇ ㄅㄚ ㄉㄞˋ ㄓ ㄕㄨㄞ)
(literally) spearheading a
literary resurgence after a
decline during the eight

dynasties—the Eastern Han
(東漢), Wei (魏), Tsin (晉),
Sung (宋), Chi (齊), Liang
(梁), Chen (陳) and Sui (隋)
Dynasties—which preceded
the Tang Dynasty—a eulogy
for Han Yü (韓愈), a great
writer of the Tang period

文契(ㄨㄣ ㄑㄧˋ)
legal papers concerning
business or property transactions

文氣(ㄨㄣ ㄑㄧˋ)
the emotional impact or
spirit of a writing

文情並茂(ㄨㄣ ㄑㄧㄥˊ ㄅㄧㄥˋ ㄇㄠˋ)
Both the language and the
content are excellent.

文曲星(ㄨㄣ ㄑㄩ ㄒㄧㄥ)
name of a constellation that
sheds particular influence on
literary geniuses

文戲(ㄨㄣ ㄒㄧˋ)
(Chinese opera) a play without war scenes

文獻(ㄨㄣ ㄒㄧㄢˋ)
records; documents; literature (in science)

文心雕龍(ㄨㄣ ㄒㄧㄣ ㄉㄧㄠ ㄌㄨㄥˊ)
*The Literary Mind and
Carving of Dragons*, a trea-
tise in literary criticism by
Liu Hsieh (劉勰), a fifth
century writer

文學(ㄨㄣ ㄒㄩㄝˊ)
literature; letters and scholarship

文學批評(ㄨㄣ ㄒㄩㄝˊ ㄆㄧ ㄆㄧㄥˊ)
literary criticism

文學革命(ㄨㄣ ㄒㄩㄝˊ ㄍㄜˊ ㄇㄧㄥˋ)
a literary revolution

文學家(ㄨㄣ ㄒㄩㄝˊ ㄐㄧㄚ)
a man of letters; a literary
man; a litterateur

文學界(ㄨㄣ ㄒㄩㄝˊ ㄐㄧㄝˋ)
the literary world, circles, or
arena

文學史(ㄨㄣ ㄒㄩㄝˊ ㄕˇ)
literary history; the history
of literature

文學士(ㄨㄣ ㄒㄩㄝˊ ㄕˋ)
Bachelor of Arts (B.A.)

文學作品(ㄨㄣ ㄒㄩㄝˊ ㄗㄨㄛˋ ㄆㄧㄣˇ)
literary works

文學研究會(ㄨㄣ ㄒㄩㄝˊ ㄧㄢˊ ㄐㄧㄡ ㄏㄨㄟˋ)
a literary society

文學院(ㄨㄣ ㄒㄩㄝˊ ㄩㄢˋ)
a college of liberal arts

文選(ㄨㄣ ㄒㄩㄢˇ)
①a selection of literary
works; an anthology ②the
title of a 60-volume work
edited by Hsiao Tung (蕭
統), prince of the Liang
Dynasty 亦作「昭明文選」

文選爛，秀才半(ㄨㄣ ㄒㄩㄢˇ ㄌㄢˋ，
ㄒㄧㄡˋ ㄘㄞˊ ㄅㄢˋ)
Extensive reading makes
one a scholar.

文職(ㄨㄣ ㄓˊ)
a civil post (as distinct from
a military post)

文質彬彬(ㄨㄣ ㄓˋ ㄅㄧㄣ ㄅㄧㄣ)
fine both in accomplish-
ments and in nature; elegant
and refined in manner

文治(ㄨㄣ ㄓˋ)
civil administration

文治武功(ㄨㄣ ㄓˋ ㄨˇ ㄍㄨㄥ)
political and military
achievements

文摘(ㄨㄣ ㄓㄞ)
an abstract; a digest

文縐縐(ㄨㄣ ㄓㄡ ㄓㄡ)or(ㄨㄣ ㄓㄡˋ ㄓㄡˋ)
showing affected elegance;
pedantic

文章(ㄨㄣ ㄓㄤ)
an article; a composition

文章憎命(ㄨㄣ ㄓㄤ ㄗㄥ ㄇㄧㄥˋ)
Literary talents are generally ill-starred in their lives.

文竹(ㄨㄣ ㄓㄨˊ)
(botany) asparagus fern

文抄公(ㄨㄣ ㄔㄠ ㄍㄨㄥ)
a plagiarist

文丑(ㄨㄣ ㄔㄡˇ)
(Chinese opera) a clown
that does not perform acro-
batics or fighting

文場(ㄨㄣ ㄔㄤˇ)or(ㄨㄣ ㄔㄤˊ)
①an examination hall (for
the civil service examination
in former times) ② music
accompanying singing and
slow-motion acting as
opposed to that accompanying fighting scenes in
Chinese opera ③the literary
arena

文石(ㄨㄣ ㄕˊ)
①stones with streaks or
mottles ②agate 亦作「瑪瑙」

文史(ㄨㄣ ㄕˇ)

the literature and history; humanities

文士(ㄨㄣˊ ㄕˋ)
a man of letters

文身(ㄨㄣˊ ㄕㄣ)
to tattoo the body

文書(ㄨㄣˊ ㄕㄨ)
①documents; records; archives ②an archivist; an office clerk

文殊(ㄨㄣˊ ㄕㄨ)
Manjusri, a Buddhist Bodhisatva, considered as an idealization of wisdom

文人(ㄨㄣˊ ㄖㄣˊ)
①a man of letters ②a man with a civilian background (as opposed to one with a military background)

文人畫(ㄨㄣˊ ㄖㄣˊ ㄏㄨㄚˋ)
a school of painting done by amateur literati

文人相輕(ㄨㄣˊ ㄖㄣˊ ㄒㄧㄤ ㄑㄧㄥ)
Men of letters tend to despise one another.

文人無行(ㄨㄣˊ ㄖㄣˊ ㄨˊ ㄒㄧㄥˊ)
Men of letters are normally Bohemians.

文弱(ㄨㄣˊ ㄖㄨㄛˋ)
effeminate; not soldierly: 他因缺少運動故看來文弱。He looks effeminate for want of exercise.

文弱書生(ㄨㄣˊ ㄖㄨㄛˋ ㄕㄨ ㄕㄥ)
an effeminate scholar

文字(ㄨㄣˊ ㄗˋ)
①a letter; a character; written language ②writing

文字交(ㄨㄣˊ ㄗˋ ㄐㄧㄠ)
friendship cemented by literature

文字學(ㄨㄣˊ ㄗˋ ㄒㄩㄝˊ)
etymology

文字處理機(ㄨㄣˊ ㄗˋ ㄔㄨˇ ㄌㄧˇ ㄐㄧ)
a word processor

文字獄(ㄨㄣˊ ㄗˋ ㄩˋ)
literary persecution

文責自負(ㄨㄣˊ ㄗㄜˊ ㄗˋ ㄈㄨˋ)
The writer is responsible for the consequences of this article. (a footnote for contributed articles published by a newspaper or magazine)

文藻(ㄨㄣˊ ㄗㄠˇ)
language or phraseology (of a poem, etc.)

diction; phraseology; language

文才(ㄨㄣˊ ㄘㄞˊ)
literary talent; literary gift: 這位青年作家很有文才。This young writer has great literary talent.

文采(ㄨㄣˊ ㄘㄞˇ)
①elegant appearances ②beautiful or gorgeous color

文從字順(ㄨㄣˊ ㄘㄨㄥˊ ㄗˋ ㄕㄨㄣˋ)
The language is idiomatic and the wording is apposite.

文思(ㄨㄣˊ ㄙ)
thoughts expressed in writing: 他的文思明朗流暢。His thoughts expressed in writing are lucid and smooth.

文案(ㄨㄣˊ ㄢˋ)
①a business communication which requires some action ②a secretary; a clerk

文以載道(ㄨㄣˊ ㄧˇ ㄗㄞˋ ㄉㄠˋ)
Writings are for conveying truth.

文義(ㄨㄣˊ ㄧˋ)
the meaning of a written article, passage, or sentence

文藝(ㄨㄣˊ ㄧˋ)
literature (as one of the fine arts); belles-lettres

文藝批評(ㄨㄣˊ ㄧˋ ㄆㄧ ㄆㄧㄥˊ)
literary criticism

文藝復興(ㄨㄣˊ ㄧˋ ㄈㄨˋ ㄒㄧㄥ)
the Renaissance

文藝節(ㄨㄣˊ ㄧˋ ㄐㄧㄝˊ)
Literature Day (falling on May 4)

文藝界(ㄨㄣˊ ㄧˋ ㄐㄧㄝˋ)
the literary circles

文藝政策(ㄨㄣˊ ㄧˋ ㄓㄥˋ ㄘㄜˋ)
a set of guiding rules laid down by the government for literary workers

文藝思潮(ㄨㄣˊ ㄧˋ ㄙ ㄔㄠˊ)
the trend of literary thoughts

文雅(ㄨㄣˊ ㄧㄚˇ)
graceful; refined; polished

文妖(ㄨㄣˊ ㄧㄠ)
a literary sorcerer

文鰩魚(ㄨㄣˊ ㄧㄠˊ ㄩˊ)
a flying fish (Cyperulus agoo) 亦作「飛魚」or「文魚」

文言(ㄨㄣˊ ㄧㄢˊ)or 文言文(ㄨㄣˊ ㄧㄢˊ ㄨㄣˊ)

the literary language used in old China which is vastly different from the modern language; classical Chinese

文無定法(ㄨㄣˊ ㄨˊ ㄉㄧㄥˋ ㄈㄚˇ)
There are no hard and fast rules one can follow in order to write well.

文武(ㄨㄣˊ ㄨˇ)
①polite letters and martial arts ②civil and military; for peace or for war

文武百官(ㄨㄣˊ ㄨˇ ㄅㄞˇ ㄍㄨㄢ)or 文武官員(ㄨㄣˊ ㄨˇ ㄍㄨㄢ ㄩㄢˊ)
all the civil and military officials

文武全才(ㄨㄣˊ ㄨˇ ㄑㄩㄢˊ ㄘㄞˊ)or 文武雙全(ㄨㄣˊ ㄨˇ ㄕㄨㄤ ㄑㄩㄢˊ)
a master of both the pen and the sword; to be well versed in both polite letters and martial arts

文武場(ㄨㄣˊ ㄨˇ ㄔㄤˇ)
musicians performing on a Peking Opera stage

文物(ㄨㄣˊ ㄨˋ)
the products of a culture; cultural artifacts

文物制度(ㄨㄣˊ ㄨˋ ㄓˋ ㄉㄨˋ)
cultural products and social institutions

文王(ㄨㄣˊ ㄨㄤˊ)
King Wen, who paved the way for the founding of the Chou Dynasty (1111—256 B. C.) by his son, King Wu

文苑(ㄨㄣˊ ㄩㄢˋ)
a writers' gathering place

文運(ㄨㄣˊ ㄩㄣˋ)
the vicissitudes of literature

【文】 2150
2. ㄨㄣˋ wenn wèn
to cover up; to conceal; to gloss over

文過(ㄨㄣˋ ㄍㄨㄛˋ)
to cover up one's fault

文過飾非(ㄨㄣˋ ㄍㄨㄛˋ ㄕˋ ㄈㄟ)
to cover up one's fault by clever use of words in writing

文飾(ㄨㄣˋ ㄕˋ)
to deceive by an impressive appearance

八畫

〔斗部〕

【斌】 2151
ㄅㄧㄣ bin bin
equally fine in external accomplishments and inter-nal qualities

【斐】 2152
ㄈㄟˇ feei fěi
1. elegant; beautiful
2. a Chinese family name

斐婓(ㄈㄟ ㄈㄟ)
(said of writing) elegant; beautiful

斐濟(ㄈㄟˇ ㄐㄧˋ)
Fiji

斐然(ㄈㄟˇ ㄖㄢˊ)
(said of results, achieve-ments, etc.) striking; bril-liant; excellent; very satis-factory

斐然成章(ㄈㄟˇ ㄖㄢˊ ㄔㄥˊ ㄓㄤ)
(said of a literary piece) to show striking literary merit; beautifully composed

【斑】 2153
ㄅㄢ ban bān
1. speckles; spots; mottles
2. mottled; variegated; motley: 這小丑穿着顏色斑駁的外衣。The jester wears a motley coat.

斑白(ㄅㄢ ㄅㄞˊ)
(said of hair) gray: 他的頭髮已變成斑白了。His hair has turned gray.

斑駁(ㄅㄢ ㄅㄛˊ)
motley (in color)

斑疹(ㄅㄢ ㄓㄣˇ)
mottled; spotted

斑點點(ㄅㄢ·ㄅㄢ ㄉㄧㄢˇ ㄉㄧㄢˇ)
mottled; speckled; spotted

斑鬢(ㄅㄢ ㄅㄧㄣˋ)
gray hair at the temples; graying temples

斑馬(ㄅㄢ ㄇㄚˇ)
a zebra

斑馬線(ㄅㄢ ㄇㄚˇ ㄒㄧㄢˋ)
a pedestrian crossing (marked with stripes like those of a zebra); a zebra crossing

斑點(ㄅㄢ ㄉㄧㄢˇ)
specks; spots; mottles: 這水果有很多的斑點。This fruit is badly specked.

斑斕(ㄅㄢ ㄌㄢˊ)
gorgeous; resplendent

斑鳩(ㄅㄢ ㄐㄧㄡ)
the ringdove; the wood pigeon; the cushat

斑晶(ㄅㄢ ㄐㄧㄥ)
phenocryst

斑疹(ㄅㄢ ㄓㄣˇ)
maculae

斑疹傷寒(ㄅㄢ ㄓㄣˇ ㄕㄤ ㄏㄢˊ)
typhus

斑竹(ㄅㄢ ㄓㄨˊ)
(botany) mottled bamboo

斑衣(ㄅㄢ ㄧ)
colorful dress (especially referring to children's wear)

斑紋(ㄅㄢ ㄨㄣˊ)
stripes; striped: 斑馬身上有斑紋。Zebras are striped.

九畫

【斒】 2154
ㄅㄢ ban bān
1. variegated; motley
2. gorgeous; resplendent

斒斕(ㄅㄢ ㄌㄢˊ)
①(said of writing) resplen-dent; gorgeous ②variegated color; multicolored

十七畫

【斕】 2155
ㄌㄢˊ lan lán
multicolored

斗 部
ㄉㄡˇ doou dǒu

【斗】 2156
ㄉㄡˇ doou dǒu
1. Chinese peck (a unit of dry measure for grain)
2. a large container for wine
3. one of the 28 constellations

斗杓(ㄉㄡˇ ㄅㄧㄠ)or 斗柄(ㄉㄡˇ ㄅㄧㄥˇ)
(astronomy) the handle of the Big Dipper

斗篷(ㄉㄡˇ ㄆㄥˊ)
a mantle; a cape

斗方名士(ㄉㄡˇ ㄈㄤ ㄇㄧㄥˊ ㄕˋ)
a pretender to refinement and elegance

斗膽(ㄉㄡˇ ㄉㄢˇ)
great intrepidity or bold-ness; to make bold: 你敢跟老板圉撞，真是斗膽。It was bold of you to contradict your boss.

斗膾(ㄉㄡˇ ㄎㄨㄞˋ)
a prime minister

斗南一人(ㄉㄡˇ ㄋㄢˊ ㄧ ㄖㄣˊ)
(literally) the only one south of the Big Dipper —one who knows no equal under the sun

斗牛(ㄉㄡˇ ㄋㄧㄡˊ)
the Big Dipper and Altair

斗笠(ㄉㄡˇ ㄌㄧˋ)
a broad-brimmed rain hat (usually worn by farmers)

斗量(ㄉㄡˇ ㄌㄧㄤˊ)
to measure with a peck

斗筲(ㄉㄡˇ ㄕㄠ)
a fingerprint (especially of the thumb)

斗酒百篇(ㄉㄡˇ ㄐㄧㄡˇ ㄅㄞˇ ㄆㄧㄢ)
great capacity for drinking and poetry (taken from a line of 杜甫:「李白斗酒詩百篇」)

斗酒隻鷄(ㄉㄡˇ ㄐㄧㄡˇ ㄓ ㄐㄧ)
some wine and a chicken —offerings to the spirit of the dead

斗帳(ㄉㄡˇ ㄓㄤˋ)
a small tent

斗轉參橫(ㄉㄡˇ ㄓㄨㄢˇ ㄕㄣ ㄏㄥˊ)
(literally) The Big Dipper has turned so that its handle is pointing horizontally. —Day is breaking.

斗食(ㄉㄡˇ ㄕˊ)
a petty official (receiving a peck of grain as pay)

斗室(ㄉㄡˇ ㄕˋ)
a little room; a small room: 他整天待在斗室之中。He stayed in a small room all day.

斗筲之人(ㄉㄡˇ ㄕㄠ ㄓ ㄖㄣˊ)
shallow common men (Con-fucius' description of offi-cials of his times)

斗粟尺布(ㄉㄡˇ ㄙㄨˋ ㄔˇ ㄅㄨˋ)
brothers at loggerheads

六畫

【料】 2157
ㄌㄧㄠˋ liaw liào
1. to conjecture; to reckon; to estimate

2. to infer; to anticipate; to foresee
3. to consider; to calculate
4. to manage; to handle; to care
5. material; stuff: 原料 raw material 燃料 fuel
6. makings; stuff: 他是讀書的料。He has got the makings of a scholar.

料到(ㄌㄧㄠˋ ㄉㄠˋ)
to foresee; to expect: 我沒料到她會遲到。I didn't expect her to be late.

料度(ㄌㄧㄠˋ ㄉㄨㄛˋ)
① to estimate; to reckon ② to infer

料理(ㄌㄧㄠˋ ㄌㄧˇ)
① to manage; to arrange; to take care of; to attend to; to dispose of: 我們能自己料理生活。We can take care of ourselves now. ② a Japanese dish; Japanese cooking

料估(ㄌㄧㄠˋ ㄍㄨ)
to estimate; to conjecture; to calculate

料峭(ㄌㄧㄠˋ ㄑㄧㄠˋ)
cold; chilly

料想(ㄌㄧㄠˋ ㄒㄧㄤˇ)
to reckon; to imagine; to expect; to presume; to suppose; to guess; to conjecture: 我料想不出那人究竟是誰。I can't imagine who that man can be. 我料想他很快就會回來。I presume that he will be back very soon. 他料想老板一定會批准他的請求。He fully expected that the boss would grant his request.

料中(ㄌㄧㄠˋ ㄓㄨㄥ)
to guess correctly

料事如神(ㄌㄧㄠˋ ㄕˋ ㄖㄨˊ ㄕㄣˊ)
to foresee with divine accuracy.

料子(ㄌㄧㄠˋ ˙ㄗ) or **料兒**(ㄌㄧㄠˋ ㄦ)
cloth; fabric; material

料算(ㄌㄧㄠˋ ㄙㄨㄢˋ)
to reckon; to estimate

七畫

【斛】 2158
ㄏㄨˊ hwu hú
a dry measure 10 or 5 times that of 斗

【斜】 2159
ㄒㄧㄝˊ shye xié
inclined; sloping; slanting; leaning; oblique; diagonal

斜邊(ㄒㄧㄝˊ ㄅㄧㄢ)
① (mathematics) the leg (of a triangle); the hypotenuse, or hypotenuse (of a right-angled triangle) ② (machinery) a bevel edge

斜坡(ㄒㄧㄝˊ ㄆㄛ)
a slope: 士兵們爬上了一個陡峭的斜坡。The soldiers climbed a steep slope.

斜面(ㄒㄧㄝˊ ㄇㄧㄢˋ)
① (mathematics) an inclined plane ② (machinery) an oblique plane; a bevel (face)

斜風細雨(ㄒㄧㄝˊ ㄈㄥ ㄒㄧˋ ㄩˇ)
light wind and drizzling rain

斜度(ㄒㄧㄝˊ ㄉㄨˋ)
gradient; the degree of inclination

斜對面(ㄒㄧㄝˊ ㄉㄨㄟˋ ㄇㄧㄢˋ) or **斜對過兒**(ㄒㄧㄝˊ ㄉㄨㄟˋ ㄍㄨㄛˋㄦ)
diagonally opposite

斜軃(ㄒㄧㄝˊ ㄊㄨㄛ)
to recline

斜體字(ㄒㄧㄝˊ ㄊㄧˇ ㄗˋ)
(printing) italics

斜睨(ㄒㄧㄝˊ ㄋㄧˋ)
to look askance—to look down upon; to despise

斜高(ㄒㄧㄝˊ ㄍㄠ)
(mathematics) a slant height

斜暉(ㄒㄧㄝˊ ㄏㄨㄟ)
the slanting beams of the setting sun

斜角(ㄒㄧㄝˊ ㄐㄧㄠˇ)
① (mathematics) an oblique angle ② (machinery) a bevel angle

斜線(ㄒㄧㄝˊ ㄒㄧㄢˋ)
an oblique line

斜照(ㄒㄧㄝˊ ㄓㄠˋ)
① to shine obliquely ② the setting sun

斜視(ㄒㄧㄝˊ ㄕˋ)
① strabismus; squint ② to look askance; to cast a side-long glance

斜視矯正手術(ㄒㄧㄝˊ ㄕˋ ㄐㄧㄠˇ ㄓㄥˋ ㄕㄡˇ ㄕㄨˋ)
strabotomy

斜眼(ㄒㄧㄝˊ ㄧㄢˇ)
① (medicine) strabismus ②

---

squint-eye or cross-eye ③ a squint-eyed or cross-eyed person

斜陽(ㄒㄧㄝˊ ㄧㄤˊ)
the declining sun; the setting sun: 斜陽將盡。The setting sun is fading away.

斜紋布(ㄒㄧㄝˊ ㄨㄣˊ ㄅㄨˋ)
(textile) twill; drill

八畫

【斝】 2160
ㄐㄧㄚˇ jea jiǎ
(archeology) a jade wine cup

九畫

【斟】 2161
ㄓㄣ jen zhēn
1. to fill a cup with (tea or wine); to pour (a beverage) into a cup: 請給我斟一杯酒。Please pour me a glass of wine.
2. to consider: 我們會將此事詳予斟議。We will carefully consider this matter.

斟滿(ㄓㄣ ㄇㄢˇ)
to fill a cup or glass to the brim

斟酒(ㄓㄣ ㄐㄧㄡˇ)
to pour wine or liquor into a cup or glass

斟酌(ㄓㄣ ㄓㄨㄛˊ)
① to fill a cup, or glass, with wine or liquor ② to consider; consideration

斟茶(ㄓㄣ ㄔㄚˊ)
to fill a cup or glass with tea: 主人斟茶待客。The host fills a cup with tea to entertain his guest.

斟情(ㄓㄣ ㄑㄧㄥˊ)
to hesitate; hesitating

十畫

【斡】 2162
ㄨㄛˋ woh wò
to revolve; to turn; to rotate

斡旋(ㄨㄛˋ ㄒㄩㄢˊ)
to mediate; to use one's good offices or influence (in settling a dispute); mediation

斡轉(ㄨㄛˋ ㄓㄨㄢˇ)

to revolve; to rotate
幹運(ㄍㄢˋ ㄩㄣˋ)
to move in a circle

【斠】 2163 ㄐㄧㄠˋ jiaw jiào
a leveling stick (used for measuring the volume of grain, etc.)

斤 部
ㄐㄧㄣ jin jīn

【斤】 2164 ㄐㄧㄣ jin jīn
1. catty (a unit of weight): 她買了十水米。She bought ten catties of rice.
2. an ax
3. discerning; keen in observation
斤兩(ㄐㄧㄣ ㄌㄧㄤˇ)
weight: 主任說的話很有斤兩。What the chief said carried a lot of weight.
斤斤較量(ㄐㄧㄣ ㄐㄧㄣ ㄐㄧㄠˋ ㄌㄧㄤˋ) or 斤斤計較(ㄐㄧㄣ ㄐㄧㄣ ㄐㄧˋ ㄐㄧㄠˋ)
to be particular about every point, detail, or trifle; to be calculating: 他斤斤計量個人得失。He is preoccupied with his personal gains and losses.
斤斤其明(ㄐㄧㄣ ㄐㄧㄣ ㄑㄧˊ ㄇㄧㄥˊ)
discerning; keen in observation; penetrating: 此人斤斤其明。This person is keen in observation.

一畫

【斥】 2165 ㄔˋ chyh chì
1. to accuse; to blame; to reproach; to reprove; to censure
2. to expel; to drive off; to banish; to eject: 他們將敵人斥逐出城。They expel the enemy from the town.
3. to survey; to observe; to reconnoiter
斥罷(ㄔˋ ㄅㄚˋ)
to dismiss (from office)
斥罵 or 叱罵(ㄔˋ ㄇㄚˋ)

to condemn; to upbraid; to denounce; to scold
斥退(ㄔˋ ㄊㄨㄟˋ)
to repel; to expel; to eject; to dismiss angrily
斥力(ㄔˋ ㄌㄧˋ)
(physics) repulsion
斥革(ㄔˋ ㄍㄜˊ)
to dismiss or remove (from office)
斥喝(ㄔˋ ㄏㄜˋ)
to scold
斥候(ㄔˋ ㄏㄡˋ)
① to reconnoiter; to patrol
② patrols
斥逐(ㄔˋ ㄓㄨˊ)
to expel; to repel; to banish; to eject
斥資(ㄔˋ ㄗ)
to contribute money
斥責 or 叱責(ㄔˋ ㄗㄜˊ)
to reprimand; to rebuke; to reprove; to reproach; to censure; to denounce

四畫

【斧】 2166 ㄈㄨˇ fuu fǔ
1. a hatchet; an ax
2. to chop; to cut
3. to trim: 請斧正拙作。Please trim and correct my work.
斧柯(ㄈㄨˇ ㄎㄜ) or 斧柄(ㄈㄨˇ ㄅㄧㄥˋ)
(literally) the handle of a hatchet—the reins of government
斧削(ㄈㄨˇ ㄒㄩㄝˋ)
(literally) to pare off with a hatchet—to correct (a composition) freely
斧鉞 or 斧質(ㄈㄨˇ ㄓˋ)
beheading by means of an ax
斧正 or 斧政(ㄈㄨˇ ㄓㄥˋ)
to correct (a composition) freely 參看「斧削」
斧石(ㄈㄨˇ ㄕˊ)
(mineral) axinite
斧子(ㄈㄨˇ ˙ㄗ) or 斧頭(ㄈㄨˇ ˙ㄊㄡ) or
an ax (axe); a hatchet
斧藻(ㄈㄨˇ ㄗㄠˇ)
to embellish; to decorate
斧鑿痕(ㄈㄨˇ ㄗㄠˋ ㄏㄣˊ)
(literally) marks of the hatchet and the chisel

—traces of laborious correction in a literary piece
斧鑕(ㄈㄨˇ ㄓˋ)
the executioner's ax — (figuratively) capital punishment

五畫

【斫】 2167 ㄓㄨㄛˊ jwo zhuó
to chop or cut (wood)
斫木(ㄓㄨㄛˊ ㄇㄨˋ)
to chop or cut wood
斫斷(ㄓㄨㄛˊ ㄉㄨㄢˋ)
to chop off; to cut off; to sever by cutting or chopping
斫頭(ㄓㄨㄛˊ ㄊㄡˊ)
to behead; to decapitate
斫斬(ㄓㄨㄛˊ ㄓㄢˇ)
to chop; to cut; to hew
斫殺(ㄓㄨㄛˊ ㄕㄚ)
to kill with a hatchet, an ax, etc.

七畫

【斬】 2168 ㄓㄢˇ jaan zhǎn
1. to cut
2. to kill; to behead
斬伐(ㄓㄢˇ ㄈㄚˊ) or (ㄓㄢˇ ㄈㄚˊ)
① to conquer; to subjugate
② to execute; to behead ③ to fell (trees); to prune
斬釘截鐵(ㄓㄢˇ ㄉㄧㄥ ㄐㄧㄝˊ ㄊㄧㄝˇ)
to speak, or act, with determination and courage
斬斷情絲(ㄓㄢˇ ㄉㄨㄢˋ ㄑㄧㄥˊ ㄙ)
to cut off the threads of love
斬頭去尾(ㄓㄢˇ ㄊㄡˊ ㄑㄩˋ ㄨㄟˇ)
to make incomplete or short by omitting the foremost and hindmost parts
斬馘(ㄓㄢˇ ㄍㄨㄛˊ)
to behead; to decapitate
斬獲(ㄓㄢˇ ㄏㄨㄛˋ)
to cause enemy troops heavy casualties and material loss; to score a victory on the battlefield
斬將搴旗(ㄓㄢˇ ㄐㄧㄤˋ ㄑㄧㄢ ㄑㄧˊ)
to behead enemy generals and capture their flags (descriptive of bravery and prowess in battle)
斬決(ㄓㄢˇ ㄐㄩㄝˊ)

to carry out an execution by beheading the criminal

斬新 or 嶄新(ㄓㄢˇ ㄒㄧㄣ)
brand-new

斬首(ㄓㄢˇ ㄕㄡˇ)
to guillotine; to behead

斬示衆(ㄓㄢˇ ㄕˋ ㄓㄨㄥˋ)
to behead a criminal and exhibit the severed head to the public as a warning to would-be offenders

斬草除根(ㄓㄢˇ ㄘㄠˇ ㄔㄨˊ ㄍㄣ)
(literally) to remove weed by rooting it out—to eliminate the cause of trouble completely

斬衰(ㄓㄢˇ ㄘㄨㄟ)
the mourning worn for one's parents or husband (the coarsest sack cloth with fringes unhemmed)

斬刈(ㄓㄢˇ ㄧˋ)
to mow down

斬妖(ㄓㄢˇ ㄧㄠ)
to exorcise evil spirits

八畫

【斮】 2169
ㄓㄨㄛˊ   *jwo zhuó*
to cut; to pare

斮脛(ㄓㄨㄛˊ ㄐㄧㄥˋ)
to cut off one's legs as punishment

斮趾(ㄓㄨㄛˊ ㄓˇ)
to cut off one's toes as punishment

斮足(ㄓㄨㄛˊ ㄗㄨˊ)
to cut off one's feet as punishment

【斯】 2170
ㄙ   *sy sī*
1. this; these; such; here
2. a connecting particle—then; thus
3. to tear; to rip; to cut away

斯巴達(ㄙ ㄅㄚ ㄉㄚˊ)
Sparta

斯磨(ㄙ ㄇㄛˊ)
to grind

斯摩棱斯克(ㄙ ㄇㄛˊ ㄌㄥˊ ㄙ ㄎㄜˋ)
Smolensk, a Russian city

斯芬克士(ㄙ ㄈㄣ ㄎㄜˋ ㄕˋ)
(Greek mythology) the Sphinx

斯德哥爾摩(ㄙ ㄉㄜˊ ㄍㄜ ㄦˇ ㄇㄛˊ)
Stockholm, capital of

Sweden

斯多噶學派(ㄙ ㄉㄨㄛ ㄍㄜˊ ㄒㄩㄝˊ ㄆㄞˋ)
the Stoics; the Stoic School

斯拉夫(ㄙ ㄌㄚ ㄈㄨ)
Slav

斯里蘭卡(ㄙ ㄌㄧˇ ㄌㄢˊ ㄎㄚˇ)
Sri Lanka

斯堪的那維亞(ㄙ ㄎㄢ ㄉㄧˊ ㄋㄚˋ ㄨㄟˊ ㄧㄚˇ)
Scandinavia

斯須之間(ㄙ ㄒㄩ ㄓ ㄐㄧㄢ)
in an instant

斯時(ㄙ ㄕˊ)
this time; such a time

斯世(ㄙ ㄕˋ)
this worldly life: 他覺得斯世恍如幻夢。He feels that this worldly life is like a dream.

斯事(ㄙ ㄕˋ)
this matter

斯人而有斯疾也(ㄙ ㄖㄣˊ ㄦˊ ㄧㄡˇ ㄙ ㄐㄧˊ ㄧㄝˇ)
That such a man should have such a sickness!—It is a pity that such a good man should contract such a disease!

斯斯文文(ㄙ ㄙ ㄨㄣˊ ㄨㄣˊ)or 斯文(ㄙ ㄨㄣˊ)
cultured; refined; elegant; gentle: 他談話斯文。His language is refined.

斯文敗類(ㄙ ㄨㄣˊ ㄅㄞˋ ㄌㄟˋ)
polished scoundrels; ruffians in scholars' gowns

斯文人(ㄙ ㄨㄣˊ ㄖㄣˊ)
a polished person; cultured people

斯文掃地(ㄙ ㄨㄣˊ ㄙㄠˇ ㄉㄧˋ)
the decadence of the intellectuals

九畫

【新】 2171
ㄒㄧㄣ   *shin xīn*
1. new; fresh; novel
2. beginning; starting
3. modern; recent
4. the prefix "neo"
5. the Hsin Dynasty (8-22 A.D.)

新版(ㄒㄧㄣ ㄅㄢˇ)
the new edition (of a book): 這本書最近有新版。The new edition of this book has been published recently.

新編(ㄒㄧㄣ ㄅㄧㄢ)
①newly compiled; a new version ②newly organized

〔斤部〕

新兵(ㄒㄧㄣ ㄅㄧㄥ)
recruits

新派(ㄒㄧㄣ ㄆㄞˋ)
the new school; the modern school

新片預告(ㄒㄧㄣ ㄆㄧㄢˋ ㄩˋ ㄍㄠˋ)
a notice announcing films to be shown

新馬(ㄒㄧㄣ ㄇㄚˇ)
Singapore and Malaysia 亦作「星馬」

新墨西哥(ㄒㄧㄣ ㄇㄛˋ ㄒㄧ ㄍㄜ)
the state of New Mexico, U.S.A.

新莽(ㄒㄧㄣ ㄇㄤˇ)
Wang Mang (王莽), 45B.C.-23A.D., who founded the short-lived Hsin Dynasty (8-22A.D.) after usurping the throne from the house of Liu of the Han Dynasty

新米(ㄒㄧㄣ ㄇㄧˇ)
fresh rice; newly-harvested rice

新苗(ㄒㄧㄣ ㄇㄧㄠˊ)or 新芽(ㄒㄧㄣ ㄧㄚˊ)
young shoots; young sprouts

新民(ㄒㄧㄣ ㄇㄧㄣˊ)
to improve the people; to introduce new life to the people

新名詞(ㄒㄧㄣ ㄇㄧㄥˊ ㄘˊ)
new terms; new terminology

新發明(ㄒㄧㄣ ㄈㄚ ㄇㄧㄥˊ)
a new invention

新法(ㄒㄧㄣ ㄈㄚˇ)
①a new method; a new technique ②new laws (particularly referring to the political renovation introduced by Wang An-shih (王安石) of the Sung Dynasty)

新房(ㄒㄧㄣ ㄈㄤˊ)
①a bridal chamber ②a new house

新婦(ㄒㄧㄣ ㄈㄨˋ)
a bride

新大陸(ㄒㄧㄣ ㄉㄚˋ ㄌㄨˋ)
the New World; the Western Hemisphere

新德里(ㄒㄧㄣ ㄉㄜˊ ㄌㄧˇ)
New Delhi, capital of India

新到(ㄒㄧㄣ ㄉㄠˋ)
having just arrived

新臺幣(ㄒㄧㄣ ㄊㄞˊ ㄅㄧˋ)
New Taiwan Dollar (NT$)

〔斤部〕

新唐書(ㄒㄧㄣ ㄊㄤ ㄕㄨ)
the *New History of Tang* (one of the *Twenty-Four Histories*), by Ou-Yang Hsiu (歐陽修), Sung Chi (宋祁), etc.

新體詩(ㄒㄧㄣ ㄊㄧ ㄕ)or 新詩(ㄒㄧㄣ ㄕ)
modern poetry, or *pai hua* poetry (in Chinese literature)

新年(ㄒㄧㄣ ㄋㄧㄢ)
New Year: 敬祝新年快樂。I wish you a happy New Year.

新娘(ㄒㄧㄣ ㄋㄧㄤ)or 新娘子(ㄒㄧㄣ ㄋㄧㄤ ˙ㄗ)or 新嫁娘(ㄒㄧㄣ ㄐㄧㄚ ㄋㄧㄤ)
a bride

新來(ㄒㄧㄣ ㄌㄞ)
having just come or arrived: 他們是新來的旅客。They are the tourists who have just arrived.

新來乍到(ㄒㄧㄣ ㄌㄞ ㄓㄚ ㄉㄠ)
being a newcomer

新郎(ㄒㄧㄣ ㄌㄤ)
a bridegroom

新浪漫主義(ㄒㄧㄣ ㄌㄤ ㄇㄢ ㄓㄨ ㄧ)
neoromanticism

新曆(ㄒㄧㄣ ㄌㄧ)
the solar calendar; the Gregorian calendar

新綠(ㄒㄧㄣ ㄌㄩ)
fresh verdure; fresh foliage

新古典主義(ㄒㄧㄣ ㄍㄨ ㄉㄧㄢ ㄓㄨ ㄧ)
neoclassicism

新鬼(ㄒㄧㄣ ㄍㄨㄟ)
the spirit of the newly deceased

新貴(ㄒㄧㄣ ㄍㄨㄟ)
a newly appointed official; a new VIP

新官上任三把火(ㄒㄧㄣ ㄍㄨㄢ ㄕㄤ ㄖㄣ ㄙㄢ ㄅㄚ ㄏㄨㄛ)
A newly inaugurated official tends to be very strict with his subordinates or enthusiastic about his job at the beginning (and is likely to relax as time goes by). 或 A new broom sweeps clean.

新宮(ㄒㄧㄣ ㄍㄨㄥ)
a newly built palace

New Caledonia

新科(ㄒㄧㄣ ㄎㄜ)
having just passed the civil service examination (in old China)

新開(ㄒㄧㄣ ㄎㄞ)
newly opened

新刊(ㄒㄧㄣ ㄎㄢ)
newly published

新罕布夏(ㄒㄧㄣ ㄏㄢ ㄅㄨ ㄒㄧㄚ)
the state of New Hampshire, U.S.A.

新歡(ㄒㄧㄣ ㄏㄨㄢ)
a new sweetheart or lover

新婚(ㄒㄧㄣ ㄏㄨㄣ)
newly married

新婚夫婦(ㄒㄧㄣ ㄏㄨㄣ ㄈㄨ ㄈㄨ)
newlyweds

新婚旅行(ㄒㄧㄣ ㄏㄨㄣ ㄌㄩ ㄒㄧㄥ)
a honeymoon tour

新幾內亞(ㄒㄧㄣ ㄐㄧ ㄋㄟ ㄧㄚ)
New Guinea

新紀錄(ㄒㄧㄣ ㄐㄧ ㄌㄨ)
a new record

新紀元(ㄒㄧㄣ ㄐㄧ ㄩㄢ)
a new era: 現在是進步的新紀元。It is a new era of progress.

新加坡(ㄒㄧㄣ ㄐㄧㄚ ㄆㄛ)
Singapore

新家庭(ㄒㄧㄣ ㄐㄧㄚ ㄊㄧㄥ)
the home of a newly married couple

新交(ㄒㄧㄣ ㄐㄧㄠ)
a new friend

新教(ㄒㄧㄣ ㄐㄧㄠ)
Protestantism

新舊交替(ㄒㄧㄣ ㄐㄧㄡ ㄐㄧㄠ ㄊㄧ)
the transition from the old to the new

新舊兒(ㄒㄧㄣ ㄐㄧㄡ ㄦ)
the degree of oldness

新金山(ㄒㄧㄣ ㄐㄧㄣ ㄕㄢ)
Melbourne, Australia

新近(ㄒㄧㄣ ㄐㄧㄣ)
recently; newly; lately: 這位詩人新近寫了不少詩。The poet has written quite a number of poems lately.

新進(人員)(ㄒㄧㄣ ㄐㄧㄣ)(ㄖㄣ ㄩㄢ)
①new employees of an organization ②a novice

新疆(ㄒㄧㄣ ㄐㄧㄤ)
Sinkiang or Chinese Turkestan

新居(ㄒㄧㄣ ㄐㄩ)

a new residence

新局面(ㄒㄧㄣ ㄐㄩ ㄇㄧㄢ)
a new situation

新句(ㄒㄧㄣ ㄐㄩ)
an original expression (in poetry)

新劇(ㄒㄧㄣ ㄐㄩ)
Western-style drama (as opposed to traditional Chinese drama or opera)

新軍(ㄒㄧㄣ ㄐㄩㄣ)
①the Western-style army organized toward the end of the Ching Dynasty ②a newly organized army

新奇(ㄒㄧㄣ ㄑㄧ)
novel; new

新氣象(ㄒㄧㄣ ㄑㄧ ㄒㄧㄤ)
a pervasive new spirit, a prevailing new atmosphere

新青年(ㄒㄧㄣ ㄑㄧㄥ ㄋㄧㄢ)
a youth with new thoughts

新晴(ㄒㄧㄣ ㄑㄧㄥ)
(said of the sky)having just cleared up

新曲(ㄒㄧㄣ ㄑㄩ)
a new song; a new musical composition; a new tune: 她以新曲娛客。She delighted her guests with her new song.

新禧(ㄒㄧㄣ ㄒㄧ)or(ㄒㄧㄣ ㄒㄧ)
Happy New Year!

新西蘭(ㄒㄧㄣ ㄒㄧ ㄌㄢ)
New Zealand 亦作「紐西蘭」

新消息(ㄒㄧㄣ ㄒㄧㄠ ㄒㄧ)
the latest news; the latest information

新秀(ㄒㄧㄣ ㄒㄧㄡ)
a person who has begun to distinguish himself in a given field

新鮮(ㄒㄧㄣ ㄒㄧㄢ)
①fresh ②new; novel; original

新星(ㄒㄧㄣ ㄒㄧㄥ)
①(astronomy) a nova; a new star ② a new cinemactor or cinemactress

新興(ㄒㄧㄣ ㄒㄧㄥ)
newly risen; rising; new and developing; burgeoning

新型(ㄒㄧㄣ ㄒㄧㄥ)
a new type; a new pattern

新學(ㄒㄧㄣ ㄒㄩㄝ)
①a young science or discipline ②newly learned

新學制(ㄒㄧㄣ ㄒㄩㄝ ㄓˋ)
a new educational system

新選(ㄒㄧㄣ ㄒㄩㄢˇ)
newly elected: 他是新選的主席。He is the newly elected president.

新知(ㄒㄧㄣ ㄓ)
① new friends ② new knowledge; new learning

新制(ㄒㄧㄣ ㄓˋ)
a new system

新政(ㄒㄧㄣ ㄓㄥˋ)
renovated government administration; the New Deal

新竹(ㄒㄧㄣ ㄓㄨˊ)
Hsinchu, Taiwan Province

新著(ㄒㄧㄣ ㄓㄨˋ)
a new work (by a writer)——本論現代藝術的新著正在銷售中。A new book on modern art is now on sale.

新妝(ㄒㄧㄣ ㄓㄨㄤ)
① the look of a woman immediately after make-up ② a new fashion in dressing

新裝(ㄒㄧㄣ ㄓㄨㄤ)
① a new dress ② newly installed

新潮派(ㄒㄧㄣ ㄔㄠˊ ㄆㄞˋ)
an avant-garde school

新潮流(ㄒㄧㄣ ㄔㄠˊ ㄌㄧㄡˊ)
a new trend

新愁(ㄒㄧㄣ ㄔㄡˊ)
fresh sorrows

新仇舊恨(ㄒㄧㄣ ㄔㄡˊ ㄐㄧㄡˋ ㄏㄣˋ)
new hatred piled on old

新陳代謝(ㄒㄧㄣ ㄔㄣˊ ㄉㄞˋ ㄒㄧㄝˋ)
① (biology) metabolism ② the new superseding the old; the replacement of the old with the new

新出土(ㄒㄧㄣ ㄔㄨ ㄊㄨˇ)
newly dug out or unearthed

新出爐(ㄒㄧㄣ ㄔㄨ ㄌㄨˊ)
① freshly baked ② newly produced or manufactured

新出手(ㄒㄧㄣ ㄔㄨ ㄕㄡˇ)
having just entered upon a career

新春(ㄒㄧㄣ ㄔㄨㄣ)
① the early spring ② the Lunar New Year

新創(ㄒㄧㄣ ㄔㄨㄤˋ)
newly devised; newly started; newly founded

free verse written in the vernacular 亦作「新體詩」

新石器時代(ㄒㄧㄣ ㄕˊ ㄑㄧˋ ㄕˊ ㄉㄞˋ)
the Neolithic Age

新時代(ㄒㄧㄣ ㄕˊ ㄉㄞˋ)
a new era: 新時代有新任務。A new era has a new task.

新式(ㄒㄧㄣ ㄕˋ)
of a new style; new model; modern: 她的服裝是新式的。Her dress is of a new style.

新世界(ㄒㄧㄣ ㄕˋ ㄐㄧㄝˋ)
the New World; the Western Hemisphere

新設(ㄒㄧㄣ ㄕㄜˋ)
newly established; newly inaugurated; newly activated

新手(ㄒㄧㄣ ㄕㄡˇ)
a new hand (at a job); a greenhorn; a novice

新生(ㄒㄧㄣ ㄕㄥ)
① newborn ② a new student ③ a new life; rebirth; regeneration

新生代(ㄒㄧㄣ ㄕㄥ ㄉㄞˋ)
the Cenozoic or Cainozoic Era

新生地(ㄒㄧㄣ ㄕㄥ ㄉㄧˋ)
reclaimed land; tidal land

新生活運動(ㄒㄧㄣ ㄕㄥ ㄏㄨㄛˊ ㄩㄣˋ ㄉㄨㄥˋ)
the New Life Movement (to modernize and discipline daily life, initiated by President Chiang Kai-shek in 1934)

新生界(ㄒㄧㄣ ㄕㄥ ㄐㄧㄝˋ)
the Cenozoic or Cainozoic group

新書(ㄒㄧㄣ ㄕㄨ)
a new book

新人(ㄒㄧㄣ ㄖㄣˊ)
① new employees; new talent; new appointees; new figures; new hands ② a bride ③ a new love ④ a man with modern thoughts

新人房(ㄒㄧㄣ ㄖㄣˊ ㄈㄤˊ)
a room of a newly married couple

新人生觀(ㄒㄧㄣ ㄖㄣˊ ㄕㄥ ㄍㄨㄢ)
a new outlook on life; a new view of life

新人物(ㄒㄧㄣ ㄖㄣˊ ㄨˋ)
a man with modern ideas

新任(ㄒㄧㄣ ㄖㄣˋ)

newly appointed; newly sworn-in

新澤西州(ㄒㄧㄣ ㄗㄜˊ ㄒㄧ ㄓㄡ)
the state of New Jersey, U.S.A.

新造(ㄒㄧㄣ ㄗㄠˋ)
newly-built; newly manufactured: 這種汽車是在德國新造的。This automobile is newly manufactured in Germany.

新村(ㄒㄧㄣ ㄘㄨㄣ)
a new residential quarter; a new housing development

新思想(ㄒㄧㄣ ㄙ ㄒㄧㄤˇ)
modern thinking; modern thoughts

新歲(ㄒㄧㄣ ㄙㄨㄟˋ)
the beginning of a new year

新藝綜合體(ㄒㄧㄣ ㄧˋ ㄗㄨㄥˇ ㄏㄜˊ ㄊㄧˇ)
(movie) CinemaScope 亦作「超視綜合體」

新印象派(ㄒㄧㄣ ㄧㄣˋ ㄒㄧㄤˋ ㄆㄞˋ)
neo-impressionism

新英格蘭(ㄒㄧㄣ ㄧㄥ ㄍㄜˊ ㄌㄢˊ)
New England

新穎(ㄒㄧㄣ ㄧㄥˇ)
novel; new; original: 這篇論文的題材新穎。The subject of this treatise is original.

新五代史(ㄒㄧㄣ ㄨˇ ㄉㄞˋ ㄕˇ)
the New History of the Five Dynasties (one of the Twenty-Four Histories), by Ou-Yang Hsiu (歐陽修)

新文化(ㄒㄧㄣ ㄨㄣˊ ㄏㄨㄚˋ)
modern culture, or culture oriented to modern science and new development in the humanities

新文化運動(ㄒㄧㄣ ㄨㄣˊ ㄏㄨㄚˋ ㄩㄣˋ ㄉㄨㄥˋ)
the New Culture Movement (around the time of the May 4th Movement in 1919)

新文學(ㄒㄧㄣ ㄨㄣˊ ㄒㄩㄝˊ)
new literature, or vernacular literature, after the May 4th Movement in 1919

新文字(ㄒㄧㄣ ㄨㄣˊ ㄗˋ)
Romanized or Latinized Chinese characters

新文藝(ㄒㄧㄣ ㄨㄣˊ ㄧˋ)
new literature, or vernacular literature

新聞(ㄒㄧㄣ ㄨㄣˊ)
news

〔斤部〕

〔斤部〕

新聞媒體(ㄒㄧㄣ ㄨㄣˊ ㄇㄟˊ ㄊㄧˇ)
news media

新聞通訊社(ㄒㄧㄣ ㄨㄣˊ ㄊㄨㄥ ㄒㄩㄣˋ ㄕㄜˋ)
a news agency

新聞稿(ㄒㄧㄣ ㄨㄣˊ ㄍㄠˇ)
a press release

新聞官(ㄒㄧㄣ ㄨㄣˊ ㄍㄨㄢ)
an information officer

新聞廣播(ㄒㄧㄣ ㄨㄣˊ ㄍㄨㄤˇ ㄅㄛˋ)
a news broadcast; a news-cast

新聞公報(ㄒㄧㄣ ㄨㄣˊ ㄍㄨㄥ ㄅㄠˋ)
a press communiqué

新聞記者(ㄒㄧㄣ ㄨㄣˊ ㄐㄧˋ ㄓㄜˇ)
a journalist; a reporter; a correspondent

新聞界(ㄒㄧㄣ ㄨㄣˊ ㄐㄧㄝˋ)
the circle of journalists; the press circle

新聞檢查(ㄒㄧㄣ ㄨㄣˊ ㄐㄧㄢˇ ㄔㄚˊ)
press censorship

新聞學(ㄒㄧㄣ ㄨㄣˊ ㄒㄩㄝˊ)
journalism

新聞紙(ㄒㄧㄣ ㄨㄣˊ ㄓˇ)
newspapers and news maga-zines

新聞處(ㄒㄧㄣ ㄨㄣˊ ㄔㄨˋ)
the information service

新聞人物(ㄒㄧㄣ ㄨㄣˊ ㄖㄣˊ ㄨˋ)
people in the news

新聞自由(ㄒㄧㄣ ㄨㄣˊ ㄗˋ ㄧㄡˊ)
freedom of the press

新聞文學(ㄒㄧㄣ ㄨㄣˊ ㄨㄣˊ ㄒㄩㄝˊ)
journalistic literature

新約全書(ㄒㄧㄣ ㄩㄝ ㄑㄩㄢˊ ㄕㄨ)
the New Testament

新月(ㄒㄧㄣ ㄩㄝˋ)
①(astronomy) a new moon
②a crescent moon; a cres-cent

新元史(ㄒㄧㄣ ㄩㄢˊ ㄕˇ)
the New History of Yüan (one of the Twenty-Five His-tories), by Ko Shao-min (柯劭忞)

十畫

【斲】 2172
(斵) ㄓㄨㄛˊ jwo zhuó

to chop; to hew

斲雕為樸(ㄓㄨㄛˊ ㄉㄧㄠ ㄨㄟˊ ㄆㄨˊ)
to do away with vanity and adopt unadorned simplicity

斲輪老手(ㄓㄨㄛˊ ㄌㄨㄣˊ ㄌㄠˇ ㄕㄡˇ)
an expert wheelwright—(fig-uratively) an old hand; an experienced man

斲喪(ㄓㄨㄛˊ ㄙㄤˋ)
①to chop down completely
②to waste one's vitality by dissipation

十四畫

【斷】 2173
ㄉㄨㄢˋ duàn duǎn

1. to cut apart; to sever
2. to give up; to abstain from
3. to judge; to decide; to con-clude: 聰明人當機立斷。 A wise man decides promptly and opportunely.
4. to break; broken: 我打斷他們的談話。 I broke off their con-versation.
5. absolutely; decidedly; cer-tainly: 這個故事斷不可信。 This story is absolutely in-credible.

斷編殘簡(ㄉㄨㄢˋ ㄅㄧㄢ ㄘㄢˊ ㄐㄧㄢˇ)
fragmentary works (of a writer) 亦作「斷簡殘編」

斷片(ㄉㄨㄢˋ ㄆㄧㄢˋ)
①fragments; disjecta mem-bra ②disruption of a movie show caused by the mechan-ical trouble of the projector

斷命(ㄉㄨㄢˋ ㄇㄧㄥˋ)
to die

斷髮文身(ㄉㄨㄢˋ ㄈㄚˇ ㄨㄣˊ ㄕㄣ)
(literally) to cut the hair and tattoo the body—to have barbarous customs

斷代(ㄉㄨㄢˋ ㄉㄞˋ)
a division of history into periods

斷電(ㄉㄨㄢˋ ㄉㄧㄢˋ)
power failure; a blackout

斷定(ㄉㄨㄢˋ ㄉㄧㄥˋ)
to determine; to conclude; to decide

斷斷不可(ㄉㄨㄢˋ ㄉㄨㄢˋ ㄅㄨˋ ㄎㄜˇ)
absolutely impermissible: 斷斷不可在此吸煙。 Smoking is absolutely impermissible here.

斷斷續續(ㄉㄨㄢˋ ㄉㄨㄢˋ ㄒㄩˋ ㄒㄩˋ)
intermittent; off and on; bro-ken: 自中午後，這裡斷斷續續地下雨。 It has been raining on and off since noon.

斷頭臺(ㄉㄨㄢˋ ㄊㄡˊ ㄊㄞˊ)
a guillotine

斷頭將軍(ㄉㄨㄢˋ ㄊㄡˊ ㄐㄧㄤ ㄐㄩㄣ)
one who would rather die than surrender

斷屠(ㄉㄨㄢˋ ㄊㄨˊ)
to prohibit the butchering of animals on certain occasions

斷奶(ㄉㄨㄢˋ ㄋㄞˇ)or斷乳(ㄉㄨㄢˋ ㄖㄨˇ)
to wean or be weaned

斷難允(ㄉㄨㄢˋ ㄋㄢˊ ㄩㄣˇ)
It is absolutely hard for one to consent....

斷爛朝報(ㄉㄨㄢˋ ㄌㄢˋ ㄔㄠˊ ㄅㄠˋ)
a worthless record or histor-ical document

斷糧(ㄉㄨㄢˋ ㄌㄧㄤˊ)
to run out of food supply

斷路(ㄉㄨㄢˋ ㄌㄨˋ)
①to break off friendly rela-tions ②to cut off a road for a retreat

斷根(ㄉㄨㄢˋ ㄍㄣ)
to be cured completely (as a disease or addiction)

斷港絕潢(ㄉㄨㄢˋ ㄍㄤˇ ㄐㄩㄝˊ ㄏㄨㄤˊ)
to reach a dead end

斷口(ㄉㄨㄢˋ ㄎㄡˇ)
(geology) a fracture

斷鶴續鳧(ㄉㄨㄢˋ ㄏㄜˋ ㄒㄩˋ ㄈㄨˊ)
(literally) to try to shorten the leg of a crane and lengthen that of an owl—to go against reason

斷後(ㄉㄨㄢˋ ㄏㄡˋ)
①to cover a retreat ②to have no offspring

斷乎(ㄉㄨㄢˋ ㄏㄨ)
absolutely; decidedly; posi-tively

斷魂(ㄉㄨㄢˋ ㄏㄨㄣˊ)
①to be entranced; to be enraptured ②overpowered by grief

斷機教子(ㄉㄨㄢˋ ㄐㄧ ㄐㄧㄠˋ ㄗˇ)or斷織(ㄉㄨㄢˋ ㄓ)
to break the loom to show one's child that the learning effort should not be inter-rupted

斷交(ㄉㄨㄢˋ ㄐㄧㄠ)
①to break off relations with someone ②to sever diplomatic relations

斷酒(ㄉㄨㄢˋ ㄐㄧㄡˇ)
①to abstain from alcohol ②

to prohibit the manufacture, transportation, and sale of alcoholic beverages

斷見(ㄉㄨㄢˋ ㄐㄧㄢˋ)
(Buddhism) the view that life ends with death

斷井頹垣(ㄉㄨㄢˋ ㄐㄧㄥˇ ㄊㄨㄟˊ ㄩㄢˊ)
(literally) The wells are dry and the fences are dilapidated.—completely deserted and in ruins

斷句(ㄉㄨㄢˋ ㄐㄩˋ)
①to punctuate the unpunctuated ancient writings when one reads them ②to punctuate

斷絕(ㄉㄨㄢˋ ㄐㄩㄝˊ)
to break off (relations); to sever

斷絕邦交(ㄉㄨㄢˋ ㄐㄩㄝˊ ㄅㄤ ㄐㄧㄠ)
to sever diplomatic ties

斷絕來往(ㄉㄨㄢˋ ㄐㄩㄝˊ ㄌㄞˊ ㄨㄤˇ)
to break off friendly relations

斷絕關係(ㄉㄨㄢˋ ㄐㄩㄝˊ (ㄍㄨㄢ‧ㄒㄧ)
to sever relations; to disown (a prodigal son)

斷七(ㄉㄨㄢˋ ㄑㄧ)
the Buddhist service on each seventh day within 49 days after one's death

斷氣(ㄉㄨㄢˋ ㄑㄧˋ)
①to breathe one's last ②to cut off the gas

斷齏畫粥(ㄉㄨㄢˋ ㄐㄧ ㄏㄨㄚˋ ㄓㄨ)
to eat sparingly because of poverty

斷袖之癖(ㄉㄨㄢˋ ㄒㄧㄡˋ ㄓ ㄆㄧˇ)
male homosexuality

斷絃(ㄉㄨㄢˋ ㄒㄧㄢˊ)
to be bereaved of one's wife

斷線(ㄉㄨㄢˋ ㄒㄧㄢˋ)
disconnection; line rupture

斷線風箏(ㄉㄨㄢˋ ㄒㄧㄢˋ ㄈㄥ ㄓㄥ)
①a blown off kite ②a thing or person that, once away, is not heard of any more. 她有如斷線風箏一般無影無蹤。She is not heard of any more, like a blown off kite.

斷續(ㄉㄨㄢˋ ㄒㄩˋ)
off and on; intermittent

斷章取義(ㄉㄨㄢˋ ㄓㄤ ㄑㄩˇ ㄧˋ)
to interpret a thing out of context

斷種(ㄉㄨㄢˋ ㄓㄨㄥˇ)

to end a family line; to have no heir

斷腸(ㄉㄨㄢˋ ㄔㄤˊ)
to break the heart; heart-broken

斷除(ㄉㄨㄢˋ ㄔㄨˊ)
to remove (obstacles, bad habits, etc.)

斷炊(ㄉㄨㄢˋ ㄔㄨㄟ)
to be so impoverished as to have to stop cooking meals

斷食(ㄉㄨㄢˋ ㄕˊ)
to starve to death voluntarily

斷水(ㄉㄨㄢˋ ㄕㄨㄟˇ)
stoppage of water supply; out of water supply; to cut off water supply

斷然(ㄉㄨㄢˋ ㄖㄢˊ)
①absolutely; definitely; positively; decidedly ②resolute; drastic

斷層(ㄉㄨㄢˋ ㄘㄥˊ)
(geology) a fault

斷送(ㄉㄨㄢˋ ㄙㄨㄥˋ)
to lose for good; 她的錯誤使她斷送了名譽。Her fault has made her lose her reputation for good.

斷案(ㄉㄨㄢˋ ㄢˋ)
①to close a legal case ②(logic) a conclusion

斷疑(ㄉㄨㄢˋ ㄧˊ)
to resolve doubts

斷崖絕壁(ㄉㄨㄢˋ ㄧㄞˊ ㄐㄩㄝˊ ㄅㄧˋ)
broken ridges and steep cliffs

斷言(ㄉㄨㄢˋ ㄧㄢˊ)
to be absolutely sure; to say with certainty: 他的朋友們斷言他是無罪的。His friends said with certainty that he was innocent.

斷無此理(ㄉㄨㄢˋ ㄨˊ ㄘˇ ㄌㄧˇ)
It is absolutely against reason. 或 It is definitely illogical.

斷語(ㄉㄨㄢˋ ㄩˇ)
judgment; a verdict; a conclusion: 慎重一點，不要遽下斷語。Be careful not to jump to conclusions.

斷獄(ㄉㄨㄢˋ ㄩˋ)
to close a trial by announcing the verdict

斷垣殘壁(ㄉㄨㄢˋ ㄩㄢˊ ㄘㄢˊ ㄅㄧˋ)
the broken fences and walls

—descriptive of a desolate scene

方 部
ㄈㄤ　fang　fāng

【方】 2174
ㄈㄤ　fang　fāng
1.square; rectangular
2.honest; morally upright: 他為人方正。He is an honest person.
3.a region; an area; a place
4.a prescription; a recipe
5.a direction
6.occultism
7.just now; just then; just: 她年方十八。She is just eighteen years old.
8.(mathematics) power
9.(classifier) short for square meter or cubic meter
10.side; party: 友誼是雙方面的事。Friendship is a two-sided affair.
11.a method; a way
12.an aspect
13.one side
14.a Chinese family name

方苞(ㄈㄤ ㄅㄠ)
Fang Pao, 1668-1749, a classical writer and originator of a school of writing known as 桐城派

方便(ㄈㄤ ㄅㄧㄢˋ)
①convenient; handy; a convenient method ②to give somebody a break; to do somebody a favor ③(colloquial) to go to the lavatory

方便之門(ㄈㄤ ㄅㄧㄢˋ ㄓ ㄇㄣˊ)
a favor or break for somebody

方步(ㄈㄤ ㄅㄨˋ)
a square pace

方袍(ㄈㄤ ㄆㄠˊ)
a Buddhist monk or priest

方帽(ㄈㄤ ㄇㄠˋ)
square caps worn by college graduates

方面(ㄈㄤ ㄇㄧㄢˋ)
①a direction; a quarter; a district; a field: 這家公司有許多方面需要改革。Reforms in many directions

〔方部〕

are needed in this company. ②(in this or that) respect; (on the one, or other) hand; (on this or that) topic, subject, etc.

方面大耳(ㄈㄤ ㄇㄧㄢˋ ㄉㄚˋ ㄦˇ)
a square face with large ears (regarded by fortune-tellers as a look of good fortune)

方命(ㄈㄤ ㄇㄧㄥˋ)
to disobey an order

方法(ㄈㄤ ㄈㄚˇ)
a method; a way; a means: 有任何方法到達那裏嗎？ Is (Are) there any means of getting there?

方法論(ㄈㄤ ㄈㄚˇ ㄌㄨㄣˋ)
methodology

方底圓蓋(ㄈㄤ ㄉㄧˇ ㄩㄢˊ ㄍㄞˋ)
A square peg cannot fit a round hole.—incompatible

方糖(ㄈㄤ ㄊㄤˊ)
cube sugar; sugar cubes

方內(ㄈㄤ ㄋㄟˋ)
within the boundaries of the country

方里(ㄈㄤ ㄌㄧˇ)
a square li (250,000 square meters)

方哩(ㄈㄤ ㄌㄧˇ)
a square mile

方領矩步(ㄈㄤ ㄌㄧㄥˇ ㄐㄩˇ ㄅㄨˋ)
dressed in scholarly clothes and showing refined manners

方略(ㄈㄤ ㄌㄩㄝˋ)
a general plan

方格(ㄈㄤ ㄍㄜˊ)
a square (in a checkerboard pattern)

方格紙(ㄈㄤ ㄍㄜˊ ㄓˇ)
graph paper

方根(ㄈㄤ ㄍㄣ)or 方程根(ㄈㄤ ㄔㄥˊ ㄍㄣ)
(mathematics) a root

方括號(ㄈㄤ ㄍㄨㄚ ㄏㄠˋ)
square brackets ([ ])

方國(ㄈㄤ ㄍㄨㄛˊ)
feudal princes who pay allegiance to a common sovereign

方軌(ㄈㄤ ㄍㄨㄟˇ)
(said of two carriages) to go abreast

方塊字(ㄈㄤ ㄎㄨㄞˋ ㄗˋ)
①Chinese characters written on square pieces of paper, used to teach a child to read ②square print

方技(ㄈㄤ ㄐㄧˋ)
(in ancient China) occultism, divination, medical practice, etc.

方劑(ㄈㄤ ㄐㄧˋ)
a medical prescription

方家(ㄈㄤ ㄐㄧㄚ)
a famous master or expert

方駕(ㄈㄤ ㄐㄧㄚˋ)
①(said of two carriages) to go abreast ②(said of two persons) evenly matched; equal in ability

方解石(ㄈㄤ ㄐㄧㄝˇ ㄕˊ)
calcite

方今(ㄈㄤ ㄐㄧㄣ)
now; at present; currently

方巾(ㄈㄤ ㄐㄧㄣ)
a kind of hood worn by intellectuals during the Ming Dynasty

方且(ㄈㄤ ㄑㄧㄝˇ)
even; still

方鉛礦(ㄈㄤ ㄑㄧㄢˊ ㄎㄨㄤˋ)
galena

方孝孺(ㄈㄤ ㄒㄧㄠˋ ㄖㄨˊ)
Fang Hsiao-ju, an upright scholar of the early Ming Dynasty, who was killed on the order of the third Ming emperor (明成祖)

方向(ㄈㄤ ㄒㄧㄤˋ)
orientation; a direction; a course: 他朝著公園的方向走去。 He went off in the direction of the park.

方向盤(ㄈㄤ ㄒㄧㄤˋ ㄆㄢˊ)
a steering wheel

方向舵(ㄈㄤ ㄒㄧㄤˋ ㄉㄨㄛˋ)
a side rudder

方興未艾(ㄈㄤ ㄒㄧㄥ ㄨㄟˋ ㄞˋ)
to be still growing; to be still making progress; to be in the ascendant: 這項社會革新運動方興未艾。 The social reform movement is still growing.

方形(ㄈㄤ ㄒㄧㄥˊ)
a rectangle

方知(ㄈㄤ ㄓ)
to know for the first time

方趾圓顱(ㄈㄤ ㄓˇ ㄩㄢˊ ㄌㄨˊ)
(literally) a creature with

rectangular feet and a round head—a human being

方志(ㄈㄤ ㄓˋ)
a geographic account

方舟(ㄈㄤ ㄓㄡ)
①(said of two ships) to sail abreast ②an ark

方針(ㄈㄤ ㄓㄣ)
a principle; a policy; a course of action

方鎮(ㄈㄤ ㄓㄣˋ)
magistrate with military power (in former times)

方丈(ㄈㄤ ㄓㄤˋ)
①(ㄈㄤ ㄓㄤˋ) a square chang (a little more than 100 square feet)
②(ㄈㄤ ·ㄓㄤ) the head priest of a Buddhist temple

方正(ㄈㄤ ㄓㄥˋ)
(said of one's conduct) irreproachable: 他是一位方正的法學專家。 He is an irreproachable jurist.

方桌(ㄈㄤ ㄓㄨㄛ)
a rectangular table

方尺(ㄈㄤ ㄔˇ)
a square chih (a little larger than a square foot)

方城之戰(ㄈㄤ ㄔㄥˊ ㄓ ㄓㄢˋ)
mah-jong game

方程式(ㄈㄤ ㄔㄥˊ ㄕˋ)
an equation

方始(ㄈㄤ ㄕˇ)
to have just begun

方士(ㄈㄤ ㄕˋ)
an occultist; an alchemist

方式(ㄈㄤ ㄕˋ)
a mode; a manner; a way

方生未死(ㄈㄤ ㄕㄥ ㄨㄟˋ ㄙˇ)
The new order has been born, but the old establishment is not yet completely dead.

方術(ㄈㄤ ㄕㄨˋ)
①(in old China) occultism, divination, or medical practice ②doctrines and policies

方枘圓鑿(ㄈㄤ ㄖㄨㄟˋ ㄩㄢˊ ㄗㄠˋ)
A square peg cannot fit a round hole.—incompatible

方字(ㄈㄤ ㄗˋ)
characters written or printed on square pieces of paper for use in teaching children to read

方子(ㄈㄤ ·ㄗ)

a medical prescription

方策(ㄈㄤ ㄘㄜˋ)
strategy; a plan

方才 or 方纔(ㄈㄤ ㄘㄞˊ)
just now; just a moment ago: 你的妹妹方才還在這兒。Your younger sister was here just a moment ago.

方寸(ㄈㄤ ㄘㄨㄣˋ)
①a square *tsun* (a little larger than a square inch）②the heart

方寸不亂(ㄈㄤ ㄘㄨㄣˋ ㄅㄨˋ ㄌㄨㄢˋ)
to remain calm; to maintain composure

方寸地(ㄈㄤ ㄘㄨㄣˋ ㄉㄧˋ)
the heart

方寸無主(ㄈㄤ ㄘㄨㄣˋ ㄨˊ ㄓㄨˇ)
bewildered; confused; dismayed

方俗(ㄈㄤ ㄙㄨˊ)
local customs

方案(ㄈㄤ ㄢˋ)
a plan; a project; a design; a scheme; a program

方以類聚(ㄈㄤ ㄧˇ ㄌㄟˋ ㄐㄩˋ)
Only people of similar character and disposition can become good friends.

方�(ㄈㄤ ㄅㄧㄢ)
the frontier region

方言(ㄈㄤ ㄧㄢˊ)
a dialect

方言字典(ㄈㄤ ㄧㄢˊ ㄗˋ ㄉㄧㄢˇ)
a dialect dictionary

方音(ㄈㄤ ㄧㄣ)
a regional accent in pronunciation

方外(ㄈㄤ ㄨㄞˋ)
beyond this world

方外之人(ㄈㄤ ㄨㄞˋ ㄓ ㄖㄣˊ)
Buddhist or Taoist priests

方位(ㄈㄤ ㄨㄟˋ)
the points of the compass; a direction; a bearing

方位角(ㄈㄤ ㄨㄟˋ ㄐㄧㄠˇ)
(surveying) azimuth, the angle measured clockwise from the south or north

方輿(ㄈㄤ ㄩˊ)
the earth

方隅(ㄈㄤ ㄩˊ)
boundaries

方圓(ㄈㄤ ㄩㄢˊ)
①neighborhood ②squares and circles

四畫

【於】 2175
1. ㄩ yu yü
1. in; on; at; by; from
2. than; then; to; with reference to
3. compared with: 他的英文優於她。Her English cannot compare with his.
4. a Chinese family name

於理甚當(ㄩˊ ㄌㄧˇ ㄕㄣˋ ㄉㄤˋ)
appropriate; proper; reasonable; justified

於後(ㄩˊ ㄏㄡˋ)
afterwards; as follows

於己無損(ㄩˊ ㄐㄧˇ ㄨˊ ㄙㄨㄣˇ)
It doesn't hurt oneself (but may do a lot of good to others).

於今(ㄩˊ ㄐㄧㄣ)
now; at present

於下(ㄩˊ ㄒㄧㄚˋ)
as follows; below

於心何忍(ㄩˊ ㄒㄧㄣ ㄏㄜˊ ㄖㄣˇ)
Where's your conscience? or How could one stand such (callousness without offering help)?

於是(ㄩˊ ㄕˋ)
then; so; thus; thereafter; thereupon: 於是我們判定他錯了。Thus we decided that he was wrong.

於是乎(ㄩˊ ㄕˋ ㄏㄨ)
then; thereupon; so; in this way; thus

於焉(ㄩˊ ㄕˋ ㄧㄢ)
thereupon

於事無補(ㄩˊ ㄕˋ ㄨˊ ㄅㄨˇ)
It doesn't help the situation. 或 It does nothing good.

於左(ㄩˊ ㄗㄨㄛˇ)
①on the left ②as follows

於此(ㄩˊ ㄘˇ)
here; in this place

於斯(ㄩˊ ㄙ)
in this place; here

於右(ㄩˊ ㄧㄡˋ)
①on the right ②as above

於焉(ㄩˊ ㄧㄢ)
①then; thereupon ②here

【於】 2175
2. ㄨ u wū
an interjection roughly equivalent to hurrah, bravo,

---

alas, etc.

於穆(ㄨ ㄇㄨˋ)
Bravo!

於乎 or 於戲(ㄨ ㄏㄨˋ)
Ah!

於皇(ㄨ ㄏㄨㄤˊ)
Wonderful!

於鑠(ㄨ ㄕㄨㄛˋ)
Hurray!

於邑(ㄨ ㄧˋ)
alas (showing anxiety or sorrow)

五畫

【施】 2176
ㄕ shy shī
1. to act; to do; to make
2. to bestow; to grant; to give (alms, etc.)
3. to apply
4. a Chinese family name

施肥(ㄕ ㄈㄟˊ)
to apply fertilizers

施粉(ㄕ ㄈㄣˇ)
to apply face powder; to powder one's face

施放(ㄕ ㄈㄤˋ)
to discharge; to fire

施耐庵(ㄕ ㄋㄞˋ ㄢ)
Shih Nai-an (c.1290-c.1365), author of *All Men Are Brothers* (水滸傳)

施禮(ㄕ ㄌㄧˇ)
to make a bow; to curtsy; to salute: 賓主互相施禮。The host and the guest saluted each other.

施工(ㄕ ㄍㄨㄥ)
to start construction or building

施工中(ㄕ ㄍㄨㄥ ㄓㄨㄥ)
under construction; abuilding: 這座橋樑正施工中。The bridge is under construction.

施加(ㄕ ㄐㄧㄚ)
to exert; to bring to bear on

施教(ㄕ ㄐㄧㄠˋ)
to teach; to educate; to instruct

施救(ㄕ ㄐㄧㄡˋ)
to rescue and resuscitate

施洗(ㄕ ㄒㄧˇ)
to baptize

施洗約翰(ㄕ ㄒㄧˇ ㄩㄝ ㄏㄢˋ)
John the Baptist

施行(ㄕ ㄒㄧㄥˊ)

〔方 部〕

①(law) to come into force; to enforce; enforcement; to put into operation; to act; to execute ② to perform

施行細則(ㄕ ㄒㄧㄥ ㄒㄧ ㄗㄜˊ)
bylaws; detailed regulations governing the implementation of a statute

施脂粉(ㄕ ㄓ ㄈㄣˇ)
to apply cosmetics

施齋(ㄕ ㄓㄞ)
to give food to a Buddhist monk or nun

施粥(ㄕ ㄓㄡ)
to offer relief to the poor by operating a soup kitchen

施展(ㄕ ㄓㄢˇ)
to display (one's feat, talent, skill, etc.); to give free play to: 他常施展他的本領。He often gives full play to his talent.

施賑(ㄕ ㄓㄣˋ)
to give to the poor

施政(ㄕ ㄓㄥˋ)
(government) to administer; to govern; to execute government orders

施政報告(ㄕ ㄓㄥˋ ㄅㄠˋ ㄍㄠˋ)
an administrative report (delivered by a head of state, province, etc. to the legislature, assembly, etc.)

施主(ㄕ ㄓㄨˇ)
one who contributes to the Buddhist faith; a term of address used by monks or nuns referring to a believer in Buddhism

施逞(ㄕ ㄔㄥˇ)
to display or exhibit (one's feat, talent, etc.)

施施(ㄕ ㄕ)
complacently; leisurely

施食(ㄕ ㄕˊ)
①to feed the poor; to give relief to the poor by feeding them ②(Buddhism) to offer food to monks or spirits of those starved to death

施捨(ㄕ ㄕㄜˇ)
to give to charity

施人慎勿念(ㄕ ㄖㄣˊ ㄕㄣˋ ㄨˋ ㄋㄧㄢˋ)
Don't try to remember the good turns one has done to others.

施恩(ㄕ ㄣ)

---

to give favors to others

施醫(ㄕ ㄧ)
to give free medical service

施藥(ㄕ ㄧㄠˋ)
to dispense medicine free of charge

施威(ㄕ ㄨㄟ)
①to impress with force ② (said of gods) to show anger or power

施為(ㄕ ㄨㄟˊ)
action; behavior; conduct

施與(ㄕ ㄩˇ)
to give to the poor; to give to charity

施用(ㄕ ㄩㄥˋ)
to use; to employ

【㳺】 2177 ㄧㄡˊ you yóu

1. to swim
2. to rove about freely
3. ornaments hanging down from banners

六畫

【旁】 2178 1.〔扇〕ㄆㄤˊ parng
péng

1. side (branches, doors, ways, etc.); the side
2. by the side of; nearby
3. other; else

旁礴(ㄆㄤˊ ㄅㄛˊ)
all-embracing; overwhelming

旁白(ㄆㄤˊ ㄅㄞˊ)
(drama) aside

旁邊(ㄆㄤˊ ㄅㄧㄢ)or 旁邊兒(ㄆㄤˊ ㄅㄧㄢㄦ)
①the side; by the side of ② nearby; in the vicinity of

旁門(ㄆㄤˊ ㄇㄣˊ)
a side door

旁門左道(ㄆㄤˊ ㄇㄣˊ ㄗㄨㄛˇ ㄉㄠˋ)
heresy; unorthodox ways

旁聽(ㄆㄤˊ ㄊㄧㄥ)
to sit at a meeting or class in the capacity as an observer, guest, auditor, etc.

旁聽席(ㄆㄤˊ ㄊㄧㄥ ㄒㄧˊ)
seats reserved for visitors or observers at a meeting or court proceeding; gallery seats

旁聽生(ㄆㄤˊ ㄊㄧㄥ ㄕㄥ)
an auditor (at a class)

旁擊(ㄆㄤˊ ㄐㄧ)

---

a son borne by one's concubine

旁觀(ㄆㄤˊ ㄍㄨㄢ)
to look on; to watch from the sidelines

旁觀者(ㄆㄤˊ ㄍㄨㄢ ㄓㄜˇ)
an onlooker; a bystander; a spectator

旁觀者清(ㄆㄤˊ ㄍㄨㄢ ㄓㄜˇ ㄑㄧㄥ)
The onlooker is clear-headed (because he can see what's going on with detachment). 或 The onlooker sees most of the game.

旁及(ㄆㄤˊ ㄐㄧˊ)
to touch on (something else) incidentally; to take up (along with something more important): 他專攻文學,也旁及藝術。He majors in literature, but also takes an interest in art.

旁妻(ㄆㄤˊ ㄑㄧ)
a concubine

旁切圓(ㄆㄤˊ ㄑㄧㄝ ㄩㄢˊ)
(geometry) an escribed circle

旁敲側擊(ㄆㄤˊ ㄑㄧㄠ ㄘㄜˋ ㄐㄧ)
to ask seemingly irrelevant questions or speak aimlessly with a hidden purpose; to teach or enlighten by indirect approach; to make oblique references

旁求(ㄆㄤˊ ㄑㄧㄡˊ)
to solicit (men of abilities, etc.) from all sides; to search everywhere 亦作「遍求」

旁系(ㄆㄤˊ ㄒㄧˋ)
a lateral family line (as distinct from the direct lineage) 參看「旁支」

旁行(ㄆㄤˊ ㄒㄧㄥˊ)
①to travel far and wide ② a written language that goes from left to right, as English, French, etc.

旁行斜上(ㄆㄤˊ ㄒㄧㄥˊ ㄒㄧㄝˊ ㄕㄤˋ)
Occidental languages

旁訓(ㄆㄤˊ ㄒㄩㄣˋ)
footnotes of scriptures or classics

旁支(ㄆㄤˊ ㄓ)
a collateral branch (of a family)

旁枝(ㄆㄤˊ ㄓ)
a side branch

旁徵曲引(ㄆㄤˊㄓㄥ ㄑㄩ ㄧㄣˇ)
to quote widely or extensively

旁證
circumstantial evidence; indirect evidence; collateral evidence

旁注 or 旁註(ㄆㄤˊㄓㄨˋ)
annotations; footnotes; notes

旁岔兒(ㄆㄤˊㄔㄚˋㄦ)
an interruption; an outgrowth or offshoot (usually undesirable)

旁出(ㄆㄤˊㄔㄨ)
an offshoot; children born of a concubine

旁生(ㄆㄤˊㄕㄥ)
①(Buddhism) domestic animals ②to occur from beside

旁人(ㄆㄤˊㄖㄣˊ)
① bystanders; onlookers; outsiders ②the others: 我必須和旁人商量. I must consult with the others.

旁若無人(ㄆㄤˊㄖㄨㄛˋㄨˊㄖㄣˊ)
to act as if there weren't any bystanders; with full composure (connoting over-confidence or arrogance)

旁坐(ㄆㄤˊㄗㄨㄛˋ)
(in ancient China) to involve one's relatives in a criminal offense

旁壓力(ㄆㄤˊㄧㄚ ㄌㄧˋ)
(physics) lateral pressure

【旁】 2178
ㄅㄤ bang bāng
參看「旁午」

旁午(ㄅㄤˊㄨˇ)
①busy; complicated ②criss-cross

【斻】 2179
ㄑㄧˊ chyi qí
a flag or streamer attached with small bells; a flag

【㫰】 2180
ㄓㄢ jan zhān
1. a flag or banner with a bent staff
2. an auxiliary particle used like 之 or 焉 to give force to the verb
3. woolen fabrics
4. a Chinese family name

【斾】 2181
ㄆㄟˋ pey pèi
a general name for flags, banners, streamers, pennons, etc.

施施(ㄊㄞ ㄊㄞ)
①(descriptive of flags) flying in the wind ②(said of plants) growing luxuriantly

【旄】 2182
1. ㄇㄠˊ mau máo
a kind of ancient flag with the oxtails set up at the top of its staff

旄車(ㄇㄠˊㄐㄩ)
an ancient war chariot

【旄】 2182
2.(舊) ㄇㄠˋ maw mào

old

旄倪(ㄇㄠˋㄋㄧˊ)
old and young

【旅】 2183
ㄌㄩˇ leu lǚ
1. to travel; to lodge: 她每年夏季去歐洲旅行. She travels in Europe every summer.
2. a traveler; a passenger; a lodger
3. a multitude; people
4. disciples; pupils; followers; subordinates
5. order; sequence; to arrange
6. (military) a brigade; troops
7. (now rarely) a sacrifice to the mountains
8. to proceed together; to do things together

旅伴(ㄌㄩˇㄅㄢˋ)
a traveling companion

旅費(ㄌㄩˇㄈㄟˋ)
traveling expenses

旅店(ㄌㄩˇㄉㄧㄢˋ)
a tavern; an inn

旅途(ㄌㄩˇㄊㄨˊ)
the route by which one travels from one place to another; on one's way to a (destination); during one's trip

旅力(ㄌㄩˇㄌㄧˋ)
① the common effort of all ② one's muscular strength

旅館(ㄌㄩˇㄍㄨㄢˇ)
a hotel; a hostel; an inn

旅客(ㄌㄩˇㄎㄜˋ)
a traveler; a passenger; a lodger

旅進旅退(ㄌㄩˇㄐㄧㄣˋㄌㄩˇㄊㄨㄟˋ)
(literally) to advance and retreat together with others —having no opinion of one's own

旅居(ㄌㄩˇㄐㄩ)
to stay in a place for a while; temporary lodging

旅行(ㄌㄩˇㄒㄧㄥˊ)
to travel; to go in a group from one place to another; travels

旅行袋(ㄌㄩˇㄒㄧㄥˊㄉㄞˋ)
a traveling bag

旅行團(ㄌㄩˇㄒㄧㄥˊㄊㄨㄢˊ)
a traveling party; a tourist group: 這個旅行團正在作環島旅行. This tourist group is going round the island.

旅行支票(ㄌㄩˇㄒㄧㄥˊㄓ ㄆㄧㄠˋ)
a traveler's check

旅行指南(ㄌㄩˇㄒㄧㄥˊㄓˇㄋㄢˊ)
a guidebook

旅行車(ㄌㄩˇㄒㄧㄥˊㄔㄜ)
a station wagon

旅行社(ㄌㄩˇㄒㄧㄥˊㄕㄜˋ)
a travel agency; a travel bureau

旅長(ㄌㄩˇㄓㄤˇ)
the commanding officer of a brigade

旅程(ㄌㄩˇㄔㄥˊ)
the route a traveler takes from one place to another; during one's trip; on one's way; a journey

旅食(ㄌㄩˇㄕˊ)
①to stay at one place as a visitor ② mess for a large group of people

旅社(ㄌㄩˇㄕㄜˋ)
a hotel; a hostel; an inn

旅生(ㄌㄩˇㄕㄥ)
(said of wild plants) to grow spontaneously

旅順(ㄌㄩˇㄕㄨㄣˋ)
Port Arthur (Lüshun), in Liaoning Province

旅人(ㄌㄩˇㄖㄣˊ)
①a traveler ②one who lives away from home

旅次(ㄌㄩˇㄘˋ)
①the place where a tourist, traveler or visitor takes up his lodgings ②during one's trip or tour

旅行軍(ㄌㄩˇㄒㄧㄥˊㄐㄩㄣ)
(said of troops) to march without taking security measures

旅遊(ㄌㄩˇㄧㄡˊ)

〔方部〕

a tour; tourism: 他們徒步旅遊
本島。They made a walking
tour of this island.

旅思(ㄌㄩˋ)
a traveler's thoughts

七畫

【旋】 2184
1. ㄒㄩㄢˊ shyuan
xuán

1. to return; to turn back: 我們
的部隊已凱旋。Our troops
have returned in triumph.

2. to revolve; to circle; to spin;
to move in an orbit: 一隻鷹在
空中盤旋。A hawk is circling
in the sky.

3. a very short while; a
moment; soon: 全部門票旋即
售罄。All tickets were soon
sold out.

4. to urinate

旋得旋失(ㄒㄩㄢˊㄉㄜˊㄒㄩㄢˊㄕ)
to gain and lose within a
short while, as playing the
stocks

旋里(ㄒㄩㄢˊㄌㄧˇ)or旋鄉(ㄒㄩㄢˊㄒㄧㄤ)
to return to one's hometown

旋螺(ㄒㄩㄢˊㄌㄨㄛˊ)
①a screw ② a variety of
the mollusk family with a
univalve shell

旋律(ㄒㄩㄢˊㄌㄩˋ)
melody: 這首歌的旋律哀怨。
This song has a doleful melody.

旋即(ㄒㄩㄢˊㄐㄧˊ)
forthwith; immediately afterwards

旋乾轉坤(ㄒㄩㄢˊㄑㄧㄢˊㄓㄨㄢˇㄎㄨㄣ)
(literally) to turn heaven
into earth and vice versa
—immense power to reverse
a situation 亦作「旋轉乾坤」

旋轉(ㄒㄩㄢˊㄓㄨㄢˇ)
to turn round and round; to
revolve; to gyrate; to rotate;
to spin: 輪子繞軸旋轉。A
wheel revolves round its
axis.

旋轉門(ㄒㄩㄢˊㄓㄨㄢˇㄇㄣˊ)
a revolving door

旋踵(ㄒㄩㄢˊㄓㄨㄥˇ)
a very short time: 他旋踵間
便把薪金花完了。He spent his
salary in a very short time.

旋繞(ㄒㄩㄢˊㄖㄠˋ)

to revolve around; to move
in an orbit; to orbit

旋窰(ㄒㄩㄢˊㄧㄠˊ)
a rotary kiln

旋渦(ㄒㄩㄢˊㄨㄛ)
①a whirlpool ② a turbulent
and difficult situation 亦作
「漩渦」

旋淵(ㄒㄩㄢˊㄩㄢ)
an abyss

【旋】 2184
2. ㄒㄩㄢˋ shiuann
xuàn

1. to whirl; a whirl
2. at the time; at the last
moment; as soon as
3. to heat wine

旋風(ㄒㄩㄢˋㄈㄥ)
a whirlwind; a cyclone

【旌】 2185
ㄐㄧㄥ jing jing

1. a kind of flag, banner, standard, etc. ornamented with
feathers: 旌旗隨風招展。Flags
are waving in the breeze.

2. to cite (one's merits, virtues, etc.); to make manifest:
政府每年旌表善人。The gov-
ernment cites the virtuous
people every year.

旌表(ㄐㄧㄥㄅㄧㄠˇ)
the honor conferred upon
the virtuous and capable (by
the emperor, etc.); to confer
such an honor

旌門(ㄐㄧㄥㄇㄣˊ)
a family cited by the government for community service or exemplary virtue,
whose door is made distinct
from others by a plaque
bearing the citation

旌銘(ㄐㄧㄥㄇㄧㄥˊ)
(during the burial cere-
mony) a flag indicating the
death of a person, usually
one known for his distin-
guished service

旌節(ㄐㄧㄥㄐㄧㄝˊ)
①a flag and staff held by a
high official in the Tang
Dynasty ② a decorated staff
used by ancient emissaries
as credentials

旌旗(ㄐㄧㄥㄑㄧˊ)
a general name for flags
and banners

旌旗蔽空(ㄐㄧㄥㄑㄧˊㄅㄧˋㄎㄨㄥ)or

旌旗蔽日(ㄐㄧㄥㄑㄧˊㄅㄧˋㄖˋ)
(literally) There are so
many flags that they cover
the whole sky (or darken
the sun).—a very large
army

旌旗所指(ㄐㄧㄥㄑㄧˊㄙㄨㄛˇㄓˇ)
wherever the army goes (the
enemy is crushed)

旌卹(ㄐㄧㄥㄒㄩˋ)
rewards given to the family
of the deceased in recognition of his meritorious service; posthumous rewards
for distinguished service

【旎】 2186
ㄋㄧˇ nii nǐ

1. romantic; tender; charming 參看「旖旎」

2. the fluttering of flags

【族】 2187
ㄗㄨˊ tzwu zú

1. a tribe; a clan; a family; relatives

2. a race (of people)

3. a class or group of things
with common features: 水族
aquatic animals

族伯(ㄗㄨˊㄅㄛˊ)
older fellow clansmen of
one's father's generation

族譜(ㄗㄨˊㄆㄨˇ)
the pedigree of a clan: 他們
詳細審查他的族譜和背景。
They scrutinized his pedigree and background.

族母(ㄗㄨˊㄇㄨˇ)
the wife of one's father's
cousin

族父(ㄗㄨˊㄈㄨˋ)
one's father's male third
cousins of the same surname

族弟(ㄗㄨˊㄉㄧˋ)
paternal male third cousins
younger than oneself

族類(ㄗㄨˊㄌㄟˋ)
of the same clan or race

族居(ㄗㄨˊㄐㄩ)
to live together as a clan

族群(ㄗㄨˊㄑㄩㄣˊ)
an ethnic group

族姓(ㄗㄨˊㄒㄧㄥˋ)
①family names in a clan ②
family standing and back-
ground

族兄(ㄗㄨˊㄒㄩㄥ)
paternal male third cousins
older than oneself

族長(ㄗㄨˊ ㄓㄤˇ)
the oldest of the highest generation in a clan; the chief of a clan

族誅(ㄗㄨˊ ㄓㄨ)
to execute all of one's relatives for his personal offense or crime

族叔(ㄗㄨˊ ㄕㄨˊ)
fellow clansmen of one's father's generation but younger than one's father

族人(ㄗㄨˊ ㄖㄣˊ)
fellow clansmen

族葬(ㄗㄨˊ ㄗㄤˋ)
to be buried with the other deceased members of the same clan

族望(ㄗㄨˊ ㄨㄤˋ)
a famous or prestigious clan

八畫

【旐】 2188
ㄓㄠˋ jaw zhǎo
(in the ancient times) a flag with tortoises and snakes emblazoned on it

九畫

【旒】 2189
ㄌㄧㄡˊ liou liú
1. a silk string used to hold a piece of jade hung on ancient ceremonial caps
2. a colored streamer hung on a flag

十畫

【旗】 2190
ㄑㄧˊ chyi qí
1. a flag; a pennant; a banner; a streamer
2. a sign; an insignia; an emblem
3. an administrative division of Mongolia (蒙古) and Tsinghai (青海)
4. the Manchus

旗袍(ㄑㄧˊ ㄆㄠˊ)
chi-pao, an all-purpose long gown worn by women in modern China (introduced by the Manchus)

旗杆 or 旗竿(ㄑㄧˊ ㄍㄢ)
a flagstaff; a flagpole; a flag

post

旗鼓(ㄑㄧˊ ㄍㄨˇ)
(military) the flags and the drums—instruments of giving orders

旗鼓相當(ㄑㄧˊ ㄍㄨˇ ㄒㄧㄤ ㄉㄤ)
of approximately equal strength, ability, etc.: 他們旗鼓相當，所以比賽十分激烈。 They were well-matched, so that the game was hotly contested.

旗開得勝(ㄑㄧˊ ㄎㄞ ㄉㄜˊ ㄕㄥˋ)
to win in the first battle, game or match; to win speedy success

旗號(ㄑㄧˊ ㄏㄠˋ)
an army signal; a flag

旗艦(ㄑㄧˊ ㄐㄧㄢˋ)
a flagship

旗槍(ㄑㄧˊ)
①banners and spears ②a kind of green tea

旗幟(ㄑㄧˊ)
flags, pennants, streamers, etc.

旗手(ㄑㄧˊ ㄕㄡˇ)
a flagman

旗人(ㄑㄧˊ ㄖㄣˊ)
a Mongol, Manchu or Chinese who was a member of any one of the twenty-four banners during the Ching Dynasty (The term is used now to refer to the Manchus exclusively.)

旗子(ㄑㄧˊ ˙ㄗ)
a flag

旗魚(ㄑㄧˊ ㄩˊ)
spearfish (*Xiphias gladius*)

旗語(ㄑㄧˊ ㄩˇ)
flag-signals

【旖】 2191
ㄧˇ yii yǐ
1. romantic; tender
2. charming; lovely; attractive; graceful
3. the fluttering of flags

旖旎(ㄧˇ ㄋㄧˇ)
①(said of flags) fluttering
②(said of scenery) enchanting

旖旎風光(ㄧˇ ㄋㄧˇ ㄈㄥ ㄍㄨㄤ)
a romantic or charming sight

十四畫

【旛】 2192
ㄈㄢ fan fān
1. a general name of flags or streamers
2. a silk (usually rectangular) pennant for hanging

十五畫

【旝】 2193
ㄎㄨㄞˋ kuay kuài
1. a flag used by a general
2. a coach used in ancient warfare for shooting stones

十六畫

【旟】 2194
ㄩˊ yu yú
1. a military flag or standard; a flag with falcons emblazoned on it
2. (said of flags) fluttering

无 部
ㄨˊ wu wú

〔无部〕

【无】 2195
ㄨˊ wu wú
the ancient form of 無—not; no; negative; without

无妄(ㄨˊ ㄨㄤˋ)
a diagram in the *Book of Changes*(易經) indicating truth and honesty

无妄之災(ㄨˊ ㄨㄤˋ ㄓ ㄗㄞ)
an unexpected trouble or bad break; a disaster brought on not by oneself

一畫

【旡】 2196
ㄐㄧˋ jih jì
to choke in eating

七畫

【既】 2197
(旣) ㄐㄧˋ jih jì
1. since ; as; now that; inasmuch as: 他既然問我，我就告訴你。 Since you ask, I will tell you.

2. already: 他的成功已是既成的事實。His success is already an accomplished fact.
3. all
4. to finish
5. a Chinese family name

既明且哲(ㄐㄧㄇㄧㄥˊㄑㄩㄝˋㄓㄜˊ)
both intelligent and wise

既得利益(ㄐㄧㄉㄜˊㄌㄧˋㄧˋ)
vested interests

既得權(ㄐㄧˋㄉㄜˊㄑㄩㄢˊ)
vested rights

既定(ㄐㄧˋㄉㄧㄥˋ)
① already decided or fixed: 那是我們的既定目標。It is our fixed goal. ② (said of a rebellion, etc.) already quelled

既來之則安之(ㄐㄧˋㄌㄞˊㄓㄓㄜˊㄢㄓ)
Since we (or you) are already here, let's make ourselves (or yourself) at home.

既成事實(ㄐㄧˋㄔㄥˊㄕˋㄕˊ)
de facto; a fact already accomplished; a *fait accompli*; an accomplished fact

既是(ㄐㄧˋㄕˋ)or 既然(ㄐㄧˋㄖㄢˊ)
since (it is so, etc.); this being the case

既然如此(ㄐㄧˋㄖㄢˊㄖㄨˊㄘˇ)
this being the case; since it is so: 既然如此，讓我們重新考慮這件事。Since it is so, let us reconsider this matter.

既遂犯(ㄐㄧˋㄙㄨㄟˋㄈㄢˋ)
a criminal who has accomplished his criminal act

既而(ㄐㄧˋㄦˊ)
then; not long afterwards; later; subsequently

既往不咎(ㄐㄧˋㄨㄤˇㄅㄨˋㄐㄧㄡˋ)
Let bygones be bygones. 或 No postmortems. 或 to forgive somebody's past misdeeds

既望(ㄐㄧˋㄨㄤˋ)
the 16th day of every month (in the lunar calendar)

日 部
(ㄖˋ) ryh rì

【日】 2198
(ㄖˋ) ryh rì
1. the sun
2. a day
3. daily; every day
4. Japan; Japanese
5. time: 往日 the past times 夏日 summertime
6. day; daytime

日薄西山(ㄖˋㄅㄛˊㄒㄧㄕㄢ)
(literally) The sun is near the west mountain.—declining rapidly; old age; approaching one's grave

日報(ㄖˋㄅㄠˋ)
a daily newspaper (especially the morning paper)

日班(ㄖˋㄅㄢ)
the day shift (in factories, etc.): 最近他輪值日班。He has been on the day shift recently.

日斑(ㄖˋㄅㄢ)
(astronomy) sunspot 亦作「太陽黑子」

日本(ㄖˋㄅㄣˇ)
Japan: 他去過日本三次。He has been to Japan three times.

日本海(ㄖˋㄅㄣˇㄏㄞˇ)
the Japan Sea

日晡(ㄖˋㄅㄨ)
dusk; sundown; sunset

日不暇給(ㄖˋㄅㄨˋㄒㄧㄚˊㄐㄧˇ)
too many things to do in a day; very busy; to wish there were 36 hours in a day

日迫(ㄖˋㄆㄛˋ)
to get closer day by day 或 Time is running out.

日偏蝕(ㄖˋㄆㄧㄢㄕˊ)
(astronomy) the partial eclipse of the sun

日平西(ㄖˋㄆㄧㄥˊㄒㄧ)
dusk; sundown

日沒(ㄖˋㄇㄛˋ)
sunset

日沒沉西(ㄖˋㄇㄛˋㄔㄣˊㄒㄧ)
sundown; sunset; dusk

日晁(ㄖˋㄇㄧㄢˇ)
(astronomy) corona, a faintly luminous envelope outside of the sun's chromosphere

日暮途窮(ㄖˋㄇㄨˋㄊㄨˊㄑㄩㄥˊ)
at the end of one's rope; at one's wits' end; in a desperate position

---

日暮途遠(ㄖˋㄇㄨˋㄊㄨˊㄩㄢˇ)
in a desperate position; having no one to turn to

日復一日(ㄖˋㄈㄨˋㄧˊㄖˋ)
day after day; day in and day out

日德蘭半島(ㄖˋㄉㄜˊㄌㄢˊㄅㄢˋㄉㄠˇ)
Jutland

日頭(ㄖˋㄊㄡˊ)
① the sun ② daytime

日圓三餐，夜圖一宿(ㄖˋㄊㄨˊㄙㄢㄘㄢ，ㄧㄝˋㄊㄨˊㄧˋㄙㄨˋ)
The people have no other ambition than food in their stomachs and a roof over their heads.

日內(ㄖˋㄋㄟˋ)
in a few days

日內瓦(ㄖˋㄋㄟˋㄨㄚˇ)
Geneva, Switzerland

日來(ㄖˋㄌㄞˊ)
in recent days; the last few days

日理萬機(ㄖˋㄌㄧˇㄨㄢˋㄐㄧ)
(literally) to manage 10,000 things in a day—very busy (said of rulers or prime ministers running the affairs of the state)

日利(ㄖˋㄌㄧˋ)or 日息(ㄖˋㄒㄧˊ)
daily interest (rate)

日曆(ㄖˋㄌㄧˋ)
a calendar

日裏(ㄖˋ·ㄌㄧ)or 日間(ㄖˋㄐㄧㄢ)
in the daytime; at daytime

日落風生(ㄖˋㄌㄨㄛˋㄈㄥㄕㄥ)
Gentle breezes come with the sunset. (an expression to describe a natural scene at dusk)

日輪(ㄖˋㄌㄨㄣˊ)
① the sun disc ② a Japanese merchantman

日晷(ㄖˋㄍㄨㄟˇ)or 日表(ㄖˋㄅㄧㄠˇ)
a sundial

日光(ㄖˋㄍㄨㄤ)
① sunshine; the light of the sun ② Nikko, a mountain resort in Japan

日光燈(ㄖˋㄍㄨㄤㄉㄥ)
a fluorescent lamp

日光能(ㄖˋㄍㄨㄤㄋㄥˊ)
solar energy

日光療法(ㄖˋㄍㄨㄤㄌㄧㄠˊㄈㄚˇ)
heliotherapy

日光節約時間(ㄖˋㄍㄨㄤㄐㄧㄝˊㄩㄝ)

ㄕㄨㄕ
daylight saving time

日光浴(日 ㄍㄨㄤ ㄩ)
sunbath

日光浴室(日《ㄨㄤ ㄩ ㄕ)
a solarium

日工(日《ㄨㄥ)
①daywork ② day labor ③ a day laborer

日課(日 ㄎㄜ)
daily courses (of study); a daily curriculum

日刊(日 ㄎㄢ)
a daily publication, newspaper, etc.

日虧(日 ㄎㄨㄟ)
(business) daily losses

日後(日 ㄏㄡ)
in the days to come; in future

日貨(日 ㄏㄨㄛ)
Japanese goods

日暉(日 ㄏㄨㄟ)
the rays of the sun

日環蝕(日 ㄏㄨㄢ ㄕ)
an annular eclipse of the sun

日機(日 ㄐㄧ)
Japanese airplanes

日積月累(日 ㄐㄧ ㄩㄝ ㄌㄟ)
day after day and month after month; gradual accumulation over a long time

日給(日 ㄐㄧ)
daily wages

日計(日 ㄐㄧ)
to calculate by the day

日計不足，歲計有餘(日 ㄐㄧ ㄅㄨ ㄗㄨ，ㄙㄨㄟ ㄐㄧ ㄧㄡ ㄩ)
Time and patience beget success.

日記(日 ㄐㄧ)
a diary

日記本(日 ㄐㄧ ㄅㄣ)
a diary book; a notebook (registering one's daily engagements or appointments)

日記帳(日 ㄐㄧ ㄓㄤ)
(accounting) daily account; day-by-day account

日久天長(日 ㄐㄧㄡ ㄊㄧㄢ ㄔㄤ)
for a long, long time; for keeps

日息人心(日 ㄐㄧㄡ ㄖㄣ ㄒㄧㄣ)
Time reveals a person's heart.

日久情生(日 ㄐㄧㄡ ㄑㄧㄥ ㄕㄥ)
Having been together for a long time, people come to have a tender feeling for each other.

日久厭生(日 ㄐㄧㄡ ㄧㄢ ㄕㄥ)
Familiarity begets contempt.

日久玩生(日 ㄐㄧㄡ ㄨㄢ ㄕㄥ)
Discipline tends to get lax as time goes by.

日就月將(日 ㄐㄧㄡ ㄩㄝ ㄐㄧㄤ)
to progress or improve with the day

日間(日 ㄐㄧㄢ)
at daytime; in the daytime: 我在日間不能睡覺。I cannot sleep in the daytime.

日見 or 日漸(日 ㄐㄧㄢ)
with each passing day; day by day: 病人的健康日見好轉。The patient is getting better day by day.

日艦(日 ㄐㄧㄢ)
a Japanese warship

日進(日 ㄐㄧㄣ)
to improve or increase with each passing day; constant improvement

日居月諸(日 ㄐㄩ ㄩㄝ ㄓㄨ)
①the sun and the moon ② the elapsing of time

日軍(日 ㄐㄩㄣ)
Japanese troops

日期 or 日子(日 ㄑㄧ)
date

日僑(日 ㄑㄧㄠ)
Japanese residents in a foreign country

日前(日 ㄑㄧㄢ)
a few days ago; recently: 日前我們曾見面。We met a few days ago.

日趨(日 ㄑㄩ)
with each passing day; gradually; day by day

日趨下流(日 ㄑㄩ ㄒㄧㄚ ㄌㄧㄡ)
to sink lower and lower with each passing day; to get meaner and more depraved with the day

日全蝕(日 ㄑㄩㄢ ㄕ)
a total eclipse of the sun

日息(日 ㄒㄧ)
interest per diem

日夕(日 ㄒㄧ)
day and night: 他日夕工作不停。He worked day and night without stopping.

日戲(日 ㄒㄧ)
a matinee

日校(日 ㄒㄧㄠ)
a day school

日新(日 ㄒㄧㄣ)or日新又新(日 ㄒㄧㄣ ㄧㄡ ㄒㄧㄣ)
daily renewal or modernization; constant progress

日新月異(日 ㄒㄧㄣ ㄩㄝ ㄧ)
continuous improvement; ever newer

日薪(日 ㄒㄧㄣ)
day wages

日行一善(日 ㄒㄧㄥ ㄧ ㄕㄢ)
to do one good deed a day

日省月試(日 ㄒㄧㄥ ㄩㄝ ㄕ)
to watch with a critical eye over a long period of time (to see if something or someone is really good)

日削月朘(日 ㄒㄩㄝ ㄩㄝ ㄗㄨㄟ)
(said of corrupt officials) to exploit the people

日誌(日 ㄓ)
a daily record

日照(日 ㄓㄠ)
①sunshine ② an umbrella

日中(日 ㄓㄨㄥ)
①high noon ② the equinox

日中則昃(日 ㄓㄨㄥ ㄗㄜ ㄗㄜ)
to decline after reaching the zenith

日中為市(日 ㄓㄨㄥ ㄨㄟ ㄕ)
①(in ancient China) to barter goods at a market at noontime ② (in modern usage) to do business during the daytime

日常(日 ㄔㄤ)
daily; usually; ordinarily; common

日常生活(日 ㄔㄤ ㄕㄥ ㄏㄨㄛ)
daily life: 健康的人過愉快的日常生活。Healthy people lead a happy daily life.

日長一線(日 ㄔㄤ ㄧ ㄒㄧㄢ)
Daytime gradually lengthens after the winter solstice.

日場(日 ㄔㄤ)or日戲(日 ㄒㄧ)
(said of shows, concerts, etc.) the morning or the afternoon show; a matinee

日程(日 ㄔㄥ)

〔日部〕

① an itinerary ② the agenda on a specific day (of a conference)

日出(日 ㄔㄨ)
sunrise: 日出時天氣變得較暖。It becomes warmer at sunrise.

日出而作(日 ㄔㄨ ㄦ ㄗㄨㄛˋ)
to start work at daybreak (and retire at sunset): 農夫們日出而作，日入而息。Farmers start work at daybreak and retire at sunset.

日戳(日 ㄔㄨㄛ)
① a date stamp; a dater ② a datemark

日蝕 or 日食(日 ㄕ)
(astronomy) solar eclipse

日食萬錢(日 ㄕ ㄨㄢˋ ㄑㄧㄢˊ)
to spend money lavishly; to live in extreme luxury

日射病(日 ㄕ ㄅㄧㄥˋ)
sunstroke

日曬雨淋(日 ㄕㄞˋ ㄩˇ ㄌㄧㄣˊ)
to be exposed to the inclemency of the elements

日甚一日(日 ㄕㄣˋ ㄧ 日)
getting more serious, painful, etc. day after day; to get worse with each passing day; to increase in intensity constantly

日上三竿(日 ㄕㄤˋ ㄙㄢ ㄍㄢ)
rather late in the morning —about 9 a.m. (often used to describe someone who gets up late)

日月月恆(日 ㄩㄝˋ ㄩㄝˋ ㄏㄥˊ)
ever increasing, growing or rising; ever prosperous

日日(日 日)
every day; daily: 他日日運動。He does exercise every day.

日日新(日 日 ㄒㄧㄣ)
daily renovation, reformation or change

日入而息(日 ㄖㄨˋ ㄦ ㄒㄧˊ)
(to start work at daybreak and) to retire at sunset

日子(日 ㄗ˙)
① time; duration ② life; living: 這些難民過著悲慘的日子。The refugees led a miserable life. ③ a day; a date

日昨(日 ㄗㄨㄛˊ)
yesterday

日坐愁城(日 ㄗㄨㄛˋ ㄔㄡˊ ㄔㄥˊ)

to be in deep worry every day; to be deeply worried every day

日俄戰爭(日 ㄜˊ ㄓㄢˋ ㄓㄥ)
the Russo-Japanese War, 1904-1905

日耳曼(日 ㄦˇ ㄇㄢˋ)
the Germans

日以繼夜(日 ㄧˇ ㄐㄧˋ ㄧㄝˋ)
day and night; continuously or incessantly

日益(日 ㄧˋ)
increasingly; day by day

日夜(日 ㄧㄝˋ)
day and night

日曜日(日 ㄧㄠˋ 日)
Sunday

日有進步(日 ㄧㄡˇ ㄐㄧㄣˋ ㄅㄨˋ)
to show improvements or progress day by day; progressing constantly

日有起色(日 ㄧㄡˇ ㄑㄧˇ ㄙㄜˋ)
improving with each passing day; turning for the better steadily

日有所思，夜有所夢(日 ㄧㄡˇ ㄙㄨㄛˇ ㄙ，ㄧㄝˋ ㄧㄡˇ ㄙㄨㄛˇ ㄇㄥˋ)
One dreams at night what one thinks in the day.

日影(日 ㄧㄥˇ)
shadows caused by the sun

日文(日 ㄨㄣˊ)
the Japanese language: 他對日文有興趣。He is much interested in Japanese.

日語(日 ㄩˇ)
the Japanese (spoken) language

日月(日 ㄩㄝˋ)
① the sun and the moon ② time ③ life; living; livelihood ④ saints and sages ⑤ emperor and empress

日月潭(日 ㄩㄝˋ ㄊㄢˊ)
Sun Moon Lake, a resort in central Taiwan

日月經天(日 ㄩㄝˋ ㄐㄧㄥ ㄊㄧㄢ)
eternal and self-evident, like the sun and the moon in the sky

日月重光(日 ㄩㄝˋ ㄔㄨㄥˊ ㄍㄨㄤ)
(literally) The sun and the moon shine again. (used figuratively to describe a joyful event such as the dawnfall of a despot, liberation from enemy occupation,

etc.)

日月如梭(日 ㄩㄝˋ ㄖㄨˊ ㄙㄨㄛ)
(literally) The sun and the moon pass over the sky as fast as a weaver's shuttle. —How fast time flies! 或 *Tempus fugit!!*

日月無光(日 ㄩㄝˋ ㄨˊ ㄍㄨㄤ)
(literally) The sun and the moon are dimmed. (often used to mean darkness in a figurative sense to describe life under tyranny, foreign occupation, etc.)

日暈(日 ㄩㄣ)
the halo of the sun; coronas

日用品(日 ㄩㄥˋ ㄆㄧㄣˇ)or 日用必需品(日 ㄩㄥˋ ㄅㄧˋ ㄒㄩ ㄆㄧㄣˇ)
daily necessities; consumer goods

一畫

【旦】 2199
　　ㄉㄢˋ　dann dòn
1. daybreak; dawn
2. day; morning
3. a female role in Chinese opera

旦不保夕(ㄉㄢˋ ㄅㄨˋ ㄅㄠˇ ㄒㄧˋ)
not knowing how the day will end; in imminent danger; precarious

旦暮(ㄉㄢˋ ㄇㄨˋ)
① morning and evening ② in a brief span of time

旦旦(ㄉㄢˋ ㄉㄢˋ)
① every day; daily ② sincerely

旦角 or 旦脚(ㄉㄢˋ ㄐㄩㄝˊ)
a female role in Chinese opera

旦夕之間(ㄉㄢˋ ㄒㄧˋ ㄓ ㄐㄧㄢ)
within a single day; between morning and evening—a very short time

旦日(ㄉㄢˋ 日)
① tomorrow ② dawn

二畫

【旨】 2200
　　ㄓˇ　jyy zhǐ
1. a purpose; will; intention; objective
2. an imperial decree
3. good; excellent; beautiful
4. tasty; pleasant to the palate:

〔日部〕

delicious

旨甘(ㄓ ㄍㄢ)
delicacies; dainties

旨歸(ㄓ ㄍㄨㄟ)
① principle ② objective

旨酒(ㄓ ㄐㄧㄡˇ)
good wine

旨趣(ㄓ ㄑㄩˋ)
purposes and intentions;
objectives and interest

旨哉斯言(ㄓ ㄗㄞ ㄙ ㄧㄢˊ)
What an admirable state-
ment (or remark)!

旨在(ㄓ ㄗㄞˋ)
with the intention of; aiming
at; designed to

旨意(ㄓ ㄧˋ)
① will; intention ② an imperial decree; God's will

【早】 2201
ㄗㄠˇ tzao zǎo

1. early; earlier; soon; beforehand; previous; premature;
in advance

2. morning

3. ago; early

4. Good morning!

早班(ㄗㄠˇ ㄅㄢ)
the morning shift

早半天兒(ㄗㄠˇ ㄅㄢˋ ㄊㄧㄢ ㄦ)or早半
晌兒(ㄗㄠˇ ㄕㄤˇ ㄦ)
morning; before noon

早眠早起(ㄗㄠˇ ㄇㄧㄢˊ ㄗㄠˇ ㄑㄧˇ)
to keep good hours; to go to
bed early and get up early
the next morning (recom-
mended as a healthy habit)

早飯(ㄗㄠˇ ㄈㄢˋ)
breakfast: 早飯已準備好了。
Breakfast is ready.

早到(ㄗㄠˇ ㄉㄠˋ)
to arrive early; to arrive
ahead of time

早稻(ㄗㄠˇ ㄉㄠˋ)
paddies that ripen early

早稻田大學(ㄗㄠˇ ㄉㄠˋ ㄊㄧㄢˊ ㄉㄚˋ
ㄒㄩㄝˊ)
Waseda University, Japan

早點(ㄗㄠˇ ㄉㄧㄢˇ)
breakfast 參看「早飯」

早點兒(ㄗㄠˇ ㄉㄧㄢˇ ㄦ)
earlier; sooner: 請早點兒來。
Please come earlier.

早退(ㄗㄠˇ ㄊㄨㄟˋ)
to retire from office or factory earlier than others

早年(ㄗㄠˇ ㄋㄧㄢˊ)
years ago; in bygone years;
many years ago

早慧(ㄗㄠˇ ㄏㄨㄟˋ)
clever in one's childhood; an
early bloomer; precocious

早婚(ㄗㄠˇ ㄏㄨㄣ)
early marriage; to marry
young

早計(ㄗㄠˇ ㄐㄧˋ)
early planning

早就(ㄗㄠˇ ㄐㄧㄡˋ)
to have already…: 他早就回
家了。He had already re-
turned home.

早期(ㄗㄠˇ ㄑㄧ)
the early stage; the early
phase: 這些小說是他的早期作
品。These novels are his
early works.

早起(ㄗㄠˇ ㄑㄧˇ)
① (ㄗㄠˇ ㄑㄧˇ) to get up early;
early to rise
② (ㄗㄠˇ ˙ㄑㄧ) early in the
morning

早些箇(ㄗㄠˇ ㄒㄧㄝ ˙ㄍㄜ)or早些兒
(ㄗㄠˇ ㄒㄧㄝ ㄦ)
sooner; earlier

早先(ㄗㄠˇ ㄒㄧㄢ)
some time ago; before

早知如此(ㄗㄠˇ ㄓ ㄖㄨˊ ㄘˇ)
If it had been known that
things would turn out this
way….

早占勿藥(ㄗㄠˇ ㄓㄢ ㄨˋ ㄧㄠˋ)
(said of a sick person) to
have gotten well early; to
get well very soon

早車(ㄗㄠˇ ㄔㄜ)
the morning train

早朝(ㄗㄠˇ ㄔㄠˊ)
(said of an emperor) to
attend the imperial court
session in the early morning

早潮(ㄗㄠˇ ㄔㄠˊ)
morning tides

早產(ㄗㄠˇ ㄔㄢˇ)
premature birth

早晨(ㄗㄠˇ ㄔㄣˊ)
morning; dawn; daybreak;
early morning

早場(ㄗㄠˇ ㄔㄤˇ)
a morning show (at a cin-
ema, theater, etc.)

早出晚歸(ㄗㄠˇ ㄔㄨ ㄨㄢˇ ㄍㄨㄟ)
(often said of a busy person,

etc.) to go out early and
return late

早春(ㄗㄠˇ ㄔㄨㄣ)
① early spring ② early
spring tea

早市(ㄗㄠˇ ㄕˋ)
a morning market

早世(ㄗㄠˇ ㄕˋ)or早夭(ㄗㄠˇ ㄊㄧㄢ)
to die very young

早熟(ㄗㄠˇ ㄕㄨˊ)or(ㄗㄠˇ ㄕㄨˊ)
① (said of plants, etc.) to
ripen early ② (said of a person) to reach puberty early
③ precocious

早上(ㄗㄠˇ ㄕㄤˋ)
early in the morning

早衰(ㄗㄠˇ ㄕㄨㄞ)
(medicine) premature senility (or decrepitude)

早睡(ㄗㄠˇ ㄕㄨㄟˋ)
to sleep early

早日(ㄗㄠˇ ㄖˋ)
at an earlier date; soon: 祝你
早日恢復健康。I hope you'll
get well soon.

早則(ㄗㄠˇ ㄗㄜˊ)
① fortunately ② already

早操(ㄗㄠˇ ㄘㄠ)
morning calisthenics; exercises before the first class in
school

早餐(ㄗㄠˇ ㄘㄢ)
breakfast

早歲(ㄗㄠˇ ㄙㄨㄟˋ)
in one's youth

早安(ㄗㄠˇ ㄢ)
Good morning!

早已(ㄗㄠˇ ㄧˇ)
to have already…: 客人早已
離去。The guests had already
left.

早晚(ㄗㄠˇ ㄨㄢˇ)
① morning and evening ②
sooner or later

【旬】 2202
ㄒㄩㄣˊ shyun xún

1. a period of ten days

2. a period of ten years (usually used to indicate a person's age)

3. widespread; throughout

4. to tour; to inspect 亦作「巡」

旬年(ㄒㄩㄣˊ ㄋㄧㄢˊ)
① a full year ② ten years

旬刊(ㄒㄩㄣˊ ㄎㄢ)
a ten-day periodical; a magazine issued once every ten

days

旬休 (ㄒㄩㄣ ㄒㄧㄡ)
(originated in the Tang Dynasty) one day of rest in ten days for government officials

旬朔 (ㄒㄩㄣ ㄕㄨㄛ)
ten days or one month

旬日 (ㄒㄩㄣ ㄖˋ)
ten days

旬歲 (ㄒㄩㄣ ㄙㄨㄟˋ)
a whole year

旬月 (ㄒㄩㄣ ㄩㄝˋ)
①a whole month ②ten months

【旭】 2203 ㄒㄩˋ shiuh xù

1. brightness or radiance of daybreak
2. the rising sun
3. proud, smug or complacent

旭旭 (ㄒㄩˋ ㄒㄩˋ)
①proud, smug or complacent ②uproarious ③description of the rising sun

旭日 (ㄒㄩˋ ㄖˋ)
the rising sun

旭日初升 (ㄒㄩˋ ㄖˋ ㄔㄨ ㄕㄥ)
early in the morning 或 The sun is rising.

【旮】 2204 《ㄚ ga gā
a corner

旮旯子 (《ㄚ ㄌㄚˊ·ㄗ)or 旮旯兒 (《ㄚ ㄌㄚˊㄦ)
a nook; a corner

【旯】 2205 ㄌㄚˊ la lá
a corner

三畫

【旰】 2206 《ㄢˋ gann gàn
evening; late

旰旰 (《ㄢˋ 《ㄢˋ)
blossoming and robust; luxuriant

旰食 (《ㄢˋ ㄕˊ)
a late meal—too busy

旰食宵衣 (《ㄢˋ ㄕˊ ㄒㄧㄠ ㄧ)
(literally) to eat late and get up early—too busy

【旱】 2207 ㄏㄢˋ hann hàn
1. drought; dry
2. (by) land route (as opposed to waterway)

旱魃 (ㄏㄢˋ ㄅㄚˊ)

the demon of drought

旱稻 (ㄏㄢˋ ㄉㄠˋ)
upland rice; dry rice

旱地 (ㄏㄢˋ ㄉㄧˋ)
nonirrigated farmland; dry land

旱天 (ㄏㄢˋ ㄊㄧㄢ)
dry days; dry weather; a drought

旱田 (ㄏㄢˋ ㄊㄧㄢˊ)
dry farmland; uplands

旱年 (ㄏㄢˋ ㄋㄧㄢˊ)
a year of drought

旱潦 (ㄏㄢˋ ㄌㄠˊ)
droughts and floods

旱路 (ㄏㄢˋ ㄌㄨˋ)or 旱道
a land route; an overland route

旱海 (ㄏㄢˋ ㄏㄞˇ)
a desert

旱荒 (ㄏㄢˋ ㄏㄨㄤ)
famine brought about by drought

旱季 (ㄏㄢˋ ㄐㄧˋ)
a dry season

旱象 (ㄏㄢˋ ㄒㄧㄤˋ)
the signs of drought

旱災 (ㄏㄢˋ ㄗㄞ)
a drought: 幾年前印度曾有嚴重的旱災。India was afflicted with a severe drought a few years ago.

旱煙 (ㄏㄢˋ ㄧㄢ)
tobacco smoked in an ordinary pipe (as contrasted with 水煙 smoked in a water pipe)

四畫

【旺】 2208 ㄨㄤˋ wang wàng
1. prosperous; to prosper; to flourish
2. vigorous; prolific; productive
3. (said of light, fires, etc.) brilliant; bright or brightly

旺地 (ㄨㄤˋ ㄉㄧˋ)
a good land; a prosperous place

旺季 (ㄨㄤˋ ㄐㄧˋ)
(said of business) a boom season; a busy season: 目前的旺季能維持多久？How long can the present boom season last?

旺盛 (ㄨㄤˋ ㄕㄥˋ)
①prosperous; prolific; productive; vigorous: 那位老人仍然精力旺盛。The old man is still vigorous. ②high (morale)

旺月 (ㄨㄤˋ ㄩㄝˋ)
a busy or boom month; the best month of the year in sales and income

旺運 (ㄨㄤˋ ㄩㄣˋ)
good fortune; good luck

【旻】 2209 ㄇㄧㄣˊ min mín
autumn

旻天 (ㄇㄧㄣˊ ㄊㄧㄢ)
①autumn ②the heavens

旻序 (ㄇㄧㄣˊ ㄒㄩˋ)
autumn festivals

【昂】 2210 ㄤˊ arng áng
1. to raise
2. lofty and proud; bold and not easily bent; straight-forward
3. high
4. expensive; costly

昂貴 (ㄤˊ ㄍㄨㄟˋ)
expensive; costly: 這部車子非常昂貴。This car is very expensive.

昂首 (ㄤˊ ㄕㄡˇ)or 昂頭 (ㄤˊ ㄊㄡˊ)
to raise one's head high

昂首闊步 (ㄤˊ ㄕㄡˇ ㄎㄨㄛˋ ㄅㄨˋ)
to stride forward with one's chin up; to stride proudly ahead

昂然 (ㄤˊ ㄖㄢˊ)
proud and bold; haughtily

昂藏 (ㄤˊ ㄘㄤˊ)
tall and elegant; dignified

昂藏六尺之軀 (ㄤˊ ㄘㄤˊ ㄌㄧㄡˋ ㄔˇ ㄓ ㄑㄩ)
a man (connoting pride, dignity, etc.)

昂昂 (ㄤˊ ㄤˊ)
proud and outstanding

昂揚 (ㄤˊ ㄧㄤˊ)
high-spirited

【昃】 2211 ㄗㄜˋ tzeh zè
after noon; afternoon; the sun on the western side of the sky

【昆】 2212 ㄎㄨㄣ kuen kūn
1. an elder brother
2. descendants; posterity
3. multitudes

4. together; in unison

昆布(ㄎㄨㄣ ㄅㄨ)
kelp (*Laminaria japonica*)亦作「海帶」

昆明(ㄎㄨㄣ ㄇㄧㄥ)
Kunming, capital of Yunnan Province

昆明湖(ㄎㄨㄣ ㄇㄧㄥ ㄏㄨ)
the Kunming Lake 亦作「滇池」or「昆明池」

昆明池(ㄎㄨㄣ ㄇㄧㄥ ㄔ)
① the Tien Lake(滇池) ② a man-made lake in Shensi Province, dug by order of Emperor Wu of the Han Dynasty

昆命 or 崑崙(ㄎㄨㄣ ㄌㄨㄣ)
the Kunlun Mountains between Tibet and Sinkiang

昆季(ㄎㄨㄣ ㄐㄧ)
brothers (the elder and younger brothers)

昆曲(ㄎㄨㄣ ㄑㄩ)
① Kun opera ② melodies for Kun opera

昆仲(ㄎㄨㄣ ㄓㄨㄥ)or 昆弟(ㄎㄨㄣ ㄉㄧ)
brothers

昆蟲(ㄎㄨㄣ ㄔㄨㄥ)
insects

昆蟲學(ㄎㄨㄣ ㄔㄨㄥ ㄒㄩㄝ)
entomology

昆蟲學家(ㄎㄨㄣ ㄔㄨㄥ ㄒㄩㄝ ㄐㄧㄚ)
an entomologist

昆玉(ㄎㄨㄣ ㄩ)
(a polite expression) your brothers

【昇】 2213
ㄕㄥ sheng shēng
1. to ascend
2. peace; peaceful
3. a Chinese family name

昇平(ㄕㄥ ㄆㄧㄥ)
time of peace

昇天(ㄕㄥ ㄊㄧㄢ)
① (Taoism) to ascend to heaven after becoming immortal ② (Christianity) the Ascension

昇格(ㄕㄥ ㄍㄜ)
to elevate status; elevation of status

昇汞(ㄕㄥ ㄍㄨㄥ)or(ㄕㄥ ㄏㄨㄥ)
(chemistry) corrosive sublimate; mercuric chloride (HgCl₂)

昇華(ㄕㄥ ㄏㄨㄚ)

① (chemistry) to sublime; sublimation ② the rising of things to a higher level; sublimation; distillation: 藝術是現實生活的昇華。Art is the distillation of real life.

昇級(ㄕㄥ ㄐㄧ)
to promote; to advance to the higher class

昇降(ㄕㄥ ㄐㄧㄤ)
promotion and demotion

昇降機(ㄕㄥ ㄐㄧㄤ ㄐㄧ)
an elevator

【昉】 2214
ㄈㄤ faang fǎng
1. dawn; daybreak
2. beginning

【昊】 2215
ㄏㄠ haw hào
1. summer time
2. the sky; the heavens

昊天(ㄏㄠ ㄊㄧㄢ)
① summer time; the summer season ② the sky; the heavens

昊天上帝(ㄏㄠ ㄊㄧㄢ ㄕㄤ ㄉㄧ)
The Reigning Sovereign in the Heavens

昊天罔極(ㄏㄠ ㄊㄧㄢ ㄨㄤ ㄐㄧ)
(said of parental love) as vast as the boundless heavens

【昌】 2216
ㄔㄤ chang chāng
1. proper; good; straight (talk)
2. prosperous; robust; vigorous; to make prosperous; to glorify
3. light; brightness
4. a Chinese family name

昌明(ㄔㄤ ㄇㄧㄥ)
① to expound and elaborate ② flourishing; advanced; developing: 現代科學昌明。Science is flourishing at the present time. ③ glorious; bright ④ name of a kind of tea produced in Szechwan (四川)

昌大(ㄔㄤ ㄉㄚ)
to increase in greatness; to make prosperous

昌期(ㄔㄤ ㄑㄧ)or 昌期(ㄔㄤ ㄑㄧ)
an era of peace and justice

昌盛(ㄔㄤ ㄕㄥ)
① powerful; prosperous; abundant: 我們的生意越來越昌盛。Our business becomes

more and more prosperous.
② glory

昌辭(ㄔㄤ ㄘ)
beautiful expressions (in writing)

昌言(ㄔㄤ ㄧㄢ)
① proper words or comments ② straight talk

【明】 2217
ㄇㄧㄥ ming míng
1. light; bright; brilliant
2. clear; understandable; to clarify; to understand; obvious; evident
3. intelligent; clever
4. eyesight; the seeing faculty
5. day; daybreak; dawn
6. to state; to show; to assert
7. next (day or year)
8. the Ming Dynasty (1368-1644 A.D.)
9. honest; aboveboard
10. a Chinese family name

明擺著(ㄇㄧㄥ ㄅㄞ ㄓㄜ)
to be clear and evident; obviously

明白(ㄇㄧㄥ ㄅㄞ)
① to understand; to know (a trick, secret, etc.) ② clever and bright; smart ③ clear and evident; obvious

明白了當(ㄇㄧㄥ ㄅㄞ ㄌㄧㄠ ㄉㄤ)
clear-cut; straightforward; distinct

明白人(ㄇㄧㄥ ㄅㄞ ㄖㄣ)
a reasonable person; a considerate person

明版(ㄇㄧㄥ ㄅㄢ)
① a printing plate engraved in the Ming Dynasty 亦作「明板」② a Ming Dynasty edition

明辨是非(ㄇㄧㄥ ㄅㄧㄢ ㄕ ㄈㄟ)
to know distinctly what is right and what is wrong; to make a clear distinction between right and wrong

明碼(ㄇㄧㄥ ㄇㄚ)
① plain code; the ordinary telegraph code ② a listed price

明媒正娶(ㄇㄧㄥ ㄇㄟ ㄓㄥ ㄑㄩ)
a formal wedding or marriage

明媚(ㄇㄧㄥ ㄇㄟ)
fair and enchanting, or bright and charming (scenery, especially referring to

〔日部〕

〔日部〕

springtime): 春日風光明媚。In spring days the landscape is bright and beautiful.

明眸皓齒(ㄇㄧㄥ ㄇㄡˊ ㄏㄠˋ ㄔˇ)
(said of a beautiful woman) with bright eyes and sparkling teeth

明眸善睞(ㄇㄧㄥ ㄇㄡˊ ㄕㄢˋ ㄌㄞˋ)
the enticing glances of a beauty

明滅(ㄇㄧㄥ ㄇㄧㄝˋ)
sometimes in view and sometimes hidden; visible and vanishing(as stars in a cloudy night or fishing lights at sea)

明明(ㄇㄧㄥ ㄇㄧㄥ)
obviously; plainly; undoubtedly: 這明明是他的錯嘛! This is obviously his fault.

明明白白(ㄇㄧㄥ ㄇㄧㄥ ㄅㄞˊ ㄅㄞˊ)
clear; clearly; obviously; evidently

明目張膽(ㄇㄧㄥ ㄇㄨˋ ㄓㄤ ㄉㄢˇ)
(to do some shameful or unlawful acts) openly or shamelessly; without caring about any onlookers; brazenly

明妃(ㄇㄧㄥ ㄈㄟ)
alias Wang Chao-chün (王昭君), a lady at the court of the early Han Dynasty who later married a chieftain of the Huns in the performance of a matrimonial diplomacy

明礬(ㄇㄧㄥ ㄈㄢˊ)
alum

明礬石(ㄇㄧㄥ ㄈㄢˊ ㄕˊ)
alumite

明分(ㄇㄧㄥ ㄈㄣˋ)
an obvious duty or obligation

明達(ㄇㄧㄥ ㄉㄚˊ)
intelligent and broad-minded

明德(ㄇㄧㄥ ㄉㄜˊ)
the highest virtue; illustrious virtu

明代(ㄇㄧㄥ ㄉㄞˋ)
the Ming Dynasty

明燈(ㄇㄧㄥ ㄉㄥ)
a bright lamp; a beacon

明斷(ㄇㄧㄥ ㄉㄨㄢˋ)
a fair and intelligent judgment; an unbiased and wise decision

明太祖(ㄇㄧㄥ ㄊㄞˋ ㄗㄨˇ)
Chu Yüan-chang (朱元璋), the founding emperor of the Ming Dynasty (1328-1398 A. D.)

明堂(ㄇㄧㄥ ㄊㄤˊ)
① a hall where solemn ceremonies were held in ancient China ②(a geomantic term) the place where water gathers before a grave

明天(ㄇㄧㄥ ㄊㄧㄢ)
tomorrow

明駝(ㄇㄧㄥ ㄊㄨㄛˊ)
a camel

明尼蘇達(ㄇㄧㄥ ㄋㄧˊ ㄙㄨ ㄉㄚˊ)
Minnesota, U. S. A.

明年(ㄇㄧㄥ·ㄋㄧㄢ)
next year; the coming year

明來暗往(ㄇㄧㄥ ㄌㄞˊ ㄢˋ ㄨㄤˇ)
to have overt and covert contacts with somebody

明朗(ㄇㄧㄥ ㄌㄤˇ)
① open-minded; straightforward ② to become clear; to clarify: 風雨後, 天色變明朗了。After the storm, the sky became clear.

明理(ㄇㄧㄥ ㄌㄧˇ)
understanding; reasonable

明麗(ㄇㄧㄥ ㄌㄧˋ)
bright and beautiful: 她喜歡明麗的秋色。She likes the bright and beautiful autumn scene.

明瞭(ㄇㄧㄥ ㄌㄧㄠˇ)
① to understand; to get a clear idea (of something): 有些人不能明瞭現代文學。Some people can't understand modern literature. ② clear and evident

明亮(ㄇㄧㄥ ㄌㄧㄤˋ)
bright (eyes, etc.); well-illuminated (rooms, etc.)

明令(ㄇㄧㄥ ㄌㄧㄥˋ)
a written order; a government order or decree

明溝(ㄇㄧㄥ ㄍㄡ)
an open ditch or gutter

明火執仗(ㄇㄧㄥ ㄏㄨㄛˇ ㄓˊ ㄓㄤˋ)
armed robbery committed openly

明慧(ㄇㄧㄥ ㄏㄨㄟˋ)
intelligent or bright

明晃晃(ㄇㄧㄥ·ㄏㄨㄤ ㄏㄨㄤˇ)
bright and shining

明鑑(ㄇㄧㄥ ㄐㄧㄢˋ)
① a clear mirror: 戲劇是人生的明鑑。Drama is the clear mirror of life. ②(your) superb intelligence; (your) penetrating judgment

明經(ㄇㄧㄥ ㄐㄧㄥ)
① a person well versed in Chinese classics ② a title for winners in the imperial examinations in the Ching Dynasty

明淨(ㄇㄧㄥ ㄐㄧㄥˋ)
bright and clean; clear and bright

明鏡高懸(ㄇㄧㄥ ㄐㄧㄥˋ ㄍㄠ ㄒㄩㄢˊ)
(literally) a clear mirror hung on high—perspicuousness or transcending intelligence in judgment

明鏡兒(ㄇㄧㄥ ㄐㄧㄥˋ ㄦˊ)
clear-minded; perspicuous

明器(ㄇㄧㄥ ㄑㄧˋ)
vessels, etc. that are buried with the deceased

明棄暗取(ㄇㄧㄥ ㄑㄧˋ ㄢˋ ㄑㄩˇ)
to discard openly but take secretly

明槍暗箭(ㄇㄧㄥ ㄑㄧㄤ ㄢˋ ㄐㄧㄢˋ)
overt and covert attack

明槍易躲, 暗箭難防(ㄇㄧㄥ ㄑㄧㄤ ㄧˋ ㄉㄨㄛˇ, ㄢˋ ㄐㄧㄢˋ ㄋㄢˊ ㄈㄤˊ)
It's easy to dodge an open attack but difficult to escape from a clandestine one.

明搶(ㄇㄧㄥ ㄑㄧㄤˇ)
open robbery

明確(ㄇㄧㄥ ㄑㄩㄝˋ)
clear and definite; unequivocal (statement, terms, etc.): 我們要求一個明確的答覆。We demand a clear and definite answer

明晰(ㄇㄧㄥ ㄒㄧ)
clear and lucid: 教師給了我們明晰的解釋。The teacher gave us a clear and lucid explanation.

明蝦(ㄇㄧㄥ ㄒㄧㄚ)
a prawn

明曉(ㄇㄧㄥ ㄒㄧㄠˇ·ㄉㄜ)
knowingly; knowing the consequences of doing something; well aware; with the full knowledge that

明效(ㄇㄧㄥ ㄒㄧㄠˋ)
obvious results; telling effects

明修棧道，暗度陳倉（ㄇㄧㄥ ㄒㄧㄡ ㄓㄢ ㄉㄠ，ㄢ ㄉㄨ ㄔㄣ ㄘㄤ）
to feign action in one place and to make the real move in another

明顯（ㄇㄧㄥ ㄒㄧㄢˇ）
evident; obvious; clear; distinct: 這很明顯是他缺席的藉口。This is evidently a pretext for his absence.

明心迹（ㄇㄧㄥ ㄒㄧㄣ ㄐㄧˋ）
to tell what's in one's mind; to get (one's purpose, intention, etc.) off one's chest

明心見性（ㄇㄧㄥ ㄒㄧㄣ ㄐㄧㄢˋ ㄒㄧㄥˋ）
to enlighten the mind and realize the Buddha-nature immanent in all beings

明信片（ㄇㄧㄥ ㄒㄧㄣˋ ㄆㄧㄢˋ）
a postcard; a postal card

明星（ㄇㄧㄥ ㄒㄧㄥ）
①a bright star ②a movie star ③Venus

明知（ㄇㄧㄥ ㄓ）
to know perfectly well; to be fully aware

明知故犯（ㄇㄧㄥ ㄓ ㄍㄨˋ ㄈㄢˋ）
to commit a crime, mistake, etc. intentionally; to run a risk, etc. even though one knows what's in store for him

明知故問（ㄇㄧㄥ ㄓ ㄍㄨˋ ㄨㄣˋ）
to ask about something one already knows

明志（ㄇㄧㄥ ㄓˋ）
to state one's own views, attitude, ambition, etc: 這位詩人寫這首詩以明志。The poet wrote this poem to state his ambition.

明智（ㄇㄧㄥ ㄓˋ）
sensible; sagacious; wise

明智之舉（ㄇㄧㄥ ㄓˋ ㄓ ㄐㄩˇ）
a wise move; an intelligent or sensible act

明治天皇（ㄇㄧㄥ ㄓˋ ㄊㄧㄢ ㄏㄨㄤˊ）
Emperor Mutsuhito of Japan whose reign, Meiji, extended from 1867 to 1912

明治維新（ㄇㄧㄥ ㄓˋ ㄨㄟˊ ㄒㄧㄣ）
the Meiji restoration, which marked the beginning of Japan's modernization

明哲（ㄇㄧㄥ ㄓㄜˊ）
a wise and virtuous person

明哲保身（ㄇㄧㄥ ㄓㄜˊ ㄅㄠˇ ㄕㄣ）
(often said of people living under tyranny) A wise person who knows what's best for himself can safeguard his personal security. 或to be worldly wise and play safe

明徵（ㄇㄧㄥ ㄓㄥ）
evident signs: 烏雲是天雨的明徵嗎? Are dark clouds the evident signs of rain?

明爭暗鬥（ㄇㄧㄥ ㄓㄥ ㄢˋ ㄉㄡˋ）
to fight overtly and covertly (often said of intramural fights)

明證（ㄇㄧㄥ ㄓㄥˋ）
irrefutable proof or evidence

明正典刑（ㄇㄧㄥ ㄓㄥˋ ㄉㄧㄢˇ ㄒㄧㄥˊ）
to execute (a criminal) openly

明珠（ㄇㄧㄥ ㄓㄨ）
①a glossy pearl ②a person of rare ability ③a beloved daughter: 她是父母的掌上明珠。She is her parents' beloved daughter.

明珠彈雀（ㄇㄧㄥ ㄓㄨ ㄊㄢˊ ㄑㄩㄝˋ）
(literally) to kill a bird with a valuable pearl—to attain an insignificant goal by costly means

明珠出老蚌（ㄇㄧㄥ ㄓㄨ ㄔㄨ ㄌㄠˇ ㄅㄤˋ）
an old couple blessed with the birth of a child

明珠入抱（ㄇㄧㄥ ㄓㄨ ㄖㄨˋ ㄅㄠˋ）
an expression for congratulating a friend on the birth of a daughter

明珠暗投（ㄇㄧㄥ ㄓㄨ ㄢˋ ㄊㄡˊ）
①to have talent but cannot find the right employment ②to take a job that's well below one's ability ③a good person joining a gang of villains

明主（ㄇㄧㄥ ㄓㄨˇ）
an enlightened ruler

明恥教戰（ㄇㄧㄥ ㄔˇ ㄐㄧㄠ ㄓㄢˋ）
to teach people ways of war to defend national honor; to train people for recovery of a lost territory

明察（ㄇㄧㄥ ㄔㄚˊ）
to be sharp and perspicacious; not to be fooled or taken in

明察秋毫（ㄇㄧㄥ ㄔㄚˊ ㄑㄧㄡ ㄏㄠˊ）
able to examine the tiniest things (as the tip of a hair)—sharp discerning intelligence

明查暗訪（ㄇㄧㄥ ㄔㄚˊ ㄢˋ ㄈㄤˇ）
to investigate openly and secretly

明澈（ㄇㄧㄥ ㄔㄜˋ）
bright and limpid; transparent

明澈如鏡（ㄇㄧㄥ ㄔㄜˋ ㄖㄨˊ ㄐㄧㄥˋ）
to be like a mirror: 湖水明澈如鏡。The lake is like a mirror.

明朝（ㄇㄧㄥ ㄔㄠˊ）
the Ming Dynasty (1368-1644 A.D.)

明成祖（ㄇㄧㄥ ㄔㄥˊ ㄗㄨˇ）
Chu Ti (朱棣), 1359-1424 A.D., the third emperor of the Ming Dynasty, who usurped the throne from his nephew

明窗淨几（ㄇㄧㄥ ㄔㄨㄤ ㄐㄧˋ ㄐㄧˇ）
a neat and well-lighted house or room

明史（ㄇㄧㄥ ㄕˇ）
the History of the Ming Dynasty, authored by Chang Ting-yü (張廷玉) and others of the Ching Dynasty under the imperial order, containing some 336 volumes

明示（ㄇㄧㄥ ㄕˋ）
clear indication; to express clearly

明室（ㄇㄧㄥ ㄕˋ）
①a well-lighted room ②the Ming Dynasty

明升暗降（ㄇㄧㄥ ㄕㄥ ㄢˋ ㄐㄧㄤˋ）
a promotion in appearance but a demotion in fact; to kick upstairs

明說（ㄇㄧㄥ ㄕㄨㄛ）
to speak frankly; to speak up

明日（ㄇㄧㄥ ㄖˋ）or 明兒（ㄇㄧㄥ ㄦˊ）
①tomorrow ②one of these days; some day

明日黃花（ㄇㄧㄥ ㄖˋ ㄏㄨㄤˊ ㄏㄨㄚ）
①outmoded; obsolete; out of fashion: 這種款式已成明日黃花。This fashion has already become outmoded. ②what has already taken place

明人不做暗事（ㄇㄧㄥ ㄖㄣˊ ㄅㄨˋ ㄗㄨㄛˋ ㄢˋ ㄕˋ）

〔日部〕

ㄋㄢˊ)
An honest man does not engage in clandestine dealings.

明若觀火(ㄇㄧㄥˊ ㄖㄨㄛˋ 《ㄨㄢ ㄏㄨㄛˇ)
as obvious as a glowing fire

明暗(ㄇㄧㄥˊ ㄢˋ)
brightness and darkness

明言(ㄇㄧㄥˊ ㄧㄢˊ)
to state clearly; to speak out

明朗人(ㄇㄧㄥˊ ㄌㄤˇ ㄖㄣˊ)
a man of clear mind and high intelligence

明瓦(ㄇㄧㄥˊ ㄨㄚˇ)
transparent tiles

明文規定(ㄇㄧㄥˊ ㄨㄣˊ 《ㄨㄟ ㄉㄧㄥˋ)
in black and white; clearly stipulated in regulations, laws, contracts, etc.

明王(ㄇㄧㄥˊ ㄨㄤˊ)
①an enlightened ruler ②(Buddhism) the rajas, mingwang or fierce spirits

【昏】 2218
ㄏㄨㄣ huen hūn
1. dusk; dark
2. confused; muddled; mixed-up; demented
3. unclear of sight; dizzy
4. (now rarely) same as婚—to marry
5. a Chinese family name

昏憊(ㄏㄨㄣ ㄅㄟˋ)
dog-tired

昏昧(ㄏㄨㄣ ㄇㄟˋ)or 昏愚(ㄏㄨㄣ ㄩˊ)
stupid; stupidity

昏迷(ㄏㄨㄣ ㄇㄧˊ)
in a coma; unconscious; delirious; stupor

昏明(ㄏㄨㄣ ㄇㄧㄥˊ)
day and night

昏倒(ㄏㄨㄣ ㄉㄠˇ)
to faint; to swoon: 她一看見血便昏倒. She swoons at the sight of blood.

昏定晨省(ㄏㄨㄣ ㄉㄧㄥˋ ㄔㄣˊ ㄒㄧㄥˇ)
to inquire after one's parents in the morning and evening—duties of a filial son; to visit or care for one's parents day and night

昏頭昏腦(ㄏㄨㄣ ㄊㄡˊ ㄏㄨㄣ ㄋㄠˇ)
to feel dizzy, confused, and mixed-up

昏天黑地(ㄏㄨㄣ ㄊㄧㄢ ㄏㄟ ㄉㄧˋ)
①very dark (as before a

storm) ②stupid or ignorant ③dizzy

昏亂(ㄏㄨㄣ ㄌㄨㄢˋ)
stupid and confused; muddled and delirious

昏聵(ㄏㄨㄣ ㄎㄨㄟˋ)
(literally) to be poor of vision and hard of hearing—muddled, confused and dizzy

昏黑(ㄏㄨㄣ ㄏㄟ)
dark

昏花(ㄏㄨㄣ ㄏㄨㄚ)
poor of vision; dim-sighted; indistinct vision: 老眼昏花 dim-sighted from old age

昏昏(ㄏㄨㄣ ㄏㄨㄣ)
slumberous

昏昏沉沉(ㄏㄨㄣ ㄏㄨㄣ ㄔㄣˊ ㄔㄣˊ)
dizzy and sleepy; slumberous

昏昏欲睡(ㄏㄨㄣ ㄏㄨㄣ ㄩˋ ㄕㄨㄟˋ)
drowsy; sleepy: 今天下午我昏昏欲睡. I was sleepy this afternoon.

昏黃(ㄏㄨㄣ ㄏㄨㄤˊ)
twilight; dim: 他在昏黃的燈光下看書. He read by a dim light.

昏厥(ㄏㄨㄣ ㄐㄩㄝˊ)
to faint; to swoon: 她突然昏厥過去. All of a sudden she fainted away.

昏君(ㄏㄨㄣ ㄐㄩㄣ)
a muddle-headed monarch

昏曉(ㄏㄨㄣ ㄒㄧㄠˇ)
morning and evening

昏眩(ㄏㄨㄣ ㄒㄩㄢˋ)
dizzy; faint; giddy

昏睡(ㄏㄨㄣ ㄕㄨㄟˋ)
deep slumber; lethargic sleep

昏暗(ㄏㄨㄣ ㄢˋ)
dim; dusky

昏暈(ㄏㄨㄣ ㄩㄣ)
dizzy; faint

昏庸(ㄏㄨㄣ ㄩㄥ)or 昏愚(ㄏㄨㄣ ㄩˊ)
stupid; imbecile; muddle-headed

【易】 2219
ㄧˋ yih yì
1. to exchange; to barter
2. to change (places, jobs, owners, etc.)
3. easy
4. amiable; lenient
5. the Book of Changes
6. a Chinese family name

易北河(ㄧˋ ㄅㄟˇ ㄏㄜˊ)

the Elbe River in Europe

易卜生(ㄧˋ ㄅㄨˇ ㄕㄥ)
Henrik Ibsen, 1828-1906, Norwegian playwright and poet

易名(ㄧˋ ㄇㄧㄥˊ)
①to change one's names ②to give a posthumous title to a person

易發難制(ㄧˋ ㄈㄚ ㄋㄢˊ ㄓˋ)
It's easier to start something than to stop it.

易放難收(ㄧˋ ㄈㄤˋ ㄋㄢˊ ㄕㄡ)
It's easier to indulge in an expensive habit than to get rid of it.

易得者易失(ㄧˋ ㄉㄜˊ ㄓㄜˇ ㄧˋ ㄕ)
Easy get, easy lose. 或Easy come, easy go.

易地皆然(ㄧˋ ㄉㄧˋ ㄐㄧㄝ ㄖㄢˊ)
(said of a universal practice, principle, etc.) It's the same everywhere.

易地而處(ㄧˋ ㄉㄧˋ ㄦˊ ㄔㄨˇ)
to look at a matter from the other fellow's viewpoint

易怒(ㄧˋ ㄋㄨˋ)
prone to anger; irascible

易開罐(ㄧˋ ㄎㄞ ㄍㄨㄢˋ)
a ring-pull can

易經(ㄧˋ ㄐㄧㄥ)
the Book of Changes

易曉(ㄧˋ ㄒㄧㄠˇ)
clear and intelligible; easy to understand: 他的解釋明白易曉. His explanation is clear and intelligible.

易行(ㄧˋ ㄒㄧㄥˊ)
easy to practice; easy to do: 這計畫簡便易行. This project is simple and easy to do.

易姓(ㄧˋ ㄒㄧㄥˋ)
①to change one's family name ②(in old China) to change dynasties

易學難精(ㄧˋ ㄒㄩㄝˊ ㄋㄢˊ ㄐㄧㄥ)
easy to learn but difficult to master: 英語易學難精. English is easy to learn but difficult to master.

易幟(ㄧˋ ㄓˋ)
(said of a city or strategic point) to change hands

易主(ㄧˋ ㄓㄨˇ)
to change owners or masters

易轍(ㄧˋ ㄔㄜˋ)
to renovate; to make a dras-

tic change

易手（ㄧˋ ㄕㄡˇ）
to change hands

易水（ㄧˋ ㄕㄨㄟˇ）
the I River in Hopeh Province

易水歌（ㄧˋ ㄕㄨㄟˇ ㄍㄜ）
the *Song of the I River*
(when Ching Ko (荆軻) was
sent to Chin (秦) to assassinate its tyrant, Shih-huang
(始皇), he was sent off with
the *Song of the I River*,
which reads: "The winds
heave as the I River turns
cold. The hero goes away
and return he will not.")

易燃物（ㄧˋ ㄖㄢˊ ㄨˋ）
combustibles; inflammables

易人（ㄧˋ ㄖㄣˊ）
to change a person (for a job)

易如反掌（ㄧˋ ㄖㄨˊ ㄈㄢˇ ㄓㄤˇ）
as easy as turning over the
palm of one's hand: 解答這個
問題易如反掌。To answer this
question is as easy as turning over the palm of one's
hand.

易子而食（ㄧˋ ㄗˇ ㄦˊ ㄕˊ）
(said of people during
severe famines) to exchange
children for eating

易俗（ㄧˋ ㄙㄨˊ）
to change practices or customs; to reform customs or
practices

易（ㄧˋ ㄧˋ）
very easy

易牙（ㄧˋ ㄧㄚˊ）
I Yah, a famous culinary
artist in the Epoch of
Spring and Autumn

易言之（ㄧˋ ㄧㄢˊ ㄓ）
in other words

易位（ㄧˋ ㄨㄟˋ）
① to change places or positions; to transpose ② to
dethrone

易於進行（ㄧˋ ㄩˊ ㄐㄧㄣˋ ㄒㄧㄥˊ）
easy to proceed; easy to
manage: 這項計畫易於進行。
The plan is easy to proceed.

易與（ㄧˋ ㄩˇ）
(said of a person) easy to
cope with; easy to get along
with

【昔】 2220　ㄒㄧ　shyi xí
1. bygone; of old; formerly;
ancient
2. a night; an evening
3. the end

昔年（ㄒㄧ ㄋㄧㄢˊ）
bygone years; past years;
former years

昔酒（ㄒㄧ ㄐㄧㄡˇ）
old wine; vintage wine

昔昔（ㄒㄧ ㄒㄧ）
every night 亦作「夕夕」

昔賢（ㄒㄧ ㄒㄧㄢˊ）
ancient sages

昔者（ㄒㄧ ㄓㄜˇ）
in former times; in ancient
times; before; formerly

昔時（ㄒㄧ ㄕˊ）
in former times; in the olden days

昔日（ㄒㄧ ㄖˋ）
in the olden days; in former
days (or times)

昔人（ㄒㄧ ㄖㄣˊ）
the ancient people

昔歲（ㄒㄧ ㄙㄨㄟˋ）
last year

【昕】 2221　ㄒㄧㄣ　shin xīn
daybreak; dawn

昕夕從公（ㄒㄧㄣ ㄒㄧ ㄘㄨㄥˊ ㄍㄨㄥ）
to devote oneself to official
duties day and night

【昀】 2222　ㄩㄣˊ　yun yún
1. daybreak; sunrise; dawn
2. sunshine

五畫

【星】 2223　ㄒㄧㄥ　shing xīng
1. any heavenly body that
shines; stars, planets, satellites, etc.
2. a spark or sparks
3. droplets; small particles of
anything; very tiny
4. name of one of the 28 constellations
5. a movie star
6. by night; nocturnal
7. an ancient percussion musical instrument consisting of
two or more brass-cup-like
pieces played by hitting
them against one another

8. a Chinese family name

星奔（ㄒㄧㄥ ㄅㄣ）
to travel, run away or
escape by night

星卜（ㄒㄧㄥ ㄅㄨˇ）
astrology and divination

星眸（ㄒㄧㄥ ㄇㄡˊ）
starry eyes; bright eyes

星芒狀（ㄒㄧㄥ ㄇㄤˊ ㄓㄨㄤˋ）
resembling a star-polygon

星命（ㄒㄧㄥ ㄇㄧㄥˋ）
astrology

星發（ㄒㄧㄥ ㄈㄚ）
to start out by night

星斗（ㄒㄧㄥ ㄉㄡˇ）
stars; heavenly bodies

星等（ㄒㄧㄥ ㄉㄥˇ）
(astronomy) visual magnitude; apparent magnitude

星探（ㄒㄧㄥ ㄊㄢˋ）
a talent scout in the movie
industry

星條旗（ㄒㄧㄥ ㄊㄧㄠˊ ㄑㄧˊ）
Stars and Stripes—the
national flag of the United
States

星團（ㄒㄧㄥ ㄊㄨㄢˊ）
(astronomy) a constellation;
a cluster

星離雨散（ㄒㄧㄥ ㄌㄧˊ ㄩˇ ㄙㄢˋ）
to separate and disperse rapidly

星曆（ㄒㄧㄥ ㄌㄧˋ）
the sidereal calendar

星列（ㄒㄧㄥ ㄌㄧㄝˋ）
arrayed like stars

星流（ㄒㄧㄥ ㄌㄧㄡˊ）
to act quickly—like a comet

星羅棋布（ㄒㄧㄥ ㄌㄨㄛˊ ㄑㄧˊ ㄅㄨˋ）
numerous and arrayed like
stars in heaven or pieces on
a chessboard (usually said
of archipelagos, etc.)

星光（ㄒㄧㄥ ㄍㄨㄤ）
starlight: 她為星光閃閃的夜晚
外出散步。She went out for a
walk on the starlight night.

星光燦爛（ㄒㄧㄥ ㄍㄨㄤ ㄘㄢˋ ㄌㄢˋ）
a star-studded gathering

星河（ㄒㄧㄥ ㄏㄜˊ）
(astronomy) the Milky Way

星號（ㄒㄧㄥ ㄏㄠˋ）
an asterisk (☆)

星漢（ㄒㄧㄥ ㄏㄢˋ）
the stars; the Milky Way

星火（ㄒㄧㄥ ㄏㄨㄛˇ）

〔日
部〕

〔日部〕

①a very urgent matter ②a spark; a small fire

星週(ㄒㄧㄥ ㄏㄨㄟˋ)
(literally) when the stars return to their old positions —A year has elapsed.

星際旅行(ㄒㄧㄥ ㄐㄧˋ ㄌㄩˇ ㄒㄧㄥˊ)
interstellar travel; space travel: 這部電影描寫星際旅行. This movie describes space travel.

星家(ㄒㄧㄥ ㄐㄧㄚ)
an astrologist

星加坡(ㄒㄧㄥ ㄐㄧㄚ ㄆㄛ)
Singapore 亦作「新加坡」or「星洲」or「星島」

星期(ㄒㄧㄥ ㄑㄧˊ)
week: 她將於一個星期後到達. She will arrive here in a week.

星期六(ㄒㄧㄥ ㄑㄧˊ ㄌㄧㄡˋ)
Saturday: 星期六是一週的第七天. Saturday is the seventh day of the week.

星期日(ㄒㄧㄥ ㄑㄧˊ ㄖˋ)or星期天(ㄒㄧㄥ ㄑㄧˊ ㄊㄧㄢ)
Sunday

星期四(ㄒㄧㄥ ㄑㄧˊ ㄙˋ)
Thursday

星期三(ㄒㄧㄥ ㄑㄧˊ ㄙㄢ)
Wednesday

星期二(ㄒㄧㄥ ㄑㄧˊ ㄦˋ)
Tuesday

星期一(ㄒㄧㄥ ㄑㄧˊ ㄧ)
Monday

星期五(ㄒㄧㄥ ㄑㄧˊ ㄨˇ)
Friday

星球(ㄒㄧㄥ ㄑㄧㄡˊ)
planets; stars: 地球是一個星球. The Earth is a planet.

星叢(ㄒㄧㄥ ㄘㄨㄥˊ)
a group of stars; a constellation

星系(ㄒㄧㄥ ㄒㄧˋ)
(astronomy) a galaxy: 星系團 a cluster of galaxies

星宿
①(ㄒㄧㄥ ㄒㄧㄡˋ) planets or stars in heaven; constellations: 十二星宿 the twelve constellations
②(ㄒㄧㄥ ㄙㄨˋ) a person who is considered an incarnation of a star

星宿海(ㄒㄧㄥ ㄒㄧㄡˋ ㄏㄞˇ)
name of a place in Chinghai,

formerly believed to be the source of the Yellow River, the second largest river in China

星象(ㄒㄧㄥ ㄒㄧㄤˋ)
to divine according to the brightness, dimness, etc. of stars—astrology

星象學(ㄒㄧㄥ ㄒㄧㄤˋ ㄒㄩㄝˊ)
astrometry 亦作「天體測定學」or「測天學」

星星
①(ㄒㄧㄥ ㄒㄧㄥ) spots, specks; a hint of grey (in the hair, etc.): 昨晚天空晴朗, 一星星雲彩也沒有. Last night the sky was clear and bright without a speck of cloud.
②(ㄒㄧㄥ ·ㄒㄧㄥ) stars, planets and satellites

星星點點(ㄒㄧㄥ ㄒㄧㄥ ㄉㄧㄢˇ ㄉㄧㄢˇ)
droplets and particles; tiny and small amounts; bit by bit; a bit

星星之火可以燎原(ㄒㄧㄥ ㄒㄧㄥ ㄓ ㄏㄨㄛˇ ㄎㄜˇ ㄧˇ ㄌㄧㄠˊ ㄩㄢˊ)
(literally) A spark may cause a conflagration. —Small things may cause big trouble.

星形(ㄒㄧㄥ ㄒㄧㄥˊ)
a star-polygon

星占學(ㄒㄧㄥ ㄓㄢ ㄒㄩㄝˊ)
astrology 亦作「占星學」or「星學」

星馳(ㄒㄧㄥ ㄔˊ)
to travel very fast like a shooting star

星辰(ㄒㄧㄥ ㄔㄣˊ)
stars; heavenly bodies

星士(ㄒㄧㄥ ㄕˋ)
an astrologist

星霜(ㄒㄧㄥ ㄕㄨㄤ)
①a whole year ②time (in terms of years)

星子(ㄒㄧㄥ ·ㄗ)or星兒(ㄒㄧㄥ ㄦ)
tiny bits, droplets or particles

星座(ㄒㄧㄥ ㄗㄨㄛˋ)
(astronomy) a constellation; a star and its satellites

星散(ㄒㄧㄥ ㄙㄢˇ)
to scatter and spread like stars

星移斗轉(ㄒㄧㄥ ㄧˊ ㄉㄡˇ ㄓㄨㄢˇ)
①A night has passed. ② the movements of the stars—the

flight of time

星翳(ㄒㄧㄥ ㄧˋ)
white spots on the cornea

星夜(ㄒㄧㄥ ㄧㄝˋ)
①night; a starlit night ②(to travel, escape, etc.) by night; by starlight

星夜奔馳(ㄒㄧㄥ ㄧㄝˋ ㄅㄣ ㄔˊ)
to travel urgently by night

星月交輝(ㄒㄧㄥ ㄩㄝˋ ㄐㄧㄠ ㄏㄨㄟ)
(literally) The moon and the stars vie for brilliance. —any gathering or congregation of famous or august personalities

星雲(ㄒㄧㄥ ㄩㄣˊ)
(astronomy) a nebula

星殞(ㄒㄧㄥ ㄩㄣˇ)
①the falling of meteoroid to the earth ②the death of a movie star or important personality

【映】 2224
(ㄧㄥˋ yìng yīng)

1. to mirror; to reflect; a reflection
2. to project (slides, pictures, etc.)
3. to shine; shining; to blind; blinding (glare, light, etc.)

映帶(ㄧㄥˋ ㄉㄞˋ)
(said of a beautiful natural scene) mountains, lakes, trees, flowers, etc. in their perspective that merge together to form an enchanting sight

映奪(ㄧㄥˋ ㄉㄨㄛˊ)
to dazzle or catch (the eyes)

映象(ㄧㄥˋ ㄒㄧㄤˋ)
image

映雪讀書(ㄧㄥˋ ㄒㄩㄝˇ ㄉㄨˊ ㄕㄨ)
to study by the glare of snow (said of Sun Kang (孫康), a poor scholar of the Tsin Dynasty)

映照(ㄧㄥˋ ㄓㄠˋ)
to shine and reflect; to combine to make a pretty scene; bright and shining

映襯(ㄧㄥˋ ㄔㄣˋ)
to set off

映山紅(ㄧㄥˋ ㄕㄢ ㄏㄨㄥˊ)
azaleas 亦作「杜鵑花」

映日(ㄧㄥˋ ㄖˋ)
bright sunlight

映眼(ㄧㄥˋ ㄧㄢˇ)

dazzling; glaring

映演 (1ㄥˋ 1ㄢˇ)
to project (a film or slide on the screen)

【春】 2225
ㄔㄨㄣ chuen chūn
1. spring, the first of the four seasons
2. sensuality; lustful; lewd; pornographic
3. alive; vitality; living: 枯木逢春. A withered tree comes to life again.
4. joyful
5. youth: 她善於保養她的青春. She keeps her youth well.
6. wine (especially in the Tang Dynasty)

春榜 (ㄔㄨㄣ ㄅㄤˇ)
the announcement of successful candidates for the national civil service examination (進士) in ancient China, which usually took place in spring

春冰 (ㄔㄨㄣ ㄅ1ㄥ)
(literally) spring ice—thin ice, implying a dangerous situation

春餅 (ㄔㄨㄣ ㄅ1ㄥˇ)
thin pancake (usually eaten in spring festivals)

春忙 (ㄔㄨㄣ ㄇㄤˊ)
the planting season

春夢 (ㄔㄨㄣ ㄇㄥˋ)
(literally) a spring dream—something that is illusory and transient

春夢無痕 (ㄔㄨㄣ ㄇㄥˋ ㄨˊ ㄏㄣˊ)
(literally) the traceless dream of spring—something that vanishes without leaving a trace

春分 (ㄔㄨㄣ ㄈㄣ)
the vernal equinox, about March 21

春方 (ㄔㄨㄣ ㄈㄤ)
aphrodisiacs; drugs that stimulate sexual desires

春風 (ㄔㄨㄣ ㄈㄥ)
① spring breezes ② good education ③ sexual intercourse ④ favor; grace ⑤ happy smiles

春風滿面 (ㄔㄨㄣ ㄈㄥ ㄇㄢˇ ㄇ1ㄢˋ)
to smile broadly; a cheerful look

春風風人 (ㄔㄨㄣ ㄈㄥ ㄈㄥ ㄖㄣˊ)
grace that has spread to all; benefits that are enjoyed by people far and wide

春風得意 (ㄔㄨㄣ ㄈㄥ ㄉㄜˊ 1ˋ)
to attain a high official rank; to ride on the crest of success

春風化雨 (ㄔㄨㄣ ㄈㄥ ㄏㄨㄚˋ ㄩˇ)
education of the young; salutary influence of education

春一度 (ㄔㄨㄣ 1 ㄉㄨˋ)
sexual intercourse

春臺 (ㄔㄨㄣ ㄊㄞˊ)
① peaceful and prosperous time ② (in ancient China) the Department of Rites ③ a dining table

春條兒 (ㄔㄨㄣ ㄊ1ㄠˊㄦ)
lucky sayings or words written on red paper hung or pasted at the doorway of a newly opened store, etc. 參看「春聯」

春天 (ㄔㄨㄣ ㄊ1ㄢ)
spring; springtime

春牛 (ㄔㄨㄣ ㄋ1ㄡˊ)
(an old Chinese custom) the Spring Ox made of clay to usher in spring

春暖花開 (ㄔㄨㄣ ㄋㄨㄢˇ ㄏㄨㄚ ㄎㄞ)
During the warmth of spring all the flowers bloom.

春女 (ㄔㄨㄣ ㄋㄩˇ)
young girls who entertain romantic thoughts

春雷 (ㄔㄨㄣ ㄌㄟˊ)
spring thunder (which is believed to awaken the wildlife from hibernation)

春蘭秋菊 (ㄔㄨㄣ ㄌㄢˊ ㄑ1ㄡ ㄐㄩˊ)
(literally) spring orchids and autumn chrysanthemums—① things grown or done at the right time ② Everything has its own proud days.

春聯 (ㄔㄨㄣ ㄌ1ㄢˊ)
New Year's couplets written on strips of red paper and pasted on doors (usually containing words of luck)

春霖 (ㄔㄨㄣ ㄌ1ㄣˊ)
spring rains; spring showers: 春霖有利於耕種. Spring rains benefit farming.

春露秋霜 (ㄔㄨㄣ ㄌㄨˋ ㄑ1ㄡ ㄕㄨㄤ)
① grace and severity ② the

flight of time

春羅 (ㄔㄨㄣ ㄌㄨㄛˊ)
a variety of silk goods

春耕 (ㄔㄨㄣ ㄍㄥ)
spring cultivation: 農夫們忙於春耕. The farmers were busy with spring cultivation.

春官 (ㄔㄨㄣ ㄍㄨㄢ)
(in the Chou Dynasty) the official in charge of rites

春光 (ㄔㄨㄣ ㄍㄨㄤ)
① spring scenes (natural charms in spring) ② lustful scenes—a sexual act

春光明媚 (ㄔㄨㄣ ㄍㄨㄤ ㄇ1ㄥˊ ㄇㄟˋ)
a sunlit and enchanting scene of spring

春光洩漏 (ㄔㄨㄣ ㄍㄨㄤ ㄒ1ㄝˋ ㄌㄡˋ)
An illicit affair became known.

春宮 (ㄔㄨㄣ ㄍㄨㄥ)
① pornographic pictures, drawings, etc. ② living quarters of the crown prince

春宮圖 (ㄔㄨㄣ ㄍㄨㄥ ㄊㄨˊ) or 春畫 (ㄔㄨㄣ ㄏㄨㄚˋ)
pornographic drawings

春困秋乏 (ㄔㄨㄣ ㄎㄨㄣˋ ㄑ1ㄡ ㄈㄚˊ)
One feels dizziness in spring and fatigue in autumn.

春寒料峭 (ㄔㄨㄣ ㄏㄢˊ ㄌ1ㄠˋ ㄑ1ㄠˋ)
the chill of early spring

春華 (ㄔㄨㄣ ㄏㄨㄚˊ)
flowers in spring—youthhood 亦作「春花」

春華秋實 (ㄔㄨㄣ ㄏㄨㄚˊ ㄑ1ㄡ ㄕˊ)
(literally) spring flowers and autumn fruits—showy appearance and virtuous substance

春花秋月 (ㄔㄨㄣ ㄏㄨㄚ ㄑ1ㄡ ㄩㄝˋ)
(literally) the spring flowers and the autumn moon—① the best things at the best time ② flight of time

春暉 (ㄔㄨㄣ ㄏㄨㄟ)
the light of the spring sun —parental love and care

春回大地 (ㄔㄨㄣ ㄏㄨㄟˊ ㄉㄚˋ ㄉ1ˋ)
Spring returns to the good earth.

春紅 (ㄔㄨㄣ ㄏㄨㄥˊ)
the flowers of spring

春季 (ㄔㄨㄣ ㄐ1ˋ)
spring

春祭 (ㄔㄨㄣ ㄐ1ˋ)

〔日部〕

春假(ㄔㄨㄣ ㄐㄧㄚˋ)
spring holidays; the spring
vacation

[日部]

春節(ㄔㄨㄣ ㄐㄧㄝˊ)
the Lunar New Year Festi-
val; the Lunar New Year's
holidays

春酒(ㄔㄨㄣ ㄐㄧㄡˇ)
feasts during the Lunar New
Year's holidays

春景(ㄔㄨㄣ ㄐㄧㄥˇ)
the beautiful scenes of
spring

春捲(ㄔㄨㄣ ㄐㄩㄢˇ)
spring rolls (meat and vegetables rolled with thin cakes
eaten as a snack)

春期(ㄔㄨㄣ ㄑㄧˊ)
puberty

春祈秋報(ㄔㄨㄣ ㄑㄧˊ ㄑㄧㄡ ㄅㄠˋ)
(in the Book of Rites) to
pray (for rain) in spring
and offer thanks (for crops)
in fall

春氣(ㄔㄨㄣ ㄑㄧˋ)
warmth given by the spring
sun—that stimulates growth
and ardor of youth

春秋(ㄔㄨㄣ ㄑㄧㄡ)
①a year; a full round of the
seasons ②spring and
autumn ③age ④annals of
any state during the period
of Warring States ⑤Spring
and Autumn Annals—a his-
tory by Confucius, based on
the annals of the state of Lu
(722-481B.C.) ⑥annals; history

春秋筆削(ㄔㄨㄣ ㄑㄧㄡ ㄅㄧˇ ㄒㄩㄝˋ)
(said of a chronicle writer)
to be keen, honest and strict
in observing and judging
things or people

春秋鼎盛(ㄔㄨㄣ ㄑㄧㄡ ㄉㄧㄥˇ ㄕㄥˋ)
in the prime of one's life

春秋時代(ㄔㄨㄣ ㄑㄧㄡ ㄕˊ ㄉㄞˋ)
the Epoch of Spring and
Autumn, approximately from
770 to 403 B. C.

春情(ㄔㄨㄣ ㄑㄧㄥˊ)
sexual desire; the longing
for the opposite sex

春情發動期(ㄔㄨㄣ ㄑㄧㄥˊ ㄈㄚ ㄉㄨㄥˋ ㄑㄧˊ)
puberty

春禊(ㄔㄨㄣ ㄒㄧˋ)
(in ancient China) a gathering by the waterside in
lunar March, where people
tried to wash away their
bad luck

春宵(ㄔㄨㄣ ㄒㄧㄠ)
①spring nights ②night rendezvous between lovers; a
wedding night

春宵苦短(ㄔㄨㄣ ㄒㄧㄠ ㄎㄨˇ ㄉㄨㄢˇ)
The night of rendezvous is
always too short (to the
lovers). 或The wedding
night is always too short (to
the newlyweds).

春宵一刻值千金(ㄔㄨㄣ ㄒㄧㄠ ㄧ ㄎㄜˋ ㄓˊ ㄑㄧㄢ ㄐㄧㄣ)
One minute in a night of
rendezvous is worth a thousand pieces of gold. 或Every
minute of the wedding night
is precious.

春晚(ㄔㄨㄣ ㄨㄢˇ)
morning in spring

春心(ㄔㄨㄣ ㄒㄧㄣ)
lustful thoughts; spring
desire

春心蕩漾(ㄔㄨㄣ ㄒㄧㄣ ㄉㄤˋ ㄧㄤˋ)
the surging of lustful desire

春汛(ㄔㄨㄣ ㄒㄩㄣˋ)
the spring flood (especially
referring to the spring inundation of the Yellow River)

春裝(ㄔㄨㄣ ㄓㄨㄤ)
spring clothes; the spring
fashion

春愁秋思(ㄔㄨㄣ ㄔㄡˊ ㄑㄧㄡ ㄙ)
spring longings and autumn
thoughts

春試(ㄔㄨㄣ ㄕˋ)or 春闈(ㄔㄨㄣ ㄨㄟˊ)
(in ancient China) the national civil service examination which usually took
place in spring

春事(ㄔㄨㄣ ㄕˋ)
spring planting

春申君(ㄔㄨㄣ ㄕㄣ ㄐㄩㄣ)
a title of Prime Minister
Huang Hsieh (黃歇) of Chu
during the period of War-
ring States

春聲(ㄔㄨㄣ ㄕㄥ)
the chirping of birds and
gurgling of streams heard in
spring

春色(ㄔㄨㄣ ㄙㄜˋ)
①spring scenery ②a joyful
appearance or expression ③
sensual or carnal scenes

春色惱人(ㄔㄨㄣ ㄙㄜˋ ㄋㄠˇ ㄖㄣˊ)
The scenes of spring are
really distracting.

春筍(ㄔㄨㄣ ㄙㄨㄣˇ)
young woman's fingers (likened to the delicate, tender
and slender spring bamboo
shoots)

春意(ㄔㄨㄣ ㄧˋ)
①spring in the air; high
spirits in spring ②thoughts
of love

春藥(ㄔㄨㄣ ㄧㄠˋ)
aphrodisiac; drugs that
induce sexual desire

春遊(ㄔㄨㄣ ㄧㄡˊ)
spring outings

春鶯(ㄔㄨㄣ ㄧㄥ)
the mango-bird; the Chinese
oriole

春雨(ㄔㄨㄣ ㄩˇ)
spring rains or showers

【昧】 2226
ㄇㄟˋ mey mèi
1. obscure; dark
2. to hide; to pocket
3. to ignore (one's conscience,
etc.)
4. blind; ignorant
5. to faint; fainting

昧昧(ㄇㄟˋ ㄇㄟˋ)
①dark; obscure ②stupid;
ignorant ③(now rarely)
deep and profound

昧瞽(ㄇㄟˋ ㄍㄨˇ)or(ㄇㄟˋ ㄍㄨˇ)
stupid and ignorant

昧旦(ㄇㄟˋ ㄉㄢˋ)
dawn; daybreak

昧良心(ㄇㄟˋ ㄌㄧㄤˊ ㄒㄧㄣ)
to ignore one's conscience;
to do evil against one's conscience; 我們決不昧着良心。
We'll never do evil against
our conscience.

昧起來(ㄇㄟˋ ㄑㄧˇ ㄌㄞˊ)
to hide another person's
things

昧下(ㄇㄟˋ ㄒㄧㄚˋ)
to hide another person's
things

昧心(ㄇㄟˋ ㄒㄧㄣ)
to ignore one's conscience

昧心錢 (ㄇㄟˋ ㄒㄧㄣ ㄑㄧㄢˊ)
money obtained by dishonest or evil means

昧覘 (ㄇㄟˋ ㄓㄢ)
to watch or inspect in secret

昧爽 (ㄇㄟˋ ㄕㄨㄤˇ)
dawn; daybreak 亦作「昧旦」

昧死 (ㄇㄟˋ ㄙˇ)
(an expression found in memorials to the emperors of the Chin and Han dynasties) to deserve death for daring to speak to Your Majesty this way

昧於事理 (ㄇㄟˋ ㄩˊ ㄕˋ ㄌㄧˇ)
to be ignorant of good reason, judgment, common practice, etc.

【昨】 2227
ㄗㄨㄛˊ tzwo zuó
yesterday; lately; past

昨非 (ㄗㄨㄛˊ ㄈㄟ)
past mistakes

昨天 (ㄗㄨㄛˊ ㄊㄧㄢ) or 昨日 (ㄗㄨㄛˊ ㄖˋ) or 昨兒 (ㄗㄨㄛˊ ㄦˊ) or 昨兒個
(ㄗㄨㄛˊ ㄦ· ㄍㄜ·)
yesterday: 昨天我很忙。I was very busy yesterday.

昨朝 (ㄗㄨㄛˊ ㄓㄠ)
yesterday morning: 昨朝下大雨。It rained hard yesterday morning.

昨死今生 (ㄗㄨㄛˊ ㄙˇ ㄐㄧㄣ ㄕㄥ)
(literally) to be dead yesterday and alive today—to be reborn; to lead a new life from now on

昨晚 (ㄗㄨㄛˊ ㄨㄢˇ) or 昨兒晚上
(ㄗㄨㄛˊ ㄦ· ㄨㄢˇ· ㄕㄤ·) or 昨夜 (ㄗㄨㄛˊ ㄧㄝˋ)
last night

【昭】 2228
ㄓㄠ jau zhāo
1. bright; brightness; luminous
2. prominent; eminent; evident; obvious
3. to make open; to show; to display: 他們對我昭示厚誼。They showed me great kindness.
4. a Chinese family name

昭明 (ㄓㄠ ㄇㄧㄥˊ)
①evident; clear ②to become bright ②(now rarely) a comet

昭明太子 (ㄓㄠ ㄇㄧㄥˊ ㄊㄞˋ ㄗˇ)
Hsiao Tung (蕭統), the eldest son of Emperor Wu of the Liang Dynasty (502-556 A.D.).

昭明文選 (ㄓㄠ ㄇㄧㄥˊ ㄨㄣˊ ㄒㄩㄢˇ)
the title of a collection of Chinese literary works edited by Hsiao Tung of the Liang Dynasty

昭穆 (ㄓㄠ ㄇㄨˋ)
(in ancient rites) a system of arranging emperors' temples

昭代 (ㄓㄠ ㄉㄞˋ)
an enlightened age or reign; (in ancient China) our dynasty or my dynasty

昭告 (ㄓㄠ ㄍㄠˋ)
to declare or announce to the public; to make known publicly

昭君 (ㄓㄠ ㄐㄩㄣ)
Wang Chiang (王嬙), a lady of the Han court, who was later married to a chieftain of a northern tribe in the performance of matrimonial diplomacy

昭顯 (ㄓㄠ ㄒㄧㄢˇ)
prominent; eminent; evident; famous

昭信中外 (ㄓㄠ ㄒㄧㄣˋ ㄓㄨㄥ ㄨㄞˋ)
to inspire confidence and faith within and without the nation

昭雪 (ㄓㄠ ㄒㄩㄝˇ)
to redress (a miscarriage of justice); to rehabilitate

昭昭 (ㄓㄠ ㄓㄠ)
clear and evident; known to all

昭彰 (ㄓㄠ ㄓㄤ)
prominent; eminent; obvious; evident: 他的罪惡昭彰。He has committed obvious crimes.

昭著 (ㄓㄠ ㄓㄨˋ)
famous; eminent: 他是一位昭著的學者。He is an eminent scholar.

昭灼 (ㄓㄠ ㄓㄨㄛˊ)
bright; shining; dazzling

昭示 (ㄓㄠ ㄕˋ)
to decree, declare, etc. officially; announcement, declaration, notice, proclamation, etc.

昭然 (ㄓㄠ ㄖㄢˊ)
clear and obvious; evident

昭然若揭 (ㄓㄠ ㄖㄢˊ ㄖㄨㄛˋ ㄐㄧㄝ)
very obvious; all too clear: 他的野心昭然若揭。His ambition is very obvious.

昭如日星 (ㄓㄠ ㄖㄨˊ ㄖˋ ㄒㄧㄥ)
as evident and obvious as the sun and the stars

昭容 (ㄓㄠ ㄖㄨㄥˊ)
①lady officials in ancient court ②a musical style in the Han Dynasty

昭蘇 (ㄓㄠ ㄙㄨ)
to wake up; to come to (from a coma, etc.)

昭儀 (ㄓㄠ ㄧˊ)
an official rank for ladies in the imperial palace

昭爛 (ㄓㄠ ㄌㄢˋ)
bright and brilliant; shining

昭陽宮 (ㄓㄠ ㄧㄤˊ ㄍㄨㄥ)
name of a palace in the Han Dynasty

【是】 2229
ㄕˋ shyh shì
1. yes; right; positive (as contrasted with negative)
2. the verb to be (for all persons and numbers): 他是我的朋友。He is my friend.
3. this, that, or which: 是日天氣晴朗。It was fine this day.
4. a Chinese family name

是必 (ㄕˋ ㄅㄧˋ)
must be; surely; certainly: 他是必疲倦了。He must be tired.

是不是 (ㄕˋ ㄅㄨˋ ㄕˋ)
Is it true or not? 或Are you ...? 或Is he...? 他是不是在這裏？Is he here?

是非 (ㄕˋ ㄈㄟ)
①right or wrong; right and wrong; yes and no ②gossip; scandal: 她太喜歡說是非。She is too fond of gossip. ③discord

是非顛倒 (ㄕˋ ㄈㄟ ㄉㄧㄢ ㄉㄠˇ)
to confound right and wrong

是非題 (ㄕˋ ㄈㄟ ㄊㄧˊ)
a true-or-false problem

是非曲直 (ㄕˋ ㄈㄟ ㄑㄩ ㄓˊ)
right and wrong, proper and improper; right and wrong, reasonable and absurd

是非之地 (ㄕˋ ㄈㄟ ㄓ ㄉㄧˋ)
a place where one is apt to

日部

〔日部〕

get into trouble

是非之心 (ㄕ ㄷㄟ ㄓ ㄒㄧㄣ)
the instinct to tell right from wrong; one's conscience; the feeling of approving and disapproving

是非人 (ㄕ ㄈㄟ ㄖㄣ)
one who stirs up strife or misunderstanding

是非自有公論 (ㄕ ㄈㄟ ㄗˋ ㄧㄡˇ ㄍㄨㄥ ㄌㄨㄣˋ)
Public opinion is the best judge of who's right and who's wrong. 或 There's always an unbiased view on the right or wrong of a matter.

是否 (ㄕ ㄈㄡˇ)
Is it...? 或 Are you...? 或 Is he...? 或 whether or not; yes or no: 他是否正在建造一所房子? Is he building a house?

是否有當 (ㄕ ㄈㄡˇ ㄧㄡˇ ㄉㄤ)
whether this is proper (I am eagerly awaiting your instruction.)

是的 (ㄕ ˙ㄉㄜ)
yes; right; correct; affirmative 或 That's it.

是古非今 (ㄕ ㄍㄨˇ ㄈㄟ ㄐㄧㄣ)
to consider anything old (to be) good and reject everything that is modern

是故 (ㄕ ㄍㄨˋ)
therefore: 她生病了，是故未能來. She was ill, and therefore could not come.

是可忍孰不可忍 (ㄕ ㄎㄜˇ ㄖㄣˇ ㄕㄨˊ ㄅㄨˋ ㄎㄜˇ ㄖㄣˇ)
If this can be endured, what else can not?

是何道理 (ㄕ ㄏㄜˊ ㄉㄠˋ ㄌㄧˇ)
Why? 或 For what reason? 他遲到是何道理? Why was he late?

是何居心 (ㄕ ㄏㄜˊ ㄐㄩ ㄒㄧㄣ)
What evil intention is this! 或 How mean you are!

是幸 (ㄕ ㄒㄧㄥˋ)
It would be fortunate indeed if you...; for which (the nation, the people, etc.) will be thankful; for which I'll be much obliged

是正 (ㄕ ㄓㄥˋ)
to check and correct

是非非 (ㄕ ㄈㄟ ㄈㄟ)

---

gossip(s); scandal(s)

是日 (ㄕ ㄖˋ)
that day; this day

是啊 (ㄕ ·ㄇㄚ)
Yeah! Oh, yes!

是所至禱 (ㄕ ㄙㄨㄛˇ ㄓˋ ㄉㄠˇ)
for which I sincerely pray; for which I'm truly obliged (an expression often used in letters)

是以 (ㄕ ㄧˇ)
therefore; hence

是耶非耶 (ㄕ ㄧㄝˊ ㄈㄟ ㄧㄝˊ)
Is it true or not? 或 Yes or no?

是樣兒 (ㄕ ㄧㄤˋㄦ)
to look good; becoming; fashionable

是味兒 (ㄕ ㄨㄟˋㄦ)
delicious; tasteful

是為 (ㄕ ㄨㄟˊ)
it is; this is

是為至要 (ㄕ ㄨㄟˊ ㄓˋ ㄧㄠˋ)
which is very important (a conventional phrase in letters addressed to one's children or people of lower position)

【昱】 2230
ㄩˋ yuh yù
1. sunshine; light; brightness; shining; dazzling
2. tomorrow

昱昱 (ㄩˋㄩˋ)
dazzling

【昴】 2231
ㄇㄠˇ mao mǎo
name of a star, one of the 28 constellations

昴星 (ㄇㄠˇ ㄒㄧㄥ)
the Pleiades

【昶】 2232
ㄔㄤˇ chaang chǎng
1. a long day
2. comfortable and easy

【昫】 2233
ㄒㄩ sheu xū
the warmth of the rising sun

昫嫗 or 昫育 (ㄒㄩˋㄩˋ)
to caress—as sunshine

【昳】 2234
1. ㄉㄧㄝˊ dye dié
the setting sun

【昳】 2234
2. ㄧˋ yih yì
bright

昳麗 (ㄧˋ ㄌㄧˋ)

---

radiantly beautiful

【昝】 2235
ㄗㄢˇ tzaan zǎn
a Chinese family name

【昪】 2236
ㄅㄧㄢˋ biann biàn
1. happy; joyful; pleasing
2. sunshine
3. light; brightness; bright

【昺】 2237
(昞) ㄅㄧㄥˇ biing bǐng
bright; glorious; brilliant; radiant

【昜】 2238
(陽) ㄧㄤ yang yáng
bright; glorious

六畫

【晏】 2239
ㄧㄢˋ yann yàn
1. clear (sky, sea, water, etc.)
2. late
3. peaceful; quiet
4. a Chinese family name

晏寂 (ㄧㄢˋㄐㄧˊ)
very quiet and silent

晏駕 (ㄧㄢˋㄐㄧㄚˋ)
the death of an emperor

晏起 (ㄧㄢˋㄑㄧˇ)
to get up late

晏寢 (ㄧㄢˋㄑㄧㄣˇ)
to sit up late

晏朝 (ㄧㄢˋㄔㄠˊ)
the evening session of the imperial court

晏然 (ㄧㄢˋㄖㄢˊ)
peaceful and easy; quiet and comfortable: 這位老者晏然自得. This old gentleman looks peaceful and easy.

晏如 (ㄧㄢˋㄖㄨˊ)
peaceful and easy

晏子 (ㄧㄢˋㄗˇ)
Yen Ying (晏嬰), prime minister of Chi (齊) in the reign of Ching Kung (景公) during the Epoch of Spring and Autumn, famous for personal integrity and hard work

晏子春秋 (ㄧㄢˋ ㄗˇ ㄔㄨㄣ ㄑㄧㄡ)
a collection of episodes of Yen Ying by an unknown author

晏晏 (ㄧㄢˋㄧㄢˋ)
mild and tender

【時】 2240 (音) ㄕ shyr shí

1. a season
2. an era; an epoch; an age; a period
3. time; fixed time
4. hours
5. often; frequently
6. fashionable
7. proper and adequate
8. opportune (moments); opportunity
9. timely; seasonable
10. now...now...; sometimes... sometimes...
11. a Chinese family name

時彥(ㄕ一ㄢˋ)
capable persons of the time

時弊(ㄕㄅㄧˋ)
current failings; present-day errors; ills of the time

時變(ㄕㄅㄧㄢˋ)
① the development of national or international events ② a change of seasons

時病(ㄕㄅㄧㄥˋ)
① the malady of the age ② (Chinese medicine) seasonal ailments

時不再來(ㄕㄅㄨˋㄗㄞˋㄌㄞˊ)
Such opportunity will not present itself again.

時不可失(ㄕㄅㄨˋㄎㄜˇㄕ)
Now or never! 或 Don't lose the opportune moment or opportunity.

時不我與(ㄕㄅㄨˋㄨㄛˇㄩˇ)
Time and tide wait for no one.

時不常見(ㄕ‧ㄅㄨˋㄔㄤˊㄐㄧㄢˋ)
often; frequently: 這事時不常見發生。It happens frequently.

時牌(ㄕㄆㄞˊ)
(in ancient China) ivory boards on which time of the day was announced

時派(ㄕㄆㄞˋ)or 時道(ㄕㄉㄠˋ)
fashionable (dress, behavior, conduct, etc.)

時評(ㄕㄆㄧㄥˊ)
news commentaries; comments on current events

時髦(ㄕㄇㄠˊ)
fashionable; modern; up-to-date: 她戴着一頂時髦的帽子。She wears a fashionable hat.

時命(ㄕㄇㄧㄥˋ)
① one's fate, fortune or luck ② current government orders

時分(ㄕㄈㄣ)
① seasons; periods ② time

時風(ㄕㄈㄥ)
timely winds

時代(ㄕㄉㄞˋ)
an era; an epoch; a period; an age; times

時代病(ㄕㄉㄞˋㄅㄧㄥˋ)
diseases of the modern times — anxiety, neurosis, suspicion, etc.

時代精神(ㄕㄉㄞˋㄐㄧㄥㄕㄣˊ)
① the spirit or aspiration of a certain period or age ② aggressive spirit

時代青年(ㄕㄉㄞˋㄑㄧㄥㄋㄧㄢˊ)
the modern youth (connoting progressiveness in outlook)

時代雜誌(ㄕㄉㄞˋㄗㄚˊㄓˋ)
Time magazine

時代錯誤(ㄕㄉㄞˋㄘㄨㄛˋㄨˋ)
anachronism

時代思潮(ㄕㄉㄞˋㄙㄔㄠˊ)
the current trend of thoughts: 現在的時代思潮是民主與科學。The current trend of thoughts is democracy and science.

時態(ㄕㄊㄞˋ)
(grammar) tense

時鳥(ㄕㄋㄧㄠˇ)
migrating birds; birds of the season 亦作「候鳥」

時來運轉(ㄕㄌㄞˊㄩㄣˋㄓㄨㄢˇ)
to get a break (after a long period of bad luck)

時令(ㄕㄌㄧㄥˋ)
time of year; seasons

時論(ㄕㄌㄨㄣˋ)
public opinion of the time

時過境遷(ㄕㄍㄨㄛˋㄐㄧㄥˋㄑㄧㄢ)
Things have changed with the passage of time.

時光(ㄕㄍㄨㄤ)
time: 時光會證明誰是對的。Time will show who is right.

時刻(ㄕㄎㄜˋ)
① time; hour ② always; constantly; continually

時刻表(ㄕㄎㄜˋㄅㄧㄠˇ)
a timetable; a schedule

時候(ㄕㄏㄡˋ)
time; hour; moment; juncture: 現在是什麼時候了? What time is it?

時貨(ㄕㄏㄨㄛˋ)
seasonable commodities

時會(ㄕㄏㄨㄟˋ)
① good luck; opportunity; the opportune moment ② (now rarely) to meet frequently

時諱(ㄕㄏㄨㄟˋ)
things or words, etc. to be avoided in conversations during a certain period of time

時機(ㄕㄐㄧ)
the opportune moment; opportunity

時機成熟(ㄕㄐㄧㄔㄥˊㄕㄨˊ)
(literally) The opportunity is ripe.—The right time has come. 或 The opportune moment is here.

時疾(ㄕㄐㄧˊ)
(Chinese medicine) seasonal ailments or diseases

時忌(ㄕㄐㄧˋ)
things, words, ideas, etc. to be avoided in conversations during certain times

時價(ㄕㄐㄧㄚˋ)
current prices; prevailing prices; (in a menu) according to the cost of the time when the dish is served

時節(ㄕㄐㄧㄝˊ)
① ⓐ occasion ⓑ a period of the year; season ② (一) 時 ⓐ time ⓑ a period of the year

時艱(ㄕㄐㄧㄢ)
perils of the time; difficult times or critical national situations

時間(ㄕㄐㄧㄢ)
① time; the hour: 時間即金錢。Time is money. ② the time —as opposed to space

時間表(ㄕㄐㄧㄢㄅㄧㄠˇ)
a timetable; a schedule

時間性(ㄕㄐㄧㄢㄒㄧㄥˋ)
the time factor: 新聞報導有時間性。News reports must be timely.

時禁(ㄕㄐㄧㄣˋ)
current prohibitions

時景(ㄕㄐㄧㄥˇ)

〔日部〕

scenery at the time or of the season

時局 (ㄕ ㄐㄩ)
the national situation; the state of national affairs; the world situation

時局平靖 (ㄕ ㄐㄩ ㄆㄧㄥˊ ㄐㄧㄥˋ)
in time of peace; a peaceful situation

時期 (ㄕ ㄑㄧˊ)
① times; a period; an age; an era ② duration

時氣 (ㄕ ㄑㄧˋ)
① (ㄕ ㄑㄧˋ) ⓐ a climate ⓑ an epidemic
② (ㄕ ㄑㄧˋ) luck of the moment

時下 (ㄕ ㄒㄧㄚˋ)
nowadays; in these days: 時下人們旅行都坐汽車了。Nowadays people travel in automobiles.

時效 (ㄕ ㄒㄧㄠˋ)
(law) prescription; the duration of validity

時鮮 (ㄕ ㄒㄧㄢ)
seasonable delicacies

時賢 (ㄕ ㄒㄧㄢˊ)
contemporary men of ability and integrity

時限 (ㄕ ㄒㄧㄢˋ)
a time limit; a deadline: 這張信用狀是有時限的。This letter of credit has a time limit.

時興 (ㄕ ㄒㄧㄥ)
fashionable or seasonable; in vogue; popular; prevailing; faddish

時行 (ㄕ ㄒㄧㄥˊ)
① fashionable or prevailing in a certain period of time; faddish ② (now rarely) to wait for the opportune moment to take action

時序 (ㄕ ㄒㄩˋ)
seasons; times

時序易遷 (ㄕ ㄒㄩˋ ㄧˋ ㄑㄧㄢ)
The seasons change.

時雪 (ㄕ ㄒㄩㄝˇ)
a timely snow

時值 (ㄕ ㄓˊ)
① the time being...; the time coincides with... 或 It happened at a time when... ② the going price

時至今日 (ㄕ ㄓˋ ㄐㄧㄣ ㄖˋ)
at this late hour; up to now

時針 (ㄕ ㄓㄣ)
the hour hand of a clock or watch

時政 (ㄕ ㄓㄥˋ)
① to take certain measures in government administration as the time demands ② government orders and regulations of the time

時症 (ㄕ ㄓㄥˋ)
(Chinese medicine) ailments or diseases caused by abnormal weather conditions; an epidemic

時裝 (ㄕ ㄓㄨㄤ)
① dresses in style or vogue; latest fashion; fashionable dresses ② (in show biz) modern dresses (as contrasted to ancient costumes)

時裝展覽 (ㄕ ㄓㄨㄤ ㄓㄢˇ ㄌㄢˇ)
a fashion show

時中 (ㄕ ㄓㄨㄥ)
propriety; proper and exact; impeccable; impeccability

時鐘 (ㄕ ㄓㄨㄥ)
a clock

時差 (ㄕ ㄔㄚ)
① (astronomy) the equation of time ② the time difference of two places located on different longitudes or time zones

時辰 (ㄕ ㄔㄣˊ)
① the 12 divisions of a day named after the 12 Terrestrial Branches: 子、丑、寅、卯、辰、巳、午、未、申、酉、戌、亥 ② the time for...; an opportunity: 這時辰起程正好。It is the right time for us to go.

時常 (ㄕ ㄔㄤˊ)
often; usually; frequently: 她時常想起往事。She often recalls the past.

時而 (ㄕ ㄦˊ)
often; usually; continually: 這種事時發生。Things like this happen frequently.

時時刻刻 (ㄕ ㄕ ㄎㄜˋ ㄎㄜˋ)
continuously; constantly; always

時⋯時⋯ (ㄕ...ㄕ...)
off and on; intermittent; now ... now ...

時食 (ㄕ ㄕˊ)
seasonable delicacies

時式 (ㄕ ㄕˋ)
the modern style; the modern fashion

時事 (ㄕ ㄕˋ)
the current state of affairs; current events

時事評論 (ㄕ ㄕˋ ㄆㄧㄥˊ ㄌㄨㄣˋ)
criticisms on current events

時勢 (ㄕ ㄕˋ)
the trend of times; the time and circumstances

時勢使然 (ㄕ ㄕˋ ㄕˇ ㄖㄢˊ)
It's the natural outcome of the time and circumstances.

時勢造英雄 (ㄕ ㄕˋ ㄗㄠˋ ㄧㄥ ㄒㄩㄥˊ)
A hero is nothing but a product of his time. 或 There would be no heroes if the time and circumstances do not give them the opportunity to distinguish themselves.

時尚 (ㄕ ㄕㄤˋ) or 時好 (ㄕ ㄏㄠˋ)
a fad; current fashion or style

時衰 (ㄕ ㄕㄨㄞ)
the decline of luck, fortune, etc.

時日 (ㄕ ㄖˋ)
① time ② an auspicious time ③ this day

時日變更線 (ㄕ ㄖˋ ㄅㄧㄢˋ ㄍㄥ ㄒㄧㄢˋ)
the international date line 亦作「國際換日線」

時人 (ㄕ ㄖㄣˊ)
contemporaries

時而 (ㄕ ㄦˊ)
from time to time; sometimes

時而後言 (ㄕ ㄦˊ ㄏㄡˋ ㄧㄢˊ)
to wait for the right moment to talk

時宜 (ㄕ ㄧˊ)
what is considered proper at the time

時疫 (ㄕ ㄧˋ)
an epidemic

時彥 (ㄕ ㄧㄢˋ)
contemporary men of ability and integrity

時諺 (ㄕ ㄧㄢˋ)
mottos or proverbs in a certain period of time

時樣 (ㄕ ㄧㄤˋ)
the vogue, style or fashion at the time

時務(ㄕ ㄨˋ)
①circumstances of the time: 他 不 識 時務。 He shows no understanding of the times.
② farm work calling for one's attention at the moment

時文(ㄕ ㄨㄣˊ)
a peculiar style of writing adopted by candidates during the civil service examinations of the Ching Dynasty known as the "eight-legged" writing (八 股 文)

時望(ㄕ ㄨㄤˋ)
①celebrities of the time ②popular fame; popular support: 這位詩人深負時望。 This poet enjoys popular fame.

時雨(ㄕ ㄩˇ)
①timely rains ② culture and education

時遇(ㄕ ㄩˋ)
favors one receives; a good break one gets; one's luck

時運不濟(ㄕ ㄩㄣˋ ㄅㄨˋ ㄐㄧˋ)
to be out of luck: 每個人都會有時運不濟的時候。 Everyone would be out of luck sometimes.

時運亨通(ㄕ ㄩㄣˋ ㄏㄥ ㄊㄨㄥ)
to be lucky; to hit the jackpot: 他近來時運亨通。 He has been lucky and prosperous recently.

【晉】 2241 (晋) ㄐㄧㄣˋ jinn jìn
1. to advance; to increase; to flourish
2. Tsin(a state during the Epoch of Spring and Autumn, occupying parts of today's Shansi and Hopeh Provinces)
3. another name for Shansi Province
4. the Tsin Dynasty (265-420 A. D.)
5. a Chinese family name

晉封(ㄐㄧㄣˋ ㄈㄥ)
(Ching Dynasty) to bestow honors on the parents, grand-parents, great-grandparents and wife of one who had rendered meritorious services to the state

晉國(ㄐㄧㄣˋ ㄍㄨㄛˊ)
the state of Tsin during the Epoch of Spring and Autumn 參看「晉 2.」

晉級(ㄐㄧㄣˋ ㄐㄧˊ)
promotion; to promote

晉接(ㄐㄧㄣˋ ㄐㄧㄝ)
to receive (visitors, etc.); to welcome

晉見(ㄐㄧㄣˋ ㄐㄧㄢˋ)
to call on (a superior) to have an audience with

晉京(ㄐㄧㄣˋ ㄐㄧㄥ)
to proceed to the national capital

晉爵(ㄐㄧㄣˋ ㄐㄩㄝˊ)
to rise in (feudal or noble) rank

晉朝(ㄐㄧㄣˋ ㄔㄠˊ)
the Tsin Dynasty (265-420 A. D.)

晉授(ㄐㄧㄣˋ ㄕㄡˋ)
(Ching Dynasty) to confer further honors on

晉升(ㄐㄧㄣˋ ㄕㄥ)
to rise in rank; to promote; to increase

晉書(ㄐㄧㄣˋ ㄕㄨ)
The History of the Tsin Dynasty, a 130-volume work compiled by 21 historians during the Tang Dynasty

晉謁(ㄐㄧㄣˋ ㄧㄝˋ)
to visit or call on (a superior or leader)

晉武帝(ㄐㄧㄣˋ ㄨˇ ㄉㄧˋ) (司馬炎), 236-290 A.D., the founding emperor of the Tsin Dynasty

晉文公(ㄐㄧㄣˋ ㄨㄣˊ ㄍㄨㄥ)
Wen Kung, a ruler of the state of Tsin in the Epoch of Spring and Autumn

晉約秦盟(ㄐㄧㄣˋ ㄩㄝ ㄑㄧㄣˊ ㄇㄥˊ)
to enter into a matrimonial contract 參看「秦晉之好」

【晃】 2242 1. ㄏㄨㄤ hoang huǎng
1. brightness
2. dazzling; glaring
3. a flash; to flash past; to appear and disappear very quickly

晃朗(ㄏㄨㄤˇ ㄌㄤˇ)
bright and brilliant

晃晃(ㄏㄨㄤˇ ㄏㄨㄤˇ)
dazzling (usually used to describe light reflected from polished metals)

晃曜 或 晃耀(ㄏㄨㄤˇ ㄧㄠˋ)
radiant

【晃】 2242 2. ㄏㄨㄤˋ huang huàng
to rock; to sway; to shake

晃蕩(ㄏㄨㄤˋ ㄉㄤˋ)
to sway; to oscillate; to shake: 旗子在風中不停地晃蕩。 The flag kept swaying in the wind.

晃動(ㄏㄨㄤˋ ㄉㄨㄥˋ)
to rock; to sway: 這船有點晃動。 The boat rocks a bit.

晃悠悠(ㄏㄨㄤˋ ㄧㄡ ㄧㄡ)
to stagger; to wobble; swaying; unstable

晃搖(ㄏㄨㄤˋ ㄧㄠˊ)
to sway; swaying; to shake; oscillating

晃漾(ㄏㄨㄤˋ ㄧㄤˋ)
to sway; swaying

【晁】 2243 ㄔㄠˊ chaur cháo
1. an ancient form of 朝
2. a Chinese family name

【晌】 2244 ㄕㄤˇ shaang shǎng
1. high noon
2. a certain duration or interval of time
3. (Northeast China dialect) a day's work

晌飯(ㄕㄤˇ ㄈㄢˋ)
(dialect) a midday meal; lunch

晌午(ㄕㄤˇ ㄨˇ)
(colloquial) high noon; midday

七畫

【晟】 2245 ㄕㄥˋ sheng shèng (又讀 ㄔㄥˊ cherng chéng)
the brightness of the sun; light; splendor

【晚】 2246 ㄨㄢˇ woan wǎn
1. sunset; evening; night: 明晚以前我不會回來。 I shan't be back before tomorrow night.
2. late: 晚做總比不做好。 Better late than never.
3. drawing toward the end
4. younger; junior

晚輩(ㄨㄢˇ ㄅㄟˋ)

〔日 部〕

〔日部〕

the younger generation; one's juniors

晚報(ㄨㄢ ㄅㄠ)
an evening paper; an afternoon paper

晚班(ㄨㄢ ㄅㄢ)
the night shift

晚半天兒(ㄨㄢ ㄅㄢ ㄊㄧㄢ儿)
late afternoon

晚半晌兒(ㄨㄢ ㄅㄢ ㄕㄤ儿)
dusk; the twilight hour

晚明小品(ㄨㄢ ㄇㄧㄥ ㄒㄧㄠ ㄆㄧㄣ)
essays of the late Ming Dynasty

晚飯(ㄨㄢ ㄈㄢ)or**晚餐**(ㄨㄢ ㄘㄢ)
dinner; supper

晚福(ㄨㄢ ㄈㄨ)
good fortune that comes late in one's life; happiness in one's closing years; old age bliss

晚達(ㄨㄢ ㄉㄚ)
to attain officialdom or get rich and well-to-do in the latter part of one's life

晚禱(ㄨㄢ ㄉㄠ)
evening prayers; vespers

晚到(ㄨㄢ ㄉㄠ)
to arrive late

晚稻(ㄨㄢ ㄉㄠ)or**晚禾**(ㄨㄢ ㄏㄜ)
a late crop of rice; the second rice crop of a year

晚唐(ㄨㄢ ㄊㄤ)
the late Tang Dynasty (often mentioned in connection with poetry)

晚年(ㄨㄢ ㄋㄧㄢ)
old age; one's later (or remaining) years

晚娘(ㄨㄢ ㄋㄧㄤ)
a stepmother

晚娘面孔(ㄨㄢ ㄋㄧㄤ ㄇㄧㄢ ㄎㄨㄥ)
(literally) a stepmother's face—an unsmiling face; a sullen look

晚了(ㄨㄢ ㄌㄜ)
It's getting late. 或 It's too late.

晚來(ㄨㄢ ㄌㄞ)
to come late

晚禮服(ㄨㄢ ㄌㄧ ㄈㄨ)
formal evening dress

晚會(ㄨㄢ ㄏㄨㄟ)
a night party; an evening gathering or meeting

晚婚(ㄨㄢ ㄏㄨㄣ)

late marriage; to marry late in one's life: 他晚婚。He married late in his life.

晚節(ㄨㄢ ㄐㄧㄝ)
① one's integrity in his closing years ② old age; one's closing years ③ closing years of a dynasty

晚間(ㄨㄢ ㄐㄧㄢ)
evening; night; nocturnal: 他習慣於晚間讀書。He is used to studying at night.

晚近(ㄨㄢ ㄐㄧㄣ)
lately; recently; modern

晚進(ㄨㄢ ㄐㄧㄣ)
a newcomer; a junior

晚景(ㄨㄢ ㄐㄧㄥ)
① scenes at sunset ② circumstances in one's old age

晚期(ㄨㄢ ㄑㄧ)
the later period

晚起(ㄨㄢ ㄑㄧ)
to rise or get up late

晚秋(ㄨㄢ ㄑㄧㄡ)
late autumn

晚霞(ㄨㄢ ㄒㄧㄚ)
rosy clouds just before sunset; sunset clouds

晚香玉(ㄨㄢ ㄒㄧㄤ ㄩ)
(botany) white lily, or tuberose (*Polianthes tuberosa*)

晚學(ㄨㄢ ㄒㄩㄝ)or**晚學生**(ㄨㄢ ㄒㄩㄝ ˙ㄕㄥ)
your pupil (a polite term referring to oneself when addressing a senior)

晚照(ㄨㄢ ㄓㄠ)
the shining of the setting sun

晚莊稼(ㄨㄢ ㄓㄨㄤ ˙ㄐㄧㄚ)
a late harvest; a late crop

晚車(ㄨㄢ ㄔㄜ)
a night train or bus: 我沒趕上往台中的晚車。I missed the night train for Taichung.

晚場(ㄨㄢ ㄔㄤ)
an evening show; an evening performance

晚食當肉(ㄨㄢ ㄕ ㄉㄤ ㄖㄡ)
Eating late is as good as enjoying meat.

晚世(ㄨㄢ ㄕ)
modern times; recent years

晚熟(ㄨㄢ ㄕㄨ)
①(said of plants) to ripen late ②(said of a person) to

mature late; a late bloomer

晚上(ㄨㄢ ㄕㄤ)
in the evening or night: 秋天晚上很涼爽。It is cool in the autumn evening.

晚生(ㄨㄢ ㄕㄥ)
a humble term referring to oneself when addressing a senior or superior

晚歲(ㄨㄢ ㄙㄨㄟ)
①in recent years; lately ② a late harvest ③ old age; one's later years

晚安(ㄨㄢ ㄢ)
Good evening! 或Good night!

晚宴(ㄨㄢ ㄧㄢ)
a dinner party

晚醵(ㄨㄢ ㄧㄢ)
①chrysanthemum ②flowers that blossom late

晚運(ㄨㄢ ㄩㄣ)
one's lot during old age

【晝】 ㄓㄡ jow zhòu ²²⁴⁷
1. day; daytime; daylight
2. a Chinese family name

晝盲(ㄓㄡ ㄇㄤ)
(medicine) hemeralopia

晝分(ㄓㄡ ㄈㄣ)
high noon

晝伏夜行(ㄓㄡ ㄈㄨ ㄧㄝ ㄒㄧㄥ)
to lie low in daytime and act at night

晝短圈(ㄓㄡ ㄉㄨㄢ ㄑㄩㄢ)
the Tropic of Capricorn 亦作「南回歸線」

晝晦(ㄓㄡ ㄏㄨㄟ)
dim sunshine (as in a cloudy day, etc.)

晝寢(ㄓㄡ ㄑㄧㄣ)
to take a nap; a siesta; to be asleep during the day

晝長圈(ㄓㄡ ㄔㄤ ㄑㄩㄢ)
the Tropic of Cancer 亦作「北回歸線」

晝日(ㄓㄡ ㄖ)
a day; daytime

晝夜(ㄓㄡ ㄧㄝ)
day and night; round the clock: 他們晝夜警戒。They were on a round-the-clock alert.

晝夜不息(ㄓㄡ ㄧㄝ ㄅㄨ ㄒㄧ)
(to work, etc.) day and night without rest or stop

晝夜平分(ㄓㄡ ㄧㄝ ㄆㄧㄥ ㄈㄣ)
the equinox

畫夜平分線(ㄓㄨˋㄧㄝˋㄆㄧㄥˊㄈㄣ
ㄒㄧㄢˋ)
the equinoctial line 亦作「赤
道」

【晞】 2248
　　ㄒㄧ shī xī
1. to dry in the sun; dry
2. sunshine at daybreak

晞髮(ㄒㄧㄈㄚˇ)
to loosen the hair in order
to dry it

【晡】 2249
　　ㄅㄨ bu bū
afternoon

晡時(ㄅㄨㄕˊ)
late afternoon (about 4 p.m.)

【晤】 2250
　　ㄨˋ wuh wù
1. to meet; to see face to face
2. enlightened; wise

晤面(ㄨˋㄇㄧㄢˋ)
to meet; to see each other

晤對(ㄨˋㄉㄨㄟˋ)
to meet face to face

晤談(ㄨˋㄊㄢˊ)
to meet and talk; to con-
verse; to discuss face to face

晤歌(ㄨˋㄍㄜ)
to sing face to face

晤商(ㄨˋㄕㄤ)
a face-to-face negotiation; to
discuss in an interview

晤言(ㄨˋㄧㄢˊ)or 晤語(ㄨˋㄩˇ)
to meet and talk

【晦】 2251
　　ㄏㄨㄟˋ huey huì
1. the last day of every month
in the lunar calendar
2. night; evening; dark
3. obscure; indistinguishable
4. unlucky; bad luck

晦盲(ㄏㄨㄟˋㄇㄤˊ)
to see nothing because of
darkness

晦蒙(ㄏㄨㄟˋㄇㄥˊ)
dark, obscure, or gloomy
(used figuratively to de-
scribe the chaos of troubled
times)

晦明(ㄏㄨㄟˋㄇㄧㄥˊ)
night and day

晦冥(ㄏㄨㄟˋㄇㄧㄥˊ)
dark and gloomy

晦匿(ㄏㄨㄟˋㄋㄧˋ)
to retire into obscurity

晦迹(ㄏㄨㄟˋㄐㄧ)
to retire into obscurity

晦氣(ㄏㄨㄟˋㄑㄧˋ)
unlucky; bad luck; to en-
counter rough going

晦氣星(ㄏㄨㄟˋㄑㄧˋㄒㄧㄥ)
the deity that metes out bad
luck to a person; a star of
ill luck

晦顯(ㄏㄨㄟˋㄒㄧㄢˇ)
obscure and obvious; obscurity and manifestation

晦朔(ㄏㄨㄟˋㄕㄨㄛˋ)
the last and first days of a
lunar month

晦暗(ㄏㄨㄟˋㄢˋ)
dark; gloomy

晦往明來(ㄏㄨㄟˋㄨㄤˇㄇㄧㄥˊㄌㄞˊ)
as day follows night and
night follows day

【皓】 2252
　　ㄏㄠˋ haw hào
1. daybreak
2. bright and brilliant

【晨】 2253
　　ㄔㄣˊ chern chén
1. morning; daybreak
2. (said of a cock) to announce
the arrival of morning; to
crow at dawn

晨風(ㄔㄣˊㄈㄥ)
① morning breezes: 我們享受
自山上吹來的晨風。We are en-
joying the morning breeze
that comes from the moun-
tain. ② name of a bird of
the hawk family

晨光(ㄔㄣˊㄍㄨㄤ)
daylight; daybreak; the dimness before dawn

晨昏(ㄔㄣˊㄏㄨㄣ)or 晨夕(ㄔㄣˊㄒㄧ)
morning and evening

晨昏顛倒(ㄔㄣˊㄏㄨㄣㄉㄧㄢㄉㄠˇ)
to mistake morning for evening and evening for morning—confused

晨昏定省(ㄔㄣˊㄏㄨㄣㄉㄧㄥˋㄒㄧㄥˇ)
to pay respects to one's
elders—especially to one's
parents—in the morning
(when they get up) and in
the evening (when they
retire)

晨雞(ㄔㄣˊㄐㄧ)
the crowing of cocks at daybreak

晨間(ㄔㄣˊㄐㄧㄢ)
in the morning: 很多人在晨間
慢跑。Many people jog in the

morning.

晨曦(ㄔㄣˊㄒㄧ)
morning light; daybreak

晨星(ㄔㄣˊㄒㄧㄥ)
① morning stars ② things
that are scarce and rare

晨鐘暮鼓(ㄔㄣˊㄓㄨㄥㄇㄨˋㄍㄨˇ)
(literally) the bell in the
morning and the drum in the
evening—bells and drums
used in Buddhist temples in
announcing time and arousing people to renewed faith
亦作「暮鼓晨鐘」

晨炊(ㄔㄣˊㄔㄨㄟ)
morning cooking; breakfast

晨操(ㄔㄣˊㄘㄠ)
morning exercise; morning
calisthenics: 晨操有益於健康。
Morning exercises are good
for the health.

八畫

【晬】 2254
　　ㄗㄨㄟˋ tzuey zuì
1. the first birth anniversary
of a child
2. anniversary

晬盤(ㄗㄨㄟˋㄆㄢˊ)
a tray holding various articles taken before a child on
the first anniversary of his
birth to see which of the
articles he grasps as a test
to determine the career he is
likely to follow in the future

【普】 2255
　　ㄆㄨˇ puu pǔ
1. universal; widespread; general; everywhere; all: 電視提
供了普遍性的娛樂。Television
provides universal entertainment.
2. Prussia
3. a Chinese family name

普遍 or 普徧(ㄆㄨˇㄅㄧㄢˋ)
universal; general; wide-
spread; everywhere; com-
mon: 運動受到普遍的喜愛。
There is a general interest
in sports.

普徧性 or 普遍性(ㄆㄨˇㄅㄧㄢˋㄒㄧㄥˋ)
universality

普法戰爭(ㄆㄨˇㄈㄚˇㄓㄢˋㄓㄥ)
the Franco-Prussian War in
1870-1871 A.D.

普汎(ㄆㄨˇㄈㄢˋ)

〔日部〕

general; widespread; universal

普渡(ㄆㄨ ㄉㄨˋ)
(Buddhism) to save all with mercy

普渡衆生(ㄆㄨ ㄉㄨˋ ㄓㄨㄥ ㄕㄥ)
(Buddhism) to deliver or save all beings: 佛教的宗旨在普渡衆生。The purpose of Buddhism is to deliver all beings.

普天同慶(ㄆㄨ ㄊㄧㄢ ㄊㄨㄥ ㄑㄧㄥˋ)
The whole world joins in the rejoicing, celebration or congratulations.

普天之下(ㄆㄨ ㄊㄧㄢ ㄓ ㄒㄧㄚˋ)
all under the heavens; all over the world

普天率土(ㄆㄨ ㄊㄧㄢ ㄕㄨㄞˋ ㄊㄨˇ)
the whole world

普陀山(ㄆㄨ ㄊㄨㄛˊ ㄕㄢ)
Mount Puto at Tinghai County (定海) of Chekiang Province, the site of one of the biggest Buddhist temples in China

普通(ㄆㄨ ㄊㄨㄥ)
ordinary; common; plain; average: 冬天禪感冒是很普通的。Colds are common in winter.

普通名詞(ㄆㄨ ㄊㄨㄥ ㄇㄧㄥˊ ㄘ)
common nouns

普通法(ㄆㄨ ㄊㄨㄥ ㄈㄚˇ)
common law

普通考試(ㄆㄨ ㄊㄨㄥ ㄎㄠˇ ㄕˋ)
the junior-grade civil service examination (in modern China)

普通會計(ㄆㄨ ㄊㄨㄥ ㄎㄨㄞˋ ㄐㄧˋ)
general accounting

普通話(ㄆㄨ ㄊㄨㄥ ㄏㄨㄚˋ)
the common dialect of the Chinese language; Mandarin

普通教育(ㄆㄨ ㄊㄨㄥ ㄐㄧㄠˋ ㄩˋ)
elementary education: 每個人都應當接受普通教育。Every one should receive elementary education.

普通心理學(ㄆㄨ ㄊㄨㄥ ㄒㄧㄣ ㄌㄧˇ ㄒㄩㄝˊ)
general psychology

普通支票(ㄆㄨ ㄊㄨㄥ ㄓ ㄆㄧㄠˋ)
an open check

普林斯頓(ㄆㄨ ㄌㄧㄣˊ ㄙ ㄉㄨㄣˋ)
① Princeton, in New Jersey
② Princeton University

普魯士(ㄆㄨ ㄌㄨˇ ㄕˋ)
Prussia

普羅文學(ㄆㄨ ㄌㄨㄛˊ ㄨㄣˊ ㄒㄩㄝˊ)
proletarian literature

普告天下(ㄆㄨ ㄍㄠˋ ㄊㄧㄢ ㄒㄧㄚˋ)
to announce to the world; to make publicly known

普及(ㄆㄨ ㄐㄧˊ)
① universal; available to all
② to popularize; to disseminate

普及本(ㄆㄨ ㄐㄧˊ ㄅㄣˇ)
a cheap edition; a paperback edition

普及教育(ㄆㄨ ㄐㄧˊ ㄐㄧㄠˋ ㄩˋ)
universal education; compulsory or mandatory education

普降甘霖(ㄆㄨ ㄐㄧㄤˋ ㄍㄢ ㄌㄧㄣˊ)
timely rain for all drought areas

普希金(ㄆㄨ ㄒㄧ ㄐㄧㄣ)
Alexander Pushkin, 1799-1837, Russian poet

普選(ㄆㄨ ㄒㄩㄢˇ)
universal suffrage; general elections

普照(ㄆㄨ ㄓㄠˋ)
(said of sunshine, God's grace, etc.) to shine upon all: 陽光普照大地。The sun shines every corner of the land.

普查(ㄆㄨ ㄔㄚˊ)
a general survey

普施(ㄆㄨ ㄕ)
to give contributions to charity in every direction

普洱茶(ㄆㄨ ㄦˇ ㄔㄚˊ)
tea brick produced at 普洱 in Yunnan Province

【景】 2256
1. ㄐㄧㄥ jǐng jīng
1. scenery; views: 我很喜歡山景。I enjoy mountain scenery very much.
2. prospects; circumstances; situations: 好景不常。The good circumstances don't last long.
3. (in motion pictures, stage shows, etc.) settings; background scenes: 休息時換景。The scenes are changed during the intervals.
4. big and strong
5. great

6. high
7. bright and luminous
8. to admire; to respect: 我們都景仰誠實的人。We all respect honest persons.
9. a Chinese family name

景命(ㄐㄧㄥˇ ㄇㄧㄥˋ)
the ruling power of the emperor (In ancient China, the emperor claimed that his ruling power was from Heaven.)

景慕(ㄐㄧㄥˇ ㄇㄨˋ)
to admire and respect: 他的聰明爲人所景慕。His cleverness is much admired and respected.

景福(ㄐㄧㄥˇ ㄈㄨˊ)
① great blessings; big happiness ② name of a reign in the Tang Dynasty (892-893A.D.)

景德鎭(ㄐㄧㄥˇ ㄉㄜˊ ㄓㄣˋ)
Ching Te Chen — a city in Kiangsi Province famous for its porcelains

景泰藍(ㄐㄧㄥˇ ㄊㄞˋ ㄌㄢˊ)
cloisonné, or Peiping enamel

景觀(ㄐㄧㄥˇ ㄍㄨㄢ)
(geography) landscape: 這地區的自然景觀很美妙。The natural landscape in this district is wonderful.

景況(ㄐㄧㄥˇ ㄎㄨㄤˋ)
(personal or general) circumstances, situations, conditions, etc.: 他的健康景況達到最佳地步。He is at the top of his condition.

景教(ㄐㄧㄥˇ ㄐㄧㄠˋ)
Nestorianism, a sect of Christianity, in the Tang Dynasty

景氣(ㄐㄧㄥˇ ㄑㄧˋ)
(economics) prosperity; booming: 和平帶來景氣。Peace brings prosperity.

景象(ㄐㄧㄥˇ ㄒㄧㄤˋ)
appearances; conditions; outlooks; scenes; sights

景星(ㄐㄧㄥˇ ㄒㄧㄥ)
auspicious stars

景星勳章(ㄐㄧㄥˇ ㄒㄧㄥ ㄒㄩㄣ ㄓㄤ)
the Order of Brilliant Star (one of the Chinese government decorations)

景行(ㄐㄧㄥˇ ㄒㄧㄥˊ)

high virtues

景致 or 景緻(ㄐㄧㄥ ㄓ)
scenery; scenes; views; pleasing views; a vista

景狀(ㄐㄧㄥ ㄓㄨㄤ)
appearances; conditions; circumstances

景色(ㄐㄧㄥ ㄙㄜ)
scenery; views; scenes; landscapes: 此山景色如畫, This mountain scenery is picturesque.

景兒(ㄐㄧㄥ ㄦ)
appearances; conditions; circumstances

景仰(ㄐㄧㄥ ㄧㄤ)
to admire and respect; to hold in deep respect; to look up to

景物(ㄐㄧㄥ ㄨ)
scenery; landscapes: 景物宜人 delightful scenery

景遇(ㄐㄧㄥ ㄩ)
(literally) circumstances; one's lot: 他目前的景遇相當不錯。His present circumstances are rather good.

景雲(ㄐㄧㄥ ㄩㄣ)
① bright clouds of many colors ② name of a reign (710-711) in the Tang Dynasty

【景】 2256
2.(影) ㄧㄥ ying yǐng
shadow; reflection; image

景附(ㄧㄥ ㄈㄨ)
to follow closely

景從(ㄧㄥ ㄘㄨㄥ)
to follow (a great master, leader, etc.) like a shadow; popular support or following 亦作「影從」

景印(ㄧㄥ ㄧㄣ)
to print with photolithographic plates; a photolithographic copy or edition

【晰】 2257
ㄒㄧ shi xī
clear; clearly; distinct: 她的口齒清晰。Her speech is distinct.

【晳】 2258
ㄒㄧ shi xī
1.(said of one's skin) fair; white: 她的皮膚白皙皙。Her skin is very white.

2. to discriminate; to distinguish or differentiate

【晴】 2259
ㄑㄧㄥ chyng qíng
1.(said of the weather) fine; fair; bright; clear; not raining

2. when the rain stops

晴天(ㄑㄧㄥ ㄊㄧㄢ)
a fine day; a cloudless day. 明天會是晴天嗎? Will it be a fine day tomorrow?

晴天霹靂(ㄑㄧㄥ ㄊㄧㄢ ㄆㄧ ㄌㄧ)
a bolt from the blue 亦作「青天霹靂」

晴朗(ㄑㄧㄥ ㄌㄤ)
(said of the sky) fine and cloudless

晴空(ㄑㄧㄥ ㄎㄨㄥ)
a clear sky; a cloudless sky

晴空萬里(ㄑㄧㄥ ㄎㄨㄥ ㄨㄢ ㄌㄧ)
The clear sky stretches thousands of miles.—a clear and boundless sky

晴和(ㄑㄧㄥ ㄏㄜ)
fine and balmy (weather)

晴雨表(ㄑㄧㄥ ㄩ ㄅㄧㄠ)or 晴雨計(ㄑㄧㄥ ㄩ ㄐㄧ)
a barometer

晴雨無阻(ㄑㄧㄥ ㄩ ㄨ ㄗㄨ)
rain or shine

【晶】 2260
ㄐㄧㄥ jing jīng
1. crystal

2. bright; clear; brilliant; radiant; glittering

晶體(ㄐㄧㄥ ㄊㄧ)
(radio) crystal

晶婚紀念(ㄐㄧㄥ ㄏㄨㄣ ㄐㄧ ㄋㄧㄢ)
the crystal (the 15th) wedding anniversary

晶晶(ㄐㄧㄥ ㄐㄧㄥ)
bright and brilliant

晶質(ㄐㄧㄥ ㄓ)
crystalloid

晶質岩(ㄐㄧㄥ ㄓ ㄧㄢ)
crystalline rocks

晶狀體(ㄐㄧㄥ ㄓㄨㄤ ㄊㄧ)
(anatomy) crystalline lens, a doubly convex, transparent body in the eye

晶簇(ㄐㄧㄥ ㄘㄨ)
crystal druse

晶瑩(ㄐㄧㄥ ㄧㄥ)
radiant; brilliant; shining

晶瑩(ㄐㄧㄥ ㄧㄥ)
sparkling; 荷葉上有晶瑩的露珠。There are sparkling dewdrops on the leaves of the lotus.

【暑】 2261
ㄍㄨㄟ goei guǐ
1. shadows caused by the sun

2. a sundial

3. time

暑刻(ㄍㄨㄟ ㄎㄜ)
① time ② a short time

暑儀(ㄍㄨㄟ ㄧ)
a sundial

暑影(ㄍㄨㄟ ㄧㄥ)
shadows

【智】 2262
ㄓ jyh zhì
1. talented; capable; intelligent; clever; wise; wisdom; knowledge; wit: 這人足智多謀。This person is wise and resourceful.

2. prudence

3. a Chinese family name

智謀(ㄓ ㄇㄡ)
cleverness; tactics; strategy; resourcefulness: 這些智謀將對他有所幫助。These tactics will help him.

智多星(ㄓ ㄉㄨㄛ ㄒㄧㄥ)
① a nickname for Wu Yung (吳用), the resourceful strategist in the *All Men Are Brothers* (水滸傳) ② a resourceful person; a mastermind

智囊(ㄓ ㄋㄤ)
a wise person; a wise advisor

智囊團(ㄓ ㄋㄤ ㄊㄨㄢ)
a brain trust; a think tank

智能(ㄓ ㄋㄥ)
intelligence and capability; knowledge and ability

智能不足(ㄓ ㄋㄥ ㄅㄨ ㄗㄨ)
mental retardation

智力(ㄓ ㄌㄧ)
intelligence: 他是一個缺乏智力的男孩。He is a boy who shows very little intelligence.

智力年齡(ㄓ ㄌㄧ ㄋㄧㄢ ㄌㄧㄥ)
mental age

智力商數(ㄓ ㄌㄧ ㄕㄤ ㄕㄨ)or 智商(ㄓ ㄕㄤ)
intelligence quotient (I.Q.)

智力測驗(ㄓ ㄌㄧ ㄘㄜ ㄧㄢ)
an intelligence test; an IQ test

智利(ㄓ ㄌㄧ)

〔日部〕

〔日部〕

Chile, or Chili
智利硝石(ㄓ ㄌㄧ ㄒㄧ ㄕˊ)
Chile saltpeter

智慮(ㄓ ㄌㄩˋ)
wisdom: 他的為人智慮深沉。
He is a man of profound
wisdom.

智略(ㄓ ㄌㄩㄝˋ)
intelligence and tact

智過萬人(ㄓ ㄍㄨㄛˋ ㄨㄢˋ ㄖㄣˊ)
(One's) intelligence is
greater than that of 10,000
men put together.—extremely intelligent

智慧(ㄓ ㄏㄨㄟˋ)
wisdom; intelligence

智慧劍(ㄓ ㄏㄨㄟˋ ㄐㄧㄢˋ)
the power of making deci-
sions which takes courage
to make

智慧財產權(ㄓ ㄏㄨㄟˋ ㄘㄞˊ ㄔㄢˇ ㄑㄩㄢˊ)
intellectual property rights

智器(ㄓ ㄑㄧˋ)
talent

智巧(ㄓ ㄑㄧㄠˇ)
brains and tact: 他們沒有智
巧。They have no brains and
tact.

智取(ㄓ ㄑㄩˇ)
to triumph by means of
strategy or tactics

智者 or 知者(ㄓ ㄓㄜˇ)
a wise man

智者千慮，必有一失(ㄓ ㄓㄜˇ
ㄑㄧㄢ ㄌㄩˋ，ㄅㄧˋ ㄧㄡˇ ㄧ ㄕ)
(literally) No matter how
hard an intelligent person
thinks, he's going to miss
something. 或 No one is in-
fallible.

智齒(ㄓ ㄔˇ)
wisdom teeth

智識(ㄓ ㄕˋ)or 知識(ㄓ ㄕˋ)
knowledge: 智識即是力量。
Knowledge is power.

智識份子(ㄓ ㄕˋ ㄈㄣˋ ㄗˇ)or 知識份
子(ㄓ ㄕˋ ㄈㄣˋ ㄗˇ)
intellectuals; educated people; the intelligentsia

智識階級(ㄓ ㄕˋ ㄐㄧㄝ ㄐㄧˊ)or 知識
階級(ㄓ ㄕˋ ㄐㄧㄝ ㄐㄧˊ)
the intelligentsia

智術(ㄓ ㄕㄨˋ)
trickery; stratagem

智仁勇(ㄓ ㄖㄣˊ ㄩㄥˇ)
wisdom, kindness and cour-

age—motto of the Chinese
boy scouts

智愚(ㄓ ㄩˊ)
the intelligent and the ignorant; the wise and the foolish

智育(ㄓ ㄩˋ)
education that aims at
cultivating one's intelligence;
mental training; intellectual
education

智圓行方(ㄓ ㄩㄢˊ ㄒㄧㄥˊ ㄈㄤ)
round in knowledge but
square in behavior—to be
quick-witted in mind and
never casual in one's behavior

智勇兼備(ㄓ ㄩㄥˇ ㄐㄧㄢ ㄅㄟˋ)or智勇
雙全(ㄓ ㄩㄥˇ ㄕㄨㄤ ㄑㄩㄢˊ)
combining the qualities of
intelligence and bravery;
both intelligent and brave;
both prudent and coura-
geous

【晾】 2263
ㄌㄧㄤˋ liang liàng
1. to dry in the air; to air; to
hang in the wind to dry
2. to dry in the sun

晾乾(ㄌㄧㄤˋ ㄍㄢ)
to dry in the air; to hang in
the wind to dry

晾曬(ㄌㄧㄤˋ ㄕㄞˋ)
to spread out to dry

晾衣服(ㄌㄧㄤˋ ㄧ ㄈㄨˊ)
to hang clothes in the wind
to dry; to dry clothes on
laundry lines; to air clothes

晾一晾(ㄌㄧㄤˋ ㄧ ㄌㄧㄤˋ)
to dry in the air

九畫

【暄】 2264
ㄒㄩㄢ shiuan xuān
1. comfortable and genial (climates); warm
2. (dialect) fluffy

暄風(ㄒㄩㄢ ㄈㄥ)
spring breeze

暄暖(ㄒㄩㄢ ㄋㄨㄢˇ)
warm and comfortable: 天氣
漸漸暄暖了。It is getting
warm and comfortable.

暄涼(ㄒㄩㄢ ㄌㄧㄤˊ)
greetings to one another

暄妍(ㄒㄩㄢ ㄧㄢˊ)

warm weather and captivating scenery (in spring)

【暇】 2265
ㄒㄧㄚˊ shiah xiá
(又讀 ㄒㄧㄚˇ shya
xiǎ)
leisure; free time; spare time

暇晷(ㄒㄧㄚˊ ㄍㄨㄟˇ)
leisure; spare time

暇時(ㄒㄧㄚˊ ㄕˊ)
leisure; spare time

暇日(ㄒㄧㄚˊ ㄖˋ)
free days; leisure; spare
time: 他們在暇日時常爬山。
They often go mountaineering in their free days.

暇逸(ㄒㄧㄚˊ ㄧˋ)
relaxation; to relax; to idle

暇裕(ㄒㄧㄚˊ ㄩˋ)
leisurely; relaxed; relaxation

【暉】 2266
ㄏㄨㄟ huei huī
1. the sunshine; the light of the
sun
2. bright; radiant

暉映(ㄏㄨㄟ ㄧㄥˋ)
(said of the sky) clear and
bright

暉夜(ㄏㄨㄟ ㄧㄝˋ)
a firefly

暉映(ㄏㄨㄟ ㄧㄥˋ)
bright and brilliant

【暈】 2267
1. ㄩㄣ iun yūn
1. to faint; to swoon
2. giddy and dizzy
3. (usually used sarcastically)
to do things without a purpose

暈倒(ㄩㄣ ㄉㄠˇ)
to faint and fall; to swoon:
她一看見血便暈倒了。She
swoons at the sight of
blood.

暈頭(ㄩㄣ ㄊㄡˊ)
①(sarcastically) a bloody
fool; a blockhead; an imbecile ②to feel dizzy

暈頭巴腦(ㄩㄣ ㄊㄡˊ ㄅㄚ ㄋㄠˇ)
to feel dizzy and giddy

暈頭轉向(ㄩㄣ ㄊㄡˊ ㄓㄨㄢˇ ㄒㄧㄤˋ)
①to feel dizzy and giddy ②
so confused that one doesn't
know what to do, say, etc.:
這門科目真難，把我搞得暈頭轉
向。This course is really difficult; it has got me confused.

【暈】 2267
2. ㄩㄣ yùnn yùn

1. (meteorology) a halo; vapors; a mist
2. dazzled; to feel faint or dizzy

暈飛機 (ㄩㄣ ㄷㄟ ㄐㄧ)
airsick

暈氣 (ㄩㄣ ㄑㄧ)
fog, mist or vapor that reflects the colors of the sun

暈車 (ㄩㄣ ㄔㄜ)
to be bussick, trainsick or carsick

暈船 (ㄩㄣ ㄔㄨㄢ)
to be seasick: 她容易暈船。
She is liable to be seasick.

【暑】 2268
ㄕㄨ shuu shǔ

1. hot; heat; the heat of summer
2. mid-summer; summer

暑伏 (ㄕㄨ ㄈㄨ)
the hottest spell of summer; dog days

暑天 (ㄕㄨ ㄊㄧㄢ)
hot days; summertime

暑假 (ㄕㄨ ㄐㄧㄚ)
summer vacation: 他們在海濱度暑假。 They spent their summer vacation at the seashore.

暑期 (ㄕㄨ ㄑㄧ)
① summer ② the summer vacation

暑期班 (ㄕㄨ ㄑㄧ ㄅㄢ)
a summer class or school

暑期學校 (ㄕㄨ ㄑㄧ ㄒㄩㄝ ㄒㄧㄠ)
a summer school

暑氣 (ㄕㄨ ㄑㄧ)
the heat of summer; the scorching heat

暑氣迫人 (ㄕㄨ ㄑㄧ ㄆㄛ ㄖㄣ)
The summer heat is very oppressive.

暑熱 (ㄕㄨ ㄖㄜ)
the scorching heat; the heat of summer

暑熱天 (ㄕㄨ ㄖㄜ ㄊㄧㄢ) or 暑天 (ㄕㄨ ㄊㄧㄢ)
hot summer days; hot

weather; dog days

暑溽 (ㄕㄨ ㄖㄨ)
hot and steamy; hot and humid

暑歲 (ㄕㄨ ㄙㄨㄟ)
a year of heat and drought

暑暍 (ㄕㄨ ㄧㄝ)
sunstroke

暑月 (ㄕㄨ ㄩㄝ)
summer months

【暗】 2269
ㄢ ann àn

1. dim; dark; obscure: 天色漸漸暗了。 It's getting dark.
2. stupid; ignorant: 他不是愚魯，祇是懶。 He's not stupid, merely lazy.
3. secret; clandestine; stealthy
4. hidden (meanings, drainage systems, rocks, etc.): 他的話另有暗義。 His words had a hidden meaning.

暗盤 (ㄢ ㄆㄢ)
a price or quotation which is kept from public knowledge but made known to selected few

暗碼 (ㄢ ㄇㄚ)
① a secret code ② secret signs used by a store to indicate the actual value of a commodity—which is not known to outsiders

暗昧 (ㄢ ㄇㄟ)
① stupid and ignorant: 這後子心智暗昧。 This boy is mentally stupid. ② stealthy or clandestine ③ obscure (due to the lapse of time)

暗門子 (ㄢ ㄇㄣ ㄗ) or 暗娼 (ㄢ ㄔㄤ)
unlicensed prostitutes

暗面描寫 (ㄢ ㄇㄧㄢ ㄇㄧㄠ ㄒㄧㄝ)
a realistic description of the seamy side of life

暗房 (ㄢ ㄈㄤ)
① (photography) a darkroom ② (now rarely) a room in which a woman gives birth to a child

暗訪 (ㄢ ㄈㄤ)
to make secret inquiries; to investigate in secret; a secret investigation

暗淡 (ㄢ ㄉㄢ) or 黯淡 (ㄢ ㄉㄢ)
① (said of colors, etc.) faded, dull and not fresh ② (said of business, future prospects, etc.) dim; dismal

a secret struggle, jockeying for power, favor, etc.

暗地揭鬼 (ㄢ ㄉㄧ ㄍㄨㄟ ㄍㄨㄟ)
to make trouble secretly

暗地裏 (ㄢ ㄉㄧ ㄌㄧ)
secretly; clandestinely; stealthily; on the sly

暗度陳倉 (ㄢ ㄉㄨ ㄔㄣ ㄘㄤ)
secret rendezvous between lovers; illicit affairs; adultery

暗探 (ㄢ ㄊㄢ)
① a plainclothes man; a detective; a spy: 他雇用一名私人暗探。 He hired a private detective. ② to spy; to investigate in secret

暗樓子 (ㄢ ㄌㄡ ㄗ)
a hidden attic or garret

暗裏 (ㄢ ㄌㄧ)
secretly; inwardly; in one's heart: 他暗裏幫助他們。 He helped them secretly.

暗裏算計 (ㄢ ㄌㄧ ㄙㄨㄢ ㄐㄧ)
to calculate in one's mind; to make calculations in secret

暗流 (ㄢ ㄌㄧㄡ)
a subterranean flow; an undercurrent

暗溝 (ㄢ ㄍㄡ)
a sewer; an underground or covered drain

暗合 (ㄢ ㄏㄜ)
an unintentional meeting of minds or agreement; agreement without prior consultation

暗害 (ㄢ ㄏㄞ)
to injure another secretly; to assassinate or murder

暗號 (ㄢ ㄏㄠ)
a secret mark, sign, signal or password

暗含著 (ㄢ ㄏㄢ ㄓㄜ)
to speak with an overtone; to convey meaning in between the lines; to insinuate; to imply

暗花兒 (ㄢ ㄏㄨㄚ ㄦ)
indistinct grains, stripes, etc. of wood, porcelain, etc.

暗火 (ㄢ ㄏㄨㄛ)
a dying fire

暗疾 (ㄢ ㄐㄧ)
ailments or diseases which

〔日部〕

are hidden from view—as piles, V. D., etc. 亦作「隱疾」

暗計 (ㄢ ㄐㄧˋ)
①to calculate or count in one's heart ②a secret design or trick; a conspiracy

暗記 (ㄢ ㄐㄧˋ)
①to memorize; to bear in mind ②a secret sign 參看「暗號」

暗礁 (ㄢ ㄐㄧㄠ)
①a submerged (or hidden) reef: 那艘船撞到暗礁沉沒。The ship was wrecked on the hidden reef. ②an unseen obstacle

暗九 (ㄢ ㄐㄧㄡˇ)
(said of one's age) a multiple of nine which begins from 18 and ends at 81

暗箭 (ㄢ ㄐㄧㄢˋ)
(literally) a secret arrow —secret activities designed to hurt somebody.

暗箭傷人 (ㄢ ㄐㄧㄢˋ ㄕㄤ ㄖㄣˊ)
to hurt another by clandestine means; to stab somebody in the back: 暗箭傷人是不道德的行為。It is immoral conduct to hurt others by clandestine means.

暗泣 (ㄢ ㄑㄧˋ)
to weep behind others' backs; to weep without uttering sound

暗器 (ㄢ ㄑㄧˋ)
(in old Chinese fighting art) hidden weapons, usually a projectile

暗喜 (ㄢ ㄒㄧˇ)
to feel happy or delighted secretly

暗笑 (ㄢ ㄒㄧㄠˋ)
to laugh in one's heart; to laugh behind another's back; to laugh up one's sleeve

暗香 (ㄢ ㄒㄧㄤ)
aroma or fragrance which is not strong but very persistent

暗香疏影 (ㄢ ㄒㄧㄤ ㄕㄨ ㄧㄥˇ)
a descriptive phrase for Chinese plum flowers (梅花)

暗箱 (ㄢ ㄒㄧㄤ)
a camera obscura

暗想 (ㄢ ㄒㄧㄤˇ)
to muse; to ponder; to turn

over in one's mind: 她把問題再暗想一次。She mused the question once more.

暗轉 (ㄢ ㄓㄨㄢˇ)
①to get a transfer or promotion in secret ②(drama) a dark change

暗中 (ㄢ ㄓㄨㄥ)
①secretly; in secret; on the sly; surreptitiously; stealthily; clandestinely; privately: 我暗中得知此事。I was told about the matter in secret. ②(to do something) in the dark or without light

暗中摸索 (ㄢ ㄓㄨㄥ ㄇㄛ ㄙㄨㄛˇ)
to grope in the dark: 他在暗中摸索着找門柄。He groped for the doorhandle in the dark.

暗嘲 (ㄢ ㄔㄠˊ)
to laugh in secret; to ridicule; to be sarcastic: 醫生常在戲劇裏被暗嘲。Doctors are often ridiculed in the plays.

暗潮 (ㄢ ㄔㄠˊ)
①an undercurrent; a hidden current of water beneath the surface ②an undercurrent; a behind-the-scenes maneuver, conflict, struggle, etc.

暗娼 (ㄢ ㄔㄤ)
unlicensed prostitutes

暗場 (ㄢ ㄔㄤˇ) or (ㄢ ㄔㄤˊ)
details in a play which are not acted out but revealed in narration, dialogues, etc.

暗處 (ㄢ ㄔㄨˋ)
①a dark place; an obscure corner ②a secret place

暗示 (ㄢ ㄕˋ)
①to hint; to suggest; to drop a hint: 我暗示他不夠謹慎。I hinted at his imprudence. ②a hint; an insinuation; a suggestion: 他們似乎沒有會我的暗示。They don't seem to take my hint.

暗室 (ㄢ ㄕˋ)
①a dark, obscure or out-of-the-way place ②a dark room for detaining rebellious prisoners ③a dark-room for developing photographs

暗事 (ㄢ ㄕˋ)
clandestine actions or illicit conduct

暗殺 (ㄢ ㄕㄚ)
assassination; to assassinate

暗殺黨 (ㄢ ㄕㄚ ㄉㄤˇ)
a gang of assassins

暗射 (ㄢ ㄕㄜˋ)
to insinuate

暗傷 (ㄢ ㄕㄤ)
①an internal injury of human body ②invisible damage of an object

暗自 (ㄢ ㄗˋ)
inwardly; to oneself; secretly: 他暗自慶幸。He considered himself lucky secretly.

暗操賤業 (ㄢ ㄘㄠ ㄐㄧㄢˋ ㄧㄝˋ)
to engage in unlicensed prostitution

暗藏 (ㄢ ㄘㄤˊ)
to hide; to conceal

暗藏春色 (ㄢ ㄘㄤˊ ㄔㄨㄣ ㄙㄜˋ)
(said of a building which usually looks respectable) to have hidden corners, cabins, etc. for amorous purposes

暗色 (ㄢ ㄙㄜˋ)
dark colors; deep colors; cold colors

暗算 (ㄢ ㄙㄨㄢˋ)
a secret plot; to plot in secret; to plot against

暗筍 (ㄢ ㄙㄨㄣˇ)
bamboo shoots which are still beneath the surface of the ground

暗送秋波 (ㄢ ㄙㄨㄥˋ ㄑㄧㄡ ㄆㄛ)
①to convey love by stealing a look at the other party ②to establish secret contact with the enemy camp, opposing faction, etc.

暗 (ㄢˋ)
①obscure ②secret

暗無天日 (ㄢ ㄨˊ ㄊㄧㄢ ㄖˋ)
①(said of a place, room, etc.) very dark ②(said of a nation, locality, etc.) where the jungle law reigns; lawlessness; total absence of justice

暗喻 (ㄢ ㄩˋ)
a concealed analogy; a metaphor

【暖】 2270

(煖) ㄋㄨㄢ noan nuan

warm, genial (weather): 天氣一天比一天暖和了。It is getting warmer day by day.

暖房(ㄋㄨㄢˇㄈㄤˊ)
① a housewarming party sponsored by friends and relatives on the eve of one's wedding or moving in ② a hothouse; a greenhouse

暖流(ㄋㄨㄢˇㄌㄧㄨˊ)
①(geography) warm ocean currents ②(meteorology) warm air currents

暖爐(ㄋㄨㄢˇㄌㄨˊ)
a stove for keeping a room warm in winter; a brazier

暖鍋(ㄋㄨㄢˇㄍㄨㄛ)
a tin, brass or pottery vessel in which food is kept steaming hot with a slow fire burning underneath; a chafing pot

暖炕(ㄋㄨㄢˇㄎㄤ)
(in North China) to warm the clay (or brick) bed by keeping a small fire under it throughout the night; such a clay (or brick) bed

暖壺(ㄋㄨㄢˇㄏㄨˊ)
① a thermos bottle ② a vessel wrapped in cloth, etc. for keeping tea warm

暖烘烘(ㄋㄨㄢˇㄏㄨㄥㄏㄨㄥ)
very warm

暖和(ㄋㄨㄢˇ˙ㄏㄨㄛ)
① warm: 她坐在暖和的陽光中。She sat in the warm sunshine. ② to warm up

暖轎(ㄋㄨㄢˇㄐㄧㄠˋ)
a sedan chair with drapes around to protect the rider from cold

暖氣(ㄋㄨㄢˇㄑㄧˋ)
warm vapor; (in air-conditioning) warm air

暖氣爐(ㄋㄨㄢˇㄑㄧˋㄌㄨˊ)
a gas heater

暖氣管(ㄋㄨㄢˇㄑㄧˋㄍㄨㄢˇ)
a heating pipe

暖氣裝置(ㄋㄨㄢˇㄑㄧˋㄓㄨㄤㄓˋ)或暖氣設備(ㄋㄨㄢˇㄑㄧˋㄕㄜˋㄅㄟˋ)
central heating installation; a heater

暖手(ㄋㄨㄢˇㄕㄡˇ)
to warm the hands: 他在冬天打字前先暖手。In winter he warms his hands before typing.

暖壽(ㄋㄨㄢˇㄕㄡˋ)

a feast or party taking place on the eve of one's birthday

暖水瓶(ㄋㄨㄢˇㄕㄨㄟˇㄆㄧㄥˊ)
a thermos bottle

暖熱(ㄋㄨㄢˇㄖㄜˋ)
very warm

暖融融(ㄋㄨㄢˇㄖㄨㄥˊㄖㄨㄥˊ)
warm, cozy and comfortable

暖翠(ㄋㄨㄢˇㄘㄨㄟˋ)
the verdant hills in the warm spring

暖色(ㄋㄨㄢˇㄙㄜˋ)
warm colors: 紅、黃、橙三色被稱為暖色。Red, yellow and orange are called warm colors.

暖酥(ㄋㄨㄢˇㄙㄨ)
a girl's breasts (which are warm and soft).

暖耳(ㄋㄨㄢˇㄦˇ)
earmuffs

【暌】 ㄎㄨㄟˊ kwei kuí 2271
1. in opposition
2. to separate; to part

暌合(ㄎㄨㄟˊㄏㄜˊ)
to meet and to part; union and separation

暌索(ㄎㄨㄟˊㄙㄨㄛˇ)
to get separated from each other

暌違(ㄎㄨㄟˊㄨㄟˊ)
(said of friends) separated; parted; separation: 我們已暌違數載。It's years since we parted.

十畫

【暝】 ㄇㄧㄥˊ ming míng 2272, 1.
obscure; dark: 天色將暝。It is getting dark.

暝濛(ㄇㄧㄥˊㄇㄥˊ)
obscure: 霧使景色暝濛不清。Mist made the view obscure.

【暝】 ㄇㄧㄥˊ ming míng 2272, 2.
night

【暢】 ㄔㄤˋ chang chàng 2273
1. smoothly; fluently
2. easily accessible
3. with gusto; to one's heart's content
4. free; expanding
5. luxuriant; luxuriance
6. (to state or elaborate) free-

ly; without restraint; clear
7. very
8. a Chinese family name

暢茂(ㄔㄤˋㄇㄠˋ)
luxuriant; prosperous; flourishing

暢達(ㄔㄤˋㄉㄚˊ)
clearly and smoothly: 譯文暢達。The translation reads clearly and smoothly.

暢談(ㄔㄤˋㄊㄢˊ)
to talk to one's heart's content

暢通(ㄔㄤˋㄊㄨㄥ)
unimpeded; unblocked: 前面的公路暢通無阻。The highway is unimpeded ahead.

暢流(ㄔㄤˋㄌㄧㄨˊ)
flowing freely

暢快(ㄔㄤˋㄎㄨㄞˋ)
cheerful and exuberant; spiritually elevated

暢懷(ㄔㄤˋㄏㄨㄞˊ)
comfortable and joyful; to one's heart's content

暢銷(ㄔㄤˋㄒㄧㄠ)
a booming sale; to sell well; to sell briskly

暢銷書(ㄔㄤˋㄒㄧㄠㄕㄨ)
a best seller

暢行無阻(ㄔㄤˋㄒㄧㄥˊㄨˊㄗㄨˇ)
to meet no obstacle wherever one goes; to pass unimpeded

暢敍(ㄔㄤˋㄒㄩˋ)
to converse joyfully; to talk to one's heart's content: 他們暢敍離情。They conversed joyfully about their separation during their separation.

暢暢(ㄔㄤˋㄔㄤˋ)
joyful and peaceful

暢然(ㄔㄤˋㄖㄢˊ)
joyfully

暢所欲言(ㄔㄤˋㄙㄨㄛˇㄩˋㄧㄢˊ)
to get something off one's chest; to talk to one's heart's content; to assert without any restraint; to speak one's mind freely

暢所欲為(ㄔㄤˋㄙㄨㄛˇㄩˋㄨㄟˊ)
to do whatever one likes

暢遂(ㄔㄤˋㄙㄨㄟˋ)
luxuriant (growth of plants, etc.); flourishing

暢遊(ㄔㄤˋㄧㄡˊ)
to enjoy a sightseeing tour:

那些旅客們暢遊名勝古蹟。The tourists enjoyed a trip to places of historic interest.

暢飲(ㄔㄤ ㄧㄣˇ)
to drink to one's heart's content: 他們通宵暢飲。They drank to their hearts' content all night.

暢旺(ㄔㄤ ㄨㄤˋ)
flourishing or prosperous; booming

暢馨(ㄔㄤ ㄊㄜˋ)
(said of plants) flourishing and prospering

暢月(ㄔㄤ ㄩㄝˋ)
the eleventh moon of the lunar year

〔日部〕

十一畫

【暮】 2274
ㄇㄨˋ muh mù

1. sunset; evening; dusk
2. closing (years); ending; late: 歲事其暮。The year is drawing to its ending.

暮年(ㄇㄨˋ ㄋㄧㄢˊ)
closing years of one's life; old age; declining years

暮齡(ㄇㄨˋ ㄌㄧㄥˊ)
closing years of one's life; aged: 他已屆暮齡。He is aged.

暮鼓晨鐘(ㄇㄨˋ ㄍㄨˇ ㄔㄣˊ ㄓㄨㄥ)
①(literally) evening drums and morning bells—used in Buddhist temples to tell time ② ringing statements or remarks which arouse the public from degeneracy or warn against lurking danger, etc.

暮景(ㄇㄨˋ ㄐㄧㄥˇ)
one's circumstances (especially, financial) during his closing years

暮氣(ㄇㄨˋ ㄑㄧˋ)
lifelessness; despondence and emaciation; gloom; dejection

暮氣沉沉(ㄇㄨˋ ㄑㄧˋ ㄔㄣˊ ㄔㄣˊ)
①(said of a person) despondent and dejected; a defeatist attitude; gloomy; indolent; lethargy ② (said of atmosphere) dead and dull; gloomy; lethargy

暮秋(ㄇㄨˋ ㄑㄧㄡ)
late autumn

暮齒(ㄇㄨˋ ㄔˇ)

late in one's life; one's closing years; aged

暮春(ㄇㄨˋ ㄔㄨㄣ)
late spring

暮世(ㄇㄨˋ ㄕˋ)
recently; the world nowadays

暮生兒(ㄇㄨˋ ㄕㄥ ㄦˊ)
a posthumous child

暮色(ㄇㄨˋ ㄙㄜˋ)
dusk; twilight; the gloaming

暮色朦朧(ㄇㄨˋ ㄙㄜˋ ㄇㄥˊ ㄌㄨㄥˊ)
glimmering twilight

暮歲(ㄇㄨˋ ㄙㄨㄟˋ)
①the end of the year ② closing years of one's life; twilight of one's life

暮靄(ㄇㄨˋ ㄞˇ)
the evening mists: 暮靄籠罩着田野。The evening mists were hovering over the field.

【暫】 2275
ㄓㄢˋ jann zhàn
(讀音 ㄗㄢˋ tzann zàn)

1. temporarily; for a short time; not lasting
2. suddenly; abruptly

暫別(ㄓㄢˋ ㄅㄧㄝˊ)
a short separation; to part for a short time

暫定(ㄓㄢˋ ㄉㄧㄥˋ)
①(said of time) tentatively set on, at, etc.: 學習限暫定一年。The term of study is tentatively set on one year. ②(said of a number, price, place, etc.)tentatively fix at

暫停(ㄓㄢˋ ㄊㄧㄥˊ)
①to stop, halt or suspend temporarily: 會議暫停了。The meeting has been suspended temporarily. ② a time-out

暫留(ㄓㄢˋ ㄌㄧㄡˊ)
to stay for a short time

暫候(ㄓㄢˋ ㄏㄡˋ)
to wait for a short time

暫緩(ㄓㄢˋ ㄏㄨㄢˇ)
to hold for a while; to postpone or delay for a while; to put off; to defer: 我們最好暫時作出決定。We had better put off (or defer) making a decision.

暫濟燃眉(ㄓㄢˋ ㄐㄧˋ ㄖㄢˊ ㄇㄟˊ)
to temporarily relieve an emergency or an urgent need (often used in asking

for a short-term loan)

暫借(ㄓㄢˋ ㄐㄧㄝˋ)
to borrow for a short time: 我可以暫借你的鋼筆嗎？May I borrow your pen for a short time?

暫且(ㄓㄢˋ ㄑㄧㄝˇ)
for the time being: 會議暫且告一段落吧，Let's stop the meeting for the time being.

暫缺(ㄓㄢˋ ㄑㄩㄝ)
①(said of a post) to be left vacant for the time being ② (said of a commodity) to run short of stock at the moment

暫歇(ㄓㄢˋ ㄒㄧㄝ)
to rest for a while; to stay for a short time

暫行(ㄓㄢˋ ㄒㄧㄥˊ)
temporary; for the time being; provisional

暫行法(ㄓㄢˋ ㄒㄧㄥˊ ㄈㄚˇ)
provisional laws; temporary laws

暫住(ㄓㄢˋ ㄓㄨˋ)
to stay for a while; to lodge temporarily at...

暫齒(ㄓㄢˋ ㄔˇ)
temporary teeth or milk teeth 亦作「乳齒」

暫時(ㄓㄢˋ ㄕˊ)
for the time being; temporarily: 那雜誌暫時停刊。The magazine temporarily suspended publication.

暫延(ㄓㄢˋ ㄧㄢˊ)
to postpone tentatively to...; to adjourn temporarily

【暴】 2276
1. ㄅㄠˋ baw bào

1. cruel; savage; fierce; atrocious; violent: 他對待犯人非常殘暴。He is very cruel to the prisoners.
2. sudden
3. short-tempered; hot-tempered: 他的脾氣暴躁。He has a hot(or quick) temper.

暴斃(ㄅㄠˋ ㄅㄧˋ)
to meet a sudden death

暴病(ㄅㄠˋ ㄅㄧㄥˋ)
a sudden illness; to fall ill suddenly: 他突發暴病。He fell ill suddenly.

暴脾氣(ㄅㄠˋ ㄆㄧˊ ㄑㄧˋ)
a hot temper

暴民(ㄅㄠ ㄇㄧㄣˊ)
mobs or mobsters; 暴民圍聚
法庭。 Mobs collected round
the court.

暴發(ㄅㄠ ㄈㄚ)
①a violent eruption; a sudden flareup ②to break out;
to erupt ③to become rich
or to attain a high position
all of a sudden

暴發戶(ㄅㄠ ㄈㄚ ㄏㄨˋ)
an upstart; a parvenu;
nouveau riche

暴風(ㄅㄠ ㄈㄥ)or 暴風雨(ㄅㄠ ㄈㄥ ㄩˇ)
a storm; a tempest: 這場暴風
雨造成很重的損害。The storm
did a lot of harm.

暴風半徑(ㄅㄠ ㄈㄥ ㄅㄢˋ ㄐㄧㄥˋ)
the radius of a typhoon or
hurricane

暴風雪(ㄅㄠ ㄈㄥ ㄒㄩㄝˇ)
a snowstorm; a blizzard

暴富(ㄅㄠ ㄈㄨˋ)
sudden wealth

暴跌(ㄅㄠ ㄉㄧㄝˊ)
(said of prices) to nose-dive;
to drop sharply; to slump: 本
公司上個月的銷售量暴跌。
Sales slumped badly in our
company last month.

暴動(ㄅㄠ ㄉㄨㄥˋ)
a riot; a rebellion; an insurrection

暴投(ㄅㄠ ㄊㄡˊ)
(baseball) a wild pitch

暴跳如雷(ㄅㄠ ㄊㄧㄠˋ ㄖㄨˊ ㄌㄟˊ)
to be infuriated; to be
enraged; furious; stamping
and roaring with anger

暴殄天物(ㄅㄠ ㄊㄧㄢˇ ㄊㄧㄢ ㄨˋ)
to waste gifts of God; a
reckless waste of grains, etc.

暴徒(ㄅㄠ ㄊㄨˊ)
a rioter; a ruffian; a thug; a
mobster; a mob; a gangster

暴怒(ㄅㄠ ㄋㄨˋ)
furious; mad; to blow one's
top; a rage

暴虐(ㄅㄠ ㄋㄩㄝˋ)
cruel; tyrannical; despotic;
brutal; atrocious

暴雷(ㄅㄠ ㄌㄟˊ)
a sudden clap of thunder

暴力(ㄅㄠ ㄌㄧˋ)
violence; brute force; naked
force

暴利(ㄅㄠ ㄌㄧˋ)
sudden huge profits

暴戾(ㄅㄠ ㄌㄧˋ)
despotic and tyrannical;
cruel and fierce

暴戾恣睢(ㄅㄠ ㄌㄧˋ ㄗ ㄙㄨㄟ)
tyrannical; despotic; cruel

暴烈(ㄅㄠ ㄌㄧㄝˋ)
violent; fierce; wild

暴斂(ㄅㄠ ㄌㄧㄢˇ)
to extort; to collect illegitimate wealth

暴亂(ㄅㄠ ㄌㄨㄢˋ)
a riot; a rebellion; a revolt

暴掠(ㄅㄠ ㄌㄩㄝˋ)
to plunder; to pillage: 敵人把
所發現之財物均暴掠而去。The
enemy plundered all the
goods they found.

暴貴者(ㄅㄠ ㄍㄨㄟˋ ㄓㄜˇ)
a parvenu; an upstart

暴客(ㄅㄠ ㄎㄜˋ)
a robber

暴橫(ㄅㄠ ㄏㄥˋ)
tyrannical; despotic; atrocious; cruel

暴忽(ㄅㄠ ㄏㄨ)
evanescent; transient

暴虎馮河(ㄅㄠ ㄏㄨˇ ㄆㄧㄥˊ ㄏㄜˊ)
(literally) to try to fight a
tiger with bare hands and
cross a river without a boat
—intrepid but foolish; foolhardy

暴桀(ㄅㄠ ㄐㄧㄝˊ)
disobedient; recalcitrant;
defiant

暴君(ㄅㄠ ㄐㄩㄣ)
a tyrant; a despot: 暴君殘虐
無度。The tyrant rioted in
cruelty.

暴棄(ㄅㄠ ㄑㄧˋ)
to despair

暴行(ㄅㄠ ㄒㄧㄥˊ)
savage acts; violence; atrocities

暴性子(ㄅㄠ ㄒㄧㄥˋ·ㄗ)
a hot temper: 他是一個暴性子
的人。He is a hot-tempered
man.

暴漲(ㄅㄠ ㄓㄤˇ)
(said of a water level or a
commodity price) to rise
sharply or quickly; to skyrocket: 河水暴漲。The river
sharply rose.

暴政(ㄅㄠ ㄓㄥˋ)
tyrannical rule; the tyranny
of the government

暴躁(ㄅㄠ ㄗㄠˋ)
irritable; fretful; irascible;
choleric

暴卒(ㄅㄠ ㄗㄨˊ)
to die of a sudden illness; to
die a violent death

暴飲暴食(ㄅㄠ ㄧㄣˇ ㄅㄠ ㄕˊ)
to eat and drink excessively

暴雨(ㄅㄠ ㄩˇ)
torrential rain; a squall: 此地
六月間常有暴雨。We often
have torrential rain here in
June.

【暴】 2276
2.(曝) ㄆㄨˋ puh pù
to expose

暴面(ㄆㄨˋ ㄇㄧㄢˋ)
to make an appearance; to
appear

暴露(ㄆㄨˋ ㄌㄨˋ)
to expose or be exposed;
exposure: 他的陰謀已暴露
無遺。His plot has been thoroughly exposed.

暴露狂(ㄆㄨˋ ㄌㄨˋ ㄎㄨㄤˊ)
(psychiatry) ①exhibition-
ism ②an exhibitionist

暴骨(ㄆㄨˋ ㄍㄨˇ)
to expose one's bones to the
elements; to die in the wilds

暴光(ㄆㄨˋ ㄍㄨㄤ)
(photography) exposure

暴章(ㄆㄨˋ ㄓㄤ)
to show

暴著(ㄆㄨˋ ㄓㄨˋ)
conspicuous; striking

暴師(ㄆㄨˋ ㄕ)
to station troops in the
wilds

暴曬(ㄆㄨˋ ㄕㄞˋ)
to expose to sunshine: 別暴
曬陽光太久。Don't expose
yourself to sunshine too
long.

暴頸龍門(ㄆㄨˋ ㄙㄢ ㄌㄨㄥˊ ㄇㄣˊ)
(formerly) to flunk the civil
service examination

【暵】 2277
ㄏㄢˋ hann hàn
to expose to sunshine; to
dry; to be scorched up; withered; wizened

暵熱(ㄏㄢˋ ㄖㄜˋ)
exposed to scorching sun-

〔日部〕

〔日部〕

shine

【暱】 2278
(昵) ㄋㄧˋ nih ni
intimate; close: 她與他很親暱. She is on intimate terms with him.

暱交 (ㄋㄧˋ ㄐㄧㄠ)
close friendship

暱就 (ㄋㄧˋ ㄐㄧㄡˋ)
to draw near to

暱嫌 (ㄋㄧˋ ㄒㄧㄢˊ)
a personal grudge

暱愛 (ㄋㄧˋ ㄞˋ)
love or affection (between opposite sexes) 亦作「昵愛」

暱友 (ㄋㄧˋ ㄧㄡˇ)
a close friend: 他們是暱友. They are close friends.

十二畫

【暹】 2279
ㄒㄧㄢ shian xiān
(said of the sun) to rise

暹羅 (ㄒㄧㄢ ㄌㄨㄛˊ)
Siam, old name of Thailand

【曇】 2280
ㄊㄢˊ tarn tán
clouds: 山巔隱在雲曇中. The summit of the mountain is lost in the clouds.

曇曇 (ㄊㄢˊ ㄊㄢˊ)
cloudy; overcast

曇花 (ㄊㄢˊ ㄏㄨㄚ)
the epiphyllum; an orchid cactus

曇花一現 (ㄊㄢˊ ㄏㄨㄚ ㄧ ㄒㄧㄢˋ)
(said of glory, favorable situation, etc.) to appear and then quickly disappear; to last for a very brief period of time like the epiphyllum blooming at night; short-lived; a flash in the pan

【暨】 2281
ㄐㄧˋ jih jì
1. and
2. to reach; to attain; to overtake
3. up to; till

暨南大學 (ㄐㄧˋ ㄋㄢˊ ㄉㄚˋ ㄒㄩㄝˊ)
National Chinan University

暨今 (ㄐㄧˋ ㄐㄧㄣ)
up to the present; till now 亦作「至今」

【曆】 2282
ㄌㄧˋ lih lì
1. a calendar
2. an era; an age
3. to calculate; to count

曆本 (ㄌㄧˋ ㄅㄣˇ)
a calendar (as a table or register)

曆法 (ㄌㄧˋ ㄈㄚˇ)
a calendar (as a system)

曆象 (ㄌㄧˋ ㄒㄧㄤˋ)
to calculate the movements of the heavenly bodies

曆書 (ㄌㄧˋ ㄕㄨ)
an almanac

曆數 (ㄌㄧˋ ㄕㄨˋ)
① Heaven's will; the determinate appointment of Heaven; fate ② farming seasons

【曄】 2283
ㄧㄝˋ yeh yè
1. bright; radiant
2. prosperous; thriving

曄然 (ㄧㄝˋ ㄖㄢˊ)
prosperous; thriving

曄曄 (ㄧㄝˋ ㄧㄝˋ)
prosperous; thriving

【曈】 2284
ㄊㄨㄥˊ torng tóng
twilight before sunrise

曈曨 (ㄊㄨㄥˊ ㄌㄨㄥˊ)
twilight before sunrise

【曉】 2285
ㄒㄧㄠˇ sheau xiǎo
1. daybreak; dawn: 天將破曉. It is now toward daybreak.
2. to tell; to explain: 他被曉示立即出發. He was told to start at once.
3. to know; to understand: 他知曉實情. He knows the truth.

曉譬 (ㄒㄧㄠˇ ㄅㄧˋ)
to explain with examples

曉風殘月 (ㄒㄧㄠˇ ㄈㄥ ㄘㄢˊ ㄩㄝˋ)
(literally) the morning breeze and the lingering moon—nature at daybreak

曉得 (ㄒㄧㄠˇ ㄉㄜˊ)
to know; to be aware of: 天曉得! God knows!

曉霞 (ㄒㄧㄠˇ ㄒㄧㄚˊ)
rosy clouds at daybreak

曉行夜宿 (ㄒㄧㄠˇ ㄒㄧㄥˊ ㄧㄝˋ ㄙㄨˋ)
to start early and stop late during a journey

曉暢 (ㄒㄧㄠˇ ㄔㄤˋ)
(said of writing) clear and fluent: 這篇文章以曉暢的文體寫成. This article is written in a clear and fluent style.

曉示 (ㄒㄧㄠˇ ㄕˋ)
to tell explicitly; to explain; to notify

曉事 (ㄒㄧㄠˇ ㄕˋ)
(said of a person) understanding and experienced

曉色 (ㄒㄧㄠˇ ㄙㄜˋ)
the scene in the early morning

曉以大義 (ㄒㄧㄠˇ ㄧˇ ㄉㄚˋ ㄧˋ)
to persuade someone to follow the right path) by telling him what is right

曉悟 (ㄒㄧㄠˇ ㄨˋ)
to understand; to realize

曉諭 (ㄒㄧㄠˇ ㄩˋ)
to explain; to tell; to give explicit instructions

【曀】 2286
ㄧˋ yih yì
dim; obscure; cloudy

【曌】 2287
ㄓㄠˋ jaw zhào
same as 照, coined by 武則天 and used as her name

【曒】 2288
ㄊㄨㄣ tuen tūn
sunrise

曒曒 (ㄊㄨㄣ ㄊㄨㄣ)
bright; glowing; blazing

十三畫

【曖】 2289
ㄞˋ ay ài
1. dim; indistinct
2. ambiguous; vague

曖昧 (ㄞˋ ㄇㄟˋ)
① ambiguous; equivocal; obscure; vague: 他的態度曖昧. He assumes an ambiguous attitude. ② a secret impropriety

曖昧行徑 (ㄞˋ ㄇㄟˋ ㄒㄧㄥˊ ㄐㄧㄥˋ)
scandals (especially illicit affairs)

曖曖 (ㄞˋ ㄞˋ)
dim; obscure; dark

【曏】 2290
ㄒㄧㄤˇ shiang xiǎng
1. a period of time
2. once upon a time

曏者 (ㄒㄧㄤˇ ㄓㄜˇ)
once upon a time

十四畫

【曙】 2291
ㄕㄨ shuh shū
dawn; daybreak

曙光 (ㄕㄨ ㄍㄨㄤ)
the first light of morning;
light at dawn

曙後星孤 (ㄕㄨ ㄏㄡˋ ㄒㄧㄥ ㄍㄨ)
an orphaned girl

曙日 (ㄕㄨ ㄖˋ)
in the morning

曙色 (ㄕㄨ ㄙㄜˋ)
light at daybreak; the light
of early dawn; the gray of
the morning

【曚】 2292
ㄇㄥˊ meng méng
dim; obscure

曚曨 (ㄇㄥˊ ㄌㄨㄥˊ)
dim; obscure: 雲遮月曚曨。
The moon was obscured by
clouds. 亦作「朦朧」

【曜】 2293
ㄧㄠˋ yaw yào
(又讀 ㄩㄝˋ yueh
yuè)
1. daylight; sunshine
2. to shine; to glisten

曜靈 (ㄧㄠˋ ㄌㄧㄥˊ)
the sun

【曛】 2294
ㄒㄩㄣ shiun xūn
1. twilight; dusk
2. the dim glow of the setting
sun

曛黑 (ㄒㄩㄣ ㄏㄟ)
dusky

曛黃 (ㄒㄩㄣ ㄏㄨㄤˊ)
sunset; dusk

十五畫

【曠】 2295
ㄎㄨㄤˋ kuang kuàng
1. open; wide; broad; empty;
vast; spacious; unoccupied
2. free from worries and petty
ideas
3. to neglect; neglect

曠廢 (ㄎㄨㄤˋ ㄈㄟˋ)
to waste

曠廢 (ㄎㄨㄤˋ ㄈㄟˋ)
to neglect; 勿曠廢你的工作和
職守。Don't neglect your
work and duty.

曠放 (ㄎㄨㄤˋ ㄈㄤˋ)
free and composed

曠夫 (ㄎㄨㄤˋ ㄈㄨ)
an unmarried man of mar-
riageable age

曠達 (ㄎㄨㄤˋ ㄉㄚˊ)
unrestrained; free; broad-
minded: 他是一位曠達的學者。
He is a broad-minded
scholar.

曠代 (ㄎㄨㄤˋ ㄉㄞˋ)
unequaled by one's contemporaries: 她是曠代佳人。She is
a beauty unequaled by her
contemporaries

曠蕩 (ㄎㄨㄤˋ ㄉㄤˋ)
①(said of space) boundless;
endless ②unrestrained; free

曠土 (ㄎㄨㄤˋ ㄊㄨˇ)
a wilderness; a wasteland

曠古未有 (ㄎㄨㄤˋ ㄍㄨˇ ㄨㄟˋ ㄧㄡˇ)
unprecedented in history

曠官 (ㄎㄨㄤˋ ㄍㄨㄢ)
a negligent official

曠工 (ㄎㄨㄤˋ ㄍㄨㄥ)
to neglect work

曠課 (ㄎㄨㄤˋ ㄎㄜˋ)
to be absent from class
without leave; to cut school;
to play truant; to truant

曠久 (ㄎㄨㄤˋ ㄐㄧㄡˇ)
lasting; long

曠學 (ㄎㄨㄤˋ ㄒㄩㄝˊ)
to neglect one's studies; to
play truant

曠職 (ㄎㄨㄤˋ ㄓˊ)
①to be absent from the
office without leave ②to
neglect official duties

曠世 (ㄎㄨㄤˋ ㄕˋ)
unequaled by one's contemporaries

曠世之才 (ㄎㄨㄤˋ ㄕˋ ㄓ ㄘㄞˊ)
a man of brilliance un-
equaled by his contempo-
raries

曠日持久 (ㄎㄨㄤˋ ㄖˋ ㄔˊ ㄐㄧㄡˇ)
to maintain a situation for a
long time to no avail; long-
drawn-out; protracted

曠逸 (ㄎㄨㄤˋ ㄧˋ)
unrestrained

曠野 (ㄎㄨㄤˋ ㄧㄝˇ)
wild plains; a prairie; the
open fields

曠原 (ㄎㄨㄤˋ ㄩㄢˊ)
wild plains; a wilderness; a

prairie; the open fields

【曝】 2296
ㄆㄨˋ puh pù
to expose to sunlight; to sun

曝背 (ㄆㄨˋ ㄅㄟˋ)
to turn the back to the sun
and enjoy its warmth

曝露 (ㄆㄨˋ ㄌㄨˋ)
to expose oneself to the
weather 亦作「暴露」

曝光 (ㄆㄨˋ ㄍㄨㄤ)
(photography) exposure

曝獻 (ㄆㄨˋ ㄒㄧㄢˋ)
to offer a humble but sincere gift or service

曝曬 (ㄆㄨˋ ㄕㄞˋ)
to expose to sunlight; to sun

曝書 (ㄆㄨˋ ㄕㄨ)
to sun books

十六畫

【曦】 2297
ㄒㄧ shi xī
sunshine; sunlight

曦光 (ㄒㄧ ㄍㄨㄤ)
sunshine; sunlight

【曨】 (曨) 2298
ㄌㄨㄥˊ long
lóng
1. vague; dim: 對於往事她僅有
曚曨的記憶。She has only a
dim recollection of the past.
2. bright

十七畫

【曩】 2299
ㄋㄤˇ naang nǎng
past; former

曩昔 (ㄋㄤˇ ㄒㄧˊ)
in the past; in former times

曩者 (ㄋㄤˇ ㄓㄜˇ)
in the past; in former times

曩時 (ㄋㄤˇ ㄕˊ)
in former times; in the past

曩日 (ㄋㄤˇ ㄖˋ)
bygone days

十九畫

【曬】 (晒) 2300
ㄕㄞˋ shay shài
to expose to sunlight; to dry
in the sun

曬不透 (ㄕㄞˋ ㄅㄨˋ ㄊㄡˋ)
impervious to sunshine

【日部】

曬棚(ㄕㄞ ㄆㄥˊ)
a drying stand or rack

曬臺(ㄕㄞ ㄊㄞˊ)
a terrace where the laundry is dried in the sun

曬太陽(ㄕㄞ ㄊㄞˋ ㄧㄤ)
to be exposed to the sun; to bask in the sun

曬圖(ㄕㄞ ㄊㄨˊ)
to make a blueprint; a blueprint 亦作「曬藍圖」

曬暖兒(ㄕㄞ ㄋㄨㄢˇ ㄦ)
to bask in the sun

曬乾(ㄕㄞ ㄍㄢ)
to dry in the sun

曬黑(ㄕㄞ ㄏㄟ)
(said of skin) darkened by overexposure to the sun

曬場(ㄕㄞ ㄔㄤˊ)or(ㄕㄞ ㄔㄤˇ)
a drying yard

曬鹽(ㄕㄞ ㄧㄢˊ)
to sun seawater to obtain salt

日 部
ㄩㄝˋ iue　yuē

【日】 2301
ㄩㄝˋ iue　yuē
1. (an archaic usage) to say
2. to call; to name

二畫

【曲】 2302
1. ㄑㄩ chiu　qū
1. bent; crooked; twisted; winding
2. little known; obscure
3. wrong; unjustifiable

曲筆(ㄑㄩ ㄅㄧˇ)
to distort facts in writing

曲庇(ㄑㄩ ㄅㄧˋ)
to conceal (another's mistake) by distortion of facts

曲阜(ㄑㄩ ㄈㄨˋ)
Chüfu, Shantung Province, where Confucius was born

曲度(ㄑㄩ ㄉㄨˋ)
(mathematics) curvature

曲突徙薪(ㄑㄩ ㄊㄨˊ ㄒㄧˇ ㄒㄧㄣ)
(literally) to bend the chimney and remove the fuel—

to take precautions before it is too late

曲撓(ㄑㄩ ㄋㄠˊ)
unjust accusation; unfair blame

曲欄(ㄑㄩ ㄌㄢˊ)
a winding balustrade

曲裏拐彎兒(ㄑㄩˋ ㄌㄧˇ ㄍㄨㄞˇ ㄨㄢ ㄦ)
winding; labyrinthine; zigzag; tortuous

曲流(ㄑㄩ ㄌㄧㄡˊ)
(geography) a meander

曲棍球(ㄑㄩ ㄍㄨㄣˋ ㄑㄧㄡˊ)
① hockey ② a hockey ball

曲肱而枕之(ㄑㄩ ㄍㄨㄥ ㄦˊ ㄓㄣˋ ㄓ)
(literally) to use one's bent arm as a pillow—to be poor but content

曲拱(ㄑㄩ ㄍㄨㄥˇ)
arched

曲解(ㄑㄩ ㄐㄧㄝˇ)
to misconstrue; to misinterpret; to twist; to distort: 這話意思很明確, 你無法曲解。These remarks are so clear that you can't distort them.

曲徑(ㄑㄩ ㄐㄧㄥˋ)
a winding path

曲徑通幽(ㄑㄩ ㄐㄧㄥˋ ㄊㄨㄥ ㄧㄡ)
a winding path leading to a secluded place

曲全(ㄑㄩ ㄑㄩㄢˊ)
to suppress one's own feelings for the sake of greater interests

曲線(ㄑㄩ ㄒㄧㄢˋ)
(mathematics) curved line; curve

曲線板(ㄑㄩ ㄒㄧㄢˋ ㄅㄢˇ)
a curved ruler

曲線美(ㄑㄩ ㄒㄧㄢˋ ㄇㄟˇ)
① linear beauty ② (said of a woman) curvaceous, or curvacious; shapely

曲直(ㄑㄩ ㄓˊ)
right and wrong: 你真是曲直不分。You really cannot distinguish between right and wrong.

曲折(ㄑㄩ ㄓㄜˊ)
① bends; turns; curves; turns and twists; tortuous: 那條路有許多曲折之處。The road is full of turns and twists. ② complications of an affair; complicated

曲折有致(ㄑㄩ ㄓㄜˊ ㄧㄡˇ ㄓˋ)
(said of a speech or literary work) delightfully complicated

曲折語(ㄑㄩ ㄓㄜˊ ㄩˇ)
inflective language 亦作「屈折語」

曲尺(ㄑㄩ ㄔˇ)
a (carpenter's) square

曲成(ㄑㄩ ㄔㄥˊ)
to fulfill somehow or other; to accomplish by hook or by crook

曲士(ㄑㄩ ㄕˋ)
an obscure person; a cramped scholar

曲室(ㄑㄩ ㄕˋ)
a secret chamber

曲射(ㄑㄩ ㄕㄜˋ)
(military) to curve fire

曲射砲(ㄑㄩ ㄕㄜˋ ㄆㄠˋ)
(military) a howitzer; a curve-fire gun

曲蟮(ㄑㄩ ㄕㄢˋ)
an earthworm

曲說(ㄑㄩ ㄕㄨㄛ)
a biased statement

曲從(ㄑㄩ ㄘㄨㄥˊ)
to obey or yield reluctantly: 他曲從她的決定。He reluctantly obeyed her decision.

曲意(ㄑㄩ ㄧˋ)
to make a special concession to achieve others' goals

曲意逢迎(ㄑㄩ ㄧˋ ㄈㄥˊ ㄧㄥˊ)
to try in every way to flatter someone; to ingratiate oneself with someone

【曲】 2302
2. ㄑㄩˇ cheu　qǔ
1. a type of verse for singing, which emerged in the Southern Sung (南宋) and Kin (金) dynasties and became popular in the Yüan Dynasty
2. a piece of music; a song: 她當衆高歌一曲。She cheerfully sang a song in public.

曲本(ㄑㄩˇ ㄅㄣˇ)
a music book

曲牌(ㄑㄩˇ ㄆㄞˊ)
names of various music tunes

曲譜(ㄑㄩˇ ㄆㄨˇ)
title of a 14-book collection of music compiled during the Ching Dynasty

曲調(ㄑㄩˇ ㄉㄧㄠˋ)

tunes; melodies

曲高和寡〈ㄑㄩˇ ㄍㄠ ㄏㄜˋ ㄍㄨㄚˇ〉
(literally) Highbrow music can be appreciated by only a few people.— caviare to the general 或 The profounder a theory is, the fewer its supporters are. 或 The more virtuous a person is, the fewer friends he has.

曲終人散〈ㄑㄩˇ ㄓㄨㄥ ㄖㄣˊ ㄙㄢˋ〉
The music is over and the people are gone.—the sadness one feels after a fanfare

曲終奏雅〈ㄑㄩˇ ㄓㄨㄥ ㄗㄡˋ ㄧㄚˇ〉
(said of a writing, speech, or performance) a brilliant conclusion

曲子〈ㄑㄩˇ ˙ㄗ〉or 曲兒〈ㄑㄩㄦˊ〉
a number; a song; a tune; a melody: 他以口哨吹流行的曲子。He whistles a popular tune.

【曳】 2303 〈ㄧˋ yih yì〉
（讀音〈ㄧㄝˋ yeh yè〉）
to haul; to tug; to drag; to trail

曳白〈ㄧˋ ㄅㄞˊ〉
(in an examination) to pass over a blank page without writing anything on it through inadvertence

曳光彈〈ㄧˋ ㄍㄨㄤ ㄉㄢˋ〉
(military) a tracer bullet

曳裾王門〈ㄧˋ ㄐㄩ ㄨㄤˊ ㄇㄣˊ〉
to live as a protégé of a feudal lord

曳杖〈ㄧˋ ㄓㄤˋ〉
to walk with a cane

曳踵〈ㄧˋ ㄓㄨㄥˇ〉or 曳足〈ㄧˋ ㄗㄨˊ〉
to drag one's feet

曳引機〈ㄧˋ ㄧㄣˇ ㄐㄧ〉
a tractor

曳尾塗中〈ㄧˋ ㄨㄟˇ ㄊㄨˊ ㄓㄨㄥ〉
(literally) to wag the tail in the mire—to live in seclusion; to lead an obscure life

三畫

【更】 2304 〈ㄍㄥ geng gēng〉
1. the watches of the night (formerly the night was divided into five periods and each covered two hours)

2. a night watchman

3. to change; to alter; to shift

4. to experience: 他少不更事。He is young and inexperienced.

5. to alternate: 日夜彼此更替。Day and night alternate with each other.

更僕難數〈ㄍㄥ ㄆㄨˊ ㄋㄢˊ ㄕㄨˇ〉
too many to enumerate

更名〈ㄍㄥ ㄇㄧㄥˊ〉
to change one's name

更番〈ㄍㄥ ㄈㄢ〉
to work by turns; to take turns: 讓我們更番做這件事。Let us take turns at doing it.

更夫〈ㄍㄥ ㄈㄨ〉or 更卒〈ㄍㄥ ㄗㄨˊ〉
a night watchman

更賦〈ㄍㄥ ㄈㄨˋ〉
(in ancient China) the tax paid to the government in lieu of frontier service

更代〈ㄍㄥ ㄉㄞˋ〉
to take turns; to work by turns

更迭〈ㄍㄥ ㄉㄧㄝˊ〉
to make a change; to alternate: 雨天與晴天交替更迭。Wet days alternate with fine days.

更訂〈ㄍㄥ ㄉㄧㄥˋ〉
to revise: 那本字典需要更訂。That dictionary needs to be revised.

更端〈ㄍㄥ ㄉㄨㄢ〉
to have a new complication

更動〈ㄍㄥ ㄉㄨㄥˋ〉
to shift; to switch; to change: 人事更動 personnel changes

更替〈ㄍㄥ ㄊㄧˋ〉
to alternate; to take turns

更年期〈ㄍㄥ ㄋㄧㄢˊ ㄑㄧˊ〉
(physiology) the menopause

更樓〈ㄍㄥ ㄌㄡˊ〉
a watchtower

更漏〈ㄍㄥ ㄌㄡˋ〉
an hourglass; a sandglass

更改〈ㄍㄥ ㄍㄞˇ〉
to change (over); to alter; to modify: 我們的決定是不能更改的。Our decision is unalterable.

更鼓〈ㄍㄥ ㄍㄨˇ〉
a night watchman's drum

更換〈ㄍㄥ ㄏㄨㄢˋ〉or 更易〈ㄍㄥ ㄧˋ〉
to change; to replace; to alter

更休〈ㄍㄥ ㄒㄧㄡ〉
to rest by turns

更新〈ㄍㄥ ㄒㄧㄣ〉
to renew; to renovate: 萬象更新。All things change from old to new.

更行〈ㄍㄥ ㄒㄧㄥˊ〉
(said of a woman) to remarry

更姓〈ㄍㄥ ㄒㄧㄥˋ〉
to change one's surname; to change one's family name

更張〈ㄍㄥ ㄓㄤ〉
to change; to alter

更正〈ㄍㄥ ㄓㄥˋ〉
to correct; to put right; correction

更始〈ㄍㄥ ㄕˇ〉
to renovate; to renew

更事〈ㄍㄥ ㄕˋ〉
experienced in affairs of the world

更深人靜〈ㄍㄥ ㄕㄣ ㄖㄣˊ ㄐㄧㄥˋ〉
The night is late and people are quiet. 或 Deep is the night and all is quiet.

更戍〈ㄍㄥ ㄕㄨˋ〉
to shift garrison forces

更次〈ㄍㄥ ㄘˋ〉
①(formerly) the watches of the night ②the time of a night watch

更衣〈ㄍㄥ ㄧ〉
① to change clothes ② to go to toilet

更衣室〈ㄍㄥ ㄧ ㄕˋ〉
a changeroom; a dressing room; a locker room; a toilet

更易〈ㄍㄥ ㄧˋ〉
to alter; to change

【更】 2304 〈ㄍㄥˋ genq gèng〉
2. more; further; to a greater degree

更妙〈ㄍㄥˋ ㄇㄧㄠˋ〉
still better; more interesting

更多〈ㄍㄥˋ ㄉㄨㄛ〉
more; still more

更好〈ㄍㄥˋ ㄏㄠˇ〉
better 或 So much the better.

更壞〈ㄍㄥˋ ㄏㄨㄞˋ〉

〔日部〕

〔日部〕

worse; even worse; worse still

更加《《ㄥ ㄐㄧㄚ》
even more

更兼《《ㄥ ㄐㄧㄢ》
in addition; furthermore; besides

更少《《ㄥ ㄕㄠˇ》
still less

更生《《ㄥ ㄕㄥ》
to start life anew; to have a new life; to regenerate; to revive: 他在病後獲得更生。 After his illness he started his life anew.

更勝一籌《《ㄥ ㄕㄥˋ ㄧˋ ㄔㄡˊ》
even better

更有甚者《《ㄥ ㄧㄡˇ ㄕㄣˋ ㄓㄜˇ》
what is more

五畫

【曷】 2305
ㄏㄜˊ her hé

1. what
2. why not
3. how

曷故《ㄏㄜˊ ㄍㄨˋ》
why; what for

曷興乎來《ㄏㄜˊ ㄒㄧㄥ ㄏㄨ ㄌㄞˊ》
Why not come and do it?

曷若《ㄏㄜˊ ㄖㄨㄛˋ》
Wouldn't it be better to…?

六畫

【書】 2306
ㄕㄨ shu shū

1. writings; a book: 她正忙於寫一本書。She is engaged in writing a book.
2. to write: 請在紙的兩面書寫。Please write on both sides of the paper.
3. a letter: 家書抵萬金。A letter from home is worth ten thousand pieces of gold.
4. a document; a certificate
5. the style of the calligraphy; script: 楷書standard script of handwriting

書包《ㄕㄨ ㄅㄠ》
a satchel; a schoolbag

書報《ㄕㄨ ㄅㄠˋ》
books and newspapers

書本《ㄕㄨ ㄅㄣˇ》or 書本兒《ㄕㄨ ㄅㄣˇㄦ》
a book

書不盡言《ㄕㄨ ㄅㄨˋ ㄐㄧㄣˋ ㄧㄢˊ》
(a sentence often used at the end of a letter) Written words are a poor vehicle of thoughts. 或 I have more to say than what is contained in this letter.

書皮《ㄕㄨ ㄆㄧˊ》
the binding of a book; book covers; a book jacket

書癖《ㄕㄨ ㄆㄧˇ》
bibliomania

書評《ㄕㄨ ㄆㄧㄥˊ》
a book review

書鋪《ㄕㄨ ㄆㄨˋ》
a bookstore

書眉《ㄕㄨ ㄇㄟˊ》
the upper margin of a book page

書面《ㄕㄨ ㄇㄧㄢˋ》
written form of communication

書面答覆《ㄕㄨ ㄇㄧㄢˋ ㄉㄚˊ ㄈㄨˋ》
a written reply; an answer in writing

書名《ㄕㄨ ㄇㄧㄥˊ》
the title of a book: 這本書的書名很奇特。The title of this book is unique.

書名號《ㄕㄨ ㄇㄧㄥˊ ㄏㄠˋ》
the "book title" mark (a punctuation mark in present-day written Chinese, consisting of a wavy line placed usually to the left of the title)

書目《ㄕㄨ ㄇㄨˋ》
a book catalogue: 參考書目 a booklist; a title catalogue

書法《ㄕㄨ ㄈㄚˇ》
calligraphy

書坊《ㄕㄨ ㄈㄤ》
a bookstore

書房《ㄕㄨ ㄈㄤˊ》
①a study: 你在她書房裏可以找到她。You will find her in her study. ②(in former times) a small private school

書獃子《ㄕㄨ ㄉㄞ ˙ㄗ》or 書呆子《ㄕㄨ ㄉㄞ ˙ㄗ》or 書癡《ㄕㄨ ㄔ》
a studious idiot; a pedant; a bookworm

書丹《ㄕㄨ ㄉㄢ》
to write an epitaph

書單《ㄕㄨ ㄉㄢ》
a booklist

書店《ㄕㄨ ㄉㄧㄢˋ》
a bookstore

書牘《ㄕㄨ ㄉㄨˊ》
letters; correspondence

書蠹《ㄕㄨ ㄉㄨˋ》
a bookworm

書皮《ㄕㄨ ㄆㄧˊ》
a book jacket; a slipcase

書攤《ㄕㄨ ㄊㄢ》or 書攤兒《ㄕㄨ ㄊㄢㄦ》
a bookstand; a bookstall

書體《ㄕㄨ ㄊㄧˇ》
calligraphic style

書僮《ㄕㄨ ㄊㄨㄥˊ》
(in former times) a boy attendant at school or in one's study

書奴《ㄕㄨ ㄋㄨˊ》
(calligraphy) a slavish imitator

書樓《ㄕㄨ ㄌㄡˊ》
a library

書林《ㄕㄨ ㄌㄧㄣˊ》
a treasury of books

書癡《ㄕㄨ ㄔ》
a learned and yet useless person

書櫥《ㄕㄨ ㄔㄨˊ 》or 書架《ㄕㄨ ㄐㄧㄚˋ》
a bookshelf

書賈《ㄕㄨ ㄍㄨˇ》
a book dealer; a bookseller

書歸正傳《ㄕㄨ ㄍㄨㄟ ㄓㄥˋ ㄓㄨㄢˋ》
Let us come back to our main story. (a phrase often used by storytellers)

書櫃《ㄕㄨ ㄍㄨㄟˋ》
a bookcase

書館《ㄕㄨ ㄍㄨㄢˇ》
①(in former times) a private school ②a bookstore

書館兒《ㄕㄨ ㄍㄨㄢˇㄦ》
a public gathering place where storytellers entertain the audience

書客《ㄕㄨ ㄎㄜˋ》
a bookseller

書口《ㄕㄨ ㄎㄡˇ》
the outer margin of a book page (where the book title and page number are printed)

書刊《ㄕㄨ ㄎㄢ》
books and magazines: 現今的書刊銷路很大。Nowadays books and magazines have a large circulation.

書庫(ㄕㄨ ㄎㄨˋ)
the stock room of a library

書債(ㄕㄨ)
a book dealer

書空咄咄(ㄕㄨ ㄎㄨㄥ ㄉㄨㄛˋ ㄉㄨㄛˋ)
(literally) to write in the air, "How strange! How strange!"—to be out of one's senses (from disappointment, etc.); in great disillusion

書後(ㄕㄨ ㄏㄡˋ)
a book review attached to a literary work, written either by the author himself or someone else

書函(ㄕㄨ ㄏㄢˊ)
a letter; correspondence

書翰(ㄕㄨ ㄏㄢˋ)
a letter; correspondence

書畫(ㄕㄨ ㄏㄨㄚˋ)
works of calligraphy and painting

書畫同源(ㄕㄨ ㄏㄨㄚˋ ㄊㄨㄥˊ ㄩㄢˊ)
Calligraphy and painting are of the same origin. (being both the products of the writing brush)—a concept among Chinese literati in former times

書畫家(ㄕㄨ ㄏㄨㄚˋ ㄐㄧㄚ)
a master in calligraphy and painting

書籍(ㄕㄨ ㄐㄧˊ)
books

書脊(ㄕㄨ ㄐㄧˇ)
the spine (of a book)

書記(ㄕㄨ ㄐㄧˋ)
a clerk

書記官(ㄕㄨ ㄐㄧˋ ㄍㄨㄢ)
a clerk of a law court

書記長(ㄕㄨ ㄐㄧˋ ㄓㄤˇ)
a secretary-general; a chief clerk

書家(ㄕㄨ ㄐㄧㄚ)or 書法家(ㄕㄨ ㄈㄚˇ ㄐㄧㄚ)
a calligraphic master; a calligrapher

書夾(ㄕㄨ ㄐㄧㄚˊ)
bookends

書架(ㄕㄨ ㄐㄧㄚˋ)
a bookshelf; a bookrack

書價(ㄕㄨ ㄐㄧㄚˋ)
book prices: 書價似乎不貴。Book prices seem reasonable.

書柬 or 書簡(ㄕㄨ ㄐㄧㄢˇ)
letters

書經(ㄕㄨ ㄐㄧㄥ)
the *Book of History* (one of the *Five Classics*)

書局(ㄕㄨ ㄐㄩˊ)
a bookstore

書卷(ㄕㄨ ㄐㄩㄢˋ)
books and scrolls

書卷氣(ㄕㄨ ㄐㄩㄢˋ ㄑㄧˋ)
bookishness; a savor of books or learning (always used in a laudatory sense)

書契(ㄕㄨ ㄑㄧˋ)
a certificate (of ownership, etc.); a deed

書篋(ㄕㄨ ㄑㄧㄝˋ)
a bookcase

書籤(ㄕㄨ ㄑㄧㄢ)
①a book label pasted on the cover ②a bookmark 亦作「書籖」

書寫(ㄕㄨ ㄒㄧㄝˇ)
to write

書信(ㄕㄨ ㄒㄧㄣˋ)
letters; correspondence

書香(ㄕㄨ ㄒㄧㄤ)
the "fragrance of books"—the general environment favorable to scholars

書香門第(ㄕㄨ ㄒㄧㄤ ㄇㄣˊ ㄉㄧˋ)
a literary family

書帙(ㄕㄨ ㄓˋ)
a book jacket

書札(ㄕㄨ ㄓㄚˊ)
letters

書齋(ㄕㄨ ㄓㄞ)
a study

書桌(ㄕㄨ ㄓㄨㄛ)
a desk; a writing desk: 她正在書桌上寫字。She is writing at her desk.

書種(ㄕㄨ ㄓㄨㄥˇ)
people given to learning

書場(ㄕㄨ ㄔㄤˊ)or(ㄕㄨ ㄔㄤˇ)
a house where stories are told

書城(ㄕㄨ ㄔㄥˊ)
a place or building in which there are a number of bookstores

書櫥(ㄕㄨ ㄔㄨˊ)
a bookcase

書生(ㄕㄨ ㄕㄥ)
a student; a scholar; a bookish person

書生本色(ㄕㄨ ㄕㄥ ㄅㄣˇ ㄙㄜˋ)

essential characteristics of a scholar (especially commendable characteristics)

書生之見(ㄕㄨ ㄕㄥ ㄓ ㄐㄧㄢˋ)
the impractical view of a bookish person; a pedantic view

書聖(ㄕㄨ ㄕㄥˋ)
a calligraphic prodigy

書册(ㄕㄨ ㄘㄜˋ)
a book (as distinct from a scroll)

書肆(ㄕㄨ ㄙˋ)
a bookstore

書案(ㄕㄨ ㄢˋ)
a desk

書衣(ㄕㄨ ㄧ)
a book jacket

書頁(ㄕㄨ ㄧㄝˋ)
a page

書業(ㄕㄨ ㄧㄝˋ)
①writing as an occupation ②book business

書院(ㄕㄨ ㄩㄢˋ)
①(in former times) a school ②a euphemism for a "brothel" in certain parts of China

七畫

【曹】 ²³⁰⁷

ㄘㄠˊ tsaur cáo

1. a plural particle: 爾曹 all of you; you
2. a Chinese family name

曹丕(ㄘㄠˊ ㄆㄧ)
Tsao Pi (187-226), poet and founder of the Wei Dynasty, son of Tsao Tsao (曹操)

曹達灰(ㄘㄠˊ ㄉㄚˊ ㄏㄨㄟ)
soda ash 亦作「蘇打灰」

曹大家(ㄘㄠˊ ㄉㄚˋ ㄍㄨ)
Pan Chao (班昭), a historian who lived in the lst century A.D., younger sister of Pan Ku(班固)

曹雪芹(ㄘㄠˊ ㄒㄩㄝˇ ㄑㄧㄣˊ)
Tsao Hsüeh-chin, also known as Tsao Chan (曹霑) (1719-1764), author of *The Dream of the Red Chamber* (紅樓夢)

曹植(ㄘㄠˊ ㄓˊ)
Tsao Chih(192-232), also known as Tsao Tze-chien (曹子建), poet and younger

 〔日部〕

日部

brother of Tsao Pi (曹丕)

曹長石 (ㄘㄠ ㄔㄤ ㄕ)
albite

曹操 (ㄘㄠ ㄘㄠ)
Tsao Tsao (155-220), father of Tsao Pi (曹丕) and Tsao Chih (曹植), skilled in strategy and versed in literature

曹魏 (ㄘㄠ ㄨㄟ)
the Wei Dynasty (220-265) of the Tsao family, as distinct from the Northern Wei Dynasty (386-534) of the Toba family

2308

【曼】 ㄇㄢ mann màn
（又讀 ㄨㄢ wàn）

1. delicately beautiful; graceful; 輕歌曼舞 soft music and graceful dances
2. long; vast; prolonged; long-drawn-out
3. a Chinese family name

曼曼 (ㄇㄢ ㄇㄢ)
long and distant

曼妙 (ㄇㄢ ㄇㄧㄠ)
(said of dancing) lithe and graceful: 她的舞姿曼妙。Her dance is lithe and graceful.

曼陀林 (ㄇㄢ ㄊㄨㄛ ㄌㄧㄣ)
(music) a mandolin

曼麗 (ㄇㄢ ㄌㄧ)
delicately beautiful

曼谷 (ㄇㄢ ㄍㄨ)
Bangkok, the capital of Thailand

曼徹斯特 (ㄇㄢ ㄔㄜ ㄙ ㄊㄜ)
Manchester, an industrial city in England

曼壽 (ㄇㄢ ㄕㄡ)
longevity

曼聲 (ㄇㄢ ㄕㄥ)
to vocalize in a prolonged tone

曼澤 (ㄇㄢ ㄗㄜ)
gorgeous; resplendent

曼辭 (ㄇㄢ ㄘ)
(in writing) ornate language

曼延 (ㄇㄢ ㄧㄢ)
to continue or extend endlessly

八畫

【曾】 2309
1. ㄗㄥ tzeng zēng

1. older or younger by three generations
2. a Chinese family name

曾母投杼 (ㄗㄥ ㄇㄨ ㄊㄡ ㄓㄨ)
Persistent rumors against someone can shake the strongest confidence in him.

曾國藩 (ㄗㄥ ㄍㄨㄛ ㄈㄢ)
Tseng Kuo-fan, 1811-1872, who helped the Manchus put down the Taiping Rebellion

曾參 (ㄗㄥ ㄕㄣ) or 曾子 (ㄗㄥ ㄗ)
Tseng Shen, a disciple of Confucius

曾祖母 (ㄗㄥ ㄗㄨ ㄇㄨ)
one's great-grandmother

曾祖父 (ㄗㄥ ㄗㄨ ㄈㄨ)
one's great-grandfather

曾孫 (ㄗㄥ ㄙㄨㄣ)
one's great-grandchild; one's great-grandchildren

曾孫女 (ㄗㄥ ㄙㄨㄣ ㄋㄩ)
one's great-granddaughter

【曾】 2309
2. ㄘㄥ tserng céng

ever; once: 數年前我曾見過他一面, I met him once a few years ago.

曾幾何時 (ㄘㄥ ㄐㄧ ㄏㄜ ㄕ)
only a short time ago; before long (an expression used in connection with drastic changes)

曾經 (ㄘㄥ ㄐㄧㄥ)
to have had the experience of; to have already: 曾經有人看見她。Somebody has already seen her.

曾經滄海 (ㄘㄥ ㄐㄧㄥ ㄘㄤ ㄏㄞ)
to have experienced great things

【替】 2310
ㄊㄧ tih tì

1. to take the place of; to replace; to substitute
2. to decay; to decline
3. to neglect
4. for; on behalf of: 別替他擔心, Don't worry about him.

替代 (ㄊㄧ ㄉㄞ)
to substitute

替代物 (ㄊㄧ ㄉㄞ ㄨ)
a substitute: 石油可製出橡膠的替代物, Substitutes for rubber can be made from petroleum.

替頭兒 (ㄊㄧ ㄊㄡ ㄦ)
(superstition) a substitute sought among the living by a haunting ghost

替工 (ㄊㄧ ㄍㄨㄥ)
a substitute worker

替壞 (ㄊㄧ ㄏㄨㄞ)
to decay; to deteriorate; to decline

替換 (ㄊㄧ ㄏㄨㄢ)
to replace; to substitute: 有甚麼東西能替換母愛嗎? Can anything replace a mother's love?

替嬭 (ㄊㄧ ㄒㄧㄝ)
to neglect

替手 (ㄊㄧ ㄕㄡ)
a substitute or alternate (worker, contestant, etc.); an understudy; a standby

替身 (ㄊㄧ ㄕㄣ)
a double; an understudy

替身演員 (ㄊㄧ ㄕㄣ ㄧㄢ ㄩㄢ)
a stunt man

替人 (ㄊㄧ ㄖㄣ)
a substitute (for another person)

替死鬼 (ㄊㄧ ㄙ ㄍㄨㄟ)
a scapegoat

2311

【最】 ㄗㄨㄟ tzuey zuì
extreme; superlative

最大 (ㄗㄨㄟ ㄉㄚ)
the biggest; the largest; the greatest; the maximum

最大公約數 (ㄗㄨㄟ ㄉㄚ ㄍㄨㄥ ㄩㄝ ㄕㄨ)
(mathematics) the greatest common divisor

最低 (ㄗㄨㄟ ㄉㄧ)
the lowest; the minimum; the least: 我們已將費用減至最低。We have reduced our expenses to the minimum.

最低工資 (ㄗㄨㄟ ㄉㄧ ㄍㄨㄥ ㄗ)
the minimum wage

最低限度 (ㄗㄨㄟ ㄉㄧ ㄒㄧㄢ ㄉㄨ)
the lowest limit ② at least

最多 (ㄗㄨㄟ ㄉㄨㄛ)
the most; at most: 錢最多的人不一定永遠是最快樂的人。Those who have the most money are not always the happiest.

最短 (ㄗㄨㄟ ㄉㄨㄢ)
the shortest

最高 (ㄗㄨㄟ ㄍㄠ)
the highest; the superlative;

the supreme; the paramount; the topmost; the uppermost; the maximum

最高法院(ㄗㄨㄟ ㄍㄠ ㄈㄚ ㄩㄢˋ)
the Supreme Court

最高峰(ㄗㄨㄟ ㄍㄠ ㄈㄥ)
the summit; the climax

最高當局(ㄗㄨㄟ ㄍㄠ ㄉㄤ ㄐㄩˊ)
the highest authorities

最高統帥(ㄗㄨㄟ ㄍㄠ ㄊㄨㄥˇ ㄕㄨㄞˋ)
the supreme commander; the commander in chief of the armed forces

最高公因數(ㄗㄨㄟ ㄍㄠ ㄍㄨㄥ ㄧㄣ ㄕㄨˋ)
(mathematics) the highest or greatest common factor

最高級(ㄗㄨㄟ ㄍㄠ ㄐㄧˊ)
①the highest; the summit ②(linguistics) the superlative degree

最高權力(ㄗㄨㄟ ㄍㄠ ㄑㄩㄢˊ ㄌㄧˋ)
the supreme power

最高學府(ㄗㄨㄟ ㄍㄠ ㄒㄩㄝˊ ㄈㄨˇ)
the highest seat of learning

最高潮(ㄗㄨㄟ ㄍㄠ ㄔㄠˊ)
the climax; the culmination: 夏天的炎熱已達最高潮。The heat of summer has reached its climax.

最好(ㄗㄨㄟ ㄏㄠˇ)
①the best: 這是我所讀過最好的書。This is the best book I have ever read. ②had better: 你最好現在就走。You had better go now.

最後(ㄗㄨㄟ ㄏㄡˋ)
last; the last; the ultimate; the final: 他是最後到達的人。He was the last man to arrive.

最後通牒(ㄗㄨㄟ ㄏㄡˋ ㄊㄨㄥ ㄉㄧㄝˊ)
an ultimatum

最後審判(ㄗㄨㄟ ㄏㄡˋ ㄕㄣˇ ㄆㄢˋ)
the Last Judgment

最後勝利(ㄗㄨㄟ ㄏㄡˋ ㄕㄥˋ ㄌㄧˋ)
the final victory

最後一滴(ㄗㄨㄟ ㄏㄡˋ ㄧ ㄉㄧ)
the last drop

最後一人(ㄗㄨㄟ ㄏㄡˋ ㄧ ㄖㄣˊ)
the last man: 他是發言的最後一人。He was the last man to speak.

最後五分鐘(ㄗㄨㄟ ㄏㄡˋ ㄨˇ ㄈㄣ ㄓㄨㄥ)
the last five minutes; the last minutes which may spell the success or failure

of an undertaking; the crucial moment

最壞(ㄗㄨㄟ ㄏㄨㄞˋ)
the worst; the meanest; the most vicious

最惠國(ㄗㄨㄟ ㄏㄨㄟˋ ㄍㄨㄛˊ)
the most favored nation

最惠國條款(ㄗㄨㄟ ㄏㄨㄟˋ ㄍㄨㄛˊ ㄊㄧㄠˊ ㄎㄨㄢˇ)
a most-favored-nation clause

最佳(ㄗㄨㄟ ㄐㄧㄚ)or**最優**(ㄗㄨㄟ ㄧㄡ)
the best; the superlative

最近(ㄗㄨㄟ ㄐㄧㄣˋ)
①the nearest; the closest; the proximate: 我們從最近的路線來的。We came by the nearest route. ②recently; recent; lately: 我最近在街上碰見了他。Recently I met him on the street.

最敬禮(ㄗㄨㄟ ㄐㄧㄥˋ ㄌㄧˇ)
the most respectful salutation; the deepest homage

最小(ㄗㄨㄟ ㄒㄧㄠˇ)
the least; the smallest; the minimum

最小公倍數(ㄗㄨㄟ ㄒㄧㄠˇ ㄍㄨㄥ ㄅㄟˋ ㄕㄨˋ)
(mathematics) the least common multiple; the lowest common multiple

最小公分母(ㄗㄨㄟ ㄒㄧㄠˇ ㄍㄨㄥ ㄈㄣ ㄇㄨˇ)
(mathematics) the least common denominator

最先(ㄗㄨㄟ ㄒㄧㄢ)
①the first; the earliest; the foremost ②at first; in the beginning

最新(ㄗㄨㄟ ㄒㄧㄣ)
the newest; the latest

最新發明(ㄗㄨㄟ ㄒㄧㄣ ㄈㄚ ㄇㄧㄥˊ)
the latest invention

最新樣式(ㄗㄨㄟ ㄒㄧㄣ ㄧㄤˋ ㄕˋ)
the latest style

最終(ㄗㄨㄟ ㄓㄨㄥ)
the final; the last; the ultimate

最長(ㄗㄨㄟ ㄔㄤˊ)
the longest

最初(ㄗㄨㄟ ㄔㄨ)
①the first; the earliest ②at first; in the beginning

最少(ㄗㄨㄟ ㄕㄠˇ)
the least; the minimum

最上乘(ㄗㄨㄟ ㄕㄤˋ ㄔㄥˊ)

first-rate; top-notch; the best

最矮(ㄗㄨㄟ ㄞˇ)
(said of stature) the shortest; (said of houses) the lowest

九畫

【會】 2312
1.ㄏㄨㄟˋ huey huì
1. to meet: 明天我將和他相會。I will meet him tomorrow.
2. to assemble; to gather; to converge
3. a meeting; a convention; a conference: 俱樂部召開一次會議。The club held a meeting.
4. an association; a society
5. a private banking cooperative
6. to be able to: 他會彈鋼琴。He is able to play the piano.
7. to understand; to comprehend; to realize
8. shall; will
9. a chief city; a capital: 省會 the provincial capital

會不會(ㄏㄨㄟˋ ㄅㄨˋ ㄏㄨㄟˋ)
①Is it likely that...? ②Can (you, he, etc.) do...or not?

會盟(ㄏㄨㄟˋ ㄇㄥˊ)
(said of feudal lords) to meet for concluding treaties

會面(ㄏㄨㄟˋ ㄇㄧㄢˋ)
to meet face to face: 我們約定了星期三和她會面。We have an appointment to meet her on Wednesday.

會費(ㄏㄨㄟˋ ㄈㄟˋ)
membership fees; dues

會典(ㄏㄨㄟˋ ㄉㄧㄢˇ)
a record of laws and systems of a dynasty

會首(ㄏㄨㄟˋ ㄕㄡˇ)
one who initiates a private banking cooperative and who receives the first payments from other members

會談(ㄏㄨㄟˋ ㄊㄢˊ)
talks: 我們已舉行了許多次會談。We've had many talks.

會通(ㄏㄨㄟˋ ㄊㄨㄥ)
to understand; to master

會同(ㄏㄨㄟˋ ㄊㄨㄥˊ)
together with

會館or**公館**(ㄏㄨㄟˋ ㄍㄨㄢˇ)
①a union building ②a club house for residents from the

〔日部〕

same province or county

會客(ㄏㄨㄟˋ ㄎㄜˋ)
to receive callers (or visitors)

會客時間(ㄏㄨㄟˋ ㄎㄜˋ ㄕˊ ㄐㄧㄢ)
the time for receiving visitors; visiting hours

會客室(ㄏㄨㄟˋ ㄎㄜˋ ㄕˋ)
a reception room

會考(ㄏㄨㄟˋ ㄎㄠˇ)
a general examination for students from various schools

會合(ㄏㄨㄟˋ ㄏㄜˊ)
to assemble; to gather; to meet; to converge; to join: 我們必須再會合討論此事。We must meet again to discuss it.

會合點(ㄏㄨㄟˋ ㄏㄜˊ ㄉㄧㄢˇ)
①a point of convergence ②(military) a meeting point

會話(ㄏㄨㄟˋ ㄏㄨㄚˋ)
a conversation; a chat; a talk; a dialogue

會集(ㄏㄨㄟˋ ㄐㄧˊ)
to assemble; to gather together

會籍(ㄏㄨㄟˋ ㄐㄧˊ)
membership (of an association)

會見(ㄏㄨㄟˋ ㄐㄧㄢˋ)
to meet (a person): 我在一個宴會上會見一個老朋友。I met with an old friend at a dinner party.

會聚(ㄏㄨㄟˋ ㄐㄩˋ)
to assemble; to flock together

會聚透鏡(ㄏㄨㄟˋ ㄐㄩˋ ㄊㄡˋ ㄐㄧㄥˋ)
convergent lenses

會聚鏡(ㄏㄨㄟˋ ㄐㄩˋ ㄐㄧㄥˋ)
a convergent mirror

會期(ㄏㄨㄟˋ ㄑㄧˊ)
①the time of a meeting ②the duration of a meeting

會齊(ㄏㄨㄟˋ ㄑㄧˊ)
to be all present at a gathering

會錢(ㄏㄨㄟˋ ㄑㄧㄢˊ)
regular payments made by members of a private banking cooperative

會銜(ㄏㄨㄟˋ ㄒㄧㄢˊ)
jointly sign an official document (other than a treaty, agreement, etc.)

會心(ㄏㄨㄟˋ ㄒㄧㄣ)
to come to an understanding without explanation; meeting of minds

會心的微笑(ㄏㄨㄟˋ ㄒㄧㄣ·ㄉㄜ ㄨㄟˊ ㄒㄧㄠˋ)
an insinuative smile; an understanding smile

會址(ㄏㄨㄟˋ ㄓˇ)
the address of an association or organization

會戰(ㄏㄨㄟˋ ㄓㄢˋ)
a major battle

會診(ㄏㄨㄟˋ ㄓㄣˇ)
(medicine) the consultation of doctors; (group) consultation

會章(ㄏㄨㄟˋ ㄓㄤ)
the charter of an association or organization

會長(ㄏㄨㄟˋ ㄓㄤˇ)
the president of an association or organization

會眼 or 會帳(ㄏㄨㄟˋ ㄓㄤˋ)
to buy one's friend a meal or a drink

會鈔(ㄏㄨㄟˋ ㄔㄠ)
to buy one's friend a meal or a drink

會場(ㄏㄨㄟˋ ㄔㄤˇ or ㄏㄨㄟˋ ㄔㄤˊ)
the place of a meeting; the site of a conference; a conference (or assembly) hall

會師(ㄏㄨㄟˋ ㄕ)
a rendezvous of friendly forces; to join forces

會試(ㄏㄨㄟˋ ㄕˋ)
(in old China) a general examination (for successful candidates from all over the country) held at the Ministry of Education prior to the imperial examination

會社(ㄏㄨㄟˋ ㄕㄜˋ)
①a company in Japan ②an association

會審(ㄏㄨㄟˋ ㄕㄣˇ)
to review or try jointly: 經過會審，這人被判決有罪。The man was tried jointly and found guilty.

會商(ㄏㄨㄟˋ ㄕㄤ)
to negotiate; to confer; to consult: 他們會商一項貸款。They negotiated a loan.

會說(ㄏㄨㄟˋ ㄕㄨㄛ)
able to talk persuasively or

eloquently

會水(ㄏㄨㄟˋ ㄕㄨㄟˇ)
able to swim

會葬(ㄏㄨㄟˋ ㄗㄤˋ)
a mass burial

會餐(ㄏㄨㄟˋ ㄘㄢ)
to dine together; to have a dinner party

會萃(ㄏㄨㄟˋ ㄘㄨㄟˋ)
to converge

會所(ㄏㄨㄟˋ ㄙㄨㄛˇ)
the office of an association or organization

會意(ㄏㄨㄟˋ ㄧˋ)
①to understand the meaning; to take a hint ②"meeting of ideas", or associative compounds, one of six categories under which Chinese characters are grouped (The meaning of a character under this category is suggested by its significant combination of two or more pictographs.)

會議(ㄏㄨㄟˋ ㄧˋ)
a conference; a meeting: 許多國際會議曾在日內瓦舉行。Many international conferences have been held in Geneva.

會議記錄(ㄏㄨㄟˋ ㄧˋ ㄐㄧˋ ㄌㄨˋ)
minutes

會要(ㄏㄨㄟˋ ㄧㄠˋ)
a record of social backgrounds of a dynasty

會友(ㄏㄨㄟˋ ㄧㄡˇ)
①a fellow member of an association or organization ②to meet a friend

會晤(ㄏㄨㄟˋ ㄨˋ)
to meet: 兩國外交官定期會晤。The diplomats of two countries meet regularly.

會務(ㄏㄨㄟˋ ㄨˋ)
the business of a meeting, conference, convention, association, etc.

會元(ㄏㄨㄟˋ ㄩㄢˊ)
the head of the successful candidates in civil service examinations in former times

會員(ㄏㄨㄟˋ ㄩㄢˊ)
a member of an association, society, etc.

會員大會(ㄏㄨㄟˋ ㄩㄢˊ ㄉㄚˋ ㄏㄨㄟˋ)

a general assembly

會員國（ㄏㄨㄟ ㄩㄢ ㄍㄨㄛ）
a member nation (or state)

【會】 2312
2. ㄏㄨㄟ hoei huì
a brief period of time; a
moment

會子（ㄏㄨㄟ·ㄗ）or 會兒（ㄏㄨㄟㄦ）
a moment: 請稍等一會兒!
Just a moment!

【會】 2312
3. ㄎㄨㄞ kuay kuài
to add; to compute

會計（ㄎㄨㄞ ㄐㄧ）
①accounting ②an account-
ant; a treasurer: 他在一家百
貨公司當會計。He works in a
department store as an
accountant.

會計部（ㄎㄨㄞ ㄐㄧ ㄅㄨ）
an accounting department

會計年度（ㄎㄨㄞ ㄐㄧ ㄋㄧㄢ ㄉㄨ）
a fiscal year (as distinct
from a calendar year)

會計學（ㄎㄨㄞ ㄐㄧ ㄒㄩㄝ）
accounting: 他主修會計學。He
majored in accounting.

會計主任（ㄎㄨㄞ ㄐㄧ ㄓㄨ ㄖㄣ）
an accountant general; a
chief accountant

會計處（ㄎㄨㄞ ㄐㄧ ㄔㄨ）
an accounting section or
department; a comptroller's
office

會計師（ㄎㄨㄞ ㄐㄧ ㄕ）
C.A.(a chartered accountant); C.P.A.(a certified public accountant)

會計室（ㄎㄨㄞ ㄐㄧ ㄕ）
an accountant's office

會計人員（ㄎㄨㄞ ㄐㄧ ㄖㄣˊ ㄩㄢˊ）
accounting personnel

【會】 2312
4. ㄍㄨㄟ guey guì

會稽（ㄍㄨㄟ ㄐㄧ）
Kueichi, Chekiang Province

十畫

【碣】 2313
ㄑㄧㄝ chieh qiè
to depart; to go; to leave

月部
ㄩㄝ yueh yuè

【月】 2314
ㄩㄝ yueh yuè
1. the moon
2. the month

月白（ㄩㄝ ㄅㄞ）
bluish white; pale blue

月白風清（ㄩㄝ ㄅㄞ ㄈㄥ ㄑㄧㄥ）
(descriptive of nocturnal
beauty) The moon is pale
and the breeze is refreshing.

月報（ㄩㄝ ㄅㄠ）
①a monthly report ②a
monthly journal

月半（ㄩㄝ ㄅㄢ）
the 15th day of a month

月表（ㄩㄝ ㄅㄧㄠ）
a monthly chronology

月餅（ㄩㄝ ㄅㄧㄥ）
a moon cake: 中國人在中秋節
吃月餅。The Chinese eat
moon cakes during the Mid-
Autumn Festival.

月票（ㄩㄝ ㄆㄧㄠ）
a monthly ticket

月杪（ㄩㄝ ㄇㄧㄠ）
the end of a month

月明星稀（ㄩㄝ ㄇㄧㄥˊ ㄒㄧㄥ ㄒㄧ）
(descriptive of nocturnal
beauty) The moon is bright
and the stars are few.

月分（ㄩㄝ ㄈㄣ）
the month; monthly

月分牌兒（ㄩㄝ ㄈㄣ ㄆㄞˊ ㄦ）
a calendar

月俸（ㄩㄝ ㄈㄥ）
a monthly salary: 你的月俸是
干? What is your monthly
salary?

月大（ㄩㄝ ㄉㄚ）
a 30-day month of the lunar
calendar; a 31-day month of
the Gregorian calendar

月底（ㄩㄝ ㄉㄧ）
the end of a month

月臺（ㄩㄝ ㄊㄞˊ）
a platform (at a railway
station): 在火車站,鐵軌旁有一
座月臺。There is a platform
beside the track at the rail-

---

way station.

月臺票（ㄩㄝ ㄊㄞˊ ㄆㄧㄠ）
a platform ticket

月老（ㄩㄝ ㄌㄠ）
a matchmaker

月曆（ㄩㄝ ㄌㄧ）
①a calendar, each page of
which is a table of the days
of a month (as distinct from
one of which each page
shows a day) ②(in ancient
China) a record of government orders to be announced
every month

月裏嫦娥（ㄩㄝ ㄌㄧ ㄔㄤˊ ㄜˊ）
a legendary fairy of the
moon—a beauty

月亮（ㄩㄝ ㄌㄧㄤ）
the moon: 那晚沒有月亮。It
was a night with no moon
visible in the sky.

月令（ㄩㄝ ㄌㄧㄥ）
a chapter of the Book of
Rites (禮記)

月桂（ㄩㄝ ㄍㄨㄟ）
a laurel (Laurus nobilis)

月光（ㄩㄝ ㄍㄨㄤ）
moonlight: 他們坐在皎潔的月
光下。They sat in the bright
moonlight.

月宮（ㄩㄝ ㄍㄨㄥ）
a legendary palace on the
moon

月刊（ㄩㄝ ㄎㄢ）
a monthly publication; a
monthly: 這雜誌是月刊。It is a
monthly magazine.

月華（ㄩㄝ ㄏㄨㄚˊ）
①brightness of the moon ②
(astronomy) the halo around
the moon; the lunar corona

月季票（ㄩㄝ ㄐㄧ ㄆㄧㄠ）
a season ticket: 他買了一張火
車的月季票。He bought a rail-
way season ticket.

月季花（ㄩㄝ ㄐㄧ ㄏㄨㄚ）
a rose (Rosa chinensis)

月經（ㄩㄝ ㄐㄧㄥ）or 月信（ㄩㄝ ㄒㄧㄣ）
or 月事（ㄩㄝ ㄕ）
menses; periods; monthlies

月經布（ㄩㄝ ㄐㄧㄥ ㄅㄨ）or 月經帶
（ㄩㄝ ㄐㄧㄥ ㄉㄞ）
a hygienic band; a sanitary
napkin; a sanitary belt

月經不調（ㄩㄝ ㄐㄧㄥ ㄅㄨ ㄊㄧㄠˊ）
irregular menses; menoxenia

〔月
部〕

〔月部〕

月經停止(ㄩㄝ ㄐㄧㄥ ㄊㄧㄥ ㄓˇ)
menopause; cessation of menses

月經過多(ㄩㄝ ㄐㄧㄥ 《ㄨㄛ ㄉㄨㄛ)
menorrhagia; the excessive menstruation

月經過少(ㄩㄝ ㄐㄧㄥ 《ㄨㄛ ㄕㄠˇ)
hypomenorrhea

月經周期(ㄩㄝ ㄐㄧㄥ ㄓㄡ ㄑㄧˊ)
menstrual cycles

月球(ㄩㄝ ㄑㄧㄡˊ)
the moon: 月球繞地球運行。The moon revolves round the earth.

月琴(ㄩㄝ ㄑㄧㄣˊ)
a four-stringed musical instrument

月息(ㄩㄝ ㄒㄧˊ)or 月利(ㄩㄝ ㄌㄧˋ)
monthly interest; monthly interest rate

月下(ㄩㄝ ㄒㄧㄚˋ)
under the moon: 他們在月下散步。They walked under the moon.

月下老人(ㄩㄝ ㄒㄧㄚˋ ㄌㄠˇ ㄖㄣˊ)
a matchmaker

月小(ㄩㄝ ㄒㄧㄠˇ)
a 29-day month of the lunar calendar; a 30-day month of the Gregorian calendar

月薪(ㄩㄝ ㄒㄧㄣ)
a monthly salary

月支(ㄩㄝ ㄓ)
①monthly expenses ②to draw (a certain amount) every month ③same as 月氏 (see below)

月氏(ㄩㄝ ㄓ)
name of a nomadic people who used to live in Central Asia

月終(ㄩㄝ ㄓㄨㄥ)or 月尾(ㄩㄝ ㄨㄟˇ)or 月底(ㄩㄝ ㄉㄧˇ)
the end of a month: 我們於月底到歐洲去。We will leave for Europe at the end of the month.

月初(ㄩㄝ ㄔㄨ)or 月頭(ㄩㄝ ㄊㄡˊ)
the beginning of a month

月蝕 or 月食(ㄩㄝ ㄕˊ)
(astronomy) a lunar eclipse

月朔(ㄩㄝ ㄕㄨㄛˋ)
the first day of each moon

月子(ㄩㄝ ㄗˇ)
the month of confinement after giving birth to a child

月色(ㄩㄝ ㄙㄜˋ)
moonlight: 美麗的湖水在燦爛的月色下閃爍如水晶。In the brilliant moonlight the beautiful lake sparkles like crystals.

月牙兒 or 月芽兒(ㄩㄝ ㄧㄚˊㄦ)
the new moon or crescent moon

月夜(ㄩㄝ ㄧㄝˋ)
a moonlight night; a moonlit night

月曜日(ㄩㄝ ㄧㄠˋ ㄖˋ)
Monday

月望(ㄩㄝ ㄨㄤˋ)
the 15th day of each moon

月餘(ㄩㄝ ㄩˊ)
more than a month

月月紅(ㄩㄝ ㄩㄝ ㄏㄨㄥˊ)
American beauty (a flower)

月圓則虧(ㄩㄝ ㄩㄢˊ ㄗㄜˊ ㄎㄨㄟ)
(literally) The moon begins to wane the moment it becomes full.—Decline inevitably follows culmination.

月暈(ㄩㄝ ㄩㄣˋ)
the halo of the moon; the lunar aureole

二畫

【有】 2315
1. (ㄧㄡˇ) yeou you
to have; to be present; to exist; there is

有把握(ㄧㄡˇ ㄅㄚˇ ㄨㄛˋ)
confident of success

有背景(ㄧㄡˇ ㄅㄟ ㄐㄧㄥˇ)
to have powerful connections

有備無患(ㄧㄡˇ ㄅㄟˋ ㄨˊ ㄏㄨㄢˋ)
There is no danger when there is preparedness.

有板有眼(ㄧㄡˇ ㄅㄢˇ ㄧㄡˇ ㄧㄢˇ)
①(said of singing performances) rhythmical; adhering to the exact rhythm ②(said of speech) the articulate ③(said of conduct) systematic

有辦法(ㄧㄡˇ ㄅㄢˋ ㄈㄚˇ)
①to have a way to solve some problem; to know how to do something ②to be resourceful

有本領(ㄧㄡˇ ㄅㄣˇ ㄌㄧㄥˇ)
capable; talented; resource-

ful: 他是一個有本領的音樂家。He is a talented musician.

有鼻子有眼兒(ㄧㄡˇ ㄅㄧˊ ˙ㄗ ㄧㄡˇ ㄧㄢˇㄦ)
①lifelike; with every detail vividly described ②plausible; convincing

有邊兒(ㄧㄡˇ ㄅㄧㄢㄦ)
to begin to take shape; likely to succeed

有病(ㄧㄡˇ ㄅㄧㄥˋ)
sick; ill; feeling unwell: 我恐怕他可能有病了。I'm afraid he may have fallen ill.

有不是(ㄧㄡˇ ㄅㄨˋ ˙ㄕ)
to have done wrong: 你們兩人都有不是。Both of you have done wrong.

有盼兒(ㄧㄡˇ ㄆㄢˋㄦ)
hopeful; promising

有憑有據(ㄧㄡˇ ㄆㄧㄥˊ ㄧㄡˇ ㄐㄩˋ)
well-founded: 這控告有憑有據。The accusation is well-founded.

有門兒(ㄧㄡˇ ㄇㄣˊㄦ)
①(said of works by beginners, etc.) to show qualities measuring up to certain standards; to get the hang of ②likely to be realized or to come true; to be hopeful (of success)

有眉目(ㄧㄡˇ ㄇㄟˊ ㄇㄨˋ)
to begin to take shape; about to materialize

有毛病(ㄧㄡˇ ㄇㄠˊ ˙ㄅㄧㄥ)
①sick; ill ②something wrong; out of order: 這車有毛病。Something is wrong with the car.

有面子(ㄧㄡˇ ㄇㄧㄢˋ ˙ㄗ)
to have one's face or honor preserved; to have one's vanity satisfied

有名(ㄧㄡˇ ㄇㄧㄥˊ)
famous; renowned; noted; well-known; illustrious; distinguished: 李白是一位有名的中國詩人。Li Po was a noted Chinese poet.

有名堂(ㄧㄡˇ ㄇㄧㄥˊ ㄊㄤˊ)
(colloqual) to be promising; to show encouraging signs

有名有姓(ㄧㄡˇ ㄇㄧㄥˊ ㄧㄡˇ ㄒㄧㄥˋ)
a person who really exists (as distinct from a fictitious character)

〔月部〕

有名無實(ㄧㄡˇㄇㄧㄥˊㄨˊㄕˊ)
to exist only in name

有名望(ㄧㄡˇㄇㄧㄥˊㄨㄤˋ)
famous; renowned; noted;
distinguished; prestigious

有命(ㄧㄡˇㄇㄧㄥˋ)
to be alive

有目共睹(ㄧㄡˇㄇㄨˋㄍㄨㄥˋㄉㄨˇ)
known to everyone with
eyes open; to be obvious to
all

有份兒 or 有分兒(ㄧㄡˇㄈㄣˋㄦ)
to have a share; to have
taken a part in; to participate in

有個大家喫(ㄧㄡˇㄇㄚˊㄍㄜˊㄐㄧㄚ)
to let everyone have a finger in the pie

有分寸(ㄧㄡˇㄈㄣㄘㄨㄣˋ)
having a sense of propriety;
knowing how far to go and
when to stop

有夫之婦(ㄧㄡˇㄈㄨㄓㄈㄨˋ)
a married woman

有福同享，有禍同當(ㄧㄡˇㄈㄨˊ
ㄊㄨㄥˊㄒㄧㄤˇ，ㄧㄡˇㄏㄨㄛˋㄊㄨㄥˊㄉㄤ)
to share bliss and misfortune together

有福氣(ㄧㄡˇㄈㄨˊㄑㄧˋ)
to be blessed or favored by
fortune: 他很有福氣，有一個好
兒子。He was fortunate
enough to have a good son.

有得(ㄧㄡˇㄉㄜˊ)
①to have learned or
acquired something ②in
store

有德(ㄧㄡˇㄉㄜˊ)
virtuous; righteous: 他是個有
德的人。He is a man of vir-
tue.

有的(ㄧㄡˇㄉㄜ˙)
①some: 有的人喜歡運動，有的
人不喜歡。Some people like
sports, and others do not. ②
Yes, there is.... 或 Yes, I
have....

有的是(ㄧㄡˇㄉㄜ˙ㄕ)
to be found everywhere; to
have plenty of: 他有的是時
間。He has all the time in the
world.

有待(ㄧㄡˇㄉㄞˋ)
①to wait until ②to require
or need (improvement, in-
vestigation, etc.)

有道(ㄧㄡˇㄉㄠˋ)

①learned and virtuous ②
reasonable; right; lawful ③
Good government prevails.

有道理(ㄧㄡˇㄉㄠˋㄌㄧˇ)
reasonable; plausible; convincing

有膽量(ㄧㄡˇㄉㄢˇㄌㄧㄤˋ)
to have the courage or guts

有敵無我(ㄧㄡˇㄉㄧˊㄨˊㄨㄛˇ)
If the enemy triumphs, there
will be no place for us.

有底(ㄧㄡˇㄉㄧˇ)
to know the true character
of a matter

有點兒(ㄧㄡˇㄉㄧㄢˇㄦ)
some; a little; somewhat;
sort of: 我對此工作有點兒厭倦
了。I am somewhat tired of
this work.

有毒(ㄧㄡˇㄉㄨˊ)
poisonous; venomous

有頭緒(ㄧㄡˇㄊㄡˊㄒㄩˋ)
to be near solution or success; to have found the clue

有頭兒(ㄧㄡˇㄊㄡˊㄦ)
to begin to show promise of
success

有頭有臉兒(ㄧㄡˇㄊㄡˊㄧㄡˇㄌㄧㄢˇㄦ)
①honored; respected ②pre-
sentable

有頭有尾(ㄧㄡˇㄊㄡˊㄧㄡˇㄨㄟˇ)
complete; finished; to do a
job from beginning to end:
這是一個有頭有尾的故事嗎？Is
this a complete story?

有頭無尾(ㄧㄡˇㄊㄡˊㄨˊㄨㄟˇ)
to leave a job incomplete or
unfinished; to quit doing
something halfway

有蹄類(ㄧㄡˇㄊㄧˊㄌㄟˋ)
(zoology) the Ungulata

有條不紊(ㄧㄡˇㄊㄧㄠˊㄅㄨˋㄨㄣˇ)
methodical; systematic;
orderly: 他的頭腦有條不紊。
He has an orderly mind.

有條件的(ㄧㄡˇㄊㄧㄠˊㄐㄧㄢˋㄉㄜ˙)
conditional; with conditions
attached: 這提議是有條件的。
The offer is conditional.

有條有理(ㄧㄡˇㄊㄧㄠˊㄧㄡˇㄌㄧˇ)
logical; orderly; systematic

有天沒日(ㄧㄡˇㄊㄧㄢㄇㄟˊㄖˋ)
(said of remarks) outra-
geous; heinous; flagrant

有天無日(ㄧㄡˇㄊㄧㄢㄨˊㄖˋ)
devoid of justice

有托而逃(ㄧㄡˇㄊㄨㄛㄦˊㄊㄠˊ)

to shirk responsibility under
an excuse

有你沒我(ㄧㄡˇㄋㄧˇㄇㄟˊㄨㄛˇ)
You and I cannot coexist.
—We are sworn enemies.

有的(ㄧㄡˇㄉㄧ˙)
①Excellent! 或 Very good!
(used in praising another's
performance) ②You'll have
your share.

有年(ㄧㄡˇㄋㄧㄢˊ)
①to have been in existence
for years ②a year of
bumper crops; a year of
plenty

有了(ㄧㄡˇㄌㄜ˙)
①to have obtained what
was wanted: 他有了些錢。He
has got some money. ②to
have found the answer or
solution 或 I've got it. ③to
become pregnant: 他的太太有
(喜)了。His wife is pregnant.

有來頭(ㄧㄡˇㄌㄞˊㄊㄡˊ)
(colloquial)not the ordinary
kind; of some special importance or distinction

有來有去的(ㄧㄡˇㄌㄞˊㄧㄡˇㄑㄩˋㄉㄜ˙)
(said of an article, a statement, a speech, etc.) to
sound reasonable, convincing, etc.

有來有往(ㄧㄡˇㄌㄞˊㄧㄡˇㄨㄤˇ)
(said of exchanging gifts or
rendering help to others)
reciprocal

有賴(ㄧㄡˇㄌㄞˋ)
to depend on; to rest on

有勞(ㄧㄡˇㄌㄠˊ)
(a conventional phrase used
in thanking for or soliciting
another's assistance)to have
troubled (you)或 Please do
me a favor by....

有落場(ㄧㄡˇㄌㄨㄛˋㄔㄤˇ)
to have found a means of
support or a way to make a
living

有禮(ㄧㄡˇㄌㄧˇ)
polite; courteous; civil; well-
mannered: 那個有禮的孩子把
座位讓給我。That polite boy
gave me his seat.

有理(ㄧㄡˇㄌㄧˇ)
①reasonable; logical: 他說的
有理。What he says is quite
reasonable. ②justified; to

〔月部〕

have justice on one's side ③ (mathematics) rational

有理無情(一ㄡ ㄌㄧˇ ㄨˊ ㄑㄧㄥˊ)
①to disregard personal feelings ②reluctantly; unwillingly

有利(一ㄡˇ ㄌㄧˋ)
profitable; advantageous; beneficial; favorable; helpful; conducive

有利必有弊(一ㄡˇ ㄌㄧˋ ㄅㄧˋ 一ㄡˇ ㄅㄧˋ)
Advantages are inevitably accompanied by disadvantages.

有利可圖(一ㄡˇ ㄌㄧˋ ㄎㄜˇ ㄊㄨˊ)
(said of material profit) profitable: 這一樁買賣大家都有利可圖。This deal is profitable to all of us.

有力者(一ㄡˇ ㄌㄧˋ ㄓㄜˇ)
a powerful person: 他在這區域是一個有力者。He is a powerful person in this neighborhood.

有例在先(一ㄡˇ ㄌㄧˋ ㄗㄞˋ ㄒㄧㄢ)
There are precedents for that.

有臉(一ㄡˇ ㄌㄧㄢˇ)
①respectable; honorable; proud: 她雖貧窮，卻是個有臉的人物。She is poor but respectable. ②favored; loved

有兩下子(一ㄡˇ ㄌㄧㄤˇ ㄒㄧㄚˋ ·ㄗ)
to have a real skill; to know one's stuff

有感(一ㄡˇ ㄍㄢˇ)
a comment on something (usually used as a suffix of a title of a literary composition)

有感地震(一ㄡˇ ㄍㄢˇ ㄉㄧˋ ㄓㄣˋ)
an earthquake that is strong enough to be felt without a seismograph

有感而發(一ㄡˇ ㄍㄢˇ ㄦˊ ㄈㄚ)
to make a comment out of personal feeling

有骨頭(一ㄡˇ ㄍㄨˇ ·ㄊㄡ)
manly; indomitable

有骨氣(一ㄡˇ ㄍㄨˇ ㄑㄧˋ)
adhering to moral principles; to have integrity

有過之無不及(一ㄡˇ ㄍㄨㄛˋ ㄓ ㄨˊ ㄅㄨˋ ㄐㄧˊ)
to go even farther than

有鬼(一ㄡˇ ㄍㄨㄟˇ)
There's something fishy.

有關(一ㄡˇ ㄍㄨㄢ)
to have something to do with; to concern

有關方面(一ㄡˇ ㄍㄨㄢ ㄈㄤ ㄇㄧㄢˋ)
the parties concerned; interested parties

有瓜葛(一ㄡˇ ㄍㄨㄚ ·ㄍㄜ)
①to have relations ②to have complications

有乖母教(一ㄡˇ ㄍㄨㄞ ㄇㄨˇ ㄐㄧㄠˋ)
(said of an independent-minded girl) to act against her mother's teachings about old virtues of women

有光紙(一ㄡˇ ㄍㄨㄤ ㄓˇ)
paper with a glossy surface; glazed paper

有功(一ㄡˇ ㄍㄨㄥ)
to have provided great services; to make contributions to

有口難言(一ㄡˇ ㄎㄡˇ ㄋㄢˊ 一ㄢˊ)
unable to speak for self-defense or self-justification under certain circumstances

有口皆碑(一ㄡˇ ㄎㄡˇ ㄐㄧㄝ ㄅㄟ)
praised by all

有口無心(一ㄡˇ ㄎㄡˇ ㄨˊ ㄒㄧㄣ)
to say what one does not mean; to be sharp-tongued but not malicious

有虧職守(一ㄡˇ ㄎㄨㄟ ㄓˊ ㄕㄡˇ)
guilty of dereliction of duty; to have neglected one's responsibility or duty

有空(一ㄡˇ ㄎㄨㄥˋ)
to have time (for doing something)

有何不可(一ㄡˇ ㄏㄜˊ ㄅㄨˋ ㄎㄜˇ)
Why not? or What's wrong with this or that?

有何為證(一ㄡˇ ㄏㄜˊ ㄨㄟˋ ㄓㄥˋ)
Can you prove it?

有害(一ㄡˇ ㄏㄞˋ)
harmful; detrimental: 酗酒對健康有害。To indulge in excessive drinking is harmful to health.

有害無益(一ㄡˇ ㄏㄞˋ ㄨˊ 一ˋ)
not helpful but harmful

有後(一ㄡˇ ㄏㄡˋ)
to have offspring (particularly male children)

有行無市(一ㄡˇ ㄏㄤˊ ㄨˊ ㄕˋ)
(said of the stock market, etc.) to have only quotations but no actual trading

有恆(一ㄡˇ ㄏㄥˊ)
persistent; persevering; tenacious

有機體(一ㄡˇ ㄐㄧ ㄊㄧˇ)
an organism

有機可乘(一ㄡˇ ㄐㄧ ㄎㄜˇ ㄔㄥˊ)
•to have loopholes to exploit

有機化合物(一ㄡˇ ㄐㄧ ㄏㄨㄚˋ ㄏㄜˊ ㄨˋ)
an organic compound

有機化學(一ㄡˇ ㄐㄧ ㄏㄨㄚˋ ㄒㄩㄝˊ)
organic chemistry

有給職(一ㄡˇ ㄐㄧˇ ㄓˊ)
a paid post

有計畫(一ㄡˇ ㄐㄧˋ ㄏㄨㄚˋ)
in a planned way; according to plan

有加利樹(一ㄡˇ ㄐㄧㄚ ㄌㄧˋ ㄕㄨˋ)
a eucalyptus

有加無已(一ㄡˇ ㄐㄧㄚ ㄨˊ 一ˇ)
to become worse or more serious: 這病人的病勢有加無已。The patient is worse than ever.

有價證券(一ㄡˇ ㄐㄧㄚˋ ㄓㄥˋ ㄑㄩㄢˋ)
securities; negotiable or marketable securities

有脚書櫥(一ㄡˇ ㄐㄧㄠˇ ㄕㄨ ㄔㄨˊ)
a walking encyclopedia

有教無類(一ㄡˇ ㄐㄧㄠˋ ㄨˊ ㄌㄟˋ)
to provide education for all people without discrimination:孔子有教無類。Confucius provided education for all people without discrimination.

有救(一ㄡˇ ㄐㄧㄡˋ)
capable of being saved; still hopeful

有舊(一ㄡˇ ㄐㄧㄡˋ)
to have had friendship in the past: 她與他們有舊。She has had friendship with them in the past.

有間(一ㄡˇ ㄐㄧㄢˋ)
①to be disloyal ②for a moment; for a little while

有見識(一ㄡˇ ㄐㄧㄢˋ ㄕˋ)
farsighted; to have an analytical mind

有鑒於此(一ㄡˇ ㄐㄧㄢˋ ㄩˊ ㄘˇ)
in view of this; because of this

有勁(一ㄡˇ ㄐㄧㄥˋ)
①strong; potent: 他已六十多歲，可是還非常有勁。He is well over sixty, but is still

going strong. ② interesting; amusing ③ full of zest or gusto

有研究(ㄧㄡ ㄐㄧㄢˇ ·ㄐㄧㄡ)
① exacting; requiring particular skill ② to stick to formalities

有經驗(ㄧㄡ ㄐㄧㄥ ㄧㄢˋ)
experienced; to have had the experience of: 這位教授對教學有經驗. This professor is experienced in teaching.

有其父必有其子(ㄧㄡ ㄑㄧˊ ㄈㄨˋ ㄅㄧˋ ㄧㄡ ㄑㄧˊ ㄗˇ)
Like father, like son.

有期徒刑(ㄧㄡ ㄑㄧˊ ㄊㄨˊ ㄒㄧㄥˊ)
(law) imprisonment for a definite term (as opposed to life imprisonment)

有起色(ㄧㄡ ㄑㄧˇ ㄙㄜˋ)
to show signs of a rise, improvement, etc.: 他的生意日有起色. His business shows signs of improvement every day.

有氣(ㄧㄡ ㄑㄧˋ)
angry; furious; indignant

有氣兒(ㄧㄡ ㄑㄧˋㄦ)
① still alive; still breathing ② angry; furious; indignant

有氣無力(ㄧㄡ ㄑㄧˋ ㄨˊ ㄌㄧˋ)
Breath is present but vigor is absent.—descriptive of a very feeble voice, half-hearted performance, etc.

有求必應(ㄧㄡ ㄑㄧㄡˊ ㄅㄧˋ ㄧㄥˋ)
unable to say no to seekers of help; to respond to every plea

有錢(ㄧㄡ ㄑㄧㄢˊ)
rich; wealthy; well-to-do; well-off

有錢能使鬼推磨(ㄧㄡ ㄑㄧㄢˊ ㄋㄥˊ ㄕ ㄍㄨㄟˇ ㄊㄨㄟ ㄇㄛˋ)
(literally) Money can make the ghost work the mill. —Money can work miracles. 或 Money makes the mare go.

有情(ㄧㄡ ㄑㄧㄥˊ)
① affected by love; to have a tender feeling for one of the opposite sex ② (Buddhism) any creature

有情人終成眷屬(ㄧㄡ ㄑㄧㄥˊ ㄖㄣˊ ㄓㄨㄥ ㄔㄥˊ ㄐㄩㄢˋ ㄕㄨˇ)
The lovers finally got married.

有頃(ㄧㄡ ㄑㄧㄥˇ)
for a moment; for a little while

有請(ㄧㄡ ㄑㄧㄥˇ)
So-and-so requests the pleasure of seeing you.

有趣(ㄧㄡ ㄑㄩˋ)
interesting; fascinating; amusing: 這個故事很有趣. This story is very interesting.

有窮(ㄧㄡ ㄑㄩㄥˊ)
to have an end; to have a limit; to be exhaustible

有喜(ㄧㄡ ㄒㄧˇ)
pregnant

有隙(ㄧㄡ ㄒㄧˋ)
to harbor a grudge

有隙可乘(ㄧㄡ ㄒㄧˋ ㄎㄜˇ ㄔㄥˊ)
There is a flaw or chance for attack.

有夏(ㄧㄡ ㄒㄧㄚˋ)
China

有些(ㄧㄡ ㄒㄧㄝ)
① some; a few ② somewhat

有血有肉(ㄧㄡ ㄒㄧㄝˇ ㄧㄡ ㄖㄡˋ)
(said of descriptions in literary works, etc.) true to life; lifelike; vivid

有效(ㄧㄡ ㄒㄧㄠˋ)
effective; effectual; valid: 這項合同在五年內有效. This contract shall be valid for five years.

有閒階級(ㄧㄡ ㄒㄧㄢˊ ㄐㄧㄝ ㄐㄧˊ)
the leisure class

有限(ㄧㄡ ㄒㄧㄢˋ)
limited; restricted; finite

有限公司(ㄧㄡ ㄒㄧㄢˋ ㄍㄨㄥ ㄙ)
a limited company; a limited-liability company

有限責任(ㄧㄡ ㄒㄧㄢˋ ㄗㄜˊ ㄖㄣˋ)
limited liability

有線(ㄧㄡ ㄒㄧㄢˋ)
wired; equipped with wires

有線電(ㄧㄡ ㄒㄧㄢˋ ㄉㄧㄢˋ)
telegraph

有心(ㄧㄡ ㄒㄧㄣ)
to have an intention; to intend; to have a mind to; to set one's mind on

有心胸(ㄧㄡ ㄒㄧㄣ ㄒㄩㄥ)
ambitious; independent-minded; to have eyesight aiming high and far

有心人(ㄧㄡ ㄒㄧㄣ ㄖㄣˊ)
① thinking people; feeling people ② a person who has a mind to do something useful

有心眼兒(ㄧㄡ ㄒㄧㄣ ㄧㄢˇㄦ)
shrewd; vigilant: 他是一個有心眼兒的商人. He is a shrewd businessman.

有形(ㄧㄡ ㄒㄧㄥˊ)
visible; tangible; concrete

有性生殖(ㄧㄡ ㄒㄧㄥˋ ㄕㄥ ㄓˊ)
sexual reproduction; gamogenesis; syngamy

有鬚眉氣(ㄧㄡ ㄒㄩ ㄇㄟˊ ㄑㄧˋ)
(said of women) to have manly qualities: 這位國會女議員有鬚眉氣. This congresswoman has manly qualities.

有學問(ㄧㄡ ㄒㄩㄝˊ ㄨㄣˋ)
learned; erudite: 他的朋友都是有學問的. His friends are all learned.

有志竟成(ㄧㄡ ㄓˋ ㄐㄧㄥˋ ㄔㄥˊ)
Where there is a will there is a way. 亦作「有志者事竟成」

有志之士(ㄧㄡ ㄓˋ ㄓ ㄕˋ)
a man of high ambitions; a man with lofty ideals; a man of noble aspirations

有志一同(ㄧㄡ ㄓˋ ㄧ ㄊㄨㄥˊ)
to be of the same mind

有法無法治(ㄧㄡ ㄈㄚˇ ㄨˊ ㄈㄚˇ ㄓˋ)
Good laws without capable law enforcers are useless.

有朝一日(ㄧㄡ ㄓㄠ ㄧ ㄖˋ)
some day in the future

有助於(ㄧㄡ ㄓㄨˋ ㄩˊ)
to be conducive to; to conduce to: 新鮮空氣有助於健康. Fresh air is conducive to health.

有著落(ㄧㄡ ㄓㄨˊ ㄌㄨㄛˋ)
to have found reliable (financial) support

有準兒(ㄧㄡ ㄓㄨㄣˇㄦ)
① aimed at a target ② confident of success ③ determined; resolute

有種(ㄧㄡ ㄓㄨㄥˇ)
to have guts

有翅難飛(ㄧㄡ ㄔˋ ㄋㄢˊ ㄈㄟ)
unable to make use of one's ability

有巢氏(ㄧㄡ ㄔㄠˊ ㄕˋ)
name of a legendary Chinese ruler who taught the people

〔月部〕

〔月部〕

to build tree houses for protection against wild beasts

有產階級 (ㄧㄡˇ ㄔㄢˇ ㄐㄧㄝ ㄐㄧ)
the propertied class; the owner class; the wealthy class; the bourgeoisie

有成 (ㄧㄡˇ ㄔㄥˊ)
to have achieved success

有出入 (ㄧㄡˇ ㄔㄨ ㄖㄨˋ)
to have discrepancy; to disagree; to be inconsistent

有失體統 (ㄧㄡˇ ㄕ ㄊㄧˇ ㄊㄨㄥˇ)
very disgraceful

有失身份 (ㄧㄡˇ ㄕ ㄕㄣ ㄈㄣˋ)
to be beneath one's dignity

有時 (ㄧㄡˇ ㄕˊ)
sometimes; occasionally; now and then: 祖父母有時會來看我們。 My grandparents occasionally visit us.

有史以來 (ㄧㄡˇ ㄕˇ ㄧˇ ㄌㄞˊ)
since the dawn of history

有始有終 (ㄧㄡˇ ㄕˇ ㄧㄡˇ ㄓㄨㄥ)
to carry out an undertaking from start to finish—not to give up halfway

有始無終 (ㄧㄡˇ ㄕˇ ㄨˊ ㄓㄨㄥ)
to give up halfway; to leave an undertaking unfinished

有事 (ㄧㄡˇ ㄕˋ)
① to be occupied; to be busy; to have business: 你今晚有事嗎? Have you any business on this evening? ② to meet with an accident; to get into trouble; if something happens

有室 (ㄧㄡˇ ㄕˋ)
to have a home; to have a wife

有識之士 (ㄧㄡˇ ㄕˋ ㄓ ㄕˋ)
knowledgeable people; far-sighted people; thinking people; a man of insight

有勢力 (ㄧㄡˇ ㄕˋ ㄌㄧˋ)
powerful; influential

有恃無恐 (ㄧㄡˇ ㄕˋ ㄨˊ ㄎㄨㄥˇ)
There is no fear when one has something to fall back upon.

有守 (ㄧㄡˇ ㄕㄡˇ)
to adhere to principles; to have moral fortitude

有守有為 (ㄧㄡˇ ㄕㄡˇ ㄧㄡˇ ㄨㄟˊ)
to uphold principles; to act according to principles

有身 (ㄧㄡˇ ㄕㄣ)
pregnant; pregnancy

有神 (ㄧㄡˇ ㄕㄣˊ)
① to show mental liveliness; spirited; full of spirit ② miraculous

有神論 (ㄧㄡˇ ㄕㄣˊ ㄌㄨㄣˋ)
theism

有傷風化 (ㄧㄡˇ ㄕㄤ ㄈㄥ ㄏㄨㄚˋ)
harmful to public morals

有傷大雅 (ㄧㄡˇ ㄕㄤ ㄉㄚˋ ㄧㄚˇ)
to constitute a breach of decorum

有傷和氣 (ㄧㄡˇ ㄕㄤ ㄏㄜˊ ㄑㄧˋ)
harmful to esprit de corps; detrimental to friendship: 爭吵有傷和氣。 Quarrels are detrimental to friendship.

有賞有罰 (ㄧㄡˇ ㄕㄤˇ ㄧㄡˇ ㄈㄚˊ)
to mete out punishments or rewards as the case demands

有聲電影 (ㄧㄡˇ ㄕㄥ ㄉㄧㄢˋ ㄧㄥˇ)
a talking picture; a talkie; a sound film

有聲有色 (ㄧㄡˇ ㄕㄥ ㄧㄡˇ ㄙㄜˋ)
(said of a description or performance) vivid; impressive:那是一場有聲有色的演講。 It was an impressive speech.

有生之年 (ㄧㄡˇ ㄕㄥ ㄓ ㄋㄧㄢˊ)
for the rest of one's life

有生以來 (ㄧㄡˇ ㄕㄥ ㄧˇ ㄌㄞˊ)
since one's birth

有數 (ㄧㄡˇ ㄕㄨˋ)
① governed by principle ② arranged by fate ③ confident; to know what one is doing

有數兒 (ㄧㄡˇ ㄕㄨˋ ㄦ)
① rare ② confident; know what one is doing ③ to know how many; to know the exact number

有說有笑 (ㄧㄡˇ ㄕㄨㄛ ㄧㄡˇ ㄒㄧㄠˋ)
to talk and laugh; cheerful; lively

有染 (ㄧㄡˇ ㄖㄢˇ)
to have an affair with

有人 (ㄧㄡˇ ㄖㄣˊ)
① some people; somebody; someone; anyone 家裏有人嗎? Is there anyone at home? ② There is somebody there. 或There are some people inside.

有人家兒 (ㄧㄡˇ ㄖㄣˊ ㄐㄧㄚ ㄦ)
(said of a girl) already betrothed

有人緣兒 (ㄧㄡˇ ㄖㄣˊ ㄩㄢˊ ㄦ)
(said of people) likable; popular

有如 (ㄧㄡˇ ㄖㄨˊ)
just like; as if; as though

有則改之,無則加勉 (ㄧㄡˇ ㄗㄜˊ 《ㄞˇ ㄓ, ㄨˊ ㄗㄜˊ ㄐㄧㄚ ㄇㄧㄢˇ)
to correct the mistakes, if any, and to keep the good record if none has been committed

有增無減 (ㄧㄡˇ ㄗㄥ ㄨˊ ㄐㄧㄢˇ)
① to increase steadily ② to get steadily worse or serious

有作為 (ㄧㄡˇ ㄗㄨㄛˋ ㄨㄟˊ)
capable of outstanding achievements

有嘴無心 (ㄧㄡˇ ㄗㄨㄟˇ ㄨˊ ㄒㄧㄣ)
to say what one does not mean 參看「有口無心」

有罪 (ㄧㄡˇ ㄗㄨㄟˋ)
guilty; sinful

有此一說 (ㄧㄡˇ ㄘˇ ㄧ ㄕㄨㄛ)
There has been such a report, theory, etc.

有才 (ㄧㄡˇ ㄘㄞˊ)
gifted; talented

有才之士 (ㄧㄡˇ ㄘㄞˊ ㄓ ㄕˋ)
a man of talent

有才無命 (ㄧㄡˇ ㄘㄞˊ ㄨˊ ㄇㄧㄥˋ)
(said of a person) gifted but out of luck—The result is failure.

有司 (ㄧㄡˇ ㄙ)
an official

有色人種 (ㄧㄡˇ ㄙㄜˋ ㄖㄣˊ ㄓㄨㄥˇ)
colored races

有素 (ㄧㄡˇ ㄙㄨˋ)
(said of friendship, training, etc.) to have a solid foundation

有所不知 (ㄧㄡˇ ㄙㄨㄛˇ ㄅㄨˋ ㄓ)
to be unaware of something

有所不為 (ㄧㄡˇ ㄙㄨㄛˇ ㄅㄨˋ ㄨㄟˊ)
There are certain things that a man of principle will not stoop to.

有礙 (ㄧㄡˇ ㄞˋ)
detrimental; harmful: 抽煙有礙健康。 Smoking is detrimental to health.

有礙觀瞻 (ㄧㄡˇ ㄞˋ 《ㄨㄢ ㄓㄢ)
to leave a very bad impression to the beholder; to be an eyesore

有案可查 (ㄧㄡˇ ㄢˋ ㄎㄜˇ ㄔㄚˊ)

to be a matter of record; to be on record

有一次(一ㄡˇ一ㄘˋ)
on one occasion; once

有一天(一ㄡˇ一ㄊㄧㄢ)
one day; someday

有一手兒(一ㄡˇ一ㄕㄡˇㄦ)
to have remarkable skill

有益(一ㄡˇ一ˋ)
profitable; beneficial; useful

有益處(一ㄡˇ一ˋㄔㄨˋ)or(一ㄡˇ一ˋ‧ㄔㄨ)
advantageous; beneficial; profitable; useful; conducive; helpful: 這字典對年輕學生非常有益處。This dictionary is very useful for (or to) young students.

有意(一ㄡˇ一ˋ)
① to intend; purposeful; intentional: 我有意於次日離去。I intended to leave the next day. ② to show interest; to be interested; to be inclined to: 你有意出去散步嗎? Do you feel inclined for a walk?

有意見(一ㄡˇ一ˋㄐㄧㄢˋ)
to have something to say; to have reservations

有意識(一ㄡˇ一ˋㄕˋ)
conscious

有意思(一ㄡˇ一ˋ‧ㄙ)
interesting; exciting; enjoyable; amusing: 他是一個很有意思的人。He's a most interesting man.

有意義的(一ㄡˇ一ˋ一ˋ‧ㄉㄜ)
meaningful; significant

有意無意之間(一ㄡˇ一ˋㄨˊ一ˋㄓㄐㄧㄢ)
between consciousness and unconsciousness; consciously or unconsciously

有要沒緊(一ㄡˇ一ㄠˋㄇㄟˊㄐㄧㄣˇ)
important but not urgent

有言在先(一ㄡˇ一ㄢˊㄗㄞˋㄒㄧㄢ)
to have agreed before; to have said previously; to have made the promise beforehand; to forewarn

有眼不識泰山(一ㄡˇ一ㄢˇㄅㄨˋㄕˋㄊㄞˋㄕㄢ)
to fail to recognize a great person

有眼無珠(一ㄡˇ一ㄢˇㄨˊㄓㄨ)
(literally) to have eyes without eyeballs—to lack discerning power

有因(一ㄡˇ一ㄣ)
There is a reason for it. 這錯誤事出有因。There is a reason for this mistake.

有癮(一ㄡˇ一ㄣˇ)
to be addicted to; to have formed a habit

有氧舞蹈(一ㄡˇ一ㄤˇㄨˇㄉㄠˋ)
aerobic dancing

有無相通(一ㄡˇㄨˊㄒㄧㄤㄊㄨㄥ)
to render financial assistance among good friends

有我無敵(一ㄡˇㄨㄛˇㄨˊㄉㄧˊ)
If we are to survive, the enemy must be vanquished.

有味兒(一ㄡˇㄨㄟˋㄦ)
① tasty; delicious: 這道餐後點心很有味兒。This dessert is delicious. ② (said of artistic works, dramatic performances, etc.) delightful ③ to stink

有外遇(一ㄡˇㄨㄞˋㄩˋ)
(said of a married person) to have an extramarital affair

有為(一ㄡˇㄨㄟˊ)
capable of great achievements

有問必錄(一ㄡˇㄨㄣˋㄅㄧˋㄌㄨˋ)
to record everything one has heard

有問必答(一ㄡˇㄨㄣˋㄅㄧˋㄉㄚˊ)
to answer all questions asked

有問題(一ㄡˇㄨㄣˋㄊㄧˊ)
questionable; doubtful; unreliable: 我的去留尚有問題。It is doubtful whether I shall go or stay.

有望(一ㄡˇㄨㄤˋ)
hopeful; promising

有餘(一ㄡˇㄩˊ)
① to have enough and to spare ② odd

有緣(一ㄡˇㄩㄢˊ)
linked by ties of fate

有孕(一ㄡˇㄩㄣˋ)
pregnant

有勇無謀(一ㄡˇㄩㄥˇㄨˊㄇㄡˊ)
to be foolhardy

有用(一ㄡˇㄩㄥˋ)
useful; practical; beneficial: 他想做社會上有用的人。He wants to be a useful member of society.

【有】 2315
2.1 ㄡˋ yow yòu
same as 又—again

四畫

【朋】 2316
ㄆㄥˊ perng péng
1. a friend; a companion: 我們是很要好的朋友。We are great friends.
2. a group; a clique

朋比為奸(ㄆㄥˊㄅㄧˇㄨㄟˊㄐㄧㄢ)
to clique together for insidious purposes; to gang up for evil doings

朋分(ㄆㄥˊㄈㄣ)
to share (profits) with each other or one another

朋黨(ㄆㄥˊㄉㄤˇ)
a faction; a clique

朋儕(ㄆㄥˊㄔㄞˊ)
a companion; a friend

朋從(ㄆㄥˊㄘㄨㄥˊ)
to stick together as a result of congenial tastes

朋友(ㄆㄥˊ一ㄡˇ)
a friend: 他是我的朋友。He is a friend of mine.

【服】 2317
1. ㄈㄨˊ fwu fú
1. clothes; dress; garments; costume
2. mourning
3. to wear (clothes)
4. to obey; to be convinced; to yield; to concede; to admit
5. to serve
6. to take (medicine)
7. to be accustomed to; to be acclimated to

服兵役(ㄈㄨˊㄅㄧㄥ一ˋ)
to undergo military service

服滿(ㄈㄨˊㄇㄢˇ)
① to complete (a period of mourning or prescribed tour of service) ② to serve up (a prison term)

服法(ㄈㄨˊㄈㄚˇ)
instructions about how to take medicine

服貼帖(ㄈㄨˊㄊㄧㄝ一ˋ一ㄝˇㄊㄧㄝˇ)or服帖(ㄈㄨˊㄊㄧㄝ一ˋ)
obedient; docile: 我的孩子都很服帖。My boys are very obedient.

服毒(ㄈㄨˊㄉㄨˊ)
to take poison

〔月部〕

服勞役(ㄈㄨˊ ㄌㄠˊ ㄧˋ)
to undergo labor service (usually as a form of punishment)

服具(ㄈㄨˊ ㄐㄩˋ)
articles for use in funeral

服氣(ㄈㄨˊ ㄑㄧˋ)
①to practice Taoist breath control ②to yield or submit willingly

服勤(ㄈㄨˊ ㄑㄧㄣˊ)
to work hard; to toil; to be on duty

服刑(ㄈㄨˊ ㄒㄧㄥˊ)
to serve a prison term

服制(ㄈㄨˊ ㄓˋ)
rules of mourning according to relationship with the deceased

服裝(ㄈㄨˊ ㄓㄨㄤ)
costumes; dress; clothes

服裝表演(ㄈㄨˊ ㄓㄨㄤ ㄅㄧㄠˇ ㄧㄢˇ)
a fashion show

服裝設計(ㄈㄨˊ ㄓㄨㄤ ㄕㄜˋ ㄐㄧˋ)
dress designing

服食(ㄈㄨˊ ㄕˊ)
①to take Taoist pills ②to take food

服式(ㄈㄨˊ ㄕˋ)
the style of dress; costume

服飾(ㄈㄨˊ ㄕˋ)
costume and accessories

服侍(ㄈㄨˊ ·ㄕ)
to wait upon; to attend on

服輸(ㄈㄨˊ ㄕㄨ)
to concede defeat

服水土(ㄈㄨˊ ㄕㄨㄟˇ ㄊㄨˇ)
①to acclimatize; to adapt oneself to the natural environment of a strange land ②(biology) adaptation

服軟(ㄈㄨˊ ㄖㄨㄢˇ)
to yield to the soft approach

服罪(ㄈㄨˊ ㄗㄨㄟˋ)
to admit one's crime

服從(ㄈㄨˊ ㄘㄨㄥˊ)
to obey; to follow; to submit to; obedience

服色(ㄈㄨˊ ㄙㄜˋ)
①the color of clothes ②colorful clothes

服喪(ㄈㄨˊ ㄙㄤ)
to remain in mourning

服餌(ㄈㄨˊ ㄦˇ)
to take Taoist pills

服役(ㄈㄨˊ ㄧˋ)
①to undergo hard labor ②to undergo military service: 他被徵召服役。He was called up for military service.

服妖(ㄈㄨˊ ㄧㄠ)
①monstrous dress; outrageous clothes ②to subjugate evil spirits

服藥(ㄈㄨˊ ㄧㄠˋ)
to take medicine

服膺(ㄈㄨˊ ㄧㄥ)
to keep (a teaching, principle, etc.) in mind and stick to (it)

服硬(ㄈㄨˊ ㄧㄥˋ)
to yield to force

服務(ㄈㄨˊ ㄨˋ)
①to render service; service ②to work as an employee: 他在一家銀行服務。He works in a bank.

服務臺(ㄈㄨˊ ㄨˋ ㄊㄞˊ)
a service desk

服務中心(ㄈㄨˊ ㄨˋ ㄓㄨㄥ ㄒㄧㄣ)
a service center

服務業(ㄈㄨˊ ㄨˋ ㄧㄝˋ)
service industry

服務員(ㄈㄨˊ ㄨˋ ㄩㄢˊ)
an attendant; a steward

服用(ㄈㄨˊ ㄩㄥˋ)
①to take (medicine, etc.): 他服用了幾片阿斯匹靈。He took down some aspirin tablets. ②clothes and tools

【服】 2317
ㄈㄨˊ　fuh fú
(Chinese medicine) a dose:
一服藥 a dose of medicine

五畫

【朏】 2318
ㄈㄟˇ　feei fěi
the light of a crescent moon

六畫

【朔】 2319
ㄕㄨㄛˋ　shuoh shuò
1. to begin
2. north
3. the first day of the month of the lunar calendar

朔邊(ㄕㄨㄛˋ ㄅㄧㄢ)
the northern frontier

朔馬(ㄕㄨㄛˋ ㄇㄚˇ)
horses of northern breeds

朔漠(ㄕㄨㄛˋ ㄇㄛˋ)
the northern deserts

朔方(ㄕㄨㄛˋ ㄈㄤ)
dreary land in the north

朔風(ㄕㄨㄛˋ ㄈㄥ)
a biting north wind

朔氣(ㄕㄨㄛˋ ㄑㄧˋ)
①the 24 solar periods of the year ②cold air

朔雪(ㄕㄨㄛˋ ㄒㄩㄝˇ)
the heavy snow in the north

朔日(ㄕㄨㄛˋ ㄖˋ)
the first day of each month of the lunar calendar

朔牖(ㄕㄨㄛˋ ㄧㄡˇ)
a northern window

朔望(ㄕㄨㄛˋ ㄨㄤˋ)
the first and the 15th days of the lunar month

朔月(ㄕㄨㄛˋ ㄩㄝˋ)
the first day of the lunar month

【脥】 2320
ㄓㄣ　jenn zhēn
1. the royal "we" (used exclusively by the emperor or king to mean "I")
2. omens; auguries; portents; signs

脥兆(ㄓㄣ ㄓㄠˋ)
omens; portents; auguries; signs: 無有脥兆可尋。There are no signs for us to read.

【朓】 2321
ㄊㄧㄠˇ　tiaw tiǎo
at the end of a lunar month when the moon is setting in the west

七畫

【朗】 2322
ㄌㄤˇ　laang lǎng
1. bright; clear: 晴朗的天空無雲。A clear sky is free from clouds.
2. resonant; sonorously; sonorous

朗讀(ㄌㄤˇ ㄉㄨˊ)
to read aloud: 請朗讀這個故事。Please read the story aloud.

朗朗(ㄌㄤˇ ㄌㄤˇ)
①bright; clear ②resonant; sonorant; sonorous

朗照(ㄌㄤˇ ㄓㄠˋ)
to shine brightly: 今晨陽光朗

照。This morning the sun shone brightly.

朗誦(ㄌㄤ ㄙㄨㄥˋ)
to recite aloud

朗月(ㄌㄤ ㄩㄝˋ)
a bright moon: 一對情侶在朗月下散步。A pair of lovers walked under the bright moon.

朗讀(ㄌㄤ ㄉㄨˊ)
to chant (verses)

【望】 2323
ㄨㄤˋ wàng wǎng

1. to view; to watch; to gaze into the distance
2. to hope; to expect
3. the 15th day of each month of the lunar calendar
4. reputation; prestige
5. to call on; to visit

望八(ㄨㄤˋ ㄅㄚ)
expecting the 80th birthday very soon

望巴巴(ㄨㄤˋ ㄅㄚ ㄅㄚ)
anxious; apprehensive: 他望巴巴會見你。He was anxious to meet you.

望不見(ㄨㄤˋ ㄅㄨˋ ㄐㄧㄢˋ)or 望不到(ㄨㄤˋ ㄅㄨˋ ㄉㄠˋ)
incapable of seeing or being seen

望梅止渴(ㄨㄤˋ ㄇㄟˊ ㄓˇ ㄎㄜˇ)
(literally) to quench one's thirst by watching plums—to have imaginary satisfaction; to console oneself with false hopes

望門投止(ㄨㄤˋ ㄇㄣˊ ㄊㄡˊ ㄓˇ)
to stop for the night at any house one happens to come across

望門寡(ㄨㄤˋ ㄇㄣˊ ㄍㄨㄚˇ)
a woman bereaved of her fiancé

望彌撒(ㄨㄤˋ ㄇㄧˊ ㄙㄚ)
to go to Mass; to attend a Mass

望風披靡(ㄨㄤˋ ㄈㄥ ㄆㄧ ㄇㄧˇ)
to flee helter-skelter at the mere sight of the oncoming force

望風撲影(ㄨㄤˋ ㄈㄥ ㄆㄨ ㄧㄥˇ)
to search without any clue; to give a wild-goose chase; to launch a witch hunt

望風逃竄(ㄨㄤˋ ㄈㄥ ㄊㄠˊ ㄘㄨㄢˋ)or 望風而逃(ㄨㄤˋ ㄈㄥ ㄦˊ ㄊㄠˊ)

to flee upon hearing the news (that a powerful enemy is approaching)

望帝(ㄨㄤˋ ㄉㄧˋ)
a cuckoo 亦作「杜鵑」

望衡對宇(ㄨㄤˋ ㄏㄥˊ ㄉㄨㄟˋ ㄩˇ)
to live near each other

望見(ㄨㄤˋ ㄐㄧㄢˋ)
to have seen; to see: 我望見有甚麼東西在動。I saw something move.

望氣(ㄨㄤˋ ㄑㄧˋ)
to read the future from the clouds (an ancient form of divination)

望秋先零(ㄨㄤˋ ㄑㄧㄡ ㄒㄧㄢ ㄌㄧㄥˊ)
to show the feebleness of old age while still young

望重士林(ㄨㄤˋ ㄓㄨㄥˋ ㄕˋ ㄌㄧㄣˊ)
to enjoy high prestige among scholars; to command respect in the academic circle

望塵莫及(ㄨㄤˋ ㄔㄣˊ ㄇㄛˋ ㄐㄧˊ)
to gaze at another's fast progress; to be left far behind; unable to compare with another's accomplishment, etc.

望穿秋水(ㄨㄤˋ ㄔㄨㄢ ㄑㄧㄡ ㄕㄨㄟˇ)
to gaze with eager expectation (until the eyes are bored through); to aspire earnestly

望日(ㄨㄤˋ ㄖˋ)
the 15th day of every lunar month

望子成龍(ㄨㄤˋ ㄗˇ ㄔㄥˊ ㄌㄨㄥˊ)
to hope one's children will have a bright future

望族(ㄨㄤˋ ㄗㄨˊ)
a respected family in a community; a family of renown

望色(ㄨㄤˋ ㄙㄜˋ)
to diagnose a disease from the patient's appearance

望歲(ㄨㄤˋ ㄙㄨㄟˋ)
to pray or hope for a bumper crop

望而卻步(ㄨㄤˋ ㄦˊ ㄑㄩㄝˋ ㄅㄨˋ)
to hesitate to approach upon seeing a difficult or dangerous situation

望而生畏(ㄨㄤˋ ㄦˊ ㄕㄥ ㄨㄟˋ)
to be awe-stricken by merely looking at it

望眼欲穿(ㄨㄤˋ ㄧㄢˇ ㄩˋ ㄔㄨㄢ)

to aspire earnestly

望洋興歎(ㄨㄤˋ ㄧㄤˊ ㄒㄧㄥ ㄊㄢˋ)
to feel powerless and frustrated in the face of a great task

望文生義(ㄨㄤˋ ㄨㄣˊ ㄕㄥ ㄧˋ)
to misconstrue the meaning of a word or phrase prima facie; to interpret without real understanding

望聞問切(ㄨㄤˋ ㄨㄣˊ ㄨㄣˋ ㄑㄧㄝˋ)
(Chinese medicine) the four essential steps a doctor takes to diagnose a disease: to observe the symptoms, to listen to the patient's description of his ailment, to ask the patient relevant questions, and to feel the patient's pulse

望月(ㄨㄤˋ ㄩㄝˋ)
the full moon 參看「滿月①」

望遠鏡(ㄨㄤˋ ㄩㄢˇ ㄐㄧㄥˋ)
a telescope: 天文望遠鏡 an astronomical telescope

八畫

【朝】 2324
1. ㄓㄠ jau zhāo
1. morning
2. a day

朝不保夕(ㄓㄠ ㄅㄨˋ ㄅㄠˇ ㄒㄧ)
(literally) One is uncertain in the morning whether one will be safe in the evening.—precarious; in constant fear; jittery

朝不謀夕(ㄓㄠ ㄅㄨˋ ㄇㄡˊ ㄒㄧ)
to fail to plan even for the immediate future

朝暮人(ㄓㄠ ㄇㄨˋ ㄖㄣˊ)
a person destined to die soon

朝發夕至(ㄓㄠ ㄈㄚ ㄒㄧ ㄓˋ)
Road condition is so good or the distance so short that one can reach one's destination in the evening if one starts out in the morning.

朝暾(ㄓㄠ ㄊㄨㄣ)
the morning sun

朝令夕改(ㄓㄠ ㄌㄧㄥˋ ㄒㄧ ㄍㄞˇ)
(literally) to issue an order in the morning and change it in the evening—to change rules very frequently; to make unforeseen changes in

〔月部〕

〔月部〕

policy

朝露(业丝 为义)
morning dew—a symbol of transience: 人生如朝露。 Human life is as evanescent as the morning dew.

朝會(业丝 厂义万)
a morning rally (in schools)

朝菌(业丝 니口万)
ephemeral fungus; morning mushrooms

朝氣(业丝 く丫)
fresh spirit; exuberance and aggressiveness: 工作要有朝氣。 Put a little more fresh spirit into your work.

朝氣蓬勃(业丝 く丫 夂丝 勺ㄛ)
full of youthful spirit; full of vigor and vitality

朝乾夕惕(业丝 くㄧㄢ Tㄧ ㄊㄧ)
diligent and alert from morning till night

朝秦暮楚(业丝 くㄧㄣ ㄇㄨ 彳ㄨ)
(literally) to support Chin in the morning and Chu in the evening—to be fickle or capricious

朝曦(业丝 Tㄧ)
the morning sun

朝夕(业丝 Tㄧ)
① day and night; always; constantly: 他們朝夕相處。 They were together from morning to night. ② a very brief period of time

朝旭(业丝 Tㄩ)
the morning sun

朝朝暮暮(业丝 业丝 ㄇㄨ ㄇㄨ)
every day; always; day and night

朝生暮死(业丝 ㄕㄥ ㄇㄨ ㄙ)
(said of life) transient; ephemeral

朝思暮想(业丝 ㄙ ㄇㄨ Tㄧㄤ)
to yearn day and night

朝三暮四(业丝 ㄙㄢ ㄇㄨ ㄙ)
to be inconsistent; to be fickle or changeable; to chop about

朝陽(业丝 ㄧㄤ)
the morning sun

朝陽鳴鳳(业丝 ㄧㄤ ㄇㄧㄥ ㄈㄥ)
outspoken admonitions

朝聞道，夕死可矣(业丝 ㄨㄣ ㄉㄠ，Tㄧ ㄙ ㄎㄜ ㄧ)
If a man in the morning hear the right way, he may

die in the evening without regret. —Truth is so valuable that one is willing to die soon after learning it.

朝夕夕殘(业丝 ㄩ ㄒㄧ ㄘㄢ)
to do nothing but eat and drink

【朝】²³²⁴
2. 彳幺 chaur choo

1. an imperial court
2. a dynasty
3. to go to imperial court
4. to face

朝拜(彳幺 ㄅㄞ)
① to worship; to pay respects to (a sovereign) ② to pilgrimage

朝報(彳幺 ㄅㄠ)
(in old China) a government bulletin

朝班(彳幺 ㄅㄢ)or 朝列(彳幺 ㄌㄧㄝ)
the assemblage of courtiers at the imperial court

朝柄(彳幺 ㄅㄧㄥ)
the power of a sovereign

朝聘(彳幺 ㄆㄧㄥ)
official intercourse among feudal princes during the Epoch of Warring States

朝冠(彳幺 ㄍㄨㄢ)
the cap worn in audience with the monarch

朝服(彳幺 ㄈㄨ)
court robes; formal dress worn in audience with the monarch

朝代(彳幺 ㄉㄞ)
a dynasty

朝天(彳幺 ㄊㄧㄢ)
① to be presented at court; to go to court ② to face upward

朝廷(彳幺 ㄊㄧㄥ)
the court (of a sovereign); an imperial court: 郢是朝廷 的意旨。 It was the wish of the court.

朝綱(彳幺 ㄍㄤ)
① rules of an imperial court ② the imperial court

朝貴(彳幺 ㄍㄨㄟ)
powerful courtiers

朝貢(彳幺 ㄍㄨㄥ)
to present tribute to the sovereign

朝考(彳幺 ㄎㄠ)
the final court examination

(under the former civil service examination system)

朝後(彳幺 ㄏㄡ)
to face backward

朝見(彳幺 ㄐㄧㄢ)
to be received in audience by a sovereign

朝覲(彳幺 ㄐㄧㄣ)
to be received in audience by a sovereign

朝前(彳幺 くㄧㄢ)
to face forward

朝鮮(彳幺 Tㄧㄢ)
an old name of Korea

朝鮮半島(彳幺 Tㄧㄢ ㄅㄢ ㄉㄠ)
the Korean Peninsula

朝獻(彳幺 Tㄧㄢ)
to offer a gift to the throne on the occasion of an audience

朝章(彳幺 业ㄤ)
rules of an imperial court

朝政(彳幺 业ㄥ)
the affairs of the state: 朝政 紊亂。 The affairs of the state were in disorder.

朝珠(彳幺 业ㄨ)
a string of 108 beads made of coral, amber, etc. worn by officials of the Ching Dynasty

朝臣(彳幺 彳ㄣ)
(collectively) the court

朝山(彳幺 ㄕㄢ)or 朝聖(彳幺 ㄕㄥ)
to go on a pilgrimage: 他們 前往聖地朝聖。 They went on a pilgrimage to a sacred place.

朝聖團(彳幺 ㄕㄥ ㄊㄨㄢ)
a pilgrimage mission; a hadji (or haji) mission

朝衣朝冠(彳幺 ㄧ 彳幺 ㄍㄨㄢ)
dressed up for audience with the emperor

朝儀(彳幺 ㄧ)
the proprieties for audience with the emperor

朝議(彳幺 ㄧ)
a civil official post in the Ching Dynasty

朝野(彳幺 ㄧㄝ)
the government and the people

朝隱(彳幺 ㄧㄣ)
a very unobtrusive or self-effacing courtier

朝陽(ㄔㄠˊ 一ㄤˊ)
① the eastern slope of a mountain ② with a sunny, usually southern, aspect: 這房屋朝陽。The house has a southern aspect.

朝望(ㄔㄠˊ ㄨㄤˋ)
respected courtiers

【期】 2325 1. ㄑㄧˊ chyi qí (又讀)ㄑㄧ chi qī

1. periods; times: 法國大革命時期 the period of the French Revolution
2. a designated time; a time limit: 計計畫必須在指定期限內實行。The project must be carried out within the designated time.
3. to expect; to hope; to wait: 勝利可期。Victory may be expected.

期票(ㄑㄧˊ ㄆㄧㄠˋ)
a time draft; a promissory note: 這是一張五百元的期票。This is a promissory note for $500.

期末考試(ㄑㄧˊ ㄇㄛˋ ㄎㄠˇ ㄕˋ) or 期考(ㄑㄧˊ ㄎㄠˇ) or 期終考試(ㄑㄧˊ ㄓㄨㄥ ㄎㄠˇ ㄕˋ)
the terminal examination; the final examination of a school term; the final 亦作「學期考試」: 他期末考試及格了。He passed the final examination.

期滿(ㄑㄧˊ ㄇㄢˇ)
The term (or period) has expired. 他的假期到星期二期滿。His vacation expires on Tuesday.

期待(ㄑㄧˊ ㄉㄞˋ)
to expect; to hope

期刊(ㄑㄧˊ ㄎㄢ)
a periodical publication; a periodical

期貨(ㄑㄧˊ ㄏㄨㄛˋ)
(economics) futures; goods to be delivered at a specified time; the future delivery

期會(ㄑㄧˊ ㄏㄨㄟˋ)
to meet at a time fixed in advance

期間(ㄑㄧˊ ㄐㄧㄢ)
a period; a term: 有很長的期間我們沒有他的消息。There were long periods when we had no news of him.

期期(ㄑㄧˊ ㄑㄧˊ)or 期期艾艾(ㄑㄧˊ ㄑㄧˊ ㄞˋ ㄞˋ)
stammering: 他期期艾艾地她道謝。He stammered his thanks to her.

期限(ㄑㄧˊ ㄒㄧㄢˋ)
a time limit; a deadline

期許(ㄑㄧˊ ㄒㄩˇ)
to expect to; expectation: 我們對你期許甚殷。We have great expectations of you.

期中報告(ㄑㄧˊ ㄓㄨㄥ ㄅㄠˋ ㄍㄠˋ)
(accounting) an interim report

期中考試(ㄑㄧˊ ㄓㄨㄥ ㄎㄠˇ ㄕˋ)
a midterm examination

期成(ㄑㄧˊ ㄔㄥˊ)
to hope for success

期日(ㄑㄧˊ ㄖˋ)
the date fixed for some purpose

期願(ㄑㄧˊ 一ˋ)
a 100-year-old person; a centenarian

期望(ㄑㄧˊ ㄨㄤˋ)
to expect; to hope: 我們都期望最好的一面。We're hoping for the best.

期約(ㄑㄧˊ ㄩㄝ)
to agree on a time for the delivery of a bribe

【期】 2325 2. (舊)ㄐㄧ ji jī
one year

期服(ㄐㄧ ㄈㄨˊ)
one-year mourning (observed for one's grandparents, father's brothers, etc.)

期年(ㄐㄧ ㄋㄧㄢˊ)
the first anniversary; a complete year

期月(ㄐㄧ ㄩㄝˋ)
① one year ② one month

十畫

【望】 2326 ㄨㄤˋ wanq wàng
the original form of 望—the 15th day of each month of the lunar calendar

十二畫

【朣】 2327 ㄊㄨㄥˊ torng tóng
the rising moon

朣朣(ㄊㄨㄥˊ ㄊㄨㄥˊ)
the appearance of the moon beginning to increase in brightness

十四畫

【朦】 2328 ㄇㄥˊ meng méng
1. the state of the moon just before setting
2. dim; vague; hazy
3. to deceive; to swindle

朦朧(ㄇㄥˊ ㄌㄨㄥˊ)
① the appearance of the moon just before setting ② dim; vague; hazy; drowsy: 他醉眼朦朧。His eyes were drowsy from drink.

十六畫

【朧】 2329 ㄌㄨㄥˊ long lóng
the moon's brightness

朧明(ㄌㄨㄥˊ ㄇㄧㄥˊ)
the moon's brightness

朧疃(ㄌㄨㄥˊ ㄊㄨㄥˇ)
the sound of a drum

朧朧(ㄌㄨㄥˊ ㄌㄨㄥˊ)
the brightness of the moon

木 部
ㄇㄨˋ muh mù

〔木部〕

【木】 2330 ㄇㄨˋ muh mù
1. a tree
2. wood; timber; lumber
3. made of wood; wooden
4. simple; honest
5. senseless; benumbed; dull: 她的手凍麻木了。Her hands were benumbed by cold.
6. a coffin

木板(ㄇㄨˋ ㄅㄢˇ)
planks; boards

木版(ㄇㄨˋ ㄅㄢˇ)
a wood engraving; a woodcut

木本(ㄇㄨˋ ㄅㄣˇ)
woody (plants)

木本水源(ㄇㄨˋ ㄅㄣˇ ㄕㄨㄟˇ ㄩㄢˊ)
(literally) A tree has its root, and a stream has its

（木
部）

木筆(ㄇㄨ ㄅㄧˇ)
(botany) a lily magnolia 亦作「辛夷」

木簰 or 木排(ㄇㄨ ㄆㄞˊ)or 木筏
(ㄇㄨ ㄈㄚˊ)
a wooden raft

木片(ㄇㄨ ㄆㄧㄢˋ)
a wood chip

木馬(ㄇㄨ ㄇㄚˇ)
(gymnastics) a horse

木棉(ㄇㄨ ㄇㄧㄢˊ)
silk cotton

木芙蓉(ㄇㄨ ㄈㄨ ㄖㄨㄥˊ)
(botany) Hibiscus mutabilis

木雕泥塑(ㄇㄨ ㄉㄧㄠ ㄋㄧˊ ㄙㄨˋ)
(literally)carved from wood and molded from clay—very stupid

木蠹(ㄇㄨ ㄉㄨˋ)
Cossus ligniperda

木鐸(ㄇㄨ ㄉㄨㄛˊ)
①a bell with a wooden clapper ②a teacher

木鐸警鐘(ㄇㄨ ㄉㄨㄛˊ ㄐㄧㄥˇ ㄓㄨㄥ)
statements that arouse the public from apathy or complacency

木頭(ㄇㄨ ·ㄊㄡ)
①wood; timber ②a stupid fellow

木頭人兒(ㄇㄨ ·ㄊㄡ ㄖㄣˊ)
a stupid fellow; an idiot

木炭(ㄇㄨ ㄊㄢˋ)
charcoal: 在火中多放些木炭。Put some more charcoal on the fire.

木炭畫(ㄇㄨ ㄊㄢˋ ㄏㄨㄚˋ)
a charcoal drawing; a fusain

木訥(ㄇㄨ ㄋㄜˋ)
honest and slow-witted; lacking the ability to talk well

木乃伊(ㄇㄨ ㄋㄞˇ ㄧ)
a mummy

木牛流馬(ㄇㄨ ㄋㄧㄡˊ ㄌㄧㄡˊ ㄇㄚˇ)
a legendary mechanical device for hauling war supplies, said to be invented by Chu-Ko Liang (諸葛亮) during the Epoch of the Three Kingdoms

木蠟(ㄇㄨ ㄌㄚˋ)
wood wax

木蘭(ㄇㄨ ㄌㄢˊ)
①a deciduous magnolia (*Magnolia obovata*) ②Hua Mu-lan(花木蘭)(circa 500 A. D.), a heroine who joined the military service in place of her sick father for 12 years without betraying her real identity

木梨(ㄇㄨ ㄌㄧˊ)
a tough pear

木料(ㄇㄨ ㄌㄧㄠˋ)
wooden material; wood; lumber: 桌子通常是木料做的。Tables are usually made of wood.

木瘤(ㄇㄨ ㄌㄧㄡˊ)
a gnarl

木蓮(ㄇㄨ ㄌㄧㄢˊ)
a magnolia

木瓜(ㄇㄨ ㄍㄨㄚ)
①a papaya (fruit) ②a papaya (tree)亦作「木瓜樹」

木棍(ㄇㄨ ㄍㄨㄣˋ)or 木棒(ㄇㄨ ㄅㄤˋ)
a wooden club: 他以木棒擊球。He hit the ball with his wooden club.

木工(ㄇㄨ ㄍㄨㄥ)
①a carpenter; a woodworker ②carpentry

木工廠(ㄇㄨ ㄍㄨㄥ ㄔㄤˇ)
a woodworking plant or shop

木刻(ㄇㄨ ㄎㄜˋ)
wood engraving; a woodcut

木化石(ㄇㄨ ㄏㄨㄚˋ ㄕˊ)
wood opal

木屐(ㄇㄨ ㄐㄧ)
clogs; pattens

木雞(ㄇㄨ ㄐㄧ)
①a simpleton ②a woodcock

木簡(ㄇㄨ ㄐㄧㄢˇ)
a wooden tablet (used as writing paper in ancient times)

木槿(ㄇㄨ ㄐㄧㄣˇ)
a hibiscus; a China rose

木漿(ㄇㄨ ㄐㄧㄤ)
(papermaking) wood pulp

木匠(ㄇㄨ ㄐㄧㄤˋ)
a carpenter; a woodworker

木強 or 木彊(ㄇㄨ ㄐㄧㄤˋ)
stiff; inexorable; uncompromising; inflexible

木精(ㄇㄨ ㄐㄧㄥ)
wood spirit; wood alcohol 亦

作「甲醇」

木器(ㄇㄨ ㄑㄧˋ)
wooden articles; wooden furniture

木器店(ㄇㄨ ㄑㄧˋ ㄉㄧㄢˋ)
a wooden article store; a wooden furniture store

木琴(ㄇㄨ ㄑㄧㄣˊ)
(music) a xylophone

木樨 or 木犀(ㄇㄨ ㄒㄧ)
(botany) Osmanthus fragrans

木屑竹頭(ㄇㄨ ㄒㄧㄝˋ ㄓㄨˊ ㄊㄡˊ)
odds and ends that may prove useful someday

木枚(ㄇㄨ ㄒㄧㄢ)
a wooden winnowing spade; a wooden shovel

木箱(ㄇㄨ ㄒㄧㄤ)
a wooden box; a wooden trunk: 他把書籍裝在木箱中。He packed the books in a wooden box.

木星(ㄇㄨ ㄒㄧㄥ)
the planet Jupiter

木札(ㄇㄨ ㄓㄚˊ)
a wooden tag

木柵(ㄇㄨ ㄓㄚˋ)
a stockade

木主(ㄇㄨ ㄓㄨˇ)
sacred wooden tablets (at temples, chapels, etc.)

木樁(ㄇㄨ ㄓㄨㄤ)
a wooden post or pile

木柴(ㄇㄨ ㄔㄞˊ)
firewood

木廠(ㄇㄨ ㄔㄤˇ)
a timber mill

木槌(ㄇㄨ ㄔㄨㄟˊ)
a gavel; a wooden hammer

木蝨(ㄇㄨ ㄕ)
a wood louse

木石(ㄇㄨ ㄕˊ)
a lifeless thing; a senseless being

木石心腸(ㄇㄨ ㄕˊ ㄒㄧㄣ ㄔㄤˊ)
flinty-hearted; unfeeling

木舌(ㄇㄨ ㄕㄜˊ)
reticent; silent

木梳(ㄇㄨ ㄕㄨ)
a wooden comb

木栓(ㄇㄨ ㄕㄨㄢ)
a cork

木然(ㄇㄨ ㄖㄢˊ)
stupefied

木人(ㄇㄨ ㄖㄣˊ)
a dull fellow; a simpleton

木人石心 (ㄇㄨ ㄖㄣˊ ㄕˊ ㄒㄧㄣ)
pitiless; unfeeling; heartless

木作 (ㄇㄨ ㄗㄨㄛˋ)
①a carpenter's shop ② a carpenter

木材 (ㄇㄨ ㄘㄞˊ)
lumber; timber: 這桌子是木材製的。This table is made of timber.

木材行 (ㄇㄨ ㄘㄞˊ ㄏㄤˊ)
a lumber company

木醋 (ㄇㄨ ㄘㄨˋ)
wood vinegar

木塞 (ㄇㄨ ㄙㄞ)
a cork

木案 (ㄇㄨ ㄢˋ)
an instrument of torture (for squeezing hands or feet)

木燧 (ㄇㄨ ㄙㄨㄟˋ)
wood for producing fire by friction

木偶 (ㄇㄨ ㄡˇ)
a puppet

木偶戲 (ㄇㄨ ㄡˇ ㄒㄧˋ)
a puppet show: 她喜歡看木偶戲。She is fond of the puppet show.

木耳 (ㄇㄨ ㄦˇ)
edible fungus from trees (Auricularia auricula)

木已成舟 (ㄇㄨ ㄧˇ ㄔㄥˊ ㄓㄡ)
(literally) The timber has been turned into a boat already.—It is irrevocable.或 It is an accomplished fact.

木曜日 (ㄇㄨ ㄧㄠˋ ㄖˋ)
Thursday

木屋 (ㄇㄨ ㄨ)
a log cabin: 他們住在一間木屋裏。They lived in a log cabin.

木碗 (ㄇㄨ ㄨㄢˇ)
a wooden bowl

木魚 (ㄇㄨ ㄩˊ)
a skull-shaped wooden drum, which a Buddhist monk or nun beats while chanting

木鳶 (ㄇㄨ ㄩㄢ)
a wooden kite (a legendary flying machine)

木俑 (ㄇㄨ ㄩㄥˇ)
a wooden image or figure to be buried with the deceased

一畫

【未】 2331
ㄨㄟˋ wey wèi

1. not yet: 這工作尚未做完。The work is not yet finished.
2. not: 我未曾見過他。I have not seen him.
3. the eighth of the Twelve Terrestrial Branches
4. 1:00-3:00 p.m.
5. a Chinese family name

未必 (ㄨㄟˋ ㄅㄧˋ)
not always; not necessarily: 那未必如此。It is not necessarily so.

未必盡然 (ㄨㄟˋ ㄅㄧˋ ㄐㄧㄣˋ ㄖㄢˊ)
not always so; not necessarily so

未便 (ㄨㄟˋ ㄅㄧㄢˋ)
not convenient; improper; inadvisable; not in a position to

未卜先知 (ㄨㄟˋ ㄅㄨˇ ㄒㄧㄢ ㄓ)
to foresee accurately

未萌 (ㄨㄟˋ ㄇㄥˊ)
yet to bud; yet to come into existence or develop

未免 (ㄨㄟˋ ㄇㄧㄢˇ)
①It must be admitted that...
②necessarily; unavoidably

未付 (ㄨㄟˋ ㄈㄨˋ)
unpaid; outstanding (debts, accounts, etc.): 他未付的帳加起來一共有七百元。His unpaid bills amounted to $700.

未到貨 (ㄨㄟˋ ㄉㄠˋ ㄏㄨㄛˋ)
goods afloat

未定 (ㄨㄟˋ ㄉㄧㄥˋ)
uncertain; unfixed; undefined: 他的行期未定。The date of his departure is uncertain.

未定之天 (ㄨㄟˋ ㄉㄧㄥˋ ㄓ ㄊㄧㄢ)
uncertainty

未定草 (ㄨㄟˋ ㄉㄧㄥˋ ㄘㄠˇ) or 未定稿 (ㄨㄟˋ ㄉㄧㄥˋ ㄍㄠˇ)
a preliminary draft

未安 (ㄨㄟˋ ㄢ)
yet to be brought to a proper state; not proper: 那樣做未安。It isn't proper to act like that.

未了 (ㄨㄟˋ ㄌㄧㄠˇ)
to fail to; cannot: 他們未能了解我的意思。They failed to

---

see what I meant.

未能免俗 (ㄨㄟˋ ㄋㄥˊ ㄇㄧㄢˇ ㄙㄨˊ)
incapable of being exempted from usual custom; unable to avoid following conventional practices

未來 (ㄨㄟˋ ㄌㄞˊ)
future; in the future: 我們的未來似難預測。Our future seems very uncertain.

未來派 (ㄨㄟˋ ㄌㄞˊ ㄆㄞˋ)
futurists; futurism

未老先衰 (ㄨㄟˋ ㄌㄠˇ ㄒㄧㄢ ㄕㄨㄞ)
to become senile before one's time

未了 (ㄨㄟˋ ㄌㄧㄠˇ)
unsettled; unfixed; unfinished: 這問題仍然未了。The problem is still unsettled.

未了公案 (ㄨㄟˋ ㄌㄧㄠˇ ㄍㄨㄥ ㄢˋ)
an unsettled problem

未了緣 (ㄨㄟˋ ㄌㄧㄠˇ ㄩㄢˊ) or 未了因 (ㄨㄟˋ ㄌㄧㄠˇ ㄧㄣ)
(Buddhism) ties carried over from the previous life

未敢苟同 (ㄨㄟˋ ㄍㄢˇ ㄍㄡˇ ㄊㄨㄥˊ)
(literary language) to beg to differ; cannot agree: 請你原諒，你的意見，我未敢苟同。I beg your pardon! I cannot agree with you.

未冠 (ㄨㄟˋ ㄍㄨㄢ)
prior to the capping ceremony which takes place when a young man is 20 years old

未可 (ㄨㄟˋ ㄎㄜˇ)
cannot: 此案未可定奪。This case cannot be decided.

未可厚非 (ㄨㄟˋ ㄎㄜˇ ㄏㄡˋ ㄈㄟ)
shouldn't be blamed too much for that—no serious mistake committed

未可知 (ㄨㄟˋ ㄎㄜˇ ㄓ)
uncertain: 他們抵達的日期尚未可知。The date of their arrival is uncertain.

未開發 (ㄨㄟˋ ㄎㄞ ㄈㄚ)
(said of land, resources, etc.) undeveloped; uncultivated

未開化的 (ㄨㄟˋ ㄎㄞ ㄏㄨㄚˋ ㄉㄜ˙)
①uncivilized ②underdeveloped

未婚 (ㄨㄟˋ ㄏㄨㄣ)
unmarried; single

未婚夫 (ㄨㄟˋ ㄏㄨㄣ ㄈㄨ)

〔木部〕

〔木 部〕

one's fiancé

未婚男子 (ㄨㄟˋ ㄏㄨㄣ ㄋㄢˊ ㄗˇ)
a bachelor

未婚妻 (ㄨㄟˋ ㄏㄨㄣ ㄑㄧ)
one's fiancée

未遑 (ㄨㄟˋ ㄏㄨㄤˊ)
busy; occupied; too busy to;
too occupied to

未及 (ㄨㄟˋ ㄐㄧˊ)
unable to make it in time;
not enough time left to do it

未幾 (ㄨㄟˋ ㄐㄧˇ)
① soon afterwards: 未幾，他
曾向我解釋。Soon afterwards
he explained it to me. ② not
many

未見 (ㄨㄟˋ ㄐㄧㄢˋ)
to have not seen; not yet
seen: 我未見過人被絞死。I've
never seen a man hanged.

未盡事宜 (ㄨㄟˋ ㄐㄧㄣˋ ㄕˋ ㄧˊ)
unfinished matters; unsettled
affairs

未經 (ㄨㄟˋ ㄐㄧㄥ)
to have not yet (gone
through)

未竟之志 (ㄨㄟˋ ㄐㄧㄥˋ ㄓ ㄓˋ)
an unfulfilled ambition: 做個
偉大的政治家是他的未竟之志。
To be a great statesman is
his unfulfilled ambition.

未決 (ㄨㄟˋ ㄐㄩㄝˊ)
undecided; uncertain; unsettled: 那仍是個未決的問題。 It
was still an undecided question.

未悉 (ㄨㄟˋ ㄒㄧ)
① not knowing; unfamiliar
② unknown

未詳 (ㄨㄟˋ ㄒㄧㄤˊ)
not knowing or known in
detail

未知鹿死誰手 (ㄨㄟˋ ㄓ ㄌㄨˋ ㄙˇ ㄕㄟˊ ㄕㄡˇ)
unable to predict who will
be the winner

未知數 (ㄨㄟˋ ㄓ ㄕㄨˋ)
①（mathematics）an un-
known number ② unknown;
uncertain

未之有焉 (ㄨㄟˋ ㄓ ㄧㄡˇ ㄧㄢ)
impossible; could not happen; never heard of: 如此意
外事件似乎未之有焉。Such an
accident seems impossible.

未嘗 (ㄨㄟˋ ㄔㄤˊ)
①（to be used before another

negative expression to form
a positive statement）not
necessarily ② never: 我生平
未嘗聽說或見過這樣的東西。
Never in my life have I
heard or seen such a thing.

未嘗不可 (ㄨㄟˋ ㄔㄤˊ ㄅㄨˋ ㄎㄜˇ)
It is not necessarily impermissible or impossible.

未成品 (ㄨㄟˋ ㄔㄥˊ ㄆㄧㄣˇ)
unfinished work

未成年 (ㄨㄟˋ ㄔㄥˊ ㄋㄧㄢˊ) or 未成人
(ㄨㄟˋ ㄔㄥˊ ㄖㄣˊ)
not yet come of age; minor

未成熟 (ㄨㄟˋ ㄔㄥˊ ㄕㄡˊ)
unripe; immature: 她是一個未
成熟的女郎。 She is an im-
mature girl.

未時 (ㄨㄟˋ ㄕˊ)
the period of the day from 1
p.m. to 3 p.m.

未始 (ㄨㄟˋ ㄕˇ)
not necessarily (used before
another negative expression
to form a positive state-
ment)

未然 (ㄨㄟˋ ㄖㄢˊ)
before it happens: 我們應防
患未然。We should prevent
trouble before it happens.

未入流 (ㄨㄟˋ ㄖㄨˋ ㄌㄧㄡˊ)
① government employees of
the lowest rank during the
Ming and Ching Dynasties
② any skill that is below the
accepted standard

未若 (ㄨㄟˋ ㄖㄨㄛˋ)
not as good as; can not be
compared with: 我的英文未若
他。My English is not as
good as his.

未曾 (ㄨㄟˋ ㄘㄥˊ)
never before: 我未曾到過那
裏。Never before have I been
there.

未曾有 (ㄨㄟˋ ㄘㄥˊ ㄧㄡˇ)
to have not happened
before; unprecedented: 這是
歷史上未曾有的奇蹟。This is a
miracle unprecedented in
history.

未遂 (ㄨㄟˋ ㄙㄨㄟˋ)
attempted without success

未遂犯 (ㄨㄟˋ ㄙㄨㄟˋ ㄈㄢˋ)
a convict guilty of an
attempted offense

未有 (ㄨㄟˋ ㄧㄡˇ)

to have never had; to have
never been; can never be: 我
對那件事從未有過懷疑。I have
never had any doubts whatever of that.

未央 (ㄨㄟˋ ㄧㄤ)
① not yet halfway through
② not exhausted

未央宮 (ㄨㄟˋ ㄧㄤ ㄍㄨㄥ)
name of a palace built in
the Han Daynasty

未完 (ㄨㄟˋ ㄨㄢˊ)
unfinished; not completed

未亡人 (ㄨㄟˋ ㄨㄤˊ ㄖㄣˊ)
a widow: 在戰爭中許多婦女成
為未亡人。 A great many
women became widows in
the war.

未雨綢繆 (ㄨㄟˋ ㄩˇ ㄔㄡˊ ㄇㄡˊ)
to take precautions before it
is too late; to take protective measures in advance

未月 (ㄨㄟˋ ㄩㄝˋ)
the sixth month of the lunar
calendar

【末】 2332
ㄇㄛˋ moh mò
1. last; final
2. late; recent
3. trivial; unimportant; insignificant
4. the end; the tip
5. the four limbs

末班 (ㄇㄛˋ ㄅㄢ)
① petty officials ② the last
scheduled bus, train, ship, or
airplane in a day

末了兒 (ㄇㄛˋ ㄌㄧㄠˇ ㄦ)
the last portion; the end

末民 (ㄇㄛˋ ㄇㄧㄣˊ)
the humblest people
laborers and traders

末代 (ㄇㄛˋ ㄉㄞˋ)
the last reign (of a dynasty)

末代孫 (ㄇㄛˋ ㄉㄞˋ ㄙㄨㄣ)
late descendants

末奈何 or 沒奈何 (ㄇㄛˋ ㄋㄞˋ ㄏㄜˊ)
Nothing can be done about
it. 或 There is no way out.

末年 (ㄇㄛˋ ㄋㄧㄢˊ)
the declining years of one's
life, a dynasty, etc.

末了 (ㄇㄛˋ ㄌㄧㄠˇ) or 末了兒 (ㄇㄛˋ
ㄌㄧㄠˇ ㄦ)
the end; the last part; last;
in the end; finally

末流 (ㄇㄛˋ ㄌㄧㄡˊ)

①later adherents (to a school of thought, religious sect, etc.) ②decadent customs or conventions of troubled times

末路 (ㄇㄜˋ ㄌㄨˋ)
a miserable end

末路窮途 (ㄇㄜˋ ㄌㄨˋ ㄑㄩㄥˊ ㄊㄨˊ)
a miserable end which one is driven to; to face a stone wall; to reach the end of the rope; to be at one's wits' end: 他到了末路窮途。He arrived at a miserable end.

末官 (ㄇㄜˋ ㄍㄨㄢ)
a petty official; a low official

末光 (ㄇㄜˋ ㄍㄨㄤ)
lingering light; dim light

末後 (ㄇㄜˋ ㄏㄡˋ)
the end; the final part

末技 (ㄇㄜˋ ㄐㄧˋ)
a trivial skill; an insignificant stunt

末季 (ㄇㄜˋ ㄐㄧˋ)
the last part of a period

末節 (ㄇㄜˋ ㄐㄧㄝˊ)
minor details

末席 (ㄇㄜˋ ㄒㄧˊ)
the least prominent seat: 他坐在末席。He took the lowest seat at table.

末行 (ㄇㄜˋ ㄒㄧㄥˊ)
minor details

末學 (ㄇㄜˋ ㄒㄩㄝˊ)
①superficial learning; insignificant learning ②a polite self-reference

末學膚受 (ㄇㄜˋ ㄒㄩㄝˊ ㄈㄨ ㄕㄡˋ)
to have acquired only skin-deep learning or superficial scholarship

末學後進 (ㄇㄜˋ ㄒㄩㄝˊ ㄏㄡˋ ㄐㄧㄣˋ)
(a polite term referring to oneself) a younger student with superficial learning

末著 (ㄇㄜˋ ㄓㄨˋ)
the last stratagem

末世 (ㄇㄜˋ ㄕˋ)
the last years (of a dynasty)

末梢 (ㄇㄜˋ ㄕㄠ)
the tip; the end

末梢神經 (ㄇㄜˋ ㄕㄠ ㄕㄣˊ ㄐㄧㄥ)
the peripheral nervous system

末日 (ㄇㄜˋ ㄖˋ)
①the last day; the end; doom ②(Christianity) Doomsday; Judgement Day; the Day of Judgement

末造 (ㄇㄜˋ ㄗㄠˋ)
the last days of a dynasty; the decaying period

末座 (ㄇㄜˋ ㄗㄨㄛˋ)
the least prominent seat 參看「敬陪末座」

末次 (ㄇㄜˋ ㄘˋ)
the last time

末俗 (ㄇㄜˋ ㄙㄨˊ)
decadent customs and practices during a period of decline

末議 (ㄇㄜˋ ㄧˋ)
trivial argument; unimportant discussion

末藝 (ㄇㄜˋ ㄧˋ)
an insignificant skill; a small skill

末業 (ㄇㄜˋ ㄧㄝˋ) or 末作 (ㄇㄜˋ ㄗㄨㄛˋ)
(in ancient China) commerce and industry which were regarded as secondary occupations; traditionally lower professions

末葉 (ㄇㄜˋ ㄧㄝˋ)
①posterity; descendants ②the last part of a dynasty ③the latter part of a century

末尾 (ㄇㄜˋ ㄨㄟˇ)
the end: 他忘記在信的末尾簽字。He's forgotten to sign his name at the end of the letter.

【本】 2333 ㄅㄣˇ been běn
1. the root of a plant
2. the root; the origin; the source; the basis; the foundation
3. original
4. a book; a copy
5. capital (in business)
6. our; this; the present
7. according to; based on
8. the beginning; the starting point

本班 (ㄅㄣˇ ㄅㄢ)
this (or our) class, squad, team, section, etc.: 他是本班第一名。He is (at the) top of this class.

本部 (ㄅㄣˇ ㄅㄨˋ)
①headquarters; the head office ②this ministry; our

ministry

本埠 (ㄅㄣˇ ㄅㄨˋ)
this city; the local area

本票 (ㄅㄣˇ ㄆㄧㄠˋ)
a cashier's check; a banker's check; a bank check

本末 (ㄅㄣˇ ㄇㄜˋ)
①the beginning and the end ②the whole story: 告訴我這故事的本末。Tell me the whole story.

本末倒置 (ㄅㄣˇ ㄇㄜˋ ㄉㄠˋ ㄓˋ)
to mistake the means for the end; to put the cart before the horse; to attend to the superficials and neglect the essentials

本名 (ㄅㄣˇ ㄇㄧㄥˊ)
one's formal name (as distinct from pen names, nicknames or other aliases)

本命年 (ㄅㄣˇ ㄇㄧㄥˋ ㄋㄧㄢˊ)
one's year of birth considered in relation to the Twelve Terrestrial Branches

本分 (ㄅㄣˇ ㄈㄣˋ)
one's part; one's role; one's duty

本俸 (ㄅㄣˇ ㄈㄥˋ) or 本薪 (ㄅㄣˇ ㄒㄧㄣ)
the basic salary (exclusive of various additional allowances)

本夫 (ㄅㄣˇ ㄈㄨ)
one's legitimate husband

本大利寬 (ㄅㄣˇ ㄉㄚˋ ㄌㄧˋ ㄎㄨㄢ)
A large capital will yield a large profit.

本當 (ㄅㄣˇ ㄉㄤ)
should have, or ought to have: 你本當在昨天就告訴我。You ought to have told me yesterday.

本黨 (ㄅㄣˇ ㄉㄤˇ)
our party; this party

本地 (ㄅㄣˇ ㄉㄧˋ)
the local area

本地風光 (ㄅㄣˇ ㄉㄧˋ ㄈㄥ ㄍㄨㄤ)
local scenery

本地貨 (ㄅㄣˇ ㄉㄧˋ ㄏㄨㄛˋ)
local goods; locally manufactured products; locally grown goods

本地人 (ㄅㄣˇ ㄉㄧˋ ㄖㄣˊ)
a native: 我父親是本地人。My father is a native of this place.

本地郵件 (ㄅㄣˇ ㄉㄧˋ ㄧㄡˊ ㄐㄧㄢˋ)

〔木部〕

〔木部〕

mail addressed to recipients within a city or community

本隊(ㄅㄣ ㄉㄨㄟˋ)
this (or our) detachment, unit, group, etc.

本題(ㄅㄣ ㄊㄧˊ)
the main subject; the point at issue; the main issue; the main question; the major theme

本體(ㄅㄣ ㄊㄧˇ)
a thing in itself; substance

本體論(ㄅㄣ ㄊㄧˇ ㄌㄨㄣˋ)
ontology

本土(ㄅㄣ ㄊㄨˇ)
the mainland; a country proper

本土文化(ㄅㄣ ㄊㄨˇ ㄨㄣˊ ㄏㄨㄚˋ)
indigenous culture

本能(ㄅㄣ ㄋㄥˊ)
instinct

本年(ㄅㄣ ㄋㄧㄢˊ)
this year; the present year; the current year

本來(ㄅㄣ ㄌㄞˊ)
① from the beginning; originally ② of course; it goes without saying

本來面目(ㄅㄣ ㄌㄞˊ ㄇㄧㄢˋ ㄇㄨˋ)
true looks; true colors; true features

本壘(ㄅㄣ ㄌㄟˇ)
(baseball) home base

本利(ㄅㄣ ㄌㄧˋ)
principal and interest

本領(ㄅㄣ ㄌㄧㄥˇ)
ability; skill; talent

本論(ㄅㄣ ㄌㄨㄣˋ)
① the main contention ② the main body of an expository writing

本該(ㄅㄣ ㄍㄞ)
ought to have; should have

本國(ㄅㄣ ㄍㄨㄛˊ)
one's home country; one's mother country

本國人(ㄅㄣ ㄍㄨㄛˊ ㄖㄣˊ)
a fellow countryman; a compatriot

本科(ㄅㄣ ㄎㄜ)
a main course (as distinct from preparatory courses)

本號(ㄅㄣ ㄏㄠˋ)
our store or company

本行(ㄅㄣ ㄏㄤˊ)
① one's trade; one's spe-

cialty: 建築是我的本行。Architecture is my speciality. ② this bank; our bank

本籍(ㄅㄣ ㄐㄧˊ)
one's original domicile; one's permanent home address: 他的本籍是紐約。His original domicile is New York.

本紀(ㄅㄣ ㄐㄧˋ)
biographic sketches of emperors

本家(ㄅㄣ ㄐㄧㄚ)
① the original home ② a reference to somebody having the same family name as one's own

本家兒(ㄅㄣ ㄐㄧㄚㄦˋ)
of one's own family

本屆(ㄅㄣ ㄐㄧㄝˋ)
current; this year's: 本屆畢業生都是女生。This year's graduates are all girls.

本金(ㄅㄣ ㄐㄧㄣ)
principal as distinct from interest

本軍(ㄅㄣ ㄐㄩㄣ)
this army; our army

本期(ㄅㄣ ㄑㄧˊ)
① this term; the current season ② the present class (of students or cadets)

本錢(ㄅㄣ ㄑㄧㄢˊ)
capital (in business)

本息(ㄅㄣ ㄒㄧˊ)
principal and interest

本校(ㄅㄣ ㄒㄧㄠˋ)
our (or this) school

本縣(ㄅㄣ ㄒㄧㄢˋ)
our (or this) county, prefecture, etc.

本心(ㄅㄣ ㄒㄧㄣ)
one's conscience

本鄉(ㄅㄣ ㄒㄧㄤ)
our (or this) village

本鄉本土(ㄅㄣ ㄒㄧㄤ ㄅㄣ ㄊㄨˇ)
one's homeland: 他的父親死於本鄉本土。His father died in his homeland.

本相(ㄅㄣ ㄒㄧㄤˋ)
the real look

本刑(ㄅㄣ ㄒㄧㄥˊ)
the standard penalty for a specific offense, to which the judge refers in meting out additional or reduced punishment

本性(ㄅㄣ ㄒㄧㄥˋ)

the real nature

本性難移(ㄅㄣ ㄒㄧㄥˋ ㄋㄢˊ ㄧˊ)
One's nature cannot be altered. 或 The leopard can't change its spots.

本質(ㄅㄣ ㄓˊ)
essential qualities; essential characteristics; essence; the intrinsic nature

本職(ㄅㄣ ㄓˊ)
one's job (or duty): 我做好本職工作。I did my own job well.

本旨(ㄅㄣ ㄓˇ)
the real intention; the real meaning

本著(ㄅㄣ ·ㄓㄜ)
in line with; in conformity with; in the light of; in accordance with

本宅(ㄅㄣ ㄓㄞˊ)
one's own residence

本週(ㄅㄣ ㄓㄡ)
this week

本州(ㄅㄣ ㄓㄡ)
Honshu, one of the principal islands of Japan

本朝(ㄅㄣ ㄔㄠˊ)
the present dynasty; our dynasty

本初子午線(ㄅㄣ ㄔㄨ ㄗˇ ㄨˇ ㄒㄧㄢˋ)
the prime meridian

本師(ㄅㄣ ㄕ)
① one's teacher ② this division; our division

本市(ㄅㄣ ㄕˋ)
this city; our city: 我住在本市。I live in this city.

本事
①(ㄅㄣ ㄕˋ) a story (or a plot) of a play, movie, etc. ②(ㄅㄣ ·ㄕ) ability; skill; talent: 他是個有本事的人。He is a man of ability.

本身(ㄅㄣ ㄕㄣ)
oneself; personally; itself; itself; per se

本生燈(ㄅㄣ ㄕㄥ ㄉㄥ)
a Bunsen burner

本省(ㄅㄣ ㄕㄥˇ)
this province; our province

本省人(ㄅㄣ ㄕㄥˇ ㄖㄣˊ)
a native of this province

本日(ㄅㄣ ㄖˋ)
today

本人(ㄅㄣ ㄖㄣˊ)

①I; me ②himself; herself; yourself ③personally

本字(ㄅㄣˇ ㄗˋ)
the standard form of a character (as distinct from the corrupted form or simplified form of the character)

本子(ㄅㄣˇ ‧ㄗ) 或 **本兒**
a book; a notebook

本草綱目(ㄅㄣˇ ㄘㄠˇ ㄍㄤ ㄇㄨˋ)
Compendium of Materia Medica, a pharmaceutical work by Li Shih-chen (李時珍) in the Ming Dynasty (1386-1644), which lists all the animals, vegetables and other objects believed to contain medicinal properties in traditional Chinese medicine

本色(ㄅㄣˇ ㄙㄜˋ)
①the original color ②the real look; the true qualities or characteristics

本訴(ㄅㄣˇ ㄙㄨˋ)
the lawsuit filed by the original plaintiff after the defendant files a countersuit

本素(ㄅㄣˇ ㄙㄨˋ)
the original element

本案(ㄅㄣˇ ㄢˋ)
the case under consideration; the present case: this case: 本案是一個特例。 This case is a special one.

本意(ㄅㄣˇ ㄧˋ)
the original intention

本義(ㄅㄣˇ ㄧˋ)
the original meaning; the real meaning

本業(ㄅㄣˇ ㄧㄝˋ)
①(in ancient China) farming which was considered the most important sector of the economy ②one's own occupation: 他更換了本業。 He changed his own occupation.

本因坊(ㄅㄣˇ ㄧㄣ ㄈㄤ)
Honinbo, one of the most coveted titles among professional go players in Japan

本銀(ㄅㄣˇ ㄧㄣˊ)
capital (in business)

本應(ㄅㄣˇ ㄧㄥ)
should have; ought to have: 你本應更加注意的。 You should have been more careful.

本務(ㄅㄣˇ ㄨˋ)
one's real duty: 保衛國家是軍人的本務。 To defend the country is soldiers' real duty.

本位(ㄅㄣˇ ㄨㄟˋ)
a standard; a basis

本位貨幣(ㄅㄣˇ ㄨㄟˋ ㄏㄨㄛˋ ㄅˋ)
standard money

本文(ㄅㄣˇ ㄨㄣˊ)
the main body of a writing

本月(ㄅㄣˇ ㄩㄝˋ)
this month

本源(ㄅㄣˇ ㄩㄢˊ)
the ultimate source

本願(ㄅㄣˇ ㄩㄢˋ)
one's real wish; long-cherished desire: 致富並非我的本願。 To become rich is not my long-cherished desire.

【札】 2334
ㄓㄚˊ *jar zhá*
1. (in ancient China) a thin wooden tablet for writing
2. correspondence; a letter
3. (in ancient China) documents or instructions to a subordinate
4. (now rarely) to die before one comes of age

札幌(ㄓㄚˊ ㄏㄨㄤˇ)
Sapporo, a city in Japan

札記(ㄓㄚˊ ㄐㄧˋ)
a notebook in which one records his comments on the book he is reading

杞子(ㄓㄚˊ ‧ㄗ)
a document sent by a superior

【朮】 2335
ㄓㄨˊ *jwu zhú*
Podophyllum versipelle, a plant with violet, green or red flowers and white roots, used in herbal medicine

朮酒(ㄓㄨˊ ㄐㄧㄡˇ)
wine in which the plant 朮 has been soaked; medicinal wine

二畫

【朱】 2336
ㄓㄨ *ju zhū*
1. red; vermilion
2. a Chinese family name

朱筆(ㄓㄨ ㄅㄧˇ)
a writing brush dipped in red ink (originally used by an emperor in signing decrees, now often used by school teachers to correct students' papers)

朱批(ㄓㄨ ㄆㄧ)
writing comments or remarks in red with a brush

朱墨本(ㄓㄨ ㄇㄛˋ ㄅㄣˇ)
editions printed during the Wan Li reign of the Ming Dynasty with dark characters and running commentaries or footnotes in red

朱墨爛然(ㄓㄨ ㄇㄛˋ ㄌㄢˋ ㄖㄢˊ)
with profuse comments written in red

朱買臣(ㄓㄨ ㄇㄞˇ ㄔㄣˊ)
Chu Mai-chen, a ranking official of the Han Dynasty, who refused to retake his wife who deserted him while he was poor

朱門(ㄓㄨ ㄇㄣˊ)
rich and influential families

朱門酒肉臭(ㄓㄨ ㄇㄣˊ ㄐㄧㄡˇ ㄖㄡˋ ㄔㄡˋ)
behind the red gate wine overflows and meat rots —The rich are excessively wealthy (while the poor suffer stark poverty).

朱邸(ㄓㄨ ㄉㄧˇ)
residence of a king or nobleman

朱樓(ㄓㄨ ㄌㄡˊ)
houses of the wealthy and influential

朱理安(ㄓㄨ ㄌㄧˇ ㄢ)
Julian or Julianus Flavius Claudius, 331-363, Roman emperor

朱理安曆(ㄓㄨ ㄌㄧˇ ㄢ ㄌㄧˋ)
the Julian calendar

朱梁(ㄓㄨ ㄌㄧㄤˊ)
the Liang Dynasty (907-923), founded by Chu Wen (朱溫)

朱輪華轂(ㄓㄨ ㄌㄨㄣˊ ㄏㄨㄚˊ ㄍㄨ)
red and ornate carriages used by noblemen in ancient times

朱古力(ㄓㄨ ㄍㄨˇ ㄌㄧˋ)
chocolate 亦作「巧克力」

朱黃(ㄓㄨ ㄏㄨㄤˊ)
red and yellow, the two colors used in proofreading

朱紅(ㄓㄨ ㄏㄨㄥˊ)

〔木部〕

【木部】

bright red; vermilion

朱槿(ㄓㄨ ㄐㄧㄣ)
(botany) Chinese hibiscus 亦作「扶桑」、「大紅花」

朱漆(ㄓㄨ ㄑㄧ)
red paint; red lacquer

朱熹(ㄓㄨ ㄒㄧ)
Chu Hsi, alias 元晦 or 晦庵 (1130-1200 A.D.), a great scholar of the Sung Dynasty, famous for his commentary on the Confucian classics which has been considered a standard exposition

朱軒
a carriage used by high officials in old China

朱陳婚姻(ㄓㄨ ㄔㄣ ㄏㄨㄣ ㄧㄣ)or **朱陳結好**(ㄓㄨ ㄔㄣ ㄐㄧㄝ ㄏㄠ)
a good matrimonial match; the two parties of a marriage

朱脣皓齒(ㄓㄨ ㄔㄨㄣ ㄏㄠ ㄔ)
(literally) red lips and sparkling teeth—a very beautiful girl

朱砂 or **硃砂**(ㄓㄨ ㄕㄚ)
cinnabar

朱儒 or **侏儒**(ㄓㄨ ㄖㄨ)
a dwarf; a pygmy or pigmy

朱衣(ㄓㄨ ㄧ)
the red robe worn by the emperor during summer

朱顏(ㄓㄨ ㄧㄢ)
①the beautiful face of a young lady ②the beautiful face of a youth

朱顏鶴髮(ㄓㄨ ㄧㄢ ㄏㄜ ㄈㄚ)
The hair is snow-white but the face is that of a young person.

朱殷(ㄓㄨ ㄧㄢ)
dark-red

朱溫(ㄓㄨ ㄨㄣ)
Chu Wen, alias 朱全忠, Emperor Tai Tsu(太祖), the founder of the Liang Dynasty

朱愚(ㄓㄨ ㄩ)
stupid; ignorant

朱元璋(ㄓㄨ ㄩㄢ ㄓㄤ)
Chu Yüan-chang, the founding emperor of the Ming Dynasty, who reigned from 1368 to 1399

【朴】 2337
1. ㄆㄛ poh pò

saltpeter

朴硝(ㄆㄛ ㄒㄧㄠ)
(Chinese medicine) saltpeter

朴資茅斯(ㄆㄛ ㄗ ㄇㄠ ㄙ)
①Portsmouth, an English naval base in Southampton ②Portsmouth, a naval base in New Hampshire, U.S.A.

朴資茅斯條約(ㄆㄛ ㄗ ㄇㄠ ㄙ ㄊㄧㄠ ㄩㄝ)
The Treaty of Portsmouth, signed between Russia and Japan in 1905, at Portsmouth, New Hampshire, U.S.A.

【朴】 2337
2. (模) ㄆㄨ pwu pú

1. (said of clothing, manner, etc.) plain; simple
2. a kind of oak (Quercus dentata)

朴茂(ㄆㄨ ㄇㄠ)
sincere and honest

朴鈍(ㄆㄨ ㄉㄨㄣ)
(said of a knife or other old weapons) blunt

朴陋(ㄆㄨ ㄌㄡ)
things in their original state—without any artificial decoration, chiseling, etc.

朴忠(ㄆㄨ ㄓㄨㄥ)
honest, loyal or faithful

朴樹(ㄆㄨ ㄕㄨ)
the hackberry

【朽】 2338
ㄒㄧㄡ sheou xiu

1. to rot; to decay; rotten; decayed: 這房子已腐朽。The house is in decay.
2. old and useless: 他老朽得不能走了。He is so old and useless that he can't walk.

朽敗(ㄒㄧㄡ ㄅㄞ)
decayed and rotten

朽邁(ㄒㄧㄡ ㄇㄞ)
(said of a person) old and useless; senile

朽木(ㄒㄧㄡ ㄇㄨ)
①rotten wood; decayed trees ②a hopeless person; a good-for-nothing

朽木不可雕(ㄒㄧㄡ ㄇㄨ ㄅㄨ ㄎㄜ ㄉㄧㄠ)
(literally) Decayed wood cannot be carved. —A congenital defeatist cannot be taught to succeed. 或 You can't teach old dogs new tricks.

朽木糞土(ㄒㄧㄡ ㄇㄨ ㄈㄣ ㄊㄨ)
decayed wood and filthy soil—a hopeless person

朽腐(ㄒㄧㄡ ㄈㄨ)
rotten; rotting

朽蠹(ㄒㄧㄡ ㄉㄨ)
①decayed and bitten by worms, etc. ②to over-hoard grains so that they rot

朽爛(ㄒㄧㄡ ㄌㄢ)
decayed and rotten

朽骨(ㄒㄧㄡ ㄍㄨ)
decaying bones

朽壞(ㄒㄧㄡ ㄏㄨㄞ)
to decay; to rot; decayed; rotten; rot: 開始朽壞了。Rot has set in.

朽穢(ㄒㄧㄡ ㄏㄨㄟ)
rotten and filthy

朽壤(ㄒㄧㄡ ㄖㄤ)
filthy earth—something that grows nothing

【朵】 2339
(朶) ㄉㄨㄛ duoo duǒ

1. a flower; a cluster of flowers; a bud
2. a lobe of the ear

朵朵(ㄉㄨㄛ ㄉㄨㄛ)
every (flower)

朵翰(ㄉㄨㄛ ㄏㄢ)or **朵雲**(ㄉㄨㄛ ㄩㄣ)
your esteemed letter

朵頤(ㄉㄨㄛ ㄧ)
the movement of the jaw in eating—the palate

三畫

【李】 2340
ㄌㄧ lii lǐ

1. plums
2. (now rare) a judge; a justice
3. a Chinese family name

李白(ㄌㄧ ㄅㄞ)or **李太白**(ㄌㄧ ㄊㄞ ㄅㄞ)
Li Po (701-762), one of the greatest Chinese poets in the Tang Dynasty

李代桃僵(ㄌㄧ ㄉㄞ ㄊㄠ ㄐㄧㄤ)
to substitute this for that

李唐(ㄌㄧ ㄊㄤ)
①the Tang Dynasty—so called because the founding emperor of the dynasty was named Li Yüan (李淵) ②name of a famous landscape painter in the Sung Dynasty

李後主(ㄌㄧ ㄏㄡ ㄓㄨ)or **李煜**

（ㄌ ㄩ）
Li Yü (937-978), the last monarch of the Southern Tang Dynasty, noted for his literary genius and was also blamed for indirectly encouraging the practice of footbinding among Chinese women

李鴻章（ㄌㄧˇ ㄏㄨㄥˊ ㄓㄤ）
Li Hung-chang (1823-1901), a prime minister in the late Ching Dynasty

李清照（ㄌㄧˇ ㄑㄧㄥ ㄓㄠˋ）
Li Ching-chao (1081-1151?), a famous woman poet of the Sung Dynasty

李下不整冠（ㄌㄧˇ ㄒㄧㄚˋ ㄅㄨˋ ㄓㄥˇ 《ㄨㄢ）
(literally) Do not adjust your hat under a plum tree. —One should avoid circumstances in which one is likely to be suspected of dishonest practices.

李下之嫌（ㄌㄧˇ ㄒㄧㄚˋ ㄓ ㄒㄧㄢˊ）
a position that invites suspicion; to be found in a suspicious position 亦作「瓜田李下」

李樹（ㄌㄧˇ ㄕㄨˋ）
the plum tree

李子（ㄌㄧˇ ˙ㄗ）
plums

李斯（ㄌㄧˇ ㄙ）
Li Ssu, a prime minister during the reign of Chin Shih Huang（秦始皇）

李耳（ㄌㄧˇ ㄦˇ）
another name of Lao-tzu（老子）, a philosopher of Confucius' time

【杉】 2341
1. ㄕㄢ shan shān
the various species of fir and pine; a China fir

杉木（ㄕㄢ ㄇㄨˋ）
fir wood

杉杆子（ㄕㄢ ㄍㄢ ˙ㄗ）or 杉篙（ㄕㄢ 《ㄠ）
straight and slender fir timber for building scaffolds and makeshift shelters

【杈】 2342
1. ㄔㄚ cha chā
1. the branches of a tree
2. a pitchfork; a fishfork; a wooden fork; a hayfork

3. any fork-like object
4. a kind of weapon in ancient China

杈枒（ㄔㄚ ㄧㄚˊ）
a forked branch

【杈】
2. ㄔㄚˋ chah chà

杈子（ㄔㄚˋ ˙ㄗ）or 杈兒（ㄔㄚˋ ㄦ）
a cheval-de-frise; chevaux-de-frise

【杌】 2343
ㄨ wuh wù
1. a tree without a branch; the stump of a tree
2. a square stool
3. worried and anxious

杌凳（ㄨ ㄉㄥˋ）
a square stool

杌陧（ㄨ ㄋㄧㄝˋ）
worried and anxious; unquiet; uneasy

杌子（ㄨ ˙ㄗ）
a stool or bench

【杏】 2344
ㄒㄧㄥˋ shinq xìng
1. an apricot
2. almonds—apricot kernels
3. apricot flowers

杏脯（ㄒㄧㄥˋ ㄈㄨˇ）
dried or preserved apricot meat

杏壇（ㄒㄧㄥˋ ㄊㄢˊ）
(originally) the site where Confucius taught his disciples—(in a broad sense) the teaching profession

杏臉（ㄒㄧㄥˋ ㄌㄧㄢˇ）
an almond-shaped face—the beautiful face of a woman

杏林（ㄒㄧㄥˋ ㄌㄧㄣˊ）
a term used in praising a good and kind physician or referring to the medical profession in general

杏酪（ㄒㄧㄥˋ ㄌㄨㄛˋ）
almond milk; a drink made from almonds

杏乾兒（ㄒㄧㄥˋ 《ㄢ ㄦ）
dried apricot meat

杏核兒（ㄒㄧㄥˋ ㄏㄜˊ ㄦ）or（ㄒㄧㄥˋ ㄏㄨˊ）
almonds

杏花（ㄒㄧㄥˋ ㄏㄨㄚ）
apricot blossoms

杏花村（ㄒㄧㄥˋ ㄏㄨㄚ ㄘㄨㄣ）
scenery of springtime in the country where apricot blossoms grow profusely (often

used in Chinese poems)

杏花雨（ㄒㄧㄥˋ ㄏㄨㄚ ㄩˇ）
the rain that usually comes in the wake of the apricot blossom season

杏黃色（ㄒㄧㄥˋ ㄏㄨㄤˊ ㄙㄜˋ）
a bright-yellow color like the apricot's, deeper than that of the orange; apricot yellow

杏實（ㄒㄧㄥˋ ㄕˊ）
the apricot fruit

杏樹（ㄒㄧㄥˋ ㄕㄨˋ）
the apricot tree

杏仁（ㄒㄧㄥˋ ㄖㄣˊ）
almonds; apricot kernels

杏仁粉（ㄒㄧㄥˋ ㄖㄣˊ ㄈㄣˇ）
almond powder; ground almonds

杏仁兒茶（ㄒㄧㄥˋ ㄖㄣˊ ㄦ ㄔㄚˊ）
almond flavored tea (with ricesoup, sugar and almond powder as chief ingredients)

杏子（ㄒㄧㄥˋ ˙ㄗ）or 杏兒（ㄒㄧㄥˋ ㄦ）
the apricot fruit

杏靨（ㄒㄧㄥˋ ㄧㄝˋ）
①apricot blossoms ②the beauty of a girl ③a beautiful oval face

杏眼（ㄒㄧㄥˋ ㄧㄢˇ）
apricot-like eyes — a woman's large eyes

杏眼桃腮（ㄒㄧㄥˋ ㄧㄢˇ ㄊㄠˊ ㄙㄞ）
large eyes and rosy cheeks (of a beauty)

杏眼圓睜（ㄒㄧㄥˋ ㄧㄢˇ ㄩㄢˊ ㄓㄥ）
the angry look of a woman: 她杏眼圓睜，She has an angry look.

杏月（ㄒㄧㄥˋ ㄩㄝˋ）
the second month of the lunar calendar

【杓】 2345
1. ㄅㄧㄠ biau biāo
name of a constellation—the handle of the Dipper

【杓】 2345
2.（ㄅㄧ）ㄕㄠˊ shaur sháo
a receptacle or container, as a cup, ladle, spoon, etc.; the handle of such

杓子（ㄕㄠˊ ˙ㄗ）
a wooden ladle

【材】 2346
ㄘㄞˊ tsair cái
1. materials—especially timber

〔木部〕

—for building houses, furniture, etc.

2. material in its broadest sense: 他就地取材。 He obtained material from local sources.

3. properties of a substance

4. ability; aptitude: 他因材施教。 He taught students in accordance with their aptitude.

5. a coffin

材木(ㄘㄞˊ ㄇㄨˋ)
timber—for building, etc.

材能 or **才能**(ㄘㄞˊ ㄋㄥˊ)
ability; capability

材吏(ㄘㄞˊ ㄌㄧˋ)
an able or capable official

材料(ㄘㄞˊ ㄌㄧㄠˋ)
①materials—for all building purposes; raw materials ②materials (such as data, statistics, figure, information for writing an article, story, novel, etc.) ③ingredients of a preparation (of food, medicine, etc.) ④makings; stuff: 他不是演戲的材料。 He hasn't the makings of an actor.

材幹(ㄘㄞˊ ㄍㄢˋ)
①gifts; talent; ability: 他的材幹過人。 His ability surpasses that of all others. ②timber

材器(ㄘㄞˊ ㄑㄧˋ)
①ability; capability; caliber (of a person) ②timber good for building purposes

材士(ㄘㄞˊ ㄕˋ)
men of ability

材人(ㄘㄞˊ ㄖㄣˊ)
①men of ability ② (in ancient China) a female court official 亦作「才人」

材藝(ㄘㄞˊ ㄧˋ)
ability and art: 他材藝兼備。 He is perfect in both ability and art.

材武(ㄘㄞˊ ㄨˇ)
①(with) both ability and courage ②military ability: 他以材武出名。 He is distinguished for military ability.

【村】 2347
(邨) ㄘㄨㄣ tsuen cūn

1. a village; the countryside; a hamlet

2. vulgar; coarse

3. naive; simple-minded

4. (now rarely) to embarrass

5. (now rarely) to scold

村夫(ㄘㄨㄣ ㄈㄨ)
①a villager ②a vulgar and naive person

村夫子(ㄘㄨㄣ ㄈㄨ ㄗˇ)
a village scholar; a pedant

村夫俗子(ㄘㄨㄣ ㄈㄨ ㄙㄨˊ ㄗˇ)
an uneducated person; an illiterate

村夫野老(ㄘㄨㄣ ㄈㄨ ㄧㄝˇ ㄌㄠˇ)
villagers and aged rustics

村婦(ㄘㄨㄣ ㄈㄨˋ)
a village woman; a country woman; a vulgar woman

村女(ㄘㄨㄣ ㄋㄩˇ)
a country girl; farmers' daughters 參看「村姑」

村落(ㄘㄨㄣ ㄌㄨㄛˋ)
a village; a hamlet: 該村落荒涼。 The village is desolate.

村姑(ㄘㄨㄣ ㄍㄨ)
village girls; farmers' daughters

村話(ㄘㄨㄣ ㄏㄨㄚˋ)
(literally) rustic talk—vulgar talk; filthy language

村居(ㄘㄨㄣ ㄐㄩ)
to live in the country; to rusticate

村氣(ㄘㄨㄣ ㄑㄧˋ)
vulgarity of the countryside

村墟(ㄘㄨㄣ ㄒㄩ)
a village market; a village marketplace

村堂(ㄘㄨㄣ ㄊㄤˊ)
(in old China) a village school

村學究(ㄘㄨㄣ ㄒㄩㄝˊ ㄐㄧㄡˋ)
a village scholar; a pedant

村鎮(ㄘㄨㄣ ㄓㄣˋ)
villages and small towns

村長(ㄘㄨㄣ ㄓㄤˇ)
the village chief

村莊(ㄘㄨㄣ ㄓㄨㄤ)
a village; a farmstead

村塾(ㄘㄨㄣ ㄕㄨˊ)
(in old China) a village school

村人(ㄘㄨㄣ ㄖㄣˊ)
villagers

村子(ㄘㄨㄣ ˙ㄗ)
a village; a hamlet

村俗(ㄘㄨㄣ ㄙㄨˊ)
village customs or traditions

【杖】 2348
ㄓㄤˋ janq zhàng

1. a stick; a staff; a cane

2. (an old punishment) to beat with a cane; flogging with a stick

3. (now rarely) a mourning staff

4. to presume on (one's connections, influence, etc.)

杖頭錢(ㄓㄤˋ ㄊㄡˊ ㄑㄧㄢˊ)
wine-money (so called because the money was usually fastened on the top of a cane or staff in old China)

杖藜(ㄓㄤˋ ㄌㄧˊ)
a staff of chenopodium; to use such a staff to help an old person in walking, etc.

杖履(ㄓㄤˋ ㄌㄩˇ)
a respectful term of address for the elders

杖期(ㄓㄤˋ ㄐㄧ)
one-year mourning after the death of one's wife or father's concubine

杖期生(ㄓㄤˋ ㄐㄧ ㄕㄥ)
a reference to the husband in an obituary announcing the death of his wife (used only when the husband's parents are dead)

杖擊(ㄓㄤˋ ㄐㄧˊ)
to hit or beat with a cane

杖刑(ㄓㄤˋ ㄒㄧㄥˊ)
(in old China) the punishment by caning

杖者(ㄓㄤˋ ㄓㄜˇ)
elders—who hold canes or staffs

杖著 or **仗著**(ㄓㄤˋ ˙ㄓㄜ)
to rely on; to presume on

杖勢 or **仗勢**(ㄓㄤˋ ㄕˋ)
to presume on one's position, connections, influence, etc.

杖責(ㄓㄤˋ ㄗㄜˊ)
to punish by caning; to flagellate; to cane

杖策(ㄓㄤˋ ㄘㄜˋ)
to hold a whip in the hand

杖義執言 or **仗義執言**(ㄓㄤˋ ㄧˋ ㄓˊ ㄧㄢˊ)
to speak out courageously for what is right

【杜】 2349
ㄉㄨˋ duh dù

1. to plug (a hole, leak, etc.); to stop; to prevent; to put an end to something
2. to shut out; to restrict; to impede
3. the russet pear (*Pyrus betulaefolia*)
4. to fabricate; to practice forgery
5. a Chinese family name

杜弊 (ㄉㄨˋ ㄅㄧˋ)
to prevent corrupt practices; to stop or put an end to illegal practices

杜門 (ㄉㄨˋ ㄇㄣˊ)
①to close one's door (and shut out visitors) ②to stay in the house

杜門卻掃 (ㄉㄨˋ ㄇㄣˊ ㄑㄩㄝˋ ㄙㄠˇ)
to shut one's door to the outside world

杜門謝客 (ㄉㄨˋ ㄇㄣˊ ㄒㄧㄝˋ ㄎㄜˋ)
to shut out visitors; to refuse to see visitors; to close one's door to visitors

杜牧 (ㄉㄨˋ ㄇㄨˋ)
Tu Mu (803-852), a famous poet of the Tang Dynasty

杜甫 (ㄉㄨˋ ㄈㄨˇ)
Tu Fu (712-770), one of the greatest poets of China in the Tang Dynasty

杜魯門 (ㄉㄨˋ ㄌㄨˇ ㄇㄣˊ)
Harry S. Truman (1884-1972), 33rd U.S. President

杜口 (ㄉㄨˋ ㄎㄡˇ)
to shut one's mouth and say nothing

杜康 (ㄉㄨˋ ㄎㄤ)
①Tu Kang, a man good at brewing wine in the Chou Dynasty ②another name of wine

杜諫 (ㄉㄨˋ ㄐㄧㄢˋ)
to persuade or advise (a superior, the emperor, etc.) to stop (a bad practice, etc.)

杜漸防微 (ㄉㄨˋ ㄐㄧㄢˋ ㄈㄤˊ ㄨㄟ)
to nip (a bad practice, etc.) in the bud

杜絕 (ㄉㄨˋ ㄐㄩㄝˊ)
①to stop (a bad practice, etc.) for good; to eradicate ②to cut off (relations with) ③irrevocable (contracts, title deeds, etc.)

杜絕後患 (ㄉㄨˋ ㄐㄩㄝˊ ㄏㄡˋ ㄏㄨㄢˋ)

---

to prevent and eliminate possible harmful consequences

杜鵑 (ㄉㄨˋ ㄐㄩㄢ)
a cuckoo 亦作「子規」

杜鵑花 (ㄉㄨˋ ㄐㄩㄢ ㄏㄨㄚ)
azaleas

杜撰 (ㄉㄨˋ ㄓㄨㄢˋ)
to fabricate (a story, etc.); to trump up; to make up: 她說的是真有其事，不是杜撰的，What she said is true, not made up.

杜松 (ㄉㄨˋ ㄙㄨㄥ)
a needle juniper (*Juniperus rigida*)

杜松子酒 (ㄉㄨˋ ㄙㄨㄥ ㄗˇ ㄐㄧㄡˇ)
gin

【杞】 2350
ㄑㄧˇ chii qǐ
1. a species of willow
2. a medlar
3. Chi, name of a state in the Chou Dynasty in today's Honan Province
4. a Chinese family name

杞柳 (ㄑㄧˇ ㄌㄧㄡˇ)
a kind of willow

杞人憂天 (ㄑㄧˇ ㄖㄣˊ ㄧㄡ ㄊㄧㄢ)
The man of Chi worried that the sky might fall down.— A man entertains imaginary or groundless fears.

杞梓 (ㄑㄧˇ ㄗˇ)
fine wood—good for carving; good timber

【束】 2351
ㄕㄨˋ shuh shù
1. to bind
2. a bunch; a bundle
3. to control; to restrain; restraint
4. a Chinese family name

束帛 (ㄕㄨˋ ㄅㄛˊ)
a bundle of silk—a betrothal present from the groom's side in ancient China

束馬懸車 (ㄕㄨˋ ㄇㄚˇ ㄒㄩㄢˊ ㄔㄜ)
(said of roads) very rugged

束髮 (ㄕㄨˋ ㄈㄚˇ)
to reach boyhood—teens or teenage

束縛 (ㄕㄨˋ ㄈㄨˊ)
restraint; restrictions; bondage; to restrain; to bind up

束縛電荷 (ㄕㄨˋ ㄈㄨˊ ㄉㄧㄢˋ ㄏㄜˋ)

(electricity) a bound charge

束躬 (ㄕㄨˋ ㄍㄨㄥ)
to restrain oneself; to control oneself; self-restraint

束脩 (ㄕㄨˋ ㄒㄧㄡ)
(literally) ten pieces of dried meat—tuition; the charge or fee given to a private tutor for instruction or teaching

束胸 (ㄕㄨˋ ㄒㄩㄥ)
(said of a woman in old China) to bind the breasts tightly with a piece of cloth (because flat-chested women were considered beautiful in those days)

束之高閣 (ㄕㄨˋ ㄓ ㄍㄠ ㄍㄜˊ)
(literally) to place (something) high in the attic—to shelve it and forget about it; to lay aside and neglect; to pigeonhole

束裝 (ㄕㄨˋ ㄓㄨㄤ)
to pack up

束裝就道 (ㄕㄨˋ ㄓㄨㄤ ㄐㄧㄡˋ ㄉㄠˋ)
to pack up for a journey

束手 (ㄕㄨˋ ㄕㄡˇ)
to have one's hands tied—no way out; powerless; at the end of the rope: 群醫束手，The doctors can do nothing to help.

束手待斃 (ㄕㄨˋ ㄕㄡˇ ㄉㄞˋ ㄅㄧˋ)
(literally) to wait for one's death with hands tied—to be a sitting duck

束手就擒 (ㄕㄨˋ ㄕㄡˇ ㄐㄧㄡˋ ㄑㄧㄣˊ)
to put up no fight and allow oneself to be caught

束手無策 (ㄕㄨˋ ㄕㄡˇ ㄨˊ ㄘㄜˋ)
no way out; powerless; at the end of the rope

束身 (ㄕㄨˋ ㄕㄣ)
self-control; to restrain oneself

束腰 (ㄕㄨˋ ㄧㄠ)
①a waist band or belt ②to tighten one's waist with a band so that it appears slender; to girdle the waist

【杠】 2352
ㄍㄤ gang gāng
1. a flag pole
2. a bridge

【杆】 2353
ㄍㄢ gan gān
1. a wooden pole; the shaft of

木部

a spear

2. rod, a unit of measurement which equals to 5.5 yards

3. a wooden fence; a balustrade; a railing

杆《ㄍㄢ》or 杆兒《ㄧㄚㄦ》

①a pole; a rod ②a gang of bandits

杆子頭《ㄍㄢ ㄗ ㄊㄡ》

the ringleader of a gang

【代】 2354 《ㄧ ㄐ yih yì》

a tiny wooden post; a boundary mark or fence

四畫

【杪】 2355 《ㄇㄧㄠ meau miǎo》

1. the tip of a small branch

2. the end (of a period)

杪末《ㄇㄧㄠ ㄇㄛ》

the endpoint; the tip

杪杪《ㄇㄧㄠ ㄇㄧㄠ》

very tiny

杪冬《ㄇㄧㄠ ㄉㄨㄥ》

the end of the winter (other seasons are spoken of in a similar manner)

杪小《ㄇㄧㄠ ㄒㄧㄠ》or 渺小《ㄇㄧㄠ ㄒㄧㄠ》

tiny

【杭】 2356 《ㄏㄤ harng háng》

1. Hangchow

2. same as 航 —to sail; to cross a stream; to navigate

3. a Chinese family name

杭州《ㄏㄤ ㄓㄡ》

Hangchow, capital city of Chekiang Province

杭州灣《ㄏㄤ ㄓㄡ ㄨㄢ》

the Gulf of Hangchow at the estuary of the Chientang River (錢塘江)

杭綢《ㄏㄤ ㄔㄡ》

silk from Hangchow (considered the best)

【杯】 2357 《ㄅㄟ bei bēi》

a cup; a tumbler; a glass; a goblet

杯盤狼藉《ㄅㄟ ㄆㄢ ㄌㄤ ㄐㄧ》

(literally) Empty glasses and plates are scattered all over. —The feast is over.

杯葛《ㄅㄟ 《ㄍㄜ》

①a boycott ②to boycott: 他們企圖杯葛他。They tried

---

to boycott him.

杯弓蛇影《ㄅㄟ ㄍㄨㄥ ㄕㄜ ㄧㄥ》

(literally) to mistake the shadow of a bow in one's cup for a snake—a false alarm; extremely suspicious

杯酒釋兵權《ㄅㄟ ㄐㄧㄡ ㄕ ㄅㄧㄥ ㄑㄩㄢ》

a stratagem used by Chao Kuang-yin (趙匡胤), founder of the Sung Dynasty (960—1279), who persuaded his generals to give up their troops during a grand feast

杯中物《ㄅㄟ ㄓㄨㄥ ㄨ》

(literally) the thing in the cup—wine; alcoholic drinks

杯水車薪《ㄅㄟ ㄕㄨㄟ ㄔㄜ ㄒㄧㄣ》

(literally) to use a cup of water to put out a cartload of burning firewood—too inadequate and useless; an utterly inadequate measure

杯子《ㄅㄟ ㄗ》

a cup; a tumbler; a glass

【杲】 2358 《ㄍㄠ gao gǎo》

1. bright—as the shining sun

2. high

杲杲《ㄍㄠ ㄍㄠ》

bright and scintillating

【杳】 2359 《ㄧㄠ yeau yǎo》

1. deep and expansive

2. quiet; silent

杳肰《ㄧㄠ ㄖㄢ》

distant and indistinguishable

杳冥《ㄧㄠ ㄇㄧㄥ》

deep, dark and obscure

杳然《ㄧㄠ ㄖㄢ》

quiet and silent; lonely

杳如黃鶴《ㄧㄠ ㄖㄨ ㄏㄨㄤ ㄏㄜ》

to disappear like the yellow crane—nowhere to be found; to disappear without leaving a trace

杳音無踪《ㄧㄠ ㄧㄣ ㄨ ㄗㄨㄥ》

gone without leaving a trace

杳無音信《ㄧㄠ ㄨ ㄧㄣ ㄒㄧㄣ》

without any news of someone for a long time

【東】 2360 《ㄉㄨㄥ dong dōng》

1. the east; eastern

2. to travel eastward

3. the host; the master; the owner

4. a Chinese family name

東北《ㄉㄨㄥ ㄅㄟ》

①northeast ②Manchuria

東半球《ㄉㄨㄥ ㄅㄢ ㄑㄧㄡ》

the Eastern Hemisphere

東奔西走《ㄉㄨㄥ ㄅㄣ ㄒㄧ ㄗㄡ》

to run about busily; to work hard for something which involves lots of leg work

東邊《ㄉㄨㄥ ㄅㄧㄢ》

the east side; on the east

東跑西顚《ㄉㄨㄥ ㄆㄠ ㄒㄧ ㄉㄧㄢ》

to run about busily; to work hard for something which involves lots of leg work

東拼西湊《ㄉㄨㄥ ㄆㄧㄣ ㄒㄧ ㄘㄡ》

to scrape (money, etc.) for a purchase, project, etc.; to patch up from bits

東普魯士《ㄉㄨㄥ ㄆㄨ ㄌㄨ ㄕ》

East Prussia

東門《ㄉㄨㄥ ㄇㄣ》

the east gate (of a city wall)

東非《ㄉㄨㄥ ㄈㄟ》

Eastern Africa

東方《ㄉㄨㄥ ㄈㄤ》

①the east ②Oriental ③a Chinese family name

東方發白《ㄉㄨㄥ ㄈㄤ ㄈㄚ ㄅㄞ》

(literally) The eastern sky is turning fish-belly gray. —daybreak: 他東方發白即起。He gets up at daybreak.

東方大港《ㄉㄨㄥ ㄈㄤ ㄉㄚ ㄍㄤ》

a projected harbor proposed by Dr. Sun Yat-sen, which is to be located on the eastern China coast

東方正敎《ㄉㄨㄥ ㄈㄤ ㄓㄥ ㄐㄧㄠ》

the Greek Orthodox Church

東方文化《ㄉㄨㄥ ㄈㄤ ㄨㄣ ㄏㄨㄚ》

Oriental culture

東風《ㄉㄨㄥ ㄈㄥ》

an east wind

東風吹馬耳《ㄉㄨㄥ ㄈㄥ ㄔㄨㄟ ㄇㄚ ㄦ》

to turn a deaf ear to; to pay no attention to; indifferent and aloof; to go in one ear and out the other

東扶西倒《ㄉㄨㄥ ㄈㄨ ㄒㄧ ㄉㄠ》

(literally) to brace up one while the others tumble down—It's difficult to educate people or to cultivate plants.

東德《ㄉㄨㄥ ㄉㄜ》

East Germany 參看「西德」

東倒西歪(ㄉㄨㄥ ㄉㄠˇ ㄒㄧ ㄨㄞ)
①(said of drunkards) to walk unsteadily ②(said of a scene, room, village, etc.) dilapidated

東道主(ㄉㄨㄥ ㄉㄠˋ ㄓㄨˇ)
the host at a dinner party; 他真是個善盼款待客人的東道主。He is such a good host.

東都(ㄉㄨㄥ ㄉㄨ)
(in ancient China) Loyang (洛陽), the eastern capital

東渡(ㄉㄨㄥ ㄉㄨˋ)
to take a sea-voyage eastward(especially referring to a trip to Japan)

東坦(ㄉㄨㄥ ㄊㄢˇ)
one's son-in-law

東塗西抹(ㄉㄨㄥ ㄊㄨˊ ㄒㄧ ㄇㄛˇ)
① (said of small children) to smear here and there ②(a polite term referring to oneself) to practice calligraphy; to write at random or without much thought

東土(ㄉㄨㄥ ㄊㄨˇ)
land in the east—Japan

東南(ㄉㄨㄥ ㄋㄢˊ)
southeast

東南西北(ㄉㄨㄥ ㄋㄢˊ ㄒㄧ ㄅㄟˇ)
(literally) east, south, west and north—all directions

東南亞(ㄉㄨㄥ ㄋㄢˊ ㄧㄚˋ)
Southeast Asia

東南亞公約組織(ㄉㄨㄥ ㄋㄢˊ ㄧㄚˋ ㄍㄨㄥ ㄩㄝ ㄗㄨˇ ㄓ)
Southeast Asia Treaty Organization (SEATO)

東挪西借(ㄉㄨㄥ ㄋㄨㄛˊ ㄒㄧ ㄐㄧㄝ)
to borrow all around; to scrape up money (for a purchase, etc.)

東拉西扯(ㄉㄨㄥ ㄌㄚ ㄒㄧ ㄔㄜˇ)
to talk aimlessly or without much thought; to ramble

東鱗西爪(ㄉㄨㄥ ㄌㄧㄣˊ ㄒㄧ ㄓㄠˇ)
odds and ends; a bit here and a bit there; fragmentary

東零西亂(ㄉㄨㄥ ㄌㄧㄥˊ ㄒㄧ ㄌㄨㄢˋ)
in complete disarray or disorder

東羅馬帝國(ㄉㄨㄥ ㄌㄨㄛˊ ㄇㄚˇ ㄉㄧˋ ㄍㄨㄛˊ)
the Eastern Roman Empire

東拐西騙(ㄉㄨㄥ ㄍㄨㄞˇ ㄒㄧ ㄆㄧㄢˋ)

---

to swindle on all sides

東宮(ㄉㄨㄥ ㄍㄨㄥ)
①the palace in which the crown prince lives ② the crown prince ③ a Chinese family name

東海(ㄉㄨㄥ ㄏㄞˇ)
the East China Sea

東海揚塵(ㄉㄨㄥ ㄏㄞˇ ㄧㄤˊ ㄔㄣˊ)
(literally) Dust rises from the East China Sea—unpredictability of world affairs

東漢(ㄉㄨㄥ ㄏㄢˋ)
the Eastern Han (25 - 220 A.D.), also known as the Later Han which began after Emperor Kuang Wu (光武帝) moved its capital to Loyang, Honan, and ended during the reign of Emperor Hsien (獻帝)

東胡(ㄉㄨㄥ ㄏㄨˊ)
ancient name of the Tungusic tribes

東加王國(ㄉㄨㄥ ㄐㄧㄚ ㄨㄤˊ ㄍㄨㄛˊ)
the Kingdom of Tonga

東家(ㄉㄨㄥ ·ㄐㄧㄚ)
①the owner of a house where one stays; the host ② the owner of a company or shop

東交民巷(ㄉㄨㄥ ㄐㄧㄠ ㄇㄧㄣˊ ㄒㄧㄤˋ)
(formerly) the Legation Quarter in Peking

東漸(ㄉㄨㄥ ㄐㄧㄢ)
(usually said of Western civilization, etc.) to gradually spread to the east

東晉(ㄉㄨㄥ ㄐㄧㄣˋ)
the Eastern Tsin Dynasty (317-420)

東進(ㄉㄨㄥ ㄐㄧㄣˋ)
to advance eastward: 大軍東進。The great army advanced eastward.

東江(ㄉㄨㄥ ㄐㄧㄤ)
the East River, a tributary of the Pearl River (珠江)

東經(ㄉㄨㄥ ㄐㄧㄥ)
longitude east of Greenwich

東京(ㄉㄨㄥ ㄐㄧㄥ)
①Tokyo ②(in the Han Dynasty) Loyang ③(in the Sung Dynasty) Kaifeng

東京灣(ㄉㄨㄥ ㄐㄧㄥ ㄨㄢ)
the Gulf of Tongking

東君(ㄉㄨㄥ ㄐㄩㄣ)

---

①the god of spring ②the sun god

東西(ㄉㄨㄥ)
①(ㄒㄧ)ⓐ east and west ⓑ from east to west ②(·ㄒㄧ)ⓐ things; objects; matters: 她愛吃甜的東西。She is too fond of sweet things. ⓑ a contemptible fellow: 他真不是東西！ What a despicable creature he is!

東周(ㄉㄨㄥ ㄓㄡ)
the Eastern Chou Dynasty (770-256 B.C.)

東張西望(ㄉㄨㄥ ㄓㄤ ㄒㄧ ㄨㄤˋ)
to look around; to gaze around; to look about furtively: 不要東張西望的。Stop gazing around.

東廠(ㄉㄨㄥ ㄔㄤˇ)
a secret police setup run by eunuchs during the Ming Dynasty

東窗事發(ㄉㄨㄥ ㄔㄨㄤ ㄕˋ ㄈㄚ)
(said of a conspiracy, secret plot, clandestine plan, etc.) to be exposed or bared; to come to light 或 The game is up.

東牀坦腹(ㄉㄨㄥ ㄔㄨㄤˊ ㄊㄢˇ ㄈㄨˋ)
an ideal son-in-law

東牀快婿(ㄉㄨㄥ ㄔㄨㄤˊ ㄎㄨㄞˋ ㄒㄩˋ)
a son-in-law

東施效顰 or 東施效矉(ㄉㄨㄥ ㄕ ㄒㄧㄠˋ ㄆㄧㄣˊ)
an ugly woman Tung Shih (東施) tried awkwardly to imitate the famous beauty Hsi Shih (西施) knitting her brows, and thus made herself even more awkward and nauseating—to imitate awkwardly

東食西宿(ㄉㄨㄥ ㄕˊ ㄒㄧ ㄙㄨˋ)
to go wherever profit is—very greedy

東沙群島(ㄉㄨㄥ ㄕㄚ ㄑㄩㄣˊ ㄉㄠˇ)
the Pratas Islands (Tungsha Chuntao)

東山再起(ㄉㄨㄥ ㄕㄢ ㄗㄞˋ ㄑㄧˇ)
(said of a retired person, etc.) to take up official duties again; to return to officialdom; to be reinstated; to stage a comeback: 他準備東山再起。He was prepared to stage a comeback.

【木部】

東人(ㄉㄨㄥ ㄖㄣˊ)
an employer; a master

東三省(ㄉㄨㄥ ㄙㄢ ㄕㄥˇ)
the Three Northeastern Provinces, in Manchuria—Heilungkiang (黑龍江), Kirin (吉林) and Liaoning (遼寧), the three provinces were redivided into nine provinces after World War II

東歐(ㄉㄨㄥ ㄡ)
Eastern Europe

東一句,西一句(ㄉㄨㄥ ㄧˋ ㄐㄩˋ,ㄒㄧ ㄧˋ ㄐㄩˋ)
①to converse completely without sequence or order; to talk incoherently ②utterances from all sides which amount to nothing; everybody talking at once

東亞(ㄉㄨㄥ ㄧㄚˇ)
East Asia

東印度公司(ㄉㄨㄥ ㄧㄣˋ ㄉㄨˋ ㄍㄨㄥ ㄙ)
East India Company

東印度羣島(ㄉㄨㄥ ㄧㄣˋ ㄉㄨˋ ㄑㄩㄣˊ ㄉㄠˇ)
the East Indies

東洋(ㄉㄨㄥ ㄧㄤˊ)
Japan

東洋車(ㄉㄨㄥ ㄧㄤˊ ㄔㄜ)
a rickshaw

東洋參(ㄉㄨㄥ ㄧㄤˊ ㄕㄣ)
a variety of ginseng grown in Japan

東洋水仙(ㄉㄨㄥ ㄧㄤˊ ㄕㄨㄟˇ ㄒㄧㄢ)
daffodils; narcissuses

東瀛(ㄉㄨㄥ ㄧㄥˊ)
Japan

東魏(ㄉㄨㄥ ㄨㄟˋ)
the Eastern Wei (534-550)

東嶽(ㄉㄨㄥ ㄩㄝˋ)
another name of Mountain Tai (泰山) in Shantung Province, one of the Five Sacred Mountains in China

【杵】 2361
　　　　ㄔㄨˇ chuu chǔ
1. a pestle; a baton used to pound the laundry: 鐵杵磨成針。An iron pestle can be ground into a needle.
2. to poke: 我用手指頭杵了他一下。I gave him a poke with a finger.

杵歌(ㄔㄨˇ ㄍㄜ)
a tune sung by the Taiwan aborigines while they are pounding grains in a mortar with a pestle

杵臼關節(ㄔㄨˇ ㄐㄧㄡˋ ㄍㄨㄢ ㄐㄧㄝˊ)
(physiology) ball-and-socket joints; enarthroses

杵臼之交(ㄔㄨˇ ㄐㄧㄡˋ ㄓ ㄐㄧㄠ)
true friendship which disregards discrepancy in wealth, influence, fame, etc.

【枇】 2362
　　　　ㄆㄧˊ pyi pí
loquats

枇杷開巷(ㄆㄧˊ ㄆㄚˊ ㄎㄞ ㄒㄧㄤˋ)
brothels; red-light districts

枇杷(ㄆㄧˊ ㄆㄚˊ)
loquats

枇杷露(ㄆㄧˊ ㄆㄚˊ ㄌㄨˋ)
diluted loquat extract (used as a medicine)

枇杷膏(ㄆㄧˊ ㄆㄚˊ ㄍㄠ)
condensed loquat extract (used as a medicine)

【杷】 2363
　　　　•ㄆㄚˊ pa pa
loquats

【杼】 2364
　　　　ㄓㄨˋ juh zhù
the shuttle of a loom

杼柚(ㄓㄨˋ ㄧㄡˋ)
looms

【板】 2365
　　　　ㄅㄢˇ baan bǎn
1. a board; a plank
2. a plate (of tin, aluminum, etc.); a slab
3. printing blocks
4. rigid; stern; straight; stiff

板板六十四(ㄅㄢˇ ㄅㄢˇ ㄌㄧㄡˋ ㄕˊ ㄙˋ)
rigid; inflexible; to stick to rules strictly

板本(ㄅㄢˇ ㄅㄣˇ)
books printed from wooden blocks

板本學(ㄅㄢˇ ㄅㄣˇ ㄒㄩㄝˊ)
textual study; a course of study to determine which age, dynasty, etc. books were printed in which age, dynasty, etc.

板壁(ㄅㄢˇ ㄅㄧˋ)
boards partitioning a house, room, etc.; wooden walls

板門店(ㄅㄢˇ ㄇㄣˊ ㄉㄧㄢˋ)
Panmunjom in Korea

板斧(ㄅㄢˇ ㄈㄨˇ)
a hatchet

板蕩(ㄅㄢˇ ㄉㄤˋ)
a world of disorder; a time of turmoil or upheavals; social confusion and chaos

板凳(ㄅㄢˇ ㄉㄥˋ)
a wooden stool

板鈦礦(ㄅㄢˇ ㄊㄞˋ ㄎㄨㄤˋ)
brookite

板栗(ㄅㄢˇ ㄌㄧˋ)
chestnuts

板畫(ㄅㄢˇ ㄏㄨㄚˋ)
a woodcut

板起面孔(ㄅㄢˇ ㄑㄧˇ ㄇㄧㄢˋ ㄎㄨㄥˇ)
to make a long face

板橋(ㄅㄢˇ ㄑㄧㄠˊ)
①a bridge built of wooden planks ②a city in Taipei Hsien, Taiwan

板球(ㄅㄢˇ ㄑㄧㄡˊ)
(sports) cricket: 板球流行於英國。Cricket is popular in England.

板滯(ㄅㄢˇ ㄓˋ)
stiff and rigid; pedantic

板著臉(ㄅㄢˇ •ㄓㄜ ㄌㄧㄢˇ)
to pull a long face; to keep a straight face

板車(ㄅㄢˇ ㄔㄜ)
a kind of hand-pulled cart for transporting heavy objects

板上釘釘(ㄅㄢˇ ㄕㄤˋ ㄉㄧㄥˋ ㄉㄧㄥ)
immovable; determined; decided

板書(ㄅㄢˇ ㄕㄨ)
writing on the blackboard

板子(ㄅㄢˇ ˙ㄗ)
①a flat bamboo, etc. for beating criminals in old China; a rod for disciplining children; a flogging board ②a printing block

板擦兒(ㄅㄢˇ ㄘㄚ ㄦˊ)
a wiper or an eraser (for a blackboard, etc.); a brush for applying whitewash

板鴨(ㄅㄢˇ ㄧㄚ)
a salted duck pressed and stretched like a plate (a specialty in Nanking)

板眼(ㄅㄢˇ ㄧㄢˇ)
①the rest and beat of music ②to be methodical in one's work; the orderly way of performing a task

【松】 2366　ㄙㄨㄥ song sōng

1. pines; firs
2. a Chinese family name

松柏(ㄙㄨㄥ ㄅㄛˊ)
① the pine and the cypress
② the conifers

松柏後凋(ㄙㄨㄥ ㄅㄛˊ ㄏㄡˋ ㄉㄧㄠ)
(literally) The leaves of pines and cypresses are always the last to fall. —Honesty and virtue will last.

松柏節操(ㄙㄨㄥ ㄅㄛˊ ㄐㄧㄝˊ ㄘㄠ)
honest and virtuous conduct; fortitude; lofty character: 他是具有松柏節操的人。He is a man of lofty character.

松柏長青(ㄙㄨㄥ ㄅㄛˊ ㄔㄤˊ ㄑㄧㄥ)or **松柏長壽**(ㄙㄨㄥ ㄅㄛˊ ㄔㄤˊ ㄕㄡˋ)
(a congratulatory expression on someone's birthday) May you live long and remain strong like the evergreen pine and cypress!

松木(ㄙㄨㄥ ㄇㄨˋ)
pine-wood boards or planks, etc. (for building purposes)

松風水月(ㄙㄨㄥ ㄈㄥ ㄕㄨㄟˇ ㄩㄝˋ)
(literally) the soughing of pines and the reflection of the moon on the water—the soothing surroundings of nature

松濤(ㄙㄨㄥ ㄊㄠˊ)
the soughing of the wind in the pines which sounds like roaring waves

松林(ㄙㄨㄥ ㄌㄧㄣˊ)
a pinery

松果(ㄙㄨㄥ ㄍㄨㄛˇ)
a strobile

松鶴遐齡(ㄙㄨㄥ ㄏㄜˋ ㄒㄧㄚˊ ㄌㄧㄥˊ)
longevity

松花(ㄙㄨㄥ ㄏㄨㄚ)
a preserved egg•

松花江(ㄙㄨㄥ ㄏㄨㄚ ㄐㄧㄤ)
the Sungari River

松花兒(ㄙㄨㄥ ㄏㄨㄚㄦ)
the fruit of a species of cypress

松節油(ㄙㄨㄥ ㄐㄧㄝˊ ㄧㄡˊ)
turpentine: 松節油是用來稀釋油漆的。Turpentine was used to mix with paints.

松江(ㄙㄨㄥ ㄐㄧㄤ)
Sungkiang, a province in Manchuria

松楸(ㄙㄨㄥ ㄑㄧㄡ)
(originally) trees planted at a tomb or grave—(figuratively) a tomb or grave

松毬(ㄙㄨㄥ ㄑㄧㄡˊ)
a pine cone

松香(ㄙㄨㄥ ㄒㄧㄤ)or **松膠**(ㄙㄨㄥ ㄐㄧㄠ)or **松脂**(ㄙㄨㄥ ㄓ)
rosin; colophony

松香油(ㄙㄨㄥ ㄒㄧㄤ ㄧㄡˊ)or **松脂油**(ㄙㄨㄥ ㄓ ㄧㄡˊ)
retinol; rosin oil

松蕈(ㄙㄨㄥ ㄒㄩㄣˋ)or **松菌**(ㄙㄨㄥ ㄐㄩㄣˋ)or **松茸**(ㄙㄨㄥ ㄖㄨㄥˊ)
pine mushrooms

松針(ㄙㄨㄥ ㄓㄣ)
pine needles

松竹梅(ㄙㄨㄥ ㄓㄨˊ ㄇㄟˊ)
the pine, the bamboo and the flowering plum—the three companions in the cold of the year

松鼠(ㄙㄨㄥ ㄕㄨˇ)
the squirrel: 這座公園以松鼠多而著名。This park is well-known for its squirrels.

松樹(ㄙㄨㄥ ㄕㄨˋ)
a pine

松仁(ㄙㄨㄥ ㄖㄣˊ)or **松仁兒**(ㄙㄨㄥ ㄖㄣˊㄦ)
the kernels in the pine cone

松子(ㄙㄨㄥ ㄗˇ)
pine nuts; pine seeds

【枏】 2367　(楠) ㄋㄢˊ nan nán

Machilus nanmu, a variety of evergreen tree, commonly known as cedar, with elliptical leaves, light green blossoms and dark, purplish fruit, even-grained, yellowish, fine wood, used for furniture or coffins which can last for hundreds of years

枏木 or 楠木(ㄋㄢˊ ㄇㄨˋ)
nanmu (*Phoebe nanmu*)

【枉】 2368　ㄨㄤˇ woang wǎng

1. to waste; useless; in vain
2. crooked
3. to wrong; to do or suffer wrong; aggrieved; oppression
4. (in polite language) to request another to deign or condescend to

枉法(ㄨㄤˇ ㄈㄚˇ)
to abuse law; to twist law to suit one's own purpose; to pervert the law: 一位重要的官員因貪賄枉法。An important official took bribes and perverted the law.

枉費(ㄨㄤˇ ㄈㄟˋ)
to waste; to try in vain; to be of no avail: 你是在枉費唇舌。You are wasting your breath.

枉費工夫(ㄨㄤˇ ㄈㄟˋ ㄍㄨㄥ ㄈㄨ)
to waste time and energy; to spend time and work in vain

枉費心機(ㄨㄤˇ ㄈㄟˋ ㄒㄧㄣ ㄐㄧ)
to scheme, plan or cudgel one's brains to no purpose or in vain; to get nowhere despite the trouble taken: 他枉費心機。He racked his brains in vain.

枉道事人(ㄨㄤˇ ㄉㄠˋ ㄕˋ ㄖㄣˊ)
to distort the truth in order to please others

枉斷(ㄨㄤˇ ㄉㄨㄢˋ)
to abuse law by distorting it; to decide unfairly

枉駕(ㄨㄤˇ ㄐㄧㄚˋ)
You have deigned to call on me.

枉己正人(ㄨㄤˇ ㄐㄧˇ ㄓㄥ ㄖㄣˊ)
a crook trying to tell others how to be a gentleman; a dishonest person telling others to behave

枉駕(ㄨㄤˇ ㄐㄧㄚˋ)
I'm honored by your visit.

枉曲(ㄨㄤˇ ㄑㄩ)
bent; crooked; warped

枉尺直尋(ㄨㄤˇ ㄔˇ ㄓˊ ㄒㄩㄣˊ)
to compromise on minor points so as to gain on the major issue; to bend in small places and straight in total

枉然(ㄨㄤˇ ㄖㄢˊ)
useless; to no purpose; in vain; futile: 我的一切工作均歸枉然。All my work was in vain.

枉撰(ㄨㄤˇ ㄓㄨㄢˋ)
tumultuous; disorderly

枉死(ㄨㄤˇ ㄙˇ)
to die through injustice; death as a result of injustice; to be wronged and

driven to death

枉死鬼 (ㄨㄤˇ ㄙˇ ㄍㄨㄟˇ)
the spirit of one who died through injustice

【枌】 2369
ㄈㄣˊ fern fén
a variety of elm with small seeds and white bark

枌楡 (ㄈㄣˊ ㄩˊ)
① a kind of elm ② (originally) the native place of the founding emperor of the Han Dynasty—one's native place or hometown

【枋】 2370
ㄈㄤ fang fāng
sandalwood

【析】 2371
ㄒㄧ shi xī
1. to split; to rip or break apart; to divide; to separate
2. to interpret; to explain; to analyze
3. a Chinese family name

析骨 (ㄒㄧ ㄍㄨˇ)
to break apart a skeleton

析居 (ㄒㄧ ㄐㄩ)
(said of brothers) to live under different roofs — to divide family property

析産 (ㄒㄧ ㄔㄢˇ)
to divide family property; to split the inheritance (among children of the deceased)

析出 (ㄒㄧ ㄔㄨ)
(chemistry) to separate out

析㸑 (ㄒㄧ ㄔㄨㄢˋ)or 析㸑 (ㄒㄧ ㄧㄢ)
(said of brothers) to divide family property and live under different roofs

析疑 (ㄒㄧ ㄧˊ)
to explain a doubt; to clarify a doubt

析義 (ㄒㄧ ㄧˋ)
interpretation and elaboration of the meaning of something

【枒】 2372
ㄧㄚˊ ya yá
1. the felloe of a wheel
2. disorderly growth of twigs

枒杈 (ㄧㄚˊ ㄔㄚ)
crotches; disorderly growth of twigs

【枕】 2373
1. ㄓㄣˇ jenn zhěn
a pillow

枕件 (ㄓㄣˇ ㄅㄨㄥˋ)

a pillow-companion—a bed fellow

枕邊人 (ㄓㄣˇ ㄅㄧㄢ ㄖㄣˊ)
wife (who shares the same pillow with her husband)

枕邊言 (ㄓㄣˇ ㄅㄧㄢ ㄧㄢˊ)
pillow talk—private talks between husband and wife

枕畔 (ㄓㄣˇ ㄆㄢˋ)
beside the pillow

枕木 (ㄓㄣˇ ㄇㄨˋ)
railroad ties; railway sleepers: 枕木支撐兩條火車軌道。Sleepers support two railway tracks.

枕簟 (ㄓㄣˇ ㄉㄧㄢˋ)
the pillow and mat—bedding

枕套 (ㄓㄣˇ ㄊㄠˋ)
a pillowcase; a pillowslip

枕頭 (ㄓㄣˇ ˙ㄊㄡ)
a pillow: 枕頭是睡覺時用來墊頭的。A pillow is used to support one's head in bed.

枕冷衾寒 (ㄓㄣˇ ㄌㄥˇ ㄑㄧㄣ ㄏㄢˊ)
the pillow is cold and the bed, chilly—after the departure or death of one's spouse

枕骨 (ㄓㄣˇ ㄍㄨˇ)
the occiput; the occipital bone

枕巾 (ㄓㄣˇ ㄐㄧㄣ)
a towel used to cover a pillow; a pillow cover

枕席 (ㄓㄣˇ ㄒㄧˊ)
① the pillow and the mat—bedding ② a mat used to cover a pillow; a pillow mat

枕席難安 (ㄓㄣˇ ㄒㄧˊ ㄋㄢˊ ㄢ)
cannot sleep—very worried and anxious

枕席之間 (ㄓㄣˇ ㄒㄧˊ ㄓ ㄐㄧㄢ)
while in bed

枕中書 (ㄓㄣˇ ㄓㄨㄥ ㄕㄨ)
① a Taoist account of immortals authored by Ko Hung (葛洪) of the Tsin Dynasty ② secret alchemistic formulas (hidden in one's pillow to prevent leakage)

【枕】 2373
枕戈待旦 (ㄓㄣˇ ㄍㄜ ㄉㄞˋ ㄉㄢˋ)
(literally) to use the spear as a pillow and wait for the morning—to be on the alert;

ever-prepared for emergency; to maintain combat readiness

枕塊 (ㄓㄣˇ ㄎㄨㄞˋ)
(literally) to pillow on a clod of earth—mourning for one's parents

枕藉 (ㄓㄣˇ ㄐㄧㄝˋ)
to lie in complete disarray or to lie about on each other

枕經史 (ㄓㄣˇ ㄐㄧㄥ ㄐㄧ ㄕˇ)or 枕經籍書 (ㄓㄣˇ ㄐㄧㄥ ㄐㄧˊ ㄕㄨ)
to be excessively fond of ancient books

枕石漱流 (ㄓㄣˇ ㄕˊ ㄕㄨˋ ㄌㄧㄡˊ)
to pillow one's head on rocks and rinse one's mouth in streams—to retire from the world

【柄】 2374
ㄖㄨㄟˋ ruey ruì
a wooden handle

枘鑿 (ㄖㄨㄟˋ ㄗㄠˋ)
(literally) a square handle and a round socket—not fitting; incompatible; cannot see eye to eye

【林】 2375
ㄌㄧㄣˊ lin lín
1. a forest; a grove; a copse
2. a collection of books, works, literary extracts, etc.
3. circles; many; numerous; a great body of (capable persons, etc.): 他081名於藝林。He was famous in the art circles.
4. a Chinese family name

林薄 (ㄌㄧㄣˊ ㄅㄛˊ)
a dense growth of trees and undergrowth; a jungle

林班 (ㄌㄧㄣˊ ㄅㄢ)
(forestry) forest divisions; forest lots; forest compartments

林表 (ㄌㄧㄣˊ ㄅㄧㄠˇ)
the edge of a forest

林逋 (ㄌㄧㄣˊ ㄅㄨ)
Lin Pu, 967-1028, a hermit poet of the Sung Dynasty 參看「梅妻鶴子」

林莽 (ㄌㄧㄣˊ ㄇㄤˇ)
trees and undergrowth; the jungle

林杪 (ㄌㄧㄣˊ ㄇㄧㄠˇ)
the edge of a forest

林木 (ㄌㄧㄣˊ ㄇㄨˋ)

a forest; woods

林帶(ㄌㄧㄣˊ ㄉㄞˋ)
a forest belt

林立(ㄌㄧㄣˊ ㄌㄧˋ)
(literally) to stand up like a forest—a great many; a forest of (stacks, derricks, etc.): 基隆港內檣檣林立。
There is a forest of masts in the Keelung harbor.

林林總總(ㄌㄧㄣˊ ㄌㄧㄣˊ ㄗㄨㄥˇ ㄗㄨㄥˇ)
numerous; multitudinous; in great abundance

林肯(ㄌㄧㄣˊ ㄎㄣˇ)
Abraham Lincoln (1809-1865), the 16th U.S. President

林整(ㄌㄧㄣˊ ㄓㄥˋ)
the tranquility of trees and valleys

林間學校(ㄌㄧㄣˊ ㄐㄧㄢ ㄒㄩㄝˊ ㄒㄧㄠˋ)
an open-air school, often located in a forest, copse, etc.

林區(ㄌㄧㄣˊ ㄑㄩ)
a forest zone; a forest region; a forest

林泉(ㄌㄧㄣˊ ㄑㄩㄢˊ)
(literally) the forest and the spring—a secluded place; an ideal spot for retirement

林泉之士(ㄌㄧㄣˊ ㄑㄩㄢˊ ㄓ ㄕˋ)
a recluse

林下(ㄌㄧㄣˊ ㄒㄧㄚˋ)
(literary) retirement

林相改良(ㄌㄧㄣˊ ㄒㄧㄤˋ《ㄞˇ ㄌㄧㄤˊ)
forest conversion

林產(ㄌㄧㄣˊ ㄔㄢˇ)
products of the forest; timber

林場(ㄌㄧㄣˊ ㄔㄤˇ)or(ㄌㄧㄣˊ ㄔㄤˊ)
① wooded land; a forest ② a logging station

林紓(ㄌㄧㄣˊ ㄕㄨˋ)or 林琴南(ㄌㄧㄣˊ ㄑㄧㄣˊ ㄋㄢˊ)
Lin Shu, 1852-1924, a writer of classic prose and translator of Western fictions

林子(ㄌㄧㄣˊ ˙ㄗ)
a grove; a clump of trees; a forest

林則徐(ㄌㄧㄣˊ ㄗㄜˊ ㄒㄩˊ)
Lin Tse-hsü, 1785-1850, whose labor on British opium import into China led to the Opium War

林藪(ㄌㄧㄣˊ ㄙㄡˇ)
a grove; rich growth of trees; woods and jungle: 我們在林藪間散步很開心。We had a pleasant walk in the rich growth of trees.

林森(ㄌㄧㄣˊ ㄙㄣ)
Lin Sen, 1868-1943, chairman of the National Government of China during 1932-1943

林業(ㄌㄧㄣˊ ㄧㄝˋ)
the forestry industry

林蔭(ㄌㄧㄣˊ ㄧㄣˋ)
the shade under trees

林蔭大道(ㄌㄧㄣˊ ㄧㄣˋ ㄉㄚˋ ㄉㄠˋ)
an avenue; a boulevard: 我們行駛在環城市區的林蔭大道上。We motored around the city on the boulevard.

林園(ㄌㄧㄣˊ ㄩㄢˊ)
wooded land; a park of trees and vegetation

【枝】2376　1. ㄓ jy zhī
1. the branches of a tree; a branch
2. limbs
3. to branch off

枝蔓(ㄓ ㄇㄢˋ)
branches and knots—complications; complexities; confused

枝頭(ㄓ ㄊㄡˊ)
on the branch

枝條(ㄓ ㄊㄧㄠˊ)
a twig

枝幹(ㄓ ㄍㄢˋ)
the trunk and the branches: 樹根支撐著枝幹。The root supports the trunk and the branches.

枝根(ㄓ ㄍㄣ)
ramose roots

枝節(ㄓ ㄐㄧㄝˊ)
①branches and knots—minor matters: 這是枝節問題。This is a minor problem. ②complications; obstacles; unexpected difficulties: 不要橫生枝節。Don't raise unexpected difficulties.

枝解 or 支解(ㄓ ㄐㄧㄝˇ)
(an ancient punishment or torture) amputation of a criminal's limbs

枝棲(ㄓ ㄑㄧ)
a roof over one's head; a place to live or make a living

枝枝節節(ㄓ ㄓ ㄐㄧㄝˊ ㄐㄧㄝˊ)
complications; complexities; diversities; minor issues: 不要太注意那些枝枝節節的問題。Don't pay too much attention to those minor issues.

枝杪(ㄓ ㄇㄧㄠˇ)
the tapering part of a branch; the tip of a branch

枝子(ㄓ ˙ㄗ)or 枝兒(ㄓ ㄦ)
a branch; a bough

枝辭(ㄓ ㄘˊ)or 枝辭蔓語(ㄓ ㄘˊ ㄇㄢˋ ㄩˇ)
incoherent speeches; unintelligible expressions

枝粗葉茂(ㄓ ㄘㄨ ㄧㄝˋ ㄇㄠˋ)
(literally) The branches are thick and the leaves are many—sturdy and vigorous; virile and prolific

枝椏(ㄓ ㄧㄚ)
branches; twigs 亦作「枝丫」

枝葉(ㄓ ㄧㄝˋ)
① children; offspring ② complications and diversities branches and leaves

枝葉扶疏(ㄓ ㄧㄝˋ ㄈㄨˊ ㄕㄨ)
(said of trees) luxuriant

【枝】2376　2. ㄑㄧˊ chyí qí
參看「枝指」

枝指(ㄓ ㄓˇ)
an additional finger; a forked finger

【果】2377　《ㄨㄛˇ guoo guǒ
1. the fruit of a tree: 他不大吃水果。He does not eat much fruit.
2. effect (in cause and effect); result; fruit; a consequence
3. surely; really; truly; exactly
4. to stuff; to fill
5. to succeed
6. a Chinese family name

果報(ㄍㄨㄛˇ ㄅㄠˋ)
(Buddhism) One reaps what he planted in his previous life. — the retribution for good or evil deeds

果不出所料(ㄍㄨㄛˇ ㄅㄨˋ ㄔㄨ ㄙㄨㄛˇ ㄌㄧㄠˋ)
as expected; as anticipated

〔木部〕

【木部】

果盤《ㄍㄨㄛ ㄆㄢˊ》
a fruit tray

果皮《ㄍㄨㄛ ㄆㄧˊ》
peel; the skin of a fruit; the pericarp or outer covering of the seed; peelings

果皮箱《ㄍㄨㄛ ㄆㄧˊ ㄒㄧㄤ》
a garbage can or box for peelings, candy wrappings, etc.

果品《ㄍㄨㄛ ㄆㄧㄣˇ》
fruits

果木《ㄍㄨㄛ ㄇㄨˋ》
a tree that bears edible fruit; fruit trees 亦作「果樹」

果脯《ㄍㄨㄛ ㄈㄨˇ》
dried or preserved fruit

果腹《ㄍㄨㄛ ㄈㄨˋ》
to fill one's stomach (usually with poor food); to feed on

果碟兒《ㄍㄨㄛ ㄉㄧㄝˊㄦ》or 果碟子
《ㄍㄨㄛ ㄉㄧㄝˊ˙ㄗ》
a small plate to hold fruit in a feast

果斷《ㄍㄨㄛ ㄉㄨㄢˋ》
decision with courage; (said of a person) of determination; resolute: 她辦事果斷。She handled affairs in a decisive manner.

果糖《ㄍㄨㄛ ㄊㄤˊ》
fructose, or fruit sugar; levulose

果嶺《ㄍㄨㄛ ㄌㄧㄥˇ》
(golf) green

果乾《ㄍㄨㄛ ㄍㄢ》
dehydrated fruit

果敢《ㄍㄨㄛ ㄍㄢˇ》
having the determination and courage to do something

果梗《ㄍㄨㄛ ㄍㄥˇ》
a fruit stem

果盒《ㄍㄨㄛ ㄏㄜˊ》
a deep tray of various shapes with matching cover for fruit and candies to be presented to guests

果核《ㄍㄨㄛ ㄏㄜˊ》
a kernel; a fruit stone; a pit

果決《ㄍㄨㄛ ㄐㄩㄝˊ》
daring and determined: 你必須果決實行你的計劃。You must carry out your plan with determination.

果心《ㄍㄨㄛ ㄒㄧㄣ》
the core (of an apple, etc.)

果汁《ㄍㄨㄛ ㄓ》
fruit juice: 他早餐喝一杯果汁。He drank a glass of fruit juice at breakfast.

果汁機《ㄍㄨㄛ ㄓ ㄐㄧ》
① a juicer 亦作「搾汁機」② a blender 亦作「攪和器」

果渣《ㄍㄨㄛ ㄓㄚ》
marc

果眞《ㄍㄨㄛ ㄓㄣ》
really; if really

果實《ㄍㄨㄛ ㄕˊ》
fruit: 這蘋果樹果實纍纍。The apple tree has fruit growing in close clusters.

果肉《ㄍㄨㄛ ㄖㄡˋ》
pulp

果然《ㄍㄨㄛ ㄖㄢˊ》
① exactly as one expected ② a kind of long-tailed monkey ③ having eaten enough

果然如此《ㄍㄨㄛ ㄖㄢˊ ㄖㄨˊ ㄘˇ》
① It happened exactly as expected. ② if really: 果然如此，你就可放心了。If this is really true, it'll take a load off your mind.

果仁《ㄍㄨㄛ ㄖㄣˊ》
the meat of a nut or in a fruit stone; a kernel

果如所料《ㄍㄨㄛ ㄖㄨˊ ㄙㄨㄛˇ ㄌㄧㄠˋ》
It happened exactly as predicted. 或 Just as one expects.

果若《ㄍㄨㄛ ㄖㄨㄛˋ》
if really

果子《ㄍㄨㄛ ˙ㄗ》
fruit: 蘋果、橙子和香蕉是果子。Apples, oranges, and bananas are fruit.

果子狸《ㄍㄨㄛ ˙ㄗ ㄌㄧˊ》
a masked (or gem-faced) civet

果子露《ㄍㄨㄛ ˙ㄗ ㄌㄨˋ》
concentrated fruit syrup

果子乾兒《ㄍㄨㄛ ˙ㄗ ㄍㄢ ㄦ》
sweetened and dried fruit boiled until thickened, to be served cool

果子醬《ㄍㄨㄛ ˙ㄗ ㄐㄧㄤˋ》
fruit jam

果子鹽《ㄍㄨㄛ ˙ㄗ ㄧㄢˊ》
fruit salt

果酸《ㄍㄨㄛ ㄙㄨㄢ》
(chemistry) tartaric acid

果阿《ㄍㄨㄛ ㄜ》
Goa, a territory of Portugal on the SW coast of India before 1962

果兒《ㄍㄨㄛ ㄦˊ》
① fruit of small size ② eggs

果爾《ㄍㄨㄛ ㄦˇ》
① if really so ② as expected or predicted

果毅《ㄍㄨㄛ ㄧˋ》
determination and fortitude

果蠅《ㄍㄨㄛ ㄧㄥˊ》
a fruit fly

果園兒《ㄍㄨㄛ ㄩㄢˊㄦ》or 果園子
《ㄍㄨㄛ ㄩㄢˊ˙ㄗ》
an orchard: 這些蘋果是由附近的果園兒生產的。These apples come from an orchard near here.

【枚】 2378　ㄇㄟˊ mei méi
1. the stalk; the trunk as opposed to branches
2. a numerary auxiliary (used in connection with coins, fruits, stamps, bombs, etc.): 她買了五枚梅子。She bought five plums.
3. a gag for troops marching at night when silence means a lot
4. a Chinese family name

枚舉《ㄇㄟˊ ㄐㄩˇ》
to enumerate; to recount one by one

【杰】 2379　(傑) ㄐㄧㄝˊ jye jié
a hero; an outstanding person

五畫

【枯】 2380　ㄎㄨ ku kū
1. withered; dry: 他的想像力好像已經枯竭了。His imagination seems to have dried up.
2. dried wood
3. ill health; emaciated

枯木發榮《ㄎㄨ ㄇㄨˋ ㄈㄚ ㄖㄨㄥˊ》
(literally) A withered old tree suddenly puts forth new sprouts.—good fortune that comes late in one's life or after a long spell of bad luck

枯木逢春《ㄎㄨ ㄇㄨˋ ㄈㄥˊ ㄔㄨㄣ》

Spring comes to the withered tree.—to get a new lease of life; good fortune that comes after a long spell of bad luck

枯橘 (ㄎㄨ ㄐㄩˊ)
①(said of a person's appearance) pale, dry and emaciated; haggard: 他的形容枯槁。He looks haggard. ②withered and dry

枯乾 (ㄎㄨ ㄍㄢ)
dry (branches, or fruit)

枯骨 (ㄎㄨ ㄍㄨˇ)
dry bones—bones or skeleton of a person dead for a long time

枯涸 (ㄎㄨ ㄏㄜˊ)
(usually said of wells, rivers, etc.) dry or waterless: 水源枯涸了。The fountainhead has dried up.

枯候 (ㄎㄨ ㄏㄡˋ)
to wait interminably

枯黃 (ㄎㄨ ㄏㄨㄤˊ)
withered and yellow: 蘋果樹葉逐漸枯黃了。The leaves of apple trees are beginning to turn yellow.

枯寂 (ㄎㄨ ㄐㄧˊ)
lonesome; lonely

枯瘠 (ㄎㄨ ㄐㄧˊ)
withered, dry and lean

枯竭 (ㄎㄨ ㄐㄧㄝˊ)
(said of source of supply) exhausted; dried up: 我們的財源枯竭了。Our financial resources were exhausted.

枯井 (ㄎㄨ ㄐㄧㄥˇ)
a dried-up well; a dry well

枯窘 (ㄎㄨ ㄐㄩㄥˇ)
dry and embarrassed — poverty-stricken

枯朽 (ㄎㄨ ㄒㄧㄡˇ)
dry and decayed; rotten: 一棵蘋果樹枯朽了。An apple tree was dry and decayed.

枯禪 (ㄎㄨ ㄔㄢˊ)
(Buddhism) to sit in meditation

枯腸 (ㄎㄨ ㄔㄤˊ)
(literally) an impoverished mind

枯瘦 (ㄎㄨ ㄕㄡˋ)
withered and thin

枯樹生花 (ㄎㄨ ㄕㄨˋ ㄕㄥ ㄏㄨㄚ)
(literally) A withered tree

suddenly blossoms.—to hit the jackpot after a long spell of bad luck

枯榮 (ㄎㄨ ㄖㄨㄥˊ)
ups and downs (of one's life); rise and fall (of a nation)

枯燥 (ㄎㄨ ㄗㄠˋ)
①dry ②uninteresting; dull

枯燥無味 (ㄎㄨ ㄗㄠˋ ㄨˊ ㄨㄟˋ)
dry and tasteless—uninteresting; monotonous

枯坐 (ㄎㄨ ㄗㄨㄛˋ)
to sit there all by oneself doing nothing

枯死 (ㄎㄨ ㄙˇ)
to wither; to dry up and die: 許多樹都枯死了。Many trees dried up.

枯索 (ㄎㄨ ㄙㄨㄛˇ)
withered and lifeless

枯葉 (ㄎㄨ ㄧㄝˋ)
dried leaves: 秋天枯葉脫落。The dried leaves fall in autumn.

枯萎 (ㄎㄨ ㄨㄟˇ)
withered: 炎熱的太陽使草都枯萎了。The hot sun withered up the grass.

枯魚 (ㄎㄨ ㄩˊ)
dried fish

【枳】 2381
ㄓˇ jyy zhǐ
1. a trifoliate orange
2. a variety of orange with a very thick skin

枳殼 (ㄓˇ ㄎㄜˊ)
the large ripe fruit of a variety of orange which is used in herbal medicine

枳棘 (ㄓˇ ㄐㄧˊ)
thorns; thorny; plants with many thorns

枳實 (ㄓˇ ㄕˊ)
the small green fruit of a variety of orange with thick skin which is used in herbal medicine

【枴】 2382
ㄍㄨㄞˇ goai guǎi
a staff for an old person; a cane: 他依靠枴杖。He leaned on his staff.

枴棒 (ㄍㄨㄞˇ ㄅㄤˋ)
a cane; an old person's staff

枴杖 (ㄍㄨㄞˇ ㄓㄤˋ)
an old person's staff; a cane

枴杖 (ㄍㄨㄞˇ ㄓㄤˋ)
an old person's staff; a cane

【枵】 2383
ㄒㄧㄠ shiau xiāo
empty

枵腹從公 (ㄒㄧㄠ ㄈㄨˋ ㄘㄨㄥˊ ㄍㄨㄥ)
to do one's duty even with an empty stomach

【枲】 2384
ㄒㄧˇ shii xǐ
the male nettle-hemp

【架】 2385
ㄐㄧㄚˋ jiah jià
1. a prop; a stand; a rack; a frame
2. to prop up; to set up; to support
3. a framework or scaffold
4. to fabricate (a charge, etc.); to fabricate
5. to lay something on
6. a quarrel

架不住 (ㄐㄧㄚˋ ㄅㄨˋ ㄓㄨˋ)
①cannot support or sustain the weight ②cannot endure any more; cannot stand (the pressure); cannot stand up again ③to be no match for

架票 (ㄐㄧㄚˋ ㄆㄧㄠˋ)
to kidnap

架得住 (ㄐㄧㄚˋ ㄉㄜˊ ㄓㄨˋ)
①able to support it; can sustain the weight: 這個輕書架，能架得住這些書嗎？Can this light shelf sustain all these books? ②able to endure it

架空 (ㄐㄧㄚˋ ㄎㄨㄥ)
①to make up; to invent (a story) ②built on stilts ③impracticable; unpractical ④to take away one's power by subtle means

架起 (ㄐㄧㄚˋ ㄑㄧˇ)
①to set up; to prop up; to support ②to put on a rack

架橋 (ㄐㄧㄚˋ ㄑㄧㄠˊ)
to build a bridge

架式 (ㄐㄧㄚˋ ㄕˋ)
a style; a manner; a pose; a stance: 這兩個男孩擺出打門的架式相互威脅。The two boys took fighting poses to threaten each other.

架勢 (ㄐㄧㄚˋ ㄕˋ)
(colloquial) a posture; a stance; a manner

架設 (ㄐㄧㄚˋ ㄕㄜˋ)

〔木 部〕

〔木

部〕

to build over something; to erect (above the ground or water level, as on stilts or posts)

架子（ㄐㄧㄚˇ）or 架兒（ㄐㄧㄚˋ）
①a rack; a stand; a frame; a scaffold ②a skeleton; an outline

架子大（ㄐㄧㄚˇ·ㄉㄚˋ）
putting on airs of self-importance; a haughty manner: 他架子大。He has a haughty manner.

架走（ㄐㄧㄚˋ ㄗㄡˇ）
to take or carry a person away by force; to kidnap: 我們把她強行架走。We carried her away by force.

架次（ㄐㄧㄚˋ ㄘˋ）
(said of planes on a bombing mission, etc.) a sortie

架訟（ㄐㄧㄚˋ ㄙㄨㄥˋ）
to persuade another to file charges in court or start a lawsuit

【枷】 2386　ㄐㄧㄚ jia jiā
a cangue; a pillory—worn by prisoners in former times: 他應受枷刑。He deserves to be put in the pillory.

枷鎖（ㄐㄧㄚ ㄙㄨㄛˇ）
①the cangue and lock ②(figuratively) bondage; shackles: 他擺脫了精神枷鎖。He was free from spiritual shackles.

【柿】 2387　ㄕˋ shyh shì
the persimmon

柿餅（ㄕˋ ㄅㄧㄥˇ）
flattened and dried persimmon

柿箱（ㄕˋ ㄒㄧㄤ）
boxes or cases made of persimmon wood

柿子（ㄕˋ·ㄗ）
the persimmon fruit: 柿子熟了。The persimmon fruit became red.

【枸】 2388　ㄍㄡˇ goou gǒu
a medlar

枸杞（ㄍㄡˇ ㄑㄧˇ）
Lycium chinense, a Chinese wolfberry

【枸】 2388　ㄍㄡ gou gōu

枸橘（ㄍㄡ ㄐㄩˊ）
a large acid orange

【枸】 2388　3. ㄐㄩˇ jeu jǔ

枸櫞（ㄐㄩ ㄩㄢˊ）
citrus medica, a citron

【枹】 2389　ㄈㄨˊ fu fú
（又讀 ㄈㄨ fwu fū）
a drumstick

枹鼓（ㄈㄨˊ ㄍㄨˇ）
①a drum beaten on the battlefield to boast morale ②a drum beaten to warn the invasion of bandits in the Han Dynasty

【柒】 2390　ㄑㄧ chi qī
another form of 七 (seven), used in writing checks, etc. to prevent fraud

【枻】 2391　ㄧˋ yih yì
1. a rowing sweep
2. an instrument for correcting a bow

【柎】 2392　ㄈㄨˊ fu fú
the calyx of a flower

【柄】 2393　ㄅㄧㄥˇ biing bǐng
（又讀 ㄅㄧㄥˋ biing bìng）
1. the handle of something
2. authority; power
3. to operate; to handle; to control
4. a handle: 刀柄the handle of a knife

柄國（ㄅㄧㄥˇ ㄍㄨㄛˊ）
to reign over a state; to hold the political power in a nation

柄臣（ㄅㄧㄥˇ ㄔㄣˊ）
a minister with full authority; a powerful minister

柄用（ㄅㄧㄥˇ ㄩㄥˋ）
to be held in esteem by the monarch and given authority

【柏】 2394　1.讀音 ㄅㄛˊ bor bó
（翻音 ㄅㄞˇ bae bǎi）
1. a cypress
2. a Chinese family name

柏府（ㄅㄛˊ ㄈㄨˇ）
the imperial censorate

柏臺（ㄅㄛˊ ㄊㄞˊ）
the imperial censorate

柏拉圖（ㄅㄛˊ ㄌㄚ ㄊㄨˊ）
Plato, 427-347 B.C., Greek philosopher

柏林（ㄅㄛˊ ㄌㄧㄣˊ）
Berlin, Germany

柏梁體（ㄅㄛˊ ㄌㄧㄤˊ ㄊㄧˇ）
a form of poetry in the Han Dynasty, originated by Emperor Wu, accentuating rhymes

柏樹（ㄅㄛˊ ㄕㄨˋ）
the cypress

柏油（ㄅㄛˊ ㄧㄡˊ）or（ㄅㄞˇ ㄧㄡˊ）
asphalt: 他們這裡有好的柏油路。They have good asphalt road here.

【某】 2395　ㄇㄡˇ moou mǒu
1. a certain person or thing
2. formerly used in place of "I": 某不敢同意。I cannot agree.

某某（ㄇㄡˇ ㄇㄡˇ）
so-and-so; a certain person

某年（ㄇㄡˇ ㄋㄧㄢˊ）
a certain year

某家（ㄇㄡˇ ㄐㄧㄚ）
a certain family; a certain household: 我知道某家。I know of a certain family.

某甲（ㄇㄡˇ ㄐㄧㄚˇ）
a certain person; a Mr. So-and-so—one whose name is unknown, unimportant, or better not to be mentioned; a pronoun referring to any third party

某些（ㄇㄡˇ ㄒㄧㄝ）
certain (things, people, etc.)

某種（ㄇㄡˇ ㄓㄨㄥˇ）
certain (reasons, results, etc.)

某處（ㄇㄡˇ ㄔㄨˋ）
a certain place; somewhere: 他住在某處。He lived in a certain place.

某時候（ㄇㄡˇ ㄕˊ·ㄏㄡ）or 某時候（ㄇㄡˇ ㄕˊ ㄏㄡˋ）
a certain time; sometime: 此事發生在上月某時。It happened sometime last month.

某數（ㄇㄡˇ ㄕㄨˋ）
a certain number or figure

某日（ㄇㄡˇ ㄖˋ）
a certain day

某人（ㄇㄡˇ ㄖㄣˊ）

①a certain person—referring to someone whose name is not mentioned for one reason or another ②a pronoun used in place of one's own name

某月(ㄇㄡˇ ㄩㄝˋ)
a certain month

【染】 2396
(ㄖㄢˇ raan răn)

1. to dye: 她把頭髮染成紅色。she dyed her hair red.

2. to soil; to pollute: 這房間一塵不染。This room was not soiled by a speck of dust.

3. to get infected; to catch a disease; infectious: 他染上了痢疾。He has caught dysentery.

4. to have an affair with

5. (in Chinese painting and calligraphy) to make strokes

染病(ㄖㄢˇ ㄅㄧㄥˋ)
to get infected; to catch a disease; to fall ill

染布(ㄖㄢˇ ㄅㄨˋ)
to dye cloth

染髮(ㄖㄢˇ ㄈㄚˇ)
to dye hair

染坊(ㄖㄢˇ ㄈㄤˊ)
a dyeing mill

染毒(ㄖㄢˇ ㄉㄨˊ)
①to be infected with venereal disease ②to use narcotics

染料(ㄖㄢˇ ㄌㄧㄠˋ)
dyestuff; dye

染缸(ㄖㄢˇ ㄍㄤ)
a dyeing tub, usually of a large size

染工(ㄖㄢˇ ㄍㄨㄥ)
a dyer

染翰(ㄖㄢˇ ㄏㄢˋ)
to soak a writing brush with ink

染化(ㄖㄢˇ ㄏㄨㄚˋ)
to educate; to exert good influence on

染疾(ㄖㄢˇ ㄐㄧˊ)
to contract a disease; to fall ill: 我怕他可能染疾了。I am afraid he may have fallen ill.

染指甲(ㄖㄢˇ ㄓˇ ㄐㄧㄚˇ)
to paint fingernails

染指(ㄖㄢˇ ㄓˇ)
to have a "cut" in illegal

profit; to encroach on

染指書(ㄖㄢˇ ㄓˇ ㄕㄨ)
finger-writing (in Chinese calligraphy)

染色(ㄖㄢˇ ㄙㄜˋ)
to dye

染色體(ㄖㄢˇ ㄙㄜˋ ㄊㄧˇ)
(genetics) a chromosome

染惡習(ㄖㄢˇ ㄜˋ ㄒㄧˊ)
to take on bad habits, practices, etc.: 有些人容易染惡習。Some people easily take on bad habits.

染污(ㄖㄢˇ ㄨ)
to stain; to smear; to make dirty; to contaminate

【柔】 2397
(ㄖㄡˊ rou róu)

1. soft and tender

2. amiable; pliant; yielding; submissive; gentle; supple

3. the new grass budding in spring

柔媚(ㄖㄡˊ ㄇㄟˋ)
amiable, pliant and yielding

柔道(ㄖㄡˊ ㄉㄠˋ)
judo

柔荑(ㄖㄡˊ ㄊㄧˊ)
the young cogongrass—(figuratively) the soft and white fingers of a woman

柔嫩(ㄖㄡˊ ㄋㄣˋ)
soft and tender

柔能克剛(ㄖㄡˊ ㄋㄥˊ ㄎㄜˋ ㄍㄤ)
(literally) The soft will conquer the hard.—Soft and subtle approach can disarm a man of hot temper.

柔和(ㄖㄡˊ ㄏㄜˊ)
soft; gentle; amiable; tender; supple

the Chinese writing brush

柔化(ㄖㄡˊ ㄏㄨㄚˋ)
to soften; to tend to become weak and lax; to melt

柔情(ㄖㄡˊ ㄑㄧㄥˊ)
soft and sentimental; tender thoughts or affection; the tender feelings of a lover

柔情似水(ㄖㄡˊ ㄑㄧㄥˊ ㄙˋ ㄕㄨㄟˇ)
tender and soft as water

柔性(ㄖㄡˊ ㄒㄧㄥˋ)
pliancy; femininity; gentleness; softness; flexibility

柔腸寸斷(ㄖㄡˊ ㄔㄤˊ ㄘㄨㄣˋ ㄉㄨㄢˋ)
brokenhearted

柔聲(ㄖㄡˊ ㄕㄥ)
a soft voice

柔順(ㄖㄡˊ ㄕㄨㄣˋ)
gentle and yielding

柔日(ㄖㄡˊ ㄖˋ)
the days that bear the even-numbered signs of the Celestial Stems (天干)—as 乙丁己辛癸

柔韌(ㄖㄡˊ ㄖㄣˋ)
pliable yet tough—as silk, leather, etc.

柔茹剛吐(ㄖㄡˊ ㄖㄨˊ ㄍㄤ ㄊㄨˇ)
to oppress the weak and fear the strong

柔弱(ㄖㄡˊ ㄖㄨㄛˋ)
weak (physique); soft and meek; low and gentle (voice, etc.); feminine

柔軟(ㄖㄡˊ ㄖㄨㄢˇ)
soft; yielding; lithe

柔軟體操(ㄖㄡˊ ㄖㄨㄢˇ ㄊㄧˇ ㄘㄠ)
calisthenics

柔魚(ㄖㄡˊ ㄩˊ)
Ommastrephes pacificus, a kind of boneless fish pale in color with light-brown dots and a triangular tail, a favorite food for people on the South China coast

柔遠(ㄖㄡˊ ㄩㄢˇ)
to apply gentleness in the policy toward frontier people (in order to win their hearts)

【柑】 2398
(ㄍㄢ gan gān)
a mandarin orange

柑橘(ㄍㄢ ㄐㄩˊ)
①oranges and tangerines ②citruses

柑子(ㄍㄢ ㄗˇ)
a mandarin orange: 他喝了一杯柑子汁。He drank a glass of mandarin orange juice.

【柳】 2399
(ㄌㄧㄡˇ leou liǔ)

1. a willow tree: 柳樹生長在河邊。Willows grew beside the stream.

2. name of one of the 28 Constellations

3. (figuratively) a singsong house; the red-light district: 紳士不逛花街柳巷。The gentlemen avoid wandering in red-light district.

4. a tumor; a swelling; a lump

〔木部〕

5. a Chinese family name

柳眉(ㄌㄧㄡ ㄇㄟˊ)
the eyebrows of a beautiful woman—like leaves of the willow

柳眉倒豎(ㄌㄧㄡ ㄇㄟˊ ㄉㄠˇ ㄕㄨˋ)
(said of a girl) to look angry; to raise eyebrows in anger

柳眉杏眼(ㄌㄧㄡ ㄇㄟˊ ㄒㄧㄥˋ ㄧㄢˇ)
graceful eyebrows and large eyes

柳體(ㄌㄧㄡ ㄊㄧˇ)or 柳字(ㄌㄧㄡ ㄗˋ)
name of a calligraphic style created by Liu Kung-chüan (柳公權) of the Tang Dynasty

柳條(ㄌㄧㄡ ㄊㄧㄠˊ)
①a withy; an osier; a willow branch ②withy-like grain, patterns, etc.

柳條籃(ㄌㄧㄡ ㄊㄧㄠˊ ㄌㄢˊ)
an osier basket; a willow basket

柳公權(ㄌㄧㄡ ㄍㄨㄥ ㄑㄩㄢˊ)
Liu Kung-chüan, A. D. 778-865, a famous calligrapher in the Tang Dynasty

柳花(ㄌㄧㄡ ㄏㄨㄚ)
the willow blossom

柳下惠(ㄌㄧㄡ ㄒㄧㄚˋ ㄏㄨㄟˋ)
another name of Chan Chin (展禽), a virtuous scholar of the Epoch of Spring and Autumn, whose name has become a synonym for fortitude against the temptation of women

柳綫(ㄌㄧㄡ ㄒㄧㄢˋ)
long withies; willow branches

柳巷花街(ㄌㄧㄡ ㄒㄧㄤˋ ㄏㄨㄚ ㄐㄧㄝ)
streets and lanes where brothels abound; the red-light district 亦作「花街柳巷」

柳絮(ㄌㄧㄡ ㄒㄩˋ)
willow catkins

柳枝(ㄌㄧㄡ ㄓ)
a withy; a willow branch

柳橙(ㄌㄧㄡ ㄔㄥˊ)
an orange

柳杉(ㄌㄧㄡ ㄕㄢ)
(botany) cryptomeria

柳宗元(ㄌㄧㄡ ㄗㄨㄥ ㄩㄢˊ)
Liu Tzung-yüan, 773-819, one of the eight greatest prose writers of the Tang and Sung Dynasties

柳絲(ㄌㄧㄡ ㄙ)
fine willow branches

柳暗花明(ㄌㄧㄡ ㄢˋ ㄏㄨㄚ ㄇㄧㄥˊ)
dense willow trees and bright flowers—an enchanting sight in springtime

柳暗花明又一村(ㄌㄧㄡ ㄢˋ ㄏㄨㄚ ㄇㄧㄥˊ ㄧㄡˋ ㄧ ㄘㄨㄣ)
Every cloud has a silver lining.

柳芽兒(ㄌㄧㄡ ㄧㄚˊ ㄦ)
willow buds or sprouts

柳葉兒(ㄌㄧㄡ ㄧㄝˋ ㄦ)
①a willow leaves ②a kind of food made of flour dough shaped like willow leaves

柳腰(ㄌㄧㄡ ㄧㄠ)
a willowy waist; a slender waist: 柳腰娉婷. A lady who has a willowy waist is elegant and graceful.

柳陰(ㄌㄧㄡ ㄧㄣ)
shade of willow trees

柳永(ㄌㄧㄡ ㄩㄥˇ)
Liu Yung, died circa A. D. 1045, the most popular writer of lyrical songs (詞) of the Sung Dynasty

【柘】 2400
ㄓㄜˋ jeh zhè
1. Cudrania tricuspidata, a thorny tree about 15 feet high whose leaves can be used in place of mulberry leaves in feeding silkworms and whose bark contains a yellow dye
2. sugarcane

柘弓(ㄓㄜˋ ㄍㄨㄥ)
a slingshot made of the tree

柘榴(ㄓㄜˋ ㄌㄧㄡˊ)
the pomegranate

柘黃(ㄓㄜˋ ㄏㄨㄤˊ)
a yellow dye made from the bark of the tree

柘蠶(ㄓㄜˋ ㄘㄢˊ)
silkworms fed on the leaves of the tree

柘蠶絲(ㄓㄜˋ ㄘㄢˊ ㄙ)
silk from worms fed on these leaves

【柙】 2401
ㄒㄧㄚˊ shya xiá
1. a cage or a pen for wild beasts, especially the fierce ones
2. a scabbard; a case for a

sword

【柚】 2402
ㄧㄡˋ yow yòu
1. a pumelo or pomelo; a shaddock
2. a teak; a teak tree

柚木(ㄧㄡˋ ㄇㄨˋ)
①a teak; a teak tree ②teak; teakwood

柚子(ㄧㄡˋ ˙ㄗ)
a pumelo or pomelo; a shaddock

【柜】 2403
ㄐㄩˇ jeu jǔ
1. a tree of the willow family
2. same as 欅, a very large tree whose beautiful fine-grained wood is good for making furniture, etc.

柜柳(ㄐㄩˇ ㄌㄧㄡ)
①a tree of the willow family ②same as above「柜2.」

【柞】 2404
ㄗㄨㄛˋ tzuoh zuò
Xylosma congesta, an evergreen thorny tree with small leaves, fine and sturdy wood; an oak

柞綢(ㄗㄨㄛˋ ㄔㄡˊ)
a tussah silk fabric

柞蠶(ㄗㄨㄛˋ ㄘㄢˊ)
tussah silkworms

柞蠶絲(ㄗㄨㄛˋ ㄘㄢˊ ㄙ)
tussah silk

【柝】 2405
ㄊㄨㄛˋ tuoh tuò
a watchman's rattle; a watchman's clapper; a knocker

【柢】 2406
ㄉㄧˇ dii dǐ
the root; the foundation; the base

【柩】 2407
ㄐㄧㄡˋ jiow jiù
a coffin with a corpse in it

柩車(ㄐㄧㄡˋ ㄔㄜ)
a hearse

【柯】 2408
ㄎㄜ ke kē
1. Pasania cuspidata, a tall evergreen tree
2. the handle of an ax
3. the stalk or the trunk of a plant
4. a Chinese family name

柯達(ㄎㄜ ㄉㄚˊ)
Kodak, a brand name

柯駕 (ㄎㄜ ㄐㄧㄚˋ)
a respectful reference to the marriage go-between

柯維納 (ㄎㄜ ㄨㄟˊ ㄋㄚˋ)
Monte Covino, A. D. 1247-1328, an Italian priest who went to China as a missionary in A. D. 1289, and later translated the *New Testament* into Chinese

【柱】 2409 ㄓㄨˋ juh zhù
1. a pillar; a post: 門廊的屋頂由磚柱支撐。The roof of the porch was supported by brick pillars.
2. a cylinder
3. to support
4. to stab; to pierce

柱面 (ㄓㄨˋ ㄇㄧㄢˋ)
(mathematics) a cylindrical surface

柱頂 (ㄓㄨˋ ㄉㄧㄥˇ)
(architecture) the uppermost portion of a column or pillar; a capital

柱頭 (ㄓㄨˋ ㄊㄡˊ)
(botany) a stigma

柱廊 (ㄓㄨˋ ㄌㄤˊ)
a colonnade

柱下史 (ㄓㄨˋ ㄒㄧㄚˋ ㄕˇ) or 柱史 (ㄓㄨˋ ㄕˇ)
an official rank originated in the Chin Dynasty, similar to that of an imperial censor

柱臣 (ㄓㄨˋ ㄔㄣˊ)
the important ministers of a nation

柱石 (ㄓㄨˋ ㄕˊ)
the pillars of a nation; the key ministers of a nation: 三軍是國家的柱石。The armed forces are the pillars of a nation.

柱石岩 (ㄓㄨˋ ㄕˊ ㄧㄢˊ)
the basalt (of a column)

柱子 (ㄓㄨˋ ˙ㄗ)
a pillar; a post

【柬】 2410 ㄐㄧㄢˇ jean jiǎn
1. a letter; an invitation or visiting card
2. to select; to pick

柬埔寨 (ㄐㄧㄢˇ ㄅㄨˇ ㄓㄞˋ)
Cambodia

柬帖 (ㄐㄧㄢˇ ㄊㄧㄝˇ)
①an invitation card ②(in old China) a red visiting card

柬請 (ㄐㄧㄢˇ ㄑㄧㄥˇ)
to invite by letter or by invitation card

柬邀 (ㄐㄧㄢˇ ㄧㄠ)
to invite by letter or by invitation card

【查】 2411 ㄔㄚˊ char chá
1. to investigate; to check; to seek out; to look into: 讓我們把這件事查個水落石出。Let's get to the bottom of the matter.
2. (used at the beginning of the official correspondence) It appears...或 It seems...或 It is known...或 It is found that...
3. a wooden raft

查辦 (ㄔㄚˊ ㄅㄢˋ)
to investigate into the irregularities (of an official or employee) and mete out due punishment: 我們將他撤職查辦。We dismiss him and have him prosecuted.

查不出來 (ㄔㄚˊ ㄅㄨˋ ㄔㄨ ㄌㄞˊ)
cannot find out (a fact); cannot check out (a figure)

查票 (ㄔㄚˊ ㄆㄧㄠˋ)
to examine or check tickets

查明 (ㄔㄚˊ ㄇㄧㄥˊ)
to investigate and clarify; to examine to the last detail; to find out: 他已查明事實真相。He has found out the truth.

查房 (ㄔㄚˊ ㄈㄤˊ)
①(said of the police) to check hotel guests at their rooms ②(said of doctors) to make the rounds of the wards: 醫生通常在上午查房間。The doctors usually make the rounds of the wards in the morning.

查訪 (ㄔㄚˊ ㄈㄤˇ)
to go around and make inquiries; to investigate

查封 (ㄔㄚˊ ㄈㄥ)
the execution of a court order by which all property of a debtor would be placed under legal custody until further action

查德 (ㄔㄚˊ ㄉㄜˊ)
Chad

查點 (ㄔㄚˊ ㄉㄧㄢˇ)
to check (the number of prisoners, students, a list of goods, etc.)

查對 (ㄔㄚˊ ㄉㄨㄟˋ)
to check or examine one by one, to verity: 查對一下這些數目字好嗎？Will you check these figures?

查理 (ㄔㄚˊ ㄌㄧˇ)
a transliteration of Charles

查理曼大帝 (ㄔㄚˊ ㄌㄧˇ ㄇㄢˋ ㄉㄚˋ ㄉㄧˋ)
Charlemagne the Great, A. D. 742-814

查理斯敦 (ㄔㄚˊ ㄌㄧˇ ㄙ ㄉㄨㄣ)
①Charleston, capital of West Virginia, U.S.A. ②a seaport in South Carolina, U.S.A.

查理所 (ㄔㄚˊ ㄌㄧˇ ㄙㄨㄛˇ)
to investigate; to examine; to ponder; to ascertain: 我想查考這所學校的建校日期。I wish to ascertain the date of the establishment of this school.

查看 (ㄔㄚˊ ㄎㄢˋ)
to examine; to investigate; to look into (a matter): 市長查看災情。The mayor looked into the extent of the disaster.

查勘 (ㄔㄚˊ ㄎㄢ)
to survey and examine; to investigate: 警方查勘犯罪的現場。The police surveyed the scene of the crime.

查庫 (ㄔㄚˊ ㄎㄨˋ)
to inspect the treasury; the inspection of the treasury

查核 (ㄔㄚˊ ㄏㄜˊ)
to check and examine; to investigate

查號台 (ㄔㄚˊ ㄏㄠˋ ㄊㄞˊ)
directory information

查戶口 (ㄔㄚˊ ㄏㄨˋ ㄎㄡˇ)
(said of the police or census officials) to make checks from house to house: 警察每年查戶口。The policemen check on household occupants every year.

查獲 (ㄔㄚˊ ㄏㄨㄛˋ)
to hunt down and seize; to ferret out; to track down: 警察查獲逃犯。The policemen

〔木部〕

〔木部〕

tracked down a fugitive criminal.

查究(彳ㄚ ㄐㄧㄡˋ)
to search into (a matter); to seek out (the cause, etc. of something): 政府查究責任。 The government found out who should be held responsible. 醫分查辦辦理。 The policemen investigate and act accordingly.

查禁(彳ㄚ ㄐㄧㄣˋ)
to prohibit or ban after investigation (usually said of pornographic books, immoral shows, gambling, etc.): 警察查禁這本書。 The policeman banned this book.

查經(彳ㄚ ㄐㄧㄥ)
to study the Bible; Bible study

查卷(彳ㄚ ㄐㄩㄢˋ)
①to check examination papers already graded to see if there is any mistake in grading ②to look into official files to find something for reference

查訖(彳ㄚ ㄑㄧˋ)
checked

查勤(彳ㄚ ㄑㄧㄣˊ)
to make the rounds and check officers, etc. to see if they are doing their duties during office hours

查清(彳ㄚ ㄑㄧㄥ)
to investigate thoroughly; to clarify: 偵探已查清他的來歷。 The detective has found out his background.

查詢(彳ㄚ ㄒㄩㄣˊ)
to inquire about; to inquire: 我向他查詢他的事。 I inquired of him about her.

查照(彳ㄚ ㄓㄠˋ)
(a documentary usage) to have learned (from your letter, etc.); to look into and act accordingly: 請查照辦理。 Please consider and act accordingly.

查賬 or 查帳(彳ㄚ ㄓㄤˋ)
to audit (accounts); an audit: 每年一次的查賬在十二月舉行。 The yearly audit takes place each December.

查賬員 or 查帳員(彳ㄚ ㄓㄤˋ ㄩㄢˊ)
an auditor

查證(彳ㄚ ㄓㄥˋ)
to investigate and verify; to check

查抄(彳ㄚ ㄔㄠ)
(in old China) to search out the property of a criminal (usually a corrupt official) and confiscate it: 法院查抄犯人財產。 The court made an inventory of a criminal's possessions and confiscated them.

查出(彳ㄚ ㄔㄨ)
to find out; to discover

查鋪(彳ㄚ ㄆㄨˋ)
(military)to check the beds at night; a bed check

查哨(彳ㄚ ㄕㄠˋ)
(military) to tour the guard posts to see if the sentries are doing their jobs; to go the rounds of guard posts; to inspect the sentries

查收(彳ㄚ ㄕㄡ)
to check the goods delivered and take them over 或 Please find....

查稅(彳ㄚ ㄕㄨㄟˋ)
tax inspection

查字典(彳ㄚ ㄗˋ ㄉㄧㄢˇ)
to consult a dictionary; to look it up in a dictionary: 我查字典。 I looked up a word in the dictionary.

查案(彳ㄚ ㄢˋ)
to investigate into a case

查夜(彳ㄚ ㄧㄝˋ)
(the police usage) to make the rounds within the beat; to go the rounds at night; night patrol

查驗(彳ㄚ ㄧㄢˋ)
to investigate; to examine; to inspect: 移民官員查驗護照。 The immigration officer examined passports.

查無實據(彳ㄚ ㄨˊ ㄕˊ ㄐㄩˋ)
(a cliché in official correspondence) It has been found that the report (or accusation) is not substantiated by facts. 或 Investigation reveals no evidence.

查問(彳ㄚ ㄨㄣˋ)or 查訊(彳ㄚ ㄒㄩㄣˋ)
to make inquiry; to look into; to investigate; to interrogate: 法官查問犯人。 The judge interrogated a pris-

oner.

查閱(彳ㄚ ㄩㄝˋ)
to consult (a book, etc.); to study (the Bible, etc.)

【查】 2411
2. ㄓㄚ ja zhā
a Chinese family name

【奈】 2412
ㄋㄞˋ nay nài
1. an apple tree
2. how
3. Then what?
4. sometimes used with a negative—(no) way out of a dilemma
5. to bear; to endure

奈何(ㄋㄞˋ ㄏㄜˊ)
①no way out; what other alternative (when there isn't any) ②to punish; to deal with; to injure 亦作「奈何」

奈花(ㄋㄞˋ ㄏㄨㄚ)
apple blossoms

奈園(ㄋㄞˋ ㄩㄢˊ) or 奈苑(ㄋㄞˋ ㄩㄢˋ)
a Buddhist temple

【柴】 2413
ㄔㄞˊ chair chái
1. firewood; brushwood; faggots
2. thin; emaciated
3. (now rarely) a fence
4. a Chinese family name

柴門(ㄔㄞˊ ㄇㄣˊ)
①a door of brushwood—a poor family②to shut one's door to all visitors

柴米(ㄔㄞˊ ㄇㄧˇ)
fuel and rice—the household needs

柴米夫妻(ㄔㄞˊ ㄇㄧˇ ㄈㄨ ㄑㄧ)
a couple who live from hand to mouth; a pair who got married for financial reasons

柴米油鹽(ㄔㄞˊ ㄇㄧˇ ㄧㄡˊ ㄧㄢˊ)
daily necessities; everyday goods

柴扉(ㄔㄞˊ ㄈㄟ)
a door of brushwood—a poor family

柴可夫(ㄔㄞˊ ㄎㄜˇ ㄈㄨ)
Anton Pavlovich Chekhov, 1860-1904, Russian writer

柴可夫斯基(ㄔㄞˊ ㄎㄜˇ ㄈㄨ ㄙ ㄐㄧ)
Peter Ilich Tchaikovsky, 1840—1893, Russian composer

柴行(ㄔㄞˊ ㄏㄤˊ)

a shop where faggots or firewood is sold

柴胡 (彳ㄞ ㄏㄨˊ)
Bupleurum falcatum, a plant about two to four inches tall with yellow flowers whose roots are used in herbal medicine

柴火 (彳ㄞ ㄏㄨㄛˇ) or 柴薪 (彳ㄞ ㄒㄧㄣ)
firewood; fuel

柴居 (彳ㄞ ㄐㄩ)
to live in the country; to rusticate

柴車 (彳ㄞ 彳ㄜ)
a crude carriage

柴窯 (彳ㄞ ㄧㄠˊ)
name of a famous pottery kiln built in Honan during the Epoch of the Five Dynasties

柴油 (彳ㄞ ㄧㄡˊ)
diesel oil

【柷】 2414
　　ㄓㄨˋ juh jhù
an ancient instrument made of wood which is played at the start of an orchestra

【柮】 2415
　　ㄉㄨㄛˊ duoh duó
firewood

【柵】 2416
　　ㄓㄚˋ jhà zhà
a fence of bamboos or wood; a palisade; a railing of posts; window-bars

柵門 (ㄓㄚˋ ㄇㄣˊ)
a door in a palisade

柵欄 (ㄓㄚˋ·ㄌㄢˊ)
a fence; a palisade; a railing: 他們住家四周有柵欄兒。 They have a fence around their house.

柵極電路 (ㄓㄚˋ ㄐㄧˊ ㄉㄧㄢˋ ㄌㄨˋ)
(electricity) a grid circuit

【柶】 2417
　　ㄙ syh sì
a dagger-shaped ritual vessel in ancient China, made of horn

【柁】 2418
1. (舵) ㄉㄨㄛˊ duoh duó
the rudder or helm of a ship; a rudder

【柁】 2418
2. ㄊㄨㄛˊ two tuó
large tie beams; girders

【枰】 2419
　　ㄆㄧㄥˊ pyng píng
1. a chessboard
2. a chess game

【柖】 2420
　　ㄊㄞˊ tair tái
1. same as 檯—a desk or table
2. an ancient unit of measurement

柖球 (ㄊㄞˊ ㄑㄧㄡˊ)
table tennis

六畫

【栓】 2421
　　ㄕㄨㄢ shuan shuān
1. a wooden pin; a peg
2. a bolt; a plug: 門栓 a door bolt
3. a stopper; a cork

栓子 (ㄕㄨㄢ ㄗˇ)
(medicine) an embolus

【柹】 2422
　　ㄕ shyh shì
1. name of a kind of tree
2. a wooden object used in divination

【栖】 2423
　　(棲) ㄑㄧ chi qī
　　(又讀 ㄒㄧ shi xī)
1. (said of birds) to roost; to perch
2. to settle; to live; to stay

栖遑 (ㄑㄧ ㄏㄨㄤˊ)
uneasy and anxious

栖栖皇皇 (ㄑㄧ ㄑㄧ ㄏㄨㄤˊ ㄏㄨㄤˊ)
vexed; rushing about

栖栖惑惑 (ㄑㄧ ㄑㄧ ㄏㄨㄛˋ ㄏㄨㄛˋ)
bustling and excited

【栝】 2424
　　ㄍㄨㄚ gua guā
1. same as 檜—a Chinese juniper
2. the pointed end of an arrow

【栩】 2425
　　ㄒㄩˇ sheu xǔ
1. a species of oak
2. glad; pleased

栩栩 (ㄒㄩˇ ㄒㄩˇ)
vivid; lively

栩栩然 (ㄒㄩˇ ㄒㄩˇ ㄖㄢˊ)
very glad and pleased

栩栩如生 (ㄒㄩˇ ㄒㄩˇ ㄖㄨˊ ㄕㄥ)
(said of a portrait, etc.) true to life; lifelike; to the life: 舅父的畫像畫得栩栩如生。 The portrait is my uncle to the life.

【栗】 2426
　　ㄌㄧˋ lih lì
1. a chestnut tree
2. strong and tough; firm; durable
3. respectful; fearful; awe-inspiring
4. to tremble: 他不寒而栗。 He trembled with fear.
5. dignified; majestic
6. a Chinese family name

栗苞 (ㄌㄧˋ ㄅㄠ)
a chestnut burr

栗木 (ㄌㄧˋ ㄇㄨˋ)
chestnut

栗犢 (ㄌㄧˋ ㄉㄨˊ)
a calf (whose horns are as large as chestnuts)

栗碌 (ㄌㄧˋ ㄌㄨˋ)
busy; pressing official duties

栗鼠 (ㄌㄧˋ ㄕㄨˇ)
a squirrel

栗子 (ㄌㄧˋ ㄗ)
chestnuts

栗色 (ㄌㄧˋ ㄙㄜˋ)
chestnut color; maroon

栗尾 (ㄌㄧˋ ㄨㄟˇ)
a Chinese writing brush

【株】 2427
　　ㄓㄨ ju zhū
1. a tree; a numerary auxiliary for counting trees or similar things
2. roots that grow above the ground

株蔓 (ㄓㄨ ㄇㄢˋ)
to involve people, relatives, etc. in a crime

株連 (ㄓㄨ ㄌㄧㄢˊ)
to involve others in a crime one committed (especially in ancient China when the friends or relatives of a person who committed treason could get such incrimination); to implicate

株戮 (ㄓㄨ ㄌㄨˋ)
to be executed for a crime committed by one's relatives or friends

株幹 (ㄓㄨ ㄍㄢˋ)
the trunk of a tree

株守 (ㄓㄨ ㄕㄡˇ)
to take no action but wish that something would come

one's way

【核】 2428
ㄏㄜˊ her hé

1. a kernel; a fruit stone; a walnut; a pit
2. to investigate; to examine; to verify; to study; to check
3. a nucleus; nuclear
4. a hard lump

核爆(ㄏㄜˊㄅㄠ)
the nuclear blast; a nuclear explosion

核辦(ㄏㄜˊㄅㄢˋ)
to study and examine (a case, etc.) and act accordingly; to consider and carry out accordingly

核膜(ㄏㄜˊㄇㄛˊ)
the membrane enclosing the nucleus of a cell

核反應(ㄏㄜˊㄈㄢˇㄧㄥˋ)
nuclear reaction

核分裂(ㄏㄜˊㄈㄣㄌㄧㄝˋ)or核子分裂(ㄏㄜˊㄗˇㄈㄣㄌㄧㄝˋ)
nuclear fission

核幅射(ㄏㄜˊㄈㄨˊㄕㄜˋ)
nuclear radiation

核覆(ㄏㄜˊㄈㄨˋ)
to make a reply after thorough investigation

核彈頭(ㄏㄜˊㄉㄢˋㄊㄡˊ)
a nuclear warhead 亦作「核子彈頭」

核彈攻擊(ㄏㄜˊㄉㄢˋㄍㄨㄥㄐㄧˊ)
nuking

核定(ㄏㄜˊㄉㄧㄥˋ)
①to decide after examination ②to fix or approve (a sum, budget, etc.) for a project, etc.; to check and ratify

核奪(ㄏㄜˊㄉㄨㄛˊ)
to make your kind decision after examination

核對(ㄏㄜˊㄉㄨㄟˋ)
to verify; to check (the facts): 將你的答案與我的核對一下。Check your answers with mine.

核桃(ㄏㄜˊㄊㄠˊ)
a walnut

核能(ㄏㄜˊㄋㄥˊ)
nuclear energy

核能發電(ㄏㄜˊㄋㄥˊㄈㄚㄉㄧㄢˋ)
nuclear power

核能電廠(ㄏㄜˊㄋㄥˊㄉㄧㄢˋㄔㄤˇ)
a nuclear power station

核果(ㄏㄜˊㄍㄨㄛˇ)
a drupe; a stone fruit

核擴散(ㄏㄜˊㄎㄨㄛˋㄙㄢˋ)
nuclear proliferation

核計(ㄏㄜˊㄐㄧˋ)
to examine and calculate

核減(ㄏㄜˊㄐㄧㄢˇ)
to cut (a budget, an estimate, etc.) after examination

核銷(ㄏㄜˊㄒㄧㄠ)
to verify accounts, budgets, etc. and find them faultless

核效應(ㄏㄜˊㄒㄧㄠˋㄧㄥˋ)
nuclear effect

核心(ㄏㄜˊㄒㄧㄣ)
①the core (of a matter, etc.) ②the inner circle (of a political party, government, etc.)

核心人物(ㄏㄜˊㄒㄧㄣㄖㄣˊㄨˋ)
a key person; a key figure

核准(ㄏㄜˊㄓㄨㄣˇ)
to approve; approval: 校長已核准有關該節日的計劃。The principal gave his approval to plans for the holiday.

核實(ㄏㄜˊㄕˊ)
to examine the facts; on-the-spot investigation

核示(ㄏㄜˊㄕˋ)
to consider or examine a matter and give instructions accordingly

核試驗(ㄏㄜˊㄕˋㄧㄢˋ)or核子試爆(ㄏㄜˊㄗˇㄕˋㄅㄠˋ)
a nuclear test

核仁(ㄏㄜˊㄖㄣˊ)
①a nucleolus ②the kernel (of a fruit stone)

核融合(ㄏㄜˊㄖㄨㄥˊㄏㄜˊ)
nuclear fusion

核子(ㄏㄜˊㄗˇ)
a nucleus; a nucleon

核子彈頭(ㄏㄜˊㄗˇㄉㄢˋㄊㄡˊ)
a nuclear warhead 亦作「核彈頭」

核子動力船(ㄏㄜˊㄗˇㄉㄨㄥˋㄌㄧˋㄔㄨㄢˊ)
a nuclear ship

核子潛艇(ㄏㄜˊㄗˇㄑㄧㄢˊㄊㄧㄥˇ)
a nuclear submarine

核子戰略(ㄏㄜˊㄗˇㄓㄢˋㄌㄩㄝˋ)
nuclear strategy

核子戰爭(ㄏㄜˊㄗˇㄓㄢˋㄓㄥ)
nuclear war

核子武器(ㄏㄜˊㄗˇㄨˇㄑㄧˋ)
nuclear weapons

核算(ㄏㄜˊㄙㄨㄢˋ)
to examine and calculate

核兒(ㄏㄜˊㄦ)or
the kernel; the fruit stone

核議(ㄏㄜˊㄧˋ)
to decide after consideration

【校】 2429
1. ㄒㄧㄠˋ shiaw xiào
1. a school: 鎮城有五所學校。There are five schools in the town.
2. field-grade (officers)

校本部(ㄒㄧㄠˋㄅㄣˇㄅㄨˋ)
the main campus of a school

校門(ㄒㄧㄠˋㄇㄣˊ)
a gate of a school or college

校風(ㄒㄧㄠˋㄈㄥ)
the characteristic of a particular school; the style of a school; the prevailing atmosphere in a school (especially referring to the conduct of the students); school tradition; school spirit: 他們學習牛津大學的優良校風。They learned from the spirit of Oxford University.

校服(ㄒㄧㄠˋㄈㄨˊ)
school uniform

校隊(ㄒㄧㄠˋㄉㄨㄟˋ)
the school team

校童(ㄒㄧㄠˋㄉㄨㄥˊ)
directors of a school

校童會(ㄒㄧㄠˋㄉㄨㄥˊㄏㄨㄟˋ)
the board of directors or trustees of a school

校內(ㄒㄧㄠˋㄋㄟˋ)
within or inside the school

校歌(ㄒㄧㄠˋㄍㄜ)
a school song; a college song

校規(ㄒㄧㄠˋㄍㄨㄟ)
school regulations; school discipline: 他違反校規。He broke school regulations.

校官(ㄒㄧㄠˋㄍㄨㄢ)
field-grade officers

校刊(ㄒㄧㄠˋㄎㄢ)
a school magazine; a school bulletin

校花(ㄒㄧㄠˋㄏㄨㄚ)
a campus queen; a school belle

校徽(ㄒㄧㄠˋㄏㄨㄟ)
a school emblem; a badge

校際(ㄒㄧㄠˋㄐㄧˋ)
interscholastic; intercolle-

giate

校警(ㄒㄧㄠ ㄐㄧㄥ)
the police guards of a school

校旗(ㄒㄧㄠ ㄑㄧˊ)
a school flag

校慶(ㄒㄧㄠ ㄑㄧㄥˋ)
anniversary celebrations of a school; 我們慶祝校慶。We celebrate the anniversary of the founding of our school.

校訓(ㄒㄧㄠ ㄒㄩㄣˋ)
a school motto

校址(ㄒㄧㄠ ㄓˇ)
the location of a school

校長(ㄒㄧㄠ ㄓㄤˇ)
a principal; a schoolmaster; the president or chancellor of a university; the commandant of a military academy

校長室(ㄒㄧㄠ ㄓㄤˇ ㄕˋ)
the schoolmaster's office; the president's office

校車(ㄒㄧㄠ ㄔㄜ)
a school bus

校舍(ㄒㄧㄠ ㄕㄜˋ)
school premises; school buildings; 他在這校舍一帶流連。He lingered about the school premises.

校醫(ㄒㄧㄠ ㄧ)
a school doctor or physician; 你如生病，即刻去看校醫。If you are ill, go to see a school doctor at once.

校友(ㄒㄧㄠ ㄧㄡˇ)
an alumnus or alumna; alumni or alumnae

校友會(ㄒㄧㄠ ㄧㄡˇ ㄏㄨㄟˋ)
an alumni association; 他們是這個校友會的會員。They are members of the alumni association.

校務(ㄒㄧㄠ ㄨˋ)
school administration; college administration

校外(ㄒㄧㄠ ㄨㄞˋ)
outside the school

校譽(ㄒㄧㄠ ㄩˋ)
the reputation or prestige of a school or college

校園(ㄒㄧㄠ ㄩㄢˊ)
the school ground; the campus

【校】 2429
2. ㄐㄧㄠˋ jiaw jiào
1. to compare

2. to proofread; proofs: 五校 the fifth proof; to proofread for the fifth time
3. to revise (books, etc.); to collate

校本(ㄒㄧㄠˋ ㄅㄣˇ)
an incomplete or deleted edition with addition of words copied from the original version

校訂(ㄒㄧㄠˋ ㄉㄧㄥˋ)
to revise: 他正在校訂手稿。He is revising a manuscript.

校訂本(ㄒㄧㄠˋ ㄉㄧㄥˋ ㄅㄣˇ)
a revised edition

校對(ㄒㄧㄠˋ ㄉㄨㄟˋ)
①to proofread; to correct proofs: 我編寫和校對這些書。I edited and proofed these books. ②a proofreader ③to calibrate

校理(ㄒㄧㄠˋ ㄌㄧˇ)
①to revise and arrange (a book, etc.) ②a secretarial rank in the Tang Dynasty

校獵(ㄒㄧㄠˋ ㄌㄧㄝˋ)
to hunt animals or birds on grounds enclosed with wooden posts or boards

校改(ㄒㄧㄠˋ ㄍㄞˇ)
to read and correct proofs

校勘(ㄒㄧㄠˋ ㄎㄢ)
to collate; to compare and correct

校正(ㄒㄧㄠˋ ㄓㄥˋ)
to correct; to correct proofs: 我校正我書中的錯字。I corrected misprints in my book.

校準(ㄒㄧㄠˋ ㄓㄨㄣˇ)
calibration: 方位校準 bearing calibration

校讐(ㄒㄧㄠˋ ㄔㄡˊ)
to collate or proofread (books, etc.)

校場(ㄒㄧㄠˋ ㄔㄤˇ)
(in ancient China) a military drill ground

校書(ㄒㄧㄠˋ ㄕㄨ)
①to proofread books ②a euphemism for "prostitute"

校樣(ㄒㄧㄠˋ ㄧㄤˋ)
galley proofs: 我已看完校樣。I have read the proofs.

校閱(ㄒㄧㄠˋ ㄩㄝˋ)
①to examine; to collate; to read and revise ②to inspect troops, honor guards, etc.: 總統校閱軍隊。The president inspected troops.

【栲】 2430
ㄎㄠˇ kao kǒo
(botany) Castanopsis hystrix

【根】 2431
ㄍㄣ gen gēn
1. the root of a plant: 他們將那樹連根拔起。They pulled up the tree by the roots.
2. a base; a foundation
3. the beginning, cause, or source of something
4. (mathematics) the root of a number: 2 是 4 的平方根。Two is the square root of four.
5. (chemistry) radical
6. a piece (of string, rope, etc.); a (stick, spear or thing of slender shape)
7. a Chinese family name

根本(ㄍㄣ ㄅㄣˇ)
①a root; a base; an origin; a foundation; a basis ②at all; basically: 這件事根本就不對。This matter is basically wrong.

根本辦法(ㄍㄣ ㄅㄣˇ ㄅㄢˋ ㄈㄚˇ)
basic principles of action; basic methods or measures

根本觀念(ㄍㄣ ㄅㄣˇ ㄍㄨㄢ ㄋㄧㄢˋ)
a radical conception

根本解決(ㄍㄣ ㄅㄣˇ ㄐㄧㄝˇ ㄐㄩㄝˊ)
a radical solution; to settle something once for all

根本上(ㄍㄣ ㄅㄣˇ ㄕㄤˋ)
basically; fundamentally; radically: 英語根本上是一種日耳曼語。English is radically a Germanic language.

根本問題(ㄍㄣ ㄅㄣˇ ㄨㄣˋ ㄊㄧˊ)
fundamental questions

根部(ㄍㄣ ㄅㄨˋ)
the root of a plant

根末(ㄍㄣ ㄇㄛˋ)
root and branch—throughout; altogether; completely

根毛(ㄍㄣ ㄇㄠˊ)
root hairs

根苗(ㄍㄣ ㄇㄧㄠˊ)
①the root, source or origin ②roots and shoots

根底(ㄍㄣ ㄉㄧˇ)
①the origin, cause and effect, or the ins and outs of something ②a basis; a foundation ③the possessions or financial standing: 她頗有根

〔木部〕

底。She is quite well-to-do. ④ background learning; early training: 你的根底很好。You have good scholastic training. ⑤ background

［木 部］

根柢《ㄍㄣ ㄉㄧˇ》
①the root of a plant ②a basis; a foundation

根瘤《ㄍㄣ ㄌㄧㄡˊ》
root nodules; root tubercles

根號《ㄍㄣ ㄏㄠˋ》
(mathematics) the radical sign

根基
①《ㄍㄣ ㄐㄧ》ⓐ foundation (in learning): 我要打好英文的根基。I want to lay a solid foundation in English.ⓑ financial standing
②《ㄍㄣ ㄐㄧ》behavior or conduct

根脚《ㄍㄣ ㄐㄧㄠˇ》
a foundation; a base

根究《ㄍㄣ ㄐㄧㄡˋ》
to go to the very root or source of something; to get to the bottom of; to probe into: 這事必須根究。This matter must be probed to the bottom.

根莖《ㄍㄣ ㄐㄧㄥ》
a rhizome; a rootstock

根據《ㄍㄣ ㄐㄩˋ》
①a basis; a root, source or origin; grounds: 毫無根據。It is utterly groundless. ②in accordance with (the regulation, etc.); on the strength of; in the light of: 根據天氣預報，將要下雨。According to the weather forecast, it will rain.

根據地《ㄍㄣ ㄐㄩˋ ㄉㄧˋ》
a base (of operations); a home base

根絕《ㄍㄣ ㄐㄩㄝˊ》
to root out (a problem, vice, etc.); to exterminate completely

根器《ㄍㄣ ㄑㄧˋ》
natural gift or inclination for (religious faith and achievement, etc.)

根鬚《ㄍㄣ ㄒㄩ》
fibrous roots

根治《ㄍㄣ ㄓˋ》
a radical treatment (for a disease, etc.); to cure (a dis-

ease) for good

根揷《ㄍㄣ ㄔㄚ》
root cutting

根除《ㄍㄣ ㄔㄨˊ》
thoroughly to do away with; to eradicate; to root out; to eliminate; to exterminate; to uproot (social evils); to effect a cure (of disease): 我們將根除水患。We'll eliminate the scourge of floods.

根深蒂固《ㄍㄣ ㄕㄣ ㄉㄧˋ ㄍㄨˋ》
deep-rooted; time-honored; firmly established; deeply entrenched

根深葉茂《ㄍㄣ ㄕㄣ ㄧㄝˋ ㄇㄠˋ》
The root is deep and leaves are many.—to be well established and vigorously developing; flourishing for a long time

根生土長《ㄍㄣ ㄕㄥ ㄊㄨˇ ㄓㄤˇ》
to be born and raised in a place: 根是生土長的中國人。He was born and raised in China.

根數《ㄍㄣ ㄕㄨˋ》
(mathematics) radical

根子《ㄍㄣ ˙ㄗ》or **根須**《ㄍㄣ ㄦ》
①the root of a plant; the base ②a source; an origin: 這個問題的根子是什麼？What's the source of the trouble?

根芽《ㄍㄣ ㄧㄚˊ》
a radicle

根由《ㄍㄣ ㄧㄡˊ》
the source, origin or cause of something

根源《ㄍㄣ ㄩㄢˊ》
the cause, source or origin of something: 貪財爲百禍之根源。The greed of money is the root of all evil.

【桁】2432 1.ㄏㄥˊ herng héng
the purlins of a roof

桁桷《ㄏㄥˊ ㄐㄩㄝˊ》
purlins and rafters

【桁】2432 2.ㄏㄤˊ harng háng
a big wooden collar (for punishing a criminal)

桁楊《ㄏㄤˊ ㄧㄤˊ》
a cangue

【桁】2432 3.ㄏㄤˋ hang hàng
a rack for hanging clothes

【格】2433 《ㄍㄜˊ ger gé
1. to correct; to adjust or regulate
2. to reach; to come or go to
3. to influence
4. to resist; to attack; to fight
5. to obstruct; to block
6. to study thoroughly; to search to the very source; to investigate
7. a standard; a form; a rule; a pattern; a style: 他的小說獨創一格。His fiction was original in style.
8. a frame; a trellis
9. squares formed by crossed lines
10.a Chinese family name

格非《ㄍㄜˊ ㄈㄟ》
to correct the wrong and evil ways

格鬥《ㄍㄜˊ ㄉㄡˋ》
a brawl; a hand-to-hand fight; a free-for-all; fisticuffs: 孩子們在格鬥。The boys are fighting hand to hand.

格調《ㄍㄜˊ ㄉㄧㄠˋ》
①literary or artistic style; form; pattern: 他的小說格調豪放。His novels have a vigorous and flowing style.

格度《ㄍㄜˊ ㄉㄨˋ》
one's moral character and bearing

格拉斯哥《ㄍㄜˊ ㄌㄚ ㄙ ㄍㄜ》
Glasgow, a city in Scotland

格蘭姆《ㄍㄜˊ ㄌㄢˊ ㄇㄨˇ》
gram, metric unit of weight 亦作「克」

格林威治《ㄍㄜˊ ㄌㄧㄣˊ ㄨㄟ ㄓˋ》
Greenwich

格林威治時間《ㄍㄜˊ ㄌㄧㄣˊ ㄨㄟ ㄓˋ ㄕ ㄐㄧㄢ》
Greenwich Mean Time (GMT)

格陵蘭《ㄍㄜˊ ㄌㄧㄥˊ ㄌㄢˊ》
Greenland

格律《ㄍㄜˊ ㄌㄩˋ》
①standard; form; pattern ②the meter of poetry, etc., with special emphasis on the number of words, rhymes, etc.

格格《ㄍㄜˊ ㄍㄜˊ》or《ㄍㄜˊ ˙ㄍㄜ》
totally incompatible with; to be out of tune with; to be

like a square peg in a round hole; cannot get along with

格格(ㄍㄜˊㄍㄜˊ)
a princess in the Ching Dynasty

格局(ㄍㄜˊㄐㄩˊ)
structure and form; style; setup

格心(ㄍㄜˊㄒㄧㄣ)
to correct one's heart (and lead him to the ways of the good)

格致(ㄍㄜˊㄓˋ)
①to investigate things and extend knowledge to the utmost ②an old name for physics

格式(ㄍㄜˊㄕ)
form; patterns; format: 他懂得公文格式。He knows of the form of an official document.

格殺(ㄍㄜˊㄕㄚ)
to kill in fighting

格殺勿論(ㄍㄜˊㄕㄚㄨˋㄌㄨㄣˋ)
to kill on sight; to shoot on sight; to execute summarily

格瑞那達(ㄍㄜˊㄖㄨㄟˋㄋㄚˋㄉㄚˊ)
Grenada

格子(ㄍㄜˊ˙ㄗ)or 格兒(ㄍㄜˊㄦ)
a square frame or blank; a trellis; a lattice

格子布(ㄍㄜˊ˙ㄗㄅㄨˋ)
checkered or checked cloth

格子窗(ㄍㄜˊ˙ㄗㄔㄨㄤ)
a lattice window

格言(ㄍㄜˊㄧㄢˊ)
a proverb; a motto; an aphorism; a maxim

格物致知(ㄍㄜˊㄨˋㄓˋㄓ)
to investigate things and to extend knowledge to the utmost

格外(ㄍㄜˊㄨㄞˋ)
exceptions; exceptional; extraordinary; unusual; exceptionally; unusually; extraordinarily; especially

格外開恩(ㄍㄜˊㄨㄞˋㄎㄞㄣ)
to pardon an offender; to punish an offender lightly

格於規定(ㄍㄜˊㄩˊㄍㄨㄟㄉㄧㄥˋ)
(not permissible) because of existing regulations; to be barred by regulations

【桀】 2434
ㄐㄧㄝˊ jye jié

1. ferocious and cruel
2. name of the last ruler of the Hsia Dynasty
3. same as 傑, outstanding and brave
4. a Chinese family name

桀犬吠堯(ㄐㄧㄝˊㄑㄩㄢˇㄈㄟˋㄧㄠˊ)
(literally) The dog of Chieh (the symbol of evil) barked at Yao (the symbol of good).—Each faithfully serves his own master.

桀黠(ㄐㄧㄝˊㄒㄧㄚˊ)
crooked and cruel; cruel and crafty

桀紂(ㄐㄧㄝˊㄓㄡˋ)
Chieh and Chou, two typical tyrants, the last rulers of the Hsia and the Shang Dynasties respectively—used as a synonymous term for a tyrant

桀驁(ㄐㄧㄝˊㄠˋ)
tyrannical and haughty

桀驁不馴(ㄐㄧㄝˊㄠˋㄅㄨˋㄒㄩㄣˊ)
obstinate and unruly; wild and intractable

【案】 2435
ㄢˋ ann àn

1. a narrow, long table
2. according to; on the strength of; following this precedent
3. a legal case; legal records; a legal offense: 此事有案可稽。This matter was on record.
4. to press 亦作「按」

案板(ㄢˋㄅㄢˇ)
a chopping or kneading board

案發(ㄢˋㄈㄚ)
a crime or conspiracy coming to the open

案奉(ㄢˋㄈㄥˋ)
(a documentary terminology used to begin a reply or a circular, etc.) on the strength of instructions from a higher government office

案牘(ㄢˋㄉㄨˊ)
official correspondence or documents

案頭(ㄢˋㄊㄡˊ)
on the desk: 案頭放着一套百科全書。There is a set of encyclopedia on the desk.

案件(ㄢˋㄐㄧㄢˋ)
a legal case; a crime: 這是民事案件。This is a civil case.

案據(ㄢˋㄐㄩˋ)
(a documentary terminology used to begin a report, etc.) according to information furnished by a subordinate government office

案卷(ㄢˋㄐㄩㄢˋ)
official files; archives

案情(ㄢˋㄑㄧㄥˊ)
the record of a case; the ins and outs of a crime

案情大白(ㄢˋㄑㄧㄥˊㄉㄚˋㄅㄞˊ)
The riddle of a puzzling case has been completely unraveled.

案桌(ㄢˋㄓㄨㄛ)
a narrow, long table

案准(ㄢˋㄓㄨㄣˇ)
a beginning term in documentary usage for correspondence, memo, etc. between government offices of the same or equal standing

案子(ㄢˋ˙ㄗ)
①a legal case; a crime: 這是一椿謀殺案子。This is a murder case. ②a large-size table (usually used in shops)

案問 or 按問(ㄢˋㄨㄣˋ)
to question; to test

案語 or 按語(ㄢˋㄩˇ)
the editor's comments or remarks

【桌】 2436
(棹) ㄓㄨㄛ juo zhuó

1. a table; a desk
2. dishes for guests around the table—usually consisting of 20 courses
3. a tableful of guests (10 to 12 persons at a round table)

桌布(ㄓㄨㄛㄅㄨˋ)
a tablecloth

桌面(ㄓㄨㄛㄇㄧㄢˋ)
the top of a table

桌燈(ㄓㄨㄛㄉㄥ)
a desk lamp

桌球(ㄓㄨㄛㄑㄧㄡˊ)
table tennis; ping-pong

桌扇(ㄓㄨㄛㄕㄢˋ)
a desk fan

桌子(ㄓㄨㄛ˙ㄗ)or 桌兒(ㄓㄨㄛㄦ)
a table; a desk

桌椅板櫈(ㄓㄨㄛㄧˇㄅㄢˇㄉㄥˋ)
tables, desks, chairs and benches—household furni-

〔木部〕

【桑】 2437
ㄙㄤ sang sāng
1. the mulberry tree: 我的花园中有一棵桑树。There is a mulberry tree in my garden.
2. a Chinese family name

桑麻(ㄙㄤ ㄇㄚˊ)
mulberry leaves and hemp —the life on a farm

桑田(ㄙㄤ ㄊㄧㄢˊ)
a plantation of mulberry trees

桑土
①(ㄙㄤ ㄊㄨˇ) mulberry fields; mulberry grounds
②(ㄙㄤ ㄉㄨˋ) the roots of the mulberry tree

桑果(ㄙㄤ ㄍㄨㄛˇ)
sorosis; the berry of a mulberry

桑间濮上(ㄙㄤ ㄐㄧㄢ ㄆㄨˊ ㄕㄤˋ)
a place notorious for profligacy

桑中之乐(ㄙㄤ ㄓㄨㄥ ㄓ ㄌㄜˋ)
illicit love

桑中之会(ㄙㄤ ㄓㄨㄥ ㄓ ㄏㄨㄟˋ)
(literally) a meeting in Sang-chung (桑中); a meeting amid mulberry trees —(figuratively) the lovers' rendezvous

桑葚(ㄙㄤ ㄖㄣˋ)
a mulberry; mulberry fruit

桑树(ㄙㄤ ㄕㄨˋ)
a mulberry tree

桑梓(ㄙㄤ ㄗˇ)
one's native place or hometown

桑梓之情(ㄙㄤ ㄗˇ ㄓ ㄑㄧㄥˊ)
the friendship of natives or inhabitants of a particular region

桑蚕(ㄙㄤ ㄘㄢˊ)
a silkworm

桑叶(ㄙㄤ ㄧㄝˋ)
mulberry leaves (for feeding silkworms)

桑榆(ㄙㄤ ㄩˊ)
①the west ②the closing years of one's life

桑榆暮景(ㄙㄤ ㄩˊ ㄇㄨˋ ㄐㄧㄥˇ)
old age; the closing years of one's life; the evening of one's life

桑园(ㄙㄤ ㄩㄢˊ)
mulberry fields

【栽】 2438
ㄗㄞ tzai zāi
1. to plant
2. to care; to assist
3. to fall; to fail
4. young trees, saplings, cuttings for planting

栽培(ㄗㄞ ㄆㄟˊ)
①to plant and cultivate; to tend ②to educate people ③to give special favor; to receive special favor

栽倒(ㄗㄞ ㄉㄠˇ)
to fall: 他从窗上栽倒下来。He fell out of the window.

栽跟头(ㄗㄞ ㄍㄣ ㄊㄡ)
①to stumble (both literally and figuratively) ②to be greatly embarrassed

栽植(ㄗㄞ ㄓˊ)
to raise: 她在花园里栽植玫瑰。She planted roses in the garden.

栽种(ㄗㄞ ㄓㄨㄥˇ)
to plant; to grow

栽赃(ㄗㄞ ㄗㄤ)
to place stolen goods in somebody's place with the intention of incriminating him; to frame somebody; to fabricate a charge against somebody; to plant: 那些毒品不是我的, 是他们栽赃给我。Those drugs aren't mine; they planted them on me.

栽秧(ㄗㄞ ㄧㄤ)
to transplant rice seedlings

【桂】 2439
ㄍㄨㄟˋ guey guì
1. cassia or cinnamon
2. a short name of Kwangsi Province
3. a Chinese family name

桂皮(ㄍㄨㄟˋ ㄆㄧˊ)
cinnamon bark

桂林(ㄍㄨㄟˋ ㄌㄧㄣˊ)
Kweilin, capital of Kwangsi Province

桂冠(ㄍㄨㄟˋ ㄍㄨㄢ)
①laurels (as an emblem of victory, success and distinction) ②a garland made of laurel flowers

桂冠诗人(ㄍㄨㄟˋ ㄍㄨㄢ ㄕ ㄖㄣˊ)
a poet laureate, or a laureate

桂花(ㄍㄨㄟˋ ㄏㄨㄚ)
sweet osmanthus

桂子(ㄍㄨㄟˋ ㄗˇ)
①cassia buds ②famous and talented sons (a polite term referring to another's children)

桂子兰孙(ㄍㄨㄟˋ ㄗˇ ㄌㄢˊ ㄙㄨㄣ)
famous and capable posterity

桂月(ㄍㄨㄟˋ ㄩㄝˋ)
the eighth month of the lunar calendar

桂圆(ㄍㄨㄟˋ ㄩㄢˊ)
①a longan ②dried longan

【桃】 2440
ㄊㄠˊ taur táo
1. a peach
2. a Chinese family name

桃符(ㄊㄠˊ ㄈㄨˊ)or 桃板(ㄊㄠˊ ㄅㄢˇ)
①the peachwood charm, used to drive away evil spirits ②couplets or scrolls pasted on Chinese New Year

桃符换春(ㄊㄠˊ ㄈㄨˊ ㄏㄨㄢˋ ㄔㄨㄣ)
the time when old "scrolls" are replaced by new ones ——the Lunar New Year's Day

桃脯(ㄊㄠˊ ㄈㄨˇ)
peaches preserved in honey

桃李(ㄊㄠˊ ㄌㄧˇ)
①(literally) peaches and plums—one's students or pupils ②the beauty of a woman

桃李不言, 下自成蹊(ㄊㄠˊ ㄌㄧˇ ㄅㄨˋ ㄧㄢˊ, ㄒㄧㄚˋ ㄗˋ ㄔㄥˊ ㄒㄧ)
Peaches and plums do not have to talk, yet people beat a path to them.—(figuratively) quiet but attractive 或 Where there is real ability, there is fame.

桃李满门(ㄊㄠˊ ㄌㄧˇ ㄇㄢˇ ㄇㄣˊ)
(said of a master) to have many pupils

桃李满天下(ㄊㄠˊ ㄌㄧˇ ㄇㄢˇ ㄊㄧㄢ ㄒㄧㄚˋ)
(said of a master or teacher) His students have spread throughout the world.

桃李门墙(ㄊㄠˊ ㄌㄧˇ ㄇㄣˊ ㄑㄧㄤˊ)
disciples and students of a master

桃李年(ㄊㄠˊ ㄌㄧˇ ㄋㄧㄢˊ)
one's youth or prime; a girl's blooming age

桃李争春(ㄊㄠˊ ㄌㄧˇ ㄓㄥ ㄔㄨㄣ)

Peaches and plums emulate each other in springtime.

桃李盈庭(ㄊㄠˊ ㄌㄧˇ ㄧㄥˊ ㄊㄧㄥˊ)
Peaches and plums fill up the courtyard. —(said of a master) to have many students

桃核(ㄊㄠˊ ㄏㄜˊ)
a peach stone

桃花(ㄊㄠˊ ㄏㄨㄚ)
the peach blossom: 人面桃花相映紅 The young girl's face and the peach flowers reflect each other's glow.

桃花臉(ㄊㄠˊ ㄏㄨㄚ ㄌㄧㄢˇ)
rosy cheeks; the peach-blossom face of a beauty

桃花心木(ㄊㄠˊ ㄏㄨㄚ ㄒㄧㄣ ㄇㄨˋ)
mahogany

桃花癬(ㄊㄠˊ ㄏㄨㄚ ㄒㄩㄢˇ)
a kind of ringworm shaped like a peach blossom, usually infecting the cheeks of young women or girls

桃花汛(ㄊㄠˊ ㄏㄨㄚ ㄒㄩㄣˋ)
spring freshets; spring floods

桃花水(ㄊㄠˊ ㄏㄨㄚ ㄕㄨㄟˇ)
spring freshets—the water from melting snow when the peach trees are in full blossom in spring

桃花源(ㄊㄠˊ ㄏㄨㄚ ㄩㄢˊ)or 桃源(ㄊㄠˊ ㄩㄢˊ)
Peach Flower Spring — a utopia (originally from a story by Tao Yüan-ming (陶淵明), one of China's most celebrated poets, where people live in peace, oblivious of the passing of time)

桃紅運(ㄊㄠˊ ㄏㄨㄥˊ ㄩㄣˋ)
a duration in a man's life when he is particularly lucky or popular with women; luck in love; a romance

桃紅(ㄊㄠˊ ㄏㄨㄥˊ)
pink; light red

桃紅柳綠(ㄊㄠˊ ㄏㄨㄥˊ ㄌㄧㄡˇ ㄌㄩˋ)
(literally) The peach blossoms and the willow turns green.—a description of the beautiful scenes of spring

桃金孃(ㄊㄠˊ ㄐㄧㄣ ㄋㄧㄤˊ)
(botany) Rhodomyrtus tomentosa, a myrtle

桃樹(ㄊㄠˊ ㄕㄨˋ)
a peach tree

桃仁(ㄊㄠˊ ㄖㄣˊ)
the dried meat of a walnut; a shelled walnut; peach kernels

桃膻兒(ㄊㄠˊ ㄖㄢ ㄦ)
the dried meat of a walnut; a shelled walnut

桃子(ㄊㄠˊ ㄗ)or 桃兒(ㄊㄠˊ ㄦ)
a peach: 我較喜歡桃子而不喜歡蘋果。I like peaches better than apples.

桃色(ㄊㄠˊ ㄙㄜˋ)
① peach color ② the symbol of romances

桃色新聞(ㄊㄠˊ ㄙㄜˋ ㄒㄧㄣ ㄨㄣˊ)
news of illicit love; newspaper stories of love and sex

桃色案(ㄊㄠˊ ㄙㄜˋ ㄢˋ)
a criminal case involving sex; crimes of passion

桃腮杏眼(ㄊㄠˊ ㄙㄞ ㄒㄧㄥˋ ㄧㄢˇ)
large eyes and rosy cheeks of a beauty

桃夭迨吉(ㄊㄠˊ ㄧㄠ ㄉㄞˋ ㄐㄧˊ)
the right age for marriage

桃月(ㄊㄠˊ ㄩㄝˋ)
the third month of the lunar year

桃園結義(ㄊㄠˊ ㄩㄢˊ ㄐㄧㄝˊ ㄧˋ)
① In the Epoch of the Three Kingdoms, the three men —Liu Pei (劉備), who later became ruler of Shu, Kuan Yü (關羽) and Chang Fei (張飛) —swore as brothers in a peach orchard. ② (said of friends) to become sworn brothers

【桄】2441 ㄍㄨㄤ guang ㄍㄨㄤˇ guǎng
1. a crossbeam
2. a reel

【桅】2442 ㄨㄟˊ wei wéi
the mast of a ship: 這船有三根桅桿。The ship has three masts.
桅竿(ㄨㄟˊ ㄍㄢ)
the mast of a boat
桅檣(ㄨㄟˊ ㄑㄧㄤˊ)
a mast

【框】2443 ㄎㄨㄤ kuang ㄎㄨㄤˋ kuàng (又讀 ㄎㄨㄤˇ kuǎng)
1. a door frame
2. a frame; to frame

3. the skeleton (of a lantern, etc.)

框框(ㄎㄨㄤ·ㄎㄨㄤ)
①a frame; a circle ② restriction; convention; to set a pattern

框子(ㄎㄨㄤ·ㄗ)or 框兒(ㄎㄨㄤ ㄦ)
a frame; a framework

【桎】2444 ㄓˋ jyh zhì
1. fetters; shackles; to fetter
2. to suffocate
桎梏(ㄓˋ ㄍㄨˋ)
shackles

【桐】2445 ㄊㄨㄥˊ torng tóng
1. a paulownia
2. a Chinese family name
桐棺(ㄊㄨㄥˊ ㄍㄨㄢ)
a coffin made of the timber of a paulownia, considered to be of very inferior quality
桐城派(ㄊㄨㄥˊ ㄔㄥˊ ㄆㄞˋ)
the Tungcheng School, a literary school in the Ching Dynasty led by Fang Pao (方苞) and Yao Nai (姚鼐) whose hometown was Tungcheng, Anhwei
桐樹(ㄊㄨㄥˊ ㄕㄨˋ)
a tung tree
桐人(ㄊㄨㄥˊ ㄖㄣˊ)
(in ancient China) carved human figures to be buried with the deceased
桐葉(ㄊㄨㄥˊ ㄧㄝˋ)
leaves of a paulownia
桐油(ㄊㄨㄥˊ ㄧㄡˊ)
tung oil; wood oil obtained from the seeds of a paulownia
桐月(ㄊㄨㄥˊ ㄩㄝˋ)
the seventh month of the lunar year

【桓】2446 ㄏㄨㄢˊ hwan huán
1. a tree with leaves like a willow and white bark
2. a Chinese family name
3. greatly; effectively
桓公(ㄏㄨㄢˊ ㄍㄨㄥ)
Duke Huan of Chi, died 643 B.C., the most celebrated among the five leading chieftains who held power in China during the 7th century B.C.

[木部]

【木部】

桓桓武夫（ㄏㄨㄢˊㄏㄨㄢˊㄨˇㄈㄨ）
a martial military man

【桔】 2447 1. ㄐㄧㄝˊ jye jié
a well sweep

桔槔（ㄐㄧㄝˊㄍㄠ）
a well sweep, a device with a water bucket raised and lowered in a well by means of a lever

桔梗（ㄐㄧㄝˊㄍㄥˇ）
Platycodon grandiflorum, a Chinese bellflower

【桔】 2447 2. ㄐㄩˊ jyu jú
an abbreviated form of 橘, a mandarin orange or tangerine

桔餅（ㄐㄩˊㄅㄧㄥ）
a dried orange flattened like a cake

桔子（ㄐㄩˊ˙ㄗ）
a small mandarin orange

【桫】 2448 （桫）ㄗㄚˊ tzar zá
（又讀）ㄗㄢ tzaan zan）
to press; to squeeze

桫指（ㄗㄚˊㄓˇ）
a torture by squeezing the fingers in former times

桫子（ㄗㄚˊ˙ㄗ）
a torture instrument for squeezing a prisoner's fingers 亦作「指枷」

【柏】 2449 ㄐㄧㄡˇ jiow jiǔ
the tallow tree (Sapium sebiferum)

【栱】 2450 ㄍㄨㄥˇ goong gǒng
a big peg or stake; a post; a prop

七畫

【桴】 2451 ㄈㄨˊ fwu fú
1. the ridge pole on a roof
2. a drumstick
3. a raft (of wood or bamboo)

桴鼓相應（ㄈㄨˊㄍㄨˇㄒㄧㄤㄧㄥˋ）
to render mutual support or assistance

桴鼓助戰（ㄈㄨˊㄍㄨˇㄓㄨˋㄓㄢˋ）
women assisting in fighting

【桫】 2452 ㄙㄨㄛ suo suō

1. a horse chestnut (Stewartia pseudocamellia)
2. sal (Cyathea spinosa)

桫欏（ㄙㄨㄛㄌㄨㄛˊ）
① the horse chestnut (Stewartia pseudocamellia) ② sal (Cyathea spinosa)

【梧】 2453 ㄨˊ wu wú
1. a firmiana (Firmiana platanifolia)
2. a support; a prop
3. to support; to prop up
4. a Chinese family name

梧桐（ㄨˊㄊㄨㄥˊ）
a firmiana; a Chinese parasol (tree)

梧州（ㄨˊㄓㄡ）
Wuchow, an important city in Kwangsi Province

梧鼠技窮（ㄨˊㄕㄨˇㄐㄧˋㄑㄩㄥˊ）
at one's wits' end; at the end of one's rope

【桶】 2454 ㄊㄨㄥˇ toong tǒng
a bucket; a tub; a pail; a barrel; a keg; a cask

桶鋪（ㄊㄨㄥˇㄆㄨˋ）
a coopery

桶匠（ㄊㄨㄥˇㄐㄧㄤˋ）
a cooper

桶子（ㄊㄨㄥˇ˙ㄗ）
a bucket; a pail; a barrel; a keg

【桷】 2455 ㄐㄩㄝˊ jyue jué
1. a rafter
2. (botany) Malus toringo

【梁】 2456 ㄌㄧㄤˊ liang liáng
1. a bridge
2. beams of a house
3. a ridge; a swelling
4. Liang, name of a dynasty (502 to 557 A.D.)
5. a state during the Epoch of Warring States, also known as Wei (魏)
6. a Chinese family name

梁孟（ㄌㄧㄤˊㄇㄥˋ）
an abbreviation for Liang Hung (梁鴻) and Meng Kuang (孟光) of the Han Dynasty, whose married life served as a paragon for all married couple

梁木其壞（ㄌㄧㄤˊㄇㄨˋㄑㄧˊㄏㄨㄞˋ）
(literally) The beams are

rotten.—the death of a virtuous person

梁麗（ㄌㄧㄤˊㄌㄧˋ）
① beams on a roof ②(now rarely) a small boat

梁惠王（ㄌㄧㄤˊㄏㄨㄟˋㄨㄤˊ）
①name of a king of the Liang State during the Epoch of Warring States ② the title of a chapter in The works of Mencius (孟子)

梁紅玉（ㄌㄧㄤˊㄏㄨㄥˊㄩˋ）
Liang Hung-yü, wife of General Han Shih-chung (韓世忠) of the Sung Dynasty (When her husband was engaged in a life-and-death battle with Nüchen troops, she beat the military drum to urge the defenders on.)

梁啓超（ㄌㄧㄤˊㄑㄧˇㄔㄠ）
Liang Chi-chao, 1873-1929, one of the major advocates of political reform in China in the late 19th century

梁山泊（ㄌㄧㄤˊㄕㄢㄆㄛ）
the home base of a gang of hero-bandits in All Men Are Brothers (水滸傳), a very popular work of fiction written by Shih Nai-an (施耐庵)

梁上君子 or 樑上君子（ㄌㄧㄤˊㄕㄤˋㄐㄩㄣㄗˇ）
(literally) gentlemen up on the beams—burglars

梁武帝（ㄌㄧㄤˊㄨˇㄉㄧˋ）
Emperor Wu of the Liang Dynasty (464 to 549 A.D.)

【梃】 2457 ㄊㄧㄥˇ tiing tǐng
1. a club; a cudgel; a stick; a cane
2. a stalk; a branch; a stem
3. straight and strong

梃杖（ㄊㄧㄥˇㄓㄤˋ）
a club; a stick

【梅】 2458 ㄇㄟˊ mei méi
1. plums; prunes
2. a Chinese family name

梅妃（ㄇㄟˊㄈㄟ）
a concubine of Emperor Ming of the Tang Dynasty, so called because she loved plum blossoms

梅毒（ㄇㄟˊㄉㄨˊ）
syphilis

梅毒菌（ㄇㄟˊㄉㄨˊㄐㄩㄣ）

［木部］

the spirochete which causes
syphilis

梅特涅(ㄇㄟ ㄊㄜ ㄋㄧㄝ)
Prince Klemens Wenzel
Metternich, 1773-1859, Aus-
trian prime minister

梅林止渴(ㄇㄟ ㄌㄧㄣ ㄓ ㄎㄜ)
When one visits the orchard
of plums, he never feels
thirsty.

梅花(ㄇㄟ ㄏㄨㄚ)
① a plum blossom ② a
wintersweet

梅花大鼓(ㄇㄟ ㄏㄨㄚ ㄉㄚ ㄍㄨ)
a kind of storytelling by
singing to the accompani-
ment of a drum and various
stringed instruments

梅花鹿(ㄇㄟ ㄏㄨㄚ ㄌㄨ)
a sika deer; a spotted deer;
a kind of deer with white
spots

梅花雀(ㄇㄟ ㄏㄨㄚ ㄑㄩㄝ)
an avadavat

梅紅(ㄇㄟ ㄏㄨㄥ)
a light red color

梅妻鶴子(ㄇㄟ ㄑㄧ ㄏㄜ ㄗ)
the story of Lin Pu (林通),
who took plum trees as his
wife and cranes for children
—the life of a hermit

梅縣(ㄇㄟ ㄒㄧㄢ)
name of a county in Kwangtung Province, home of the
Hakkas

梅香(ㄇㄟ ㄒㄧㄤ)
a name usually given to a
maid or slave-girl in former
times, now used as a synonym for a maid servant

梅子(ㄇㄟ ㄗ)
plums: 我喜歡梅子腾子桃子。I
like plums better than
peaches.

梅雨(ㄇㄟ ㄩ)
the rainy season in early
summer when plums are
ripening

梅月(ㄇㄟ ㄩㄝ)
the fourth month of the
lunar year

【梓】 2459
ㄗ tzyy zǐ
1. *Catalpa ovata*, a tall, stately
tree with palm-shaped
leaves and yellow flowers in
summer

2. one's native place or hometown
3. to make furniture; furniture
4. to carve words on a wood-
board; printing blocks: 他最
近的著作已付梓。His latest
work has been sent to the
printers.
5. (now rarely) a Chinese family name

梓里(ㄗ ㄌㄧ)
one's native place or hometown

梓宮(ㄗ ㄍㄨㄥ)
the coffin for an emperor

梓匠輪輿(ㄗ ㄐㄧㄤ ㄌㄨㄣ ㄩ)
carpenters and wheelwrights

梓器(ㄗ ㄑㄧ)
a coffin

梓人(ㄗ ㄖㄣ)
a carpenter; a wood engraver; a builder; an architect

【梏】 2460
1. ㄍㄨ guh guh
1. hand-shackles; handcuffs;
manacles
2. to detain; to imprison

梏亡(ㄍㄨ ㄨㄤ)
to be fettered in mind by
greed

【梏】 2460
2. ㄐㄩㄝ jyue jué
1. great
2. straightforward; upright

【梔】 2461
(栀) ㄓ jy zhī

梔子(ㄓ ㄗ)
a gardenia

梔子花(ㄓ ㄗ ㄏㄨㄚ)
Cape jasmine

【梗】 2462
ㄍㄥ geeng gěng
1. the branch or stem of a
plant
2. to prick or pierce with a
thorn; thorny
3. an outline; a synopsis; a
summary
4. to block; to obstruct: 他從中
作梗。He placed obstacles in
the way.
5. stubborn; stiff
6. fierce and fearless
7. an ailment; bane; distress
8. to straighten: 他梗着脖子,He
straightened up his neck.
9. honest; straight

梗概(ㄍㄥ ㄍㄞ)
an outline; a summary; a
synopsis

梗化(ㄍㄥ ㄏㄨㄚ)
to obstruct education; to hinder cultural development

梗直(ㄍㄥ ㄓ)
straight and honest; outspoken

梗阻(ㄍㄥ ㄗㄨ)
to block; to obstruct; to
hamper: 他梗阻我們的計劃。
He obstructed our plan.

梗塞(ㄍㄥ ㄙㄜ)
to obstruct; to block

梗礙(ㄍㄥ ㄞ)
to obstruct: 樹木梗礙了視野。
Trees obstructed the view.

梗兒(ㄍㄥ ㄦ)
a stem or branch

【條】 2463
ㄊㄧㄠ tyau tiáo
1. an article, section, clause,
etc. of an agreement, pact,
treaty, law, etc.
2. in good order; (to present)
one by one
3. a numerary adjunct for
something narrow and long,
as roads, fish, ropes, dogs,
snakes, etc.
4. stripes

條碼(ㄊㄧㄠ ㄇㄚ)
(computers) a bar code

條目(ㄊㄧㄠ ㄇㄨ)
clauses or articles of an
agreement, etc.; particulars
or details

條分縷析(ㄊㄧㄠ ㄈㄣ ㄌㄩ ㄒㄧ)
to analyze to the last detail;
detailed presentation

條幅(ㄊㄧㄠ ㄈㄨ)
a vertical hanging scroll of
calligraphy or painting

條達(ㄊㄧㄠ ㄉㄚ)
① reasonable; logical; orderly ② a bracelet

條對(ㄊㄧㄠ ㄉㄨㄟ)
to give answers to every
question asked

條頓(ㄊㄧㄠ ㄉㄨㄣ)
the Teutons

條條(ㄊㄧㄠ ㄊㄧㄠ)
in good order; reasonable;
logical

條條大道通羅馬(ㄊㄧㄠ ㄊㄧㄠ ㄉㄚ ㄉㄠ
ㄊㄨㄥ ㄌㄨㄛ ㄇㄚ)

Every road leads to Rome.

條理(ㄊㄧㄠˊ ㄌㄧˇ)
①reasonable; logical ②orderly; (to present) in good order; methodical: 他的文章條理清楚。His articles are well-organized.

條理井然(ㄊㄧㄠˊ ㄌㄧˇ ㄐㄧㄥˇ ㄖㄢˊ)
in good order and with good reasoning

條例(ㄊㄧㄠˊ ㄌㄧˋ)
rules, regulations, or laws

條列(ㄊㄧㄠˊ ㄌㄧㄝˋ)
to list item by item

條規(ㄊㄧㄠˊ ㄍㄨㄟ)
rules and regulations: 遵守這遊戲的條規。Obey the rules and regulations of the game.

條貫(ㄊㄧㄠˊ ㄍㄨㄢˋ)
to present reasons, analyses, etc. in good order and with logic

條款(ㄊㄧㄠˊ ㄎㄨㄢˇ)
an article of laws; a section, chapter, or clause of agreements, regulations, provisions, etc.

條件(ㄊㄧㄠˊ ㄐㄧㄢˋ)
①conditions; conditional; terms: 才能與努力是成功的條件。Ability and effort are conditions of success. ②articles, clauses, etc. in an agreement, etc.

條件句(ㄊㄧㄠˊ ㄐㄧㄢˋ ㄐㄩˋ)
(grammar) a conditional clause

條陳(ㄊㄧㄠˊ ㄔㄣˊ)
①to present item by item ②such a written presentation

條暢 or **條鬯**(ㄊㄧㄠˊ ㄔㄤˋ)
clear and smooth (writing, etc.)

條子(ㄊㄧㄠˊ ˙ㄗ)
①a short letter; a note ②an order; a memo (often from a superior): 我們老板給我們下條子。Our boss gave us a written order. ③a summons for prostitutes

條案(ㄊㄧㄠˊ ㄢˋ)
a long and narrow table

條文(ㄊㄧㄠˊ ㄨㄣˊ)
the text of a treaty, regulation, law, etc.

條紋(ㄊㄧㄠˊ ㄨㄣˊ)
stripes; streaks; the grain

(of wood)

條約(ㄊㄧㄠˊ ㄩㄝ)
a treaty (between nations)

條約港(ㄊㄧㄠˊ ㄩㄝ ㄍㄤˇ)
a treaty port

條約國(ㄊㄧㄠˊ ㄩㄝ ㄍㄨㄛˊ)
Treaty Powers

梟　2464
　　ㄒㄧㄠ　shiau xiāo
1. an owl; a legendary bird said to eat its own mother
2. a smuggler of contraband, narcotics, etc.
3. brave and unscrupulous

梟捕(ㄒㄧㄠ ㄈㄨˇ)
a reformed son

梟匪(ㄒㄧㄠ ㄈㄟˇ) or **梟販**(ㄒㄧㄠ ㄈㄢˋ)
smugglers of contraband, narcotics, etc.

梟鳥(ㄒㄧㄠ ㄋㄧㄠˇ)
an owl

梟亂(ㄒㄧㄠ ㄌㄨㄢˋ)
to confuse; to cause turmoil

梟騎(ㄒㄧㄠ ㄐㄧˋ)
elite cavalry units: 梟騎騎馬進入市區。The elite cavalry rode into the city.

梟將(ㄒㄧㄠ ㄐㄧㄤˋ)
a brave leader of troops; a brave general: 他是一員梟將。He was a brave general.

梟獍(ㄒㄧㄠ ㄐㄧㄥˋ)
(literally) the mother-eater and the father-eater—disobedient children; ungrateful persons

梟雄(ㄒㄧㄠ ㄒㄩㄥˊ)
an unscrupulous, brave and capable person; a fierce, ambitious man: 他是一代梟雄。He was a fierce and ambitious person in his time.

梟示(ㄒㄧㄠ ㄕˋ)
to display the head of a decapitated person (as a warning to others)

梟首(ㄒㄧㄠ ㄕㄡˇ)
to decapitate a person and hang his head on a pole

梵　2465
　　ㄈㄢˋ　fann fàn
1. clean and pure
2. Sanskrit
3. a Brahman
4. anything pertaining to Buddhism

梵唄(ㄈㄢˋ ㄅㄞˋ)

Buddhist chanting of prayers

梵諦崗(ㄈㄢˋ ㄉㄧˋ ㄍㄤ)《地》
the Vatican

梵諦崗城(ㄈㄢˋ ㄉㄧˋ ㄍㄤ ㄔㄥˊ)
the Vatican City

梵宮(ㄈㄢˋ ㄍㄨㄥ)
a Buddhist temple

梵學(ㄈㄢˋ ㄒㄩㄝˊ)
Buddhism (as a kind of learning)

梵眾(ㄈㄢˋ ㄓㄨㄥˋ)
Buddhist monks

梵刹(ㄈㄢˋ ㄔㄚˋ)
a Buddhist temple: 我們參觀了一座梵刹。We visited a Buddhist temple.

梵唱(ㄈㄢˋ ㄔㄤˋ)
Buddhist chanting

梵師(ㄈㄢˋ ㄕ)
a salutation for a Buddhist monk

梵書(ㄈㄢˋ ㄕㄨ)
①Buddhist scriptures ②the Sanskrit

梵字(ㄈㄢˋ ㄗˋ)
the written Sanskrit

梵音(ㄈㄢˋ ㄧㄣ)
the chanting of the Buddhist scriptures

梵文(ㄈㄢˋ ㄨㄣˊ)
the written Sanskrit

梵字(ㄈㄢˋ ㄗˋ)
a Buddhist temple

梵語(ㄈㄢˋ ㄩˇ)
the spoken Sanskrit

梯　2466
　　ㄊㄧ　ti tī
1. a ladder; steps; stairs: 這段短樓梯通到二樓。The short stair leads to the second floor.
2. something to lean or depend on
3. terraced
4. private; intimate
5. a phase (in the induction of military draftees)

梯隊(ㄊㄧ ㄉㄨㄟˋ)
echelon formation; echelon

梯田(ㄊㄧ ㄊㄧㄢˊ)
terraced paddies on a slope

梯級(ㄊㄧ ㄐㄧˊ)
a stair; a step

梯己(ㄊㄧ ㄐㄧˇ)
①private property that is not known to others ②by

〔木部〕

and intimate conversations or persons 亦作「體己」

梯階 (ㄊㄧ ㄐㄧㄝ)
①steps of a ladder ②keys to accomplish something; means to achieve a result

梯形 (ㄊㄧ ㄒㄧㄥ)
①(geometry) trapezoid ②a flat raised piece of land in gardens

梯山航海 (ㄊㄧ ㄕㄢ ㄏㄤ ㄏㄞ)
scaling mountains and crossing seas—to travel along a long and difficult road 亦作「梯航」

梯子 (ㄊㄧ ˙ㄗ)
a ladder or steps; a step-ladder

梯次 (ㄊㄧ ˙ㄘ)
phases (in the induction of military draftees)

【械】 ㄒㄧㄝ shieh xiè
（又讀 ㄐㄧㄝ jieh jiè）
1. weapons
2. implements; machinery; machines
3. shackles; fetters
4. to arrest and put in prison

械鬥 (ㄒㄧㄝ ㄉㄡ)
(said of mobs or gangsters) to fight with arms or implements; to fight with weapons between groups of people

械彈 (ㄒㄧㄝ ㄉㄢ)
weapons and ammunition

械繫 (ㄒㄧㄝ ㄒㄧ)
to shackle a prisoner

械用 (ㄒㄧㄝ ㄩㄥ)
implements

【梲】 2468 ㄓㄨㄛ jwo zhuó
1. a joist
2. a club or cane

【桷】 2469 ㄐㄩㄝ leu lǚ
a small beam supporting the rafters at the eaves

【梢】 2470 ㄕㄠ shau shāo
1. the tip of a branch or things of similar shape
2. the end of something—the result, etc.
3. the rudder
4. (now rarely) the sound of wind

梢婆 (ㄕㄠ ㄆㄛ)
a boatwoman

梢末 (ㄕㄠ ㄇㄛ)
the extreme end of a thing

梢頭 (ㄕㄠ ㄊㄡ)
①the tip of a tree: 一隻鳥棲在樹梢頭。A bird perched on the tip of a tree. ②the close of spring

梢公 or 艄公 (ㄕㄠ ㄍㄨㄥ)
a helmsman; a boatman; a rudder: 梢公帶旅客過渡頭。The boat rudder rowed the travelers over the ferry.

梢長大漢 (ㄕㄠ ㄔㄤ ㄉㄚ ㄏㄢ)
a tall and big fellow

梢子 (ㄕㄠ ˙ㄗ)or 梢兒 (ㄕㄠ ㄦ)
①the tip of a branch or anything of similar shape ②short pants

【梭】 ㄙㄨㄛ suo suō
1. a weaver's shuttle
2. to move to and fro; to shuttle: 飛機穿梭於波士頓與紐約之間。The airplane shuttles from Boston to New York.
3. swift

梭哈 (ㄙㄨㄛ ㄏㄚ)
a kind of card game

梭巡 (ㄙㄨㄛ ㄒㄩㄣ)
to patrol to and fro

梭子 (ㄙㄨㄛ ˙ㄗ)
a weaver's shuttle

【梆】 2472 ㄅㄤ bang bāng
a watchman's rattle made of wood or bamboo

梆子 (ㄅㄤ ˙ㄗ)
①a watchman's rattle ②a kind of Chinese opera originated in Shensi (陝西)

梆子腔 (ㄅㄤ ˙ㄗ ㄑㄧㄤ)
a type of Chinese opera originated in Shensi (陝西)

【梳】 2473 （櫛）ㄕㄨ shu shū
1. a comb; a coarse comb
2. to comb: 他用手指頭梳他紅長的鬍子。He was combing his fingers through his long red beard.

梳篦 (ㄕㄨ ㄅㄧ)
to dress up one's hair

梳頭 (ㄕㄨ ㄊㄡ)
to comb one's hair

梳理 (ㄕㄨ ㄌㄧ)

---

①(textile) carding ②combing

梳攏 (ㄕㄨ ㄌㄨㄥ)
(said of a maiden sold to a warehouse) to receive patron for the first time

梳裹 (ㄕㄨ ㄍㄨㄛ)
(formerly) to comb the hair and bind the feet (referring to women's small feet)

梳洗 (ㄕㄨ ㄒㄧ)
to comb one's hair and wash up

梳粧 (ㄕㄨ ㄓㄨㄤ)
(said of a woman) to doll up; to dress and make up

梳粧打扮 (ㄕㄨ ㄓㄨㄤ ㄉㄚ ㄅㄢ)
to dress smartly; to be dressed up

梳粧臺 (ㄕㄨ ㄓㄨㄤ ㄊㄞ)
a dressing table where cosmetics, toilet requisites, etc. are laid out for use

梳齒 (ㄕㄨ ㄔ)
the teeth of a comb

梳子 (ㄕㄨ ˙ㄗ)or 梳頭 (ㄕㄨ ㄦ)
a comb

【桿】 2474 ㄍㄢ gaan gǎn
a wooden pole, cane, stick, or club

桿撥 (ㄍㄢ ㄅㄛ)
a thin piece of wood for plucking a pi-pa (琵琶) or a Chinese moon guitar (月琴), now fingers are used instead

桿棒 (ㄍㄢ ㄅㄤ)
a club used as a weapon in ancient warfare

桿弟 (ㄍㄢ ㄉㄧ)
a caddy; a caddie

桿菌 (ㄍㄢ ㄐㄩㄣ)or 桿狀菌 (ㄍㄢ ㄓㄨㄤ ㄐㄩㄣ)
a bacillus; bacilli

桿子 (ㄍㄢ ˙ㄗ)
a club; a stick

八畫

【棃】 2475 （梨）ㄌㄧ li lí
1. a pear
2. Chinese opera

棃乾 (ㄌㄧ ㄍㄢ)
a variety of small pear

棃乾兒 (ㄌㄧ ㄍㄢ ㄦ)
dried pears

〔木部〕

〔木部〕

梨膏(ㄌㄧˊ ㄍㄠ)
a heavy syrup of pear juice
and honey

梨糕(ㄌㄧˊ ㄍㄠ)
hard candy with malt sugar
and sesame as main ingredients

梨果(ㄌㄧˊ ㄍㄨㄛˇ)
(botany) pome

梨花大鼓(ㄌㄧˊ ㄏㄨㄚ ㄉㄚˋ ㄍㄨˇ)
a type of folksong in
Shantung Province, usually
accompanied by a drum and
two brass pieces to punctuate the narrative song

梨花簡(ㄌㄧˊ ㄏㄨㄚ ㄐㄧㄢˇ)
the crescent brass pieces
used in 梨花大鼓

梨花槍(ㄌㄧˊ ㄏㄨㄚ ㄑㄧㄤ)
a set of combat techniques
featuring the use of spear in
ancient China

梨樹(ㄌㄧˊ ㄕㄨˋ)
the pear tree

梨棗(ㄌㄧˊ ㄗㄠˇ)
the pear and the date, whose
wood is used for cutting
printing blocks; printing
blocks

梨兒(ㄌㄧˊ ㄦ)
pears

梨渦(ㄌㄧˊ ㄨㄛ)
dimples: 這個美麗的女子兩頰
都有梨渦。This pretty girl
has dimples on her cheeks.

梨園(ㄌㄧˊ ㄩㄢˊ)
the operatic circle

梨園子弟(ㄌㄧˊ ㄩㄢˊ ㄗˇ ㄉㄧˋ)
operatic players

【棄】 2476
(弃) (ㄑㄧˋ) chih tì
1. to discard; to cast aside
2. to reject; to abandon; to desert; to forsake: 他放棄運動
研究醫學。He forsook sports
to study medicine.
3. to forget
4. to throw away one's own
life

棄背(ㄑㄧˋ ㄅㄟˋ)
the death of one's parents;
to suffer loss of one's parents

棄婦(ㄑㄧˋ ㄈㄨˋ)
a woman who is divorced or
deserted by her husband

棄短取長(ㄑㄧˋ ㄉㄨㄢˇ ㄑㄩˇ ㄔㄤˊ)
to eliminate the defects or
shortcomings and adopt the
good points of others

棄官(ㄑㄧˋ ㄍㄨㄢ)
to give up one's office; to
abandon official life

棄甲曳兵(ㄑㄧˋ ㄐㄧㄚˇ ㄧˋ ㄅㄧㄥ)
(said of military troops) to
be totally defeated; to throw
away their armor and trail
their weapons behind them

棄舊迎新(ㄑㄧˋ ㄐㄧㄡˋ ㄧㄥˊ ㄒㄧㄣ)
to reject the old and welcome the new—as in the case
of taking a second wife

棄井(ㄑㄧˋ ㄐㄧㄥˇ)
(literally) to stop the digging of a well before water
is reached—all the past
accomplishments coming to
naught

棄捐(ㄑㄧˋ ㄐㄩㄢ)
to cast aside; to reject; to
abandon; to fall out of
favor; to be neglected

棄妻(ㄑㄧˋ ㄑㄧ)
① a woman divorced by her
husband ②(formerly) to divorce one's wife

棄權(ㄑㄧˋ ㄑㄩㄢˊ)
(in voting) to abstain; to
waive a right; a waiver

棄邪歸正(ㄑㄧˋ ㄒㄧㄝˊ ㄍㄨㄟ ㄓㄥˋ)
to reject evil ways and start
on the right track

棄之可惜(ㄑㄧˋ ㄓ ㄎㄜˇ ㄒㄧˊ)
It is a waste to discard it.

棄之如敝屣(ㄑㄧˋ ㄓ ㄖㄨˊ ㄅㄧˋ ㄒㄧˇ)
to reject something as if it
were worthless

棄職潛逃(ㄑㄧˋ ㄓˊ ㄑㄧㄢˊ ㄊㄠˊ)
to desert one's post and take
flight

棄置(ㄑㄧˋ ㄓˋ)
to cast aside

棄世(ㄑㄧˋ ㄕˋ)
①to die ②to lift one's head
above ordinary things; to
look far and high; to abandon worldly life

棄市(ㄑㄧˋ ㄕˋ)
to be executed; public execution

棄暗投明(ㄑㄧˋ ㄢˋ ㄊㄡˊ ㄇㄧㄥˊ)
(literally) to forsake darkness and come to the light
—to renounce a bad cause

and join the camp of justice
(often used by defectors for
self-justification)

棄兒(ㄑㄧˋ ㄦˊ)
an abandoned child; a foundling

棄言(ㄑㄧˋ ㄧㄢˊ)
① to be unable to keep one's
promise ② words which
have become obsolete and
no longer in circulation

棄養(ㄑㄧˋ ㄧㄤˇ)
the death of one's parents

棄嬰(ㄑㄧˋ ㄧㄥ)
an abandoned infant; a foundling

棄物(ㄑㄧˋ ㄨˋ)
trash; discarded useless
things

棄文就武(ㄑㄧˋ ㄨㄣˊ ㄐㄧㄡˋ ㄨˇ)
to quit civilian life and join
the military

【棉】 2477
ㄇㄧㄢˊ mian miản
cotton: 這件襯衫是棉製品。
This shirt is made of cotton.

棉薄 or 緜薄(ㄇㄧㄢˊ ㄅㄛˊ)
meager or trivial: 他靠每月棉
薄的薪資過生活。He lives on
his meager pay per month.

棉被(ㄇㄧㄢˊ ㄅㄟˋ)
a cotton quilt

棉布(ㄇㄧㄢˊ ㄅㄨˋ)
a cotton cloth

棉袍(ㄇㄧㄢˊ ㄆㄠˊ)
a cotton-wadded long gown

棉毛衫(ㄇㄧㄢˊ ㄇㄠˊ ㄕㄢ)
a cotton sweater or T-shirt;
a cotton jersey

棉紡(ㄇㄧㄢˊ ㄈㄤˇ)
cotton spinning

棉紡廠(ㄇㄧㄢˊ ㄈㄤˇ ㄔㄤˇ)
a cotton spinning and weaving mill; a cotton mill

棉套(ㄇㄧㄢˊ ㄊㄠˋ)
a cotton-wadded covering
for keeping something warm

棉條(ㄇㄧㄢˊ ㄊㄧㄠˊ)
a sliver

棉田(ㄇㄧㄢˊ ㄊㄧㄢˊ)
cotton fields

棉褲(ㄇㄧㄢˊ ㄎㄨˋ)
cotton-padded trousers

棉花(ㄇㄧㄢˊ ㄏㄨㄚ)
cotton: 他們把棉花紡成紗。
They spun cotton into yarn.

棉線(ㄇㄧㄢˊㄒㄧㄢˋ)
cotton thread; cotton

棉絮(ㄇㄧㄢˊㄒㄩˋ)
fluffed cotton; cotton batting

棉織物(ㄇㄧㄢˊㄓㄨ×)or 棉織品(ㄇㄧㄢˊ ㄓㄨˋㄆㄧㄣˇ)
cotton goods or cotton piece goods; cotton textiles; cotton fabrics

棉紙(ㄇㄧㄢˊㄓ)
a kind of thin and soft paper

棉紗(ㄇㄧㄢˊㄕㄚ)
cotton yarn

棉繩(ㄇㄧㄢˊㄕㄥˊ)
cotton cord

棉子油(ㄇㄧㄢˊㄗ·ㄧㄡˊ)
cottonseed oil

棉襖(ㄇㄧㄢˊㄠˇ)
a cotton-padded Chinese jacket

棉衣(ㄇㄧㄢˊㄧ)
cotton clothes: 他花費很多錢在棉衣上。He spends a lot of money on cotton clothes.

【棋】 2478 (綦·暴) ㄑㄧˊ chyi qí
1. any piece used in the game of chess
2. chess or other similar games

棋卜(ㄑㄧˊㄅㄨˇ)
to divine with chess

棋布(ㄑㄧˊㄅㄨˋ)
to spread out (something) in great numbers like stones or chessmen on a chessboard

棋盤(ㄑㄧˊㄆㄢˊ)or 棋枰(ㄑㄧˊㄆㄧㄥˊ)
a chessboard

棋品(ㄑㄧˊㄆㄧㄣˇ)
one's demeanor while playing chess; character of a chess player

棋譜(ㄑㄧˊㄆㄨˇ)
a manual on chess; a collection of records of famous chess plays between experts, contemporary and ancient

棋迷(ㄑㄧˊㄇㄧˊ)
a chess fan; a chess enthusiast

棋逢敵手(ㄑㄧˊㄈㄥˊㄉㄧˊㄕㄡˇ)
a good match; to be well-matched in a contest

棋段(ㄑㄧˊㄉㄨㄢˋ)
grades of the skill of chess playing

棋列(ㄑㄧˊㄌㄧㄝˋ)
to spread out (something) in great numbers like stones or chessmen on a chessboard

棋格(ㄑㄧˊㄍㄜˊ)
one's rating in chess-playing skill

棋高一著(ㄑㄧˊㄍㄠ ㄧㄓㄨˋ)
to be superior in intelligence, stratagem, skill, etc. than one's opponent

棋局(ㄑㄧˊㄐㄩˊ)
①the chessboard with the pieces arranged ②a game of chess

棋峙(ㄑㄧˊㄓˋ)
(said of partitioning of land by warlords, etc.) to exist side by side; to confront each other; to match in power as rivals (as in the Epoch of the Three Kingdoms)

棋戰(ㄑㄧˊㄓㄢˋ)
to fight it out in chess; a game of chess

棋士(ㄑㄧˊㄕˋ)
a professional chess player

棋手(ㄑㄧˊㄕㄡˇ)
a high-graded chess player

棋聖(ㄑㄧˊㄕㄥˋ)
an expert among chess experts; a national champion at chess

棋子(ㄑㄧˊㄗˇ)
chess pieces

棋子兒(ㄑㄧˊㄗ·ㄦ)
chessmen; stones (in go game)

棋王(ㄑㄧˊㄨㄤˊ)
a chess champion

【棍】 2479 ㄍㄨㄣˋ guenn gùn
1. a club; a stick; a cudgel; a truncheon
2. a rascal; a villain; a ruffian: 他被一群惡棍攻擊。He was attacked by a band of ruffians.

棍棒(ㄍㄨㄣˋㄅㄤˋ)
clubs; sticks: 他用棍棒打人。He beat the man with a stick.

棍騙(ㄍㄨㄣˋㄆㄧㄢˋ)
to swindle; to cheat; to wheedle

棍徒(ㄍㄨㄣˋㄊㄨˊ)
rascals, villains, ruffians, rowdies, etc.

棍子(ㄍㄨㄣˋ·ㄗ)or 棍兒(ㄍㄨㄦˋ)
①a club, stick, cudgel, etc. ②(when preceded by a noun, as party, information, etc.) an unprincipled small fry; a paw

【棒】 2480 ㄅㄤˋ banq bàng
1. a club; a stick; a truncheon
2. to hit with a club
3. good; strong; wonderful: 她字寫得真棒。She writes a good hand.

棒棒糖(ㄅㄤˋ·ㄅㄤ ㄊㄤˊ)
a lollipop

棒棒雞(ㄅㄤˋ·ㄅㄤ ㄐㄧ)
boneless chicken with heavy seasoning (a specialty in Szechwan restaurants)

棒冰(ㄅㄤˋㄅㄧㄥ)
an ice-cream stick, usually a sherbet stick

棒打薄情郎(ㄅㄤˋㄉㄚˇㄅㄛˊㄑㄧㄥˊㄌㄤˊ)
to hit a fickle male lover with a club

棒頭出孝子(ㄅㄤˋㄊㄡˊㄔㄨ ㄒㄧㄠˋㄗˇ)
(a Chinese saying) Dutiful sons are the products of the rod.—Children must be disciplined whenever necessary. 或 Parents must be very severe while educating their children.

棒喝(ㄅㄤˋㄏㄜˋ)
①to bang and bawl in rebuke of a student ②to arouse a person from his evil ways—as if by using a club: 給他來個當頭棒喝。Let's give him a direct sharp warning.

棒喝圖(ㄅㄤˋㄏㄜˋㄊㄨˊ)
another name for Fascisti, an Italian political organization (1919 to 1943) founded by Benito Mussolini

棒球(ㄅㄤˋㄑㄧㄡˊ)
baseball: 棒球是美國全國性的運動。Baseball is the national game of the U.S.A.

棒球場(ㄅㄤˋㄑㄧㄡˊㄔㄤˇ)or(ㄅㄤˋㄑㄧㄡˊ ㄔㄤˊ)
a baseball diamond; a baseball stadium

〔木部〕

〔木部〕

棒杵(ㄅㄤˋ ㄔㄨˇ)or 棒槌(ㄅㄤˋ ㄔㄨㄟˊ)
a club used to pound clothes

棒瘡(ㄅㄤˋ ㄔㄨㄤ)
inflammations, lesions, etc. as a result of punishment by caning

棒子(ㄅㄤˋ ·ㄗ)
① a short and thick club: 他用棒子打我。He hit me with a club. ② Indian corn

棒子麵(ㄅㄤˋ ·ㄗ ㄇㄧㄢˋ)
cornmeal 亦作「玉米麵」

【棗】 2481
ㄗㄠˇ tzao zǎo
1. jujube (Zizyphus vulgaris), commonly called date
2. a Chinese family name

棗木(ㄗㄠˇ ㄇㄨˋ)
jujube (trees)

棗脯(ㄗㄠˇ ㄈㄨˇ)
dried dates preserved in honey; dried dates

棗泥(ㄗㄠˇ ㄋㄧˊ)
jujube paste, used as stuffing for pastry or dumplings

棗(兒)糕(ㄗㄠˇ(ㄦ)ㄍㄠ)
date-dumplings; steamed cake with dates

棗核兒(ㄗㄠˇ ㄏㄜˊㄦ)
date stones

棗樹(ㄗㄠˇ ㄕㄨˋ)
a jujube tree

棗仁(ㄗㄠˇ ㄖㄣˊ)
kernels of the date

棗子(ㄗㄠˇ ·ㄗ)or 棗兒(ㄗㄠˇㄦ)
dates

【棘】 2482
ㄐㄧˊ jyi jí
1. buckthorns; thorny brambles: 小心,那刑棘叢。Be careful of that thorn bush.
2. urgent
3. a Chinese family name

棘皮動物(ㄐㄧˊ ㄆㄧˊ ㄉㄨㄥˋ ㄨˋ)
an echinoderm

棘林(ㄐㄧˊ ㄌㄧㄣˊ)
a forest of buckthorns, brambles, etc.

棘卿(ㄐㄧˊ ㄑㄧㄥ)
(in ancient China) the president of the Supreme Court

棘心(ㄐㄧˊ ㄒㄧㄣ)
a term of self-reference for a son when speaking of his parents

棘針(ㄐㄧˊ ㄓㄣ)
buckthorns

棘楚(ㄐㄧˊ ㄔㄨˇ)
troubles; problems; thorns

棘手(ㄐㄧˊ ㄕㄡˇ)
thorny (matters); difficult to handle

棘人(ㄐㄧˊ ㄖㄣˊ)
a term of self-reference during the mourning period for one's parent

棘闈(ㄐㄧˊ ㄨㄟˊ)or 棘院(ㄐㄧˊ ㄩㄢˋ)
the examination hall in old China—the surrounding walls were covered with thorns

【根】 2483
ㄍㄣ cheng chéng
1. doorposts
2. to stop
3. to touch
4. a Chinese family name

根撥(ㄍㄣ ㄅㄛ)
to push aside

根觸(ㄍㄣ ㄔㄨˋ)
① to be sentimentally moved or touched ② to touch with one's hand

【棧】 2484
ㄓㄢˋ jann zhàn
1. a storehouse; a warehouse: 他把商品儲存於貨棧中。He stored the goods in the warehouse.
2. a tavern; an inn
3. a road made along a cliff
4. (now rarely) a pen or stable
5. a Chinese family name

棧房(ㄓㄢˋ ㄈㄤˊ)
① a storehouse; a warehouse; a godown ② a tavern; an inn

棧道(ㄓㄢˋ ㄉㄠˋ)or 棧閣(ㄓㄢˋ ㄍㄜˊ)
a log-formed road along a steep cliff

棧單(ㄓㄢˋ ㄉㄢ)
a warrant (a receipt for goods in storage)

棧橋(ㄓㄢˋ ㄑㄧㄠˊ)
a pier for loading and unloading purposes; a landing pier

【棟】 2485
ㄉㄨㄥˋ donq dòng
the main beam of a house

棟梁 or 棟樑(ㄉㄨㄥˋ ㄌㄧㄤˊ)
① the ridgepole and beams ② (figuratively) a man of great ability 參看「棟梁之才」

棟梁之器 or 棟樑之器(ㄉㄨㄥˋ ㄌㄧㄤˊ ㄓ ㄑㄧˋ)

a man of great ability and tremendous promise

棟梁之才 or 棟樑之才(ㄉㄨㄥˋ ㄌㄧㄤˊ ㄓ ㄘㄞˊ)
a man of tremendous promise; a man of great statesmanship

棟折榱崩(ㄉㄨㄥˋ ㄓㄜˊ ㄘㄨㄟ ㄅㄥ)
(literally) The beams are broken and rafters destroyed.—The state is falling apart.

棟宇(ㄉㄨㄥˋ ㄩˇ)
a house

【棚】 2486
ㄆㄥˊ perng péng
a tent; a shed; an awning; a mat awning

棚鋪(ㄆㄥˊ ㄆㄨˋ)
a tent shop

棚戶(ㄆㄥˊ ㄏㄨˋ)
(literally) people who live in tents—refugees or poor families; squatters; slum dwellers

棚匠(ㄆㄥˊ ㄐㄧㄤˋ)
a person who erects tents or mat awnings as a profession

棚車(ㄆㄥˊ ㄔㄜ)
a covered cart (usually with canvas, etc.); a wagon (used by early Americans in their travel to the West)

棚子(ㄆㄥˊ ·ㄗ)or 棚兒(ㄆㄥˊㄦ)
a small tent; a shed

【棣】 2487
ㄉㄧˋ dih dì
1. a mountain tree, as a cherry, etc.
2. same as 弟—a kid brother
3. a Chinese family name

棣棠(ㄉㄧˋ ㄊㄤˊ)
a shrub with yellow flowers (Kerria japonica)

棣華(ㄉㄧˋ ㄏㄨㄚˊ)
brothers

棣鄂 or 棣萼(ㄉㄧˋ ㄜˋ)
love between brothers; fraternity

【棠】 2488
ㄊㄤˊ tarng táng
the sweet pear tree; the wild plum

棠棣(ㄊㄤˊ ㄉㄧˋ)
① Prunus japonica, the wild plum ② brothers

【棨】 2489
ㄑㄧˇ chii qǐ

(in ancient China) a tally or wooden pass used by a messenger as his credentials in passing through a guarded gate, checkpoint, etc.

榮楬(くｆ ㄨ丫)

(in ancient China) a black cloth draped over a spear used to herald the arrival of an official so that people will step aside to let him pass

【棻】 2490

ㄈㄣ fen fēn

a kind of fragrant tree used to produce perfume by burning it

【棐】 2491

ㄈㄟ feei fěi

1. a species of yew found in North China
2. bamboo products
3. to assist

【棼】 2492

ㄈㄣ fen fén

1. beams on the roof of a house
2. a kind of linen
3. confused; disarrayed; disordered

棼亂(ㄈㄣ ㄌㄨㄢ)
in confusion

【森】 2493

ㄙㄣ sen sēn

1. luxuriant vegetation or luxuriant growth of trees
2. dark and obscure; severe
3. serene; majestic

森巴舞(ㄙㄣ ㄅㄚ ㄨ)
samba, a ballroom dance that originated in Brazil

森列(ㄙㄣ ㄌㄧㄝ)
(said of mountain peaks) rising in ranks

森林(ㄙㄣ ㄌㄧㄣ)
forest

森林資源(ㄙㄣ ㄌㄧㄣ ㄗ ㄩㄢ)
forest reserves

森林浴(ㄙㄣ ㄌㄧㄣ ㄩ)
a green shower

森羅殿(ㄙㄣ ㄌㄨㄛ ㄉㄧㄢ)
(in Chinese mythology) the palace of the ruler of the underworld; the palace of the King of Hell

森羅萬象(ㄙㄣ ㄌㄨㄛ ㄨㄢ ㄒㄧㄤ)
the phenomena of the universe

森竪(ㄙㄣ ㄕㄨ)
one's hair standing on end—for fear

森然(ㄙㄣ ㄖㄢ)
① (said of tall trees) dense; thick: 郎公園林木森然。 The park is thickly wooded with tall trees. ② awe inspiring; trembling

森森(ㄙㄣ ㄙㄣ)
① luxuriant growth of vegetation; dense; thick ② trembling; fearful; dark: 開鬼的古堡險森森的。 The haunted castle was very dark.

森聳(ㄙㄣ ㄙㄨㄥ)
to rise high and majestic

森嚴(ㄙㄣ ㄧㄢ)
stern and severe; forbidden (looks); awe-inspiring

森衛(ㄙㄣ ㄨㄟ)
closely guarded

森鬱(ㄙㄣ ㄩ)
thickly overgrown; dense

【椒】 2494

ㄐㄧㄠ jiau jiāo

1. pepper: 在菜裡加點胡椒。 Add some pepper to the dish.
2. mountaintops

椒餅(ㄐㄧㄠ ㄅㄧㄥ)
pepper cake

椒目(ㄐㄧㄠ ㄇㄨ)
the dark seeds of pepper fruit

椒粉(ㄐㄧㄠ ㄈㄣ)
pepper

椒房(ㄐㄧㄠ ㄈㄤ)or 椒屋(ㄐㄧㄠ ㄨ)or 椒殿(ㄐㄧㄠ ㄉㄧㄢ)
the palace of the queen; private apartments of the empress

椒闈(ㄐㄧㄠ ㄨㄟ)
① persons of low moral standing; unprincipled persons ② relatives of the nobility

椒酒(ㄐㄧㄠ ㄐㄧㄡ)
wine soaked with pepper which one used to offer his seniors on the Lunar New Year's Day in former times

椒鹽(ㄐㄧㄠ ㄧㄢ)
a condiment made of powdered roast prickly ash and salt

【棫】 2495

ㄩ yuh yù

a thorny shrub with yellow flowers and dark fruit

椵(ㄐㄧㄚ)
① the title of a poem in *The Book of Poetry* ② a multitude of talented persons ③ names of two kinds of trees *yu* and *jia*

【棬】 2496

ㄑㄩㄢ chiuan quān

a wooden bowl; crooked wood

棬樞(ㄑㄩㄢ ㄕㄨ)
(literally) a door made of warped wood—a very poor family

【棲】 2497

ㄑㄧ chi qī (又讀 ㄒㄧ shi xī)

1. to rest; to stay; to perch; to settle: 一隻烏鴉棲息在樹頂。 A crow perched on the treetop.
2. the place one stays
3. (now rarely) a bed

棲遁 or 棲遯(ㄑㄧ ㄉㄨㄣ)
to live in seclusion: 她遠離朋友, 過棲遁生活。 She lives in seclusion apart from her friends.

棲流所(ㄑㄧ ㄌㄧㄡ ㄙㄨㄛ)
a refuge for vagrants or the homeless (mostly for women)

棲棲(ㄑㄧ ㄏㄨㄤ)
in a hurry; hasty

棲居(ㄑㄧ ㄐㄩ)
to dwell; to live

棲棲(ㄑㄧ ㄑㄧ)
anxious; jittery; jumpy

棲棲遑遑(ㄑㄧ ㄑㄧ ㄏㄨㄤ ㄏㄨㄤ)
anxious; nervous; jumpy

棲息(ㄑㄧ ㄒㄧ)
to rest; to stay; to perch: 有許多麻雀棲息在電線上。 A great number of sparrows perched on the wires.

棲止(ㄑㄧ ㄓ)
to settle (at a place)

棲遲(ㄑㄧ ㄔ)
to sojourn; to travel and rest

棲處(ㄑㄧ ㄔㄨ)
① (ㄑㄧ ㄔㄨ) to stay (at a place)
② (ㄑㄧ ㄔㄨ) an abode (usually temporarily)

棲身(ㄑㄧ ㄕㄣ)
to live; to stay; to dwell: 這

【木部】

些離民無處棲身。These refugees have no place to stay.

棲神（ㄒㄧㄣ ㄕㄣˊ）
(Taoism) a way to discipline one's mind

棲宿（ㄒㄧㄙㄨˋ）
to rest or stay for the night

棲泊（ㄒㄧ ㄅㄛˊ）
to come to anchor; to stay temporarily

【棺】 2498
《ㄍㄨㄢ guan guān》
a coffin (usually made of wood in China)

棺木（《ㄍㄨㄢㄇㄨˋ）
a coffin 亦作「棺材」:他們把棺木放進墓穴。They lowered the coffin into the grave.

棺殮（《ㄍㄨㄢㄌㄧㄢˋ）
① coffin and graveclothes ② to put a shrouded corpse into a coffin

棺蓋（《ㄍㄨㄢㄍㄞˋ）
the lid of a coffin

棺槨（《ㄍㄨㄢㄍㄨㄛˇ）
inner and outer coffins in ancient times

棺罩（《ㄍㄨㄢㄓㄠˋ）
a pall (for covering a coffin)

棺材（《ㄍㄨㄢ・ㄘㄞ）
a coffin:他用釘子釘自己的棺材(他自尋滅亡)。He drove a nail into his coffin.

【棵】 2499
ㄎㄜ ke kē
a numeray adjunct for trees: 一棵大樹遮著房子。A large tree shaded the house.

【植】 2500
ㄓ jyr zhí
1. to plant; to set up; to erect
2. (now rarely) to lean on
3. plants; vegetation

植病害（ㄓㄅㄧㄥˋㄏㄞˋ）
plant disease

植黨營私（ㄓㄉㄤˇㄧㄥˊㄙ）
to form a faction for selfish ends: 他們植黨營私。They form political cliques for the benefit of themselves.

植立（ㄓㄌㄧˋ）
to set up; to erect

植樹（ㄓㄕㄨˋ）
to plant trees: 他在花園裡植樹。He planted trees in his garden.

植樹節（ㄓㄕㄨˋㄐㄧㄝˊ）
Arbor Day on March 12, death anniversary of Dr. Sun Yat-sen

植字（ㄓㄗˋ）
to set type for printing

植字板（ㄓㄗˋㄅㄢˇ）
a printing plate of setting type

植物（ㄓㄨˋ）
vegetables; plants; flora: 樹是大型植物。Trees are large plants.

植物標本（ㄓㄨˋㄅㄧㄠㄅㄣˇ）
a herbarium; a botanical specimen

植物病理學（ㄓㄨˋㄅㄧㄥˋㄌㄧˇㄒㄩㄝˊ）
phytopathology

植物胚學（ㄓㄨˋㄆㄟㄒㄩㄝˊ）
vegetable embryology

植物分類學（ㄓㄨˋㄈㄣㄌㄟˋㄒㄩㄝˊ）
classificatory botany

植物化學（ㄓㄨˋㄏㄨㄚˋㄒㄩㄝˊ）
phytochemistry

植物界（ㄓㄨˋㄐㄧㄝˋ）
the vegetable kingdom

植物群落（ㄓㄨˋㄑㄩㄣˊㄌㄨㄛˋ）
a plant community

植物形態學（ㄓㄨˋㄒㄧㄥˊㄊㄞˋㄒㄩㄝˊ）
morphological botany

植物學（ㄓㄨˋㄒㄩㄝˊ）
botany: 他研究植物學。He studies botany.

植物學家（ㄓㄨˋㄒㄩㄝˊㄐㄧㄚ）
a botanist: 他父親是植物學家。His father was a botanist.

植物生態學（ㄓㄨˋㄕㄥㄊㄞˋㄒㄩㄝˊ）
plantation ecology; vegetable ecology

植物人（ㄓㄨˋㄖㄣˊ）
a vegetable

植物油（ㄓㄨˋㄧㄡˊ）
vegetable oil

植物岩（ㄓㄨˋㄧㄢˊ）
phytogenic rocks

植物園（ㄓㄨˋㄩㄢˊ）
a botanical garden; an arboretum: 台北有一座植物園。There is an arboretum in Taipei.

【椎】 2501
ㄓㄨㄟ juei zhuī
（又讀 ㄔㄨㄟˊ chwei chuí）
1. a hammer; a mallet; a bludgeon; a mace
2. to beat; to hammer; to hit; to strike
3. a vertebra

椎剝（ㄓㄨㄟ ㄅㄛ）
to kill a person and rob him

椎埋（ㄓㄨㄟ ㄇㄞˊ）
① to kill someone and bury his body ② to dig graves

椎牛（ㄓㄨㄟ ㄋㄧㄡˊ）
to kill an ox

椎魯（ㄓㄨㄟ ㄌㄨˇ）
dull and stupid

椎輪（ㄓㄨㄟ ㄌㄨㄣˊ）
a wheel without the hub—something at its initial state and leaving much to be desired or done

椎骨（ㄓㄨㄟ ㄍㄨˇ）
a vertebra: 他椎骨痛。He has a pain in his vertebrae.

椎擊（ㄓㄨㄟ ㄐㄧˊ）
to strike with a mallet, hammer, etc.

椎髻（ㄓㄨㄟ ㄐㄧˋ）
(in hairdressing) a tiny bum shaped like a mallet

椎心泣血（ㄓㄨㄟ ㄒㄧㄣ ㄑㄧˋ ㄒㄩㄝˋ）
deep sorrow; extreme grief; excruciating pains

椎殺（ㄓㄨㄟ ㄕㄚ）
to kill with a mallet, hammer, etc.

【桌】 2502
1.（桌）ㄓㄨㄛ juo zhuō
a table

【棹】 2502
2.（櫂）ㄓㄠˋ jaw zhào
1. an oar or scull
2. a boat: 他鼓棹而進。He rowed his boat forward.

【椅】 2503
1. ㄧˇ yii yǐ
1. a chair; a bench: 他們坐在公園的長椅上。They sat on the bench in the park.
2. Idesia polycarpa 即「山桐子」

椅背（ㄧˇㄅㄟˋ）
the back of a chair

椅披（ㄧˇㄆㄧ）
a colorful silk drapery at the back of a chair

椅墊子（ㄧˇㄉㄧㄢˋ・ㄗ）
a chair cushion

椅套（ㄧˇㄊㄠˋ）
chair covers

椅靠 (ǐ ㄎㄠˋ)
the back of a chair 參看「椅背」

【椅】(ǐ, ㄹ)
a chair

【橔】2504 (槨) ㄍㄨㄛˇ guǒ guǒ
an outer coffin

【椏】2505
ㄧㄚ ia yā
the forking branch of a tree

椏枝 (ㄧㄚ ㄓ)
a forking branch

【椓】2506 ㄓㄨㄛˊ jwo zhuó
1. to strike; to hammer
2. (an ancient punishment) to castrate; castration
3. to slander; to injury

【棕】2507 (椶) ㄗㄨㄥ tzong zōng
the palm tree

棕綳兒 (ㄗㄨㄥ ㄅㄥ)
a wooden frame with stretched coir ropes to be placed on a bedstead

棕毛 (ㄗㄨㄥ ㄇㄠˊ)
palm coir or fibers

棕毯 (ㄗㄨㄥ ㄊㄢˇ)
coir matting

棕櫚 (ㄗㄨㄥ ㄌㄩˊ)or棕櫚樹(ㄗㄨㄥ ㄌㄩˊ ㄕㄨˋ)
the palm tree

棕櫚科 (ㄗㄨㄥ ㄌㄩˊ ㄎㄜ)
Palmae

棕竹 (ㄗㄨㄥ ㄓㄨˊ)
Rhapis humilis, a variety of black bamboo

棕種 (ㄗㄨㄥ ㄓㄨㄥˇ)
the Brown Race

棕繩 (ㄗㄨㄥ ㄕㄥˊ)
coir rope

棕樹 (ㄗㄨㄥ ㄕㄨˋ)
a palm

棕色 (ㄗㄨㄥ ㄙㄜˋ)
brown, the color of palm fibers; 我有一套棕色的衣服。I have a brown suit.

棕簑 (ㄗㄨㄥ ㄙㄨㄛ)
a coir rain-cape; a coir rain-coat

棕筍 (ㄗㄨㄥ ㄙㄨㄣˇ)
clusters of the flower buds of palms

九畫

【椹】2508 ㄓㄣ jen zhēn
a chopping board; a block

椹板 (ㄓㄣ ㄅㄢˇ)
a chopping board

椹質 (ㄓㄣ ㄓˋ)
a wooden block used in beheading a death convict

【椳】2509
ㄨㄟ uei wēi
sockets which hold doors in place

【械】2510
1. ㄐㄧㄢ jian jiān
1. a wooden box or chest
2. same as 緘—a letter

【械】2510
2. ㄒㄧㄢˊ shyan xián
a goblet

【椽】2511 ㄔㄨㄢˊ chwan chuán
a beam; a rafter

椽筆 (ㄔㄨㄢˊ ㄅㄧˇ)
your masterly writing

椽柱 (ㄔㄨㄢˊ ㄓㄨˋ)
a pillar

椽子 (ㄔㄨㄢˊ ˙ㄗ)
a beam; a rafter

【椰】2512
ㄧㄝ ye yé
a coconut; a coconut palm; a coconut tree

椰乾 (ㄧㄝ ㄍㄢ)
copra, coppra, coprah, or copperah

椰殼 (ㄧㄝ ㄎㄜˊ)
a coconut shell

椰肉 (ㄧㄝ ㄖㄡˋ)
coconut meat: 椰肉用來做蛋糕。The coconut meat is used for making a cake.

椰子 (ㄧㄝ ˙ㄗ)
a coconut

椰菜 (ㄧㄝ ㄘㄞˋ)
a savoy

椰油 (ㄧㄝ ㄧㄡˊ)
coconut oil; coconut butter

【椿】2513
ㄔㄨㄣ chuen chūn
1. one's father
2. Cedrela sinensis

椿庭 (ㄔㄨㄣ ㄊㄧㄥˊ)
one's father

椿齡 (ㄔㄨㄣ ㄌㄧㄥˊ)or椿壽 (ㄔㄨㄣ ㄕㄡˋ)or椿年(ㄔㄨㄣ ㄋㄧㄢˊ)
venerable age; great age; long life

椿象 (ㄔㄨㄣ ㄒㄧㄤˋ)
Aenaria lewisi, a kind of beetle sucking the juice from rice and wheat stalks; a stink-bug; a shieldbug

椿萱 (ㄔㄨㄣ ㄒㄩㄢ)
one's parents

椿萱並茂 (ㄔㄨㄣ ㄒㄩㄢ ㄅㄧㄥˋ ㄇㄠˋ)
Both parents are alive and well.

【楂】2514
ㄓㄚ ja zhā
1. a species of hawthorn
2. a wooden raft

楂楂 (ㄓㄚ ㄓㄚ)
the sound of magpies crowing

【楓】2515
ㄈㄥ feng fēng
a maple

楓糖 (ㄈㄥ ㄊㄤˊ)
maple sugar

楓橋 (ㄈㄥ ㄑㄧㄠˊ)
name of a bridge at Soo-chow, Kiangsu Province

楓宸 (ㄈㄥ ㄔㄣˊ)
an emperor's residence

楓樹 (ㄈㄥ ㄕㄨˋ)
a maple: 楓樹到秋天就變紅了。Maples turn red in fall.

【楊】2516
ㄧㄤˊ yang yáng
1. a poplar
2. a willow
3. a Chinese family name

楊白頭 (ㄧㄤˊ ㄅㄞˊ ㄊㄡˊ)
an albino

楊朱 (ㄧㄤˊ ㄓㄨ)
Yang Chu, an egoist, and Mo Ti, a philanthropist, both were contemporaries of Mencius

楊梅 (ㄧㄤˊ ㄇㄟˊ)
(botany) an arbutus

楊梅瘡 (ㄧㄤˊ ㄇㄟˊ ㄔㄨㄤ)
syphilis 亦作「梅毒」

楊太真 (ㄧㄤˊ ㄊㄞˋ ㄓㄣ)or楊玉環 (ㄧㄤˊ ㄩˋ ㄏㄨㄢˊ)
Yang Yü-huan (719-756), a concubine of Emperor Hsüan Tsung of the Tang Dynasty 亦作「楊貴妃」

楊桃 (ㄧㄤˊ ㄊㄠˊ)
a carambola or star fruit

楊柳 (ㄧㄤˊ ㄌㄧㄡˇ)
a willow

楊花 (ㄧㄤˊ ㄏㄨㄚ)
poplar blossoms; poplar fila-

〔木部〕

ments

楊朱（ㄧㄤ ㄓㄨ）
Yang Chu, a contemporary of Mencius and advocate of egoism

【木部】

【楔】 2517
ㄒㄧㄝ shieh xiē
1. to wedge
2. a gatepost
3. a wedge

楔緊（ㄒㄧㄝ ㄐㄧㄣ）
to wedge it tight

楔形葉（ㄒㄧㄝ ㄒㄧㄥˊ ㄧㄝˋ）
a cuneate leaf

楔形文字（ㄒㄧㄝ ㄒㄧㄥˊ ㄨㄣˊ ㄗˋ）
cuneiform; sphenogram

楔子（ㄒㄧㄝ ˙ㄗ）
①a wedge ②a preface; a foreword; a prologue

【楙】 2518
ㄇㄠˊ maw mào
1. (said of vegetation) luxuriant; lush
2. name of a plant

【楛】
1. ㄏㄨˋ huh hù
the arrow-thorn—name of a plant

楛矢（ㄏㄨˋ ㄕ）
an arrow with a shaft made of this particular wood

【楛】 2519
2. ㄎㄨˇ kuu kǔ
crude and easy to break

【楞】 2520
1. ㄌㄥˊ leng léng
1. angular
2. an edge
3. Ceylon (used in Buddhist books)

楞伽（ㄌㄥˊ ㄑㄧㄝ）
①Lanka, a mountain in the southeast part of Ceylon, now called Adam's Peak ②the island of Ceylon

楞伽經（ㄌㄥˊ ㄑㄧㄝ ㄐㄧㄥ）
the Lankavatara sutra

楞嚴經（ㄌㄥˊ ㄧㄢˊ ㄐㄧㄥ）
the Surangama sutra

【楞】 2520
2. (楞) ㄌㄥˋ lenq lèng
stupid; imbecile; rude

【楡】 2521
ㄩˊ yu yú
an elm

楡皮（ㄩˊ ㄆㄧˊ）
elm bark (used as medicine)

楡林港（ㄩˊ ㄌㄧㄣˊ ㄍㄤˇ）
Yülin, a seaport on Hainan Island

楡關（ㄩˊ ㄍㄨㄢ）
Elm Pass, another name of Shanhaikwan（山海關）, eastern end of the Great Wall

楡科（ㄩˊ ㄎㄜ）
Ulmaceae, the elm family

楡火（ㄩˊ ㄏㄨㄛˇ）
a fire produced by rubbing pieces of elm wood

楡莢（ㄩˊ ㄐㄧㄚˊ）
elm seeds

楡莢雨（ㄩˊ ㄐㄧㄚˊ ㄩˇ）
spring rain

楡錢兒糕（ㄩˊ ㄑㄧㄢˊ ㄦ ㄍㄠ）
elm-seed cake

楡錢兒（ㄩˊ ㄑㄧㄢˊ ㄦ）or 楡錢兒（ㄩˊ ㄑㄧㄢˊ ㄦ）
elm seeds 參看「楡莢」

楡樹（ㄩˊ ㄕㄨˋ）
an elm; an elm tree

楡塞（ㄩˊ ㄙㄞ）
a frontier stronghold

【楝】 2522
ㄌㄧㄢˋ liann liàn
a kind of tree (Melia azedarach); chinaberry

楝樹（ㄌㄧㄢˋ ㄕㄨˋ）
chinaberry

【栖】 2523
ㄧㄡˊ you yóu
a kind of tree (Quercus glandulifera)

【楰】 2524
ㄩˊ yu yú
Yü (name of a plant)

【楚】 2525
ㄔㄨˇ chuu chǔ
1. name of a powerful feudal state which existed 740-330 B. C.
2. a Chinese family name
3. clear; neat
4. distress; suffering

楚霸王（ㄔㄨˇ ㄅㄚˋ ㄨㄤˊ）
the title adopted by Hsiang Yü（項羽）, who overthrew the Chin Dynasty

楚歌（ㄔㄨˇ ㄍㄜ）
the songs of the people of Chu（楚）參看「四面楚歌」

楚國（ㄔㄨˇ ㄍㄨㄛˊ）
a powerful feudal state that existed 740-330 B. C.

楚館秦樓（ㄔㄨˇ ㄍㄨㄢˇ ㄑㄧㄣˊ ㄌㄡˊ）
places for pleasure; brothels

楚弓楚得（ㄔㄨˇ ㄍㄨㄥ ㄔㄨˇ ㄉㄜˊ）
Loss of a possession within one's own state is no cause for regret because it will come into the possession of a fellow countryman, not of an alien.

楚狂（ㄔㄨˇ ㄎㄨㄤˊ）
a lunatic

楚河漢界（ㄔㄨˇ ㄏㄜˊ ㄏㄢˋ ㄐㄧㄝˋ）
the border of two opposing powers

楚囚（ㄔㄨˇ ㄑㄧㄡˊ）
①a prisoner ②a man in great straits

楚囚對泣（ㄔㄨˇ ㄑㄧㄡˊ ㄉㄨㄟˋ ㄑㄧˋ）
to lament a common misery

楚楚（ㄔㄨˇ ㄔㄨˇ）
①touching; pathetic ②bright and clear ③tidy; neat

楚楚動人（ㄔㄨˇ ㄔㄨˇ ㄉㄨㄥˋ ㄖㄣˊ）
(said of a young woman) lovingly pathetic; delicate and attractive

楚楚可憐（ㄔㄨˇ ㄔㄨˇ ㄎㄜˇ ㄌㄧㄢˊ）
pathetically delicate; tender and pathetic: 那女孩子楚楚可憐. That girl was delicate and touching.

楚聲（ㄔㄨˇ ㄕㄥ）
the songs of the people of Chu（楚）

楚辭（ㄔㄨˇ ㄘˊ）
a collection of poems compiled by Liu Hsiang（劉向）

楚材晉用（ㄔㄨˇ ㄘㄞˊ ㄐㄧㄣˋ ㄩㄥˋ）
(literally) Chu's talents are employed by Tsin—(figuratively) Talents of one country are employed by other countries.

楚騷（ㄔㄨˇ ㄙㄠ）
Li-sao, a representative work by the patriotic poet Chü Yüan（屈原）of the state of Chu

楚腰（ㄔㄨˇ ㄧㄠ）
(literally) the waist of Chu—the slim waist of a woman

【業】 2526
ㄧㄝˋ yeh yè
1. work; occupations; professions; vocations; callings; trades: 他已經失業一年了. He has been out of work for a year.
2. estate; property
3. already

業荒於嬉(ㄧㄝˋㄏㄨㄤㄩㄒㄧ)
Distraction deprives work of excellence.

業績(ㄧㄝˋㄐㄧ)
the track record

業經(ㄧㄝˋㄐㄧㄥ)
to have already been: 你的求職申請書業經批准。Your application for the position has already been approved.

業精於勤(ㄧㄝˋㄐㄧㄥㄩㄑㄧㄣˊ)
Excellence in work is possible only with diligence.

業障(ㄧㄝˋㄓㄤ)
(Buddhism) the past sin as a present obstacle; karma

業主(ㄧㄝˋㄓㄨˇ)
the proprietor; the owner

業種(ㄧㄝˋㄓㄨㄥˇ)
son of a concubine; a bastard

業師(ㄧㄝˋㄕ)
one's teacher

業已(ㄧㄝˋㄧˇ)
already: 他的老板業已病故。His boss has already died of illness.

業務(ㄧㄝˋㄨˋ)
official functions; business activities: 這家公司恢復正常業務。This company resumed normal business.

業餘(ㄧㄝˋㄩˊ)
① nonprofessional; amateur ② spare time: 他利用業餘時間幫朋友修手錶。He repaired wrist watches for his friends during his spare time.

【楣】 2527
ㄇㄟˊ mei méi
the lintel (over a door)

楣式(ㄇㄟˊㄕˋ)
the lintel style

【楨】 2528
ㄓㄣ jen zhēn
(又讀 ㄓㄥ jeng zhēng)

1. sturdy wood
2. posts at ends of walls

【楫】 2529
ㄐㄧˊ jyi jí
1. an oar
2. a boat

楫師(ㄐㄧˊㄕ)
a boatman; a ferryman

【楬】 2530
ㄐㄧㄝˊ jye jié
a signpost

【極】 2531
ㄐㄧˊ jyi jí

1. to exhaust
2. extreme; extremely; highest; topmost; farthest; utmost: 此事極爲重要。This is a matter of the utmost importance.
3. poles: 北極與南極 the North and South Poles
4. to reach; to arrive at

極表同情(ㄐㄧˊㄅㄧㄠˇㄊㄨㄥˊㄑㄧㄥˊ)
very sympathetic

極品(ㄐㄧˊㄆㄧㄣˇ)
a thing of the highest grade

極目(ㄐㄧˊㄇㄨˋ)
to look as far as possible

極峯(ㄐㄧˊㄈㄥ)
the topmost figure (of a nation)

極大(ㄐㄧˊㄉㄚˋ)
maximum

極地(ㄐㄧˊㄉㄧˋ)
the polar regions

極點(ㄐㄧˊㄉㄧㄢˇ)or極頂(ㄐㄧˊㄉㄧㄥˇ)
an extremity; the topmost point; the zenith; the apex; the height; the climax: 他走到了極點。He was at the apex of his fortunes.

極度(ㄐㄧˊㄉㄨˋ)
extremely; exceedingly: 我極度疲勞。I was extremely tired.

極多(ㄐㄧˊㄉㄨㄛ)
extremely numerous

極端(ㄐㄧˊㄉㄨㄢ)
an extreme; an extreme act; extremely: 他極端負責的態度令老闆讚賞。His extreme sense of responsibility was appreciated by his boss.

極東(ㄐㄧˊㄉㄨㄥ)
the Far East

極樂世界(ㄐㄧˊㄌㄜˋㄕˋㄐㄧㄝˋ)
(Buddhism) Paradise; Pure Land

極力(ㄐㄧˊㄌㄧˋ)
to make every effort: 我們應極力避免犯錯。We ought to make the utmost effort to avoid mistakes.

極流(ㄐㄧˊㄌㄧㄡˊ)
polar currents 亦作「寒流」

極量(ㄐㄧˊㄌㄧㄤˋ)
(pharmacology) the maximum dose

極光(ㄐㄧˊㄍㄨㄤ)
the auroras (or aurorae); the polar lights: 北極光 the northern lights 南極光 the southern lights

極口稱讚(ㄐㄧˊㄎㄡˇㄔㄥㄗㄢˋ)
to speak in the highest terms; to praise lavishly

極好(ㄐㄧˊㄏㄠˇ)
very good; extremely good; superb; excellent: 這演員表演得極好。The actor gave a superb performance.

極化(ㄐㄧˊㄏㄨㄚˋ)
polarization; to polarize: 社會極化成兩個階級。Society has polarized into two classes.

極壞(ㄐㄧˊㄏㄨㄞˋ)
the worst

極盡(ㄐㄧˊㄐㄧㄣˋ)
to use to the utmost

極距(ㄐㄧˊㄐㄩˋ)
(astronomy) polar distance

極其(ㄐㄧˊㄑㄧˊ)
very; exceedingly; highly: 王小姐是一個極其美麗的女孩。Miss Wang is a girl of exceeding beauty.

極圈(ㄐㄧˊㄑㄩㄢ)
the polar circles

極權國家(ㄐㄧˊㄑㄩㄢˊㄍㄨㄛˊㄐㄧㄚ)
a dictatorial nation; a dictatorship; a totalitarian nation

極權主義(ㄐㄧˊㄑㄩㄢˊㄓㄨˇㄧˋ)
dictatorship; totalitarianism

極限(ㄐㄧˊㄒㄧㄢˋ)
(mathematics) a limit

極刑(ㄐㄧˊㄒㄧㄥˊ)
death penalty; capital punishment

極行(ㄐㄧˊㄒㄧㄥˊ)
the best deed

極選(ㄐㄧˊㄒㄩㄢˇ)
the best choice

極致(ㄐㄧˊㄓˋ)
the ultimate attainment; acme

極軸(ㄐㄧˊㄓㄡˊ)
(mathematics) a polar axis

極處(ㄐㄧˊㄔㄨˋ)
extremity; the farthest point

極盛(ㄐㄧˊㄕㄥˋ)
the heyday; the prime; the zenith; the acme; the golden age: 羅馬在極盛時期統治了整個文明的歐洲。Rome ruled all of civilized Europe at the

〔木部〕

〔木部〕

zenith of its power.

極尊 (ㄐㄧˊ ㄗㄨㄣ)
parents

極惡 (ㄐㄧˊ ㄜˋ)
extreme atrocity

極為 (ㄐㄧˊ ㄨㄟˊ)
extremely; exceedingly; highly

【楮】 2532
ㄔㄨ chuu chǔ
paper mulberry

楮幣 (ㄔㄨˇ ㄅㄧˋ)or 楮券 (ㄔㄨˇ ㄑㄩㄢˋ)
(formerly) a bank note

楮墨 (ㄔㄨˇ ㄇㄛˋ)
paper and ink

楮錢 (ㄔㄨˇ ㄑㄧㄢˊ)or 楮鏹 (ㄔㄨˇ ㄑㄧㄤˇ)
imitation paper money burned for the dead

楮知白 (ㄔㄨˇ ㄓ ㄅㄞˊ)
another name of paper

【楷】 2533
ㄎㄞˇ kae kǎi
1. regular; standard
2. a model; a norm
3. (calligraphy) standard script: 請用正楷寫你的名字。Please write your name in standard script.

楷模 (ㄎㄞˇ ㄇㄛˊ)
a model (for imitation)：他是勤勞的楷模。He's a model of industry.

楷法 (ㄎㄞˇ ㄈㄚˇ)
techniques of standard handwriting

楷範 (ㄎㄞˇ ㄈㄢˋ)
a model for others in conduct, etc.

楷書 (ㄎㄞˇ ㄕㄨ)
the standard style of handwriting in Chinese, as block letters in English

楷書 (ㄎㄞˇ ㄕㄨ)
standard script of handwriting; regular script

楷則 (ㄎㄞˇ ㄗㄜˊ)
a model; a norm

【楸】 2534
ㄑㄧㄡ chiou qiū
Chinese catalpa (Mallotus japonicus)，a kind of hard wood used for making chessboards

楸枰 (ㄑㄧㄡ ㄆㄧㄥˊ)
a chessboard

【楹】 2535
ㄧㄥˊ yng yíng

a pillar; a column:

楹聯 (ㄧㄥˊ ㄌㄧㄢˊ)
the scrolls hung on a pillar; the literary couplet on a pillar or wall

楹鼓 (ㄧㄥˊ ㄍㄨˇ)
a large drum strengthened with a cross bar

楹柱 (ㄧㄥˊ ㄓㄨˋ)
a pillar; a column

【楯】 2536
ㄕㄨㄣˇ shoen shǔn
1. the horizontal bar of a railing
2. same as 盾—a shield used in battle

【梗】 2537
ㄆㄧㄢˊ pyan pián
a kind of tree

十畫

【榕】 2538
ㄖㄨㄥˊ rong róng
a banyan tree

榕城 (ㄖㄨㄥˊ ㄔㄥˊ)
another name of Foochow (福州)，noted for its banyan trees

榕樹 (ㄖㄨㄥˊ ㄕㄨˋ)
a banyan tree

【榔】 2539
ㄌㄤˊ lang láng
1. a betel palm
2. a betel nut

榔頭 (ㄌㄤˊ ㄊㄡˊ)
a hammer

【榛】 2540
ㄓㄣ jen zhēn
a hazel

榛莽 (ㄓㄣ ㄇㄤˇ)
thickets; bushes; thick underbrush or undergrowth

榛蕪 (ㄓㄣ ㄨˊ)
overgrown with wild plants

榛子 (ㄓㄣ ㄗ)
a hazelnut

榛蕪 (ㄓㄣ ㄨˊ)
①bushy and weedy ②a wilderness ③humble; inferior

【榦】 2541
1．(幹) ㄍㄢˋ gann gàn
1. a tree trunk
2. posts, or supports, at ends of walls

2．(幹) ㄏㄢˋ harn hàn
railings around a well

【榖】 2542
ㄨˊ guu gǔ
a kind of tree (Broussonetia papyrifera)

【橰】 2543
ㄍㄠ gau gāo
a well sweep

【榭】 2544
ㄒㄧㄝˋ shieh xiè
a pavilion; an arbor; a kiosk: 水榭 a pavilion surrounded by water

【榫】 2545
ㄙㄨㄣˇ soen sǔn
tenon and mortise

榫頭 (ㄙㄨㄣˇ ㄊㄡˊ)
a tenon

榫子 (ㄙㄨㄣˇ ㄗ)or 榫兒 (ㄙㄨㄣˇㄦ)
tenon and mortise

榫牙 (ㄙㄨㄣˇ ㄧㄚˊ)
a tenon

榫眼 (ㄙㄨㄣˇ ㄧㄢˇ)
a mortise

【榨】 2546
ㄓㄚˋ jah zhà
to squeeze or press (for juice); to extract: 他把檸檬榨乾。He squeezed a lemon dry.

榨取 (ㄓㄚˋ ㄑㄩˇ)
exploitation; to exploit; to extort; to squeeze: 榨取遊客會破壞商業。Exploitation of the tourist destroys trade.

榨牀 (ㄓㄚˋ ㄔㄨㄤˊ)
a press for extracting oil or juice

榨菜 (ㄓㄚˋ ㄘㄞˋ)
preserved mustard seasoned with salt and hot pepper

榨油 (ㄓㄚˋ ㄧㄡˊ)
to extract oil: 我們可自橄欖中榨油。We can extract oil from olives.

榨油水 (ㄓㄚˋ ㄧㄡˊ ㄕㄨㄟˇ)
to extort money from people

【榜】 2547
1．ㄅㄤˇ baang bǎng
a publicly posted roll of successful examinees

榜牌 (ㄅㄤˇ ㄆㄞˊ)
a bulletin board

榜帖 (ㄅㄤˇ ㄊㄧㄝˇ)
①a list of successful examinees ②a bulletin; a public

notice

榜示（ㄅㄤˇ ㄕˋ）
to post for public attention

榜首（ㄅㄤˇ ㄕㄡˇ）
the top candidate of an examination

榜上無名（ㄅㄤˇ ㄕㄤˋ ㄨˊ ㄇㄧㄥˊ）
to fail in an examination

榜額（ㄅㄤˇ ㄜˊ）
a horizontal tablet

榜眼（ㄅㄤˇ ㄧㄢˇ）
the second best of the successful examinees in the imperial examination

榜樣（ㄅㄤˇ ㄧㄤˋ）
an example; a model

榜文（ㄅㄤˇ ㄨㄣˊ）
the writing in a public notice

【榜】 2547
2. ㄅㄥˋ beng bèng
1. to oar
2. a whip; a rod

榜女（ㄅㄥˋ ㄋㄩˇ）
a boatwoman

榜掠（ㄅㄥˋ ㄌㄩㄝˋ）
to whip; to flog

榜歌（ㄅㄥˋ ㄍㄜ）
a boatman's song

榜笞（ㄅㄥˋ ㄔ）
to beat; to flog; to whip

榜楚（ㄅㄥˋ ㄔㄨˇ）
to beat; to flog; to whip

榜箠（ㄅㄥˋ ㄔㄨㄟˊ）
a cane for torturing criminals

榜人（ㄅㄥˋ ㄖㄣˊ）
a boatman; a ferryman

【榱】 2548
ㄘㄨㄟ tsuei cuī
a rafter

【榻】 2549
ㄊㄚˋ tah tà
a couch; a bed

榻布（ㄊㄚˋ ㄅㄨˋ）
a kind of coarse cloth

榻登（ㄊㄚˋ ㄉㄥ）
a rug placed on a low-legged stool beside a bed

榻榻米（ㄊㄚˋ ㄊㄚˋ ㄇㄧˇ）
(Japanese) tatami—① any of a number of thick, woven straw mats of uniform dimensions, about three feet by six feet, used in Japanese houses ② a measure of living space equal to about 18

square feet

【榴】 2550
ㄌㄧㄡˊ liou liú
a pomegranate

榴彈（ㄌㄧㄡˊ ㄉㄢˋ）
a grenade; a high explosive shell

榴彈砲（ㄌㄧㄡˊ ㄉㄢˋ ㄆㄠˋ）
a howitzer

榴火（ㄌㄧㄡˊ ㄏㄨㄛˇ）
fiery red of pomegranate blossoms

【榮】 2551
ㄖㄨㄥˊ rong róng
1. glory; honor: 他是讓全國引以爲榮的人。 He is an honor to his country.
2. luxuriant; lush; teeming; leafy: 草春榮冬枯。 Grass grows in spring and withers in winter.
3. a Chinese family name

榮民（ㄖㄨㄥˊ ㄇㄧㄣˊ）
retired servicemen; veterans

榮名（ㄖㄨㄥˊ ㄇㄧㄥˊ）
honor and fame

榮典（ㄖㄨㄥˊ ㄉㄧㄢˇ）
a honorary reward

榮祿（ㄖㄨㄥˊ ㄌㄨˋ）
Jung Lu, a high ranking Manchu official, who helped Empress Dowager Tzu Hsi thwart the political reform movement during the last years of the 19th century

榮祿大夫（ㄖㄨㄥˊ ㄌㄨˋ ㄉㄚˋ ㄈㄨ）
a rank in government service in former times

榮歸（ㄖㄨㄥˊ ㄍㄨㄟ）
①(said of a high official) to retire in glory ②to return home in triumph

榮光（ㄖㄨㄥˊ ㄍㄨㄤ）
glory; splendor

榮枯（ㄖㄨㄥˊ ㄎㄨ）
①(said of vegetation) flourishing and withering ②rise and fall; ups and downs; vicissitudes: 我們應該榮枯與共。 We should share our vicissitudes.

榮華富貴（ㄖㄨㄥˊ ㄏㄨㄚˊ ㄈㄨˋ ㄍㄨㄟˋ）
honor and wealth

榮獲（ㄖㄨㄥˊ ㄏㄨㄛˋ）
to get or win the honor : 此次比賽他榮獲冠軍。 He won the championship in the con-

test.

榮顯（ㄖㄨㄥˊ ㄒㄧㄢˇ）
honor and high position

榮幸（ㄖㄨㄥˊ ㄒㄧㄥˋ）
honored; to have the honor of: 很榮幸能與你共餐。 It is a great honor to dine with you.

榮恥（ㄖㄨㄥˊ ㄔˇ）
honor and dishonor

榮寵（ㄖㄨㄥˊ ㄔㄨㄥˇ）
glorious favor

榮施（ㄖㄨㄥˊ ㄕ）
glorious giving

榮任（ㄖㄨㄥˊ ㄖㄣˋ）
to have the honor of being appointed (to a post)

榮辱（ㄖㄨㄥˊ ㄖㄨˇ）
honor and dishonor

榮宗耀祖（ㄖㄨㄥˊ ㄗㄨㄥ ㄧㄠˋ ㄗㄨˇ）
to bring glory to one's family and ancestors; to redound to the glory of one's ancestors

榮悴（ㄖㄨㄥˊ ㄘㄨㄟˋ）
①flourishing and withering (of vegetation) ②ups and downs; vicissitudes

榮哀錄（ㄖㄨㄥˊ ㄞ ㄌㄨˋ）
a collection of eulogies and commemorative writings in honor of an illustrious figure

榮耀（ㄖㄨㄥˊ ㄧㄠˋ）
glory; honor; splendor

榮養（ㄖㄨㄥˊ ㄧㄤˇ）
to support one's parents

榮膺（ㄖㄨㄥˊ ㄧㄥ）
to have the honor of being appointed (to a post)

榮譽（ㄖㄨㄥˊ ㄩˋ）
honor: 他的成功爲學校贏得榮譽。 His success won honor for his school.

榮譽軍人（ㄖㄨㄥˊ ㄩˋ ㄐㄩㄣ ㄖㄣˊ）
servicemen wounded in action

【槃】 2552
（盤）ㄆㄢˊ parn pán
1. a wooden tray
2. great

槃根錯節（ㄆㄢˊ ㄍㄣ ㄘㄨㄛˋ ㄐㄧㄝˊ）
① very complicated; difficult to solve or explain ② (said of old social forces) deep-rooted 亦作「盤根錯節」

槃才（ㄆㄢˊ ㄘㄞˊ）
a person of great talent

槃匜（ㄆㄢˊ ㄧˊ）

【木部】

a basin; a tray; a washing-bowl

【槊】 2553
ㄕㄨㄛˋ shuoh shuò
a spear; a lance

【槁】 2554
(槀)《ㄍㄠˇ gao gǎo
withered; dead; rotten: 長期臥病使這病人形容枯槁。A long illness has emaciated the invalid.

槁木死灰《ㄍㄠ ㄇㄨˋ ㄙˇ ㄏㄨㄟ》
(literally) rotten wood and cold ashes—a person utterly without vitality or ambition; completely apathetic

槁骨《ㄍㄠˇ ㄍㄨˇ》
bones of the deceased

槁梧《ㄍㄠˇ ㄨˊ》
name of a stringed instrument in Chinese music

【構】 2555
《ㄍㄡˋ gow gòu
to frame; to form; to build; to establish; to constitute; to scheme: 雙親與孩子構成一個家庭。Parents and children form a family.

構兵《ㄍㄡˋ ㄅㄧㄥ》
to be at war; to have a clash of arms; to wage war

構圖《ㄍㄡˋ ㄊㄨˊ》
composition (in drawing): 他的畫構圖甚美。The composition of his picture is beautiful.

構難《ㄍㄡˋ ㄋㄢˊ》
to bring trouble

構亂《ㄍㄡˋ ㄌㄨㄢˋ》
to stir up disorder

構禍《ㄍㄡˋ ㄏㄨㄛˋ》
to bring disaster

構會《ㄍㄡˋ ㄏㄨㄟˋ》
to incriminate unjustly

構精《ㄍㄡˋ ㄐㄧㄥ》
① to have sexual union ② to concentrate attention

構陷《ㄍㄡˋ ㄒㄧㄢˋ》
to frame a charge against someone; to incriminate unjustly

構釁《ㄍㄡˋ ㄒㄧㄣˋ》
to be at feud

構想《ㄍㄡˋ ㄒㄧㄤˇ》
an idea; a conception; a plan; a scheme

構築《ㄍㄡˋ ㄓㄨˋ》
to construct; to build: 我們構築防禦工事。We construct our fortifications.

構成《ㄍㄡˋ ㄔㄥˊ》
to constitute; to form; to contexture

構造《ㄍㄡˋ ㄗㄠˋ》
structure; construction; organization: 人體是巧妙的構造。Human body is a wonderful structure.

構造心理學《ㄍㄡˋ ㄗㄠˋ ㄒㄧㄣ ㄌㄧˇ ㄒㄩㄝˊ》
structural psychology

構造式《ㄍㄡˋ ㄗㄠˋ ㄕˋ》
constitutional formula (of a chemical compound)

構思《ㄍㄡˋ ㄙ》
① to weigh something mentally ② to plot; a plot

構怨《ㄍㄡˋ ㄩㄢˋ》
to be at feud; to contract hatred against

【槌】 2556
ㄔㄨㄟˊ chwei chuí
a hammer

槌兒《ㄔㄨㄟˊ ㄦˊ》
a hammer

槌骨《ㄔㄨㄟˊ ㄍㄨˇ》
a malleus

槌鼓《ㄔㄨㄟˊ ㄍㄨˇ》
to beat a drum

槌擊《ㄔㄨㄟˊ ㄐㄧ》
to beat with a hammer

槌球《ㄔㄨㄟˊ ㄑㄧㄡˊ》
croquet

【槍】 2557
ㄑㄧㄤ chiang qiāng
1. a spear; a lance; a javelin
2. a rifle; a pistol; a gun

槍斃《ㄑㄧㄤ ㄅㄧˋ》or槍決《ㄑㄧㄤ ㄐㄩㄝˊ》
to execute by shooting; to shoot to death

槍炮《ㄑㄧㄤ ㄆㄠˋ》
firearms; guns

槍法《ㄑㄧㄤ ㄈㄚˇ》
① marksmanship ② art of using spears

槍刀劍戟《ㄑㄧㄤ ㄉㄠ ㄐㄧㄢˋ ㄐㄧˇ》
arms; weapons

槍彈《ㄑㄧㄤ ㄉㄢˋ》
a cartridge; a shell; a bullet

槍頭兒《ㄑㄧㄤ ㄊㄡˊ ㄦˊ》
a spearhead

槍膛《ㄑㄧㄤ ㄊㄤˊ》
a bore

槍替《ㄑㄧㄤ ㄊㄧˋ》
to serve as a substitute examinee; to take an examination in place of the real examinee

槍托《ㄑㄧㄤ ㄊㄨㄛ》
the rifle butt; the gun stock

槍榴彈《ㄑㄧㄤ ㄌㄧㄡˊ ㄉㄢˋ》
a rifle grenade

槍林彈雨《ㄑㄧㄤ ㄌㄧㄣˊ ㄉㄢˋ ㄩˇ》
a fierce battle (in which one faces a rain of bullets and artillery shells): 戰士們冒著槍林彈雨衝鋒陷陣。The soldiers charged under a hail of bullets.

槍桿《ㄑㄧㄤ ㄍㄢˇ》
① the shaft of a spear ② a rifle; arms

槍口《ㄑㄧㄤ ㄎㄡˇ》
a muzzle (of a rifle, pistol, etc.)

槍機《ㄑㄧㄤ ㄐㄧ》
a trigger

槍尖《ㄑㄧㄤ ㄐㄧㄢ》
a spearhead

槍械《ㄑㄧㄤ ㄒㄧㄝˋ》
weapons

槍枝《ㄑㄧㄤ ㄓ》
rifles

槍戰《ㄑㄧㄤ ㄓㄢˋ》
a gun battle; exchange of fire; a shootout: 他們都是在槍戰中受傷。They are all wounded in the gun battle.

槍殺《ㄑㄧㄤ ㄕㄚ》
to shoot

槍手《ㄑㄧㄤ ㄕㄡˇ》
① 《ㄑㄧㄤ ㄕㄡˇ》a rifleman; a gunman; a hired gunman ② 《ㄑㄧㄤ ㄕㄡˇ》③ a substitute examinee; a hired examinee; one who takes an examination in place of the real examinee ⑤ a ghost writer

槍傷《ㄑㄧㄤ ㄕㄤ》
bullet (or gunshot) wounds

槍擊《ㄑㄧㄤ ㄐㄧ》
the report or crack of a gun; a shot

槍刺《ㄑㄧㄤ ㄘˋ》
to thrust with a spear

【槐】 2558
ㄏㄨㄞˊ hwai huái
a locust tree (Sophora japonica) similar to the ash; an

acacia; a Chinese scholar-tree

槐鼎 (ㄏㄨㄞˊ ㄉㄧㄥˇ)
the three top officials of the state in ancient times

槐火 (ㄏㄨㄞˊ ㄏㄨㄛˇ)
a fire made by drilling a piece of locust wood

槐序 (ㄏㄨㄞˊ ㄒㄩˋ)
summer

槐月 (ㄏㄨㄞˊ ㄩㄝˋ)
the fourth moon of the lunar year

【槎】 2559 ㄔㄚˊ char chá
1. a raft
2. to hew; to chop; to cut

【槓】 2560 ㄍㄤˋ gang gàng
1. a lever; a carrying pole
2. (sports) a bar
3. to sharpen (a knife)
4. to argue; to dispute
5. to cross out

槓夫 (ㄍㄤˋ ㄈㄨ)
a coffin bearer

槓刀 (ㄍㄤˋ ㄉㄠ)
to sharpen a knife

槓刀布 (ㄍㄤˋ ㄉㄠ ㄅㄨˋ)
a coarse cloth for sharpening a razor

槓頭 (ㄍㄤˋ ㄊㄡˊ)
①the head coffin bearer ②
an argumentative person

槓鈴 (ㄍㄤˋ ㄌㄧㄥˊ)
(sports) a barbell

槓桿 (ㄍㄤˋ ㄍㄢˇ)
a lever; a pry: 工人用槓桿移動巖石。The worker is levering at the rock.

槓桿定律 (ㄍㄤˋ ㄍㄢˇ ㄉㄧㄥˋ ㄌㄩˋ)
(physics) law of lever

槓子 (ㄍㄤˋ ˙ㄗ)
①horizontal or parallel bars: 他會玩槓子。He can take gymnastic exercises on bars. ②a stout carrying pole

【榷】 2561 ㄑㄩㄝˋ chiueh què
1. to monopolize
2. to levy taxes

榷利 (ㄑㄩㄝˋ ㄌㄧˋ)
to enjoy monopoly

榷酤 (ㄑㄩㄝˋ ㄍㄨ)
to monopolize the sale of alcoholic beverages

榷茶 (ㄑㄩㄝˋ ㄔㄚˊ)
to levy tea taxes

榷鹽 (ㄑㄩㄝˋ ㄧㄢˊ)
to levy salt taxes

榷運司 (ㄑㄩㄝˋ ㄩㄣˋ ㄙ)
a government agency in charge of salt taxes

【榧】 2562 ㄈㄟˇ feei fěi
a species of yew (Torreya nucifera)

【榾】 2563 ㄍㄨˇ guu gǔ
chopped pieces of wood

榾柮 (ㄍㄨˇ ㄉㄨㄛˋ)
chopped pieces of wood

【槅】 2564 ㄍㄜˊ ger gé
a semicircular wooden collar at the end of the shafts of a large carriage; a yoke for harnessing animals

十一畫

【槥】 2565 ㄏㄨㄟˋ huey huì
a small coffin

【槭】 2566 ㄗㄨˊ tzwu zú
a kind of maple (Acer palmatum)

槭樹 (ㄗㄨˊ ㄕㄨˋ)
a maple

【橚】 2567 ㄧㄡˇ yeou yǒu
1. an ancient rite of building fires in worship
2. to supply firewood for building fires

【概】 2568 (槩) (ㄍㄞˋ) gay gài
1. general; overall; roughly: 大概地說物價仍在上漲。Overall, prices are rising.
2. without exception; categorically
3. the manner of carrying oneself; deportment

概不考慮 (ㄍㄞˋ ㄅㄨˋ ㄎㄠˇ ㄌㄩˋ)
No consideration will be given to all requests, suggestions, etc.

概不除欠 (ㄍㄞˋ ㄅㄨˋ ㄔㄨˊ ㄑㄧㄢˋ)
No sale on credit under all circumstances, conditions, etc. No chits.

概不容情 (ㄍㄞˋ ㄅㄨˋ ㄖㄨㄥˊ ㄑㄧㄥˊ)
No leniency toward any offence, mistake, etc.

概貌 (ㄍㄞˋ ㄇㄠˋ)
a general picture

概念 (ㄍㄞˋ ㄋㄧㄢˋ)
a concept; a conception; a general idea

概論 (ㄍㄞˋ ㄌㄨㄣˋ)
a general discussion; an outline

概略 (ㄍㄞˋ ㄌㄩㄝˋ)
an outline; a summary: 他已告訴我這篇故事的概略。He has already told me the outline of the story.

概觀 (ㄍㄞˋ ㄍㄨㄢ)
a general view; a bird's-eye view; a conspectus

概括 (ㄍㄞˋ ㄎㄨㄛˋ)
to summarize; to sum up; to generalize: 我把我的看法概括地講一講。I'll give my views in broad outline.

概括性 (ㄍㄞˋ ㄎㄨㄛˋ ㄒㄧㄥˋ)
generality

概況 (ㄍㄞˋ ㄎㄨㄤˋ)
a general situation; an overall condition: 我把前線的概況報告他了。I have reported the general situation of the front to him.

概見 (ㄍㄞˋ ㄐㄧㄢˋ)
to have a general look

概算 (ㄍㄞˋ ㄙㄨㄢˋ)
①to compute roughly; to make a rough estimate of ②
a preliminary government budget; a rough estimate

概而不論 (ㄍㄞˋ ㄦˊ ㄅㄨˋ ㄌㄨㄣˋ)
to do without careful consideration; to be headlong

概要 (ㄍㄞˋ ㄧㄠˋ)
a summary; an outline; a synopsis; a résumé

概行 (ㄍㄞˋ ㄒㄧㄥˊ) or 概施 (ㄍㄞˋ ㄒㄧ)
to do something without exception

【槧】 2569 ㄑㄧㄢˋ chiann qiàn
1. a wooden tablet for writing
2. an edition, or version, of a book
3. a letter

槧本 (ㄑㄧㄢˋ ㄅㄣˇ)
a book printed by engravings

〔木部〕

〔木部〕

【樂】 2570 ㄐㄧㄤ jeang jiāng
an oar

【樂】 2571
1. ㄩㄝˋ yueh yuè
1. music: 她喜愛各種音樂。She likes every kind of music.
2. a Chinese family name

樂譜(ㄩㄝˋ ㄆㄨˇ)
a score (of music); musical notes; music: 他一張一張地翻樂譜。He leafed through the music.

樂府(ㄩㄝˋ ㄈㄨˇ)
①(in ancient times) a government agency for collecting songs ②a collection of songs and poems

樂隊(ㄩㄝˋ ㄉㄨㄟˋ)
a band; an orchestra: 我們學校的樂隊是新組成的。The band of our school is newly organized.

樂團(ㄩㄝˋ ㄊㄨㄢˊ)
①a philharmonic society ②a philharmonic orchestra

樂理(ㄩㄝˋ ㄌㄧˇ)
musicology

樂歌(ㄩㄝˋ ㄍㄜ)
playing music and singing songs

樂官(ㄩㄝˋ ㄍㄨㄢ)
(formerly) the official in charge of music

樂工(ㄩㄝˋ ㄍㄨㄥ)
a musician

樂戶(ㄩㄝˋ ㄏㄨˋ)
(formerly) a government-operated whorehouse

樂經(ㄩㄝˋ ㄐㄧㄥ)
the *Book of Music* (one of the *Six Classics*, supposedly lost when the First Emperor of the Chin Dynasty burned books)

樂器(ㄩㄝˋ ㄑㄧˋ)
a musical instrument

樂曲(ㄩㄝˋ ㄑㄩ)
a piece of music; a musical composition

樂章(ㄩㄝˋ ㄓㄤ)
a movement (of a symphony, sonata, etc.)

樂師(ㄩㄝˋ ㄕ)
musicians

樂音(ㄩㄝˋ ㄧㄣ)
a musical tone; a musical sound

樂舞(ㄩㄝˋ ㄨˇ)
a dance accompanied by music

【樂】 2571 ㄌㄜˋ leh lè
1. happy; glad; joyful; joyous; cheerful; elated; content; delighted; pleased; willing: 孩子們似乎很快樂。The children seem very happy.
2. pleasant; agreeable; enjoyable; pleasing; comfortable

樂不可支(ㄌㄜˋ ㄅㄨˋ ㄎㄜˇ ㄓ)
to be beside oneself with happiness; to be overwhelmed with joy

樂不思蜀(ㄌㄜˋ ㄅㄨˋ ㄙ ㄕㄨˇ)
too happy to think of home — an allusion to Liu Chan (劉禪), who felt happy in Loyang (洛陽) after he was captured as a prisoner by Ssu-Ma Chao (司馬昭)

樂得(ㄌㄜˋ ㄉㄜˊ)
to be very glad to; to do something willingly (because of sure reward for doing it)

樂陶陶(ㄌㄜˋ ㄊㄠˊ ㄊㄠˊ)
cheerful; happy; joyful

樂天(ㄌㄜˋ ㄊㄧㄢ)
to be content with one's lot; to be optimistic; to be easy-going; happy-go-lucky

樂天派(ㄌㄜˋ ㄊㄧㄢ ㄆㄞˋ)
an optimist; an easygoing person; a happy-go-lucky person

樂天知命(ㄌㄜˋ ㄊㄧㄢ ㄓ ㄇㄧㄥˋ)
to be content with what one is; happy-go-lucky: 樂天知命的人沒煩惱。Those who are contented with their lot have nothing to worry about.

樂天主義(ㄌㄜˋ ㄊㄧㄢ ㄓㄨˇ ㄧˋ)
optimism

樂土(ㄌㄜˋ ㄊㄨˇ)
a land of comfort; a paradise

樂觀(ㄌㄜˋ ㄍㄨㄢ)
optimistic: 我們對國家的前途很樂觀。We are optimistic about the future of our country.

樂觀主義(ㄌㄜˋ ㄍㄨㄢ ㄓㄨˇ ㄧˋ)
optimism

樂呵呵(ㄌㄜˋ ㄏㄜ ㄏㄜ)
buoyant; happy and gay: 他成天總是樂呵呵的。He is always cheerful and gay.

樂禍(ㄌㄜˋ ㄏㄨㄛˋ)
to take delight in others' disaster

樂壞了(ㄌㄜˋ ㄏㄨㄞˋ ㄌㄜ)
very happy: 他樂壞了。He was very happy.

樂極生悲(ㄌㄜˋ ㄐㄧˊ ㄕㄥ ㄅㄟ)
Happiness is followed by sorrow when it reaches an extreme.

樂境(ㄌㄜˋ ㄐㄧㄥˋ)
state of happiness; happiness

樂捐(ㄌㄜˋ ㄐㄩㄢ)
to donate voluntarily

樂趣(ㄌㄜˋ ㄑㄩˋ)
delight; pleasure; joy; fun

樂嘻嘻(ㄌㄜˋ ㄒㄧ ㄒㄧ)
pleased; delighted; glad; joyous

樂助(ㄌㄜˋ ㄓㄨˋ)
willing to help

樂處(ㄌㄜˋ ㄔㄨˋ)
a source of delight; pleasures; happiness

樂施(ㄌㄜˋ ㄕ)
willing to give to the poor; charitable; generous; benevolent

樂事(ㄌㄜˋ ㄕˋ)
a pleasant thing or matter; a source of joy: 他以助人為樂事。He found a source of joy in helping others.

樂善好施(ㄌㄜˋ ㄕㄢˋ ㄏㄠˋ ㄕ)
willing to do good and give help to the poor; fond of doing philanthropic work; charitable; benevolent

樂輸(ㄌㄜˋ ㄕㄨ)
willing to pay or contribute

樂滋滋(ㄌㄜˋ ㄗ ㄗ)
contented; pleased

樂子(ㄌㄜˋ ㄗˇ)
①joy; fun; joy derived from a joke: 他尋我的樂子。He joked with me. ②an awkward predicament

樂此不疲(ㄌㄜˋ ㄘˇ ㄅㄨˋ ㄆㄧˊ)or 樂此不倦(ㄌㄜˋ ㄘˇ ㄅㄨˋ ㄐㄩㄢˋ)
to delight in a thing and never get tired of it

樂從(ㄌㄜˋ ㄘㄨㄥˊ)

willing to obey; obedient; willing to follow

樂兒(ㄌㄜˋㄦ)
①happy laughter ②an enjoyable thing: 這不是什麼樂兒. This is nothing enjoyable.

樂而不淫(ㄌㄜˋㄦˊㄅㄨˋㄧㄣˊ)
pleasant but not obscene

樂而忘返(ㄌㄜˋㄦˊㄨㄤˋㄈㄢˇ)
to be a slave of pleasure

樂以忘憂(ㄌㄜˋㄧˇㄨㄤˋㄧㄡ)
to seek pleasure in order to free oneself from care

樂易(ㄌㄜˋㄧˋ)
pleasant; agreeable

樂意(ㄌㄜˋㄧˋ)
①willing: 我樂意幫你的忙. I am willing to help you. ②pleased: 她聽了這話有點樂意. She seemed somewhat pleased with that remark.

樂業(ㄌㄜˋㄧㄝˋ)
to like one's job or trade

樂紋兒(ㄌㄜˋㄨㄣˊㄦ)
a dimple

樂聞(ㄌㄜˋㄨㄣˊ)
happy to hear about

樂於(ㄌㄜˋㄩ)
to like or love (doing something): 他樂於幫助他人. He likes to help others.

樂育(ㄌㄜˋㄩˋ)
to be happy in teaching

樂園(ㄌㄜˋㄩㄢˊ)
a paradise; Eden; Elysium: 香港是購物者的樂園. Hong Kong is a paradise for shoppers.

【樂】 2571
3. ㄧㄠˋ yaw yào
to love; to be fond of; to delight in

樂羣(ㄧㄠˋㄑㄩㄣˊ)or(ㄌㄜˋㄑㄩㄣˊ)
fond of company and learning from one's friends

【槲】 2572
ㄏㄨˊ hwu hú
a species of oak (Quercus dentata)

【槿】 2573
ㄐㄧㄣˇ jiin jǐn
1. a hibiscus
2. as in 朝槿—morning-glories

【槽】 2574
ㄘㄠˊ tsaur cáo
1. a manger

2. a trough; a flume; a chute
3. as in 跳槽—to jump on another bandwagon

槽櫪(ㄘㄠˊㄌㄧˋ)
a stable

槽子(ㄘㄠˊㄗ)
a trough; a manger 亦作「槽頭」

槽兒(ㄘㄠˊㄦ)
①a depression or groove in a surface ②(formerly) a term for addressing the wine waiter

【樁】 2575
ㄓㄨㄤ juang zhuāng
1. a stake; a post; a pile
2. a numeral auxiliary for affairs or matters

【樅】 2576
ㄘㄨㄥ tsong cōng
a fir; a fir tree (Abies firma): 樅木是一種常綠樹. The fir is an evergreen tree.

【樟】 2577
ㄓㄤ jang zhāng
a camphor tree

樟木(ㄓㄤㄇㄨˋ)
①a camphor tree ②the wood of a camphor tree

樟腦(ㄓㄤㄋㄠˇ)
camphor

樟腦酊(ㄓㄤㄋㄠˇㄉㄧㄥ)
tincture of camphor

樟腦精(ㄓㄤㄋㄠˇㄐㄧㄥ)
camphene; spirit of camphor; essence of camphor

樟腦油(ㄓㄤㄋㄠˇㄧㄡˊ)
camphor oil

樟腦丸(ㄓㄤㄋㄠˇㄨㄢˊ)
a camphor ball; a mothball

樟科(ㄓㄤㄎㄜ)
the camphor family (Lauraceae)

樟樹(ㄓㄤㄕㄨˋ)
a camphor tree

樟蠶(ㄓㄤㄘㄢˊ)
Caligula japonica, a kind of silkworm

【樗】 2578
ㄕㄨ shu shū
Ailanthus altissima

樗蒲(ㄕㄨㄆㄨˊ)
an ancient gambling game

樗櫟之材(ㄕㄨㄌㄧˋㄓㄘㄞˊ)
the timber of the ailanthus and the chestnut oak —a use-

less person

樗材(ㄕㄨㄘㄞˊ)
(a self-reference in polite conversation) a useless person; a good-for-nothing

樗散(ㄕㄨㄙㄢˇ)
to have talent without being recognized or employed

【樊】 2579
ㄈㄢˊ farn fán
1. a bird cage
2. disorderly; confused; messy
3. a Chinese family name

樊籬(ㄈㄢˊㄌㄧˊ)
①the fence ②(figuratively) something preventing progress or approach, etc.

樊籠(ㄈㄢˊㄌㄨㄥˊ)
①a cage to confine birds or wild beasts ②(figuratively) the place or condition of confinement

樊然(ㄈㄢˊㄖㄢˊ)
disorderly; confused; messy

【樓】 2580
ㄌㄡˊ lou lóu
a building of two stories or more; a tower

樓板(ㄌㄡˊㄅㄢˇ)
wooden planks used to build a floor (above the ground floor)

樓房(ㄌㄡˊㄈㄤˊ)
a building of two stories or more

樓底下(ㄌㄡˊㄉㄧˇㄒㄧㄚˋ)
the ground floor; downstairs

樓頂(ㄌㄡˊㄉㄧㄥˇ)
the top of a tall building

樓臺(ㄌㄡˊㄊㄞˊ)
a tower

樓梯(ㄌㄡˊㄊㄧ)
a staircase: 外邊的樓梯通到花園. The outside staircase leads to the garden.

樓櫓(ㄌㄡˊㄌㄨˇ)
a watchtower; a donjon

樓鴿(ㄌㄡˊㄍㄜ)
pigeons nesting in buildings

樓閣(ㄌㄡˊㄍㄜˊ)
a tower

樓下(ㄌㄡˊㄒㄧㄚˋ)
downstairs: 她在樓下等候. She is waiting downstairs.

樓船(ㄌㄡˊㄔㄨㄢˊ)
a large turreted boat

樓上(ㄌㄡˊㄕㄤˋ)

〔木部〕

upstairs: 樓上住着一位退休的老工人。A retired worker lives upstairs.

【標】 2581
ㄅㄧㄠ biau biāo

1. to show; to indicate; to mark; to symbolize; to put a mark, tag or label on: 這藥的成分標在瓶上。The ingredients of the medicine are marked on the bottle.
2. a mark; a sign; a symbol; an indication; a label
3. a model; a paragon
4. to bid; to tender

標本(ㄅㄧㄠㄅㄣˇ)
①a specimen ②appearance and substance

標榜(ㄅㄧㄠㄅㄤˇ)
①to glorify; to uphold: 他們標榜自由平等。They uphold liberty and equality. ②to profess; to declare ③to boost: 他們互相標榜。They boosted each other.

標賣(ㄅㄧㄠㄇㄞˋ)
to sell by tender

標名(ㄅㄧㄠㄇㄧㄥˊ)
a label; a title

標明(ㄅㄧㄠㄇㄧㄥˊ)
to label; to indicate; to mark clearly: 紙箱上標明「小心輕放」。The carton is marked "Handle with care."

標的(ㄅㄧㄠ˙ㄉㄜ)
a target; an objective; a purpose; an aim

標點(ㄅㄧㄠㄉㄧㄢˇ)
punctuation

標點符號(ㄅㄧㄠㄉㄧㄢˇㄈㄨˊㄏㄠˋ)
a punctuation mark

標題(ㄅㄧㄠㄊㄧˊ)
a heading; a title; a headline

標題音樂(ㄅㄧㄠㄊㄧˊㄧㄣㄩㄝˋ)
program music

標統(ㄅㄧㄠㄊㄨㄥˇ)
(Ching Dynasty) a regiment commander

標格(ㄅㄧㄠㄍㄜˊ)
an example; a model

標高(ㄅㄧㄠㄍㄠ)
elevation; the vertical distance between the top of an object and the sea level: 此山標高是五千呎。The elevation of the mountain is 5,000 feet.

標購(ㄅㄧㄠㄍㄡˋ)
to buy at public bidding

標竿(ㄅㄧㄠㄍㄢ)
a guidepost

標會(ㄅㄧㄠㄏㄨㄟˋ)
to draw lots to determine who should get the loan from a private loan association

標記(ㄅㄧㄠㄐㄧˋ)
a mark; an indication; a sign: 他已在有地雷的地方做了一個標記。He has put a mark on the spot where there is a land mine.

標價(ㄅㄧㄠㄐㄧㄚˋ)
①the tag price; the listed price ②to indicate the price of a commodity on a tag

標籤(ㄅㄧㄠㄑㄧㄢ)
a label; a tag: 我在盒子上貼了一張標籤。I put a label on the box.

標槍(ㄅㄧㄠㄑㄧㄤ)
a javelin; a spear; a lance

標新立異(ㄅㄧㄠㄒㄧㄣㄌㄧˋㄧˋ)
to try to be fanciful; to try to be original; to do something unconventional or unorthodox

標致(or 標緻)(ㄅㄧㄠㄓˋ)
(said of females) good-looking; handsome

標幟(ㄅㄧㄠㄓˋ)
a mark or sign made for distinction

標識(or 標誌)(ㄅㄧㄠㄓˋ)
a mark; a symbol; a sign

標注(ㄅㄧㄠㄓㄨˋ)
to mark (for calling attention or avoiding confusion)

標準(ㄅㄧㄠㄓㄨㄣˇ)
①a standard; a criterion: 我們學校有極高的教學標準。Our school has high standards of teaching. ②typical

標準桿(ㄅㄧㄠㄓㄨㄣˇㄍㄢ)
(golf) par

標準國語(ㄅㄧㄠㄓㄨㄣˇㄍㄨㄛˊㄩˇ)or 標準語(ㄅㄧㄠㄓㄨㄣˇㄩˇ)
Mandarin Chinese; Mandarin

標準化(ㄅㄧㄠㄓㄨㄣˇㄏㄨㄚˋ)
to standardize; standardization: 汽車零件是標準化的。The parts of an automobile are standardized.

標準局(ㄅㄧㄠㄓㄨㄣˇㄐㄩˊ)
the National Bureau of Standards

標準氣壓(ㄅㄧㄠㄓㄨㄣˇㄑㄧˋㄧㄚ)
standard atmospheric pressure

標準制(ㄅㄧㄠㄓㄨㄣˇㄓˋ)
the metric system

標準燭光(ㄅㄧㄠㄓㄨㄣˇㄓㄨˊㄍㄨㄤ)
standard (or mean) candle power: 標準燭光測量光之強度。A standard candle measures the intensity of a light.

標準時(ㄅㄧㄠㄓㄨㄣˇㄕˊ)
standard time

標準音(ㄅㄧㄠㄓㄨㄣˇㄧㄣ)
standard pronunciation

標售(ㄅㄧㄠㄕㄡˋ)
to sell by tender: 這些貨物要公開標售。These goods are to be sold through open tender.

標語(ㄅㄧㄠㄩˇ)
a slogan; a motto: 他們在牆上張貼標語。They paste up slogans on the wall.

【樛】 2582
ㄐㄧㄡ jiou jiū

1. drooping branches
2. twisted; distorted

樛木(ㄐㄧㄡㄇㄨˋ)
①a tree with hanging branches ②(figuratively) a man of position who is benevolent to the humble and the underprivileged

樛結(ㄐㄧㄡㄐㄧㄝˊ)
twisted; entangled

【樞】 2583
ㄕㄨ shu shū

1. a hinge; a pivot
2. a kind of tree

樞密使(ㄕㄨㄇㄧˋㄕˇ)or 樞使(ㄕㄨㄕˇ)or 樞相(ㄕㄨㄒㄧㄤ)
a lord chancellor, or prime minister, of the late Tang Dynasty and the Sung Dynasty

樞院(ㄕㄨㄩㄢˋ)or 樞府(ㄕㄨㄈㄨˇ)
the Privy Council, or Cabinet, of the late Tang Dynasty and the Sung Dynasty

樞紐(ㄕㄨㄋㄧㄡˇ)
the vital point; the key; the pivot: 這火車站是這個小鎮的交通樞紐。The railway sta-

樞路（ㄕㄨ ㄌㄨˋ）
a key road

樞紐（ㄕㄨ ㄋㄧㄡˇ）
①the vital element ②
important government posts
亦作「樞衡」

樞機主教（ㄕㄨ ㄐㄧ ㄓㄨˇ ㄐㄧㄠˋ）
a cardinal of the Catholic
Church

樞軸（ㄕㄨ ㄓㄡˊ）
the center of administration

樞臣（ㄕㄨ ㄔㄣˊ）
a chief courtier; a prime
minister; a premier

樞奧（ㄕㄨ ㄠˋ）
confidential information or
affairs

樞要（ㄕㄨ ㄧㄠˋ）
the center of administration

樞務（ㄕㄨ ㄨˋ）
the duty of the premier;
state affairs

【模】 2584
1. ㄇㄛˊ mo mó
1. a model; a norm: 我給他買了
一個船模型。I bought him a
model of a ship.
2. to imitate; to copy

模表（ㄇㄛˊ ㄅㄧㄠˇ）
an exemplary thing; an
example; a model

模糊糊的（ㄇㄛˊ ㄏㄨ ㄏㄨ˙ ㄉㄜ˙）
vague; ambiguous; dim;
hazy; unintelligible: 在霧中一
切東西都顯得模模糊糊的。In a
fog everything looks vague.

模範（ㄇㄛˊ ㄈㄢˋ）
an exemplary thing; an
example; a model

模範生（ㄇㄛˊ ㄈㄢˋ ㄕㄥ）
a model student

模仿（ㄇㄛˊ ㄈㄤˇ）
to imitate; to copy; to model
oneself on: 這小男孩模仿他的
父親。The little boy imitated
his father.

模倣性（ㄇㄛˊ ㄈㄤˇ ㄒㄧㄥˋ）
imitativeness

模特兒（ㄇㄛˊ ㄊㄜˋ ㄦˊ）
a model (for artists, photog-
raphers, etc.); a manikin or
mannequin

模擬（ㄇㄛˊ ㄋㄧˇ）
to simulate; to imitate

模稜兩可（ㄇㄛˊ ㄌㄥˊ ㄌㄧㄤˇ ㄎㄜˇ）
equivocal; ambiguous

模里西斯（ㄇㄛˊ ㄌㄧˇ ㄒㄧ ㄙ）
Mauritius

模楷（ㄇㄛˊ ㄎㄞˇ）
a model; a norm; an exem-
plary thing; an example; to
take something as a model
亦作「楷模」: 這個學生是勤勉的
模楷。The student is a model
of diligence.

模糊（ㄇㄛˊ ㄏㄨˊ）
①dim; vague; ambiguous;
unintelligible: 此句意義模糊。
This sentence is ambiguous
in sense. ②to obscure; to
blur: 眼淚使我視線模糊。Tears
blurred my sight.

模寫（ㄇㄛˊ ㄒㄧㄝˇ）
to transcribe; to copy

模範教授（ㄇㄛˊ ㄈㄢˋ ㄐㄧㄠ ㄕㄡˋ）
presentative instruction

模型（ㄇㄛˊ ㄒㄧㄥˊ）
a miniature; a model

模式（ㄇㄛˊ ㄕˋ）
a model; a formula; a pattern

模數（ㄇㄛˊ ㄕㄨˋ）
(mathematics) modulus

模造紙（ㄇㄛˊ ㄗㄠˋ ㄓˇ）
simile paper: 我要買一張模造
紙。I want to buy a piece of
simile paper.

模斯（ㄇㄛˊ ㄙ）
Samuel F.B. Morse (1791-
1872), inventor of telegraph

【模】 2584
2. ㄇㄨˊ mu mú
a mold; a form; a matrix

模子（ㄇㄨˊ ㄗˇ）
a mold; a form

模樣（ㄇㄨˊ ㄧㄤˋ）
①appearances; looks: 他的
模樣很高尚。He is a man of
noble appearance. ②about;
around: 那女的有 30 歲模樣。
The woman was around
thirty.

【樣】 2585
ㄧㄤˋ yang yàng
1. appearances; looks
2. a style; a pattern; a mode; a
form
3. a sort; a kind; a variety
4. a sample

樣板（ㄧㄤˋ ㄅㄢˇ）
①a sample plate ②a tem-

plet ③a model; a prototype;
an example

樣本（ㄧㄤˋ ㄅㄣˇ）
a sample (of printed material): 它和樣本相符。It comes
up to sample.

樣品（ㄧㄤˋ ㄆㄧㄣˇ）
a specimen; a sample (of a
commodity); 讓我看看布疋的
樣品。Show me samples of
cloths.

樣張（ㄧㄤˋ ㄓㄤ）
a specimen sheet

樣冊子（ㄧㄤˋ ㄘㄜˋ ㄗˇ）or 樣冊兒
（ㄧㄤˋ ㄘㄜˋ ㄦ）
a book used to hold patterns
for embroidery

樣式（ㄧㄤˋ ㄕˋ）
style; modes; patterns

樣子（ㄧㄤˋ ㄗˇ）or 樣兒（ㄧㄤˋ ㄦ）
①appearances; looks ②
style; modes; patterns ③a
sample ④a proof sheet

樣樣（ㄧㄤˋ ㄧㄤˋ）
each and every; all; every
kind: 那孩子樣樣都好。That
child is developing in every
way.

樣樣宗宗（ㄧㄤˋ ㄧㄤˋ ㄗㄨㄥ ㄗㄨㄥ）
of all sorts; varied; diversified

樣樣兒（ㄧㄤˋ ㄧㄤˋ ㄦ）
every sort; every variety

【楠】 2586
ㄋㄢˊ man mán
a kind of tree

十二畫

【樸】 2587
ㄆㄨˊ pwu pú
1. (said of dress, clothing, literary style, etc.) plain; simple
2. the substance of things;
things in the rough
3. honest; sincere; simple
4. Aphananthe aspera, a tree of
the elm family

樸樸實實（ㄆㄨˊ ㄆㄨˊ ㄕˊ ㄕˊ）or 樸實
（ㄆㄨˊ ㄕˊ）
①(said of dresses, style,
etc.) simple; plain ②honest;
sincere; simple in taste

樸馬（ㄆㄨˊ ㄇㄚˇ）
an untrained horse; a horse
that has not been broken in

樸鈍（ㄆㄨˊ ㄉㄨㄣˋ）

〔木部〕

①(said of tools, knives, etc.) blunt ②(said of one's natural endowments) dull; slow; stupid

模厚(ㄇㄨˊ ㄏㄡˋ)
simple and sincere; simple-mindedness: 此地民風模厚。 The people here are simple and sincere.

模學(ㄇㄨˊ ㄒㄩㄝˊ)
textual study of the Chinese classics, advocated by scholars during the Han Dynasty 亦作「漢學」

模直(ㄇㄨˊ ㄓˊ)
simple-minded; honest; sincerity

模質(ㄇㄨˊ ㄓˊ)
not ornamented; unadorned

模拙(ㄇㄨˊ ㄓㄨㄛ)
simple and naive

模素(ㄇㄨˊ ㄙㄨˋ)
(said of dresses, etc.) simple and plain: 她的衣着模素。 She dresses simply.

模野(ㄇㄨˊ ㄧㄝˇ)
simple; rustic

【樵】 2588
ㄑㄧㄠˊ chyau qiáo

1. firewood; fuel
2. to gather fuel or firewood
3. a woodcutter
4. to burn
5. a tower; a lookout

樵夫(ㄑㄧㄠˊ ㄈㄨ)or樵客(ㄑㄧㄠˊ ㄎㄜˋ) or樵子(ㄑㄧㄠˊ ㄗˇ)
a woodcutter

樵斧(ㄑㄧㄠˊ ㄈㄨˇ)
an axe

樵歌(ㄑㄧㄠˊ ㄍㄜ)
①songs of the woodcutters 亦作「樵唱」②the title of a three-volume collection of poems, etc. by Chu Tun-ju (朱敦儒) of the Sung Dynasty 亦作「太平樵唱」

樵戶(ㄑㄧㄠˊ ㄏㄨˋ)
a family which lives on woodcutting or gathering firewood

樵薪(ㄑㄧㄠˊ ㄒㄧㄣ)
to gather fuel or firewood

樵叟(ㄑㄧㄠˊ ㄙㄡˇ)
an old woodcutter

樵蘇(ㄑㄧㄠˊ ㄙㄨ)
to gather firewood and weed

樵隱(ㄑㄧㄠˊ ㄧㄣˇ)
a recluse or hermit who leads a woodcutter's life

【樺】 2589
ㄏㄨㄚˋ huah huà

a birch

樺木(ㄏㄨㄚˋ ㄇㄨˋ)
Betulaceae

樺燭(ㄏㄨㄚˋ ㄓㄨˊ)
a torch or candle made by rolling the bark of birch around beeswax

【樨】 2590
ㄒㄧ shí xì

a cassia tree

【橄】 2591
ㄍㄢˇ gaan gǎn

an olive

橄欖(ㄍㄢˇ ㄌㄢˇ)
olives: 橄欖是和平的象徵。 An olive is the symbol of peace.

橄欖球(ㄍㄢˇ ㄌㄢˇ ㄑㄧㄡˊ)
American football; rugby: 你喜歡玩橄欖球嗎? Do you like playing American football?

橄欖枝(ㄍㄢˇ ㄌㄢˇ ㄓ)
the olive branch (a symbol of peace)

橄欖油(ㄍㄢˇ ㄌㄢˇ ㄧㄡˊ)
olive oil

【樾】 2592
ㄩㄝˋ yueh yuè

the shade of trees

樾蔭(ㄩㄝˋ ㄧㄣˋ)
the protection from the powerful

【樽】 2593
ㄗㄨㄣ tzuen zūn

1. a wine vessel; a goblet; a bottle; a wine jar
2. (said of vegetation) luxuriant

樽俎(ㄗㄨㄣ ㄗㄨˇ)
a goblet; a wine vessel (used in rituals)

樽俎折衝(ㄗㄨㄣ ㄗㄨˇ ㄓㄜˊ ㄔㄨㄥ)
to talk or negotiate over cups of wine—to discharge the duties of a diplomat

【橐】 2594
ㄊㄨㄛˊ two tuó

a bag or sack

橐筆(ㄊㄨㄛˊ ㄅㄧˇ)
living on writing

橐駝(ㄊㄨㄛˊ ㄊㄨㄛˊ)
①a camel ②a hunchback

橐橐(ㄊㄨㄛˊ ㄊㄨㄛˊ)
the sound of footsteps or rattles

橐囊(ㄊㄨㄛˊ ㄋㄤˊ)
sacks or bags

橐中裝(ㄊㄨㄛˊ ㄓㄨㄥ ㄓㄨㄤ)
gems; jewels; valuables

橐筍(ㄊㄨㄛˊ ㄙㄨㄣˇ)
a bag; a satchel

橐籥(ㄊㄨㄛˊ ㄩㄝˋ)
a tube for blowing up the fire in a furnace, etc.

【樹】 2595
ㄕㄨˋ shuh shù

1. trees
2. to plant; to cultivate; to grow: 十年樹木，百年樹人。 It takes ten years to grow trees, but a hundred years to rear people.
3. to erect; to establish
4. (now rarely) a door screen

樹碑(ㄕㄨˋ ㄅㄟ)
to erect a memorial tablet

樹碑立傳(ㄕㄨˋ ㄅㄟ ㄌㄧˋ ㄓㄨㄢˋ)
to erect a monument and write a biography to glorify somebody—to build up somebody's public image

樹本(ㄕㄨˋ ㄅㄣˇ)
①the root of a tree ②to build a good foundation for something

樹皮(ㄕㄨˋ ㄆㄧˊ)
bark

樹末(ㄕㄨˋ ㄇㄛˋ)or樹梢(ㄕㄨˋ ㄕㄠ)
the tip of a tree 亦作「樹杪」

樹苗(ㄕㄨˋ ㄇㄧㄠˊ)
a seedling; a sapling

樹木(ㄕㄨˋ ㄇㄨˋ)
①trees ②to plant a tree

樹大根深(ㄕㄨˋ ㄉㄚˋ ㄍㄣ ㄕㄣ)
(literally) The tree is big, and the root, deep.—①A famous personality wields great and deep-rooted influence. ②This big concern has a good foundation of long standing.

樹大招風(ㄕㄨˋ ㄉㄚˋ ㄓㄠ ㄈㄥ)
(literally) High trees attract the wind.—Famous persons attract criticisms easily.

樹大蔭大(ㄕㄨˋ ㄉㄚˋ ㄧㄣˋ ㄉㄚˋ)
(literally) The bigger the tree, the bigger the shade. —A powerful man can easily help or shield his follower.

樹德(ㄕㄨˋ ㄉㄜˊ)

to establish one's virtues; to exemplify one's integrity

樹倒猢猻散(ㄕㄨ ㄉㄠˇ ㄏㄨˊ ㄙㄨㄣ ㄙㄢˋ)
(literally) When a big tree comes down, all the monkeys on it will disperse. —When a big family fortune comes to nil, all who live on it will run away. 或 When a high official is dismissed from office, all his underlings will break up and run away.

樹黨(ㄕㄨˋ ㄉㄤˇ)
to form a clique, gang, faction, party, etc.

樹敵(ㄕㄨˋ ㄉ一ˊ)
to make an enemy of; to make enemy; to antagonize: 我們不應樹敵太多。We should not make too many enemies.

樹顚(ㄕㄨˋ ㄉ一ㄢ)
the top of a tree; the highest point of a tree 亦作「樹頂」

樹梃(ㄕㄨˋ ㄊ一ㄥˇ)
the trunk of a tree

樹立(ㄕㄨˋ ㄌ一ˋ)
to establish (a reputation, etc.)

樹林(ㄕㄨˋ ㄌ一ㄣˊ)
a forest; a grove of trees; woods

樹幹(ㄕㄨˋ ㄍㄢˋ)
the trunk of a tree

樹根(ㄕㄨˋ ㄍㄣ)
the root of a tree

樹節(ㄕㄨˋ ㄐ一ㄝˊ)
to establish one's virtue; to preserve one's integrity

樹介(ㄐ一ㄝˋ ㄐ一ㄝˋ)
icicles on a tree

樹膠(ㄕㄨˋ ㄐ一ㄠ)
resin; gum

樹教(ㄕㄨˋ ㄐ一ㄠˋ)
to establish a religion

樹起筋骨(ㄕㄨˋ ㄑ一ˇ ㄐ一ㄣ ㄍㄨˇ)
to pull oneself together (for a task, etc.)

樹下(ㄕㄨˋ ㄒ一ㄚˋ)
under the tree

樹勳(ㄕㄨˋ ㄒㄩㄣ)
to establish one's name by great accomplishments

樹汁(ㄕㄨˋ ㄓ)
sap

樹枝(ㄕㄨˋ ㄓ)

boughs or branches of a tree: 樹枝在微風中搖曳。The branches waved in the breeze.

樹脂(ㄕㄨˋ ㄓ)
resin

樹椿子(ㄕㄨˋ ㄔㄨㄣ ˙ㄗ)
the stump of a tree: 獵人坐在樹椿子上。The hunter sat on a stump.

樹杈兒(ㄕㄨˋ ㄔㄚˋㄦ)
the fork of a tree; a crotch: 她正坐在一棵樹杈兒上。She is sitting in the crotch of a tree.

樹身(ㄕㄨˋ ㄕㄣ)
①the trunk of a tree ②to establish a tree's virtue; to preserve one's integrity

樹上(ㄕㄨˋ ㄕㄤˋ)
on the tree; above the tree: 鳥兒棲息於樹上。The bird perched on the tree.

樹薯粉(ㄕㄨˋ ㄕㄨˊ ㄈㄣˇ)
cassava

樹人(ㄕㄨˋ ㄖㄣˊ)
to cultivate young persons; to educate the young

樹叢(ㄕㄨˋ ㄘㄨㄥˊ)
a grove of trees

樹恩(ㄕㄨˋ ㄣ)
to give favors; to befriend

樹葉(ㄕㄨˋ 一ㄝˋ)or樹葉子(ㄕㄨˋ 一ㄝˋ ˙ㄗ)or樹葉兒(ㄕㄨˋ 一ㄝˋㄦ)
the leaves of a tree; foliage

樹腰(ㄕㄨˋ 一ㄠ)
the middle of a tree trunk

樹陰(ㄕㄨˋ 一ㄣ)or樹蔭(ㄕㄨˋ 一ㄣˋ)
the shade of a tree: 我在樹蔭下休息。I took a rest in the shade of a tree.

樹影(ㄕㄨˋ 一ㄥˇ)
the shadow of a tree

樹威(ㄕㄨˋ ㄨㄟ)
to establish one's reputation, awe-inspiring name, or great influence

樹欲靜而風不止(ㄕㄨˋ ㄩˋ ㄐ一ㄥˋ ㄦˊ ㄈㄥ ㄅㄨˋ ㄓˇ)
(literally) The tree wants to remain quiet, but the winds won't stop.—I'd like to do something, but circumstances won't allow it.

樹怨(ㄕㄨˋ ㄩㄢˋ)
to make an enemy of; to

make enemy; to antagonize: 他的政策使得市民和他樹怨。His policy antagonized the people of the town.

【橇】2596
ㄑ一ㄠˊ tsuey cui
(又讀ㄑ一ㄠˊ chiau qiáo)
a sledge for transportation over mud or snow; a sleigh

【橈】2597
ㄋㄠˊ nau náo
1. crooked or bent wood
2. to enfeeble; to weaken; to sap; to devitalize
3. to disperse; to scatter
4. to wrong or be wronged

橈敗(ㄋㄠˊ ㄅㄞˋ)
defeated as troops

橈骨(ㄋㄠˊ ㄍㄨˇ)
(anatomy) the radius of the forearm

橈足(ㄋㄠˊ ㄗㄨˊ)
(zoology) pleopod, a swim-meret 亦作「腹肢」

橈足類(ㄋㄠˊ ㄗㄨˊ ㄌㄟˋ)
(zoology) copepoda

【橋】2598
ㄑ一ㄠˊ chyau qiáo
1. a bridge; any bridge-like structure: 河上架着一座橋。A bridge was built across the river.
2. beams of a structure
3. (now rarely) cross-grained
4. tall; high; elevated
5. a Chinese family name

橋牌(ㄑ一ㄠˊ ㄆㄞˊ)
(card games) bridge

橋墩(ㄑ一ㄠˊ ㄉㄨㄣ)
the buttresses of a bridge

橋洞(ㄑ一ㄠˊ ㄉㄨㄥˋ)
the arches of a bridge

橋頭(ㄑ一ㄠˊ ㄊㄡˊ)
either end of a bridge

橋頭堡(ㄑ一ㄠˊ ㄊㄡˊ ㄅㄠˇ)
①(military) a bridgehead ②(construction) a bridge tower

橋欄杆(ㄑ一ㄠˊ ㄌㄢˊ ㄍㄢ)
railings or balustrades of a bridge

橋梁(ㄑ一ㄠˊ ㄌ一ㄤˊ)
any material which forms the span of a bridge

橋拱(ㄑ一ㄠˊ ㄍㄨㄥˇ)
a bridge arch

橋下(ㄑ一ㄠˊ ㄒ一ㄚˋ)

below the bridge
橋上（ㄑㄧㄠˊ ㄕㄤˋ）
on the bridge

2599
【橙】 cherng chéng
（語音 ㄔㄥˊ chén chén）
the orange: 柳橙產於溫暖的地
方。Oranges are produced in
warm districts.
橙皮（ㄔㄥˊ ㄆㄧˊ）
orange peel—used in
Chinese herbal medicine
橙皮菓醬（ㄔㄥˊ ㄆㄧˊ《ㄨㄛˇ ㄐㄧㄤˋ）
marmalade
橙黃橘綠（ㄔㄥˊ ㄏㄨㄤˊ ㄐㄩˊ ㄌㄨˋ）
the autumn season (when
the oranges mellow)
橙黃色（ㄔㄥˊ ㄏㄨㄤˊ ㄙㄜˋ）
orange (color)
橙汁（ㄔㄥˊ ㄓ）
orange juice
橙子（ㄔㄥˊ ㄗ）
oranges

【橘】 2600 ㄐㄩˊ jyu jú
the mandarin orange; the
Chinese orange; a tangerine
橘餅（ㄐㄩˊ ㄅㄧㄥˇ）
flattened orange seasoned
with honey
橘皮（ㄐㄩˊ ㄆㄧˊ）or 橘紅（ㄐㄩˊ ㄏㄨㄥˊ）
the peel of mandarin orange
—used in Chinese herbal
medicine
橘化為枳（ㄐㄩˊ ㄏㄨㄚˋ ㄨㄟˊ ㄓˇ）
The orange in the south of
the River Huai becomes its
another variety when it is
transplanted into the north
of the River Huai.—(figuratively) Things will turn out
differently in different localities or surroundings.
橘黃（ㄐㄩˊ ㄏㄨㄤˊ）
an orange color
橘紅（ㄐㄩˊ ㄏㄨㄥˊ）
①tangerine (color)②
(Chinese medicine) dried tangerine peel
橘樹（ㄐㄩˊ ㄕㄨˋ）
the mandarin orange tree
橘子（ㄐㄩˊ ㄗˇ）
mandarin oranges; tange-
rines
橘子汁（ㄐㄩˊ ㄗˇ ㄓ）
orange juice: 我喜歡喝橘子

汁。I like orange juice.

【橡】 2601 ㄒㄧㄤˋ shiang xiàng
an acorn
橡皮（ㄒㄧㄤˋ ㄆㄧˊ）
①a rubber; an eraser: 這枝
鉛筆有橡皮。The pencil has a
rubber.②rubber
橡皮圖章（ㄒㄧㄤˋ ㄆㄧˊ ㄊㄨˊ ㄓㄤ）
a rubber stamp
橡皮膏（ㄒㄧㄤˋ ㄆㄧˊ ㄍㄠ）
adhesive plaster
橡皮筋（ㄒㄧㄤˋ ㄆㄧˊ ㄐㄧㄣ）
rubber bands
橡栗（ㄒㄧㄤˋ ㄌㄧˋ）
oak chestnuts
橡膠（ㄒㄧㄤˋ ㄐㄧㄠ）
rubber
橡膠樹（ㄒㄧㄤˋ ㄐㄧㄠ ㄕㄨˋ）
a rubber tree
橡膠園（ㄒㄧㄤˋ ㄐㄧㄠ ㄩㄢˊ）
a plantation of trees that
produce latex
橡實（ㄒㄧㄤˋ ㄕˊ）or 橡子（ㄒㄧㄤˋ ㄗˇ）
an acorn
橡樹（ㄒㄧㄤˋ ㄕㄨˋ）
an oak

【橢】 2602 ㄊㄨㄛˇ tuoo tuǒ
oval; oblong; elliptical
橢圓（ㄊㄨㄛˇ ㄩㄢˊ）
(mathematics) an ellipse
橢圓體（ㄊㄨㄛˇ ㄩㄢˊ ㄊㄧˇ）
an ellipsoid
橢圓規（ㄊㄨㄛˇ ㄩㄢˊ ㄍㄨㄟ）
an ellipsograph; elliptical
compasses
橢圓形的（ㄊㄨㄛˇ ㄩㄢˊ ㄒㄧㄥˊ ㄉㄜ）
oval; elliptical

【橦】 2603 ㄊㄨㄥˊ torng tóng
a species of tree grown in
Yunnan (雲南) whose flow-
ers are used to make a kind
of cloth
橦布（ㄊㄨㄥˊ ㄅㄨˋ）
the cloth made from the
flowers of 橦

【樣】 2604 ㄇㄤˋ maang màng
a mango

【機】 2605 ㄐㄧ ji jī
1. mechanics; machinery
2. opportune; opportunity
3. a crucial point; a pivot
4. tricky; cunning

5. an aircraft; a plane; an airplane: 你要坐飛機去嗎？Are
you going by plane?
機梭（ㄐㄧ ㄙㄨㄛ）
revetment (for parking an
airplane)
機變（ㄐㄧ ㄅㄧㄢˋ）
①to adapt oneself to environment, etc.; flexibility ②
cunning and shrewd; contriv-
ances and versatile schemes
機變百出（ㄐㄧ ㄅㄧㄢˋ ㄅㄞˇ ㄔㄨ）
with a thousand tricks up
one's sleeves
機謀（ㄐㄧ ㄇㄡˊ）
①shrewdness; cunning;
quick-witted and full of
tricks; tricky ② a stratagem
機米（ㄐㄧ ㄇㄧˇ）
machine-polished rice
機密（ㄐㄧ ㄇㄧˋ）
secret; confidential; classified: 我們應嚴守國防機密。We
should strictly guard
national defense secrets.
機密消息（ㄐㄧ ㄇㄧˋ ㄒㄧㄠ ㄒㄧ）
classified information
機密文件（ㄐㄧ ㄇㄧˋ ㄨㄣˊ ㄐㄧㄢˋ）
secret or confidential documents: 這是絕對機密文件。
This is strictly confidential
documents.
機敏（ㄐㄧ ㄇㄧㄣˇ）
sharp; quick-witted; shrewdness; cleverness; perspicac-
ity; resourceful
機房（ㄐㄧ ㄈㄤˊ）
①a storage for textile
machinery ② an engine room
機動（ㄐㄧ ㄉㄨㄥˋ）
mobile
機動性（ㄐㄧ ㄉㄨㄥˋ ㄒㄧㄥˋ）
(military) mobility
機動車（ㄐㄧ ㄉㄨㄥˋ ㄔㄜ）
motorized vehicles
機頭（ㄐㄧ ㄊㄡˊ）
the nose section of an airplane
機能（ㄐㄧ ㄋㄥˊ）
functions; functional (ailments, etc.)
機鈕（ㄐㄧ ㄋㄧㄡˇ）
①a button that controls a
machine ② a key point in
something or development
機靈（ㄐㄧ ㄌㄧㄥˊ）
clever; smart; sharp; intelli-

［木部］

gent: 她是一個機靈的學生。She is a smart student.

機伶(ㄐㄧ ㄌㄧㄥ)
quick-witted; clever; readily responsive 參看「機靈」

機伶鬼兒(ㄐㄧ ㄌㄧㄥ ㄍㄨㄟˇ ㄦ)
a quick-witted or clever fellow

機率(ㄐㄧ ㄌㄩˋ)
the probability 亦作「或然率」

機構(ㄐㄧ ㄍㄡˋ)
an organization

機關(ㄐㄧ ㄍㄨㄢ)
①an organization; an institution ②a machine ③a stratagem; an intrigue

機關報(ㄐㄧ ㄍㄨㄢ ㄅㄠˋ)
a government party paper; an official mouthpiece

機關槍(ㄐㄧ ㄍㄨㄢ ㄑㄧㄤ)
a machine gun

機關車(ㄐㄧ ㄍㄨㄢ ㄔㄜ)
a locomotive; an engine

機工(ㄐㄧ ㄍㄨㄥ)
①a mechanic; a worker in a textile mill ②short for mechanical engineering

機庫(ㄐㄧ ㄎㄨˋ)
a hangar

機括(ㄐㄧ ㄍㄨㄚ)
①a mechanism; a mechanical contrivance ②a catch or trigger

機會(ㄐㄧ ㄏㄨㄟˋ)
opportunity: 此種機會不應失去。Such opportunities should not be missed.

機會均等(ㄐㄧ ㄏㄨㄟˋ ㄐㄩㄣ ㄉㄥˇ)
equal opportunity

機會主義(ㄐㄧ ㄏㄨㄟˋ ㄓㄨˇ ㄧˋ)
opportunism

機會主義者(ㄐㄧ ㄏㄨㄟˋ ㄓㄨˇ ㄧˋ ㄓㄜˇ)
an opportunist

機捷(ㄐㄧ ㄐㄧㄝˊ)
witty; quick-witted; cleverness

機件(ㄐㄧ ㄐㄧㄢˋ)
machine parts or works; component parts of a machine

機近(ㄐㄧ ㄐㄧㄣˋ)
secret and strategic (positions, places, points, etc.)

機警(ㄐㄧ ㄐㄧㄥˇ)
alert; alertness; sharp and quick-witted: 他很機警。He has an alert mind.

機器(ㄐㄧ ㄑㄧˋ)
machinery; a machine: 一個工廠有許多機器。A factory contains much machinery.

機器人(ㄐㄧ ㄑㄧˋ ㄖㄣˊ)
a robot

機巧(ㄐㄧ ㄑㄧㄠˇ)
tact; tactful; clever; cleverness; shrewd; shrewdness

機槍(ㄐㄧ ㄑㄧㄤ)
a machine gun

機槍手(ㄐㄧ ㄑㄧㄤ ㄕㄡˇ)
a machine gunner

機羣(ㄐㄧ ㄑㄩㄣˊ)
an air armada; a fleet of airplanes

機械(ㄐㄧ ㄒㄧㄝˋ)
①a machine; machinery ②mechanical. 我不喜歡機械的勞動。I don't like mechanical labor. ③(said of persons) cunning or shrewd

機械工程(ㄐㄧ ㄒㄧㄝˋ ㄍㄨㄥ ㄔㄥˊ)
mechanical engineering

機械化(ㄐㄧ ㄒㄧㄝˋ ㄏㄨㄚˋ)
mechanization

機械化部隊(ㄐㄧ ㄒㄧㄝˋ ㄏㄨㄚˋ ㄅㄨˋ ㄉㄨㄟˋ)
motorized troops; mechanized troops

機械性(ㄐㄧ ㄒㄧㄝˋ ㄒㄧㄥˋ)
of a mechanical nature; mechanical: 她的誦讀很機械性。Her reading is very mechanical.

機械學(ㄐㄧ ㄒㄧㄝˋ ㄒㄩㄝˊ)
mechanics

機械油(ㄐㄧ ㄒㄧㄝˋ ㄧㄡˊ)
lubricants for machines

機先(ㄐㄧ ㄒㄧㄢ)
(to take) the initiative or steps in advance

機心(ㄐㄧ ㄒㄧㄣ)
a shrewd and cunning mind: 他是個有機心的政客。He is a shrewd politician.

機型(ㄐㄧ ㄒㄧㄥˊ)
①the type (of an aircraft) ②the model (of a machine): 他的車子是去年的機型。His car is last year's model.

機織(ㄐㄧ ㄓ)
machine-woven; woven by a machine

機製(ㄐㄧ ㄓˋ)
made by a machine; machine-

made

機智(ㄐㄧ ㄓˋ)
alertness; quick wit; ready responsiveness; skillful; tact: 簡潔乃機智的靈魂。Brevity is the soul of wit.

機詐(ㄐㄧ ㄓㄚˋ)
cunningness; cunning; tricky; crafty; sly

機軸(ㄐㄧ ㄓㄡˊ)
a pivot; an axis

機長(ㄐㄧ ㄓㄤˇ)
an aircraft (or crew) commander

機杼(ㄐㄧ ㄓㄨˋ)
①the shuttle of a loom ②the construction of an essay

機車(ㄐㄧ ㄔㄜ)
①motorcycles: 他騎機車上工。He goes to work by motorcycle. ②a locomotive

機場(ㄐㄧ ㄔㄤˇ)
an airport; an airfield

機床(ㄐㄧ ㄔㄨㄤˊ)
a machine tool

機師(ㄐㄧ ㄕ)
a pilot (of an airplane)

機身(ㄐㄧ ㄕㄣ)
the fuselage

機組(ㄐㄧ ㄗㄨˇ)
①(machinery) a unit; a set ②the aircrew; the flight crew

機座(ㄐㄧ ㄗㄨㄛˋ)
machine base; machine foundation

機艙(ㄐㄧ ㄘㄤ)
the cockpit of a small airplane; the cabin of an airliner

機宜(ㄐㄧ ㄧˊ)
a matter and its arrangements; a line of action; guidelines; a policy

機翼(ㄐㄧ ㄧˋ)
wings of an airplane: 機翼在飛行中折斷。The wings of an airplane were broken in the flight.

機要(ㄐㄧ ㄧㄠˋ)
confidential and important (matters, etc.)

機要秘書(ㄐㄧ ㄧㄠˋ ㄇㄧˋ ㄕㄨ)
a confidential secretary

機油(ㄐㄧ ㄧㄡˊ)
lubricating oil; lubricant: 上

（木部）

〔木部〕

油的時候試試這種機油。When it's time to lubricate, try this lubricant.

機務(ㄐㄧ ㄨ)
①important matters ② mechanical work

機尾(ㄐㄧ ㄨㄟˇ)
the tail section of an airplane

機遇(ㄐㄧ ㄩˋ)
chance; opportunity; luck

機員(ㄐㄧ ㄩㄢˊ)
a member of an aircraft crew

機緣(ㄐㄧ ㄩㄢˊ)
chance and opportunity: 偶然的機緣導致鑽石礦的發現。Chance led to the finding of the diamond mine.

機運(ㄐㄧ ㄩㄣˋ)
luck; fate: 凡事都有機運。There is luck in everything.

【橫】 2606

1. ㄏㄥˊ herng héng
1. horizontal; crosswise; lateral
2. east to west or vice versa
3. by the side of; sideways
4. to move crosswise; to traverse: 這條鐵路橫貫沙漠數百哩。This railway traverses hundreds of miles of the desert.
5. unrestrainedly; turbulently: 江河橫溢。Waters overflow turbulently.
6. a Chinese family name

橫波(ㄏㄥˊ ㄅㄛ)
①the sideway glances (of a beauty, etc.)②a transverse wave

橫濱(ㄏㄥˊ ㄅㄧㄣ)
Yokohama, Japan

橫披(ㄏㄥˊ ㄆㄧ)
the horizontal scroll of painting or calligraphy work

橫眉瞪眼(ㄏㄥˊ ㄇㄟˊ ㄉㄥˋ ㄧㄢˇ)
angry looks; to look angrily at 亦作「橫眉立目」

橫目(ㄏㄥˊ ㄇㄨˋ)
①angry eyes; to look angrily at ②(now rarely) human kind

橫幅(ㄏㄥˊ ㄈㄨˊ)
①a horizontal scroll of painting or calligraphy ②a banner

橫刀奪愛(ㄏㄥˊ ㄉㄠ ㄉㄨㄛˊ ㄞˋ)
to take away another's woman by force

橫笛(ㄏㄥˊ ㄉㄧˊ)
the common flute (to be played horizontally)

橫渡(ㄏㄥˊ ㄉㄨˋ)
to cross (a river, ocean, etc.)

橫隊(ㄏㄥˊ ㄉㄨㄟˋ)
a rank; a row

橫斷面(ㄏㄥˊ ㄉㄨㄢˋ ㄇㄧㄢˋ)
the cross section

橫斷山脈(ㄏㄥˊ ㄉㄨㄢˋ ㄕㄢ ㄇㄞˋ)or 橫貫山脈(ㄏㄥˊ ㄍㄨㄢˋ ㄕㄢ ㄇㄞˋ)
①a mountain range that runs from east to west ② name of a mountain range in Sikang (西康) stretching to Szechwan (四川) and Yunnan (雲南)

橫躺豎臥(ㄏㄥˊ ㄊㄤˇ ㄕㄨˋ ㄨㄛˋ)
(said of persons) lying in total disorder

橫了心(ㄏㄥˊ ˙ㄌㄜ ㄒㄧㄣ)
to steel one's heart (as a result of determination, etc.); in desperation

橫攔豎遮(ㄏㄥˊ ㄌㄢˊ ㄕㄨˋ ㄓㄜ)
to place obstructions at every possible point

橫列(ㄏㄥˊ ㄌㄧㄝˋ)
to arrange in a horizontal line

橫流(ㄏㄥˊ ㄌㄧㄡˊ)
(said of a river) to overflow; to run out of the accustomed course

橫樑(ㄏㄥˊ ㄌㄧㄤˊ)
a crossbeam

橫膈膜(ㄏㄥˊ ㄍㄜˊ ㄇㄛˊ)
the diaphragm

橫瓦(ㄏㄥˊ ㄨㄚˇ)
①crosswise; horizontal; from east to west or vice versa ②to span; to traverse: 一座美麗的大橋橫亙在河上。A beautiful bridge traversed the river.

橫貫公路(ㄏㄥˊ ㄍㄨㄢˋ ㄍㄨㄥ ㄌㄨˋ)
①any highway that runs from east to west ②the Cross-Island or East-West Highway in Taiwan

橫跨(ㄏㄥˊ ㄎㄨㄚˋ)
to stretch over or across: 一

道彩虹橫跨天際。A rainbow stretched across the sky.

橫截(ㄏㄥˊ ㄐㄧㄝˊ)
to cut across

橫截面(ㄏㄥˊ ㄐㄧㄝˊ ㄇㄧㄢˋ)
a cross section

橫七豎八(ㄏㄥˊ ㄑㄧ ㄕㄨˋ ㄅㄚ)
in total disorder or disarray; to be cluttered: 那房間橫七豎八地堆滿了書和雜誌。The room was cluttered up with books and magazines.

橫起來(ㄏㄥˊ ㄑㄧˇ ˙ㄌㄞ)
①to place things horizontally ②to shoulder the responsibility of

橫渠學派(ㄏㄥˊ ㄑㄩˊ ㄒㄩㄝˊ ㄆㄞˋ)
a school of learning founded by Chang Tsai (張載) of the Northern Sung Dynasty stressing on emulating ancient styles

橫寫(ㄏㄥˊ ㄒㄧㄝˇ)
to write horizontally (as distinct from the traditional Chinese way of writing from top to bottom)

橫行(ㄏㄥˊ ㄒㄧㄥˊ)
①to run wild; to proceed on ways other than proper (usually evil) ②to move sideways—as crabs

橫行霸道(ㄏㄥˊ ㄒㄧㄥˊ ㄅㄚˋ ㄉㄠˋ)
to bully; to terrorize; to act tyrannically; to behave in total disregard of law

橫行介士(ㄏㄥˊ ㄒㄧㄥˊ ㄐㄧㄝˋ ㄕˋ)
the crab

橫行文字(ㄏㄥˊ ㄒㄧㄥˊ ㄨㄣˊ ㄗˋ)
the Romanized languages —English, French, German, etc. that go horizontally

橫須賀(ㄏㄥˊ ㄒㄩ ㄏㄜˋ)
Yokosuka, the biggest Japanese naval base

橫軸(ㄏㄥˊ ㄓㄡˊ)
①a horizontal scroll (of calligraphy, picture, etc.) ② a transversal axis, or the axis of an abscissa

橫振動(ㄏㄥˊ ㄓㄣˋ ㄉㄨㄥˋ)
transverse vibration

橫征暴歛(ㄏㄥˊ ㄓㄥ ㄅㄠˋ ㄌㄧㄢˋ)
to impose or force unbearable taxes on the people: 國王橫征暴歛。A king imposed unbearable taxes on the peo-

ple.

横陳(ㄏㄥˊ ㄔㄣˊ)
to lie down with limbs fully stretched

横衝直撞(ㄏㄥˊ ㄔㄨㄥ ㄓˊ ㄓㄨㄤˋ)
(said of a bull, car, truck, etc.) to bump; to jostle and elbow one's way right and left

横生(ㄏㄥˊ ㄕㄥ)
①to arise from every side ②to be full of; to brim (with happiness, interest, etc.): 他的演說妙趣横生。His speech was full of wit and humor. ③all beings except human beings

横枝節(ㄏㄥˊ ㄓ ㄐㄧㄝˊ)
①side issues or new problems that come or appear unexpectedly ②to raise obstacles; to complicate an issue deliberately

横豎(ㄏㄥˊ ㄕㄨˋ)
①(ㄏㄥˊ ㄕㄨˋ) in any case; anyway
②(ㄏㄥˊ ㄕㄨˋ) horizontal and perpendicular; in every direction

横豎豎說(ㄏㄥˊ ㄕㄨㄛˋ ㄕㄨˋ ㄕㄨㄛˋ)
to persuade repeatedly and insistently; to exhaust oneself with persuasion

横槊賦詩(ㄏㄥˊ ㄕㄨㄛˋ ㄈㄨˋ ㄕ)
(literally) to compose poems while holding the lance horizontally in the saddle—to indulge in literary pursuits while in war

横閂(ㄏㄥˊ ㄔㄨㄢ)
a door latch or bolt

横肉(ㄏㄥˊ ㄖㄡˋ)
(said of a person's appearance) fierce-looking: 他一臉横肉。He is fierce-looking.

横坐標(ㄏㄥˊ ㄗㄨㄛˋ ㄅㄧㄠ)
(mathematics) an abscissa

横財(ㄏㄥˊ ㄘㄞˊ)
a fortune which one doesn't deserve; a windfall; illegal gains: 他發了横財。He made a windfall.

横掃(ㄏㄥˊ ㄙㄠˇ)
to sweep away; to make a clean sweep of; to roll back

横三豎四(ㄏㄥˊ ㄙㄢ ㄕㄨˋ ㄙˋ)
disorderly; in disarray; con-

---

fusion

横兒(ㄏㄥˊ ㄦˊ)
①(calligraphy) a horizontal stroke ②a horizontal scroll or picture

横溢(ㄏㄥˊ ㄧˋ)
①brimming; overflowing; abundant ②to brim; to overflow: 河水横溢兩岸。The river overflowed its banks.

横紋肌(ㄏㄥˊ ㄨㄣˊ ㄐㄧ)
the striped muscle

【横】 2606
2. ㄏㄥˋ hèng **héng**

1. cross-grained; perverse
2. presumptuous and unreasonable
3. unexpected; uncalled for
4. violent; cross

横暴(ㄏㄥˋ ㄅㄠˋ)
perverse and tyrannical

横逆(ㄏㄥˋ ㄋㄧˋ)
perverse and unreasonable; unreasonableness

横流(ㄏㄥˋ ㄌㄧㄡˊ)
water flowing out of its proper course; an overflowing of (evil tides, etc.)

横話(ㄏㄥˋ ㄏㄨㄚˋ)
①unlucky words or utterances ②stiff and stern language; harsh words

横禍(ㄏㄥˋ ㄏㄨㄛˋ)
unexpected misfortune or disaster

横政(ㄏㄥˋ ㄓㄥˋ)
tyrannical rule or administration

横事(ㄏㄥˋ ㄕˋ)
a bad accident; unlucky happenings

横恣(ㄏㄥˋ ㄗˋ)
arrogant and presumptuous

横死(ㄏㄥˋ ㄙˇ)
an unnatural death; a violent death; to meet with a sudden death

横議(ㄏㄥˋ ㄧˋ)
extreme views; radical statements; far-fetched arguments

横夭(ㄏㄥˋ ㄧㄠ)
an unnatural death

十三畫

【檀】 2607
ㄊㄢˊ tarn **tán**

---

1. sandalwood
2. a Chinese family name

檀板(ㄊㄢˊ ㄅㄢˇ)
pieces (usually three) of hardwood for beating time; castanets

檀島(ㄊㄢˊ ㄉㄠˇ)
the Hawaiian Islands

檀郎(ㄊㄢˊ ㄌㄤˊ)
(formerly) a term of address for one's husband or lover

檀林(ㄊㄢˊ ㄌㄧㄣˊ)
a Buddhist monastery

檀口(ㄊㄢˊ ㄎㄡˇ)
the red lips of a pretty girl

檀香(ㄊㄢˊ ㄒㄧㄤ)
①incense made of sandalwood ②*Santalum album*

檀香山(ㄊㄢˊ ㄒㄧㄤ ㄕㄢ)
Honolulu

檀越(ㄊㄢˊ ㄩㄝˋ)
Danapati, an almsgiver, or a patron (a salutation used by Buddhist monks in addressing one who bestows alms)

【檄】 2608
ㄒㄧˊ shyi **xí**

a summons to arms in ancient times

檄文(ㄒㄧˊ ㄨㄣˊ)
a written summons to arms for a cause; a manifesto listing the crimes of a tyrant

【檐】 2609
(簷) ㄧㄢˊ yan **yán**

1. eaves of a house
2. the brim: 請抓住你的帽檐兒。Please hold the brim of your cap.

【檔】 2610
ㄉㄤˋ daang **dàng**
(又讀 ㄉㄤˇ danq)

1. an abbreviation for 檔案 (files)
2. shelves; pigeonholes
3. a wooden crosspiece, as the rung of a ladder, etc.
4. (now rarely) a wooden support

檔卷(ㄉㄤˋ ㄐㄩㄢˋ)
official files

檔期(ㄉㄤˋ ㄑㄧˊ)
a schedule for showing motion pictures in a theater

檔子(ㄉㄤˋ ㄗ˙) or 檔兒(ㄉㄤˋ ㄦ)
①one (thing, matter) ②a group of (persons, etc.)

〔木部〕

檔册（ㄉㄤ ㄘㄜˋ）
records; files

檔案（ㄉㄤ ㄢˋ）
official files (of government offices); archives: 他們調閱了所有檔案. They consulted all the files.

【檉】 2611
ㄔㄥ cheng chēng
a tamarisk

檉柳（ㄔㄥ ㄌㄧㄡˇ）
a tamarisk

【檜】 2612
ㄎㄨㄞˋ kuay kuài
（又讀 ㄍㄨㄟˋ guey guì）
the Chinese juniper or cypress

檜柏（ㄎㄨㄞˋ ㄅㄛˊ）
a Chinese cypress

檜木（ㄏㄨㄞˋ ㄇㄨˋ）
timber of a Chinese cypress or juniper

【檎】 2613
ㄑㄧㄣˊ chyn qín
a small red apple (Malus asiatica)

【檟】 2614
ㄐㄧㄚˇ jea jiǎ
1. an ancient version of 茶, tea
2. a small evergreen shrub (Mallotus japonicus)

【檢】 2615
ㄐㄧㄢˇ jean jiǎn
1. a book label
2. to sort; to gather
3. to inspect; to check up; to collate
4. to discuss thoroughly: 我們檢討利弊得失. We discussed thoroughly the merits and demerits.
5. a form; a pattern
6. to restrict; to regulate

檢波器（ㄐㄧㄢˇ ㄅㄛ ㄑㄧˋ）
a detector (for testing conductivity of electric currents)

檢點（ㄐㄧㄢˇ ㄉㄧㄢˇ）
①to behave (oneself) ②to inspect and arrange; to check ③(in ancient China) a bodyguard; an orderly ④to be cautious; to be careful: 他的言行有失檢點. He was careless about his words and acts.

檢定（ㄐㄧㄢˇ ㄉㄧㄥˋ）
①to inspect and approve (or sanction) ②inspection

檢定考試（ㄐㄧㄢˇ ㄉㄧㄥˋ ㄎㄠˇ ㄕˋ）
an examination held to determine the qualification of government employees and teachers who have not received regular training for the posts they are to hold

檢討（ㄐㄧㄢˇ ㄊㄠˇ）
to review and discuss (past performances, etc.); to make self-examination or soul-searching

檢討會（ㄐㄧㄢˇ ㄊㄠˇ ㄏㄨㄟˋ）
a conference held for reviewing and discussing past performances, plans, etc.

檢校（ㄐㄧㄢˇ ㄐㄧㄠˋ）
①to collate and correct; to examine ②to evaluate or grade the performance of government officials

檢舉（ㄐㄧㄢˇ ㄐㄩˇ）
to lay bare evidences of a corrupt official, etc.; to inform the authorities of an unlawful act, plot, etc.; to inform against an offender, etc.: 人人應該檢舉罪犯. Everyone should inform against a criminal.

檢修（ㄐㄧㄢˇ ㄒㄧㄡ）
to examine and repair; to overhaul: 他正在檢修汽車引擎. He is overhauling the engine of a car.

檢查（ㄐㄧㄢˇ ㄔㄚˊ）
to inspect; to examine; to test (a machine, etc.); (physical) checkup: 我已作了身體檢查. I have had a physical examination.

檢查站（ㄐㄧㄢˇ ㄔㄚˊ ㄓㄢˋ）
a checkpoint; an inspection station

檢查人員（ㄐㄧㄢˇ ㄔㄚˊ ㄖㄣˊ ㄩㄢˊ）
an inspector (as a customs officer, etc.); a person authorized to search, inspect, etc.

檢察（ㄐㄧㄢˇ ㄔㄚˊ）
①to inspect ②inspection

檢察官（ㄐㄧㄢˇ ㄔㄚˊ ㄍㄨㄢ）
a court prosecutor; an attorney general; a procurator

檢察長（ㄐㄧㄢˇ ㄔㄚˊ ㄓㄤˇ）
the procurator general (of the Supreme Court)

檢察處（ㄐㄧㄢˇ ㄔㄚˊ ㄔㄨˋ）
a judicial office where court prosecutors institute prosecutions in criminal cases; a procuratorate

檢束（ㄐㄧㄢˇ ㄕㄨˋ）
to discipline; to restrain: 她無法檢束孩子們惡作劇. She could not restrain her children from mischief.

檢字（ㄐㄧㄢˇ ㄗˋ）
①a table or index in a dictionary to help find a word ②to censor or screen writings

檢字法（ㄐㄧㄢˇ ㄗˋ ㄈㄚˇ）
the method for using the table or index in a dictionary for finding words

檢疫（ㄐㄧㄢˇ ㄧˋ）
quarantine

檢疫所（ㄐㄧㄢˇ ㄧˋ ㄙㄨㄛˇ）
the quarantine office

檢驗（ㄐㄧㄢˇ ㄧㄢˋ）
to inspect and examine; inspection

檢溫器（ㄐㄧㄢˇ ㄨㄣ ㄑㄧˋ）
a medical thermometer

檢閱（ㄐㄧㄢˇ ㄩㄝˋ）
to inspect or review (troops); a military review: 將軍正在檢閱儀仗隊. The general is reviewing a guard of honor.

【檣】 2616
ㄑㄧㄤˊ chyang qiáng
the mast of a ship: 道船有三根檣櫓. The ship has three masts.

檣傾楫摧（ㄑㄧㄤˊ ㄑㄧㄥ ㄐㄧˊ ㄘㄨㄟ）
a totally wrecked boat

【檁】 2617
ㄌㄧㄣˇ liin lǐn
a crossbeam in a house

檁子（ㄌㄧㄣˇ ㄗ˙）
purlins; crossbeams

【樣】 2618
ㄧ yii yì
to moor a boat to the bank

【檝】 2619
（楫）ㄐㄧˊ jyi jí
an oar or paddle

十四畫

【檸】2620 ㄋㄧㄥˊ ning níng

檸檬(ㄋㄧㄥˊ ㄇㄥˊ)
lemon: 我喜歡在茶裡加檸檬。I
like lemon in my tea.

檸檬水(ㄋㄧㄥˊ ㄇㄥˊ ㄕㄨㄟˇ)
lemonade

檸檬色(ㄋㄧㄥˊ ㄇㄥˊ ㄙㄜˋ)
citrine

檸檬素(ㄋㄧㄥˊ ㄇㄥˊ ㄙㄨˋ)
citrin

檸檬酸(ㄋㄧㄥˊ ㄇㄥˊ ㄙㄨㄢ)
citric acid

檸檬酸鹽(ㄋㄧㄥˊ ㄇㄥˊ ㄙㄨㄢ ㄧㄢˊ)
citrate

【檬】2621 ㄇㄥˊ meng méng
1. a kind of locust or acacia
2. lemon

檬果(ㄇㄥˊ ㄍㄨㄛˇ)
a mango 亦作「芒果」

【檮】2622 ㄊㄠˊ taur táo
ignorant and stupid; a blockhead

檮昧(ㄊㄠˊ ㄇㄟˋ)
ignorant and naive; dull and
stupid

檮杌(ㄊㄠˊ ㄨˋ)
① a legendary fierce animal
② villainous

【檻】2623 ㄐㄧㄢˋ jiann jiàn
railings; bars, as window or
door bars

檻車(ㄐㄧㄢˋ ㄔㄜ)
a cart with a cage for animals or prisoners

檻羊(ㄐㄧㄢˋ ㄧㄤˊ)
(figuratively)at the mercy
of others like a caged lamb

【檻】2623 ㄎㄢˇ kaan kǎn
a doorsill; a threshold

【櫃】2624 ㄍㄨㄟˋ guey guì
1. a cabinet; a wardrobe; a
cupboard
2. a shop counter

櫃面(ㄍㄨㄟˋ ㄇㄧㄢˋ)
the counter in a store: 店員
站在櫃臺後面。The clerk
stood behind the counter.

櫃(ㄍㄨㄟˋ)
a cabinet; a cupboard; a
sideboard

櫃子(ㄍㄨㄟˋ ˙ㄗ)or 櫃(ㄍㄨㄟˋ)
a cabinet; a sideboard

【檯】2625 ㄊㄞˊ tair tái
a table

檯布(ㄊㄞˊ ㄅㄨˋ)
a tablecloth

檯面(ㄊㄞˊ ㄇㄧㄢˋ)
(gambling) stakes

檯燈(ㄊㄞˊ ㄉㄥ)
a table lamp: 請打開檯燈。
Please turn on the table
lamp.

檯球(ㄊㄞˊ ㄑㄧㄡˊ)
table tennis

【檳】2626 ㄅㄧㄣ bin bīn
the areca; the betel; the
areca nut; the betel nut

檳榔(ㄅㄧㄣ ㄌㄤˊ)
the areca nut; the betel nut

檳榔糕(ㄅㄧㄣ ㄌㄤˊ ㄍㄠ)
sweets made of betel nut
and sugar

檳榔嶼(ㄅㄧㄣ ㄌㄤˊ ㄩˇ)
Penang, Malaysia

【櫂】2627 (櫂) ㄓㄠˋ jaw zhào
1. an oar; a paddle
2. to row
3. a general name of boat

櫂歌(ㄓㄠˋ ㄍㄜ)
a boat-song; to chant a
boat-song

櫂槳(ㄓㄠˋ ㄐㄧㄤˇ)
to pull an oar

櫂船(ㄓㄠˋ ㄔㄨㄢˊ)
to row a boat

十五畫

【櫚】2628 ㄌㄩˊ liu lǘ
a palm; the Chinese coir
palm

【櫟】2629 ㄌㄧˋ lih lì
the chestnut-leaved oak
(Quercus chinensis and serrata)

櫟散(ㄌㄧˋ ㄙㄢ)
useless materials

【櫓】2630 ㄌㄨˇ luu lǔ
1. an oar; a scull; a sweep
2. (in ancient warfare) a big
shield; a long spear
3. (now rarely) a lookout
tower on a city wall

櫓夫(ㄌㄨˇ ㄈㄨ)
an oarsman

【櫛】2631 ㄐㄧㄝˊ jye jié
1. a comb; a comb of many
fine teeth
2. to comb the hair
3. to weed out; to eliminate; to
delete

櫛比(ㄐㄧㄝˊ ㄅㄧˇ)
(said of houses) placed
closely together like the
teeth of a comb; joined
closely together: 那些房子鱗
次櫛比。Those houses close
together in serrated formation.

櫛風沐雨(ㄐㄧㄝˊ ㄈㄥ ㄇㄨˋ ㄩˇ)
(literally) combed by the
wind and bathed by the rain
—to be exposed to hard-
ships; hardworking; industrious

櫛工(ㄐㄧㄝˊ ㄍㄨㄥ)
a barber; a hairdresser

櫛櫛(ㄐㄧㄝˊ ㄐㄧㄝˊ)
placed very closely together
as teeth of a comb (often
said of masts of boats in a
fishing harbor, etc.)

【櫝】2632 ㄉㄨˊ dwu dú
1. a closet; a wardrobe; a cabinet; a sideboard or cup-
board
2. a coffin
3. a scabbard
4. to hide; to conceal

【櫥】2633 (櫉) ㄔㄨˊ chwu chú
a closet; a cabinet; a sideboard; a cupboard, etc.

櫥櫃(ㄔㄨˊ ㄍㄨㄟˋ)
a closet; a cabinet; a night
table with drawers, etc.

櫥窗(ㄔㄨˊ ㄔㄨㄤ)
a show window; a show-
case; a display window

十六畫

【木部】

【櫪】 2634 ㄌㄧˋ lih lì
1. a stable; a manger
2. *Quercus serrata*
3. a wooden device used to torture a criminal by pressing his fingers

櫪馬(ㄌㄧˋ ㄇㄚˇ)
stablehorse

櫪梏(ㄌㄧˋ ㄍㄨˋ)
a wooden device used to torture a criminal by pressing his fingers

【櫬】 2635 ㄔㄣˋ chenn chèn
1. a coffin
2. a tung tree

【櫨】 2636 ㄌㄨˊ lu lú
1. the square peck-shaped box half way up a staff or mast
2. the name of a plant

櫨(ㄌㄨˊ ㄉㄡˇ)
the square peck-shaped box half way up a staff or mast

【櫳】 2637 (櫳) ㄌㄨㄥˊ long lóng
1. window with bars
2. a pen or cage for animals

櫳檻(ㄌㄨㄥˊ ㄐㄧㄢ)
a pen or cage for animals

【櫱】 2638 ㄋㄧㄝˋ nieh niè
sprouts grown from the stump of a tree

【橥】 2639 ㄓㄨ ju zhū
a wooden peg; a post; a stalk or stick

十七畫

【櫺】 2640 ㄌㄧㄥˊ ling líng
1. carved or patterned window-railings, sills
2. the wooden planks which join eaves with a house

櫺牀(ㄌㄧㄥˊ ㄔㄨㄤ)
a bed with railings

【欄】 2641 ㄌㄢˇ lan lǎn
1. a railing; a balustrade; a fence: 此馬跳過了欄柵。The horse jumped over the fence.
2. a pen for domesticated animals

【欄杆】(ㄌㄢˊ ㄍㄢ)
① a railing; a balustrade ② silk trimming for girls

欄杆兒(ㄌㄢˊ ㄍㄢˊ)
① a railing or balustrade ② (in Chinese opera company) a horizontal bar for developing muscular strength of players

【櫻】 2642 ㄧㄥ ing yīng
the cherry; the cherry blossoms

櫻桃(ㄧㄥ ㄊㄠˊ)
cherries

櫻脣(ㄧㄥ ㄔㄨㄣˊ)
the small, beautiful mouth of a woman

櫻草(ㄧㄥ ㄘㄠˇ)or 櫻草花(ㄧㄥ ㄘㄠˇ ㄏㄨㄚ)
a primrose

【欅】 2643 ㄐㄩˇ jeu jǔ
a kind of elm, with fine-grained wood (*Zelkova serrata*)

【檀】 2644 ㄔㄢˊ charn chán
1. sandalwood
2. a comet

【欂】 2645 ㄅㄛˊ bor bó
參看「檽櫨」
a square wooden block at the top of a column

【櫽】 2646 ㄧㄣˇ yiin yǐn
1. to straighten bent wood (by heat, etc.)
2. to correct or adjust

櫽括(ㄧㄣˇ ㄍㄨㄚ)
a piece of wood used in straightening bent wood

十八畫

【權】 2647 ㄑㄩㄢˊ chyuan quán
1. to weigh (the significance, etc.); to assess
2. power; authority; inherent rights; jurisdiction; influence
3. an expedient way; expediency; alternative
4. temporarily; for the time being

5. a Chinese family name

權變(ㄑㄩㄢˊ ㄅㄧㄢˋ)
to adjust oneself to changing situations, conditions, etc.

權柄(ㄑㄩㄢˊ ㄅㄧㄥˇ)or(ㄑㄩㄢˊ ㄅㄧㄥˋ)
authority; power: 我掌握權柄。I was in power.

權謀(ㄑㄩㄢˊ ㄇㄡˊ)
schemes and power; the use of schemes and power

權門(ㄑㄩㄢˊ ㄇㄣˊ)
powerful families; the households of powerful ministers

權代(ㄑㄩㄢˊ ㄉㄞˋ)
to act in another's place temporarily; to substitute for another for the time being: 他權代經理。He acted as manager for the time being.

權典(ㄑㄩㄢˊ ㄉㄧㄢˇ)
a provisional law; temporary regulations

權能(ㄑㄩㄢˊ ㄋㄥˊ)
① authority; powers and functions ②(law) the exercise of one's rights

權利分開(ㄑㄩㄢˊ ㄌㄧˋ ㄈㄣ ㄎㄞ)
the division of people's rights and the powers of the government in a democratic constitution

權倿(ㄑㄩㄢˊ ㄋㄧㄥˋ)
a mean politician in power

權利(ㄑㄩㄢˊ ㄌㄧˋ)
rights; some right or advantage enjoyed by common consent

權利法案(ㄑㄩㄢˊ ㄌㄧˋ ㄈㄚˇ ㄢˋ)
Bill of Rights

權力(ㄑㄩㄢˊ ㄌㄧˋ)
power; authority

權力結構(ㄑㄩㄢˊ ㄌㄧˋ ㄐㄧㄝˊ ㄍㄡˋ)
power structure

權略(ㄑㄩㄢˊ ㄌㄩㄝˋ)
schemes or measures to meet exigencies

權貴(ㄑㄩㄢˊ ㄍㄨㄟˋ)
highly-placed personalities; ranking officials; influential figures; the mighty

權衡(ㄑㄩㄢˊ ㄏㄥˊ)
to weigh, consider or assess: 我們權衡利弊。We weighed the advantages and disadvantages.

權且(ㄑㄩㄢˊ ㄑㄧㄝˇ)
for the time being; temporarily; in the mean time; interim: 我們權且如此辦理。Let's carry it out as interim measure.

權限(ㄑㄩㄢˊ ㄒㄧㄢˋ)
limitation of power or authority; jurisdiction within certain limits

權宜(ㄑㄩㄢˊ ㄧˊ)
crafty and dishonest; expediency in disregard of morality

權杖(ㄑㄩㄢˊ ㄓㄤˋ)
a baton or staff borne as a symbol of office

權重(ㄑㄩㄢˊ ㄓㄨㄥˋ)
to be in power

權臣(ㄑㄩㄢˊ ㄔㄣˊ)
powerful courtiers: 權臣欺君。Powerful courtiers insult their king.

權寵(ㄑㄩㄢˊ ㄔㄨㄥˇ)
to gain powers through favor from the emperor, etc.

權勢(ㄑㄩㄢˊ ㄕˋ)
power and influence

權術(ㄑㄩㄢˊ ㄕㄨˋ)
craft or tact (in handling political things, etc.); political trickery; politics: 他喜歡玩弄權術。He likes to play politics.

權數(ㄑㄩㄢˊ ㄕㄨˋ)
the talent to meet exigencies

權宜(ㄑㄩㄢˊ ㄧˊ)
expedient; temporary (measures, etc.)

權宜之計(ㄑㄩㄢˊ ㄧˊ ㄓ ㄐㄧˋ)
an expedient; a makeshift

權益(ㄑㄩㄢˊ ㄧˋ)
rights and interests

權要(ㄑㄩㄢˊ ㄧㄠˋ)
①bigwigs; top dogs; powerful persons ②confidential matter

權右(ㄑㄩㄢˊ ㄧㄡˋ)
bigwigs; top dogs; highly-placed personalities

權威(ㄑㄩㄢˊ ㄨㄟ)
①an authority (in certain sphere of knowledge): 他是一個語音學權威。He is an authority on phonetics. ②power and prestige

權輿(ㄑㄩㄢˊ ㄩˊ)
the beginning

十九畫

【欒】 2648
ㄌㄨㄢˊ luan luán
1. *Koelreuteria paniculata*, name of a small tree with tiny leaves and yellow flowers
2. the two corners at the mouth of a Chinese bell
3. a Chinese family name

二十一畫

【欖】 2649
ㄌㄢˇ laan lǎn
the olive

欠 部
ㄑㄧㄢ chiann qiàn

【欠】 2650
ㄑㄧㄢˋ chiann qiàn
1. to owe; to owe money
2. deficient; lacking; short of; not enough: 他的寫作文字欠佳。His writing is not good enough.
3. to raise slightly (a part of the body)
4. to yawn

欠安(ㄑㄧㄢˋ ㄢ)
not very proper or appropriate; not satisfactory or dependable: 他的文章措詞欠妥。His essay was not properly worded.

欠款(ㄑㄧㄢˋ ㄎㄨㄢˇ)
①to owe money ②debts; the amount of money owed

欠佳(ㄑㄧㄢˋ ㄐㄧㄚ)
not satisfactory: 結果欠佳。The result was not satisfactory.

欠繳(ㄑㄧㄢˋ ㄐㄧㄠˇ)
to have not paid (one's due, tax, etc.)

欠據(ㄑㄧㄢˋ ㄐㄩˋ)
an I.O.U. note

欠錢(ㄑㄧㄢˋ ㄑㄧㄢˊ)
①to owe money ②to be short of money

欠情(ㄑㄧㄢˋ ㄑㄧㄥˊ)
to owe favors; favors not returned or repaid

欠缺(ㄑㄧㄢˋ ㄑㄩㄝ)
①to lack; deficient; short of: 他們欠缺經驗。They are still lacking in experience. ②shortcomings: 我的工作還有很多欠缺。There are still many shortcomings in my job.

欠薪(ㄑㄧㄢˋ ㄒㄧㄣ)
overdue wages; back pay

欠債(ㄑㄧㄢˋ ㄓㄞˋ)
to be in debt; to owe money

欠賬(ㄑㄧㄢˋ ㄓㄤˋ)
①to owe money; to buy on credit ②overdue bills

欠伸(ㄑㄧㄢˋ ㄕㄣ)
to yawn

欠身(ㄑㄧㄢˋ ㄕㄣ)
to get ready to stand up as a gesture of courtesy

欠稅(ㄑㄧㄢˋ ㄕㄨㄟˋ)
tax arrears

欠資郵票(ㄑㄧㄢˋ ㄗ ㄧㄡˊ ㄆㄧㄠˋ)
a postage-due stamp

欠安(ㄑㄧㄢˋ ㄢ)
not at ease at heart; not feeling well physically

二畫

【次】 2651
ㄘ tsyh cì
1. the next in order; secondary
2. inferior; lower
3. vice or deputy (ministers, etc.)
4. a place where one stops for rest on a trip; a place
5. to stop at a place
6. by; at (the feast, table, etc.); in the midst
7. a grade; grading; order; sequence
8. (chemistry) the prefix "hypo"
9. time (each occasion of a recurring action or event)

次品(ㄘˋ ㄆㄧㄣˇ)
goods of inferior quality

次等(ㄘˋ ㄉㄥˇ)or 次一等(ㄘˋ ㄧ ㄉㄥˇ)
a lower or inferior class or category; of the second grade or quality

次等貨(ㄘˋ ㄉㄥˇ ㄏㄨㄛˋ)
seconds

次第(ㄘˋ ㄉㄧˋ)

（欠 部）

〔欠〕部

①order; grade; sequence ②in order; one by one; one after another

次年(ㄘ ㄋㄧㄢˊ)
the next year; the following year

次女(ㄘ ㄋㄩˇ)
the second daughter

次女高音(ㄘ ㄋㄩˇ ㄍㄠ ㄧㄣ)
a mezzo-soprano

次席(ㄘ ㄒㄧˊ)
①the seat next to the guest of honor or the person in command ②a bamboo mat

次序(ㄘ ㄒㄩˋ)
order, sequence, succession, etc.: 這些書是按照大小次序排列的。The books are arranged in order of size.

次殖民地(ㄘ ㄓˊ ㄇㄧㄣˊ ㄉㄧˋ)
a country with the important part of its sovereignty usurped by foreign powers and is therefore in a worse situation than a colony

次長(ㄘ ㄓㄤˇ)
a vice minister; a deputy minister: 他是參謀次長。He is a Deputy Chief of the General Staff.

次中音(ㄘ ㄓㄨㄥ ㄧㄣ)
(music) submedant

次室(ㄘ ㄕˋ)
a concubine

次數(ㄘ ㄕㄨˋ)
the number of times

次日(ㄘ ㄖˋ)
the next day; the following day: 他於次日來見我。He came to see me the next day.

次子(ㄘ ㄗˇ)or 次男(ㄘ ㄋㄢˊ)
the second son

次早(ㄘ ㄗㄠˇ)
the next morning

次次(ㄘ ㄘˋ)
①every time ②uneasy

次要(ㄘ ㄧㄠˋ)
secondary; not very important: 你使這個問題退居次要地位。You relegated the problem to a secondary position.

次於(ㄘ ㄩˊ)
next to...; inferior to...

次韻(ㄘ ㄩㄣˋ)
(poetry) to rhyme one's poem in accordance with another's

四畫

【欣】 2652
ㄒㄧㄣ shin xīn
glad; gladly; joyful; joyfully; delighted; happy: 這消息使全國歡欣鼓舞。The news delighted the whole nation.

欣忭(ㄒㄧㄣ ㄅㄧㄢˋ)
delight; joy

欣逢(ㄒㄧㄣ ㄈㄥˊ)
happy to be present (on a joyful occasion)

欣戴(ㄒㄧㄣ ㄉㄞˋ)
to support (a leader, cause, etc.) gladly

欣悅(ㄒㄧㄣ ㄒㄧˇ)
delighted to learn; to have happily learned that

欣喜(ㄒㄧㄣ ㄒㄧˇ)or 欣懌(ㄒㄧㄣ ㄧˋ)
joyful; happy; delight

欣喜欲狂(ㄒㄧㄣ ㄒㄧˇ ㄩˋ ㄎㄨㄤˊ)or 欣喜若狂(ㄒㄧㄣ ㄒㄧˇ ㄖㄨㄛˋ ㄎㄨㄤˊ)
to be beside oneself with joy: 他欣喜若狂。He was beside himself with joy.

欣羨(ㄒㄧㄣ ㄒㄧㄢˋ)
to admire or envy

欣欣向榮(ㄒㄧㄣ ㄒㄧㄣ ㄒㄧㄤˋ ㄖㄨㄥˊ)
①(said of flowers in spring) blossoming ②(said of business, financial situations, etc.) prospering; flourishing; thriving: 我國國民經濟正欣欣向榮。Our national economy is prospering.

欣欣然(ㄒㄧㄣ ㄒㄧㄣ ㄖㄢˊ)
happy; joyful; complacent

欣賞(ㄒㄧㄣ ㄕㄤˇ)
to appreciate; to enjoy; to admire: 她欣賞藝術與音樂。She has an appreciation of art and music.

欣然(ㄒㄧㄣ ㄖㄢˊ)
gladly; with pleasure: 他欣然接受禮物。He accepted the present with pleasure.

欣慰(ㄒㄧㄣ ㄨㄟˋ)
gratified; delighted; satisfied; comforted; contented; satisfaction; to joy: 我看到你如此成功而感欣慰。I joy to see you so successful.

欣悅(ㄒㄧㄣ ㄩㄝˋ)
delighted; joyous; joyful; glad; happy

欣躍(ㄒㄧㄣ ㄩㄝˋ)
dancing with glee

六畫

【欬】 2653
1.(咳)ㄎㄜˊ ker kè
1.to cough: 他欬得很厲害。He coughs badly.
2. the sound of laughing

【欬】 2653
2.ㄎㄞˋ kay kài
asthma and coughing

七畫

【欲】 2654
ㄩˋ yuh yù
1. to desire; to intend; to long for; to want; wish; desire; expectation; longing: 他暢所欲言。He poured out what he wished to say.
2. (now rarely) love; to love
3. (now rarely) genial and amiable
4. about to; on the point of; to the verge of: 這座大廟, 搖搖欲墜。This temple is on the verge of collapse.

欲罷不能(ㄩˋ ㄅㄚˋ ㄅㄨˋ ㄋㄥˊ)
unable to stop even if one wants to

欲不可從 or 欲不可縱(ㄩˋ ㄅㄨˋ ㄎㄜˇ ㄗㄨㄥˋ)
Desire must be kept under control.

欲的(ㄩˋ ㄉㄜ)
to intend to; to want to

欲蓋彌彰(ㄩˋ ㄍㄞˋ ㄇㄧˊ ㄓㄤ)
The more one tries to cover up (a secret, etc.), the better-known it will become.

欲海難填(ㄩˋ ㄏㄞˇ ㄋㄢˊ ㄊㄧㄢˊ)
One's desires are insatiable.

欲火 or 慾火(ㄩˋ ㄏㄨㄛˇ)
the fire of desire—sexual desire

欲加之罪, 何患無詞(ㄩˋ ㄐㄧㄚ ㄓ ㄗㄨㄟˋ, ㄏㄜˊ ㄏㄨㄢˋ ㄨˊ ㄘˊ)
If you want to condemn somebody, you can always trump up a charge.

欲界(ㄩˋ ㄐㄧㄝˋ)
(Buddhism) Kamadhatu; the realm or realms of desire for food, sleep and sex

欲箭(ㄩ ㄐㄧㄢˋ)
(Buddhism) the arrow of five desires—that can harm all living beings

欲壑(ㄩ ㄏㄜˋ)
the gulf of human desires
—deep and hard to get across

欲擒故縱(ㄩ ㄑㄧㄣˊ ㄍㄨˋ ㄗㄨㄥˋ)
(literally) If one wants to catch somebody, he may need to let loose the noose for a while.—to try to get something by feigning uninterestedness or making concessions

欲心(ㄩ ㄒㄧㄣ)
one's desires

欲想(ㄩ ㄒㄧㄤˇ)
desires for wealth and women

欲障(ㄩ ㄓㄤˋ)
desires that pose as one's obstacles to salvation

欲速不達(ㄩ ㄙㄨˋ ㄅㄨˋ ㄉㄚˊ)
Haste makes waste. 或 More haste, less speed.

欲火(ㄩ ㄏㄨㄛˇ)
passion-love; love inspired by desire, through any of the five senses

欲要(ㄩ ㄧㄠˋ)
to desire; to want to

欲言又止(ㄩ ㄧㄢˊ ㄧㄡˋ ㄓˇ)
to wish to speak but keep silent on second thought

欲望(ㄩ ㄨㄤˋ)
desires; to long for; longings: 這年輕人有求名的欲望。The young man had a desire for fame.

【欸】 2655_{1.} ㄞ ae ai
1. the sound of answering
2. sighs
3. the sound of rowing a boat

欸乃(ㄞ ㄋㄞˇ)
the sound of rowing a boat

【欸】 2655_{2.} ㄟˋ ey èi
an exclamation indicating promise or affirmation: 欸，我就來! Yes, I'll come in a moment.

【欷】 2656 ㄒㄧ shi xī
to sob

欷歔(ㄒㄧ ㄒㄩ)
to sob

八畫

【款】 2657
(欵) ㄎㄨㄢˇ koan kuǎn
1. sincerity; sincere; sincerely
2. an article, an item, etc. (in a contract, treaty, etc.)
3. to entertain; to treat well
4. slowly; slow
5. to knock (at a door)
6. a fund; a sum of money; money
7. empty (words, etc.)

款步(ㄎㄨㄢˇ ㄅㄨˋ)
(often said of women) to move or proceed slowly; to walk in slow steps: 她款步而行。She walked in slow steps.

款門(ㄎㄨㄢˇ ㄇㄣˊ)
to knock at the door

款密(ㄎㄨㄢˇ ㄇㄧˋ)
intimate

款目(ㄎㄨㄢˇ ㄇㄨˋ)
①an article or item in a contract, treaty, etc. ②an entry in an account; a sum of money

款伏(ㄎㄨㄢˇ ㄈㄨˊ)
to submit to or obey willingly; to admire

款附(ㄎㄨㄢˇ ㄈㄨˋ)
to submit to or obey with true loyalty; to follow willingly

款待(ㄎㄨㄢˇ ㄉㄞˋ)
to entertain with courtesy and warmth; hospitality

款段(ㄎㄨㄢˇ ㄉㄨㄢˋ)
(said of horses) to proceed slowly

款冬(ㄎㄨㄢˇ ㄉㄨㄥ)
(botany) a coltsfoot (*Tussilago farfara*)

款留(ㄎㄨㄢˇ ㄌㄧㄡˊ)
to try sincerely to make a guest stay longer in order to offer greater hospitality

款客(ㄎㄨㄢˇ ㄎㄜˋ)
to entertain guests

款款(ㄎㄨㄢˇ ㄎㄨㄢˇ)
①sincerely ②slowly

款接(ㄎㄨㄢˇ ㄐㄧㄝ)
to entertain (guests, etc.); to receive (visitors, etc.)

款交(ㄎㄨㄢˇ ㄐㄧㄠ)
sincere friendship

款襟(ㄎㄨㄢˇ ㄐㄧㄣ)
to talk to one's heart's content

款啟(ㄎㄨㄢˇ ㄑㄧˇ)
limited views; provincialism

款洽(ㄎㄨㄢˇ ㄑㄧㄚˋ)or(ㄎㄨㄢˇ ㄒㄧㄚˊ)
a meeting of minds; on very agreeable terms

款曲(ㄎㄨㄢˇ ㄑㄩ)
①secrets in one's heart; heartfelt feelings ②to conduct oneself with great tact in social gatherings

款項(ㄎㄨㄢˇ ㄒㄧㄤˋ)
a sum of money; a fund; money: 他出一大筆款項買了這幢房子。He paid a large sum for the house.

款識(ㄎㄨㄢˇ ㄓˋ)
①words engraved on tripods, bells, etc. ②the name, signature, etc. in a painting or calligraphy

款式(ㄎㄨㄢˇ ㄕˋ)
fashions; styles; patterns: 這些皮鞋是最新的款式。These are the latest style in shoes.

款子(ㄎㄨㄢˇ ˙ㄗ)
money; a sum of money

款額(ㄎㄨㄢˇ ㄜˊ)
the amount of money involved

款言(ㄎㄨㄢˇ ㄧㄢˊ)
empty words: 款言不聽。Do not listen to empty words.

款引(ㄎㄨㄢˇ ㄧㄣˇ)
to confess; to admit

款語(ㄎㄨㄢˇ ㄩˇ)
gentle and persuasive conversation

【欽】 2658 ㄑㄧㄣ chin qīn
1. to respect; respectful; to admire
2. a term used to address a monarch in ancient China—Your Majesty
3. a Chinese family name

欽佩(ㄑㄧㄣ ㄆㄟˋ)

to admire; to respect; to agree wholeheartedly: 我欽佩你的坦白。I admire your frankness.

欽命(ㄑㄧㄣ ㄇㄧㄥˋ)

①(by) imperial orders ②an

【欠部】

imperial emissary

欽慕(ㄑㄧㄣ ㄇㄨˋ)
to admire; to look up to: 他的聰明為人所欽慕。His cleverness is much admired.

欽點
designated by the emperor as members of the Imperial Academy

欽定(ㄑㄧㄣ ㄉㄧㄥˋ)
(said of books, etc.) compiled and published by imperial orders; compiled or edited by the emperor

欽天監(ㄑㄧㄣ ㄊㄧㄢ ㄐㄧㄢ)
(in old China) a government post in charge of astronomy, astrology, divination and related sciences

欽敬(ㄑㄧㄣ ㄐㄧㄥˋ)
to admire and respect

欽遲(ㄑㄧㄣ ㄔˊ)
to admire; to look up to

欽差大臣(ㄑㄧㄣ ㄔㄞ ㄉㄚˋ ㄔㄣˊ)
(in old China) officials sent to the provinces on specific missions by order of the emperor; imperial inspector generals

欽此(ㄑㄧㄣ ㄘˇ)
an expression making the end of imperial orders in old China

欽賜(ㄑㄧㄣ ㄙˋ)
granted or bestowed by the emperor (for meritorious service, etc.)

欽挹(ㄑㄧㄣ ㄧˋ)
to admire and respect; to look up to

欽仰(ㄑㄧㄣ ㄧㄤˇ)
to admire and respect; to look up to

【欺】 2659 ㄑㄧ chi qī
1. to cheat; to deceive; to swindle; to impose on; to take advantage of
2. to disregard the dictates of one's own conscience
3. to insult; to bully

欺詐(ㄑㄧ ㄊㄡˊ)
to cheat; to deceive; to swindle

欺瞞(ㄑㄧ ㄇㄢˊ)
to deceive; to cheat

欺朦(ㄑㄧ ㄇㄥˊ)

to cheat; to defraud; to hide the truth (from superiors, etc.)

欺負(ㄑㄧ ㄈㄨˋ)
to bully; to oppress; to insult; to ridicule

欺誕(ㄑㄧ ㄉㄢˋ)
to cheat by exaggerating

欺凌(ㄑㄧ ㄌㄧㄥˊ)
to mistreat; to insult; to bully

欺君(ㄑㄧ ㄐㄩㄣ)
to withhold truth from emperor

欺下罔上(ㄑㄧ ㄒㄧㄚˋ ㄨㄤˇ ㄕㄤˋ)
to oppress the people and hide the truth from higher authorities

欺心(ㄑㄧ ㄒㄧㄣ)
to disregard the dictates of one's own conscience; unconscionable

欺詐(ㄑㄧ ㄓㄚˋ)
to swindle; to defraud; to cheat: 誠實的商人不欺詐顧客。Honest merchants do not swindle their customers.

欺世盜名(ㄑㄧ ㄕˋ ㄉㄠˋ ㄇㄧㄥˊ)
to win fame by cheating the world

欺善怕惡(ㄑㄧ ㄕㄢˋ ㄆㄚˋ ㄜˋ)
to oppress the good and timid and fear the wicked

欺上瞞下(ㄑㄧ ㄕㄤˋ ㄇㄢˊ ㄒㄧㄚˋ)
to cheat one's superiors and defraud one's subordinates

欺人太甚(ㄑㄧ ㄖㄣˊ ㄊㄞˋ ㄕㄣˋ)
It's really too much! 或 You have insulted me beyond the limit.或 That's going too far.

欺人之談(ㄑㄧ ㄖㄣˊ ㄓ ㄊㄢˊ)
a lie

欺人自欺(ㄑㄧ ㄖㄣˊ ㄗˋ ㄑㄧ)
to cheat oneself and others

欺軟怕硬(ㄑㄧ ㄖㄨㄢˇ ㄆㄚˋ ㄧㄥˋ)
to bully the weak and fear the strong

欺壓(ㄑㄧ ㄧㄚˋ)
to cheat and oppress

欺侮(ㄑㄧ ㄨˇ)
to insult or ridicule; to bully: 他欺侮他的弟弟。He bullies his younger brother.

欺罔(ㄑㄧ ㄨㄤˇ)or 欺誑(ㄑㄧ ㄎㄨㄤˊ)

【欻】 2660 1. ㄏㄨ hu hū

sudden; suddenly; abruptly

欻忽(ㄈㄨˊ ㄈㄨˊ)
quickly; swiftly

【欻】 2660 2. ㄔㄨㄚ chua chuā
descriptive of the sound

【欿】 2661 ㄎㄢˇ kaan kǎn
1. discontented with oneself
2. sad and gloomy

欿然(ㄎㄢˇ ㄖㄢˊ)
① dissatisfied; discontented
② without elation

【欸】 2662 (欸) ㄧ i yī
an interjection of pleasure
—Bravo! Good!

欸乃盛哉(ㄧˋ ㄋㄞˇ ㄕㄥˋ ㄗㄞ)
What a grand occasion! 或 What a grand sight!

九畫

【歇】 2663 ㄒㄧㄝ shie xiē
1. to rest
2. to sleep
3. to come to an end; to stop
4. to lodge

歇泊(ㄒㄧㄝ ㄅㄛˊ)
to lie at anchor

歇拍(ㄒㄧㄝ ㄆㄞ)
the ending of a lyrical song (詞)

歇馬(ㄒㄧㄝ ㄇㄚˇ)
① to dismount and take a rest ② to stop working

歇乏(ㄒㄧㄝ ㄈㄚˊ)
a rest after toiling

歇店(ㄒㄧㄝ ㄉㄧㄢˋ)
to stay or lodge at an inn: 他歇店住了一星期。He stayed at an inn for a week. ② an inn

歇頂(ㄒㄧㄝ ㄉㄧㄥˇ)
to get bald as one gets older

歇腳兒(ㄒㄧㄝ ㄐㄧㄠˇㄦ)
① to rest one's feet after a long walk ② to stay at a place; to stay at an inn

歇工(ㄒㄧㄝ ㄍㄨㄥ)
to stop work

歇後(ㄒㄧㄝ ㄏㄡˋ)
to omit the last part of a common expression

歇後語(ㄒㄧㄝ ㄏㄡˋ ㄩˇ)
a common expression whose

last part is omitted; a riddle thus made, for example, 泥菩薩過河—自身難保。A clay idol fords a river.—It is hard for one to save himself (let alone help others).

歇脚(ㄒㄧㄝ ㄐㄧㄠˇ)
to rest the feet after walking

歇息(ㄒㄧㄝ ㄒㄧˊ)
①to take a rest ②to put up for the night; to stay at an inn

歇夏(ㄒㄧㄝ ㄒㄧㄚˋ)
(said of an opera company, etc.) to stop performance in summer; to take a vacation in summer

歇歇兒(ㄒㄧㄝ ·ㄒㄧㄝ ㄦ)
to take a little rest: 勞苦工作後歇歇兒是必須的。Rest is necessary after hard work.

歇心(ㄒㄧㄝ ㄒㄧㄣ)
not to indulge in fancy or desire; not to worry or care

歇手(ㄒㄧㄝ ㄕㄡˇ)
to discontinue (an operation, work, etc.); to stop doing something

歇晌兒(ㄒㄧㄝ ㄕㄤˇㄦ)
a rest after lunch; to take a nap or siesta after noon: 他每天午後歇晌兒。He takes a nap every afternoon.

歇坐(ㄒㄧㄝ ㄗㄨㄛˋ)
(in a Chinese feast) to take a brief rest after three rounds of drink

歇嘴(ㄒㄧㄝ ㄗㄨㄟˇ)
to stop talking; to shut up

歇斯的里(ㄒㄧㄝ ㄙ ㄉㄧˋ ㄌㄧˇ)
hysteria

歇宿(ㄒㄧㄝ ㄙㄨˋ)
to spend the night; to stay for the night; to make an overnight stop: 他來此歇宿。He came here to make an overnight stop.

歇一宿(ㄒㄧㄝ ㄧˋ ㄒㄧㄡˇ)
to stay or rest for the night

歇一歇(ㄒㄧㄝ ·ㄧ ·ㄒㄧㄝ)or 歇歇(ㄒㄧㄝ·ㄒㄧㄝ)
to take a rest or break

歇業(ㄒㄧㄝ ㄧㄝˋ)
to close shop

【歆】 2664
ㄒㄧㄣ shin xīn

1. (said of gods, etc.) to accept offerings, etc.
2. to admire; to submit to willingly
3. to move

歆慕 or 欣慕(ㄒㄧㄣ ㄇㄨˋ)
to cherish

歆羨(ㄒㄧㄣ ㄒㄧㄢˋ)
to admire; to envy (another's beauty or luck)

歆艷(ㄒㄧㄣ ㄧㄢˋ)
to envy; to admire

【歃】 2665
ㄕㄚˋ shah shà

to drink blood; to smear the mouth with blood of an animal in oath-taking

歃血(ㄕㄚˋ ㄒㄩㄝˋ)
(an ancient practice) to smear the mouth with blood in oath-taking

十畫

【歉】 2666
ㄑㄧㄢˋ chiann qiàn

1. deficient; insufficient; deficiency
2. a poor crop or harvest
3. to regret; sorry
4. an apology; apologetic

歉收(ㄑㄧㄢˋ ㄕㄡ)
a bad harvest

歉然(ㄑㄧㄢˋ ㄖㄢˊ)
to regret; to feel sorry

歉仄(ㄑㄧㄢˋ ㄗㄜˋ)
very sorry; regrettable

歉歲(ㄑㄧㄢˋ ㄙㄨㄟˋ)
a year of poor harvest

歉意(ㄑㄧㄢˋ ㄧˋ)
regrets; apologies: 我表示歉意。I expressed my regret.

【歌】 2667
ㄍㄜ ge gē

1. to sing; to chant
2. to praise
3. a song
4. poems with rhythms and rhymes suitable for use as lyrics in songs

歌譜(ㄍㄜ ㄆㄨˇ)
music scores

歌德(ㄍㄜ ㄉㄜˊ)
① to praise the virtues, achievements, etc. of someone (often one's superior) ② Johann Wolfgang von Goethe (1749-1832), German poet and dramatist

歌臺舞樹(ㄍㄜ ㄊㄞˊ ㄨˇ ㄊㄨˋ)
the stage—where songs and dances are performed; places of amusement

歌廳(ㄍㄜ ㄊㄧㄥ)
an entertainment establishment where popular songs are sung by professional singers

歌女(ㄍㄜ ㄋㄩˇ)
a songstress; a female singer

歌功頌德(ㄍㄜ ㄍㄨㄥ ㄙㄨㄥˋ ㄉㄜˊ)
①to praise another (usually one's superior) for his achievements and virtues ② to flatter; to give undeserved praises

歌喉(ㄍㄜ ㄏㄡˊ)
one's singing voice; one's vocal talent as a singer

歌后(ㄍㄜ ㄏㄡˋ)
a very accomplished female vocalist

歌集(ㄍㄜ ㄐㄧˊ)or 歌本(ㄍㄜ ㄅㄣˇ)
a collection of songs; a songbook

歌妓(ㄍㄜ ㄐㄧˋ)
(formerly) female entertainers somewhat like the geisha girls in Japan

歌劇(ㄍㄜ ㄐㄩˋ)
operas

歌曲(ㄍㄜ ㄑㄩˇ)
a song; a tune; a ballad: 她唱了一首流行歌曲。She sang a popular song.

歌星(ㄍㄜ ㄒㄧㄥ)
a singing star; an accomplished vocalist

歌詩(ㄍㄜ ㄕ)
①songs ②to sing poems

歌唱(ㄍㄜ ㄔㄤˋ)
to sing; to chant

歌唱家(ㄍㄜ ㄔㄤˋ ㄐㄧㄚ)
a vocalist; an acclaimed singer

歌吹(ㄍㄜ ㄔㄨㄟˋ)
singing and musical accompaniments; the singing and the playing of musical instruments

歌手(ㄍㄜ ㄕㄡˇ)
a songster; a vocalist

歌聲(ㄍㄜ ㄕㄥ)
the singing voice; the vocal part in a performance: 歌聲

〔欠部〕

〔欠 部〕

盈耳。The sound of singing fills the ear.

歌聲繞梁(《さ アム 日幺 カlた)
The voice of singing reverberates round the beams of a house for days. (an expression to describe the superb performance of a vocalist)

歌詞(《さ ち)
lyrics or words of a song

歌頌(《さ ムメム)
to sing praises: 我們歌頌她的美德。We chant the praise of her virtues.

歌讀(《さ ムメム)
① to read a book aloud musically ② to sing praises

歌兒(《さ ル)
a song; a tune

歌謠(《さ lㄠ)
a ballad; a folk song

歌筵(《さ lㄢ)
a feast enlivened by a singing performance

歌舞(《さ メ)
singing and dancing; song and dance

歌舞伎(《さ メ ㄐl)
a geisha (especially in Japan)

歌舞劇(《さ メ ㄐㄩ)
a light opera; a musical; operetta

歌舞場(《さ メ ㄔㄤ)
places of amusement or entertainment—stages and cabarets

歌舞昇平(《さ メ アム ㄆlㄥ)
reign of peace and prosperity (when people can rejoice with singing and dancing)

歌王(《さ メㄤ)
a very accomplished male vocalist

歌詠(《さ ㄩㄥ)
to sing praises; to sing; to eulogize: 他們歌詠聖賢。They eulogized the sages.

十一畫

【歎】 2668 (嘆) ㄊㄢ tann tòn
to sigh in wonderment or lamentation; to exclaim

歎美(ㄊㄢ ㄇㄟ)

to praise

歎服(ㄊㄢ ㄈㄨ)
to praise and admire

歎號(ㄊㄢ ㄏㄠ)
(punctuation) the exclamation mark (!)

歎氣(ㄊㄢ ㄑl)
to sigh: 那老人唉聲嘆氣。The old man sighed in despair.

歎息(ㄊㄢ ㄒl)
① to sigh in lamentation; to lament ② to exclaim ③ a sigh: 他深深發出一聲歎息。He heaved a great sigh.

歎惜(ㄊㄢ ㄒl)
to sigh with regret; to lament

歎傷(ㄊㄢ アㄤ)
to lament: 她為何歎傷? Why does she lament?

歎賞(ㄊㄢ アㄤ)
to praise and admire; to exclaim in appreciation

歎詞(ㄊㄢ ち)
(grammar) an interjection

歎愕(ㄊㄢ ㄜ)
to exclaim in surprise or wonder

歎一口氣(ㄊㄢ lㄎㄡ ㄑl)
to heave a sigh

歎為觀止(ㄊㄢ ㄨㄟ ㄍㄨㄢ ㄓ)
the most magnificent sight of all; an unrivaled sight; a sight never to be forgotten

歎惋(ㄊㄢ ㄨㄢ)
to sigh in lamentation; to sigh with regret

【歐】 2669 ㄡ ou ōu
1. Europe; European
2. same as 嘔—to vomit
3. same as 毆—to beat
4. same as 謳—to sing
5. (electricity) ohm, the SI unit of electrical resistance
6. a Chinese family name

歐美(ㄡ ㄇㄟ)
Europe and America—the West; Western

歐姆(ㄡ ㄇㄨ)
Georg Simon Ohm (1787–1854), German physicist

歐姆定律(ㄡ ㄇㄨ ㄉlㄥ ㄌㄩ)
Ohm's law

歐風美雨(ㄡ ㄈㄥ ㄇㄟ ㄩ)
the influences of Western culture and civilization

歐羅巴(ㄡ ㄌㄨㄛ ㄅㄚ)
① the European continent ② (Greek mythology) Europa

歐化(ㄡ ㄏㄨㄚ)
Europeanization; westernized

歐幾里得(ㄡ ㄐl ㄌl ㄉㄜ)
Euclid (330-275 B.C.?), Greek mathematician

歐幾里得原理(ㄡ ㄐl ㄌl ㄉㄜ ㄩㄢ ㄌl)
the Elements of Euclid

歐西(ㄡ ㄒl)
the Western world; the West

歐洲(ㄡ ㄓㄡ)
Europe

歐洲共同市場(ㄡ ㄓㄡ ㄍㄨㄥ ㄊㄨㄥ ㄕ ㄔㄤ)
European Common Market (ECM)

歐戰(ㄡ ㄓㄢ)
World War I (which was largely confined in Europe)

歐氏管(ㄡ ㄕ ㄍㄨㄢ)
(anatomy) the Eustachian tube 亦作「耳氣管」

歐亞(ㄡ lㄚ)
Europe and Asia; Eurasia

歐亞混血兒(ㄡ lㄚ ㄏㄨㄣ ㄒㄩㄝ ㄦ)
a Eurasian

歐陽(ㄡ lㄤ)
a Chinese family name

歐陽修(ㄡ lㄤ ㄒlㄡ)
Ou-Yang Hsiu (1007-1072), a famous conservative official and man of letters of the Sung Dynasty

【歔】 2670 ㄏㄨ hu hū
to blow; to exhale

【歙】 2671 lㄣ yiin yín
the ancient version of 飲—to drink

十二畫

【歃】 2672 1. ㄒl shih xī
to suck; to inhale

【歃】 2672 2. アㄜ sheh shè
name of a county in Anhwei Province

【歔】 2673 ㄒㄩ shiu xū
1. to exhale from the nose

2. to sob

歇歇 (ㄒㄩ ㄒㄧ)
to sob; to sniffle —as after crying

【歔】 (嘘) ㄒㄧㄠˇ 2674
shiaw
xiǎo
1. to scream or whistle; a whistling or hissing sound
2. to sigh; to groan

十三畫

【歕】 (噴) ㄆㄣ pen pēn 2675
1. to spurt; to blow
2. to snort; to puff

【歜】 ㄔㄨ chuh chù 2676
furious; wrathful

【斂】 ㄌㄧㄢ liann liàn 2677
1. to collect; to gather
2. to hold together
3. to deduct; to subtract
4. to desire; to ask for something

十四畫

【歟】 ㄩ yu yú 2678
a final particle indicating doubt, surprise, exclamation, etc.

十五畫

【歠】 ㄔㄨㄛ chuoh chuò 2679
to drink; to sip; to suck

十八畫

【歡】 ㄏㄨㄢ huan huān 2680
1. pleased; glad; jubilant
2. pleasures; joys
3. a lover
4. active and energetic; quick; in full swing
5. a Chinese family name

歡伯 (ㄏㄨㄢ ㄅㄛˊ)
wine and liquor

歡蹦亂跳 (ㄏㄨㄢ ㄅㄥˋ ㄌㄨㄢˋ ㄊㄧㄠˋ)
skipping or jumping about with joy; gamboling

歡抃 (ㄏㄨㄢ ㄅㄧㄢˋ)
happy; joyful

歡抃
to clap hands as a result of joy

歡騰 (ㄏㄨㄢ ㄊㄥˊ)
great rejoicing; jubilation

歡天喜地 (ㄏㄨㄢ ㄊㄧㄢ ㄒㄧˇ ㄉㄧˋ)
overjoyed; very much pleased: 我們歡天喜地的迎接國慶。We greeted National Day with boundless joy.

歡樂 (ㄏㄨㄢ ㄌㄜˋ)
joy; happiness; gaiety

歡樂場 (ㄏㄨㄢ ㄌㄜˋ ㄔㄤˇ) or 歡場
gay establishments; places where people seek carnal pleasure

歡呼 (ㄏㄨㄢ ㄏㄨ)
to cheer with jubilation; to shout for joy; to hurrah

歡會 (ㄏㄨㄢ ㄏㄨㄟˋ)
a happy reunion

歡聚 (ㄏㄨㄢ ㄐㄩˋ)
① a happy reunion; a joyful meeting; a happy get-together ② to gather together happily: 我們歡聚一堂。We happily gathered under the same roof.

歡喜 (ㄏㄨㄢ ㄒㄧˇ)
joyful; happy: 小孩子歡喜喜的過新年。Children spent a joyful New Year.

歡喜佛 (ㄏㄨㄢ ㄒㄧˇ ㄈㄛˊ) or 歡喜天 (ㄏㄨㄢ ㄒㄧˇ ㄊㄧㄢ)
devas of pleasure; two human figures with elephant heads, one a male and the other a female, shown in an obscene act, which are found in the secret chambers of some Lamaist temples—a symbol of the good, represented by the female, subduing the forces of evil and violence, represented by the male

歡喜錢兒 (ㄏㄨㄢ ㄒㄧˇ ㄑㄧㄢˊㄦ)
money given on happy occasions, such as a wedding, birthday party, etc.

歡洽 (ㄏㄨㄢ ㄒㄧㄚˋ)
friendly; harmoniously

歡笑 (ㄏㄨㄢ ㄒㄧㄠˋ)
cheer and laughter—great joy; jubilation

歡心 (ㄏㄨㄢ ㄒㄧㄣ)
(to win another's) favor or heart; love

歡欣 (ㄏㄨㄢ ㄒㄧㄣ)
jubilation; joy

歡欣鼓舞 (ㄏㄨㄢ ㄒㄧㄣ ㄍㄨˇ ㄨˇ)
to be overjoyed; very pleased; to be beside oneself with joy; dancing with joy; to be filled with exultation

歡敘 (ㄏㄨㄢ ㄒㄩˋ)
to meet in joy; to talk about old times happily

歡暢 (ㄏㄨㄢ ㄔㄤˋ)
thoroughly delighted; elated

歡聲雷動 (ㄏㄨㄢ ㄕㄥ ㄌㄟˊ ㄉㄨㄥˋ)
to cheer thunderously; roaring applause: 全場觀眾歡聲雷動。The audience broke into roaring applause.

歡送 (ㄏㄨㄢ ㄙㄨㄥˋ)
to send off; to give a farewell party

歡顏 (ㄏㄨㄢ ㄧㄢˊ)
happy looks or appearances

歡宴 (ㄏㄨㄢ ㄧㄢˋ)
to dine a guest in a friendly manner

歡迎 (ㄏㄨㄢ ㄧㄥˊ)
to welcome; a welcome

歡愉 (ㄏㄨㄢ ㄩˊ)
joy and pleasure

歡悅 (ㄏㄨㄢ ㄩㄝˋ)
joy and happiness; very pleased

歡躍 (ㄏㄨㄢ ㄩㄝˋ)
overjoyed; very pleased; dancing with joy: 母親對她兒子的成功十分歡躍。The mother is very pleased with her son's success.

止部
ㄓˇ jyy zhǐ

【止】 ㄓˇ jyy zhǐ 2681
1. to stop; to desist; to still: 他停止吸煙。He stopped smoking.
2. to rest in; to stay
3. deportment
4. to detain
5. to prohibit
6. to come to; to arrive at

〔止部〕

〔正
部〕

7. still; calm; stagnant

8. only

止泊(ㄓ ㄅㄛ)
　to stay and rest

止謗(ㄓ ㄅㄤˋ)
　to stop libels or slanders

止步(ㄓ ㄅㄨˋ)
　to stop; to stand still; to go no further: 遊客止步。No visitors. 或 Out of bounds.

止付(ㄓ ㄈㄨˋ)
　(economics) to stop payment

止妒(ㄓ ㄉㄨˋ)
　to suppress jealousy

止痛(ㄓ ㄊㄨㄥˋ)
　to stop pain; to kill pain

止痛藥(ㄓ ㄊㄨㄥˋ ㄧㄠˋ)
　the anodyne drug; the anodyne; the painkiller

止怒(ㄓ ㄋㄨˋ)
　to stop or check anger

止戈為武(ㄓ ㄍㄜ ㄨㄟˊ ㄨˇ)
　Military forces are to be used for the maintenance of peace and order.

止咳(ㄓ ㄎㄜˊ)
　to stop coughing

止渴(ㄓ ㄎㄜˇ)
　to quench thirst

止境(ㄓ ㄐㄧㄥˋ)
　limits; the terminal point; the end: 他的貪心是無止境的。His greed knows no limits.

止息(ㄓ ㄒㄧˊ)
　to cease; to stop

止血(ㄓ ㄒㄧㄝˇ)
　to stop bleeding or hemorrhage

止血帶(ㄓ ㄒㄧㄝˇ ㄉㄞˋ)
　a tourniquet

止血藥(ㄓ ㄒㄧㄝˇ ㄧㄠˋ)
　a styptic

止瀉(ㄓ ㄒㄧㄝˋ)
　to stop diarrhea

止住(ㄓ ㄓㄨˋ)
　to stop; to halt; to desist

止是 or 衹是(ㄓ ㄕˋ)
　only that; it is only

止水(ㄓ ㄕㄨㄟˇ)
　stagnant water; still water

止詞(ㄓ ㄘˊ)
　(grammar) the object of a preposition or transitive verb

止宿(ㄓ ㄙㄨˋ)

---

to stay at

止遏(ㄓ ㄜˋ)
　to stop; to suppress; to quench (thirst); to put (a fire) under control; to ward off (the enemy attack)

止癢(ㄓ ㄧㄤˇ)
　to stop or alleviate itching

止於(ㄓ ㄩˊ)
　to stop at; this far and no further

止於至善(ㄓ ㄩˊ ㄓˋ ㄕㄢˋ)
　to arrive at supreme goodness; to attain perfection or *summum bonum*

一畫

【正】 2682
1. ㄓㄥˋ jenq zhèng

1. the obverse side; the right side

2. appropriate; proper

3. formal

4. to rectify; to correct

5. pure; not contaminated

6. straightforward and unbending; honest and virtuous

7. the person in charge; the principal (as against the secondary)

8. to mete out punishment for a criminal

9. original (texts, etc.)

10. exactly; just; right: 這正是你們所需要的東西。This is exactly what you want.

11. positively

12. main; principal

13. sharp; punctually: 九點正來。Come at nine o'clock sharp.

14. just; unbiased

15. a Chinese family name

正北(ㄓㄥˋ ㄅㄟˇ)
　due north: 這風是向正北吹。The wind is due north.

正本(ㄓㄥˋ ㄅㄣˇ)
　the original copy: 我已將正本送到檔案庫存放了。I deposited the original in the archives.

正本清源(ㄓㄥˋ ㄅㄣˇ ㄑㄧㄥ ㄩㄢˊ)
　to effect radical reform; to overhaul thoroughly

正比例(ㄓㄥˋ ㄅㄧˇ ㄌㄧˋ)or 正比(ㄓㄥˋ ㄅㄧˇ)
　direct proportion

正步(ㄓㄥˋ ㄅㄨˋ)

---

　the goose step; the parade step: 正步走! Parade step, march!

正牌兒(ㄓㄥˋ ㄆㄞˊ ㄦˊ)
　the original or real thing; the original brand (as distinct from the imitation product)

正派(ㄓㄥˋ ㄆㄞˋ)
　honest, proper and straightforward; virtuous; upright

正門(ㄓㄥˋ ㄇㄣˊ)
　the front door; the front gate; the main entrance

正面(ㄓㄥˋ ㄇㄧㄢˋ)
　① the right side; the obverse side; the head (of a coin); the front directly: 有建議請正面提出來。Please offer your suggestion directly. ③ positive

正面攻擊(ㄓㄥˋ ㄇㄧㄢˋ ㄍㄨㄥ ㄐㄧˊ)
　a frontal attack

正名(ㄓㄥˋ ㄇㄧㄥˊ)
　to give a right or good name to a cause; rectification of name

正法(ㄓㄥˋ ㄈㄚˇ)
　① the proper law or rule ② to execute (a death convict); execution

正反(ㄓㄥˋ ㄈㄢˇ)
　positive and negative

正反合(ㄓㄥˋ ㄈㄢˇ ㄏㄜˊ)
　(dialectic) thesis-antithesis-synthesis

正犯(ㄓㄥˋ ㄈㄢˋ)
　the principal criminal (as opposed to accessories): 正犯被警察逮捕。The principal criminal was arrested by the policeman.

正方(ㄓㄥˋ ㄈㄤ)
　① to adjust to the right course ② a square

正方形(ㄓㄥˋ ㄈㄤ ㄒㄧㄥˊ)
　(geometry) a square

正房(ㄓㄥˋ ㄈㄤˊ)
　① the main rooms in a compound with houses around a courtyard ② one's legal wife (as contrasted with a concubine) 參看「上房」

正負(ㄓㄥˋ ㄈㄨˋ)
　positive and negative

正大(ㄓㄥˋ ㄉㄚˋ)
　just and fair; honest; above-

board

正大光明(ㄓㄥ ㄉㄚ ㄍㄨㄤ ㄇㄧㄥ)
fair and frank; just and pure of mind; open and above-board

正道(ㄓㄥ ㄉㄠ)or 正路(ㄓㄥ ㄌㄨ)
the right course; the proper way; the correct path

正旦(ㄓㄥ ㄉㄢ)
①the female role in Chinese opera; the prima donna virtuoso ②the first day of a year

正當
①(ㄓㄥ ㄉㄤ)just at that time; right at that time; just when: 正當秋收之時。It is just the time for autumn harvest.
②(ㄓㄥ ㄉㄤ)proper; appropriate; justifiable; legitimate

正當年(ㄓㄥ ㄉㄤ ㄋㄧㄢˊ)
in the prime of one's life; the golden years of one's life

正當中(ㄓㄥ ㄉㄤ ㄓㄨㄥ)
right in the middle

正當理由(ㄓㄥ ㄉㄤ ㄌㄧ ㄧㄡˊ)
proper reasons

正當行為(ㄓㄥ ㄉㄤ ㄒㄧㄥˊ ㄨㄟˊ)
proper conduct

正當要求(ㄓㄥ ㄉㄤ ㄧㄠ ㄑㄧㄡˊ)
an appropriate request; a justifiable demand

正殿(ㄓㄥ ㄉㄧㄢˋ)
the main hall; the hall in the middle

正對(ㄓㄥ ㄉㄨㄟˋ)
directly across; face to face; directly opposite: 太陽光正對著我們照射。The sun was shining in our faces.

正東(ㄓㄥ ㄉㄨㄥ)
due east

正頭香主(ㄓㄥ ㄊㄡˊ ㄒㄧㄤ ㄓㄨˇ)
one's male heirs

正題(ㄓㄥ ㄊㄧˊ)
①the subject (or topic) of a talk or an essay: 他的演說轉入正題。His speech came to the subject. ②(philosophy) a thesis

正體字(ㄓㄥ ㄊㄧˇ ㄗ)
the standard Chinese character (as distinct from the simplified character and the running and manuscript styles of writing)

正廳(ㄓㄥ ㄊㄧㄥ)
①the main hall ②stalls (in a theater)

正途(ㄓㄥ ㄊㄨˊ)
the proper way or course: 他偏離正途。He digressed from the proper way.

正統(ㄓㄥ ㄊㄨㄥˇ)
orthodox; authorized

正統派(ㄓㄥ ㄊㄨㄥˇ ㄆㄞˋ)
the orthodox school (of thought)

正南(ㄓㄥ ㄋㄢˊ)
due south

正路(ㄓㄥ ㄌㄨˋ)
the right path; the straight path

正論(ㄓㄥ ㄌㄨㄣˋ)
the reasonable or appropriate opinion; the sound statement

正割(ㄓㄥ ㄍㄜ)
(mathematics) secant

正格(ㄓㄥ ㄍㄜˊ)
the orthodox style of Chinese poetry

正該(ㄓㄥ ㄍㄞ)
should; must; it's proper...

正趕上(ㄓㄥ ㄍㄢˇ ㄕㄤˋ)
just in time for...: 我昨天正趕上汽船。I was just in time for the steamer yesterday.

正果(ㄓㄥ ㄍㄨㄛˇ)
(Buddhism) spiritual progress through practicing Buddhism

正規軍(ㄓㄥ ㄍㄨㄟ ㄐㄩㄣ)
the regular army: 他加入正規軍。He entered the regular army.

正軌(ㄓㄥ ㄍㄨㄟˇ)
the right track; the proper way or course

正宮(ㄓㄥ ㄍㄨㄥ)
①the queen's apartment in the palace ②the queen consort

正宮娘娘(ㄓㄥ ㄍㄨㄥ ㄋㄧㄤˊ ㄋㄧㄤˊ)
the queen consort; the emperor's legal wife

正課(ㄓㄥ ㄎㄜˋ)
taxes and revenues

正楷(ㄓㄥ ㄎㄞˇ)
the standard script (in Chinese calligraphy)

正合式 or 正合適(ㄓㄥ ㄏㄜˊ ㄕˋ)

exactly right or appropriate; to fit exactly; to fit like a glove

正合我意(ㄓㄥ ㄏㄜˊ ㄨㄛˇ ㄧˋ)
It's exactly what I am hoping for. 他的回答正合我意。His answer was exactly what I was hoping.

正好(ㄓㄥ ㄏㄠˇ)
exactly (at the right moment); exactly right; it just happened that...; just enough: 這套衣服我穿正好。This suit fits me nicely.

正號(ㄓㄥ ㄏㄠˋ)
(mathematics) the plus sign, or the positive sign

正貨(ㄓㄥ ㄏㄨㄛˋ)
the legal tender; the hard currency

正極(ㄓㄥ ㄐㄧˊ)
(electricity) the positive electrode; the positive pole; the anode

正襟危坐(ㄓㄥ ㄐㄧㄣ ㄨㄟˊ ㄗㄨㄛˋ)
to straighten one's lapels and sit up stiffly; to sit upright and look straight ahead

正經(ㄓㄥ ㄐㄧㄥ)
(said of manners, conduct, etc.) very proper; respectable; serious

正經八百(ㄓㄥ ㄐㄧㄥ ㄅㄚ ㄅㄞˇ)
serious; earnest: 選擇職業是件正經八百的事。The selection of one's occupation is a serious matter.

正妻(ㄓㄥ ㄑㄧ)
one's legal wife

正氣(ㄓㄥ ㄑㄧˋ)
righteousness; the spiritual strength for the right and just

正氣歌(ㄓㄥ ㄑㄧˋ ㄍㄜ)
The Song of Righteousness—authored by Wen Tien-hsiang (文天祥) of the Sung Dynasty after being taken prisoner by the Mongols

正切(ㄓㄥ ㄑㄧㄝ)
(mathematics) tangent

正巧(ㄓㄥ ㄑㄧㄠˇ)
exactly; it happens that...; exactly when...; coincidence: 他來訪時，正巧我出去了。I happened to be out when he

〔正 部〕

called.

正寢(ㄓㄥ ㄑㄧㄣˇ)
the main room in a house

正取(ㄓㄥ ㄑㄩˇ)
(said of students, etc. through entrance or qualifying examinations) to be formally admitted, as contrasted to those admitted on the list of alternative candidates

正取生(ㄓㄥ ㄑㄩˇ ㄕㄥ)
a student formally admitted 參看「正取」

正確(ㄓㄥ ㄑㄩㄝˋ)
accurate; correct; right; proper; appropriate

正確性(ㄓㄥ ㄑㄩㄝˋ ㄒㄧㄥˋ)
accuracy; correctness

正西(ㄓㄥ ㄒㄧ)
due west

正席(ㄓㄥ ㄒㄧˊ)
the table of honor in a grand feast

正弦(ㄓㄥ ㄒㄧㄢˊ)
(mathematics) sine

正相反(ㄓㄥ ㄒㄧㄤ ㄈㄢˇ)
on the contrary

正學(ㄓㄥ ㄒㄩㄝˊ)
the orthodox learning

正直(ㄓㄥ ㄓˊ)
upright and honest; straightforward and unbiased; candid and fair: 他為人正直。He is straightforward and unbiased.

正值(ㄓㄥ ㄓˊ)
just at that time; exactly during; it happened just when...

正著(ㄓㄥ ㄓㄠˊ)
(to run into somebody) face to face; (to score) the bull's eye; (to smash) right into something

正中(ㄓㄥ ㄓㄨㄥ)
right in the middle; right in the center: 請把花瓶放在桌子的正中。Please put the vase right in the middle of the table.

正中下懷(ㄓㄥ ㄓㄨㄥ ㄒㄧㄚˋ ㄏㄨㄞˊ)
to fit in exactly with one's wishes; exactly as one wishes or hopes for: 此事正中下懷。It is just what I hope for.

正常(ㄓㄥ ㄔㄤˊ)

normal; normally; common; commonly; usual; usually: 機器運轉正常。The machine is functioning normally.

正常價格(ㄓㄥ ㄔㄤˊ ㄐㄧㄚˋ ㄍㄜˊ)
regular price

正長石(ㄓㄥ ㄔㄤˊ ㄕˊ)
orthoclase

正出(ㄓㄥ ㄔㄨ)
children born by the legal wife

正史(ㄓㄥ ㄕˇ)
official history as contrasted to legends, etc.

正是(ㄓㄥ ㄕˋ)
①yes, exactly so: 正是如此。Just so! ②an expression introducing a common saying which ends a chapter in the old Chinese novel

正式(ㄓㄥ ㄕˋ)
formal; formally; official; officially; legally or lawfully: 他們正式宣告訂婚。They formally announced their engagement.

正室(ㄓㄥ ㄕˋ)
①one's legal wife ②one's male heir

正事(ㄓㄥ ㄕˋ)
①one's job; one's duty or obligation ②serious business: 我們開始談正事吧。Let's begin to talk business.

正視(ㄓㄥ ㄕˋ)
to look straight in the eye; to look at something without bias or distortion: 我們應該正視現實。We should look at the facts without bias.

正身(ㄓㄥ ㄕㄣ)
one's real self; one's real person

正數(ㄓㄥ ㄕㄨˋ)
a positive number

正人君子(ㄓㄥ ㄖㄣˊ ㄐㄩㄣ ㄗˇ)
a gentleman; a just and upright man

正字(ㄓㄥ ㄗˋ)
①to correct a wrongly written character ②the standard script

正則(ㄓㄥ ㄗㄜˊ)
①the proper ways or methods ②to adjust the rules and regulations, etc.

正在(ㄓㄥ ㄗㄞˋ)

①(said of a position) exactly at ②used before a verb to form a progressive tense: 我們正在聊天。We're having a chat.

正坐(ㄓㄥ ㄗㄨㄛˋ)
to sit straight

正宗(ㄓㄥ ㄗㄨㄥ)
orthodox; handed down directly from the founder, master, etc.

正色(ㄓㄥ ㄙㄜˋ)
①stern and serious facial expression ②cardinal colors —blue, yellow, red, white and black

正義(ㄓㄥ ㄧˋ)
righteousness; justice: 我們為正義而戰。We fight for justice.

正義感(ㄓㄥ ㄧˋ ㄍㄢˇ)
the sense of justice or righteousness: 這年輕人具有正義感。The young man has a sense of justice.

正業(ㄓㄥ ㄧㄝˋ)
①a respectable job; a regular occupation; proper duties: 他的兒子不務正業。His son didn't attend to his duties. ②one's main job as contrasted to his side-jobs

正顏厲色(ㄓㄥ ㄧㄢˊ ㄌㄧˋ ㄙㄜˋ)
a stern and severe look; a serious manner

正音(ㄓㄥ ㄧㄣ)
to correct pronunciation: 他為我正音。He corrected my pronunciation.

正午(ㄓㄥ ㄨˇ)
high noon; noon

正誤(ㄓㄥ ㄨˋ)
to correct mistakes

正味(ㄓㄥ ㄨㄟˋ)
the original and unmodified taste

正位(ㄓㄥ ㄨㄟˋ)
the principal seat; the seat of honor

正文(ㄓㄥ ㄨㄣˊ)
text; key paragraphs of an article

正用(ㄓㄥ ㄩㄥˋ)
(for) legitimate or proper use

【正】 2682
2. ㄓㄥ jeng zhēng

the first in the lunar calendar

正朔 (ㄓㄥˋ ㄕㄨㄛˋ)
① the first day of the first lunar month ②(formerly) the calendar officially promulgated by the emperor

正月 (ㄓㄥ ㄩㄝˋ)
the first month of the lunar year

二畫

【此】 2683
ㄘˇ tsyy cǐ
1. this; these
2. such; thus: 他用功讀書,因此獲得高分數。 He studied hard; thus he got high marks.
3. if so; in this case
4. here

此輩 (ㄘˇ ㄅㄟˋ)
people of this type; such people

此仆彼起 (ㄘˇ ㄆㄨ ㄅㄧˇ ㄑㄧˇ)
here falling and there rising (said of the voices of chanting crowds, jumping fish, etc.)

此番 (ㄘˇ ㄈㄢ)
this time

此覆 (ㄘˇ ㄈㄨˋ)
I hereby reply as above. (an expression used at the end of the official correspondence addressed to a man of the equal footing)

此道 (ㄘˇ ㄉㄠˋ)
(often used derogatively) things like this; this pursuit, hobby, work, etc.

此種 (ㄘˇ ㄓㄨㄥˇ)
this kind; this type; such

此地 (ㄘˇ ㄉㄧˋ)
this place; here

此地無銀三百兩 (ㄘˇ ㄉㄧˋ ㄨˊ ㄧㄣˊ ㄙㄢ ㄅㄞˇ ㄌㄧㄤˇ)
In a folk tale, a person buried 300 taels of silver in the ground and posted a sign there declaring, "No 300 taels of silver buried here."

此老 (ㄘˇ ㄌㄠˇ)
this old man (used in a comic sense)

此路不通 (ㄘˇ ㄌㄨˋ ㄅㄨˋ ㄊㄨㄥ)
This road is blocked.—

please detour

此公 (ㄘˇ ㄍㄨㄥ)
this fellow

此刻 (ㄘˇ ㄎㄜˋ)
at this moment; at present; presently

此後 (ㄘˇ ㄏㄡˋ)
from now on; hereafter; henceforth

此際 (ㄘˇ ㄐㄧˋ)
at this time; at the moment

此間 (ㄘˇ ㄐㄧㄢ)
this place; within this; here: 此間已有傳聞。 It has been so rumored here.

此舉 (ㄘˇ ㄐㄩˇ)
this action; this undertaking; this move

此君 (ㄘˇ ㄐㄩㄣ)
① this gentleman ② bamboo (from 晉書王羲之傳—徽之征嘯咏, 指竹曰「何可一日無此君耶!」)

此起彼落 (ㄘˇ ㄑㄧˇ ㄅㄧˇ ㄌㄨㄛˋ)
(said of voices) rising and falling; continuously

此致 (ㄘˇ ㄓˋ)
(the form closing a letter) Thus I inform you.

此中 (ㄘˇ ㄓㄨㄥ)
in this

此處 (ㄘˇ ㄔㄨˋ)
this place; here: 請從此處走。 Come this way, please.

此時此地 (ㄘˇ ㄕˊ ㄘˇ ㄉㄧˋ)
here and now; under the present circumstances

此時此刻 (ㄘˇ ㄕˊ ㄘˇ ㄎㄜˋ)
at the (very) moment

此事 (ㄘˇ ㄕˋ)
this matter: 此事無關緊要。 This matter is not important.

此上 (ㄘˇ ㄕㄤˋ)
I hereby submit the above. (an expression used at the end of a letter addressed to a superior or an elder)

此生 (ㄘˇ ㄕㄥ)
(in) this life: 他此生很有成就。 He has had a successful life.

此日 (ㄘˇ ㄖˋ)
this day; this very day

此人 (ㄘˇ ㄖㄣˊ)
this man; this fellow: 此人是誰? Who is this?

此一時,彼一時 (ㄘˇ ㄧ ㄕˊ, ㄅㄧˇ ㄧ ㄕˊ)
Time has changed. (Therefore, one must think or do things differently.) or Circumstances have changed with the passage of time.

此外 (ㄘˇ ㄨㄞˋ)
besides; aside from this; in addition: 此外你還需要努力。 You need money and effort. In addition, you need diligence.

三畫

【步】 2684
ㄅㄨˋ buh bù
1. a pace; a step: 這是邁向成功的第一步。 It was the first step toward success.
2. to walk; on foot: 他經常在公園散步。 He often walks in the park.
3. situation; state; degree: 事情怎麼會發展到如此駭人的地步? How did things get into such an appalling state?
4. banks of rivers, ponds, etc.
5. fortune; doom
6. a unit of length in ancient China of about 5.5 feet
7. a Chinese family name

步兵 (ㄅㄨˋ ㄅㄧㄥ)
foot soldiers; infantry

步步 (ㄅㄨˋ ㄅㄨˋ)
① step by step; pace after pace ② gradually; progressively; steadily: 敵軍正在步步逼進中。 Our enemy troops are pressing forward steadily.

步步高陞 (ㄅㄨˋ ㄅㄨˋ ㄍㄠ ㄕㄥ)
to get promotion step by step or continuously; to attain eminence step by step

步步生蓮花 (ㄅㄨˋ ㄅㄨˋ ㄕㄥ ㄌㄧㄢˊ ㄏㄨㄚ)
the mincing steps of a beautiful woman (a term in reference to the concubine of 南齊東昏侯 who was made to walk on the golden lotus flowers laid on the floor)

步步為營 (ㄅㄨˋ ㄅㄨˋ ㄨㄟˊ ㄧㄥˊ)
to consolidate every position occupied before the troops push forward again; to move carefully every step on the way

【正部】

步伐(ㄅㄨˋ ㄈㄚˊ)or(ㄅㄨˋ ㄈㄚ)
steps or paces (in the military drill, parade, review, etc.): 他們以一致的步伐行走。They were walking in step.

步法(ㄅㄨˋ ㄈㄚˇ)
(dancing) footwork

步道(ㄅㄨˋ ㄉㄠˋ)
a sidewalk; a footpath

步調(ㄅㄨˋ ㄉㄧㄠˋ)
marching order; gaits: 他以快速的步調行走。He took a fast gait.

步調一致(ㄅㄨˋ ㄉㄧㄠˋ ㄧ ㄓˋ)
to be united in action; to act in unison; to keep in step

步隊(ㄅㄨˋ ㄉㄨㄟˋ)
a formation of foot soldiers; infantry

步態(ㄅㄨˋ ㄊㄞˋ)
a gait; a pace

步履(ㄅㄨˋ ㄌㄩˇ)
to walk; to move on foot

步履維艱(ㄅㄨˋ ㄌㄩˇ ㄨㄟˊ ㄐㄧㄢ)
to walk with difficulty

步鎗 or 步槍(ㄅㄨˋ ㄑㄧㄤ)
a rifle

步趨(ㄅㄨˋ ㄑㄩ)
to follow or pattern after (an example, etc.)

步行(ㄅㄨˋ ㄒㄧㄥˊ)
to walk; to march on foot

步哨(ㄅㄨˋ ㄕㄠˋ)
a sentry; the watch; a guard

步人後塵(ㄅㄨˋ ㄖㄣˊ ㄏㄡˋ ㄔㄣˊ)
to follow in another's footsteps; to trail along behind others 亦作「步人後廛」

步子(ㄅㄨˋ ˙ㄗ)
a step; a pace; 他們步子輕快。They walked with springy steps.

步驟(ㄅㄨˋ ㄗㄡˋ)
procedure, or sequence of doing something; measures or steps taken: 他們正在採取適當的步驟。They are taking proper steps.

步測(ㄅㄨˋ ㄘㄜˋ)
to measure distance by counting paces; to pace off

步搖(ㄅㄨˋ ㄧㄠˊ)
a dangling ornament worn by women in ancient China (which sways when the wearer walks)亦作「步步搖」

步月(ㄅㄨˋ ㄩㄝˋ)
to stroll under the moon

步韻(ㄅㄨˋ ㄩㄣˋ)
to compose a poem by using the rhymes of a poem by another

四畫

【歧】 2685
  ㄑㄧˊ chyi qí
1. a path branching out from the main road; a forked road
2. forked; divergent; strayed: 他們的意見分歧。They are divided in opinion.
3. anything that goes astray

歧途(ㄑㄧˊ ㄊㄨˊ)or 歧路(ㄑㄧˊ ㄌㄨˋ)
①a path branching out from the main road ②the wrong way; the road of evil

歧念(ㄑㄧˊ ㄋㄧㄢˋ)
evil thoughts or ideas

歧路徬徨(ㄑㄧˊ ㄌㄨˋ ㄆㄤˊ ㄏㄨㄤˊ)
to be hesitant or indecisive at a road junction

歧路亡羊(ㄑㄧˊ ㄌㄨˋ ㄨㄤˊ ㄧㄤˊ)
(literally) Sheep will easily get lost when there're too many forked roads.—One who seeks truth is apt to get lost when confronted with too many choices.

歧黃 or 岐黃(ㄑㄧˊ ㄏㄨㄤˊ)
①medical science ②names of two legendary herb doctors — Chi Po (歧伯) and Huang Ti (黃帝)

歧見(ㄑㄧˊ ㄐㄧㄢˋ)
different opinions or interpretations; conflicting ideas

歧出(ㄑㄧˊ ㄔㄨ)
①branching out ②conflicting and confusing

歧視(ㄑㄧˊ ㄕˋ)
to give different kinds of treatment to people; to act biasedly; to discriminate against; discrimination

歧義(ㄑㄧˊ ㄧˋ)
ambiguity; different meanings; various interpretations

歧異(ㄑㄧˊ ㄧˋ)
different; discrepancies; conflicts

【武】 2686
  ㄨˇ wuu wǔ
1. force; military
2. warlike; martial
3. footprints; steps
4. the length of half a pace
5. the string of an ancient hat
6. to inherit
7. a Chinese family name

武備(ㄨˇ ㄅㄟˋ)
armaments and military provisions

武編(ㄨˇ ㄅㄧㄢ)
the title of a 10-volume book in two parts on major wars in Chinese history and military strategies and tactics, authored by Tang Shun-chih (唐順之) of the Ming Dynasty

武弁(ㄨˇ ㄅㄧㄢˋ)
①a hat for a military man ②a military man

武廟(ㄨˇ ㄇㄧㄠˋ)
temples built in honor of Generals Kuan Yü (關羽) and Yüeh Fei (岳飛)

武夫(ㄨˇ ㄈㄨ)
a person of great physical strength; military men; a warrior: 他乃一介武夫。He was a warrior.

武德(ㄨˇ ㄉㄜˊ)
soldierly virtues

武門(ㄨˇ ㄇㄣˊ)
to resort to violence; to use force

武旦(ㄨˇ ㄉㄢˋ)
a Chinese opera actress who plays the role of a lady warrior

武當派(ㄨˇ ㄉㄤ ㄆㄞˋ)
the Wutang School of Chinese boxing, which stresses the use of internal force (內功)

武斷(ㄨˇ ㄉㄨㄢˋ)
to jump to a conclusion without regard to reason, logic, propriety, etc.; to decide arbitrarily

武力(ㄨˇ ㄌㄧˋ)
military might; naked power; (by) force; force of arms

武力干涉(ㄨˇ ㄌㄧˋ ㄍㄢ ㄕㄜˋ)
to interfere through the use of force

武力解決(ㄨˇ ㄌㄧˋ ㄐㄧㄝˇ ㄐㄩㄝˊ)

solution through the use of force; to settle differences through force

武力鎮壓 (ㄨㄌㄧˋ ㄓㄣˋ ㄧㄚ)
armed suppression

武林 (ㄨˇ ㄌㄧㄣˊ)
the circle of boxers

武官 (ㄨˇ ㄍㄨㄢ)
① a military officer ② a military attaché in an embassy: 他是一位海軍武官。He is a naval attaché.

武工 (ㄨˇ ㄍㄨㄥ)
(usually said of players in Chinese operas) acrobatic skills

武功 (ㄨˇ ㄍㄨㄥ)
① military achievements ② fighting skills; a feat of arms ③ name of a county and a mountain in Shensi Province

武科 (ㄨˇ ㄎㄜ)
(formerly) subjects used to test or qualify military personnel

武庫 (ㄨˇ ㄎㄨˋ)
① an arsenal or a general storeroom in ancient China ② name of a constellation, also known as 奎

武侯 (ㄨˇ ㄏㄡˊ)
the Count of Wu, Chu-Ko Liang (諸葛亮), in the Epoch of the Three Kingdoms

武漢 (ㄨˇ ㄏㄢˋ)
Wuhan—Wuchang (武昌) and Hankow (漢口), sometimes the city of Hanyang (漢陽) is included

武行 (ㄨˇ ㄏㄤˊ)
(in Chinese opera) actors and actresses who play acrobatic roles or the role of warriors

武將 (ㄨˇ ㄐㄧㄤˋ)
field commanders; ranking military officers

武舉 (ㄨˇ ㄐㄩˇ) or 武舉人 (ㄨˇ ㄐㄩˇ ㄖㄣˊ)
(formerly) successful candidates of provincial examinations of military officers

武器 (ㄨˇ ㄑㄧˋ)
weapons; arms

武戲 (ㄨˇ ㄒㄧˋ)
a Chinese opera that consists chiefly of fighting scenes

武俠 (ㄨˇ ㄒㄧㄚˊ)
chivalry

武俠小說 (ㄨˇ ㄒㄧㄚˊ ㄒㄧㄠˇ ㄕㄨㄛ)
a novel of swordsmen

武俠片 (ㄨˇ ㄒㄧㄚˊ ㄆㄧㄢˋ)
motion pictures depicting the chivalry and prowess of ancient swordsmen

武秀才 (ㄨˇ ㄒㄧㄡˋ ㄘㄞˊ)
a county qualified military officer

武仙座 (ㄨˇ ㄒㄧㄢ ㄗㄨㄛˋ)
(astronomy) Hercules

武訓 (ㄨˇ ㄒㄩㄣˋ)
Wu Hsün, 1838-1896, a beggar who founded several schools with his savings from mendicancy

武職 (ㄨˇ ㄓˊ)
military offices or posts

武裝 (ㄨˇ ㄓㄨㄤ)
① armed; to arm; armament ② military uniform

武裝部隊 (ㄨˇ ㄓㄨㄤ ㄅㄨˋ ㄉㄨㄟˋ)
armed forces

武裝和平 (ㄨˇ ㄓㄨㄤ ㄏㄜˊ ㄆㄧㄥˊ)
armed peace; peace maintained precariously by the balance of power

武裝侵略 (ㄨˇ ㄓㄨㄤ ㄑㄧㄣ ㄌㄩㄝˋ)
armed aggression

武裝衝突 (ㄨˇ ㄓㄨㄤ ㄔㄨㄥ ㄊㄨˊ)
an armed conflict; open hostilities; an armed clash

武狀元 (ㄨˇ ㄓㄨㄤˋ ㄩㄢˊ)
the candidate who came out top in Imperial Examinations for military personnel in old China

武昌 (ㄨˇ ㄔㄤ)
Wuchang, one of the three cities in the Wuhan (武漢) industrial complex in central China

武昌起義 (ㄨˇ ㄔㄤ ㄑㄧˇ ㄧˋ)
The Wuchang Uprising on October 10, 1911, which led to the downfall of the Ching Dynasty and the birth of the Republic of China

武場 (ㄨˇ ㄔㄤˇ)
①(in Chinese opera) music produced by percussion instruments such as gongs, drums and cymbals, which accompanies fighting scenes,

gestures, etc. 參看「文場」②a practicing ground in a military camp in old China

武師 (ㄨˇ ㄕ)
① a person skilled in martial arts ② troops

武士 (ㄨˇ ㄕˋ)
① a brave man of fighting skill; a warrior ② a samurai ③ a knight or cavalier: 他頗有武士氣概。He had knightly qualities.

武士道 (ㄨˇ ㄕˋ ㄉㄠˋ)
the samurai spirit; the samurai code; (Japanese) Bushido

武生 (ㄨˇ ㄕㄥ)
a male actor in Peking opera who plays the role of a young warrior or acrobat

武術 (ㄨˇ ㄕㄨˋ)
martial arts; skills in boxing, fencing, etc.; fighting skills or feats

武人 (ㄨˇ ㄖㄣˊ)
① an army man 參看「文人」② a warlord; a warrior; a leader

武則天 (ㄨˇ ㄗㄜˊ ㄊㄧㄢ) or 武后 (ㄨˇ ㄏㄡˋ)
Empress Wu (625-705) of the Tang Dynasty, who usurped the throne, famous for her lasciviousness and statecraft

武夷 (ㄨˇ ㄧˊ)
Mount Wu Yi in Fukien, where the famous black tea *Bohea* (Fukienese pronunciation of Wu Yi) is grown

武藝 (ㄨˇ ㄧˋ)
fighting skills or feats

五畫

【歪】 2687 ㄨㄞ uai wāi
1. aslant; askew; crooked; tilted; awry; out of the perpendicular: 那道牆歪了。The wall is out of the perpendicular.
2. depraved; evil
3. to lie down on one side for a brief nap
4. to shirk one's responsibility and try to involve others

歪愍 (ㄨㄞ ㄑㄧㄝˊ)
to make trouble

〔止 部〕

【止部】

歪門邪道(ㄨㄞ ㄇㄣˊ ㄒㄧㄝˊ ㄉㄠˋ)
crooked ways; dishonest practices 亦作「邪魔外道」。

歪風(ㄨㄞ ㄈㄥ)
an evil wind; an unhealthy trend

歪打正著(ㄨㄞ ㄉㄚˇ ㄓㄥˋ ㄓㄠ)
to do something unintentionally, but harvest exactly what one wishes; to hit the mark by a fluke

歪念頭(ㄨㄞ ㄋㄧㄢˋ ˙ㄊㄡ)or 歪主意(ㄨㄞ ㄓㄨˇ ㄧˋ)
evil ideas; crooked ideas; depraved thoughts

歪貨(ㄨㄞ ㄏㄨㄛˋ)
a rotten apple; fallen angels or wanton girls

歪七扭八(ㄨㄞ ㄑㄧ ㄋㄧㄡˇ ㄅㄚ)
not straight or upright; aslant; askew; very untidy; to twist around

歪曲(ㄨㄞ ㄑㄩ)
to twist or confuse (things, facts, etc.) intentionally; to distort: 他歪曲我的話，以便造成一種錯誤印象。He twisted what I said so as to give a wrong impression.

歪曲事實(ㄨㄞ ㄑㄩ ㄕˋ ㄕˊ)
to twist or distort facts; fact-fudging; to fudge a fact: 他歪曲事實，使之聳人聽聞。He distorted the fact to make it sensational.

歪斜(ㄨㄞ ㄒㄧㄝˊ)
aslant; askew; crooked

歪心(ㄨㄞ ㄒㄧㄣ)
a twisted mind; a crooked mind; an evil mind

歪纏(ㄨㄞ ㄔㄢˊ)
to tangle people with lengthy and nonsensical talks; to harass another (with endless and meaningless conversation)

歪詩(ㄨㄞ ㄕ)
doggerel; inelegant verses

歪嘴(ㄨㄞ ㄗㄨㄟˇ)
a wry mouth; wry-mouthed

歪歪扭扭(ㄨㄞ ˙ㄨㄞ ㄋㄧㄡˇ ㄋㄧㄡˇ)
crooked and twisted; not straight

九畫

【歲】 2688 ㄙㄨㄟˋ suey suì
1. a year; age (of a person): 一個人到二十一歲即成年。A man comes of age at twenty-one.
2. harvest

歲不我與(ㄙㄨㄟˋ ㄅㄨˋ ㄨㄛˇ ㄩˇ)
I can't help getting old.或 Time and tide wait for no one.

歲杪(ㄙㄨㄟˋ ㄇㄧㄠˇ)
the end of a year

歲暮(ㄙㄨㄟˋ ㄇㄨˋ)
①the late season of a year: 歲暮天寒。Cold weather sets in as the year draws to its end. ②the closing years of one's life

歲闌(ㄙㄨㄟˋ ㄌㄢˊ)
the late season of a year

歲貢(ㄙㄨㄟˋ ㄍㄨㄥˋ)
(in ancient China) the annual tribute offered by a vassal state or protectorate, etc.

歲寒三友(ㄙㄨㄟˋ ㄏㄢˊ ㄙㄢ ㄧㄡˇ)
the three friends in the cold of the year—the pine, the bamboo, and the plum, which do not wither in winter

歲寒松柏(ㄙㄨㄟˋ ㄏㄢˊ ㄙㄨㄥ ㄅㄛˊ)
virtuous persons (whose fortitude and uprightness are best revealed in time of trouble or when the going is rough)

歲華(ㄙㄨㄟˋ ㄏㄨㄚˊ)
time of year; the procession of the seasons

歲計(ㄙㄨㄟˋ ㄐㄧˋ)
the annual budget

歲夕(ㄙㄨㄟˋ ㄒㄧˋ)
New Year's Eve

歲差(ㄙㄨㄟˋ ㄔㄞ)
the precession of the equinoxes

歲出(ㄙㄨㄟˋ ㄔㄨ)
annual expenditures

歲除(ㄙㄨㄟˋ ㄔㄨˊ)
the close of a year; New Year's Eve

歲時(ㄙㄨㄟˋ ㄕˊ)
time of year; times and seasons

歲收(ㄙㄨㄟˋ ㄕㄡ)
the annual income

歲首(ㄙㄨㄟˋ ㄕㄡˇ)
the beginning of a year

歲數(ㄙㄨㄟˋ ㄕㄨˋ)
age (of a person); years: 他看來比其實際歲數年輕。He looks young for his age.

歲入(ㄙㄨㄟˋ ㄖㄨˋ)
the annual income

歲次(ㄙㄨㄟˋ ㄘˋ)
the year of (followed by the year identified by its cyclic name consisting of a celestial stem (天干) and a terrestrial branch (地支)

歲歲年年(ㄙㄨㄟˋ ㄙㄨㄟˋ ㄋㄧㄢˊ ㄋㄧㄢˊ)
year after year; every year

歲夜(ㄙㄨㄟˋ ㄧㄝˋ)
New Year's Eve

歲月(ㄙㄨㄟˋ ㄩㄝˋ)
times and seasons; time;歲月會證明誰是對的。Time will show who is right.

歲月如流(ㄙㄨㄟˋ ㄩㄝˋ ㄖㄨˊ ㄌㄧㄡˊ)
歲月不居(ㄙㄨㄟˋ ㄩㄝˋ ㄅㄨˋ ㄐㄩ)or 歲月無情(ㄙㄨㄟˋ ㄩㄝˋ ㄨˊ ㄑㄧㄥˊ)
Time and tide wait for no man. 或 Time flies! 或 Tempus fugit.

歲運(ㄙㄨㄟˋ ㄩㄣˋ)
the luck for the year

十二畫

【歷】 2689 ㄌㄧˋ lih lì
1. to pass; to elapse
2. to undergo; to go through; to experience: 探險者經歷很多痛苦。The explorers underwent much suffering.
3. things or duration that had come to pass
4. all previous (occasions, sessions); what has taken place
5. through; throughout; successive: 他歷任五年市長。He has been mayor for five successive years.
6. to last (a certain period of time)

歷代(ㄌㄧˋ ㄉㄞˋ)
successive generations; throughout the ages; the dynasties in their successive order: 這些是歷代名畫。These are famous paintings through the ages.

歷年(ㄌㄧˋ ㄋㄧㄢˊ)
through the years; in the years past

歷來(ㄌㄧˋ ㄌㄞˊ)
hitherto; till now; heretofore; from the old days; since a long time ago. 這是一個歷來無人知道的事實。It is a fact hitherto unknown.

歷覽(ㄌㄧˋ ㄌㄢˇ)
to travel and see; to view during a tour; to visit

歷歷(ㄌㄧˋ ㄌㄧˋ)
distinctly; clearly; vividly: 往事歷歷在心頭。Past events remain fresh in my memory.

歷歷如繪(ㄌㄧˋ ㄌㄧˋ ㄖㄨˊ ㄏㄨㄟˋ)
(to tell a story or experience) vividly; distinctly

歷歷在目(ㄌㄧˋ ㄌㄧˋ ㄗㄞˋ ㄇㄨˋ)
(said of recollecting a past event or experience) as if it were taking place right before one's eyes; vividly

歷練(ㄌㄧˋ ㄌㄧㄢˋ)
to practice and experience

歷落(ㄌㄧˋ ㄌㄨㄛˋ)
① noisy ② disorderly; disarray ③ dashing and elegant (manner, deportment, etc.)

歷亂(ㄌㄧˋ ㄌㄨㄢˋ)
confused and disorderly; in turmoil

歷劫(ㄌㄧˋ ㄐㄧㄝˊ)
① to experience many mishaps and misfortunes; to pass through one crisis after another ② to pass through years and decades

歷屆(ㄌㄧˋ ㄐㄧㄝˋ)
successive (or all) previous (meetings, games, elections, etc.): 那是個歷屆畢業生的聚會。It's a party for graduates of all previous years.

歷久不變(ㄌㄧˋ ㄐㄧㄡˇ ㄅㄨˋ ㄅㄧㄢˋ)
(said of writing, reputation, a school of thought, etc.) long-lasting

歷久彌堅(ㄌㄧˋ ㄐㄧㄡˇ ㄇㄧˊ ㄐㄧㄢ)
(said of one's faith, belief, conviction, etc.) to remain unshakable and become even firmer as time goes by

歷盡艱難(ㄌㄧˋ ㄐㄧㄣˋ ㄐㄧㄢ ㄋㄢˊ)
to have gone through all kinds of hardships and difficulties.

歷經(ㄌㄧˋ ㄐㄧㄥ)
to have experienced, undergone or encountered many times. 他們歷經千辛萬苦。They have experienced great hardships and pains.

歷險(ㄌㄧˋ ㄒㄧㄢˇ)
to undergo or experience adventures and dangers; to have had a narrow escape

歷朝(ㄌㄧˋ ㄔㄠˊ)
down through the dynasties; through the successive dynasties

歷程(ㄌㄧˋ ㄔㄥˊ)
process; course: 他們回顧戰爭的歷程。They looked back on the course of the war.

歷時(ㄌㄧˋ ㄕˊ)
to last (a certain period of time): 會議歷時三個鐘頭。The meeting lasted three hours.

歷史(ㄌㄧˋ ㄕˇ)
history: 中國是歷史悠久的國家。China is a richly historical land.

歷史的(ㄌㄧˋ ㄕˇ ㄉㄜ˙)
historical: 這些是歷史的真實事件和人物。These are historical events and people.

歷史的真實性(ㄌㄧˋ ㄕˇ ㄉㄜ˙ ㄓㄣ ㄕˊ ㄒㄧㄥˋ)
historicity

歷史地理(ㄌㄧˋ ㄕˇ ㄉㄧˋ ㄌㄧˇ)
historical geography

歷史觀(ㄌㄧˋ ㄕˇ ㄍㄨㄢ)
the historical view or concept

歷史家(ㄌㄧˋ ㄕˇ ㄐㄧㄚ)
a historian; a historiographer: 他是位著名的歷史家。He is an eminent historian.

歷史性的(ㄌㄧˋ ㄕˇ ㄒㄧㄥˋ ㄉㄜ˙)
historic: 那是一場歷史性的勝利。It's a historic victory.

歷史學(ㄌㄧˋ ㄕˇ ㄒㄩㄝˊ)
the science of history; historiography

歷史眼光(ㄌㄧˋ ㄕˇ ㄧㄢˇ ㄍㄨㄤ)
in the light of history; historically

歷稔(ㄌㄧˋ ㄖㄣˇ)
down through the years

歷任(ㄌㄧˋ ㄖㄣˋ)
① to have held the following posts ② (those who) have held the same post

歷次(ㄌㄧˋ ㄘˋ)
all previous or past (occasions, etc.)

歷有年所(ㄌㄧˋ ㄧㄡˇ ㄋㄧㄢˊ ㄙㄨㄛˇ)
It has been many years (since a certain event occurred).

十四畫

【歸】2690
《ㄍㄨㄟ guei guī
1. to come back; to return: 他下班運歸。He returned from work late.
2. to return (something to its owner): 物歸原主。Return the thing to its rightful owner.
3. (said of a woman) to marry
4. to pledge allegiance to
5. to belong; to attribute: 這些書歸我所有。These books belong to me.
6. to turn over to; to put in somebody's charge: 這事應歸他管。This matter should be turned over to him.
7. a Chinese family name

歸併(ㄍㄨㄟ ㄅㄧㄥˋ)
to merge into; to unite with; to put together; to annex; to incorporate into一些小銀行歸併成一個大組織。The small banks are merged into one large organization.

歸附(ㄍㄨㄟ ㄈㄨˋ)
to follow (a leader in a revolution, etc.); to pledge allegiance to

歸檔(ㄍㄨㄟ ㄉㄤˋ)
to return (a document, materials, etc.) back to file; to file away: 把這些信件仔細地歸檔。File these letters carefully.

歸隊(ㄍㄨㄟ ㄉㄨㄟˋ)
(said of stragglers, individual members of an organization) to return to the ranks; to rejoin the group; to go back to the unit

歸天(ㄍㄨㄟ ㄊㄧㄢ)or歸西(ㄍㄨㄟ ㄒㄧ)
(literally) to return to heaven—to pass away

正部]

歸田《ㄍㄨㄟ ㄊㄧㄢˊ》
①(in ancient China) one was allotted farmland at 20 and would return the land to the state at 60—having reached 60 years of age ②to return to one's hometown after serving the government for years—to retire from public life

歸途《ㄍㄨㄟ ㄊㄨˊ》
on the way home; the homeward journey: 我在歸途中遇到他。I met him on my way home.

歸納《ㄍㄨㄟ ㄋㄚˋ》
to induct (a theory, natural law, etc.); to sum up: 他歸納出一些自然法則。He inducted some physical laws.

歸納法《ㄍㄨㄟ ㄋㄚˋ ㄈㄚˇ》
the inductive method; induction: 所有歸納法的推論都是一種猜測。Every induction is a speculation.

歸寧《ㄍㄨㄟ ㄋㄧㄥˊ》
(said of a woman) to visit her parents after marriage

歸類《ㄍㄨㄟ ㄌㄟˋ》
to categorize; to classify

歸老《ㄍㄨㄟ ㄌㄠˇ》
to retire on account of age

歸攏《ㄍㄨㄟ ㄌㄨㄥˇ》
to unite with; to collaborate with: 請把東西歸攏起來。Please put the things together.

歸根結底《ㄍㄨㄟ ㄍㄣ ㄐㄧㄝˊ ㄉㄧˇ》
fundamentally; basically; finally; in the end; in the final analysis: 歸根結底, 和平豈非即爲人權? Is not peace, in the final analysis, a matter of human rights?

歸耕《ㄍㄨㄟ ㄍㄥ》
to retire from public service and return home

歸骨《ㄍㄨㄟ ㄍㄨˇ》
to bring home one's remains for burial

歸國《ㄍㄨㄟ ㄍㄨㄛˊ》
to return to one's fatherland

歸功於《ㄍㄨㄟ ㄍㄨㄥ ㄩˊ》
to give the credit to; to attribute the success to: 我們一切的成就都歸功於他的幫忙。We attribute all our achieve-ments to his help.

歸戶《ㄍㄨㄟ ㄏㄨˋ》
(said of tax officials) to add undivided dividend to the income of a taxpayer

歸化《ㄍㄨㄟ ㄏㄨㄚˋ》
①to be naturalized as a citizen: 他歸化爲中國人。He was naturalized as a Chinese citizen. ②(said of a protectorate state, etc.) to pledge allegiance to

歸還《ㄍㄨㄟ ㄏㄨㄢˊ》
①to return (something to its owner): 請把那本書歸還圖書館。Return that book to the library, please. ②to come home

歸寂《ㄍㄨㄟ ㄐㄧˊ》
(Buddhism) to die

歸計《ㄍㄨㄟ ㄐㄧˋ》
plans for going home; to go home

歸家《ㄍㄨㄟ ㄐㄧㄚ》
to return home; homecoming

歸結《ㄍㄨㄟ ㄐㄧㄝˊ》
the end or conclusion of a matter; to sum up; to put in a nutshell: 歸結來 (一句話), 我們結婚了。In a nutshell, we got married.

歸咎《ㄍㄨㄟ ㄐㄧㄡˋ》
to lay the blame on…; to impute: 不要把你的貧窮歸咎於運氣不好。Don't impute your poverty to bad luck.

歸期《ㄍㄨㄟ ㄑㄧˊ》
the date of one's return

歸齊《ㄍㄨㄟ ㄑㄧˊ》
①to amount to; to total ②in the end; fundamentally; basically

歸僑《ㄍㄨㄟ ㄑㄧㄠˊ》
returned overseas Chinese 亦作「歸國華僑」

歸休《ㄍㄨㄟ ㄒㄧㄡ》
①to take a leave for rest ②to die

歸心《ㄍㄨㄟ ㄒㄧㄣ》
①to submit heart and soul (to a cause, leader, etc.) ②the thought or idea of returning home; homesickness

歸心似箭《ㄍㄨㄟ ㄒㄧㄣ ㄙˋ ㄐㄧㄢˋ》
to be anxious or eager to return home; with one's heart set on speeding home:

他歸心似箭。He was anxious to return home as soon as possible.

歸降《ㄍㄨㄟ ㄒㄧㄤˊ》
to yield; to pledge allegiance; to surrender

歸向《ㄍㄨㄟ ㄒㄧㄤˋ》
①the direction of movement ②to turn toward (the righteous side); to incline to

歸省《ㄍㄨㄟ ㄒㄧㄥˇ》
to return home to visit one's parents

歸趙《ㄍㄨㄟ ㄓㄠˋ》
to return something to its rightful owner

歸眞《ㄍㄨㄟ ㄓㄣ》
①to revert to one's natural self ②(in Buddhist terminology) to die

歸正《ㄍㄨㄟ ㄓㄥˋ》
to return to the right cause; (said of rebellious elements, etc.) to return to the side of the government

歸主《ㄍㄨㄟ ㄓㄨˇ》
to return to the Lord—conversion

歸著《ㄍㄨㄟ ㄓㄨㄛˊ》
①《ㄍㄨㄟ ㄓㄨㄛˊ》a place to stay, develop, etc.; a home base ②《ㄍㄨㄟ ㄓㄨˋ》to make arrangements; to put in order; to tidy up

歸程《ㄍㄨㄟ ㄔㄥˊ》
the homeward journey

歸除《ㄍㄨㄟ ㄔㄨˊ》
(in abacus calculation) division of a number consisting of three or more digits

歸屬《ㄍㄨㄟ ㄕㄨˇ》
①ownership ②to belong

歸順《ㄍㄨㄟ ㄕㄨㄣˋ》
①to yield; to submit; to surrender ②name of an old region in Yunnan Province

歸入《ㄍㄨㄟ ㄖㄨˋ》
to classify; to include: 這些書可歸入同一類。These books may be classified in the same category.

歸葬《ㄍㄨㄟ ㄗㄤˋ》
to bring back one's remains home for burial

歸罪《ㄍㄨㄟ ㄗㄨㄟˋ》
to lay the blame on another; to hold someone responsible

for a mistake; to impute: 他
把你的失敗歸罪於懶惰。He
imputed your failure to laziness.

歸宗(ㄍㄨㄟ ㄗㄨㄥ)
to return an adopted son to
his original ancestral lineage

歸宿(ㄍㄨㄟ ㄙㄨˋ)
①one's final settling place;
a home to return to ②(said
of a woman) marriage: 她終
於找到歸宿了。She was finally
married. ③ conclusions

歸綏(ㄍㄨㄟ ㄙㄨㄟ)
Kweisui, capital city of
Suiyüan Province

歸案(ㄍㄨㄟ ㄢˋ)
to arrest a criminal and
bring him to court for prosecution: 他已被緝拿歸案。He
was arrested and brought to
justice.

歸依(ㄍㄨㄟ ㄧ)
to follow Buddhist faith; to
become a Buddhist disciple,
monk or nun 亦作「皈依」: 他
已經歸依佛教。He has become
a Buddhist disciple.

歸隱(ㄍㄨㄟ ㄧㄣˇ)
to retire; retirement

歸於(ㄍㄨㄟ ㄩˊ)
① to belong to; to be at-
tributed to ② to result in;
to end in

歸獄(ㄍㄨㄟ ㄩˋ)
(said of prisoners) to return
to jail after a home leave

歹 部

ㄉㄞˇ dae dǎi

【歹】 2691
1. ㄉㄞˇ dae dǎi
bad; wicked; evil; crooked;
depraved; vicious: 他常為非
作歹。He often did evil.

歹毒(ㄉㄞˇ ㄉㄨˊ)
vicious; viciousness; malicious; malice

歹徒(ㄉㄞˇ ㄊㄨˊ)
hoodlums; bad guys; ruf-
fians; scoundrels; evil fellows

歹念(ㄉㄞˇ ㄋㄧㄢˋ)
evil thoughts: 歹念佔據了他
的心。Evil thoughts occupy
his mind.

歹心(ㄉㄞˇ ㄒㄧㄣ)
evil intent

歹人(ㄉㄞˇ ㄖㄣˊ)
① evil persons ② thieves or
burglars

歹意(ㄉㄞˇ ㄧˋ)
malice; malicious intent; bad
intentions

【歹】 2691
2. (歹) ㄜ eh ě
(now rarely) the remains of
a person

二畫

【死】 2692
1. ㄙˇ syy sǐ
1. to die; to die for; dead;
death: 人皆有死。Death comes
to all men.
2. used as an intensive or
superlative; very; extremely:
她高興死了。She was extreme-
ly happy.
3. condemned (persons whose
lives are numbered, as criminals on the death row)
4. inanimate; dull and stupid;
inert; insensible; lifeless
5. obstinate or stubborn; persevering; resolute; resolutely
6. rigid, fixed or unchangeable
(regulations, etc.); immovable (drawers, etc.): 那是個
死規矩。It's a rigid rule.
7. impassable; closed

死板(ㄙˇ ㄅㄢˇ)
wooden (persons); rigid
(regulations); fixed and unchangeable (methods, etc.);
monotonous(work, life, etc.):
他辦事死板板的。He worked
in a mechanical way.

死別(ㄙˇ ㄅㄧㄝˊ)
to be parted by death;
death-partings

死不瞑目(ㄙˇ ㄅㄨˋ ㄇㄧㄥˊ ㄇㄨˋ)
to be unwilling to die (because of some unfinished
tasks, unfulfilled wishes,
intensive grudges, etc.)

死不悔改(ㄙˇ ㄅㄨˋ ㄏㄨㄟˇ ㄍㄞˇ)
cannot die; will not die

absolutely unrepentant; incorrigible

死不認錯(ㄙˇ ㄅㄨˋ ㄖㄣˋ ㄘㄨㄛˋ)
stubbornly refuse to admit
one's guilt or mistake

死不足惜(ㄙˇ ㄅㄨˋ ㄗㄨˊ ㄒㄧˊ)
Death is not to be regretted
(if it serves a purpose).

死不要臉(ㄙˇ ㄅㄨˋ ㄧㄠˋ ㄌㄧㄢˇ)
extremely shameless; utterly
shameless; brazen-faced

死皮賴臉(ㄙˇ ㄆㄧˊ ㄌㄞˋ ㄌㄧㄢˇ)
brazen-faced and unreasonable; to importune shame-
lessly

死拼(ㄙˇ ㄆㄧㄣ)
to fight to the death: 他們將
死拼到底。They will fight to
the death.

死馬當作活馬醫(ㄙˇ ㄇㄚˇ ㄉㄤ ㄏㄨㄛˊ
ㄇㄚˇ ㄧ)
to do what one can to solve
an apparently unsolvable
problem or reverse a seemingly hopeless situation

死眉瞪眼(ㄙˇ ㄇㄟˊ ㄉㄥˋ ㄧㄢˇ)
① a wooden expression that
infuriates ② inanimate

死命(ㄙˇ ㄇㄧㄥˋ)
① with all the power and
strength at one's command;
desperately: He
struggled desperately.② to
cause to die: 他制敵於死命。
He sent the enemy to his
doom.

死法子(ㄙˇ ㄈㄚˇ ˙ㄗ)
a rigid and unimaginative
way of doing things

死得其所(ㄙˇ ㄉㄜˊ ㄑㄧˊ ㄙㄨㄛˇ)
to die a worthy death

死鬥(ㄙˇ ㄉㄡˋ)
to fight to death

死黨(ㄙˇ ㄉㄤˇ)
sworn confederates; sworn
followers; a gang of die-
hards sticking together till
death shall they part

死擋(ㄙˇ ㄉㄤˇ)
to resist to death

死等(ㄙˇ ㄉㄥˇ)
to wait indefinitely without
giving up hope; to wait forever

死敵(ㄙˇ ㄉㄧˊ)
a mortal enemy; an arch
adversary; an implacable

〔歹
部〕

【歹部】

foe; a deadly enemy

死地（ㄙ ㄉㄧ）
①a hopeless situation ②a "dead" locality or site (in the geomantic sense) ③the place of death

死店活人開（ㄙ ㄉㄧㄢˋ ㄏㄨㄛˊ ㄖㄣˊ ㄎㄞ）
Everything depends on how one manages it. 或 Man's action and thought determine the success of an endeavor.

死讀書（ㄙ ㄉㄨˊ ㄕㄨ）
to study mechanically; to read (a book) without thinking

死對頭（ㄙ ㄉㄨㄟˋ ·ㄊㄡ）
arch enemies or rivals; bitter opponents

死胎（ㄙ ㄊㄞ）
a stillbirth; a dead fetus

死腦筋（ㄙ ㄋㄠˇ ㄐㄧㄣ）
a one-track mind

死難（ㄙ ㄋㄢˋ）
to die a martyr's death

死拉活拽（ㄙ ㄌㄚ ㄏㄨㄛˊ ㄓㄨㄞˋ）
to drag and pull with all one's strength

死裏逃生（ㄙ ㄌㄧˇ ㄊㄠˊ ㄕㄥ）
to escape death by a narrow margin; to have a close bout with death; to escape by the skin of one's teeth

死力（ㄙ ㄌㄧˋ）
to strive with all one's efforts

死路（ㄙ ㄌㄨˋ）
①a blind alley; a dead end ②a fatal route

死路一條（ㄙ ㄌㄨˋ ㄧ ㄊㄧㄠˊ）
no way out; doomed

死溝（ㄙ ㄍㄡ）
a blocked up ditch or gutter

死狗（ㄙ ㄍㄡˇ）
a dead dog (a term used in name-calling)

死規矩（ㄙ ㄍㄨㄟ ·ㄐㄩ）
rigid, stiff, unchangeable, and sometimes unreasonable rules

死鬼（ㄙ ㄍㄨㄟˇ）
You devil! (a term often used by Chinese women to scold their husbands)

死光（ㄙ ㄍㄨㄤ）
① death rays ② all dead; without survivors

死工夫（ㄙ ㄍㄨㄥ ·ㄈㄨ）
sheer hard work (in which luck or talent plays no part)

死摳兒（ㄙ ㄎㄡ ㄦ）
①obstinate; stubborn ②to dedicate oneself (to a study) ③stingy; tight-fisted

死海（ㄙ ㄏㄞˇ）
Dead Sea between Israel and Jordan

死後（ㄙ ㄏㄡˋ）
after death; postmortem

死衚衕（ㄙ ㄏㄨˊ ㄊㄨㄥˋ）
a dead-end alley

死活（ㄙ ㄏㄨㄛˊ）
① dead or alive ② no matter what; in any case; anyway; simply

死火山（ㄙ ㄏㄨㄛˇ ㄕㄢ）
an extinct volcano

死灰（ㄙ ㄏㄨㄟ）
cold ashes of a fire—(figuratively) discouraged or lonely

死灰復燃（ㄙ ㄏㄨㄟ ㄈㄨˋ ㄖㄢˊ）
(said of emotion, especially love, crushed rebellious force, dormant ideas, etc.) rekindled; rejuvenated

死肌（ㄙ ㄐㄧ）
muscles that have lost functioning power due to rheumatism, etc.

死寂（ㄙ ㄐㄧˋ）
deathly stillness

死忌（ㄙ ㄐㄧˋ）
death anniversaries

死記（ㄙ ㄐㄧˋ）
to memorize by rote; mechanical memorizing

死勁（ㄙ ㄐㄧㄣˋ）
①all one's strength; all one's might ②with all one's strength (or might); for all one is worth: 她死勁兒跑。She ran for all she was worth.

死節（ㄙ ㄐㄧㄝˊ）
to die a martyr's death; to die for honor

死結（ㄙ ㄐㄧㄝˊ）
①a fast knot (as opposed to slip knots) ②a problem or issue that defies solution; an impasse

死角（ㄙ ㄐㄧㄠˇ）
a dead angle; the defiladed space

死諫（ㄙ ㄐㄧㄢˋ）
to risk one's life in pressing a point on the emperor

死井（ㄙ ㄐㄧㄥˇ）
a dried-up well

死期（ㄙ ㄑㄧ）
the time of death; the hour of doom

死棋（ㄙ ㄑㄧˊ）
①a dead piece in a game of chess ②(figuratively)a hopeless case

死乞白賴（ㄙ ㄑㄧ ㄅㄞˊ ㄌㄞˋ）
to entangle without stop; to be importunate; to lie shamelessly

死氣沉沉（ㄙ ㄑㄧˋ ㄔㄣˊ ㄔㄣˊ）
a dead atmosphere; hopeless and gloomy; dull and despondent; lifeless air; stagnant: 那是場死氣沉沉的表演。It's a lifeless performance.

死囚（ㄙ ㄑㄧㄡˊ）
a death convict

死前（ㄙ ㄑㄧㄢˊ）
before death; before one dies: 他死前立下遺言。He made a will before his death.

死去活來（ㄙ ㄑㄩˋ ㄏㄨㄛˊ ㄌㄞˊ）
in extreme pain or distress; half dead

死心（ㄙ ㄒㄧㄣ）
to give up one's hope for good; to think no more of something

死心塌地（ㄙ ㄒㄧㄣ ㄊㄚ ㄉㄧˋ）
unreservedly; wholeheartedly; to be dead set; head over heels

死心眼兒（ㄙ ㄒㄧㄣ ㄧㄢˇㄦ）
obstinate and simple-minded

死信（ㄙ ㄒㄧㄣˋ）
undeliverable letters; dead letters

死巷（ㄙ ㄒㄧㄤˋ）or 死胡同（ㄙ ㄏㄨˊ ·ㄊㄨㄥ）
a dead-end alley (also used figuratively)

死相（ㄙ ㄒㄧㄤˋ）
(literally) a cadaverous look—a dull and inanimate look (often used by a wife to scold her husband)

死刑（ㄙ ㄒㄧㄥˊ）
a capital punishment; a death penalty

死性（ㄙ ·ㄒㄧㄥ）

① obstinacy; stubbornness
② an over-candid disposition that knows neither refinement nor tact in dealing with people

死訊(ㄙ ㄒㄩㄣˋ)
news of someone's death

死者(ㄙ ㄓㄜˇ)
the dead; the deceased; the departed soul: 他們哀悼死者。 They mourned for the dead.

死戰(ㄙ ㄓㄢˋ)
to battle to the last

死中求生(ㄙ ㄓㄨㄥ ㄑㄧㄡˊ ㄕㄥ)
to struggle in a desperate or hopeless situation for survival

死纏活纏(ㄙ ㄔㄢˊ ㄏㄨㄛˊ ㄔㄢˊ)
to importune or entangle a person incessantly

死屍(ㄙ ㄕ)
a corpse

死守(ㄙ ㄕㄡˇ)
to defend (a position, city, etc.) to the last: 英勇的戰士死守陣地。 The brave soldiers defended the position to the last.

死傷(ㄙ ㄕㄤ)
the dead and wounded; casualties

死傷枕藉(ㄙ ㄕㄤ ㄓㄣˇ ㄐㄧˊ)
heavy casualties

死生有命(ㄙ ㄕㄥ ㄧㄡˇ ㄇㄧㄥˋ)
Life and death are predetermined. 或 Life and death lie in the lap of the gods.或 A person's life and death are matters of fate.

死說活說(ㄙ ㄕㄨㄛ ㄏㄨㄛˊ ㄕㄨㄛ)
to persuade by all means; to importune incessantly

死水(ㄙ ㄕㄨㄟˇ)
stagnant water; stagnating water

死水坑子(ㄙ ㄕㄨㄟˇ ㄎㄥ˙ ㄗ)
a low-lying point where drainage of water is difficult

死人(ㄙ ㄖㄣˊ)
① a dead person ② You blockhead! 或 You stupid! 或 You fool!

死字(ㄙ ㄗˋ)
a word which is no longer in use or circulation; an obsolete word

死罪(ㄙ ㄗㄨㄟˋ)

① the capital punishment; sentence of death ②(in ancient China) a term of apology used in correspondence ③(in ancient China) a conventional phrase used in writing memorials to the emperor

死喪(ㄙ ㄙㄤˋ)
death and burial

死而復甦(ㄙ ㄦˊ ㄈㄨˋ ㄙㄨ)
to wake up from death; to resurrect

死而後已(ㄙ ㄦˊ ㄏㄡˋ ㄧˇ)
to stop only upon death

死而無怨(ㄙ ㄦˊ ㄨˊ ㄩㄢˋ)
to die without a grudge

死要面子(ㄙ ㄧㄠˋ ㄇㄧㄢˋ ˙ㄗ)
to try to preserve one's face at all costs

死有餘辜(ㄙ ㄧㄡˇ ㄩˊ ㄍㄨ)
Death will not expiate all his crimes. 他真是死有餘辜。 He deserves to die many times for his crimes.

死因(ㄙ ㄧㄣ)
the cause of death: 他的死因不明。 The cause of his death is still unknown.

死樣(ㄙ ˙ㄧㄤ)
stupid and dull; wooden; doltish

死硬(ㄙ ㄧㄥˋ)
intransigent; very obstinate; irreconcilable; stiff and unbending

死硬派(ㄙ ㄧㄥˋ ㄆㄞˋ)
diehards

死無對證(ㄙ ㄨˊ ㄉㄨㄟˋ ㄓㄥˋ)
to lack evidence because of the death of a principal witness

死無葬身之地(ㄙ ㄨˊ ㄗㄤˋ ㄕㄣ ㄓ ㄉㄧˋ)
to die without a place for burial (a phrase usually used as a warning to somebody)

死無遺憾(ㄙ ㄨˊ ㄧˊ ㄏㄢˋ)
to die without regret

死文字(ㄙ ㄨㄣˊ ㄗˋ)
dead languages—languages which are no longer in common usage, as Greek, Latin, etc.

死亡(ㄙ ㄨㄤˊ)
to die; death: 他因傷死亡。 He died from a wound.

死亡保險(ㄙ ㄨㄤˊ ㄅㄠˇ ㄒㄧㄢˇ)
life insurance 亦作「壽險」or「人壽保險」

死亡通告(ㄙ ㄨㄤˊ ㄊㄨㄥ ㄍㄠˋ)
an obituary; a death notice 亦作「訃聞」

死亡率(ㄙ ㄨㄤˊ ㄌㄩˋ)
death rate; mortality

死亡學(ㄙ ㄨㄤˊ ㄒㄩㄝˊ)
thanatology

死亡證書(ㄙ ㄨㄤˊ ㄓㄥˋ ㄕㄨ)
a death certificate

死於非命(ㄙ ㄩˊ ㄈㄟ ㄇㄧㄥˋ)
to die an unnatural death: 他昨夜死於非命。 He died an unnatural death last night.

四畫

【歿】 2693
(歿) ㄇㄛˋ moh mò
to die; death: 他於一九五六年病歿。 He died of illness in 1956.

歿世不忘(ㄇㄛˋ ㄕˋ ㄅㄨˋ ㄨㄤˋ)
shall never forget

歿存均感(ㄇㄛˋ ㄘㄨㄣˊ ㄐㄩㄣ ㄍㄢˇ)
Both the dead and the living shall be grateful.

【殀】 2694
ㄧㄠˇ yeau yǎo
1. to die young or untimely
2. to be wronged or aggrieved

五畫

【殆】 2695
ㄉㄞˋ day dài
1. precarious; dangerous; danger; perilous: 他處於危殆之中。 He is in great danger.
2. tired
3. afraid
4. nearly; almost: 存款殆盡。 The cash is almost exhausted.
5. only; merely; even

殆不可能(ㄉㄞˋ ㄅㄨˋ ㄎㄜˇ ㄋㄥˊ)
almost impossible

殆矣哉(ㄉㄞˋ ㄧˇ ㄗㄞ)
in grave danger; very dangerous indeed

殆已無望(ㄉㄞˋ ㄧˇ ㄨˊ ㄨㄤˋ)
nearly hopeless

【殄】 2696
ㄊㄧㄢˇ tean tiǎn
1. to end; to terminate
2. to exterminate; to exterpate;

〔歹部〕

to weed out; to wipe out
3. to waste

殄滅(ㄊㄧㄢˇ ㄇㄧㄝˋ)
to exterminate thoroughly;
to extirpate; to commit genocide

殄難(ㄊㄧㄢˇ ㄋㄢˊ)
to exterminate dangers; to
eliminate dangers and hardships

殄絕(ㄊㄧㄢˇ ㄐㄩㄝˊ)
to bring to termination; to
bring to an end

殄殲(ㄊㄧㄢˇ ㄐㄧㄢ)
(said of a dynasty, reign,
etc.) to be eliminated; to
come to an end

殄瘁(ㄊㄧㄢˇ ㄘㄨㄟˋ)
misfortune and poverty; ruin

【殃】 2697
ㄧㄤ iang yāng
1. disaster; misfortune; calamities: 戰爭是可怕的災殃。War
is a frightful calamity.
2. the return of the spirit of
the deceased

殃民(ㄧㄤ ㄇㄧㄣˊ)
to wrong and suppress the
people; to bring disaster to
the people

殃禍(ㄧㄤ ㄏㄨㄛˋ)
disasters and calamities

殃及池魚(ㄧㄤ ㄐㄧˊ ㄔˊ ㄩˊ)
(literally) (When the city
gate catches fire,) the disaster even extends to the fish
in the moat—to cause trouble or bring disaster to innocent people

殃及無辜(ㄧㄤ ㄐㄧˊ ㄨˊ ㄍㄨ)
Trouble involves the innocent people.

【殂】 2698
ㄘㄨ tswu cú
to die; dead; death

殂沒(ㄘㄨ ㄇㄛˋ)
to die; to perish; death

殂落(ㄘㄨ ㄌㄨㄛˋ) or 殂謝(ㄘㄨ ㄒㄧㄝˋ)
to pass away; to demise

殂殞(ㄘㄨ ㄩㄣˇ)
to die; death (of usually an
eminent figure)

六畫

【殉】 2699
ㄒㄩㄣˋ shiunn xùn

1. to die for a cause
2. (originally) to be buried
with the dead (usually said
of slaves, loyal servants,
concubines, etc.)

殉名(ㄒㄩㄣˋ ㄇㄧㄥˊ)
to win fame at the expense
of one's life

殉道(ㄒㄩㄣˋ ㄉㄠˋ)
to die for the right cause; to
die a martyr's death

殉道精神(ㄒㄩㄣˋ ㄉㄠˋ ㄐㄧㄥ ㄕㄣˊ)
martyrdom

殉道者(ㄒㄩㄣˋ ㄉㄠˋ ㄓㄜˇ)
a martyr

殉難(ㄒㄩㄣˋ ㄋㄢˊ)
to die for one's country: 他
父親爲國殉難。His father died
for his country.

殉利(ㄒㄩㄣˋ ㄌㄧˋ) or 殉財(ㄒㄩㄣˋ ㄘㄞˊ)
to die for money

殉國(ㄒㄩㄣˋ ㄍㄨㄛˊ)
to die for one's country; to
die a martyr's death

殉節(ㄒㄩㄣˋ ㄐㄧㄝˊ)
to die to protect one's virtue
or for the sake of honor

殉教(ㄒㄩㄣˋ ㄐㄧㄠˋ)
to die for a religious cause

殉情(ㄒㄩㄣˋ ㄑㄧㄥˊ)
to die for love

殉職(ㄒㄩㄣˋ ㄓˊ)
to die on one's job; to die
while performing one's
work: 他因公殉職了。He died
at his post.

殉身(ㄒㄩㄣˋ ㄕㄣ)
to die for a cause, faith, etc.

殉葬(ㄒㄩㄣˋ ㄗㄤˋ)
to bury the living, jewels,
vessels, etc. with the dead

【殊】 2700
ㄕㄨ shu shū

1. different; special; strange
2. distinguished; outstanding
3. extremely; very
4. really; indeed: 此事殊難解決。
This matter is indeed difficult to settle.
5. still; yet
6. exceed; over

殊不可解(ㄕㄨ ㄅㄨˋ ㄎㄜˇ ㄐㄧㄝˇ)
really difficult to understand

殊不知(ㄕㄨ ㄅㄨˋ ㄓ)
Who knows that....; really
don't know

殊方(ㄕㄨ ㄈㄤ)

strange lands; foreign lands

殊途同歸(ㄕㄨ ㄊㄨˊ ㄊㄨㄥˊ ㄍㄨㄟ)
to reach the same destination (or goal) by different
routes; to reach the same
decision or conclusion by
different means or ways

殊禮(ㄕㄨ ㄌㄧˇ)
a very polite reception;
utmost courtesy

殊功(ㄕㄨ ㄍㄨㄥ)
extraordinary achievements;
distinguished services

殊堪嘉尚(ㄕㄨ ㄎㄢ ㄐㄧㄚ ㄕㄤˋ)
richly deserving commendation (a cliché often found in
official citations)

殊行(ㄕㄨ ㄒㄧㄥˊ)
remarkable behavior or conduct; extraordinary actions

殊勳(ㄕㄨ ㄒㄩㄣ)
extraordinary achievements
or merits

殊寵(ㄕㄨ ㄔㄨㄥˇ)
special favor

殊深(ㄕㄨ ㄕㄣ)
extremely; profoundly; deeply

殊勝(ㄕㄨ ㄕㄥˋ)
remarkable and outstanding

殊容(ㄕㄨ ㄖㄨㄥˊ)
a stunningly beautiful face;
extraordinary beauty

殊榮(ㄕㄨ ㄖㄨㄥˊ)
special honors

殊死(ㄕㄨ ㄙˇ)
desperate; life-and-death: 那
是一場殊死的搏鬥。That was
a life-and-death struggle.

殊死戰(ㄕㄨ ㄙˇ ㄓㄢˋ)
to fight to the last man; a
life-or-death battle; a desperate fight: 他們作殊死戰。
They fought a last-ditch battle.

殊俗(ㄕㄨ ㄙㄨˊ)
① strange customs ② different from common practices;
extraordinary

殊異(ㄕㄨ ㄧˋ)
special; extraordinary

殊末(ㄕㄨ ㄇㄛˋ)
not yet

殊文(ㄕㄨ ㄨㄣˊ)
a strange language (espe-
cially written); a different
language

殊遇(ㄕㄨ ㄩ)
special treatment; special kindness

殊域(ㄕㄨ ㄩˋ)
strange lands

七畫

【殍】 2701 ㄆㄧㄠˇ peau piǎo
1. to starve to death
2. a person who died from starvation 亦作「莩」

八畫

【殖】 2702 ㄓˊ jyr zhí
1. to grow in abundance; to prosper; to reproduce; to propagate: 大多數植物靠種子繁殖。Most plants reproduce by seeds.
2. to plant
3. to become wealthy
4. to colonize; colonization

殖民(ㄓˊ ㄇㄧㄣˊ)
to colonize; to settle people in a less developed area

殖民地(ㄓˊ ㄇㄧㄣˊ ㄉㄧˋ)
a colony

殖民教育(ㄓˊ ㄇㄧㄣˊ ㄐㄧㄠˋ ㄩˋ)
colonial education

殖民政策(ㄓˊ ㄇㄧㄣˊ ㄓㄥˋ ㄘㄜˋ)
the colonial policy; colonialism

殖利(ㄓˊ ㄌㄧˋ)
to make profits

殖穀(ㄓˊ ㄍㄨˇ)
to plant rice

殖貨(ㄓˊ ㄏㄨㄛˋ)
to prosper in commercial dealings; to increase one's possessions in property and goods

殖產(ㄓˊ ㄔㄢˇ)
to increase one's property and holdings

【殘】 2703 ㄘㄢˊ tsarn cán
1. to destroy; to injure; to damage; to spoil
2. to wither
3. cruel and fierce; heartless and relentless: 他生性凶殘。He was cruel by nature.
4. crippled; disfigured: 他在一次車禍中變成殘廢。He was

crippled in a motorcar accident.
5. remnants or residues; the little amount of something left
6. incomplete: 這是他的殘稿。This is his incomplete manuscript.
7. to kill

殘杯冷炙(ㄘㄢˊ ㄅㄟ ㄌㄥˇ ㄓˋ)
the dregs of wine and cold meat—what is left of a feast

殘暴(ㄘㄢˊ ㄅㄠˋ)
cruel and heartless; cold-blooded; cruelty; ruthlessness; brutal: 殘暴的士兵，毆打他們的俘虜。Brutal soldiers beat their prisoners.

殘兵敗將(ㄘㄢˊ ㄅㄧㄥ ㄅㄞˋ ㄐㄧㄤˋ)
the remnants of a defeated army

殘部(ㄘㄢˊ ㄅㄨˋ)
the remnants of defeated troops, bandit groups, etc.

殘破(ㄘㄢˊ ㄆㄛˋ)
① damaged; spoiled; dilapidated: 傢俱由於使用而殘破。Furniture is dilapidated by use. ② not complete; deficient

殘篇斷簡(ㄘㄢˊ ㄆㄧㄢ ㄉㄨㄢˋ ㄐㄧㄢˇ)
books with missing pages, chapters, volumes, etc.; fragments

殘夢(ㄘㄢˊ ㄇㄥˋ)
an unfinished dream

殘民自肥(ㄘㄢˊ ㄇㄧㄣˊ ㄗˋ ㄈㄟˊ)
to fatten oneself by exploiting the people

殘廢(ㄘㄢˊ ㄈㄟˋ)
crippled, maimed, or disabled: 他在戰事中受重傷而殘廢。He was seriously maimed in the war.

殘燈燭明(ㄘㄢˊ ㄉㄥ ㄈㄨˊ ㄇㄧㄥˊ)
(figuratively) the last flicker of life in a dying man

殘冬(ㄘㄢˊ ㄉㄨㄥ)
the last days of winter

殘年(ㄘㄢˊ ㄋㄧㄢˊ)or 殘歲(ㄘㄢˊ ㄙㄨㄟˋ)
① the closing days of the year ② one's closing years; the evening of life

殘虐(ㄘㄢˊ ㄋㄩㄝˋ)
cruelty and torture; cold-bloodedness

殘留(ㄘㄢˊ ㄌㄧㄡˊ)
to remain; to be left over

殘藥剩飯(ㄘㄢˊ ㄧㄠˋ ㄕㄥˋ ㄈㄢˋ)
the remains of a meal; left-overs

殘酷(ㄘㄢˊ ㄎㄨˋ)
cruelty; heartlessness; cold-bloodedness; savagery: 那是一場殘酷的戰事。That was a cruel war.

殘骸(ㄘㄢˊ ㄏㄞˊ)
① incomplete remains ② the wreckage (of an airplane, ship or truck): 那是飛機的殘骸。It was the wreckage of an airplane.

殘害(ㄘㄢˊ ㄏㄞˋ)
to oppress cruelly; to injure heartlessly; to slaughter

殘痕(ㄘㄢˊ ㄏㄣˊ)
traces or marks left

殘花敗柳(ㄘㄢˊ ㄏㄨㄚ ㄅㄞˋ ㄌㄧㄡˇ)
(literally) faded flowers and withered willows—fallen angels; prostitutes

殘紅(ㄘㄢˊ ㄏㄨㄥˊ)
fallen flowers

殘疾(ㄘㄢˊ ㄐㄧˊ)
physical deformity—crippled, deformed, maimed, etc.

殘局(ㄘㄢˊ ㄐㄩˊ)
① the aftermath of war, revolution or great upheaval ② an unfinished chess game

殘卷(ㄘㄢˊ ㄐㄩㄢˋ)
a volume with many missing pages; a volume that used to be part of a complete book

殘缺 or 殘闕(ㄘㄢˊ ㄑㄩㄝ)
incomplete; fragmentary

殘席(ㄘㄢˊ ㄒㄧˊ)
a table after a feast

殘照(ㄘㄢˊ ㄓㄠˋ)
① the setting sun ② the evening glow

殘燭(ㄘㄢˊ ㄓㄨˊ)
an expiring candle

殘喘(ㄘㄢˊ ㄔㄨㄢˇ)
agonized breathing just before dying

殘春(ㄘㄢˊ ㄔㄨㄣ)
the last days of spring

殘殺(ㄘㄢˊ ㄕㄚ)
to kill indiscriminately or savagely; to massacre; to slaughter

【歹部】

殘山賸水(ㄘㄢ ㄕㄢ ㄕㄥˋ ㄕㄨㄟˇ)
the reduced territories of a nation after aggression by a foreign power

殘生(ㄘㄢ ㄕㄥ)
the closing years of one's life; one's remaining years

殘暑(ㄘㄢ ㄕㄨˇ)
the lingering heat of late summer

殘忍(ㄘㄢ ㄖㄣˇ)
cruelty; heartlessness; brutality; cruel; heartless; brutal; savage: 我不喜歡殘忍的人。I do not like cruel people.

殘賊(ㄘㄢ ㄗㄜˊ)
①to injure; to spoil ②a ravening thief

殘存(ㄘㄢ ㄘㄨㄣˊ)
surviving

殘而不廢(ㄘㄢ ㄦˊ ㄅㄨˋ ㄈㄟˋ)
disabled but useful; crippled but leading an active life

殘陽(ㄘㄢ ㄧㄤˊ)
the setting sun; the evening glow

殘餘(ㄘㄢ ㄩˊ)
remnants; survivals; remains; vestiges; residues

殘月(ㄘㄢ ㄩㄝˋ)
the waning moon

九畫

【殛】 2704
ㄐㄧˊ jyi jí
to put to death

十畫

【殞】 2705
ㄩㄣˇ yeun yún
1. to die; to perish
2. same as 隕—to fall

殞沒(ㄩㄣˇ ㄇㄛˋ)
to perish; to die

殞滅(ㄩㄣˇ ㄇㄧㄝˋ)
to exterminate; to annihilate; to wipe out

殞命(ㄩㄣˇ ㄇㄧㄥˋ)
to perish; to die

殞落(ㄩㄣˇ ㄌㄨㄛˋ)or 殞墜(ㄩㄣˇ ㄓㄨㄟˋ)
to fall

殞石(ㄩㄣˇ ㄕˊ)
a meteorite

十一畫

【殣】 2706
ㄐㄧㄣˇ jiin jín
1. to starve to death
2. to bury

【殤】 2707
ㄕㄤ shang shāng
1. to die young; to die prematurely
2. national mourning

【殢】 2708
ㄊㄧˋ tih tì
greatly distressed

殢酒
to suffer from alcoholism

十二畫

【殪】 2709
ㄧˋ yih yì
1. to die
2. to kill

【殫】 2710
ㄉㄢ dan dān
to use up; to exhaust

殫悶(ㄉㄢ ㄇㄣˋ)
to swoon; to lose consciousness; to faint

殫力(ㄉㄢ ㄌㄧˋ)
to strive; to endeavor

殫竭其力(ㄉㄢ ㄐㄧㄝˊ ㄑㄧˊ ㄌㄧˋ)
to give all of one's strength

殫見洽聞(ㄉㄢ ㄐㄧㄢˋ ㄒㄧㄚˊ ㄨㄣˊ)
to have vast knowledge and experience; to have seen all and heard all

殫精竭慮(ㄉㄢ ㄐㄧㄥ ㄐㄧㄝˊ ㄌㄩˋ)
to devote one's entire energy and thought; to think with all one's energies or powers

殫洽(ㄉㄢ ㄒㄧㄚˊ)
very erudite

殫心(ㄉㄢ ㄒㄧㄣ)
to devote one's entire mind

殫殘(ㄉㄢ ㄘㄢˊ)
to destroy

殫思極慮(ㄉㄢ ㄙ ㄐㄧˊ ㄌㄩˋ)or 殫精極慮(ㄉㄢ ㄐㄧㄥ ㄐㄧˊ ㄌㄩˋ)
to devote one's entire thought; to rack one's brains

十三畫

【殭】 2711
ㄐㄧㄤ jiang jiāng

dead and stiff

殭巴(ㄐㄧㄤ ㄅㄚˋ)
shriveled

殭尸 or 殭屍(ㄐㄧㄤ ㄕ)
a vampire; a reanimated corpse

殭蠶(ㄐㄧㄤ ㄘㄢˊ)
the silkworm dead before producing the cocoon; a stiffened silkworm

殭硬(ㄐㄧㄤ ㄧㄥˋ)
stiff

【殮】 2712
ㄌㄧㄢˋ liann liàn
to prepare a body for the coffin; to encoffin

殮埋(ㄌㄧㄢˋ ㄇㄞˊ)or 殮葬(ㄌㄧㄢˋ ㄗㄤˋ)
to shroud and bury

殮具(ㄌㄧㄢˋ ㄐㄩˋ)
articles for preparing the body for the coffin

十四畫

【殯】 2713
ㄅㄧㄣˋ binn bìn
1. to lay a coffin in a memorial hall
2. to carry to the grave

殯殮(ㄅㄧㄣˋ ㄌㄧㄢˋ)
a funeral

殯車(ㄅㄧㄣˋ ㄔㄜ)
a hearse

殯葬(ㄅㄧㄣˋ ㄗㄤˋ)
a burial; a funeral

殯儀館(ㄅㄧㄣˋ ㄧˊ ㄍㄨㄢˇ)
a funeral parlor

十七畫

【殲】 2714
ㄐㄧㄢ jian jiān
to annihilate; to exterminate; to destroy

殲滅(ㄐㄧㄢ ㄇㄧㄝˋ)
to annihilate; to exterminate; to wipe out

殲滅戰(ㄐㄧㄢ ㄇㄧㄝˋ ㄓㄢˋ)
a large-scale military operation designed to wipe out enemy forces; a war or battle of annihilation

殲敵(ㄐㄧㄢ ㄉㄧˊ)
to destroy the enemy

殳 部
ㄕㄨ shu shū

【殳】 2715
ㄕㄨ shu shū
a halberd; a kind of ancient weapon made of bamboo

殳書(ㄕㄨ ㄕㄨ)
a style of handwriting in Chin (秦) Dynasty (used for inscriptions on weapons)

五畫

【段】 2716
ㄉㄨㄢˋ duann duàn
1. a section; a division; a part; a paragraph
2. a stage
3. a Chinese family name

段落(ㄉㄨㄢˋ ㄌㄨㄛˋ)
①end (of a paragraph, stage, etc.): 這事已暫告一段落。This matter has come to an end for the time being. ② a paragraph ③ a phase

六畫

【殷】 2717
1. ㄧㄣ in yīn
1. abundant; flourishing; thriving; prosperous; rich
2. polite; courteous; civil; hospitable
3. sad; sorrowful; mournful
4. eager; eagerly
5. an alternative name for the latter half of the Shang (商) Dynasty

殷富(ㄧㄣ ㄈㄨˋ)
wealthy; prosperous; well-off

殷鑑(ㄧㄣ ㄐㄧㄢˋ)
(literally) a warning for the Yin people—a predecessor's failure as a warning

殷鑑不遠(ㄧㄣ ㄐㄧㄢˋ ㄅㄨˋ ㄩㄢˇ)
The beacon of Yin is not far distant.—(figuratively) The lesson (of failure) can be found in recent time. 或 One need not look far for a lesson.

殷契(ㄧㄣ ㄑㄧˋ)
the oracle-bone writing

殷切(ㄧㄣ ㄑㄧㄝˋ)

ardent; eager

殷勤 or 慇懃(ㄧㄣ ㄑㄧㄣˊ)
courteous; polite; civil: 他們對客人很慇懃。They are very courteous to their guests.

殷墟(ㄧㄣ ㄒㄩ)
the dwelling place of the Yin people (before 1200 B.C.) found in what is today's Anyang County (安陽縣), Honan Province (河南省), once the capital of the Yin Dynasty

殷墟書契(ㄧㄣ ㄒㄩ ㄕㄨ ㄑㄧˋ)or 殷墟文字(ㄧㄣ ㄒㄩ ㄨㄣˊ ㄗˋ)
the oracle-bone writing found in the dwelling place of the Yin people

殷實(ㄧㄣ ㄕˊ)
prosperous; well-off; substantial: 這是家殷實商店。It's a substantial store.

殷商(ㄧㄣ ㄕㄤ)
① the Shang Dynasty (c. 1800-1200 B.C.) was later renamed Yin Dynasty ② a prosperous merchant: 他是一名殷商。He is a prosperous merchant.

殷盛(ㄧㄣ ㄕㄥˋ)
thriving; flourishing; prosperous; abundant

殷憂啟聖(ㄧㄣ ㄧㄡ ㄑㄧˇ ㄕㄥˋ)
Deep sorrow leads to enlightenment.

殷殷(ㄧㄣ ㄧㄣ)
① prosperous; thriving; rich; abundant ② courteous; polite; civil ③ sorrowful; sad; mournful

殷殷垂誡(ㄧㄣ ㄧㄣ ㄔㄨㄟˊ ㄐㄧㄝˋ)
to admonish sincerely

【殷】 2717
2. ㄧㄢˇ ian yǎn
dark red

殷紅(ㄧㄢˇ ㄏㄨㄥˊ)
dark red

七畫

【殺】 2718
1. ㄕㄚ sha shā
1. to kill; to put to death; to slaughter; to destroy: 殺生容易，回生難。It's easy to kill, but impossible to restore life.
2. exceedingly; extremely: 他的

行爲眞是笑殺人。His conduct is extremely ridiculous.
3. to weaken; to deflate: 你最好殺殺他的威風。You'd better deflate his arrogance.
4. to fight: 他殺出敵人重圍。He fought his way out of the enemy's heavy siege.

殺伐(ㄕㄚ ㄈㄚˊ)or(ㄕㄚ ㄈㄚ)
fighting; war: 殺伐之聲 a noise of fighting

殺風景(ㄕㄚ ㄈㄥ ㄐㄧㄥˇ)
to dampen interest; to make dull; to spoil or ruin happiness; to kill joy; to do something to spoil one's enthusiasm

殺敵(ㄕㄚ ㄉㄧˊ)
to fight the enemy

殺敵致果(ㄕㄚ ㄉㄧˊ ㄓˋ ㄍㄨㄛˇ)
to serve with distinction in war

殺頭(ㄕㄚ ㄊㄡˊ)
to perform decapitation; to behead: 他因叛國罪被殺頭。He was beheaded for high treason.

殺退(ㄕㄚ ㄊㄨㄟˋ)
to put to flight; to rout

殺(ㄕㄚ ㄍㄨˋ)
to kill; to slay

殺掠(ㄕㄚ ㄌㄩㄝˋ)
to kill and plunder

殺光(ㄕㄚ ㄍㄨㄤ)
to kill all

殺害(ㄕㄚ ㄏㄞˋ)
to murder; to kill: 她被殺害了。She was murdered.

殺機(ㄕㄚ ㄐㄧ)
intention to murder

殺雞儆猴(ㄕㄚ ㄐㄧ ㄐㄧㄥˇ ㄏㄡˊ)
to kill the chicken to intimidate the monkey to punish somebody as a warning to others 亦作「殺雞駭猴」

殺雞取卵(ㄕㄚ ㄐㄧ ㄑㄩˇ ㄌㄨㄢˇ)
to kill the hen to get eggs —a very foolish act

殺雞焉用牛刀(ㄕㄚ ㄐㄧ ㄧㄢ ㄩㄥˋ ㄋㄧㄡˊ ㄉㄠ)
(literally) Why use a cattle knife for a chicken?—Great talent can be used for better purposes or for greater results.

殺價(ㄕㄚ ㄐㄧㄚˋ)
to reduce prices; to cut price

down

殺戒(ㄕㄚ ㄐㄧㄝˋ)
the Buddhist prohibition against killing

殺盡斬絕(ㄕㄚ ㄐㄧㄣˋ ㄓㄢˇ ㄐㄩㄝˊ)
to kill all; to give no quarter

殺菌(ㄕㄚ ㄐㄩㄣˋ)
to kill germs; to sterilize; to decontaminate; to disinfect

殺菌燈(ㄕㄚ ㄐㄩㄣˋ ㄉㄥ)
an ultraviolet lamp

殺氣(ㄕㄚ ㄑㄧˋ)
① (said of a sight or scene) a very severe or chilling appearance ② a murderous atmosphere; a furious look

殺氣騰騰(ㄕㄚ ㄑㄧˋ ㄊㄥˊ ㄊㄥˊ)
There is a prevailing thirst for blood.—with a murderous look on one's face

殺青(ㄕㄚ ㄑㄧㄥ)
(said of films, books, etc.) to be completed: 這部電影將於明年六月殺青。 The movie will be completed next June.

殺蟲劑(ㄕㄚ ㄔㄨㄥˊ ㄐㄧˋ)
the insecticide

殺蟲藥(ㄕㄚ ㄔㄨㄥˊ ㄧㄠˋ)
anthelmintic (against intestinal parasites)

殺手(ㄕㄚ ㄕㄡˇ)
a hit man; a killer

殺身之禍(ㄕㄚ ㄕㄣ ㄓ ㄏㄨㄛˋ)
a fatal disaster; a lethal misfortune: 他的財富和聲望招致殺身之禍。 His wealth and reputation caused a fatal misfortune to him.

殺身成仁(ㄕㄚ ㄕㄣ ㄔㄥˊ ㄖㄣˊ)
to fulfil justice at the cost of one's own life; to sacrifice one's own life for justice

殺傷(ㄕㄚ ㄕㄤ)
to kill and wound; to inflict wounds upon: 這種地雷殺傷力很強。 This is a powerful antipersonnel mine.

殺生(ㄕㄚ ㄕㄥ)
killing

殺牲(ㄕㄚ ㄕㄥ)
to butcher domestic animals other than cats and dogs

殺人(ㄕㄚ ㄖㄣˊ)
to kill a person; to murder: 汝不可殺人！ Thou shalt not kill!

殺人不見血(ㄕㄚ ㄖㄣˊ ㄅㄨˋ ㄐㄧㄢˋ ㄒㄧㄝˋ)
(said of a devious act) able to kill without bloodshed —to kill with subtle means

殺人不眨眼(ㄕㄚ ㄖㄣˊ ㄅㄨˋ ㄓㄚˇ ㄧㄢˇ)
capable of killing without even a blink of the eyes —hardhearted, cold-blooded, or very cruel

殺人犯(ㄕㄚ ㄖㄣˊ ㄈㄢˋ)
a murder convict; a murderer; a homicide

殺人者死(ㄕㄚ ㄖㄣˊ ㄓㄜˇ ㄙˇ)
Murder is punishable by death.

殺人如麻(ㄕㄚ ㄖㄣˊ ㄖㄨˊ ㄇㄚˊ)
to kill people as if they were just hemp; to have killed many people

殺人罪(ㄕㄚ ㄖㄣˊ ㄗㄨㄟˋ)
homicide; murder

殺人盈野(ㄕㄚ ㄖㄣˊ ㄧㄥˊ ㄧㄝˇ)
Bodies of the killed lie everywhere.

殺人未遂(ㄕㄚ ㄖㄣˊ ㄨㄟˋ ㄙㄨㄟˊ)
an attempted murder

殺人越貨(ㄕㄚ ㄖㄣˊ ㄩㄝˋ ㄏㄨㄛˋ)
to kill and rob

殺死(ㄕㄚ ㄙˇ)
to kill; to slay; to murder

殺一警百(ㄕㄚ ㄧ ㄐㄧㄥˇ ㄅㄞˇ)
to kill one as a warning to a hundred

殺威棒(ㄕㄚ ㄨㄟ ㄅㄤˋ)
a flogging administered to a culprit upon his first appearance before the magistrate with the intention of crushing his spirit

殺尾(ㄕㄚ ㄨㄟˇ)
to come to a conclusion

【殺】2718
2. ㄕㄞˋ shay shài
to degrade; to decline; to diminish; to abate: 風勢稍殺。 The winds have abated.

八畫

2719
(彀,亮,殻) ㄑㄩㄝˋ chiueh
（又讀 ㄎㄜˊ ker kě)
（語音 ㄑㄧㄠˋ chiaw qiào)
shells; husks; coverings

殼斗(ㄎㄜˊ ㄉㄡˇ)
cupule

殼果(ㄎㄜˊ ㄍㄨㄛˇ)
a nut

殼子(ㄎㄜˊ ˙ㄗ) or 殼兒(ㄎㄜˊ ㄦ)
a shell; a hard covering (of an animal, or of an egg, fruit, nut or seed); the outer surface (as opposed to the contents or substance)

殼菜(ㄎㄜˊ ㄘㄞˋ)
a kind of mussel with edible meat (Mytilus crassitesta) 亦作「淡菜」

【殽】2720
ㄧㄠˊ yau yáo
1. confusion; disorder; mess
2. dishes

殽亂(ㄧㄠˊ ㄌㄨㄢˋ)
disorderly; confused; messy

殽核(ㄧㄠˊ ㄏㄜˊ)
dishes and fruit

殽舛(ㄧㄠˊ ㄔㄨㄢˇ)
disorderly; confused; messy

殽雜(ㄧㄠˊ ㄗㄚˊ)
disorderly; messy

九畫

【殿】2721
ㄉㄧㄢˋ diann diàn
1. a palace; a palace hall; a temple; a sanctuary; 神殿 the temple of gods
2. the rear; the rear guard

殿版(ㄉㄧㄢˋ ㄅㄢˇ)
the edition of classics and other works printed by imperial decree in the early Ching Dynasty

殿本(ㄉㄧㄢˋ ㄅㄣˇ)
a copy or the edition of classics and other works printed by imperial order in the early Ching Dynasty

殿堂(ㄉㄧㄢˋ ㄊㄤˊ) or 殿庭(ㄉㄧㄢˋ ㄊㄧㄥˊ)
a palace; a palace hall; a temple; a sanctuary

殿後(ㄉㄧㄢˋ ㄏㄡˋ)
the rear, or rear guard (of marching troops); to bring up the rear

殿軍(ㄉㄧㄢˋ ㄐㄩㄣ)
① the rear guard (of marching troops) ② the last-placed winner in a contest

殿下(ㄉㄧㄢˋ ㄒㄧㄚˋ)

① Your, His, or Her Highness ② Your, or His Majesty (in the Wei and Tsin Dynasties)

殿試（ㄉㄧㄢ ㄕ）
the civil service examination held in the presence of the emperor at his court

殿元（ㄉㄧㄢ ㄩㄢ）
the candidate who won the first place in a civil service examination held in the presence of the emperor

【毀】 2722 ㄏㄨㄟ huei huǐ
1. to destroy; to ruin; to damage; to injure: 他自毀前程。He destroyed his own career.
2. to libel; to slander; to abuse; to revile; to defame; to blame excessively

毀敗（ㄏㄨㄟ ㄅㄞ）
to destroy; to ruin

毀謗（ㄏㄨㄟ ㄅㄤ）
to libel; to slander; to malign; a libel or slander; calumniation: 他不在乎他人惡意的毀謗。He doesn't care about others' malicious slanders.

毀滅（ㄏㄨㄟ ㄇㄧㄝ）
to destroy; to ruin; to demolish: 你將毀滅你的前途。You will ruin your prospects.

毀詆（ㄏㄨㄟ ㄉㄧ）
to slander; to libel

毀短（ㄏㄨㄟ ㄉㄨㄢ）
to disparage; to denounce; to run down; to speak ill of

毀害（ㄏㄨㄟ ㄏㄞ）
to injure; to damage: 不要毀害他人。Don't injure other people.

毀壞（ㄏㄨㄟ ㄏㄨㄞ）
to destroy; to injure; to damage

毀家紓難（ㄏㄨㄟ ㄐㄧㄚ ㄕㄨ ㄋㄢ）
to donate all one has for the sake of the nation in a crisis; to offer all one has for charity

毀棄（ㄏㄨㄟ ㄑㄧ）
to abrogate; to repeal; to dissolve; to annul; to rescind

毀傷（ㄏㄨㄟ ㄕㄤ）
to damage; to injure: 他的名譽受到毀傷。He has a damaged reputation.

毀容（ㄏㄨㄟ ㄖㄨㄥ）
to disfigure

毀詈（ㄏㄨㄟ ㄌㄧ）
to revile; to abuse

毀損（ㄏㄨㄟ ㄙㄨㄣ）
to damage; to injure; to disfigure

毀於一旦（ㄏㄨㄟ ㄩ ㄧ ㄉㄢ）
to be ruined or destroyed in one day

毀譽（ㄏㄨㄟ ㄩ）
praise and dispraise: 他不計毀譽。He was indifferent to people's praise or dispraise.

毀譽參半（ㄏㄨㄟ ㄩ ㄘㄢ ㄅㄢ）
to give a mixture of praise and dispraise; to draw both praises and criticisms; to be as much censured as praised: 此人毀譽參半。The man got both praise and dispraise.

毀約（ㄏㄨㄟ ㄩㄝ）
to break one's promise: 他從不毀約。He never breaks his promise.

十一畫

【毅】 2723 ㄧ yih yì
firm; resolute; endurance; fortitude

毅力（ㄧ ㄌㄧ）
perseverance; determination; resoluteness; indomitability; firmness; stamina: 這個年輕人缺乏毅力。The youth lacks stamina.

毅然（ㄧ ㄖㄢ）
firmly; courageously

毅然決然（ㄧ ㄖㄢ ㄐㄩㄝ ㄖㄢ）
in a determined manner; with determination; resolutely; firmly

毅勇（ㄧ ㄩㄥ）
firm courage; fortitude

【毆】 2724 ㄡ ou ōu
to beat; to hit; a blow: 他們吵嘴後互毆。They exchanged blows after a hot argument.

毆斃（ㄡ ㄅㄧ）
to beat to death

毆鬥（ㄡ ㄉㄡ）
to have a fist fight; to fisticuff; to beat a person with fists or clubs; to come to blows: 他用拳頭毆打我。He struck me with his fist.

毆擊（ㄡ ㄐㄧ）
to fisticuff; to beat someone with fists or clubs

毆殺（ㄡ ㄕㄚ）
to beat to death 參看「毆斃」

毆傷（ㄡ ㄕㄤ）
to injure by beating

毆辱（ㄡ ㄖㄨ）
to beat and insult

毋 部
ㄨ wu wú

【毋】 2725 ㄨ wu wú
1. (imperative) do not; no: 毋誤前途。Do not hurt your career.
2. a Chinese family name

毋寧（ㄨ ㄋㄧㄥ）
rather... (than); (not so much...) as: 與其說他是學者,毋寧說他是個教師。He is rather a teacher than a scholar.

毋需（ㄨ ㄒㄩ）
do not need: 你今天毋需工作。You do not need to work today.

毋忘在莒（ㄨ ㄨㄤ ㄗㄞ ㄐㄩ）
Do not forget national humiliation in time of peace and security.

毋庸（ㄨ ㄩㄥ）
need not: 應毋庸議。This need not be considered.

毋庸諱言（ㄨ ㄩㄥ ㄏㄨㄟ ㄧㄢ）
There's no need for reticence.

一畫

【母】 2726 ㄇㄨ muu mǔ
1. one's mother; one's female parent: 家母今年八十歲。My mother is 80 years old.
2. mother—(figuratively) the origin: 需要為發明之母。Necessity is the mother of invention.

（毋 部）

3. female

母馬(ㄇㄨˇ ㄇㄚˇ)
a mare

母貓(ㄇㄨˇ ㄇㄠ)
a tabby (as opposed to a tomcat)

母法(ㄇㄨˇ ㄈㄚˇ)
a foreign law from which a domestic law is copied or patterned after

母範(ㄇㄨˇ ㄈㄢˋ)
a model for mothers

母的(ㄇㄨˇ ·ㄉㄜ)
female

母黨(ㄇㄨˇ ㄉㄤˇ)
maternal relatives

母弟(ㄇㄨˇ ㄉㄧˋ)
one's younger brother born of the same mother

母體(ㄇㄨˇ ㄊㄧˇ)
the mother body

母兔(ㄇㄨˇ ㄊㄨˋ)
a doe

母難日(ㄇㄨˇ ㄋㄢˊ ㄖˋ)
my birthday (a day when mother underwent a crisis and excruciating pains in giving birth)

母牛(ㄇㄨˇ ㄋㄧㄡˊ)
a cow

母女(ㄇㄨˇ ㄋㄩˇ)
mother and daughter

母老虎(ㄇㄨˇ ㄌㄠˇ ㄏㄨˇ)
① a shrew; a termagant ② a tigress

母狼(ㄇㄨˇ ㄌㄤˊ)
a she-wolf

母鹿(ㄇㄨˇ ㄌㄨˋ)
a roe deer; a roe

母狗(ㄇㄨˇ ㄍㄡˇ)
a bitch

母國(ㄇㄨˇ ㄍㄨㄛˊ)
one's mother country; one's motherland

母公司(ㄇㄨˇ ㄍㄨㄥ ㄙ)
a parent company

母后(ㄇㄨˇ ㄏㄡˋ)
① the queen ② the queen mother

母機(ㄇㄨˇ ㄐㄧ)
a mother machine; a machine that makes other machines

母雞(ㄇㄨˇ ㄐㄧ)
a hen

母姊會(ㄇㄨˇ ㄐㄧˇ ㄏㄨㄟˋ)
a mother-sister conference

母教(ㄇㄨˇ ㄐㄧㄠˋ)
one's mother's teachings

母舅(ㄇㄨˇ ㄐㄧㄡˋ)
a maternal uncle; one's mother's brother

母艦(ㄇㄨˇ ㄐㄧㄢˋ)
mother ship; a carrier: 航空母艦 an aircraft carrier

母錢(ㄇㄨˇ ㄑㄧㄢˊ)
capital (for business)

母親(ㄇㄨˇ ㄑㄧㄣ)
mother

母親節(ㄇㄨˇ ㄑㄧㄣ ㄐㄧㄝˊ)
Mother's Day, on the second Sunday in May

母權(ㄇㄨˇ ㄑㄩㄢˊ)
matriarchal power

母系(ㄇㄨˇ ㄒㄧˋ)
① the maternal side ② matriarchal

母系制度(ㄇㄨˇ ㄒㄧˋ ㄓˋ ㄉㄨˋ)
matriarchy

母系社會(ㄇㄨˇ ㄒㄧˋ ㄕㄜˋ ㄏㄨㄟˋ)
a matriarchal society

母校(ㄇㄨˇ ㄒㄧㄠˋ)
one's alma mater; Alma Mater: 我們必須為母校爭光。 We must try to reflect credit on our alma mater.

母象(ㄇㄨˇ ㄒㄧㄤˋ)
a female elephant

母性(ㄇㄨˇ ㄒㄧㄥˋ)
motherliness; maternity; maternal instinct; the mother: 那件事引出了她的母性。It brought out the mother in her.

母兄(ㄇㄨˇ ㄒㄩㄥ)
one's elder brother born of the same mother

母豬(ㄇㄨˇ ㄓㄨ)
a sow

母獅(ㄇㄨˇ ㄕ)
a lioness

母山羊(ㄇㄨˇ ㄕㄢ ㄧㄤˊ)
a she-goat, or nanny goat

母數(ㄇㄨˇ ㄕㄨˋ)
a denominator (in arithmetic)

母子(ㄇㄨˇ ㄗˇ)
① mother and son ② principal and interest

母子之情(ㄇㄨˇ ㄗˇ ㄓ ㄑㄧㄥˊ)
love between mother and son

母鵝(ㄇㄨˇ ㄜˊ)
a goose (as opposed to a gander)

母愛(ㄇㄨˇ ㄞˋ)
mother love; maternal affection; maternal love

母儀(ㄇㄨˇ ㄧˊ)
the paragon of motherhood

母以子貴(ㄇㄨˇ ㄧˇ ㄗˇ ㄍㄨㄟˋ)
A mother's social position is elevated by the success of her sons.

母鴨(ㄇㄨˇ ㄧㄚ)
a duck (as opposed to a drake)

母液(ㄇㄨˇ ㄧㄝˋ)
(chemistry) mother liquid

母夜叉(ㄇㄨˇ ㄧㄝˋ ㄔㄚ)
① an ugly female devil ② an ugly and fierce woman

母岩(ㄇㄨˇ ㄧㄢˊ)
mother rock

母音(ㄇㄨˇ ㄧㄣ)
a vowel 亦作「元音」

母羊(ㄇㄨˇ ㄧㄤˊ)
a ewe

母語(ㄇㄨˇ ㄩˇ)
① one's mother tongue; one's native language ② a parent language

三畫

【每】 2727
ㄇㄟˇ meei mei
every; each; per: 我們每人都有自己的責任。Each one of us has his duty.

每每(ㄇㄟˇ ㄇㄟˇ)
repeatedly; often: 他每每不在家。He is often not at home.

每飯不忘(ㄇㄟˇ ㄈㄢˋ ㄅㄨˋ ㄨㄤˋ)
to be remembered at every meal

每逢(ㄇㄟˇ ㄈㄥˊ)
every time or whenever (a season, festival or some specific occasion comes)

每逢佳節倍思親(ㄇㄟˇ ㄈㄥˊ ㄐㄧㄚ ㄐㄧㄝˊ ㄅㄟˋ ㄙ ㄑㄧㄣ)
On the happy festival, more than ever we think of our relatives far away.

每當(ㄇㄟˇ ㄉㄤ)
whenever; every time

每天(ㄇㄟˇ ㄊㄧㄢ)

every day; daily: 他們每天
見面。They saw each other
every day.

每年(ㄇㄟ ㄋㄧㄢ)
every year; annually; per
annum; yearly; each year

每隔(ㄇㄟ ㄍㄜ)
every (three hours, five
days, two feet, etc): 他們每
隔二週見一次面。They saw
each other every two weeks.

每下愈況(ㄇㄟ ㄒㄧㄚ ㄩˋ ㄎㄨㄤˋ)or 每
況愈下(ㄇㄟ ㄎㄨㄤˋ ㄩˋ ㄒㄧㄚˋ)
progressively worse; steadily
worse; getting worse and
worse; going from bad to
worse: 現在一切的事情每況愈
下。Things are going from
bad to worse nowadays.

每處(ㄇㄟ ㄔㄨˋ)
everywhere

每日(ㄇㄟ ㄖˋ)
every day; daily: 大多數的報
紙每日出版。Most newspapers
appear daily.

每人(ㄇㄟ ㄖㄣˊ)
everybody; each one; everyone: 每人可以試兩次。Each
man may try twice.

每次(ㄇㄟ ㄘˋ)
every time; each time: 他常
常聽到這個故事, 但他每次都
笑。He has heard the story
often but he laughs every
time.

每月(ㄇㄟ ㄩㄝˋ)
each month; every month;
monthly: 他每月來一次。He
comes here monthly.

【每】 2728
ㄞˇ ae ǎi
adulterous

四畫

【毒】 2729
ㄉㄨˊ dwu dú
1. poison; toxins: 對甲是良藥對
乙卻是劇毒。One man's meat
is another man's poison.
2. poisonous; noxious: 那是隻毒
蜘蛛。It's a poisonous spider.
3. to poison

毒品(ㄉㄨˊ ㄆㄧㄣˇ)
narcotic drugs; narcotics

毒罵(ㄉㄨˊ ㄇㄚˋ)
to scold ferociously and
maliciously; to revile; to rail

at madly

毒打(ㄉㄨˊ ㄉㄚˇ)
to beat cruelly or savagely

毒辣(ㄉㄨˊ ㄌㄚˋ)
cruel; malicious; spiteful: 他
這樣謀害孩童真是毒辣。It's
cruel of him to murder the
child.

毒瘡(ㄉㄨˊ ㄔㄨㄤ)
① an ulcer ② an epidemic

毒瘤(ㄉㄨˊ ㄌㄧㄡˊ)
malignant growth; cancer
growth

毒害(ㄉㄨˊ ㄏㄞˋ)
to injure atrociously; to murder

毒狠(ㄉㄨˊ ㄏㄣˇ)
atrocious; heinous; cruel: 他
真兇狠! How cruel he is!

毒卉(ㄉㄨˊ ㄏㄨㄟˋ)
the poppy

毒計(ㄉㄨˊ ㄐㄧˋ)
a malicious scheme; a deadly trap

毒酒(ㄉㄨˊ ㄐㄧㄡˇ)
poisoned wine

毒氣(ㄉㄨˊ ㄑㄧˋ)
poisonous gas; noxious gas

毒氣彈(ㄉㄨˊ ㄑㄧˋ ㄉㄢˋ)
a gas bomb

毒刑(ㄉㄨˊ ㄒㄧㄥˊ)
cruel punishment; brutal torture

毒性(ㄉㄨˊ ㄒㄧㄥˋ)
toxicity; poisonousness: 他正
在研究殺蟲劑的毒性。He is
studying the toxicity of
insecticides.

毒汁(ㄉㄨˊ ㄓ)
poisonous fluid

毒質(ㄉㄨˊ ㄓˊ)
poisonous matter

毒著兒(ㄉㄨˊ ㄓㄨㄛ ㄦ)
a dirty trick; an odious
scheme; venomous means; a
murderous plan

毒瘴(ㄉㄨˊ ㄓㄤˋ)
miasmas 亦作「瘴氣」

毒蟲(ㄉㄨˊ ㄔㄨㄥˊ)
a poisonous insect

毒殺(ㄉㄨˊ ㄕㄚ)
to poison to death; to kill by
poisoning

毒砂(ㄉㄨˊ ㄕㄚ)
(mining) arsenopyrite

毒蛇(ㄉㄨˊ ㄕㄜˊ)or 毒虺(ㄉㄨˊ ㄏㄨㄟˇ)

a venomous snake: 他被毒蛇
咬傷了。He was bitten by a
venomous snake.

毒手(ㄉㄨˊ ㄕㄡˇ)
an atrocious act; a venomous action; a murderous
scheme (or hand): 他對她下
了毒手。She laid murderous
hands on her.

毒刺(ㄉㄨˊ ㄘˋ)
a venomous sting; a poisonous prick

毒草(ㄉㄨˊ ㄘㄠˇ)
poisonous herbs

毒死(ㄉㄨˊ ㄙˇ)or 毒斃(ㄉㄨˊ ㄅㄧˋ)
to poison to death

毒素(ㄉㄨˊ ㄙㄨˋ)
poisonous matter; toxins

毒餌(ㄉㄨˊ ㄦˇ)
poison bait

毒牙(ㄉㄨˊ ㄧㄚˊ)
a poison fang

毒藥(ㄉㄨˊ ㄧㄠˋ)
poisonous drugs; poison

毒物(ㄉㄨˊ ㄨˋ)
poisonous substance; poison

毒瓦斯(ㄉㄨˊ ㄨㄚˇ ㄙ)
toxic gas; poison gas

九畫

【毓】 2730
ㄩˋ yuh yù
1. to bring up; to rear; to nurture; to nurse
2. to grow

比 部
ㄅㄧˇ bii bǐ

【比】 2731
ㄅㄧˇ bii bǐ
1. to compare with; to be
comparable to: 我的畫不能與
你的比。My painting cannot
be compared with yours.
2. to liken; to compare to: 人生
常被比擬爲朝聖之旅程。Life is
often likened to a pilgrimage.
3. to compete
4. than: 我比他年輕。I am
younger than he.
5. to: 我隊以五比三勝他隊。Our

【比部】

比team beat their team (by a score of) five to two.
比
to liken; to compare to

比不得(ㄅㄧˇ ㄅㄨˋ ㄉㄜˊ)
not to be compared; beyond all comparison

比不上(ㄅㄧˇ ㄅㄨˋ ㄕㄤˋ)
to be inferior to; to be no peer for: 我的英文比不上他。 My English cannot compare with his.

比目魚(ㄅㄧˇ ㄇㄨˋ ㄩˊ)
a flatfish; a sole

比分(ㄅㄧˇ ㄈㄣ)
(sports) score: 現在比分是六比五。 The score is 6 to 5.

比方(ㄅㄧˇ ㄈㄤ)
to liken; to compare to

比方說(ㄅㄧˇ ㄈㄤ ㄕㄨㄛ)
for example; for instance

比附(ㄅㄧˇ ㄈㄨˋ)
to liken; to compare to

比對(ㄅㄧˇ ㄉㄨㄟˋ)
to compare and check; to collate

比擬(ㄅㄧˇ ㄋㄧˇ)
①to liken; to compare to: 她把他的詩比擬彎曲的溪流。 She compared his poetry to a meandering stream. ②a parallel: 這種比擬是不當的。 It is improper to draw such a parallel.

ratio; proportion: 人的智慧和年齡成比例嗎? Are men wise in proportion to their age?

比例尺(ㄅㄧˇ ㄌㄧˋ ㄔˇ)
scale (of a map, model, etc.)

比率(ㄅㄧˇ ㄌㄩˋ)
ratio; proportion: 出生與人口的比率 the proportion of births to the population

比個高低(ㄅㄧˇ ㄍㄜˋ ㄍㄠ ㄉㄧ)
to determine by competition who is the better or stronger of two or more contestants

比號(ㄅㄧˇ ㄏㄠˋ)
the sign of ratio(:)

比畫(ㄅㄧˇ ㄏㄨㄚˋ)
①to gesticulate; to gesture; to use sign language 亦作「比手畫脚」: 她比手畫脚地說著。 She made herself understood

with the help of gestures. ②
to come to blows

比基尼(ㄅㄧˇ ㄐㄧ ㄋㄧˊ)
Bikini Island, a site of many atomic tests

比基尼泳裝(ㄅㄧˇ ㄐㄧ ㄋㄧˊ ㄩㄥˇ ㄓㄨㄤ)
bikini (a very small 2-piece bathing suit for women)

比加(ㄅㄧˇ ㄐㄧㄚ)
belga (a former monetary unit of Belgium)

比價(ㄅㄧˇ ㄐㄧㄚˋ)
to compare prices or bids

比較(ㄅㄧˇ ㄐㄧㄠˋ)or(ㄅㄧˇ ㄐㄧㄠˇ)
①comparative; comparatively; relatively: 近來他的生活過得比較舒適。 He lived in comparative comfort recently.②to compare: 把你的車跟他的車比較一下。 Compare your car with his.

比較級(ㄅㄧˇ ㄐㄧㄠˋ ㄐㄧˊ)
(grammar) the comparative degree

比較值(ㄅㄧˇ ㄐㄧㄠˋ ㄓˊ)
comparative value

比較文學(ㄅㄧˇ ㄐㄧㄠˋ ㄨㄣˊ ㄒㄩㄝˊ)
comparative literature: 嚴先生專攻比較文學。 Mr. Yen majors in comparative literature.

比較語言學(ㄅㄧˇ ㄐㄧㄠˋ ㄩˇ ㄧㄢˊ ㄒㄩㄝˊ)
comparative linguistics

比丘(ㄅㄧˇ ㄑㄧㄡ)
a Buddhist monk

比丘尼(ㄅㄧˇ ㄑㄧㄡ ㄋㄧˊ)
a Buddhist nun

比照(ㄅㄧˇ ㄓㄠˋ)
according to; in the light of: 我們可以比照他們的經驗來擬定我們的計畫。 We can draw up our plan in the light of their experience.

比重(ㄅㄧˇ ㄓㄨㄥˋ)
specific gravity

比重瓶(ㄅㄧˇ ㄓㄨㄥˋ ㄆㄧㄥˊ)
a pycnometer

比重計(ㄅㄧˇ ㄓㄨㄥˋ ㄐㄧˋ)
a hydrometer

比試(ㄅㄧˇ ㄕˋ)
①have a competition ②to measure with one's hand or arm; to make a gesture of measuring

比上不足，比下有餘(ㄅㄧˇ ㄕㄤˋ ㄅㄨˋ ㄗㄨˊ, ㄅㄧˇ ㄒㄧㄚˋ ㄧㄡˇ ㄩˊ)

to be worse off than some but better off than many; to fall short of the best but be better than the worst

比熱(ㄅㄧˇ ㄖㄜˋ)
(physics) specific heat

比如(ㄅㄧˇ ㄖㄨˊ)
such as; like

比薩斜塔(ㄅㄧˇ ㄙㄚ ㄒㄧㄝˊ ㄊㄚˇ)
the (Leaning) Tower of Pisa

比賽(ㄅㄧˇ ㄙㄞˋ)
a contest; a match; a tournament; to compete in contest: 他參加了射擊比賽。 He took part in the shooting contest.

比塞大(ㄅㄧˇ ㄙㄞˋ ㄉㄚˋ)
Bizerta or Bizerte, a North African seaport

比翼(ㄅㄧˇ ㄧˋ)
(to fly) wing to wing—inseparable (said of lovers, or a married couple)

比翼鳥(ㄅㄧˇ ㄧˋ ㄋㄧㄠˇ)
①a spoonbill 亦作「鶼鶼」 a pair of lovebirds; a pair of birds with the wings of one—a devoted couple

比翼雙飛(ㄅㄧˇ ㄧˋ ㄕㄨㄤ ㄈㄟ)
to fly side by side

比一比(ㄅㄧˇ ㄧ ㄅㄧˇ)
①to make a comparison ②to engage in a contest; to have a contest

比武(ㄅㄧˇ ㄨˇ)
to demonstrate fighting skills in a tournament; to contest in physical prowess

比喻(ㄅㄧˇ ㄩˋ)
①a metaphor; a figure of speech; a simile: 這不過是個比喻之辭。 This is just a figure of speech. ②to compare to; to liken: 人生常被比喻成海上的旅程。 Man's life is often likened to a sea voyage.

【比】 2731
2. ㄅㄧˋ bih bì
1. close; near; neighboring
2. to stand side by side

比比皆是(ㄅㄧˇ ㄅㄧˇ ㄐㄧㄝ ㄕˋ)
to be found or seen everywhere—very common; a common sight: 中國的名詩人比比皆是。 Famous Chinese poets can be found everywhere.

比匪(ㄅㄧˇ ㄈㄟˇ)
to associate with bad characters

比年(ㄅㄧˇ ㄋㄧㄢˊ)or 比歲(ㄅㄧˇ ㄙㄨㄟˋ)
① recent years ② every year

比來(ㄅㄧˇ ㄌㄞˊ)
recently; lately

比聯(ㄅㄧˇ ㄌㄧㄢˊ)
to adjoin each other (as lands, etc.)

比鄰(ㄅㄧˇ ㄌㄧㄣˊ)
close neighbors

比及(ㄅㄧˇ ㄐㄧˊ)
up to the time when; by the time when

比肩(ㄅㄧˇ ㄐㄧㄢ)
side by side; shoulder to shoulder: 他們比肩而行。They walked side by side.

比肩作戰(ㄅㄧˇ ㄐㄧㄢ ㄗㄨㄛˋ ㄓㄢˋ)
to fight shoulder to shoulder

比親(ㄅㄧˇ ㄑㄧㄣ)
intimate; close

比舍(ㄅㄧˇ ㄕㄜˋ)
the next-door house; the neighboring house; the adjacent house

比屋(ㄅㄧˇ ㄨ)
houses adjoining each other

五畫

【毖】 2732
ㄅㄧˋ bih bì
1. cautious; caution; to guard against; judicious
2. (said of springs) flowing; gushing

【毗】 2733
ㄆㄧˊ pyi pí
1. to assist
2. to adjoin: 運動場與學校毗連。The playing field adjoins the school.

毗尼(ㄆㄧˊ ㄋㄧˊ)
(Buddhism) vinaya; the precepts and commands of moral asceticism and monastic discipline (said to have been given by Buddha)

毗連(ㄆㄧˊ ㄌㄧㄢˊ)
(of lands) to adjoin each other; adjacent to: 加拿大和美國毗連。Canada adjoins the United States.

毗倚(ㄆㄧˊ ㄧˇ)
to depend upon; to rely upon

十三畫

【毚】 2734
ㄔㄢˊ charn chán
1. cunning; crafty
2. greedy

毚兔(ㄔㄢˊ ㄊㄨˋ)
a crafty hare

毚欲(ㄔㄢˊ ㄩˋ)
greed; avarice

毛 部
ㄇㄠˊ mau máo

【毛】 2735
ㄇㄠˊ mau máo
1. hair; fur; feathers; down: 我的狗長得一身好毛。My dog has a good coat of hair.
2. vegetation
3. ten cents; a dime: 他們幾乎連一毛錢也沒有賺到。They made hardly a dime.
4. gross; untouched; unpolished
5. panic-stricken; scared; flurried: 他心裡直發毛。He felt scared.
6. very young; little: 他只是個毛孩子。He's only a little child.
7. a Chinese family name

毛玻璃(ㄇㄠˊ ㄅㄛ ㄌㄧ)
frosted glass

毛包(ㄇㄠˊ ㄅㄠ)
a simple, unpolished person

毛筆(ㄇㄠˊ ㄅㄧˇ)
a writing brush; a hair pencil

毛筆畫(ㄇㄠˊ ㄅㄧˇ ㄏㄨㄚˋ)
drawings done with a writing brush

毛邊紙(ㄇㄠˊ ㄅㄧㄢ ㄓˇ)
a kind of paper made from bamboo pulp, which was widely used in old China

毛病(ㄇㄠˊ ㄅㄧㄥˋ)
① fault; defects; shortcoming; blemish: 這篇文章有小毛病。There are some small mistakes in the article.② trouble; disorder: 這架電視機有點毛病。There's something wrong with the television.③ disease; illness; trouble: 她胃有毛病。She has stomach trouble.

毛病百出(ㄇㄠˊ ㄅㄧㄥˋ ㄅㄞˇ ㄔㄨ)
glitched-filled

毛坯(ㄇㄠˊ ㄆㄧ)
① earthenware that is not baked yet ② a half-finished product; raw products

毛皮(ㄇㄠˊ ㄆㄧˊ)
fur; pelt

毛毛蟲(ㄇㄠˊ ㄇㄠˊ ㄔㄨㄥˊ)
a caterpillar 亦作「毛蟲」

毛毛雨(ㄇㄠˊ ㄇㄠˊ ㄩˇ)
drizzle

毛髮(ㄇㄠˊ ㄈㄚˇ)
body hairs and hair

毛紡廠(ㄇㄠˊ ㄈㄤˇ ㄔㄤˇ)
a woolen textile mill

毛豆(ㄇㄠˊ ㄉㄡˋ)
① green or tender soybeans ② young soybeans

毛桃(ㄇㄠˊ ㄊㄠˊ)
a kind of small peach; a wild peach

毛頭(ㄇㄠˊ ㄊㄡˊ)
a youngster; a child

毛毯(ㄇㄠˊ ㄊㄢˇ)
a woolen blanket: 他圍著一條毛毯。He wrapped his woolen blanket around him.

毛里斯(ㄇㄠˊ ㄌㄧˇ ㄙ)
Mauritius Island, off the east African coast 亦作「模里西斯」

毛利(ㄇㄠˊ ㄌㄧˋ)
gross earnings; gross profit

毛料(ㄇㄠˊ ㄌㄧㄠˋ)
woolen material

毛驢(ㄇㄠˊ ㄌㄩˊ)
a young donkey

毛茛(ㄇㄠˊ ㄍㄣˋ)
(botany) a crowfoot; a buttercup

毛骨悚然(ㄇㄠˊ ㄍㄨˇ ㄙㄨㄥˇ ㄖㄢˊ)
to shudder with fear; to be horror-stricken; to make one's hair stand on end

毛公鼎(ㄇㄠˊ ㄍㄨㄥ ㄉㄧㄥˇ)
name of a bronze tripod cast in the Chou Dynasty, famed for its inscribed characters

毛褲(ㄇㄠˊ ㄎㄨˋ)
long woolen underwear

毛孔(ㄇㄠˊ ㄎㄨㄥˇ)
pores (of the skin): 汗由皮膚上的毛孔流出來。Sweat comes through the pores in the

〔毛部〕

skin.

毛孩子(ㄇㄠˊ ㄏㄞ ·ㄗ)
a child

【毛】部

毛巾(ㄇㄠˊ ㄐㄧㄣ)
①a towel: 我用毛巾擦乾自己。I dried myself on a towel. ②a woolen muffler

毛舉(ㄇㄠˊ ㄐㄩˇ)
①to cite at random ②to list or cite trifles

毛奇(ㄇㄠˊ ㄑㄧˊ)
Helmuth Karl Bernhard, Count von Moltke, 1800-1891, a famous Prussian general

毛嬙西施(ㄇㄠˊ ㄑㄧㄤˊ ㄒㄧ ㄕ)
Mao Chiang and Hsi Shih, famous beauties in ancient China, now used as synonymous terms of very beautiful women

毛細管(ㄇㄠˊ ㄒㄧˋ ㄍㄨㄢˇ)
a capillary tube; a capillary

毛細現象(ㄇㄠˊ ㄒㄧˋ ㄒㄧㄢˋ ㄒㄧㄤˋ)
capillary action; capillary attraction and repulsion

毛線(ㄇㄠˊ ㄒㄧㄢˋ)
woolen yarn; knitting wool

毛線衣(ㄇㄠˊ ㄒㄧㄢˋ ㄧ)
a knitted woolen garment; a sweater; wool: 他冬天穿毛線衣。He wears wool in winter.

毛織物(ㄇㄠˊ ㄓ ㄨˋ)or 毛織品(ㄇㄠˊ ㄓ ㄆㄧㄣˇ)
woolen textiles; woolen goods; woolen stuff; woolen fabrics; wool: 我們通常在冬天穿毛織品。We usually wear wool in winter.

毛氈(ㄇㄠˊ ㄓㄢ)
①a woolen carpet ②felt: 那是用毛氈製的。It is made of felt.

毛蟲(ㄇㄠˊ ㄔㄨㄥˊ)
①a caterpillar ②wild beasts

毛蝨(ㄇㄠˊ ㄕ)
a crab louse

毛詩(ㄇㄠˊ ㄕ)
the Book of Odes as edited by Mao Heng (毛亨)in the Han Dynasty

毛手毛腳(ㄇㄠˊ ㄕㄡˇ ㄇㄠˊ ㄐㄧㄠˇ)
①restless; uneasy; unquiet ②to take liberties with a woman by the actions of one's hands

hair on a plant

毛茸茸(ㄇㄠˊ ㄖㄨㄥˊ ㄖㄨㄥˊ)
hairy; downy: 他有雙毛茸茸的手。He has hairy hands.

毛子(ㄇㄠˊ ·ㄗ)
①a hairy fellow—a Westerner ②the tuft of hair on a child's head

毛躁(ㄇㄠˊ ㄗㄠˋ)
①irritable: 她近來毛躁得很。She has been very irritable lately. ②rash and restless: 他是毛躁的年輕人。He's a rash young man.

毛瑟(ㄇㄠˊ ㄙㄜˋ ㄑㄧˇ)
a mauser

毛遂自薦(ㄇㄠˊ ㄙㄨㄟˋ ㄗˋ ㄐㄧㄢˋ)
to recommend oneself, to volunteer for a task—a common allusion to Mao Sui (毛遂) of the Warring States Period, who recommended himself to a post

毛筍(ㄇㄠˊ ㄙㄨㄣˇ)
the shoot of a variety of bamboo

毛髮(ㄇㄠˊ ㄈㄚˇ)
hairs

毛衣(ㄇㄠˊ ㄧ)
woolen sweaters; sweaters: 我的毛衣是羊毛製的。My sweater is made of wool.

毛丫頭(ㄇㄠˊ ㄧㄚ ·ㄊㄡ)
a little girl

毛穎(ㄇㄠˊ ㄧㄥˇ)
a writing brush

毛襪(ㄇㄠˊ ㄨㄚˋ)
woolen stockings

毛羽(ㄇㄠˊ ㄩˇ)
fur and feathers

六畫

【毬】 2736
ㄖㄨㄥˊ rong róng
1. fine hair; down
2. felt

毬帽(ㄖㄨㄥˊ ㄇㄠˋ)
a felt cap or hat

毬鞋(ㄖㄨㄥˊ ㄒㄧㄝˊ)
felt shoes

七畫

【毫】 2737
ㄏㄠˊ haur hóo

1. fine hair
2. a measure of length
3. a writing brush: 狼毫a writing brush made of wolf's hair
4. a dime
5. a measure of weight
6. a Chinese family name

毫巴(ㄏㄠˊ ㄅㄚ)
(meteorology) millibar, a unit of atmospheric pressure

毫不(ㄏㄠˊ ㄅㄨˋ)
not at all; not in the least: 這消息毫不足怪。This news is not at all surprising.

毫不相干(ㄏㄠˊ ㄅㄨˋ ㄒㄧㄤ ㄍㄢ)
totally unrelated; completely irrelevant

毫不在乎(ㄏㄠˊ ㄅㄨˋ ㄗㄞˋ ㄏㄨ ·ㄈㄨˊ)
completely unperturbed; not at all perturbed; do not mind or care at all

毫末(ㄏㄠˊ ㄇㄛˋ)
extremely small parts; minute elements

毫毛(ㄏㄠˊ ㄇㄠˊ)
the fine hair on human skin: 他們的威脅無損於我們一根毫毛。Their threats can't harm a single hair of our head.

毫芒(ㄏㄠˊ ㄇㄤˊ)
extremely tiny parts

毫米(ㄏㄠˊ ㄇㄧˇ)
millimeter (mm.), a unit of length

毫秒(ㄏㄠˊ ㄇㄧㄠˇ)
a millisecond

毫髮(ㄏㄠˊ ㄈㄚˇ)
extremely little

毫髮不爽(ㄏㄠˊ ㄈㄚˇ ㄅㄨˋ ㄕㄨㄤˇ ㄇㄜˋ)
There is not even slightest deviation. 或 It does not deviate a hair's breath. 或It's perfectly accurate.

毫釐(ㄏㄠˊ ㄌㄧˊ)
extremely small space; hair-breadth; an iota

毫釐不差(ㄏㄠˊ ㄌㄧˊ ㄅㄨˋ ㄔㄚ)
without the slightest error

毫釐千里(ㄏㄠˊ ㄌㄧˊ ㄑㄧㄢ ㄌㄧˇ)
An error by a hairbreadth may eventually result in an error of a thousand miles.

毫克(ㄏㄠˊ ㄎㄜˋ)
milligram (mg.), a unit of mass or weight

毫升(ㄏㄠˊ ㄕㄥ)

milliliter (ml.), a unit of capacity

毫素 (ㄏㄠˊ ㄙㄨˋ)
the writing brush and writing paper

毫無 (ㄏㄠˊ ㄨˊ)
not at all; not in the least

毫無可取 (ㄏㄠˊ ㄨˊ ㄎㄜˇ ㄑㄩˇ)
totally worthless

毫無價值 (ㄏㄠˊ ㄨˊ ㄐㄧㄚˋ ㄓˊ)
good for nothing: 一支破了的溫度計是毫無價值的。 A broken thermometer is good for nothing.

毫無誠意 (ㄏㄠˊ ㄨˊ ㄔㄥˊ ㄧˋ)
to have no sincerity at all

毫無疑問 (ㄏㄠˊ ㄨˊ ㄧˊ ㄨㄣˋ)
There is no doubt.

【毬】 2738
ㄑㄧㄡˊ chyou qiú
a ball; a sphere

毬果 (ㄑㄧㄡˊ ㄍㄨㄛˇ)
cones (of pines, spruces, etc.); strobiles

八畫

【毯】 2739
ㄊㄢˇ taan tǎn
a rug; a carpet; a blanket: 地板上鋪着地毯。 The floor is covered with a carpet.

毯子 (ㄊㄢˇ ˙ㄗ)
a rug; a carpet; a blanket: 他肩上一條厚毛毯子。 He wrapped a woolen rug around him.

【毳】 2740
ㄘㄨㄟˋ tsuey cuì
fine feathers or fur

毳毛 (ㄘㄨㄟˋ ㄇㄠˊ)
fine feathers or fur

毳冕 (ㄘㄨㄟˋ ㄇㄧㄢˇ)
imperial costume for worship of nature

毳幕 (ㄘㄨㄟˋ ㄇㄨˋ)or 毳帳 (ㄘㄨㄟˋ ㄓㄤˋ)
a felt curtain; a felt tent

毳衣 (ㄘㄨㄟˋ ㄧ)
① a kind of elaborate garment woven of down or fur ② a garment woven of feathers and worn by Buddhist monks

九畫

【毽】 2741
ㄐㄧㄢˋ jiann jiàn
a shuttlecock: 雞毛毽 a shuttlecock made of chicken feathers

毽子 (ㄐㄧㄢˋ ˙ㄗ)
a shuttlecock

十一畫

【氂】 2742
ㄌㄧ li lí
ㄇㄠ mau máo
1. a horse tail
2. long hair; thick hair
3. a yak

氂牛 (ㄇㄠˊ ㄋㄧㄡˊ)
a yak 亦作「犛牛」

十二畫

【氅】 2743
ㄔㄤˇ chaang chǎng
a garment woven of down

氅衣 (ㄔㄤˇ ㄧ)
① an outer garment; a coat ② the costume of the Taoist priest

【氄】 2744
ㄖㄨㄥˇ roong rǒng
1. fine hair
2. fine; soft

氄毛兒 (ㄖㄨㄥˇ ㄇㄠˊ ㄦ)
fine hair

氄刺 (ㄖㄨㄥˇ ㄘˋ)
fine fishbones

十三畫

【氈】 2745
(毡、氊) ㄓㄢ jan zhān
1. felt
2. a blanket

氈帽 (ㄓㄢ ㄇㄠˋ)
a felt cap or hat

氈帳 (ㄓㄢ ㄓㄤˋ)
a felt tent

氈毯 (ㄓㄢ ㄊㄢˇ)
a felt rug

氈笠 (ㄓㄢ ㄌㄧˋ)
a felt hat with broad rim

氈裘 (ㄓㄢ ㄑㄧㄡˊ)
① a felt garment worn by the nomad people in the north ② the chieftain of the nomads

氈裘之君 (ㄓㄢ ㄑㄧㄡˊ ㄓ ㄐㄩㄣ)
a nomad chieftain

氈鞋 (ㄓㄢ ㄒㄧㄝˊ)
felt shoes

氈子 (ㄓㄢ ˙ㄗ)
felt

氏 部
ㄕˋ shyh shì

【氏】 2746
1. ㄕˋ shyh shì
1. family name; surname: 陳氏兄弟 the Chen brothers
2. a character placed after a married woman's maiden name; nee: 夫人林氏 his wife née Lin
3. the title of a government position in former times

氏譜 (ㄕˋ ㄆㄨˇ)
a family tree; lineage; a genealogy

氏族 (ㄕˋ ㄗㄨˊ)
a family; a clan

氏族制度 (ㄕˋ ㄗㄨˊ ㄓˋ ㄉㄨˋ)
the clan system

【氏】 2746
2. ㄓ jy zhī
name of an ancient barbarian tribe 參看「月氏」

一畫

【氐】 2747
1. ㄉㄧ di dī
1. name of an ancient barbarian tribe to the west
2. same as 低—low

氐羌 (ㄉㄧ ㄑㄧㄤ)
ancient barbarian tribes to the west

【氐】 2747
2. ㄉㄧˇ dii dǐ
1. foundation
2. same as 抵—on the whole

【民】 2748
ㄇㄧㄣˊ min mín
1. the people; the subject; the populace; the public: 他們爲民除害。 They rid the people of a scourge.
2. civilians: 我們實施軍民聯防。 We are making joint defense by army and civilians.

〔氏部〕

〔氏部〕

3. a Chinese family name

民胞物與(ㄇㄧㄣ ㄅㄠ ㄨˋ ㄩˇ)
to be kind to people and animals

民辦(ㄇㄧㄣ ㄅㄢˋ)
privately operated; privately owned; nongovernmental: 那是一所民辦中學。That is a high school run by the local people.

民本主義(ㄇㄧㄣ ㄅㄣˇ ㄓㄨˇ ㄧˋ)
democracy

民兵(ㄇㄧㄣ ㄅㄧㄥ)
① a militiaman ② a militia force

民不聊生(ㄇㄧㄣ ㄅㄨˋ ㄌㄧㄠˊ ㄕㄥ)
The people cannot live in peace. 或 The people are living in misery.

民不堪命(ㄇㄧㄣ ㄅㄨˋ ㄎㄢ ㄇㄧㄥˋ)
The people cannot stand the pressure of the government. 或 The people are hard pressed.

民瘼(ㄇㄧㄣ ㄇㄛˋ)
sufferings of the people

民母(ㄇㄧㄣ ㄇㄨˇ)
① the queen ② my mother (a reference used in speaking to judges in former times)

民法(ㄇㄧㄣ ㄈㄚˇ)
the civil law; the civil code

民憤(ㄇㄧㄣ ㄈㄣˋ)
public wrath; popular hatred: 此事引起極大的民憤。It has aroused the bitter indignation of the people.

民房(ㄇㄧㄣ ㄈㄤˊ)
a private house; a civilian house

民風(ㄇㄧㄣ ㄈㄥ)
customs of the people; popular customs

民夫(ㄇㄧㄣ ㄈㄨ)
① a laborer drafted for government service ② my husband (a reference used in speaking to judges in former times)

民田(ㄇㄧㄣ ㄊㄧㄢˊ)
people's farmland

民庭(ㄇㄧㄣ ㄊㄧㄥˊ)
a civil court 亦作「民事法庭」

民團(ㄇㄧㄣ ㄊㄨㄢˊ)
a posse; a paramilitary unit organized by a community for self-defense

民力(ㄇㄧㄣ ㄌㄧˋ)
① the means of the people ② people's labor

民歌(ㄇㄧㄣ ㄍㄜ)
a folk song; a ballad

民國(ㄇㄧㄣ ㄍㄨㄛˊ)
① a republic; a democracy ② the Republic of China, founded in 1912

民貴君輕(ㄇㄧㄣ ㄍㄨㄟˋ ㄐㄩㄣ ㄑㄧㄥ)
The people are more important than the ruler. (a concept upheld by Mencius)

民可使由之，不可使知之(ㄇㄧㄣ ㄎㄜˇ ㄕˇ ㄧㄡˊ ㄓ，ㄅㄨˋ ㄎㄜˇ ㄕˇ ㄓ ㄓ)
The people should be told to do this or that without telling them why.

民瘼(ㄇㄧㄣ ㄏㄠˋ)
a scourge or calamity to the people; evils to the common people

民航(ㄇㄧㄣ ㄏㄤˊ)
civil aviation

民航機(ㄇㄧㄣ ㄏㄤˊ ㄐㄧ)
an airliner; a civil airplane (or aircraft)

民航局(ㄇㄧㄣ ㄏㄤˊ ㄐㄩˊ)
Civil Aeronautics Administration (CAA)

民間(ㄇㄧㄣ ㄐㄧㄢ)
among the people: 這首歌謠長久地在民間流傳。For generations this ballad has circulated among the people.

民間故事(ㄇㄧㄣ ㄐㄧㄢ ㄍㄨˋ ㄕˋ)
folktales; folklore

民間疾苦(ㄇㄧㄣ ㄐㄧㄢ ㄐㄧˊ ㄎㄨˇ)
the hardships of the people: 他深知民間疾苦。He understood the hardships of the people.

民間藝術(ㄇㄧㄣ ㄐㄧㄢ ㄧˋ ㄕㄨˋ)
folk art

民間音樂(ㄇㄧㄣ ㄐㄧㄢ ㄧㄣ ㄩㄝˋ)
folk music

民間文學(ㄇㄧㄣ ㄐㄧㄢ ㄨㄣˊ ㄒㄩㄝˊ)
folk literature; popular literature

民妻(ㄇㄧㄣ ㄑㄧ)
my wife (a reference used in speaking to judges in former times)

民氣(ㄇㄧㄣ ㄑㄧˋ)
morale or spirit of the people

民情(ㄇㄧㄣ ㄑㄧㄥˊ)
the condition of the people

民權(ㄇㄧㄣ ㄑㄩㄢˊ)
civil rights; people's rights

民權主義(ㄇㄧㄣ ㄑㄩㄢˊ ㄓㄨˇ ㄧˋ)
The Principle of the People's Rights (one of The Three Principles of the People)

民權初步(ㄇㄧㄣ ㄑㄩㄢˊ ㄔㄨ ㄅㄨˋ)
The Fundamental Knowledge in Democracy, a book dealing with the procedures of the parliamentary rule, authored by Dr. Sun Yat-sen

民窮財盡(ㄇㄧㄣ ㄑㄩㄥˊ ㄘㄞˊ ㄐㄧㄣˋ)
The means of the people have been used up (due to government exploitation or heavy spending).

民心(ㄇㄧㄣ ㄒㄧㄣ)
popular sentiments; popular support: 他深得民心。He wins the ardent support of the people.

民選(ㄇㄧㄣ ㄒㄩㄢˇ)
popularly elected

民脂民膏(ㄇㄧㄣ ㄓ ㄇㄧㄣ ㄍㄠ)
the hard-won possessions of the people; the fruits of people's toil

民治(ㄇㄧㄣ ㄓˋ)
government by the people

民智(ㄇㄧㄣ ㄓˋ)
intelligence of the people

民政(ㄇㄧㄣ ㄓㄥˋ)
civil administration

民政廳(ㄇㄧㄣ ㄓㄥˋ ㄊㄧㄥ)
Department of Civil Affairs

民主(ㄇㄧㄣ ㄓㄨˇ)
democratic; democracy: 美國的學校是民主的。Schools in the United States are democratic.

民主黨(ㄇㄧㄣ ㄓㄨˇ ㄉㄤˇ)
Democratic Party (of the United States)

民主政體(ㄇㄧㄣ ㄓㄨˇ ㄓㄥˋ ㄊㄧˇ)
democratic government; democracy

民主政治(ㄇㄧㄣ ㄓㄨˇ ㄓㄥˋ ㄓˋ)
democracy

民主主義(ㄇㄧㄣ ㄓㄨˇ ㄓㄨˇ ㄧˋ)
democratism

民主潮流(ㄇㄧㄣ ㄓㄨˇ ㄔㄠˊ ㄌㄧㄡˊ)
the tide of democracy

民主社會黨(ㄇㄧㄣ ㄓㄨˇ ㄕㄜˋ ㄏㄨㄟˋ)or民社黨(ㄇㄧㄣ ㄕㄜˋ ㄉㄤˇ)
China Democratic Socialist Party

民眾(ㄇㄧㄣ ㄓㄨˋ)
the people; the common people; the multitude; the masses; the populace

民眾團體(ㄇㄧㄣ ㄓㄨˋ ㄊㄨㄢˊ ㄊㄧˇ)
a civic organization; a mass organization; a civic body

民眾教育(ㄇㄧㄣ ㄓㄨˋ ㄐㄧㄠˋ ㄩˋ)
education of the masses; adult education

民初(ㄇㄧㄣ ㄔㄨ)
in the early republican years; in the early days of the Republic of China

民師(ㄇㄧㄣ ㄕ)
a model or teacher of the people

民食(ㄇㄧㄣ ㄕˊ)
foodstuff for the people; provisions for the people

民時(ㄇㄧㄣ ㄕˊ)
the farming season

民事(ㄇㄧㄣ ㄕˋ)
① civil affairs ② agricultural affairs

民事訴訟法(ㄇㄧㄣ ㄕˋ ㄙㄨˋ ㄙㄨㄥˋ ㄈㄚˇ)
the code of civil procedures

民生(ㄇㄧㄣ ㄕㄥ)
the people's livelihood: 戰爭使得民生凋敝。The war has reduced the people to destitution.

民生主義(ㄇㄧㄣ ㄕㄥ ㄓㄨˇ ㄧˋ)
The Principle of the People's Livelihood (one of The Three Principles of the People)

民生在勤(ㄇㄧㄣ ㄕㄥ ㄗㄞˋ ㄑㄧㄣˊ)
To live well, one must work diligently.

民生物資(ㄇㄧㄣ ㄕㄥ ㄨˋ ㄗ)
daily necessities; goods essential to daily living

民生問題(ㄇㄧㄣ ㄕㄥ ㄨㄣˋ ㄊㄧˊ)
problems of the people's livelihood

民賊(ㄇㄧㄣ ㄗㄟˊ)
a public enemy; a traitor to the people

民族(ㄇㄧㄣ ㄗㄨˊ)
a nation; a people: 中國人是個勤勞的民族。The Chinese are a hard-working people.

民族革命(ㄇㄧㄣ ㄗㄨˊ ㄍㄜˊ ㄇㄧㄥˋ)
a national revolution

民族性(ㄇㄧㄣ ㄗㄨˊ ㄒㄧㄥˋ)
national character

民族學(ㄇㄧㄣ ㄗㄨˊ ㄒㄩㄝˊ)
ethnology

民族至上(ㄇㄧㄣ ㄗㄨˊ ㄓˋ ㄕㄤˋ)
(slogan) the nation above all

民族主義(ㄇㄧㄣ ㄗㄨˊ ㄓㄨˇ ㄧˋ)
① The Principle of Nationalism (one of The Three Principles of the People) ② nationalism

民族自決(ㄇㄧㄣ ㄗㄨˊ ㄗˋ ㄐㄩㄝˊ)
national self-determination

民族意識(ㄇㄧㄣ ㄗㄨˊ ㄧˋ ㄕˋ)
national consciousness

民族英雄(ㄇㄧㄣ ㄗㄨˊ ㄧㄥ ㄒㄩㄥˊ)
a national hero: 他是位民族英雄。He was a national hero.

民族舞蹈(ㄇㄧㄣ ㄗㄨˊ ㄨˇ ㄉㄠˋ)
race dance

民族運動(ㄇㄧㄣ ㄗㄨˊ ㄩㄣˋ ㄉㄨㄥˋ)
a national movement

民俗(ㄇㄧㄣ ㄙㄨˊ)
folkways; customs and practices of the people

民俗學(ㄇㄧㄣ ㄙㄨˊ ㄒㄩㄝˊ)
folklore

民以食為天(ㄇㄧㄣ ㄧˇ ㄕˊ ㄨㄟˊ ㄊㄧㄢ)
To the people foodstuff is all-important.

民意(ㄇㄧㄣ ㄧˋ)
popular sentiments; public opinion; the will of the people

民意代表(ㄇㄧㄣ ㄧˋ ㄉㄞˋ ㄅㄧㄠˇ)
people's representatives; parliamentarians

民意機關(ㄇㄧㄣ ㄧˋ ㄐㄧ ㄍㄨㄢ)
the people's representative body

民意測驗(ㄇㄧㄣ ㄧˋ ㄘㄜˋ ㄧㄢˋ)
a poll; polltaking; a public opinion survey

民謠(ㄇㄧㄣ ㄧㄠˊ)
a folk song

民有,民治,民享(ㄇㄧㄣ ㄧㄡˇ, ㄇㄧㄣ ㄓˋ, ㄇㄧㄣ ㄒㄧㄤˇ)
of the people, by the people, and for the people

民隱(ㄇㄧㄣ ㄧㄣˇ)
the distress of the people unknown to the authorities

民營(ㄇㄧㄣ ㄧㄥˊ)
privately owned

民惟邦本 or 民為邦本(ㄇㄧㄣ ㄨㄟˊ ㄅㄤ ㄅㄣˇ)
The people are the foundation of the state.

民望(ㄇㄧㄣ ㄨㄤˋ)
① popular expectation; popularity among the people ② an example to be observed by people

民約論(ㄇㄧㄣ ㄩㄝ ㄌㄨㄣˋ)
the Doctrine of Social Contract by Jean Jacques Rousseau

民怨沸騰(ㄇㄧㄣ ㄩㄢˋ ㄈㄟˋ ㄊㄥˊ)
Discontent among the people is boiling. 或 Public resentment is seething.

民運(ㄇㄧㄣ ㄩㄣˋ)
① civil transport ② democratic movement

民用機場(ㄇㄧㄣ ㄩㄥˋ ㄐㄧ ㄔㄤˇ)or(ㄇㄧㄣ ㄩㄥˋ ㄐㄧ ㄔㄤˇ)
a civil airport

四畫

【氓】 2749
1. (ㄇㄥˊ) ㄇㄥˊ meng ㄇㄥˊ méng
the people; the populace

氓隷(ㄇㄥˊ ㄌㄧˋ)
people who are engaged in laborious work

【氓】 2749
2. ㄇㄤˊ mang máng
a rascal; a vagabond: 他們是城裏的流氓。They are city rascals.

气 部
ㄑㄧˋ chih qì

二畫

【氖】 2750
ㄋㄞˇ nae nǎi
neon

氖燈(ㄋㄞˇ ㄉㄥ)
a neon lamp; a neon light; a neon sign 亦作「霓虹燈」

【气部】

四畫

【氛】 2751
ㄈㄣ fen fēn
air; atmosphere; prevailing mood: 鄉下有一種寧靜的氣氛。There's an atmosphere of peace in the country.

氛厲(ㄈㄣ ㄌㄧ)
disasters; calamities

氛邪(ㄈㄣ ㄒㄧㄝˊ)
an evil air

氛翳(ㄈㄣ ㄧˋ)
an inauspicious and foreboding atmosphere

氛圍(ㄈㄣ ㄨㄟˊ)
air; atmosphere; mood

氛氳(ㄈㄣ ㄩㄣ)
the spirit, or atmosphere, of prosperity or propitiousness; a vigorous spirit; a vigorous atmosphere

五畫

【氟】 2752
ㄈㄨ fwu fú
fluorine

氟化作用(ㄈㄨ ㄏㄨㄚˋ ㄗㄨㄛˋ ㄩㄥˋ)
fluorination

氟化物(ㄈㄨ ㄏㄨㄚˋ ㄨˋ)
(chemistry) fluoride

六畫

【氣】 2753
ㄑㄧˋ chih qì
1. air; gas; vapor; the atmosphere: 我們必須呼吸新鮮空氣。We must breathe fresh air.
2. breath: 他深沉地吸了一口氣。He took a deep breath.
3. spirit; morale: 士氣消沉(or 極佳)。The morale of the troops is low (or perfect).
4. influence
5. bearing; manner
6. smells; odors: 玫瑰發出香味。Roses smell sweet.
7. to be angry; to be indignant; rage; anger: 他氣得直哆嗦。He trembled with rage.
8. to provoke; to goad; to make angry; to annoy: 他故意氣你一下。He was deliberately to annoy you.
9. weather: 秋高氣爽 fine

autumn weather

氣瓣(ㄑㄧˋ ㄅㄢˋ)
an air valve

氣不平(ㄑㄧˋ ㄅㄨˋ ㄆㄧㄥˊ)
to be indignant about unfairness or injustice

氣魄(ㄑㄧˋ ㄆㄛˋ)
spirit; vigor; broadness of mind; moral strength

氣派(ㄑㄧˋ ㄆㄞˋ)
a dignified air; an impressive style or manner

氣泡(ㄑㄧˋ ㄆㄠˋ)
air bubbles: 氣泡破了。The bubble has burst.

氣門(ㄑㄧˋ ㄇㄣˊ)
①an air valve; an air escape ②(zoology) a stigma

氣悶(ㄑㄧˋ ㄇㄣ)
stifling; sultry; oppressive

氣氛(ㄑㄧˋ ㄈㄣ)
atmosphere; mood: 研討會的氣氛始終很熱烈。The atmosphere was lively throughout the seminar.

氣忿 or 氣憤(ㄑㄧˋ ㄈㄣˋ)
to be angry; to be furious; to be enraged; to be indignant: 大家對這樣的誣告感到氣憤。Everybody was indignant at such a false accusation.

氣忿忿(ㄑㄧˋ ㄈㄣˋ ㄈㄣˋ)
furious; angry; enraged; mad; wrathful

氣墊(ㄑㄧˋ ㄉㄧㄢˋ)
an air cushion (or mattress)

氣度(ㄑㄧˋ ㄉㄨˋ)
①spirit; air; bearing; manner: 氣度非凡。He has an impressive manner.②capacity for tolerance

氣短(ㄑㄧˋ ㄉㄨㄢˇ)
①to be short of breath; to pant ②to be disappointed; to be discouraged: 失敗並未使林先生氣短。Mr. Lin was not discouraged by failure.

氣頭上(ㄑㄧˋ ㄊㄡˊ ㄕㄤ)
right in the middle of one's fit of rage

氣體(ㄑㄧˋ ㄊㄧˇ)
gas; the gaseous body; vapor: 空氣是許多氣體的混合物。Air is a mixture of gases.

氣體動力論(ㄑㄧˋ ㄊㄧˇ ㄉㄨㄥˋ ㄌㄧˋ ㄌㄨㄣˋ)
the kinetic theory of gases

氣體動力學(ㄑㄧˋ ㄊㄧˇ ㄉㄨㄥˋ ㄌㄧˋ ㄒㄩㄝˊ)or 氣體力學(ㄑㄧˋ ㄊㄧˇ ㄌㄧˋ ㄒㄩㄝˊ)
aerodynamics; pneumatics

氣團(ㄑㄧˋ ㄊㄨㄢˊ)
a mass of cold or hot air: 冷氣團 a cold air mass

氣吞山河(ㄑㄧˋ ㄊㄨㄣ ㄕㄢ ㄏㄜˊ)
(descriptive of warriors) to be filled with vehemence that can conquer mountains and rivers—full of daring

氣筒(ㄑㄧˋ ㄊㄨㄥˇ)or 氣筒子(ㄑㄧˋ ㄊㄨㄥˇ ㄗˇ)
an air pump; an inflator; a bicycle pump

氣餒(ㄑㄧˋ ㄋㄟˇ)
discouraged; despondent; crestfallen: 失敗並沒有使她氣餒。She was not discouraged by failure.

氣惱(ㄑㄧˋ ㄋㄠˇ)
to be sulky; to be sullen; to take offense; to be resentful: 不要因細故而氣惱。Don't be sulky about trifles.

氣囊(ㄑㄧˋ ㄋㄤˊ)
the air bladder (of fish); the air sac (of birds or plants); the gasbag or envelope (of a dirigible)

氣逆(ㄑㄧˋ ㄋㄧˋ)
(Chinese herb medicine) the supposed upward motion of the spirit

氣力(ㄑㄧˋ ㄌㄧˋ)
strength; effort; energy: 他們花了很大的氣力完成了這項任務。They exerted great efforts to accomplish the duty.

氣流(ㄑㄧˋ ㄌㄧㄡˊ)
an airflow; an air current; an atmospheric current

氣量大(ㄑㄧˋ ㄌㄧㄤˋ ㄉㄚˋ)
magnanimous; generous; tolerant; broad-minded: 他是一位氣量大的統治者。He was a magnanimous ruler.

氣量小(ㄑㄧˋ ㄌㄧㄤˋ ㄒㄧㄠˇ)
narrow-minded: 他是個氣量小的法官。He is a narrow-minded judge.

氣格(ㄑㄧˋ ㄍㄜˊ)
character; personality

氣概(ㄑㄧˋ ㄍㄞˋ)
spirit; air; bearing; manner;

他具有英雄氣概。He is a man of heroic spirit.

氣根〈くì ㄍㄣ〉
a clinging root; an aerial root

氣骨〈くì ㄍㄨˇ〉
one's natural character

氣管〈くì ㄍㄨㄢˇ〉
trachea; windpipe

氣管炎〈くì ㄍㄨㄢ ㄧㄢˊ〉
tracheitis

氣貫長虹〈くì ㄍㄨㄢˋ ㄔㄤˊ ㄏㄨㄥˊ〉
(descriptive of warriors) to be filled with a spirit as lofty as the rainbow spanning the sky—full of noble aspiration and daring

氣功〈くì ㄍㄨㄥ〉
(Chinese boxing) the ability to use one's inner strength such as control of muscle and breathing; a system of deep breathing exercises

氣孔〈くì ㄎㄨㄥˇ〉
pores (on the skin); stomas (on a leaf); the spiracle or blowhole (of a whale); vesicles (of the igneous rock)

氣候〈くì ㄏㄡˋ〉
①climate; weather: 我喜歡乾燥氣候。I like an arid climate. ②situations: 政治氣候 the political situation (or climate)

氣候學〈くì ㄏㄡˋ ㄒㄩㄝˊ〉
climatology

氣憤〈くì ㄈㄣˋ〉
to be angry; to be resentful; to be hateful; to be bitter

氣哼哼〈くì ㄏㄥ ㄏㄥ〉
angry; mad; enraged; furious

氣呼呼〈くì ㄏㄨ ㄏㄨ〉
panting with rage

氣化〈くì ㄏㄨㄚˋ〉
to evaporate; to gasify; to vaporize; gasification

氣化熱〈くì ㄏㄨㄚˋ ㄖㄜˋ〉
evaporation heat

氣昏了〈くì ㄏㄨㄣ ·ㄌㄜ〉
to be driven mad by anger

氣急敗壞〈くì ㄐ í ㄅㄞˋ ㄏㄨㄞˋ〉
desperate and low-spirited

氣結〈くì ㄐㄧㄝˊ〉
①(Chinese herb medicine) supposed clogging of the spirit ②depressed; despondent; low-spirited

氣節〈くì ㄐㄧㄝˊ〉
①moral principle; righteousness: 他的確是個有氣節的人。He is indeed a man of righteousness. ②a season; the 24 solar periods of the year

氣界〈くì ㄐㄧㄝˋ〉
the atmosphere (surrounding the earth)

氣盡〈くì ㄐㄧㄣˋ〉
to run out of vitality

氣沮〈くì ㄐㄩˇ〉
dispirited; depressed

氣絕〈くì ㄐㄩㄝˊ〉
to breathe one's last; at one's last gasp: 他到達時，他父親剛剛氣絕了。He arrived just after his father had breathed his last.

氣球〈くì ㄑㄧㄡˊ〉
a balloon

氣槍〈くì ㄑㄧㄤ〉
an air gun; an air rifle: 你能用氣槍打下一隻鳥嗎？Can you shoot down a bird with an air gun?

氣圈〈くì ㄑㄩㄢ〉
the atmosphere (around the earth)

氣息〈くì ㄒ í 〉
①breath: 今天有點春天的氣息。There is a breath of spring in the air today.②the spirit (of writings): 他的作品毫無氣息。His writings totally lack of spirit.

氣息奄奄〈くì ㄒ í ㄧㄢ ㄧㄢ〉
The breath is dying out.—dying; at one's last gasp

氣象〈くì ㄒㄧㄤˋ〉
①meteorology; weather; climates ②the prevailing spirit; atmosphere: 這是生氣蓬勃的萬象氣象。This is a new and dynamic atmosphere.

氣象報告〈くì ㄒㄧㄤˋ ㄅㄠˋ ㄍㄠˋ〉or
氣象預報〈くì ㄒㄧㄤˋ ㄩˋ ㄅㄠˋ〉
a weather forecast

氣象臺〈くì ㄒㄧㄤˋ ㄊㄞˊ〉
a weather station; a meteorological observatory

氣象局〈くì ㄒㄧㄤˋ ㄐㄩˊ〉
a weather bureau

氣象學〈くì ㄒㄧㄤˋ ㄒㄩㄝˊ〉
meteorology

氣象衛星〈くì ㄒㄧㄤˋ ㄨㄟˋ ㄒㄧㄥ〉
a weather satellite

氣象萬千〈くì ㄒㄧㄤˋ ㄨㄢˋ ㄑㄧㄢ〉
Nature abounds in changes. 或 Things change in countless ways.

氣性〈くì ㄒㄧㄥˋ〉
temper; dispositions

氣虛〈くì ㄒㄩ〉
physically weak; deficiency of vital energy

氣吁吁〈くì ㄒㄩ ㄒㄩ〉
gasping for breath

氣質〈くì ㄓˊ〉
dispositions; temperament: 這兩兄弟的氣質完全不同。The two brothers have entirely different temperaments.

氣壯山河〈くì ㄓㄨㄤˋ ㄕㄢ ㄏㄜˊ〉
The spirit is so vigorous that it affects even the mountains and the rivers.

氣成岩〈くì ㄔㄥˊ ㄧㄢˊ〉
aerial rock

氣喘〈くì ㄔㄨㄢˇ〉
①to pant; to gasp; to be out of breath: 他跑得太快，而氣喘不已。He ran so fast that he was out of breath.②asthma: 陣發性氣喘 spasmodic asthma

氣喘如牛〈くì ㄔㄨㄢˇ ㄖㄨˊ ㄋㄧㄡˊ〉
to pant like an ox

氣窗〈くì ㄔㄨㄤ〉
a transom; a ventilation window; a louver window; a fanlight

氣沖斗牛〈くì ㄔㄨㄥ ㄉㄡˇ ㄋㄧㄡˊ〉
(literally) The anger even affects the northern stars.—very angry

氣沖沖〈くì ㄔㄨㄥ ㄔㄨㄥ〉
furious; to fly into a rage

氣勢〈くì ㄕˋ〉
vehemence; fervor; imposing manner: 明年我想參觀氣勢雄偉的萬里長城。I wish to visit the imposing Great Wall next year.

氣勢磅礴〈くì ㄕˋ ㄆㄤˊ ㄅㄛˊ〉
of great momentum; powerful

氣盛〈くì ㄕㄥˋ〉
overbearing; arrogant

氣數〈くì ㄕㄨˋ〉or 氣運〈くì ㄩㄣˋ〉
destiny; fate; fortune

氣層〈くì ㄘㄥˊ〉
the atmosphere (around the earth)

〔气部〕

〔水部〕

氣死人(くî ㄙˇ ㄖㄣˊ)
infuriating; maddening; exasperating

氣色(くî ㄙㄜˋ)
complexion; color: 他的氣色很好。He has a good complexion. 或 He has a rosy complexion. 他的氣色不好。He looks pale.

氣昂昂(くî ㄤˊ ㄤˊ)
in high spirits; elated

氣壓(くî ㄧㄚ)
air pressure; atmospheric pressure; barometric pressure: 高氣壓 high pressure

氣壓計(くî ㄧㄚ ㄐㄧˋ)
a barometer; an air gauge 亦作「風雨表」or「晴雨表」

氣燄(くî ㄧㄢˋ)
hauteur; arrogance: 他的氣燄囂張。He was swollen with arrogance.

氣味(くî ㄨㄟˋ)or氣味兒(くî ㄨㄟ ㄦ)
smacks; smells; odors: 這氣味真好! What a nice smell!

氣味相投(くî ㄨㄟˋ ㄒㄧㄤ ㄊㄡˊ)
having the same tastes and temperament; congenial; to be birds of a feather

氣溫(くî ㄨㄣ)
the atmospheric temperature; the temperature

氣宇(くî ㄩˇ)
dignified and inspiring looks; the manner of a person's carriage

氣宇軒昂(くî ㄩˇ ㄒㄩㄢ ㄤˊ)
dignified; exalted; manly

氣韻(くî ㄩㄣˋ)
the tone or style (of a work of art, literature, etc.)

【氤】 2754
ㄧㄣ in yin
the spirit of harmony (between heaven and earth) 參看「氤氳」

氤氳(ㄧㄣ ㄩㄣ)
①the spirit of harmony (between heaven and earth)
②misty; dense; thick
③the spirit of vigor or prosperity

【氧】 2755
ㄧㄤˇ yeang yǎng
oxygen: 水含有氫和氧。Water contains hydrogen and oxygen.

氧化(ㄧㄤˇ ㄏㄨㄚˋ)
to oxidize or be oxidized; oxidation

氧化碳(ㄧㄤˇ ㄏㄨㄚˋ ㄊㄢˋ)
carbon oxide

氧化鐵(ㄧㄤˇ ㄏㄨㄚˋ ㄊㄧㄝˇ)
ferric oxide

氧化銅(ㄧㄤˇ ㄏㄨㄚˋ ㄊㄨㄥˊ)
cupric oxide; cuprite

氧化鋁(ㄧㄤˇ ㄏㄨㄚˋ ㄌㄩˇ)
aluminum oxide

氧化鈣(ㄧㄤˇ ㄏㄨㄚˋ ㄍㄞˋ)
calcium oxide

氧化汞(ㄧㄤˇ ㄏㄨㄚˋ ㄍㄨㄥˇ)
mercuric oxide

氧化劑(ㄧㄤˇ ㄏㄨㄚˋ ㄐㄧˋ)
an oxidizing agent; an oxidizer

氧化金(ㄧㄤˇ ㄏㄨㄚˋ ㄐㄧㄣ)
gold oxide

氧化鉛(ㄧㄤˇ ㄏㄨㄚˋ ㄑㄧㄢ)
plumbic oxide

氧化錫(ㄧㄤˇ ㄏㄨㄚˋ ㄒㄧˊ)
stannic oxide

氧化矽(ㄧㄤˇ ㄏㄨㄚˋ ㄒㄧ)
silica

氧化鋅(ㄧㄤˇ ㄏㄨㄚˋ ㄒㄧㄣ)
zinc oxide

氧化焰(ㄧㄤˇ ㄏㄨㄚˋ ㄧㄢˋ)
oxidizing flame

氧化銀(ㄧㄤˇ ㄏㄨㄚˋ ㄧㄣˊ)
oxidized silver

氧化物(ㄧㄤˇ ㄏㄨㄚˋ ㄨˋ)
the oxide

氧氣(ㄧㄤˇ くî)
oxygen

【氦】 2756
ㄏㄞˋ hay hài
helium

七畫

【氫】 2757
くㄧㄥ ching qing
hydrogen

氫彈(くㄧㄥ ㄉㄢˋ)
hydrogen bombs

氫化(くㄧㄥ ㄏㄨㄚˋ)
hydrogenation

氫化作用(くㄧㄥ ㄏㄨㄚˋ ㄗㄨㄛˋ ㄩㄥˋ)
hydrogenation

氫化物(くㄧㄥ ㄏㄨㄚˋ ㄨˋ)
the hydride

氫氣(くㄧㄥ くî)
hydrogen

氫酸(くㄧㄥ ㄙㄨㄢ)
hydracid

氫氧化鈉(くㄧㄥ ㄧㄤˇ ㄏㄨㄚˋ ㄋㄚˋ)
sodium hydroxide

氫氧化鈣(くㄧㄥ ㄧㄤˇ ㄏㄨㄚˋ ㄍㄞˋ)
calcium hydroxide

氫氧化物(くㄧㄥ ㄧㄤˇ ㄏㄨㄚˋ ㄨˋ)
hydroxide

氫氧基(くㄧㄥ ㄧㄤˇ ㄐㄧ)or氫氧根(くㄧㄥ ㄧㄤˇ ㄍㄣ)
hydroxyl

氫氧吹管(くㄧㄥ ㄧㄤˇ ㄔㄨㄟ ㄍㄨㄢˇ)
an oxyhydrogen blowpipe

八畫

【氯】 2758
ㄌㄩˋ liuh lǜ
chlorine

氯化鈉(ㄌㄩˋ ㄏㄨㄚˋ ㄋㄚˋ)
sodium chloride

氯化鈣(ㄌㄩˋ ㄏㄨㄚˋ ㄍㄞˋ)
calcium chloride

氯化鉀(ㄌㄩˋ ㄏㄨㄚˋ ㄐㄧㄚˇ)
potassium chloride

氯化金(ㄌㄩˋ ㄏㄨㄚˋ ㄐㄧㄣ)
auric chloride

氯化物(ㄌㄩˋ ㄏㄨㄚˋ ㄨˋ)
the chloride

氯氣(ㄌㄩˋ くî)
chlorine; chlorine gas

氯水(ㄌㄩˋ ㄕㄨㄟˇ)
chlorine water

【氮】 2759
ㄉㄢˋ dann dàn
nitrogen

氮肥(ㄉㄢˋ ㄈㄟˊ)
nitrogenous fertilizers

氮氣固定法(ㄉㄢˋ くî ㄍㄨˋ ㄉㄧㄥˋ ㄈㄚˇ)
the nitrogen fixation

十畫

【氳】 2760
ㄩㄣ iun yūn
the atmosphere of harmony; the spirit of prosperity or vigor 參看「氤氳」

水 部
ㄕㄨㄟˇ　shoei shuǐ

【水】 2761 ㄕㄨㄟˇ shoei shuǐ

1. water: 活水 flowing water 死水 stagnant water
2. a general term for seas, lakes, rivers, etc.
3. liquid; juice: 檸檬水 lemonade 墨水 ink
4. flood disaster; flood
5. a Chinese family name

水壩(ㄕㄨㄟˇ ㄅㄚˋ)
a dam: 尼羅河上有好幾個水壩。There are several dams across the Nile.

水玻璃(ㄕㄨㄟˇ ㄅㄛ ㄌㄧ)
sodium silicate; water glass

水表(ㄕㄨㄟˇ ㄅㄧㄠˇ)
a water meter; a hydrometer; a water gauge

水濱(ㄕㄨㄟˇ ㄅㄧㄣ)or 水邊(ㄕㄨㄟˇ ㄅㄧㄢ)
the waterside; the shore

水兵(ㄕㄨㄟˇ ㄅㄧㄥ)
① a sailor; a bluejacket ② an old name of the navy

水波(ㄕㄨㄟˇ ㄅㄛ)
ripples of water

水牌(ㄕㄨㄟˇ ㄆㄞˊ)
a blackboard in stores for temporary recording of bills

水泡(ㄕㄨㄟˇ ㄆㄠˋ)
① foam; a bubble ② a blister; to blister 亦作「水皰」; 她的腳很嬌嫩,容易起水泡。Her feet are tender and blister easily.

水畔(ㄕㄨㄟˇ ㄆㄢˋ)
beside of the water; the shore

水盆(ㄕㄨㄟˇ ㄆㄣˊ)
a basin: 在水盆內洗手。Wash your hands in the basin.

水瓢(ㄕㄨㄟˇ ㄆㄧㄠˊ)
a dipper; a water ladle

水萍(ㄕㄨㄟˇ ㄆㄧㄥˊ)
(botany) duckweed

水平(ㄕㄨㄟˇ ㄆㄧㄥˊ)
horizontal

水平面(ㄕㄨㄟˇ ㄆㄧㄥˊ ㄇㄧㄢˋ)
a level surface

水平舵(ㄕㄨㄟˇ ㄆㄧㄥˊ ㄉㄨㄛˋ)
a horizontal rudder; a stabilizer

水平線(ㄕㄨㄟˇ ㄆㄧㄥˊ ㄒㄧㄢˋ)
a horizontal line

水瓶座(ㄕㄨㄟˇ ㄆㄧㄥˊ ㄗㄨㄛˋ)
(astrology) Aquarius (or Water Carrier) 亦作「寶瓶座」

水平儀(ㄕㄨㄟˇ ㄆㄧㄥˊ ㄧˊ)
leveling instrument; a level

水磨(ㄕㄨㄟˇ ㄇㄛˋ)
① (ㄕㄨㄟˇ ㄇㄛˋ) fine work on jade, etc. polished with waterstone
② (ㄕㄨㄟˇ ㄇㄛˋ) a water mill

水磨工夫(ㄕㄨㄟˇ ㄇㄛˋ «ㄨㄥ ·ㄈㄨ)
the fine workmanship

水脈(ㄕㄨㄟˇ ㄇㄛˋ)or(ㄕㄨㄟˇ ㄇㄞˋ)
river channel; stream course

水墨畫(ㄕㄨㄟˇ ㄇㄛˋ ㄏㄨㄚˋ)
a painting done with ink and water to bring out different shades of darkness

水沫子(ㄕㄨㄟˇ ㄇㄛˋ ·ㄗ)
foam; froth

水門(ㄕㄨㄟˇ ㄇㄣˊ)
a floodgate; a water gate; a sluice

水門汀(ㄕㄨㄟˇ ㄇㄣˊ ㄊㄧㄥ)
cement 亦作「水泥」

水蜜桃(ㄕㄨㄟˇ ㄇㄧˋ ㄊㄠˊ)
a honey peach

水面(ㄕㄨㄟˇ ㄇㄧㄢˋ)
the water surface; the water level

水母(ㄕㄨㄟˇ ㄇㄨˇ)
Aurelia aurita, a jellyfish

水肥(ㄕㄨㄟˇ ㄈㄟˊ)
collected human body waste (used as fertilizer)

水分(ㄕㄨㄟˇ ㄈㄣˋ)
moisture; dampness; water content; humidity: 海上吹來的風通常含有水分。Winds from the sea are usually moist.

水夫(ㄕㄨㄟˇ ㄈㄨ)
a water bearer

水道(ㄕㄨㄟˇ ㄉㄠˋ)
① a watercourse; a waterway ② (by) water: 這回我想打水道去花蓮。This time I'll go to Hualien by water.

水稻(ㄕㄨㄟˇ ㄉㄠˋ)
aquatic rice (as opposed to hill rice)

水到渠成(ㄕㄨㄟˇ ㄉㄠˋ ㄑㄩˊ ㄔㄥˊ)
(literally) As water comes, it forms a channel automatically.—When conditions are ripe, success will come. 或 The thing takes care of it-

self.

水痘(ㄕㄨㄟˇ ㄉㄡˋ)
chicken pox; varicella

水滴(ㄕㄨㄟˇ ㄉㄧ)
water drops

水滴石穿(ㄕㄨㄟˇ ㄉㄧ ㄕˊ ㄔㄨㄢ)
(literally) Dripping water can wear through a stone.—Persistent effort can solve any problem. 或 Constant effort brings success.

水底(ㄕㄨㄟˇ ㄉㄧˇ)
at the bottom of water

水底電纜(ㄕㄨㄟˇ ㄉㄧˇ ㄉㄧㄢˋ ㄌㄢˇ)
cable (laid across oceans); submarine cable

水電(ㄕㄨㄟˇ ㄉㄧㄢˋ)
water and electricity

水電費(ㄕㄨㄟˇ ㄉㄧㄢˋ ㄈㄟˋ)
charges for water and electricity

水碓(ㄕㄨㄟˇ ㄉㄨㄟˋ)
a rice-polishing device using water power

水塔(ㄕㄨㄟˇ ㄊㄚˇ)
a water tower

水獺(ㄕㄨㄟˇ ㄊㄚˇ)
an otter (Lutra lutra)

水潭(ㄕㄨㄟˇ ㄊㄢˊ)
a pool; a pond

水塘(ㄕㄨㄟˇ ㄊㄤˊ)
a pool; a pond: 一隻青蛙跳入水塘中。A frog jumped into the pond.

水天一色(ㄕㄨㄟˇ ㄊㄧㄢ ㄧˋ ㄙㄜˋ)
The water and the sky merge in one color. 或 A vast expanse of blue water directly adjoins the blue sky.

水田(ㄕㄨㄟˇ ㄊㄧㄢˊ)
the paddy field; the rice field

水土(ㄕㄨㄟˇ ㄊㄨˇ)
① the natural environment ② soil and water

水土保持(ㄕㄨㄟˇ ㄊㄨˇ ㄅㄠˇ ㄔˊ)
soil conservation

水土不服(ㄕㄨㄟˇ ㄊㄨˇ ㄅㄨˋ ㄈㄨˊ)
one's system disagreeing with a new natural environment; to fail to acclimate oneself in a new natural environment

水桶(ㄕㄨㄟˇ ㄊㄨㄥˇ)
a bucket; a pail: 他們用水桶提水。They carried water in

〔水部〕

buckets.

水泥(ㄕㄨㄟˇ ㄋㄧˊ)
cement: 水泥是由石灰石做的。
Cement is made from limestone.

水泥攪拌機(ㄕㄨㄟˇ ㄋㄧˊ ㄐㄧㄠˇ ㄅㄢˋ ㄐㄧ)
a concrete mixer

水鳥(ㄕㄨㄟˇ ㄋㄧㄠˇ)
water birds; waterfowls; aquatic birds

水牛(ㄕㄨㄟˇ ㄋㄧㄡˊ)
a water buffalo: 這農夫有三隻水牛。The farmer has three water buffaloes.

水牛城(ㄕㄨㄟˇ ㄋㄧㄡˊ ㄔㄥˊ)
Buffalo, a port in West New York

水牛兒(ㄕㄨㄟˇ ㄋㄧㄡˊㄦ)
a snail

水來土掩(ㄕㄨㄟˇ ㄌㄞˊ ㄊㄨˇ ㄧㄢˇ)
to attempt to stop any onslaught

水雷(ㄕㄨㄟˇ ㄌㄟˊ)
a mine (against the ship): 水雷用以炸敵船。A mine is used to blow up enemy ships.

水雷艇(ㄕㄨㄟˇ ㄌㄟˊ ㄊㄧㄥˇ)
①a minelayer ②a torpedo boat

水漏(ㄕㄨㄟˇ ㄌㄡˋ)
a water clock; a clepsydra

水力(ㄕㄨㄟˇ ㄌㄧˋ)
hydraulic power; water power

水力發電(ㄕㄨㄟˇ ㄌㄧˋ ㄈㄚ ㄉㄧㄢˋ)
hydraulic power generation

水力發電廠(ㄕㄨㄟˇ ㄌㄧˋ ㄈㄚ ㄉㄧㄢˋ ㄔㄤˇ)
a hydraulic power plant

水力起重機(ㄕㄨㄟˇ ㄌㄧˋ ㄑㄧˇ ㄓㄨㄥˋ ㄐㄧ)
a hydraulic crane

水力學(ㄕㄨㄟˇ ㄌㄧˋ ㄒㄩㄝˊ)
hydraulics

水力昇降機(ㄕㄨㄟˇ ㄌㄧˋ ㄕㄥ ㄐㄧㄤˋ ㄐㄧ)
a hydraulic lift

水利(ㄕㄨㄟˇ ㄌㄧˋ)
water conservancy

水利工程(ㄕㄨㄟˇ ㄌㄧˋ ㄍㄨㄥ ㄔㄥˊ) or
水利工程學(ㄕㄨㄟˇ ㄌㄧˋ ㄍㄨㄥ ㄔㄥˊ ㄒㄩㄝˊ)
hydraulic engineering

水利局(ㄕㄨㄟˇ ㄌㄧˋ ㄐㄩˊ)
Water Conservancy Bu-

reau

水利設施(ㄕㄨㄟˇ ㄌㄧˋ ㄕㄜˋ ㄕ)
water conservancy facilities

水療(ㄕㄨㄟˇ ㄌㄧㄠˊ)
hydrotherapy; hydropathic treatment

水流(ㄕㄨㄟˇ ㄌㄧㄡˊ)
water current; water flow: 他順著水流游泳。He swam with the current.

水瀑(ㄕㄨㄟˇ ㄆㄨˋ)
a waterfall; a cascade

水量(ㄕㄨㄟˇ ㄌㄧㄤˋ)
water volume; amount of water

水靈(ㄕㄨㄟˇ ㄌㄧㄥˊ)
①(said of fruit, vegetables, etc.) fresh and juicy ②(said of appearances) bright and beautiful; radiant and vivacious

水路(ㄕㄨㄟˇ ㄌㄨˋ)
①a waterway; a watercourse ②(by) water: 那批貨物是由水路運送的。The goods were shipped by water.

水路圖(ㄕㄨㄟˇ ㄌㄨˋ ㄊㄨˊ)
a hydrographic map

水陸(ㄕㄨㄟˇ ㄌㄨˋ)
land and water

水陸並進(ㄕㄨㄟˇ ㄌㄨˋ ㄅㄧㄥˋ ㄐㄧㄣˋ)
to send troops to a place by sea and over land simultaneously

水陸兩棲動物(ㄕㄨㄟˇ ㄌㄨˋ ㄌㄧㄤˇ ㄑㄧ ㄉㄨㄥˋ ㄨˋ)
an amphibian.

水陸兩用(ㄕㄨㄟˇ ㄌㄨˋ ㄌㄧㄤˇ ㄩㄥˋ)
amphibious: 那是一輛水陸兩用坦克。It's an amphibious tank.

水淥淥的(ㄕㄨㄟˇ ㄌㄨˋ ㄌㄨˋ˙ㄉㄜ)
drenched; wet all over; dripping: 他一身水淥淥的。He is drenched to the skin.

水落石出(ㄕㄨㄟˇ ㄌㄨㄛˋ ㄕˊ ㄔㄨ)
(literally) Stones come into view with the drop of the water surface.—The truth comes into light eventually. 眞象一定會水落石出的。Doubts will clear up when facts are known.

水輪(ㄕㄨㄟˇ ㄌㄨㄣˊ)
a water wheel

水輪機(ㄕㄨㄟˇ ㄌㄨㄣˊ ㄐㄧ)
a machine powered by

water wheels

水龍(ㄕㄨㄟˇ ㄌㄨㄥˊ)
①a fire engine ②a kind of water plant

水龍頭(ㄕㄨㄟˇ ㄌㄨㄥˊ ㄊㄡˊ)
a faucet; a cock; a tap: 請打開水龍頭。Please turn the tap on.

水綠(ㄕㄨㄟˇ ㄌㄩˋ)
light green

水閣(ㄕㄨㄟˇ ㄍㄜˊ)
a pavilion or tower by the water

水溝(ㄕㄨㄟˇ ㄍㄡ)
a ditch; a drain; a gutter

水缸(ㄕㄨㄟˇ ㄍㄤ)
a large pottery jug for holding water

水耕法(ㄕㄨㄟˇ ㄍㄥ ㄈㄚˇ)
hydroponics 亦作「無土栽培法」

水國(ㄕㄨㄟˇ ㄍㄨㄛˊ)
a watery region

水果(ㄕㄨㄟˇ ㄍㄨㄛˇ)
fruit: 那些是多汁的水果。They are juicy fruits.

水鬼(ㄕㄨㄟˇ ㄍㄨㄟˇ)
①a water goblin ②(slang) a frogman

水管(ㄕㄨㄟˇ ㄍㄨㄢˇ)
a water pipe

水罐(ㄕㄨㄟˇ ㄍㄨㄢˋ)
a water pot; a canteen

水光(ㄕㄨㄟˇ ㄍㄨㄤ)
the light on the water

水坑(ㄕㄨㄟˇ ㄎㄥ)
a water hole; a pool: 汙水坑 a cesspit or cesspool

水庫(ㄕㄨㄟˇ ㄎㄨˋ)
a reservoir

水痕(ㄕㄨㄟˇ ㄏㄣˊ)
water stains; watermarks

水壺(ㄕㄨㄟˇ ㄏㄨˊ)
a canteen: 那是個軍人的水壺。That's a soldier's canteen.

水滸傳(ㄕㄨㄟˇ ㄏㄨˇ ㄓㄨㄢˋ)
All Men Are Brothers, a popular novel by Shih Nai-an (施耐庵)

水花(ㄕㄨㄟˇ ㄏㄨㄚ)
①foam; froth; spray: 瀑布的水花 the spray of a waterfall ②a flower blooming in water

水火(ㄕㄨㄟˇ ㄏㄨㄛˇ)
①water and fire — essen-

〔水部〕

tials of life ② incompatible (things) ③disaster; miseries: 他們生活於水火之中。They live in untold miseries.

水火不相容(ㄕㄨㄟˇ ㄏㄨㄛˇ ㄅㄨˋ ㄒㄧㄤ ㄖㄨㄥˊ)
Water and fire cannot co-exist. —(figuratively) incompatible; irreconcilable: 他們兩人水火不相容。Both of them are incompatible as fire and water.

水火無情(ㄕㄨㄟˇ ㄏㄨㄛˇ ㄨˊ ㄑㄧㄥˊ)
Water and fire are merciless. 或 Floods and fires have no mercy for anybody.

水患(ㄕㄨㄟˇ ㄏㄨㄢˋ)
floods; flood disaster: 豪雨在這城的低窪處造成水患。The rainstorm caused floods in the low-lying parts of the town.

水紅(ㄕㄨㄟˇ ㄏㄨㄥˊ)
pink

水解(ㄕㄨㄟˇ ㄐㄧㄝˇ)
hydrolysis

水腳(ㄕㄨㄟˇ ㄐㄧㄠˇ)
freight

水餃(ㄕㄨㄟˇ ㄐㄧㄠˇ)
Chinese ravioli; boiled dumplings

水酒(ㄕㄨㄟˇ ㄐㄧㄡˇ)
diluted wine

水晶(ㄕㄨㄟˇ ㄐㄧㄥ)
crystal; crystallized quartz

水晶體(ㄕㄨㄟˇ ㄐㄧㄥ ㄊㄧˇ)
①(anatomy) the lens (of eyes) ② the crystalline lens

水晶宮(ㄕㄨㄟˇ ㄐㄧㄥ ㄍㄨㄥ)
the crystal palace, abode of the legendary Dragon King

水晶球(ㄕㄨㄟˇ ㄐㄧㄥ ㄑㄧㄡˊ)
a crystal ball

水晶石(ㄕㄨㄟˇ ㄐㄧㄥ ㄕˊ)
cryolite

水精鹽(ㄕㄨㄟˇ ㄐㄧㄥ ㄧㄢˊ)
natural salt

水井(ㄕㄨㄟˇ ㄐㄧㄥˇ)
a well: 這口水井乾涸了。The well is dry.

水居(ㄕㄨㄟˇ ㄐㄩ)
①(said of person) to make one's home on rivers, lakes, or waterways ② fishes and mollusks

水軍(ㄕㄨㄟˇ ㄐㄩㄣ)
(formerly) the navy; naval

units

水汽(ㄕㄨㄟˇ ㄑㄧˋ)
water vapor; moisture; steam

水球(ㄕㄨㄟˇ ㄑㄧㄡˊ)
(sports) water polo

水鉛鑛(ㄕㄨㄟˇ ㄑㄧㄢˊ ㄎㄨㄤˋ)
wulfenite

水禽(ㄕㄨㄟˇ ㄑㄧㄣˊ)
aquatic birds; waterfowls

水芹(ㄕㄨㄟˇ ㄑㄧㄣˊ)
water celery

水槍(ㄕㄨㄟˇ ㄑㄧㄤ)
a squirt gun

水清無魚(ㄕㄨㄟˇ ㄑㄧㄥ ㄨˊ ㄩˊ)
(literally) There is no fish in clear water.—An overly pure-minded person has few friends.

水螅(ㄕㄨㄟˇ ㄒㄧ)
a polyp; a hydra

水系(ㄕㄨㄟˇ ㄒㄧˋ)
the river system; the hydrographic net

水下(ㄕㄨㄟˇ ㄒㄧㄚˋ)
under water; submerged: 潛艇潛入水下去了。The submarine submerged.

水蝎(ㄕㄨㄟˇ ㄒㄧㄝ)
a water scorpion

水榭(ㄕㄨㄟˇ ㄒㄧㄝˋ)
a pavilion or bower surrounded by water

水瀉(ㄕㄨㄟˇ ㄒㄧㄝˋ)
diarrhoea

水泄不通(ㄕㄨㄟˇ ㄒㄧㄝˋ ㄅㄨˋ ㄊㄨㄥ)
so crowded, or so carefully guarded, that it is impossible even for water to seep through: 此路擠得水泄不通。The road is so crowded as to be impassable.

水袖(ㄕㄨㄟˇ ㄒㄧㄡˋ)
the long white fabric sewed to the lower end of sleeves of robes worn in Chinese opera

水銹(ㄕㄨㄟˇ ㄒㄧㄡˋ)
①rust; watermarks ② scale; incrustation

水仙花(ㄕㄨㄟˇ ㄒㄧㄢ ㄏㄨㄚ)
a narcissus; a daffodil

水險(ㄕㄨㄟˇ ㄒㄧㄢˇ)
marine insurance

水鄉(ㄕㄨㄟˇ ㄒㄧㄤ)
a place near a lake, sea or

river; swampy regions

水箱(ㄕㄨㄟˇ ㄒㄧㄤ)
a water tank

水星(ㄕㄨㄟˇ ㄒㄧㄥ)
the planet Mercury

水性(ㄕㄨㄟˇ ㄒㄧㄥˋ)
①an unpredictable temperament ②the water condition (of a river, etc., as affecting a swimmer): 他不習水性。He was an inexperienced swimmer.

水性楊花(ㄕㄨㄟˇ ㄒㄧㄥˋ ㄧㄤˊ ㄏㄨㄚ)
(said of women) fickle and lascivious

水質(ㄕㄨㄟˇ ㄓˊ)
properties of particular specimens of water

水蛭(ㄕㄨㄟˇ ㄓˋ)
a leech

水閘(ㄕㄨㄟˇ ㄓㄚˊ)
a floodgate; a water gate; a sluice; a lock (of a canal)

水柵(ㄕㄨㄟˇ ㄓㄚˋ)
a water barrier; a weir

水戰(ㄕㄨㄟˇ ㄓㄢˋ)
a naval warfare

水漲船高(ㄕㄨㄟˇ ㄓㄤˇ ㄔㄨㄢˊ ㄍㄠ)
(literally) When water rises, the boat rises with it.— ① When the person one relies on rises in the world, one rises with him. ② When the production cost rises, the commodity price rises with it.

水腫(ㄕㄨㄟˇ ㄓㄨㄥˇ)
(medicine) edema

水蒸氣(ㄕㄨㄟˇ ㄓㄥ ㄑㄧˋ)
water vapor; steam; vapor: 水蒸氣推動機器。Steam drives machinery.

水珠子(ㄕㄨㄟˇ ㄓㄨ ˙ㄗ)
(colloquial) drops of water

水柱(ㄕㄨㄟˇ ㄓㄨˋ)
a water column

水準(ㄕㄨㄟˇ ㄓㄨㄣˇ)
a standard; a level

水準器(ㄕㄨㄟˇ ㄓㄨㄣˇ ㄑㄧˋ)
a level (an instrument)

水中撈月(ㄕㄨㄟˇ ㄓㄨㄥ ㄌㄠ ㄩㄝˋ)
(literally) to try to fish the moon out of water—to make obviously futile efforts

水腫(ㄕㄨㄟˇ ㄓㄨㄥˇ)
dropsy; hydrophilic swelling

【水部】

水池(ㄕㄨㄟ ㄔˊ)or 水池子(ㄕㄨㄟ ㄔˊ ˙ㄗ)
a pool; a pond; a water tank: 他在野外跌入水池中。He fell into the pool in the field.

水車(ㄕㄨㄟ ㄔㄜ)
①a water wheel ②a water-cart; a water wagon

水產(ㄕㄨㄟ ㄔㄢˇ)
marine products

水產學(ㄕㄨㄟ ㄔㄢˇ ㄒㄩㄝˊ)
fishery science

水產學校(ㄕㄨㄟ ㄔㄢˇ ㄒㄩㄝˊ ㄒㄧㄠˋ)
the school for training of fishery workers

水產資源(ㄕㄨㄟ ㄔㄢˇ ㄗ ㄩㄢˊ)
aquatic resources

水產業(ㄕㄨㄟ ㄔㄢˇ ㄧㄝˋ)
fishery; fishing industry

水廠(ㄕㄨㄟ ㄔㄤˇ)
waterworks

水程(ㄕㄨㄟ ㄔㄥˊ)
sea voyage; voyage by water

水成岩(ㄕㄨㄟ ㄔㄥˊ ㄧㄢˊ)
sedimentary rock; aqueous rock

水師(ㄕㄨㄟ ㄕ)
①(formerly) the navy; naval units ②a sailor; a boat-man

水蝕(ㄕㄨㄟ ㄕˊ)
water erosion

水勢(ㄕㄨㄟ ㄕˋ)
①the flow of the water ②the direction of flowing water

水蛇(ㄕㄨㄟ ㄕㄜˊ)
a water snake; an aquatic snake

水蛇腰(ㄕㄨㄟ ㄕㄜˊ ㄧㄠ)
an extremely slender waist

水手(ㄕㄨㄟ ㄕㄡˇ)
a sailor; a mariner

水深(ㄕㄨㄟ ㄕㄣ)
the depth of water

水深火熱(ㄕㄨㄟ ㄕㄣ ㄏㄨㄛˇ ㄖㄜˋ)
an abyss of suffering; misery caused by government oppression: 他們過去生活在水深火熱之中。They lived in an abyss of misery in the past.

水上芭蕾舞(ㄕㄨㄟ ㄕㄤˋ ㄅㄚ ㄌㄟˇ ㄨˇ)
water ballet; synchronized swimming

a seaplane; a hydroplane

水上警察(ㄕㄨㄟ ㄕㄤˋ ㄐㄧㄥˇ ㄔㄚˊ)
or 水警(ㄕㄨㄟ ㄐㄧㄥˇ)
the water police; the marine police

水上人家(ㄕㄨㄟ ㄕㄤˋ ㄖㄣˊ ㄐㄧㄚ)
boat dwellers

水上運動(ㄕㄨㄟ ㄕㄤˋ ㄩㄣˋ ㄉㄨㄥˋ)
water sports; aquatic sports

水生植物(ㄕㄨㄟ ㄕㄥ ㄓˊ ㄨˋ)
the aquatic plants

水栓(ㄕㄨㄟ ㄕㄨㄢ)
a hydrant

水乳交融(ㄕㄨㄟ ㄖㄨˇ ㄐㄧㄠ ㄖㄨㄥˊ)
in harmony like water and milk

水溶性(ㄕㄨㄟ ㄖㄨㄥˊ ㄒㄧㄥˋ)
water soluble; solubility

水漬(ㄕㄨㄟ ㄗ)
①to drench ②water stains; watermarks

水漬貨(ㄕㄨㄟ ㄗ ㄏㄨㄛˋ)
goods with water stains; water damaged commodities

水災(ㄕㄨㄟ ㄗㄞ)
flood disaster; floods: 在水災地區建立臨時流動餐館。Canteens were set up in the flooded areas.

水藻(ㄕㄨㄟ ㄗㄠˇ)
algae

水葬(ㄕㄨㄟ ㄗㄤˋ)
burial at sea; burial in the sea

水族(ㄕㄨㄟ ㄗㄨˊ)
aquatic animals

水族館(ㄕㄨㄟ ㄗㄨˊ ㄍㄨㄢˇ)
an aquarium

水鑽(ㄕㄨㄟ ㄗㄨㄢˋ)
①a hydraulic drill ②a diamond

水彩(ㄕㄨㄟ ㄘㄞˇ)
watercolor

水彩畫(ㄕㄨㄟ ㄘㄞˇ ㄏㄨㄚˋ)
a watercolor painting; a watercolor

水彩畫家(ㄕㄨㄟ ㄘㄞˇ ㄏㄨㄚˋ ㄐㄧㄚ)
a watercolorist

水槽(ㄕㄨㄟ ㄘㄠˊ)
a water trough; a water tank

水草(ㄕㄨㄟ ㄘㄠˇ)
①waterweeds; water plants ②water and grass

水蔥(ㄕㄨㄟ ㄘㄨㄥ)
a water onion

水蔥兒似的(ㄕㄨㄟ ㄘㄨㄥ ㄦ ㄕˋ ˙ㄉㄜ)

(said of girls) bright and beautiful

水速(ㄕㄨㄟ ㄙㄨˋ)
the speed of a water current

水速表(ㄕㄨㄟ ㄙㄨˋ ㄅㄧㄠˇ)
a tachometer

水鴨(ㄕㄨㄟ ㄧㄚ)
a teal

水鴨子(ㄕㄨㄟ ㄧㄚ ˙ㄗ)
(slang) a small naval craft for beach operations

水壓(ㄕㄨㄟ ㄧㄚ)
water pressure

水壓機(ㄕㄨㄟ ㄧㄚ ㄐㄧ)
a hydraulic press

水杓子(ㄕㄨㄟ ㄕㄠˊ ˙ㄗ)
a dipper; a ladle

水曜日(ㄕㄨㄟ ㄧㄠˋ ㄖˋ)
Wednesday

水煙(ㄕㄨㄟ ㄧㄢ)
tobacco for the hookah

水煙袋(ㄕㄨㄟ ㄧㄢ ㄉㄞˋ)
a hookah; a hubble-bubble

水銀(ㄕㄨㄟ ㄧㄣˊ)
mercury (an element)

水銀燈(ㄕㄨㄟ ㄧㄣˊ ㄉㄥ)
a mercury lamp

水銀柱(ㄕㄨㄟ ㄧㄣˊ ㄓㄨˋ)
a mercury column

水印(ㄕㄨㄟ ㄧㄣˋ)
the seal or chop of a business firm

水污染(ㄕㄨㄟ ㄨ ㄖㄢˇ)
water pollution

水位(ㄕㄨㄟ ㄨㄟˋ)
the water stage; the water level; the watermark

水文(ㄕㄨㄟ ㄨㄣˊ)or 水文學(ㄕㄨㄟ ㄨㄣˊ ㄒㄩㄝˊ)
hydrology

水汪汪的(ㄕㄨㄟ ㄨㄤ ㄨㄤ ˙ㄉㄜ)
(said of women's eyes) bright and attractive

水芋(ㄕㄨㄟ ㄩˋ)
a calla (or calla lily)

水域(ㄕㄨㄟ ㄩˋ)
waters; a water area: 熱帶水域 a tropical water area

水源(ㄕㄨㄟ ㄩㄢˊ)
①the riverhead; the waterhead; headwaters ②a source of water: 他們正在尋找新水源。They were seeking new sources of water.

水運(ㄕㄨㄟ ㄩㄣˋ)
transportation by water

一畫

【永】 2762
ㄩㄥˇ yeong yǒng
long in time; everlasting;
eternal; permanent

永保太平(ㄩㄥˇ ㄅㄠˇ ㄊㄞˋ ㄆㄧㄥˊ)
to remain peaceful for all
time

永保青春(ㄩㄥˇ ㄅㄠˇ ㄑㄧㄥ ㄔㄨㄣ)
to remain youthful forever

永別(ㄩㄥˇ ㄅㄧㄝˊ)
to part for good; to die

永不(ㄩㄥˇ ㄅㄨˋ)
will never: 他永不改變心意。
He will never change his
mind.

永不分離(ㄩㄥˇ ㄅㄨˋ ㄈㄣ ㄌㄧˊ)
never to be separated

永不錄用(ㄩㄥˇ ㄅㄨˋ ㄌㄨˋ ㄩㄥˋ)
(said of a disgraced official)
never to be employed again

永命(ㄩㄥˇ ㄇㄧㄥˋ)
a long life; longevity

永斷葛藤(ㄩㄥˇ ㄉㄨㄢˋ ㄍㄜˊ ㄊㄥˊ)
to sever relations forever

永年(ㄩㄥˇ ㄋㄧㄢˊ)
a long life; longevity

永樂大典(ㄩㄥˇ ㄌㄜˋ ㄉㄚˋ ㄉㄧㄢˇ)
Encyclopedia Sinica, a 22,877-
volume collection of books
compiled by order of Emper-
or Cheng Tsu of the Ming
Dynasty (明成祖)

永古(ㄩㄥˇ ㄍㄨˇ)
time immemorial

永固(ㄩㄥˇ ㄍㄨˋ)
to remain secure forever

永恆(ㄩㄥˇ ㄏㄥˊ)
eternity; eternal; perpetual;
everlasting

永久(ㄩㄥˇ ㄐㄧㄡˇ)
permanent; perpetual; eternal; lasting; everlasting; un-
ending; endless

永久地址(ㄩㄥˇ ㄐㄧㄡˇ ㄉㄧˋ ㄓˇ)
a permanent address

永久和平(ㄩㄥˇ ㄐㄧㄡˇ ㄏㄜˊ ㄆㄧㄥˊ)
everlasting peace; permanent
peace

永久中立國(ㄩㄥˇ ㄐㄧㄡˇ ㄓㄨㄥ ㄌㄧˋ
ㄍㄨㄛˊ)
a permanent neutral power

永久齒(ㄩㄥˇ ㄐㄧㄡˇ ㄔˇ)
permanent teeth

永久組織(ㄩㄥˇ ㄐㄧㄡˇ ㄗㄨˇ ㄓ)
a permanent organization

永訣(ㄩㄥˇ ㄐㄩㄝˊ)
to be gone forever—to die

永享(ㄩㄥˇ ㄒㄧㄤˇ)
to enjoy forever

永誌不忘(ㄩㄥˇ ㄓˋ ㄅㄨˋ ㄨㄤˋ)
to bear in mind forever; to
remember forever

永晝(ㄩㄥˇ ㄓㄡˋ)
a long day

永垂不朽(ㄩㄥˇ ㄔㄨㄟˊ ㄅㄨˋ ㄒㄧㄡˇ)
to be remembered forever
by posterity; immortal (fame,
accomplishment, etc.): 他已獲得
永垂不朽的聲名。 He has
achieved immortality.

永世(ㄩㄥˇ ㄕˋ)
① forever; eternity: 我對那事
永世難忘。I will never forget
it for my life. ② the whole
lifetime

永逝(ㄩㄥˇ ㄕˋ)
to be gone forever—to die

永生(ㄩㄥˇ ㄕㄥ)
①for ever: 我將永生永世愛
她。I shall love her for ever
and ever. ② eternal life:
基督教許諾永生嗎? Does the
Christian religion promise
eternal life?

永日(ㄩㄥˇ ㄖˋ)
a long day; all the day

永字八法(ㄩㄥˇ ㄗˋ ㄅㄚ ㄈㄚˇ)
the eight representative
strokes as contained in the
character 永 (側, 勒, 努, 趯,
策, 掠, 啄, 磔)

永存(ㄩㄥˇ ㄘㄨㄣˊ)
to remain forever; to live
for ever and ever

永逸(ㄩㄥˇ ㄧˋ)
to be at ease and free from
trouble forever: 一勞永逸to
do all that is required so
that one never has to do it
again

永夜(ㄩㄥˇ ㄧㄝˋ)
a long night

永言(ㄩㄥˇ ㄧㄢˊ)
to be remembered forever

永無寧日(ㄩㄥˇ ㄨˊ ㄋㄧㄥˊ ㄖˋ)
Never will there be days of
peace.

永遠(ㄩㄥˇ ㄩㄢˇ)
forever; eternally; perpetu-
ally: 他永遠離開了。He went

away forever.

二畫

【氽】 2763
1. ㄊㄨㄣˇ toen tǔn
the action of water moving
or pushing an object

【氽】 2763
2. ㄘㄨㄢˊ tsuan
cuān
(cooking) to boil (food)

氽湯(ㄘㄨㄢˊ ㄊㄤ)
to prepare a soup

氽子(ㄘㄨㄢˊ ·ㄗ)or 氽兒(ㄘㄨㄢˊ ㄦˊ)
a kind of metal kettle

【氾】 2764
ㄈㄢˋ fann fàn
1. to spread; to fill everywhere
2. extensive; vast; boundless
3. floating

氾博(ㄈㄢˋ ㄅㄛˊ)
vast; broad; extensive;
immense

氾氾(ㄈㄢˋ ㄈㄢˋ)
afloat

氾濫(ㄈㄢˋ ㄌㄢˋ)
① to overflow; in flood: 湖水
氾濫。The lake overflowed.②
to spread far and wide

氾論(ㄈㄢˋ ㄌㄨㄣˊ)
general discussion

【汁】 2765
ㄓ jy zhī
juice; the natural fluid; sap

汁水兒(ㄓ ㄕㄨㄟˇㄦˊ)
juice; fluid; sap: 這種水果汁
水兒很多。This fruit is juicy.

汁液(ㄓ ㄧㄝˋ)
juice; sap

【汀】 2766
ㄊㄧㄥ ting tīng
1. a low, level land along a
river; beach
2. a shoal

汀曲(ㄊㄧㄥ ㄑㄩ)
a bend in a stream

汀洲(ㄊㄧㄥ ㄓㄡ)
an islet in a stream; a shoal

汀渚(ㄊㄧㄥ ㄓㄨˇ)
an islet in a stream; a shoal

【求】 2767
ㄑㄧㄡˊ chyou qiú
1. to solicit; to ask for; to
pray for; to beg: 求您幫個忙,
好嗎? May I ask you a
favor?
2. demand: 供不應求。The sup-

〔水部〕

（水
部）

ply falls short of the demand.

3. to seek: 大多數人尋求財富，每個人都追求幸福。Most men seek wealth; all men seek happiness.

4. to covet; to desire

求備（ㄑㄧㄡˊ ㄅㄟˋ）
to seek completeness

求名求利（ㄑㄧㄡˊ ㄇㄧㄥˊ ㄑㄧㄡˊ ㄌㄧˋ）
to seek fame and wealth

求福免禍（ㄑㄧㄡˊ ㄈㄨˊ ㄇㄧㄢˇ ㄏㄨㄛˋ）
to seek happiness and avoid calamity

求代（ㄑㄧㄡˊ ㄉㄞˋ）
to seek a substitute to do a duty

求貸（ㄑㄧㄡˊ ㄉㄞˋ）
to ask for loan

求田問舍（ㄑㄧㄡˊ ㄊㄧㄢˊ ㄨㄣˋ ㄕㄜˇ）
interested exclusively in the acquisition of one's estate—not interested in more ambitious things

求告（ㄑㄧㄡˊ ㄍㄠˋ）
to implore; to beseech; to entreat; to supplicate

求過於供（ㄑㄧㄡˊ ㄍㄨㄛˋ ㄩˊ ㄍㄨㄥˋ）
The demand exceeds the supply.

求和（ㄑㄧㄡˊ ㄏㄜˊ）or 求成（ㄑㄧㄡˊ ㄔㄥˊ）
to seek peace with an enemy; to try to end hostilities

求化（ㄑㄧㄡˊ ㄏㄨㄚˋ）
(said of Buddhist monks) to beg for alms: 僧侶們沿街求化。The monks beg for alms from street to street.

求歡（ㄑㄧㄡˊ ㄏㄨㄢ）
to seek the consent of a woman for a sexual intercourse

求婚（ㄑㄧㄡˊ ㄏㄨㄣ）or 求親（ㄑㄧㄡˊ ㄑㄧㄣ）
to propose (to a woman): 他已下定決心要向她求婚。He has made up his mind to propose marriage to her.

求凰（ㄑㄧㄡˊ ㄏㄨㄤˊ）
to seek a wife

求解（ㄑㄧㄡˊ ㄐㄧㄝˇ）
①to seek help in distress ②to seek the solution to a mathematical problem

求教（ㄑㄧㄡˊ ㄐㄧㄠˋ）
to seek instruction; to seek

advice: 向他求教。Ask him for advice.

求救（ㄑㄧㄡˊ ㄐㄧㄡˋ）
to seek relief; to ask for rescue: 他們發出求救信號。They signaled for help.或 They signaled an SOS.

求見（ㄑㄧㄡˊ ㄐㄧㄢˋ）
to seek an interview

求壞得隴（ㄑㄧㄡˊ ㄐㄧㄝˊ ㄉㄜˊ ㄌㄨㄥˇ）
to get more than one has asked for

求乞（ㄑㄧㄡˊ ㄑㄧˇ）
to beg for food or money: 他沿門求乞。He begs his bread from door to door.

求籤（ㄑㄧㄡˊ ㄑㄧㄢ）
to seek divine guidance by drawing lots

求親（ㄑㄧㄡˊ ㄑㄧㄣ）
①to seek a marriage alliance ②to ask for help from relatives

求親告友（ㄑㄧㄡˊ ㄑㄧㄣ ㄍㄠˋ ㄧㄡˇ）
to ask favors of relatives and friends

求情（ㄑㄧㄡˊ ㄑㄧㄥˊ）
①to ask for mercy or leniency; to intercede; to plead ②to ask for a favor

求全（ㄑㄧㄡˊ ㄑㄩㄢˊ）
①to seek a satisfactory result; to demand perfection: 萬事莫求全。Don't ask for perfection. ②to try to preserve oneself

求全之毀（ㄑㄧㄡˊ ㄑㄩㄢˊ ㄓ ㄏㄨㄟˇ）
to try to be perfect only to receive reproaches

求全責備（ㄑㄧㄡˊ ㄑㄩㄢˊ ㄗㄜˊ ㄅㄟˋ）
to criticize so that everything will become perfect; to demand perfection: 他事事求全責備。He demands perfection in everything.

求仙（ㄑㄧㄡˊ ㄒㄧㄢ）
to seek an immortal (usually in mountains)

求賢若渴（ㄑㄧㄡˊ ㄒㄧㄢˊ ㄖㄨㄛˋ ㄎㄜˇ）
to seek talent with eagerness

求心力（ㄑㄧㄡˊ ㄒㄧㄣ ㄌㄧˋ）
centripetal force

求學（ㄑㄧㄡˊ ㄒㄩㄝˊ）
to receive education; to study

求知（ㄑㄧㄡˊ ㄓ）

to seek knowledge

求知慾（ㄑㄧㄡˊ ㄓ ㄩˋ）
a thirst(or craving) for knowledge

求之不得（ㄑㄧㄡˊ ㄓ ㄅㄨˋ ㄉㄜˊ）
to be exactly what has been sought eagerly; most welcome: 這是求之不得的好機會。This is a most welcome opportunity.

求職（ㄑㄧㄡˊ ㄓˊ）
positions wanted

求證（ㄑㄧㄡˊ ㄓㄥˋ）
to seek verification or confirmation

求助（ㄑㄧㄡˊ ㄓㄨˋ）
to resort to; to seek help; to seek aid

求成（ㄑㄧㄡˊ ㄔㄥˊ）
①to hope for success: 他急於求成。He is impatient for success. ②to seek peace with an enemy 參看「求和」

求神問卜（ㄑㄧㄡˊ ㄕㄣˊ ㄨㄣˋ ㄅㄨˇ）
to seek divine advice

求生（ㄑㄧㄡˊ ㄕㄥ）
to seek to survive; to try to remain alive

求勝（ㄑㄧㄡˊ ㄕㄥˋ）
to strive for victory: 他們求勝心切。They strove to gain victory.

求饒（ㄑㄧㄡˊ ㄖㄠˊ）
to ask for forgiveness; to seek pardon; to beg for mercy

求人（ㄑㄧㄡˊ ㄖㄣˊ）
①to ask for help ②to look for talents

求人不如求己（ㄑㄧㄡˊ ㄖㄣˊ ㄅㄨˋ ㄖㄨˊ ㄑㄧㄡˊ ㄐㄧˇ）
Relying upon oneself is better than relying upon others.

求仁得仁（ㄑㄧㄡˊ ㄖㄣˊ ㄉㄜˊ ㄖㄣˊ）
to seek for virtue and get virtue—to want something and succeed in getting it

求容（ㄑㄧㄡˊ ㄖㄨㄥˊ）
to seek room or space for oneself

求子（ㄑㄧㄡˊ ㄗˇ）
(said of a childless couple) to pray for a son

求才（ㄑㄧㄡˊ ㄘㄞˊ）
positions vacant

求愛（ㄑㄧㄡˊ ㄞˋ）
to woo; to court

求偶(く1ㄡˇ)
to seek a spouse

求雨(く1ㄩˇ)
to pray for rain

求援(く1ㄡ ㄩㄢˊ)
to seek relief; to ask for help

三畫

【汉】 2768
彳ㄚˊ chah chá
a branching stream

汉流(彳ㄚˊ ㄌ1ㄡˊ)
a tributary of a river or current

汉港(彳ㄚˊ ㄍㄤˇ)
a branching point of a stream

【汎】 2769
ㄈㄢˋ fann fàn

1. afloat; to float
2. extensive; widespread

汎美航空公司(ㄈㄢˋ ㄇㄟˇ ㄏㄤˊ ㄎㄨㄥ ㄍㄨㄥ ㄙ)
Pan American World Airways

汎美洲主義(ㄈㄢˋ ㄇㄟˇ ㄓㄡ ㄓㄨˇ 1ˋ)
Pan-Americanism

汎汎(ㄈㄢˋ ㄈㄢˋ)
going downstream smoothly

汎濫(ㄈㄢˋ ㄌㄢˋ)
to overflow; to spread; to flood; to inundate

汎理論(ㄈㄢˋ ㄌ1ˇ ㄌㄨㄣˊ)
panlogism

汎論(ㄈㄢˋ ㄌㄨㄣˊ)
general discussion

汎心論(ㄈㄢˋ ㄒ1ㄣ ㄌㄨㄣˊ)
panpsychism

汎舟(ㄈㄢˋ ㄓㄡ)
to row a boat; boating: 他喜歡汎舟和游泳。 He enjoys boating and swimming.

汎稱(ㄈㄢˋ ㄔㄥ)
a collective name; generally called

汎愛(ㄈㄢˋ ㄞˋ)
philanthropy; to overflow in love to all

【油】 2770
ㄕㄢ shann shān
a basket for catching fish

油頭(ㄕㄢ ㄊㄡˊ)
Swatow, a city in Kwangtung Province

【汐】 2771
ㄒ1ˋ shih xì
the flow of the tide at night

【汗】 2772
1. ㄏㄢˋ hann hàn
sweat; perspiration

汗斑(ㄏㄢˋ ㄅㄢ)
dark spots on the skin supposed to be caused by obstructed perspiration

汗馬功勞(ㄏㄢˋ ㄇㄚˇ ㄍㄨㄥ ㄌㄠˊ)
distinguished services in war

汗毛(ㄏㄢˋ ㄇㄠˊ)
down; the soft, fine hair on the human body

汗毛孔(ㄏㄢˋ ㄇㄠˊ ㄎㄨㄥˇ)
pores in the skin

汗漫(ㄏㄢˋ ㄇㄢˋ)
① a wide expanse of water ② large but empty ③ unconventional and uninhibited

汗牛充棟(ㄏㄢˋ ㄋ1ㄡˊ ㄔㄨㄥ ㄉㄨㄥˋ)
(said of books, particularly those dealing with the same subject) numerous; overabundant; truckload of

汗流滿面(ㄏㄢˋ ㄌ1ㄡˊ ㄇㄢˇ ㄇ1ㄢˋ)
to perspire all over one's face

汗流浹背(ㄏㄢˋ ㄌ1ㄡˊ ㄐ1ㄚ ㄅㄟˋ)
to perspire all over (because of fear of punishment); bathed in sweat; soaked with sweat (from fear or physical exertion): 他全身汗流浹背。 He was bathed in sweat.

汗垢(ㄏㄢˋ ㄍㄡˇ)
sweat mixed with dirt

汗脚(ㄏㄢˋ ㄐ1ㄠˇ)
feet that tend to perspire

汗巾(ㄏㄢˋ ㄐ1ㄣ)
a girdle; a sash

汗青(ㄏㄢˋ ㄑ1ㄥ)
(literally) to sweat bamboo pieces by heat for use in writing—① to put something in writing ② history

汗腺(ㄏㄢˋ ㄒ1ㄢˋ)
a sweat gland

汗疹(ㄏㄢˋ ㄓㄣˇ)
sudamina

汗珠子(ㄏㄢˋ ㄓㄨ ˙ㄗ)
beads of sweat

汗手(ㄏㄢˋ ㄕㄡˇ)
hands wet with perspiration

汗衫(ㄏㄢˋ ㄕㄢ)
a T-shirt

汗如雨下(ㄏㄢˋ ㄖㄨˊ ㄩˇ ㄒ1ㄚˋ)
to sweat profusely

汗液(ㄏㄢˋ 1ㄝˋ)
perspiration; sweat: 胖人流汗多汗液。 Fat persons perspire heavily.

汗顏(ㄏㄢˋ 1ㄢˊ)
to perspire from embarrassment or shame

【汗】 2772
2. ㄏㄢˊ harn hán
as in 可汗—a khan

【池】 2773
ㄔˊ chyr chí

1. a pond; a pool; a moat: 我們學校有一游泳池。 Our school has a swimming pool.
2. an enclosed space with raised sides: 舞池 a dance floor
3. a Chinese family name

池塘(ㄔˊ ㄊㄤˊ)
a pond: 綠色的浮渣漂在池塘上面。 Green scum floated on the top of the pond.

池隍(ㄔˊ ㄏㄨㄤˊ)
a moat

池榭(ㄔˊ ㄒ1ㄝˋ)
a bower or pavilion on a pond

池心(ㄔˊ ㄒ1ㄣ)
the middle or center of a pond

池沼(ㄔˊ ㄓㄠˇ)
ponds and swamps

池中物(ㄔˊ ㄓㄨㄥ ㄨˋ)
(literally) common stuff that can be found in a pond—a mediocre person

池水(ㄔˊ ㄕㄨㄟˇ)
pond water

池子(ㄔˊ ˙ㄗ)
① a pond ② orchestra stalls in a theater

池鹽(ㄔˊ 1ㄢˊ)
lake salt

池魚(ㄔˊ ㄩˊ)
the fish in the moat—According to the folktale, when the gate of a city in the State of Sung was on fire, people drew water from the moat to put out the fire. Therefore, the moat was soon dried and the fish in the moat died.

〔水 部〕

池魚之殃（ㄔ ㄩ ㄓ ㄧㄤ）
disasters suffered by outsiders or innocent people; disasters brought on by others 參看「池魚」

【氾】 2774 ㄈㄢˋ syh sì
a stream that branches and afterwards merges again

【汝】 2775 ㄖㄨˇ ruu rǔ
you; thou; thee; thy: 汝意爲何? What do you aim at?

汝輩（ㄖㄨˇ ㄅㄟˋ）or 汝曹（ㄖㄨˇ ㄘㄠˊ）or 汝等（ㄖㄨˇ ㄉㄥˇ）
(plural) ye (used in addressing inferiors); you: 汝曹好學。You all are fond of studying.

汝窰（ㄖㄨˇ ㄧㄠˋ）
name of a famous porcelain kiln in the Sung Dynasty at Juchou (汝州), in Honan

【江】 2776 ㄐㄧㄤ jiang jiāng
1. a large river
2. the Yangtze River
3. a Chinese family name

江北（ㄐㄧㄤ ㄅㄟˇ）
the area north of the Yangtze River (particularly referring to northern Kiangsu)

江表（ㄐㄧㄤ ㄅㄧㄠˇ）
the area south of the Yangtze River

江畔（ㄐㄧㄤ ㄆㄢˋ）
the river bank; beside the river

江防（ㄐㄧㄤ ㄈㄤˊ）
① river control works for the Yangtze River ② defense works along the Yangtze River

江東（ㄐㄧㄤ ㄉㄨㄥ）
the Kiangsu area; the lower reaches of the Yangtze River

江南（ㄐㄧㄤ ㄋㄢˊ）
the entire area south of the Yangtze River (particularly referring to southern Kiangsu)

江郎才盡（ㄐㄧㄤ ㄌㄤˊ ㄘㄞˊ ㄐㄧㄣˋ）
to have used up one's literary talent or energy—the reference is about Chiang Yen (江淹)

江輪（ㄐㄧㄤ ㄌㄨㄣˊ）
a river steamship

江河行地（ㄐㄧㄤ ㄏㄜˊ ㄒㄧㄥˊ ㄉㄧˋ）
unalterable (like rivers flowing through on the surface of the earth)

江河日下（ㄐㄧㄤ ㄏㄜˊ ㄖˋ ㄒㄧㄚˋ）
to decline steadily (as river water flows downstream); to go from bad to worse

江湖（ㄐㄧㄤ ㄏㄨˊ）
① rivers and lakes ② wandering; vagrant; vagabond: 他曾流落江湖。He once lived a vagabond life. ③ sophisticated and shrewd ④ practicing quackery; a quack

江湖客（ㄐㄧㄤ ㄏㄨˊ ㄎㄜˋ）
an itinerant

江湖氣（ㄐㄧㄤ ㄏㄨˊ ㄑㄧˋ）
insincere; sly; sleekly

江淮（ㄐㄧㄤ ㄏㄨㄞˊ）
① the Yangtze River and the Huai River (淮河) ② Kiangsu and Anhwei provinces

江西（ㄐㄧㄤ ㄒㄧ）
Kiangsi Province

江心（ㄐㄧㄤ ㄒㄧㄣ）
the middle of a river (as opposed to portions near the banks)

江心補漏（ㄐㄧㄤ ㄒㄧㄣ ㄅㄨˇ ㄌㄡˋ）
(literally) to mend a leak in midstream—to try to prevent a disaster when it is too late

江浙（ㄐㄧㄤ ㄓㄜˋ）
Kiangsu (江蘇) and Chekiang (浙江)

江浙菜（ㄐㄧㄤ ㄓㄜˋ ㄘㄞˋ）
cuisine of the Kiangsu-Chekiang area

江山（ㄐㄧㄤ ㄕㄢ）
the mountains and rivers of a country—the land; the throne; the national territory or authority over it: 那君王已失江山。That King has lost his political power.

江山美人（ㄐㄧㄤ ㄕㄢ ㄇㄟˇ ㄖㄣˊ）
the land and the beauty

江山易改, 本性難移（ㄐㄧㄤ ㄕㄢ ㄧˋ ㄍㄞˇ, ㄅㄣˇ ㄒㄧㄥˋ ㄋㄢˊ ㄧˊ）
Changing one's nature is harder than changing mountains and rivers. 或 A fox may grow gray, but never

good. 或 A leopard never changes his spots.

江水（ㄐㄧㄤ ㄕㄨㄟˇ）
river water

江左（ㄐㄧㄤ ㄗㄨㄛˇ）
the Kiangsu area

江蘇（ㄐㄧㄤ ㄙㄨ）
Kiangsu Province

江瑤柱（ㄐㄧㄤ ㄧㄠˊ ㄓㄨˋ）
a scallop

江右（ㄐㄧㄤ ㄧㄡˋ）
the Kiangsi area

江淹（ㄐㄧㄤ ㄧㄢ）
Chiang Yen (444-505), famous for his achievement in literature, but his talent exhausted in old age

江洋大盜（ㄐㄧㄤ ㄧㄤˊ ㄉㄚˋ ㄉㄠˋ）
a notorious bandit leader

江月（ㄐㄧㄤ ㄩㄝˋ）
the moon's reflection on a river

【汛】 2777 ㄒㄩㄣˋ shiunn xùn
1. to sprinkle
2. abundant water; a flood
3. menses; menstruation

汛期（ㄒㄩㄣˋ ㄑㄧˊ）
(irrigation) the flood season

【汞】 2778 《ㄨㄥˇ goong gǒng（又讀 ㄏㄨㄥˊ hong hóng）
mercury (an element)

汞粉（《ㄨㄥˇ ㄈㄣˇ）
calomel

汞齊（《ㄨㄥˇ ㄐㄧˋ）
amalgam 亦作「賔齊」

汞化物（《ㄨㄥˇ ㄏㄨㄚˋ ㄨˋ）
mercuride

汞養 or 汞氧（《ㄨㄥˇ ㄧㄤˋ）
oxide of mercury

【污】 2779（汗,汙）ㄨ u wū
1. dirty; filthy
2. to stain; to mar; to insult; to slander: 殘曝玷污了他的品性。His character was stained by cruelty.
3. corrupt: 污吏接受了該貪款。The corrupt official accepted the money.

污衊（ㄨ ㄇㄧㄝˋ）
to libel; to slander

污名（ㄨ ㄇㄧㄥˊ）
infamy; dishonor

污點（ㄨ ㄉㄧㄢˇ）

a blot; a stain; a smear; a
flaw; a defect: 他的品性是沒
有污點的。His character is
without a stain.

污泥（ㄨ ㄋㄧˊ）
mud: 他的上衣染有污泥。He
has mud stains on his coat.

污吏（ㄨ ㄌㄧˋ）
a corrupt official

污垢（ㄨ ㄍㄡˋ）
dirt; filth: 我怎樣除去牆上的
污垢呢？How can I get the
dirt off the walls?

污穢（ㄨ ㄏㄨㄟˋ）
dirty; filthy: 那是條污穢的街
道。That's a filthy street.

污穢不堪（ㄨ ㄏㄨㄟˋ ㄅㄨˋ ㄎㄢ）
intolerably dirty or filthy

污跡（ㄨ ㄐㄧ）
stains; smears; smudges

污臭（ㄨ ㄔㄡˋ）
a foul odor

污濁（ㄨ ㄓㄨㄛˊ）
muddy; dirty; foul; filthy: 那
是條污濁的溪流。It is a
muddy stream.

污水（ㄨ ㄕㄨㄟˇ）
sewage; filthy water

污水處理（ㄨ ㄕㄨㄟˇ ㄔㄨˇ ㄌㄧˇ）
sewage disposal; sewage
treatment

污染（ㄨ ㄖㄢˇ）
to stain; to contaminate; to
pollute; contamination; pollution: 我們應謹慎避免供水的
污染。We must be careful to
avoid contamination of our
water supply.

污辱（ㄨ ㄖㄨˇ）
①to insult; to shame; to
humiliate ②to rape

污俗（ㄨ ㄙㄨˊ）
vulgar custom

污損（ㄨ ㄙㄨㄣˇ）
to stain and damage; to contaminate

四畫

【汨】 2780
（ㄇㄧˋ mih mi）
name of a river in Hunan
Province

汨羅（ㄇㄧˋ ㄌㄨㄛˊ）or 汨羅江（ㄇㄧˋ
ㄌㄨㄛˊ ㄐㄧㄤ）
a river in Hunan Province
(where the ancient poet, Chü

Yüan（屈原）drowned him-
self)

【汩】 2781
1.《ㄍㄨˇ guu gǔ》
1. to dredge (a channel, etc.)
2. confused; disorderly
3. the sound of waves
4. a Chinese family name

汩沒（ㄍㄨˇ ㄇㄛˋ）
to sink; to decline

汩亂（ㄍㄨˇ ㄌㄨㄢˋ）
to cause disorder

汩汩（ㄍㄨˇ ㄍㄨˇ）
①the sound of waves: 那溪
流繞著石頭汩汩地流著。The
stream gurgled around the
rocks. ②panicky; in confusion

【汩】 2781
2.《ㄩˋ yuh yù》
rapid; fleeting

汩流（ㄩˋ ㄌㄧㄡˊ）
rapids

【汭】 2782
ㄖㄨㄟˋ ruey ruì
a bend in a stream

【汰】 2783
ㄊㄞˋ tay tài
1. excessive
2. to sift; to eliminate; to
remove

汰揀（ㄊㄞˋ ㄐㄧㄢˇ）
to wash and polish

汰去（ㄊㄞˋ ㄑㄩˋ）
to eliminate; to remove

汰侈（ㄊㄞˋ ㄔˇ）
excessive luxury; too extravagant

汰沙（ㄊㄞˋ ㄕㄚ）
①to sift sand ②to elimi-
nate useless stuff

汰弱留強（ㄊㄞˋ ㄖㄨㄛˋ ㄌㄧㄡˊ ㄑㄧㄤˊ）
to weed out the weak and
retain the strong

【汪】 2784
ㄨㄤ uang wāng
1. (said of water) deep and
extensive
2. a puddle: 一汪雨水 a puddle
of rainwater
3. (said of liquid) to soak; to
collect; to accumulate: 連那
子都汪著水。Even the straw
mat was soaked.
4. a Chinese family name

汪達爾（ㄨㄤ ㄉㄚˊ ㄦˇ）
the Vandals

汪精衛（ㄨㄤ ㄐㄧㄥ ㄨㄟˋ）

Wang Ching-wei, 1883-1944,
who once tried to assassinate Tsai Li（載澧）, the
regent of the Ching Dynasty,
and was thus put in prison
until the revolution of 1911
in Wuchang

汪洋（ㄨㄤ ㄧㄤˊ）
a vast expanse of water,
汪洋浩瀚the vast expanse of
the ocean

汪洋大海（ㄨㄤ ㄧㄤˊ ㄉㄚˋ ㄏㄞˇ）
the vast expanse of sea
or ocean

汪汪（ㄨㄤ ㄨㄤ）
①(said of water)deep and
extensive ②the barking of
dogs; a bowwow: 這隻黑狗汪
汪地叫著。The black dog is
barking. ③ brimming with
tears: 一股油然而生的憐憫之
情使他淚眼汪汪。Sudden pity
teared his sight.

【汲】 2785
ㄐㄧˊ jyi jí
1. to draw water or liquid: 他
從池裡汲水。He drew water
from the pond.
2. a Chinese family name

汲道（ㄐㄧˊ ㄉㄠˋ）
a road for drawing water

汲古（ㄐㄧˊ ㄍㄨˇ）
to explore the classics

汲古閣（ㄐㄧˊ ㄍㄨˇ ㄍㄜˊ）
the library of Mao Chin（毛
晉）in the Ming Dynasty,
with a collection of more
than 80,000 volumes, besides
many books reprinted under
his personal supervision

汲汲（ㄐㄧˊ ㄐㄧˊ）
anxious; avid; restless(ly);
to crave: 勿汲汲於個人名利。
Do not crave personal fame
and gain.

汲酒（ㄐㄧˊ ㄐㄧㄡˇ）
to draw wine from a barrel

汲取（ㄐㄧˊ ㄑㄩˇ）
to draw; to derive: 他由讀書
中汲取快樂。He derived pleas-
ure from reading.

汲水（ㄐㄧˊ ㄕㄨㄟˇ）
to draw water

汲水機（ㄐㄧˊ ㄕㄨㄟˇ ㄐㄧ）
a device for drawing water

汲水唧筒（ㄐㄧˊ ㄕㄨㄟˇ ㄐㄧ ㄊㄨㄥˇ）
a pump

汲引(ㄐㄧˊ ㄧㄣˇ)
to employ people of talent:
汲引後進 to employ and pro-
mote younger talents to
higher positions

(水部)

2786
【決】 (決) ㄐㄩㄝˊ jyue
　　　　　 jué

1. to decide; to conclude; to
judge: 他將決定誰先去。He'll
decide who goes first.
2. (said of a dike) to burst; to
break
3. certain; sure; definite
4. to put someone to death; to
execute a person: 他們槍決了
那個犯人。They executed that
prisoner by shooting.

決不(ㄐㄩㄝˊ ㄅㄨˋ)
never: 我們決不退讓。We will
never give in.

決不寬貸(ㄐㄩㄝˊ ㄅㄨˋ ㄎㄨㄢ ㄉㄞˋ)
On no account will leniency
be shown.

決不至於(ㄐㄩㄝˊ ㄅㄨˋ ㄓˋ ㄩˊ)
will certainly not be so (bad
or good)

決不食言(ㄐㄩㄝˊ ㄅㄨˋ ㄕˊ ㄧㄢˊ)
never to break a promise

決非(ㄐㄩㄝˊ ㄈㄟ)
by no means; in no way: 他
們臉色黝黑, 但決非難看。They
are dark-faced, but by
no means bad-looking.

決防(ㄐㄩㄝˊ ㄈㄤˊ)
the breach or rupture of a
dike

決門or **決鬥**(ㄐㄩㄝˊ ㄉㄡˋ)
a duel; to fight a duel: 我向
你挑戰作一決鬥。I challenge
you to a duel.

決定(ㄐㄩㄝˊ ㄉㄧㄥˋ)
to determine; to decide; to
resolve; a decision: 他決定更
用功。He resolved to work
harder.

決定權(ㄐㄩㄝˊ ㄉㄧㄥˋ ㄑㄩㄢˊ)
the say; the power to make
decisions

決定性的(ㄐㄩㄝˊ ㄉㄧㄥˋ ㄒㄧㄥˋ ˙ㄉㄜ)
decisive: 我們贏得決定性的戰
役。We won a decisive battle.

決斷(ㄐㄩㄝˊ ㄉㄨㄢˋ)
to decide; to make a decision; to conclude

決堤(ㄐㄩㄝˊ ㄊㄧˊ)
the collapse of an embankment or a dyke

決裂(ㄐㄩㄝˊ ㄌㄧㄝˋ)
①to burst open; to suffer a
rupture ②to break; to break
off relations; a rupture: 他們
的友情決裂了。Their friend-
ship was broken off.

決口(ㄐㄩㄝˊ ㄎㄡˇ)
a rupture; an opening

決計(ㄐㄩㄝˊ ㄐㄧˋ)
①to make up one's mind; to
decide: 我決計要去加拿大。I
have decided to leave for
Canada. ② absolutely; certainly: 他這麼辦決計沒錯兒。
We absolutely can't go
wrong if we do it this way.

決絕(ㄐㄩㄝˊ ㄐㄩㄝˊ)
①to sever relations firmly
②to part forever

決心(ㄐㄩㄝˊ ㄒㄧㄣ)
to make up one's mind; to
resolve; determination; determined: 他決心改正自己的錯
誤。He is determined to correct his own mistakes.

決選(ㄐㄩㄝˊ ㄒㄩㄢˇ)
a runoff election; a runoff

決戰(ㄐㄩㄝˊ ㄓㄢˋ)
a decisive battle; to fight a
decisive battle

決勝(ㄐㄩㄝˊ ㄕㄥˋ)
①certain to bring victory
②to decide a contest

決然(ㄐㄩㄝˊ ㄖㄢˊ)
resolutely; firmly; in a determined manner

決眥(ㄐㄩㄝˊ ㄗˋ)
to have a lesion in the eye
(in consequence of an angry
stare)

決擇(ㄐㄩㄝˊ ㄗㄜˊ)
to make a final resolution
between possible alterna-
tives

決雌雄(ㄐㄩㄝˊ ㄘ ㄒㄩㄥˊ)
to fight a decisive battle

決策(ㄐㄩㄝˊ ㄘㄜˋ)
an adopted policy; a decision

決策機構(ㄐㄩㄝˊ ㄘㄜˋ ㄐㄧ ㄍㄡˋ)
a policy-making agency

決死(ㄐㄩㄝˊ ㄙˇ)
life-and-death: 那是一場決死
的戰鬥。That was a life-and-
death struggle.

決賽(ㄐㄩㄝˊ ㄙㄞˋ)
the final (of a contest, race,
etc.): 他將參加網球決賽。He
will take part in the tennis
finals.

決算(ㄐㄩㄝˊ ㄙㄨㄢˋ)
a final financial statement

決疑(ㄐㄩㄝˊ ㄧˊ)
to settle a doubtful point; to
dispel doubts

決意(ㄐㄩㄝˊ ㄧˋ)
to make up one's mind; to
decide; to resolve

決議(ㄐㄩㄝˊ ㄧˋ)
a resolution (reached at a
meeting); a decision; to
decide; to resolve

決議案(ㄐㄩㄝˊ ㄧˋ ㄢˋ)
a resolution (reached at a
meeting)

決無(ㄐㄩㄝˊ ㄨˊ)
never; by no means; impossible: 那是決無可能的事啊!
What an impossible story!

決獄(ㄐㄩㄝˊ ㄩˋ)
to decide a legal case

2787
【汶】 ㄨㄣˊ wenn wèn
name of a river in Shantung

汶水(ㄨㄣˊ ㄕㄨㄟˇ)
name of a river in Shantung

2788
【汴】 ㄅㄧㄢˋ biann biàn
1. an alternative name for
Honan
2. the ancient name of a river
in Honan

汴京(ㄅㄧㄢˋ ㄐㄧㄥ)or **汴梁**(ㄅㄧㄢˋ
ㄌㄧㄤˊ)
the capital of the Northern
Sung Dynasty, at what is
Kaifeng (開封) today

汴水(ㄅㄧㄢˋ ㄕㄨㄟˇ)
the ancient name of a river
in Honan

2789
【汾】 ㄈㄣˊ fern fén
name of a tributary of the
Yellow River

汾酒(ㄈㄣˊ ㄐㄧㄡˇ)
kaoliang wine made in the
Fen River (汾水) area

汾水(ㄈㄣˊ ㄕㄨㄟˇ)or **汾河**(ㄈㄣˊ ㄏㄜˊ)
name of a tributary of the
Yellow River

2790
【沁】 ㄑㄧㄣˋ chinn qìn
to soak; to seep; to perco-

late; to permeate; to ooze; to exude: 他的額上沁出了汗珠。His forehead was oozing sweat.

沁水（くⅠㄣ ㄕㄨㄟˇ）
a county in Shansi Province

沁人心脾（くⅠㄣ ㄖㄣˊ ㄒⅠㄣ ㄆⅠˊ）
to affect people deeply; to touch one's heart

沁入（くⅠㄣ ㄖㄨˋ）
to soak into; to soak through; to permeate: 水會沁入土中。Water will soak through the earth.

【沂】 2791
　Ⅰˊ yi yí
names of four rivers originating in Shantung

沂水（Ⅰˊ ㄕㄨㄟˇ）
①name of a county in Shantung ②names of the rivers originating in Shantung

【沅】 2792
　ㄩㄢˊ yuan yuán
name of a river flowing through Hunan

沅水（ㄩㄢˊ ㄕㄨㄟˇ）or 沅江（ㄩㄢˊ ㄐⅠㄤ）
name of a river flowing through Hunan

【沃】 2793
　ㄨㄛˋ woh wò
1. to irrigate: 沃田 to irrigate farmland
2. (said of land) fertile: 這塊土地很肥沃。The land is fertile.

沃土（ㄨㄛˋ ㄊㄨˇ）
fertile land

沃饒（ㄨㄛˋ ㄖㄠˊ）
fertile and productive

沃壤（ㄨㄛˋ ㄖㄤˇ）
fertile soil

沃潤（ㄨㄛˋ ㄖㄨㄣˋ）
fertile and moist

沃野千里（ㄨㄛˋ Ⅰㄝˇ くⅠㄢ ㄌⅠˇ）
an endless expanse of fertile land

沃衍（ㄨㄛˋ Ⅰㄢˇ）
a fertile area

沃腴（ㄨㄛˋ ㄩˊ）
fertile

【汽】 2794
　くⅠˋ chìh qì
gas; steam; vapor

汽表（くⅠˋ ㄅⅠㄠˇ）
a steam gauge

汽泡（くⅠˋ ㄆㄠˋ）
bubbles

汽門（くⅠˋ ㄇㄣˊ）
a steam valve

汽笛（くⅠˋ ㄉⅠˊ）
a steam whistle; a siren

汽艇（くⅠˋ ㄊⅠㄥˇ）
a motorboat; a steam launch

汽缸（くⅠˋ ㄍㄤ）
cylinders (in automobiles, motorcycles, etc.)

汽鍋（くⅠˋ ㄍㄨㄛ）
a boiler; a steam boiler

汽管（くⅠˋ ㄍㄨㄢˇ）
a steam pipe

汽焊（くⅠˋ ㄏㄢˋ）
oxyacetylene welding

汽化（くⅠˋ ㄏㄨㄚˋ）
vaporization; to vaporize: 水煮沸時就汽化。Water vaporizes when boiled.

汽機（くⅠˋ ㄐⅠ）
a steam engine

汽槍（くⅠˋ くⅠㄤ）
an air gun

汽車（くⅠˋ ㄔㄜ）
an automobile: 警察吹警笛令汽車停止。The policeman whistled for the automobile to stop.

汽車旅館（くⅠˋ ㄔㄜ ㄌㄩˇ ㄍㄨㄢˇ）
a motel

汽車工業（くⅠˋ ㄔㄜ ㄍㄨㄥ Ⅰㄝˋ）
the auto industry

汽車間（くⅠˋ ㄔㄜ ㄐⅠㄢ）
a garage: 我租了一幢有汽車間的房子。I rented a house with a garage.

汽船（くⅠˋ ㄔㄨㄢˊ）
a steamship; a steamboat; a steamer

汽水（くⅠˋ ㄕㄨㄟˇ）or 汽水兒（くⅠˋ ㄕㄨㄟˇㄦ）
soda water; soft drinks or soda pop: 她喝了一杯汽水。She drank a glass of soda.

汽壓（くⅠˋ Ⅰㄚ）
steam pressure

汽油（くⅠˋ Ⅰㄡˊ）
gasoline; gas: 我的汽油用完了。I've run out of gas.

汽油彈（くⅠˋ Ⅰㄡˊ ㄉㄢˋ）
①a napalm bomb ②a fire bomb or Molotov cocktail

汽油引擎（くⅠˋ Ⅰㄡˊ Ⅰㄣˇ くⅠㄥˊ）
a gasoline engine

【沇】 2795
　Ⅰㄢˇ yean yǎn
flowing and engulfing; overflowing and brimming

沇水（Ⅰㄢˇ ㄕㄨㄟˇ）
①the Chi River (濟水), in Honan (河南) ②the Yen River in Shansi (山西)

【沆】 2796
　ㄏㄤˊ harng háng
to ferry; a ferry

【沆】 2796
　ㄏㄤˋ hanq hàng
1. a vast expanse of water
2. mist; fog
3. flowing

沆茫（ㄏㄤˋ ㄇㄤˊ）or 沆漭（ㄏㄤˋ ㄇㄤˇ）
an expanse of water; water immeasurable

沆瀣（ㄏㄤˋ ㄒⅠㄝˋ）
moderately flowing waters

沆瀣一氣（ㄏㄤˋ ㄒⅠㄝˋ Ⅰ くⅠˋ）
(to talk, think, etc.) in the same vein; the meeting of minds; to gang up for an objective

沆濭（ㄏㄤˋ ㄞˋ）
expansive waters

【沌】 2797
　ㄉㄨㄣˋ duenn dùn
turbid; unclear; chaotic: 混沌 the chaotic world in prehistoric times

【沈】 2798
　1. （沉）ㄔㄣˊ chern chén
1. to sink; to be drawn deep into; to submerge; to set: 太陽沈到山後。The sun sank behind the mountain.
2. to indulge in; to be addicted to: 他沈迷於吸煙。He is addicted to smoking.
3. (said of sleep) deep; sound; fast: 他睡得很沈。He was in a deep sleep.
4. persistent and lasting; for a long time
5. delaying; postponement
6. heavy (in weight): 這包沙太沈了。This sack of sand is too heavy.
7. latent; hidden
8. to straighten (one's face); to put on a grave expression: 他那臉一沈。He put on a grave expression.
9. to retain (one's composure); to restrain (oneself from

（水部）

沈得住氣，He contained his anger.

沈博絕麗(ㄕㄣˊ ㄅㄛˊ ㄐㄩㄝˊ ㄌㄧˋ)
(said of literary works) profound in substance and beautiful in style

沈不住氣(ㄕㄣˊ·ㄅㄨ ㄓㄨˋ ㄑㄧˋ)
to be rash; easily excited; excitable; cannot remain calm

沈沒(ㄕㄣˊ ㄇㄛˋ)
to sink

沈默(ㄕㄣˊ ㄇㄛˋ)
silence; silent; reticent: 沈默即同意, Silence gives consent.

沈默寡言(ㄕㄣˊ ㄇㄛˋ ㄍㄨㄚˇ ㄧㄢˊ)
taciturn; reticent: 他是個沈默寡言的人. He is a taciturn person.

沈默是金(ㄕㄣˊ ㄇㄛˋ ㄕˋ ㄐㄧㄣ)
Silence is golden.

沈悶(ㄕㄣˊ ㄇㄣˋ)
①depressed; heavy at heart: 他的心情沈悶. He felt depressed. ②dull and heavy (atmosphere); hot and humid

沈迷(ㄕㄣˊ ㄇㄧˊ)
to indulge in; to wallow in: 他沈迷於金錢. He is wallowing in money.

沈迷不醒(ㄕㄣˊ ㄇㄧˊ ㄅㄨˋ ㄒㄧㄥˇ) or 沈迷不悟(ㄕㄣˊ ㄇㄧˊ ㄅㄨˋ ㄨˋ)
deeply addicted to, imbibed or infatuated in (vice, sinful ways, etc.)

沈綿(ㄕㄣˊ ㄇㄧㄢˊ)
chronic (diseases); persistent and lasting

沈湎(ㄕㄣˊ ㄇㄧㄢˇ)
to wallow in; to be abandoned (or given) to: 他沈湎於賭博. He was given to gambling.

沈湎酒色(ㄕㄣˊ ㄇㄧㄢˇ ㄐㄧㄡˇ ㄙㄜˋ)
to overindulge oneself in wine and women; to sink deeply into the world of wine and sex

沈冥(ㄕㄣˊ ㄇㄧㄥˊ)
to leave without a trace; traceless

沈伏(ㄕㄣˊ ㄈㄨˊ)
①latent; hidden; not obvious ②dull and slow ③a low official rank that does not command attention

沈浮(ㄕㄣˊ ㄈㄨˊ)
①ups and downs in a person's life ②to follow or change with prevailing customs, practices, etc. ③(now rarely) very many

沈達(ㄕㄣˊ ㄉㄚˊ)
quiet and understanding; silent but aboveboard

沈得住氣(ㄕㄣˊ ㄉㄜˊ ㄓㄨˋ ㄑㄧˋ)
to retain one's composure; to be able to restrain oneself even in an emotional crisis; calm: 他總是沈得住氣. He always keeps his composure.

沈甸甸(ㄕㄣˊ ㄉㄧㄢˋ ㄉㄧㄢˋ·ㄉㄜ)
①(said of swords, pens, chopsticks or tools) heavy and not easy to wield ②heavy: 這一袋麵粉沈甸甸的. This sack of flour is pretty heavy. ③heavy (at heart); serious (looks)

沈澱(ㄕㄣˊ ㄉㄧㄢˋ)
to precipitate; to settle; sediment

沈澱物(ㄕㄣˊ ㄉㄧㄢˋ ㄨˋ)
sediment: 茶中有沈澱物. There's some sediment in the tea.

沈痛(ㄕㄣˊ ㄊㄨㄥˋ)
①to be deeply grieved; to be heavy or painful at heart: 她母親的去世使她感到非常沈痛. She was deeply grieved at her mother's death. ②bitter: 這是個沈痛的教訓. It is a bitter lesson.

沈溺(ㄕㄣˊ ㄋㄧˋ)
①to be imbibed or to indulge in (vices, etc.); to immerse in: 他沈溺於一本書中. He was immersed in a book. ②to sink and submerge in water

沈落(ㄕㄣˊ ㄌㄨㄛˋ)
to sink; to fall down

沈淪(ㄕㄣˊ ㄌㄨㄣˊ)
to drown and perish (in water, sins, etc.)

沈痼(ㄕㄣˊ ㄍㄨˋ)
①a chronic disease or ailment; a serious illness ②a bad habit from which one cannot withdraw

沈厚(ㄕㄣˊ ㄏㄡˋ)
①calm and sincere ②profundity

沈酣(ㄕㄣˊ ㄏㄢ)
①to be comfortably drunk ②to indulge oneself or be imbibed in (an amusement, pastime, hobby, etc.)

沈酣經史(ㄕㄣˊ ㄏㄢ ㄐㄧㄥ ㄕˇ)
deeply absorbed in the study of classics

沈積岩(ㄕㄣˊ ㄐㄧ ㄧㄢˊ)
sedimentary rocks

沈機觀變(ㄕㄣˊ ㄐㄧ ㄍㄨㄢ ㄅㄧㄢˋ)
to watch calmly the changes and turns of affairs

沈寂(ㄕㄣˊ ㄐㄧˊ)
①quiet; silent; hush; hushed: 房間陷入一片沈寂. A hush fell over the room. ②newsless; traceless ③to lie low

沈浸(ㄕㄣˊ ㄐㄧㄣˋ)
①to permeate; to be immersed in; to submerge; to be steeped in: 她沈浸在快樂的回憶裏. She was immersed in happy memories. ②very erudite

沈降(ㄕㄣˊ ㄐㄧㄤˋ)
to subside

沈靜(ㄕㄣˊ ㄐㄧㄥˋ)
calm; quiet; placid: 他心情沈靜. He was in a placid mood.

沈潛(ㄕㄣˊ ㄑㄧㄢˊ)
of a thoughtful and calm disposition; reserved and retiring

沈西(ㄕㄣˊ ㄒㄧ)
(literally) to sink in the west—sunset

沈下臉來(ㄕㄣˊ ㄒㄧㄚˋ ㄌㄧㄢˇ ㄌㄞˊ)
to straighten one's face—to turn on an angry look; to pull a long face

沈陷(ㄕㄣˊ ㄒㄧㄢˋ)
①to sink; to cave in: 地震使土地沈陷了. The earthquake made the ground cave in. ②(construction) settlement

沈心(ㄕㄣˊ ㄒㄧㄣ)
①to get angry through misunderstanding ②to think deeply and consider carefully

沈香(ㄕㄣˊ ㄒㄧㄤ) or 沈香木(ㄕㄣˊ ㄒㄧㄤ ㄇㄨˋ)
aloeswood; agalloch eaglewood

沈酗(ㄕㄣˊ ㄒㄩˋ)
to be addicted to liquor;

alcoholism; dead drunk

沈滯(ㄕㄣ ㄓ)
①stagnant; stalemated ②to feel bad and miserable ③to remain in an inferior position for a long time

沈舟破釜(ㄕㄣ ㄓㄡ ㄆㄛ ㄈㄨ)
to cast the dice; to reach the point of no return; to cross the Rubicon 參看「破斧沈舟」

沈佳氣(ㄕㄣ ㄓㄚ ㄑㄧˋ)
Steady (on)! 或 to restrain oneself; to control one's temper; to remain calm or composed

沈著(ㄕㄣ ㄓㄜˊ)
calm and steady; slow but sure; serene; composed

沈重(ㄕㄣ ㄓㄨㄥˋ)
①heavy (in weight)② heavy (at heart); serious (looks)③ calm, steady and graceful; dignified

沈沈(ㄕㄣ ㄕㄣ)
①heavy: 玉蜀黍穗沈沈地垂下來。The ears of corn hang heavy on the stalks. ② deep: 他已沈沈入睡。He has sunk into a deep sleep. ③ dull; gloomy; dark; dreary: 暮氣沈沈 lifeless; lethargic

沈船(ㄕㄣ ㄔㄨㄢˊ)
①a sunken ship; a shipwreck ②to scuttle a ship

沈睡(ㄕㄣ ㄕㄨㄟˋ)or 沈眠(ㄕㄣ ㄇㄧㄢˊ)
deep slumber; sound sleep

沈醉(ㄕㄣ ㄗㄨㄟˋ)
①dead-drunk ②to become intoxicated

沈猜(ㄕㄣ ㄘㄞ)
to be very suspicious

沈思(ㄕㄣ ㄙ)
to ponder; to meditate; to contemplate; meditation; contemplation

沈思凝想(ㄕㄣ ㄙ ㄋㄧㄥˊ ㄒㄧㄤˇ)
to ponder; to think deeply or profoundly

沈邃(ㄕㄣ ㄙㄨㄟˋ)
deep and profound; deep and obscure

沈疴(ㄕㄣ ㄎㄜ)or 沈痼(ㄕㄣ ㄍㄨˋ)
a chronic disease; a serious ailment of long standing

沈疑(ㄕㄣ ㄧˊ)
hesitant, suspicious and deep-thinking

沈抑(ㄕㄣ ㄧˋ)
(said of talents, etc.) buried or submerged

沈毅(ㄕㄣ ㄧˋ)
steady and sturdy; fortitude

沈壓(ㄕㄣ ㄧㄚ)
buried and submerged (talents, etc.)

沈憂(ㄕㄣ ㄧㄡ)
deep worries and anxiety; melancholic

沈吟(ㄕㄣ ㄧㄣˊ)
①to hesitate ②to ponder; to think deeply

沈飲(ㄕㄣ ㄧㄣˇ)
to drink heavily

沈魚落雁(ㄕㄣ ㄩˊ ㄌㄨㄛˋ ㄧㄢˋ)
(said of women) extremely beautiful

沈鬱(ㄕㄣ ㄩˋ)
deeply depressed; downcast; gloomy

沈鬱頓挫(ㄕㄣ ㄩˋ ㄉㄨㄣˋ ㄘㄨㄛˋ)
(said of literary works) profound and forceful

沈冤(ㄕㄣ ㄩㄢ)
an unredressed wrong or grievance of long standing; a grievous wrong: 他沈冤莫白。He suffered a grievous wrong.

沈遠(ㄕㄣ ㄩㄢˇ)
far and great (ambitions, objectives, etc.)

沈勇(ㄕㄣ ㄩㄥˇ)
calm, steady and courageous

【沈】 2798
2. ㄕㄣˊ sheen shén
a Chinese family name

沈周(ㄕㄣˊ ㄓㄡ)or 沈石田(ㄕㄣˊ ㄕˊ ㄊㄧㄢˊ)
Shen Chou, 1472-1509, a noted landscape painter in the Ming Dynasty

沈腰(ㄕㄣˊ ㄧㄠ)
slender waist—the reference is about Shen Yüeh (沈約)

沈腰潘鬢(ㄕㄣˊ ㄧㄠ ㄆㄢ ㄅㄧㄣˋ)
to have a slender waist and hoary hair, the reference is about Shen Yüeh (沈約) and Pan Yüeh (潘岳)

沈約(ㄕㄣˊ ㄩㄝ)
Shen Yüeh, 441-513, an official and scholar of the Liang Dynasty, best remembered for his 四聲譜, an epoch-making work in phonology

【沐】 2799
ㄇㄨˋ muh mù
1. to shampoo; to wash; to bathe; to cleanse
2. a holiday; a leave; to take a leave
3. to receive favor
4. a Chinese family name

沐猴(ㄇㄨˋ ㄏㄡˊ)
a macaque

沐猴而冠(ㄇㄨˋ ㄏㄡˊ ㄦˊ ㄍㄨㄢ)
(literally) to dress up a monkey, trying to fool people into believing that it's a man—A worthless fellow is a worthless fellow, no matter what he wears. 或 Beautiful clothes can't hide one's ugliness inside. 或 Clothes do not make the man.

沐櫛(ㄇㄨˋ ㄐㄧㄝˊ)
to shampoo and comb

沐日(ㄇㄨˋ ㄖˋ)
①a day of rest; a holiday ②sunbathing

沐恩(ㄇㄨˋ ㄣ)
①to receive favor ②(formerly) a self reference used by low-ranking officers in speaking to their superiors

沐雨櫛風(ㄇㄨˋ ㄩˇ ㄐㄧㄝˊ ㄈㄥ)
to work and toil; to work very hard regardless of weather

沐浴(ㄇㄨˋ ㄩˋ)or 沐洗(ㄇㄨˋ ㄒㄧˇ)
①to bathe ②to steep in or receive favor ③to soak in

沐浴淸化(ㄇㄨˋ ㄩˋ ㄑㄧㄥ ㄏㄨㄚˋ)
enriched by your kindness and transformed by your purity

【沔】 2800
ㄇㄧㄢˇ mean miǎn
1. overflowing (water); a flood
2. name of a river

沔水(ㄇㄧㄢˇ ㄕㄨㄟˇ)
Mian River, or Han River, in Shansi Province

【沖】 2801
(冲) ㄔㄨㄥ chong chōng
1. to wash away; to wash with running water; to rinse; to flush: 這艘船被沖上岸來。The boat was washed ashore.

〔水
部〕

2. to soar; to rise rapidly or shoot up
3. to pour water (to powder, etc.); to make beverages, etc.; to infuse: 沖泡茶水 to infuse tea leaves in hot water to make tea
4. empty; void
5. to dash against; to clash with
6. childhood
7. to neutralize; to make void

沖犯(ㄔㄨㄥ ㄈㄢ)
to offend (a superior, an elder, etc.): 我希望我一點也沒有沖犯了你。 I hope I haven't offended you in any way.

沖服(ㄔㄨㄥ ㄈㄨ)
(medicine) to infuse with water and drink

沖倒(ㄔㄨㄥ ㄉㄠ)
to be crushed or knocked down by flood

沖淡(ㄔㄨㄥ ㄉㄢ)
① to dilute with water, etc.
② to play down; to mitigate the intensity of a situation or statement ③ to make few demands on life

沖塌(ㄔㄨㄥ ㄊㄚ)
to be destroyed by floods

沖天(ㄔㄨㄥ ㄊㄧㄢ)or 沖霄(ㄔㄨㄥ ㄒㄧㄠ)
to shoot up to the sky

沖退(ㄔㄨㄥ ㄊㄨㄟ)
to defer to; to be submissive

沖牛奶(ㄔㄨㄥ ㄋㄧㄡˊ ㄋㄞˇ)
to make milk from powdered milk by pouring boiling water

沖齡(ㄔㄨㄥ ㄌㄧㄥ)
childhood

沖開水(ㄔㄨㄥ ㄎㄞ ㄕㄨㄟ)
① to pour boiled water on; to infuse (tea, etc.); to pour boiling water in a thermos bottle ② (Shanghai dialect) to buy boiling water from a shop

沖口而出(ㄔㄨㄥ ㄎㄡˇ ㄦˊ ㄔㄨ)
to say something without thinking; to blurt out

沖和(ㄔㄨㄥ ㄏㄜˊ)
to diffuse; to dilute; to mix liquids

沖壞(ㄔㄨㄥ ㄏㄨㄞ)
to be damaged or destroyed by lashing waters or by

flood: 堤防被暴風雨沖壞了。 The embankment was washed out by the storm.

沖昏頭腦(ㄔㄨㄥ ㄏㄨㄣ ㄊㄡˊ ㄋㄠˇ)
to turn someone's head; dizzy

沖積(ㄔㄨㄥ ㄐㄧ)
alluviation

沖積期(ㄔㄨㄥ ㄐㄧ ㄑㄧˊ)
the alluvial epoch

沖積扇(ㄔㄨㄥ ㄐㄧ ㄕㄢ)
(geology) alluvial fan

沖積層(ㄔㄨㄥ ㄐㄧ ㄘㄥˊ)
an alluvium; an alluvial stratum; alluvial deposits

沖積物(ㄔㄨㄥ ㄐㄧ ㄨˋ)
sediment; deposit

沖擊(ㄔㄨㄥ ㄐㄧ)
(said of waves or floods) to lash or pound against: 海浪不斷地沖擊岩石。 The sea waves continuously lashed at the rocks.

沖襟(ㄔㄨㄥ ㄐㄧㄣ)
open-minded and at peace with oneself and the world

沖洗(ㄔㄨㄥ ㄒㄧˇ)
① to flush; to wash with running water; flush: 這水管堵住了，好好把它沖洗一下。 The pipe is blocked; give it a good flush. ② (photography) to develop or process negatives: 他在暗室沖洗底片。 He was in the darkroom developing his films.

沖喜(ㄔㄨㄥ ㄒㄧˇ)
(an old Chinese custom) to arrange a wedding for a young man who was seriously ill with the hope that the "event of great joy" would drive away his bad luck and hasten his recovery

沖虛(ㄔㄨㄥ ㄒㄩ)
① carefree; devoid of ambition ② to soar; to rise high

沖帳(ㄔㄨㄥ ㄓㄤˋ)or 沖賬(ㄔㄨㄥ ㄓㄤˋ)
(accounting) to cancel out an expenditure

沖撞(ㄔㄨㄥ ㄓㄨㄤ)
to offend (especially a superior, an elder, etc.): 你說的話真的沖撞了你的上司。 What you said really offended your boss.

沖茶(ㄔㄨㄥ ㄔㄚˊ)

to make tea

沖沖(ㄔㄨㄥ ㄔㄨㄥ)
① tinklings of pendants ② the sound of breaking ice ③ an infuriated expression

沖繩(ㄔㄨㄥ ㄕㄥ)
Okinawa

沖刷(ㄔㄨㄥ ㄕㄨㄚ)
erosion; to scour; to wash out (or away): 將鏽跡沖刷掉。 Scour the rust off.

沖散(ㄔㄨㄥ ㄙㄢ)
to disperse by the use of force; (said of a family in war or other great upheaval) to be scattered or separated in confusion: 警察將人羣沖散。 The police dispersed the crowd.

〔沙〕 2802

ㄕㄚ sha ㄕㄚˋ shà

1. sand; tiny gravel or pebbles: 孩子們喜歡在沙地上玩。 Children enjoy playing on the sands.
2. the land around water; a beach; a sandbank; a desert
3. to pick, select, sort or sift
4. (said of fruit, especially melons) overripe
5. (said of the human voice) hoarse: 他一直喊叫到聲音沙啞了。 He shouted until he was hoarse.
6. sandy—not glossy or smooth; granular
7. a kind of clay for making utensils, vessels, etc.
8. a Chinese family name

沙巴(ㄕㄚ ㄅㄚ)
Sabah, a state of Malaysia

沙包(ㄕㄚ ㄅㄠ)
① sandbags ② a porcelain vessel shaped like a small jug

沙暴(ㄕㄚ ㄅㄠˋ)
a sandstorm

沙盤演習(ㄕㄚ ㄆㄢˊ ㄧㄢˇ ㄒㄧˊ)or 沙盤作業(ㄕㄚ ㄆㄢˊ ㄗㄨㄛˋ ㄧㄝˋ)
(military) sand table exercises

沙模(ㄕㄚ ㄇㄛˊ)
a sand mold

沙漠(ㄕㄚ ㄇㄛˋ)
a desert: 那是沙漠中的綠洲。 That is an oasis in the desert.

沙漠之舟(ㄕㄚ ㄇㄛˋ ㄓ ㄓㄡ)

the ship of the desert—the camel

沙門(ㄕㄚ ㄇㄣˊ)
①(Buddhism) a monk or a nun ②name of an islet off the Shantung coast

沙彌(ㄕㄚ ㄇㄧˊ)or 沙彌僧(ㄕㄚ ㄇㄧ ㄙㄥ)
a Buddhist novice

沙彌子(ㄕㄚ ㄇㄧˊ ㄗ˙)
a monk who entered the temple or monastery at a very young age; a Buddhist novice

沙發(ㄕㄚ ㄈㄚ)
a sofa: 她在裝沙發套。She was upholstering the sofa.

沙袋(ㄕㄚ ㄉㄞˋ)
① sandbags ② an instrument of torture in ancient China made of layers of leather sewed together and stuffed with sand

沙丁魚(ㄕㄚ ㄉㄧㄥ ㄩˊ)
a sardine: 他們擠得像沙丁魚一樣。They were packed like sardines.

沙堆(ㄕㄚ ㄉㄨㄟ)
a sand dune; a sand hill

沙汰(ㄕㄚ ㄊㄞˋ)
to sift; to eliminate (as in a contest)

沙灘(ㄕㄚ ㄊㄢ)
a piece of sandy land around water; a sandbank; a sandy beach

沙糖(ㄕㄚ ㄊㄤˊ)
crystal sugar; granular sugar; brown sugar; powdered sugar

沙陸(ㄕㄚ ㄌㄨˋ)
a sand bar

沙田(ㄕㄚ ㄊㄧㄢˊ)
farmland converted from tideland

沙田柚(ㄕㄚ ㄊㄧㄢˊ ㄧㄡˋ)
pomelos produced in Kwangsi, especially in Junghsien (容縣)

沙土(ㄕㄚ ㄊㄨˇ)
a mixture of sand and clay; sandy soil

沙拉(ㄕㄚ ㄌㄚ)
salad: 水果沙拉 fruit salad

沙拉醬(ㄕㄚ ㄌㄚ ㄐㄧㄤˋ)
salad dressing

沙拉油(ㄕㄚ ㄌㄚ ㄧㄡˊ)
salad oil

沙勞越(ㄕㄚ ㄌㄠˊ ㄩㄝˋ)
Sarawak, a state of Malaysia

沙漏(ㄕㄚ ㄌㄡˋ)
① an hourglass ② a sand filter

沙裏淘金(ㄕㄚ ㄌㄧˇ ㄊㄠˊ ㄐㄧㄣ)
①to sift gold from sand ② to pick the best from a vast quantity ③ time-consuming

沙粒(ㄕㄚ ㄌㄧˋ)
sand grains

沙礫(ㄕㄚ ㄌㄧˋ)
pebbles; gravel; grit: 沙礫跑進我的鞋子裏。I have got grit in my shoe.

沙龍(ㄕㄚ ㄌㄨㄥˊ)
a salon

沙籠(ㄕㄚ ㄌㄨㄥˊ)
a sarong

沙濾(ㄕㄚ ㄌㄩˋ)or 沙濾器(ㄕㄚ ㄌㄩˋ ㄑㄧˋ)
a sand filter

沙鍋(ㄕㄚ ㄍㄨㄛ)
① an earthenware cooking pot ② food cooked and served in such a pot

沙果兒(ㄕㄚ ㄍㄨㄛˇ ㄦ)
a kind of small apples; the crab apple

沙坑(ㄕㄚ ㄎㄥ)
a sand pit

沙皇(ㄕㄚ ㄏㄨㄤˊ)
a czar or a tsar (of Russia)

沙金(ㄕㄚ ㄐㄧㄣ)
alluvial gold

沙磧(ㄕㄚ ㄑㄧˋ)
a desert

沙丘(ㄕㄚ ㄑㄧㄡ)
a sand dune; a sand hill

沙紙(ㄕㄚ ㄓˇ)
sandpaper; emery paper

沙洲(ㄕㄚ ㄓㄡ)
a shoal; a sand bar; a sandbank

沙渚(ㄕㄚ ㄓㄨˇ)
a sandy islet; a sandbank; a sand bar

沙場(ㄕㄚ ㄔㄤˇ)
a battlefield: 他戰死於沙場。He died on the battlefield.

沙石(ㄕㄚ ㄕˊ)
① gravel ② sandstone

沙士(ㄕㄚ ㄕˋ)
sarsaparilla

沙沙(ㄕㄚ ㄕㄚ)

to rustle; a rustle: 樹葉在微風中發出沙沙聲。Leaves rustled in the breeze.

沙沙聲響(ㄕㄚ ㄕㄚ ㄕㄥ ㄒㄧㄤˇ)
a light chafing sound; a rustle: 我們聽見樹葉的沙沙聲響。We have heard a rustle of leaves.

沙手(ㄕㄚ ㄕㄡˇ)
(Chinese boxing) hands toughened by rubbing daily with green beans and then iron sand, which are capable of performing unusual feats

沙子(ㄕㄚ ㄗ˙)
sand

沙俄(ㄕㄚ ㄜˊ)
czarist Russia

沙鷗(ㄕㄚ ㄡ)
a sea gull

沙啞(ㄕㄚ ㄧㄚˇ)
(said of the voice) husky; hoarse: 他唱了一小時後嗓子都沙啞了。He is hoarse after singing for an hour.

沙燕兒(ㄕㄚ ㄧㄢˋ ㄦ)
the common kite, looking like a swallow

沙岩(ㄕㄚ ㄧㄢˊ)
sandstone

沙眼(ㄕㄚ ㄧㄢˇ)
trachoma

沙烏地阿拉伯(ㄕㄚ ㄨ ㄉㄧ ㄚ ㄌㄚ ㄅㄛˊ)
Saudi Arabia

沙文主義(ㄕㄚ ㄨㄣˊ ㄓㄨˇ ㄧˋ)
chauvinism

沙魚(ㄕㄚ ㄩˊ)
the shark

【沒】 2803
1. ㄇㄛˋ moh mò
1. to sink; to submerge: 潛艇沒入水中。The submarine submerged.
2. to overflow; to rise beyond
3. to disappear
4. to go into oblivion: 在我們的歷史中,許多英雄被埋沒了。Many heroes went into oblivion.
5. none; exhausted
6. eliminated
7. finished; completed
8. to take property away from another; to confiscate
9. to die; dead

沒沒無聞(ㄇㄛˋ ㄇㄛˋ ㄨˊ ㄨㄣˊ)

【水

部】

(said of a person) unknown; nameless; obscure: 他是個沒沒無聞的作家。He was a nameless writer.

沒頂 (ㄇㄛ ㄉㄧㄥˇ)
to drown

沒奈何 (ㄇㄛ ㄋㄞˋ ㄏㄜˊ) or (ㄇㄟˊ ㄋㄞˋ ㄏㄜˊ)
to have no alternative; to have to; cannot but(do)

沒落 (ㄇㄛ ㄌㄨㄛˋ)
① to sink ② the fall or decline (of an empire, etc.): 羅馬帝國的沒落 the decline of the Rome Empire

沒骨畫 (ㄇㄛ ㄍㄨˇ ㄏㄨㄚˋ)
(in old China) a school of painting resembling today's watercolor

沒官 (ㄇㄛ ㄍㄨㄢ)
to be confiscated by the government

沒齒 (ㄇㄛ ㄔˇ)
to the end of one's life

沒齒難忘 (ㄇㄛ ㄔˇ ㄋㄢˊ ㄨㄤˋ)
to remember (a favor) as long as one lives: 你這個恩情叫我沒齒難忘。I always feel indebted to you for this favor.

沒世 (ㄇㄛ ㄕˋ)
① through one's lifetime ② eternal; forever; everlasting

沒收 (ㄇㄛ ㄕㄡ)
to confiscate; confiscation: 政府將所有叛國者的財產沒收了。The government confiscated the property of all traitors.

沒入 (ㄇㄛ ㄖㄨˋ)
to confiscate

【沒】 *2803*
2. (ㄇㄟˊ) mei méi
1. none; nothing; no: 我的財富一點也沒給我帶來快樂。I am none the happier for my wealth.
2. not yet; negative

沒把鼻 (ㄇㄟˊ ㄅㄚˇ ㄅㄧˊ)
groundless; without a basis; without any hold on (another, etc.)

沒把握 (ㄇㄟˊ ㄅㄚˇ ㄨㄛˋ)
not sure; not certain; uncertain: 他沒把握會成功。He is uncertain of success.

沒皮沒臉 (ㄇㄟˊ ㄆㄧˊ ㄇㄟˊ ㄌㄧㄢˇ)
shameless; shamelessly

沒皮賴臉 (ㄇㄟˊ ㄆㄧˊ ㄌㄞˋ ㄌㄧㄢˇ)
brazen-faced; brazen-facedly

沒譜兒 (ㄇㄟˊ ㄆㄨˇ ㄦ)
without any standard or criterion; to be unsure; to have no idea: 關於如何幫助他,我們還沒譜兒呢! We have no idea yet as to how to help him.

沒門兒 (ㄇㄟˊ ㄇㄣˊ ㄦ)
① to have no access to something; to have no means of doing something ② no go

沒命 (ㄇㄟˊ ㄇㄧㄥˋ)
① regardless of life; with one's all-out effort ② to die; dead

沒法兒 (ㄇㄟˊ ㄈㄚˇ ㄦ) or 沒法子 (ㄇㄟˊ ㄈㄚˇ ˙ㄗ)
no way out; no alternative (but⋯); without a way; to have to

沒分曉 (ㄇㄟˊ ㄈㄣ ㄒㄧㄠˇ)
foolish

沒縫兒 (ㄇㄟˊ ㄈㄥˋ ㄦ)
without a crack or loophole

沒大沒小 (ㄇㄟˊ ㄉㄚˋ ㄇㄟˊ ㄒㄧㄠˇ)
ill-mannered or rude to one's elders

沒道理 (ㄇㄟˊ ㄉㄠˋ ㄌㄧˇ)
unreasonable; not justified

沒地兒 (ㄇㄟˊ ㄉㄧˋ ㄦ)
no seat or place for

沒多少 (ㄇㄟˊ ㄉㄨㄛ ㄕㄠˇ)
not much; not many

沒對兒 (ㄇㄟˊ ㄉㄨㄟˋ ㄦ)
matchless; peerless

沒斷 (ㄇㄟˊ ㄉㄨㄢˋ)
incessant; continuous; continuously; ceaselessly: 雨沒斷地下了一星期。We've had a week of incessant rain.

沒頭沒腦 (ㄇㄟˊ ㄊㄡˊ ㄇㄟˊ ㄋㄠˇ)
(to utter, do, etc. something) all of a sudden; abruptly; inexplicably; illogical

沒頭帖 (ㄇㄟˊ ㄊㄡˊ ㄊㄧㄝˇ)
an unsigned or unnamed (invitation, etc.) card

沒頭腦 (ㄇㄟˊ ㄊㄡˊ ㄋㄠˇ)
without brains; stupid; ignorant

沒頭案子 (ㄇㄟˊ ㄊㄡˊ ㄢˋ ˙ㄗ)
a criminal case without a clue for the police to work on

沒聽提 (ㄇㄟˊ ㄊㄧㄥ ㄊㄧˊ)
to take no notice of; to pay no attention to

沒了 (ㄇㄟˊ ㄌㄜ˙)
① to disappear; to vanish ② without: 我們沒了他不成。We cannot do without him.

沒來 (ㄇㄟˊ ㄌㄞˊ)
to have not come; to fail to show up: 她還沒來。She has not come yet.

沒來由 (ㄇㄟˊ ㄌㄞˊ ㄧㄡˊ)
without any cause or reason; uncalled-for; unprovoked

沒落子 (ㄇㄟˊ ㄌㄨㄛˋ ˙ㄗ) or 沒落兒 (ㄇㄟˊ ㄌㄨㄛˋ ㄦ)
with no means of making a living

沒了期 (ㄇㄟˊ ㄌㄧㄠˇ ㄑㄧˊ)
(said of misery or misfortune) to have no end; endless

沒臉 (ㄇㄟˊ ㄌㄧㄢˇ)
too ashamed to (do a thing); to lose face

沒良心 (ㄇㄟˊ ㄌㄧㄤˊ ㄒㄧㄣ)
without conscience; unconscionable; ungrateful

沒轍 (ㄇㄟˊ ㄓㄜˋ)
at the end of one's rope; at one's wits' end

沒籠頭的馬 (ㄇㄟˊ ㄌㄨㄥˊ ˙ㄊㄡ ˙ㄉㄜ ㄇㄚˇ)
unharnessed horse—(figuratively)without restraints of any kind; unbridled

沒骨頭 (ㄇㄟˊ ㄍㄨˇ ˙ㄊㄡ) or 沒骨氣 (ㄇㄟˊ ㄍㄨˇ ㄑㄧˋ)
spineless; chicken-hearted

沒規矩 (ㄇㄟˊ ㄍㄨㄟ ㄐㄩ)
not observing proper rules or manners; improper; inappropriate; impudent

沒關係 (ㄇㄟˊ ㄍㄨㄢ ˙ㄒㄧ)
It does not matter. or Never mind.

沒見過眼 (ㄇㄟˊ ㄐㄧㄢˋ ˙ㄍㄨㄛ ㄧㄢˇ)
rustic; unsophisticated; to have seen little of the world

沒勁兒 (ㄇㄟˊ ㄐㄧㄥˋ ㄦ)
① to have no interest in, or desire for anything ② listless

沒結沒完 (ㄇㄟˊ ㄐㄧㄝˊ ㄇㄟˊ ㄨㄢˊ)

incessant and continuous;
endless

沒見過世面 (ㄇㄟˊ ㄐㄧㄢˋ ‧ㄍㄨㄛ ‧ㄕˋ ㄇㄧㄢˋ)
green and inexperienced; unsophisticated

沒見識 (ㄇㄟˊ ㄐㄧㄢˋ ‧ㄕ)
inexperienced and ignorant;
unlearned and provincial

沒講究 (ㄇㄟˊ ㄐㄧㄤˇ ‧ㄐㄧㄡ)
①nothing particular to
think about ②to discard
formalities

沒精打彩 (ㄇㄟˊ ㄐㄧㄥ ㄉㄚˇ ㄘㄞˇ)
listless; dispirited; 病後幾週
他一直沒精打彩。He remained
listless for weeks after his
illness.

沒輕沒重 (ㄇㄟˊ ㄑㄧㄥ ㄇㄟˊ ㄓㄨㄥˋ)
①(said of behavior) without
manners ②(said of utterances) untimely or thoughtless; rash and rude

沒去 (ㄇㄟˊ ㄑㄩ)
didn't go; to have not left;
他沒去那裏。He did not go
there.

沒趣兒 (ㄇㄟˊ ㄑㄩˋㄦ)
①uninteresting; unpleasant
or awkward situation ②
rebuke; snub; rebuff; reprimand: 他自討沒趣兒。He
received a rebuff.

沒下downloaded場 (ㄇㄟˊ ㄒㄧㄚˋ ㄔㄤˇ)
to have a tragic end; to
have no happy ending

沒羞沒臊 (ㄇㄟˊ ㄒㄧㄡ ㄇㄟˊ ㄙㄠˋ)
brazen-faced; shameless

沒心沒肺 (ㄇㄟˊ ㄒㄧㄣ ㄇㄟˊ ㄈㄟˋ)
careless; inattentive

沒心腸 (ㄇㄟˊ ㄒㄧㄣ ‧ㄔㄤ)
no heart for; not interested
in

沒心眼兒 (ㄇㄟˊ ㄒㄧㄣ ㄧㄢˇㄦ)
①careless ②frank; candid

沒想到 (ㄇㄟˊ ㄒㄧㄤˇ ㄉㄠˋ)
to have not expected; to
have not thought about; unexpectedly

沒指望 (ㄇㄟˊ ㄓˇ ㄨㄤˋ)
hopeless: 這情況似乎已沒指
望。It seems to be a hopeless
case.

沒志氣 (ㄇㄟˊ ㄓˋ ㄑㄧˋ)
(said of a person) without
ambition; marked by defeatism

沒轍 (ㄇㄟˊ ㄓㄜˋ)
Nothing can be done about
it.

沒治兒 (ㄇㄟˊ ㄓˋㄦ)
unmanageable

沒主意 (ㄇㄟˊ ㄓㄨˇ ‧ㄧ)or(ㄇㄟˊ ㄓㄨˇ ㄧˋ)
to lose one's head; cannot
make up one's mind

沒準兒 (ㄇㄟˊ ㄓㄨㄣˇㄦ)
uncertain; unsure; doubtful;
maybe

沒種 (ㄇㄟˊ ㄓㄨㄥˇ)
cowardly

沒尺寸 (ㄇㄟˊ ㄔˇ ‧ㄘㄨㄣ)
rash and thoughtless; illmannered

沒出息 (ㄇㄟˊ ㄔㄨ ‧ㄒㄧ)
(said of persons) not promising; useless; good-fornothing

沒事兒 (ㄇㄟˊ ㄕˋㄦ)or沒事兒(ㄇㄟˊ ㄕˋㄦ)
①nothing wrong; all right;
O.K.: 我保你沒事。I guarantee
that nothing will happen to
you. ②without anything to
do; nothing important

沒事找事 (ㄇㄟˊ ㄕˋ ㄓㄠˇ ㄕˋ)
①to ask for trouble; to ask
for it ②to try hard to find
fault; to cavil

沒甚麼 (ㄇㄟˊ ㄕㄜˊ ‧ㄇㄜ)
① Nothing! or Never mind!
或It's all right.②not important; not difficult, bad, etc.:
這事對我們沒甚麼重要的。The
matter is of little importance to us.

沒深沒淺 (ㄇㄟˊ ㄕㄣ ㄇㄟˊ ㄑㄧㄢˇ)
ignorant and rash; impudent
and thoughtless

沒商量 (ㄇㄟˊ ㄕㄤ ‧ㄌㄧㄤ)
nothing to discuss or negotiate—already decided

沒日沒夜 (ㄇㄟˊ ㄖˋ ㄇㄟˊ ㄧㄝˋ)
day and night

沒日子 (ㄇㄟˊ ㄖˋ ‧ㄗ)
①the date not set yet; the
time undecided ②not long
in the future; in the near
future

沒早沒晚 (ㄇㄟˊ ㄗㄠˇ ㄇㄟˊ ㄨㄢˇ)
day and night; without
regard to the time of day

沒造化 (ㄇㄟˊ ㄗㄠˋ ‧ㄏㄨㄚ)
unlucky; out of luck

沒詞兒 (ㄇㄟˊ ㄘˊㄦ)
to be short of words—un-

able to respond; to lose in a
debate, an argument, etc.

沒錯兒 (ㄇㄟˊ ㄘㄨㄛˋㄦ)
①I'm quite sure. 或You can
rest assured. ②can't go
wrong

沒意思 (ㄇㄟˊ ㄧˋ ‧ㄙ)
weary; bored; not interesting

沒有 (ㄇㄟˊ ㄧㄡˇ)
no; not; not yet; do not have;
without: 教室裡沒有人。There
isn't anyone in the classroom.

沒有的話 (ㄇㄟˊ ㄧㄡˇ ‧ㄉㄜ ㄏㄨㄚˋ)
not true; nothing of the
kind; it can not be

沒有的事兒 (ㄇㄟˊ ㄧㄡˇ ‧ㄉㄜ ㄕˋㄦ)
Nothing of that sort! 或It's
impossible.

沒有說的 (ㄇㄟˊ ㄧㄡˇ ㄕㄨㄛ ‧ㄉㄜ)
①really good ②it goes
without saying; needless to
say

沒影兒 (ㄇㄟˊ ㄧㄥˇㄦ)
①not even a shadow—without trace ②groundless; not
true ③to vanish ④to get
far away

沒味兒 (ㄇㄟˊ ㄨㄟˋㄦ)
(literally) tasteless — ①not
delicious ②not interesting

沒胃口 (ㄇㄟˊ ㄨㄟˋ ㄎㄡˇ)
①to have lost one's appetite
②to have no interest in
something

沒完 (ㄇㄟˊ ㄨㄢˊ)
①incessant; continuous;
without end: 他的困苦經歷好
像沒完完了似的。The story of
his troubles seemed (to be)
endless. ② There will be no
end to this.

沒王法 (ㄇㄟˊ ㄨㄤˊ ㄈㄚˇ)
lawless; without justice; to
act lawlessly

沒緣 (ㄇㄟˊ ㄩㄢˊ)
Fate has decided against
(people's meeting again,
etc.). 或no opportunity of

沒用 (ㄇㄟˊ ㄩㄥˋ)
useless; of no use: 抱怨也沒
用。It's no use complaining
(or to complain).

【汕】 2804
　　　jyy zhǐ
a sandy islet in a stream; a
small sandbank

〔水部〕

【沏】 2805
1. くｌ chi qī
1. to infuse
2. (said of the flowing water) rapidly; turbulently

沏茶（くｌ ｲｙ）
to infuse tea; to make tea; 她用開水沏茶。She was infusing tea leaves in boiling water to make tea.

【沏】 2805
2. くｕ chiu qù
to drench with water

【沓】 2806
ㄊˋ tah tà
1. repeated; reiterated
2. crowded together; joined or connected; piled up
3. lax
4. talkative

沓沓（ㄊˋ ㄊˋ）
①lax ②chattering and talkative ③running quickly

沓合（ㄊˋ ㄏㄜˊ）
to pile one upon another; to superimpose

沓至（ㄊˋ ㄓˋ）
to come one after another without stop

沓雜（ㄊˋ ㄗㄚˊ）
crowded and mixed; confused

【沛】 2807
ㄆㄟ pey pèi
1. copious; abundance; full of; much: 他活力充沛。He is full of vitality.
2. quickly; rapidly; sudden
3. to fall prostrate
4. to reserve water for irrigation
5. tall; high; great

沛流（ㄆㄟˋ ㄌㄧㄡˊ）
a great flow of water; flowing copiously

沛公（ㄆㄟˋ ㄍㄨㄥ）
Liu Pang (劉邦), the founding emperor of the Han Dynasty, who started his uprising at his native town of Pei (沛)

沛然（ㄆㄟˋ ㄖㄢˊ）
①(said of rain) copious ②great or vast

沛澤（ㄆㄟˋ ㄗㄜˊ）
thickets and marshes

沛艾（ㄆㄟˋ ㄞˋ）
(said of horses) tall and

strong

五畫

【沫】 2808
ㄇㄛˋ moh mò
1. tiny bubbles on the surface of water; froth; suds; lather: 啤酒倒出時起泡沫。Beer froths when it is poured out.
2. saliva
3. (now rarely) to end; to finish

沫子（ㄇㄛˋ ˙ㄗ）or 沫兒（ㄇㄛˋㄦ）
froth; suds; tiny bubbles

沫雨（ㄇㄛˋ ㄩˇ）
rains that cause floods

【沬】 2809
ㄇㄟˊ mey mèi
1. dusk
2. name of a river
3. (in ancient China) name of a town in the state of Wei, in today's Honan Province

沬血（ㄇㄟˋ ㄒㄧㄝˇ）
blood flowing in one's face; a bleeding face

【沮】 2810
1. ㄐㄩ jiu jū
1. name of a river in Shantung Province; name of a river in Shansi Province
2. a Chinese family name

沮蒼（ㄐㄩ ㄘㄤ）
Chü Sung (沮誦) and Tsang Chieh (倉頡), legendary figures credited with the invention of Chinese characters

沮誦 or 沮頌（ㄐㄩ ㄙㄨㄥˋ）
name of a legendary person in the reign of Huang Ti (Yellow Emperor), who helped create the Chinese written language

【沮】 2810
2. ㄐㄩˇ jeu jǔ
1. to stop; to abate
2. to lose; to be defeated
3. to spoil; to injure; to destroy or damage

沮短（ㄐㄩˇ ㄉㄨㄢˇ）
to slander; to gossip; to backbite

沮駭（ㄐㄩˇ ㄏㄞˋ）
to frighten by a threat of destruction; to intimidate

沮壞（ㄐㄩˇ ㄏㄨㄞˋ）
ruined; damaged

沮泄（ㄐㄩˇ ㄒㄧˋ）
to leak (secrets, information, etc.)

沮舍（ㄐㄩˇ ㄕㄜˋ）
a damaged, ruined or dilapidated house

沮喪（ㄐㄩˇ ㄙㄤˋ）
discouraged and disappointed; crestfallen; despondent; downcast; low-spirited

【沮】 2810
3. ㄐㄩˋ jiuh jù
damp, low-lying land; marshy

沮洳（ㄐㄩˋ ㄖㄨˋ）
damp, low-lying land

沮澤（ㄐㄩˋ ㄗㄜˊ）
swamps; marsh

【沭】 2811
ㄕㄨˋ shuh shù
short for 沭水

沭水（ㄕㄨˋ ㄕㄨㄟˇ）
name of a river in Shantung Province

【沱】 2812
ㄊㄨㄛˊ two tuó
1. waterways; rivers; streams
2. name of a river
3. continuous heavy rains

沱茶（ㄊㄨㄛˊ ㄔㄚˊ）
a bowl-shaped compressed mass of tea leaves

沱若（ㄊㄨㄛˊ ㄖㄨㄛˋ）
(said of tears, etc.) flowing down

【沴】 2813
ㄌㄧˋ lih lì
1. miasmas; foul and poisonous air
2. dislocation

沴孽（ㄌㄧˋ ㄋㄧㄝˋ）
evil spirits

沴氣（ㄌㄧˋ ㄑㄧˋ）
miasmas; poisonous vapor

【沸】 2814
ㄈㄟˋ fey fèi
1. boiling (water, etc.)
2. to gush; bubbling up

沸沸（ㄈㄟˋ ㄈㄟˋ）
water gushing out from a spring (usually used figuratively)

沸沸揚揚（ㄈㄟˋ ㄈㄟˋ ㄧㄤˊ ㄧㄤˊ）
to bubble with noise; in a hubbub

沸點（ㄈㄟˋ ㄉㄧㄢˇ）
the boiling point

〔水 部〕

沸鼎(ㄈㄟ ㄉㄧㄥ)
a cauldron holding boiling water

沸湯(ㄈㄟ ㄊㄤ)
boiling water

沸騰(ㄈㄟ ㄊㄥ)
①boiling—when liquid turn to steam: 香水因沸騰而溢出。 The pot is boiling over.② bubbling and boiling—unrest; seething: 他的熱血沸騰。 His blood is bubbling and boiling.

沸泉(ㄈㄟ ㄑㄩㄢ)
a bubbling spring

沸石(ㄈㄟ ㄕ)
zeolite

沸水(ㄈㄟ ㄕㄨㄟ)
boiling water; boiled water

【油】 ²⁸¹⁵ (ㄧㄡ you yóu)

1.a general name for oil, fat, grease, either animal or vegetable: 油水不相容。 Oil and water have an antipathy.
2. anything in liquid form which is inflammable, as petroleum, gasoline, etc.
3. to oil: 他給腳踏車上油。 He oiled his bicycle.
4. to varnish; to paint: 請油一油大門。 Varnish the gate, please.
5. greasy: 她不喜歡油膩的食物。 She disliked greasy food.
6.polished and over-experienced; sly; sleeky
7. luxuriant; prospering; flourishing

油杯(ㄧㄡ ㄅㄟ)or 油壺(ㄧㄡ ㄏㄨ)
an oilcup

油餅(ㄧㄡ ㄅㄧㄥˇ)
fried salty pancakes

油布(ㄧㄡ ㄅㄨ)
oilcloth (used as a water-proof covering)

油瓶(ㄧㄡ ㄆㄧㄥ)
①a bottle for storing oil ② a woman's children by previous marriage

油墨(ㄧㄡ ㄇㄛ)
printing ink

油門(ㄧㄡ ㄇㄣ)
①a throttle ② an accelerator: 公車司機踩油門加速。 The bus driver stepped on the accelerator.

油坊(ㄧㄡ ㄈㄤ)
an oil extracting mill

油豆腐(ㄧㄡ ㄉㄡˋ ㄈㄨ)
fried bean curd

油燈(ㄧㄡ ㄉㄥ)
an oil lamp

油點子(ㄧㄡ ㄉㄧㄢˇ ˙ㄗ)or 油點兒(ㄧㄡ ㄉㄧㄚㄦ)
greasy spots; oil stains

油頭粉面(ㄧㄡ ㄊㄡˊ ㄈㄣˇ ㄇㄧㄢ)
pomaded hair and powdered face – descriptive of a frivolous youngster

油頭滑腦(ㄧㄡ ㄊㄡˊ ㄏㄨㄚˊ ㄋㄠˇ)
slick; flippant

油條(ㄧㄡ ㄊㄧㄠˊ)
①fritters of twisted dough —a Chinese specialty usually for breakfast ② a suave, well-oiled person, long on experience but short on sincerity: 他是個老油條。 He is a well-oiled fellow.

油田(ㄧㄡ ㄊㄧㄢˊ)
an oil field

油桶(ㄧㄡ ㄊㄨㄥˇ)
an oil drum

油泥(ㄧㄡ ㄋㄧˊ)
greasy dirt: 擦掉你手錶上的油泥。 Clean the greasy dirt on your watch.

油膩(ㄧㄡ ㄋㄧ)
(said of food) fatty; oily; greasy: 這食物油膩。 The food was greasy.

油簍(ㄧㄡ ㄌㄡˇ)
a willow basket covered with oilcloth, etc. for storage of liquids

油料(ㄧㄡ ㄌㄧㄠ)
petroleum, oil and lubricant (POL)

油料庫(ㄧㄡ ㄌㄧㄠ ㄎㄨ)
an oil depot; a POL depot

油亮(ㄧㄡ ㄌㄧㄤ)
glossy; shiny: 這桌面非常的油亮。 The top of this table is very glossy.

油輪(ㄧㄡ ㄌㄨㄣˊ)
an oil tanker; a tanker; an oiler

油綠(ㄧㄡ ㄌㄩˋ)
dark green

油膏(ㄧㄡ ㄍㄠ)
ointment

油鍋(ㄧㄡ ㄍㄨㄛ)

①an oil pan for frying or cooking ②a cauldron of oil —a punishment for evil spirits in the legendary hell

油管(ㄧㄡ ㄍㄨㄢˇ)
oil pipes; oil pipelines: 他們在鋪設油管。 They were laying oil pipes.

油罐(ㄧㄡ ㄍㄨㄢ)
an oilcan; an oil tank

油光(ㄧㄡ ㄍㄨㄤ)
glossy; shiny; varnished: 他的鞋子油光晶亮。 His shoes are shiny.

油礦(ㄧㄡ ㄎㄨㄤ)
an oil field; oil deposit

油葫蘆(ㄧㄡ ㄏㄨˊ ㄌㄨˊ)
a kind of cricket (Gryllodes miltratus)

油滑(ㄧㄡ ㄏㄨㄚˊ)
slippery and sly; suave and crafty; sleeky: 他是個油滑的政客。 He is a crafty politician.

油畫(ㄧㄡ ㄏㄨㄚ)
oil paintings

油灰(ㄧㄡ ㄏㄨㄟ)
putty

油跡(ㄧㄡ ㄐㄧ)
oil stains; greasy spots: 油跡易除。 Oil stains are easy to remove.

油煎(ㄧㄡ ㄐㄧㄢ)
to fry in oil or fat

油井(ㄧㄡ ㄐㄧㄥˇ)
an oil well: 他們鑽了一口油井。 They drilled (or bored) an oil well.

油漆(ㄧㄡ ㄑㄧ)
①paint; varnish; oil paint: 油漆未乾! Wet (or Fresh) Paint! ② to paint: 請把大門油漆一下。 Please have the gate painted.

油漆匠(ㄧㄡ ㄑㄧ ㄐㄧㄤ)
a house painter; an oil painter

油腔滑調(ㄧㄡ ㄑㄧㄤ ㄏㄨㄚˊ ㄉㄧㄠ)
oily and fishy; polished and slippery; suave and sly; utterly insincere; glib

油裙(ㄧㄡ ㄑㄩㄣˊ)
an apron used during cooking

油箱(ㄧㄡ ㄒㄧㄤ)
a fuel tank

油星(子)(ㄧㄡ ㄒㄧㄥ ˙ㄗ)or 油杵

〔水部〕

子(一ㄡ ˙ㄗ)
droplets of oil, that may shoot out during frying, etc.

油脂(一ㄡ ㄓ)
① (chemistry) olein ② oil and grease; fats

油紙(一ㄡ ㄓˇ)
oilpaper

油渣(一ㄡ ㄓㄚ)
① dregs of fat ② oil residue

油渣餅(一ㄡ ㄓㄚ ㄅㄧㄥˇ)
oil cake

油渣粉(一ㄡ ㄓㄚ ㄈㄣˇ)
oil meal

油炸果(一ㄡ ㄓㄚˊ ㄍㄨㄛˇ)or 油炸鬼
(一ㄡ ㄓㄚˊ ㄍㄨㄟˇ)
fritters of twisted dough

油榨機(一ㄡ ㄓㄚˋ ㄐㄧ)
an oil press

油氈(一ㄡ ㄓㄢ)
asphalt roofing

油廠(一ㄡ ㄔㄤˇ)
① an oil refinery ② an oil extracting mill

油商(一ㄡ ㄕㄤ)
an oil dealer; an oil businessman; an oilman

油水兒(一ㄡ ㄕㄨㄟˇㄦ)
① the cream or essence of something ② side profit or outside profit in a deal—as kickbacks, etc.

油然(一ㄡ ㄖㄢˊ)
① copious; luxuriant; flourishing; abundantly ② (now rarely) not moving ahead; halting

油然而生(一ㄡ ㄖㄢˊ ㄦˊ ㄕㄥ)
(said of love, admiration, sympathy, etc.) to grow in abundance and somewhat suddenly; to well up: 同情之心，油然而生。Sympathy wells up in one's heart.

油子(一ㄡ ˙ㄗ)
① a sleeky person; a sly fellow ② any black sticky substance

油嘴(一ㄡ ㄗㄨㄟˇ)
glib-tongued; oily-tongued

油嘴滑舌(一ㄡ ㄗㄨㄟˇ ㄏㄨㄚˊ ㄕㄜˊ)
sweet and smooth words which are not backed by sincerity: 他是個油嘴滑舌的政客。He was a politician with a well-oiled tongue.

油彩(一ㄡ ㄘㄞˇ)
greasepaint; paint

油菜(一ㄡ ㄘㄞˋ)
rape

油層(一ㄡ ㄘㄥˊ)
an oil reservoir; an oil layer; an oil horizon

頁岩(一ㄡ ㄧㄝˊㄢˊ)
oil shale

油油(一ㄡ 一ㄡ)
① luxuriant and glossy—as new leaves in spring ② (said of water) flowing

油煙(一ㄡ 一ㄢ)
lamp soot; lampblack

油煙子(一ㄡ 一ㄢ ˙ㄗ)
greasy dirt produced from heating oil

油鹽店(一ㄡ 一ㄢˊ ㄉㄧㄢˋ)
a grocery store

油鹽醬醋(一ㄡ 一ㄢˊ ㄐㄧㄤˋ ㄘㄨˋ)
oils, salt, soybean sauce and vinegar—daily necessaries

油印(一ㄡ 一ㄣˋ)
to mimeograph: 他油印了六十份宣傳資料。He mimeographed sixty copies of propaganda.

油印本(一ㄡ 一ㄣˋ ㄅㄣˇ)
a mimeographed booklet, pamphlet, etc.

油印機(一ㄡ 一ㄣˋ ㄐㄧ)
a mimeograph

油污(一ㄡ ㄨ)
greasy dirt

〔河〕 ㄏㄜˊ her hé 2816

1. a general name for rivers, streams, and waterways: 這河注入湖內。The river runs into a lake.

2. Ho, the Yellow River in northern China, 2,700 miles long

河壩(ㄏㄜˊ ㄅㄚˋ)
dikes; embankments; levees

河伯娶婦(ㄏㄜˊ ㄅㄛˊ ㄑㄩˇ ㄈㄨˋ)
(in ancient China) a local custom of offering a young girl to the god of the Yellow River as his bride—by throwing her into the river

河北(ㄏㄜˊ ㄅㄟˇ)
① north of the river ② Hopeh Province

河蚌(ㄏㄜˊ ㄅㄤˋ)
bivalves grown in rivers and lakes; mussels

河邊(ㄏㄜˊ ㄅㄧㄢ)or 河邊兒(ㄏㄜˊ ㄅㄧㄢㄦ)
the riverside; by the side of the river: 我們沿著河邊走。We walked along the riverside.

河邊的(ㄏㄜˊ ㄅㄧㄢ ˙ㄉㄜ)
riverain; riverine: 河邊的村落顯得特別的寧靜。Riverine villages appear especially calm.

河濱(ㄏㄜˊ ㄅㄧㄣ)
the riverbanks; the riverside; the waterfront

河畔(ㄏㄜˊ ㄆㄢˋ)
riverbanks; by the side of the river; the riverside

河馬(ㄏㄜˊ ㄇㄚˇ)
a hippopotamus, or a hippo

河防(ㄏㄜˊ ㄈㄤˊ)
embankments or levees along the Yellow River

河道(ㄏㄜˊ ㄉㄠˋ)
the course of a river; a waterway; the channel of a river: 他們沿該國的河道逆游而上。They went up the riverways of the country.

河隄(ㄏㄜˊ ㄉㄧ)or 河堤(ㄏㄜˊ ㄉㄧ)
embankments; dikes; levees

河東(ㄏㄜˊ ㄉㄨㄥ)
① the area east of the Yellow River in Shansi Province (山西) ② the southwestern part of Shansi Province

河東獅吼(ㄏㄜˊ ㄉㄨㄥ ㄕ ㄏㄡˇ)
the display of shrewishness; the outburst of a virago

河東獅子(ㄏㄜˊ ㄉㄨㄥ ㄕ ˙ㄗ)
a shrew; a virago; a fishwife

河套(ㄏㄜˊ ㄊㄠˋ)
the Great Bend of the Yellow River Inner in Mongolia

河壋(ㄏㄜˊ ㄊㄤˊ)
the sand dune along a river

河圖洛書(ㄏㄜˊ ㄊㄨˊ ㄌㄨㄛˋ ㄕㄨ)
(according to Chinese legends) mystic signs and markings revealed to Fu Hsi (伏羲) and Yü the Great (大禹) thousands of years ago

河豚(ㄏㄜˊ ㄊㄨㄣˊ)
the globefish; a blowfish; a puffer

河內(ㄏㄜˊ ㄋㄟˋ)
① Hanoi, North Vietnam ② the old name of a region

〔水
部〕

north of the Yellow River, including the northern part of Honan and the southern part of Shansi

河南(ㄏㄜˊㄋㄢˊ)
Honan Province

河南墜子(ㄏㄜˊㄋㄢˊㄓㄨㄟˋ)
Honan opera featuring narration and singing to the accompaniment of stringed and percussion instruments

河流(ㄏㄜˊㄌㄧㄨˊ)
streams, waterways, rivers or channels of water

河梁(ㄏㄜˊㄌㄧㄤˊ)
①a bridge spanning a river ②the parting place

河洛(ㄏㄜˊㄌㄨㄛˋ)
①the basin between the Yellow River and the River Lo ②short for 河圖洛書

河工(ㄏㄜˊㄍㄨㄥ)
river engineering; river works

河公(ㄏㄜˊㄍㄨㄥ)or 河伯(ㄏㄜˊㄅㄛˊ)
the god of the Yellow River

河口(ㄏㄜˊㄎㄡˇ)
a river mouth; a stream outlet

河海不擇細流(ㄏㄜˊㄏㄞˇㄅㄨˋㄗㄜˊㄒㄧˋㄌㄧㄨˊ)
Profound learning is an accumulation of bits of knowledge.

河漢(ㄏㄜˊㄏㄢˋ)
the Milky Way

河漢斯言(ㄏㄜˊㄏㄢˋㄙㄧㄢˊ)
statements that are too far-fetched to gain credulity

河清(ㄏㄜˊㄑㄧㄥ)
clear water in the Yellow River (which is always muddy), regarded as a harbinger of some great happy event

河清難俟(ㄏㄜˊㄑㄧㄥㄋㄢˊㄙˋ)
It takes too long to wait, and life is short.

河清海晏(ㄏㄜˊㄑㄧㄥㄏㄞˇㄧㄢˋ)
halcyon days; time of peace and prosperity

河渠(ㄏㄜˊㄑㄩˊ)
the place where water is reserved; a reservoir; waterways

河西(ㄏㄜˊㄒㄧ)
west of the Yellow River

河心(ㄏㄜˊㄒㄧㄣ)
the middle of a river

河州 or 河洲(ㄏㄜˊㄓㄡ)
a sand bar or islet in a river

河牀(ㄏㄜˊㄔㄨㄤˊ)
the riverbed; the floor of a river

河山(ㄏㄜˊㄕㄢ)
rivers and mountains—the territory of a country

河山變色(ㄏㄜˊㄕㄢㄅㄧㄢˋㄙㄜˋ)
The situation of the land is greatly changed.

河身(ㄏㄜˊㄕㄣ)
water volume of a river

河神(ㄏㄜˊㄕㄣˊ)
a river-god

河朔(ㄏㄜˊㄕㄨㄛˋ)
①the northern bank of the Yellow River ②the part of China north of the Yellow River

河水不犯井水(ㄏㄜˊㄕㄨㄟˇㄅㄨˋㄈㄢˋㄐㄧㄥˇㄕㄨㄟˇ)
not to interfere with one another; Everyone minds his own business.

河沿(ㄏㄜˊㄧㄢˊ)
the riverbank; the riverside

河魚腹疾(ㄏㄜˊㄩˊㄈㄨˋㄐㄧˊ)or 河魚之疾(ㄏㄜˊㄩˊㄓㄐㄧˊ)
diarrhea

河嶽(ㄏㄜˊㄩㄝˋ)
the Yellow River and the Five Sacred Mountains of China

河源(ㄏㄜˊㄩㄢˊ)
①the source of the Yellow River—in Tsinghai Province ②name of a county in Kwangtung Province

〔沼〕 2817
ㄓㄠˇ **jao zhǎo**

a lake; a pond; a pool; a marsh

沼氣(ㄓㄠˇㄑㄧˋ)
marsh gas; methane

沼澤(ㄓㄠˇㄗㄜˊ)
a marsh; a swamp; a bog; lakes and ponds

〔沽〕 2818
ㄍㄨ **gu gū**

1. to buy
2. to sell
3. crude; inferior (quality)
4. (now rare) negligent

沽名釣譽(ㄍㄨㄇㄧㄥˊㄉㄧㄠˋㄩˋ)

to do something, not for the sake of achievement, but for the sake of fishing for a good reputation or fame; to seek publicity

沽河(ㄍㄨㄏㄜˊ)
also known as the Pai River (白河) near Tientsin

沽激(ㄍㄨㄐㄧ)
to behave unnaturally for the sake of a good reputation

沽酒(ㄍㄨㄐㄧㄨˇ)
①to buy wine ②wine or spirits bought from stores

沽售(ㄍㄨㄕㄡˋ)
to buy and sell

〔治〕 2819
ㄓˋ **jyh zhì**
(動詞讀音 ㄔˊ chyr chí)

1. to administer; to control; to govern; to manage; to rule:
他統治這國家有二十年。He ruled the country for twenty years.

2. to regulate; to harness (a river)

3. the seat of the local government: 縣治 the county seat

4. to treat (a disease); to cure: 牙醫師在治療我的牙齒。The dentist is treating my teeth.

5. to study; to research: 他專治農業。He makes a study in agriculture.

6. to punish

7. peaceful and orderly

8. a Chinese family name

治辦(ㄓˋㄅㄢˋ)
successful discharge of duties

治本(ㄓˋㄅㄣˇ)
to deal with (or cure) a trouble, etc. at the source; to treat a matter thoroughly

治標(ㄓˋㄅㄧㄠ)
to cope with the symptoms only (as opposed to 治本)

治兵(ㄓˋㄅㄧㄥ)
to lead troops; to direct military affairs

治病(ㄓˋㄅㄧㄥˋ)
to treat a disease or ailment: 我是來治病的。I am here to cure.

治平(ㄓˋㄆㄧㄥˊ)
①to govern the nation and

〔水部〕

bring peace to the world ②
peace and prosperity as a
result of enlightened government

治命 (坐 ㄇㄧㄥ)
the sensible orders or instructions left by a dead man

治理 (坐 ㄌㄧ)
① to administer; to regulate;
to manage; to govern: 總統治
理國家. The President gov-
erns the country. ② to harness; to regulate; to bring
under control; to put in
order

治療 (坐 ㄌㄧㄠ)
to treat or cure (a disease);
cure; treatment; therapy

治亂 (坐 ㄌㄨㄢ)
order and disorder; peace
and upheaval

治亂興亡 (坐 ㄌㄨㄢ ㄒㄧㄥ ㄨㄤ)
the rise and fall of a nation;
order and prosperity on the
one hand and confusion and
decline on the other

治亂之道 (坐 ㄌㄨㄢ ㄓ ㄉㄠ)
the proper way of govern-
ment

治國 (坐 ㄍㄨㄛ)
to govern a nation; to
administer national affairs;
to rule a country: 治國平天下
to rule the country and give
peace to the world

治功 (坐 ㄍㄨㄥ)
the achievement of manag-
ing national affairs

治好了 (坐 ㄏㄠˇ·ㄌㄜ)
(said of a disease) cured: 她
的病不久就治好了. She was
soon cured of her illness.

治化 (坐 ㄏㄨㄚ)
to train the people with better (or more civilized) ways
of life with enlightened government

治淮 (坐 ㄏㄨㄞ)
to regulate the Huai River
(which is particularly troublesome)

治黃 (坐 ㄏㄨㄤ)
to regulate the Yellow River
(which is particularly troublesome)

治績 (坐 ㄐㄧ)
the merits or achievements

of an administration

治家 (坐 ㄐㄧㄚ)
to manage a household; to
regulate a family

治經 (坐 ㄐㄧㄥ)
to study classics

治軍 (坐 ㄐㄩㄣ)
to direct military affairs; to
direct troops

治權 (坐 ㄑㄩㄢ)
the power of governing, as
opposed to people's political
rights

治下 (坐 ㄒㄧㄚ)
① under the rule, control, or
jurisdiction of ② a self-
reference when reporting to
a superior or a local chief

治學 (坐 ㄒㄩㄝ)
to study; to devote oneself
to learning

治裝 (坐 ㄓㄨㄤ)
to pack or arrange one's
baggage before taking a
trip; to buy new clothing
before embarking on a long
journey

治產 (坐 ㄔㄢ)
to manage property; to buy
real estate

治世 (坐 ㄕ)
a time of peace and order as
a result of enlightened government

治事 (坐 ㄕ)
to transact business

治生 (坐 ㄕㄥ)
to make a living

治術 (坐 ㄕㄨ)
the ways and means of a
good government

治水 (坐 ㄕㄨㄟ)
to regulate waterways,
rivers, etc. to prevent them
from flooding; river control;
flood control

治戎 (坐 ㄖㄨㄥ)
to use the military forces

治罪 (坐 ㄗㄨㄟ)
to punish a criminal according to law; to bring to justice

治絲而棼 (坐 ㄙ ㄦ ㄈㄣ)
to mess up something
because of mishandling

治喪 (坐 ㄙㄤ)
to manage a funeral; to take

care of the funeral rites

治喪委員會 (坐 ㄙㄤ ㄨㄟ ㄩㄢ ㄏㄨㄟ)
a funeral committee

治安 (坐 ㄢ)
public security; peace and
order of a society or a
nation

治安機關 (坐 ㄢ ㄐㄧ ㄍㄨㄢ)
the public-security organization; law-enforcement agencies

治外法權 (坐 ㄨㄞ ㄈㄚ ㄑㄩㄢ)
extraterritoriality; extrality

治愈 or 治癒 (坐 ㄩ)
to succeed in curing a disease; to restore health to a
patient; to heal: 此病很快就治
愈了. It soon healed up.

【沾】 2820 (坐ㄢ) jan zhān

1. to moisten; to wet
2. to tinge; to stain; to contaminate
3. to be imbued with; to be infected with
4. to benefit from
5. to touch: 他煙酒不沾. He
touched neither tobacco nor
alcohol.

沾邊 (坐ㄢ ㄅㄧㄢ)
① to touch on (or upon)
only lightly: 別和那種事沾邊.
Don't touch that kind of
business. ② to be close to
what it should be; to be relevant: 你講的一點兒也不沾邊。
What you say is not rele-
vant at all.

沾便宜 (坐ㄢ ㄅㄧㄢ ㄧ)
① to reap benefits from a
deal etc.; to gain small
advantage or profit ② to
tease someone in order to
get some verbal advantage

沾溉 (坐ㄢ ㄍㄞ)
① to moisten and irrigate
(the land) ② favors

沾光 (坐ㄢ ㄍㄨㄤ)
to benefit from the support
or influence of someone; to
ride on someone's coattails
to success

沾花惹草 (坐ㄢ ㄏㄨㄚ ㄖㄜˇ ㄘㄠˇ)
to fool around with women

沾襟 (坐ㄢ ㄐㄧㄣ)
to moisten sleeves with
tears

沾親帶故 (坐ㄢ ㄑㄧㄣ ㄉㄞ ㄍㄨ)

① with blood or marital relationship; having personal connections, close or remote ② to rub off some glory on friends and relatives

沾沾自喜 (ㄓㄢ ㄓㄢ ㄗˋ ㄒˇ)
smug and complacent

沾溼 (ㄓㄢ ㄕ)
① to make wet; to moisten; damp or wet ② steeped in; imbued with

沾手 (ㄓㄢ ㄕㄡˇ)
① to touch with the hand ② to play a role in something; to have a finger in the pie

沾水 (ㄓㄢ ㄕㄨㄟˇ)
to soak in water

沾脣 (ㄓㄢ ㄔㄨㄣˊ)
(said of food or drink) to touch the lips: 她一向酒不沾脣。She has never let wine touch her lips.

沾染 (ㄓㄢ ㄖㄢˇ)
to be steeped in; to become addicted to (bad habits, practices, etc.): 他 沾染了 惡習。He was steeped in vice.

沾染習氣 (ㄓㄢ ㄖㄢˇ ㄒㄧˊ ㄑㄧˋ)
to be corrupted by prevailing bad customs or practices

沾染世俗 (ㄓㄢ ㄖㄢˇ ㄕˋ ㄙㄨˊ)
corrupted by worldly ways

沾潤 (ㄓㄢ ㄖㄨㄣˋ)
① to moisten; to wet ② to harvest benefits from the side

沾濡 (ㄓㄢ ㄖㄨˊ)
imbued with; to soak in

【況】 2821
(況) ㄎㄨㄤˋ kuàng

1. moreover; in addition; not to mention...

2. to compare; comparative: 以古況今 to compare the present with the past

3. situations; conditions; circumstances: 您的近況如何？How have you been recently?

4. to visit; to call on

5. a Chinese family name

況兼 (ㄎㄨㄤˋ ㄐㄧㄢ)
besides; moreover; in addition; not to mention the fact that...

況且 (ㄎㄨㄤˋ ㄑㄧㄝˇ)
moreover; besides; furthermore: 我太疲倦不能出去, 況且時候也太晚了。I am too tired to go; besides, it's too late.

況又 (ㄎㄨㄤˋ ㄧㄡˋ)
furthermore

況味 (ㄎㄨㄤˋ ㄨㄟˋ)
① situations; conditions; circumstances ② flavor

【泂】 2822
ㄐㄩㄥˇ jeong jiǒng

1. (said of water) clear and deep

2. far and wide

泂泂 (ㄐㄩㄥˇ ㄐㄩㄥˇ)
clear and deep

【沿】 2822
1. ㄧㄢˊ yan yán

1. to follow; to go along; along: 我沿着街道走。I walked along the street.

2. to hand down; to continue: 相沿成習。A custom has come down from the past and become customary.

3. successive; continuous

沿波討源 (ㄧㄢˊ ㄅㄛ ㄊㄠˇ ㄩㄢˊ)
(literally) to trace the water and search for its source—to get into the very source of something

沿邊兒 (ㄧㄢˊ ㄅㄧㄢ ㄦ)
along the edge

沿門托鉢 (ㄧㄢˊ ㄇㄣˊ ㄊㄨㄛ ㄅㄛ)
(Buddhism) to beg for alms from door to door

沿途 (ㄧㄢˊ ㄊㄨˊ)
along the way; throughout the journey: 我們沿途受到熱情的接待。We were warmly received throughout our journey.

沿例 (ㄧㄢˊ ㄌㄧˋ)
to follow a precedent or prevailing practice

沿路 (ㄧㄢˊ ㄌㄨˋ)
along the road; along the way: 我們沿路看到許多野生動物。We saw many wild animals along the way.

沿革 (ㄧㄢˊ ㄍㄜˊ)
successive changes; vicissitudes or history (of a system, institution, etc.); evolution: 社會風習的沿革 the evolution of social customs

沿河 (ㄧㄢˊ ㄏㄜˊ)
along the river

沿海 (ㄧㄢˊ ㄏㄞˇ)
① along the coast ② offshore

沿海一帶 (ㄧㄢˊ ㄏㄞˇ ㄧ ㄉㄞˋ)
along the coastal region; in the seaboard region or coastal area

沿襲 (ㄧㄢˊ ㄒㄧˊ)
to follow the old or traditional (practices, customs, precedents, etc.): 切勿沿襲陳規。Do not follow the old conventions.

沿線 (ㄧㄢˊ ㄒㄧㄢˋ)
along a railway or highway: 這些是鐵路沿線的村鎮。These are the villages and towns along the railway.

沿着 (ㄧㄢˊ ㄓㄜ)
to follow or go along …: 我們沿着河岸走。We went along the riverside.

沿才授職 (ㄧㄢˊ ㄘㄞˊ ㄕㄡˋ ㄓˊ)
to confer an office, position, etc. on a person according to his ability; assignment on merit basis

沿岸 (ㄧㄢˊ ㄢˋ)
along the coast of…; littoral: 我們沿岸散步。We take a walk along the shore.

沿用 (ㄧㄢˊ ㄩㄥˋ)
to continue following the old practices, customs, etc.: 我們仍沿用着舊有的習俗。We continued following the old customs.

【沿】 2823
2. ㄧㄢˋ yann yàn

the edge of something; the brim: 邊沿 the edge or border of anything

〔水部〕

【泄】 2824
1. ㄒㄧㄝˋ shieh xiè

1. to leak out; to reveal

2. to vent

3. to scatter; to disperse

4. a Chinese family name

泄憤 (ㄒㄧㄝˋ ㄈㄣˋ)
to vent one's anger

泄涕 (ㄒㄧㄝˋ ㄊㄧˋ)
to come to tears; to cry

泄漏 (ㄒㄧㄝˋ ㄌㄡˋ) or 泄露 (ㄒㄧㄝˋ ㄌㄡˋ)
to leak out (secrets, etc.): 消息已泄漏出去了。The information has leaked out.

泄瀉 (ㄒㄧㄝˋ ㄒㄧㄝˋ)
diarrhoea 參看「泄瀉」

泄露 (ㄒㄧㄝˋ ㄌㄡˋ)

（水部）

to leak out (information, secrets, etc.); to reveal or expose unintentionally

泄恨（ㄒㄧㄝˋ ㄏㄣˋ）
to vent one's hatred or anger

泄勁（ㄒㄧㄝˋ ㄐㄧㄣˋ）
to be discouraged; to be disheartened; to slacken one's efforts

泄瀉（ㄒㄧㄝˋ ㄒㄧㄝˋ）
diarrhoea; to have loose bowels

泄水（ㄒㄧㄝˋ ㄕㄨˇ）
(said of water) to seep out from cracks; sluicing

泄水道（ㄒㄧㄝˋ ㄕㄨˇ ㄉㄠˋ）
sluiceway

【泄】 2824
ㄧˋ yih yì
1. mild and easy
2. many; crowded
泄沓（ㄧˋ ㄊㄚˋ）
①garrulous and disorderly
②easygoing; lax in moral attitude 亦作「泄沓沓者」
泄泄（ㄧˋ）
①to flap wings ②many (people); crowded

【洪】 2825
ㄧˋ yih yì
1. dissipated and licentious; libertine
2. flooding; overflowing

【泐】 2826
ㄌㄜˋ leh lè
1. rocks splitting
2. to write letters
3. to carve
4. to condense; to coagulate
泐布（ㄌㄜˋ ㄅㄨˋ）
to report by letter
泐覆（ㄌㄜˋ ㄈㄨˋ）
to reply by letter
泐達（ㄌㄜˋ ㄉㄚˊ）
to notify or report by letter
泐石（ㄌㄜˋ ㄕˊ）
①to carve on a rock ②rock splitting up
泐此（ㄌㄜˋ ㄘˇ）
a concluding expression used at the end of a letter in old China

【泊】 2827
ㄆㄛˋ bor bó
（又讀ㄆㄛˊ poh pó）
1. to stay; to anchor a ship; to moor: 這船停泊在岸邊。The

ship anchored along the shore.
2. to drift
3. tranquil and quiet
4. a lake; a body of water: 此一湖泊魚產甚豐。The lake teems with fish.
泊泊（ㄆㄛˋ ㄆㄛˋ）
ripples (of water)
泊船（ㄆㄛˋ ㄔㄨㄢˊ）
to moor a boat
泊岸（ㄆㄛˋ ㄢˋ）
to anchor alongside the river

【泅】 2828
ㄑㄧㄡˊ chyou qiú
to swim: 他不費力地泅過這條河。He swam across the river easily.
泅渡（ㄑㄧㄡˊ ㄉㄨˋ）
to swim across
泅水（ㄑㄧㄡˊ ㄕㄨˇ）
to swim

【泌】 2829
ㄅㄧˋ bih bì
1. swift and easy gushing of water
2. name of a river in Honan Province
泌水（ㄅㄧˋ ㄕㄨㄟˇ）
the Pi River in Honan Province

【泌】 2829
ㄇㄧˋ mih mì
to seep out; to excrete; to secrete
泌尿管（ㄇㄧˋ ㄋㄧㄠˋ ㄍㄨㄢˇ）or（ㄇㄧˋ ㄌㄨㄟˋ ㄍㄨㄢˇ）
the uropoietic passage; the urinary canal
泌尿科（ㄇㄧˋ ㄋㄧㄠˋ ㄎㄜ）or（ㄇㄧˋ ㄌㄨㄟˋ ㄎㄜ）
the urological department
泌尿器官（ㄇㄧˋ ㄋㄧㄠˋ ㄑㄧˋ ㄍㄨㄢ）or（ㄇㄧˋ ㄌㄨㄟˋ ㄑㄧˋ ㄍㄨㄢ）
(physiology) uropoietic organs; urinary organs
泌尿學（ㄇㄧˋ ㄋㄧㄠˋ ㄒㄩㄝˊ）
urology

【泔】 2830
ㄍㄢ gan gān
1. the water from washing rice
2. a way of cooking
3. (said of food) stale
泔水（ㄍㄢ ㄕㄨㄟˇ）
the water from washing rice; hogwash
泔水桶（ㄍㄢ ㄕㄨㄟˇ ㄊㄨㄥˇ）

a bucket for hogwash

【泓】 2831
ㄏㄨㄥˊ horng hóng
1. clear, deep water; limpid water
2. the ancient form of a stream in Honan Province
泓泓（ㄏㄨㄥˊ ㄏㄨㄥˊ）
very deep
泓宏（ㄏㄨㄥˊ ㄏㄨㄥˊ）
very loud; roaring

【法】 2832
1.（礻）ㄈㄚˇ faa fǎ
1. an institution
2. law; regulations; rules; the statutes; legal: 守法是人人的義務。It is the duty of everybody to obey the law.
3. methods; ways of doing things: 他的教法很好。His teaching method is very good.
4. to pattern or model after; to emulate: 他勤讀以效法那位名作家。He studied hard in emulating the famous writer.
5. (Buddhism) the "way"—doctrines, etc.
6. tricks; magic arts: 請解釋這戲法。Please explain the trick.
7. expert or standard (calligraphy, painting, etc.)
8. penalty; punishment
9. a Chinese family name
法寶（ㄈㄚˇ ㄅㄠˇ）
① dharmaratna, one of the three Buddhist treasures ② something of uncanny or occult power—for killing or subduing the enemy ③ a standby; something that one always brings along—as saw, nails, hammer to a carpenter; pencil and paper to a reporter: 這字典是他的隨身法寶。This dictionary is his standby.
法辦（ㄈㄚˇ ㄅㄢˋ）
to bring (someone) to justice; to punish according to the law: 謀殺兇手已送法辦。The murderer was brought to justice.
法幣（ㄈㄚˇ ㄅㄧˋ）
the legal tender
法部（ㄈㄚˇ ㄅㄨˋ）or 法務部（ㄈㄚˇ ㄨˋ ㄅㄨˋ）

the Ministry of Justice

法碼(ㄈㄚˇ ㄇㄚˇ)
standard weights

法門(ㄈㄚˇ ㄇㄣˊ)
①(in ancient China) the south gate ② dharmaparyaya; the doctrines or wisdom of Buddha regarded as the door to enlightenment ③ the way, or method of learning something。動像是成功的不二法門。 Industry and thrift are the only correct method to success.

法名(ㄈㄚˇ ㄇㄧㄥˊ)
the name one assumes upon becoming a Buddhist monk or nun

法服(ㄈㄚˇ ㄈㄨˊ)
①ceremonial dress; dress for official functions ② gowns or robes worn by Buddhist monks or nuns

法典(ㄈㄚˇ ㄉㄧㄢˇ)
①a code of laws; a statute book ②the scriptures of Buddhism

法定(ㄈㄚˇ ㄉㄧㄥˋ)
stipulated by law; legal; legally-provided; determined or prescribed by law

法定代理人(ㄈㄚˇ ㄉㄧㄥˋ ㄉㄞˋ ㄌㄧˇ ㄖㄣˊ)
a legal representative

法定年齡(ㄈㄚˇ ㄉㄧㄥˋ ㄋㄧㄢˊ ㄌㄧㄥˊ)
legal age

法定人數(ㄈㄚˇ ㄉㄧㄥˋ ㄖㄣˊ ㄕㄨˋ)
a quorum—the number of members of a group or organization required to be present to transact business legally, usually a majority: 我們現在已足法定人數。 We have a quorum now.

法度(ㄈㄚˇ ㄉㄨˋ)
laws and institutions

法臺(ㄈㄚˇ ㄊㄞˊ)
a platform on which a Buddhist monk or Taoist priest performs rites

法堂(ㄈㄚˇ ㄊㄤˊ)
a court of law in former times

法帖(ㄈㄚˇ ㄊㄧㄝˋ)
a model copy book of calligraphy

法條(ㄈㄚˇ ㄊㄧㄠˊ)
items or articles of law

法庭(ㄈㄚˇ ㄊㄧㄥˊ)
a law court; a courtroom; a tribunal: 此事將由法庭裁決。 The court will rule on the matter.

法徒(ㄈㄚˇ ㄊㄨˊ)
the Buddhist monk

法統(ㄈㄚˇ ㄊㄨㄥˇ)
the system of justice

法臘(ㄈㄚˇ ㄌㄚˋ)
the end of the Buddhist monk's year after the summer retreat; a Buddhist year (the number of 夏臘 or 戒臘 or discipline years, indicating the years since a monk's ordination)

法老(ㄈㄚˇ ㄌㄠˇ)
Pharaoh, title of an ancient Egyptian king

法理(ㄈㄚˇ ㄌㄧˇ)
①the principle or theory of law ②the doctrines of Buddhism

法理學(ㄈㄚˇ ㄌㄧˇ ㄒㄩㄝˊ)
jurisprudence

法力(ㄈㄚˇ ㄌㄧˋ)
①power of Buddhist doctrines ②black magic; supernatural power

法吏(ㄈㄚˇ ㄌㄧˋ)
a warden; a prison-guard; court clerks

法令(ㄈㄚˇ ㄌㄧㄥˋ)
a general term for laws and regulations

法螺(ㄈㄚˇ ㄌㄨㄛˊ)
①a horn made of sea shell, used originally in the ancient army, now also used in Buddhist and Taoist rituals ②(figuratively) as in 吹法螺—to brag; to boast; to make boasts

法輪(ㄈㄚˇ ㄌㄨㄣˊ)
(Buddhism) dharmacakra; the Wheel of the Law; the Buddha truth which is capable of crushing all evil and all opposition, like Indra's wheel, and which rolls on from man to man, place to place, age to age

法律(ㄈㄚˇ ㄌㄩˋ)
laws

法律顧問(ㄈㄚˇ ㄌㄩˋ ㄍㄨˋ ㄨㄣˋ)
a legal advisor

法律行為(ㄈㄚˇ ㄌㄩˋ ㄒㄧㄥˊ ㄨㄟˊ)
a legal act

法律學(ㄈㄚˇ ㄌㄩˋ ㄒㄩㄝˊ)
jurisprudence; law; the science of law 亦作「法學」

法律學系(ㄈㄚˇ ㄌㄩˋ ㄒㄩㄝˊ ㄒㄧˋ)or法律系(ㄈㄚˇ ㄌㄩˋ ㄒㄧˋ)
the Department of Law (at a university)

法律制裁(ㄈㄚˇ ㄌㄩˋ ㄓˋ ㄘㄞˊ)
legal sanctions

法規(ㄈㄚˇ ㄍㄨㄟ)
laws and regulations

法官(ㄈㄚˇ ㄍㄨㄢ)
a judge (at court); a judicial official; a justice: 這法官很仁慈。 The judge was very kind.

法冠(ㄈㄚˇ ㄍㄨㄢ)
①a cap worn by judicial officials in ancient times ② the cap of a Taoist high priest

法科(ㄈㄚˇ ㄎㄜ)
the law department of a college; the department of human sciences—including law, economics, political science

法號(ㄈㄚˇ ㄏㄠˋ)
the religious name of a Buddhist monk or nun

法籍(ㄈㄚˇ ㄐㄧˊ)
law books

法紀(ㄈㄚˇ ㄐㄧˋ)
law and discipline: 他目無法紀。 He acted in utter disregard of law and discipline.

法家(ㄈㄚˇ ㄐㄧㄚ)
①the Legalist School, one of the nine schools of learning in ancient China, stressing law and punishment ②a great master; a leading authority

法家拂士(ㄈㄚˇ ㄐㄧㄚ ㄈㄨˊ ㄕˋ)
(originally in Mencius) officials and advisors of high moral standing and ability

法警(ㄈㄚˇ ㄐㄧㄥˇ)
①the judicial police ②a bailiff

法器(ㄈㄚˇ ㄑㄧˋ)
①implements used in worship ②one who obeys Buddha ③a vessel of the law

法權(ㄈㄚˇ ㄑㄩㄢˊ)
jurisdiction

〔水部〕

〔水部〕

法新(ㄈㄚˋㄒㄧㄣ)
(British coin) a farthing

法相(ㄈㄚˋㄒㄧㄤˋ)
(Buddhism) the aspects or characteristics of things — All things are of monadic nature but differ in form.

法學博士(ㄈㄚˋㄒㄩㄝˊㄅㄛˊㄕˋ)
a Doctor of Laws (L.L.D.)

法學家(ㄈㄚˋㄒㄩㄝˊㄐㄧㄚ)
a jurist

法學士(ㄈㄚˋㄒㄩㄝˊㄕˋ)
a Bachelor of Laws (LL.B.)

法治(ㄈㄚˋㄓˋ)
rule of law

法制(ㄈㄚˋㄓˋ)
the legal system; laws and institutions: 我們要加強民主法制。Let's strengthen the democratic legal system.

法制室(ㄈㄚˋㄓˋㄕˋ)
a bureau in the early days of the Republic responsible for the drafting of statutes and laws

法場(ㄈㄚˋㄔㄤˇ)or(ㄈㄚˋㄔㄤˊ)
①an execution ground; the place of execution ②any place set aside for religious practices

法師(ㄈㄚˋㄕ)
①a salutation for a Buddhist monk ②a Taoist high priest

法施(ㄈㄚˋㄕ)
to teach the principles of Buddhism

法式(ㄈㄚˋㄕˋ)
①a pattern; a model; something to emulate; a standard ②legal ways or forms

法事(ㄈㄚˋㄕˋ)
Buddhist rituals performed on special occasions

法身(ㄈㄚˋㄕㄣ)
(Buddhism) dharmakaya; embodiment of truth and law; the spiritual or true body; essential Buddhahood; the essence of being; the absolute; the norm of the universe

法書(ㄈㄚˋㄕㄨ)
①masterpieces of calligraphy ②a volume on institutions and systems

法術(ㄈㄚˋㄕㄨˋ)
①an uncanny, occult, or supernatural feat, usually performed by a Buddhist or Taoist, for a purpose—as curing of the sick, etc. ②the black art

法數(ㄈㄚˋㄕㄨˋ)
(mathematics) an addend, subtrahend, multiplier or divisor

法人(ㄈㄚˋㄖㄣˊ)
a juridical person; a corporate person; a legal person; legalis homo

法則(ㄈㄚˋㄗㄜˊ)
①a way or method; a pattern or model considered as a standard ②a formula in mathematics ③an agreement which has the same binding force as law

法藏(ㄈㄚˋㄘㄤˊ)
the doctrines in Buddhist scriptures

法座(ㄈㄚˋㄗㄨㄛˋ)
①the seat of the chief, as a throne in court ②a rendezvous for listening to Buddhist's lecture

法曹(ㄈㄚˋㄘㄠˊ)
judges

法案(ㄈㄚˋㄢˋ)
a bill which has been passed by parliament; a law; a statute

法衣(ㄈㄚˋㄧ)
robes or gowns worn by Buddhist monks or judges or lawyers

法醫(ㄈㄚˋㄧ)
an expert in forensic medicine employed by a court of law, such as a coroner

法醫學(ㄈㄚˋㄧㄒㄩㄝˊ)
forensic medicine; medical jurisprudence

法益(ㄈㄚˋㄧˋ)
interests provided in the law or protected by the law

法外施恩(ㄈㄚˋㄨㄞˋㄕㄣ)
to be lenient within the limits of the law

法網(ㄈㄚˋㄨㄤˇ)
the dragnet or the arms of law

法院(ㄈㄚˋㄩㄢˋ)
a court of justice; a court of

law: 犯人被押到法院受審。The prisoner was brought to court for trial.

【法】   2832
  2.ㄈㄚˋ far fà

法碼兒(ㄈㄚˋ·ㄇㄚㄦ)
weights of a scale 亦作「砝碼」

法子(ㄈㄚˋ·ㄗ)
a method; a way: 他採用同一法子。He adopted the same method.

【法】   2832
  3.ㄈㄚ fa fā
a way, especially used in 沒法兒"No way out."

【法】   2832
  4.ㄈㄚˊ fah fá
1. the Frank
2. France; French

法蘭西(ㄈㄚˊㄌㄢˊㄒㄧ)
France

法蘭絨(ㄈㄚˊㄌㄢˊㄖㄨㄥˊ)
flannel

法郎(ㄈㄚˊㄌㄤˊ)
(a monetary unit of France) franc 亦作「佛郎」: 這本書值十五法郎。This book costs 15 francs.

法國(ㄈㄚˊㄍㄨㄛˊ)
France: 法國的首都是巴黎。The capital of France is Paris.

法國大革命(ㄈㄚˊㄍㄨㄛˊㄉㄚˋㄍㄜˊㄇㄧㄥˋ)
the French Revolution (1789-1799)

法國人(ㄈㄚˊㄍㄨㄛˊㄖㄣˊ)
the French; a Frenchman

法籍(ㄈㄚˊㄐㄧˊ)
of French nationality

法西斯分子(ㄈㄚˊㄒㄧㄙㄈㄣˋㄗˇ)
Fascists

法西斯主義(ㄈㄚˊㄒㄧㄙㄓㄨˇㄧˋ)
Fascism

法新社(ㄈㄚˊㄒㄧㄣㄕㄜˋ)
Agence France Presse (AFP)

法文(ㄈㄚˊㄨㄣˊ)
the French language

法語(ㄈㄚˊㄩˇ)
the spoken French; French: 我母親會說法語。My mother speaks French.

【泗】   2833
  ㄙˋ syh sì
1. snivel; nasal mucus

2. name of a river
3. name of a county

泗水 (ㄙ ㄕㄨㄟ)
①name of a county in Shantung ②Surabaya, a seaport on Java

【泖】 2834
ㄇㄠˇ mao mǎo
1. still waters
2. name of a river in Kiangsu Province

【泚】 2835
ㄘˇ tsyy cǐ
1. clear waters
2. bright and brilliant
3. sweating

【泝】 2836
ㄙㄨˋ suh sù
same as 溯—to go upstream or to trace up to the source

泝流 (ㄙㄨˋ ㄌㄧㄡˊ)
to go against the current; to go upstream

泝洄 (ㄙㄨˋ ㄏㄨㄟˊ)
to go against the stream

泝游 (ㄙㄨˋ ㄧㄡˊ)
to go down the stream

泝沿 (ㄙㄨˋ ㄧㄢˊ)
①to follow the stream or current ②to follow along a course

泝源 (ㄙㄨˋ ㄩㄢˊ)
to trace up to the source

【泠】 2837
ㄌㄧㄥˊ ling líng
1. clear sounds
2. mild and comfortable
3. same as 伶—a drama performer; an actor; an actress
4. a Chinese family name

泠風 (ㄌㄧㄥˊ ㄈㄥ)
mild winds; breezes

泠冽 (ㄌㄧㄥˊ ㄌㄧㄝˋ)
clear

泠泠 (ㄌㄧㄥˊ ㄌㄧㄥˊ)
①gurgling sound ②cool clear and crisp sound

泠然 (ㄌㄧㄥˊ ㄖㄢˊ)
①gentle and charming ②to understand; to realize ③cool ④a clear and crisp sound

【泛】 2838
ㄈㄢˋ fann fàn
1. to float; to drift
2. not exact or precise; not practical
3. not sincere; not intimate

4. generally (speaking); as a whole; pan-: 泛美 Pan-American
5. to be suffused with

泛美航空公司 (ㄈㄢˋ ㄇㄟˇ ㄏㄤˊ ㄎㄨㄥ ㄍㄨㄥ ㄙ)
the Pan American World Airways Inc.

泛泛 (ㄈㄢˋ ㄈㄢˋ)
①not close or intimate ②in generalities ③to float

泛泛之交 (ㄈㄢˋ ㄈㄢˋ ㄓ ㄐㄧㄠ)
a nodding acquaintance; a casual acquaintance

泛覽 (ㄈㄢˋ ㄌㄢˇ) or 泛觀 (ㄈㄢˋ ㄍㄨㄢ)
a quick and general glance; to see or view briefly

泛濫成災 (ㄈㄢˋ ㄌㄢˋ ㄔㄥˊ ㄗㄞ)
a disaster caused by flooding waters; a disastrous flood

泛論 (ㄈㄢˋ ㄌㄨㄣˋ)
to discuss generally; a general survey or review

泛指 (ㄈㄢˋ ㄓˇ)
to generally indicate; vague reference or allusion: 他的說明是泛指一般人的。His explanation refers to people in general.

泛舟 (ㄈㄢˋ ㄓㄡ)
to row a boat; boating: 我們去泛舟。Let's go boating now.

泛常 (ㄈㄢˋ ㄔㄤˊ)
①usually; frequently; often ②not close or intimate

泛稱 (ㄈㄢˋ ㄔㄥ)
generally called···

泛神論 (ㄈㄢˋ ㄕㄣˊ ㄌㄨㄣˋ)
pantheism

泛音 (ㄈㄢˋ ㄧㄣ)
(music) overtones

泛問 (ㄈㄢˋ ㄨㄣˋ)
a question which does not concern a particular person or thing

【波】 2839
ㄅㄛ bo bō
(又讀 ㄆㄛ po pō)
1. waves; breakers: 波浪很高。The waves were high.
2. to undulate; undulation; to fluctuate; fluctuations
3. to affect; to involve; to implicate; to entangle

波峯 (ㄅㄛ ㄈㄥ)
the wave crest

波幅 (ㄅㄛ ㄈㄨˊ)
the range of undulations or fluctuations

波蕩 (ㄅㄛ ㄉㄤˋ)
unstable; turmoil

波多黎各 (ㄅㄛ ㄉㄨㄛ ㄌㄧˊ ㄍㄜˋ)
Puerto Rico

波段 (ㄅㄛ ㄉㄨㄢˋ)
a wave band

波動 (ㄅㄛ ㄉㄨㄥˋ)
①undulation ②(said of prices) fluctuations; to fluctuate: 物價年年波動。Prices fluctuate from year to year.

波濤 (ㄅㄛ ㄊㄠˊ)
billows; breakers; large waves

波濤起伏 (ㄅㄛ ㄊㄠˊ ㄑㄧˇ ㄈㄨˊ)
(said of sea waves) swelling, heaving and subsiding—also used figuratively to describe tumultuous situations, instability, etc.

波濤洶湧 (ㄅㄛ ㄊㄠˊ ㄒㄩㄥ ㄩㄥˇ)
roaring waves and billows that swell up to heaven; to billow—a term used figuratively to describe tumultuous situations

波累 (ㄅㄛ ㄌㄟˇ)
to involve in a trouble

波蘭 (ㄅㄛ ㄌㄢˊ)
Poland: 華沙是波蘭的首都。Warsaw is the capital of Poland.

波蘭人 (ㄅㄛ ㄌㄢˊ ㄖㄣˊ)
a Pole; the Poles

波瀾 (ㄅㄛ ㄌㄢˊ)
①waves or billows ②the turns and twists of a piece of writing

波瀾起伏 (ㄅㄛ ㄌㄢˊ ㄑㄧˇ ㄈㄨˊ)
(said of a piece of writing) with one climax following another

波瀾壯闊 (ㄅㄛ ㄌㄢˊ ㄓㄨㄤˋ ㄎㄨㄛˋ)
surging forward with great momentum; unfolding on a magnificent scale

波浪 (ㄅㄛ ㄌㄤˋ)
billows; breakers; waves: 波浪在岸邊起伏。The waves rose and fell on the shore.

波浪鼓 (ㄅㄛ ㄌㄤˋ ㄍㄨˇ)
a kind of toy-drum for children with a long handle and

【水部】

（水部）

one pendant on each side which hits the drum when the handle is twisted 亦作「博浪鼓」

波羅門 (ㄅㄛ ㄌㄨㄛˊ ㄇㄣˊ)
(Hinduism) Brahman, or Brahmin, a member of the highest, or priestly, class among the Hindus

波羅的海 (ㄅㄛ ㄌㄨㄛˊ ㄉㄜ˙ ㄏㄞˇ)
the Baltic Sea, in northern Europe

波谷 (ㄅㄛ ㄍㄨˇ)
the trough of the waves

波光 (ㄅㄛ ㄍㄨㄤ)
the glistening light of waves

波河 (ㄅㄛ ㄏㄜˊ)
the Po River, in northern Italy

波及 (ㄅㄛ ㄐㄧˊ)
①to affect; to involve: 經濟危機波及了全世界。The economic crisis affected the entire world. ②(said of a fire) to engulf; to spread to

波心 (ㄅㄛ ㄒㄧㄣ)
①the center of a water-ring ②the heart of a trouble, instability, etc.

波札那 (ㄅㄛ ㄓㄚˊ ㄋㄚˋ)
Botswana

波折 (ㄅㄛ ㄓㄜˊ)
twists and turns of a matter; obstructions or obstacles: 事情發生了波折。Things took an unexpected turn.

波磔 (ㄅㄛ ㄓㄜˊ)
(Chinese calligraphy) a downward stroke to the left or right

波狀葉 (ㄅㄛ ㄓㄨㄤˋ ㄧㄝˋ)
sinuate leaves

波臣 (ㄅㄛ ㄔㄣˊ)
①denizens of water ②victims of drowning

波長 (ㄅㄛ ㄔㄤˊ)
(physics) wavelength

波士頓 (ㄅㄛ ㄕˋ ㄉㄨㄣˋ)
Boston

波神 (ㄅㄛ ㄕㄣˊ)
a nymph; the deity of a river

波茨坦宣言 (ㄅㄛ ㄘˊ ㄊㄢˇ ㄒㄩㄢ ㄧㄢˊ)
the Potsdam Declaration signed by China, Great Britain and the U.S. in 1945

波斯 (ㄅㄛ ㄙ)
Persia

波斯貓 (ㄅㄛ ㄙ ㄇㄠ)
a Persian cat

波斯帝國 (ㄅㄛ ㄙ ㄉㄧˋ ㄍㄨㄛˊ)
the Persian Empire

波斯菊 (ㄅㄛ ㄙ ㄐㄩˊ)
coreopsis

波斯灣 (ㄅㄛ ㄙ ㄨㄢ)
the Persian Gulf

波昂 (ㄅㄛ ㄤˊ)
Bonn, capital of West Germany

波義耳定律 (ㄅㄛ ㄧˋ ㄦˇ ㄉㄧㄥˋ ㄌㄩˋ)
Boyle's Law

波紋 (ㄅㄛ ㄨㄣˊ)
ripples; a water-ring

【泣】 2840
(ㄑㄧˋ) chih qì
to weep; to come to tears without crying: 她泣不成聲。She choked with sobs.

泣別 (ㄑㄧˋ ㄅㄧㄝˊ)
to part in tears

泣涕 (ㄑㄧˋ ㄊㄧˋ)
to come to tears for sorrow; to weep

泣辜 (ㄑㄧˋ ㄍㄨ)
to commiserate a criminal as Yü the Great (大禹) did, descending from the carriage to do so 參看「泣罪」

泣鬼神 (ㄑㄧˋ ㄍㄨㄟˇ ㄕㄣˊ)
to move, or touch not only men, but the spirits and gods as well: 動天地而泣鬼神 to move the universe and cause the gods to weep—very moving

泣叩 (ㄑㄧˋ ㄎㄡˋ)
a concluding expression used after one's name in a mourning notice

泣諫 (ㄑㄧˋ ㄐㄧㄢˋ)
to counsel (a superior, king, or emperor) in tears indicating absolute sincerity

泣下沾襟 (ㄑㄧˋ ㄒㄧㄚˋ ㄓㄢ ㄐㄧㄣ)
to weep so much that the tears make the front part of the garment dripping wet

泣下數行 (ㄑㄧˋ ㄒㄧㄚˋ ㄕㄨˋ ㄏㄤˊ)
tears coursing down the cheeks

泣下如雨 (ㄑㄧˋ ㄒㄧㄚˋ ㄖㄨˊ ㄩˇ)
One's tears fall down like rain.

泣血 (ㄑㄧˋ ㄒㄩㄝˋ)
to weep blood (an expression used especially after one's name in a mourning notice for one's parents)

泣血稽顙 (ㄑㄧˋ ㄒㄩㄝˋ ㄐㄧ ㄙㄤˇ)
weeping blood and knocking the head—in mourning for one's parents (an expression used in an obituary)

泣血三年 (ㄑㄧˋ ㄒㄩㄝˋ ㄙㄢ ㄋㄧㄢˊ)
to mourn for one's parents for three years

泣杖 (ㄑㄧˋ ㄓㄤˋ)
to cry over the stick (said of a filial son, Han Po-yü (韓伯兪) of the Han Dynasty, who wept because the stick used by his mother to punish him was making lighter strokes and he drew the conclusion that his mother was getting weaker)

泣珠 (ㄑㄧˋ ㄓㄨ)
to weep pearly tears—with reference to a Chinese mythical tale of how a generous person repaid his host by weeping pearls instead of tears to be presented to the host

泣罪 (ㄑㄧˋ ㄗㄨㄟˋ)
to weep for a criminal's evildoing 亦作「泣辜」

泣訴 (ㄑㄧˋ ㄙㄨˋ)
to tell one's sorrows or grievances in tears; to accuse while weeping

【泡】 2841
1. ㄆㄠˋ paw pào
1. bubbles; suds; froth; foam: 他用肥皂水吹氣泡。He blows bubbles with soap water.
2. a blister
3. to steep; to soak; to dip; to infuse (tea, etc.): 她把麵包泡在牛奶中。She soaked bread in milk.
4. (slang) to dawdle; to fool around (especially with women)

泡泡糖 (ㄆㄠˋ ㄆㄠˋ ㄊㄤˊ)
bubble gum

泡沫 (ㄆㄠˋ ㄇㄛˋ)
suds; foam; froth: 浪花衝擊海岸造成泡沫。The foam is made by waves breaking on the shore.

泡沫乳膠 (ㄆㄠˋ ㄇㄛˋ ㄖㄨˇ ㄐㄧㄠ)

〔水部〕

foam rubber

泡飯 (ㄆㄠ ㄈㄢ)
to heat cooked rice with boiling water for eating

泡湯 (ㄆㄠ ㄊㄤ)
①to make soup by infusing in hot water ②(said of a dream) busted; (said of money) wasted; (said of hope) dashed

泡沫 (ㄆㄠ ㄇㄛ)
visionary; empty bubbles

泡茶 (ㄆㄠ ㄔㄚ)
to infuse tea; to make tea

泡水 (ㄆㄠ ㄕㄨㄟ)
to soak in water

泡菜 (ㄆㄠ ㄘㄞ)
vegetables preserved in salted water; Chinese pickles

泡泡 (ㄆㄠ ㄆㄠ)
①bubbles; foam: 水開時就起氣泡泡。When water boils, bubbles form. ②blisters: 我的腳起泡泡了。I've got blisters on my feet.

泡影 (ㄆㄠ ㄧㄥ)
the shadow of bubbles—unreality; pie in the sky

【泡】 2841
2. ㄆㄠ pau p'ao
1. loose and soft; spongy
2. an amount of excrement or urine: 小孩子撒一泡尿。The child urinated.

【泥】 2842
1. ㄋㄧ ní
1. mud; mire; earth; soil; clay: 我的上衣沾滿污泥。My coat is covered with mud.
2. to paste; to plaster: 這工人正在泥牆。The worker was plastering the wall.
3. mashed vegetables or fruit; paste: 棗泥 jujube paste

泥巴 (ㄋㄧˊ ㄅㄚ)
mud; mire; earth; clay

泥盆紀 (ㄋㄧˊ ㄆㄣˊ ㄐㄧˋ)
(geology) the Devonian Period

泥菩薩 (ㄋㄧˊ ㄆㄨˊ ㄙㄚˋ)
a clay idol: 他像泥菩薩過江, 自身難保。He is like a clay idol wading across a river—hardly able to save himself (let alone anyone else).

泥封 (ㄋㄧˊ ㄈㄥ)
to seal (a wine jug, jars, etc.) with mud or clay

泥點兒 (ㄋㄧˊ ㄉㄧㄢˇ ㄦ) or 泥點子 (ㄋㄧˊ ㄉㄧㄢˇ ㄗ)
droplets of mud

泥多佛大 (ㄋㄧˊ ㄉㄨㄛ ㄈㄛˊ ㄉㄚˋ)
(literally) The more the clay, the bigger the statue of Buddha.—The more the supporters, the greater the achievements of the leader.

泥胎 (ㄋㄧˊ ㄊㄞ)
statues of gods made of mud

泥炭 (ㄋㄧˊ ㄊㄢˋ)
peat 亦作「泥煤」

泥塘 (ㄋㄧˊ ㄊㄤˊ) or 泥潭 (ㄋㄧˊ ㄊㄢˊ)
a pond of mire; a morass

泥淖 (ㄋㄧˊ ㄋㄠˋ)
①the ground soaked in rain water; mire ②filthy; dirty ③the masses; the unknown; the humble

泥土 (ㄋㄧˊ ㄊㄨˇ)
mud; clay; earth; soil: 把它埋在泥土裏。Bury it in the earth.

泥淖 (ㄋㄧˊ ㄋㄠˋ)
mud; quagmires: 車子陷在泥淖中。The cart was bogged in the mud.

泥牛入海 (ㄋㄧˊ ㄋㄧㄡˊ ㄖㄨˋ ㄏㄞˇ)
(literally) A mud ox goes into the sea.—never to return

泥濘 (ㄋㄧˊ ㄋㄧㄥˋ)
muddy: 那是一條泥濘的路。It is a muddy road.

泥濘 (ㄋㄧˊ ㄋㄧㄥˋ)
a marshy ground; a quagmire

泥垢 (ㄋㄧˊ ㄍㄡˋ)
mud and dirt—especially those on the human body: 洗掉你手上的泥垢。Wash the dirt off your hands.

泥坑 (ㄋㄧˊ ㄎㄥ)
a mud pit; a quagmire; a morass: 不要陷入悲觀主義的泥坑裏。Don't fall into the quagmire of pessimism.

泥灰土 (ㄋㄧˊ ㄏㄨㄟ ㄊㄨˇ)
marly soil

泥漿 (ㄋㄧˊ ㄐㄧㄤ)
mire: 我們在滿是泥漿的足球場上踢球。We played on a football field that was thick with mire.

泥鰍 (ㄋㄧˊ ㄑㄧㄡ) or 泥鰌 (ㄋㄧˊ ㄑㄧㄡ)
a loach; a mudfish

泥像 (ㄋㄧˊ ㄒㄧㄤˋ)

a statue or image of a god, made of mud or clay

泥沼 (ㄋㄧˊ ㄓㄠˇ)
mire; swamp; morasses; sloughs

泥磚 (ㄋㄧˊ ㄓㄨㄢ)
sun-dried mud bricks

泥船渡河 (ㄋㄧˊ ㄔㄨㄢˊ ㄉㄨˋ ㄏㄜˊ)
(originally in the Buddhist scripture) to cross a river in a boat of mud—How dangerous is the world where temptations lurk everywhere.

泥沙 (ㄋㄧˊ ㄕㄚ)
①mud and sand; silt ②something worthless ③to sink to the bottom

泥沙俱下 (ㄋㄧˊ ㄕㄚ ㄐㄩˋ ㄒㄧㄚˋ)
Mud and sand are carried along.—There is a mingling of good and bad.

泥首 (ㄋㄧˊ ㄕㄡˇ)
to kowtow with the head touching the ground

泥水活 (ㄋㄧˊ ㄕㄨㄟˇ ㄏㄨㄛˊ)
the work of a bricklayer and plasterer

泥水匠 (ㄋㄧˊ ㄕㄨㄟˇ ㄐㄧㄤˋ)
a bricklayer; a plasterer

泥人 (ㄋㄧˊ ㄖㄣˊ)
a clay doll

泥滓 (ㄋㄧˊ ㄗˇ)
①dirty or filthy ②low and inferior ③the world

泥足深陷 (ㄋㄧˊ ㄗㄨˊ ㄕㄣ ㄒㄧㄢˋ)
to sink deep in the mire; to get into real trouble; to bog down

泥醉 (ㄋㄧˊ ㄗㄨㄟˋ)
dead drunk

泥塑 (ㄋㄧˊ ㄙㄨˋ)
a clay sculpture

泥塑木雕 (ㄋㄧˊ ㄙㄨˋ ㄇㄨˋ ㄉㄧㄠ)
(literally) made of clay or carved from wood—①idols ②one who is devoid of emotions

泥塑人 (ㄋㄧˊ ㄙㄨˋ ㄖㄣˊ)
(literally) a person of clay—a person without motion of any kind, as after a shock or in great embarrassment

泥娃娃 (ㄋㄧˊ ㄨㄚˊ ·ㄨㄚ)
a clay doll (often found in the temple of the goddess of

〔水部〕

propagation ready to be stolen by those women believers who wish to beget a son)

【泥】 2842
ㄋㄧˊ ㄋㄧˇ nih ní

1. to be tied down by conventions, old practices; very conservative
2. to request with sweet words
3. inapplicable

泥古(ㄋㄧˊ ㄍㄨˇ)
very conservative; to stick to ancient ways and thoughts

泥滯(ㄋㄧˊ ㄓˋ)
①bigoted and conservative ②to stay somewhere without obvious reason ③to be mired

泥飲(ㄋㄧˊ ㄧㄣˇ)
to compel others to drink

【泮】 2843
ㄆㄢˋ pann pàn

1. (in ancient China) an institution of higher learning
2. (now rarely) to dissolve; to melt

泮宮(ㄆㄢˋ ㄍㄨㄥ)
an institution of higher learning in ancient China

泮汗(ㄆㄢˋ ㄏㄢˋ)
(said of flooding waters) expansive

泮渙(ㄆㄢˋ ㄏㄨㄢˋ)
to dissolve (like floes)

泮水(ㄆㄢˋ ㄕㄨㄟˇ)
a semicircular pool on the premises of an institution of higher learning in former times

【泯】 2844
ㄇㄧㄣˊ ㄇㄧㄣˇ miin mín
to destroy; to eliminate; to put an end to; to vanish

泯滅(ㄇㄧㄣˇ ㄇㄧㄝˋ)or泯沒(ㄇㄧㄣˇ ㄇㄛˋ)
to vanish without a trace; to sink into oblivion: 他們的貢獻永遠不會泯沒的。Their contributions will never sink into oblivion.

泯泯(ㄇㄧㄣˇ ㄇㄧㄣˇ)
①vague and gloomy; very low visibility ②clear (water) ③tumultuous; confusing and disorderly

泯絕(ㄇㄧㄣˇ ㄐㄩㄝˊ)
to be lost for ever; extinguished

【注】 2845
ㄓㄨˋ juh zhù

1. to pour (liquid): 雷電過後,大雨如注。After lightning and thunder came a heavy downpour.
2. to concentrate; to engross; preoccupation: 她全神貫注於一篇有趣的故事。She was engrossed in an interesting story.
3. same as 註—to annotate: 有的人一面讀書一面做批註。Some people annotate as they read.
4. stakes (in gambling): 孤注一擲 to stake all on a single throw of the dice.

注明(ㄓㄨˋ ㄇㄧㄥˊ)
to make a footnote; to mark out 亦作「註明」: 你應該注明出處 You should give sources of your quotations.

注目(ㄓㄨˋ ㄇㄨˋ)
to look attentively; to focus one's look on; to gaze at; to stare at

注目禮(ㄓㄨˋ ㄇㄨˋ ㄌㄧˇ)
(military) parade salute

注册(ㄓㄨˋ ㄘㄜˋ)
casting

注定(ㄓㄨˋ ㄉㄧㄥˋ)
to be doomed; to be destined: 他注定要失敗。He is doomed to failure.

注解(ㄓㄨˋ ㄐㄧㄝˇ)
①to annotate ②footnotes; annotations 亦作「註解」

注脚(ㄓㄨˋ ㄐㄧㄠˇ)
footnotes; annotations 亦作「註脚」

注銷(ㄓㄨˋ ㄒㄧㄠ)
to make void; to nullify; to annul; to cancel; to be written off: 賬已注銷。The account has been written off.

注心(ㄓㄨˋ ㄒㄧㄣ)
to concentrate attention; to focus attention

注重(ㄓㄨˋ ㄓㄨㄥˋ)
to attach great importance to; to consider to be important; to lay stress on; to emphasize: 本辭典特別注重文法。This dictionary puts a special emphasis on grammar.

注釋(ㄓㄨˋ ㄕˋ)
①to annotate ②footnotes; annotations 亦作「註釋」

注視(ㄓㄨˋ ㄕˋ)
to look attentively; to watch; to focus one's look on: 他注視著太陽漸漸落到樹後。He watched the sun setting behind the trees.

注射(ㄓㄨˋ ㄕㄜˋ)
to inject; injection; to get a shot: 傷寒預防注射 a typhoid shot

注射器(ㄓㄨˋ ㄕㄜˋ ㄑㄧˋ)
a syringe (for injection)

注疏(ㄓㄨˋ ㄕㄨ)or(ㄓㄨˋ ㄕㄨˋ)
notes and commentaries

注水(ㄓㄨˋ ㄕㄨㄟˇ)
water flooding

注入(ㄓㄨˋ ㄖㄨˋ)
to pour into; to empty into: 河水注入海。The waters of the river pour into the sea.

注入式(ㄓㄨˋ ㄖㄨˋ ㄕˋ)
(education) a spoonfeeding method or a cramming method (as opposed to a developmental method)

注子(ㄓㄨˋ ㄗˇ)
a wine vessel

注意(ㄓㄨˋ ㄧˋ)
to pay attention to; to watch: 過街時要注意車輛。Watch out for cars when you cross the street.

注意力(ㄓㄨˋ ㄧˋ ㄌㄧˋ)
attention

注音(ㄓㄨˋ ㄧㄣ)
to make phonetic transcriptions: 本文有注音嗎? Is the text marked with phonetic symbols?

注音符號(ㄓㄨˋ ㄧㄣ ㄈㄨˊ ㄏㄠˋ)
the National Phonetic Symbols (for Mandarin)

【決】 2846
ㄐㄧㄤ iang yāng

1. great; profound
2. (said of clouds)turbulent

泱漭無際(ㄧㄤ ㄇㄤˇ ㄨˊ ㄐㄧˋ)
vast without limit

泱泱(ㄧㄤ ㄧㄤ)
①great; magnificent; broad and deep ②(said of clouds) turbulent

泱泱大風(ㄧㄤ ㄧㄤ ㄉㄚˋ ㄈㄥ)
the impressive manner of a

great country

央泱大國(ㄧㄤ ㄧㄤ ㄉㄚˋ ㄍㄨㄛˊ)
a great country

【泳】 2847
ㄩㄥˋ yeong yǒng

1. to swim: 他游泳過河。He swam across the river.
2. types or methods of swimming: 蛙泳 breaststroke

【泉】 2848
ㄑㄩㄢˊ chyuan quán

1. a spring; a fountain
2. money (archaic)
3. a Chinese family name

泉幣(ㄑㄩㄢˊ ㄅㄧˋ)or泉布(ㄑㄩㄢˊ ㄅㄨˋ)
money, or currency (archaic terms)

泉脈(ㄑㄩㄢˊ ㄇㄞˋ)or(ㄑㄩㄢˊ ㄇㄛˋ)
ground water channels

泉臺(ㄑㄩㄢˊ ㄊㄞˊ)
a grave; a tomb

泉林(ㄑㄩㄢˊ ㄌㄧㄣˊ)
①natural scenery ②the abode of a recluse

泉路(ㄑㄩㄢˊ ㄌㄨˋ)
the way to Hades

泉下(ㄑㄩㄢˊ ㄒㄧㄚˋ)
the world of the dead; Hades

泉州(ㄑㄩㄢˊ ㄓㄡ)
Chuanchow, Fukien Province

泉州灣(ㄑㄩㄢˊ ㄓㄡ ㄨㄢ)
name of the estuary of the Tsin River in Fukien

泉石(ㄑㄩㄢˊ ㄕˊ)
springs and rocks—the beauty of nature

泉石膏肓(ㄑㄩㄢˊ ㄕˊ ㄍㄠ ㄏㄨㄤ)
inveterate love of outing; an obsession with nature

泉水(ㄑㄩㄢˊ ㄕㄨㄟˇ)
spring water

泉壤(ㄑㄩㄢˊ ㄖㄤˇ)
the world of the dead; Hades

泉源(ㄑㄩㄢˊ ㄩㄢˊ)
a fountainhead; a springhead; a source; a wellspring; 知識是智慧的泉源。Knowledge is the source of wisdom.

【泰】 2849
ㄊㄞˋ tay tài

1. great; big
2. quiet; calm; peace; ease: 國泰民安。The country is prosperous at peace, and the

people live in happiness.
3. Thailand
4. good luck
5. same as 太—very; much; too; excessive

泰半(ㄊㄞˋ ㄅㄢˋ)
more than half; the greater part; the majority

泰斗(ㄊㄞˋ ㄉㄡˇ)
①Mountain Tai and the Dipper ②a leading authority (in certain field or discipline)

泰戈爾(ㄊㄞˋ ㄍㄜ ㄦˇ)
Rabindranath Tagore, 1861-1941, an Indian poet

泰國(ㄊㄞˋ ㄍㄨㄛˊ)
Thailand: 泰國首都是曼谷。The capital of Thailand is Bangkok.

泰國人(ㄊㄞˋ ㄍㄨㄛˊ ㄖㄣˊ)
a Thai; a Thailander

泰西(ㄊㄞˋ ㄒㄧ)
the Western countries; the West; the Occident

泰山(ㄊㄞˋ ㄕㄢ)
①Mountain Tai (in Shantung, one of the Five Sacred Mountains)②(figuratively) great importance ③one's father-in-law (one's wife's father) ④ Tarzan

泰山北斗(ㄊㄞˋ ㄕㄢ ㄅㄟˇ ㄉㄡˇ)
①Mountain Tai and the Dipper ②an eminent authority (in a learned field)

泰山不讓土壤(ㄊㄞˋ ㄕㄢ ㄅㄨˋ ㄖㄤˋ ㄊㄨˇ ㄖㄤˇ)
A learned man never stops his pursuit of knowledge.

泰山梁木(ㄊㄞˋ ㄕㄢ ㄌㄧㄤˊ ㄇㄨˋ)
a sage

泰山刻石(ㄊㄞˋ ㄕㄢ ㄎㄜˋ ㄕˊ)
the Mountain Tai inscription (attributed to 秦始皇)

泰山鴻毛(ㄊㄞˋ ㄕㄢ ㄏㄨㄥˊ ㄇㄠˊ)
the difference between Mountain Tai and a feather — very great difference (especially used in describing the manner of one's death—to die for a noble cause or for a trifle reason)

泰山其頹(ㄊㄞˋ ㄕㄢ ㄑㄧˊ ㄊㄨㄟˊ)
The revered man is dead.

泰山壓卵(ㄊㄞˋ ㄕㄢ ㄧㄚ ㄌㄨㄢˋ)or泰山壓頂(ㄊㄞˋ ㄕㄢ ㄧㄚ ㄉㄧㄥˇ)

(literally) It is like Mountain Tai crushing an egg.— It is a big mismatch. 或 overwhelming force

泰水(ㄊㄞˋ ㄕㄨㄟˇ)
one's mother-in-law (one's wife's mother)

泰然(ㄊㄞˋ ㄖㄢˊ)or泰然自若(ㄊㄞˋ ㄖㄢˊ ㄗˋ ㄖㄨㄛˋ)
unperturbed; unagitated; unalarmed; self-possessed; composed; equanimous

泰晤士報(ㄊㄞˋ ㄨˋ ㄕˋ ㄅㄠˋ)
the *Times*, published in London since 1785

泰晤士河(ㄊㄞˋ ㄨˋ ㄕˋ ㄏㄜˊ)
the Thames River

六畫

【洄】 2850
ㄏㄨㄟˊ hwei huí

(said of water) whirling

洄洑(ㄏㄨㄟˊ ㄈㄨˊ)
(said of water) whirling

洄瀾(ㄏㄨㄟˊ ㄌㄢˊ)
eddies

【洎】 2851
ㄐㄧˋ jih jì

1. until; till; up to
2. soup; meat broth
3. to soak; to drench

洎乎(ㄐㄧˋ ㄏㄨ)
until; till; up to

【洑】 2852
ㄈㄨˊ fwu fú

1. a whirlpool; a vortex
2. an undercurrent

【洌】 2853
ㄌㄧㄝˋ lieh liè

(said of liquid) clear and transparent

【洋】 2854
ㄧㄤˊ yang yáng

1. an ocean
2. foreign; Western; Occidental
3. imported

洋布(ㄧㄤˊ ㄅㄨˋ)
machine-made piece goods

洋房(ㄧㄤˊ ㄈㄤˊ)
a Western-style house

洋服(ㄧㄤˊ ㄈㄨˊ)
Western clothes; Occidental dress

洋釘(ㄧㄤˊ ㄉㄧㄥ)
a nail

〔水 部〕

〔水部〕

洋鐵(1ㄤ ㄊㄧㄝˇ)
tin plate; galvanized iron

洋鐵罐兒(1ㄤ ㄊㄧㄝˇ ㄍㄨㄢˋㄦ)
a tin, or tin can

洋奴(1ㄤ ㄋㄨˊ)
a slave of a foreign master; a flunkey of the Occident; a worshipper of everything foreign

洋蠟(1ㄤ ㄌㄚˋ)
a candle

洋樓(1ㄤ ㄌㄡˊ)
a Western-style building of two stories or more

洋流(1ㄤ ㄌㄧㄡˊ)
the marine current

洋狗(1ㄤ ㄍㄡˇ)
a dog of foreign breed

洋鬼子(1ㄤ ㄍㄨㄟˇ·ㄗ)
a foreign devil (a derogatory term referring to a foreigner, especially a Westerner)

洋廣雜貨(1ㄤ ㄍㄨㄤˇ ㄗㄚˊ ㄏㄨㄛˋ)
foreign goods (imported through Kwangtung)

洋行(1ㄤ ㄏㄤˊ)
a foreign business firm

洋化(1ㄤ ㄏㄨㄚˋ)
to be westernized

洋火(1ㄤ ㄏㄨㄛˇ)
matches (for making a fire)
亦作「火柴」

洋貨(1ㄤ ㄏㄨㄛˋ)
foreign goods; imported products

洋槐(1ㄤ ㄏㄨㄞˊ)
an acacia; a locust tree

洋灰(1ㄤ ㄏㄨㄟ)
cement

洋紅(1ㄤ ㄏㄨㄥˊ)
carmine

洋酒(1ㄤ ㄐㄧㄡˇ)
imported wine and spirits

洋涇浜(1ㄤ ㄐㄧㄥ ㄅㄤ)
①the concessions in Shanghai before World War II ②pidgin English 亦作「洋涇浜英語」

洋錢(1ㄤ ㄑㄧㄢˊ)
silver dollars; Mexican dollars

洋琴(1ㄤ ㄑㄧㄣˊ)
a piano

洋務鬼(1ㄤ ㄑㄧㄣˊ ㄍㄨㄟˇ)
(derogatory term) a bands-man

洋鎗大砲(1ㄤ ㄑㄧㄤ ㄉㄚˋ ㄆㄠˋ)
firearms; guns

洋繡球(1ㄤ ㄒㄧㄡˋ ㄑㄧㄡˊ)
a hydrangea

洋相(1ㄤ ㄒㄧㄤˋ)
to make an exhibition of oneself: 你是在當衆出洋相。You are making an exhibition of yourself.

洋裝(1ㄤ ㄓㄨㄤ)
① Western dress ② Western binding (for books)

洋車(1ㄤ ㄔㄜ)
a rickshaw or ricksha

洋場(1ㄤ ㄔㄤˇ)
①old foreign settlement, usually referring to old Shanghai ②a prosperous metropolis

洋式(1ㄤ ㄕˋ)
the Western style

洋水仙(1ㄤ ㄕㄨㄟˇ ㄒㄧㄢ)
hyacinth (an aquatic plant)
亦作「風信子」

洋人(1ㄤ ㄖㄣˊ)
a Westerner; a foreigner

洋財(1ㄤ ㄘㄞˊ)
a big fortune; a windfall

洋菜(1ㄤ ㄘㄞˋ)
thin strips of agar-agar extracted from Gracilaria, used as a dish; agar 亦作「石花菜」

洋葱(1ㄤ ㄘㄨㄥ)
an onion: 我們在後院種洋葱。We grow onions in the backyard.

洋傘(1ㄤ ㄙㄢˇ)
an (Western-style) umbrella

洋溢(1ㄤ ㄧˋ)
to be filled or fraught with; to brim with

洋油(1ㄤ ㄧㄡˊ)
kerosene

洋煙(1ㄤ 1ㄢ)or洋烟捲兒(1ㄤ 1ㄢ ㄐㄩㄢˇㄦ)
cigarettes; imported cigarettes or tobacco

洋銀(1ㄤ 1ㄣˊ)
German silver, the alloy of Cu 40-65%, Ni 6-35%, Zn 15-35%

洋洋(1ㄤ 1ㄤ)
①full of water ②vast; extensive; great ③in high spirits; elated

洋洋大觀(1ㄤ 1ㄤ ㄉㄚˋ ㄍㄨㄢ)
imposing; grand; magnificent

洋洋得意(1ㄤ 1ㄤ ㄉㄜˊ ㄧˋ)
in high spirits; proud and happy; elated: 他聽到這消息而洋洋得意。He was elated over the news.

洋洋自得(1ㄤ 1ㄤ ㄗˋ ㄉㄜˊ)
self-satisfied

洋洋灑灑(1ㄤ 1ㄤ ㄙㄚˇ ㄙㄚˇ)
(said of expository writing, etc.) copious and fluent

洋務(1ㄤ ㄨˋ)
foreign affairs or business

洋娃娃(1ㄤ ㄨㄚˊ·ㄨㄚ)
a doll: 這女孩有個漂亮的洋娃娃。The little girl has a pretty doll.

洋爲中用(1ㄤ ㄨㄟˊ ㄓㄨㄥ ㄩㄥˋ)
to make foreign things serve China

洋文(1ㄤ ㄨㄣˊ)
a foreign language

洋芋(1ㄤ ㄩˋ)
a potato: 洋芋長在地下。Potatoes grow under the ground.

【洒】 2855
1. ㄙㄚˇ saa sǎ
1. I; me
2. to pour; to sprinkle

洒家(ㄙㄚˇ ㄐㄧ)
I; me

洒掃(ㄙㄚˇ ㄙㄠˋ)
to sprinkle water and sweep away the dirt; to clean up 亦作「灑掃」

【洒】 2855
1. ㄒㄧㄢˇ shean xiǎn
1. respectful
2. deep
3. alarmed; surprised

洒然(ㄒㄧㄢˇ ㄖㄢˊ)
①alarmed; surprised ②cold

洒如(ㄒㄧㄢˇ ㄖㄨˊ)
respectful; deferential

【洒】 2855
3. ㄒㄧˇ shii xǐ
same as 洗—to wash

【洗】 2856
1. ㄒㄧˇ shii xǐ
1. to wash; to rinse; to clean; to clear: 飯前把手洗乾淨。Wash your hands clean before each meal.
2. to baptize: 他受洗禮入基督教。He was baptized into the

Christian faith.

洗不掉 (ㄒㄧˇ ㄅㄨˋ ㄉㄧㄠˋ)
incapable of being washed off; indelible

洗不清 (ㄒㄧˇ ㄅㄨˋ ㄑㄧㄥ)
unable to vindicate oneself

洗牌 (ㄒㄧˇ ㄆㄞˊ)
to shuffle playing cards or mah-jong pieces; a shuffle

洗髮粉 (ㄒㄧˇ ㄈㄚˇ ㄈㄣˇ)
shampoo powder

洗髮水 (ㄒㄧˇ ㄈㄚˇ ㄕㄨㄟˇ)
liquid shampoo

洗盪 (ㄒㄧˇ ㄉㄤˋ)
to wash or purify

洗滌 (ㄒㄧˇ ㄉㄧˊ)
to wash; to cleanse; to rinse

洗滌劑 (ㄒㄧˇ ㄉㄧˊ ㄐㄧˋ)
a detergent; washing fluid

洗頭 (ㄒㄧˇ ㄊㄡˊ)or 洗頭髮 (ㄒㄧˇ ㄊㄡˊ ㄈㄚˇ)
to shampoo; to wash one's hair; to have one's hair washed

洗腦 (ㄒㄧˇ ㄋㄠˇ)
to brainwash; to indoctrinate

洗禮 (ㄒㄧˇ ㄌㄧˇ)
① to baptize or be baptized; baptism: 他受洗禮成爲天主教徒。 He was baptized a Catholic. ② a severe test: 他受過戰爭的洗禮。 He has gone through the test of battle.

洗臉 (ㄒㄧˇ ㄌㄧㄢˇ)
to wash one's face; to wash oneself: 他在洗臉。 He's washing his face now.

洗臉盆 (ㄒㄧˇ ㄌㄧㄢˇ ㄆㄣˊ)
a washbasin 亦作「臉盆」

洗煉 (ㄒㄧˇ ㄌㄧㄢˋ)
(said of literary writings) refined; polished; elegant

洗刮 (ㄒㄧˇ ㄍㄨㄚ)
to wash and scrape

洗甲 (ㄒㄧˇ ㄐㄧㄚˇ)or 洗兵 (ㄒㄧˇ ㄅㄧㄥ)
to end hostilities; to have a truce

洗劫 (ㄒㄧˇ ㄐㄧㄝˊ)
to sack everything; to sack a place without leaving anything behind: 士兵洗劫這城。 The soldiers sacked the town.

洗腳 (ㄒㄧˇ ㄐㄧㄠˇ)
to wash one's feet

洗淨 (ㄒㄧˇ ㄐㄧㄥˋ)
to wash something until it's clean: 把它們洗(乾)淨。 Wash them clean.

洗錢 (ㄒㄧˇ ㄑㄧㄢˊ)
to launder money; money laundering

洗心革面 (ㄒㄧˇ ㄒㄧㄣ ㄍㄜˊ ㄇㄧㄢˋ)
to reform oneself; to reform: 如果給他機會，他答應洗心革面。 He promised to reform if given a chance.

洗削 (ㄒㄧˇ ㄒㄩㄝ)
to wipe away (disgrace, etc.)

洗雪 (ㄒㄧˇ ㄒㄩㄝˇ)or (ㄒㄧˇ ㄒㄩㄝˋ)
① to cleanse (both literally and figuratively) ② to revenge; to vindicate

洗濯 (ㄒㄧˇ ㄓㄨㄛˊ)
to wash; to rinse

洗塵 (ㄒㄧˇ ㄔㄣˊ)or 洗泥 (ㄒㄧˇ ㄋㄧˊ)
to give a welcome dinner (for someone arriving after a long trip)

洗腸 (ㄒㄧˇ ㄔㄤˊ)
to purge the bowels; to remove poison from one's stomach by means of laxatives or saline

洗晒 (ㄒㄧˇ ㄕㄞˋ)
to wash and dry in the sun

洗手 (ㄒㄧˇ ㄕㄡˇ)
① to wash one's hands: 你飯前要洗手。 You have to wash (your hands) before dinner. ② to wash one's hands of evil ways

洗手不幹 (ㄒㄧˇ ㄕㄡˇ ㄅㄨˋ ㄍㄢˋ)
to wash one's hands of an evil practice; to quit committing crimes

洗手間 (ㄒㄧˇ ㄕㄡˇ ㄐㄧㄢ)
a toilet; a water closet; a rest room; a lavatory

洗腎 (ㄒㄧˇ ㄕㄣˋ)
dialysis or hemodialysis

洗刷 (ㄒㄧˇ ㄕㄨㄚ)
① a scrub; to scrub; to clean: 他將地板洗刷乾淨。 He scrubbed the floor clean ② to vindicate oneself

洗刷不清 (ㄒㄧˇ ㄕㄨㄚ ㄅㄨˋ ㄑㄧㄥ)
unable to vindicate oneself

洗澡 (ㄒㄧˇ ㄗㄠˇ)
to take a bath: 我們在湖裡洗澡。 We bathed in the lake.

洗澡盆 (ㄒㄧˇ ㄗㄠˇ ㄆㄣˊ)
a bathtub 亦作「浴盆」

洗澡塘 (ㄒㄧˇ ㄗㄠˇ ㄊㄤˊ)
a bath pool

洗澡間 (ㄒㄧˇ ㄗㄠˇ ㄐㄧㄢ)
a bathroom 亦作「浴室」: 我能借用你的洗澡間嗎？ May I use your bathroom?

洗擦 (ㄒㄧˇ ㄘㄚ)
to wash and scrub

洗耳恭聽 (ㄒㄧˇ ㄦˇ ㄍㄨㄥ ㄊㄧㄥ)
to listen respectfully

洗衣 (ㄒㄧˇ ㄧ)or 洗衣服 (ㄒㄧˇ ㄧ ㄈㄨˊ)
to wash clothes; to do one's washing: 她每天上午洗衣。 She does her washing every morning.

洗衣店 (ㄒㄧˇ ㄧ ㄉㄧㄢˋ)
a laundry shop: 將這些襯衫送到洗衣店去。 Send these shirts to the laundry.

洗衣機 (ㄒㄧˇ ㄧ ㄐㄧ)
a washing machine; a laundry machine

洗衣作 (ㄒㄧˇ ㄧ ㄗㄨㄛˋ)
a laundry shop

洗胃 (ㄒㄧˇ ㄨㄟˋ)
(medicine) gastric lavage

洗碗盤 (ㄒㄧˇ ㄨㄢˇ ㄆㄢˊ)
to do the dishes

洗碗機 (ㄒㄧˇ ㄨㄢˇ ㄐㄧ)
a dishwasher

洗浴 (ㄒㄧˇ ㄩˋ)
to take a bath

洗冤 (ㄒㄧˇ ㄩㄢ)
to clear oneself of a false charge; to vindicate oneself: 見證人的證詞爲被告洗冤。 The testimony of witnesses vindicated the defendant.

洗熨 (ㄒㄧˇ ㄩㄣˋ)
to launder; to wash and iron (clothes)

2856
【洗】 2. ㄒㄧㄢˇ shean xian
a Chinese family name

洗馬 (ㄒㄧㄢˇ ㄇㄚˇ)
an official title given to the crown prince's herald

2857
【洙】 ㄓㄨ ju zhū
(又讀 ㄕㄨ shu shú)
name of a river in Shantung

洙水 (ㄓㄨ ㄕㄨㄟˇ)
name of a river in Shantung

洙泗 (ㄓㄨ ㄙˋ)
names of two rivers in

〔水部〕

Shantung

【洟】 2858
ㄧ yí yǐ
nasal mucus; snivel

涕洟(ㄊㄧˋ ㄊㄧˋ)
nasal mucus; snivel

【洞】 2859
ㄉㄨㄥˋ dòng dòng
1. a cave; a hole: 我的鞋子破了個洞。 There is a hole in my shoe.
2. to penetrate; to see through

洞房(ㄉㄨㄥˋ ㄈㄤˊ)
①an inner chamber ②a nuptial chamber

洞房花燭夜(ㄉㄨㄥˋ ㄈㄤˊ ㄏㄨㄚ ㄓㄨˊ ㄧㄝˋ)
wedding night; the night of wedding

洞府(ㄉㄨㄥˋ ㄈㄨˇ)
the abode of a mountain genie or a Taoist priest

洞達(ㄉㄨㄥˋ ㄉㄚˊ)
having insight; to understand thoroughly

洞天(ㄉㄨㄥˋ ㄊㄧㄢ)
①a hidden but beautiful spot (or world) ②a cavern as the abode of the fairies

洞天福地(ㄉㄨㄥˋ ㄊㄧㄢ ㄈㄨˊ ㄉㄧˋ)
mountains inhabited by Taoist priests

洞庭(ㄉㄨㄥˋ ㄊㄧㄥˊ)or洞庭湖(ㄉㄨㄥˋ ㄊㄧㄥˊ ㄏㄨˊ)
Lake Tungting (in northern Hunan)

洞貫(ㄉㄨㄥˋ ㄍㄨㄢˋ)
①to penetrate through ②to understand fully

洞開(ㄉㄨㄥˋ ㄎㄞ)
wide open

洞窟(ㄉㄨㄥˋ ㄎㄨ)
a cave; a cavern

洞鑒(ㄉㄨㄥˋ ㄐㄧㄢˋ)
to see clearly

洞見癥結(ㄉㄨㄥˋ ㄐㄧㄢˋ ㄓㄥ ㄐㄧㄝˊ)
to see clearly the hidden cause of a problem; to get to the heart of the problem

洞悉(ㄉㄨㄥˋ ㄒㄧ)
to see clearly and understand thoroughly

洞悉無遺(ㄉㄨㄥˋ ㄒㄧ ㄨˊ ㄧˊ)
to see and know completely

洞簫(ㄉㄨㄥˋ ㄒㄧㄠ)
a kind of flute; a bamboo flageolet

洞曉(ㄉㄨㄥˋ ㄒㄧㄠˇ)
to know clearly

洞僊(ㄉㄨㄥˋ ㄒㄧㄢ)
genies living in caves

洞穴(ㄉㄨㄥˋ ㄒㄩㄝˋ)
a cave; a cavern

洞察(ㄉㄨㄥˋ ㄔㄚˊ)
to see and understand clearly; to have an insight into: 他能洞察那些事件的是非。He saw clearly the rights and wrongs of the case.

洞徹(ㄉㄨㄥˋ ㄔㄜˋ)
to understand thoroughly

洞穿(ㄉㄨㄥˋ ㄔㄨㄢ)
to pierce through: 子彈洞穿了他的帽子。The shot pierced his hat.

洞若觀火(ㄉㄨㄥˋ ㄖㄨㄛˋ ㄍㄨㄢ ㄏㄨㄛˇ)
to see clearly as if one were seeing fire

洞兒(ㄉㄨㄥˋ ㄦ)
a cave; a hole; a pit

【洛】 2860
ㄌㄨㄛˋ luò luò
name of a river

洛克斐勒(ㄌㄨㄛˋ ㄎㄜˋ ㄈㄟ ㄌㄜˋ)
John D. Rockefeller, 1839-1937, American oil magnate and philanthropist

洛迦諾(ㄌㄨㄛˋ ㄐㄧㄚ ㄋㄨㄛˋ)
Locarno, Switzerland

洛神(ㄌㄨㄛˋ ㄕㄣˊ)
the Goddess of the Lo River

洛神賦(ㄌㄨㄛˋ ㄕㄣˊ ㄈㄨˋ)
Ode to the Goddess of the Lo River, by Tsao Chih (曹植) (192-232 A.D.)

洛書(ㄌㄨㄛˋ ㄕㄨ)
the characters supposedly devised by Emperor Yü (禹) of the Hsia Dynasty (2205-1782 B.C.) in imitation of the shell pattern of a divine tortoise in the Lo River

洛桑(ㄌㄨㄛˋ ㄙㄤ)
Lausanne, Switzerland

洛誦(ㄌㄨㄛˋ ㄙㄨㄥˋ)
to read repeatedly in order to commit to memory

洛邑(ㄌㄨㄛˋ ㄧˋ)
an ancient city in what is Loyang, Honan, today

洛陽(ㄌㄨㄛˋ ㄧㄤˊ)
Loyang, in Honan, capital of the Eastern Han Dynasty

洛陽花(ㄌㄨㄛˋ ㄧㄤˊ ㄏㄨㄚ)
a white peony

洛陽紙貴(ㄌㄨㄛˋ ㄧㄤˊ ㄓˇ ㄍㄨㄟˋ)
to become a best seller

【津】 2861
ㄐㄧㄣ jīn jīn
1. a ferry
2. juicy; tasty
3. saliva
4. to sweat; to perspire
5. as in 指點迷津 (to show one how to get to the right path)
6. short for Tientsin

津巴布韋(ㄐㄧㄣ ㄅㄚ ㄅㄨˋ ㄨㄟˊ)
Zimbabwe 亦作「辛巴威」

津浦鐵路(ㄐㄧㄣ ㄆㄨˇ ㄊㄧㄝˇ ㄌㄨˋ)
the Tientsin-Pukou Railway

津門(ㄐㄧㄣ ㄇㄣˊ)
①a checkpoint at a ferry ②another name of Tientsin (天津)

津筏(ㄐㄧㄣ ㄈㄚˊ)
a ferry raft; a ferryboat

津達(ㄐㄧㄣ ㄉㄚˊ)
to arrive at a place through a ferry

津渡(ㄐㄧㄣ ㄉㄨˋ)
a ferry

津貼(ㄐㄧㄣ ㄊㄧㄝ)
an allowance; a subsidy; to subsidize; to help out with money: 他們受到政府的津貼。They were subsidized by the government.

津梁(ㄐㄧㄣ ㄌㄧㄤˊ)
a bridge (both literally and figuratively)

津隘(ㄐㄧㄣ ㄍㄨㄢ)
a checkpoint

津津樂道(ㄐㄧㄣ ㄐㄧㄣ ㄌㄜˋ ㄉㄠˋ)
to talk with great relish: 這他對自己的成就津津樂道。He relishes talking about his achievement.

津津有味(ㄐㄧㄣ ㄐㄧㄣ ㄧㄡˇ ㄨㄟˋ)
①(to do something) with great relish or interest; with gusto ②very tasty; very agreeable to the palate

津人(ㄐㄧㄣ ㄖㄣˊ)
a ferryman

津潤(ㄐㄧㄣ ㄖㄨㄣˋ)
juicy and nourishing

津涯(ㄐㄧㄣ ㄧㄚˊ)
the waterside; shores

津液(ㄐㄧㄣ ㄧㄝˋ)
saliva

【水部】

津要(ㄐㄧㄣ ㄧㄠ)
① key places or locations ②
key posts

【洧】 2862
ㄨㄟˇ woei wěi
name of a river in Honan

洧水(ㄨㄟˇ ㄕㄨㄟˇ)or 洧河(ㄨㄟˇ ㄏㄜˊ)
name of a river in Honan

【洫】 2863
ㄒㄩˋ shiuh xù
a ditch; a moat

【洩】 2864
ㄒㄧㄝˋ shieh xiè
to drain; to vent; to let out;
to dissipate; to leak out: 秘
密已經外洩。The secret has
leaked out.

洩忿 or 洩憤(ㄒㄧㄝˋ ㄈㄣˋ)
to give vent to one's anger

洩底(ㄒㄧㄝˋ ㄉㄧˇ)
to disclose a secret

洩漏(ㄒㄧㄝˋ ㄌㄡˋ)
to make known; to disclose;
to divulge; to reveal; to leak
out; leakage: 這消息洩漏出去
了。The news has leaked out.

洩漏秘密(ㄒㄧㄝˋ ㄌㄡˋ ㄇㄧˋ ㄇㄧˋ)
to disclose a secret; to
divulge a secret

洩漏天機(ㄒㄧㄝˋ ㄌㄡˋ ㄊㄧㄢ ㄐㄧ)
to disclose a divine secret

洩露(ㄒㄧㄝˋ ㄌㄨˋ)
to disclose; to reveal; to
divulge: 永不要洩露我的秘密。
Never reveal my secret.

洩恨(ㄒㄧㄝˋ ㄏㄣˋ)
to give vent to one's resentment; to vent one's grudge

洩洪(ㄒㄧㄝˋ ㄏㄨㄥˊ)
to let water flow out from
the reservoir; to release
excessive water from a reservoir

洩氣(ㄒㄧㄝˋ ㄑㄧˋ)
① to lose strength, momentum, etc. ② discouraging;
disappointing; discouraged;
disappointed: 再試試！不要因
爲一次失敗就洩氣。Try again!
Don't let one failure discourage you. ③ to give vent to
one's pent-up resentment,
frustration, etc.

【洪】 2865
ㄏㄨㄥˊ horng hóng
1. great; immense; magnificent
2. floods; turbulent waters; torrents: 山洪淹沒了田野。The

mountain torrent flooded the
fields.
3. a Chinese family name

洪波(ㄏㄨㄥˊ ㄅㄛ)or洪濤(ㄏㄨㄥˊ
ㄊㄠˊ)
turbulent waves; big waves

洪門(ㄏㄨㄥˊ ㄇㄣˊ)
a secret society originally
dedicated to the cause of
overthrowing the Manchus
and the restoration of the
Ming Dynasty 亦作「紅幫」

洪峯(ㄏㄨㄥˊ ㄈㄥ)
the high point of a flood

洪福(ㄏㄨㄥˊ ㄈㄨˊ)
great happiness; bliss; blessing

洪福齊天(ㄏㄨㄥˊ ㄈㄨˊ ㄑㄧˊ ㄊㄧㄢ)
great happiness; boundless
bliss

洪大(ㄏㄨㄥˊ ㄉㄚˋ)
great; massive; immense

洪流(ㄏㄨㄥˊ ㄌㄧㄡˊ)
① a torrent ② a powerful
current: 民主的洪流洶湧澎湃。
The powerful current of
democracy is surging for-
ward.

洪亮(ㄏㄨㄥˊ ㄌㄧㄤˋ)
loud and clear; sonorous: 這
歌者的桑音洪亮。The singer
has a sonorous voice.

洪量(ㄏㄨㄥˊ ㄌㄧㄤˋ)
① magnanimity ② great
capacity for drinking

洪鑪 or 洪爐(ㄏㄨㄥˊ ㄌㄨˊ)
① a large furnace; a smelting oven ② (figuratively)
mighty furnace

洪荒(ㄏㄨㄥˊ ㄏㄨㄤ)
primitive; chaotic

洪積期(ㄏㄨㄥˊ ㄐㄧ ㄑㄧˊ)
(geology) the Pleistocene
Epoch; the Diluvial Epoch

洪積層(ㄏㄨㄥˊ ㄐㄧ ㄘㄥˊ)
(geology) diluviums

洪秀全(ㄏㄨㄥˊ ㄒㄧㄡˋ ㄑㄩㄢˊ)
Hung Hsiu-chüan, 1812-1864,
leader of the Taiping rebels

洪憲(ㄏㄨㄥˊ ㄒㄧㄢˋ)
the reigning title adopted by
Yüan Shih-kai (袁世凱),
which lasted less than three
months in 1915

洪鐘(ㄏㄨㄥˊ ㄓㄨㄥ)
① a large bell ② (said of a
voice) stentorian; very loud

or powerful: 他聲如洪鐘。He
has a stentorian voice.

洪水(ㄏㄨㄥˊ ㄕㄨㄟˇ)
a flood; a deluge: 洪水淹沒了
整個地區。The flood inundat-
ed the whole district.

洪水猛獸(ㄏㄨㄥˊ ㄕㄨㄟˇ ㄇㄥˇ ㄕㄡˋ)
disaster; calamity; a catastrophe

洪水位(ㄏㄨㄥˊ ㄕㄨㄟˇ ㄨㄟˋ)
the high water mark; the
high water level; the flood
level

洪澤湖(ㄏㄨㄥˊ ㄗㄜˊ ㄏㄨˊ)
name of a lake between Anhwei and Kiangsu

洪大略(ㄏㄨㄥˊ ㄉㄚˋ ㄌㄩㄝˋ)
a great mind with great
schemes

洪儒(ㄏㄨㄥˊ ㄖㄨˊ)
a great scholar

洪恩(ㄏㄨㄥˊ ㄣ)
great kindness

洪楊之亂(ㄏㄨㄥˊ ㄧㄤˊ ㄓ ㄌㄨㄢˋ)
the Taiping Rebellion
(1851-1864), led by Hung
Hsiu-chüan (洪秀全) and
Yang Hsiu-ching (楊秀清)

【洱】 2866
ㄦˇ eel ěr
1. name of a lake in Yunnan
2. name of a river in Yunnan

洱海(ㄦˇ ㄏㄞˇ)
name of a lake in Yunnan

洱水(ㄦˇ ㄕㄨㄟˇ)
name of a river in Yunnan

【洳】 2867
ㄖㄨˋ ruh rù
damp; moist; oozy

【洲】 2868
ㄓㄡ jou zhōu
1. an island in a river
2. a continent

洲汀(ㄓㄡ ㄊㄧㄥ)
an island in a river

洲際彈道飛彈(ㄓㄡ ㄐㄧˋ ㄉㄢˋ ㄉㄠˋ
ㄈㄟ ㄉㄢˋ)
the intercontinental ballistic
missile; the ICBM

洲沚(ㄓㄡ ㄓˇ)
an island in a river

洲渚(ㄓㄡ ㄓㄨˇ)
an island in a river

洲嶼(ㄓㄡ ㄩˇ)
an island in a river

【洮】 2869
1. ㄊㄠˊ taur táo

〔水部〕

〔水部〕

name of a river in Kansu

洮河（ㄊㄠˊ ㄏㄜˊ）
name of a river in Kansu

【洮】 2869
2. ㄧㄠˊ yau yóo
name of a lake in Kiangsu

洮湖（ㄧㄠˊ ㄏㄨˊ）
name of a lake in Kiangsu

【洵】 2870
ㄒㄩㄣˊ shyun xún
true; real; truly; really; certainly

洵河（ㄒㄩㄣˊ ㄏㄜˊ）
name of a river in Shensi

洵屬（ㄒㄩㄣˊ ㄕㄨˇ）
truly; certainly

【洶】 2871
ㄒㄩㄥ shiong xiōng
1. unquiet; restless; turbulent; tumultuous
2. noisy; uproarious; clamorous

洶動（ㄒㄩㄥ ㄉㄨㄥˋ）
unquiet; restless; disturbed

洶洶（ㄒㄩㄥ ㄒㄩㄥ）
tumultuous; turbulent; agitated; truculent

洶湧 或 洶涌（ㄒㄩㄥ ㄩㄥˇ）
(said of water) tumultuous; turbulent: 河流洶湧地滾滾流去。The river rolls turbulently.

洶湧澎湃（ㄒㄩㄥ ㄩㄥˇ ㄆㄥˊ ㄆㄞˋ）
surging; turbulent; tempestuous

【洽】 2872
ㄒㄧㄚˊ shya xiá
（又讀 ㄑㄧㄚˋ chiah qià）
1. to spread; to diffuse
2. harmony; agreement
3. to negotiate; to consult

洽博（ㄒㄧㄚˊ ㄅㄛˊ）
of wide experience and knowledge

洽辦（ㄒㄧㄚˊ ㄅㄢˋ）
to handle an assignment through negotiation

洽談（ㄒㄧㄚˊ ㄊㄢˊ）
to discuss or consult (problems) together

洽化（ㄒㄧㄚˊ ㄏㄨㄚˋ）
to diffuse virtuous influence

洽商（ㄒㄧㄚˊ ㄕㄤ）
to discuss (details of a contract, etc.)

洽聞（ㄒㄧㄚˊ ㄨㄣˊ）
of wide knowledge; learned; widely read

【活】 2873
ㄏㄨㄛˊ hwo huó
1. to live; to survive; to be alive
2. to save the life of
3. active; lively; vivacious
4. movable; mobile; flexible
5. work

活靶（ㄏㄨㄛˊ ㄅㄚˇ）
a maneuvering target

活剝生吞（ㄏㄨㄛˊ ㄅㄛ ㄕㄥ ㄊㄨㄣ）
(literally) to skin an animal alive and eat the meat raw without chewing—to make unimaginative use of ready-made ideas (especially in writing)

活寶（ㄏㄨㄛˊ ㄅㄠˇ）
a lively person; one who behaves clownishly

活版（ㄏㄨㄛˊ ㄅㄢˇ）
a printing plate with movable type

活不了（ㄏㄨㄛˊ ㄅㄨˋ ㄌㄧㄠˇ）
unlikely to survive

活不下去（ㄏㄨㄛˊ ㄅㄨˋ ㄒㄧㄚˋ ㄑㄩˋ）
to lack the means, strength, or courage to live on

活潑潑地（ㄏㄨㄛˊ ㄆㄛ ㄆㄛ ˙ㄉㄜ）
actively; vivaciously; with sprightliness

活潑（ㄏㄨㄛˊ ㄆㄛ）
active; lively; sprightly; full of life; vivacious (especially said of children): 她是個活潑的小孩。She is a lively child.

活埋（ㄏㄨㄛˊ ㄇㄞˊ）
to bury alive

活賣（ㄏㄨㄛˊ ㄇㄞˋ）
to pawn; to pledge; to mortgage

活門（ㄏㄨㄛˊ ㄇㄣˊ）or 活瓣（ㄏㄨㄛˊ ㄅㄢˋ）
a valve

活命（ㄏㄨㄛˊ ㄇㄧㄥˋ）
①to survive; to live ②life

活佛（ㄏㄨㄛˊ ㄈㄛˊ）
(Lamaism) a Buddha incarnate

活的（ㄏㄨㄛˊ ˙ㄉㄜ）
living; live; alive: 它是條活的魚。It's a living fish.

活得不耐煩（ㄏㄨㄛˊ ㄉㄜˊ ㄅㄨˋ ㄋㄞˋ ㄈㄢˊ）
getting tired of living (a sarcastic expression)

活到老，學不了（ㄏㄨㄛˊ ㄉㄠˋ ㄌㄠˇ，ㄒㄩㄝˊ ㄅㄨˋ ㄌㄧㄠˇ）
There is still much to learn after one has grown old. 或 The pursuit of knowledge is an endless effort.

活到老，學到老（ㄏㄨㄛˊ ㄉㄠˋ ㄌㄠˇ，ㄒㄩㄝˊ ㄉㄠˋ ㄌㄠˇ）
One is never too old to learn. 或 No dog is too old to learn new tricks.

活動房屋（ㄏㄨㄛˊ ㄉㄨㄥˋ ㄈㄤˊ ㄨ）
a movable building

活動（ㄏㄨㄛˊ ㄉㄨㄥˋ）
①activities: 我們喜歡戶外活動。We are fond of outdoor activities. ②active; lively ③to try to get help or support for an objective; to lobby; to canvass: 他正在替她活動。He is trying to get help for her. ④movable; mobile ⑤loose ⑥to exercise; to limber; to move about: 站起來活動活動。Stand up and move about.

活脫（ㄏㄨㄛˊ ㄊㄨㄛ）
(to be) remarkably like

活力（ㄏㄨㄛˊ ㄌㄧˋ）
vitality; vigor

活力素（ㄏㄨㄛˊ ㄌㄧˋ ㄙㄨˋ）
vitamins 亦作「維生素」

活靈活現（ㄏㄨㄛˊ ㄌㄧㄥˊ ㄏㄨㄛˊ ㄒㄧㄢˋ）
vivid; lifelike: 他說得活靈活現的。He gave a vivid description. 亦作「活龍活現」

活路（ㄏㄨㄛˊ ㄌㄨˋ）
①an unblocked passage or a feasible approach or course of action; a way out ③a way to make a living

活絡（ㄏㄨㄛˊ ㄌㄨㄛˋ）
①loose ②noncommittal; indefinite

活龍活現（ㄏㄨㄛˊ ㄌㄨㄥˊ ㄏㄨㄛˊ ㄒㄧㄢˋ）
vividly; as if it were taking place here and now

活該（ㄏㄨㄛˊ ㄍㄞ）
It serves you (him, them) right. 要是她不再跟你講話，那是你活該。It will serve you right if she never speaks to you again.

活口（ㄏㄨㄛˊ ㄎㄡˇ）
①a captive; a prisoner ②to support a dependent or dependents

活（ㄏㄨㄛˊ ㄉㄜ）or 活的（ㄏㄨㄛˊ ㄉㄜ）

〔水部〕

活 ㄏㄨㄛ ·ㄎㄜ
alive; live; living: 他們被活活燒死了。They were burnt alive.

活火山 (ㄏㄨㄛ ㄏㄨㄛ ㄕㄢ)
an active volcano

活計 (ㄏㄨㄛ ㄐㄧ˙)
①one's way to make a living ②needlework; handiwork: 她喜歡坐著做活計。She likes to sit at needlework.

活見鬼 (ㄏㄨㄛ ㄐㄧㄢˋ ㄍㄨㄟˇ)
absurd; preposterous

活劇 (ㄏㄨㄛ ㄐㄩˋ)
a living drama; a drama in real life

活期 (ㄏㄨㄛ ㄑㄧ)
due on demand

活期存款 (ㄏㄨㄛ ㄑㄧ ㄘㄨㄣˊ ㄎㄨㄢˇ)
a demand deposit; a current deposit

活期存款帳戶 (ㄏㄨㄛ ㄑㄧ ㄘㄨㄣˊ ㄎㄨㄢˇ ㄓㄤˋ ㄏㄨˋ)
a current account

活現 (ㄏㄨㄛ ㄒㄧㄢˋ)
to appear vividly; to come alive

活性碳 (ㄏㄨㄛ ㄒㄧㄥˋ ㄊㄢˋ)
active carbon

活像 (ㄏㄨㄛ ㄒㄧㄤˋ)
to look like a reincarnation of; to be quite like; the image of: 長得活像他父親。He is the image of his father.

活捉 (ㄏㄨㄛ ㄓㄨㄛ)
to catch alive; to capture alive: 他們被活捉。They were captured alive.

活世壽人 (ㄏㄨㄛ ㄕˋ ㄕㄡˋ ㄖㄣˊ)
to benefit the world and mankind

活受罪 (ㄏㄨㄛ ㄕㄡˋ ㄗㄨㄟˋ)
to feel as if one were just living to suffer; to suffer greatly

活生生 (ㄏㄨㄛ ㄕㄥ ㄕㄥ)
very much living; alive and kicking: 它是個活生生的例子。It's a living example.

活水 (ㄏㄨㄛ ㄕㄨㄟˇ)
flowing water; running water

活人 (ㄏㄨㄛ ㄖㄣˊ)
a living person; a person who is still alive

活人無算 (ㄏㄨㄛ ㄖㄣˊ ㄨˊ ㄙㄨㄢˋ)
(especially said of a doctor) to have saved innumerable lives

活字版 (ㄏㄨㄛ ㄗˋ ㄅㄢˇ)
movable type

活字金 (ㄏㄨㄛ ㄗˋ ㄐㄧㄣ)
type metal

活死人 (ㄏㄨㄛ ㄙˇ ㄖㄣˊ)
a living corpse

活塞 (ㄏㄨㄛ ㄙㄞ)
a piston

活兒 (ㄏㄨㄛ ㄦ)
①jobs; work; labor: 他一個人做兩個人的活兒。He does the work of two men. ②products: 這些活兒做得好。These products is well made.

活頁 or 活葉 (ㄏㄨㄛ ㄧㄝˋ)
loose or detachable leaves (of notebooks, etc.)

活躍 (ㄏㄨㄛ ㄩㄝˋ)or (ㄏㄨㄛ ㄧㄠˋ)
active; actively: 市面很活躍。The market is very active.

活用 (ㄏㄨㄛ ㄩㄥˋ)
to use or apply knowledge with imagination or ingenuity

【派】 2874
ㄆㄞˋ pay pài
1. a tributary; a branch
2. a division; a school (of philosophy, art, etc.); a sect: 他是一個老派人物。He is a gentleman of the old school.
3. a faction: 該黨分為幾個小派系。The party split into petty factions.
4. to assign; to dispatch; to send: 他派女僕去請醫生。He sent the maid for a doctor.

派別 (ㄆㄞˋ ㄅㄧㄝˊ)
①factions ②schools (of thought)

派兵 (ㄆㄞˋ ㄅㄧㄥ)
to send troops; to dispatch troops

派兵遣將 (ㄆㄞˋ ㄅㄧㄥ ㄑㄧㄢˇ ㄐㄧㄤˋ)
to dispatch troops and send generals

派不是 (ㄆㄞˋ ㄅㄨˋ ˙ㄕ)
to criticize one for a mistake; to blame one for a fault: 他們派他不是。They blame him for his faults.

派發 (ㄆㄞˋ ㄈㄚ)
to distribute

派代表 (ㄆㄞˋ ㄉㄞˋ ㄅㄧㄠˇ)
to send a delegate; to dispatch a representative

派對 (ㄆㄞˋ ㄉㄨㄟˋ)
a party (for social entertainment)

派頭 (ㄆㄞˋ ㄊㄡˊ)
manner; air; the way one acts and speaks: 我叔父派頭十足。My uncle has a conceited manner.

派令 (ㄆㄞˋ ㄌㄧㄥˋ)
orders of appointment in written form

派遣 (ㄆㄞˋ ㄑㄧㄢˇ)
to dispatch: 美國派遣使者到中國。The United States dispatched a messenger to China.

派遣軍 (ㄆㄞˋ ㄑㄧㄢˇ ㄐㄩㄣ)
an expeditionary force

派系 (ㄆㄞˋ ㄒㄧˋ)
①factions (within a political party, etc.)②affiliation with (a school or party)

派駐 (ㄆㄞˋ ㄓㄨˋ)
to accredit

派差 (ㄆㄞˋ ㄔㄞ)
to assign work; to send one on an errand

派出所 (ㄆㄞˋ ㄔㄨ ㄙㄨㄛˇ)
a police station

派司 (ㄆㄞˋ ㄙ)
a pass; a safe-conduct

派員 (ㄆㄞˋ ㄩㄢˊ)
to send a staffer or officer

派用場 (ㄆㄞˋ ㄩㄥˋ ㄔㄤˇ)or (ㄆㄞˋ ㄩㄥˋ ㄔㄤˇ)
to assign work; to use something for a specific purpose

【流】 2875
ㄌㄧㄡˊ liou liú
1. to flow; to discharge: 水向低處流。Water flows to the lowest level.
2. to wander; to stray
3. a branch; a division
4. a class; a rank: 上流人士和普通民眾都喜歡他。He is liked by the classes and the masses.
5. unsettled; unfixed; mobile

流波 (ㄌㄧㄡˊ ㄅㄛ)
①(said of a beautiful woman) a turn of the eyes in one direction ②flowing water; current

〔水部〕

流輩(ㄌㄧㄡ ㄅㄟˋ)
people of the same rank

流弊(ㄌㄧㄡ ㄅㄧˋ)
long accumulated evil effect;
abuses

流別(ㄌㄧㄡ ㄅㄧㄝˊ)
branches; schools; divisions

流變(ㄌㄧㄡ ㄅㄧㄢˋ)
later developments

流通(ㄌㄧㄡ ㄊㄨㄥ)
to be exiled

流布(ㄌㄧㄡ ㄅㄨˋ)
to be transmitted; to spread

流派(ㄌㄧㄡ ㄆㄞˋ)
①branches; divisions;
schools ②a tributary

流配(ㄌㄧㄡ ㄆㄟˋ)
to banish; to exile

流盼(ㄌㄧㄡ ㄆㄢˋ)
to turn the eyes

流品(ㄌㄧㄡ ㄆㄧㄣˇ)
social status

流馬(ㄌㄧㄡ ㄇㄚˇ)
a device for hauling supplies
devised by Chu-Ko Liang
(諸葛亮) in the Epoch of the
Three Kingdoms

流沫(ㄌㄧㄡ ㄇㄛˋ)
foam; froth

流氓(ㄌㄧㄡ ㄇㄤˊ)
a hoodlum; a hooligan; a villain; a rascal: 他在耍流氓。He
behaved like a hoodlum.

流湎(ㄌㄧㄡ ㄇㄧㄢˇ)
①to be addicted to alco-
holic drinks ②to indulge

流眄(ㄌㄧㄡ ㄇㄧㄢˇ)or 流目(ㄌㄧㄡ
ㄇㄨˋ)
to turn the eyes

流民(ㄌㄧㄡ ㄇㄧㄣˊ)
refugees

流芳(ㄌㄧㄡ ㄈㄤ)
to hand down a fine reputation through history; to be
honored by posterity

流芳百世(ㄌㄧㄡ ㄈㄤ ㄅㄞˇ ㄕˋ)or 流
芳千古(ㄌㄧㄡ ㄈㄤ ㄑㄧㄢ ㄍㄨˇ)
to hand down a fine reputation through generations;
to be honored by all generations

流放(ㄌㄧㄡ ㄈㄤˋ)
to exile; to banish: 他被流放
到西伯利亞。He was banished
to Siberia.

流風(ㄌㄧㄡ ㄈㄥ)
traditional customs

流彈(ㄌㄧㄡ ㄉㄢˋ)
a stray bullet

流宕(ㄌㄧㄡ ㄉㄤˋ)
①to loaf about ②(said of a
piece of writing) fluent and
uninhibited

流蕩(ㄌㄧㄡ ㄉㄤˋ)
to loaf about; to roam

流當(ㄌㄧㄡ ㄉㄤ)
to fail to reclaim pawned
articles within the specified
time

流當品(ㄌㄧㄡ ㄉㄤ ㄆㄧㄣˇ)
unclaimed or unredeemed
articles in a pawnshop

流電(ㄌㄧㄡ ㄉㄧㄢˋ)
lightning speed; extreme
swiftness

流毒(ㄌㄧㄡ ㄉㄨˊ)
detrimental effect; harm

流動(ㄌㄧㄡ ㄉㄨㄥˋ)
①to be in flowing motion:
河水緩緩地流動。The river is
flowing sluggishly ②on the
move ③mobile; itinerant;
going from place to place

流動投資(ㄌㄧㄡ ㄉㄨㄥˋ ㄊㄡˊ ㄗ)
current investment

流動戶口(ㄌㄧㄡ ㄉㄨㄥˋ ㄏㄨˋ ㄎㄡˇ)
the registered temporary
domicile

流動金(ㄌㄧㄡ ㄉㄨㄥˋ ㄐㄧㄣ)or 流動
基金(ㄌㄧㄡ ㄉㄨㄥˋ ㄐㄧ ㄐㄧㄣ)
revolving funds; working
capital

流動性(ㄌㄧㄡ ㄉㄨㄥˋ ㄒㄧㄥˋ)
mobility; fluidity

流動商店(ㄌㄧㄡ ㄉㄨㄥˋ ㄕㄤ ㄉㄧㄢˋ)
a mobile shop

流動人口(ㄌㄧㄡ ㄉㄨㄥˋ ㄖㄣˊ ㄎㄡˇ)
transient population or residents; the floating population

流動資本(ㄌㄧㄡ ㄉㄨㄥˋ ㄗ ㄅㄣˇ)
floating capital; circulating
capital

流動資產(ㄌㄧㄡ ㄉㄨㄥˋ ㄗ ㄔㄢˇ)
(accounting) accrued assets;
circulating assets

流體(ㄌㄧㄡ ㄊㄧˇ)
fluid: 空氣是流體，不是液體。
Air is a fluid but not a liquid.

流涕(ㄌㄧㄡ ㄊㄧˋ)
to shed tears

流鐵槽(ㄌㄧㄡ ㄊㄧㄝˇ ㄘㄠˊ)
(metallurgy) an iron runner

流通(ㄌㄧㄡ ㄊㄨㄥ)
in circulation; to circulate;
to ventilate: 我們開窗以使空
氣流通。We ventilate a room
by opening windows.

流年(ㄌㄧㄡ ㄋㄧㄢˊ)
①years that flow by one
after another; fleeting time:
似水流年。Time passes swift-
ly like flowing water. ②the
change of one's fortune in a
given year

流年不利(ㄌㄧㄡ ㄋㄧㄢˊ ㄅㄨˋ ㄌㄧˋ)
to have a year of ill luck; an
unlucky year

流淚(ㄌㄧㄡ ㄌㄟˋ)
to shed tears: 這女孩流淚了。
The girl shed tears.

流覽(ㄌㄧㄡ ㄌㄢˇ)
①to take a comprehensive
look; to survey ②to skim
over; to read through

流浪(ㄌㄧㄡ ㄌㄤˋ)
to wander about; to roam
about; to rove: 這小女孩流浪
街頭。The little girl wan-
dered the street.

流浪漢(ㄌㄧㄡ ㄌㄤˋ ㄏㄢˋ)
a vagabond; a bum; a
drifter: 他是個無家可歸的流浪
漢。He is a homeless vaga-
bond.

流離失所(ㄌㄧㄡ ㄌㄧˊ ㄕ ㄙㄨㄛˇ)
homeless and wandering
from place to place: 戰爭使
許多人流離失所。The war
forced thousands of people
to wander about as refugees.

流理台(ㄌㄧㄡ ㄌㄧˇ ㄊㄞˊ)
a set of kitchen units including such items as a kitchen
sink, a range, etc.

流利(ㄌㄧㄡ ㄌㄧˋ)
flowing smoothly; fluent: 你
的英語相當流利。Your English
is rather fluent.

流麗(ㄌㄧㄡ ㄌㄧˋ)
(said of literary writings)
fluent and elegant

流里流氣(ㄌㄧㄡ ㄌㄧˇ ㄌㄧㄡ ㄑㄧˋ)
rascally

流連(ㄌㄧㄡ ㄌㄧㄢˊ)
reluctant to leave; reluctant
to end a pleasant experi-
ence; to tarry; to linger on

【水部】

流連忘返(ㄌㄧㄡ ㄌㄧㄢ ㄨㄤˋ ㄈㄢˇ)
to forget to go home because of pleasures elsewhere

流量(ㄌㄧㄡ ㄌㄧㄤˋ)
(hydrology) flow capacity; discharge

流露(ㄌㄧㄡ ㄌㄨˋ)
to reveal unknowingly; to betray; to manifest: 他真情流露。He revealed his sentiment.

流落(ㄌㄧㄡ ㄌㄨㄛˋ)
to become an outcast in a strange land; to become a wanderer in a faraway land owing to lack of money for the home trip: 她流落異鄉。She wandered destitute far from home.

流丐(ㄌㄧㄡ ㄍㄞˋ)
a vagrant beggar; a vagabond

流官(ㄌㄧㄡ ㄍㄨㄢ)
(during the Ching Dynasty) a local official appointed by the Central Government (as opposed to those holding inherited titles)

流光(ㄌㄧㄡ ㄍㄨㄤ)
①the swift flow of time ②moonlight reflected on flowing water

流寇(ㄌㄧㄡ ㄎㄡˋ)
wandering bandits; bandits without a permanent base

流汗(ㄌㄧㄡ ㄏㄢˋ)
to perspire; to sweat: 天氣很熱時，我們會流汗。We sweat when it is very hot.

流戶(ㄌㄧㄡ ㄏㄨˋ)
homeless families

流滑(ㄌㄧㄡ ㄏㄨㄚˊ)
crafty; cunning

流火(ㄌㄧㄡ ㄏㄨㄛˇ)
①summer heat ②(Chinese medicine) inflammatory disease with redness of skin

流金鑠石(ㄌㄧㄡ ㄐㄧㄣ ㄕㄨㄛˋ ㄕˊ)
scorching heat in the summer sun

流氣(ㄌㄧㄡ ㄑㄧˋ)
hooliganism; rascally behavior

流徙(ㄌㄧㄡ ㄒㄧˇ)
to exile

流霞(ㄌㄧㄡ ㄒㄧㄚˊ)

flowing vapor

流血(ㄌㄧㄡ ㄒㄧㄝˇ)
to shed blood; to bleed; bloodshed; bleeding: 有人說政治是不流血的戰爭。It is said politics is war without bloodshed.

流涎(ㄌㄧㄡ ㄒㄧㄢˊ)
to drivel; to drool

流線型(ㄌㄧㄡ ㄒㄧㄢˋ ㄒㄧㄥˊ)
streamlined

流星(ㄌㄧㄡ ㄒㄧㄥ)
(astronomy) a meteor

流星雨(ㄌㄧㄡ ㄒㄧㄥ ㄩˇ)
a meteoric shower

流刑(ㄌㄧㄡ ㄒㄧㄥˊ)
(in old China) banishment or exile as a form of punishment

流行(ㄌㄧㄡ ㄒㄧㄥˊ)
①to be in fashion; to be popular; to be in vogue; fashionable; prevalent:這是現今流行的論調。This argument is prevalent now. ②(said of a contagious disease) to spread, rage, or be rampant: 疾病在該村流行著。Sickness was rampant in the village.

流行病(ㄌㄧㄡ ㄒㄧㄥˊ ㄅㄧㄥˋ)
an epidemic (disease)

流行性感冒(ㄌㄧㄡ ㄒㄧㄥˊ ㄒㄧㄥˋ ㄍㄢˇ ㄇㄠˋ)
influenza; flu; epidemic catarrh

流質(ㄌㄧㄡ ㄓˊ)
liquid

流注(ㄌㄧㄡ ㄓㄨˋ)
(said of a river) to flow into a lake or sea

流轉(ㄌㄧㄡ ㄓㄨㄢˇ)
①to wander about; to move from place to place ②to spread; to transmit, or be transmitted (from person to person, or from generation to generation) ③to alternate

流產(ㄌㄧㄡ ㄔㄢˇ)
①to have a miscarriage; abortion ②to prove abortive; to fail to materialize: 她的計劃流產了。Her plan proved abortive.

流娼(ㄌㄧㄡ ㄔㄤ)
a streetwalker

流暢(ㄌㄧㄡ ㄔㄤˋ)

(usually said of the style of writing) fluent; smooth

流程(ㄌㄧㄡ ㄔㄥˊ)
①technological process ②(mining) circuits

流傳(ㄌㄧㄡ ㄔㄨㄢˊ)
to transmit, or be transmitted, from person to person, or from generation to generation; to spread: 這消息很快地流傳開來。The news soon spread.

流失(ㄌㄧㄡ ㄕ)
to run off; to be washed away

流逝(ㄌㄧㄡ ㄕˋ)
(said of time) to pass; to elapse; passage

流沙(ㄌㄧㄡ ㄕㄚ)
①sediment (in rivers) ②the quicksand

流說(ㄌㄧㄡ ㄕㄨㄛ)
heretical assertion

流水(ㄌㄧㄡ ㄕㄨㄟˇ)
flowing water; current: 他順著流水游泳。He swam with the current.

流水賬(ㄌㄧㄡ ㄕㄨㄟˇ ㄓㄤˋ)
running account; journal account

流人(ㄌㄧㄡ ㄖㄣˊ)
①a refugee ②an exile

流刺網(ㄌㄧㄡ ㄘˋ ㄨㄤˇ)
a drift net

流竄(ㄌㄧㄡ ㄘㄨㄢˋ)
(said of bandits or rebel troops) to roam about

流蘇(ㄌㄧㄡ ㄙㄨ)
tassels (of flags)

流俗(ㄌㄧㄡ ㄙㄨˊ)
popular customs

流速(ㄌㄧㄡ ㄙㄨˋ)
the speed of current; current velocity

流速計(ㄌㄧㄡ ㄙㄨˋ ㄐㄧˋ)
a current meter

流言(ㄌㄧㄡ ㄧㄢˊ)
groundless statement; idle talk; rumor; hearsay

流言止於智者(ㄌㄧㄡ ㄧㄢˊ ㄓˇ ㄩˊ ㄓˋ ㄓㄜˇ)
A wise man does not believe in rumors.

流音(ㄌㄧㄡ ㄧㄣ)
(phonetics) a glide; the transitional sound

〔水部〕

流鴬 (ㄌ丨ㄡˊㄇㄥ)
a streetwalker

流螢 (ㄌ丨ㄡˊ丨ㄥˊ)
a firefly

流亡 (ㄌ丨ㄡˊㄨㄤˊ)
to be exiled; to wander in a strange land: 他繼生流亡國外。He was exiled for life.

流亡政府 (ㄌ丨ㄡˊㄨㄤˊㄓㄥˋㄈㄨˇ)
a government in exile

流於形式 (ㄌ丨ㄡˊㄩˊㄒ丨ㄥˊㄕˋ)
to have become a matter of formality

流域 (ㄌ丨ㄡˊㄩˋ)
drainage basin; drainage area; catchment area; catchment basin; river basin; valley

流寓 (ㄌ丨ㄡˊㄩˋ)
to live here and there in a strange land; to have no permanent home

流用 (ㄌ丨ㄡˊㄩㄥˋ)
to put a thing to a use not originally intended

【洏】 2876 (ㄦˊ erl ér)
1. tearful; weeping
2. to cook food thoroughly

【洸】 2877 (ㄍㄨㄤ guang guāng)
1. name of a river in Shantung
2. (said of water) to glitter
3. cavalierly; bravely; to be martial-looking

七畫

【浙】 2878 (ㄓㄜˋ jeh zhè)
1. Chekiang
2. name of a river

浙東 (ㄓㄜˋㄉㄨㄥ)
eastern Chekiang

浙江 (ㄓㄜˋㄐ丨ㄤ)
①Chekiang Province ②name of a river in Chekiang

浙江潮 (ㄓㄜˋㄐ丨ㄤㄔㄠˊ)
the tide at the mouth of the Chientang River (錢塘江) in Chekiang

浙西 (ㄓㄜˋㄒ丨)
western Chekiang

【浚】 2879 (ㄐㄩㄣˋ jiunn jùn)
1. to dredge
2. deep

浚泥機 (ㄐㄩㄣˋㄋ丨ˊㄐ丨)
a dredge

浚利 (ㄐㄩㄣˋㄌ丨ˋ)
(said of a waterway) unobstructed

【浜】 2880 (ㄅㄤ bang bāng)
a small stream

【浡】 2881 (ㄅㄛˊ bor bó)
to rise; excited

浡然 (ㄅㄛˊㄖㄢˊ)
① rising ② flourishingly

【浣】 2882 (ㄏㄨㄢˇ hoan huǎn)
(又讀 ㄨㄢˋ woan wàn)
1. to wash; to rinse
2. ten days; any of the three ten-day divisions of a month: 上浣 the first ten days of a month

浣滌 (ㄏㄨㄢˇㄉ丨ˊ)
to wash; to rinse

浣花溪 (ㄏㄨㄢˇㄏㄨㄚㄒ丨)
name of a place in Szechwan (四川), known as the home of the poet Tu Fu

浣熊 (ㄏㄨㄢˇㄒㄩㄥˊ)
a racoon

浣濯 (ㄏㄨㄢˇㄓㄨㄛˊ)
to wash; to rinse

浣紗溪 (ㄏㄨㄢˇㄕㄚㄒ丨)
name of a river in Chekiang, where the famed beauty, Hsi Shih (西施), washed cotton yarn when she was a country girl

浣衣 (ㄏㄨㄢˇ丨)
to wash clothes

【浩】 2883 (ㄏㄠˋ haw hào)
1. massive; great; vast
2. many; much
3. a Chinese family name

浩博 (ㄏㄠˋㄅㄛˊ)
many; much

浩漫 (ㄏㄠˋㄇㄢˋ)
many; numerous

浩茫 (ㄏㄠˋㄇㄤˊ)
(said of a body of water) vast or extensive

浩渺 or 浩淼 (ㄏㄠˋㄇ丨ㄠˇ)
(said of a body of water) vast or extensive; extending into the distance

浩繁 (ㄏㄠˋㄈㄢˊ)
① many; numerous ② (said of duties, etc.) heavy: 這是一筆浩繁的開銷。This is a heavy expenditure.

浩大 (ㄏㄠˋㄉㄚˋ)
great; vast

浩蕩 (ㄏㄠˋㄉㄤˋ)
vast and restless

浩歎 (ㄏㄠˋㄊㄢˋ)
to give a deep emotional sigh; to heave a deep sigh

浩歌 (ㄏㄠˋㄍㄜ)
to sing aloud

浩浩 (ㄏㄠˋㄏㄠˋ)
①(said of water) vast ②(said of time) infinitive ③(said of the heaven) vast

浩浩蕩蕩 (ㄏㄠˋㄏㄠˋㄉㄤˋㄉㄤˋ)
(said of an army in march) moving in an imposing manner; surging ahead; overwhelming

浩瀚 (ㄏㄠˋㄏㄢˋ)
huge quantities; vast

浩劫 (ㄏㄠˋㄐ丨ㄝˊ)
great disaster; a catastrophe; a calamity

浩氣 (ㄏㄠˋㄑ丨ˋ)
the Great Spirit (the aim of self-cultivation preached by Mencius)

浩氣長存 (ㄏㄠˋㄑ丨ˋㄔㄤˊㄘㄨㄣˊ)
imperishable noble spirit

浩然 (ㄏㄠˋㄖㄢˊ)
great; overwhelming

浩然之氣 (ㄏㄠˋㄖㄢˊㄓㄑ丨ˋ)
the Great Spirit (the aim of self-cultivation preached by Mencius)

浩壤 (ㄏㄠˋㄖㄤˇ)
vast land

浩如烟海 (ㄏㄠˋㄖㄨˊ丨ㄢㄏㄞˇ)
as vast as a misty ocean

浩飲 (ㄏㄠˋ丨ㄣˇ)
to drink without inhibition; to drink like a fish

【浥】 2884 (丨ˋ yih yì)
wet, moist; to moisten

浥濕 (丨ˋㄕ)
wet; moist

浥潤 (丨ˋㄖㄨㄣˋ)
wet; moist

浥浥 (丨ˋ丨ˋ)
moist

【浦】 2885 (ㄆㄨˇ puu pǔ)
1. the shore; the beach; the

riverside
2. a Chinese family name

浦東（ㄆㄨ ㄉㄨㄥ）
that part of Shanghai east
of the Huangpu River

浦口（ㄆㄨ ㄎㄡ）
a city opposite Nanking on
the Yangtze River

【浬】 2886
（ㄌㄧ）
(a unit of distance used
chiefly in navigation) a
nautical mile; a geographic
mile; a sea mile

【浪】 2887
1. （ㄌㄤ lang lǎng）
1. waves; billows; breakers: 白
浪滔天 white breakers sweep-
ing across the sea 巨浪打在
我們身上 Great waves surged
over us. 海浪拍擊著海岸。The
waves beat upon the shore.
2. dissolute; debauched; unrestrained; rash

浪板（ㄌㄤ ㄅㄢˇ）
a plastic roofing board

浪婆（ㄌㄤ ㄆㄛˊ）
the goddess of the waves

浪漫（ㄌㄤ ㄇㄢˋ）
①dissolute; debauched ②
romantic

浪漫派（ㄌㄤ ㄇㄢˋ ㄆㄞˋ）
romanticism

浪漫的（ㄌㄤ ㄇㄢˋ ·ㄉㄜ）
romantic

浪漫主義（ㄌㄤ ㄇㄢˋ ㄓㄨˇ ㄧˋ）
romanticism

浪莽（ㄌㄤ ㄇㄤˇ）
unrestrained

浪盂（ㄌㄤ ㄋˇ）
①discouraged; dejected ②
aloud

浪費（ㄌㄤ ㄈㄟˋ）
to waste; to lavish; waste: 他
在不重要的事情上面浪費許多
時間。He wastes a lot of
time on things that have no
importance.

浪放（ㄌㄤ ㄈㄤˋ）
uninhibited; unrestrained 亦
作「放浪」

浪蕩（ㄌㄤ ㄉㄤˋ）
to debauch; to dissipate: 他
的生活浪蕩。He led a de-
bauched life.

浪頭（ㄌㄤ ㄊㄡˊ）
the crest of a wave: 此時浪

頭很高。Now the crests of the
waves are high.

浪花（ㄌㄤ ㄏㄨㄚ）
spray of breaking waves: 我
們被海水的浪花濺濕。We were
wet with the sea spray.

浪迹（ㄌㄤ ㄐㄧ）
wandering; vagrant

浪迹天涯（ㄌㄤ ㄐㄧ ㄊㄧㄢ ㄧㄚˊ）
to wander about far away
from home

浪橋（ㄌㄤ ㄑㄧㄠˊ）
a swing bridge

浪信（ㄌㄤ ㄒㄧㄣˋ）
gullible; to believe unwisely:
他浪信人言。He unwisely
believed in others' words.

浪職（ㄌㄤ ㄓˊ）
to neglect one's duty

浪潮（ㄌㄤ ㄔㄠˊ）
①tide; waves ②(figuratively) tide; tendency

浪闖（ㄌㄤ ㄔㄨㄤˇ）
to beat about pointlessly

浪士（ㄌㄤ ㄕˋ）
a debauchee

浪人（ㄌㄤ ㄖㄣˊ）
①a vagrant ②a dismissed
courtier ③an unemployed
person; a jobless person

浪子（ㄌㄤ ㄗˇ）
a prodigal; a debauchee; a
loafer

浪子回頭（ㄌㄤ ㄗˇ ㄏㄨㄟˊ ㄊㄡˊ）
the return of the prodigal
son

浪遊（ㄌㄤ ㄧㄡˊ）
to roam for pleasure; to
make a tour: 那攝影家浪遊世
界。The photographer roamed
about the world.

浪語（ㄌㄤ ㄩˇ）
a nonsensical joke

【浪】 2887
2. （ㄌㄤ lang lǎng）
flowing; fluent

浪浪（ㄌㄤ ㄌㄤ）
flowing

【浭】 2888
（ㄍㄥ geng gēng）
name of a river in Hopeh

浭水（ㄍㄥ ㄏㄨㄟˇ）
a river in Hopeh

【浴】 2889
（ㄩˋ yuh yù）
1.to bathe; a bath: 他用熱水沐
浴。He bathed himself in hot

water.
2. to wash

浴盆（ㄩˋ ㄆㄣˊ）
a bath; a bathtub

浴佛（ㄩˋ ㄈㄛˊ）
to bathe Buddha's image (as
a Buddhist rite in celebration of the Buddha's birthday)

浴佛節（ㄩˋ ㄈㄛˊ ㄐㄧㄝˊ）
the Buddha Bathing Festival
(on the eighth day of the
fourth moon, when Buddha's
image is bathed in celebration of his birthday)

浴德（ㄩˋ ㄉㄜˊ）
to cultivate one's virtue

浴室（ㄩˋ ㄕˋ）
a bathhouse; a public bath

浴巾（ㄩˋ ㄐㄧㄣ）
a bath towel

浴像（ㄩˋ ㄒㄧㄤˋ）
to bathe Buddha's image (as
a Buddhist rite)

浴血苦戰（ㄩˋ ㄒㄧㄝˇ ㄎㄨˇ ㄓㄢˋ）
to be at bay in a fierce battle; to fight a bloody battle

浴池（ㄩˋ ㄔˊ）
a bath pool

浴場（ㄩˋ ㄔㄤˇ）or（ㄩˋ ㄔㄤˋ）
a bathing beach: 去年夏天他
常去那個海水浴場。Last sum-
mer he often went to that
bathing beach.

浴屍（ㄩˋ ㄕ）
to bathe a corpse (in preparation for funeral service)

浴室（ㄩˋ ㄕˋ）
a bathroom

浴日（ㄩˋ ㄖˋ）
①bright sunrise ②great
distinction; great exploits;
eminent contributions

浴衣（ㄩˋ ㄧ）
a bathrobe; bathing dress;
bathing costume; a bathing
gown

【浮】 2890
ㄈㄨˊ fwu fú
（又讀 ㄈㄡˊ four fóu）
1. to float; to waft
2. to overflow; to exceed
3. empty; superficial; unsubstantial; unfounded; groundless

浮薄（ㄈㄨˊ ㄅㄛˊ）
insincere; untruthful; unsta-

〔水
部〕

【水部】

ble; frivolous; flippant: 他是個浮薄少年。He's an unstable youth.

浮報(ㄈㄨˊ ㄅㄠˋ)
to report more than the actual amount spent

浮標(ㄈㄨˊ ㄅㄧㄠ)
a buoy

浮冰(ㄈㄨˊ ㄅㄧㄥ)
floating ice; (ice) floes

浮萍(ㄈㄨˊ ㄆㄧㄥˊ)
duckweed

浮冒(ㄈㄨˊ ㄇㄠˋ)
reckless and untruthful (in accounts)

浮靡(ㄈㄨˊ ㄇㄧˊ)
decadent

浮面(ㄈㄨˊ ㄇㄧㄢˋ)
the surface: 他把浮面的一層泥刮去。He scraped the mud off the surface.

浮名(ㄈㄨˊ ㄇㄧㄥˊ)
an empty name or honor

浮費(ㄈㄨˊ ㄈㄟˋ)
to waste; to lavish

浮泛(ㄈㄨˊ ㄈㄢˋ)
① to boat ② superficial: 他的報告內容浮泛。His report was superficial and full of generalities.

浮雕(ㄈㄨˊ ㄉㄧㄠ)
(sculpture) relief

浮動(ㄈㄨˊ ㄉㄨㄥˋ)
① to waft; to float; to drift ② to be unsteady; to fluctuate

浮屠 or 浮圖(ㄈㄨˊ ㄊㄨˊ)
① Buddha ② a pagoda; a stupa

浮浪(ㄈㄨˊ ㄌㄤˋ)
to loaf about

浮浪人(ㄈㄨˊ ㄌㄤˋ ㄖㄣˊ)
a loafer

浮浪子弟(ㄈㄨˊ ㄌㄤˋ ㄗˇ ㄉㄧˋ)
vagrant or unemployed persons

浮力(ㄈㄨˊ ㄌㄧˋ)
(physics) buoyancy: 木頭的浮力大於鐵。Wood has more buoyancy than iron.

浮利(ㄈㄨˊ ㄌㄧˋ)
empty profit

浮梗(ㄈㄨˊ ㄍㄥˇ)
duckweed stalks

浮瓜沈李(ㄈㄨˊ ㄍㄨㄚ ㄔㄣˊ ㄌㄧˇ)
to pursue summer joys or

pleasures

浮光掠影(ㄈㄨˊ ㄍㄨㄤ ㄌㄩㄝˋ ㄧㄥˇ)
floating light and passing shadow—superficial opinions, descriptions, sketches, etc.

浮誇(ㄈㄨˊ ㄎㄨㄚ)
boastfully vain; vainglorious: 他很浮誇地說他所做過的事。He speaks boastfully of what he has done.

浮華(ㄈㄨˊ ㄏㄨㄚˊ)
vanity; superficial beauty: 他過著浮華的人生。He led a life of vanity.

浮滑(ㄈㄨˊ ㄏㄨㄚˊ)
fickle and crafty

浮家泛宅(ㄈㄨˊ ㄐㄧㄚ ㄈㄢˋ ㄓㄞˋ)
to dwell on a boat

浮氣(ㄈㄨˊ ㄑㄧˋ)
flippancy; frivolity

浮橋(ㄈㄨˊ ㄑㄧㄠˊ) or 浮梁(ㄈㄨˊ ㄌㄧㄤˊ)
a pontoon bridge

浮簽(ㄈㄨˊ ㄑㄧㄢ)
a piece of paper intended to be detached eventually

浮淺(ㄈㄨˊ ㄑㄧㄢˇ)
superficial; shallow

浮囂(ㄈㄨˊ ㄒㄧㄠ)
fickle and excitable: 他們是浮囂之輩。They are fickle and excitable fellows.

浮現(ㄈㄨˊ ㄒㄧㄢˋ)
(said of memories, etc.) to rise before one's mind; to appear in one's mind's eye

浮腫(ㄈㄨˊ ㄓㄨㄥˇ)
① (medicine) dropsy; edema ② bloated; swollen; dropsical swelling

浮沈(ㄈㄨˊ ㄔㄣˊ)
① rise and fall; vicissitudes ② to follow the trend: 他與世浮沈。He followed the crowd without his own principles.

浮沈子(ㄈㄨˊ ㄔㄣˊ ㄗˇ)
(physics) a Cartesian diver

浮塵(ㄈㄨˊ ㄔㄣˊ) or 浮埃(ㄈㄨˊ ㄞ)
floating dust

浮秤(ㄈㄨˊ ㄔㄥˋ)
a hydrometer

浮屍(ㄈㄨˊ ㄕ)
a floating corpse

浮石(ㄈㄨˊ ㄕˊ)
(mining) pumice (stone)

浮士德(ㄈㄨˊ ㄕˋ ㄉㄜˊ)
① Johann Faust, German magician, ?-C.1538 ② Faust (in medieval legend, a philosopher, represented as selling his soul to a devil, Mephistopheles, for wisdom and power, the main character of Goethe's Faust and Marlowe's Dr. Faustus.)

浮世繪(ㄈㄨˊ ㄕˋ ㄏㄨㄟˋ)
a (Japanese) woodcut

浮生六記(ㄈㄨˊ ㄕㄥ ㄌㄧㄡˋ ㄐㄧˋ)
Six Unforgettable Chapters of My Life, by Shen San-pai (沈三白) of the Ching Dynasty

浮生若夢(ㄈㄨˊ ㄕㄥ ㄖㄨㄛˋ ㄇㄥˋ)
Life is like a dream.

浮說(ㄈㄨˊ ㄕㄨㄛ)
groundless remarks

浮水(ㄈㄨˊ ㄕㄨㄟˇ)
(dialect) to float; to waft; to swim

浮榮(ㄈㄨˊ ㄖㄨㄥˊ)
vanity

浮躁(ㄈㄨˊ ㄗㄠˋ)
restless; impatient; rash

浮辭(ㄈㄨˊ ㄘˊ)
untruthful remarks; unfounded statements; high-sounding remarks

浮財(ㄈㄨˊ ㄘㄞˊ)
wealth (which is transient and has no intrinsic value)

浮額(ㄈㄨˊ ㄜˊ)
an amount in excess; an extra number or sum

浮一大白(ㄈㄨˊ ㄧ ㄉㄚˋ ㄅㄞˊ)
to empty a full glass of wine or liquor at one drink

浮游(ㄈㄨˊ ㄧㄡˊ)
an ephemera

浮游生物(ㄈㄨˊ ㄧㄡˊ ㄕㄥ ㄨˋ)
plankton

浮言(ㄈㄨˊ ㄧㄢˊ)
unfounded remarks; groundless statements

浮艷(ㄈㄨˊ ㄧㄢˋ)
pompous and unsubstantial

浮揚(ㄈㄨˊ ㄧㄤˊ)
to soar

浮影(ㄈㄨˊ ㄧㄥˇ)
floating shadows; visions

浮文(ㄈㄨˊ ㄨㄣˊ)
empty writing

浮譽(ㄈㄨ ㄩ)
empty honor

浮雲(ㄈㄨ ㄩㄣ)
floating clouds

浮雲朝露(ㄈㄨ ㄩㄣ ㄓㄠ ㄌㄨ)
(literally) floating cloud and morning dew—fleeting; ephemeral; brief

【海】2891
ㄏㄞ hae hǎi
1. the sea; the ocean:我在海中游泳. I swam in the sea.
2. a great number of people or things coming together—(figuratively) a huge gathering
3. an area; a field: 學海無涯. The field of learning is boundless.
4. great; unlimited
5. a Chinese family name

海拔(ㄏㄞ ㄅㄚˊ)
the elevation or height above sea level: 這山高海拔三千九百米. The mountain is 3,900 meters above sea level.

海豹(ㄏㄞ ㄅㄠˋ)
a seal (a sea animal): 某些種類的海豹已近乎絕種. Some kinds of seals are nearly extinct.

海報(ㄏㄞ ㄅㄠˋ)
a theater poster

海邦(ㄏㄞ ㄅㄤ)
a maritime nation

海表(ㄏㄞ ㄅㄧㄠˇ)
overseas lands

海邊(ㄏㄞ ㄅㄧㄢ)or 海邊兒(ㄏㄞ ㄅㄧㄚˇㄦ)
the seashore; the seaside; the beach: 孩子們在海邊到處奔跑. Children were running about on the beach.

海濱(ㄏㄞ ㄅㄧㄣ)
the seashore; the beach: 我們在海濱度假. We spent our holidays by the seashore.

海不揚波(ㄏㄞ ㄅㄨˋ ㄧㄤˊ ㄅㄛ)
The sea is calm.—The world is in peace.

海派(ㄏㄞ ㄆㄞˋ)
the Shanghai style (of opera, living, etc.), as opposed to the Peking style

海泡石(ㄏㄞ ㄆㄠˋ ㄕˊ)
(mining) sepiolite

海盤車(ㄏㄞ ㄆㄢˊ ㄔㄜ)
an asteroid; a starfish

海平面(ㄏㄞ ㄆㄧㄥˊ ㄇㄧㄢˋ)
sea level: 這座山高出海平面一萬英尺. The mountain is 10,000 feet above sea level.

海埔(ㄏㄞ ㄆㄨˇ)
the seaside

海埔新生地(ㄏㄞ ㄆㄨˇ ㄒㄧㄣ ㄕㄥ ㄉㄧˋ)
the tidal land

海馬(ㄏㄞ ㄇㄚˇ)
① hippocampus ② a sea horse

海罵(ㄏㄞ ㄇㄚˋ)
to accuse or slander an unnamed person

海鰻(ㄏㄞ ㄇㄢˊ)
a conger pike; a sea eel

海綿(ㄏㄞ ㄇㄧㄢˊ)
sponge

海面(ㄏㄞ ㄇㄧㄢˋ)
the sea surface

海防(ㄏㄞ ㄈㄤˊ)
① coastal defense: 海防十分鞏固. The coastal defense is very strong. ② Haiphong, North Viet Nam

海防部隊(ㄏㄞ ㄈㄤˊ ㄅㄨˋ ㄉㄨㄟˋ)
coastal defense forces

海風(ㄏㄞ ㄈㄥ)
a sea wind; a sea breeze: 海風自北方吹來. A sea wind was blowing from the north.

海帶(ㄏㄞ ㄉㄞˋ)
kelp; a sea tangle

海島(ㄏㄞ ㄉㄠˇ)
an island (in the sea): 臺灣是一個海島. Taiwan is an island.

海盜(ㄏㄞ ㄉㄠˋ)
a pirate; a sea rover; a sea robber

海盜船(ㄏㄞ ㄉㄠˋ ㄔㄨㄢˊ)
a pirate ship; a sea rover

海膽(ㄏㄞ ㄉㄢˇ)
a sea urchin

海底(ㄏㄞ ㄉㄧˇ)
the bed or bottom of the sea

海底電線(ㄏㄞ ㄉㄧˇ ㄉㄧㄢˋ ㄒㄧㄢˋ)or 海底電纜(ㄏㄞ ㄉㄧˇ ㄉㄧㄢˋ ㄌㄢˇ)
a submarine cable

海底撈針(ㄏㄞ ㄉㄧˇ ㄌㄠ ㄓㄣ)
(literally) to try to recover a needle from the bottom of the sea—to make a futile search

海底撈月(ㄏㄞ ㄉㄧˇ ㄌㄠ ㄩㄝ)
to try to fish out the moon from the bottom of the sea —to strive in vain

海底鑽探(ㄏㄞ ㄉㄧˇ ㄗㄨㄢ ㄊㄢˋ)
offshore drilling

海地(ㄏㄞ ㄉㄧˋ)
Haiti

海地人(ㄏㄞ ㄉㄧˋ ㄖㄣˊ)
a Haitian

海釣(ㄏㄞ ㄉㄧㄠˋ)
offshore angling

海頓(ㄏㄞ ㄉㄨㄣˋ)
Franz Joseph Haydn, 1732-1809, Austrian composer

海獺(ㄏㄞ ㄊㄚˇ)
a sea otter; a beaver: 動物園裡有三隻海獺. There are three beavers in the zoo.

海濤(ㄏㄞ ㄊㄠˊ)
sea waves; billows

海灘(ㄏㄞ ㄊㄢ)
the seashore; the beach

海棠(ㄏㄞ ㄊㄤˊ)
Malus spectabilis; Chinese flowering apple

海塘(ㄏㄞ ㄊㄤˊ)or 海堤(ㄏㄞ ㄊㄧˊ)
sea wall; sea embankment

海圖(ㄏㄞ ㄊㄨˊ)
a sea or marine chart

海豚(ㄏㄞ ㄊㄨㄣˊ)
a dolphin

海內(ㄏㄞ ㄋㄟˋ)
within the four seas; within the country

海內清平(ㄏㄞ ㄋㄟˋ ㄑㄧㄥ ㄆㄧㄥˊ)
The country is in peace and good order.

海內存知己(ㄏㄞ ㄋㄟˋ ㄘㄨㄣˊ ㄓ ㄐㄧˇ)
"A real friend cannot be wanting in this wide world." (a line from 王勃)

海內晏如(ㄏㄞ ㄋㄟˋ ㄧㄢˋ ㄖㄨˊ)
Peace reigns throughout the land.

海內無雙(ㄏㄞ ㄋㄟˋ ㄨˊ ㄕㄨㄤ)
unequaled or peerless in the whole country

海南島(ㄏㄞ ㄋㄢˊ ㄉㄠˇ)
Hainan (an island off South China)

海難(ㄏㄞ ㄋㄢˋ)
a disaster at sea; a wreck: 那次暴風雨引起了許多海難. The storm caused many

【水 部】

wrecks.

海鳥(ㄏㄞˇ ㄋㄧㄠˇ)
a seafowl; a sea crow

海蘭泡(ㄏㄞˇ ㄌㄢˊ ㄆㄠˋ)
Blagoveshchensk

海浪(ㄏㄞˇ ㄌㄤˋ)
seas; sea waves: 海浪很高。
Sea waves are very high.

海狸(ㄏㄞˇ ㄌㄧˊ)
a beaver

海里(ㄏㄞˇ ㄌㄧˇ)
nautical mile, a unit of distance used chiefly in navigation

海流(ㄏㄞˇ ㄌㄧㄡˊ)
the ocean current

海量(ㄏㄞˇ ㄌㄧㄤˋ)
① a mind with the broadness of the sea; great magnanimity; magnanimous ② great capacity for alcoholic drinks

海路(ㄏㄞˇ ㄌㄨˋ)
a sea route; a sea lane; a seaway

海螺(ㄏㄞˇ ㄌㄨㄛˊ)
a sea univalve; a conch

洛洛因(ㄏㄞˇ ㄌㄨㄛˋ ㄧㄣ)
heroin

海輪(ㄏㄞˇ ㄌㄨㄣˊ)
a seagoing (or oceangoing) ship

海倫凱勒(ㄏㄞˇ ㄌㄨㄣˊ ㄎㄞˇ ㄌㄜˋ)
Helen Adams Keller, 1880–1968

海龍王(ㄏㄞˇ ㄌㄨㄥˊ ㄨㄤˊ)
Dragon King, the Chinese equivalent of Neptune

海溝(ㄏㄞˇ ㄍㄡ)
(oceanic) trenches

海狗(ㄏㄞˇ ㄍㄡˇ)
a seal

海港(ㄏㄞˇ ㄍㄤˇ)
a seaport; a harbor: 這島上有個良好的海港。The island has a fine harbor.

海國(ㄏㄞˇ ㄍㄨㄛˊ)
a maritime nation

海龜(ㄏㄞˇ ㄍㄨㄟ)
a green turtle (Chelonia mydas)

海關(ㄏㄞˇ ㄍㄨㄢ)
the customs; a custom house: 通過海關的檢查花了一小時。It took an hour to pass the customs.

海關檢查(ㄏㄞˇ ㄍㄨㄢ ㄐㄧㄢˇ ㄔㄚˊ)
customs inspection

海關人員(ㄏㄞˇ ㄍㄨㄢ ㄖㄣˊ ㄩㄢˊ)
customs officers

海口(ㄏㄞˇ ㄎㄡˇ)
① a seaport ② bragging; exaggerated statements

海枯石爛(ㄏㄞˇ ㄎㄨ ㄕˊ ㄌㄢˋ)
(I will remain faithful to you) even if the sea dries and stones rot

海闊天空(ㄏㄞˇ ㄎㄨㄛˋ ㄊㄧㄢ ㄎㄨㄥ)
endlessly vast; boundless

海葵(ㄏㄞˇ ㄎㄨㄟˊ)
(zoology) a sea anemone

海涵(ㄏㄞˇ ㄏㄢˊ)
great magnanimity; broadmindedness; forgiveness

海話(ㄏㄞˇ ㄏㄨㄚˋ)
boasts; exaggerations; bragging

海貨(ㄏㄞˇ ㄏㄨㄛˋ)
marine goods

海岬(ㄏㄞˇ ㄐㄧㄚˇ)
a cape

海角天涯(ㄏㄞˇ ㄐㄧㄠˇ ㄊㄧㄢ ㄧㄚˊ)
the farthest end of the earth

海徼(ㄏㄞˇ ㄐㄧㄠˋ)
remote coastal regions

海禁(ㄏㄞˇ ㄐㄧㄣˋ)
restrictions at ports of entry and exit

海禁大開(ㄏㄞˇ ㄐㄧㄣˋ ㄉㄚˋ ㄎㄞ)
to drastically ease restrictions at ports of entry and exit

海疆(ㄏㄞˇ ㄐㄧㄤ)
coastal areas and territorial seas

海(ㄏㄞˇ ㄐㄧㄥˇ)
the seascape: 海景悅目。The seascape pleases the eyes.

海軍(ㄏㄞˇ ㄐㄩㄣ)
the navy; naval: 他服務於海軍。He serves in the navy.

海軍部(ㄏㄞˇ ㄐㄩㄣ ㄅㄨˋ)
Department of the Navy (especially of the United States)

海軍部長(ㄏㄞˇ ㄐㄩㄣ ㄅㄨˋ ㄓㄤˇ)
the Secretary of the Navy (especially of the United States)

海軍陸戰隊(ㄏㄞˇ ㄐㄩㄣ ㄌㄨˋ ㄓㄢˋ ㄎㄨㄟˋ)

the Marine Corps

海軍陸戰隊司令(ㄏㄞˇ ㄐㄩㄣ ㄌㄨˋ ㄓㄢˋ ㄎㄨㄟˋ ㄙ ㄌㄧㄥˋ)
the commandant of the Marine Corps

海軍官校(ㄏㄞˇ ㄐㄩㄣ ㄍㄨㄢ ㄒㄧㄠˋ)
a naval academy: 他在海軍官校讀書。He studies at the naval academy now.

海軍中將(ㄏㄞˇ ㄐㄩㄣ ㄓㄨㄥ ㄐㄧㄤˋ)
vice-admiral

海軍准將(ㄏㄞˇ ㄐㄩㄣ ㄓㄨㄣˇ ㄐㄧㄤˋ)
commander (above lieutenant commander)

海軍中尉(ㄏㄞˇ ㄐㄩㄣ ㄓㄨㄥ ㄨㄟˋ)
lieutenant junior grade

海軍少將(ㄏㄞˇ ㄐㄩㄣ ㄕㄠˇ ㄐㄧㄤˋ)
rear admiral

海軍少校(ㄏㄞˇ ㄐㄩㄣ ㄕㄠˇ ㄒㄧㄠˋ)
lieutenant commander

海軍少尉(ㄏㄞˇ ㄐㄩㄣ ㄕㄠˇ ㄨㄟˋ)
ensign

海軍上將(ㄏㄞˇ ㄐㄩㄣ ㄕㄤˋ ㄐㄧㄤˋ)
admiral

海軍上校(ㄏㄞˇ ㄐㄩㄣ ㄕㄤˋ ㄒㄧㄠˋ)
captain (just below rear admiral)

海軍上尉(ㄏㄞˇ ㄐㄩㄣ ㄕㄤˋ ㄨㄟˋ)
lieutenant (just below lieutenant commander)

海軍總司令(ㄏㄞˇ ㄐㄩㄣ ㄗㄨㄥˇ ㄙ ㄌㄧㄥˋ)
the commander in chief of the navy; (in the U.S.) the chief of naval operations

海軍演習(ㄏㄞˇ ㄐㄩㄣ ㄧㄢˇ ㄒㄧˊ)
naval maneuvers

海蛸(ㄏㄞˇ ㄑㄧㄠˋ)
a sea squirt

海權(ㄏㄞˇ ㄑㄩㄢˊ)
sea power

海峽(ㄏㄞˇ ㄒㄧㄚˊ)
straits; a channel: 台灣海峽 the Taiwan Straits

海嘯(ㄏㄞˇ ㄒㄧㄠˋ)
a tidal wave; a tsunami

海鮮(ㄏㄞˇ ㄒㄧㄢ)
fresh seafood; marine delicacies: 我喜歡吃海鮮。I like seafood.

海象(ㄏㄞˇ ㄒㄧㄤˋ)
a sea elephant; a walrus

海星(ㄏㄞˇ ㄒㄧㄥ)
the starfish

海蜇(ㄏㄞˇ ㄓㄜˊ)
a sea blubber; a jellyfish

海戰（ㄏㄞˇ ㄓㄢˋ）
a naval battle; a sea en-
counter

海潮（ㄏㄞˇ ㄔㄠˊ）
ocean tides

海產（ㄏㄞˇ ㄔㄢˇ）
marine products; seafood

海船（ㄏㄞˇ ㄔㄨㄢˊ）
a seagoing ship

海獅（ㄏㄞˇ ㄕ）
a sea lion

海事（ㄏㄞˇ ㄕˋ）
marine affairs; maritime
affairs

海誓山盟（ㄏㄞˇ ㄕˋ ㄕㄢ ㄇㄥˊ）
to vow eternal love

海市蜃樓（ㄏㄞˇ ㄕˋ ㄕㄣˋ ㄌㄡˊ）
a mirage

海蛇（ㄏㄞˇ ㄕㄜˊ）
a sea serpent

海獸（ㄏㄞˇ ㄕㄡˋ）
a sea animal

海扇（ㄏㄞˇ ㄕㄢˋ）
a scallop

海參（ㄏㄞˇ ㄕㄣ）
a trepang; a sea cucumber; a
sea slug; *bêche-de-mer*

海參崴（ㄏㄞˇ ㄕㄣ ㄨㄞ）
Vladivostok

海神（ㄏㄞˇ ㄕㄣˊ）
Neptune; Poseidon

海商（ㄏㄞˇ ㄕㄤ）
marine commerce

海上保險（ㄏㄞˇ ㄕㄤˋ ㄅㄠˇ ㄒㄧㄢˇ）
marine insurance

海上保險單（ㄏㄞˇ ㄕㄤˋ ㄅㄠˇ ㄒㄧㄢˇ ㄉㄢ）
a marine policy

海上貿易（ㄏㄞˇ ㄕㄤˋ ㄇㄠˋ ㄧˋ）
seaborne commerce

海上法（ㄏㄞˇ ㄕㄤˋ ㄈㄚˇ）or 海洋法
（ㄏㄞˇ ㄧㄤˊ ㄈㄚˇ）
marine law; maritime law;
the law of the sea

海上作業（ㄏㄞˇ ㄕㄤˋ ㄗㄨㄛˋ ㄧㄝˋ）
operations on the sea

海上運輸（ㄏㄞˇ ㄕㄤˋ ㄩㄣˋ ㄕㄨ）
marine transportation

海水不可斗量（ㄏㄞˇ ㄕㄨㄟˇ ㄅㄨˋ ㄎㄜˇ
ㄉㄡˇ ㄌㄧㄤˊ）
Sea water is immeasurable —
Great minds cannot be fath-
omed.

海水污染（ㄏㄞˇ ㄕㄨㄟˇ ㄨ ㄖㄢˇ）
sea water pollution

海水浴（ㄏㄞˇ ㄕㄨㄟˇ ㄩˋ）

sea bathing

海藻（ㄏㄞˇ ㄗㄠˇ）
seaweed

海葬（ㄏㄞˇ ㄗㄤˋ）
burial at sea

海菜（ㄏㄞˇ ㄘㄞˋ）
(botany) an edible seaweed

海鷗（ㄏㄞˇ ㄡ）
a sea gull

海岸（ㄏㄞˇ ㄢˋ）
the coast; the seaside; the
seashore: 海岸的土地貧瘠。
The land is barren on the
coast.

海岸線（ㄏㄞˇ ㄢˋ ㄒㄧㄢˋ）
the coastal line

海牙（ㄏㄞˇ ㄧㄚˊ）
The Hague: 國際法庭位於海
牙。The International Court
of Justice is at The Hague.

海鹽（ㄏㄞˇ ㄧㄢˊ）
sea salt

海燕（ㄏㄞˇ ㄧㄢˋ）
a petrel

海晏河清（ㄏㄞˇ ㄧㄢˋ ㄏㄜˊ ㄑㄧㄥ）
time of peace and calm

海洋（ㄏㄞˇ ㄧㄤˊ）
seas and oceans; the ocean

海洋大學（ㄏㄞˇ ㄧㄤˊ ㄉㄚˋ ㄒㄩㄝˊ）
a university on the sea

海洋童子軍（ㄏㄞˇ ㄧㄤˊ ㄊㄨㄥˊ ㄗˇ ㄐㄩㄣ）
a sea scout

海洋公約（ㄏㄞˇ ㄧㄤˊ ㄍㄨㄥ ㄩㄝ）
a maritime convention

海洋性氣候（ㄏㄞˇ ㄧㄤˊ ㄒㄧㄥˋ ㄑㄧˋ ㄏㄡˋ）
the oceanic (or marine) climate

海洋學（ㄏㄞˇ ㄧㄤˊ ㄒㄩㄝˊ）
oceanography

海洋洲（ㄏㄞˇ ㄧㄤˊ ㄓㄡ）
Oceania

海洋生物（ㄏㄞˇ ㄧㄤˊ ㄕㄥ ㄨˋ）
a marine organism

海洋資源（ㄏㄞˇ ㄧㄤˊ ㄗ ㄩㄢˊ）
marine resources

海屋添籌（ㄏㄞˇ ㄨ ㄊㄧㄢ ㄔㄡˊ）
(literally) to add another
counter as the ocean once
again turned into dry land
—a conventional phrase for
wishing an aged person a
happy birthday

海霧（ㄏㄞˇ ㄨˋ）
sea fog

海外（ㄏㄞˇ ㄨㄞˋ）
overseas; abroad

海外僑胞（ㄏㄞˇ ㄨㄞˋ ㄑㄧㄠˊ ㄅㄠ）
overseas Chinese: 海外僑胞慶
祝雙十節國慶日。Overseas
Chinese celebrate the Double
Tenth, our National Day.

海味（ㄏㄞˇ ㄨㄟˋ）
seafood

海灣（ㄏㄞˇ ㄨㄢ）
a bay; a gulf

海碗（ㄏㄞˇ ㄨㄢˇ）
a big bowl

海王（ㄏㄞˇ ㄨㄤˊ）
a dominant sea power; the
king of the sea

海王星（ㄏㄞˇ ㄨㄤˊ ㄒㄧㄥ）
the planet Neptune

海隅（ㄏㄞˇ ㄩˊ）
remote regions by the sea

海芋（ㄏㄞˇ ㄩˋ）
a common calla; a lily-of-
the-Nile 亦作「馬蹄蓮」

海域（ㄏㄞˇ ㄩˋ）
a sea area; a marine area;
sea waters

海員（ㄏㄞˇ ㄩㄢˊ）
a sailor; a seaman; a mariner

海員法庭（ㄏㄞˇ ㄩㄢˊ ㄈㄚˇ ㄊㄧㄥˊ）
a marine court

海運（ㄏㄞˇ ㄩㄣˋ）
marine transportation; sea
transportation

【浸】2892 ㄐㄧㄣˋ jinn jìn
1. to dip; to immerse; to soak;
to permeate; to percolate
2. gradual; gradually

浸不透（ㄐㄧㄣˋ ㄅㄨˋ ㄊㄡˋ）
impervious to water; cannot
be soaked through

浸泡（ㄐㄧㄣˋ ㄆㄠˋ）
to soak; to immerse

浸透（ㄐㄧㄣˋ ㄊㄡˋ）
to permeate; to percolate;
soaked through: 雨水浸透了
她的衣裳。Her clothes were
soaked with rain.

浸禮（ㄐㄧㄣˋ ㄌㄧˇ）
baptism by immersion (not
by sprinkling)

浸禮會（ㄐㄧㄣˋ ㄌㄧˇ ㄏㄨㄟˋ）
the Baptist Church

浸假（ㄐㄧㄣˋ ㄐㄧㄚˇ）
gradually

浸漸（ㄐㄧㄣˋ ㄐㄧㄢˋ）
gradually; step by step; little

【水部】

by little: 他浸漸致富。He has become rich little by little.

浸信會(ㄐㄧㄣ ㄒㄧㄣ ㄏㄨㄟˋ)
the Baptist Church

浸尋(ㄐㄧㄣ ㄒㄩㄣˊ)
gradually

浸濕(ㄐㄧㄣ ㄕ)
to soak: 洗衣前先將衣服浸濕。Soak clothes before washing.

浸蝕(ㄐㄧㄣ ㄕˊ)
erosion; to erode: 流水浸蝕土壤與巖石。Running water erodes soil and rocks.

浸水(ㄐㄧㄣ ㄕㄨㄟˇ)
to immerse or dip in water; flooded; deluged; inundated: 她頭浸水。She dipped her head in the water.

浸染(ㄐㄧㄣ ㄖㄢˇ)
to contaminate or be contaminated gradually

浸入(ㄐㄧㄣ ㄖㄨˋ)
to permeate; to percolate: 水能浸入吸墨紙中。Water will permeate blotting paper.

浸潤(ㄐㄧㄣ ㄖㄨㄣˋ)
to pass in gradually; to soak: 雨水浸潤著大地。The rain is soaking into the earth.

浸漬(ㄐㄧㄣ ㄗˋ)
to soak or be soaked

浸淫(ㄐㄧㄣ ㄧㄣˊ)
①to stain gradually ②to be familiar with

浸淫羣籍(ㄐㄧㄣ ㄧㄣˊ ㄑㄩㄣˊ ㄐㄧˊ)
to read extensively over a long period of time

【浼】 2893
ㄇㄟˇ meei mei

1. to stain; to soil; to contaminate; to defile
2. full of water
3. to entrust

浼人說項(ㄇㄟˇ ㄖㄣˊ ㄕㄨㄛ ㄒㄧㄤˋ)
to request one to say a good word for

浼污(ㄇㄟˇ ㄨ)
to soil, besmirch (someone's reputation, etc.)

【涇】 2894
ㄐㄧㄥ jing jing

name of a river in Shensi (陝西)

涇河(ㄐㄧㄥ ㄏㄜˊ)
name of a river in Shensi (陝

西)

涇渭(ㄐㄧㄥ ㄨㄟˋ)
two merging rivers in Shensi, of which one is muddy and the other is clear

涇渭不分(ㄐㄧㄥ ㄨㄟˋ ㄅㄨˋ ㄈㄣ)
unable to distinguish between the clear and the muddy; unable to distinguish between good and evil

涇渭分明(ㄐㄧㄥ ㄨㄟˋ ㄈㄣ ㄇㄧㄥˊ)
as different as the waters of the Ching and the Wei—to be entirely different

【涅】 2895
(湼) ㄋㄧㄝˋ nieh niè

1. to blacken; to dye black
2. to block up

涅白(ㄋㄧㄝˋ ㄅㄞˊ)
opaque

涅槃(ㄋㄧㄝˋ ㄆㄢˊ)
Nirvana

涅面(ㄋㄧㄝˋ ㄇㄧㄢˋ)
to tattoo the face

涅齒(ㄋㄧㄝˋ ㄔˇ)
to blacken the teeth

涅字(ㄋㄧㄝˋ ㄗˋ)
tattooed letters or characters

【涉】 2896
ㄕㄜˋ sheh shè

1. to wade: 他們涉水過河。They waded across the river.
2. to cross
3. to experience
4. to involve; to entangle; to implicate
5. a Chinese family name

涉筆(ㄕㄜˋ ㄅㄧˇ)
to start to write

涉覽(ㄕㄜˋ ㄌㄢˇ)
to read casually; to skim

涉獵羣書(ㄕㄜˋ ㄌㄧㄝˋ ㄑㄩㄣˊ ㄕㄨ)
to read widely

涉歷(ㄕㄜˋ ㄌㄧˋ)
one's past experience

涉獵(ㄕㄜˋ ㄌㄧㄝˋ)
to study haphazardly; to dabble in; to browse; to read cursorily

涉及(ㄕㄜˋ ㄐㄧˊ)
to involve; to relate to; to deal with

涉禽類(ㄕㄜˋ ㄑㄧㄣˊ ㄌㄟˋ)
Gallatores

涉嫌(ㄕㄜˋ ㄒㄧㄢˊ)
to come under suspicion; to

be involved (in a crime)

涉險(ㄕㄜˋ ㄒㄧㄢˇ)
to be engaged in an adventure; to adventure: 除了他以外，沒有人敢涉險做這件事。No man would adventure it except him.

涉想(ㄕㄜˋ ㄒㄧㄤˇ)
to think about

涉事(ㄕㄜˋ ㄕˋ)
to give a narration

涉世(ㄕㄜˋ ㄕˋ)
to make one's way through the world; to get along in the world

涉世未深(ㄕㄜˋ ㄕˋ ㄨㄟˋ ㄕㄣ)
inexperienced in affairs of the world

涉足(ㄕㄜˋ ㄗㄨˊ)
to set foot in: 永遠不要涉足我們的地產。Never set foot in our property again.

涉足花叢(ㄕㄜˋ ㄗㄨˊ ㄏㄨㄚ ㄘㄨㄥˊ)
to fool around with women; to visit brothels

涉足其間(ㄕㄜˋ ㄗㄨˊ ㄑㄧˊ ㄐㄧㄢ)
to set foot there

涉訟(ㄕㄜˋ ㄙㄨㄥˋ)
to get involved in a lawsuit

【消】 2897
ㄒㄧㄠ shiau xiāo

1. to vanish; to disappear; to die out
2. to disperse; to eliminate; to remove; to alleviate; to allay; to extinguish; to quench
3. to need; to take: 來回只消三天。It takes only three days to get there and back.

消磨(ㄒㄧㄠ ㄇㄛˊ)
to while away (time): 孩子們在海灘上消磨許多下午。The children while away many afternoons on the beach.

消磨時間(ㄒㄧㄠ ㄇㄛˊ ㄕˊ ㄐㄧㄢ)
to kill time; to pass the time

消弭(ㄒㄧㄠ ㄇㄧˇ)
to put an end to; to terminate; to bring to an end

消弭禍患(ㄒㄧㄠ ㄇㄧˇ ㄏㄨㄛˋ ㄏㄨㄢˋ)
to soothe catastrophes

消滅(ㄒㄧㄠ ㄇㄧㄝˋ)
①to annihilate; to exterminate; to destroy; extermination; annihilation ②to die out

消費(ㄒㄧㄠㄈㄟˋ)
consumption; to consume

消費品(ㄒㄧㄠㄈㄟˋㄆㄧㄣˇ)
consumer goods; expendable materials

消費合作社(ㄒㄧㄠㄈㄟˋㄏㄜˊㄗㄨㄜˋㄕㄜˋ)
a consumers' cooperative

消費者(ㄒㄧㄠㄈㄟˋㄓㄜˇ)
a consumer; 生產者設法供應消費者的需要。Producers try to supply the demand of consumers.

消費水準(ㄒㄧㄠㄈㄟˋㄕㄨㄟˇㄓㄨㄣˇ)
the standard of consumption

消防(ㄒㄧㄠㄈㄤˊ)
fire fighting; prevention and extinction of fires

消防隊(ㄒㄧㄠㄈㄤˊㄉㄨㄟˋ)
a fire brigade; a fire department

消防隊員(ㄒㄧㄠㄈㄤˊㄉㄨㄟˋㄩㄢˊ)or 消防人員(ㄒㄧㄠㄈㄤˊㄖㄣˊㄩㄢˊ)
a fireman; a fire fighter

消防車(ㄒㄧㄠㄈㄤˊㄔㄜ)
a fire engine

消防雲梯(ㄒㄧㄠㄈㄤˊㄩㄣˊㄊㄧ)
a ladder truck

消毒(ㄒㄧㄠㄉㄨˊ)
to disinfect; to sterilize; to pasteurize; to decontaminate

消毒劑(ㄒㄧㄠㄉㄨˊㄐㄧˋ)
disinfectant

消毒水(ㄒㄧㄠㄉㄨˊㄕㄨㄟˇ)
antiseptic solution

消毒藥(ㄒㄧㄠㄉㄨˊㄧㄠˋ)
disinfectant; antiseptic

消停(ㄒㄧㄠㄊㄧㄥˊ)
to stop; to pause

消耗(ㄒㄧㄠㄏㄠˋ)
to consume; to expend; to exhaust

消耗品(ㄒㄧㄠㄏㄠˋㄆㄧㄣˇ)
expendables; consumables

消耗戰(ㄒㄧㄠㄏㄠˋㄓㄢˋ)
a war of attrition

消化(ㄒㄧㄠㄏㄨㄚˋ)
①to digest (food); digestion: 有些食物比其他食物容易消化。Some foods are digested more easily than others. ②to absorb mentally

消化不良(ㄒㄧㄠㄏㄨㄚˋㄅㄨˋㄌㄧㄤˊ)
indigestion; dyspepsia: 他患消化不良症。He suffers from indigestion.

消化道(ㄒㄧㄠㄏㄨㄚˋㄉㄠˋ)
the alimentary canal; the digestive tract

消化器官(ㄒㄧㄠㄏㄨㄚˋㄑㄧˋㄍㄨㄢ)
the digestive organs

消化系統(ㄒㄧㄠㄏㄨㄚˋㄒㄧˋㄊㄨㄥˇ)
the digestive apparatus or system

消火唧筒(ㄒㄧㄠㄏㄨㄛˇㄐㄧㄊㄨㄥˇ)
a fire engine

消火劑(ㄒㄧㄠㄏㄨㄛˇㄐㄧˋ)
fire-extinguishing chemicals

消火器(ㄒㄧㄠㄏㄨㄛˇㄑㄧˋ)
a fire extinguisher

消火栓(ㄒㄧㄠㄏㄨㄛˇㄕㄨㄢ)or 消防栓(ㄒㄧㄠㄈㄤˊㄕㄨㄢ)
a fireplug; a hydrant

消魂 or 銷魂(ㄒㄧㄠㄏㄨㄣˊ)
to be held spellbound (by a beautiful woman)

消極(ㄒㄧㄠㄐㄧˊ)
negative; pessimistic; passive

消極抵抗(ㄒㄧㄠㄐㄧˊㄉㄧˇㄎㄤˋ)
passive resistance

消極主義(ㄒㄧㄠㄐㄧˊㄓㄨˇㄧˋ)
pessimism; negativism; passivism

消解(ㄒㄧㄠㄐㄧㄝˇ)
to clear up; to dispel

消滅(ㄒㄧㄠㄇㄧㄝˋ)
to decrease; to lessen; to diminish; to abate; to reduce: 他的興趣消滅。His interest decreases.

消金窟(ㄒㄧㄠㄐㄧㄣㄎㄨ)
cabarets or brothels (where money is spent freely)

消氣(ㄒㄧㄠㄑㄧˋ)
to allay one's anger

消遣(ㄒㄧㄠㄑㄧㄢˇ)
pastimes; diversions; recreation: 他有時打牌消遣。He sometimes plays cards as a pastime.

消卻(ㄒㄧㄠㄑㄩㄝˋ)
to eliminate; to get rid of

消息(ㄒㄧㄠㄒㄧˊ)
news; tidings; information: 我很久沒他的消息了。I have had no news from him for a long time.

消夏(ㄒㄧㄠㄒㄧㄚˋ)
to relieve summer heat; to take a summer vacation 亦作「消暑」

消歇(ㄒㄧㄠㄒㄧㄝ)
to become extinct; to subside: 暴風雨已消歇。The storm has subsided.

消閒(ㄒㄧㄠㄒㄧㄢˊ)
to kill the leisure time: 他藉著看小說來消閒。He kills the leisure time by reading a novel.

消長(ㄒㄧㄠㄓㄤˇ)
rise and fall; vicissitudes; ups and downs; waning and waxing

消腫(ㄒㄧㄠㄓㄨㄥˇ)
to remove or reduce a swelling

消愁解悶(ㄒㄧㄠㄔㄡˊㄐㄧㄝˇㄇㄣˋ)
to quench sorrow and dissipate worry

消沉(ㄒㄧㄠㄔㄣˊ)
depressed; dejected; low-spirited: 雨天總是使我消沉。The rainy days always depressed me.

消除(ㄒㄧㄠㄔㄨˊ)
to eliminate; to get rid of

消除噪音(ㄒㄧㄠㄔㄨˊㄗㄠˋㄧㄣ)
abatement of noise

消失(ㄒㄧㄠㄕ)
to vanish; to disappear; to die out: 船漸失於地平線之外。The ship vanished beyond the horizon.

消石灰(ㄒㄧㄠㄕˊㄏㄨㄟ)
slaked lime

消逝(ㄒㄧㄠㄕˋ)
to die away; to vanish; to elapse: 音樂慢慢消逝了。The music slowly died away.

消釋(ㄒㄧㄠㄕˋ)
to clear up; to dispel

消受(ㄒㄧㄠㄕㄡˋ)
①to endure: 我無法消受他。I can't endure him. ②to enjoy

消瘦(ㄒㄧㄠㄕㄡˋ)
skinny; emaciated; wasted

消暑(ㄒㄧㄠㄕㄨˇ)
to relieve summer heat; to take a summer vacation

消暑止渴(ㄒㄧㄠㄕㄨˇㄓˇㄎㄜˇ)
(said of a drink) to relieve summer heat and quench thirst

消鎔 or 消溶(ㄒㄧㄠㄖㄨㄥˊ)

〔水部〕

〔水部〕

(said of substances) to melt

消融 (ㄒㄧㄠ ㄖㄨㄥˊ)
to melt: 在溫暖的春天冰雪全消融了。The ice melts in the warmth of spring.

消災 (ㄒㄧㄠ ㄗㄞ)
to prevent or forestall calamities

消散 (ㄒㄧㄠ ㄙㄢˋ)
to scatter and disappear; to dissipate

消夜 or 宵夜 (ㄒㄧㄠ ㄧㄝˋ)
a midnight snack

消炎 (ㄒㄧㄠ ㄧㄢˊ)
to reduce or eliminate inflammation

消炎片 (ㄒㄧㄠ ㄧㄢˊ ㄆㄧㄢˋ)
sulfaguanidine tablets; anti-inflammation pills

消炎粉 (ㄒㄧㄠ ㄧㄢˊ ㄈㄣˇ)
sulfadiazine powder; anti-inflammation powder

消音器 (ㄒㄧㄠ ㄧㄣ ㄑㄧˋ)
a silencer; a muffler 亦作「消聲器」

【涑】 2898
ㄙㄨˋ suh sù
name of a tributary of the Yellow River

涑水 (ㄙㄨˋ ㄕㄨㄟˇ)
name of a tributary of the Yellow River

【涓】 2899
ㄐㄩㄢ jiuan juān
a small stream; a rivulet; a brook

涓滴 (ㄐㄩㄢ ㄉㄧ)
trickles; drips

涓滴歸公 (ㄐㄩㄢ ㄉㄧ ㄍㄨㄟ ㄍㄨㄥ)
(said of an honest official) to hand over every cent of public money to the government treasury

涓流 (ㄐㄩㄢ ㄌㄧㄡˊ)
a small stream; a rivulet; a brook

涓毫 (ㄐㄩㄢ ㄏㄠˊ)
a modicum; a drop or a grain

涓滴 (ㄐㄩㄢ ㄉㄧ)
trickles; a small stream

涓塵 (ㄐㄩㄢ ㄔㄣˊ) or 涓埃 (ㄐㄩㄢ ㄞ)
① tiny fragments; particles ② insignificant; negligible; the least

【涎】 2900
ㄒㄧㄢˊ shyan xián

saliva

涎皮賴臉 (ㄒㄧㄢˊ ㄆㄧˊ ㄌㄞˋ ㄌㄧㄢˇ) or 涎皮涎臉 (ㄒㄧㄢˊ ㄆㄧˊ ㄒㄧㄢˊ ㄌㄧㄢˇ)
shameless; brazen

涎沫 (ㄒㄧㄢˊ ㄇㄛˋ)
saliva 亦作「涎水」

涎臉 (ㄒㄧㄢˊ ㄌㄧㄢˇ)
shameless; brazen

涎涎 (ㄒㄧㄢˊ ㄒㄧㄢˊ)
shiny; glossy

【涔】 2901
ㄘㄣˊ tsern cén
1. a puddle
2. tearful

涔涔 (ㄘㄣˊ ㄘㄣˊ)
① rainy ② distressed ③ dusky; shadowy ④ tearful

涔涔淚下 (ㄘㄣˊ ㄘㄣˊ ㄌㄟˋ ㄒㄧㄚˋ)
in tears: 我發覺她涔涔淚下。I found her in tears.

【涕】 2902
ㄊㄧˋ tih tì
1. tears
2. snivel

涕淚 (ㄊㄧˋ ㄌㄟˋ)
tears: 涕淚從她的面頰流下。The tears rolled down her cheeks.

涕零 (ㄊㄧˋ ㄌㄧㄥˊ)
to shed tears

涕泗如雨 (ㄊㄧˋ ㄙˋ ㄖㄨˊ ㄩˇ)
tears streaming down like raindrops

涕泣 (ㄊㄧˋ ㄑㄧˋ)
to weep; to cry: 她為她悲慘的命運而涕泣。She wept her sad fate.

涕泣沾襟 (ㄊㄧˋ ㄑㄧˋ ㄓㄢ ㄐㄧㄣ)
to wet the front part of one's garment with tears

涕泗滂沱 (ㄊㄧˋ ㄙˋ ㄆㄤ ㄊㄨㄛˊ)
drenched with tears and snivel

涕泗交流 (ㄊㄧˋ ㄙˋ ㄐㄧㄠ ㄌㄧㄡˊ)
Tears and snivel fall down at the same time.—crying bitterly

涕洟 (ㄊㄧˋ ㄧˊ)
tears and snivel

【浆】 2903
ㄐㄧㄤ jiang jiāng
a flood

浆水 (ㄐㄧㄤ ㄕㄨㄟˇ)
floodwater; a flood

【泣】 2904
ㄌㄧˋ lih lì
1. to arrive

2. the murmur of flowing water

涖止 (ㄌㄧˋ ㄓˇ) or 涖臨 (ㄌㄧˋ ㄌㄧㄣˊ)
to arrive; to be present

涖政 (ㄌㄧˋ ㄓㄥˋ)
to administer the government

【浞】 2905
ㄓㄨㄛˊ jwo zhuó
to soak

【浯】 2906
ㄨˊ wu wú
name of a river in Shantung

浯水 (ㄨˊ ㄕㄨㄟˇ)
name of a river in Shantung

【涌】 2907
ㄩㄥˇ yeong yǒng
to rise; to spring; to gush out; to pour out; to surge

涌湍 (ㄩㄥˇ ㄊㄨㄢ)
(said of flowing water) rapid and turbulent

涌進 (ㄩㄥˇ ㄐㄧㄣˋ)
to rush into; to swarm into

涌泉 (ㄩㄥˇ ㄑㄩㄢˊ)
a bubbling fountain

涌出 (ㄩㄥˇ ㄔㄨ)
to gush out

八畫

【涯】 2908
ㄧㄚˊ ya yá
1. water's edge; waterfront; a bank
2. a limit
3. faraway places

涯際 (ㄧㄚˊ ㄐㄧˋ)
the edge; the limit: 他的貪心是無涯際的。His greed knows no limits.

涯涘 (ㄧㄚˊ ㄙˋ)
① the edge of a body of water ② limits

涯岸 (ㄧㄚˊ ㄢˋ)
the edge; the limit: 別走得太近涯岸。Don't walk too near the edge.

【液】 2909
ㄧㄝˋ yeh yè
(讀音ㄧˋ yih yì)
liquid; juices; secretions; sap

液態 (ㄧㄝˋ ㄊㄞˋ)
(physics) the liquid state

液體 (ㄧㄝˋ ㄊㄧˇ)
liquid

液體比重計 (ㄧㄝˋ ㄊㄧˇ ㄅㄧˇ ㄓㄨㄥˋ ㄐㄧˋ)

液體動力學(ㄧㄝˋ ㄊㄧˇ ㄉㄨㄥˋ ㄌㄧˊ ㄒㄩㄝˊ)
hydrodynamics

液體靜力學(ㄧㄝˋ ㄊㄧˇ ㄐㄧㄥˋ ㄌㄧˊ ㄒㄩㄝˊ)
hydrostatics

液體燃料(ㄧㄝˋ ㄊㄧˇ ㄖㄢˊ ㄌㄧㄠˋ)
liquid fuel

液化(ㄧㄝˋ ㄏㄨㄚˋ)
to liquefy or be liquefied;
liquefaction

液化天然氣(ㄧㄝˋ ㄏㄨㄚˋ ㄊㄧㄢ ㄖㄢˊ ㄑㄧˋ)
liquefied natural gas

液汁(ㄧㄝˋ ㄓ)
liquid; fluid; juices; sap

【涪】 2910
ㄈㄨˊ fwu fú
1. name of a river in Szechwan
Province
2. name of an old administrative district

涪江(ㄈㄨˊ ㄐㄧㄤ)
name of a river in Szechwan
Province

【涵】 2911
ㄏㄢˊ harn hán
1. wet, damp and marshy
2. to contain
3. lenient and broad-minded

涵洞(ㄏㄢˊ ㄉㄨㄥˋ)
a culvert

涵管(ㄏㄢˊ ㄍㄨㄢˇ)
a drainage pipe

涵煦(ㄏㄢˊ ㄒㄩˋ)
to protect and raise (children, etc.); to cherish and
nourish

涵蓄 or 含蓄(ㄏㄢˊ ㄒㄩˋ)
(said of manners, speeches,
etc.) reserved

涵濡(ㄏㄢˊ ㄖㄨˊ)
to set a good moral example
to the younger generation

涵容(ㄏㄢˊ ㄖㄨㄥˊ)
①to contain; capable of
holding ②tolerant

涵義(ㄏㄢˊ ㄧˋ)
meaning; implication 亦作「含
義」

涵養(ㄏㄢˊ ㄧㄤˇ)
①capability to be kind,
patient, lenient, tolerant or
broad-minded under all circumstances ②to cherish and
nourish

涵泳(ㄏㄢˊ ㄩㄥˇ)
to swim

【涸】 2912
ㄏㄜˊ her hé
(舊音 ㄏㄠˋ haw hào)
drying up; dried-up; ex-
hausted

涸鮒(ㄏㄜˊ ㄈㄨˋ)
in dire poverty

涸轍(ㄏㄜˊ ㄓㄜˊ)
(literally) fish in a dried rut
—men in dire poverty

涸澤(ㄏㄜˊ ㄗㄜˊ)
a dried-up lake; to dry up a
lake: 久旱涸澤。The long
drought dried up a lake.

涸乾(ㄏㄜˊ ㄍㄢ)
dried-up; exhausted

【涿】 2913
ㄓㄨㄛ juo zhuó
1. to drip; to trickle
2. old and current names of
counties, rivers, mountains
in various places

涿鹿(ㄓㄨㄛ ㄌㄨˋ)
①name of a county in Cha-
har(察哈爾) ②name of a
mountain southeast of the
county mentioned above,
where Huang Ti (黃帝) or
the Yellow Emperor, killed
Chih Yu (蚩尤), the enemy
chieftain, after a decisive
battle

涿水(ㄓㄨㄛ ㄕㄨㄟˇ)
ancient name of a river west
of today's Cho County(涿縣)
in Hopeh Province

【淀】 2914
ㄉㄧㄢˋ diann diàn
shallow water

淀河(ㄉㄧㄢˋ ㄏㄜˊ)
also known as Ta Ching
River (大清河) in Hopeh
Province

【淄】 2915
ㄗ tzy zī
1. black
2. name of a river in Shantung
Province

淄水(ㄗ ㄕㄨㄟˇ)
a river in Shantung Prov-
ince

【涼】 2916
ㄌㄧㄤˊ liang liáng
1. cool; chilly; cold
2. thin
3. discouraged; disappointed

4. name of one of the 16 states
during the Eastern Tsin
5. a Chinese family name

涼拌(ㄌㄧㄤˊ ㄅㄢˋ)
(said of food) cold and
dressed with sauce

涼棚(ㄌㄧㄤˊ ㄆㄥˊ)
a shed, awning, etc. to provide shade in the sun: 他們
近蓋了一個涼棚。They built a
shed recently.

涼帽(ㄌㄧㄤˊ ㄇㄠˋ)
a straw hat; a summer hat:
他戴上涼帽出去了。He put on
his straw hat and went out.

涼粉兒(ㄌㄧㄤˊ ㄈㄣˇ ㄦ)
gelatin or jelly made from
agar-agar, bean flour, etc.

涼風(ㄌㄧㄤˊ ㄈㄥ)
a cool breeze; a cool wind
from the southwest

涼德(ㄌㄧㄤˊ ㄉㄜˊ)
(having) very little virtue

涼臺(ㄌㄧㄤˊ ㄊㄞˊ)
a balcony; a veranda

涼亭(ㄌㄧㄤˊ ㄊㄧㄥˊ)
(formerly) a shed along a
highway or country road, to
provide a place of rest for
travelers

涼了(ㄌㄧㄤˊ ㄌㄜ˙)
①became cold ②disap-
pointed or discouraged

涼了半截兒(ㄌㄧㄤˊ ㄌㄜ˙ ㄅㄢˋ ㄐㄧㄝˊ ㄦ)
to be greatly disappointed
or discouraged; half-beaten
psychologically

涼糕(ㄌㄧㄤˊ ㄍㄠ)
a kind of cake made of glutinous rice served cold in
summer

涼開水(ㄌㄧㄤˊ ㄎㄞ ㄕㄨㄟˇ)
cold boiled water: 我喜歡涼
開水。I like cold boiled
water.

涼快(ㄌㄧㄤˊ ㄎㄨㄞˋ)
①cool and comfortable ②
to cool oneself

涼氣(ㄌㄧㄤˊ ㄑㄧˋ)
chilly air

涼蓆(ㄌㄧㄤˊ ㄒㄧˊ)
a sleeping mat (usually
made of straw or bamboo)
used in summer

涼鞋(ㄌㄧㄤˊ ㄒㄧㄝˊ)
sandals; summer shoes; slippers

〔水
部〕

涼著了 (ㄌㄧㄤ ㄓㄜ ·ㄌㄜ)
to have caught cold: 我涼著了。I have caught cold.

涼州 (ㄌㄧㄤ ㄓㄡ)
name of the former capital of Kansu Province

涼茶 (ㄌㄧㄤ ㄔㄚˊ)
①cold tea ②(Chinese medicine) a concoction drink of many herbal ingredients to drive off the "heat" in human body

涼水 (ㄌㄧㄤ ㄕㄨㄟˇ)
cold water

涼爽 (ㄌㄧㄤ ㄕㄨㄤ)
cool and comfortable; refreshing

涼菜 (ㄌㄧㄤ ㄘㄞˋ)
vegetables eaten uncooked; cold dishes

涼颼颼 (ㄌㄧㄤ ㄙㄡ ·ㄌㄜ)
chilly: 不穿外套，我覺得涼颼颼的。Without my coat I feel chilly.

涼傘 (ㄌㄧㄤ ㄙㄢˇ)
a parasol

涼陰 (ㄌㄧㄤ ㄧㄣ)
(said of an emperor) in mourning; royal mourning 亦作「諒闇」

涼意 (ㄌㄧㄤ ㄧˋ)
to be getting chilly

【淅】 2917 ㄒㄧ shi xī
1. water for washing rice; to wash rice
2. name of a river in Honan Province

淅米 (ㄒㄧ ㄇㄧˇ)
to wash rice

淅瀝 (ㄒㄧ ㄌㄧˋ)
①the pattering of sleet; the sound of raindrops ②the sound of falling leaves in the wind

淅淅 (ㄒㄧ ㄒㄧ)
the sound of the mild wind

淅颯 (ㄒㄧ ㄙㄚˋ)
the sound of light or gentle movements

【淆】 2918 ㄧㄠˊ yau yáo
confused and disorderly; mixed

淆亂 (ㄧㄠˊ ㄌㄨㄢˋ)
to confuse; to mislead

淆亂視聽 (ㄧㄠˊ ㄌㄨㄢˋ ㄕ ㄊㄧㄥ)
to confuse and muddle the truth; to mislead the public 亦作「混淆視聽」

淆雜 (ㄧㄠˊ ㄗㄚ)
mixed; miscellaneous

【洴】 2919 ㄆㄧㄥˊ pyng píng
1. the sound of silk, etc. floating in the wind
2. to wash; to bleach

洴澼 (ㄆㄧㄥˊ ㄆㄧˋ)
the sound of silk flapping in the wind

洴澼絖 (ㄆㄧㄥˊ ㄆㄧˋ ㄎㄨㄤˋ)
to float silk on water; the washing of silk

【淌】 2920 ㄊㄤˇ taang tǎng
to flow down; to trickle; to drip

淌汗 (ㄊㄤˇ ㄏㄢˋ)
to perspire

淌眼抹淚 (ㄊㄤˇ ㄧㄢˇ ㄇㄛˇ ㄌㄟˋ)
to cry; to weep

淌眼淚 (ㄊㄤˇ ㄧㄢˇ ㄌㄟˋ)
to shed tears; to be in tears

【淖】 2921 ㄋㄠˋ naw nào
slush; mud

淖濘 (ㄋㄠˋ ㄋㄧㄥˋ)
slushy mud

【淑】 2922 ㄕㄨˊ shwu shú
1. good; pure; virtuous
2. (said of women) beautiful or charming
3. clear

淑美 (ㄕㄨˊ ㄇㄟˇ)
beautiful; beautiful and virtuous

淑妃 (ㄕㄨˊ ㄈㄟ)
a general name for the emperor's concubines

淑範 (ㄕㄨˊ ㄈㄢˋ)
a paragon of female virtues

淑德 (ㄕㄨˊ ㄉㄜˊ)
female virtues—especially chastity

淑弟 (ㄕㄨˊ ㄉㄧˋ)
my good kid brother

淑女 (ㄕㄨˊ ㄋㄩˇ)
gentlewomen; ladies; unmarried girls of respectable reputation

淑夫人 (ㄕㄨˊ ㄈㄨ ㄖㄣˊ)
a greeting (used in letters addressed to women)

淑華 (ㄕㄨˊ ㄏㄨㄚˊ)
fine and outstanding

淑化 (ㄕㄨˊ ㄏㄨㄚˋ)
teachings of virtues and goodness

淑景 (ㄕㄨˊ ㄐㄧㄥˇ)
beautiful scenery

淑均 (ㄕㄨˊ ㄐㄩㄣ)
fine and fair

淑氣 (ㄕㄨˊ ㄑㄧˋ)
the mild air in spring

淑清 (ㄕㄨˊ ㄑㄧㄥ)
(said of the sun, the moon, the sky, etc.) clear and bright

淑心 (ㄕㄨˊ ㄒㄧㄣ)
a pure heart

淑行 (ㄕㄨˊ ㄒㄧㄥˊ)
virtuous conduct or behavior

淑性 (ㄕㄨˊ ㄒㄧㄥˋ)
a gentle disposition or temperament

淑善君子 (ㄕㄨˊ ㄕㄢˋ ㄐㄩㄣ ㄗˇ)
a good man; a gentleman; a virtuous man

淑慎 (ㄕㄨˊ ㄕㄣˋ)
(said of women) gentle and respectful: 那護士甚爲淑慎。The nurse is very gentle and respectful.

淑人 (ㄕㄨˊ ㄖㄣˊ)
①a good man; a virtuous man②an honorary title bestowed on wives of ranking officials in ancient China

淑姿 (ㄕㄨˊ ㄗ)
graceful manner; graceful deportment

淑儀 (ㄕㄨˊ ㄧˊ)
a rank of court ladies in ancient China

淑婉 (ㄕㄨˊ ㄨㄢˇ)
good and gentle; elegant; refined

淑郁 (ㄕㄨˊ ㄩˋ)
aromatic

淑媛 (ㄕㄨˊ ㄩㄢˊ)
①a rank of court ladies in ancient China ②ladies; gentlewomen; virtuous women

【凄】 2923 ㄑㄧ chi qī
1. cloudy and rainy
2. cold and chilly
3. sorrow; sorrowful; miserable; desolate

凄迷（ㄑㄧ ㄇㄧˊ）
①(said of sights) cheerless; desolate; dreary ②(said of the mood) despondent; depressed

凄風苦雨（ㄑㄧ ㄈㄥ ㄎㄨˇ ㄩˇ）
chilly winds and cold rains that inspire sadness in a person's mind

凄冷（ㄑㄧ ㄌㄥˇ）
desolate; bleak

凄厲（ㄑㄧ ㄌㄧˋ）
① sad and sorrowful ② bleak and harsh

凄涼（ㄑㄧ ㄌㄧㄤˊ）or 凄凄涼涼（ㄑㄧ ㄑㄧ ㄌㄧㄤˊ ㄌㄧㄤˊ）
desolate and sorrowful; lonely; lonesome: 這個老人過着凄涼的生活。 The old man led a lonesome life.

凄惶（ㄑㄧ ㄏㄨㄤˊ）
very anxious about

凄緊（ㄑㄧ ㄐㄧㄣˇ）
harsh blowing of chilly winds

凄凄（ㄑㄧ ㄑㄧ）
①descriptive of the coldness of wind and rain; chilly ②the rising of clouds ③flowing (tears, etc.)

凄其（ㄑㄧ ㄑㄧˊ）
cold and chilly

凄切（ㄑㄧ ㄑㄧㄝˋ）or 凄凄切切（ㄑㄧ ㄑㄧ ㄑㄧㄝˋ ㄑㄧㄝˋ）
bitter and sorrowful

凄切動人（ㄑㄧ ㄑㄧㄝˋ ㄉㄨㄥˋ ㄖㄣˊ）
sadly moving

凄楚（ㄑㄧ ㄔㄨˇ）
sad and sorrowful; heartrending; heartbreaking

凄愴（ㄑㄧ ㄔㄨㄤˋ）
heartrending; heartbreaking 亦作「悽愴」

凄然（ㄑㄧ ㄖㄢˊ）
very sorrowful; very sad

凄慘（ㄑㄧ ㄘㄢˇ）or 凄凄慘慘（ㄑㄧ ㄑㄧ ㄘㄢˇ ㄘㄢˇ）
heartrending; heartbreaking

凄咽（ㄑㄧ ㄧㄝˋ）
a low and sad voice; to sob while speaking

凄豔（ㄑㄧ ㄧㄢˋ）
(said of a love story) sad and beautiful

【淋】 2924
1. （ㄌㄧㄣˊ linn lín）

1. to soak with water; to drip
2. gonorrhea

淋巴（ㄌㄧㄣˊ ㄅㄚ）
lymph

淋巴管（ㄌㄧㄣˊ ㄅㄚ ㄍㄨㄢˇ）
lymphatic ducts; lymphatics

淋巴腺（ㄌㄧㄣˊ ㄅㄚ ㄒㄧㄢˋ）
lymphatic glands

淋巴腺結核（ㄌㄧㄣˊ ㄅㄚ ㄒㄧㄢˋ ㄐㄧㄝˊ ㄏㄜˊ）
lymphadenitis tuberculosis

淋巴腺炎（ㄌㄧㄣˊ ㄅㄚ ㄒㄧㄢˋ ㄧㄢˊ）
lymphadenitis

淋病（ㄌㄧㄣˊ ㄅㄧㄥˋ）
gonorrhea 亦作「淋症」

淋漓（ㄌㄧㄣˊ ㄌㄧˊ）
dripping wet

淋漓（ㄌㄧㄣˊ ㄌㄧˊ）
①dripping wet ②(now rarely) long

淋漓盡致（ㄌㄧㄣˊ ㄌㄧˊ ㄐㄧㄣˋ ㄓˋ）
(to narrate, describe, argue, etc.) thoroughly; completely

淋淋（ㄌㄧㄣˊ ㄌㄧㄣˊ）
dripping wet; pouring (rain, etc.)

淋鈴（ㄌㄧㄣˊ ㄌㄧㄥˊ）
the sound of splattering rains

淋漉（ㄌㄧㄣˊ ㄌㄨˋ）
dripping wet; pouring (rain, etc.)

淋菌（ㄌㄧㄣˊ ㄐㄩㄣˋ）
gonococci

淋濕（ㄌㄧㄣˊ ㄕ）or（ㄌㄧㄣˊ ㄕ）
to be soaked, splashed wet (by rain, etc.): 我們課身淋濕了。 Our clothes were soaked through.

淋雨（ㄌㄧㄣˊ ㄩˇ）or（ㄌㄧㄣˊ ㄩˇ）
to get wet in the rain; to be exposed to the rain

淋浴（ㄌㄧㄣˊ ㄩˋ）
a shower; a shower bath: 他們生早晨淋浴。 They have a shower in the morning.亦作「淋浴浴」

【淋】 2924
2. （ㄌㄧㄣˋ linn lìn）
to filter; to strain

淋酒（ㄌㄧㄣˋ ㄐㄧㄡˇ）
to strain wine

【淘】 2925
ㄊㄠˊ taur táo
1. to wash (especially rice); to wash in a sieve
2. to dredge; to scour

3. to eliminate the inferior (by exams, contests, etc.)

淘米（ㄊㄠˊ ㄇㄧˇ）
to wash rice

淘汰（ㄊㄠˊ ㄊㄞˋ）
①to eliminate inferior contestants, goods, etc. ②elimination

淘汰法（ㄊㄠˊ ㄊㄞˋ ㄈㄚˇ）
(mining) concentration

淘汰賽（ㄊㄠˊ ㄊㄞˋ ㄙㄞˋ）
elimination series

淘淘（ㄊㄠˊ ㄊㄠˊ）
①water flowing ②to wash

淘濾（ㄊㄠˊ ㄌㄩˋ）
①to dredge ②to wash

淘換（ㄊㄠˊ ㄏㄨㄢˋ）
to search for; to select; to choose

淘金（ㄊㄠˊ ㄐㄧㄣ）
①to pan gold ②to make quick bucks or high profits

淘金者（ㄊㄠˊ ㄐㄧㄣ ㄓㄜˇ）
a gold digger

淘井（ㄊㄠˊ ㄐㄧㄥˇ）
to wash or scour a well

淘氣（ㄊㄠˊ ㄑㄧˋ）
naughty, mischievous or annoying (children): 他弟弟像猴子一樣淘氣。 His brother is as mischievous as a monkey.

淘氣鬼（ㄊㄠˊ ㄑㄧˋ ㄍㄨㄟˇ）
a mischievous imp

淘沙揀金（ㄊㄠˊ ㄕㄚ ㄐㄧㄢˇ ㄐㄧㄣ）
to wash the sand for gold —to choose or search for the very best

淘神（ㄊㄠˊ ㄕㄣˊ）
①annoyed as a result of a child's naughtiness or mischief ②worrying; irritating; troublesome

【淚】 2926
（ㄌㄟˋ）ley lèi
tears

淚滴（ㄌㄟˋ ㄉㄧ）
teardrops 亦作「淚點」

淚囊（ㄌㄟˋ ㄋㄤˊ）
a lachrymal sac

淚河（ㄌㄟˋ ㄏㄜˊ）
a river of tears—very sad; deep sorrow

淚痕（ㄌㄟˋ ㄏㄣˊ）
traces of tears

淚下沾襟（ㄌㄟˋ ㄒㄧㄚˋ ㄓㄢ ㄐㄧㄣ）

〔水部〕

（水部）

to wet the front part of one's garment with tears

淚腺(カㄟ ㄒ ㄧㄢˋ)
a lachrymal gland

淚珠(カㄟ ㄓㄨ)
teardrops: 淚珠從她臉頰流下。
Teardrops fell down her cheeks.

淚竹(カㄟ ㄓㄨˊ)
another name of 斑竹. the speckled bamboo

淚水(カㄟ ㄕㄨㄟˇ)
tears

淚人兒(カㄟ ㄖㄣˊ ㄦ)
one who is crying bitterly; a weeping Niobe; one who is all tears

淚如泉湧(カㄟ ㄖㄨˊ ㄑㄩㄢˊ ㄩㄥˇ)
tears welling up like a fountain: 她淚如泉湧。Her tears well up like a fountain.

淚如雨下(カㄟ ㄖㄨˊ ㄩˇ ㄒㄧㄚˋ)
The tears come down like rain.

淚容滿面(カㄟ ㄖㄨㄥˊ ㄇㄢˇ ㄇㄧㄢˋ)
tearful look; lachrymal countenance

淚潸潸(カㄟ ㄕㄢ ㄕㄢ)
tears falling down abundantly

淚眼(カㄟ ㄧㄢˇ)
teary eyes

淚眼模糊(カㄟ ㄧㄢˇ ㄇㄛˊ ㄏㄨˊ)
eyes blurred by tears

淚汪汪的(カㄟ ㄨㄤ ㄨㄤ ˙ㄉㄜ)
tearful; brimming with tears

【淝】 2927
ㄈㄟˊ feir féi
name of a river in Anhwei Province

淝水(ㄈㄟˊ ㄕㄨㄟˇ)
the Fei River in Anhwei Province

淝水之戰(ㄈㄟˊ ㄕㄨㄟˇ ㄓ ㄓㄢˋ)
the Battle of the Fei River in which Hsieh Hsüan (謝玄) defeated Fu Chien (苻堅), thus ensuring the security of the Eastern Tsin (東晉) Dynasty against invasion from the north

【淙】 2928
ㄘㄨㄥˊ tsorng cóng
the sound of flowing water; water flowing

淙琤(ㄘㄨㄥˊ ㄔㄥ) or 淙靜(ㄘㄨㄥˊ ㄐㄧㄥˋ)

the tinkling sound of gems

淙淙(ㄘㄨㄥˊ ㄘㄨㄥˊ)
①the gurgling sound of flowing water—especially a creek ②the tinkling sound of metals or gems

【湍】 2929
ㄊㄨㄢ tean tuān
turbid; muddy

湍汩(ㄊㄨㄢ ㄍㄨˇ)
to submerge

湍涊(ㄊㄨㄢ ㄋㄧㄢˇ)
dirty; filthy

【淞】 2930
ㄙㄨㄥ song sōng
name of a river in Kiangsu Province

淞江(ㄙㄨㄥ ㄐㄧㄤ)
the Sung River in Kiangsu

【淡】 2931
ㄉㄢˋ dann dàn
1. weak or thin (tea, coffee, etc.)
2. tasteless; without enough salt; insipid
3. off-season—when business is poor; dull; slack
4. light (in color); slight
5. without worldly desires
6. same as 氮—nitrogen

淡泊(ㄉㄢˋ ㄅㄛˊ)
to lead a tranquil life without worldly desires

淡泊名利(ㄉㄢˋ ㄅㄛˊ ㄇㄧㄥˊ ㄌㄧˋ)
to be indifferent to fame and wealth 亦作「澹泊名利」

淡薄(ㄉㄢˋ ㄅㄛˊ)
①thin; weak; deficient; light ②to become indifferent; to flag ③dim; faint

淡漠(ㄉㄢˋ ㄇㄛˋ)
indifference; aloofness; not interested or enthusiastic: 她對他很淡漠。She treated him with indifference.

淡墨(ㄉㄢˋ ㄇㄛˋ)
light ink

淡飯(ㄉㄢˋ ㄈㄢˋ)
simple food

淡淡(ㄉㄢˋ ㄉㄢˋ)
①light; slight ②(now rarely) water flowing smoothly

淡綠(ㄉㄢˋ ㄌㄩˋ)
light green

淡化(ㄉㄢˋ ㄏㄨㄚˋ)
①desalination ②to play down; to water down

淡話(ㄉㄢˋ ㄏㄨㄚˋ)
an insipid talk or conversation

淡黃(ㄉㄢˋ ㄏㄨㄤˊ)
light yellow

淡紅(ㄉㄢˋ ㄏㄨㄥˊ)
light red; pink: 她穿淡紅色的衣服。She is dressed in pink

淡紅銀礦(ㄉㄢˋ ㄏㄨㄥˊ ㄧㄣˊ ㄎㄨㄤˋ)
proustite

淡季(ㄉㄢˋ ㄐㄧˋ)
slack seasons or off seasons (for business): 淡季旅館收費較低。Hotel charges are lower in the slack season.

淡酒(ㄉㄢˋ ㄐㄧㄡˇ)
weak wine

淡江大學(ㄉㄢˋ ㄐㄧㄤ ㄉㄚˋ ㄒㄩㄝˊ)
Tamkang University

淡妝濃抹(ㄉㄢˋ ㄓㄨㄤ ㄋㄨㄥˊ ㄇㄛˇ)
a woman's make-up—originally from a line of a poem by Su Shih (蘇軾): "Whether in light or heavy make-up, she looks as becoming as ever."

淡水(ㄉㄢˋ ㄕㄨㄟˇ)
①fresh water—as opposite to salt water or seawater ②Tamsui, a seaside resort in northern Taiwan

淡水湖(ㄉㄢˋ ㄕㄨㄟˇ ㄏㄨˊ)
freshwater lakes

淡水魚(ㄉㄢˋ ㄕㄨㄟˇ ㄩˊ)
fishes grown in fresh water

淡水漁業(ㄉㄢˋ ㄕㄨㄟˇ ㄩˊ ㄧㄝˋ)
freshwater fishing

淡然(ㄉㄢˋ ㄖㄢˊ)
indifferent; not to care

淡然置之(ㄉㄢˋ ㄖㄢˊ ㄓˋ ㄓ)
to care very little about the matter; to take it easy; unruffled

淡菜(ㄉㄢˋ ㄘㄞˋ)
dried meat of a species of mussel, Mytilus crassitesta

淡色(ㄉㄢˋ ㄙㄜˋ)
a light color; light-colored: 他喜歡淡色的衣服。He likes light-colored clothes.

淡掃蛾眉(ㄉㄢˋ ㄙㄠˇ ㄜˊ ㄇㄟˊ)
(said of a woman)to apply a light make-up

淡而無味(ㄉㄢˋ ㄦˊ ㄨˊ ㄨㄟˋ)
①tasteless (food, etc.)②insipid (stories, talks, conversations, etc.)

淡雅（ㄉㄢ ㄧㄚˇ）
(said of attire, decoration, etc.) light, simple but graceful or elegant

淡忘（ㄉㄢ ㄨㄤˋ）
to fade from one's memory

淡月（ㄉㄢ ㄩㄝˋ）
a slack month (for business, etc.)

【淤】 2932　ㄩ iu yü
1. muddy sediment; mud; sediment
2. stalemated; blocked; to silt up

淤點（ㄩ ㄉㄧㄢˇ）
(pathology) petechiae

淤泥（ㄩ ㄋㄧˊ）
sediment at the bottom of a river, ditch, etc.; silt: 港口為淤泥所塞。 The harbor is being choked up with silt.

淤溉（ㄩ ㄍㄞˋ）
to irrigate farmland with muddy water which is nourishing to the plants

淤河（ㄩ ㄏㄜˊ）
rivers or streams choked up by silt of mud and sand

淤積（ㄩ ㄐㄧ）
to silt up; to clog up: 沙土淤積於麥田上。 Sand silted over wheat fields.

淤血（ㄩ ㄒㄧㄝˇ）
blood clot

淤滯（ㄩ ㄓˋ）
clogged; choked

淤濁（ㄩ ㄓㄨㄛˊ）
muddy and turbid

淤沙（ㄩ ㄕㄚ）
silt

淤塞（ㄩ ㄙㄜˋ）
to silt up; to block; blocked or choked by silt

淤關（ㄩ ㄍㄨㄢ）
blocked or choked by silt

淤塞（ㄩ ㄙㄜˋ）
silted; blocked

【淦】 2933　ㄍㄢˋ gann gòn
1. water leaking into a boat
2. name of a river in Kiangsi Province

【漻】 2934　ㄌㄨˊ luh lú
1. clear water
2. to drip; to strain

3. name of a tributary of the Hsiang River (湘江) in Hunan Province
4. a Chinese family name

漻漻
damp and wet; dripping

漻水（ㄌㄨˊ ㄕㄨㄟˇ）
name of a tributary of the Hsiang River (湘江) in Hunan Province

【淩】 2935　ㄌㄧㄥˊ ling líng
1. to pass; to traverse; to cross
2. to intrude; to insult or bully
3. a Chinese family name

【淪】 2936　ㄌㄨㄣˊ luen lún
1. to sink into oblivion, ruin, etc.; to fall; engulfed or lost; submerged
2. ripples; eddying water

淪敗（ㄌㄨㄣˊ ㄅㄞˋ）
(said of a nation) to fall; lost or ruined

淪滅（ㄌㄨㄣˊ ㄇㄧㄝˋ）
totally lost or ruined; to sink into total disintegration

淪替（ㄌㄨㄣˊ ㄊㄧˋ）
to get weaker and disintegrate gradually

淪落（ㄌㄨㄣˊ ㄌㄨㄛˋ）
to get lost (in a strange land, etc.)

淪迴（ㄌㄨㄣˊ ㄏㄨㄟˊ）
an eddy

淪棄（ㄌㄨㄣˊ ㄑㄧˋ）
rejected and discarded

淪陷（ㄌㄨㄣˊ ㄒㄧㄢˋ）
(said of a territory) occupied by or lost to the enemy

淪陷區（ㄌㄨㄣˊ ㄒㄧㄢˋ ㄑㄩ）
territory occupied by the enemy; enemy occupied area

淪胥（ㄌㄨㄣˊ ㄒㄩ）
to drag each other to total ruin; to be involved in ruin together

淪入風塵（ㄌㄨㄣˊ ㄖㄨˋ ㄈㄥ ㄔㄣˊ）
(said of women) to fall into professions not socially respectable—as prostitution, etc.

淪喪（ㄌㄨㄣˊ ㄙㄤˋ）
to be lost or ruined

淪為（ㄌㄨㄣˊ ㄨㄟˊ）
to become what is way

below the social position one used to occupy

淪亡（ㄌㄨㄣˊ ㄨㄤˊ）
lost or ruined

【淨】 2937　ㄐㄧㄥˋ jinq jìng
1. clean; pure; to cleanse; to purify
2. empty; vain
3. a role in Chinese opera with a heavily painted face
4. completely; clean
5. only; merely; nothing but
6. net (income, profit, etc.)

淨本（ㄐㄧㄥˋ ㄅㄣˇ）
(Tang Dynasty) a clean and neat copy of an original work

淨瓶（ㄐㄧㄥˋ ㄆㄧㄥˊ）
a vessel used by Buddhists for washing hands

淨面（ㄐㄧㄥˋ ㄇㄧㄢˋ）
to wash one's face

淨土（ㄐㄧㄥˋ ㄊㄨˇ）
sukhavati; the land of the pure—the land of Buddha

淨土宗（ㄐㄧㄥˋ ㄊㄨˇ ㄗㄨㄥ）
the Pure-land Sect of Buddhism whose chief tenet is salvation by faith in Amitabha, also known as the Lotus Sect (蓮花宗 or 蓮宗)

淨利（ㄐㄧㄥˋ ㄌㄧˋ）
net profit

淨化（ㄐㄧㄥˋ ㄏㄨㄚˋ）
to purify

淨價（ㄐㄧㄥˋ ㄐㄧㄚˋ）
a net price

淨角（ㄐㄧㄥˋ ㄐㄧㄠˇ）
a male role in Chinese opera with a heavily painted face

淨盡（ㄐㄧㄥˋ ㄐㄧㄣˋ）
completely exhausted (as stocks, supplies, etc.)

淨君（ㄐㄧㄥˋ ㄐㄩㄣ）
another name of a broom

淨值（ㄐㄧㄥˋ ㄓˊ）
net value

淨宅（ㄐㄧㄥˋ ㄓㄞˊ）
to exorcize evil spirits from a haunted house

淨賺（ㄐㄧㄥˋ ㄓㄨㄢˋ）
net earnings

淨重（ㄐㄧㄥˋ ㄓㄨㄥˋ）
net weight 亦作「淨量」

淨手（ㄐㄧㄥˋ ㄕㄡˇ）
①to wash one's hands ②to

（水部）

淨身(ㄐㄧㄥ ㄕㄣ)
to castrate; castration

淨身人(ㄐㄧㄥ ㄕㄣ ㄖㄣˊ)
a castrated man

淨剩(ㄐㄧㄥ ㄕㄥˋ)
only: 屋裡淨剩他一個人。Only he is left in the room.

淨水(ㄐㄧㄥ ㄕㄨㄟˇ)
clean water

淨存(ㄐㄧㄥ ㄘㄨㄣˊ)or淨餘(ㄐㄧㄥ ㄩˊ)
net balance

淨眼(ㄐㄧㄥ ㄧㄢˇ)
eyes which can see gods and deities

【淬】 2938
ㄘㄨㄟˋ tsuey cuì

1. to temper iron or steel for making swords, etc. (also used figuratively)

2. to dip into water; to soak; to dye

淬勉(ㄘㄨㄟˋ ㄇㄧㄢˇ)
to persuade; to urge and advise; to arouse to action: 他淬勉我努力用功。He persuaded me to work hard.

淬勵(ㄘㄨㄟˋ ㄌㄧˋ)
to arouse to action; to encourage

淬礪(ㄘㄨㄟˋ ㄌㄧˋ)
①to temper and grind ②to train or discipline oneself (toward a goal)

【淮】 2939
ㄏㄨㄞˊ hwai huái

name of a river flowing from West China into the Gulf of Pohai

淮南(ㄏㄨㄞˊ ㄋㄢˊ)
the region south of the Huai River

淮南鷄犬(ㄏㄨㄞˊ ㄋㄢˊ ㄐㄧ ㄑㄩㄢˇ)
humble followers waiting for a pull from their superior—Legend has it that Liu An, King of Huai Nan(淮南王劉安), achieved immortality and that his chickens and dogs, having eaten the leftovers of his elixir, followed him into heaven.

淮南子(ㄏㄨㄞˊ ㄋㄢˊ ㄗˇ)
the title of a book on philosophy by Liu An, King of Huai Nan (淮南王劉安)of the Han Dynasty

淮軍(ㄏㄨㄞˊ ㄐㄩㄣ)
a military force trained and commanded by Li Hungchang (李鴻章), which played a major role in the suppression of the Taiping Rebellion (so named because the soldiers were recruited in the valley of the Huai River)

淮枳(ㄏㄨㄞˊ ㄓˇ)
Things appear differently under different situations.

淮水(ㄏㄨㄞˊ ㄕㄨㄟˇ)or淮河(ㄏㄨㄞˊ ㄏㄜˊ)
the Huai River, which begins in Honan Province, runs through Anhwei and empties into the sea on the Kiangsu coast

淮鹽(ㄏㄨㄞˊ ㄧㄢˊ)
salt produced in the Huai region

淮陰侯(ㄏㄨㄞˊ ㄧㄣ ㄏㄡˊ)
General Han Hsin (韓信) of the Han Dynasty, who was conferred the title Marquis of Huai Yin

【淫】 2940
ㄧㄣˊ yn yín

1. licentious; lewd; lascivious; libidinous; dissolute

2. obscene; pornographic

3. to seduce; to debauch; to tempt; temptation

4. things related to sexual desire and behavior

淫奔(ㄧㄣˊ ㄅㄣ)
to elope; elopement

淫朋狎友(ㄧㄣˊ ㄆㄥˊ ㄒㄧㄚˊ ㄧㄡˇ)
debauching company

淫靡(ㄧㄣˊ ㄇㄧˊ)
extravagant; extravagance

淫放(ㄧㄣˊ ㄈㄤˋ)
to give free rein to the passion

淫風(ㄧㄣˊ ㄈㄥ)
wanton customs; libidinous practices; dissoluteness and debauchery that prevail

淫風甚熾(ㄧㄣˊ ㄈㄥ ㄕㄣˋ ㄔˋ)
Wanton custom is in a blaze.

淫夫淫婦(ㄧㄣˊ ㄈㄨ ㄧㄣˊ ㄈㄨˋ)
a man and a woman having illicit liaison; adulterers and adulteresses

淫蕩(ㄧㄣˊ ㄉㄤˋ)
(especially said of women) lewd and libidinous; lascivious and wanton; profligate

淫愚(ㄧㄣˊ ㄩˋ)
wanton and debauching

淫念(ㄧㄣˊ ㄋㄧㄢˋ)
carnal desires; lust

淫謔(ㄧㄣˊ ㄒㄩㄝˋ)
obscene jesting

淫樂(ㄧㄣˊ ㄌㄜˋ)
to give free rein to sexual desire; wantonness; carnal pleasures

淫潦(ㄧㄣˊ ㄌㄠˇ)
floods caused by excessive rains or overflowing rivers

淫亂(ㄧㄣˊ ㄌㄨㄢˋ)
debauchery

淫畫(ㄧㄣˊ ㄏㄨㄚˋ)
pornographic or obscene pictures

淫穢(ㄧㄣˊ ㄏㄨㄟˋ)
dirty (books, pictures, language, scenes); obscene

淫巧(ㄧㄣˊ ㄑㄧㄠˇ)
clever in improper ways; lewdly suave

淫戲(ㄧㄣˊ ㄒㄧˋ)
①sexual intercourse ②pornographic plays, shows, etc.

淫刑(ㄧㄣˊ ㄒㄧㄥˊ)
to mete out punishments freely or without any consideration; punishments meted out in this manner

淫行(ㄧㄣˊ ㄒㄧㄥˊ)
licentious conduct

淫學(ㄧㄣˊ ㄒㄩㄝˊ)
improper learning; unorthodox learning

淫視(ㄧㄣˊ ㄕˋ)
to make sheep's eyes; a come-hither look; lascivious looks

淫書(ㄧㄣˊ ㄕㄨ)
obscene books

淫泆(ㄧㄣˊ ㄧˋ)
①flooding waters ②saliva-like excretion during or before sexual intercourse

淫人妻女(ㄧㄣˊ ㄖㄣˊ ㄑㄧ ㄋㄩˇ)
to violate another's wife and daughters (will have one's own violated)

淫辭(ㄧㄣˊ ㄘˊ)

obscene expressions; wanton language

淫洗(ㄧㄣ ㄒㄧˇ)
debauchery; wantonness

淫業(ㄧㄣ ㄧㄝˋ)
the profession of prostitution

淫娃蕩子(ㄧㄣ ㄨㄚˊ ㄉㄤˋ ㄗˇ)
fast women and lewd men

淫威(ㄧㄣ ㄨㄟ)
① imposing or awe-inspiring power ② excessive use of powers and punishments

淫雨(ㄧㄣ ㄩˇ)
incessant rains; excessive rains: 淫雨為災。Excessive rains become a calamity.

淫慾(ㄧㄣ ㄩˋ)
wanton desires; sexual desire

淫慾過度(ㄧㄣ ㄩˋ ㄍㄨㄛˋ ㄉㄨˋ)
to abandon oneself to the passion; excessive indulgence in the pursuit of pleasures

【淳】 2941
ㄔㄨㄣˊ chwen chún

1. pure; clean; simple; sincere; honest
2. a couple or pair (of chariots)
3. big; great

淳樸(ㄔㄨㄣˊ ㄆㄨˊ)
sincere and simple (villagers, etc.); honest; unsophisticated: 他是個淳樸的莊稼人。He is an honest peasant.

淳風(ㄔㄨㄣˊ ㄈㄥ)
simple and sincere tradition or custom

淳良(ㄔㄨㄣˊ ㄌㄧㄤˊ)
pure, simple and honest

淳古(ㄔㄨㄣˊ ㄍㄨˇ)
as simple and pure as in ancient times

淳和(ㄔㄨㄣˊ ㄏㄜˊ)
simple and gentle

淳厚(ㄔㄨㄣˊ ㄏㄡˋ)
simple and sincere

淳質(ㄔㄨㄣˊ ㄓˊ)
the quality of being simple and pure

淳粹(ㄔㄨㄣˊ ㄘㄨㄟˋ)
pure; unadulterated

【淵】 2942
ㄩㄢ iuan yuān

1. deep waters; a gulf; an abyss
2. profound (learning); depth; profundity; erudition; extensive
3. a Chinese family name

淵博(ㄩㄢ ㄅㄛˊ)
(said of learning) erudite; erudition; profound and extensive: 他的學問淵博。He has profound and extensive knowledge.

淵海(ㄩㄢ ㄏㄞˇ)
(literally) deep sea—deep and vast; profound and extensive

淵泓(ㄩㄢ ㄏㄨㄥˊ)
profound and vast; deep and extensive

淵玄(ㄩㄢ ㄒㄩㄢˊ)
profundity; depth

淵沖(ㄩㄢ ㄔㄨㄥ)
deep but open-minded

淵識(ㄩㄢ ㄕˋ)
erudite and sophisticated; well versed in learning and rich in experience

淵藪(ㄩㄢ ㄙㄡˇ)
the place where things or persons flock together—a haunt or hotbed

淵詣(ㄩㄢ ㄧˋ)
deep or profound meaning

淵源(ㄩㄢ ㄩㄢˊ)
① the source; the origin or background ② relationship

淵深(ㄩㄢ ㄕㄣ)
deep; profound

【深】 2943
ㄕㄣ shen shēn

1. deep; depth
2. profound; mysterious; difficult; abstruse
3. close; intimate
4. very; extremely

深壁高壘(ㄕㄣ ㄅㄧˋ ㄍㄠ ㄌㄟˇ)
strong defense works

深表同情(ㄕㄣ ㄅㄧㄠˇ ㄊㄨㄥˊ ㄑㄧㄥˊ)
to sympathize with; very sympathetic to; to express deep sympathy: 我對你的傷心事深表同情。I sympathize with you in your grief.

深不可測(ㄕㄣ ㄅㄨˋ ㄎㄜˇ ㄘㄜˋ)
immeasurable depth or profundity; extremely abstruse; unfathomable; to be an enigma

深謀遠慮(ㄕㄣ ㄇㄡˊ ㄩㄢˇ ㄌㄩˋ)
to think and plan far ahead; great prudence; foresight

深莽(ㄕㄣ ㄇㄤˇ)
land with dense tall grass

深渺(ㄕㄣ ㄇㄧㄠˇ)
deep and far

深妙(ㄕㄣ ㄇㄧㄠˋ)
abstruse and uncanny; profound

深明大義(ㄕㄣ ㄇㄧㄥˊ ㄉㄚˋ ㄧˋ)
to have a firm grasp of what is right and wrong; to forget self-interest in the face of an event of great significance

深得民心(ㄕㄣ ㄉㄜˊ ㄇㄧㄣˊ ㄒㄧㄣ)
well-received; to win strong popular support: 我們政府深得民心。Our government wins strong popular support.

深度(ㄕㄣ ㄉㄨˋ)
① depth (of a river, box, tank, etc.) ② profundity (of learning, etc.) ③ understanding (of the ways of the world); sophistication

深談(ㄕㄣ ㄊㄢˊ)
intimate talks

深痛(ㄕㄣ ㄊㄨㄥˋ)
deep grief; to lament deeply

深念(ㄕㄣ ㄋㄧㄢˋ)
to remember or consider; to think deeply

深藍(ㄕㄣ ㄌㄢˊ)
dark blue

深慮(ㄕㄣ ㄌㄩˋ)
deep worry or consideration; to think far ahead

深溝高壘(ㄕㄣ ㄍㄡ ㄍㄠ ㄌㄟˇ) or 深塹高壘
a deep ditch and a high wall—strong defense works or fortifications

深感(ㄕㄣ ㄍㄢˇ)
to feel keenly or deeply

深耕(ㄕㄣ ㄍㄥ)
to plow deep

深更半夜(ㄕㄣ ㄍㄥ ㄅㄢˋ ㄧㄝˋ)
deep in the night; midnight: 他們工作至深更半夜。They worked until midnight.

深痼(ㄕㄣ ㄍㄨˋ)
chronic or deep-rooted (disease, habit, etc.)

〔水部〕

〔水部〕

深閨 (アㄣ «ㄍㄟ)
inner chambers or apartments where the women of the house live

深宮 (アㄣ «ㄨㄥ)
the forbidden palace; the harem

深刻 (アㄣ ㄎㄜ)
①deeply meaningful; profound significance (views, comments, etc.); poignant; incisive: 他的批評很深刻. His criticism is very penetrating. ②to carve deep (in my heart); deep (impression, etc.)

深坑 (アㄣ ㄎㄥ)
a deep pit; an abyss

深海 (アㄣ ㄏㄞˇ)
deep sea

深海動物 (アㄣ ㄏㄞˇ ㄉㄨㄥˋ ㄨˋ)
abyssal faunae

深海漁業 (アㄣ ㄏㄞˇ ㄩˊ ㄧㄝˋ)
deep-sea fishery

深厚 (アㄣ ㄏㄡˋ)
①long and close (friendship, relationship, etc.): 我們有深厚的友誼. We have long and close friendship. ②profound (learning, training, etc.) ③deep-seated; solid

深恨 (アㄣ ㄏㄣˋ)
①deep hatred ②to regret very much

深呼吸 (アㄣ ㄏㄨ ㄒㄧ)
a deep breath; to breathe deeply

深紅 (アㄣ ㄏㄨㄥˊ)
dark red

深交 (アㄣ ㄐㄧㄠ)
long, intimate friendship

深究 (アㄣ ㄐㄧㄡˋ)
to study, deliberate, search or delve into something deeply: 對這個問題不必深究. You don't have to delve into the subject deeply.

深井 (アㄣ ㄐㄧㄥˇ)
a deep well

深居簡出 (アㄣ ㄐㄩ ㄐㄧㄢˇ ㄔㄨ)
to lead a secluded life; to live in seclusion or solitude

深切 (アㄣ ㄑㄧㄝˋ)
deeply; sincerely; penetrating; intensively; thorough; intensely

深秋 (アㄣ ㄑㄧㄡ)
late fall; late autumn

深淺 (アㄣ ㄑㄧㄢˇ)
①deep or shallow; depth ②(said of colors) deep or light ③(good or evil) intentions

深情 (アㄣ ㄑㄧㄥˊ)
deep affection or love: 他對他太太懷著深情. He has deep affection for his wife.

深情厚誼 (アㄣ ㄑㄧㄥˊ ㄏㄡˋ ㄧˋ)
long and close friendship

深趣 (アㄣ ㄑㄩˋ)
deep interest; enthusiasm: 我對音樂有深趣. I have deep interest in music.

深悉 (アㄣ ㄒㄧ)
to realize fully; to know thoroughly; fully aware

深宵 (アㄣ ㄒㄧㄠ)
deep in the night

深心 (アㄣ ㄒㄧㄣ)
deep in one's heart; deep thoughts; profound meaning

深信 (アㄣ ㄒㄧㄣˋ)
to believe strongly; deep faith; firmly convinced

深信不疑 (アㄣ ㄒㄧㄣˋ ㄅㄨˋ ㄧˊ)
to believe without a shadow of doubt

深省 (アㄣ ㄒㄧㄥˇ)
to understand after soul-searching; to make a thorough self-examination

深知 (アㄣ ㄓ)
to know thoroughly; well aware; to realize fully: 他深知其錯. He fully realizes his error.

深致 (アㄣ ㄓˋ)
to convey or express sincerely or deeply

深摯 (アㄣ ㄓˋ)
close or intimate (friendship, etc.); deep (affection); sincere: 他們兩友誼深摯. There was intimate friendship between them.

深宅大院 (アㄣ ㄓㄞˊ ㄉㄚˋ ㄩㄢˋ)
a large house and a big yard —the house of the wealthy

深池 (アㄣ ㄔˊ)
①a deep pond ②a deep moat

深讎 or 深仇 (アㄣ ㄔㄡˊ)
deep animosity or hatred

深仇大恨 (アㄣ ㄔㄡˊ ㄉㄚˋ ㄏㄣˋ)
a deep-seated hatred

深沈 (アㄣ ㄔㄣˊ)
①dark: 天色漸深沈. It is getting dark. ②(said of a person) reserved; impenetrable; unfathomable; calm; composed; serious: 她這人很深沈. She is impenetrable.

深長 (アㄣ ㄔㄤˊ)
profound (significance, meaning, etc.): 這篇文章意義深長. This article is profound in meaning.

深成岩 (アㄣ ㄔㄥˊ ㄧㄢˊ)
plutonic rocks

深處 (アㄣ ㄔㄨˋ)
the deep, inner or obscure part (of woods, heart, etc.)

深識 (アㄣ ㄕˊ)
farsight; profound understanding: 他是有深識的人. He is a man of farsight.

深室 (アㄣ ㄕˋ)
a prison cell

深山 (アㄣ ㄕㄢ)
deep in the mountain

深深 (アㄣ ㄕㄣ)
very deeply

深水 (アㄣ ㄕㄨㄟˇ)
deep waters

深水炸彈 (アㄣ ㄕㄨㄟˇ ㄓㄚˋ ㄉㄢˋ)
a depth charge bomb

深入 (アㄣ ㄖㄨˋ)
(to research, study, delve, etc.) deeply or thoroughly into something; to reach or penetrate deep (into enemy territory)

深入不毛 (アㄣ ㄖㄨˋ ㄅㄨˋ ㄇㄠˊ)
to penetrate deep into wilderness or uncivilized regions

深入淺出 (アㄣ ㄖㄨˋ ㄑㄧㄢˇ ㄔㄨ)
to explain in everyday language the results of a profound study, research, etc.

深入人心 (アㄣ ㄖㄨˋ ㄖㄣˊ ㄒㄧㄣ)
to impress deeply upon everyone's mind: 這觀念深入人心. The idea impressed deeply upon everyone's mind.

深造 (アㄣ ㄗㄠˋ)
to pursue advanced study

深藏不露 (アㄣ ㄘㄤˊ ㄅㄨˋ ㄌㄡˋ)
Real knowledge is not showy.

深懷若虛 (アㄣ ㄏㄨㄞˊ ㄖㄨㄛˋ ㄒㄩ)
(literally) to bosom a trea-

sure and act as if one had nothing with him—very reserved and humble

深籟(ㄕㄣ ㄒㄥˊ)
deep in the woods

深思(ㄕㄣ ㄙ)
deep thought; contemplation; to think deeply; to ponder: 他坐在那裏深思。He sat there deep in contemplation.

深思熟慮(ㄕㄣ ㄙ ㄕㄡˊ ㄌㄩˋ)
careful deliberation; to think and contemplate thoroughly; to ponder: 他對此事深思熟慮。He ponders deeply over the matter.

深邃(ㄕㄣ ㄙㄨㄟˋ)
deep and far; profound and abstruse

深算(ㄕㄣ ㄙㄨㄢˋ)
careful deliberation, calculation or planning

深奧(ㄕㄣ ㄠˋ)
deep; abstruse; profound; recondite: 這是一本深奧的書。This is a profound book.

深暗(ㄕㄣ ㄢˋ)
dark; dark and obscure: 顏色深黯。The color is dark.

深恩(ㄕㄣ ㄣ)
great favors: 他的深恩令人難忘。His great favors are unforgettable.

深意(ㄕㄣ ㄧˋ)
deep or abstruse meaning

深夜(ㄕㄣ ㄧㄝˋ)
deep in the night

深憂(ㄕㄣ ㄧㄡ)
deep worries: 深憂使他不能入睡。Deep worries kept him awake.

深言(ㄕㄣ ㄧㄢˊ)or 深語(ㄕㄣ ㄩˇ)
a confidential or intimate talk

深惡痛絕(ㄕㄣ ㄨ ㄊㄨㄥˋ ㄐㄩㄝˊ)
to shun like poison; to detest extremely; to have a great aversion(to something or someone): 他對酗酒深惡痛絕。He regards drunkenness with great aversion.

深為(ㄕㄣ ㄨㄟˊ)
greatly; deeply; highly: 他深為吃驚。He was greatly surprised.

深文奧義(ㄕㄣ ㄨㄣˊ ㄠˋ ㄧˋ)
(said of writings) hard to understand; abstruse

深淵(ㄕㄣ ㄩㄢ)
an abyss; a very dangerous place: 他陷入苦難的深淵。He fell into the abyss of misery.

深遠(ㄕㄣ ㄩㄢˇ)
deep and far (in meaning, significance, etc.)

深院(ㄕㄣ ㄩㄢˋ)
a large courtyard—the house of a rich family

深願(ㄕㄣ ㄩㄢˋ)
to be very willingly; would be very glad to…

【淶】 2944
ㄌㄞˊ lái lói
name of a river in Hopeh Province 亦作「淶水」

淶水(ㄌㄞˊ ㄕㄨㄟˇ)
參看「淶」

【混】 2945
1. ㄏㄨㄣˋ huenn
hùn
1. disorderly; confused
2. to mix; mixed; to mingle or blend
3. to fool around; just to get along
4. to do things at random or without purpose

混不過去(ㄏㄨㄣˋ ㄅㄨˊ ㄍㄨㄛˋ ㄑㄩˋ)
unable to fool others

混不下去(ㄏㄨㄣˋ ㄅㄨˊ ㄒㄧㄚˋ ㄑㄩˋ)
cannot stay on the job any longer; unable to get along smoothly due to many handicaps, etc.

混飯吃(ㄏㄨㄣˋ ㄈㄢˋ ㄔ)
just to make ends meet; just to get along

混紡(ㄏㄨㄣˋ ㄈㄤˇ)
(said of textiles) mixture of natural and synthetic fibers

混沌(ㄏㄨㄣˋ ㄉㄨㄣˋ)or 混沌沌沌
(ㄏㄨㄣˋ ㄏㄨㄣˋ ㄉㄨㄣˋ ㄉㄨㄣˋ)
①the chaotic world in prehistoric times ②ignorant and dumb

混沌初開(ㄏㄨㄣˋ ㄉㄨㄣˋ ㄔㄨ ㄎㄞ)
at the dawn of civilization

混同(ㄏㄨㄣˋ ㄊㄨㄥˊ)
to merge; to combine: 油和水不容易混同。Oil and water do not readily combine.

混凝土(ㄏㄨㄣˋ ㄋㄧㄥˊ ㄊㄨˇ)
concrete

混亂(ㄏㄨㄣˋ ㄌㄨㄢˋ)

〔水部〕

confusion; chaos: 軍隊陷於混亂。The army were thrown into confusion.

混汞法(ㄏㄨㄣˋ ㄍㄨㄥˇ ㄈㄚˇ)
(chemistry) amalgamation

混合(ㄏㄨㄣˋ ㄏㄜˊ)
to mix together; to mingle or blend together

混合法(ㄏㄨㄣˋ ㄏㄜˊ ㄈㄚˇ)
syncretic theories; mixture

混合列車(ㄏㄨㄣˋ ㄏㄜˊ ㄌㄧㄝˋ ㄔㄜ)
a mixed train (with both freight cars and passenger coaches)

混合花序(ㄏㄨㄣˋ ㄏㄜˊ ㄏㄨㄚ ㄒㄩˋ)
mixed inflorescence

混合機(ㄏㄨㄣˋ ㄏㄜˊ ㄐㄧ)
a concrete mixer; a mixer

混合雙打(ㄏㄨㄣˋ ㄏㄜˊ ㄕㄨㄤ ㄉㄚˇ)
mixed doubles

混合物(ㄏㄨㄣˋ ㄏㄜˊ ㄨˋ)
a mixture; a blend: 空氣是氣體的混合物,不是化合物。Air is a mixture, not a compound of gases.

混號(ㄏㄨㄣˋ ㄏㄠˋ)or 混名(ㄏㄨㄣˋ ㄇㄧㄥˊ)
a nickname

混混(ㄏㄨㄣˋ ㄏㄨㄣˋ)
①dark; opaque; blackened ②to drift through(life) ③a hoodlum; a hooligan; a villain; a rascal

混跡(ㄏㄨㄣˋ ㄐㄧ)
to mix or hide oneself in a company, crowd, society, organization, etc: 他正混跡人群中。He is hiding himself in the crowd.

混進(ㄏㄨㄣˋ ㄐㄧㄣˋ)
to infiltrate; to sneak into

混血(ㄏㄨㄣˋ ㄒㄧㄝˋ)
hybridization

混血兒(ㄏㄨㄣˋ ㄒㄧㄝˋ ㄦˊ)
a human hybrid; a mixed-blood; a child of an interracial marriage

混戰(ㄏㄨㄣˋ ㄓㄢˋ)
a melee; a wild battle

混帳 or 混賬(ㄏㄨㄣˋ ㄓㄤˋ)
That good-for-nothing! 或 That s.o.b! 或 Scoundrel! 或 Rascal!

混成(ㄏㄨㄣˋ ㄔㄥˊ)
to mix together; to blend together

〔水部〕

混成旅 (ㄏㄨㄣˋ ㄔㄥˊ ㄌㄩˇ)
(military) a mixed or composite brigade

混充 (ㄏㄨㄣˋ ㄔㄨㄥ)
to pretend to be (someone else); to masquerade or pose (as someone else): 他混充音樂家。He pretends to be a musician.

混世魔王 (ㄏㄨㄣˋ ㄕˋ ㄇㄛˊ ㄨㄤˊ)
a fiendish person who causes an upheaval in the world—like Hitler, etc.

混說 (ㄏㄨㄣˋ ㄕㄨㄛ)
to talk nonsense; to talk at random: 別混說! Don't talk nonsense!

混日子 (ㄏㄨㄣˋ ㄖˋ ˙ㄗ)
just to make a living; just to get along (without any plan, ambition, etc. for the future)

混然 (ㄏㄨㄣˋ ㄖㄢˊ)
mixed and indistinguishable

混入 (ㄏㄨㄣˋ ㄖㄨˋ)
to mix oneself inside a body of people, an organization; to get into an organization or restricted area without undergoing the proper procedures

混資格 (ㄏㄨㄣˋ ㄗ ㄍㄜˊ)
to study or receive a training not for the sake of knowledge but for the academic degree or diploma

混子 (ㄏㄨㄣˋ ˙ㄗ)
one who fools around in a respectable profession; a quack

混雜 (ㄏㄨㄣˋ ㄗㄚˊ)
①to blend; to mix: 不要把糖和沙混雜在一起。Don't mix sand with the sugar. ②motley; heterogeneous; mixed ③disorderly; chaotic; confused

混一 (ㄏㄨㄣˋ ㄧ)
unification

混一混 (ㄏㄨㄣˋ ㄧ ㄏㄨㄣˋ)or 混混 (ㄏㄨㄣˋ ㄏㄨㄣˋ)
just to get along

混為一談 (ㄏㄨㄣˋ ㄨㄟˊ ㄧ ㄊㄢˊ)
to lump together; to confuse something with something else

【混】 2945
2. (諢) ㄏㄨㄣˋ **hwen hún**

turbid; muddy; not clear

混蛋 (ㄏㄨㄣˋ ㄉㄢˋ)
Bloody fool!!

混濁 (ㄏㄨㄣˋ ㄓㄨㄛˊ)
turbid; not clean or pure: 這是條混濁的河。This is a turbid river.

混水 (ㄏㄨㄣˋ ㄕㄨㄟˇ)
①turbid water ②troubled waters ③improper undertakings; illegal activities

混水摸魚 (ㄏㄨㄣˋ ㄕㄨㄟˇ ㄇㄛ ㄩˊ)
to fish in troubled waters

【混】 2945
3. ㄏㄨㄣˊ **hoen hún**
confused and not distinguishable

混亂 (ㄏㄨㄣˋ ㄌㄨㄢˋ)
confusion; disorder; chaos: 他的房間一片混亂。His room was in great disorder.

混淆 (ㄏㄨㄣˋ ㄒㄧㄠˊ)
mixed, confused and indistinguishable

混淆是非 (ㄏㄨㄣˋ ㄒㄧㄠˊ ㄕˋ ㄈㄟ)
to confound right and wrong

混淆視聽 (ㄏㄨㄣˋ ㄒㄧㄠˊ ㄕˋ ㄊㄧㄥ)
to confuse public opinion

【清】 2946
ㄑㄧㄥ **ching qīng**
1. pure; clean; clear
2. brief; scarce
3. virtuous; honest
4. to arrange; to place in order
5. to conclude; to terminate; to repay (debts); to settle
6. clear, simple and easily understandable
7. Ching Dynasty (1644-1911)
8. to clean

清白 (ㄑㄧㄥ ㄅㄞˊ)
(said of a person's character, family background) clean; unsoiled; unimpeachable; innocent

清班 (ㄑㄧㄥ ㄅㄢ)or 清秩 (ㄑㄧㄥ ㄓˋ)
virtuous officials collectively

清標 (ㄑㄧㄥ ㄅㄧㄠ)
①a pure and austere look ②the bright moon

清兵 (ㄑㄧㄥ ㄅㄧㄥ)
Manchu troops

清貧 (ㄑㄧㄥ ㄆㄧㄣˊ)
poor and virtuous: 他很清貧。He is very poor and virtuous.

清平 (ㄑㄧㄥ ㄆㄧㄥˊ)

①peace and justice ②(said of a disposition) pure, honest and peace-loving ③name of counties in Shantung and Kweichow

清平世界 (ㄑㄧㄥ ㄆㄧㄥˊ ㄕˋ ㄐㄧㄝˋ)
a peaceful and orderly world

清門 (ㄑㄧㄥ ㄇㄣˊ)
a poor family

清廟 (ㄑㄧㄥ ㄇㄧㄠˋ)
①(Chou Dynasty) the temple for worshipping King Wen (文王) ②an ancestral shrine

清名 (ㄑㄧㄥ ㄇㄧㄥˊ)
an unimpeachable reputation; an unsoiled name

清明 (ㄑㄧㄥ ㄇㄧㄥˊ)
①clean and just (administration) ②one of the 24 solar periods in a year which falls on April 5 or 6 when people visit their ancestral tombs, also known as Tomb-Sweeping Day

清芬 (ㄑㄧㄥ ㄈㄣ)
①soothing aroma ②virtues

清風 (ㄑㄧㄥ ㄈㄥ)
①cool breezes; soothing wind ②(said of an official) to remain poor and clean at retirement

清風明月 (ㄑㄧㄥ ㄈㄥ ㄇㄧㄥˊ ㄩㄝˋ)
(literally) the soothing wind and the bright moon —aloof

清風兩袖 (ㄑㄧㄥ ㄈㄥ ㄌㄧㄤˇ ㄒㄧㄡˋ)
(said of an honest official) to remain poor upon retirement

清風徐來 (ㄑㄧㄥ ㄈㄥ ㄒㄩˊ ㄌㄞˊ)
The soothing breezes slowly blow this way.

清福 (ㄑㄧㄥ ㄈㄨˊ)
a kind of happiness with the absence of worries and cares; an easy and carefree life

清道 (ㄑㄧㄥ ㄉㄠˋ)
①to sweep the road; to clear the way ②(in former times) before the passing of the sedan chair of a high official, magistrate, etc. guardsmen would first clear the way and warn the peo-

ple of his imminent arrival

清道夫（くlㄥ ㄉㄠ ㄈㄨ）
a scavenger

清單（くlㄥ ㄉㄢ）
a detailed list of items which serves as a receipt, statement, etc.; a statement of account

清淡（くlㄥ ㄉㄢ）
①not enthusiastic; calm ②dull or sluggish (markets); slack: 這一季生意清淡。Business is slack at this season. ③(said of food) simple; without grease or heavy seasoning

清黨（くlㄥ ㄉㄤ）
a purge within a political party; to purge undesirable elements from a political party

清點（くlㄥ ㄉlㄢ）
to check; to make an inventory; to sort and count

清燉（くlㄥ ㄉㄨㄣ）
to stew or steam meat without seasoning

清談（くlㄥ ㄊㄢ）
①pure theoretical talks based on the teachings of Lao-tzu (老子) ②a polite reference to the utterances of others

清談誤國（くlㄥ ㄊㄢ ㄨˋ ㄍㄨㄛˊ）
(said of intellectuals) Pure theories and talks without action will get the nation into trouble.

清湯（くlㄥ ㄊㄤ）
consommé; clear soup; light soup

清天（くlㄥ ㄊlㄢ）
①a clear sky: 清天無雲。There were no clouds in the clear sky. ②a virtuous official (often used as a salutation to the judge in former times)

清恬（くlㄥ ㄊlㄢˊ）
pure and quiet (life); tranquil and comfortable

清聽（くlㄥ ㄊlㄥ）
your kind listening

清廷（くlㄥ ㄊlㄥˊ）
the Ching government; the Manchu court

清通（くlㄥ ㄊㄨㄥ）
(said of writings, etc.) clear

and smooth style; clearly understandable

清朗（くlㄥ ㄌㄤˇ）
①clear and loud (sound, voice, etc.) ②clear and crisp (weather): 天氣清朗。The weather is clear and crisp.

清冷（くlㄥ ㄌㄥˇ）
①cool; refreshing ②deserted

清理（くlㄥ ㄌlˇ）
①to settle (accounts, etc.); clearance (of sales, etc.) ②to arrange; to tidy up

清麗（くlㄥ ㄌlˋ）
(said of writings, etc.) a clear and attractive style

清冽（くlㄥ ㄌlㄝˋ）
clear and cold (water): 水甚清冽。The water is clear and cold.

清寮（くlㄥ ㄌlㄠˊ）
clear and open (space, fields, etc.)

清流（くlㄥ ㄌlㄡˊ）
①a clear stream ②virtuous scholars ③(now rarely) an air current ④name of a county in Fukien Province

清漣（くlㄥ ㄌlㄢˊ）
clear, rippled waters in a pond, etc.

清廉（くlㄥ ㄌlㄢˊ）
clean, honest and capable (officials, etc.); free from corruption

清涼（くlㄥ ㄌlㄤˊ）
①nice and cool; refreshing (weather, water, etc.): 天氣清涼。It is nice and cool. ②name of a hill in Nanking

清涼劑（くlㄥ ㄌlㄤˊ ㄐlˋ）
a herbal concoction that is supposed to relieve the latent "heat" in the human body

清涼飲料（くlㄥ ㄌlㄤˊ lㄣˇ ㄌlㄠˋ）
a cold drink; a cooler

清亮（くlㄥ ㄌlㄤˋ）
clear and bright (eyes): 她眼睛清亮。Her eyes are clear and bright.

清歌（くlㄥ ㄍㄜ）
singing without an instrumental accompaniment

清歌妙舞（くlㄥ ㄍㄜ ㄇlㄠˋ ㄨˇ）
good songs and wonderful

dances—the stage; a good song-and-dance performance

清高（くlㄥ ㄍㄠ）
morally lofty or upright; not interested in politics or other worldly things

清高絕俗（くlㄥ ㄍㄠ ㄐㄩㄝˊ ㄙㄨˊ）
extremely aloof from mundane affairs

清規（くlㄥ ㄍㄨㄟ）
Buddhist rules; discipline among Buddhist monks and nuns

清貴（くlㄥ ㄍㄨㄟˋ）
①pure and valuable ②the Hanlin Academy (翰林院), often referred to as 清貴衙門

清官（くlㄥ ㄍㄨㄢ）
honest officials

清宮（くlㄥ ㄍㄨㄥ）
①to clean or sweep the palace' chambers ②the palace of the Ching rulers

清客（くlㄥ ㄎㄜˋ）
①proteges of the powerful who stay with their benefactors like parasites ②another name of plum blossoms

清苦（くlㄥ ㄎㄨˇ）
poor but clean and honest

清寒（くlㄥ ㄏㄢˊ）
①poor but clean and honest ②(said of weather, etc.) cold and crisp ③(said of moonlight) cold and bright

清華（くlㄥ ㄏㄨㄚˊ）
①(literary style) outstanding and beautiful ②eminent and honest gentlemen ③moonlight ④enchanting views

清華大學（くlㄥ ㄏㄨㄚˊ ㄉㄚˋ ㄒㄩㄝˊ）
National Tsing Hua University

清華園（くlㄥ ㄏㄨㄚˊ ㄩㄢˊ）
name of a garden in suburban Peking

清化（くlㄥ ㄏㄨㄚˋ）
moral influence or education

清季（くlㄥ ㄐlˋ）
the last years of the Ching Dynasty

清潔（くlㄥ ㄐlㄝˊ）
clean; sanitary

清潔隊（くlㄥ ㄐlㄝˊ ㄉㄨㄟˋ）
a cleaning squad

【水部】

清潔工人(ㄑㄧㄥ ㄐㄧㄝˊ ㄍㄨㄥ ㄖㄣˊ)
sanitation workers; street cleaners

清潔劑(ㄑㄧㄥ ㄐㄧㄝˊ ㄐㄧˋ)
a detergent

清介(ㄑㄧㄥ ㄐㄧㄝˋ)
pure, virtuous and not mixing with the ordinary run of life

清剿(ㄑㄧㄥ ㄐㄧㄠˇ)
to wipe out (bandits or rebel troops) completely

清教徒(ㄑㄧㄥ ㄐㄧㄠˋ ㄊㄨˊ)
the Puritans

清酒(ㄑㄧㄥ ㄐㄧㄡˇ)
①wine used in ancestral worshiping or in offerings; pure spirits ②a kind of rice wine; sake

清減(ㄑㄧㄥ ㄐㄧㄢˇ)
to get thin; to lose weight

清淨(ㄑㄧㄥ ㄐㄧㄥˋ)
clean and pure

清淨無為(ㄑㄧㄥ ㄐㄧㄥˋ ㄨˊ ㄨㄟˊ)
to discard all desires and worries from one's mind —Taoist teachings

清靜(ㄑㄧㄥ ㄐㄧㄥˋ)
quiet (houses, surroundings, etc.)。咱們找個清靜的地方休息。Let's find a quiet place for a rest.

清欠(ㄑㄧㄥ ㄑㄧㄢˋ)
to repay all one's debts

清癯(ㄑㄧㄥ ㄑㄩˊ)
thin but healthy; lean and sprightly

清曲(ㄑㄧㄥ ㄑㄩˇ)
singing without dialogues 亦作「散曲」

清泉(ㄑㄧㄥ ㄑㄩㄢˊ)
①a crystal-clear fountain ②old name of a county in Hunan, now merged into Hengyang city

清晰(ㄑㄧㄥ ㄒㄧ)
①loud and clear (in radio reception, talking, listening, etc.): 這小女孩發音清晰。The little girl's pronunciation is clear. ②clearly

清洗(ㄑㄧㄥ ㄒㄧˇ)
to wash clean: 他在清洗炊具。He is cleaning cooking utensils.

清曉(ㄑㄧㄥ ㄒㄧㄠˇ)
dawn: 他清曉即起。He got up

at dawn.

清修(ㄑㄧㄥ ㄒㄧㄡ)
to lead a life of few wants and ambitions

清秀(ㄑㄧㄥ ㄒㄧㄡˋ)
good-looking; with clear-cut features; well-shaped; handsome without the aid of cosmetics

清閒(ㄑㄧㄥ ㄒㄧㄢˊ)
at leisure; to have all the time one needs

清新(ㄑㄧㄥ ㄒㄧㄣ)
refreshing (style, fashion, etc.); fresh

清心寡慾(ㄑㄧㄥ ㄒㄧㄣ ㄍㄨㄚˇ ㄩˋ)
to purge one's mind of desires and ambitions

清香(ㄑㄧㄥ ㄒㄧㄤ)
mild fragrance (as distinct from strong aroma)

清香撲鼻(ㄑㄧㄥ ㄒㄧㄤ ㄆㄨ ㄅㄧˊ)
A sweet scent assails one's nostrils.

清鄉(ㄑㄧㄥ ㄒㄧㄤ)
to get rid of bandits from the countryside

清醒(ㄑㄧㄥ ㄒㄧㄥˇ)
①to come to; wide awake: 病人已經清醒過來。The patient has come to. ②clear-minded; sober

清興(ㄑㄧㄥ ㄒㄧㄥˋ)
pleasure: 他一直過着清興的生活。He has always lived a life of pleasure.

清虛(ㄑㄧㄥ ㄒㄩ)
high and mild; refined and nonaggressive

清眞(ㄑㄧㄥ ㄓㄣ)
①Mohammedan or Islamic ②pure; purity

清眞館(ㄑㄧㄥ ㄓㄣ ㄍㄨㄢˇ)or 清眞食堂(ㄑㄧㄥ ㄓㄣ ㄕˊ ㄊㄤˊ)
a Mohammedan restaurant where no pork is served

清眞教(ㄑㄧㄥ ㄓㄣ ㄐㄧㄠˋ)
Mohammedanism or Islamism

清眞寺(ㄑㄧㄥ ㄓㄣ ㄙˋ)
a mosque

清賬(ㄑㄧㄥ ㄓㄤˋ)
to pay off all one's debts; to settle all one's accounts

清蒸(ㄑㄧㄥ ㄓㄥ)
(a form of cooking) to steam; steamed

清正(ㄑㄧㄥ ㄓㄥˋ)
clean, honest and just

清濁(ㄑㄧㄥ ㄓㄨㄛˊ)
①(some water) clear and (some water) turbid ②(said of people) honest and dishonest

清濁不分(ㄑㄧㄥ ㄓㄨㄛˊ ㄅㄨˋ ㄈㄣ)
to be unable to distinguish the clear from the muddy

清茶(ㄑㄧㄥ ㄔㄚˊ)
①green tea ②(to entertain) with nothing but tea

清查(ㄑㄧㄥ ㄔㄚˊ)
to check, investigate, survey thoroughly; a thorough check-up

清澈(ㄑㄧㄥ ㄔㄜˋ)
crystal-clear; limpid (water)

清朝(ㄑㄧㄥ ㄔㄠˊ)
①the Ching or Manchu Dynasty (1644-1911) ②an enlightened reign

清晨(ㄑㄧㄥ ㄔㄣˊ)
early in the morning; dawn: 我清晨起床。I got up at dawn.

清償(ㄑㄧㄥ ㄔㄤˊ)
to pay off all one's debts

清場(ㄑㄧㄥ ㄔㄤˇ)or(ㄑㄧㄥ ㄔㄤˇ)
(said of movie theaters) to have every moviegoer out before the next show starts

清唱(ㄑㄧㄥ ㄔㄤˋ)
to sing Chinese opera without wearing costume or makeup

清除(ㄑㄧㄥ ㄔㄨˊ)
①to eliminate, rid of, clear away, liquidate, purge, or remove ②to clean or tidy up (a house)

清楚(ㄑㄧㄥ ㄔㄨˇ)or 清清楚楚(ㄑㄧㄥ ㄑㄧㄥ ㄔㄨˇ ㄔㄨˇ)
①clear; without ambiguity ②to know thoroughly; to understand: 這個問題你清楚嗎? Do you understand this question?

清創術(ㄑㄧㄥ ㄔㄨㄤ ㄕㄨˋ)
(medicine) *débridement*

清士(ㄑㄧㄥ ㄕˋ)
a man of honesty and unimpeachable integrity

清室(ㄑㄧㄥ ㄕˋ)
the royal family of the Ching Dynasty

清瘦(ㄑㄧㄥ ㄕㄡˋ)

thin and lean: 你看起來很清瘦。 You look rather thin.

清尚（ㄑㄧㄥ ㄕㄤˋ）
high-class; high-society

清聲（ㄑㄧㄥ ㄕㄥ）
voiceless consonants

清水（ㄑㄧㄥ ㄕㄨㄟˇ）
clear (or fresh) water

清水貨（ㄑㄧㄥ ㄕㄨㄟˇ ㄏㄨㄛˋ）
① unadulterated goods ②
(slang) a virgin

清爽（ㄑㄧㄥ ㄕㄨㄤˇ）
① sober ② quiet and comfortable; cooling and refreshing ③ clear and easy to understand ④ to have everything (debts, etc.) settled; relieved; relaxed

清早（ㄑㄧㄥ ㄗㄠˇ）
early in the morning; dawn

清册（ㄑㄧㄥ ㄘㄜˋ）
a long list or volume containing all details or items to be handed over to the successor, to an office, etc.

清操（ㄑㄧㄥ ㄘㄠ）
virtuous disposition and behavior

清查盤庫（ㄑㄧㄥ ㄔㄚˊ ㄆㄢˊ ㄎㄨˋ）
to make an inventory of warehouses

清脆（ㄑㄧㄥ ㄘㄨㄟˋ）
clear and crisp (note, sound, etc.); sharp and loud (slapping sound, etc.)

清掃戰場（ㄑㄧㄥ ㄙㄠˇ ㄓㄢˋ ㄔㄤˊ）or
（ㄑㄧㄥ ㄙㄠˇ ㄓㄢˋ ㄔㄤˇ）
to mop up the remnants of the enemy on battlefield

清算（ㄑㄧㄥ ㄙㄨㄢˋ）
① to liquidate; liquidation ② to purge

清一色（ㄑㄧㄥ ㄧ ㄙㄜˋ）
① (in mah-jong) the series of 13 or 16 blocks belonging to the same pattern which is equivalent to a hand of royal flush in poker and a grand slam in bridge ② uniformly; homogeneous

清議（ㄑㄧㄥ ㄧˋ）
comments among the honest and scholarly

清雅（ㄑㄧㄥ ㄧㄚˇ）
neat and refined (taste, adornment, etc.); graceful

此爲清雅設計。It is a neat and refined design.

清夜（ㄑㄧㄥ ㄧㄝˋ）
in the still of the night

清夜捫心（ㄑㄧㄥ ㄧㄝˋ ㄇㄣˊ ㄒㄧㄣ）
to make self-examination in the still of the night

清幽（ㄑㄧㄥ ㄧㄡ）
quiet and secluded: 此地十分清幽。This place is quiet and secluded.

清油（ㄑㄧㄥ ㄧㄡˊ）
(dialect) ① vegetable oil ② tea oil

清揚（ㄑㄧㄥ ㄧㄤˊ）
① fine-featured; beautiful or handsome (especially said of eyes and eyebrows) ② (Buddhism) clear and resonant

清玩（ㄑㄧㄥ ㄨㄢˊ）
curios; small decorative articles

清望（ㄑㄧㄥ ㄨㄤˋ）
fine prestige; untarnished reputation

【淺】 2947
ㄑㄧㄢˇ chean qiǎn
1. shallow; superficial
2. easy; simple
3. (color) light
4. (said of land) narrow and small

淺薄（ㄑㄧㄢˇ ㄅㄛˊ）
superficial; superficiality; shallow; meager

淺謀（ㄑㄧㄢˇ ㄇㄡˊ）
a scheme which can be easily detected or discovered

淺明（ㄑㄧㄢˇ ㄇㄧㄥˊ）
easy and clear (readings, ideas, etc.): 他的思想淺明。His ideas are easy and clear.

淺灘（ㄑㄧㄢˇ ㄊㄢ）
a shoal: 該船在淺灘失事。The ship was wrecked on the shoals.

淺陋（ㄑㄧㄢˇ ㄌㄡˋ）
vulgar; crude; shallow

淺陋不堪（ㄑㄧㄢˇ ㄌㄡˋ ㄅㄨˋ ㄎㄢ）
very shallow and detestable

淺海（ㄑㄧㄢˇ ㄏㄞˇ）
a shallow sea; an epeiric sea

淺紅（ㄑㄧㄢˇ ㄏㄨㄥˊ）
light red

淺交（ㄑㄧㄢˇ ㄐㄧㄠ）
not on intimate terms

淺見（ㄑㄧㄢˇ ㄐㄧㄢˋ）
① a superficial or shallow view; a short-sighted view ② (a polite expression) my shallow view: 這是我的淺見。This is my shallow view.

淺近（ㄑㄧㄢˇ ㄐㄧㄣˋ）
easy to understand; fundamental; simple

淺笑（ㄑㄧㄢˇ ㄒㄧㄠˋ）
a smile; to smile

淺鮮（ㄑㄧㄢˇ ㄒㄧㄢ）
slight; insignificant

淺顯（ㄑㄧㄢˇ ㄒㄧㄢˇ）
obvious; easily understandable: 這是很淺顯的。It is quite obvious.

淺學（ㄑㄧㄢˇ ㄒㄩㄝˊ）
shallow or superficial learning

淺斟低唱（ㄑㄧㄢˇ ㄓㄨㄣ ㄉㄧ ㄔㄤˋ）
(literally) to drink light and hum low—a scene of a merrymaking party in the company of prostitutes or disreputable women

淺嘗輒止（ㄑㄧㄢˇ ㄔㄤˊ ㄓㄜˊ ㄓㄧˇ）
(literally) to stop after a sip or nibble—to refuse to make a deeper study; do not study further or deeper; to make a superficial study only

淺說（ㄑㄧㄢˇ ㄕㄨㄛ）
a layman's description or talk; an explanation of a theory, etc. in layman's language

淺睡（ㄑㄧㄢˇ ㄕㄨㄟˋ）
a dogsleep 亦作「假寐」

淺人（ㄑㄧㄢˇ ㄖㄣˊ）
a shallow or superficial person; a person without much deep thought

淺色（ㄑㄧㄢˇ ㄙㄜˋ）
light colors: 她穿著一件淺色的衣服。She wore a light-colored dress.

淺而易見（ㄑㄧㄢˇ ㄦˊ ㄧˋ ㄐㄧㄢˋ）
apparent; obvious; easily understood

淺易（ㄑㄧㄢˇ ㄧˋ）
very easy or simple (to learn, understand, etc.)

淺閱（ㄑㄧㄢˇ ㄩㄝˋ）
narrow or shallow learning or experience

〔水 部〕

〔水
部〕

【淹】 2948
ㄧㄢ ian yān

1. to submerge; to drown; to soak; to steep in; to flood
2. to delay; to procrastinate
3. to stay; to be stranded
4. (now rarely) deep; well-versed; erudite; profound
5. (now rarely) discomfort caused by perspiration or liquids on skin

淹博〔ㄧㄢ ㄅㄛˊ〕
erudite; erudition

淹沒〔ㄧㄢ ㄇㄛˋ〕
① submerged; inundated; drowned ② to waste a talent as if by submerging it

淹通〔ㄧㄢ ㄊㄨㄥ〕
to be well-versed; to have attained profundity or depth

淹通古今〔ㄧㄢ ㄊㄨㄥ ㄍㄨˇㄐㄧㄣ〕
to be thoroughly acquainted with the old and modern

淹留〔ㄧㄢ ㄌㄧㄡˊ〕
to stay for a long period

淹該〔ㄧㄢ ㄍㄞ〕
erudite and well-versed

淹貫〔ㄧㄢ ㄍㄨㄢˋ〕
well-versed; widely-read

淹滯〔ㄧㄢ ㄓˋ〕
talented persons holding inferior posts

淹遲〔ㄧㄢ ㄔˊ〕
slow; dilatory

淹沈〔ㄧㄢ ㄔㄣˊ〕
① to be bed-ridden for a long time ② to procrastinate

淹識〔ㄧㄢ ㄕˋ〕
profundity; erudition

淹潤〔ㄧㄢ ㄖㄨㄣˋ〕
intimate but shy; amiable but timid

淹死〔ㄧㄢ ㄙˇ〕
drowned: 他跌入海裡淹死了。He fell into the sea and was drowned.

淹雅〔ㄧㄢ ㄧㄚˇ〕
(said of a scholar of profound learning) deep and refined

【添】 2949
ㄊㄧㄢ tian tiān

1. to add to; to increase; to replenish (stock, etc.)
2. to have a baby

添本〔ㄊㄧㄢ ㄅㄣˇ〕
to increase capital: 他們決定

添本。They decided to increase capital.

添兵〔ㄊㄧㄢ ㄅㄧㄥ〕
to reinforce

添補〔ㄊㄧㄢ ㄅㄨˇ〕
to make complete; to complete what is lacking

添飯〔ㄊㄧㄢ ㄈㄢˋ〕
to have another helping (or bowl) of rice

添墳〔ㄊㄧㄢ ㄈㄣˊ〕
to add earth to the graves of the deceased, especially on the Tomb-Sweeping Day (清明)

添房〔ㄊㄧㄢ ㄈㄤˊ〕
(old usage) presents sent to the family which is marrying off a daughter

添福添壽〔ㄊㄧㄢ ㄈㄨˊㄊㄧㄢ ㄕㄡˋ〕
(a well-wishing expression) to add to your happiness and your longevity

添附〔ㄊㄧㄢ ㄈㄨˋ〕
to enclose; to supplement; to add to; additional

添丁〔ㄊㄧㄢ ㄉㄧㄥ〕
to beget a son: 他添丁了。He begot a son.

添丁發財〔ㄊㄧㄢ ㄉㄧㄥ ㄈㄚ ㄘㄞˊ〕
May you have an increase in your family and be prosperous by becoming wealthy.

添多〔ㄊㄧㄢ ㄉㄨㄛ〕
to add more; to increase: 這城市人口添多了。The town is increasing in population.

添改〔ㄊㄧㄢ ㄍㄞˇ〕
to add and change; to make additions and alterations

添購〔ㄊㄧㄢ ㄍㄡˋ〕
to purchase; to make additional purchase of: 她添購了許多新衣服。She purchases a lot of new dresses.

添貨〔ㄊㄧㄢ ㄏㄨㄛˋ〕
(said of a store) to replenish stock

添加〔ㄊㄧㄢ ㄐㄧㄚ〕
to add to; to increase

添加劑〔ㄊㄧㄢ ㄐㄧㄚ ㄐㄧˋ〕
(chemistry) an additive

添價〔ㄊㄧㄢ ㄐㄧㄚˋ〕
to raise the price (of something): 商人添價。Merchants raise prices.

添箱〔ㄊㄧㄢ ㄒㄧㄤ〕or 添妝〔ㄊㄧㄢ ㄓ〕

wedding presents sent to the bride's family

添枝添葉〔ㄊㄧㄢ ㄓ ㄊㄧㄢ ㄧㄝˋ〕or 添枝加葉〔ㄊㄧㄢ ㄓ ㄐㄧㄚ ㄧㄝˋ〕
(literally) to add branches and leaves—to blow up or embellish a story, report, etc.

添置〔ㄊㄧㄢ ㄓˋ〕
to purchase additionally: 我要添置家具。I want to buy more furniture.

添製衣服〔ㄊㄧㄢ ㄓˋ ㄧ ˙ㄈㄨ〕
to make or purchase additional clothes

添註〔ㄊㄧㄢ ㄓㄨˋ〕
to fill (a blank form, etc.)

添設〔ㄊㄧㄢ ㄕㄜˋ〕
to set up additionally

添上〔ㄊㄧㄢ ˙ㄕㄤˋ〕
① to add to ② besides; in addition to

添造〔ㄊㄧㄢ ㄗㄠˋ〕
to build more; to construct; to expand

添菜〔ㄊㄧㄢ ㄘㄞˋ〕
to have additional dishes

添油加醋〔ㄊㄧㄢ ㄧㄡˊ ㄐㄧㄚ ㄘㄨˋ〕or 添油加醬〔ㄊㄧㄢ ㄧㄡˊ ㄐㄧㄚ ㄐㄧㄤˋ〕
(literally) to add oil and vinegar—to embellish or blow up a story or report with something which is usually not true

【涴】 2950
ㄨㄛ woh wò
to stain; to soil

【淇】 2951
ㄑㄧˊ chyi qí
name of a river in Honan

淇〔ㄑㄧˊ ㄏㄜˊ〕
name of a river in Honan

【涮】 2952
ㄕㄨㄢ shuann shuàn

1. to rinse (a container, etc.)
2. to boil in a chafing pot
3. to cheat with lies

涮洗〔ㄕㄨㄢ ㄒㄧˇ〕
to rinse

涮羊肉〔ㄕㄨㄢ ㄧㄤˊ ㄖㄡˋ〕or 涮鍋子〔ㄕㄨㄢ ㄍㄨㄛ ˙ㄗ〕
mutton cooked in a chafing pot

【淴】 2953
ㄏㄨ hu hū

the sound of flowing waters

渝浴(ㄗㄨˋㄩˋ)
(dialect) to take a bath

【淼】 2954
ㄇㄧㄠˇ meau miǎo
(said of water) extensive or overwhelming

淼茫(ㄇㄧㄠˇㄇㄤˊ)or 淼漫(ㄇㄧㄠˇㄇㄢˋ) or 淼淼(ㄇㄧㄠˇㄇㄧㄠˇ)
(said of an expanse of water) stretching as far as the eye can see

九畫

【渙】 2955
ㄏㄨㄢˋ huann huàn
1. scattered; dispersed
2. name of a river

渙發(ㄏㄨㄢˋㄈㄚ)
high-spirited

渙然(ㄏㄨㄢˋㄖㄢˊ)
scattered; dispersed

渙然冰釋(ㄏㄨㄢˋㄖㄢˊㄅㄧㄥㄕˋ)
(said of a grudge, misunderstanding, etc.) to disappear as melting ice; to vanish: 他的疑慮渙然冰釋。His misgivings have melted away.

渙散(ㄏㄨㄢˋㄙㄢˋ)
①lacking concentration or organization ②(said of morale) to collapse

【渚】 2956
ㄓㄨˇ juu zhǔ
a sand bar in river

【淳】 2957
ㄊㄧㄥˊ tyng tíng
1. (said of water) not flowing; still
2. (said of water) clear

【渝】 2958
ㄩˊ yu yú
1. to change one's mind
2. another name of Chungking
3. another name of the Chialing River in Szechwan

【減】 2959
ㄐㄧㄢˇ jean jiǎn
1. to decrease; to reduce; to lessen; to diminish; to subtract; to deduct; to cut
2. a Chinese family name

減半(ㄐㄧㄢˇㄅㄢˋ)
to reduce to a half

減筆字(ㄐㄧㄢˇㄅㄧˇㄗˋ)
a simplified Chinese character

減免(ㄐㄧㄢˇㄇㄧㄢˇ)
①to mitigate or annul (a punishment) ②to reduce or remit (taxation, etc.)

減法(ㄐㄧㄢˇㄈㄚˇ)
(arithmetic) subtraction

減肥(ㄐㄧㄢˇㄈㄟˊ)
to reduce (weight); to lose weight

減俸(ㄐㄧㄢˇㄈㄥˋ)or 減薪(ㄐㄧㄢˇㄒㄧㄣ)
a pay cut; a salary reduction

減低(ㄐㄧㄢˇㄉㄧ)
to decrease; to reduce; to lessen; to lower

減退(ㄐㄧㄢˇㄊㄨㄟˋ)
to reduce; to fall; to abate; to decrease; to lessen; to diminish

減號(ㄐㄧㄢˇㄏㄠˋ)
the minus sign (−)

減緩(ㄐㄧㄢˇㄏㄨㄢˇ)
to retard; to slow down

減價(ㄐㄧㄢˇㄐㄧㄚˋ)
to cut down prices; to reduce prices; to mark down

減輕(ㄐㄧㄢˇㄑㄧㄥ)
to lighten; to lessen; to reduce; to diminish; to mitigate

減去(ㄐㄧㄢˇㄑㄩˋ)
to subtract; to deduct; to take away

減息(ㄐㄧㄢˇㄒㄧˊ)
to lower interest rate

減刑(ㄐㄧㄢˇㄒㄧㄥˊ)
①to commute a sentence ② a commutation of sentence; mitigation of penalty

減產(ㄐㄧㄢˇㄔㄢˇ)
to cut production or output; a drop in production or output

減少(ㄐㄧㄢˇㄕㄠˇ)
to decrease; to diminish; to lessen; to reduce

減收(ㄐㄧㄢˇㄕㄡ)
①a decrease in income or receipt ②a drop in harvest

減省(ㄐㄧㄢˇㄕㄥˇ)
to reduce waste; to save; to be frugal; to economize

減數(ㄐㄧㄢˇㄕㄨˋ)
(mathematics) subtrahend

減稅(ㄐㄧㄢˇㄕㄨㄟˋ)
to reduce, cut, or lower taxes

減弱(ㄐㄧㄢˇㄖㄨㄛˋ)
to weaken; to subside; to reduce in strength or intensity: 風勢減弱了。The wind has subsided.

減竈(ㄐㄧㄢˇㄗㄠˋ)
to make a deceptive show of weakness or decline, as Sun Pin (孫臏) of the Epoch of Warring States did by leaving fewer and fewer cooking ovens behind as his troops retreated

減租(ㄐㄧㄢˇㄗㄨ)
to reduce, cut, or lower rent

減色(ㄐㄧㄢˇㄙㄜˋ)
to fade or pale (literally and figuratively); to impair the excellence of

減速(ㄐㄧㄢˇㄙㄨˋ)
to slow down; to decelerate

減縮(ㄐㄧㄢˇㄙㄨㄛˋ)
①to retrench ②to abbreviate

【渡】 2960
ㄉㄨˋ duh dù
1. to cross (a river or ocean)
2. a ferry

渡頭(ㄉㄨˋㄊㄡˊ)
a ferry

渡輪(ㄉㄨˋㄌㄨㄣˊ)
a ferry steamer

渡過難關(ㄉㄨˋㄍㄨㄛˋㄋㄢˊㄍㄨㄢ)
to tide over a difficulty

渡口(ㄉㄨˋㄎㄡˇ)
a ferry

渡河(ㄉㄨˋㄏㄜˊ)
to cross a river: 我們可以用渡船渡河。We can cross the river by ferry.

渡海(ㄉㄨˋㄏㄞˇ)
to sail across a sea

渡航(ㄉㄨˋㄏㄤˊ)
to sail across a river or a sea

渡假(ㄉㄨˋㄐㄧㄚˋ)
to spend one's holidays

渡江(ㄉㄨˋㄐㄧㄤ)
to cross a large river

渡船(ㄉㄨˋㄔㄨㄢˊ)
a ferryboat

【渣】 2961
ㄓㄚ ja zhā
dregs; lees; grounds; sediment

渣滓(ㄓㄚㄗˇ)

〔水部〕

dregs; lees; grounds; sediment

渣子(ㄓㄚ·ㄗ)or 渣兒(ㄓㄚㄦ)
dregs; lees; grounds; sediment

【渠】 2962
ㄑㄩ chyu qú
1. a drain; a channel; a ditch
2. great; deep
3. he; she
4. a Chinese family name

渠輩(ㄑㄩㄅㄟ)
they; them

渠道(ㄑㄩㄉㄠ)
①an irrigation ditch ②a medium of communication; a channel

渠魁(ㄑㄩ ㄎㄨㄟ)or 渠帥(ㄑㄩ ㄕㄨㄞ)
chief criminals

【渤】 2963
ㄅㄛ bor bó
(said of water) swelling or rising

渤海(ㄅㄛ ㄏㄞ)
Pohai, a gulf of the Yellow Sea

【渥】 2964
ㄨㄛ woh wò
1. to dye
2. great (kindness)

渥丹(ㄨㄛ ㄉㄢ)
①to dye red ②deep red; vermilion

渥太華(ㄨㄛ ㄊㄞ ㄏㄨㄚ)
Ottawa, capital of Canada

渥惠(ㄨㄛ ㄏㄨㄟ)
great kindness; profound benefaction

渥澤(ㄨㄛ ㄗㄜ)
great kindness; profound benefaction

渥恩(ㄨㄛ ㄣ)
profound benefaction; great kindness

渥味(ㄨㄛ ㄨㄟ)
strong flavor

【渦】 2965
1. ㄨㄛ uo wō
a whirlpool; an eddy

渦電流(ㄨㄛ ㄉㄧㄢ ㄌㄧㄡ)
eddy current

渦流(ㄨㄛ ㄌㄧㄡ)
①(geography)the circular movement of a fluid; a whirling fluid; an eddy ②(physics) eddy current; vortex flow

渦輪發電機(ㄨㄛ ㄌㄨㄣ ㄈㄚ ㄉㄧㄢ ㄐㄧ)
a turbine generator

渦輪機(ㄨㄛ ㄌㄨㄣ ㄐㄧ)
a turbine

渦旋(ㄨㄛ ㄒㄩㄢ)
to whirl: 樹葉在風中渦旋。The leaves whirled in the wind.

【渦】 2965
2.《ㄨㄛ guo guō
name of a river

渦河(ㄍㄨㄛ ㄏㄜ)
name of a river flowing through Anhwei (安徽)

【渭】 2966
ㄨㄟ wey wèi
name of a river

渭河(ㄨㄟ ㄏㄜ)
Wei River, a tributary of the Yellow River

【港】 2967
《ㄤ gaang gǎng
1. a harbor; a seaport
2. a bay; a gulf
3. short for Hongkong

港幣(《ㄤ ㄅㄧ)
Hongkong currency

港督(《ㄤ ㄉㄨ)
the governor of Hongkong

港口(《ㄤ ㄎㄡ)
a harbor; a seaport; a port

港九(《ㄤ ㄐㄧㄡ)
Hongkong and Kowloon

港警(《ㄤ ㄐㄧㄥ)
the harbor police

港紙(《ㄤ ㄓ)
paper money circulated in Hongkong

港市(《ㄤ ㄕ)
a port

港澳(《ㄤ ㄠ)
Hongkong and Macao

港務局(《ㄤ ㄨ ㄐㄩ)
the harbor bureau

港灣(《ㄤ ㄨㄢ)
①a harbor ②a bay; a gulf

【渲】 2968
ㄒㄩㄢ shiuann
xuàn
to color with paint

渲染(ㄒㄩㄢ ㄖㄢ)
①to color with paint ②to make exaggerated additions in a story or report; to play up

【測】 2969
ㄘㄜ tseh cè

to measure; to survey

測不透(ㄘㄜ ·ㄅㄨ ㄊㄡ)
hard to understand; incomprehensible; unable to understand; unable to figure out

測地學(ㄘㄜ ㄉㄧ ㄒㄩㄝ)
geodesy

測定(ㄘㄜ ㄉㄧㄥ)
to determine

測度(ㄘㄜ ㄉㄨㄛ)
to infer; to speculate; to conjecture; to guess

測雷器(ㄘㄜ ㄌㄟ ㄑㄧ)
a mine detector

測力計(ㄘㄜ ㄌㄧ ㄐㄧ)
a hand-dynamometer 亦作「握力計」

測量(ㄘㄜ ㄌㄧㄤ)
①geodetic survey ②to survey

測量地形(ㄘㄜ ㄌㄧㄤ ㄉㄧ ㄒㄧㄥ)
to survey the topography

測量隊(ㄘㄜ ㄌㄧㄤ ㄉㄨㄟ)
a survey party

測量局(ㄘㄜ ㄌㄧㄤ ㄐㄩ)
a survey office

測量學(ㄘㄜ ㄌㄧㄤ ㄒㄩㄝ)
surveying

測量術(ㄘㄜ ㄌㄧㄤ ㄕㄨ)
geodetic surveying; surveying

測量水深(ㄘㄜ ㄌㄧㄤ ㄕㄨㄟ ㄕㄣ)
to strike soundings

測量員(ㄘㄜ ㄌㄧㄤ ㄩㄢ)
a land surveyor; a surveyor 亦作「測繪員」

測候(ㄘㄜ ㄏㄡ)
astronomical or meteorological observation

測繪(ㄘㄜ ㄏㄨㄟ)
to survey and map

測繪員(ㄘㄜ ㄏㄨㄟ ㄩㄢ)
a land surveyor; a surveyor

測謊(ㄘㄜ ㄏㄨㄤ)
a polygraph test

測謊器(ㄘㄜ ㄏㄨㄤ ㄑㄧ)
a lie detector; a polygraph

測角器(ㄘㄜ ㄐㄧㄠ ㄑㄧ)
a goniometer; a protractor

測徑器(ㄘㄜ ㄐㄧㄥ ㄑㄧ)
calipers

測深器(ㄘㄜ ㄕㄣ ㄑㄧ)
a sounder

測字(ㄘㄜ ㄗ)
to tell someone's fortune by analyzing the component

parts of the character he picks at random 亦作「拆字」

測字攤 (ㄘㄜˋ ㄗˋ ㄊㄢ)
a curbside stand where a fortuneteller tells customers' fortune by 測字

測驗 (ㄘㄜˋ ㄧˋ)
①to test; to examine ②a quiz or test: 老師明天要測驗我們算術。The teacher will give us a test in arithmetic tomorrow.

測音器 (ㄘㄜˋ ㄧㄣ ㄑㄧˋ)
a sound locator; an ˈacousti-timeter

測面法 (ㄘㄜˋ ㄇㄧㄢˋ ㄈㄚˇ)
cyclometry

測圓器 (ㄘㄜˋ ㄩㄢˊ ㄑㄧˋ)
a cyclometer

【渴】 2970
ㄎㄜˇ kee kě

1. thirsty
2. to long; to crave; to pine

渴筆 (ㄎㄜˇ ㄅㄧˇ)
①a dry brush ②a style in Chinese landscape painting done with a dry brush

渴病 (ㄎㄜˇ ㄅㄧㄥˋ)
diabetes

渴慕 (ㄎㄜˇ ㄇㄨˋ)
to long for; to aspire after

渴得很 (ㄎㄜˇ ˙ㄉㄜ ㄏㄣˇ)
very thirsty: 我覺得渴得很。I feel very thirsty.

渴念 (ㄎㄜˇ ㄋㄧㄢˋ)
to miss very much; to yearn for

渴求 (ㄎㄜˇ ㄑㄧㄡˊ)
to search for earnestly; to crave for

渴想 (ㄎㄜˇ ㄒㄧㄤˇ)
to miss very much; to long for; to crave for

渴賞 (ㄎㄜˇ ㄕㄤˇ)
eager for a reward

渴睡 (ㄎㄜˇ ㄕㄨㄟˋ)
①a doze; a cat nap; to doze ②sleepy

渴死 (ㄎㄜˇ ㄙˇ)
extremely thirsty

渴仰 (ㄎㄜˇ ㄧㄤˇ)
to adore; to admire

渴望 (ㄎㄜˇ ㄨㄤˋ)
to long for; to be thirsty for; to crave for; to aspire to: 他們渴望發財。They aspire after wealth.

渴雨 (ㄎㄜˇ ㄩˇ)
(said of land) thirsty for rain

渴欲 (ㄎㄜˇ ㄩˋ)
to aspire to

【湃】 2971
ㄆㄞˋ pay pài
billowy; turbulent

【湣】 2972
ㄇㄧㄣˇ miin mǐn
mixed; confused

【渺】 2973
ㄇㄧㄠˇ meau miǎo
1. endlessly long or vast; far
2. tiny; infinitesimal
3. indistinct; blurred

渺不足道 (ㄇㄧㄠˇ ㄅㄨˋ ㄗㄨˊ ㄉㄠˋ)
too small for mention

渺漫 (ㄇㄧㄠˇ ㄇㄢˋ)
endlessly long or vast

渺茫 (ㄇㄧㄠˇ ㄇㄤˊ)
①endlessly vast; boundless ②remote and vague; indistinct

渺渺 (ㄇㄧㄠˇ ㄇㄧㄠˇ)
blurred; indistinct

渺乎其微 (ㄇㄧㄠˇ ㄏㄨ ㄑㄧˊ ㄨㄟˊ)
too small to be measured; infinitesimal

渺小 (ㄇㄧㄠˇ ㄒㄧㄠˇ)
very small; tiny; infinitesimal; insignificant

渺然 (ㄇㄧㄠˇ ㄖㄢˊ)
vast; boundless; endless

渺無人跡 (ㄇㄧㄠˇ ㄨˊ ㄖㄣˊ ㄐㄧ)
remote and uninhabited

【游】 2974
ㄧㄡˊ you yóu
1. to swim; to float; to waft; to drift
2. same as 遊—to wander about
3. part of a river
4. a Chinese family name

游民 (ㄧㄡˊ ㄇㄧㄣˊ)
idle people; idlers

游牧 (ㄧㄡˊ ㄇㄨˋ)
nomadic

游牧民族 (ㄧㄡˊ ㄇㄨˋ ㄇㄧㄣˊ ㄗㄨˊ)
nomadic people; nomads

游目騁懷 (ㄧㄡˊ ㄇㄨˋ ㄔㄥˇ ㄏㄨㄞˊ)
to feel spiritual uplift before a thrilling view of nature

游蕩 (ㄧㄡˊ ㄉㄤˋ)
to loaf; loafing

游動 (ㄧㄡˊ ㄉㄨㄥˋ)
to move about

游談 (ㄧㄡˊ ㄊㄢˊ)

游離 (ㄧㄡˊ ㄌㄧˊ)
(of a radical, valency, nucleus, etc., in chemistry) free; ionization; liberation

游離分子 (ㄧㄡˊ ㄌㄧˊ ㄈㄣˋ ㄗˇ)
one who quits the collective

游宦 (ㄧㄡˊ ㄏㄨㄢˋ)
to serve as an official away from home

游擊 (ㄧㄡˊ ㄐㄧ)
①a military rank in former times ②a guerrilla attack; a hit-and-run attack

游擊隊 (ㄧㄡˊ ㄐㄧ ㄉㄨㄟˋ)
a guerrilla band; guerrillas

游擊戰 (ㄧㄡˊ ㄐㄧ ㄓㄢˋ)
a guerrilla warfare

游擊手 (ㄧㄡˊ ㄐㄧ ㄕㄡˇ)
(baseball) a shortstop

游騎兵 (ㄧㄡˊ ㄑㄧˊ ㄅㄧㄥ)
a ranger

游戲 (ㄧㄡˊ ㄒㄧˋ)
a game; play (also written 遊戲)

游戲人間 (ㄧㄡˊ ㄒㄧˋ ㄖㄣˊ ㄐㄧㄢ)
①to play through life ②a world of fun and frolic

游俠 (ㄧㄡˊ ㄒㄧㄚˊ)
a traveling swordsman; a traveling champion of justice

游學 (ㄧㄡˊ ㄒㄩㄝˊ)
to study in a strange land

游塵 (ㄧㄡˊ ㄔㄣˊ)
①floating particles of dust ②trivial things

游食 (ㄧㄡˊ ㄕˊ)
to live like a parasite

游士 (ㄧㄡˊ ㄕˋ)
a free-lancing scholar

游手好閒 (ㄧㄡˊ ㄕㄡˇ ㄏㄠˋ ㄒㄧㄢˊ)
loitering about and doing nothing; loafing 亦作「遊手好閒」

游山玩水 (ㄧㄡˊ ㄕㄢ ㄨㄢˊ ㄕㄨㄟˇ)
to roam in hills and play with water

游說 (ㄧㄡˊ ㄕㄨㄟˋ)
to lobby; to canvass (for a cause, project, etc.); to drum up support

游刃有餘 (ㄧㄡˊ ㄖㄣˋ ㄧㄡˇ ㄩˊ)
more than capable of doing something; highly competent

〔水部〕

to go canvassing; to canvass ②to play and talk

〔水 部〕

游資(١ㄡ ㄗ)
　idle capital; idle money

游子(١ㄡ ㄗˇ)
　①an ion ②a wandering son

游子思親(١ㄡ ㄗˇ ㄙ ㄑ١ㄣ)
　A wandering son thinks of
　his parents.

游辭(١ㄡ ㄘˊ)
　①unfounded remarks; a
　groundless statement ②a
　joke; a jest

游絲(١ㄡ ㄙ)
　gossamer

游移不定(١ㄡˊ ١ˊ ㄅㄨˋ ㄉ١ㄥˋ)
　undecided; wavering; hesitat-
　ing; vacillating

游移其詞(١ㄡˊ ١ˊ ㄑ١ˊ ㄘˊ)
　to hesitate in words

游弋 or 游奕(١ㄡˊ ١ˋ)
　(said of naval vessels) to
　patrol

游言(١ㄡˊ ١ㄢˊ)
　unfounded remarks; rumors

游泳(١ㄡˊ ㄩㄥˇ) or 游水(١ㄡˊ ㄕㄨㄟˇ)
　swimming

游泳池(١ㄡˊ ㄩㄥˇ ㄔˊ)
　a swimming pool

游泳衣(١ㄡˊ ㄩㄥˇ ١)
　a swimming suit

【渾】 1. ㄏㄨㄣˊ   hwen
　　　　　　　　　hún
1. entire; complete
2. to blend; to merge
3. muddy; turbid

渾名(ㄏㄨㄣˊ ㄇ١ㄥˊ)
　a nickname

渾蛋(ㄏㄨㄣˊ ㄉㄢˋ)
　"rotten egg"—(abusive lan-
　guage) a blackguard; a
　wretch; a scoundrel; a bas-
　tard; a skunk 亦作「混蛋」

渾天儀(ㄏㄨㄣˊ ㄊ١ㄢ ١ˊ)
　(astronomy) an armillary
　sphere

渾厚(ㄏㄨㄣˊ ㄏㄡˋ)
　①(said of one's character)
　simple and honest ②(said of
　writing, painting, etc.) sim-
　ple and vigorous

渾涵(ㄏㄨㄣˊ ㄏㄢˊ)
　to include; to contain; to
　embrace

渾渾噩噩(ㄏㄨㄣˊ ㄏㄨㄣˊ ㄜˋ ㄜˋ) or 渾
　噩(ㄏㄨㄣˊ ㄜˋ)
　①simple and honest ②igno-

rant; muddle-headed

渾家(ㄏㄨㄣˊ ㄐ١ㄚ)
　①the whole family ②(a
　polite expression) my wife

渾球(ㄏㄨㄣˊ ㄑ١ㄡˊ)
　a zany

渾象(ㄏㄨㄣˊ ㄒ١ㄤˋ)
　(astronomy) a celestial
　globe

渾濁(ㄏㄨㄣˊ ㄓㄨㄛˊ)
　turbid; muddy

渾成(ㄏㄨㄣˊ ㄔㄥˊ)
　to blend or merge into
　(something new)

渾身(ㄏㄨㄣˊ ㄕㄣ)
　one's entire body; from head
　to toe: 他渾身是傷。He was
　wounded from head to toe.

渾身解數(ㄏㄨㄣˊ ㄕㄣ ㄐ١ㄝˇ ㄕㄨˋ)
　①every means of solution
　②charm (of women)

渾身是膽(ㄏㄨㄣˊ ㄕㄣ ㄕˋ ㄉㄢˇ)
　very daring; fearless

渾水(ㄏㄨㄣˊ ㄕㄨㄟˇ)
　muddy water

渾水摸魚(ㄏㄨㄣˊ ㄕㄨㄟˇ ㄇㄛ ㄩˊ)
　to fish in troubled waters

渾然(ㄏㄨㄣˊ ㄖㄢˊ)
　①completely: 我渾然不覺冷。
　I don't feel cold at all. ②
　without leaving a trace

渾然一體(ㄏㄨㄣˊ ㄖㄢˊ ١ˋ ㄊ١ˇ)
　a unified entity; an integral
　whole

渾人(ㄏㄨㄣˊ ㄖㄣˊ)
　an unreasonable fellow

渾似(ㄏㄨㄣˊ ㄙˋ)
　as if; as though; very much
　alike

渾圓(ㄏㄨㄣˊ ㄩㄢˊ)
　①tactful; sophisticated ②a
　sphere ③perfectly round

【渾】 2. ㄏㄨㄣˋ   huenn
　　　　　　　　　hùn
chaotic; confused; messy

渾沌(ㄏㄨㄣˋ ㄉㄨㄣˋ)
　chaos; confusion; mess

渾沌初開(ㄏㄨㄣˋ ㄉㄨㄣˋ ㄔㄨ ㄎㄞ)
　when the universe was tak-
　ing shape

渾天儀(ㄏㄨㄣˋ ㄊ١ㄢ ١ˊ)
　a celestial globe; an armil-
　lary sphere

【湄】 ㄇㄟˊ   mei   méi
　shore; bank; the margin (of

the water)

湄公河(ㄇㄟˊ ㄍㄨㄥ ㄏㄜˊ)
　the Mekong River

【湊】 (湊) ㄘㄡˋ   tsow   còu   2977
1. to put together
2. to raise (fund)
3. to happen by chance
4. to move close to; to press
　near

湊不齊(ㄘㄡˋ ㄅㄨˋ ㄑ١ˊ)
　①unable to gather enough
　people together for a game
　②unable to get all the parts
　together to form the whole

湊不出(ㄘㄡˋ ㄅㄨˋ ㄔㄨ)
　unable to get a necessary
　sum of money ready; unable
　to raise the amount of
　(money)

湊分子(ㄘㄡˋ ㄈㄣˋ ㄗ)
　to raise money from among
　several people for a joint
　gift or a social party

湊膽子(ㄘㄡˋ ㄉㄢˇ ㄗ)
　to seek company so as to
　lessen fear or to boost cour-
　age

湊攏(ㄘㄡˋ ㄌㄨㄥˇ)
　to manage to collect or
　gather together

湊空兒(ㄘㄡˋ ㄎㄨㄥˋㄦ)
　to take advantage of leisure
　to do something

湊合(ㄘㄡˋ ㄏㄜˊ)
　①to manage to collect or
　gather together ②to make
　do with what is available ③
　to improvise ④not too bad;
　passable

湊集(ㄘㄡˋ ㄐ١ˊ)
　to scrape together; to man-
　age to gather or collect
　together

湊近(ㄘㄡˋ ㄐ١ㄣˋ)
　to get near; to approach; to
　come closer

湊齊(ㄘㄡˋ ㄑ١ˊ)
　①to manage to line up
　enough people for a game ②
　to manage to collect all the
　parts to form the whole

湊巧(ㄘㄡˋ ㄑ١ㄠˇ)
　by chance; by coincidence:
　我湊巧遇到他。I met him by
　chance.

湊趣兒(ㄘㄡˋ ㄑㄩˋㄦ)

①to make fun; to poke fun:
別拿他湊趣兒。Don't poke fun
at him. ② to cater to
another's taste

湊成(ㄘㄡˋ ㄔㄥˊ)
to succeed in putting
together

湊數(ㄘㄡˋ ㄕㄨˋ)
①to make up the proper
number ②to play second
fiddle; to play an unimportant role

湊熱鬧(ㄘㄡˋ ㄖㄜ˙ ·ㄋㄠ)
①to take part in merriment;
to help make merry ②to
add trouble to

湊在一起(ㄘㄡˋ ㄗㄞˋ ㄧˋ ㄑㄧˇ)
①to put together ②(said of
people) to gang up; to team
up

湊足(ㄘㄡˋ ㄗㄨˊ)
①to manage to raise
enough money for a purpose
②to manage to line up
enough people for a game

【湎】 2978
ㄇㄧㄢˇ mean miǎn
1. drunk
2. unaware
3. changing

湎於酒(ㄇㄧㄢˇ ㄩˊ ㄐㄧㄡˇ)
to be addicted to intoxicants

【湍】 2979
ㄊㄨㄢ tuan tuān
rapidly flowing

湍瀨(ㄊㄨㄢ ㄌㄞˋ)
shallow rapids

湍流(ㄊㄨㄢ ㄌㄧㄡˊ)
rapids; torrent; swift current: 他逆著湍流游泳。He
swam against the swift current.

湍疾(ㄊㄨㄢ ㄐㄧˊ)
(said of water) rapid

湍急(ㄊㄨㄢ ㄐㄧˊ)
(said of water) swift; rapid:
水流湍急。The current is
rapid.

【溢】 2980
ㄅㄣˋ pern pèn
name of a river in Kiangsi

溢水(ㄅㄣˋ ㄕㄨㄟˇ)
name of a river in Kiangsi

【湔】 2981
ㄐㄧㄢ jian jiān
to wash

湔洗(ㄐㄧㄢ ㄒㄧˇ)
to wash

湔雪(ㄐㄧㄢ ㄒㄩㄝˇ)
to wipe away (disgrace,
etc.)

湔濯(ㄐㄧㄢ ㄓㄨㄛˊ)
to wash

【湜】 2982
ㄕˊ shyr shí
(said of water) transparent

【湧】 2983
ㄩㄥˇ yeong yǒng
1. to gush; to pour
2. to rise

湧進(ㄩㄥˇ ㄐㄧㄣˋ)
to swarm into; to sweep
into: 人們湧進電影院。People
swarmed into the cinema.

湧泉(ㄩㄥˇ ㄑㄩㄢˊ)
a fountain; a spring

湧現(ㄩㄥˇ ㄒㄧㄢˋ)
to crop up (in one's mind,
etc.); to emerge: 新問題不斷
湧現。New problems are con-
stantly emerging.

湧至(ㄩㄥˇ ㄓˋ)
to arrive like a flood

湧出(ㄩㄥˇ ㄔㄨ)
to well out; to spring out

湧上來(ㄩㄥˇ ㄕㄤˋ ㄌㄞˊ)
①to well up: 她的眼淚湧上
來。Tears welled up in her
eyes. ②to come in a sweep

湧上心來(ㄩㄥˇ ㄕㄤˋ ㄒㄧㄣ ·ㄌㄞ)
to come up in the mind like
a ground swell

【湖】 2984
ㄏㄨˊ hwu hú
1. a lake
2. a Chinese family name

湖泊(ㄏㄨˊ ㄆㄛˊ)
lakes

湖北(ㄏㄨˊ ㄅㄟˇ)
Hupeh Province

湖筆(ㄏㄨˊ ㄅㄧˇ)
a writing brush made at Hu-
chow(湖州), Chekiang

湖邊(ㄏㄨˊ ㄅㄧㄢ)or 湖畔(ㄏㄨˊ ㄆㄢˋ)
beside the lake; the shore of
a lake

湖畔詩人(ㄏㄨˊ ㄆㄢˋ ㄕ ㄖㄣˊ)
the Lake Poets (in English
literature)

湖南(ㄏㄨˊ ㄋㄢˊ)
Hunan Province

湖光山色(ㄏㄨˊ ㄍㄨㄤ ㄕㄢ ㄙㄜˋ)
the natural beauty of lakes
and mountains

湖廣(ㄏㄨˊ ㄍㄨㄤˇ)
name of an ancient province
covering parts of Hunan,
Hupeh, Kwangtung and
Kwangsi

湖廣熟天下足(ㄏㄨˊ ㄍㄨㄤˇ ㄕㄡˊ ㄊㄧㄢ ㄒㄧㄚˋ ㄗㄨˊ)
When Hukwang has a
bumper crop, the country
will be free from hunger.

湖海之士(ㄏㄨˊ ㄏㄞˇ ㄓ ㄕˋ)
a man with a great mind

湖心(ㄏㄨˊ ㄒㄧㄣ)
the middle of a lake

湖心亭(ㄏㄨˊ ㄒㄧㄣ ㄊㄧㄥˊ)
a pavilion in the middle of a
lake

湖沼(ㄏㄨˊ ㄓㄠˇ)
lakes and marshes

湖州(ㄏㄨˊ ㄓㄡ)
Huchow, an old prefecture
in Chekiang

湖縐(ㄏㄨˊ ㄓㄡˋ)
a kind of silk produced at
Huchow(湖州), Chekiang

湖水(ㄏㄨˊ ㄕㄨㄟˇ)
lake water: 湖水甚清。The
lake water is clear.

湖澤(ㄏㄨˊ ㄗㄜˊ)
lakes

湖煙(ㄏㄨˊ ㄧㄢ)
mist on a lake

【湘】 2985
ㄒㄧㄤ shiang xiāng
1. name of a river flowing
through Hunan
2. an alternative name of
Hunan

湘妃(ㄒㄧㄤ ㄈㄟ)
the two wives of the legendary Emperor Shun (舜)

湘妃竹(ㄒㄧㄤ ㄈㄟ ㄓㄨˊ)
speckled bamboo

湘夫人(ㄒㄧㄤ ㄈㄨ ㄖㄣˊ)
the nymph of the Hsiang
River

湘女多情(ㄒㄧㄤ ㄋㄩˇ ㄉㄨㄛ ㄑㄧㄥˊ)
Girls of Hunan are affec-
tionate.

湘簾(ㄒㄧㄤ ㄌㄧㄢˊ)
a bamboo curtain made of
speckled bamboo

湘江(ㄒㄧㄤ ㄐㄧㄤ)or 湘水(ㄒㄧㄤ ㄕㄨㄟˇ)
the Hsiang River, flowing
through Hunan

湘君(ㄒㄧㄤ ㄐㄩㄣ)

〔水部〕

a deity of the Hsiang River in Hunan

湘軍(ㄒㄧㄤ ㄐㄩㄣ)
the army organized by Tseng Kuo-fan (曾國藩) toward the end of the Ching Dynasty to put down the Taiping Rebellion, so called because the soldiers were from Hunan

湘繡(ㄒㄧㄤ ㄒㄧㄡˋ)
embroideries from Hunan; Hunan-style embroideries

湘竹(ㄒㄧㄤ ㄓㄨˊ)
speckled bamboo

湘中(ㄒㄧㄤ ㄓㄨㄥ)
an alternative name of Hunan

【湛】 2986 ㄓㄢ jann zhàn
1. dewy
2. deep; profound
3. same as 沈—to sink
4. a Chinese family name

湛藍(ㄓㄢ ㄌㄢˊ)
dark blue; azure

湛新(ㄓㄢ ㄒㄧㄣ)
brand-new: 這是湛新的車子。 This is a brand-new car.

湛湛(ㄓㄢ ㄓㄢ)
①dewy ②deep; profound

湛然(ㄓㄢ ㄖㄢˊ)
①(said of water) transparent: 水清湛然。 The water is clean and transparent. ②quiet; calm

湛恩(ㄓㄢ ㄣ)
great kindness

湛憂(ㄓㄢ ㄧㄡ)
deep worry

【湮】 2987 ㄧㄣ in yīn
1. to bury
2. to block
3. long (in time)

湮沒(ㄧㄣ ㄇㄛˋ)
to bury or be buried

湮沒不彰(ㄧㄣ ㄇㄛˋ ㄅㄨˋ ㄓㄤ)
to fall into the shade

湮沒無聞(ㄧㄣ ㄇㄛˋ ㄨˊ ㄨㄣˊ)
to remain unknown; to remain obscure; to pass into oblivion

湮滅(ㄧㄣ ㄇㄧㄝˋ)
to bury; to destroy (evidence): 他們湮滅證據。 They destroyed the evidence.

湮沈(ㄧㄣ ㄔㄣˊ)
to have no chance to rise in the world

湮阨(ㄧㄣ ㄜˋ)
clogged; blocked

湮遠(ㄧㄣ ㄩㄢˇ)
very long (in time)

【湫】 2988 ㄐㄧㄡ jiou jiū
1. name of a river in Kansu Province
2. a small pond

【湫】 2988 ㄐㄧㄠˇ jeau jiǎo
damp and narrow

湫隘(ㄐㄧㄠˇ ㄞˋ)
a damp and narrow place

【湯】 2989 ㄊㄤ tang
tāng
1. hot water
2. soup; broth
3. a Chinese family name

湯餅筵(ㄊㄤ ㄅㄧㄥˇ ㄧㄢˊ)
a dinner party given on the third day after the birth of a baby 亦作「湯餅之喜」

湯婆子(ㄊㄤ ㄆㄛˊ ˙ㄗ)
a hot-water bedwarmer, made of copper or pewter 亦作「湯婆」

湯麵(ㄊㄤ ㄇㄧㄢˋ)
noodles with soup

湯沐(ㄊㄤ ㄇㄨˋ)
to bathe; to take a bath: 他每晨湯沐。 He takes a bath every morning.

湯頭(ㄊㄤ ㄊㄡˊ)
a prescription of herbal medicines

湯糰(ㄊㄤ ㄊㄨㄢˊ)
balls of glutinous rice

湯鍋(ㄊㄤ ㄍㄨㄛ)
a soup pot

湯火(ㄊㄤ ㄏㄨㄛˇ)
hot water and burning fire —dangerous things

湯鑊(ㄊㄤ ㄏㄨㄛˋ)
a cauldron for boiling criminals in ancient China

湯池(ㄊㄤ ㄔˊ)
①(literally) a city moat filled with boiling water —impenetrable defense works ②hot springs

湯池之固(ㄊㄤ ㄔˊ ㄓ ㄍㄨˋ)
impenetrable defense works

湯匙(ㄊㄤ ㄔˊ)
a spoon

湯勺(ㄊㄤ ㄕㄠˊ)
a soup ladle

湯水(ㄊㄤ ㄕㄨㄟˇ)
①name of a river in Honan ②soup ③financial means ④troublesome

湯若望(ㄊㄤ ㄖㄨㄛˋ ㄨㄤˋ)
Joannes Adam Schall von Bell (1591-1666), German Jesuit missionary who introduced the solar calendar to China

湯藥(ㄊㄤ ㄧㄠˋ)
decoction of Chinese medicine 亦作「湯液」

湯武(ㄊㄤ ㄨˇ)
Tang and Wu, founders of the Shang and Chou dynasties respectively

湯武革命(ㄊㄤ ㄨˇ ㄍㄜˊ ㄇㄧㄥˋ)
the revolutions by which Tang founded the Dynasty Shang and Wu founded the Dynasty Chou

湯碗(ㄊㄤ ㄨㄢˇ)
a large bowl for holding soup

湯圓(ㄊㄤ ㄩㄢˊ)
balls of glutinous rice

【湯】 2989 2.ㄕㄤ shang
shāng
(said of water) flowing

湯湯(ㄕㄤ ㄕㄤ)
(said of water) flowing turbulently

【湟】 2990 ㄏㄨㄤˊ hwang
huáng
1. a mean, dirty place
2. name of a river

【渫】 2991 ㄒㄧㄝˋ shieh xiè
to remove; to eliminate

【湲】 2992 ㄩㄢˊ yuan yuán
(said of water) flowing

【湑】 2993 ㄒㄩˇ sheu xǔ
luxuriant; rich

【湢】 2994 ㄅㄧˋ bih bì
1. a bathroom
2. neat; orderly

【湋】 2995 ㄨㄟˊ uei wéi

a bend on a river

【涴】 2996
ㄩㄢ yean yǔn
(said of clouds) forming or rising

【湉】 2997
ㄊㄧㄢ tyan tien
to flow placidly

十畫

【溫】 2998
(溫) ㄨㄣ uen wēn
1. warm; mild; lukewarm; to warm: 請把酒溫一下。Please warm up the wine.
2. to review; to revise
3. temperature
4. a Chinese family name

溫飽(ㄨㄣ ㄅㄠ)
adequately fed and clothed

溫帶(ㄨㄣ ㄉㄞ)
the Temperate Zone

溫帶氣候(ㄨㄣ ㄉㄞ ㄑㄧ ㄏㄡ)
temperate climate

溫帶植物(ㄨㄣ ㄉㄞ ㄓ ㄨ)
the flora of the Temperate Zone

溫度(ㄨㄣ ㄉㄨ)
temperature

溫度計(ㄨㄣ ㄉㄨ ㄐㄧ)or 溫度表
(ㄨㄣ ㄉㄨ ㄅㄧㄠ)
a thermometer: 華氏溫度表 the Fahrenheit thermometer 攝氏溫度表 the Celsius thermometer

溫尼伯(ㄨㄣ ㄋㄧ ㄅㄛ)
Winnipeg, a city in Canada

溫暖(ㄨㄣ ㄋㄨㄢ)
warm; warmth: 這件外衣可以使你保持溫暖。This coat will keep you warm.

溫良(ㄨㄣ ㄌㄧㄤ)
good-natured

溫哥華(ㄨㄣ ㄍㄜ ㄏㄨㄚ)
Vancouver, a city in Canada

溫故知新(ㄨㄣ ㄍㄨ ㄓ ㄒㄧㄣ)
to learn new things by reviewing old things

溫恭自虛(ㄨㄣ ㄍㄨㄥ ㄗ ㄒㄩ)
gentle and modest

溫開水(ㄨㄣ ㄎㄞ ㄕㄨㄟ)
lukewarm boiled water

溫炕(ㄨㄣ ㄎㄤ)
a brick or earthen bed warmed by a fire underneath (in North China)

溫和(ㄨㄣ ㄏㄜ)
gentle; mild; temperate; warm: 天氣還溫和呢。The weather is still warm.

溫和派(ㄨㄣ ㄏㄜ ㄆㄞ)
the moderate faction; a moderate (as opposed to a radical)

溫厚(ㄨㄣ ㄏㄡ)
gentle and sincere

溫酒(ㄨㄣ ㄐㄧㄡ)
to heat wine; lukewarm wine

溫居(ㄨㄣ ㄐㄩ)
① to congratulate someone on moving into a new residence ② a housewarming

溫覺(ㄨㄣ ㄐㄩㄝ)
the faculty to feel hot or cold

溫情(ㄨㄣ ㄑㄧㄥ)
kindness; warm-heartedness; a warm feelings

溫情主義(ㄨㄣ ㄑㄧㄥ ㄓㄨ ㄧ)
① paternalism ② soft-heartedness; excessive tender-heartedness

溫泉(ㄨㄣ ㄑㄩㄢ)
a hot spring; a mineral spring; a spa

溫泉浴(ㄨㄣ ㄑㄩㄢ ㄩ)
a hot-spring bath

溫習(ㄨㄣ ㄒㄧ)
to review (what has been learned): 他溫習功課。He reviews his lessons.

溫血動物(ㄨㄣ ㄒㄧㄝ ㄉㄨㄥ ㄨ)
a warm-blooded animal

溫馨(ㄨㄣ ㄒㄧㄣ)
warm and fragrant

溫煦(ㄨㄣ ㄒㄩ)
mild and warm

溫馴(ㄨㄣ ㄒㄩㄣ)
easily controlled; docile; meek; tame

溫州(ㄨㄣ ㄓㄡ)
Wenchow, Chekiang

溫州灣(ㄨㄣ ㄓㄡ ㄨㄢ)
Wenchow Bay (off Wenchow, Chekiang)

溫差(ㄨㄣ ㄔㄞ)
difference in temperature; the range of temperature

溫床(ㄨㄣ ㄔㄨㄤ)
a hotbed

溫室(ㄨㄣ ㄕ)
a greenhouse

溫書(ㄨㄣ ㄕㄨ)
to read familiar books again

溫水(ㄨㄣ ㄕㄨㄟ)
lukewarm water

溫水浴(ㄨㄣ ㄕㄨㄟ ㄩ)
a warm water bath; a hot water bath

溫順(ㄨㄣ ㄕㄨㄣ)
gentle; good-natured; docile; obedient: 她常常騎溫順的馬。She always rides a docile horse.

溫柔(ㄨㄣ ㄖㄡ)
warm and tender; sweet-natured

溫柔敦厚(ㄨㄣ ㄖㄡ ㄉㄨㄣ ㄏㄡ)
tender and gentle

溫柔鄉(ㄨㄣ ㄖㄡ ㄒㄧㄤ)
(literally) land of the tender — ① a brothel ② the enthralling experience of enjoying female charms in an intimate manner

溫潤(ㄨㄣ ㄖㄨㄣ)
① mild and smooth ② beautiful and tender

溫辭(ㄨㄣ ㄘ)
mild or gentle words

溫存(ㄨㄣ ㄘㄨㄣ)
tender; loving; caressing

溫存話兒(ㄨㄣ ㄘㄨㄣ ㄏㄨㄚㄦ)
loving words

溫雅(ㄨㄣ ㄧㄚ)
gentle and graceful

溫顏(ㄨㄣ ㄧㄢ)
a happy and agreeable look

溫婉(ㄨㄣ ㄨㄢ)
gentle; obedient

溫文(ㄨㄣ ㄨㄣ)
gentle and polite

溫文爾雅(ㄨㄣ ㄨㄣ ㄦ ㄧㄚ)
gentle and graceful

【源】 2999
ㄩㄢ yuan yuán
a source; a head (of a stream)

源頭(ㄩㄢ ㄊㄡ)
a head or a source (of a stream)

源流(ㄩㄢ ㄌㄧㄡ)
full particulars; all the details; the whole story

源源流流(ㄩㄢ ㄑㄧㄥ ㄌㄧㄡ ㄑㄧㄥ)or
源清流潔(ㄩㄢ ㄑㄧㄥ ㄌㄧㄡ ㄐㄧㄝ)
(literally) If a stream is

（水部）

（水
部）

clear, it is because the
source is clear.—If the
leader is good, his followers
will be good.

源泉(ㄩㄢˊ ㄑㄩㄢˊ)
an original source; a
fountainhead

源水(ㄩㄢˊ ㄕㄨㄟˇ)
a fountainhead

源委 or 原委(ㄩㄢˊ ㄨㄟˇ)
full particulars; all the
details; the whole story: 請你
告訴我源委。Please let me
know all the details.

源源本本 or 元元本本(ㄩㄢˊ ㄩㄢˊ
ㄅㄣˇ ㄅㄣˇ)
from beginning to end; without omissions; the whole
story

源源不絕(ㄩㄢˊ ㄩㄢˊ ㄅㄨˋ ㄐㄩㄝˊ)
to continue without end

源遠而來(ㄩㄢˊ ㄩㄢˇ ㄦˊ ㄌㄞˊ)
to come in an endless flow

源遠流長(ㄩㄢˊ ㄩㄢˇ ㄌㄧㄡˊ ㄔㄤˊ)
(literally) to have a long
course originating in a
remote source—to have a
long history

【溘】 3000
ㄎㄜˋ keh kè
sudden; abrupt; unexpected

溘謝(ㄎㄜˋ ㄒㄧㄝˋ)
to die suddenly

溘逝(ㄎㄜˋ ㄕˋ)or 溘然長逝(ㄎㄜˋ ㄖㄢˊ
ㄔㄤˊ ㄕˋ)
to die suddenly: 他溘然長逝。
He died suddenly.

溘然(ㄎㄜˋ ㄖㄢˊ)
suddenly; unexpectedly; all
of a sudden

【溟】 3001
ㄇㄧㄥˊ ming míng
1. drizzle
2. vast; boundless
3. the sea; the ocean

溟滓(ㄇㄧㄥˊ ㄗˇ)
endlessly vast; boundless

溟濛(ㄇㄧㄥˊ ㄇㄥˊ)
①drizzle ②gloomy; dim;
obscure

溟溟(ㄇㄧㄥˊ ㄇㄧㄥˊ)
①drizzling ②gloomy; dim;
dark

溟島(ㄇㄧㄥˊ ㄉㄠˇ)
an island in the sea

溟海(ㄇㄧㄥˊ ㄏㄞˇ)
a dark sea

溟池(ㄇㄧㄥˊ ㄔˊ)
the northern sea

【溝】 3002
《ㄡ gou gōu
1. a ditch; a waterway; a moat
2. a groove; a rut

溝瀆(《ㄡ ㄉㄨˊ)
a ditch; a channel; a drain

溝通(《ㄡ ㄊㄨㄥ)
to bring about an unob-
structed interflow of (feelings, ideas, etc.); to act as
an intermediary for the promotion of mutual under-
standing; to facilitate the
flow of (culture, etc.)

溝壑(《ㄡ ㄏㄨㄛˋ)
a valley, gorge, or canyon

溝渠(《ㄡ ㄑㄩˊ)
a ditch; a drain; a channel; a
drain

溝洫(《ㄡ ㄒㄩˋ)
an irrigation ditch

溝中瘠(《ㄡ ㄓㄨㄥ ㄐㄧˊ)
a poor person found dead in
a ditch

溝子(《ㄡ ˙ㄗ)or 溝兒(《ㄡ ㄦ)
①a ditch; a drain; a channel; a gutter ②a groove

【溜】 3003
1. ㄌㄧㄡˋ liow liù
1. rapids
2. a row; a column
3. surroundings; neighborhood

溜溜 or 溜溜(ㄌㄧㄡˋ ㄌㄧㄡˋ)
①to take a stroll; to stroll;
to ramble: 我們溜溜去。Let's
take a stroll. ②the murmur
of flowing waters

溜兒(ㄌㄧㄡˋ ㄦ)
a row; a column

【溜】 3003
2. ㄌㄧㄡ liou liū
1. to go secretly and quietly
2. to slip; to slide

溜邊兒(ㄌㄧㄡ ㄅㄧㄢ ㄦ)
to go stealthily

溜冰(ㄌㄧㄡ ㄅㄧㄥ)
to skate; skating

溜冰鞋(ㄌㄧㄡ ㄅㄧㄥ ㄒㄧㄝˊ)
a pair of skates; skating
shoes; roller skates: 他買了一
雙溜冰鞋。He bought a pair
of skates.

溜冰場(ㄌㄧㄡ ㄅㄧㄥ ㄔㄤˇ)or(ㄌㄧㄡ
ㄅㄧㄥ ㄔㄤˊ)
a skating rink

溜門子的(ㄌㄧㄡ ㄇㄣˊ ˙ㄗ ˙ㄉㄜ)
a sneak thief

溜達(ㄌㄧㄡ ˙ㄉㄚ)or(ㄌㄧㄡ ㄉㄚˊ)
to stroll; to ramble: 我們在
鎮上溜達溜達。We rambled
about the town.

溜光(ㄌㄧㄡ ㄍㄨㄤ)
①smooth ②(said of people)
to have all gone away

溜口(ㄌㄧㄡ ㄎㄡˇ)
a slip of the tongue; to
divulge a secret unintentionally; to blurt out

溜滑(ㄌㄧㄡ ㄏㄨㄚˊ)
①slippery ②cunning; crafty

溜滑板(ㄌㄧㄡ ㄏㄨㄚˊ ㄅㄢˇ)
to skate with a skateboard

溜之大吉(ㄌㄧㄡ ㄓ ㄉㄚˋ ㄐㄧˊ)
to leave stealthily; to leave
without notifying others; to
slip out

溜走(ㄌㄧㄡ ㄗㄡˇ)
to leave stealthily; to slip
away: 他偷偷地溜走沒被人看
見。He slipped away without
being seen.

【準】 3004
ㄓㄨㄣˇ joen zhǔn
1. level; even
2. a rule; a criterion; a standard; accurate; accuracy: 你的
工作未達標準。Your work is
below (the) standard.
3. to aim; to sight
4. would-be (bride, son-in-law,
etc.); to-be
5. (law) quasi-
6. certainly: 他明天準去。He'll
certainly be there tomorrow.

準兒(ㄓㄨㄣˇ ㄦ)
certain; sure: 這種天氣沒準
兒。No one can be sure
about this kind of weather.

準備(ㄓㄨㄣˇ ㄅㄟˋ)
①to prepare; to get ready;
preparation: 妳準備好了嗎？
Are you ready? ②to plan:
他們準備下星期三開始試驗。
They plan to start the
experiment next Wednesday.

準備活動(ㄓㄨㄣˇ ㄅㄟˋ ㄏㄨㄛˊ ㄉㄨㄥˋ)
a warming-up exercise; a
limbering-up exercise

準備金(ㄓㄨㄣˇ ㄅㄟˋ ㄐㄧㄣ)
①preparatory funds ②
(banking) reserve

準不準(ㄓㄨㄣˇ ㄅㄨˋ ㄓㄨㄣˇ)

Is it accurate? 或 Is it correct? 或 Is it true? 或 Does the clock keep good time?

準犯罪 (ㄓㄨㄣ ㄈㄢ ㄗㄨㄟ)
(law) quasi-offense

準的 (ㄓㄨㄣ ㄉㄧ)
a standard; a criterion

準定 (ㄓㄨㄣ ㄉㄧㄥ)
definitely 亦作「一定」

準頭 (ㄓㄨㄣ ˙ㄊㄡ)
accuracy; a standard: 他做事沒有準頭。 There is no standard in what he does.

準禁治産者 (ㄓㄨㄣ ㄐㄧㄣ ㄓ ㄙㄢ ㄓㄜ)
(law) a quasi-incompetent person

準據 (ㄓㄨㄣ ㄐㄩ)
a basis: 這信念沒任何科學的準據。The belief has no scientific basis whatever.

準確 (ㄓㄨㄣ ㄑㄩㄝ)
correct; accurate; precise; exact: 這句子不大準確。This sentence is not quite correct.

準確性 (ㄓㄨㄣ ㄑㄩㄝ ㄒㄧㄥ)
accuracy

準新娘 (ㄓㄨㄣ ㄒㄧㄣ ㄋㄧㄤ)
a would-be bride; a bride-to-be

準新郎 (ㄓㄨㄣ ㄒㄧㄣ ㄌㄤ)
a would-be bridegroom; a bridegroom-to-be

準星 (ㄓㄨㄣ ㄒㄧㄥ)
the front sight (of a gun)

準成 (ㄓㄨㄣ ㄔㄥ)
reliable; dependable

準時 (ㄓㄨㄣ ㄕ)
punctual; punctually; punctuality; on time: 請準時出席。You are requested to come punctually.

準式 (ㄓㄨㄣ ㄕ)
a rule; a regulation; a criterion

準繩 (ㄓㄨㄣ ㄕㄥ)
①(carpenter's) marking line ②a criterion; a standard: 我們學校有很高的教學準繩。Our school has a high standard of teaching.

準則 (ㄓㄨㄣ ㄗㄜ)
a rule; a criterion; a standard

【溢】 3005
ㄧ yih yì
1. to flow over; to brim over
2. excessive

溢美 (ㄧ ㄇㄟ)
to praise excessively

溢美之言 (ㄧ ㄇㄟ ㄓ ㄧㄢ)
words of fulsome praise

溢滿 (ㄧ ㄇㄢ)
to brim over; to overflow

溢目 (ㄧ ㄇㄨ)
to crowd one's sight; to be too numerous to be fully seen

溢洪道 (ㄧ ㄏㄨㄥ ㄉㄠ)
a spillway

溢價 (ㄧ ㄐㄧㄚ)
to soar beyond the original price

溢出 (ㄧ ㄔㄨ)
to brim over; to flow over; to overflow; to spill over: 這河水溢出兩岸。The river flowed over its banks.

溢收 (ㄧ ㄕㄡ)
to earn more than planned

溢額 (ㄧ ㄜ)
the amount in excess; excess; overage

溢惡 (ㄧ ㄜ)
to be excessively abusive

溢於言表 (ㄧ ㄩ ㄧㄢ ㄅㄧㄠ)
(said of emotions or inner feelings) to show clearly in one's utterances and manners

溢譽 (ㄧ ㄩ)
flattery; excessive praises; to flatter; to praise excessively: 別爲她的溢譽所騙。Don't be deceived by her flatteries.

【溥】 3006
ㄆㄨ puu pǔ
1. great; wide; vast
2. universal

溥博 (ㄆㄨ ㄅㄛ)
inclusive and extensive

溥被 (ㄆㄨ ㄅㄟ)
to spread widely

溥天同慶 (ㄆㄨ ㄊㄧㄢ ㄊㄨㄥ ㄑㄧㄥ)
simultaneously celebrated everywhere under the sun, universally celebrated

溥天之下 (ㄆㄨ ㄊㄧㄢ ㄓ ㄒㄧㄚ)
everywhere under the sun

溥儀 (ㄆㄨ ㄧ)
Pu-yi, the last emperor of the Ching Dynasty

溥原 (ㄆㄨ ㄩㄢ)
an extensive plain; a prairie

【溧】 3007
ㄌㄧ lih lì
1. name of a river flowing through Anhwei and Kiangsu
2. name of a county in Kiangsu

溧烈 (ㄌㄧ ㄌㄧㄝ)
biting cold

溧水 (ㄌㄧ ㄕㄨㄟ)
name of a county and a river in Kiangsu

【溯】 3008
ㄙㄨ suh sù
1. to go upstream; to go against a stream
2. to recall

溯洄 (ㄙㄨ ㄏㄨㄟ)
to go upstream

溯江而上 (ㄙㄨ ㄐㄧㄤ ㄦ ㄕㄤ)
to go upstream in a boat

溯自 (ㄙㄨ ㄗ)
ever since

溯溯 (ㄙㄨ ㄧㄣ)
to go upstream

溯源 (ㄙㄨ ㄩㄢ)
to trace back to the source

【溪】 3009
ㄒㄧ shi xī
(又讀 ㄑㄧ chi qī)
a mountain stream

溪流 (ㄒㄧ ㄌㄧㄡ)
a (mountain) stream; a brook

溪谷 (ㄒㄧ ㄍㄨ)
a valley; a dale; a canyon; a gorge

溪口 (ㄒㄧ ㄎㄡ)
a town in Chekiang, where President Chiang Kai-shek was born

溪澗 (ㄒㄧ ㄐㄧㄢ)
a mountain stream

溪水 (ㄒㄧ ㄕㄨㄟ)
the water of a mountain stream; mountain streams

【溲】 3010
ㄙㄡ sou sōu
1. to urinate
2. to immerse; to soak; to drench

溲便 (ㄙㄡ ㄅㄧㄢ)
to urinate

溲溺 (ㄙㄡ ㄋㄧㄠ)
to urinate

溲箕 (ㄙㄡ ㄐㄧ)
a basket for washing rice

溲器 (ㄙㄡ ㄑㄧ)

【水部】

a urinal

【溴】 3011 ㄒㄧㄡˋ shiow xiù

bromine

溴化鈉(ㄒㄧㄡˋ ㄏㄨㄚˋ ㄋㄚˋ)
sodium bromide

溴化鉀(ㄒㄧㄡˋ ㄏㄨㄚˋ ㄐㄧㄚˇ)
potassium bromide

溴化氫(ㄒㄧㄡˋ ㄏㄨㄚˋ ㄑㄧㄥ)
hydrogen bromide

溴化銀(ㄒㄧㄡˋ ㄏㄨㄚˋ ㄧㄣˊ)
silver bromide

溴水(ㄒㄧㄡˋ ㄕㄨㄟˇ)
bromine water

溴酸(ㄒㄧㄡˋ ㄙㄨㄢ)
bromic acid

【溷】 3012 ㄏㄨㄣˋ huenn hùn
1. dirty
2. messy

溷跡(ㄏㄨㄣˋ ㄐㄧ)
to conceal

溷汁(ㄏㄨㄣˋ ㄓ)
dirty water; sewage

溷濁(ㄏㄨㄣˋ ㄓㄨㄛˊ)
dirty; muddy

溷廁(ㄏㄨㄣˋ ㄘˋ)
a water closet; a lavatory

溷看(ㄏㄨㄣˋ ㄎㄢˋ)
messy; confused; chaotic: 他已經溷看了。He became confused.

【溺】 3013 ㄋㄧˋ nih nì
1. to drown
2. to indulge

溺女(ㄋㄧˋ ㄋㄩˇ)
to drown a daughter at birth (in former times when daughters were unwanted in poor families)

溺鬼(ㄋㄧˋ ㄍㄨㄟˇ)
the ghost of the drowned

溺職(ㄋㄧˋ ㄓ)
to neglect one's duty

溺志(ㄋㄧˋ ㄓˋ)
to indulge (in an enjoyment, pursuit, etc.)

溺死(ㄋㄧˋ ㄙˇ)or溺斃(ㄋㄧˋ ㄅㄧˋ)
to be drowned: 那男人溺死了。The man was drowned.

溺愛(ㄋㄧˋ ㄞˋ)
to lavish one's love upon (a child); to pamper: 他溺愛孩子。He pampers his child.

溺於酒色(ㄋㄧˋ ㄩˊ ㄐㄧㄡˇ ㄙㄜˋ)
to indulge in wine and

women

【溺】 3013 ㄋㄧㄠˋ niaw niào
to urinate

溺褲(ㄋㄧㄠˋ ㄎㄨˋ)
to wet oneself

溺器(ㄋㄧㄠˋ ㄑㄧˋ)
a urinal; a bedpan

溺牀(ㄋㄧㄠˋ ㄔㄨㄤˊ)
to wet the bed

溺尿(ㄋㄧㄠˋ ㄙㄨㄟ)or(ㄋㄧㄠˋ ㄋㄧㄠˋ)
to urinate; to make water

【溶】 3014 ㄖㄨㄥˊ rong róng
1. to dissolve; to melt
2. (said of rivers) having much water

溶媒(ㄖㄨㄥˊ ㄇㄟˊ)
a solvent

溶點(ㄖㄨㄥˊ ㄉㄧㄢˇ)
the melting point

溶化(ㄖㄨㄥˊ ㄏㄨㄚˋ)
to dissolve; to melt: 冰全溶化了。The ice had all melted.

溶劑(ㄖㄨㄥˊ ㄐㄧˋ)
a dissolvent; a solvent: 水是糖及鹽的溶劑。Water is a solvent of suger and salt.

溶解(ㄖㄨㄥˊ ㄐㄧㄝˇ)
to dissolve; to melt

溶解度(ㄖㄨㄥˊ ㄐㄧㄝˇ ㄉㄨˋ)
solubility

溶解力(ㄖㄨㄥˊ ㄐㄧㄝˇ ㄌㄧˋ)
(chemistry) solvency

溶解性(ㄖㄨㄥˊ ㄐㄧㄝˇ ㄒㄧㄥˋ)
solvability

溶解熱(ㄖㄨㄥˊ ㄐㄧㄝˇ ㄖㄜˋ)
the heat of dissolution

溶質(ㄖㄨㄥˊ ㄓˊ)
a solute: 鹽是海水中的溶質。Salt is a solute in sea water.

溶入(ㄖㄨㄥˊ ㄖㄨˋ)
to dissolve into

溶溶(ㄖㄨㄥˊ ㄖㄨㄥˊ)
①(said of a river) having much water; full of water ② vast; extensive; broad

溶液(ㄖㄨㄥˊ ㄧㄝˋ)
(chemistry) solution

【溽】 3015 ㄖㄨˋ ruh rù
moist; humid

溽氣(ㄖㄨˋ ㄑㄧˋ)
the muggy vapor

溽氣蒸騰(ㄖㄨˋ ㄑㄧˋ ㄓㄥ ㄊㄥˊ)
sweltering

溽暑(ㄖㄨˋ ㄕㄨˇ)
sweltering summer weather

【滁】 3016 ㄔㄨˊ chwu chú
name of a tributary of the Yangtze River

滁河(ㄔㄨˊ ㄏㄜˊ)
name of a tributary of the Yangtze River

滁水(ㄔㄨˊ ㄕㄨㄟˇ)
name of a river in Anhwei

【滃】 3017 ㄨㄥˇ woeng wěng
(said of rivers and clouds) swelling or rising

滃鬱(ㄨㄥˇ ㄩˋ)
filled with vapor

【滂】 3018 ㄆㄤ pang pāng
torrential; overwhelming

滂渤(ㄆㄤ ㄅㄛˊ)
(said of moving water) turbulent

滂沛(ㄆㄤ ㄆㄟˋ)
torrential; overwhelming; surging

滂沛(ㄆㄤ ㄆㄟˋ)
①(said of rain) torrential ② surging; sweeping

滂沱(ㄆㄤ ㄊㄨㄛˊ)
①(said of rain) torrential: 大雨滂沱。The rain came down in torrents. ②(said of tears) streaming

滂澤(ㄆㄤ ㄗㄜˊ)
great kindness

滂洋(ㄆㄤ ㄧㄤˊ)
vast; extensive

【滄】 3019 ㄘㄤ tsang cāng
blue; azure; green

滄波(ㄘㄤ ㄅㄛ)
the blue waves

滄茫(ㄘㄤ ㄇㄤˊ)
endlessly vast; boundless; blurred by vast distance

滄溟(ㄘㄤ ㄇㄧㄥˊ)
the blue sea

滄浪(ㄘㄤ ㄌㄤˊ)
azure water

滄海(ㄘㄤ ㄏㄞˇ)
the blue sea

滄海橫流(ㄘㄤ ㄏㄞˇ ㄏㄥˊ ㄌㄧㄡˊ)
the chaos of the world

滄海桑田(ㄘㄤ ㄏㄞˇ ㄙㄤ ㄊㄧㄢˊ)or滄桑(ㄘㄤ ㄙㄤ)
the swift changes of the

world; the vicissitudes of life

滄海遺珠 (ㄘㄤ ㄏㄞˇ ㄧˊ ㄓㄨ)
a pearl left in the boundless sea—undiscovered talent

滄海一粟 (ㄘㄤ ㄏㄞˇ ㄧ ㄙㄨˋ)
a grain in the boundless sea: a pebble in the boundless ocean—infinitely small

滄江 (ㄘㄤ ㄐㄧㄤ)
the blue river

滄洲 (ㄘㄤ ㄓㄡ)
the silvan waterside (often in reference to the abode of a hermit)

滄滄涼涼 (ㄘㄤ ㄘㄤ ㄌㄧㄤˊ ㄌㄧㄤˊ)
(said of atmosphere) cold

滄溟 (ㄘㄤ ㄇㄧˊ)
the blue sea

【滅】 3020
ㄇㄧㄝˋ mieh miè

1. to destroy; to ruin; to wipe out; to exterminate
2. to put out; to extinguish; to go out

滅沒 (ㄇㄧㄝˋ ㄇㄛˋ)
to vanish; to disappear

滅門 (ㄇㄧㄝˋ ㄇㄣˊ)
to put a whole family to death

滅門之禍 (ㄇㄧㄝˋ ㄇㄣˊ ㄓ ㄏㄨㄛˋ)
(in ancient China) the disaster of having a whole family beheaded when a member of the family committed high treason, rebellion, etc.

滅燈 (ㄇㄧㄝˋ ㄉㄥ)
to turn off lights; to blow out the lamp: 別滅燈。Don't blow out the lamp.

滅掉 (ㄇㄧㄝˋ ㄉㄧㄠˋ)
to destroy; to ruin

滅頂 (ㄇㄧㄝˋ ㄉㄧㄥˇ)
to be drowned

滅度 (ㄇㄧㄝˋ ㄉㄨˋ)
(Buddhism) *Nirvana*

滅裂 (ㄇㄧㄝˋ ㄌㄧㄝˋ)
to manage things in a slapdash, irresponsible manner

滅良心 (ㄇㄧㄝˋ ㄌㄧㄤˊ ㄒㄧㄣ)
to go against conscience

滅口 (ㄇㄧㄝˋ ㄎㄡˇ)
to kill a person to prevent him from disclosing a secret

滅族 (ㄇㄧㄝˋ ㄗㄨˊ)
to exterminate a family

滅火劑 (ㄇㄧㄝˋ ㄏㄨㄛˇ ㄐㄧˋ)
fire-extinguishing chemicals

(or agents)

滅火器 (ㄇㄧㄝˋ ㄏㄨㄛˇ ㄑㄧˋ)
a fire extinguisher

滅火沙 (ㄇㄧㄝˋ ㄏㄨㄛˇ ㄕㄚ)
sand for extinguishing a fire

滅跡 (ㄇㄧㄝˋ ㄐㄧ)
to destroy evidence

滅盡天良 (ㄇㄧㄝˋ ㄐㄧㄣˋ ㄊㄧㄢ ㄌㄧㄤˊ)
to destroy utterly one's conscience

滅絕 (ㄇㄧㄝˋ ㄐㄩㄝˊ)
to exterminate; to annihilate; to wipe out

滅心 (ㄇㄧㄝˋ ㄒㄧㄣ)
to go against conscience

滅性 (ㄇㄧㄝˋ ㄒㄧㄥˋ)
to lose life

滅種 (ㄇㄧㄝˋ ㄓㄨㄥˇ)
to commit genocide

滅屍 (ㄇㄧㄝˋ ㄕ)
to destroy a corpse so as to leave no traces of the crime

滅族 (ㄇㄧㄝˋ ㄗㄨˊ)
to wipe out an entire clan; genocide

滅此朝食 (ㄇㄧㄝˋ ㄘˇ ㄓㄠ ㄕ)
eager to destroy the enemy

滅音器 (ㄇㄧㄝˋ ㄧㄣ ㄑㄧˋ)
the muffler (of an engine)

滅亡 (ㄇㄧㄝˋ ㄨㄤˊ)
(said of a country) to lose independence status and become a mere geographic name; to perish; to be doomed

【滇】 3021
ㄉㄧㄢ dian diān
(又讀 ㄊㄧㄢˊ tyan tián)
an alternative name of Yünnan

滇湎鐵路 (ㄉㄧㄢ ㄇㄧㄢˇ ㄊㄧㄝˇ ㄌㄨˋ)
a railway linking Yünnan and Burma

滇緬公路 (ㄉㄧㄢ ㄇㄧㄢˇ ㄍㄨㄥ ㄌㄨˋ)
the Burma Road (from Kunming to Ledo)

滇池 (ㄉㄧㄢ ㄔˊ)
name of a lake in Yünnan

滇越鐵路 (ㄉㄧㄢ ㄩㄝˋ ㄊㄧㄝˇ ㄌㄨˋ)
a railway linking Yünnan and Vietnam

【滋】 3022
ㄗ tzy zī

1. to grow
2. to increase; to multiply
3. to nourish

4. to give rise to
5. to spurt out
6. juice; sap

滋補 (ㄗ ㄅㄨˇ)
to nourish; nutritious; tonic: 人參是滋補身體的名藥。Ginseng is a famous tonic medicine.

滋茂 (ㄗ ㄇㄠˋ)
luxuriant; lush; teeming: 兩岸草木滋茂。Lush grass grows along the river banks.

滋蔓 (ㄗ ㄇㄢˋ)
lush; teeming; to grow and spread: 田裏雜草滋蔓。Weeds grow and spread in the field.

滋蔓難圖 (ㄗ ㄇㄢˋ ㄋㄢˊ ㄊㄨˊ)
It will be too late to deal with an enemy if he is allowed to grow in strength.

滋多 (ㄗ ㄉㄨㄛ)
to increase; to multiply

滋息 (ㄗ ㄒㄧˊ)
to bear interest

滋殖 (ㄗ ㄓˊ)
to reproduce in large numbers

滋長 (ㄗ ㄓㄤˇ)
to grow; to thrive: 花沒有日光就不會滋長。Flowers will not thrive without sunshine.

滋事 (ㄗ ㄕˋ)
to create trouble; to disturb peace: 他因滋事被捕。He was arrested for disturbing peace.

滋生 (ㄗ ㄕㄥ)
to reproduce in large numbers; to multiply

滋擾 (ㄗ ㄖㄠˇ)
to disturb peace and order; to harass

滋潤 (ㄗ ㄖㄨㄣˋ)
① to freshen; to enrich ② to moisten; moist; juicy

滋嘴兒 (ㄗ ㄗㄨㄟˇㄦ)
to smile; to grin

滋芽兒 (ㄗ ㄧㄚˊㄦ)
to sprout

滋養 (ㄗ ㄧㄤˇ)
to nourish: 用牛奶滋養嬰孩。Babies are nourished with milk.

滋養品 (ㄗ ㄧㄤˇ ㄆㄧㄣˇ)
nourishing food; nutritive food; nutrient; nourishment

【水部】

【水部】

滋養分(ㄗ ㄧㄤ ㄈㄣ)or 滋養料(ㄗ
ㄧㄤ ㄌㄧㄠ)
nourishment; nutrition

滋味(ㄗ ㄨㄟ)
taste; flavor

滋膩(ㄗ ㄋㄧ)
greasy food

滋育(ㄗ ㄩ)
to reproduce in large numbers; to multiply

3023
【滑】 ㄏㄨㄚˊ hwa huá
1. to slip; to glide
2. smooth; slippery
3. insincere; dishonest; cunning

滑板(ㄏㄨㄚˊ ㄅㄢ)
①(machinery) a slide ②
(table tennis) feint play ③ a
skateboard

滑瓣(ㄏㄨㄚˊ ㄅㄢˋ)
a sliding valve

滑冰(ㄏㄨㄚˊ ㄅㄧㄥ)
to skate

滑冰場(ㄏㄨㄚˊ ㄅㄧㄥ ㄔㄤˇ)
a skating rink

滑坡(ㄏㄨㄚˊ ㄆㄛ)
landslide; landslip

滑門(ㄏㄨㄚˊ ㄇㄣˊ)
a sliding door

滑倒(ㄏㄨㄚˊ ㄉㄠˇ)
to slip and fall: 他在冰上滑
倒。He slipped on the ice.

滑道(ㄏㄨㄚˊ ㄉㄠˋ)
a chute; a slide

滑頂(ㄏㄨㄚˊ ㄉㄧㄥˇ)
the sliding roof (of an automobile)

滑動(ㄏㄨㄚˊ ㄉㄨㄥˋ)
(physics) to slide

滑頭(ㄏㄨㄚˊ ㄊㄡˊ)
a crafty person; a cunning person

滑頭滑腦(ㄏㄨㄚˊ ㄊㄡˊ ㄏㄨㄚˊ ㄋㄠˇ)
sly; crafty; guile

滑梯(ㄏㄨㄚˊ ㄊㄧ)
a slideway (for children's amusement)

滑鐵盧(ㄏㄨㄚˊ ㄊㄧㄝˇ ㄌㄨˊ)
Waterloo, a village in central Belgium (Napoleon decisively defeated here on June 18, 1815)

滑膩(ㄏㄨㄚˊ ㄋㄧˋ)
smooth and lustrous

滑了一跤(ㄏㄨㄚˊ ㄌㄜ‧ㄧ ㄐㄧㄠ)
to have a slip when walking

滑壘(ㄏㄨㄚˊ ㄌㄟˇ)
(baseball) base sliding

滑溜兒(ㄏㄨㄚˊ ㄌㄧㄡ ㄦ)
smooth and shiny

滑輪(ㄏㄨㄚˊ ㄌㄨㄣˊ)
① a roller ② a pulley

滑竿(ㄏㄨㄚˊ ㄍㄢ)
an uncovered sedan chair in Szechwan

滑桿(ㄏㄨㄚˊ ㄍㄢˇ)
(mechanics) a sliding bar

滑口(ㄏㄨㄚˊ ㄎㄡˇ)
glib; voluble

滑稽(ㄏㄨㄚˊ ㄐㄧ)or(ㄍㄨˇ ㄐㄧ)
ludicrous; funny; comical; ridiculous: 多麼滑稽的故事!
What a funny story!

滑稽劇(ㄏㄨㄚˊ ㄐㄧ ㄐㄩˋ)or(ㄍㄨˇ
ㄐㄧ ㄐㄩˋ)
comedy; burlesque; farce

滑劑(ㄏㄨㄚˊ ㄐㄧˋ)
lubricant

滑精(ㄏㄨㄚˊ ㄐㄧㄥ)
involuntary emission of semen; spermatorrhea

滑翔(ㄏㄨㄚˊ ㄒㄧㄤˊ)
to glide

滑翔機(ㄏㄨㄚˊ ㄒㄧㄤˊ ㄐㄧ)
a glider

滑翔翼(ㄏㄨㄚˊ ㄒㄧㄤˊ ㄧˋ)
a hang glider

滑翔運動(ㄏㄨㄚˊ ㄒㄧㄤˊ ㄩㄣˋ ㄉㄨㄥˋ)
exercise in glider manipulation; glider sports

滑行(ㄏㄨㄚˊ ㄒㄧㄥˊ)
to slide; to coast; to taxi

滑雪(ㄏㄨㄚˊ ㄒㄩㄝˇ)
to ski; to slide or travel on skis

滑車(ㄏㄨㄚˊ ㄔㄜ)
a pulley; a winch

滑石(ㄏㄨㄚˊ ㄕˊ)
talc or talcum

滑石粉(ㄏㄨㄚˊ ㄕˊ ㄈㄣˇ)
talcum powder

滑水(ㄏㄨㄚˊ ㄕㄨㄟˇ)
water skiing

滑潤(ㄏㄨㄚˊ ㄖㄨㄣˋ)
smooth; well-lubricated

滑澤(ㄏㄨㄚˊ ㄗㄜˊ)
smooth and lustrous

滑草運動(ㄏㄨㄚˊ ㄘㄠˇ ㄩㄣˋ ㄉㄨㄥˋ)
grass skiing

3024
【滔】 ㄊㄠ tau tāo
1. fluent

2. to fill; to prevail

滔滔(ㄊㄠ ㄊㄠ)
flowing smoothly; fluent

滔滔不絶(ㄊㄠ ㄊㄠ ㄅㄨˋ ㄐㄩㄝˊ)
talking fluently and endlessly

滔滔善辯(ㄊㄠ ㄊㄠ ㄕㄢˋ ㄅㄧㄢˋ)
eloquent; skilled in debating

滔天大罪(ㄊㄠ ㄊㄧㄢ ㄉㄚˋ ㄗㄨㄟˋ)
heinous crimes; an extremely serious offense

3025
【滓】 ㄗˇ tzyy zǐ
dregs; lees; sediment

3026
【滎】 ㄧㄥˊ yng yíng
(said of waves) rising

滎陽(ㄧㄥˊ ㄧㄤˊ)
name of an ancient lake in Honan

滎澤(ㄧㄥˊ ㄗㄜˊ)
name of a county in Honan

3027
【溈】 ㄍㄨㄟ guey guī
name of a river

3028
【滕】 ㄊㄥˊ terng téng
name of a state during the Spring and Autumn Age

滕文公(ㄊㄥˊ ㄨㄣˊ ㄍㄨㄥ)
name of a king of the state of 滕 during the Spring and Autumn Age

滕王閣(ㄊㄥˊ ㄨㄤˊ ㄍㄜˊ)
a renowned tower in Nanchang, Kiangsi, built in the Tang Dynasty

十一畫

3029
【滬】 ㄏㄨˋ huh hù
an alternative name of Shanghai

滬寧鐵路(ㄏㄨˋ ㄋㄧㄥˊ ㄊㄧㄝˇ ㄌㄨˋ)
old name of the Shanghai-Nanking Railway

滬杭鐵路(ㄏㄨˋ ㄏㄤˊ ㄊㄧㄝˇ ㄌㄨˋ)
the Shanghai-Hangchow Railway

滬杭甬鐵路(ㄏㄨˋ ㄏㄤˊ ㄩㄥˇ ㄊㄧㄝˇ ㄌㄨˋ)
the Shanghai-Hangchow-Ningpo Railway

滬江(ㄏㄨˋ ㄐㄧㄤ)
an alternative name of Shanghai

滬市(ㄏㄨˋ ㄕˋ)

Shanghai

【滌】 3030 ㄉㄧˊ dyi díi
1. to wash; to cleanse
2. to sweep

滌蕩(ㄉㄧˊ ㄉㄤˋ)
①to wash off ②to spread out

滌慮(ㄉㄧˊ ㄌㄩˋ)
to free the mind from worries

滌去(ㄉㄧˊ ㄑㄩˋ)
to wash off; to wash away: 滌去牆上的污跡。Wash those dirty marks off the wall.

滌瑕(ㄉㄧˊ ㄒㄧㄚˊ)
to cleanse away a stain; to mend one's ways

滌塵(ㄉㄧˊ ㄔㄣˊ)
to wash off dust

滌場(ㄉㄧˊ ㄔㄤˊ)or滌場(ㄔㄤˊ)
to sweep the yard

滌除(ㄉㄧˊ ㄔㄨˊ)
①to wash off; to wash away ②to sweep away ③to do away with

滌硯(ㄉㄧˊ ㄧㄢˋ)
to wash the ink-slab—to prepare for study

【滯】 3031 ㄓˋ jyh zhì
at a standstill; stagnant; impeded; blocked; stationary

滯悶(ㄓˋ ㄇㄣˋ)
to have pent-up feeling

滯伏(ㄓˋ ㄈㄨˊ)
①to lie hidden ②to lack ambition

滯泥(ㄓˋ ㄋㄧˊ)
to adhere too closely; stubborn and inflexible

滯累(ㄓˋ ㄌㄟˊ)
the burden of the temporal world

滯留(ㄓˋ ㄌㄧㄡˊ)
①to remain at a standstill ②to loiter; to detain: 他因事滯留在辦公室。He was detained in the office by business. ③to overstay

滯留鋒(ㄓˋ ㄌㄧㄡˊ ㄈㄥ)
stagnant atmospheric masses; stationary front

滯固(ㄓˋ ㄍㄨˋ)
obstinate; inflexible

滯貨(ㄓˋ ㄏㄨㄛˋ)or滯銷貨(ㄓˋ ㄒㄧㄠ ㄏㄨㄛˋ)

unsaleable goods; dead stock

滯氣(ㄓˋ ㄑㄧˋ)
stagnant humor

滯銷(ㄓˋ ㄒㄧㄠ)
sales slump

滯住(ㄓˋ ㄓㄨˋ)
impeded; stopped; detained

滯塞不通(ㄓˋ ㄙㄜˋ ㄅㄨˋ ㄊㄨㄥ)
obstructed and impeded

滯訟(ㄓˋ ㄙㄨㄥˋ)or滯獄(ㄓˋ ㄩˋ)
a prolonged lawsuit

滯礙(ㄓˋ ㄞˋ)
to obstruct; to impede: 他工作受到滯礙。He was impeded in his work.

滯淹(ㄓˋ ㄧㄢ)
to remain at a standstill

滯淀(ㄓˋ ㄉㄧㄢˋ)
①to remain at a standstill ②stagnation; stagnancy

滯胃(ㄓˋ ㄨㄟˋ)
indigestion

滯運(ㄓˋ ㄩㄣˋ)
bad fortune; adversity

【滲】 3032 ㄕㄣˋ shenn shèn
to permeate; to percolate; to infiltrate; to seep; to ooze: 雨水滲入砂中。The rain has permeated the sand.

滲透(ㄕㄣˋ ㄊㄡˋ)
to infiltrate; to permeate; to percolate; to seep through: 水滲透到泥土裏面。The water permeated through the soil.

滲透性(ㄕㄣˋ ㄊㄡˋ ㄒㄧㄥˋ)
permeability; osmosis (or osmose)

滲透作用(ㄕㄣˋ ㄊㄡˋ ㄗㄨㄛˋ ㄩㄥˋ)
osmosis; permeation

滲透壓力(ㄕㄣˋ ㄊㄡˋ ㄧㄚ ㄌㄧˋ)
osmotic pressure

滲漏(ㄕㄣˋ ㄌㄡˋ)
to seep out; to ooze out

滲出(ㄕㄣˋ ㄔㄨ)
to seep out; to ooze out: 泉水自石中滲出。The spring oozes out of a rock.

滲入(ㄕㄣˋ ㄖㄨˋ)
①to permeate; to seep into: 雨水滲入地下。The rain permeated the ground. ②(said of influence, etc.) to penetrate; to infiltrate

【滴】 3033 ㄉㄧ di dī
1. water drops

2. to drip

滴答(ㄉㄧ ㄉㄚˊ)
ticktack (or other similar recurring sound)

滴滴(ㄉㄧ ㄉㄧ)
in drops; drop by drop

滴答(ㄉㄧ ㄉㄚˊ)
to ticktack; ticktack: 霰滴滴答答地打在窗上。Sleet ticktacked against the window panes.

滴定法(ㄉㄧ ㄉㄧㄥˋ ㄈㄚˇ)
(chemistry) titration

滴瀝(ㄉㄧ ㄌㄧˋ)
the pattering sound of rain-drops

滴里搭拉的(ㄉㄧ ㄌㄧˇ ㄉㄚ ㄌㄚ ˙ㄉㄜ)
the pattering of raindrops

滴溜溜(ㄉㄧ ㄌㄧㄡ ㄌㄧㄡ)
round; going round and round

滴管(ㄉㄧ ㄍㄨㄢˇ)
a medicine dropper; a pipette

滴灌(ㄉㄧ ㄍㄨㄢˋ)
(agriculture) drip irrigation; trickle irrigation

滴下(ㄉㄧ ㄒㄧㄚˋ)
to drip: 雨從傘上滴下。Rain drips from the umbrella.

滴血(ㄉㄧ ㄒㄧㄝˇ)
(in former times) to drop blood in water in a test to decide kinship

滴水穿石(ㄉㄧ ㄕㄨㄟˇ ㄔㄨㄢ ㄕˊ)
(literally) Constant dropping wears away a stone. Persistent efforts can overcome any difficulty.

【滹】 3034 ㄏㄨ hu hū
name of a river flowing through Hopeh

滹沱(ㄏㄨ ㄊㄨㄛˊ)
name of a river flowing through Hopeh

【滸】 3035 ㄏㄨˇ huu hǔ
waterside; shore

【滾】 3036 (滾) ㄍㄨㄣˇ goen gǔn
1. to turn round and round; to roll; to rotate: 很多石頭從山坡上滾下來。Many stones came rolling down the slope.
2. boiling: 茶壺裏的水滾了。The

（水部）

pot is boiling.

滾邊 《《ㄨㄣˇ ㄅㄧㄢ》
①an embroidered hem ②to stitch a hem around a border

滾翻 《《ㄨㄣˇ ㄈㄢ》
(sports) a roll; to roll

滾蛋 《《ㄨㄣˇ ㄉㄢˋ》
Get out! 或 Go to hell! 或 Beat it!

滾地球 《《ㄨㄣˇ ㄉㄧˋ ㄑㄧㄡˊ》
(baseball) ground ball

滾動摩擦 《《ㄨㄣˇ ㄉㄨㄥˋ ㄇㄛˊ ㄘㄚ》
rolling friction

滾湯 《《ㄨㄣˇ ㄊㄤ》
boiled water

滾燙 《《ㄨㄣˇ ㄊㄤˋ》
boiling; steaming hot; piping hot: 水滾燙。The water is steaming hot.

滾筒印刷機 《《ㄨㄣˇ ㄊㄨㄥˇ ㄧㄣˋ ㄕㄨㄚ ㄐㄧ》
a rotary press

滾利 《《ㄨㄣˇ ㄌㄧˋ》
to yield compound interest

滾路機 《《ㄨㄣˇ ㄌㄨˋ ㄐㄧ》
a road roller

滾瓜爛熟 《《ㄨㄣˇ ㄍㄨㄚ ㄌㄢˋ ㄕㄡˊ》
learned very thoroughly; committed to memory firmly

滾滾 《《ㄨㄣˇ 《《ㄨㄣˇ》
①(said of flowing waters) rolling; torrential; billowing: 滾滾的濃煙向上升起。The billowing smoke rose up. ②to pour into: 財源滾滾到我家。Profits pour into my home from all sides.

滾滾東流 《《ㄨㄣˇ 《《ㄨㄣˇ ㄉㄨㄥ ㄌㄧㄡˊ》
rolling eastward (as most rivers in China)

滾滾流出 《《ㄨㄣˇ 《《ㄨㄣˇ ㄌㄧㄡˊ ㄔㄨ》
to flow out plentifully; to gush out

滾滾而來 《《ㄨㄣˇ 《《ㄨㄣˇ ㄦˊ ㄌㄞˊ》
to come in torrents

滾開 《《ㄨㄣˇ ㄎㄞ》
Get away! 或 Get out! 或 Beat it!

滾起來 《《ㄨㄣˇ ㄑㄧˇ ㄌㄞˊ》
①to start a fist fight ②Get up! (used abusively) ③to start boiling

滾球兒 《《ㄨㄣˇ ㄑㄧㄡˊ ㄦ》
Go away!

滾下去 《《ㄨㄣˇ ㄒㄧㄚˋ ㄑㄩ》
①to roll down ②Get out! 或

Beat it!

滾雪球 《《ㄨㄣˇ ㄒㄩㄝˇ ㄑㄧㄡˊ》
①to roll a snowball ②to snowball

滾出去 《《ㄨㄣˇ ㄔㄨ ㄑㄩˋ》
①to roll out ②Get out!

滾石不生苔 《《ㄨㄣˇ ㄕˊ ㄅㄨˋ ㄕㄥ ㄊㄞˊ》
A rolling stone gathers no moss.

滾水 《《ㄨㄣˇ ㄕㄨㄟˇ》
boiling water

滾熱 《《ㄨㄣˇ ㄖㄜˋ》or滾熱兒的 《《ㄨㄣˇ ㄖㄜˋ ㄦ ㄉㄜ》
piping hot

滾子 《《ㄨㄣˇ ˙ㄗ》
a roller

滾兒 《《ㄨㄣˇ ㄦ》
a turn; a roll

滾圓 《《ㄨㄣˇ ㄩㄢˊ》
perfectly round

【滿】 3037
ㄇㄢˇ maan mǎn

1. full; filled: 這箱子滿了。The box is full.
2. plentiful; abundant
3. proud; haughty
4. to expire: 他的任期將滿。His term of office will soon expire.
5. completely; entirely; perfectly
6. Manchu
7. a Chinese family name

滿杯 《ㄇㄢˇ ㄅㄟ》
a full cup: 他喝滿杯的酒。He drank a full cup of wine.

滿不在乎 《ㄇㄢˇ ㄅㄨˋ ㄗㄞˋ ㄏㄨ》
completely unperturbed; do not care at all; nonchalant

滿瓶不動半瓶搖 《ㄇㄢˇ ㄆㄧㄥˊ ㄅㄨˋ ㄉㄨㄥˋ ㄅㄢˋ ㄆㄧㄥˊ ㄧㄠˊ》
Full vessels give the least sound.

滿沒聽提 《ㄇㄢˇ ㄇㄟˊ ㄊㄧㄥ ㄊㄧˊ》or滿不聽提 《ㄇㄢˇ ㄅㄨˋ ㄊㄧㄥ ㄊㄧˊ》
to pay no attention at all

滿滿的 《ㄇㄢˇ ㄇㄢˇ ㄉㄜ》
full to the brim; brimful: 杯子滿滿的。The glass is full to the brim.

滿當當 《ㄇㄢˇ ㄉㄤ ㄉㄤ》
full; plentiful

滿門 《ㄇㄢˇ ㄇㄣˊ》
the whole family

滿門桃李 《ㄇㄢˇ ㄇㄣˊ ㄊㄠˊ ㄌㄧˇ》
a lot of students

滿面怒容 《ㄇㄢˇ ㄇㄧㄢˋ ㄋㄨˋ ㄖㄨㄥˊ》
red with anger; to look furious

滿面笑容 《ㄇㄢˇ ㄇㄧㄢˋ ㄒㄧㄠˋ ㄖㄨㄥˊ》
looking happy and cheerful; all smiles

滿面春風 《ㄇㄢˇ ㄇㄧㄢˋ ㄔㄨㄣ ㄈㄥ》
looking happy and cheerful; beaming with pleasure

滿目蕭然 《ㄇㄢˇ ㄇㄨˋ ㄒㄧㄠ ㄖㄢˊ》
Desolation spreads as far as the eye can reach.

滿目瘡痍 《ㄇㄢˇ ㄇㄨˋ ㄔㄨㄤ ㄧˊ》
Misery and suffering greets the eye everywhere.

滿帆 《ㄇㄢˇ ㄈㄢˊ》
full sails

滿分 《ㄇㄢˇ ㄈㄣ》or滿分兒 《ㄇㄢˇ ㄈㄣ ㄦ》
a perfect score; full marks

滿服 《ㄇㄢˇ ㄈㄨˊ》
to complete a mourning period

滿腹牢騷 《ㄇㄢˇ ㄈㄨˋ ㄌㄠˊ ㄙㄠ》
to have a heart full of discontents, grievances, complaints, etc.

滿腹狐疑 《ㄇㄢˇ ㄈㄨˋ ㄏㄨˊ ㄧˊ》
to be filled with suspicion; extremely suspicious

滿腹經綸 《ㄇㄢˇ ㄈㄨˋ ㄐㄧㄥ ㄌㄨㄣˊ》
very erudite; very much learned

滿打算 《ㄇㄢˇ ㄉㄚˇ ㄙㄨㄢˋ》
to have intended

滿地 《ㄇㄢˇ ㄉㄧˋ》
all over the ground; everywhere

滿頭大汗 《ㄇㄢˇ ㄊㄡˊ ㄉㄚˋ ㄏㄢˋ》
with one's brow beaded with perspiration

滿堂紅 《ㄇㄢˇ ㄊㄤˊ ㄏㄨㄥˊ》
①conventional decorations in red for the drawing room on an auspicious occasion ②all-round victory; success in every field

滿天下 《ㄇㄢˇ ㄊㄧㄢ ㄒㄧㄚˋ》
all over the world; everywhere

滿天星 《ㄇㄢˇ ㄊㄧㄢ ㄒㄧㄥ》
①(botany) Serissa foetida; Enkianthus japonicus ②the sky filled with stars

滿天星斗 《ㄇㄢˇ ㄊㄧㄢ ㄒㄧㄥ ㄉㄡˇ》
a clear sky full of stars

滿腦子 《ㄇㄢˇ ㄋㄠˇ ˙ㄗ》

to have one's mind stuffed with

滿擬 (ㄇㄢˇ ㄋㄧˊ)
to have had the intention of

滿壘 (ㄇㄢˇ ㄌㄟˇ)
bases loaded; full base

滿臉風塵 (ㄇㄢˇ ㄌㄧㄢˇ ㄈㄥ ㄔㄣˊ)
a face covered with traveling dust—the indication of having undergone hardship

滿臉通紅 (ㄇㄢˇ ㄌㄧㄢˇ ㄊㄨㄥ ㄏㄨㄥˊ)
The face reddens all over.

滿臉晦氣 (ㄇㄢˇ ㄌㄧㄢˇ ㄏㄨㄟˋ ㄑㄧˋ)
to look very depressed

滿臉殺氣 (ㄇㄢˇ ㄌㄧㄢˇ ㄕㄚ ㄑㄧˋ)
to look like one in a murderous mood

滿臉俗氣 (ㄇㄢˇ ㄌㄧㄢˇ ㄙㄨˊ ㄑㄧˋ)
to look very vulgar: 那記者滿臉俗氣. The reporter looks very vulgar.

滿貫 (ㄇㄢˇ ㄍㄨㄢˋ)
①to reach the utmost ②(mah-jong game) full marks; a perfect score

滿口胡說 (ㄇㄢˇ ㄎㄡˇ ㄏㄨˊ ㄕㄨㄛ)
to talk irresponsibly; to talk nonsense或Nonsense! 或Rubbish! 或Baloney!

滿口稱讚 (ㄇㄢˇ ㄎㄡˇ ㄔㄥ ㄗㄢˋ)
to praise unreservedly

滿口應承 (ㄇㄢˇ ㄎㄡˇ ㄧㄥˋ ㄔㄥˊ)or滿口答應 (ㄇㄢˇ ㄎㄡˇ ㄉㄚˊ ㄧㄥˋ)
to promise with great readiness

滿坑滿谷 (ㄇㄢˇ ㄎㄥ ㄇㄢˇ ㄍㄨˇ)
(literally)numerous enough to fill the pit or the valley—exceedingly numerous

滿漢 (ㄇㄢˇ ㄏㄢˋ)
the Manchus and the Chinese

滿漢全席 (ㄇㄢˇ ㄏㄢˋ ㄑㄩㄢˊ ㄒㄧˊ)
the complete Manchu and Chinese banquet, featuring numerous courses and delicacies, which lasts as long as one or two days

滿懷 (ㄇㄢˇ ㄏㄨㄞˊ)
a heart full of (enthusiasm, sorrow, etc.)

滿假 (ㄇㄢˇ ㄐㄧㄚˇ)
Leave of absence expires.

滿街 (ㄇㄢˇ ㄐㄧㄝ)
all over the street

滿江紅 (ㄇㄢˇ ㄐㄧㄤ ㄏㄨㄥˊ)
①a kind of flowerless plant (Azolla imbricata) ②a poetic form (made famous by Gen. Yüeh Fei of the Sung Dynasty)

滿期 (ㄇㄢˇ ㄑㄧˊ)
the expiration of a given period; to expire

滿腔熱血 (ㄇㄢˇ ㄑㄧㄤ ㄖㄜˋ ㄒㄧㄝˇ)
full of patriotic fervor

滿腔熱忱 (ㄇㄢˇ ㄑㄧㄤ ㄖㄜˋ ㄔㄣˊ)
to be filled with ardor and sincerity

滿清 (ㄇㄢˇ ㄑㄧㄥ)
the Ching Dynasty (1644-1911)

滿孝 (ㄇㄢˇ ㄒㄧㄠˋ)
to complete a period of mourning

滿限 (ㄇㄢˇ ㄒㄧㄢˋ)
to have reached the deadline

滿心 (ㄇㄢˇ ㄒㄧㄣ)
wholeheartedly

滿心歡喜 (ㄇㄢˇ ㄒㄧㄣ ㄏㄨㄢ ㄒㄧˇ)
to be filled with joy

滿紙 (ㄇㄢˇ ㄓˇ)
all over a page or letter sheet

滿招損，謙受益 (ㄇㄢˇ ㄓㄠ ㄙㄨㄣˇ，ㄑㄧㄢ ㄕㄡˋ ㄧˋ)
Haughtiness invites losses while modesty brings profits.

滿洲 (ㄇㄢˇ ㄓㄡ)
Manchuria

滿洲八旗 (ㄇㄢˇ ㄓㄡ ㄅㄚ ㄑㄧˊ)
the eight army divisions organized by the Manchus during the Ching Dynasty with each division identified by the color of its banner

滿洲國 (ㄇㄢˇ ㄓㄡ ㄍㄨㄛˊ)
the puppet Manchukuo set up by the Japanese in Manchuria, lasting from 1932 to 1945

滿洲語 (ㄇㄢˇ ㄓㄡ ㄩˇ)
Manchu (the Tungusic language of the Manchus)

滿張羅 (ㄇㄢˇ ㄓㄤ ㄌㄨㄛˊ)
very thoughtful in the reception of guests

滿裝 (ㄇㄢˇ ㄓㄨㄤ)
①Manchu clothing ②filled with; loaded with: 貨車滿裝着貨物. The cart was loaded with goods.

滿朝文武 (ㄇㄢˇ ㄔㄠˊ ㄨㄣˊ ㄨˇ)
all the ministers and generals in the imperial court

滿場 (ㄇㄢˇ ㄔㄤˇ)or滿座 (ㄇㄢˇ ㄗㄨㄛˋ)
①the whole assembly ②Tickets sold out!

滿城風雨 (ㄇㄢˇ ㄔㄥˊ ㄈㄥ ㄩˇ)
widespread excitement over a scandal, an incident, etc.; the talk of the town

滿處 (ㄇㄢˇ ㄔㄨˋ)
all over the place: 滿處是人. People are everywhere.

滿市街 (ㄇㄢˇ ㄕˋ ㄐㄧㄝ)
all over the city; everywhere

滿身 (ㄇㄢˇ ㄕㄣ)
the whole body

滿身是汗 (ㄇㄢˇ ㄕㄣ ㄕˋ ㄏㄢˋ)
to sweat all over

滿人 (ㄇㄢˇ ㄖㄣˊ)
①the Manchus ②(Buddhism) a perfect man; one who does good deeds

滿載 (ㄇㄢˇ ㄗㄞˋ)
fully laden

滿載而歸 (ㄇㄢˇ ㄗㄞˋ ㄦˊ ㄍㄨㄟ)
to return home fully laden with riches, gifts, etc.

滿足 (ㄇㄢˇ ㄗㄨˊ)
to satisfy or be satisfied; to gratify or be gratified; to meet; content; satisfaction; gratification

滿族 (ㄇㄢˇ ㄗㄨˊ)
the Manchu people; the Manchus

滿座 (ㄇㄢˇ ㄗㄨㄛˋ)
①all the people present; all the audience; all the attendants ②a capacity audience

滿座高朋 (ㄇㄢˇ ㄗㄨㄛˋ ㄍㄠ ㄆㄥˊ)
The whole audience is lofty and intelligent.

滿嘴 (ㄇㄢˇ ㄗㄨㄟˇ)
to have a mouthful of (food, honeyed words, etc.)

滿額 (ㄇㄢˇ ㄜˊ)
to have reached the fixed amount or quota

滿而不溢 (ㄇㄢˇ ㄦˊ ㄅㄨˋ ㄧˋ)
(literally) full without flowing over—very much accomplished but behaving modestly

滿耳 (ㄇㄢˇ ㄦˇ)
to have one's ears filled

〔水部〕

〔水部〕

with (sound or voice)

滿以為(ㄇㄢˇ ㄧˇ ㄨㄟˊ)
to have counted on or expected something to happen (but it did not)

滿意(ㄇㄢˇ ㄧˋ)
satisfied; content: 大家對你的進步都很滿意。Everyone was satisfied with your progress.

滿眼(ㄇㄢˇ ㄧㄢˇ)
① to have one's eyes filled with ②to meet the eye on every side

滿文(ㄇㄢˇ ㄨㄣˊ)or 滿洲文字(ㄇㄢˇ ㄓㄨ ㄨㄣˊ ㄗˋ)
written Manchu language

滿月(ㄇㄢˇ ㄩㄝˋ)
① a full moon 亦作「望月」 ② (of a baby) to be one month old

滿園春色(ㄇㄢˇ ㄩㄢˊ ㄔㄨㄣ ㄙㄜˋ)
The garden is filled with the brightness of spring.

【漁】 3038
ㄩˊ yú yù
1. to fish
2. to seek; to pursue
3. to seize; to acquire forcibly

漁婆(ㄩˊ ㄆㄛˊ)
a fisherwoman

漁民(ㄩˊ ㄇㄧㄣˊ)
the fishing population; fishermen

漁夫(ㄩˊ ㄈㄨ)
a fisherman: 漁夫捉到一條大魚。The fisherman caught a big fish.

漁艇(ㄩˊ ㄊㄧㄥˇ)
a fishing boat: 我們乘漁艇去吧。Let us go by fishing boat.

漁撈科(ㄩˊ ㄌㄠ ㄎㄜ)
the department of fishery

漁郎(ㄩˊ ㄌㄤˊ)
a fisherman

漁利(ㄩˊ ㄌㄧˋ)
to seek profits or gains by unethical means; profiteering

漁獵(ㄩˊ ㄌㄧㄝˋ)
① fishing and hunting ② to seek (illegal gains)

漁獵時代(ㄩˊ ㄌㄧㄝˋ ㄕˊ ㄉㄞˋ)
the fishing and hunting age

漁歌(ㄩˊ ㄍㄜ)
fishermen's songs 參看「漁唱」

漁港(ㄩˊ ㄍㄤˇ)
a fishing harbor

漁戶(ㄩˊ ㄏㄨˋ)
fishing families; fishermen

漁火(ㄩˊ ㄏㄨㄛˇ)
lights on fishing boats

漁獲量(ㄩˊ ㄏㄨㄛˋ ㄌㄧㄤˋ)
a catch

漁會(ㄩˊ ㄏㄨㄟˋ)
a fishermen's association

漁家(ㄩˊ ㄐㄧㄚ)
fishing families; fishermen

漁具(ㄩˊ ㄐㄩˋ)
a fishing outfit

漁樵耕讀(ㄩˊ ㄑㄧㄠˊ ㄍㄥ ㄉㄨˊ)
the fisherman, the wood-cutter, the farmer, and the scholar (the four respectable occupations in old China)

漁權(ㄩˊ ㄑㄩㄢˊ)
a piscary 亦作「捕漁權」

漁汛(ㄩˊ ㄒㄩㄣˋ)
fishing seasons

漁舟(ㄩˊ ㄓㄡ)or 漁船(ㄩˊ ㄔㄨㄢˊ)
a fishing boat

漁產(ㄩˊ ㄔㄢˇ)
aquatic products

漁場(ㄩˊ ㄔㄤˇ)or 漁區(ㄩˊ ㄑㄩ)
fishing grounds

漁唱(ㄩˊ ㄔㄤˋ)
fishermen's songs 參看「漁歌」

漁食(ㄩˊ ㄕˊ)
to get sustenance forcibly as a fisherman gets fish

漁人(ㄩˊ ㄖㄣˊ)
a fisherman

漁人得利(ㄩˊ ㄖㄣˊ ㄉㄜˊ ㄌㄧˋ)or 漁翁得利(ㄩˊ ㄨㄥ ㄉㄜˊ ㄌㄧˋ)
The fisherman catches both (while the snipe and the clam are locked in a fight). 或(While two dogs fight for a bone,) a third runs away with it.

漁村(ㄩˊ ㄘㄨㄣ)
a fishing village

漁色(ㄩˊ ㄙㄜˋ)
to seek carnal pleasure

漁色之徒(ㄩˊ ㄙㄜˋ ㄓ ㄊㄨˊ)
a fellow of excessive lust

漁業(ㄩˊ ㄧㄝˋ)
fishery

漁業公司(ㄩˊ ㄧㄝˋ ㄍㄨㄥ ㄙ)
a fishing company; a marine products company

漁業區(ㄩˊ ㄧㄝˋ ㄑㄩ)
a fishing zone

漁網(ㄩˊ ㄨㄤˇ)
a fishing net

漁翁(ㄩˊ ㄨㄥ)or 漁父(ㄩˊ ㄈㄨˋ)
an old fisherman

【澩】 3039
ㄐㄧ jih jī
shore; waterside

【漉】 3040
ㄌㄨˋ luh lù
1. to remove sediment by filtering
2. wet; dripping

【漂】 3041
1. ㄆㄧㄠ piau piāo
to drift; to float; to be tossed about

漂泊(ㄆㄧㄠ ㄅㄛˊ)
to drift; to wander: 我像朵孤雲般漂泊。I wandered lonely as a cloud.

漂泊異鄉(ㄆㄧㄠ ㄅㄛˊ ㄧˋ ㄒㄧㄤ)
to wander in a strange land

漂苹(ㄆㄧㄠ ㄆㄧㄥˊ)
duckweed

漂浮(ㄆㄧㄠ ㄈㄨˊ)
to drift; to float

漂蕩(ㄆㄧㄠ ㄉㄤˋ)
① to drift about; to be tossed (by waves): 船在波浪中漂蕩。The ship is tossed by the wave. ②to wander; to ramble about

漂流(ㄆㄧㄠ ㄌㄧㄡˊ)
to drift

漂流無定(ㄆㄧㄠ ㄌㄧㄡˊ ㄨˊ ㄉㄧㄥˋ)
to drift about; to wander aimlessly

漂流物(ㄆㄧㄠ ㄌㄧㄡˊ ㄨˋ)
flotsam

漂零(ㄆㄧㄠ ㄌㄧㄥˊ)
①(said of leaves) to be scattered about ②to live a lone wandering life

漂淪(ㄆㄧㄠ ㄌㄨㄣˊ)
to be a pitiable lone wanderer

漂海(ㄆㄧㄠ ㄏㄞˇ)
to take a long voyage

漂絮(ㄆㄧㄠ ㄒㄩˋ)
to wander like catkins floating in the air

漂兒(ㄆㄧㄠ ㄦ)
a buoy; afloat

漂搖(ㄆㄧㄠ ㄧㄠˊ)
to be tossed about in wind or water; to wave; to flutter

漂洋(ㄆㄧㄠ ㄧㄤˊ)

to take a long voyage

漂絮(ㄆ一ㄠ ㄒㄩ)
to wander about like catkins
floating in the air

漂兒(ㄆ一ㄠ ㄦ)
a buoy; a float

漂搖(ㄆ一ㄠ 一ㄠ)
to be tossed about in wind
or water; to wave; to flutter

漂洋(ㄆ一ㄠ 一ㄤ)
to take a long voyage

漂洋過海(ㄆ一ㄠ 一ㄤ ㄍㄨㄛ ㄏㄞ)
to sail across an ocean

【漂】3041
2. ㄆ一ㄠ peau piǎo
to bleach

漂白(ㄆ一ㄠ ㄅㄞ)
to bleach

漂白粉(ㄆ一ㄠ ㄅㄞ ㄈㄣ)
bleaching powder

漂白劑(ㄆ一ㄠ ㄅㄞ ㄐㄧ)
a bleaching agent; a decolor-
ant

漂布(ㄆ一ㄠ ㄅㄨ)
①to bleach linen ②bleached
linen

【漂】3041
3. ㄆ一ㄠ piaw piào
pretty; nice; sleek

漂亮(ㄆ一ㄠ ㄌ一ㄤ)
①pretty; handsome ②wise
in worldly ways ③brilliant;
beautiful

【漆】3042
1. ㄑ一 chi qī
1. a varnish tree; a lacquer
tree
2. varnish; lacquer
3. to varnish; to lacquer; to
paint: 他把門漆成紅色。He
painted the door red.

漆工(ㄑ一 ㄍㄨㄥ)or 漆匠(ㄑ一 ㄐ一ㄤ)
a painter; a varnisher: 他是
個房屋漆工。He is a house
painter.

漆器(ㄑ一 ㄑ一)
lacquer wares: 小販廉價出售
漆器。The peddler sold his
lacquer wares cheap.

漆書(ㄑ一 ㄕㄨ)
to write in varnish on bamboo tablets

漆樹(ㄑ一 ㄕㄨ)
the varnish tree

【漆】3042
2. ㄑㄩ chiuh qù
pitch-black

漆黑(ㄑ一 ㄏㄟ)
pitch-black; coal black;
raven

漆黑一團(ㄑ一 ㄏㄟ 一 ㄊㄨㄢ)
complete darkness

【漏】3043
1. to divulge; to disclose: 他洩
漏了秘密。He disclosed the
secret.
2. leak; to leak: 管子在漏水。
Water is leaking out of the
pipe.
3. to slip or omit unintentionally; to neglect; to forget; to
be missing: 漏了兩行。Two
lines are missing.
4. a water clock; an hourglass

漏報(ㄌㄡ ㄅㄠ)
to fail to include something
in a report intentionally or
unintentionally

漏排(ㄌㄡ ㄆㄞ)
to omit some words or passages in printing due to
carelessness

漏風(ㄌㄡ ㄈㄥ)
not airtight: 風箱漏風了。The
bellows is not airtight.

漏風聲(ㄌㄡ ㄈㄥ ㄕㄥ)
to disclose a secret; to leak
out a secret: 這封信漏了風聲。
This letter discloses a
secret.

漏脯充飢(ㄌㄡ ㄈㄨ ㄔㄨㄥ ㄐ一)
to care only for the present
regardless of future consequences

漏斗(ㄌㄡ ㄉㄡ)
a funnel

漏斗狀花冠(ㄌㄡ ㄉㄡ ㄓㄨㄤ ㄏㄨㄚ ㄍㄨㄢ)
funnel-shaped corolla

漏底(ㄌㄡ ㄉㄧ)
①a leak in the bottom of a
vessel for liquids ②to disclose a secret

漏掉(ㄌㄡ ㄉㄧㄠ)
to be missing or left out

漏電(ㄌㄡ ㄉㄧㄢ)
electric leakage

漏洞(ㄌㄡ ㄉㄨㄥ)
a shortcoming; a loophole:
任何法律都有漏洞。Every law
has a loophole.

漏脫(ㄌㄡ ㄊㄨㄛ)
to be left out inadvertently

漏列(ㄌㄡ ㄌ一ㄝ)
to fail to include or list due
to oversight

漏鼓(ㄌㄡ ㄍㄨ)
a drum for announcing the
watches or hours of the day

漏刻(ㄌㄡ ㄎㄜ)
a water clock; a clepsydra

漏孔(ㄌㄡ ㄎㄨㄥ)
a small hole through which
air or water leaks out

漏壺(ㄌㄡ ㄏㄨ)
a water clock; a clepsydra

漏接(ㄌㄡ ㄐ一ㄝ)
(baseball) passed ball

漏箭(ㄌㄡ ㄐ一ㄢ)
an arrow, or a needle, for
indicating time in a clepsydra

漏盡(ㄌㄡ ㄐ一ㄣ)
The night has run its
course.

漏精(ㄌㄡ ㄐ一ㄥ)
involuntary emission of
semen; spermatorrhea

漏氣(ㄌㄡ ㄑ一)
(said of air) to leak out; not
airtight

漏洩 or 漏泄(ㄌㄡ ㄒ一ㄝ)
to leak out: 這消息已漏洩出
去了。The news has leaked
out.

漏巵(ㄌㄡ ㄓ)
①a leaky wine-cup ②leak-
age of interest ③one who
can drink much liquor

漏出來(ㄌㄡ ㄔㄨ ㄌㄞ)
to leak out

漏師(ㄌㄡ ㄕ)
to leak out military secrets

漏杓(ㄌㄡ ㄕㄠ)
a skimmer; a skimming
ladle

漏水(ㄌㄡ ㄕㄨㄟ)
(said of containers, holds,
etc.) leaking: 這船漏水了。
This boat leaks.

漏稅(ㄌㄡ ㄕㄨㄟ)
tax evasion; to evade tax
payment

漏子(ㄌㄡ ㄗ)
①a funnel ②a shortcoming;
a weak point 亦作「漏兒」

漏夜(ㄌㄡ 一ㄝ)
in the dead of night: 他們漏
夜工作。They worked in the

〔水
部〕

〔水
部〕

dead of night.

漏屋 (ㄌㄚˋ ㄨ)
a leaky house

漏網之魚 (ㄌㄚˋ ㄨㄤˇ ㄓ ㄩˊ)
a fish that has escaped the net—a criminal who has escaped punishment

漏雨 (ㄌㄚˋ ㄩˇ)
(said of a roof) leaking

【漓】 3044 (ㄌㄧˊ)
1. dripping wet
2. thin

【溉】 3045 《ㄍㄞ gay gài》
1. to water; to irrigate
2. to wash

溉滌 (ㄍㄞˋ ㄉㄧˊ)
to wash

溉田 《ㄍㄞˋ ㄊㄧㄢˊ》
to irrigate fields: 農夫溉田。
The farmers irrigate fields.

【漚】 3046 (ㄡ ou ōu)
foam; bubbles; froth

【漚】 3046 (ㄡ ow òu)
to soak

漚麻 (ㄡˋ ㄇㄚˊ)
to soak hemp in water (so that it can be split easily)

漚鬱 (ㄡˋ)
(said of fragrance) rich

【演】 3047 (ㄧㄢˇ yean yǎn)
1. to perform for entertainment; to act; to play
2. to expound
3. to exercise; to practice
4. to evolve; to develop

演變 (ㄧㄢˇ ㄅㄧㄢˋ)
to develop and change; to evolve; evolutionary changes

演練 (ㄧㄢˇ ㄌㄧㄢˋ)
drill

演化 (ㄧㄢˇ ㄏㄨㄚˋ)
to develop and change; to evolve; evolution

演技 (ㄧㄢˇ ㄐㄧˋ)
acting

演進 (ㄧㄢˇ ㄐㄧㄣˋ)
to evolve; to develop

演講 (ㄧㄢˇ ㄐㄧㄤˇ)
to deliver a speech; to orate; to speak; to address

演講比賽 (ㄧㄢˇ ㄐㄧㄤˇ ㄅㄧˇ ㄙㄞˋ)
an oratorical contest

演講稿 (ㄧㄢˇ ㄐㄧㄤˇ ㄍㄠˇ)
written text of a speech

演劇 (ㄧㄢˇ ㄐㄩˋ)
① drama ② to act in a play

演習 (ㄧㄢˇ ㄒㄧˊ)
military exercises; maneuvers; a war game

演戲 (ㄧㄢˇ ㄒㄧˋ)
① to act in a play ② to play-act: 別再演戲了。Stop playacting.

演唱 (ㄧㄢˇ ㄔㄤˋ)
to sing before an audience; to sing onstage

演出 (ㄧㄢˇ ㄔㄨ)
(said of entertainers) to perform; to present (a play): 我們班上演出一劇。Our class presented a play.

演示 (ㄧㄢˇ ㄕˋ)
to demonstrate (skills, techniques, etc.)

演說 (ㄧㄢˇ ㄕㄨㄛ)
to give a speech; to deliver a speech; to speak; to address; to orate

演說家 (ㄧㄢˇ ㄕㄨㄛ ㄐㄧㄚ)
an orator

演說者 (ㄧㄢˇ ㄕㄨㄛ ㄓㄜˇ)
a speaker

演奏 (ㄧㄢˇ ㄗㄡˋ)
(said of musicians) to perform

演奏會 (ㄧㄢˇ ㄗㄡˋ ㄏㄨㄟˋ)
a concert; a recital

演算 (ㄧㄢˇ ㄙㄨㄢˋ)
mathematical exercises; to do mathematical problems

演義 (ㄧㄢˇ ㄧˋ)
a historical novel

演繹 (ㄧㄢˇ ㄧˋ)
to deduce

演繹法 (ㄧㄢˇ ㄧˋ ㄈㄚˇ)
deduction; the deductive method

演武場 (ㄧㄢˇ ㄨˇ ㄔㄤˇ) or (ㄧㄢˇ ㄨˋ ㄔㄤˇ)
a parade ground

演員 (ㄧㄢˇ ㄩㄢˊ)
an actor or actress

【漕】 3048 (ㄘㄠˊ tsaur cáo)
to transport grain by water

漕糧 (ㄘㄠˊ ㄌㄧㄤˊ)
rice transported to the capital by water as farm tax in kind during the Ching Dynasty

漕溝 (ㄘㄠˊ ㄍㄡ)
a canal

漕轉 (ㄘㄠˊ ㄓㄨㄢˇ)
transportation of rice to the capital by water and by land

漕司 (ㄘㄠˊ ㄙ)
(Sung Dynasty) an official post in charge of water transportation of rice to the capital

漕銀 (ㄘㄠˊ ㄧㄣˊ)
money paid to the government in place of tribute rice

漕運 (ㄘㄠˊ ㄩㄣˋ)
to transport grain to the capital by water

【漠】 3049 (ㄇㄛˋ moh mò)
1. a desert
2. indifferent; unconcerned
3. quiet; silent

漠北 (ㄇㄛˋ ㄅㄟˇ)
north of the Gobi Desert —Outer Mongolia

漠不關心 (ㄇㄛˋ ㄅㄨˋ ㄍㄨㄢ ㄒㄧㄣ)
to pay no attention at all; do not care at all; completely indifferent

漠不相關 (ㄇㄛˋ ㄅㄨˋ ㄒㄧㄤ ㄍㄨㄢ)
totally unrelated

漠漠 (ㄇㄛˋ ㄇㄛˋ)
① overcast ② silent; quiet ③ misty; foggy ④ vast and lonely

漠南 (ㄇㄛˋ ㄋㄢˊ)
south of the Gobi Desert —Inner Mongolia

漠視 (ㄇㄛˋ ㄕˋ)
① to despise; to hold in contempt ② to ignore; to pay no heed to ③ to consider unimportant; to underestimate; to treat with indifference

漠然 (ㄇㄛˋ ㄖㄢˊ)
① indifferent; unaffected; unmoved ② completely ignorant; at a loss

漠然不動 (ㄇㄛˋ ㄖㄢˊ ㄅㄨˋ ㄉㄨㄥˋ)
not in the least moved; quite unaffected; completely indifferent

【漣】 3050 (ㄌㄧㄢˊ lian lián)
1. ripples
2. weeping

連連(ㄌㄧㄢ ㄌㄧㄢ)
weeping

連洳(ㄌㄧㄢ ㄖㄨ)
weeping

漣漪(ㄌㄧㄢ ㄧ)
ripples: 月光在漣漪上閃耀。
The moon danced on the
ripples.

【漪】 3051
ㄧ i yi
ripples

漪瀾(ㄧ ㄌㄢ)
ripples

【漩】 3052
ㄒㄩㄢ shyuan xuan
(又讀 ㄒㄩㄢ shiuann
xuann)
a whirlpool

漩渦(ㄒㄩㄢ ㄨㄛ)
①a whirlpool ②a dispute; a
quarrel

【漢】 3053
ㄏㄢˋ hann hàn
1. of the Han Dynasty (206 B.
C.-220 A.D.)
2. of the Chinese people or
language
3. a man; a fellow
4. name of a tributary of the
Yangtze River

漢碑(ㄏㄢˋ ㄅㄟ)
tablets with inscriptions of
the Han Dynasty

漢堡(ㄏㄢˋ ㄅㄠˇ)
①Hamburg, Germany ②a
hamburger

漢方(ㄏㄢˋ ㄈㄤ)
Chinese medicinal art

漢代(ㄏㄢˋ ㄉㄞˋ)
the Han Dynasty (206 B.C.-
220 A.D.)

漢調(ㄏㄢˋ ㄉㄧㄠˋ)
a style of Chinese opera
prevalent in Hupeh

漢土(ㄏㄢˋ ㄊㄨˇ)
the land of the Han people
—China

漢尼拔(ㄏㄢˋ ㄋㄧˊ ㄅㄚˊ)
Hannibal, 247-183B.C., general of Carthage

漢女(ㄏㄢˋ ㄋㄩˇ)
the goddess of the Han
River (a tributary of the
Yangtze)

漢高祖(ㄏㄢˋ ㄍㄠ ㄗㄨˇ)
the dynastic title of Liu
Pang (劉邦), 247-195B.C.,

founder of the Han Dynasty
(206 B.C.-220 A.D.)

漢光武帝(《ㄨㄤ ㄨˇ ㄉㄧˋ)
Emperor Kuang Wu, who re-
stored the Han Dynasty in 25
A.D. after the usurpation by
Wang Mang (王莽)

漢口(ㄏㄢˋ ㄎㄡˇ)
Hankow, Hupeh

漢化(ㄏㄢˋ ㄏㄨㄚˋ)
sinicized; assimilated by the
Chinese

漢奸(ㄏㄢˋ ㄐㄧㄢ)
a traitor (to China)

漢江(ㄏㄢˋ ㄐㄧㄤ)
the Han River

漢軍(ㄏㄢˋ ㄐㄩㄣ)
the Manchu troops com-
posed of defected Chinese
people in the early Ching
Dynasty

漢獻帝(ㄏㄢˋ ㄒㄧㄢˋ ㄉㄧˋ)
Emperor Hsien (181-234 A.
D.), the last ruler of the
Eastern Han Dynasty

漢姓(ㄏㄢˋ ㄒㄧㄥˋ)
a Chinese surname adopted
by an alien

漢學(ㄏㄢˋ ㄒㄩㄝˊ)
①Sinology: 他專攻漢學。He
majors in Sinology. ②tex-
tual study of classics (prevalent in the Han Dynasty)

漢學家(ㄏㄢˋ ㄒㄩㄝˊ ㄐㄧㄚ)
①a Sinologue or Sinologist
②an expert in the textual
study of classics

漢朝(ㄏㄢˋ ㄔㄠˊ)
the Han Dynasty (206 B.C.-
220 A.D.)

漢城(ㄏㄢˋ ㄔㄥˊ)
Seoul, capital of South
Korea

漢室(ㄏㄢˋ ㄕˋ)
the House of Liu, which
ruled China during the Han
Dynasty (206 B.C.-220 A.D.)

漢書(ㄏㄢˋ ㄕㄨ)
the *History of the Han
Dynasty*, prepared by Pan Ku
(班固) during the latter half
of the Han Dynasty (also
known as 前漢書, covering
the 239 years from 漢高祖 to
the death of 王莽)

漢水(ㄏㄢˋ ㄕㄨㄟˇ)
the Han River, a tributary

of the Yangtze

漢人(ㄏㄢˋ ㄖㄣˊ)
the Han people—the pre-
dominant ethnic group in
China

漢字(ㄏㄢˋ ㄗˋ)
the Chinese characters

漢子(ㄏㄢˋ ˙ㄗ)
①a man ②a husband

漢族(ㄏㄢˋ ㄗㄨˊ)
the Han people—the largest
ethnic group of the Chinese
race

漢醫(ㄏㄢˋ ㄧ)
①a Chinese medicine ②a
Chinese herb doctor

漢譯(ㄏㄢˋ ㄧˋ)
translated into Chinese; a
Chinese rendering of a book:
這是哈姆雷特的漢譯。This is a
Chinese translation of *Hamlet*.

漢陽(ㄏㄢˋ ㄧㄤˊ)
Hanyang, a city on the Yangtze River opposite Hankow

漢英詞典(ㄏㄢˋ ㄧㄥ ㄘˊ ㄉㄧㄢˇ)
a Chinese-English dictionary

漢武帝(ㄏㄢˋ ㄨˇ ㄉㄧˋ)
Emperor Wu (157-87 B.C.),
whose reign marked the culmination of the Han Dynasty

漢文(ㄏㄢˋ ㄨㄣˊ)
①written Chinese ② the Chinese language or literature

漢語(ㄏㄢˋ ㄩˇ)
the Chinese language

【漫】 3054
ㄇㄢˋ mann màn
1. overflowing
2. uncontrolled; uninhibited
3. reckless; wild
4. unsystematic; aimless
5. to spread or extend over
6. all over the place; everywhere
7. a Chinese family name

漫筆(ㄇㄢˋ ㄅㄧˇ)
a familiar essay; a causerie

漫步(ㄇㄢˋ ㄅㄨˋ)
to ramble; to stroll

漫不經心(ㄇㄢˋ ㄅㄨˋ ㄐㄧㄥ ㄒㄧㄣ)
heedless; unmindful; inattentive; unconcerned

漫評(ㄇㄢˋ ㄆㄧㄥˊ)
rambling comments

漫罵(ㄇㄢˋ ㄇㄚˋ)

〔水
部〕

（水
部）

to abuse or slander with abandon

漫漫 (ㄇㄢˋ ㄇㄢˋ)
unrestrained; uninhibited

漫談 (ㄇㄢˋ ㄊㄢˊ) or 慢條斯理 (ㄇㄢˋ ㄊㄧㄠˊ ㄙ ㄌㄧˇ)
casual comments; rambling talks

漫條斯理 or 慢條斯理 (ㄇㄢˋ ㄊㄧㄠˊ ㄙ ㄌㄧˇ)
leisurely; calmly

漫浪 (ㄇㄢˋ ㄌㄤˋ)
morally reckless or loose

漫汗 (ㄇㄢˋ ㄏㄢˋ)
vast; boundless

漫畫 (ㄇㄢˋ ㄏㄨㄚˋ)
a cartoon; a caricature

漫畫家 (ㄇㄢˋ ㄏㄨㄚˋ ㄐㄧㄚ)
a cartoonist; a caricaturist

漫漶 (ㄇㄢˋ ㄏㄨㄢˋ)
indecipherable; illegible

漫長 (ㄇㄢˋ ㄔㄤˊ)
endless; infinite

漫射 (ㄇㄢˋ ㄕㄜˋ)
diffused reflection or diffusion

漫山遍野 (ㄇㄢˋ ㄕㄢ ㄅㄧㄢˋ ㄧㄝˇ)
so numerous as to cover the mountains and the plains; to be found everywhere

漫溢 (ㄇㄢˋ ㄧˋ)
to overflow; to brim over

漫遊 (ㄇㄢˋ ㄧㄡˊ)
to tour without a serious purpose; to travel about for pleasure

漫言 (ㄇㄢˋ ㄧㄢˊ)
words uttered without much thought; unsupported remarks

漫衍 (ㄇㄢˋ ㄧㄢˇ)
①to extend endlessly ②to wander from place to place; to have no fixed home

漫無邊際 (ㄇㄢˋ ㄨˊ ㄅㄧㄢ ㄐㄧˋ)
①boundless; limitless ②straying far from the point; rambling; discursive

漫無目標 (ㄇㄢˋ ㄨˊ ㄇㄨˋ ㄅㄧㄠ)
aimless; at random

漫無限制 (ㄇㄢˋ ㄨˊ ㄒㄧㄢˋ ㄓˋ)
with no restrictions whatsoever

漫無止境 (ㄇㄢˋ ㄨˊ ㄓˇ ㄐㄧㄥˋ)
extending or continuing endlessly; boundless

漫語 (ㄇㄢˋ ㄩˇ)
words uttered without much thought; unsupported or unfounded remarks

【漫】3054　ㄇㄢˋ man màn
(said of an expanse of water) vast or endless

漫漫 (ㄇㄢˋ ㄇㄢˋ)
extending endlessly

漫漫長夜 (ㄇㄢˋ ㄇㄢˋ ㄔㄤˊ ㄧㄝˋ)
a long, long night which seems to have no end

漫天 (ㄇㄢˋ ㄊㄧㄢ)
so vast as to cover the heavens

漫天大謊 (ㄇㄢˋ ㄊㄧㄢ ㄉㄚˋ ㄏㄨㄤˇ)
a monstrous lie

漫天討價 (ㄇㄢˋ ㄊㄧㄢ ㄊㄠˇ ㄐㄧㄚˋ) or 漫天要價 (ㄇㄢˋ ㄊㄧㄢ ㄧㄠˋ ㄐㄧㄚˋ)
to quote an exorbitant price in anticipation of haggling

【漬】3055　ㄗˋ tzyh zì
1. to soak
2. to dye
3. to be caked with

漬痕 (ㄗˋ ㄏㄣˊ)
a stain; a spot; a smear

漬染 (ㄗˋ ㄖㄢˇ)
to dye: 這布容易漬染。 This cloth dyes easily.

【漯】3056　ㄊㄚˋ tah tà
name of a river flowing through Shantung

漯河 (ㄊㄚˋ ㄏㄜˊ)
name of a river flowing through Shantung

【漱】3057　ㄕㄨˋ shuh shù
(讀音 ㄙㄡˋ sow sòu)
1. to rinse; to gargle
2. to wash

漱口 (ㄕㄨˋ ㄎㄡˇ)
to rinse the mouth; to gargle the throat

漱口水 (ㄕㄨˋ ㄎㄡˇ ㄕㄨㄟˇ)
a gargle; a mouthwash

漱口藥水 (ㄕㄨˋ ㄎㄡˇ ㄧㄠˋ ㄕㄨㄟˇ)
a mouthwash

漱口盂 (ㄕㄨˋ ㄎㄡˇ ㄩˊ) or 漱口杯 (ㄕㄨˋ ㄎㄡˇ ㄅㄟ)
a mouth washing cup; a mug

漱滌 (ㄕㄨˋ ㄉㄧˊ)
to wash; to rinse

【潊】3058　ㄒㄩˋ shiuh xù
name of a river in Hunan

【漳】3059　ㄓㄤ jang zhāng
1. name of a river in Fukien
2. name of a river in Honan

漳緞 (ㄓㄤ ㄉㄨㄢˋ)
brocade produced in Changchou, Fukien

漳泥 (ㄓㄤ ㄋㄧˊ)
seal ink produced in Changchou

漳河 (ㄓㄤ ㄏㄜˊ)
name of a river in Honan

漳廈鐵路 (ㄓㄤ ㄒㄧㄚˋ ㄊㄧㄝˇ ㄌㄨˋ)
the Changchou-Amoy Railway in Fukien

漳州 (ㄓㄤ ㄓㄡ)
Changchou, Fukien

【漲】3060　1. ㄓㄤˇ janq zhǎng
to swell; to expand

漲潮 (ㄓㄤˇ ㄔㄠˊ)
(said of the tide) to flow

漲水 (ㄓㄤˇ ㄕㄨㄟˇ)
the swell of a river; to swell: 河因下雨而漲水。 The river is swollen by rain.

漲縮 (ㄓㄤˇ ㄙㄨㄛˋ)
swelling and shrinking; elasticity

漲溢 (ㄓㄤˇ ㄧˋ)
(said of a river) to overflow

【漲】3060　2. ㄓㄤˋ jaang zhàng
to go up or rise (as prices, water, etc.): 河水暴漲。 The river suddenly rose.

漲風 (ㄓㄤˋ ㄈㄥ)
the upward trend of commodity prices and service charges

漲落 (ㄓㄤˋ ㄌㄨㄛˋ)
(said of commodity prices, stocks, etc.) the rate of increase or rise

漲跌 (ㄓㄤˋ ㄉㄧㄝˊ)
price fluctuation

漲落 (ㄓㄤˋ ㄌㄨㄛˋ)
①price fluctuation ②rising and dropping (of water stage)

漲價 (ㄓㄤˋ ㄐㄧㄚˋ)
to register a price hike; to raise prices; appreciation

【漾】3061　ㄧㄤˋ yanq yàng
1. to ripple

2. to brim over
3. to throw up; to vomit

漾波(|ㅊ ㄅㄛ)
ripples

漾舟(|ㅊ ㅛㄨ)
to enjoy boating

漾漾(|ㅊ |ㅊ)
rippling

【漸】 3062
1. ㅐ|ㄢ jiann jiàn
gradually; little by little; by degrees

漸減(ㅐ|ㄢ ㅐ|ㄢ)
to decrease gradually: 他對 這科目的興趣漸減. His interest in this subject gradually decreases.

漸漸(ㅐ|ㄢ ㅐ|ㄢ)
gradually; little by little: 你 會漸漸習慣它的. You will get used to it gradually.

漸進(ㅐ|ㄢ ㅐ|ㄣ)
to advance little by little; to make gradual progress

漸強音(ㅐ|ㄢ ㄑ|ㅊ |ㄣ)
(music) a crescendo

漸入佳境(ㅐ|ㄢ ㄖㄨ ㅐ|ㄚ ㅐ|ㄥ)
to get better and better

漸增(ㅐ|ㄢ ㄗㄥ)
to increase gradually: 駕駛員 漸增速度. The driver increased speed gradually.

漸次(ㅐ|ㄢ ㄘ)
gradually; little by little; by degrees: 水面漸次上升. The water level rose little by little.

【漸】 3062
2. ㅐ|ㄢ jian jiān
1. to soak; to permeate
2. (said of the territory) to reach

漸染(ㅐ|ㄢ ㅁㄢ)
to soak; to imbue

漸洳(ㅐ|ㄢ ㅁㄨ)
to soak

漸漬(ㅐ|ㄢ ㄗ)
to soak; to imbue

【漶】 3063
ㄏㄨㄢ huann huàn
to wear out beyond recognition

【滷】 3064
ㄌㄨ luu lǔ
1. gravy; broth; sauce
2. salty; salted

滷麵(ㄌㄨ ㄇ|ㄢ)
noodles served with gravy

滷蛋(ㄌㄨ ㄉㄢ)
a hard-boiled egg stewed in gravy; a marinated egg

滷湖(ㄌㄨ ㄏㄨ)
a salt lake

滷鷄(ㄌㄨ ㅐ|)
chicken stewed in soybean sauce; marinated chicken

滷蝦(ㄌㄨ ㄒ|ㄚ)
salted shrimp gravy

滷汁(ㄌㄨ ㄓ)
marinade

滷水(ㄌㄨ ㄕㄨㄟ)
salt brine

滷肉(ㄌㄨ ㅁㄡ)
meat stewed in soybean sauce; marinated meat

滷菜(ㄌㄨ ㄘㄞ)
marinated vegetables, meat, etc.

滷鴨(ㄌㄨ |ㄚ)
marinated duck

【潊】 3065
|ㄡ iou yōu
(said of water) flowing

【潃】 3066
ㄌ|ˇ lǐ
1. saliva; spittle
2. flowing downstream

【漿】 3067
ㅐ|ㅊ jiang jiāng
1. thick fluid; starch
2. to starch

漿果(ㅐ|ㅊ ㄍㄨㄛ)
a berry

漿糊(ㅐ|ㅊ ㄏㄨ)
paste: 他用漿糊把信封封住.
He sealed the envelope with paste.

漿洗衣服(ㅐ|ㅊ ㄒ| |ㄈㄨ)
to wash and starch clothes

漿水(ㅐ|ㅊ ㄕㄨㄟ)
starch solution; mixed starch

【潁】 3068
|ㄥ yiing yǐng
name of a river and a place in Anhwei

潁河(|ㄥ ㄏㄜ)
name of a river in Anhwei

潁上(|ㄥ ㄕㄤ)
name of a county in Anhwei

【潦】 3069
ㄌ|ㄠ liau liǎo
deep and clear

十二畫

【漭】 3070
ㄇㄤ maang mǎng
vast; expansive

【潔】 3071
ㅐ|ㄝ jye jié
1. clean; spotless; pure; stainless; immaculate: 他心地純潔. He is pure in heart.
2. to clean; to keep clean

潔白(ㅐ|ㄝ ㄅㄞ)
clean and white; immaculate; spotless

潔癖(ㅐ|ㄝ ㄆ|)
a morbid fear of getting dirty; mysophobia

潔婦(ㅐ|ㄝ ㄈㄨ)
a chaste woman

潔朗(ㅐ|ㄝ ㄌㄤ)
clean and bright

潔廉(ㅐ|ㄝ ㄌ|ㄢ)
incorruptible; clean: 潔廉的人 不會受賄. The incorruptible man could not be bribed.

潔己(ㅐ|ㄝ ㅐ|)
to keep oneself free from immorality

潔淨(ㅐ|ㄝ ㅐ|ㄥ)
clean; untarnished; untainted; stainless: 他雙手潔淨. His hands are clean.

潔身自好(ㅐ|ㄝ ㄕㄣ ㄗ ㄏㄠ)or 潔身自愛(ㅐ|ㄝ ㄕㄣ ㄗ ㄞ)
to exercise self-control so as to protect oneself from immorality

潔樽候敎(ㅐ|ㄝ ㄗㄨㄣ ㄏㄡ ㅐ|ㄠ)
I am looking forward to your visit with wine-cups washed clean. (a conventional phrase often printed on an invitation to dinner)

【潑】 3072
ㄆㄛ po pō
1. to pour; to sprinkle; to spill
2. ferocious; fierce; spiteful; villainous

潑皮(ㄆㄛ ㄆ|)
a ruffian; a villain

潑墨山水(ㄆㄛ ㄇㄛ ㄕㄢ ㄕㄨㄟ)
landscape painting done with splashes of ink; splashink landscape

潑婦(ㄆㄛ ㄈㄨ)
a virago; a shrew; a termagant

潑婦罵街(ㄆㄛ ㄈㄨ ㄇㄚ ㅐ|ㄝ)
(literally) a virago yelling

〔水
部〕

in the street—to utter abusive language loudly and freely without much provocation or justification

潑天富貴(ㄆㄛ ㄊㄧㄢ ㄈㄨˋ ㄍㄨㄟˋ)
extreme wealth

潑天大禍(ㄆㄛ ㄊㄧㄢ ㄉㄚˋ ㄏㄨㄛˋ)
extreme disaster

潑剌(ㄆㄛ ㄌㄚˊ)
splashing sound of fish jumping out of water

潑辣(ㄆㄛ ㄌㄚˊ)
① fierce; ferocious; spiteful ② pungent: 這份評論寫得很潑辣。The critique is written in a pungent style.

潑辣貨(ㄆㄛ ㄌㄚˊ ㄏㄨㄛˋ)
a ferocious woman; 她是個潑辣貨。She is a ferocious woman.

潑賴(ㄆㄛ ㄌㄞˋ)
villainous; knavish

潑冷水(ㄆㄛ ㄌㄥˇ ㄕㄨㄟˇ)
to pour or to throw cold water on—(figuratively) to dampen the enthusiasm of

潑街(ㄆㄛ ㄐㄧㄝ)
to water the street

潑水難收(ㄆㄛ ㄕㄨㄟˇ ㄋㄢˊ ㄕㄡ)
(literally) Spilled water cannot be retrieved.—One cannot undo an accomplished fact.

潑水節(ㄆㄛ ㄕㄨㄟˇ ㄐㄧㄝˊ)
the Water-Sprinkling Festival of Thailand, Laos, Burma and some minority nationalities in China

【潛】 3073
ㄑㄧㄢˊ chyan *qián*
1. to hide; to conceal
2. to dive
3. hidden; secret; latent

潛伏(ㄑㄧㄢˊ ㄈㄨˊ)
① to be in hiding; to lie hidden ② latent; hidden; concealed

潛伏期(ㄑㄧㄢˊ ㄈㄨˊ ㄑㄧˊ)
an incubation period; a latent period

潛伏性(ㄑㄧㄢˊ ㄈㄨˊ ㄒㄧㄥˋ)
latency

潛德(ㄑㄧㄢˊ ㄉㄜˊ)
hidden virtues; unnoticed virtues

潛邸(ㄑㄧㄢˊ ㄉㄧˇ)
the residence of an emperor

before ascending the throne

潛逃(ㄑㄧㄢˊ ㄊㄠˊ)
to escape secretly; to slip away: 他們潛逃了。They slipped away.

潛逃(ㄑㄧㄢˊ ㄊㄠˊ)
to flee secretly; to slip away; to abscond

潛艇(ㄑㄧㄢˊ ㄊㄧㄥˇ)
a submarine

潛艇補給艦(ㄑㄧㄢˊ ㄊㄧㄥˇ ㄅㄨˇ ㄐㄧ ㄐㄧㄢˋ)
a submarine tender

潛能(ㄑㄧㄢˊ ㄋㄥˊ)
potential energy; potentiality

潛匿(ㄑㄧㄢˊ ㄋㄧˋ)
to go into hiding; to hide oneself

潛力(ㄑㄧㄢˊ ㄌㄧˋ)
potential; hidden force; unused strength: 他似乎具有領導者的潛力。He seems to have potential as a leader.

潛龍(ㄑㄧㄢˊ ㄌㄨㄥˊ)
a hidden dragon—an unrecognized sage

潛居(ㄑㄧㄢˊ ㄐㄩ)
to live in seclusion; to live in a hiding place

潛修(ㄑㄧㄢˊ ㄒㄧㄡ)
to cultivate oneself in quiet privacy

潛心(ㄑㄧㄢˊ ㄒㄧㄣ)
to have a quiet concentrated mind

潛心研究(ㄑㄧㄢˊ ㄒㄧㄣ ㄧㄢˊ ㄐㄧㄡˋ)
to study diligently with a quiet mind: 他潛心研究歷史。He devotes himself to the study of history.

潛行(ㄑㄧㄢˊ ㄒㄧㄥˊ)
to go secretly

潛虛(ㄑㄧㄢˊ ㄒㄩ)
to live in seclusion

潛師(ㄑㄧㄢˊ ㄕ)
to move troops secretly

潛勢力(ㄑㄧㄢˊ ㄕˋ ㄌㄧˋ)
latent power

潛水(ㄑㄧㄢˊ ㄕㄨㄟˇ)
① to dive ② name of a river flowing through Anhwei (安徽) and Kiangsu (江蘇)

潛水底(ㄑㄧㄢˊ ㄕㄨㄟˇ ㄉㄧˇ)
to explore a riverbed, sea bottom, etc., by diving

潛水艇(ㄑㄧㄢˊ ㄕㄨㄟˇ ㄊㄧㄥˇ)

a submarine: 潛水艇潛水了。The submarine dived.

潛水炸彈(ㄑㄧㄢˊ ㄕㄨㄟˇ ㄓㄚˋ ㄉㄢˋ)
a depth charge

潛水衣(ㄑㄧㄢˊ ㄕㄨㄟˇ ㄧ)
a diving suit

潛水員(ㄑㄧㄢˊ ㄕㄨㄟˇ ㄩㄢˊ)or 潛水夫(ㄑㄧㄢˊ ㄕㄨㄟˇ ㄈㄨ)
a diver

潛熱(ㄑㄧㄢˊ ㄖㄜˋ)
latent heat

潛入(ㄑㄧㄢˊ ㄖㄨˋ)
① to enter secretly; to slip in ② to dive into (water)

潛滋暗長(ㄑㄧㄢˊ ㄗ ㄢˋ ㄓㄤˇ)
to grow and develop secretly

潛在(ㄑㄧㄢˊ ㄗㄞˋ)
latent

潛在能力(ㄑㄧㄢˊ ㄗㄞˋ ㄋㄥˊ ㄌㄧˋ)or 潛力(ㄑㄧㄢˊ ㄌㄧˋ)
potentiality

潛在意識(ㄑㄧㄢˊ ㄗㄞˋ ㄧˋ ㄕˋ)or 潛意識(ㄑㄧㄢˊ ㄧˋ ㄕˋ)
subconsciousness

潛藏(ㄑㄧㄢˊ ㄘㄤˊ)
to be in hiding

潛移默化(ㄑㄧㄢˊ ㄧˊ ㄇㄛˋ ㄏㄨㄚˋ)
to change and influence unobtrusively and imperceptibly

潛望鏡(ㄑㄧㄢˊ ㄨㄤˋ ㄐㄧㄥˋ)
a periscope

【潘】 3074
ㄆㄢ pan *pān*
1. a Chinese family name
2. water in which rice has been washed

潘金蓮(ㄆㄢ ㄐㄧㄣ ㄌㄧㄢˊ)
Pan Chin-lien, a female character of loose morals in the novel All Men Are Brothers (水滸傳)

【潟】 3075
ㄒㄧˋ shih *xì*
saline land

潟湖(ㄒㄧˋ ㄏㄨˊ)
(geography) a lagoon

【潞】 3076
ㄌㄨˋ luh *lù*
name of several rivers in Northern China

【潢】 3077
ㄏㄨㄤˊ hwang *huáng*
a lake or a pond

潢池(ㄏㄨㄤˊ ㄔˊ)
a pond

潏洋（ㄏㄨㄟㄧㄤˊ）
deep and expansive

潏潏（ㄏㄨㄟˋ）
(said of a body of water)
boundless

【潪】3078 ㄐㄧㄢ jiann jiān
a mountain stream

潏流（ㄐㄧㄢ ㄌㄧㄡˊ）
a mountain stream; a stream
in a valley

潏河（ㄐㄧㄢ ㄏㄜˊ）
name of a river originating
in Honan

潏壑（ㄐㄧㄢ ㄏㄨㄛˋ）
a valley; a ravine

潏溪（ㄐㄧㄢ ㄒㄧ）
a mountain stream; a stream
in a valley: 我們順着潏溪而
下. We went down the moun-
tain stream.

潏峽（ㄐㄧㄢ ㄒㄧㄚˊ）
a gorge

潏過（ㄐㄧㄢ ㄍㄨㄛˋ）
a mountain stream: 他跳過潏
水. He jumped across the
mountain stream.

【潦】3079 1. （潦）ㄌㄠˊ law láo
to flood; floods

【潦】3079 2. ㄌㄠˇ lao lǎo
a puddle

【潦】3079 3. ㄌㄧㄠˊ liau liáo
1. disheartened; disappointed
2. without care

潦倒（ㄌㄧㄠˊ ㄉㄠˇ）
disappointed; unhappy; down
in luck: 他過着潦倒的生活.
He led an unhappy life.

潦草（ㄌㄧㄠˊ ㄘㄠˇ）or潦潦草草（ㄌㄧㄠˊ
ㄌㄧㄠˊ ㄘㄠˇ ㄘㄠˇ）
①in a careless, irrespon-
sible manner; perfunctory ②
(said of handwriting) hasty
and careless; illegible

潦草塞責（ㄌㄧㄠˊ ㄘㄠˇ ㄙㄜˋ ㄗㄜˊ）
to do a duty perfunctorily

【潤】3080 ㄖㄨㄣˋ ruenn rùn
1. moist; glossy; fresh
2. to moisten; to freshen
3. to enrich; to benefit
4. to embellish

潤筆（ㄖㄨㄣˋ ㄅㄧˇ）or潤毫（ㄖㄨㄣˋ

ㄏㄠˊ）
remuneration（or fee）for
writing or painting

潤肺（ㄖㄨㄣˋ ㄈㄟˋ）
(Chinese herb medicine) to
moisten supposedly dry
lungs

潤膩（ㄖㄨㄣˋ ㄋㄧˋ）
fine and smooth

潤滑（ㄖㄨㄣˋ ㄏㄨㄚˊ）
①to lubricate ②smooth

潤滑劑（ㄖㄨㄣˋ ㄏㄨㄚˊ ㄐㄧˋ）
a lubricant

潤滑油（ㄖㄨㄣˋ ㄏㄨㄚˊ ㄧㄡˊ）
lubricating oil

潤腸（ㄖㄨㄣˋ ㄔㄤˊ）
(Chinese herb medicine) to
moisten the supposedly dry
digestive apparatus

潤濕（ㄖㄨㄣˋ ㄕ）
moist and fresh: 草因露水而
潤濕. Grasses were moist
with dew.

潤飾（ㄖㄨㄣˋ ㄕˋ）
to add color; to embellish
or polish a writing

潤飾之詞（ㄖㄨㄣˋ ㄕˋ ㄓ ㄘˊ）
ornamental words that gloss
over fault

潤身（ㄖㄨㄣˋ ㄕㄣ）
to invigorate or enrich oneself with virtues

潤資（ㄖㄨㄣˋ ㄗ）
fee for writing or painting

潤澤（ㄖㄨㄣˋ ㄗㄜˊ）
①moist and glossy; fresh;
vigorous: 她有一頭潤澤有光的
頭髮. She has sleek and
glossy hair. ② to moisten;
to freshen; to invigorate

潤色（ㄖㄨㄣˋ ㄙㄜˋ）
to add color; to embellish or
polish a writing: 你的作文需
要潤色一下. Your composi-
tion needs polishing.

潤益（ㄖㄨㄣˋ ㄧˋ）
profit; benefit; dividend

潤屋（ㄖㄨㄣˋ ㄨ）
to enrich the house with
material wealth

【潭】3081 ㄊㄢˊ tarn tán
1. deep water; a deep pool
2. deep; profound

潭府（ㄊㄢˊ ㄈㄨˇ）
your residence or house (a
polite expression)

潭第（ㄊㄢˊ ㄉㄧˋ）
your mansion (a polite
expression)

潭腿（ㄊㄢˊ ㄊㄨㄟˇ）
one of the northern schools
of boxing, founded by the
monks of the Temple of
Dragon Pond (龍潭寺)

潭祉（ㄊㄢˊ ㄓˇ）
great happiness (a term
used in letter writing)

潭水（ㄊㄢˊ ㄕㄨㄟˇ）
deep water

潭奧（ㄊㄢˊ ㄠˋ）
profound; deep

潭影（ㄊㄢˊ ㄧㄥˇ）
the reflection in a deep pond

【潮】3082 ㄔㄠˊ chaur cháo
1. the tide
2. damp; moist; wet
3. (now rarely, said of gold,
silver, etc.) inferior in skill
or fineness

潮流（ㄔㄠˊ ㄌㄧㄡˊ）
①tides; tidal currents ②a
current; a trend; a tendency

潮解（ㄔㄠˊ ㄐㄧㄝˇ）
to deliquesce; deliquescence

潮氣（ㄔㄠˊ ㄑㄧˋ）
dampness; high humidity;
moist; moisture

潮汐（ㄔㄠˊ ㄒㄧˋ）
morning tide and evening
tide; tides

潮信（ㄔㄠˊ ㄒㄧㄣˋ）
①the fixed time of the tides
②menstruation; period; the
time of menstruating

潮州（ㄔㄠˊ ㄓㄡ）
Chaochow, Kwantung Prov-
ince

潮濕（ㄔㄠˊ ㄕ）
humid; damp: 我不喜歡潮濕的
天氣. I don't like damp
weather.

潮水（ㄔㄠˊ ㄕㄨㄟˇ）
the tide

潮音（ㄔㄠˊ ㄧㄣ）
the chanting of Buddhist
scriptures by the monks

【潯】3083 ㄒㄩㄣˊ shyun xún
1. a steep bank by the stream
2. an alternative name of Chiuchiang (九江) in Kiangsi

潯江（ㄒㄩㄣˊ ㄐㄧㄤ）

【水部】

溹陽(ㄙㄨㄛ ㄧㄤ)
name of a river in Kwangsi

溹溪(ㄙㄨㄛ ㄒㄧ)
name of a river near Chiuchiang

【潼】 3084 ㄊㄨㄥˊ torng tóng
1. high and lofty
2. a tributary of the Yellow River
3. a county in Shensi Province

潼關(ㄊㄨㄥˊ ㄍㄨㄢ)
name of a strategic point and a county in Shensi Province, a gateway between Northwest and Central China

【潺】 3085 ㄔㄢˊ charn chán
the sound of water flowing

潺潺(ㄔㄢˊ ㄔㄢˊ)
the gurgling of water flowing; the murmuring of flowing water

潺湲(ㄔㄢˊ ㄩㄢˊ)
①water flowing ②tears streaming down

【潸】 3086 ㄕㄢ shan shān
tears flowing; to weep

潸然(ㄕㄢ ㄖㄢˊ)
tears flowing; weeping

潸潸(ㄕㄢ ㄕㄢ)
to weep continually

潸然(ㄕㄢ ㄖㄢˊ)
tears falling

【潰】 3087 ㄎㄨㄟˋ kuey kuì
1. a river overflowing its banks
2. broken up; scattered
3. (military) defeated
4. (said of a dike or dam) to burst

潰敗(ㄎㄨㄟˋ ㄅㄞˋ)
(military) defeated and scattered; routed; a rout: 撤退變成潰敗。The retreat became a rout.

潰不成軍(ㄎㄨㄟˋ ㄅㄨˋ ㄔㄥˊ ㄐㄩㄣ)
defeated and broken up to such a state that it can no longer be called an army; completely routed

潰破(ㄎㄨㄟˋ ㄆㄛˋ)
(said of dikes) broken up; (said of the army) defeated; (said of abscesses) bursting

潰盟(ㄎㄨㄟˋ ㄇㄥˊ)
to violate an agreement or treaty; a breach of faith

潰敵(ㄎㄨㄟˋ ㄉㄧˊ)
to defeat the enemy; to put the enemy to rout

潰逃(ㄎㄨㄟˋ ㄊㄠˊ)
to escape in disorder; to flee pell-mell; to run helter-skelter: 敵人潰逃。The enemies fled pell-mell.

潰退(ㄎㄨㄟˋ ㄊㄨㄟˋ)
to retreat as a result of defeat

潰爛(ㄎㄨㄟˋ ㄌㄢˋ)
bursting of an abscess; inflamed; inflammation

潰決(ㄎㄨㄟˋ ㄐㄩㄝˊ)
floods overflowing or breaking up levees, embankments, etc.

潰走(ㄎㄨㄟˋ ㄗㄡˇ)
(said of a defeated army) to scatter and run for life

潰散(ㄎㄨㄟˋ ㄙㄢˇ)
defeated and dispersed

潰瘍(ㄎㄨㄟˋ ㄧㄤˊ)
an ulcer

潰圍(ㄎㄨㄟˋ ㄨㄟˊ)
to break the enemy encirclement and get away

【澄】 3088 ㄔㄥˊ cherng chéng
(籀音 ㄉㄥˋ denq dèng)
1. clear and still (water)
2. to purify water by letting the impurities settle down to the bottom
3. to pacify

澄明(ㄔㄥˊ ㄇㄧㄥˊ)
clear and bright

澄空(ㄔㄥˊ ㄎㄨㄥ)
a clear sky

澄清(ㄔㄥˊ ㄑㄧㄥ)
①to purify water by letting the impurities settle down to the bottom ② to quell disturbances in the world; to put in order; to set right ③ to clarify ④ clear

澄清天下(ㄔㄥˊ ㄑㄧㄥ ㄊㄧㄢ ㄒㄧㄚˋ)
to rid the world of all troubles and disturbances

澄清事實(ㄔㄥˊ ㄑㄧㄥ ㄕˋ ㄕˊ)
to clarify some facts

澄心(ㄔㄥˊ ㄒㄧㄣ)
to calm one's mind

澄澈(ㄔㄥˊ ㄔㄜˋ)
crystal clear

澄淵(ㄔㄥˊ ㄩㄢ)
clear, deep water

【澈】 3089 ㄔㄜˋ cheh chè
1. thoroughly; completely
2. clear water
3. to understand

澈底(ㄔㄜˋ ㄉㄧˇ)
thoroughly; completely; thoroughgoing

澈頭澈尾(ㄔㄜˋ ㄊㄡˊ ㄔㄜˋ ㄨㄟˇ)
out and out; thoroughly

澈查(ㄔㄜˋ ㄔㄚˊ)
to investigate thoroughly

澈悟(ㄔㄜˋ ㄨˋ)
to realize or understand completely

【澎】 3090 ㄆㄥ peng pēng
the roaring of colliding billows

澎湃(ㄆㄥ ㄆㄞˋ)
the roaring of billows; to surge: 大海中波濤澎湃。Waves surge in the sea.

【澎】 3090 ㄆㄥˊ perng péng
the Pescadores

澎湖(ㄆㄥˊ ㄏㄨˊ)
the Penghus, or the Pescadores, in the Taiwan Straits

【澍】 3091 ㄕㄨˋ shuh shù
1. seasonal rains; timely rain
2. (said of plants, etc.) saturated with rainwater

【澆】 3092 ㄐㄧㄠ jiau jiāo
1. to water (plants, flowers, etc.)
2. to sprinkle water on
3. perfidious; faithless; ungrateful

澆薄(ㄐㄧㄠ ㄅㄛˊ)
rash and perfidious; faithless and ungrateful

澆漓之世(ㄐㄧㄠ ㄌㄧˊ ㄓ ㄕˋ)
the age of demoralization

澆浮(ㄐㄧㄠ ㄈㄨˊ)
rash and faithless

澆奠(ㄐㄧㄠ ㄉㄧㄢˋ)
to pour out a libation

澆冷水(ㄐㄧㄠ ㄌㄥˇ ㄕㄨㄟˇ)
to dampen enthusiasm; to discourage; to throw cold water on

澆灌（ㄐㄧㄠ ㄍㄨㄢ）
to water (plants, etc.); to pour water: 她每天早晨澆灌花草。 She waters plants every morning.

澆花
to water flowers: 那女孩正在澆花。 The girl is watering flowers.

澆愁（ㄐㄧㄠ ㄔㄡ）
to wash away sorrows with wine

澆水（ㄐㄧㄠ ㄕㄨㄟˇ）
to water; to pour water on

【潲】 3093
ㄕㄠ ㄕㄠˋ shaw shàu
(said of rain) to fall slantwise

潲進來（ㄕㄠˋ ㄐㄧㄣ ㄌㄞˊ）
(said of the rainwater) splashing in with the wind

潲濕了（ㄕㄠˋ ㄕ ˙ㄌㄜ）
to get wet by the rainwater splashing in with the wind

潲雨（ㄕㄠˋ ㄩˇ）
①rain slanted by wind ②to get wet by the slanting rain

【澇】 3094
ㄌㄠ law lào
1. (said of farm crops) to rot in the field owing to floods; waterlogged
2. torrents; floods

【潙】 3095
ㄍㄨㄟ guei guī
name of a river in Yung-chi County（永濟縣）Shansi Province

【澌】 3096
ㄙ sy sī
1. to exhaust; to drain out
2. the sound of breaking or scattering

澌滅（ㄙ ㄇㄧㄝˋ）
to vanish

澌盡（ㄙ ㄐㄧㄣˋ）
to exhaust; to drain out

澌澌（ㄙ ㄙ）
the sound of the pouring rain or the heaving wind

【澉】 3097
ㄍㄢˇ gaan gǎn
to wash

澉浦（ㄍㄢˇ ㄆㄨˇ）
name of a town in Chekiang（浙江）

【滈】 3098
ㄏㄠˋ haw hào

radiance of gems

【澂】 3099
ㄔㄥˊ cherng chéng
same as 澄—clear and still water

澂江（ㄔㄥˊ ㄐㄧㄤ）
name of a county in Yunnan Province

十三畫

【澠】 3100
1. ㄕㄥˊ sherng
shéng
name of a river in Shantung Province

澠水（ㄕㄥˊ ㄕㄨㄟˇ）
name of a river in Shantung Province

【澠】 3100
2. ㄇㄧㄢˇ miin miǎn
1. the ancient name of a place in Honan Province where the kings of Chin（秦）and Chao（趙）of the Epoch of Warring States held their summit conference
2. name of a river and a county in Honan Province

澠河（ㄇㄧㄢˇ ㄏㄜˊ）
name of a river in Honan Province

【澥】 3101
ㄒㄧㄝˋ shieh xiè
1. a blocked stream
2. to stop the flow of water
3. another name of Pohai（渤海）

【澡】 3102
ㄗㄠˇ tzao zǎo
to wash; to bathe

澡盆（ㄗㄠˇ ㄆㄣˊ）
a bathtub

澡堂 or 澡塘（ㄗㄠˇ ㄊㄤˊ）
a bathhouse; a public bath

澡身（ㄗㄠˇ ㄕㄣ）
to take a bath

澡身浴德（ㄗㄠˇ ㄕㄣ ㄩˋ ㄉㄜˊ）
(literally) to bathe oneself in water and in virtues—to cleanse both physically and morally

【澧】 3103
ㄌㄧˇ lii lǐ
1. a fountain; a spring
2. name of a county in Hunan Province

【澮】 3104
ㄎㄨㄞˋ kuay kuài
1. ditches on farmland
2. name of a river in Shansi and Honan provinces

澮水（ㄎㄨㄞˋ ㄕㄨㄟˇ）
①name of a river in Shansi
②name of a river in Honan

【澨】 3105
ㄕˋ shyh shì
1. the waterside; the waterfront
2. name of a river in Hupeh Province

澨水（ㄕˋ ㄕㄨㄟˇ）
name of a river in Hupeh Province

【澤】 3106
ㄗㄜˊ tzer zé
1. the place where water gathers; a marsh
2. grace; favors; kindness
3. brilliance; radiance; luster; bright; glossy; smooth
4. to benefit; to enrich

澤被（ㄗㄜˊ ㄅㄟˋ）
to extend benefit

澤被天下（ㄗㄜˊ ㄅㄟˋ ㄊㄧㄢ ㄒㄧㄚˋ）
Benefits spread to all people.

澤民（ㄗㄜˊ ㄇㄧㄣˊ）
to benefit the people

澤鹵（ㄗㄜˊ ㄌㄨˇ）
salty land that grows no crops

澤國（ㄗㄜˊ ㄍㄨㄛˊ）
land submerged or inundated by water; a marsh or swamp

澤及枯骨（ㄗㄜˊ ㄐㄧˊ ㄎㄨ ㄍㄨˇ）
to benefit even the dead

澤及萬世（ㄗㄜˊ ㄐㄧˊ ㄨㄢˋ ㄕˋ）
The good grace or benevolence will be felt for countless generations to come.

【澱】 3107
ㄉㄧㄢˋ diann diàn
1. sediment; dregs; precipitate
2. indigo

澱粉（ㄉㄧㄢˋ ㄈㄣˇ）
starch

【澳】 3108
ㄠˋ aw ào
1. deep waters—where sea-going vessels can moor
2. name of various places (see below)

澳門（ㄠˋ ㄇㄣˊ）
Macao

〔水部〕

澳大利亞（ㄠ ㄉㄚˋ ㄌㄧˋ ㄧˋㄚ）
Australia

澳洲（ㄠˋ ㄓㄡ）
Australia 參看「澳大利亞」

【澼】 3109
ㄆㄧˋ pih pì
to wash; to launder

【澹】 1. ㄉㄢˋ dann dàn
quiet and tranquil

澹泊（ㄉㄢˋ ㄅㄛˊ）
having no worldly desires or
ambitions 亦作「淡泊」

澹泊名利（ㄉㄢˋ ㄅㄛˊ ㄇㄧㄥˊ ㄌㄧˋ）
to be indifferent toward
fame and wealth

澹泊明志（ㄉㄢˋ ㄅㄛˊ ㄇㄧㄥˊ ㄓˋ）
to live a simple life to show
one's will and moral fortitude

澹漠（ㄉㄢˋ ㄇㄛˋ）
indifference; indifferent;
placid and dispassionate

澹澉（ㄉㄢˋ ㄍㄢˇ）
to wash

澹然（ㄉㄢˋ ㄖㄢˊ）
tranquil and calm

澹雅（ㄉㄢˋ ㄧㄚˇ）
quiet and refined

【澹】 3110
2. ㄊㄢˊ tarn tán

澹臺（ㄊㄢˊ ㄊㄞˊ）
①a double-surname ②name
of a lake in Kiangsu（江蘇）

【潭】 3111
ㄔㄢˊ charn chán
1. (said of the water) placid,
calm and tranquil
2. name of a river

潭州（ㄔㄢˊ ㄓㄡ）
the ancient name of a politi-
cal region in the Tang
Dynasty in today's Ching
Feng County（清豐縣）of
Hopeh Province

【激】 3112
ㄐㄧ ji jī
1. to stir up; to rouse; to
arouse; to urge; to excite
2. sudden; great; very
3. heated (debate, battle, etc.);
fierce; angry; vexed
4. abnormal; unusual; drastic
5. to turn back the current—as
a dike

激變（ㄐㄧ ㄅㄧㄢˋ）
an upheaval; a sudden
change of a situation (such

as mutiny, coup, etc.)

激辯（ㄐㄧ ㄅㄧㄢˋ）
a heated argument or debate

激發（ㄐㄧ ㄈㄚ）
to stir up; to arouse; to spur
to action

激發天良（ㄐㄧ ㄈㄚ ㄊㄧㄢ ㄌㄧㄤˊ）
to arouse one's conscience

激憤（ㄐㄧ ㄈㄣˋ）
wrathful; indignant: 群眾心情
激憤。The crowd are filled
with indignation.

激盪（ㄐㄧ ㄉㄤˋ）
to surge, turmoil; stirring; in
drastic motion or change

激動（ㄐㄧ ㄉㄨㄥˋ）
aroused; stimulated; excited;
agitated

激湍（ㄐㄧ ㄊㄨㄢ）
(said of the flow of water)
swift and torrential

激痛（ㄐㄧ ㄊㄨㄥˋ）
very painful; severe pain;
painfully excited or stimulated

激怒（ㄐㄧ ㄋㄨˋ）
to irritate; to infuriate; to
provoke; to enrage

激浪（ㄐㄧ ㄌㄤˋ）
heaving breakers or billows

激厲（ㄐㄧ ㄌㄧˋ）
to arouse to high emotional
response; to stimulate and
urge

激勵（ㄐㄧ ㄌㄧˋ）
to arouse and encourage ; to
impel: 他的一番演說激勵我們
更加努力。His speech impelled
us to greater efforts.

激勵士氣（ㄐㄧ ㄌㄧˋ ㄕˋ ㄑㄧˋ）
to boost the morale (of the
army or people)

激烈（ㄐㄧ ㄌㄧㄝˋ）
heated (debates, battles,
etc.); drastic (measures,
means, etc.); violent
(actions, speeches, etc.); radical or extremist (parties,
etc.); fierce (combats)

激烈手段（ㄐㄧ ㄌㄧㄝˋ ㄕㄡˇ ㄉㄨㄢˋ）
drastic actions or measures;
violent means

激流（ㄐㄧ ㄌㄧㄡˊ）
strong currents; rapids

激論（ㄐㄧ ㄌㄨㄣˋ）
heated discussions or comments

激聒（ㄐㄧ 《ㄨㄚ）
to chatter incessantly

激減（ㄐㄧ ㄐㄧㄢˇ）
to decrease or lessen drastically

激進（ㄐㄧ ㄐㄧㄣˋ）
radical

激進派（ㄐㄧ ㄐㄧㄣˋ ㄆㄞˋ）
a radical or extremist party
or faction

激進分子（ㄐㄧ ㄐㄧㄣˋ ㄈㄣ ㄗˇ）or 激烈
分子（ㄐㄧ ㄌㄧㄝˋ ㄈㄣ ㄗˇ）
radicals; extremists

激將（ㄐㄧ ㄐㄧㄤˋ）
to taunt someone into doing
something which he will not
do under ordinary circum-
stances

激將法（ㄐㄧ ㄐㄧㄤˋ ㄈㄚˇ）
urging or prodding some-
body by derision, sarcasm,
etc.

激劇（ㄐㄧ ㄐㄩˋ）
very excited; extremely
agitated

激起（ㄐㄧ ㄑㄧˇ）
to arouse; to excite; to stir
up

激起公憤（ㄐㄧ ㄑㄧˇ ㄍㄨㄥ ㄈㄣˋ）
to arouse public indignation

激切（ㄐㄧ ㄑㄧㄝˋ）
to talk so candidly and honestly that it hurts

激情（ㄐㄧ ㄑㄧㄥˊ）
fervor; ardor; passion; enthusiasm

激勸（ㄐㄧ ㄑㄩㄢˋ）
to arouse and encourage; to
arouse and persuade

激戰（ㄐㄧ ㄓㄢˋ）
a heated battle; a fierce
combat

激濁揚清（ㄐㄧ ㄓㄨㄛˊ ㄧㄤˊ ㄑㄧㄥ）
to rid of the evil and hail
the virtuous

激楚（ㄐㄧ ㄔㄨˇ）
voices that rend the heart
and rouse the spirit

激賞（ㄐㄧ ㄕㄤˇ）
to appreciate tremendously;
to heap high praise on (a
work, person, etc.)

激增（ㄐㄧ ㄗㄥ）
to shoot up; to increase
sharply

激素（ㄐㄧ ㄙㄨˋ）

**〔水
部〕**

(physiology) hormone 亦作
「荷爾蒙」

激昂(ㄐㄧ ㄤ)or激昂慷慨(ㄐㄧ ㄤ ㄎㄤ
ㄎㄞ)
high-spirited; tremendously
excited; passionate

激揚(ㄐㄧ ㄧㄤ)
to be moved to renewed
courage or determination; to
be aroused to a new lease of
spirit

激於義憤(ㄐㄧ ㄩ ㄧ ㄈㄣ)
to be aroused by one's sense
of justice

激越(ㄐㄧ ㄩㄝ)
sonorous; stentorian

【濁】 ³¹¹³ ㄓㄨㄛˊ jwo zhuó
1. (said of water) turbid or
muddy
2. (said of the world) tumultuous, evil, corrupt
3. (said of a person) stupid
and idiotic
4. name of a constellation

濁醪(ㄓㄨㄛˊ ㄌㄠˊ)
unstrained wine

濁浪(ㄓㄨㄛˊ ㄌㄤ)
muddy waves

濁流(ㄓㄨㄛˊ ㄌㄧㄡˊ)
a turbid stream

濁酒(ㄓㄨㄛˊ ㄐㄧㄡˇ)
unstrained wine or liquor

濁井(ㄓㄨㄛˊ ㄐㄧㄥˇ)
a muddy well

濁氣(ㄓㄨㄛˊ ㄑㄧ)
foul smell, breath or air;
bad breath

濁漳(ㄓㄨㄛˊ ㄓㄤ)
another name of the Chang
River in Honan Province

濁世(ㄓㄨㄛˊ ㄕ)
①(Buddhism) the human
world ②the tumultuous
world

濁聲(ㄓㄨㄛˊ ㄕㄥ)
voiced sounds

濁水(ㄓㄨㄛˊ ㄕㄨㄟˇ)
turbid or muddy water

濁水溪(ㄓㄨㄛˊ ㄕㄨㄟˇ ㄒㄧ)
①a muddy river ②name of
a river in Taiwan

濁人(ㄓㄨㄛˊ ㄖㄣˊ)
a stupid, mixed-up person; a
muddle-headed person

濁音(ㄓㄨㄛˊ ㄧㄣ)
a voiced sound

濁物(ㄓㄨㄛˊ ㄨˋ)
a bloody fool; an idiot; a
blockhead

【濂】 ³¹¹⁴ ㄌㄧㄢˊ lian lián
name of a river in Hunan
Province

濂洛關閩(ㄌㄧㄢˊ ㄌㄨㄛˋ ㄍㄨㄢ ㄇㄧㄣˊ)
the four most influential
branches of the Li School of
Thought (理學), led by Chou
Tun-yi of Lien-hsi (濂溪周敦
頤), Cheng Hao & Cheng Yi
of Loyang (洛陽程顥程頤),
Chang Tsai of Kuan-chung
(關中張載)and Chu Hsi of
Min (閩中朱熹), in the Sung
Dynasty

濂溪(ㄌㄧㄢˊ ㄒㄧ)
the River Lien, in Hunan
Province

濂學學派(ㄌㄧㄢˊ ㄒㄩㄝˊ ㄒㄩㄝˊ ㄆㄞˋ)
the Lien Hsi branch of the
Li School 參看「濂洛關閩」

【濃】 ³¹¹⁵ ㄋㄨㄥˊ nong nóng
1. (said of drinks, liquids, etc.)
thick; strong; heavy; concentrated: 血濃於水。Blood is
thicker than water.
2. (said of colors) deep; dark
3. dense
4. (said of a smell) strong;
heavy: 梔子花香味很濃。The
capejasmine has a heavy
fragrance.

濃抹(ㄋㄨㄥˊ ㄇㄛˋ)
to wear heavy make-up

濃墨(ㄋㄨㄥˊ ㄇㄛˋ)
heavy (Chinese) ink; thick
ink

濃眉大眼(ㄋㄨㄥˊ ㄇㄟˊ ㄉㄚˋ ㄧㄢˇ)
bushy eyebrows and big
eyes

濃密(ㄋㄨㄥˊ ㄇㄧˋ)
(said of the growth of vegetation, beard, hair, etc.)
dense; thick; luxuriant: 她有
一頭濃密的頭髮。She has
thick hair.

濃淡(ㄋㄨㄥˊ ㄉㄢˋ)
①(said of color) deep or
light ②(said of drinks)
strong or weak ③(said of
make-up) heavy or light ④
(said of liquid generally)
concentrated or diluted

濃度(ㄋㄨㄥˊ ㄉㄨˋ)

①(chemistry) concentration
②density

濃湯(ㄋㄨㄥˊ ㄊㄤ)
thick soup

濃綠(ㄋㄨㄥˊ ㄌㄩˋ)
dark green

濃厚(ㄋㄨㄥˊ ㄏㄡˋ)
①(said of material things)
thick and ②(said of
feelings, interest, etc.) deep;
great

濃酒(ㄋㄨㄥˊ ㄐㄧㄡˇ)
strong drink

濃情(ㄋㄨㄥˊ ㄑㄧㄥˊ)
passionate feeling; affectionate regard

濃情蜜意(ㄋㄨㄥˊ ㄑㄧㄥˊ ㄇㄧˋ ㄧˋ)
strong affection and deep
love

濃妝 or 濃粧(ㄋㄨㄥˊ ㄓㄨㄤ)
heavy make-up; gorgeously
dressed

濃妝艷抹(ㄋㄨㄥˊ ㄓㄨㄤ ㄧㄢˋ ㄇㄛˋ)
to wear heavy make-up

濃茶(ㄋㄨㄥˊ ㄔㄚˊ)
strong tea

濃睡(ㄋㄨㄥˊ ㄕㄨㄟˋ)
a sound sleep; deep slumbers

濃縮(ㄋㄨㄥˊ ㄙㄨㄛ)
①to condense; condensed; to
concentrate: 他把一段濃縮為
一句。He condensed the para-
graph into one line. ② to
enrich; enriched

濃縮果汁(ㄋㄨㄥˊ ㄙㄨㄛ ㄍㄨㄛˇ ㄓ)
condensed fruit juices

濃煙(ㄋㄨㄥˊ ㄧㄢ)
thick smoke; heavy smoke

濃艷(ㄋㄨㄥˊ ㄧㄢˋ)
gorgeous; bright-colored

濃陰(ㄋㄨㄥˊ ㄧㄣ)
the dark shade under a big
tree with thick foliage or in
a dense forest

濃陰蔽空(ㄋㄨㄥˊ ㄧㄣ ㄅㄧˋ ㄎㄨㄥ)
The thick branches and
leaves seem to blot out the
sky.

濃霧(ㄋㄨㄥˊ ㄨˋ)
heavy fog; dense mist: 倫敦
以濃霧聞名。London is fa-
mous for its dense fog.

濃郁(ㄋㄨㄥˊ ㄩˋ)
strong; heavy; rich: 這些故事
具有濃郁的浪漫氣息。These
stories have a strong flavor

〔水部〕

of romance.

【濃】 3116
濃雲密佈 (ㄋㄨㄥ ㄩㄣ ㄇㄧˋ ㄅㄨˋ)
Dark clouds stretch all over
the sky.--a sign of an
impending storm

【濊】 3116
1. ㄏㄨㄟˋ huey huì
water plentiful

【濊】 3116
1. ㄨㄟˋ wey wèi
1. deep and expansive
2. dirty
3. name of a river

濊水 (ㄨㄟˋ ㄕㄨㄟˇ)
name of an old river in
Hopeh, now silted

【凜】 3117
1. ㄌㄧㄣˇ liin lǐn
1. desolate; deserted
2. cold; chilly

凜水 (ㄌㄧㄣˇ ㄕㄨㄟˇ)
ice-cold; bone-chilling: 北風
凜水. The north wind is ice-
cold.

凜然 (ㄌㄧㄣˇ ㄖㄢˊ)
awe-inspiring; commanding
respect

3118
【澣】 (浣) ㄏㄨㄢˇ hoan
ㄏㄨㄢˋ huàn
(又讀) ㄨㄢˇ woan
wàn
1. to wash
2. (Tang Dynasty) ten days

十四畫

【濘】 3119
1. ㄋㄧㄥˊ ㄋㄧㄥˇ ninq níng
muddy; miry

濘淖 (ㄋㄧㄥˊ ㄋㄠˋ)
mud; muddy; covered with
mud: 汽車陷入濘淖中。 The
car stuck in the mud of the
road.

濘滯 (ㄋㄧㄥˊ ㄓˋ)
muddy roads that make
traveling difficult

【濘】 3119
2. ㄋㄥˊ nenq néng
pasty; soft and mashy

濘泥 (ㄋㄥˊ ㄋㄧˊ)
mire; mud

【濛】 3120
ㄇㄥˊ meng méng
misty; drizzly

濛濛 (ㄇㄥˊ ㄇㄥˊ)
misty

濛濛細雨 (ㄇㄥˊ ㄇㄥˊ ㄒㄧˋ ㄩˇ)
drizzle; to drizzle

濛鬆雨 (ㄇㄥˊ ㄙㄨㄥ ㄩˇ)
drizzle

濛霧 (ㄇㄥˊ ㄨˋ)
mist; fog: 濛霧全消散了。 The
mist has entirely cleared off.

【澀】 3121
(澁); ㄙㄜˋ seh sè
1. rough; harsh; not smooth
2. a slightly bitter taste that
numbs the tongue—as some
unripened fruits; puckery
3. (said of writing, reading,
etc.) difficult or jolting
4. slow of tongue

澀體 (ㄙㄜˋ ㄊㄧˇ)
(Tang Dynasty) a style of
literary writing which is difficult to read

澀訥 (ㄙㄜˋ ㄋㄜˋ) or 澀吶 (ㄙㄜˋ ㄋㄚˋ)
slow of tongue

澀滯 (ㄙㄜˋ ㄓˋ)
not smooth; obstructed

澀暖 (ㄙㄜˋ ㄓㄤˋ) or 澀帳 (ㄙㄜˋ ㄓㄤˋ)
bad debts

澀縮 (ㄙㄜˋ ㄙㄨㄛ)
not straightforward

澀味 (ㄙㄜˋ ㄨㄟˋ)
astringent taste

【濠】 3122
ㄏㄠˊ haur háo
a moat; a trench or ditch

濠梁 (ㄏㄠˊ ㄌㄧㄤˊ)
a bridge spanning a small
creek

濠溝 (ㄏㄠˊ ㄍㄡ)
a trench: 他們挖條濠溝。 They
dug a trench.

濠塹 (ㄏㄠˊ ㄑㄧㄢˋ)
a moat; a canal or ditch
around the city wall

【濟】 3123
1. ㄐㄧˋ jih jì
1. to relieve; to aid: 同舟共濟.
Being in the same boat, the
refugees help one another.
2. to cross a stream
3. to succeed; to be up to standard
4. to benefit; benefits
5. a ford

濟貧 (ㄐㄧˋ ㄆㄧㄣˊ)
to aid or relieve the poor

濟度 (ㄐㄧˋ ㄉㄨˋ)
(Buddhism) to provide salvation for the masses

濟溺 (ㄐㄧˋ ㄋㄧˋ)
to help or relieve others in
great difficulty

濟困扶危 (ㄐㄧˋ ㄎㄨㄣˋ ㄈㄨˊ ㄨㄟˊ)
(literally) to relieve the less
privileged and help the
endangered—philanthropic;
compassionate

濟急 (ㄐㄧˋ ㄐㄧˊ)
to aid the people in urgent
need

濟世 (ㄐㄧˋ ㄕˋ)
to benefit the world

濟世安民 (ㄐㄧˋ ㄕˋ ㄢ ㄇㄧㄣˊ)
to benefit the age and pacify
the masses

濟事 (ㄐㄧˋ ㄕˋ)
to help the matter; to be useful in coping with a situation, etc.: 光哭是不濟事的.
Crying won't help the matter.

濟燃眉之急 (ㄐㄧˋ ㄖㄢˊ ㄇㄟˊ ㄓ ㄐㄧˊ)
to help meet an urgent need

濟弱扶傾 (ㄐㄧˋ ㄖㄨㄛˋ ㄈㄨˊ ㄑㄧㄥ)
to help the weak and aid the
needy

濟私 (ㄐㄧˋ ㄙ)
to benefit one's own end; to
serve a selfish purpose

濟惡 (ㄐㄧˋ ㄜˋ)
to help an evil cause

濟危 (ㄐㄧˋ ㄨㄟˊ)
to aid the endangered or
needy

【濟】 3123
2. ㄐㄧˇ jii jǐ
1. various; varied; numerous
2. elegant and dignified
3. name of various counties
and a river

濟南 (ㄐㄧˇ ㄋㄢˊ)
Tsinan, capital of Shantung
Province

濟濟 (ㄐㄧˇ ㄐㄧˇ)
① multitudinous; numerous
② magnificent ③ beautiful

濟濟多士 (ㄐㄧˇ ㄐㄧˇ ㄉㄨㄛ ㄕˋ)
Numerous are talented persons.

濟濟一堂 (ㄐㄧˇ ㄐㄧˇ ㄧ ㄊㄤˊ)
to gather together or congregate in this hall

濟水 (ㄐㄧˇ ㄕㄨㄟˇ)
name of a stream which
empties into the Yellow
River from Honan Province

【濤】 3124
ㄊㄠ taur tāo
(又讀 ㄊㄠ tau tóo)
a big wave; a billow; a
heavy swell

濤波(ㄊㄠ ㄅㄛ)or 濤瀾(ㄊㄠ ㄌㄢ)
billows; great waves

濤聲(ㄊㄠ ㄕㄥ)
the sound of roaring billows:
我們聽到遠處的濤聲。We
heard the sound of roaring
billows in the distance.

【濡】 3125
ㄖㄨ ru rú
1. to moisten; to immerse; to
wet
2. to linger; to procrastinate
3. glossy; smooth
4. to tolerate; to endure

濡筆(ㄖㄨ ㄅ一)or 濡毫(ㄖㄨ ㄏㄠ)
to moisten the (Chinese)
writing or painting brush

濡翰(ㄖㄨ ㄏㄢ)
to moisten the brush

濡跡(ㄖㄨ ㄐ一)
to linger at (a place, etc.)

濡滯(ㄖㄨ ㄓ)
slow; to procrastinate

濡濕(ㄖㄨ ㄕ)
to soak by immersion; to
make wet

濡染(ㄖㄨ ㄖㄢˇ)
to dye; to be imbued with

濡忍(ㄖㄨ ㄖㄣˇ)
to endure; to bear with
patience

濡潤(ㄖㄨ ㄖㄨㄣˋ)
glossy

【濫】 3126
ㄌㄢˋ lann làn
1. to overflow; to flood; to
inundate; inundation
2. to do things without plans;
reckless
3. to practice no self-restraint;
to give way to unbridled
license
4. to abuse (one's power, influence, etc.)
5. false; not true
6. superfluous words or expressions

濫發(ㄌㄢˋ ㄈㄚ)
to issue an excessive
amount of (bank notes, invitations, etc.)

濫罰(ㄌㄢˋ ㄈㄚˊ)
excessive or undue penalty

or punishment

濫伐(ㄌㄢˋ ㄈㄚˊ)
excessive felling of trees

濫伐森林(ㄌㄢˋ ㄈㄚˊ ㄙㄣ ㄌㄧㄣˊ)
to log without (or not
according to) plan; excessive felling of trees

濫費(ㄌㄢˋ ㄈㄟˋ)
to go to excess in expenditure; to waste (money)

濫調(ㄌㄢˋ ㄉㄧㄠˋ)
platitudes; clichés; hackneyed expressions; worn-out
themes

濫套(ㄌㄢˋ ㄊㄠˋ)
truisms; clichés; trite or
superfluous expressions

濫頭寸(ㄌㄢˋ ㄊㄡˊ ㄘㄨㄣ)
idle money in the bank

濫墾(ㄌㄢˋ ㄎㄣˇ)
to cultivate farms in areas
where soil conservation
should be maintained

濫交(ㄌㄢˋ ㄐㄧㄠ)
to befriend at random; to
make friends indiscriminately

濫竽(ㄌㄢˋ ㄩˊ)
to take what one does not
deserve; to take excessively

濫刑(ㄌㄢˋ ㄒㄧㄥˊ)
excessive punishment

濫殺(ㄌㄢˋ ㄕㄚ)
to kill at random; to kill indiscriminately

濫收(ㄌㄢˋ ㄕㄡ)
to receive or take what one
should not; to receive or
take too much; to charge
too much

濫觴(ㄌㄢˋ ㄕㄤ)
the very origin or source (of
a practice, tradition, etc.);
the beginning

濫惡(ㄌㄢˋ ㄜˋ)
big evils

濫污(ㄌㄢˋ ㄨ)
dirty; tricky; unchaste

濫竽充數(ㄌㄢˋ ㄩˊ ㄔㄨㄥ ㄕㄨˋ)
to hold a post without the
necessary qualifications just
to make up the number

濫用(ㄌㄢˋ ㄩㄥˋ)
①to spend excessively; to
expend too much ②to mis-
use; to abuse

濫用公款(ㄌㄢˋ ㄩㄥˋ ㄍㄨㄥ ㄎㄨㄢˇ)

irregularities in use of public funds

濫用職權(ㄌㄢˋ ㄩㄥˋ ㄓˊ ㄑㄩㄢˊ)
to misuse one's powers; to
abuse one's authority

濫用藥物(ㄌㄢˋ ㄩㄥˋ 一ㄠˋ ㄨˋ)
drug abuse

【濯】 3127
ㄓㄨㄛˊ jwo zhuó
1. to wash
2. to eliminate vices
3. grand; magnificent
4. a Chinese family name

濯濯(ㄓㄨㄛˊ ㄓㄨㄛˊ)
①bright and brilliant ②
(said of mountains) denud-
ed; bare; bald: 童山濯濯。
That mountain is bald. ③to
be fat and sleek

濯纓濯足(ㄓㄨㄛˊ 一ㄥ ㄓㄨㄛˊ ㄗㄨˊ)
Whether one is received
with respect or despite depends on one's own conduct.

【濮】 3128
ㄆㄨˊ pwu pú
1. name of an ancient river in
today's Honan Province
2. name of an ancient barbarian tribe
3. a Chinese family name

濮上(ㄆㄨˊ ㄕㄤˋ)
a place where debauchery is
prevalent

濮上之音(ㄆㄨˊ ㄕㄤˋ ㄓ 一ㄣ)
lewd and debauching music

濮水(ㄆㄨˊ ㄕㄨㄟˇ)
name of an ancient stream
in Honan and Hupeh

【濬】 3129
ㄐㄩㄣˋ jiunn jùn
1. to dredge a waterway; to
dig or wash (a well, etc.)
2. deep; profound

濬哲(ㄐㄩㄣˋ ㄓㄜˊ)
profound wisdom: 他的言行
表現其濬哲。He showed great
wisdom in what he said and
did.

【濰】 3130
ㄨㄟˊ wei wéi
name of a river in Shantung
Province

濰水(ㄨㄟˊ ㄕㄨㄟˇ)
the Wei River, in Shantung
Province

【濱】 3131
ㄅㄧㄣ bin bīn
1. water's edge; to border on

〔水部〕

2. same as 瀕—near at hand
3. (military) a low, level sea-coast

濱臨大海(ㄅㄧㄣㄌㄧㄣㄉㄚˋㄏㄞˇ)
on the brink of the sea

濱海地區(ㄅㄧㄣㄏㄞˇㄉㄧˋㄑㄩ)
the coastal region; the coast

濱近(ㄅㄧㄣㄐㄧㄣˋ)
close to; near to: 我家濱近車站。My house is close to the station.

濱江(ㄅㄧㄣㄐㄧㄤ)
the former name of Harbin (哈爾濱), capital of Sung-kiang Province

濱死(ㄅㄧㄣㄙˇ)
to be near to death; dying; to have one foot in the grave

濱危(ㄅㄧㄣㄨㄟˊ)
to have a close encounter with great danger; dying; close to death

【濩】 3132 ㄏㄨㄛˋ huoh huò
1. turbulent water
2. (now rarely) to cook; to boil

【濕】 3133 (濕) ㄕ shy shī
1. damp; moist; wet; humid; to get wet
2. (Chinese medicine) ailments caused by high humidity

濕地(ㄕㄉㄧˋ)
a damp place; a marsh or swamp: 濕地有很多青蛙。There are a lot of frogs in the marsh.

濕電池(ㄕㄉㄧㄢˋㄔˊ)
a galvanic battery

濕度(ㄕㄉㄨˋ)
humidity

濕度表(ㄕㄉㄨˋㄅㄧㄠˇ)
a hygrometer

濕透(ㄕㄊㄡˋ)
to be drenched; dripping wet; soaking wet: 你的上裝濕透了。Your coat is dripping wet.

濕漉漉(ㄕㄌㄨˋㄌㄨˋ)
dripping wet

濕季(ㄕㄐㄧˋ)
a rainy season; a monsoon

濕津津(ㄕㄐㄧㄣㄐㄧㄣ)
damp and wet: 我不喜歡濕津津的天氣。I don't like damp and wet weather.

濕氣(ㄕㄑㄧˋ)
①(Chinese medicine) ailments caused by high humidity, such as rashes, pustules, rheumatism, athlete's foot, etc. ② humidity; dampness; moisture

濕疹(ㄕㄓㄣˇ)
eczema

濕熱(ㄕㄖㄜˋ)
damp and hot

濕潤(ㄕㄖㄨㄣˋ)
damp, to moisten

濕窪(ㄕㄨㄚ)
swampy regions; swamp

十五畫

【濺】 3134 ㄐㄧㄢˋ jiann jiàn
to splash; to sprinkle; to spray; to spill: 我被濺了一身水。I was splashed with water all over.

濺沫(ㄐㄧㄢˋㄇㄛˋ)
to splash saliva around (especially when one talks excitedly or vehemently)

濺泥(ㄐㄧㄢˋㄋㄧˊ)
to splash mud

濺濺(ㄐㄧㄢˋㄐㄧㄢˋ)
the gurgling sound of flowing water

濺血(ㄐㄧㄢˋㄒㄩㄝˋ)
to splash with drops of blood

濺水(ㄐㄧㄢˋㄕㄨㄟˇ)
to splash water

【濼】 3135 1. ㄌㄨㄛˊ luoh luó
name of a stream in Shantung Province

【濼】 3135 2. ㄅㄛˊ bor bó
a lake

【瀆】 3136 ㄉㄨˊ dwu dú
1. a ditch
2. a river
3. to desecrate; to profane; to blaspheme; to be rude and disrespectful
4. to annoy

瀆犯(ㄉㄨˊㄈㄢˋ)
to be rude and profane; to desecrate; to be sacrilegious

瀆職(ㄉㄨˊㄓˊ)
malfeasance; irregularity or misconduct in office; dereliction of duty

瀆職罪(ㄉㄨˊㄓˊㄗㄨㄟˋ)
guilt for malfeasance

瀆神(ㄉㄨˊㄕㄣˊ)
①to desecrate the god ② to disturb (your) peace of mind (an expression often used in asking someone for a favor)

【濾】 3137 ㄌㄩˋ liuh lǜ
to filter; to strain out

濾波器(ㄌㄩˋㄅㄛㄑㄧˋ)
a wave filter

濾過性病毒(ㄌㄩˋㄍㄨㄛˋㄒㄧㄥˋㄅㄧㄥˋㄉㄨˊ)or濾過性病原體(ㄌㄩˋㄍㄨㄛˋㄒㄧㄥˋㄅㄧㄥˋㄩㄢˊㄊㄧˇ)
virus—a living thing even smaller than bacteria which causes infectious disease in the body, in plants, etc.

濾管(ㄌㄩˋㄍㄨㄢˇ)
a filter pipe

濾器(ㄌㄩˋㄑㄧˋ)
a filter: 用濾器把水濾清。Clean the water with a filter.

濾紙(ㄌㄩˋㄓˇ)
a filter paper

濾水池(ㄌㄩˋㄕㄨㄟˇㄔˊ)
a settling pond; a depositing reservoir; a filter bed

濾嘴香烟(ㄌㄩˋㄗㄨㄟˇㄒㄧㄤㄧㄢ)
filter-tipped cigarettes

【瀑】 3138 1. ㄆㄨˋ puh pù
a waterfall; a cascade; a cataract

瀑布(ㄆㄨˋㄅㄨˋ)
a waterfall; a cascade; a cataract

瀑流(ㄆㄨˋㄌㄧㄡˊ)
a cascade; a waterfall; a cataract

【瀑】 3138 2. ㄅㄠˋ baw bào
a pouring rain which comes all of a sudden; a sudden shower

【瀉】 3139 ㄒㄧㄝˋ shieh xiè
1. to drain; water flowing down: 一瀉千里 to flow a thousand li at one plunge
2. diarrhea; to have loose

〔水部〕

bowels

瀉肚(ㄒㄧㄝˋㄉㄨˋ)or 瀉肚子(ㄒㄧㄝˋㄉㄨˋ·ㄗ)
diarrhea; to have loose bowels: 他瀉肚子。He has diarrhea.

瀉痢(ㄒㄧㄝˋㄌㄧˋ)
diarrhea

瀉鹽(ㄒㄧㄝˋㄧㄢˊ)
Epsom salts (magnesium sulfate)

瀉鹵(ㄒㄧㄝˋㄌㄨˇ)
barren, salty land

瀉出(ㄒㄧㄝˋㄔㄨ)
to leak out; to spurt out: 汽油瀉出。The gasoline leaks out.

瀉藥(ㄒㄧㄝˋㄧㄠˋ)or 瀉劑(ㄒㄧㄝˋㄐㄧˋ)
cathartics, laxatives or purgatives

瀉鹽(ㄒㄧㄝˋㄧㄢˊ)
Epsom salts (magnesium sulfate) 亦作「瀉利鹽」

【瀋】 3140 ㄕㄣˇ sheen shěn
1. juice; fluid; liquid; water
2. short for Shenyang (Mukden), capital of Liaoning Province

瀋陽(ㄕㄣˇㄧㄤˊ)
Mukden (Shenyang), capital of Liaoning Province

瀋陽事變(ㄕㄣˇㄧㄤˊㄕˋㄅㄧㄢˋ)
The Mukden Incident on September 18, 1931, which ended in the occupation of Manchuria by the Japanese militarists

【瀏】 3141 ㄌㄧㄡˊ liou liú
1. (said of water) clear; bright and clear; the appearance of a clear stream
2. a fast-blowing wind; a cool wind
3. to get away secretly; to take French leave

瀏覽(ㄌㄧㄡˊㄌㄢˇ)
to glance over; to thumb through; to take a casual look at (a scene); to skim through

瀏亮(ㄌㄧㄡˊㄌㄧㄤˋ)
(said of the sky, etc.) bright and clear

【瀅】 3142 ㄧㄥˊ yng yíng
(said of water) clear; bright

and clear; glossy

【瀍】 3143 ㄔㄢˊ charn chán
name of a river in Honan

瀍水(ㄔㄢˊㄕㄨㄟˇ)
the Chan River, a tributary of the Lo River in Honan

【瀁】 3144 ㄧㄤ yeang yǎng
1. water in motion
2. to move a boat or something in water
3. ripples; waves; rapids
4. to overflow—too much or too many
5. name of a stream in Shensi Province

十六畫

【瀘】 3145 ㄌㄨˊ lu lú
1. name of a river in Yunnan Province
2. name of a river in Szechwan Province

瀘水(ㄌㄨˊㄕㄨㄟˇ)
①name of a river in Szechwan Province ②name of a river in Yunnan Province

【瀕】 3146 ㄅㄧㄣ bin bīn
1. near; close to; to border
2. water's edge

瀕臨(ㄅㄧㄣㄌㄧㄣˊ)
near; on the brink of

瀕河(ㄅㄧㄣㄏㄜˊ)
on the bank of the river; riverside

瀕海(ㄅㄧㄣㄏㄞˇ)
close to the sea; along the coast

瀕行(ㄅㄧㄣㄒㄧㄥˊ)
upon leaving; about to leave

瀕死(ㄅㄧㄣㄙˇ)or 瀕於死亡(ㄅㄧㄣㄩˊㄙˇㄨㄤˊ)
on the brink of death

瀕危(ㄅㄧㄣㄨㄟ)
on the verge of death or great danger

瀕於破產(ㄅㄧㄣㄩˊㄆㄛˋㄔㄢˇ)
on the verge of bankruptcy

瀕於毀滅(ㄅㄧㄣㄩˊㄏㄨㄟˇㄇㄧㄝˋ)
on the brink of ruin

瀕於絕境(ㄅㄧㄣㄩˊㄐㄩㄝˊㄐㄧㄥˋ)
to face an impasse

【瀚】 3147 ㄏㄢˋ hann hàn

vast; expansive

瀚海(ㄏㄢˋㄏㄞˇ)
the Gobi Desert

瀚瀚(ㄏㄢˋㄏㄢˋ)
vast and expansive

【瀝】 3148 ㄌㄧˋ lih lì
1. to fall down by drops; to drip; to trickle
2. remaining drops of wine
3. to strain water or liquids

瀝膽披肝(ㄌㄧˋㄉㄢˇㄆㄧㄍㄢ)《借》
absolutely sincere and loyal

瀝瀝(ㄌㄧˋㄌㄧˋ)
①the sound of flowing waters ②the sound of heaving wind ③to drip; to trickle

瀝懇(ㄌㄧˋㄎㄣˇ)
to beseech; to request earnestly

瀝酒(ㄌㄧˋㄐㄧㄡˇ)
to strain wine

瀝青(ㄌㄧˋㄑㄧㄥ)
①asphalt; pitch ②another name of resin

瀝青路(ㄌㄧˋㄑㄧㄥㄌㄨˋ)
a bituminous road; an asphalt road

瀝青岩(ㄌㄧˋㄑㄧㄥㄧㄢˊ)
a pitchstone 亦作「松脂岩」

瀝血(ㄌㄧˋㄒㄧㄝˇ)
①to drip blood ②to take a blood-oath ③very loyal and sincere

瀝陳(ㄌㄧˋㄔㄣˊ)
to state honestly in detail

瀝液(ㄌㄧˋㄧㄝˋ)
a small amount of flowing waters

【瀟】 3149 ㄒㄧㄠ shiau xiāo
1. the sound of beating rain and whistling wind; the roar of a strong wind
2. name of a stream in Hunan

瀟瀟(ㄒㄧㄠㄒㄧㄠ)
a rushing rain and whistling wind; the roar of gusts

瀟湘(ㄒㄧㄠㄒㄧㄤ)
①the Hsiao River and Hsiang River ②name of a town in Hunan, north of Ling Ling, where the two rivers meet

瀟灑 or 瀟洒(ㄒㄧㄠㄙㄚˇ)
(usually said of a man's

〔水部〕

manner) casual and elegant; dashing and refined

【瀛】 3150
ㄧㄥ yng yíng
1. the sea; the ocean
2. within the lake

瀛臺 (ㄧㄥ ㄊㄞ)
a spot within the Forbidden City in Peking, which was surrounded on three sides by water, where the young Emperor Kuang Hsü (光緒) was imprisoned by Queen Dowager Tzu Hsi (慈禧太后) after the abortive political reform movement in the late 19th century

瀛海 (ㄧㄥ ㄏㄞ)
the sea; the ocean

瀛寰 (ㄧㄥ ㄏㄨㄢ)
the globe; the world

瀛眷 (ㄧㄥ ㄐㄩㄢ)
your dependents; your family (a polite expression)

瀛洲 (ㄧㄥ ㄓㄡ)
(in old Chinese legend) the Holy Mountain in the East Sea, where the immortals dwell

【瀨】 3151
ㄌㄞ lay lài
1. a torrent; a swift current
2. water flowing over shallows
3. name of a stream in Kwangsi, also known as the River Li
4. name of a stream in Kiangsu

瀨水 (ㄌㄞ ㄕㄨㄟ)
①also known as the River Li (荔江), a stream in Kwangsi ②name of a stream in Kiangsu

【瀧】 3152
1. ㄌㄨㄥ long lóng
1. raining; rainy
2. wet; soaked; saturated
3. a swift current
4. (in Japanese) a waterfall

【瀧】 3152
2. ㄕㄨㄤ shuang shuāng
name of a river in Hunan

瀧岡 (ㄕㄨㄤ ㄍㄤ)
name of a hill in Yung-feng County (永豐縣) of Kiangsi

【瀣】 3153
ㄒㄧㄝ shieh xiè
mist; vapor

【瀦】 3154
ㄓㄨ ju zhū
a pool; a pond

【瀠】 3155
ㄧㄥ yng yíng
參看「瀠洄」

瀠洄 (ㄧㄥ ㄏㄨㄟ)
the whirling of water

十七畫

【瀰】 3156
ㄇㄧ mi mí
(said of water) brimming; overflowing

瀰漫 (ㄇㄧ ㄇㄢ)
① brimming, overflowing water ② to permeate

【瀹】 3157
ㄩㄝ yueh yuè
1. to cook or to boil with soup
2. to soak
3. to clear the courses of rivers

【瀾】 3158
1. ㄌㄢ lan lán
a great wave; a huge billow

瀾翻 (ㄌㄢ ㄈㄢ)
(said of a piece of writing or a speech) with numerous turns and twists

瀾滄江 (ㄌㄢ ㄘㄤ ㄐㄧㄤ)
the Lantsang River in Yunnan, one of the tributaries of the Mekong River

【瀾】 3158
2. ㄌㄢ lann làn
1. overflowing; dripping wet; a vast expanse of water
2. thin rice paste

瀾漫 (ㄌㄢ ㄇㄢ)
① overflowing; inundating ② dripping wet; wet through ③ sprightly; carefree: 這些孩子天真瀾漫。These childern are innocent and carefree. ④ disorderly

瀾汗 (ㄌㄢ ㄏㄢ)
descriptive of a vast expanse of water

【瀲】 3159
ㄌㄧㄢ liann liàn
1. (said of water) overflowing
2. the edge of a large body of water

瀲灔 (ㄌㄧㄢ ㄧㄢ)
overflowing; inundating

(said of water or wine) overflowing

十八畫

【瀝】 3160
ㄩㄥ iong yǒng
1. the flowing back of flooding waters
2. name of a stream in Shantung Province

瀝水 (ㄩㄥ ㄕㄨㄟ)
name of a stream in Shantung Province

【灃】 3161
ㄈㄥ feng fēng
name of a river in Shensi Province

灃沛 (ㄈㄥ ㄆㄟ)
① brimming; overflowing; abundant ② copious rain

灃水 (ㄈㄥ ㄕㄨㄟ)
the Feng River, in Shensi Province

【灌】 3162
ㄍㄨㄢ guann guàn
1. to water; to fill; to pour (on, into, at); to irrigate
2. to offer a libation
3. shrubs; bushy clumps

灌唱片 (ㄍㄨㄢ ㄔㄤ ㄆㄧㄢ·ㄦ) or 灌唱片
to cut a record

灌莽 (ㄍㄨㄢ ㄇㄤ)
grassy and bushy land

灌迷湯 (ㄍㄨㄢ ㄇㄧ ㄊㄤ)
to flatter; (said of a woman) to utter sweet words to a man for ulterior purposes

灌木 (ㄍㄨㄢ ㄇㄨ)
shrubs

灌佛 (ㄍㄨㄢ ㄈㄛ)
to wash a Buddha's image with scented water

灌奠 (ㄍㄨㄢ ㄉㄧㄢ)
to offer a libation by pouring wine on the ground

灌頂 (ㄍㄨㄢ ㄉㄧㄥ)
(Buddhism) abhisecani; murdhabhisitka (inauguration or consecration by sprinkling or pouring water on the head)

灌溉 (ㄍㄨㄢ ㄍㄞ)
to irrigate; irrigation

灌溉渠 (ㄍㄨㄢ ㄍㄞ ㄑㄩ)

灌溉系統(ㄍㄨㄢ ㄍㄞ ㄒㄧˋ ㄊㄨㄥˇ)
an irrigation system

灌救(ㄍㄨㄢ ㄐㄧㄡˋ)
to save life by forcing medicine down the throat of a dying person

灌漿(ㄍㄨㄢ ㄐㄧㄤ)
to fill the crevices between bricks, etc. with mortar to make the foundation, wall, or pavement secure

灌注(ㄍㄨㄢ ㄓㄨˋ)
①to pour into ②to teach; to inculcate; to instill ③to concentrate (attention) on

灌腸(ㄍㄨㄢ ㄔㄤˊ)
to give an enema or clyster

灌腸劑(ㄍㄨㄢ ㄔㄤˊ ㄐㄧˋ)
a clyster; an enema

灌腸器(ㄍㄨㄢ ㄔㄤˊ ㄑㄧˋ)
an enema syringe; a clyster pipe

灌唱片(ㄍㄨㄢ ㄔㄤˋ ㄆㄧㄢˋ)
參看「灌片子」

灌輸(ㄍㄨㄢ ㄕㄨ)
to instill; to teach; to impart (knowledge to someone); to inculcate

灌水(ㄍㄨㄢ ㄕㄨㄟˇ)
to inject water into (meat, chicken, etc.) so as to increase weight before marketing; to pour water into something

灌醉(ㄍㄨㄢ ㄗㄨㄟˋ)
to force someone to drink until he is drunk

灌叢(ㄍㄨㄢ ㄘㄨㄥˊ)
dense shrubs and thick undergrowth

灌藥(ㄍㄨㄢ ㄧㄠˋ)
to force one to take medicine

灌音(ㄍㄨㄢ ㄧㄣ)
to cut a record

十九畫

【灑】 3163
(洒) ㄙㄚˇ saa sǎ
1. to splash; to spill; to sprinkle (liquids)
2. to wash

灑脫(ㄙㄚˇ ㄊㄨㄛ)
casual and carefree; graceful; free and easy

灑淚(ㄙㄚˇ ㄌㄟˋ)
to shed tears: 她灑淚公堂。
She shed tears in court.

灑落(ㄙㄚˇ ㄌㄨㄛˋ)
①casual and elegant ②desolate; dilapidated ③to give the cold shoulder to; to be rude to

灑汗(ㄙㄚˇ ㄏㄢˋ)
to perspire; to sweat

灑家(ㄙㄚˇ ㄐㄧㄚ)
I; me 亦作「洒家」

灑泣(ㄙㄚˇ ㄑㄧˋ)
to shed tears

灑水(ㄙㄚˇ ㄕㄨㄟˇ)
to spill water; to sprinkle water: 他灑水於街上。He sprinkles the street with water.

灑水車(ㄙㄚˇ ㄕㄨㄟˇ ㄔㄜ)
a sprinkler truck

灑然(ㄙㄚˇ ㄖㄢˊ)
shocked; frightened

灑灑(ㄙㄚˇ ㄙㄚˇ)
continuously; incessantly

灑掃(ㄙㄚˇ ㄙㄠˋ)
to sprinkle water and sweep

【灘】 3164
ㄊㄢ tan tān
a beach; a sandbank; a shoal

灘頭陣地(ㄊㄢ ㄊㄡˊ ㄓㄣˋ ㄉㄧˋ)or 灘頭堡(ㄊㄢ ㄊㄡˊ ㄅㄠˇ)
a beachhead

灘黄(ㄊㄢ ㄏㄨㄤˊ)
Soochow opera

灘船(ㄊㄢ ㄔㄨㄢˊ)
a small boat without an awning or cover

二十一畫

【灝】 3165
ㄏㄠˇ haw hǎo
bean soup

【灞】 3166
ㄅㄚˋ bah bà
name of a river in Shensi

灞橋(ㄅㄚˋ ㄑㄧㄠˊ)
name of a bridge over the Pa River, where ancient people in Changan (長安), the old capital, often bade their friends good-bye

灞橋折柳(ㄅㄚˋ ㄑㄧㄠˊ ㄓㄜˊ ㄌㄧㄡˇ)
to part from friends; to bid farewell

灞水(ㄅㄚˋ ㄕㄨㄟˇ)
name of a river near Chang-an (長安), Shensi (陝西)

二十二畫

【灣】 3167
ㄨㄢ uan wān
1. a bay; a gulf; a cove
2. the bend of a stream
3. to anchor; to moor

灣流(ㄨㄢ ㄌㄧㄡˊ)
a gulf stream

灣轉(ㄨㄢ ‧ㄓㄨㄢˇ)
to get by indirect means; to hunt for (something) in a painstaking way

灣子(ㄨㄢ ‧ㄗ)
a curve

二十三畫

【灤】 3168
ㄌㄨㄢˊ luan luán
name of a river in northern China

灤河(ㄌㄨㄢˊ ㄏㄜˊ)
name of a river in northern China

二十四畫

【灨】 3169
ㄍㄢˋ gann gàn
the Kan River in Kiangsi (江西) Province

灨江(ㄍㄢˋ ㄐㄧㄤ)
the Kan River in Kiangsi (江西) Province

二十八畫

【灩】 3170
(灎) ㄧㄢˋ yann yàn
overflowing; inundating

灩澦堆(ㄧㄢˋ ㄩˋ ㄉㄨㄟ)
a steep cliff in the middle of the Yangtze River in Szechwan (四川), a navigator's nightmare

火 部

ㄏㄨㄛˇ huoo huǒ

〔火部〕

【火】 3171 ㄏㄨㄛˇ huǒ huǒ

1. fire; flames; to burn with fire
2. fury; anger; temper
3. urgency; urgent; imminent; pressing
4. (Chinese herbal medicine) the latent "heat" in human body
5. (now rarely) a group (of people)
6. a Chinese family name

〔火部〕

火拔子 (ㄏㄨㄛˇ ㄅㄚˊ ˙ㄗ)
(Chinese medicine) cupping; a suction cup (used to suck "moisture" from the human body, with the cup made vacuum by burning thin paper, etc. inside) 亦作「拔火罐兒」

火把 (ㄏㄨㄛˇ ㄅㄚˇ)
a torch: 火把點燃了。The torch was lighted.

火鉢 (ㄏㄨㄛˇ ㄅㄛ)
a brazier; a fire pan; a fire pan

火玻璃 (ㄏㄨㄛˇ ㄅㄛ ˙ㄌㄧ)
flint glass; fireproof glass

火爆 (ㄏㄨㄛˇ ㄅㄠˋ)
(dialect) fiery; irritable

火伴 or 伙伴 (ㄏㄨㄛˇ ㄅㄢˋ) or 伙伴兒 (ㄏㄨㄛˇ ㄅㄢˋㄦ)
buddies; companions

火棒 (ㄏㄨㄛˇ ㄅㄤˋ)
①a torch made of a club tipped with alcohol-drenched cloth for twirling in darkness ②a poker

火併 (ㄏㄨㄛˇ ㄅㄧㄥˋ)
an intramural fight

火砲 (ㄏㄨㄛˇ ㄆㄠˋ)
artillery pieces

火盆 (ㄏㄨㄛˇ ㄆㄣˊ)
a brazier; a fire pan

火門 (ㄏㄨㄛˇ ㄇㄣˊ)
a fire hole

火苗子 (ㄏㄨㄛˇ ㄇㄧㄠˊ ˙ㄗ) or 火苗兒 (ㄏㄨㄛˇ ㄇㄧㄠˊㄦ)
tongues of flame; flames

火棉 (ㄏㄨㄛˇ ㄇㄧㄢˊ) or 火藥棉 (ㄏㄨㄛˇ ㄧㄠˋ ㄇㄧㄢˊ)
guncotton

火房 or 伙房 (ㄏㄨㄛˇ ㄈㄤˊ)
a kitchen: 她在火房裏烹飪。She is cooking in the kitchen.

火夫 or 火伕 (ㄏㄨㄛˇ ㄈㄨ)
a kitchen assistant; (military) a cook

火底 (ㄏㄨㄛˇ ㄉㄧˇ)
ashes, etc. after a fire

火頭 (ㄏㄨㄛˇ ㄊㄡˊ)
①the person responsible for the start of a fire ②(in old China) a cook ③the duration and degree of heating, cooking, etc.

火頭軍 (ㄏㄨㄛˇ ㄊㄡˊ ㄐㄩㄣ)
a mess sergeant; a military cook

火腿 (ㄏㄨㄛˇ ㄊㄨㄟˇ)
Chinese ham

火腿蛋 (ㄏㄨㄛˇ ㄊㄨㄟˇ ㄉㄢˋ)
ham and egg

火腿三明治 (ㄏㄨㄛˇ ㄊㄨㄟˇ ㄙㄢ ㄇㄧㄥˊ ㄓˋ)
a ham sandwich

火牛 (ㄏㄨㄛˇ ㄋㄧㄡˊ)
(in ancient China) to attach burning reeds, etc. to the tails of oxen to overwhelm the enemy defense 參看「火牛計」

火牛計 (ㄏㄨㄛˇ ㄋㄧㄡˊ ㄐㄧˋ)
tactics in this manner used by General Tien Tan (田單) of Chi (齊) during the Warring States period 參看「火牛」

火奴魯魯 (ㄏㄨㄛˇ ㄋㄨˊ ㄌㄨˇ ㄌㄨˇ)
Honolulu 亦作「檀香山」

火辣辣 (ㄏㄨㄛˇ ㄌㄚˋ ㄌㄚˋ)
burning

火力 (ㄏㄨㄛˇ ㄌㄧˋ)
①firepower: 砲兵的火力比步兵的大。The artillery has more firepower than the infantry. ②thermal

火力發電廠 (ㄏㄨㄛˇ ㄌㄧˋ ㄈㄚ ㄉㄧㄢˋ ㄔㄤˇ)
a thermoelectric plant; a thermo-power plant

火力集中 (ㄏㄨㄛˇ ㄌㄧˋ ㄐㄧˊ ㄓㄨㄥ)
concentration of fire

火爐子 (ㄏㄨㄛˇ ㄌㄨˊ ˙ㄗ)
a stove

火輪 (ㄏㄨㄛˇ ㄌㄨㄣˊ)
①a steamship ②the sun

火龍 (ㄏㄨㄛˇ ㄌㄨㄥˊ) or 火蛇 (ㄏㄨㄛˇ ㄕㄜˊ)
a firedrake; a mythical fiery dragon

火耕水耨 (ㄏㄨㄛˇ ㄍㄥ ㄕㄨㄟˇ ㄋㄡˋ)
to burn straws and weeds and water the land--an ancient way to fertilize the land

火鍋 (ㄏㄨㄛˇ ㄍㄨㄛ)
a chafing pot; a chafing dish

火光 (ㄏㄨㄛˇ ㄍㄨㄤ)
the light or glow of fire

火光冲天 (ㄏㄨㄛˇ ㄍㄨㄤ ㄔㄨㄥ ㄊㄧㄢ)
The glow of fire lit up the sky.

火攻 (ㄏㄨㄛˇ ㄍㄨㄥ)
to attack by setting fire to enemy ships or camps

火口 (ㄏㄨㄛˇ ㄎㄡˇ)
a volcanic crater

火炕 (ㄏㄨㄛˇ ㄎㄤˋ)
(in North China) a bed of bricks with a fire built underneath to keep warm

火坑 (ㄏㄨㄛˇ ㄎㄥ)
①a situation of extreme hardship or difficulty ②prostitution: 她墮入火坑。She has fallen into prostitution.

火筷子 (ㄏㄨㄛˇ ㄎㄨㄞˋ ˙ㄗ)
a pair of fire-tongs; a poker

火鶴 (ㄏㄨㄛˇ ㄏㄜˋ)
a flamingo

火海 (ㄏㄨㄛˇ ㄏㄞˇ)
a great fire; a conflagration

火海戰術 (ㄏㄨㄛˇ ㄏㄞˇ ㄓㄢˋ ㄕㄨˋ)
the tactics featuring intensive firepower to counter the human-sea tactics

火候 (ㄏㄨㄛˇ ㄏㄡˋ)
①the time used in cooking a certain food ②scholastic achievement ③Taoist alchemy

火候未到 (ㄏㄨㄛˇ ㄏㄡˋ ㄨㄟˋ ㄉㄠˋ)
(said of cooking time, training, etc.) not yet up to the required standard

火狐 (ㄏㄨㄛˇ ㄏㄨˊ)
a red fox

火花 (ㄏㄨㄛˇ ㄏㄨㄚ)
sparks: 火花從營火中迸出。Sparks were flying from the campfire.

火花放電 (ㄏㄨㄛˇ ㄏㄨㄚ ㄈㄤˋ ㄉㄧㄢˋ)
spark discharge

火花四濺 (ㄏㄨㄛˇ ㄏㄨㄚ ㄙˋ ㄐㄧㄢˋ)
Sparks fly off in all directions.

火化 (ㄏㄨㄛˇ ㄏㄨㄚˋ)
to cremate; cremation

火患(ㄏㄨㄛˇ ㄏㄨㄢˋ)
　fire hazards

火紅(ㄏㄨㄛˇ ㄏㄨㄥˊ)
　red as fire; fiery; flaming

火雞(ㄏㄨㄛˇ ㄐㄧ)
　a turkey

火急(ㄏㄨㄛˇ ㄐㄧˊ)
　very urgent; imminent

火計 or 伙計(ㄏㄨㄛˇ ˙ㄐㄧ)
　waiters; assistants in a
　store; salesmen; shop clerks

火教(ㄏㄨㄛˇ ㄐㄧㄠˋ)
　Parseeism

火酒(ㄏㄨㄛˇ ㄐㄧㄡˇ)
　alcohol

火剪(ㄏㄨㄛˇ ㄐㄧㄢˇ)
　① a pair of fire-tongs for
　poking or moving burning
　coals ②(formerly) a pair of
　fire-tongs for curling hair

火箭(ㄏㄨㄛˇ ㄐㄧㄢˋ)
　① a rocket: 火箭被發射到月
　球. The rocket was launched
　to the moon. ② an arrow
　with a burning substance
　attached

火箭砲(ㄏㄨㄛˇ ㄐㄧㄢˋ ㄆㄠˋ)
　a bazooka; a rocket launch-
　er

火箭發射臺(ㄏㄨㄛˇ ㄐㄧㄢˋ ㄈㄚ ㄕㄜˋ
ㄊㄞˊ)
　a rocket launching pad

火箭飛機(ㄏㄨㄛˇ ㄐㄧㄢˋ ㄈㄟ ㄐㄧ)
　a rocket-propelled plane

火警(ㄏㄨㄛˇ ㄐㄧㄥˇ) or 火警警報
(ㄏㄨㄛˇ ㄐㄧㄥˇ ㄐㄧㄥˇ ㄅㄠˋ)
　a fire alarm; a signal that
　warns that a fire has started

火炬(ㄏㄨㄛˇ ㄐㄩˋ)
　a torch; a link

火漆(ㄏㄨㄛˇ ㄑㄧ)
　sealing wax

火氣(ㄏㄨㄛˇ ㄑㄧˋ)
　①(Chinese medicine) inter-
　nal heat (as a cause of dis-
　ease) ② temper; the boiling
　point (of a person): 他火氣很
　大. He has a quick temper.

火器(ㄏㄨㄛˇ ㄑㄧˋ)
　firearms

火球(ㄏㄨㄛˇ ㄑㄧㄡˊ)
　a meteor; a fireball

火鉗(ㄏㄨㄛˇ ㄑㄧㄢˊ)
　a pair of fire-tongs; fire
　irons 亦作「火箸」

火槍(ㄏㄨㄛˇ ㄑㄧㄤ)
　a firelock; a flintlock

火線(ㄏㄨㄛˇ ㄒㄧㄢˋ)
　the battlefront; a firing line;
　a fighting line

火巷(ㄏㄨㄛˇ ㄒㄧㄤˋ)
　a fire lane

火星(ㄏㄨㄛˇ ㄒㄧㄥ)
　① the planet Mars ② sparks

火星人(ㄏㄨㄛˇ ㄒㄧㄥ ㄖㄣˊ)
　a Martian

火刑(ㄏㄨㄛˇ ㄒㄧㄥˊ)
　death by fire

火性(ㄏㄨㄛˇ ㄒㄧㄥˋ)
　quick-tempered; the low
　boiling point (of a person)

火紙媒兒(ㄏㄨㄛˇ ㄓˇ ㄇㄟˊ)or 火紙
捻兒(ㄏㄨㄛˇ ㄓˇ ㄋㄧㄢˇ)
　a thin roll of touch paper
　used for lighting in water-
　pipe smoking

火燭(ㄏㄨㄛˇ ㄓㄨˊ)
　① candlelight ② an inflam-
　mable substance; a combus-
　tible substance

火燭小心(ㄏㄨㄛˇ ㄓㄨˊ ㄒㄧㄠˇ ㄒㄧㄣ)
　Be careful with fire!

火主(ㄏㄨㄛˇ ㄓㄨˇ)
　the owner or lodger of a
　house where a fire first start-
　ed

火磚(ㄏㄨㄛˇ ㄓㄨㄢ)
　firebricks

火中取栗(ㄏㄨㄛˇ ㄓㄨㄥ ㄑㄩˋ ㄌㄧˋ)
　to pull chestnuts out of the
　fire

火種(ㄏㄨㄛˇ ㄓㄨㄥˇ)
　① tinder; embers kept for
　starting a new fire ② any
　burning object which causes
　a fire disaster

火熾(ㄏㄨㄛˇ ㄔˋ)
　white-hot (also used figura-
　tively to describe passion)

火車(ㄏㄨㄛˇ ㄔㄜ)
　a train

火車票(ㄏㄨㄛˇ ㄔㄜ ㄆㄧㄠˋ)
　train tickets: 請替我買火車
　票. Please buy the train
　tickets for me.

火車頭(ㄏㄨㄛˇ ㄔㄜ ㄊㄡˊ)
　a locomotive; a railway
　engine for drawing a train

火車站(ㄏㄨㄛˇ ㄔㄜ ㄓㄢˋ)
　a railway station

火車時間表(ㄏㄨㄛˇ ㄔㄜ ㄕˊ ㄐㄧㄢ
ㄅㄧㄠˇ)

a railway schedule; a train
schedule

火柴(ㄏㄨㄛˇ ㄔㄞˊ)
　a match

火柴盒(ㄏㄨㄛˇ ㄔㄞˊ ㄏㄜˊ)
　a matchbox

火場(ㄏㄨㄛˇ ㄔㄤˇ)or 火災(ㄏㄨㄛˇ ㄗㄞ)
　the scene of a fire

火成岩(ㄏㄨㄛˇ ㄔㄥˊ ㄧㄢˊ)
　igneous rocks

火石(ㄏㄨㄛˇ ㄕˊ)
　flint

火勢(ㄏㄨㄛˇ ㄕˋ)
　the intensity and scope of a
　fire

火食 or 伙食(ㄏㄨㄛˇ ˙ㄕ)
　meals; board

火食費(ㄏㄨㄛˇ ㄕ ㄈㄟˋ)
　a boarding fee

火舌(ㄏㄨㄛˇ ㄕㄜˊ)
　licking flame; tongues of
　flame

火燒(ㄏㄨㄛˇ ㄕㄠ)
　①(ㄏㄨㄛˇ ㄕㄠ)a fire disaster
　②(ㄏㄨㄛˇ ˙ㄕㄠ)baked wheaten
　cake

火燒眉毛(ㄏㄨㄛˇ ㄕㄠ ㄇㄟˊ ㄇㄠˊ)
　(literally) like fire burning
　the eyebrows—very urgent
　or imminent

火燒心(ㄏㄨㄛˇ ㄕㄠ ㄒㄧㄣ)
　(literally) like fire burning
　the heart—very anxious or
　worried

火燒雲(ㄏㄨㄛˇ ㄕㄠ ㄩㄣˊ)
　red clouds—as at sunset

火首(ㄏㄨㄛˇ ㄕㄡˇ)
　one whose house is the first
　to catch fire

火山(ㄏㄨㄛˇ ㄕㄢ)
　a volcano

火山爆發(ㄏㄨㄛˇ ㄕㄢ ㄅㄠˋ ㄈㄚ)
　a volcanic eruption

火山脈(ㄏㄨㄛˇ ㄕㄢ ㄇㄞˋ)
　a volcanic range

火山地震(ㄏㄨㄛˇ ㄕㄢ ㄉㄧˋ ㄓㄣˋ)
　an earthquake caused by the
　eruption of a volcano

火山口(ㄏㄨㄛˇ ㄕㄢ ㄎㄡˇ)
　a volcanic crater

火山灰(ㄏㄨㄛˇ ㄕㄢ ㄏㄨㄟ)
　volcanic ashes; lapillus

火山熔岩(ㄏㄨㄛˇ ㄕㄢ ㄖㄨㄥˊ ㄧㄢˊ)
　lava

火山岩(ㄏㄨㄛˇ ㄕㄢ ㄧㄢˊ)
　volcanic rocks

〔火
部〕

〔火部〕

火神(ㄏㄨㄛˇ ㄕㄣˊ)
(Chinese mythology) the god of fire

火傷(ㄏㄨㄛˇ ㄕㄤ)
a burn; a blister caused by burning

火上加油(ㄏㄨㄛˇ ㄕㄤ ㄐㄧㄚ ㄧㄡˊ)
(literally) to pour oil on the flame—to make things worse; to aggravate

火樹銀花(ㄏㄨㄛˇ ㄕㄨˋ ㄧㄣˊ ㄏㄨㄚ)
spluttering fireworks—bright lights and illuminations of a big city at night

火熱(ㄏㄨㄛˇ ㄖㄜˋ)
passionate; enthusiastic; intimate

火災(ㄏㄨㄛˇ ㄗㄞ)
a fire disaster

火災保險(ㄏㄨㄛˇ ㄗㄞ ㄅㄠˇ ㄒㄧㄢˇ)or 火險(ㄏㄨㄛˇ ㄒㄧㄢˇ)
fire insurance

火災保險費(ㄏㄨㄛˇ ㄗㄞ ㄅㄠˇ ㄒㄧㄢˇ ㄈㄟˋ)
a premium for fire insurance

火災保險單(ㄏㄨㄛˇ ㄗㄞ ㄅㄠˇ ㄒㄧㄢˇ ㄉㄢ)or 火險保單(ㄏㄨㄛˇ ㄒㄧㄢˇ ㄅㄠˇ ㄉㄢ)
a fire insurance policy

火葬(ㄏㄨㄛˇ ㄗㄤˋ)
to cremate; cremation

火葬爐(ㄏㄨㄛˇ ㄗㄤˋ ㄌㄨˊ)
a cremator

火葬場(ㄏㄨㄛˇ ㄗㄤˋ ㄔㄤˇ)or火葬場(ㄏㄨㄛˇ ㄗㄤˋ ㄔㄤˇ)
a crematory; a crematorium

火傘(ㄏㄨㄛˇ ㄙㄢˇ)
the white-hot sunshine in summer

火傘高張(ㄏㄨㄛˇ ㄙㄢˇ ㄍㄠ ㄓㄤ)《文言文》
the scorching sunshine in summer—like a fully spread umbrella of fire

火速(ㄏㄨㄛˇ ㄙㄨˋ)
urgently; with the greatest urgency; imminent; urgent; posthaste: 食物必須火速送給那些災民. It's urgent that food must be sent to the sufferers.

火兒(ㄏㄨㄛˇ ㄦ)
①fire ②anger

火兒了(ㄏㄨㄛˇ ㄦ ˙ㄌㄜ)or 火了(ㄏㄨㄛˇ ˙ㄌㄜ)
to get mad; to become angry

火藥(ㄏㄨㄛˇ ㄧㄠˋ)
gunpowder: 我們需要火藥.
We are in need of gunpowder.

火藥庫(ㄏㄨㄛˇ ㄧㄠˋ ㄎㄨˋ)
a powder magazine; an ammunition depot

火藥味(ㄏㄨㄛˇ ㄧㄠˋ ㄨㄟˋ)or 火藥氣息(ㄏㄨㄛˇ ㄧㄠˋ ㄑㄧˋ ㄒㄧˊ)
the smell of gunpowder—a tense situation which can easily erupt into open hostilities

火曜日(ㄏㄨㄛˇ ㄧㄠˋ ㄖˋ)
Tuesday

火油(ㄏㄨㄛˇ ㄧㄡˊ)
kerosene

火眼金睛(ㄏㄨㄛˇ ㄧㄢˇ ㄐㄧㄣ ㄐㄧㄥ)
fierce-looking; awe-inspiring (looks)

火燄(ㄏㄨㄛˇ ㄧㄢˋ)
flames

火燄噴射器(ㄏㄨㄛˇ ㄧㄢˋ ㄆㄣ ㄕㄜˋ ㄑㄧˋ)
a flame thrower

火印(ㄏㄨㄛˇ ㄧㄣˋ)
a firemark; a seal made by hot iron; a brand

火網(ㄏㄨㄛˇ ㄨㄤˇ)
(literally) the net of fire —intense shooting in battle; cross fire

二畫

【灰】 3172
ㄏㄨㄟ huei huī
1. ashes; dust
2. lime
3. gray (color)
4. disheartened; disappointed or discouraged
5. (now rarely) to break into tiny pieces or particles

灰白(ㄏㄨㄟ ㄅㄞˊ)
pale; ashen: 她臉色灰白. She turned pale.

灰白質(ㄏㄨㄟ ㄅㄞˊ ㄓˊ)
the gray matter (the outer cortex of nerve cells) and the white matter (the inner mass of nerve fibers); the cinereum matter

灰濛濛(ㄏㄨㄟ ㄇㄥˊ ㄇㄥˊ)
dusky; overcast: 灰濛濛的夜色 a dusky night scene

灰錳氧(ㄏㄨㄟ ㄇㄥˇ ㄧㄤˇ)
potassium permanganate

灰滅(ㄏㄨㄟ ㄇㄧㄝˋ)
to destroy; to wipe out; to vanish: 他所有的希望都灰滅了. All his hopes were destroyed.

灰分(ㄏㄨㄟ ㄈㄣ)
(biology) inorganic substance in a plant; ashes

灰頭土面(ㄏㄨㄟ ㄊㄡˊ ㄊㄨˇ ㄇㄧㄢˋ)
dusty and dirty in appearance—a sloven

灰頭土臉兒(ㄏㄨㄟ ㄊㄡˊ ㄊㄨˇ ㄌㄧㄢˇ ㄦ)
①to be covered with dust all over the face ②to lose face

灰錦礦(ㄏㄨㄟ ㄊㄧ ㄎㄨㄤˋ)
gray antimony

灰土(ㄏㄨㄟ ㄊㄨˇ)
dust; dirt

灰姑娘(ㄏㄨㄟ ㄍㄨ ㄋㄧㄤˊ)《文言》
①Cinderella, the heroine of a fairy tale ②a person who achieves unexpected or sudden success or recognition, especially after obscurity, neglect or misery

灰燼(ㄏㄨㄟ ㄐㄧㄣˋ)
ashes; ember

灰心(ㄏㄨㄟ ㄒㄧㄣ)
disappointed; discouraged; disheartened: 不要因一次失敗而灰心. Don't be disheartened by a single failure.

灰心喪氣(ㄏㄨㄟ ㄒㄧㄣ ㄙㄤˋ ㄑㄧˋ)
crestfallen and disheartened

灰汁(ㄏㄨㄟ ㄓ)or灰水(ㄏㄨㄟ ㄕㄨㄟˇ)
lye

灰指甲(ㄏㄨㄟ ㄓˇ ㄐㄧㄚˇ)
leuconychia

灰塵(ㄏㄨㄟ ㄔㄣˊ)
dust: 馬路上積了厚厚的灰塵. Dust lay thick on the road.

灰長石(ㄏㄨㄟ ㄔㄤˊ ㄕˊ)
anorthite

灰吹法(ㄏㄨㄟ ㄔㄨㄟ ㄈㄚˇ)
cupellation

灰石(ㄏㄨㄟ ㄕˊ)
limestone

灰沙(ㄏㄨㄟ ㄕㄚ)
sand and dust

灰鼠(ㄏㄨㄟ ㄕㄨˇ)
the squirrel

灰曹長石(ㄏㄨㄟ ㄘㄠˊ ㄔㄤˊ ㄕˊ)
labradorite

灰色(ㄏㄨㄟ ㄙㄜˋ)or(ㄏㄨㄟˋ ㄙㄜˋ)
gray color

灰色人生觀(ㄏㄨㄟ ㄙㄜˋ ㄖㄣˊ ㄕㄥ ㄍㄨㄢ)

pessimistic attitude toward life

灰暗（ㄏㄨㄟ ㄢˋ）
murky gray; gloomy: 灰暗的天空使人發愁。The gloomy sky makes people sad.

三畫

【灸】 3173 ㄐㄧㄡˇ jeou jiǔ
(Chinese medicine) to cauterize by burning moxa; moxa cautery; moxibustion

灸治（ㄐㄧㄡˋㄓˋ）
to treat by moxa cautery or moxibustion

灸刺（ㄐㄧㄡˋ ㄘˋ）
cautery and acupuncture

【灼】 3174 ㄓㄨㄛˊ jwo zhuó
1. to burn; to cauterize
2. bright; clear; luminous; brilliant
3. flowers in full bloom

灼爛（ㄓㄨㄛˊㄌㄢˋ）
badly burned

灼骨（ㄓㄨㄛˊㄍㄨˇ）
to burn the bones—a method of divination in ancient times

灼見（ㄓㄨㄛˊ ㄐㄧㄢˋ）
brilliant views; clear views: 你對這一題目有何灼見？What are your brilliant views on the subject?

灼灼（ㄓㄨㄛˊㄓㄨㄛˊ）
①bright and brilliant ② blooming ③(figuratively) of uncommon brilliance

灼焃（ㄓㄨㄛˊ ㄕˋ）
burn

灼爍（ㄓㄨㄛˊ ㄕㄨㄛˋ）
①bright and luminous ② splendorous

灼熱（ㄓㄨㄛˊㄖㄜˋ）
intense heat; red-hot

灼然（ㄓㄨㄛˊㄖㄢˊ）
crystal-clear; obvious

【災】 3175 （災,烖,裁）ㄗㄞ tzai zāi
a disaster; a calamity; a catastrophe

災變（ㄗㄞ ㄅㄧㄢˋ）
a disaster; a calamity

災民（ㄗㄞㄇㄧㄣˊ）
refugees created by disasters

災難（ㄗㄞ ㄋㄢˋ）
disasters; calamities; catastrophes

災黎（ㄗㄞ ㄌㄧˊ）
refugees created by disasters or calamities

災黎遍野（ㄗㄞ ㄌㄧˊ ㄅㄧㄢˋ ㄧㄝˇ）
The land is filled with disaster-stricken refugees.

災戾（ㄗㄞ ㄌㄧˋ）
disasters; calamities: 戰爭是可怕的災戾。War is a frightful calamity.

災沴（ㄗㄞ ㄌㄧˋ）
disasters (like droughts or floods)

災害（ㄗㄞ ㄏㄞˋ）
disasters; calamities; damage or casualties caused by disasters

災禍（ㄗㄞ ㄏㄨㄛˋ）
disasters or calamities; catastrophes

災禍臨頭（ㄗㄞ ㄏㄨㄛˋㄌㄧㄣˊㄊㄡˊ）
A great disaster is imminent.

災患（ㄗㄞ ㄏㄨㄢˋ）
disasters or calamities

災荒（ㄗㄞ ㄏㄨㄤ）
famine caused by floods or droughts

災情（ㄗㄞ ㄑㄧㄥˊ）
the extent of a disaster or calamity

災情慘重（ㄗㄞ ㄑㄧㄥˊ ㄘㄢˇ ㄓㄨㄥˋ）
①The situation in the afflicted area is serious. ② (now often used comically) heavy losses; big damages

災區（ㄗㄞ ㄑㄩ）
the area affected by a disaster or calamity; the afflicted area; the disaster area

災祥（ㄗㄞ ㄒㄧㄤˊ）
an omen of good or bad; a disaster or blessing

災星（ㄗㄞ ㄒㄧㄥ）
(literally) the star of calamity—disasters or calamities

災疫（ㄗㄞ ㄧˋ）
a pestilence: 災疫正在東方肆虐。A pestilence is raging in the East.

災殃（ㄗㄞ ㄧㄤ）
a disaster; a calamity; a catastrophe

災阨（ㄗㄞ ㄜˋ）
disasters or calamities; catastrophes

四畫

【炎】 3176 ㄧㄢˊ yan yán
1. burning; hot; sultry
2. to blaze; to flame; to flare up
3. inflammation

炎方（ㄧㄢˊㄈㄤ）
the south (where the weather is very hot)

炎帝（ㄧㄢˊㄉㄧˋ）
Yen Ti, who supposedly lived from 2737 to 2697 B. C. 亦作「神農」

炎天（ㄧㄢˊㄊㄧㄢ）
a hot day; dog days

炎土（ㄧㄢˊㄊㄨˇ）
the region in the southwestern China, where the weather is very hot

炎涼（ㄧㄢˊㄌㄧㄤˊ）
①(said of weather) hot and cold ② snobbishness

炎涼世態（ㄧㄢˊㄌㄧㄤˊㄕˋㄊㄞˋ）
the aspect of worldly affairs, now hot and now cold

炎漢（ㄧㄢˊ ㄏㄢˋ）or 炎劉（ㄧㄢˊㄌㄧㄡˊ）
the Han Dynasty (206 B. C. to 220 A. D.)

炎荒（ㄧㄢˊ ㄏㄨㄤ）
the southern frontiers, where the weather is very hot

炎黃（ㄧㄢˊ ㄏㄨㄤˊ）
Yen Ti and Huang Ti (or the Yellow Emperor), two of the earliest rulers of China

炎黃子孫（ㄧㄢˊ ㄏㄨㄤˊ ㄗˇ ㄙㄨㄣ）
the Chinese people, who are supposed to be descendants of Yen Ti (炎帝) and Huang Ti (黃帝)

炎徼（ㄧㄢˊ ㄐㄧˋ）
the southern frontiers

炎夏（ㄧㄢˊ ㄒㄧㄚˋ）
hot summer; summer at its hottest

炎瘴（ㄧㄢˊ ㄓㄤˋ）
the far south frontiers where miasma and malaria prevail

炎症（ㄧㄢˊ ㄓㄥˋ）

〔火部〕

（火部）

inflammation

炎暑（ㄧㄢˊ ㄕㄨˇ）
hot summer; summer heat;
summer at its hottest

炎熱（ㄧㄢˊ ㄖㄜˋ）
(said of weather) very hot:
天氣炎熱。The weather has
been very hot.

炎宋（ㄧㄢˊ ㄙㄨㄥˋ）
the Sung Dynasty (the
House of Chao)

炎炎（ㄧㄢˊ ㄧㄢˊ）
①impressive and imposing;
awe-inspiring ②very hot

炎陽（ㄧㄢˊ ㄧㄤˊ）
the scorching sun

炎威（ㄧㄢˊ ㄨㄟ）
oppressively imposing; op-
pressiveness

【炊】 3177
ㄔㄨㄟ chuei chuī
to cook: 巧婦難為無米之炊。
Even a skillful wife cannot
cook a meal without rice.

炊餅（ㄔㄨㄟ ㄅㄧㄥˇ）
steamed cake

炊骨易子（ㄔㄨㄟ ㄍㄨˇ ㄧˋ ㄗˇ）
(literally) to cook with the
bones as fuel and to ex-
change children for eating
—sufferings during a severe
famine

炊桂（ㄔㄨㄟ ㄍㄨㄟˋ）
scarcity of firewood

炊火（ㄔㄨㄟ ㄏㄨㄛˇ）
a cooking fire which indicates presence of human
habitation

炊金饌玉（ㄔㄨㄟ ㄐㄧㄣ ㄓㄨㄢˋㄩˋ）
the finest delicacies—as
expensive as gold and gems

炊具（ㄔㄨㄟ ㄐㄩˋ）
cooking utensils 亦作「炊事
具」

炊帚（ㄔㄨㄟ ㄓㄡˇ）
a brush for washing kitchen
utensils

炊事（ㄔㄨㄟ ㄕˋ）
cooking

炊事兵（ㄔㄨㄟ ㄕˋ ㄅㄧㄥ）
a military cook

炊沙作飯（ㄔㄨㄟ ㄕㄚ ㄗㄨㄛˋ ㄈㄢˋ）
(literally) to cook the sand
for food—a useless or meaningless attempt

炊爨（ㄔㄨㄟ ㄘㄨㄢˋ）
to prepare meals

炊烟（ㄔㄨㄟ ㄧㄢ）
the smoke from a kitchen
fire

炊烟裊裊（ㄔㄨㄟ ㄧㄢ ㄋㄧㄠˇ ㄋㄧㄠˇ）
smoke spiraling from kitch-
ens

炊烟四起（ㄔㄨㄟ ㄧㄢ ㄙˋ ㄑㄧˇ）
cooking smoke all around
—It's about mealtime.

【炕】 3178
ㄎㄤˋ kang kàng
1. dry; to dry
2. hot
3. kang, a brick bed warmed
by a fire underneath (in
North China)

炕面甎（ㄎㄤˋ ㄇㄧㄢˋ ㄓㄨㄢ）
square bricks that surface a
brick bed

炕洞（ㄎㄤˋ ㄉㄨㄥˋ）
the hole under the brick bed
for taking out or putting in
the stove that warms; the
flue of a brick bed

炕爐子（ㄎㄤˋ ㄌㄨˊ ㄗ˙）
a squat stove or oven used
specially for warming the
brick bed

炕淋（ㄎㄤˋ ㄌㄧㄣˊ）
a brick bed warmed by a
fire underneath

炕沿兒（ㄎㄤˋ ㄧㄢˊ ㄦ）
the outer edge of a brick
bed

【炖】 3179
ㄉㄨㄣˋ duenn dùn
fire burning intensely

【炘】 3180
ㄒㄧㄣ shin xīn
1. brilliant and bright
2. to scorch; scorching hot

炘炘（ㄒㄧㄣ ㄒㄧㄣ）
brilliant and bright

【炙】 3181
ㄓˋ jyh zhì
to burn; to cauterize; to
roast; to broil; to heat

炙背（ㄓˋ ㄅㄟˋ）
to expose the back to the
sun

炙乾（ㄓˋ ㄍㄢ）
to dry by applying heat

炙炒（ㄓˋ ㄔㄠˇ）
to broil

炙手可熱（ㄓˋ ㄕㄡˇ ㄎㄜˇ ㄖㄜˋ）
very influential and powerful

【炒】 3182
ㄔㄠˇ chao chǎo
to fry; to stir-fry

炒米粉（ㄔㄠˇ ㄇㄧˇ ㄈㄣˇ）
to fry rice noodles; fried rice
noodles

炒麵（ㄔㄠˇ ㄇㄧㄢˋ）
to fry noodles; fried noodles

炒飯（ㄔㄠˇ ㄈㄢˋ）
to fry rice; fried rice

炒蛋（ㄔㄠˇ ㄉㄢˋ）
scrambled eggs

炒地皮（ㄔㄠˇ ㄉㄧˋ ㄆㄧˊ）
to engage in land speculation

炒冷飯（ㄔㄠˇ ㄌㄥˇ ㄈㄢˋ）
to fry leftover rice—to do
the same old thing without
new contents

炒肝兒（ㄔㄠˇ ㄍㄢ ㄦ）
stir-fried liver

炒股票（ㄔㄠˇ ㄍㄨˇ ㄆㄧㄠˋ）
(colloquial) to manipulate
stock trading

炒勺（ㄔㄠˇ ㄕㄠˊ）
a flat cooking ladle

炒熱（ㄔㄠˇ ㄖㄜˋ）
①to jack up the price of
stocks by manipulation ②to
make an ordinary news
event a top story by sensational reporting

炒肉絲（ㄔㄠˇ ㄖㄡˋ ㄙ）
stir-fried meat slices; to
stir-fry meat slices

炒菜（ㄔㄠˇ ㄘㄞˋ）
to fry vegetables or meat;
fried dishes (as distinct
from steamed or stewed
dishes)

炒魷魚（ㄔㄠˇ ㄧㄡˊ ㄩˊ）
(slang) to be fired: 他因不識
實而被炒魷魚。He was fired
for dishonesty.

五畫

【炫】 3183
ㄒㄩㄢˋ shiuann xuàn
1. to show off; to display; to
flaunt
2. dazzling; bright; shining

炫目（ㄒㄩㄢˋ ㄇㄨˋ）
to dazzle the eyes

炫怪（ㄒㄩㄢˋ ㄍㄨㄞˋ）
to try to attract others'
attention by sensationalism

炫惑 (ㄒㄩㄢˋ ㄏㄨㄛˋ)
to dazzle and confuse

炫晝縞夜 (ㄒㄩㄢˋ ㄓㄡˋ ㄍㄠˇ 一ㄝˋ)
to illuminate day and night

炫耀 (ㄒㄩㄢˋ 一ㄠˋ)
to show off; to flaunt

炫耀 (ㄒㄩㄢˋ 一ㄠˋ)
①to flaunt; to show off; 這女孩炫耀她的新衣服。The girl flaunted her new clothes. ②bright and brilliant

【炬】 3184 ㄐㄩˋ jiuh jù
1. a torch
2. fire

【炮】 3185 1. ㄆㄠˊ paur páo
to refine medicinal herbs

炮鳳烹龍 (ㄆㄠˊ ㄈㄥˋ ㄆㄥ ㄌㄨㄥˊ)
to cook a pheasant and a white horse as sacrifices when the emperors of old China officiated at grand ceremonies

炮煉 (ㄆㄠˊ ㄌㄧㄢˋ)
to refine or decoct (medicine) by applying heat

炮烙 (ㄆㄠˊ ㄌㄨㄛˋ)
an ancient Chinese torture

炮烙之刑 (ㄆㄠˊ ㄌㄨㄛˋ ㄓ ㄒㄧㄥˊ)
an ancient torture or punishment by ordering a prisoner to walk on a slippery metal beam kept hot by coal underneath

炮製 (ㄆㄠˊ ㄓˋ)
to refine or decoct (herbal medicine); the process of refining herbal medicine

【炮】 3185 2. (砲) ㄆㄠˋ paw pào
a big gun, cannon, etc.

炮火 (ㄆㄠˋ ㄏㄨㄛˇ)
gunfire 亦作「砲火」

【炮】 3185 3. (炰) ㄅㄠ bau bāo
1. to roast or bake
2. to dry by heat

炮肉 (ㄅㄠ ㄖㄡˋ)
roasted meat; to roast or barbecue meat

【炯】 3186 (烱) ㄐㄩㄥˇ jeong jiǒng
bright; brightness; clear

炯見 (ㄐㄩㄥˇ ㄐㄧㄢˋ)
bright and clear

炯戒 (ㄐㄩㄥˇ ㄐㄧㄝˋ)
a clear warning

炯鑒 (ㄐㄩㄥˇ ㄐㄧㄢˋ)
clear reflection; clear understanding

炯炯 (ㄐㄩㄥˇ ㄐㄩㄥˇ)
①clear and bright (eyes, etc.): 他有一雙炯炯有神的眼睛。He has a pair of bright piercing eyes. ②discerning

炯心 (ㄐㄩㄥˇ ㄒㄧㄣ)
clear conscience

【炳】 3187 ㄅㄧㄥˇ biing bǐng
bright; luminous

炳燭 或 秉燭 (ㄅㄧㄥˇ ㄓㄨˊ)
(to take a night trip, stroll, etc.) by the bright candle-light

炳著 (ㄅㄧㄥˇ ㄓㄨˋ)
eminent; renowned

炳然 (ㄅㄧㄥˇ ㄖㄢˊ)
bright

炳耀 (ㄅㄧㄥˇ 一ㄠˋ)
bright and luminous

炳蔚 (ㄅㄧㄥˇ ㄨㄟˋ)
deep and luminous

【炷】 3188 ㄓㄨˋ juh jù
1. the wick (of a candle, lamp, etc.)
2. a stick (of incense, etc.)
3. to burn; to cauterize

炷香 (ㄓㄨˋ ㄒㄧㄤ)
①to burn incense ②a stick of incense

【炸】 3189 1. ㄓㄚˋ jah zhà
1. to explode; to burst; to bomb
2. to get mad
3. to disperse boisterously; to flee in terror

炸彈 (ㄓㄚˋ ㄉㄢˋ)
bombs

炸裂 (ㄓㄚˋ ㄌㄧㄝˋ)
to split, blast or break by explosion or bombing; to develop cracks as a result of explosion

炸毀 (ㄓㄚˋ ㄏㄨㄟˇ)
to destroy by bombing or explosion; to blow up; to blast

炸傷 (ㄓㄚˋ ㄕㄤ)
to be injured in bombing or explosion

炸死 (ㄓㄚˋ ㄙˇ)
to kill by bombing; to be killed in bombing or explosion

炸藥 (ㄓㄚˋ 一ㄠˋ)
dynamite; explosives

【炸】 3189 2. ㄓㄚˊ jar zhá
to fry in oil or fat; to deep-fry

炸麻花兒 (ㄓㄚˊ ㄇㄚˊ ㄏㄨㄚ ㄦ)
sweet twisted pastry-strips fried in oil

炸糕 (ㄓㄚˊ ㄍㄠ)
stuffed glutinous rice cakes fried in oil

炸雞 (ㄓㄚˊ ㄐㄧ)
fry chicken; fried chicken

炸醬 (ㄓㄚˊ ㄐㄧㄤˋ)
fried bean sauce (usually with mince-meat)

炸醬麵 (ㄓㄚˊ ㄐㄧㄤˋ ㄇㄧㄢˋ)
a kind of noodles served with fried bean sauce and mince-meat

炸圈兒 (ㄓㄚˊ ㄑㄩㄢ ㄦ)
fried large hog intestines

炸油條 (ㄓㄚˊ 一ㄡˊ ㄊㄧㄠˊ)
to fry twisted dough-strips

炸丸子 (ㄓㄚˊ ㄨㄢˊ ㄗ˙)
fried meat balls; to fry meat balls

【炭】 3190 ㄊㄢˋ tann tàn
1. charcoal
2. coal
3. (chemistry) C—carbon

炭筆 (ㄊㄢˋ ㄅㄧˇ)
charcoal for drawing

炭田 (ㄊㄢˋ ㄊㄧㄢˊ)
a coal field

炭爐 (ㄊㄢˋ ㄌㄨˊ)
a charcoal stove

炭坑 (ㄊㄢˋ ㄎㄥ)
(mining) a coal pit

炭化 (ㄊㄢˋ ㄏㄨㄚˋ)
to carbonize; carbonization; to carburet; carburetion

炭化鈣 (ㄊㄢˋ ㄏㄨㄚˋ ㄍㄞˋ)
calcium carbide (CaC₂)

炭化作用 (ㄊㄢˋ ㄏㄨㄚˋ ㄗㄨㄛˋ ㄩㄥˋ)
carbonization

炭化物 (ㄊㄢˋ ㄏㄨㄚˋ ㄨˋ)
carbides

炭畫 (ㄊㄢˋ ㄏㄨㄚˋ)
charcoal drawings

炭火 (ㄊㄢˋ ㄏㄨㄛˇ)

〔火部〕

〔火部〕

charcoal fires

炭灰（ㄊㄢ ㄏㄨㄟ）
ashes

炭精（ㄊㄢ ㄐㄧㄥ）
pure carbon

炭紙（ㄊㄢ ㄓˇ）or炭精紙（ㄊㄢ ㄐㄧㄥ ㄓˇ）
carbon paper 亦作「複寫紙」

炭商（ㄊㄢ ㄕㄤ）
a coal or charcoal dealer

炭水化合物（ㄊㄢ ㄕㄨㄟˇ ㄏㄨㄚˋ ㄏㄜˊ ㄨˋ）
carbohydrate

炭素（ㄊㄢ ㄙㄨˋ）
carbon

炭酸（ㄊㄢ ㄙㄨㄢ）
carbonic acid

炭酸飽和（ㄊㄢ ㄙㄨㄢ ㄅㄠˇ ㄏㄜˊ）
carbonation

炭酸氣（ㄊㄢ ㄙㄨㄢ ㄑㄧˋ）
carbonic-acid gas

炭酸石灰（ㄊㄢ ㄙㄨㄢ ㄕˊ ㄏㄨㄟ）
carbonate of lime

炭酸水（ㄊㄢ ㄙㄨㄢ ㄕㄨㄟˇ）
carbonated water; soda water; aerated water

炭酸鹽（ㄊㄢ ㄙㄨㄢ ㄧㄢˊ）
carbonate

【炤】 3191
ㄓㄠ jaw zhào
formerly interchangeable with 照—to shine

【為】 3192
1. ㄨㄟˊ wéi wěi
simplified form of 爲—to be; to do; to make

【為】 3192
2. ㄨㄟˋ wèy wèi
simplified form of 爲—for

六畫

【烏】 3193
ㄨ u wū
1. a crow, raven or rook
2. dark color
3. how; what; when
4. Alas!
5. (now rarely) the sun
6. a Chinese family name

烏鬢（ㄨ ㄅㄧㄣ）
young people (whose hair is black)

烏哺（ㄨ ㄅㄨˇ）
to provide for or support one's parents when they get old (According to Chinese

legend, the raven feeds its parents when they get too old to find food outside.)

烏梅（ㄨ ㄇㄟˊ）
dried plums

烏帽（ㄨ ㄇㄠˋ）
the costume of a hermit or of one who chooses to live in seclusion

烏木（ㄨ ㄇㄨˋ）
ebony

烏髮（ㄨ ㄈㄚˇ）
① dark hair; raven hair ② to dye the hair black

烏飛兔走（ㄨ ㄈㄟ ㄊㄨˋ ㄗㄡˇ）
How time flies!

烏豆（ㄨ ㄉㄡˋ）
the black beans—a variety of soybeans, usually used in herbal medicine

烏兔（ㄨ ㄊㄨˋ）
the sun and the moon

烏托邦（ㄨ ㄊㄨㄛ ㄅㄤ）
① utopia—an ideal place or state; any visionary system of political or social perfection ② *Utopia*

烏托邦社會主義（ㄨ ㄊㄨㄛ ㄅㄤ ㄕㄜˋ ㄏㄨㄟˋ ㄓㄨˇ ㄧˋ）
utopian socialism

烏私情（ㄨ ㄙ ㄑㄧㄥˊ）
filial piety 參看「烏哺」

烏拉圭（ㄨ ㄌㄚ ㄍㄨㄟ）
Uruguay

烏拉山（ㄨ ㄌㄚ ㄕㄢ）
the Ural Mountains

烏拉草（ㄨ ㄌㄚ ㄘㄠˇ）
name of a reed produced in Kirin Province, usually used as lining or padding in winter shoes to warm the feet

烏裏烏塗（ㄨ.ㄌㄧ ㄨ.ㄊㄨ）or烏塗（ㄨ.ㄊㄨ）
① lukewarm ② (said of persons) dumb and dull ③ vain (effort); in vain ④ tangled; muddled; ambiguous

烏溜溜（ㄨ ㄌㄧㄡ ㄌㄧㄡ）
(said of eyes) dark and liquid: 她有一雙烏溜溜的眼睛。She has dark and liquid eyes.

烏梁海（ㄨ ㄌㄧㄤˊ ㄏㄞˇ）
Uriankhai, a Mongolian tribe 亦作「兀良哈」

烏亮（ㄨ ㄌㄧㄤˋ）
glossy black; jet-black: 烏亮

的頭髮 jet-black hair

烏魯木齊（ㄨ ㄌㄨˇ ㄇㄨˋ ㄑㄧˊ）
Urumchi, old name of Tihwa (迪化), in Sinkiang (新疆)

烏龍茶（ㄨ ㄌㄨㄥˊ ㄔㄚˊ）
oolong (a variety of semifermented brown or amber tea from Taiwan)

烏干達（ㄨ ㄍㄢ ㄉㄚˊ）
Uganda

烏龜（ㄨ ㄍㄨㄟ）
① a turtle; a tortoise ② a cuckold; a man who is two-timed by his wife

烏克蘭（ㄨ ㄎㄜˋ ㄌㄢˊ）
Ukraine, Russia

烏合之眾（ㄨ ㄏㄜˊ ㄓ ㄓㄨㄥˋ）
a band of rebels or bandits characterized by lack of discipline and tight organization; a mob; a rabble

烏黑（ㄨ ㄏㄟ）
pitch-dark (night); raven black (hair)

烏呼（ㄨ ㄏㄨ）or烏虖（ㄨ ㄏㄨ）or烏嘑（ㄨ ㄏㄨ）or嗚呼（ㄨ ㄏㄨ）
Alas!

烏鷄（ㄨ ㄐㄧ）or烏骨鷄（ㄨ ㄍㄨˇ ㄐㄧ）
dark-boned and dark-skinned chicken (believed to be of more nutritious value than the ordinary species)

烏脚病（ㄨ ㄐㄧㄠˇ ㄅㄧㄥˋ）
the black foot disease, a kind of endemic ailment in southern Taiwan

烏桕（ㄨ ㄐㄧㄡˋ）or烏臼（ㄨ ㄐㄧㄡˋ）
Sapium sebiferum, the Chinese tallow tree

烏巾（ㄨ ㄐㄧㄣ）
a hat worn by an official in ancient China

烏江（ㄨ ㄐㄧㄤ）
① name of a stream in Anhwei, where Hsiang Yü (項羽), an arch rival of Liu Pang (劉邦), committed suicide ② former name of chien-chiang (黔江), the biggest river in Kweichow Province

烏七八糟（ㄨ ㄑㄧ ㄅㄚ ㄗㄠ）
in total disorder, confusion or pandemonium

烏騅（ㄨ ㄓㄨㄟ）
a dark stallion

烏紗帽（ㄨ ㄕㄚ ㄇㄠˋ）
a hat worn by officials in

ancient China (now used as a synonym of a government post)

烏賊（ㄨ ㄗˊ）
the cuttlefish; the inkfish

烏蘇里江（ㄨㄨ ㄌㄧˇ ㄐㄧㄤ）
the Ussuri River, a tributary of Heilungkiang

烏孫（ㄨ ㄙㄨㄣ）
name of an ancient state, west of the Han Empire

烏衣巷（ㄨ ㄧ ㄒㄧㄤˋ）
Black Gown Lane, a special residential area of the nobility in the Tsin (晉) Dynasty, southeast of today's Nanking

烏鴉（ㄨ ㄧㄚ）
a crow; a raven

烏鴉座（ㄨ ㄧㄚ ㄗㄨㄛˋ）
(astronomy) Corvus

烏有（ㄨ ㄧㄡˇ）
nothingness

烏有先生（ㄨ ㄧㄡˇ ㄒㄧㄢ ㄕㄥ）
Mr. Nobody—a fictitious character created by Su-Ma Hsiang-ju (司馬相如)

烏煙瘴氣（ㄨ ㄧㄢ ㄓㄤˋ ㄑㄧˋ）
(said of air) heavily polluted; now also used figuratively to indicate corruption, confusion, etc.

烏焉成馬（ㄨ ㄧㄢ ㄔㄥˊ ㄇㄚˇ）
Copying begets mistakes, as 烏 and 焉 are erroneously written as 馬 after being copied repeatedly.

烏魚（ㄨ ㄩˊ）
black mullet

烏魚子（ㄨ ㄩˊ ㄗˇ）
mullet's roe

烏雲（ㄨ ㄩㄣˊ）
①dark clouds ②(figuratively) a woman's black hair

烏雲密佈（ㄨ ㄩㄣˊ ㄇㄧˋ ㄅㄨˋ）
as dark clouds mass up—A heavy downpour is in the making or the situation is getting dangerous or imminent.

【烈】 3194
ㄌㄧㄝˋ lieh liè
1. fiery; acute; vehement; fierce; strong; violent
2. honest and virtuous; just and straightforward; chaste
3. merits; achievements

4. a Chinese family name

烈風（ㄌㄧㄝˋ ㄈㄥ）
a strong wind

烈婦（ㄌㄧㄝˋ ㄈㄨˋ）
①a woman who kills herself after her husband's death ②a woman or girl who dies to defend her chastity

烈女（ㄌㄧㄝˋ ㄋㄩˇ）
a girl of virtuous upbringing

烈烈（ㄌㄧㄝˋ ㄌㄧㄝˋ）
①majestic and imposing ②sad ③cold ④blazing

烈火（ㄌㄧㄝˋ ㄏㄨㄛˇ）
a blazing fire; a fierce fire

烈火轟雷（ㄌㄧㄝˋ ㄏㄨㄛˇ ㄏㄨㄥ ㄌㄟˊ）
quick-tempered; violent; ferocious

烈火見眞金（ㄌㄧㄝˋ ㄏㄨㄛˇ ㄐㄧㄢˋ ㄓㄣ ㄐㄧㄣ）
Pure gold proves its worth in a blazing fire.—Truth is ultimately clear; lies or slanders.或 True loyalty can stand the test of adversity.

烈酒（ㄌㄧㄝˋ ㄐㄧㄡˇ）
strong drink; a stiff drink

烈性（ㄌㄧㄝˋ ㄒㄧㄥˋ）
a straightforward but violent disposition

烈士（ㄌㄧㄝˋ ㄕˋ）or 烈漢（ㄌㄧㄝˋ ㄏㄢˋ）
martyrs; noble-hearted men who bow to neither intimidation nor temptation: 他們是革命烈士。They are revolutionary martyrs.

烈士殉名（ㄌㄧㄝˋ ㄕˋ ㄒㄩㄣˋ ㄇㄧㄥˊ）
An upright man dies in defense of his name.

烈暑（ㄌㄧㄝˋ ㄕㄨˇ）
summer at its hottest

烈日（ㄌㄧㄝˋ ㄖˋ）
the scorching sun

烈日當空（ㄌㄧㄝˋ ㄖˋ ㄉㄤ ㄎㄨㄥ）
the scorching sun high up in the sky

烈祖（ㄌㄧㄝˋ ㄗㄨˇ）
an illustrious ancestor

烈焰（ㄌㄧㄝˋ ㄧㄢˋ）
blazing flames; a violent or fierce fire

【烝】 3195
ㄓㄥ jeng zhēng
1. to rise—as steam
2. many; numerous

3. lewdness, incest, etc. among the older generation
4. to steam 亦作「蒸」

烝民（ㄓㄥ ㄇㄧㄣˊ）
the people; the masses

烝黎（ㄓㄥ ㄌㄧˊ）
the people; the masses

烝烝（ㄓㄥ ㄓㄥ）
①rising and flourishing ②(now rarely) sincere and filial

〔火部〕

【烊】 3196
ㄧㄤˊ yang yáng
to smelt; to melt

烊金（ㄧㄤˊ ㄐㄧㄣ）
molten metal; molten metal ores

【烘】 3197
ㄏㄨㄥ hong hōng
1. to bake; to roast
2. to dry or warm near a fire

烘焙（ㄏㄨㄥ ㄅㄟˋ）
to dry (herbal medicine) over a fire

烘托（ㄏㄨㄥ ㄊㄨㄛ）
(said of writing or painting) to make conspicuous by contrast

烘暖（ㄏㄨㄥ ㄋㄨㄢˇ）
to warm by fire

烘爐（ㄏㄨㄥ ㄌㄨˊ）
a baking oven; a portable stove or furnace

烘乾（ㄏㄨㄥ ㄍㄢ）
to dry beside or over a fire

烘乾機（ㄏㄨㄥ ㄍㄢ ㄐㄧ）
a clothing dryer

烘烤（ㄏㄨㄥ ㄎㄠˇ）or 烘焙（ㄏㄨㄥ ㄅㄟˋ）
to bake; to roast; to warm or dry by the fire

烘烘（ㄏㄨㄥ ㄏㄨㄥ）
①warm and cozy ②(said of a fire) blazing ③(said of a crowd) noisy and jubilant

烘焦（ㄏㄨㄥ ㄐㄧㄠ）
(said of cloth, paper, etc.) to get partially burned because of over-heating near the fire

烘襯（ㄏㄨㄥ ㄔㄣˋ）
(said of writing or painting) to make conspicuous by contrast or other means

烘染（ㄏㄨㄥ ㄖㄢˇ）
to emphasize the most important point by elaboration

〔火部〕

烘雲托月(ㄏㄨㄥ ㄩㄣ ㄊㄨㄛ ㄩㄝ)
to bring something out with the help of a favorable background; to make something more noticeable by contrast

【烤】 3198 (ㄎㄠ kao kǎo)
1. to roast; to bake; to toast
2. to warm by a fire
3. scorching

烤餅(ㄎㄠ ㄅㄧˇ)
to bake a cake

烤麵包(ㄎㄠ ㄇㄧㄢˋ ㄅㄠ)
to bake bread; to toast bread

烤麵包機(ㄎㄠ ㄇㄧㄢˋ ㄅㄠ ㄐㄧ)
a toaster

烤爐(ㄎㄠ ㄌㄨˊ)
an oven

烤火(ㄎㄠ ㄏㄨㄛˇ)
to warm by the fire

烤焦(ㄎㄠ ㄐㄧㄠ)
burned in roasting or baking

烤箱(ㄎㄠ ㄒㄧㄤ)
an oven for baking

烤肉(ㄎㄠ ㄖㄡˋ)
①to roast meat; to barbecue: 我們烤肉和馬鈴薯。We roasted meat and potatoes.
②barbecue; meat roasted on an open fire

烤一烤(ㄎㄠ ㄧ ㄎㄠ)
①to warm or dry near a fire ②to roast for a little while

烤鴨(ㄎㄠ ㄧㄚ)
①to roast duck ②roasted duck

【烟】 3199 (ㄧㄢ ian yān)
simplified form of 煙

【烙】 3200 (ㄌㄠˋ law lào)
(讀音 ㄌㄨㄛˋ luoò luò)
1. to burn
2. to brand; to iron
3. to bake in a pan

烙餅(ㄌㄠˋ ㄅㄧˇ)
a kind of thick, hard pancake ②the baking of such a cake

烙鐵(ㄌㄠˋ ㄊㄧㄝˇ)
an iron; a branding iron

烙印(ㄌㄠˋ ㄧㄣˋ)
to brand; a brand

七畫

【烽】 3201 (ㄈㄥ feng fēng)
(in ancient China) a tall structure (on a city wall, etc.) where fire was made to signal enemy invasion or presence of bandits

烽鼓(ㄈㄥ ㄍㄨˇ)
signal fires and drums—war

烽候(ㄈㄥ ㄏㄡˋ)
to erect a watchtower to detect enemy's presence

烽火(ㄈㄥ ㄏㄨㄛˇ)
signal fires; beacon fires

烽火臺(ㄈㄥ ㄏㄨㄛˇ ㄊㄞˊ)
a tall structure for lighting a signal or beacon fire

烽火連年(ㄈㄥ ㄏㄨㄛˇ ㄌㄧㄢˊ ㄋㄧㄢˊ)
continuous wars

烽燧(ㄈㄥ ㄙㄨㄟˋ)
fire and smoke used as warning signals during night and day respectively

烽煙(ㄈㄥ ㄧㄢ)
smoke used as a warning signal

烽煙遍地(ㄈㄥ ㄧㄢ ㄅㄧㄢˋ ㄉㄧˋ)
Beacon fires are found everywhere.

烽煙四起(ㄈㄥ ㄧㄢ ㄙˋ ㄑㄧˇ)
a land or country beset by war

【烹】 3202 (ㄆㄥ peng pēng)
1. to cook; to boil; to decoct
2. (cooking) to add bean sauce and dressing after frying
3. (slang) to frighten (away)

烹調(ㄆㄥ ㄊㄧㄠˊ)
to cook or prepare (food); cooking

烹醢(ㄆㄥ ㄏㄞˇ)
the most frightening tortures for prisoners in ancient China

烹煮(ㄆㄥ ㄓㄨˇ)
to cook; to boil

烹茶(ㄆㄥ ㄔㄚˊ)
to make tea: 她為客人烹茶。She makes tea for the guests.

烹飪(ㄆㄥ ㄖㄣˋ)
to cook; cooking

烹飪法(ㄆㄥ ㄖㄣˋ ㄈㄚˇ)
a culinary art; cookery; a recipe

【焄】 3203 (ㄒㄩㄣ shiun xūn)
1. rising flames or fumes
2. aroma

【焉】 3204 (ㄧㄢ ian yān)
1. an interrogative—how, why, when, etc.
2. a pronoun—it
3. an adverb—there; here
4. a conjunctive—and so; so that
5. a final particle indicating numerous senses

焉得(ㄧㄢ ㄉㄜˊ)
How can one be (or attain)...?

焉能(ㄧㄢ ㄋㄥˊ)
How can (one do it, succeed,etc.)?

焉敢(ㄧㄢ ㄍㄢˇ)
How dare...?

焉支(ㄧㄢ ㄓ)
name of a mountain in Kansu Province

焉知(ㄧㄢ ㄓ)
How could one know...?

焉知非福(ㄧㄢ ㄓ ㄈㄟ ㄈㄨˊ)
How could you know it is not a blessing?

焉有(ㄧㄢ ㄧㄡˇ)
How could there be such...?

焉用(ㄧㄢ ㄩㄥˋ)
Why is it necessary to use...? 或 Is it needed?

【烺】 3205 (ㄌㄤˇ laang lǎng)
(said of fire) bright

【烷】 3206 (ㄨㄢˊ wan wán)
1. fire
2. alkane

烷基(ㄨㄢˊ ㄐㄧ)
(chemistry) alkyl

【烯】 3207 (ㄒㄧ shi xī)
1.the color of fire
2.alkene

八畫

【焙】 3208 (ㄅㄟˋ bey bèi)
to dry or heat near a fire; to toast; to bake

焙粉(ㄅㄟˋ ㄈㄣˇ)

baking powder 亦作「發粉」

焙爐（ㄆㄟ ㄌㄨ）
an oven; a toaster

焙乾（ㄆㄟ ㄍㄢ）
to dry by fire

焙茶（ㄆㄟ ㄔㄚ）
to dry tea by fire

【焮】 3209
ㄒㄧㄣ shinn xin
1. to burn; to heat; to cauterize
2. "heat" in Chinese medicine

焮天（ㄒㄧㄣ ㄊㄧㄢ）
(said of a big fire) fiercely burning

焮腫（ㄒㄧㄣ ㄓㄨㄥˇ）
(medicine) a skin swelling or inflammation

【焯】 3210
ㄓㄨㄛ jwo zhuó
1. same as 灼—to burn
2. bright and brilliant

【焚】 3211
ㄈㄣˊ fern fén
to burn; to set fire to

焚斃（ㄈㄣˊ ㄅㄧˋ）
to burn to death; to be burned to death

焚滅（ㄈㄣˊ ㄇㄧㄝˋ）
to burn down to nothing; to destroy by fire

焚溺（ㄈㄣˊ ㄋㄧˋ）
to be burned or drowned—to be in great difficulty

焚掠（ㄈㄣˊ ㄌㄩㄝˋ）
to burn and loot; burning and pillaging

焚膏繼晷（ㄈㄣˊ ㄍㄠ ㄐㄧˋ ㄍㄨㄟˇ）
to burn the midnight oil —(figuratively) to be very diligent in study

焚化（ㄈㄣˊ ㄏㄨㄚˋ）
①to cremate ②to burn (offerings, etc.) for the dead ③to put to fire

焚化爐（ㄈㄣˊ ㄏㄨㄚˋ ㄌㄨˊ）
an incinerator

焚毀（ㄈㄣˊ ㄏㄨㄟˇ）
to burn up; to destroy by fire; to consume by burning

焚掠（ㄈㄣˊ ㄐㄩㄝˋ）
to burn and loot; burning and pillaging

焚琴煮鶴（ㄈㄣˊ ㄑㄧㄣˊ ㄓㄨˇ ㄏㄜˋ）
to burn the *chin* (a musical instrument) and cook the crane—(figuratively). to

pour cold water on something interesting or exciting; to spoil the fun

焚修（ㄈㄣˊ ㄒㄧㄡ）
to burn incense and discipline oneself according to the strict rules of Buddhism or Taoism

焚香（ㄈㄣˊ ㄒㄧㄤ）
to burn incense (in worship, offering, etc.)

焚香膜拜（ㄈㄣˊ ㄒㄧㄤ ㄇㄛˊ ㄅㄞˋ）
to worship at temples

焚芝（ㄈㄣˊ ㄓ）
good people or virtuous persons being involved in trouble or incriminated with trumped-up charges

焚舟（ㄈㄣˊ ㄓㄡ）
to burn the boat after crossing the river; to cross the Rubicon—There's no going back.

焚燒（ㄈㄣˊ ㄕㄠ）
to consume by fire; to burn; to destroy by burning: 他焚燒他所有的信。He burned all his letters.

焚身（ㄈㄣˊ ㄕㄣ）
to bring ruin to oneself because of greediness

焚書坑儒（ㄈㄣˊ ㄕㄨ ㄎㄥ ㄖㄨˊ）
to burn the books and bury the scholars alive—said of Shih Huang of the Chin (秦) Dynasty

焚如（ㄈㄣˊ ㄖㄨˊ）
a fire disaster

焚硯 or **焚研**（ㄈㄣˊ ㄧㄢˋ）
to destroy the ink-slab—to write no more because others write so much better

【焱】 3212
(簡) ㄧㄢˋ yann yàn
flames

【焦】 3213
ㄐㄧㄠ jiau jiāo
1. scorched or burned; charred
2. the smell or stench of things burned
3. worried and anxious
4. a Chinese family name

焦不離孟，孟不離焦（ㄐㄧㄠ ㄅㄨˋ ㄌㄧˊ ㄇㄥˋ，ㄇㄥˋ ㄅㄨˋ ㄌㄧˊ ㄐㄧㄠ）
Damon and Pythias

焦平面（ㄐㄧㄠ ㄆㄧㄥˊ ㄇㄧㄢˋ）
a focal plane

焦煤（ㄐㄧㄠ ㄇㄟˊ）
coke

焦悶（ㄐㄧㄠ ㄇㄣˋ）
①(said of weather) hot and humid or oppressive ②worried and anxious; harassed; a depressive mood

焦點（ㄐㄧㄠ ㄉㄧㄢˇ）
① focus ② a burning point; a point of tremendous significance; a focal point

焦頭爛額（ㄐㄧㄠ ㄊㄡˊ ㄌㄢˋ ㄜˊ）
(literally) to suffer burns on head and forehead when fighting a fire—in great trouble or difficulty; in straits; in bad shape

焦炭（ㄐㄧㄠ ㄊㄢˋ）
coke

焦土（ㄐㄧㄠ ㄊㄨˇ）
scorched earth—ravages of war

焦土抗戰（ㄐㄧㄠ ㄊㄨˇ ㄎㄤˋ ㄓㄢˋ）
to adopt a scorched earth policy in fighting the invading enemy

焦土政策（ㄐㄧㄠ ㄊㄨˇ ㄓㄥˋ ㄘㄜˋ）
the scorched earth policy

焦桐（ㄐㄧㄠ ㄊㄨㄥˊ）
a Chinese lute or lyre

焦勞（ㄐㄧㄠ ㄌㄠˊ）
worried and worn down by hard work

焦慮（ㄐㄧㄠ ㄌㄩˋ）
deeply worried and anxious

焦慮不安（ㄐㄧㄠ ㄌㄩˋ ㄅㄨˋ ㄢ）
to be on pins and needles

焦渴（ㄐㄧㄠ ㄎㄜˇ）
① very thirsty ② very anxious

焦枯（ㄐㄧㄠ ㄎㄨ）
withered (by heat)

焦黃（ㄐㄧㄠ ㄏㄨㄤˊ）
pale yellow

焦急（ㄐㄧㄠ ㄐㄧˊ）
very anxious; in deep anxiety

焦竭（ㄐㄧㄠ ㄐㄧㄝˊ）
worried and exhausted

焦距（ㄐㄧㄠ ㄐㄩˋ）
(physics) focal length or focal distance; focus: 這相片對準了焦距。This photograph is in focus.

焦心（ㄐㄧㄠ ㄒㄧㄣ）
anxious; worried

〔火 部〕

〔火部〕

焦灼(ㄐㄧㄠ ㄓㄨㄛ)
①burned by fire ②anxious; worried

焦熱(ㄐㄧㄠ ㄖㄜˋ)
burning heat; scorching hot

焦熱電現象(ㄐㄧㄠ ㄖㄜˋ ㄉㄧㄢˋ ㄒㄧㄢˋ)
pyroelectricity

焦棗兒(ㄐㄧㄠ ㄗㄠˇ)
fire-dried dates—a specialty in Northern China

焦躁(ㄐㄧㄠ ㄗㄠˋ)
worried, anxious and getting impatient; getting restless because of anxiety

焦思(ㄐㄧㄠ ㄙ)
deep worry: 焦思使她不能入睡。 Deep worry kept her awake.

焦散面(ㄐㄧㄠ ㄙㄢˋ ㄇㄧㄢˋ)
(optics) the caustic surface

焦爾定律 or 焦耳定律(ㄐㄧㄠ ㄦˇ ㄉㄧㄥˋ ㄌㄩˋ)
(physics) Joule's Law

焦爾熱 or 焦耳熱(ㄐㄧㄠ ㄦˇ ㄖㄜˋ)
Joule's heat

焦油(ㄐㄧㄠ ㄧㄡˊ)
tar

焦油腦(ㄐㄧㄠ ㄧㄡˊ ㄋㄠˇ)
naphthalene

【無】 3214
ㄨˊ wu wú

1. negative; not; no; none
2. without; destitute of; wanting; to lack; to have not
3. no matter what (or how); not yet
4. a Chinese family name

無巴鼻(ㄨˊ ㄅㄚ ㄅㄧˊ)
to have nothing to hold on; unreal

無備(ㄨˊ ㄅㄟˋ)
unprepared; without preparation

無被花(ㄨˊ ㄅㄟˋ ㄏㄨㄚ)
an achlamydeous flower

無報酬(ㄨˊ ㄅㄠˋ ㄔㄡˊ)
without pay, recompense or reward; gratuitous

無比(ㄨˊ ㄅㄧˇ)
incomparable; incomparably; extremely; without peer; peerless; matchless

無裨(ㄨˊ ㄅㄧˋ)
won't help; useless

無邊(ㄨˊ ㄅㄧㄢ)

limitless; vast and expansive

無邊風月(ㄨˊ ㄅㄧㄢ ㄈㄥ ㄩㄝˋ)
boundless natural charms

無邊無際(ㄨˊ ㄅㄧㄢ ㄨˊ ㄐㄧˋ)
boundless; limitless; vast

無邊無涯(ㄨˊ ㄅㄧㄢ ㄨˊ ㄧㄚˊ)
without restraints of any sort

無病呻吟(ㄨˊ ㄅㄧㄥˋ ㄕㄣ ㄧㄣˊ)
(literally) to groan when there is no physical pain—① to groan for no reason; to complain without a cause ② (said of writing) affected sentimentality

無病自炙(ㄨˊ ㄅㄧㄥˋ ㄗˋ ㄐㄧˋ)
to bring trouble to oneself by making uncalled-for moves

無補(ㄨˊ ㄅㄨˇ)
useless; of no avail or use; won't help: 空談無補於事實。 Mere words won't help facts.

無不(ㄨˊ ㄅㄨˋ)
all without exception; invariably

無不如意(ㄨˊ ㄅㄨˋ ㄖㄨˊ ㄧˋ)
to have everything go one's way

無朋(ㄨˊ ㄆㄥˊ)
incomparable; incomparably; peerless; matchless

無偏無頗(ㄨˊ ㄆㄧㄢ ㄨˊ ㄆㄛ)
very just; unbiased; impartial: 法律應該一視同仁無偏無頗。 Law shall be uniform and impartial.

無米之炊(ㄨˊ ㄇㄧˇ ㄓ ㄔㄨㄟ)
(Even a capable woman cannot prepare) a meal without rice—impossible for lacking the most essential

無明(ㄨˊ ㄇㄧㄥˊ)
(Buddhism) avidya, ignorance, nescience, unknowing—the primary or fundamental root of all evil and suffering in the world

無明火(ㄨˊ ㄇㄧㄥˊ ㄏㄨㄛˇ)
fury; wrath; anger

無名小卒(ㄨˊ ㄇㄧㄥˊ ㄒㄧㄠˇ ㄗㄨˊ)
a nobody; an unimportant person; small fry

無名指(ㄨˊ ㄇㄧㄥˊ ㄓˇ)
the ring finger

無名氏(ㄨˊ ㄇㄧㄥˊ ㄕˋ)

Mr. Anonymous—usually used by a person who contributes to a charitable cause without revealing his name

無名作家(ㄨˊ ㄇㄧㄥˊ ㄗㄨㄛˋ ㄐㄧㄚ)
①an anonymous writer ② an unknown writer

無名業火(ㄨˊ ㄇㄧㄥˊ ㄧㄝˋ ㄏㄨㄛˇ)
irrepressible anger

無名英雄(ㄨˊ ㄇㄧㄥˊ ㄧㄥ ㄒㄩㄥˊ)
an unsung hero; an unknown soldier (for a cause)

無目的(ㄨˊ ㄇㄨˋ ㄉㄧˋ)
aimless; without objective; at random: 他過着無目的的生活。 He leads an aimless life.

無法(ㄨˊ ㄈㄚˇ)
unable; incapable: 我們無法應付困難。 We are unable to cope with difficulties.

無法可想(ㄨˊ ㄈㄚˇ ㄎㄜˇ ㄒㄧㄤˇ)
no way out; no alternative; at the end of one's rope; powerless

無法形容(ㄨˊ ㄈㄚˇ ㄒㄧㄥˊ ㄖㄨㄥˊ)
beyond description

無法可施(ㄨˊ ㄈㄚˇ ㄎㄜˇ ㄕ)
unable to do anything about it

無法無天(ㄨˊ ㄈㄚˇ ㄨˊ ㄊㄧㄢ)
lawless and godless; to be totally devoid of conscience and respect for law; recklessly

無非(ㄨˊ ㄈㄟ)
no other than; only; no more than; nothing but: 無非是好壞兩種後果。There are only two consequences, a good one and a bad one.

無分彼此(ㄨˊ ㄈㄣ ㄅㄧˇ ㄘˇ)
one for all and all for one

無分軒輊(ㄨˊ ㄈㄣ ㄒㄩㄢ ㄓˋ)
a draw or tie; well-matched

無分(ㄨˊ ㄈㄣˋ)
①to have nothing to do with it ②to be denied a share

無方(ㄨˊ ㄈㄤ)
①no set rules, regulations, or precedents; no set pattern ②not the right method; the wrong way (of bringing up a child)

無妨(ㄨˊ ㄈㄤˊ)
①doesn't matter; unimpor-

tant ② do not constitute an obstacle or obstruction; there's no harm

無風(ㄨㄈㄥ)
(meteorology) calm: 昨天海上無風。The sea was calm yesterday.

無風不起浪(ㄨㄈㄥㄅㄨˋㄑㄧˇㄌㄤˋ)
(literally) There won't be billows when there's no wind.—There must be a cause or reason for this.

無風起浪(ㄨㄈㄥㄑㄧˇㄌㄤˋ)
to start a big trouble out of nothing

無風三尺浪(ㄨㄈㄥㄙㄢㄔˇㄌㄤˋ)
(literally) There are billows three feet high (on the sea) even if there is no wind.—A sea voyage is full of risks.

無道(ㄨㄉㄠˋ)
tyranny; tyrannical; injustice; unjust

無黨無派(ㄨㄉㄤˇㄨㄆㄞˋ)
without party affiliation of any sort; nonpartisan

無敵(ㄨㄉㄧˊ)
without match; matchless; invincible

無敵不克(ㄨㄉㄧˊㄅㄨˋㄎㄜˋ)
to make conquests on all sides; to smash whoever stands in the way

無敵艦隊(ㄨㄉㄧˊㄐㄧㄢˋㄉㄨㄟˋ)
the Invincible Armada

無底洞(ㄨㄉㄧˇㄉㄨㄥˋ)
(literally) the bottomless pit—human greed or desires (which can never be fully satisfied); any hobby or pursuit which requires an inexhaustible supply of funds

無抵抗主義(ㄨㄉㄧˇㄎㄤˋㄓㄨˇㄧˋ)
the Principle of Non-resistance, initiated by Lev Nikolaevich Tolstoy, 1828-1910, also known as Tolstoyism

無的放矢(ㄨㄉㄧˋㄈㄤˋㄕˇ)
(literally) to shoot without a target—indiscriminate; to attack without a cause; to make unfounded charges or accusations

無地自容(ㄨㄉㄧˋㄗˋㄖㄨㄥˊ)
(literally) no place to hide—extremely embarrassed or

ashamed: 他因他所做的事無地自容。He is extremely ashamed of what he did.

無定形(ㄨㄉㄧㄥˋㄒㄧㄥˊ)
amorphous; formless

無毒(ㄨㄉㄨˊ)
poisonless; harmless: 有些蛇無毒。Some snakes are poisonless.

無毒不丈夫(ㄨㄉㄨˊㄅㄨˋㄓㄤˋㄈㄨ)
Ruthlessness is the mark of a truly great man. 或 One who is not ruthless is not a truly great man.

無獨有偶(ㄨㄉㄨˊㄧㄡˇㄡˇ)
It happens that there is a similar case. 或 by coincidence

無度(ㄨㄉㄨˋ)
without restraints; very indulgent: 他飲酒無度。He drank without restraints.

無多有少(ㄨㄉㄨㄛㄧㄡˇㄕㄠˇ)
(said of a contribution to a charity) It doesn't matter how much.

無端(ㄨㄉㄨㄢ)
without cause or reason; unprovoked; unjustified: 他無端生氣。He was angry without cause.

無多冬夏(ㄨㄉㄨㄛㄉㄨㄥㄒㄧㄚˋ)
It doesn't matter whether it is summer or winter.

無動於衷(ㄨㄉㄨㄥˋㄩˊㄓㄨㄥ)
①unmoved; flinty-hearted; callous: 她對我的忠告無動於衷。She is callous to my advice. ②to remain firm; to stand pat

無頭案(ㄨㄊㄡˊㄢˋ)
a criminal case without any clues

無頭無腦(ㄨㄊㄡˊㄨㄋㄠˇ)
disorderly and confused; muddled and mixed-up

無頭無尾(ㄨㄊㄡˊㄨㄨㄟˇ)
without head or tail—confused, muddled or mixed-up

無題(ㄨㄊㄧˊ)
(usually serving as a title of a poem) "Without a Title"—a poem which says more than a title can contain

無條件投降(ㄨㄊㄧㄠˊㄐㄧㄢˋㄊㄡˊㄒㄧㄤˊ)
unconditional surrender: 中

國接受日本無條件投降。China accepted Japan's unconditional surrender.

無忝所生(ㄨㄊㄧㄢˇㄙㄨㄛˇㄕㄥ)
Don't do anything to bring shame on your parents!

無他(ㄨㄊㄚ)
①nothing else; for no other reason than ②loyal; dedicated ③in good health; safe 亦作[無恙]

無痛分娩法(ㄨㄊㄨㄥˋㄈㄣㄇㄧㄢˇㄈㄚˇ)
painless delivery

無奈(ㄨㄋㄞˋ)
can't help it; having no alternative

無能(ㄨㄋㄥˊ)
incompetent; inefficient; incapable; without talent

無能為力(ㄨㄋㄥˊㄨㄟˊㄌㄧˋ)
unable to help; can't do anything about it; powerless

無寧(ㄨㄋㄧㄥˊ)
to prefer; rather...

無賴(ㄨㄌㄞˋ)
a villain; a rascal

無漏(ㄨㄌㄡˋ)
(Buddhism) anasrava, no drip, leak or flow—passionless; outside the passion stream

無理(ㄨㄌㄧˇ)
unreasonable; unjustifiable

無理方程式(ㄨㄌㄧˇㄈㄤㄔㄥˊㄕˋ)
an irrational equation

無理函數(ㄨㄌㄧˇㄏㄢˊㄕㄨˋ)
(mathematics) an irrational quantity

無理取鬧(ㄨㄌㄧˇㄑㄩˇㄋㄠˋ)
to make trouble without a cause; to make trouble out of nothing

無理要求(ㄨㄌㄧˇㄧㄠˋㄑㄧㄡˊ)
unjustifiable demands

無力(ㄨㄌㄧˋ)
①feeble; weak ②cannot afford; too poor to do something: 我無力在台北購買房子。I cannot afford to buy a house in Taipei.

無利可圖(ㄨㄌㄧˋㄎㄜˇㄊㄨˊ)
profitless: 這是無利可圖的買賣。This is a profitless business.

無立錐之地(ㄨㄌㄧˋㄓㄨㄟㄓㄉㄧˋ)
very poor; stark poverty: 他

〔火部〕

〔火部〕

窮得無立錐之地。He is very poor.

無聊(ㄨ ㄌㄧㄠ)
①listless; ennui; boring; boredom; (feeling) indifferent and uninteresting ②nonsensical; silly: 不要講這種無聊話。Don't make such silly remarks.

無聊賴(ㄨ ㄌㄧㄠ ㄌㄞˋ)
disappointed and discouraged

無良(ㄨ ㄌㄧㄤˊ)
no good; without virtue or principle

無兩(ㄨ ㄌㄧㄤˇ)or 無二(ㄨ ㄦˋ)
matchless; without match; unique: 這幅圖畫被認為是獨一無二的。The picture is thought to be unique.

無量(ㄨ ㄌㄧㄤˋ)
limitless; boundless

無量佛(ㄨ ㄌㄧㄤˋ ㄈㄛˊ)or 無量壽(ㄨ ㄌㄧㄤˋ ㄕㄡˋ)
①boundless, infinite life ②a name of Amitabha

無路可走(ㄨ ㄌㄨˋ ㄎㄜˇ ㄗㄡˇ)
at the end of one's rope; at one's wit's end; no way out; to come to a dead end

無論(ㄨ ㄌㄨㄣˋ)
①no matter; whatever; regardless: 無論誰都不能違法。Nobody is supposed to break laws, no matter who he is. ②not to mention the fact that; let alone; to say nothing of

無論如何(ㄨ ㄌㄨㄣˋ ㄖㄨˊ ㄏㄜˊ)
no matter what; anyway; in any case; under all circumstances; come what may

無告(ㄨ ㄍㄠˋ)
with no one to turn to for help

無垢(ㄨ ㄍㄡˋ)
spotless

無干(ㄨ ㄍㄢ)
no concern (of mine, yours, etc.); nothing to do (with you, me, him, etc.): 這事與我無干。It has nothing to do with me.

無根無蒂(ㄨ ㄍㄣ ㄨ ㄉㄧˋ)
without ground; groundless; with nothing to rely on

---

innocent; guiltless; the innocent: 這司機並非無辜。The driver was not guiltless.

無骨(ㄨ ㄍㄨˇ)
①(literally) without a bone —without the backbone ②(said of a girl dancing, etc.) soft and graceful (as if she were without a bone in her body)

無故(ㄨ ㄍㄨˋ)
without cause or reason; uncalled-for: 學生不得無故缺席。Students may not be absent without reason.

無怪(ㄨ ㄍㄨㄞˋ)or 無怪乎(ㄨ ㄍㄨㄞˋ ㄏㄨ)
It's not strange that... 或no wonder that; naturally: 無怪乎他會失敗。No wonder that he has failed.

無軌電車(ㄨ ㄍㄨㄟˇ ㄉㄧㄢˋ ㄔㄜ)
a trolley car; a trolley bus

無軌可循(ㄨ ㄍㄨㄟˇ ㄎㄜˇ ㄒㄩㄣˊ)
no precedent to follow

無鬼論(ㄨ ㄍㄨㄟˇ ㄌㄨㄣˋ)
a theory refuting the existence of ghosts or spirits advanced by Juan Chan (阮瞻) of the Tsin Dynasty

無關(ㄨ ㄍㄨㄢ)
no relationship; no concern; no connection; irrelevant; to have nothing to do with: 此事與我們無關。It has nothing to do with us.

無關痛癢(ㄨ ㄍㄨㄢ ㄊㄨㄥˋ ㄧㄤˇ)
not important at all; of no concern or consequence

無關宏旨(ㄨ ㄍㄨㄢ ㄏㄨㄥˊ ㄓˇ)
insignificant; of no consequence; unimportant

無關緊要(ㄨ ㄍㄨㄢ ㄐㄧㄣˇ ㄧㄠˋ)
not important; of no consequence or significance: 這事無關緊要。This matter is not important.

無官一身輕(ㄨ ㄍㄨㄢ ㄧ ㄕㄣ ㄑㄧㄥ)
One feels carefree when he is relieved of official duties.

無功受祿(ㄨ ㄍㄨㄥ ㄕㄡˋ ㄌㄨˋ)
to get the reward without real achievements or contributions

無可奈何(ㄨ ㄎㄜˇ ㄋㄞˋ ㄏㄜˊ)or 無可如何(ㄨ ㄎㄜˇ ㄖㄨˊ ㄏㄜˊ)
having no alternative; to

---

have to; powerless

無可厚非(ㄨ ㄎㄜˇ ㄏㄡˋ ㄈㄟ)
shouldn't be blamed too much for that—no serious mistakes committed

無可救藥(ㄨ ㄎㄜˇ ㄐㄧㄡˋ ㄧㄠˋ)
incorrigible; incurable

無可置疑(ㄨ ㄎㄜˇ ㄓˋ ㄧˊ)
beyond doubt; cannot be doubted: 他的誠懇是無可置疑的。His honesty is beyond doubt.

無可爭辯(ㄨ ㄎㄜˇ ㄓㄥ ㄅㄧㄢˋ)
indisputable: 這是無可爭辯的事實。This is an indisputable fact.

無可無不可(ㄨ ㄎㄜˇ ㄨ ㄅㄨˋ ㄎㄜˇ)
yes and no (an expression used to indicate an ambiguous attitude)

無愧(ㄨ ㄎㄨㄟˋ)
with a clear conscience; able to look people straight in the eye

無愧色(ㄨ ㄎㄨㄟˋ ㄙㄜˋ)
without any expression of shame, regret or embarrassment

無孔不入(ㄨ ㄎㄨㄥˇ ㄅㄨˋ ㄖㄨˋ)
to let no opportunity slip by (in the pursuit of one's selfish ends); (to serve self-interest) by hook or by crook; to exploit every crack or loophole one can find

無何有之鄉(ㄨ ㄏㄜˊ ㄧㄡˇ ㄓ ㄒㄧㄤ)
(originally from *Chuang Tzu*) a world where nothing really exists

無害(ㄨ ㄏㄞˋ)
harmless; not injurious

無後(ㄨ ㄏㄡˋ)
heirless; without posterity

無後座力砲(ㄨ ㄏㄡˋ ㄗㄨㄛˋ ㄌㄧˋ ㄆㄠˋ)
a recoilless gun

無後為大(ㄨ ㄏㄡˋ ㄨㄟˊ ㄉㄚˋ)
Having no male heir is the gravest of the three cardinal offenses against filial piety. 參看「不孝有三」。

無恆(ㄨ ㄏㄥˊ)or 無恆心(ㄨ ㄏㄥˊ ㄒㄧㄣ)
lacking perseverance; without persistency; without patience; without consistency

無花果(ㄨ ㄏㄨㄚ ㄍㄨㄛˇ)

the fig

無話不談 (ㄨˊ ㄏㄨㄚˋ ㄅㄨˋ ㄊㄢˊ)
to keep no secrets from each other

無毀無譽 (ㄨˊ ㄏㄨㄟˇ ㄨˊ ㄩˋ)
(literally) neither criticism nor praise—just so-so; passable; merely acceptable

無稽 (ㄨˊ ㄐㄧ)
wild (talks, rumors, etc.); groundless

無稽之談 (ㄨˊ ㄐㄧ ㄓ ㄊㄢˊ)or 無稽之言 (ㄨˊ ㄐㄧ ㄓ ㄧㄢˊ)
groundless utterances; wild talks; rumors; sheer nonsense

無機 (ㄨˊ ㄐㄧ)
(chemistry) inorganic

無機體 (ㄨˊ ㄐㄧ ㄊㄧˇ)or無機物 (ㄨˊ ㄐㄧ ㄨˋ)
inorganic matters; inorganic substances

無機化合物 (ㄨˊ ㄐㄧ ㄏㄨㄚˋ ㄏㄜˊ ㄨˋ)
inorganic compounds

無機化學 (ㄨˊ ㄐㄧ ㄏㄨㄚˋ ㄒㄩㄝˊ)
inorganic chemistry

無極 (ㄨˊ ㄐㄧˊ)
① a mind completely devoid of worries, thought or desires (a philosophical theory initiated by Chou Tun-yi (周敦頤) of the Sung Dynasty) ②name of a county in Hopeh Province

無疾而終 (ㄨˊ ㄐㄧˊ ㄦˊ ㄓㄨㄥ)
to die without any apparent ailment or disease

無籍游民 (ㄨˊ ㄐㄧˊ ㄧㄡˊ ㄇㄧㄣˊ)
vagrants without homes

無幾 (ㄨˊ ㄐㄧˇ)
① not much; not many; little; almost the same: 我們兩人年齡相差無幾。We are almost the same age. ②not long afterwards; shortly

無給職 (ㄨˊ ㄐㄧˇ ㄓˊ)
a position without pay; an honorary post

無際 (ㄨˊ ㄐㄧˋ)
(said of space)boundless: 我喜歡一望無際的海洋。I like the boundless ocean.

無記 (ㄨˊ ㄐㄧˋ)
(Buddhism) unrecordable (either as good or bad)

無記名投票 (ㄨˊ ㄐㄧˋ ㄇㄧㄥˊ ㄊㄡˊ ㄆㄧㄠˋ)
secret ballot

無計可施 (ㄨˊ ㄐㄧˋ ㄎㄜˇ ㄕ)
at the end of one's rope; helpless; powerless; at one's wit's end: 我對此事無計可施。I am quite powerless in the matter.

無濟於事 (ㄨˊ ㄐㄧˋ ㄩˊ ㄕˋ)
won't help the matter; not enough by a long shot; inadequate; to no avail; to no effect; of no avail

無家可歸 (ㄨˊ ㄐㄧㄚ ㄎㄜˇ ㄍㄨㄟ)
homeless; without a home to go back to

無價之寶 (ㄨˊ ㄐㄧㄚˋ ㄓ ㄅㄠˇ)
a priceless treasure; an invaluable asset: 那件藝術品是無價之寶。That is a priceless work of art.

無解 (ㄨˊ ㄐㄧㄝˇ)
insolvable

無噍類 (ㄨˊ ㄐㄧㄠˋ ㄌㄟˋ)
all dead—no survivors

無堅不摧 (ㄨˊ ㄐㄧㄢ ㄅㄨˋ ㄘㄨㄟ)
to overrun all fortifications; to be all-conquering

無間 (ㄨˊ ㄐㄧㄢ)
① nonstop; continuous: 兩國合作無間。The two countries cooperated continuously. ② close and intimate

無盡藏 (ㄨˊ ㄐㄧㄣˋ ㄗㄤˋ)
(Buddhism)virtue that encompasses all

無盡無休 (ㄨˊ ㄐㄧㄣˋ ㄨˊ ㄒㄧㄡ)
continuous; endlessly; boundless; limitless

無疆 (ㄨˊ ㄐㄧㄤ)
boundless; limitless

無精打采 (ㄨˊ ㄐㄧㄥ ㄉㄚˇ ㄘㄞˇ)
listless; indifferent; low-spirited; not interested; discouraged or disappointed; despondent; dejected: 他們無精打采地握著手。They shook hands rather listlessly.

無莖植物 (ㄨˊ ㄐㄧㄥ ㄓˊ ㄨˋ)
plants without stems—a general name for all varieties of fungi and algae

無拘無束 (ㄨˊ ㄐㄩ ㄨˊ ㄕㄨˋ)or無拘束 (ㄨˊ ㄐㄩ ㄕㄨˋ)
unconstrained; carefree; without a worry or care in the world; to feel at home; to have a completely free hand in...; completely with-

out restraints; freely

無期 (ㄨˊ ㄑㄧˊ)
no definite term or date; with no end in sight

無期徒刑 (ㄨˊ ㄑㄧˊ ㄊㄨˊ ㄒㄧㄥˊ)
life imprisonment: 他被判無期徒刑。He was sentenced to imprisonment for life.

無奇不有 (ㄨˊ ㄑㄧˊ ㄅㄨˋ ㄧㄡˇ)
Nothing is too strange (in the world, this school, etc.).

無巧不巧 (ㄨˊ ㄑㄧㄠˇ ㄅㄨˋ ㄑㄧㄠˇ)
by coincidence; coincidentally

無巧不成書 (ㄨˊ ㄑㄧㄠˇ ㄅㄨˋ ㄔㄥˊ ㄕㄨ)
There would have been no story to tell if not for that coincidence.—It happened that....

無牽無掛 (ㄨˊ ㄑㄧㄢ ㄨˊ ㄍㄨㄚˋ)
to have no cares

無前 (ㄨˊ ㄑㄧㄢˊ)
(used to describe a brave and skillful fighter)matchless; peerless

無情 (ㄨˊ ㄑㄧㄥˊ)
callous; heartless; ruthless; devoid of emotions or feelings: 他是無情的人。He is a heartless man.

無情無緒 (ㄨˊ ㄑㄧㄥˊ ㄨˊ ㄒㄩˋ)
listless and indifferent; bored

無權 (ㄨˊ ㄑㄩㄢˊ)
to have no right

無拳無勇 (ㄨˊ ㄑㄩㄢˊ ㄨˊ ㄩㄥˇ)
to have neither fighting skill nor courage—a weakling

無窮 (ㄨˊ ㄑㄩㄥˊ)
endless; boundless; limitless; inexhaustible; interminable; infinite: 他似乎有無窮的智慧和力量。It seems that he has inexhaustible wisdom and power.

無窮大 (ㄨˊ ㄑㄩㄥˊ ㄉㄚˋ)
(mathematics)infinite; infinitely great

無窮小 (ㄨˊ ㄑㄩㄥˊ ㄒㄧㄠˇ)
(mathematics)infinitesimal

無窮無盡 (ㄨˊ ㄑㄩㄥˊ ㄨˊ ㄐㄧㄣˋ)
endless; infinite; boundless; limitless; interminable

無錫 (ㄨˊ ㄒㄧˊ)
name of a county in Kiangsu Province famous for its production of wheat flour,

〔火部〕

（火
部）

cotton yarn and farm products

無息貸款(ㄨㄒㄧˊ ㄌㄞˋ ㄎㄨㄢˇ)
an interest-free loan

無隙可乘(ㄨㄒㄧˊ ㄎㄜˇ ㄔㄥˊ)
to have no vulnerability or weakness to exploit; to have no loophole to exploit

無瑕(ㄨㄒㄧㄚˊ)
without blemish, defect or fault—perfect: 他的行為無瑕。His behavior was perfect.

無暇(ㄨㄒㄧㄚˊ)
to have no time; without leisure

無下箸處(ㄨㄒㄧㄚˋ ㄓㄨˋ ㄔㄨˋ)
(literally) no place to ply the chopsticks (said of the rich who are too particular about their food)

無懈可擊(ㄨㄒㄧㄝˋ ㄎㄜˇ ㄐㄧˊ)
flawless; unimpeachable; unassailable; invulnerable

無效(ㄨㄒㄧㄠˋ)
①ineffective; useless; to no avail ②invalid; not valid; null and void: 他們宣佈合約無效。They declared the contract invalid.

無休止(ㄨㄒㄧㄡ ㄓˇ)
ceaseless; endless; on and on: 他們無休止地爭論。They argued on and on.

無限(ㄨㄒㄧㄢˋ)
limitless; boundless; infinite; unlimited; immeasurable: 他是個有無限野心的獨裁者。He is a dictator with limitless ambitions.

無限公司(ㄨㄒㄧㄢˋ ㄍㄨㄥ ㄙ)
an unlimited company

無限花序(ㄨㄒㄧㄢˋ ㄏㄨㄚ ㄒㄩˋ)
indefinite inflorescence

無限制(ㄨㄒㄧㄢˋ ㄓˋ)
unlimited; without qualifications or restrictions; unbridled

無線電(ㄨㄒㄧㄢˋ ㄉㄧㄢˋ)
radio; wireless

無線電報(ㄨㄒㄧㄢˋ ㄉㄧㄢˋ ㄅㄠˋ)
a telegram; a wireless cable

無線電變壓器(ㄨㄒㄧㄢˋ ㄉㄧㄢˋ ㄅㄧㄢˋ ㄧㄚ ㄑㄧˋ)
a radio transformer

無線電天線(ㄨㄒㄧㄢˋ ㄉㄧㄢˋ ㄊㄧㄢ ㄒㄧㄢˋ)
a radio antenna

無線電桿(ㄨㄒㄧㄢˋ ㄉㄧㄢˋ ㄍㄢˇ)
a wireless mast

無線電廣播站(ㄨㄒㄧㄢˋ ㄉㄧㄢˋ ㄍㄨㄤˇ ㄅㄛˋ ㄓㄢˋ)
a radio station

無線電廣播員(ㄨㄒㄧㄢˋ ㄉㄧㄢˋ ㄍㄨㄤˇ ㄅㄛˋ ㄩㄢˊ)
a radiobroadcaster

無線電擴大器(ㄨㄒㄧㄢˋ ㄉㄧㄢˋ ㄎㄨㄛˋ ㄉㄚˋ ㄑㄧˋ)
a radio amplifier

無線電話(ㄨㄒㄧㄢˋ ㄉㄧㄢˋ ㄏㄨㄚˋ)
radiophone

無線電傳眞(ㄨㄒㄧㄢˋ ㄉㄧㄢˋ ㄔㄨㄢˊ ㄓㄣ)
fax (facsimile)

無心(ㄨㄒㄧㄣ)
①unintentional; unintentionally; inadvertently ②in no mood

無信(ㄨㄒㄧㄣˋ)
faithless; devoid of faith

無形(ㄨㄒㄧㄥˊ)
without leaving a trace; without taking a form; invisible

無形中(ㄨㄒㄧㄥˊ ㄓㄨㄥ)
imperceptibly; insidiously; unknowingly: 這形中成了慣例。This has imperceptibly become a common practice.

無行為能力人(ㄨㄒㄧㄥˊ ㄨㄟˊ ㄋㄥˊ ㄌㄧˋ ㄖㄣˊ)
(law) a person without disposing capacity

無行(ㄨㄒㄧㄥˊ)
indulgent in evil ways; to have no moral scruples

無性(ㄨㄒㄧㄥˋ)
(biology) asexual

無性生殖(ㄨㄒㄧㄥˋ ㄕㄥ ㄓˊ)
(biology) asexual reproduction or propagation; cloning

無須(ㄨㄒㄩ)or無須乎(ㄨㄒㄩ ㄏㄨˊ)
unnecessary; not necessary; no need to: 無須解釋。It's unnecessary to explain it.

無知(ㄨㄓ)
ignorant; ignorance; (said of a child) innocent

無止境(ㄨㄓˇ ㄐㄧㄥˋ)
to have no limits or boundary; (said of knowledge) to know no end: 他的貪心是無止境的。His greed has no limits.

無遮大會(ㄨㄓㄜ ㄉㄚˋ ㄏㄨㄟˋ)
(Buddhism) panca (varsika)-parisad, the quinquennial assembly for having all things in common, and for confession, penance and remission

無照(ㄨㄓㄠˋ)
(to engage in a business) without a license: 無照駕駛是違法的。It is illegal to drive without a license.

無長物(ㄨㄓㄤˇ ㄨˋ)
to have no extra things

無徵不信(ㄨㄓㄥ ㄅㄨˋ ㄒㄧㄣˋ)
not credible unless supported by evidence or reference

無政府主義(ㄨㄓㄥˋ ㄈㄨˇ ㄓㄨˇ ㄧˋ)
anarchism

無政府狀態(ㄨㄓㄥˋ ㄈㄨˇ ㄓㄨㄤˋ ㄊㄞˋ)
anarchy

無主見(ㄨㄓㄨˇ ㄐㄧㄢˋ)
indecisive; cannot make up one's mind about anything

無著(ㄨㄓㄨˊ)
①cannot locate; cannot find ②(Buddhism) name of Buddhist saint Asanga, brother of Vasubandhu ③a term referring to Buddha

無狀(ㄨㄓㄨㄤˋ)
ill-mannered

無中生有(ㄨㄓㄨㄥ ㄕㄥ ㄧㄡˇ)
(literally) to make something out of nothing—to fabricate; to imagine; to invent; to frame up; purely fictitious

無恥(ㄨㄔˇ)
shameless; brazen; impudent

無恥之尤(ㄨㄔˇ ㄓ ㄧㄡˊ)
utterly shameless; most brazen; completely devoid of a sense of shame

無產階級(ㄨㄔㄢˇ ㄐㄧㄝ ㄐㄧˊ)
the proletarian class; the proletariat

無產階級專政(ㄨㄔㄢˇ ㄐㄧㄝ ㄐㄧˊ ㄓㄨㄢ ㄓㄥˋ)
the dictatorship of the proletariat; proletarian dictatorship

無產階級文化大革命(ㄨㄔㄢˇ ㄐㄧㄝ ㄐㄧˊ ㄨㄣˊ ㄏㄨㄚˋ ㄉㄚˋ ㄍㄜˊ ㄇㄧㄥˋ)
the Great Proletarian Cultural Revolution on the Chinese mainland (1966-1976)

無常(ㄨㄔㄤˊ)

① ever-changing; capricious; variable: 他是個反覆無常的人。He is a man of capricious temper. ②(Buddhism) *anitya*, impermanent ③ (Chinese mythology) name of a ghost or spirit that heralds a person's death ④ death

無腸公子(ㄨˊㄔㄤˊ《ㄨㄥㄗˇ)
a crab

無出(ㄨˊㄔㄨ)
without any offspring or children

無出其右(ㄨˊㄔㄨㄑㄧˊㄧㄡˋ)
Nobody can better him. or second to none; peerless; matchless; unequaled

無師自通(ㄨˊㄕㄗˋㄊㄨㄥ)
to acquire a skill without being taught

無時無地(ㄨˊㄕˊㄨˊㄉㄧˋ)
every minute and everywhere

無時無刻(ㄨˊㄕˊㄨˊㄎㄜˋ)
every minute and every moment; always; constantly; all the time

無始(ㄨˊㄕˇ)
(Buddhism) without beginning, as is the chain of transmigration

無始無邊(ㄨˊㄕˇㄨˊㄅㄧㄢ)
vastly expansive and ever-lasting

無視(ㄨˊㄕˋ)
to consider as unimportant; to pay no attention to; to have no high opinion of; to disregard

無事不登三寶殿(ㄨˊㄕˋㄅㄨˋㄉㄥㄙㄢㄅㄠˇㄉㄧㄢˋ)
One never goes to a Buddhist temple for nothing. —One would not go to somebody's place except on business or for help. so I wouldn't come to you if I hadn't something to ask of you.

無事忙(ㄨˊㄕˋㄇㄤˊ)
to be busy for nothing; a busybody

無事生非(ㄨˊㄕˋㄕㄥㄈㄟ)
to make trouble out of nothing

無涉(ㄨˊㄕㄜˋ)
no concern; no business(of his, yours, mine, etc.); not involved; to have nothing to do with

無神論(ㄨˊㄕㄣˊㄌㄨㄣˋ)
atheism

無神論者(ㄨˊㄕㄣˊㄌㄨㄣˋㄓㄜˇ)
an atheist

無傷(ㄨˊㄕㄤ)
no harm; doesn't matter

無傷大雅(ㄨˊㄕㄤㄉㄚˋㄧㄚˇ)
No serious harm is done. or It means no offense. or It doesn't matter. 他們說的話無傷大雅. What they said means no offense.

無上光榮(ㄨˊㄕㄤˋㄍㄨㄤ日ㄨㄥˊ)
matchless honor; the highest honor

無生(ㄨˊㄕㄥ)
(Buddhism) immortal; subject neither to birth nor to death

無生物(ㄨˊㄕㄥㄨˋ)
an inanimate object; a non-living matter

無聲(ㄨˊㄕㄥ)
noiseless; silent: 鳥在樹上悄然無聲。The birds were silent in the trees.

無聲電影(ㄨˊㄕㄥㄉㄧㄢˋㄧㄥˇ)
a silent movie (or film)

無聲無臭(ㄨˊㄕㄥㄨˊㄒㄧㄡˋ)
① a nobody; small fry or potatoes ② quietly and without leaving a trace

無殊(ㄨˊㄕㄨ)
not different from; tantamount to

無數(ㄨˊㄕㄨˋ)
① countless; numerous ② an uncertain number of; do not know for certain

無雙(ㄨˊㄕㄨㄤ)or 無二(ㄨˊㄦˋ)
peerless; matchless; unique; unrivaled; unparalleled: 他的辯才無雙。His eloquence is unrivaled.

無雙國士(ㄨˊㄕㄨㄤㄍㄨㄛˊㄕˋ)
a man of superior talent or ability

無日(ㄨˊㄖˋ)
① not a single day ② soon

無人過問(ㄨˊㄖㄣˊㄍㄨㄛˋㄨㄣˋ)
(literally) Nobody asks about it. or Nobody cares about it. or Nobody shows any interest in it.

無人駕駛飛機(ㄨˊㄖㄣˊㄐㄧㄚˋㄕˇㄈㄟㄐㄧ)
a pilotless plane

無任感激(ㄨˊㄖㄣˋㄍㄢˇㄐㄧ)
to appreciate very much

無任歡迎(ㄨˊㄖㄣˋㄏㄨㄢㄧㄥˊ)
most welcome: 無蒙光臨,無任歡迎。Your visit will be most welcome.

無任所大使(ㄨˊㄖㄣˋㄙㄨㄛˇㄉㄚˋㄕˇ)
a roving ambassador

無如(ㄨˊㄖㄨˊ)
It's a pity that....or couldn't help that...

無足輕重(ㄨˊㄗㄨˊㄑㄧㄥㄓㄨㄥˋ)
of little significance; of no consequence; of little importance

無罪(ㄨˊㄗㄨㄟˋ)
innocent; guiltless; not guilty

無統(ㄨˊㄘ)
flawless; without blemish or defect: 他的推理完美無統。His reasoning is flawless.

無猜(ㄨˊㄘㄞ)
childlike innocence; unsuspicious

無措(ㄨˊㄘㄨㄛˋ)
① to act strangely, without propriety, etc. ② jumpy

無從(ㄨˊㄘㄨㄥˊ)
to have no place (or no way) to lay hands on or begin with

無私(ㄨˊㄙ)
selfless; disinterested; unselfish: 他是個無私的官員。He is a selfless official.

無私有弊(ㄨˊㄙㄧㄡˇㄅㄧˋ)
(said of the performance of government officials) susceptible to accusations of irregularities owing to careless handling although no irregularities are involved

無所不至(ㄨˊㄙㄨㄛˇㄅㄨˋㄓˋ)
① omnipresent; omnipresence; ubiquitous; present everywhere ② very thorough; very attentive; very thoughtful

無所不在(ㄨˊㄙㄨㄛˇㄅㄨˋㄗㄞˋ)
omnipresent; ubiquitous

無所不用其極(ㄨˊㄙㄨㄛˇㄅㄨˋㄩㄥˋㄑㄧˊㄐㄧˊ)
to go to extremes in every

〔火部〕

〔火部〕

measure or on every count; to pursue everything to its brutal end; to stop at nothing

無所不包(ㄨㄙㄨㄅㄨㄅㄠ)
Nothing is left out. 或 all-encompassing; all-embracing

無所不能(ㄨㄙㄨㄅㄨㄋㄥ)
omnipotence; omnipotent; almighty; capable of doing anything: 沒有人是無所不能的。None is omnipotent.

無所不知(ㄨㄙㄨㄅㄨㄓ)
omniscient; omniscience; to know everything

無所不有(ㄨㄙㄨㄅㄨㄧㄡ)
omnifarious; to have all

無所不爲(ㄨㄙㄨㄅㄨㄨㄟ)
ready to do anything, however bad it may be; to stop at nothing 或 No act is considered too evil or too cruel.

無所住(ㄨㄙㄨㄛㄓㄨ)
(Buddhism) apratisthita, no means of staying; non-abiding

無所事事(ㄨㄙㄨㄛㄕㄕ)
to do nothing; to be at a loose end; to idle away one's time

無所適從(ㄨㄙㄨㄛㄕㄘㄨㄥ)
don't know where to turn to; indecisive; no set plan or principle to follow; don't know whose suggestion to follow

無所謂(ㄨㄙㄨㄛㄨㄟ)
don't mind—one way or the other; do not care: 他來不來我都無所謂。I don't mind whether he comes or not.

無所畏懼(ㄨㄙㄨㄛㄨㄟㄐㄩ)
fearless; dauntless

無算(ㄨㄙㄨㄢ)
①countless; cannot be counted ②of an uncertain number

無惡不作(ㄨㄜㄅㄨㄗㄨㄛ)
capable of committing every crime under the sun; to stop at nothing in doing evil

無礙(ㄨㄞ)
①do not matter; no harm; not in the way; all right ②(Buddhism) apratihata (un-hindered; without obstacle; permeating everywhere)

無一不備(ㄨㄧㄅㄨㄅㄟ)
Everything is available. 或 Nothing is missing.

無一不通(ㄨㄧㄅㄨㄊㄨㄥ)
to know all; extremely versatile

無一不能(ㄨㄧㄅㄨㄋㄥ)
almighty; extremely versatile; to be able to handle everything (at hand)

無一不精(ㄨㄧㄅㄨㄐㄧㄥ)
to be an expert in everything; versatility plus virtuosity

無依無靠(ㄨㄧㄨㄎㄠ)
with no one to turn to or rely on; completely helpless

無疑(ㄨㄧ)
without doubt; undoubtedly; unquestionably: 那無疑是眞的。That is undoubtedly true.

無已(ㄨㄧ)
①endlessly ②cannot help but...

無以復加(ㄨㄧㄈㄨㄐㄧㄚ)
extremely; utterly; utmost; cannot be surpassed; the last word in (beauty, brutality, etc.)

無以自解(ㄨㄧㄗㄐㄧㄝ)
unable to explain oneself away; cannot extricate oneself from; unable to give an excuse

無以爲繼(ㄨㄧㄨㄟㄐㄧ)
to be hard put to find a sequel

無益(ㄨㄧ)
won't serve any purpose; useless; without benefit; unprofitable; no good: 多談無益。It is useless to keep talking.

無異(ㄨㄧ)
not different from; tantamount to; the same as: 你的回答無異是拒絕。Your answer is tantamount to a refusal.

無異議(ㄨㄧㄧ)
without a dissenting voice; unanimous

無異議通過(ㄨㄧㄧㄊㄨㄥㄍㄨㄛ)
to pass unanimously

無意(ㄨㄧ)
to have no interest in; have no intention (of doing something)

無意犯(ㄨㄧㄈㄢ)
a person who commits an offense unintentionally

無意中(ㄨㄧㄓㄨㄥ)or 無意間(ㄨㄧㄐㄧㄢ)
unexpectedly; unintentionally; accidentally; by accident

無意識(ㄨㄧㄕ)
①(psychology) unconsciousness ②unintentional

無涯(ㄨㄧㄚ)
boundless; limitless; endless

無業遊民(ㄨㄧㄝㄧㄡㄇㄧㄣ)
a vagrant

無憂無慮(ㄨㄧㄡㄨㄌㄩ)
carefree; without a worry and care in the world

無由(ㄨㄧㄡ)
no way to; in no position to; unable to

無有(ㄨㄧㄡ)
none; nothing

無煙煤(ㄨㄧㄢㄇㄟ)
anthracite, or hard coal

無煙火藥(ㄨㄧㄢㄏㄨㄛㄧㄠ)
smokeless powder; ballistite

無顏見江東父老(ㄨㄧㄢㄐㄧㄢㄐㄧㄤㄉㄨㄥㄈㄨㄌㄠ)
to have no face or to be too ashamed to go back home to see one's elders (after defeat, failure, etc.)

無厭(ㄨㄧㄢ)
insatiable (as man's greed, desires, etc.); never tire of

無因(ㄨㄧㄣ)
①without cause or reason ②no way to; in no position to; unable to

無垠(ㄨㄧㄣ)
(said of space) boundless; limitless; extremely expansive: 我們看到了一望無垠的草原。We saw a boundless prairie.

無恙(ㄨㄧㄤ)
to feel well; all right; (usually used in the opening paragraph of a letter); in good health; safe: 別來無恙? Have you been all right since we last met?

無影無踪(ㄨㄧㄥㄨㄗㄨㄥ)
(to vanish or disappear) without a trace

無誤(ㄨㄨ)

correct; right; verified and
found correct

無我(ㄨ ㄨㄛ)
(Buddhism) *anatman*, no
individual independent existence

無為(ㄨ ㄨㄟ)
to let things take their own
course; inaction; inactivity

無為而治(ㄨ ㄨㄟ ㄦ ㄓ)
(literally) to govern by
doing nothing—according to
Lao-tzu(老子), enlightened
administration is possible
only when the ruler can set
a good example for the people to follow instead of proclaiming restrictive laws
and regulations which tend
to interfere with the orderly
life of the masses

無微不至(ㄨ ㄨㄟ ㄅㄨ ㄓ)
down to the very last detail;
very thoughtful; to considerate in every way

無味(ㄨ ㄨㄟ)
①tasteless; not interesting;
dull; dry; unattractive
(offers, etc.)②unpalatable;
unappetizing

無謂(ㄨ ㄨㄟ)
①don't presume ②sense-
less; meaningless; pointless

無畏(ㄨ ㄨㄟ)
dauntless; without fear

無畏艦(ㄨ ㄨㄟ ㄐㄧㄢ)
Dreadnaught (name of a
class of warships)

無畏施(ㄨ ㄨㄟ ㄕ)
abhayyapradana, the bestow-
ing of confidence by every
true Buddhist, i.e. that none
may fear him

無往不利(ㄨ ㄨㄤ ㄅㄨ ㄌㄧ)
lucky in every endeavor;
successful in whatever one
does

無望(ㄨ ㄨㄤ)
①hopeless; to despair of;
without hope ②do not
expect that... ③without
boundary line or marks

無妄之災(ㄨ ㄨㄤ ㄓ ㄗㄞ)
unexpected misfortunes; uncalled-for disasters or calamities

無虞匱乏(ㄨ ㄩ ㄎㄨㄟ ㄈㄚ)
no fear of deficiency; sufficient; abundant

無與倫比(ㄨ ㄩ ㄌㄨㄣ ㄅㄧ)
beyond comparison; peerless;
head and shoulders above
others; without equal;
unique; unparalleled

無欲則剛(ㄨ ㄩ ㄗㄜ ㄍㄤ)
One can be upright if he has
no selfish desires.

無緣(ㄨ ㄩㄢ)
①no opportunity or chance
②no way to; unable to ③
an inexplicable animosity
toward somebody

無緣無故(ㄨ ㄩㄢ ㄨ ㄍㄨ)
without cause or reason;
uncalled-for; for no reason
at all

無遠弗屆(ㄨ ㄩㄢ ㄈㄨ ㄐㄧㄝ)
No place is too far away to
be reached.或to reach everywhere: 他的美名傳遍天下，無
遠弗屆。His good reputation
reached everywhere.

無韻詩(ㄨ ㄩㄣ ㄕ)
(poetry) blank verse: 這個劇
本是用無韻詩寫的。The play
is written in blank verse.

無庸(ㄨ ㄩㄥ)
no need to; unnecessary

無庸置疑(ㄨ ㄩㄥ ㄓ ㄧ)
unquestionable

無用(ㄨ ㄩㄥ)
useless; of no use: 汽車沒有
汽油即無用。A car is useless
without gasoline.

【然】 3215 ㄖㄢ ran rán
1.yes; most certainly; permission; right; correct
2. however; but; still; nevertheless; on the other hand
3. really; if so
4. same as 燃—to burn
5. a Chinese family name

然眉之急(ㄖㄢ ㄇㄟ ㄓ ㄐㄧ)
extremely urgent—as if the
eyebrows were on fire 亦作
「燃眉之急」

然否(ㄖㄢ ㄈㄡ)
Yes or no?或Is it correct?或
Is it so?

然諾(ㄖㄢ ㄋㄨㄛ)
a promise; to give one's
word: 他是重然諾的人。He is
serious about making and
keeping a promise.

然後(ㄖㄢ ㄏㄡ)
then; afterward; later

然乎(ㄖㄢ ㄏㄨ)
Isn't it so?

然信(ㄖㄢ ㄒㄧㄣ)
to pledge to keep a promise

然則(ㄖㄢ ㄗㄜ)
but; but then; in that case

然而(ㄖㄢ ㄦ)
however; but; nevertheless;
on the other hand

【焰】 3216 (燄) ㄧㄢ yann yàn
(又讀)ㄧㄢ yan yàn
1. flames; blazes
2. glowing; brilliant

焰火(ㄧㄢ ㄏㄨㄛ)
fireworks 亦作「煙火」

焰焰(ㄧㄢ ㄧㄢ)
blazing

九畫

【煌】 3217 ㄏㄨㄤ hwang huáng
bright and brilliant

煌煌(ㄏㄨㄤ ㄏㄨㄤ)
(said of stars, etc.)bright
and scintillating

【煉】 3218 ㄌㄧㄢ liann liàn
1. to smelt; to refine; to condense (milk); to temper (a
metal) with fire
2. (Chinese medicine) to keep
herbs, etc. boiling for a long
time
3. to train; to form character
by hardship

煉丹(ㄌㄧㄢ ㄉㄢ)
(Taoism) to refine (by heating) concoctions for special
purposes; to make pills of
immortality

煉鐵法(ㄌㄧㄢ ㄊㄧㄝ ㄈㄚ)
puddling

煉鐵爐(ㄌㄧㄢ ㄊㄧㄝ ㄌㄨ)
a bloomery; a puddling furnace

煉鐵廠(ㄌㄧㄢ ㄊㄧㄝ ㄔㄤ)
a blooming mill; an iron-
works

煉鋼(ㄌㄧㄢ ㄍㄤ)
to refine steel; steelmaking

煉鋼廠(ㄌㄧㄢ ㄍㄤ ㄔㄤ)
a steel refinery; a steel mill

煉焦(ㄌㄧㄢ ㄐㄧㄠ)

〔火部〕

【火部】

to make coke

煉焦爐(ㄌㄧㄢˋ ㄐㄧㄠ ㄌㄨˊ)
a coke furnace

煉指(ㄌㄧㄢˋ ㄓˇ)
finger-burning (an ascetic act of Buddhists)

煉製(ㄌㄧㄢˋ ㄓˋ)
to refine

煉石補天 or 鍊石補天(ㄌㄧㄢˋ ㄕˊ ㄅㄨˇ ㄊㄧㄢ)
to smelt stones to mend the sky (a feat performed by 女媧氏, a mythological character)

煉乳(ㄌㄧㄢˋ ㄖㄨˇ)
condensed milk

煉油廠(ㄌㄧㄢˋ ㄧㄡˊ ㄔㄤˇ)
an oil refinery

煉獄(ㄌㄧㄢˋ ㄩˋ)
the purgatory

【煒】 3219
ㄨㄟˇ woei wěi
1. dark red
2. glowing; bright

【煖】 3220
(暖) ㄋㄨㄢˇ noan nuǎn
warm; to warm; genial (weather)

煖風徐來(ㄋㄨㄢˇ ㄈㄥ ㄒㄩˊ ㄌㄞˊ)
The genial breeze blows gently.

煖衣飽食(ㄋㄨㄢˇ ㄧ ㄅㄠˇ ㄕˊ)
well-clad and well-fed

【煜】 3221
ㄩˋ yuh yù
1. bright and brilliant
2. flames or blazes
3. to illuminate; to shine

煜煜(ㄩˋ ㄩˋ)
bright and shining

【煙】 3222
(烟) ㄧㄢ ian yān
1. smoke; fumes
2. tobacco; a smoke; a cigarette
3. mist; vapor
4. opium
5. a Chinese family name

煙波(ㄧㄢ ㄅㄛ)
lakes; mist-covered waters

煙煤(ㄧㄢ ㄇㄟˊ)
bituminous coal; soft coal

煙幕(ㄧㄢ ㄇㄨˋ)
①a smoke screen ②(figuratively) anything that serves to hide a ship, airplane, etc. from the enemy

煙幕彈(ㄧㄢ ㄇㄨˋ ㄉㄢˋ)
a smoke bomb

煙袋(ㄧㄢ ㄉㄞˋ)
a smoking pipe: 水煙袋 a pipe with a water compartment for filtering tobacco

煙袋荷包(ㄧㄢ ㄉㄞˋ ㄏㄜˊ·ㄅㄠ)
a tobacco pouch

煙斗(ㄧㄢ ㄉㄡˇ)
a pipe (for smoking)

煙燈(ㄧㄢ ㄉㄥ)
a tiny lamp for opium-smoking

煙蒂(ㄧㄢ ㄉㄧˋ)
a cigarette butt: 不要到處亂丟煙蒂，Don't throw away cigarette butts anywhere.

煙毒(ㄧㄢ ㄉㄨˊ)
the poisoning effect of opium-smoking

煙臺(ㄧㄢ ㄊㄞˊ)
Yentai, or Chefoo, in Shantung

煙頭(ㄧㄢ ㄊㄡˊ)
a cigarette butt (or end, stub, stump)

煙突(ㄧㄢ ㄊㄨˊ)
a pipe; a chimney

煙土(ㄧㄢ ㄊㄨˇ)
raw or crude opium

煙筒(ㄧㄢ ㄊㄨㄥˊ)
a chimney; a ventilating pipe for a stove; a funnel; a stovepipe

煙嵐(ㄧㄢ ㄌㄢˊ)
mountain mists or vapor

煙膏(ㄧㄢ ㄍㄠ)
processed opium in paste form

煙鬼(ㄧㄢ ㄍㄨㄟˇ)
an opium smoker or addict; a heavy smoker

煙館(ㄧㄢ ㄍㄨㄢˇ)
a house for opium smoking

煙海(ㄧㄢ ㄏㄞˇ)
(literally) mists over the sea —many, numerous; huge and voluminous: 我們的資料浩如煙海，We have a huge amount of data.

煙花(ㄧㄢ ㄏㄨㄚ)
① prostitutes ② fanfare; prosperity ③a mist of flowers—beautiful scenery of spring flowers

煙花巷(ㄧㄢ ㄏㄨㄚ ㄒㄧㄤˋ) or 煙花柳巷(ㄧㄢ ㄏㄨㄚ ㄌㄧㄡˇ ㄒㄧㄤˋ)
a red-light district; a zone where brothels are located

煙火(ㄧㄢ ㄏㄨㄛˇ)
①kitchen smoke which suggests presence of humans ② cooked food (as distinct from herbs and fruits which are supposed to be the food of immortals) ③a signal fire or beacon ④fireworks: 他們在廣場放煙火。They put on a display of fireworks in the square. ⑤smoke and fire: 嚴禁煙火。Smoking or lighting fires strictly forbidden.

煙火(ㄧㄢ ㄏㄨㄛˇ)
(Taoism) the worldly ways, customs, etc.

煙灰(ㄧㄢ ㄏㄨㄟ)
cigarette ashes; cigar ashes

煙灰缸(ㄧㄢ ㄏㄨㄟ ㄍㄤ)
an ashtray

煙酒稅(ㄧㄢ ㄐㄧㄡˇ ㄕㄨㄟˋ) or 菸酒稅(ㄧㄢ ㄐㄧㄡˇ ㄕㄨㄟˋ)
wine and tobacco tax

煙鹼(ㄧㄢ ㄐㄧㄢˇ)
nicotine

煙禁(ㄧㄢ ㄐㄧㄣˋ)
prohibition of opium smoking

煙景(ㄧㄢ ㄐㄧㄥˇ)
①beautiful scenes of a fine day ②changing clouds and mists ③vapor over a lake

煙捲兒(ㄧㄢ ㄐㄩㄢˇㄦ)
a cigarette

煙槍(ㄧㄢ ㄑㄧㄤ)
①a pipe for opium smoking; an opium pipe ②a chain smoker

煙霞癖(ㄧㄢ ㄒㄧㄚˊ ㄆㄧˇ)
①a deep love for natural charms—mountains, lakes, etc. ②(comically) opium addiction

煙霞痼疾(ㄧㄢ ㄒㄧㄚˊ ㄍㄨˋ ㄐㄧˊ)
a deep-rooted love for natural charms

煙消火滅(ㄧㄢ ㄒㄧㄠ ㄏㄨㄛˇ ㄇㄧㄝˋ)
to vanish or disappear; to come to an end

煙消雲散(ㄧㄢ ㄒㄧㄠ ㄩㄣˊ ㄙㄢˇ)
to vanish like mist and smoke—to vanish completely; to disappear

煙瘴(ㄧㄢ ㄓㄤˋ)

〔火部〕

miasmas

煙塵(ㄧㄢ ㄔㄣ)
①smoke and dust; air pollution ②the smoke and dust of battle

煙士披利純(ㄧㄢ ㄕ ㄆㄧ ㄌㄧ ㄔㄨㄣ)
inspiration 亦作「靈感」

煙嘴兒(ㄧㄢ ㄗㄨㄟˇㄦ)
a cigarette holder

煙草 or 菸草(ㄧㄢ ㄘㄠˇ)
tobacco; the tobacco plant

煙囪(ㄧㄢ ㄔㄨㄥ)
a chimney; a stack; a funnel; a stovepipe

煙絲(ㄧㄢ ㄙ)
cut-tobacco for pipe smoking

煙靄(ㄧㄢ ㄞˇ)
mist and vapor; clouds

煙兒(ㄧ ㄦ)
smoke

煙葉(ㄧㄢ ㄧㄝˋ)
tobacco (leaves)

煙癮(ㄧㄢ ㄧㄣˇ)
①opium or tobacco addiction ②a craving for tobacco

煙霧(ㄧㄢ ㄨˋ)
smoke; mist; vapor; misty; smog

煙雲過眼(ㄧㄢ ㄩㄣˊ ㄍㄨㄛˋ ㄧㄢˇ)
ephemeral; transient

【煤】 3223
ㄇㄟˊ mei méi
1. coal; charcoal; coke
2. carbon; soot

煤末(ㄇㄟˊ ㄇㄛˋ)
coal dust

煤袋(ㄇㄟˊ ㄉㄞˋ)
a coal sack

煤毒(ㄇㄟˊ ㄉㄨˊ)
carbon monoxide (CO)

煤炭(ㄇㄟˊ ㄊㄢˋ)
coal; anthracite; hard coal; coke: 我們貯備煤炭過冬。We lay in coals for the winter.

煤炭店(ㄇㄟˊ ㄊㄢˋ ㄉㄧㄢˋ)
a shop selling coal, firewood, etc.

煤田(ㄇㄟˊ ㄊㄧㄢˊ)
a coal field; a coal bed

煤爐子(ㄇㄟˊ ㄌㄨˊ ㄗ˙)
a coal stove

煤坑(ㄇㄟˊ ㄎㄥ)
a coal pit

煤礦(ㄇㄟˊ ㄎㄨㄤˋ)
①a coal mine: 他們在地裏開

採煤礦。They mined the earth for coal. ②a coal shaft

煤礦工人(ㄇㄟˊ ㄎㄨㄤˋ ㄍㄨㄥ ㄖㄣˊ)
a coal miner: 他的父親是煤礦工人。His father is a coal miner.

煤焦油(ㄇㄟˊ ㄐㄧㄠ ㄧㄡˊ)
coal tar

煤氣(ㄇㄟˊ ㄑㄧˋ)
gas (for lighting or heating); coal gas

煤氣表(ㄇㄟˊ ㄑㄧˋ ㄅㄧㄠˇ)
a gas meter 亦作「瓦斯表」

煤氣燈(ㄇㄟˊ ㄑㄧˋ ㄉㄥ)
a gas lamp; a gas light

煤氣炭(ㄇㄟˊ ㄑㄧˋ ㄊㄢˋ)
gas carbon

煤氣爐(ㄇㄟˊ ㄑㄧˋ ㄌㄨˊ)
a gas stove; a gas furnace

煤氣管(ㄇㄟˊ ㄑㄧˋ ㄍㄨㄢˇ)
gas pipes

煤氣公司(ㄇㄟˊ ㄑㄧˋ ㄍㄨㄥ ㄙ)
a gas company

煤氣機(ㄇㄟˊ ㄑㄧˋ ㄐㄧ)
a coal gas engine

煤氣中毒(ㄇㄟˊ ㄑㄧˋ ㄓㄨㄥ ㄉㄨˊ)
carbon monoxide poisoning; gas poisoning

煤球(ㄇㄟˊ ㄑㄧㄡˊ)
coal balls (made of coal dust and clay); briquets

煤屑(ㄇㄟˊ ㄒㄧㄝˋ)
coal dust; coal splinters

煤箱(ㄇㄟˊ ㄒㄧㄤ)
a coal scuttle; a coal hod

煤渣(ㄇㄟˊ ㄓㄚ)
coal cinders; coal slag

煤車(ㄇㄟˊ ㄔㄜ)
a coal car

煤塵爆炸(ㄇㄟˊ ㄔㄣˊ ㄅㄠˋ ㄓㄚˋ)
a coal-dust explosion

煤商(ㄇㄟˊ ㄕㄤ)
a coal dealer; a coalman

煤倉(ㄇㄟˊ ㄘㄤ)
a coal bunker

煤層(ㄇㄟˊ ㄘㄥˊ)
a coal seam; a coal bed; coal measures

煤油(ㄇㄟˊ ㄧㄡˊ)
kerosene: 這個爐子燒煤油。This stove burns kerosene.

煤油燈(ㄇㄟˊ ㄧㄡˊ ㄉㄥ)
a kerosene lamp

煤油爐(ㄇㄟˊ ㄧㄡˊ ㄌㄨˊ)
a kerosene stove

煤油罐(ㄇㄟˊ ㄧㄡˊ ㄍㄨㄢˋ)
a kerosene can or container

煤煙(ㄇㄟˊ ㄧㄢ)
soot

【煥】 3224
ㄏㄨㄢˋ huann huàn
1. bright; brilliant; lustrous; luminous
2. (said of an appearance) shining; vigorous and elegant

煥發(ㄏㄨㄢˋ ㄈㄚ)
brilliant and luminous; scintillating; shining; radiant; vivacious; glowing: 他容光煥發。His face is glowing with health.

煥爛(ㄏㄨㄢˋ ㄌㄢˋ)
very bright and luminous; shining and flourishing

煥煥(ㄏㄨㄢˋ ㄏㄨㄢˋ)
①bright and shining; scintillating ②glorious; remarkable; prominent

煥然一新(ㄏㄨㄢˋ ㄖㄢˊ ㄧ ㄒㄧㄣ)
brand-new; renovated from top to bottom; to take on an entirely new look

煥耀(ㄏㄨㄢˋ ㄧㄠˋ)
bright and luminous; shining and flourishing

【煨】 3225
ㄨㄟ uei wēi
to bake; to stew; to simmer; to burn in ashes; to roast (sweet potatoes, etc.) in fresh cinders

煨乾避濕(ㄨㄟ ㄍㄢ ㄅㄧˋ ㄕ)
(literally) to sleep on a bed sheet wet by a child and let the child sleep where the sheet is dry—the loving care a mother gives to her child

煨燼(ㄨㄟ ㄐㄧㄣˋ)
ashes

煨肉(ㄨㄟ ㄖㄡˋ)
to stew meat

【煩】 3226
ㄈㄢˊ farn fán
1. to vex; to annoy; to worry
2. annoying
3. to trouble
4. superfluous and confusing

煩悶 or 煩懣(ㄈㄢˊ ㄇㄣˋ)
annoyed; vexed; depressed; downcast; bored; worried: 他爲何那麼煩悶? Why is he so worried?

【火 部】

煩法(ㄈㄢ ㄈㄚˇ)
irritating petty laws and regulations; red tape

煩費(ㄈㄢ ㄈㄟˋ)
to cause trouble and expenses

煩惱(ㄈㄢ ㄋㄠˇ)
worries; cares; worried

煩難(ㄈㄢ ㄋㄢˊ)
complicated and difficult to handle

煩了(ㄈㄢ ．ㄌㄜ)
tired of; bored

煩勞(ㄈㄢ ㄌㄠˊ)
to ask someone to do something

煩亂(ㄈㄢ ㄌㄨㄢˋ)
confusing

煩苛(ㄈㄢ ㄎㄜ)
petty and harassing (regulations, taxation, etc.)

煩交(ㄈㄢ ㄐㄧㄠ)
please deliver to

煩請(ㄈㄢ ㄑㄧㄥˇ)
Would you mind...? 或 Please be so kind as to....

煩細(ㄈㄢ ㄒㄧˋ)
petty details; petty and detailed

煩囂(ㄈㄢ ㄒㄧㄠ)
①the hubbub of a noisy place ②cares and worries of this world

煩心(ㄈㄢ ㄒㄧㄣ)
to trouble or worry the mind; vexation

煩想(ㄈㄢ ㄒㄧㄤˇ)
worries

煩累(ㄈㄢ ㄌㄟˇ)
verbose; verbosity; long-winded; prolix

煩數(ㄈㄢ ㄕㄨㄛˋ)
frequency

煩熱(ㄈㄢ ㄖㄜˋ)
oppressively hot; oppressive heat; sultry

煩擾(ㄈㄢ ㄖㄠˇ)
to trouble with petty things; to annoy; to harass; to feel disturbed: 蚊子在夏天煩擾我們。Mosquitoes annoy us in the summer.

煩冗(ㄈㄢ ㄖㄨㄥˇ)
lengthy and tedious; petty, disorderly and busy; diverse and complicated

煩雜(ㄈㄢ ㄗㄚˊ)
petty and varied; confusing and disorderly

煩躁(ㄈㄢ ㄗㄠˋ)
annoyed and impatient; vexed; short-tempered; agitated

煩瑣(ㄈㄢ ㄙㄨㄛˇ)
petty and multitudinous; tedious

煩碎(ㄈㄢ ㄙㄨㄟˋ)
petty and overdetailed

煩言(ㄈㄢ ㄧㄢˊ)
complaints

煩猥(ㄈㄢ ㄨㄟˇ)
multitudinous and petty

煩文縟節(ㄈㄢ ㄨㄣˊ ㄖㄨˋ ㄐㄧㄝˊ)
petty formalities; red tape

【煬】 3227
1.(ㄧㄤˊ) yang yáng
same as 烊—to smelt or melt (metals)

煬帝(ㄧㄤˊ ㄉㄧˋ)
Emperor Yang of the Sui Dynasty, who ordered the digging of the Grand Canal in the early seventh century

【煬】 3227
2.(ㄧㄤˋ) yang yàng
1.(said of fire) roaring or blazing
2. to put before the fire

【煮】 3228
(煑) ㄓㄨˇ juu zhǔ
to cook; to boil; to stew; to decoct

煮茗(ㄓㄨˇ ㄇㄧㄥˇ)
to boil tea; to infuse tea

煮沸(ㄓㄨˇ ㄈㄟˋ)
to boil; to heat water or soup until it boils

煮飯(ㄓㄨˇ ㄈㄢˋ)
to cook rice; to cook meals

煮豆燃萁(ㄓㄨˇ ㄉㄡˋ ㄖㄢˊ ㄑㄧˊ)
(literally) to make a fire of beanstalks for boiling beans — fraternal persecution; the conflict among brothers

煮爛(ㄓㄨˇ ㄌㄢˋ)
to stew something until it's tender

煮鶴焚琴(ㄓㄨˇ ㄏㄜˋ ㄈㄣˊ ㄑㄧㄣˊ)
to destroy something fine by behaving rudely

煮海為鹽(ㄓㄨˇ ㄏㄞˇ ㄨㄟˊ ㄧㄢˊ)
to boil seawater for salt

煮餃子(ㄓㄨˇ ㄐㄧㄠˇ ·ㄗ)
to boil ravioli (or stuffed dumplings)

煮粥(ㄓㄨˇ ㄓㄡ)
to cook congee

煮熟(ㄓㄨˇ ㄕㄨˊ)
to cook thoroughly

煮肉(ㄓㄨˇ ㄖㄡˋ)
to cook meat

煮字療飢(ㄓㄨˇ ㄗˋ ㄌㄧㄠˊ ㄐㄧ)
to live on writing; to have a writer's career

煮菜(ㄓㄨˇ ㄘㄞˋ)
to prepare food or dishes

煮鹽(ㄓㄨˇ ㄧㄢˊ)
to get salt by evaporation of seawater

【煎】 3229
ㄐㄧㄢ jian jiān
1. to fry in fat or oil
2. to decoct
3. (figuratively)to torment; to kill

煎逼(ㄐㄧㄢ ㄅㄧ)or 煎迫(ㄐㄧㄢ ㄆㄛˋ)
to torture; to persecute

煎餅(ㄐㄧㄢ ·ㄅㄧㄥ)
pancakes: 他常以煎餅當早餐。He usually has pancakes for breakfast.

煎蛋(ㄐㄧㄢ ㄉㄢˋ)
①to fry eggs: 他正用平底鍋煎蛋。He is frying the egg in the pan. ② fried eggs

煎心(ㄐㄧㄢ ㄒㄧㄣ)
(literally) to fry the heart —very worried

煎炒(ㄐㄧㄢ ㄔㄠˇ)
to fry; to stir-fry

煎熬(ㄐㄧㄢ ㄠˊ)
①to decoct until almost dry ②to put somebody in hot water; to make someone suffer; to torture; to torment

煎藥(ㄐㄧㄢ ㄧㄠˋ)
to make a decoction of herbal medicines

煎魚(ㄐㄧㄢ ㄩˊ)
to fry fish

【煞】 3230
ㄕㄚˋ shah shà
1. a fierce god; a malignant deity; an evil spirit; a goblin
2. very; much; extremely
3. to bring to an end; to conclude

煞筆(ㄕㄚˋ ㄅㄧˇ)
(said of a piece of writing or a speech) ①to come to a

conclusion; to write the final line ②concluding lines of an article

煞費工夫(ㄕㄚ ㄈㄟ ㄍㄨㄥ ㄈㄨ)
to take much trouble

煞費苦心(ㄕㄚ ㄈㄟ ㄎㄨ ㄒㄧㄣ)
to have made painstaking effort; to take great pains: 他為此事煞費苦心. He did the work with great pains.

煞風景(ㄕㄚ ㄈㄥ ㄐㄧㄥ)
to throw a wet blanket; to spoil pleasure

煞後兒(ㄕㄚ ㄏㄡ ㄦ)
timid; shy; not aggressive

煞脚(ㄕㄚ ㄐㄧㄠ)
to stop or halt; to come to a conclusion

煞氣(ㄕㄚ ㄑㄧ)
a fierce attitude; an ominous look

煞星(ㄕㄚ ㄒㄧㄥ)
a malignant star—(usually said of a person) that brings wars, deaths, calamities, disasters

煞緊步兒(ㄕㄚ ㄐㄧㄣ ㄅㄨ ㄦ)
to halt one's pace

煞是(ㄕㄚ ㄕ)
very (interesting, encouraging, etc.): 他的話煞是有趣. What he said was very funny.

煞神(ㄕㄚ ㄕㄣ)
an ominous deity or malignant god who brings catastrophes

煞尾(ㄕㄚ ㄨㄟ)
①the conclusion or ending paragraph of an article ②a final stage, an end; an ending ③to come to an end; to wind up

【煞】 3230
2. ㄕㄚ　sha shà
1. to tighten; to bind
2. to offset; to reduce; to mitigate
3. an auxiliary particle in old usage
4. to brake; to stop; to bring to a close

煞氣(ㄕㄚ ㄑㄧ)
to vent one's anger on an innocent party; to take it out on somebody or something

煞性子(ㄕㄚ ㄒㄧㄥ ˙ㄗ)

to vent one's anger on an innocent party

煞賬(ㄕㄚ ㄓㄤ)
(said of an accountant) to make out a statement

煞住(ㄕㄚ ㄓㄨ)
to stop; to hold it

煞車(ㄕㄚ ㄔㄜ)
①to fasten goods on a truck or cart with ropes ②to apply the brakes; to brake

【煦】 3231
ㄒㄩ　sheu xu
1. warm and cozy
2. favors; kindness; good graces; kind and gracious

煦沫(ㄒㄩ ㄇㄛ)
to drool

煦煦(ㄒㄩ ㄒㄩ)
①kind; gracious; benevolent ②(said of weather) warm and fine; balmy: 煦煦春風使人昏昏欲睡. The balmy spring breeze makes us sleepy.

煦日(ㄒㄩ ㄖ)
①the warm sun ②a warm and fine day

【照】 3232
ㄓㄠ　jaw zhào
1. to shine upon; to light or illumine
2. a certificate or license
3. in accordance with; according to; to pattern on or after
4. to compare, collate, survey, etc.
5. to photograph; to take a picture; to shoot
6. to look after; to take care of
7. to notify or proclaim
8. sunshine
9. a picture
10. a Chinese family name

照搬(ㄓㄠ ㄅㄢ)
to imitate; to copy

照辦(ㄓㄠ ㄅㄢ)
to take actions, etc. accordingly; to act upon; to comply with; to manage, or handle something according to instructions, orders, etc.

照本宣科(ㄓㄠ ㄅㄣ ㄒㄩㄢ ㄎㄜ)
to read item by item from the text; to repeat what the book says

照本出售(ㄓㄠ ㄅㄣ ㄔㄨ ㄕㄡ)
to sell at cost price (a common sales slogan in a Chinese shop)

照壁(ㄓㄠ ㄅㄧ)
a wall immediately outside the front door

照片(ㄓㄠ ㄆㄧㄢ)
a photograph; a snapshot

照碼對折(ㄓㄠ ㄇㄚ ㄉㄨㄟ ㄓㄜ)
(a common sales slogan) to offer a 50 percent discount on the tagged prices

照面(ㄓㄠ ㄇㄧㄢ)
to meet; to come face to face: 讓我們彼此打個照面. Let's come face to face with each other.

照明(ㄓㄠ ㄇㄧㄥ)
(said of photography, etc.) lighting

照明彈(ㄓㄠ ㄇㄧㄥ ㄉㄢ)
a flare

照明設備(ㄓㄠ ㄇㄧㄥ ㄕㄜ ㄅㄟ)
illuminating equipment; photo flash equipment

照看(ㄓㄠ ㄎㄢ)
to look after; to care for: 請多照拂她. Please be so kind as to take good care of her.

照付(ㄓㄠ ㄈㄨ)
to pay the full amount according to the price tag, receipt, notice, IOU, etc.

照度(ㄓㄠ ㄉㄨ)
(physics) illumination

照例(ㄓㄠ ㄌㄧ)
to follow precedents or usual practices; as a rule

照料(ㄓㄠ ㄌㄧㄠ)
to take care of; to look after: 你不在時家裏的事有我們照料. We'll take care of things at home while you're away.

照臨(ㄓㄠ ㄌㄧㄣ)
①(polite usage, said of a guest) your much honored arrival (at our place) ②the visits of a king or emperor ③to shine on: 曙光照臨大地. The early sun shines on the land. ④(figuratively) to enlighten and rule

照錄(ㄓㄠ ㄌㄨ) or 照抄(ㄓㄠ ㄔㄠ)
to record or copy exactly as what is said or written

〔火部〕

〔火部〕

照顧(ㄓㄠˋ ㄍㄨˋ)
①to look after; to take care of; care ②to patronize ③to give consideration to; to consider; to take something into account

照管(ㄓㄠˋ ㄍㄨㄢˇ)
to take care of; to manage; to be in charge of; to look after: 她在家照管孩子。She looks after children at home.

照看(ㄓㄠˋ ㄎㄢˋ)
to look after; to keep an eye on: 請幫我照看一下小孩。Will you please keep an eye on my child?

照空燈(ㄓㄠˋ ㄎㄨㄥ ㄉㄥ)
a searchlight

照會(ㄓㄠˋ ㄏㄨㄟˋ)
diplomatic notes; memoranda: 提出照會 to present a note

照價收買(ㄓㄠˋ ㄐㄧㄚˋ ㄕㄡ ㄇㄞˇ)
to buy or requisition (land) according to the price declared by the owner

照繳(ㄓㄠˋ ㄐㄧㄠˇ)
to pay (taxes, fines, etc.) according to the stipulated amount

照舊(ㄓㄠˋ ㄐㄧㄡˋ)
as usual; as before: 他照舊在晚餐前回了家。He came home before dinner as usual.

照鏡自憐(ㄓㄠˋ ㄐㄧㄥˋ ㄗˋ ㄌㄧㄢˊ)
to sympathize with oneself in the mirror

照鏡子(ㄓㄠˋ ㄐㄧㄥˋ ˙ㄗ)
to see oneself in the mirror

照牆(ㄓㄠˋ ㄑㄧㄤˊ)
a wall immediately outside the front door

照相(ㄓㄠˋ ㄒㄧㄤˋ)
to take a picture or photograph: 我們週末照相去。Let's go and take photographs this weekend.

照相板(ㄓㄠˋ ㄒㄧㄤˋ ㄅㄢˇ)
a phototype; a photogravure

照相館(ㄓㄠˋ ㄒㄧㄤˋ ㄍㄨㄢˇ)
a photostudio

照相機(ㄓㄠˋ ㄒㄧㄤˋ ㄐㄧ)
a camera

照相師(ㄓㄠˋ ㄒㄧㄤˋ ㄕ)
a photographer

照相術(ㄓㄠˋ ㄒㄧㄤˋ ㄕㄨˋ)
photography

照直說(ㄓㄠˋ ㄓˊ ㄕㄨㄛ)
to speak frankly; to talk bluntly

照章辦理(ㄓㄠˋ ㄓㄤ ㄅㄢˋ ㄌㄧˇ)
to carry on, operate, or manage according to rules, regulations, etc.

照准(ㄓㄠˋ ㄓㄨㄣˇ)
to approve (a request); to grant; to give approval (to a request); approved: 請假一天照准。Your request for a day off is granted.

照常(ㄓㄠˋ ㄔㄤˊ)
as usual

照射(ㄓㄠˋ ㄕㄜˋ)
to shine or light upon; to illuminate; to radiate; to irradiate

照收(ㄓㄠˋ ㄕㄡ)
①to duly receive; duly received ②to accept accordingly

照身鏡(ㄓㄠˋ ㄕㄣ ㄐㄧㄥˋ)
a cheval glass; a long mirror that reflects the whole length of the body

照數(ㄓㄠˋ ㄕㄨˋ)
according to the listed sum, number, etc.

照說(ㄓㄠˋ ㄕㄨㄛ)
as a rule: 照說這時候該冷了。As a rule, it should be cold by now.

照此類推(ㄓㄠˋ ㄘˇ ㄌㄟˋ ㄊㄨㄟ)
to draw analogous conclusions

照算(ㄓㄠˋ ㄙㄨㄢˋ)
①to calculate or charge (the listed items) accordingly ②to charge without deduction, discount, etc.

照妖鏡(ㄓㄠˋ ㄧㄠ ㄐㄧㄥˋ)
①(a Taoist superstition) a tiny mirror hung on the back to frighten away evil spirits ②a mirror said to make evil spirits appearing in human form show their original forms

照耀(ㄓㄠˋ ㄧㄠˋ)
to radiate; to light up; to shine; to illuminate: 那是陽光照耀的美麗早晨。It was a beautiful morning with the sun shining.

照樣(ㄓㄠˋ ㄧㄤˋ)

①to pattern after; to copy ②as usual; in the old manner; all the same

照應(ㄓㄠˋ ㄧㄥˋ)
①to take care of; to look after: 請照應一下我的小孩。Please take care of my child for a moment. ②to correlate

照原價(ㄓㄠˋ ㄩㄢˊ ㄐㄧㄚˋ)
according to the old price (although there has been a price hike)

【煢】 3233
ㄑㄩㄥˊ　chyong qiong
to be all alone; without friends or relatives; solitary

煢煢(ㄑㄩㄥˊ ㄑㄩㄥˊ)
to be all alone in the whole wide world

煢獨(ㄑㄩㄥˊ ㄉㄨˊ)
alone; friendless and childless

煢居(ㄑㄩㄥˊ ㄐㄩ)
to live alone

煢煢(ㄑㄩㄥˊ ㄑㄩㄥˊ)
desolate and alone; lonely

十畫

【熙】 3234
ㄒㄧ　shi xi
1. bright and brilliant; glorious
2. expansive; spacious
3. flourishing; prosperous; booming
4. peaceful and happy

熙來壤往 or 熙來攘往(ㄒㄧ ㄌㄞˊ ㄖㄤˇ ㄨㄤˇ)
the hustle and bustle of large crowds

熙熙(ㄒㄧ ㄒㄧ)
peaceful and happy

熙熙壤壤 or 熙熙攘攘(ㄒㄧ ㄒㄧ ㄖㄤˇ ㄖㄤˇ)
coming and going busily; crowded and noisy; hustle and bustle

熙洽(ㄒㄧ ㄒㄧㄚˊ)
(said of times) peaceful and prosperous

熙笑(ㄒㄧ ㄒㄧㄠˋ)
to laugh happily

熙朝(ㄒㄧ ㄔㄠˊ)
a prosperous reign or age (in old China, a reference to

〔火部〕

the dynasty in which one lived)

照春(ㄓㄠ ㄔㄨㄣ)
spring; springtime

照怡(ㄓㄠ 一ˊ)
amiable and cordial

【熊】 3235
ㄒㄩㄥˊ shyong xióng

1. a bear
2. shining bright
3. a Chinese family name

熊白(ㄒㄩㄥˊ ㄅㄞˊ)
the fatty portion on the back of a bear which tastes delicious

熊羆(ㄒㄩㄥˊ ㄆㄧˊ)
①name of two fierce animals used as a synonym of men of enormous strength ② name of an ancient Chinese (in the *Book of Shu*)

熊羆入夢(ㄒㄩㄥˊ ㄆㄧˊ ㄖㄨˋ ㄇㄥˋ)
May you bear a son!—a congratulatory greeting to a friend when he begets a son

熊貓(ㄒㄩㄥˊ ㄇㄠ)
a panda

熊蹯(ㄒㄩㄥˊ ㄈㄢˊ)
the palm of a bear (a rare delicacy in Chinese feasts)亦作「熊掌」

熊膽(ㄒㄩㄥˊ ㄉㄢˇ)
the gall secretion of a bear (used in Chinese medicine)

熊虎(ㄒㄩㄥˊ ㄏㄨˇ)
the bear and the tiger —intrepid; fierce

熊心豹膽(ㄒㄩㄥˊ ㄒㄧㄣ ㄅㄠˋ ㄉㄢˇ)
(literally) the heart of a bear and the gall of a leopard — tremendous bravery or courage

熊熊(ㄒㄩㄥˊ ㄒㄩㄥˊ)
bright and brilliant; flaming and glorious; shining

熊熊大火(ㄒㄩㄥˊ ㄒㄩㄥˊ ㄉㄚˋ ㄏㄨㄛˇ)
a blazing fire

熊掌(ㄒㄩㄥˊ ㄓㄤˇ)
the palms or soles of a bear (a rare delicacy in Chinese feasts)

熊腰虎背(ㄒㄩㄥˊ ㄧㄠ ㄏㄨˇ ㄅㄟˋ)
the waist of a bear and the back of a tiger—heavy and muscular build of the body

【熏】 3236
(燻)ㄒㄩㄣ shiun xūn

1. smoke; to smoke; to burn; smoked (meat, fish, etc.)
2. (said of smell) to assail nostrils: 臭氣熏人。The stench is assailing our nostrils.
3. warm; mild
4. to move or touch
5. same as 曛 or 薰
6. to scent; to fumigate

熏沐(ㄒㄩㄣ ㄇㄨˋ)
to bathe and apply perfume

熏風(ㄒㄩㄣ ㄈㄥ)
southeast (warm) winds

熏天(ㄒㄩㄣ ㄊㄧㄢ)
overwhelming

熏爐(ㄒㄩㄣ ㄌㄨˊ)
a portable stove for burning incense or warming; a brazier

熏黑(ㄒㄩㄣ ㄏㄟ)
to blacken by smoke

熏夕(ㄒㄩㄣ ㄒㄧˋ)
evening time; dusk

熏香(ㄒㄩㄣ ㄒㄧㄤ)
a kind of incense used especially for perfuming clothing, bedding, rooms, etc.

熏炙(ㄒㄩㄣ ㄓˋ)
to cauterize

熏灼四方(ㄒㄩㄣ ㄓㄨㄛˊ ㄙˋ ㄈㄤ)
(said of powerful officials) to terrorize or bully people

熏肉(ㄒㄩㄣ ㄖㄡˋ)
to smoke meat; smoked meat; bacon

熏染(ㄒㄩㄣ ㄖㄢˇ)
to influence

熏死(ㄒㄩㄣ ㄙˇ)
suffocated to death (by fumes, stench, etc.)

熏衣(ㄒㄩㄣ ㄧ)
to fumigate clothing with aromatic smoke

熏魚(ㄒㄩㄣ ㄩˊ)
to smoke fish; smoked fish

【熄】 3237
ㄒㄧˊ shyi xí

1. to extinguish (a fire); to put out (a light): 把燈熄了。Put out the light.
2. to quash; to destroy; to obliterate

熄滅(ㄒㄧˊ ㄇㄧㄝˋ)
to extinguish (a fire); to put out (a light); to die out

熄燈(ㄒㄧˊ ㄉㄥ)
to put out the light; to turn

or switch off the light: 你離開時請熄燈。Please turn off the light (or lamp) as you leave.

熄火(ㄒㄧˊ ㄏㄨㄛˇ)
①(usually said of factories, steamships, etc.) to stop the fire (in the boiler)—to stop operation ②to turn off the lamp or light

熄火器(ㄒㄧˊ ㄏㄨㄛˇ ㄑㄧˋ)
a fire extinguisher 亦作「滅火器」

【熗】 3238
ㄑㄧㄤˋ chiang qiàng

1. a way of cooking in which foods (especially bivalves and some vegetables) are eaten right after being brought to a boil
2. to fry something quickly in hot oil, then cook it with sauce and water
3. same as 嗆—to choke with smoke, etc.

【煽】 3239
ㄕㄢ shan shān

1. to stir up; to instigate; to incite; to fan
2. flaming; blazing; to flame

煽動(ㄕㄢ ㄉㄨㄥˋ)
to incite; to stir up (a strike, uprising, etc.): 他們企圖煽動群衆。They tried to stir up trouble among the masses.

煽火(ㄕㄢ ㄏㄨㄛˇ)
to fan the fire; to fan the flame

煽惑(ㄕㄢ ㄏㄨㄛˋ)
to incite; to agitate; to rouse with words or lies: 不要煽惑人心。Don't agitate people by demagogy

【熔】 3240
(鎔)ㄖㄨㄥˊ rong róng

1. to smelt; to weld or fuse metals; to melt
2. a die; a mold
3. a spear-like weapon

熔點(ㄖㄨㄥˊ ㄉㄧㄢˇ)
a melting or fusion point

熔度(ㄖㄨㄥˊ ㄉㄨˋ)
fusibility

熔爐(ㄖㄨㄥˊ ㄌㄨˊ)
a smelting furnace; a melting pot: 美國常被稱爲熔爐。America is often called a

melting pot.

熔化（ㄖㄨㄥˊ ㄏㄨㄚˋ）
to turn metals into liquid by heating; to smelt; to melt

〔火部〕

熔劑（ㄖㄨㄥˊ ㄐㄧˋ）
flux

熔接（ㄖㄨㄥˊ ㄐㄧㄝ）
to weld; to solder. 銅很容易熔接。Copper welds easily.

熔解（ㄖㄨㄥˊ ㄐㄧㄝˇ）
to turn metals into liquid by heating; to smelt; to melt; to fuse; fusion or melting

熔解熱（ㄖㄨㄥˊ ㄐㄧㄝˇ ㄖㄜˋ）
①the quantity of heat energy needed to turn a cubic centimeter of solid metals into liquid ②latent heat of fusion

熔鑄（ㄖㄨㄥˊ ㄓㄨˋ）
founding; casting

熔冶（ㄖㄨㄥˊ ㄧㄝˇ）
to smelt; to melt

熔岩（ㄖㄨㄥˊ ㄧㄢˊ）
lava

【熒】3241
　ㄧㄥˊ yng yíng
1. bright; shining; luminous
2. dazzling; glittering; sparkling; glimmering
3. to doubt; to suspect

熒爆（ㄧㄥˊ ㄅㄠˋ）
light of fire

熒光（ㄧㄥˊ ㄍㄨㄤ）
(physics) fluorescence; fluorescent light

熒惑（ㄧㄥˊ ㄏㄨㄛˋ）
①to confuse or fool others with smooth talks, etc. ②the god of fire ③another name of Mars

熒熒（ㄧㄥˊ ㄧㄥˊ）
①bright and brilliant; luminous ②twinkling; glimmering; sparkling

十一畫

【熠】3242
　ㄧˋ yih yì
bright and brilliant; luminous

熠熠（ㄧˋ ㄧˋ）
bright and luminous. 星光熠熠。The stars are bright and luminous.

熠燿（ㄧˋ ㄧㄠˋ）

①bright and luminous ②a glowworm; a firefly

3243
【熟】
　ㄕㄨˊ shwu shú
（讀音 ㄕㄡˊ shour shóu
1. cooked or well-done (as opposed to raw); prepared or processed
2. ripe (fruit); to ripen
3. very familiar; well versed; experienced; conversant
4. careful or painstaking survey, study, inspection, etc.
5. deep or sound (sleep)

熟皮（ㄕㄨˊ ㄆㄧˊ）
leather; processed hides

熟寐（ㄕㄨˊ ㄇㄟˋ）
a sound sleep or slumber

熟苗（ㄕㄨˊ ㄇㄧㄠˊ）
the part of Miao people (a minority race in China) who have been assimilated to the Han (Chinese) ways of life and observe government laws

熟眠（ㄕㄨˊ ㄇㄧㄢˊ）
a deep sleep or slumber; 嬰兒在搖籃裏熟眠。The baby slumbered in his cradle.

熟番（ㄕㄨˊ ㄈㄢ）
assimilated border tribes

熟飯（ㄕㄨˊ ㄈㄢˋ）or（ㄕㄨˊ ㄈㄢˋ）
cooked rice

熟道（ㄕㄨˊ ㄉㄠˋ）or 熟路（ㄕㄨˊ ㄌㄨˋ）
a familiar road or route

熟地（ㄕㄨˊ ㄉㄧˋ）
the root of foxglove —Rehmannia glutinosa — used in Chinese medicine ②cultivated land

熟讀（ㄕㄨˊ ㄉㄨˊ）or（ㄕㄨˊ ㄉㄡˊ）
to be well versed in; to read thoroughly; to memorize by rote

熟透（ㄕㄨˊ ㄊㄡˋ）or（ㄕㄨˊ ㄊㄡˋ）
①well-cooked ②thoroughly ripe ③very familiar with

熟炭（ㄕㄨˊ ㄊㄢˋ）
coke; charcoal

熟鐵（ㄕㄨˊ ㄊㄧㄝˇ）
wrought iron

熟脫（ㄕㄨˊ ㄊㄨㄛ）
well versed; very familiar with

熟銅（ㄕㄨˊ ㄊㄨㄥˊ）
wrought brass or copper

熟能生巧（ㄕㄨˊ ㄋㄥˊ ㄕㄥ ㄑㄧㄠˇ）
Skill comes from long experience. 或 Dexterity is the product of long practice. 或 Practice makes perfect.

熟年（ㄕㄨˊ ㄋㄧㄢˊ）
a plentiful year; a year of good harvests

熟了（ㄕㄨˊ •ㄌㄜ）or（ㄕㄨˊ •ㄌㄜ）
①ripe: 蘋果已經熟了。The apple is ripe. ②well prepared (lessons) ③well cooked or done: 肉已經煮熟了。The meat is well cooked.

熟臉兒（ㄕㄨˊ ㄌㄧㄢˇ ㄦ）or 熟面孔（ㄕㄨˊ ㄇㄧㄢˋ ㄎㄨㄥˇ）
a familiar face

熟料（ㄕㄨˊ ㄌㄧㄠˋ）
①timber which has been sawed and cut to required sizes for construction purposes ②cooked or prepared ingredients

熟練（ㄕㄨˊ ㄌㄧㄢˋ）
experienced, skilled or dexterous

熟練工人（ㄕㄨˊ ㄌㄧㄢˋ ㄍㄨㄥ ㄖㄣˊ）
experienced or skilled workers

熟路（ㄕㄨˊ ㄌㄨˋ）
a familiar route

熟慮（ㄕㄨˊ ㄌㄩˋ）
to consider or ponder carefully

熟客（ㄕㄨˊ ㄎㄜˋ）or（ㄕㄨˊ ㄎㄜˋ）
an old customer or patron; a frequent visitor

熟貨（ㄕㄨˊ ㄏㄨㄛˋ）or（ㄕㄨˊ ㄏㄨㄛˋ）
processed commodities or goods; finished products

熟悉（ㄕㄨˊ ㄒㄧ）
very familiar with; conversant with; to have an intimate knowledge of: 他熟悉此事。He has an intimate knowledge of the matter.

熟習（ㄕㄨˊ ㄒㄧˊ）
to learn by heart; to be well versed in; to be skilled in

熟知（ㄕㄨˊ ㄓ）
well acquainted or familiar with; to be well versed in; to know well

熟主顧（ㄕㄨˊ ㄓㄨˇ ㄍㄨˋ）
an old customer or patron

熟食（ㄕㄨˊ ㄕˊ）

① cooked food ② the habit of eating cooked food instead of raw or uncooked food

熟石灰 (ㄕㄨˊ ㄕˊ ㄏㄨㄟ)
slaked lime

熟視 (ㄕㄨˊ ㄕˋ)
to look carefully and for a long time; to scrutinize

熟視無睹 (ㄕㄨˊ ㄕˋ ㄨˊ ㄉㄨˇ)
to look at but pay no attention to; to regard as of no consequence; to turn a blind eye to

熟識 (ㄕㄨˊ ㄕˋ)
to know well; very familiar with

熟手 (ㄕㄨˊ ㄕㄡˇ) or (ㄕㄨˊ ㄕㄡˇ)
an experienced or skilled hand

熟睡 (ㄕㄨˊ ㄕㄨㄟˋ)
a sound sleep; to sleep soundly

熟肉 (ㄕㄨˊ ㄖㄡˋ) or (ㄕㄨˊ ㄖㄡˋ)
cooked meat; well-done meat

熟人 (ㄕㄨˊ ㄖㄣˊ) or (ㄕㄨˊ ㄖㄣˊ)
an old acquaintance

熟字 (ㄕㄨˊ ㄗˋ) or (ㄕㄨˊ ㄗˋ)
a familiar word; a word one knows

熟思 (ㄕㄨˊ ㄙ)
to think over or consider carefully; to ponder deeply; to deliberate: 答覆之前, 他熟思這問題。He deliberated the question before he made an answer.

熟菜 (ㄕㄨˊ ㄘㄞˋ) or (ㄕㄨˊ ㄘㄞˋ)
cooked dishes or food

熟諳 (ㄕㄨˊ ㄢ)
well-experienced; to be well versed in; to be an expert in: 他熟諳水性。He is an expert in swimming.

【熬】 3244
1. ㄠˊ aur áo

1. to extract (oil, etc.) by applying heat
2. to cook; to stew or simmer
3. to endure with perseverance; to suffer with patience (an ordeal, etc.); to sustain

熬不過 (ㄠˊ ㄅㄨˋ ㄍㄨㄛˋ)
to be unable to sustain or endure; cannot survive a grave illness (after a given time)

熬頭兒 (ㄠˊ ㄊㄡˊㄦ)
the reward obtained from long ordeals, sufferings, etc.

熬湯 (ㄠˊ ㄊㄤ)
to stew or simmer (meat) for broth

熬煉 (ㄠˊ ㄌㄧㄢˋ)
to boil and smelt—strict discipline

熬膏 (ㄠˊ ㄍㄠ)
① to simmer (raw opium) to paste, readying it for smoking ②to prepare (herbal medicine) in paste form, mostly for external use

熬枯受淡 (ㄠˊ ㄎㄨ ㄕㄡˋ ㄉㄢˋ)
to have undergone the whole ordeal of ennui and dull life

熬煎 (ㄠˊ ㄐㄧㄢ)
a tremendous ordeal; suffering

熬刑 (ㄠˊ ㄒㄧㄥˊ)
(said of a prisoner) to insist on innocence under torture

熬粥 (ㄠˊ ㄓㄡ)
to cook congee or gruel by simmering

熬出來 (ㄠˊ ㄔㄨ ㄌㄞˊ) or 熬出頭 (ㄠˊ ㄔㄨ ㄊㄡˊ)
to have gone through all sorts of ordeal

熬日子 (ㄠˊ ㄖˋ ㄗ˙)
to go through hard times

熬夜 (ㄠˊ ㄧㄝˋ)
to work (or gamble) until deep into the night; to burn the midnight oil

熬藥 (ㄠˊ ㄧㄠˋ)
to decoct medicinal herbs

熬油 (ㄠˊ ㄧㄡˊ)
① to waste lamp oil by staying up at night ② to extract oil (as lard, etc.) by heating

【熝】 3244
1. ㄠ au áo

1. to cook; to stew
2. to be worn down by worries, cares; discouraged or despondent; dejected

熝惱 (ㄠ ㄋㄠˇ)
unhappy and dejected

熝心 (ㄠ ㄒㄧㄣ)
annoying; vexing; unhappy

熝菜 (ㄠ ㄘㄞˋ)
to cook food (with water)

【熱】 3245
ㄖㄜˋ reh rè

〔火部〕

1. hot; heated; burning; to heat: 房間熱得像火爐。The room was as hot as an oven.
2. fever
3. earnest; ardent; zealous; enthusiastic; passionate: 他是個熱心的工作者。He is a zealous worker.

熱病 (ㄖㄜˋ ㄅㄧㄥˋ)
fever

熱門 (ㄖㄜˋ ㄇㄣˊ)
something very much in vogue or fashion; something everyone is after or interested in; a craze: 駕滑翔機是最近的熱門玩意兒。Gliding is the latest craze.

熱門貨 (ㄖㄜˋ ㄇㄣˊ ㄏㄨㄛˋ)
a commodity which is enjoying a brisk sale

熱敷法 (ㄖㄜˋ ㄈㄨ ㄈㄚˇ)
(medicine) hot compresses

熱帶 (ㄖㄜˋ ㄉㄞˋ)
the tropics; the Torrid Zone: 熱帶地方是很熱的。It's hot in the tropics.

熱帶植物 (ㄖㄜˋ ㄉㄞˋ ㄓˊ ㄨˋ)
tropical plants

熱帶魚 (ㄖㄜˋ ㄉㄞˋ ㄩˊ)
tropical fish

熱帶雨林 (ㄖㄜˋ ㄉㄞˋ ㄩˇ ㄌㄧㄣˊ)
a tropical rain forest

熱度 (ㄖㄜˋ ㄉㄨˋ)
① heat; temperature: 他的熱度降下去了嗎? Has his temperature come down? ② enthusiasm

熱湯 (ㄖㄜˋ ㄊㄤ)
hot soup

熱騰騰 (ㄖㄜˋ ㄊㄥˊ ㄊㄥˊ)
piping hot; steaming hot

熱天 (ㄖㄜˋ ㄊㄧㄢ)
hot weather; dog days

熱那亞 (ㄖㄜˋ ㄋㄚˇ ㄧㄚˇ)
Genoa, Italy

熱鬧 (ㄖㄜˋ ㄋㄠˋ)
① bustling; thronged; populous; noisy; hustle and bustle: 這個市場很熱鬧。The market is bustling with activity. ② prosperous; flourishing; thriving ③ lively; animated; cheerful; cheery; merry; gay

熱鬧兒 (ㄖㄜˋ ㄋㄠˋㄦ)
merriment; merrymaking;

〔火 部〕

mirth; fun; hilarity

熱能(ㄖㄜˋ ㄋㄥˊ)
thermal energy

熱刺刺的(ㄖㄜˋ ㄘˋ ㄘˋ ·ㄉㄜ)
①impassioned; passionate
②burning hot; scorching: 太陽熱刺刺的。The sun is burning hot.

熱淚盈眶(ㄖㄜˋ ㄌㄟˋ ㄧㄥˊ ㄎㄨㄤˋ)
tearful; eyes moistening

熱浪(ㄖㄜˋ ㄌㄤˋ)
a heat wave; a hot wave

熱力(ㄖㄜˋ ㄌㄧˋ)
a heat energy; thermal energy

熱力學(ㄖㄜˋ ㄌㄧˋ ㄒㄩㄝˊ)
thermodynamics

熱烈(ㄖㄜˋ ㄌㄧㄝˋ)
fervent; passionate; vehement; fiery; enthusiastic; rousing (welcomes): 大家對他的建議反應很熱烈。Everybody responded enthusiastically to his proposal.

熱戀(ㄖㄜˋ ㄌㄧㄢˋ)
to be passionately in love; to be head over heels in love

熱量(ㄖㄜˋ ㄌㄧㄤˋ)
the quantity of heat; calories

熱絡(ㄖㄜˋ ㄌㄨㄛˋ)
very intimate; on friendly terms: 他們是很熱絡的朋友。They are very intimate friends.

熱狗(ㄖㄜˋ ㄍㄡˇ)
a hot dog

熱鍋上的螞蟻(ㄖㄜˋ ㄍㄨㄛ ·ㄕㄤ ·ㄉㄜ ㄇㄚˇ ·ㄧˇ)
(literally) an ant on a hot pan—one in extreme anxiety; restless or fidgeting due to deep worry: 他們急得像熱鍋上的螞蟻。They were as restless as ants on a hot pan.

熱炕(ㄖㄜˋ ㄎㄤˋ)
a brick bed warmed by fire

熱狂(ㄖㄜˋ ㄎㄨㄤˊ)
wild with excitement; hotheaded; frantic; fanatical

熱河(ㄖㄜˋ ㄏㄜˊ)
Jehol Province

熱海(ㄖㄜˋ ㄏㄞˇ)
①Issiq Köl, or Issyk-Kul, a lake in Soviet Central Asia ② Atami, Japan

熱呼呼的(ㄖㄜˋ ㄏㄨ ㄏㄨ ·ㄉㄜ)
piping hot; warm: 他心裏感到

熱呼呼的。He felt it heart-warming.

熱和(ㄖㄜˋ ·ㄏㄨㄛ)
①warm ②gentle; friendly; amiable ③intimate; close

熱烘烘的(ㄖㄜˋ ㄏㄨㄥ ㄏㄨㄥ ·ㄉㄜ)
glowing with heat; red-hot; white-hot

熱氣(ㄖㄜˋ ㄑㄧˋ)
hot vapor; hot gas; hot air; heat

熱氣騰騰(ㄖㄜˋ ㄑㄧˋ ㄊㄥˊ ㄊㄥˊ)
piping hot; steaming hot

熱切(ㄖㄜˋ ㄑㄧㄝˋ)
fervent; earnest; sincerely; earnestly

熱情(ㄖㄜˋ ㄑㄧㄥˊ)
passion; ardor; fervor; passionate; fervent; ardent

熱血(ㄖㄜˋ ㄒㄧㄝˋ)
hot-blooded; fiery-spirited; fervent; zealous; righteous ardor

熱血沸騰(ㄖㄜˋ ㄒㄧㄝˋ ㄈㄟˋ ㄊㄥˊ)
to seethe with fervor; to have a boiling passion

熱血動物(ㄖㄜˋ ㄒㄧㄝˋ ㄉㄨㄥˋ ㄨˋ)
a warm-blooded animal

熱心(ㄖㄜˋ ㄒㄧㄣ)或熱心腸兒(ㄖㄜˋ ㄒㄧㄣ ㄔㄤˊㄦ)
enthusiastic; eager; ardent; zealous; warm-hearted: 他熱心公益事業。He is enthusiastic in promoting public welfare.

熱暑(ㄖㄜˋ ㄕㄨˇ)
to suffer heatstroke

熱戰(ㄖㄜˋ ㄓㄢˋ)
a hot war; a shooting war (as distinct from a cold war)

熱漲冷縮(ㄖㄜˋ ㄓㄤˋ ㄌㄥˇ ㄙㄨㄛ)
to expand when hot and to shrink when cold

熱中名利(ㄖㄜˋ ㄓㄨㄥ ㄇㄧㄥˊ ㄌㄧˋ)
to pursue fame and wealth with fervor

熱潮(ㄖㄜˋ ㄔㄠˊ)
①great mass fervor ②an upsurge

熱忱(ㄖㄜˋ ㄔㄣˊ)
enthusiasm; sincerity; earnest: 我們受到熱忱的歡迎。We are received with great enthusiasm.

熱腸(ㄖㄜˋ ㄔㄤˊ)
enthusiastic; eager; ardent;

zealous

熱誠(ㄖㄜˋ ㄔㄥˊ)
eager devotion; earnestness; sincerity

熱身運動(ㄖㄜˋ ㄕㄣ ㄩㄣˋ ㄉㄨㄥˋ)
warm-up exercise

熱水瓶(ㄖㄜˋ ㄕㄨㄟˇ ㄆㄧㄥˊ)
a thermos (bottle); a thermos flask

熱水器(ㄖㄜˋ ㄕㄨㄟˇ ㄑㄧˋ)
a water heater

熱容量(ㄖㄜˋ ㄖㄨㄥˊ ㄌㄧㄤˋ)
heat capacity

熱竈(ㄖㄜˋ ㄗㄠˋ)
(figuratively) a man in power

熱愛(ㄖㄜˋ ㄞˋ)
to love passionately; to love fervently; passionate love; deep attachment

熱一句，冷一句(ㄖㄜˋ ㄧˋ ㄐㄩˋ，ㄌㄥˇ ㄧˋ ㄐㄩˋ)
to fling hot words and cold words alternately

熱飲(ㄖㄜˋ ㄧㄣˇ)
hot drinks

熱望(ㄖㄜˋ ㄨㄤˋ)
to hope earnestly; to wish ardently: 我們熱望他會成功。We hoped earnestly that he would succeed.

【樵】 3246
(樵)ㄧㄡˊ ㄧㄡˇ
to burn piled firewood

【熨】 3247
1. ㄩㄣˋ yunn yùn
to iron (clothes or cloth)

熨平(ㄩㄣˋ ㄆㄧㄥˊ)
to iron (clothes or cloth)

熨斗(ㄩㄣˋ ㄉㄡˇ)
an iron (for pressing clothes)

熨衣服(ㄩㄣˋ ㄧ ·ㄈㄨ)
to iron clothes: 她一下午都在熨衣服。She's been ironing all afternoon.

【熨】 3247
2. ㄩˋ yuh yù
to settle (matters)

熨貼(ㄩˋ ㄊㄧㄝ)
(said of matters) settled, or taken care of

【麃】 3248
ㄅㄧㄠ biau biāo
1. to cultivate fields
2. valiant; vigorous

十二畫

【熾】 3249
彳 chyh chì

1. intense; vigorous; energetic
2. burning hot; flaming

熾茂
luxuriant; teeming; lush

熾烈(彳 ㄌ一ㄝ)
blazing; burning vigorously:
爐火熾烈。The stove is burning fiercely.

熾盛(彳 ㄕㄥ)
thriving; flourishing

熾熱(彳 ㄖㄜ)
intense heat; intensely hot;
blazing: 工人在熾熱的陽光下
辛苦工作。The workers
labored under a blazing sun.

【燈】 3250
ㄉㄥ deng dēng

1. a lamp; a lantern; a burner
2. Buddha dharma; the Buddhist doctrine
3. a valve; a tube

燈泡兒(ㄉㄥ ㄆㄠ ㄦ)
an electric bulb; a light bulb

燈謎(ㄉㄥ ㄇㄧˊ)or燈虎(ㄉㄥ ㄏㄨˇ)
riddles written on lanterns
(in public contests in which
prizes are offered); lantern
riddles

燈塔(ㄉㄥ ㄊㄚˇ)
a lighthouse

燈臺(ㄉㄥ ㄊㄞˊ)
① a lighthouse ② a lampstand

燈頭(ㄉㄥ ㄊㄡˊ)
a socket for an electric bulb

燈籠褲(ㄉㄥ ㄌㄨㄥ ㄎㄨˋ)
baggy pants worn by athletes; knickerbockers

燈籠(ㄉㄥ ㄌㄨㄥ)
a lantern

燈光(ㄉㄥ ㄍㄨㄤ)
lamplight; lights; illumination

燈花(ㄉㄥ ㄏㄨㄚ)
snuff (of wick)

燈火(ㄉㄥ ㄏㄨㄛˇ)
lamplight; lights; illumination

燈火管制(ㄉㄥ ㄏㄨㄛˇ ㄍㄨㄢˇ ㄓˋ)
a blackout or dim-out (against air raiders, etc.)

燈紅酒綠(ㄉㄥ ㄏㄨㄥˊ ㄐㄧㄡˇ ㄌㄩˋ)
(literally) red lanterns and
green wine—a scene of
debauchery

燈架(ㄉㄥ ㄐㄧㄚˋ)
a lamp holder

燈節(ㄉㄥ ㄐㄧㄝˊ)
the Lantern Festival (falling
on the 15th day of the first
lunar month)

燈下(ㄉㄥ ㄒㄧㄚˋ)
by lamplight—by night

燈心(ㄉㄥ ㄒㄧㄣ)or燈蕊(ㄉㄥ ㄖㄨㄟˇ)
lampwick; candlewick; wick

燈心絨(ㄉㄥ ㄒㄧㄣ ㄖㄨㄥˊ)
corduroy

燈心草(ㄉㄥ ㄒㄧㄣ ㄘㄠˇ)
a rush

燈罩(ㄉㄥ ㄓㄠˋ)
a lampshade: 燈罩上灰塵積
聚。Dust accumulated on the
lampshade.

燈盞(ㄉㄥ ㄓㄢˇ)
oil lamps

燈燭輝煌(ㄉㄥ ㄓㄨˊ ㄏㄨㄟ ㄏㄨㄤˊ)
blazing with lights or The
lights are glittering with
splendor.

燈船(ㄉㄥ ㄔㄨㄢˊ)
a lightship

燈座(ㄉㄥ ㄗㄨㄛˋ)
a lampstand

燈蛾(ㄉㄥ ㄜˊ)
moths attracted by lamplight

燈蛾撲火(ㄉㄥ ㄜˊ ㄆㄨ ㄏㄨㄛˇ)
(literally) Moths dash into
the flame.—an act of self-destruction; a suicidal act

燈油(ㄉㄥ ㄧㄡˊ)
lamp oil

【燃】 3251
ㄖㄢˊ ran rán

to burn; to ignite; to light

燃眉之急(ㄖㄢˊ ㄇㄟˊ ㄓ ㄐㄧˊ)
a matter as urgent as if the
eyebrows had caught fire

燃放(ㄖㄢˊ ㄈㄤˋ)
to set off (fireworks, etc.)

燃燈(ㄖㄢˊ ㄉㄥ)
to light a lamp

燃料(ㄖㄢˊ ㄌㄧㄠˋ)
fuel: 汽油不再是廉價燃料。Gasoline is no longer a cheap
fuel.

燃料庫(ㄖㄢˊ ㄌㄧㄠˋ ㄎㄨˋ)
a fuel depot; a fuel reservoir

燃料礦物(ㄖㄢˊ ㄌㄧㄠˋ ㄎㄨㄤˋ ㄨˋ)
mineral fuels

燃燭(ㄖㄢˊ ㄓㄨˊ)
to light a candle

燃燒(ㄖㄢˊ ㄕㄠ)
to burn; to be on fire; to be
in flames; combustion: 乾柴
容易燃燒。Dry wood burns
easily.

燃燒彈(ㄖㄢˊ ㄕㄠ ㄉㄢˋ)
an incendiary shell or bomb

燃燒點(ㄖㄢˊ ㄕㄠ ㄉㄧㄢˇ)
the point of combustion

燃燒熱(ㄖㄢˊ ㄕㄠ ㄖㄜˋ)
heat of combustion

【燎】 3252
ㄌㄧㄠˊ liaw liáo

1. to burn over a wider and
wider area; to set fire to
2. to be brilliant

燎朗(ㄌㄧㄠˊ ㄌㄤˇ)
bright; luminous

燎獵(ㄌㄧㄠˊ ㄌㄧㄝˋ)
to hunt by setting fire to the
bushes in the field

燎炬(ㄌㄧㄠˊ ㄐㄩˋ)
a torch

燎原(ㄌㄧㄠˊ ㄩㄢˊ)
① to set the prairie ablaze:
星星之火可以燎原。A little
spark can set a blazing prairie fire. ② to get out of control like a prairie fire

【燎】 3252. ㄌㄧㄠˇ leau liǎo
to singe

燎毛(ㄌㄧㄠˇ ㄇㄠˊ)
to singe hair—a thing that
can be done very easily

燎髮(ㄌㄧㄠˇ ㄈㄚˇ)
to singe hair—a thing that
can be done very easily

【燉】 3253
ㄉㄨㄣˋ duenn dùn

1. to stew; to simmer
2. to warm

燉爛(ㄉㄨㄣˋ ㄌㄢˋ)
to stew until it is soft

燉雞(ㄉㄨㄣˋ ㄐㄧ)
① to stew chicken ② stewed
chicken

燉熟(ㄉㄨㄣˋ ㄕㄡˊ)
to stew until it is done

燉肉(ㄉㄨㄣˋ ㄖㄡˋ)
① stewed meat ② to stew
meat

燉藥(ㄉㄨㄣˋ ㄧㄠˋ)

〔火部〕

〔火部〕

to make concoction by simmering

【燉】 3253
ㄉㄨㄣ ㄉㄨㄣˊ duèn dūn
Tunhwang, Kansu 參看「燉煌」

燉煌 or 敦煌 (ㄉㄨㄣ ㄏㄨㄤˊ)
Tunhwang, Kansu (甘肅), a site of many caves housing vast quantities of Buddhist arts and scriptures of ancient China

【燒】 3254
ㄕㄠ shau shāo
1. to burn
2. to roast; to stew
3. to boil; to heat: 水燒開了。The water is boiling.
4. to run a fever; to have a temperature
5. a fever: 他的燒退了。His fever is down.

燒杯 (ㄕㄠ ㄅㄟ)
a beaker

燒餅 (ㄕㄠ ㄅㄧㄥˇ)
a sesame seed cake

燒盤兒 (ㄕㄠ ㄆㄢˊㄦ)
(figuratively) a face red with shame or embarrassment

燒瓶 (ㄕㄠ ㄆㄧㄥˊ)
a flask

燒賣 (ㄕㄠ ·ㄇㄞ)
a kind of steamed pie stuffed with meat

燒刀子 (ㄕㄠ ㄉㄠ ·ㄗ)
a kind of strong alcoholic drink

燒頭香 (ㄕㄠ ㄊㄡˊ ㄒㄧㄤ)
to burn the first incense stick of the day (at a temple on a festival)

燒鳥 (ㄕㄠ ㄋㄧㄠˇ)
roast bird

燒冷竈 (ㄕㄠ ㄌㄥˇ ㄗㄠˋ)
to engage in an unpopular activity or to cultivate the friendship of someone temporary out of luck in the hope of eventually profiting therefrom

燒煉 (ㄕㄠ ㄌㄧㄢˋ)
Taoist technique of making the elixir of life; to practice alchemy

燒烤 (ㄕㄠ ㄎㄠˇ)
to roast

燒化 (ㄕㄠ ㄏㄨㄚˋ)
to reduce to ashes; to melt down by fire; to cremate

燒活 (ㄕㄠ ㄏㄨㄛˊ)
paper structures burned in a funeral

燒火 (ㄕㄠ ㄏㄨㄛˇ)
to build a fire; to make a fire

燒灰 (ㄕㄠ ㄏㄨㄟ)
to reduce to ashes

燒燬 (ㄕㄠ ㄏㄨㄟˇ)
to burn down; to destroy in fire

燒焦 (ㄕㄠ ㄐㄧㄠ)
to scorch; to sear; to singe

燒酒 (ㄕㄠ ㄐㄧㄡˇ)
a kind of strong alcoholic drink; white spirits

燒鹼 or 燒碱 (ㄕㄠ ㄐㄧㄢˇ)
caustic soda

燒錢化紙 (ㄕㄠ ㄑㄧㄢˊ ㄏㄨㄚˋ ㄓˇ)
to perform the rite of burning imitation paper money for the dead

燒心 (ㄕㄠ ㄒㄧㄣ)
fretful; uneasy; anxious; apprehensive

燒香 (ㄕㄠ ㄒㄧㄤ)
to burn joss sticks in worship

燒指 (ㄕㄠ ㄓˇ)
to burn fingers in the Buddhist rite of self-torture

燒紙引鬼 (ㄕㄠ ㄓˇ ㄧㄣˇ ㄍㄨㄟˇ)
(literally) to invite ghosts unintentionally by burning imitation paper money—to invite trouble by showing civility or kindness

燒殺 (ㄕㄠ ㄕㄚ)
burning and killing; atrocities committed by enemy troops, bandits, etc.

燒傷 (ㄕㄠ ㄕㄤ)
burns: 他受到三級燒傷。He suffered from third-degree burns.

燒水 (ㄕㄠ ㄕㄨㄟˇ)
to boil water; to heat water

燒死 (ㄕㄠ ㄙˇ) or (ㄕㄠ ·ㄙ)
to burn to death

燒夷彈 (ㄕㄠ ㄧˊ ㄉㄢˋ)
an incendiary shell or bomb

燒窰 (ㄕㄠ ㄧㄠˊ)
to build fire in a pottery or

porcelain kiln

燒尾 (ㄕㄠ ㄨㄟˇ)
celebrating banquets held by the scholars of the Tang and Sung dynasties who had just passed the imperial civil service examination

【燐】 3255
(磷) ㄌㄧㄣˊ lín lín
phosphorus

燐肥 (ㄌㄧㄣˊ ㄈㄟˊ)
phosphorus fertilizer; phosphorite

燐光 (ㄌㄧㄣˊ ㄍㄨㄤ)
phosphorescence

燐火 (ㄌㄧㄣˊ ㄏㄨㄛˇ)
a jack-o'-lantern; a will-o'-the-wisp; a phosphorescent light

燐灰石 (ㄌㄧㄣˊ ㄏㄨㄟ ㄕˊ)
apatite

燐酸 (ㄌㄧㄣˊ ㄙㄨㄢ)
phosphoric acid

燐酸鈣 (ㄌㄧㄣˊ ㄙㄨㄢ ㄍㄞˇ)
calcium phosphate

【燔】 3256
ㄈㄢˊ farn fán
1. roast meat for offering
2. to burn; to roast

燔柴 (ㄈㄢˊ ㄔㄞˊ)
a holocaust (an ancient rite of worshiping Heaven)

燔肉 (ㄈㄢˊ ㄖㄡˋ)
roast meat for offering

【熹】 3257
(爔) ㄒㄧ shi xī
1. faint sunlight; dawn
2. giving out faint light

熹微 (ㄒㄧ ㄨㄟˊ)
①faint light at dawn ②(said of morning sunlight) dim; pale

【燕】 3258
ㄧㄢˋ yann yàn
1. a swallow
2. comfort; ease
3. to feast; to enjoy

燕麥 (ㄧㄢˋ ㄇㄞˋ)
oats

燕麥片 (ㄧㄢˋ ㄇㄞˋ ㄆㄧㄢˋ)
oatmeal

燕婉之私 (ㄧㄢˋ ㄨㄢˇ ㄓ ㄙ)
conjugal happiness

燕女 (ㄧㄢˋ ㄋㄩˇ)
to delight in women

燕樂
①(ㄧㄢˋ ㄌㄜˋ) to entertain; to

please

燕②(丨ㄢㄩˋ) ⓐ music played in the banquet ⓑ popular music (as distinct from classical music)

燕侶(丨ㄢㄌㄩˇ)
a married couple; husband and wife

燕侶鶯儔(丨ㄢㄌㄩˇㄧㄥㄔㄡˊ)
a happily married couple; a devoted couple

燕賀(丨ㄢㄏㄜˋ)
to offer congratulations on the completion of a new residence

燕好(丨ㄢㄏㄠˇ)
(said of husband and wife) very fond of each other

燕頷虎頸(丨ㄢㄏㄢˋㄏㄨˇㄐㄧㄥˇ)
a noble look; a dignified appearance

燕几(丨ㄢㄐㄧˇ)
a stool much used at one's leisure

燕居(丨ㄢㄐㄩ)
to live at leisure; to live at ease

燕雀兒(丨ㄢㄑㄩㄝˋㄦ)
a finch

燕寢(丨ㄢㄑㄧㄣˇ)
a place for rest

燕雀處堂(丨ㄢㄑㄩㄝˋㄔㄨˇㄊㄤˊ)
to be oblivious of danger in the comfort of an easy life

燕雀安知鴻鵠志(丨ㄢㄑㄩㄝˋㄢㄓ ㄏㄨㄥˊㄏㄨˊㄓˋ)
(literally) How can a swallow understand the mind of a swan?—How can a common fellow read the mind of a great man?

燕巢幕上(丨ㄢㄔㄠˊㄇㄨˋㄕㄤˋ)
(literally) a swallow's nest built on a curtain—a very precarious situation

燕出(丨ㄢㄔㄨ)
(said of a ruler) to go out in secrecy

燕瘦環肥(丨ㄢㄕㄡˋㄏㄨㄢˊㄈㄟˊ)
(literally) Chao Fei-yen (趙飛燕) was skinny while Yang Yü-huan (楊玉環) was plump. (Both were imperial concubines of unusual beauty.) —beautiful women, each of whom is attractive in her own way

燕子(丨ㄢ˙ㄗ)or 燕兒(丨ㄢˊㄦ)
a swallow

燕子磯(丨ㄢˇㄗㄐㄧ)
name of a hill to the north of Nanking overlooking the Yangtze River

燕窩(丨ㄢㄨㄛ)
a rare delicacy prepared from swallows' nests found on seaside cliffs, etc., built of seaweed and a certain secretion from swallows

燕安(丨ㄢㄢ)
comfort; ease; peace

燕爾新婚(丨ㄢˇㄦˇㄒㄧㄣㄏㄨㄣ)
marital happiness; conjugal bliss

燕遊(丨ㄢˊㄧㄡˊ)
to make pleasure trips

燕燕于飛(丨ㄢˋㄧㄢˋㄩˊㄈㄟ)
The swallows go flying together.— (said of husband and wife) deeply attached to each other

燕飲(丨ㄢˋㄧㄣˇ)
to feast: 他們坐在那裏, 燕飲終日。 They sat there feasting all day long.

燕窩(丨ㄢㄨㄛ)
swallows' nests found on seaside cliffs, etc., built of seaweed and a certain secretion by swallows, used as an ingredient for a highly valued Chinese dish

燕尾服(丨ㄢㄨㄟˇㄈㄨˊ)
a swallow-tailed coat; a swallowtail; a tailcoat; a full-dress coat; tails

燕婉(丨ㄢㄨㄢˇ)
friendly; genial

燕語(呢喃)(丨ㄢˇㄩˇ(ㄋㄧˊㄋㄢˊ))
the soft chirping of swallows

【燕】 3258
         2. 丨ㄢ ian yān
a state in what is Hopeh (河北) today during the Epoch of Warring States

燕京(丨ㄢㄐㄧㄥ)
ancient name of Peking

燕京大學(丨ㄢㄐㄧㄥㄉㄚˋㄒㄩㄝˊ)
Yenching University, Peking

燕趙(丨ㄢㄓㄠˋ)
the state of Yen and the state of Chao, now used in reference to northern China

燕山(丨ㄢㄕㄢ)
a mountain range in Hopeh

燕說(丨ㄢㄕㄨㄛ)
distorted remarks; slanted views; twisted interpretations

燕然山(丨ㄢㄖㄢˊㄕㄢ)
ancient name of what is today's Hangai Mountain (杭愛山) in Outer Mongolia

燕雲十六州(丨ㄢㄩㄣˊㄕˊㄌㄧㄡˋㄓㄡ)
the 16 provinces roughly corresponding to what is today's Hopeh (河北), northern Shensi (陝西) and Chahar (察哈爾) that were ceded to the Kitans in the 10th century A.D. by Shih Ching-tang (石敬塘), the first ruler of the Later Tsin Dynasty, as a price for their assistance in obtaining his throne

【燙】 3259
      ㄊㄤˋ tang tàng
1. to scald; to burn
2. to heat; to warm
3. very hot: 這湯眞燙。The soup is boiling hot.
4. to iron

燙麵(ㄊㄤˋㄇㄧㄢˋ)
dough kneaded with hot water; to knead dough with hot water

燙髮(ㄊㄤˋㄈㄚˇ)
to have a permanent wave; to have a permanent

燙酒(ㄊㄤˋㄐㄧㄡˇ)
to heat wine or liquor in hot water

燙金(ㄊㄤˋㄐㄧㄣ)
gilding; bronzing

燙手(ㄊㄤˋㄕㄡˇ)
①to scald one's hand ②difficult to handle or manage

燙傷(ㄊㄤˋㄕㄤ)
a burn; a scald: 他被熱水燙傷。He was scalded with hot water.

燙衣服(ㄊㄤˋ丨˙ㄈㄨ)
to iron clothes

燙一燙(ㄊㄤˋ丨ˋ˙ㄊㄤ)
to have (something) heated, scalded, or ironed

【燊】 3260
      ㄕㄣ shen shēn
vigorous

〔火部〕

【火部】

【燋】 3261
1. ㄐㄧㄠ jiau jiāo
1. a torch
2. same as 焦 — to scorch; to scald

【燋】 3261
2.(憔) ㄑㄧㄠˊ chyan qiáo
haggard; worn; emaciated

【燜】 3262
ㄇㄣ menn mèn
(又讀 ㄇㄣˊ mhen mén)
to cook with mild heat in a closed vessel; to cook in a casserole
燜飯(ㄇㄣ ㄈㄢˋ)
to cook rice over a slow fire
燜肉(ㄇㄣ ㄖㄡˋ)
meat cooked in a casserole

【燁】 3263
ㄧㄝˋ yeh yè
blazing; splendid; glorious

十三畫

【營】 3264
ㄧㄥˊ yng yíng
1. military barracks; a camp: 集中營 a concentration camp
2. a battalion: 騎兵營 a cavalry battalion
3. to manage; to administer; to handle; to operate; to run
營販(ㄧㄥˊ ㄈㄢˋ)
to manage sale business
營房(ㄧㄥˊ ㄈㄤˊ)
barracks
營地(ㄧㄥˊ ㄉㄧˋ)
a campsite; a camping ground
營田(ㄧㄥˊ ㄊㄧㄢˊ)
①to engage in farming ②to employ refugees or vagrants to cultivate public land
營利(ㄧㄥˊ ㄌㄧˋ)
to engage in making profit
營火(ㄧㄥˊ ㄏㄨㄛˇ)
a campfire—an outdoor fire in a camp for warmth or cooking
營火會(ㄧㄥˊ ㄏㄨㄛˇ ㄏㄨㄟˋ)
a campfire —a social gathering of soldiers, scouts, etc.
營妓(ㄧㄥˊ ㄐㄧˋ)
publicly provided prostitutes at military barracks; a camp follower

營救(ㄧㄥˊ ㄐㄧㄡˋ)
to rescue or deliver
營建(ㄧㄥˊ ㄐㄧㄢˋ)
to manage or handle the construction of; to construct
營求(ㄧㄥˊ ㄑㄧㄡˊ)
to seek
營寨(ㄧㄥˊ ㄓㄞˋ)
barracks; a military post
營長(ㄧㄥˊ ㄓㄤˇ)
a battalion commander
營帳(ㄧㄥˊ ㄓㄤˋ)
tents used as military barracks
營造(ㄧㄥˊ ㄗㄠˋ)
civil engineering activities
營生(ㄧㄥˊ ㄕㄥ)
to make a living: 他靠賣水果營生。He earns a living as a fruiterer.
營造(ㄧㄥˊ ㄗㄠˋ)
to construct; to build: 建築者職司營造。A builder is one who builds.
營造尺(ㄧㄥˊ ㄗㄠˋ ㄔˇ)
the standard foot adopted by the Public Works Ministry during the Ming and Ching dynasties
營造廠(ㄧㄥˊ ㄗㄠˋ ㄔㄤˇ)
a construction firm; a building contractor; a contractor
營造商(ㄧㄥˊ ㄗㄠˋ ㄕㄤ)
a building contractor; a contractor
營葬(ㄧㄥˊ ㄗㄤˋ)
to manage a funeral
營私(ㄧㄥˊ ㄙ)
to seek personal gain (especially through a public post)
營私舞弊(ㄧㄥˊ ㄙ ㄨˇ ㄅㄧˋ)
to seek personal gain illicitly while holding a public post; to practice graft
營業(ㄧㄥˊ ㄧㄝˋ)
to engage in business; business operation
營業開支(ㄧㄥˊ ㄧㄝˋ ㄎㄞ ㄓ)
management and general expenses
營業執照(ㄧㄥˊ ㄧㄝˋ ㄓˊ ㄓㄠˋ)
a business license
營業時間(ㄧㄥˊ ㄧㄝˋ ㄕˊ ㄐㄧㄢ)
business hours: 營業時間是上午八時到下午六時。Business

hours, 8 a.m. to 6 p.m.
營業收入(ㄧㄥˊ ㄧㄝˋ ㄕㄡ ㄖㄨˋ)
operating revenue
營業稅(ㄧㄥˊ ㄧㄝˋ ㄕㄨㄟˋ)
business tax
營業額(ㄧㄥˊ ㄧㄝˋ ㄜˊ)
the volume of business
營養(ㄧㄥˊ ㄧㄤˇ)
nutrition; nourishment: 均衡的飲食使你的身體獲得營養。A balanced diet provides nutrition for your body.
營養不良(ㄧㄥˊ ㄧㄤˇ ㄅㄨˋ ㄌㄧㄤˊ)
malnutrition; undernourishment: 不適當的食物會引起營養不良。Improper food can cause malnutrition.
營養品(ㄧㄥˊ ㄧㄤˇ ㄆㄧㄣˇ)
nutriment
營養價值(ㄧㄥˊ ㄧㄤˇ ㄐㄧㄚˋ ㄓˊ)
nutritive value
營養學(ㄧㄥˊ ㄧㄤˇ ㄒㄩㄝˊ)
nutriology
營養素(ㄧㄥˊ ㄧㄤˇ ㄙㄨˋ)
nutrients (a collective term for protein, carbonhydrates, fat, vitamins, and minerals)
營務(ㄧㄥˊ ㄨˋ)
military matters

【燧】 3265
ㄙㄨㄟˋ suey suì
1. a flint
2. a beacon
燧石(ㄙㄨㄟˋ ㄕˊ)
flint
燧人氏(ㄙㄨㄟˋ ㄖㄣˊ ㄕˋ)
a legendary ruler said to be the first to discover fire

【燠】 3266
1. ㄩˋ yuh yù
warm

【燠】 3266
2. ㄠˋ aw ào
very hot; sweltering
燠熱(ㄠˋ ㄖㄜˋ)
very hot: 天氣這麼燠熱，我什麼事也不想做。It's so hot that I do not want to do anything.

【燠】 3266
3. ㄧㄡˋ iou yòu
as in 燠休 — to comfort or to soothe (the distressed or afflicted)

【燦】 3267
ㄘㄢˋ tsann càn
bright; brilliant; resplendent

燦爛 (ㄘㄢ ㄌㄢˋ)
resplendent; brilliant; glorious: 金剛鑽閃耀著燦爛的光輝。 The diamond sparkles with brilliant light.

燦然
brilliantly; brightly; gloriously

【燬】 3268 ㄏㄨㄟˇ　hoei huǐ
1. fire; a blaze
2. to destroy by fire; to burn away; to burn down: 這幢房子燬燬了。 The house was burnt down.

【燥】 3269 ㄗㄠˋ　tzaw zào
1. arid; dry; parched: 天氣發燥。 The weather is dry.
2. impatient; restless

燥烈 (ㄗㄠˋ ㄌㄧㄝˋ)
(said of food or drug) burning

燥渴 (ㄗㄠˋ ㄎㄜˇ)
very thirsty

燥灼 (ㄗㄠˋ ㄓㄨㄛˊ)
very uneasy; very anxious

燥濕 (ㄗㄠˋ ㄕ)
dryness and wetness

燥熱 (ㄗㄠˋ ㄖㄜˋ)
dry and hot: 這些時天氣很燥熱。 The weather has been very dry and hot.

【燴】 3270 ㄏㄨㄟˋ　huey huì
1. to put (a variety of materials) together and cook; to braise
2. to serve (noodles, rice, etc.) with a topping of meat, vegetables, etc., in gravy

【燭】 3271 ㄓㄨˊ　jwu zhú
1. a candle
2. to illuminate; to shine upon: 火光燭天。 Leaping flames lit up the sky.

燭臺 (ㄓㄨˊ ㄊㄞˊ)
a candlestick; a candlestand

燭奴 (ㄓㄨˊ ㄋㄨˊ)
a large wooden candlestand carved in the shape of a boy

燭淚 (ㄓㄨˊ ㄌㄟˋ)
the guttering of a candle

燭光 (ㄓㄨˊ ㄍㄨㄤ)
①(physics) candle power: 這是六十燭光的燈泡。 This is a 60-watt bulb. ② candlelight

燭花 (ㄓㄨˊ ㄏㄨㄚ)
snuff: 她在剪燭花。 She is trimming off the snuff.

燭架 (ㄓㄨˊ ㄐㄧㄚˋ)
a candlestick; a candlestand

燭心 or 燭芯 (ㄓㄨˊ ㄒㄧㄣ)
candlewick

【燮】 3272 ㄒㄧㄝˋ　shieh xiè
to blend; to harmonize; harmonious

燮理 (ㄒㄧㄝˋ ㄌㄧˇ)
to harmonize; to adapt; to adjust; well-regulated

燮和 (ㄒㄧㄝˋ ㄏㄜˊ)
to harmonize; living in harmony

燮友 (ㄒㄧㄝˋ ㄧㄡˇ)
gentle; good-natured

十四畫

【燹】 3273 ㄒㄧㄢˇ　shean xiǎn
1. fires set off by troops or shells
2. outdoor fire

【燾】 3274 ㄊㄠˋ　taur tào
（又讀 ㄉㄠˋ daw dào）
1. to illuminate extensively
2. to cover like a canopy

燾育 (ㄊㄠˋ ㄩˋ)
(said of Heaven) to nurse all the things on earth

【燼】 3275 ㄐㄧㄣˋ　jinn jìn
1. embers; ashes; cinders
2. victims of disasters

【燿】 3276 ㄧㄠˋ　yaw yào
same as 耀—to shine brilliantly

十五畫

【爆】 3277 ㄅㄠˋ　baw bào
1. to explode; to burst; to crack; to pop
2. to quick-boil; to quick-fry

爆破 (ㄅㄠˋ ㄆㄛˋ)
to demolish by explosives; demolition

爆米花 (ㄅㄠˋ ㄇㄧˇ ㄏㄨㄚ)
popcorn

爆發 (ㄅㄠˋ ㄈㄚ)
① to explode; to blow up ②

to break out; to erupt; to flare up: 抗日戰爭在一九三七年爆發。 The war of Resistance against Japan broke out in 1937.

爆肚兒 (ㄅㄠˋ ㄉㄨˇ)
cooked tripe of sheep (regarded as a delicacy in North China)

爆裂 (ㄅㄠˋ ㄌㄧㄝˋ)
to burst; to erupt; to pop open; to crack

爆性 (ㄅㄠˋ ㄒㄧㄥˋ)
quick-tempered; hot-tempered

爆炸 (ㄅㄠˋ ㄓㄚˋ)
to explode; to blow up; explosion; blast

爆炸力 (ㄅㄠˋ ㄓㄚˋ ㄌㄧˋ)
explosive force; the impact of explosion

爆炸物 (ㄅㄠˋ ㄓㄚˋ ㄨˋ)
an explosive

爆仗 (ㄅㄠˋ ㄓㄤˋ)
firecrackers

爆竹 (ㄅㄠˋ ㄓㄨˊ)
firecrackers: 孩子們在燃放爆竹。 The children are letting off firecrackers.

【爍】 3278 ㄕㄨㄛˋ　shuoh shuò
1. to glitter; to glisten; to sparkle
2. to melt: 衆口爍金。 People's gossip is enough to melt metals.—People's gossip is enough to destroy anybody.

爍亮 (ㄕㄨㄛˋ ㄌㄧㄤˋ)
glittering; glistening; sparkling

爍爍 (ㄕㄨㄛˋ ㄕㄨㄛˋ)
glittering; glistening; sparkling

【爇】 3279 ㄖㄨㄛˋ　ruoh ruò
（又讀 ㄖㄜˋ reh rè）
to burn

十六畫

【爐】 3280 ㄌㄨˊ　lu lú
a stove; an oven; a furnace; a fireplace; a hearth

爐邊 (ㄌㄨˊ ㄅㄧㄢ)
the fireside; a hearth

爐邊談話 (ㄌㄨˊ ㄅㄧㄢ ㄊㄢˊ ㄏㄨㄚˋ)
a fireside chat

【爐】部

爐餅(ㄌㄨˊ ㄅㄧㄥˇ)
a kind of baked cake

爐門(ㄌㄨˊ ㄇㄣˊ)
the draft and ash hole of a stove

爐臺兒(ㄌㄨˊ ㄊㄞˊ ㄦ)
a mantel

爐條(ㄌㄨˊ ㄊㄧㄠˊ)
the grill of a stove or oven

爐坑(ㄌㄨˊ ㄎㄥ)
space for collecting ashes in a stove

爐火純青(ㄌㄨˊ ㄏㄨㄛˇ ㄔㄨㄣˊ ㄑㄧㄥ)
(literally) The stove fire for concocting the elixir of life begins to give a pure glow. — The skill is mature. 或 the consummation of skill or learning

爐灰(ㄌㄨˊ ㄏㄨㄟ)
ashes from a stove

爐子(ㄌㄨˊ ˙ㄗ)
a stove; a fireplace; a furnace; a kiln

爐竈(ㄌㄨˊ ㄗㄠˋ)
①a cooking stove; a cooking range ②(figuratively) a start; an enterprise: 你計畫另起爐竈嗎? Do you plan to make a fresh start?

爐鴨(ㄌㄨˊ ㄧㄚ)
a roast duck

爐冶(ㄌㄨˊ ㄧㄝˇ)
metallurgical works

十七畫

【爛】 3281　ㄌㄢˋ lann làn
1. overripe; rotten; to rot; to fester: 傷口爛了。The wound is festering.
2. cooked soft; well cooked: 肉煮爛了。The meat is boiled soft.
3. bright; brilliant
4. to scald; to burn; to scorch
5. worn-out: 鞋子穿爛了。The shoes are worn-out.
6. dissolute; messy

爛漫(ㄌㄢˋ ㄇㄢˋ)
①brilliant; resplendent: 山花爛漫。The bright mountain flowers are in full bloom. ②dissipated; debauched ③fast asleep ④naive; simple-minded: 她是個天真爛漫的小

女孩。She is a naive (or an innocent) little girl.

爛得很(ㄌㄢˋ ˙ㄉㄜ ㄏㄣˇ)
lousy

爛攤子(ㄌㄢˋ ㄊㄢ ˙ㄗ)
a shambles

爛泥(ㄌㄢˋ ㄋㄧˊ)
soft mud; mire

爛爛(ㄌㄢˋ ㄌㄢˋ)
bright; brilliant

爛好人(ㄌㄢˋ ㄏㄠˇ ㄖㄣˊ)
one who cannot say no to requests for help or favor; one who is ever ready to help others indiscriminately; a goody-goody: 他真是個爛好人。He is such a goody-goody fellow.

爛糊(ㄌㄢˋ ㄏㄨˊ)
(said of food) very soft, well cooked, or overripe

爛貨(ㄌㄢˋ ㄏㄨㄛˋ)
①(abusive language) a fast woman; a woman of easy virtue ②worthless goods; goods of poor quality

爛紙(ㄌㄢˋ ㄓˇ)
wastepaper

爛賬(ㄌㄢˋ ㄓㄤˋ)
①very well cooked; very ripe ②thoroughly familiar: 她的台詞背得爛熟。She learns her lines thoroughly.

爛然(ㄌㄢˋ ㄖㄢˊ)
bright; brilliant

爛醉(ㄌㄢˋ ㄗㄨㄟˋ)
dead drunk

爛醉如泥(ㄌㄢˋ ㄗㄨㄟˋ ㄖㄨˊ ㄋㄧˊ)
dead drunk; drunk as a lord

爛羊頭(ㄌㄢˋ ㄧㄤˊ ˙ㄊㄡ)
(literally) a rotten sheep head—official titles that are wantonly conferred upon unworthy persons

十八畫

【爝】 3282　ㄐㄩㄝˊ jyue jué
a torch

爝火(ㄐㄩㄝˊ ㄏㄨㄛˇ)
torch fire

二十五畫

【爨】 3283　ㄘㄨㄢˋ tsuann cuàn
1. to cook
2. a cooking stove

爨婢(ㄘㄨㄢˋ ㄅㄧˋ)
a kitchenmaid

爨婦(ㄘㄨㄢˋ ㄈㄨˋ)
a female cook

爨室(ㄘㄨㄢˋ ㄕˋ)
a kitchen

爪 部
ㄓㄠˇ jao zhǎo

【爪】 3284　1. ㄓㄠˇ jao zhǎo
1. a nail
2. a claw; a talon

爪士(ㄓㄠˇ ㄕˋ)
retainers; lackeys

爪牙(ㄓㄠˇ ㄧㄚˊ)
nails and teeth — retainers; lackeys; cat's-paws

爪牙吏(ㄓㄠˇ ㄧㄚˊ ㄌㄧˋ)
officials serving as tools of a tyrannical ruler

爪牙官(ㄓㄠˇ ㄧㄚˊ ㄍㄨㄢ)
lackeys of a ruthless ruler

爪牙鷹犬(ㄓㄠˇ ㄧㄚˊ ㄧㄥ ㄑㄩㄢˇ)
lackeys and hired ruffians

爪印(ㄓㄠˇ ㄧㄣˋ)
a nail mark; a trace; a print

爪哇(ㄓㄠˇ ㄨㄚ)
Java, island of Indonesia

【爪】 3284　2. ㄓㄨㄚˇ joa zhuǎ
claw

爪子(ㄓㄨㄚˇ ˙ㄗ)
a claw; a paw; a talon

四畫

【爬】 3285　ㄆㄚˊ par pá
1. to creep; to crawl
2. to climb; to clamber
3. to scratch
4. to lie face downwards

爬不動(ㄆㄚˊ ㄅㄨˋ ㄉㄨㄥˋ)
unable to crawl or climb

爬不起來(ㄆㄚˊ ㄅㄨˋ ㄑㄧˇ ˙ㄌㄞ)
unable to get up (from a lying position or a bed)

爬飯(ㄆㄚˊ ㄈㄢˋ)
to rake rice into the mouth with chopsticks

爬得高跌得重(ㄆㄚˊ ㄉㄜˊ ㄍㄠ ㄉㄧㄝ ㄉㄜˊ ㄓㄨㄥˋ)
The higher one climbs, the harder one falls.

爬剔(ㄆㄚˊ ㄐㄧ)
to exploit; to squeeze

爬羅剔抉(ㄆㄚˊ ㄌㄨㄛˊ ㄊㄧ ㄐㄩㄝˊ)
to dig up and rake up everything—to exploit thoroughly

爬高枝兒(ㄆㄚˊ ㄍㄠ ㄓㄦ)
to be a hanger-on of glory; to jump on the bandwagon of the powerful; to cling to the wealthy and influential

爬梳(ㄆㄚˊ ㄕㄨ)
to comb; to straighten out; to put in order

爬起來(ㄆㄚˊ ㄑㄧˇ ㄌㄞˊ)
to get up

爬牆(ㄆㄚˊ ㄑㄧㄤˊ)
to climb a fence; to scale a wall

爬行(ㄆㄚˊ ㄒㄧㄥˊ)
①to crawl; to creep ②a crawl

爬行運動(ㄆㄚˊ ㄒㄧㄥˊ ㄩㄣˋ ㄉㄨㄥˋ)
creeping movement

爬出來(ㄆㄚˊ ㄔㄨ ㄌㄞˊ)
to climb out: 小孩從車子裏爬出來。The child climbed out of the car.

爬蟲(ㄆㄚˊ ㄔㄨㄥˊ)
a reptile

爬蟲類(ㄆㄚˊ ㄔㄨㄥˊ ㄌㄟˋ)
Reptilia

爬山(ㄆㄚˊ ㄕㄢ)
to climb mountains

爬山虎(ㄆㄚˊ ㄕㄢ ㄏㄨˇ)
(botany) Virginia creeper

爬山者(ㄆㄚˊ ㄕㄢ ㄓㄜˇ)
an alpinist; a mountaineer: 他是老經驗的爬山者。He is an experienced mountaineer.

爬山鼠(ㄆㄚˊ ㄕㄢ ㄕㄨˇ)
a field mouse

爬山運動(ㄆㄚˊ ㄕㄢ ㄩㄣˋ ㄉㄨㄥˋ)
mountain climbing; mountaineering; alpinism

爬上(ㄆㄚˊ ㄕㄤˋ)
to climb up: 我看見他爬上一棵樹。I saw him climbing up a tree.

爬梳(ㄆㄚˊ ㄕㄨ)
to comb; to straighten out; to tidy up

爬搔(ㄆㄚˊ ㄙㄠ)
to scratch

【爭】　3286
　　ㄓㄥ jeng zhēng
1. to contend; to struggle; to strive
2. to fight; to dispute; to argue; to quarrel: 他們在爭什麼？What are they arguing about?
3. short of; to lack; to be deficient in
4. same as 怎—how; why

爭霸(ㄓㄥ ㄅㄚˋ)
to contend (or struggle) for hegemony; to scramble (or strive) for supremacy

爭霸戰(ㄓㄥ ㄅㄚˋ ㄓㄢˋ)
a struggle for power; a power struggle; a fight for hegemony

爭辯(ㄓㄥ ㄅㄧㄢˋ)
to argue; to debate; to dispute

爭面子(ㄓㄥ ㄇㄧㄢˋ ˙ㄗ)
to try to win or excel for the sake of face

爭鳴(ㄓㄥ ㄇㄧㄥˊ)
to contend

爭名奪利(ㄓㄥ ㄇㄧㄥˊ ㄉㄨㄛˊ ㄌㄧˋ)
to struggle for fame and wealth

爭風吃醋(ㄓㄥ ㄈㄥ ㄔ ㄘㄨˋ)
to quarrel from jealousy; to fight for the affection of a man or woman

爭得(ㄓㄥ ㄉㄜˊ)
①to win ②How can it be?

爭鬥 or 爭闘(ㄓㄥ ㄉㄡˋ)
to struggle; to contend; to conflict

爭奪(ㄓㄥ ㄉㄨㄛˊ)
to struggle for; to contend for; to scramble for; to fight for; to vie with somebody for something

爭奪戰(ㄓㄥ ㄉㄨㄛˊ ㄓㄢˋ)
a battle over a city, strategic point, etc.

爭端(ㄓㄥ ㄉㄨㄢ)
the cause of dispute, quarrel, or fight

爭論(ㄓㄥ ㄌㄨㄣˋ)
to argue; to dispute; debate; dispute

爭光(ㄓㄥ ㄍㄨㄤ)
to win glory

爭功(ㄓㄥ ㄍㄨㄥ)
to contend for credit

爭衡(ㄓㄥ ㄏㄥˊ)
to vie for superiority; to scramble for advantage

爭競(ㄓㄥ ㄐㄧㄥˋ)
to compete; to vie

爭氣(ㄓㄥ ㄑㄧˋ)
don't let down; to strive to excel; to try to win credit for

爭強(ㄓㄥ ㄑㄧㄤˊ)
to struggle for supremacy

爭強鬥勝(ㄓㄥ ㄑㄧㄤˊ ㄉㄡˋ ㄕㄥˋ)
to desire to excel over others; to fight for the leading role

爭取(ㄓㄥ ㄑㄩˇ)
to try to get; to win over; to strive for; to compete for

爭取時間(ㄓㄥ ㄑㄩˇ ㄕˊ ㄐㄧㄢ)
①to endeavor to avoid waste of time; to act quickly ②to stall for time

爭權奪利(ㄓㄥ ㄑㄩㄢˊ ㄉㄨㄛˊ ㄌㄧˋ)
to fight for selfish gains; to scramble for personal gains

爭席(ㄓㄥ ㄒㄧˊ)
to contend for a seat

爭先恐後(ㄓㄥ ㄒㄧㄢ ㄎㄨㄥˇ ㄏㄡˋ)
anxious to be ahead of others; afraid to fall behind others

爭閒氣(ㄓㄥ ㄒㄧㄢˊ ㄑㄧˋ)
to argue or dispute over trifles

爭相羅致(ㄓㄥ ㄒㄧㄤ ㄌㄨㄛˊ ㄓˋ)
engaged in a frantic competition to secure employment of (talent); to compete for the service of (a capable person)

爭雄(ㄓㄥ ㄒㄩㄥˊ)
to struggle or contend for supremacy

爭執(ㄓㄥ ㄓˊ)or 爭持(ㄓㄥ ㄔˊ)
to contest; to argue or dispute obstinately; to wrangle; to refuse to give in; argument; wrangling dispute

爭執不下(ㄓㄥ ㄓˊ ㄅㄨˋ ㄒㄧㄚˋ)
Each sticks to his own stand.

爭吵(ㄓㄥ ㄔㄠˇ)

〔爪部〕

to quarrel; to wrangle; to altercate; to squabble

爭產(ㄓㄥ ㄔㄢˇ)
(especially said of brothers) to fight for inheritance

爭長競短(ㄓㄥ ㄔㄤˊ ㄐㄧㄥˋ ㄉㄨㄢˇ)
to squabble over trifles

爭城奪地(ㄓㄥ ㄔㄥˊ ㄉㄨㄛˊ ㄉㄧˋ)
to conquer cities and capture territories by force of arms

爭勝(ㄓㄥ ㄕㄥˋ)
to struggle or contend for the upper hand

爭嘴(ㄓㄥ ㄗㄨㄟˇ)
①to fight for food ②to argue in self-defense

爭訟(ㄓㄥ ㄙㄨㄥˋ)
to dispute through a lawsuit; litigation

爭議(ㄓㄥ ㄧˋ)
to engage in a controversy; to dispute; to argue

爭一口氣(ㄓㄥ ㄧˋ ㄎㄡˇ ㄑㄧˋ)
to strive for a vindication; to struggle for honor or success to prove one's worth

爭妍鬥麗(ㄓㄥ ㄧㄢˊ ㄉㄡˋ ㄌㄧˋ)
to contend in beauty and fascination

五畫

【爰】 3287
ㄩㄢˊ yuan yúan
thereupon; therefore; accordingly

爰歷(ㄩㄢˊ ㄌㄧˋ)
an ancient wordbook by Chao Kao (趙高)of the Chin (秦)Dynasty

爰於(ㄩㄢˊ ㄩˊ)
Accordingly, (I took such and such an action on a certain date.)

八畫

【爲】 3288
1.(為)ㄨㄟˊ wei wéi
1. to do; to act
2. to manage; to handle; to exercise; to administer; to govern
3. to serve as
4. to become
5. to be

爲盼(ㄨㄟˊ ㄆㄢˋ)
That is what I, or we, expect. (a conventional phrase often used to close a formal letter)

爲證(ㄨㄟˊ ㄓㄥˋ)or 爲據(ㄨㄟˊ ㄐㄩˋ)
to use as proof; to use as evidence: 以郵戳爲憑. The postmark will serve as a proof.

爲民前鋒(ㄨㄟˊ ㄇㄧㄣˊ ㄑㄧㄢˊ ㄈㄥ)
to be the vanguard of the people

爲法自斃(ㄨㄟˊ ㄈㄚˇ ㄗˋ ㄅㄧˋ)
to suffer from one's own schemes

爲非作歹(ㄨㄟˊ ㄈㄟ ㄗㄨㄛˋ ㄉㄞˇ)
to do evil; to perpetrate outrages

爲富不仁(ㄨㄟˊ ㄈㄨˋ ㄅㄨˋ ㄖㄣˊ)
wealthy but unkind; rich but immoral

爲禱(ㄨㄟˊ ㄉㄠˇ)
That is what I, or we, humbly pray for. (a conventional phrase frequently used to close a formal letter）

爲頭(ㄨㄟˊ ㄊㄡˊ)or 爲首(ㄨㄟˊ ㄕㄡˇ)
①to be the head or leader ②headed by; led by

爲難(ㄨㄟˊ ㄋㄢˊ)
①awkward; troubled; distressed; in difficulties or a dilemma: 他問了個很爲難的問題. He asked a very awkward question. ②to make things difficult (for another): 他似乎故意爲難我. It seems that he deliberately makes things difficult for me.

爲力(ㄨㄟˊ ㄌㄧˋ)
to endeavor; to make efforts; to strive

爲鬼爲蜮(ㄨㄟˊ ㄍㄨㄟˇ ㄨㄟˊ ㄩˋ)
to injure others in secret

爲荷(ㄨㄟˊ ㄏㄜˋ)or 爲感(ㄨㄟˊ ㄍㄢˇ)
I, or we, will highly appreciate your kindness. (a conventional phrase frequently used to close a formal letter of request)

爲患(ㄨㄟˊ ㄏㄨㄢˋ)or 爲害(ㄨㄟˊ ㄏㄞˋ)
to be a cause of trouble; to bring trouble

爲期(ㄨㄟˊ ㄑㄧˊ)
to serve as the date (for an

occasion) or deadline: 展覽爲期一週. The exhibition is scheduled to last a week.

爲期不遠(ㄨㄟˊ ㄑㄧˊ ㄅㄨˋ ㄩㄢˇ)
in the near future; soon

爲限(ㄨㄟˊ ㄒㄧㄢˋ)
to serve as a limit; exclusively; not to exceed

爲幸(ㄨㄟˊ ㄒㄧㄥˋ)
It would be fortunate indeed. (a conventional phrase often used to close a formal letter of request)

爲學(ㄨㄟˊ ㄒㄩㄝˊ)
to engage in studies

爲止(ㄨㄟˊ ㄓˇ)
①until; till; up to: 他賭到把錢都輸光爲止. He gambled till he had lost all his money. ②no further: 我們的討論到此爲止. That's all for our discussion.

爲證(ㄨㄟˊ ㄓㄥˋ)
to serve as proof; to serve as evidence

爲政不在多言(ㄨㄟˊ ㄓㄥˋ ㄅㄨˋ ㄗㄞˋ ㄉㄨㄛ ㄧㄢˊ)
Acts speak louder than words in government administration. 或 True statesmanship does not lie in empty talks. 或 Mere talking does not give birth to efficient administration.

爲主(ㄨㄟˊ ㄓㄨˇ)
mainly; to be the most important; to be the chief or principal (element, component, etc.)

爲重(ㄨㄟˊ ㄓㄨㄥˋ)
to attach most importance to: 你必須以大局爲重. You must put the general interest first.

爲時過早(ㄨㄟˊ ㄕˊ ㄍㄨㄛˋ ㄗㄠˇ)
earlier than is expected; premature; too early; too soon: 現在下結論爲時過早. It's still too early to reach a conclusion.

爲壽(ㄨㄟˊ ㄕㄡˋ)
to offer congratulations on birthdays

爲山九仞，功虧一簣(ㄨㄟˊ ㄕㄢ ㄐㄧㄡˇ ㄖㄣˋ ㄍㄨㄥ ㄎㄨㄟ ㄧ ㄎㄨㄟˋ)
(literally) The lack of one basketful of earth spoils the

entire effort to build a nine-*jen* mountain.—The whole plan is ruined by a last-minute mistake or negligence.

爲善 (ㄨㄟ ㄕㄢˋ)
to do good

爲善最樂 (ㄨㄟ ㄕㄢˋ ㄗㄨㄟˋ ㄌㄜˋ)
Doing good is the greatest source of happiness.

爲生 (ㄨㄟˊ ㄕㄥ)
to make a living: 他以當店員爲生。 He makes a living as a salesman.

爲數不多 (ㄨㄟˊ ㄕㄨˋ ㄅㄨˋ ㄉㄨㄛ)
limited in number; not many: 我有幾個，但爲數不多。 I have a few, but not many.

爲數不少 (ㄨㄟˊ ㄕㄨˋ ㄅㄨˋ ㄕㄠˇ)
many; quite a number of: 考試不及格的學生爲數不少。 Many a student fails to pass in the examination.

爲人 (ㄨㄟˊ ㄖㄣˊ)
one's personality, temperament, or character; to behave; to conduct oneself: 他爲人高尚。 He conducts himself nobly.

爲人師表 (ㄨㄟˊ ㄖㄣˊ ㄕ ㄅㄧㄠˇ)
to be a model of virtue for others

爲人在世 (ㄨㄟˊ ㄖㄣˊ ㄗㄞˋ ㄕˋ)
to live in this world

爲所欲爲 (ㄨㄟˊ ㄙㄨㄛˇ ㄩˋ ㄨㄟˊ)
to have one's way; to do as one pleases; unscrupulous

爲惡 (ㄨㄟˊ ㄜˋ)
to do evil

爲業 (ㄨㄟˊ ㄧㄝˋ)
as a means of livelihood

爲要 (ㄨㄟˊ ㄧㄠˋ)
It's very important that you do what I have told you. (a conventional phrase for closing a formal letter of injunction)

爲伍 (ㄨㄟˊ ㄨˇ)
to associate or mix (with)

【爲】 3288
2.(爲) ㄨㄟˋ **wey wèi**
for; for the good of; for the sake of

爲民喉舌 (ㄨㄟˋ ㄇㄧㄣˊ ㄏㄡˊ ㄕㄜˊ)
to speak for the people

爲民請命 (ㄨㄟˋ ㄇㄧㄣˊ ㄑㄧㄥˇ ㄇㄧㄥˋ)
to plead for the people; to

appeal for the people

爲民除害 (ㄨㄟˋ ㄇㄧㄣˊ ㄔㄨˊ ㄏㄞˋ)
to remove the evils from the people; to eliminate a public scourge; to destroy a public enemy

爲名爲利 (ㄨㄟˋ ㄇㄧㄥˊ ㄨㄟˋ ㄌㄧˋ)
for fame and for wealth

爲的是 (ㄨㄟˋ ㄉㄜˊ ㄕˋ)
for the sake of; for the purpose of

爲了 (ㄨㄟˋ ㄌㄜˊ)
for; for the sake of: 爲了和平，我們必須有耐心。 We must be patient for the sake of peace.

爲國捐軀 (ㄨㄟˋ ㄍㄨㄛˊ ㄐㄩㄢ ㄑㄩ)
to sacrifice one's life for the fatherland

爲國爭光 (ㄨㄟˋ ㄍㄨㄛˊ ㄓㄥ ㄍㄨㄤ)
to struggle for the glory of one's country

爲公 (ㄨㄟˋ ㄍㄨㄥ)
for public good

爲何 (ㄨㄟˋ ㄏㄜˊ)
What for? 或 Why? 或 for what reason? 你知道他爲何遲到嗎? Do you know why he was late?

爲虎傅翼 (ㄨㄟˋ ㄏㄨˇ ㄈㄨˋ ㄧˋ) or 爲虎添翼 (ㄨㄟˋ ㄏㄨˇ ㄊㄧㄢ ㄧˋ)
(literally) to give wings to a tiger—to help a villain do evil

爲虎作倀 (ㄨㄟˋ ㄏㄨˇ ㄗㄨㄛˋ ㄔㄤ)
to help an evil person do evil; to make common cause with an evildoer

爲己 (ㄨㄟˋ ㄐㄧˇ)
for personal interest

爲…起見 (ㄨㄟˋ…ㄑㄧˇ ㄐㄧㄢˋ)
in order to…; for the purpose of…

爲小失大 (ㄨㄟˋ ㄒㄧㄠˇ ㄕ ㄉㄚˋ)
to lose a pound in trying to save a penny

爲之動容 (ㄨㄟˋ ㄓ ㄉㄨㄥˋ ㄖㄨㄥˊ)
to show interest in (something)

爲甚麼 (ㄨㄟˋ ㄕㄜˊ ㄇㄜ)
What for? 或 Why? 爲甚麼猶豫不決呢? Why hesitate?

爲人 (ㄨㄟˋ ㄖㄣˊ)
for others' interest; for the sake of others

爲人說項 (ㄨㄟˋ ㄖㄣˊ ㄕㄨㄛ ㄒㄧㄤˋ)
to say a good word for

someone

爲人作伐 (ㄨㄟˋ ㄖㄣˊ ㄗㄨㄛˋ ㄈㄚˊ)
to act as a matchmaker

爲人作嫁 (ㄨㄟˋ ㄖㄣˊ ㄗㄨㄛˋ ㄐㄧㄚˋ)
to work for others without profiting oneself

爲此 (ㄨㄟˋ ㄘˇ)
because of this; for this reason: 我們都爲此感動不已。 We all were deeply moved by this.

爲私 (ㄨㄟˋ ㄙ)
for one's personal interest

爲我 (ㄨㄟˋ ㄨㄛˇ)
egoistic; selfish

(爪部)

十四畫

【爵】 3289
ㄐㄩㄝˊ **jyue jué**
1. a degree or a title of nobility; peerage; the rank or dignity of a peer
2. an ancient wine pitcher with three legs and a loop handle

爵弁 (ㄐㄩㄝˊ ㄅㄧㄢ)
a kind of ceremonial cap in the Chou Dynasty

爵服 (ㄐㄩㄝˊ ㄈㄨˊ)
the degree and costume of nobility

爵土 (ㄐㄩㄝˊ ㄊㄨˇ)
land conferred along with a degree of nobility

爵祿 (ㄐㄩㄝˊ ㄌㄨˋ)
the degree and emolument of nobility

爵高者憂深 (ㄐㄩㄝˊ ㄍㄠ ㄓㄜˇ ㄧㄡ ㄕㄣ)
The higher one's position is, the greater one's care will be. 或 *noblesse oblige*

爵章 (ㄐㄩㄝˊ ㄓㄤ)
badges of nobility conferred on noblemen in Mongolia, Tibet and Mohammedan districts after the birth of the Republic

爵主 (ㄐㄩㄝˊ ㄓㄨˇ)
an heir apparent to a title of nobility

爵士 (ㄐㄩㄝˊ ㄕˋ)
Sir (a title of nobility)

爵士音樂 (ㄐㄩㄝˊ ㄕˋ ㄧㄣ ㄩㄝˋ)
jazz; jazz music

爵士樂隊 (ㄐㄩㄝˊ ㄕˋ ㄩㄝˋ ㄉㄨㄟˋ)
a jazz band

爵位 (ㄐㄩㄝˊ ㄨㄟˋ)

〔父・爻部〕

父 部
ㄈㄨ fuh fù

a degree of nobility

【父】 3290
1. ㄈㄨ fuh fù
1. father: 有其父必有其子。 Like father, like son.
2. a male relative of an elder generation: 伯父 uncle 祖父 grandfather
3. to do father's duties
父輩(ㄈㄨ ㄅㄟ)
the elder generation; the senior generation
父不父，子不子(ㄈㄨ ㄅㄨ ㄈㄨ，ㄗ ㄅㄨ ㄗ)
Fathers neglect their duties as fathers while sons neglect their duties as sons.
父命(ㄈㄨ ㄇㄧㄥ)
father's orders; father's commands: 父命不可違。 Father's orders must be obeyed.
父母(ㄈㄨ ㄇㄨ)
parents; father and mother
父母國(ㄈㄨ ㄇㄨ ㄍㄨㄛ)
fatherland; mother country
父母官(ㄈㄨ ㄇㄨ ㄍㄨㄢ)
a local official; a magistrate
父母劬勞(ㄈㄨ ㄇㄨ ㄑㄩ ㄌㄠ)
the hardships of parents in bringing up children
父母之邦(ㄈㄨ ㄇㄨ ㄓ ㄅㄤ)
one's own country; one's native land
父父子子(ㄈㄨ ㄈㄨ ㄗ ㄗ)
Fathers do their duties as fathers and sons do their duties as sons.
父黨(ㄈㄨ ㄉㄤ)
one's kinsfolk on the paternal side
父臺(ㄈㄨ ㄊㄞ)
a polite way of addressing a local official in former times
父天母地(ㄈㄨ ㄊㄧㄢ ㄇㄨ ㄉㄧ)
the son of Heaven and Earth—the emperor
父老(ㄈㄨ ㄌㄠ)
elders
父親(ㄈㄨ ㄑㄧㄣ)
father: 他一直像父親一般待我。 He has been like a father to me.
父親節(ㄈㄨ ㄑㄧㄣ ㄐㄧㄝ)
Father's Day (falling on August 8)
父權(ㄈㄨ ㄑㄩㄢ)
paternal power; patriarchate
父系制度(ㄈㄨ ㄒㄧ ㄓ ㄉㄨ)
patriarchy
父兄(ㄈㄨ ㄒㄩㄥ)
male seniors in a family; father and elder brothers
父執(ㄈㄨ ㄓ)
father's friends
父債子還(ㄈㄨ ㄓㄞ ㄗ ㄏㄨㄢ)
According to Chinese customs, the son is bound to pay his father's debts.
父事(ㄈㄨ ㄕ)
to attend upon someone as one attends upon one's own father
父子(ㄈㄨ ㄗ)
father and son
父子兵(ㄈㄨ ㄗ ㄅㄧㄥ)
troops bound together like father and son
父子相傳(ㄈㄨ ㄗ ㄒㄧㄤ ㄔㄨㄢ)
passed down through generations by fathers to sons
父作子述(ㄈㄨ ㄗㄨㄛ ㄗ ㄕㄨ)
What the father founded, the son developed.
父慈子孝(ㄈㄨ ㄘ ㄗ ㄒㄧㄠ)
The father is affectionate and the son is filial.
父嚴母慈(ㄈㄨ ㄧㄢ ㄇㄨ ㄘ)
The father is stern and the mother is gentle.
父蔭(ㄈㄨ ㄧㄣ)
father's influence and protection
父王(ㄈㄨ ㄨㄤ)
my imperial father

【父】 3290
2. ㄈㄨ fuu fǔ
a respectful term for an elderly man in ancient times: 漁父 a fisherman

四畫

【爸】 3291
ㄅㄚ bah bà
father
爸爸(ㄅㄚ ·ㄅㄚ)

father; papa

六畫

【爹】 3292
ㄉㄧㄝ die diē
father: 乾爹 an adoptive father
爹媽(ㄉㄧㄝ ㄇㄚ)
father and mother; parents
爹爹(ㄉㄧㄝ ㄉㄧㄝ)
father
爹娘 or 爹孃(ㄉㄧㄝ ㄋㄧㄤ)
father and mother; parents

九畫

【爺】 3293
ㄧㄝ ye yé
1. father
2. master; sir
3. god: 老天爺 God; Heaven
爺們(ㄧㄝ ㄇㄣ)
men; gentlemen
爺娘 or 爺孃(ㄧㄝ ㄋㄧㄤ)
father and mother; parents
爺兒們(ㄧㄝㄦ ㄇㄣ)
men and boys
爺兒倆(ㄧㄝㄦ ㄌㄧㄚ)
father and son; father and daughter
爺爺(ㄧㄝ ·ㄧㄝ)
① grandfather; grandpa ② sir

爻 部
ㄧㄠ yau yáo

【爻】 3294
ㄧㄠ yau yáo
(讀音 ㄒㄧㄠ shyau xiáo)
single and divided lines in eight groups of three lines each as specified in the Book of Changes: 陽爻 yang yao—the long line (—) 陰爻 yin yao—two broken short lines (- -)
爻象(ㄧㄠ ㄒㄧㄤ)
diagrams for divination
爻辭(ㄧㄠ ㄘ)
explanations of diagrams for divination

七畫

【爽】 3295
ㄕㄨㄤ shoang
shuang

1. refreshing; bracing; crisp;
agreeable; pleasant; brisk: 秋
高氣爽 the clear and crisp
autumn climate
2. to feel well: 他感到身體不爽。
He does not feel well.
3. straightforward; frank; open-
hearted: 他為人豪爽。He is
straightforward.
4. to fail; to miss; to lose
5. to be in error

爽法 (ㄕㄨㄤ ㄈㄚˇ)
to break regulations; to disregard the law; to violate
the law

爽德 (ㄕㄨㄤ ㄉㄜˊ)
to lose virtue; to depart
from virtue; to forfeit one's
virtue

爽當 (ㄕㄨㄤ ㄉㄤ)
brisk; agile

爽朗 (ㄕㄨㄤ ㄌㄤˇ)
①(said of weather, etc.)
refreshing: 我喜歡鄉間爽朗的
天氣。I like the refreshing
weather in the countryside.
②open-minded; straight-
forward

爽利 (ㄕㄨㄤ ㄌㄧˋ)
agile; brisk and neat;
speedy; alert: 他辦事爽利。He
is brisk and neat in his
work.

爽塏 (ㄕㄨㄤ ㄎㄞˇ)
high and dry ground

爽口 (ㄕㄨㄤ ㄎㄡˇ)
palatable; tasty

爽快 (ㄕㄨㄤ ㄎㄨㄞˋ)
①straightforward; frank;
open-hearted: 他對人很爽快。
He is open-hearted with
everybody. ②readily and
briskly; with alacrity ③
comfortable; pleasant;
refreshing

爽氣 (ㄕㄨㄤ ㄑㄧˋ)
①refreshing air; a bracing
atmosphere ②straight-
forward; open-hearted

爽心 (ㄕㄨㄤ ㄒㄧㄣ)
gratified; satisfied; pleased;
cheerful

爽心悅目 (ㄕㄨㄤ ㄒㄧㄣ ㄩㄝˋ ㄇㄨˋ)
refreshing to the heart and
pleasing to the eye

爽信 (ㄕㄨㄤ ㄒㄧㄣˋ)
to fail to keep a promise: 不
可爽信於人。One should not
fail to keep one's promise.

爽性 (ㄕㄨㄤ ㄒㄧㄥˋ)
might just as well: 我們爽性
做完再休息。We might as
well finish it before we have
a rest.

爽直 (ㄕㄨㄤ ㄓˊ)
outspoken; frank; straightforward; open-hearted: 他說
話很爽直。He is very outspo-
ken.

爽失 (ㄕㄨㄤ ㄕ)
to fail to keep or honor (a
pledge, etc.)

爽身粉 (ㄕㄨㄤ ㄕㄣ ㄈㄣˇ)
talcum powder

爽神 (ㄕㄨㄤ ㄕㄣˊ)
refreshing

爽然 (ㄕㄨㄤ ㄖㄢˊ)
discouraged; disappointed;
dejected

爽然若失 (ㄕㄨㄤ ㄖㄢˊ ㄖㄨㄛˋ ㄕ)
dejected as if one had made
a mistake

爽脆 (ㄕㄨㄤ ㄘㄨㄟˋ)
brisk; keen and energetic

爽約 (ㄕㄨㄤ ㄩㄝ)
to fail to keep a promise; to
break an appointment

十畫

【爾】 3296
ㄦˇ eel ěr

1. you; thou
2. that; this; those; these; such;
so: 果爾 if so
3. after adjectives: 率爾 hastily;
thoughtless
4. only

爾等 (ㄦˇ ㄉㄥˇ)
you all

爾來 (ㄦˇ ㄌㄞˊ)
until now; up to the present

爾後 (ㄦˇ ㄏㄡˋ)
thereafter; afterwards; subsequently

爾時 (ㄦˇ ㄕˊ)
at that time; then

爾日 (ㄦˇ ㄖˋ)
that day

爾汝 (ㄦˇ ㄖㄨˇ)
to address each other intimately; on first name basis

爾汝交 (ㄦˇ ㄖㄨˇ ㄐㄧㄠ)
intimate friendship

爾曹 (ㄦˇ ㄘㄠˊ)
you all; you people

爾爾 (ㄦˇ ㄦˇ)
so-so; not so outstanding: 生
意不過爾爾。Business is only
just so-so.

爾雅 (ㄦˇ ㄧㄚˇ)
①an ancient book contain-
ing commentaries on clas-
sics, names, etc. ②graceful
and correct

爾為爾，我為我 (ㄦˇ ㄨㄟˊ ㄦˇ, ㄨㄛˇ
ㄨㄟˊ ㄨㄛˇ)
(literally) You are you and
I am I. —(figuratively) Let
everybody mind his own
business.

爿 部
ㄑㄧㄤˊ chyang qiáng

四畫

【牀】 3297
(床) ㄔㄨㄤˊ chwang
chuáng

1. a bed; a couch: 單人牀 a single bed 雙人牀 a double bed
2. the ground under a body of
water: 河床 a riverbed

牀鋪 (ㄔㄨㄤˊ ㄆㄨ)
a bed and bedding

牀單 (ㄔㄨㄤˊ ㄉㄢ)
bed linen; a bedsheet; sheets

牀墊 (ㄔㄨㄤˊ ㄉㄧㄢˋ)
a mattress

牀榻 (ㄔㄨㄤˊ ㄊㄚˋ)
a bed; a couch

牀頭 (ㄔㄨㄤˊ ㄊㄡˊ)
the head of a bed; bedside

牀頭金盡 (ㄔㄨㄤˊ ㄊㄡˊ ㄐㄧㄣ ㄐㄧㄣˋ)
impoverished by frequent
visits to whorehouses or by
association with disrepu-
table women

牀頭人 (ㄔㄨㄤˊ ㄊㄡˊ ㄖㄣˊ)
one's wife

牀公牀婆 (ㄔㄨㄤˊ ㄍㄨㄥ ㄔㄨㄤˊ ㄆㄛˊ)

爿部

牀部

the god and goddess of the bed

牀架(ㄔㄨㄤˊ ㄐㄧㄚˋ)
a bedstead

牀脚(ㄔㄨㄤˊ ㄐㄧㄠˇ)
the foot of the bed

牀罩(ㄔㄨㄤˊ ㄓㄠˋ)
a bedspread

牀帳子(ㄔㄨㄤˊ ㄓㄤˋ ˙ㄗ)
a mosquito net 亦作「帳子」

牀蝨(ㄔㄨㄤˊ ㄕ)
bedbugs; a cimex

牀上(ㄔㄨㄤˊ ㄕㄤˋ)
on a bed or a couch: 他還在牀上睡覺。He is still in bed.

牀上安牀(ㄔㄨㄤˊ ㄕㄤˋ ㄢ ㄔㄨㄤˊ)
duplication; overlapping; to duplicate; to overlap

牀蓐(ㄔㄨㄤˊ ㄖㄨˋ)
bedding; bedclothes

牀褥子(ㄔㄨㄤˊ ㄖㄨˋ ˙ㄗ)
a mattress

牀第(ㄔㄨㄤˊ ㄉㄧˋ)
privacy of the bed

牀第之間(ㄔㄨㄤˊ ㄉㄧˋ ㄓ ㄐㄧㄢ)
on the conjugal bed

牀第之私(ㄔㄨㄤˊ ㄉㄧˋ ㄓ ㄙ)
private talks between husband and wife

牀沿(ㄔㄨㄤˊ ㄧㄢˊ)
edge of the bed

牀位(ㄔㄨㄤˊ ㄨㄟˋ)
berths or bunks (in a ship or on a train)

五畫

【牁】 3298
《ㄜ ge gē
a stake to which a boat may be moored

六畫

【牂】 3299
ㄗㄤ tzang zāng
a ewe

牂牁(ㄗㄤ ㄍㄜ)
① ancient name of Kwei-chow (貴州) and its vicinity today ② stakes to which boats are moored

牂雲(ㄗㄤ ㄩㄣˊ)
dog-shaped clouds

十三畫

【牆】 3300
(墻) ㄑㄧㄤˊ chyang
                    qiáng
a wall; a fence: 隔牆有耳。Walls have ears.

牆壁(ㄑㄧㄤˊ ㄅㄧˋ)
a wall (of a building)

牆頭(ㄑㄧㄤˊ ㄊㄡˊ)
the top or crest of a fence or wall

牆頭草,風吹兩邊倒(ㄑㄧㄤˊ ㄊㄡˊ ㄘㄠˇ,ㄈㄥ ㄔㄨㄟ ㄌㄧㄤˇ ㄅㄧㄢ ㄉㄠˇ)
The grass on the top of a wall sways with every wind.—A person acts as the occasion dictates.

牆根(ㄑㄧㄤˊ ㄍㄣ)
the foot of a wall or fence; foundations of a wall

牆角(ㄑㄧㄤˊ ㄐㄧㄠˇ)
a corner between two walls: 他們躲在牆角裏。They hid in the corner between two walls.

牆脚(ㄑㄧㄤˊ ㄐㄧㄠˇ)
the foot of a wall

牆外漢(ㄑㄧㄤˊ ㄨㄞˋ ㄏㄢˋ)
an outsider; an amateur

牆宇(ㄑㄧㄤˊ ㄩˇ)
① dwelling; walled building ② capacity for tolerance

牆垣(ㄑㄧㄤˊ ㄩㄢˊ)
a wall; a fence: 有些古老的城市周圍有牆垣。Some old towns have walls right round them.

片 部
ㄆㄧㄢˋ piann piàn

【片】 3301
1. ㄆㄧㄢˋ piann
        piàn
a piece; a slice; a fragment; a chip

片片(ㄆㄧㄢˋ ㄆㄧㄢˋ)
in pieces; in fragments

片麻岩(ㄆㄧㄢˋ ㄇㄚˊ ㄧㄢˊ)
(geology) gneiss

片面(ㄆㄧㄢˋ ㄇㄧㄢˋ)
① unilateral: 他們片面撕毀協議。They tore up the agreement unilaterally. ② unfair: 你不能片面地看問題。You should not take an unfair approach to problems.

片面之交(ㄆㄧㄢˋ ㄇㄧㄢˋ ㄓ ㄐㄧㄠ)
a casual acquaintance

片面之言(ㄆㄧㄢˋ ㄇㄧㄢˋ ㄓ ㄧㄢˊ)or 片面之詞(ㄆㄧㄢˋ ㄇㄧㄢˋ ㄓ ㄘˊ)
one-sided remarks

片名(ㄆㄧㄢˋ ㄇㄧㄥˊ)
title of a motion picture

片段(ㄆㄧㄢˋ ㄉㄨㄢˋ)
① passages or fragments of a writing; extracts ② parts; fragments: 生活的片段 a part of life

片頭(ㄆㄧㄢˋ ㄊㄡˊ)
titles (of a motion picture)

片刻(ㄆㄧㄢˋ ㄎㄜˋ)
a little while; a brief space of time; a moment; an instant: 請稍候片刻。Please wait for a little while.

片甲不留(ㄆㄧㄢˋ ㄐㄧㄚˇ ㄅㄨˋ ㄌㄧㄡˊ)
(literally) to have not even a fragment of armor remaining.— ① to wipe out the enemy to a man ② to suffer a crushing defeat

片假名(ㄆㄧㄢˋ ㄐㄧㄚˇ ㄇㄧㄥˊ)
the square Japanese syllabary; katakana

片紙隻字(ㄆㄧㄢˋ ㄓˇ ㄓ ㄗˋ)
a brief piece of writing; a brief note or letter

片酬(ㄆㄧㄢˋ ㄔㄡˊ)
remuneration for a movie actor or actress for starring in a film

片長(ㄆㄧㄢˋ ㄔㄤˊ)
the length of a motion picture in terms of showing time

片時(ㄆㄧㄢˋ ㄕˊ)
a brief space of time; a short while: 我片時即回。I'll be back in a short while.

片晌(ㄆㄧㄢˋ ㄕㄤˇ)
a short space of time; a short while

片子(ㄆㄧㄢˋ ˙ㄗ)
① a motion picture or a film ② a calling card

片租(ㄆㄧㄢˋ ㄗㄨ)
a film rent

片兒(ㄆㄧㄢˋ ㄦˊ)
① a thin flat piece ② a calling card; a visiting card 亦

作「名片」

片兒湯(ㄆㄧㄢˋㄦㄊㄤ)
flat pieces of dough served with soup

片岩(ㄆㄧㄢˋㄧㄢˊ)
schistose rocks

片言(ㄆㄧㄢˋㄧㄢˊ)
a few words: 他能片言解紛。
He can settle a dispute with just a few words.

片言折獄(ㄆㄧㄢˋㄧㄢˊㄓㄜˊㄩˋ)
A single word uttered by a wise man can decide a legal case.

【片】 3301
ㄆㄧㄢˋ　2. ㄆㄧㄢ pian piàn
1. a photograph
2. a phonograph record

四畫

【版】 3302
ㄅㄢˇ baan bǎn
1. household registers
2. printing plate
3. edition: 平裝版 a paperback edition 精裝版 a hardback edition
4. supporting boards used in building walls

版版六十四(ㄅㄢˇㄅㄢˇㄌㄧㄡˋㄕˊㄙˋ)
very conservative; inflexible

版本(ㄅㄢˇㄅㄣˇ)
edition: 這是最新的版本。This is the newest edition.

版面(ㄅㄢˇㄇㄧㄢˋ)
①space of a whole page ②layout of a printed sheet

版圖(ㄅㄢˇㄊㄨˊ)
①household registers and maps; population and territory ②territory; dominion: 南沙群島是中國的版圖。The Spratly Islands are Chinese territory.

版畫(ㄅㄢˇㄏㄨㄚˋ)
a picture printed from an engraved or etched plate; a print

版籍(ㄅㄢˇㄐㄧˊ)
①books ②household registers; a census

版權(ㄅㄢˇㄑㄩㄢˊ)
copyright

版權法(ㄅㄢˇㄑㄩㄢˊㄈㄚˇ)
copyright law

版權所有(ㄅㄢˇㄑㄩㄢˊㄙㄨㄛˇㄧㄡˇ)
all rights reserved (as stated by the publisher in a book)

版築(ㄅㄢˇㄓㄨˊ)
①to build (walls with the aid of supporting boards) ②to build; to construct

版稅(ㄅㄢˇㄕㄨㄟˋ)
royalties (on books)

八畫

【牌】 3303
ㄆㄞˊ pair pái
1. a bulletin board
2. a tablet; a signboard; a plate: 門牌 a doorplate 招牌 a signboard
3. a card; a tag; a label
4. a trademark; a brand: 他喜歡買名牌貨。He likes to buy goods of a well-known brand.

牌榜(ㄆㄞˊㄅㄤˇ)
a bulletin board

牌匾(ㄆㄞˊㄅㄧㄢˇ)
a tablet; a signboard; a plaque

牌坊(ㄆㄞˊㄈㄤ)
an honorific arch or portal

牌樓(ㄆㄞˊㄌㄡˊ)
a celebration arch; a ceremonial arch

牌號(ㄆㄞˊㄏㄠˋ)
a store name appearing on the signboard; a trademark; a brand

牌九(ㄆㄞˊㄐㄧㄡˇ)
Chinese dominoes

牌局(ㄆㄞˊㄐㄩˊ)
a gambling game

牌照(ㄆㄞˊㄓㄠˋ)
a license plate; a license

牌示(ㄆㄞˊㄕˋ)
a public notice; a bulletin

牌子(ㄆㄞˊㄗ˙)
①a bulletin board ②a card; a tag; a label ③a brand (of commodities): 這是牌子極好的咖啡。This is an excellent brand of coffee. ④reputation ⑤a signboard; a plate

牌子老(ㄆㄞˊㄗ˙ㄌㄠˇ)
a brand or a trademark which has been in use for a long time (which means the merchandise concerned must be very good)

牌額(ㄆㄞˊㄜˊ)
a tablet (bearing inscriptions, written characters, etc.)

牌位(ㄆㄞˊㄨㄟˋ)
an ancestral tablet; a memorial tablet

九畫

【牒】 3304
ㄉㄧㄝˊ dye dié
1. official documents
2. certificates
3. records of a family pedigree

牒籍(ㄉㄧㄝˊㄐㄧˊ)
ancient books and records: 牒籍上有記載。It was recorded in the ancient books.

牒狀(ㄉㄧㄝˊㄓㄨㄤˋ)
documents pertaining to a lawsuit

牒文(ㄉㄧㄝˊㄨㄣˊ)
official dispatches

十畫

【牓】 3305
(榜) ㄅㄤˇ baang bǎng
1. a tablet; a plaque
2. a public notice

牓示(ㄅㄤˇㄕˋ)
to announce by putting up a notice

牓書(ㄅㄤˇㄕㄨ)
large characters on a tablet

牓子(ㄅㄤˇㄗ˙)
folded paper listing one's biographic data or the reason for calling when he is about to be received by a superior or ruler

十一畫

【牖】 3306
ㄧㄡˇ yeou yǒu
1. a window
2. to guide; to educate; to enlighten

牖民(ㄧㄡˇㄇㄧㄣˊ)
to guide the people; to educate the people

牖里(ㄧㄡˇㄌㄧˇ)
the place where King Wen of the Chou Dynasty (周文王) was held prisoner by King Chou of the Shang Dynasty

〔片部〕

（簡牘）

（牙‧牛部）

十五畫

【牘】 3307
ㄉㄨˊ dwu dú
1. a wooden writing tablet
2. documents; archives; letters
3. a hollow pole used to strike the ground to mark the beat of music in ancient times
牘箋(ㄉㄨˊ ㄐㄧㄢ)
letters
牘尾(ㄉㄨˊ ㄨㄟˇ)
the closing part of a letter

牙 部
ㄧㄚˊ ya yá

【牙】 3308
ㄧㄚˊ ya yá
1. teeth: 蛀牙 a decayed tooth
2. to bite
3. ivory articles
4. a broker
牙白口清(ㄧㄚˊ ㄅㄞˊ ㄎㄡˇ ㄑㄧㄥ)
able to speak articulately
牙買加(ㄧㄚˊ ㄇㄞˇ ㄐㄧㄚ)
Jamaica
牙粉(ㄧㄚˊ ㄈㄣˇ)
dentifrice; tooth powder
牙縫兒(ㄧㄚˊ ㄈㄥˋㄦ)
space between the teeth
牙疼(ㄧㄚˊ ㄊㄥˊ)or 牙痛(ㄧㄚˊ ㄊㄨㄥˋ)
toothache
牙帖(ㄧㄚˊ ㄊㄧㄝˇ)
a business license of a brokerage firm
牙膏(ㄧㄚˊ ㄍㄠ)
toothpaste
牙垢(ㄧㄚˊ ㄍㄡˋ)
tartar on the teeth
牙根(ㄧㄚˊ ㄍㄣ)
base of the teeth
牙關(ㄧㄚˊ ㄍㄨㄢ)
a mandibular joint
牙科(ㄧㄚˊ ㄎㄜ)
dentistry
牙科醫生(ㄧㄚˊ ㄎㄜ ㄧ ㄕㄥ)or 牙醫(ㄧㄚˊ ㄧ)
a dentist: 我明天跟牙醫有約。 I have an appointment with the dentist tomorrow.

牙行(ㄧㄚˊ ㄏㄤˊ)
a commission agency of a broker; a brokerage firm
牙慧(ㄧㄚˊ ㄏㄨㄟˋ)
what others have said or written; a stale expression
牙祭(ㄧㄚˊ ㄐㄧˋ)
as in 打牙祭—to have a rare sumptuous meal; to have something special to eat
牙將(ㄧㄚˊ ㄐㄧㄤˋ)
a low-ranking military officer
牙籤(兒)(ㄧㄚˊ ㄑㄧㄢ (ㄦ))
a toothpick
牙線(ㄧㄚˊ ㄒㄧㄢˋ)
dental floss
牙周病(ㄧㄚˊ ㄓㄡ ㄅㄧㄥˋ)
periodontosis; rapidly advancing juvenile periodontitis
牙章(ㄧㄚˊ ㄓㄤ)
an ivory seal or chop
牙筋(ㄧㄚˊ ㄓㄨˋ)or 牙筷(ㄧㄚˊ ㄓㄨˋㄎㄨㄞˋ)
chopsticks made of ivory
牙齒(ㄧㄚˊ ㄔˇ)
a tooth or teeth: 我昨天拔了一顆牙齒。 I had a tooth pulled out yesterday.
牙牀(ㄧㄚˊ ㄔㄨㄤˊ)
①teethridge; gum　②an ivory bedstead
牙刷(ㄧㄚˊ ㄕㄨㄚ)
a toothbrush: 你每餐之後都要用牙刷刷牙。 Brush your teeth with a toothbrush after every meal.
牙人(ㄧㄚˊ ㄖㄣˊ)
a sales agent; a broker
牙磁(ㄧㄚˊ ㄘˊ)
enamel
牙牙學語(ㄧㄚˊ ㄧㄚˊ ㄒㄩㄝˊ ㄩˇ)
(said of an infant) to begin to babble, prattle, or lisp
牙音(ㄧㄚˊ ㄧㄣ)
gutturals or velars (in traditional Chinese phonology)
牙齦(ㄧㄚˊ ㄧㄣˊ)
gums

八畫

【撐】 3309
（撐）ㄔㄥ cheng
chēng
to prop; to support

牛 部
ㄋㄧㄡˊ niou niú

【牛】 3310
ㄋㄧㄡˊ niou niú
1. an ox; cattle; a cow; a bull: 水牛 a water buffalo 乳牛 a milk cow
2. a Chinese family name
3. (said of a person) stubborn; headstrong
牛排(ㄋㄧㄡˊ ㄆㄞˊ)
steak; beefsteak
牛皮(ㄋㄧㄡˊ ㄆㄧˊ)
①cowhide　②as in 吹牛皮—to talk big; to brag
牛脾氣(ㄋㄧㄡˊ ㄆㄧˊ ㄑㄧˋ)
stubbornness; obstinacy
牛皮紙(ㄋㄧㄡˊ ㄆㄧˊ ㄓˇ)
kraft paper; brown paper
牛馬(ㄋㄧㄡˊ ㄇㄚˇ)
①cattle and horses　②people who are being overworked like beasts of burden: 莫為兒孫作牛馬。 Do not slave for your children.
牛馬不如(ㄋㄧㄡˊ ㄇㄚˇ ㄅㄨˋ ㄖㄨˊ)
to be worked even harder than cattle and horses
牛馬生活(ㄋㄧㄡˊ ㄇㄚˇ ㄕㄥ ㄏㄨㄛˊ)
a life of drudgery
牛毛(ㄋㄧㄡˊ ㄇㄠˊ)
hairs of an ox—numerous: 他的問題多如牛毛。 He has numerous problems.
牛毛雨(ㄋㄧㄡˊ ㄇㄠˊ ㄩˇ)or 牛毛細雨(ㄋㄧㄡˊ ㄇㄠˊ ㄒㄧˋ ㄩˇ)
fine drizzling rain
牛蝱 or 牛虻(ㄋㄧㄡˊ ㄇㄥˊ)
a gadfly
牛眠吉壤(ㄋㄧㄡˊ ㄇㄧㄢˊ ㄐㄧˊ ㄖㄤˇ)
an ideal burial ground (in the superstitious sense)
牛糞(ㄋㄧㄡˊ ㄈㄣˋ)
cow dung
牛蜂(ㄋㄧㄡˊ ㄈㄥ)
a hornet
牛刀(ㄋㄧㄡˊ ㄉㄠ)
a butcher knife for cattle
牛刀小試(ㄋㄧㄡˊ ㄉㄠ ㄒㄧㄠˇ ㄕˋ)
①(literally) to use a large butcher knife to cut a little

thing—to try to kill a fly with a long spear ②the first small display of a master hand

牛痘(ㄋㄧㄡˊㄉㄡˋ)
cowpox; vaccinia

牛鼎烹雞(ㄋㄧㄡˊㄉㄧㄥˇㄆㄥ ㄐㄧ)
(literally) to boil a fowl in the great cauldron for cooking an ox—to kill a fly with a long spear; to employ a steam hammer to crack a nut

牛犢(子)(ㄋㄧㄡˊㄉㄨˊ·ㄗˇ)
a calf

牛肚子(ㄋㄧㄡˊㄉㄨˇ·ㄗˇ)
the stomach of an ox

牛頓(ㄋㄧㄡˊㄉㄨㄣˋ)
Sir Isaac Newton (1642-1727), English philosopher and mathematician

牛頓運動定律(ㄋㄧㄡˊㄉㄨㄣˋㄩㄣˋㄉㄨㄥˋㄉㄧㄥˋㄌㄩˋ)
Newton's law of motion

牛頭不對馬嘴(ㄋㄧㄡˊㄊㄡˊㄅㄨˊㄉㄨㄟˋㄇㄚˇㄗㄨㄟˇ)
(literally) The head of an ox does not match the mouth of a horse—irrelevant; not to the point; unconnected; incongruous

牛頭馬面(ㄋㄧㄡˊㄊㄡˊㄇㄚˇㄇㄧㄢˋ)
ox-headed and horse-faced demons in Hades

牛奶(ㄋㄧㄡˊㄋㄞˇ)
(cow's) milk

牛奶糖(ㄋㄧㄡˊㄋㄞˇㄊㄤˊ)
butter candy; toffee; taffy

牛奶公司(ㄋㄧㄡˊㄋㄞˇㄍㄨㄥㄙ)
a dairy company

牛腩(ㄋㄧㄡˊㄋㄢˇ)
sirloin; tenderloin

牛酪(ㄋㄧㄡˊㄌㄠˋ)
butter and cheese; yogurt

牛郎(ㄋㄧㄡˊㄌㄤˊ)
a cowboy: 他在電影裏飾演牛郎。He acted as a cowboy in the film.

牛郎織女(ㄋㄧㄡˊㄌㄤˊㄓ ㄋㄩˇ)
the Cowherd and the Weaving Maid who, according to Chinese folklore, meet once a year on the seventh day of the seventh moon over a bridge across the Milky Way formed by sympathetic magpies 亦作「牽牛織女」

牛骨(ㄋㄧㄡˊㄍㄨˇ)
bones of an ox

牛鬼蛇神(ㄋㄧㄡˊㄍㄨㄟˇㄕㄜˊㄕㄣˊ)
(literally) demons with the head of an ox and spirits with the body of a serpent —①absurdities ②forces of evil

牛後(ㄋㄧㄡˊㄏㄡˋ)
(literally) buttocks of an ox—people content to follow the great: 寧為雞口, 毋為牛後. Better to reign in hell than serve in heaven.

牛黃(ㄋㄧㄡˊㄏㄨㄤˊ)
bezoar taken from an ox (used as a medicine)

牛驥同皁(ㄋㄧㄡˊㄐㄧˋㄊㄨㄥˊㄗㄠˋ)
(literally) a cow and a thoroughbred horse sharing the same trough—to make no distinction between the wise and the foolish

牛角(ㄋㄧㄡˊㄐㄧㄠˇ)
horns of cattle

牛角尖(ㄋㄧㄡˊㄐㄧㄠˇㄐㄧㄢ)
the tip of a horn—an insignificant problem: 鑽牛角尖 to get oneself into a dead-end alley through sheer stubbornness

牛津(ㄋㄧㄡˊㄐㄧㄣ)
Oxford, a city in England

牛津大學(ㄋㄧㄡˊㄐㄧㄣ ㄉㄚˋㄒㄩㄝˊ)
Oxford University

牛筋(ㄋㄧㄡˊㄐㄧㄣ)
a cattle tendon

牛勁(ㄋㄧㄡˊㄐㄧㄥˋ)or 牛勁兒(ㄋㄧㄡˊㄐㄧㄥˋㄦ)
①very stubborn; stubbornness; headstrong: 這小伙子有股牛勁. The lad is headstrong. ②great strength

牛氣(ㄋㄧㄡˊㄑㄧˋ)
self-conceit; pride; haughtiness

牛群(ㄋㄧㄡˊㄑㄩㄣˊ)
a herd of cattle

牛心(ㄋㄧㄡˊㄒㄧㄣ)
①the heart of an ox ②stubbornness

牛性(ㄋㄧㄡˊㄒㄧㄥˋ)
stubbornness

牛車(ㄋㄧㄡˊㄔㄜ)
an oxcart; an ox-drawn cart

牛舌(ㄋㄧㄡˊㄕㄜˊ)
the tongue of an ox

牛舍(ㄋㄧㄡˊㄕㄜˋ)or 牛棚(ㄋㄧㄡˊㄆㄥˊ)or 牛欄(ㄋㄧㄡˊㄌㄢˊ)
a cattle pen, shed, or yard

牛山濯濯(ㄋㄧㄡˊㄕㄢ ㄓㄨㄛˊㄓㄨㄛˊ)
(literally) a treeless mountain—a bald head

牛肉(ㄋㄧㄡˊㄖㄡˋ)
beef

牛肉麵(ㄋㄧㄡˊㄖㄡˋㄇㄧㄢˋ)
noodles served with stewed beef

牛肉店(ㄋㄧㄡˊㄖㄡˋㄉㄧㄢˋ)
a beef store

牛肉湯(ㄋㄧㄡˊㄖㄡˋㄊㄤ)
beef soup

牛肉乾(ㄋㄧㄡˊㄖㄡˋㄍㄢ)
dried roast beef

牛肉汁(ㄋㄧㄡˊㄖㄡˋㄓ)
beef extract

牛乳(ㄋㄧㄡˊㄖㄨˇ)
cow milk

牛仔(ㄋㄧㄡˊㄗㄞˇ)
a cowboy

牛仔褲(ㄋㄧㄡˊㄗㄞˇㄎㄨˋ)
blue jeans; jeans: 男孩子穿着牛仔褲或卡其褲. The boys wore jeans or khakis.

牛溲馬勃(ㄋㄧㄡˊㄙㄡ ㄇㄚˇㄅㄛˊ)
trivial but useful things

牛耳(ㄋㄧㄡˊㄦˇ)
the ears of a bull: 執牛耳 to hold the bull's ear—to play the leading role; to be in a dominant position

牛衣對泣(ㄋㄧㄡˊㄧ ㄉㄨㄟˋㄑㄧˋ)
(literally) to weep together in coarse clothes—(said of a married couple) to live in extreme poverty

牛疫(ㄋㄧㄡˊㄧˋ)or 牛瘟(ㄋㄧㄡˊㄨㄣ)
rinderpest; a cattle plague

牛腰(ㄋㄧㄡˊㄧㄠ)
kidneys of an ox

牛油(ㄋㄧㄡˊㄧㄡˊ)
①butter ②tallow ③butter oil

牛油麵包(ㄋㄧㄡˊㄧㄡˊㄇㄧㄢˋㄅㄠ)
butter and bread

牛飲(ㄋㄧㄡˊㄧㄣˇ)
to drink heavily; to drink like a fish

牛蛙(ㄋㄧㄡˊㄨㄚ)
a bullfrog

牛尾湯(ㄋㄧㄡˊㄨㄟˇㄊㄤ)
an oxtail broth

〔牛部〕

〔牛部〕

二畫

【牝】 3311 ㄆㄧㄣˋ pinn, pìn
female of an animal

牝馬(ㄆㄧㄣˋ ㄇㄚˇ)
a mare

牝貓(ㄆㄧㄣˋ ㄇㄠ)
a tabby (as distinct from a tomcat)

牝牡驪黄(ㄆㄧㄣˋ ㄇㄨˇ ㄌㄧˊ ㄏㄨㄤˊ)
One's real worth is more valuable than his looks. 或 to judge not by the superficial aspects of things

牝犢(ㄆㄧㄣˋ ㄉㄨˊ)
a female calf; a young cow; a heifer

牝兔(ㄆㄧㄣˋ ㄊㄨˋ)
a female rabbit; a doe

牝鹿(ㄆㄧㄣˋ ㄌㄨˋ)
a female deer; a doe, a roe, or a roe deer

牝雞(ㄆㄧㄣˋ ㄐㄧ)
a hen: 我們養牝雞生蛋。 We raised hens to get eggs.

牝雞司晨(ㄆㄧㄣˋ ㄐㄧ ㄙ ㄔㄣˊ)
(literally) the hen crowing at dawn—a woman usurping man's power 或 The gray mare is the better horse.

牝豬(ㄆㄧㄣˋ ㄓㄨ)
a she-pig; a sow

牝朝(ㄆㄧㄣˋ ㄔㄠˊ)
the Female Era (the reign of Empress Wu from 690 to 705 A.D.)

牝鵝(ㄆㄧㄣˋ ㄜˊ)
a goose (as opposed to a gander)

牝羊(ㄆㄧㄣˋ ㄧㄤˊ)
a ewe

【牟】 3312 ㄇㄡˊ mou, móu
1. to seek
2. to bellow(or low)
3. a Chinese family name

牟尼(ㄇㄡˊ ㄋㄧˊ)
(Buddhism) muni; peace

牟利(ㄇㄡˊ ㄌㄧˋ)
to seek profits

牟取(ㄇㄡˊ ㄑㄩˇ)
to seek; to obtain: 有些商人牟取暴利。 Some merchants seek exorbitant profits.

三畫

【牡】 3313 ㄇㄨˇ muu, mǔ
(又讀 ㄇㄡˇ moou, mǒou)
a male animal

牡馬(ㄇㄨˇ ㄇㄚˇ)
a stallion

牡丹(ㄇㄨˇ ㄉㄢ)
a peony

牡丹江(ㄇㄨˇ ㄉㄢ ㄐㄧㄤ)
the Mutankiang (a river in Kirin Province(吉林省))

牡牛(ㄇㄨˇ ㄋㄧㄡˊ)
a bull; an ox

牡蠣(ㄇㄨˇ ㄌㄧˋ)
an oyster

牡鹿(ㄇㄨˇ ㄌㄨˋ)
a stag

牡齒(ㄇㄨˇ ㄔˇ)
lower teeth

3314
【牠】 ㄊㄚ ta tā
(讀音 ㄊㄨㄛ tuo tuō)
(又讀 ㄊㄜ te tē)
it

【牢】 3315 ㄌㄠˊ lau, láo
1. a pen; a stable; a cage
2. a jail; a prison
3. secure; stable; firm; fast
4. worried; concerned
5. sacrifice

牢不可破(ㄌㄠˊ ㄅㄨˋ ㄎㄜˇ ㄆㄛˋ)
impregnable; invulnerable; very secure; unbreakable; unshakable

牢牢(ㄌㄠˊ ㄌㄠˊ)
firmly; fast: 我把小船牢牢繫在木柱上。 I made the boat fast to the post.

牢籠(ㄌㄠˊ ㄌㄨㄥˊ)
①to cover; to include ②to captivate; to ensnare; to win over by schemes ③a pen; a cage; a prison

牢籠計(ㄌㄠˊ ㄌㄨㄥˊ ㄐㄧˋ)
a scheme to entrap; a trick

牢固(ㄌㄠˊ ㄍㄨˋ)
secure; firm

牢靠(ㄌㄠˊ ㄎㄠˋ)
①firm; stable; secure; sturdy ②reliable; trustworthy; dependable

牢記(ㄌㄠˊ ㄐㄧˋ)
to keep firmly in mind

牢檻(ㄌㄠˊ ㄐㄧㄢˋ)
a jail; a prison

牢什子(ㄌㄠˊ ㄕ˙ㄗ)
a nuisance; an eyesore

牢卒(ㄌㄠˊ ㄗㄨˊ)
a jailer

牢騷(ㄌㄠˊ ㄙㄠ)
discontent; grumbling; complaint: 不要發牢騷。 Don't grumble!

牢穩(ㄌㄠˊ ㄨㄣˇ)
secure; stable; firm: 這門牢穩嗎? Is the door secure?

牢獄(ㄌㄠˊ ㄩˋ)
a jail; a prison

四畫

【牧】 3316 ㄇㄨˋ muh, mù
1. to pasture; to shepherd
2. pasture
3. to govern
4. a magistrate; a public administrator

牧馬(ㄇㄨˋ ㄇㄚˇ)
to pasture horses

牧馬中原(ㄇㄨˋ ㄇㄚˇ ㄓㄨㄥ ㄩㄢˊ)
to become master of the country

牧民(ㄇㄨˋ ㄇㄧㄣˊ)
to shepherd the people; to govern the people

牧夫(ㄇㄨˋ ㄈㄨ)
officials in charge of civil administration

牧笛(ㄇㄨˋ ㄉㄧˊ)
a shepherd's pipe

牧地(ㄇㄨˋ ㄉㄧˋ)
a pasture; a grazing area

牧童(ㄇㄨˋ ㄊㄨㄥˊ)
a cowboy; a shepherd boy

牧牛(ㄇㄨˋ ㄋㄧㄡˊ)
to pasture cattle; to herd cows: 他在草地上牧牛。 He pastured cattle.

牧歌(ㄇㄨˋ ㄍㄜ)
a pastoral song; a shepherd song

牧者(ㄇㄨˋ ㄓㄜˇ)
a shepherd

牧豬奴(ㄇㄨˋ ㄓㄨ ㄋㄨˊ)
①a swineherd ②a gambler

牧場(ㄇㄨˋ ㄔㄤˇ)

a pasture; a ranch; a stock farm

牧畜(ㄇㄨˋㄔㄨˋ)
pasturage; stock farming

牧師(ㄇㄨˋㄕ)
a pastor; a preacher; a clergyman

牧守(ㄇㄨˋㄕㄡˇ)
a provincial magistrate during the Han Dynasty

牧草(ㄇㄨˋㄘㄠˇ)
herbage; pasture: 這些地方有好的牧草。These lands afford good pasture.

牧羊(ㄇㄨˋㄧㄤˊ)
to pasture sheep; to tend sheep

牧羊犬(ㄇㄨˋㄧㄤˊㄑㄩㄢˇ)
a shepherd dog; a collie

牧羊人(ㄇㄨˋㄧㄤˊㄖㄣˊ)
a shepherd: 牧羊人帶羊下山。The shepherd guided his sheep down the hill.

【物】 3317
ㄨˋ　wù　wu

1. a thing; matter; a being
2. content; substance: 他的演說言之無物。There was no substance in his speech.
3. the physical world; nature
4. other people

物薄情厚(ㄨˋㄅㄛˊㄑㄧㄥˊㄏㄡˋ)
The gift is of small value but the thoughtfulness behind it is immense.

物品(ㄨˋㄆㄧㄣˇ)
things; articles

物莫如新，友莫如故(ㄨˋㄇㄛˋㄖㄨˊㄒㄧㄣ，ㄧㄡˇㄇㄛˋㄖㄨˊㄍㄨˋ)
Things are good when new, but friendship is good when old.

物美價廉(ㄨˋㄇㄟˇㄐㄧㄚˋㄌㄧㄢˊ)
(said of merchandise) excellent quality and reasonable price

物腐蟲生(ㄨˋㄈㄨˇㄔㄨㄥˊㄕㄥ)
(literally) Worms breed only when things have already started rotting. —Ruin befalls only those who have weaknesses. 或 A nation falls only when it has already been on the decline.

物阜民康(ㄨˋㄈㄨˋㄇㄧㄣˊㄎㄤ)
Goods are plentiful and the people are happy.

物體(ㄨˋㄊㄧˇ)
(physics) a body; a substance; an object

物累(ㄨˋㄌㄟˋ)
the burden of material things

物離鄉貴(ㄨˋㄌㄧˊㄒㄧㄤㄍㄨㄟˋ)
A commodity commands a higher price where it is not grown or manufactured.

物理(ㄨˋㄌㄧˇ)
①the law of nature ②physics

物理變化(ㄨˋㄌㄧˇㄅㄧㄢˋㄏㄨㄚˋ)
physical changes

物理學(ㄨˋㄌㄧˇㄒㄩㄝˊ)
physics

物理學家(ㄨˋㄌㄧˇㄒㄩㄝˊㄐㄧㄚ)
a physicist

物力(ㄨˋㄌㄧˋ)
material means or resources: 我們要節約財力物力。We must use financial and material resources sparingly.

物料(ㄨˋㄌㄧㄠˋ)
materials; stuff

物論(ㄨˋㄌㄨㄣˋ)
public opinion

物各有主(ㄨˋㄍㄜˋㄧㄡˇㄓㄨˇ)
Everything has its owner.

物故(ㄨˋㄍㄨˋ)
dead; deceased; to pass away; to die: 這位小說家已物故多年。The novelist has been dead for several years.

物歸原主(ㄨˋㄍㄨㄟㄩㄢˊㄓㄨˇ)
Things return to their proper owners.

物華(ㄨˋㄏㄨㄚˊ)
①the essence of things ②beautiful scenes

物華天寶(ㄨˋㄏㄨㄚˊㄊㄧㄢㄅㄠˇ)
Good products from the earth are nature's treasures.

物化(ㄨˋㄏㄨㄚˋ)
①changes of matters in nature ②death

物換星移(ㄨˋㄏㄨㄢˋㄒㄧㄥㄧˊ)
(literally) Things change and stars move.—vicissitudes of human affairs with the elapse of time

物極則反(ㄨˋㄐㄧˊㄗㄜˊㄈㄢˇ)or **物極必反**(ㄨˋㄐㄧˊㄅㄧˋㄈㄢˇ)
As soon as a thing reaches its extremity, it reverses its

course.

物價(ㄨˋㄐㄧㄚˋ)
commodity prices: 物價平落。Prices drop to normal.

物價波動(ㄨˋㄐㄧㄚˋㄅㄛㄉㄨㄥˋ)
price fluctuations

物價指數(ㄨˋㄐㄧㄚˋㄓˇㄕㄨˋ)
a price index

物價穩定(ㄨˋㄐㄧㄚˋㄨㄣˇㄉㄧㄥˋ)
stability of commodity prices; price stability

物件(ㄨˋㄐㄧㄢˋ)
articles; things

物盡其用(ㄨˋㄐㄧㄣˋㄑㄧˊㄩㄥˋ)
The utility of things should be exhausted.

物鏡(ㄨˋㄐㄧㄥˋ)
the objective (of a microscope)

物競天擇(ㄨˋㄐㄧㄥˋㄊㄧㄢㄗㄜˊ)
the struggle for survival among things by the law of natural selection

物象(ㄨˋㄒㄧㄤˋ)
①physical phenomena; natural phenomena ②the shape and appearance of things

物質(ㄨˋㄓˊ)
(physics) matter

物質不滅律(ㄨˋㄓˊㄅㄨˋㄇㄧㄝˋㄌㄩˋ)
the law of conservation of matter

物質名詞(ㄨˋㄓˊㄇㄧㄥˊㄘˊ)
a material noun

物質建設(ㄨˋㄓˊㄐㄧㄢˋㄕㄜˋ)
material development or progress (of a community, country, etc.)

物質生活(ㄨˋㄓˊㄕㄥㄏㄨㄛˊ)
physical life; material life

物質三態(ㄨˋㄓˊㄙㄢㄊㄞˋ)
the three states of matter —solid, liquid and gas

物質文明(ㄨˋㄓˊㄨㄣˊㄇㄧㄥˊ)
material civilization

物證(ㄨˋㄓㄥˋ)
material evidence

物主(ㄨˋㄓㄨˇ)
the owner (of a thing): 誰是這些物品的物主？Who is the owner of these articles?

物產(ㄨˋㄔㄢˇ)
natural resources

物傷其類(ㄨˋㄕㄤㄑㄧˊㄌㄟˋ)
All beings grieve for the death of their fellow beings.

〔牛部〕

〔牛部〕

物資 (ㄨ ㄗ)
materials; supplies; goods.

物色 (ㄨ ㄙㄜˋ)
to seek (talent); to scout for (talent); to look for (a son-in-law, mate, etc.)

物以類聚
Birds of a feather flock together.

物以稀爲貴 (ㄨ ㄧˇ ㄒㄧ ㄨㄟˊ ㄍㄨㄟˋ)
A thing is valued if it is rare. 或 When a thing is scarce, it is precious.

物役 (ㄨ ㄧˋ)
to be a slave of material things

物議 (ㄨ ㄧˋ)
public criticisms; public censure

物有本末，事有終始 (ㄨ ㄧㄡˇ ㄅㄣˇ ㄇㄛˋ, ㄕˋ ㄧㄡˇ ㄓㄨㄥ ㄕˇ)
Things have their root and branches; affairs have their end and beginning.

物物交換 (ㄨ ㄨ ㄐㄧㄠ ㄏㄨㄢˋ)
to barter one thing for another

物我兩忘 (ㄨ ㄨㄛˇ ㄌㄧㄤˇ ㄨㄤˋ)
to become unconscious of the boundary between oneself and the external world

物外 (ㄨ ㄨㄞˋ)
beyond the physical world

物望 (ㄨ ㄨㄤˋ)
the object of popular admiration

物慾 (ㄨ ㄩˋ)
worldly desires; craving for material things

五畫

【牯】3318 《ㄨˇ guu gǔ
1. a cow
2. a castrated bull

牯牛 (《ㄨˇ ㄋㄧㄡˊ)
① a cow ② a castrated bull

牯嶺 (《ㄨˇ ㄌㄧㄥˇ)
Kuling, a summer resort in Kiangsi

【牲】3319 ㄕㄥ sheng shēng
livestock

牲口 (ㄕㄥ ·ㄎㄡ)
livestock

牲畜 (ㄕㄥ ㄔㄨˋ)
livestock

【牴】3320 ㄉㄧˇ dii dǐ
to gore

牴觸 (ㄉㄧˇ ㄔㄨˋ)
to contradict; to conflict

牴牾 (ㄉㄧˇ ㄨˇ)
to contradict; to conflict 參看「牴觸」

六畫

【特】3321 ㄊㄜˋ teh tè
1. special; unique; peculiar; particular; extraordinary; unusual; outstanding; distinguished; exclusive: 這種食物有奇特的味道。This food has a peculiar taste.
2. just; merely; only: 不特如此 not only that
3. a bull

特別 (ㄊㄜˋ ㄅㄧㄝˊ)
① special; peculiar; particular; unique; unusual; extraordinary: 嬰兒需要特別的食物。Babies need special food. ② especially; particularly

特別法 (ㄊㄜˋ ㄅㄧㄝˊ ㄈㄚˇ)
special law

特別費 (ㄊㄜˋ ㄅㄧㄝˊ ㄈㄟˋ)
extraordinary expenses; special expenses

特別黨部 (ㄊㄜˋ ㄅㄧㄝˊ ㄉㄤˇ ㄅㄨˋ)
non-regional party headquarters of the Kuomintang formed in the various professions or various branches of government-operated enterprises

特別開支 (ㄊㄜˋ ㄅㄧㄝˊ ㄎㄞ ㄓ)
special expenses

特別快車 (ㄊㄜˋ ㄅㄧㄝˊ ㄎㄨㄞˋ ㄔㄜ) or 特別快車 (ㄊㄜˋ ㄅㄧㄝˊ ㄎㄞˋ)
a special express train; a special express: 這是上午八時去台北的特別快車。This is the 8:00 a.m. special express to Taipei.

特別區域 (ㄊㄜˋ ㄅㄧㄝˊ ㄑㄩ ㄩˋ)
special administrative districts (such as Jehol, Suiyüan, etc. before they became provinces)

特別市 (ㄊㄜˋ ㄅㄧㄝˊ ㄕˋ)
a special municipality (directly under the jurisdic-

tion of the Central Government)

特派 (ㄊㄜˋ ㄆㄞˋ)
specially despatched or appointed; to commission specially

特派記者 (ㄊㄜˋ ㄆㄞˋ ㄐㄧˋ ㄓㄜˇ)
a special correspondent; an accredited journalist

特派員 (ㄊㄜˋ ㄆㄞˋ ㄩㄢˊ)
a correspondent (of a news agency, newspaper etc.): 王先生是我們駐倫敦的特派員。Mr. Wang is our London correspondent.

特命全權大使 (ㄊㄜˋ ㄇㄧㄥˋ ㄑㄩㄢˊ ㄑㄩㄢˊ ㄉㄚˋ ㄕˇ)
an ambassador extraordinary and plenipotentiary

特命全權公使 (ㄊㄜˋ ㄇㄧㄥˋ ㄑㄩㄢˊ ㄑㄩㄢˊ ㄍㄨㄥ ㄕˇ)
an envoy extraordinary and minister plenipotentiary

特大 (ㄊㄜˋ ㄉㄚˋ)
exceptionally big; the most

特大號 (ㄊㄜˋ ㄉㄚˋ ㄏㄠˋ)
king-size; extra large size: 我們都很羨慕他那特大號的床。We all admire his king-size bed.

特等 (ㄊㄜˋ ㄉㄥˇ)
of the special class or grade

特等艙 (ㄊㄜˋ ㄉㄥˇ ㄘㄤ)
a stateroom

特地 (ㄊㄜˋ ㄉㄧˋ)
on purpose; specially; designedly; exclusively: 我們是特地來向你學習的。We came specially to learn from you.

特點 (ㄊㄜˋ ㄉㄧㄢˇ)
special features; peculiarities; characteristics

特定 (ㄊㄜˋ ㄉㄧㄥˋ)
① specially designated ② specific; specified; given

特拉瓦 (ㄊㄜˋ ㄌㄚ ㄨㄚˇ)
Delaware, a state in U.S.A.

特拉維夫 (ㄊㄜˋ ㄌㄚ ㄨㄟˊ ㄈㄨ)
Tel Aviv

特例 (ㄊㄜˋ ㄌㄧˋ)
a special case; a special instance; an exceptional case

特立獨行 (ㄊㄜˋ ㄌㄧˋ ㄉㄨˊ ㄒㄧㄥˊ)
to be self-reliant; to be one's own master

特洛伊 (ㄊㄜˋ ㄌㄨㄛˋ ㄧ)
Troy

特故(ㄊㄜ ㄍㄨ)
on purpose; intentionally

特工(ㄊㄜ ㄍㄨㄥ)
secret service

特攻隊(ㄊㄜ ㄍㄨㄥ ㄉㄨㄟˋ)
commando units; rangers

特工人員(ㄊㄜ ㄍㄨㄥ ㄖㄣˊ ㄩㄢˊ)
a special agent

特刊(ㄊㄜ ㄎㄢ)
the extra edition, special edition or special supplement (of a newspaper or magazine)

特惠關稅(ㄊㄜ ㄏㄨㄟˋ ㄍㄨㄢ ㄕㄨㄟˋ)
preferential tariffs

特急(ㄊㄜ ㄐㄧˊ)
of special urgency

特級(ㄊㄜ ㄐㄧˊ)
of the special class or grade; superfine. 他送我一些特級烏龍茶。He gave me some superfine oolong tea.

特級上將(ㄊㄜ ㄐㄧˊ ㄕㄤ ㄐㄧㄤ)
a five-star general or admiral

特技(ㄊㄜ ㄐㄧˋ)
special skills; stunts; aerobatics

特家新聞(ㄊㄜ ㄐㄧㄚ ㄒㄧㄣ ㄨㄣˊ)or 特家報導(ㄊㄜ ㄐㄧㄚ ㄅㄠˋ ㄉㄠˇ)
an exclusive report or story by a news medium; a scoop 亦作「獨家報導」

特價(ㄊㄜ ㄐㄧㄚˋ)
a specially reduced price; a bargain price. 我們這些東西都是特價出售的。We'll sell these articles at a bargain price.

特獎(ㄊㄜ ㄐㄧㄤˇ)
a special prize; a grand prize

特遣隊(ㄊㄜ ㄑㄧㄢˇ ㄉㄨㄟˋ)
a task force

特權(ㄊㄜ ㄑㄩㄢˊ)
privileges; 繳半費之特權 the privilege of paying half fare

特權階級(ㄊㄜ ㄑㄩㄢˊ ㄐㄧㄝ ㄐㄧˊ)
the privileged class

特寫(ㄊㄜ ㄒㄧㄝˇ)
①a feature story (in a newspaper or magazine) ② a close-up (in a movie)

特效(ㄊㄜ ㄒㄧㄠˋ)
special virtue or efficacy (of a medicine, etc.)

特效藥(ㄊㄜ ㄒㄧㄠˋ ㄧㄠˋ)
a specific; a wonder drug; a patent medicine

特性(ㄊㄜ ㄒㄧㄥˋ)
characteristics; peculiarities; distinctive features; defining features: Every region has its own 性。Every region has its own characteristics.

特許(ㄊㄜ ㄒㄩˇ)
to permit as a special case; to charter; special mission

特許權(ㄊㄜ ㄒㄩˇ ㄑㄩㄢˊ)
a patent

特許狀(ㄊㄜ ㄒㄩˇ ㄓㄨㄤˋ)
a charter

特選(ㄊㄜ ㄒㄩㄢˇ)
carefully chosen; hand-picked

特支費(ㄊㄜ ㄓ ㄈㄟˋ)
a special allowance for a government agency or its chief to meet contingent expenses

特質(ㄊㄜ ㄓˊ)
special qualities; characteristics; peculiarities

特指(ㄊㄜ ㄓˇ)
to refer particularly to

特製(ㄊㄜ ㄓˋ)
manufactured for a specific purpose; manufactured with a special process or extra care

特徵(ㄊㄜ ㄓㄥ)
defining qualities; distinctive features; characteristics; unique qualities: 他們有一同的特徵。They have one characteristic in common.

特准(ㄊㄜ ㄓㄨㄣˇ)
a special permit; to permit as a special case

特種(ㄊㄜ ㄓㄨㄥˇ)
of a special kind

特種部隊(ㄊㄜ ㄓㄨㄥˇ ㄅㄨˋ ㄉㄨㄟˋ)
special forces

特種營業(ㄊㄜ ㄓㄨㄥˇ ㄧㄥˊ ㄧㄝˋ)
special business operations (such as cabarets, bars, wine-houses, etc.)

特產(ㄊㄜ ㄔㄢˇ)
unique or special products (of a place)

特長(ㄊㄜ ㄔㄤˊ)
special merits; strong points; a specialty; a special skill:

舞蹈是我的特長。Dancing is my strong point.

特稱(ㄊㄜ ㄔㄥ)
(logic) particular (as opposed to universal)

特出(ㄊㄜ ㄔㄨ)
outstanding; distinguished; eminent; prominent: 他證明自己是位傑出的政治家。He proved himself an eminent statesman.

特使(ㄊㄜ ㄕˇ)or(ㄊㄜ ㄕˋ)
a special envoy

特赦(ㄊㄜ ㄕㄜˋ)
special pardon; an amnesty

特殊(ㄊㄜ ㄕㄨ)
special; unusual; unique: 在我的一生中,這是一個特殊的日子。This is a special day in my life.

特殊分子(ㄊㄜ ㄕㄨ ㄈㄣˋ ㄗˇ)
special members

特殊教育(ㄊㄜ ㄕㄨ ㄐㄧㄠˋ ㄩˋ)
special education (as for the blind, etc.)

特任(ㄊㄜ ㄖㄣˋ)
special appointment rank, the highest of the four civil service grades in China

特任官(ㄊㄜ ㄖㄣˋ ㄍㄨㄢ)
an official holding a post of the special appointment rank

特操(ㄊㄜ ㄘㄠ)
extraordinary moral conduct or righteousness

特色(ㄊㄜ ㄙㄜˋ)
unique features; special features; characteristics: 你的計劃有何特色? What are the unique features of your plan?

特恩(ㄊㄜ ㄣ)
special favor or kindness

特意(ㄊㄜ ㄧˋ)
on purpose; intentionally

特異(ㄊㄜ ㄧˋ)
peculiar; singular; unusual; strange

特藝彩色(ㄊㄜ ㄧˋ ㄘㄞˇ ㄙㄜˋ)
deluxe colors (of motion pictures)

特優(ㄊㄜ ㄧㄡ)
(said of performance) excellent; extraordinary

特有(ㄊㄜ ㄧㄡˇ)
to have exclusively; unique;

【牛部】

peculiar; special: 香蕉有其特有的香味。Bananas have their own special smell.

特宥(ㄊㄜˋ ㄧㄡˋ)
special pardon or leniency

特務(ㄊㄜˋ ㄨˋ)
a secret agent

特為(ㄊㄜˋ ㄨㄟˋ)
for this particular reason; particularly for the sake of: 我特為此事而來。I come specially for this purpose.

特約(ㄊㄜˋ ㄩㄝ)
①a special agreement or contract ②specially or exclusively engaged

特約記者(ㄊㄜˋ ㄩㄝ ㄐㄧˋ ㄓㄜˇ)
a stringer or a special correspondent (of a newspaper, etc.)

特約診所(ㄊㄜˋ ㄩㄝ ㄓㄣˇ ㄙㄨㄛˇ)
a clinic exclusively engaged by an organization

特約撰稿人(ㄊㄜˋ ㄩㄝ ㄓㄨㄢˋ ㄍㄠˇ ㄖㄣˊ)
a special contributor

特約醫院(ㄊㄜˋ ㄩㄝ ㄧ ㄩㄢˋ)
a hospital exclusively engaged by an organization

【牷】 3322
ㄑㄩㄢˊ chyuan quán
1. an ox of one color
2.(said of a sacrifice) intact

【牸】 3323
ㄗˋ tzyh zì
1. female animals
2. a cow

七畫

【牽】 3324
ㄑㄧㄢ chian qiān
1. to lead along; to drag; to pull; to tug; to haul
2. to involve; to affect
3. to control; to restrain

牽動(ㄑㄧㄢ ㄉㄨㄥˋ)
to affect as if a tugging action had been applied; to influence

牽牛花(ㄑㄧㄢ ㄋㄧㄡˊ ㄏㄨㄚ)
morning glory

牽牛星(ㄑㄧㄢ ㄋㄧㄡˊ ㄒㄧㄥ)
the star Altair

牽念(ㄑㄧㄢ ㄋㄧㄢˋ)
to feel anxious about; to be concerned for: 我如晚回, 請勿牽念。Don't be anxious if I am late.

牽累(ㄑㄧㄢ ㄌㄟˇ)
to drag (into trouble); to involve

牽連(ㄑㄧㄢ ㄌㄧㄢˊ)
to involve (in trouble); to implicate

牽蘿補屋(ㄑㄧㄢ ㄌㄨㄛˊ ㄅㄨˇ ㄨ)
(literally) to mend a leaky roof with vines—in financial straits

牽掛(ㄑㄧㄢ ㄍㄨㄚˋ)
to be concerned for; to feel anxious about; to worry about: 她牽掛她丈夫的安危。She worried about her husband's safety.

牽合(ㄑㄧㄢ ㄏㄜˊ)
to couple by force; to match by force

牽強(ㄑㄧㄢ ㄑㄧㄤˇ)
(said of an interpretation, etc.) forced; unnatural; far-fetched: 他的比喻有些牽強。His comparison is somewhat far-fetched.

牽強附會(ㄑㄧㄢ ㄑㄧㄤˇ ㄈㄨˋ ㄏㄨㄟˋ)
to give a forced interpretation; to distort the meaning; to make a far-fetched interpretation; to draw a forced analogy

牽線(ㄑㄧㄢ ㄒㄧㄢˋ)
①to pull strings; to use indirect influence to gain one's ends, etc.; to control from behind the scenes ②to act as a go-between

牽制(ㄑㄧㄢ ㄓˋ)
①to restrain; to curb; to check: 戰爭牽制了我們的計劃。The war gave a check to our plan.②to divert (enemy attention)

牽制行動(ㄑㄧㄢ ㄓˋ ㄒㄧㄥˊ ㄉㄨㄥˋ)
(military) a diversionary action or move

牽著鼻子走(ㄑㄧㄢ ·ㄓㄜ ㄅㄧˊ ·ㄗ ㄗㄡˇ)
to lead by the nose: 不要讓任何人牽著鼻子走。Don't let anyone lead you by the nose.

牽扯(ㄑㄧㄢ ㄔㄜˇ)
complication (of a matter); to involve; to implicate

牽掣(ㄑㄧㄢ ㄔㄜˋ)
to restrain; to get bogged

down; to curb; to check; to impede: 不要被枝節問題牽掣住。Don't get bogged down in minor issues.

牽腸掛肚(ㄑㄧㄢ ㄔㄤˊ ㄍㄨㄚˋ ㄉㄨˋ)or
牽腸割肚(ㄑㄧㄢ ㄔㄤˊ ㄍㄜ ㄉㄨˋ)
to be deeply concerned; to be very worried about

牽涉(ㄑㄧㄢ ㄕㄜˋ)
to involve; to affect; to implicate

牽手(ㄑㄧㄢ ㄕㄡˇ)
①to lead by the hand ②one's wife

牽絲(ㄑㄧㄢ ㄙ)
①to enter government service (in days of feudalism) ②to draw lots by pulling at one of the silk threads

牽絲扳藤(ㄑㄧㄢ ㄙ ㄅㄢ ㄊㄥˊ)
to harass or annoy persistently

牽一髮而動全身(ㄑㄧㄢ ㄧ ㄈㄚˋ ㄦˊ ㄉㄨㄥˋ ㄑㄩㄢˊ ㄕㄣ)
The pull of one hair may move the whole body. —What happens to a small part may affect the whole.

牽引(ㄑㄧㄢ ㄧㄣˇ)
①to involve (in trouble); to drag (into trouble) ②to draw

牽引機(ㄑㄧㄢ ㄧㄣˇ ㄐㄧ)
a tractor

牽挽(ㄑㄧㄢ ㄨㄢˇ)
to drag; to tug; to pull

【牾】 3325
ㄨˇ wuu wù
1. to oppose
2. to gore

八畫

【犁】 3326
(犂)ㄌㄧˊ lí
1. to till; to plough
2. a plough

犁田(ㄌㄧˊ ㄊㄧㄢˊ)
to plough (or plow) a field

犁庭掃穴(ㄌㄧˊ ㄊㄧㄥˊ ㄙㄠˇ ㄒㄩㄝˋ)or
犁庭掃閭(ㄌㄧˊ ㄊㄧㄥˊ ㄙㄠˇ ㄌㄩˊ)
to annihilate the enemy

【犀】 3327
ㄒㄧ shi xī
1.(said of armor, weapons, etc.) sharp-edged and hard
2. a rhinoceros

犀兵(ㄒㄧ ㄅㄧㄥ)
sharp weapons

犀牛(ㄒㄧ ㄋㄧㄡ)
the rhinoceros

犀利(ㄒㄧ ㄌㄧ)
①hard and sharp ②trenchant; sharp: 他的文筆犀利。
He has a trenchant pen.

犀甲(ㄒㄧ ㄐㄧㄚˇ)
armor made of rhinoceros
hide

犀角(ㄒㄧ ㄐㄧㄠˇ)
①a rhinoceros horn ②bone
of the forehead

犀照(ㄒㄧ ㄓㄠˋ)
very discerning

【觭】 3328
ㄐㄧ ji jī
a horn

觭角(ㄐㄧ ㄐㄧㄠˇ)
①a horn ②a corner: 屋子觭
角裏有一張書桌。 There is a
desk in a corner of the
room.

【犉】 3329
ㄖㄨㄣˊ ruen rún
1. an ox with yellow hair and
a black mouth
2. an ox seven feet tall

【犇】 3330
ㄅㄣ ben bēn
an ancient variant of 奔 —
to run away; to be in a hurry

九畫

【犍】 3331
ㄐㄧㄢ jian jiān
a castrated bull

犍牛(ㄐㄧㄢ ㄋㄧㄡˊ)
a bullock

十畫

【犒】 3332
ㄎㄠˋ kaw kào
to reward (soldiers, laborers,
etc.)

犒勞(ㄎㄠˋ ㄌㄠˊ)
①to reward or cheer troops
with food, money, gifts. etc.
②food, money, gifts. etc.
used to cheer troops

犒師(ㄎㄠˋ ㄕ)or 犒軍(ㄎㄠˋ ㄐㄩㄣ)
to cheer troops with material
gifts

犒賞(ㄎㄠˋ ㄕㄤˇ)
to reward (one for contributions) with money or gifts

【犖】
ㄌㄨㄛˊ luoh luò
1. a spotted ox
2. of many colors

犖犖(ㄌㄨㄛˊ ㄌㄨㄛˊ)
clear; evident; apparent

犖犖大者(ㄌㄨㄛˊ ㄌㄨㄛˊ ㄉㄚˋ ㄓㄜˇ)
the evident and major
instances, cases, examples,
etc.

犖确(ㄌㄨㄛˊ ㄑㄩㄝˋ)
rugged or craggy (mountains)

十一畫

【犛】 3334
ㄌㄧˊ li lí
1. a black ox
2. a yak

犛牛(ㄌㄧˊ ㄋㄧㄡˊ)
a yak

十五畫

【犢】 3335
ㄉㄨˊ dwu dú
a calf: 初生之犢不畏虎。 A
newborn calf fears not the
tiger.

犢鼻(ㄉㄨˊ ㄅㄧˊ)
(Chinese herb medicine) a
point susceptible to acupuncture under the kneecap

犢鼻褌(ㄉㄨˊ ㄅㄧˊ ㄎㄨㄣˊ)
knee breeches; shorts

十六畫

【犧】 3336
ㄒㄧ shi xī
1. sacrifice (as homage to a
deity); a beast of a uniform
color for sacrifice
2. to give up (for the sake of
something of greater value);
to sacrifice

犧牲(ㄒㄧ ㄕㄥ)
①sacrifice (offered to a
deity) ②to sacrifice (something valued for the sake of
something else): 他英勇爲國
犧牲。 He died a heroic death
for his country.

犧牲品(ㄒㄧ ㄕㄥ ㄆㄧㄣˇ)

①a loss leader—a popular
article sold for a fraction of
its normal price ②a sacrificial lamb

犧牲打(ㄒㄧ ㄕㄥ ㄉㄚˇ)
a sacrifice hit

犧牲者(ㄒㄧ ㄕㄥ ㄓㄜˇ)
victim(s)

犧尊(ㄒㄧ ㄗㄨㄣ)
a wooden wine cup shaped
like an ox

【犨】 3337
ㄔㄡ chou chōu
the panting of an ox

犬 部
ㄑㄩㄢˇ cheuan quǎn

【犬】 3338
ㄑㄩㄢˇ cheuan quǎn
a dog; a canine

犬鋪(ㄑㄩㄢˇ ㄆㄨˋ)or 犬窩(ㄑㄩㄢˇ ㄨㄛ)
a doghouse; a kennel

犬馬之勞(ㄑㄩㄢˇ ㄇㄚˇ ㄓ ㄌㄠˊ)
(literally) labor of a dog or
a horse—one's own service
(a self-depreciatory term):
我願效犬馬之勞。 I'll serve you
loyally.

犬吠(ㄑㄩㄢˇ ㄈㄟˋ)
the bark of a dog

犬禍(ㄑㄩㄢˇ ㄏㄨㄛˋ)
prevalence of rabies

犬豸(ㄑㄩㄢˇ ㄓ)
a beast or brute (used as a
term of abuse)

犬齒(ㄑㄩㄢˇ ㄔˇ)or 犬牙(ㄑㄩㄢˇ ㄧㄚˊ)
a cuspid; a canine tooth

犬儒學派(ㄑㄩㄢˇ ㄖㄨˊ ㄒㄩㄝˊ ㄆㄞˋ)
the Cynics (in Greek philosophy)

犬儒主義(ㄑㄩㄢˇ ㄖㄨˊ ㄓㄨˇ ㄧˋ)
Cynicism

犬戎(ㄑㄩㄢˇ ㄖㄨㄥˊ)
name of a barbarian tribe to
the west in ancient times

犬子(ㄑㄩㄢˇ ㄗˇ)
my son (a self-depreciatory
term): 請原諒犬子無知。 Please
excuse my son's ignorance.

犬牙相制(ㄑㄩㄢˇ ㄧㄚˊ ㄒㄧㄤ ㄓˋ)
①(said of two countries) to
adjoin each other along a

【犬 部】

zigzag borderline ②(said of two forces) to face each other across a zigzag front

犬牙相錯(ㄑㄩㄢ ㄧㄚˊ ㄒㄧㄤ ㄘㄨㄛˋ)or 犬牙交錯(ㄑㄩㄢ ㄧㄚˊ ㄐㄧㄠ ㄘㄨㄛˋ)
to adjoin each other along a zigzag borderline; interlocking

一畫

【犮】 3339
ㄅㄛˊ bor bó
the way a dog walks

二畫

【犯】 3340
ㄈㄢˋ fann fàn
1. to violate; to offend; to break (regulations or laws)
2. to commit (crimes, etc.)
3. to invade; to attack; to work against
4. a criminal
5. to have a recurrence of; to revert to

犯病(ㄈㄢˋ ㄅㄧㄥˋ)
to fall back into an old illness or a bad habit; to have a relapse: 他昨天又犯病了。He had a relapse yesterday.

犯不著(ㄈㄢˋ ㄅㄨˋ ㄓㄠˊ)or 犯不上(ㄈㄢˋ ㄅㄨˋ ㄕㄤˋ)
not worthwhile: 犯不著和這小孩爭辯。It is not worthwhile arguing with this child.

犯脾氣(ㄈㄢˋ ㄆㄧˊ ㄑㄧˋ)
to lose one's temper

犯法(ㄈㄢˋ ㄈㄚˇ)
to violate the law; to break the law

犯得著(ㄈㄢˋ ㄉㄜˊ ㄓㄠˊ)or 犯得上(ㄈㄢˋ ㄉㄜˊ ㄕㄤˋ)
worthwhile: 犯得著跟他吵嗎? Is it worthwhile quarreling with him?

犯土(ㄈㄢˋ ㄊㄨˇ)
to offend the deity of a locality (as through some construction project)

犯難(ㄈㄢˋ ㄋㄢˊ)
to risk danger

犯顏(ㄈㄢˋ ㄍㄢˇ)
to advise or admonish the emperor bluntly

犯規(ㄈㄢˋ ㄍㄨㄟ)

(sports) to commit a foul; to violate a rule or regulation

犯規者(ㄈㄢˋ ㄍㄨㄟ ㄓㄜˇ)
an offender

犯科(ㄈㄢˋ ㄎㄜ)
to break the law; to commit an offense

犯諱(ㄈㄢˋ ㄏㄨㄟˋ)
(in old China) to use a word which is part of the name of an emperor or an elder

犯忌諱(ㄈㄢˋ ㄐㄧˋ ㄏㄨㄟˋ)
to violate a taboo; to do something proscribed by superstitions

犯戒(ㄈㄢˋ ㄐㄧㄝˋ)
to violate a religious prohibition

犯界(ㄈㄢˋ ㄐㄧㄝˋ)
to cross the frontiers of another country illegally or by force

犯禁(ㄈㄢˋ ㄐㄧㄣˋ)
to violate prohibitions (laid down by the proper authorities)

犯境(ㄈㄢˋ ㄐㄧㄥˋ)
to invade the territory; to aggress upon the territory of another country

犯闕(ㄈㄢˋ ㄑㄩㄝˋ)
(said of rebels) to invade the imperial palace; to attack the capital

犯舌(ㄈㄢˋ ㄕㄜˊ)
to talk too much; to blab

犯上(ㄈㄢˋ ㄕㄤˋ)
to offend against one's superiors

犯上作亂(ㄈㄢˋ ㄕㄤˋ ㄗㄨㄛˋ ㄌㄨㄢˋ)
to rebel against authority

犯人(ㄈㄢˋ ㄖㄣˊ)
a criminal; a prisoner

犯罪(ㄈㄢˋ ㄗㄨㄟˋ)
(to commit) a crime, an offense or a sin: 他因犯罪而下獄。He was sent to prison for his crimes.

犯罪心理學(ㄈㄢˋ ㄗㄨㄟˋ ㄒㄧㄣ ㄌㄧˇ ㄒㄩㄝˊ)
criminal psychology

犯罪行爲(ㄈㄢˋ ㄗㄨㄟˋ ㄒㄧㄥˊ ㄨㄟˊ)
a criminal act; a criminality; crime: 謀殺和詐騙是犯罪行爲。Murder and swindling are

criminal acts.

犯罪學(ㄈㄢˋ ㄗㄨㄟˋ ㄒㄩㄝˊ)
criminology

犯錯誤(ㄈㄢˋ ㄘㄨㄛˋ ㄨˋ)or 犯錯(ㄈㄢˋ ㄘㄨㄛˋ)
to make a mistake; to err: 犯錯是人之常情,寬恕是超凡的。To err is human, to forgive divine.

犯死罪(ㄈㄢˋ ㄙˇ ㄗㄨㄟˋ)
to commit a crime punishable by death

犯案(ㄈㄢˋ ㄢˋ)
to commit a crime; to commit an offense

犯疑(ㄈㄢˋ ㄧˊ)or 犯疑心(ㄈㄢˋ ㄧˊ ㄒㄧㄣ)
to be suspicious: 無知者犯疑。The ignorant are suspicious.

犯意(ㄈㄢˋ ㄧˋ)
criminal intent

犯顏(ㄈㄢˋ ㄧㄢˊ)
to incur the displeasure of an elder or a superior with words

三畫

【犴】 3341
ㄢˋ ann àn
1. a prison; a jail
2. a species of dog with black mouth and nose

四畫

【狀】 3342
ㄓㄨㄤˋ juang zhuàng
1. appearance; look; shape; form
2. condition; state; situation
3. written appeal
4. a certificate: 獎狀 a certificate of commendation
5. to describe; to narrate; description

狀貌(ㄓㄨㄤˋ ㄇㄠˋ)
appearance; look

狀態(ㄓㄨㄤˋ ㄊㄞˋ)
situation; state; condition: 我們處於戰爭狀態。We are in a state of war.

狀況(ㄓㄨㄤˋ ㄎㄨㄤˋ)
situation; circumstances; condition

狀況證據(ㄓㄨㄤˋ ㄎㄨㄤˋ ㄓㄥˋ ㄐㄩˋ)
circumstantial evidence

〔犬 部〕

狀紙 (ㄓㄨㄤˋ ㄓˇ)
an official form for filing a lawsuit

狀子 (ㄓㄨㄤˋ ·ㄗ)
a written complaint; a plaint

狀詞 (ㄓㄨㄤˋ ㄘˊ)
the contents of an accusation

狀元 (ㄓㄨㄤˋ ㄩㄢˊ) or 狀頭 (ㄓㄨㄤˋ ㄊㄡˊ)
①the top successful candidate in the imperial examination ②the very best: 行行出狀元。 Every trade has its master. 或 One may distinguish himself in any trade.

狀元紅 (ㄓㄨㄤˋ ㄩㄢˊ ㄏㄨㄥˊ)
a kind of high-quality Shaohsing wine

【狂】 3343
ㄎㄨㄤˊ kwang kuáng
1. crazy; mad; mentally deranged
2. violent
3. unrestrained; uninhibited; wild
4. haughty

狂暴 (ㄎㄨㄤˊ ㄅㄠˋ)
wild; fierce; furious; ferocious; brutal

狂奔 (ㄎㄨㄤˊ ㄅㄣ)
to run about wildly; to run about madly

狂飆 (ㄎㄨㄤˊ ㄅㄧㄠ)
a hurricane

狂吠 (ㄎㄨㄤˊ ㄈㄟˋ)
①to bark wildly ②to utter wild words; to yell like a mad dog; to yell nonsense

狂放 (ㄎㄨㄤˊ ㄈㄤˋ)
wild; unrestrained

狂風暴雨 (ㄎㄨㄤˊ ㄈㄥ ㄅㄠˋ ㄩˇ)
violent wind and rain; a violent storm: 這場狂風暴雨造成很大的損害。 The violent storm did a lot of harm.

狂風怒號 (ㄎㄨㄤˊ ㄈㄥ ㄋㄨˋ ㄏㄠˊ)
A violent wind is howling wildly.

狂蜂浪蝶 (ㄎㄨㄤˊ ㄈㄥ ㄌㄤˋ ㄉㄧㄝˊ)
lascivious men

狂夫 (ㄎㄨㄤˊ ㄈㄨ)
a bohemian; one who cares nothing about conventions or decorum

狂瀾 (ㄎㄨㄤˊ ㄌㄢˊ)
to debauch; to dissipate; debauchery

狂態 (ㄎㄨㄤˊ ㄊㄞˋ)
①a scandalous scene; a display of wild manners ②insolent and conceited manners

狂瀾 (ㄎㄨㄤˊ ㄌㄢˊ)
①violent waves ②violent disturbances: 力挽狂瀾 to do one's utmost to stem violent disturbances

狂亂 (ㄎㄨㄤˊ ㄌㄨㄢˋ)
wild; frenzied; frantic; mad; frenzy

狂歌 (ㄎㄨㄤˊ ㄍㄜ)
to sing with wild joy

狂客 (ㄎㄨㄤˊ ㄎㄜˋ)
①a bohemian ②poplar catkins ③peach blossoms

狂呼 (ㄎㄨㄤˊ ㄏㄨ)
to shout in wild excitement

狂歡 (ㄎㄨㄤˊ ㄏㄨㄢ)
to rejoice with wild excitement; to be carried away by wild pleasure or joy; to revel

狂歡節 (ㄎㄨㄤˊ ㄏㄨㄢ ㄐㄧㄝˊ)
a carnival 亦作「嘉年華會」

狂狷 (ㄎㄨㄤˊ ㄐㄩㄢˋ)
radicals and ultraconservatives

狂犬病 (ㄎㄨㄤˊ ㄑㄩㄢˇ ㄅㄧㄥˋ)
rabies; hydrophobia

狂喜 (ㄎㄨㄤˊ ㄒㄧˇ)
to show wild joy; to rejoice with wild excitement

狂笑 (ㄎㄨㄤˊ ㄒㄧㄠˋ)
to give wild laughter

狂想曲 (ㄎㄨㄤˊ ㄒㄧㄤˇ ㄑㄩˇ)
(music) a rhapsody

狂相 (ㄎㄨㄤˊ ㄒㄧㄤˋ)
a display of unrestraint, or excessive haughtiness, or of excessive frivolity

狂士 (ㄎㄨㄤˊ ㄕˋ)
an idiosyncratic gentleman; a bohemian scholar; a self-conceited scholar

狂生 (ㄎㄨㄤˊ ㄕㄥ)
a bohemian young scholar

狂熱 (ㄎㄨㄤˊ ㄖㄜˋ)
fanatical; feverish; unreasonably enthusiastic; wildly zealous

狂人 (ㄎㄨㄤˊ ㄖㄣˊ)
①a lunatic ②an extremely conceited fellow

狂恣 (ㄎㄨㄤˊ ㄗˋ)
unrestrained; uninhibited; dissolute; profligate

狂走 (ㄎㄨㄤˊ ㄗㄡˇ)
to run about madly; to run about wildly

狂草 (ㄎㄨㄤˊ ㄘㄠˇ)
a wild scribble; an excessively free cursive style (in Chinese calligraphy)

狂傲 (ㄎㄨㄤˊ ㄠˋ)
unreasonably haughty; improperly domineering

狂藥 (ㄎㄨㄤˊ ㄧㄠˋ)
alcoholic beverages

狂言 (ㄎㄨㄤˊ ㄧㄢˊ)
wild words; boastful talks; brag

狂妄 (ㄎㄨㄤˊ ㄨㄤˋ)
①wild; irrational; crazy; mentally deranged; out of one's right mind ②extremely conceited: 他是個狂妄的畫家。 He is an extremely conceited painter.

狂妄無知 (ㄎㄨㄤˊ ㄨㄤˋ ㄨˊ ㄓ)
conceited and ignorant

【狄】 3344
ㄉㄧˊ dyi dí
1. name of a barbarian tribe to the north of ancient China
2. a Chinese family name

狄更斯 (ㄉㄧˊ ㄍㄥ ㄙ)
Charles Dickens, 1812-1870, English novelist

狄克推多 (ㄉㄧˊ ㄎㄜˋ ㄊㄨㄟ ㄉㄨㄛ)
①a dictator 亦作「獨裁者」 ②dictatorship 亦作「獨裁」

狄青 (ㄉㄧˊ ㄑㄧㄥ)
Ti Ching, 1008-1057, a general in the Sung Dynasty

狄斯耐樂園 (ㄉㄧˊ ㄙ ㄋㄞˋ ㄌㄜˋ ㄩㄢˊ)
Disneyland, U. S. A.

狄斯可 (ㄉㄧˊ ㄙ ㄎㄜˇ)
disco 亦作「迪斯可」

【犾】 3345
ㄩㄢˊ yeun yún
name of a barbarian tribe to the north of ancient China

【狃】 3346
ㄋㄧㄡˇ neou niǔ
1. to covet
2. to be accustomed to
3. to hold the post of
4. avaricious; greedy

狃於陋習 (ㄋㄧㄡˇ ㄩˊ ㄌㄡˋ ㄒㄧˊ)

to be accustomed to bad habits

狃於成見 (ㄋㄧㄡˇ ㄩˊ ㄔㄥˊ ㄐㄧㄢˋ)
to be a slave of preconceived ideas; opinionated

〔犬 部〕

五畫

【狎】 3347
ㄒㄧㄚˊ shya xiá
to show familiarity, intimacy, or disrespect

狎昵 (ㄒㄧㄚˊ ㄋㄧˋ)
very intimate; very familiar

狎弄 (ㄒㄧㄚˊ ㄋㄨㄥˋ)
to show improper familiarity with; to be rude to; to be impolite to

狎客 (ㄒㄧㄚˊ ㄎㄜˋ)
① a rude person; an impolite person; a disrespectful person ② prostitute's customers

狎妓 (ㄒㄧㄚˊ ㄐㄧˋ)
to visit a brothel

狎近 (ㄒㄧㄚˊ ㄐㄧㄣˋ)
to be very intimate; to be very familiar

狎邪 (ㄒㄧㄚˊ ㄒㄧㄝˊ)
① to indulge in vice; to visit a brothel ② improper

狎侮 (ㄒㄧㄚˊ ㄨˇ)
to show improper intimacy with; to be impolite to; to treat with disrespect

狎翫 (ㄒㄧㄚˊ ㄨㄢˋ)
to show disrespect from familiarity

【狗】 3348
ㄍㄡˇ goou gǒu
1. a dog
2. (figuratively) a lackey; a footman; a servile person; a follower
3. damned; cursed

狗屁 (ㄍㄡˇ ㄆㄧˋ)or 狗屁不通 (ㄍㄡˇ ㄆㄧˋ ㄅㄨˋ ㄊㄨㄥ)
Nonsense! 或 Rubbish! 或 Baloney!

狗命 (ㄍㄡˇ ㄇㄧㄥˋ)
a life worth as little as a dog's; a life of little worth

狗母 (ㄍㄡˇ ㄇㄨˇ)
lizard fish 亦作「蜥蜴魚」

狗吠 (ㄍㄡˇ ㄈㄟˋ)
the bark of a dog

狗膽 (ㄍㄡˇ ㄉㄢˇ)or 狗膽包天 (ㄍㄡˇ ㄉㄢˇ ㄅㄠ ㄊㄧㄢ)
monstrous audacity; boldness; bold; daring

狗顛屁股 (ㄍㄡˇ ㄉㄧㄢ ㄆㄧˋ ㄍㄨ)
obsequious; subservient

狗頭 (ㄍㄡˇ ㄊㄡˊ)
a dog's head (a term of abuse)

狗頭軍師 (ㄍㄡˇ ㄊㄡˊ ㄐㄩㄣ ㄕ)
a person who offers bad advice; a good-for-nothing adviser

狗腿子 (ㄍㄡˇ ㄊㄨㄟˇ ˙ㄗ)
a dog's leg—(figuratively) a person who slavishly does legwork for others; a hired thug; a henchman

狗拿耗子，多管閒事 (ㄍㄡˇ ㄋㄚˊ ㄏㄠˋ˙ㄗ, ㄉㄨㄛ ㄍㄨㄢˇ ㄒㄧㄢˊ ㄕˋ)
a dog trying to catch mice —to meddle; to poke one's nose into other's business

狗男女 (ㄍㄡˇ ㄋㄢˊ ㄋㄩˇ)
adulterers and adulteresses

狗急跳牆 (ㄍㄡˇ ㄐㄧˊ ㄊㄧㄠˋ ㄑㄧㄤˊ)
A cornered beast will do something desperate.—A person takes desperate measures in a critical situation.

狗監 (ㄍㄡˇ ㄐㄧㄢ)
an emperor's attendant in charge of hunting dogs (during the Han Dynasty)

狗氣 (ㄍㄡˇ ㄑㄧˋ)
(literally) a dog's temperament—the attitude of flattering superiors and bullying subordinates

狗血噴頭 (ㄍㄡˇ ㄒㄧㄝˇ ㄆㄣ ㄊㄡˊ)
(literally) to get a spray of dog's blood on the head—to be scolded in a very humiliating fashion

狗熊 (ㄍㄡˇ ㄒㄩㄥˊ)
① a bear ② (figuratively) a coward

狗彘不若 (ㄍㄡˇ ㄓˋ ㄅㄨˋ ㄖㄨㄛˋ)
even more despicable than a beast

狗彘不如 (ㄍㄡˇ ㄓˋ ㄅㄨˋ ㄖㄨˊ)
a very bad man (so bad that even beasts avoid eating his flesh after his death)

狗仗人勢 (ㄍㄡˇ ㄓㄤˋ ㄖㄣˊ ㄕˋ)
(literally) to behave like a dog relying upon the power of its master—to use the influence of one's master in

bullying others

狗吃屎 (ㄍㄡˇ ㄔ ㄕˇ)
a dog eating dung—(figuratively) face down: 他跌了個狗吃屎。He stumbled and fell to the ground face down.

狗食 (ㄍㄡˇ ㄕˊ)
dog food (a term of abuse)

狗屎 (ㄍㄡˇ ㄕˇ)
(literally) dog's droppings —utterly worthless

狗肉 (ㄍㄡˇ ㄖㄡˋ)
dog meat

狗嘴呂不出象牙來 (ㄍㄡˇ ㄗㄨㄟˇ ㄌㄧˇ ㄅㄨˋ ㄔㄨ ㄒㄧㄤˋ ㄧㄚˊ ㄌㄞˊ)
(literally) One cannot expect to find elephant tusks in the mouth of a dog.—A mean fellow never speaks nice things.

狗才 (ㄍㄡˇ ㄘㄞˊ)
(literally) a man with a dog's talent—a man of little competence

狗咬呂洞賓 (ㄍㄡˇ ㄧㄠˇ ㄌㄩˇ ㄉㄨㄥˋ ㄅㄧㄣ)
to snarl and snap at Lü Tung-pin (one of the Eight Immortals of Taoism)—to mistake a good man for a bad one

狗眼看人低 (ㄍㄡˇ ㄧㄢˇ ㄎㄢˋ ㄖㄣˊ ㄉㄧ)
to act like a snob

狗尾續貂 (ㄍㄡˇ ㄨㄟˇ ㄒㄩˋ ㄉㄧㄠ)
(literally) to put a dog's tail to a marten's body—to complete a masterpiece with poor writing (a self-depreciatory expression)

狗尾草 (ㄍㄡˇ ㄨㄟˇ ㄘㄠˇ)
foxtail

【狐】 3349
ㄏㄨˊ hwu hú
the fox

狐步舞 (ㄏㄨˊ ㄅㄨˋ ㄨˇ)
a fox trot

狐朋狗友 (ㄏㄨˊ ㄆㄥˊ ㄍㄡˇ ㄧㄡˇ)
a bunch of rogues

狐埋狐搰 (ㄏㄨˊ ㄇㄞˊ ㄏㄨˊ ㄏㄨˊ)
to be hesitant to achieve success

狐媚 (ㄏㄨˊ ㄇㄟˋ)
to charm by flattery; to be sycophantic; to bewitch by cajolery

狐狸 (ㄏㄨˊ ㄌㄧ)
a fox

狐狸狗(ㄏㄨˊ·ㄌㄧ ㄍㄡˇ)
a spitz, or Pomeranian

狐狸精(ㄏㄨˊ·ㄌㄧ ㄐㄧㄥ)
a woman of easy virtue (supposed to be a fox in disguise); an enchantress; a vixen

狐狸尾巴(ㄏㄨˊ·ㄌㄧ ㄨㄟˇ·ㄅㄚ)
a fox's tail—something that reveals one's true form or evil intentions; a cloven hoof: 狐狸尾巴總是要露出來的。The devil can't hide his cloven hoof.

狐猴(ㄏㄨˊ ㄏㄡˊ)
a lemur

狐假虎威(ㄏㄨˊ ㄐㄧㄚˇ ㄏㄨˇ ㄨㄟ)
(literally) to behave like the fox that borrowed the terror of the tiger—to be an ass in a lion's skin; to bully the weak because of one's association with the powerful

狐裘羔袖(ㄏㄨˊ ㄑㄧㄡˊ ㄍㄠ ㄒㄧㄡˋ)
(literally) a fox-fur robe with lamb-skin sleeves—good on the whole but not perfect

狐羣狗黨(ㄏㄨˊ ㄑㄩㄣˊ ㄍㄡˇ ㄉㄤˇ)
a bunch of rogues; a gang of scoundrels

狐仙(ㄏㄨˊ ㄒㄧㄢ)
a fairy fox

狐臭(ㄏㄨˊ ㄔㄡˋ) or 狐騷(ㄏㄨˊ ㄙㄠ)
an armpit odor

狐死兔泣(ㄏㄨˊ ㄙˇ ㄊㄨˋ ㄑㄧˋ)or 狐死兔悲(ㄏㄨˊ ㄙˇ ㄊㄨˋ ㄅㄟ)
When the fox dies, the hare grieves.—One grieves for one's kind.

狐疑(ㄏㄨˊ ㄧˊ)
suspicious; doubt; suspicion: 他似乎滿腹狐疑。He seemed to be very suspicious.

狐疑不決(ㄏㄨˊ ㄧˊ ㄅㄨˋ ㄐㄩㄝˊ)
hesitant; undecided

【狒】 3350
ㄈㄟˋ fey fèi
the baboon

狒狒(ㄈㄟˋ ㄈㄟˋ)
the baboon

【狙】 3351
ㄐㄩ jiu jū
1. a monkey; an ape
2. to lie in ambush

狙伏(ㄐㄩ ㄈㄨˊ)
to lie in ambush

狙擊(ㄐㄩ ㄐㄧˊ)
to launch a sneak attack; to attack by surprise; to snipe

狙擊手(ㄐㄩ ㄐㄧˊ ㄕㄡˇ)
a sniper

狙詐(ㄐㄩ ㄓㄚˋ)
a trick; a ruse; a wile: 不可狙詐待人。You should not treat others with tricks.

狙伺(ㄐㄩ ㄙˋ)
to spy; to reconnoiter in secret

六畫

【狠】 3352
ㄏㄣˇ heen hěn
1. vicious; cruel; atrocious
2. severe(ly); extreme(ly)

狠命(ㄏㄣˇ ㄇㄧㄥˋ)
to make a desperate effort; to use all the strength

狠毒(ㄏㄣˇ ㄉㄨˊ)
atrocious; cruel; brutal; malicious: 他對待犯人非常狠毒。He is very brutal to the prisoners.

狠戾(ㄏㄣˇ ㄌㄧˋ)
vicious; cruel; atrocious

狠狠地(ㄏㄣˇ ㄏㄣˇ·ㄉㄜ)
in cold blood; mercilessly; cruelly; brutally; severely

狠心(ㄏㄣˇ ㄒㄧㄣ)
heartless; pitiless; merciless; cruel

【狡】 3353
ㄐㄧㄠˇ jeau jiǎo
1. cunning; crafty; sly; wily; artful; shrewd
2. suspicion; to suspect

狡辯(ㄐㄧㄠˇ ㄅㄧㄢˋ)
to use sophisticated argument in self-defense; to defend oneself in a devious way; artful self-defense; to quibble

狡憤(ㄐㄧㄠˇ ㄈㄣˋ)
to fly into a rage; to rage

狡徒(ㄐㄧㄠˇ ㄊㄨˊ)
a swindler; a crook; a crafty person

狡兔死，走狗烹(ㄐㄧㄠˇ ㄊㄨˋ ㄙˇ，ㄗㄡˇ ㄍㄡˇ ㄆㄥ)
(literally) After the cunning hare is killed, the hound is boiled.—After work is done, those who did the work are discarded.

狡兔三窟(ㄐㄧㄠˇ ㄊㄨˋ ㄙㄢ ㄎㄨ)
(literally) A wily rabbit has three burrows. — elaborate precautions made for self-protection

狡脫(ㄐㄧㄠˇ ㄊㄨㄛ)
to evade smartly

狡童(ㄐㄧㄠˇ ㄊㄨㄥˊ)
① a crafty youth ② a youth handsome but worthless

狡賴(ㄐㄧㄠˇ ㄌㄞˋ)
to prevaricate; to give a false alibi

狡獪(ㄐㄧㄠˇ ㄎㄨㄞˋ)
crafty; cunning; deceitful; treacherous; artful

狡猾(ㄐㄧㄠˇ ㄏㄨㄚˊ)
cunning; crafty; sly; wily; artful

狡計(ㄐㄧㄠˇ ㄐㄧˋ)
a clever scheme; a cunning plot

狡黠(ㄐㄧㄠˇ ㄒㄧㄚˊ)
deceitful; treacherous; sly; crafty

狡詐(ㄐㄧㄠˇ ㄓㄚˋ)
deceitful; cunning; swindling; wily

狡飾(ㄐㄧㄠˇ ㄕˋ)
to cover up the truth; to deceive; to lie

狡偽(ㄐㄧㄠˇ ㄨㄟˇ)
deceitful; treacherous; crafty

【狩】 3354
ㄕㄡˋ show shòu
1. to hunt in winter
2. an imperial tour

狩獵(ㄕㄡˋ ㄌㄧㄝˋ)
hunting; to hunt or trap game

七畫

【猈】 3355
ㄅㄧˋ bih bì
1. a legendary beast looking like a tiger
2. a prison

猈性(ㄅㄧˋ ㄒㄧㄥˋ)
① a legendary beast looking like a tiger ② a prison or penitentiary

【狼】 3356
ㄌㄤˊ lang láng
1. the wolf
2. a heartless, cruel person;

[犬部]

〔犬部〕

cruel and heartless; cunning and crafty
3. name of a constellation
4. a Chinese family name

狼狽 (ㄌㄤˊ ㄅㄟˋ)
①helplessly dependent; desperate ②in a difficult position: 他們處境狼狽。 They are in a difficult position. ③ill at ease; embarrassed: 他感到很狼狽。 He felt quite embarrassed. ④ heartless and cruel persons

狼狽不堪 (ㄌㄤˊ ㄅㄟˋ ㄅㄨˋ ㄎㄢ)
in utter disorder or confusion; to be in great distress or embarrassment; very troubled

狼狽為奸 (ㄌㄤˊ ㄅㄟˋ ㄨㄟˊ ㄐㄧㄢ)
to work hand in glove with somebody; to gang up with evil ways); to gang up with somebody

狼多肉少 (ㄌㄤˊ ㄉㄨㄛ ㄖㄡˋ ㄕㄠˇ)
(literally) There is too little meat for so many wolves. —too many looters for the limited wealth, resources, etc.

狼貪 (ㄌㄤˊ ㄊㄢ)
greedy; avaricious

狼吞虎嚥 (ㄌㄤˊ ㄊㄨㄣ ㄏㄨˇ ㄧㄢˋ)
to devour (food) like a wolf and a tiger—to gobble up; to wolf down; to devour ravenously

狼狗 (ㄌㄤˊ ㄍㄡˇ)
a German shepherd; a wolf hound

狼毫 (ㄌㄤˊ ㄏㄠˊ)
a Chinese writing brush made of wolf's hair

狼嚎鬼叫 (ㄌㄤˊ ㄏㄠˊ ㄍㄨㄟˇ ㄐㄧㄠˋ)
pathetic cries; bloodcurdling shrieks

狼藉 or 狼籍 (ㄌㄤˊ ㄐㄧˊ)
①in total disorder or disarray; in pandemonium: 杯盤狼藉。 Empty glasses and plates are scattered all over. ②為非狼藉—notorious

狼犬 (ㄌㄤˊ ㄑㄩㄢˇ)
the German shepherd dog; a police dog

狼心狗肺 (ㄌㄤˊ ㄒㄧㄣ ㄍㄡˇ ㄈㄟˋ)
heartless and cruel; rotten to the core

狼人 (ㄌㄤˊ ㄖㄣˊ)
a wolf man

狼子野心 (ㄌㄤˊ ㄗˇ ㄧㄝˇ ㄒㄧㄣ)
a cruel and heartless character

狼崽子 (ㄌㄤˊ ㄗㄞˇ ˙ㄗ)
an ingrate; a greedy and coldblooded s.o.b.

狼煙 (ㄌㄤˊ ㄧㄢ)
(in ancient China) a smoke signal; smoke from burning wolf excrement as a signal to alert troops against invaders

【狽】 3357
ㄅㄟˋ bey bèi
a kind of wolf with shorter forelegs

【狷】 3358
ㄐㄩㄢˋ jiuann juàn
1. rash; quick-tempered
2. honest and straightforward

狷急 (ㄐㄩㄢˋ ㄐㄧˊ)
easily impatient and angry

狷急 (ㄐㄩㄢˋ ㄐㄧˊ)
a rigid and candid disposition which cannot be easily bent

狷介 (ㄐㄩㄢˋ ㄐㄧㄝˋ)
honest and straightforward; incorruptible; upright

狷狹 (ㄐㄩㄢˋ ㄒㄧㄚˊ) or 狷隘 (ㄐㄩㄢˋ ㄞˋ)
narrow-minded; parochial; narrow

【狸】 3359
(貍) ㄌㄧˊ lí
1. a fox
2. a racoon dog

狸貓 (ㄌㄧˊ ㄇㄠ)
a kind of wild cat

狸德 (ㄌㄧˊ ㄉㄜˊ)
as greedy as a fox

【狹】 3360
ㄒㄧㄚˊ shya xiá
narrow; narrow-minded

狹窄 (ㄒㄧㄚˊ ㄓㄞˇ)
(usually said of a house, room, etc.) narrow and dingy

狹路 (ㄒㄧㄚˊ ㄌㄨˋ) or 狹徑 (ㄒㄧㄚˊ ㄐㄧㄥˋ)
a narrow path or road

狹路相逢 (ㄒㄧㄚˊ ㄌㄨˋ ㄒㄧㄤ ㄈㄥˊ)
(literally) to meet on a narrow path—enemies or rivals

coming face to face

狹小 (ㄒㄧㄚˊ ㄒㄧㄠˇ)
(said of rooms, etc.) narrow and small: 他正想走出狹小的圈子。 He is trying to step out of his narrow circle.

狹心症 (ㄒㄧㄚˊ ㄒㄧㄣ ㄓㄥˋ)
angina pectoris

狹窄 (ㄒㄧㄚˊ ㄓㄞˇ)
narrow; cramped: 他的見識狹窄。 He is limited in knowledge and narrow in experience.

狹長 (ㄒㄧㄚˊ ㄔㄤˊ)
long and narrow

狹隘 (ㄒㄧㄚˊ ㄞˋ)
narrow-minded; narrow; parochial: 我不喜歡你狹隘的看法。 I don't like your narrow view.

狹義 (ㄒㄧㄚˊ ㄧˋ)
the narrow sense

狹韻 (ㄒㄧㄚˊ ㄩㄣˋ)
a rhyme that encompasses only a few characters

【狺】 3361
ㄧㄣˊ yn yín
the snarling of dogs

狺狺 (ㄧㄣˊ ㄧㄣˊ)
to yelp

八畫

【猖】 3362
ㄔㄤ chang chāng
wild; mad; impudent; unruly; reckless

猖披 (ㄔㄤ ㄆㄧ)
to act wildly as one pleases; to act without restraints of any sort; unbridled and ungovernable

猖厲 (ㄔㄤ ㄌㄧˋ)
wild and severe; mad and violent

猖亂 (ㄔㄤ ㄌㄨㄢˋ)
wild and disorderly

猖狂 (ㄔㄤ ㄎㄨㄤˊ)
wild; ungovernable; unrestrained; unbridled; unruly: 我們擊退猖狂的敵人。 We defeated unrestrained enemy.

猖獗 (ㄔㄤ ㄐㄩㄝˊ)
rampant; on the rampage; raging

〔犬部〕

【猗】 3363
ㄧ　ī yī
1. an exclamation indicating admiration
2. an adverbial particle

猗靡(ㄧ ㄇㄧˊ)
flowing and fluttering with the wind

猗猗(ㄧ ㄧ)
splendid and flourishing

【猗】 3363
ㄜ　ē ee
gentle, soft and pliant

猗儺(ㄜ ㄋㄨㄛˊ)
gentle; soft and pliant

【猊】 3364
ㄋㄧˊ ní ni
1. the lion
2. a wild beast or wild horse

【猙】 3365
ㄓㄥ jeng zheng
fierce-looking; hideous; repulsive

猙獰(ㄓㄥ ㄋㄧㄥˊ)
fierce-looking; hideous; repulsive: 那人看起來相貌猙獰。 That man looks hideous.

【猛】 3366
ㄇㄥˇ meong meng
1. bold; brave; fierce; violent
2. sudden and quick (strikes, thrusts, etc.)
3. severe; strict; stringent
4. a Chinese family name

猛不防(ㄇㄥˇ ㄅㄨˋ ㄈㄤˊ)
unexpectedly; unawares

猛扑(ㄇㄥˇ ㄆㄨ)
to lunge at something with force; to attack fiercely

猛力(ㄇㄥˇ ㄌㄧˋ)
vigorously; with great force

猛戾(ㄇㄥˇ ㄌㄧˋ)
fierce and violent; ferocious and unruly

猛烈(ㄇㄥˇ ㄌㄧㄝˋ)
fierce; violent and savage

猛攻(ㄇㄥˇ ㄍㄨㄥ)
a powerful or fierce attack; to attack in full force or savagely; a furious assault

猛可(ㄇㄥˇ ㄎㄜˇ)
suddenly; all of a sudden: 他猛可想起他的母親。 All of a sudden he thought of his mother.

猛虎(ㄇㄥˇ ㄏㄨˇ)
a ferocious tiger

猛火(ㄇㄥˇ ㄏㄨㄛˇ)
a raging fire

猛擊(ㄇㄥˇ ㄐㄧˊ)
a furious blow; a sudden and violent attack or thrust; to attack with full force

猛劑(ㄇㄥˇ ㄐㄧˋ)
very potent drugs

猛進(ㄇㄥˇ ㄐㄧㄣˋ)
to advance in quick and big strides; remarkable improvement or progress: 我們正在突飛猛進。 We are advancing by leaps and bounds.

猛將(ㄇㄥˇ ㄐㄧㄤˋ)
a brave or courageous general: 我們的猛將如雲。 We have a great many brave generals.

猛決(ㄇㄥˇ ㄐㄩㄝˊ)
brave and determined

猛禽(ㄇㄥˇ ㄑㄧㄣˊ)
fierce birds (as eagles, hawks, etc.); birds of prey: 鷹是一種猛禽。 The eagle is a bird of prey.

猛犬(ㄇㄥˇ ㄑㄩㄢˇ)
fierce dogs; vicious dogs; bulldogs

猛襲(ㄇㄥˇ ㄒㄧˊ)
to attack ferociously

猛醒(ㄇㄥˇ ㄒㄧㄥˇ)
a sudden realization; to awake or realize all of a sudden

猛追(ㄇㄥˇ ㄓㄨㄟ)
to be in hot pursuit of: 狗猛追兔子。 The dog is in hot pursuit of the rabbits.

猛撞(ㄇㄥˇ ㄓㄨㄤˋ)
to ram or bump suddenly and with force: 那輛卡車猛撞他的汽車。 That truck bumped his car with force.

猛士(ㄇㄥˇ ㄕˋ)
brave men; warriors

猛獸(ㄇㄥˇ ㄕㄡˋ)
fierce wild beasts

猛然(ㄇㄥˇ ㄖㄢˊ)
suddenly; abruptly: 他的聲音和態度猛然改變。 His voice and manner changed suddenly.

猛以濟寬(ㄇㄥˇ ㄧˇ ㄐㄧˋ ㄎㄨㄢ)
Strictness is to correct the weakness of laxity.

【猜】 3367
ㄘㄞ tsai cāi
1. to guess; to suspect; to doubt: 她猜對了。 She guessed right.
2. cruel and suspicious

猜不透(ㄘㄞ ㄅㄨˋ ㄊㄡˋ)
unable to guess; unable to make out (what's on his mind, etc.)

猜不著(ㄘㄞ ㄅㄨˋ ㄓㄠˊ)or 猜不出(ㄘㄞ ㄅㄨˋ ㄔㄨ)
cannot guess; unable to make out or find the right answer

猜破(ㄘㄞ ㄆㄛˋ)
to make out or unearth mentally what's on another's mind

猜謎(ㄘㄞ ㄇㄧˊ)or 猜謎兒(ㄘㄞ ㄇㄧˊㄦ)
① to solve riddles ② to guess

猜防(ㄘㄞ ㄈㄤˊ)
to suspect and be on guard

猜燈(ㄘㄞ ㄉㄥ)
to solve riddles (on Lantern Festival)

猜度(ㄘㄞ ㄉㄨㄛˋ)
to guess and assess; to surmise; to conjecture

猜忌(ㄘㄞ ㄐㄧˋ)
to be jealous and suspicious

猜懼(ㄘㄞ ㄐㄩˋ)
to suspect and fear; suspicious and apprehensive

猜拳(ㄘㄞ ㄑㄩㄢˊ)
to play the finger-guessing game (usually in drinking)

猜嫌(ㄘㄞ ㄒㄧㄢˊ)
jealous and suspicious

猜想(ㄘㄞ ㄒㄧㄤˇ)
to guess; to conjecture; to surmise

猜著(ㄘㄞ ㄓㄠˊ)or 猜中(ㄘㄞ ㄓㄨㄥˋ)
to guess correctly; to make out; to solve (a riddle)

猜測(ㄘㄞ ㄘㄜˋ)
to guess; to assess; to surmise; to speculate; to conjecture: 這個謠言引起很多的猜測。 The rumor raised much conjecture.

猜疑(ㄘㄞ ㄧˊ)
to suspect; suspicion; to doubt

猜嫌(ㄘㄞ ㄧˊ)
suspicion; to suspect; to

〔犬 部〕

doubt: 甚至他母親也有猜疑。 Even his mother suspected him.

【猓】 3368
《ㄨㄛ guoo guǒ
name of a tribe spread over Yunnan, Kweichow and Szechwan provinces

猓玀 (《ㄨㄛ ㄌㄨㄛ)
參看「猓」

【猝】 3369
ㄘㄨ tsuh cù
sudden; abrupt; hurried; unexpected

猝不及防(ㄘㄨ ㄅㄨ ㄐㄧˊ ㄈㄤ)
to be caught unprepared; to be caught off one's guard

猝然(ㄘㄨ ㄖㄢˊ)
sudden; suddenly; abruptly; unexpectedly: 天氣猝然起變化。 There was a sudden change in the weather.

【猋】 3370
ㄅㄧㄠ biau biāo
1. same as 飆—a storm, gale or hurricane
2. (said of dogs) running fast
3. swift; quick; rapid

九畫

【猢】 3371
ㄏㄨ hwu hú
a monkey

猢猻(ㄏㄨˊㄙㄨㄣ)
monkeys (also used figuratively); 樹倒猢猻散。When the tree falls, the monkeys scatter. — When a person falls from power, his followers leave him.

猢猻入布袋(ㄏㄨˊㄙㄨㄣ ㄖㄨˋ ㄅㄨˋ ㄉㄞˋ)
to submit to discipline reluctantly (like monkeys being confined in a bag)

猢猻王(ㄏㄨˊㄙㄨㄣ ㄨㄤˊ)
(literally) the king of monkeys—(formerly) a teacher of a private village school

【猥】 3372
ㄨㄟˇ woei wěi
1. vulgar; wanton; low; lewd and licentious
2. many; numerous; varied; multitudinous
3. the bark of a dog

猥官(ㄨㄟˇ ㄍㄨㄢ)
low-ranking officials at various levels

猥妓(ㄨㄟˇ ㄐㄧˋ)
prostitutes

猥賤(ㄨㄟˇ ㄐㄧㄢˋ)
low and vulgar; lowly; humble: 他出身猥賤。 He is a man of humble birth.

猥褻(ㄨㄟˇ ㄒㄧㄝˋ)
obscene; obscenity; lewd; to act indecently toward (a woman): 他的想法猥褻。What an obscene mind he has!

猥褻行爲(ㄨㄟˇ ㄒㄧㄝˋ ㄒㄧㄥˊ ㄨㄟˊ)
obscene or indecent acts (or behavior)

猥雜(ㄨㄟˇ ㄗㄚˊ)
numerous and varied

猥瑣(ㄨㄟˇ ㄙㄨㄛˇ)
low and petty

【猶】 3373
ㄧㄡˊ you yóu
1. like; similar to; tantamount to; as if
2. still; yet; even; especially; while: 此事記憶猶新。It is still fresh in my memory.
3. a kind of monkey
4. a Chinese family name
5. strategy; scheme; plot

猶大(ㄧㄡˊ ㄉㄚˋ)
Judas

猶他(ㄧㄡˊ ㄊㄚ)
the state of Utah, U. S. A.

猶太(ㄧㄡˊ ㄊㄞˋ)
①Jews or Hebrews; Jewish ②Judaea, name of an ancient state in today's Southern Palestine ③(comically) stingy or tight-fisted; miserly; parsimonious

猶太的(ㄧㄡˊ ㄊㄞˋ ˙ㄉㄜ)
Jewish

猶太教(ㄧㄡˊ ㄊㄞˋ ㄐㄧㄠˋ)
Judaism

猶太人(ㄧㄡˊ ㄊㄞˋ ㄖㄣˊ)
the Jewish people; Jews

猶女(ㄧㄡˊ ㄋㄩˇ)
a niece

猶可(ㄧㄡˊ ㄎㄜˇ)
still all right; probably (negotiable, etc.)

猶之乎(ㄧㄡˊ ㄓ ㄏㄨ)
like; similar to

猶如(ㄧㄡˊ ㄖㄨˊ)
①just like; just as if ②still ③(now rarely) easy-going; lax ④(now rarely) laughing-

ly; smiling

猶如(ㄧㄡˊ ㄖㄨˊ)
just like: 教室燈火輝煌，猶如白晝。 The classroom was lit up as bright as day.

猶若(ㄧㄡˊ ㄖㄨㄛˋ)
just like; almost like; tantamount to

猶子(ㄧㄡˊ ㄗˇ)
①a nephew ②just like a son

猶自(ㄧㄡˊ ㄗˋ)
still (as an adverb)

猶孫(ㄧㄡˊ ㄙㄨㄣ)
sons of a nephew

猶疑(ㄧㄡˊ ㄧˊ)
undecided; to hesitate: 猶疑不決的人不會成功。 He who hesitates is lost.

猶有可爲(ㄧㄡˊ ㄧㄡˇ ㄎㄜˇ ㄨㄟˊ)
(said of a bad situation) still retrievable, reversible, salvable, etc.

猶有餘悸(ㄧㄡˊ ㄧㄡˇ ㄩˊ ㄐㄧˋ)
Even now I am scared.

猶未定(ㄧㄡˊ ㄨㄟˋ ㄉㄧㄥˋ)
not decided yet

猶未知(ㄧㄡˊ ㄨㄟˋ ㄓ)
do not know yet; maybe

猶豫(ㄧㄡˊ ㄩˋ)or 猶豫豫像(ㄧㄡˊ ㄧㄡˋ ㄩˋ)
hesitant; undecided

【猩】 3374
ㄒㄧㄥ shing xīng
1. scarlet; red
2. a yellow-haired ape

猩紅(ㄒㄧㄥ ㄏㄨㄥˊ)
scarlet

猩紅熱(ㄒㄧㄥ ㄏㄨㄥˊ ㄖㄜˋ)
scarlet fever

猩猩(ㄒㄧㄥ ㄒㄧㄥ)
a yellow-haired ape; a chimpanzee; an orangutan

猩猩能言，不離禽獸(ㄒㄧㄥ ㄒㄧㄥ ㄋㄥˊ ㄧㄢˊ, ㄅㄨˋ ㄌㄧˊ ㄑㄧㄣˊ ㄕㄡˋ)
Though a chimpanzee is able to talk, it is still an animal.

猩脣(ㄒㄧㄥ ㄔㄨㄣˊ)
①red lips ②the ape's lips (one of the eight rare delicacies in Chinese cookery)

【猱】 3375
ㄋㄠˊ nau náo
1. a yellow-haired monkey
2. to scratch

猱升(ㄋㄠˊ ㄕㄥ)

the monkey climbs a tree

猱雜 (ㄋㄠˊ ㄗㄚˊ)
noisily and cynically; comical and restless

猱兒 (ㄋㄠˊ ㄦˊ)
prostitutes

【猴】 3376 ㄏㄡˊ hour hóu
1. the monkey
2. naughty or impish (child)

猴類 (ㄏㄡˊ ㄌㄟˋ)
quadrumana

猴急 (ㄏㄡˊ ㄐㄧˊ)
very impatient: 你為何如此猴急? Why are you so impatient?

猴戲 (ㄏㄡˊ ㄒㄧˋ)
a monkey show (in a circus, a zoo, etc.)

猴子 (ㄏㄡˊ ˙ㄗ) or 猴兒 (ㄏㄡˊ ㄦˊ)
①a monkey ②a clever person with a glib and sharp tongue

猴棗 (ㄏㄡˊ ㄗㄠˇ)
①a kind of bezoar taken from monkeys ② a kind of persimmon

猴猻王 (ㄏㄡˊ ㄙㄨㄣ ㄨㄤˊ)
(literally) the king of the monkeys—a satirical term referring to village tutors in ancient China

【猷】 3377 ㄧㄡˊ you yóu
1. a plan; a program; a scheme
2. a way or path
3. to draw or paint
4. like; similar to
5. (now rarely) an opening particle

十畫

【猺】 3378 (傜) ㄧㄠˊ yau yáo
1. a jackal
2. name of a tribe in Kwangtung, Hunan, Kwangsi and Yunnan

猺峒 (ㄧㄠˊ ㄉㄨㄥˋ)
caves in which the Yao tribesmen live

猺山 (ㄧㄠˊ ㄕㄢ)
name of a mountain range in Kwangsi

猺族 (ㄧㄠˊ ㄗㄨˊ)
the Yao tribe in Kwangtung, Hunan and Yun-

nan

【猿】 3379 (猨) ㄩㄢˊ yuan yuán
an ape; a gibbon

猿臂 (ㄩㄢˊ ㄅㄧˋ)
①the ape's arms ②long arms

猿啼 (ㄩㄢˊ ㄊㄧˊ)
the gibbon's howling

猿類 (ㄩㄢˊ ㄌㄟˋ)
anthropoid

猿號 (ㄩㄢˊ ㄏㄠˊ)
an ape's call; a gibbon's howls

猿猴 (ㄩㄢˊ ㄏㄡˊ)
apes and monkeys

猿人 (ㄩㄢˊ ㄖㄣˊ)
the ape; anthropoid apes; a gorilla

【獅】 3380 ㄕ shy shī
the lion: 獅子是萬獸之王。The lion is the king of beasts.

獅猴 (ㄕ ㄏㄡˊ)
a kind of lion-like animal with a roundish head and long, soft and thick hair

獅身人面像 (ㄕ ㄕㄣ ㄖㄣˊ ㄇㄧㄢˋ ㄒㄧㄤˋ)
the Sphinx

獅子 (ㄕ ˙ㄗ)
the lion

獅子搏兔 (ㄕ ˙ㄗ ㄅㄛˊ ㄊㄨˋ)
(literally) a lion fights a hare.—to use a lot of strength to perform a small feat

獅子鼻 (ㄕ ˙ㄗ ㄅㄧˊ)
a snub nose

獅子猫 (ㄕ ˙ㄗ ㄇㄠ)
the Siamese cat

獅子頭 (ㄕ ˙ㄗ ㄊㄡˊ)
stewed meat balls

獅子狗 (ㄕ ˙ㄗ ㄍㄡˇ)
a poodle

獅子國 (ㄕ ˙ㄗ ㄍㄨㄛˊ)
Ceylon or Sri Lanka

獅子吼 (ㄕ ˙ㄗ ㄏㄡˇ)
①the howls of a shrew ② (Buddhism) the preaching of Buddha that shakes the world—like a lion's roars

獅子會 (ㄕ ˙ㄗ ㄏㄨㄟˋ)
International Association of Lions Clubs 亦作「國際獅子會」

獅子山 (ㄕ ˙ㄗ ㄕㄢ)

①Sierra Leone ②name of a strategic hill overlooking the Yangtze River, northwest of Nanking

獅子座 (ㄕ ˙ㄗ ㄗㄨㄛˋ)
①(astronomy) Leo ②(Buddhism) the Lion's Seat—where Buddha sat

獅子鷹 (ㄕ ˙ㄗ ㄧㄥ)
the screech-owl

【猾】 3381 ㄏㄨㄚˊ hwa huá
cunning; shrewd; crafty: 他狡猾如狐狸。He is as cunning as a fox.

猾手 (ㄏㄨㄚˊ ㄕㄡˇ)
a master in cunningness

猾吏 (ㄏㄨㄚˊ ㄌㄧˋ)
a cunning and wicked official

猾亂 (ㄏㄨㄚˊ ㄌㄨㄢˋ)
to cause turmoil or upheaval

猾賊 (ㄏㄨㄚˊ ㄗㄟˊ)
a glib rascal

【猻】 3382 ㄙㄨㄣ suen sūn
a monkey

【獃】 3383 (呆) ㄉㄞ dai dāi
(又讀) ㄞˊ air ái
1. stupid; silly; foolish; idiotic; a fool: 你 真 是 獃! What a fool you were!
2. maladroit; awkward; clumsy; bungling
3. to stay: 我每天都獃在家裏。I stay at home every day.

獃板 (ㄉㄞ ㄅㄢˇ)
dull and mechanical; without flexibility

獃獃地 (ㄉㄞ ㄉㄞ ˙ㄉㄜ)
stupidly; idiotically

獃頭獃腦 (ㄉㄞ ㄊㄡˊ ㄉㄞ ㄋㄠˇ)
a silly or clumsy appearance; a rustic and stupid look; looking like an idiot

獃磕磕 (ㄉㄞ ㄎㄜ ˙ㄎㄜ)
vacant and stupid; dumbfounded

獃話 (ㄉㄞ ㄏㄨㄚˋ)
stupid nonsense: 不要聽他的獃話。Don't listen to his stupid nonsense.

獃氣 (ㄉㄞ ㄑㄧˋ)
a silly look; idiotic

獃相 (ㄉㄞ ㄒㄧㄤˋ)
a silly look

〔犬部〕

〔犬部〕

獃住了 (ㄉㄞ ㄓㄨˋ·ㄌㄜ)
dumbfounded: 聽他這麼說，她獃住了。She was dumbfounded to hear him say so.

獃若木雞 (ㄉㄞˊ ㄖㄨㄛˋ ㄇㄨˋ ㄐㄧ)
as dull as a wooden chicken —very dull or stupid

獃子 (ㄉㄞˊ·ㄗ)
an idiot; a stupid person

【獄】 3384　ㄩˋ yuh yù
1. jail; prison
2. a lawsuit: 折獄 to decide a lawsuit

獄吏 (ㄩˋ ㄌㄧˋ)
a jailer; a warden

獄官 (ㄩˋ ㄍㄨㄢ)
a warden: 他當了二十年的獄官。He has been a warden for twenty years.

獄警 (ㄩˋ ㄐㄧㄥˇ)
the prison police; prison guards

獄囚 (ㄩˋ ㄑㄧㄡˊ)
prisoners

獄卒 (ㄩˋ ㄗㄨˊ) or 獄吏 (ㄩˋ ㄌㄧˋ)
low-ranking employees who help run a prison; jailers; gaolers

獄訟 (ㄩˋ ㄙㄨㄥˋ)
a lawsuit

十一畫

【獒】 3385　ㄠˊ aur áo
a large fierce dog; a mastiff

【獏】 3386　ㄇㄨˊ mu mú
Mu, name of a tribe in Hopu, Kwangtung Province 亦作「獏瑤」

【獐】 3387　ㄓㄤ jang zhāng
the roe deer; the hornless river deer

獐頭鼠目 (ㄓㄤ ㄊㄡˊ ㄕㄨˇ ㄇㄨˋ)
facial features suggesting cunning and meanness

十二畫

【獠】 3388　ㄌㄧㄠˊ liau liáo
1. also known as 夷, a primitive tribe in Southwest China
2. (said of one's looks) fierce

3. nocturnal hunting
4. a monster; a wicked person

獠面 (ㄌㄧㄠˊ ㄇㄧㄢˋ)
a fierce appearance; terrifying looks

獠牙 (ㄌㄧㄠˊ ㄧㄚˊ)
long protruding teeth; buckteeth; fangs: 青面獠牙 with a green face and ferocious fangs

【獞】 3389 (僮) ㄊㄨㄥˊ torng tóng
Tung, name of a primitive tribe in Kwangtung and Kwangsi

獞人 (ㄊㄨㄥˊ ㄖㄣˊ)
the tribesmen of Tung

獞族 (ㄊㄨㄥˊ ㄗㄨˊ)
the Tung tribe

【獗】 3390　ㄐㄩㄝˊ jue jué
unruly; lawless and wild; rampant

十三畫

【獨】 3391　ㄉㄨˊ dwu dú
1. alone; solitary; single
2. only
3. to monopolize
4. to be old and without a son
5. how; Is it possible?

獨霸一方 (ㄉㄨˊ ㄅㄚˋ ㄧ ㄈㄤ)
to wield absolute power in a part of a country, province, etc.

獨白 (ㄉㄨˊ ㄅㄞˊ)
(dramatics) monologue; soliloquy

獨臂盜 (ㄉㄨˊ ㄅㄧˋ ㄉㄠˋ)
a one-armed robber

獨步 (ㄉㄨˊ ㄅㄨˋ)
unrivaled; peerless; without match; unique

獨步古今 (ㄉㄨˊ ㄅㄨˋ ㄍㄨˇ ㄐㄧㄣ)
to be equaled neither in ancient times nor in modern times

獨排眾議 (ㄉㄨˊ ㄆㄞˊ ㄓㄨㄥˋ ㄧˋ)
to hold one's own opinion against that of the majority (often said of a person of unique ability)

獨門兒 (ㄉㄨˊ ㄇㄣˊ·ㄦ)
the special skill transmitted from generation to generation exclusively inside a

family

獨門獨院 (ㄉㄨˊ ㄇㄣˊ ㄉㄨˊ ㄩㄢˋ)
a single house which has its own entrance and courtyard (as distinct from apartment houses)

獨木不成林 (ㄉㄨˊ ㄇㄨˋ ㄅㄨˋ ㄔㄥˊ ㄌㄧㄣˊ)
(literally) A single tree can not make a forest.—One person cannot handle all the tasks by himself.

獨木難支 (ㄉㄨˊ ㄇㄨˋ ㄋㄢˊ ㄓ)
One cannot sustain or stem the adversity all by himself.

獨幕劇 (ㄉㄨˊ ㄇㄨˋ ㄐㄩˋ)
a one-act play

獨木橋 (ㄉㄨˊ ㄇㄨˋ ㄑㄧㄠˊ)
a single-plank bridge

獨木舟 (ㄉㄨˊ ㄇㄨˋ ㄓㄡ)
a canoe

獨峯駝 (ㄉㄨˊ ㄈㄥ ㄊㄨㄛˊ)
the single-humped camel —the dromedary

獨夫 (ㄉㄨˊ ㄈㄨ)
a merciless autocrat; a cruel ruler

獨到 (ㄉㄨˊ ㄉㄠˋ)
original: 他有很多獨到的見解。He is rich in original views.

獨到之處 (ㄉㄨˊ ㄉㄠˋ ㄓ ㄔㄨˋ)
originality (of ideas); special merits

獨當一面 (ㄉㄨˊ ㄉㄤ ㄧ ㄇㄧㄢˋ)
to handle a major task or assignment unaided; to head a large organization: 她已經可以獨當一面了。She can now handle a major task by herself.

獨斷獨行 (ㄉㄨˊ ㄉㄨㄢˋ ㄉㄨˊ ㄒㄧㄥˊ)
to decide and act on one's own; to act arbitrarily

獨特 (ㄉㄨˊ ㄊㄜˋ)
unique

獨吞 (ㄉㄨˊ ㄊㄨㄣ)
to pocket (profit) without sharing (it) with anyone else

獨攬大權 (ㄉㄨˊ ㄌㄢˇ ㄉㄚˋ ㄑㄩㄢˊ)
to grasp at authority by oneself; to arrogate all power to oneself

獨立 (ㄉㄨˊ ㄌㄧˋ)
independence; independent

獨立旅 (ㄉㄨˊ ㄌㄧˋ ㄌㄩˇ)
(military) a brigade which forms an independent fight-

獨立國(ㄉㄨˊㄌㄧˋㄍㄨㄛˊ)or 獨立國家(ㄉㄨˊㄌㄧˋㄍㄨㄛˊㄐㄧㄚ)
an independent nation or country

獨立紀念日(ㄉㄨˊㄌㄧˋㄐㄧˋㄋㄧㄢˋㄖˋ)
Independence Day (U.S.), the Fourth of July, the anniversary of the adoption of the Declaration of Independence

獨立精神(ㄉㄨˊㄌㄧˋㄐㄧㄥㄕㄣˊ)
the spirit of independence; independent-minded

獨立宣言(ㄉㄨˊㄌㄧˋㄒㄩㄢㄧㄢˊ)
the Declaration of Independence of the U.S.A.

獨立師(ㄉㄨˊㄌㄧˋㄕ)
(military) a division as an independent fighting force which is not subordinate to the command of a corps

獨立自主(ㄉㄨˊㄌㄧˋㄗˋㄓㄨˇ)
① the independence of sovereignty ② to act independently and with the initiative in one's own hands

獨力(ㄉㄨˊㄌㄧˋ)
single-handed; all by yourself; on one's own: 你能獨力做此工作嗎? Can you do the work on your own?

獨力支持(ㄉㄨˊㄌㄧˋㄓㄔˊ)
to support single-handedly

獨輪車(ㄉㄨˊㄌㄨㄣˊㄔㄜ)
a monocycle

獨家經營(ㄉㄨˊㄐㄧㄚㄐㄧㄥㄧㄥˊ)
to engage in a line of business without competition

獨家新聞(ㄉㄨˊㄐㄧㄚㄒㄧㄣㄨㄣˊ)
an exclusive news report; a scoop

獨腳戲(ㄉㄨˊㄐㄧㄠˇㄒㄧˋ)
a one-man show

獨角獸(ㄉㄨˊㄐㄧㄠˇㄕㄡˋ)
a unicorn (a legendary animal)

獨居(ㄉㄨˊㄐㄩ)
to live alone

獨居石(ㄉㄨˊㄐㄩㄕˊ)
(mineral) monazite

獨具匠心(ㄉㄨˊㄐㄩˋㄐㄧㄤˋㄒㄧㄣ)
to have originality

獨具隻眼(ㄉㄨˊㄐㄩˋㄓㄧㄢˇ)or 獨具慧眼(ㄉㄨˊㄐㄩˋㄏㄨㄟˋㄧㄢˇ)

to have a remarkable view; to have clairvoyance; to see things in a different light

獨清獨醒(ㄉㄨˊㄑㄧㄥㄉㄨˊㄒㄧㄥˇ)
to remain sane and sober and realize the lurking dangers in time of outward peace and prosperity when others live in a false sense of security

獨秀(ㄉㄨˊㄒㄧㄡˋ)
to be outstanding at a given time

獨弦哀歌(ㄉㄨˊㄒㄧㄢˊㄞㄍㄜ)
to pretend to be unique and outstanding in one's statements or actions

獨行(ㄉㄨˊㄒㄧㄥˊ)
① to walk alone ② to insist on one's ways in doing things

獨行盜(ㄉㄨˊㄒㄧㄥˊㄉㄠˋ)
a lone robber; a robber who acts alone

獨占 or 獨佔(ㄉㄨˊㄓㄢˋ)
to monopolize; monopoly

獨占花魁(ㄉㄨˊㄓㄢˋㄏㄨㄚㄎㄨㄟˊ)
to be the lucky man in winning the pretty courtesan's hand

獨占鰲頭(ㄉㄨˊㄓㄢˋㄠˊㄊㄡˊ)
① to emerge first in the civil service examination in former times ② to come out first; to be the champion

獨筆(ㄉㄨˊㄅㄧˇ)
to head or to be in charge of (a department, etc.)

獨酌(ㄉㄨˊㄓㄨㄛˊ)
to drink without company

獨持異議(ㄉㄨˊㄔˊㄧˋㄧˋ)
to hold an opinion different from that of the majority on a controversial issue

獨唱(ㄉㄨˊㄔㄤˋ)
singing solo; a vocal recital

獨出心裁(ㄉㄨˊㄔㄨㄒㄧㄣㄘㄞˊ)
to be unique or original in one's planning and design

獨處(ㄉㄨˊㄔㄨˇ)
to stay alone

獨創(ㄉㄨˊㄔㄨㄤˋ)
(literally) to create all by oneself—unique; original

獨善其身(ㄉㄨˊㄕㄢˋㄑㄧˊㄕㄣ)
to keep oneself clean and pure; to conduct oneself virtuously

獨身(ㄉㄨˊㄕㄣ)
unmarried; single

獨身主義(ㄉㄨˊㄕㄣㄓㄨˇㄧˋ)
the belief in the merits of remaining unmarried (as distinct from religious celibacy)

獨生女(ㄉㄨˊㄕㄥㄋㄩˇ)
the only daughter

獨生子(ㄉㄨˊㄕㄥㄗˇ)or 獨子(ㄉㄨˊㄗˇ)
the only son

獨樹一幟(ㄉㄨˊㄕㄨˋㄧˋㄓˋ)
(literally) to set up a separate flag—to take a distinctive course or attitude of one's own

獨資經營(ㄉㄨˊㄗㄐㄧㄥㄧㄥˊ)
to operate a business setup entirely with one's own capital: 他獨資經營這家商店。He is the sole owner of the store.

獨自(ㄉㄨˊㄗˋ)or 獨自個(ㄉㄨˊㄗˋㄍㄜ)
alone; single-handedly; personally

獨奏(ㄉㄨˊㄗㄡˋ)
(music) a solo performance: 他將獨奏喇叭。He's going to solo on the trumpet.

獨坐(ㄉㄨˊㄗㄨㄛˋ)
to sit all by oneself

獨裁(ㄉㄨˊㄘㄞˊ)
dictatorship; dictatorial

獨裁政治(ㄉㄨˊㄘㄞˊㄓㄥˋㄓˋ)
dictatorship; autocracy

獨一無二(ㄉㄨˊㄧㄨˊㄦˋ)
the one and the only one; unique; to stand alone

獨眼龍(ㄉㄨˊㄧㄢˇㄌㄨㄥˊ)
(comically) a one-eyed person or a person with a defective eye

獨往獨來(ㄉㄨˊㄨㄤˇㄉㄨˊㄌㄞˊ)
(literally) to come and go alone—to act independently without seeking company

【獷】 3392
ㄍㄨㄤˇ kuay kuǎi
cunning; artful; crafty; 狐狸非常狡獷。A fox has a great deal of cunning.

獷猾(ㄍㄨㄤˇㄏㄨㄚˊ)
cunning: 他是個狡獷的政客。He is a crafty politician.

【獬】 3393
ㄒㄧㄝˋ shieh xiè

1. a Pekingese dog
2. a mythical animal which was supposed to know the difference between right and wrong

〔犬 部〕

十四畫

【獲】 3394
ㄏㄨㄛˊ huoh huó

1. to get; to obtain; to incur; to capture; to catch; to reap: 我們去年喜獲豐收。We happily reaped a bumper harvest last year.
2. can; able: 不獲善終 to be not able to die a natural death
3. a slave-girl

獲得(ㄏㄨㄛˊ ㄉㄜˊ)
to get or obtain; to acquire: 他將獲得所要的東西。He will obtain what he wants.

獲麟(ㄏㄨㄛˊ ㄌㄧㄣˊ)
① the capture of a unicorn (When Confucius had written about the capture of a *lin* (a female unicorn), he concluded his *Spring and Autumn Annals*—the only book he authored). ② (figuratively) All affairs come to an end.

獲咎(ㄏㄨㄛˊ ㄐㄧㄡˋ)
to incur blame

獲救(ㄏㄨㄛˊ ㄐㄧㄡˋ)
to be rescued or saved from (death, disaster, etc.)

獲獎(ㄏㄨㄛˊ ㄐㄧㄤˇ)
to win a prize

獲赦(ㄏㄨㄛˊ ㄕㄜˋ)
to be pardoned

獲勝(ㄏㄨㄛˊ ㄕㄥˋ)
to triumph; to obtain victory; to win: 甲隊以三比一獲勝。Team A won the match three to one.

獲罪(ㄏㄨㄛˊ ㄗㄨㄟˋ)
to be blamed; to offend; to commit a crime or sin

獲益(ㄏㄨㄛˊ ㄧˋ)
to get profit: 他學習英文頗有獲益。He has studied English to his profit.

【獮】 3395
ㄒㄧㄢˇ shean xiǎn

1. to hunt; to kill
2. autumn hunting by ancient emperors

【獯】 3396
ㄒㄩㄣ shiun xūn

name of a northern barbarian tribe in ancient China known as the Huns (匈奴) during the Han Dynasty

獯鬻(ㄒㄩㄣˊ ㄩˋ)
參看「獯」

【獰】 3397
ㄋㄧㄥˊ ning níng

a fierce appearance; an awe-inspiring look

獰笑(ㄋㄧㄥˊ ㄒㄧㄠˋ)
① a laugh with malignant intent; a frightening laugh ② to laugh malignantly

獰惡可怖(ㄋㄧㄥˊ ㄜˋ ㄎㄜˇ ㄅㄨˋ)
(said of a person's appearance) fierce and terrifying

十五畫

【獵】 3398
ㄌㄧㄝˋ lieh liè

to hunt; to chase; field sports

獵名(ㄌㄧㄝˋ ㄇㄧㄥˊ)
to hunt for a good name or a good reputation; to be after fame: 他此舉乃為獵名。He did this to hunt for a good name.

獵狗(ㄌㄧㄝˋ ㄍㄡˇ)
a pointer; a hunting dog; a hound: 獵狗追近獵物。The hounds got nearer to their game.

獵戶(ㄌㄧㄝˋ ㄏㄨˋ)
hunters; huntsmen

獵戶座(ㄌㄧㄝˋ ㄏㄨˋ ㄗㄨㄛˋ)
(astronomy) Orion

獵獲(ㄌㄧㄝˋ ㄏㄨㄛˊ)
to catch in hunting; to bag: 我們昨天獵獲兩三隻野兔。We bagged a couple of hares yesterday.

獵奇(ㄌㄧㄝˋ ㄑㄧˊ)
① to hunt for the strange or uncommon ② a record of what is strange or uncommon

獵槍(ㄌㄧㄝˋ ㄑㄧㄤ)
a hunting gun; a fowling piece; a shotgun

獵取(ㄌㄧㄝˋ ㄑㄩˇ)
to chase after; to pursue; to hunt

獵取功名(ㄌㄧㄝˋ ㄑㄩˇ ㄍㄨㄥ ㄇㄧㄥˊ)
to try to win a degree in civil examination

獵犬(ㄌㄧㄝˋ ㄑㄩㄢˇ)
a hunting dog; a pointer, dachshund, etc.: 獵犬追逐野獸。The hunting dogs chased wild animals.

獵犬座(ㄌㄧㄝˋ ㄑㄩㄢˇ ㄗㄨㄛˋ)
Canes Venatici

獵裝(ㄌㄧㄝˋ ㄓㄨㄤ)
hunting dress

獵場(ㄌㄧㄝˋ ㄔㄤˇ)
a hunting ground; a hunting field

獵食(ㄌㄧㄝˋ ㄕˊ)
to hunt for food: 狼成群獵食。Wolves hunt in packs.

獵人(ㄌㄧㄝˋ ㄖㄣˊ)
a hunter; a huntsman

獵艷(ㄌㄧㄝˋ ㄧㄢˋ)
to chase after pretty women

獵鷹(ㄌㄧㄝˋ ㄧㄥ)
a falcon

獵物(ㄌㄧㄝˋ ㄨˋ)
game; a quarry

【獷】 3399
ㄍㄨㄤˇ goang guǎng

fierce and rude; uncivilized

獷敵(ㄍㄨㄤˇ ㄉㄧˊ)
a savage enemy; a deadly rival

獷悍(ㄍㄨㄤˇ ㄏㄢˋ)
rude and brutal

獷俗(ㄍㄨㄤˇ ㄙㄨˊ)
uncivilized customs; barbarian ways

【獸】 3400
ㄕㄡˋ show shòu

1. a general name for quadruped; a beast or animal
2. bestial; beastly

獸皮(ㄕㄡˋ ㄆㄧˊ)
animal skin or hide

獸面(ㄕㄡˋ ㄇㄧㄢˋ)
(in ancient China) a mask of an animal head worn by a player

獸類(ㄕㄡˋ ㄌㄟˋ)
animals; beasts

獸力(ㄕㄡˋ ㄌㄧˋ)
animal power (especially said of beasts of burden)

獸爐(ㄕㄡˋ ㄌㄨˊ)
a vessel for burning incense usually shaped like an animal

〔犬 部〕

獸工(ㄕㄡ ㄍㄨㄥ)
a tanner

獸環(ㄕㄡ ㄏㄨㄢ)
a doorknob shaped like the head of an animal with a ring for a knocking purpose

獸姦(ㄕㄡ ㄐㄧㄢ)
sodomy; buggery

獸檻(ㄕㄡ ㄐㄧㄢ)
a pen or cage for animals 亦作「獸圈」

獸聚鳥散(ㄕㄡ ㄐㄩˋ ㄋㄧㄠˇ ㄙㄢˋ)
(usually said of bandits, etc.) to get together and disperse like animals and birds

獸圈(ㄕㄡ ㄐㄩㄢˋ)
a pen or cage for animals

獸心(ㄕㄡ ㄒㄧㄣ)
bestiality; beastliness

獸行(ㄕㄡ ㄒㄧㄥˊ)
bestial or beastly acts or conduct; atrocities

獸性(ㄕㄡ ㄒㄧㄥˋ)
①bestiality; beastliness ②animal passions or desires

獸性大發(ㄕㄡ ㄒㄧㄥˋ ㄉㄚˋ ㄈㄚ)
to raise one's animal disposition

獸中之王(ㄕㄡ ㄓㄨㄥ ㄓ ㄨㄤˊ)
the king of beasts—the lion

獸醫(ㄕㄡ ㄧ)
a veterinarian

獸醫學(ㄕㄡ ㄧ ㄒㄩㄝˊ)
veterinary science; zoopathology

獸慾(ㄕㄡ ㄩˋ)
carnal desire; lust; bestial urge (especially referring to rape)

十六畫

【獺】 3401
ㄊㄚˇ tah tǎ
an otter

獺祭(ㄊㄚˇ ㄐㄧ)
to write an article by heaping up quotations and allusions from a large number of books

【獻】 3402
ㄒㄧㄢˋ shiann xiàn
1. to present; to forward; to offer; to dedicate; to donate
2. to display; to show; to stage
3. to curry (favor, etc.); to flatter or cater to

獻寶(ㄒㄧㄢˋ ㄅㄠˇ)
①to present a treasure ②to offer a scheme or one's valuable experience ③to show off what one treasures

獻曝(ㄒㄧㄢˋ ㄆㄨˋ)
(a polite expression) to offer my humble gift or advice

獻媚(ㄒㄧㄢˋ ㄇㄟˋ)
①to act coquettishly ②to curry favor; to toady; to act obsequiously

獻俘(ㄒㄧㄢˋ ㄈㄨˊ)
(in ancient China) to offer prisoners of war at the national shrine after the triumphal conclusion of a war

獻禮(ㄒㄧㄢˋ ㄌㄧˇ)
①the ceremony of offering presents ②to present a gift

獻花(ㄒㄧㄢˋ ㄏㄨㄚ)
to present flowers or bouquets; to lay a wreath: 小姐們向英雄獻花。 The girls presented flowers to the heroes.

獻機(ㄒㄧㄢˋ ㄐㄧ)
to contribute money for the procurement of warplanes as a gift to the country

獻技(ㄒㄧㄢˋ ㄐㄧˋ)
to display one's feat; to stage a performance of special skills or feats: 他到國外獻技去了。 He went abroad to perform feats.

獻計(ㄒㄧㄢˋ ㄐㄧˋ)
to present or offer advice or a scheme for adoption; to make suggestions

獻捷(ㄒㄧㄢˋ ㄐㄧㄝˊ)
to send prisoners of war to an ally as a gesture of friendship upon the victorious conclusion of a war

獻酒(ㄒㄧㄢˋ ㄐㄧㄡˇ)
to offer wine

獻艦(ㄒㄧㄢˋ ㄐㄧㄢˋ)
to contribute money for the procurement of warships as a gift to the country

獻金(ㄒㄧㄢˋ ㄐㄧㄣ)
①to contribute (money) ②money contributed

獻旗(ㄒㄧㄢˋ ㄑㄧˊ)
to present flags or pennants

獻芹(ㄒㄧㄢˋ ㄑㄧㄣˊ)
to offer my humble gift

獻醜(ㄒㄧㄢˋ ㄔㄡˇ)or 獻拙(ㄒㄧㄢˋ ㄓㄨㄛˊ)
to show my poor skill or talent (a polite expression)

獻身(ㄒㄧㄢˋ ㄕㄣ)
to offer or dedicate oneself (to a cause, one's nation, etc.): 他一生獻身學術。 He dedicated all his life to learning.

獻身社會(ㄒㄧㄢˋ ㄕㄣ ㄕㄜˋ ㄏㄨㄟˋ)
to offer oneself to social work; to dedicate oneself to public services

獻詞(ㄒㄧㄢˋ ㄘˊ)
a dedication; a dedication speech

獻策(ㄒㄧㄢˋ ㄘㄜˋ)
①to offer a plan, scheme, etc.; to advise ②a plan; advice

獻歲(ㄒㄧㄢˋ ㄙㄨㄟˋ)
the beginning of a new year

獻藝(ㄒㄧㄢˋ ㄧˋ)
①to exhibit one's skill ②(said of actors) to appear on stage for performances: 電影明星將來此登臺獻藝。 The movie star will come here and appear on stage.

獻殷勤(ㄒㄧㄢˋ ㄧㄣ ㄑㄧㄣˊ)
to flatter; to make oneself liked; to ingratiate

十七畫

【獼】 3403
ㄇㄧˊ mi mí
a rhesus monkey

獼猴(ㄇㄧˊ ㄏㄡˊ)
a rhesus monkey; a macaque

十九畫

【玀】 3404
ㄌㄨㄛˊ luo luó
a primitive tribe 參看「猓玀」

二十畫

【玁】 3405
(獫)ㄒㄧㄢˇ shean xiǎn
a dog with a long snout or muzzle

玁狁(ㄒㄧㄢˇ ㄩㄣˇ)

Hsien-yūn, a barbarian tribe known as the Huns (匈奴) during the Chin and the Han dynasties

〔玄部〕

玄部
ㄒㄩㄢ shyuan xuán

【玄】 3406
ㄒㄩㄢ shyuan xuán

1. far and obscure; occult or mystic
2. dark or black
3. deep and profound; abstruse and subtle: 這太玄了。 This is getting too abstruse.
4. silent and meditative
5. pretending
6. a Chinese family name

玄默(ㄒㄩㄢ ㄇㄛˋ)
taciturn and meditative

玄謨(ㄒㄩㄢ ㄇㄛˊ)
a subtle and profound scheme

玄門(ㄒㄩㄢ ㄇㄣˊ)
①Buddhism ②Taoism

玄妙(ㄒㄩㄢ ㄇㄧㄠˋ)
profound, abstruse and subtle; mysterious: 這些是很玄妙的問題。 These are very abstruse questions.

玄服(ㄒㄩㄢ ㄈㄨˊ)
dark dress or clothing

玄德(ㄒㄩㄢ ㄉㄜˊ)
①latent or hidden virtues ②(Buddhism) the fabulous and subtle faith

玄談(ㄒㄩㄢ ㄊㄢˊ)
①the profound, abstruse words of Lao-tzu ②the foreword or introduction to a Buddhist scripture

玄鳥(ㄒㄩㄢ ㄋㄧㄠˇ)
①a swallow ②a crane

玄覽(ㄒㄩㄢ ㄌㄢˇ)
to view all with a tranquil mind

玄理(ㄒㄩㄢ ㄌㄧˇ)
profound or abstruse reasoning or theory

玄關(ㄒㄩㄢ ㄍㄨㄢ)
①the entrance to Buddhism ②the door of a house ③a vestibule

玄黃(ㄒㄩㄢ ㄏㄨㄤˊ)
①heaven and earth ②dark yellow

玄機(ㄒㄩㄢ ㄐㄧ)
(Taoism) the profound and mysterious truth

玄教(ㄒㄩㄢ ㄐㄧㄠˋ)
Taoism

玄酒(ㄒㄩㄢ ㄐㄧㄡˇ)
①(in ancient China) the water used in worshiping ②diluted wine

玄穹(ㄒㄩㄢ ㄑㄩㄥˊ)
the sky; heaven

玄象(ㄒㄩㄢ ㄒㄧㄤˋ)
the phenomena of celestial bodies

玄虛(ㄒㄩㄢ ㄒㄩ)
①empty and without substance; mysterious; mystic: 他爲何故弄玄虛? Why was he deliberately mysterious? ②cunning and evil schemes; tricks

玄學(ㄒㄩㄢ ㄒㄩㄝˊ)
①metaphysics: 玄學討論抽象的概念。 Metaphysics deals with abstractions. ②Taoism ③Buddhism ④spiritualism (as opposed to materialism)

玄學家(ㄒㄩㄢ ㄒㄩㄝˊ ㄐㄧㄚ)
a spiritualist; a metaphysicist

玄之又玄(ㄒㄩㄢ ㄓ ㄧㄡˋ ㄒㄩㄢ)
①occult; the most mysterious of the mysterious ②nonsense

玄眞(ㄒㄩㄢ ㄓㄣ)
jade

玄著(ㄒㄩㄢ ㄓㄨˋ)
profound or abstruse writings

玄奘(ㄒㄩㄢ ㄗㄤˋ)
Hsüan Tsang, 596-664, a Buddhist monk in the Tang Dynasty, who toured India for more than 10 years and brought back 600-odd Buddhist scriptures, 75 of which he and his disciples translated into Chinese

玄宗(ㄒㄩㄢ ㄗㄨㄥ)
the Buddhist religion

玄孫(ㄒㄩㄢ ㄙㄨㄣ)
great-great-grandson

玄奧(ㄒㄩㄢ ㄠˋ)
①abstruse and subtle; difficult to comprehend ②mys-

teries; profundities

玄武湖(ㄒㄩㄢ ㄨˇ ㄏㄨˊ)
a famous lake in Nanking

玄武岩(ㄒㄩㄢ ㄨˇ ㄧㄢˊ)
basalt

玄悟(ㄒㄩㄢ ㄨˋ)
a profound understanding of an abstruse theory

玄月(ㄒㄩㄢ ㄩㄝˋ)
the ninth moon in the lunar calendar

六畫

【率】 3407
1. ㄕㄨㄞˋ shuay shuài

1. to lead (troops, a team, etc.); to command
2. to follow; to act in accordance with
3. rash and hasty
4. generally; in general; usually
5. simple and candid; frank; straightforward; to the point
6. (said of men) dashing

率部(ㄕㄨㄞˋ ㄅㄨˋ)or率兵(ㄕㄨㄞˋ ㄅㄧㄥ)
to lead troops

率土之濱(ㄕㄨㄞˋ ㄊㄨˇ ㄓ ㄅㄧㄣ)
within the sea-boundaries of the land—within the territory of a state

率同(ㄕㄨㄞˋ ㄊㄨㄥˊ)
accompanied by; to lead all the others in (visiting, inspecting, etc.)

率領(ㄕㄨㄞˋ ㄌㄧㄥˇ)
to lead (troops, a team, etc.); to head (a mission, etc.): 將軍率領軍隊衝鋒。 The general led his armies in the charge.

率先(ㄕㄨㄞˋ ㄒㄧㄢ)
to be the first; to take the lead: 由誰率先開始? Who takes the lead?

率性(ㄕㄨㄞˋ ㄒㄧㄥˋ)
①one's natural disposition ②to act according to the dictates of one's conscience

率直(ㄕㄨㄞˋ ㄓˊ)
candid; frank; straight; honest

率眞(ㄕㄨㄞˋ ㄓㄣ)
candid; frank; honest

率索(ㄕㄨㄞˋ ㄙㄨㄛˇ)

to lead a crowd; to lead a large group of people

率師 (ㄌㄨㄞ ㄕ)
to lead troops

率獸食人 (ㄌㄨㄞ ㄕㄡ ㄕ ㄖㄣ)
to lead on beasts to devour men—tyranny of government

率然 (ㄌㄨㄞ ㄖㄢ)
randomly; casually

率爾 (ㄌㄨㄞ ㄦ)
casually; rashly; at random: 你不應該率爾行事。You should not do everything rashly.

率爾操觚 (ㄌㄨㄞ ㄦ ㄘㄠ ㄍㄨ)
to write at random or desultorily

率意 (ㄌㄨㄞ ㄧ)
①to act on the spur of the moment; to follow one's inclination: 不可率意孤行。You should not act on the spur of the moment. ② with all one's sincerity

率由 (ㄌㄨㄞ ㄧㄡ)
to follow; to act according to

率由舊章 (ㄌㄨㄞ ㄧㄡ ㄐㄧㄡ ㄓㄤ)
to follow old practices or precedents

率允 (ㄌㄨㄞ ㄩㄣ)
to promise at random or carelessly

【率】 3407
2. ㄌㄩ　liuh lü
1. (mathematics) ratio
2. a suffix used to indicate a measure or rate
3. to calculate

玉 部
ㄩ yuh yǔ

【玉】 3408
ㄩ yuh yǔ
1. a precious stone—especially jade; a gem
2. a polite expression for "your"
3. a designation of things belonging to a girl or young woman
4. (said of a person, especially a woman) pure; fair; beauti-

ful
5. a Chinese family name

玉撥 (ㄩ ㄅㄛ)
a jade hairpin

玉帛 (ㄩ ㄅㄛ)
①gems and silk (used as state gifts in ancient China) ②(figuratively) friendship

玉杯 (ㄩ ㄅㄟ)
①a jade cup ②name of a book authored by Tung Chung-shu (董仲舒) of the Han Dynasty

玉臂 (ㄩ ㄅㄧ)
a girl's arms; a pretty woman's arms

玉陛 (ㄩ ㄅㄧ)
the steps of white jade leading to the throne

玉鬢 (ㄩ ㄅㄧㄣ)
white hair

玉步 (ㄩ ㄅㄨ)
①your footsteps ②the footsteps of a pretty girl

玉不琢不成器 (ㄩ ㄅㄨ ㄓㄨㄛ ㄅㄨ ㄔㄥ ㄑㄧ)
(literally) Jade must be cut and chiseled to make it a useful vessel.—A person must be disciplined and educated to be a useful citizen.

玉佩 (ㄩ ㄆㄟ)
jade pendants on a girdle

玉盤 (ㄩ ㄆㄢ)
①a jade plate or tray ②(figuratively) a variety of chrysanthemum with protruding yellow center and whitish green edge

玉貌 (ㄩ ㄇㄠ) or 玉面 (ㄩ ㄇㄧㄢ)
①a face; the face of a pretty girl ②your face

玉門關 (ㄩ ㄇㄣ ㄍㄨㄢ) or 玉塞 (ㄩ ㄙㄞ)
the Yü-men Pass—a gate on the Great Wall in Kansu Province, a strategic gateway to the Western Regions (西域)

玉米 (ㄩ ㄇㄧ)
Indian corn; maize

玉米花 (ㄩ ㄇㄧ ㄏㄨㄚ)
popcorn

玉面朱唇 (ㄩ ㄇㄧㄢ ㄓㄨ ㄔㄨㄣ)
a beautiful and fashionable woman

玉帶 (ㄩ ㄉㄞ)

a jade-studded belt worn by high-ranking officials in ancient China

玉雕 (ㄩ ㄉㄧㄠ)
jade carving; jade sculpture

玉敦 (ㄩ ㄉㄨㄣ)
a jade vessel used to hold blood during the oath-taking ceremony in ancient China

玉堂 (ㄩ ㄊㄤ)
①a rich and powerful family ②an imperial harem ③name of an office in the Han Dynasty

玉體 (ㄩ ㄊㄧ)
①yourself; your person: 請保重玉體。Please take good care of yourself. ② the nude body of a girl

玉體橫陳 (ㄩ ㄊㄧ ㄏㄥ ㄔㄣ)
(said of a girl or a young woman) the beautiful nude body lying in full view

玉體違和 (ㄩ ㄊㄧ ㄨㄟ ㄏㄜ)
a term referring to someone who is out of sorts

玉兔 (ㄩ ㄊㄨ)
①(Chinese mythology) the jade hare in the moon ②the moon

玉兔東升 (ㄩ ㄊㄨ ㄉㄨㄥ ㄕㄥ)
The moon rises in the east.

玉輦 (ㄩ ㄌㄧㄢ)
the imperial carriage

玉女 (ㄩ ㄋㄩ)
①a young and beautiful girl ②your daughter ③an angel in the fairyland

玉樓 (ㄩ ㄌㄡ)
①the fairyland; paradise ②a jade tower ③(Taoism) the shoulder

玉樓赴召 (ㄩ ㄌㄡ ㄈㄨ ㄓㄠ)
(said of a young scholar) to die

玉漏 (ㄩ ㄌㄡ)
a jade hourglass

玉蘭 (ㄩ ㄌㄢ)
a magnolia

玉露 (ㄩ ㄌㄨ)
①dewdrops ②the best green tea

玉鈎 or 玉鉤 (ㄩ ㄍㄡ)
①the crescent moon; the new moon ②the jade hook

玉梗 (ㄩ ㄍㄥ)
a neat row of sparkling

teeth

玉骨冰肌(ㄩˋ ㄍㄨˇ ㄅㄧㄥ ㄐㄧ)
elegant demeanor and high personality

玉衡(ㄩˋ ㄏㄥˊ)
an ancient instrument for observing heavenly bodies

玉卮(ㄩˋ ㄓㄨ)
①a jade wine-cup, symbolic of spiritual purity ②honest and virtuous ③a jade hour-glass

玉笏(ㄩˋ ㄏㄨˋ)
a jade tablet held by a high official to attend the imperial court session in the early morning

玉環(ㄩˋ ㄏㄨㄢˊ)
①jade rings or bracelets ②the moon

玉皇大帝(ㄩˋ ㄏㄨㄤˊ ㄉㄚˋ ㄉㄧˋ)or 玉帝(ㄩˋ ㄉㄧˋ)
the Jade Emperor, the supreme deity in Taoism

玉潔冰清(ㄩˋ ㄐㄧㄝˊ ㄅㄧㄥ ㄑㄧㄥ)
pure like jade, clear like ice—pure and virtuous

玉尖(ㄩˋ ㄐㄧㄢ)
①tapering fingers of a beautiful woman ②mountain peaks

玉減香消(ㄩˋ ㄐㄧㄢˇ ㄒㄧㄤ ㄒㄧㄠ)
(said of a beauty) to become emaciated

玉漿(ㄩˋ ㄐㄧㄤ)
good wine

玉器(ㄩˋ ㄑㄧˋ)
jade articles

玉磬(ㄩˋ ㄑㄧㄥˋ)
an ancient musical instrument

玉闕(ㄩˋ ㄑㄩㄝˋ)
①the holy city ②the gate to a holy land

玉泉山(ㄩˋ ㄑㄩㄢˊ ㄕㄢ)
name of a hill northwest of Peking, near the Summer Palace

玉璽(ㄩˋ ㄒㄧˇ)
the imperial seal

玉匣(ㄩˋ ㄒㄧㄚˊ)
①a jade box for jewels ②a coffin for emperors in the Han Dynasty

玉屑(ㄩˋ ㄒㄧㄝˋ)
①broken jade ②snow ③exquisite writing

玉簫(ㄩˋ ㄒㄧㄠ)
a jade flute

玉心(ㄩˋ ㄒㄧㄣ)
a heart as pure as jade

玉虛(ㄩˋ ㄒㄩ)
the fairyland

玉卮(ㄩˋ ㄓ)
a jade cup

玉質(ㄩˋ ㄓˊ)
of jade

玉趾(ㄩˋ ㄓˇ)
(a term of respect) your footsteps

玉札(ㄩˋ ㄓㄚˊ)
name of a herb used in Chinese medicine

玉照(ㄩˋ ㄓㄠˋ)
your photograph or picture

玉展(ㄩˋ ㄓㄢˇ)
for your perusal (a polite expression following the name of a person to whom a letter is addressed)

玉筯(ㄩˋ ㄓㄨˋ)
①chopsticks made of jade ②snivel; tears ③a style of calligraphy known as "small seal" (小篆)

玉鐲(ㄩˋ ㄓㄨㄛˊ)
a jade bracelet

玉池(ㄩˋ ㄔˊ)
(Taoism) the mouth

玉齒(ㄩˋ ㄔˇ)
sparkling teeth

玉蟾(ㄩˋ ㄔㄢˊ)
the jade toad—the moon

玉成其事(ㄩˋ ㄔㄥˊ ㄑㄧˊ ㄕˋ)
to assist another in accomplishing a task or attaining a goal

玉食(ㄩˋ ㄕˊ)
delicacies; dainties

玉食錦衣(ㄩˋ ㄕˊ ㄐㄧㄣˇ ㄧ)
sumptuous food and luxurious clothing

玉石俱焚(ㄩˋ ㄕˊ ㄐㄩˋ ㄈㄣˊ)
to destroy indiscriminately, be it jade or rock

玉手(ㄩˋ ㄕㄡˇ)
fair hands; hands of a pretty lady

玉手纖纖(ㄩˋ ㄕㄡˇ ㄒㄧㄢ ㄒㄧㄢ)
the slender hands of a pretty young woman

玉山(ㄩˋ ㄕㄢ)
①Mt. Yu, the highest mountain peak in Taiwan ②elegant and majestic ③name of a county in Kiangsi

玉蜀黍(ㄩˋ ㄕㄨˇ ㄕㄨˇ)
Indian corn; maize: 玉蜀黍差不多可以收成了。The corn is nearly ready for harvesting.

玉樹(ㄩˋ ㄕㄨˋ)
①a young person with talent and good looks ②a locust tree

玉人(ㄩˋ ㄖㄣˊ)
①a beautiful woman ②a lapidary

玉潤珠圓(ㄩˋ ㄖㄨㄣˋ ㄓㄨ ㄩㄢˊ)
(said of a singing voice) smooth and soft

玉容(ㄩˋ ㄖㄨㄥˊ)
a beautiful face

玉容花貌(ㄩˋ ㄖㄨㄥˊ ㄏㄨㄚ ㄇㄠˋ)
a fair face and elegant form

玉簪(ㄩˋ ㄗㄢ)
①a jade hairpin ②(botany) tuberose

玉慘花愁(ㄩˋ ㄘㄢˇ ㄏㄨㄚ ㄔㄡˊ)
(said of a pretty woman) sad; crying

玉色(ㄩˋ ㄙㄜˋ)
①a color that never changes as jade ②virtuous and pure ③fair (faces) ④(color) jade green

玉搔頭(ㄩˋ ㄙㄠ ㄊㄡˊ)
a jade hairpin 亦作「玉簪」

玉髓(ㄩˋ ㄙㄨㄟˇ)
①exquisite wine ②(mineral) chalcedony

玉碎珠沉(ㄩˋ ㄙㄨㄟˋ ㄓㄨ ㄔㄣˊ)
the death of a beauty

玉筍(ㄩˋ ㄙㄨㄣˇ)
①fingers of a beautiful woman ②talents as many as bamboo shoots

玉案(ㄩˋ ㄢˋ)
①a jade plate for food ②narrow jade table ③name of a mountain in Yunnan Province

玉儀(ㄩˋ ㄧˊ)
①a complexion as smooth as jade ②a jade-ornamented instrument for observing heavenly bodies

玉液瓊漿(ㄩˋ ㄧㄝˋ ㄑㄩㄥˊ ㄐㄧㄤ)or 玉液(ㄩˋ ㄧㄝˋ)
top-quality wine

玉顏(ㄩˋ ㄧㄢˊ)

a fair complexion

玉靨(ㄩˋ｜ㄝˋ)
a complexion as smooth as jade

玉音(ㄩˋ｜ㄣ)
①valuable words ②imperial decrees ③your esteemed reply ④jadelike music—beautiful sound

玉英(ㄩˋ｜ㄥ)
①jade of best quality ②cactus flowers

玉腕(ㄩˋ ㄨㄢˋ)
the wrist and forearm of a beautiful woman

玉宇(ㄩˋ ㄩˇ)
①a splendid hall—as if made of jade ②the palace of the legendary Jade Emperor

玉殞香消(ㄩˋ ㄩㄣˇ ㄒ｜ㄤ ㄒ｜ㄠ)
the death of a woman

【王】 3409
1. ㄨㄤˊ　wang wáng
1. a king; a ruler
2. a prince, the highest rank of nobility
3. great; of a tremendous size
4. the strongest or most powerful
5. a salutation of respect
6. an audience with the ruler or emperor
7. a Chinese family name

王八 or 忘八(ㄨㄤˊ ㄅㄚ)
①a turtle; a tortoise ②a cuckold ③a man who works in a brothel ④a s.o.b.

王八蛋(ㄨㄤˊ ㄅㄚ ㄉㄢˋ)
a term of revilement similar to "s.o.b."

王八羔子(ㄨㄤˊ ㄅㄚ ㄍㄠ ˙ㄗ)
a term of revilement similar to "s.o.b."

王霸(ㄨㄤˊ ㄅㄚˋ)
the business of being a king or ruler

王牌(ㄨㄤˊ ㄆㄞˊ)
a trump card

王莽(ㄨㄤˊ ㄇㄤˇ)
Wang Mang (45 B.C.- 23 A.D.), a prime minister of the Western Han Dynasty who introduced many reforms after he usurped the throne

王命(ㄨㄤˊ ㄇ｜ㄥˋ)
the emperor's orders; the

royal decrees

王母(ㄨㄤˊ ㄇㄨˇ)
①the grandmother ②the leading Taoist goddess

王法(ㄨㄤˊ ㄈㄚˇ)
the King's law—the laws of the land; the law

王妃(ㄨㄤˊ ㄈㄟ)
a prince's concubine

王府(ㄨㄤˊ ㄈㄨˇ)
the palace of a prince

王父(ㄨㄤˊ ㄈㄨˋ)
the grandfather

王大父(ㄨㄤˊ ㄉㄚˋ ㄈㄨˋ)
the great grandfather

王道(ㄨㄤˊ ㄉㄠˋ)
the ways of an enlightened ruler; an enlightened reign of righteousness (as opposed to tyranny); royal government

王庭(ㄨㄤˊ ㄊ｜ㄥˊ)
the king's court; the imperial court

王綱(ㄨㄤˊ ㄍㄤ)
laws, regulations, institutions, etc. of a reign

王國(ㄨㄤˊ ㄍㄨㄛˊ)
a kingdom

王冠(ㄨㄤˊ ㄍㄨㄢ)
a crown

王宮(ㄨㄤˊ ㄍㄨㄥ)
a royal palace

王公(ㄨㄤˊ ㄍㄨㄥ)or 王公大人(ㄨㄤˊ ㄍㄨㄥ ㄉㄚˋ ㄖㄣˊ)
princes and nobles

王侯(ㄨㄤˊ ㄏㄡˊ)
princes and marquises—the nobility

王侯將相(ㄨㄤˊ ㄏㄡˊ ㄐ｜ㄤ ㄒ｜ㄤˋ)
princes, nobles, generals and ministers—the ruling class

王后(ㄨㄤˊ ㄏㄡˋ)
the queen

王化(ㄨㄤˊ ㄏㄨㄚˋ)
civilizing influence; sovereign grace

王畿(ㄨㄤˊ ㄐ｜)
the suburbs of the capital of an empire

王駕(ㄨㄤˊ ㄐ｜ㄚˋ)
①the king's carriage ②the king or emperor

王權(ㄨㄤˊ ㄑㄩㄢˊ)
the authority of a king; imperial powers; the throne

王羲之(ㄨㄤˊ ㄒ｜ ㄓ)
Wang Hsi-chih (321-379), the greatest of Chinese calligraphers

王謝(ㄨㄤˊ ㄒ｜ㄝˋ)
Wang and Hsieh, both prospering families during the period of the Six Dynasties, now used as a synonym of influential families

王者(ㄨㄤˊ ㄓㄜˇ)
①an emperor or king ②a true royal sovereign

王昭君(ㄨㄤˊ ㄓㄠ ㄐㄩㄣ)
another name for Wang Chiang (王嬙), a court lady during the Han Dynasty, who was given to the chieftain of a barbarian tribe as his wife in the performance of matrimonial diplomacy

王朝(ㄨㄤˊ ㄔㄠˊ)
a dynasty

王臣(ㄨㄤˊ ㄔㄣˊ)
king's servants

王儲(ㄨㄤˊ ㄔㄨˊ)
a crown prince

王師(ㄨㄤˊ ㄕ)
the king's troops; the emperor's troops

王事(ㄨㄤˊ ㄕˋ)
royal affairs

王室(ㄨㄤˊ ㄕˋ)
①the royal family; the ruling house ②the imperial or royal court

王水(ㄨㄤˊ ㄕㄨㄟˇ)
(chemistry) aqua regia

王子(ㄨㄤˊ ㄗˇ)
a prince

王族(ㄨㄤˊ ㄗㄨˊ)
the royal family; persons of royal lineage

王佐之才(ㄨㄤˊ ㄗㄨㄛˇ ㄓ ㄘㄞˊ)
the capabilities of a prime minister: 此人具有王佐之才. This man has the capabilities of a prime minister.

王孫(ㄨㄤˊ ㄙㄨㄣ)
①descendants of the nobility ②a cricket ③a monkey ④a Chinese family name

王孫公子(ㄨㄤˊ ㄙㄨㄣ ㄍㄨㄥ ˙ㄗ)
blue-blooded young men; aristocrats

王安石(ㄨㄤˊ ㄢ ㄕˊ)

〔玉部〕

（玉部）

Wang An-shih (1021-1086), a prime minister during the reign of Emperor Shen Tzung (神宗), part of whose "new deal" is still being practiced today

王爾德(ㄨㄤ ㄦˇ ㄉㄜˊ)
Oscar Wilde (1856-1900), English novelist and playwright

王業(ㄨㄤ ㄧㄝˋ)
the country (regarded as the monarch's private property)

王爺(ㄨㄤ ㄧㄝˊ)
① a nobleman ② Your Imperial Highness

王陽明(ㄨㄤ ㄧㄤˊ ㄇㄧㄥˊ)or 王守仁(ㄨㄤ ㄕㄡˇ ㄖㄣˊ)
Wang Yang-ming (1472-1528), who advocated the theory that action should go along with knowledge or theory

王維(ㄨㄤ ㄨㄟˊ)
Wang Wei (699-759), a famous painter and poet in the Tang Dynasty

王位(ㄨㄤ ㄨㄟˋ)
the throne; the crown

【王】 3409
2. ㄨㄤˋ wanq wàng
to rule; to govern

王天下(ㄨㄤ ㄊㄧㄢ ㄒㄧㄚˋ)
to rule over the empire

二畫

【玎】 3410
ㄉㄧㄥ ding dīng
the jingling or tinkling sound

玎璫(ㄉㄧㄥ ㄉㄤ)
ding-dong; the jingling or tinkling sound: 鐘玎璫地響。
The bell goes ding-dong.

玎玲(ㄉㄧㄥ ㄌㄧㄥˊ)
the jingling or tinkling sound

三畫

【玕】 3411
《ㄢ gan gān
a kind of inferior gem; a stone slightly inferior in quality to jade

【玖】 3412
ㄐㄧㄡˇ jeou jiǔ
1. a black jade stone

2. an elaborate form of 九, nine, used in checks, etc. to prevent fraud

四畫

【玫】 3413
ㄇㄟˊ mei méi
1. the rose
2. another name of black mica —a sparkling red gem

玫瑰(ㄇㄟˊ ㄍㄨㄟ)
① the rose (blossoms) ② black mica—a sparkling red gem

玫瑰酒(ㄇㄟˊ ㄍㄨㄟ ㄐㄧㄡˇ)
mild and sweetened kaoliang wine

玫瑰紅(ㄇㄟˊ ㄍㄨㄟ ㄏㄨㄥˊ)
① rose red ② rose-red: 她穿上玫瑰紅的衣服。She put on rose-red clothes.

玫瑰紫(ㄇㄟˊ ㄍㄨㄟ ㄗˇ)
dark red; rose purple

玫瑰油(ㄇㄟˊ ㄍㄨㄟ ㄧㄡˊ)
attar of roses

【玦】 3414
ㄐㄩㄝˊ jyue jué
a jade ring with a small segment cut off

【玩】 3415
1. ㄨㄢˊ wan wán
1. to play with; to play; to toy with: 孩子們在玩。The children are at play.
2. to amuse oneself with; to find pleasure in

玩兒(ㄨㄢˊㄦ)
to play; to play or toy with

玩兒票(ㄨㄢˊㄦ ㄆㄧㄠˋ)or 玩票(ㄨㄢˊ ㄆㄧㄠˋ)
① to amuse oneself by playing parts in Chinese operas as an amateur ② to do a payless job

玩兒命(ㄨㄢˊㄦ ㄇㄧㄥˋ)
to play with one's life at stake; to do daredevil tricks; to toy with one's life

玩兒話(ㄨㄢˊㄦ ㄏㄨㄚˋ)
jokes; utterances which are not said or taken seriously

玩把戲(ㄨㄢˊ ㄅㄚˇ ㄒㄧˋ)
to play little tricks; to juggle

玩不得(ㄨㄢˊ ·ㄅㄨ ㄉㄜˊ)
(literally) (It's) not something to play with—something serious or important

玩不動(ㄨㄢˊ ㄅㄨˋ ㄉㄨㄥˋ)
too exhausted or too weak to play

玩弄(ㄨㄢˊ ㄋㄨㄥˋ)
to toy with: 她玩弄她的一串珠子。She toyed with her string of beads.

玩花樣(ㄨㄢˊ ㄏㄨㄚ ㄧㄤˋ)
to play tricks; to cheat

玩火(ㄨㄢˊ ㄏㄨㄛˇ)
to play with fire—a dangerous game

玩火自焚(ㄨㄢˊ ㄏㄨㄛˇ ㄗˋ ㄈㄣˊ)
Whoever plays with fire will get burnt. 或 Whoever plays with fire will perish by fire.

玩具(ㄨㄢˊ ㄐㄩˋ)
toys

玩具店(ㄨㄢˊ ㄐㄩˋ ㄉㄧㄢˋ)
a toy shop

玩笑(ㄨㄢˊ ㄒㄧㄠˋ)
① jokes; jesting ② to take something less seriously than it deserves

玩手段(ㄨㄢˊ ㄕㄡˇ ㄉㄨㄢˋ)
to resort to scheming; to manipulate

玩賞(ㄨㄢˊ ㄕㄤˇ)
to amuse by viewing; to enjoy or appreciate the beauty of something

玩耍(ㄨㄢˊ ㄕㄨㄚˇ)
to play; to have fun

玩偶(ㄨㄢˊ ㄡˇ)
dolls

玩意兒(ㄨㄢˊ ㄧˋㄦ)or 玩藝兒(ㄨㄢˊ ㄧˋㄦ)
① toys ② activities for entertainment or relaxation ③ a thing ④ (slang) a louse

玩物(ㄨㄢˊ ㄨˋ)
a plaything; something to play with; a toy

【玩】 3415
2. ㄨㄢˋ wann wàn
1. to joke; to take things lightly; to toy with
2. something to amuse oneself —as antiques, etc.
3. (now rarely) to learn

玩法(ㄨㄢˋ ㄈㄚˇ)
to toy with laws; to take laws and regulations lightly

玩弄(ㄨㄢˋ ㄋㄨㄥˋ)
① to juggle with: 他喜歡玩弄詞句。He likes to juggle with words. ② to play jokes on;

to fool: 不要再玩弄他。Don't fool him any longer.

玩愒(ㄨㄢˊ ㄎㄞˋ)or 玩歲愒日(ㄨㄢˊ ㄙㄨㄟˋ ㄎㄞˋ ㄖˋ)
to fritter away one's time

玩好(ㄨㄢˊ ㄏㄠˋ)
something one adopts as a hobby or one amuses oneself with

玩忽(ㄨㄢˊ ㄏㄨ)
to take things lightly; to neglect (official duties, laws and regulations)

玩習(ㄨㄢˊ ㄒㄧˊ)
to learn and practice

玩視(ㄨㄢˊ ㄕˋ)
to take laws and regulations lightly as if they were something to toy with

玩世不恭(ㄨㄢˊ ㄕˋ ㄅㄨˋ ㄍㄨㄥ)
to be a cynic, beatnik or hippie; to take everything lightly; to disdain worldly affairs

玩物喪志(ㄨㄢˊ ㄨˋ ㄙㄤˋ ㄓˋ)
to apply oneself too much to trifles, petty amusements, etc. so that one's fortitude and will power are eroded away 或 Riding a hobby saps one's will to make progress. 或 Excessive attention to trivia saps the will.

玩味(ㄨㄢˊ ㄨㄟˋ)
to ponder; to digest food for thought: 這個問題頗值玩味。This problem is worth pondering.

玩月(ㄨㄢˊ ㄩㄝˋ)
to enjoy the moonlight

【玨】3416
(珏) ㄐㄩㄝˊ jue jué
two pieces of jade fastened together

【玠】3417
ㄐㄧㄝˋ jieh jiè
a large jade tablet

五畫

【玲】3418
ㄌㄧㄥˊ ling líng
the tinkling of jade pendants

玲玎(ㄌㄧㄥˊ ㄉㄧㄥ)
①the tinkling of jade pendants ②the sound of waves pounding on rocks

玲琅(ㄌㄧㄥˊ ㄌㄤˊ)
the tinkling of jades

玲玲(ㄌㄧㄥˊ ㄌㄧㄥˊ)
the tinkling of jade pendants

玲瓏(ㄌㄧㄥˊ ㄌㄨㄥˊ)
① pleasing; delicate; cute; fine; regular ② bright ③ tinkling of jades

玲瓏剔透(ㄌㄧㄥˊ ㄌㄨㄥˊ ㄊㄧ ㄊㄡˋ)
①exquisitely carved ②(said of a person) very bright

【玷】3419
ㄉㄧㄢˋ diann diàn
1. a flaw or blemish in a piece of jade; a stain; a defect; a spot
2. to stain; to blemish; to disgrace

玷辱(ㄉㄧㄢˋ ㄖㄨˋ)
to disgrace (one's family name, etc.)

玷汙(ㄉㄧㄢˋ ㄨ)
a stain (in one's reputation, etc.); a blot on the scutcheon; to stain: 殘暴玷汙他的品性。His character was stained by cruelty.

【玳】3420
ㄉㄞˋ day dài
the tortoise shell

玳瑁(ㄉㄞˋ ㄇㄠˋ)
a hawksbill turtle, or hawksbill

玳瑁眼鏡(ㄉㄞˋ ㄇㄠˋ ㄧㄢˇ ㄐㄧㄥˋ)
hawksbill shell-rimmed eyeglasses

【珉】3421
ㄇㄧㄣˊ min mín
a stone resembling jade

【珂】3422
ㄎㄜ ke kē
1. a stone resembling jade
2. a decorative article on a bridle
3. a kind of cowry

珂里(ㄎㄜ ㄌㄧˇ)or 珂鄉(ㄎㄜ ㄒㄧㄤ)
(a polite expression) your hometown

珂羅版(ㄎㄜ ㄌㄨㄛˊ ㄅㄢˇ)
collotype

【玼】3423
ㄘˇ tsyy cǐ
1. a blemish; a flaw
2. brilliant

【珊】3424
ㄕㄢ shan shān
1. coral
2. the tinkling of pendants

珊瑚(ㄕㄢ ㄏㄨˊ)
coral: 她戴着珊瑚戒指。She wears a coral ring.

珊瑚島(ㄕㄢ ㄏㄨˊ ㄉㄠˇ)
a coral island; an atoll

珊瑚礁(ㄕㄢ ㄏㄨˊ ㄐㄧㄠ)
coral reefs

珊瑚蟲(ㄕㄢ ㄏㄨˊ ㄔㄨㄥˊ)
a coral polyp

珊瑚樹(ㄕㄢ ㄏㄨˊ ㄕㄨˋ)
a kind of evergreen tree (Viburnum odoratissimum)

珊珊(ㄕㄢ ㄕㄢ)
the tinkling of jade pendants

【珍】3425
ㄓㄣ jen zhēn
1. precious; rare; very valuable
2. valuables; treasures
3. delicacies; dainties

珍寶(ㄓㄣ ㄅㄠˇ)
jewelry and valuables

珍本(ㄓㄣ ㄅㄣˇ)
a rare or precious edition of an ancient book; a rare book

珍品(ㄓㄣ ㄆㄧㄣˇ)
delicacies; treasures or valuables; precious objects

珍祕(ㄓㄣ ㄇㄧˋ)
a treasure or precious thing which one is reluctant to let others know

珍怪(ㄓㄣ ㄍㄨㄞˋ)
rarities; strange happenings

珍貴(ㄓㄣ ㄍㄨㄟˋ)
valuable; treasurable; precious

珍奇(ㄓㄣ ㄑㄧˊ)
rare and precious

珍禽(ㄓㄣ ㄑㄧㄣˊ)
a rare bird

珍禽異獸(ㄓㄣ ㄑㄧㄣˊ ㄧˋ ㄕㄡˋ)
rare birds and animals

珍惜(ㄓㄣ ㄒㄧ)
to treasure; to consider very precious; to prize

珍羞 or 珍饈(ㄓㄣ ㄒㄧㄡ)
rare delicacies; dainties

珍珠(ㄓㄣ ㄓㄨ)
pearls

珍珠米(ㄓㄣ ㄓㄨ ㄇㄧˇ)
maize; (Indian) corn

珍珠港(ㄓㄣ ㄓㄨ ㄍㄤˇ)
Pearl Harbor

珍重(ㄓㄣ ㄓㄨㄥˋ)
to take good care of (your-

〔玉部〕

〔玉部〕

self); to think much of; to
value highly

珍藏(ㄓㄣ ㄘㄤˊ)
to value highly; to have a
high opinion of (something);
to treasure

珍攝(ㄓㄣ ㄕㄜˋ)
to take good care of one's
health

珍賞(ㄓㄣ ㄕㄤˇ)
to treasure and enjoy (a collection, etc.)

珍惜(ㄓㄣ ㄒㄧ)
to treasure; to keep something as a treasure (usually
said of rare books and
works of art)

珍藏密歛(ㄓㄣ ㄘㄤˊ ㄇㄧˋ ㄌㄧㄢˋ)
to hide or keep in a very
safe place

珍愛(ㄓㄣ ㄞˋ)
to value; to treasure; to love
dearly: 她珍愛她媽媽送給她的
針線包。She treasures the
sewing kit her mother gave
her.

珍異(ㄓㄣ ㄧˋ)
rare and precious

珍物(ㄓㄣ ㄨˋ)
① treasures; valuables: 她將
珍物藏在保險箱裏。She kept
her valuables in a safe. ②
delicacies

珍味(ㄓㄣ ㄨㄟˋ)
rare delicacies

珍玩(ㄓㄣ ㄨㄢˊ)
curios of great value: 他買了
許多珍玩。He bought a lot of
curios.

珍聞(ㄓㄣ ㄨㄣˊ)
rare news or information;
very valuable information

珍御(ㄓㄣ ㄩˋ)
expensive items of clothing

【玻】3426
ㄅㄛ bo bō
glass

玻璃(ㄅㄛ ·ㄌㄧ)
glass: 玻璃易碎。Glass breaks
easily.

玻璃杯(ㄅㄛ ·ㄌㄧ ㄅㄟ)
a glass; a tumbler

玻璃版(ㄅㄛ ·ㄌㄧ ㄅㄢˇ)
collotype

玻璃板(ㄅㄛ ·ㄌㄧ ㄅㄢˇ)
a glass plate; plate glass

玻璃片(ㄅㄛ ·ㄌㄧ ㄆㄧㄢˋ)

window glass; sheet glass

玻璃瓶(ㄅㄛ ·ㄌㄧ ㄆㄧㄥˊ)
a glass bottle

玻璃體(ㄅㄛ ·ㄌㄧ ㄊㄧˇ)
(anatomy) vitreous body

玻璃匠(ㄅㄛ ·ㄌㄧ ㄐㄧㄤˋ)
① a glassblower ② a gla-
zier; a glass cutter; a workman who fixes window glass
or plate glass

玻璃球(ㄅㄛ ·ㄌㄧ ㄑㄧㄡˊ)
glass beads; glass balls

玻璃圈(ㄅㄛ ·ㄌㄧ ㄑㄩㄢ)
(slang) the gay circle; the
world of male homosexuals

玻璃紙(ㄅㄛ ·ㄌㄧ ㄓˇ)
cellophane

玻璃窗(ㄅㄛ ·ㄌㄧ ㄔㄨㄤ)
a glass window

玻利維亞(ㄅㄛ ㄌㄧˋ ㄨㄟˊ ㄧㄚˋ)
Bolivia

【珀】3427
ㄆㄛˋ poh pò
amber

【珈】3428
ㄐㄧㄚ jia jiā
a kind of jewelry

六畫

【珙】3429
ㄍㄨㄥˇ goong gǒng
a large piece of jadestone

【珥】3430
ㄦˇ eel ěr
1. an ear ornament of pearl or
jade
2. to stick; to insert

【珞】3431
ㄌㄨㄛˋ luoh luò
jade ornaments for the neck

【珠】3432
ㄓㄨ ju zhū
1. a pearl
2. a bead; a drop
3. the pupil of the eye
4. a Chinese family name

珠箔(ㄓㄨ ㄅㄛˊ)
a curtain of pearls; a screen
of beads

珠寶(ㄓㄨ ㄅㄠˇ)
jewelry; pearls and valu-
ables; gems

珠蚌(ㄓㄨ ㄅㄤˋ)
the oysters or mollusks that
produce pearls; the pearl
oyster

珠母(ㄓㄨ ㄇㄨˇ)

the pearl oyster

珠胎暗結(ㄓㄨ ㄊㄞ ㄢˋ ㄐㄧㄝˊ)
to be pregnant (as a result
of a love affair)

珠淚(ㄓㄨ ㄌㄟˋ)
tears

珠簾(ㄓㄨ ㄌㄧㄢˊ)
a curtain or screen of pearls
or beads

珠聯璧合(ㄓㄨ ㄌㄧㄢˊ ㄅㄧˋ ㄏㄜˊ)
an excellent match (espe-
cially referring to mar-
riage); a perfect pair; a
happy combination

珠履(ㄓㄨ ㄌㄩˇ)
shoes with pearls as ornament

珠光寶氣(ㄓㄨ ㄍㄨㄤ ㄅㄠˇ ㄑㄧˋ)
(said of wealthy women)
sparkling with pearls and
precious stones; to be richly
bejeweled

珠宮貝闕(ㄓㄨ ㄍㄨㄥ ㄅㄟˋ ㄑㄩㄝˋ)
the palace for the god of
water

珠喉(ㄓㄨ ㄏㄡˊ)
the smooth and sweet voice
of a vocalist

珠汗(ㄓㄨ ㄏㄢˋ)
beads of perspiration

珠還合浦(ㄓㄨ ㄏㄨㄢˊ ㄏㄜˊ ㄆㄨˇ)
the return of a valuable
thing to its rightful owner

珠鷄(ㄓㄨ ㄐㄧ)
a guinea fowl (Numida
meleagris)

珠璣(ㄓㄨ ㄐㄧ)
exquisite or excellent wording of a piece of writing

珠江(ㄓㄨ ㄐㄧㄤ)
the Pearl River in Kwang-
tung Province

珠江三角洲(ㄓㄨ ㄐㄧㄤ ㄙㄢ ㄐㄧㄠˇ ㄓㄡ)
the delta of the Pearl River

珠子(ㄓㄨ ·ㄗ)
pearls; beads: 這串珠子多少
錢? How much is this string
of beads?

珠翠(ㄓㄨ ㄘㄨㄟˋ)
pearls and jades—head ornaments of a woman

珠算(ㄓㄨ ㄙㄨㄢˋ)
calculation with an abacus

珠兒(ㄓㄨ ㄦ)
beads

珠圍翠繞(ㄓㄨ ㄨㄟ ㄘㄨㄟ ㄖㄠˋ)
①(said of women) richly ornamented ②surrounded by pretty waiting maids

珠玉(ㄓㄨ ㄩˋ)
①beautifully written verses or articles ②elegant and stately (in appearance)

珠圓玉潤(ㄓㄨ ㄩㄢˊ ㄩˋ ㄖㄨㄣˋ)
①smooth and sweet (voice) ②smooth and easy (style in writing)

【珩】 3433
ㄏㄥˊ herng héng
the top gem of the pendants from a girdle

【班】 3434
ㄅㄢ ban bān
1. a grade; a rank or position
2. a class or company; a set; a group
3. a squad (of soldiers)
4. to distribute
5. to return
6. same as 斑 — variegated; of different colors
7. of equal rank, same generation, etc.
8. a shift; duty
9. scheduled runs (of the bus, etc.)
10. a Chinese family name

班駁(ㄅㄢ ㄅㄛˊ)or 班駁陸離(ㄅㄢ ㄅㄛˊ ㄌㄨˋ ㄌㄧˊ)
variegated; of different colors

班白 or 斑白(ㄅㄢ ㄅㄞˊ)or(ㄅㄢ ㄅㄞˊ)
gray-headed; graying: 他的頭髮已經班白。His hair has turned gray.

班班(ㄅㄢ ㄅㄢ)
①clear and apparent ②the noise of moving wagons

班門弄斧(ㄅㄢ ㄇㄣˊ ㄋㄨㄥˋ ㄈㄨˇ)
to show off one's talent or skill before an expert: 我不敢在他面前班門弄斧。I dare not show off my skill before him.

班底(ㄅㄢ ㄉㄧˇ)
①ordinary members of a theatrical troupe ②(in politics, etc.) loyal supporters; hard-core followers

班頭(ㄅㄢ ㄊㄡˊ)
the leader of longshoremen or pedicab drivers at a specific locality

班列(ㄅㄢ ㄌㄧㄝˋ)
relative ranks; order or sequence

班固(ㄅㄢ ㄍㄨˋ)
Pan Ku (32-92 A.D.), who completed the *History of the Han Dynasty* begun by his father

班行(ㄅㄢ ㄏㄤˊ)
in the same rank

班機(ㄅㄢ ㄐㄧ)
an airliner on the scheduled flight: 這是快速班機。This is a fast airliner.

班級(ㄅㄢ ㄐㄧˊ)
a grade; a form; a class

班昭(ㄅㄢ ㄓㄠ)
Pan Chao (c. 49-120), sister of 班固, a famous authoress

班長(ㄅㄢ ㄓㄤˇ)
①(military) a squad leader ②(in school) the leader of a class; a dux; a class monitor

班車(ㄅㄢ ㄔㄜ)
a regular bus

班超(ㄅㄢ ㄔㄠ)
Pan Ch'ao (32-102 A.D.), a younger brother of Pan Ku (班固), known for his exploits in the Western Regions (西域)

班禪(ㄅㄢ ㄔㄢˊ)
the Panchen Lama (of Tibet)

班師(ㄅㄢ ㄕ)
to withdraw troops after a victorious campaign

班子(ㄅㄢ ㄗˇ)
①an operatic company ②a brothel

班次(ㄅㄢ ㄘˋ)
①the flight number of an airliner ②the designated number of a scheduled train ③the grade or class (of a student): 在學校時, 他的班次比我高。At school he is in a higher class than I. ④ sequence

【珪】 3435
ㄍㄨㄟ guei guī
a jade tablet worn by feudal princes as a symbol of authority

【珣】 3436
ㄒㄩㄣˊ shyun xún
name of a kind of jade

【珮】 3437
(佩) ㄆㄟˋ pey pèi
jade pendants

【琉】 3438
ㄌㄧㄡˊ liou liú
1. a glossy and bright stone
2. glazed

琉璃(ㄌㄧㄡˊ ㄌㄧˊ)
①glass ②a glasslike substance; porcelain ③colored glaze ④glossy gems

琉璃廠(ㄌㄧㄡˊ ㄌㄧˊ ㄔㄤˇ)
a place in Peking where bookstores are concentrated —so named because it was originally the site of a porcelain kiln

琉璃草(ㄌㄧㄡˊ ㄌㄧˊ ㄘㄠˇ)
a forget-me-not 亦作「毋忘我草」

琉璃瓦(ㄌㄧㄡˊ ㄌㄧˊ ㄨㄚˇ)
encaustic tiles; glazed tiles

琉球(ㄌㄧㄡˊ ㄑㄧㄡˊ)
Ryukyu

七畫

【現】 3439
ㄒㄧㄢˋ shiann xiàn
1. to emerge; to appear; to reveal
2. current; now; present; modern
3. in time of need; extempore
4. cash
5. ready; available
6. actual

現批(ㄒㄧㄢˋ ㄆㄧ)
to make purchases in cash

現買現賣(ㄒㄧㄢˋ ㄇㄞˇ ㄒㄧㄢˋ ㄇㄞˋ)
to sell something right after it is bought

現代(ㄒㄧㄢˋ ㄉㄞˋ)
modern; current; present; in modern times; the present world; the present age

現代化(ㄒㄧㄢˋ ㄉㄞˋ ㄏㄨㄚˋ)
to modernize; modernization

現代史(ㄒㄧㄢˋ ㄉㄞˋ ㄕˇ)
contemporary history; modern history

現代作家(ㄒㄧㄢˋ ㄉㄞˋ ㄗㄨㄛˋ ㄐㄧㄚ)
a contemporary writer; a modern writer

現代音樂(ㄒㄧㄢˋ ㄉㄞˋ ㄧㄣ ㄩㄝˋ)
modern music

現代五項運動(ㄒㄧㄢˋ ㄉㄞˋ ㄨˇ ㄒㄧㄤˋ

〔玉部〕

【玉部】

現代五項 (ㄒㄧㄢˋ ㄉㄞˋ)
modern pentathlon

現代文學 (ㄒㄧㄢˋ ㄉㄞˋ ㄨㄣˊ ㄒㄩㄝˊ)
contemporary literature;
modern literature

現露 (ㄒㄧㄢˋ ㄌㄨˋ)
to reveal; to come to the
open; to unveil

現款 (ㄒㄧㄢˋ ㄎㄨㄢˇ)
cash; ready money

現貨 (ㄒㄧㄢˋ ㄏㄨㄛˋ)
stock goods; goods on hand;
spots

現貨交易 (ㄒㄧㄢˋ ㄏㄨㄛˋ ㄐㄧㄠ ㄧˋ)
spot transactions

現貨市場 (ㄒㄧㄢˋ ㄏㄨㄛˋ ㄕˋ ㄔㄤˇ)
the spot market

現階段 (ㄒㄧㄢˋ ㄐㄧㄝ ㄉㄨㄢˋ)
the present stage

現今 (ㄒㄧㄢˋ ㄐㄧㄣ)
nowadays; at present; now

現金 (ㄒㄧㄢˋ ㄐㄧㄣ)
cash; ready money

現金買賣 (ㄒㄧㄢˋ ㄐㄧㄣ ㄇㄞˇ ㄇㄞˋ) or
現金交易 (ㄒㄧㄢˋ ㄐㄧㄣ ㄐㄧㄠ ㄧˋ)
business transactions in
cash; cash transactions

現錢 (ㄒㄧㄢˋ ㄑㄧㄢˊ)
ready money; cash

現下 (ㄒㄧㄢˋ ㄒㄧㄚˋ)
now; at present

現象 (ㄒㄧㄢˋ ㄒㄧㄤˋ)
phenomena; appearances

現象界 (ㄒㄧㄢˋ ㄒㄧㄤˋ ㄐㄧㄝˋ)
the phenomenal world

現象學 (ㄒㄧㄢˋ ㄒㄧㄤˋ ㄒㄩㄝˊ)
the phenomenology

現形 (ㄒㄧㄢˋ ㄒㄧㄥˊ)
to reveal one's true colors,
form, character, etc.

現行 (ㄒㄧㄢˋ ㄒㄧㄥˊ)
existing; presently valid or
effective; in force: 我們將維
持現行政策。 We'll maintain
the existing policies.

現行法 (ㄒㄧㄢˋ ㄒㄧㄥˊ ㄈㄚˇ)
the law actually in force;
the existing law

現行犯 (ㄒㄧㄢˋ ㄒㄧㄥˊ ㄈㄢˋ)
a person *flagrante delicto*

現職 (ㄒㄧㄢˋ ㄓˊ)
the present job; a current
post or position

現狀 (ㄒㄧㄢˋ ㄓㄨㄤˋ)
things as they are; the *status
quo*: 他們企圖維持現狀。 They

seek to preserve the *status
quo*.

現場 (ㄒㄧㄢˋ ㄔㄤˇ)
the scene (of an incident);
a site; a spot: 警察匆忙趕到
作案現場。 The police hurried
to the scene of the crime.

現場表演 (ㄒㄧㄢˋ ㄔㄤˇ ㄅㄧㄠˇ ㄧㄢˇ)
① to reenact a crime by a
criminal at the same scene
after he is caught ② a live
show

現場採訪 (ㄒㄧㄢˋ ㄔㄤˇ ㄘㄞˇ ㄈㄤˇ)
spot coverage

現成 (ㄒㄧㄢˋ ㄔㄥˊ)
ready; ready-made; at hand:
他常買現成的衣服。 He often
buys ready-made clothes.

現成飯 (ㄒㄧㄢˋ ㄔㄥˊ ㄈㄢˋ)
(literally) food which has
already been prepared—benefits, etc. that one can readily reap without exertion

現成話 (ㄒㄧㄢˋ ㄔㄥˊ ㄏㄨㄚˋ)
I-told-you-so remarks; an onlooker's unsolicited com-
ments

現實 (ㄒㄧㄢˋ ㄕˊ)
① reality; things as they are:
你不知道人生的現實。 You do
not know the realities of
life. ② practical; pragmatic;
real; actual

現實主義 (ㄒㄧㄢˋ ㄕˊ ㄓㄨˇ ㄧˋ)
realism; pragmatism

現實生活 (ㄒㄧㄢˋ ㄕˊ ㄕㄥ ㄏㄨㄛˊ)
the real life; the actual life

現勢 (ㄒㄧㄢˋ ㄕˋ)
the present situation; the
current situation

現世 (ㄒㄧㄢˋ ㄕˋ)
① the present nowadays; present; this life ② to be disgraced; to bring shame on
oneself

現世報 (ㄒㄧㄢˋ ㄕˋ ㄅㄠˋ)
retribution in one's own lifetime

現身說法 (ㄒㄧㄢˋ ㄕㄣ ㄕㄨㄛ ㄈㄚˇ)
to act as an example to
others; to give a demonstration in person

現任 (ㄒㄧㄢˋ ㄖㄣˋ)
present (position, job, or
employment); incumbent: 現
任校長過去是教師。 The pres-
ent principal used to be a

teacher.

現在 (ㄒㄧㄢˋ ㄗㄞˋ)
now; at present

現在完成式 (ㄒㄧㄢˋ ㄗㄞˋ ㄨㄢˊ ㄔㄥˊ ㄕˋ)
(English grammar) the present perfect tense

現存 (ㄒㄧㄢˋ ㄘㄨㄣˊ)
in stock; on hand; available

現役 (ㄒㄧㄢˋ ㄧˋ)
active (military) service;
active duty

現役軍人 (ㄒㄧㄢˋ ㄧˋ ㄐㄩㄣ ㄖㄣˊ)
military personnel on active
service

現有 (ㄒㄧㄢˋ ㄧㄡˇ)
to have on hand; available;
existing

現眼 (ㄒㄧㄢˋ ㄧㄢˇ)
to lose face; to be embarrassed; to make a scene; to
cut a sorry figure: 他在眾人
面前丟人現眼。 He made a
fool of himself in public.

現銀 (ㄒㄧㄢˋ ㄧㄣˊ)
ready cash (originally referring to silver coins)

現洋 (ㄒㄧㄢˋ ㄧㄤˊ)
① silver dollars 亦作「現大洋」
② ready cash

【球】 3440
ㄑㄧㄡˊ chyou qiú

1. a ball or anything shaped
like a ball: 請把球傳給我。
Please pass the ball.

2. the globe; the earth: 全球戰
略 the global strategy

球板 (ㄑㄧㄡˊ ㄅㄢˇ)
paddles (for hitting ping-
pong, etc.)

球拍 (ㄑㄧㄡˊ ㄆㄞ)
rackets (for tennis, etc.)

球門 (ㄑㄧㄡˊ ㄇㄣˊ)
(in football, etc.) the goal

球門球 (ㄑㄧㄡˊ ㄇㄣˊ ㄑㄧㄡˊ)
(football) goal kick

球迷 (ㄑㄧㄡˊ ㄇㄧˊ)
fans of ball games: 我弟弟是
棒球迷。 My younger brother
is a baseball fan.

球面 (ㄑㄧㄡˊ ㄇㄧㄢˋ)
(mathematics) spherical surface

球面幾何學 (ㄑㄧㄡˊ ㄇㄧㄢˋ ㄐㄧ ㄏㄜˊ ㄒㄩㄝˊ)
spherical geometry

球房 (ㄑㄧㄡˊ ㄈㄤˊ)
a gym where ball games

(especially table tennis) are played

球膽(ㄑㄧㄡˊ ㄉㄢˇ)
a ball bladder

球隊(ㄑㄧㄡˊ ㄉㄨㄟˋ)
teams for playing ball games: 我不是任何球隊的球員。I am not on any football team.

球僮(ㄑㄧㄡˊ ㄊㄨㄥˊ)
a caddy

球類(ㄑㄧㄡˊ ㄌㄟˋ)
kinds of balls—football, basketball, baseball, etc.

球根(ㄑㄧㄡˊ ㄍㄣ)
bulbous roots

球莖(ㄑㄧㄡˊ ㄐㄧㄥ)
bulbs or corms

球徑(ㄑㄧㄡˊ ㄐㄧㄥˋ)
the diameter of a sphere

球徑計(ㄑㄧㄡˊ ㄐㄧㄥˋ ㄐㄧˋ)
a spherometer

球戲(ㄑㄧㄡˊ ㄒㄧˋ)
a ball game

球鞋(ㄑㄧㄡˊ ㄒㄧㄝˊ)
tennis shoes; sneakers: 她每天都穿球鞋。She wears a pair of tennis shoes every day.

球形(ㄑㄧㄡˊ ㄒㄧㄥˊ)
spherical; globular; bulbous: 他建了一棟球形小屋。He has built a little globular house.

球穴(ㄑㄧㄡˊ ㄒㄩㄝˊ)
a hole

球證(ㄑㄧㄡˊ ㄓㄥˋ)
a referee or an umpire of a ball game

球狀花序(ㄑㄧㄡˊ ㄓㄨㄤˋ ㄏㄨㄚ ㄒㄩˋ)
(botany) strobilus

球狀菌(ㄑㄧㄡˊ ㄓㄨㄤˋ ㄐㄩㄣˋ)or 球菌(ㄑㄧㄡˊ ㄐㄩㄣˋ)
(microbiology) coccus

球場(ㄑㄧㄡˊ ㄔㄤˇ)or(ㄑㄧㄡˊ ㄔㄤˇ)
a playground for ball games

球賽(ㄑㄧㄡˊ ㄙㄞˋ)
a ball game

球兒(ㄑㄧㄡˊ ㄦ)
a ball: 他把球兒踢開。He kicked the ball away.

球衣(ㄑㄧㄡˊ ㄧ)
the jacket for a ballplayer

球員(ㄑㄧㄡˊ ㄩㄢˊ)
a ballplayer

球運(ㄑㄧㄡˊ ㄩㄣˋ)
①the luck of a team during a ball game ②movements

or drives for the promotion of ball games

【理】 3441
ㄌㄧˇ lǐ
1. reason; logic; cause; truth; right; righteousness
2. law; principles; doctrine; theory; science
3. to arrange
4. to administer; to govern; to operate; to regulate; to manage; to run
5. to reply or answer; to respond
6. texture; grain (in wood, skin, etc.)
7. name of a religious sect
8. a Chinese family name

理賠(ㄌㄧˇ ㄆㄟˊ)
(insurance) adjustment

理髮(ㄌㄧˇ ㄈㄚˇ)
to cut the hair, to have a haircut: 他昨天去理髮。He had his hair cut yesterday.

理髮店(ㄌㄧˇ ㄈㄚˇ ㄉㄧㄢˋ)or 理髮廳(ㄌㄧˇ ㄈㄚˇ ㄊㄧㄥ)or 理髮館(ㄌㄧˇ ㄈㄚˇ ㄍㄨㄢˇ)
a barbershop: 昨天我到理髮店理髮。I had a haircut at the barbershop yesterday.

理髮小姐(ㄌㄧˇ ㄈㄚˇ ㄒㄧㄠˇ ㄐㄧㄝˇ)
a woman barber

理髮師(ㄌㄧˇ ㄈㄚˇ ㄕ)
a barber; a hairdresser

理藩院(ㄌㄧˇ ㄈㄢˊ ㄩㄢˋ)
the Ministry of Tribal Affairs in the Ching Dynasty, roughly equivalent to the Commission on Mongolian and Tibetan Affairs of the republican era

理當(ㄌㄧˇ ㄉㄤ)
ought to; to be obliged to; should; duty-bound: 理當如此。That's just as it should be.

理短(ㄌㄧˇ ㄉㄨㄢˇ)
to be on the wrong side; to have no justification

理念(ㄌㄧˇ ㄋㄧㄢˋ)
a rational concept; an idea

理路(ㄌㄧˇ ㄌㄨˋ)
logical thinking

理歸(ㄌㄧˇ ㄍㄨㄟ)
①to put in order; to wipe out confusion with sound administration ②orderliness

and confusion; peace and turmoil

理論(ㄌㄧˇ ㄌㄨㄣˋ)
①theory; theoretical ②to argue; to debate: 我和我的老闆理論。I argued with my boss.

理論科學(ㄌㄧˇ ㄌㄨㄣˋ ㄎㄜ ㄒㄩㄝˊ)
theoretical or pure sciences

理論家(ㄌㄧˇ ㄌㄨㄣˋ ㄐㄧㄚ)
theoreticians: 他是軍事理論家。He is a military theoretician.

理論與實際(ㄌㄧˇ ㄌㄨㄣˋ ㄩˇ ㄕˊ ㄐㄧˋ)
theory and reality; ideals and facts

理該(ㄌㄧˇ ㄍㄞ)
duty-bound; should; ought to: 他理該幫助他兄弟。He was duty-bound to help his brother.

理工科(ㄌㄧˇ ㄍㄨㄥ ㄎㄜ)
departments of natural sciences and engineering in a college

理科(ㄌㄧˇ ㄎㄜ)
departments of natural sciences in a college or university

理虧(ㄌㄧˇ ㄎㄨㄟ)
to be on the wrong side; to be in the wrong; to have no justification: 他承認自己理虧。He admitted that he was in the wrong

理合(ㄌㄧˇ ㄏㄜˊ)
good reasons dictate that…; (in documentary usage) ought to…; duty-bound; as a matter of course

理化(ㄌㄧˇ ㄏㄨㄚˋ)
①physics and chemistry ②politics and education; to govern and educate

理會(ㄌㄧˇ ㄏㄨㄟˋ)
①to understand; to comprehend: 這很難理會。It's difficult to understand. ②to care; to heed; to take notice of; to pay attention to: 不要理會他們。Don't pay attention to them.

理家(ㄌㄧˇ ㄐㄧㄚ)
to manage domestic affairs; to housekeep

理解(ㄌㄧˇ ㄐㄧㄝˇ)
to comprehend; to under-

(與)

stand: 請用孩子能夠理解的字眼。Please use words that the child can comprehend.

理解力 (ㄌㄧˇ ㄐㄧㄝˇ ㄌㄧˋ)
the faculty of comprehension; understanding; perception: 這問題超出我的理解力。The problem is beyond my comprehension.

理教 (ㄌㄧˇ ㄐㄧㄠˋ)
name of a religious sect founded by Yang lai-ju (羊來如) of the early Ching Dynasty, which advocates clean living

理屈 (ㄌㄧˇ ㄑㄩ)
to be on the wrong side; cannot appeal to good reasoning

理屈詞窮 (ㄌㄧˇ ㄑㄩ ㄘˊ ㄑㄩㄥˊ)
to be on the wrong side and unable to say a word in self-defense

理想 (ㄌㄧˇ ㄒㄧㄤˇ)
① ideal: 這種天氣玩棒球很理想。This weather is ideal for playing baseball. ② ideas; thought

理想的 (ㄌㄧˇ ㄒㄧㄤˇ ·ㄉㄜ)
ideal; ideally; theoretically

理想國 (ㄌㄧˇ ㄒㄧㄤˇ ㄍㄨㄛˊ)
① Utopia, an imaginary island described in Sir Thomas More's *Utopia* ② a utopia; an ideal state

理想化 (ㄌㄧˇ ㄒㄧㄤˇ ㄏㄨㄚˋ)
to idealize

理想家 (ㄌㄧˇ ㄒㄧㄤˇ ㄐㄧㄚ)
idealists

理想主義 (ㄌㄧˇ ㄒㄧㄤˇ ㄓㄨˇ ㄧˋ)
idealism

理性 (ㄌㄧˇ ㄒㄧㄥˋ)
(philosophy) reason; rationality: 他似乎失去理性。It seems that he has lost his reason.

理性主義 (ㄌㄧˇ ㄒㄧㄥˋ ㄓㄨˇ ㄧˋ)
rationalism

理學 (ㄌㄧˇ ㄒㄩㄝˊ)
① natural sciences ② a school of learning in the Sung Dynasty devoted to the study of the classics with a rational approach

理學博士 (ㄌㄧˇ ㄒㄩㄝˊ ㄅㄛˊ ㄕˋ)
Doctor of Science (D. Sc.)

理學家 (ㄌㄧˇ ㄒㄩㄝˊ ㄐㄧㄚ)
a scholar devoted to the study of the classics with a philosophical approach

理學學士 (ㄌㄧˇ ㄒㄩㄝˊ ㄒㄩㄝˊ ㄕˋ)
Bachelor of Science (B. Sc.)

理學碩士 (ㄌㄧˇ ㄒㄩㄝˊ ㄕㄨㄛˋ ㄕˋ)
Master of Science (M. Sc.)

理直氣壯 (ㄌㄧˇ ㄓˊ ㄑㄧˋ ㄓㄨㄤˋ)
(to speak, act, etc.) with confidence for one knows that he is in the right; to be fearless with the knowledge that one is on the side of justice: 他理直氣壯地回答。He replied with perfect assurance.

理智 (ㄌㄧˇ ㄓˋ)
intellect; reason (as opposed to emotion): 他已喪失理智。He has lost his reason.

理查 (ㄌㄧˇ ㄔㄚˊ)
transliteration of Richard

理查遜 (ㄌㄧˇ ㄔㄚˊ ㄒㄩㄣˋ)
transliteration of Richardson

理事 (ㄌㄧˇ ㄕˋ)
① to manage or administer affairs: 他病得太嚴重,理事。He is too sick to manage affairs. ② an administrator ③ board directors (of a company)

理事國 (ㄌㄧˇ ㄕˋ ㄍㄨㄛˊ)
a member country of the Security Council of the United Nations

理事會 (ㄌㄧˇ ㄕˋ ㄏㄨㄟˋ)
the board of directors; a council

理事長 (ㄌㄧˇ ㄕˋ ㄓㄤˇ)
the board chairman; chairman of the board of directors

理則學 (ㄌㄧˇ ㄗㄜˊ ㄒㄩㄝˊ)
logic 亦作「邏輯學」

理財 (ㄌㄧˇ ㄘㄞˊ)
to manage or administer finances; to conduct financial transactions

理財家 (ㄌㄧˇ ㄘㄞˊ ㄐㄧㄚ)
a financier

理睬 (ㄌㄧˇ ㄘㄞˇ)
to pay attention to; to care; to heed: 沒人理睬他。Nobody pays any attention to him.

理塞 (ㄌㄧˇ ㄙㄜˋ)
to be in the wrong; to have no excuse

理所當然 (ㄌㄧˇ ㄙㄨㄛˇ ㄉㄤ ㄖㄢˊ)
as a matter of course; naturally; natural

理由 (ㄌㄧˇ ㄧㄡˊ)
reasons; grounds; causes; explanations: 我有充分理由相信你是對的。I have every reason to believe that you are right.

理由書 (ㄌㄧˇ ㄧㄡˊ ㄕㄨ)
(law) a statement in which one states one's reasons, causes or grounds for a certain action

理當 (ㄌㄧˇ ㄉㄤ)
duty-bound; as a matter of course; ought to; obliged to: 我理應向他致謝。I'm in duty-bound to thank him.

理諭 (ㄌㄧˇ ㄩˋ)
to appeal with reason

【琅】 3442
ㄌㄤˊ lang láng
1. a kind of stone resembling jade
2. clean and white; pure; spotless
3. a Chinese family name

琅璫入獄 (ㄌㄤˊ ㄉㄤ ㄖㄨˋ ㄩˋ)
to be put in jail clanking with manacles

琅琅 (ㄌㄤˊ ㄌㄤˊ)
the tinkling or jingling of metals and jades

琅琅書聲 (ㄌㄤˊ ㄌㄤˊ ㄕㄨ ㄕㄥ)
the sound of reading aloud

琅玕 (ㄌㄤˊ ㄍㄢ)
a stone resembling jade

琅函 (ㄌㄤˊ ㄏㄢˊ)
① a bookcase ② (a polite expression) your letter

琅簡蘂書 (ㄌㄤˊ ㄐㄧㄢˇ ㄖㄨㄟˇ ㄕㄨ)
Taoist scriptures

琅書 (ㄌㄤˊ ㄕㄨ)
Taoist scriptures

琅邪 or 琅琊 (ㄌㄤˊ ㄧㄝˊ)
ancient name of Chiaochou (膠州), including the eastern part of Shantung (山東)

【邪】 3443
ㄧㄝˊ ye yé
used in 琅邪, ancient name of the eastern portion of Shantung (山東); also name of a mountain in eastern Shantung

八畫

【瑓】 3444
(盞) ㄓㄢ jaan zhǎn
a jade wine-cup or chalice

【琛】 3445
ㄔㄣ chen chēn
treasures; jewelry or valuables

【琢】 3446
ㄓㄨㄛ jwo zhuó
1. to cut, chisel or polish jade, gems
2. to improve (literary works); to polish; to refine

琢磨(ㄓㄨㄛ ㄇㄛ)
① to cut and polish ② to study and improve; to mold (oneself) ③ to ponder over; to consider

琢句(ㄓㄨㄛ ㄐㄩ)
sentence formation; to write and polish phrases and sentences

【琚】 3447
ㄐㄩ jiu jū
a gem worn at the girdle-pendant

【琤】 3448
ㄔㄥ cheng chēng
a tinkling sound—descriptive of jangling, twanging, or gurgling (of flowing water)

琤琤(ㄔㄥ ㄔㄥ)
① the sound of plucking stringed musical instrument ② the sound of flowing water or stream

琤瑽(ㄔㄥ ㄘㄨㄥ)
the tinkling of jade pendants

【琦】 3449
ㄑㄧ chyi qí
1. a kind of jade
2. same as 奇—strange
3. outstanding; extraordinary; distinguished; admirable

琦瑋(ㄑㄧ ㄨㄟ)
① fine jades ② distinguished

【琨】 3450
ㄎㄨㄣ kuen kūn
fine rocks next to jade in quality

琨庭(ㄎㄨㄣ ㄊㄧㄥ)
a yard dotted with white stones

【琪】 3451
ㄑㄧ chyi qí
a piece of jade; a jadelike precious stone; a white gem

琪花瑤草(ㄑㄧ ㄏㄨㄚ ㄧㄠ ㄘㄠ)
blossoms and vegetation in the fairyland

琪樹(ㄑㄧ ㄕㄨ)
① a jade tree in myth ② a tree whose branches hang down like willows and bear berries

【琥】 3452
ㄏㄨ huu hǔ
1. a jade ornament in the shape of a tiger
2. amber

琥珀(ㄏㄨ ㄆㄛ)
amber

琥珀酸(ㄏㄨ ㄆㄛ ㄙㄨㄢ)
succinic acid

【琺】 3453
ㄈㄚ fah fà
enamel; enamelware

琺瑯(ㄈㄚ ㄌㄤ)
enamel

琺瑯質(ㄈㄚ ㄌㄤ ㄓ)
enamel—especially referring to the hard, white glossy coating of teeth

【琬】 3454
ㄨㄢ woan wǎn
1. a kind of jade tablet slightly tapering at the top
2. the virtue of a gentleman

琬圭(ㄨㄢ ㄍㄨㄟ)
a kind of jade tablet held by feudal princes during the audience with the emperor

琬琰之章(ㄨㄢ ㄧㄢ ㄓ ㄓㄤ)
an esteemed letter

【琮】 3455
ㄘㄨㄥ tsong cóng
an octagonal jade piece with a round hole in the center

【琴】 3456
ㄑㄧㄣ chyn qín
1. *chin*, a Chinese fretted instrument with seven or five strings somewhat similar to the zither
2. a musical instrument—especially stringed, as the piano, the violin, etc.
3. a Chinese family name

琴譜(ㄑㄧㄣ ㄆㄨ)
a score for the lute, the guitar, the piano or other stringed instruments

琴囊(ㄑㄧㄣ ㄋㄤ)
a cloth bag for a *chin* (琴)

琴鳥(ㄑㄧㄣ ㄋㄧㄠ)
a lyrebird (*Menura superba*)

琴歌(ㄑㄧㄣ ㄍㄜ)
① a tune for stringed instruments ② to play stringed instruments and sing

琴鍵(ㄑㄧㄣ ㄐㄧㄢ)
a key

琴劍飄零(ㄑㄧㄣ ㄐㄧㄢ ㄆㄧㄠ ㄌㄧㄥ)
(said of impoverished men of letters) wandering from place to place

琴棋書畫(ㄑㄧㄣ ㄑㄧ ㄕㄨ ㄏㄨㄚ)
music, chess, calligraphy and painting—the secondary accomplishments of an all-round scholar

琴弦(ㄑㄧㄣ ㄒㄧㄢ)
the string of a stringed instrument: 她將小提琴的琴弦上緊。 She tightened the strings of her violin.

琴心(ㄑㄧㄣ ㄒㄧㄣ)
the emotional appeal through lute playing

琴心劍膽(ㄑㄧㄣ ㄒㄧㄣ ㄐㄧㄢ ㄉㄢ)
music and swordsmanship—the qualities of an accomplished scholar

琴床(ㄑㄧㄣ ㄔㄨㄤ)
a stand or prop for a stringed instrument

琴師(ㄑㄧㄣ ㄕ)
a player of the stringed instrument; a pianist

琴手(ㄑㄧㄣ ㄕㄡ)
a player of the stringed instrument

琴書(ㄑㄧㄣ ㄕㄨ)
① the music of a lute ② title of a music book ③ name of a prostitute in the Sung Dynasty

琴瑟(ㄑㄧㄣ ㄙㄜ)
① *chin* and *se*, two Chinese instruments ② a married couple

琴瑟不調(ㄑㄧㄣ ㄙㄜ ㄅㄨ ㄊㄧㄠ)
discord between husband and wife; a marriage on the rocks

琴瑟調和(ㄑㄧㄣ ㄙㄜ ㄊㄧㄠ ㄏㄜ)
a happy married life; conjugal harmony

【玉部】

琴瑟和鳴(ㄑㄧㄣˊ ㄙㄜˋ ㄏㄜˊ ㄇㄧㄥˊ)
marital harmony; conjugal
bliss

【琵】 3457
ㄆㄧˊ pyi pí
the four-stringed guitar or
the balloon-guitar

琵琶(ㄆㄧˊ ·ㄆㄚˊ)
pi-pa—a short-necked fretted
lute of Chinese origin

琵琶撥(ㄆㄧˊ ·ㄆㄚˊ ㄅㄛ)
a plectrum

琵琶別抱(ㄆㄧˊ ·ㄆㄚˊ ㄅㄧㄝˊ ㄅㄠˋ)
the remarriage of a woman;
to marry another husband

琵琶骨(ㄆㄧˊ ·ㄆㄚˊ ㄍㄨˇ)
the collarbone

琵琶記(ㄆㄧˊ ·ㄆㄚˊ ㄐㄧˋ)
name of a well-known
Chinese drama

【琶】 3458
ㄆㄚˊ par pá
(顧音 ·ㄆㄚˊ ·pa
po)
a four-stringed guitar or
balloon-guitar

【琳】 3459
ㄌㄧㄣˊ lin lín
a fine piece of jade; a gem

琳琅 or 琳瑯(ㄌㄧㄣˊ ㄌㄤˊ)
① fine jades ② people of
outstanding talent ③ pre-
cious collection of books ④
the tinkling of jade pendants

琳琅滿目(ㄌㄧㄣˊ ㄌㄤˊ ㄇㄢˇ ㄇㄨˋ)
(literally) Good gems fill
the eyes.—a vast array of
beautiful and fine things

琳宮(ㄌㄧㄣˊ ㄍㄨㄥ)or 琳宇(ㄌㄧㄣˊ ㄩˇ)
a Taoist monastery

【琰】 3460
ㄧㄢˇ yean yǎn
the glitter of gems

琰圭(ㄧㄢˇ ㄍㄨㄟ)
a jade tablet with a pointed
top

【琯】 3461
ㄍㄨㄢˇ goan guǎn
1. a jade tube used as an
instrument in ancient times
2. to polish precious metals or
stones

九畫

【瑟】 3462
ㄙㄜˋ seh sè
1. se, a large horizontal musi-

cal instrument, about nine
feet long, originally with 50
strings which was later
reduced to 25 with movable
bridges for tuning
2. varied and many
3. elegant and stately; majestic
4. bright and clear; pure and
clean
5. same as 索—alone; lonely;
solitary

瑟堡(ㄙㄜˋ ㄅㄠˇ)
Cherbourg, a French port

瑟調(ㄙㄜˋ ㄉㄧㄠˋ)
a form in Chinese "Collection of Tunes" (樂府) consisting of 38 tunes, played with
seven musical instruments

瑟瑟(ㄙㄜˋ ㄙㄜˋ)
① the heaving sound of
wind ② the turquoise

瑟縮(ㄙㄜˋ ㄙㄨˋ)
① stiff and numb—as from
cold ② timid and trembling;
to shrink—as from fear ③
the heaving sound of wind

【瑁】 3463
ㄇㄟˋ mey mèi
a tortoise shell

【瑁】 3463
ㄇㄠˋ maw mào
a very precious piece of jade
worn by ancient emperors to
match tablets borne by the
nobles

【瑋】 3464
ㄨㄟˇ woei wěi
1. a kind of jade
2. rare; precious; splendorous

【瑄】 3465
ㄒㄩㄢ shiuan xuān
an ornamental piece of jade
about 6.5 inches in diameter

【瑑】 3466
ㄓㄨㄢˋ juann zhuàn
engraving on a jade tablet

【瑕】 3467
ㄒㄧㄚˊ shya xiá
1. a flaw, spot, or blemish in a
piece of jade
2. a fault, error, blemish or
flaw

瑕病(ㄒㄧㄚˊ ㄅㄧㄥˋ)
a blemish; a flaw

瑕不掩瑜(ㄒㄧㄚˊ ㄅㄨˋ ㄧㄢˇ ㄩˊ)
The defects do not outweigh
the merits.

瑕玷(ㄒㄧㄚˊ ㄉㄧㄢˋ)
flaws and defects

瑕釁(ㄒㄧㄚˊ ㄒㄧㄣˋ)
faults and errors

瑕謫(ㄒㄧㄚˊ ㄓㄜˊ)
blemishes and flaws; errors

瑕疵(ㄒㄧㄚˊ ㄘ)
defects; flaws; blemishes

瑕瑜(ㄒㄧㄚˊ ㄩˊ)
good and bad points; virtues
and flaws

瑕瑜互見(ㄒㄧㄚˊ ㄩˊ ㄏㄨˋ ㄐㄧㄢˋ)
(said of a single person) to
have both good and bad
qualities; (said of two measures, persons, etc.) each
having strong and weak
points

【瑙】 3468
ㄋㄠˇ nao nǎo
agate; cornelian

【瑛】 3469
ㄧㄥ ing yīng
1. the glitter or sheen of jade
2. a transparent piece of jade;
a crystal

【瑜】 3470
ㄩˊ yu yú
1. a fine and flawless piece of
jade; a perfect gem
2. the brilliancy of jade; the
luster of gems
3. excellencies; virtues
4. yoga, a mystic and ascetic
practice in Hindu philosophy

瑜不掩瑕(ㄩˊ ㄅㄨˋ ㄧㄢˇ ㄒㄧㄚˊ)
The merits do not outweigh
the defects.

瑜伽(ㄩˊ ㄑㄧㄝ)
yoga, a mystic and ascetic
practice in Hindu philosophy 亦作「瑜珈」

瑜伽派(ㄩˊ ㄑㄧㄝ ㄆㄞˋ)
the yoga sect of the Hindu
philosophy 亦作「瑜珈派」

瑜伽宗(ㄩˊ ㄑㄧㄝ ㄗㄨㄥ)
the Yogācara, or esoteric
sect (The principles of yoga
are accredited to Patanjali
in the second century B.C.,
later founded as a school in
Buddhism by Asanga, fourth
century A.D. Hstan Tsang
(玄奘) became a disciple
and advocate of this
school.) 亦作「瑜珈宗」

【瑞】 3471
ㄖㄨㄟˋ ruey ruì
1. something portending good

luck or fortune; good omen :
吉瑞 signs of good luck
2. lucky; auspicious; fortunate
3. a jade tablet given to feudal princes on their investiture, as a sign of authority and rank
4. a Chinese family name

瑞符 (ㄖㄨㄟˋ ㄈㄨˊ)
a credential tally in ancient China issued to the commander, etc. authorizing him to launch military operations

瑞典 (ㄖㄨㄟˋ ㄉㄧㄢˇ)
Sweden

瑞典人 (ㄖㄨㄟˋ ㄉㄧㄢˇ ㄖㄣˊ)
the Swedes

瑞圖 (ㄖㄨㄟˋ ㄊㄨˊ)
a drawing, or picture portending luck, good fortune, etc.

瑞腦 (ㄖㄨㄟˋ ㄋㄠˇ)
camphor from Borneo

瑞鳥 (ㄖㄨㄟˋ ㄋㄧㄠˇ)
an auspicious bird—a bird of good omen (in Chinese legends, known as 鸞)

瑞禾 (ㄖㄨㄟˋ ㄏㄜˊ)
an excellent crop 亦作「嘉禾」

瑞祥 (ㄖㄨㄟˋ ㄒㄧㄤˊ)
good luck; good fortune; good omen ; auspiciousness

瑞雪 (ㄖㄨㄟˋ ㄒㄩㄝˇ)
①a timely snow in late winter or early spring; a seasonable snow that will kill pests and that portends a bumper crop in the coming year ②a Chinese medicinal herb 亦作「桔梗根」

瑞雪兆豐年 (ㄖㄨㄟˋ ㄒㄩㄝˇ ㄓㄠˋ ㄈㄥ ㄋㄧㄢˊ)
A timely snow promises a good harvest.

瑞士 (ㄖㄨㄟˋ ㄕˋ)
Switzerland

瑞士人 (ㄖㄨㄟˋ ㄕˋ ㄖㄣˊ)
a Swiss; the Swiss people

瑞草 (ㄖㄨㄟˋ ㄘㄠˇ)
a legendary shrub, regarded as a good omen; the shrub of luck-tea

瑞應 (ㄖㄨㄟˋ ㄧㄥˋ)
the appearance of precious, rare and auspicious things as Heaven's response to the high virtue of the reigning monarch

瑞玉 (ㄖㄨㄟˋ ㄩˋ)
a piece of jade serving as the credentials of a feudal lord

瑞雲 (ㄖㄨㄟˋ ㄩㄣˊ)
auspicious clouds

【瑚】 3472
　ㄏㄨˊ hwu hú
coral

瑚璉 (ㄏㄨˊ ㄌㄧㄢˇ)
a sacrificial vessel for grains in the imperial ancestral shrine–a person of virtue and quality

【琿】 3473
　ㄏㄨㄣˊ hwen hún
a kind of precious jade

【瑗】 3474
　ㄩㄢˋ yuann yuàn
1. a huge ring of fine jade
2. name of a kind of jade

【瑀】 3475
　ㄩˇ yeu yǔ
a jadelike stone

十畫

【瑩】 3476
　ㄧㄥˊ yng yíng
1. the luster of jade
2. a jadelike pebble
3. smooth and glossy; clean and shining; bright and brilliant
4. transparent; pure
5. (said of a person) bright and clever

瑩潔 (ㄧㄥˊ ㄐㄧㄝˊ)
clean and lustrous; pure and clear

瑩鏡 (ㄧㄥˊ ㄐㄧㄥˋ)
a clear mirror

瑩徹 (ㄧㄥˊ ㄔㄜˋ)
clear and transparent

瑩潤 (ㄧㄥˊ ㄖㄨㄣˋ)
polished and glossy; clear and lustrous

瑩澤 (ㄧㄥˊ ㄗㄜˊ)
transparent and shiny

【瑤】 3477
　ㄧㄠˊ yau yáo
1. a precious jade or stone
2. clean, pure and white
3. treasurable; valuable; precious

瑤碧 (ㄧㄠˊ ㄅㄧˋ)
agate with a greenish luster

瑤圃 (ㄧㄠˊ ㄆㄨˇ)
the place where immortals live; a fairyland

瑤臺 (ㄧㄠˊ ㄊㄞˊ)
①a towerlike building or namented with gems ②a fairyland ③a beautiful terrace

瑤花 (ㄧㄠˊ ㄏㄨㄚ)
rare flowers

瑤華 (ㄧㄠˊ ㄏㄨㄚˊ)
①(ㄧㄠˊ ㄏㄨㄚ) blossoms as white and pure as jade ②(ㄧㄠˊ ㄏㄨㄚˊ) ⓐ treasurable; precious ⓑ fine jade

瑤箋 (ㄧㄠˊ ㄐㄧㄢ) or 瑤函 (ㄧㄠˊ ㄏㄢˊ)
(a polite expression) your letter

瑤琴 (ㄧㄠˊ ㄑㄧㄣˊ)
a lute studded or ornamented with gems

瑤池 (ㄧㄠˊ ㄔˊ)
the place where immortals live; a fairyland

瑤觴 (ㄧㄠˊ ㄕㄤ)
a jade wine-cup

瑤芙 (ㄧㄠˊ ㄈㄨ)
the most precious kind of jade

【瑣】 3478
　ㄙㄨㄛˇ suoo suǒ
1. trifles; petty; frivolous; trifling
2. troublesome; annoying
3. a jade chain
4. a palace gate

瑣瀆 (ㄙㄨㄛˇ ㄉㄨˊ)
to bother others with trifle matters

瑣細 (ㄙㄨㄛˇ ㄒㄧˋ)
①petty; trifling; frivolous ②troublesome

瑣屑 (ㄙㄨㄛˇ ㄒㄧㄝˋ)
petty; unimportant; insignificant; small

瑣事 (ㄙㄨㄛˇ ㄕˋ)
trifles; trivial matters

瑣辭 (ㄙㄨㄛˇ ㄘˊ)
petty or trivial talks; superfluous wording; annoying and uncalled-for utterances

瑣才 (ㄙㄨㄛˇ ㄘㄞˊ)
(said of persons) of little capability or talent

瑣碎 (ㄙㄨㄛˇ ㄙㄨㄟˋ)
①trifling; petty and varied;

〔玉部〕

〔玉部〕

他認爲那是瑣碎之事。He takes it as a trifling matter. ② a slight indisposition or ailment

瑣務
trifling matters

瑣尾流離 (ㄙㄨㄛ ㄨㄟ ㄌㄧㄡ ㄌㄧ)
to begin (a career, life, etc.) happily but end in failure

瑣聞 (ㄙㄨㄛ ㄨㄣ)
bits of unimportant information; sundry news or anecdotes

【瑯】 3479
　(瑯) ㄌㄤ lang lǎng
a stone resembling jade, pure and white

瑯嬛福地 (ㄌㄤ ㄏㄨㄢ ㄈㄨ ㄉㄧ)
library of a fairyland, where rare ancient books were stored

瑯琊 (ㄌㄤ ㄧㄝ)
① name of an ancient region in today's eastern Shantung Province ② name of a mountain in Shantung

【瑰】 3480
　ㄍㄨㄟ guei guī
1. fabulous; great; extraordinary
2. a stone which is a little less valuable than jade; a kind of jasper

瑰寶 (ㄍㄨㄟ ㄅㄠ)
a treasure; a gem

瑰麗 (ㄍㄨㄟ ㄌㄧ)
fabulously beautiful; magnificent: 這座宮殿眞是雄偉瑰麗。The palace is indeed magnificent.

瑰姿 (ㄍㄨㄟ ㄗ)
(said of a person) extraordinary or preeminent appearance

瑰岸 (ㄍㄨㄟ ㄢ)
tall and strong

瑰異 (ㄍㄨㄟ ㄧ)
fabulous and extraordinary things

瑰意琦行 (ㄍㄨㄟ ㄧ ㄑㄧ ㄒㄧㄥ)
outstanding in thinking and action

瑰瑋 (ㄍㄨㄟ ㄨㄟ)
rare and precious; treasurable

【瑱】 3481
　1. ㄊㄧㄢ tiann tiàn
earplugs of jade

【瑱】 3481
　2. ㄓㄣ jenn zhèn
to weight; to press

【瑪】 3482
　ㄇㄚ maa mǎ
agate; cornelian

瑪瑙 (ㄇㄚ ㄋㄠ)
agate; cornelian

瑪麗 or 瑪利 (ㄇㄚ ㄌㄧ)
Mary

瑪志尼 (ㄇㄚ ㄓ ㄋㄧ)
Giuseppe Mazzini (1805-1872), Italian patriot 亦作[馬志尼]

瑪賽克 (ㄇㄚ ㄙㄞ ㄎㄜ)
mosaic 亦作 [馬賽克]

瑪雅人 (ㄇㄚ ㄧㄚ ㄖㄣ)
Maya

【瑳】 3483
　ㄘㄨㄛ tsuoo cuǒ
1. the luster and purity of jade
2. bright and flourishing
3. the brilliant white appearance of the teeth

【瑲】 3484
　ㄑㄧㄤ chiang qiāng
the tinkling of jade pendants

瑲瑲 (ㄑㄧㄤ ㄑㄧㄤ)
the jingling or chiming of bells

【瑨】 3485
　ㄐㄧㄣ jinn jìn
a fine piece of jade

十一畫

【瑽】 3486
　ㄘㄨㄥ tsong cōng
the tinkling of metal ornaments and jade pendants

【瑾】 3487
　ㄐㄧㄣ jiin jǐn
fine jade

瑾瑜 (ㄐㄧㄣ ㄩ)
a fine piece of jade

瑾瑜匿瑕 (ㄐㄧㄣ ㄩ ㄋㄧ ㄒㄧㄚ)
flaws hidden in a beautiful gem

【璀】 3488
　ㄘㄨㄟ tsoei cuǐ
the luster or glitter of jade and gems

璀璨 (ㄘㄨㄟ ㄘㄢ)
the brilliancy and luster of pearls and precious stones: 她的鑽戒璀璨奪目。Her diamond ring dazzled with brilliancy.

璀錯 (ㄘㄨㄟ ㄘㄨㄛ)
many and varied

璀璨 (ㄘㄨㄟ ㄘㄢ)
bright and clear

【璇】 3489
　ㄒㄩㄢ shyuan xuán
1. fine jade
2. name of a constellation

璇閨 (ㄒㄩㄢ ㄍㄨㄟ)
an exquisite, cozy boudoir ornamented with fine jade

璇宮 (ㄒㄩㄢ ㄍㄨㄥ)
an exquisite room ornamented with fine gems; a swanky palace; a luxuriously-furnished hall

璇花 (ㄒㄩㄢ ㄏㄨㄚ)
blossoms as pure and white as jade

璇璣 (ㄒㄩㄢ ㄐㄧ)
① the North Star ② an ancient astronomical instrument of the time of Shun (舜) (2255-2205 B.C.)

璇室 (ㄒㄩㄢ ㄕ)
a gem-studded room

【璃】 3490
　ㄌㄧ li
glass; a glassy substance 參看 [琉璃]

【璉】 3491
　ㄌㄧㄢ lian
a vessel to hold grain offerings for the imperial sacrifice

【璈】 3492
　ㄠ aur áo
name of an ancient musical instrument

【璋】 3493
　ㄓㄤ jang zhāng
an ancient jade ornament used in state ceremonies; a jade tablet

【璁】 3494
　ㄘㄨㄥ tsong cōng
a jadelike stone

璁琤 (ㄘㄨㄥ ㄔㄥ)
the sound of music instruments; the tinkling of jades

十二畫

【璟】 3495
　ㄐㄧㄥ jiing jǐng
the luster of jade

【璘】 3496
　ㄌㄧㄣ lin

the brilliance of jade

【璜】 3497 ㄏㄨㄤ hwang
huáng

an ancient jade ornament, semicircular in shape, hung up as a tinkling pendant

【璞】 3498 ㄆㄨ pwu pú
1. an uncarved or unpolished jade or gem
2. (figuratively): natural; unadorned: 返璞歸真 to revert to one's natural self

璞玉渾金 (ㄆㄨ ㄩˋ ㄏㄨㄣˊ ㄐㄧㄣ)
(literally) uncarved jade and unrefined gold—The real value of things lies in what they are made of, not what they appear to be.

【璣】 3499 ㄐㄧ ji jī
1. pearls, jade, etc. which are not quite circular
2. as in 璇璣 or 璿璣—an ancient astronomical instrument
3. name of a constellation

【璠】 3500 ㄈㄢˊ farn fán
a piece of precious jade

【璐】 3501 ㄌㄨˋ luh lù
fine jade

十三畫

【璦】 3502 ㄞˇ ay ài
fine jade

璦琿 (ㄞˇ ㄏㄨㄣˊ)
Ai Hun, a county in Heilungkiang (黑龍江) in Northeast China

璦琿條約 (ㄞˇ ㄏㄨㄣˊ ㄊㄧㄠˊ ㄩㄝ)
the Sino-Russian treaty concluded in 1858 at Ai Hun, in which the present boundaries between the two nations were defined

【璧】 3503 ㄅㄧˋ bih bì
1. a round and flat piece of jade with a circular hole in it
2. a general name of all kinds of jade, jade-wares and ornaments

璧田 (ㄅㄧˋ ㄊㄧㄢˊ)
good farmland

璧合 (ㄅㄧˋ ㄏㄜˊ)
a perfect match

璧還 (ㄅㄧˋ ㄏㄨㄢˊ)
to return a gift or present; to decline a present with thanks

璧謝 (ㄅㄧˋ ㄒㄧㄝˋ)
to return a present with thanks

璧趙 (ㄅㄧˋ ㄓㄠˋ)
to return something valuable to its original owner

璧水 (ㄅㄧˋ ㄕㄨㄟˇ)
(in ancient China) a semicircular pool within the precincts of a college

璧人 (ㄅㄧˋ ㄖㄣˊ)
a person as beautiful or handsome as jade; a fine-looking person

璧玉 (ㄅㄧˋ ㄩˋ)
a round and flat piece of jade with a circular hole in it

璧月 (ㄅㄧˋ ㄩㄝˋ)
a full moon

【環】 3504 ㄏㄨㄢˊ hwan huán
1. a jade ring or bracelet; a ring; a bracelet
2. earrings for women; ear-ornaments
3. around; round; to surround; surrounding; to encircle: 台北四面環山。 Taipei is surrounded by mountains.
4. a link: 這是最弱的一環。 This is the weakest link.
5. (sports) a ring: 命中三環 to hit the three-point ring
6. A Chinese family name

環拜 (ㄏㄨㄢˊ ㄅㄞˋ)
to bow around

環保 (ㄏㄨㄢˊ ㄅㄠˇ)
short for 環境保護

環保局 (ㄏㄨㄢˊ ㄅㄠˇ ㄐㄩˊ)
the Bureau of Environmental Protection (BEP) in the local government

環保署 (ㄏㄨㄢˊ ㄅㄠˇ ㄕㄨˇ)
the Environmental Protection Agency (EPA) in the Central Government

環抱 (ㄏㄨㄢˊ ㄅㄠˋ)
to surround; to encircle; to hem in; to encincture: 羣山環

抱著村莊。 A ring of hills encinctured the village.

環佩 (ㄏㄨㄢˊ ㄆㄟˋ)
ornaments for women

環肥燕瘦 (ㄏㄨㄢˊ ㄈㄟˊ ㄧㄢ ㄕㄡˋ)
(literally) Yang Yü-huan (楊玉環)was plump, while Chao Fei-yen (趙飛燕)was skinny. (Both were imperial concubines of unusual beauty.)— beautiful women, each of whom is attractive in her own way 亦作「燕瘦環肥」

環島 (ㄏㄨㄢˊ ㄉㄠˇ)
around-the-island

環堵蕭然 (ㄏㄨㄢˊ ㄉㄨˇ ㄒㄧㄠ ㄖㄢˊ)
(literally) nothing within the four walls—abject poverty

環列 (ㄏㄨㄢˊ ㄌㄧㄝˋ)
to place in a circle; to surround on all sides

環流 (ㄏㄨㄢˊ ㄌㄧㄡˊ)
① to flow or travel around in circles ② circulation; circumfluence

環顧 (ㄏㄨㄢˊ ㄍㄨˋ)
① to look around ② to review; to take stock of: 環顧國際局勢 to take stock of the world situation

環繞四週 (ㄏㄨㄢˊ ㄖㄠˋ ㄙˋ ㄓㄡˋ)
to look around

環河 (ㄏㄨㄢˊ ㄏㄜˊ)
along a river bend

環海 (ㄏㄨㄢˊ ㄏㄞˇ)
within the seven seas —China

環節 (ㄏㄨㄢˊ ㄐㄧㄝˊ)
a segment; a link: 這不是主要的環節。 This is not the key link.

環節動物 (ㄏㄨㄢˊ ㄐㄧㄝˊ ㄉㄨㄥˋ ㄨˋ)
the annulata

環境 (ㄏㄨㄢˊ ㄐㄧㄥˋ)
surroundings; environment; circumstances

環境保護 (ㄏㄨㄢˊ ㄐㄧㄥˋ ㄅㄠˇ ㄏㄨˋ)
environmental protection

環境污染 (ㄏㄨㄢˊ ㄐㄧㄥˋ ㄨ ㄖㄢˇ)
pollution of the environment; environmental pollution

環境衛生 (ㄏㄨㄢˊ ㄐㄧㄥˋ ㄨㄟˋ ㄕㄥ)
environmental sanitation

環球 (ㄏㄨㄢˊ ㄑㄧㄡˊ)

〔玉部〕

around the globe; through-out the world; universal

環城(ㄏㄨㄢˊ ㄔㄥˊ)
around the city

環蝕(ㄏㄨㄢˊ ㄕˊ)
(astronomy) annular eclipse

環視(ㄏㄨㄢˊ ㄕˋ)
to look around

環繞(ㄏㄨㄢˊ ㄖㄠˋ)
to revolve round; to circle; to move round; to surround

環子(ㄏㄨㄢˊ ˙ㄗ)或環兒(ㄏㄨㄢˊㄦˊ)
a ring

環遊世界(ㄏㄨㄢˊ ㄧㄡˊ ㄕˋ ㄐㄧㄝˋ)
to take a round-the-world tour

環衛(ㄏㄨㄢˊ ㄨㄟˋ)
the imperial guards

環暈(ㄏㄨㄢˊ ㄩㄣˋ)
the lunar or solar halo

【璨】 3505
ㄘㄢˋ tsann cǎn
bright and brilliant; lustrous and luminous

【璫】 3506
ㄉㄤ dang dāng
1. richly ornamented
2. pearls for filling up ear punctures to prevent the holes from closing
3. ancient headgear

【璩】 3507
ㄑㄩˊ chyu qú
1. a ringed ornament—ear-rings, rings for fingers
2. a Chinese family name

十四畫

【璽】 3508
ㄒㄧˇ shii xǐ
1. the seal of an emperor or a king
2. the formal seal of a state; the national emblem

璽綬(ㄒㄧˇ ㄕㄡˋ)
the imperial seal and the at-tached cordon

璽書(ㄒㄧˇ ㄕㄨ)
documents sealed with per-sonal or official seals

【璵】 3509
ㄩˊ yu yú
fine jade

【璿】 3510
ㄒㄩㄢˊ shyuan xuán
fine jade

璿圖(ㄒㄩㄢˊ ㄊㄨˊ)

the state; the nation

璿宮(ㄒㄩㄢˊ ㄍㄨㄥ)
a gem-studded chamber

璿璣玉衡(ㄒㄩㄢˊ ㄐㄧ ㄩˋ ㄏㄥˊ)
an ancient astronomical instrument

【璺】 3511
ㄨㄣˋ wenn wèn
a crack in jade (or on glass-ware or earthenware)

十五畫

【瓊】 3512
ㄑㄩㄥˊ chyong qióng
1. fine jade or agate
2. excellent; beautiful; fabulous

瓊杯(ㄑㄩㄥˊ ㄅㄟ)
a jade wine-cup

瓊葩(ㄑㄩㄥˊ ㄆㄚ)
blossoms as pure and white as jade

瓊蔴(ㄑㄩㄥˊ ㄇㄚˊ)
sisal; 這條繩子是用瓊蔴製成的。The rope is made of sisal.

瓊島(ㄑㄩㄥˊ ㄉㄠˇ)
① Hainan Island (海南島) ② also known as Chiung Hua Islet (瓊華島), one of the eight scenic spots in Peking

瓊樓玉宇(ㄑㄩㄥˊ ㄌㄡˊ ㄩˋ ㄩˇ)
①(Chinese mythology) the Palace of the Moon ②a magnificent or splendid building

瓊粒(ㄑㄩㄥˊ ㄌㄧˋ)
ricegrains in a year of fam-ine (which are as precious as jade)

瓊林(ㄑㄩㄥˊ ㄌㄧㄣˊ)
a collection of rare and val-uable things (usually refer-ring to books)

瓊林宴(ㄑㄩㄥˊ ㄌㄧㄣˊ ㄧㄢˋ)
(in the Ching Dynasty) a feast hosted by the emperor in honor of the successful candidates of imperial examination the day after the examination

瓊花(ㄑㄩㄥˊ ㄏㄨㄚ)
a rare flower said to confer immortality when eaten

瓊華(ㄑㄩㄥˊ ㄏㄨㄚˊ)
fine jade; beautiful gems

瓊玖(ㄑㄩㄥˊ ㄐㄧㄡˇ)
fine jade

瓊漿(ㄑㄩㄥˊ ㄐㄧㄤ)
good wine

瓊琚(ㄑㄩㄥˊ ㄐㄩ)
fine jade

瓊枝玉葉(ㄑㄩㄥˊ ㄓ ㄩˋ ㄧㄝˋ)
lineal imperial descendants

瓊州海峽(ㄑㄩㄥˊ ㄓㄡ ㄏㄞˇ ㄒㄧㄚˊ)
the Hainan Straits

瓊姿(ㄑㄩㄥˊ ㄗ)
an elegant or a graceful appearance

瓊斯(ㄑㄩㄥˊ ㄙ)
transliteration of Jones

瓊瑤(ㄑㄩㄥˊ ㄧㄠˊ)
① fine jade ② your letter ③ a gift or literary piece writ-ten for others

瓊筵(ㄑㄩㄥˊ ㄧㄢˊ)
a banquet; an elaborate feast

瓊音(ㄑㄩㄥˊ ㄧㄣ)
a clear and crisp sound

瓊英(ㄑㄩㄥˊ ㄧㄥ)
a beautiful stone resembling jade

十六畫

【瓏】 3513
ㄌㄨㄥˊ long lóng
1. a clear and crisp sound
2. dry; parched
3. the rumbling of cart
4. the tinkling of metals or jades
5. dusky

【瓌】 3514
ㄍㄨㄟ guei guī
1. same as 瑰, a kind of jasper
2. extraordinary; fabulous or admirable

瓌寶(ㄍㄨㄟ ㄅㄠˇ)
an extraordinary treasure

瓌奇(ㄍㄨㄟ ㄑㄧˊ)
rare and precious things

十七畫

【瓔】 3515
ㄧㄥ ing yīng
a necklace of precious stones

瓔珞(ㄧㄥ ㄌㄨㄛˋ)
a necklace of precious stones

瓔珞棗兒(ㄧㄥ ㄌㄨㄛ ㄗㄠˇㄦ)
a kind of oblong jujube

瓜 部
《ㄍㄨㄚ gua guā》

【瓜】 3516
《ㄍㄨㄚ gua guā
melons, gourds, cucumbers, etc.

瓜瓣(《ㄍㄨㄚ ㄅㄢˋ)
melon seed

瓜剖豆分(《ㄍㄨㄚ ㄆㄡˇ ㄉㄡˋ ㄈㄣ)
(said of a country) to be divided or split like a melon or a bean; to be partitioned

瓜棚(《ㄍㄨㄚ ㄆㄥˊ)
the framework for melon vines

瓜皮帽(《ㄍㄨㄚ ㄆㄧˊ ㄇㄠˋ)
a small round skullcap much worn in former times

瓜皮艇(《ㄍㄨㄚ ㄆㄧˊ ㄊㄧㄥˇ)
a small skiff

瓜縣(《ㄍㄨㄚ ㄇㄧㄢˊ)
to have prosperous descendants 參看「瓜瓞綿綿」

瓜分(《ㄍㄨㄚ ㄈㄣ)
to divide and distribute; to apportion; to partition; to dismember

瓜達康納爾(《ㄍㄨㄚ ㄉㄚˊ ㄎㄤ ㄋㄚˋ ㄦˇ)
Guadalcanal Island in the Pacific

瓜代(《ㄍㄨㄚ ㄉㄞˋ)
to relieve or replace (an official) upon the expiration of his term of office

瓜地馬拉(《ㄍㄨㄚ ㄉㄧˋ ㄇㄚˇ ㄌㄚ)
Guatemala

瓜瓞綿綿(《ㄍㄨㄚ ㄉㄧㄝˊ ㄇㄧㄢˊ ㄇㄧㄢˊ)
to have prosperous descendants (an expression of felicitation printed on a marriage certificate) 亦作「綿綿瓜瓞」

瓜條(《ㄍㄨㄚ ㄊㄧㄠˊ)
melon rind cut into thin strips and sweetened

瓜田李下(《ㄍㄨㄚ ㄊㄧㄢˊ ㄌㄧˇ ㄒㄧㄚˋ)
(literally) in a melon field (where one may be suspected of stealing melons if one ties one's shoestrings) and under a plum tree (where

one may be suspected of stealing plums if one arranges one's hat)—a position that invites suspicion

瓜葛(《ㄍㄨㄚ ㄍㄜˊ)
melon vines—a multitude of relatives; to get mixed up; connected; involved; related; complications

瓜果(《ㄍㄨㄚ ㄍㄨㄛˇ)
melons and fruits: 瓜果有益健康. Melons and fruits are good for the health.

瓜熟蒂落(《ㄍㄨㄚ ㄕㄨˊ ㄉㄧˋ ㄌㄨㄛˋ)
(literally) When a melon is ripe, it falls of its own accord.—Things take care of themselves when the right time comes. 或 Everything can be done easily at the right time.

瓜仁(《ㄍㄨㄚ ㄖㄣˊ)or 瓜仁兒(《ㄍㄨㄚ ㄖㄣˊㄦ)
the edible part of a melon seed; the kernel of a melon seed

瓜瓤(《ㄍㄨㄚ ㄖㄤˊ)
the pulp of a melon

瓜子(《ㄍㄨㄚ ㄗˇ)or 瓜子兒(《ㄍㄨㄚ ㄗˇㄦ)
melon seeds

瓜子臉(《ㄍㄨㄚ ㄗˇ ㄌㄧㄢˇ)
an oval face (usually said of a pretty woman): 這女孩有張瓜子臉. The girl has an oval face.

五畫

【瓞】 3517
ㄉㄧㄝ dye diē
a kind of small melons

六畫

【瓠】 3518
ㄏㄨˋ huh hù
a gourd; a calabash

瓠肥(ㄏㄨˋ ㄈㄟˊ)
obese; fat

瓠落(ㄏㄨˋ ㄌㄨㄛˋ)
(said of a vessel) flat and shallow—large but useless

瓠果(ㄏㄨˋ ㄍㄨㄛˇ)
pepos

十一畫

【瓢】 3519
ㄆㄧㄠˊ pyau piáo
a ladle (often made of a dried calabash or gourd)

瓢蟲(ㄆㄧㄠˊ ㄔㄨㄥˊ)
a ladybug; a ladybird

瓢兒(ㄆㄧㄠˊㄦ)
① a ladle (often made of a dried calabash or gourd) ② (jocular usage) human head

十四畫

【瓣】 3520
ㄅㄢˋ bann bàn
1. petals (of a flower)
2. sections (as of oranges)
3. a valve; a lamella
4. fragments; pieces

瓣兒(ㄅㄢˋㄦ)
① petals (of flowers) ② sections (as of oranges)

瓣香(ㄅㄢˋ ㄒㄧㄤ)
① petallike incense used in worship of Buddha ② the worship or admiration of someone

十七畫

【瓤】 3521
ㄖㄤˊ rang ráng
1. the pulp of a fruit; a section of an orange, a tangerine, etc.
2. the interior part of certain things

瓤兒(ㄖㄤˊㄦ)
the pulp of a fruit; a section of an orange, a tangerine, etc.

瓦 部
ㄨㄚˇ woa wǎ

【瓦】 3522
1. ㄨㄚˇ woa wǎ
1. earthenware; pottery
2. a tile
3. watt, the SI unit of power
4. a Chinese family name

瓦房(ㄨㄚˇ ㄈㄤˊ)
a tiled house: 他住在一所瓦房子裏. He lives in a tiled

【瓦部】

house.

瓦釜雷鳴(ㄨㄚ ㄈㄨˇ ㄌㄟˊ ㄇㄧㄥˊ)
(literally) an earthen pot sounding like thunder—an unworthy man creating sensations and enjoying popularity

瓦當(ㄨㄚˇ ㄉㄤ)
tiles with a circular facade at one end used along the edge of palace eaves during the Han Dynasty

瓦當文(ㄨㄚˇ ㄉㄤ ㄨㄣˊ)
inscriptions on the circular facade of a tile 參看「瓦當」

瓦特(ㄨㄚˇ ㄊㄜˋ)
①James Watt, 1736-1819, Scottish inventor ②(electricity) watt

瓦楞紙(ㄨㄚˇ ㄌㄥ ㄓˇ)
corrugated paper

瓦礫(ㄨㄚˇ ㄌㄧˋ)
①rubble; ruin ②worthless things

瓦裂(ㄨㄚˇ ㄌㄧㄝˋ)
broken like a tile

瓦鱗(ㄨㄚˇ ㄌㄧㄣˊ)
tiles overlapping like scales

瓦鍋(ㄨㄚˇ ㄍㄨㄛ)
an earthen pot

瓦棺(ㄨㄚˇ ㄍㄨㄢ)
a pottery coffin

瓦罐(ㄨㄚˇ ㄍㄨㄢˋ)
an earthen jar; a pottery container

瓦塊(ㄨㄚˇ ㄎㄨㄞˋ)
fragments of a tile

瓦合(ㄨㄚˇ ㄏㄜˊ)
loosely put together

瓦解(ㄨㄚˇ ㄐㄧㄝˇ)
to fall apart; to disintegrate; to collapse; to crumble

瓦解冰消(ㄨㄚˇ ㄐㄧㄝˇ ㄅㄧㄥ ㄒㄧㄠ)
to disintegrate like tiles and to dissolve like ice

瓦解土崩(ㄨㄚˇ ㄐㄧㄝˇ ㄊㄨˇ ㄅㄥ)
to fall completely apart; to disintegrate completely

瓦匠(ㄨㄚˇ ㄐㄧㄤˋ)
a bricklayer; a plasterer

瓦器(ㄨㄚˇ ㄑㄧˋ)
earthenware; pottery

瓦全(ㄨㄚˇ ㄑㄩㄢˊ)
to choose life rather than death when it would be more honorable to die; to

---

compromise one's principles for self-preservation: 寧爲玉碎, 不爲瓦全。One would rather be a broken piece of jade than be a whole piece of tile.—One would rather die with honor than survive with dishonor.

瓦時(ㄨㄚˇ ㄕˊ)
(electricity) watt-hour

瓦時計(ㄨㄚˇ ㄕˊ ㄐㄧˋ)
a watt-hour meter

瓦作(ㄨㄚˇ ·ㄗㄨㄛ)
a bricklayer; a plasterer

瓦斯(ㄨㄚˇ ㄙ)
gas; poisonous gas used in war

瓦斯彈(ㄨㄚˇ ㄙ ㄉㄢˋ)
a gas bomb; a gas shell

瓦斯筒(ㄨㄚˇ ㄙ ㄊㄨㄥˇ)
a gas cylinder

瓦窰(ㄨㄚˇ ㄧㄠˊ)
a pottery or tile kiln

【瓦】 3522
2. ㄨㄚˋ wah wà
to cover a roof with tiles; to tile

五畫

【瓴】 3523
ㄌㄧㄥˊ ling líng
1.the concave channels of tiling
2. a bottle with a handle

六畫

【瓷】 3524
ㄘˊ tsyr cí
porcelain; chinaware

瓷胎(ㄘˊ ㄊㄞ)
porcelain not yet baked

瓷土(ㄘˊ ㄊㄨˇ)
kaolin(e); porcelain clay

瓷器(ㄘˊ ㄑㄧˋ)
porcelain; porcelain ware; chinaware; china: 她買了一套精美的瓷器。She bought a set of fine china.

瓷甎 or 瓷磚(ㄘˊ ㄓㄨㄢ)
small porcelain tiles used for wall paneling or floor pavement

瓷窰(ㄘˊ ㄧㄠˊ)
a porcelain kiln

瓷瓦兒(ㄘˊ ㄨㄚˇㄦ)

---

fragments of porcelain

八畫

【瓿】 3525
ㄆㄡˇ poou pǒu
a jar; a pot

【瓶】 3526
(瓶、缾) ㄆㄧㄥˊ pyng píng
a bottle; a pitcher; a jug; a vase

瓶鉢(ㄆㄧㄥˊ ㄅㄛ)
a Buddhist monk's rice bowl

瓶頸(ㄆㄧㄥˊ ㄐㄧㄥˇ)
a bottleneck

瓶裝(ㄆㄧㄥˊ ㄓㄨㄤ)
bottled

瓶子(ㄆㄧㄥˊ ·ㄗ)or 瓶兒(ㄆㄧㄥˊㄦ)
a bottle; a jar; a vase

瓶塞兒(ㄆㄧㄥˊ ㄙㄞ ㄦ)
a bottle stopper or plug; a cork

九畫

【甄】 3527
ㄓㄣ jen zhēn
1. a potter's wheel
2. to make pottery ware
3. to examine; to discern
4. to grade (competence, etc.) by examinations
5. to make clear
6. a Chinese family name

甄拔(ㄓㄣ ㄅㄚˊ)
to select (talent) by a competitive examination

甄別(ㄓㄣ ㄅㄧㄝˊ)
to grade (competence, aptitude, etc.) by an examination); to screen

甄別考試(ㄓㄣ ㄅㄧㄝˊ ㄎㄠˇ ㄕˋ)
an examination for grading abilities, screening, etc.

甄汰(ㄓㄣ ㄊㄞˋ)
to eliminate by an examination

甄選(ㄓㄣ ㄒㄩㄢˇ)
to select (talented people, etc.)

甄審(ㄓㄣ ㄕㄣˇ)
to screen and select (candidates)

甄用(ㄓㄣ ㄩㄥˋ)
to employ by an examination

【甃】 3528
ㄓㄡ jow zhòu
1. the brick wall of a well; a tile
2. to build a well
3. to construct with bricks

十一畫

【甌】 3529
ㄡ ou ōu
1. a cup; a bowl
2. a Chinese family name

甌脫(ㄡ ㄊㄨㄛ)
①entrenchments on the frontiers ②no man's land on the border

甌越(ㄡ ㄩㄝˋ)
eastern Chekiang

【甎】 3530
(磚,塼) ㄓㄨㄢ juan zhuān
brick

甎頭(ㄓㄨㄢ ㄊㄡ) bricks: 他們用甎頭造房子。 They built their houses with bricks.

甎廠(ㄓㄨㄢ ㄔㄤˇ)
a brickfield; a brickyard

甎窰(ㄓㄨㄢ ㄧㄠˊ)
a brick kiln

甎瓦(ㄓㄨㄢ ㄨㄚˇ)
bricks and tiles

【甍】 3531
ㄇㄥˊ meng méng
rafters

十二畫

【甌】 3532
ㄗㄥˋ tzeng zèng
earthenware for cooking

甑塵釜魚(ㄗㄣˊ ㄔㄣˊ ㄈㄨˇ ㄩˊ)
(literally) Dust has covered kitchen utensils and fish has spawned in cooking vessels because of long disuse.—a state of stark poverty

甑兒糕(ㄗㄣˊ ㄦˊ ㄍㄠ)
a kind of steamed rice cake with stuffing

十三畫

【甕】 3533
ㄨㄥˋ wenq wèng
a jar; a jug; a pot; an urn

甕天(ㄨㄥˋ ㄊㄧㄢ)
(literally) to see the sky from inside a jar—to know very little of the world

甕計(ㄨㄥˋ ㄐㄧˋ)
counting chickens before they are hatched

甕中之鼈(ㄨㄥˋ ㄓㄨㄥ ㄓ ㄅㄧㄝˋ)
(literally) the turtle inside a jar—something that can be caught easily

甕中捉鼈(ㄨㄥˋ ㄓㄨㄥ ㄓㄨㄛ ㄅㄧㄝˋ)
(literally) to catch the turtle inside a jar—to catch something that has no way of escape

甕牖(ㄨㄥˋ ㄧㄡˇ)
(literally) a small round window like the mouth of a jar; a window made of the mouth of a broken jar—the mark of a needy family

【甓】 3534
ㄆㄧˊ pih pí
a brick; a tile

十六畫

【甗】 3535
ㄧㄢˇ yean yǎn
an earthenware vessel in two parts, of which one is for steaming and the other is for boiling; an ancient double boiler

甘 部
《ㄢ gan gān

【甘】 3536
《ㄢ gan gān
1. tasty; luscious; delicious
2. sweet
3. willing: 我不甘落後。 I was unwilling to lag behind.
4. to enjoy
5. pleasant; pleasing
6. a Chinese family name

甘拜下風(《ㄢ ㄅㄞˋ ㄒㄧㄚˋ ㄈㄥ)
willing to take an inferior position; to admit defeat willingly

甘比亞(《ㄢ ㄅㄧˇ ㄧㄚˇ)
Gambia, a river in W Africa, flowing W to the Atlantic

甘美(《ㄢ ㄇㄟˇ)
delicious; tasty; palatable

甘地(《ㄢ ㄉㄧˋ)
Mahatma Gandhi (Mohandas Karamchand Gandhi), 1869-1948, the spiritual leader of India in its independence movement

甘地主義(《ㄢ ㄉㄧˋ ㄓㄨˇ ㄧˋ)
Gandhism

甘棠遺愛(《ㄢ ㄊㄤˊ ㄧˊ ㄞ)
the memory left behind by a virtuous and capable official

甘迺迪(《ㄢ ㄋㄞˋ ㄉㄧˊ)
John Fitzgerald Kennedy, 1917-1963, the 35th President of the United States

甘藍(《ㄢ ㄌㄢˊ)or甘藍菜(《ㄢ ㄌㄢˊ ㄘㄞˋ)
a kale; cabbage: 他在菜園種甘藍菜。He grows cabbages in his garden.

甘霖(《ㄢ ㄌㄧㄣˊ)
a seasonable rain; a timely rain

甘霖普降(《ㄢ ㄌㄧㄣˊ ㄆㄨˇ ㄐㄧㄤˋ)
Seasonable rain has fallen everywhere.

甘露(《ㄢ ㄌㄨˋ)
sweet dew

甘露(《ㄢ ㄌㄨˋ)
Kan Lo, a child prodigy in the state of Chin, who was given a high official rank at the age of 12 in the Epoch of Warring States

甘瓜苦蒂(《ㄢ ㄍㄨㄚ ㄎㄨˇ ㄉㄧˋ)
(literally) a sweet melon with a bitter peduncle—a flaw in a precious stone 或 Nothing can be perfect.

甘汞(《ㄢ ㄍㄨㄥˇ)
calomel

甘苦(《ㄢ ㄎㄨˇ)
①sweetness and bitterness; happiness and suffering; prosperity and adversity ②hardships and difficulties experienced in work

甘苦備嘗(《ㄢ ㄎㄨˇ ㄅㄟˋ ㄔㄤˊ)
to have tasted both sweetness and bitterness; to have known both happiness and suffering

甘苦同受(《ㄢ ㄎㄨˇ ㄊㄨㄥˊ ㄕㄡˋ)
to share not only the sweets but also the bitters; to share both enjoyment and suffer-

〔甘部〕

ing
甘結《《ㄢ ㄐㄧㄝˊ》
an affidavit pledging that
what is stated therein is
absolutely true
甘蕉《《ㄢ 亦作「香蕉」
a banana 亦作「香蕉」
甘井先竭《《ㄢ ㄐㄧㄥ ㄒㄧㄢ ㄐㄧㄝˊ》
(literally) A sweet well
dries early.—Men of talent
decay faster.
甘寢《《ㄢ ㄑㄧㄣˇ》
to sleep soundly
甘泉《《ㄢ ㄑㄩㄢˊ》
① a fresh spring ② name of
a county in Shensi
甘休《《ㄢ ㄒㄧㄡ》
willing to stop or halt: 他不
肯與他們善罷甘休. He won't
stop quarreling with them.
甘心《《ㄢ ㄒㄧㄣ》
① willingly; willing ② joyous; happy ③ to be wearied
in mind
甘心瞑目《《ㄢ ㄒㄧㄣ ㄇㄧㄥˊ ㄇㄨˋ》
to die without dissatisfaction
甘心情願《《ㄢ ㄒㄧㄣ ㄑㄧㄥˊ ㄩㄢˋ》
perfectly willing
甘心忍受《《ㄢ ㄒㄧㄣ ㄖㄣˇ ㄕㄡˋ》
willing to endure
甘之如飴《《ㄢ ㄓ ㄖㄨˊ ㄧˊ》
to be quite content even in
adversity
甘旨《《ㄢ ㄓˇ》
delicious or tasty food
甘蔗《《ㄢ ㄓㄜˋ》
sugarcane: 甘蔗沒有兩頭甜.
A sugarcane is never sweet
at both ends.—One can't
have it both ways.
甘蔗板《《ㄢ ㄓㄜˋ ㄅㄢˇ》
a bagasse board
甘薯 or 甘藷《《ㄢ ㄕㄨˇ》
sweet potatoes
甘草《《ㄢ ㄘㄠˇ》
licorice
甘脆《《ㄢ ㄘㄨㄟˋ》
delicacies
甘肅《《ㄢ ㄙㄨˋ》
Kansu Province
甘油《《ㄢ ㄧㄡˊ》
glycerine
甘言《《ㄢ ㄧㄢˊ》
honeyed words
甘為戎首《《ㄢ ㄨㄟˊ ㄖㄨㄥˊ ㄕㄡˇ》

not to hesitate in starting a
war
甘味《《ㄢ ㄨㄟˋ》
sweetness; lusciousness
甘心《《ㄢ ㄒㄧㄣ》
to be willing to; to be happy
to
甘雨《《ㄢ ㄩˇ》
a seasonable rain
甘願《《ㄢ ㄩㄢˋ》
willing; willingly; readily: 他
甘願做任何事情. He was will-
ing to do anything.

四畫

【甚】 1. ㄕㄣˋ shenn shèn
1. to a great extent; to a high
degree; very; exceedingly
2. more than
甚多《ㄕㄣˋ ㄉㄨㄛ》
very much or many
甚好《ㄕㄣˋ ㄏㄠˇ》or 甚佳《ㄕㄣˋ ㄐㄧㄚ》
very good; very well
甚急《ㄕㄣˋ ㄐㄧˊ》
① very anxious ② very
urgent
甚囂塵上《ㄕㄣˋ ㄒㄧㄠ ㄔㄣˊ ㄕㄤˋ》
(literally) much noise amid
a cloud of dust—very much
talked about; widely reported or speculated
甚至《ㄕㄣˋ ㄓˋ》 or 甚至於《ㄕㄣˋ ㄓˋ ㄩˊ》
though it may seem improbable (emphasizing the limit
of what is possible or probable); even; even to the
extent that...; to go so far
as...
甚是《ㄕㄣˋ ㄕˋ》
very; exceedingly; extremely
甚少《ㄕㄣˋ ㄕㄠˇ》
very few; very little: 甚少人
知道他的名字. Very few peo-
ple know his name.
甚早《ㄕㄣˋ ㄗㄠˇ》
very early
甚而《ㄕㄣˋ ㄦˊ》
so much so that...
甚殷《ㄕㄣˋ ㄧㄣ》
very sincerely; very badly
甚為《ㄕㄣˋ ㄨㄟˊ》
very; much: 我聞此消息甚為欣
喜. I was very pleased to
hear the news.
甚為不解《ㄕㄣˋ ㄨㄟˊ ㄅㄨˋ ㄐㄧㄝˇ》

much perplexed; completely
at a loss
甚於《ㄕㄣˋ ㄩˊ》
(to be worse, harder, better,
etc.) than...
甚遠《ㄕㄣˋ ㄩㄢˇ》
very far

【甚】 2.(什) ㄕㄜˊ sher shé
what
甚麼《ㄕㄜˊ ㄇㄛˊ》
what: 你讀過甚麼書? What
books have you read?
甚麼的《ㄕㄜˊ ㄇㄛˊ ˙ㄉㄜ》
① and what not; and so
forth 亦作「等等」 ② what
甚麼地方《ㄕㄜˊ ㄇㄛˊ ㄉㄧˋ ㄈㄤ》
where: 你住在甚麼地方?
Where do you live?
甚麼話《ㄕㄜˊ ㄇㄛˊ ㄏㄨㄚˋ》
What nonsense! 或 Bosh!
甚麼事《ㄕㄜˊ ㄇㄛˊ ㄕˋ》
① What's the matter? ② no
matter what; whatever it is
甚麼人《ㄕㄜˊ ㄇㄛˊ ㄖㄣˊ》
① Who? 還有甚麼人在那裡?
Who else was there? ② no
matter who; whoever it is
甚麼樣《ㄕㄜˊ ㄇㄛˊ ㄧㄤˋ》
What kind? 或 What sort? 他
是甚麼樣的人? What is he
like?

六畫

【甜】 3538 ㄊㄧㄢˊ tyan tián
1. sweet; luscious: 這蛋糕太甜
了. This cake is too sweet.
2. agreeable; pleasant
甜美《ㄊㄧㄢˊ ㄇㄟˇ》
① sweet; luscious ② pleasant; refreshing
甜蜜《ㄊㄧㄢˊ ㄇㄧˋ》
sweet as honey; honeyed;
affectionate; fond; happy
甜麵醬《ㄊㄧㄢˊ ㄇㄧㄢˋ ㄐㄧㄤˋ》
sweetened soybean paste
甜點《ㄊㄧㄢˊ ㄉㄧㄢˇ》
sweet; dessrrt: 甜點隨後就
送來. The sweets will be
served next.
甜頭《ㄊㄧㄢˊ ㄊㄡˊ》
① sweet taste; pleasant flavor ② good; benefit
甜甘《ㄊㄧㄢˊ ㄍㄢ》
sweet, honeyed, or pleasing:

這種茶甜甘。This kind of tea is sweet.

甜瓜(ㄊㄧㄢ ㄍㄨㄚ)
a sweet melon

甜酒釀(ㄊㄧㄢ ㄐㄧㄡˇ ㄧㄤˋ)
fermented rice

甜津津(ㄊㄧㄢ ㄐㄧㄣ ㄐㄧㄣ‧ㄉㄜ)
very sweet; very agreeable

甜情蜜意(ㄊㄧㄢ ㄑㄧㄥˊ ㄇㄧˋ ㄧˋ)
tender affections or love between man and woman

甜心(ㄊㄧㄢ ㄒㄧㄣ)
a sweetheart

甜香(ㄊㄧㄢ ㄒㄧㄤ)
sweet and fragrant

甜食(ㄊㄧㄢ ㄕˊ)
sweet food; sweetmeats: 她愛吃甜食。She likes sweet things.

甜睡(ㄊㄧㄢ ㄕㄨㄟˋ)
sleeping soundly

甜菜(ㄊㄧㄢ ㄘㄞˋ)
a sugar beet

甜菜糖(ㄊㄧㄢ ㄘㄞˋ ㄊㄤˊ)
beet sugar

甜酸苦辣(ㄊㄧㄢ ㄙㄨㄢ ㄎㄨˇ ㄌㄚˋ)
(literally) sweetness, sourness, bitterness and hotness —all sorts of joys and sorrows: 我嘗遍了人生的甜酸苦辣。I have experienced all sorts of joys and sorrows.

甜言蜜語(ㄊㄧㄢ ㄧㄢˊ ㄇㄧˋ ㄩˇ)
honeyed words; cajolery; flattery

甜玉米(ㄊㄧㄢ ㄩˋ ㄇㄧˇ)
sweet corn; sugar corn

甜味(ㄊㄧㄢ ㄨㄟˋ)
sweet taste: 這麵包有點甜味。This bread tastes sweet.

生 部
ㄕㄥ sheng shēng

【生】 3539
ㄕㄥ sheng shēng
1. to live; life; living; livelihood; alive: 她過着幸福的生活。She leads a happy life.
2. to be born; to come into being; to come into existence: 我在台北出生和長大。I was born and bred in Taipei.
3. to breed; to bear; to beget;

to produce; to create; to give rise to; to cause
4. uncooked; raw; unripe; crude: 蕃茄可以生吃。Tomatoes can be eaten raw.
5. unfamiliar; strange; unknown: 這小孩不會認生。This child is not shy with strangers.
6. savage; untamed; barbarian; uncultured
7. a pupil; a student
8. the male character type in Chinese opera
9. creatures
10. a Chinese family name

生病(ㄕㄥ ㄅㄧㄥˋ)
to get sick; to fall ill: 她正照料着生病的父親。She is taking care of her sick father.

生不帶來，死不帶去(ㄕㄥ ㄅㄨˋ ㄉㄞˋ ㄌㄞˊ，ㄙˇ ㄅㄨˋ ㄉㄞˋ ㄑㄩˋ)
One does not bring anything when one comes into this world, nor does one take anything when one leaves it.

生不逢辰(ㄕㄥ ㄅㄨˋ ㄈㄥˊ ㄔㄣˊ)
to be born at a wrong time; luckless; unlucky: 我生不逢辰。I was born under an unlucky star.

生怕(ㄕㄥ ㄆㄚˋ)
very anxious; very apprehensive

生皮(ㄕㄥ ㄆㄧˊ)
raw hide; untanned hide

生啤酒(ㄕㄥ ㄆㄧˊ ㄐㄧㄡˇ)
draught beer

生僻(ㄕㄥ ㄆㄧˋ)
not frequently seen; strange; unusual; uncommon

生平(ㄕㄥ ㄆㄧㄥˊ)
①one's brief biographical sketch ②in the course of life

生煤(ㄕㄥ ㄇㄟˊ)
bituminous coal; soft coal

生米煮成熟飯(ㄕㄥ ㄇㄧˇ ㄓㄨˇ ㄔㄥˊ ㄕㄡˊ ㄈㄢˋ)
(literally) The rice has been boiled.—What is done cannot be undone.

生苗(ㄕㄥ ㄇㄧㄠˊ)
the savage Miao people in remote southwestern China as distinct from those relatively cultured

生民(ㄕㄥ ㄇㄧㄣˊ)
the people; the populace

生命(ㄕㄥ ㄇㄧㄥˋ)
life: 生命短促，藝術流長。Art is long; life is short.

生命力(ㄕㄥ ㄇㄧㄥˋ ㄌㄧˋ)
vitality: 她的生命力因為病痛而減弱了。Her vitality was lessened by illness.

生命線(ㄕㄥ ㄇㄧㄥˋ ㄒㄧㄢˋ)
a lifeline (in a figurative sense)

生母(ㄕㄥ ㄇㄨˇ)
a real mother (as distinct from a foster mother)

生髮油(ㄕㄥ ㄈㄚˋ ㄧㄡˊ)
hair tonic

生佛(ㄕㄥ ㄈㄛˊ)
①all living creatures and Buddha ②a living Buddha

生番(ㄕㄥ ㄈㄢ)
savages; barbarians

生飯(ㄕㄥ ㄈㄢˋ)
(Buddhism) symbolic offering of food to all creatures before a meal

生分(ㄕㄥ ㄈㄣ)
unfriendly; strange; unfamiliar

生父(ㄕㄥ ㄈㄨˋ)
a real father (as distinct from a foster father): 他是我的生父。He is my real father.

生旦淨末丑(ㄕㄥ ㄉㄢˋ ㄐㄧㄥˋ ㄇㄛˋ ㄔㄡˇ)
the major types of characters in Chinese opera—the male roles, female roles, painted-face roles, and clownish roles

生的米突(ㄕㄥ ㄉㄜ˙ ㄇㄧˇ ㄊㄨˊ)
centimeter 亦作「公分」

生動(ㄕㄥ ㄉㄨㄥˋ)
vivid; lively; lifelike

生態(ㄕㄥ ㄊㄞˋ)
the relations and interactions between organisms and their environment, including other organisms

生態學(ㄕㄥ ㄊㄞˋ ㄒㄩㄝˊ)
ecology

生疼(ㄕㄥ ㄊㄥˊ)
very painful

生鐵(ㄕㄥ ㄊㄧㄝˇ)
pig iron; crude iron

生徒(ㄕㄥ ㄊㄨˊ)
pupils; students

〔生 部〕

生吞活剝(ㄕㄥ ㄊㄨㄣ ㄏㄨㄛˊ ㄅㄛ)
to make awkward use of stock expressions in one's compositions; to use someone's ideas without fully understanding them

生銅(ㄕㄥ ㄊㄨㄥˊ)
unprocessed copper; brass: 這是生銅製的。This is made of unprocessed copper.

生年月日(ㄕㄥ ㄋㄧㄢˊ ㄩㄝˋ ㄖˋ)
the date of birth

生拉硬拽(ㄕㄥ ㄌㄚ ㄧㄥˋ ㄓㄨㄞˋ)
① to obtain reluctant obedience or compliance ② irrelevant; far-fetched; unnatural

生來(ㄕㄥ ㄌㄞˊ)
① since one's birth ② by nature; inborn: 他們是生來就喜歡惡作劇的孩子。They are children with an inborn love of mischief.

生老病死(ㄕㄥ ㄌㄠˇ ㄅㄧㄥˋ ㄙˇ)
(Buddhism) birth, age, disease, and death—the four miseries, or sufferings in the course of human life

生冷(ㄕㄥ ㄌㄥˇ)
(said of food) uncooked and cold

生離死別(ㄕㄥ ㄌㄧˊ ㄙˇ ㄅㄧㄝˊ)
separation in life and parting at death—the bitterest sorrows to man

生理(ㄕㄥ ㄌㄧˇ)
physiological functions and processes; physiology: 消化是一種生理過程。Digestion is a physiological process.

生理學(ㄕㄥ ㄌㄧˇ ㄒㄩㄝˊ)
physiological science; physiology

生利息(ㄕㄥ ㄌㄧˋ ·ㄒㄧ)
to bear interest; to yield interest

生力軍(ㄕㄥ ㄌㄧˋ ㄐㄩㄣ)
fresh troops; a vital new force: 他們是文藝界的一支生力軍。They are a vital new force in the field of art and literature.

生料(ㄕㄥ ㄌㄧㄠˋ)
unprocessed goods

生靈塗炭(ㄕㄥ ㄌㄧㄥˊ ㄊㄨˊ ㄊㄢˋ)
The people are suffering from extreme privation (during wartime).

生路(ㄕㄥ ㄌㄨˋ)
① a way to make a living; a way to survive: 他不得不另謀生路。He cannot but try to find another job. ② an unfamiliar road; a strange road

生龍活虎(ㄕㄥ ㄌㄨㄥˊ ㄏㄨㄛˊ ㄏㄨˇ)
(like) a live dragon or a live tiger—full of vigor and vitality: 年青人幹起活來眞是生龍活虎。When the youth work, they do it with furious energy.

生根(ㄕㄥ ㄍㄣ)
to root: 植物很快地生根。The plant roots quickly.

生公說法(ㄕㄥ ㄍㄨㄥ ㄕㄨㄛ ㄈㄚˇ)
(said of orations) very touching or convincing; emotion-arousing

生客(ㄕㄥ ㄎㄜˋ)
a new guest; an unfamiliar guest

生恐(ㄕㄥ ㄎㄨㄥˇ)
very anxious; very apprehensive

生虎子(ㄕㄥ ㄏㄨˇ ·ㄗ)
a beginner; a novice; a greenhorn

生花妙筆(ㄕㄥ ㄏㄨㄚ ㄇㄧㄠˋ ㄅㄧˇ)
ability for exquisite writing; admirable writing skill

生活(ㄕㄥ ㄏㄨㄛˊ)
① life; 日常生活 daily life ② to live: 我與我太太幸福地生活著。I live happily with my wife.

生活必需品(ㄕㄥ ㄏㄨㄛˊ ㄅㄧˋ ㄒㄩ ㄆㄧㄣˇ)
necessities of life: 這些是生活必需品。These are necessities of life.

生活費(ㄕㄥ ㄏㄨㄛˊ ㄈㄟˋ)
living expenses

生活方式(ㄕㄥ ㄏㄨㄛˊ ㄈㄤ ㄕˋ)
the ways of living; the modes of living

生活指數(ㄕㄥ ㄏㄨㄛˊ ㄓˇ ㄕㄨˋ)
the index of living cost

生活程度(ㄕㄥ ㄏㄨㄛˊ ㄔㄥˊ ㄉㄨˋ)
① the standard of living ② the cost of living: 東京生活程度高。The cost of living in Tokyo is high.

生活水準(ㄕㄥ ㄏㄨㄛˊ ㄕㄨㄟˇ ㄓㄨㄣˇ)
the standard of living

生活問題(ㄕㄥ ㄏㄨㄛˊ ㄨㄣˋ ㄊㄧˊ)
the problems of livelihood

生火(ㄕㄥ ㄏㄨㄛˇ)
to make a fire; to build a fire: 生火吧！Make a fire.

生還(ㄕㄥ ㄏㄨㄢˊ)
to come back alive; to survive

生還者(ㄕㄥ ㄏㄨㄢˊ ㄓㄜˇ)
a survivor

生機(ㄕㄥ ㄐㄧ)
① vitality; liveliness: 整個天地間似乎充滿了生機。All nature seemed to be full of life. ② the chance of survival

生計(ㄕㄥ ㄐㄧˋ)
livelihood; living: 我另謀生計。I tried to find some other means of livelihood.

生寄死歸(ㄕㄥ ㄐㄧˋ ㄙˇ ㄍㄨㄟ)
To live is like being a lodger in the world, and to die is like returning home.

生就的(ㄕㄥ ㄐㄧㄡˋ ·ㄉㄜ)
inborn; by nature: 他生就的懶。He is lazy by nature.

生薑(ㄕㄥ ㄐㄧㄤ)
green ginger

生聚教訓(ㄕㄥ ㄐㄩˋ ㄐㄧㄠˋ ㄒㄩㄣˋ)
the pooling and training of manpower (for a sacred war)

生絹(ㄕㄥ ㄐㄩㄢ)
raw silk

生漆(ㄕㄥ ㄑㄧ)
crude lacquer

生氣(ㄕㄥ ㄑㄧˋ)
① vitality; liveliness: 年輕人充滿了生氣。Young people are full of vitality. ② to get angry; to get mad

生氣蓬勃(ㄕㄥ ㄑㄧˋ ㄆㄥˊ ㄅㄛˊ)
vigorous; active; lively: 那老人依然生氣蓬勃。The old man is still vigorous and lively.

生前(ㄕㄥ ㄑㄧㄢˊ)
during one's lifetime; before one's death; while one was alive

生擒(ㄕㄥ ㄑㄧㄣˊ)
to take (a prisoner) alive; to capture alive

生趣(ㄕㄥ ㄑㄩˋ)
the pleasure of life

生全(ㄕㄥ ㄑㄩㄢˊ)
the salvation of life

生息(ㄕㄥ ㄒㄧˊ)
①to bear interest; to yield interest ②to reproduce and multiply ③to live; living

生肖(ㄕㄥ ㄒㄧㄠˋ)
the relation of the year of one's birth to one of the 12 animals (the mouse, the ox, the tiger, the rabbit, the dragon, the snake, the horse, the sheep, the monkey, the fowl, the dog, and the pig)亦作[屬相]

生效(ㄕㄥ ㄒㄧㄠˋ)
to go into effect; to be effective or valid

生銹(ㄕㄥ ㄒㄧㄡˋ)
to rust: 我的刀生銹了。My knife rusted.

生性(ㄕㄥ ㄒㄧㄥˋ)
①natural disposition; nature ②aloof; unfriendly

生殖(ㄕㄥ ㄓˊ)
(biology) reproduction

生殖力(ㄕㄥ ㄓˊ ㄌㄧˋ)
fecundity

生殖器(ㄕㄥ ㄓˊ ㄑㄧˋ)
reproductive organs; genitals

生張熟魏(ㄕㄥ ㄓㄤ ㄕㄡˊ ㄨㄟˋ)
①old acquaintances and new customers received alike by the prostitutes — promiscuous ②to be unacquainted with each other

生長(ㄕㄥ ㄓㄤˇ)
to grow; to develop; growth

生長激素(ㄕㄥ ㄓㄤˇ ㄐㄧ ㄙㄨˋ)
growth hormone

生衆食寡(ㄕㄥ ㄓㄨㄥˋ ㄕˊ ㄍㄨㄚˇ)
Production surpasses consumption.

生吃(ㄕㄥ ㄔ)
to eat (something) raw; to eat (something) without cooking: 他生吃蔬菜。He eats vegetables raw.

生產(ㄕㄥ ㄔㄢˇ)
①to produce; production: 這個工廠生產汽車。This factory produces cars.②to give birth to; childbirth: 我姐姐快生產了。My sister will be having her baby soon.

生產部(ㄕㄥ ㄔㄢˇ ㄅㄨˋ)
a productive department

生產力(ㄕㄥ ㄔㄢˇ ㄌㄧˋ)
productivity

生產量(ㄕㄥ ㄔㄢˇ ㄌㄧㄤˋ)
the productive output

生產率(ㄕㄥ ㄔㄢˇ ㄌㄩˋ)
the production rate

生產過程(ㄕㄥ ㄔㄢˇ ㄍㄨㄛˋ ㄔㄥˊ)
production process

生產過剩(ㄕㄥ ㄔㄢˇ ㄍㄨㄛˋ ㄕㄥˋ)
overproduction

生產合作社(ㄕㄥ ㄔㄢˇ ㄏㄜˊ ㄗㄨㄛˋ ㄕㄜˋ)
a producers' guild; a producers' cooperative

生產機關(ㄕㄥ ㄔㄢˇ ㄐㄧ ㄍㄨㄢ)
①production organization ②(economics) the means of production

生產計畫(ㄕㄥ ㄔㄢˇ ㄐㄧˋ ㄏㄨㄚˋ)
a production technique

生產技術(ㄕㄥ ㄔㄢˇ ㄐㄧˋ ㄕㄨˋ)
production technique

生產效率(ㄕㄥ ㄔㄢˇ ㄒㄧㄠˋ ㄌㄩˋ)
production efficiency

生產線(ㄕㄥ ㄔㄢˇ ㄒㄧㄢˋ)
production line

生產中心(ㄕㄥ ㄔㄢˇ ㄓㄨㄥ ㄒㄧㄣ)
a production center

生產成本(ㄕㄥ ㄔㄢˇ ㄔㄥˊ ㄅㄣˇ)
(accounting) the cost of production; production cost

生產額(ㄕㄥ ㄔㄢˇ ㄜˊ)
(accounting) the volume of production

生辰(ㄕㄥ ㄔㄣˊ)
birthday

生成(ㄕㄥ ㄔㄥˊ)
①to grow to ②inborn; by nature

生石灰(ㄕㄥ ㄕˊ ㄏㄨㄟ)
quicklime; unslaked lime

生事(ㄕㄥ ㄕˋ)
①to create trouble; to give rise to disturbance ②livelihood

生殺予奪(ㄕㄥ ㄕㄚ ㄩˇ ㄉㄨㄛˊ)
to spare, kill, give, and take at will; to wield absolute power

生手(ㄕㄥ ㄕㄡˇ)
a beginner; a novice: 生手很可能出錯。Novices are likely to make some mistakes.

生身父母(ㄕㄥ ㄕㄣ ㄈㄨˋ ㄇㄨˇ)
real parents (as distinct from foster parents)

生生不息(ㄕㄥ ㄕㄥ ㄅㄨˋ ㄒㄧˊ)or 生生不已(ㄕㄥ ㄕㄥ ㄅㄨˋ ㄧˇ)
to multiply endlessly; to

breed in endless succession

生疏 or 生疎(ㄕㄥ ㄕㄨ)
①unfamiliar; unskilled; pretty rusty ②strange; not on intimate terms: 我在此人地生疏。I'm quite strange here.

生水(ㄕㄥ ㄕㄨㄟˇ)
unboiled water

生日(ㄕㄥ ㄖˋ)
birthday: 我的生日是五月二十日。My birthday is May 20.

生人(ㄕㄥ ㄖㄣˊ)
①a living person ②a stranger: 一個陌生人和我講話。A stranger spoke to me.

生榮死哀(ㄕㄥ ㄖㄨㄥˊ ㄙˇ ㄞ)
respected while living and mourned when dead

生字(ㄕㄥ ㄗˋ)
a new word; an unfamiliar word: 不要用艱澀的生字。Do not use difficult new words.

生詞(ㄕㄥ ㄘˊ)
a new word

生財(ㄕㄥ ㄘㄞˊ)
the furniture and office equipment of a shop or business firm

生財有道(ㄕㄥ ㄘㄞˊ ㄧㄡˇ ㄉㄠˋ)
to be expert in making money

生菜(ㄕㄥ ㄘㄞˋ)
raw vegetables; salad: 我點了一份生菜沙拉。I ordered a helping of vegetable salad.

生存(ㄕㄥ ㄘㄨㄣˊ)
to survive; survival; existence

生存空間(ㄕㄥ ㄘㄨㄣˊ ㄎㄨㄥ ㄐㄧㄢ)
living space; lebensraum

生存競爭(ㄕㄥ ㄘㄨㄣˊ ㄐㄧㄥˋ ㄓㄥ)
the struggle for existence

生存權(ㄕㄥ ㄘㄨㄣˊ ㄑㄩㄢˊ)
the right to life

生絲(ㄕㄥ ㄙ)
raw silk

生死關頭(ㄕㄥ ㄙˇ ㄍㄨㄢ ㄊㄡˊ)
a life-and-death crisis

生死之交(ㄕㄥ ㄙˇ ㄓ ㄐㄧㄠ)
deep friendship (implying the sharing of each other's fate)

生死肉骨(ㄕㄥ ㄙˇ ㄖㄡˋ ㄍㄨˇ)
(literally) to revive the dead and flesh a skeleton—to provide miraculous relief

〔生部〕

〔生部〕

生死以之(ㄕㄥ ㄙ ㄧˇ ㄓ)
willing to sacrifice one's life for the attainment of an objective

生色(ㄕㄥ ㄙㄜˋ)
①to add color; to add splendor ②a mild harmony appearing in the countenance

生澀(ㄕㄥ ㄙㄜˋ)
(said of a piece of writing) difficult to read or understand

生而知之(ㄕㄥ ㄦˊ ㄓ ㄓ)
to know from birth; to know without learning

生兒育女(ㄕㄥ ㄦˊ ㄩˋ ㄋㄩˇ)
to give birth to children and rear them

生疑(ㄕㄥ ㄧˊ)
to become suspicious

生意(ㄕㄥ ㄧˋ)
①business; trade: 生意清淡。 Business is dull. ②vitality: 春天的大地充滿生意。 Spring has filled the earth with vitality.

生意經(ㄕㄥ ㄧˋ ㄐㄧㄥ)
businessmen's talk

生涯(ㄕㄥ ㄧㄚˊ)
①a career; a life ②livelihood

生油(ㄕㄥ ㄧㄡˊ)
①uncooked edible oil ②peanut oil

生厭(ㄕㄥ ㄧㄢˋ)
to become bored or tired of something

生硬(ㄕㄥ ㄧㄥˋ)
awkward; stiff: 她生硬地鞠躬。 She made a stiff bow.

生物(ㄕㄥ ㄨˋ)
①a living thing; animal and plant life; an organism ②biology

生物標本(ㄕㄥ ㄨˋ ㄅㄧㄠˇ ㄅㄣˇ)
a biological specimen

生物化學(ㄕㄥ ㄨˋ ㄏㄨㄚˋ ㄒㄩㄝˊ)
biochemistry

生物界(ㄕㄥ ㄨˋ ㄐㄧㄝˋ)
the biological world; the kingdom of fauna and flora; the world of living things

生物圈(ㄕㄥ ㄨˋ ㄑㄩㄢ)
the biosphere

生物學(ㄕㄥ ㄨˋ ㄒㄩㄝˊ)
biology: 植物學和動物學是生物學的部分。Botany and zoology are branches of biology.

生於憂患，死於安樂(ㄕㄥ ㄩˊ ㄧㄡ ㄏㄨㄢˋ，ㄙˇ ㄩˊ ㄢ ㄌㄜˋ)
Life springs from sorrow and calamity, and death from ease and pleasure.—to thrive in adversity and to perish in soft living

生育(ㄕㄥ ㄩˋ)
to give birth to; childbirth

生育限制(ㄕㄥ ㄩˋ ㄒㄧㄢˋ ㄓˋ)
birth control; family planning

生員(ㄕㄥ ㄩㄢˊ)
①successful candidates in local examinations under the former civil service system ②(in old times) students

五畫

【牲】 3540
ㄕㄥ shen shēn
1. numerous; many
2. crowded

六畫

【產】 3541
ㄔㄢˇ chaan chǎn
1. to bear (offspring); to lay (eggs)
2. to produce; to bring about: 耕作是有生產價值的勞動。 Farming is productive labor.

產婆(ㄔㄢˇ ㄆㄛˊ)
a midwife

產品(ㄔㄢˇ ㄆㄧㄣˇ)
products

產品成本(ㄔㄢˇ ㄆㄧㄣˇ ㄔㄥˊ ㄅㄣˇ)
product cost

產門(ㄔㄢˇ ㄇㄣˊ)
(anatomy) the vagina

產房(ㄔㄢˇ ㄈㄤˊ)
a lying-in room; a maternity room; a delivery ward

產婦(ㄔㄢˇ ㄈㄨˋ)
a lying-in woman; a woman who has just given birth to a baby

產地(ㄔㄢˇ ㄉㄧˋ)
a producing center; a growing district; a breeding center

產地證明書(ㄔㄢˇ ㄉㄧˋ ㄓㄥˋ ㄇㄧㄥˊ ㄕㄨ)
the certificate of origin

產量(ㄔㄢˇ ㄌㄧㄤˋ)
production; output; yield: 過去三十年中農產品產量劇增。 Over the last thirty years crop yields have increased sharply.

產卵(ㄔㄢˇ ㄌㄨㄢˇ)
to lay eggs; to spawn

產卵管(ㄔㄢˇ ㄌㄨㄢˇ ㄍㄨㄢˇ)or產卵器(ㄔㄢˇ ㄌㄨㄢˇ ㄑㄧˋ)
(zoology) the ovipositor

產卵期(ㄔㄢˇ ㄌㄨㄢˇ ㄑㄧˊ)
the breeding season; the spawning season

產科(ㄔㄢˇ ㄎㄜ)
obstetrics

產科醫生(ㄔㄢˇ ㄎㄜ ㄧ ㄕㄥ)
an obstetrician

產科醫院(ㄔㄢˇ ㄎㄜ ㄧ ㄩㄢˋ)
a lying-in hospital; a maternity hospital

產後(ㄔㄢˇ ㄏㄡˋ)
after childbirth; postnatal

產假(ㄔㄢˇ ㄐㄧㄚˋ)
maternity leave: 她請產假。 She asked for maternity leave.

產期(ㄔㄢˇ ㄑㄧ)
time of childbirth

產前(ㄔㄢˇ ㄑㄧㄢˊ)
before childbirth; prenatal

產權(ㄔㄢˇ ㄑㄩㄢˊ)
ownership (of real estate)

產銷(ㄔㄢˇ ㄒㄧㄠ)
production and marketing

產銷合一(ㄔㄢˇ ㄒㄧㄠ ㄏㄜˊ ㄧ)or產銷一元化(ㄔㄢˇ ㄒㄧㄠ ㄧ ㄩㄢˊ ㄏㄨㄚˋ)
integration of production and marketing operations

產生(ㄔㄢˇ ㄕㄥ)
to produce; to give rise to; to cause; to bring about: 那一世紀產生的偉人很少。 The century produced few great men.

產蓐 or 產褥(ㄔㄢˇ ㄖㄨˋ)
lying-in

產褥熱(ㄔㄢˇ ㄖㄨˋ ㄖㄜˋ)
puerperal fever

產額(ㄔㄢˇ ㄜˊ)
the amount of production; output

產兒(ㄔㄢˇ ㄦˊ)
a newborn infant

產業(ㄔㄢˇ ㄧㄝˋ)

①property; estate: 他有一大片產業。He has a large estate. ②industry

產業革命(ㄔㄢˇ ㄧㄝˋ ㄍㄜˊ ㄇㄧㄥˋ)
the Industrial Revolution

產物(ㄔㄢˇ ㄨˋ)
products; outcomes

七畫

【甥】 3542
ㄕㄥ shēng shēng
1. a nephew (son of a sister)
2. a son-in-law who assumes one's own name and lives under one's own roof

甥女(ㄕㄥ ㄋㄩˇ)
a niece (daughter of a sister)

甥舘(ㄕㄥ ㄍㄨㄢˇ)
the room for a son-in-law who assumes his father-in-law's name and lives under his father-in-law's roof

甥兒(ㄕㄥ ㄦˊ)
a nephew; a sister's son

【甦】 3543
ㄙㄨ su sū
to come back to life; to rise from the dead; to revive; to resurrect; to regain consciousness

甦醒(ㄙㄨ ㄒㄧㄥˇ)
to come back to life; to revive; to come to: 他使昏迷的孩子甦醒。He revived a senseless child.

【甤】 3544
ㄖㄨㄟˊ ruei ruí
(plants) drooping with fruit

用 部
ㄩㄥˋ yonq yòng

【用】 3545
ㄩㄥˋ yonq yòng
1. to use; to employ: 誰都不應使用暴力。Nobody should use force.
2. to exert
3. use: 那架電視仍在使用。The television set is still in use.
4. effect
5. finance
6. to need; need: 不用擔心。Do not worry.
7. to eat; to drink: 請用甜點。Have some sweets, please.

用畢(ㄩㄥˋ ㄅㄧˋ)
after using (durable articles)

用兵(ㄩㄥˋ ㄅㄧㄥ)
to make use of troops; to manipulate troops: 他善於用兵。He is well versed in the art of war.

用不得(ㄩㄥˋ ㄅㄨˋ ㄉㄜˊ)
①unfit for use ②(said of a person) cannot be employed without resulting in harm

用不了(ㄩㄥˋ ㄅㄨˋ ㄌㄧㄠˇ)
①more than enough for the purpose: 我把用不了的錢放在銀行裏。I put the spare money in the bank. ②can be done with less

用不慣(ㄩㄥˋ ㄅㄨˋ ㄍㄨㄢˋ)
unaccustomed to the use of

用不著(ㄩㄥˋ ㄅㄨˋ ㄓㄠˊ)
①to have no use for ②there is no need to; it is unnecessary to

用不盡(ㄩㄥˋ ㄅㄨˋ ㄐㄧㄣˋ)
too many or too much for use; cannot be used up

用品(ㄩㄥˋ ㄆㄧㄣˇ)
articles for use: 這些是辦公用品。These are articles for office use.

用命(ㄩㄥˋ ㄇㄧㄥˋ)
to obey orders

用法(ㄩㄥˋ ㄈㄚˇ)
the way to use a thing; directions for using or operating something

用非所學(ㄩㄥˋ ㄈㄟ ㄙㄨㄛˇ ㄒㄩㄝˊ)
to be engaged in an occupation not related to one's training

用非所長(ㄩㄥˋ ㄈㄟ ㄙㄨㄛˇ ㄔㄤˊ)
to be engaged in an occupation having nothing to do with one's speciality

用飯(ㄩㄥˋ ㄈㄢˋ)
to have a meal; to take a meal; to eat a meal

用得着(ㄩㄥˋ ㄉㄜˊ ㄓㄠˊ)
①to find something useful; to need ②there is need to; it is necessary to: 你用得着立刻出發嗎? Is it necessary that you start at once?

用地(ㄩㄥˋ ㄉㄧˋ)
land for a specific use

用度(ㄩㄥˋ ㄉㄨˋ)
expenses; expenditure: 他的用度浩繁。His expenditure is multifarious.

用特(ㄩㄥˋ ㄊㄜˋ)
Therefore, I specially.... (a conventional phrase in formal letters)

用頭(ㄩㄥˋ ㄊㄡˊ)
use (to which a thing can be put); a purpose (for which a thing may be employed)

用途(ㄩㄥˋ ㄊㄨˊ)
a purpose (for which a thing may be employed); use: 今日石油的用途很廣。Nowadays petroleum has many uses.

用力(ㄩㄥˋ ㄌㄧˋ)
to exert oneself; to make an effort; to put forth one's strength: 我用力把車推了一下。I gave the car a hard push.

用力過度(ㄩㄥˋ ㄌㄧˋ ㄍㄨㄛˋ ㄉㄨˋ)
to exert oneself too strenuously; to make too strenuous efforts

用光(ㄩㄥˋ ㄍㄨㄤ)
to use up; to run out of; to exhaust: 他用光了所有的錢。He exhausted all his money.

用功(ㄩㄥˋ ㄍㄨㄥ)
to study diligently; to work hard; to study hard

用工夫(ㄩㄥˋ ㄍㄨㄥ ㄈㄨ)
to practice or study diligently; to work hard

用戶(ㄩㄥˋ ㄏㄨˋ)
a customer (of a utility); a consumer: 公司徵求用戶意見。The company asked for consumers' opinions.

用計(ㄩㄥˋ ㄐㄧˋ)
to use tricks; to employ schemes: 他用計騙害人。He used tricks for getting another in trouble.

用盡(ㄩㄥˋ ㄐㄧㄣˋ)
to exhaust (strength, etc.)

用盡方法(ㄩㄥˋ ㄐㄧㄣˋ ㄈㄤ ㄈㄚˇ)
to exhaust one's wits; to resort to every available means; to do something by hook or by crook

〔用部〕

〔田部〕

用盡心機(ㄩㄥ ㄐㄧㄣ ㄒㄧㄣ ㄐㄧ)
to have tried every means; to have left no stone unturned: 他用盡心機賺錢。He has tried every means to earn money.

用具(ㄩㄥ ㄐㄩ)
a tool; an appliance; an implement

用錢(ㄩㄥ ㄑㄧㄢ)
① to spend money ② middleman's fees; commission

用錢如水(ㄩㄥ ㄑㄧㄢ ㄖㄨ ㄕㄨㄟ)
to spend money like water; to spend money carelessly or extravagantly

用情(ㄩㄥ ㄑㄧㄥ)
to appeal to emotion; to feel serious about a love affair

用情不專(ㄩㄥ ㄑㄧㄥ ㄅㄨ ㄓㄨㄢ)
to be frivolous in affairs of the heart

用去(ㄩㄥ ㄑㄩ)
to have spent or used

用賢(ㄩㄥ ㄒㄧㄢ)
to employ men of wisdom and virtue

用心(ㄩㄥ ㄒㄧㄣ)
to be careful; to exercise caution; to take care; to pay attention: 你讀用心讀書。You must pay attention to your study.

用心良苦(ㄩㄥ ㄒㄧㄣ ㄌㄧㄤ ㄎㄨ)
well-intentioned but little understood; to lay oneself out

用刑(ㄩㄥ ㄒㄧㄥ)
to torture

用之不竭(ㄩㄥ ㄓ ㄅㄨ ㄐㄧㄝ)
It cannot be used up. 或It is inexhaustible.

用場(ㄩㄥ ㄔㄤ)or用處(ㄩㄥ ㄔㄨ)
a purpose (for which a thing may be employed); use: 用處甚大。The usefulness is great.

用世(ㄩㄥ ㄕ)
to be employed in a way in which one can do good to the world

用事(ㄩㄥ ㄕ)
① to be in power ② to manage things; to handle things; to act: 你別意氣用事。Don't be swayed by your feelings and act rashly.

用是(ㄩㄥ ㄕ)
therefore; for this reason

用水(ㄩㄥ ㄕㄨㄟ)
① to use water ② water for a specific use

用人(ㄩㄥ ㄖㄣ)
① to employ people ② a servant

用字(ㄩㄥ ㄗ)
wording

用以(ㄩㄥ ㄧ)
in order to; so as to

用意(ㄩㄥ ㄧ)
an intention; a purpose; an idea: 他用意甚善。He is well-intended.

用印(ㄩㄥ ㄧㄣ)
to put a stamp or seal on a document; to stamp

用武(ㄩㄥ ㄨ)
① to resort to force; to use violence ② to display one's abilities or talents

用完(ㄩㄥ ㄨㄢ)
to use up; to exhaust

用語(ㄩㄥ ㄩ)
terminology; phraseology: 我不懂法律用語。I don't understand legal phraseology.

用韻(ㄩㄥ ㄩㄣ)
to use rhyme

【甩】 3546
ㄕㄨㄞ shoai shuai
1. to throw away; to discard; to cast away
2. to leave (somebody) behind
3. to swing: 不要用你的手臂。Don't swing your arms.

用不掉(ㄕㄨㄞ ㄅㄨ ㄉㄧㄠ)or甩不脫(ㄕㄨㄞ ㄅㄨ ㄊㄨㄛ)
cannot get rid of; cannot shake off

甩了(ㄕㄨㄞ ㄌㄜ)
to have thrown away; to have cast away: 他被女朋友甩了。He was thrown overboard by his girl friend.

甩手(ㄕㄨㄞ ㄕㄡ)
to take no heed; to ignore; to wash one's hands of

二畫

【甫】 3547
ㄈㄨ fuu fǔ
1. (euphemism) a man
2. (euphemism) father

3. then and only then
4. just; immediately after; a short while ago
5. barely
6. a Chinese family name

甫能(ㄈㄨ ㄋㄥ)
able then and only then

【甬】 3548
ㄩㄥ yeong yǒng
1. a measure of capacity (equal to 10 斗)
2. alternative name of Ningpo, Chekiang

甬道(ㄩㄥ ㄉㄠ)or甬路(ㄩㄥ ㄌㄨ)
① the central path in a hall
② a road flanked by walls
③ a corridor

四畫

【甭】 3549
ㄅㄥ berng béng
unnecessary; do not have to: 甭再說了。Don't say anymore.

七畫

【甯】 3550
1. ㄋㄧㄥ ninq níng
a Chinese family name

【甯】 3550
2. ㄋㄧㄥ ning níng
same as 寧—peaceful; rather

田 部
ㄊㄧㄢ tyan tián

【田】 3551
ㄊㄧㄢ tyan tián
1. agricultural land; cultivated land; a field; a rice field; farmland; cropland: 他星期天在田地裏工作。He works in the field on Sunday.
2. to hunt game
3. a Chinese family name

田夫(ㄊㄧㄢ ㄈㄨ)
a farmer; a husbandman

田父(ㄊㄧㄢ ㄈㄨ)
an old farmer; an aged farmer

田賦(ㄊㄧㄢ ㄈㄨ)
taxes on agricultural land

田單(ㄊㄧㄢ ㄉㄢ)
① title deeds (for agricul-

tural land) ②General Tien Tan of the Chi State (齊國) during the Epoch of War-ring States, who recovered his fatherland from the hands of Yen (燕) invaders

田地(ㄊㄧㄢˊㄉㄧˋ)
①agricultural land ②posi-tion; condition; state of affairs; a plight: 我怎麼落到這步田地。How did I get into such a plight?

田頭
a manager of agricultural land

田納西(ㄊㄧㄢˊㄋㄚˋㄒㄧ)
Tennessee, U.S.A.

田里(ㄊㄧㄢˊㄌㄧˇ)
a rural area; a rural commu-nity

田獵
to hunt game

田廬(ㄊㄧㄢˊㄌㄨˊ)
a farmhouse

田螺(ㄊㄧㄢˊㄌㄨㄛˊ)
a mud-snail; a pond-snail

田埂(ㄊㄧㄢˊㄍㄥˇ)
ridges between plots of farmland

田戶(ㄊㄧㄢˊㄏㄨˋ)
a land tiller; a farmer

田雞(ㄊㄧㄢˊㄐㄧ)
a frog

田家(ㄊㄧㄢˊㄐㄧㄚ)
a farming family; a peasant family; a cottage

田家子(ㄊㄧㄢˊㄐㄧㄚˊㄗˇ)
farmers; farming people; peasants

田間(ㄊㄧㄢˊㄐㄧㄢ)
in the field

田徑賽(ㄊㄧㄢˊㄐㄧㄥˋㄙㄞˋ)
track and field events

田契(ㄊㄧㄢˊㄑㄧˋ)
a title deed for agricultural land

田器(ㄊㄧㄢˊㄑㄧˋ)
agricultural tools; farming implements

田主(ㄊㄧㄢˊㄓㄨˇ)
a landlord (of agricultural land)

田莊(ㄊㄧㄢˊㄓㄨㄤ)
a farmhouse; a farmstead: 我祖父有一座田莊。My grand-father had a farmhouse.

田中義一(ㄊㄧㄢˊㄓㄨㄥㄧˋㄧ)
Giichi Tanaka (1863-1929), Japanese prime minister (1927-1929), a military and political leader known for masterminding the invasion of China

田疇(ㄊㄧㄢˊㄔㄡˊ)
agricultural land; farmland

田產(ㄊㄧㄢˊㄔㄢˇ)
real estate

田舍(ㄊㄧㄢˊㄕㄜˋ)
a farmhouse

田舍奴(ㄊㄧㄢˊㄕㄜˋㄋㄨˊ)or 田舍漢
(ㄊㄧㄢˊㄕㄜˋㄏㄢˋ)or 田舍兒(ㄊㄧㄢˊ
ㄕㄜˋㄦˊ)
a country bumpkin; a yokel; a rustic

田舍翁(ㄊㄧㄢˊㄕㄜˋㄨㄥ)
an old countryman

田鼠(ㄊㄧㄢˊㄕㄨˇ)
the field mouse

田租(ㄊㄧㄢˊㄗㄨ)
the land rental paid by a tenant farmer

田賽(ㄊㄧㄢˊㄙㄞˋ)
field sports; field events

田叟(ㄊㄧㄢˊㄙㄡˇ)
old farmers; aged farmers

田岸(ㄊㄧㄢˊㄢˋ)
ridges between plots of farmland

田野(ㄊㄧㄢˊㄧㄝˇ)
fields; cultivated lands

田月桑時(ㄊㄧㄢˊㄩㄝˋㄙㄤㄕˊ)
the farming season

田園(ㄊㄧㄢˊㄩㄢˊ)
①fields and gardens ②rural; pastoral; bucolic

田園詩人(ㄊㄧㄢˊㄩㄢˊㄕㄖㄣˊ)
a pastoral poet; an idyllist

田園文學(ㄊㄧㄢˊㄩㄢˊㄨㄣˊㄒㄩㄝˊ)
pastoral literature; idyllic literature

【由】 3552
　　ㄧˊ you yóu
1. reason; cause; a source; deri-vation
2. from: 鋼是由鐵製成的。Steel is made from iron.
3. up to (someone to make a decision): 事不由己。Things are getting out of hand.
4. by; through: 請由大門出去。Please exit by the main door.

---

5. a Chinese family name

由不得(ㄧˊㄅㄨˋㄉㄜˊ)
involuntarily; unable to do as one pleases: 這件事由不得你。The matter is not up to you.

由他去罷(ㄧˊㄊㄚㄑㄩˋㄅㄚˋ)
Leave him alone. 或 Let him be.

由天而降(ㄧˊㄊㄧㄢㄦˊㄐㄧㄤˋ)
to come down from heaven; to come from nowhere

由你(ㄧˊㄋㄧˇ)
as you please; as you like; whatever you say

由你決定(ㄧˊㄋㄧˇㄐㄩㄝˊㄉㄧㄥˋ)
It's up to you to make the decision. 此事由你決定。This matter is up to you to make the decision.

由來(ㄧˊㄌㄞˊ)
①derivation; a source ②so far; up to now

由來已久(ㄧˊㄌㄞˊㄧˇㄐㄧㄡˇ)
It has been so for quite some time. 或 long-standing; time-honored: 這種風俗由來已久。This is a long-standing custom.

由儉入奢易(ㄧˊㄐㄧㄢˇㄖㄨˋㄕㄜㄧˋ)
It is easy to go from frugal-ity to extravagance.

由簡而繁(ㄧˊㄐㄧㄢˇㄦˊㄈㄢˊ)
to go from the simple to the complex

由近及遠(ㄧˊㄐㄧㄣˋㄐㄧˊㄩㄢˇ)
to go from the near to the distant

由淺入深(ㄧˊㄑㄧㄢˇㄖㄨˋㄕㄣ)
to go from the easy to the difficult and complicated

由衷(ㄧˊㄓㄨㄥ)
from the depth of one's heart; heartfelt: 我們表示由衷的感激。We extended our heartfelt thanks.

由衷之言(ㄧˊㄓㄨㄥㄓㄧㄢˊ)
words uttered in sincerity; words spoken from the bot-tom of one's heart

由奢入儉難(ㄧˊㄕㄜㄖㄨˋㄐㄧㄢˇㄋㄢˊ)
It is difficult to go from extravagance to frugality.

由此(ㄧˊㄘˇ)
hence; from this; therefore

由此觀之(ㄧˊㄘˇㄍㄨㄢㄓ)
judging from this; looking at

〔田部〕

【田部】

the matter from this viewpoint

由此可見(ㄧㄡˊ ㄘˇ ㄎㄜˇ ㄐㄧㄢˋ)
thus it can be seen; this shows; that proves

由此前往(ㄧㄡˊ ㄘˇ ㄑㄧㄢˊ ㄨㄤˇ)
to go from here

由於(ㄧㄡˊ ㄩˊ)
because of; owing to; due to; as a result of: 由於你的協助，工作進行得很順利。Owing to your assistance, work is going on smoothly.

【甲】 3553
ㄐㄧㄚˇ jea jiǎ

1. the first of the Ten Celestial Stems
2. armor; shell; crust
3. most outstanding
4. a measure of land in Taiwan (equal to 0.97 hectare)
5. a tithing—a group of ten families under the Tithing System introduced by Wang An-shih(王安石)of the Sung Dynasty

甲板(ㄐㄧㄚˇ ㄅㄢˇ)
the deck (of a ship)

甲苯(ㄐㄧㄚˇ ㄅㄣˇ)
toluene, or methylbenzene

甲榜(ㄐㄧㄚˇ ㄅㄤˇ)
a successful candidate in an imperial examination under the former civil service examination system

甲兵(ㄐㄧㄚˇ ㄅㄧㄥ)or 甲士(ㄐㄧㄚˇ ㄕˋ) or 甲卒(ㄐㄧㄚˇ ㄗㄨˊ)
an armed soldier

甲部(ㄐㄧㄚˇ ㄅㄨˋ)
the Classics (one of the four traditional library divisions) 亦作「經部」

甲等(ㄐㄧㄚˇ ㄉㄥˇ)
grade-A (said of student papers scoring 80 points or more)

甲第(ㄐㄧㄚˇ ㄉㄧˋ)
①a mansion; a hall: 甲第連雲。Large and high houses are towering to the clouds. ②a top successful candidate in an examination

甲天下(ㄐㄧㄚˇ ㄊㄧㄢ ㄒㄧㄚˋ)
to be unequaled in the world: 桂林山水甲天下。The mountains and rivers of Kweilin are the finest under heaven.

甲骨文(ㄐㄧㄚˇ ㄍㄨˇ ㄨㄣˊ)
oracle-bone scriptures

甲科(ㄐㄧㄚˇ ㄎㄜ)
the highest category in the civil service examinations before the Republic

甲殼(ㄐㄧㄚˇ ㄎㄜˊ)
a shell

甲殼類(ㄐㄧㄚˇ ㄎㄜˊ ㄌㄟˋ)
the crustacean: 螃蟹、龍蝦、蝦子等是甲殼類。Crabs, lobsters, shrimps, etc. are crustaceans.

甲基(ㄐㄧㄚˇ ㄐㄧ)
methyl

甲醛(ㄐㄧㄚˇ ㄑㄩㄢˊ)
formaldehyde, or methanal

甲冑(ㄐㄧㄚˇ ㄓㄡˋ)
armor; a panoply

甲長(ㄐㄧㄚˇ ㄓㄤˇ)
a head of a tithing

甲狀腺(ㄐㄧㄚˇ ㄓㄨㄤˋ ㄒㄧㄢˋ)
thyroid

甲狀腺切除手術(ㄐㄧㄚˇ ㄓㄨㄤˋ ㄒㄧㄢˋ ㄑㄧㄝ ㄔㄨˊ ㄕㄡˇ ㄕㄨˋ)
thyroidectomy

甲狀腺腫(ㄐㄧㄚˇ ㄓㄨㄤˋ ㄒㄧㄢˋ ㄓㄨㄥˇ)
goiter

甲狀腺素(ㄐㄧㄚˇ ㄓㄨㄤˋ ㄒㄧㄢˋ ㄙㄨˋ)
thyroxine; thyroiodine

甲狀腺炎(ㄐㄧㄚˇ ㄓㄨㄤˋ ㄒㄧㄢˋ ㄧㄢˊ)
thyroiditis

甲狀軟骨(ㄐㄧㄚˇ ㄓㄨㄤˋ ㄖㄨㄢˇ ㄍㄨˇ)
the thyroid cartilage

甲醇(ㄐㄧㄚˇ ㄔㄨㄣˊ)
methyl alcohol or methanol

甲蟲(ㄐㄧㄚˇ ㄔㄨㄥˊ)
a beetle

甲申之役(ㄐㄧㄚˇ ㄕㄣ ㄓ ㄧˋ)
the Sino-French War (in 1884)

甲子(ㄐㄧㄚˇ ㄗˇ)
①the first year in a sexagenary cycle of which each year is designated by a combination of one of the Ten Celestial Stems and one of the Twelve Terrestrial Branches ②one's age

甲族(ㄐㄧㄚˇ ㄗㄨˊ)
influential families of long standing

甲乙(ㄐㄧㄚˇ ㄧˇ)
the first and second of the Ten Celestial Stems—the sequence or order of things

甲午之戰(ㄐㄧㄚˇ ㄨˇ ㄓ ㄓㄢˋ)
the Sino-Japanese War of 1894

甲烷(ㄐㄧㄚˇ ㄨㄢˊ)
methane

甲魚(ㄐㄧㄚˇ ㄩˊ)
a green turtle (Trionyx sinensis)

甲於天下(ㄐㄧㄚˇ ㄩˊ ㄊㄧㄢ ㄒㄧㄚˋ)
unequaled in the world

【申】 3554
ㄕㄣ shen shēn

1. the ninth of the Twelve Terrestrial Branches
2. to appeal; to plead
3. to state; to set forth; to explain; to explicate
4. to extend; to expand
5. to inculcate (especially repeatedly)
6. a brief name of Shanghai
7. a Chinese family name

申包胥(ㄕㄣ ㄅㄠ ㄒㄩ)
a minister of the state of Chu(楚) during the Epoch of Spring and Autumn, whose real name was Kung - Sun Pao-hsü (公孫包胥)

申報(ㄕㄣ ㄅㄠˋ)
①to declare; to file (tax returns) ②name of a newspaper formerly published in Shanghai

申報戶口(ㄕㄣ ㄅㄠˋ ㄏㄨˋ ㄎㄡˇ)
to report one's address for the domiciliary register

申辯(ㄕㄣ ㄅㄧㄢˋ)
to argue; to contend; to defend oneself; to explain one's conduct: 你將需要律師為你申辯。You will need lawyers to defend you.

申明(ㄕㄣ ㄇㄧㄥˊ)
to set forth; to explain; to expound; to explicate

申覆(ㄕㄣ ㄈㄨˋ)
to reply to a superior

申旦(ㄕㄣ ㄉㄢˋ)
from night till morning

申討(ㄕㄣ ㄊㄠˇ)
openly condemn; to denounce

申理(ㄕㄣ ㄌㄧˇ)
to redress wrong

申令(ㄕㄣ ㄌㄧㄥˋ)
to decree; to order

申告(ㄕㄣ ㄍㄠˋ)
to file a complaint (in a

court of law); to appeal to a court of law

申告鈴(ㄕㄣ ㄍㄠ ㄌㄧㄥ)
a bell to be rung when appealing to a court of law

申斥(ㄕㄣ ㄔ)
①a reprimand; a rebuke ②to rebuke; to reprimand

申請(ㄕㄣ ㄑㄧㄥ)
to request or to apply (to some authorities for something); application; request: 他向銀行申請貸款。He applied to the bank for a loan.

申請書(ㄕㄣ ㄑㄧㄥ ㄕㄨ)
an application form; a written request

申請人(ㄕㄣ ㄑㄧㄥ ㄖㄣ)
an applicant; one who makes a request to the higher authorities

申謝(ㄕㄣ ㄒㄧㄝ)
to extend one's thanks; to express gratitude

申斥(ㄕㄣ ㄔ)
to reprimand; to rebuke

申飭(ㄕㄣ ㄔ)
to reprimand; to rebuke

申時(ㄕㄣ ㄕ)
3-5 p.m.

申述(ㄕㄣ ㄕㄨ)
to state; to explain in detail

申說(ㄕㄣ ㄕㄨㄛ)
to explain; to explicate; to set forth; to expound

申訴(ㄕㄣ ㄙㄨ)
to present one's case (in a law court, etc.); to appeal; to lodge a complaint: 我向上級法院提出申訴。I appealed to the higher court.

申冤(ㄕㄣ ㄩㄢ)
to appeal for justice regarding a false charge

二畫

【男】 3555
ㄋㄢ nan nán

1. a human male; a man; a boy; a son
2. a baron

男扮女裝(ㄋㄢ ㄅㄢ ㄋㄩ ㄓㄨㄤ)
disguised as a woman

男儐相(ㄋㄢ ㄅㄧㄣ ㄒㄧㄤ)
a best man (at a wedding)

男朋友(ㄋㄢ ㄆㄥ ㄧㄡ)
a boyfriend: 從來沒有人看見她有男朋友。She is never seen with a boy.

男僕(ㄋㄢ ㄆㄨ)
a male servant

男方(ㄋㄢ ㄈㄤ)
the bridegroom's family, relatives and friends collectively

男大當婚，女大當嫁(ㄋㄢ ㄉㄚ ㄉㄤ ㄏㄨㄣ，ㄋㄩ ㄉㄚ ㄉㄤ ㄐㄧㄚ)
Upon growing up, every male should take a wife and every female should take a husband.

男盜女娼(ㄋㄢ ㄉㄠ ㄋㄩ ㄔㄤ)
The male are robbers and the female harlots.

男低音(ㄋㄢ ㄉㄧ ㄧㄣ)
(music)①bass (the lowest male voice) ②a bass (a singer with the lowest male voice)

男女(ㄋㄢ ㄋㄩ)
①male and female; men and women; both sexes ②one's children ③attendants; servants

男女平等(ㄋㄢ ㄋㄩ ㄆㄧㄥ ㄉㄥ)
equal rights for both sexes

男女同校(ㄋㄢ ㄋㄩ ㄊㄨㄥ ㄒㄧㄠ)
coeducation

男女老幼(ㄋㄢ ㄋㄩ ㄌㄠ ㄧㄡ)
males and females of all ages; all people regardless of age and sex

男女關係(ㄋㄢ ㄋㄩ ㄍㄨㄢ ㄒㄧ)
relations between the two sexes

男女授受不親(ㄋㄢ ㄋㄩ ㄕㄡ ㄕㄡ ㄅㄨ ㄑㄧㄣ)
A man and a woman unless related by blood or marriage should not touch hands when giving and taking things. (according to the code of conduct before the republican era)

男女有別(ㄋㄢ ㄋㄩ ㄧㄡ ㄅㄧㄝ)
Males and females should be treated differently. 或 Males and females should be distinguished.

男高音(ㄋㄢ ㄍㄠ ㄧㄣ)
(music)①tenor (the highest male voice) ②a tenor (a singer with the highest male voice)

男耕女織(ㄋㄢ ㄍㄥ ㄋㄩ ㄓ)
(said of an agricultural society) The men plow and the women weave.

男孩子(ㄋㄢ ㄏㄞˊ ㄗ)or 男孩兒(ㄋㄢ ㄏㄞㄦ)
a boy

男歡女愛(ㄋㄢ ㄏㄨㄢ ㄋㄩ ㄞ)
The couple are enraptured with love.

男婚女嫁(ㄋㄢ ㄏㄨㄣ ㄋㄩ ㄐㄧㄚ)
A man should take a wife and a woman should take a husband.

男家(ㄋㄢ ㄐㄧㄚ)
the bridegroom's family

男爵(ㄋㄢ ㄐㄩㄝ)
a baron

男爵夫人(ㄋㄢ ㄐㄩㄝ ㄈㄨ ㄖㄣ)
a baroness

男系(ㄋㄢ ㄒㄧ)
the male line; the spear side

男性(ㄋㄢ ㄒㄧㄥ)
①the male sex ②the masculine gender

男性荷爾蒙(ㄋㄢ ㄒㄧㄥ ㄏㄜ ㄦ ㄇㄥ)
(biochemistry) androgen

男性化(ㄋㄢ ㄒㄧㄥ ㄏㄨㄚ)
(said of a girl or a woman) acting or behaving like a man

男裝(ㄋㄢ ㄓㄨㄤ)
male costume; men's clothing

男中音(ㄋㄢ ㄓㄨㄥ ㄧㄣ)
(music)①baritone, or barytone (the male singing voice lower than tenor and higher than bass) ②a baritone, or a barytone (a man with such a singing voice)

男生(ㄋㄢ ㄕㄥ)
a boy student

男子(ㄋㄢ ㄗ)or 男人(ㄋㄢ ㄖㄣ)
a man: 他沒有男子氣。He's only half a man.

男子漢(ㄋㄢ ㄗ ㄏㄢ)
a manly man: 我們怎樣使他成為男子漢? How can we make a man of him?

男子生殖器(ㄋㄢ ㄗ ㄕㄥ ㄓ ㄑㄧ)
the male genitals; the male reproductive organs

男左女右(ㄋㄢ ㄗㄨㄛ ㄋㄩ ㄧㄡ)
(a popular concept) The left

〔田部〕

represents the male and the right represents the female.

男尊女卑(ㄋㄢ ㄗㄨㄣ ㄋㄩ ㄅㄟ)
the treatment of females as inferior to males

男廁所(ㄋㄢ ㄘㄜ ㄙㄨㄛ)
men's room

男才女貌(ㄋㄢ ㄘㄞ ㄋㄩ ㄇㄠ)
The man is able and the woman is beautiful. —an ideal couple

男色(ㄋㄢ ㄙㄜ)or 男寵(ㄋㄢ ㄔㄨㄥ)
sodomy; buggery

男兒(ㄋㄢ ㄦ)
① a boy; a son ② a man (emphasizing the manliness)

男兒本色(ㄋㄢ ㄦ ㄅㄣ ㄙㄜ)
the manliness of a man

【甸】 3556
ㄉㄧㄢ diann diàn
1. suburbs or outskirts of the capital
2. to govern; to rule
3. farm crops

甸服(ㄉㄧㄢ ㄈㄨ)
areas within 500 *li* of the capital in the Hsia Dynasty

甸地(ㄉㄧㄢ ㄉㄧ)
the suburbs or outskirts of the capital

甸甸(ㄉㄧㄢ ㄉㄧㄢ)
the sound of horses and carriages in motion

甸侯(ㄉㄧㄢ ㄏㄡ)
feudal lord within 500 *li* of the imperial capital in the Hsia Dynasty

甸人(ㄉㄧㄢ ㄖㄣ)
an ancient official title

甸役(ㄉㄧㄢ ㄧ)
hunting

甸萬姓(ㄉㄧㄢ ㄨㄢ ㄒㄧㄥ)
to govern the people

【町】 3557
ㄊㄧㄥ tiing tǐng
the boundary between agricultural land

町畦(ㄊㄧㄥ ㄓㄨㄟ)
waste land; a paddock

町畦(ㄊㄧㄥ ㄒㄧ)
a low bank of earth between fields

【町】 3557
ㄉㄧㄥ ding dǐng
(in Japan) a street; a city block

三畫

【甿】 3558
ㄇㄥ meng méng
farming population

【畁】 3559
ㄅㄧ bih bì
to confer; to bestow; to give to

四畫

【界】 3560
ㄐㄧㄝ jieh jiè
1. a boundary
2. to limit; to demarcate; to define; to delimit
3. world

界碑(ㄐㄧㄝ ㄅㄟ)
a landmark; a boundary stone

界畫(ㄐㄧㄝ ㄏㄨㄚ)
to draw lines with the aid of a ruler in drawing palatial buildings 亦作「匠畫」

界限(ㄐㄧㄝ ㄒㄧㄢ)
① outer limits; a border ② to limit; to restrict

界線(ㄐㄧㄝ ㄒㄧㄢ)
a boundary; a borderline; a dividing line; a demarcation line

界尺(ㄐㄧㄝ ㄔ)
a ruler (for ruling a line)

界石(ㄐㄧㄝ ㄕ)
a boundary stone; a landmark

界說(ㄐㄧㄝ ㄕㄨㄛ)
a definition

界外球(ㄐㄧㄝ ㄨㄞ ㄑㄧㄡ)
(sports) out-of-bounds

界約(ㄐㄧㄝ ㄩㄝ)
a frontier agreement (between two countries)

【畏】 3561
ㄨㄟ wey wèi
1. to stand in awe of; to fear; to dread; to be afraid of; to be scared of
2. to revere; to respect

畏避(ㄨㄟ ㄅㄧ)
to evade because of fear

畏怕(ㄨㄟ ㄆㄚ)
to fear; to dread; to stand in awe of

畏法(ㄨㄟ ㄈㄚ)
to fear the law

畏服(ㄨㄟ ㄈㄨ)
to submit from fear; to yield from awe

畏憚(ㄨㄟ ㄉㄢ)
to have scruples about

畏途(ㄨㄟ ㄊㄨ)
① a difficult path deserving fear; a dangerous path ② a task shirked by everybody

畏難(ㄨㄟ ㄋㄢ)
to fear difficulty

畏光(ㄨㄟ ㄍㄨㄤ)
(medicine) photophobia

畏忌(ㄨㄟ ㄐㄧ)
to have scruples about

畏敬(ㄨㄟ ㄐㄧㄥ)
to stand in awe of

畏懼(ㄨㄟ ㄐㄩ)
to dread; to be scared of; to fear

畏怯(ㄨㄟ ㄑㄧㄝ)
to fear; to be scared of

畏葸退縮(ㄨㄟ ㄒㄧ ㄊㄨㄟ ㄙㄨㄛ)
to recoil from fear

畏首畏尾(ㄨㄟ ㄕㄡ ㄨㄟ ㄨㄟ)
to have too many fears; to harbor fear fore and aft

畏日(ㄨㄟ ㄖ)
the scorching sun in summer

畏罪(ㄨㄟ ㄗㄨㄟ)
to be afraid of punishment

畏罪自殺(ㄨㄟ ㄗㄨㄟ ㄗ ㄕㄚ)
to kill oneself from fear of punishment

畏死(ㄨㄟ ㄙ)
to be afraid of dying; to fear death

畏縮(ㄨㄟ ㄙㄨㄛ)
to shrink; to recoil; to cringe; to flinch

畏友(ㄨㄟ ㄧㄡ)
a friend of stern moral integrity; a respectable friend

【畋】 3562
ㄊㄧㄢ tyan tián
1. to cultivate land
2. to hunt game

畋獵(ㄊㄧㄢ ㄌㄧㄝ)
hunting

【畎】 3563
ㄑㄩㄢ cheuan quǎn
1. an irrigation ditch
2. a valley; a dale; a canyon

畎畝(ㄑㄩㄢ ㄇㄨ)

〔田 部〕

the fields

畎澮 (ㄑㄩㄢ ㄏㄨㄞ)
ditches in the fields

五畫

【畔】 3564 ㄆㄢ pann pàn
1. a boundary between fields
2. a side; a bank
3. same as 叛 — to rebel; to betray

畔岸 (ㄆㄢ ㄢ)
①limits; a boundary ②self-indulgent

【畛】 3565 ㄓㄣ jeen zhěn
1. footpathes between fields; dikes along watercourses in fields
2. a boundary; limits

畛域 (ㄓㄣ ㄩ)
range; scope; a boundary; (figuratively) distinction: 我們不分畛域. We make no distinctions.

【畚】 3566 ㄅㄣ been běn
a bamboo basket for carrying earth

畚箕 (ㄅㄣ ㄐㄧ)
a bamboo basket for carrying earth or dirt

【畜】 3567 1. ㄔㄨ chuh chù
1. a dumb creature; an animal
2. livestock

畜類 (ㄔㄨ ㄌㄟˋ)
dumb creatures; animals

畜力 (ㄔㄨ ㄌㄧˋ)
animal power

畜生 (ㄔㄨ ㄕㄥ)
①dumb creatures; animals ②a beast (a reviling term)

畜疫 (ㄔㄨ ㄧˋ)
epidemic disease of domestic animals

【畜】 3567 2. ㄒㄩ shiuh xù
1. to rear or raise (livestock or children)
2. a Chinese family name

畜牧 (ㄒㄩ ㄇㄨˋ)
animal husbandry; livestock industry

畜牧學 (ㄒㄩ ㄇㄨˋ ㄒㄩㄝˊ)
animal husbandry; zootechny

畜牧場 (ㄒㄩ ㄇㄨˋ ㄔㄤˇ) or (ㄒㄩ ㄇㄨˋ ㄔㄤˇ)
a livestock farm; a range; a grazing ground

畜牧時代 (ㄒㄩ ㄇㄨˋ ㄕˊ ㄉㄞˋ)
the pastoral age

畜產 (ㄒㄩ ㄔㄢˇ)
products of animal husbandry

畜養 (ㄒㄩ ㄧㄤˇ)
to rear or raise (livestock): 他畜養家畜. He raised domestic animals.

【畝】 3568 ㄇㄨˇ muu mǔ
mu, a Chinese land measure (equal to 733 ½ square yards)

【留】 3569 (圖) ㄌㄧㄡˊ liou liú
1. to remain; to stay; to be at a standstill
2. to ask somebody to stay
3. to detain; to obstruct; to keep; to delay
4. to leave
5. to preserve; to reserve

留別 (ㄌㄧㄡˊ ㄅㄧㄝˊ)
to give something to (or to write a poem for) a friend as a souvenir on parting

留念紀念 (ㄌㄧㄡˊ ㄐㄧˋ ㄋㄧㄢˋ)
a souvenir or keepsake

留步 (ㄌㄧㄡˊ ㄅㄨˋ)
(Please) do not trouble yourself by accompanying me to the door (a visitor's remark to the host on leaving)

留不住 (ㄌㄧㄡˊ ㄅㄨˋ ㄓㄨˋ)
unable to detain; unable to make someone stay

留得 (ㄌㄧㄡˊ ㄉㄜˊ)
to leave behind a good reputation

留得青山在，不愁沒柴燒。(ㄌㄧㄡˊ ㄉㄜˊ ㄑㄧㄥ ㄕㄢ ㄗㄞˋ, ㄅㄨˋ ㄔㄡˊ ㄇㄟˊ ㄔㄞˊ ㄕㄠ)
As long as the mountain is green, there will be firewood.—As long as there is life, there is hope.

留到 (ㄌㄧㄡˊ ㄉㄠˋ)
to wait until

留地步 (ㄌㄧㄡˊ ㄉㄧˋ ㄅㄨˋ)
not to push one's advantage too far; not to go to ex-

tremes

留頭髮 (ㄌㄧㄡˊ ㄊㄡˊ ㄈㄚˇ)
to allow the hair to grow

留退步 (ㄌㄧㄡˊ ㄊㄨㄟˋ ㄅㄨˋ) or 留後步 (ㄌㄧㄡˊ ㄏㄡˋ ㄅㄨˋ)
to leave ground for retreat

留難 (ㄌㄧㄡˊ ㄋㄢˊ)
to make things difficult (for another); to put obstacles in somebody's way: 他老是留難我。He always puts obstacles in my way.

留鳥 (ㄌㄧㄡˊ ㄋㄧㄠˇ)
a stationary bird; a resident bird

留念 (ㄌㄧㄡˊ ㄋㄧㄢˋ)
as a keepsake or souvenir

留連 (ㄌㄧㄡˊ ㄌㄧㄢˊ)
reluctant to leave; unwilling to part with

留連忘返 (ㄌㄧㄡˊ ㄌㄧㄢˊ ㄨㄤˋ ㄈㄢˇ)
so enchanted as to forget about home

留戀 (ㄌㄧㄡˊ ㄌㄧㄢˋ)
unwilling to leave; reluctant to part with

留客 (ㄌㄧㄡˊ ㄎㄜˋ)
to detain a guest; to ask a guest to stay

留侯 (ㄌㄧㄡˊ ㄏㄡˊ)
the title conferred upon Chang Liang (張良), the strategist who played a significant role in the founding of the Han Dynasty

留後路 (ㄌㄧㄡˊ ㄏㄡˋ ㄌㄨˋ)
to keep a way open for retreat; to leave a way out: 你該給自己留條後路. You should leave yourself a way out.

留鬍子 (ㄌㄧㄡˊ ㄏㄨˊ ㄗ)
to grow a mustache or a beard

留話 (ㄌㄧㄡˊ ㄏㄨㄚˋ)
to leave a message

留級 (ㄌㄧㄡˊ ㄐㄧˊ)
to repeat the year's work; to fail to get promoted to the next grade at school

留居 (ㄌㄧㄡˊ ㄐㄩ)
to stay on or settle down in a place

留情 (ㄌㄧㄡˊ ㄑㄧㄥˊ)
to show mercy; to relent: 他對別人毫不留情。He shows others no mercy.

田部

留取 (ㄌㄧㄡ ㄑㄩ)
to preserve; to leave

留下 (ㄌㄧㄡ ㄒㄧㄚˋ)
①to leave: 那傷口留下一個疤。The wound left a scar. ②to detain; to stop ③to remain; to stay ④to preserve

留校察看 (ㄌㄧㄡ ㄒㄧㄠˋ ㄔㄚˊ ㄎㄢˋ)
(said of a misbehaving student) to be kept in school but placed under surveillance

留心 (ㄌㄧㄡ ㄒㄧㄣ)
to pay attention; to take heed; to be careful; to exercise caution

留鬚 (ㄌㄧㄡ ㄒㄩ)
to grow a beard: 那老人留鬚。That old man grows a beard.

留學 (ㄌㄧㄡ ㄒㄩㄝˊ)
to study abroad; to study in a foreign country

留學生 (ㄌㄧㄡ ㄒㄩㄝˊ ㄕㄥ)
a student studying abroad

留職停薪 (ㄌㄧㄡ ㄓˊ ㄊㄧㄥˊ ㄒㄧㄣ)
leave without pay

留置 (ㄌㄧㄡ ㄓˋ)
to detain; to put aside

留滯 (ㄌㄧㄡ ㄓˋ)
to remain at a standstill; to stay

留中不發 (ㄌㄧㄡ ㄓㄨㄥ ㄅㄨˋ ㄈㄚ)
(said of a memorial 奏摺) to be kept at the imperial palace without an answer; to be shelved

留住 (ㄌㄧㄡ ‧ㄓㄨˋ)
to succeed in making someone stay

留呈 (ㄌㄧㄡ ㄔㄥˊ)
to leave (a written message) behind for an elder or superior

留守 (ㄌㄧㄡ ㄕㄡˇ)
①to act for the emperor during his absence from the capital ②(said of troops) to remain stationed at a camp in the rear

留守處 (ㄌㄧㄡ ㄕㄡˇ ㄔㄨˋ)
a liaison office left in the rear by troops fighting on the front

留神 (ㄌㄧㄡ ㄕㄣˊ)
to pay attention; to be care-

---

ful; to exercise caution: 過街時要留神。Be careful when you are crossing the street.

留聲機 (ㄌㄧㄡ ㄕㄥ ㄐㄧ)
a phonograph

留任 (ㄌㄧㄡ ㄖㄣˋ)
to stay in a position for another term

留存 (ㄌㄧㄡ ㄘㄨㄣˊ)
①to preserve; to keep ②to remain; to be extant

留宿 (ㄌㄧㄡ ㄙㄨˋ)
to keep (a guest) overnight

留意 (ㄌㄧㄡ ㄧˋ)
to pay attention to be careful; to be cautious; to take care; to exercise caution

留一手 (ㄌㄧㄡ ㄧ ㄕㄡˇ)or留後手 (ㄌㄧㄡ ㄏㄡˋ ㄕㄡˇ)
to hold back a trick or two (in teaching a trade or skill)

留言 (ㄌㄧㄡ ㄧㄢˊ)
to leave one's comments; to leave a message

留養 (ㄌㄧㄡ ㄧㄤˇ)
to stay at home to look after one's parents

留影 (ㄌㄧㄡ ㄧㄥˇ)
to take a photo as a memento; to have a picture taken as a souvenir

留餘地 (ㄌㄧㄡ ㄩˊ ㄉㄧˋ)
to refrain from going to extremes; not to push one's advantage too far; to allow for unforeseen circumstances

留寓 (ㄌㄧㄡ ㄩˋ)
to be long absent from home

留用 (ㄌㄧㄡ ㄩㄥˋ)
①to give employment to someone ②to keep for use by oneself

六畫

【畦】 3570
ㄒㄧ shî xî
(舊音 ㄑㄧˊ chyí qí)
1. land of 50 畝 (畝) 畝
2. a plot, piece, or parcel of land
3. a farmer; a laborer

畦徑 (ㄒㄧ ㄐㄧㄥˋ)
a way; a method; a bypath

畦畛 (ㄒㄧ ㄓㄣˇ)
①scope; range ②prejudice

【時】 3571
ㄓ jyh zhî
a place for worshipping Heaven, Earth, and the five sage kings in ancient times

【略】 3572
(畧) ㄌㄩㄝˋ liueh lüè
1. approximate; rough; brief
2. slight; small in extent
3. to scheme; to plan
4. strategy: 他是一個戰略家。He is a person skilled in strategy.
5. to invade; to seize
6. to omit; to leave out: 這一章可以略去。This chapter may be omitted.
7. to survey the boundaries
8. a Chinese family name

略賣 (ㄌㄩㄝˋ ㄇㄞˋ)
to sell women or children kidnapped or seduced from their homes

略地 (ㄌㄩㄝˋ ㄉㄧˋ)
①to invade territory ②to inspect a frontier

略奪 (ㄌㄩㄝˋ ㄉㄨㄛˊ)
to rob; to take by force

略圖 (ㄌㄩㄝˋ ㄊㄨˊ)
a rough drawing; a sketch; a rough sketch; a sketch map; a rough plan: 他畫了一張這鎮的略圖。He made a sketch of the town.

略同 (ㄌㄩㄝˋ ㄊㄨㄥˊ)
approximately the same; about the same; similar

略歷 (ㄌㄩㄝˋ ㄌㄧˋ)
a brief personal record; a biographical sketch

略略 (ㄌㄩㄝˋ ㄌㄩㄝˋ)
briefly; slightly; a little; somewhat

略可 (ㄌㄩㄝˋ ㄎㄜˇ)
acceptable in general; all right on the whole

略取 (ㄌㄩㄝˋ ㄑㄩˇ)
to take by force

略去 (ㄌㄩㄝˋ ㄑㄩˋ)
to omit; to leave out; to delete

略知一二 (ㄌㄩㄝˋ ㄓ ㄧ ㄦˋ)
to know or understand just a little

略傳 (ㄌㄩㄝˋ ㄓㄨㄢˋ)
a biographical sketch; a brief personal history

略識之無 (ㄌㄩㄝˋ ㄕˊ ㄓ ㄨˊ)

only slightly literate

略勝一籌(ㄌㄩㄝ ㄕㄥ ㄧ ㄔㄡ)
slightly better; slightly superior; a cut above

略述(ㄌㄩㄝ ㄕㄨ)
to describe briefly; to give a short description of; to outline

略說(ㄌㄩㄝ ㄕㄨㄛ)
to say a few words about; briefly refer to

略字(ㄌㄩㄝ ㄗ)
abbreviated form of a word; abbreviation

略有門徑(ㄌㄩㄝ ㄧㄡ ㄇㄣ ㄐㄧㄥ)
to have some rough understanding of a subject

略有所聞(ㄌㄩㄝ ㄧㄡ ㄙㄨㄛ ㄨㄣ)
to have heard something (about it): 此事我略有所聞。I have heard something about this matter.

略誘(ㄌㄩㄝ ㄧㄡ)
(law) to seduce or force a minor to leave his family or guardian; abduction; kidnapping

略言之(ㄌㄩㄝ ㄧㄢ ㄓ)
to state briefly; in short: 略言之, 他不接受我的勸告。In short, he did not take my advice.

略微(ㄌㄩㄝ ㄨㄟ)
slightly; a little; somewhat: 她略微有點頭痛。She has a slight headache.

【畢】 *3573*
ㄅㄧˋ bih bì
1. to complete; to finish; to end
2. whole; total; complete
3. a Chinese family name

畢命(ㄅㄧ ㄇㄧㄥ)
to end one's life; to die

畢達哥拉斯(ㄅㄧ ㄉㄚˊ ㄍㄜ ㄌㄚ ㄙ)
Pythagoras, 582-500 B.C., Greek philosopher and mathematician

畢卡索(ㄅㄧ ㄎㄚˇ ㄙㄨㄛ)
Pablo Picasso, 1881-1973, Spanish painter

畢集(ㄅㄧ ㄐㄧ)
to gather or assemble completely

畢竟(ㄅㄧ ㄐㄧㄥ)
after all; in the long run; ultimately

畢其功於一役(ㄅㄧ ㄑㄧˊ ㄍㄨㄥ ㄩˊ ㄧ ㄧ)
to accomplish the whole task at one stroke

畢肖(ㄅㄧ ㄒㄧㄠ)
similar; completely alike; closely resembling

畢生(ㄅㄧ ㄕㄥ)
in one's whole life; throughout one's lifetime; lifelong: 他以畢生的精力從事語言研究。He devoted a lifetime to the study of language.

畢昇(ㄅㄧ ㄕㄥ)
Pi Sheng (c. 11th century), an inventor of the movable type during the Sung Dynasty

畢業(ㄅㄧ ㄧㄝ)
to be graduated; to graduate; graduation: 在牛津大學讀了三年, 他畢業了。After three years at Oxford, he graduated.

畢業班(ㄅㄧ ㄧㄝ ㄅㄢ)
the graduating class

畢業典禮(ㄅㄧ ㄧㄝ ㄉㄧㄢˇ ㄌㄧˇ)
commencement exercises; commencement 亦作「畢業式」

畢業年限(ㄅㄧ ㄧㄝ ㄋㄧㄢˊ ㄒㄧㄢ)
a required number of years for graduation

畢業論文(ㄅㄧ ㄧㄝ ㄌㄨㄣˊ ㄨㄣˊ)
a thesis

畢業考試(ㄅㄧ ㄧㄝ ㄎㄠˇ ㄕ)
a graduation examination

畢業照片(ㄅㄧ ㄧㄝ ㄓㄠ ㄆㄧㄢˋ)
a photograph of all the graduating students and their teachers taken together on the commencement day

畢業證書(ㄅㄧ ㄧㄝ ㄓㄥ ㄕㄨ)or 畢業文憑(ㄅㄧ ㄧㄝ ㄨㄣˊ ㄆㄧㄥˊ)
a diploma

畢業式(ㄅㄧ ㄧㄝ ㄕ)
commencement exercises; a commencement

畢業生(ㄅㄧ ㄧㄝ ㄕㄥ)
a graduate: 我是耶魯大學的畢業生。I'm a graduate of Yale University.

【異】 *3574*
(異) ㄧˋ yih yì
1. different; difference
2. peculiar; extraordinary; unusual; strange; uncommon
3. foreign; unfamiliar; unknown

4. to marvel; to wonder
5. to separate
a foreign country

異邦(ㄧ ㄅㄤ)
a foreign country

異稟(ㄧ ㄅㄧㄥˇ)
extraordinary endowments; extraordinary talent

異名(ㄧ ㄇㄧㄥˊ)
a different name

異母兄弟(ㄧ ㄇㄨˇ ㄒㄩㄥ ㄉㄧˋ)
brothers born of different mothers; half brothers

異方殊俗(ㄧ ㄈㄤ ㄕㄨ ㄙㄨˊ)
different customs in alien countries

異服(ㄧ ㄈㄨˊ)
outlandish costume; strange clothing: 他喜歡穿奇裝異服。He likes to wear an outlandish dress.

異代(ㄧ ㄉㄞˋ)
a different age or era

異代交(ㄧ ㄉㄞˋ ㄐㄧㄠ)
admiration for historical personalities

異地(ㄧ ㄉㄧˋ)
a strange land; a foreign land

異端(ㄧ ㄉㄨㄢ)
strange doctrines

異端邪說(ㄧ ㄉㄨㄢ ㄒㄧㄝˊ ㄕㄨㄛ)
heretical beliefs; heresy

異態(ㄧ ㄊㄞˋ)
strange bearing or manner

異體字(ㄧ ㄊㄧˇ ㄗ)
a variant form of a Chinese character

異途同歸(ㄧ ㄊㄨˊ ㄊㄨㄥˊ ㄍㄨㄟ)
(literally) to arrive at an identical point through different courses—to reach an identical conclusion through different procedures of separate studies; to attain the same objective through different efforts

異同(ㄧ ㄊㄨㄥˊ)
① differences and similarities ② inconsistent

異能(ㄧ ㄋㄥˊ)
extraordinary talent; genius: 他是一個有奇才異能的人。He has extraordinary talents and abilities.

異類(ㄧ ㄌㄟˋ)
① those of a different class or kind ② nonhuman ③

〔田
部〕

aliens; a different tribe or race

異國(ㄧˋ ㄍㄨㄛˊ)
a foreign country

異國情調(ㄧˋ ㄍㄨㄛˊ ㄑㄧㄥˊ ㄉㄧㄠˋ)
an exotic touch or mood on a foreign land

異客(ㄧˋ ㄎㄜˋ)
a stranger

異口同聲(ㄧˋ ㄎㄡˇ ㄊㄨㄥˊ ㄕㄥ)or**異口同音**(ㄧˋ ㄎㄡˇ ㄊㄨㄥˊ ㄧㄣ)
The same thing is said by different mouths. 或 People are unanimous in their opinion.

異乎尋常(ㄧˋ ㄏㄨ ㄒㄩㄣˊ ㄔㄤˊ)
unusual; extraordinary

異花受精(ㄧˋ ㄏㄨㄚ ㄕㄡˋ ㄐㄧㄥ)
allogamy; cross-fertilization

異化(ㄧˋ ㄏㄨㄚˋ)
①(philosophy) alienation ②(linguistics) dissimilation

異化作用(ㄧˋ ㄏㄨㄚˋ ㄗㄨㄛˋ ㄩㄥˋ)
catabolism

異己(ㄧˋ ㄐㄧˇ)
those who differ from or disagree with oneself; a dissident

異教(ㄧˋ ㄐㄧㄠˋ)
heathenism; paganism

異教徒(ㄧˋ ㄐㄧㄠˋ ㄊㄨˊ)
a heathen; a pagan

異軍突起(ㄧˋ ㄐㄩㄣ ㄊㄨˊ ㄑㄧˇ)
(literally) A new army appears all of a sudden (to change the situation).—the unexpected appearance of a new talent, factor, stratagem, etc. that upsets the status quo

異曲同工(ㄧˋ ㄑㄩˇ ㄊㄨㄥˊ ㄍㄨㄥ)
(literally) Different songs are sung with the same excellence.—The writings are different, but the excellence is the same.

異趣(ㄧˋ ㄑㄩˋ)
①different tastes or interests ②extraordinary taste

異心(ㄧˋ ㄒㄧㄣ)
dishonesty; infidelity; disloyalty; insincerity; treachery

異香(ㄧˋ ㄒㄧㄤ)
rare fragrance; unusually sweet smell

異香異氣(ㄧˋ ㄒㄧㄤ ㄧˋ ㄑㄧˋ)
an unusual kind of pleasant smell

異鄉(ㄧˋ ㄒㄧㄤ)
a strange community; a strange land; a foreign land; away from one's home

異想天開(ㄧˋ ㄒㄧㄤˇ ㄊㄧㄢ ㄎㄞ)
to have fantastic notions

異相(ㄧˋ ㄒㄧㄤˋ)
①a strange physiognomy ②to differ in appearance

異象(ㄧˋ ㄒㄧㄤˋ)
strange phenomena

異形(ㄧˋ ㄒㄧㄥˊ)
a strange form or shape

異性(ㄧˋ ㄒㄧㄥˋ)
①of the other sex; the opposite sex ②of a different nature

異性戀(ㄧˋ ㄒㄧㄥˋ ㄌㄧㄢˋ)
heterosexuality

異姓(ㄧˋ ㄒㄧㄥˋ)
those with different surnames

異質(ㄧˋ ㄓˊ)
of a different nature; of a different quality

異體(ㄧˋ ㄊㄧˇ)
a heterogeneous body

異質同像(ㄧˋ ㄓˊ ㄊㄨㄥˊ ㄒㄧㄤˋ)
isomorphism

異常(ㄧˋ ㄔㄤˊ)
extraordinary; unusual; strange: 天氣異常寒冷。It was unusually cold.

異事(ㄧˋ ㄕˋ)
①a peculiar affair ②a different matter; another affair ③to be engaged in different occupations

異數(ㄧˋ ㄕㄨˋ)
①different rank ②courteous reception; unusual favor

異說(ㄧˋ ㄕㄨㄛ)
①heresies ②a different interpretation; a different theory

異日(ㄧˋ ㄖˋ)
①another day; some other day ②bygone days

異人(ㄧˋ ㄖㄣˊ)
①an extraordinary person; an idiosyncratic person ②a stranger ③another person; somebody else

異哉(ㄧˋ ㄗㄞ)
How strange! 或 What a strange thing it is!

異族(ㄧˋ ㄗㄨˊ)
a different clan, tribe, or race

異辭(ㄧˋ ㄘˊ)
dissenting statements

異才(ㄧˋ ㄘㄞˊ)
unusual talent; genius

異彩(ㄧˋ ㄘㄞˇ)
extraordinary (or radiant) splendor

異爨(ㄧˋ ㄘㄨㄢˋ)
(said of brothers) to form separate families

異俗(ㄧˋ ㄙㄨˊ)
①different custom ②bad custom

異議(ㄧˋ ㄧˋ)
dissent; objections

異議分子(ㄧˋ ㄧˋ ㄈㄣˋ ㄗˇ)
a dissident

異樣(ㄧˋ ㄧㄤˋ)
unusual; extraordinary; peculiar; strange; differences

異物(ㄧˋ ㄨˋ)
①a rare treasure; an extremely valuable object ②a peculiar thing; a strange thing; an uncommon thing ③the dead

異味(ㄧˋ ㄨㄟˋ)
extraordinarily pleasant flavor; uncommonly sweet taste

異聞(ㄧˋ ㄨㄣˊ)
①unusual news; a strange story; a strange tale ②a different report

異域(ㄧˋ ㄩˋ)
a foreign land; a strange land

七畫

【番】 3575
1. ㄈㄢ　fan　fān
1. to take turns
2. order in series
3. a time: 他三番兩次的打擾她。He disturbed her time and again.
4. a kind of; a sort of
5. barbarians

番邦(ㄈㄢ ㄅㄤ)
a barbarian state

番代(ㄈㄢ ㄉㄞˋ)
to take turns

番地(ㄈㄢ ㄉㄧˋ)

〔田 部〕

a strange land; a foreign land

番瓜（ㄈㄢ ㄍㄨㄚ）
a pumpkin 亦作「南瓜」: 番瓜
用來做餅。A pumpkin is used for making pies.

番鬼（ㄈㄢ ㄍㄨㄟ）
a foreign devil (an abusive term)

番號（ㄈㄢ ㄏㄠˋ）
a numerical designation of a military unit

番紅花（ㄈㄢ ㄏㄨㄥˊ ㄏㄨㄚ）
a saffron

番椒（ㄈㄢ ㄐㄧㄠ）
pepper; capsicum 亦作「辣椒」

番茄（ㄈㄢ ㄑㄧㄝˊ）
a tomato

番茄醬（ㄈㄢ ㄑㄧㄝˊ ㄐㄧㄤˋ）
tomato ketchup

番茄汁（ㄈㄢ ㄑㄧㄝˊ ㄓ）
tomato juice

番休（ㄈㄢ ㄒㄧㄡ）
to take a leave by turns 亦作「輪休」

番石榴（ㄈㄢ ㄕˊ ㄌㄧㄡ）
a guava

番薯（ㄈㄢ ㄕㄨˇ）
a sweet potato

番戍（ㄈㄢ ㄕㄨˋ）
to keep watch by turns

番人（ㄈㄢ ㄖㄣˊ）
aborigines; savages; barbarians

番子（ㄈㄢ ˙ㄗ）
a barbarian—a foreigner; an alien

番菜（ㄈㄢ ㄘㄞˋ）
western-style meals

番銀（ㄈㄢ ㄧㄣˊ）
Mexican silver dollars

番語（ㄈㄢ ㄩˇ）
foreign languages

【番】 3575
2. ㄆㄢ pan pān
1. a county in Kwangtung
2. a Chinese family name

番禺（ㄆㄢ ㄩˊ）
a county in Kwangtung（廣東）

【番】 3575
3. ㄅㄛ bo bō
martial-like

【畬】 3576
ㄩˊ yu yú
land cultivated for two or three years

【畬】 3577
ㄕㄜ she shē
1. name of a backward people in southern China
2. to cultivate land by first setting fire to it

畬蠻（ㄕㄜ ㄇㄢˊ）
name of a backward people in southern China

【畫】 3578
ㄏㄨㄚˋ huà huà
1. to paint or draw (a picture); a painting; a drawing: 牆上有幅畫。There's a painting on the wall.
2. to mark off; to delimit
3. to plan; to design; a plan
4. a stroke in a Chinese character

畫報（ㄏㄨㄚˋ ㄅㄠˋ）
a pictorial

畫板（ㄏㄨㄚˋ ㄅㄢˇ）
a drawing board; a drafting board

畫筆（ㄏㄨㄚˋ ㄅㄧˇ）
a painting brush

畫壁（ㄏㄨㄚˋ ㄅㄧˋ）
a wall with murals

畫餅（ㄏㄨㄚˋ ㄅㄧㄥˇ）
pie in the sky; illusion

畫餅充飢（ㄏㄨㄚˋ ㄅㄧㄥˇ ㄔㄨㄥ ㄐㄧ）
(literally) to try to satisfy hunger by drawing cakes—to value empty names; empty solace

畫布（ㄏㄨㄚˋ ㄅㄨˋ）
a canvas (for painting)

畫癖（ㄏㄨㄚˋ ㄆㄧˇ）
a craze for painting

畫片兒（ㄏㄨㄚˋ ㄆㄧㄢˋ ㄦ）
printed pictures; picture postcards

畫品（ㄏㄨㄚˋ ㄆㄧㄣˇ）
the grade of paintings

畫屏（ㄏㄨㄚˋ ㄆㄧㄥˊ）
a screen decorated with paintings

畫譜（ㄏㄨㄚˋ ㄆㄨˇ）
① a picture copybook ② commentaries on painting

畫眉（ㄏㄨㄚˋ ㄇㄟˊ）
① to blacken eyebrows ② the thrush

畫眉鳥（ㄏㄨㄚˋ ㄇㄟˊ ㄋㄧㄠˇ）
the thrush

畫卯（ㄏㄨㄚˋ ㄇㄠˇ）
(said of officials in former

times) to report for work early in the morning

畫面（ㄏㄨㄚˋ ㄇㄧㄢˋ）
① the full length and breadth of a picture ② (geometry) a picture plane

畫法（ㄏㄨㄚˋ ㄈㄚˇ）
a method of painting or drawing

畫分 or 劃分（ㄏㄨㄚˋ ㄈㄣ）
to mark off; to divide; to demarcate

畫舫（ㄏㄨㄚˋ ㄈㄤˇ）
a pleasure boat decorated with pictures and elaborate wood lacework

畫符（ㄏㄨㄚˋ ㄈㄨˊ）
(said of Taoist priests) to draw spells or charms

畫符念咒（ㄏㄨㄚˋ ㄈㄨˊ ㄋㄧㄢˋ ㄓㄡˋ）
(said of Taoist priests) to draw spells and mumble incantations

畫到（ㄏㄨㄚˋ ㄉㄠˋ）
(said of an employee) to sign one's name in the roll when reporting for work in the morning; to clock in

畫荻教子（ㄏㄨㄚˋ ㄉㄧˊ ㄐㄧㄠˋ ㄗˇ）
(literally) to teach the child by drawing characters on the ground with a reed (the story is about the mother of Ou-Yang Hsiu（歐陽修）—to teach one's children with great maternal patience

畫地自限（ㄏㄨㄚˋ ㄉㄧˋ ㄗˋ ㄒㄧㄢˋ）
to try to limit oneself; to impose restrictions on oneself

畫地為牢（ㄏㄨㄚˋ ㄉㄧˋ ㄨㄟˊ ㄌㄠˊ）
to draw a circle on the ground to serve as a prison

畫棟雕梁（ㄏㄨㄚˋ ㄉㄨㄥˋ ㄉㄧㄠ ㄌㄧㄤˊ）
(said of ornate buildings) painted rafters and carved beams

畫堂（ㄏㄨㄚˋ ㄊㄤˊ）
a beautifully decorated room or house

畫帖（ㄏㄨㄚˋ ㄊㄧㄝˋ）
a copybook for art students

畫圖（ㄏㄨㄚˋ ㄊㄨˊ）
① to paint pictures; to draw pictures ② a picture; a painting; a drawing

畫圖器（ㄏㄨㄚˋ ㄊㄨˊ ㄑㄧˋ）

【田部】

drawing instruments

畫諾(ㄏㄨㄚˋ ㄋㄨㄛˋ)
to sign one's name to
express consent; to endorse
a document

畫廊(ㄏㄨㄚˋ ㄌㄤˊ)
a gallery (for paintings)

畫龍點睛(ㄏㄨㄚˋ ㄌㄨㄥˊ ㄉㄧㄢˇ ㄐㄧㄥ)
(literally) to add eyeballs to
the picture of a dragon—to
enliven the whole composition by the skillful use of a
couple of sentences; to add
the punch line; to add the
finishing touch

畫稿(ㄏㄨㄚˋ ㄍㄠˇ)
①drafts for paintings or
drawings: 他正在做畫稿。He's
making a draft for his painting. ②to endorse the draft
of a document

畫工(ㄏㄨㄚˋ ㄍㄨㄥ)
a painter (in the sense of a
craftsman as distinct from
an accomplished artist)

畫供(ㄏㄨㄚˋ ㄍㄨㄥˋ)
to sign a written confession
to a crime by the accused

畫刊(ㄏㄨㄚˋ ㄎㄢ)
a pictorial magazine

畫框(ㄏㄨㄚˋ ㄎㄨㄤˋ)
a picture frame

畫虎類狗(ㄏㄨㄚˋ ㄏㄨˇ ㄌㄟˋ ㄍㄡˇ)
(literally) to try to draw a
tiger and end up with a dog
—to fail because of undue
ambition

畫畫兒(ㄏㄨㄚˋ ㄏㄨㄚˋ ㄦ)
to paint pictures; to draw
pictures: 他的孩子會畫畫兒。
His child can paint pictures.

畫戟(ㄏㄨㄚˋ ㄐㄧˇ)
a halberd decorated with
pictures

畫家(ㄏㄨㄚˋ ㄐㄧㄚ)
a painter; an artist

畫架(ㄏㄨㄚˋ ㄐㄧㄚˋ)
an easel

畫界(ㄏㄨㄚˋ ㄐㄧㄝˋ)
to delimit; to mark boundaries; to demarcate

畫匠(ㄏㄨㄚˋ ㄐㄧㄤˋ)
a painter (in the sense of a
craftsman as distinct from
an artist) 參看「畫工」

畫境(ㄏㄨㄚˋ ㄐㄧㄥˋ)
the world created by the

painter

畫具(ㄏㄨㄚˋ ㄐㄩˋ)
articles used for painting;
painting tools

畫像(ㄏㄨㄚˋ ㄒㄧㄤˋ)
①to paint a portrait ②a
portrait ③a portrayal in
words

畫行(ㄏㄨㄚˋ ㄒㄧㄥˊ)
to write down the character
行 on a document to show
one's approval

畫學(ㄏㄨㄚˋ ㄒㄩㄝˊ)
①a painting school; an art
school ②the art of painting

畫展(ㄏㄨㄚˋ ㄓㄢˇ)
an art exhibition; a painting
exhibition

畫中有詩(ㄏㄨㄚˋ ㄓㄨㄥ ㄧㄡˇ ㄕ)
There is poetry in a painting.

畫師(ㄏㄨㄚˋ ㄕ)
a painter; an artist

畫史(ㄏㄨㄚˋ ㄕˇ)
a book by Mi Fei (米芾) of
the Sung Dynasty comment-
ing on the authenticity of
well-known paintings

畫室(ㄏㄨㄚˋ ㄕˋ)
an artist's studio

畫蛇添足(ㄏㄨㄚˋ ㄕㄜˊ ㄊㄧㄢ ㄗㄨˊ)
(literally) to add feet to a
snake while painting it—to
make undesirable additions;
superfluous

畫聖(ㄏㄨㄚˋ ㄕㄥˋ)
the Divine Master of Painting, the title accorded by
posterity to the Tang
Dynasty painter Wu Tao-tzu
(吳道子)

畫册(ㄏㄨㄚˋ ㄘㄜˋ)
a picture or painting album

畫策(ㄏㄨㄚˋ ㄘㄜˋ)
to plan; to scheme

畫兒(ㄏㄨㄚˋ ㄦ)
a painting; a drawing: 這是
一張好畫兒。This is a good
drawing.

畫一 or 劃一(ㄏㄨㄚˋ ㄧ)
①uniform ②to make uni-
form

畫一組織 or 劃一組織(ㄏㄨㄚˋ ㄧ
ㄗㄨ ㄓ)
to have a uniform organization

畫意(ㄏㄨㄚˋ ㄧˋ)

the mood of a painting

畫押(ㄏㄨㄚˋ ㄧㄚ)
to sign a contract or agreement

畫頁(ㄏㄨㄚˋ ㄧㄝˋ)
a picture sheet; a picture
page

畫影圖形(ㄏㄨㄚˋ ㄧㄥˇ ㄊㄨˊ ㄒㄧㄥˊ)
to draw the likenesses of a
criminal at large for posting
in various places

【畯】 3579
ㄐㄩㄣˋ jiunn jŭn
1. the official in charge of
farmland in ancient times
2. rustic; crude

八畫

【畹】 3580
ㄨㄢˇ woan wăn
a measure of land equaling
12 or 30 mu (畝)

【畸】 3581
ㄐㄧ jī jī
1. fields with irregular boundaries
2. malformed; misshapen;
deformity
3. fractional remainders

畸態(ㄐㄧ ㄊㄞˋ)
abnormality; oddity

畸零(ㄐㄧ ㄌㄧㄥˊ)
①fractional remainders ②a
solitary person; a lonely person

畸角子(ㄐㄧ ㄐㄧㄠˇ ㄗ)or 畸角兒
(ㄐㄧ ㄐㄧㄠˇ ㄦ)
a corner

畸輕畸重(ㄐㄧ ㄑㄧㄥ ㄐㄧ ㄓㄨㄥˋ)
to place either too little or
too great emphasis on a
matter; to attach too much
weight to this and too little
weight to that

畸形(ㄐㄧ ㄒㄧㄥˊ)
malformation; deformity;
abnormality; abnormal;
deformed

畸形發展(ㄐㄧ ㄒㄧㄥˊ ㄈㄚ ㄓㄢˇ)
abnormal development

畸人(ㄐㄧ ㄖㄣˊ)
an odd person; an idiosyncratic person

【當】 3582
1. ㄉㄤ dang dāng
1. to undertake or assume
(responsibilities, etc.); to

accept
2. to face: 他當著我的面扯了個謊。He told me a lie to my face.
3. equal; well-matched: 我們實力相當。We are well-matched in strength.
4. the very same (place, year, day, etc.)
5. ought to; should; must: 你當遵守諾言。You should keep your promise.
6. just at (a time or a place)
7. to work as; to serve as

當班(ㄉㄤ ㄅㄢ)
to be on duty by turns

當兵(ㄉㄤ ㄅㄧㄥ)
to serve in the army; to be a soldier

當兵的(ㄉㄤ ㄅㄧㄥ ㄉㄜ)
a soldier; a serviceman

當不起(ㄉㄤ ㄅㄨ ㄑㄧ)
unequal to (a responsibility, honor, etc.); dare not accept: 我當不起這樣的獎賞。I just don't deserve such a prize.

當面(ㄉㄤ ㄇㄧㄢ)
right in one's face; right in one's presence; face to face: 他當面說好話，背後中傷我。He says nice things to my face, then stabs me in the back.

當面鑼對面鼓(ㄉㄤ ㄇㄧㄢ ㄌㄨㄛ ㄉㄨㄟ ㄇㄧㄢ ㄍㄨ)
right in one's face; in one's presence

當面言明(ㄉㄤ ㄇㄧㄢ ㄧㄢ ㄇㄧㄥ)
to state clearly in one's presence

當番(ㄉㄤ ㄈㄢ)
to do a duty by turns; to be on duty

當代(ㄉㄤ ㄉㄞ)
in the present age

當道(ㄉㄤ ㄉㄠ)
①men holding the reins of government; to be in power ②to block one's way

當地(ㄉㄤ ㄉㄧ)
this place; local

當斷不斷(ㄉㄤ ㄉㄨㄢ ㄅㄨ ㄉㄨㄢ)
to be indecisive when decision is needed

當頭(ㄉㄤ ㄊㄡ)
①right overhead; right on somebody's head; head-on ②to face with (difficulties, etc.); imminent

當頭棒喝(ㄉㄤ ㄊㄡ ㄅㄤ ㄏㄜ)
①to arouse a person from stupidity by drastic means ②to give an aggressor a stunning blow at the start

當頭人(ㄉㄤ ㄊㄡ ㄖㄣ)
husband (used by wives in speaking of their husbands)

當天(ㄉㄤ ㄊㄧㄢ)
on the same day; on that very day: 這事必須當天做完。The work must be done on the very day.

當年(ㄉㄤ ㄋㄧㄢ)
①that year; the year in question ②bygone years; in those days: 她的美貌不減當年。She is as beautiful as ever.

當量(ㄉㄤ ㄌㄧㄤ)
(chemistry) equivalent

當令(ㄉㄤ ㄌㄧㄥ)
seasonable; fashionable

當爐 or 當壚(ㄉㄤ ㄌㄨ)
to sell alcoholic drinks

當爐(ㄉㄤ ㄌㄨ)
to sit before a fire

當路(ㄉㄤ ㄌㄨ)
①people holding the reins of government ②to obstruct one's way

當國(ㄉㄤ ㄍㄨㄛ)
to hold the reins of government; to rule the country

當歸(ㄉㄤ ㄍㄨㄟ)
ligusticum, or levisticum, whose root is used as medicine

當歸鴨(ㄉㄤ ㄍㄨㄟ ㄧㄚ)
a dish of duck seasoned with ligusticum

當官(ㄉㄤ ㄍㄨㄢ)
①to fill an office; to be an official: 他已不當官了。He is no longer in office. ②in the presence of an official

當關(ㄉㄤ ㄍㄨㄢ)
①to guard a pass or checkpoint ②a doorkeeper

當口(ㄉㄤ ㄎㄡ)
the critical moment; the crucial point

當行出色(ㄉㄤ ㄏㄤ ㄔㄨ ㄙㄜ)
excellent and opportune; to be an expert; to be in one's element

當機立斷(ㄉㄤ ㄐㄧ ㄌㄧ ㄉㄨㄢ)
to make quick decisions in the face of problems

當即(ㄉㄤ ㄐㄧ)
immediately; with dispatch; promptly; right away: 我當即表示贊同。I gave my approval immediately.

當家(ㄉㄤ ㄐㄧㄚ)
to housekeep; to manage household affairs; to be the master of a family, an organization, etc.

當家的(ㄉㄤ ㄐㄧㄚ ㄉㄜ)
①my husband ②a housekeeper ③the head monk of a temple

當間兒(ㄉㄤ ㄐㄧㄢ ㄦ)
in the middle

當街(ㄉㄤ ㄐㄧㄝ)
in the street: 他當街行乞。He begs in the street.

當今(ㄉㄤ ㄐㄧㄣ)
①the present time; today ②the reigning emperor

當局(ㄉㄤ ㄐㄩ)
the authorities

當局者迷，旁觀者清(ㄉㄤ ㄐㄩ ㄓㄜ ㄇㄧ，ㄆㄤ ㄍㄨㄢ ㄓㄜ ㄑㄧㄥ)
The onlooker sees the game more clearly than the players. 或 Those who are involved cannot see things as clearly as outsiders do.

當前(ㄉㄤ ㄑㄧㄢ)
①before one; facing one ②present; current

當權(ㄉㄤ ㄑㄩㄢ)
to exercise authority; to be in power

當下(ㄉㄤ ㄒㄧㄚ)
presently; immediately

當先(ㄉㄤ ㄒㄧㄢ)
①to be in the front ②formerly; previously

當心(ㄉㄤ ㄒㄧㄣ)
to be careful; to be cautious; to take care: 當心不要打破雞蛋。Be careful not to break the eggs.

當心扒手(ㄉㄤ ㄒㄧㄣ ㄆㄚ ㄕㄡ)
Watch out for pickpockets! 或 Beware of pickpockets!

當心火車(ㄉㄤ ㄒㄧㄣ ㄏㄨㄛ ㄔㄜ)
Beware of trains!

當選(ㄉㄤ ㄒㄩㄢ)
to get elected; to be elected;

〔田部〕

to win an election: 他當選為主席。He was elected chairman.

當選證書(ㄉㄤ ㄒㄩㄢ ㄓㄥ ㄕㄨ)
certificates issued to the successful candidates of an election

當選人(ㄉㄤ ㄒㄩㄢ ㄖㄣ)
as in 總統當選人 (the president-elect)

當之無愧(ㄉㄤ ㄓ ㄨ ㄎㄨㄟ)
fully deserve (a title, an honor, etc.); to be worthy of: 英雄的稱號, 他當之無愧。He fully deserves the title of a hero.

當值(ㄉㄤ ㄓ)
to take one's turn on duty; to be on duty by turns

當中(ㄉㄤ ㄓㄨㄥ)
right in the middle

當眾(ㄉㄤ ㄓㄨㄥ)
in the presence of all

當眾宣佈(ㄉㄤ ㄓㄨㄥ ㄒㄩㄢ ㄅㄨ)
to announce before a crowd; to announce publicly

當差(ㄉㄤ ㄔㄞ)
to do a duty; to be on duty

當差(ㄉㄤ ㄔㄞ/ㄉㄤ ㄔ)
①a servant ②a government employee

當朝(ㄉㄤ ㄔㄠ)
①during the present reign ②the present emperor

當娼(ㄉㄤ ㄔㄤ)
to be a prostitute

當場(ㄉㄤ ㄔㄤ/ㄉㄤ ㄔㄤ)
on the spot; then and there: 我當場拒絕了他們的幫助。I turned down their help on the spot.

當場交貨(ㄉㄤ ㄔㄤ ㄐㄧㄠ ㄏㄨㄛ/ㄉㄤ ㄔㄤ ㄐㄧㄠ ㄏㄨㄛ)
delivery on the spot upon payment

當場出醜(ㄉㄤ ㄔㄤ ㄔㄨ ㄔㄡ/ㄉㄤ ㄔㄤ ㄔㄨ ㄔㄡ)
to suffer embarrassment right before a crowd

當初(ㄉㄤ ㄔㄨ)
at first; in the beginning

當時(ㄉㄤ ㄕ)
①at that time; then; in those days ②at the very moment; immediately

當世(ㄉㄤ ㄕ)
①the present age; the present time ②to be a ruler

當事(ㄉㄤ ㄕ)
①to deal with a matter; to take charge of a matter ②the authorities

當事者(ㄉㄤ ㄕ ㄓㄜ)or 當事人(ㄉㄤ ㄕ ㄖㄣ)
the party concerned; those directly involved

當日(ㄉㄤ ㄖ)
on the same day; on that very day: 此文件當日有效。This document is valid on the same day.

當然(ㄉㄤ ㄖㄢ)
①of course; naturally ②as it should be; only natural: 那是理所當然。That is just as it should be.

當然委員(ㄉㄤ ㄖㄢ ㄨㄟ ㄩㄢ)
an ex-officio member of a committee, council or commission

當仁不讓(ㄉㄤ ㄖㄣ ㄅㄨ ㄖㄤ)
①to yield to nobody when one is doing what is right ②do not refuse to accept a reward or position which one deserves ③to be behind none in the desire to benefit mankind

當夜(ㄉㄤ ㄧㄝ)
on the same night; on that very night

當陽(ㄉㄤ ㄧㄤ)
①(literally) to face the sun or the south—to rule ②a county in Hupeh

當午(ㄉㄤ ㄨ)
noon; noontide; midday

當務之急(ㄉㄤ ㄨ ㄓ ㄐㄧ)
a business or task of the greatest urgency at present

當晚(ㄉㄤ ㄨㄢ)
on the same night; on that very night

〔當〕 3582
ㄉㄤ　dang　dǎng
1. proper; appropriate
2. to pawn; to mortgage; to pledge
3. to take as; to regard as; to consider as

當票(ㄉㄤ ㄆㄧㄠ)
a pawn ticket

當鋪(ㄉㄤ ˙ㄆㄨ)
a pawnbroker's shop; a pawnshop

當鋪(ㄉㄤ ˙ㄆㄨ)
to pawn something at a pawnshop

當頭(ㄉㄤ ㄊㄡ)
something pawned; a pledge

當真(ㄉㄤ ㄓㄣ)
①true; real; really: 這話當真? Is it really true? ②to be serious; no joking

當作 or 當做(ㄉㄤ ㄗㄨㄛ)
to regard as; to treat as

當耳邊風(ㄉㄤ ㄦ ㄅㄧㄢ ㄈㄥ)
(literally) to regard as nothing but a wind blowing past the ear—to take no serious heed to (advice, etc.)

當押(ㄉㄤ ㄧㄚ)
to pawn; to mortgage

〔當〕 3582
3. ㄉㄤ　daang　dǒng
to mistake something for another

當是(ㄉㄤ ㄕ)
to mistake something for another; to think that...: 我把她當是她的姐姐。I mistook her for her sister.

十畫

〔畿〕 3583
ㄐㄧ　ji　jī
(又讀 ㄑㄧ　chyi　qí)
areas near the capital; the royal domain

畿輔(ㄐㄧ ㄈㄨ)or 畿甸(ㄐㄧ ㄉㄧㄢ)
areas near the capital

畿甸(ㄐㄧ ㄉㄧㄢ)
the capital

十四畫

〔疆〕 3584
ㄐㄧㄤ　jiang　jiāng
1. the boundary; the border; the frontier
2. a limit

疆土(ㄐㄧㄤ ㄊㄨ)
territory

疆吏(ㄐㄧㄤ ㄌㄧ)
a frontier official

疆界(ㄐㄧㄤ ㄐㄧㄝ)
borders; frontiers

疆徼(ㄐㄧㄤ ㄐㄧㄠ)
frontiers; borders

疆場(ㄐㄧㄤ ㄔㄤ)
a battlefield: 他戰死疆場。He
died on the battlefield.

疆界(ㄐㄧㄤ ㄐㄧㄝ)
①national borders ②field
borders

疆域(ㄐㄧㄤ ㄩ)
territory

【疇】 3585 ㄔㄡ chour chóu
1. agricultural land; fields
2. who
3. formerly; previously
4. a class; a category; a rank

疇輩(ㄔㄡ ㄅㄟ)
people of the same generation or position

疇類(ㄔㄡ ㄌㄟ)
of the same class or category

疇昔(ㄔㄡ ㄒㄧ)
formerly; previously; in the
past; yesterday

疇日(ㄔㄡ ㄖ)
in the past; in former times

疇人(ㄔㄡ ㄖㄣ)
an astrologist

十七畫

【疊】 3586 (疊) ㄉㄧㄝ dye dié
1. to fold up
2. to pile up
3. to repeat; to duplicate
4. a stack of (bank notes)

疊羅漢(ㄉㄧㄝ ㄌㄨㄛ ㄏㄢ)
(sports) pyramid

疊騎(ㄉㄧㄝ ㄐㄧ)
to ride side by side

疊句(ㄉㄧㄝ ㄐㄩ)
a refrain

疊起(ㄉㄧㄝ ㄑㄧ)
①to fold up: 百葉窗可以疊起
來。The window shutters fold
back. ②to pile up

疊置法(ㄉㄧㄝ ㄓ ㄈㄚ)
(mathematics) superposition

疊嶂(ㄉㄧㄝ ㄓㄤ)
rows of peaks

疊牀架屋(ㄉㄧㄝ ㄔㄨㄤ ㄐㄧㄚ ㄨ)
to be repetitious; redundant;
overlapping

疊字(ㄉㄧㄝ ㄗ)
(linguistics) reiterative locu-
tion; reduplication

疊韻(ㄉㄧㄝ ㄩㄣ)
①two words of the same
rhyme ②to repeat a rhyme

疋　部
ㄆㄧ pii pǐ

【疋】 3587 ㄆㄧ pii pǐ
a roll (of cloth); a bolt (of
cloth)

疋頭(ㄆㄧ ㄊㄡ)
cloth; fabrics; piece goods

疋練(ㄆㄧ ㄌㄧㄢ)
a cascade

六畫

【疏】 3588 (疎，或疏，七畫)
1. ㄕㄨ shu shū
1. thin; sparse; few: 那老人有疏
疏的幾根鬍子。That old man
has a sparse beard.
2. unfamiliar; distant; unfriendly: 他們在台北人地生疏。They
are unfamiliar with Taipei
and its people.
3. careless; neglectful: 他疏忽了
他的健康。He neglected his
health.
4. to channel; to remove obstructions
5. coarse

疏布(ㄕㄨ ㄅㄨ)
coarse cloth

疏慢(ㄕㄨ ㄇㄢ)
to neglect inadvertently

疏密(ㄕㄨ ㄇㄧ)
①looseness and density ②
neglect and watchfulness

疏防(ㄕㄨ ㄈㄤ)or疏於防範(ㄕㄨ ㄩ
ㄈㄤ ㄈㄢ)
to fail to take precautions;
to be neglectful of necessary
precautions

疏放(ㄕㄨ ㄈㄤ)
careless; lax; loose

疏導(ㄕㄨ ㄉㄠ)or(ㄕㄨ ㄉㄠ)
①to channel ②to enlighten

疏宕(ㄕㄨ ㄉㄤ)
open-minded; carefree; free
and easy

疏通(ㄕㄨ ㄊㄨㄥ)
①to clean or dredge (a

waterway) ②to improve
(relations, etc.); to bring
about an understanding or
reconciliation; to bridge different views

疏漏(ㄕㄨ ㄌㄡ)
careless omissions; slips;
oversights

疏懶(ㄕㄨ ㄌㄢ)
idle; lazy; loose; lax: 他是一
個疏懶的人。He is an idle
fellow.

疏朗(ㄕㄨ ㄌㄤ)
clear

疏理(ㄕㄨ ㄌㄧ)
①to dredge and improve (a
waterway) ②to put (mat-
ters) in order

疏落(ㄕㄨ ㄌㄨㄛ)or疏疏落落(ㄕㄨ
ㄕㄨ ㄌㄨㄛ ㄌㄨㄛ)
sparse; few
to neglect inadvertently

疏闊(ㄕㄨ ㄎㄨㄛ)
①lacking precision; inaccurate; rough ②(said of relations); distant; cold; to
estrange; to alienate

疏狂(ㄕㄨ ㄎㄨㄤ)
unrestrained; uninhibited

疏忽(ㄕㄨ ㄏㄨ)
carelessness; careless; inadvertent; remiss; negligent;
oversight; to neglect: 他一時
疏忽，弄錯了。He made the
mistake through an over-
sight.

疏濬(ㄕㄨ ㄐㄩㄣ)
to clean or dredge (waterways): 港口正在疏濬中。The
harbor is being dredged.

疏懈(ㄕㄨ ㄒㄧㄝ)
negligent; neglectful; idle;
lazy

疏星(ㄕㄨ ㄒㄧㄥ)
sparse stars

疏失(ㄕㄨ ㄕ)
remiss; at fault; negligent;
negligence

疏食(ㄕㄨ ㄕ)
coarse meal

疏神(ㄕㄨ ㄕㄣ)
careless; inadvertent; inadvertence: 他的錯誤只是一時
疏神。His error was a mere
inadvertence.

疏率(ㄕㄨ ㄕㄨㄞ)

〔疋部〕

【疋部】

careless and rash; heedless

疏財仗義(ㄕㄨ ㄘㄞˊ ㄓㄤˋ ㄧˋ)
to give generously and be a champion of justice; generous and ready to extend a helping hand

疏散(ㄕㄨ ㄙㄢˇ)
to disperse; dispersion

疏鬆(ㄕㄨ ㄙㄨㄥ)
① loose: 土質疏鬆。The soil is loose. ② to loosen ③ puffy

疏而不漏(ㄕㄨ ㄦˊ ㄅㄨˋ ㄌㄡˋ)
(said of the meshes of justice) to be loose but never miss

疏野(ㄕㄨ ㄧㄝˇ)
rude; impolite

疏影(ㄕㄨ ㄧㄥˇ)
scatterd shadows as of plum blossoms

疏於職守(ㄕㄨ ㄩˊ ㄓˊ ㄕㄡˇ)
to neglect one's duty

疏濬(ㄕㄨ ㄐㄩㄣˋ)
to clean or dredge (waterways)

疏遠(ㄕㄨ ㄩㄢˇ) or 疏逖(ㄕㄨ ㄊㄧˋ)
(said of relations) not close; cold; to make a stranger of; to alienate or estrange: 爭吵使他與其家人疏遠。A quarrel had estranged him from his family.

【疏】 3588
2. ㄕㄨ shuh shū
1. to present point by point
2. to explicate; to annotate

九畫

【疑】 3589
ㄧˊ yi yí
1. doubtful; dubious; skeptical; doubt; to doubt; to question
2. suspicious; to suspect
3. strange; incomprehensible; mysterious; questionable
4. sham; dummy; false

疑謗(ㄧˊ ㄅㄤˋ)
suspected and slandered

疑兵(ㄧˊ ㄅㄧㄥ)
troops deployed to mislead the enemy

疑犯(ㄧˊ ㄈㄢˋ)
a criminal suspect

疑竇(ㄧˊ ㄉㄡˋ)
suspicion; doubt: 此事啓人疑

竇。This matter aroused our suspicion.

疑點(ㄧˊ ㄉㄧㄢˇ)
① a doubtful or questionable point ② a suspicious point

疑團(ㄧˊ ㄊㄨㄢˊ)
clogging suspicions; a maze of suspicions: 他滿腹疑團。He was full of doubts and suspicions.

疑團冰釋(ㄧˊ ㄊㄨㄢˊ ㄅㄧㄥ ㄕˋ)
The suspicions have dissolved completely.

疑難(ㄧˊ ㄋㄢˊ)
a question; a problem; a puzzle; things one cannot understand or problems one cannot solve; uncertainty

疑慮(ㄧˊ ㄌㄩˋ)
apprehension; anxiety; misgivings; to misgive: 他憂得疑慮不安。His mind misgave him.

疑古(ㄧˊ ㄍㄨˇ)
to be skeptical of antiquity

疑惑(ㄧˊ ㄏㄨㄛˋ)
① to doubt ② to suspect ③ to puzzle

疑忌(ㄧˊ ㄐㄧˋ)
suspicious and jealous

疑懼(ㄧˊ ㄐㄩˋ)
suspicious and fearful

疑心(ㄧˊ ㄒㄧㄣ)
① to doubt ② suspicion: 我對他起疑心。I have a feeling of suspicion about him.

疑心病(ㄧˊ ㄒㄧㄣ ㄅㄧㄥˋ)
① hypochondria ② skepticism

疑心生暗鬼(ㄧˊ ㄒㄧㄣ ㄕㄥ ㄢˋ ㄍㄨㄟˇ)
A suspicious heart will see imaginary ghosts. 或 Suspicions create imaginary fears.

疑信參半(ㄧˊ ㄒㄧㄣˋ ㄘㄢ ㄅㄢˋ)
half in belief and half in doubt; do not believe entirely

疑兇(ㄧˊ ㄒㄩㄥ)
a suspected murderer or assailant: 警察逮捕了疑兇。The police have arrested this suspected murderer.

疑塚(ㄧˊ ㄓㄨㄥˇ)
false graves (for distracting the attention of body snatchers or tomb sackers)

疑城(ㄧˊ ㄔㄥˊ)
sham castles (for deceiving the enemy)

疑神疑鬼(ㄧˊ ㄕㄣˊ ㄧˊ ㄍㄨㄟˇ)
to have unnecessary suspicions; to be even afraid of one's own shadow: 他終日疑神疑鬼的。He was even afraid of his own shadow all day.

疑則勿用，用則勿疑(ㄧˊ ㄗㄜˊ ㄨˋ ㄩㄥˋ, ㄩㄥˋ ㄗㄜˊ ㄨˋ ㄧˊ)
Do not employ a person one distrusts, but one must trust the person one employs.

疑猜(ㄧˊ ㄘㄞ)
to suspect; to guess; to conjecture

疑似(ㄧˊ ㄙˋ)
could be; suspected to be

疑案(ㄧˊ ㄢˋ)
an unsettled case; an uncertain case; a puzzling case

疑貳(ㄧˊ ㄦˋ)
to become double-minded because of suspicion

疑義(ㄧˊ ㄧˋ)
dubious interpretation

疑問(ㄧˊ ㄨㄣˋ)
a question; doubt; uncertainty: 你有什麼疑問? Do you have any questions?

疑問代名詞(ㄧˊ ㄨㄣˋ ㄉㄞˋ ㄇㄧㄥˊ ㄘˊ)
interrogative pronouns

疑問號(ㄧˊ ㄨㄣˋ ㄏㄠˋ)
a question mark

疑問句(ㄧˊ ㄨㄣˋ ㄐㄩˋ)
an interrogative sentence

疑獄(ㄧˊ ㄩˋ)
an uncertain criminal case; a mysterious criminal case; a puzzling case

疑雲(ㄧˊ ㄩㄣˊ)
clouds of suspicion or misgivings (darkening one's mind): 疑雲頃刻消散。The misgivings were dispelled at once.

【躓】 3590
ㄓˋ jyh zhì
to suffer a fall; to fall; to trip; to stumble

疒 部
彳ㄨㄤ chwang chuáng

二畫

【疔】3591
ㄉㄧㄥ ding dīng
a boil; a carbuncle

疔毒(ㄉㄧㄥ ㄉㄨˊ)
carbincular infection

疔瘡(ㄉㄧㄥ ㄔㄨㄤ)
(pathology) a boil; a carbuncle; furuncle

三畫

【疙】3592
《ㄜ ge gē
a wart; a pustule; a pimple

疙瘩(《ㄜ ˙ㄉㄚ)
① a wart; a pustule; a pimple ② a round lump; a knot (of rope, string, thread,etc.) ③ a knot in one's heart; hang-up: 他的勸告解開了我心上的疙瘩。His advice got rid of my hang-up.

疙瘩兒湯(《ㄜ ˙ㄉㄚ ㄦ ㄊㄤ)
small round lumps of dough served with soup

疙裏疙瘩的(《ㄜ ˙ㄌㄧ 《ㄜ ˙ㄉㄚ ˙ㄉㄜ)
① troublesome; not smooth ② faultfinding; hard to please

疙瘩瘩瘩(《ㄜ ˙《ㄜ ㄉㄚ ㄉㄚ)
rough; bumpy

【疚】3593
ㄐㄧㄡˋ jiow jiù
1. prolonged illness
2. mental discomfort
3. a guilty conscience

疚懷(ㄐㄧㄡˋ ㄏㄨㄞˊ)
ashamed

疚心(ㄐㄧㄡˋ ㄒㄧㄣ)
ashamed

【疝】3594
ㄕㄢˋ shann shàn
hernia

疝痛(ㄕㄢˋ ㄊㄨㄥˋ)
colic

疝氣(ㄕㄢˋ ˙ㄑㄧ)
hernia

四畫

【疤】3595
ㄅㄚ ba bā
1. a scar
2. a birthmark

疤(ㄅㄚ ˙ㄍㄚ)
① a scar ② a birthmark

疤瘌鬢(ㄅㄚ ˙ㄍㄚ ㄅㄧㄣ)
a birthmark at the temple (considered undesirable for a woman)

疤瘌眼(ㄅㄚ ˙ㄍㄚ ㄧㄢˇ)
a scarred eyelid

疤臉(ㄅㄚ ㄌㄧㄢˇ)
a scarred face

疤痕(ㄅㄚ ㄏㄣˊ)
a scar

【疥】3596
ㄐㄧㄝˋ jieh jiè
scabies

疥癬(ㄐㄧㄝˋ ㄒㄩㄢˇ)
scabies; the itch; mange; ringworm

疥癬蟲(ㄐㄧㄝˋ ㄒㄩㄢˇ ㄔㄨㄥˊ)
a scab mite; an itch mite

疥瘡(ㄐㄧㄝˋ ㄔㄨㄤ)
sores from scabies

【疫】3597
ㄧˋ yih yì
an epidemic; a plague; a pestilence

疫病傳染(ㄧˋ ㄅㄧㄥˋ ㄔㄨㄢˊ ㄖㄢˇ)
contagion

疫苗(ㄧˋ ㄇㄧㄠˊ)
vaccine

疫癘(ㄧˋ ㄌㄧˋ)
bubonic plague; a plague; pestilence

疫症(ㄧˋ ㄓㄥˋ)
an epidemic

疫症學(ㄧˋ ㄓㄥˋ ㄒㄩㄝˊ)
epidemiology

【疣】3598
ㄧㄡˊ you yóu
a wart; a papule

五畫

【疲】3599
ㄆㄧˊ pyi pí
weary; tired; fatigued; exhausted

疲憊(ㄆㄧˊ ㄅㄟˋ)
fatigued; tired; weary

疲憊不堪(ㄆㄧˊ ㄅㄟˋ ㄅㄨˋ ㄎㄢ)
extremely tired; about to collapse from exhaustion

疲敝(ㄆㄧˊ ㄅㄧˋ)
weak from exhaustion; weary and weak

疲乏(ㄆㄧˊ ㄈㄚˊ)
tired; weary; exhausted: 我太疲乏,不能再向前走了。I'm too tired to go any further.

疲鈍(ㄆㄧˊ ㄉㄨㄣˋ)
weary and slow; slothful from exhaustion

疲勞(ㄆㄧˊ ㄌㄠˊ)
fatigue; exhaustion; weariness: 他很疲勞。He suffered fatigue.

疲勞過度(ㄆㄧˊ ㄌㄠˊ 《ㄨㄛˋ ㄉㄨˋ)
excessive fatigue

疲勞轟炸(ㄆㄧˊ ㄌㄠˊ ㄏㄨㄥ ㄓㄚˋ)
① harassing air raids ② a long and tedious harangue

疲倦(ㄆㄧˊ ㄐㄩㄢˋ)
weary; tired; fatigued

疲弱(ㄆㄧˊ ㄖㄨㄛˋ)
① weary and weak; weak from exhaustion ② (of commodities) to decrease in demand

疲軟(ㄆㄧˊ ㄖㄨㄢˇ)
① tired and feeble ② (of commodities) to decrease in demand ③ (of finance) to weaken

疲玩(ㄆㄧˊ ㄨㄢˊ)
remiss; negligent; not alert

疲於奔命(ㄆㄧˊ ㄩˊ ㄅㄣ ㄇㄧㄥˋ)
tired from running around —wearied of coping with many problemes at the same time

【疳】3600
《ㄢ gan gān
1. a kind of infantile disease caused by digestive trouble or malnutrition
2. a kind of infectious venereal disease

疳積(《ㄢ ㄐㄧ)
an infantile disease caused by digestive trouble or malnutrition

【疸】3601
ㄉㄢˇ daan dǎn
jaundice

【疴】3602
(痾)ㄜ e ē
(又讀 ㄎㄜ ke kē)

（疒
部）

sickness; disease

【疹】 3603
ㄓㄣ jeen zhěn
rashes

疹子（ㄓㄣ·ㄗ）
measles; carbuncles

【疽】 3604
ㄐㄩ jiu jū
ulcer

【疼】 3605
ㄊㄥ terng téng
1. to ache; to hurt; pain; sore:
她的腿疼。She has a pain in
the leg.
2. to dote on; to be fond of (a
child)

疼痛（ㄊㄥ ㄊㄨㄥ）
to ache

疼熱（ㄊㄥ ㄖㄜ）
to suffer pain and fever

疼愛（ㄊㄥ ㄞ）
to be fond of (a child): 她非
常疼愛她的小孩。She is very
fond of her children.

【疾】 3606
ㄐㄧ jyi jí
1. disease; suffering: 疾病通常
由病菌而起。Disease is usu-
ally caused by germs.
2. to hate; to detest
3. swift; rapid; quick; fast

疾病（ㄐㄧ ㄅㄧㄥ）
diseases: 醫生的職責為預防和
治療疾病。The business of
doctors is to prevent and
cure diseases.

疾風知勁草（ㄐㄧ ㄈㄥ ㄓ ㄐㄧㄥ ㄘㄠˇ）
(literally) Strong winds test
the sturdiness of grass.
—Adversity tests the character of a man.

疾雷（ㄐㄧ ㄌㄟ）
①a sudden clap of thunder
②a swift action

疾雷不及掩耳（ㄐㄧ ㄌㄟ ㄅㄨ ㄐㄧ
ㄧㄢˇ ㄦˇ）
(literally) a clap of thunder
so sudden that there is no
time for covering one's ears
—an action so swift that
there is no time to prepare
to meet it

疾苦（ㄐㄧ ㄎㄨˇ）
suffering (especially under
an oppressive government)

疾呼（ㄐㄧ ㄏㄨ）
to call out loudly; to shout

疾駛（ㄐㄧ ㄕˇ）or 疾馳（ㄐㄧ ㄔˊ）

to move swiftly; to dart; to
fleet; to drive very fast: 船乘
風疾駛。The ship was driving
very fast before the wind.

疾視（ㄐㄧ ㄕˋ）
to look at someone angrily

疾首（ㄐㄧ ㄕㄡˇ）
headache caused by rage

疾甚（ㄐㄧ ㄕㄣˋ）
to be seriously ill

疾走（ㄐㄧ ㄗㄡˇ）
to move or march swiftly; to
walk quickly; to run

疾足先登（ㄐㄧ ㄗㄨˊ ㄒㄧㄢ ㄉㄥ）
He who has fast legs will
get there first. 或 He who
acts fast will succeed first.亦
作「捷足先登」

疾惡如仇（ㄐㄧ ㄜˋ ㄖㄨˊ ㄔㄡˊ）
to hate evil as much as one
hates an enemy

疾言厲色（ㄐㄧ ㄧㄢˊ ㄌㄧˋ ㄙㄜˋ）
(literally) to speak fast with
a harsh look—to lecture severely

疾言遽色（ㄐㄧ ㄧㄢˊ ㄐㄩˋ ㄙㄜˋ）
speaking hastily and looking
flurried

【病】 3607
ㄅㄧㄥ binq bìng
1. illness; disease; ailment
2. to be ill
3. blemish; fault: 此不足為病。It
cannot be counted as a fault.
4. to injure; to harm
5. to worry
6. to hate
7. to insult

病包兒（ㄅㄧㄥ ㄅㄠ ㄦ）
a sickly person

病變（ㄅㄧㄥ ㄅㄧㄢˋ）
pathological changes

病魔（ㄅㄧㄥ ㄇㄛˊ）
the demon of ill health; the
curse of disease

病沒 or 病歿（ㄅㄧㄥ ㄇㄛˋ）
to die of illness; to succumb
to a disease

病發（ㄅㄧㄥ ㄈㄚ）
to fall ill

病廢（ㄅㄧㄥ ㄈㄟˋ）
to be disabled by disease

病房（ㄅㄧㄥ ㄈㄤˊ）
a sickroom; a ward: 醫生正在
巡查病房。The doctor is visit-
ing the ward.

病夫（ㄅㄧㄥ ㄈㄨ）

a man who is sick most of
the time

病倒（ㄅㄧㄥ ㄉㄠˇ）
to fall ill; to be confined in
bed due to illness: 他的妻子
病倒了。His wife fell sick.

病毒（ㄅㄧㄥ ㄉㄨˊ）
viruses

病篤（ㄅㄧㄥ ㄉㄨˇ）
dying of illness: 這老人病篤。
The old man was dying of
illness.

病榻（ㄅㄧㄥ ㄊㄚˋ）
a sickbed 參看「病床」

病態（ㄅㄧㄥ ㄊㄞˋ）
morbid (or abnormal) state

病痛（ㄅㄧㄥ ㄊㄨㄥˋ）
slight illness; indisposition

病理學（ㄅㄧㄥ ㄌㄧˇ ㄒㄩㄝˊ）
pathology

病例（ㄅㄧㄥ ㄌㄧˋ）
number of cases of a particular disease

病歷（ㄅㄧㄥ ㄌㄧˋ）
case history; medical history
(of a patient)

病根（ㄅㄧㄥ ㄍㄣ）
①cause of a disease; the
origin of a disease ②the
cause of trouble: 自私是他的
病根。Selfishness is the cause
of his trouble.

病根子（ㄅㄧㄥ ㄍㄣ·ㄗ）
a constitutional disease;
a chronic disease; an old
complaint

病骨（ㄅㄧㄥ ㄍㄨˇ）
to get skinny due to a disease; to be emaciated from
disease

病故（ㄅㄧㄥ ㄍㄨˋ）
to die of illness: 她父親病故
於中風。Her father died of
apoplexy.

病國殃民（ㄅㄧㄥ ㄍㄨㄛˊ ㄧㄤ ㄇㄧㄣˊ）
to injure both the state and
the people

病況（ㄅㄧㄥ ㄎㄨㄤˋ）
the condition of a patient

病號（ㄅㄧㄥ ㄏㄠˋ）
a hospitalized patient who is
numbered for easy identification

病後（ㄅㄧㄥ ㄏㄡˋ）
after an illness; during convalescence

病革（ㄅㄧㄥ ㄐㄧˊ）

about to die of an illness

病疾(ㄅㄧㄥˋ ㄐㄧˊ)
sickness; disease; illness

病急亂投醫(ㄅㄧㄥˋ ㄐㄧˊ ㄌㄨㄢˋ ㄊㄡˊ ㄧ)
to turn to any doctor or prescription one can find when critically ill—to try anything when in a desperate situation

病家(ㄅㄧㄥˋ ㄐㄧㄚ)
a patient

病假(ㄅㄧㄥˋ ㄐㄧㄚˋ)
sick leave: 她請病假. She asked for sick leave.

病劇(ㄅㄧㄥˋ ㄐㄩˋ)
seriously ill; far advanced in one's illness; in a critical condition

病菌(ㄅㄧㄥˋ ㄐㄩㄣˋ)
germs; bacteria; viruses: 這牛奶沒有病菌嗎? Is this milk free from germs?

病情(ㄅㄧㄥˋ ㄑㄧㄥˊ)
the condition of a patient: 這嬰兒的病情有好轉. The baby's condition took a favorable turn.

病軀(ㄅㄧㄥˋ ㄑㄩ)
a sick body

病徵(ㄅㄧㄥˋ ㄓㄥ)
symptoms of a disease

病症(ㄅㄧㄥˋ ㄓㄥˋ)
①a disease; an ailment ②symptoms of a disease

病狀(ㄅㄧㄥˋ ㄓㄨㄤˋ)
symptoms of a disease

病重(ㄅㄧㄥˋ ㄓㄨㄥˋ)
seriously ill; in a critical condition

病牀(ㄅㄧㄥˋ ㄔㄨㄤˊ)
a sickbed: 這所醫院有五百張病牀. The hospital has five hundred sickbeds.

病蟲害(ㄅㄧㄥˋ ㄔㄨㄥˊ ㄏㄞˋ)
blight

病室(ㄅㄧㄥˋ ㄕˋ)
a sickroom; a ward

病勢(ㄅㄧㄥˋ ㄕˋ)
the condition of a patient

病人(ㄅㄧㄥˋ ㄖㄣˊ)
a sick man; a patient

病入膏肓(ㄅㄧㄥˋ ㄖㄨˋ ㄍㄠ ㄏㄨㄤ)
so advanced in one's disease as to be past remedy

病容(ㄅㄧㄥˋ ㄖㄨㄥˊ)
a sickly look; an emaciated

look

病從口入(ㄅㄧㄥˋ ㄊㄨㄥˊ ㄎㄡˇ ㄖㄨˋ)
Diseases enter by the mouth. (Therefore, one should be careful in his diet or eating habits.): 病從口入, 禍從口出. Diseases enter by the mouth; misfortunes issue from it.

病死(ㄅㄧㄥˋ ㄙˇ)
to die of an illness

病因(ㄅㄧㄥˋ ㄧㄣ)
the cause of a disease; the origin of a disease

病危(ㄅㄧㄥˋ ㄨㄟˊ)
dying of an illness; about to die of an illness

病愈 or 病癒(ㄅㄧㄥˋ ㄩˋ)
to recover from illness; to get well

病原(ㄅㄧㄥˋ ㄩㄢˊ)
the cause of a disease; the origin of a disease

病原體(ㄅㄧㄥˋ ㄩㄢˊ ㄊㄧˇ)
viruses

病院(ㄅㄧㄥˋ ㄩㄢˋ)
a hospital: 他仍在精神病院裡. He is still in a mental hospital.

【症】 3608
ㄓㄥˋ jenq zhèng
1. sickness; an ailment
2. symptoms or manifestations of a disease

症候(ㄓㄥˋ ㄏㄡˋ)or 症狀(ㄓㄥˋ ㄓㄨㄤˋ)
symptoms or manifestations of a disease

【痃】 3609
ㄒㄧㄢˊ shyan xián
(pathology) bubo

【痀】 3610
ㄐㄩ jiu jū
a hunchback; a humpback

痀僂(ㄐㄩ ㄌㄡˊ)or 痀瘻(ㄐㄩ ㄌㄡˊ)
hunchback; humpback

【痂】 3611
ㄐㄧㄚ jia jiā
scab over a sore

【疱】 3612
(同) ㄆㄠˋ paw pào
acne

疱疹(ㄆㄠˋ ㄓㄣˇ)
①a bleb ②herpes

【痁】 3613
ㄉㄧㄢ diann diàn
chronic malaria

【痄】 3614
ㄓㄚˋ jah zhà
scrofulous swellings and

sores

痄腮(ㄓㄚˋ ㄙㄞ)
mumps

ㄘ tsy cí
(又讀) ㄘˇ tsyr cǐ
a defect; a flaw; a mistake

疵累(ㄘ ㄌㄟˋ)
a flaw; a fault; a defect

疵癘(ㄘ ㄌㄧˋ)
①disease ②disaster

疵瑕(ㄘ ㄒㄧㄚˊ)
a fault; a mistake; an error

六畫

【痌】 3616
ㄊㄨㄥ tong tōng
aching; painful

痌瘝(ㄊㄨㄥ ㄍㄨㄢ)
suffering; disease

痌瘝在抱(ㄊㄨㄥ ㄍㄨㄢ ㄗㄞˋ ㄅㄠˋ)
to have a constant concern for the suffering of the people

【痍】 3617
ㄧˊ yí yí
a wound; a bruise; a sore

【痊】 3618
ㄑㄩㄢˊ chyuan quán
healed; cured; recovery

痊可(ㄑㄩㄢˊ ㄎㄜˇ)
to have been cured; to have recovered from illness

痊愈 or 痊癒(ㄑㄩㄢˊ ㄩˋ)
to have been cured; to have recovered from illness

【痏】 3619
ㄨㄟˇ woei wěi
a mark on the skin; a scar

【痕】 3620
ㄏㄣˊ hern hén
a mark; a scar; a trace: 他的面頰上有一道傷痕. He had a scar on his cheek.

痕跡(ㄏㄣˊ ㄐㄧ)
a trace: 露營者除去所有營火的痕跡. The campers removed all traces of their fire.

【痔】 3621
ㄓˋ jyh zhì
piles; hemorrhoids

痔漏(ㄓˋ ㄌㄡˋ)or 痔瘻(ㄓˋ ㄌㄡˋ)
an anal fistula

痔核(ㄓˋ ㄏㄜˊ)
blind piles

痔瘡(㞢·ㄔㄨㅊ)
piles; hemorrhoids

七畫

【痛】 3622
ㄊㄨㄥ tòng tōng
1. painful; aching
2. sorrowful; sad; bitter; poignant; bitterly
3. heartily; to one's heart's content

痛不欲生(ㄊㄨㄥ ㄅㄨˋ ㄩˋ ㄕㄥ)
to grieve to the extent of wishing to die

痛罵(ㄊㄨㄥ ㄇㄚˋ)
to berate; to revile; to vituperate; to give a good dressing-down

痛風(ㄊㄨㄥ ㄈㄥ)
gout (a disease)

痛打(ㄊㄨㄥ ㄉㄚˇ)
to beat soundly; to give a severe thrashing

痛悼(ㄊㄨㄥ ㄉㄠˋ)
to grieve over the death of someone bitterly

痛詆(ㄊㄨㄥ ㄉㄧˇ)
to berate; to revile; to vituperate: 他痛詆他兒子。He berated his son.

痛定思痛(ㄊㄨㄥ ㄉㄧㄥˋ ㄙ ㄊㄨㄥ)
to recall the past with pangs in the heart; to feel pangs over a past defeat, failure, etc.

痛改前非(ㄊㄨㄥ ㄍㄞˇ ㄑㄧㄢˊ ㄈㄟ)
to repent past mistakes

痛哭(ㄊㄨㄥ ㄎㄨ)
to weep bitterly: 她痛哭。She wept bitter tears.

痛哭流涕(ㄊㄨㄥ ㄎㄨ ㄌㄧㄡˊ ㄊㄧˋ)
to shed tears in bitter sorrow; to shed tears of anguish

痛苦(ㄊㄨㄥ ㄎㄨˇ)
painful; suffering; pain; anguish

痛快(ㄊㄨㄥ ㄎㄨㄞˋ)or 痛痛快快(ㄊㄨㄥ ㄊㄨㄥ ㄎㄨㄞˋ ㄎㄨㄞˋ)
①delighted; very happy ②straightforward ③ to one's heart's content

痛快淋漓(ㄊㄨㄥ ㄎㄨㄞˋ ㄌㄧㄣˊ ㄌㄧˊ)
satisfying in every respect

痛恨(ㄊㄨㄥ ㄏㄣˋ)
to detest; to hate deeply

痛悔(ㄊㄨㄥ ㄏㄨㄟˇ)
to repent bitterly

痛擊(ㄊㄨㄥ ㄐㄧˊ)
to give a hard blow

痛覺(ㄊㄨㄥ ㄐㄩㄝˊ)
a sense of pain

痛切(ㄊㄨㄥ ㄑㄧㄝˋ)
sharply painful to the feelings; poignant; pungent

痛惜(ㄊㄨㄥ ㄒㄧ)
to regret deeply

痛心(ㄊㄨㄥ ㄒㄧㄣ)
heartbroken; very sorry

痛心疾首(ㄊㄨㄥ ㄒㄧㄣ ㄐㄧˊ ㄕㄡˇ)
to hate deeply; to feel bitter about...

痛斥(ㄊㄨㄥ ㄔˋ)
to scold severely; scathingly denounce

痛楚(ㄊㄨㄥ ㄔㄨˇ)
pain; suffering; anguish

痛處(ㄊㄨㄥ ㄔㄨˋ)
a sore spot; a tender spot

痛入骨髓(ㄊㄨㄥ ㄖㄨˋ ㄍㄨˇ ㄙㄨㄟˇ)
The pain penetrates even into the marrow.

痛自悔改(ㄊㄨㄥ ㄗˋ ㄏㄨㄟˇ ㄍㄞˇ)
to show deep repentance

痛責(ㄊㄨㄥ ㄗㄜˊ)
to scold severely

痛愛(ㄊㄨㄥ ㄞˋ)
to love deeply; to love passionately

痛毆(ㄊㄨㄥ ㄡ)
to beat savagely; to give a sounding beating

痛飲(ㄊㄨㄥ ㄧㄣˇ)
to drink to one's heart's content

痛飲黃龍(ㄊㄨㄥ ㄧㄣˇ ㄏㄨㄤˊ ㄌㄨㄥˊ)
to drink for victory in the heart of conquered enemy territory

痛癢(ㄊㄨㄥ ㄧㄤˇ)
①sufferings; difficulties ②importance: 那無關痛癢。It is of no importance.

痛癢相關(ㄊㄨㄥ ㄧㄤˇ ㄒㄧㄤ ㄍㄨㄢ)
to have loving concern for each other; to share a common lot: 我們痛癢相關。We shared a common lot.

痛恨(ㄊㄨㄥ ㄏㄣˋ)
to hate bitterly; to detest; to abhor; disgusting: 我痛恨每天必須早起。I detest having to

rise early every day.

【痘】 3623
ㄉㄡˋ dòu dòu
smallpox 亦作「天花」

痘疤(ㄉㄡˋ ㄅㄚ)
smallpox scabs

痘苗(ㄉㄡˋ ㄇㄧㄠˊ)
vaccine; lymph

痘瘡(ㄉㄡˋ ㄔㄨㄤ)
smallpox

【痙】 3624
ㄐㄧㄥˋ jìng jīng
spasm; convulsions

痙攣(ㄐㄧㄥˋ ㄌㄨㄢˊ)
convulsions; spasm; cramp; a jerk

【痢】 3625
ㄌㄧˋ lìh lì
dysentery; diarrhea

痢疾(ㄌㄧˋ ㄐㄧˊ)
dysentery; diarrhea: 他患痢疾。He has diarrhea.

【痧】 3626
ㄕㄚ sha shā
1. cholera
2. measles

痧子(ㄕㄚˇ ·ㄗ)
measles

【痣】 3627
ㄓˋ jyh zhì
moles; nevus: 她下巴上有顆痣。She has a mole on her chin.

【痠】 3628
ㄙㄨㄢ suan suān
muscular pains

痠痛(ㄙㄨㄢ ㄊㄨㄥˋ)or 痠疼(ㄙㄨㄢ ㄊㄨㄥˊ)
(said of muscles, bones, etc.) to ache 參看「痠疼」: 我的骨頭痠痛。My bones ache.

痠懶(ㄙㄨㄢ ㄌㄢˇ)
sore and weary

痠軟(ㄙㄨㄢ ㄖㄨㄢˇ)
sore and weak: 我的四肢痠軟。My limbs are sore and weak.

【痡】 3629
ㄆㄨ pu pū
a disease; an ailment

【痞】 3630
ㄆㄧˇ pǐi pǐ
1. dyspepsia; a spleen infection
2. a ruffian; a scoundrel

痞棍(ㄆㄧˇ ㄍㄨㄣˋ)or 痞子(ㄆㄧˇ ·ㄗ)
a rascal; a scoundrel

痞塊(ㄆㄧˇ ㄎㄨㄞˋ)
a swelling of the abdomen due to constipation

【痤】 3631
ㄘㄨㄛˊ tswo cuó
1. a boil or carbuncle on the face
2. minor swelling; an abscess

八畫

【痰】 3632
ㄊㄢˊ tarn tán
phlegm; expectoration; sputum

痰迷心竅(ㄊㄢˊ ㄇㄧˊ ㄒㄧㄣ ㄑㄧㄠˋ)
confused; foolish; befuddled

痰桶(ㄊㄢˊ ㄊㄨㄥˇ)
a spittoon

痰涎(ㄊㄢˊ ㄒㄧㄢˊ)
phlegm; spittle; expectoration

痰喘(ㄊㄢˊ ㄔㄨㄢˇ)
asthma

痰盂(ㄊㄢˊ ㄩˊ)or痰罐(ㄊㄢˊ ㄍㄨㄢˋ)
a spittoon

【痱】 3633
(痱) ㄈㄟˋ fey fèi
heat rashes; heat spots; prickly heat

痱子(ㄈㄟˋ ㄗˇ)
heat rashes; heat spots; prickly heat: 這孩子生痱子。
The child has heat rashes.

痱子粉(ㄈㄟˋ ㄗˇ ㄈㄣˇ)
talcum powder; baby powder

【痳】 3634
(痳) ㄌㄧㄣˊ lin lín
gonorrhea

痳病(ㄌㄧㄣˊ ㄅㄧㄥˋ)
gonorrhea 參看「淋病」

痳症(ㄌㄧㄣˊ ㄓㄥˋ)
gonorrhea

【痲】 3635
ㄇㄚˊ ma má
1. measles
2. leprosy
3. to stupefy; to benumb; to anesthetize; to paralyze
4. a pockmark

痲痹(ㄇㄚˊ ㄅㄧˋ)
paralysis; palsy; numbness

痲面(ㄇㄚˊ ㄇㄧㄢˋ)
a pockmarked face

痲瘋(ㄇㄚˊ ㄈㄥ)
leprosy

痲瘋院(ㄇㄚˊ ㄈㄥ ㄩㄢˋ)
a leprosarium; a lazaretto; a leper house

痲臉婆(ㄇㄚˊ ㄌㄧㄢˇ ㄆㄛˊ)
a woman with a pock-marked face

痲疹(ㄇㄚˊ ㄓㄣˇ)
measles: 痲疹是小孩生的病。
Measles is a children's disease.

痲子(ㄇㄚˊ ㄗˇ)
① pockmarks ② a person with a pockmarked face

【痺】 3636
ㄅㄧˋ bih bì
paralysis

【痼】 3637
《ㄨˋ guh gù
a chronic disease: 痼疾不治。
A chronic disease is incurable.

痼癖(《ㄨˋ ㄆㄧˇ)
an addiction; a fondness

痼疾(《ㄨˋ ㄐㄧˊ)
an incurable chronic disease: 我是來治痼疾的。I am here to cure my chronic disease

痼習(《ㄨˋ ㄒㄧˊ)
a deep-rooted habit

【瘀】 3638
ㄩ iu yū
a hematoma

瘀膿(ㄩ ㄋㄨㄥˊ)
pus

瘀血(ㄩ ㄒㄧㄝˇ)
a hematoma

瘀傷(ㄩ ㄕㄤ)
a contusion, a bruise: 他的腿瘀傷了。He received a bruise on his leg.

瘀肉(ㄩ ㄖㄡˋ)
gangrene

【痿】 3639
ㄨㄟˇ woei wěi
paralysis; impotent

痿痹(ㄨㄟˇ ㄅㄧˋ)
paralysis

痿症(ㄨㄟˇ ㄓㄥˋ)
(Chinese medicine) the flaccidity-syndrome; flaccid paralysis

【瘁】 3640
ㄘㄨㄟˋ tsuey cuì
1. disease; illness
2. overfatigued; toil

【痴】 3641
ㄔ chy chī
the simplified form of 癡, 參看「癡」

九畫

【瘍】 3642
ㄧㄤˊ yang yáng
skin diseases or infections; sores; an ulcer

【瘋】 3643
ㄈㄥ feng fēng
insane; crazy; mad; mentally deranged; lunatic; wild

瘋癲(ㄈㄥ ㄉㄧㄢ)or瘋瘋癲癲(ㄈㄥ ㄈㄥ ㄉㄧㄢ ㄉㄧㄢ)
mentally deranged; insane

瘋狗(ㄈㄥ ㄍㄡˇ)or瘋犬(ㄈㄥ ㄑㄩㄢˇ)
a mad dog; a rabid dog

瘋狂(ㄈㄥ ㄎㄨㄤˊ)
crazy; mad; insane; wild; irrational: 她因過分悲傷而導致瘋狂。She went insane from the tragedy.

瘋話(ㄈㄥ ㄏㄨㄚˋ)
gibberish; jargon

瘋犬病(ㄈㄥ ㄑㄩㄢˇ ㄅㄧㄥˋ)
rabies; hydrophobia

瘋人(ㄈㄥ ㄖㄣˊ)or瘋子(ㄈㄥ ㄗˇ)
a lunatic; a madman; a maniac

瘋人院(ㄈㄥ ㄖㄣˊ ㄩㄢˋ)
a mental hospital; a mental institution; an insane asylum

【瘓】 3644
ㄏㄨㄢˋ huann huàn
paralysis: 他的左臂瘓瘓了。His left arm was paralyzed.

【瘖】 3645
ㄧㄣ in yīn
dumb; mute

瘖啞(ㄧㄣ ㄧㄚˇ)
dumb; mute

【痢】 3646
ㄌㄚˋ lah là
favus

痢痢 or 鬎鬁(ㄌㄚˋ ㄌㄧˋ)
favus

痢痢頭(ㄌㄚˋ ㄌㄧˋ ㄊㄡˊ)
a head made bald by favus

【瘉】 3647
ㄩˋ yuh yù
1. same as 愈—healed; cured
2. ill; sick

【瘧】 3648
ㄋㄩㄝˋ niueh nüè
malaria

瘧疾(ㄋㄩㄝˋ ㄐㄧˊ)
malaria

瘧疾原蟲(ㄋㄩㄝˋ ㄐㄧˊ ㄩㄢˊ ㄔㄨㄥˊ)

a plasmodium

糖蚊 (ㄊㄤˊ ㄨㄣˊ)
an anopheles

十畫

【瘝】 3649
《ㄍㄨㄢ guan guān
sick; ill; ailing

【瘟】 3650
ㄨㄣ uen wēn
an epidemic; a plague; a pestilence

瘟氣 (ㄨㄣ ㄑㄧˋ)
pestilential vapor

瘟神 (ㄨㄣ ㄕㄣˊ)
① the god of pestilence ② a fellow who brings disaster to mankind

瘟生 (ㄨㄣ ㄕㄥ)
(Shanghai dialect) a sucker

瘟疫 (ㄨㄣ ㄧˋ)
an epidemic; a plague; a pestilence: 瘟疫正流行於那個城。 The plague is now prevailing in that city.

【瘡】 3651
ㄔㄨㄤ chuang chuāng
1. an ulcer; a sore; a boil
2. a wound

瘡疤 (ㄔㄨㄤ ㄅㄚ)
the scar of an ulcer; wound scars

瘡痨 (ㄔㄨㄤ ㄌㄠˊ)
a chronic ulcer

瘡口 (ㄔㄨㄤ ㄎㄡˇ)
an opening of an ulcer or a sore

瘡痍 (ㄔㄨㄤ ㄧˊ) or 瘡痏 (ㄔㄨㄤ ㄨㄟˇ)
① an ulcer; a sore ② suffering; hardship; privation

瘡痍滿目 (ㄔㄨㄤ ㄧˊ ㄇㄢˇ ㄇㄨˋ)
One sees suffering everywhere.

【瘦】 3652
ㄕㄡˋ show shòu
thin; lean; slim; meager; scrawny; emaciated

瘦巴 (ㄕㄡˋ ㄅㄚ)
skinny; lean

瘦馬 (ㄕㄡˋ ㄇㄚˇ)
a lean horse

瘦骨嶙峋 (ㄕㄡˋ ㄍㄨˇ ㄌㄧㄣˊ ㄒㄩㄣˊ)
very skinny

瘦果 (ㄕㄡˋ ㄍㄨㄛˇ)
an achene

瘦瘠 (ㄕㄡˋ ㄐㄧˊ)

(said of soil) unproductive; barren

瘦筋巴骨 (ㄕㄡˋ ㄐㄧㄣ ㄅㄚ ㄍㄨˇ)
skinny; very lean; very thin

瘦金書 (ㄕㄡˋ ㄐㄧㄣ ㄕㄨ)
a style of Chinese calligraphy, originated by Emperor Hui Tsung (徽宗) of the Sung Dynasty, featuring slim and sturdy strokes

瘦小 (ㄕㄡˋ ㄒㄧㄠˇ)
thin and small

瘦削 (ㄕㄡˋ ㄒㄩㄝ)
slim: 胖的女孩羨慕瘦削的女孩。 Fat girls envy slim girls.

瘦長 (ㄕㄡˋ ㄔㄤˊ)
skinny and tall; tall and lean

瘦肉 (ㄕㄡˋ ㄖㄡˋ)
lean meat

瘦弱 (ㄕㄡˋ ㄖㄨㄛˋ)
thin and weak; emaciated and frail: 生病後,她看來瘦弱。 She looked thin and weak after her illness.

瘦子 (ㄕㄡˋ ˙ㄗ)
a thin person; a living skeleton

瘦硬 (ㄕㄡˋ ㄧㄥˋ)
(said of a handwriting) fine and forceful

【瘠】 3653
ㄐㄧˊ jyi jí
1. thin; lean; meager; emaciated
2. (said of land) sterile, infertile, or unproductive; barren

瘠地 (ㄐㄧˊ ㄉㄧˋ)
sterile, or unproductive land

瘠土 (ㄐㄧˊ ㄊㄨˇ)
sterile soil; infertile soil

瘠瘦 (ㄐㄧˊ ㄕㄡˋ)
emaciated; lean and weak

【瘢】 3654
ㄅㄢ ban bān
a scar; a freckle

瘢點 (ㄅㄢ ㄉㄧㄢˇ)
a black spot on the skin; a scar

瘢痕 (ㄅㄢ ㄏㄣˊ)
a scar

【瘥】 3655
1. ㄔㄞ chay chāi
cured; healed; recovered

【瘥】 3655
2. ㄘㄨㄛˋ tswo cuò
sick; ill; ailing; affliction

【瘩】 3656
˙ㄉㄚ da da
a boil; a pimple; a wart

【瘞】 3657
ㄧˋ yih yì
to bury

【瘤】 3658
(瘤) ㄌㄧㄡˊ liou liú
a tumor; a swelling; a lump

瘤胃 (ㄌㄧㄡˊ ㄨㄟˋ)
a rumen

十一畫

【瘴】 3659
ㄓㄤˋ janq zhàng
miasma; swamp vapor

瘴母 (ㄓㄤˋ ㄇㄨˇ)
masses of miasma

瘴地 (ㄓㄤˋ ㄉㄧˋ)
a miasmal place

瘴癘 (ㄓㄤˋ ㄌㄧˋ)
disease or epidemic attributed to miasma; poisonous vapor

瘴氣 (ㄓㄤˋ ㄑㄧˋ)
miasma; pestilential vapor

瘴煙毒霧 (ㄓㄤˋ ㄧㄢ ㄉㄨˊ ㄨˋ)
clouds of pestilential vapor; miasmal clouds

瘴雨蠻煙 (ㄓㄤˋ ㄩˇ ㄇㄢˊ ㄧㄢ)
pestilential rain and unhealthy mist

【瘳】 3660
ㄔㄡ chou chōu
1. cured; healed
2. to harm; to hurt

【瘵】 3661
ㄓㄞˋ jay zhài
1. tuberculosis
2. distress

【瘺】 3662
1. ㄌㄧㄡˊ liou liú
a hunchback; a humpback

【瘺】 3662
2. ㄌㄡˊ low lóu
goiter; scrofula

【瘸】 3663
ㄑㄩㄝˊ chyue qué
1. a cripple
2. to be lame: 我的右腿瘸了。 I am lame in the right leg.

瘸腿 (ㄑㄩㄝˊ ㄊㄨㄟˇ)
crippled; lame

瘸子 (ㄑㄩㄝˊ ˙ㄗ)
a lame man; a cripple

【瘼】 3664
ㄇㄛ moh mò
1. disease; illness; an ailment
2. suffering; hardship; privation

十二畫

【療】 3665
ㄌㄧㄠ liau liáo
to treat (a disease); to relieve; to heal

療貧(ㄌㄧㄠ ㄆㄧㄣ)
to relieve the poor

療法(ㄌㄧㄠ ㄈㄚ)
a cure; a therapy

療毒(ㄌㄧㄠ ㄉㄨˊ)
to remove poison from human body

療妒(ㄌㄧㄠ ㄉㄨˋ)
to cure jealousy

療飢(ㄌㄧㄠ ㄐㄧ)
to relieve hunger

療效(ㄌㄧㄠ ㄒㄧㄠ)
curative effect

療治(ㄌㄧㄠ ㄓˋ)
to treat (a disease)

療養(ㄌㄧㄠ ㄧㄤ)
to recuperate; to convalesce: 他正在療養中。He is convalescent now.

療養院(ㄌㄧㄠ ㄧㄤ ㄩㄢ)
a sanatorium; a sanitarium; a rest home

【癃】 3666
ㄌㄨㄥ long lóng
1. humping of the back in old age
2. anuria

癃疾(ㄌㄨㄥ ㄐㄧ)
①humping of the back in old age ②anuria

【癌】 3667
ㄧㄢ yan yán
(又讀 ㄞ air ái)
cancer: 他死於胃癌。He died of stomach cancer.

癌細胞(ㄧㄢ ㄒㄧ ㄅㄠ)
cancer cells

癌症(ㄧㄢ ㄓㄥ)
cancer

癌腫(ㄧㄢ ㄓㄨㄥ)
a malignant tumor; cancer

【癆】 3668
ㄌㄠ lau láo
tuberculosis; consumption

癆病(ㄌㄠ ㄅㄧㄥ)or 癆症(ㄌㄠ ㄓㄥ)

tuberculosis; consumption

癆傷(ㄌㄠ ㄕㄤ)
weakened by overexertion

【癇】 3669
ㄒㄧㄢ shyan xián
epilepsy

癇風(ㄒㄧㄢ ㄈㄥ)
epilepsy

【癉】 3670
ㄉㄢ dann dàn
1. to hate bitterly; to detest
2. illness caused by over-exhaustion; distress

【瘢】 3671
ㄅㄢ ban bān
unhealthy marks on the skin; a blotch

十三畫

【癖】 3672
ㄆㄧˇ pii pǐ
1. chronic swelling of the spleen
2. addiction; a habitual inclination

癖好(ㄆㄧˇ ㄏㄠ)
a habitual inclination; addiction; a propensity

癖性(ㄆㄧˇ ㄒㄧㄥ)
a propensity; a habitual inclination; a habitual tendency

【癘】 3673
ㄌㄧ lih lì
1. an ulcer
2. pestilential vapor; pestilence

【癒】 3674
(瘉) ㄩ yuh yù
healed; cured

十四畫

【癟】 3675
(癟) ㄅㄧㄝ biee biě
flat; (sunken); not full

癟螺痧(ㄅㄧㄝ ㄌㄨㄛ ㄕㄚ)
cholera

癟著肚子(ㄅㄧㄝ ㄓㄜ ㄉㄨ ㄗ)
with an empty stomach

癟子(ㄅㄧㄝ ㄗ)
a setback; a blow

癟嘴子(ㄅㄧㄝ ㄗㄨㄟ ㄗ)
a person who has lost all teeth

癟三(ㄅㄧㄝ ㄙㄢ)
(Wu or Shanghai dialect) a bum; a tramp

【癡】 3676
(痴) ㄔ chy chī
1. idiotic; silly; foolish; stupid; senseless; crazy; insane
2. to beset: 她的美麗使他如醉如癡。Her beauty besotted him.

癡迷(ㄔ ㄇㄧ)
infatuated; besotted

癡肥(ㄔ ㄈㄟ)
very fat and looking stupid; obese

癡福(ㄔ ㄈㄨ)
the bliss of imbecility; idiotic happiness

癡鈍(ㄔ ㄉㄨㄣ)
dull; imbecile; stupid

癡男(ㄔ ㄋㄢ)
a man blinded by love; an infatuated man

癡念(ㄔ ㄋㄧㄢ)
stupid notions; foolish ideas; idiotic thoughts

癡狂(ㄔ ㄎㄨㄤ)
nonsensical; irrational; silly; senseless; idiotic

癡漢(ㄔ ㄏㄢ)
a fool; a simpleton; an idiot

癡情(ㄔ ㄑㄧㄥ)
blind love; blind passion; infatuation

癡笑(ㄔ ㄒㄧㄠ)
to giggle; to titter

癡心(ㄔ ㄒㄧㄣ)
①blind love; blind passion; infatuation ②a silly wish

癡心女子負心漢(ㄔ ㄒㄧㄣ ㄋㄩˇ ㄗ ㄈㄨ ㄒㄧㄣ ㄏㄢ)
the common story of an infatuated girl deserted by a heartless man

癡想妄想(ㄔ ㄒㄧㄤ ㄨㄤ ㄒㄧㄤ)
silly and fantastic notions; daydreaming: 許多人喜歡癡心妄想。There are people who are fond of daydreaming.

癡想(ㄔ ㄒㄧㄤ)
silly thoughts; idiotic ideas; to daydream; to indulge in wishful thinking

癡人(ㄔ ㄖㄣ)
an idiot; a fool; a foolish man

癡人說夢(ㄔ ㄖㄣ ㄕㄨㄛ ㄇㄥ)
an idiot's gibberish; nonsense

癡子(ㄔ ㄗ)
an idiot; a simpleton; a fool

（疒部）

癡獃(ㄔ ㄞ)or 癡呆(ㄔ ㄉㄞ)
stupid; foolish; imbecile; idiotic; dull; silly

癡物(ㄔ ㄨ)
a fool; an idiot; a simpleton

〔疒部〕

十五畫

【癢】 3677
(癢)〔ㄧ yeang yǎng〕
to itch; to tickle: 我的鼻子癢。
My nose tickles.

癢癢(ㄧ尤˙ㄧ尤)
itchy; ticklish; to itch terribly

【癤】 3678
1. ㄐㄧㄝ jye jié
a small sore; a pimple

【癤】 3678
2. ㄐㄧㄝ jie jié
a gnarl

癤子(ㄐㄧㄝ˙ㄗ)
a gnarl

【癥】 3679
ㄓㄥ jeng zhēng
obstruction of the bowels

癥結(ㄓㄥ ㄐㄧㄝ)
① obstruction of the bowels ② a difficult point (of a problem); a bottleneck; the ultimate source of trouble; a crux, a basic problem: 問題的癥結在此。The crux of the matter is this.

十六畫

【癩】 3680
ㄌㄞ lay lài
1. leprosy
2. favus; scabies
3. bad

癩皮狗(ㄌㄞ ㄆㄧˊ ㄍㄡ)
① a mangy dog ② a disgusting creature

癩頭(ㄌㄞ ㄊㄡˊ)
a favus-infected head

癩頭瘡(ㄌㄞ ㄊㄡˊ ㄔㄨㄤ)
scabies on the head

癩蝦蟆(ㄌㄞ ㄏㄚˊ˙ㄇㄚ)
the toad

癩蝦蟆想吃天鵝肉(ㄌㄞ ㄏㄚˊ˙ㄇㄚ ㄒㄧㄤˇㄔㄕㄊㄧㄢㄜˊㄖㄡˋ)
(literally) for a toad to think of eating a swan's meat—to have wishes above one's social or financial position, or beyond one's ability to realize (especially said of a man's marital aspiration)

【癬】(ㄒㄩㄢ)
favus; ringworm

癬瘡(ㄒㄩㄢ ㄔㄨㄤ)
scabies

癬子(ㄒㄩㄢ˙ㄗ)
one whose head is made bald or scarred by favus

十七畫

【癭】 3681
ㄧㄥˇ yiing yǐng
1. a reddish swelling on the neck
2. a gnarl

【癮】 3682
ㄧㄣˇ yiin yǐn
1. addiction; a habitual craving: 他是一個有毒癮的人。He is a drug addict.
2. strong interest (in a sport or pastime): 她看電影看上癮了。She takes a strong interest in movies.

癮頭(ㄧㄣˇ ㄊㄡˊ)
addiction

癮君子(ㄧㄣˇ ㄐㄩㄣ˙ㄗ)
an opium eater; a heavy smoker

【癣】 3683
ㄒㄩㄢ sheuan xuān
(讀音 ㄒㄧㄢ shean xiān)
ringworm; tetter

十八畫

【癰】 3684
ㄩㄥ iong yōng
a carbuncle

癰疽(ㄩㄥ ㄐㄩ)
a carbuncle

癰腫(ㄩㄥ ㄓㄨㄥˇ)
an abscess

癰瘡(ㄩㄥ ㄔㄨㄤ)
a carbuncle

【癯】 3685
ㄑㄩ chyu qú
emaciated; thin; lean

十九畫

【癲】 3686
ㄉㄧㄢ dian diān

mentally deranged; insane; mad; crazy; lunatic

癲狂(ㄉㄧㄢ ㄎㄨㄤˊ)
mentally deranged; insane; mad; crazy; lunatic

癲癇(ㄉㄧㄢ ㄒㄧㄢˊ)
epilepsy

【癱】 3687
ㄊㄢ tan tān
paralysis

癱瘓(ㄊㄢ ㄏㄨㄢˋ)
paralyzed; standstill

癱軟(ㄊㄢ ㄖㄨㄢˇ)
(said of arms, legs, etc.) weak and limp

癱子(ㄊㄢ˙ㄗ)
a paralytic

癶 部
ㄅㄛ bo bō

四畫

【癸】 3688
ㄍㄨㄟˇ goei guǐ
the last of the Ten Celestial Stems

七畫

【登】 3689
ㄉㄥ deng dēng
1. to ascend; to climb; to rise
2. to record; to register; to enter
3. to take; to employ
4. to board
5. to step on; to tread

登報(ㄉㄥ ㄅㄠˋ)
to make an announcement in the newspaper

登報聲明(ㄉㄥ ㄅㄠˋ ㄕㄥ ㄇㄧㄥˊ)
to clarify or announce by a newspaper advertisement

登榜(ㄉㄥ ㄅㄤˇ)
to succeed, or be announced as a successful candidate (in a competitive examination); to pass a competitive examination

登陴(ㄉㄥ ㄆㄧˊ)
to guard the city wall

登門(ㄉㄥ ㄇㄣˊ)

to pay a special visit to another's house

登門拜訪(ㄉㄥ ㄇㄣˊ ㄅㄞˋ ㄈㄤˇ)
to make a special call on another at his house; to visit

登門答謝(ㄉㄥ ㄇㄣˊ ㄉㄚˊ ㄒㄧㄝˋ)
to make a special call on another at his house to express gratitude

登峰造極(ㄉㄥ ㄈㄥ ㄗㄠˋ ㄐㄧˊ)
to reach the summit of achievement; to reach the acme; to achieve the highest attainments

登第(ㄉㄥ ㄉㄧˋ)
to pass a competitive examination; to succeed in a competitive examination

登臺(ㄉㄥ ㄊㄞˊ)
① to mount a platform ② to go on the stage: 她要登臺。 She wants to go on the stage.

登臺演說(ㄉㄥ ㄊㄞˊ ㄧㄢˇ ㄕㄨㄛ)
to deliver a speech from a platform

登壇拜將(ㄉㄥ ㄊㄢˊ ㄅㄞˋ ㄐㄧㄤˋ)
(in ancient times) to go through the ceremonies of appointing a commander-in-chief

登堂入室(ㄉㄥ ㄊㄤˊ ㄖㄨˋ ㄕ)
to ascend to the hall and reach the inner room — to master learning or skill

登天(ㄉㄥ ㄊㄧㄢ)
(literally) climbing to heaven—something very difficult

登徒子(ㄉㄥ ㄊㄨˊ ㄗ)
a lecher; a debauchee

登樓(ㄉㄥ ㄌㄡˊ)
to climb a flight of stairs; to go toward an upper floor; to go upstairs

登臨(ㄉㄥ ㄌㄧㄣˊ)
to climb a hill, a tall building, etc. which commands a broad view

登陸(ㄉㄥ ㄌㄨˋ)
to go ashore; to land: 敵軍登陸我海岸。 The enemy landed on our shore.

登陸部隊(ㄉㄥ ㄌㄨˋ ㄅㄨˋ ㄉㄨㄟˋ)
landing troops

登陸艇(ㄉㄥ ㄌㄨˋ ㄊㄧㄥˇ)
landing craft; landing ship

tank (LST)

登陸戰(ㄉㄥ ㄌㄨˋ ㄓㄢˋ)
landing operations

登錄(ㄉㄥ ㄌㄨˋ)
to register

登錄號(ㄉㄥ ㄌㄨˋ ㄏㄠˋ)
the registered mark or number

登輪(ㄉㄥ ㄌㄨㄣˊ)
to board a steamship

登龍門(ㄉㄥ ㄌㄨㄥˊ ㄇㄣˊ)
to enter a successful career with the help of an influential person

登龍有術(ㄉㄥ ㄌㄨㄥˊ ㄧㄡˇ ㄕㄨˋ)
very skillful in finding a powerful patron to advance one's career

登革熱(ㄉㄥ ㄍㄜˊ ㄖㄜˋ)
(medicine) dengue fever

登高(ㄉㄥ ㄍㄠ)
to ascend heights; to climb mountains

登高節(ㄉㄥ ㄍㄠ ㄐㄧㄝˊ)
the Mountain Climbing Festival (on the 9th of the 9th moon)

登高自卑(ㄉㄥ ㄍㄠ ㄗˋ ㄅㄟ)
To reach a high position, one must start from a low position.

登高一呼(ㄉㄥ ㄍㄠ ㄧ ㄏㄨ)
to rally for a just cause; to arouse for action

登科(ㄉㄥ ㄎㄜ)
to pass the civil service examination in former times

登科錄(ㄉㄥ ㄎㄜ ㄌㄨˋ)
a roster of successful candidates of the civil service examination in former times

登基(ㄉㄥ ㄐㄧ)
to ascend the throne

登機(ㄉㄥ ㄐㄧ)
to board a plane

登極(ㄉㄥ ㄐㄧˊ)
to ascend the throne

登記(ㄉㄥ ㄐㄧˋ)
to register; to check in; to enter one's name; registration

登記簿(ㄉㄥ ㄐㄧˋ ㄅㄨˋ)
a register

登記處(ㄉㄥ ㄐㄧˋ ㄔㄨˋ)
a registry; a registration office

登進(ㄉㄥ ㄐㄧㄣˋ)
to be promoted in rank; to get a promotion

登遐(ㄉㄥ ㄒㄧㄚˊ)
the death of the emperor

登仙(ㄉㄥ ㄒㄧㄢ)
① to become an immortal ② to die

登舟(ㄉㄥ ㄓㄡ)
to take a boat ride

登賬 or 登帳(ㄉㄥ ㄓㄤˋ)
to enter in the accounts

登場(ㄉㄥ ㄔㄤˇ)
① (said of actors, entertainers, etc.) to appear on the stage ② (said of products) to appear in the market ③ to be gathered and taken to the threshing ground

登程(ㄉㄥ ㄔㄥˊ)
to start a journey; to set out

登船(ㄉㄥ ㄔㄨㄢˊ)
to take a boat; to take a ride aboard a ship: 我在高雄登船往歐洲。 At Kaohsiung I took a boat for Europe.

登春臺(ㄉㄥ ㄔㄨㄣ ㄊㄞˊ)
the peace and happiness of people in a prosperous age

登時(ㄉㄥ ㄕˊ)
immediately; forthwith; at once

登山(ㄉㄥ ㄕㄢ)
to climb a mountain; to mountaineer: 他很喜歡登山。 He is very fond of mountaineering.

登山隊(ㄉㄥ ㄕㄢ ㄉㄨㄟˋ)
a mountaineering party

登山協會(ㄉㄥ ㄕㄢ ㄒㄧㄝˊ ㄏㄨㄟˋ)
an alpine club or association

登山陟嶺(ㄉㄥ ㄕㄢ ㄓˋ ㄌㄧㄥˇ)
to go over hills and mountains

登載(ㄉㄥ ㄗㄞˋ)
(said of a periodical or newspaper) to carry (an article); to publish (a news story)

登岸(ㄉㄥ ㄢˋ)
to go ashore; to land: 乘客均已登岸。 The passengers have landed.

登瀛州(ㄉㄥ ㄧㄥˊ ㄓㄡ)
to reach the paradise of immortals

登位(ㄉㄥ ㄨㄟˋ)

〔癶

部〕

to ascend the throne
登庸人才(カノ ㄩㄥ ㄖㄣ ㄘㄞ)
to employ talents

【發】 3690
ㄈㄚ fa fā
1. to shoot; to launch
2. to issue; to publish
3. to begin; to start; to initiate; to originate
4. to reveal; to disclose; to uncover
5. to become; to come to be
6. to utter; to express; to speak
7. to set off; to set out
8. to illuminate; to help out
發白(ㄈㄚ ㄅㄞˊ)
to turn white; to turn pale:
她的臉色發白。She turns pale.
發包(ㄈㄚ ㄅㄠ)
to contract with a contractor for a construction program
發報(ㄈㄚ ㄅㄠˋ)
to transmit messages
發報機(ㄈㄚ ㄅㄠˋ ㄐㄧ)
a telegraph transmitter
發榜(ㄈㄚ ㄅㄤˇ)
to publish the result of a competitive examination
發表(ㄈㄚ ㄅㄧㄠˇ)
to make (a statement); to make known; to make public; to publish; to announce; to deliver (a speech)
發邊(ㄈㄚ ㄅㄧㄢ)
to banish to the frontiers
發兵(ㄈㄚ ㄅㄧㄥ)
to dispatch troops
發病(ㄈㄚ ㄅㄧㄥˋ)
to get sick; to fall ill
發布 or 發佈(ㄈㄚ ㄅㄨˋ)
to announce; to promulgate:
國王發布了一項命令。The king promulgated a decree.
發排(ㄈㄚ ㄆㄞˊ)
to send (manuscripts) to the composing room
發牌(ㄈㄚ ㄆㄞˊ)
to deal cards: 是誰發的牌?
Who dealt the cards?
發配(ㄈㄚ ㄆㄟˋ)
to banish (a criminal) to a frontier garrison
發砲(ㄈㄚ ㄆㄠˋ)
to fire artillery pieces
發胖(ㄈㄚ ㄆㄤˋ)

to put on (or gain) weight;
to get fat
發脾氣(ㄈㄚ ㄆㄧˊ ㄑㄧˋ)
to lose one's temper; to get angry; to get mad
發票(ㄈㄚ ㄆㄧㄠˋ)
a bill of sale; an invoice
發麻(ㄈㄚ ㄇㄚˊ)
numb; benumbed: 我的雙手因冷而發麻。My hands are numb with cold.
發賣(ㄈㄚ ㄇㄞˋ)
to put on sale
發邁(ㄈㄚ ㄇㄞˋ)
to embark on a long journey
發霉(ㄈㄚ ㄇㄟˊ)
to get mildewed; to mildew
發毛(ㄈㄚ ㄇㄠˊ)
to feel a shudder; to have the feeling of the hair standing on end (with horror, etc.): 他看見血便發毛。He felt a shudder at the sight of blood.
發悶(ㄈㄚ ㄇㄣˋ)
①(ㄈㄚ ㄇㄣˋ)(said of the weather) to become oppressive
②(ㄈㄚ ㄇㄣˋ) to become depressed, dejected, or low-spirited
發蒙(ㄈㄚ ㄇㄥˊ)
①to teach a child to read and write ②to enlighten
發麵(ㄈㄚ ㄇㄧㄢˋ)
①to make dough rise; to leaven dough ②leavened dough
發明(ㄈㄚ ㄇㄧㄥˊ)
①to invent; to innovate; to devise: 蒸汽機是何時發明的?When was the steam engine invented? ②an invention
發明家(ㄈㄚ ㄇㄧㄥˊ ㄐㄧㄚ)
an inventor: 愛迪生是一個著名的發明家。Edison was a famous inventor.
發命令(ㄈㄚ ㄇㄧㄥˋ ㄌㄧㄥˋ)
to issue orders; to give orders
發木(ㄈㄚ ㄇㄨˋ)
to be numbed; to be benumbed; to be inactive
發凡(ㄈㄚ ㄈㄢˊ)
an introduction; a preface; a foreword
發煩(ㄈㄚ ㄈㄢˊ)

to get impatient; to become irritable; to feel annoyed
發粉(ㄈㄚ ㄈㄣˇ)or發酵粉(ㄈㄚ ㄒㄧㄠˋ ㄈㄣˇ)
baking powder
發憤(ㄈㄚ ㄈㄣˋ)
to be roused to action; to be spurred
發憤圖強(ㄈㄚ ㄈㄣˋ ㄊㄨˊ ㄑㄧㄤˊ)
(said of a nation) to strive for progress with determination 亦作「發奮圖強」
發憤忘食(ㄈㄚ ㄈㄣˋ ㄨㄤˋ ㄕˊ)
to be roused to such diligence as to forget one's meals
發放(ㄈㄚ ㄈㄤˋ)
①to issue; to distribute; to provide; to extend ②to dispose of
發瘋(ㄈㄚ ㄈㄥ)
to go mad; to lose one's senses; to lose one's mind; to become insane
發福(ㄈㄚ ㄈㄨˊ)
①to become rich and happy ②(jocularly) to become fat
發付(ㄈㄚ ㄈㄨˋ)
to send on an errand; to dispatch
發達(ㄈㄚ ㄉㄚˊ)
to develop; to evolve; to grow; developed; prosperous; thriving; booming
發獃(ㄈㄚ ㄉㄞ)
to look absent-minded; to look like an idiot; to be lost in reverie
發抖(ㄈㄚ ㄉㄡˇ)
to tremble; to shudder; to shiver
發單(ㄈㄚ ㄉㄢ)
an invoice; a bill of sale
發電(ㄈㄚ ㄉㄧㄢˋ)
①to generate electric power ②to send a telegram
發電體(ㄈㄚ ㄉㄧㄢˋ ㄊㄧˇ)
a charged body; an electrified body
發電機(ㄈㄚ ㄉㄧㄢˋ ㄐㄧ)
a generator; a dynamo: 發電機產生電力。A dynamo generates electricity.
發電廠(ㄈㄚ ㄉㄧㄢˋ ㄔㄤˇ)
a power plant
發電所(ㄈㄚ ㄉㄧㄢˋ ㄙㄨㄛˇ)

a powerhouse

發端(ㄈㄚ ㄉㄨㄢ)
to originate; to begin; to stem

發動(ㄈㄚ ㄉㄨㄥˋ)
to start; to launch; to initiate: 我不能使它發動。I can't make it start.

發動機(ㄈㄚ ㄉㄨㄥˋ ㄐㄧ)
a motor; an engine

發條(ㄈㄚ ㄊㄧㄠˊ)
a spring (of a mechanical device): 這玩具是用發條轉動。The toy is worked by a spring.

發難(ㄈㄚ ㄋㄢˋ)
①to spearhead a rebellion or revolution ②to ask difficult questions

發黏(ㄈㄚ ㄋㄧㄢˊ)
to become sticky

發怒(ㄈㄚ ㄋㄨˋ)
to become angry; to get mad; to lose one's temper

發擂(ㄈㄚ ㄌㄟˊ)
to start beating (drums, gongs, etc.)

發牢騷(ㄈㄚ ㄌㄠˊ ㄙㄠ)
to grumble; to complain: 不要發牢騷! Don't grumble!

發懶(ㄈㄚ ㄌㄢˇ)
to become indolent or lazy

發冷(ㄈㄚ ㄌㄥˇ)
to feel a chill; to feel chilly

發楞(ㄈㄚ ㄌㄥˋ)
to stare vacantly into space

發利市(ㄈㄚ ㄌㄧˋ ㄕˋ)
to do a good business; to do a brisk business

發亮(ㄈㄚ ㄌㄧㄤˋ)
to shine; to glitter; to shimmer; to gleam: 她的黑髮閃閃發亮。Her black hair shone glisteningly.

發落(ㄈㄚ ㄌㄨㄛˋ)
to deal with (an offender): 法官對少年犯從輕發落。The judge dealt with the juvenile delinquent leniently.

發給(ㄈㄚ ㄍㄟˇ)
to issue (supplies, allowances, etc.): 將口糧發給士兵們了。Food rations were issued to the soldiers.

發糕(ㄈㄚ ㄍㄠ)
a steamed sponge cake (usually sweetened)

發稿(ㄈㄚ ㄍㄠˇ)
(journalism) to send out a story or report for publication

發乾(ㄈㄚ ㄍㄢ)
to become dry

發光(ㄈㄚ ㄍㄨㄤ)
to shine; to glitter; to twinkle; to gleam; to emit light

發光體(ㄈㄚ ㄍㄨㄤ ㄊㄧˇ)
a luminous body: 太陽與星星都是發光體。The sun and stars are luminous bodies.

發光顏料(ㄈㄚ ㄍㄨㄤ ㄧㄢˊ ㄌㄧㄠˋ)
luminescent pigment

發刊(ㄈㄚ ㄎㄢ)
to start or launch (a magazine, newspaper, etc.); to bring out the first issue

發刊詞(ㄈㄚ ㄎㄢ ㄘˊ)
editor's opening statement for a new magazine, newspaper, etc.

發狂(ㄈㄚ ㄎㄨㄤˊ)
to go crazy; to become mentally deranged

發號施令(ㄈㄚ ㄏㄠˋ ㄕ ㄌㄧㄥˋ)
to give commands; to issue orders

發汗(ㄈㄚ ㄏㄢˋ)
①to perspire or sweat ②diaphoresis; to induce perspiration (as by drugs)

發汗劑(ㄈㄚ ㄏㄢˋ ㄐㄧˋ)
a diaphoretic; a sudorific

發狠(ㄈㄚ ㄏㄣˇ)
①to make a tremendous effort; to exert oneself ②to show anger

發橫(ㄈㄚ ㄏㄥˋ)
to turn villainous

發乎情，止乎禮(ㄈㄚ ㄏㄨ ㄑㄧㄥˊ，ㄓˇ ㄏㄨ ㄌㄧˇ)
An action impelled by emotion should stop within the limit of propriety.

發話器(ㄈㄚ ㄏㄨㄚˋ ㄑㄧˋ)
a telephone transmitter

發火(ㄈㄚ ㄏㄨㄛˇ)
①to become angry; to show anger; to get mad ②to burst into flames ③to go off

發火點(ㄈㄚ ㄏㄨㄛˇ ㄉㄧㄢˇ)
a flash point; an ignition point

發貨(ㄈㄚ ㄏㄨㄛˋ)
to send off goods; to send out goods; to forward goods

發揮(ㄈㄚ ㄏㄨㄟ)
to bring (skill, talent, etc.) into full play: 我們應該發揮集體智慧。We should bring our collective wisdom into full play.

發揮作用(ㄈㄚ ㄏㄨㄟ ㄗㄨㄛˋ ㄩㄥˋ)
to produce a marked effect; to be effective; to produce a result; (said of effect) to tell

發回(ㄈㄚ ㄏㄨㄟˊ)
to send back; to return

發回更審(ㄈㄚ ㄏㄨㄟˊ ㄍㄥ ㄕㄣˇ)
to order a lower court to make a new trial

發還(ㄈㄚ ㄏㄨㄢˊ)
to send back; to return

發昏(ㄈㄚ ㄏㄨㄣ)
①to be giddy; to faint ②to lose one's head; to become confused

發慌(ㄈㄚ ㄏㄨㄤ)
to lose one's composure; to become panicky; to be jittery; to feel nervous; to get flustered; to get flurried

發皇(ㄈㄚ ㄏㄨㄤˊ)
to flourish; to thrive; to prosper

發洪(ㄈㄚ ㄏㄨㄥˊ)
to swell into a flood

發迹(ㄈㄚ ㄐㄧ)
to rise (in business, career, etc.); to gain fame and fortune

發急(ㄈㄚ ㄐㄧˊ)
to become nervous; to fret; to chafe; to grow impatient: 我等朋友等得發急。I am impatient for a friend's arrival.

發交(ㄈㄚ ㄐㄧㄠ)
to hand over; to turn over; to deliver

發酒瘋(ㄈㄚ ㄐㄧㄡˇ ㄈㄥ)
to get drunk and behave irrationally

發姦擿伏(ㄈㄚ ㄐㄧㄢ ㄊㄧˋ ㄈㄨˊ)
to uncover hidden iniquities

發掘(ㄈㄚ ㄐㄩㄝˊ)
to unearth; to dig out; to excavate: 我由一大堆的報告中發掘眞象。I dug out the truth from a mass of information.

發噱(ㄈㄚ ㄐㄩㄝˊ)

〔癶
部〕

to laugh

發覺(ㄈㄚ ㄐㄩㄝ)
①to realize; to come to know; to discover; to find: 我們發覺我們做錯了。We found that we had made a mistake. ②(said of crimes, plots, etc.) to be brought to light; to be uncovered

發起(ㄈㄚ ㄑㄧˇ)
to initiate; to start; to originate: 這計畫是誰發起的? With whom did the scheme originate?

發起人(ㄈㄚ ㄑㄧˇ ㄖㄣˊ)
an originator; an initiator; a promoter

發球(ㄈㄚ ㄑㄧㄡˊ)
to serve a ball (in tennis, handball, etc.): 該你發球了。It's your turn to serve the ball.

發遣(ㄈㄚ ㄑㄧㄢˇ)
to send away

發情期(ㄈㄚ ㄑㄧㄥˊ ㄑㄧˊ)
①puberty ②rut or heat of some animals)

發下(ㄈㄚ ㄒㄧㄚˋ)
to issue (orders, supplies, etc.)

發泄 or 發洩(ㄈㄚ ㄒㄧㄝˋ)
to give vent to; to vent; to let out

發笑(ㄈㄚ ㄒㄧㄠˋ)
to laugh

發酵(ㄈㄚ ㄒㄧㄠˋ)
to ferment; fermentation

發酵乳(ㄈㄚ ㄒㄧㄠˋ ㄖㄨˇ)
ferment milk; yogurt

發現 or 發見(ㄈㄚ ㄒㄧㄢˋ)
to discover; to find; discovery: 在他和我的交往中, 我發現他是誠實的。I've found him honest in his dealings with me.

發薪水(ㄈㄚ ㄒㄧㄣ ㄕㄨㄟˇ)
to hand out paychecks to employees

發信(ㄈㄚ ㄒㄧㄣˋ)
to mail a letter; to send or post a letter: 他發信給他的朋友。He sent a letter to his friend.

發祥地(ㄈㄚ ㄒㄧㄤˊ ㄉㄧˋ)
the place of a thing's beginning or early development; the cradle; a birthplace

發餉(ㄈㄚ ㄒㄧㄤˇ)

to issue pay (especially to soldiers)

發行(ㄈㄚ ㄒㄧㄥˊ)
①(ㄈㄚ ㄒㄧㄥˊ) (said of currency, bonds, books, etc.) to issue; to publish; to distribute; to put on sale; to release: 政府發行債券。The government issues bonds. ②(ㄈㄚ ㄒㄧㄥˊ) to sell wholesale ⑤ a wholesaler

發行量(ㄈㄚ ㄒㄧㄥˊ ㄌㄧㄤˋ)
the volume of circulation

發行人(ㄈㄚ ㄒㄧㄥˊ ㄖㄣˊ) or 發行者(ㄈㄚ ㄒㄧㄥˊ ㄓㄜˇ)
a publisher

發咒(ㄈㄚ ㄓㄡˋ)
to take an oath; to vow; to swear

發展(ㄈㄚ ㄓㄢˇ)
to develop; to grow; to expand; development

發展中國家(ㄈㄚ ㄓㄢˇ ㄓㄨㄥ ㄍㄨㄛˊ ㄐㄧㄚ)
a developing country

發顫(ㄈㄚ ㄓㄢˋ)
to tremble; to shudder; to shiver

發疹子(ㄈㄚ ㄓㄣˇ ·ㄗ)
to have rashes; to have measles

發脹(ㄈㄚ ㄓㄤˋ)
①to swell; to bloat ②to have a glutted feeling

發冢(ㄈㄚ ㄓㄨㄥˇ)
to open graves

發呆(ㄈㄚ ㄉㄞ)
to stare vacantly into space; to appear absent-minded

發潮(ㄈㄚ ㄔㄠˊ)
to become damp: 我的襯衫有點兒發潮。My shirt became a bit damp.

發愁(ㄈㄚ ㄔㄡˊ)
to worry; to be anxious or troubled: 他為還債的事發愁。He was worried about paying the debts.

發出(ㄈㄚ ㄔㄨ)
to send forth; to generate; to issue; to emit: 玫瑰花發出宜人的香氣。The roses send forth delightful fragrance.

發怵(ㄈㄚ ㄔㄨˋ)
to become fearful; to be seized with fear

發喘(ㄈㄚ ㄔㄨㄢˇ)

to run short of breath

發矢(ㄈㄚ ㄕˇ)
to shoot an arrow; to discharge an arrow

發市(ㄈㄚ ㄕˋ)
to begin business

發誓(ㄈㄚ ㄕˋ)
to vow; to swear; to take an oath: 他發誓效忠國王。He vowed that he would be loyal to the king.

發痧(ㄈㄚ ㄕㄚ)
to contract cholera

發射(ㄈㄚ ㄕㄜˋ)
to launch; to shoot; to catapult: 我們將發射人造衛星。We will launch a man-made satellite.

發射臺(ㄈㄚ ㄕㄜˋ ㄊㄞˊ)
a launching pad

發燒(ㄈㄚ ㄕㄠ)
to have a temperature; to run a temperature; to have a fever

發售(ㄈㄚ ㄕㄡˋ)
to go on sale

發身(ㄈㄚ ㄕㄣ)
to reach puberty

發神經(ㄈㄚ ㄕㄣˊ ㄐㄧㄥ)
to go crazy; to lose sanity

發生(ㄈㄚ ㄕㄥ)
to happen; to occur; to arise: 可能有什麼重要發生。Something is likely to happen.

發生關係(ㄈㄚ ㄕㄥ ㄍㄨㄢ ㄒㄧˋ)
①to establish relationship; to have something to do with ②to have an affair with

發生心理學(ㄈㄚ ㄕㄥ ㄒㄧㄣ ㄌㄧˇ ㄒㄩㄝˊ)
genetic psychology

發生學(ㄈㄚ ㄕㄥ ㄒㄩㄝˊ)
embryology

發生衝突(ㄈㄚ ㄕㄥ ㄔㄨㄥ ㄊㄨˊ)
to have a conflict; to come to a clash; to develop into a fight

發聲(ㄈㄚ ㄕㄥ)
to give off sound

發聲器(ㄈㄚ ㄕㄥ ㄑㄧˋ)
①a vocal organ ②a sounder (of a telegraph)

發揮(ㄈㄚ ㄈㄨㄟ)
to bring into full play

發熱(ㄈㄚ ㄖㄜˋ)

to have a temperature; to run a temperature; to have a fever

發人深省(ㄈㄚ ㄖㄣ ㄕㄣ ㄒㄧㄥˇ)
to stimulate deep thought; to provide food for thought

發軔(ㄈㄚ ㄖㄣˋ)
the beginning (or origin) of a thing

發躁(ㄈㄚ ㄗㄠˋ)
to become irritable; to get impatient

發作(ㄈㄚ ㄗㄨㄛˋ)
①to go into action; to show effect; to break out: 毒性開始發作。The poison began to show its effect. ②to have a fit (of anger)③(said of illness) to have a relapse; to have an attack of disease: 他的心臟病又發作了。He's had another heart attack. ④(said of a crime or a plot) to be exposed

發慈悲(ㄈㄚ ㄘˊ ㄅㄟ)
to show mercy or pity

發財(ㄈㄚ ㄘㄞˊ)
to make a fortune; to acquire wealth; to become rich

發散(ㄈㄚ ㄙㄢˇ)
to disperse; to dissipate; to scatter

發散透鏡(ㄈㄚ ㄙㄢˇ ㄊㄡˋ ㄐㄧㄥˋ)
a divergent lens

發喪(ㄈㄚ ㄙㄤ)
to inform relatives and friends of a death

發酸(ㄈㄚ ㄙㄨㄢ)
①to become sour; to sour ②(said of muscles) to ache from exertion

發送(ㄈㄚ ㄙㄨㄥˋ)
①to send: 報務員會發送密碼電報。Telegraphists can transmit a coded message. ②to hold a funeral service

發呆(ㄈㄚ ㄉㄞ)or(ㄈㄚ ㄉㄞˊ)
to look absent-minded; to stare vacantly

發芽(ㄈㄚ ㄧㄚˊ)
to sprout: 雨水使小麥發芽。The rain has sprouted the wheat.

發啞(ㄈㄚ ㄧㄚˇ)
to become hoarse: 他由於傷風而聲音發啞。He was hoarse

from a cold.

發瘧子(ㄈㄚ ㄧㄠˋ ˙ㄗ)
to have an attack of malaria

發煙硫酸(ㄈㄚ ㄧㄢ ㄌㄧㄡˊ ㄙㄨㄢ)
fuming sulfuric acid

發煙硝酸(ㄈㄚ ㄧㄢ ㄒㄧㄠ ㄙㄨㄢ)
fuming nitric acid

發炎(ㄈㄚ ㄧㄢˊ)
to become inflamed; to become infected: 我的傷口發炎了。My wound has become inflamed.

發言(ㄈㄚ ㄧㄢˊ)
to speak; to voice one's views: 我要求發言。I ask to be heard.

發言權(ㄈㄚ ㄧㄢˊ ㄑㄩㄢˊ)
right of speaking; voice (in a conference or meeting)

發言人(ㄈㄚ ㄧㄢˊ ㄖㄣˊ)
a spokesman: 他是政府發言人。He was the government spokesman.

發音(ㄈㄚ ㄧㄣ)
to pronounce; pronunciation; articulation; to enunciate; enunciation

發音器官(ㄈㄚ ㄧㄣ ㄑㄧˋ ㄍㄨㄢ)
vocal organs

發音學(ㄈㄚ ㄧㄣ ㄒㄩㄝˊ)
orthoepy

發引(ㄈㄚ ㄧㄣˇ)
(said of a funeral procession) to leave for the place of burial

發揚(ㄈㄚ ㄧㄤˊ)
to exalt; to enhance; to encourage; to add glory to

發揚蹈厲(ㄈㄚ ㄧㄤˊ ㄉㄠˋ ㄌㄧˋ)
to show a dauntless spirit

發揚光大(ㄈㄚ ㄧㄤˊ ㄍㄨㄤ ㄉㄚˋ)
to enhance and glorify

發洋財(ㄈㄚ ㄧㄤˊ ㄘㄞˊ)
to make a big fortune; to make a strike

發癢(ㄈㄚ ㄧㄤˇ)
to itch: 我的背部發癢。My back itches.

發威(ㄈㄚ ㄨㄟ)
to fly into a rage; to rage

發問(ㄈㄚ ㄨㄣˋ)
to ask questions; to raise questions

發往(ㄈㄚ ㄨㄤˇ)
to send or dispatch to (a place)

發語詞(ㄈㄚ ㄩˇ ㄘˊ)
an introductory particle

發育(ㄈㄚ ㄩˋ)
①to grow up; to develop: 植物是由種子發育而成的。Plants develop from seeds. ②to send forth and nourish

發育不良(ㄈㄚ ㄩˋ ㄅㄨˋ ㄌㄧㄤˊ)
maldevelopment

發越(ㄈㄚ ㄩㄝˋ)
①swift; quick ②(said of a pleasant smell, etc.) to diffuse

發源(ㄈㄚ ㄩㄢˊ)
①an origin; a source: 這河發源於這湖。The river takes its source from the lake. ②to originate

發源地(ㄈㄚ ㄩㄢˊ ㄉㄧˋ)
(said of rivers, etc.) the place of origin

發願(ㄈㄚ ㄩㄢˋ)
to vow to achieve an objective

發牢騷(ㄈㄚ ㄌㄠˊ ㄙㄠ)
to grumble; to complain

發暈(ㄈㄚ ㄩㄣˋ)
to feel dizzy or giddy

九畫

【凳】 3691 (櫈) ㄉㄥˋ denq dèng
a stool

凳子(ㄉㄥˋ ˙ㄗ)or凳兒(ㄉㄥˋㄦ)
a stool

白 部
ㄅㄛˊ bor bó

【白】 3692 ㄅㄞˊ bair bái
(讀音 ㄅㄛˊ bor bó)
1. white; clear; bright; clean; pure; plain
2. empty; blank
3. in vain; for nothing
4. free of charge; gratis
5. the spoken part in an opera, etc.
6. to state; to explain
7. a Chinese family name

白白地(ㄅㄞˊ ㄅㄞˊ ㄉㄧˋ)
in vain; to no purpose; to

〔白 部〕

(or of) no avail; for nothing

白百合花(ㄅㄞ ㄅㄞ ㄏㄜˊ ㄏㄨㄚ)or白水仙(ㄅㄞ ㄕㄨㄟˇ ㄒㄧㄢ)
a Madonna lily

白斑(ㄅㄞ ㄅㄢ)
white specks; white spots

白斑症(ㄅㄞ ㄅㄢ ㄓㄥˋ)
vitiligo; leukoderma

白璧微瑕(ㄅㄞ ㄅㄧˋ ㄨㄟ ㄒㄧㄚˊ)
a trivial flaw on a jade; a small defect

白布(ㄅㄞ ㄅㄨˋ)
plain white cloth; calico

白跑一趟(ㄅㄞ ㄆㄠˇ ㄧ ㄊㄤ)
to make a futile trip

白砒(ㄅㄞ ㄆㄧˊ)
arsenic 亦作「砒霜」

白皮書(ㄅㄞ ㄆㄧˊ ㄕㄨ)
a white paper (in the sense of an official government report)

白葡萄酒(ㄅㄞ ㄆㄨˊ ㄊㄠˊ ㄐㄧㄡˇ)
sherry: 白葡萄酒是由葡萄做成的。Sherry is made from grapes.

白馬非馬論(ㄅㄞ ㄇㄚˇ ㄈㄟ ㄇㄚˇ ㄌㄨㄣˋ)
the argument that a white horse is not entirely the same as a horse, advanced by Kung-Sun Lung (公孫龍) of the Epoch of Warring States

白馬寺(ㄅㄞ ㄇㄚˇ ㄙˋ)
the White Horse Temple, the oldest Buddhist temple in China (in Honan) built in the first century

白螞蟻(ㄅㄞ ㄇㄚˇ ㄧˇ)
a termite

白墨(ㄅㄞ ㄇㄛˋ)
chalk

白沫子(ㄅㄞ ㄇㄛˋ ㄗˇ)
white froth or foam: 啤酒倒出時會起白沫子。Beer froths when it is poured out.

白煤(ㄅㄞ ㄇㄟˊ)
anthracite; hard coal; smokeless coal

白黴(ㄅㄞ ㄇㄟˊ)
mold; mildew

白茅(ㄅㄞ ㄇㄠˊ)or(ㄅㄞ ㄇㄠˊ)
an edible wild grass (*Imperata cylindrica*), whose root is used in Chinese herbal medicine

white dog

白忙(ㄅㄞ ㄇㄤˊ)
to busy oneself to no purpose

白茫茫(ㄅㄞ ㄇㄤˊ ㄇㄤˊ)
showing a vast expanse of whiteness

白米(ㄅㄞ ㄇㄧˇ)or(ㄅㄞ ㄇㄧˇ)
white polished rice

白蜜(ㄅㄞ ㄇㄧˋ)or(ㄅㄞ ㄇㄧˋ)
whitish honey

白粉兒(ㄅㄞ ㄈㄣˇ ㄦ)
heroin 亦作「海洛因」

白描(ㄅㄞ ㄇㄧㄠˊ)or(ㄅㄞ ㄇㄧㄠˊ)
a kind of Chinese outline drawing; a sketch

白面書生(ㄅㄞ ㄇㄧㄢˋ ㄕㄨ ㄕㄥ)
①a fair-complexioned young scholar ②an inexperienced young scholar

白牡丹(ㄅㄞ ㄇㄨˇ ㄉㄢ)
a white peony: 我們園中有棵白牡丹。There is a white peony in our garden.

白木耳(ㄅㄞ ㄇㄨˋ ㄦˇ)
a kind of white-colored edible fungus (*Tremella fuciformis*)亦作「銀耳」

白髮蒼蒼(ㄅㄞ ㄈㄚˇ ㄘㄤ ㄘㄤ)
hoary-headed

白費(ㄅㄞ ㄈㄟˋ)
to use up or spend without profit; to waste: 我白費力氣。I waste my energy.

白費心機(ㄅㄞ ㄈㄟˋ ㄒㄧㄣ ㄐㄧ)
to scheme in vain; to make plans to no avail

白礬(ㄅㄞ ㄈㄢˊ)or(ㄅㄞ ㄈㄢˊ)
alum 亦作「明礬」

白飯(ㄅㄞ ㄈㄢˋ)or(ㄅㄞ ㄈㄢˋ)
cooked white rice (especially if not mixed with any other food): 中國人喜吃白飯。The Chinese like to eat cooked white rice.

白搭(ㄅㄞ ㄉㄚ)
futile; fruitless; in vain; to no avail; no use: 和她辯也是白搭。It is no use arguing with her.

白帶(ㄅㄞ ㄉㄞˋ)
(medicine) leucorrhea; white flow

白刀子進, 紅刀子出(ㄅㄞ ㄉㄠ ·ㄗ ㄐㄧㄣˋ, ㄏㄨㄥˊ ㄉㄠ ·ㄗ ㄔㄨ)
(literally) The knife is white upon entry and red upon exit. —A murder takes place.

白帝城(ㄅㄞ ㄉㄧˋ ㄔㄥˊ)
White God City—a strategic point in Szechwan during the Epoch of the Three Kingdoms

白丁(ㄅㄞ ㄉㄧㄥ)or白民(ㄅㄞ ㄇㄧㄣˊ)
a commoner

白頭(ㄅㄞ ㄊㄡˊ)
a hoary head

白頭偕老(ㄅㄞ ㄊㄡˊ ㄒㄧㄝˊ ㄌㄠˇ)
(said of a married couple) to stick to each other to the end of their lives

白頭如新(ㄅㄞ ㄊㄡˊ ㄖㄨˊ ㄒㄧㄣ)
to remain aloof from each other though associated for a long time

白頭翁(ㄅㄞ ㄊㄡˊ ㄨㄥ)
①(zoology) a grackle; a grey starling ②(botany) an anemone (*Anemone camphor*)

白糖(ㄅㄞ ㄊㄤˊ)
white sugar; refined sugar: 在咖啡中加些白糖。Put some refined sugar in the coffee.

白鐵(ㄅㄞ ㄊㄧㄝˇ)
galvanized iron; tinplate

白天(ㄅㄞ ㄊㄧㄢ)
daytime

白兔(ㄅㄞ ㄊㄨˋ)or(ㄅㄞ ㄊㄨˋ)
①a white rabbit ②the rabbit in the moon—the moon

白銅(ㄅㄞ ㄊㄨㄥˊ)
tutenag

白內障(ㄅㄞ ㄋㄟˋ ㄓㄤˋ)
(medicine) cataract

白鑞(ㄅㄞ ㄌㄚˋ)
pewter; solder

白蠟(ㄅㄞ ㄌㄚˋ)
white wax (*Cire blanche*), a kind of insect secretion

白蠟蟲(ㄅㄞ ㄌㄚˋ ㄔㄨㄥˊ)
a lanternfly (*Flata limbata*)

白蘭地(ㄅㄞ ㄌㄢˊ ㄉㄧˋ)
brandy

白浪滔天(ㄅㄞ ㄌㄤˋ ㄊㄠ ㄊㄧㄢ)
white breakers sweeping across the sky

白梨(ㄅㄞ ㄌㄧˊ)
a kind of light-skinned pear (grown in the Peking area)

白痢(ㄅㄞ ㄌㄧˋ)
white dysentery (dysentery characterized by white mucous stool)

白蓮教(ㄅㄞ ㄌㄧㄢˊ ㄐㄧㄠˋ)

the White Lotus Society, set up near the end of the Yüan Dynasty, announcing the coming of Maitreya, the opening of his white lotus, and the day of salvation at hand (It developed into a revolution which resulted in the expulsion of the Mongols and establishment of the Ming Dynasty. Under the Ching Dynasty it was resurrected under a variety of names, and caused various uprisings.)

白蓮社(ㄅㄞ ㄌㄧㄢˊ ㄕㄜˋ)
a society formed in the Tsin Dynasty early in the fourth century A.D. by Hui Yüan (慧遠), who with 123 notable literati, swore to a life of purity before the image of Amitabha, and planted white lotuses in symbol

白練(ㄅㄞˊ ㄌㄧㄢˋ)
① white silk ② a cascade

白領階級(ㄅㄞˊ ㄌㄧㄥˇ ㄐㄧㄝ ㄐㄧˊ)
the white-collar class

白令海峽(ㄅㄞˊ ㄌㄧㄥˋ ㄏㄞˇ ㄒㄧㄚˊ)
the Bering Strait

白露(ㄅㄞˊ ㄌㄨˋ)or(ㄅㄞˊ ㄌㄡˋ)
① one of the 24 climatic periods of the lunar year (beginning on September 8 or 9) ② white dew

白鷺(ㄅㄞˊ ㄌㄨˋ)or(ㄅㄞˊ ㄌㄡˋ)
an egret

白鹿洞(ㄅㄞˊ ㄌㄨˋ ㄉㄨㄥˋ)
a place in Kiangsi where Confucian scholar Chu Hsi (朱熹) of the Sung Dynasty ran his school

白龍魚服(ㄅㄞˊ ㄌㄨㄥˊ ㄩˊ ㄈㄨˊ)
a ranking government official in ordeal while traveling incognito

白乾兒 or 白干兒(ㄅㄞˊ ㄍㄢ ㄦ)
pure kaoliang wine

白鴿(ㄅㄞˊ ㄍㄜ)
a pigeon

白給(ㄅㄞˊ ㄍㄟˇ)
to give for nothing

白骨(ㄅㄞˊ ㄍㄨˇ)
bones of the dead

白果(ㄅㄞˊ ㄍㄨㄛˇ)
a ginkgo nut, or a gingko nut

白圭之玷(ㄅㄞˊ ㄍㄨㄟ ㄓ ㄉㄧㄢˋ)
(literally) a flaw in a piece of jade—damage suffered through careless speech

白桂油(ㄅㄞˊ ㄍㄨㄟˋ ㄧㄡˊ)
canella

白宮(ㄅㄞˊ ㄍㄨㄥ)
the White House, Washington D.C.

白開水(ㄅㄞˊ ㄎㄞ ㄕㄨㄟˇ)
boiled water

白喉(ㄅㄞˊ ㄏㄡˊ)
diphtheria

白喉菌(ㄅㄞˊ ㄏㄡˊ ㄐㄩㄣˋ)
a diphtherial bacillus

白虎(ㄅㄞˊ ㄏㄨˇ)
① general name of seven stars in the western sky ② (slang) a woman's reproductive organ without hairs

白虎星(ㄅㄞˊ ㄏㄨˇ ㄒㄧㄥ)
(said of a woman) a jinx

白花(ㄅㄞˊ ㄏㄨㄚ)
①(ㄅㄞˊ ㄏㄨㄚ) ⓐ to spend (time, or money) without results ⓑ white flowers
②(ㄅㄞˊ ㄏㄨㄚˋ) sweet words to console

白花狗(ㄅㄞˊ ㄏㄨㄚ ㄍㄡˇ)
Dalmatian (a dog)

白花花(ㄅㄞˊ ㄏㄨㄚ ㄏㄨㄚ)
shining white

白花蛇(ㄅㄞˊ ㄏㄨㄚ ㄕㄜˊ)
a spotted venomous snake (Agkistrodon acutus)

白話(ㄅㄞˊ ㄏㄨㄚˋ)
spoken Chinese; vernacular Chinese: 這故事以白話寫成。The story is written in spoken Chinese.

白話小說(ㄅㄞˊ ㄏㄨㄚˋ ㄒㄧㄠˇ ㄕㄨㄛ)
novels in vernacular Chinese

白話詩(ㄅㄞˊ ㄏㄨㄚˋ ㄕ)
verses in vernacular Chinese

白話詞(ㄅㄞˊ ㄏㄨㄚˋ ㄘˊ)
verses of irregular lines in vernacular Chinese

白話文(ㄅㄞˊ ㄏㄨㄚˋ ㄨㄣˊ)
writing in vernacular Chinese

白話文學(ㄅㄞˊ ㄏㄨㄚˋ ㄨㄣˊ ㄒㄩㄝˊ)
vernacular Chinese literature; vernacular literature

白樺(ㄅㄞˊ ㄏㄨㄚˋ)
the white birch

白灰(ㄅㄞˊ ㄏㄨㄟ)or(ㄅㄞˊ ㄏㄨㄟˋ)
lime

白芥子(ㄅㄞˊ ㄐㄧㄝˋ ㄗˇ)
mustard seed

白酒(ㄅㄞˊ ㄐㄧㄡˇ)
spirits usually distilled from sorghum or maize; white spirits

白金(ㄅㄞˊ ㄐㄧㄣ)
① platinum ② silver

白金漢宮(ㄅㄞˊ ㄐㄧㄣ ㄏㄢˋ ㄍㄨㄥ)
Buckingham Palace, England

白淨(ㄅㄞˊ ㄐㄧㄥˋ)
perfectly clean; immaculate

白駒過隙(ㄅㄞˊ ㄐㄩ ㄍㄨㄛˋ ㄒㄧˋ)
(literally) a fleeting horse seen from a crevice—the swiftness of the lapse of time

白居易(ㄅㄞˊ ㄐㄩ ㄧˋ)
Pai Chü-i (772-846), a poet of the Tang Dynasty

白菊花(ㄅㄞˊ ㄐㄩˊ ㄏㄨㄚ)
a feverfew

白卷兒(ㄅㄞˊ ㄐㄩㄢˋ ㄦ)or白卷子(ㄅㄞˊ ㄐㄩㄢˋ ˙ㄗ)
an examination paper handed in with all the questions unanswered: 他繳白卷子。He handed in a blank examination paper.

白鉛礦(ㄅㄞˊ ㄑㄧㄢ ㄎㄨㄤˋ)
cerussite

白屈菜(ㄅㄞˊ ㄑㄩ ㄘㄞˋ)
a celandine

白晳(ㄅㄞˊ ㄒㄧ)
white-skinned: 他有白晳的皮膚。He is a white-skinned person.

白血病(ㄅㄞˊ ㄒㄧㄝˇ ㄅㄧㄥˋ)
leukemia

白血球(ㄅㄞˊ ㄒㄧㄝˇ ㄑㄧㄡˊ)
white blood cells; leucocytes

白信石(ㄅㄞˊ ㄒㄧㄣˋ ㄕˊ)
white arsenic

白相(ㄅㄞˊ ㄒㄧㄤˋ)or(ㄅㄞˊ ㄒㄧㄤ)
(the Wu or Shanghai dialect) to play

白相人(ㄅㄞˊ ㄒㄧㄤˋ ㄖㄣˊ)
(the Wu or Shanghai dialect) a loafer

白鮮(ㄅㄞˊ ㄒㄧㄢ)
favus; honeycomb ringworm

白熊(ㄅㄞˊ ㄒㄩㄥˊ)or(ㄅㄞˊ ㄒㄩㄥˊ)
a polar bear: 白熊生活在北極區。Polar bears are living in the arctic regions.

〔白部〕

〔白
部〕

白芷(ㄅㄞˊ ㄓˇ)
dahurian angelica (root)

白摺子(ㄅㄞˊ ㄓㄜˊ ·ㄗ)
a writing pad of plain white
paper used for practicing
calligraphy

白齋(ㄅㄞˊ ㄓㄞ)
a diet of unflavored food

白晝(ㄅㄞˊ ㄓㄡˋ)
broad daylight: 他們在白晝搶
劫他。They robbed him in
broad daytime.

白晝見鬼(ㄅㄞˊ ㄓㄡˋ ㄐㄧㄢˋ ㄍㄨㄟˇ)
to see a ghost in broad daylight; to have a fantasy

白晝宣淫(ㄅㄞˊ ㄓㄡˋ ㄒㄩㄢ ㄧㄣˊ)
to indulge in lascivious acts
in broad daylight

白煮(ㄅㄞˊ ㄓㄨˇ)
to boil in plain water

白紵(ㄅㄞˊ ㄓㄨˋ)or(ㄅㄜˊ ㄓㄨˋ)
fine white linen: 那一家備有
很多白紵織物。The house has
a good stock of fine white
linen.

白濁(ㄅㄞˊ ㄓㄨㄛˊ)
gonorrhea; gonoblennorrhoea
亦作「淋病」

白賺(ㄅㄞˊ ㄓㄨㄢˋ)
to earn with little or no
effort

白種人(ㄅㄞˊ ㄓㄨㄥˇ ㄖㄣˊ)
the white people; the
Caucasians

白吃(ㄅㄞˊ ㄔ)
to eat without payment: 他出
吃了一頓大餐。He ate a big
dinner without payment.

白癡(ㄅㄞˊ ㄔ)or(ㄅㄜˊ ㄔ)
an idiot: 他的舉動像白癡。He
is behaving like an idiot.

白菖蒲(ㄅㄞˊ ㄔㄤ ㄆㄨˊ)
Acorus calamus, a sweet flag

白氅(ㄅㄞˊ ㄔㄤˇ)or(ㄅㄜˊ ㄔㄤˇ)
a uniform made of down
worn by a guard in ancient
times

白食(ㄅㄞˊ ㄕˊ)
a free meal

白士(ㄅㄞˊ ㄕˋ)or(ㄅㄜˊ ㄕˋ)
a needy but morally clean
scholar

白蛇傳(ㄅㄞˊ ㄕㄜˊ ㄓㄨㄢˋ)
a legend of a white-snake
fairy Pai Su-chen (白素貞),
who fell in love with and

married a mortal man Hsü
Hsien (許仙)

白首(ㄅㄞˊ ㄕㄡˇ)or(ㄅㄜˊ ㄕㄡˇ)
a hoary head—the old age

白首窮經(ㄅㄞˊ ㄕㄡˇ ㄑㄩㄥˊ ㄐㄧㄥ)
to continue to study even in
old age

白手成家(ㄅㄞˊ ㄕㄡˇ ㄔㄥˊ ㄐㄧㄚ)or白
手起家(ㄅㄞˊ ㄕㄡˇ ㄑㄧˇ ㄐㄧㄚ)
to rise in life by one's own
efforts; to become rich from
scratch; from rags to riches

白山黑水(ㄅㄞˊ ㄕㄢ ㄏㄟ ㄕㄨㄟˇ)
Mt. Changpai (長白山) and
the Amur River (黑龍江), which
dominate the landscape of
Manchuria

白身(ㄅㄞˊ ㄕㄣ)or(ㄅㄜˊ ㄕㄣ)
not holding any government
office

白鼠(ㄅㄞˊ ㄕㄨˇ)
a white mouse (commonly
believed to be divine); an
albino rat: 我以白鼠做實驗。I
made experiments on white
mice.

白薯(ㄅㄞˊ ㄕㄨˇ)
a sweet potato

白蜀葵(ㄅㄞˊ ㄕㄨˇ ㄎㄨㄟˊ)
candytuft

白說(ㄅㄞˊ ㄕㄨㄛ)
to waste one's breath; to
speak in vain

白水(ㄅㄞˊ ㄕㄨㄟˇ)or(ㄅㄜˊ ㄕㄨㄟˇ)
plain water

白日(ㄅㄞˊ ㄖˋ)or(ㄅㄜˊ ㄖˋ)
① daytime; daylight ② the
sun

白日夢(ㄅㄞˊ ㄖˋ ㄇㄥˋ)
a daydream; reverie

白日鬼(ㄅㄞˊ ㄖˋ ㄍㄨㄟˇ)
a swindler; a cheater; a
trickster; a burglar

白日昇天(ㄅㄞˊ ㄖˋ ㄕㄥ ㄊㄧㄢ)
① to become an immortal ②
to rise abruptly in the world

白熱(ㄅㄞˊ ㄖㄜˋ)
white-hot

白熱化(ㄅㄞˊ ㄖㄜˋ ㄏㄨㄚˋ)
(said of a contest, move-
ment, etc.) to reach the white-
hot point; to reach the climax

白人(ㄅㄞˊ ㄖㄣˊ)
a white man or woman

白刃(ㄅㄞˊ ㄖㄣˋ)or(ㄅㄜˊ ㄖㄣˋ)

naked blades

白刃戰(ㄅㄞˊ ㄖㄣˋ ㄓㄢˋ)
a bayonet fight; a hand-to-
hand combat

白扔(ㄅㄞˊ ㄖㄥ)
to spend without proper
return; to waste

白字(ㄅㄞˊ ㄗˋ)
misused homophonous char-
acters; wrongly written or
mispronounced characters:
他寫得白字連篇。He wrote
pages and pages of wrongly
written characters.

白菜(ㄅㄞˊ ㄘㄞˋ)
① Brassica pekinensis;
Chinese cabbage ② white
rape

白醋(ㄅㄞˊ ㄘㄨˋ)
plain vinegar

白色(ㄅㄞˊ ㄙㄜˋ)
white

白色人種(ㄅㄞˊ ㄙㄜˋ ㄖㄣˊ ㄓㄨㄥˇ)
the white race

白松香(ㄅㄞˊ ㄙㄨㄥ ㄒㄧㄤ)
galbanum

白送(ㄅㄞˊ ㄙㄨㄥˋ)
to give away; to give gratis;
to send (a gift) with nothing
in return

白鵝(ㄅㄞˊ ㄜˊ)
a white goose

白俄(ㄅㄞˊ ㄜˊ)
White Russian; Byelorussian

白俄羅斯(ㄅㄞˊ ㄜˊ ㄌㄨㄛˊ ㄙ)
White Russia; Byelorussia

白堊(ㄅㄞˊ ㄜˋ)
(geology) chalk

白堊紀(ㄅㄞˊ ㄜˋ ㄐㄧˋ)
the Cretaceous period

白皚皚(ㄅㄞˊ ㄞˊ ㄞˊ)
(usually said of snow) white
and clean

白衣大士(ㄅㄞˊ ㄧ ㄉㄚˋ ㄕˋ)
the Goddess of Mercy (in
Buddhism)

白衣天使(ㄅㄞˊ ㄧ ㄊㄧㄢ ㄕˇ)
angels in white—nurses

白蟻(ㄅㄞˊ ㄧˇ)
a termite

白眼(ㄅㄞˊ ㄧㄢˇ)or(ㄅㄜˊ ㄧㄢˇ)
① the whites of the eyes ②
disdain; contempt: 他遭人白
眼。He was treated with disdain.

白眼圈(ㄅㄞˊ ㄧㄢˇ ㄑㄩㄢ)

〔白部〕

the white-eye (a bird)

白眼珠兒(ㄅㄞ 一ㄢ ㄓㄨ ㄦ)
the whites of the eye

白銀(ㄅㄞ 一ㄣ)or(ㄅㄜ 一ㄣ)
silver; 這或指是白銀製的。The
ring is made of silver.

白楊(ㄅㄞ 一ㄤ)or(ㄅㄜ 一ㄤ)
a poplar; an aspen; an abele

白鸚鵡(ㄅㄞ 一ㄥ ㄨˇ)
a cacatua; a kakatoe

白尾鷹(ㄅㄞ ㄨㄟˇ 一ㄥ)
a sea eagle

白文(ㄅㄞ ㄨㄣˊ)or(ㄅㄜ ㄨㄣˊ)
plain text without annotations

白榆(ㄅㄞ ㄩˊ)or(ㄅㄜ ㄩˊ)
an elm with whitish bark

白玉(ㄅㄞ ㄩˋ)or(ㄅㄜ ㄩˋ)
white jade

白玉微瑕(ㄅㄞ ㄩˋ ㄨㄟ ㄒㄧㄚˊ)
(literally) a tiny flaw in a
piece of white jade—a small
defect

白雲(ㄅㄞ ㄩㄣˊ)
white clouds

白雲母(ㄅㄞ ㄩㄣˊ ㄇㄨˇ)
white mica; muscovite

白雲觀(ㄅㄞ ㄩㄣˊ ㄍㄨㄢ)or(ㄅㄜ
ㄩㄣˊ ㄍㄨㄢ)
a Taoist temple near Peking

白雲石(ㄅㄞ ㄩㄣˊ ㄕˊ)
dolomite

白雲蒼狗(ㄅㄞ ㄩㄣˊ ㄘㄤ ㄍㄡˇ)
(literally) A white cloud at
one moment may look like a
gray dog the next moment.
—Things change in an un-
predictable manner.

白用心機(ㄅㄞ ㄩㄥˋ ㄒㄧㄣ ㄐㄧ)
to scheme in vain; to fail in
one's designs

一畫

〔百〕 3693
ㄅㄞˇ bae bǎi
(讀音 ㄅㄜˊ bor bó)

1. hundred
2. many; numerous
3. all

百拜(ㄅㄞˇ ㄅㄞ)
much courtesy

百倍(ㄅㄞˇ ㄅㄟˋ)
one hundred times

百寶箱(ㄅㄞˇ ㄅㄠˇ ㄒㄧㄤ)
a jewel case; a jewel box

百般(ㄅㄞˇ ㄅㄢ)
all sorts; every kind

百般殷勤(ㄅㄞˇ ㄅㄢ 一ㄣ ㄑㄧㄣˊ)
courtesy expressed in nu-
merous ways

百弊(ㄅㄞˇ ㄅㄧˋ)
all the ill effects

百弊叢生(ㄅㄞˇ ㄅㄧˋ ㄘㄨㄥˊ ㄕㄥ)
All the ill effects appear.

百不得一(ㄅㄞˇ ㄅㄨˋ ㄉㄜˊ 一)
Not one out of a hundred is
acceptable. 或 Less than 1%
is qualified.

百不失一(ㄅㄞˇ ㄅㄨˋ ㄕ 一)
There is not a single miss in
a hundred tries.

百步穿楊(ㄅㄞˇ ㄅㄨˋ ㄔㄨㄢ 一ㄤˊ)
(archery) superior marks-
manship: 他是一個百步穿楊的
射手。He is a superior marksman.

百朋之錫(ㄅㄞˇ ㄆㄥˊ ㄓ 一)
a very expensive gift; a
handsome reward

百美圖(ㄅㄞˇ ㄇㄟˇ ㄊㄨˊ)
a picture showing large
numbers of beautiful women

百米賽跑(ㄅㄞˇ ㄇㄧˇ ㄙㄞˋ ㄆㄠˇ)
the 100-meter dash

百慕達羣島(ㄅㄞˇ ㄇㄨˋ ㄉㄚˊ ㄑㄩㄣˊ ㄉㄠˇ)
the Bermuda Islands

百發百中(ㄅㄞˇ ㄈㄚ ㄅㄞˇ ㄓㄨㄥˋ)
to hit the target at every
shot: 那射手百發百中。That
archer hits the target at
every shot.

百廢待興(ㄅㄞˇ ㄈㄟˋ ㄉㄞˋ ㄒㄧㄥ)
(said of government administration) All neglected matters are yet to be dealt with.

百廢俱舉(ㄅㄞˇ ㄈㄟˋ ㄐㄩ ㄐㄩˇ)or(ㄅㄞˇ
ㄈㄟˋ ㄐㄩˋ ㄐㄩˇ)
(said of government administration) All neglected matters have been taken care
of.

百分比(ㄅㄞˇ ㄈㄣ ㄅㄧˇ)or百分率(ㄅㄞˇ
ㄈㄣ ㄌㄩˋ)
a percentage

百分法(ㄅㄞˇ ㄈㄣ ㄈㄚˇ)
statement or expression in
percentage

百分之百(ㄅㄞˇ ㄈㄣ ㄓ ㄅㄞˇ)
a hundred per cent; out and
out; absolutely

百分數(ㄅㄞˇ ㄈㄣ ㄕㄨˋ)
a percentage

百夫長(ㄅㄞˇ ㄈㄨ ㄓㄤˇ)
①a centurion (of the
Roman Empire) ②a low-
ranking military officer (in
ancient China)

百讀不厭(ㄅㄞˇ ㄉㄨˊ ㄅㄨˋ 一ㄢˋ)
(said of a book)not boring
even after repeated reading;
very interesting: 這本書百讀
不厭。I never get tired of
reading this book.

百端(ㄅㄞˇ ㄉㄨㄢ)
all matters

百聽不厭(ㄅㄞˇ ㄊㄧㄥ ㄅㄨˋ 一ㄢˋ)
worth hearing a hundred
times: 這個故事我百聽不厭。
I never get tired of hearing
this story.

百衲(ㄅㄞˇ ㄋㄚˋ)
full of patches—said of a
Buddhist monk's robe

百衲本(ㄅㄞˇ ㄋㄚˋ ㄅㄣˇ)
a book made complete by
assembling many different
rare editions or fragments

百衲衣(ㄅㄞˇ ㄋㄚˋ 一)
①clothes with many patches
② a Buddhist monk's robe
full of patches

百鳥(ㄅㄞˇ ㄋㄧㄠˇ)
all species of birds

百年(ㄅㄞˇ ㄋㄧㄢˊ)
①a hundred years; a cen-
tury: 這是百年罕見的大水災。
It's the biggest flood in the
century. ②a lifetime

百年大計(ㄅㄞˇ ㄋㄧㄢˊ ㄉㄚˋ ㄐㄧˋ)
a project of vital and lasting
importance; a great plan
covering a very long period;
a long-range program

百年好合(ㄅㄞˇ ㄋㄧㄢˊ ㄏㄠˇ ㄏㄜˊ)
a harmonious union lasting
a hundred years (a conventional congratulatory message on a wedding)

百年後(ㄅㄞˇ ㄋㄧㄢˊ ㄏㄡˋ)
after death

百年紀念(ㄅㄞˇ ㄋㄧㄢˊ ㄐㄧˋ 一ㄢˋ)
the centennial, or centenary

百年戰爭(ㄅㄞˇ ㄋㄧㄢˊ ㄓㄢˋ ㄓㄥ)
the Hundred Years' War,
1337-1453, between England
and France

百年樹人(ㄅㄞˇ ㄋㄧㄢˊ ㄕㄨˋ ㄖㄣˊ)
It takes one hundred years
to cultivate a man. 或 Educa-

〔白

部〕

tion of the people takes a hundred years to bear fruit.

百裏挑一(ㄅㄞ ㄌㄧˇ ㄊㄧㄠ ㄧ)
(literally) to pick one out of a hundred—very few

百里侯(ㄅㄞ ㄌㄧˇ ㄏㄡˊ)
the magistrate of a county in former times

百里才(ㄅㄞ ㄌㄧˇ ㄘㄞˊ)
talent barely good enough for a county magistrate

百僚(ㄅㄞ ㄌㄧㄠˊ)
all the officials

百鍊鋼 or 百鍊剛(ㄅㄞ ㄌㄧㄢˋ ㄍㄤ)
well-tempered steel

百鍊金(ㄅㄞ ㄌㄧㄢˋ ㄐㄧㄣ)
well-tempered gold

百鍊成鋼(ㄅㄞ ㄌㄧㄢˋ ㄔㄥˊ ㄍㄤ)
Mastery comes from long training. 或 Expertise is the result of long and hard practice.

百伶百俐(ㄅㄞ ㄌㄧㄥˊ ㄅㄞ ㄌㄧˋ)
very clever; very intelligent

百靈鳥(ㄅㄞ ㄌㄧㄥˊ ㄋㄧㄠˇ)
a lark; the Mongolian lark

百感交集(ㄅㄞ ㄍㄢˇ ㄐㄧㄠ ㄐㄧˊ)
Lots of emotions crowd into the heart.

百穀(ㄅㄞ ㄍㄨˇ)
all kinds of grain

百果(ㄅㄞ ㄍㄨㄛˇ)
all kinds of fruits

百官(ㄅㄞ ㄍㄨㄢ)
officials of all ranks and descriptions

百工(ㄅㄞ ㄍㄨㄥ)
①all sorts of officers ②all sorts of handicraftsmen

百科全書(ㄅㄞ ㄎㄜ ㄑㄩㄢˊ ㄕㄨ)or 百科辭典(ㄅㄞ ㄎㄜ ㄘˊ ㄉㄧㄢˇ)
an encyclopedia

百口莫辯(ㄅㄞ ㄎㄡˇ ㄇㄛˋ ㄅㄧㄢˋ)
There is no room for verbal defense.—unable to give a convincing explanation for self-defense

百揆(ㄅㄞ ㄎㄨㄟˊ)or(ㄅㄞ ㄎㄨㄟ)
the chief minister of a state

百孔千瘡(ㄅㄞ ㄎㄨㄥˇ ㄑㄧㄢ ㄔㄨㄤ)
(literally) honeycombed or riddled with holes—in a state of ruin or extreme distress; in very bad shape

百合(ㄅㄞ ㄏㄜˊ)
the lily

百合花(ㄅㄞ ㄏㄜˊ ㄏㄨㄚ)
the lily

百花(ㄅㄞ ㄏㄨㄚ)
all sorts of flowers

百花齊放(ㄅㄞ ㄏㄨㄚ ㄑㄧˊ ㄈㄤˋ)
All flowers are in bloom.

百花洲(ㄅㄞ ㄏㄨㄚ ㄓㄡ)
a place in Nanchang, Kiangsi, a naval training center during the Sung Dynasty

百花生日(ㄅㄞ ㄏㄨㄚ ㄕㄥ ㄖˋ)
the birthday of all flowers (the 12th day of the second lunar month)

百花王(ㄅㄞ ㄏㄨㄚ ㄨㄤˊ)
the Queen of Flowers—the peony

百貨公司(ㄅㄞ ㄏㄨㄛˋ ㄍㄨㄥ ㄙ)
a department store

百貨商場(ㄅㄞ ㄏㄨㄛˋ ㄕㄤ ㄔㄤˇ)or
(ㄅㄞ ㄏㄨㄛˋ ㄕㄤ ㄔㄤ)
an emporium

百計千方(ㄅㄞ ㄐㄧˋ ㄑㄧㄢ ㄈㄤ)
all sorts of tricks and stratagems

百家(ㄅㄞ ㄐㄧㄚ)
①the various schools of thinkers ②various families

百家姓(ㄅㄞ ㄐㄧㄚ ㄒㄧㄥˋ)
the Book of Family Names

百家爭鳴(ㄅㄞ ㄐㄧㄚ ㄓㄥ ㄇㄧㄥˊ)
All schools of thoughts contend for attention.

百結衣(ㄅㄞ ㄐㄧㄝˊ ㄧ)
clothes full of patches

百星不如一月(ㄅㄞ ㄒㄧㄥ ㄅㄨˋ ㄖㄨˊ ㄧ ㄩㄝˋ)
(literally) A single moon is better than one hundred stars.—Quality is more important than quantity.

百姓(ㄅㄞ ㄒㄧㄥˋ)
①the common people; the people ②all existing family names

百折不撓(ㄅㄞ ㄓㄜˊ ㄅㄨˋ ㄋㄠˊ)
unflinching despite repeated setbacks; indomitable; unswerving; unshakable

百折不回(ㄅㄞ ㄓㄜˊ ㄅㄨˋ ㄏㄨㄟˊ)
pushing forward despite repeated frustrations

百褶裙(ㄅㄞ ㄓㄜˇ ㄑㄩㄣˊ)or 百襇裙
(ㄅㄞ ㄐㄧㄢˇ ㄑㄩㄣˊ)
a pleated skirt

百戰百勝(ㄅㄞ ㄓㄢˋ ㄅㄞ ㄕㄥˋ)

victorious in every battle

百中無一(ㄅㄞ ㄓㄨㄥ ㄨˊ ㄧ)
not one in a hundred; very few

百尺竿頭(ㄅㄞ ㄔˇ ㄍㄢ ㄊㄡˊ)
(literally) the top of a hundred-foot pole—the highest achievement

百尺竿頭，更進一步(ㄅㄞ ㄔˇ ㄍㄢ ㄊㄡˊ，ㄍㄥˋ ㄐㄧㄣˋ ㄧ ㄅㄨˋ)
to make still further progress

百川滙宗(ㄅㄞ ㄔㄨㄢ ㄏㄨㄟˋ ㄗㄨㄥ)
(literally) A hundred rivers may merge in one.—Divergence ends in uniformity or agreement.

百十來個(ㄅㄞ ㄕˊ ㄌㄞˊ ㄍㄜˋ)
around a hundred; a hundred or so

百世(ㄅㄞ ㄕˋ)
a period of a hundred generations—a very long period of time

百世師(ㄅㄞ ㄕˋ ㄕ)
a teacher for a hundred generations—a sage

百事通(ㄅㄞ ㄕˋ ㄊㄨㄥ)
an expert in everything; an all-rounder; a knowledgeable person

百事俱廢(ㄅㄞ ㄕˋ ㄐㄩ ㄈㄟˋ)
Everything is neglected.

百舌(ㄅㄞ ㄕㄜˊ)or(ㄅㄞ ㄕㄜˋ)or 百舌鳥(ㄅㄞ ㄕㄜˊ ㄋㄧㄠˇ)
a shrike 亦作「反舌鳥」或「伯勞鳥」

百壽圖(ㄅㄞ ㄕㄡˋ ㄊㄨˊ)
a pattern composed of a hundred different styles of the character 壽 and presented as a birthday gift

百獸之王(ㄅㄞ ㄕㄡˋ ㄓ ㄨㄤˊ)
the king of all animals—the lion

百善孝爲先(ㄅㄞ ㄕㄢˋ ㄒㄧㄠˋ ㄨㄟˊ ㄒㄧㄢ)
Filial piety is the most important of all virtues.

百身莫贖(ㄅㄞ ㄕㄣ ㄇㄛˋ ㄕㄨˊ)
A dead person cannot be made alive again by any means.

百乘之家(ㄅㄞ ㄕㄥˋ ㄓ ㄐㄧㄚ)
a house with a hundred carriages—a family of an official during the Chou Dynas-

ty
百日(ㄅㄞˇ ㄖˋ)
the hundredth day after
one's death

百日咳(ㄅㄞˇ ㄖˋ ㄎㄜˊ)
whooping cough

百日紅(ㄅㄞˇ ㄖˋ ㄏㄨㄥˊ)
crape myrtle

百日草(ㄅㄞˇ ㄖˋ ㄘㄠˇ)
(botany) youth-and-old-age

百忍(ㄅㄞˇ ㄖㄣˇ)
great endurance; great forbearance

百子圖(ㄅㄞˇ ㄗˇ ㄊㄨˊ)
a picture showing numerous
children either drawn or embroidered (given as a wish
that the recipient will have
numerous offspring)

百子全書(ㄅㄞˇ ㄗˇ ㄑㄩㄢˊ ㄕㄨ)
a complete collection of all
schools of thoughts from
ancient times, compiled during the Ching Dynasty

百足之蟲，死而不殭(ㄅㄞˇ ㄗㄨˊ ㄓ
ㄔㄨㄥˊ，ㄙˇ ㄦˊ ㄅㄨˋ ㄐㄧㄤ)
(literally) A centipede dies
hard.—The influence of a
powerful man lingers on
after his downfall.

百縱千隨(ㄅㄞˇ ㄗㄨㄥˋ ㄑㄧㄢ ㄙㄨㄟˊ)
to yield to all the wishes of
a child, etc.)

百思莫解(ㄅㄞˇ ㄙ ㄇㄛˋ ㄐㄧㄝˇ)
incomprehensible; inexplicable: 此事我百思莫解。I
remain puzzled after pondering over the matter a hundred times.

百依百順(ㄅㄞˇ ㄧ ㄅㄞˇ ㄕㄨㄣˋ)
to yield to all the wishes of
a child, etc.) 亦作「百縱千隨」

百葉箱(ㄅㄞˇ ㄧㄝˋ ㄒㄧㄤ)
a thermometer screen

百葉窗(ㄅㄞˇ ㄧㄝˋ ㄔㄨㄤ)
Venetian blinds

百憂(ㄅㄞˇ ㄧㄡ)
all worries or sorrows

百無聊賴(ㄅㄞˇ ㄨˊ ㄌㄧㄠˊ ㄌㄞˋ)
very much bored

百無禁忌(ㄅㄞˇ ㄨˊ ㄐㄧㄣˋ ㄐㄧˋ)
There are no taboos or
restrictions at all.

百無一長(ㄅㄞˇ ㄨˊ ㄧ ㄔㄤˊ)
skilled in nothing; good-for-
nothing

百無一失(ㄅㄞˇ ㄨˊ ㄧ ㄕ)

(literally) There is not a
single miss in a hundred
tries.—sure to succeed if certain rules are followed

百物(ㄅㄞˇ ㄨˋ)
all things

百萬(ㄅㄞˇ ㄨㄢˋ)
a million

百萬富翁(ㄅㄞˇ ㄨㄢˋ ㄈㄨˋ ㄨㄥ)
a millionaire

百聞不如一見(ㄅㄞˇ ㄨㄣˊ ㄅㄨˋ ㄖㄨˊ
ㄧ ㄐㄧㄢˋ)
There is nothing like seeing
for oneself. 或 Seeing is believing.

百喻經(ㄅㄞˇ ㄩˋ ㄐㄧㄥ)
the sutra of the 100 par-
ables, translated by Gunard-
dhi, in the late fifth century

百越(ㄅㄞˇ ㄩㄝˋ)
Yüeh—ancient name of the
area of what is Chekiang,
Fukien, and Kwangtung today

二畫

【皂】 3694
(皂) ㄗㄠˋ tzaw zào
1. black
2. menial labor
3. a lictor
4. soap

皂白(ㄗㄠˋ ㄅㄞˊ)
black and white—right and
wrong

皂白不分(ㄗㄠˋ ㄅㄞˊ ㄅㄨˋ ㄈㄣ)
to fail to distinguish between right and wrong

皂隸(ㄗㄠˋ ㄌㄧˋ)
a government-employed
laborer, messenger, etc. in
ancient times

皂櫪(ㄗㄠˋ ㄌㄧˋ)
a stable 亦作「馬廄」

皂莢(ㄗㄠˋ ㄐㄧㄚˊ)
a honey locust

【皁】 3695
ㄗㄠˋ tzaw zào
soap

三畫

【的】 3696
1. ㄉㄧˊ dih dí
1. clear; manifest
2. a target; a goal
的的(ㄉㄧˊ ㄉㄧˊ)

clear; distinct

的皪 or 的礫(ㄉㄧˊ ㄌㄧˋ)
bright; lustrous

【的】 3696
2. ㄉㄧˋ dyi dì
accurate; exact; proper

的當(ㄉㄧˋ ㄉㄤ)
accurate; proper

的款(ㄉㄧˋ ㄎㄨㄢˇ)
a surely available sum of
money

的確(ㄉㄧˋ ㄑㄩㄝˋ)
certainly; surely

【的】 3696
3. •ㄉㄜ •de de
1. a bound subordinate particle translatable by "'s"
or with terms interchanged
by "of": 這是我姊姊的皮包。
This is my elder sister's
purse.
2. by "-ly"
3. by an adjectival ending, a
prepositional phrase, or a
relative: 玫瑰花開了，有紅
的，有黃的。The roses are in
bloom; some are red and
some yellow.

四畫

【皆】 3697
ㄐㄧㄝ jie jiē
all; every; entire: 四海之內，
皆兄弟也。Within the four
seas all people are brothers.

皆大歡喜(ㄐㄧㄝ ㄉㄚˋ ㄏㄨㄢ ㄒㄧˇ)
Everybody is satisfied.

皆可(ㄐㄧㄝ ㄎㄜˇ)
all acceptable

皆知(ㄐㄧㄝ ㄓ)
all aware

皆是(ㄐㄧㄝ ㄕˋ)
(they) all are

皆屬(ㄐㄧㄝ ㄕㄨˇ)
(they) all belong to

皆因(ㄐㄧㄝ ㄧㄣ)
only because; just because;
all because

【皇】 3698
ㄏㄨㄤˊ hwang huáng
1. imperial; royal
2. an emperor
3. beautiful; brilliant
4. uneasy; anxious
5. a term of respect for an
ancestor

皇妣(ㄏㄨㄤˊ ㄅㄧˇ)
one's deceased mother

〔百部〕

〔白
部〕

皇辟（ㄏㄨㄤˊ ㄅㄧˋ）
①the emperor ②my late husband

皇甫（ㄏㄨㄤˊ ㄈㄨˇ）
a Chinese family name

皇帝（ㄏㄨㄤˊ ㄉㄧˋ）
an emperor

皇都（ㄏㄨㄤˊ ㄉㄨ）
the imperial capital

皇太后（ㄏㄨㄤˊ ㄊㄞˋ ㄏㄡˋ）
the empress dowager

皇太子（ㄏㄨㄤˊ ㄊㄞˋ ㄗˇ）
the crown prince 參看「皇儲」

皇天后土（ㄏㄨㄤˊ ㄊㄧㄢ ㄏㄡˋ ㄊㄨˇ）
Heaven and Earth

皇圖（ㄏㄨㄤˊ ㄊㄨˊ）
the domain of an empire

皇統（ㄏㄨㄤˊ ㄊㄨㄥˇ）
imperial lineage

皇陵（ㄏㄨㄤˊ ㄌㄧㄥˊ）
an imperial mausoleum

皇冠（ㄏㄨㄤˊ ㄍㄨㄢ）
an imperial crown

皇宮（ㄏㄨㄤˊ ㄍㄨㄥ）
an imperial palace

皇考（ㄏㄨㄤˊ ㄎㄠˇ）
one's deceased father

皇后（ㄏㄨㄤˊ ㄏㄡˋ）
an empress

皇皇（ㄏㄨㄤˊ ㄏㄨㄤˊ）
①brilliant ②uneasy; anxious; restless

皇皇巨著（ㄏㄨㄤˊ ㄏㄨㄤˊ ㄐㄩˋ ㄓㄨˋ）
a great brilliant work

皇極（ㄏㄨㄤˊ ㄐㄧˊ）
the rules established by the emperor for public observance

皇家（ㄏㄨㄤˊ ㄐㄧㄚ）
the imperial family (or house)

皇親國戚（ㄏㄨㄤˊ ㄑㄧㄣ ㄍㄨㄛˊ ㄑㄧ）
relatives of the emperor

皇清經解（ㄏㄨㄤˊ ㄑㄧㄥ ㄐㄧㄥ ㄐㄧㄝˇ）
a huge collection of commentaries on classics compiled by Juan Yüan (阮元) during the Ching Dynasty

皇城（ㄏㄨㄤˊ ㄔㄥˊ）
the Imperial City (the inner part of Peking)

皇儲（ㄏㄨㄤˊ ㄔㄨˊ）
the crown prince 亦作「皇太子」

皇室（ㄏㄨㄤˊ ㄕˋ）
the imperial household; the royal household

皇上（ㄏㄨㄤˊ ㄕㄤˋ）
His Majesty

皇族（ㄏㄨㄤˊ ㄗㄨˊ）
the imperial family; the royal family

皇祖（ㄏㄨㄤˊ ㄗㄨˇ）
the imperial ancestors before the founder of the dynasty

皇祖姒（ㄏㄨㄤˊ ㄗㄨˇ ㄙ）
one's deceased grandmother

皇祖考（ㄏㄨㄤˊ ㄗㄨˇ ㄎㄠˇ）
one's deceased grandfather

皇恩（ㄏㄨㄤˊ ㄣ）
imperial favor or kindness

【皈】 3699
《ㄍㄨㄟ guei guī》
to follow

皈依（ㄍㄨㄟ ㄧ）
to be converted to (Buddhism)

五畫

【皋】 3700
（臯）《ㄍㄠ gau gāo》
1. a marsh; a swamp
2. a shore

皋比（ㄍㄠ ㄆㄧˊ）
①a tiger's skin ②a teacher's seat; a teacher's position

皋門（ㄍㄠ ㄇㄣˊ）
a palace gate

皋隰（ㄍㄠ ㄒㄧˊ）
a swamp; a marsh

皋壤（ㄍㄠ ㄖㄤˇ）
land by a marsh or swamp

皋陶（ㄍㄠ ㄊㄠˊ）
name of the man who served as a chief judicial officer for the legendary ruler Shun (舜)

皋月（ㄍㄠ ㄩㄝˋ）
the fifth month of the lunar year

六畫

【皎】 3701
ㄐㄧㄠˇ jeau jiǎo
1. white; clean
2. bright; lustrous; brilliant: 皎月當空. The bright moon hung in the sky.

皎白（ㄐㄧㄠˇ ㄅㄞˊ）
brightly white

皎厲（ㄐㄧㄠˇ ㄌㄧˋ）
proud

皎潔（ㄐㄧㄠˇ ㄐㄧㄝˊ）
brightly clean

皎皎（ㄐㄧㄠˇ ㄐㄧㄠˇ）
①very white ②bright

皎如日月（ㄐㄧㄠˇ ㄖㄨˊ ㄖˋ ㄩㄝˋ）
as bright as the heavenly bodies

七畫

【皓】 3702
ㄏㄠˋ haw hào
white and bright

皓魄（ㄏㄠˋ ㄆㄛˋ）
the moon or moonlight

皓礬（ㄏㄠˋ ㄈㄢˊ）
white vitriol or goslarite

皓天 or 昊天（ㄏㄠˋ ㄊㄧㄢ）
①a summer sky ②the sky; heaven

皓皓（ㄏㄠˋ ㄏㄠˋ）
bright; brilliant; glistening; gleaming

皓齒（ㄏㄠˋ ㄔˇ）
white teeth; sparkling teeth

皓首（ㄏㄠˋ ㄕㄡˇ）
a hoary head—old age

皓首窮經（ㄏㄠˋ ㄕㄡˇ ㄑㄩㄥˊ ㄐㄧㄥ）
to continue to study even in old age

皓腕（ㄏㄠˋ ㄨㄢˋ）
an attractive white arm (of a woman)

皓月當空（ㄏㄠˋ ㄩㄝˋ ㄉㄤ ㄎㄨㄥ）
The bright moon hangs in the sky.

【皖】 3703
ㄨㄢˇ woan wǎn
1. name of an ancient state in what is today's Anhwei
2. an alternative name of Anhwei

皖北（ㄨㄢˇ ㄅㄟˇ）
the part of Anhwei north of the Yangtze River

皖南（ㄨㄢˇ ㄋㄢˊ）
the part of Anhwei south of the Yangtze River

皖水（ㄨㄢˇ ㄕㄨㄟˇ）
a tributary of the Yangtze River originating in Anhwei

【皕】 3704
ㄅㄧˋ bih bì
two hundred

八畫

【皙】 3705
ㄒㄧ shi xi
1. white skin
2. a kind of dates

十畫

【皚】 3706
ㄞ air ái
pure white; white and clean; brightly white

皚皚(ㄞˊㄞˊ)
brightly white: 白雪皚皚 an expanse of white snow

【皜】 3707
ㄏㄠˋ haw hào
white; bright

皜皜(ㄏㄠˋㄏㄠˋ)
white and glistening

十二畫

【皤】 3708
ㄆㄛˊ por pó
1. (said of an old man) hoary-headed
2. white
3. a vast belly

皤皤(ㄆㄛˊㄆㄛˊ)
white; hoary

皤然(ㄆㄛˊㄖㄢˊ)
white; hoary

皮 部
ㄆㄧˊ pyi pí

【皮】 3709
ㄆㄧˊ pyi pí
1. skin; fur; hide; leather; rind; peltry; bark
2. a thin sheet
3. naughty
4. a Chinese family name

皮包(ㄆㄧˊㄅㄠ)
a handbag or purse (especially one made of leather); 她從皮包裡拿出錢來。She took money from her handbag.

皮包骨(ㄆㄧˊㄅㄠㄍㄨˇ)or 皮包骨頭
(ㄆㄧˊㄅㄠㄍㄨˇ·ㄊㄡ)
skinny; only skin and bones:

他瘦得皮包骨頭。He is only skin and bones.

皮弁(ㄆㄧˊㄅㄧㄢˋ)
an ancient cap made of a deer's hide

皮破血流(ㄆㄧˊㄆㄛˋㄒㄩㄝˋㄌㄧㄡˊ)
wounded and bleeding

皮袍(ㄆㄧˊㄆㄠˊ)
a fur gown

皮膜組織(ㄆㄧˊㄇㄛˊㄗㄨˇㄓ)
(anatomy) epithelium

皮毛(ㄆㄧˊㄇㄠˊ)
superficial knowledge

皮毛之見(ㄆㄧˊㄇㄠˊㄓㄐㄧㄢˋ)
a superficial view or opinion

皮面(ㄆㄧˊㄇㄧㄢˋ)
①the outer skin; epidermis ②to remove the skin; to skin ③a leather cover

皮筏(ㄆㄧˊㄈㄚˊ)
a kayak

皮膚(ㄆㄧˊㄈㄨ)
skin

皮膚病(ㄆㄧˊㄈㄨㄅㄧㄥˋ)
skin disease

皮膚科(ㄆㄧˊㄈㄨㄎㄜ)
dermatology

皮膚科醫生(ㄆㄧˊㄈㄨㄎㄜㄧㄕㄥ)
a dermatologist

皮膚科醫院(ㄆㄧˊㄈㄨㄎㄜㄧㄩㄢˋ)
a dermatological clinic

皮膚炎(ㄆㄧˊㄈㄨㄧㄢˊ)
dermatitis

皮膚癌(ㄆㄧˊㄈㄨㄞˊ)
skin cancer

皮袋(ㄆㄧˊㄉㄞˋ)
a leather bag or purse

皮帶(ㄆㄧˊㄉㄞˋ)
a leather belt

皮蛋(ㄆㄧˊㄉㄢˋ)
duck's eggs preserved in lime

皮條(ㄆㄧˊㄊㄧㄠˊ)
thongs

皮條客(ㄆㄧˊㄊㄧㄠˊㄎㄜˋ)
a pimp

皮條客(ㄆㄧˊㄊㄧㄠˊㄎㄜˋㄑㄧㄡ)
the service rendered by a pander

皮艇(ㄆㄧˊㄊㄧㄥˇ)
a skin boat

皮囊(ㄆㄧˊㄋㄤˊ)
a leather bag

皮裡抽肉(ㄆㄧˊㄌㄧˇㄔㄡㄖㄡˋ)
skinny; emaciated

皮裡春秋(ㄆㄧˊㄌㄧˇㄔㄨㄣㄑㄧㄡ)or
皮裡陽秋(ㄆㄧˊㄌㄧˇㄧㄤˊㄑㄧㄡ)
to have an unexpressed opinion about the worth of a person or thing; to criticize mentally

皮臉(ㄆㄧˊㄌㄧㄢˇ)
shameless; brazen

皮革(ㄆㄧˊㄍㄜˊ)
leather

皮革工廠(ㄆㄧˊㄍㄜˊㄍㄨㄥㄔㄤˇ)
a tannery

皮開肉綻(ㄆㄧˊㄎㄞㄖㄡˋㄓㄢˋ)
The skin ruptures and the flesh bursts.—the effect of severe beating

皮厚(ㄆㄧˊㄏㄡˋ)
thick-skinned: 她剝了一個皮厚的柳橙。She peeled a thick-skinned orange.

皮花科(ㄆㄧˊㄏㄨㄚㄎㄜ)
the department of dermatology and syphilology

皮貨(ㄆㄧˊㄏㄨㄛˋ)
furs

皮黃(ㄆㄧˊㄏㄨㄤˊ)
a Peking opera tune; Peking opera

皮夾(ㄆㄧˊㄐㄧㄚˊ·ㄗ)or 皮夾兒
(ㄆㄧˊㄐㄧㄚˊㄦ)
a wallet (especially of leather)

皮夾克(ㄆㄧˊㄐㄧㄚˊㄎㄜˋ)
a leather jacket, or Wind-breaker

皮匠(ㄆㄧˊㄐㄧㄤˋ)
a cobbler

皮球(ㄆㄧˊㄑㄧㄡˊ)
a rubber ball

皮下注射(ㄆㄧˊㄒㄧㄚˋㄓㄨˋㄕㄜˋ)
①a hypodermic injection, or subcutaneous injection ②to skin-pop

皮鞋(ㄆㄧˊㄒㄧㄝˊ)
leather shoes

皮笑肉不笑(ㄆㄧˊㄒㄧㄠˋㄖㄡˋㄅㄨˋㄒㄧㄠˋ)
treacherous; crafty; putting on a false smile

皮箱(ㄆㄧˊㄒㄧㄤ)
a suitcase or valise (especially of leather)

皮相(ㄆㄧˊㄒㄧㄤˋ)
an external appearance

皮相之談(ㄆㄧˊㄒㄧㄤˋㄓㄊㄢˊ)
a superficial talk or opinion

皮靴(ㄆㄧ ㄒㄩㄝ)
leather boots: 她穿着一雙長筒的皮靴。She was in a pair of leather boots.

皮之不存，毛將焉附(ㄆㄧ ㄓ ㄅㄨ ㄘㄨㄣ，ㄇㄠ ㄐㄧㄤ ㄧㄢ ㄈㄨ)
(literally) Where can the hair grow when there is no skin?—How can one live as a free man when one's country loses its sovereignty?

皮紙(ㄆㄧ ㄓˇ)
heavy wrapping paper

皮裝書(ㄆㄧ ㄓㄨㄤ ㄕㄨ)
a leather-bound book

皮尺(ㄆㄧ ㄔˇ)
a tape measure; a tape

皮肉生涯(ㄆㄧ ㄖㄡ ㄕㄥ ㄧㄚˊ)
prostitution

皮子(ㄆㄧ ˙ㄗ)
①skin; rind ②leather; hide ③the cover or jacket (of a book)

皮草(ㄆㄧ ㄘㄠˇ)
furs

皮層(ㄆㄧ ㄘㄥˊ)
a cortex

皮鬆肉緊(ㄆㄧ ㄙㄨㄥ ㄖㄡˋ ㄐㄧㄣˇ)
idle; inactive

皮襖(ㄆㄧ ㄠˇ)
a fur coat; a leather coat

皮衣(ㄆㄧ ㄧ)
fur clothing: 她穿着非常昂貴的皮衣。She was wearing very expensive furs.

皮影戲(ㄆㄧ ㄧㄥˇ ㄒㄧˋ)
the shadow show

五畫

【皰】 3710
(疱) ㄆㄠˋ paw pào
pimples

七畫

【皴】 3711
ㄘㄨㄣ tsuen cūn
1. (said of the skin) to crack or chap from cold
2. (Chinese painting) a technique of representing irregular surfaces

皴法(ㄘㄨㄣ ㄈㄚˇ)
(Chinese painting) a technique of representing irregular surfaces

九畫

【皸】 3712
ㄐㄩㄣ jiun jūn
(said of the skin) to crack or chap from cold or dryness

皸裂(ㄐㄩㄣ ㄌㄧㄝˋ)
(said of the skin) to chap or crack from cold or dryness

十畫

【皺】 3713
ㄓㄡ jow zhòu
1. wrinkles; creases; folds; rumples
2. to wrinkle; to fold; to contract; to crease; to crumple

皺鷲(ㄓㄡˋ ㄐㄩ)
unpleasantly narrow; close; confining

皺眉(ㄓㄡˋ ㄇㄟˊ)or 皺眉頭(ㄓㄡˋ ㄇㄟˊ ˙ㄊㄡ)
to frown; to knit the brows

皺摺(ㄓㄡˋ ㄓㄜˊ)
creases; folds

皺皺巴巴(ㄓㄡˋ ㄓㄡˋ ㄅㄚ ㄅㄚ)
not smooth; full of creases; creasy; crumpled; shriveled

皺胃(ㄓㄡˋ ㄨㄟˋ)
an abomasum

皺紋(ㄓㄡˋ ㄨㄣˊ)
wrinkles; creases; folds; rumples

皿 部
ㄇㄧㄢˇ miin mǐn

【皿】 3714
ㄇㄧㄢˇ miin mǐn
(又讀 ㄇㄧㄥˊ miing míng)
a shallow container (such as a dish, plate, saucer, etc.)

三畫

【盂】 3715
ㄩˊ yu yú
1. a basin; a broad-mouthed receptacle for holding liquid; a jar

2. a party for hunting

盂蘭盆會(ㄩˊ ㄌㄢˊ ㄆㄣˊ ㄏㄨㄟˋ)
the Buddhist name of the Ghost Festival (the 15th of the seventh moon), being a transliteration from Sanskrit ullambana (deliverance)

四畫

【盅】 3716
ㄓㄨㄥ jong zhōng
a small cup

【盆】 3717
ㄆㄣˊ pern pén
a bowl; a basin; a tub

盆地(ㄆㄣˊ ㄉㄧˋ)
(geology) a basin

盆景(ㄆㄣˊ ㄐㄧㄥˇ)
a potted plant; a bonsai

盆子(ㄆㄣˊ ˙ㄗ)or 盆兒(ㄆㄣˊ ㄦ)
a bowl; a basin; a tub

盆栽(ㄆㄣˊ ㄗㄞ)
a potted plant; to plant in a pot; a bonsai 亦作「盆景」

【盈】 3718
ㄧㄥˊ yng yíng
to fill; to become full

盈把(ㄧㄥˊ ㄅㄚˇ)
a handful

盈滿(ㄧㄥˊ ㄇㄢˇ)
filled; full

盈利(ㄧㄥˊ ㄌㄧˋ)
profit; gains: 盈利一百萬元 to net a profit of one million dollars

盈貫(ㄧㄥˊ ㄍㄨㄢˋ)
(said of a bow)drawn to the fullest extent

盈虧(ㄧㄥˊ ㄎㄨㄟ)
①(said of the moon) waxing and waning ②profits and losses

盈千累萬(ㄧㄥˊ ㄑㄧㄢ ㄌㄟˇ ㄨㄢˋ)
thousands upon thousands

盈缺(ㄧㄥˊ ㄑㄩㄝ)
(said of the moon) waxing and waning

盈箱累篋(ㄧㄥˊ ㄒㄧㄤ ㄌㄟˇ ㄑㄧㄝˋ)
(said of treasures, etc.) to fill boxes and baskets to the brim

盈虛(ㄧㄥˊ ㄒㄩ)
waxing and waning; fullness and emptiness; ups and downs

盈則必虧(ㄧㄥˊ ㄗㄜˊ ㄅㄧˋ ㄎㄨㄟ)

When the fullest extent is reached, the decline begins.

盈溢(ㄧㄥˊㄧˋ)
to brim over

盈盈(ㄧㄥˊㄧㄥˊ)
①(said of water) clear and abundant②(said of a woman's bearing) easy and graceful

盈餘(ㄧㄥˊㄩˊ)
a surplus; profit

盈餘滾入(ㄧㄥˊㄩˊㄍㄨㄣˇㄖㄨˋ)
to enter the surplus in the accounts

盈月(ㄧㄥˊㄩㄝˋ)
a full moon

【盃】3719
(杯)ㄅㄟ bei bēi
a cup; a tumbler

五畫

【益】3720
ㄧˋ yih yì
1. to increase; to add to; to augment
2. in a higher degree; to a greater extent; more
3. benefit; profit; advantage: 這是對他有益的。It is to his advantage.

益發(ㄧˋㄈㄚ)
increasingly; more and more; all the more; ever more: 工作益發困難了。The work is getting increasingly difficult.

益鳥(ㄧˋㄋㄧㄠˇ)
beneficial birds; insectivorous birds

益加(ㄧˋㄐㄧㄚ)
increasingly; more and more; all the more; ever more

益智(ㄧˋㄓˋ)
①to grow in intelligence or wisdom ②the longan

益者三友(ㄧˋㄓㄜˇㄙㄢㄧㄡˇ)
There are three kinds of beneficial friends—honest friends, understanding friends, and learned friends.

益州(ㄧˋㄓㄡ)
an ancient province in what is Szechwan today

益處(ㄧˋㄔㄨˋ)or(ㄧˋ•ㄔㄨ)
advantages; benefit; profit

益蟲(ㄧˋㄔㄨㄥˊ)
beneficial insects

益壽(ㄧˋㄕㄡˋ)
to lengthen or prolong one's life: 據說此藥可延年益壽。It is said that the medicine may prolong one's life.

益友(ㄧˋㄧㄡˇ)
helpful friends; beneficial friends; useful friends

【盍】3721
ㄏㄜˊ her hé
1. what
2. why not
3. to get together

盍興乎來(ㄏㄜˊㄒㄧㄥㄏㄨㄌㄞˊ)
Why not rise and join us?

【盎】3722
ㄤˋ anq àng
1. a basin; a pot; a bowl
2. abundant; plentiful; rich

盎格羅薩克森(ㄤˋㄍㄜˊㄌㄨㄛˊㄙㄚˋㄎㄜˋㄙㄣ)
the Anglo-Saxons

盎然(ㄤˋㄖㄢˊ)
abundant; full; exuberant: 趣味盎然 full of interest

盎斯(ㄤˋㄙ)
an ounce 亦作「盎司」

盎盎(ㄤˋㄤˋ)
plentiful; full

【盌】3723
ㄨㄢˇ woan wǎn
same as 碗—a bowl

六畫

【盒】3724
ㄏㄜˊ her hé
a small box; a case: 他吃了一盒盒糖。He ate a whole box of candy.

盒子(ㄏㄜˊ•ㄗ)or 盒兒(ㄏㄜˊㄦ)
a small case; a small box

盒子槍(ㄏㄜˊ•ㄗㄑㄧㄤ)
a mauser pistol

【盔】3725
ㄎㄨㄟ kuei kuī
1. a helmet
2. a basin; a pot

盔頭(ㄎㄨㄟㄊㄡˊ)
caps formerly worn by actors in Chinese opera

盔甲(ㄎㄨㄟㄐㄧㄚˇ)
helmets and mail; armor

七畫

【盛】3726
ㄕㄥˋ sheng shèng
1. abundant; rich; exuberant; flourishing; prosperous
2. (said of fire, storm, etc.)to rage: 火勢盛盛。The fire is raging.
3. a Chinese family name

盛名(ㄕㄥˋㄇㄧㄥˊ)
a glorious name; great reputation

盛名難副(ㄕㄥˋㄇㄧㄥˊㄋㄢˊㄈㄨˋ)
to have a fame greater than one deserves 或 It is hard to live up to a great reputation.

盛名之累(ㄕㄥˋㄇㄧㄥˊㄓㄌㄟˋ)
the trouble of being a famous personality

盛服(ㄕㄥˋㄈㄨˊ)
in all one's robes; in full dress

盛大(ㄕㄥˋㄉㄚˋ)
grand; magnificent; majestic

盛德大業(ㄕㄥˋㄉㄜˊㄉㄚˋㄧㄝˋ)
great virtues and magnificent achievements (of a ruler, etc.)

盛典(ㄕㄥˋㄉㄧㄢˇ)
a grand occasion; a big ceremony

盛多(ㄕㄥˋㄉㄨㄛ)
midwinter

盛唐(ㄕㄥˋㄊㄤˊ)
the period of full literary grandeur in the Tang Dynasty, corresponding to most of the 8th century

盛年(ㄕㄥˋㄋㄧㄢˊ)
the prime of one's life: 他在盛年時期去世。He died in the prime of his life.

盛怒(ㄕㄥˋㄋㄨˋ)
in great anger; wrath

盛開(ㄕㄥˋㄎㄞ)
in full bloom: 櫻花盛開。The cherry trees are in full bloom.

盛況空前(ㄕㄥˋㄎㄨㄤˋㄎㄨㄥㄑㄧㄢˊ)
unprecedented in grandeur, festivity, etc.

盛會(ㄕㄥˋㄏㄨㄟˋ)
a grand gathering; a magnificent assembly

盛極必衰(ㄕㄥˋㄐㄧˊㄅㄧˋㄕㄨㄞ)
Everything starts to fall after it has reached the ze-

（皿部）

nith.

盛極一時(ㄕㄥˊ ㄐㄧˊ ㄧˋ ㄕˊ)
to be in vogue for a time; to
be all the rage at the moment

皿部

盛舉(ㄕㄥˊ ㄐㄩˇ)
a great undertaking or
enterprise; a worthy project:
讓我們共襄盛舉. Let's cooperated in this great project.

盛氣(ㄕㄥˊ ㄑㄧˋ)
①exploding anger or rage
②arrogant; haughty ③full of
spirit

盛氣凌人(ㄕㄥˊ ㄑㄧˋ ㄌㄧㄥˊ ㄖㄣˊ)
to treat others rudely
through arrogance

盛情(ㄕㄥˊ ㄑㄧㄥˊ)
warm thoughtfulness; a very
warm heart; utmost sincerity

盛情難卻(ㄕㄥˊ ㄑㄧㄥˊ ㄋㄢˊ ㄑㄩㄝˋ)
It is hard to turn down the
offer made with such warmheartedness.

盛夏(ㄕㄥˊ ㄒㄧㄚˋ)
midsummer

盛行(ㄕㄥˊ ㄒㄧㄥˊ)
(said of things) to be popular or in vogue: 這些衣服曾經
盛行一時。These clothes were
in vogue for a time.

盛饌(ㄕㄥˊ ㄓㄨㄢˋ)
a sumptuous meal; a feast

盛裝(ㄕㄥˊ ㄓㄨㄤ)
in full dress; in rich attire

盛產(ㄕㄥˊ ㄔㄢˇ)
to abound in; to teem with;
to be rich in: 中東盛產石油。
The Middle East is rich in
oil.

盛世(ㄕㄥˊ ㄕˋ)
a prosperous age or period;
halcyon days

盛事(ㄕㄥˊ ㄕˋ)
a grand affair or occasion

盛暑(ㄕㄥˊ ㄕㄨˇ)
midsummer; intense heat

盛衰(ㄕㄥˊ ㄕㄨㄞ)
rise and fall; ups and downs;
vicissitudes

盛衰興廢(ㄕㄥˊ ㄕㄨㄞ ㄒㄧㄥ ㄈㄟˋ)
vicissitudes; ups and downs;
waning and waxing; rise
and fall

盛讚(ㄕㄥˊ ㄗㄢˋ)
to praise profusely; to pay

high compliments

盛意(ㄕㄥˊ ㄧˋ)
warm-heartedness; thoughtfulness; generosity: 我們對他
的盛意表示感謝。We thanked
him for his generosities.

盛顏(ㄕㄥˊ ㄧㄢˊ)
one's look in the prime of
his life

盛筵(ㄕㄥˊ ㄧㄢˊ)
a sumptuous feast: 我們參加
了那個盛筵。We went to the
sumptuous feast.

盛筵難再(ㄕㄥˊ ㄧㄢˊ ㄋㄢˊ ㄗㄞˋ)
Sumptuous feasts are not
repeated often. 或 Grand
gatherings do not take place
every day.

盛宴(ㄕㄥˊ ㄧㄢˋ)
a grand banquet; a splendid
meal 亦作「盛筵」

盛王(ㄕㄥˊ ㄨㄤˊ)
a ruler of great virtue

盛譽(ㄕㄥˊ ㄩˋ)
great fame; high reputation

3726
盛 2. ㄔㄥˊ cherng
                   chéng
to take (loose material) into
a bowl or basin; to hold; to
contain

盛飯(ㄔㄥˊ ㄈㄢˋ)
to take cooked rice out of a
cooker into a bowl

盛殮(ㄔㄥˊ ㄌㄧㄢˋ)
to place a body in a coffin

3727
盜 ㄉㄠˋ daw dào
to steal; to rob; to misappropriate

盜版(ㄉㄠˋ ㄅㄢˇ)
a pirated edition

盜賣(ㄉㄠˋ ㄇㄞˋ)
to misappropriate and sell

盜名(ㄉㄠˋ ㄇㄧㄥˊ)
to steal glory one does not
deserve; to seek undeserved
publicity

盜墓(ㄉㄠˋ ㄇㄨˋ)
to steal from graves; to sack
tombs; to plunder graves

盜伐(ㄉㄠˋ ㄈㄚˊ)
to fell trees unlawfully

盜匪(ㄉㄠˋ ㄈㄟˇ)
robbers; bandits; brigands

盜壘(ㄉㄠˋ ㄌㄟˇ)
base stealing (as of base-

ball)

盜錄(ㄉㄠˋ ㄌㄨˋ)
to pirate (a videocassette,
record, etc.)

盜魁(ㄉㄠˋ ㄎㄨㄟˊ)or 盜首(ㄉㄠˋ ㄕㄡˇ)
the leader of a gang of robbers or bandits; a ringleader

盜汗(ㄉㄠˋ ㄏㄢˋ)
(pathology) night sweats

盜竊(ㄉㄠˋ ㄑㄧㄝˋ)
theft; larceny; misappropriation: 他因盜竊而被關進獄中。
He was put in prison for
theft.

盜取(ㄉㄠˋ ㄑㄩˇ)
to take unlawfully; to steal;
to pilfer; to purloin

盜儒(ㄉㄠˋ ㄖㄨˊ)
a corrupt scholar; an immoral intellectual

盜賊(ㄉㄠˋ ㄗㄟˊ)
a thief; a robber; a bandit

盜賊蠭起(ㄉㄠˋ ㄗㄟˊ ㄈㄥ ㄑㄧˇ)
to be infested with robbers
and thieves

盜憎主人(ㄉㄠˋ ㄗㄥ ㄓㄨˇ ㄖㄣˊ)
①to bully the weak; to
usurp power ② Thieves are
angry with the master.

盜藪(ㄉㄠˋ ㄙㄡˇ)
a den of robbers

盜案(ㄉㄠˋ ㄢˋ)
a theft case

盜亦有道(ㄉㄠˋ ㄧˋ ㄧㄡˇ ㄉㄠˋ)
Even robbers have a code of
conduct.

盜印(ㄉㄠˋ ㄧㄣˋ)
to pirate; piracy

盜用(ㄉㄠˋ ㄩㄥˋ)
to embezzle; to usurp

八畫

3728
盞 ㄓㄢˇ jaan zhǎn
1. a small shallow container; a
small cup
2. a numerical adjunct denoting lamps

3729
盟 ㄇㄥˊ meng méng
1. a covenant; an oath; a vow;
to covenant; to ally: 許多國
家將與我國締盟。Many foreign powers will ally with
us.
2. a Mongol league

盟邦(ㄇㄥˊ ㄅㄤ)
　an allied country; allies

盟府(ㄇㄥˊ ㄈㄨˇ)
　(in ancient China) the repository of covenants; a place for safekeeping records of an alliance

盟國(ㄇㄥˊ ㄍㄨㄛˊ)
　allied powers; allies

盟機(ㄇㄥˊ ㄐㄧ)
　allied warplanes

盟軍(ㄇㄥˊ ㄐㄩㄣ)
　allied troops; allied forces

盟心(ㄇㄥˊ ㄒㄧㄣ)
　to swear mutual devotion

盟兄弟(ㄇㄥˊ ㄒㄩㄥ ㄉㄧˋ)
　sworn brothers (not linked by kinship)

盟長(ㄇㄥˊ ㄓㄤˇ)
　the chief of a Mongol league composed of several tribes

盟主(ㄇㄥˊ ㄓㄨˇ)
　the leader of an alliance

盟誓(ㄇㄥˊ ㄕˋ)
　an oath of mutual devotion; to take an oath; to make a pledge

盟友(ㄇㄥˊ ㄧㄡˇ)
　an ally

盟約(ㄇㄥˊ ㄩㄝ)
　a treaty of alliance

九畫

【盡】 ³⁷³⁰
　ㄐㄧㄣˋ jinn jìn
1. to exhaust; to use up
2. to put to the best use
3. to complete; to finish; to accomplish
4. all; entirely; totally; completely; wholly
5. the utmost

盡本分(ㄐㄧㄣˋ ㄅㄣˇ ㄈㄣˋ)
　to play one's proper role; to do what one is supposed to do, no more and no less

盡命(ㄐㄧㄣˋ ㄇㄧㄥˋ)
　to sacrifice one's own life

盡付東流(ㄐㄧㄣˋ ㄈㄨˋ ㄉㄨㄥ ㄌㄧㄡˊ)
　(literally) all gone with the eastward stream—all in vain

盡頭(ㄐㄧㄣˋ ㄊㄡˊ)
　the extremity; the end

盡年(ㄐㄧㄣˋ ㄋㄧㄢˊ)
　to live out a natural life span; to complete the whole

of the allotted span of life

盡禮(ㄐㄧㄣˋ ㄌㄧˇ)
　very polite; the full observance of the rules of propriety

盡力(ㄐㄧㄣˋ ㄌㄧˋ)
　to make efforts; to exert oneself; to do all one can; to do one's best: 我們將盡力支援你。We'll do our best to help you.

盡力而為(ㄐㄧㄣˋ ㄌㄧˋ ㄦˊ ㄨㄟˊ)or盡力為之(ㄐㄧㄣˋ ㄌㄧˋ ㄨㄟˊ ㄓ)
　to execute or perform with effort; to do one's best

盡量(ㄐㄧㄣˋ ㄌㄧㄤˋ)
　as much as possible; to the utmost 亦作「儘量」

盡歡而散(ㄐㄧㄣˋ ㄏㄨㄢ ㄦˊ ㄙㄢˋ)
　to leave only after each has enjoyed himself to the utmost

盡節(ㄐㄧㄣˋ ㄐㄧㄝˊ)
　to die for chastity

盡淨(ㄐㄧㄣˋ ㄐㄧㄥˋ)
　completely; all together

盡其在我(ㄐㄧㄣˋ ㄑㄧˊ ㄗㄞˋ ㄨㄛˇ)
　to do one's best; to do what one can (and leave the rest to God or Heaven)

盡其所長(ㄐㄧㄣˋ ㄑㄧˊ ㄙㄨㄛˇ ㄔㄤˊ)
　to work or endeavor to the best of one's ability

盡其所有(ㄐㄧㄣˋ ㄑㄧˊ ㄙㄨㄛˇ ㄧㄡˇ)
　to give all one has

盡棄(ㄐㄧㄣˋ ㄑㄧˋ)
　① all wasted; all in vain ② all forgotten

盡情(ㄐㄧㄣˋ ㄑㄧㄥˊ)
　to one's heart's content

盡孝(ㄐㄧㄣˋ ㄒㄧㄠˋ)
　to do one's filial duty: 不要忘記對父母盡孝。Don't forget your duty to your parents.

盡心(ㄐㄧㄣˋ ㄒㄧㄣ)
　to devote all one's energies: 他盡心做一件工作。He devoted his energies to a task.

盡心竭力(ㄐㄧㄣˋ ㄒㄧㄣ ㄐㄧㄝˊ ㄌㄧˋ)
　to devote all the mental and physical energy one can muster; to do one's utmost

盡信書則不如無書(ㄐㄧㄣˋ ㄒㄧㄣˋ ㄕㄨ ㄗㄜˊ ㄅㄨˋ ㄖㄨˊ ㄨˊ ㄕㄨ)
　Believing everything in books is worse than having no books at all.

盡性(ㄐㄧㄣˋ ㄒㄧㄥˋ)
　to fulfill one's nature

盡興(ㄐㄧㄣˋ ㄒㄧㄥˋ)
　to enjoy to one's heart's content: 我們盡興而歸。We returned after thoroughly enjoying ourselves.

皿
部

盡職(ㄐㄧㄣˋ ㄓˊ)
　to do one's duty; having a sense of responsibility; conscientious: 她工作很盡職。She is a conscientious worker.

盡忠(ㄐㄧㄣˋ ㄓㄨㄥ)
　to do one's duty as a subject; to be loyal to the ruler: 他為國盡忠。He was loyal to his country.

盡忠報國(ㄐㄧㄣˋ ㄓㄨㄥ ㄅㄠˋ ㄍㄨㄛˊ)
　to devote oneself to one's country

盡是(ㄐㄧㄣˋ ㄕˋ)
　all are; without exception; to be full of

盡善盡美(ㄐㄧㄣˋ ㄕㄢˋ ㄐㄧㄣˋ ㄇㄟˇ)
　perfectly satisfactory; perfectly good; flawless; perfect

盡述(ㄐㄧㄣˋ ㄕㄨˋ)
　to tell a complete story

盡數(ㄐㄧㄣˋ ㄕㄨˋ)
　fully; the whole; the whole amount

盡日(ㄐㄧㄣˋ ㄖˋ)
　the whole day; all day long

盡人倫(ㄐㄧㄣˋ ㄖㄣˊ ㄌㄨㄣˊ)
　to do what friendship or other human relations dictate

盡人事(ㄐㄧㄣˋ ㄖㄣˊ ㄕˋ)
　to do everything one ought to do (and hope that fate will take care of the rest)

盡人事以聽天命(ㄐㄧㄣˋ ㄖㄣˊ ㄕˋ ㄧˇ ㄊㄧㄥ ㄊㄧㄢ ㄇㄧㄥˋ)
　One does one's best and leaves the rest to Heaven.

盡責任(ㄐㄧㄣˋ ㄗㄜˊ ㄖㄣˋ)
　to do one's duty: 每個人都應該盡責任。Every man should do his duty.

盡瘁(ㄐㄧㄣˋ ㄘㄨㄟˋ)
　to exhaust one's mental energy

盡意(ㄐㄧㄣˋ ㄧˋ)
　① to give full expression to one's ideas ② to one's heart's content

盡義務(ㄐㄧㄣˋ ㄧˋ ㄨˋ)

【皿部】

①to fulfill one's duty; 我們
應盡義務。We should fulfill
our duty. ②to work without
pay

盡言(ㄐㄧㄣˋㄧㄢˊ)
to speak out; to speak up; to
admonish without reserve

【監】 3731
1. ㄐㄧㄢ jian jiān
1. to supervise; to superintend;
to oversee; to direct; to
inspect
2. to confine; to keep in custody; to imprison

監謗(ㄐㄧㄢㄅㄤˋ)
to watch over libelers or
detractors

監票(ㄐㄧㄢㄆㄧㄠˋ)
(in elections) to watch for
irregularities in a voting; to
scrutinize a ballot

監票人(ㄐㄧㄢㄆㄧㄠˋㄖㄣˊ)or 監票員
(ㄐㄧㄢㄆㄧㄠˋㄩㄢˊ)
a ballot supervisor; a scruti-
neer

監犯(ㄐㄧㄢㄈㄢˋ)
a prisoner; a jailbird

監房(ㄐㄧㄢㄈㄤˊ)
a prison cell

監督(ㄐㄧㄢㄉㄨ)
to supervise; to superintend;
to oversee

監盤(ㄐㄧㄢㄅㄢˋ)
to monitor

監牢(ㄐㄧㄢㄌㄠˊ)
a prison; a jail

監臨(ㄐㄧㄢㄌㄧㄣˊ)
to supervise or proctor (a
civil service examination in
former times)

監國(ㄐㄧㄢㄍㄨㄛˊ)
a regent

監管(ㄐㄧㄢㄍㄨㄢˇ)
to take charge of

監工(ㄐㄧㄢㄍㄨㄥ)
① a superintendent or su-
pervisor of a construction
project ②to superintend or
supervise work: 他親自監工。
He superintended all their
work personally.

監考(ㄐㄧㄢㄎㄠˇ)
to proctor or invigilate an
examination

監考員(ㄐㄧㄢㄎㄠˇㄩㄢˊ)
a proctor; an invigilator

監護(ㄐㄧㄢㄏㄨˋ)

custody; to act as the guardian of: 父母對年幼兒女有監護
之責。Parents have the cus-
tody of their young children.

監護人(ㄐㄧㄢㄏㄨˋㄖㄣˊ)
a guardian (of a minor)

監交(ㄐㄧㄢㄐㄧㄠ)
to supervise or witness the
handover (of duties or public property between officials)

監禁(ㄐㄧㄢㄐㄧㄣˋ)
①to confine; to imprison; to
immure ②custody; confine-
ment; imprisonment

監軍(ㄐㄧㄢㄐㄩㄣ)
an inspector—the general of
an army in former times

監修(ㄐㄧㄢㄒㄧㄡ)
①to direct or supervise the
compilation or editing (of
books) ②to direct or supervise repair work

監製(ㄐㄧㄢㄓˋ)
to direct or supervise the
manufacture of

監斬(ㄐㄧㄢㄓㄢˇ)
to supervise the decapitation
of criminals in former times

監察(ㄐㄧㄢㄔㄚˊ)
to supervise; to control; control

監察權(ㄐㄧㄢㄔㄚˊㄑㄩㄢˊ)
the power of control (one of
the five powers of the government specified in the
Constitution of the Republic
of China)

監察使(ㄐㄧㄢㄔㄚˊㄕˇ)or(ㄐㄧㄢㄔㄚˊㄕˇ)
a controlling inspector (appointed to help exercise
the power of control in the
early years of the Republic
of China)

監察人(ㄐㄧㄢㄔㄚˊㄖㄣˊ)
an auditor (in a corpora-
tion)

監察委員(ㄐㄧㄢㄔㄚˊㄨㄟˇㄩㄢˊ)
a member of the Control
Yüan: 他父親做過監察委員。
His father was a member of
the Control Yüan.

監察御史(ㄐㄧㄢㄔㄚˊㄩˋㄕˇ)
an official in charge of the
discipline of public functionaries in former times

監察員(ㄐㄧㄢㄔㄚˊㄩㄢˊ)
an inspector

監察院(ㄐㄧㄢㄔㄚˊㄩㄢˋ)
Control Yüan (one of the
five major branches of the
government of the Republic
of China)

監場(ㄐㄧㄢㄔㄤˊ)or(ㄐㄧㄢㄔㄤˇ)
①to proctor or invigilate an
examination ②a proctor; an
invigilator

監視(ㄐㄧㄢㄕˋ)
①to keep a watchful eye
on; to watch; to keep under
surveillance: 警察嚴密監視那
罪犯。The police kept the
criminal under strict surveillance. ② to monitor

監視器(ㄐㄧㄢㄕˋㄑㄧˋ)
a watchdog

監試(ㄐㄧㄢㄕˋ)
to invigilate; to keep watch
over students at an examination

監事(ㄐㄧㄢㄕˋ)
a supervisor (of a corporation)

監事會(ㄐㄧㄢㄕˋㄏㄨㄟˋ)
a board of supervisors (of a
corporation)

監守自盜(ㄐㄧㄢㄕㄡˇㄗˋㄉㄠˋ)
embezzlement; to pilfer public property one is entrusted
to safeguard

監押(ㄐㄧㄢㄧㄚ)
to keep(a person)in custody

監印(ㄐㄧㄢㄧㄣˋ)
an official in charge of the
official seal

監獄(ㄐㄧㄢㄩˋ)
a prison; a jail: 他們因偷錢被
送進監獄。They were taken
to prison for stealing money.

【監】 3731
2. ㄐㄧㄢˋ jiann jiàn
1. an official position in former times
2. a government establishment
(such as a school) in former
times
3. a eunuch

監本(ㄐㄧㄢˋㄅㄣˇ)
books issued by the Imperial
Academy (國子監) during the
various dynasties

監生(ㄐㄧㄢˋㄕㄥ)

a student of the Imperial Academy (國子監) during the Ming and Ching dynasties

十畫

【盤】 3732
ㄆㄢ parn pán
1. a tray; a plate; a dish
2. twisted; entangled; entwined; intricate; winding; to entangle; to entwine
3. to investigate; to interrogate
4. (said of a chess match, etc.) a round

盤剝剝利(ㄆㄢ ㄅㄛ ㄌㄧˋ ㄌㄧˋ)
to be a Shylock; to exploit

盤駁(ㄆㄢ ㄅㄛˊ)
to interrogate and refute

盤礴(ㄆㄢ ㄅㄛˊ)
vast; extensive

盤馬彎弓(ㄆㄢ ㄇㄚˇ ㄨㄢ ㄍㄨㄥ)
to make a show of readiness to fight; to rattle the saber

盤費(ㄆㄢ ㄈㄟˋ)
traveling expenses

盤點(ㄆㄢ ㄉㄧㄢˇ)
to check; to make an inventory of

盤腿(ㄆㄢ ㄊㄨㄟˇ)
to sit with the legs crossed

盤尼西林(ㄆㄢ ㄋㄧˊ ㄒㄧ ㄌㄧㄣˊ)
penicillin

盤弄(ㄆㄢ ㄋㄨㄥˋ)
①to tamper with ②to provoke

盤根錯節(ㄆㄢ ㄍㄣ ㄘㄨㄛˋ ㄐㄧㄝˊ)
(literally) twisted roots and intricate gnarls—great complexity; very complicated

盤庚(ㄆㄢ ㄍㄥ)
name of a ruler in the Shang Dynasty

盤古(ㄆㄢ ㄍㄨˇ)
Pan Ku, the legendary creator and first ruler of the universe

盤互(ㄆㄢ ㄏㄨˋ)
to entangle each other

盤貨(ㄆㄢ ㄏㄨㄛˋ)
to make an inventory of stock; to take stock

盤獲(ㄆㄢ ㄏㄨㄛˋ)
to catch (a criminal) through investigation

盤桓(ㄆㄢ ㄏㄨㄢˊ)
to linger; 我們在東京盤桓了幾

天,遊覽了各處名勝。We lingered a few days sightseeing in Tokyo.

盤結(ㄆㄢ ㄐㄧㄝˊ)
to join in a coil

盤詰(ㄆㄢ ㄐㄧㄝˊ)
to interrogate closely

盤踞(ㄆㄢ ㄐㄩ)
①to squat with the legs crossed ②to take a fixed position; to be entrenched; to occupy; 敵人盤踞我們的堡壘。The enemy occupied our fort.

盤據(ㄆㄢ ㄐㄩˋ)
to occupy and hold a place (usually said of enemy troops, rebels or bandits)

盤曲(ㄆㄢ ㄑㄩ)
winding; spiraling; coiling

盤膝(ㄆㄢ ㄒㄧ)
to sit with the legs crossed: 他盤膝而坐。He sat with his legs crossed.

盤香(ㄆㄢ ㄒㄧㄤ)
coiled incense

盤旋(ㄆㄢ ㄒㄩㄢˊ)
to circle; to hover around: 兩隻鷹在頭頂盤旋。Two hawks were hovering overhead.

盤眼(ㄆㄢ ㄧㄢˇ)
to examine the account

盤查(ㄆㄢ ㄔㄚˊ)
to question; to cross-examine; to interrogate and search: 警察盤查我疑的人。The policeman questioned a suspicious person.

盤纏(ㄆㄢ ·ㄔㄢ)
traveling expenses

盤川(ㄆㄢ ㄔㄨㄢ)
traveling expenses

盤石(ㄆㄢ ㄕˊ)
a huge circular stone

盤繞(ㄆㄢ ㄖㄠˋ)
to twine; to wind round: 藤葛盤繞在樹幹上。The vines twine round the tree trunk.

盤子(ㄆㄢ ·ㄗ)or 盤兒(ㄆㄢˊㄦ)
a tray; a plate; a dish

盤餐(ㄆㄢ ㄘㄢ)
dishes of food

盤錯(ㄆㄢ ㄘㄨㄛˋ)
entwined; entangled

盤存(ㄆㄢ ㄘㄨㄣˊ)

to take an inventory of

盤算(ㄆㄢ ㄙㄨㄢˋ)
to make a mental calculation; to figure

盤飧(ㄆㄢ ㄙㄨㄣ)
dishes; the food in a dish

盤渦(ㄆㄢ ㄨㄛ)
a whirlpool; an eddy

盤問(ㄆㄢ ㄨㄣˋ)
to interrogate closely

盤紆(ㄆㄢ ㄩ)
winding; circuitous

盤鬱(ㄆㄢ ㄩˋ)
(said of scenic spots) winding and enchanting

盤運(ㄆㄢ ㄩㄣˋ)
to convey; to transport

十一畫

【盥】 3733
ㄍㄨㄢˇ guann guàn
1. to wash one's hands
2. to wash

盥櫛(ㄍㄨㄢˇ ㄐㄧㄝˊ)
to wash one's face and comb one's hair

盥洗(ㄍㄨㄢˇ ㄒㄧˇ)
to wash oneself

盥洗室(ㄍㄨㄢˇ ㄒㄧˇ ㄕˋ)
a washroom; a restroom; a lavatory

盥濯(ㄍㄨㄢˇ ㄓㄨㄛˊ)
to wash; to rinse

盥漱(ㄍㄨㄢˇ ㄕㄨˋ)
to wash the hands and rinse the mouth

【盦】 3734
ㄢ an ān
1. the lid of a caldron
2. a Buddhist cloister for nuns 亦作「庵」

【盧】 3735
ㄌㄨˊ lu lú
1. black
2. a Chinese family name

盧比(ㄌㄨˊ ㄅㄧˇ)
rupee (a monetary unit of India, etc.)

盧布(ㄌㄨˊ ㄅㄨˋ)
ruble (a monetary unit of the Soviet Union)

盧溝橋 or 蘆溝橋(ㄌㄨˊ ㄍㄡ ㄑㄧㄠˊ)
the Marco Polo Bridge (near Peking, where on July 7, 1937, a clash between the Japanese and Chinese troops

皿部

〔目部〕

triggered the Sino-Japanese War of 1937-1945)

盧森堡 (ㄌㄨ ㄙㄣ ㄅㄠˇ)
Luxemburg, Europe

盧梭 (ㄌㄨ ㄙㄨㄛ)
Jean Jacques Rousseau, 1712-1778, French philosopher

盧安達 (ㄌㄨ ㄢ ㄉㄚˊ)
Rwanda

盧昂 (ㄌㄨ ㄤˊ)
Rouen, France

十二畫

【盩】 3736
　　ㄓㄡ **jou zhōu**
the turn of a mountain range

盩厔 (ㄓㄡ ㄓˋ)
name of a county in Shensi

【盪】 3737
　　ㄉㄤˋ **dang dàng**
1. to toss about; to swing
2. to wash

盪盪 (ㄉㄤˋ ㄉㄤˋ)
vast; extensive

盪滌 (ㄉㄤˋ ㄉㄧˊ)
to wash; to rinse; to refresh: 美景可以盪滌你心。The beautiful scenery can refresh your mind.

盪槳 (ㄉㄤˋ ㄐㄧㄤˇ)
to row a boat

盪秋千 (ㄉㄤˋ ㄑㄧㄡ ㄑㄧㄢ)
to swing (in a swing)

盪舟 (ㄉㄤˋ ㄓㄡ)
① to boat ② to move a boat along upon the land

盪漾 (ㄉㄤˋ ㄧㄤˋ)
① to be gently tossed about ② to ripple: 綠油油的稻子在微風中盪漾。The green rice rippled in the breeze.

十四畫

【蠱】 3738
　　ㄍㄨˇ **guu gǔ**
1. a salt pit
2. incompact
3. leisure
4. to drink by sucking

目 部
ㄇㄨˋ **muh mù**

【目】 3739
　　ㄇㄨˋ **muh mù**
1. the eye: 他雙目失明。He is blind in both eyes.
2. to look; to regard; to see: 此事被目為奇蹟。It was regarded as a miracle.
3. a table of contents; a category

目波 (ㄇㄨˋ ㄅㄛ)
glances as bright as dancing waves

目標 (ㄇㄨˋ ㄅㄧㄠ)
① an objective; a target; to target ② an aim; a goal: 他的人生目標是當個大作家。His goal in life is to become a great writer.

目不窺園 (ㄇㄨˋ ㄅㄨˋ ㄎㄨㄟ ㄩㄢˊ)
completely absorbed in study

目不交睫 (ㄇㄨˋ ㄅㄨˋ ㄐㄧㄠ ㄐㄧㄝˊ)
to go completely without sleep

目不見睫 (ㄇㄨˋ ㄅㄨˋ ㄐㄧㄢˋ ㄐㄧㄝˊ)
(literally) The eyes cannot see the eyelashes.—One does not have a correct appraisal of his own ability.

目不暇給 (ㄇㄨˋ ㄅㄨˋ ㄒㄧㄚˊ ㄐㄧˇ)or 目不暇接 (ㄇㄨˋ ㄅㄨˋ ㄒㄧㄚˊ ㄐㄧㄝ)
So many things come into sight that the eyes are kept fully occupied.

目不斜視 (ㄇㄨˋ ㄅㄨˋ ㄒㄧㄝˊ ㄕˋ)
to look steadily forward; to look straight ahead

目不轉睛 (ㄇㄨˋ ㄅㄨˋ ㄓㄨㄢˇ ㄐㄧㄥ)
to gaze steadily; to look attentively

目不識丁 (ㄇㄨˋ ㄅㄨˋ ㄕˋ ㄉㄧㄥ)
(literally) to recognize not even the character 丁—completely illiterate

目迷五色 (ㄇㄨˋ ㄇㄧˊ ㄨˇ ㄙㄜˋ)
so dazzled as to lose clear vision; bewildered by a complicated situation

目瞪口呆 (ㄇㄨˋ ㄉㄥˋ ㄎㄡˇ ㄉㄞ)
dumbfounded; stupefied

目的 (ㄇㄨˋ ㄉㄧˋ)
a purpose; an objective; an end; an aim

目的地 (ㄇㄨˋ ㄉㄧˋ ㄉㄧˋ)
a destination

目的論 (ㄇㄨˋ ㄉㄧˋ ㄌㄨㄣˊ)
(philosophy) teleology

目的物 (ㄇㄨˋ ㄉㄧˋ ㄨˋ)
an objective; an aim

目睹 or 目覩 (ㄇㄨˋ ㄉㄨˇ)
to see directly; to witness; to see with one's own eyes: 他目睹此意外事件。He witnessed the accident.

目逃 (ㄇㄨˋ ㄊㄠˊ)
to look away in shame or awe

目挑心招 (ㄇㄨˋ ㄊㄧㄠ ㄒㄧㄣ ㄓㄠ)
(said of prostitutes) to seduce; to behave coquettishly

目聽 (ㄇㄨˋ ㄊㄧㄥ)
(literally) to hear with the eyes—to know what one is about to say by looking at him

目逆 (ㄇㄨˋ ㄋㄧˋ)
to greet someone with the eyes on his (or her) approach

目力 (ㄇㄨˋ ㄌㄧˋ)
eyesight; vision: 我的目力不佳。I have poor eyesight.

目連救母 (ㄇㄨˋ ㄌㄧㄢˊ ㄐㄧㄡˋ ㄇㄨˇ)
the legend of Moginlin (目犍連), a disciple of Buddha, entering Hell to rescue his own mother

目錄 (ㄇㄨˋ ㄌㄨˋ)
① a table of contents; contents ② a list; a catalogue

目錄學 (ㄇㄨˋ ㄌㄨˋ ㄒㄩㄝˊ)
bibliography

目耕 (ㄇㄨˋ ㄍㄥ)
to read as diligently as someone plows the field

目光 (ㄇㄨˋ ㄍㄨㄤ)
insight; vision; sight: 那是目光短淺的計畫。It is a short-sighted plan.

目光炯炯 (ㄇㄨˋ ㄍㄨㄤ ㄐㄩㄥˇ ㄐㄩㄥˇ)
to have eyes with a piercing gleam

目光如豆 (ㄇㄨˋ ㄍㄨㄤ ㄖㄨˊ ㄉㄡˋ)
to lack insight or vision; shortsighted: 目光如豆的人永不會成功。Those who are shortsighted will never suc-

ceed.

目如炬(ㄇㄨ《ㄨㄜ ㄇㄨ ㄐㄩ)
to have great insight or vision; farsighted

目光銳利(ㄇㄨ《ㄨㄤ ㄖㄨㄟ ㄌㄧ)
to have a penetrating sight; sharp-eyed; sharp-sighted: 他是目光銳利的人。He is a sharp-eyed person.

目眶(ㄇㄨ ㄎㄨㄤ)
the eye sockets

目空一切(ㄇㄨ ㄎㄨㄥ ㄧ ㄑㄧㄝ)
so self-conceited that nothing enters one's eyes; to consider everybody and everything beneath one's notice; to look down on everyone or everything; to be supercilious or arrogant

目擊(ㄇㄨ ㄐㄧ)
to see personally; to witness: 他目擊此意外。He witnessed the accident.

目今(ㄇㄨ ㄐㄧㄣ)
now; the present

目禁(ㄇㄨ ㄐㄧㄣ)
to restrain (someone) by winks or blinks

目鏡(ㄇㄨ ㄐㄧㄥ)
the ocular, or eyepiece (of a microscope)

目前(ㄇㄨ ㄑㄧㄢ)
now; at present: 到目前爲止，我沒有得到他一點音信。I have heard nothing from him up to now.

目下(ㄇㄨ ㄒㄧㄚ)
at the moment; now; at present

目笑(ㄇㄨ ㄒㄧㄠ)
to cast a derisive look

目眩(ㄇㄨ ㄒㄩㄢ)
dazzled

目指氣使(ㄇㄨ ㄓ ㄑㄧ ㄕ)
arrogant; haughty

目中無人(ㄇㄨ ㄓㄨㄥ ㄨ ㄖㄣ)
so arrogant that no one is important in his eyes; to be supercilious; to be overweening

目使頤令(ㄇㄨ ㄕ ㄧ ㄌㄧㄥ)
(literally) giving orders by a look or glance—arrogant; conceited

目濡耳染(ㄇㄨ ㄖㄨ ㄦ ㄖㄢ)
to become familiar with something because of long exposure to it

目眥欲裂(ㄇㄨ ㄗ ㄩ ㄌㄧㄝ)
to show such anger in the eyes that it appears as if they were bursting

目次(ㄇㄨ ㄘ)
a table of contents

目測(ㄇㄨ ㄘㄜ)
to measure distance with the eyes

目送(ㄇㄨ ㄙㄨㄥ)
to follow with the eyes; to gaze after

目迎目送(ㄇㄨ ㄧㄥ ㄇㄨ ㄙㄨㄥ)
to salute an officer with the eyes

目無法紀(ㄇㄨ ㄨ ㄈㄚ ㄐㄧ)
to disregard all laws and regulations; lawless

目無全牛(ㄇㄨ ㄨ ㄑㄩㄢ ㄋㄧㄡ)
(said of an experienced butcher) to see an ox not as a whole (but only as parts to be cut)—to be supremely skilled; dexterous

目無尊長(ㄇㄨ ㄨ ㄗㄨㄣ ㄓㄤ)
to show no respect to elders and superiors

目無餘子(ㄇㄨ ㄨ ㄩ ㄗ)
to despise all others

目語(ㄇㄨ ㄩ)
to converse with the eyes for fear of speaking out under tyranny

二畫

【盯】 3740
ㄉㄧㄥ ding dīng
to stare at; to gaze at; to fix one's eyes on; to keep a close watch: 他兩眼盯着電視。His eyes were fixed on the TV.

盯梢(ㄉㄧㄥ ㄕㄠ)
to shadow somebody; to tail somebody

三畫

【盱】 3741
ㄒㄩ shiu xū
1. to open the eyes wide
2. worried; uneasy; anxious

盱衡(ㄒㄩ ㄏㄥ)
①to look with eyes wide open ②to make a general survey

盯盯(ㄒㄩ ㄒㄩ)
①staring with eyes wide open ②proud and haughty

【盲】 3742
ㄇㄤ mang máng
1. blind; to blind
2. deluded

盲目(ㄇㄤ ㄇㄨ)
①blind ②lacking insight or understanding ③ reckless; aimless

盲目不盲心(ㄇㄤ ㄇㄨ ㄅㄨ ㄇㄤ ㄒㄧㄣ)
blind in the eye but not in the mind

盲目飛行(ㄇㄤ ㄇㄨ ㄈㄟ ㄒㄧㄥ)
instrument flying

盲點(ㄇㄤ ㄉㄧㄢ)or盲斑(ㄇㄤ ㄅㄢ)
(anatomy) a blind spot; a scotoma

盲動(ㄇㄤ ㄉㄨㄥ)
to act blindly or rashly

盲腸(ㄇㄤ ㄔㄤ)
the cecum, or caecum; the vermiform appendix

盲腸割除手術(ㄇㄤ ㄔㄤ ㄍㄜ ㄔㄨ ㄕㄡ ㄕㄨ)
an appendectomy 亦作「闌尾切除手術」

盲腸炎(ㄇㄤ ㄔㄤ ㄧㄢ)
appendicitis

盲人(ㄇㄤ ㄖㄣ)
a blind person

盲人摸象(ㄇㄤ ㄖㄣ ㄇㄛ ㄒㄧㄤ)
to draw a conclusion from incomplete data (as some blind men did about the elephant, each touching merely a small part of the elephant's body)

盲人教育(ㄇㄤ ㄖㄣ ㄐㄧㄠ ㄩ)
the education of the blind

盲人騎瞎馬(ㄇㄤ ㄖㄣ ㄑㄧ ㄒㄧㄚ ㄇㄚ)
(literally) A blind man rides a blind horse.—a very dangerous act

盲從(ㄇㄤ ㄘㄨㄥ)
to follow blindly: 他們盲從他們的領袖。They followed their leaders blindly.

盲啞學校(ㄇㄤ ㄧㄚ ㄒㄩㄝ ㄒㄧㄠ)
a school for the blind and the mute

盲文(ㄇㄤ ㄨㄣ)or盲字(ㄇㄤ ㄗ)
braille 亦作「點字」

【直】 3743
ㄓ jyr zhí

（目部）

1. straight; to straighten: 站直。
Stand up straight!
2. upright and honest; fair; unbiased
3. vertical; longitudinal; from top to bottom
4. outspoken; frank; straightforward: 請你直說吧。Please speak frankly.
5. directly; firsthand: 我直接獲知此事。I learned it firsthand.
6. continuous; uninterrupted
7. stiff; numb: 天太冷，手指都凍直了。It was so cold that my fingers were frozen stiff.
8. just; simply; only; merely
9. a vertical stroke (in Chinese characters)

直筆 (ㄓ ㄅㄧˇ)
unprejudiced or straightforward writing; to write in an unprejudiced or straightforward way

直布羅陀 (ㄓ ㄅㄨˋ ㄌㄨㄛˊ ㄊㄨㄛˊ)
Gibraltar

直布羅陀海峽 (ㄓ ㄅㄨˋ ㄌㄨㄛˊ ㄊㄨㄛˊ ㄏㄞˇ ㄒㄧㄚˊ)
Strait of Gibraltar

直脾氣 (ㄓ ㄆㄧˊ ㄑㄧˋ)
outspoken; frank

直眉瞪眼 (ㄓ ㄇㄟˊ ㄉㄥˋ ㄧㄢˇ)
① to look angry ② to look stupid; to stare blankly; to be stupefied

直髮種 (ㄓ ㄈㄚˇ ㄓㄨㄥˇ)
the Mongolian race (characterized by straight hair)

直奉戰爭 (ㄓ ㄈㄥˋ ㄓㄢˋ ㄓㄥ)
the war between warlords, Tsao Kun (曹錕) and Chang Tso-lin (張作霖) in 1923-1924

直達 (ㄓ ㄉㄚˊ)
to go nonstop to; through: 請買兩張直達車票。Please buy two through tickets.

直達車 (ㄓ ㄉㄚˊ ㄔㄜ)
a nonstop express; a through train, bus, etc.

直待 (ㄓ ㄉㄞˋ)
to go on waiting

直搗黃龍 (ㄓ ㄉㄠˇ ㄏㄨㄤˊ ㄌㄨㄥˊ)
to march to the enemy's heartland

直到 (ㄓ ㄉㄠˋ)
① till; until ② up to

直挺挺 (ㄓ ㄊㄧㄥˇ ㄊㄧㄥˇ)
stiff; straight; stiffly: 他直挺挺地站着。He stands straight.

直通 (ㄓ ㄊㄨㄥ)
to lead directly to; to reach directly

直隸 (ㄓ ㄌㄧˋ)
① to be directly under the jurisdiction of ② former name of Hopeh (河北)

直立 (ㄓ ㄌㄧˋ)
to stand erect

直立莖 (ㄓ ㄌㄧˋ ㄐㄧㄥ)
(botany) an erect stem

直流 (ㄓ ㄌㄧㄡˊ)
(electricity) direct current

直流發電機 (ㄓ ㄌㄧㄡˊ ㄈㄚ ㄉㄧㄢˋ ㄐㄧ)
a direct-current dynamo; a direct-current generator

直流電 (ㄓ ㄌㄧㄡˊ ㄉㄧㄢˋ)
direct current (D.C.)

直話 (ㄓ ㄏㄨㄚˋ)
outspoken remarks; a frank speech

直接 (ㄓ ㄐㄧㄝ)
direct; firsthand; directly: 火車直接開往那裏。The train goes there direct.

直接推理 (ㄓ ㄐㄧㄝ ㄊㄨㄟ ㄌㄧˇ)
immediate reasoning

直接交涉 (ㄓ ㄐㄧㄝ ㄐㄧㄠ ㄕㄜˋ)
direct negotiations: 他們直接交涉和約。They negotiated a peace treaty directly.

直接交易 (ㄓ ㄐㄧㄝ ㄐㄧㄠ ㄧˋ)
direct transaction

直接教學法 (ㄓ ㄐㄧㄝ ㄐㄧㄠˋ ㄒㄩㄝˊ ㄈㄚˇ)
(pedagogy) the direct method

直接選舉 (ㄓ ㄐㄧㄝ ㄒㄩㄢˇ ㄐㄩˇ)
direct election (as distinct from election by an electoral college)

直接證據 (ㄓ ㄐㄧㄝ ㄓㄥˋ ㄐㄩˋ)
direct evidence

直接政治 (ㄓ ㄐㄧㄝ ㄓㄥˋ ㄓˋ)
direct government

直接稅 (ㄓ ㄐㄧㄝ ㄕㄨㄟˋ)
a direct tax: 所得稅是一種直接稅。A tax on income is a direct tax.

直捷 (ㄓ ㄐㄧㄝˊ)
simple and direct; straightforward

直截了當 (ㄓ ㄐㄧㄝˊ ㄌㄧㄠˇ ㄉㄤˋ)
straightforward; flatly; blunt; simple and direct: 你直截了當地說好了。Come

straight to the point.

直交 (ㄓ ㄐㄧㄠ)
(mathematics) orthogonal

直角 (ㄓ ㄐㄧㄠˇ)
a right angle: 那汽車向北作直角轉彎。The car right-angled sharply north.

直角體 (ㄓ ㄐㄧㄠˇ ㄊㄧˇ)
(mathematics) a cuboid

直角三角形 (ㄓ ㄐㄧㄠˇ ㄙㄢ ㄐㄧㄠˇ ㄒㄧㄥˊ)
a right-angled triangle

直諫 (ㄓ ㄐㄧㄢˋ)
to admonish without reserve

直講 (ㄓ ㄐㄧㄤˇ)
to explain (classics) in the vernacular

直徑 (ㄓ ㄐㄧㄥˋ)
① a diameter ② a straight path

直覺 (ㄓ ㄐㄩㄝˊ)
intuition: 她憑著女人的直覺去了解他。She understood him by woman's intuition.

直前 (ㄓ ㄑㄧㄢˊ)
to go straightforward

直去直來 (ㄓ ㄑㄩˋ ㄓ ㄌㄞˊ)
to go and return without undue delay

直系親屬 (ㄓ ㄒㄧˋ ㄑㄧㄣ ㄕㄨˇ)
a direct or lineal relation (as opposed to a collateral relation): 孫子是祖父的直系親屬。A grandson is a lineal descendant of his grandfather.

直轄 (ㄓ ㄒㄧㄚˊ)
to be under the direct control or jurisdiction of

直轄市 (ㄓ ㄒㄧㄚˊ ㄕˋ)
a special municipality (under the direct jurisdiction of the Central Government like a province)

直下 (ㄓ ㄒㄧㄚˋ)
to deteriorate steadily

直銷 (ㄓ ㄒㄧㄠ)
to sell directly or direct sale by a manufacturer instead of through an agent

直線 (ㄓ ㄒㄧㄢˋ)
① a straight line ② steep; sharp: 現在物價直線上漲。Nowadays, prices rise sharply.

直線形 (ㄓ ㄒㄧㄢˋ ㄒㄧㄥˊ)
a rectilinear figure

直心眼兒(ㄓ ㄒㄧㄣ ㄧㄢˇ ㄦ)
honest; upright

直性兒(ㄓ ㄒㄧㄥˋ ㄦ)or直性子(ㄓ ㄒㄧㄥˋ •ㄗ)
straightforward; honest; frank

直須(ㄓ ㄒㄩ)
should then; should immediately

直腰腰兒(ㄓ •ㄧㄠ ㄧㄦ)
to give the waist a stretch —to take a rest

直尺(ㄓ ㄔˇ)
a straightedge

直臣(ㄓ ㄔㄣˊ)
an outspoken subject or courtier

直陳(ㄓ ㄔㄣˊ)
to describe truthfully; to state frankly

直腸(ㄓ ㄔㄤˊ)
the rectum

直腸直肚(ㄓ ㄔㄤˊ ㄓ ㄉㄨˋ)
outspoken; straightforward; frank

直腸癌(ㄓ ㄔㄤˊ ㄞˊ)
cancer of the rectum

直腸炎(ㄓ ㄔㄤˊ ㄧㄢˊ)
rectitis; proctitis

直是(ㄓ ㄕˋ)
it is always

直視(ㄓ ㄕˋ)
to look steadily at

直受(ㄓ ㄕㄡˋ)
①to accept oppression meekly ②to fail to return a salutation or gift

直上青雲(ㄓ ㄕㄤˋ ㄑㄧㄥ ㄩㄣˊ)
to hit the highest literary honors

直上直下(ㄓ ㄕㄤˋ ㄓ ㄒㄧㄚˋ)
very steep

直昇機(ㄓ ㄕㄥ ㄐㄧ)
a helicopter

直昇機坪(ㄓ ㄕㄥ ㄐㄧ ㄆㄧㄥˊ)or直昇機場(ㄓ ㄕㄥ ㄐㄧ ㄔㄤˇ)
a heliport; a helipad

直書(ㄓ ㄕㄨ)
to write straightforwardly

直抒己見(ㄓ ㄕㄨ ㄐㄧˇ ㄐㄧㄢˋ)
to state one's opinions straightforwardly

直屬(ㄓ ㄕㄨˇ)
to be under the direct control or jurisdiction of

直率(ㄓ ㄕㄨㄞˋ)

frank; outspoken; straightforward; candid: 請直率地告訴我。Please tell me frankly.

直爽(ㄓ ㄕㄨㄤˇ)
straightforward; frank; forthright: 他的性格直爽。He has a forthright character.

直認不諱(ㄓ ㄖㄣˋ ㄅㄨˋ ㄏㄨㄟˋ)
to plead guilty to a charge

直入(ㄓ ㄖㄨˋ)
to go right in

直譯(ㄓ ㄧˋ)
literal translation; verbatim translation; word-for-word translation

直言(ㄓ ㄧㄢˊ)
①to speak out; to speak bluntly: 恕我直言。Excuse me for speaking bluntly. ②outspoken remarks; frank statement

直言不諱(ㄓ ㄧㄢˊ ㄅㄨˋ ㄏㄨㄟˋ)
to speak plainly and frankly; not to mince words

直言無隱(ㄓ ㄧㄢˊ ㄨˊ ㄧㄣˇ)
to tell the truth without reservation

直皖戰爭(ㄓ ㄨㄢˇ ㄓㄢˋ ㄓㄥ)
the war between warlords Tsao Kun (曹錕) and Tuan Chi-jui (段祺瑞) in 1920

直喻(ㄓ ㄩˋ)
a simile 亦作「明喻」

四畫

【相】 3744
1. ㄒㄧㄤ shiang xiāng
1. each other; one another; mutually; reciprocal: 我們兩人素不相識。We do not know each other.
2. substance

相伴(ㄒㄧㄤ ㄅㄢˋ)
to accompany somebody; to be a companion of each other

相比(ㄒㄧㄤ ㄅㄧˇ)
to compare with each other: 兩者相差懸殊，無法相比。There's no comparison between the two.

相並(ㄒㄧㄤ ㄅㄧㄥˋ)
abreast; side by side

相陪(ㄒㄧㄤ ㄆㄟˊ)
in the company of; accompanied by

相配(ㄒㄧㄤ ㄆㄟˋ)
to match well: 他們是很相配的一對夫妻。They are a well-matched couple.

相撲(ㄒㄧㄤ ㄆㄨ)
to wrestle with each other

相罵(ㄒㄧㄤ ㄇㄚˋ)
to revile each other; to abuse each other

相煩(ㄒㄧㄤ ㄈㄢˊ)
to trouble someone with requests; to ask for a favor

相反(ㄒㄧㄤ ㄈㄢˇ)
contrary; opposed to each other; contradictory: 結果與我們預期的相反。The result was contrary to our expectations.

相反相成(ㄒㄧㄤ ㄈㄢˇ ㄒㄧㄤ ㄔㄥˊ)
(said of two things) to be both contrary and complementary to each other; to oppose each other and yet also complement each other

相反詞(ㄒㄧㄤ ㄈㄢˇ ㄘˊ)
an antonym

相仿(ㄒㄧㄤ ㄈㄤˇ)
alike; similar: 他們年紀相仿。They are about the same age.

相逢(ㄒㄧㄤ ㄈㄥˊ)
to meet each other; to come across: 他們的車子在狹路相逢。Their cars met on the narrow road.

相符(ㄒㄧㄤ ㄈㄨˊ)
to tally; to correspond; to agree; to match: 他的陳述與事實相符。His statement tallies with the facts.

相輔相成(ㄒㄧㄤ ㄈㄨˇ ㄒㄧㄤ ㄔㄥˊ)
to complement each other; to reciprocate and complement

相打(ㄒㄧㄤ ㄉㄚˇ)
to have a fight: 你們爲何又相打了？Why did you have a fight again?

相得(ㄒㄧㄤ ㄉㄜˊ)
harmonious; friendly

相得益彰(ㄒㄧㄤ ㄉㄜˊ ㄧˋ ㄓㄤ)
Each gains in appearance from the presence of the other. 或 Each complements the other.

相待(ㄒㄧㄤ ㄉㄞˋ)
to treat (a person): 請別把我

〔目部〕

〔目部〕

當小孩相待。Please don't treat me as a child.

相當 (ㄒㄧㄤ ㄉㄤ)
①to balance; equivalent; to match; to correspond to: 得失相當。The gains balance the losses. ②considerable; to a great extent ③appropriate; fit; suitable

相等 (ㄒㄧㄤ ㄉㄥˇ)
equal; equivalent: 他把蛋糕切成相等的兩分。He divided the cake into two equal parts.

相抵 (ㄒㄧㄤ ㄉㄧˇ)
to offset; to cancel each other; to counterbalance: 這兩個數彼此相抵。These two figures cancel each other.

相對 (ㄒㄧㄤ ㄉㄨㄟˋ)
①corresponding ②relative ③opposite; face to face: 這兩個男孩相對而坐。The two boys sit opposite each other.

相對論 (ㄒㄧㄤ ㄉㄨㄟˋ ㄌㄨㄣˊ)
the theory of relativity

相對基金 (ㄒㄧㄤ ㄉㄨㄟˋ ㄐㄧ ㄐㄧㄣ)
a counterpart fund

相投 (ㄒㄧㄤ ㄊㄡˊ)
congenial; compatible

相談 (ㄒㄧㄤ ㄊㄢˊ)
to converse; to talk together: 他們相談了一會兒。They talked together for a short time.

相提並論 (ㄒㄧㄤ ㄊㄧˊ ㄅㄧㄥˋ ㄌㄨㄣˊ)
mentioned and discussed as related things; to mention (two things or persons of different worth) in the same breath: 這兩件事不能相提並論。These two things cannot be mentioned in the same breath.

相托 (ㄒㄧㄤ ㄊㄨㄛ)
to entrust

相通 (ㄒㄧㄤ ㄊㄨㄥ)
to communicate with each other; to be interlinked: 這兩個房間有門相通。The two rooms open into each other.

相同 (ㄒㄧㄤ ㄊㄨㄥˊ)
①the same; identical: 這兩個學生在這個問題上觀點相同。The two students have the same views on this question. ②similar; alike

相賴 (ㄒㄧㄤ ㄌㄞˋ)
to depend on each other

相連 (ㄒㄧㄤ ㄌㄧㄢˊ)
connected; joined; linked: 兩地有橋樑相連。The two places are linked by a bridge.

相隔 (ㄒㄧㄤ ㄍㄜˊ)
to be separated by; to be apart; to be at a distance of: 這個小鎮與市區相隔十哩。The small town is ten miles apart from downtown.

相告 (ㄒㄧㄤ ㄍㄠˋ)
to tell; to pass information

相干 (ㄒㄧㄤ ㄍㄢ)
related; connected; to have to do with: 這兩個問題互不相干。The two problems are not related to each other.

相顧失色 (ㄒㄧㄤ ㄍㄨˋ ㄕ ㄙㄜˋ)
to look at each other in dismay

相關 (ㄒㄧㄤ ㄍㄨㄢ)
related; connected: 公共衛生和國民健康密切相關。Public health has a direct bearing on the citizens' health.

相尅 (ㄒㄧㄤ ㄎㄜˋ)
mutually destructive

相看 (ㄒㄧㄤ ㄎㄢˋ)
①to look at each other ②to appraise each other (said of a man and a woman in a meeting arranged by the matchmaker)

相好 (ㄒㄧㄤ ㄏㄠˇ)
①to be on friendly terms ②a good friend; a lover; a sweetheart ③to have an affair with

相互 (ㄒㄧㄤ ㄏㄨˋ)
each other; one another; mutually; reciprocally; mutual; reciprocal: 這次的討論會增進相互的了解。The discussion meeting promoted mutual understanding.

相互關係 (ㄒㄧㄤ ㄏㄨˋ ㄍㄨㄢ ㄒㄧˋ)
mutual relation; correlation: 氣候與農作物間有極密切的相互關係。There is a close correlation between climate and crops.

相互信任 (ㄒㄧㄤ ㄏㄨˋ ㄒㄧㄣˋ ㄖㄣˋ)
mutual credits

相會 (ㄒㄧㄤ ㄏㄨㄟˋ)
to meet together; to meet each other

相繼 (ㄒㄧㄤ ㄐㄧˋ)

in succession; one after another: 代表們相繼發言。The representatives spoke in succession.

相偕 (ㄒㄧㄤ ㄐㄧㄝ) or (ㄒㄧㄤ ㄐㄧㄝˊ)
both; together

相交 (ㄒㄧㄤ ㄐㄧㄠ)
①to intersect: 這條路與主要街道相交。This road intersects main streets. ②to make friends with each other; to become associated with each other: 他們相交有年。They have made friends with each other for years.

相較 (ㄒㄧㄤ ㄐㄧㄠˋ)
to compare with each other

相救 (ㄒㄧㄤ ㄐㄧㄡˋ)
to rescue; to help out of difficulty

相煎太急 (ㄒㄧㄤ ㄐㄧㄢ ㄊㄞˋ ㄐㄧˊ)
to torment a person too hard

相間 (ㄒㄧㄤ ㄐㄧㄢˋ)
spaced in-between; to alternate

相見恨晚 (ㄒㄧㄤ ㄐㄧㄢˋ ㄏㄣˋ ㄨㄢˇ)
to regret having not met earlier

相近 (ㄒㄧㄤ ㄐㄧㄣˋ)
close (in amount, degree, quality, etc.); approximate: 得分相近。The score was very close.

相將 (ㄒㄧㄤ ㄐㄧㄤ)
together; both

相敬如賓 (ㄒㄧㄤ ㄐㄧㄥˋ ㄖㄨˊ ㄅㄧㄣ)
(said of a married couple) to respect each other as if the other were a guest

相距 (ㄒㄧㄤ ㄐㄩˋ)
distance between two points; away from: 這兩棵樹相距二十公尺。The distance between the two trees is 20 meters.

相聚 (ㄒㄧㄤ ㄐㄩˋ)
to meet together; to assemble

相切 (ㄒㄧㄤ ㄑㄧㄝ)
(geometry) to be tangent

相求 (ㄒㄧㄤ ㄑㄧㄡˊ)
to ask for a favor; to beg; to entreat: 他有事相求於我。He entreated a favor of me.

相親相愛 (ㄒㄧㄤ ㄑㄧㄣ ㄒㄧㄤ ㄞˋ)
to be kind to each other and love each other

相去無幾(ㄒㄧㄤ ㄑㄩˋ ㄨˊ ㄐㄧˇ)
The difference is insignificant.

相覷(ㄒㄧㄤ ㄑㄩˋ)
to look at each other

相勸(ㄒㄧㄤ ㄑㄩㄢˋ)
to persuade; to offer advice:
我昨天對他好言相勸。She offered him well-meaning advice yesterday.

相信(ㄒㄧㄤ ㄒㄧㄣˋ)
to believe；to have faith in:
我不十分相信他。I can't quite believe him.

相向(ㄒㄧㄤ ㄒㄧㄤˋ)
to face each other

相像(ㄒㄧㄤ ㄒㄧㄤˋ)
to resemble; to be similar; to be alike: 這兩幅畫很相像。These two pictures are very much alike.

相形見絀(ㄒㄧㄤ ㄒㄧㄥˊ ㄐㄧㄢˋ ㄔㄨˋ)
found to be inferior by comparison; to be outshone

相形之下(ㄒㄧㄤ ㄒㄧㄥˊ ㄓ ㄒㄧㄚˋ)
by comparison; when compared; in comparison with

相繼(ㄒㄧㄤ ㄐㄧˋ)
①to inherit ②to continue or succeed one after another

相知(ㄒㄧㄤ ㄓ)
①bosom friends; great friends ②to know each other well: 相知恨晚。It is much regretted that we have not known earlier.

相爭(ㄒㄧㄤ ㄓㄥ)
to fight each other over something; to quarrel; to argue vehemently

相助(ㄒㄧㄤ ㄓㄨˋ)
to help; to help each other:
多謝你大力相助。Thank you very much for your great help.

相撞(ㄒㄧㄤ ㄓㄨㄤˋ)
to collide with each other

相持不下(ㄒㄧㄤ ㄔˊ ㄅㄨˋ ㄒㄧㄚˋ)
persistently opposing each other with neither giving way; to be at a stalemate (or deadlock): 這兩派相持不下。The two parties are at a deadlock.

相差(ㄒㄧㄤ ㄔㄚ)
to differ

相稱(ㄒㄧㄤ ㄔㄣˋ)
to fit each other; to match each other; to be symmetrical: 這兩種布配在一起很相稱。The two kinds of cloth match very well.

相處(ㄒㄧㄤ ㄔㄨˇ)
to spend time together; to live together; to get along with: 他這個人不好相處。He is difficult to get along with.

相傳(ㄒㄧㄤ ㄔㄨㄢˊ)
①(said of a report) to be transmitted from person to person或It is said that.... or Legend has it that.... ②to be passed or handed down from generation to generation

相視(ㄒㄧㄤ ㄕˋ)
to look at each other

相識(ㄒㄧㄤ ㄕˊ)
①to know each other; to be acquainted with each other:
我們素不相識。We are not acquainted with each other.
②an acquaintance: 他是我們的老相識。He is our old acquaintance.

相善(ㄒㄧㄤ ㄕㄢˋ)
on friendly terms; on good terms

相商(ㄒㄧㄤ ㄕㄤ)
to confer; to exchange views; to consult: 我有要事相商。I have something important to consult with you.

相生相剋(ㄒㄧㄤ ㄕㄥ ㄒㄧㄤ ㄎㄜˋ)
mutual production and destruction (as among the five elements); mutual promotion and restraint

相率(ㄒㄧㄤ ㄕㄨㄞˋ)
leading one another; together

相濡以沫(ㄒㄧㄤ ㄖㄨˊ ㄧˇ ㄇㄛˋ)
to help each other when both are in humble circumstances

相若(ㄒㄧㄤ ㄖㄨㄛˋ)
similar; alike: 這兩兄弟長相相若。The two brothers look alike.

相贈(ㄒㄧㄤ ㄗㄥˋ)
to present a gift; to give a present: 他以金錢相贈。He presented me with a gold watch.

相左(ㄒㄧㄤ ㄗㄨㄛˇ)
to disagree; to differ; to be at odds with; to conflict with each other

相思(ㄒㄧㄤ ㄙ)
to pine for each other; to miss each other; to be in love with each other

相思病(ㄒㄧㄤ ㄙ ㄅㄧㄥˋ)
lovesickness

相思鳥(ㄒㄧㄤ ㄙ ㄋㄧㄠˇ)
a lovebird (any of small parrots that show great affection for their mates)

相思樹(ㄒㄧㄤ ㄙ ㄕㄨˋ)
①Abrus precatorius ②an acacia

相思子(ㄒㄧㄤ ㄙ ㄗˇ)or相思豆(ㄒㄧㄤ ㄙ ㄉㄡˋ)
red beans; seeds of Abrus precatorius; jequirities; love peas 亦作「紅豆」

相似(ㄒㄧㄤ ㄙˋ)
alike; similar: 他們面貌相似。They look alike.

相似字(ㄒㄧㄤ ㄙˋ ㄗˋ)
a synonym

相似詞(ㄒㄧㄤ ㄙˋ ㄘˊ)
a synonymous phrase; a synonym

相愛(ㄒㄧㄤ ㄞˋ)
to love each other

相安無事(ㄒㄧㄤ ㄢ ㄨˊ ㄕˋ)
at peace with each other

相依(ㄒㄧㄤ ㄧ)
to depend on each other; to be interdependent: 我們唇齒相依。We are as closely related to each other as lips and teeth.

相依為命(ㄒㄧㄤ ㄧ ㄨㄟˊ ㄇㄧㄥˋ)
to rely upon each other for life

相宜(ㄒㄧㄤ ㄧˊ)
fitting; proper; appropriate

相邀(ㄒㄧㄤ ㄧㄠ)
to invite

相沿(ㄒㄧㄤ ㄧㄢˊ)
to pass down from generation to generation without change

相沿成習(ㄒㄧㄤ ㄧㄢˊ ㄔㄥˊ ㄒㄧˊ)
to have come down from the past and become customary

相印(ㄒㄧㄤ ㄧㄣˋ)
①to bear testimony or witness for each other ②to fit

〔目部〕

〔目部〕

or match each other completely (as two hearts)

相迎(ㄒㄧㄤ ㄧㄥˊ)
to welcome; to greet

相應(ㄒㄧㄤ ㄧㄥˋ)
①(documentary usage) should ②to support each other ③corresponding; relevant

相應不理(ㄒㄧㄤ ㄧㄥˋ ㄅㄨˋ ㄌㄧˇ)
to disregard another's request (a phrase common in official communications); to ignore; to pay no heed to

相映成趣(ㄒㄧㄤ ㄧㄥˋ ㄔㄥˊ ㄑㄩˋ)
to form an interesting or delightful contrast

相違(ㄒㄧㄤ ㄨㄟˊ)
①to disagree; to differ ②to be parted; to be separated

相維(ㄒㄧㄤ ㄨㄟˊ)
to support each other

相與(ㄒㄧㄤ ㄩˇ)
①to get along with: 他這個人難相與。He is extremely difficult to get along with. ②a friend ③together

相遇(ㄒㄧㄤ ㄩˋ)
to meet each other

相約(ㄒㄧㄤ ㄩㄝ)
to reach an agreement; to make an appointment

【相】 3744
2. ㄒㄧㄤ shiang xiàng
1. to examine; to study; to read
2. a countenance; facial features; looks; appearance; bearing; posture: 這個人一臉福相。The man has a countenance of good luck.
3. the prime minister (in feudal times)
4. to assist; to help

相片(ㄒㄧㄤˋ ㄆㄧㄢ)
a photograph; a photo

相貌(ㄒㄧㄤˋ ㄇㄠˋ)
a countenance; a physiognomy; a face; facial features: 他的相貌很端正。He has very regular features.

相貌堂堂(ㄒㄧㄤˋ ㄇㄠˋ ㄊㄤˊ ㄊㄤˊ)
to have a dignified appearance

相面(ㄒㄧㄤˋ ㄇㄧㄢˋ)
to practice physiognomy; to tell somebody's fortune by

reading his face

相命(ㄒㄧㄤˋ ㄇㄧㄥˋ)
fortunetelling

相法(ㄒㄧㄤˋ ㄈㄚˇ)
physiognomy

相夫教子(ㄒㄧㄤˋ ㄈㄨ ㄐㄧㄠˋ ㄗˇ)
to help the husband and teach the children—the duty of a wife

相府(ㄒㄧㄤˋ ㄈㄨˇ)
an influential courtier's mansion; a prime minister's residence

相臺(ㄒㄧㄤˋ ㄊㄞˊ)
a tower built by Tsao Tsao (曹操) in what is Honan today

相體裁衣(ㄒㄧㄤˋ ㄊㄧˇ ㄘㄞˊ ㄧ)
to decide the quantity of materials needed before proceeding to do something

相女配夫(ㄒㄧㄤˋ ㄋㄩˇ ㄆㄟˋ ㄈㄨ)
Study your own daughter properly when finding her a husband.

相國(ㄒㄧㄤˋ ㄍㄨㄛˊ)
the prime minister (a term of respect)

相公(ㄒㄧㄤˋ ㄍㄨㄥ)
①(ㄒㄧㄤˋ ㄍㄨㄥ) the premier ②(ㄒㄧㄤˋ ㄍㄨㄥ) ⓐ a young gentleman (a term common in operas and old novels) ⓑ (slang) a catamite ⓒ a mahjong player who unintentionally takes in the wrong number of dominos and is thus disqualified in a game

相機(ㄒㄧㄤˋ ㄐㄧ)
①to watch for the good chance for action ②a camera

相機行事(ㄒㄧㄤˋ ㄐㄧ ㄒㄧㄥˊ ㄕˋ)
to act as circumstances dictate

相親(ㄒㄧㄤˋ ㄑㄧㄣ)
an interview prior to marriage; to size up a prospective mate in an arranged meeting

相紙(ㄒㄧㄤˋ ㄓˇ)
(photography) printing paper; photographic paper

相士(ㄒㄧㄤˋ ㄕˋ)
①a fortune-teller: 他從不相信相士的話。He never believes the fortune-teller's

words. ②to appraise a person's latent ability

相手術(ㄒㄧㄤˋ ㄕㄡˇ ㄕㄨˋ)
palmistry

相聲(ㄒㄧㄤˋ ㄕㄥ)
a Chinese comic dialogue; a cross talk

相術(ㄒㄧㄤˋ ㄕㄨˋ)
physiognomy

相人(ㄒㄧㄤˋ ㄖㄣˊ)
to practice physiognomy

相爺(ㄒㄧㄤˋ ㄧㄝˊ)
the prime minister

相印(ㄒㄧㄤˋ ㄧㄣˋ)
the prime minister's seal

【眄】 3745
ㄒㄧˋ shih xì
to look in anger

【盼】 3746
ㄆㄢˋ pann pàn
1. to look
2. (descriptive of the black and white of the eyes) well defined
3. to hope; to look for; to expect

盼禱(ㄆㄢˋ ㄉㄠˇ)
(a conventional phrase in formal letters) to hope

盼頭(ㄆㄢˋ ·ㄊㄡ)
hope; good prospects 亦作「盼兒」: 我覺得這事有盼頭了。I feel this business is looking hopeful now.

盼念(ㄆㄢˋ ㄋㄧㄢˋ)
to hope; to long for

盼望(ㄆㄢˋ ㄨㄤˋ)
to hope; to wish

【眄】 3747
ㄇㄧㄢˇ mean miǎn
1. to look askance; to ogle
2. to look

眄盹(ㄇㄧㄢˇ ㄇㄧㄢˇ)
①looking askance ②looking dull

眄眠(ㄇㄧㄢˇ ㄋㄧˋ)
to look askance

眄睞(ㄇㄧㄢˇ ㄌㄞˋ)
looking concerned

【眇】 3748
ㄇㄧㄠˇ meau miǎo
1. tiny; fine; small; unimportant
2. blind in one eye

眇眇(ㄇㄧㄠˇ ㄇㄧㄠˇ)
①tiny ②far; distant; high

眇眇忽忽(ㄇㄧㄠˇ ㄇㄧㄠˇ ㄏㄨ ㄏㄨ)

indistinct; too small to identify

眇乎其小(ㄇㄧㄠˇ ㄏㄨ ㄑㄧ ㄒㄧㄠˇ)
How small it is! or How insignificant it is!

眇小(ㄇㄧㄠˇ ㄒㄧㄠˇ)
very small; tiny; insignificant: 他們成功的希望很眇小。
There is small hope of success for them.

【眈】 3749
ㄉㄢ dan dān
to look downward

眈眈(ㄉㄢ ㄉㄢ)
eyeing gloatingly; looking at greedily; staring

【眊】 3750
ㄇㄠˋ maw mào
1. dim-sighted; eyes not seeing very clearly; dull and mixed-up
2. same as 耄—aged

眊眊(ㄇㄠˋ ㄇㄠˋ)
①unable to see clearly ②dull and mixed-up, probably because of old age

眊瞆(ㄇㄠˋ ㄍㄨㄟˋ)
dim-sighted and hard of hearing

【眕】 3751
ㄉㄨㄣˇ doen dǔn
to doze: 他伏在書上打眕。He dozed over a book.

眕兒(ㄉㄨㄣˇㄦ)
a doze; a nap: 他總是在上課時打眕兒。He always fell into a doze in his classes.

眕睡(ㄉㄨㄣˇ ㄕㄨㄟˋ)
to doze; to nod; a nap

【盾】 3752
ㄕㄨㄣˇ shoen shǔn
(又讀 ㄉㄨㄣˇ duenn dǔn)
1. a shield; a buckler
2. a guilder, a monetary unit in Holland

盾牌(ㄉㄨㄣˇ ㄆㄞˊ)
①a shield ②(figuratively) a pretext; an excuse

【省】 3753
1. ㄕㄥˇ sheeng shěng
1. a province; provincial
2. economical; frugal; to economize: 學生應當能省則省。Students should economize wherever possible.
3. to save; to omit; to reduce; to avoid; to abridge: 這個字

不能省。The word cannot be omitted.

省不了(ㄕㄥˇ ㄅㄨˋ ㄌㄧㄠˇ)
unable to economize any further

省分(ㄕㄥˇ ㄈㄣ)
a province

省得(ㄕㄥˇ ㄉㄜ˙)
①lest ②to avoid; to save (trouble, etc.)

省道(ㄕㄥˇ ㄉㄠˋ)
a provincial highway; an interprovincial highway

省黨部(ㄕㄥˇ ㄉㄤˇ ㄅㄨˋ)
provincial headquarters of a political party

省力(ㄕㄥˇ ㄌㄧˋ)
to save energy or labor; labor-saving: 這種機器省力不少。The machine saves a lot of labor.

省立學校(ㄕㄥˇ ㄌㄧˋ ㄒㄩㄝˊ ㄒㄧㄠˋ)
a provincial school

省料(ㄕㄥˇ ㄌㄧㄠˋ)
to save material

省令(ㄕㄥˇ ㄌㄧㄥˋ)
orders issued by the provincial government

省略(ㄕㄥˇ ㄌㄩㄝˋ)
to omit; to abridge; omission; abridgment

省略符號(ㄕㄥˇ ㄌㄩㄝˋ ㄈㄨˊ ㄏㄠˋ)
①an ellipsis (...); an apostrophe (') ②(music) an abbreviation

省略推理(ㄕㄥˇ ㄌㄩㄝˋ ㄊㄨㄟ ㄌㄧˇ)
(logic) an enthymeme

省略算(ㄕㄥˇ ㄌㄩㄝˋ ㄙㄨㄢˋ)
(mathematics) an approximation

省工夫是(ㄕㄥˇ ㄍㄨㄥ ㄈㄨ˙)
to save time

省會(ㄕㄥˇ ㄏㄨㄟˋ)
the seat of the provincial government; a provincial capital; the capital city of a province

省界(ㄕㄥˇ ㄐㄧㄝˋ)
provincial boundaries

省減(ㄕㄥˇ ㄐㄧㄢˇ)
to reduce; to cut (expenses, a budget, etc.); to lessen; to practice austerity; to economize

省儉(ㄕㄥˇ ㄐㄧㄢˇ)
frugal; frugality; thrifty

省錢(ㄕㄥˇ ㄑㄧㄢˊ)
to save money; economical

省卻(ㄕㄥˇ ㄑㄩㄝˋ)
to avoid (trouble, etc.); to save (time, etc.): 此書爲教師省卻許多麻煩。The book saves the teacher much trouble.

省下(ㄕㄥˇ ㄒㄧㄚˋ)
to save (money)

省心(ㄕㄥˇ ㄒㄧㄣ)
to save cares or worries; to save further thought

省治(ㄕㄥˇ ㄓˋ)
the seat of the provincial government; the capital city of a province

省長(ㄕㄥˇ ㄓㄤˇ)
the governor of a province in the early republican years

省政府(ㄕㄥˇ ㄓㄥˋ ㄈㄨˇ)
the provincial government

省主席(ㄕㄥˇ ㄓㄨˇ ㄒㄧˊ)
the governor of a province

省吃儉用(ㄕㄥˇ ㄔ ㄐㄧㄢˇ ㄩㄥˋ)
frugal and thrifty; to practice austerity in every respect

省城(ㄕㄥˇ ㄔㄥˊ)
the city in which the provincial government is located; a provincial capital

省時(ㄕㄥˇ ㄕˊ)
to save time; timesaving: 開車比走路省時。It will save time if we drive the car instead of walking.

省事(ㄕㄥˇ ㄕˋ)
①to save trouble: 這樣可以省事不少。This can save me a lot of trouble. ②easy

省試(ㄕㄥˇ ㄕˋ)
a provincial examination (for civil officials, etc.)

省議會(ㄕㄥˇ ㄧˋ ㄏㄨㄟˋ)
the provincial assembly

省議員(ㄕㄥˇ ㄧˋ ㄩㄢˊ)
a provincial assemblyman; a member of a provincial assembly

省油(ㄕㄥˇ ㄧㄡˊ)
low in fuel consumption; to save fuel

省油燈(ㄕㄥˇ ㄧㄡˊ ㄉㄥ)
(slang) an oil-saving lamp —a fellow who causes the least trouble

〔目部〕

【目部】

省文(ㄕㄥ ㄨㄣˊ)
an abridged expression; elliptical

省垣(ㄕㄥ ㄩㄢˊ)
the seat of the provincial government; the capital city of a province

省用(ㄕㄥ ㄩㄥˋ)
to save; to economize

【省】 3753
2. ㄒㄧㄥˇ shiing xíng

1. to examine (oneself, etc.); to reflect; to introspect; to consider
2. to understand; to know
3. to visit (one's seniors, etc.)
4. to test; an examination
5. memory

省墓(ㄒㄧㄥˇ ㄇㄨˋ)
to visit the graves of one's ancestors

省會(ㄒㄧㄥˇ ㄏㄨㄟˋ)
① to instruct; to exhort ② to understand; to know

省親(ㄒㄧㄥˇ ㄑㄧㄣ)
to visit one's senior relatives —especially parents

省察(ㄒㄧㄥˇ ㄔㄚˊ)
① to examine; to study; to observe ② to introspect; to make self-examination

省事(ㄒㄧㄥˇ ㄕˋ)
clever and understanding; perceptive and alert—observant; conscious

省視(ㄒㄧㄥˇ ㄕˋ)
to examine; to survey; to inspect; to visit

省悟(ㄒㄧㄥˇ ㄨˋ)
to realize; realization; to awaken to (truth, etc.); awakening

【眉】 3754
ㄇㄟˊ mei méi

1. eyebrows
2. the side
3. the top margin of a printed page in a book
4. a rare Chinese family name

眉筆(ㄇㄟˊ ㄅㄧˇ)
an eyebrow pencil

眉批(ㄇㄟˊ ㄆㄧ)
the running comment on the upper margin of a printed page in a book

眉毛(ㄇㄟˊ ㄇㄠˊ)
the eyebrows

眉目(ㄇㄟˊ ㄇㄨˋ)
① a general facial appearance ② arrangement, order or sequence of things; a general sketch or idea of things: 我的論文已有眉目了。I have had a general sketch for my treatise. ③ close or near at hand ④ the sign of a positive outcome: 我的計畫有眉目了。My plan is beginning to take shape.

眉目傳情(ㄇㄟˊ ㄇㄨˋ ㄔㄨㄢˊ ㄑㄧㄥˊ)
to make sheep's eyes (at someone); to converse with eyes (between a man and a woman); eloquent eyes

眉目如畫(ㄇㄟˊ ㄇㄨˋ ㄖㄨˊ ㄏㄨㄚˋ)
as pretty as a picture

眉飛色舞(ㄇㄟˊ ㄈㄟ ㄙㄜˋ ㄨˇ)
to be beside oneself with joy; to be overjoyed; to be enraptured; to be exultant

眉黛(ㄇㄟˊ ㄉㄞˋ)
painted eyebrows; pretty eyebrows

眉頭(ㄇㄟˊ ㄊㄡˊ)
the space between the eyebrows

眉頭不展(ㄇㄟˊ ㄊㄡˊ ㄅㄨˋ ㄓㄢˇ)
with knitted brows—worried; unhappy

眉來眼去(ㄇㄟˊ ㄌㄞˊ ㄧㄢˇ ㄑㄩˋ)
(between a man and a woman) to converse with eyes; to make passes both ways

眉高眼低(ㄇㄟˊ ㄍㄠ ㄧㄢˇ ㄉㄧ)
a kind of facial expression

眉開眼笑(ㄇㄟˊ ㄎㄞ ㄧㄢˇ ㄒㄧㄠˋ) or 眉花眼笑(ㄇㄟˊ ㄏㄨㄚ ㄧㄢˇ ㄒㄧㄠˋ)
very happy, joyful or jubilant

眉急(ㄇㄟˊ ㄐㄧˊ)
very urgent or imminent (predicaments)

眉睫(ㄇㄟˊ ㄐㄧㄝˊ)
① very close, imminent or urgent: 這危險迫在眉睫。This is an imminent danger. ② eyebrows and eyelashes

眉蹙(ㄇㄟˊ ㄐㄧˋ)
to knit one's eyebrows—pensive, sad or worried

眉清目秀(ㄇㄟˊ ㄑㄧㄥ ㄇㄨˋ ㄒㄧㄡˋ) or 眉目清秀(ㄇㄟˊ ㄇㄨˋ ㄑㄧㄥ ㄒㄧㄡˋ)
good-looking; to look clean and pretty; pleasant facial features

眉心(ㄇㄟˊ ㄒㄧㄣ)
the space between the eyebrows

眉史(ㄇㄟˊ ㄕˇ)
(euphemism) a prostitute

眉梢(ㄇㄟˊ ㄕㄠ)
the ends of the eyebrows

眉壽(ㄇㄟˊ ㄕㄡˋ)
bushy eyebrows—longevity; a long life

眉山(ㄇㄟˊ ㄕㄢ)
Meishan, a county in Szechwan Province

眉眼(ㄇㄟˊ ㄧㄢˇ)
facial expression

眉宇(ㄇㄟˊ ㄩˇ)
① a facial appearance ② the forehead

眉語(ㄇㄟˊ ㄩˇ)
(literally) to speak with the eyebrows—to signal with eyebrows

眉月(ㄇㄟˊ ㄩㄝˋ)
crescent-shaped eyebrows

【看】 3755
1. ㄎㄢ kann kàn

1. to see; to look at; to observe; to watch; to look in the direction of; to read: 她看書看得睡著了。She read herself to sleep.
2. to examine; to consider; to think: 我看他這個人不可靠。I don't think he is reliable.
3. to visit; to call on: 我下週會去看你的。I will visit you next week.
4. to present (tea, wine, etc.)
5. to depend on

看病(ㄎㄢ ㄅㄧㄥˋ)
① to see a doctor: 他明天要去看病。He's going to see a doctor tomorrow. ② to examine the patient; to take a look at the patient; to practice medicine: 醫生出門給人看病去了。The doctor's gone to see a patient.

看不得(ㄎㄢ ㄅㄨˋ ㄉㄜˊ)
① should not see ② unnecessary to see; not worth seeing

看不出(ㄎㄢ ㄅㄨˋ ㄔㄨ)
① unable to see through; unable to understand or gain a full understanding of something or somebody; unable to assess the full (potential,

etc.) ② unable to face a situation or accept a fact with resignation

看不來(ㄎㄢ ㄅㄨˋ ㄌㄞˊ)
① not willing to see ② unable to see

看不過(ㄎㄢ ㄅㄨˋ ㄍㄨㄛˋ)
(in a case of exceptionally intolerable, cruel, etc. situation) cannot help but (give him a helping hand, etc.); one's heart is not steely enough to see

看不慣(ㄎㄢ ㄅㄨˋ ㄍㄨㄢˋ)
to detest; to disdain

看不起(ㄎㄢ ㄅㄨˋ ㄑㄧˇ)
to look down upon; to despise

看不下去(ㄎㄢ ㄅㄨˋ ㄒㄧㄚˋ ㄑㄩˋ)
① unable to continue seeing ② cannot help but...亦作「看不過」 ③ ugly; utterly not worth seeing

看不出(ㄎㄢ ㄅㄨˋ ㄔㄨ)
unable to perceive, detect, foresee, etc.

看不上(ㄎㄢ ㄅㄨˋ ㄕㄤˋ)或看不上眼(ㄎㄢ ㄅㄨˋ ㄕㄤˋ ㄧㄢˇ)
① not up to one's standard; not to one's taste ② to detest; to disdain; to despise

看破(ㄎㄢ ㄆㄛˋ)
① to see through a thing ② to be resigned to what is inevitable

看破紅塵(ㄎㄢ ㄆㄛˋ ㄏㄨㄥˊ ㄔㄣˊ)
to see through the vanity of life (and to become a Buddhist monk or nun); to be disillusioned with the mortal world

看面子(ㄎㄢ ㄇㄧㄢˋ ˙ㄗ)
for the sake of (a person who recommended, requested, etc.)

看法(ㄎㄢ ㄈㄚˇ)
an opinion; a viewpoint

看風頭(ㄎㄢ ㄈㄥ ㄊㄡˊ)
to see which way the wind blows (so that one can manage to stay in an advantageous position)

看風轉舵(ㄎㄢ ㄈㄥ ㄓㄨㄢˇ ㄉㄨㄛˋ)或看風使帆(ㄎㄢ ㄈㄥ ㄕˇ ㄈㄢˊ)
to adapt oneself to circumstances; to trim one's sails

看風水(ㄎㄢ ㄈㄥ ㄕㄨㄟˇ)

to practice geomancy (in selecting a site for a tomb or building)

看得透(ㄎㄢ ㄉㄜˊ ㄊㄡˋ)
① to be able to see through or understand: 這個人我看得透. I can see through the man. ② to be able to face a situation or accept a fact with resignation

看得來(ㄎㄢ ㄉㄜˊ ㄌㄞˊ)
worth seeing; presentable

看得過(ㄎㄢ ㄉㄜˊ ㄍㄨㄛˋ)
presentable; passable

看得過去(ㄎㄢ ㄉㄜˊ ㄍㄨㄛˋ ㄑㄩˋ)
barely presentable; barely worth seeing

看得起(ㄎㄢ ㄉㄜˊ ㄑㄧˇ)
to think highly of; to have a high opinion of; to respect

看得上(ㄎㄢ ㄉㄜˊ ㄕㄤˋ)
to one's taste; presentable; up to standard

看待(ㄎㄢ ㄉㄞˋ)
to treat (another, a child, friend, etc.); treatment

看到(ㄎㄢ ㄉㄠˋ)
to catch sight of; to see

看臺(ㄎㄢ ㄊㄞˊ)
(sports) a deck or stand for observers or spectators; bleachers

看透(ㄎㄢ ㄊㄡˋ)
① to see through (a trick, conspiracy, etc.) ② to be resigned to what is inevitable

看頭兒(ㄎㄢ ㄊㄡˊㄦ)或看頭(ㄎㄢ ㄊㄡˊ)
that which is worth seeing or reading: 這篇報導很有看頭. This report is well worth reading.

看天田(ㄎㄢ ㄊㄧㄢ ㄊㄧㄢˊ)
paddies without dependable irrigation water

看膩了(ㄎㄢ ㄋㄧˋ ˙ㄌㄜ)
to be tired of seeing or watching

看來(ㄎㄢ ㄌㄞˊ)
it looks as if; evidently: 這工作看來今天可以做完. It looks as if we'll be able to finish this job today.

看個飽(ㄎㄢ ˙ㄍㄜ ㄅㄠˇ)或看個夠(ㄎㄢ ˙ㄍㄜ ㄍㄡˋ)
to see or watch to one's

heart's content

看顧(ㄎㄢ ㄍㄨˋ)
to look after

看過(ㄎㄢ ㄍㄨㄛˋ)
① to take a look at ② to make a perusal of ③ to have seen or read: 你看過這新戲沒有? Have you seen the new play?

看官(ㄎㄢ ㄍㄨㄢ)
① (in old Chinese novels) dear readers ② the audience

看慣(ㄎㄢ ㄍㄨㄢˋ)
to be used to seeing; to become accustomed to seeing

看看(ㄎㄢ ㄎㄢˋ)
① to take a look at: 仔細看看. Watch me carefully. ② to examine and survey ③ to visit or call on: 我想你應該去看他. I think you ought to call on him. ④ to see the sights ⑤ to thumb through (a book, etc.)

看機會(ㄎㄢ ㄐㄧ ㄏㄨㄟˋ)
to look for a chance or an opportunity; to watch for an opportunity

看見(ㄎㄢ ㄐㄧㄢˋ)
to see (with one's eyes); to catch sight of: 我們看見有人站在門口. We saw someone standing in the doorway.

看齊(ㄎㄢ ㄑㄧˊ)
① (military) to dress: 向右看齊! Face right! Right, dress! ② to follow the example of; to emulate (someone)

看輕(ㄎㄢ ㄑㄧㄥ)
to despise; to underestimate

看清楚(ㄎㄢ ㄑㄧㄥ ˙ㄔㄨ)
to see clearly; to have a clear look at

看情形(ㄎㄢ ㄑㄧㄥˊ ㄒㄧㄥˊ)
depending on circumstances

看取(ㄎㄢ ㄑㄩˇ)
Let's see....

看戲(ㄎㄢ ㄒㄧˋ)
to watch a show: 我們去看戲吧. Let's go to the play.

看相(ㄎㄢ ㄒㄧㄤˋ)
① to visit a physiognomist or fortuneteller ② to practice physiognomy

看著辦(ㄎㄢ ˙ㄓㄜ ㄅㄢˋ)
to see what happens and act accordingly; to manage

〔目部〕

things according to the prevailing situation

看朱成碧(ㄎㄢ ㄓㄨ ㄔㄥˊ ㄅㄧˋ)
(literally) to take red for green—dim-sighted; dazzled

看中(ㄎㄢ ㄓㄨㄥˋ)
to feel satisfied with; to favor (a choice); to choose; to settle on; to prefer; to like

看重(ㄎㄢ ㄓㄨㄥˋ)
to esteem; to respect; to regard as important; to value

看成(ㄎㄢ ㄔㄥˊ)
to look upon as; to regard as

看出(ㄎㄢ ㄔㄨ)
to make out; to see: 我已看出問題在那裏。 I have seen where the trouble is.

看穿(ㄎㄢ ㄔㄨㄢ)
to see through (a trick); 我們立即看穿他的詭計。 We at once saw through his trick.

看事做事(ㄎㄢ ㄕˋ ㄗㄨㄛˋ ㄕˋ)
to make no decision beforehand but take appropriate actions as the situation warrants

看手相(ㄎㄢ ㄕㄡˇ ㄒㄧㄤˋ)
to read palms as a means of fortunetelling; to practice palmistry

看上(ㄎㄢ ㄕㄤˋ)
①to favor; to be satisfied with; to choose ②to be absorbed in (reading, etc.) ③to take a fancy to: 他看上一位美麗的姑娘。 He took a fancy to a beautiful girl.

看書(ㄎㄢ ㄕㄨ)
to read a book: 我沒有足夠的時間看書。 I haven't enough time to read.

看熱鬧(ㄎㄢ ㄖㄜˋ ㄋㄠˋ)
①to go where the crowds are (for fun or excitement): 他不喜歡看熱鬧。 He hates to go where the crowds are. ②to watch others' failure with secret delight

看人(ㄎㄢ ㄖㄣˊ)
①depending on who the person is②to visit or see someone

看人眉睫(ㄎㄢ ㄖㄣˊ ㄇㄟˊ ㄐㄧㄝˊ)

to be subservient as a yes-man; to watch for the expression of another so that one knows how to act to please him

看人嘴臉(ㄎㄢ ㄖㄣˊ ㄗㄨㄟˇ ㄌㄧㄢˇ)
to be subservient or obedient; to live on another's favor; to depend on another

看作(ㄎㄢ ㄗㄨㄛˋ)
to regard as; to consider to be; to treat as

看錯(ㄎㄢ ㄘㄨㄛˋ)
①to mistake someone or something for another ②to misjudge someone's ability, character, etc.

看醫生(ㄎㄢ ㄧ ㄕㄥ)
to consult a doctor or physician

看一看(ㄎㄢ ㄧ˙ ㄎㄢ)
to take a look; to have a look: 讓我看一看你的字典。 Let's have a look at your dictionary.

看樣子(ㄎㄢ ㄧㄤˋ ˙ㄗ)
it seems; it looks as if: 看樣子, 他是不會來了。 It seems that he will not come.

看望(ㄎㄢ ㄨㄤˋ)
to visit or call on

【看】 3755
    2. ㄎㄢ kan kàn
1. to watch; to mind; to look after
2. to guard; to keep under surveillance

看馬(ㄎㄢ ㄇㄚˇ)
to tend horses; to look after horses

看門(ㄎㄢ ㄇㄣˊ)
①a doorkeeper or gate-keeper; a watchman; a janitor ②to watch or guard the door

看牛(ㄎㄢ ㄋㄧㄡˊ)
①a cowherd ②to herd or take care of cattle

看更(ㄎㄢ ㄍㄥ)
①to beat the night watch ②a night watchman

看管(ㄎㄢ ㄍㄨㄢˇ)
①to take into custody; to guard; to safeguard ②a custodian

看護(ㄎㄢ ㄏㄨˋ)
①to nurse; to take care: 她

看護病人。 She nursed the sick. ②a nurse (in hospital)

看護婦(ㄎㄢ ㄏㄨˋ ㄈㄨˋ)
a hospital nurse

看家(ㄎㄢ ㄐㄧㄚ)
①to stay at home and look after the house ②a house-guard③(money, etc.) saved for a rainy day

看家本領(ㄎㄢ ㄐㄧㄚ ㄅㄣˇ ㄌㄧㄥˇ)
one's specialty or special skill

看家狗(ㄎㄢ ㄐㄧㄚ ㄍㄡˇ)
a watchdog

看守(ㄎㄢ ㄕㄡˇ)
①to watch or guard: 這條狗日夜看守著這個小孩。 The dog guarded the child day and night. ②to detain

看守所(ㄎㄢ ㄕㄡˇ ㄙㄨㄛˇ)
a detention house for prisoners awaiting trials

看座兒的(ㄎㄢ ㄗㄨㄛˋ ㄦ ˙ㄉㄜ)
a steward in a Chinese opera theater

看財奴(ㄎㄢ ㄘㄞˊ ㄋㄨˊ)
a miser

看押(ㄎㄢ ㄧㄚ)
to detain (for questioning, awaiting trial, etc.); to put under guard or custody

五畫

【眙】 3756
    1. ㄔ chyh chì
1. to stare; to look in the face
2. to look in astonishment; to look with the eyes wide open

【眙】 3756
    2. ㄧˊ yi yí
as in 盱眙—name of a county

【眣】 3757
    ㄉㄧㄝˊ dye diè
squinting eyes

【眛】 3758
    ㄇㄟˋ mey mèi
dim-sighted; poor visioned

眛良心(ㄇㄟˋ ㄌㄧㄤˊ ㄒㄧㄣ)
to disregard one's conscience

眛於(ㄇㄟˋ ㄩˊ)
blind to: 他們眛於事實。 They are blind to the facts.

【眠】 3759
    ㄇㄧㄢˊ mian mián

1. to sleep; sleep: 那晚我失眠通
青。I lay all that night sleepless.
2. to hibernate; hibernation: 有
些熊冬眠。Some bears hibernate.

眠花宿柳 (ㄇㄧㄢˊㄏㄨㄚˋㄙㄨˋㄌㄧㄡˇ)
to sleep with prostitutes; to
visit a brothel

眠思夢想 (ㄇㄧㄢˊㄙㄇㄥˋㄒㄧㄤˇ)
to think day and night

眠雲 (ㄇㄧㄢˊㄩㄣˊ)
(literally) to sleep in the
cloud—to live in a hill or
mountain

【眩】 3760
ㄒㄩㄢˋ shiuann xuàn
1. to confuse; to dazzle
2. dizzy; giddy; confused vision

眩惑 (ㄒㄩㄢˋㄏㄨㄛˋ)
to confuse and cheat (the
people); to mislead

眩耀 (ㄒㄩㄢˋㄧㄠˋ)
dazzling; to dazzle

眩暈 (ㄒㄩㄢˋㄩㄣˊ)
vertigo; giddiness; dizziness

【眨】 3761
ㄓㄚˇ jaa zhǎ
to wink; to blink: 那女孩對我
眨了眨眼。The girl winked at
me.

眨巴眼兒 (ㄓㄚˇㄅㄚ˙ㄧㄢˇㄦ)
to wink one's eyes in quick
succession

眨眼 (ㄓㄚˇㄧㄢˇ)
to wink

眨眼間 (ㄓㄚˇㄧㄢˇㄐㄧㄢ)
in the twinkling of an eye; a
very short time: 這種事情眨
眼間就過去了。It will pass
away in a very short while.

【眞】 3762
ㄓㄣ jen zhēn
(眞) ㄓㄣ
1. true; real; factual; genuine;
actual; substantial; really;
truly: 美即是眞, 眞即是美。
Beauty is truth, truth
beauty.
2. the highest sincerity one is
capable of
3. a Chinese family name

眞皮 (ㄓㄣㄆㄧˊ)
①dermis ②genuine leather

眞憑實據 (ㄓㄣㄆㄧㄥˊㄕˊㄐㄩˋ)
concrete proof and genuine
evidence; indisputable proof

眞面目 (ㄓㄣㄇㄧㄢˋㄇㄨˋ)
(literally) the real face

—true colors; true character;
the actual thing behind a
false front: 我已認清他的眞面
目。I see him in his true
colors.

眞分數 (ㄓㄣㄈㄣㄕㄨˋ)
a proper fraction

眞刀眞槍 (ㄓㄣㄉㄠㄓㄣㄑㄧㄤ)
genuine swords and spears
(in theatrical performance
or stage show)—the real
thing: 他們眞刀眞槍地幹起來
了。They started in real earnest.

眞諦 (ㄓㄣㄉㄧˋ)
the real meaning; the
essence: 他要講人生的眞諦。
He will speak on the real
meaning of life.

眞理 (ㄓㄣㄌㄧˇ)
① truth ② righteousness

眞格的 (ㄓㄣㄍㄜˊㄉㄜ˙)
real; true: 別再開玩笑吧, 說眞
格的吧。Stop making a joke
and tell me the truth.

眞箇 (ㄓㄣㄍㄜˋ)
really; actually: 他眞箇了不
起。He is really wonderful.

眞果 (ㄓㄣㄍㄨㄛˇ)
(botany) true fruit

眞工夫 (ㄓㄣㄍㄨㄥ˙ㄈㄨ)
a true skill or accomplishment

眞空 (ㄓㄣㄎㄨㄥ)
vacuum

眞空地帶 (ㄓㄣㄎㄨㄥㄉㄧˋㄉㄞˋ)
① a region where no authority is exercised by any party
② (military) no man's land

眞空管 (ㄓㄣㄎㄨㄥㄍㄨㄢˇ)
① a vacuum tube ② tubes
used in radio receivers, etc.

眞空計 (ㄓㄣㄎㄨㄥㄐㄧˋ)
a vacuum gauge

眞空吸塵器 (ㄓㄣㄎㄨㄥㄒㄧㄔㄣˊㄑㄧˋ)
a vacuum cleaner

眞話 (ㄓㄣㄏㄨㄚˋ)
the truth; true or factual
statements: 他說的根本不是眞
話。There is not a particle of
truth in what he says.

眞迹 (ㄓㄣㄐㄧ)
real handwriting, paintings,
etc. (as opposed to forgeries
or fakes); authentic works

眞假 (ㄓㄣㄐㄧㄚˇ)
true and false; real and fake

眞金不怕火煉 (ㄓㄣㄐㄧㄣㄅㄨˊㄆㄚˋㄏㄨㄛˇㄌㄧㄢˋ)
(literally) Genuine gold is
not afraid of fire.—Truth is
ultimately louder than lies
or slanders. 或 True loyalty
can stand the test of adversity.

眞君 (ㄓㄣㄐㄩㄣ)
a deferential title of an immortal

眞切 (ㄓㄣㄑㄧㄝˋ)
① true and concise; vivid ②
(to see or hear) clearly

眞槍實彈 (ㄓㄣㄑㄧㄤㄕˊㄉㄢˋ)
real guns and bullets; live
ammunition

眞情 (ㄓㄣㄑㄧㄥˊ)
① actual happenings (of an
incident, etc.); the true state
of affairs ② real affections;
true feelings; sincerity: 她的
信真情流露。Her letter re-
veals her true feelings.

眞確 (ㄓㄣㄑㄩㄝˋ)
authentic; true; real; accurate; clear; distinct: 他帶來眞
確的消息。He brought authen-
tic news.

眞詮 (ㄓㄣㄑㄩㄢˊ)
the correct meaning or
explanation

眞心 (ㄓㄣㄒㄧㄣ)
from the bottom of one's
heart; real or actual intention; sincere; sincerity;
wholehearted

眞心話 (ㄓㄣㄒㄧㄣㄏㄨㄚˋ)
sincere talks; words from
the bottom of one's heart

眞心實意 (ㄓㄣㄒㄧㄣㄕˊㄧˋ) 或 眞心
誠意 (ㄓㄣㄒㄧㄣㄔㄥˊㄧˋ)
genuinely and sincerely; truly and wholeheartedly; wholeheartedly; sincerely

眞相 (ㄓㄣㄒㄧㄤˋ)
the truth (about a happening, etc.); the real situation;
the actual state of affairs:
他掩蓋眞相。He covered up
the facts.

眞相畢露 (ㄓㄣㄒㄧㄤˋㄅㄧˋㄌㄨˋ)
to have one's true face or
colors completely exposed

眞相大白 (ㄓㄣㄒㄧㄤˋㄉㄚˋㄅㄞˊ)
The truth is out.

眞像 (ㄓㄣㄒㄧㄤˋ)

〔目
部〕

（optics）the real image

眞性(ㄓㄣ ㄒㄧㄥ)
①the natural property ②
one's natural disposition

眞知灼見(ㄓㄣ ㄓ ㄓㄨㄛ ㄐㄧㄢ)
correct and penetrating
views

眞摯(ㄓㄣ ㄓ)
sincere; sincerity; faithful;
true; truly: 他們的友誼是眞摯
的。Their friendship is sincere.

眞正(ㄓㄣ ㄓㄥ)
①actual; actually; real;
really; precisely ②genuine

眞珠(ㄓㄣ ㄓㄨ)
natural pearls (as distinct
from cultured pearls or imitation pearls)

眞珠岩(ㄓㄣ ㄓㄨ ㄧㄢ)
perlite, or pearlite

眞誠(ㄓㄣ ㄔㄥ)
sincere; genuine; true: 眞誠的
友誼應永恆不渝。True friend-
ship should last forever.

眞除(ㄓㄣ ㄔㄨ)
the formal appointment to
an office (as opposed to an
acting capacity)

眞實(ㄓㄣ ㄕ)
actual; true; truth; real; factual: 這是一篇眞實的故事。
This is a story of real life.

眞實性(ㄓㄣ ㄕ ㄒㄧㄥ)
reliability; truthfulness

眞善美(ㄓㄣ ㄕㄢ ㄇㄟ)
truth, goodness and beauty;
the true, the good, and the
beautiful

眞書(ㄓㄣ ㄕㄨ)
the standard or regular style
of Chinese calligraphy 亦作
「楷書」

眞率(ㄓㄣ ㄕㄨㄞ)
frank and honest; straightforward; unaffected

眞人(ㄓㄣ ㄖㄣ)
①(Taoism) the Immortal
—also used as a title of
respect in addressing
Taoists ②a real person

眞人不露相(ㄓㄣ ㄖㄣ ㄅㄨ ㄌㄨ ㄒㄧㄤ)
A man of substance does
not like to show off (or
reveal his true worth)

眞人眞事(ㄓㄣ ㄖㄣ ㄓㄣ ㄕ)
The characters are real, and

the story is true. 或 real people and real events

眞宰(ㄓㄣ ㄗㄞ)
the Almighty; Heaven; the
true lord of the universe

眞贓(ㄓㄣ ㄗㄤ)
stolen goods; loot

眞贓實犯(ㄓㄣ ㄗㄤ ㄕ ㄈㄢ)
concrete evidence; irrefutable proof of guilt

眞材實料(ㄓㄣ ㄘㄞ ㄕ ㄌㄧㄠ)
genuine material and solid
substance

眞才實學(ㄓㄣ ㄘㄞ ㄕ ㄒㄩㄝ)
①solid learning; genuine
talent ②truly learned; highly competent

眞草(ㄓㄣ ㄘㄠ)
the standard style and script
style in Chinese calligraphy

眞愛(ㄓㄣ ㄞ)
true love

眞意(ㄓㄣ ㄧ)
true intent and real meaning

眞贗(ㄓㄣ ㄧㄢ)
true or false; genuine or
fake

眞僞(ㄓㄣ ㄨㄟ)
true and false

眞僞莫辨(ㄓㄣ ㄨㄟ ㄇㄛ ㄅㄧㄢ)
cannot distinguish whether
it's genuine or fake, true or
false

【眚】 3763
ㄕㄥ sheeng shĕng
1. an eye-ailment or disease
2. a blunder; a fault; a mistake;
an error
3. corruption
4. to reduce; to save (the trouble, etc.)
5. calamity; disaster

眚災(ㄕㄥ ㄗㄞ)
faults and misfortunes

【眥】 3764
(眦) ㄗ tzyh zì
eye sockets

眥目(ㄗ ㄇㄨ)
to open eyes wide

眥裂(ㄗ ㄌㄧㄝ)
to open eyes wide, as in
anger

六畫

【眯】 3765
ㄇㄧ mii mí
1. a foreign body getting into
the eye
2. to close one's eyes into narrow slits

【睞】 3766
ㄧ yi yì
to stare at someone for a
long time without talking

【眶】 3767
ㄎㄨㄤ kuang kuàng
the socket of the eye; the
rim of the eye: 她熱淚盈眶。
Her eyes filled with tears.

【眸】 3768
ㄇㄡ mou móu
the pupil of the eye — the
eyes

眸子(ㄇㄡ ㄗ)
the eyes; the pupil of the eye

【眼】 3769
ㄧㄢ yean yǎn
1. the eye: 我親眼看見了。I saw
it with my own eyes.
2. a look; a glance: 她瞪了我一
眼。She gave me a hard look.
3. a tiny hole; an opening; an
orifice; an aperture
4. a key point

眼巴巴(ㄧㄢ ㄅㄚ ㄅㄚ)
①expectantly; anxiously;
eagerly: 大家眼巴巴盼着你的
來臨。We were eagerly look-
ing forward to your arrival.
②helplessly (watching something unpleasant happen)

眼波(ㄧㄢ ㄅㄛ)
eyesight; vision; bright-eyed
—like the ripples on a
stream

眼不見，心不煩(ㄧㄢ ㄅㄨ ㄐㄧㄢ，
ㄒㄧㄣ ㄅㄨ ㄈㄢ)
One who avoids seeing trouble does not have to worry
about trouble.

眼不見爲淨(ㄧㄢ ㄅㄨ ㄐㄧㄢ ㄨㄟ
ㄐㄧㄥ)
If one wants to avoid seeing
dirtiness, he should turn his
eyes away.—a passive way
to stay out of trouble 或 Out
of sight, out of mind.

眼不觀邪(ㄧㄢ ㄅㄨ ㄍㄨㄢ ㄒㄧㄝ)
to see no evil; to turn eyes
away from evils

眼皮(ㄧㄢ ㄆㄧ)
eyelids

眼明手快(一ㄢ ㄇ一ㄥˊ ㄕㄡˇ ㄎㄨㄞˋ)
to be sharp of sight and quick of hand; to see things clearly and act speedily; sharp-eyed and quick-moving

眼目(一ㄢˇ ㄇㄨˋ)
① the eyes ② to serve as the eye of another; a spy ③ essential points or parts

眼福(一ㄢˇ ㄈㄨˊ)
a feast to the eye; joy to the eye; delight to the eye

眼到手到(一ㄢˇ ㄉㄠˋ ㄕㄡˇ ㄉㄠˋ)
to take down notes while reading, as a diligent scholar does

眼跳(一ㄢˇ ㄊㄧㄠˋ)
twitching of the eyelid (believed to portend trouble or disaster)

眼淚(一ㄢˇ ㄌㄟˋ)
tears: 擦乾你的眼淚。 Wipe away your tears.

眼淚汪汪(一ㄢˇ ㄌㄟˋ ㄨㄤ ㄨㄤ)
eyes brimming with tears; tearful

眼裏(一ㄢˇ ㄌㄧˇ)
within one's vision; in one's eyes: 他看在眼裏，記在心裏。 He bears in mind what he sees.

眼力(一ㄢˇ ㄌㄧˋ)
① eyesight; vision ② discerning ability; the power of judgment

眼簾(一ㄢˇ ㄌㄧㄢˊ)
the iris

眼亮(一ㄢˇ ㄌㄧㄤˋ)
clear-sighted; sharp-sighted

眼高手低(一ㄢˇ ㄍㄠ ㄕㄡˇ ㄉㄧ)
to criticize the performance of others when oneself cannot equal or exceed; to have great aims but poor abilities; to be conceited but incompetent

眼觀鼻，鼻觀心(一ㄢˇ ㄍㄨㄢ ㄅㄧˊ, ㄅㄧˊ ㄍㄨㄢ ㄒㄧㄣ)
to sit quietly without looking sideways

眼光(一ㄢˇ ㄍㄨㄤ)
sight; insight; vision; eye —discerning ability; power of judgment: 我們的眼光都集中到她身上。 We turned our eyes on her.

眼光短淺(一ㄢˇ ㄍㄨㄤ ㄉㄨㄢˇ ㄑㄧㄢˇ)
shortsighted

眼光遠大(一ㄢˇ ㄍㄨㄤ ㄩㄢˇ ㄉㄚˋ)
farsighted

眼科(一ㄢˇ ㄎㄜ)
ophthalmology

眼科大夫(一ㄢˇ ㄎㄜ ㄉㄞˋㄈㄨ)or 眼科醫生(一ㄢˇ ㄎㄜ 一 ㄕㄥ)
an ophthalmologist; an oculist; an eye doctor

眼科醫院(一ㄢˇ ㄎㄜ 一 ㄩㄢˋ)
a hospital of ophthalmology

眼看(一ㄢˇ ㄎㄢˋ)or 眼看着(一ㄢˇ ㄎㄢˋ ·ㄓㄜ)
① imminent; soon: 眼看天就要黑了。 It'll be dark soon. ② to see something happening ③ to watch helplessly

眼庫(一ㄢˇ ㄎㄨˋ)
an eye bank

眼眶(一ㄢˇ ㄎㄨㄤˋ)
an eye socket: 她眼眶裏含着熱淚。 Her eyes were filled with tears.

眼孔(一ㄢˇ ㄎㄨㄥˇ)
an eyelet; an orifice

眼黑(一ㄢˇ ㄏㄟ)
greedy; avarice

眼花(一ㄢˇ ㄏㄨㄚ)
eyesight blurred; dim of sight; giddy or dizzy

眼花撩亂(一ㄢˇ ㄏㄨㄚ ㄌㄧㄠˊ ㄌㄨㄢˋ)
(scenes so varied and confusing as) to dazzle the eyes

眼紅(一ㄢˇ ㄏㄨㄥˊ)
① red-eyed ② covetous; envious ③ angry

眼睫毛(一ㄢˇ ㄐㄧㄝˊ ㄇㄠˊ)
eyelashes

眼界(一ㄢˇ ㄐㄧㄝˋ)
one's field of vision; an outlook

眼界高(一ㄢˇ ㄐㄧㄝˋ ㄍㄠ)
to have one's standard set high

眼尖(一ㄢˇ ㄐㄧㄢ)
sharp-eyed; quick of sight

眼瞼(一ㄢˇ ㄐㄧㄢˇ)
eyelids

眼鏡(一ㄢˇ ㄐㄧㄥˋ)
glasses; spectacles

眼鏡鋪子(一ㄢˇ ㄐㄧㄥˋ ㄆㄨˋ ·ㄗ)
an optician's shop

眼鏡盒(一ㄢˇ ㄐㄧㄥˋ ㄏㄜˊ)
a case for glasses

眼鏡蛇(一ㄢˇ ㄐㄧㄥˋ ㄕㄜˊ)
a cobra

眼睛(一ㄢˇ ·ㄐㄧㄥ)
the eyes

眼球(一ㄢˇ ㄑㄧㄡˊ)
eyeballs

眼球筋(一ㄢˇ ㄑㄧㄡˊ ㄐㄧㄣ)
ocular muscles

眼前(一ㄢˇ ㄑㄧㄢˊ)
① right before one's eyes: 眼前是一片水域。 Before our eyes was a stretch of water. ② at this moment; now; at present

眼圈子(一ㄢˇ ㄑㄩㄢ ·ㄗ)or 眼圈兒(一ㄢˇ ㄑㄩㄢ ㄦ)
the rim of the eye; an eye socket

眼下(一ㄢˇ ㄒㄧㄚˋ)
at present; currently; at the moment: 眼下我們必須安於現狀。 At present, we must be content with matters as they stand.

眼線(一ㄢˇ ㄒㄧㄢˋ)
(said of crime investigation) a contact, a stool pigeon, or an informer

眼罩(一ㄢˇ ㄓㄠˋ)
① an eyeshade ② blinkers (for a horse)

眼睜睜(一ㄢˇ ㄓㄥ ㄓㄥ)
① right before one's eyes; publicly; openly; in broad daylight ② watchful; attentively ③ to watch helplessly

眼珠(一ㄢˇ ㄓㄨ)
eyeballs

眼珠子(一ㄢˇ ㄓㄨ ·ㄗ)or 眼珠兒(一ㄢˇ ㄓㄨㄦ)
① eyeballs ② (figuratively) vision

眼拙(一ㄢˇ ㄓㄨㄛ)
(usually a polite expression) dim or shortsighted (for not knowing you before)

眼中釘(一ㄢˇ ㄓㄨㄥ ㄉㄧㄥ)or 眼中刺(一ㄢˇ ㄓㄨㄥ ㄘˋ)
(literally) a thorn in the eye —the most hated person; an eyesore

眼中人(一ㄢˇ ㄓㄨㄥ ㄖㄣˊ)
the loved one; the person after one's heart

眼中無人(一ㄢˇ ㄓㄨㄥ ㄨˊ ㄖㄣˊ)
haughty; arrogant

眼岔(一ㄢˇ ㄔㄚˋ)

目部

confusing vision; eyesight blurred; to mistake one for another

眼饞(一ㄢˊ)
covetous; envious

眼穿(一ㄓㄨㄢ)
anxiously awaiting; eagerly expecting

眼屎(一ㄕ)
secretions of the eyes

眼神(一ㄕㄣˊ)
expression of the eyes; gleams of the eyes

眼生(一ㄕㄥ)
unfamiliar by sight: 這個人我覺得眼生。The man is unfamiliar to me.

眼熟(一ㄕㄨˊ)
to seem to know; seemingly familiar by sight: 來客看來很眼熟。The visitor looks familiar.

眼如秋水(一ㄖㄨˊㄑㄧㄡㄕㄨㄟˇ)
bright-eyed

眼子(一˙ㄗ)
a small hole; an orifice

眼色(一ㄙㄜˋ)
the expression of one's eyes (indicating one's intention, wish, etc.); a hint or a cue given with the eyes

眼兒(一ㄦˊ)
① the eye ② a tiny hole; an orifice

眼藥水(一ㄧㄠˋㄕㄨㄟˇ)
eyewash; eyewater; eyedrops

眼窩(一ㄨㄛ)
an orbit; an eye socket

眼語(一ㄩˇ)
(literally) the eye-talk—to indicate or hint with one's eyes

眼暈(一ㄩㄣˋ)
① dazzled; blurring vision; dizzy ② (cosmetics) eye-shadow

【眺】 ㄊㄧㄠˋ tiaw **tiào** 3770
to look far away; to take a look at faraway things; to look far into the distance

眺望(一ㄨㄤˋ)
to look far away

【眵】 ㄔ chy **chī** 3771
caking of eye secretions; secretions

【眾】 (衆) ㄓㄨㄥˋ jonq **zhòng** 3772
1. many; numerous
2. a crowd; a multitude; all; the masses
3. public or popular (opinion, views, etc.)

眾叛親離(ㄓㄨㄥˋㄆㄢˋㄑㄧㄣㄌㄧˊ)
(said of a dictator at his downfall) opposed by the masses and deserted by followers—to be utterly isolated

眾目睽睽(ㄓㄨㄥˋㄇㄨˋㄎㄨㄟˊㄎㄨㄟˊ)
the glare of the public; the public gaze

眾目昭彰(ㄓㄨㄥˋㄇㄨˋㄓㄠㄓㄤ)
the stare or watchful eyes of the public

眾多(ㄓㄨㄥˋㄉㄨㄛ)
numerous

眾怒難犯(ㄓㄨㄥˋㄋㄨˋㄋㄢˊㄈㄢˋ)
It's unwise to offend the public. 或 It's dangerous to antagonize the masses.

眾寡不敵(ㄓㄨㄥˋㄍㄨㄚˇㄅㄨˋㄉㄧˊ)
One is no match for a crowd. 或 being outnumbered

眾寡懸殊(ㄓㄨㄥˋㄍㄨㄚˇㄒㄩㄢˊㄕㄨ)
The disparity of numerical strength is too great.

眾口難調(ㄓㄨㄥˋㄎㄡˇㄋㄢˊㄊㄧㄠˊ)
It's difficult to obtain unanimity from a crowd.

眾口鑠金(ㄓㄨㄥˋㄎㄡˇㄕㄨㄛˋㄐㄧㄣ)
Too many rumors can confuse what is right or wrong.

眾口一詞(ㄓㄨㄥˋㄎㄡˇㄧ ㄘˊ)
(said of many persons) to speak out with one voice; unanimously

眾擎易舉(ㄓㄨㄥˋㄑㄧㄥˊㄧˋㄐㄩˇ)
Cooperation and unity make difficult things easy.

眾志成城(ㄓㄨㄥˋㄓˋㄔㄥˊㄔㄥˊ)or 眾心成城(ㄓㄨㄥˋㄒㄧㄣㄔㄥˊㄔㄥˊ)
Unity of purpose is a formidable force.

眾矢之的(ㄓㄨㄥˋㄕˇㄓ ㄉㄧˋ)
(literally) the target of many arrows—the target of public attacks (or censure)

眾生(ㄓㄨㄥˋㄕㄥ)
① all living creatures ② beasts or animals

眾生相(ㄓㄨㄥˋㄕㄥㄒㄧㄤˋ)
(Buddhism) the idea that all

the living are produced by the *skandhas*

眾庶(ㄓㄨㄥˋㄕㄨˋ)
the masses; the people

眾說紛紜(ㄓㄨㄥˋㄕㄨㄛㄈㄣㄩㄣˊ)
Opinions vary. 眾說紛紜,莫衷一是。As opinions vary, no conclusion can be reached.

眾人(ㄓㄨㄥˋㄖㄣˊ)
many people; all people; the multitude: 這是一齣吸引眾人的戲劇。It's a play that appeals to the multitude.

眾所周知(ㄓㄨㄥˋㄙㄨㄛˇㄓㄡㄓ)
universally known; as everyone knows; as is known to all; it is common knowledge that

眾議紛紜(ㄓㄨㄥˋㄧˋㄈㄣㄩㄣˊ)
Public opinions or views are divergent. 或 There's no agreement among many views.

眾議院(ㄓㄨㄥˋㄧˋㄩㄢˋ)or 眾院(ㄓㄨㄥˋㄩㄢˋ)
the Lower House of a Parliament; the House of Commons; the House

眾望(ㄓㄨㄥˋㄨㄤˋ)
public support or confidence; popularity (of a leader); people's expectations: 這位領袖不孚眾望。The leader fell short of people's confidence.

眾望所歸(ㄓㄨㄥˋㄨㄤˋㄙㄨㄛˇㄍㄨㄟ)
to enjoy public confidence; to command public respect and support

【眷】 ㄐㄩㄢˋ jiuann **juàn** 3773
1. to look back—to regard; to care for; to concern
2. to admire; to love
3. relatives; dependents

眷念(ㄐㄩㄢˋㄋㄧㄢˋ)
to think of or remember with affection; to feel nostalgic about

眷戀(ㄐㄩㄢˋㄌㄧㄢˋ)
to admire; to be attached to someone

眷糧(ㄐㄩㄢˋㄌㄧㄤˊ)
food allowances for dependents or military personnel or public functionaries

眷顧(ㄐㄩㄢˋㄍㄨˋ)
to care for; to concern; to

〔目部〕

regard; regards

眷口 (ㄐㄩㄢˋ ㄎㄡˇ)
family; dependents

眷懷 (ㄐㄩㄢˋ ㄏㄨㄞˊ)
to remember; to cherish the memory of

眷眷 (ㄐㄩㄢˋ ㄐㄩㄢˋ)
to remember with tender feelings

眷注 (ㄐㄩㄢˋ ㄓㄨˋ)
to concern with affection; to care for

眷屬 (ㄐㄩㄢˋ ㄕㄨˇ)
dependents; family

眷村 (ㄐㄩㄢˋ ㄘㄨㄣ)
a military dependents' village

眷愛 (ㄐㄩㄢˋ ㄞˋ)
to care for; to love; to regard with affection

眷佑 (ㄐㄩㄢˋ ㄧㄡˋ)
to care for and assist

七畫

【睇】 3774
ㄉㄧˋ dih dì
1. to take a casual look at
2. to look sideways; to look askance; to cast a sidelong glance

【睏】 3775
ㄎㄨㄣˋ kuenn kùn
drowsy; sleepy

【着】 3776
ㄓㄨㄛˊ jwo zhuó
ㄓㄠ jaur zhāo
ㄓㄠ jau zhǎo
·ㄓㄜ ·je zhe
same as 著

八畫

【睛】 3777
ㄐㄧㄥ jing jīng
1. the pupil of the eye
2. eyes

睛球 (ㄐㄧㄥ ㄑㄧㄡˊ)
the eyeball; the pupil of the eye

睛珠 (ㄐㄧㄥ ㄓㄨ)
the eyeball; the pupil of the eye

【睞】 3778
ㄌㄞˋ lay lài
1. to look at; to glance
2. to squint; cockeyed

【睡】 3779
ㄕㄨㄟˋ shuey shuì
to sleep; to rest with eyes closed: 柔和的音樂使他入睡。
The soft music put him to sleep.

睡袍 (ㄕㄨㄟˋ ㄆㄠˊ)
a sleeping gown

睡魔 (ㄕㄨㄟˋ ㄇㄛˊ)
extreme sleepiness

睡美人 (ㄕㄨㄟˋ ㄇㄟˇ ㄖㄣˊ)
a sleeping beauty

睡夢 (ㄕㄨㄟˋ ㄇㄥˋ)
in sleep; in one's dreams

睡眠 (ㄕㄨㄟˋ ㄇㄧㄢˊ)
sleep: 你需要幾小時的睡眠？
How many hours' sleep do you need?

睡眠不足 (ㄕㄨㄟˋ ㄇㄧㄢˊ ㄅㄨˋ ㄗㄨˊ)
insufficient sleep; want of sleep

睡眠曲 (ㄕㄨㄟˋ ㄇㄧㄢˊ ㄑㄩˇ)
a lullaby

睡眠時間 (ㄕㄨㄟˋ ㄇㄧㄢˊ ㄕˊ ㄐㄧㄢ)
①the length of one's sleep
②one's bedtime

睡袋 (ㄕㄨㄟˋ ㄉㄞˋ)
a sleeping bag

睡懶覺 (ㄕㄨㄟˋ ㄌㄢˇ ㄐㄧㄠˋ)
to get up late; to sleep in

睡蓮 (ㄕㄨㄟˋ ㄌㄧㄢˊ)
a water lily

睡覺 (ㄕㄨㄟˋ ㄐㄧㄠˋ)
to sleep; to go to bed: 你該睡覺了。It's time for you to go to bed.

睡鄉 (ㄕㄨㄟˋ ㄒㄧㄤ)
dreamland

睡醒 (ㄕㄨㄟˋ ㄒㄧㄥˇ)
to wake up from sleep

睡著 (ㄕㄨㄟˋ ㄓㄠˊ)
to have fallen asleep: 小嬰兒已經睡著了。The little baby has fallen asleep.

睡車 (ㄕㄨㄟˋ ㄔㄜ)
a sleeping car; a sleeper

睡獅 (ㄕㄨㄟˋ ㄕ)
(literally) a sleeping lion—a big country lacking vitality

睡熟 (ㄕㄨㄟˋ ㄕㄨˊ) or (ㄕㄨㄟˋ ㄕㄡˊ)
to sleep soundly

睡衣 (ㄕㄨㄟˋ ㄧ)
pajamas; a sleeping gown; night clothes

睡意 (ㄕㄨㄟˋ ㄧˋ)
sleepiness; drowsiness: 他似

乎已有幾分睡意。He seems to be somewhat sleepy.

睡遊病 (ㄕㄨㄟˋ ㄧㄡˊ ㄅㄧㄥˋ)
somnambulism

睡眼朦朧 (ㄕㄨㄟˋ ㄧㄢˇ ㄇㄥˊ ㄌㄨㄥˊ)
sleepy-eyed; eyes heavy with slumber

睡眼惺忪 (ㄕㄨㄟˋ ㄧㄢˇ ㄒㄧㄥ ㄙㄨㄥ)
to have a drowsy look

睡午覺 (ㄕㄨㄟˋ ㄨˇ ㄐㄧㄠˋ)
to take a siesta or afternoon nap

【睢】 3780
ㄙㄨㄟ suei suī
1. to raise one's eyes
2. freely or without thought of others; at random
3. a Chinese family name

睢 (ㄙㄨㄟ suī)
name of an ancient region in today's Shangchiu County (商邱) of Honan Province—It was defended to the last man against rebels led by An Lu-shan (安祿山) in the Tang Dynasty.

【睜】 3781
ㄓㄥ jeng zhēng
to open the eyes

睜開眼睛 (ㄓㄥ ㄎㄞ ㄧㄢˇ ㄐㄧㄥ)
to open the eyes

睜開眼睛說謊話 (ㄓㄥ ㄎㄞ ㄧㄢˇ ㄐㄧㄥ ㄕㄨㄛ ㄏㄨㄤˇ ㄏㄨㄚˋ)
to tell a barefaced lie

睜眼 (ㄓㄥ ㄧㄢˇ)
to open the eyes

睜一隻眼，閉一隻眼 (ㄓㄥ ㄧˋ ㄓ ㄧㄢˇ，ㄅㄧˋ ㄧˋ ㄓ ㄧㄢˇ)
to turn a blind eye to something; to pretend not to see —to overlook purposely

【睥】 3782
ㄅㄧˋ bih bì
1. to look askance; a scornful look
2. battlements atop city walls

睥睨 (ㄅㄧˋ ㄋㄧˋ)
to look askance—an expression of disdain; overweening

【睨】 3783
ㄋㄧˋ nih nì
1. to look askance—an expression of disdain or arrogance
2. to slant

【睦】 3784
ㄇㄨˋ muh mù
1. friendly; amiable; to befriend; to be on friendly

目部

terms
2. a Chinese family name

睦鄰（ㄇㄨˋ ㄌㄧㄣˊ）
to remain on friendly terms with the neighbors (often referring to neighboring countries)

睦親（ㄇㄨˋ ㄑㄧㄣ）
close relatives

睦誼（ㄇㄨˋ ㄧˋ）
cordiality or friendship (usually referring to that between nations)

【睫】 3785 ㄐㄧㄝˊ jye jié
1. eyelashes
2. to blink; to wink

睫毛（ㄐㄧㄝˊ ㄇㄠˊ）
eyelashes

【睬】 3786 ㄘㄞˇ tsae cǎi
1. to look; to watch
2. to notice; to pay attention to

【督】 3787 ㄉㄨ du dū
1. to oversee; to superintend; to supervise
2. to reprove; to censure
3. a marshal; a general
4. a viceroy or governor-general
5. a Chinese family name

督辦（ㄉㄨ ㄅㄢˋ）
①to superintend an operation; to supervise and manage ②an official rank—a director, superintendent, or supervisor

督撫（ㄉㄨ ㄈㄨˇ）
the viceroy and inspector-general

督導（ㄉㄨ ㄉㄠˇ）or（ㄉㄨ ㄉㄠˋ）
to direct and supervise

督理（ㄉㄨ ㄌㄧˇ）
to supervise and manage

督勸（ㄉㄨ ㄑㄩㄢˋ）
to urge and encourage

督過（ㄉㄨ ㄍㄨㄛˋ）
to reprove; to censure

督工（ㄉㄨ ㄍㄨㄥ）
①to oversee working; to superintend workers ②an overseer; a foreman 亦作「監工」

督課（ㄉㄨ ㄎㄜˋ）
to supervise one's work; to direct a job or task

督軍（ㄉㄨ ㄐㄩㄣ）
(in the early days of the Republic) the highest military commander as well as the governor in a province

督學（ㄉㄨ ㄒㄩㄝˊ）
an inspector of educational establishments

督戰（ㄉㄨ ㄓㄢˋ）
to direct military operations

督飭（ㄉㄨ ㄔˋ）
to supervise and direct

督察（ㄉㄨ ㄔㄚˊ）
①to superintend and oversee; to act as a watchdog ②an inspector

督師（ㄉㄨ ㄕ）
to lead the army

督署（ㄉㄨ ㄕㄨˇ）
the office of the viceroy, governor, etc.

督率（ㄉㄨ ㄕㄨㄞˋ）
to direct and lead

督責（ㄉㄨ ㄗㄜˊ）
to supervise and urge on

督造（ㄉㄨ ㄗㄠˋ）
to supervise the manufacture of (weapons, cars, etc.)

督促（ㄉㄨ ㄘㄨˋ）
to urge; to press (a person to complete a task in time, etc.): 工頭督促工人努力工作。 The foreman urged his workmen on.

督郵（ㄉㄨ ㄧㄡˊ）
(in ancient China) an assistant to the chief of a prefecture

【睪】 3788 （睾）《ㄍㄠ gau gāo
1. the marsh 亦作「皐」
2. high; lofty
3. the testicle, or testis

睪丸（ㄍㄠ ㄨㄢˊ）
the testicle, or testis

【睠】 3789 ㄐㄩㄢˋ jiuann juàn
1. to look back
2. same as眷—to care for

九畫

【睹】 3790 （覩）ㄉㄨˇ duu dǔ
to witness; to see; to look at; to observe; to gaze at

睹物思人（ㄉㄨˇ ㄨˋ ㄙ ㄖㄣˊ）
to see the things one is reminded of the owner; to think of a person as one sees the thing(s) he has left behind

【睽】 3791 ㄎㄨㄟˊ kwei kuí
1. separated 亦作「暌」
2. in opposition
3. to squint
4. to stare at
5. unusual; strange

睽離（ㄎㄨㄟˊ ㄌㄧˊ）
long separation; separated for a long time: 她睽離母親二十年。 She was separated from her mother for twenty years.

睽隔（ㄎㄨㄟˊ ㄍㄜˊ）
sundered; separated

睽孤（ㄎㄨㄟˊ ㄍㄨ）
eccentric and unsociable

睽睽（ㄎㄨㄟˊ ㄎㄨㄟˊ）
to stare; staring

睽疑（ㄎㄨㄟˊ ㄧˊ）
to suspect; to feel strange

睽違（ㄎㄨㄟˊ ㄨㄟˊ）
to separate; separation

【瞅】 3792 ㄔㄡˇ choou chǒu
to look at; to see; to gaze

瞅不得（ㄔㄡˇ ㄅㄨˋ ㄉㄜˊ）
①should not be seen ②not worth seeing

瞅不見（ㄔㄡˇ ㄅㄨˋ ㄐㄧㄢˋ）
unable to see; to look but unable to see

瞅了一眼（ㄔㄡˇ ㄌㄜˊ ㄧ ㄧㄢˇ）
to take a look at

瞅見（ㄔㄡˇ ㄐㄧㄢˋ）
to see

瞅瞅（ㄔㄡˇ ㄔㄡˇ）
to notice; to look: 她全不睬瞅他。 She won't pay any attention to him.

【瞄】 3793 ㄇㄧㄠˊ miau miǎo
to aim at; to take aim; to look at attentively

瞄準（ㄇㄧㄠˊ ㄓㄨㄣˇ）
to take aim; to aim at; to train upon; to take sight: 把砲瞄準敵人的船隻。 Train guns upon the enemy ships.

瞄準器（ㄇㄧㄠˊ ㄓㄨㄣˇ ㄑㄧˋ）
a sighting device; gun sights

【睿】 3794
ㄖㄨㄟˋ ruey ruì

1. to understand thoroughly; quick or keen of perception
2. wise and clever; astute and discreet; perspicacious
3. the profoundest (learning); the divine sagacity of sages

睿圖(ㄖㄨㄟˋ ㄊㄨˊ)
①plans designed by the emperor ②a portrait of Confucius

睿覽(ㄖㄨㄟˋ ㄌㄢˇ)
for the emperor's perusal

睿智 or 睿知(ㄖㄨㄟˋ ㄓˋ)
the divine sagacity of sages; superior intelligence

睿哲(ㄖㄨㄟˋ ㄓㄜˊ)
①saintly wisdom; superior intelligence ②His Majesty

睿藻(ㄖㄨㄟˋ ㄗㄠˇ)
poems or articles written by the emperor, the empress or imperial concubines

【瞀】 3795
ㄇㄠˋ maw mào
(又讀 ㄇㄡˊ mow móu)

1. dim-sighted; nearsighted; indistinct vision
2. illiterate; ignorant; feeble-minded
3. confused; confusion; dazzled

瞀亂(ㄇㄠˋ ㄌㄨㄢˋ)
confused and feeble-minded

瞀儒(ㄇㄠˋ ㄖㄨˊ)
a stupid or ignorant scholar

十畫

【瞋】 3796
ㄔㄣ chen chēn

1. angry; anger 亦作「嗔」
2. to open the eyes

瞋目(ㄔㄣ ㄇㄨˋ)
①to glare; an angry look; angry eyes ②to open one's eyes wide

瞋怒(ㄔㄣ ㄋㄨˋ)
to be beside oneself with anger

瞋視(ㄔㄣ ㄕˋ)
to look with angry eyes; to look angrily at

【瞎】 3797
ㄒㄧㄚ shia xiā

1. blind; blindly
2. reckless; heedless; rash; (to do things, etc.) without purpose or reason; at random; groundlessly
3. (dialect) to become tangled (said of thread, etc.)

瞎辦(ㄒㄧㄚ ㄅㄢˋ)
to make a futile effort; to work to no avail

瞎捧(ㄒㄧㄚ ㄆㄥˇ)
to heap praises on someone blindly

瞎貓逮死耗子(ㄒㄧㄚ ㄇㄠ ㄙˇ ㄏㄠˋ ˙ㄗ)
(literally) A blind cat caught a dead rat.—a pure coincidence; a lucky hit

瞎忙(ㄒㄧㄚ ㄇㄤˊ)
to mess about; to be busy for nothing; to be busy without purpose or objective

瞎鬧(ㄒㄧㄚ ㄋㄠˋ)
to make nonsense; to cause meaningless trouble; to make a loud fuss over nothing; to fool around: 別瞎鬧，趕快往前走。Go ahead quickly and don't fool around.

瞎弄(ㄒㄧㄚ ㄋㄨㄥˋ)
to throw into disorder or confusion; to manage or operate without any method or plan

瞎了(ㄒㄧㄚ ˙ㄌㄜ)
to be blinded; to lose one's vision

瞎了眼睛(ㄒㄧㄚ ˙ㄌㄜ ㄧㄢˇ ㄐㄧㄥ)
①Blind fool! ②to become blind

瞎賴(ㄒㄧㄚ ㄌㄞˋ)
to put blame on others without the slightest justification

瞎聊(ㄒㄧㄚ ㄌㄧㄠˊ)
to converse at random; to talk nonsense; to jaw; to chat idly

瞎搞 or 瞎搗(ㄒㄧㄚ ㄍㄠˇ)
to do a thing without any plan or method

瞎話(ㄒㄧㄚ ㄏㄨㄚˋ)
lies; a nonsensical remark

瞎抓(ㄒㄧㄚ ㄓㄨㄚ)
to grasp anything within reach without knowing what to do with it

瞎扯(ㄒㄧㄚ ㄔㄜˇ)
to talk recklessly; to tell lies; to speak nonsense

瞎吹(ㄒㄧㄚ ㄔㄨㄟ)
to brag; to make wild boasts

瞎闖(ㄒㄧㄚ ㄔㄨㄤˇ)
to move ahead without a set direction or purpose; to make reckless or rash moves

瞎說(ㄒㄧㄚ ㄕㄨㄛ)
to speak groundlessly; to talk nonsense; wild talks: 別瞎說。Don't speak groundlessly.

瞎說八道(ㄒㄧㄚ ㄕㄨㄛ ㄅㄚ ㄉㄠˋ)
to talk through one's hat; to make reckless or irresponsible utterances; to tell lies or talk nonsense

瞎字不識(ㄒㄧㄚ ㄗˋ ㄅㄨˋ ㄕˊ)
illiterate; unable to read a single word

瞎子(ㄒㄧㄚ ˙ㄗ)
a blind man

瞎子摸象(ㄒㄧㄚ ˙ㄗ ㄇㄛ ㄒㄧㄤˋ)
(literally) The blindman feels an elephant.— unable to learn the whole picture

瞎猜(ㄒㄧㄚ ㄘㄞ)
to guess wildly; to make a wild guess; to make a random guess

瞎眼(ㄒㄧㄚ ㄧㄢˇ)
blind

【瞍】 3798
ㄙㄡˇ soou sǒu
to have eyes without pupils; blind

【瞑】 3799
1. ㄇㄧㄥˊ ming míng
(又讀 ㄇㄧㄥˋ miìng mìng)
to close the eyes

瞑瞑(ㄇㄧㄥˊ ㄇㄧㄥˊ)
to look but see nothing; vision obscured

瞑目(ㄇㄧㄥˊ ㄇㄨˋ)
①to close the eyes ②to die without regret or in peace

【瞑】 3799
2. ㄇㄧㄢˇ miann miǎn
to throw into a state of confusion 參看「瞑眩」

瞑眩(ㄇㄧㄢˇ ㄒㄩㄢˋ)
①to feel dizzy and upset ②medicine in its beneficial operation, yet causing distress; dizziness, nausea, etc. as a side effect of drugs

【瞌】 3800
ㄎㄜ ke kē

（目部）

【目部】

to be tired and to doze off

瞌睡(ㄎㄜ ㄕㄨㄟˋ)
to doze off while sitting: 他伏在書上打瞌睡。He dozed over a book.

【眯】 3801
ㄇㄧˊ mhi mi

1. to keep one's eyes half closed; to narrow the eyes: 她瞇着眼睛笑。She narrowed her eyes into a smile.

2. (dialect) to take a nap; to deceive: 我剛才眯了一會兒。I took a short nap just now.

眯縫眼兒(ㄇㄧˋ·ㄈㄥ ㄧㄢˇ)
①slit eyes ②slit-eyed; half-closed (eyes)

十一畫

【瞞】 3802
ㄇㄢˊ man mán

1. to hide the truth; to fool others by lying; to deceive

2. dim-sighted; poor vision

瞞不了人(ㄇㄢˊ ㄅㄨˋ ㄌㄧㄠˇ ㄖㄣˊ)
cannot hide the truth from others; cannot deceive others

瞞騙(ㄇㄢˊ ㄆㄧㄢˋ)
to deceive and lie; to hide the truth by lying

瞞得過(ㄇㄢˊ ㄉㄜˊ ㄍㄨㄛˋ)
(said of secrets, truth, etc.) can be concealed or hidden —with lies, etc.

瞞天過海(ㄇㄢˊ ㄊㄧㄢ ㄍㄨㄛˋ ㄏㄞˇ)
very clever and daring in deceiving others

瞞哄(ㄇㄢˊ ㄏㄨㄥˇ)
to deceive and cheat; to hide (the truth) and cheat

瞞心昧己(ㄇㄢˊ ㄒㄧㄣ ㄇㄟˋ ㄐㄧˇ)
unconscionable and self-deceiving; very mean

瞞上欺下(ㄇㄢˊ ㄕㄤˋ ㄑㄧ ㄒㄧㄚˋ)
to hide the truth from higher authorities and oppress the people

【瞟】 3803
ㄆㄧㄠˇ peau piǎo
to look askance at

瞟眇(ㄆㄧㄠˇ ㄇㄧㄠˇ)
①obscure and indistinct —due to distance, mists, etc. ②very undependable or unreliable ③having little chance 亦作「縹緲」

瞟了他一眼(ㄆㄧㄠˇ·ㄌㄜ ㄊㄚ ㄧ ㄧㄢˇ)
to give him a side glance

【瞠】 3804
ㄔㄥ cheng chēng
to look straight at; to stare at

瞠目(ㄔㄥ ㄇㄨˋ)
to gaze at fixedly; wide-eyed

瞠目結舌(ㄔㄥ ㄇㄨˋ ㄐㄧㄝˊ ㄕㄜˊ)
wide-eyed and tongue-tied; amazed and speechless

瞠乎其後(ㄔㄥ ㄏㄨˊ ㄑㄧˊ ㄏㄡˋ)
far behind, without any hope of catching up

【瞢】 3805
ㄇㄥˊ meng méng

1. dim-sighted; poor vision

2. obscure; not bright

3. ashamed

4. grief

瞢然(ㄇㄥˊ ㄖㄢˊ)
dark and obscure

【瞖】 3806
ㄧˋ yih yì
cataract

十二畫

【瞬】 3807
ㄕㄨㄣˋ shuenn shùn

1. to blink, wink or twinkle

2. a very short time; in the twinkling of an eye

瞬華(ㄕㄨㄣˋ ㄏㄨㄚˊ)
time flying away; ephemeral

瞬間(ㄕㄨㄣˋ ㄐㄧㄢ)
in the twinkling of an eye; in an instant: 就在那一瞬間，電話響了。At that instant the telephone rang.

瞬息(ㄕㄨㄣˋ ㄒㄧˊ)or瞬息之間(ㄕㄨㄣˋ ㄒㄧˊ ㄓ ㄐㄧㄢ)
in a wink; in the twinkling of an eye

瞬息萬變(ㄕㄨㄣˋ ㄒㄧˊ ㄨㄢˋ ㄅㄧㄢˋ)
(literally) ten thousand changes in the twinkling of an eye—many changes within a short time

瞬瞬(ㄕㄨㄣˋ ㄕㄨㄣˋ)
in a blink; in a twinkling

【瞰】 3808
ㄎㄢˋ kann kàn

1. to watch; to look far away

2. to overlook (from a high ground)

瞰視(ㄎㄢˋ ㄕˋ)
to overlook; to watch from above

瞰望(ㄎㄢˋ ㄨㄤˋ)
to overlook; to observe (or look from above; to have a bird's-eye view

【瞳】 3809
ㄊㄨㄥˊ torng tóng

1. the pupil of the eye

2. stupid; ignorant

瞳矇(ㄊㄨㄥˊ ㄇㄥˊ)
ignorant

瞳孔(ㄊㄨㄥˊ ㄎㄨㄥˇ)
the pupil of the eye

瞳孔散大(ㄊㄨㄥˊ ㄎㄨㄥˇ ㄙㄢˇ ㄉㄚˋ)
mydriasis (the dilation of the pupil)

瞳孔縮小(ㄊㄨㄥˊ ㄎㄨㄥˇ ㄙㄨㄛ ㄒㄧㄠˇ)
the contraction of the pupil

瞳人(ㄊㄨㄥˊ ㄖㄣˊ)
the pupil of the eye

瞳子(ㄊㄨㄥˊ ㄗˇ)
the pupil of the eye

【瞪】 3810
ㄉㄥˋ denq dèng
to stare at; to open (one's eyes) wide; to glare at

瞪視(ㄉㄥˋ ㄕˋ)
to stare one in the face

瞪眼(ㄉㄥˋ ㄧㄢˇ)
①to stare at angrily ②to look straight ahead; to make a fishy glance

【瞭】 3811
1. ㄌㄧㄠˇ leau liǎo

1. to understand

2. clear and bright

瞭亮(ㄌㄧㄠˇ ㄌㄧㄤˋ)
to understand; to be clear about

瞭解(ㄌㄧㄠˇ ㄐㄧㄝˇ)
to comprehend; to understand; understanding

瞭然(ㄌㄧㄠˇ ㄖㄢˊ)
clear and evident; plain and fully understandable

瞭如指掌(ㄌㄧㄠˇ ㄖㄨˊ ㄓˇ ㄓㄤˇ)
to know or understand thoroughly—as clear as if one were looking at one's own palms and fingers

【瞭】 3811
2. ㄌㄧㄠˋ liaw liào
to look down from a higher place

瞭望(ㄌㄧㄠˋ ㄨㄤˋ)
to look down from a higher place

瞭望臺(ㄌㄧㄠˋ ㄨㄤˋ ㄊㄞˊ)

a watchtower; a lookout (post)

【瞡】3812 《ㄨㄟ guey guì
1. a blind man
2. stupid; ignorant

【瞧】3813 《ㄑㄧㄠˊ chyau qiáo
1. to see; to look at: 等着瞧吧。
Wait and see.
2. to steal a glance; to glance quickly

瞧病《ㄑㄧㄠˊ ㄅㄧㄥˋ》
①(said of a patient) to see a doctor ②(said of a doctor) to take a look at a patient

瞧不見《ㄑㄧㄠˊ ㄅㄨˋ ㄐㄧㄢˋ》
should not be seen; not worth seeing; unnecessary to see

瞧不透《ㄑㄧㄠˊ ㄅㄨˋ ㄊㄡˋ》
unable to see through; not able to understand: 我真瞧不透他爲何如此做。I can't understand why he did so.

瞧不過《ㄑㄧㄠˊ ㄅㄨˋ ㄍㄨㄛˋ》
(in the case of exceptionally cruel, etc. scenes) not hardhearted enough to see something to its brutal end

瞧不慣《ㄑㄧㄠˊ ㄅㄨˋ ㄍㄨㄢˋ》
not used to seeing or witnessing (cruel scenes, practices, etc.)

瞧不起《ㄑㄧㄠˊ ㄅㄨˋ ㄑㄧˇ》
to look down upon; to despise; to hold in contempt: 我們都瞧不起他。We all look down upon him.

瞧不上眼《ㄑㄧㄠˊ ㄅㄨˋ ㄕㄤˋ ㄧㄢˇ》
not worth seeing — well beneath one's standard or ideal ①(said of commodities, etc.) not up to one's (fine) taste ②(said of a person) to turn one's nose up at

瞧得透《ㄑㄧㄠˊ ㄉㄜˊ ㄊㄡˋ》
to see through; to understand thoroughly

瞧得起《ㄑㄧㄠˊ ㄉㄜˊ ㄑㄧˇ》
to esteem or respect; to value; to think much (or highly) of somebody

瞧得上《ㄑㄧㄠˊ ㄉㄜˊ ㄕㄤˋ》
good enough to suit one's taste

瞧見《ㄑㄧㄠˊ ㄐㄧㄢˋ》
to see; to catch sight of

瞧著《ㄑㄧㄠˊ ㄓㄜ˙》
①while looking ②Let's see. 或Let's consider. 或Let's wait and see.

瞧著辦《ㄑㄧㄠˊ ㄓㄜ˙ ㄅㄢˋ》
Let's wait and see what happens and plan our strategy, countermeasure, etc. then.

瞧熱鬧兒《ㄑㄧㄠˊ ㄖㄜˋ ㄋㄠˋ ㄦ》
①to go and see where the fanfare is—as in a festival, etc. ②to be a bystander in fights, fires, etc. ③to watch the failure or disaster of others with secret delight

瞧一瞧《ㄑㄧㄠˊ ㄧˋ ㄑㄧㄠˊ》
to take a look: 讓我們瞧一瞧你的字典。Let's have a look at your dictionary.

【瞵】3814 ㄌㄧㄣˊ lin lín
1. to look at; to stare at
2.(said of eyes) clear and bright

瞵盼《ㄌㄧㄣˊ ㄆㄢˋ》
to look around

【瞥】3815 ㄆㄧㄝ piē
to have a casual and short glance; to catch a glimpse of

瞥一眼《ㄆㄧㄝ ㄧˋ ㄧㄢˇ》
to cast a casual and brief glance

瞥見《ㄆㄧㄝ ㄐㄧㄢˋ》
to catch a glimpse of; to catch sight of

十三畫

【瞻】3816 ㄓㄢ jan zhān
1. to look; to look up
2. to regard respectfully; to reverence

瞻對《ㄓㄢ ㄉㄨㄟˋ》
①to respond to the emperor during a court audience ②name of a tribal district in Sikang (西康)

瞻禮日《ㄓㄢ ㄌㄧˇ ㄖˋ》
Sunday

瞻前顧後《ㄓㄢ ㄑㄧㄢˊ ㄍㄨˋ ㄏㄡˋ》
(literally) to look forward and backward—very cautious: 做這種工作不要太過瞻前顧後。Don't be too cautious over this work.

瞻徇《ㄓㄢ ㄒㄩㄣˋ》
to practice favoritism; to be unduly lenient in the enforcement of law

瞻視《ㄓㄢ ㄕˋ》
to look; to behold; to look up to

瞻依《ㄓㄢ ㄧ》
to look up to one's father as an example and to depend on one's mother while one is growing up

瞻仰 or 瞻卬《ㄓㄢ ㄧㄤˇ》
①to look up respectfully; to pay respects to ②to look up to

瞻望《ㄓㄢ ㄨㄤˋ》
①to look forward to a faraway place; to raise one's head and look far ahead ②to adore; to worship

【瞼】3817 ㄐㄧㄢˇ jean jiǎn
the eyelids

【瞽】3818 《ㄨˇ guu gǔ
1. blind
2.(in ancient China) blind musicians
3. having no discerning ability; lacking the power of judgment

瞽矇《ㄍㄨˇ ㄇㄥ》
the official rank of court musicians in ancient China

瞽者《ㄍㄨˇ ㄓㄜˇ》
the blind; a blind person

瞽史《ㄍㄨˇ ㄕˇ》
the two official posts in the Chou Dynasty, one in charge of music, and the other in charge of rites and astrology

瞽說《ㄍㄨˇ ㄕㄨㄛ》or 瞽言《ㄍㄨˇ ㄧㄢˊ》
shallow and unreasonable talks; wild talks

瞽瞍《ㄍㄨˇ ㄙㄡˇ》
Ku-sou—"The Blind Man", a nickname for the father of Shun (舜), so called for his attempt to kill his son who eventually became a sage king

瞽議《ㄍㄨˇ ㄧˋ》
wild talks; groundless statements

〔矛部〕

【瞿】 3819
1. ㄑㄩ chiu qū
(又讀 ㄑㄩ chyu qú)
a Chinese family name

瞿曇(ㄑㄩ ㄊㄢˊ)
Gautama, the family name
of Buddha

瞿唐峽(ㄑㄩ ㄊㄤˊ ㄒㄧㄚˊ)
the Chü Tang Gorge, one of
the three gorges along the
Yangtze River and a gate-
way to Szechwan

【瞿】 3819
2. ㄐㄩˋ jiuh jù
1. shocked or scared
2. (said of hawks and falcons)
to look around

瞿然(ㄐㄩˋ ㄖㄢˊ)
alarmed

十四畫

【矇】 3820
1. ㄇㄥˊ meng méng
1. blind
2. (figuratively) ignorant; stupid and obstinate

矇藏(ㄇㄥˊ ㄘㄤˊ)
to hide the truth from a
superior

矇昧(ㄇㄥˊ ㄇㄟˋ)
① stupid and obstinate ②
dim-sighted

矇矓(ㄇㄥˊ ㄌㄨㄥˊ)
obscure and dim; unclear

矇矓(ㄇㄥˊ ㄏㄨㄥˊ)
① hazy; sight-blurred: 矇矓的
景色頗有詩意。A hazy view is
quite poetic. ② half-asleep;
drowsy; somnolent

矇瞶(ㄇㄥˊ ㄍㄨㄟˋ)
① blind and deaf ② ignorant
and stupid

矇瞍(ㄇㄥˊ ㄙㄡˇ)
① a blind person ② blind
musicians in ancient China

【矇】 3820
2. ㄇㄥ mheng mēng
1. to deceive; to cheat
2. lucky

矇騙(ㄇㄥ ㄆㄧㄢˋ)
to deceive and cheat

矇混(ㄇㄥ ㄏㄨㄣˋ)
to fake and cheat

矇住(ㄇㄥ ㄓㄨˋ)
to obtain or achieve something through sheer luck

矇住(ㄇㄥ ㄓㄨˋ)
① to hide the truth and
deceive others ② to get confused or befuddled

十五畫

【矍】 3821
ㄐㄩㄝˊ jyue jué
1. to watch in fright; scared
2. old but healthy

矍鑠(ㄐㄩㄝˊ ㄕㄨㄛˋ)
to be old but healthy and
spry; to be hale and hearty

矍矍(ㄐㄩㄝˊ ㄐㄩㄝˊ)
looking around in fear

十六畫

【矓】 3822
ㄌㄨㄥˊ long lóng
hazy; blurred: 霧氣使群山矓
矓不清。Mists blurred the
hills.

十九畫

【矗】 3823
ㄔㄨˋ chuh chù
1. rising sharply; steep
2. lofty; upright; straight
3. luxuriant growth

矗立(ㄔㄨˋ ㄌㄧˋ)
rising up steeply; to stand
high; to stick up; to tower
up

矗矗(ㄔㄨˋ ㄔㄨˋ)
steep and lofty

二十畫

【矙】 3824
ㄎㄢˋ kann kàn
1. to watch; to spy
2. to overlook; to look downward

二十一畫

【矚】 3825
ㄓㄨˇ juu zhǔ
to watch; to observe or gaze
at carefully or steadily; to
pay attention

矚目(ㄓㄨˇ ㄇㄨˋ)
to watch or stare at with
great interest; to look at
eagerly; to be the focus of
attention

矚望(ㄓㄨˇ ㄨㄤˋ)
to watch and expect eagerly;
to look forward to

矛 部
ㄇㄠˊ mau máo

【矛】 3826
ㄇㄠˊ mau máo
a lance; a spear

矛兵(ㄇㄠˊ ㄅㄧㄥ)
a lancer; a pikeman

矛盾(ㄇㄠˊ ㄉㄨㄣˋ) or (ㄇㄠˊ ㄕㄨㄣˋ)
to contradict; contradiction;
inconsistency: 他的話與事實
矛盾。His statement contra-
dicts with the facts.

矛盾律(ㄇㄠˊ ㄉㄨㄣˋ ㄌㄩˋ)
the law of contradiction

矛頭(ㄇㄠˊ ㄊㄡˊ)
a spearhead

矛戟(ㄇㄠˊ ㄐㄧˇ)
lances and spears

矛槍(ㄇㄠˊ ㄑㄧㄤ)
spears and javelins

四畫

【矜】 3827
1. ㄐㄧㄣ jin jīn
1. to feel sorry for; to pity; to
commiserate with; to be
sympathetic with; to com-
passionate
2. to brag; to boast; arrogant;
conceited: 他的行為舉止顯現
驕矜之氣。His manner
revealed his arrogant airs.
3. self-esteem; self-control;
self-discipline; dignified
4. to emulate

矜宥(ㄐㄧㄣ ㄧㄡˋ)
to commute the sentence of
a criminal for humanitarian
reasons

矜憫(ㄐㄧㄣ ㄇㄧㄣˇ)
to pity; to sympathize; to
compassionate

矜伐(ㄐㄧㄣ ㄈㄚˊ)
to be arrogant due to one's
accomplishments

矜大(ㄐㄧㄣ ㄉㄚˋ)
proud and bragging; arro-
gant and exaggerative

矜憐(ㄐㄧㄣ ㄌㄧㄢˊ)
to commiserate with; to pity; to feel sorry for

矜貴(ㄐㄧㄣ ㄍㄨㄟˋ)
to boast of one's high position, blue blood, etc.

矜誇(ㄐㄧㄣ ㄎㄨㄚ)
to brag or boast about one's accomplishments: 她從不矜誇自己的才能。She never boasted about her talent.

矜惜(ㄐㄧㄣ ㄒㄧˊ)
to value; to treasure

矜恤(ㄐㄧㄣ ㄒㄩˋ)
to sympathize with; to have pity on

矜重(ㄐㄧㄣ ㄓㄨㄥˋ)
dignified; self-control or self-esteem

矜持(ㄐㄧㄣ ㄔˊ)
to carry oneself with dignity and reserve; to conduct oneself with circumspection: 他的舉止矜持。He conducted himself with circumspection.

矜寵(ㄐㄧㄣ ㄔㄨㄥˇ)
to presume on the favor of the boss

矜式(ㄐㄧㄣ ㄕˋ)
to emulate or pattern after; to respect as a model

矜飾(ㄐㄧㄣ ㄕˋ)
to brag and pretend

矜人(ㄐㄧㄣ ㄖㄣˊ)
men in a pitiable case

【矜】 3827
2.《ㄍㄨㄢ guan guān
a widower 亦作「鰥」

矜寡孤獨(《ㄍㄨㄢ ㄍㄨㄚˇ ㄍㄨ ㄉㄨˊ)
(literally) the widower, the widow, the orphan and the childless—the less privileged group or unfortunate lot

七畫

【矞】 3828
ㄩˋ yuh yù
1. bright and brilliant; charming
2. nature bursting into life
3. clouds of many hues

矞皇(ㄩˊ ㄏㄨㄤˊ)
①bright and beautiful ②name of a deity

矞矞(ㄩˊ ㄩˋ)
nature bursting into life

矞雲(ㄩˊ ㄩㄣˊ)
clouds of many hues

矢 部
ㄕˇ　shyy　shǐ

【矢】 3829
ㄕˇ shyy shǐ
1. an arrow; a dart
2. to vow; to take an oath; to pledge
3. to display
4. straightforward

矢服(ㄕˇ ㄈㄨˊ)
a quiver for holding arrows

矢口不移(ㄕˇ ㄎㄡˇ ㄅㄨˋ ㄧˊ)
to stick to one's original statement

矢口否認(ㄕˇ ㄎㄡˇ ㄈㄡˇ ㄖㄣˋ)
to deny flatly

矢志不移(ㄕˇ ㄓˋ ㄅㄨˋ ㄧˊ)
to swear that one will stick to something; to take an oath not to change one's mind: 我對妳的愛矢志不移。I swear I'll love you forever.

矢志靡他(ㄕˇ ㄓˋ ㄇㄧˊ ㄊㄚ)
to swear that one would stick it out

矢車菊(ㄕˇ ㄔㄜ ㄐㄩˊ)
bluebottle; cornflower; bachelor's button

矢石(ㄕˇ ㄕˊ)
arrows and rocks used as weapons in ancient warfare; bullets and bombs in modern warfare

矢誓(ㄕˇ ㄕˋ)
to take an oath

矢人(ㄕˇ ㄖㄣˊ)
a maker of arrows

矢石雨下(ㄕˇ ㄕˊ ㄩˇ ㄒㄧㄚˋ)
The arrows come down like a shower.

矢在弦上(ㄕˇ ㄗㄞˋ ㄒㄧㄢˊ ㄕㄤˋ)
(literally) The arrow is on the strained cord.—imminent; cannot be stopped

矢言(ㄕˇ ㄧㄢˊ)
an oath; a solemn vow; to make a vow

二畫

【矣】 3830
ㄧˇ yii yǐ
1. a final particle denoting the perfect tense: 悔之晚矣。It's too late to repent.
2. an auxiliary denoting determination
3. (in usage) both particles or auxiliaries indicating exclamations or questions 亦作「哉」or「乎」

三畫

【知】 3831
1. ㄓ jy zhī
1. knowledge
2. to know; to understand; to feel; to recognize; to be aware of: 若要人不知，除非己莫為。If you don't want others to know it, don't do it.
3. to acquaint; to be familiar with; to befriend
4. to control; to operate; to direct
5. to wait on

知白守黑(ㄓ ㄅㄞˊ ㄕㄡˇ ㄏㄟ)
(literally) to stick to obscurity for a reason, even if one knows that light is something valuable (from Lao-tzu)—to be content with retirement and to let others enjoy the limelight

知賓(ㄓ ㄅㄧㄣ)
a receptionist

知兵(ㄓ ㄅㄧㄥ)
to be well versed in military arts

知名(ㄓ ㄇㄧㄥˊ)
well-known

知名度(ㄓ ㄇㄧㄥˊ ㄉㄨˋ)
name recognition; name familiarity

知名之士(ㄓ ㄇㄧㄥˊ ㄓ ㄕˋ)or 知名人士(ㄓ ㄇㄧㄥˊ ㄖㄣˊ ㄕˋ)
a well-known personality; a famous person; a public figure; a celebrity

知命之年(ㄓ ㄇㄧㄥˋ ㄓ ㄋㄧㄢˊ)
50 years of age

知法犯法(ㄓ ㄈㄚˇ ㄈㄢˋ ㄈㄚˇ)
to transgress a law knowingly

知府(ㄓ ㄈㄨˇ)
the magistrate of a prefec-

〔矢部〕

ture

知道(ㄓ ㄉㄠˋ)
to know; to realize; to understand: 他真的不知道這件事。He really knows nothing about it.

知難行易(ㄓ ㄋㄢˊ ㄒㄧㄥˊ ㄧˋ)
It's easier to do a thing than to know the why. (a theory advanced by Dr. Sun Yat-sen, in rebutting the popular belief to the contrary)

知難而退(ㄓ ㄋㄢˊ ㄦˊ ㄊㄨㄟˋ)
to withdraw or quit after learning of the difficulties, hardships, etc. involved

知禮(ㄓ ㄌㄧˇ)
to say and act in proper manners; to know the rules of propriety

知了(ㄓ ㄌㄧㄠˇ)
the cicada, or broad locust

知根知底(ㄓ ㄍㄣ ㄓ ㄉㄧˇ)
to know (somebody or something) to the very root or source; to know through and through

知更雀(ㄓ ㄍㄥ ㄑㄩㄝˋ)or 知更鳥(ㄓ ㄍㄥ ㄋㄧㄠˇ)
the robin

知過(ㄓ ㄍㄨㄛˋ)
to realize (or know) one's mistake

知過必改(ㄓ ㄍㄨㄛˋ ㄅㄧˋ ㄍㄞˇ)
One should correct his faults once he is aware of them.

知客(ㄓ ㄎㄜˋ)
①a reception monk in a Buddhist temple ②a person in charge of reception at ceremonies

知幾(ㄓ ㄐㄧ)
to know or detect something before it takes shape; to discover something at its very beginning

知己(ㄓ ㄐㄧˇ)
①a close or intimate friend: 他是我的知己。He is my bosom (or intimate) friend. ②intimate: 我和她很知己。I am on intimate terms with her. ③to know oneself

知己知彼，百戰百勝(ㄓ ㄐㄧˇ ㄓ ㄅㄧˇ，ㄅㄞˇ ㄓㄢˋ ㄅㄞˇ ㄕㄥˋ)
Knowing one's own situation and that of the enemy

guarantees victory in every battle.

知交(ㄓ ㄐㄧㄠ)
intimate and close friends: 他和我父親是多年知交。He and my father are intimate friends for many years.

知覺(ㄓ ㄐㄩㄝˊ)
①consciousness: 我們在睡眠時沒有知覺。We have no consciousness during sleep. ②perception

知覺神經(ㄓ ㄐㄩㄝˊ ㄕㄣˊ ㄐㄧㄥ)
sensory nerves

知其不可爲而爲之(ㄓ ㄑㄧˊ ㄅㄨˋ ㄎㄜˇ ㄨㄟˊ ㄦˊ ㄨㄟˊ ㄓ)
to do something even though one knows it is impossible to succeed

知一不知其二(ㄓ ㄧ ㄅㄨˋ ㄓ ㄑㄧˊ ㄦˋ)
to know only a part of the story; to have only a partial understanding of a situation

知情(ㄓ ㄑㄧㄥˊ)
to be aware of (usually referring to a secret, plot, etc.); to be in the know: 知情不報將受罰。Those who conceal what they know of a case will be punished.

知趣(ㄓ ㄑㄩˋ)
sensible; having a sense of propriety; knowing what to do in a delicate situation

知悉(ㄓ ㄒㄧ)
to know; to learn of; to be aware of：我們尚未知悉他是否安全到達。We have not yet learned whether he arrived safely.

知曉(ㄓ ㄒㄧㄠˇ)
to know; to be aware of; to learn of; to understand

知縣(ㄓ ㄒㄧㄢˋ)
a county magistrate in former times

知心(ㄓ ㄒㄧㄣ)
①meeting of minds; bosom (friends) ②to know what's on the mind of another person

知心話(ㄓ ㄒㄧㄣ ㄏㄨㄚˋ)
intimate talks or words; secrets from the bottom of one's heart

知心人(ㄓ ㄒㄧㄣ ㄖㄣˊ)

a bosom friend: 她終於找到知心人了。She has finally found a bosom friend.

知行合一(ㄓ ㄒㄧㄥˊ ㄏㄜˊ ㄧ)
(literally) Knowledge and action should go hand in hand.—Action without knowledge serves no purpose, while knowledge without action is futile. (a theory advocated by Wang Yang-ming (王陽明) of the Ming Dynasty)

知之爲知之，不知爲不知，是知也(ㄓ ㄓ ㄨㄟˊ ㄓ ㄓ，ㄅㄨˋ ㄓ ㄨㄟˊ ㄅㄨˋ ㄓ，ㄕˋ ㄓ ㄧㄝˇ)
When you know a thing, to hold that you know it; and when you do not know a thing, to allow that you do not know it;—this is knowledge. (論語·爲政)

知止(ㄓ ㄓˇ)
to know where to stop

知制誥(ㄓ ㄓˋ ㄍㄠˋ)
an official in ancient China in charge of secretarial matters

知照(ㄓ ㄓㄠˋ)
①to notify; to tell ②(a Chinese documentary usage to a subordinate organization) for your information

知州(ㄓ ㄓㄡ)
(in ancient China) the chief of a prefecture

知政(ㄓ ㄓㄥˋ)
to administer the government; to handle state affairs

知恥(ㄓ ㄔˇ)
to have a sense of shame

知恥近乎勇(ㄓ ㄔˇ ㄐㄧㄣˋ ㄏㄨ ㄩㄥˇ)
Knowing shame is akin to courage.

知事(ㄓ ㄕˋ)
①a former official post equivalent to today's county magistrate ②to know things when one grows up

知識(ㄓ ㄕˋ)
knowledge; learning; information: 知識即力量。Knowledge is power.

知識分子(ㄓ ㄕˋ ㄈㄣˋ ㄗˇ)
intellectuals; the intelligentsia

知識論(ㄓ ㄕˋ ㄌㄨㄣˋ)
(philosophy)epistemology;

the theory of knowledge 亦作「認識論」

知識階級(ㄓ ㄕˊ ㄐㄧㄝˊ ㄐㄧˊ)
the intelligentsia; the intellectual class

知人(ㄓ ㄖㄣˊ)
to know people—the ability to understand people, their moral standing, integrity, ability, etc.

知人知面不知心(ㄓ ㄖㄣˊ ㄓ ㄇㄧㄢˋ ㄅㄨˋ ㄓ ㄒㄧㄣ)
(literally) One may know a person by his face, but one cannot read his mind.—Do not trust people too easily.

知人善任(ㄓ ㄖㄣˊ ㄕㄢˋ ㄖㄣˋ)
to be expert in judging people's worth and to know how to employ them to the best advantage

知子莫若父(ㄓ ㄗˇ ㄇㄛˋ ㄖㄨㄛˋ ㄈㄨˋ)
Father knows his sons best.

知足(ㄓ ㄗㄨˊ)
to be content with what one has had

知足常樂(ㄓ ㄗㄨˊ ㄔㄤˊ ㄌㄜˋ)
Contentment brings happiness.

知友(ㄓ ㄧㄡˇ)
a close or intimate friend

知言(ㄓ ㄧㄢˊ)
①words of wisdom ②to know the true meaning of one's words

知音(ㄓ ㄧㄣ)
①a close or intimate friend ②one who is well versed in music

知無不言(ㄓ ㄨˊ ㄅㄨˋ ㄧㄢˊ)
to hide nothing; to be very frank

知無不言，言無不盡(ㄓ ㄨˊ ㄅㄨˋ ㄧㄢˊ ㄧㄢˊ ㄨˊ ㄅㄨˋ ㄐㄧㄣˋ)
One says all one knows and says it without reserve.

知我罪我(ㄓ ㄨㄛˇ ㄗㄨㄟˋ ㄨㄛˇ)
If you understand me, well and good. If not, I don't care a bit.

知遇(ㄓ ㄩˋ)
to have found a patron or superior who appreciates one's ability

知遇之恩(ㄓ ㄩˋ ㄓ ㄣ)
the debt one owes to somebody who understands him

and has treated him well

【知】 3831
2. (智) ㄓ jyh zhì
the learned; the wise; brains

知能(ㄓ ㄋㄥˊ)
intellectual capacity

知者不惑(ㄓ ㄓㄜˇ ㄅㄨˋ ㄏㄨㄛˋ)
The wise harbor no doubts.

知者樂水(ㄓ ㄓㄜˇ ㄧㄠˋ ㄕㄨㄟˇ)
The wise enjoy water.

四畫

【矧】 3832 ㄕㄣˇ sheen shěn
1. still more
2. also
3. gums

【矦】 3833
1. (侯) ㄏㄡˊ hour hóu
the second of the five grades of the nobility; a marquis
2. a bull's-eye
3. beautiful
4. an opening particle—but
5. why
6. a Chinese family name

五畫

【矩】 3834 ㄐㄩˇ jeu jǔ
1. a carpenter's square
2. a rule; a regulation; a pattern
3. to carve

矩步(ㄐㄩˇ ㄅㄨˋ)
to behave in a cautious manner

矩度(ㄐㄩˇ ㄉㄨˋ)
laws and regulations; a pattern or model

矩矱(ㄐㄩˇ ㄏㄨㄛˋ)
regulations; rules

矩形(ㄐㄩˇ ㄒㄧㄥˊ)
a rectangle; rectangular

矩形體(ㄐㄩˇ ㄒㄧㄥˊ ㄊㄧˇ)
a rectangular parallelepiped

矩尺(ㄐㄩˇ ㄔˇ)
a carpenter's square

七畫

【矬】 3835 ㄘㄨㄛˊ tswo cuó
short; dwarf

矬子(ㄘㄨㄛˊ ㄗˇ)

a dwarf; a shortie

【短】 3836 ㄉㄨㄢˇ doan duǎn
1. short; brief; 多季晝短夜長。In winter the days are short and the nights long.
2. to be deficient; to want; to lack; to owe
3. shortcomings; faults; mistakes: 勿道人之短。Don't talk about people's shortcomings.

短波(ㄉㄨㄢˇ ㄅㄛ)
(said of radio, etc.) short-wave

短兵(ㄉㄨㄢˇ ㄅㄧㄥ)
knives and swords, etc. (as opposed to lances and spears)

短兵相接(ㄉㄨㄢˇ ㄅㄧㄥ ㄒㄧㄤ ㄐㄧㄝ)
(military) to fight at close quarters; hand-to-hand combat

短不了(ㄉㄨㄢˇ ㄅㄨˋ ㄌㄧㄠˇ)
①cannot do without: 人類不了水。People cannot do without water. ②cannot avoid; to have to

短跑(ㄉㄨㄢˇ ㄆㄠˇ)
a short-distance race; a sprint; a dash

短跑健將(ㄉㄨㄢˇ ㄆㄠˇ ㄐㄧㄢˋ ㄐㄧㄤˋ)
a sprinter; a short-distance runner: 他弟弟是著名的短跑健將。His younger brother is a famous sprinter.

短篇小說(ㄉㄨㄢˇ ㄆㄧㄢ ㄒㄧㄠˇ ㄕㄨㄛ)
short stories: 我喜歡有關科學的短篇小說。I like short stories about science.

短片(ㄉㄨㄢˇ ㄆㄧㄢˋ)
(film) a short film

短評(ㄉㄨㄢˇ ㄆㄧㄥˊ)
a short comment or critique; a brief commentary

短命(ㄉㄨㄢˇ ㄇㄧㄥˋ)
to die early; short-lived; to die young

短打(ㄉㄨㄢˇ ㄉㄚˇ)
①short clothes (as opposed to long gowns) ②(drama)a hand-to-hand fight in tights ③(baseball)to bunt; a bunt

短大衣(ㄉㄨㄢˇ ㄉㄚˋ ㄧ)
a short overcoat

短刀(ㄉㄨㄢˇ ㄉㄠ)
a short sword; a dagger

短笛(ㄉㄨㄢˇ ㄉㄧˊ)

〔矢部〕

【矢部】

a piccolo

短短(ㄉㄨㄢˇ ㄉㄨㄢˇ)
brief; short: 她給他寫了一封短短的謝信。She wrote him a brief letter of thanks.

短噸(ㄉㄨㄢˇ ㄉㄨㄣ)
short ton

短亭長亭(ㄉㄨㄢˇ ㄊㄧㄥˊ ㄔㄤˊ ㄊㄧㄥˊ)
small pavilions outside every city in ancient China, a smaller one in every 5 *li*, and a larger one in every 10 *li*

短禮(ㄉㄨㄢˇ ㄌㄧˇ)
to lack courtesy

短路(ㄉㄨㄢˇ ㄌㄨˋ)
①an improper or unlawful way of making a living—as robbery, burglary, etc. ②(electricity) short circuit

短綆汲深(ㄉㄨㄢˇ ㄍㄥˇ ㄐㄧˊ ㄕㄣ)
(literally) to draw water from a deep well with a short rope—to do something beyond one's capability

短工(ㄉㄨㄢˇ ㄍㄨㄥ)
a temporary worker; a handy man; a temporary employee: 他要我幫他找一位短工。He asked me to find a temporary worker for him.

短褲(ㄉㄨㄢˇ ㄎㄨˋ)
knee pants; shorts; short pants

短褐(ㄉㄨㄢˇ ㄏㄜˊ)
the clothing of the poor

短計(ㄉㄨㄢˇ ㄐㄧˋ)
unsound plans or measures; bad policies

短見(ㄉㄨㄢˇ ㄐㄧㄢˋ)
①shortsightedness ②suicide: 老人昨晚尋短見。The old man attempted suicide last night.

短劍(ㄉㄨㄢˇ ㄐㄧㄢˋ)
a dagger

短距離(ㄉㄨㄢˇ ㄐㄩˋ ㄌㄧˊ)
short distance; close range

短期(ㄉㄨㄢˇ ㄑㄧˊ)
short-term (bonds, loans, etc.); a short period: 我要申請一筆短期貸款。I want to apply for a short-term loan.

短期投資(ㄉㄨㄢˇ ㄑㄧˊ ㄊㄡˊ ㄗ)
liquid investment; temporary investment; short-term investment

短期計劃(ㄉㄨㄢˇ ㄑㄧˊ ㄐㄧˋ ㄏㄨㄚˋ)
a short-term project

短期信貸(ㄉㄨㄢˇ ㄑㄧˊ ㄒㄧㄣˋ ㄉㄞˋ)
short-term credit

短期銀行貸款(ㄉㄨㄢˇ ㄑㄧˊ ㄧㄣˊ ㄏㄤˊ ㄉㄞˋ ㄎㄨㄢˇ)
short-term bank loans

短氣(ㄉㄨㄢˇ ㄑㄧˋ)
to lose courage or heart; despondent and discouraged; depressed; in low spirits

短欠(ㄉㄨㄢˇ ㄑㄧㄢˋ)
to be short by...; to fall short; to owe

短缺(ㄉㄨㄢˇ ㄑㄩㄝ)
to fall short; deficient; deficiency; shortage: 在戰時，常常發生糧食短缺的情形。Food shortages often occur in time of war.

短小(ㄉㄨㄢˇ ㄒㄧㄠˇ)
short and small: 他的身材短小。He is a person of short and small stature.

短小精悍(ㄉㄨㄢˇ ㄒㄧㄠˇ ㄐㄧㄥ ㄏㄢˋ)
short but energetic; short in physical stature but long in stamina

短訓班(ㄉㄨㄢˇ ㄒㄩㄣˋ ㄅㄢ)
a short-term training course

短折(ㄉㄨㄢˇ ㄓㄜˊ)
to die young; short-lived

短暫(ㄉㄨㄢˇ ㄓㄢˋ)
transient; brief; a short period: 這數學天才的一生是短暫而光榮的。The mathematical genius' life was short but glorious.

短針(ㄉㄨㄢˇ ㄓㄣ)
the hour hand

短裝(ㄉㄨㄢˇ ㄓㄨㄤ)
short clothes

短長(ㄉㄨㄢˇ ㄔㄤˊ)
①shortcomings and good points ②good and evil ③life and death

短程(ㄉㄨㄢˇ ㄔㄥˊ)
short distance; short range

短絀(ㄉㄨㄢˇ ㄔㄨˋ)
to fall short by...; deficient; deficiency

短處(ㄉㄨㄢˇ ㄔㄨˋ)
shortcomings; faults; defects; weak points: 不守時間是他最大的短處。Not being punctual is his greatest shortcoming.

短時間(ㄉㄨㄢˇ ㄕˊ ㄐㄧㄢ)
a short time or period

短視(ㄉㄨㄢˇ ㄕˋ)
shortsighted; to lack foresight: 政府的政策是短視的。The government's policy is shortsighted.

短少(ㄉㄨㄢˇ ㄕㄠˇ)
to fall short by...; deficient; deficiency; missing: 這本書短少一頁。There is one page missing in this book.

短衫(ㄉㄨㄢˇ ㄕㄢ)
a shirt; a jacket

短促(ㄉㄨㄢˇ ㄘㄨˋ)
①(said of time) short; brief; transient; ephemeral ②of short duration: 如是結束了這個短促的旅程。Thus ended the journey of short duration.

短音階(ㄉㄨㄢˇ ㄧㄣ ㄐㄧㄝ)
(music) the minor scale

短音程(ㄉㄨㄢˇ ㄧㄣ ㄔㄥˊ)
(music) a minor interval

短襪(ㄉㄨㄢˇ ㄨㄚˋ)
socks

短文(ㄉㄨㄢˇ ㄨㄣˊ)
a short essay

短語(ㄉㄨㄢˇ ㄩˇ)
phrases

八畫

【矮】 3837
ㄞˇ ae ǎi

1. a short person; a dwarf
2. short; low; low-ranking: 他比他姐姐矮一個頭。He's a head shorter than his sister.

矮柏(ㄞˇ ㄅㄞˇ)
a tree resembling a cedar or a cypress but much shorter, usually planted in gardens

矮胖(ㄞˇ ㄆㄤˋ)
short and fat

矮櫈子(ㄞˇ ㄉㄥˋ ˙ㄗ)or矮櫈(ㄞˇ ㄉㄥˋ)
a low bench or stool

矮奴(ㄞˇ ㄋㄨˊ)
①(derogatively) the Japs ②Ainus (a race of dwarfs)

矮個兒(ㄞˇ ㄍㄜˋ ˙ㄦ)or矮個子(ㄞˇ ㄍㄜˋ ˙ㄗ)
a person of short stature; short-statured

矮牆淺屋(ㄞˇ ㄑㄧㄤˊ ㄑㄧㄢˇ ㄨ)
The wall is low and house small.—a poor family

矮小(ㄞˇ ㄒㄧㄠˇ)

short-statured; undersized; low (houses, trees, etc.): 他的身材矮小。He is short and slight in figure.

矮樹 (ㄞˇ ㄕㄨˋ)
a low tree; bushes

矮人觀場 (ㄞˇ ㄖㄣˊ《ㄨㄢ ㄔㄤˇ)or 矮人看場 (ㄞˇ ㄖㄣˊ ㄎㄢˋ ㄔㄤˇ)
(literally) the dwarf seeing a show—seeing nothing but applauding with the others

矮子 (ㄞˇ ˙ㄗ)
a short person; a dwarf

矮子看戲 (ㄞˇ ˙ㄗ ㄒㄧˋ)
to follow the reaction of others without an opinion of one's own 參看「矮人看場」

矮娃子 (ㄞˇ ㄨㄚˊ ˙ㄗ)
a short person; a dwarf

矮屋 (ㄞˇ)
a house with a low ceiling; a low house

十二畫

【矯】 3838
ㄐㄧㄠˇ jeau jiǎo
1. to straighten; to correct; to rectify
2. to falsify; to forge; to fake; to pretend
3. strong and powerful; vigorous; brave
4. to raise (one's head) high
5. a Chinese family name

矯託 (ㄐㄧㄠˇ ㄊㄨㄛ)
to fake; to take...as an excuse or a pretext

矯亢 (ㄐㄧㄠˇ ㄎㄤˋ)
to affect superiority by acting or talking in a manner different from others'

矯捷 (ㄐㄧㄠˇ ㄐㄧㄝˊ)
agile; vigorous and nimble; brisk

矯矯不羣 (ㄐㄧㄠˇ ㄐㄧㄠˇ ㄅㄨˋ ㄑㄩㄣˊ)
outstanding; peerless; remarkable

矯健 (ㄐㄧㄠˇ ㄐㄧㄢˋ)
strong and vigorous: 他踏著矯健的步伐。He walks with vigorous strides.

矯情 (ㄐㄧㄠˇ ㄑㄧㄥˊ)
to talk or act against customs or common practices in order to advertise one's self-styled superiority; to be

affectedly unconventional

矯形 (ㄐㄧㄠˇ ㄒㄧㄥˊ)
(medicine) orthopaedic

矯制 (ㄐㄧㄠˇ ㄓˋ)
to fake orders from above

矯詔 (ㄐㄧㄠˇ ㄓㄠˋ)
to forge or fake an imperial decree

矯正 (ㄐㄧㄠˇ ㄓㄥˋ)
to correct or rectify

矯世 (ㄐㄧㄠˇ ㄕˋ)
to reform or correct social customs or practices by personally setting examples

矯飾 (ㄐㄧㄠˇ ㄕˋ)
to affect; affected; affectation

矯揉造作 (ㄐㄧㄠˇ ㄖㄡˊ ㄗㄠˋ ㄗㄨㄛˋ)
affectation; to behave in an affected manner

矯枉過正 (ㄐㄧㄠˇ ㄨㄤˇ ㄍㄨㄛˋ ㄓㄥˋ)
to be overstrict in correcting mistakes, faults, etc.; to exceed the proper limits in righting a wrong

【矰】 3839
ㄗㄥ tzeng zēng
an arrow, dart, etc. attached to a silk cord or string for shooting birds, etc.

矰繳 (ㄗㄥ ㄓㄨㄛˊ)
a bird-shooting device (see above)

十四畫

【矱】 3840
ㄏㄨㄛˋ huoh huò
a measure; a criterion

石 部
ㄕˊ shyr shí

【石】 3841
1. ㄕˊ shyr shí
1. rocks; stones; minerals, etc.: 滾石不生苔。A rolling stone gathers no moss.
2. a calculus, as a kidney calculus (commonly known as a kidney stone)
3. stone tablets
4. medicines
5. barren, as a barren woman

6. name of an ancient musical instrument
7. a Chinese family name

石碑 (ㄕˊ ㄅㄟ)
a stone tablet; a stele

石斑魚 (ㄕˊ ㄅㄢ ㄩˊ)
a spotted grouper; a cabrilla

石板 (ㄕˊ ㄅㄢˇ)
a slate; a stone slab; a flagstone

石版 (ㄕˊ ㄅㄢˇ)
① a lithographic stoneplate
② stone slabs or slates—usually for construction purposes ③ a slate

石版畫 (ㄕˊ ㄅㄢˇ ㄏㄨㄚˋ)
a lithograph

石版石 (ㄕˊ ㄅㄢˇ ㄕˊ)
a lithographic stone

石本 (ㄕˊ ㄅㄣˇ)
rubbing from stone inscriptions

石筆 (ㄕˊ ㄅㄧˇ)
a slate pencil

石壁 (ㄕˊ ㄅㄧˋ)
a stone wall; a precipice

石破天驚 (ㄕˊ ㄆㄛˋ ㄊㄧㄢ ㄐㄧㄥ)
(said of music, statements, writings, etc.) world-shaking; sensational; remarkably original and forceful

石癖 (ㄕˊ ㄆㄧˇ)
a love for rocks and stones

石馬 (ㄕˊ ㄇㄚˇ)
stone horses — as those beside a grave or tomb

石墨 (ㄕˊ ㄇㄛˋ)
graphite; black lead; plumbago

石磨 (ㄕˊ ㄇㄛˋ)
a millstone; a grindstone

石煤 (ㄕˊ ㄇㄟˊ)
hard coal; stone coal; bone coal

石門水庫 (ㄕˊ ㄇㄣˊ ㄕㄨㄟˇ ㄎㄨˋ)
the Shih-men Reservoir in northern Taiwan

石綿 (ㄕˊ ㄇㄧㄢˊ)
asbestos

石綿板 (ㄕˊ ㄇㄧㄢˊ ㄅㄢˇ)
an asbestos board

石綿瓦 (ㄕˊ ㄇㄧㄢˊ ㄨㄚˇ)
an asbestos shingle; an asbestos tile

石民 (ㄕˊ ㄇㄧㄣˊ)
civilians

〔石 部〕

〔石部〕

石縫(ㄕ ㄈㄥˊ)
a crevice in stone or between rocks

石達開(ㄕ ㄉㄚˊ ㄎㄞ)
Shih Ta-kai (?-1863) a scholar-general who fought the Manchus during the Taiping Rebellion

石埭(ㄕ ㄉㄞˋ)
①a dike or embankment of stone ②name of a county in Anhwei Province

石磴(ㄕ ㄉㄥˋ)
stone steps

石雕(ㄕ ㄉㄧㄠ)
①stone carving ②carved stone

石墩(ㄕ ㄉㄨㄣ)
①a stone pier ②a block of stone used as a seat

石洞(ㄕ ㄉㄨㄥˋ)
a stone cave

石頭(ㄕ ㄊㄡˊ)or(ㄕˊ·ㄊㄡ)
stone; a rock

石頭記(ㄕ ㄊㄡˊ ㄐㄧˋ)
another title of the Chinese novel 紅樓夢 (The Dream of the Red Chamber)

石頭城(ㄕ ㄊㄡˊ ㄔㄥˊ)
name of an ancient city west of Nanking

石炭(ㄕ ㄊㄢˋ)
coal

石炭酸(ㄕ ㄊㄢˋ ㄙㄨㄢ)
carbolic acid; phenol

石田(ㄕ ㄊㄧㄢˊ)
barren land; a field which is not arable

石楠(ㄕ ㄋㄢˊ)
a rhododendron

石女(ㄕ ㄋㄩˇ)
a barren woman; a woman with a defective reproductive organ

石蠟(ㄕ ㄌㄚˋ)
paraffin (wax)

石礫(ㄕ ㄌㄧˋ)
gravel

石榴(ㄕ ㄌㄧㄡˊ)or(ㄕ ㄌㄧㄡˊ)
a pomegranate

石榴裙(ㄕ ㄌㄧㄡˊ ㄑㄩㄣˊ)
①a red skirt; a woman's petticoat ②(now figuratively) feminine charms

石榴石(ㄕ ㄌㄧㄡˊ ㄕˊ)
a garnet

石路(ㄕ ㄌㄨˋ)
a stone-paved road; a pebble road; a gravel road

石膏(ㄕ ㄍㄠ)
gypsum; plaster

石膏像(ㄕ ㄍㄠ ㄒㄧㄤˋ)
a plaster bust; a plaster statue

石敢當(ㄕ ㄍㄢˇ ㄉㄤ)
a stone tablet, erected at the entrance of a lane, etc, to drive away misfortune or evil spirits

石鼓(ㄕ ㄍㄨˇ)
drum-shaped stones of the Epoch of Warring States, ten of which have been preserved

石鼓文(ㄕ ㄍㄨˇ ㄨㄣˊ)
ancient characters engraved on the drum-shaped stones

石棺(ㄕ ㄍㄨㄢ)
a stone coffin; a sarcophagus

石工(ㄕ ㄍㄨㄥ)
a mason; masonry: 他的職業是石工。 He's a mason by trade.

石刻(ㄕ ㄎㄜˋ)
stone engraving; stone carving; stone inscriptions

石窟(ㄕ ㄎㄨ)
a grotto

石塊(ㄕ ㄎㄨㄞˋ)
a piece of stone or rock; a pebble; a boulder: 石塊與碎石正自山上滾下。 Rocks and stones were rolling down the hill.

石斛蘭(ㄕ ㄏㄨˊ ㄌㄢˊ)
dendrobium

石花菜(ㄕ ㄏㄨㄚ ㄘㄞˋ)
Gelidium amansii, a gelatinous seaweed which is used as a dish after cooking 亦作「洋菜」

石化工業(ㄕ ㄏㄨㄚˋ ㄍㄨㄥ ㄧㄝˋ)
the petrochemical industries

石灰(ㄕ ㄏㄨㄟ)
lime: 熟石灰 slaked lime 生石灰 quick lime

石灰粉末(ㄕ ㄏㄨㄟ ㄈㄣˇ ㄇㄛˋ)
slaked lime

石灰岩(ㄕ ㄏㄨㄟ ㄧㄢˊ)
limestone

石灰水(ㄕ ㄏㄨㄟ ㄕㄨㄟˇ)
limewater; aqua calcis

石灰岩(ㄕ ㄏㄨㄟ ㄧㄢˊ)
limestone

石黃(ㄕ ㄏㄨㄤˊ)
hartite

石階(ㄕ ㄐㄧㄝ)
stone steps: 一段石階往上通到房子。 A flight of stone steps leads up to the house.

石交(ㄕ ㄐㄧㄠ)
friendship or ties as strong as stone; close and intimate friendship

石鹼(ㄕ ㄐㄧㄢˇ)
soap

石鹼石(ㄕ ㄐㄧㄢˇ ㄕˊ)
soapstone

石匠(ㄕ ㄐㄧㄤˋ)
a stonemason: 蘇格拉底曾做過石匠和雕刻匠。 Socrates was a stonemason and carver.

石晶(ㄕ ㄐㄧㄥ)
rock crystal

石經(ㄕ ㄐㄧㄥ)
classics engraved on stone tablets in various dynasties after exhaustive verification and research, made usually by orders of the emperors

石決明(ㄕ ㄐㄩㄝˊ ㄇㄧㄥˊ)
an abalone; the shell of an abalone or sea-ear

石器(ㄕ ㄑㄧˋ)
stoneware; stone implements; a stone artifact; a stone vessel

石器時代(ㄕ ㄑㄧˋ ㄕˊ ㄉㄞˋ)
the Stone Age

石牆(ㄕ ㄑㄧㄤˊ)
a stone wall

石像(ㄕ ㄒㄧㄤˋ)
a statue or bust of stone

石竹(ㄕ ㄓㄨˊ)
a carnation

石柱(ㄕ ㄓㄨˋ)
a stone pillar

石鐘乳(ㄕ ㄓㄨㄥ ㄖㄨˇ)or(ㄕ ㄖㄨˇ)
stalactites 亦作「鐘乳石」

石沈大海(ㄕ ㄔㄣˊ ㄉㄚˋ ㄏㄞˇ)
(literally) rocks falling into the sea—completely without information or response; no news at all; without a trace; to disappear forever

石室(ㄕ ㄕˋ)
①a stone house—very

strong and safe ② a stone
chamber for keeping books
③ a stone tomb or vault

石蕊試紙(ㄕ ㄖㄨㄟˇ ㄕˋ ㄓˇ)
litmus paper

石蕊試藥(ㄕ ㄖㄨㄟˇ ㄕˋ ㄧㄠˋ)
litmus

石綿(ㄕ ㄇㄧㄢˋ)
asbestos

石子(ㄕ ㄗˇ)or石子兒(ㄕ ㄗˇ ㄦ)or
石頭子兒(ㄕ ㄊㄡˊ ㄗˇ ㄦ)
pieces of stone; pebbles

石子路(ㄕ ㄗˇ ㄌㄨˋ)
a graveled path; a macadam
road: 有一條石子路通到花園。
There is a graveled path
leading to the garden.

石髓(ㄕ ㄙㄨㄟˇ)
stalactites

石筍(ㄕ ㄙㄨㄣˇ)
a stalagmite: 這個洞裏有許多
石筍。There are many stalag-
mites in the cave.

石油(ㄕ ㄧㄡˊ)
crude oil; petroleum: 石油價
格又上漲了。The price of pe-
troleum has gone up again.

石油公司(ㄕ ㄧㄡˊ ㄍㄨㄥ ㄙ)
a petroleum company

石油工業(ㄕ ㄧㄡˊ ㄍㄨㄥ ㄧㄝˋ)
petroleum industry

石油化工廠(ㄕ ㄧㄡˊ ㄏㄨㄚˋ ㄍㄨㄥ ㄔㄤˇ)
a petrochemical works

石油化學(ㄕ ㄧㄡˊ ㄏㄨㄚˋ ㄒㄩㄝˊ)
petrochemistry

石油化學工業(ㄕ ㄧㄡˊ ㄏㄨㄚˋ ㄒㄩㄝˊ ㄍㄨㄥ ㄧㄝˋ)
the petrochemical industries

石油精(ㄕ ㄧㄡˊ ㄐㄧㄥ)
benzine

石油井(ㄕ ㄧㄡˊ ㄐㄧㄥˇ)
(petroleum) an oil well

石鹽(ㄕ ㄧㄢˊ)
mineral salt; rock salt

石印(ㄕ ㄧㄣˋ)
lithography

石印本(ㄕ ㄧㄣˋ ㄅㄣˇ)
a lithographic edition or
copy

石英(ㄕ ㄧㄥ)
quartz

石英鐘(ㄕ ㄧㄥ ㄓㄨㄥ)
a quartz clock

石屋(ㄕ ㄨ)
a stone house

【石】 3841
2. ㄉㄢˋ dann dàn
1. a dry measure for grains
roughly equivalent to 120-
160 pounds; picul
2. a weight measure equivalent
to about 110 pounds

三畫

【矽】 3842
ㄒㄧ shih xī
silicon (Si)

矽鋼(ㄒㄧ ㄍㄤ)
silicon steel

矽谷(ㄒㄧ ㄍㄨˇ)
Silicon Valley in California

矽石(ㄒㄧ ㄕˊ)
silex

矽砂(ㄒㄧ ㄕㄚ)
quartz sand

矽藻(ㄒㄧ ㄗㄠˇ)
diatom

矽酸(ㄒㄧ ㄙㄨㄢ)
silicic acid

矽酸鈉(ㄒㄧ ㄙㄨㄢ ㄋㄚˋ)
sodium silicate

矽酸鋁(ㄒㄧ ㄙㄨㄢ ㄌㄩˇ)
aluminium silicate

矽酸鈣(ㄒㄧ ㄙㄨㄢ ㄍㄞˋ)
calcium silicate

矽酸鉀(ㄒㄧ ㄙㄨㄢ ㄐㄧㄚˇ)
potassium silicate

矽酸鹽(ㄒㄧ ㄙㄨㄢ ㄧㄢˊ)
silicate

【砑】 3843
ㄎㄨ kuh kū
1. stone
2. diligent; industrious
3. very tired

砑砑(ㄎㄨ ㄎㄨ)
①diligent; industrious ②
very tired

四畫

【砉】 3844
ㄏㄨㄛ huoh huò
a splitting sound; a cracking
sound

【砂】 3845
ㄕㄚ sha shā
1. sand; coarse sand; gravel:
孩子們喜歡在砂裏玩。Children
enjoy playing on the sands.
2. coarse--not smooth
3. infinitesimal

砂布(ㄕㄚ ㄅㄨˋ)
emery cloth; abrasive cloth

砂糖(ㄕㄚ ㄊㄤˊ)
crude sugar; brown sugar

砂鐵(ㄕㄚ ㄊㄧㄝˇ)
magnetic sand

砂土(ㄕㄚ ㄊㄨˇ)
a sandy soil

砂囊(ㄕㄚ ㄋㄤˊ)
a gizzard

砂礫(ㄕㄚ ㄌㄧˋ)
gravel; pebbles

砂輪(ㄕㄚ ㄌㄨㄣˊ)
an emery wheel; grindstone

砂濾器(ㄕㄚ ㄌㄩˋ ㄑㄧˋ)
a sand filter

砂礦(ㄕㄚ ㄎㄨㄤˋ)
minerals in the form of sand

砂碛(ㄕㄚ ㄐㄧˋ)
sandy shoals

砂金(ㄕㄚ ㄐㄧㄣ)
gold dust; placer gold; alluvial gold

砂金石(ㄕㄚ ㄐㄧㄣ ㄕˊ)
aventurine

砂質(ㄕㄚ ㄓˊ)
sandy: 這條河流是砂質底。The
river is of a sandy bottom.

砂紙(ㄕㄚ ㄓˇ)
sandpaper; emery paper

砂岩(ㄕㄚ ㄧㄢˊ)
sandstone

砂眼(ㄕㄚ ㄧㄢˇ)
(medicine) trachoma 亦作
「沙眼」

砂浴(ㄕㄚ ㄩˋ)
(chemistry) sand bath

【砌】 3846
ㄑㄧˋ chih qì
1. to lay (bricks, etc.); to
pave; to raise in layers; to
build
2. steps

砌路(ㄑㄧˋ ㄌㄨˋ)
to build or pave a road

砌牆(ㄑㄧˋ ㄑㄧㄤˊ)
to build a wall

砌磚工人(ㄑㄧˋ ㄓㄨㄢ ㄍㄨㄥ ㄖㄣˊ)
a bricklayer

砌詞捏控(ㄑㄧˋ ㄘˊ ㄋㄧㄝ ㄎㄨㄥˋ)
to fabricate or trump up
charges; to frame

【砍】 3847
ㄎㄢˇ kaan kǎn
1. to chop; to hack; to fell
(trees, etc.); to cut down:

〔石部〕

〔石部〕

他們把路邊的樹砍倒。They felled these roadside trees.
2. to throw at

砍伐(ㄎㄢ ㄈㄚˊ)
to fell (trees, etc.)

砍斷(ㄎㄢ ㄉㄨㄢˋ)
to break apart by chopping; to cut something in two

砍頭(ㄎㄢ ㄊㄡˊ)
to behead; to decapitate

砍下來(ㄎㄢ ㄒㄧㄚˋ ㄌㄞˊ)
to chop or cut down: 他把這些樹枝砍下來。He chops down the branches.

砍柴(ㄎㄢ ㄔㄞˊ)
to chop or cut firewood

砍殺(ㄎㄢ ㄕㄚ)
to hack to death; to hack and kill

砍傷(ㄎㄢ ㄕㄤ)
to wound by hacking or cutting

砍死(ㄎㄢ ㄙˇ)
to hack to death: 他被強盜砍死。He was hacked to death by a robber.

【砒】 3848 ㄆㄧ pi pī
arsenic

砒霜(ㄆㄧ ㄕㄨㄤ)
arsenic trioxide(As₂O₃)

砒酸(ㄆㄧ ㄙㄨㄢ)
arsenic acid

五畫

【砥】 3849 ㄉㄧˇ dii dǐ
(又讀 ㄓˇ jyy zhǐ)
1. a whetstone; a grindstone
2. to discipline; to polish

砥礪(ㄉㄧˇ ㄌㄧˋ)
to discipline and polish; to temper; to encourage

砥柱(ㄉㄧˇ ㄓㄨˋ)
①name of a mountain through which the Yellow River was supposedly channeled ②an indomitable person

砥石(ㄉㄧˇ ㄕˊ)
a fine grindstone; a whetstone

【砧】 3850 ㄓㄣ jen jēn
1. a rock with a flat top on which the laundry is beaten

and washed; an anvil
2. an ancient instrument for torture

砧板(ㄓㄣ ㄅㄢˇ)
a chopping block

砧斧(ㄓㄣ ㄈㄨˇ)
ancient weapons or instruments for killing

砧骨(ㄓㄣ ㄍㄨˇ)
(anatomy) an incus

砧鑕(ㄓㄣ ㄓˋ)
an ancient instrument for torture

砧杵(ㄓㄣ ㄔㄨˇ)
the stone block and wooden club for laundering clothes; anvil and pestle

【砭】 3851 ㄅㄧㄢ bian biān
1. a stone probe; a stone needle used in acupuncture in ancient China
2. to advise or exhort; to admonish
3. to pierce

砭骨(ㄅㄧㄢ ㄍㄨˇ)
(literally) to pierce the bone —extremely painful or cold

砭灸(ㄅㄧㄢ ㄐㄧㄡˇ)
to acupuncture and cauterize

砭人肌骨(ㄅㄧㄢ ㄖㄣˊ ㄐㄧ ㄍㄨˇ)
(said of cold, pain, etc.) bone-piercing

【砰】 3852 ㄆㄥ peng pēng
1. the sound of crashing stones
2. Bang! a loud sound; deafening: 他們的一聲把門關上。He shut the door with a bang.

砰磅(ㄆㄥ ㄆㄤ)
①Bing-bang!—the sound of falling stones ②the roars of raging water

砰砰(ㄆㄥ ㄆㄥ)
①the sound of drumbeats ②Bang! Bang!—the sound of gunfire

砰磷(ㄆㄥ ㄌㄧㄣˊ)
①high and steep ②thunder

砰訇(ㄆㄥ ㄏㄨㄥˊ)
loud or deafening

砰然(ㄆㄥ ㄖㄢˊ)
loud; deafening; roaring; banging

【砝】 3853 ㄈㄚ far fó
standard weights used in

scales; steelyard weights

砝碼(兒)(ㄈㄚˇ ㄇㄚˇ(ㄦ))
standard weights used in scales; steelyard weights

【破】 3854 ㄆㄛˋ poh pò
1. to break
2. dilapidated; ruined; destroyed
3. to defeat; to beat (the enemy); to capture (enemy territory)
4. to expose; exposed; to lay bare; (to see) through
5. to spend (money, etc.)
6. to solve or break (a murder case, etc.); to analyze
7. to come to an end
8. paltry

破敗(ㄆㄛˋ ㄅㄞˋ)
destroyed; ruined; dilapidated; beaten: 這棟房子已經破敗不堪。The house is dilapidated.

破壁飛去(ㄆㄛˋ ㄅㄧˋ ㄈㄟ ㄑㄩˋ)
to rocket into fame and fortune; to become wealthy and influential all of a sudden

破冰船(ㄆㄛˋ ㄅㄧㄥ ㄔㄨㄢˊ)
an icebreaker

破布(ㄆㄛˋ ㄅㄨˋ)
rags

破破爛爛(ㄆㄛˋ ㄆㄛˋ ㄌㄢˋ ㄌㄢˋ)
tattered; tumble-down; dilapidated: 他穿著破破爛爛的衣服。He is dressed in tatters.

破盤(ㄆㄛˋ ㄆㄢˊ)
①broken dishes ②the baring of a secret or plot

破片(ㄆㄛˋ ㄆㄧㄢˋ)
fragments; broken pieces

破門(ㄆㄛˋ ㄇㄣˊ)
excommunication

破門而入(ㄆㄛˋ ㄇㄣˊ ㄦˊ ㄖㄨˋ)
to break into a house; to force one's way into a house

破謎兒(ㄆㄛˋ ㄇㄧˊ ㄦˊ)
to solve a riddle

破滅(ㄆㄛˋ ㄇㄧㄝˋ)
to come to nil; ruined or destroyed; to fall through; to be shattered; to disillusion: 我們的希望破滅了。Our hopes were shattered.

破廟(ㄆㄛˋ ㄇㄧㄠˋ)
a dilapidated temple

破費(ㄆㄛˋ ㄈㄟˋ)

to spend money; to go to some expense; (used in polite conversation) to waste your money

破釜沈舟 (ㄆㄛ ㄈㄨˇ ㄔㄣˊ ㄓㄡ)
(literally) to destroy the cooking pots and scuttle the ships—no turning back; determined; to cut off all means of retreat 參看「沈舟破釜」

破腹 (ㄆㄛˋ ㄈㄨˋ)
diarrhea

破膽 (ㄆㄛˋ ㄉㄢˇ)
to be scared out of one's wits; very frightened

破敵 (ㄆㄛˋ ㄉㄧˊ)
to defeat the enemy (or one's opponents)

破的 (ㄆㄛˋ ㄉㄧˋ)
to the point; to hit the bull's eye; to hit the nail on the head

破題 (ㄆㄛˋ ㄊㄧˊ)
to analyze the meaning of the title or subject' (of a composition) in the first two sentences of their writings by writers of the eight-legged essays (八股文) in the Ming and Ching dynasties

破題兒第一遭 (ㄆㄛˋ ㄊㄧˊ ㄦ ㄉㄧˋ ㄧ ㄗㄠ)
for the first time

破體字 (ㄆㄛˋ ㄊㄧˇ ㄗˋ)
a character written in an unorthodox form

破涕爲笑 (ㄆㄛˋ ㄊㄧˋ ㄨㄟˊ ㄒㄧㄠˋ)
to break into laughter while still crying (upon learning of cheering news, etc.); to smile through tears

破天荒 (ㄆㄛˋ ㄊㄧㄢ ㄏㄨㄤ)
never before—for the first time; unprecedented; history-making

破土 (ㄆㄛˋ ㄊㄨˇ)
①to break the ground (for a building project) ②(said of a seedling) to break through the soil

破土典禮 (ㄆㄛˋ ㄊㄨˇ ㄉㄧㄢˇ ㄌㄧˇ)
a ground-breaking ceremony

破爛兒 (ㄆㄛˋ ㄌㄢˋ ㄦ)
rags and rubbish; wastes or refuse; junk

破浪 (ㄆㄛˋ ㄌㄤˋ)

(literally) to break the waves—to set sail; to embark on a sea voyage

破例 (ㄆㄛˋ ㄌㄧˋ)
to make an exception (to a rule, common practices, etc.); to break a rule

破裂 (ㄆㄛˋ ㄌㄧㄝˋ)
①to end in a rupture; to break off; rupture; severance ②broken; cracked; rupture; 洪水導致大壩破裂。The flood led to the rupture of the dam.

破臉 (ㄆㄛˋ ㄌㄧㄢˇ)
to quarrel openly; to turn against (an acquaintance or associate); to fall out: 我 不顧同朋友破臉。I don't like to fall out with my friends.

破落 (ㄆㄛˋ ㄌㄨㄛˋ)
the decline (of wealth and position, etc.); to fall into reduced circumstances

破落戶 (ㄆㄛˋ ㄌㄨㄛˋ ㄏㄨˋ)
①a fallen family ②rascals or vagrants coming from once wealthy and influential families

破格 (ㄆㄛˋ ㄍㄜˊ)
exceptions to a rule or practice; to make an exception

破格錄用 (ㄆㄛˋ ㄍㄜˊ ㄌㄨˋ ㄩㄥˋ)
to employ (usually a person of remarkable ability) in defiance of rules, practices, etc.

破瓜 (ㄆㄛˋ ㄍㄨㄚ)or 破瓜之年 (ㄆㄛˋ ㄍㄨㄚ ㄓ ㄋㄧㄢˊ)
①(said of a girl) reaching 16 years of age ②to deflower a virgin ③(said of a man) 64 years of age

破罐子 (ㄆㄛˋ ㄍㄨㄢˋ ㄗ)
(literally) a broken vessel, jar, etc.—①an unchaste woman ②a person of poor health

破工夫 (ㄆㄛˋ ㄍㄨㄥ ㄈㄨ)
to take time

破口大罵 (ㄆㄛˋ ㄎㄡˇ ㄉㄚˋ ㄇㄚˋ)
to abuse freely and loudly; to shout with abuse; to let loose a torrent of invective

破獲 (ㄆㄛˋ ㄏㄨㄛˋ)
to break (into a secret hide-out) and capture (criminals,

loots, etc.); to uncover (a plot, criminal activities, etc.)

破壞 (ㄆㄛˋ ㄏㄨㄞˋ)
to ruin; to destroy; to violate; to break

破壞名譽 (ㄆㄛˋ ㄏㄨㄞˋ ㄇㄧㄥˊ ㄩˋ)
to ruin one's reputation; to libel; to slander

破壞力 (ㄆㄛˋ ㄏㄨㄞˋ ㄌㄧˋ)
destructive power

破壞秩序 (ㄆㄛˋ ㄏㄨㄞˋ ㄓˋ ㄒㄩˋ)
to cause damage or disruption to public order; the violation of public order

破壞中立 (ㄆㄛˋ ㄏㄨㄞˋ ㄓㄨㄥ ㄌㄧˋ)
the violation of neutrality

破紀錄 (ㄆㄛˋ ㄐㄧˋ ㄌㄨˋ)
to break a record; record-breaking; record-shattering

破家 (ㄆㄛˋ ㄐㄧㄚ)
①to exhaust one's family property ②to ruin one's family

破戒 (ㄆㄛˋ ㄐㄧㄝˋ)
①(usually said of monks, nuns, etc.) to break the rules; to break a religious precept ②to make an exception; to break one's vow

破舊 (ㄆㄛˋ ㄐㄧㄡˋ)
shabby; worn-out; disreputable; dilapidated

破鏡重圓 (ㄆㄛˋ ㄐㄧㄥˋ ㄔㄨㄥˊ ㄩㄢˊ)
(said of a divorced or separated couple) reunion and reconciliation

破鞋 (ㄆㄛˋ ㄒㄧㄝˊ)
(literally) worn-out shoes—unlicensed prostitutes; loose women

破曉 (ㄆㄛˋ ㄒㄧㄠˇ)
daybreak; dawn

破相 (ㄆㄛˋ ㄒㄧㄤˋ)
①(said of facial features) to be marred by a scar, etc. ②to make a fool of oneself

破折號 (ㄆㄛˋ ㄓㄜˊ ㄏㄠˋ)
a dash (a punctuation mark)

破綻 (ㄆㄛˋ ㄓㄢˋ)
a slip, flaw or weak point; a loophole: 他們的證詞破綻百出。Their testimony is full of flaws.

破竹之勢 (ㄆㄛˋ ㄓㄨˊ ㄓ ㄕˋ)
overwhelming force; irresistible; able to overcome all

〔石部〕

〔石部〕

obstacles with great ease
—as splitting a bamboo pole

破鈔(ㄆㄛ ㄔㄠ)or(ㄆㄛ ㄔㄠ)
to spend money; (in polite usage) to waste your money

破產(ㄆㄛ ㄔㄢ)
① bankruptcy; insolvency; to go bankrupt; to bankrupt; insolvent; to go bust: 胡亂的花費將使他破產。Foolish expenditures will bankrupt him. ② to come to naught; to fall through

破除(ㄆㄛ ㄔㄨ)
to eliminate; to get rid of

破除迷信(ㄆㄛ ㄔㄨ ㄇㄧ ㄒㄧㄣ)
to get rid of superstition

破船(ㄆㄛ ㄔㄨㄢ)
a broken-down ship

破船偏遇打頭風(ㄆㄛ ㄔㄨㄢ ㄆㄧㄢ ㄩ ㄉㄚ ㄊㄡ ㄈㄥ)
(literally) As luck would have it, a broken-down ship should encounter a headwind. —dogged by evil on the fire of misfortune

破身(ㄆㄛ ㄕㄣ)
the first sexual intercourse of a man or woman

破傷風(ㄆㄛ ㄕㄤ ㄈㄥ)
tetanus

破財(ㄆㄛ ㄘㄞ)
to lose money

破財消災(ㄆㄛ ㄘㄞ ㄒㄧㄠ ㄗㄞ)
to suffer unexpected financial losses and forestall calamities

破碎(ㄆㄛ ㄙㄨㄟ)
①broken (heart, hope, etc.) ②to come to pieces; to shatter

破損(ㄆㄛ ㄙㄨㄣ)
broken or damaged; ruined: 這棟房子已經破損了。This house has been damaged.

破案(ㄆㄛ ㄢ)
to break a criminal case; to solve a case

破衣裳(ㄆㄛ ㄧ ㄕㄤ)or 破衣(ㄆㄛ ㄧ)
rags; ragged garments or clothing: 他穿著破衣。He was clad in rags.

破顏(ㄆㄛ ㄧㄢ)
to break into a smile

破音字(ㄆㄛ ㄧㄣ ㄗ)or 破音字(ㄆㄛ ㄗ)
or 破音(ㄆㄛ ㄧㄣ)

---

a character which is not pronounced in the usual way because of a different meaning it carries

【砷】 3855
ㄕㄣ shen shēn
arsenic

砷化氫(ㄕㄣ ㄏㄨㄚ ㄑㄧㄥ)
hydrogen arsenide

【砸】 3856
ㄗㄚ tzar zá
1. to crash and break; to squash; to smash; to knock; to pound: 玻璃杯掉在地板上砸了。The glass smashed on the floor.

2. to ruin; to fail; to be bungled: 他把事情搞砸了。The job was bungled by him.

3. to mash; to beat to a pulp

砸飯碗(ㄗㄚ ㄈㄢ ㄨㄢ)
(literally) to break one's rice bowl—to lose one's job

砸了(ㄗㄚ ㄌㄜ)
① to knock and break: 她把茶壺砸了。She dropped the teapot and broke it. ② to fail; to bungle; busted

砸爛(ㄗㄚ ㄌㄢ)
to crush to a mash

砸鍋(ㄗㄚ ㄍㄨㄛ)
to fail in a task or an attempt

砸傷(ㄗㄚ ㄕㄤ)
to be injured by a crashing object

砸死(ㄗㄚ ㄙ)
① to be crushed to death ② (used comically) to hand a person an impossible task to perform

砸碎(ㄗㄚ ㄙㄨㄟ)
to break to pieces; to smash

【砮】 3857
ㄋㄨ nuu nǔ
flint arrowheads

【砦】 3858
ㄓㄞ jay zhài
a stockade; a military outpost

【砲】 3859
ㄆㄠ paw pào
a simplified form of 礮 —artillery

砲艦(ㄆㄠ ㄐㄧㄢ)
a gunboat

六畫

【硃】 3860
ㄓㄨ ju zhū
1. vermilion
2. imperial (the signature and instructions of an emperor were written in red)

硃筆(ㄓㄨ ㄅㄧ)
a vermilion writing brush

硃批(ㄓㄨ ㄆㄧ)
an imperial rescript

硃卷(ㄓㄨ ㄩㄢ)
the red-ink copy of test papers used in civil service examinations in former times

硃砂(ㄓㄨ ㄕㄚ)
cinnabar

硃砂痣(ㄓㄨ ㄕㄚ ㄓ)
a red mole

硃諭(ㄓㄨ ㄩ)or 硃批諭旨(ㄓㄨ ㄆㄧ ㄩ ㄓ)
imperial decrees, mandates, instructions, etc.

【硌】 3861
ㄍㄜ geh gè
damage or injuries caused by being squeezed or pressed on a rough surface

硌得慌(ㄍㄜ ㄉㄜ ㄏㄨㄤ)
to feel uncomfortable over some bumpy surface

【硒】 3862
ㄒㄧ shi xī
selenium (Se)

【硫】 3863
ㄌㄧㄡ liou liú
sulphur, or sulfur

硫苦土(ㄌㄧㄡ ㄎㄨ ㄊㄨ)or 硫酸鎂(ㄌㄧㄡ ㄙㄨㄢ ㄇㄟ)
magnesium sulfate

硫化物(ㄌㄧㄡ ㄏㄨㄚ ㄨ)
a sulfide; a sulfuret

硫磺(ㄌㄧㄡ ㄏㄨㄤ)
sulphur, or sulfur; brimstone

硫磺島(ㄌㄧㄡ ㄏㄨㄤ ㄉㄠ)
Iwo Jima, one of the Volcano Islands

硫磺礦(ㄌㄧㄡ ㄏㄨㄤ ㄎㄨㄤ)
a sulfur or brimstone mine: 陽明山有豐富的硫磺礦。Yangmingshan is rich in sulfur mines.

硫磺泉(ㄌㄧㄡ ㄏㄨㄤ ㄑㄩㄢ)
a sulfur spring

硫酸(ㄌㄧㄡ ㄙㄨㄢ)
sulfuric acid

硫酸鎂(ㄌㄧㄡㄙㄨㄢㄇㄟˇ)
magnesium sulfate (MgSO₄)

硫酸銅(ㄌㄧㄡㄙㄨㄢㄊㄨㄥˊ)
cupric sulfate (CuSO₄) 亦作
「膽礬」

硫酸鈉(ㄌㄧㄡㄙㄨㄢㄋㄚˋ)
sodium sulfate (Na₂SO₄)

硫酸化合物(ㄌㄧㄡㄙㄨㄢㄏㄨㄚˋㄏㄜˊㄨˋ)
sulfates

硫酸銨(ㄌㄧㄡㄙㄨㄢㄢˇ)
ammonium sulfate

硫酸鹽(ㄌㄧㄡㄙㄨㄢㄧㄢˊ)
sulfate

【研】 3864
(研) ㄧㄢˊ yán yàn

1. to go to the very source; to study; to investigate; to research; to examine; to search into carefully
2. to grind; to powder

研磨(ㄧㄢˊㄇㄛˊ)
① to grind; to pestle ② to abrade; to polish

研墨(ㄧㄢˊㄇㄛˋ)
to rub an ink stick on an ink-slab (for brush writing)

研討(ㄧㄢˊㄊㄠˇ)
to study and discuss; to investigate and research

研討會(ㄧㄢˊㄊㄠˇㄏㄨㄟˋ)
a study group; a workshop; a seminar; a symposium

研究(ㄧㄢˊㄐㄧㄡ)
to study and research; studies; researches; to go to the very source of: 他的研究工作很成功。His researches have been successful.

研究費(ㄧㄢˊㄐㄧㄡㄈㄟˋ)
research funds; research expenditure

研究計畫(ㄧㄢˊㄐㄧㄡㄐㄧˋㄏㄨㄚˋ)
a research project

研究室(ㄧㄢˊㄐㄧㄡㄕˋ)
a research laboratory; a research chamber

研究生(ㄧㄢˊㄐㄧㄡㄕㄥ)
a graduate student

研究所(ㄧㄢˊㄐㄧㄡㄙㄨㄛˇ)
a research laboratory; a research institute; a graduate school

研究員(ㄧㄢˊㄐㄧㄡㄩㄢˊ)
a researcher; a research

worker; a research fellow: 研究員正在研究此問題。Research workers are examining the problem.

研究院(ㄧㄢˊㄐㄧㄡㄩㄢˋ)
a research institute

研求(ㄧㄢˊㄑㄧㄡˊ)
to research and examine; to study; to examine into; to explore

研習(ㄧㄢˊㄒㄧˊ)
to research and study; to examine and study

研習會(ㄧㄢˊㄒㄧˊㄏㄨㄟˋ)
a study meeting or conference; a symposium; a seminar; a workshop

研製(ㄧㄢˊㄓˋ)
① to prepare; to manufacture; to develop ② (Chinese medicine) to prepare medicinal powder by grinding

研鑽(ㄧㄢˊㄗㄨㄢ)
to examine into; to closely study and investigate; to research into

研碎(ㄧㄢˊㄙㄨㄟˋ)
to grind to pieces: 他們將咖啡豆研碎。They grind coffee beans to pieces.

七畫

【硜】 3865
ㄎㄥ keng kēng
the sound of pebbles or stones rubbing or knocking together

硜硜(ㄎㄥㄎㄥ)
stubborn; obstinate

硜硜自守(ㄎㄥㄎㄥㄗˋㄕㄡˇ)
shallow and obstinate

【硬】 3866
ㄧㄥˋ yìng yìng

1. hard; stiff; solid; firm
2. stiff; rigid; inflexible; obstinate; very insistent; unyielding
3. to harden; to solidify; to stiffen
4. by force
5. to manage to do something in a forced manner
6. (said of quality) good
7. able (person)

硬玻璃(ㄧㄥˋㄅㄛ·ㄌㄧ)
hard glass

硬幫幫(ㄧㄥˋㄅㄤㄅㄤ)

① hard and firm ② rigid and inflexible; stiff: 這些規則硬幫幫的。The rules are rigid and inflexible.

硬逼(ㄧㄥˋㄅㄧ)
to compel or force; to press hard; hard-pressed

硬幣(ㄧㄥˋㄅㄧˋ)
hard money (as opposed to paper money); coins; specie

硬碰硬(ㄧㄥˋㄆㄥˋㄧㄥˋ)
① to meet force with force ② 100 per cent (genuine) ③ extremely rigid or inflexible; fixed ④ (said of a job) tough; painstaking: 這是硬碰硬的差事。This is an extremely tough job.

硬煤(ㄧㄥˋㄇㄟˊ)
hard coal; anthracite

硬木(ㄧㄥˋㄇㄨˋ)
hardwood

硬度(ㄧㄥˋㄉㄨˋ)
hardness: 這塊板子的硬度不夠。The board is not hard enough.

硬頭貨(ㄧㄥˋㄊㄡˊㄏㄨㄛˋ)
① foods not easily digested ② money (especially hard cash)

硬體(ㄧㄥˋㄊㄧˇ)
(computers) hardware

硬挺(ㄧㄥˋㄊㄧㄥˇ)
to endure with one's best; to put up with all one's might; to stick out

硬來(ㄧㄥˋㄌㄞˊ)
to do something forcibly: 他做事常常硬來。He often does things forcibly.

硬朗(ㄧㄥˋㄌㄤˇ)
(said of the aged) sturdy and strong: 他七十多了，身體還很硬朗。He's over seventy but still sturdy and strong.

硬裏子(ㄧㄥˋㄌㄧˇ·ㄗ)
a good supporting player, actor, or actress

硬領子(ㄧㄥˋㄌㄧㄥˇ·ㄗ)
a hard collar starched or lined with celluloid

硬幹(ㄧㄥˋㄍㄢˋ)
to do something in disregard of obstacles

硬骨頭(ㄧㄥˋㄍㄨˇ·ㄊㄡ)
a hard bone—an incorrupt-

〔石部〕

〔石 部〕

ible person; a person of moral fortitude; a dauntless, unyielding person

硬漢(ㄧㄥˋ ㄏㄢˋ)
a hardened man; a courageous man; a man of fortitude

硬話(ㄧㄥˋ ㄏㄨㄚˋ)
a defiant talk; a big talk

硬化(ㄧㄥˋ ㄏㄨㄚˋ)
①to harden; to stiffen; to solidify ②(medicine) sclerosis; cirrhosis

硬氣(ㄧㄥˋ ㄑㄧˋ)
①to feel no qualm in the knowledge that one is on the side of righteousness ②firm and manly; sportsman-like

硬橡皮(ㄧㄥˋ ㄒㄧㄤˋ ㄆㄧˊ)
ebonite; hard rubber

硬性(ㄧㄥˋ ㄒㄧㄥˋ)
①a stubborn or obstinate disposition ②(said of materials) hardness

硬性規定(ㄧㄥˋ ㄒㄧㄥˋ ㄍㄨㄟ ㄉㄧㄥˋ)
rigid and inflexible ruling; hard-and-fast rules

硬脂(ㄧㄥˋ ㄓ)
stearin

硬脂酸(ㄧㄥˋ ㄓ ㄙㄨㄢ)
stearic acid

硬紙板(ㄧㄥˋ ㄓˇ ㄅㄢˇ)
cardboard

硬著頭皮(ㄧㄥˋ ㄓㄜ ㄊㄡˊ ㄆㄧˊ)
to do something against one's will; to force oneself to: 我硬著頭皮去見她。I forced myself to see her.

硬起心(ㄧㄥˋ ㄑㄧˇ ㄒㄧㄣ)
to steel one's heart

硬仗(ㄧㄥˋ ㄓㄤˋ)
a showdown battle; a formidable task; a fierce fight; an all-out battle

硬撐(ㄧㄥˋ ㄔㄥ)
to hold on firmly despite extreme adversity, pain, etc.; to keep on doing something without regard to one's own strength

硬石膏(ㄧㄥˋ ㄕˊ ㄍㄠ)
anhydrite

硬是(ㄧㄥˋ ㄕˋ)
(dialect)①actually; really ②just; simply

硬手(ㄧㄥˋ ㄕㄡˇ)

an expert; an efficient or capable person

硬說(ㄧㄥˋ ㄕㄨㄛ)
to insist on saying; to assert; to stand on one's views: 他硬說自己的判斷是對的。He obstinately asserted that his judgment was right.

硬水(ㄧㄥˋ ㄕㄨㄟˇ)
hard water

硬彩(ㄧㄥˋ ㄘㄞˇ)
deep or dark colors on porcelain

硬要(ㄧㄥˋ ㄧㄠˋ)
to want or demand insistently: 他們硬要我收下這些禮物。They demanded insistently that I accept these gifts.

硬文學(ㄧㄥˋ ㄨㄣˊ ㄒㄩㄝˊ)
(literally) hard literature—academic writings; literature with a bold and raw style that stirs up the inner feelings or fighting spirit of the readers

硬玉(ㄧㄥˋ ㄩˋ)
jadeite

【硝】 3867 ㄒㄧㄠ shiau xiāo
1. niter; saltpeter
2. to tan leather

硝化(ㄒㄧㄠ ㄏㄨㄚˋ)
nitration

硝化甘油(ㄒㄧㄠ ㄏㄨㄚˋ ㄍㄢ ㄧㄡˊ)
nitroglycerine

硝基(ㄒㄧㄠ ㄐㄧ)
nitro

硝鏹水(ㄒㄧㄠ ㄑㄧㄤˇ ㄕㄨㄟˇ)or **硝酸**(ㄒㄧㄠ ㄙㄨㄢ)
nitric acid

硝石(ㄒㄧㄠ ㄕˊ)
saltpeter, or niter

硝酸鈉(ㄒㄧㄠ ㄙㄨㄢ ㄋㄚˋ)
sodium nitrate

硝酸鉀(ㄒㄧㄠ ㄙㄨㄢ ㄐㄧㄚˇ)
potassium nitrate

硝酸鹽(ㄒㄧㄠ ㄙㄨㄢ ㄧㄢˊ)
nitrate

【硯】 3868 ㄧㄢˋ yann yàn
an inkstone

硯臺(ㄧㄢˋ ㄊㄞˊ)
an ink-slab; an inkstone

硯田(ㄧㄢˋ ㄊㄧㄢˊ)
(literally) the ink-slab farm—writing as a means of making a living

硯耕(ㄧㄢˋ ㄍㄥ)
(literally) to plough the field of the ink-slab—to live by writing

硯盒(ㄧㄢˋ ㄏㄜˊ)or **硯室**(ㄧㄢˋ ㄕˋ)
a case for an ink-slab

硯兄(ㄧㄢˋ ㄒㄩㄥ)
a polite reference to fellow students who are older than oneself

硯池(ㄧㄢˋ ㄔˊ)
①the depression for water on an ink-slab ②a pool for washing the ink-slab

硯友(ㄧㄢˋ ㄧㄡˇ)
fellow students; classmates

硯瓦(ㄧㄢˋ ㄨㄚˇ)
an ink-slab

【硭】 3869 ㄇㄤˊ mang máng
sodium sulphate

硭硝(ㄇㄤˊ ㄒㄧㄠ)
sodium sulphate

【确】 3870 ㄑㄩㄝˋ chiueh què
1. hard stone
2. (said of land) barren; unproductive

八畫

【硎】 3871 ㄒㄧㄥˊ shyng xíng
a whetstone; a grindstone

【硼】 3872 1. ㄆㄥˊ perng péng boron 2. borax

硼化物(ㄆㄥˊ ㄏㄨㄚˋ ㄨˋ)
boride

硼砂(ㄆㄥˊ ㄕㄚ)
borax

硼酸(ㄆㄥˊ ㄙㄨㄢ)
boric acid

硼酸綿(ㄆㄥˊ ㄙㄨㄢ ㄇㄧㄢˊ)
cotton immersed in boric acid

硼酸鹽(ㄆㄥˊ ㄙㄨㄢ ㄧㄢˊ)
borate

【硼】 3872 2. ㄆㄥ peng pēng
the sound of splashing

硼砰(ㄆㄥ ㄆㄥ)
the sound of water splashing or sloshing

【碌】 3873 ㄌㄨˋ luh lù

1. mediocre; common
2. busy; occupied
3. a kind of stone roller

碌碡(ㄌㄨ ㄓㄡ)
a kind of stone roller

碌碌(ㄌㄨ ㄌㄨ)
① mediocre; commonplace; incompetent: 他是個碌碌無能的辦事員。He is an incompetent clerk. ② busy; occupied: 他整天忙忙碌碌的。He is busy going about his work all day long. ③ the color of jade

【碑】 3874
ㄅㄟ bei bēi
a stone tablet

碑版(ㄅㄟ ㄅㄢ)
stone tablets; steles

碑銘(ㄅㄟ ㄇㄧㄥ)
a part of an inscription on a tablet, usually in rhyme

碑帖(ㄅㄟ ㄊㄧㄝ)
the rubbings of inscriptions from stone tablets used as calligraphic models

碑亭(ㄅㄟ ㄊㄧㄥ)
a pavilion built over a stone tablet

碑林(ㄅㄟ ㄌㄧㄣ)
a large collection of stone tablets, especially that of Sian (西安) which includes more than 600 items

碑記(ㄅㄟ ㄐㄧ)
an inscriptional record; an inscription

碑碣(ㄅㄟ ㄐㄧㄝ)
stone tablets; steles

碑誌(ㄅㄟ ㄓ)
an inscription on a tablet

碑額(ㄅㄟ ㄜ)
the head of a stone tablet; the top part of a tablet

碑陰(ㄅㄟ ㄧㄣ)
the back of a stone tablet

碑文(ㄅㄟ ㄨㄣ)
an inscription on a tablet

【碎】 3875
ㄙㄨㄟ suey suì
1. broken; smashed; torn; to break to pieces; to smash
2. trivial; unimportant; trifling
3. garrulous; gabby

碎水斧(ㄙㄨㄟ ㄕㄨㄟ ㄈㄨ)
an ice ax

碎冰船(ㄙㄨㄟ ㄅㄧㄥ ㄔㄨㄢ)
an icebreaker

碎步兒(ㄙㄨㄟ ㄅㄨ ㄦ)
short quick steps

碎片(ㄙㄨㄟ ㄆㄧㄢ)
fragments; splinters; shreds; chips: 鏡子破成碎片。The mirror broke into splinters.

碎煤(ㄙㄨㄟ ㄇㄟ)
slack coal

碎密(ㄙㄨㄟ ㄇㄧ)
complicated and disorderly

碎紛紛(ㄙㄨㄟ ㄈㄣ ㄈㄣ)
broken to pieces

碎爛(ㄙㄨㄟ ㄌㄢ)
smashed or broken beyond recognition

碎裂(ㄙㄨㄟ ㄌㄧㄝ)
torn or broken to pieces

碎工(ㄙㄨㄟ ㄍㄨㄥ)
odd jobs

碎貨(ㄙㄨㄟ ㄏㄨㄛ)
retail goods

碎金(ㄙㄨㄟ ㄐㄧㄣ)
brief literary masterpieces

碎屑(ㄙㄨㄟ ㄒㄧㄝ)
very small broken pieces

碎小(ㄙㄨㄟ ㄒㄧㄠ)
one's dependents

碎屍萬段(ㄙㄨㄟ ㄕ ㄨㄢ ㄉㄨㄢ)
(literally) to tear the body to thousands of pieces—to inflict severe punishment

碎石(ㄙㄨㄟ ㄕ)
(construction) macadam; crushed stones; broken stones

碎石路(ㄙㄨㄟ ㄕ ㄌㄨ)
a macadam pavement; a gravel road; a broken stone road

碎石機(ㄙㄨㄟ ㄕ ㄐㄧ)
a crusher; a stone breaker

碎石子(ㄙㄨㄟ ㄕ ㄗ)
gravel; macadam

碎嘴子(ㄙㄨㄟ ㄗㄨㄟ ㄗ)
① a chatterbox; a garrulous person ② to chatter; to talk too much; to prate

碎瓷(ㄙㄨㄟ ㄘ)
the crackleware; the porcelainware with a smashed-ice design

碎銀(ㄙㄨㄟ ㄧㄣ)
small bits of silver

碎務(ㄙㄨㄟ ㄨ)
chores

碎玉(ㄙㄨㄟ ㄩ)
① broken jade ② beautiful white teeth

【碉】 3876
ㄉㄧㄠ diau diāo
a stone chamber

碉堡(ㄉㄧㄠ ㄅㄠ)
a fort; a pillbox; a blockhouse

【碓】 3877
ㄉㄨㄟ duey duì
a pestle (for husking grain)

碓房(ㄉㄨㄟ ㄈㄤ)
an establishment for hulling grain

碓臼(ㄉㄨㄟ ㄐㄧㄡ)
pestles and mortars

【碇】 3878
ㄉㄧㄥ dinq dìng
an anchor (for a ship)

【碰】 3879
(撞) ㄆㄥ penq pèng
1. to collide; to hit; to touch; to bump: 我用力碰他。I hit hard against him.
2. to meet unexpectedly; to run into: 我沒碰着她。I didn't meet her.
3. to take one's chance: 我要去那兒碰碰機會。I want to go there to take a chance.

碰杯(ㄆㄥ ㄅㄟ)
to clink glasses

碰壁(ㄆㄥ ㄅㄧ)
① to meet rejection ② to encounter difficulties; to run into a blind alley

碰面(ㄆㄥ ㄇㄧㄢ)
to meet; to come face to face

碰翻(ㄆㄥ ㄈㄢ)
to tip over after being hit by something

碰倒(ㄆㄥ ㄉㄠ)
to tumble down after being hit by something

碰到(ㄆㄥ ㄉㄠ)
① to meet someone unexpectedly ② to touch something

碰釘子(ㄆㄥ ㄉㄧㄥ ㄗ)
to meet rejection; to be rebuffed; to be rebuked

碰頭(ㄆㄥ ㄊㄡ)
① to meet someone; to rendezvous ② to have one's head hit accidentally

碰壞(ㄆㄥ ㄏㄨㄞ)

〔石部〕

〔石部〕

to be damaged by collision

碰見 (ㄆㄥˋ ㄐㄧㄢˋ)
to meet or encounter someone unexpectedly; to run into

碰巧 (ㄆㄥˋ ㄑㄧㄠˇ)
by coincidence; accidentally; to happen to: 我碰巧在公車上遇见她。I happened to meet her in the bus.

碰撞 (ㄆㄥˋ ㄓㄨㄤˋ)
to hit; to run into: 一輛巴士從後面碰撞了一部汽車。A bus ran into a car from behind.

碰傷 (ㄆㄥˋ ㄕㄤ)
to be injured or damaged after being hit by something

碰一鼻子灰 (ㄆㄥˋ ㄧˋ ㄅㄧˊ·ㄗㄏㄨㄟ)
to meet rejection; to meet with a rebuff

碰運氣 (ㄆㄥˋ ㄩㄣˋ·ㄑㄧ)
①to try one's luck ②sheer luck; a lucky stroke; a fluke

【碚】 3880
ㄅㄟˋ bey bèi
1. as in 蝦蟆碚—a place in Hupeh
2. as in 碚礧—a bud

【碘】 3881
ㄉㄧㄢˇ dean diǎn
iodine

碘化物 (ㄉㄧㄢˇ ㄏㄨㄚˋ ㄨˋ)
an iodide

碘酒 (ㄉㄧㄢˇ ㄐㄧㄡˇ) or 碘酊 (ㄉㄧㄢˇ ㄉㄧㄥˇ)
iodine tincture: 他在傷口上擦些碘酒。He applied some iodine tincture on the wound.

碘酸 (ㄉㄧㄢˇ ㄙㄨㄢ)
iodic acid

碘銀礦 (ㄉㄧㄢˇ ㄧㄣˊ ㄎㄨㄤˋ)
iodyrite

【碏】 3882
ㄑㄩㄝˋ chiueh què
(said of stone) many-colored

【碡】 3883
ㄉㄨˊ dwu dú
a kind of stone roller

【碁】 3884
(棋) ㄑㄧˊ chyi qí
1. any Oriental game played on a checkered board, like Chinese chess, go, etc.
2. any piece used in the game of chess

【碍】 3885
ㄞˋ ay ài

a simplified form of 礙—to obstruct; to hinder; 無知爲進步之障礙。Ignorance is an obstruction to progress.

【碗】 3886
(盌、椀) ㄨㄢˇ woan wǎn
a bowl (especially a small one): 他把碗打破了。He broke his bowl.

碗碟 (ㄨㄢˇ ㄉㄧㄝˊ)
bowls and dishes

碗櫃 (ㄨㄢˇ 《ㄨㄟˋ) or 碗碟櫃 (ㄨㄢˇ ㄉㄧㄝˊ 《ㄨㄟˋ)
a cupboard

碗筷 (ㄨㄢˇ ㄎㄨㄞˋ)
bowls and chopsticks

九畫

【碧】 3887
ㄅㄧˋ bih bì
1. green; blue; verdant; emerald green
2. jasper; emerald

碧桃 (ㄅㄧˋ ㄊㄠˊ)
a kind of peach tree that does not bear fruit 亦作「千葉桃」

碧潭 (ㄅㄧˋ ㄊㄢˊ)
the Green Lake (in suburban Taipei, Taiwan)

碧落 (ㄅㄧˋ ㄌㄨㄛˋ)
the sky; the blue realm

碧綠 (ㄅㄧˋ ㄌㄩˋ)
verdant; emerald green: 田野長滿碧綠的青草。The field was covered with verdant grass.

碧空 (ㄅㄧˋ ㄎㄨㄥ)
a blue sky; an azure sky

碧海青天 (ㄅㄧˋ ㄏㄞˇ ㄑㄧㄥ ㄊㄧㄢ)
the emerald sea under the blue sky

碧漢 (ㄅㄧˋ ㄏㄢˋ)
a blue sky; an azure sky

碧血 (ㄅㄧˋ ㄒㄧㄝˋ) or (ㄅㄧˋ ㄒㄩㄝˋ)
bloodshed for patriotism or loyalty, from the legend of Chang Hung (萇弘) of the Chou Dynasty whose blood turned to jasper three years after his death in battle

碧血丹心 (ㄅㄧˋ ㄒㄧㄝˋ ㄉㄢ ㄒㄧㄣ) or
(ㄅㄧˋ ㄒㄩㄝˋ ㄉㄢ ㄒㄧㄣ)
deep patriotism

碧水 (ㄅㄧˋ ㄕㄨㄟˇ)

blue waters

碧草 (ㄅㄧˋ ㄘㄠˇ)
verdant grass; green grass

碧草如茵 (ㄅㄧˋ ㄘㄠˇ ㄖㄨˊ ㄧㄣ)
The expanse of verdant grass seems like a pleasant mat. 或 a carpet of green grass

碧眼兒 (ㄅㄧˋ ㄧㄢˇ ㄦ)
(literally) men with blue eyes—Westerners

碧瑤 (ㄅㄧˋ ㄧㄠˊ)
Baguio, the Philippines

碧眼 (ㄅㄧˋ ㄧㄢˇ)
blue-eyed

碧瓦 (ㄅㄧˋ ㄨㄚˇ)
emerald green glazed tiles

碧玉 (ㄅㄧˋ ㄩˋ)
jasper; emerald

碧雲寺 (ㄅㄧˋ ㄩㄣˊ ㄙˋ)
a famed Buddhist temple in the Western Hills (西山) near Peking

【碣】 3888
ㄐㄧㄝˊ jye jié
a stone tablet (especially one with a round outline)

【碩】 3889
ㄕˋ shyr shì
(語音 ㄕㄨㄛˋ shuò)
great; large

碩大無朋 (ㄕˋ ㄉㄚˋ ㄨˊ ㄆㄥˊ)
unequaled in huge size; mammoth; gigantic

碩老 (ㄕˋ ㄌㄠˇ)
a learned elder; an old venerable scholar

碩果僅存 (ㄕˋ ㄍㄨㄛˇ ㄐㄧㄣˇ ㄘㄨㄣˊ)
the only remaining of the great; the only one of its kind to have survived; the rare survival

碩學通儒 (ㄕˋ ㄒㄩㄝˊ ㄊㄨㄥ ㄖㄨˊ) or 碩學鴻儒 (ㄕˋ ㄒㄩㄝˊ ㄏㄨㄥˊ ㄖㄨˊ)
an erudite and wise scholar

碩士
①(ㄕˋ ㄕˋ) a wise man
②(ㄕㄨㄛˋ ㄕˋ) a holder of the master's degree

碩儒 (ㄕˋ ㄖㄨˊ)
a great Confucian scholar; a great scholar

碩言 (ㄕˋ ㄧㄢˊ)
boastful talks; grand words

碩彥 (ㄕˋ ㄧㄢˋ)

a man of great talent; a learned scholar

碩望〔ㄕ ㄨㄤˋ〕
a much respected man; a man of great fame

【碳】3890 ㄊㄢˋ tann tàn
carbon 亦作「炭」

碳化〔ㄊㄢˋ ㄏㄨㄚˋ〕
to carbonize; to carbonate; carbonization

碳化物〔ㄊㄢˋ ㄏㄨㄚˋ ㄨˋ〕
carbide

碳水化合物〔ㄊㄢˋ ㄕㄨㄟˇ ㄏㄨㄚˋ ㄏㄜˊ ㄨˋ〕
carbohydrate

碳酸〔ㄊㄢˋ ㄙㄨㄢ〕
carbonic acid

碳酸鈉〔ㄊㄢˋ ㄙㄨㄢ ㄋㄚˋ〕
sodium carbonate

碳酸鈣〔ㄊㄢˋ ㄙㄨㄢ ㄍㄞˇ〕
calcium carbonate

碳酸氣〔ㄊㄢˋ ㄙㄨㄢ ㄑㄧˋ〕
carbonic-acid gas; carbon dioxide 亦作「二氧化碳」

碳酸中毒〔ㄊㄢˋ ㄙㄨㄢ ㄓㄨㄥ ㄉㄨˊ〕
poisoning from carbonic acid

【碴】3891 ㄔㄚˊ char chá
1. chips, fragments or splinters (of glass, china, etc.)
2. to be cut (by broken glass, china, etc.)

碴兒〔ㄔㄚˊㄦ〕
①chips, fragments or splinters (of glass, china, etc.) ② the cause of a trouble; a quarrel: 別找他的碴兒。Do not pick a quarrel with him.

【碟】3892 ㄉㄧㄝˊ dye dié
a dish or plate (especially a small one)

碟兒〔ㄉㄧㄝˊㄦ〕or碟子〔ㄉㄧㄝˊ ㄗ〕
a dish or plate (especially a small one)

碟影片〔ㄉㄧㄝˊ ㄧㄥˇ ㄆㄧㄢˋ〕
a videodisc

碟影機〔ㄉㄧㄝˊ ㄧㄥˇ ㄐㄧ〕
a videodisc player

十畫

【確】3893 ㄑㄩㄝˋ chiueh què
1. sure; certain; secure; real; true; valid: 我確信他會來。I

am sure that he will come.
2. firm; firmly

確保〔ㄑㄩㄝˋ ㄅㄠˇ〕
to secure; to insure; to be sure to

確非〔ㄑㄩㄝˋ ㄈㄟ〕
actually not; really not; truly not

確否待考〔ㄑㄩㄝˋ ㄈㄡˇ ㄉㄞˋ ㄎㄠˇ〕or確否待查〔ㄑㄩㄝˋ ㄈㄡˇ ㄉㄞˋ ㄔㄚˊ〕
Whether it's true or not remains to be verified.

確當〔ㄑㄩㄝˋ ㄉㄤˋ〕
true; proper and correct

確定〔ㄑㄩㄝˋ ㄉㄧㄥˋ〕
① to decide; to fix; to settle; to determine ② certain; sure; definite

確立〔ㄑㄩㄝˋ ㄌㄧˋ〕
to establish firmly

確論〔ㄑㄩㄝˋ ㄌㄨㄣˋ〕
a sound statement; a definite view

確耗〔ㄑㄩㄝˋ ㄏㄠˋ〕
reliable information

確乎〔ㄑㄩㄝˋ ㄏㄨ〕
certainly; surely; assuredly; undoubtedly

確據〔ㄑㄩㄝˋ ㄐㄩˋ〕
sure proof; reliable evidence

確切〔ㄑㄩㄝˋ ㄑㄧㄝˋ〕
valid; sound; right; accurate; exact; precise; clear and unambiguous: 你必須確切地執行命令。You must carry out an order exactly to the letter.

確信〔ㄑㄩㄝˋ ㄒㄧㄣˋ〕
to be convinced; to believe firmly; to be certain of: 我確信他會成功。I was certain of his succeeding.

確訊〔ㄑㄩㄝˋ ㄒㄩㄣˋ〕
reliable information; reliable report

確知〔ㄑㄩㄝˋ ㄓ〕
to know for sure: 你確知全部實情嗎? Do you know the whole truth for sure?

確證〔ㄑㄩㄝˋ ㄓㄥˋ〕
convincing proof; conclusive evidence; ironclad proof

確實〔ㄑㄩㄝˋ ㄕˊ〕
real; true; certain: 這確實是個好主意。This is really a good idea.

確實性〔ㄑㄩㄝˋ ㄕˊ ㄒㄧㄥˋ〕
reliability; authenticity

確然〔ㄑㄩㄝˋ ㄖㄢˊ〕
certain; sure; without doubt

確認〔ㄑㄩㄝˋ ㄖㄣˋ〕
to certify; to identify with certainty; to affirm; to confirm

確鑿〔ㄑㄩㄝˋ ㄗㄨㄛˊ〕
accurate; precise; beyond any doubt; authentic; conclusive; irrefutable: 你能提出確鑿證據嗎? Can you give me conclusive proof?

確有其事〔ㄑㄩㄝˋ ㄧㄡˇ ㄑㄧˊ ㄕˋ〕
It actually happened.

確有其人〔ㄑㄩㄝˋ ㄧㄡˇ ㄑㄧˊ ㄖㄣˊ〕
There is (or was) indeed such a person.

【碾】3894 ㄋㄧㄢˇ nean niǎn
1. a stone roller
2. to mill; to roll; to crush

碾米〔ㄋㄧㄢˇ ㄇㄧˇ〕
to husk rice

碾米機〔ㄋㄧㄢˇ ㄇㄧˇ ㄐㄧ〕
a rice-husking machine

碾米廠〔ㄋㄧㄢˇ ㄇㄧˇ ㄔㄤˇ〕
a rice-husking mill

碾子〔ㄋㄧㄢˇ ㄗ〕
a stone roller for hulling grain, etc.

碾碎〔ㄋㄧㄢˇ ㄙㄨㄟˋ〕
to pulverize

【碼】3895 ㄇㄚˇ maa mǎ
1. yard (a measure of length)
2. a symbol; a code; a sign or thing indicating number

碼頭〔ㄇㄚˇ ㄊㄡˊ〕
① a dock; a quay; a wharf; a pier ② a port city ③ bailiwick or sphere of influence (of gangsters)

碼頭工人〔ㄇㄚˇ ㄊㄡˊ ㄍㄨㄥ ㄖㄣˊ〕
a stevedore; a longshoreman

碼頭稅〔ㄇㄚˇ ㄊㄡˊ ㄕㄨㄟˋ〕or碼頭費〔ㄇㄚˇ ㄊㄡˊ ㄈㄟˋ〕
wharfage; quayage; pier dues

碼子〔ㄇㄚˇ ㄗ〕or碼兒〔ㄇㄚˇㄦ〕
a system of numerical symbols used in business

【磁】3896 ㄘˊ tsyr cí
1. magnetic; magnetism
2. porcelain; china

磁暴〔ㄘˊ ㄅㄠˋ〕
(physics) a magnetic storm

〔石部〕

【石
部】

磁片(ㄘ ㄆㄧㄢ)or 磁碟片(ㄘ ㄉㄧㄝ/ ㄆㄧㄢ)
(computers) a diskette; a floppy disc

磁帶(ㄘ ㄉㄞ)
a magnetic tape

磁頭(ㄘ ㄊㄡ/)
a magnetic head

磁鐵(ㄘ ㄊㄧㄝ)
a magnet; magnetic iron

磁鐵礦(ㄘ ㄊㄧㄝ ㄎㄨㄤ)
magnetite; loadstone

磁力(ㄘ ㄌㄧ)
magnetic force; magnetism: 這塊鐵已失去磁力。The iron has lost its magnetic force.

磁感應(ㄘ ㄍㄢ ㄧㄥ)
magnetic induction

磁化(ㄘ ㄏㄨㄚ)
to magnetize; magnetization

磁婚(ㄘ ㄏㄨㄣ)
china wedding, the 20th wedding anniversary

磁極(ㄘ ㄐㄧ/)
magnetic poles

磁圈(ㄘ ㄑㄩㄢ)
the magnetic field

磁性(ㄘ ㄒㄧㄥ)
magnetism

磁針(ㄘ ㄓㄣ)
a magnetic needle: 磁針指向南方。The magnetic needle points south.

磁場(ㄘ ㄔㄤ/)or(ㄘ ㄔㄤ)
the magnetic field

磁石(ㄘ ㄕ/)
a magnet; a loadstone: 地球中心是一塊天然磁石。The center of the earth is a natural magnet.

【磋】 3897　ㄘㄨㄛ tsuo cuō
to file; to polish (jade, stone, horn, etc.)

磋磨(ㄘㄨㄛ ㄇㄛ/)
①to polish (jade, horn, stone, etc.) ②to learn through discussions with others

磋商(ㄘㄨㄛ ㄕㄤ)
to exchange views; to hold a discussion or consultation

【磅】 3898　1. ㄅㄤ banq bàng
1. a pound
2. scales

3. to weigh

磅秤(ㄅㄤ ㄔㄥ)
scales giving the weight in avoirdupois

【磅】 3898　2. ㄆㄤ pang páng
the noise of stone crashing

磅礴(ㄆㄤ ㄅㄛ/)
boundless; majestic; extensive; filling all space

【磔】 3899　ㄓㄜ/ jer zhé
1. to dismember a human being (an ancient punishment)
2. (Chinese calligraphy) a downward stroke sliding to the right

【磕】 3900　ㄎㄜ ke kē
to strike; to bump; to collide; to knock

磕碰(ㄎㄜ ㄆㄥ)
to bump against; to hit against; to collide with

磕頭(ㄎㄜ ㄊㄡ/)
to kowtow

磕頭碰腦(ㄎㄜ ㄊㄡ/ ㄆㄥ ㄋㄠ/)
to bump against things on every side (as in a room full of furniture); to bump against one another (as in a crowd)

磕磕巴巴(ㄎㄜ· ㄎㄜ· ㄅㄚ ㄅㄚ)
stammering; stuttering

磕磕撞撞(ㄎㄜ· ㄎㄜ· ㄓㄨㄤ ㄓㄨㄤ)
to walk unsteadily; to stumble or stagger along

磕牙(ㄎㄜ ㄧㄚ/)
to chat; to jabber; to gossip: 別坐在那裏與她們磕牙兒了。Don't sit there prating and making fun of her.

【磊】 3901　ㄌㄟ/ leei lěi
1. a heap of stones
2. great; massive

磊磊(ㄌㄟ/ ㄌㄟ/)
①(said of stones) innumerable ②rolling

磊落落(ㄌㄟ/ ㄌㄨㄛ ㄌㄨㄛ/)
①clear; distinct ②open-hearted; candid; unaffected; free and easy

磊落(ㄌㄟ/ ㄌㄨㄛ/)
①a lot of ②open-hearted; candid; unaffected; open and

aboveboard; free and easy: 他的行爲光明磊落。He acts openly and aboveboard.

磊塊or 壘塊(ㄌㄟ/ ㄎㄨㄞ)
one's grievances

【磒】 3902　ㄩㄣ/ yeun yǔn
to fall down

磒石(ㄩㄣ/ ㄕ/)or 磒星(ㄩㄣ/ ㄒㄧㄥ)
a meteor; a meteorite: 無聲的磒石滑過夜空。The silent meteor slides in the night sky.

【磐】 3903　ㄆㄢ/ parn pán
1. a massive rock
2. to linger around
3. to league together

磐礴(ㄆㄢ/ ㄅㄛ/)
extensive; vast; imposing; great

磐石(ㄆㄢ/ ㄕ/)
a massive rock: 他們的愛情堅若磐石。Their love is as steady as a massive rock.

磐石之安(ㄆㄢ/ ㄕ/ ㄓ ㄢ)
as stable and secure as a massive rock

磐牙(ㄆㄢ/ ㄧㄚ/)or 盤牙(ㄆㄢ/ ㄧㄚ/)
to league together (as bandits)

十一畫

【磨】 3904　1. ㄇㄛ/ mo mó
1. to dawdle; to waste time; to while away
2. to rub; to grind; to polish; to wear: 我的脚上磨了泡。My feet were blistered from the rubbing.
3. sufferings; obstacles; setbacks: 好事多磨。The road to happiness is strewn with setbacks.

磨墨(ㄇㄛ/ ㄇㄛ)
to prepare liquid ink from an ink stick; to rub down an ink stick

磨滅(ㄇㄛ/ ㄇㄧㄝ)
①to wear out ②to obliterate; delible: 他在我心中留下不可磨滅的印象。He left an indelible impression on my mind.

磨刀(ㄇㄛ/ ㄉㄠ)
to sharpen a knife

磨刀石(ㄇㄜ ㄉㄠ ㄕ)
a whetstone; a grindstone

磨難(ㄇㄜ ㄋㄢ)
① sufferings; privations; tribulations; difficulties; obstacles ② to cause to suffer; to give a hard time

磨礪 or 磨厲(ㄇㄜ ㄌ一)
① to sharpen (a knife) ② to train; to harden; to temper; to discipline oneself

磨礪以須 or 磨厲以須(ㄇㄜ ㄌ一 一 ㄒㄩ)
to be combat-ready; to sharpen weapons in anticipation of war

磨鍊(ㄇㄜ ㄌ一ㄢ)
① to forge or temper (metal) ② to train; to harden; to discipline

磨光(ㄇㄜ ㄍㄨㄤ)
to polish; to burnish

磨功夫(ㄇㄜ ㄍㄨㄥ ㄈㄨ)
to waste time; time-consuming; 刺繡是件磨功夫的活兒. Embroidering is a time-consuming job.

磨勘(ㄇㄜ ㄎㄢ)
① to grade; to rate ② to review (examination papers under the former civil service examination system) ③ to study hard in search of truth

磨勁兒(ㄇㄜ ㄐ一ㄣㄦ)
persistence; perseverance; persistent; persevering

磨鏡(ㄇㄜ ㄐ一ㄥ)
to polish pieces of metal into mirrors

磨鏡子(ㄇㄜ ㄐ一ㄥ ˙ㄗ)
(slang) homosexual act between two women; lesbianism

磨拳擦掌(ㄇㄜ ㄑㄩㄢ ㄘㄚ ㄓㄤ)
saber-rattling; ready for fight

磨折(ㄇㄜ ㄓㄜ)
tribulations; privations; sufferings; to cause to suffer; to give a hard time; to wear down; to reduce (a person) to a worse condition

磨琢(ㄇㄜ ㄓㄨㄛ)
(literally) to grind and to carve—to educate; to train; to study

磨杵成針(ㄇㄜ ㄔㄨ ㄔㄥ ㄓㄣ)
(literally) A pestle can be rubbed into a needle.—Persistent efforts can achieve difficult things.

磨穿鐵硯(ㄇㄜ ㄔㄨㄢ ㄊ一ㄝ一ㄢ)
(literally) to wear through an iron ink-slab—to apply oneself to literary work with persistent efforts

磨石子地(ㄇㄜ ㄕˊ˙ㄗ ㄉ一)
terrazzo floor

磨擦(ㄇㄜ ㄘㄚ)
① to rub ② friction

磨蹭(ㄇㄜ ˙ㄘㄥ)
to be tardy; to be slow; to dawdle; 不要磨磨蹭蹭的, 趕快做你的事. Stop dawdling and do your work quickly.

磨損(ㄇㄜ ㄙㄨㄣ)
wear and tear; to wear away

磨牙(ㄇㄜ 一ㄚ)
to be talkative and argumentative ② to grind one's teeth

【磨】 3904 ㄇㄜ moh mò
1. a mill
2. to turn around
3. to grind (grain, etc.)

磨磐(ㄇㄜ ㄆㄢ)
a millstone; a mill

磨坊(ㄇㄜ ㄈㄤ)or 磨房(ㄇㄜ ㄈㄤ)
a mill (referring to the building)

磨豆腐(ㄇㄜ ㄉㄡ ˙ㄈㄨ)
to grind beans to make bean curd

【磬】 3905 ㄑ一ㄥ chìng qìng
a kind of musical instrument (made by hollowing out a hard sonorous stone, etc.); a musical stone

磬竭(ㄑ一ㄥ ㄐ一ㄝ)
used up; exhausted; emptied

磬折(ㄑ一ㄥ ㄓㄜ)
humpbacked or bent as a chiming-stone

磬氏(ㄑ一ㄥ ㄕ)
a workman who makes musical stones

【磧】 3906 ㄑ一 chìh qì
1. gravel and sand in shallow waters

2. a desert

磧鹵(ㄑ一 ㄌㄨ)
sandy and saline land; barren land

【磚】 3907 ㄓㄨㄢ juan zhuān
bricks 亦作「甎」

十二畫

【磯】 3908 ㄐ一 jī jī
1. a rocky cliff on the water's edge; water-surrounded rocks
2. rocks that water pounds against; stones in a river, interrupting and fretting the current

【磴】 3909 ㄉㄥ dēng dèng
steps on rock

磴道(ㄉㄥ ㄉㄠ)
a rocky mountain path

【磷】 3910 1. ㄌ一ㄣ lín lín
1. phosphorus 亦作「燐」
2. water flowing between stones

磷磷(ㄌ一ㄣ ㄌ一ㄣ)
① the sound of water and stone beating against each other ② brilliance of precious stones

磷礦(ㄌ一ㄣ ㄎㄨㄤ)
phosphate rock

【磷】 3910 2. ㄌ一ㄣ linn lìn
thin (as opposed to thick)

【磺】 3911 ㄏㄨㄤ hwang huáng
sulfur; brimstone

磺酸(ㄏㄨㄤ ㄙㄨㄢ)
sulfonic acid

磺胺藥類(ㄏㄨㄤ ㄢ一ㄠ ㄌㄟ)
sulfa drugs

【磽】 3912 ㄑ一ㄠ chiau qiāo
hard barren land; poor in soil

磽薄(ㄑ一ㄠ ㄅㄜ)
hard and barren; hard and infertile

磽瘠(ㄑ一ㄠ ㄐ一)
hard and barren; hard and infertile

磽埆(ㄑ一ㄠ ㄑㄩㄝ)
① hard and barren land ②

〔石部〕

〔石部〕

hard (as opposed to soft)

【礁】 3913　ㄐㄧㄠ jiau jiāo
a reef

礁石 (ㄐㄧㄠ ㄕ)
a reef

十三畫

【礎】 3914　ㄔㄨ chuu chǔ
a plinth

礎石 (ㄔㄨ ㄕ)
the stone base of a column

礎潤而雨 (ㄔㄨ ㄖㄨㄣ ㄦ ㄩ)
(literally) A damp plinth foretells rain.—Insignificant signs reveal big events ahead.

十四畫

【礙】 3915　(碍) ㄞ ay ài
1. to obstruct; to hinder; to be in the way of
2. harmful; detrimental: 缺乏睡眠有礙身體健康。Lack of sleep is detrimental to one's health.

礙道 (ㄞ ㄉㄠ)
to obstruct the way

礙口 (ㄞ ㄎㄡ)
unpleasant to talk about: 這種事有點礙口。It is unpleasant to talk about such a thing.

礙事 (ㄞ ㄕ)
to be in the way; to be an obstacle to work; to be a problem: 只擦破皮，不礙事，it is just a graze, nothing serious.

礙手礙腳 (ㄞ ㄕㄡ ㄞ ㄐㄧㄠ)
to be very much in the way

礙眼 (ㄞ ㄧㄢ) or 礙目 (ㄞ ㄇㄨ)
unpleasant to the eye; to offend the eye; to be an eyesore

礙於情面 (ㄞ ㄩ ㄑㄧㄥ ㄇㄧㄢ)
for fear of hurting somebody's feelings

十五畫

【礫】 3916　ㄌㄧ lih lì
gravel; a pebble; shingle

礫石 (ㄌㄧ ㄕ)
gravel; a pebble

礫岩 (ㄌㄧ ㄧㄢ)
(geology) conglomerate

【礪】 3917　ㄌㄧ lih lì
1. a whetstone
2. to sharpen (a knife)

礪石 (ㄌㄧ ㄕ)
a whetstone

【礬】 3918　ㄈㄢˊ farn fán
alum; vitriol

礬土 (ㄈㄢˊ ㄊㄨ)
alumina

礬石 (ㄈㄢˊ ㄕ)
alunite

【礦】 3919　(鑛) ㄎㄨㄤ kuang kuàng
1. a mineral; ore
2. mining
3. a mine—(figuratively) a rich source

礦脈 (ㄎㄨㄤ ㄇㄞ)
an ore vein; an ore lode

礦苗 (ㄎㄨㄤ ㄇㄧㄠ)
the outcrop of a mineral; ore

礦工 (ㄎㄨㄤ ㄍㄨㄥ) or 礦夫 (ㄎㄨㄤ ㄈㄨ)
a miner

礦坑 (ㄎㄨㄤ ㄎㄥ)
a mining shaft; a pit: 這附近有一個舊礦坑。There's an old pit near here.

礦區 (ㄎㄨㄤ ㄑㄩ)
a mining district; an ore field

礦泉 (ㄎㄨㄤ ㄑㄩㄢ)
a mineral spring

礦產 (ㄎㄨㄤ ㄔㄢ)
mineral resources: 臺灣礦產並不豐富。Taiwan is not rich in mineral resources.

礦床 (ㄎㄨㄤ ㄔㄨㄤ)
the bed (of a mineral); mineral deposit; ore beds

礦石 (ㄎㄨㄤ ㄕ)
a mineral; ore

礦石收音機 (ㄎㄨㄤ ㄕ ㄕㄡ ㄧㄣ ㄐㄧ)
a crystal radio set

礦砂 (ㄎㄨㄤ ㄕㄚ)
the ore in sand form

礦山 (ㄎㄨㄤ ㄕㄢ)
mountains containing mineral deposits; a mine

礦層 (ㄎㄨㄤ ㄘㄥ)
the bed or stratum (of a mineral); mineral deposits; a seam

礦業 (ㄎㄨㄤ ㄧㄝ)
mining industry; mining

礦物 (ㄎㄨㄤ ㄨ)
a mineral

礦物學 (ㄎㄨㄤ ㄨ ㄒㄩㄝ)
mineralogy

礦物學家 (ㄎㄨㄤ ㄨ ㄒㄩㄝ ㄐㄧㄚ)
a mineralogist

礦物油 (ㄎㄨㄤ ㄨ ㄧㄡ)
mineral oil

十六畫

【礮】 3920　(砲) ㄆㄠ paw pào
1. a catapult
2. an artillery piece; a cannon; a gun

礮兵 (ㄆㄠ ㄅㄧㄥ)
①an artilleryman; a gunner
②artillery (as a branch of the armed forces): 礮兵轟擊該城。The artillery bombarded the town.

礮兵部隊 (ㄆㄠ ㄅㄧㄥ ㄅㄨ ㄉㄨㄟ)
artillery units

礮兵陣地 (ㄆㄠ ㄅㄧㄥ ㄓㄣ ㄉㄧ)
an artillery position or emplacement

礮彈 (ㄆㄠ ㄉㄢ)
a cannon ball; a shell; a cannon shot

礮塔 (ㄆㄠ ㄊㄚ)
a turret; a barbette; a gunhouse: 他們極力守護著礮塔。They tried hard to guard the turret.

礮臺 (ㄆㄠ ㄊㄞ)
a gun emplacement; a battery; a fort

砲艇(ㄆㄠˋ ㄊㄧㄥˇ)
a gunboat

砲火(ㄆㄠˋ ㄏㄨㄛˇ)
artillery fire; gunfire

砲灰(ㄆㄠˋ ㄏㄨㄟ)
cannon fodder

砲轟(ㄆㄠˋ ㄏㄨㄥ)
① to bombard with artillery fire; to cannonade ② concentrated verbal attacks

砲擊(ㄆㄠˋ ㄐㄧ)
a cannonade; bombardment; to bombard with artillery fire; to shell: 我們的戰艦砲擊他們的堡壘。Our ships bombarded their fortress.

砲艦(ㄆㄠˋ ㄐㄧㄢˋ)
a gunboat

砲車(ㄆㄠˋ ㄔㄜ)
a gun carriage

砲手(ㄆㄠˋ ㄕㄡˇ)
a gunner; a cannoneer; an artilleryman: 他在戰時是砲手。He was a gunner during the war.

砲身(ㄆㄠˋ ㄕㄣ)
the gun barrel

砲聲(ㄆㄠˋ ㄕㄥ)
the roaring of artillery pieces; the thunder of cannonade

砲座(ㄆㄠˋ ㄗㄨㄛˋ)
a gun platform; a barbette

砲衣(ㄆㄠˋ ㄧ)
canvas covering of an artillery piece; a gun cover

砲位(ㄆㄠˋ ㄨㄟˋ)
an artillery park; a gun pit; an emplacement

【礱】 3921
　　ㄌㄨㄥˊ　long lóng
1. to grind
2. a kind of mill

十七畫

【礴】 3922
　　ㄅㄛˊ　bor bó
filling all space; extensive

示 部
ㄕ shyh shì

【示】 3923
　　ㄕ shyh shì
1. to show; to indicate
2. to make known; to notify; a notice
3. to instruct
4. to demonstrate

示範(ㄕ ㄈㄢˋ)
① to set an example ② to demonstrate (how a thing works, etc.)

示範表演(ㄕ ㄈㄢˋ ㄅㄧㄠˇ ㄧㄢˇ)
demonstration (of a skill)

示覆(ㄕ ㄈㄨˋ)
to reply to an inquiry (a conventional phrase in formal communications when asking the other party to reply)

示疾(ㄕ ㄐㄧˊ)
illness (of a Buddhist priest)

示寂(ㄕ ㄐㄧˋ)
(said of a Buddhist priest) to indicate the way to Nirvana; to die

示警(ㄕ ㄐㄧㄥˇ)
to give a warning: 他們在街上鳴鑼示警。They gave a warning by beating gongs in the street.

示知(ㄕ ㄓ)
to inform; to notify

示眾(ㄕ ㄓㄨㄥˋ)
to exhibit to the public; to show to the public

示人(ㄕ ㄖㄣˊ)
to make known; to show others; to let others have a look at

示弱(ㄕ ㄖㄨㄛˋ)
to show weakness; to yield; to give in: 他不甘示弱而再試一次。He didn't give in and tried again.

示愛(ㄕ ㄞˋ)
to show one's tender feeling to one of the opposite sex

示意(ㄕ ㄧˋ)
to indicate one's wish or intention (usually by facial expressions or gestures); to drop a hint; to motion: 他示意我進去。He motioned me to enter.

示威(ㄕ ㄨㄟ)
① to demonstrate (by a mass meeting or parade) ②

to make a show of force

示威遊行(ㄕ ㄨㄟ ㄧㄡˊ ㄒㄧㄥˊ)
demonstration

示威運動(ㄕ ㄨㄟ ㄩㄣˋ ㄉㄨㄥˋ)
demonstration (by a mass meeting or parade)

二畫

【礽】 3924
　　ㄖㄥˊ　reng réng
a blessing; happiness; bliss

三畫

【社】 3925
　　ㄕㄜˋ sheh shè
1. the god of land
2. an association; an organization; a corporation; an agency
3. society; a community

社評(ㄕㄜˋ ㄆㄧㄥˊ)
an editorial

社土(ㄕㄜˋ ㄊㄨˇ)
land conferred upon a feudal lord by the emperor

社團(ㄕㄜˋ ㄊㄨㄢˊ)
an association; a corporation; a civic organization: 他們組成協助盲人的社團。They formed an association to help blind people.

社論(ㄕㄜˋ ㄌㄨㄣˋ)
an editorial

社會(ㄕㄜˋ ㄏㄨㄟˋ)
society; community: 他為社會的利益而做那件事。He did it for the interests of society.

社會變遷(ㄕㄜˋ ㄏㄨㄟˋ ㄅㄧㄢˋ ㄑㄧㄢ)
social change

社會名流(ㄕㄜˋ ㄏㄨㄟˋ ㄇㄧㄥˊ ㄌㄧㄡˊ)
noted public figures; socialites

社會發展(ㄕㄜˋ ㄏㄨㄟˋ ㄈㄚ ㄓㄢˇ)
social development

社會福利(ㄕㄜˋ ㄏㄨㄟˋ ㄈㄨˊ ㄌㄧˋ)
social welfare

社會福利事業保險(ㄕㄜˋ ㄏㄨㄟˋ ㄈㄨˊ ㄌㄧˋ ㄕˋ ㄧㄝˋ ㄅㄠˇ ㄒㄧㄢˇ)
social welfare insurance

社會服務(ㄕㄜˋ ㄏㄨㄟˋ ㄈㄨˊ ㄨˋ)
social services

社會黨(ㄕㄜˋ ㄏㄨㄟˋ ㄉㄤˇ)
Socialist Party

社會地位(ㄕㄜˋ ㄏㄨㄟˋ ㄉㄧˋ ㄨㄟˋ)
social status; social position;

（示 部）

〔示 部〕

社會標準
social standing

社會倫理(ㄕㄜˋ ㄏㄨㄟˋ ㄌㄨㄣˊ ㄌㄧˇ)
social ethics

社會改革(ㄕㄜˋ ㄏㄨㄟˋ ㄍㄞˇ ㄍㄜˊ)
social reform

社會工作(ㄕㄜˋ ㄏㄨㄟˋ ㄍㄨㄥ ㄗㄨㄛˋ)
social work

社會工作者(ㄕㄜˋ ㄏㄨㄟˋ ㄍㄨㄥ ㄗㄨㄛˋ ㄓㄜˇ)
a social worker

社會科學(ㄕㄜˋ ㄏㄨㄟˋ ㄎㄜ ㄒㄩㄝˊ)
social science

社會教育(ㄕㄜˋ ㄏㄨㄟˋ ㄐㄧㄠˋ ㄩˋ)
social education

社會進步(ㄕㄜˋ ㄏㄨㄟˋ ㄐㄧㄣˋ ㄅㄨˋ)
social progress

社會進化(ㄕㄜˋ ㄏㄨㄟˋ ㄐㄧㄣˋ ㄏㄨㄚˋ)
social evolution

社會局(ㄕㄜˋ ㄏㄨㄟˋ ㄐㄩˊ)
the bureau of social affairs
(under a city or county government)

社會角色(ㄕㄜˋ ㄏㄨㄟˋ ㄐㄩㄝˊ ㄙㄜˋ)
a social role

社會現象(ㄕㄜˋ ㄏㄨㄟˋ ㄒㄧㄢˋ ㄒㄧㄤˋ)
social phenomena

社會心理(ㄕㄜˋ ㄏㄨㄟˋ ㄒㄧㄣ ㄌㄧˇ)
social psychology (as a phenomenon)

社會心理學(ㄕㄜˋ ㄏㄨㄟˋ ㄒㄧㄣ ㄌㄧˇ ㄒㄩㄝˊ)
social psychology (as a science)

社會新聞(ㄕㄜˋ ㄏㄨㄟˋ ㄒㄧㄣ ㄨㄣˊ)
human interest stories or crime stories (as distinct from political, military, or educational news items)

社會學(ㄕㄜˋ ㄏㄨㄟˋ ㄒㄩㄝˊ)
sociology

社會秩序(ㄕㄜˋ ㄏㄨㄟˋ ㄓˋ ㄒㄩˋ)
social order

社會主義(ㄕㄜˋ ㄏㄨㄟˋ ㄓㄨˇ ㄧˋ)
socialism

社會事業(ㄕㄜˋ ㄏㄨㄟˋ ㄕˋ ㄧㄝˋ)
social work; social service; public welfare projects

社會生活(ㄕㄜˋ ㄏㄨㄟˋ ㄕㄥ ㄏㄨㄛˊ)
social life; community life

社會組織(ㄕㄜˋ ㄏㄨㄟˋ ㄗㄨˇ ㄓ)
social organization

社會壓力(ㄕㄜˋ ㄏㄨㄟˋ ㄧㄚ ㄌㄧˋ)
social pressure

社會問題(ㄕㄜˋ ㄏㄨㄟˋ ㄨㄣˋ ㄊㄧˊ)
a social problem

社會運動(ㄕㄜˋ ㄏㄨㄟˋ ㄩㄣˋ ㄉㄨㄥˋ)

社會運動
social movement

社稷(ㄕㄜˋ ㄐㄧˋ)
the god of land and the god of grain—a country

社稷之臣(ㄕㄜˋ ㄐㄧˋ ㄓ ㄔㄣˊ)
a key minister; an important courtier

社交(ㄕㄜˋ ㄐㄧㄠ)
social intercourse; sociality

社交公開(ㄕㄜˋ ㄐㄧㄠ ㄍㄨㄥ ㄎㄞ)
free social intercourse between men and women

社交生活(ㄕㄜˋ ㄐㄧㄠ ㄕㄥ ㄏㄨㄛˊ)
social life

社交舞(ㄕㄜˋ ㄐㄧㄠ ㄨˇ)
social dancing; ballroom dancing

社區(ㄕㄜˋ ㄑㄩ)
a community

社區發展(ㄕㄜˋ ㄑㄩ ㄈㄚ ㄓㄢˇ)
community development

社區規劃(ㄕㄜˋ ㄑㄩ ㄍㄨㄟ ㄏㄨㄚˋ)
community planning

社學(ㄕㄜˋ ㄒㄩㄝˊ)
a community school (in the Ming and Ching dynasties)

社長(ㄕㄜˋ ㄓㄤˇ)
the president or director of an association, newspaper, etc.): 他已經當了六年的社長了。He has been the president of the association for six years.

社鼠(ㄕㄜˋ ㄕㄨˇ)
(literally) mice in a temple —wicked people under the protection of a powerful man

社友(ㄕㄜˋ ㄧㄡˇ)
a fellow member (of a society, association, etc.): 歡迎所有社友參加此一活動。All fellow members are welcome to take part in the activity.

社務(ㄕㄜˋ ㄨˋ)
affairs or business of an association, newspaper office, etc.

社員(ㄕㄜˋ ㄩㄢˊ)
a member (of an association, society, etc.)

社員大會(ㄕㄜˋ ㄩㄢˊ ㄉㄚˋ ㄏㄨㄟˋ)
a general convention of an association, society, etc.

【祁】 3926
(ㄑㄧˊ chyi qí)
vigorous; thriving; to be

large

祁門(ㄑㄧˊ ㄇㄣˊ)
name of a county in Anhwei, famous for its black tea

祁連山(ㄑㄧˊ ㄌㄧㄢˊ ㄕㄢ)
name of a mountain in Kansu

祁寒酷暑(ㄑㄧˊ ㄏㄢˊ ㄎㄨˋ ㄕㄨˇ)
severe cold and intense heat

祁山(ㄑㄧˊ ㄕㄢ)
name of a mountain in Kansu used as a staging area by Chu-Ko Liang (諸葛亮) in the war against Wei (魏) during the Epoch of the Three Kingdoms

【祀】 3927
(ㄙˋ syh sì)
to worship; to offer sacrifices to

祀奉(ㄙˋ ㄈㄥˋ)
to worship: 中國人祀奉祖先。The Chinese worship their ancestors.

祀典(ㄙˋ ㄉㄧㄢˇ)
religious rites or services; rites of offering sacrifices

祀天(ㄙˋ ㄊㄧㄢ)
to worship, or offer sacrifices to Heaven

祀孔(ㄙˋ ㄎㄨㄥˇ)
to worship Confucius in ceremonies held on his birth anniversary on September 28

祀事(ㄙˋ ㄕˋ)
religious rites or services

祀神(ㄙˋ ㄕㄣˊ)
to worship gods

祀竈(ㄙˋ ㄗㄠˋ)
to worship the kitchen god (done on the 23rd of the 12th moon)

祀祖(ㄙˋ ㄗㄨˇ)
to worship ancestors

四畫

【祆】 3928
(ㄒㄧㄢ shian xiān)
Ormazd, the supreme deity in Zoroastrianism

祆教(ㄒㄧㄢ ㄐㄧㄠˋ)
Zoroastrianism

【祅】 3929
(ㄧㄠ iau yāo)

1. calamity due to terrestrial disturbances (as distinct from 災—disaster which is sent down from above)
2. bizarre

【祇】 3930 くí chyi qí
1. the god of the earth
2. peace; serenity; to be at rest
祇悔(くⁱ ㄏㄨㄟˇ)
  great regret; deep remorse

【祇】 3930 2.(只,祇) ㄓ jyy zhī (原讀ㄓ jy zhī)
  only; merely
祇得(ㄓ ㄉㄜˊ)
  to have to; to have no alternative
祇好(ㄓ ㄏㄠˇ)
  to have to; to have no other choice
祇要(ㄓ ㄧㄠˋ)
  only if

【祈】 3931 くí chyi qí
1. to pray
2. to beg; to entreat; to beseech; to supplicate; to request respectfully: 敬祈指導。We respectfully request your guidance.
祈福(くí ㄈㄨˊ)
  to pray for blessings
祈禱(くí ㄉㄠˇ)
  to pray, to offer a prayer
祈禱者(くí ㄉㄠˇ ㄓㄜˇ)
  a person praying; a prayer
祈禱文(くí ㄉㄠˇ ㄨㄣˊ)
  prayers
祈年(くí ㄋㄧㄢˊ)
  to pray for a bumper crop
祈年殿(くí ㄋㄧㄢˊ ㄉㄧㄢˋ)or祈穀壇(くí ㄍㄨˇ ㄊㄢˊ)
  name of a shrine in the Temple of Heaven in Peking
祈年宮(くí ㄋㄧㄢˊ ㄍㄨㄥ)
  name of an ancient palace in Shensi
祈(くí)
  slowly
祈求(くí くㄧㄡˊ)
  to pray for; to appeal for; to ask humbly for; to supplicate for: 他祈求上帝幫助。He prayed to God for help.
祈請(くí くㄧㄥˇ)

  to beg; to beseech; to entreat
祈禳(くí ㄖㄤˊ)
  to pray for protection against calamities
祈雨(くí ㄩˇ)
  to pray for rain: 農民正在祈雨。The farmers are praying for rain.

【祉】 3932 ㄓ jyy zhǐ
  happiness; blessings; blessedness; welfare
祉祿(ㄓ ㄌㄨˋ)
  happiness and wealth

五畫

【祐】 3933 ㄧㄡˋ yow yòu
  divine help
祐助(ㄧㄡˋ ㄓㄨˋ)
  (said of a deity) to help (a mortal)

【祓】 3934 ㄈㄨˊ fwu fú
1. to exorcise
2. to cleanse; to clean
祓禊(ㄈㄨˊ ㄒㄧˋ)
  exorcism by a bath; ablutions
祓濯(ㄈㄨˊ ㄓㄨㄛˊ)
  to cleanse; to purify
祓除(ㄈㄨˊ ㄔㄨˊ)
  to exorcise
祓飾(ㄈㄨˊ ㄕˋ)
  to refresh; to renew

【祔】 3935 ㄈㄨˋ fuh fù
1. to enshrine in the ancestral temple
2. to bury in the family tomb

【祕】 3936 (祕) ㄇㄧˋ mih mì (又讀ㄅㄧˋ bih bì)
  secret; confidential; hidden; unknown; mysterious: 你必須爲此事保守祕密。You must keep the matter a secret.
祕寶(ㄇㄧˋ ㄅㄠˇ)
  a rare treasure
祕本(ㄇㄧˋ ㄅㄣˇ)
  ①a rare book ②a secret book
祕密(ㄇㄧˋ ㄇㄧˋ)
  secret; confidential; hidden; clandestine; a secret
祕密投票(ㄇㄧˋ ㄇㄧˋ ㄊㄡˊ ㄆㄧㄠˋ)

  a secret ballot
祕密條約(ㄇㄧˋ ㄇㄧˋ ㄊㄧㄠˊ ㄩㄝ)
  a secret treaty
祕密會議(ㄇㄧˋ ㄇㄧˋ ㄏㄨㄟˋ ㄧˋ)
  a secret conference; a closed-door meeting; a conclave; a clandestine meeting: 他們在祕密會議裏碰頭。They met at a clandestine meeting.
祕密結婚(ㄇㄧˋ ㄇㄧˋ ㄐㄧㄝˊ ㄏㄨㄣ)
  a secret wedding; a clandestine marriage
祕密結社(ㄇㄧˋ ㄇㄧˋ ㄐㄧㄝˊ ㄕㄜˋ)
  to form a secret society
祕密警察(ㄇㄧˋ ㄇㄧˋ ㄐㄧㄥˇ ㄔㄚˊ)
  the secret police; the Gestapo
祕密消息(ㄇㄧˋ ㄇㄧˋ ㄒㄧㄠ ㄒㄧˊ)
  confidential information; classified information
祕密外交(ㄇㄧˋ ㄇㄧˋ ㄨㄞˋ ㄐㄧㄠ)
  secret diplomacy
祕密文件(ㄇㄧˋ ㄇㄧˋ ㄨㄣˊ ㄐㄧㄢˋ)
  a secret document; a classified document
祕方(ㄇㄧˋ ㄈㄤ)
  a secret recipe
祕府(ㄇㄧˋ ㄈㄨˇ)
  ①a secret repository ②a secretariat in former times
祕魯(ㄇㄧˋ ㄌㄨˇ)or(ㄅㄧˋ ㄌㄨˇ)
  Peru; Peruvian
祕閣(ㄇㄧˋ ㄍㄜˊ)
  ①a place in the imperial palace to file confidential documents ②an armrest (used when one is writing)
祕笈(ㄇㄧˋ ㄐㄧˊ)
  an extraordinary book
祕籍(ㄇㄧˋ ㄐㄧˊ)
  ①a rare book ②a secret book
祕訣(ㄇㄧˋ ㄐㄩㄝˊ)
  a knack; secrets (of success, etc.); the key (to the solution of a problem): 你能否告訴我們你的成功祕訣? Can you tell us the secret of your success?
祕製(ㄇㄧˋ ㄓˋ)
  to prepare from a secret recipe
祕傳(ㄇㄧˋ ㄔㄨㄢˊ)
  to transmit from generation to generation exclusively inside a family

〔示部〕

祕書(ㄇㄧˋㄕㄨ)
a secretary: 他是董事長的祕
書。He is secretary to the
President.

祕書長(ㄇㄧˋㄕㄨㄓㄤˇ)
the emperor's secretariat

祕奧(ㄇㄧˋㄠˋ)
the inner mysteries

祕而不宣(ㄇㄧˋㄦˊㄅㄨˋㄒㄩㄢ)
to keep (things) secret; to
refrain from making an
announcement

祕要(ㄇㄧˋㄧㄠˋ)
(said of government papers,
etc.) classified

祕文(ㄇㄧˋㄨㄣˊ)
secret writing; a secret book

祕聞(ㄇㄧˋㄨㄣˊ)
exclusively inmost news

【祖】 3937
ㄗㄨˇ tzuu zǔ
1. one's grandfather or grandmother: 外祖 one's maternal
grandfather
2. ancestors; forebears: 遠祖
remote ancestors
3. a founder; an originator
4. to follow the example of; to
imitate
5. a Chinese family name

祖輩(ㄗㄨˇㄅㄟˋ)
ancestors; forefathers

祖妣(ㄗㄨˇㄅㄧˇ)
one's deceased grandmother

祖構(ㄗㄨˇㄍㄡˋ)
to strive for achievements
(a reference to 祖逖)

祖廟(ㄗㄨˇㄇㄧㄠˋ)
an ancestral shrine or temple

祖母(ㄗㄨˇㄇㄨˇ)
one's grandmother: 他小時候
住在祖母家。He lived in his
grandmother's home when
he was young.

祖墳(ㄗㄨˇㄈㄣˊ)
an ancestral grave

祖父(ㄗㄨˇㄈㄨˋ)
one's grandfather: 他已經當
祖父了。He's a grandfather
now.

祖德(ㄗㄨˇㄉㄜˊ)
the virtuous deeds of one's
ancestors

祖逖(ㄗㄨˇㄊㄧˋ)
Tsu Ti, 266-321 A.D., a
patriotic general of the Tsin

Dynasty

祖國(ㄗㄨˇㄍㄨㄛˊ)
one's fatherland; one's
mother country; one's homeland

祖考(ㄗㄨˇㄎㄠˇ)
①one's deceased grand-
father ②ancestors

祖籍(ㄗㄨˇㄐㄧˊ)
one's ancestral home; the
land of one's ancestors: 我們
祖籍廣東。Our ancestral home
is in Kwangtung.

祖餞(ㄗㄨˇㄐㄧㄢˋ)
to give a farewell dinner or
luncheon

祖居(ㄗㄨˇㄐㄩ)
one's ancestral home

祖先(ㄗㄨˇㄒㄧㄢ)
ancestors; forebears; forefathers

祖帳(ㄗㄨˇㄓㄤˋ)
to give a farewell dinner or
luncheon

祖產(ㄗㄨˇㄔㄢˇ)
ancestral estate

祖傳(ㄗㄨˇㄔㄨㄢˊ)
handed down by one's ancestors; inherited from one's
ancestors; hereditary

祖沖之(ㄗㄨˇㄔㄨㄥㄓ)
Tsu Chung-chih, 429-500, a
scholar and inventor

祖師(ㄗㄨˇㄕ)
①the founder of a sect,
especially Bodhidharma. (達
摩) of the Zen sect ②the
originator of a craft or
trade

祖上(ㄗㄨˇㄕㄤˋ)
ancestors; forebears; forefathers

祖述(ㄗㄨˇㄕㄨˋ)
to hand down as if from
one's ancestors

祖宗(ㄗㄨˇㄗㄨㄥ)
ancestors; forefathers; forebears

祖孫(ㄗㄨˇㄙㄨㄣ)
ancestors and descendants

祖送(ㄗㄨˇㄙㄨㄥˋ)
to give a farewell luncheon
or dinner party

祖業(ㄗㄨˇㄧㄝˋ)
①property inherited from
one's ancestors ②a trade or
business inherited from one's

ancestors

【祇】 3938
ㄓ jy zhī
1. to respect; to revere
2. only; but; just 亦作「祇」

祇奉(ㄓㄈㄥˋ)
①to respect; to hold in
great respect ②to accept
with respect

祇候(ㄓㄏㄡˋ)
①to wait upon respectfully
②an official receptionist in
the Sung Dynasty

祇承(ㄓㄔㄥˊ)
to accept with respect

祇避(ㄓㄅㄧˋ)
to observe or follow with
respect

祇肅(ㄓㄙㄨˋ)
respectful; reverent

祇仰(ㄓㄧㄤˇ)
to respect; to revere; to hold
in high esteem

【祜】 3939
ㄏㄨˋ huh hù
a blessing

【祛】 3940
ㄑㄩ chiu qū
to dispel; to expel; to
remove

祛祛(ㄑㄩㄑㄩ)
healthy and strong; stout

祛災(ㄑㄩㄗㄞ)
to dispel disasters

祛疑(ㄑㄩㄧˊ)
to dispel doubt

【祚】 3941
ㄗㄨㄛˋ tzuoh zuò
1. a blessing
2. the throne
3. the year

祚命(ㄗㄨㄛˋㄇㄧㄥˋ)
a heavenly blessing

祚胤(ㄗㄨㄛˋㄧㄣˋ)
to grant happiness and dignity to one's posterity

【祝】 3942
ㄓㄨˋ juh zhù
1. to wish someone happiness;
to pray for happiness: 祝你
旅途愉快。I wish you a pleas-
ant journey. 或 Bon voyage!
2. to congratulate; to felicitate
3. to celebrate
4. a Chinese family name

祝福(ㄓㄨˋㄈㄨˊ)
①to bless ②to wish happi-
ness to ③new year's sacri-

fice (an old custom in certain parts of Chekiang Province)

祝典(ㄓㄨ ㄉㄧㄢˇ)
a celebration

祝告(ㄓㄨ ㄍㄠˋ)
to invoke; to implore in prayer

祝嘏(ㄓㄨ ㄍㄨˇ)
to wish someone a happy birthday

祝賀(ㄓㄨ ㄏㄜˋ)
congratulations; to congratulate; to felicitate: 謹接受我的祝賀。Please accept my congratulations.

祝捷(ㄓㄨ ㄐㄧㄝˊ)
to celebrate victory; to send a congratulatory message to a victorious army or sports team

祝壽(ㄓㄨ ㄕㄡˋ)
to celebrate someone's birthday; to wish someone a happy birthday

祝融(ㄓㄨ ㄖㄨㄥˊ)
the god of fire

祝融爲虐(ㄓㄨ ㄖㄨㄥˊ ㄨㄟˊ ㄋㄩㄝˋ)
The god of fire wrought great havoc.

祝詞 or 祝辭(ㄓㄨ ㄘˊ)
① a congratulatory message ② prayers at sacrificial rites in ancient times

祝頌(ㄓㄨ ㄙㄨㄥˋ)
to congratulate and commend

祝文(ㄓㄨ ㄨㄣˊ)
a congratulatory message

【神】 3943
ㄕㄣˊ shern shén
1. gods; deities; immortals; spiritual beings
2. soul; mind; spirit
3. appearances; looks; expressions; airs
4. supernatural; marvelous; wondrous; miraculous; mysterious; mystical
5. smart; clever

神兵(ㄕㄣˊ ㄅㄧㄥ)
divine troops

神不知鬼不覺(ㄕㄣˊ ㄅㄨˋ ㄓ ㄍㄨㄟˇ ㄅㄨˋ ㄐㄩㄝˊ)
unknown even to gods and spirits—cloaked in extreme secrecy; extremely stealthy

神不守舍(ㄕㄣˊ ㄅㄨˋ ㄕㄡˇ ㄕㄜˋ)
out of one's wits; mentally wandering; delirious

神品(ㄕㄣˊ ㄆㄧㄣˇ)
sublime works (of art, literature, etc.); works of genius

神謀魔道(ㄕㄣˊ ㄇㄡˊ ㄇㄛˊ ㄉㄠˋ)
as if urged by gods or demons

神秘 or 神祕(ㄕㄣˊ ㄇㄧˋ)
mysterious; mystical; mystery: 他是位神秘人物。He's a mysterious person.

神妙(ㄕㄣˊ ㄇㄧㄠˋ)
marvelous; wondrous; wonderful: 他的筆法神妙。His style of writing is wonderful.

神廟(ㄕㄣˊ ㄇㄧㄠˋ)
a temple of the gods

神明(ㄕㄣˊ ㄇㄧㄥˊ)
the gods; deities; divinities

神明保佑(ㄕㄣˊ ㄇㄧㄥˊ ㄅㄠˇ ㄧㄡˋ)
to have divine help

神木(ㄕㄣˊ ㄇㄨˋ)
a divine tree

神峯(ㄕㄣˊ ㄈㄥ)
outstanding dignity

神鋒(ㄕㄣˊ ㄈㄥ)
a sword

神風隊(ㄕㄣˊ ㄈㄥ ㄉㄨㄟˋ)or 神風特攻隊(ㄕㄣˊ ㄈㄥ ㄊㄜˋ ㄍㄨㄥ ㄉㄨㄟˋ)
kamikaze, Japan's suicide pilots at the end of World War II

神福(ㄕㄣˊ ㄈㄨˊ)
①to pray for happiness ② offerings to the gods

神父(ㄕㄣˊ ㄈㄨˋ)
a Catholic father 亦作「神甫」

神殿(ㄕㄣˊ ㄉㄧㄢˋ)
a sanctuary

神都(ㄕㄣˊ ㄉㄨ)
① China ② the imperial capital

神態(ㄕㄣˊ ㄊㄞˋ)
looks; appearances; airs; facial expressions: 他的神態悠閒。He looks perfectly relaxed.

神頭鬼臉(ㄕㄣˊ ㄊㄡˊ ㄍㄨㄟˇ ㄇㄧㄢˇ)
monstrosities

神通(ㄕㄣˊ ㄊㄨㄥ)
ubiquitous supernatural power, especially of the Buddha

神通廣大(ㄕㄣˊ ㄊㄨㄥ ㄍㄨㄤˇ ㄉㄚˋ)
possessing marvelous abilities; very resourceful

神童(ㄕㄣˊ ㄊㄨㄥˊ)
a child prodigy

神鳥(ㄕㄣˊ ㄋㄧㄠˇ)
the phoenix

神農(ㄕㄣˊ ㄋㄨㄥˊ)
Shen Nung, a legendary ruler supposed to have introduced agriculture and herbal medicine

神女(ㄕㄣˊ ㄋㄩˇ)
a prostitute; a harlot

神來之筆(ㄕㄣˊ ㄌㄞˊ ㄓ ㄅㄧˇ)
a stroke of genius (as if it were the result of divine inspiration)

神力(ㄕㄣˊ ㄌㄧˋ)
divine power; marvelous ability; supernatural strength

神靈(ㄕㄣˊ ㄌㄧㄥˊ)
① gods; spirits ② marvelous; prodigious

神怪(ㄕㄣˊ ㄍㄨㄞˋ)
mysterious; mystical; supernatural

神龜(ㄕㄣˊ ㄍㄨㄟ)
a supernatural tortoise

神鬼(ㄕㄣˊ ㄍㄨㄟˇ)
gods and ghosts

神功(ㄕㄣˊ ㄍㄨㄥ)
a prodigious feat; a supernatural accomplishment; a miracle

神工鬼斧(ㄕㄣˊ ㄍㄨㄥ ㄍㄨㄟˇ ㄈㄨˇ)
prodigious skill; supernatural skill 參看「鬼斧神工」

神龕(ㄕㄣˊ ㄎㄢ)
a sanctuary; a shrine for idols or ancestral tablets

神乎其神(ㄕㄣˊ ㄏㄨ ㄑㄧˊ ㄕㄣˊ)
How marvelous! 或 How wondrous! 或 fantastic; wonderful; miraculous

神戶(ㄕㄣˊ ㄏㄨˋ)
Kobe, Japan

神化(ㄕㄣˊ ㄏㄨㄚˋ)
to deify; deified; deification; to make a god of

神話(ㄕㄣˊ ㄏㄨㄚˋ)
a myth; mythology

神話學(ㄕㄣˊ ㄏㄨㄚˋ ㄒㄩㄝˊ)
mythology

神話時代(ㄕㄣˊ ㄏㄨㄚˋ ㄕˊ ㄉㄞˋ)
the mythological age

〔示部〕

（示部）

神魂(ㄕㄣ ㄏㄨㄣˊ)
①the soul ②a state of mind: 他顯得神魂不定。He appeared to be deeply perturbed.

神魂顛倒(ㄕㄣ ㄏㄨㄣˊ ㄉㄧㄢ ㄉㄠˇ)
to be fascinated head over heels; to be carried away: to be transported; to be infatuated; to be held spellbound

神迹 or 神蹟(ㄕㄣ ㄐㄧ)
a marvelous event; a miracle: 過去從未發生這種神蹟。Such a miracle has never occurred before.

神機(ㄕㄣ ㄐㄧ)
①a God-given chance ②the divine plan

神機妙算(ㄕㄣ ㄐㄧ ㄇㄧㄠˋ ㄙㄨㄢˋ)
①stratagems so wonderful that they seem to be conceived by divine beings ②wonderful foresight (in military operations, etc.)

神交(ㄕㄣ ㄐㄧㄠ)
①friendship grown out of mutual admiration without having met once ②spiritual communication

神經(ㄕㄣ ㄐㄧㄥ)
nerve, any of the threadlike parts of the body which form a system to carry feelings and messages to and from the brain

神經病(ㄕㄣ ㄐㄧㄥ ㄅㄧㄥˋ)
①neurosis; mental disorder ②a neurotic

神經痛(ㄕㄣ ㄐㄧㄥ ㄊㄨㄥˋ)
neuralgia

神經過敏(ㄕㄣ ㄐㄧㄥ ㄍㄨㄛˋ ㄇㄧㄣˇ)
①morbidly sensitive; excessively sensitive ②(medicine) hyperaesthesia

神經緊張(ㄕㄣ ㄐㄧㄥ ㄐㄧㄣˇ ㄓㄤ)
nervous: 有些人在黑暗處會神經緊張。Some are nervous in the dark.

神經系(ㄕㄣ ㄐㄧㄥ ㄒㄧˋ)
the nervous system

神經細胞(ㄕㄣ ㄐㄧㄥ ㄒㄧˋ ㄅㄠ)
nerve cells; neurocyte

神經纖維(ㄕㄣ ㄐㄧㄥ ㄒㄧㄢ ㄨㄟˊ)
nerve fibers

神經質(ㄕㄣ ㄐㄧㄥ ㄓˊ)
a nervous temperament; ner-

vosity: 她的母親是個神經質的人。Her mother has a nervous temperament.

神經戰(ㄕㄣ ㄐㄧㄥ ㄓㄢˋ)
a war of nerves; psychological warfare

神經中樞(ㄕㄣ ㄐㄧㄥ ㄓㄨㄥ ㄕㄨ)
the nerve center: 腦是身體的神經中樞。The brain is the nerve center of the body.

神經梢(ㄕㄣ ㄐㄧㄥ ㄕㄠ)
nerve endings

神經衰弱(ㄕㄣ ㄐㄧㄥ ㄕㄨㄞ ㄖㄨㄛˋ)
neurasthenia

神經組織(ㄕㄣ ㄐㄧㄥ ㄗㄨˇ ㄓ)
nerve tissue

神經錯亂(ㄕㄣ ㄐㄧㄥ ㄘㄨㄛˋ ㄌㄨㄢˋ)
nervous disorder; mental disorder

神經炎(ㄕㄣ ㄐㄧㄥ ㄧㄢˊ)
neuritis

神劇(ㄕㄣ ㄐㄩˋ)
an oratorio

神奇(ㄕㄣ ㄑㄧˊ)
marvelous; wondrous; mysterious; miraculous

神祇(ㄕㄣ ㄑㄧˊ)
the gods; the spirits

神氣
①(ㄕㄣ ㄑㄧˋ) divine atmosphere ②(ㄕㄣ ˙ㄑㄧ) ① dignified; imposing ⓐ to put on airs; overweening: 呵！這老人倒神氣起來了。Humph! What airs the old man gives himself!ⓑ an appearance; an air; an expression: 男孩臉上顯出得意的神氣。The boy had an air of complacency.

神氣活現(ㄕㄣ ㄑㄧˋ ㄏㄨㄛˊ ㄒㄧㄢˋ)
very cocky; as proud as a peacock

神器(ㄕㄣ ㄑㄧˋ)
the throne

神槍手(ㄕㄣ ㄑㄧㄤ ㄕㄡˇ)
a sharpshooter; a marksman

神情(ㄕㄣ ㄑㄧㄥˊ)
a facial expression; a look; an appearance; an air: 他臉上露出愉快的神情。He wore a happy expression.

神曲(ㄕㄣ ㄑㄩˇ)
the *Divine Comedy*, by Dante Alighieri, 1265-1321

神權(ㄕㄣ ㄑㄩㄢˊ)
①the divine right (of kings) ②religious authority

神效(ㄕㄣ ㄒㄧㄠˋ)
marvelous effect; wondrous efficacy

神仙(ㄕㄣ ㄒㄧㄢ)
an immortal; a supernatural being; a celestial being

神仙魚(ㄕㄣ ㄒㄧㄢ ㄩˊ)
an angelfish (a species of tropical fish)

神像(ㄕㄣ ㄒㄧㄤˋ)
①an image of a dead person ②an idol; the picture or the statue of a god or the Buddha

神學(ㄕㄣ ㄒㄩㄝˊ)
theology: 他是研究神學的學生。He is a student of theology.

神學博士(ㄕㄣ ㄒㄩㄝˊ ㄅㄛˊ ㄕˋ)
a doctor of divinity (D.D.)

神學院(ㄕㄣ ㄒㄩㄝˊ ㄩㄢˋ)
a seminary (for training priests or ministers)

神職人員(ㄕㄣ ㄓˊ ㄖㄣˊ ㄩㄢˊ)
the clergy

神紙(ㄕㄣ ㄓˇ)
paper burned in worship

神志(ㄕㄣ ㄓˋ)
①mind ②consciousness

神志不清(ㄕㄣ ㄓˋ ㄅㄨˋ ㄑㄧㄥ)
unconscious; in a state of a coma

神智(ㄕㄣ ㄓˋ)
①mind ②intelligence

神智不清(ㄕㄣ ㄓˋ ㄅㄨˋ ㄑㄧㄥ)
clouded in the mind; incapable of clear thinking; muddleheaded

神州(ㄕㄣ ㄓㄡ)
①China ②the imperial capital

神主(ㄕㄣ ㄓㄨˇ)
a wooden tablet used as a symbol of the deceased

神馳(ㄕㄣ ㄔˊ)
to allow the thoughts to fly to an adored person

神差鬼使(ㄕㄣ ㄔㄞ ㄍㄨㄟˇ ㄕˇ)
as though urged by gods and demons (said of someone doing something explicably)

神出鬼沒(ㄕㄣ ㄔㄨ ㄍㄨㄟˇ ㄇㄛˋ)
to appear and disappear quite unpredictably like gods and demons; to appear unexpectedly in a moment

and to disappear completely in the next (usually said of guerrillas); to come and go like a shadow: 這個間諜神出鬼沒的。The spy comes and goes like a shadow.

神社(ㄕㄣ ㄕㄜˋ)
a Shinto shrine

神聖(ㄕㄣ ㄕㄥˋ)
holy; sacred; divine: 保護國土是軍人的神聖職責。Defending territory is soldiers' sacred duty.

神聖不可侵犯(ㄕㄣ ㄕㄥˋ ㄅㄨˋ ㄎㄜˇ ㄑㄧㄣ ㄈㄢˋ)
sacred and not to be violated; holy and inviolable

神聖羅馬帝國(ㄕㄣ ㄕㄥˋ ㄌㄨㄛˊ ㄇㄚˇ ㄉㄧˋ ㄍㄨㄛˊ)
the Holy Roman Empire

神術(ㄕㄣ ㄕㄨˋ)
marvelous technique; wondrous tricks

神人(ㄕㄣ ㄖㄣˊ)
①one who has discovered truth; a holy man ②man with a very dignified look ③gods and men

神人共憤(ㄕㄣ ㄖㄣˊ ㄍㄨㄥˋ ㄈㄣˋ)
to be hated by immortals and mortals alike—to incur the wrath or indignation of all

神彩(ㄕㄣ ㄘㄞˇ)
a countenance; a look; an expression

神采煥發(ㄕㄣ ㄘㄞˇ ㄏㄨㄢˋ ㄈㄚ)
a happy look; gay

神采奕奕(ㄕㄣ ㄘㄞˇ ㄧˋ ㄧˋ)
①beaming; in high spirits ②glowing with health and radiating vigor

神思(ㄕㄣ ㄙ)
thoughts; a state of mind; a mental state

神似(ㄕㄣ ㄙˋ)
lifelike; to be alike in spirit; to be an excellent likeness

神色(ㄕㄣ ㄙㄜˋ)
a look; an expression

神色自若(ㄕㄣ ㄙㄜˋ ㄗˋ ㄖㄨㄛˋ)
to look unperturbed

神速(ㄕㄣ ㄙㄨˋ)
marvelously fast; wondrously quick; lightning speed: 收效神速 to yield marvelously quick results

神髓(ㄕㄣ ㄙㄨㄟˇ)
essence; quintessence

神算(ㄕㄣ ㄙㄨㄢˋ)
①a very clever plan ②miraculous foresight; marvelous prediction

神恩(ㄕㄣ ㄣ)
divine favor

神兒(ㄕㄣˊ ㄦ)
a look; an expression; an air

神醫(ㄕㄣ ㄧ)
a marvelous physician; a great doctor

神異(ㄕㄣ ㄧˋ)
①miraculous; marvelous; wondrous ②gods and spirits

神意(ㄕㄣ ㄧˋ)
the will of God; divine will

神遊(ㄕㄣ ㄧㄡˊ)
to tour (a place) by imagination; to make a mental travel

神佑(ㄕㄣ ㄧㄡˋ)
divine help

神鷹(ㄕㄣ ㄧㄥ)
①(literally) a divine eagle —a patriotic way of saying "our air force" or "our air force planes" ②a condor

神武(ㄕㄣ ㄨˇ)
intelligent and courageous

神物(ㄕㄣ ㄨˋ)
①a supernatural being; an immortal; a deity ②a wonder; a prodigy; a phenomenon

神悟(ㄕㄣ ㄨˋ)
marvelously quick understanding

神位(ㄕㄣ ㄨㄟˋ)
a sacred tablet used as the symbol of a deity

神往(ㄕㄣ ㄨㄤˇ)
to have one's thoughts or imagination absorbed in some wonderful thing or place: 日月潭的景色令人神往。The scenery of the Sun Moon Lake is enchanting.

神宇(ㄕㄣ ㄩˇ)
an appearance; a look

神韻(ㄕㄣ ㄩㄣˋ)
①(said of a person) an appearance and a carriage; an impression; an air ②(said of paintings or calligraphic works) poetic quality; charm

神勇(ㄕㄣ ㄩㄥˇ)
superhuman bravery; extraordinarily brave

【祠】 3944 ㄘˊ tsyr cí
1. a temple; a shrine
2. the spring worship

祠堂(ㄘˊ ㄊㄤˊ)
a shrine; an ancestral hall (or temple); a memorial temple

祠官(ㄘˊ ㄍㄨㄢ)
an official in charge of the spring worship

祠祀(ㄘˊ ㄙˋ)
a custodian of a temple or shrine

祠宇(ㄘˊ ㄩˇ)
a shrine; a temple

【祟】 3945 ㄙㄨㄟˋ suey suì
1. the evil influence of gods or demons
2. (said of ghosts or evil spirits) to haunt; to afflict

祟惑(ㄙㄨㄟˋ ㄏㄨㄛˋ)
to confuse by evil influence

六畫

【祥】 3946 ㄒㄧㄤˊ shyang xiáng
auspicious; propitious; favorable

祥麟(ㄒㄧㄤˊ ㄌㄧㄣˊ)
a legendary horse-like animal resembling the unicorn, whose appearance was regarded in ancient times as an auspicious omen

祥兆(ㄒㄧㄤˊ ㄓㄠˋ)
a good omen

祥瑞(ㄒㄧㄤˊ ㄖㄨㄟˋ)
a good omen; an auspicious omen; auspiciousness

祥雲(ㄒㄧㄤˊ ㄩㄣˊ)
auspicious clouds

【祧】 3947 ㄊㄧㄠ tiau tiāo
1. an ancestral temple (especially of distant ancestors)
2. to be or become heir to

【票】 3948 ㄆㄧㄠˋ piaw piào
1. a bill; a note

[示 部]

2.a ticket: 憑票入場。Admission by ticket only.
3.a ballot
4.a hostage
5.amateur performance

票面(ㄆㄧㄠˋ ㄇㄧㄢˋ)
the face value of a note, bond, etc.

票面值(ㄆㄧㄠˋ ㄇㄧㄢˋ ㄓˊ)or 票面額(ㄆㄧㄠˋ ㄇㄧㄢˋ ㄜˊ)
face value; nominal value; par value

票房(ㄆㄧㄠˋ ㄈㄤˊ)
①a box office; a ticket window ②a club of amateur Peking opera actors ③box office—(figuratively) the power of a show or performer to attract an audience

票根(ㄆㄧㄠˋ ㄍㄣ)
a ticket stub; a counterfoil

票匭(ㄆㄧㄠˋ ㄍㄨㄟˇ)
①a ticket box ②a ballot box

票價(ㄆㄧㄠˋ ㄐㄧㄚˋ)
the price of a ticket; an admission (or entrance) fee

票據(ㄆㄧㄠˋ ㄐㄩ)
negotiable instruments; bills; notes; vouchers; receipts

票據法(ㄆㄧㄠˋ ㄐㄩ ㄈㄚˇ)
Law of Negotiable Instruments

票據交換所(ㄆㄧㄠˋ ㄐㄩ ㄐㄧㄠ ㄏㄨㄢˋ ㄙㄨㄛˇ)
a clearing house

票決(ㄆㄧㄠˋ ㄐㄩㄝˊ)
to decide by casting ballots. 讓我們付諸票決。Let's decide by casting ballots.

票箱(ㄆㄧㄠˋ ㄒㄧㄤ)
a ballot box

票選(ㄆㄧㄠˋ ㄒㄩㄢˇ)
to elect by casting ballots

票傳(ㄆㄧㄠˋ ㄔㄨㄢˊ)
to serve a summons on someone

票數(ㄆㄧㄠˋ ㄕㄨˋ)
the number of votes or ballots

票子(ㄆㄧㄠˋ ˙ㄗ)or 票兒(ㄆㄧㄠˋ ㄦ)
a ticket; a note; a bill; paper money: 我有許多票子要付款。I have many bills to pay.

票存(ㄆㄧㄠˋ ㄘㄨㄣˊ)
cash reserves against notes

issued

票額(ㄆㄧㄠˋ ㄜˊ)
the sum stated on a check or bill; face value

票友(ㄆㄧㄠˋ ㄧㄡˇ)
an amateur actor or actress of Peking opera

【祭】 3949　ㄐㄧˋ jih jì
1. to worship; to offer sacrifices to; to honor by a rite or service
2. to wield

祭品(ㄐㄧˋ ㄆㄧㄣˇ)
offerings; sacrificial articles; sacrifices

祭服(ㄐㄧˋ ㄈㄨˊ)
a robe worn for a religious rite

祭地(ㄐㄧˋ ㄉㄧˋ)
annual services of offering sacrifices to the earth

祭典(ㄐㄧˋ ㄉㄧㄢˇ)
services or ceremonies of offering sacrifices

祭奠(ㄐㄧˋ ㄉㄧㄢˋ)
to offer sacrifices to the spirit of a deceased person

祭壇(ㄐㄧˋ ㄊㄢˊ)
an altar

祭天(ㄐㄧˋ ㄊㄧㄢ)
annual services of offering sacrifices to Heaven

祭田(ㄐㄧˋ ㄊㄧㄢˊ)
fields set apart for maintaining annual sacrifices

祭禮(ㄐㄧˋ ㄌㄧˇ)
sacrifices offered to gods or the deceased; sacrificial offerings

祭告(ㄐㄧˋ ㄍㄠˋ)
to inform (the gods of important national events) through a rite or service

祭冠(ㄐㄧˋ ㄍㄨㄢ)
a cap worn in a major religious service

祭酒(ㄐㄧˋ ㄐㄧㄡˇ)
①(in ancient times) the person who performs the libation before a banquet ②a respectable elder; the most senior and respected person of a profession

祭獻(ㄐㄧˋ ㄒㄧㄢˋ)
to offer (sacrifices)

祭主(ㄐㄧˋ ㄓㄨˇ)

an officiant at a religious rite or service

祭竈(ㄐㄧˋ ㄗㄠˋ)
the worship of the kitchen god (performed on the 23rd day of the 12th lunar month)

祭祖(ㄐㄧˋ ㄗㄨˇ)
to perform rites in honor of ancestors

祭司(ㄐㄧˋ ㄙ)or 祭師(ㄐㄧˋ ㄕ)
an officiant at a religious service; a high priest

祭祀(ㄐㄧˋ ㄙˋ)
to worship; to honor by a service or rite; to offer sacrifices to

祭掃(ㄐㄧˋ ㄙㄠˇ)
to clean and offer sacrifices at a tomb

祭物(ㄐㄧˋ ㄨˋ)
sacrifices

祭文(ㄐㄧˋ ㄨㄣˊ)
a written message offered (to the gods and the deceased, etc.) in worship; sacrificial writing; an elegiac address

七畫

【祲】 3950　ㄐㄧㄣ jin jìn
1. ominous or sinister spirits
2. vigorous

八畫

【祺】 3951　ㄑㄧˊ chyi qí
1. lucky; propitious; auspicious
2. peaceful; serene

祺祥(ㄑㄧˊ ㄒㄧㄤˊ)
fortunate; lucky; auspicious; propitious

祺然(ㄑㄧˊ ㄖㄢˊ)
peaceful; serene

【祿】 3952　ㄌㄨˋ luh lù
1. happiness; prosperity
2. official pay; salary

祿命(ㄌㄨˋ ㄇㄧㄥˋ)
a person's lot through life

祿俸(ㄌㄨˋ ㄈㄥˋ)
official pay

祿蠹(ㄌㄨˋ ㄉㄨˋ)
a sinecurist

祿秩(ㄌㄨˋ ㄓˋ)
official rank and pay

祿食(ㄌㄨˋ ㄕˊ)
official pay

祿餌(ㄌㄨˋ ㄦˇ)
official pay as a bait (for talent)

祿養(ㄌㄨˋ ㄧㄤˇ)
to support (dependents) with official pay

祿位(ㄌㄨˋ ㄨㄟˋ)
official salary and rank

【祼】3953
《ㄍㄨㄢˋ guann guàn》
to pour out a libation

【禁】3954 1. ㄐㄧㄣˋ jinn jìn
1. to prohibit; to forbid; to ban: 禁止在湖內游泳。Swimming is banned in this lake.
2. to confine; to imprison; to detain: 他們把我監禁起來。They imprisoned me.
3. secret
4. a royal residence: 紫禁城 the Forbidden City in Peking

禁閉(ㄐㄧㄣˋ ㄅㄧˋ)
①to prohibit entry into government services ②to imprison; to confine; to lock up: 他被關禁閉。He was placed in confinement.

禁閉室(ㄐㄧㄣˋ ㄅㄧˋ ㄕˋ)
a confinement cell

禁品(ㄐㄧㄣˋ ㄆㄧㄣˇ)
contraband; prohibited merchandise

禁方(ㄐㄧㄣˋ ㄈㄤ)
a secret medical prescription

禁地(ㄐㄧㄣˋ ㄉㄧˋ)
a forbidden ground; an area declared out of bounds

禁賭(ㄐㄧㄣˋ ㄉㄨˇ)
to prohibit gambling

禁屠(ㄐㄧㄣˋ ㄊㄨˊ)
to prohibit slaughter of animals

禁例(ㄐㄧㄣˋ ㄌㄧˋ)
an official prohibition or restraint; an interdict

禁獵(ㄐㄧㄣˋ ㄌㄧㄝˋ)
a ban on hunting

禁令(ㄐㄧㄣˋ ㄌㄧㄥˋ)
a prohibition; a ban; an interdict

禁臠(ㄐㄧㄣˋ ㄌㄨㄢˊ)
①a forbidden thing; one's

exclusive domain ②a precious thing

禁臠(ㄐㄧㄣˋ)
①confinement; imprisonment ②to prohibit entry into government services

禁菓(ㄐㄧㄣˋ ㄍㄨㄛˇ)
the forbidden fruit: 夏娃吃了禁菓。Eve ate the forbidden fruit.

禁火(ㄐㄧㄣˋ ㄏㄨㄛˇ)
to prohibit cooking (on March 3 in the lunar calendar)

禁忌(ㄐㄧㄣˋ ㄐㄧˋ)
①a taboo; to taboo ②to avoid; to abstain from

禁酒(ㄐㄧㄣˋ ㄐㄧㄡˇ)
to prohibit the use of alcoholic drinks

禁軍(ㄐㄧㄣˋ ㄐㄩㄣ)
imperial guards

禁區(ㄐㄧㄣˋ ㄑㄩ)
①a forbidden region; a restricted zone ②a preserve; a reserve ③(football) the penalty area ④(basketball) the restricted area

禁止(ㄐㄧㄣˋ ㄓˇ)
to forbid; to prohibit; to ban; to taboo: 禁止在火車內吸煙。Smoking is banned in the train.

禁止倒垃圾(ㄐㄧㄣˋ ㄓˇ ㄉㄠˋ ㄌㄜˋ ㄙㄜˋ)
Do not leave garbage here.

禁止停車(ㄐㄧㄣˋ ㄓˇ ㄊㄧㄥˊ ㄔㄜ)
No parking.

禁止關稅(ㄐㄧㄣˋ ㄓˇ ㄍㄨㄢ ㄕㄨㄟˋ)
a prohibitive tariff

禁止吸煙(ㄐㄧㄣˋ ㄓˇ ㄒㄧ ㄧㄢ)
No smoking.

禁止招貼(ㄐㄧㄣˋ ㄓˇ ㄓㄠ ㄊㄧㄝ)
Post no bills.

禁止車輛通行(ㄐㄧㄣˋ ㄓˇ ㄔㄜ ㄌㄧㄤˋ ㄊㄨㄥ ㄒㄧㄥˊ)
No vehicles allowed. 或 No thoroughfare. 或 Closed to traffic.

禁止設攤(ㄐㄧㄣˋ ㄓˇ ㄕㄜˋ ㄊㄢ)
Do not set up stands here.

禁止入內(ㄐㄧㄣˋ ㄓˇ ㄖㄨˋ ㄋㄟˋ)
No admittance.

禁止按喇叭(ㄐㄧㄣˋ ㄓˇ ㄢˋ ㄌㄚ ˙ㄅㄚ)
Do not sound horns. 或 No honking.

禁治產(ㄐㄧㄣˋ ㄓˋ ㄔㄢˇ)

(law) incompetency (to manage one's own property)

禁中(ㄐㄧㄣˋ ㄓㄨㄥ)
the emperor's living quarters

禁城(ㄐㄧㄣˋ ㄔㄥˊ)
the forbidden city

禁食(ㄐㄧㄣˋ ㄕˊ)
fast; to fast

禁書(ㄐㄧㄣˋ ㄕㄨ)
banned books

禁足(ㄐㄧㄣˋ ㄗㄨˊ)
to forbid a soldier to leave the barracks on holidays as a form of punishment

禁坐(ㄐㄧㄣˋ ㄗㄨㄛˋ)
the throne

禁夜(ㄐㄧㄣˋ ㄧㄝˋ)
the curfew

禁煙(ㄐㄧㄣˋ ㄧㄢ)
①to prohibit opium ②to prohibit cooking ③smoke rising from the imperial palace

禁煙節(ㄐㄧㄣˋ ㄧㄢ ㄐㄧㄝˊ)
Opium Prohibition Day, on June 3

禁衛軍(ㄐㄧㄣˋ ㄨㄟˋ ㄐㄩㄣ)
imperial guards 亦作「禁軍」

禁慾(ㄐㄧㄣˋ ㄩˋ)
to be ascetic; abstinence

禁苑(ㄐㄧㄣˋ ㄩㄢˋ)
an imperial garden

禁運(ㄐㄧㄣˋ ㄩㄣˋ)
to embargo; an embargo

【禁】3954 2. ㄐㄧㄣ jin
to endure; to bear; to withstand; to stand

禁不起(ㄐㄧㄣ ㄅㄨˋ ㄑㄧˇ)
unable to endure; unable to withstand; unable to help; unable to stand: 他禁不起誘惑。He failed to withstand the temptation.

禁不住(ㄐㄧㄣ ㄅㄨˋ ㄓㄨˋ)
①unable to endure; unable to withstand; unable to stand; unable to avoid: 他禁不住一點批評。He can't stand a little bit of criticism. ②can not help: 她禁不住哭了起來。She could not help crying.

禁得起(ㄐㄧㄣ ˙ㄉㄜ ㄑㄧˇ)
able to withstand; able to stand; able to endure; able to avoid: 他禁得起嚴厲的考

驗。He was able to stand severe tests.

禁得住(ㄐㄧㄣˋ·ㄉㄜ ㄓㄨˋ)
able to withstand; able to endure; able to refrain from

九畫

【示部】

【禍】 3955
ㄏㄨㄛˋ huoh huò

1. calamity; disaster; misfortune; evil: 戰爭是可怕的災禍。War is a frightful calamity.
2. to bring disaster upon; to harm; to injure; to do evil to
3. to punish

禍不單行(ㄏㄨㄛˋ ㄅㄨˋ ㄉㄢ ㄒㄧㄥˊ)
Misfortunes never come singly(or single).

禍福倚伏(ㄏㄨㄛˋ ㄈㄨˊ ㄧˇ ㄈㄨˊ)
Fortune and misfortune are interrelated.

禍福無門(ㄏㄨㄛˋ ㄈㄨˊ ㄨˊ ㄇㄣˊ)
(literally) Fortune and misfortune do not come through a definite door.—The arrival of fortune or misfortune is unpredictable.

禍端(ㄏㄨㄛˋ ㄉㄨㄢ)
the cause of a misfortune or disaster

禍胎(ㄏㄨㄛˋ ㄊㄞ)
a source of disaster

禍亂(ㄏㄨㄛˋ ㄌㄨㄢˋ)
disturbances; disastrous disorder

禍根(ㄏㄨㄛˋ ㄍㄣ)
seeds of misfortune; a source of disaster

禍國殃民(ㄏㄨㄛˋ ㄍㄨㄛˊ ㄧㄤ ㄇㄧㄣˊ)
to bring disaster upon the state and the people; to harm the state and injure the people

禍害(ㄏㄨㄛˋ ㄏㄞˋ)
harm; injury; evil

禍患(ㄏㄨㄛˋ ㄏㄨㄢˋ)
misfortune; disaster; harm; evil

禍起蕭牆(ㄏㄨㄛˋ ㄑㄧˇ ㄒㄧㄠ ㄑㄧㄤˊ)
Disaster arises from the very inside.

禍心(ㄏㄨㄛˋ ㄒㄧㄣ)
evil intention; malice: 此人包藏禍心。This man harbors evil intentions (or thoughts).

禍兆(ㄏㄨㄛˋ ㄓㄠˋ)
evil omens or portents

禍種(ㄏㄨㄛˋ ㄓㄨㄥˇ)
seeds of trouble in the future

禍事(ㄏㄨㄛˋ ㄕˋ)
disaster; calamity; mishap; misfortune; catastrophe

禍首(ㄏㄨㄛˋ ㄕㄡˇ)
the one who starts the trouble; a chief culprit

禍水(ㄏㄨㄛˋ ㄕㄨㄟˇ)
a woman who is often the source of troubles

禍棗災梨(ㄏㄨㄛˋ ㄗㄠˇ ㄗㄞ ㄌㄧˊ)
to print worthless writings; to publish useless books

禍從天降(ㄏㄨㄛˋ ㄘㄨㄥˊ ㄊㄧㄢ ㄐㄧㄤˋ)
(literally) A calamity descended from the sky.—an unexpected disaster

禍從口出(ㄏㄨㄛˋ ㄘㄨㄥˊ ㄎㄡˇ ㄔㄨ)
(literally) The mouth is the primary source of calamities.—Careless talks may land one in trouble.

【福】 3956
ㄈㄨˊ fwu fú

happiness; good fortune; good luck; a blessing; bliss: 我祝你婚姻幸福。I wish you felicity in marriage.

福薄(ㄈㄨˊ ㄅㄛˊ)
luckless; unlucky; hapless; unfortunate

福庇(ㄈㄨˊ ㄅㄧˋ)
(a complimentary phrase) your fortunate protection

福命(ㄈㄨˊ ㄇㄧㄥˋ)
one's lot through life

福分(ㄈㄨˊ ·ㄈㄣ)
share of happiness allotted by destiny

福地洞天(ㄈㄨˊ ㄉㄧˋ ㄉㄨㄥˋ ㄊㄧㄢ)
a paradise

福特(ㄈㄨˊ ㄊㄜˋ)
①Henry Ford, 1863-1947, American inventor of the automobile and philanthropist ②Gerald Rudolph Ford, born 1913, 38th U.S. President (1974-77)

福特基金會(ㄈㄨˊ ㄊㄜˋ ㄐㄧ ㄐㄧㄣ ㄏㄨㄟˋ)
Ford Foundation

福體(ㄈㄨˊ ㄊㄧˇ)
your health (a respectful expression used in address-

ing one's elders)

福利(ㄈㄨˊ ㄌㄧˋ)
welfare; good; prosperity; well-being; fringe benefits for employees: 我們要為人民謀福利。We should work for the well-being of the people.

福利社(ㄈㄨˊ ㄌㄧˋ ㄕㄜˋ)
a store doing business on the premises of a school, factory, government agency, etc.

福祿特爾(ㄈㄨˊ ㄌㄨˋ ㄊㄜˋ ㄦˇ)
Marie Arouet Voltaire, 1694-1778, French thinker and writer

福祿壽(ㄈㄨˊ ㄌㄨˋ ㄕㄡˋ)
happiness, wealth, and longevity (which are the ingredients of a happy life)

福過災生(ㄈㄨˊ ㄍㄨㄛˋ ㄗㄞ ㄕㄥ)
When fortune passes, misfortune follows.

福躬(ㄈㄨˊ ㄍㄨㄥ)
(a complimentary phrase) your happy or fortunate person

福克蘭群島(ㄈㄨˊ ㄎㄜˋ ㄌㄢˊ ㄑㄩㄣˊ ㄉㄠˇ)
the Falkland Islands

福建(ㄈㄨˊ ㄐㄧㄢˋ)
Fukien Province

福晉(ㄈㄨˊ ㄐㄧㄣˋ)
a Manchurian term for "wife"

福氣(ㄈㄨˊ ·ㄑㄧ)
good luck

福相(ㄈㄨˊ ㄒㄧㄤˋ)
a countenance of good luck

福星高照(ㄈㄨˊ ㄒㄧㄥ ㄍㄠ ㄓㄠˋ)
The lucky star is in the ascendant.—to ride the high tide of good luck

福至心靈(ㄈㄨˊ ㄓˋ ㄒㄧㄣ ㄌㄧㄥˊ)
The mind works more efficiently when good fortune comes.

福州(ㄈㄨˊ ㄓㄡ)
Foochow, Fukien

福壽全歸(ㄈㄨˊ ㄕㄡˋ ㄑㄩㄢˊ ㄍㄨㄟ)
to have enjoyed both happiness and longevity (a laudatory expression about a person who died at a venerable age)

福壽雙全(ㄈㄨˊ ㄕㄡˋ ㄕㄨㄤ ㄑㄩㄢˊ)
to enjoy both happiness and longevity

福善禍淫(ㄈㄨ ㄕㄢ ㄏㄨㄛˋ ㄧㄣˊ)
Heaven blesses the virtuous and punishes the evil.

福如東海(ㄈㄨˊ ㄖㄨˊ ㄉㄨㄥ ㄏㄞˇ)
happiness as immense as the eastern sea

福澤(ㄈㄨˊ ㄗㄜˊ)
good fortune; happiness; blessedness

福音(ㄈㄨˊ ㄧㄣ)
① good news; welcome news
② the gospel: 他是個福音傳道者。He's a minister of the gospel.

福音堂(ㄈㄨˊ ㄧㄣ ㄊㄤˊ)
a chapel

福音主義(ㄈㄨˊ ㄧㄣ ㄓㄨˇ ㄧˋ)
evangelism

福蔭(ㄈㄨˊ ㄧㄣ)
(a complimentary phrase) your fortunate protection

福無雙至(ㄈㄨˊ ㄨˊ ㄕㄨㄤ ㄓˋ)
Blessings never come in pairs.

福王(ㄈㄨˊ ㄨㄤˊ)
one of the last princes of the Ming Dynasty, executed by the Manchus

【禋】 3957
ㄧㄣ in yīn
1. to worship with sincerity and reverence
2. to offer sacrifices to Heaven

【禊】 3958
ㄒㄧˋ shih xì
semiannual exorcism performed at the water's edge in ancient times

禊帖(ㄒㄧˋ ㄊㄧㄝˇ)
the "Gathering at Orchid Pavilion" (蘭亭帖) by Wang Hsi-chih (王羲之), considered to be the most valuable calligraphic work

【禔】 3959
ㄊㄧˊ tyi tí
happiness; good fortune; good luck; blessings

【禎】 3960
ㄓㄣ jen zhēn
1. auspicious; a good omen
2. a Chinese family name

禎祥(ㄓㄣ ㄒㄧㄤˊ)
a good omen; a lucky omen

【禕】 3961
ㄧ iyī
excellent

【禘】 3962
ㄉㄧˋ dih dì
imperial sacrifice made once every five years

禘郊(ㄉㄧˋ ㄐㄧㄠ)
imperial sacrifice held in the countryside

十畫

【禡】 3963
ㄇㄚˋ mah mò
sacrifice to the god of war offered by troops on the eve of a battle

禡祭(ㄇㄚˋ ㄐㄧˋ)
the ritual of offering sacrifices to the god of war by troops on the eve of a battle

【禛】 3964
ㄓㄣ jen zhēn
to be blessed because of one's sincerity

十一畫

【禦】 3965
ㄩˋ yuh yù
to guard against; to take precautions against: 攻擊爲最佳之防禦。The best defense is to attack.

禦敵(ㄩˋ ㄉㄧˊ)
to guard against the enemy

禦寇(ㄩˋ ㄎㄡˋ)
to guard against bandits; to take precautions against invaders

禦寒(ㄩˋ ㄏㄢˊ)
to protect oneself from cold; to take precautions against cold

禦侮(ㄩˋ ㄨˇ)
to guard against the insults of foreign powers

【禩】 3966
ㄙˋ syh
same as 祀—to worship; to offer sacrifices

十二畫

【禧】 3967
ㄒㄧˇ shi xǐ
(又讀 ㄒㄧ shii xī)
happiness; blessings; auspiciousness: 恭賀新禧。Happy New Year!

【禪】 3968
ㄔㄢˊ charn chán
1. Zen Buddhism
2. meditation; intense contemplation

禪房(ㄔㄢˊ ㄈㄤˊ)
a hermitage; a monastery

禪堂(ㄔㄢˊ ㄊㄤˊ)
a meditation hall or room

禪林(ㄔㄢˊ ㄌㄧㄣˊ)
a grove of meditation—a monastery

禪機(ㄔㄢˊ ㄐㄧ)
subtleties of Zen principles

禪寂(ㄔㄢˊ ㄐㄧˊ)
(Buddhism) the ideal peace of mind

禪偈(ㄔㄢˊ ㄐㄧˋ)
utterances of a Zen master, in the form of verse, often a recapitulation of what he has just said

禪牀(ㄔㄢˊ ㄔㄨㄤˊ)
(Buddhism) a seat for meditation

禪師(ㄔㄢˊ ㄕ)
a master, or teacher, of meditation, or of the Zen school

禪宗(ㄔㄢˊ ㄗㄨㄥ)
the Zen sect of Buddhism, said to be established in China by Bodhidharma (達摩)

禪寺(ㄔㄢˊ ㄙˋ)
a Buddhist temple

禪椅(ㄔㄢˊ ㄧˇ)
(Buddhism) a seat for meditation

禪悟(ㄔㄢˊ ㄨˋ)
to realize truth through meditation; a full realization of truth through meditation

禪味(ㄔㄢˊ ㄨㄟˋ)
(Buddhism) pleasant effect of meditation

禪悅(ㄔㄢˊ ㄩㄝˋ)
(Buddhism) joy of the mystic trance

【禪】 3968
ㄕㄢˋ shann shàn
to abdicate (the throne)

禪讓(ㄕㄢˋ ㄖㄤˋ)
to abdicate the throne

禪位(ㄕㄢˋ ㄨㄟˋ)
to abdicate the throne

【禨】 3969
ㄐㄧ ji jī

to seek blessings from ghosts

十三畫

〔示部〕

【禮】 3970 （ㄌㄧˇ）lǐ
1. courtesy; propriety; decorum; politeness; civility; etiquette: 他對老師總是彬彬有禮。He is always courteous to the teachers.
2. rites; ceremony
3. a gift; a present
4. a Chinese family name

禮拜（ㄌㄧˇ ㄅㄞˋ）
①church service; worship ②a week: 她生病臥床已經一個禮拜了。She has been sick in bed for a week.

禮拜堂（ㄌㄧˇ ㄅㄞˋ ㄊㄤˊ）
a chapel; a church

禮拜天（ㄌㄧˇ ㄅㄞˋ ㄊㄧㄢ）or 禮拜日（ㄌㄧˇ ㄅㄞˋ ㄖˋ）
Sunday 亦作「星期天」

禮拜寺（ㄌㄧˇ ㄅㄞˋ ㄙˋ）
a mosque

禮部（ㄌㄧˇ ㄅㄨˋ）
(in former times) Ministry of Rites and Education

禮部試（ㄌㄧˇ ㄅㄨˋ ㄕˋ）
general civil service examinations in former times, administered by the Ministry of Rites and Education

禮砲 or 禮礮（ㄌㄧˇ ㄆㄠˋ）
a gun salute; a salvo

禮品（ㄌㄧˇ ㄆㄧㄣˇ）
a gift; a present

禮聘（ㄌㄧˇ ㄆㄧㄣˋ）
to cordially invite the service of; to enlist the service of someone with handsome gifts

禮帽（ㄌㄧˇ ㄇㄠˋ）
a ceremonial hat or cap; a hat or cap worn by men on a formal occasion or ceremony

禮貌（ㄌㄧˇ ㄇㄠˋ）
etiquette; politeness; good manners; civility; decorum; 對人要有禮貌。Be polite to others.

禮門義路（ㄌㄧˇ ㄇㄣˊ ㄧˋ ㄌㄨˋ）
Decorum is an obligatory road to all men.

禮法（ㄌㄧˇ ㄈㄚˇ）
decorum; rules of politeness

禮服（ㄌㄧˇ ㄈㄨˊ）
ceremonial dress; full dress; a dress suit; a formal dress: 她穿著一件漂亮的禮服。She wears a beautiful formal dress.

禮單（ㄌㄧˇ ㄉㄢ）
a list of presents

禮度（ㄌㄧˇ ㄉㄨˋ）
rules of decorum; etiquette

禮多人不怪（ㄌㄧˇ ㄉㄨㄛ ㄖㄣˊ ㄅㄨˋ ㄍㄨㄞˋ）
Nobody blames excessive politeness.

禮堂（ㄌㄧˇ ㄊㄤˊ）
①an auditorium ②a hall decorated for a wedding ceremony or funeral service

禮記（ㄌㄧˇ ㄐㄧˋ）
the *Book of Rites*, one of the Thirteen Classics

禮節（ㄌㄧˇ ㄐㄧㄝˊ）
etiquette; requirements of decorum; rules of politeness; courtesy; protocol; civility

禮教（ㄌㄧˇ ㄐㄧㄠˋ）
ethical education

禮金（ㄌㄧˇ ㄐㄧㄣ）
a cash gift

禮器（ㄌㄧˇ ㄑㄧˋ）
instruments for sacrificial ceremonies

禮輕人意重（ㄌㄧˇ ㄑㄧㄥ ㄖㄣˊ ㄧˋ ㄓㄨㄥˋ）
The thoughtfulness is worth far more than the gift itself. 或 The gift is trifling, but the feeling is profound.

禮券（ㄌㄧˇ ㄑㄩㄢˋ）
gift coupons sold by a shop, which the recipient may convert into goods (or cash) at the shop in question

禮賢下士（ㄌㄧˇ ㄒㄧㄢˊ ㄒㄧㄚˋ ㄕˋ）
(said of a ruler) courteous to the wise and condescending to the scholarly

禮制（ㄌㄧˇ ㄓˋ）
a system of ceremonial forms

禮成（ㄌㄧˇ ㄔㄥˊ）
Ceremony is over.

禮尚往來（ㄌㄧˇ ㄕㄤˋ ㄨㄤˇ ㄌㄞˊ）
Courtesy emphasizes reciprocity.

禮數（ㄌㄧˇ ㄕㄨˋ）
different grades of courtesy due to differences in rank

禮讓（ㄌㄧˇ ㄖㄤˋ）
to make way humbly or modestly

禮讚（ㄌㄧˇ ㄗㄢˋ）
to praise; to worship; to idolize; to adore; to glorify: 他們唱聖詩禮讚上帝。They sing hymns to glorify God.

禮葬（ㄌㄧˇ ㄗㄤˋ）
to bury with pomp

禮俗（ㄌㄧˇ ㄙㄨˊ）
manners and custom (of a people)

禮所當然（ㄌㄧˇ ㄙㄨㄛˇ ㄉㄤ ㄖㄢˊ）
Etiquette requires it.

禮儀（ㄌㄧˇ ㄧˊ）
ceremonies for courtesy; etiquette; protocol; decorum

禮義之邦（ㄌㄧˇ ㄧˋ ㄓ ㄅㄤ）
a state of ceremonies

禮義廉恥（ㄌㄧˇ ㄧˋ ㄌㄧㄢˊ ㄔˇ）
propriety, justice, honesty, and a sense of shame—the four cardinal virtues of the people

禮無不答（ㄌㄧˇ ㄨˊ ㄅㄨˋ ㄉㄚˊ）
Courtesy must be reciprocated.

禮物（ㄌㄧˇ ㄨˋ）
①a gift; a present: 我有一份禮物送給您。I have a present for you. ②products of a culture

禮遇（ㄌㄧˇ ㄩˋ）
to treat with courtesy; to treat with respect: 他受到禮遇。He was accorded courteous reception.

禮樂射御書數（ㄌㄧˇ ㄩㄝˋ ㄕㄜˋ ㄩˋ ㄕㄨ ㄕㄨˋ）
rites, music, archery, driving a chariot, learning and mathematics (known together as "six arts", which ancient scholars were required to master)

十四畫

【禰】 3971 （ㄋㄧˇ）1. nǐ
the shrine where one's father's sacred tablet is kept

【禰】 3971 （ㄇㄧˊ）2. mí

a Chinese family name

【禱】 3972
ㄉㄠ dao dǎo
to pray; to beseech; to plead;
to entreat: 她新禱兒子歸來.
She prayed for her son's
return.

禱告(ㄉㄠ ㄍㄠ)
a prayer; to pray: 他向上帝禱
告求助. He prayed to God
for help.

禱祀(ㄉㄠ ㄙ)
to perform a sacrifice and
pray for happiness

十七畫

【禳】 3973
ㄖㄤ rang rǎng
1. a form of sacrifice performed for exorcism
2. to exorcise

【禴】 3974
ㄩㄝ yueh yuè
a kind of annual sacrifice

内 部
ㄖㄡ rou róu

四畫

【禹】 3975
ㄩ yeu yǔ
1. Yü, the legendary founder
of the Hsia (夏) Dynasty
(21st-16th century B.C.)
2. a Chinese family name

禹碑(ㄩ ㄅㄟ)
a tablet with inscriptions
supposedly set up by the legendary ruler Yü (禹)

禹甸(ㄩ ㄉㄧㄢ)
the domain of China in prehistoric times

禹陵(ㄩ ㄌㄧㄥ)
the monument of the legendary ruler Yü (禹) (in Che-
kiang)

禹貢(ㄩ ㄍㄨㄥ)
China's oldest known book of
geography

禹跡(ㄩ ㄐㄧ)
the area where the legend-

ary ruler Yü (禹) traversed

禹穴(ㄩ ㄒㄩㄝ)
①a cave in Chekiang sup-
posedly used as a repository
of books by the legendary
ruler Yü (禹) ②a place in
Shensi supposedly used as
an abode by the legendary
ruler Yü (禹) when he
tamed the Yellow River

【禺】 3976
1. ㄩ yu yú
name of a mountain in Chekiang

【禺】 3976
2. ㄩ yuh yù
a monkey

八畫

【禽】 3977
ㄑㄧㄣ chyn qín
1. birds; fowls
2. same as 擒 — to catch; to
capture

禽鳥(ㄑㄧㄣ ㄋㄧㄠ)
birds; fowls

禽獵(ㄑㄧㄣ ㄌㄧㄝ)
to hunt

禽荒(ㄑㄧㄣ ㄏㄨㄤ)
obsessed with hunting

禽獸(ㄑㄧㄣ ㄕㄡ)
①dumb creatures ②birds and
beasts

禾 部
ㄏㄜ her hé

【禾】 3978
ㄏㄜ her hé
1. grains still on the stalk
2. the rice crop

禾本科(ㄏㄜ ㄅㄣ ㄎㄜ)
the grass family

禾苗(ㄏㄜ ㄇㄧㄠ)
rice seedlings

禾稈(ㄏㄜ ㄍㄢ)
the stalk of a rice plant

禾黍(ㄏㄜ ㄕㄨ)
millet; corn

禾穗(ㄏㄜ ㄙㄨㄟ)
an ear of grain

二畫

【禿】 3979
(禿) ㄊㄨ tu tū
bald; bare: 這棵樹光禿禿的.
This tree is bare (or leaf-
less).
①a worn-down writing
brush ②(a self-depreciatory
term) poor writing skill

禿髮症(ㄊㄨ ㄈㄚ ㄓㄥ)
alopecia 亦作「禿髮病」

禿頂(ㄊㄨ ㄉㄧㄥ)
bald at the top of the head;
baldheaded

禿頭(ㄊㄨ ㄊㄡ)
baldheaded; bald; a bald head

禿驢(ㄊㄨ ㄌㄩ)
a bald ass (an abusive term
applied to a Buddhist monk)

禿鷲(ㄊㄨ ㄐㄧㄡ)
a vulture; a condor

禿瘡(ㄊㄨ ㄔㄨㄤ)
(pathology) favus

禿山(ㄊㄨ ㄕㄢ)
a bare hill; a barren hill

禿子(ㄊㄨ ˙ㄗ)
a baldhead; a baldpate

禿友(ㄊㄨ ㄧㄡ)
a pen or writing brush

【秀】 3980
ㄒㄧㄡ shiow xiù
1. brilliant; excellent; competent; outstanding
2. beautiful; elegant; graceful;
delicate; fine
3. (said of grain crops) to put
forth new flowers or ears

秀拔(ㄒㄧㄡ ㄅㄚ)
(said of a calligraphic style)
fine

秀眉(ㄒㄧㄡ ㄇㄟ)
long hairs in the eyebrows
of an aged person

秀美(ㄒㄧㄡ ㄇㄟ)
elegant; graceful; beautiful;
fine: 她寫的字極爲秀美. Her
handwriting is very beautiful.

秀發(ㄒㄧㄡ ㄈㄚ)
①blooming ②good-looking;
fine-looking; handsome

秀頂(ㄒㄧㄡ ㄉㄧㄥ)
a bald head; baldheaded

秀女(ㄒㄧㄡ ㄋㄩ)
(during the Ching Dynasty)
women in the emperor's

【禾·部】

harem

秀麗(ㄒㄧㄡˋ ㄌㄧˋ)
elegant; beautiful; graceful; fine

秀氣
①(ㄒㄧㄡˋ ㄑㄧˋ) the invigorating sight of a marvelous landscape
②(ㄒㄧㄡ ·ㄑㄧˋ) fine; elegant; graceful

秀出(ㄒㄧㄡˋ ㄔㄨ)
outstanding

秀士(ㄒㄧㄡˋ ㄕˋ)
①a man of outstanding ability and virtue ②the lowest degree conferred upon successful candidates under the former civil service examination system

秀才(ㄒㄧㄡˋ ㄘㄞˊ)
the lowest degree conferred upon successful candidates under the former civil service examination system ②fine talent③a scholar; a skillful writer

秀才人情紙半張(ㄒㄧㄡˋ ㄘㄞˊ ㄖㄣˊ ㄑㄧㄥˊ ㄓˇ ㄅㄢˋ ㄓㄤ)
(literally) A gift costs a scholar no more than a half sheet of paper.—Because scholars value literary products as gifts, their friendship is inexpensive.

秀色可餐(ㄒㄧㄡˋ ㄙㄜˋ ㄎㄜˇ ㄘㄢ)
(said of a woman) beauty that is the feast of the eye—very attractive

秀而不實(ㄒㄧㄡˋ ㄦˊ ㄅㄨˋ ㄕˊ)
(literally) flowering but bearing no fruit—beautiful in appearance but empty in substance

秀異(ㄒㄧㄡˋ ㄧˋ)
outstanding; striking

秀雅(ㄒㄧㄡˋ ㄧㄚˇ)
graceful; elegant; fine

秀外慧中(ㄒㄧㄡˋ ㄨㄞˋ ㄏㄨㄟˋ ㄓㄨㄥ)
beautiful and intelligent: 她是位秀外慧中的女孩。She's a beautiful and intelligent girl.

【私】 3981
ㄙ sy sī
1. private; personal; person-to-person
2. secret; clandestine
3. to have illicit relations or an affair with

4. contraband
5. prejudice; biased; to favor
6. selfish; selfishly
7. reproductive organs of both sexes

私奔(ㄙ ㄅㄣ)
to elope; elopement: 那女孩子與情人私奔。That girl eloped with her lover.

私弊(ㄙ ㄅㄧˋ)
dishonest practice; irregularities

私門(ㄙ ㄇㄣˊ)
①powerful or influential families ②one's home or hometown ③an unlicensed brothel

私名號(ㄙ ㄇㄧㄥˊ ㄏㄠˋ)
(in Chinese punctuation marks) the line along either side of a word or words to indicate a proper noun

私販(ㄙ ㄈㄢˋ)
dealers in contraband goods; smugglers

私房(ㄙ ㄈㄤˊ)
①private or personal (pocket, etc.) ②personal or private savings (usually of married women)

私房錢(ㄙ ㄈㄤˊ ㄑㄧㄢˊ)
private savings (usually of married women)

私訪(ㄙ ㄈㄤˇ)
(said of officials in old times) to travel incognito in order to get in touch with the public for its opinions, views, etc.

私德(ㄙ ㄉㄜˊ)
personal virtue; private conduct; personal morals

私鬥(ㄙ ㄉㄡˋ)
a private or personal fight; a brawl

私底下(ㄙ ㄉㄧˇ ·ㄒㄧㄚˋ)
privately; secretly

私第(ㄙ ㄉㄧˋ)
a private residence

私定終身(ㄙ ㄉㄧㄥˋ ㄓㄨㄥ ㄕㄣ)
(in old China) to pledge to marry without the permission of parents

私逃(ㄙ ㄊㄠˊ)
to escape or run away secretly; to elope; to abscond

to talk in private; private talks; confidential talks

私帑(ㄙ ㄊㄤˇ)
personal or private property of the emperor

私田(ㄙ ㄊㄧㄢˊ)
privately owned farmland

私通(ㄙ ㄊㄨㄥ)
①to collaborate with enemy forces or a foreign country ②to have an illicit affair with parties other than one's spouse; adultery

私囊(ㄙ ㄋㄤˊ)
private pocket (as opposed to the public coffers)

私暱(ㄙ ㄋㄧˋ)
to favor privately; to have an affair with

私釀(ㄙ ㄋㄧㄤˋ)
to bootleg; to brew alcoholic drinks illegally

私累(ㄙ ㄌㄟˇ)
a personal burden—such as the family

私立(ㄙ ㄌㄧˋ)
(usually said of schools, hospitals, etc.) established and operated by private funds: 他在一所私立學校求學。He studies at a private school.

私利(ㄙ ㄌㄧˋ)
private interests; personal gains: 只圖個人私利是自私的行為。It is selfish to pursue only private ends.

私和(ㄙ ㄏㄜˊ)
private settlement of a criminal case

私語(ㄙ ㄩˇ)
secret or personal words or talks; confidential talks

私貨(ㄙ ㄏㄨㄛˋ)
①smuggled goods ②goods whose source cannot be traced, usually referring to stolen articles

私會(ㄙ ㄏㄨㄟˋ)
a secret rendezvous

私積(ㄙ ㄐㄧ)
private savings

私家偵探(ㄙ ㄐㄧㄚ ㄓㄣ ㄊㄢˋ)
a private detective; a private eye

私家車(ㄙ ㄐㄧㄚ ㄔㄜ)
a private car

私交(ㄙ ㄐㄧㄠ)

personal friendship (as distinct from official association)

私酒(ㄙ ㄐㄧㄡˇ)
alcoholic beverages produced by unlicensed breweries; untaxed liquors; bootleg; moonshine

私見(ㄙ ㄐㄧㄢˋ)
a personal opinion or view; bias

私情(ㄙ ㄑㄧㄥˊ)
① private feelings; personal preference ② illicit love

私下(ㄙ ㄒㄧㄚˋ)or 私下裏(ㄙ ㄒㄧㄚˋ ㄌㄧˇ)
privately; secretly: 我希望私下同你談談。I wish to talk with you in private.

私梟(ㄙ ㄒㄧㄠ)
a smuggler

私心(ㄙ ㄒㄧㄣ)
selfishness; private or selfish motive; favoritism: 他腦裏充滿著私心雜念。He was full of selfish ideas and personal considerations.

私信(ㄙ ㄒㄧㄣˋ)
personal letters, mail or correspondence

私相授受(ㄙ ㄒㄧㄤ ㄕㄡˋ ㄕㄡˋ)
to transfer offices or ownership of public properties without going through legal procedure: 不可拿公家的東西私相授受。There must be no illicit transfer of public property.

私刑(ㄙ ㄒㄧㄥˊ)
to lynch; lynching

私蓄(ㄙ ㄒㄩˋ)
personal savings

私宅(ㄙ ㄓㄞˊ)
a private residence

私債(ㄙ ㄓㄞˋ)
personal debts

私章(ㄙ ㄓㄤ)
a personal seal; a private chop

私鑄(ㄙ ㄓㄨˋ)
(in old China) to mint coins illegally

私衷(ㄙ ㄓㄨㄥ)
a private view; a personal wish 亦作「私悃」

私仇(ㄙ ㄔㄡˊ)
a personal grudge

私產(ㄙ ㄔㄢˇ)
private property; personal estate

私娼(ㄙ ㄔㄤ)
unlicensed prostitutes or brothels

私處(ㄙ ㄔㄨˋ)
private parts; reproductive organs of both sexes

私室(ㄙ ㄕˋ)
a private room

私事(ㄙ ㄕˋ)or 私務(ㄙ ㄨˋ)
personal affairs; private affairs: 不要干涉我的私事。Don't interfere in my personal affairs.

私設(ㄙ ㄕㄜˋ)
established without authorization

私生活(ㄙ ㄕㄥ ㄏㄨㄛˊ)
one's private life

私生子(ㄙ ㄕㄥ ㄗˇ)
an illegitimate child; a bastard; a bastard son

私塾(ㄙ ㄕㄨˊ)
(formerly) a village school supported by private means

私淑(ㄙ ㄕㄨˊ)
to learn not directly from the master himself

私淑弟子(ㄙ ㄕㄨˊ ㄉㄧˋ ㄗˇ)
a disciple who has not taken lessons directly under the master himself

私人(ㄙ ㄖㄣˊ)
① individual; personal; private: 別問私人的事。Don't ask personal questions. ② persons employed not because of their merits but because of their personal relationship with the boss

私人秘書(ㄙ ㄖㄣˊ ㄇㄧˋ ㄕㄨ)
a private secretary; a personal secretary

私人企業(ㄙ ㄖㄣˊ ㄑㄧˇ ㄧㄝˋ)
private enterprises

私人資格(ㄙ ㄖㄣˊ ㄗ ㄍㄜˊ)
in one's personal capacity; as an individual

私自(ㄙ ㄗˋ)
personally; privately; doing something without permission

私藏(ㄙ ㄘㄤˊ)
① private collection ② to keep something against the

law

私謁(ㄙ ㄧㄝˋ)
to call on someone to ask for a personal favor

私有(ㄙ ㄧㄡˇ)
privately-owned; private: 這部車是他的私有財產。The car is his private property.

私有土地(ㄙ ㄧㄡˇ ㄊㄨˇ ㄉㄧˋ)
privately-owned land; private land

私有林(ㄙ ㄧㄡˇ ㄌㄧㄣˊ)
privately-owned forests or woodland

私有公物(ㄙ ㄧㄡˇ ㄍㄨㄥ ㄨˋ)
(law) to offer private possessions for public uses

私有制(ㄙ ㄧㄡˇ ㄓˋ)
private ownership of property

私有財產(ㄙ ㄧㄡˇ ㄘㄞˊ ㄔㄢˇ)
private property or possessions

私鹽(ㄙ ㄧㄢˊ)
untaxed salt

私印(ㄙ ㄧㄣˋ)
a private seal; a personal chop

私營(ㄙ ㄧㄥˊ)
privately-operated; privately-run

私語(ㄙ ㄩˇ)
① private talks; intimate and soothing words ② to whisper or talk in a very low voice: 他們在竊竊私語。They were talking in whispers.

私欲(ㄙ ㄩˋ)or 私慾(ㄙ ㄩˋ)
① personal or selfish desires ② greediness

私怨(ㄙ ㄩㄢˋ)
a personal grudge: 我對你沒有私怨。I owe you no grudge.

私願(ㄙ ㄩㄢˋ)
a personal wish or desire

私運(ㄙ ㄩㄣˋ)
to smuggle

私用(ㄙ ㄩㄥˋ)
①(for) personal use ② illegal use (of public property, etc.)

三畫

【秉】 *3982* ㄅㄧㄥˇ biing bǐng

〔禾部〕

1. to hold in hand
2. to take charge of; to rule
3. authority
4. an ancient grain measure; a measure for liquid
5. a Chinese family name

秉筆 (ㄅㄧㄥˇ ㄅㄧˇ)
to hold a pen

秉賦 (ㄅㄧㄥˇ ㄈㄨˋ)
one's natural endowments

秉鐸 (ㄅㄧㄥˇ ㄉㄨㄛˊ)
an instructor

秉國 (ㄅㄧㄥˇ 《ㄨㄛˊ)
to rule a nation; to exercise authority over a nation

秉公辦理 (ㄅㄧㄥˇ 《ㄨㄥ ㄅㄢˋ ㄌㄧˇ)
① to act strictly according to official procedures ② to handle a matter impartially

秉鈞 (ㄅㄧㄥˇ ㄐㄩㄣ) or 秉軸 (ㄅㄧㄥˇ ㄓㄡˊ)
to be in power; to rule a nation

秉性 or 稟性 (ㄅㄧㄥˇ ㄒㄧㄥˋ)
nature; a natural disposition or temperament

秉直 (ㄅㄧㄥˇ ㄓˊ)
① to adhere to correct principles ② frank and honest

秉燭夜遊 (ㄅㄧㄥˇ ㄓㄨˊ ㄧㄝˋ ㄧㄡˊ)
(literally) to hold a candle for a night excursion—Life being short, one cannot afford to let time flee without making use of it.

秉持 (ㄅㄧㄥˇ ㄔˊ)
① to hold on to or to adhere to (one's principles, etc.) ② to hold in hand (a spear, etc.)

秉鉞 (ㄅㄧㄥˇ ㄩㄝˋ)
to wield military power

四畫

【秋】 3983
(秌) (ㄑㄧㄡ chiou qiū)

1. autumn; fall: 秋去冬來。Winter comes after autumn.
2. time; a period: 多事之秋 an eventful period
3. a season
4. a year: 千秋萬歲 for thousands of years
5. ripening of grains; a harvest
6. a Chinese family name

秋波 (ㄑㄧㄡ ㄅㄛ)
bewitching eyes of a woman

秋波暗送 (ㄑㄧㄡ ㄅㄛ ㄢˋ ㄙㄨㄥˋ)
to send silent and endearing messages with bewitching eyes 亦作「暗送秋波」

秋波微轉 (ㄑㄧㄡ ㄅㄛ ㄨㄟˊ ㄓㄨㄢˇ)
a slight turn of her bewitching eyes; eloquent eyes that send a silent message

秋末 (ㄑㄧㄡ ㄇㄛˋ)
late autumn; the last days of autumn

秋分 (ㄑㄧㄡ ㄈㄣ)
the autumnal equinox (or point), one of the 24 climatic transitions in a lunar year, which falls on September 23 or 24

秋風 (ㄑㄧㄡ ㄈㄥ)
① autumn wind ② presents or gift money obtained on pretexts, such as one's birthday, etc.

秋風過耳 (ㄑㄧㄡ ㄈㄥ ㄍㄨㄛˋ ㄦˇ)
like an autumn breeze passing by the ear—something heard but not given much attention

秋刀魚 (ㄑㄧㄡ ㄉㄠ ㄩˊ)
a saury

秋天 (ㄑㄧㄡ ㄊㄧㄢ)
autumn; fall

秋娘 (ㄑㄧㄡ ㄋㄧㄤˊ)
an aged woman (whose beauty has disappeared with youth)

秋老虎 (ㄑㄧㄡ ㄌㄠˇ ㄏㄨˇ)
scorching heat in early autumn

秋涼 (ㄑㄧㄡ ㄌㄧㄤˊ)
chilliness in autumn

秋羅 (ㄑㄧㄡ ㄌㄨㄛˊ)
a kind of thin, light and striped silk fabric

秋高馬肥 (ㄑㄧㄡ 《ㄠ ㄇㄚˇ ㄈㄟˊ)
(literally) when the autumn skies are high and the horses are fat—time fit for starting a campaign in ancient times

秋高氣爽 (ㄑㄧㄡ 《ㄠ ㄑㄧˋ ㄕㄨㄤˇ)
the clear and crisp autumn climate

秋海棠 (ㄑㄧㄡ ㄏㄞˇ ㄊㄤˊ)
(botany) a begonia

秋毫 (ㄑㄧㄡ ㄏㄠˊ)
① a very tiny thing; trifles

② a writing brush

秋毫無犯 (ㄑㄧㄡ ㄏㄠˊ ㄨˊ ㄈㄢˋ)
(said of troops) not to cause the slightest trouble to the people

秋後 (ㄑㄧㄡ ㄏㄡˋ)
after the "Beginning of Autumn", one of the 24 climatic transitions in a lunar year which falls on August 7 or 8

秋季 (ㄑㄧㄡ ㄐㄧˋ)
autumn (season)

秋節 (ㄑㄧㄡ ㄐㄧㄝˊ)
① the Moon Festival on the 15th of the eighth lunar month ② the Mountain Climbing Festival on the ninth of the ninth lunar month

秋瑾 (ㄑㄧㄡ ㄐㄧㄣˇ)
Chiu Chin (1875-1907), a woman revolutionary executed by the Manchus

秋氣 (ㄑㄧㄡ ㄑㄧˋ)
① the desolate air of autumn ② dilapidated or desolate

秋千 or 鞦韆 (ㄑㄧㄡ ㄑㄧㄢ)
a swing: 他在那兒打秋千。He was having a swing over there.

秋汛 (ㄑㄧㄡ ㄒㄩㄣˋ)
the overflowing of rivers in the early part of autumn

秋蟬 (ㄑㄧㄡ ㄔㄢˊ)
the autumn cicada which hums in the evening

秋成 (ㄑㄧㄡ ㄔㄥˊ)
the autumn harvest

秋蟲 (ㄑㄧㄡ ㄔㄨㄥˊ)
autumn insects—often referring to crickets

秋實 (ㄑㄧㄡ ㄕˊ)
fruits in autumn (as a result of flowering in spring)

秋試 (ㄑㄧㄡ ㄕˋ) or 秋闈 (ㄑㄧㄡ ㄨㄟˊ)
(in ancient China) the civil service examination held in autumn

秋事 (ㄑㄧㄡ ㄕˋ)
the autumn harvest

秋社 (ㄑㄧㄡ ㄕㄜˋ)
Chinese Thanksgiving Day in autumn

秋收 (ㄑㄧㄡ ㄕㄡ)
the autumn harvest

秋扇(ㄑㄧㄡ ㄕㄢˋ)
(literally) fans in autumn
—deserted women

秋扇見捐(ㄑㄧㄡ ㄕㄢˋ ㄐㄧㄢˋ ㄐㄩㄢ)
(said of women) to be
deserted as fans are cast
away in autumn

秋聲(ㄑㄧㄡ ㄕㄥ)
the sound of winds sweeping
through withered leaves in
autumn; the autumnal sough

秋水(ㄑㄧㄡ ㄕㄨㄟˇ)
① autumn waters—clear and
bright ② the bewitching
eyes of a woman ③(said of
complexion) clear and bright
④ the flashing of swords

秋水伊人(ㄑㄧㄡ ㄕㄨㄟˇ ㄧ ㄖㄣˊ)
thinking of an old acquaintance on seeing a familiar
scene

秋霜(ㄑㄧㄡ ㄕㄨㄤ)
① autumn frost—(figuratively)snowy hair ② severity;
sternness

秋思(ㄑㄧㄡ ㄙ)
(literally) autumn thought
—a lonesome and desolate
mood

秋色(ㄑㄧㄡ ㄙㄜˋ)
autumn scenes; autumnal
colors

秋色宜人(ㄑㄧㄡ ㄙㄜˋ ㄧ ㄖㄣˊ)
delightful autumn scenery

秋意(ㄑㄧㄡ ㄧˋ)
cool and a little chilly, indicating the presence of
autumn

秋顏(ㄑㄧㄡ ㄧㄢˊ)
fading beauty

秋雨(ㄑㄧㄡ ㄩˇ)
autumn rain

秋月春風(ㄑㄧㄡ ㄩㄝˋ ㄔㄨㄣ ㄈㄥ)
(literally) the autumn moon
and spring breezes—the
beauty of nature

【科】 3984
ㄎㄜ ke ke
1. a department
2. a section
3. a class; a variety; a family
(of plants or animals)
4. rules; laws
5. the action in Chinese opera
6. a subject in the civil service
examination of former times
7. a branch of academic or

vocational studies
8. to mete out (prison terms,
etc.); to levy (taxes, etc.); to
fine someone

科白(ㄎㄜ ㄅㄞˊ)
dialogue and acting in
Chinese opera

科班(ㄎㄜ ㄅㄢ)
① a Chinese operatic com-
pany which operates a class
to train young pupils ② very
formal or orthodox training
one received when young

科班出身(ㄎㄜ ㄅㄢ ㄔㄨ ㄕㄣ)
having received professional
training for what one is
doing

科名(ㄎㄜ ㄇㄧㄥˊ)
to establish one's name and
position under the civil service examination system in
monarchical China

科目(ㄎㄜ ㄇㄨˋ)
① subjects, courses, classifications of academic studies
② the civil examination system in former times

科斗 or 蝌蚪(ㄎㄜ ㄉㄡˇ)
the tadpole

科斗文(ㄎㄜ ㄉㄡˇ ㄨㄣˊ)
Chinese characters in the
Chou Dynasty (1125-255B.C.)
which resemble tadpoles in
shape

科令(ㄎㄜ ㄌㄧㄥˋ)
laws and regulations

科羅拉多(ㄎㄜ ㄌㄨㄛ ㄌㄚ ㄉㄨㄛ)
the state of Colorado, U.S.A.

科倫坡(ㄎㄜ ㄌㄨㄣˊ ㄆㄛ)
Colombo, the capital of Sri
Lanka 今譯作「可倫坡」

科隆(ㄎㄜ ㄌㄨㄥˊ)
Cologne, a German city

科幻小說(ㄎㄜ ㄏㄨㄢˋ ㄒㄧㄠˇ ㄕㄨㄛ)
science fiction 亦作「科學幻想
小說」

科諢(ㄎㄜ ㄏㄨㄣˋ)
(Chinese opera) a comical
part—including jokes and
clownish acts

科技(ㄎㄜ ㄐㄧˋ)
science and technology

科際整合(ㄎㄜ ㄐㄧˋ ㄓㄥˇ ㄏㄜˊ)
interdisciplinary integration

科舉(ㄎㄜ ㄐㄩˇ) or 科甲(ㄎㄜ ㄐㄧㄚˇ)
or 科第(ㄎㄜ ㄉㄧˋ)
the civil service examination

system in ancient China

科西嘉(ㄎㄜ ㄒㄧ ㄐㄧㄚ)
Corsica

科刑(ㄎㄜ ㄒㄧㄥˊ)or 科罪(ㄎㄜ ㄗㄨㄟˋ)
to mete out punishment

科學(ㄎㄜ ㄒㄩㄝˊ)
science: 他決定研究科學。He
decided to study science.

科學方法(ㄎㄜ ㄒㄩㄝˊ ㄈㄤ ㄈㄚˇ)
scientific methods, ways or
approaches

科學的(ㄎㄜ ㄒㄩㄝˊ ㄉㄜ˙)
scientific: 她具有科學的頭腦。
She has a scientific mind.

科學管理(ㄎㄜ ㄒㄩㄝˊ ㄍㄨㄢˇ ㄌㄧˇ)or
科學化管理(ㄎㄜ ㄒㄩㄝˊ ㄏㄨㄚˋ
ㄍㄨㄢˇ ㄌㄧˇ)
scientific management

科學工業園區(ㄎㄜ ㄒㄩㄝˊ ㄍㄨㄥ ㄧㄝˋ
ㄩㄢˊ ㄑㄩ)
the Science Industrial District

科學化(ㄎㄜ ㄒㄩㄝˊ ㄏㄨㄚˋ)
scientific

科學家(ㄎㄜ ㄒㄩㄝˊ ㄐㄧㄚ)
scientists

科學界(ㄎㄜ ㄒㄩㄝˊ ㄐㄧㄝˋ)
① the world of science ② the
community of scientists

科學教育(ㄎㄜ ㄒㄩㄝˊ ㄐㄧㄠˋ ㄩˋ)
science education

科學知識(ㄎㄜ ㄒㄩㄝˊ ㄓ ㄕˋ)
scientific knowledge

科學時代(ㄎㄜ ㄒㄩㄝˊ ㄕˊ ㄉㄞˋ)
the era of science

科學儀器(ㄎㄜ ㄒㄩㄝˊ ㄧˊ ㄑㄧˋ)
scientific instruments

科學萬能(ㄎㄜ ㄒㄩㄝˊ ㄨㄢˋ ㄋㄥˊ)
There is nothing science
cannot accomplish.

科長(ㄎㄜ ㄓㄤˇ)
a section chief in various
government agencies

科場(ㄎㄜ ㄔㄤˇ)
a site of the civil service
examination in ancient
China

科任教員(ㄎㄜ ㄖㄣˋ ㄐㄧㄠˋ ㄩㄢˊ)
a teacher who is employed
to teach a specific subject or
course of study, as math.,
literature, etc. (as opposed
to those employed to oversee a class)

科則(ㄎㄜ ㄗㄜˊ)
classifications, grades, etc.

〔禾部〕

（禾
部）

in taxation and compulsory services, etc.

科以罰金（ㄎㄜ ㄧ ㄈㄚˊ ㄐㄧㄣ）
to impose a fine on someone

科威特（ㄎㄜ ㄨㄟ ㄊㄜˋ）
Kuwait

科員（ㄎㄜ ㄩㄢˊ）
a junior government employee

【秒】 3985
ㄇㄧㄠˇ meau miǎo
1. (said of time or a degree) a second
2. the beard of grain

秒錶（ㄇㄧㄠˇ ㄅㄧㄠˇ）
a stopwatch; a chronograph
亦作「錶錶」

秒忽（ㄇㄧㄠˇ ㄏㄨ）
an infinitesimal number

秒針（ㄇㄧㄠˇ ㄓㄣ）
the second hand (on the dial of a clock or watch)

【秕】 3986
ㄅㄧˇ bii bǐ
1. husks; grains not fully grown; blasted grains
2. mean; no good; not qualified or competent

秕謬（ㄅㄧˇ ㄇㄧㄡˋ）
to go against good reasoning or sense; mistaken; erroneous

秕穀（ㄅㄧˇ ㄍㄨˇ）
rice grains not fully grown

秕糠 or 秕穅（ㄅㄧˇ ㄎㄤ）
①chaff ②worthless stuff; leavings

秕政（ㄅㄧˇ ㄓㄥˋ）
bad administration or government

秕滓（ㄅㄧˇ ㄗˇ）
husks, chaff or refuse

【种】 3987
ㄔㄨㄥˊ chorng chóng
1. naive; naivete
2. a Chinese family name
3. a simplified form of 種

【秔】 3988
（粳、稉）（ㄍㄥ）geng
（籼音 ㄐㄧㄥ）jing
jing
non-glutinous rice

秔米（ㄍㄥ ㄇㄧˇ）
non-glutinous rice 亦作「粳米」

秔稻（ㄍㄥ ㄉㄠˋ）
non-glutinous rice which

ripens a little late 亦作「粳稻」

五畫

【秦】 3989
ㄑㄧㄣˊ chyn qín
1. the feudal state of Chin (879-221 B.C.) in the Chou Dynasty, which later unified the whole country under the Chin Dynasty (221-206 B.C.)
2. another name of Shensi Province
3. the ancient name of China as known to the people of the Western Region (西域)
4. a Chinese family name

秦庭之哭（ㄑㄧㄣˊ ㄊㄧㄥˊ ㄓ ㄎㄨ）
begging in tears for assistance in desperation (a reference to the episode of Shen Pao-hsü（申包胥）in the Epoch of Warring States）

秦樓楚館（ㄑㄧㄣˊ ㄌㄡˊ ㄔㄨˇ ㄍㄨㄢˇ）
brothels

秦良玉（ㄑㄧㄣˊ ㄌㄧㄤˊ ㄩˋ）
Chin Liang-yü, the wife of Ma Chien-cheng（馬千乘）, a ranking military officer in the Ming Dynasty, whose military acumen was so superb that she was given a field command in her own right

秦嶺（ㄑㄧㄣˊ ㄌㄧㄥˇ）
also known as Mt. Chin（秦山）, or the Southern Mountain（終南山）, which soars up in Kansu and ends in Honan

秦觀（ㄑㄧㄣˊ ㄍㄨㄢ）
Chin Kuan, alias Shao-yü（少游）, 1049-1100, a famous poet and essayist in the Sung Dynasty

秦檜（ㄑㄧㄣˊ ㄏㄨㄟˋ）or（ㄑㄧㄣˊ ㄎㄨㄞˋ）
Chin Kuei (1090-1155), a prime minister of the Sung Dynasty, regarded as a traitor by posterity for his part in executing General Yüeh Fei（岳飛）, an outstanding field commander

秦火（ㄑㄧㄣˊ ㄏㄨㄛˇ）
the fire of Chin—a reference to the burning of books ordered by the First Emperor

（始皇帝）

秦淮（ㄑㄧㄣˊ ㄏㄨㄞˊ）
the Chinhuai River that flows through Nanking City, formerly, a merrymaking center

秦皇島（ㄑㄧㄣˊ ㄏㄨㄤˊ ㄉㄠˇ）
Chinhuangtao, a port in Hopeh Province, which was opened as a commercial port in 1898

秦晉之好（ㄑㄧㄣˊ ㄐㄧㄣˋ ㄓ ㄏㄠˇ）
Chin and Tsin, the two powerful states in the Epoch of Warring States, which maintained close ties for generations through matrimonial diplomacy—a phrase now used as a congratulatory expression on wedding

秦鏡高懸（ㄑㄧㄣˊ ㄐㄧㄥˋ ㄍㄠ ㄒㄩㄢˊ）
(literally) The all-discerning mirror in the palace of Chin hangs high.— Nothing escapes the discerning eyes of the presiding judge.

秦腔（ㄑㄧㄣˊ ㄑㄧㄤ）
a kind of opera popular in part of northern China, also known as 梆子

秦中（ㄑㄧㄣˊ ㄓㄨㄥ）
another name of Shensi Province

秦始皇（ㄑㄧㄣˊ ㄕˇ ㄏㄨㄤˊ）
Chin Shih Huang, or the First Emperor of Chin, 259-210 B.C., who unified China under the Chin Dynasty, which he hoped to last forever

秦聲（ㄑㄧㄣˊ ㄕㄥ）
tunes and songs of Chin

秦二世（ㄑㄧㄣˊ ㄦˋ ㄕˋ）
the second son of the First Emperor, who was killed after a three-year reign

【租】 3990
ㄗㄨ tzu zū
1. to rent; to lease; to let; to hire; to charter
2. rent; rental
3. taxes; to tax

租米（ㄗㄨ ㄇㄧˇ）
the percentage of a crop yield given to the landlord as farm rental

租稅（ㄗㄨ ㄕㄨㄟˋ）
royalties

租賃（ㄗㄨ ㄌㄧㄣˋ）

to rent (a house, etc.); to lease: 他租賃了服裝和道具。He rented costumes and stage properties.

租賃契約(ㄗㄨ ㄌㄧㄣˋ ㄑㄧˋ ㄩㄝ)
a lease contract

租戶(ㄗㄨ ㄏㄨˋ)
a tenant

租價(ㄗㄨ ㄐㄧㄚˋ)
rent, or rental

租界(ㄗㄨ ㄐㄧㄝˋ)
a foreign settlement or concession

租借(ㄗㄨ ㄐㄧㄝˋ)
lend-lease; to rent: 我們租借公寓。We rented an apartment.

租借法案(ㄗㄨ ㄐㄧㄝˋ ㄈㄚˇ ㄢˋ)
the Lend-Lease Act of the U.S. in World War II

租借地(ㄗㄨ ㄐㄧㄝˋ ㄉㄧˋ)
a settlement or concession granted to a foreign nation (usually as a result of military defeat) for a specified time; leased territory

租金(ㄗㄨ ㄐㄧㄣ)or租錢(ㄗㄨ ㄑㄧㄢˊ)
rent or rental: 我得去收租金。I must collect the rent.

租金收入(ㄗㄨ ㄐㄧㄣ ㄕㄡ ㄖㄨˋ)
rental receipts

租契(ㄗㄨ ㄑㄧˋ)
a lease or rental agreement

租出(ㄗㄨ ㄔㄨ)
to let

租借(ㄗㄨ ㄕㄡˋ)
for rent or sale

租書處(ㄗㄨ ㄕㄨ ㄔㄨˋ)
a rental library

租稅(ㄗㄨ ㄕㄨㄟˋ)
taxes paid to the government

租徭(ㄗㄨ ㄧㄠˊ)
taxes and compulsory services

租約(ㄗㄨ ㄩㄝ)
a lease: 租約何時期滿？When does the lease expire?

租用(ㄗㄨ ㄩㄥˋ)
to rent for use; to rent from others; to be tenanted: 我租用她的房子。I rented the house from her.

【秧】 3991
ㄧㄤ iang yāng
1. rice seedlings
2. tree saplings; very young

plants for transplanting
3. fry
4. (now rarely) to cultivate; to grow

秧苗(ㄧㄤ ㄇㄧㄠˊ)
rice seedlings: 農夫在移植秧苗。The farmer was setting out rice seedlings.

秧田(ㄧㄤ ㄊㄧㄢˊ)
a water field for the cultivation of rice seedlings

秧歌(ㄧㄤ ㄍㄜ)
songs sung by farmers when transplanting rice seedlings

秧針(ㄧㄤ ㄓㄣ)
the first sprouts of rice seedlings

【秤】 3992
ㄔㄥˋ cheng chèng
1. a weighing scale; a balance; a steelyard
2. to weigh with a scale, etc.

秤平斗滿(ㄔㄥˋ ㄆㄧㄥˊ ㄉㄡˇ ㄇㄢˇ)
(literally) even balances and full measures—fair dealings; honest business transactions

秤量貨幣(ㄔㄥˋ ㄌㄧㄤˊ ㄏㄨㄛˋ ㄅㄧˋ)
money by weight (used before the appearance of standardized coins)

秤桿兒(ㄔㄥˋ ㄍㄢˇ ㄦ)
the beam of a steelyard

秤鉤兒(ㄔㄥˋ ㄍㄡ ㄦ)
the hook at the end of a steelyard

秤而斛(ㄔㄥˋ ㄦˊ ㄏㄨˊ)
① extremely stingy ② over-emphasis on trifles

秤星(ㄔㄥˋ ㄒㄧㄥ)
the brass marks on a steelyard

秤錘(ㄔㄥˋ ㄔㄨㄟˊ)or秤砣(ㄔㄥˋ ㄊㄨㄛˊ)
the weight used with a steelyard; the sliding weight of a steelyard

【秤】 3992
2. ㄆㄧㄥˊ pyng píng
scales for measuring weight

【秩】 3993
ㄓˋ jyh zhì
1. order; orderly
2. official ranks
3. official salaries
4. a decade

秩滿(ㄓˋ ㄇㄢˇ)
to have completed the tenure of a public post

秩祿(ㄓˋ ㄌㄨˋ)

official salaries

秩序(ㄓˋ ㄒㄩˋ)
① order ② arrangement

秩序大亂(ㄓˋ ㄒㄩˋ ㄉㄚˋ ㄌㄨㄢˋ)
in pandemonium; in total (or great) disorder

秩序井然(ㄓˋ ㄒㄩˋ ㄐㄧㄥˇ ㄖㄢˊ)
in perfect or apple-pie order

秩然有序(ㄓˋ ㄖㄢˊ ㄧㄡˇ ㄒㄩˋ)
orderly; neat and well arranged; shipshape

【秣】 3994
ㄇㄛˋ moh mò
1. horse feed; fodder
2. to feed a horse

秣馬厲兵(ㄇㄛˋ ㄇㄚˇ ㄌㄧˋ ㄅㄧㄥ)
(literally) to feed the horses and drill the soldiers—to prepare for war

秣陵(ㄇㄛˋ ㄌㄧㄥˊ)
name of an old city near Nanking

【秭】 3995
ㄗˇ tzyy zǐ
one trillion—1,000,000,000,000

【秬】 3996
ㄐㄩˋ jiuh jù
the black millet

秬酒(ㄐㄩˋ ㄐㄧㄡˇ)
liquor made from black millet

秬鬯(ㄐㄩˋ ㄔㄤˋ)
a sacrificial wine made from millet and fragrant herbs, and given as an imperial favor

【秫】 3997
ㄕㄨˊ shwu shú
a glutinous variety of millet; kaoliang; sorghum

秫米(ㄕㄨˊ ㄇㄧˇ)
another name of glutinous rice; husked sorghum

秫稭(ㄕㄨˊ ㄐㄧㄝ)or秫秸(ㄕㄨˊ ㄅㄚ)
the stalk of millet

秫酒(ㄕㄨˊ ㄐㄧㄡˇ)
wine made from glutinous rice

六畫

【移】 3998
ㄧˊ yi yí
1. to change; to alter; to influence; to affect
2. to shift; to move: 他把沙發移到左邊。He moved the sofa to the left.

〔禾部〕

〔禾部〕

3. to forward; to transmit; to transfer; to transplant; to convey: 工廠將被移至基隆。The factory will be transferred to Keelung.
4. to give; to endow

移步(ㄧ ㄅㄨˋ)
to move one's steps; to walk

移民(ㄧ ㄇㄧㄣˊ)
① to immigrate; immigration ② to emigrate; to settle people (in a new region, etc.); to colonize ③ an immigrant; an immigration ④ an emigrant

移民法(ㄧ ㄇㄧㄣˊ ㄈㄚˇ)
the immigration laws

移民局(ㄧ ㄇㄧㄣˊ ㄐㄩˊ)
the immigration office

移民區(ㄧ ㄇㄧㄣˊ ㄑㄩ)
a settlement; a colony

移民政策(ㄧ ㄇㄧㄣˊ ㄓㄥˋ ㄘㄜˋ)
an emigration or immigration policy; a colonization policy

移風易俗(ㄧ ㄈㄥ ㄧˋ ㄙㄨˊ)
to make changes in customs and traditions; to improve public morals

移牒(ㄧ ㄉㄧㄝˊ)
a formal notification addressed to another government organization of corresponding level in a foreign country

移調(ㄧ ㄉㄧㄠˋ)
(music) transposition

移鼎(ㄧ ㄉㄧㄥˇ)
the change of a regime or dynasty

移東就西(ㄧ ㄉㄨㄥ ㄐㄧㄡˋ ㄒㄧ)
to make up a deficit or insufficiency in one place with a surplus from somewhere else

移動(ㄧ ㄉㄨㄥˋ)
to move; to shift; to change: 不要移動我桌上的東西。Don't move the things on my table.

移天易日(ㄧ ㄊㄧㄢ ㄧˋ ㄖˋ)
to usurp political power; to usurp the throne

移挪(ㄧ ㄋㄨㄛˊ)
to use money for a purpose not originally intended

移靈(ㄧ ㄌㄧㄥˊ)
to move a corpse to a funeral parlor

移國(ㄧ ㄍㄨㄛˊ)
to usurp the political power of a nation; to usurp the throne

移晷(ㄧ ㄍㄨㄟˇ)
the moving of shadows under the sun–(figuratively) the passage of time

移宮換羽(ㄧ ㄍㄨㄥ ㄏㄨㄢˋ ㄩˇ)
the variation of a musical composition

移開(ㄧ ㄎㄞ)
to move away: 他們把桌子移開了。They moved the table away.

移花接木(ㄧ ㄏㄨㄚ ㄐㄧㄝ ㄇㄨˋ)
① to cheat by sleight of hand ② to graft; to graft one twig on another

移禍(ㄧ ㄏㄨㄛˋ)
to shift trouble or calamity to another; to shirk one's responsibility, etc. by incriminating another person

移交(ㄧ ㄐㄧㄠ)
to turn over; to hand over (responsibility, public property, etc.) to another person or organization: 這些儀器已經移交給學校了。These instruments have been turned over to the school.

移居(ㄧ ㄐㄩ)
to move one's place of dwelling; to move to another town, country, etc. for settlement: 他們已移居鄉下。They moved to the country.

移情別戀(ㄧ ㄑㄧㄥˊ ㄅㄧㄝˊ ㄌㄧㄢˋ)
to shift one's love to another person; to have a new sweetheart

移徙(ㄧ ㄒㄧˇ)
to move and settle (people) in an undeveloped place

移孝作忠(ㄧ ㄒㄧㄠˋ ㄗㄨㄛˋ ㄓㄨㄥ)
to replace filial piety with loyalty to the country

移植(ㄧ ㄓˊ)
① to transplant: 我們把花移植到花園裡。We transplanted the flowers to the garden. ② grafting; transplanting

移殖(ㄧ ㄓˊ)
to move people for coloniza-

-tion

移住(ㄧ ㄓㄨˋ)
to change one's place of dwelling; to move and settle down in another land

移轉(ㄧ ㄓㄨㄢˇ)
to transfer (certain rights, holdings, etc.)

移充(ㄧ ㄔㄨㄥ)
to use money or something for a purpose not originally intended

移時(ㄧ ㄕˊ)
a little while; a brief period of time

移山倒海(ㄧ ㄕㄢ ㄉㄠˇ ㄏㄞˇ)
very capable; very resourceful

移審(ㄧ ㄕㄣˇ)
to transfer a legal case to an appellate court

移書(ㄧ ㄕㄨ)
to write a letter to someone

移樽就教(ㄧ ㄗㄨㄣ ㄐㄧㄡˋ ㄐㄧㄠˋ)
① to go to another's place in order to seek his advice ② accommodating

移液管(ㄧ ㄧㄝˋ ㄍㄨㄢˇ)
a pipette

移玉(ㄧ ㄩˋ)
(a polite expression in a letter of invitation) May I request your company at…?

七畫

【稍】 3999
ㄕㄠ shāu shǎo
1. slightly; a little; slight: 你不要稍待片刻嗎? Won't you stay a little while?
2. somewhat; rather: 天氣稍熱。The weather is rather hot.
3. gradually

稍淡(ㄕㄠ ㄉㄢˋ)
(said of a liquid) a little too thin; (said of taste) a little too weak; (said of a color) a little too pale

稍濃(ㄕㄠ ㄋㄨㄥˊ)
(said of a color or liquid) a little too thick; (said of smell or taste) rather strong

稍可(ㄕㄠ ㄎㄜˇ)
slightly better; moderately successful

稍可即止(ㄕㄠ ㄎㄜˇ ㄐㄧˊ ㄓˇ)

to stop after being moderately successful—don't be too ambitious for...

稍後 (ㄕㄠ ㄏㄡˋ)
shortly afterward; soon afterward: 我稍後寫了一封信給他。 I wrote him a letter soon afterward.

稍候 (ㄕㄠ ㄏㄡˋ)
to wait for a while (or moment) 亦作「稍等」: 請稍候一會兒。 Please wait a moment.

稍緩 (ㄕㄠ ㄏㄨㄢˇ)
a little slower; not so fast; to put off for a while

稍加 (ㄕㄠ ㄐㄧㄚ)
slightly more; to make some addition

稍佳 (ㄕㄠ ㄐㄧㄚ)
a little better

稍覺 (ㄕㄠ ㄐㄩㄝˊ)
to feel slightly

稍息 (ㄕㄠ ㄒㄧ)
(military) to stand at ease; 稍息! (a word of command) At ease!

稍暇 (ㄕㄠ ㄒㄧㄚˊ)
to have a little leisure

稍懈 (ㄕㄠ ㄒㄧㄝˋ)
①to relax a little ②to slow down slightly

稍嫌 (ㄕㄠ ㄒㄧㄢˊ)
slightly more or less than the ideal state or amount

稍稍 (ㄕㄠ ㄕㄠ)
①briefly ②gradually ③just a little

稍縱即逝 (ㄕㄠ ㄗㄨㄥˋ ㄐㄧˊ ㄕˋ)
transient; fleeting: 莫錯失了這稍縱即逝的機會。 Don't miss this fleeting opportunity.

稍次 (ㄕㄠ ㄘˋ)
slightly inferior in quality

稍異 (ㄕㄠ ㄧˋ)
slightly different; somewhat different

稍有更動 (ㄕㄠ ㄧㄡˇ ㄍㄥ ㄉㄨㄥˋ)
some slight changes

稍微 (ㄕㄠ ㄨㄟˊ) or 稍許 (ㄕㄠ ㄒㄩˇ)
slightly; a little; a bit; rather: 明天會稍微有點冷。 It will be rather chilly tomorrow.

【稀】 4000
ㄒㄧ shi xī
thin (liquids, etc.); watery;

diluted: 這酒精加水變稀了。 The alcohol is diluted with water.

2. rare; scarce; uncommon: 物以稀為貴。 A thing is valued if it is rare.
3. scattered; sparse
4. open; loose (as texture)

稀薄 (ㄒㄧ ㄅㄛˊ)
①(said of air) thin or rare: 高地空氣稀薄。 The air is thin on heights. ②(said of liquids) diluted

稀飯 (ㄒㄧ ㄈㄢˋ)
congee; gruel; porridge

稀爛 (ㄒㄧ ㄌㄢˋ)
①completely mashed; like paste; pulpy ②crumbled; smashed to pieces

稀硫酸 (ㄒㄧ ㄌㄧㄡˊ ㄙㄨㄢˋ)
diluted sulphuric acid

稀亂八糟 (ㄒㄧ ㄌㄨㄢˋ ㄅㄚ ㄗㄠ)
in total disorder; in a pandemonium

稀客 (ㄒㄧ ㄎㄜˋ)
a guest who seldom comes to visit; a visitor who hasn't seen the host for a long time

稀罕 (ㄒㄧ ㄏㄢˇ)
①rare; rarity; scarce: 在那個國家，雪是稀罕的。 Snow is a rarity in that country. ②to care: 誰稀罕？ Who cares?

稀奇 (ㄒㄧ ㄑㄧˊ)
①strange; rare: 他的拜訪實屬稀奇。 His visits are rather rare. ②to care

稀奇古怪 (ㄒㄧ ㄑㄧˊ ㄍㄨˇ ㄍㄨㄞˋ)
strange; bizarre; odd

稀世 (ㄒㄧ ㄕˋ)
extremely rare or precious

稀釋 (ㄒㄧ ㄕˋ)
to dilute (liquids)

稀少 (ㄒㄧ ㄕㄠˇ)
few; little; scarce; rare; sparse: 聽眾稀少。 The audience was few.

稀疏 (ㄒㄧ ㄕㄨ)
scattered or dispersed; thin; sparse

稀爛 (ㄒㄧ ㄌㄢˋ)
extremely rotten; very bad

稀鬆 (ㄒㄧ ㄙㄨㄥ)
①indifferent; not interested: 他把那話兒看得稀鬆。 He is indifferent to the work. ②not important; common; triv-

ial ③loose

稀有 (ㄒㄧ ㄧㄡˇ)
rare; one in a million: 她是世上稀有的美女。 She is a rare beauty.

稀鹽酸 (ㄒㄧ ㄧㄢˊ ㄙㄨㄢˋ)
diluted hydrochloric acid

【稅】 4001
ㄕㄨㄟˋ shuey shuì

1. taxes; duties on commodities: 他們被課以重稅。 They are heavily taxed.
2. (now rarely) to lay; to place
3. (now rarely) to present another with

稅票 (ㄕㄨㄟˋ ㄆㄧㄠˋ)
receipts for taxes paid

稅目 (ㄕㄨㄟˋ ㄇㄨˋ)
a tax designation

稅法 (ㄕㄨㄟˋ ㄈㄚˇ)
tax law

稅單 (ㄕㄨㄟˋ ㄉㄢ)
①a transit pass for imports; a tax invoice ②a tax form

稅吏 (ㄕㄨㄟˋ ㄌㄧˋ)
tax collectors; tax officials 亦作「稅務員」

稅率 (ㄕㄨㄟˋ ㄌㄩˋ)
tax rates; duty rates

稅關 (ㄕㄨㄟˋ ㄍㄨㄢ)
the customhouse; the Customs

稅款 (ㄕㄨㄟˋ ㄎㄨㄢˇ)
tax money

稅金 (ㄕㄨㄟˋ ㄐㄧㄣ)
tax money; tax dues

稅捐 (ㄕㄨㄟˋ ㄐㄩㄢ)
taxes and surtaxes

稅捐稽徵處 (ㄕㄨㄟˋ ㄐㄩㄢ ㄐㄧ ㄓㄥ ㄔㄨˋ)
a tax collection office

稅契 (ㄕㄨㄟˋ ㄑㄧˋ)
receipts issued by a tax office for taxes paid on deeds to newly purchased real estate

稅制 (ㄕㄨㄟˋ ㄓˋ)
the tax system: 累進稅制 progressive taxation

稅收 (ㄕㄨㄟˋ ㄕㄡ)
tax revenue

稅則 (ㄕㄨㄟˋ ㄗㄜˊ)
a customs tariff; a customs order; a customs table

稅額 (ㄕㄨㄟˋ ㄜˊ)
an amount of tax

〔禾 部〕

税務(ㄕㄨㄟˋ ㄨˋ)
tax administration; affairs pertaining to taxation

税務機關(ㄕㄨㄟˋ ㄨˋ ㄐㄧ ㄍㄨㄢ)
tax offices

税務員(ㄕㄨㄟˋ ㄨˋ ㄩㄢˊ)or 税務人員(ㄕㄨㄟˋ ㄨˋ ㄖㄣˊ ㄩㄢˊ)
revenue officers; tax collectors; tax officials 参看「税吏」

【稊】 4002
ㄊㄧˊ tyi tí
darnels; tares

【稈】 4003
ㄍㄢˇ gaan gǎn
the stalk of grain; straw: 高粱稈 a sorghum stalk 麥稈床 a bed of straw

稈子(ㄍㄢˇ ˙ㄗ)
the stalk of a rice plant; straw

【稂】 4004
ㄌㄤˊ lang láng
weeds or grass which are particularly harmful to the growth of rice seedlings; wolf's-tail grass

稂莠(ㄌㄤˊ ㄧㄡˇ)
weeds and grass

【程】 4005
ㄔㄥˊ cherng chéng
1. a form; a pattern
2. degree; extent
3. a schedule; an agenda; order
4. a course
5. to measure; to assess
6. a journey; a road
7. distance
8. a general name of measurements of all kinds
9. a Chinese family name

程墨(ㄔㄥˊ ㄇㄛˋ)
published standard test papers of civil service examination in former times

程門立雪(ㄔㄥˊ ㄇㄣˊ ㄌㄧˋ ㄒㄩㄝˇ)
(said of pupils) to serve and learn from the master with reverence—a reference to Yu Tso (游酢) and Yang Shih (楊時), who waited at the gate of Cheng Yi (程頤) in snow until it was one foot deep

程邈(ㄔㄥˊ ㄇㄧㄠˇ)
Cheng Miao, a jailer-turned prisoner in the Chin Dynasty, who created the "clerical style" (隸書) of Chinese calligraphy

程度(ㄔㄥˊ ㄉㄨˋ)
①degree; extent; a stage, a state or condition: 學生們表現出不同程度的技巧。The students show various degrees of skill. ②standard; required qualifications or attainments ③general achievement in academic studies

程顥(ㄔㄥˊ ㄏㄠˋ)
Cheng Hao (1032—1085), a famous scholar in the Sung Dynasty

程序(ㄔㄥˊ ㄒㄩˋ)
procedures; processes: 他熟悉出口程序。He is familiar with export procedure.

程朱(ㄔㄥˊ ㄓㄨ)
Cheng Hao (程顥), Cheng Yi (程頤) and Chu Hsi (朱熹), all famous scholars of the Sung Dynasty

程式(ㄔㄥˊ ㄕˋ)
①standard forms or patterns; standard procedures ②(computers) a program

程式設計(ㄔㄥˊ ㄕˋ ㄕㄜˋ ㄐㄧˋ)
programing

程子(ㄔㄥˊ ˙ㄗ)
the Cheng brothers—Cheng Hao (程顥) and Cheng Yi (程頤)—of the Sung Dynasty

程儀(ㄔㄥˊ ㄧˊ)
presents or gifts for a friend embarking on a journey

程頤(ㄔㄥˊ ㄧˊ)
Cheng Yi (1033-1107), a famous scholar of the Sung Dynasty 亦作「伊川先生」

【稌】 4006
ㄊㄨˊ twu tú
(glutinous) rice

八畫

【稟】 4007
ㄅㄧㄥˇ biing bǐng
1. to report to a superior or one's seniors; to petition; to appeal
2. to receive commands; at the behest of
3. one's natural endowments or gifts

稟白(ㄅㄧㄥˇ ㄅㄞˊ)or 稟報(ㄅㄧㄥˇ ㄅㄠˋ)
to report to a superior 参看「稟告」

稟明(ㄅㄧㄥˇ ㄇㄧㄥˊ)
to explain to a superior or elder; to clarify a matter to a superior or elder

稟命(ㄅㄧㄥˇ ㄇㄧㄥˋ)
at the behest of; by order of

稟賦(ㄅㄧㄥˇ ㄈㄨˋ)
a natural endowment, gift or disposition: 他稟賦聰明。He is gifted with keen intelligence.

稟覆(ㄅㄧㄥˇ ㄈㄨˋ)
to make a (verbal or written) reply to a superior

稟告(ㄅㄧㄥˇ ㄍㄠˋ)
to report (to one's superior)

稟性(ㄅㄧㄥˇ ㄒㄧㄥˋ)
a natural disposition or temperament: 此人稟性純厚。The man is simple and honest by nature.

稟陳(ㄅㄧㄥˇ ㄔㄣˊ)
to report to a superior 参看「稟告」

稟承(ㄅㄧㄥˇ ㄔㄥˊ)
(to do something) according to orders of a superior or higher office; to take (orders); to receive (commands): 他稟承其父的旨意。He acted on the orders of his father.

稟受(ㄅㄧㄥˇ ㄕㄡˋ)
①to endure ②nature

【稔】 4008
ㄖㄣˇ reen rěn
1. the ripening of paddy or rice; a harvest
2. a year
3. used to; often
4. to accumulate; to hoard
5. to be familiar with somebody

稔亂(ㄖㄣˇ ㄌㄨㄢˋ)
the turmoil that has been brewed for a long time

稔知(ㄖㄣˇ ㄓ)
to know well; familiar

稔熟(ㄖㄣˇ ㄕㄨˊ)
(said of grain) ripe

稔色(ㄖㄣˇ ㄙㄜˋ)
①beauty or charms ②to have a weakness for women

【稚】 4009
(俗)ㄓˋ jyh zhì
young and tender; small; delicate; immature; childish

稚嫩(ㄓ ㄋㄣˋ)
①tender and delicate ②
young and tender

稚女(ㄓ ㄋㄩˇ)
young girls

稚齡(ㄓ ㄌㄧㄥˊ)
tender age (or years)

稚氣(ㄓ ㄑㄧˋ)
innocence of a child; childishness

稚氣(ㄓ ㄑㄧˋ)
young people; children; tod-
dlers

稚(ㄓ ㄇㄛˋ)
tender and delicate

稚子(ㄓ ˙ㄗ)
①young children ②bamboo
shoots

【稜】 4010
ㄌㄥˊ leng léng
1. a corner; an angle; an edge
2. a square piece of wood
3. an awe-inspiring air

稜角(ㄌㄥˊ ㄐㄧㄠˇ)
①chilly or frosty ②awe-
inspiring

稜角(ㄌㄥˊ ㄐㄧㄠˇ)
①an angle; a corner ②
pointed; pointedness: 性拆可
以把你的稜角磨掉。 Frustra-
tions could eliminate your
pointedness.

稜鏡(ㄌㄥˊ ㄐㄧㄥˋ)
a prism: 三稜鏡 a triangular
prism

稜晰(ㄌㄥˊ ㄌㄥˊ)or稜角睜睜(ㄌㄥˊ ㄌㄥˊ
ㄓㄥ ㄓㄥ)
①rash; rude ②very cold

稜柱體(ㄌㄥˊ ㄓㄨˋ ㄊㄧˇ)
(mathematics) a prism

稜錐體(ㄌㄥˊ ㄓㄨㄟ ㄊㄧˇ)
a pyramid

稜子(ㄌㄥˊ ·ㄗ)or稜兒(ㄌㄥˊ ㄦ)
an angle; a right angle; a
corner

【稗】 4011
ㄅㄞˋ bay bài
1. barnyard grass
2. small; little
3. novels, legends, etc.

稗販(ㄅㄞˋ ㄈㄢˋ)
peddlers or hawkers

稗官(ㄅㄞˋ ㄍㄨㄢ)
officials of low ranks

稗官野史(ㄅㄞˋ ㄍㄨㄢ ㄧㄝˇ ㄕˇ)
unofficial historical writings; historical novels

稗史(ㄅㄞˋ ㄕˇ)
unofficial historical writings

稗說(ㄅㄞˋ ㄕㄨㄛ)
novels; stories

稗子(ㄅㄞˋ ·ㄗ)
barnyard grass

【稠】 4012
ㄔㄡˊ chour chóu
1. dense; closely crowded
together
2. (said of liquids) thick; viscous
3. a Chinese family name

稠密(ㄔㄡˊ ㄇㄧˋ)
crowded; dense: 這是個人煙稠
密的城市。 This is a thickly
populated city.

稠疊(ㄔㄡˊ ㄉㄧㄝˊ)
overlapping

稠濁(ㄔㄡˊ ㄓㄨㄛˊ)
wordy and confused

稠人廣衆(ㄔㄡˊ ㄖㄣˊ ㄍㄨㄤˇ ㄓㄨㄥˋ)
a large audience; a sea of
people

稠雲(ㄔㄡˊ ㄩㄣˊ)
dense clouds

【稞】 4013
ㄎㄜ ke kē
wheat or barley

九畫

【種】 4014
1. ㄓㄨㄥˇ joong
zhǒng
1. seeds of grain
2. races (of human beings)
3. descendants; posterity
4. a species; a genus; a kind or
sort: 這是柳橙的一種。 This is
a species of orange.
5. guts; grit: 他沒種做這件事。
He has no guts for it.

種別(ㄓㄨㄥˇ ㄅㄧㄝˊ)
classification

種皮(ㄓㄨㄥˇ ㄆㄧˊ)
a seed coat

種馬(ㄓㄨㄥˇ ㄇㄚˇ)
a studhorse; a stallion

種類(ㄓㄨㄥˇ ㄌㄟˋ)
a sort; a kind; a variety; a
class: 他有不同種類的玩具。 He
has toys of different kinds.

種切(ㄓㄨㄥˇ ㄑㄧㄝ)
and so on; etc.

種種(ㄓㄨㄥˇ ㄓㄨㄥˇ)
①various kinds ②short-

cropped hair ③simple and
sincere (as rural people)

種畜(ㄓㄨㄥˇ ㄒㄩˋ)
domestic animals raised for
a breeding purpose

種人(ㄓㄨㄥˇ ㄖㄣˊ)
people of the same race

種子(ㄓㄨㄥˇ ㄗˇ)
a seed

種子隊(ㄓㄨㄥˇ ㄗˇ ㄉㄨㄟˋ)
(sports meetings) a seed
team

種族(ㄓㄨㄥˇ ㄗㄨˊ)
(said of people) a race, or
tribe

種族革命(ㄓㄨㄥˇ ㄗㄨˊ ㄍㄜˊ ㄇㄧㄥˋ)
racial revolution

種族隔離(ㄓㄨㄥˇ ㄗㄨˊ ㄍㄜˊ ㄌㄧˊ)
racial segregation; apartheid
(in South Africa)

種族歧視(ㄓㄨㄥˇ ㄗㄨˊ ㄑㄧˊ ㄕˋ)
racial discrimination

種原論(ㄓㄨㄥˇ ㄩㄢˊ ㄌㄨㄣˋ)
Origin of Species, by
Charles R. Darwin

【種】 4014
2. ㄓㄨㄥˋ jonq
zhòng
1. to plant; to sow; to cultivate: 農夫在田裏種小麥。 The
farmer sowed the field with
wheat.
2. to vaccinate

種麥得麥(ㄓㄨㄥˋ ㄇㄞˋ ㄉㄜˊ ㄇㄞˋ)
As a man sows, so shall he
reap. 或A man reaps what
he sows.

種德(ㄓㄨㄥˋ ㄉㄜˊ)
to accumulate virtuous
deeds; to cultivate virtues

種痘(ㄓㄨㄥˋ ㄉㄡˋ)or種牛痘(ㄓㄨㄥˋ
ㄋㄧㄡˊ ㄉㄡˋ)
to vaccinate; vaccination
(against smallpox): 這小孩已
經種痘了。 The child has been
vaccinated.

種地(ㄓㄨㄥˋ ㄉㄧˋ)
to farm; to cultivate the
land

種田(ㄓㄨㄥˋ ㄊㄧㄢˊ)
to farm; to till the land

種田的(ㄓㄨㄥˋ ㄊㄧㄢˊ ·ㄉㄜ)
a farmer

種瓜得瓜，種豆得豆(ㄓㄨㄥˋ ㄍㄨㄚ
ㄉㄜˊ ㄍㄨㄚ，ㄓㄨㄥˋ ㄉㄡˋ ㄉㄜˊ ㄉㄡˋ)
One reaps what he sows. 或
You must reap what you

〔禾
部〕

【禾 部】

have sown.

種花 (ㄓㄨㄥ ㄏㄨㄚ)
to raise, grow or cultivate flowers

種禍 (ㄓㄨㄥ ㄏㄨㄛˋ)
to sow the seeds of calamity or misfortune

種植 (ㄓㄨㄥ ㄓˊ)
to plant; to raise or grow (plants); to cultivate

種莊稼 (ㄓㄨㄥ ㄓㄨㄤ ·ㄐㄧㄚ)
to till the land; to be a farmer

種菜 (ㄓㄨㄥ ㄘㄞˋ)
to grow vegetables

種因 (ㄓㄨㄥ ㄧㄣ)
to do something which eventually becomes the cause of some development (usually undesirable development) in the future

【稱】 4015 1. ㄔㄥ cheng
chēng

1. to weigh; to measure weight
2. to claim; to report; to declare
3. to call; to name; a name; an appellation
4. to offer as an excuse (as illness)
5. to say; to tell; to state
6. to speak laudatory words; to praise
7. to take up (arms, etc.)
8. a Chinese family name

稱霸 (ㄔㄥ ㄅㄚˋ)
to become the most powerful nation in the world or part of the world; to hold an undisputed position of strength; to occupy the leading position (in certain field of sports, etc.)

稱便 (ㄔㄥ ㄅㄧㄢˋ)
(said of new facilities or better services) hailed as a great service to the public; to commend something

稱兵 (ㄔㄥ ㄅㄧㄥ)
to take up arms; to be on the warpath; to commence hostilities with

稱病 (ㄔㄥ ㄅㄧㄥˋ)
to offer illness as an excuse; to malinger

稱道 (ㄔㄥ ㄉㄠˋ)
to praise or acclaim

稱孤道寡 (ㄔㄥ ㄍㄨ ㄉㄠˋ ㄍㄨㄚˇ)
to declare or call oneself king or emperor; to claim imperial authority

稱快 (ㄔㄥ ㄎㄨㄞˋ)
to express one's gratification; to feel jubilant

稱號 (ㄔㄥ ㄏㄠˋ)
an appellation; a title; a designation: 他贏得了多產作家的稱號。He has won the title of prolific writer.

稱呼 (ㄔㄥ ㄏㄨ)
a name by which one addresses another; to address; to name: 你怎麼稱呼市長? How do you address the mayor?

稱慶 (ㄔㄥ ㄑㄧㄥˋ)
to congratulate; to express joy

稱謝 (ㄔㄥ ㄒㄧㄝˋ)
to express thanks: 他對她的幫助稱謝不止。He thanked her again and again for her help.

稱羨不置 (ㄔㄥ ㄒㄧㄢˋ ㄅㄨˋ ㄓˋ)
to envy to no end; to admire greatly

稱羨不已 (ㄔㄥ ㄒㄧㄢˋ ㄅㄨˋ ㄧˇ)
to express profuse admiration

稱許 (ㄔㄥ ㄒㄩˇ)
to approve and praise; approval and praise

稱兄道弟 (ㄔㄥ ㄒㄩㄥ ㄉㄠˋ ㄉㄧˋ)
on first-name terms; very intimate

稱雄 (ㄔㄥ ㄒㄩㄥˊ)
to claim leadership; to occupy a dominating position; to hold sway over

稱制 (ㄔㄥ ㄓˋ)
(said of an empress dowager) to act as regent; to assume regency

稱臣 (ㄔㄥ ㄔㄣˊ)
(literally) to declare oneself a vassal—to be subjugated; to concede defeat; to submit to the victor

稱述 (ㄔㄥ ㄕㄨˋ)
to praise or laud someone's deeds

稱說 (ㄔㄥ ㄕㄨㄛ)
to narrate; to state; to tell

稱字 (ㄔㄥ ㄗˋ)
to address another person by his style as a token of respect

稱讚 (ㄔㄥ ㄗㄢˋ)
to praise; to acclaim: 老師讚他的勤勞。The teacher praised him for his diligence.

稱頌 (ㄔㄥ ㄙㄨㄥˋ)
to praise; to extol: 大多數人喜歡被稱頌。Most people like to receive praises.

稱一稱 (ㄔㄥ ·ㄧ ·ㄔㄥ)
to weigh (something)

稱引 (ㄔㄥ ㄧㄣˇ)
to adduce; to cite as an example or precedent

稱揚 (ㄔㄥ ㄧㄤˊ)
to praise and extol

稱為 (ㄔㄥ ㄨㄟˊ)
to call; to designate

稱謂 (ㄔㄥ ㄨㄟˋ)
name or appellation of a person or thing

稱譽 (ㄔㄥ ㄩˋ)
to praise; to acclaim; to extol

【稱】 4015 2. ㄔㄥˋ chenq
chèng

1. a steelyard; a weighing machine
2. fit; proper; suitable; well-matched
3. symmetrical; to be equal to; corresponding to

稱不離砣 (ㄔㄥˋ ㄅㄨˋ ㄌㄧˊ ㄊㄨㄛˊ)
(literally) The steelyard never goes without the weight.—inseparable 亦作「秤不離鉈」

稱體裁衣 (ㄔㄥˋ ㄊㄧˇ ㄘㄞˊ ㄧ)
exactly matching; perfectly suitable

稱職 (ㄔㄥˋ ㄓˊ)
well qualified; competent; equal to the job one is doing: 他是一位稱職的教師。He is a competent teacher.

稱旨 (ㄔㄥˋ ㄓˇ)
to be in full accordance with the ideas of the emperor

稱身 (ㄔㄥˋ ㄕㄣ)
(said of dresses) to fit perfectly: 這件夾克你穿了挺稱身的。This jacket fits you perfectly.

【稱】 4015
ㄔ ㄣ chenn chèn
fit; suitable; in accordance with

稱錢(ㄔㄥ ㄑㄧㄢ)
rich

稱心(ㄔㄥ ㄒㄧㄣ)
to find something satisfactory; to have something as one's wish 亦作「愜心」；這部車實在很稱心。This car is quite satisfactory—just the thing I want.

稱心如意(ㄔㄥ ㄒㄧㄣ ㄖㄨ ㄧˋ)
very gratifying and satisfactory; happy and contented

稱意(ㄔㄥ ㄧˋ)
agreeable; gratifying; satisfactory

稱願(ㄔㄥ ㄩㄢˋ)
just as one wishes

【稽】 4016
ㄐㄧㄝ jie jiē
the stalk of corn, hemp, etc.

稭稈(ㄐㄧㄝ ㄍㄢˇ)
straw

【稨】 4017
ㄅㄧㄢˇ bean biǎn
a lentil

十畫

【穀】 4018
ㄍㄨˇ guu gǔ
1. grain; corn; cereals
2. lucky; happy; favorable; good
3. to live; while alive

穀道(ㄍㄨˇ ㄉㄠˋ)
① the rectum, or alimentary canal ② to stop eating grain as a means to attain immortality

穀旦(ㄍㄨˇ ㄉㄢˋ)
an auspicious (lucky) day; a good day

穀類(ㄍㄨˇ ㄌㄟˋ)
grain and corn; cereals

穀梁傳(ㄍㄨˇ ㄌㄧㄤˊ ㄓㄨㄢˋ)
one of the three expansions of Confucius' *Spring and Autumn Annals*

穀賤傷農(ㄍㄨˇ ㄐㄧㄢˋ ㄕㄤ ㄋㄨㄥˊ)
Low grain price hurts the farmer.—a theory advanced by Chao Tso (晁錯) of the Han Dynasty

穀場(ㄍㄨˇ ㄔㄤˇ)or(ㄍㄨˇ ㄔㄤˊ)
a yard for sunning or drying grain, corn, etc.

穀日(ㄍㄨˇ ㄖˋ)
the eighth day of the first month in the lunar calendar

穀子(ㄍㄨˇ ˙ㄗ)
millet 亦作「粟」or「小米」

穀倉(ㄍㄨˇ ㄘㄤ)
a barn for storing grain; a granary

穀物(ㄍㄨˇ ㄨˋ)
cereals; grain

穀雨(ㄍㄨˇ ㄩˇ)
Grain rains—one of the 24 climatic transitions in a lunar year, which falls on April 20 or 21

【稿】 4019
(稾)ㄍㄠˇ gao gǎo
1. a manuscript; a sketch; a rough draft or copy: 這是演說的草稿。This is a draft for a speech.
2. a pattern or copy book for drawing
3. straw; a stalk of grain

稿本(ㄍㄠˇ ㄅㄣˇ)
① a manuscript or draft of a literary work ② a pattern or copy book for drawing

稿費(ㄍㄠˇ ㄈㄟˋ)
fees paid to the contributor of a published article; payment to a writer on a piecework basis; contribution fees

稿底(ㄍㄠˇ ㄉㄧˇ)
a rough draft of a piece of writing

稿件(ㄍㄠˇ ㄐㄧㄢˋ)
① contribution to a publication; writings ② manuscripts; a sketch; a rough draft

稿紙(ㄍㄠˇ ㄓˇ)
manuscript or draft paper

稿酬(ㄍㄠˇ ㄔㄡˊ)
fees paid to a writer on a piecework basis

稿子(ㄍㄠˇ ˙ㄗ)or 稿兒(ㄍㄠˇㄦ)
① manuscripts; drafts: 他正在起個稿子。He is making a draft. ② plans in one's mind; a plan formulated beforehand; a plan or precedent

【稷】 4020
ㄐㄧˋ jih jì
paniceled millet

【稼】 4021
ㄐㄧㄚˋ jiah jià
1. to farm, plant, sow or cultivate
2. grain; crops

稼穡(ㄐㄧㄚˋ ㄙㄜˋ)
planting and harvesting of grain; farming; agricultural operations

稼穡艱難(ㄐㄧㄚˋ ㄙㄜˋ ㄐㄧㄢ ㄋㄢˊ)
the toil and hardship of a farmer's life

【稻】 4022
ㄉㄠˋ daw dào
paddy or rice

稻米(ㄉㄠˋ ㄇㄧˇ)
rice or paddy: 中國人以稻米為主食。The Chinese live on rice.

稻飯(ㄉㄠˋ ㄈㄢˋ)
cooked rice

稻田(ㄉㄠˋ ㄊㄧㄢˊ)
a paddy field; a rice field

稻穀(ㄉㄠˋ ㄍㄨˇ)
paddy

稻場(ㄉㄠˋ ㄔㄤˇ)or(ㄉㄠˋ ㄔㄤˊ)
a yard for sunning or drying unhulled rice

稻熱病(ㄉㄠˋ ㄖˋ ㄅㄧㄥˋ)
rice blast

稻子(ㄉㄠˋ ˙ㄗ)
unhulled rice

稻草(ㄉㄠˋ ㄘㄠˇ)
rice straw

稻草堆(ㄉㄠˋ ㄘㄠˇ ㄉㄨㄟ)
a straw stack

稻草人(ㄉㄠˋ ㄘㄠˇ ㄖㄣˊ)
a scarecrow; a jack of straw

稻草褥(ㄉㄠˋ ㄘㄠˇ ㄖㄨˋ)
a straw mattress

稻穗(ㄉㄠˋ ㄙㄨㄟˋ)
the ear or spike of the rice plant

稻孫(ㄉㄠˋ ㄙㄨㄣ)
the aftergrowth of rice plants

稻秧(ㄉㄠˋ ㄧㄤ)
rice seedlings; rice shoots

【稽】 4023
1. ㄐㄧ ji jī
1. to investigate; to examine; to inspect; to verify: 有案可稽的。It can be verified. 或 It's verifiable.

(禾部)

〔禾部〕

2. to stay; to delay or procrastinate

3. a Chinese family name

稽留(ㄐㄧㄌㄧㄡˊ)
①to stay; to stay for a long time ②another name of the prison in the Chou Dynasty

稽留熱(ㄐㄧㄌㄧㄡˊㄖㄜˋ)
remittent fever

稽古(ㄐㄧㄍㄨˇ)
to examine and study ancient ways, matters, etc.

稽考(ㄐㄧㄎㄠˇ)
to examine; to verify: 無引稽考. It cannot be verified.

稽核(ㄐㄧㄏㄜˊ)
to examine and audit; to inspect and audit: 王先生在稽核帳目, Mr. Wang was auditing the accounts.

稽數(ㄐㄧㄕㄨˋ)
to check; to investigate or verify

稽徵處(ㄐㄧㄓㄥㄔㄨˋ)
an office for auditing (accounts) and levying (taxes)

稽遲(ㄐㄧㄔˊ) or 稽滯(ㄐㄧㄓˋ)
to be delayed or detained; to procrastinate

稽查(ㄐㄧㄔㄚˊ) or 稽察(ㄐㄧㄔㄚˊ)
to examine and investigate

稽程(ㄐㄧㄔㄥˊ)
①the delay in presenting documents, formal reports, etc. ②to delay journey

稽疑(ㄐㄧㄧˊ)
to solve doubt by means of divination; to examine by divination

稽延(ㄐㄧㄧㄢˊ)
to delay; to procrastinate

【稽】 4023
②. ㄑㄧˇ chii qǐ
to kowtow; to bow to the ground

稽首(ㄑㄧˇㄕㄡˇ)
to kowtow—an expression of great respect

稽顙(ㄑㄧˇㄙㄤˇ)
to kowtow to those who attend the funeral service of one's parent with one's forehead touching the ground

【稹】 4024
ㄓㄣˋ jeen zhěn
1. circumspect

2. (said of roots) entwined

十一畫

【穈】 4025
ㄇㄣˊ men mén
large-grained millet with red seedlings

【穌】 4026
ㄙㄨ su sú
1. to mow grass
2. to revive; to come to; to rise again

【穎】 4027
(穎) ㄧㄥˇ yiing yǐng
1. outstanding; remarkable; talented; distinguished
2. a sharp point of an awl
3. the point of a writing brush
4. the ears of grain hanging down with their own weight

穎脫(ㄧㄥˇㄊㄨㄛ)
to distinguish oneself in performance

穎果(ㄧㄥˇㄍㄨㄛˇ)
a caryopsis

穎花(ㄧㄥˇㄏㄨㄚ)
Glumales, a glume flower

穎慧(ㄧㄥˇㄏㄨㄟˋ)
clever; bright; intelligent

穎秀(ㄧㄥˇㄒㄧㄡˋ)
outstandingly talented

穎哲(ㄧㄥˇㄓㄜˊ)
clever and wise

穎悟(ㄧㄥˇㄨˋ)
very bright; unusually intelligent

【穆】 4028
ㄇㄨˋ muh mù
1. peaceful; serene
2. respectful; reverent
3. profound
4. majestic; solemn
5. the right side of an ancestral shrine
6. a Chinese family name

穆卜(ㄇㄨˋㄅㄨˇ)
to consult the oracle reverently

穆民(ㄇㄨˋㄇㄧㄣˊ)
a name which the Mohammedans call themselves

穆穆(ㄇㄨˋㄇㄨˋ)
①profound ②respectable; majestic; very admirable

穆罕默德(ㄇㄨˋㄏㄢˇㄇㄛˋㄉㄜˊ)
Mohammed (c.570-632), the founder of Mohammedanism

穆清(ㄇㄨˋㄑㄧㄥ)
①the Heaven ②peaceful and orderly (world, etc.)

穆然(ㄇㄨˋㄖㄢˊ)
①peaceful and respectful ②meditative

【積】 4029
ㄐㄧ ji jī
1. to accumulate; to store up; to amass
2. long (time); old; deep-rooted; longstanding
3. (mathematics) product

積弊(ㄐㄧㄅㄧˋ)
deep-rooted evils or corrupt ways

積弊難返(ㄐㄧㄅㄧˋㄋㄢˊㄈㄢˇ)
It's very difficult to uproot deep-entrenched evils or shortcomings.

積水(ㄐㄧㄕㄨㄟˇ)
ice which exists for a long time

積木(ㄐㄧㄇㄨˋ)
building blocks, or wooden blocks (a kind of children's toy)

積分(ㄐㄧㄈㄣ)
①accumulated points ②integral calculus

積分學(ㄐㄧㄈㄣㄒㄩㄝˊ)
(mathematics) integral calculus

積福(ㄐㄧㄈㄨˊ)
to accumulate or store up happiness by charitable deeds

積德(ㄐㄧㄉㄜˊ)
to make it a point to do good deeds whenever possible

積年累月(ㄐㄧㄋㄧㄢˊㄌㄟˇㄩㄝˋ)
for years and months—a long time

積累(ㄐㄧㄌㄟˇ)
to accumulate: 他已積累了豐富的經驗. He has accumulated a wealth of experience

積勞成疾(ㄐㄧㄌㄠˊㄔㄥˊㄐㄧˊ)
to fall sick from persistent overwork

積穀防饑(ㄐㄧㄍㄨˇㄈㄤˊㄐㄧ)
to store up food in anticipation of famine; to get prepared for a rainy day

積毀銷骨(ㄐㄧㄏㄨㄟˇㄒㄧㄠㄍㄨˇ)
Libels can destroy strong

family ties.

積極(ㄐㄧ ㄐㄧˊ)
active(ly); positive(ly); persistent(ly): 他們採取了積極的措施。 They adopted active measures.

積極分子(ㄐㄧ ㄐㄧˊ ㄈㄣ ㄗˇ)
an activist; an enthusiast; a radical

積久(ㄐㄧ ㄐㄧㄡˇ)
over a long time

積漸(ㄐㄧ ㄐㄧㄢˋ)
gradually; little by little

積聚(ㄐㄧ ㄐㄩˋ)
to accumulate; to amass; to pile; to store up

積欠(ㄐㄧ ㄑㄧㄢˋ)
accumulated debts; outstanding debts; arrears: 他還清了積欠的錢。 He cleared up all outstanding debts.

積習(ㄐㄧ ㄒㄧˊ)
a deep-rooted practice; an old habit

積習難改(ㄐㄧ ㄒㄧˊ ㄋㄢˊ ㄍㄞˇ)
It's very difficult to get rid of an old habit.

積薪(ㄐㄧ ㄒㄧㄣ)
a pile of firewood; the piling of firewood

積蓄(ㄐㄧ ㄒㄩˋ)
savings: 他失去了所有的積蓄。 He lost all his savings.

積雪(ㄐㄧ ㄒㄩㄝˇ)
accumulated snow: 積雪盈尺。 Accumulated snow is over a foot.

積貯(ㄐㄧ ㄓㄨˋ)
①savings ②to store up

積重難返(ㄐㄧ ㄓㄨㄥˋ ㄋㄢˊ ㄈㄢˇ)
It is very difficult to break a habit of long standing.

積食(ㄐㄧ ㄕˊ)
(medicine) dyspepsia; indigestion

積少成塔(ㄐㄧ ㄕㄠˇ ㄔㄥˊ ㄊㄚˇ)
Great things rise from small beginnings.

積少成多(ㄐㄧ ㄕㄠˇ ㄔㄥˊ ㄉㄨㄛ)
Economy in trifles will ensure abundance. 或 Many buckets of water will make a river. 或 Many feathers make a bed.

積善餘慶(ㄐㄧ ㄕㄢˋ ㄩˊ ㄑㄧㄥˋ)
If one does (or accumulates) enough good deeds, one will

have more than enough blessings to spare.

積水(ㄐㄧ ㄕㄨㄟˇ)
to accumulate water; accumulated water (in low-lying areas after a shower)

積攢(ㄐㄧ ㄗㄢˇ)
①savings ②to save bit by bit

積存(ㄐㄧ ㄘㄨㄣˊ)
to save; to store; to lay up (or in): 有些動物會積存食物過冬。 Some animals store food for the winter.

積惡(ㄐㄧ ㄜˋ)
to practice evils day in and day out; to indulge in evil ways; to commit many crimes

積壓(ㄐㄧ ㄧㄚ)
to neglect handling official papers, legal cases, etc.; to accumulate and hold up official documents

積雨(ㄐㄧ ㄩˇ)
to rain for a long time

積羽沈舟(ㄐㄧ ㄩˇ ㄔㄣˊ ㄓㄡ)
Accumulation of feathers may sink a boat. 或 Accumulation of small particles results in a mountain.

積怨(ㄐㄧ ㄩㄢˋ)
to accumulate animus, malice or hatred; accumulated or deep-rooted animus, malice or hatred: 消除你心中的積怨。 Get rid of your accumulated hatred.

【稯】 ㄐㄧ jih jí   4030
same as 穖—panicled millet

十二畫

【穗】 ㄙㄨㄟˋ suey suì   4031
1. fruits or grains in a cluster grown at the tip of a stem or stalk
2. the ear of grain
3. another name of Canton
4. a candle snuff; a candlewick

穗狀花序(ㄙㄨㄟˋ ㄓㄨㄤˋ ㄏㄨㄚ ㄒㄩˋ)
the spikes (of flowers)

穗子(ㄙㄨㄟˋ ‧ㄗ) 或 穗兒(ㄙㄨㄟㄦ)
the ear of grain

十三畫

【穡】 ㄙㄜˋ seh sè   4032
1. to harvest grain; to gather in the harvest; to reap
2. same as 嗇—thrifty; stingy; tight-fisted

穡夫(ㄙㄜˋ ㄈㄨ)or 穡人(ㄙㄜˋ ㄖㄣˊ)
a farmer

穡臣(ㄙㄜˋ ㄔㄣˊ)
an official in charge of agriculture in ancient times

穡事(ㄙㄜˋ ㄕˋ)
farming; husbandry

【穢】 ㄏㄨㄟˋ huey huì   4033
1. vile; wicked
2. dirty; filthy
3. obscene; wanton (ways or conduct)
4. ugly and abominable
5. weeds on a farm

穢名(ㄏㄨㄟˋ ㄇㄧㄥˊ)
a notorious reputation

穢德(ㄏㄨㄟˋ ㄉㄜˊ)
debauched ways; filthy deeds

穢土(ㄏㄨㄟˋ ㄊㄨˇ)
①dirty or unclean earth ②(Buddhism) the human world

穢亂(ㄏㄨㄟˋ ㄌㄨㄢˋ)
debauched; wanton

穢氣(ㄏㄨㄟˋ ㄑㄧˋ)
foul air

穢褻(ㄏㄨㄟˋ ㄒㄧㄝˋ)
obscene; pornographic

穢行(ㄏㄨㄟˋ ㄒㄧㄥˊ)
debauched or vile behavior; scandalous conduct

穢史(ㄏㄨㄟˋ ㄕˇ)
①a record of someone's scandalous acts ②the title of a libelous book by Wei Shou (魏收)

穢物(ㄏㄨㄟˋ ㄨˋ)
filth

【穠】 ㄋㄨㄥˊ nong nóng   4034
luxuriant growth of plants

穠纖合度(ㄋㄨㄥˊ ㄒㄧㄢ ㄏㄜˊ ㄉㄨˋ)
(said of a girl's figure) well-proportioned: 她個子雖小，但長得穠纖合度。 She is rather small but well-proportioned.

穠艷(ㄋㄨㄥˊ ㄧㄢˋ)

beautiful and glamorous

十四畫

〔穴 部〕

【穩】 4035
ㄨㄣˇ woen wén

1. stable; stability; steady; firm: 他把桌子放穩。He made the table steady.
2. sure; certain: 這事你拿得穩嗎? Are you quite sure of it?
3. secure; security

穩便(ㄨㄣˇ ㄅㄧㄢˋ)
①safe and convenient ②at will; to proceed as one wishes

穩婆(ㄨㄣˇ ㄆㄛˊ)
a midwife

穩當(ㄨㄣˇ·ㄉㄤ)
proper and secure; safe and sound: 他想到一個穩當的辦法。He thinks of a proper and secure method.

穩定(ㄨㄣˇ ㄉㄧㄥˋ)
①to stabilize: 政府設法穩定物價。The government tries to stabilize prices. ②stable; steady: 全世界需要穩定的和平。The whole world needs a stable peace.

穩定平衡(ㄨㄣˇ ㄉㄧㄥˋ ㄆㄧㄥˊ ㄏㄥˊ)
(physics) stable equilibrium

穩貼(ㄨㄣˇ ㄊㄧㄝ)
proper and secure; safe and sound

穩妥(ㄨㄣˇ ㄊㄨㄛˇ)
secure and dependable; proper and sure: 他認爲那樣辦更穩妥。He thinks it's safer to do it that way.

穩固(ㄨㄣˇ ㄍㄨˋ)
stable and firm; secure: 它具有穩固的基礎。It has a firm (or solid) foundation.

穩健(ㄨㄣˇ ㄐㄧㄢˋ)
firm and steady (as opposed to rash or whimsical): 他是個穩健的青年。He is a steady young man.

穩健派(ㄨㄣˇ ㄐㄧㄢˋ ㄆㄞˋ)
the moderates (as opposed to radicals)

穩下(ㄨㄣˇ ㄒㄧㄚˋ)
to calm down: 我們試着穩下那個人的怒氣。We tried to calm down the angry man.

穩紮穩打(ㄨㄣˇ ㄓㄚˊ ㄨㄣˇ ㄉㄚˇ)

to proceed steadily and step by step; to do things steadily without hurrying; to go ahead steadily and strike sure blows

穩住(ㄨㄣˇ ㄓㄨˋ)
①to hold back someone from intervening in one's plans—sometimes with tricks, etc. ②(said of contests, games, battle, etc.) to hold stable or consolidate; to make secure or stable (a situation, etc.)

穩重(ㄨㄣˇ ㄓㄨㄥˋ)
steady, calm, and dignified

穩如泰山(ㄨㄣˇ ㄖㄨˊ ㄊㄞˋ ㄕㄢ)
as stable as Mount Tai --(figuratively) to be in an invincible position

穩穩當當(ㄨㄣˇ ㄨㄣˇ ㄉㄤ ㄉㄤ)
①safe and secure; proper and dependable ②sure and certain

【穫】 4036
ㄏㄨㄛˋ huoh huò
to reap or harvest; to cut grain

十七畫

【穰】 4037
ㄖㄤˊ rang ráng
1. crowded
2. confusing; mixed-up; disturbed (mind, etc.)
3. stalks of cereal grasses
4. luxuriant

穰田(ㄖㄤˊ ㄊㄧㄢˊ)
to offer sacrifices to gods for a good harvest

穰穰(ㄖㄤˊ ㄖㄤˊ)
①in abundant measure ②confused and disturbed ③luxuriant

穴 部
ㄒㄩㄝ shiueh xué

【穴】 4038
ㄒㄩㄝ shiueh xué
1. a cave; a den; a hole: 老鼠在牆上挖洞穴。The mouse made a hole in the wall.
2. points in the human body

where acupuncture can be applied
3. (Chinese boxing) points in the human body where nerve centers are supposed to be located, a strike at which may cause paralysis or even death

穴道(ㄒㄩㄝ ㄉㄠˋ)
① see 2. and 3. ② an underground channel

穴見(ㄒㄩㄝ ㄐㄧㄢˋ)
limited views or horizons

穴居(ㄒㄩㄝ ㄐㄩ)
to live in a cave; cave-dwelling

穴居野處(ㄒㄩㄝ ㄐㄩ ㄧㄝˇ ㄔㄨˋ)
(said of primitive people) to live in caves in the wilderness

穴隙(ㄒㄩㄝ ㄒㄧˋ)
a hole; a crack

二畫

【究】 4039
ㄐㄧㄡ jiow jiū
(又讀 ㄐㄧㄡˇ jiou jiǔ)

1. to examine; to study; to investigate exhaustively; to dig into
2. finally; in the end; after all
3. actually; really

究辦(ㄐㄧㄡ ㄅㄢˋ)
to investigate and punish

究根問底(ㄐㄧㄡ ㄍㄣ ㄨㄣˋ ㄉㄧˇ)
to get to the bottom of something; to investigate exhaustively

究詰(ㄐㄧㄡ ㄐㄧㄝˊ)
to interrogate; to question closely; to cross-examine

究竟(ㄐㄧㄡ ㄐㄧㄥˋ)
①the very truth; the very source; the very end; the outcome: 我們都想知道這個究竟。We want to know the outcome. ②after all; in the end; finally; at last ③actually; exactly; on earth: 他究竟到那兒去了? Where on earth has he gone?

究細兒(ㄐㄧㄡ ㄒㄧˋ〔ㄦˊ〕)or(ㄐㄧㄡ ㄒㄧˋ〔ㄦ·〕)
to dig into; to scrutinize

究查(ㄐㄧㄡ ㄔㄚˊ)

to examine; to investigate; to probe

究問（ㄐㄧㄡˋ ㄨㄣˊ）
to study and question; to dig into; to cross-examine

三畫

【穸】 4040
ㄒㄧˋ shih hsi
1. a tomb or grave 參看「窀穸」
2. the dead of night

【穹】 4041
ㄑㄩㄥ chiong qióng （又讀 ㄑㄩㄥˊ chyong qióng）
1. high and vast
2. arched; vaulted
3. deep and spacious
4. the sky

穹冥（ㄑㄩㄥ ㄇㄧㄥˊ）
the sky; the heavens

穹地（ㄑㄩㄥ ㄉㄧˋ）
an area with an elevated center (the opposite of a basin); an elevation

穹靈（ㄑㄩㄥ ㄌㄧㄥˊ）
gods high above

穹廬（ㄑㄩㄥ ㄌㄨˊ）
the Mongolian felt tents with rounded tops; a yurt

穹隆（ㄑㄩㄥ ㄌㄨㄥˊ）
①the arched firmament; vault 亦作「穹窿」②long and winding

穹谷（ㄑㄩㄥ ㄍㄨˇ）
a deep valley or ravine

穹嵌（ㄑㄩㄥ ㄑㄧㄢ）
places high up on a steep hill

穹蒼（ㄑㄩㄥ ㄘㄤ）
the sky; the firmament; the azure vault

【空】 4042
1. ㄎㄨㄥ kong kòng
1. empty; hollow; void: 那箱子完全是空的。The box is quite empty.
2. to empty; to exhaust; to reduce to extremity
3. fictitious; unreal; impractical
4. vain and useless (efforts, etc.); ineffective; fruitless: 她空忙了一陣。She made fruitless efforts.
5. high and vast
6. the sky; space: 天空無雲。There were no clouds in the sky.
7. (Buddhism) sunyata; empty; void; vacant; non-existent
8. merely; only
9. a Chinese family name

空跑一趟（ㄎㄨㄥ ㄆㄠˇ ㄧ ㄊㄤˋ）
to take a trip without achieving the purpose: 他空跑一趟。He made a journey for nothing.

空盤（ㄎㄨㄥ ㄆㄢˊ）
①to buy long or sell short; to speculate on the market ②nominal prices

空門（ㄎㄨㄥ ㄇㄣˊ）
①Buddhism ②the teachings which regard everything as unreal, or immaterial ③the school of unreality, one of the four divisions made by Tien-tai (天台)

空濛（ㄎㄨㄥ ㄇㄥˊ）
the misty atmosphere of rainy days

空明（ㄎㄨㄥ ㄇㄧㄥˊ）
glittering of reflected moonlight in water

空費（ㄎㄨㄥ ㄈㄟˋ）
to waste (time or money) in vain

空泛（ㄎㄨㄥ ㄈㄢˋ）
①hollow; not practical ②too general—not specific

空防（ㄎㄨㄥ ㄈㄤˊ）
air defense

空腹（ㄎㄨㄥ ㄈㄨˋ）
on an empty stomach

空腹高心（ㄎㄨㄥ ㄈㄨˋ ㄍㄠ ㄒㄧㄣ）
poor in talent but very ambitious

空蕩蕩（ㄎㄨㄥ ㄉㄤˋ ㄉㄤˋ）
empty; deserted

空對地飛彈（ㄎㄨㄥ ㄉㄨㄟˋ ㄉㄧˋ ㄈㄟ ㄉㄢˋ）
air-to-ground missiles

空對空飛彈（ㄎㄨㄥ ㄉㄨㄟˋ ㄎㄨㄥ ㄈㄟ ㄉㄢˋ）
air-to-air missiles

空洞（ㄎㄨㄥ ㄉㄨㄥˋ）
①vast and empty ②(said of writings, thought, etc.) empty; hollow; shallow: 那只不過是個空洞的理論。That is nothing but an empty theory.

空投（ㄎㄨㄥ ㄊㄡˊ）
airdrop; to make airdrop; to airdrop

空頭（ㄎㄨㄥ ㄊㄡˊ）or（ㄎㄨㄥ ㄊㄡ）
①(stock market) to sell short ②phony; armchair: 他是個空頭戰略家。He's an armchair strategist.

空頭支票（ㄎㄨㄥ ㄊㄡˊ ㄓ ㄆㄧㄠˋ）or（ㄎㄨㄥ ㄊㄡ ㄓ ㄆㄧㄠˋ）
①a rubber check; a check that bounces; a bad check; a dishonored check ②an empty promise; lip service

空頭人情（ㄎㄨㄥ ㄊㄡˊ ㄖㄣˊ ㄑㄧㄥˊ）or（ㄎㄨㄥ ㄊㄡ ㄖㄣˊ ㄑㄧㄥˊ）
to offer lip service; a friendly gesture which neither costs nor helps anything

空談（ㄎㄨㄥ ㄊㄢˊ）
empty talks; academic talks in total disregard of reality; idle chatter

空談誤國（ㄎㄨㄥ ㄊㄢˊ ㄨˋ ㄍㄨㄛˊ）
(usually said of intellectuals) Empty talks jeopardize national interests.

空桶子（ㄎㄨㄥ ㄊㄨㄥˇ ·ㄗ）or 空桶兒（ㄎㄨㄥ ㄊㄨㄥˇ ㄦ）
(literally) an empty bucket or barrel—a blockhead

空難（ㄎㄨㄥ ㄋㄢˊ）
an air disaster; a plane crash or collision: 他在一次空難中喪生。He was killed in an air disaster.

空靈（ㄎㄨㄥ ㄌㄧㄥˊ）
cute; lovely; artistic

空論（ㄎㄨㄥ ㄌㄨㄣˋ）
empty talks; shallow talks; impractical statements

空谷足音（ㄎㄨㄥ ㄍㄨˇ ㄗㄨˊ ㄧㄣ）
(literally) the sound of footsteps in an empty valley—a person of unusual talent or virtue who can seldom be found, or a remarkable statement which one does not hear often

空閨獨守（ㄎㄨㄥ ㄍㄨㄟ ㄉㄨˊ ㄕㄡˇ）
to lead the lonely life of a widow or of a deserted wife

空口說白話（ㄎㄨㄥ ㄎㄡˇ ㄕㄨㄛ ㄅㄞˊ ㄏㄨㄚˋ）
to talk without taking action

空口無憑（ㄎㄨㄥ ㄎㄡˇ ㄨˊ ㄆㄧㄥˊ）
(said of a promise or

〔穴部〕

［穴部］

pledge) Mere verbal statement has no binding force.

空闊(ㄎㄨㄥ ㄎㄨㄛˋ)
spacious; broad; as far as eyes can reach; open

空匱(ㄎㄨㄥ ㄎㄨㄟˋ)
poor; needy; deficient

空曠(ㄎㄨㄥ ㄎㄨㄤˋ)
expansive; vast and boundless: 那是一片空曠的草原。It's a vast expanse of prairie.

空空(ㄎㄨㄥ ㄎㄨㄥ)
①empty; nothing: 他兩手空空的。His hands are empty.
②(Buddhism) unreality of unreality (When all has been regarded as illusion, or unreal, the abstract idea of unreality itself must be destroyed.)

空空洞洞(ㄎㄨㄥ ㄎㄨㄥ ㄉㄨㄥˋ ㄉㄨㄥˋ)
empty; hollow; nothing or nobody in there

空空如也(ㄎㄨㄥ ㄎㄨㄥ ㄖㄨˊ ㄧㄝˇ)
empty; nothing left

空函(ㄎㄨㄥ ㄏㄢˊ)
①a letter without words ②a letter asking for books or samples, etc. without enclosing return postage

空話(ㄎㄨㄥ ㄏㄨㄚˋ)
empty talks; talks without content: 沒有人喜歡空話。Nobody likes empty talks.

空歡喜(ㄎㄨㄥ ㄏㄨㄢ ㄒㄧˇ)
joy that ends in disappointment

空幻(ㄎㄨㄥ ㄏㄨㄢˋ)
illusory; visionary; unreal; intangible: 海市蜃樓是一空幻景象。A mirage is an illusion.

空際(ㄎㄨㄥ ㄐㄧˋ)
the sky; the horizon

空即是色(ㄎㄨㄥ ㄐㄧˊ ㄕˋ ㄙㄜˋ)
The immaterial is the material. (Sunyata is rupa.)

空架子(ㄎㄨㄥ ㄐㄧㄚˋ˙ㄗ)
a bold front with nothing behind it; a deceptive appearance of power or influence which no longer exists

空劫(ㄎㄨㄥ ㄐㄧㄝˊ)
(Buddhism) the empty kalpa, one of the Four Calamities, which will reduce the world to nothing

空界(ㄎㄨㄥ ㄐㄧㄝˋ)
(Buddhism) the realm of space, one of the Six Realms: earth, water, fire, wind, space and knowledge

空間(ㄎㄨㄥ ㄐㄧㄢ)
space (in the sense of dimensions)

空降(ㄎㄨㄥ ㄐㄧㄤˋ)
to land troops by parachutes

空降部隊(ㄎㄨㄥ ㄐㄧㄤˋ ㄅㄨˋ ㄉㄨㄟˋ)
airborne troops

空降陣地(ㄎㄨㄥ ㄐㄧㄤˋ ㄓㄣˋ ㄉㄧˋ)
an airhead

空軍(ㄎㄨㄥ ㄐㄩㄣ)
the air force

空軍基地(ㄎㄨㄥ ㄐㄩㄣ ㄐㄧ ㄉㄧˋ)
an air base

空軍中將(ㄎㄨㄥ ㄐㄩㄣ ㄓㄨㄥ ㄐㄧㄤˋ)
a lieutenant general of the air force

空軍中校(ㄎㄨㄥ ㄐㄩㄣ ㄓㄨㄥ ㄒㄧㄠˋ)
a lieutenant colonel of the air force

空軍中尉(ㄎㄨㄥ ㄐㄩㄣ ㄓㄨㄥ ㄨㄟˋ)
a first lieutenant of the air force

空軍少將(ㄎㄨㄥ ㄐㄩㄣ ㄕㄠˋ ㄐㄧㄤˋ)
a major general of the air force

空軍少校(ㄎㄨㄥ ㄐㄩㄣ ㄕㄠˋ ㄒㄧㄠˋ)
a major of the air force; a squadron leader

空軍少尉(ㄎㄨㄥ ㄐㄩㄣ ㄕㄠˋ ㄨㄟˋ)
a second lieutenant of the air force

空軍上將(ㄎㄨㄥ ㄐㄩㄣ ㄕㄤˋ ㄐㄧㄤˋ)
a general of the air force

空軍上校(ㄎㄨㄥ ㄐㄩㄣ ㄕㄤˋ ㄒㄧㄠˋ)
an air-force colonel

空軍上尉(ㄎㄨㄥ ㄐㄩㄣ ㄕㄤˋ ㄨㄟˋ)
an air-force captain

空軍武官(ㄎㄨㄥ ㄐㄩㄣ ㄨˇ ㄍㄨㄢ)
an air attaché

空氣(ㄎㄨㄥ ㄑㄧˋ)
air or atmosphere (also used figuratively): 我們必須呼吸新鮮空氣。We must breathe the fresh air.

空氣墊(ㄎㄨㄥ ㄑㄧˋ ㄉㄧㄢˋ)
an air mattress

空氣調節(ㄎㄨㄥ ㄑㄧˋ ㄊㄧㄠˊ ㄐㄧㄝˊ)
air conditioning

空氣囊(ㄎㄨㄥ ㄑㄧˋ ㄋㄤˊ)
an air bag

空氣流通(ㄎㄨㄥ ㄑㄧˋ ㄌㄧㄡˊ ㄊㄨㄥ)

air ventilation; well ventilated; airy; air circulation: 他的房間空氣流通。His room is well ventilated.

空氣傳染(ㄎㄨㄥ ㄑㄧˋ ㄔㄨㄢˊ ㄖㄢˇ)
airborne infection

空氣污染(ㄎㄨㄥ ㄑㄧˋ ㄨ ㄖㄢˇ)
air pollution

空前(ㄎㄨㄥ ㄑㄧㄢˊ)
unprecedented

空前絕後(ㄎㄨㄥ ㄑㄧㄢˊ ㄐㄩㄝˊ ㄏㄡˋ)
(said of a remarkable achievement, masterpiece, etc.) not equaled before or after

空拳(ㄎㄨㄥ ㄑㄩㄢˊ)
to hold nothing in the hand; barehanded

空襲(ㄎㄨㄥ ㄒㄧˊ)
an air raid; an air attack

空襲警報(ㄎㄨㄥ ㄒㄧˊ ㄐㄧㄥˇ ㄅㄠˋ)
an air-raid alert; an air-raid alarm

空心(ㄎㄨㄥ ㄒㄧㄣ)
①hollow: 這是一株空心的樹。This is a hollow tree. ②nothing in mind

空心大老官(ㄎㄨㄥ ㄒㄧㄣ ㄉㄚˋ ㄌㄠˇ 《ㄨㄢ)
a vainglorious person without the means or ability to back up his pretensions

空心菜(ㄎㄨㄥ ㄒㄧㄣ ㄘㄞˋ)
a water convolvulus 亦作「蕹菜」

空想(ㄎㄨㄥ ㄒㄧㄤˇ)
①an impractical thought or idea; a daydream ②to daydream

空虛(ㄎㄨㄥ ㄒㄩ)
empty; void; emptiness

空穴來風(ㄎㄨㄥ ㄒㄩㄝˋ ㄌㄞˊ ㄈㄥ)
(said of news, or information) groundless or baseless

空戰(ㄎㄨㄥ ㄓㄢˋ)
an air battle

空中(ㄎㄨㄥ ㄓㄨㄥ)
in the air; in the sky

空中巴士(ㄎㄨㄥ ㄓㄨㄥ ㄅㄚ ㄕˋ)
an air bus

空中飛人(ㄎㄨㄥ ㄓㄨㄥ ㄈㄟ ㄖㄣˊ)
a trapeze show

空中大學(ㄎㄨㄥ ㄓㄨㄥ ㄉㄚˋ ㄒㄩㄝˊ)
an open university

空中樓閣(ㄎㄨㄥ ㄓㄨㄥ ㄌㄡˊ 《ㄜˊ)
a castle in the air—illusion

空中纜車(ㄎㄨㄥ ㄓㄨㄥ ㄌㄢ ㄔㄜ)
a cable car

空中花園(ㄎㄨㄥ ㄓㄨㄥ ㄏㄨㄚ ㄩㄢ)
hanging gardens

空中加油(ㄎㄨㄥ ㄓㄨㄥ ㄐㄧㄚ ㄧㄡ)
refueling in midair; in-flight refueling

空中陷阱(ㄎㄨㄥ ㄓㄨㄥ ㄒㄧㄢ ㄐㄧㄥ)
(aviation) an air pocket

空中小姐(ㄎㄨㄥ ㄓㄨㄥ ㄒㄧㄠ ㄐㄧㄝ)
a stewardess (of a passenger plane); an air hostess

空中學校(ㄎㄨㄥ ㄓㄨㄥ ㄒㄩㄝ ㄒㄧㄠ)
a school on the air

空中少爺(ㄎㄨㄥ ㄓㄨㄥ ㄕㄠ ㄧㄝ)
(informal) a male flight attendant

空中預警機(ㄎㄨㄥ ㄓㄨㄥ ㄩ ㄐㄧㄥ ㄐㄧ)
airborne warning and control system (AWACS)

空城計(ㄎㄨㄥ ㄔㄥ ㄐㄧ)
①a bluff ②nobody left behind to guard the house

空手(ㄎㄨㄥ ㄕㄡ)
empty-handed; unarmed: 他空手而來。He came empty-handed.

空手道(ㄎㄨㄥ ㄕㄡ ㄉㄠ)
karate, a type of Oriental boxing

空身(ㄎㄨㄥ ㄕㄣ)
to carry nothing except oneself; to carry no baggage, etc.

空身人兒(ㄎㄨㄥ ㄕㄣ ㄖㄣ ㄦ)
a person without any string attached

空說(ㄎㄨㄥ ㄕㄨㄛ)
empty talks; useless talks

空宗(ㄎㄨㄥ ㄗㄨㄥ)
(Buddhism) the Sunyat sects, i.e. those which make the unreality of the ego and things their fundamental tenet

空言(ㄎㄨㄥ ㄧㄢ)
empty talks; mere talks

空運(ㄎㄨㄥ ㄩㄣ)
air transportation; air freight; an airlift; to transport by air: 裝備將予空運歐洲。The equipment will be airlifted to Europe.

【空】 4042
2. ㄎㄨㄥ kòng kōng
1. leisure; free time; spare

time. 他現在有空。He is at leisure now.
2. blank (space); vacant; vacancy; to leave blank or vacant
3. spacious—implying a sense of awe
4. a chance; an opportunity
5. wanting; deficient; impoverished

空白(ㄎㄨㄥ ㄅㄞ)
a blank in a paper or form

空白支票(ㄎㄨㄥ ㄅㄞ ㄓ ㄆㄧㄠ)
a blank check

空乏(ㄎㄨㄥ ㄈㄚ)
wanting; impoverished

空房(ㄎㄨㄥ ㄈㄤ)
an unoccupied house or room

空檔(ㄎㄨㄥ ㄉㄤ)
①vacant space in a movie theater schedule②free time; spare time

空地(ㄎㄨㄥ ㄉㄧ)
a vacant area; a vacant lot; a vacancy

空肚兒(ㄎㄨㄥ ㄉㄨ ㄦ)
empty-stomached

空格兒(ㄎㄨㄥ ㄍㄜ ㄦ)
the blank in a form (for filling)

空缺(ㄎㄨㄥ ㄑㄩㄝ)
①a vacant position; a vacancy: 我們有些空缺的職位。We have some vacant positions. ②scarcity (of food, money, etc.)

空隙(ㄎㄨㄥ ㄒㄧ)
a vacant space; a crevice; a gap; a loophole

空暇(ㄎㄨㄥ ㄒㄧㄚ)
free time; spare time; leisure; time free from work

空閒(ㄎㄨㄥ ㄒㄧㄢ)
leisure; spare time: 我沒有空閒看書。I have no leisure to read.

空額(ㄎㄨㄥ ㄜ)
a vacancy; an opening; a deficit: 空額已經補上。The vacancy has already been filled.

空兒(ㄎㄨㄥ ㄦ)
①leisure; spare time ②a vacant space; a gap ③an opportunity

空位(ㄎㄨㄥ ㄨㄟ)or 空座兒(ㄎㄨㄥ ㄗㄨㄛ ㄦ)
a vacant or unoccupied seat: 戲院裏有許多空座兒。There are many vacant seats in the theater.

四畫

【穿】 4043
ㄔㄨㄢ chuān chuàn
1. to wear (clothes, shoes, etc.)
2. to pierce through; to penetrate or bore through; to thread
3. to cross (a street, etc.)
4. to see through; to bare a secret, etc.)

穿幫(ㄔㄨㄢ ㄅㄤ)
(informal) accidentally reveal something very embarrassing which one has tried to conceal

穿鼻(ㄔㄨㄢ ㄅㄧ)
to pierce the nose (of a cow, etc.)

穿壁引光(ㄔㄨㄢ ㄅㄧ ㄧㄣ ㄍㄨㄤ)
(literally) to bore a hole through the wall so that light from the neighbor can be used for studying—very studious and diligent under financial pressure

穿不得(ㄔㄨㄢ ㄅㄨ ㄉㄜ)
(said of clothing, etc.) cannot or shouldn't be worn (because of unfitness or impropriety)

穿不起(ㄔㄨㄢ ㄅㄨ ㄑㄧ)
cannot afford to wear it—too expensive

穿不住(ㄔㄨㄢ ㄅㄨ ㄓㄨ)
①cannot stand a lot of wear—poor quality ②cannot wear it any longer—due to a rise in temperature

穿房過屋(ㄔㄨㄢ ㄈㄤ ㄍㄨㄛ ㄨ)
intimate and close (friends)

穿戴(ㄔㄨㄢ ㄉㄞ)
to wear (clothes, ornaments, etc.): 他們穿戴整齊。They are neatly dressed.

穿透(ㄔㄨㄢ ㄊㄡ)
to penetrate; to pierce through: 子彈穿透木板。The bullet penetrated the board.

穿堂(ㄔㄨㄢ ㄊㄤ)

【穴部】

a small room, etc. serving as a passageway in a house

穿堂門兒(ㄔㄨㄢ ㄊㄤˊ ㄇㄣˊ)
a passageway

穿廊(ㄔㄨㄢ ㄌㄤˊ)
a corridor; a covered passageway

穿過去(ㄔㄨㄢ ㄍㄨㄛˋ ㄑㄩˋ)
to penetrate; to thread through: 子彈從他胸膛穿過去。A bullet penetrated his chest.

穿孔(ㄔㄨㄢ ㄎㄨㄥˇ)
①to bore a hole; to perforate; to punch ②(medicine) perforation: 他患了胃穿孔的病。He suffered from gastric perforation.

穿孔機(ㄔㄨㄢ ㄎㄨㄥˇ ㄐㄧ)
a punch; a perforator

穿甲彈(ㄔㄨㄢ ㄐㄧㄚˇ ㄉㄢˋ)
armor-piercing shells

穿鞋(ㄔㄨㄢ ㄒㄧㄝˊ)
to put on shoes

穿孝(ㄔㄨㄢ ㄒㄧㄠˋ)
to wear or put on mourning (clothing)

穿線(ㄔㄨㄢ ㄒㄧㄢˋ)
①to thread a needle: 能幫我穿線嗎? Will you thread this needle for me? ②to serve as a go-between

穿心槓(ㄔㄨㄢ ㄒㄧㄣ ㄍㄤˋ)
a pole with which two persons lift a coffin

穿針(ㄔㄨㄢ ㄓㄣ)
to thread a needle

穿針引線(ㄔㄨㄢ ㄓㄣ ㄧㄣˇ ㄒㄧㄢˋ)
to serve as a go-between

穿著(ㄔㄨㄢ ㄓㄨㄛˊ)
①attire; dress: 他不講究穿著。He is not particular about his dress. ②dressed in: 她穿著黑色衣服。She was dressed in black.

穿插(ㄔㄨㄢ ㄔㄚ)
①to serve as a go-between ②the insertion of an episode or interlude

穿山甲(ㄔㄨㄢ ㄕㄢ ㄐㄧㄚˇ)
① Manis pentadactyla, the pangolin 亦作「鯪鯉」②(Chinese medicine) pangolin scales

穿鑿附會(ㄔㄨㄢ ㄗㄠˋ ㄈㄨˋ ㄏㄨㄟˋ)
to offer far-fetched or dubious explanations

穿刺(ㄔㄨㄢ ㄘˋ)
a puncture

穿素(ㄔㄨㄢ ㄙㄨˋ)
(said of descendants of a deceased person) to wear clothes of subdued colors for some time just after the mourning period

穿梭(ㄔㄨㄢ ㄙㄨㄛ)
①busy comings and goings of people ②to shuttle back and forth

穿耳(ㄔㄨㄢ ㄦˇ)
to pierce the ears(for wearing earrings)

穿衣鏡(ㄔㄨㄢ ㄧ ㄐㄧㄥˋ)
a dressing glass; a cheval glass

穿眼(ㄔㄨㄢ ㄧㄢˇ)
to bore a hole; to perforate

穿窬之盜(ㄔㄨㄢ ㄩˊ ㄓ ㄉㄠˋ)
a burglar; a thief

穿越(ㄔㄨㄢ ㄩㄝˋ)
to pass through; to cross (a bridge, street, tunnel, etc.)

【突】 4044
ㄊㄨ twu tú
1. abrupt; sudden; unexpected; suddenly; unexpectedly
2. to offend; to go against
3. to break through (enemy encirclement)
4. to project or jut out
5. a chimney

突變(ㄊㄨ ㄅㄧㄢˋ)
①an unexpected change ②mutation

突變說(ㄊㄨ ㄅㄧㄢˋ ㄕㄨㄛ)
(biology) the mutation theory

突破(ㄊㄨ ㄆㄛˋ)
①to break or smash (old records, etc.) ②to break through

突飛猛進(ㄊㄨ ㄈㄟ ㄇㄥˇ ㄐㄧㄣˋ)
to advance (or go ahead) by leaps and bounds; to progress rapidly

突突(ㄊㄨ ㄊㄨ)
the throbs of heartbeats

突尼西亞(ㄊㄨ ㄋㄧˊ ㄒㄧ ㄧㄚˋ)
Tunisia, a country in North Africa, capital Tunis

突感(ㄊㄨ ㄍㄢˇ)
to feel suddenly

突擊(ㄊㄨ ㄐㄧˊ)
to attack (or assault) sud-

denly; to make a surprise attack; to raid: 警察突擊賭窟。The police raided a gambling house.

突擊隊(ㄊㄨ ㄐㄧˊ ㄉㄨㄟˋ)
shock troops; commando units; a shock brigade

突擊檢查(ㄊㄨ ㄐㄧˊ ㄐㄧㄢˇ ㄔㄚˊ)
to make a search without prior notice or announcement

突騎(ㄊㄨ ㄐㄧˋ)
the sallying cavalry

突將(ㄊㄨ ㄐㄧㄤˋ)
a bold general of unusual fighting skill or stamina

突厥(ㄊㄨ ㄐㄩㄝˊ)
an ancient name of the Turks

突起(ㄊㄨ ㄑㄧˇ)
①to rise up all of a sudden; to rise high; to tower: 奇峰突起。Peaks tower magnificently. ②to break out; suddenly appear: 戰事突起。Hostilities broke out.

突出(ㄊㄨ ㄔㄨ)
①outstanding; remarkable ②to jut out

突然(ㄊㄨ ㄖㄢˊ)
suddenly; abruptly; unexpectedly; abrupt; sudden: 突然下起雨來。Suddenly it began to rain.

突如其來(ㄊㄨ ㄖㄨˊ ㄑㄧˊ ㄌㄞˊ)
suddenly; abruptly; unexpectedly

突兀(ㄊㄨ ㄨˋ)
①lofty and steep; high ②suddenly; abruptly; unexpectedly

突圍(ㄊㄨ ㄨㄟˊ)
to break through enemy encirclement or siege

【窀】 4045
ㄓㄨㄣ juen zhun
a pit for the coffin

五畫

【窅】 4046
ㄧㄠˇ yeau yǎo
1. far and deep; mysterious
2. sad

窅眇(ㄧㄠˇ ㄇㄧㄠˇ)
deep; far and deep

窅冥(ㄧㄠˇ ㄇㄧㄥˊ)

①far and deep; obscure and mysterious ②sunken eyes

眢然(ㄩㄢ ㄖㄢˊ)
sad; touched

眢邃(ㄩㄢ ㄙㄨㄟˋ)
far and deep

眢窅(ㄩㄢ ㄧㄠˇ)
①somber ②deep

【窈】 4047　ㄧㄠˇ yeau yǎo
1. deep; obscure; secluded
2. tranquil

窈冥(ㄧㄠˇ ㄇㄧㄥˊ)
①obscure; dusky ②deep; profound; mysterious

窈窕(ㄧㄠˇ ㄊㄧㄠˇ)
①(said of young women) quiet and modest; attractive and charming ②far and deep

窈窕淑女(ㄧㄠˇ ㄊㄧㄠˇ ㄕㄨˊ ㄋㄩˇ)
a quiet and modest maiden

窈藹(ㄧㄠˇ ㄞˇ)
deep, far or obscure

窈窈(ㄧㄠˇ ㄧㄠˇ)
①obscure; dusky ②far and deep; profound

【窄】 4048　ㄓㄞˇ jae zhǎi
（又讀 ㄗㄜˋ tzer zè）
1. narrow; contracted; tight
2. narrow-minded; mean: 他心胸狹窄。He is narrow-minded.

窄門(ㄓㄞˇ ㄇㄣˊ)
a narrow door or gate

窄道(ㄓㄞˇ ㄉㄠˋ)
a narrow path

窄小(ㄓㄞˇ ㄒㄧㄠˇ)
①(said of a dress) tight and small ②(said of a room, etc.) narrow and small

窄巷(ㄓㄞˇ ㄒㄧㄤˋ)
a narrow lane

窄韻(ㄓㄞˇ ㄩㄣˋ)
difficult rhyme; the rarest rhyme in verses

【窆】 4049　ㄅㄧㄢˇ bean biǎn
to put the coffin in the grave; to bury

窆石(ㄅㄧㄢˇ ㄕˊ)
(in ancient China) stones used in gliding a coffin down a tunnel

六畫

【窒】 4050　ㄓˋ jhy zhì
to block; to stop up; to obstruct; to stuff up

窒悶(ㄓˋ ㄇㄣˋ)
close; stuffy; badly ventilated

窒息(ㄓˋ ㄒㄧˊ)
to asphyxiate; to suffocate; to smother; asphyxiation; asphyxia; suffocation: 我幾乎被煙窒息了。I am almost suffocated with smoke.

窒息藥(ㄓˋ ㄒㄧˊ ㄧㄠˋ)
an asphyxiant

窒塞(ㄓˋ ㄙㄜˋ)
to block; to obstruct: 大雪窒塞道路。The heavy snowfall blocked the roads.

窒礙(ㄓˋ ㄞˋ)
to obstruct; an obstacle: 樹木窒礙了視野。Trees obstructed the view.

窒欲 or 窒慾(ㄓˋ ㄩˋ)
to restrain one's lusts

【窕】 4051　ㄊㄧㄠˇ teau tiǎo
1. slender
2. quiet and modest; charming and attractive
3. beautiful; wonderful; good

七畫

【窖】 4052　ㄐㄧㄠˋ jiao jiào
1. a cellar; a vault; a pit: 他食物貯藏在地窖裏。He stored food in the cellar.
2. to store things in a cellar, etc.

窖冰(ㄐㄧㄠˋ ㄅㄧㄥ)
to keep ice in a cellar, vault or pit

窖果子(ㄐㄧㄠˋ ㄍㄨㄛˇ ˙ㄗ)
to keep fruits in a cellar

窖藏(ㄐㄧㄠˋ ㄘㄤˊ)
to store things in a cellar

【窗】 4053　（窓、窻、牕）ㄔㄨㄤ chuang chuāng
1. a window; a skylight: 誰打破窗戶? Who broke the window?
2. a place where one studies

窗板(ㄔㄨㄤ ㄅㄢˇ)
window shutters

窗櫺(ㄔㄨㄤ ㄌㄧㄥˊ)

the lintel of a window

窗幔(ㄔㄨㄤ ㄇㄢˋ)or窗帷(ㄔㄨㄤ ㄨㄟˊ)
a window curtain or screen

窗明几淨(ㄔㄨㄤ ㄇㄧㄥˊ ㄐㄧ ㄐㄧㄥˋ)
(said of rooms) neat and bright

窗臺(ㄔㄨㄤ ㄊㄞˊ)
a window sill

窗簾 or 窗帘(ㄔㄨㄤ ㄌㄧㄢˊ)
a window curtain, screen or blind

窗櫺(ㄔㄨㄤ ㄌㄧㄥˊ)
the window lattice

窗口(ㄔㄨㄤ ㄎㄡˇ)
①a window: 她坐在窗口。She sat at (or by) the window. ②a wicket; a window

窗框(ㄔㄨㄤ ㄎㄨㄤ)
a window frame

窗戶(ㄔㄨㄤ ˙ㄏㄨ)
a window: 請打開窗戶。Open the window, please.

窗戶紙(ㄔㄨㄤ ˙ㄏㄨ ㄓˇ)
①a kind of thin semi-transparent paper used to cover a window in place of glass ②(said of a person's complexion)pale ③ a thin veil(in a figurative sense)

窗下(ㄔㄨㄤ ㄒㄧㄚˋ)
to study (before the window)

窗紗(ㄔㄨㄤ ㄕㄚ)
gauze used to cover a window

窗子(ㄔㄨㄤ ˙ㄗ)or窗兒(ㄔㄨㄤ ㄦ)
a window: 他把窗子關起來然後離開。He shut the window and then left.

窗友(ㄔㄨㄤ ㄧㄡˇ)
fellow students; schoolmates

窗牖(ㄔㄨㄤ ㄧㄡˇ)
windows

窗外(ㄔㄨㄤ ㄨㄞˋ)
outside the window

【窘】 4054　ㄐㄩㄥˇ jeong jiǒng
1. hard-pressed; poverty-stricken
2. to embarrass
3. afflicted; distressed

窘步(ㄐㄩㄥˇ ㄅㄨˋ)
to walk awkwardly because of being hard-pressed

窘迫(ㄐㄩㄥˇ ㄆㄛˋ)
hard-pressed; afflicted in a predicament: 他的處境窘迫。

【穴部】

He found himself in a predicament.

窘態 (ㄐㄩㄥˇ ㄊㄞˋ)
an embarrassed look; a distressed look; 她露出窘態。She showed signs of embarrassment.

窘急 (ㄐㄩㄥˇ ㄐㄧˊ)
afflicted; in great difficulty; hard-pressed

窘境 (ㄐㄩㄥˇ ㄐㄧㄥˋ)
an awkward situation; a predicament; a plight

窘住 (ㄐㄩㄥˇ ˙ㄓㄨ)
embarrassed; distressed; to embarrass

窘蹙 (ㄐㄩㄥˇ ㄊㄨˋ)
hard-pressed; urgent

八畫

【窟】 4055
ㄎㄨ ku kū
1. a hole; a cave; a pit
2. to dig the ground and build underground living quarters
3. a den for wild animals (now also used figuratively, as a gambling den, an opium-smoking den, etc.)

窟窿 (ㄎㄨ ˙ㄌㄨㄥ) or 窟窿洞 (ㄎㄨ ˙ㄌㄨㄥ ㄌㄨㄥˊ) or 窟洞 (ㄎㄨ ㄌㄨㄥˊ)
holes: 他的鞋底磨了個窟窿。He has worn a hole in the sole of his shoe.

窟窿眼兒 (ㄎㄨ ˙ㄌㄨㄥ ㄧㄢˇ ㄦ)
tiny holes

窟窖 (ㄎㄨ ㄐㄧㄠˋ)
a cellar or vault: 他放了些酒在窟窖裏。He stored some wine in the cellar.

窟居 (ㄎㄨ ㄐㄩ)
to live in caves

窟穴 (ㄎㄨ ㄒㄩㄝˋ)
holes

窟宅 (ㄎㄨ ㄓㄞˊ)
an underground chamber

窟室 (ㄎㄨ ㄕˋ)
an underground room or chamber; a cellar

【窠】 4056
ㄎㄜ ke kē
1. a den; a burrow
2. a nest
3. a hole
4. a dwelling for people

窠臼 (ㄎㄜ ㄐㄧㄡˋ)
a set pattern or rule; a stereotype

窠巢 (ㄎㄜ ㄔㄠˊ)
a nest

九畫

【窩】 4057
ㄨㄛ uo wō
1. a cave; a den; a nest
2. an apartment; living quarters; a house
3. to hide; to harbor (a criminal, etc.)
4. to bend; to crease
5. a litter; a brood
6. to block; to hold in; to check
7. a hollow part of the human body; a pit

窩風 (ㄨㄛ ㄈㄥ)
to shelter or protect from the wind

窩囊 (ㄨㄛ ˙ㄋㄤ)
① stupid, cowardly and timid; good-for-nothing; useless (person) ② to feel vexed; to be annoyed: 我不願受他的窩囊氣。I'll not put up with his petty annoyances.

窩囊廢 (ㄨㄛ ˙ㄋㄤ ㄈㄟˋ)
a stupid, cowardly good-for-nothing; a worthless wretch

窩膿 (ㄨㄛ ㄋㄨㄥˊ)
to suppurate

窩裏窩囊 (ㄨㄛ ㄌㄧˇ ㄨㄛ ˙ㄋㄤ)
stupid and cowardly

窩囊眼 (ㄨㄛ ˙ㄋㄤ ㄧㄢˇ)
a person with sunken eyes

窩家 (ㄨㄛ ㄐㄧㄚ)
a house where stolen goods are hidden—the house of an evil person

窩心 (ㄨㄛ ㄒㄧㄣ)
① to suffer an insult which one is powerless to avenge ② (Shanghai dialect) gratifying

窩主 (ㄨㄛ ㄓㄨˇ)
one who harbors criminals or keeps stolen goods

窩藏 (ㄨㄛ ㄘㄤˊ)
to harbor (outlaws); to keep (stolen goods)

窩兒 (ㄨㄛㄦ)
① a place or den one occupies ② a cave, a pit

窩兒裏反 (ㄨㄛ ㄦ ㄌㄧˇ ㄈㄢˇ)
an intramural fight

窩窩頭 (ㄨㄛ ㄨㄛ ㄊㄡˊ) or 窩頭 (ㄨㄛ ㄊㄡˊ)
a kind of steamed dumpling made of corn meal or other cheap cereals and eaten by the poor in northern China

【窪】 4058
ㄨㄚ ua wā
1. deep; hollow; low-lying
2. a pit; a hole; a hollow; a depression: 這些路滿是坑窪。These roads are full of holes.

窪地 (ㄨㄚ ㄉㄧˋ)
marsh land; low-lying land

窪田 (ㄨㄚ ㄊㄧㄢˊ)
a low-lying field or plantation; marsh land

【窨】 4059
1. ㄧㄣˋ yinn yìn
a cellar; an underground storeroom

【窨】 2. ㄒㄩㄣ shiun xūn
to add aroma to tea by mixing it with jasmine

【窬】 4060
ㄩˊ yu yú
1. a hole in the wall; a small door or window
2. to climb over a wall

十畫

【窮】 4061
ㄑㄩㄥˊ chyong qióng
1. poor; impoverished; destitute: 他窮得沒錢上學。He was too poor to go to school.
2. to exhaust; to trace to the very source
3. distress; affliction
4. the extreme; the farthest; an end
5. thoroughly

窮北 (ㄑㄩㄥˊ ㄅㄟˇ)
the extreme north; the farthest north

窮兵黷武 (ㄑㄩㄥˊ ㄅㄧㄥ ㄉㄨˊ ㄨˇ)
to wage war frequently; to follow a policy of expansionism by military means; to be a warmonger

窮忙 (ㄑㄩㄥˊ ㄇㄤˊ)
to toil all day long just to make both ends meet; to be

〔穴部〕

busy for nothing: 你整天在窮
忙什麼? What are you busy
for all day long?

窮民〈くuź ㄇㄧㄣ〉
poor people; the destitute

窮目〈くuź ㄇㄨ〉
to see as far as one can

窮乏〈くuź ㄈㄚ〉
destitute; wanting; poverty-
stricken

窮達〈くuź ㄉㄚˊ〉
to remain obscure or to
become distinguished; ob-
scurity or eminence

窮大手〈くuź ㄉㄚˋ ㄕㄡˇ〉
poor but putting on a bold
front by spending lavishly

窮到骨〈くuź ㄉㄠˋ ㄍㄨˇ〉
stark poverty; extremely
poor

窮當益堅〈くuź ㄉㄤ ㄧˋ ㄐㄧㄢ〉
The greater one's adversity
is, the stronger his fortitude
should be.

窮滴滴〈くuź ㄉㄧ ㄉㄧ〉
destitute; poor

窮冬〈くuź ㄉㄨㄥ〉
deep in winter; winter at its
coldest

窮途〈くuź ㄊㄨˊ〉or 窮途末路〈くuź
ㄊㄨˊ ㄇㄛˋ ㄌㄨˋ〉
extremely distressed or difficult state; in straits; at the
end of one's rope

窮通〈くuź ㄊㄨㄥ〉
failure or success

窮鳥入懷〈くuź ㄋㄧㄠˇ ㄖㄨˋ ㄏㄨㄞˊ〉
to become somebody's pro-
tégé when one is down in
his luck

窮年累月〈くuź ㄋㄧㄢˊ ㄌㄟˇ ㄩㄝˋ〉
for a very long time; for
years on end; year after
year

窮老〈くuź ㄌㄠˇ〉
①till one's death ② old and
poor; aged and destitute

窮里〈くuź ㄌㄧˇ〉
obscure or out-of-the-way
places

窮理〈くuź ㄌㄧˇ〉
to probe into or trace to the
very root of things

窮骨頭〈くuź ㄍㄨˇ ㄊㄡˊ〉
(abusively) a poor or stingy
person

窮鬼〈くuź ㄍㄨㄟˇ〉
a poverty-stricken fellow

窮光蛋〈くuź ㄍㄨㄤ ㄉㄢˋ〉
a destitute fellow; a penniless vagrant; a pauper; a
poor wretch

窮逛〈くuź ㄍㄨㄤˋ〉
to fool around without
spending money

窮開心〈くuź ㄎㄞ ㄒㄧㄣ〉
to enjoy moments of happiness even in poverty

窮寇勿追〈くuź ㄎㄡˋ ㄨˋ ㄓㄨㄟ〉
(originally from Sun Tzu's
The Art of War) Don't pursue a desperate enemy (lest
he should put up a life-or-
death fight that would make
the pursuer pay dearly).

窮坑難滿〈くuź ㄎㄥ ㄋㄢˊ ㄇㄢˇ〉
The pit of avarice can never
be filled.

窮苦〈くuź ㄎㄨˇ〉
destitute; poverty; poverty-
stricken

窮困〈くuź ㄎㄨㄣˋ〉
poverty-stricken; to be beset
by poverty; distressed and
afflicted: 這對年輕夫婦極為窮
困。The young couple are as
poor as church mice.

窮困潦倒〈くuź ㄎㄨㄣˋ ㄌㄧㄠˊ ㄉㄠˇ〉
to be penniless and frustrated

窮漢〈くuź ㄏㄢˋ〉
a poor man

窮歡樂〈くuź ㄏㄨㄢ ㄌㄜˋ〉
to find moments of rejoicing
in poverty

窮極〈くuź ㄐㄧˊ〉
①extremely; in the extreme
② abjectly poor

窮極思變〈くuź ㄐㄧˊ ㄙ ㄅㄧㄢˋ〉
One will start thinking
about changes when he is in
extreme poverty.

窮極無聊〈くuź ㄐㄧˊ ㄨˊ ㄌㄧㄠˊ〉
①to do very foolish things
in desperation ② to be utterly bored ③ absolutely senseless; disgusting

窮家富路〈くuź ㄐㄧㄚ ㄈㄨˋ ㄌㄨˋ〉
to practice thrift at home
but be amply provided while
traveling

窮究〈くuź ㄐㄧㄡˋ〉
to examine, inquire, study or

trace to the very source of
something; to make a thorough inquiry

窮盡〈くuź ㄐㄧㄣˋ〉
to come to an end; to
exhaust: 戰場戰爭窮盡了我們
的國力。The war exhausted
our country.

窮經〈くuź ㄐㄧㄥ〉
to study classics exhaustively

窮氣〈くuź ㄑㄧˋ〉
an appearance or look of
poverty

窮小子〈くuź ㄒㄧㄠˇ ㄗ˙〉
a poor bum (a contempt-
ous expression)

窮嫌富不要〈くuź ㄒㄧㄢˊ ㄈㄨˋ ㄅㄨˋ
ㄧㄠˋ〉
(said of a commodity, etc.)
The poor shun it because of
its high price, and the rich
dislike it because of its poor
quality.

窮鄉僻壤〈くuź ㄒㄧㄤ ㄆㄧˋ ㄖㄤˇ〉
out-of-the-way regions;
remote areas

窮相〈くuź ㄒㄧㄤˋ〉
an appearance or manners,
indicating poverty

窮巷〈くuź ㄒㄧㄤˋ〉
a lane in a slum area

窮形盡相〈くuź ㄒㄧㄥˊ ㄐㄧㄣˋ ㄒㄧㄤˋ〉
① to give a vivid description
of something ② mean and
distasteful language or conduct

窮凶極惡〈くuź ㄒㄩㄥ ㄐㄧˊ ㄜˋ〉
extremely violent and wicked;
utterly evil; atrocious; dia-
bolical

窮治〈くuź ㄓˋ〉
to manage a matter by first
examining into it thoroughly

窮追不捨〈くuź ㄓㄨㄟ ㄅㄨˋ ㄕㄜˇ〉
to pursue relentlessly; to go
in hot pursuit

窮愁〈くuź ㄔㄡˊ〉
dejection caused by poverty
and sorrow

窮愁潦倒〈くuź ㄔㄡˊ ㄌㄧㄠˊ ㄉㄠˇ〉
to crack up under the strain
of poverty and sorrow

窮奢極侈〈くuź ㄕㄜ ㄐㄧˊ ㄔˇ〉or 窮
奢極欲〈くuź ㄕㄜ ㄐㄧˊ ㄩˋ〉
to go to the extreme of
extravagance: 他們過着窮奢

〔穴部〕

極侈的生活。They live a life of wanton extravagance.

窮山惡水（くⅠ½ アㄢ ㄜ ㄕㄨㄟ）
a barren and unwholesome view; the poor, barren land

窮書生（くⅠ½ ㄕㄨ ㄕㄥ）
a poor scholar; a destitute student

窮鼠齧貓（くⅠ½ ㄕㄨ ㄋⅠㄝ ㄇㄠ）
（literally）A desperate rat will turn back to bite the pursuing cat.—One will fight back out of desperation.

窮日子（くⅠ½ ㄖ˙ ㄗ）
poverty-stricken days; the miserable life of a poor fellow

窮人（くⅠ½ ㄖㄣ）
destitute people; the poor

窮則變，變則通（くⅠ½ ㄗㄜˊ ㄅⅠㄢˋ，ㄅⅠㄢˋ ㄗㄜˊ ㄊㄨㄥ）
Impasse is followed by change, and change will lead to solution.

窮措大（くⅠ½ ㄘㄨㄛˋ ㄉㄚˋ）
a poor scholar

窮酸（くⅠ½ ㄙㄨㄢ）
（said of a scholar）poor, jealous and pedantic

窮酸相（くⅠ½ ㄙㄨㄢ ㄒⅠㄤˋ）
the manners of a destitute scholar

窮源溯流（くⅠ½ ㄩㄢˊ ㄙㄨˋ ㄌⅠㄡˊ）
（literally）to follow a stream to its very source—to trace to the very source of something

【窯】 4062
（窰）｜ㄠˊ yau yáo

1. a kiln; a brick furnace
2. pottery
3. a pit in a coal mine; a coal shaft
4. a cave—for human dwelling
5. a brothel

窯洞（Ⅰㄠˊ ㄉㄨㄥˋ）
①a cave for human dwelling ②the opening of a kiln

窯坑（Ⅰㄠˊ ㄎㄥ）
a pit formed by digging for clay in making pottery

窯黑兒（Ⅰㄠˊ ㄏㄟ ㄦ）
coal miners

窯姐兒（Ⅰㄠˊ ㄐⅠㄝˇ ㄦ）
prostitutes

窯子（Ⅰㄠˊ ㄗˇ）
①a brothel ②a prostitute

【窳】 4063
ㄩˇ yeu yǔ

1. coarse; crude; of inferior quality
2. lazy
3. weak; fragile
4. bad; mean

窳敗（ㄩˇ ㄅㄞˋ）
to rot; to fall

窳惰（ㄩˇ ㄉㄨㄛˋ）
lazy and dissipated; weak and indolent

窳陋（ㄩˇ ㄌㄡˋ）
crude; coarse; inferior（quality）

窳劣（ㄩˇ ㄌⅠㄝˋ）
bad; poor （quality）

窳楛（ㄩˇ ㄏㄨˋ）
coarse and fragile

十一畫

【窺】 4064
ㄎㄨㄟ kuei kuī

to watch or see in secret; to spy; to peep; to pry into

窺豹一斑（ㄎㄨㄟ ㄅㄠˋ Ⅰ ㄅㄢ）
（literally）to see only one spot of the leopard—to have only a limited view

窺探（ㄎㄨㄟ ㄊㄢˋ）
to spy on; to peep; to pry into: 不要窺探他人事物。Don't spy into other people's affairs.

窺天鏡（ㄎㄨㄟ ㄊⅠㄢ ㄐⅠㄥˋ）
a telescope

窺見（ㄎㄨㄟ ㄐⅠㄢˋ）
to get（or catch）a glimpse of; to detect

窺察（ㄎㄨㄟ ㄔㄚˊ）
to spy on; to watch

窺視（ㄎㄨㄟ ㄕˋ）
to peep at; to spy on; to watch secretly

窺測（ㄎㄨㄟ ㄘㄜˋ）
to watch and assess（a situation, development, etc.）

窺伺（ㄎㄨㄟ ㄙˋ）
to watch and wait （for a chance to attack, etc.）

窺隙（ㄎㄨㄟ ㄒⅠˋ）
to watch for a weakness （of the adversary）

窺園（ㄎㄨㄟ ㄩㄢˊ）
（literally）to look out occasionally at the garden—to

lack concentration while studying

【窶】 4065
ㄐㄩˋ jiuh jù

impoverished; straitened; destitute

窶人子（ㄐㄩˋ ㄖㄣˊ ㄗˇ）
a son from an impoverished family

十二畫

【窾】 4066
ㄎㄨㄢˇ koan kuǎn

1. a hollow; an opening
2. empty; hollow

窾竅（ㄎㄨㄢˇ くⅠㄠˋ）or 窾要（ㄎㄨㄢˇ Ⅰㄠˋ）
the main points or the crux of a matter

【窿】 4067
ㄌㄨㄥˊ long lóng

a hole; a cavity

十三畫

【竄】 4068
ㄘㄨㄢˋ tsuann cuàn

1. to escape; to run away; to flee
2. to change or alter（the wording）
3. to banish; to execute

竄伏（ㄘㄨㄢˋ ㄈㄨˊ）
to lie low; to skulk

竄定（ㄘㄨㄢˋ ㄉⅠㄥˋ）
to change or alter the wording of writings for the last time before publication

竄逃（ㄘㄨㄢˋ ㄊㄠˊ）
to flee in disorder: 敵人兵敗竄逃。The enemy was defeated and fled in disorder.

竄匿（ㄘㄨㄢˋ ㄋⅠˋ）
to flee and hide

竄改（ㄘㄨㄢˋ ㄍㄞˇ）
to make changes and alterations in a piece of writing （especially without authority）; to interpolate; to tamper

竄改帳目（ㄘㄨㄢˋ ㄍㄞˇ ㄓㄤˋ ㄇㄨˋ）
to fake accounts; to falsify accounts

竄擾（ㄘㄨㄢˋ ㄖㄠˇ）
①（said of bandits）to harass the people ②（said of the enemy）to intrude

竄入(ㄘㄨㄢ ㄖㄨˋ)
①to interpolate ②to flee to

竄逸(ㄘㄨㄢ ㄧˋ)
to escape; to take to one's
heels

【竅】 4069
ㄑㄧㄠˋ chiaw qiào
1. a hole; a cavity
2. apertures
3. the crux, key points, gist of
a matter; a knack

竅門(ㄑㄧㄠˋ ㄇㄣˊ)
the secret of doing some-
thing successfully; the right
way to do something; the
key to something; a knack

十五畫

【竇】 4070
ㄉㄡˋ dow dòu
1. a hole; a cavity; a burrow
2. a corrupt practice
3. a Chinese family name

十六畫

【竈】 4071
(竈) ㄗㄠˋ tzaw zào
1. a place for cooking; a
kitchen
2. a cooking stove or furnace

竈頭(ㄗㄠˋ ㄊㄡˊ)
a kitchen place

竈間(ㄗㄠˋ ㄐㄧㄢ)
the kitchen

竈君(ㄗㄠˋ ㄐㄩㄣ)or 竈神(ㄗㄠˋ ㄕㄣˊ)
or 竈王爺(ㄗㄠˋ ㄨㄤˊ ㄧㄝˊ)
the god of the kitchen

十七畫

【竊】 4072
ㄑㄧㄝˋ chieh qiè
1. to steal; to burglarize
2. a thief; a burglar
3. to usurp
4. stealthy
5. a self-derogatory way of
saying "I"

竊柄(ㄑㄧㄝˋ ㄅㄧㄥˋ)
to usurp the power of the
state

竊犯(ㄑㄧㄝˋ ㄈㄢˋ)
a thief; a burglar

竊盜狂(ㄑㄧㄝˋ ㄉㄠˋ ㄎㄨㄤˊ)
kleptomania

竊盜罪(ㄑㄧㄝˋ ㄉㄠˋ ㄗㄨㄟˋ)

theft; larceny: 他因竊盜罪被
關入獄中。He was put in
prison for theft.

竊聽(ㄑㄧㄝˋ ㄊㄧㄥ)
to eavesdrop; eavesdropping

竊聽器(ㄑㄧㄝˋ ㄊㄧㄥ ㄑㄧˋ)
a bugging device; a tapping
device; a listening-in device;
a bug

竊鉤竊國(ㄑㄧㄝˋ ㄍㄡ ㄑㄧㄝˋ ㄍㄨㄛˊ)
(originally, from *Chuang
Tzu* 莊子) Those who steal a
hook would be executed,
while those who steal
(usurp) the throne would
become kings.—punishment
or reward not depending
on the things one does

竊看(ㄑㄧㄝˋ ㄎㄢˋ)
to peep; to look at some-
thing stealthily

竊窺(ㄑㄧㄝˋ ㄨㄟ)
to steal a glance; to spy; to
watch stealthily; to peep

竊號(ㄑㄧㄝˋ ㄏㄠˋ)
to usurp the name of the
emperor

竊據(ㄑㄧㄝˋ ㄐㄩˋ)
the occupation of an area,
or a city by rebels

竊竊私議(ㄑㄧㄝˋ ㄑㄧㄝˋ ㄙ ㄧˋ)
to discuss something in
secret; to comment on something in whispers

竊竊私語(ㄑㄧㄝˋ ㄑㄧㄝˋ ㄙ ㄩˇ)
to talk stealthily or in a
very low voice; to whisper

竊取(ㄑㄧㄝˋ ㄑㄩˇ)
to steal; to take something
which does not lawfully
belong to one: 這間諜想竊
取機密情報。The spy tried to
steal secret information.

竊笑(ㄑㄧㄝˋ ㄒㄧㄠˋ)
to laugh behind another's
back; to laugh in secret

竊視(ㄑㄧㄝˋ ㄕˋ)
to peep

竊賊(ㄑㄧㄝˋ ㄗㄟˊ)
a thief; a burglar: 昨夜竊賊闖
入他家。Burglars broke into
his house last night.

竊思(ㄑㄧㄝˋ ㄙ)
I think personally that.... 或
My personal view is that....
或 in my personal opinion

竊案(ㄑㄧㄝˋ ㄢˋ)

a theft or larceny case

竊衣(ㄑㄧㄝˋ ㄧ)
(botany) torilis

竊以為(ㄑㄧㄝˋ ㄧˇ ㄨㄟˊ)
in my humble opinion; I presume that....

竊謂(ㄑㄧㄝˋ ㄨㄟˋ)
I should say that.... 或 Personally, I am inclined to
think that....

竊位(ㄑㄧㄝˋ ㄨㄟˋ)
to occupy a very powerful
position without the required
talent

竊位素餐(ㄑㄧㄝˋ ㄨㄟˋ ㄙㄨˋ ㄘㄢ)
to hold a high position but
do nothing for public interest

竊玉偷香(ㄑㄧㄝˋ ㄩˋ ㄊㄡ ㄒㄧㄤ)
to have an affair with a
girl; the ways of Don Juan,
or Casanova with women

立 部
ㄌㄧˋ lih lì

【立】 4073
ㄌㄧˋ lih lì
1. to stand
2. to establish; to found; to
build; to erect; to create; to
start
3. to stand on one's own feet;
to live
4. immediately; at once
5. a Chinese family name

立碑(ㄌㄧˋ ㄅㄟ)
to erect a monument

立逼(ㄌㄧˋ ㄅㄧ)
to force someone to do
something right away

立品(ㄌㄧˋ ㄆㄧㄣˇ)
to cultivate one's moral
character

立馬(ㄌㄧˋ ㄇㄚˇ)
to stop a horse; to rein in a
horse

立眉立眼(ㄌㄧˋ ㄇㄟˊ ㄌㄧˋ ㄧㄢˇ)
to get angry; to become furious

立名(ㄌㄧˋ ㄇㄧㄥˊ)
to distinguish oneself; to
achieve fame

立命(ㄌㄧˋ ㄇㄧㄥˋ)

〔立部〕

to establish one's Heaven-ordained being

立法(ㄌㄧˋ ㄈㄚˇ)
to legislate; to make laws; to enact laws

立法機關(ㄌㄧˋ ㄈㄚˇ ㄐㄧ ㄍㄨㄢ)
a legislative organ

立法權(ㄌㄧˋ ㄈㄚˇ ㄑㄩㄢˊ)
legislative power

立法委員(ㄌㄧˋ ㄈㄚˇ ㄨㄟˇ ㄩㄢˊ)
a legislator; a lawmaker

立法院(ㄌㄧˋ ㄈㄚˇ ㄩㄢˋ)
Legislative Yuan

立方(ㄌㄧˋ ㄈㄤ)
(mathematics) cube; cubic power

立方根(ㄌㄧˋ ㄈㄤ ㄍㄣ)
(mathematics) a cube root

立方體(ㄌㄧˋ ㄈㄤ ㄊㄧˇ)
(geometry) a cube

立方形的(ㄌㄧˋ ㄈㄤ ㄒㄧㄥˊ·ㄉㄜ)
cuboid

立德(ㄌㄧˋ ㄉㄜˊ)
to achieve virtue

立等(ㄌㄧˋ ㄉㄥˇ)or立揀(ㄌㄧˋ ㄉㄤˇ)
immediately; at once

立地成佛(ㄌㄧˋ ㄉㄧˋ ㄔㄥˊ ㄈㄛˊ)
to become a Buddha immediately (as soon as one lays down the butcher's knife)

立定(ㄌㄧˋ ㄉㄧㄥˋ)
(word of command) Halt!

立定主意(ㄌㄧˋ ㄉㄧㄥˋ ㄓㄨˇ ㄧˋ)
to make up one's mind; to make a decision: 我已立定主意個醫生。I've made up my mind to be a doctor.

立冬(ㄌㄧˋ ㄉㄨㄥ)
the Beginning of Winter (the date marking the beginning of one of the 24 seasonal periods in a year, falling normally on November 7 or 8 in the lunar calendar)或 Winter begins.

立陶宛(ㄌㄧˋ ㄊㄠˊ ㄨㄢˇ)
Lithuania

立談之間(ㄌㄧˋ ㄊㄢˊ ㄓ ㄐㄧㄢ)
in a moment; in an instant; in a jiffy

立體(ㄌㄧˋ ㄊㄧˇ)
①a solid body; a solid ②three-dimensional

立體電影(ㄌㄧˋ ㄊㄧˇ ㄉㄧㄢˋ ㄧㄥˇ)
a wide-angle motion picture; a 3-D motion picture; a

Cinerama

立體感(ㄌㄧˋ ㄊㄧˇ ㄍㄢˇ)
three-dimensional effects

立體化學(ㄌㄧˋ ㄊㄧˇ ㄏㄨㄚˋ ㄒㄩㄝˊ)
stereochemistry

立體幾何(ㄌㄧˋ ㄊㄧˇ ㄐㄧ ㄏㄜˊ)
solid geometry, stereometry, or geometry of space

立體戰爭(ㄌㄧˋ ㄊㄧˇ ㄓㄢˋ ㄓㄥ)
three-dimensional warfare

立體聲音(ㄌㄧˋ ㄊㄧˇ ㄕㄥ ㄧㄣ)
stereophonically reproduced sound; stereophony; stereo: 這是一臺立體聲音唱機。This is a stereo record player.

立體藝術(ㄌㄧˋ ㄊㄧˇ ㄧˋ ㄕㄨˋ)
plastic arts

立突(ㄌㄧˋ ㄊㄨˋ)or立脫爾(ㄌㄧˋ ㄊㄨㄛ ㄦˇ)
a liter (or litre) 亦作「公升」

立論(ㄌㄧˋ ㄌㄨㄣˊ)
an assertion made; a reasoning advanced; to set forth one's views; to present one's argument

立竿見影(ㄌㄧˋ ㄍㄢ ㄐㄧㄢˋ ㄧㄥˇ)
(literally) The moment a pole is erected, it throws its shadow upon the ground. —The outcome may be known immediately.

立國(ㄌㄧˋ ㄍㄨㄛˊ)
to found a state

立櫃(ㄌㄧˋ ㄍㄨㄟˋ)
a chest of drawers; a closet

立功(ㄌㄧˋ ㄍㄨㄥ)
to render distinguished service; to achieve distinction

立功贖罪(ㄌㄧˋ ㄍㄨㄥ ㄕㄨˊ ㄗㄨㄟˋ)
to render meritorious services to make repayment for one's crimes

立刻(ㄌㄧˋ ㄎㄜˋ)or立即(ㄌㄧˋ ㄐㄧˊ)or立時(ㄌㄧˋ ㄕˊ)
at once; immediately; promptly; right away: 我立刻就去。I'll be there right away.

立合同(ㄌㄧˋ ㄏㄜˊ ㄊㄨㄥˊ)
to conclude a contract

立候(ㄌㄧˋ ㄏㄡˋ)
to wait for something to happen immediately

立後(ㄌㄧˋ ㄏㄡˋ)
to adopt an heir

立婚書(ㄌㄧˋ ㄏㄨㄣ ㄕㄨ)

to draw up a marriage contract

立界(ㄌㄧˋ ㄐㄧㄝˋ)
to erect boundary markers; to mark boundary lines

立脚(ㄌㄧˋ ㄐㄧㄠˇ)
to have a footing; to have a standing space: 立脚之處。There was no footing on the cliff.

立脚點(ㄌㄧˋ ㄐㄧㄠˇ ㄉㄧㄢˇ)or立足點(ㄌㄧˋ ㄗㄨˊ ㄉㄧㄢˇ)
a footing; a foothold

立見(ㄌㄧˋ ㄐㄧㄢˋ)
can be seen immediately

立決(ㄌㄧˋ ㄐㄩㄝˊ)
to sentence and execute summarily

立契(ㄌㄧˋ ㄑㄧˋ)
to make a contract; to conclude an agreement

立秋(ㄌㄧˋ ㄑㄧㄡ)
the Beginning of Autumn (the date marking the beginning of one of the 24 seasonal periods in a year, falling normally on August 8 or 9 in the lunar calendar)或 Autumn begins.

立泉(ㄌㄧˋ ㄑㄩㄢˊ)
a waterfall; a cascade

立下(ㄌㄧˋ ㄒㄧㄚˋ)
to draw up (a legal document,etc.): 我將替你立下這事的計畫,I'll draw up a scheme of it for you.

立夏(ㄌㄧˋ ㄒㄧㄚˋ)
the Beginning of Summer (the date marking the beginning of one of the 24 seasonal periods in a year, falling normally on May 6 or 7 in the lunar calendar)或 Summer begins.

立效(ㄌㄧˋ ㄒㄧㄠˋ)
①to have a desired effect immediately ②to render meritorious service

立憲國(ㄌㄧˋ ㄒㄧㄢˋ ㄍㄨㄛˊ)
a constitutional state

立憲政體(ㄌㄧˋ ㄒㄧㄢˋ ㄓㄥˋ ㄊㄧˇ)
a constitutional government

立像(ㄌㄧˋ ㄒㄧㄤˋ)
①to erect a statue ②a statue in a standing position

立志(ㄌㄧˋ ㄓˋ)
to set an object of pursuit;

to make up one's mind to pursue some object; to resolve; to be determined: 他立志做大事不做大官。 He is determined to do great service, not to be an official.

立正(ㄌㄧˋ ㄓㄥˋ)
to stand at attention 或 Attention!

立軸(ㄌㄧˋ ㄓㄡˊ)
①a hanging scroll (of painting or calligraphy) ② (machinery) a vertical shaft; an upright shaft

立錐之地(ㄌㄧˋ ㄓㄨㄟ ㄓ ㄉㄧˋ)
space just enough for the point of a drill—very small space

立朝(ㄌㄧˋ ㄔㄠˊ)
to serve as a courtier

立場(ㄌㄧˋ ㄔㄤˇ)
a position; a stand; an attitude: 他對這件事表明立場。 He made his stand clear on this.

立儲(ㄌㄧˋ ㄔㄨˊ)
to designate the crown prince

立春(ㄌㄧˋ ㄔㄨㄣ)
the Beginning of Spring (the date marking the beginning of one of the 24 seasonal periods in a year, falling normally on February 4 or 5 in the lunar calendar) 或 Spring begins.

立誓(ㄌㄧˋ ㄕˋ)
to take an oath; to vow; to swear: 他立誓戒酒。 He is under a vow to drink no wine.

立身處世(ㄌㄧˋ ㄕㄣ ㄔㄨˇ ㄕˋ)
to establish oneself and manage to get along in the world

立字(ㄌㄧˋ ㄗˋ)
to make a contract in writing

立足地(ㄌㄧˋ ㄗㄨˊ ㄉㄧˋ)
a foothold; a footing: 我無法在此處得立足地。 I can't gain a foothold here.

立嗣(ㄌㄧˋ ㄙˋ)
to adopt an heir

立案(ㄌㄧˋ ㄢˋ)
to accredit (a school, etc.); to place a case on file for investigation and prosecution

立遺囑(ㄌㄧˋ ㄧˊ ㄓㄨˇ)
to make one's last will and testament

立意(ㄌㄧˋ ㄧˋ)
①to make up one's mind; to resolve ②intention or purpose; conception

立異(ㄌㄧˋ ㄧˋ)
①to dissent ② to be different

立業(ㄌㄧˋ ㄧㄝˋ)
to establish a business; to get a respectable career

立言(ㄌㄧˋ ㄧㄢˊ)
to leave worthy writings to posterity; to achieve glory by writing

立於不敗之地(ㄌㄧˋ ㄩˊ ㄅㄨˋ ㄅㄞˋ ㄓ ㄉㄧˋ)
to establish oneself in an unassailable position

立愈 or 立癒(ㄌㄧˋ ㄩˋ)
to be cured immediately

立約(ㄌㄧˋ ㄩㄝ)
to conclude a treaty; to contract

五畫

【站】 4074
ㄓㄢˋ jann zhàn
1. to stand: 往後站! Stand back!
2. a station; a stop; a center for rendering certain services

站班(ㄓㄢˋ ㄅㄢ)
(said of guards, etc.) to be on duty; to stand guard

站不起來(ㄓㄢˋ ㄅㄨˋ ㄑㄧˇ ㄌㄞˊ)
unable to stand up

站不住(ㄓㄢˋ ㄅㄨˋ ㄓㄨˋ)
①unable to keep standing ②(said of a theory) disputable; full of loopholes

站不住腳(ㄓㄢˋ ㄅㄨˋ ㄓㄨˋ ㄐㄧㄠˇ)
unable to hold one's position

站不穩(ㄓㄢˋ ㄅㄨˋ ㄨㄣˇ)
unable to stand firmly

站排(ㄓㄢˋ ㄆㄞˊ)
to line up

站票(ㄓㄢˋ ㄆㄧㄠˋ)
a ticket for standing room; an SRO (standing room only) ticket

站夫(ㄓㄢˋ ㄈㄨ)
a porter at a railway station

站得住(ㄓㄢˋ ㄉㄜˊ ㄓㄨˋ)
①able to stand; able to hold one's position ②(said of a theory) sound; irrefutable

站定(ㄓㄢˋ ㄉㄧㄥˋ)
to stand still

站隊(ㄓㄢˋ ㄉㄨㄟˋ)
to queue up; to line up; to stand in line

站臺(ㄓㄢˋ ㄊㄞˊ)
a platform (at a railway station)

站立(ㄓㄢˋ ㄌㄧˋ)
to stand

站籠(ㄓㄢˋ ㄌㄨㄥˊ)
a wooden cage for torturing convicts as a form of punishment in former times 亦作「立枷」

站崗(ㄓㄢˋ ㄍㄤˇ)
to stand guard; to act as a sentry; to stand sentry

站起來(ㄓㄢˋ ㄑㄧˇ ㄌㄞˊ)
to stand up; to rise

站長(ㄓㄢˋ ㄓㄤˇ)
the head of a station; a stationmaster; a station agent

站住(ㄓㄢˋ ㄓㄨˋ)
(word of command) Halt! 或 to stop; to stand: 我聽到有人叫我站住。 I heard someone calling to me to stop.

站穩(ㄓㄢˋ ㄨㄣˇ)
to stand firm; to take a firm stand

【竚】 4075
(佇) ㄓㄨˋ juh zhù
to stand for a long time

竚候(ㄓㄨˋ ㄏㄡˋ)
to stand and wait

【並】 4076
(並) ㄅㄧㄥˋ bìng bìng
1. also; and
2. to combine; to join

六畫

【竟】 4077
ㄐㄧㄥˋ jìng jìng
1. to come to an end; to terminate; to go through the whole course; to finish; to complete
2. rather unexpectedly; some-

〔立 部〕

立部

what to one's surprise; in a way thought to be rather unlikely

竟敢 (ㄐㄧㄥˋ ㄍㄢˇ)
to dare somewhat to one's surprise; to have the audacity: 他竟敢侮辱我。He dared to insult me.

竟是 (ㄐㄧㄥˋ ㄕˋ)
to turn out to be

竟日 (ㄐㄧㄥˋ ㄖˋ)
the whole day; all day long

竟然 (ㄐㄧㄥˋ ㄖㄢˊ)
in a way thought to be rather unlikely; somewhat unexpectedly; somewhat to one's surprise

竟然不理 (ㄐㄧㄥˋ ㄖㄢˊ ㄅㄨˋ ㄌㄧˇ)
to pay no heed, somewhat to another's surprise

竟然如此 (ㄐㄧㄥˋ ㄖㄢˊ ㄖㄨˊ ㄘˇ)
to be so, somewhat to one's surprise

竟自 (ㄐㄧㄥˋ ㄗˋ)
somewhat to one's surprise

竟夜 (ㄐㄧㄥˋ ㄧㄝˋ)
all night; the whole night

竟有此事 (ㄐㄧㄥˋ ㄧㄡˇ ㄘˇ ㄕˋ)
To everyone's surprise, it did happen.

【章】 4078 ㄓㄤ jang zhāng
1. a piece of writing; a chapter; a main division of a book: 全書共三十章。The book has thirty chapters.
2. a system; a statute; an organized body
3. an emblem; a seal; a stamp
4. to make clear; to make known
5. a pattern; an example
6. a Chinese family name

章法 (ㄓㄤ ㄈㄚˇ)
① the presentation of ideas in a piece of writing; the art of composition ② orderly ways: 他辦事很有章法。He does everything in orderly ways.

章服 (ㄓㄤ ㄈㄨˊ)
ceremonial dress with distinctive colors and designs for rulers and courtiers in ancient times

章臺 (ㄓㄤ ㄊㄞˊ)
(euphemism) a brothel; a house of ill fame

章回小說 (ㄓㄤ ㄏㄨㄟˊ ㄒㄧㄠˇ ㄕㄨㄛ)
a serial novel; a type of old Chinese novel with each chapter headed by a couplet giving the main points of its content

章節 (ㄓㄤ ㄐㄧㄝˊ)
chapters and sections (of a piece of writing)

章句 (ㄓㄤ ㄐㄩˋ)
proper division (of an unpunctuated ancient text) into chapters and sentences

章程 (ㄓㄤ ㄔㄥˊ)
① a set of regulation; constitution ② a solution; a way

章奏 (ㄓㄤ ㄗㄡˋ)
an appeal or report presented to the emperor

章草 (ㄓㄤ ㄘㄠˇ)
a style of cursive writing of the "script" type, originated by Shih-yu (史游) of the Han Dynasty, so named because it was chiefly used in 章奏

章魚 (ㄓㄤ ㄩˊ)
an octopus

七畫

【童】 4079 ㄊㄨㄥˊ torng tóng
1. a child; a minor; a virgin
2. (said of land, etc.) bare; barren
3. a Chinese family name

童便 (ㄊㄨㄥˊ ㄅㄧㄢˋ)
(Chinese medicine) urine of boys

童僕 (ㄊㄨㄥˊ ㄆㄨˊ)
a boy servant; a boy; a houseboy; a manservant

童蒙 (ㄊㄨㄥˊ ㄇㄥˊ)
innocent childhood; childish ignorance

童男 (ㄊㄨㄥˊ ㄋㄢˊ)
a virgin man

童男女 (ㄊㄨㄥˊ ㄋㄢˊ ㄋㄩˇ)
minors of both sexes

童牛角馬 (ㄊㄨㄥˊ ㄋㄧㄡˊ ㄐㄧㄠˇ ㄇㄚˇ)
(literally) a hornless ox and a horned horse—common practice; abnormal phenomenon

童年 (ㄊㄨㄥˊ ㄋㄧㄢˊ)
childhood; youth: 他們自童年起即感好友。They are good

friends since childhood.

童女 (ㄊㄨㄥˊ ㄋㄩˇ)
a virgin

童工 (ㄊㄨㄥˊ ㄍㄨㄥ)
child labor; a child laborer

童話 (ㄊㄨㄥˊ ㄏㄨㄚˋ)
nursery stories; juvenile stories; fairy tales

童昏 (ㄊㄨㄥˊ ㄏㄨㄣ)
young and ignorant; naive and ignorant

童心 (ㄊㄨㄥˊ ㄒㄧㄣ)
a childish heart

童心未泯 (ㄊㄨㄥˊ ㄒㄧㄣ ㄨㄟˋ ㄇㄧㄣˇ)
to retain a childish heart; still to keep traces of childishness or childlike innocence

童稚 (ㄊㄨㄥˊ ㄓˋ)
children

童貞 (ㄊㄨㄥˊ ㄓㄣ)
virginity; chastity

童真 (ㄊㄨㄥˊ ㄓㄣ)
a Buddhist novice; a monk (who should have a child's nature of simplicity)

童裝 (ㄊㄨㄥˊ ㄓㄨㄤ)
children's garments

童山 (ㄊㄨㄥˊ ㄕㄢ)
a bare hill

童山濯濯 (ㄊㄨㄥˊ ㄕㄢ ㄓㄨㄛˊ ㄓㄨㄛˊ)
① an unforested mountain ② baldheaded

童身 (ㄊㄨㄥˊ ㄕㄣ)
(said of a male adult) to have had no sexual intercourse with a woman

童生 (ㄊㄨㄥˊ ㄕㄥ)
a candidate for the lowest degree under the former civil service examination system

童豎 (ㄊㄨㄥˊ ㄕㄨˋ)
a toddler

童子 (ㄊㄨㄥˊ ㄗˇ) or 童蒲 (ㄊㄨㄥˊ ㄖㄨˊ)
a minor; a child; a boy; a lad

童子軍 (ㄊㄨㄥˊ ㄗˇ ㄐㄩㄣ) or 童軍 (ㄊㄨㄥˊ ㄐㄩㄣ)
a boy scout

童子軍大露營 (ㄊㄨㄥˊ ㄗˇ ㄐㄩㄣ ㄉㄚˋ ㄌㄨˋ ㄧㄥˊ)
a camporee; a jamboree

童叟 (ㄊㄨㄥˊ ㄙㄡˇ)
children and aged people

童叟無欺 (ㄊㄨㄥˊ ㄙㄡˇ ㄨˊ ㄑㄧ)

We are honest even to children and aged people. (a shop sign meaning "We are honest with all customers.")

童騃(ㄊㄨㄥˊ ㄞˊ)
young and ignorant

童謠(ㄊㄨㄥˊ ㄧㄠˊ)
nursery rhymes; nursery songs

童幼(ㄊㄨㄥˊ ㄧㄡˋ)
childhood

童顏鶴髮(ㄊㄨㄥˊ ㄧㄢˊ ㄏㄜˋ ㄈㄚˇ)
(literally) a ruddy complexion and a hoary head—to look youthful at an advanced age

童養媳(ㄊㄨㄥˊ ㄧㄤˇ ㄒㄧˊ)
a girl brought up in the family of her future husband; a child daughter-in-law

【竣】 4080
(ㄐㄩㄣˋ) jiunn jùn
accomplished; completed

竣工(ㄐㄩㄣˋ ㄍㄨㄥ)
(said of a construction project) to be completed

竣事(ㄐㄩㄣˋ ㄕˋ)
(said of a plan, etc.) having been completed

【竦】 4081
(ㄙㄨㄥˇ) soong sǒng
1. respectful
2. awed

竦然(ㄙㄨㄥˇ ㄖㄢˊ)
fearful; scared

九畫

【竭】 4082
(ㄐㄧㄝˊ) jye jié
1. to devote, or put forth (efforts, etc.)
2. to exhaust; to use up

竭力(ㄐㄧㄝˊ ㄌㄧˋ)
to do one's utmost; to do one's best; to exert one's utmost strength: 我們竭力幫助他。We do our best to help him.

竭誠(ㄐㄧㄝˊ ㄔㄥˊ)
to devote one's mental energy to the full

竭盡(ㄐㄧㄝˊ ㄐㄧㄣˋ)
to devote to the full; to exhaust; to use up

竭盡棉薄(ㄐㄧㄝˊ ㄐㄧㄣˋ ㄇㄧㄢˊ ㄅㄛˊ)
to do all one can (a polite expression)

竭蹶(ㄐㄧㄝˊ ㄐㄩㄝˊ)
①to stagger; to totter ②to proceed with difficulty ③destitute; impoverished

竭智盡力(ㄐㄧㄝˊ ㄓˋ ㄐㄧㄣˋ ㄌㄧˋ)or 竭智(ㄐㄧㄝˊ ㄓˋ)
to devote one's mental resources to the full

竭誠(ㄐㄧㄝˊ ㄔㄥˊ)
wholeheartedly; with all sincerity: 我們竭誠擁護我們的領袖。We support our leader with all sincerity.

竭澤而漁(ㄐㄧㄝˊ ㄗㄜˊ ㄦˊ ㄩˊ)
(literally) to fish by emptying the water of a pond—to make a thorough but unwise exploitation

【端】 4083
(ㄉㄨㄢ) duan duān
1. an extreme; an end
2. a beginning
3. correct; proper; upright
4. leads; a clue
5. to carry carefully
6. cause

端木(ㄉㄨㄢ ㄇㄨˋ)
a Chinese double family name

端方(ㄉㄨㄢ ㄈㄤ)
upright; righteous

端底(ㄉㄨㄢ ㄉㄧˇ)
after all; in the long run; ultimately: 他雖浪費，端底不失為一好人。He is a spendthrift. After all, he is a good man.

端的(ㄉㄨㄢ ㄉㄧˋ)
①indeed; actually; as expected ②after all; in the long run

端倪(ㄉㄨㄢ ㄋㄧˊ)
general shape; an outline; a clue; signs: 我們找到這祕密的一點端倪。We found a clue to the mystery.

端凝(ㄉㄨㄢ ㄋㄧㄥˊ)
solemn; dignified

端賴(ㄉㄨㄢ ㄌㄞˋ)
to rely entirely upon

端麗(ㄉㄨㄢ ㄌㄧˋ)
neat and beautiful; graceful; comely

端拱(ㄉㄨㄢ ㄍㄨㄥˇ)
(said of a monarch) to rule without actually governing

端揆(ㄉㄨㄢ ㄎㄨㄟˊ)
a prime minister

端詳(ㄉㄨㄢ ㄒㄧㄤˊ)
①to study or examine in detail; to scrutinize ②details; the whole story: 告訴我事情的端詳吧。Tell me all the details. ③dignified and serene: 她舉止端詳。She behaves with serene dignity.

端相(ㄉㄨㄢ ㄒㄧㄤˋ)
to look at carefully

端行(ㄉㄨㄢ ㄒㄧㄥˊ)
upright behavior

端緒(ㄉㄨㄢ ㄒㄩˋ)
clues to the handling of a thing

端正(ㄉㄨㄢ ㄓㄥˋ)
①correct; proper ②to correct; to rectify: 我們端正學習態度。We correct our attitude toward study. ③regular; well-formed; symmetric: 他的五官端正。He has regular features.

端莊(ㄉㄨㄢ ㄓㄨㄤ)
sober; dignified

端重(ㄉㄨㄢ ㄓㄨㄥˋ)
serious; sober; sedate

端士(ㄉㄨㄢ ㄕˋ)
a high-principled man

端視(ㄉㄨㄢ ㄕˋ)
to look steadily

端上(ㄉㄨㄢ ㄕㄤˋ)
to carry (a tray of food, etc.) carefully

端然(ㄉㄨㄢ ㄖㄢˊ)
neat; symmetrical

端坐(ㄉㄨㄢ ㄗㄨㄛˋ)
to sit properly; to sit straight

端陽節(ㄉㄨㄢ ㄧㄤˊ ㄐㄧㄝˊ)or 端午節(ㄉㄨㄢ ㄨˇ ㄐㄧㄝˊ)
the Dragon-Boat Festival (falling on the fifth day of the fifth lunar month)

端陽競渡(ㄉㄨㄢ ㄧㄤˊ ㄐㄧㄥˋ ㄉㄨˋ)
a dragon-boat race on the Dragon-Boat Festival

端委(ㄉㄨㄢ ㄨㄟˇ)
ceremonial robes or dress

端月(ㄉㄨㄢ ㄩㄝˋ)
the first lunar month; the first moon

十五畫

〔立部〕

【競】 4084 ㄐㄧㄥˋ jìnq jìng
to compete; to vie

競賣(ㄐㄧㄥˋ ㄇㄞˋ)
an auction; to auction off: 他
競賣他的傢俱。He auctioned
off his furniture.

競渡(ㄐㄧㄥˋ ㄉㄨˋ)
a boat race (especially the
one on the Dragon-Boat Festival)

競技(ㄐㄧㄥˋ ㄐㄧˋ)
a race; a contest; a tournament

競進(ㄐㄧㄥˋ ㄐㄧㄣˋ)
to advance side by side

競選(ㄐㄧㄥˋ ㄒㄩㄢˇ)
to vie in an election; to campaign; to run for: 他 競選總統。He ran for the presidency.

競爭(ㄐㄧㄥˋ ㄓㄥ)
to compete; to vie; competition

競爭心(ㄐㄧㄥˋ ㄓㄥ ㄒㄧㄣ)
competitive spirit; the spirit to excel

競爭性(ㄐㄧㄥˋ ㄓㄥ ㄒㄧㄥˋ)
competitiveness

競爭者(ㄐㄧㄥˋ ㄓㄥ ㄓㄜˇ)
a competitor

競走(ㄐㄧㄥˋ ㄗㄡˇ)
a foot race; a walkathon

競賽(ㄐㄧㄥˋ ㄙㄞˋ)
a race; a contest

竹 部
ㄓㄨˊ jwu zhú

【竹】 4085
ㄓㄨˊ jwu zhú
1. bamboo
2. slips of bamboo for writing
3. a Chinese family name

竹帛(ㄓㄨˊ ㄅㄛˊ)
①bamboo tablets and textiles (both used as paper in ancient times) ②books

竹報平安(ㄓㄨˊ ㄅㄠˋ ㄆㄧㄥˊ ㄢ)
to report in a letter home that everything is well

竹布(ㄓㄨˊ ㄅㄨˋ)
starched light-blue cotton cloth

竹批兒(ㄓㄨˊ ㄆㄧ ㄦ)
bamboo strips (as material for making baskets, etc.)

竹馬(ㄓㄨˊ ㄇㄚˇ)
a bamboo hobbyhorse: 兒童
騎竹馬玩。Children rode on a bamboo hobbyhorse to play.

竹篾(ㄓㄨˊ ㄇㄧㄝˋ)
thin and flat slips of bamboo used for weaving purpose

竹幕(ㄓㄨˊ ㄇㄨˋ)
the Bamboo Curtain (a derogatory reference to socialist states)

竹筏(ㄓㄨˊ ㄈㄚˊ)
a bamboo raft: 他乘竹筏順流
而下。He went down the river on a bamboo raft.

竹夫人(ㄓㄨˊ ㄈㄨ ㄖㄣˊ)
a large pillow-shaped bamboo ware used as an armrest and footrest in bed during summer

竹頭木屑(ㄓㄨˊ ㄊㄡˊ ㄇㄨˋ ㄒㄧㄝˋ)
(literally) odd pieces of bamboo and wood—seemingly unimportant but useful things

竹筒(ㄓㄨˊ ㄊㄨㄥˊ)
a bamboo tube

竹籃(ㄓㄨˊ ㄌㄢˊ)
a bamboo basket: 她買了一個
竹籃。She bought a bamboo basket.

竹籬茅舍(ㄓㄨˊ ㄌㄧˊ ㄇㄠˊ ㄕㄜˋ)
(literally) a bamboo fence around a thatched cottage —a simple dwelling

竹笠(ㄓㄨˊ ㄌㄧˋ)
a bamboo hat

竹簾(ㄓㄨˊ ㄌㄧㄢˊ)
a bamboo curtain or screen

竹林(ㄓㄨˊ ㄌㄧㄣˊ)
a bamboo grove

竹林七賢(ㄓㄨˊ ㄌㄧㄣˊ ㄑㄧ ㄒㄧㄢˊ)
山濤、阮籍、嵇康、向秀、劉伶、阮咸、王戎, known as the Seven Wise Men of the Bamboo Grove (a group of seven men of letters in the 3th century)

竹林之遊(ㄓㄨˊ ㄌㄧㄣˊ ㄓ ㄧㄡˊ)
association with learned scholars

竹籠(ㄓㄨˊ ㄌㄨㄥˊ)
a bamboo cage; a bamboo

basket with a narrow opening

竹竿(ㄓㄨˊ ㄍㄢ)or 竹竿兒(ㄓㄨˊ ㄍㄚㄦ)
a bamboo pole or cane

竹槓(ㄓㄨˊ ㄍㄤˋ)
a bamboo carrying pole

竹工(ㄓㄨˊ ㄍㄨㄥ)
bamboo works

竹雞(ㄓㄨˊ ㄐㄧ)
a bamboo partridge

竹節(ㄓㄨˊ ㄐㄧㄝˊ)
bamboo joints

竹簡(ㄓㄨˊ ㄐㄧㄢˇ)
slips of bamboo for writing

竹器(ㄓㄨˊ ㄑㄧˋ)
bamboo ware

竹蓆子(ㄓㄨˊ ㄒㄧˊ ㄗ)
a mat made of split bamboo

竹枝詞(ㄓㄨˊ ㄓ ㄘˊ)
a kind of verse mainly about the life of the common people, originating in the Tang Dynasty

竹紙(ㄓㄨˊ ㄓˇ)
bamboo paper

竹製品(ㄓㄨˊ ㄓˋ ㄆㄧㄣˇ)
bamboo articles

竹實(ㄓㄨˊ ㄕˊ)
bamboo seeds

竹書(ㄓㄨˊ ㄕㄨ)
a collection of ancient bamboo books, supposedly unearthed from a prince's grave in the 4th century

竹書紀年(ㄓㄨˊ ㄕㄨ ㄐㄧˋ ㄋㄧㄢˊ)
a chronicle book among a collection of ancient bamboo books, supposedly discovered in a prince's grave in the 4th century

竹子(ㄓㄨˊ ㄗˇ)
bamboo

竹孫(ㄓㄨˊ ㄙㄨㄣ)
bamboo growing out of a side root

竹蓀(ㄓㄨˊ ㄙㄨㄣ)
an edible whitish fungus

竹笋 or 竹筍(ㄓㄨˊ ㄙㄨㄣˇ)
bamboo shoots

竹椅(ㄓㄨˊ ㄧˇ)
a bamboo chair

竹葉青(ㄓㄨˊ ㄧㄝˋ ㄑㄧㄥ)
①three-year-old Shaohsing wine ②a kind of venomous snake

竹輿(ㄓㄨˊ ㄩˊ)
a bamboo sedan chair

二畫

【竺】 4086
ㄓㄨ jwu zhú
1. ancient name of India 參看
「天竺」
2. a Chinese family name
竺經(ㄓㄨ ㄐㄧㄥ)
the Buddhist scriptures; Indian sutras
竺學(ㄓㄨ ㄒㄩㄝˊ)
the study of Buddhism

三畫

【竽】 4087
ㄩˊ yu yú
a kind of musical instrument with 36 reeds

【竿】 4088
《ㄍㄢ gan gān
1. a bamboo pole; a bamboo rod
2. slips of bamboo for writing
竿頭日上(《ㄢ ㄊㄡˊ ㄖˋ ㄕㄤˋ)
to make constant progress in one's studies 亦作竿頭日進」
竿子(《ㄢ ˙ㄗ)or竿兒(《ㄢˊ)
a bamboo pole

四畫

【笆】 4089
ㄅㄚ ba bā
a bamboo fence
笆斗(ㄅㄚ ㄉㄡˇ)
a willow basket for holding grains

【笊】 4090
ㄓㄠˋ jaw zhào
a bamboo skimmer
笊籬(ㄓㄠˋ ㄌㄧˊ)
a bamboo skimmer; a wire strainer; a fisherman's rake for catching clam, etc.

【笏】 4091
ㄏㄨˋ huh hù
a tablet held by a civil official during an audience with the monarch

【笈】 4092
ㄐㄧˊ jyi jí
a bamboo bookcase

【笑】 4093
ㄒㄧㄠˋ shiaw xiào
1. to laugh; to smile; to grin;

to giggle; to titter; to chuckle; to snicker
2. to ridicule; to deride; to jeer: 她剛開始學，別笑她。She has just started learning. Don't jeer at her.
笑柄(ㄒㄧㄠˋ ㄅㄧㄥˇ)
a laughingstock; a joke
笑不可仰(ㄒㄧㄠˋ ㄅㄨˋ ㄎㄜˇ ㄧㄤˇ)
to roll with laughter
笑破肚皮(ㄒㄧㄠˋ ㄆㄛˋ ㄉㄨˋ ㄆㄧˊ)
to be overwhelmed with laughter; to roll with laughter
笑罵由他(ㄒㄧㄠˋ ㄇㄚˋ ㄧㄡˊ ㄊㄚ)
Let him ridicule and revile as he likes. (I don't care a bit about his ridicule and abuse.)
笑貌(ㄒㄧㄠˋ ㄇㄠˋ)
a smiling face
笑眯眯(ㄒㄧㄠˋ ㄇㄧ ˙ㄇㄧ)
to be all smiles; beaming
笑面虎(ㄒㄧㄠˋ ㄇㄧㄢˋ ㄏㄨˇ)
a smiling tiger—(figuratively) a friendly-looking villain; a wolf in sheep's clothing; a treacherous fellow
笑掉大牙(ㄒㄧㄠˋ ㄉㄧㄠˋ ㄉㄚˋ ㄧㄚˊ)
to burst out laughing over the absurdity, ludicrousness, etc. of something
笑談(ㄒㄧㄠˋ ㄊㄢˊ)
① a laughingstock ② laughing conversation; gay conversation ③ to laugh over
笑納(ㄒㄧㄠˋ ㄋㄚˋ)
to accept (a gift) with a laugh over its worthlessness (a conventional expression for asking another to accept a gift): 請笑納, Please accept this small gift of mine.
笑裏藏刀(ㄒㄧㄠˋ ㄌㄧˇ ㄘㄤˊ ㄉㄠ)
(literally) to conceal a dagger behind a smile—very treacherous
笑臉(ㄒㄧㄠˋ ㄌㄧㄢˇ)
a smiling face: 我們對他笑臉相迎。We greeted him with a smiling face.
笑口常開(ㄒㄧㄠˋ ㄎㄡˇ ㄔㄤˊ ㄎㄞ)
grinning all the time
笑哈哈(ㄒㄧㄠˋ ㄏㄚ ㄏㄚ)or笑呵呵(ㄒㄧㄠˋ ㄏㄜ ㄏㄜ)
to laugh heartily
笑話百出(ㄒㄧㄠˋ ㄏㄨㄚˋ ㄅㄞˇ ㄔㄨ)

to make many ridiculous mistakes
笑話(ㄒㄧㄠˋ ˙ㄏㄨㄚˋ)or笑話兒(ㄒㄧㄠˋ ˙ㄏㄨㄚˊ)
① a joke; a funny story: 那是個有趣的笑話。That's a good joke. ② a ridiculous error; a laughable mistake ③ Nonsense! ④ to laugh at; to ridicule: 可別笑話我的表演。Please do not laugh at my performance.
笑氣(ㄒㄧㄠˋ ㄑㄧˋ)
(chemistry) laughing gas; nitrous oxide
笑嘻嘻(ㄒㄧㄠˋ ㄒㄧ ㄒㄧ)
to be all smiles; to look very happy
笑逐顏開(ㄒㄧㄠˋ ㄓㄨˊ ㄧㄢˊ ㄎㄞ)
to beam with smiles; to be wreathed in smiles
笑場(ㄒㄧㄠˋ ㄔㄤˇ)or笑誤(ㄒㄧㄠˋ ㄒㄧˇ)
an entertainer's silly laughter during performance
笑出眼淚(ㄒㄧㄠˋ ㄔㄨ ㄧㄢˇ ㄌㄟˋ)
to laugh until tears come
笑殺(ㄒㄧㄠˋ ㄕㄚ)or笑煞(ㄒㄧㄠˋ ㄕㄚ)
to be overwhelmed with laughter
笑聲(ㄒㄧㄠˋ ㄕㄥ)
sound of laughter
笑容(ㄒㄧㄠˋ ㄖㄨㄥˊ)
a smile; happy expression; a smiling countenance
笑容可掬(ㄒㄧㄠˋ ㄖㄨㄥˊ ㄎㄜˇ ㄐㄩ)
to show pleasant smiles; to be all smiles; to be radiant with smiles
笑死人(ㄒㄧㄠˋ ㄙˇ ㄖㄣˊ)
to make one laugh to death; extremely ridiculous; ludicrous to the utmost degree
笑一笑(ㄒㄧㄠˋ ㄧˋ ㄒㄧㄠˋ)
to give a smile
笑靨(ㄒㄧㄠˋ ㄧㄝˋ)or笑渦(ㄒㄧㄠˋ ㄨㄛ)
dimples appearing with a smile
笑微微(ㄒㄧㄠˋ ㄨㄟ ㄨㄟ)
smiling

五畫

【笙】 4094
ㄕㄥ sheng shēng
a kind of panpipe with 13 reeds

【竹部】

笙歌(ㄕㄥ《ㄜ)
music and songs

笙管(ㄕㄥ《ㄨㄢˇ)
pipes of a panpipe

笙簧(ㄕㄥ ㄏㄨㄤˊ)
reeds of a panpipe

笙磬同音(ㄕㄥ ㄑㄧㄥˋ ㄊㄨㄥˊ ㄧㄣ)
in complete harmony

【笠】 4095
ㄌㄧˋ lih lì
1. a bamboo hat
2. a bamboo shade or covering

【笛】 4096
ㄉㄧˊ dyi dí
a flute

笛卡兒(ㄉㄧˊ ㄎㄚˇ ㄦˊ)
Daniel Defoe, 1659? —1731,
English writer and political
commentator

笛卡爾(ㄉㄧˊ ㄎㄚˇ ㄦˇ)
René Descartes, 1596-1650,
French philosopher and
mathematician

笛子(ㄉㄧˊ ㆍ)
a flute: 他在吹笛子。He plays
(on) the flute.

【笨】 4097
ㄅㄣˋ benn bèn
1. stupid; dull: 他笨透了。He is
as stupid as an owl.
2. clumsy; awkward: 你這人笨
手笨腳的。You are clumsy.

笨伯(ㄅㄣˋ ㄅㄛˊ)
a fool; a simpleton

笨蛋(ㄅㄣˋ ㄉㄢˋ)
a fool; a simpleton

笨頭笨腦(ㄅㄣˋ ㄊㄡˊ ㄅㄣˋ ㄋㄠˇ)
stupid; muddleheaded; dull;
blockheaded

笨瓜(ㄅㄣˋ ㄍㄨㄚ)
a fool

笨工(ㄅㄣˋ ㄍㄨㄥ)
an unskilled workman

笨漢(ㄅㄣˋ ㄏㄢˋ)
a clumsy fellow: 他是個笨漢。
He's a clumsy fellow.

笨貨(ㄅㄣˋ ㄏㄨㄛˋ)
a fool; a simpleton; a dullard

笨像伙(ㄅㄣˋ ㄒㄧㄤˋ˙ㄏㄨㄛˇ)
a fool; a simpleton; a clumsy
fellow

笨拙(ㄅㄣˋ ㄓㄨㄛˊ)
unskilled; clumsy; awkward:
他行動笨拙。He is clumsy in
movement.

笨重(ㄅㄣˋ ㄓㄨㄥˋ)

①cumbersome; heavy; too
heavy for convenient han-
dling ② clumsy

笨車(ㄅㄣˋ ㄔㄜ)
a heavy wagon; a heavy
cart

笨手笨腳(ㄅㄣˋ ㄕㄡˇ ㄅㄣˋ ㄐㄧㄠˇ)
acting clumsily; all thumbs

笨人(ㄅㄣˋ ㄖㄣˊ)
a fool; a simpleton; a dullard; an idiot

笨賊(ㄅㄣˋ ㄗㄟˊ)
①a fool; a simpleton; a dullard; an idiot ②a stupid burglar

【答】 4098
ㄔ chy chī
1. a bamboo whip
2. to whip; to flog

笞背(ㄔ ㄅㄟˋ)
to flog the back; to whip the
back

笞罵(ㄔ ㄇㄚˋ)
to whip and revile

笞臀(ㄔ ㄊㄨㄣˊ)
to whip the buttocks; to flog
the buttocks

笞刑(ㄔ ㄒㄧㄥˊ)
cane punishment; whipping,
or flogging (as a form of
punishment in former times)

笞辱(ㄔ ㄖㄨˋ)
to whip and insult

【笥】 4099
ㄙ syh sì
a bamboo box or chest

笥匱蕁空(ㄙㄨㄟˋ ㄎㄨㄟˋ ㄐㄩㄢˋ ㄎㄨㄥ)
(literally) All the boxes and
bags are empty.—extremely
destitute; dead broke

【第】 4100
ㄗ tzyy zì
a bed

【符】 4101
ㄈㄨˊ fwu fú
1. a tally carried for identification, as a warrant, etc.; an
identification tag or label
2. an auspicious omen
3. a charm; a talisman; a spell:
有些人信符咒。Some people
believe in charms.
4. to match; to tally; to correspond; to accord: 他言不符
實。His statement does not
tally with facts.
5. a symbol; a sign
6. a Chinese family name

符命(ㄈㄨˊ ㄇㄧㄥˋ)
auspicious omen sent down
upon a prince as a token of
his appointment to the
throne

符頭(ㄈㄨˊ ㄊㄡˊ)
heads of musical notes

符籙(ㄈㄨˊ ㄌㄨˋ)
Taoist secret talismanic
writing

符合(ㄈㄨˊ ㄏㄜˊ)
to correspond; to match; to
tally: 你的帳目和我的符合。
Your account tallies with
mine.

符號(ㄈㄨˊ ㄏㄠˋ)
a symbol; a sign: 文字是思想
的符號。Words are the signs
of ideas.

符號邏輯(ㄈㄨˊ ㄏㄠˋ ㄌㄨㄛˊ ㄐㄧ)
symbolic logic

符璽(ㄈㄨˊ ㄒㄧˇ)
a tally or a seal consisting
of two halves carried for
identification, as a warrant,
etc.

符璽(ㄈㄨˊ ㄒㄧˇ)
an imperial seal or stamp

符信(ㄈㄨˊ ㄒㄧㄣˋ)
①an identification tag, sign,
etc. ② to certify authenticity
by matching the tallies

符咒(ㄈㄨˊ ㄓㄡˋ)
a charm; a spell; an amulet:
他被符咒鎮住。He was bound
by a spell.

符讖(ㄈㄨˊ ㄔㄣˋ)
Taoist omens and proph-
ecies

符水(ㄈㄨˊ ㄕㄨㄟˇ)
magic words and water for
curing diseases

符籙(ㄈㄨˊ ㄖㄨˋ)
auspices; an auspicious
omen

符驗(ㄈㄨˊ ㄧㄢˋ)
to verify through a tally, a
sign

符應(ㄈㄨˊ ㄧㄥˋ)
agreement of an omen with
the fact

符尾(ㄈㄨˊ ㄨㄟˇ)
tails of musical notes

【第】 4102
ㄉㄧˋ dih dì
1. sequence; order
2. rank; grade; degree

3. a mansion; a residence
4. a Chinese family name

第八藝術(ㄉㄧˋ ㄅㄚ ㄧˋ ㄕㄨˋ)
the eighth art—the movies

第六感(ㄉㄧˋ ㄌㄧㄡˋ ㄍㄢˇ)
the sixth sense; extrasensory perception (ESP)

第宅(ㄉㄧˋ ㄓㄞˊ)
a mansion

第三(ㄉㄧˋ ㄙㄢ)
third; tertiary: 在賽跑中我得到第三名。I got the third prize in the race.

第三帝國(ㄉㄧˋ ㄙㄢ ㄉㄧˋ ㄍㄨㄛˊ)
the Third Reich; the Nazi Germany

第三國際(ㄉㄧˋ ㄙㄢ ㄍㄨㄛˊ ㄐㄧˋ)
the Third International

第三者(ㄉㄧˋ ㄙㄢ ㄓㄜˇ)
a third person; a disinterested person; a third party

第三世界(ㄉㄧˋ ㄙㄢ ㄕˋ ㄐㄧㄝˋ)
the third world (including the developing countries in Asia, Africa, Latin America and elsewhere)

第三人稱(ㄉㄧˋ ㄙㄢ ㄖㄣˊ ㄔㄥ)
(grammar) the third person

第二(ㄉㄧˋ ㄦˋ)
second; secondary: 她是第二個出去的人。She was the second person to go out.

第二國際(ㄉㄧˋ ㄦˋ ㄍㄨㄛˊ ㄐㄧˋ)
the Second International

第二人稱(ㄉㄧˋ ㄦˋ ㄖㄣˊ ㄔㄥ)
(grammar) the second person

第二次世界大戰(ㄉㄧˋ ㄦˋ ㄘˋ ㄕˋ ㄐㄧㄝˋ ㄉㄚˋ ㄓㄢˋ)
the Second World War; World War Ⅱ

第一(ㄉㄧˋ ㄧ)
first; primary: 他在全班是第一。He is the first in his class.

第一排(ㄉㄧˋ ㄧ ㄆㄞˊ)
the first row

第一天(ㄉㄧˋ ㄧ ㄊㄧㄢ)
the first day

第一流(ㄉㄧˋ ㄧ ㄌㄧㄡˊ)
first-rate; first-class: 他是第一流的作家。He is a first-rate writer.

第一國際(ㄉㄧˋ ㄧ ㄍㄨㄛˊ ㄐㄧˋ)
the First International

第一泉(ㄉㄧˋ ㄧ ㄑㄩㄢˊ)
spring water of the top quality

第一線(ㄉㄧˋ ㄧ ㄒㄧㄢˋ)
the foremost line; the first line; the front

第一手資料(ㄉㄧˋ ㄧ ㄕㄡˇ ㄗ ㄌㄧㄠˋ)
the firsthand material

第一審(ㄉㄧˋ ㄧ ㄕㄣˇ)
the first instance; the first trial; the first hearing

第一人稱(ㄉㄧˋ ㄧ ㄖㄣˊ ㄔㄥ)
(grammar) the first person

第一次(ㄉㄧˋ ㄧ ㄘˋ)
the first time: 這是我生平第一次搭飛機。I took an airplane for the first time.

第一次世界大戰(ㄉㄧˋ ㄧ ㄘˋ ㄕˋ ㄐㄧㄝˋ ㄉㄚˋ ㄓㄢˋ)
the First World War; World War Ⅰ

第一義(ㄉㄧˋ ㄧ ㄧˋ)
the primary sense

第五縱隊(ㄉㄧˋ ㄨˇ ㄗㄨㄥˋ ㄉㄨㄟˋ)
the fifth column

【筊】 4103
ㄐㄧㄠˇ jia jiǎ
a reed leaf whistle; the Tartar pipe

【筊】 4104
ㄋㄨˇ nu nǔ
a bird cage

【笴】 4105
《ㄜ gee ge
the stem of an arrow

【笤】 4106
ㄊㄧㄠˊ tyau tiáo
a bamboo broom

笤帚(ㄊㄧㄠˊ ㄓㄡˇ)
a bamboo broom

【笮】 4107
1. ㄗㄜˊ tzer zé
1. pressing
2. boards laid across rafters
3. an arrow bag

【榨】 4107
2. ㄓㄚˊ jah zhá
1. a kind of liquor container
2. to squeeze; to press

【笵】 4108
ㄈㄢˋ fann fàn
1. a bamboo form
2. same as 範—a model

六畫

【筆】 4109
ㄅㄧˇ bii bǐ
1. a writing brush; a pen; a

pencil
2. writer's skill or style
3. to write
4. a stroke; a touch
5. a unit of amount
6. (formerly) prose
7. a Chinese family name

筆墨(ㄅㄧˇ ㄇㄛˋ)
①pen and ink ②writing; words: 他們激動的心情難以用筆墨來形容。Words can hardly describe how excited they were.

筆墨生涯(ㄅㄧˇ ㄇㄛˋ ㄕㄥ ㄧㄚˊ)
a writing career: 她放棄了筆墨生涯。She abandoned her writing career.

筆帽(ㄅㄧˇ ㄇㄠˋ)
the cap of a pen or writing brush

筆名(ㄅㄧˇ ㄇㄧㄥˊ)
a pen name; nom de plume; a pseudonym

筆伐(ㄅㄧˇ ㄈㄚˊ)or(ㄅㄧˇ ㄈㄚˊ)
to attack in writings

筆法(ㄅㄧˇ ㄈㄚˇ)
①a calligraphic style ②a writing style

筆鋒(ㄅㄧˇ ㄈㄥ)
①a penpoint ②forcefulness of writing

筆答(ㄅㄧˇ ㄉㄚˊ)
written answers (in an examination)

筆底下(ㄅㄧˇ ㄉㄧˇ ·ㄒㄧㄚ)
under the sweep of a writer's pen — (figuratively) ability to write: 他筆底下不錯。He wrote well.

筆底生花(ㄅㄧˇ ㄉㄧˇ ㄕㄥ ㄏㄨㄚ)
(literally) to make flowers bloom under one's pen—to produce very fine writings

筆調(ㄅㄧˇ ㄉㄧㄠˋ)
the tone or style (of a writer)

筆套(ㄅㄧˇ ㄊㄠˋ)
the cap of a pen or writing brush

筆頭兒(ㄅㄧˇ ㄊㄡˊㄦ)
①a penpoint; the point of a writing brush ②ability to write; writing skill: 你筆頭兒很好。Your writing skill is very good.

筆談(ㄅㄧˇ ㄊㄢˊ)
to confer by writing

【竹部】

筆挺(ㄅㄧˇ ㄊㄧㄥˇ)
(said of dress) smooth ironed; spick-and-span; trim: 他穿着一身筆挺的制服。 He was dressed in a trim uniform.

筆禿墨乾(ㄅㄧˇ ㄊㄨ ㄇㄛˋ ㄍㄢ)
(literally) The writing brush is worn out and the ink slab is dry.—to have written a great deal

筆筒(ㄅㄧˇ ㄊㄨㄥˇ)
a tubular penrack or penholder; a pen container

筆難盡述(ㄅㄧˇ ㄋㄢˊ ㄐㄧㄣˇ ㄕㄨˋ)
to defy full description in writing; too many to be put down in writing

筆力(ㄅㄧˇ ㄌㄧˋ)
① the vigor of style in literary composition ② the vigor of strokes in calligraphy or drawing

筆桿(ㄅㄧˇ ㄍㄢˇ)or筆管(ㄅㄧˇ ㄍㄨㄢˇ)
the handle of a pen; a penholder

筆耕(ㄅㄧˇ ㄍㄥ)
to make a living by writing

筆酣墨飽(ㄅㄧˇ ㄏㄢˊ ㄇㄛˋ ㄅㄠˇ)
(literally) The pen is in full swing and the ink is plentiful.—to be in the middle of a creative writing mood

筆畫(ㄅㄧˇ ㄏㄨㄚˋ)
the number of strokes in (a character)

筆會(ㄅㄧˇ ㄏㄨㄟˋ)
P.E.N. (the International Association of Poets, Playwrights, Editors, Essayists, and Novelists)

筆跡(ㄅㄧˇ ㄐㄧ)
one's handwriting: 我核對他的筆跡。 I identified his handwriting.

筆記(ㄅㄧˇ ㄐㄧˋ)
notes taken (of lectures, speeches, etc.)

筆記簿(ㄅㄧˇ ㄐㄧˋ ㄅㄨˋ)
a notebook

筆記小說(ㄅㄧˇ ㄐㄧˋ ㄒㄧㄠˇ ㄕㄨㄛ)
literary sketches; a sketchbook

筆架(ㄅㄧˇ ㄐㄧㄚˋ)
a penrack; a penholder

筆尖(ㄅㄧˇ ㄐㄧㄢ)
a penpoint; the point of a writing brush

筆鉛(ㄅㄧˇ ㄑㄧㄢ)
graphite; the lead in a pencil

筆洗(ㄅㄧˇ ㄒㄧˇ)or筆海(ㄅㄧˇ ㄏㄞˇ)
a writing-brush washer

筆下留情(ㄅㄧˇ ㄒㄧㄚˋ ㄌㄧㄡˊ ㄑㄧㄥˊ)
to have some restraint when attacking others in writing; to be merciful in writing: 請您筆下留情。 Please spare me in critical attacks.

筆下超生(ㄅㄧˇ ㄒㄧㄚˋ ㄔㄠ ㄕㄥ)
to relent when writing a verdict (a phrase for asking a judge to refrain from passing a death sentence)

筆心(ㄅㄧˇ ㄒㄧㄣ)
① pencil lead ② a refill (for a ball-point pen)

筆削(ㄅㄧˇ ㄒㄩㄝˋ)
to correct or improve (a composition)

筆之於書(ㄅㄧˇ ㄓ ㄩˊ ㄕㄨ)
to commit it to writing

筆直(ㄅㄧˇ ㄓˊ)
perfectly straight: 他的身子挺得筆直。 He stood straight as a ramrod.

筆札(ㄅㄧˇ ㄓㄚˊ)
① writing materials ② records

筆者(ㄅㄧˇ ㄓㄜˇ)
the (present) writer: 〈本文〉筆者對它無記憶。 It eludes this writer's memory.

筆戰(ㄅㄧˇ ㄓㄢˋ)
① a paper battle; paper warfare; a war of the pen ② to write polemics against (someone)

筆陣(ㄅㄧˇ ㄓㄣˋ)
a pen with a force as overwhelming as battle array

筆床(ㄅㄧˇ ㄔㄨㄤˊ)
a penrack; a penholder

筆試(ㄅㄧˇ ㄕˋ)
a written examination: 他筆試及格了。 He passed the written examination.

筆勢(ㄅㄧˇ ㄕˋ)
the force (of a calligraphy or writing style)

筆述(ㄅㄧˇ ㄕㄨˋ)
to narrate or describe in writing; narration or description in writing

筆順(ㄅㄧˇ ㄕㄨㄣˋ)
stroke order (for characters)

筆資(ㄅㄧˇ ㄗ)or筆潤(ㄅㄧˇ ㄖㄨㄣˋ)
writer's fees; remuneration for writing

筆走龍蛇(ㄅㄧˇ ㄗㄡˇ ㄌㄨㄥˊ ㄕㄜˊ)
(literally) Dragons and snakes follow his writing brush.— a vigorous calligraphic style

筆算(ㄅㄧˇ ㄙㄨㄢˋ)
arithmetic worked out on paper; written calculation: 他的筆算有錯誤。 He made a mistake in his written calculation.

筆意(ㄅㄧˇ ㄧˋ)
① a calligraphic style ② the meaning of a passage or sentence

筆譯(ㄅㄧˇ ㄧˋ)
written translation: 這本書筆譯有錯誤。 This book has errors in written translation.

筆友(ㄅㄧˇ ㄧㄡˇ)
pen pals; friends among fellow writers

筆誤(ㄅㄧˇ ㄨˋ)
a slip of the pen: 這篇文章有筆誤。 This essay has a slip of the pen.

【筇】 4110
ㄑㄩㄥˊ chyong qióng
a kind of bamboo (commonly used to make walking sticks)

筇杖(ㄑㄩㄥˊ ㄓㄤˋ)
a kind of bamboo stick

【筌】 4111
ㄑㄩㄢˊ chyuan quán
a bamboo fish trap

【筍】 4112
(筍) ㄙㄨㄣˇ soen sǔn
bamboo shoots or sprouts

筍鞭(ㄙㄨㄣˇ ㄅㄧㄢ)
the subterranean stem of bamboo

筍皮(ㄙㄨㄣˇ ㄆㄧˊ)or筍殼(ㄙㄨㄣˇ ㄎㄜˊ)
the scale-like outer skin of a bamboo shoot

筍乾(ㄙㄨㄣˇ ㄍㄢ)
bamboo shoots cooked and dried for preservation

筍雞(ㄙㄨㄣˇ ㄐㄧ)
a young chicken

筍尖(ㄙㄨㄣˇ ㄐㄧㄢ)
the tip, or upper part of tender bamboo shoots

筍衣(ㄙㄨㄣ ㄧ)
the shell of a bamboo shoot

筍鴨(ㄙㄨㄣ ㄧㄚ)
a young duck; a duckling

筍芽(ㄙㄨㄣ ㄧㄚ)
sprouting bamboo shoots

【等】 4113
ㄉㄥˇ deeng děng

1. rank; grade
2. same; equal
3. to wait: 請 等 一 下。Would you mind waiting a moment?
4. when; till: 等你做完再走,Stay till you're through.
5. and so on; etc.; and the like
6. common

等比(ㄉㄥˇ ㄅㄧˇ)
geometric ratio; the ratio of equality

等比級數(ㄉㄥˇ ㄅㄧˇ ㄐㄧˊ ㄕㄨˋ)
geometric progression

等邊三角形(ㄉㄥˇ ㄅㄧㄢ ㄙㄢ ㄐㄧㄠˇ ㄒㄧㄥˊ)
an equilateral triangle

等不及(ㄉㄥˇ ㄅㄨˋ ㄐㄧˊ)
①too impatient to wait ②unable to wait any longer

等偏線(ㄉㄥˇ ㄆㄧㄢ ㄒㄧㄢˋ)
an isogonic line; isogonics

等分
①(ㄉㄥˇ ㄈㄣ) division into equal parts; to divide into equal parts
②(ㄉㄥˇ ㄈㄣˋ) equal in quantities

等待(ㄉㄥˇ ㄉㄞˋ)
to wait for; to await

等到(ㄉㄥˇ ㄉㄠˋ)
by the time; when

等等(ㄉㄥˇ ㄉㄥˇ)
and so forth; et cetera; etc.

等等兒(ㄉㄥˇ ㄉㄥˇ ㄦ)
to wait a while

等第(ㄉㄥˇ ㄉㄧˋ)
rank; grade

等同(ㄉㄥˇ ㄊㄨㄥˊ)
to equate; to be equal

等列(ㄉㄥˇ ㄌㄧㄝˋ)
①grade; rank ②to rank with

等量齊觀(ㄉㄥˇ ㄌㄧㄤˋ ㄑㄧˊ ㄍㄨㄢ)
to regard, or treat indiscriminately; to equate

等高線(ㄉㄥˇ ㄍㄠ ㄒㄧㄢˋ)
a contour

等號(ㄉㄥˇ ㄏㄠˋ)
the equal mark or sign(=)

等候(ㄉㄥˇ ㄏㄡˋ)
to wait; to await; to expect: 你們等候命令。You waited for instructions.

等級(ㄉㄥˇ ㄐㄧˊ)
grade; rank: A 等級牛奶品質最好。Grade A milk is the best milk.

等價(ㄉㄥˇ ㄐㄧㄚˋ)
equal in value or prices

等角線(ㄉㄥˇ ㄐㄧㄠˇ ㄒㄧㄢˋ)
an isogonal line

等角形(ㄉㄥˇ ㄐㄧㄠˇ ㄒㄧㄥˊ)
isogonal figures

等角三角形(ㄉㄥˇ ㄐㄧㄠˇ ㄙㄢ ㄐㄧㄠˇ ㄒㄧㄥˊ)
an equiangular triangle

等距(ㄉㄥˇ ㄐㄩˋ)
equal distance; equidistance

等情(ㄉㄥˇ ㄑㄧㄥˊ)
a phrase conventionally used in official communications immediately after a quotation from a letter by a lower agency

等閒(ㄉㄥˇ ㄒㄧㄢˊ)
①negligent; careless; aimlessly: 大好時光, 不可等閒度過。Don't waste your precious time aimlessly. ②common; ordinary; usual; commonplace

等閒度過(ㄉㄥˇ ㄒㄧㄢˊ ㄉㄨˋ ㄍㄨㄛˋ)
to pass days in a useless or common way

等閒視之(ㄉㄥˇ ㄒㄧㄢˊ ㄕˋ ㄓ)
to regard it as of no importance

等著(ㄉㄥˇ ㄓㄜˋ)
waiting for: 一封信等著你 (來看)。A letter is waiting for you.

等要(ㄉㄥˇ ㄓㄜˋ ㄧㄠˋ)
①waiting to (do a thing) ②to want (something) immediately

等差(ㄉㄥˇ ㄔㄚ)
equal difference

等差級數(ㄉㄥˇ ㄔㄚ ㄐㄧˊ ㄕㄨˋ)
arithmetic progression

等式(ㄉㄥˇ ㄕˋ)
an equation; equality

等身(ㄉㄥˇ ㄕㄣ)
equal to one's height; as high as oneself: 他的著作等身。His works piled up as high as himself.

等人(ㄉㄥˇ ㄖㄣˊ)
①people of the same rank or grade ②to wait for someone ③and others

等子(ㄉㄥˇ ㄗˇ)
small weights used in measuring precious metals, medicines, etc.

等次(ㄉㄥˇ ㄘˋ)
①rank; grade: 我們的產品分等次出售。Our products are sold in grades. ②sequence; order

等速度(ㄉㄥˇ ㄙㄨˋ ㄉㄨˋ)
uniform velocity

等速運動(ㄉㄥˇ ㄙㄨˋ ㄩㄣˋ ㄉㄨㄥˋ)
(physics) uniform motion

等而下(ㄉㄥˇ ㄦˊ ㄒㄧㄚˋ)
from that grade down

等一會兒(ㄉㄥˇ ㄧ ㄏㄨㄟˋ ㄦ)
①to wait a little while: 不要走那麼快! 等我一會兒。Don't go so fast! Wait up for me! ②after a little while

等一等(ㄉㄥˇ ㄧ·ㄉㄥˇ)or 等一下(ㄉㄥˇ ㄧ ㄒㄧㄚˋ)
to wait a little while

等腰三角形(ㄉㄥˇ ㄧㄠ ㄙㄢ ㄐㄧㄠˇ ㄒㄧㄥˊ)
an isosceles triangle

等由(ㄉㄥˇ ㄧㄡˊ)
a phrase conventionally used in official communications immediately after a quotation from a letter by an agency of the same rank

等因(ㄉㄥˇ ㄧㄣ)
a conventional phrase used in official communications immediately after a quotation from a letter by an agency of a higher rank or the same rank

等因奉此(ㄉㄥˇ ㄧㄣ ㄈㄥˋ ㄘˇ)
①a conventional phrase used in official communications immediately after a quotation from a letter by a superior agency and before a comment thereupon ②to handle official writings; to serve as a common civil servant

等位(ㄉㄥˇ ㄨㄟˋ)
grade; rank

等溫線(ㄉㄥˇ ㄨㄣ ㄒㄧㄢˋ)

〔竹部〕

〔竹部〕

isotherms

等於(ㄉㄥˇ ㄩˊ)
①to be equal to: 十角等於一元。 Ten dimes are equal to one dollar. ②tantamount to; the same as: 這等於拒絕幫助我們。 This is tantamount to refusal to help us.

【筏】 4114
　　ㄈㄚˊ far fá
a raft: 他乘木筏順流而下。 He went down the river on a raft.

筏子(ㄈㄚˊ·ㄗ)
a raft

【筑】 4115
　　ㄓㄨˊ jwu zhú
a kind of ancient string instrument with five strings, thirteen strings, or twenty-one strings

【筐】 4116
　　ㄎㄨㄤ kuang kuāng
a rectangular chest or box woven from bamboo strips (or wicker); a shallow basket

筐篋(ㄎㄨㄤ ㄑㄧㄝˋ)
a rectangular box or chest

筐篋中物(ㄎㄨㄤ ㄑㄧㄝˋ ㄓㄨㄥ ㄨˋ)
a commonplace thing

筐子(ㄎㄨㄤ·ㄗ) or 筐兒(ㄎㄨㄤㄦ)
a bamboo chest; a wicker chest

【筒】 4117
　　ㄊㄨㄥˊ toong tóng
　　(又讀 ㄊㄨㄥˇ torng tǒng)
a tube; a pipe; a cylinder: 這圓筒的容積是多少？ What is the volume of this cylinder?

筒狀花冠(ㄊㄨㄥˊ ㄓㄨㄤˋ ㄏㄨㄚ ㄍㄨㄢ)
tubiflora

筒子(ㄊㄨㄥˊ·ㄗ)
a tube; a pipe

【筋】 4118
　　ㄐㄧㄣ jin jīn
1. tendons; sinews; muscles
2. veins that stand out under the skin
3. plant fibers resembling a tendon

筋疲力竭(ㄐㄧㄣ ㄆㄧˊ ㄌㄧˋ ㄐㄧㄝˊ)
to be completely exhausted; to have used up all energy

筋斗(ㄐㄧㄣ ㄉㄡˇ)
a somersault 亦作「跟頭」

筋骨(ㄐㄧㄣ ㄍㄨˇ)
①bones and muscles—physique; build (of one's body): 練功夫可以鍛鍊筋骨。 Practicing kung fu strengthens the physique. ②strength

筋節(ㄐㄧㄣ ㄐㄧㄝˊ)
①tendons and joints ②forceful transitions between passages in a piece of writing

筋肉(ㄐㄧㄣ ㄖㄡˋ)
muscle

筋肉組織(ㄐㄧㄣ ㄖㄡˋ ㄗㄨˇ ㄓ)
muscular tissue

【答】 4119
　　1. ㄉㄚˊ dar dá
1. to answer; to reply: 他答覆了我的問題。 He answered my question.
2. to reciprocate; to return

答拜(ㄉㄚˊ ㄅㄞˋ)
①to return a courtesy call
②to return a salutation

答辯(ㄉㄚˊ ㄅㄧㄢˋ)
to reply (to a verbal attack); to speak in self-defense; to defend oneself: 這被告有一律師替他答辯。 The accused man had a lawyer to defend him.

答辯書(ㄉㄚˊ ㄅㄧㄢˋ ㄕㄨ)
a written answer, reply, or refutation (to a verbal attack or charge)

答不上來(ㄉㄚˊ ㄅㄨˋ ㄕㄤˋ ㄌㄞˊ)
unable to answer; at a loss to answer

答非所問(ㄉㄚˊ ㄈㄟ ㄙㄨㄛˇ ㄨㄣˋ)
to give an irrelevant answer

答覆(ㄉㄚˊ ㄈㄨˋ)
to reply to, or answer (an inquiry, etc.); an answer; a reply: 我等候你的答覆。 I wait for your reply.

答禮(ㄉㄚˊ ㄌㄧˇ)
to reciprocate another's courtesy; to return a salute

答錄機(ㄉㄚˊ ㄌㄨˋ ㄐㄧ)
an answering machine

答話(ㄉㄚˊ ㄏㄨㄚˋ)
to reply orally; an oral reply or answer

答謝(ㄉㄚˊ ㄒㄧㄝˋ)
to acknowledge; to convey one's thanks (for a favor, etc.)

答數(ㄉㄚˊ ㄕㄨˋ)
an answer (to an arithmetic problem)

答辭 or 答詞(ㄉㄚˊ ㄘˊ)
a thank-you speech; an address in reply; an answering speech

答案(ㄉㄚˊ ㄢˋ)
solution, answers (to examination questions, puzzles, etc.): 我找不到問題的答案。 I seek no solution for the problem.

答問(ㄉㄚˊ ㄨㄣˋ)
questions and answers; catechism

【答】 4119
　　2. ㄉㄚ da dā
a variant of 答(ㄉㄚˊ)used only in some phrases

答答(ㄉㄚ ㄉㄚ)
①a crackling sound ②shy; bashful

答理(ㄉㄚ ㄌㄧˇ)
to answer a person; to respond

答腔(ㄉㄚ ㄑㄧㄤ)
a reply; words uttered in reply; to reply; to answer

答碴兒(ㄉㄚ ㄔㄚ ㄦ)
to continue another's utterance or speech

答應(ㄉㄚ ㄧㄥ)
①to assent or agree to (a request); to promise (to do something) ②an answer: 他們按鈴但沒人答應。 They rang but got no answer.

【筈】 4120
　　ㄍㄨㄚ gua guā
the end of an arrow

【笄】 4121
　　(笄) ㄐㄧ ji jī
a hairpin for fastening the hair (used by women in former times)

笄年(ㄐㄧ ㄋㄧㄢˊ)
(said of a woman) the age to begin wearing the hairpin—the beginning of maturity at 15

笄冠(ㄐㄧ ㄍㄨㄢ)
having just attained maturity

【策】 4122
　　ㄘㄜˋ tseh cè
1. a whip (for goading horses)
2. expository writings on government affairs
3. orders of appointment

4. a plan; a scheme; a stratagem
5. to whip; to spur; to urge; to
impel
6. a Chinese family name

策馬 (ㄘㄜˋ ㄇㄚˇ)
to whip a horse; to spur a
horse

策命 (ㄘㄜˋ ㄇㄧㄥˋ)
orders of appointment to or
removal from an office

策反 (ㄘㄜˋ ㄈㄢˇ)
to instigate defection in the
enemy camp

策動 (ㄘㄜˋ ㄉㄨㄥˋ)
to machinate; to maneuver;
to instigate

策勵 (ㄘㄜˋ ㄌㄧˋ)
to urge; to impel; to spur

策令 (ㄘㄜˋ ㄌㄧㄥˋ)
presidential appointment to
an office (in the early years
of the Republic of China)

策論 (ㄘㄜˋ ㄌㄨㄣˋ)
questions and themes (given
in former civil service examinations)

策略 (ㄘㄜˋ ㄌㄩㄝˋ)
a stratagem; a scheme;
tactics

策畫 (ㄘㄜˋ ㄏㄨㄚˋ)
to plan; to make plans

策杖 (ㄘㄜˋ ㄓㄤˋ)
to use a walking stick

策士 (ㄘㄜˋ ㄕˋ)
a scheming person; a
schemer; a member of a
brain trust

試試 (ㄘㄜˋ ㄕˋ)
to test (candidates under the
former civil service examination system)

策應 (ㄘㄜˋ ㄧㄥˋ)
to act in concert with each
other

策源地 (ㄘㄜˋ ㄩㄢˊ ㄉㄧˋ)
①a (military) base ②the
source (of a stream) ③the
place of origin

【筴】 4123
ㄐㄧㄚˊ jeau jiáo
1. a rope made of bamboo
strips
2. a kind of bamboo device
used in divination

七畫

【筠】 4124
ㄩㄣˊ yun yún
the skin of the bamboo

【筥】 4125
ㄐㄩˇ jeu jǔ
a round bamboo basket for
holding rice

【筦】 4126
ㄍㄨㄢˇ goan guǎn
1. same as 管—a pipe; a tube
2. a key
3. to be in charge
4. wind instruments made of
bamboo (such as flutes, etc.)
5. a Chinese family name

【筩】 4127
ㄊㄨㄥˊ torng tóng
1. a bamboo pipe
2. a hook for fishing

【筮】 4128
ㄕˋ shyh shì
to divine by means of the
stalks of the milfoil

筮人 (ㄕˋ ㄖㄣˊ)
a fortuneteller

【筯】 4129
ㄓㄨˋ juh jhù
1. chopsticks
2. tongs

【筱】 4130
ㄒㄧㄠˇ sheau xiǎo
1. little slender bamboo
2. little; small

【筲】 4131
ㄕㄠ shau shāo
a basket for holding cooked
rice

筲箕 (ㄕㄠ ㄐㄧ)
a basket for washing rice

【筴】 4132
1. ㄘㄜˋ tseh cè
1. the milfoil used for divination in ancient times
2. same as 策

【筴】 4132
ㄐㄧㄚˊ jya jiá
tongs

【筳】 4133
ㄊㄧㄥˊ tyng tíng
little slender bamboo

【筵】 4134
ㄧㄢˊ yan yán
1. a bamboo mat
2. a feast; a banquet

筵席 (ㄧㄢˊ ㄒㄧˊ)
①a mat for sitting on ②a
feast; a banquet

【算】 4135
ㄙㄨㄢˋ suann suàn

1. an ancient device for working with numbers
2. a scheme

【筷】 4136
ㄎㄨㄞˋ kuay kuài
chopsticks

筷子 (ㄎㄨㄞˋ·ㄗ)
chopsticks

【筧】 4137
ㄐㄧㄢˇ jean jiǎn
a bamboo water pipe

筧橋 (ㄐㄧㄢˇ ㄑㄧㄠˊ)
a town north of Hangchow,
Chekiang, the site of an airfield and an aviation school

八畫

【箋】 4138
(牋) ㄐㄧㄢ jian jiān
1. a commentary; a note
2. fancy note paper, letter
paper, or stationery: 蠟箋
glazed note paper
3. letters; correspondence: 我有
許多信箋。I have a good deal
of correspondence.

箋牘 (ㄐㄧㄢ ㄉㄨˊ)
letters; correspondence

箋紙 (ㄐㄧㄢ ㄓˇ)
stationery; letter paper

箋札 (ㄐㄧㄢ ㄓㄚˊ)
letters; correspondence

箋注 (ㄐㄧㄢ ㄓㄨˋ)
notes and commentaries

【箏】 4139
ㄓㄥ jeng jhēng
1. a plucked stringed instrument in some ways similar
to the zither
2. a kite: 他在放風箏。He is
flying a kite.

【箑】 4140
ㄕㄚˋ shah shà
(又讀 ㄐㄧㄝˊ jye jié)
a fan

【箍】 4141
ㄍㄨ gu gū
1. a hoop
2. to bind round; to hoop

箍桶 (ㄍㄨ ㄊㄨㄥˇ)
to fix hoops on a barrel

箍桶店 (ㄍㄨ ㄊㄨㄥˇ ㄉㄧㄢˋ)
a coopery

【箔】 4142
ㄅㄛˊ bor bó
1. foil; gilt
2. a curtain

(竹
部)

【竹部】

3. a frame for raising silk-worms
4. paper tinsel burnt as offerings to the dead。

【箕】 4143 ㄐㄧ jī jí

1. a winnowing basket; a sieve:
竹箕 a bamboo winnowing basket
2. a dust basket; a garbage basket; a dustpan
3. nonspiral lines on a finger-tip

箕斗 (ㄐㄧ ㄉㄡ)
spiral and nonspiral lines on the fingertips

箕斂 (ㄐㄧ ㄌㄧㄢ) or 箕會 (ㄐㄧ ㄏㄨㄟ)
to exploit or squeeze by ruthless taxation

箕踞 (ㄐㄧ ㄐㄩ)
(said of a person) to sit with legs sprawled out

箕裘 (ㄐㄧ ㄑㄧㄡ)
to carry on the trade of one's father (from 良弓之子之必學爲箕，良冶之子必學爲裘, a passage in the Book of Rites)

箕帚 (ㄐㄧ ㄓㄡˋ)
(literally) a dustpan and a broom—a wife or a concubine

箕張 (ㄐㄧ ㄓㄤ)
wide in the front and narrow in the rear

箕山之志 (ㄐㄧ ㄕㄢ ㄓ ㄓˋ)
the desire to live the life of a recluse

箕子 (ㄐㄧ ㄗˇ)
Chi Tzu, a righteous courtier in the Yin Dynasty, who incurred the displeasure of his monarch Chou(紂王) and feigned madness

箕坐 (ㄐㄧ ㄗㄨㄛˋ)
to sit with legs sprawled out

箕尾 (ㄐㄧ ㄨㄟˇ)
the constellations Sagittarius and Scorpio

【算】 4144 ㄙㄨㄢˋ suann suàn

1. to count; to figure; to reckon; to compute; to calculate
2. to plan; to scheme
3. to infer; to guess; to foretell
4. to regard; to consider; to deem; to count
5. to be of importance; to be

of consequence; to matter
6. a Chinese family name

算不得 (ㄙㄨㄢˋ ㄅㄨˋ ㄉㄜˊ)
not to be counted or regarded

算不了 (ㄙㄨㄢˋ ㄅㄨˋ ㄌㄧㄠˇ)
not to be counted or regard-ed

算不了什麼 (ㄙㄨㄢˋ ㄅㄨˋ ㄌㄧㄠˇ ㄕㄜˊ ˙ㄇㄜ)
①not so serious or impor-tant; nothing to be alarmed or excited about ②not very impressive

算不清 (ㄙㄨㄢˋ ㄅㄨˋ ㄑㄧㄥ)
innumerable; uncountable

算盤 (ㄙㄨㄢˋ ㄆㄢˊ)
an abacus

算盤脂袋 (ㄙㄨㄢˋ ㄆㄢˊ ㄗˇ ㄉㄞˋ)
a miser

算盤疙瘩 (ㄙㄨㄢˋ ㄆㄢˊ ㄍㄜ ˙ㄉㄚ)
a kind of ornamental knots made in laces or ropes, look-ing like abacus beads

算盤子兒 (ㄙㄨㄢˋ ㄆㄢˊ ㄗˇ ㄦ)
abacus beads

算命 (ㄙㄨㄢˋ ㄇㄧㄥˋ)
to tell one's fortune

算命的 (ㄙㄨㄢˋ ㄇㄧㄥˋ ˙ㄉㄜ) or 算命先生 (ㄙㄨㄢˋ ㄇㄧㄥˋ ㄒㄧㄢ ˙ㄙㄥ)
a fortuneteller

算法 (ㄙㄨㄢˋ ㄈㄚˇ)
arithmetic; a method of cal-culation

算得甚麼 (ㄙㄨㄢˋ ㄉㄜˊ ㄕㄜˊ ˙ㄇㄜ) or 不得甚麼 (ㄙㄨㄢˋ ㄅㄨˋ ㄉㄜˊ ㄕㄜˊ ˙ㄇㄜ)
of no special account or con-sequence; trifling; trivial say It's nothing. 那算不得甚麼。實在是容易的事。 That does not bother me, it's quite simple.

算題 (ㄙㄨㄢˋ ㄊㄧˊ)
an arithmetic problem

算了 (ㄙㄨㄢˋ ˙ㄌㄜ)
①Forget about it. 或That's enough! ②settled; (said of a case) concluded

算來 (ㄙㄨㄢˋ ㄌㄞˊ)
by counting (often used in connection with time or money)

算來算去 (ㄙㄨㄢˋ ㄌㄞˊ ㄙㄨㄢˋ ㄑㄩˋ)
to compute or count over and over again

算曆 (ㄙㄨㄢˋ ㄌㄧˋ)
arithmetic and the calendar

算卦 (ㄙㄨㄢˋ ㄍㄨㄚˋ)
to tell one's fortune

算卦的 (ㄙㄨㄢˋ ㄍㄨㄚˋ ˙ㄉㄜ)
a fortuneteller

算計 (ㄙㄨㄢˋ ㄐㄧˋ)
①to consider; to plan: 我正算計著要去歐洲。I am plan-ning a trip to Europe. ②to plot against someone

算計人 (ㄙㄨㄢˋ ㄐㄧˋ ㄖㄣˊ)
to plot against a person: 他暗中算計人。He secretly plot-ted against others.

算起來 (ㄙㄨㄢˋ ㄑㄧˇ ㄌㄞˊ)
in total; all told; in all; in the aggregate

算清 (ㄙㄨㄢˋ ㄑㄧㄥ)
to find out the sum, ratio, etc. of

算學 (ㄙㄨㄢˋ ㄒㄩㄝˊ)
mathematics

算賬 (ㄙㄨㄢˋ ㄓㄤˋ)
①to compute income and expense; to settle an account: 他算帳算得很快。He is quick at accounts. ②to get even (with a person): 回同同那壞蛋算眼。The scoun-drel will pay for this.

算籌 (ㄙㄨㄢˋ ㄔㄡˊ)
tallies used for working with numbers

算式 (ㄙㄨㄢˋ ㄕˋ)
a mathematical formula

算上 (ㄙㄨㄢˋ ㄕㄤˋ)
to count in; to include: 我們今天宴會也算上她。We includ-ed her in today's party.

算數 (ㄙㄨㄢˋ ㄕㄨˋ)
①to be of importance ②to count; to stand; to mean what one says; valid: 我說話是算數的。I mean what I say.

算術 (ㄙㄨㄢˋ ㄕㄨˋ)
arithmetic

算術級數 (ㄙㄨㄢˋ ㄕㄨˋ ㄐㄧˊ ㄕㄨˋ)
an arithmetic progression

算無遺策 (ㄙㄨㄢˋ ㄨˊ ㄧˊ ㄘㄜˋ)
to plan very carefully with every conceivable possibility taken into account

【箠】 4145 ㄔㄨㄟˊ chwei chuí

1. a whip (for goading horses)
2. whipping or flogging (as a punishment)

箠罵 (ㄔㄨㄟˊ ㄇㄚˋ)

to flog and curse

箠楚（ㄓㄨㄟˊ ㄔㄨˇ）
whipping or flogging as a punishment

【箅】 4146
　　ㄅㄧˋ bih bì
a bamboo grid for steaming food

【箜】 4147
　　ㄎㄨㄥ kong kōng
a kind of ancient plucked stringed instrument

箜篌（ㄎㄨㄥ ㄏㄡˊ）
a kind of ancient musical instrument with 23 strings

【箝】 4148
　　ㄑㄧㄢˊ chyan qián
1. tongs; pincers; tweezers: 火箝 firetongs
2. to tweezer

箝口（ㄑㄧㄢˊ ㄎㄡˇ）
① to keep one's mouth shut; to keep silent ② to prevent from talking; to fort to keep silent; to gag

箝口結舌（ㄑㄧㄢˊ ㄎㄡˇ ㄐㄧㄝˊ ㄕㄜˊ）
① to keep silent ② to be forced to keep silent

箝緊（ㄑㄧㄢˊ ㄐㄧㄣˇ）
to clasp tightly

箝形攻勢（ㄑㄧㄢˊ ㄒㄧㄥˊ ㄍㄨㄥ ㄕˋ）
(military operations) a pincers movement

箝制（ㄑㄧㄢˊ ㄓˋ）
to use pressure upon; to force; to pin down

箝子（ㄑㄧㄢˊ ·ㄗ）
tongs; tweezers; pincers

箝語（ㄑㄧㄢˊ ㄩˇ）
to restrict freedom of speech

【管】 4149
　　ㄍㄨㄢˇ goan guǎn
1. a tube; a pipe; a duct
2. a wind instrument
3. to control; to manage; to take care of; to keep: 他把工廠管得井井有條。He keeps the factory in good order.
4. to heed; to pay attention to
5. to provide
6. to guarantee: 此照相機管用一年。This camera is guaranteed for one year.
7. to meddle in; to interfere in; to bother about: 別管我。Do not interfere with me.
8. a key
9. a Chinese family name

管保（ㄍㄨㄢˇ ㄅㄠˇ）
to guarantee: 我管保他不知道。I'm sure that he does not know.

管鮑（ㄍㄨㄢˇ ㄅㄠˋ）
Kuan Chung (管仲) and Pao Shu-ya (鮑叔牙) of the Epoch of Warring States (equivalent to Damon and Pythias, or David and Jonathan)

管鮑分金（ㄍㄨㄢˇ ㄅㄠˋ ㄈㄣ ㄐㄧㄣ）
a friendship so close as to make no distinction between each other's wealth 參看「管鮑」

管不了（ㄍㄨㄢˇ ·ㄅㄨ ㄌㄧㄠˇ）
to lack the capacity to control

管不着（ㄍㄨㄢˇ ·ㄅㄨ ㄓㄠˊ）
to have no authority to interfere in: 我怎麼管不着? Why shouldn't I interfere?

管不住（ㄍㄨㄢˇ ·ㄅㄨ ㄓㄨˋ）
to be incapable of controlling

管飯（ㄍㄨㄢˇ ㄈㄢˋ）
(said of an employer, etc.) to provide meals: 這雇主不管飯。This employer does not provide meals.

管待（ㄍㄨㄢˇ ㄉㄞˋ）
to entertain; to fete; to show hospitality to

管道（ㄍㄨㄢˇ ㄉㄠˋ）
① a pipeline; piping; a conduit; tubing: 煤氣管道 gas piping ② a channel for communication, consultation, etc.

管寧（ㄍㄨㄢˇ ㄋㄧㄥˊ）
Kuan Ning, 158-241, a hermit during the Epoch of the Three Kingdoms

管理（ㄍㄨㄢˇ ㄌㄧˇ）
to manage; to administer; to handle; to take care of; management; administration: 在他的管理下，公司發展得很快。The company developed rapidly under his administration.

管理顧問（ㄍㄨㄢˇ ㄌㄧˇ ㄍㄨˋ ㄨㄣˋ）
a management consultant

管理局（ㄍㄨㄢˇ ㄌㄧˇ ㄐㄩˊ）or 管理處
（ㄍㄨㄢˇ ㄌㄧˇ ㄔㄨˋ）
a government agency in charge of the administration of national railways, highways, forestry, etc.; a special administration

管理人（ㄍㄨㄢˇ ㄌㄧˇ ㄖㄣˊ）
an administrator; a manager; a supervisor; a superintendent; a caretaker; a trustee; a custodian; a keeper

管理員（ㄍㄨㄢˇ ㄌㄧˇ ㄩㄢˊ）
a keeper; a caretaker; an administrator; a manager; a custodian; a janitor

管窺蠡測（ㄍㄨㄢˇ ㄎㄨㄟ ㄌㄧˊ ㄘㄜˋ）
(literally) to view the sky through a tube and measure the sea with a calabash — restricted in vision and shallow in understanding

管伙食（ㄍㄨㄢˇ ㄏㄨㄛˇ ㄕˊ）
① to take charge of meals for a whole organization or a group of people ② (said of an employer) to provide meals

管換（ㄍㄨㄢˇ ㄏㄨㄢˋ）
(a phrase commonly used by shopkeepers) responsible for replacing defective merchandise

管家（ㄍㄨㄢˇ ㄐㄧㄚ）
① to housekeep; to run a home
② a housekeeper

管家婆（ㄍㄨㄢˇ ㄐㄧㄚ ㄆㄛˊ）
a housekeeper

管教
① （ㄍㄨㄢˇ ㄐㄧㄠˋ）sure to make (a person feel or act in some predicted way): 聽我的話管教你成功。Surely you will succeed if you follow my advice.
② （ㄍㄨㄢˇ ·ㄐㄧㄠ）to direct and teach (children, students, etc.); to discipline and educate

管見（ㄍㄨㄢˇ ㄐㄧㄢˋ）
my narrow view or opinion; my humble opinion: 請容陳管見。Please allow me to state my humble opinion.

管轄（ㄍㄨㄢˇ ㄒㄧㄚˊ）
to have jurisdiction over; to have control over

管轄權（ㄍㄨㄢˇ ㄒㄧㄚˊ ㄑㄩㄢˊ）
jurisdiction

【竹部】

管下《ㄍㄨㄢ ㄒㄧㄚˋ》
subordinates

管絃 or 管弦《ㄍㄨㄢ ㄒㄧㄢˊ》
①wind and stringed instruments ②piping and fiddling

管絃樂《ㄍㄨㄢ ㄒㄧㄢˊ ㄩㄝˋ》
orchestral music

管絃樂團《ㄍㄨㄢ ㄒㄧㄢˊ ㄩㄝˋ ㄊㄨㄢˊ》
an orchestra

管閒事《ㄍㄨㄢ ㄒㄧㄢˊ ㄕˋ》
nosy; to meddle; to poke one's nose into others' business

管制《ㄍㄨㄢ ㄓˋ》
to control; control

管賬的《ㄍㄨㄢ ㄓㄤˋ ·ㄉㄜ》
a bookkeeper

管狀花《ㄍㄨㄢ ㄓㄨㄤˋ ㄏㄨㄚ》
flowers of tubuliflorous plants

管中窺豹《ㄍㄨㄢ ㄓㄨㄥ ㄎㄨㄟ ㄅㄠˋ》
(literally) to look at the spots of a leopard through a tube—to have partial knowledge of something

管仲《ㄍㄨㄢ ㄓㄨㄥˋ》
Kuan Chung, ?-644 B.C., prime minister of the state of Chi (齊) during the Epoch of Warring States

管事《ㄍㄨㄢ ㄕˋ》
①a housekeeper or shopkeeper ②effective; useful; to work ③to take care of; to administer; to be in charge: 那裡誰管事? Who is in charge there?

管事的《ㄍㄨㄢ ㄕˋ ·ㄉㄜ》
a butler

管束《ㄍㄨㄢ ㄕㄨˋ》
to control; to restrain; to discipline

管子《ㄍㄨㄢ ·ㄗ》
①《ㄍㄨㄢ ㄗˇ》ⓐ a book authored by Kuan Chung (管仲) and later expanded by others ⓑ Kuan Chung (管仲), ?-644B.C. 亦作「管氏」②《ㄍㄨㄢˇ ·ㄗ》a tube; a pipe; a duct

管兒《ㄍㄨㄚㄦ》
a tube; a pipe; a duct

管晏《ㄍㄨㄢ ㄧㄢˋ》
Kuan Chung (管仲) and Yen Ying (晏嬰), both famed statesmen in the state of Chi

(齊) during the Epoch of Warring States

管籥《ㄍㄨㄢ ㄩㄝˋ》
①a flute; a pipe ②a key

管樂《ㄍㄨㄢ ㄩㄝˋ》
wind music

管樂隊《ㄍㄨㄢ ㄩㄝˋ ㄉㄨㄟˋ》
a wind band; a band

管樂器《ㄍㄨㄢ ㄩㄝˋ ㄑㄧˋ》
wind instruments; the wind

管用《ㄍㄨㄢ ㄩㄥˋ》
useful; effective; to work: 這藥挺管用。This medicine is very effective.

【箚】 4150
ㄓㄚˊ jar zhá
1. correspondence; letters
2. (in former times) written directives or instructions to a lower government agency

箚記《ㄓㄚˊ ㄐㄧˋ》
①a notebook ②to put down by items

箚子《ㄓㄚˊ ·ㄗ》
(in former times) written directives or instructions from a higher office

【箙】 4151
ㄈㄨˊ fwu fú
a quiver

【箇】 4152
ㄍㄜˋ geh gè
same as 個—a numeracy adjunct for practically everything

箇別《ㄍㄜˋ ㄅㄧㄝˊ》
individually; separately

箇體《ㄍㄜˋ ㄊㄧˇ》
an entity

箇性《ㄍㄜˋ ㄒㄧㄥˋ》
individuality; individual traits; personality

箇中秘密《ㄍㄜˋ ㄓㄨㄥ ㄇㄧˋ ㄇㄧˋ》
the inside story

箇人《ㄍㄜˋ ㄖㄣˊ》
①an individual ②I

箇子《ㄍㄜˋ ·ㄗ》
a person's stature

箇案《ㄍㄜˋ ㄢˋ》
(social work) an individual case as a subject of study

箇位《ㄍㄜˋ ㄨㄟˋ》
a unit

九畫

【箬】 4153
(篛) ㄖㄨㄛˋ ruoh ruò
1. the bamboo cuticle
2. a kind of bamboo with broad leaves which are often used to make various coverings

箬篷《ㄖㄨㄛˋ ㄆㄥˊ》
a hood, or top, made of bamboo leaves (usually for boats)

箬帽芒鞋《ㄖㄨㄛˋ ㄇㄠˋ ㄇㄤˊ ㄒㄧㄝˊ》
a bamboo hat and straw sandals—the clothing of a farmer or hermit

箬笠《ㄖㄨㄛˋ ㄌㄧˋ》or 箬帽《ㄖㄨㄛˋ ㄇㄠˋ》
a wide, conical bamboo hat

箬竹《ㄖㄨㄛˋ ㄓㄨˊ》
a variety of bamboo, with broad leaves that are often used to make hats, etc.

【箱】 4154
ㄒㄧㄤ shiang xiāng
1. a box; a chest; a trunk: 把行李放在行李箱內。Put the baggage in the trunk.
2. the box or body of a carriage

箱底兒《ㄒㄧㄤ ㄉㄧˇ ㄦ》
minor actors and actresses in a dramatic troupe

箱籠《ㄒㄧㄤ ㄌㄨㄥˊ》
boxes; chests; trunks: 我給他兩箱籠蜜柑. I gave him two boxes of oranges.

箱根《ㄒㄧㄤ ㄍㄣ》
Hakone, Japan

箱匧《ㄒㄧㄤ ㄑㄧㄝˋ》
boxes; chests

箱屍案《ㄒㄧㄤ ㄕ ㄢˋ》
a murder case with the victim's body found in a trunk

箱子《ㄒㄧㄤ ·ㄗ》
a box; a chest; a trunk: 他用紙板做一個箱子。He made a box with paperboard.

【箭】 4155
ㄐㄧㄢˋ jiann jiàn
1. an arrow
2. a sign which is like an arrow
3. Sinarundinaria nitida, a variety of bamboo

箭靶《ㄐㄧㄢˋ ㄅㄚˇ》
a target for archery

箭風《ㄐㄧㄢˋ ㄈㄥ》
a destructive wind

箭搭上弓《ㄐㄧㄢˋ ㄉㄚ ㄕㄤˋ ㄍㄨㄥ》

(literally) The arrow is fitted to the string.—① ready to go ② imminent

箭袋(ㄐㄧㄢˋ ㄉㄞˋ)or 箭壺(ㄐㄧㄢˋ ㄏㄨˊ)
a quiver

箭頭子(ㄐㄧㄢˋ ㄊㄡˊ ˙ㄗ)
an arrowhead—(figuratively) speedily; fast

箭頭文字(ㄐㄧㄢˋ ㄊㄡˊ ㄨㄣˊ ㄗˋ)
cuneiform characters

箭箙(ㄐㄧㄢˋ ㄊㄡˊ ㄒㄥˊ)or 箭简(ㄐㄧㄢˋ ㄐㄧㄢˇ)
a quiver

箭樓(ㄐㄧㄢˋ ㄌㄡˊ)
battlements

箭豬(ㄐㄧㄢˋ ㄓㄨ)
a porcupine

箭如雨下(ㄐㄧㄢˋ ㄖㄨˊ ㄩˇ ㄒㄧㄚˋ)
Arrows descend like a shower.

箭在弦上(ㄐㄧㄢˋ ㄗㄞˋ ㄒㄧㄢˊ ㄕㄤˋ)
(literally) The arrow is already fitted to the string.—① imminent action expected ② There can be no turning back.

箭鏃(ㄐㄧㄢˋ ㄗㄨˊ)
an arrowhead

箭筍(ㄐㄧㄢˋ ㄙㄨㄣˇ)
small bamboo shoots

箭衣(ㄐㄧㄢˋ ㄧ)
uniform for an archer

箭無虛發(ㄐㄧㄢˋ ㄨˊ ㄒㄩ ㄈㄚ)or 箭無空發(ㄐㄧㄢˋ ㄨˊ ㄎㄨㄥ ㄈㄚ)
(literally) No arrow that is shot is wasted.—excellent marksmanship: 他是位箭無虛發的射手。 He is an accurate marksman.

【篹】 4156 ㄅㄧㄢ biān biàn
a bamboo sedan chair

【箸】 4157 ㄓㄨˋ juh zhù
chopsticks

【箴】 4158 ㄓㄣ jen zhēn
1. a probe; a needle
2. to warn; to admonish

箴砭(ㄓㄣ ㄅㄧㄢ)
stone probes (used in acupuncture)

箴銘(ㄓㄣ ㄇㄧㄥˊ)
admonitions or warnings carved on a stone

箴規(ㄓㄣ ㄍㄨㄟ)
warnings; admonitions; to

admonish; to exhort: 傳道者箴規其聽衆爲善。 The preacher exhorted his congregation to do good.

箴諫(ㄓㄣ ㄐㄧㄢˋ)
to admonish; to exhort; to caution against

箴石(ㄓㄣ ㄕˊ)
stone probes or needles (used in acupuncture)

箴言(ㄓㄣ ㄧㄢˊ)
admonitions; warning words; a maxim:「三思而後行」是一句箴言。 "Look before you leap" is a maxim.

【節】 4159 ㄐㄧㄝˊ jye jié
1. a node; a knot; a joint
2. a passage; a paragraph; a section
3. principles; integrity; fidelity; constancy; uprightness
4. a festival; a holiday
5. seasons
6. (music) beats; rhythm; time
7. to restrain; to control; to restrict
8. to curtail; to economize

節本(ㄐㄧㄝˊ ㄅㄣˇ)
an abridged edition

節拍(ㄐㄧㄝˊ ㄆㄞ)
(music) beats, rhythm or time: 他用快節拍演奏。 He played in quick rhythm.

節旄(ㄐㄧㄝˊ ㄇㄠˊ)
tassels on a tally

節目(ㄐㄧㄝˊ ㄇㄨˋ)
the events of an entertainment or the like; a program; items on a program: 整個節目都很令人愉快。 The entire program was delightful.

節目單(ㄐㄧㄝˊ ㄇㄨˋ ㄉㄢ)
a program (of a concert, show, etc.)

節婦(ㄐㄧㄝˊ ㄈㄨˋ)
① a woman adhering to widowhood ② a woman who dies for protecting her chastity

節電(ㄐㄧㄝˊ ㄉㄧㄢˋ)
to save electricity; to cut down power consumption: 我們應該節電。 We should cut down power consumption.

節度使(ㄐㄧㄝˊ ㄉㄨˋ ㄕˇ)
an official in charge of military supply (set up in the

kingdom of Wu during the Epoch of Three Kingdoms)

節度使(ㄐㄧㄝˊ ㄉㄨˋ ㄕˇ)or(ㄐㄧㄝˊ ㄉㄨˋ ㄕˋ)
a governor of one or more provinces in charge of both civil and military affairs during the Tang Dynasty

節勞(ㄐㄧㄝˊ ㄌㄠˊ)
to conserve one's energy

節禮(ㄐㄧㄝˊ ㄌㄧˇ)
presents sent on a festival

節流(ㄐㄧㄝˊ ㄌㄧㄡˊ)
to curtail expenditures; to cut down expenses: 我們必須開源節流。 We have to earn more income and cut down expenses.

節令(ㄐㄧㄝˊ ㄌㄧㄥˋ)
festivals

節錄(ㄐㄧㄝˊ ㄌㄨˋ)
① to excerpt ② an excerpt

節略(ㄐㄧㄝˊ ㄌㄩㄝˋ)
an outline; a summary

節概(ㄐㄧㄝˊ ㄍㄞˋ)
principles; integrity; uprightness

節骨眼(ㄐㄧㄝˊ ㄍㄨˊ ㄧㄢˇ)
a critical juncture; a critical moment

節節敗退(ㄐㄧㄝˊ ㄐㄧㄝˊ ㄅㄞˋ ㄊㄨㄟˋ)
to suffer one defeat after another

節節勝利(ㄐㄧㄝˊ ㄐㄧㄝˊ ㄕㄥˋ ㄌㄧˋ)
to score one victory after another

節儉(ㄐㄧㄝˊ ㄐㄧㄢˇ)
to be frugal; to practice austerity; to economize

節敬(ㄐㄧㄝˊ ㄐㄧㄥˋ)
presents sent on festivals

節氣(ㄐㄧㄝˊ ㄑㄧˋ)
the 24 seasonal periods into which the lunar year is divided, each consisting of 15 days

節孝(ㄐㄧㄝˊ ㄒㄧㄠˋ)
wifely fidelity and filial piety

節制(ㄐㄧㄝˊ ㄓˋ)
to restrict; to hold down; to keep within limits; to limit; to control: 他不能節制他的脾氣。 He lost control of his temper.

節制生育(ㄐㄧㄝˊ ㄓˋ ㄕㄥ ㄩˋ)
to practice birth control;

〔竹部〕

birth control 亦作「節育」

節制資本 (ㄐㄧㄝˊ ㄓˋ ㄗ ㄅㄣˇ)
the restriction of private
capital (one of the measures
under *The Three Principles
of the People* by Dr. Sun
Yat-sen)

節食 (ㄐㄧㄝˊ ㄕˊ)
to go on a diet: 她太胖, 故須
節食。 She got so fat that she
had to diet.

節上生枝 (ㄐㄧㄝˊ ㄕㄤˋ ㄕㄥ ㄓ)
one complication arising
from another

節省 (ㄐㄧㄝˊ ㄕㄥˇ)
to economize; to save; to use
with thrift: 機械節省勞工。
Machines save labor.

節省費用 (ㄐㄧㄝˊ ㄕㄥˇ ㄈㄟˋ ㄩㄥˋ) or 節
省開支 (ㄐㄧㄝˊ ㄕㄥˇ ㄎㄞ ㄓ)
to cut down expenses; to
practice economy; to economize; to be frugal; to be
thrifty

節省時間 (ㄐㄧㄝˊ ㄕㄥˇ ㄕˊ ㄐㄧㄢ)
to save time

節日 (ㄐㄧㄝˊ ㄖˋ)
a festival; a holiday

節子 (ㄐㄧㄝˊ ㄗ)
a node; a joint; a knot

節奏 (ㄐㄧㄝˊ ㄗㄡˋ)
rhythm: 他以緩慢的節奏演奏。
He played in slow rhythm.

節奏樂器 (ㄐㄧㄝˊ ㄗㄡˋ ㄩㄝˋ ㄑㄧˋ)
rhythmical instruments (such
as drums, triangles, etc.)

節足動物 (ㄐㄧㄝˊ ㄗㄨˊ ㄉㄨㄥˋ ㄨˋ)
an arthropod

節操 (ㄐㄧㄝˊ ㄘㄠ)
constancy; fidelity; integrity;
chastity; moral fortitude

節哀 (ㄐㄧㄝˊ ㄞ)
to restrain grief

節哀順變 (ㄐㄧㄝˊ ㄞ ㄕㄨㄣˋ ㄅㄧㄢˋ)
to restrain grief and accept
the change (common advice
to the bereaved)

節兒 (ㄐㄧㄝˊ ㄦ)
①a node; a joint; a knot ②
a section or passage (of a
piece of writing) ③a festival

節衣縮食 (ㄐㄧㄝˊ ㄧ ㄙㄨㄛ ㄕˊ)
to economize clothing and
food; to live a frugal life

節義 (ㄐㄧㄝˊ ㄧˋ)
integrity; constancy;

chastity

節外生枝 (ㄐㄧㄝˊ ㄨㄞˋ ㄕㄥ ㄓ)
to bring about extra complications; to run into un-
expected difficulty; to hit a
snag

節育 (ㄐㄧㄝˊ ㄩˋ)
to practice birth control;
birth control

節慾 (ㄐㄧㄝˊ ㄩˋ)
to restrain or control one's
desires; to be ascetic; to
practice abstinence

節約 (ㄐㄧㄝˊ ㄩㄝ)
to economize; to be frugal;
to use with thrift; to save:
我們需厲行節約。 We should
practice strict economy.

節用 (ㄐㄧㄝˊ ㄩㄥˋ)
to cut down expenses; to
economize; to practice econom
y

【篁】 4160
ㄏㄨㄤˊ hwang huáng
bamboo; a bamboo bush; a
clump of bamboos; a bam-
boo grove

【範】 4161
ㄈㄢˋ fann fàn
1. a model; a form; an example; a pattern: 這學生是勤勉
的模範。 This student is a
model of diligence.
2. range; scope; limits
3. to observe the proper rules
4. a Chinese family name

範本 (ㄈㄢˋ ㄅㄣˇ)
①a copy or copybook (for
penmanship, calligraphy,
painting, etc.) ②a model; an
example

範例 (ㄈㄢˋ ㄌㄧˋ)
an example; a model: 把這個
當範例用。 Use this as a
model.

範疇 (ㄈㄢˋ ㄔㄡˊ)
category

範圍 (ㄈㄢˋ ㄨㄟˊ)
range; scope; a sphere: 這件
事超過我的能力範圍。 It is
beyond the range of my ability.

範文 (ㄈㄢˋ ㄨㄣˊ)
a model essay

【篇】 4162
ㄆㄧㄢ pian piān
1. a numeral adjunct for
compositions, poems, etc.: 這

是一篇不朽的文章。 This is an
immortal composition.
2. a chapter; a section; a part
3. a page
4. books; volumes

篇章 (ㄆㄧㄢ ㄓㄤ)
①a piece (of poetry, etc.);
an article ②a page

篇目 (ㄆㄧㄢ ㄇㄨˋ)
titles; headings

篇幅 (ㄆㄧㄢ ㄈㄨˊ)
①the length (of a piece of
writing) ②space (of a periodical or newspaper)

篇籍 (ㄆㄧㄢ ㄐㄧˊ)
books

篇章 (ㄆㄧㄢ ㄓㄤ)
books; literary compositions;
poems

篇什 (ㄆㄧㄢ ㄕˊ)
poems

【篆】 4163
ㄓㄨㄢˋ juann zhuàn
1. the seal type, an ancient calligraphic style
2. a seal
3. a Chinese family name

篆刻 (ㄓㄨㄢˋ ㄎㄜˋ)
to cut a seal in the seal type

篆章 (ㄓㄨㄢˋ ㄓㄤ)
a seal; a chop

篆書 (ㄓㄨㄢˋ ㄕㄨ)
the seal type, an ancient calligraphic style

篆字 (ㄓㄨㄢˋ ㄗˋ) or 篆文 (ㄓㄨㄢˋ ㄨㄣˊ)
characters written in the
seal type

篆額 (ㄓㄨㄢˋ ㄜˊ)
to inscribe characters on the
top of a tablet in the seal
type

篆務 (ㄓㄨㄢˋ ㄨˋ)
official affairs

【篋】 4164
ㄑㄧㄝˋ chieh qiè
a chest; a box; a trunk

篋篋 (ㄑㄧㄝˋ ㄑㄧㄝˋ)
long and thin; slender

篋笥 (ㄑㄧㄝˋ ㄙ)
a bamboo box for holding
books and clothes, etc.

【篌】 4165
ㄏㄡˊ hour hóu
a kind of ancient musical
instrument like a lute 參看
「箜篌」

十畫

【築】 4166
ㄓㄨ jwu zhú
1. to build (out of earth, rock, etc.)
2. a house; a room

築壇(ㄓㄨ ㄊㄢˊ)
to build an altar

築堤(ㄓㄨ ㄊㄧˊ)
to build a dike or embankment

築土(ㄓㄨ ㄊㄨˇ)
to build an earth-fill structure

築路(ㄓㄨ ㄌㄨˋ)
to build roads

築路機(ㄓㄨ ㄌㄨˋ ㄐㄧ)
a road-building machine; a grader (for grading a roadway)

築牆(ㄓㄨ ㄑㄧㄤˊ)
to build walls

築巢(ㄓㄨ ㄔㄠˊ)
to build a nest

築城(ㄓㄨ ㄔㄥˊ)
to build a castle or city wall

築室道謀(ㄓㄨ ㄕˋ ㄉㄠˋ ㄇㄡˊ)
(literally) to consult passersby about building a house —to seek the advice of those who have little concern for one's problem

【籌】 4167
《ㄡ gou gōu
a basket; a cage

【篚】 4168
ㄈㄟˇ feei fěi
a square bamboo basket

【篡】 4169
ㄘㄨㄢˋ tsuann cuàn
to seize (power, the throne, etc.); to usurp

篡奪(ㄘㄨㄢˋ ㄉㄨㄛˊ)
to seize (power, the throne, etc.); to usurp

篡逆(ㄘㄨㄢˋ ㄋㄧˋ)
to rebel; to revolt

篡立(ㄘㄨㄢˋ ㄌㄧˋ)
to become an unlawful ruler

篡改(ㄘㄨㄢˋ ㄍㄞˇ)
to alter a piece of writing with an evil intent; to tamper (with a document, etc.)

篡弒(ㄘㄨㄢˋ ㄕˋ)
to commit regicide

篡賊(ㄘㄨㄢˋ ㄗㄟˊ)
a usurper

篡位(ㄘㄨㄢˋ ㄨㄟˋ)
to seize the throne

【篤】 4170
ㄉㄨ duu dǔ
1. deep; much; great; profound
2. dangerous; serious
3. generous
4. to consolidate; to make solid
5. to limit

篤定(ㄉㄨ ㄉㄧㄥˋ)
(informally) very confident; assured

篤老(ㄉㄨ ㄌㄠˇ)
very old; of a venerable age

篤癃(ㄉㄨ ㄌㄨㄥˊ)
an invalid or disabled person

篤厚(ㄉㄨ ㄏㄡˋ)
very sincere

篤疾(ㄉㄨ ㄐㄧˊ)
a fatal illness; a serious disease

篤敬(ㄉㄨ ㄐㄧㄥˋ)
sincerely respectful

篤劇(ㄉㄨ ㄐㄩˋ)
seriously ill

篤信(ㄉㄨ ㄒㄧㄣˋ)
① to have sincere faith in ② honest; trustworthy

篤行(ㄉㄨ ㄒㄧㄥˊ)
honest in behavior

篤學(ㄉㄨ ㄒㄩㄝˊ)
to study diligently

篤志(ㄉㄨ ㄓˋ)
firm determination

篤實(ㄉㄨ ㄕˊ)
① sincere; honest; candid; faithful ② solid; sound

篤守(ㄉㄨ ㄕㄡˇ)
to give careful attention to; to observe with great care

篤生(ㄉㄨ ㄕㄥ)
to be much blessed by Heaven—much gifted

篤愛(ㄉㄨ ㄞˋ)
deep affection

【篙】 4171
《ㄠ gau gāo
the pole for punting a boat; a boat pole

篙工(《ㄠ ㄍㄨㄥ)
a boatman (who punts a boat)

篙師(《ㄠ ㄕ)
a boatman (especially a skilled one) who punts a boat

篙人(《ㄠ ㄖㄣˊ)
a boatman

【篩】 4172
ㄕㄞ shai shāi
1. a sieve; a screen; a sifter; a strainer
2. to sieve; to screen; to sift; to strain

篩分(ㄕㄞ ㄈㄣ)or 篩選(ㄕㄞ ㄒㄩㄢˇ)
screening; sieving; sifting

篩鑼(ㄕㄞ ㄌㄨㄛˊ)
① a small gong ② to beat a gong

篩骨(ㄕㄞ ㄍㄨˇ)
an ethmoid bone

篩管(ㄕㄞ ㄍㄨㄢˇ)
(botany) sieve tubes

篩孔(ㄕㄞ ㄎㄨㄥˇ)
sieve meshes

篩子(ㄕㄞ ·ㄗ)
a sieve; a sifter

【篦】 4173
ㄅㄧ bih bì
a comb (especially a fine-toothed one)

篦櫛(ㄅㄧ ㄐㄧㄝˊ)
a fine-toothed comb, usually made of bamboo

篦子(ㄅㄧ ·ㄗ)
a double-edged, fine-toothed comb

【篪】 4174
(箎) ㄔˊ chyr chí
a kind of bamboo flute 亦作「笹」

【篨】 4175
ㄔㄨˊ chwu chú
1. a coarse bamboo mat
2. an ugly bloated mass

【箱】 4176
ㄕㄠ shau shāo
a bamboo tube for holding chopsticks

【篘】 4177
ㄔㄡ chou chōu
1. a wine filter
2. to filter wine

【篛】 4178
ㄖㄨㄛˋ ruoh ruò
same as 箬—a kind of broad-leaved bamboo

【簑】 4179
ㄙㄨㄛ suo suō
same as 蓑—a coir raincoat (or cape)

十一畫

（竹部）

【篠】 4180
ㄒㄧㄠˇ sheau xiǎo
1. a variety of bamboo with thin and short stems
2. a bamboo basket

【篳】 4181
ㄅㄧˋ bih bì
bamboo, wicker, etc. which can be used to make baskets, bags, etc.
篳門圭竇（ㄅㄧˋ ㄇㄣˊ ㄍㄨㄟ ㄉㄡˋ）
a humble dwelling
篳路藍縷（ㄅㄧˋ ㄌㄨˋ ㄌㄢˊ ㄌㄩˇ）
(literally) firewood carts and rags—the hard life of pioneers

【篼】 4182
ㄉㄡ dou dōu
a mountain sedan chair made of bamboo
篼子（ㄉㄡ ˙ㄗ）
a mountain sedan chair

【篾】 4183
（䈼）ㄇㄧㄝˋ mieh miè
1. a thin and long strip of bamboo for making baskets, etc.; thin (bamboo) laths
2. name of a variety of bamboo
篾片（ㄇㄧㄝˋ ㄆㄧㄢˋ）
①a thin and long strip of bamboo ②protégés who are good at pleasing the patron
篾匠（ㄇㄧㄝˋ ㄐㄧㄤˋ）
a bamboo craftsman
篾席（ㄇㄧㄝˋ ㄒㄧˊ）
a bamboo bed mat

【篷】 4184
ㄆㄥˊ perng péng
1. a covering; an awning; a tent
2. a sail; a boat
篷布（ㄆㄥˊ ㄅㄨˋ）
a tarpaulin
篷車（ㄆㄥˊ ㄔㄜ）
a wagon
篷窗（ㄆㄥˊ ㄔㄨㄤ）
windows in a boat

【簌】 4185
ㄙㄨˋ suh sù
(said of flower petals) falling in great quantities
簌地（ㄙㄨˋ ㄉㄧˋ）
(said of tears) flowing
簌簌（ㄙㄨˋ ㄙㄨˋ）

①luxuriant growth (of vegetation) ②(onomatopoeia) a very slight sound ③to shower down
簌簌地（ㄙㄨˋ ㄙㄨˋ ˙ㄉㄧ）
a very slight sound of something moving stealthily, flowing, or dropping—as droplets of water, tears, etc.

【簏】 4186
ㄌㄨˋ luh lù
a bamboo trunk
簏簌（ㄌㄨˋ ㄙㄨˋ）
hanging down

【簇】 4187
ㄘㄨˋ tsuh cù
1. a cluster; a crowd; crowded: 有些花是簇生的, Some flowers grow in clusters.
2. an arrowhead
3. a framework on which silkworms spin
4. to crowd together; to cluster together
簇聚（ㄘㄨˋ ㄐㄩˋ）
to cluster or crowd together: 他們簇聚在火爐邊。They crowded round the stove.
簇新（ㄘㄨˋ ㄒㄧㄣ）
brand-new
簇簇（ㄘㄨˋ ㄘㄨˋ）
piled up; in array
簇擁（ㄘㄨˋ ㄩㄥˇ）
attended by a crowd: 他前後簇擁着一大羣人。He was attended by a large crowd in front and behind.

【篕】 4188
ㄧˋ yì
a small house attached to a pavilion

【簀】 4189
ㄗㄜˊ tzer zé
1. a bamboo bed mat
2. to be densely collected together

【簋】 4190
ㄍㄨㄟˇ goei guǐ
a round bamboo vessel for holding grains in ancient offerings or feasts; a bronze vessel for holding food in ancient times

【簉】 4191
ㄗㄠˋ tzaw zòu
1. deputy; a deputy; an attendant
2. an escorting vehicle
3. a concubine

簜弄（ㄕㄤˇ ㄋㄨㄥˋ）
a ditty; a little tune
簜室（ㄕㄤˇ ㄕˋ）
a concubine

【簨】 4192
1. ㄓㄨㄢˋ juann zhuàn
same as 撰—to collect, edit or write

【簨】 4192
2. ㄙㄨㄢˇ soan suǎn
（又讀 ㄗㄨㄢˋ tzoan zuàn）
a splint basket; a bamboo basket

【簍】 4193
ㄌㄡˇ loou lǒu
a basket made by weaving bamboo slats, wickers or twigs
簍子（ㄌㄡˇ ˙ㄗ）
a basket made of bamboo, wickers or twigs
簍兒（ㄌㄡˇ ㄦ）
①a basket ②a kind of dumpling with stuffing

【簿】 4194
ㄅㄨˋ buh bù
1. a bamboo basket
2. same as 簿—books, volumes, or letters

【艄】 4195
ㄕㄠ shau shāo
1. the tail of a helm
2. to flutter in the wind

【簰】 4196
ㄆㄞˊ pair pái
a raft; a bamboo raft

【篲】 4197
ㄏㄨㄟˋ huey huì
a broom; a bamboo broom

十二畫

【簞】 4198
ㄉㄢ dan dān
a kind of round bamboo ware for holding cooked rice
簞瓢屢空（ㄉㄢ ㄆㄧㄠˊ ㄌㄩˇ ㄎㄨㄥ）
(literally) The basket and gourd are frequently empty. —with no food and water; stark poverty
簞笥（ㄉㄢ ㄙˋ）
①a bamboo box ②vessels for holding food
簞食瓢飲（ㄉㄢ ㄙˋ ㄆㄧㄠˊ ㄧㄣˇ）

to lead a simple life

簞食壺漿(ㄉㄢ ㄙˋ ㄏㄨˊ ㄐㄧㄤ)
(said of the populace) to cheer the troops with food and drink

【簟】 4199
ㄉㄧㄢˋ diann diàn
a bamboo mat

簞竹(ㄉㄧ ㄓㄨˊ)
a variety of giant bamboo

【簡】 4200
(簡) ㄐㄧㄢˇ jean
jiǎn

1. brief; succinct; terse; simple:
他給了我一個簡潔的答覆。He gave me a terse reply.
2. (in ancient China) a slip or tablet of bamboo for writing
3. a letter; a note
4. to treat coolly or impolitely
5. to designate or appoint (an official)
6. to select; to choose
7. a Chinese family name

簡拔(ㄐㄧㄢˇ ㄅㄚˊ)
to select and designate (someone for a post)

簡報(ㄐㄧㄢˇ ㄅㄠˋ)
a briefing

簡筆字(ㄐㄧㄢˇ ㄅㄧˇ ㄗˋ)or **簡體字**(ㄐㄧㄢˇ ㄊㄧˇ ㄗˋ)
an abbreviated or simplified form of a character, such as 体 for 體

簡編(ㄐㄧㄢˇ ㄅㄧㄢ)
books; volumes

簡便(ㄐㄧㄢˇ ㄅㄧㄢˋ)
simple and convenient

簡樸(ㄐㄧㄢˇ ㄆㄨˊ)
simple and unadorned; plain:
他過著簡樸生活。He led a simple life.

簡慢(ㄐㄧㄢˇ ㄇㄢˋ)
(a polite expression to say to a guest) to treat impolitely or coolly

簡明(ㄐㄧㄢˇ ㄇㄧㄥˊ)
brief and clear; terse and to the point; concise: 他對會議作了一個簡明的報告。He gave a concise report of the meeting.

簡分數(ㄐㄧㄢˇ ㄈㄣ ㄕㄨˋ)
a simple fraction

簡單(ㄐㄧㄢˇ ㄉㄢ)
①simple; brief: 這個解釋十分簡單。The explanation was

quite simple. ② ordinary

簡單明瞭(ㄐㄧㄢˇ ㄉㄢ ㄇㄧㄥˊ ㄌㄧㄠˇ)
brief and clear; simple and to the point

簡單生活(ㄐㄧㄢˇ ㄉㄢ ㄕㄥ ㄏㄨㄛˊ)
a simple life

簡牘(ㄐㄧㄢˇ ㄉㄨˊ)
①books and volumes ②letters or correspondence

簡短(ㄐㄧㄢˇ ㄉㄨㄢˇ)
brief; succinct; terse; short:
林肯的蓋茨堡演講辭簡短有力。Lincoln's Gettysburg Address is terse.

簡圖(ㄐㄧㄢˇ ㄊㄨˊ)
a sketch; a diagram

簡陋(ㄐㄧㄢˇ ㄌㄡˋ)
simple and crude: 這所學校設備簡陋。This school has simple and crude equipment.

簡練(ㄐㄧㄢˇ ㄌㄧㄢˋ)
①to select and study thoroughly ②(said of a piece of writing) refined; succinct

簡略(ㄐㄧㄢˇ ㄌㄩㄝˋ)
brief; sketchy

簡括(ㄐㄧㄢˇ ㄍㄨㄚ)
brief but to the point; succinct

簡忽(ㄐㄧㄢˇ ㄏㄨ)
to slight; to treat coolly

簡化(ㄐㄧㄢˇ ㄏㄨㄚˋ)
to simplify; simplification:
這故事已由王先生簡化了。The story has been simplified by Mr. Wang.

簡潔(ㄐㄧㄢˇ ㄐㄧㄝˊ)
(said of a piece of writing) simple and perspicuous; brief and to the point; succinct

簡介(ㄐㄧㄢˇ ㄐㄧㄝˋ)
a brief introduction; a synopsis

簡寫(ㄐㄧㄢˇ ㄒㄧㄝˇ)
①to write a Chinese character in a simplified form ②to simplify a book for beginners

簡直(ㄐㄧㄢˇ ㄓˊ)
①simply; outright; at all: 那簡直是不可能的。That's simply impossible. ②honest; unaffected

簡札(ㄐㄧㄢˇ ㄓㄚˊ)
letters; correspondence

簡章(ㄐㄧㄢˇ ㄓㄤ)

a brief and concise statement of regulations, procedures, etc.

簡擢(ㄐㄧㄢˇ ㄓㄨㄛˊ)
to select and designate (a person for a post)

簡稱(ㄐㄧㄢˇ ㄔㄥ)
to be called or known as... for short

簡任(ㄐㄧㄢˇ ㄖㄣˋ)
the selected appointment rank (the second highest of the four grades in modern Chinese civil service)

簡字(ㄐㄧㄢˇ ㄗˋ)
①an abbreviated or simplified form of a character ②a kind of phonetic signs devised by Lao Nai-hsüan (勞乃宣) of the Ching Dynasty

簡冊(ㄐㄧㄢˇ ㄘㄜˋ)
books

簡而言之(ㄐㄧㄢˇ ㄦˊ ㄧㄢˊ ㄓ)
in short; briefly; in a word

簡易(ㄐㄧㄢˇ ㄧˋ)
simple; easy; simple and convenient

簡易科(ㄐㄧㄢˇ ㄧˋ ㄎㄜ)
a short course; a snap course

簡要(ㄐㄧㄢˇ ㄧㄠˋ)
brief and concise; brief and to the point

簡約(ㄐㄧㄢˇ ㄩㄝ)
brief; terse; succinct

【簣】 4201
ㄎㄨㄟˋ kuey kuì
a bamboo basket for carrying earth

【簦】 4202
ㄉㄥ dēng
a kind of umbrella used in ancient China

簦笠(ㄉㄥ ㄌㄧˋ)
a kind of large umbrella with a long handle, used for street stalls

【簠】 4203
ㄈㄨˇ fuu fǔ
a square vessel for containing the cooked grain at sacrifices or feasts

簠簋不飭(ㄈㄨˇ ㄍㄨㄟˇ ㄅㄨˋ ㄔˋ)
(literally) Sacrificial items are not laid out in good order. —the abuse of powers

〔竹部〕

by greedy officials

【簨】 4204 ㄙㄨㄣˇ soen sǔn
a beam for hanging bells or chime stone

簨虡（ㄙㄨㄣˇ ㄐㄩˋ）
a beam for hanging bells or chime stone

【簪】 4205 ㄗㄢ tzan zān
（又讀 ㄗㄣ tzen zēn）
1. a clasp for clipping the cap and hair together
2. a hairpin for women
3. to stick (in the hair, etc.); to wear

簪筆（ㄗㄢ ㄅㄧˇ）
(said of ancient courtiers) to stick the writing brush in one's hair or behind the ear

簪紱（ㄗㄢ ㄈㄨˊ）
(literally) a cap clasp and hat tassels for an official seal—high position and wealth

簪笏（ㄗㄢ ㄏㄨˋ）
(literally) the cap clasp and the jade tablet (used during an audience with the emperor, etc.)—high officials

簪花（ㄗㄢ ㄏㄨㄚ）
to wear a flower; to stick a flower on one's cap or hat

簪環首飾（ㄗㄢ ㄏㄨㄢˊ ㄕㄡˇ ㄕˋ）
women's hairpins, rings, jewels, etc.

簪纓（ㄗㄢ ㄧㄥ）
dresses and ornaments of the nobility

簪子（ㄗㄢ ˙ㄗ）or 簪兒（ㄗㄢㄦ）
a woman's hairpin

簪纓世冑（ㄗㄢ ㄧㄥ ㄕˋ ㄓㄡˋ）
a family producing public officials for successive generations 亦作「華冑」

【簧】 4206 ㄏㄨㄤˊ hwang huáng
1. a reed; the metal tongue in a reed organ
2. a reed organ
3. a spring or catch in a machine: 這沙發裝有鐵絲彈簧。The sofa has wire springs.

簧片（ㄏㄨㄤˊ ㄆㄧㄢˋ）
the metal tongue in a reed organ; a reed

簧鼓（ㄏㄨㄤˊ ㄍㄨˇ）
to dazzle people with sweet talks

簧樂器（ㄏㄨㄤˊ ㄩㄝˋ ㄑㄧˋ）
the reed instruments (in a symphony orchestra)

【簙】 4207 ㄅㄛˊ bor bó
a kind of chess game

【簫】 4208 ㄒㄧㄠ shiau xiāo
a vertical flute of bamboo: 他在吹簫。He plays on the vertical bamboo flute.

簫管（ㄒㄧㄠ ㄍㄨㄢˇ）
a panpipe and a double flute

簫韶（ㄒㄧㄠ ㄕㄠˊ）
the name of the music created by Emperor Shun (舜), 2255 B.C.

十三畫

【簷】 4209 ㄧㄢˊ yan yán
1. the eaves of a house
2. the edge or brim of anything sloping downward—as that of a hat, umbrella, etc.

簷馬（ㄧㄢˊ ㄇㄚˇ）or 簷鐵馬（ㄧㄢˊ ㄊㄧㄝˇ ㄇㄚˇ）
tiny metallic ornaments, bells, etc., hanging down from the eaves and tinkling in the wind

簷溜（ㄧㄢˊ ㄌㄧㄡˋ）or 簷滴（ㄧㄢˊ ㄉㄧ）
dripping water from the eaves

簷前（ㄧㄢˊ ㄑㄧㄢˊ）
the front of the eaves; in front of the eaves

簷下（ㄧㄢˊ ㄒㄧㄚˋ）
under the eaves: 燕子築巢於簷下。The swallows nested under the eaves.

簷牙（ㄧㄢˊ ㄧㄚˊ）
the projecting tiles on the eaves (for the ornamental purpose)

【簸】 4210
1. ㄅㄛˇ boo bǒ
to winnow; to sift (especially rice)

簸蕩（ㄅㄛˇ ㄉㄤˋ）
the rocking of a boat; to roll: 那船在浪上簸蕩得很厲害。That ship was rolling heavily on the waves.

簸弄（ㄅㄛˇ ㄋㄨㄥˋ）
①to play jokes on; to deceive ②to spread rumors or tell tales; to start rumors and incite incidents

簸揚（ㄅㄛˇ ㄧㄤˊ）
to winnow; to sift

2. ㄅㄛˋ boh bò
a winnow

簸箕（ㄅㄛˋ ˙ㄐㄧ）
①a winnow ②a container for dust; a dustpan

【簽】 4211 ㄑㄧㄢ chian qiān
1. to sign one's name; to put down one's signature; to subscribe; to endorse: 他忘記簽名。He's forgotten to sign his name.
2. bamboo slips used for drawing lots or divination
3. a label

簽名（ㄑㄧㄢ ㄇㄧㄥˊ）
to sign; to put down one's signature; to autograph; a signature

簽名簿（ㄑㄧㄢ ㄇㄧㄥˊ ㄅㄨˋ）
a book for putting down autographs (of visitors, guests, etc.); a guest book: 這是來賓簽名簿。This is a book for signatures of visitors.

簽到（ㄑㄧㄢ ㄉㄠˋ）
to sign on an attendance book of an office, firm or factory

簽到簿（ㄑㄧㄢ ㄉㄠˋ ㄅㄨˋ）
a book where employees or workers put down their signatures or initials to indicate their presence in time; an attendance book

簽訂（ㄑㄧㄢ ㄉㄧㄥˋ）
to conclude and sign (a treaty, etc.): 昨天晚上他們簽訂了一份合約。They signed an agreement last night.

簽訂條約（ㄑㄧㄢ ㄉㄧㄥˋ ㄊㄧㄠˊ ㄩㄝ）
to sign a treaty

簽訂合同（ㄑㄧㄢ ㄉㄧㄥˋ ㄏㄜˊ ㄊㄨㄥˊ）
to sign a contract

簽條（ㄑㄧㄢ ㄊㄧㄠˊ）
①a label ②an office note; a memo

簽知（ㄑㄧㄢ ㄓ）
to sign or initial on a docu-

ment, etc. to show that one has read the contents therein

簽證〔ㄑㄧㄢ ㄓㄥˋ〕
a visa; to visa: 他持有過境簽證. He holds a transit visa.

簽註〔ㄑㄧㄢ ㄓㄨˋ〕or 簽註意見〔ㄑㄧㄢ ㄓㄨˋ ㄧˋ ㄐㄧㄢˋ〕
to attach a slip of paper to a document with comments on it; to put down one's comments on a document or official correspondence

簽呈〔ㄑㄧㄢ ㄔㄥˊ〕
a written report addressed to a superior

簽收〔ㄑㄧㄢ ㄕㄡ〕
to sign after receiving something

簽署〔ㄑㄧㄢ ㄕㄨˇ〕
to sign or initial (a document)

簽字〔ㄑㄧㄢ ㄗˋ〕
a signature; to sign or initial: 這合約簽字後立即生效. The contract came into force upon signature.

簽字筆〔ㄑㄧㄢ ㄗˋ ㄅㄧˇ〕
a felt pen; a felt-tip pen; a felt marker

簽字國〔ㄑㄧㄢ ㄗˋ ㄍㄨㄛˊ〕
a signatory country

簽押〔ㄑㄧㄢ ㄧㄚˊ〕
to sign one's name or put a seal on

簽印〔ㄑㄧㄢ ㄧㄣˋ〕
to sign or put a seal on

簽約〔ㄑㄧㄢ ㄩㄝ〕
to sign a contract, treaty, etc.

【簾】 4212 〔ㄌㄧㄢˊ lian lián〕
1. a loose hanging screen for a door or window, usually made of stringed beads, bamboo slabs, etc.; blinds; a curtain: 請掛窗簾拉上。Please draw the window curtains.
2. a flag as a shop sign: 酒簾 a wineshop sign

簾幕〔ㄌㄧㄢˊ ㄇㄨˋ〕
screens and blinds

簾內簾外〔ㄌㄧㄢˊ ㄋㄟˋ ㄌㄧㄢˊ ㄨㄞˋ〕
(literally) within and without the curtain—private and public

簾櫳〔ㄌㄧㄢˊ ㄌㄨㄥˊ〕

the windows, doors and the screens

簾官〔ㄌㄧㄢˊ ㄍㄨㄢ〕
officials in charge of the civil service examination in former times

簾眷〔ㄌㄧㄢˊ ㄐㄩㄢˋ〕
to win the favor of the queen dowager when she acts as regent in the emperor's childhood

簾政〔ㄌㄧㄢˊ ㄓㄥˋ〕
the regency of an empress-dowager

簾子〔ㄌㄧㄢˊ ˙ㄗ〕or 簾兒〔ㄌㄧㄚˊㄦ〕
a screen; a curtain; blinds

簾押〔ㄌㄧㄢˊ ㄧㄚ〕
a curtain ballast

【簨】 4213 〔ㄙㄨㄣˇ jiuh jǔ〕
pillars beside the crossbeam for hanging bells or drums

【簿】 4214 〔ㄅㄨˋ buh bù〕
1. books: 支票簿 a checkbook
2. to record; to register

簿歷〔ㄅㄨˋ ㄌㄧˋ〕
a person's records, qualifications, etc.

簿錄〔ㄅㄨˋ ㄌㄨˋ〕
① to confiscate property ② a catalogue of books: 她做了一本簿錄。She makes a catalogue of books.

簿籍〔ㄅㄨˋ ㄐㄧˊ〕
① a domiciliary register ② account books

簿記〔ㄅㄨˋ ㄐㄧˋ〕
bookkeeping: 單（複）式簿記 bookkeeping by single (double) entry

簿記學〔ㄅㄨˋ ㄐㄧˋ ㄒㄩㄝˊ〕
bookkeeping (as a course of study)

簿記學校〔ㄅㄨˋ ㄐㄧˋ ㄒㄩㄝˊ ㄒㄧㄠˋ〕
a bookkeeping school

簿記員〔ㄅㄨˋ ㄐㄧˋ ㄩㄢˊ〕
a bookkeeper; a ledger clerk: 她是本公司的簿記員。She is a bookkeeper of our company.

簿子〔ㄅㄨˋ ˙ㄗ〕
a blank book for writing; an exercise book; a notebook

簿冊〔ㄅㄨˋ ㄘㄜˋ〕
books (for record, registration, etc.) and files; lists or

registers

【簳】 4215 〔ㄍㄢˇ gaan gǎn〕
young bamboo

【籀】 4216 〔ㄓㄡˋ jow zhòu〕
1. a type of Chinese calligraphy, also known as 大篆—the large seal
2. to deduce

籀篆〔ㄓㄡˋ ㄓㄨㄢˋ〕or 籀書〔ㄓㄡˋ ㄕㄨ〕or 籀文〔ㄓㄡˋ ㄨㄣˊ〕
the "large seal" type of Chinese calligraphy, initiated during the Chou Dynasty by Historian Chou (史籀)

十四畫

【籃】 4217 〔ㄌㄢˊ lan lán〕
a basket: 她買了一籃桃子。She bought a basket of peaches.

籃板球〔ㄌㄢˊ ㄅㄢˇ ㄑㄧㄡˊ〕
(basketball) rebounds

籃球〔ㄌㄢˊ ㄑㄧㄡˊ〕
basketball

籃球架〔ㄌㄢˊ ㄑㄧㄡˊ ㄐㄧㄚˋ〕
basketball back stops; basketball stands

籃球賽〔ㄌㄢˊ ㄑㄧㄡˊ ㄙㄞˋ〕
a basketball game

籃子〔ㄌㄢˊ ˙ㄗ〕or 籃兒〔ㄌㄢˊㄦ〕
baskets

籃輿〔ㄌㄢˊ ㄩˊ〕
a bamboo sedan chair

【籌】 4218 〔ㄔㄡˊ chour chóu〕
1. chips, tallies, etc. for calculating purposes
2. to plan; to prepare
3. to raise (money)
4. to assess or estimate

籌備〔ㄔㄡˊ ㄅㄟˋ〕
to prepare and plan; to arrange

籌備費〔ㄔㄡˊ ㄅㄟˋ ㄈㄟˋ〕
preliminary expenditure

籌備會〔ㄔㄡˊ ㄅㄟˋ ㄏㄨㄟˋ〕
a preparatory meeting, committee, etc.; an organizing committee

籌備處〔ㄔㄡˊ ㄅㄟˋ ㄔㄨˋ〕
a preparatory office

籌備委員〔ㄔㄡˊ ㄅㄟˋ ㄨㄟˇ ㄩㄢˊ〕
members on a preparatory committee

〔竹 部〕

〔竹部〕

籌辦(ㄔㄡ ㄅㄢ)
to plan and sponsor (a show, sports event, school, etc.)

籌邊(ㄔㄡ ㄅㄧㄢ)
to make plans for affairs pertaining to a nation's borders

籌碼(ㄔㄡ ㄇㄚˇ)
chips (in gambling, etc.); a counter: 這是政治交易的籌碼。This is a bargaining counter in political deals.

籌募(ㄔㄡ ㄇㄨˋ)
to raise; to collect (funds)

籌度(ㄔㄡ ㄉㄨㄛˊ)
to plan and estimate

籌略(ㄔㄡ ㄌㄩㄝˋ)
strategy; plans; tactics

籌款(ㄔㄡ ㄎㄨㄢˇ)
to procure money; to raise funds: 他為一新事業籌款。He raises money for a new undertaking.

籌劃(ㄔㄡ ㄏㄨㄚˋ)
to deliberate and plan; a layout

籌建(ㄔㄡ ㄐㄧㄢˋ)
to prepare the construction of

籌餉(ㄔㄡ ㄒㄧㄤˇ)
to raise money or funds for military payroll

籌商(ㄔㄡ ㄕㄤ)or 籌議(ㄔㄡ ㄧˋ)
to plan and discuss (means to cope with a certain problem, etc.)

籌策(ㄔㄡ ㄘㄜˋ)
to prepare and plan

籌措(ㄔㄡ ㄘㄨㄛˋ)
to raise (funds)

籌算(ㄔㄡ ㄙㄨㄢˋ)
to calculate with chips marked with figures

籌安會(ㄔㄡ ㄢ ㄏㄨㄟˋ)
a political body founded in 1915, whose aim was to make Yüan Shih-kai (袁世凱) emperor

【籍】 4219 (ㄐㄧˊ jyi jí)
1. books; volumes; reading materials
2. a record or register of population
3. one's hometown or native place: 祖籍 the native land of one's ancestors
4. a Chinese family name

籍沒(ㄐㄧ ㄇㄛˋ)
to confiscate someone's possessions

籍隸(ㄐㄧ ㄌㄧˋ)
to be a native of; to hail from

籍斂(ㄐㄧ ㄌㄧㄢˋ)
to demand or collect illegal taxes

籍貫(ㄐㄧ ㄍㄨㄢˋ)
one's native place or hometown: 你的籍貫是那裡? What is your hometown?

籍籍(ㄐㄧˊ ㄐㄧˊ)
①confusing; disorderly ②noisy; vociferous

籍甚(ㄐㄧ ㄕㄣˋ)
(said of reputation) widespread

十五畫

【籐】 4220 (ㄊㄥˊ terng téng)
same as 藤—vines; canes; climbing plants; rattans

籐椅(ㄊㄥˊ ㄧˇ)
a rattan armchair

十六畫

【籙】 4221 (ㄌㄨˋ luh lù)
1. lists or registers
2. a Taoist amulet or charm

【籜】 4222 (ㄊㄨㄛˋ tuoh tuò)
the shell of bamboo shoots

【籟】 4223 (ㄌㄞˋ lay lài)
1. a kind of pipe
2. unspecified sounds

【籠】 4224 (ㄌㄨㄥˊ long lóng) (又讀 ㄌㄨㄥˇ loong long)
1. a cage; a coop
2. a tight, storied cagelike bamboo ware for steaming dumplings, etc.; a bamboo food steamer
3. to include; to encompass

籠頭
①(ㄌㄨㄥˊ ㄊㄡˊ) the leader of prisoners in a jail
②(ㄌㄨㄥˇ ㄊㄡˊ) the halter of an animal

籠統(ㄌㄨㄥˇ ㄊㄨㄥˇ)
generalized; general; sweeping; indiscriminate: 這篇敘述太籠統了。The statement is too general.

籠利(ㄌㄨㄥˇ ㄌㄧˋ)
to amass gains; to make profit

籠絡(ㄌㄨㄥˇ ㄌㄨㄛˋ)or(ㄌㄨㄥˇ ㄌㄨㄛˋ)
①to entice, tempt, ensnare or cajole ②to befriend another with a view to winning him over

籠括(ㄌㄨㄥˇ ㄍㄨㄚ)
to encompass; to seize all

籠罩(ㄌㄨㄥˇ ㄓㄠˋ)or(ㄌㄨㄥˇ ㄓㄠˋ)
to cover completely; to permeate; to shroud: 晨霧籠罩着山頭。The mountain is shrouded in morning mist.

籠中鳥(ㄌㄨㄥˊ ㄓㄨㄥ ㄋㄧㄠˇ)
(literally) a bird in a cage—restricted and confined; without much freedom

籠子(ㄌㄨㄥˊ ˙ㄗ)
①a cage; a coop ②a bamboo ware

【籞】 4225 (ㄩˋ yuh yù)
1. the forbidden garden in a palace
2. a fenced place in a pond for keeping fish

十七畫

【籤】 4226 (籖)(ㄑㄧㄢ chian qiān)
1. a slip of bamboo engraved with signs to be used in gambling or divination; a lot
2. a label
3. a small sharp-pointed stick

籤兒(ㄑㄧㄢ ㄦ)
①a gambling slip of bamboo engraved with spots to determine the winner ②sticks with pointed ends, used to pierce into bags, etc. to find out the contents therein ③a label

籤詩(ㄑㄧㄢ ㄕ)or 籤語(ㄑㄧㄢ ㄩˇ)
a doggerel poem or quote foretelling one's fortune as denoted by a divination lot drawn by oneself

【籥】 4227
ㄩㄝ yueh yuè
1. a short flute or pipe used in ancient China
2. a key

【籧】 4228
1. ㄑㄩ chyu qú
a crude bamboo mat

籧除〈ㄑㄩˊㄔㄨˊ〉
a kind of ailment, probably of a rheumatic nature, which causes stiff neck and backbone; a vicious bloated mass

【籧】 4228
2. ㄐㄩ jeu jǔ
a vessel for raising silkworms

十九畫

【籩】 4229
ㄅㄧㄢ bian biān
a bamboo container for food, also used to hold fruit or dried meat, etc. in sacrifices

籩豆〈ㄅㄧㄢ ㄉㄡˋ〉
two ancient food containers used at sacrifices

【籬】 4230
ㄌㄧˊ li lí
a bamboo fence; a hedge

籬笆〈ㄌㄧˊ ㄅㄚ〉
a bamboo fence: 那匹馬跳過了籬笆。 That horse jumped over the fence.

籬落〈ㄌㄧˊ ㄌㄨㄛˋ〉
a fence; a hedge

籬根〈ㄌㄧˊ ㄍㄣ〉
the lower part of a fence

籬菊〈ㄌㄧˊ ㄐㄩˊ〉
chrysanthemums beside the fence

籬竹〈ㄌㄧˊ ㄓㄨˊ〉
a fence formed by living bamboos

籬垣〈ㄌㄧˊ ㄩㄢˊ〉
a fence; a hedge: 在他家前面有一道籬垣。 There is a hedge in front of his house.

【籮】 4231
ㄌㄨㄛˊ luo luó
1. a bamboo basket with a square or rectangular bottom and a round top
2. a piece of sieve-like ware with a broad edge

籮筐〈ㄌㄨㄛˊ ㄎㄨㄤ〉
a large basket made of bamboo

二十六畫

【籲】 4232
ㄩˋ yuh yù
to appeal; to request; to urge; to ask; to implore; to beseech

籲天〈ㄩˋ ㄊㄧㄢ〉
to cry to Heaven; to appeal to God

籲求〈ㄩˋ ㄑㄧㄡˊ〉
to urge; to implore

籲請〈ㄩˋ ㄑㄧㄥˇ〉
to request; to beseech; to urge

米部
ㄇㄧˇ mii mǐ

【米】 4233
ㄇㄧˇ mii mǐ
1. hulled or husked rice; uncooked rice: 中國人靠米為生。 The Chinese live on rice.
2. a shelled or a husked seed: 花生米 a peanut; a peanut kernel
3. meter (the fundamental unit of length in the metric system)
4. a Chinese family name

米芾〈ㄇㄧˇ ㄈㄨˊ〉or 米南宮《ㄨㄥ》
Mi Fei, a renowned painter and calligrapher of the Sung Dynasty

米飯〈ㄇㄧˇ ㄈㄢˋ〉
rice; cooked rice: 中國人喜歡吃米飯。 The Chinese like to eat cooked rice.

米粉〈ㄇㄧˇ ㄈㄣˇ〉
① rice flour ② thin noodles made of rice flour; rice-flour noodles: 你喜歡吃米粉嗎? Do you like rice-flour noodles?

米粉肉〈ㄇㄧˇ ㄈㄣˇ ㄖㄡˋ〉
(Chinese cooking) a dish prepared by steaming meat mixed with rice flour; pork steamed with ground glutinous rice

米店〈ㄇㄧˇ ㄉㄧㄢˋ〉
a shop selling rice (usually along with other kinds of grain)

米湯〈ㄇㄧˇ ㄊㄤ〉
① rice soup ② flattering words

米突〈ㄇㄧˇ ㄊㄨˊ〉
① meter, the fundamental unit of length in the metric system ② metric

米突制〈ㄇㄧˇ ㄊㄨˊ ㄓˋ〉
the metric system 亦作「米制」or「公制」

米突尺〈ㄇㄧˇ ㄊㄨˊ ㄔˇ〉
a metric ruler

米蘭〈ㄇㄧˇ ㄌㄢˊ〉
Milan, an industrial city in central Lombardy, in N Italy

米粒〈ㄇㄧˇ ㄌㄧˋ〉or 米粒兒〈ㄇㄧˇ ㄌㄧˋ ㄦˊ〉
a grain of rice

米糧〈ㄇㄧˇ ㄌㄧㄤˊ〉
rice and food supplies; provisions

米糕〈ㄇㄧˇ ㄍㄠ〉
rice cake; rice pudding

米糠〈ㄇㄧˇ ㄎㄤ〉
rice bran; paddy chaff

米黃〈ㄇㄧˇ ㄏㄨㄤˊ〉
cream-colored; cream: 她穿着米黃色衣服。 She wore a cream dress.

米價〈ㄇㄧˇ ㄐㄧㄚˋ〉
the price of rice

米酒〈ㄇㄧˇ ㄐㄧㄡˇ〉
rice wine; rice beer

米粥〈ㄇㄧˇ ㄓㄡ〉
congee; rice gruel

米珠薪桂〈ㄇㄧˇ ㄓㄨ ㄒㄧㄣ ㄍㄨㄟˋ〉
(literally) rice as precious as pearls and firewood as expensive as cinnamon—the high cost of living

米食〈ㄇㄧˇ ㄕˊ〉
a rice diet

米色〈ㄇㄧˇ ㄙㄜˋ〉
a very light chocolate brown color; cream

三畫

【籽】 4234
ㄗˇ tzyy zǐ
seeds of plants

四畫

【粉】 4235
ㄈㄣˇ feen fěn

1. flour
2. powder
3. white (color)
4. to whitewash; to plaster
5. to make up; to doll up; to powder

粉白黛黑(ㄈㄣˇ ㄅㄞˊ ㄉㄞˋ ㄏㄟ)or 粉紅黛綠(ㄈㄣˇ ㄏㄨㄥˊ ㄉㄞˋ ㄌㄩˋ)
①a beauty ②heavy make-up

粉筆(ㄈㄣˇ ㄅㄧˇ)
chalk

粉壁(ㄈㄣˇ ㄅㄧˋ)
a whitewashed wall

粉皮(ㄈㄣˇ ㄆㄧˊ)
①a thin, almost transparent sheet made with ground green beans ②the sheepskin without wool on it

粉撲兒(ㄈㄣˇ ㄆㄨ ㄦˊ)
a powder puff

粉末(ㄈㄣˇ ㄇㄛˋ)
fine dust of anything; powder

粉末檢波器(ㄈㄣˇ ㄇㄛˋ ㄐㄧㄢˇ ㄅㄛ ㄑㄧˋ)
a coherer

粉墨(ㄈㄣˇ ㄇㄛˋ)
①(said of theatrical players) to apply make-up ②to polish up or gloss over (a piece of writing)

粉墨登場(ㄈㄣˇ ㄇㄛˋ ㄉㄥ ㄔㄤˊ)
①to make up and go on stage ②(said of a puppet regime) to assume an air of legality

粉面(ㄈㄣˇ ㄇㄧㄢˋ)
①a fair complexion ②a powdered face

粉黛(ㄈㄣˇ ㄉㄞˋ)
①beauties

粉蝶(ㄈㄣˇ ㄉㄧㄝˊ)
a white butterfly (Pieris rapae)

粉頭(ㄈㄣˇ ㄊㄡˊ)
①prostitutes ②(Chinese opera) white make-up for male players, denoting a crafty or cunning character

粉條兒(ㄈㄣˇ ㄊㄧㄠˊ ㄦˊ)
①a food item made with ground green beans ②chalk or crayons for writing

粉團(ㄈㄣˇ ㄊㄨㄢˊ)
fried glutinous rice cakes (usually covered with sesame)

粉嫩(ㄈㄣˇ ㄋㄣˋ)
(usually said of the skin of women or children) fair and tender; blooming and soft

粉盒(ㄈㄣˇ ㄏㄜˊ)
a powder box; a vanity case

粉紅(ㄈㄣˇ ㄏㄨㄥˊ)
pink

粉箋(ㄈㄣˇ ㄐㄧㄢ)
a kind of pink-colored paper

粉牆(ㄈㄣˇ ㄑㄧㄤˊ)
①to plaster or whitewash a wall ②a white wall

粉紙(ㄈㄣˇ ㄓˇ)
①powder paper (a cosmetic item of women) ②a kind of white paper made of bamboo pulp

粉裝玉琢(ㄈㄣˇ ㄓㄨㄤ ㄩˋ ㄓㄨㄛˊ)
(descriptive of a lady) lovely and white-skinned

粉飾(ㄈㄣˇ ㄕˋ)
①to whitewash; to embellish; to touch up ②to make up

粉飾太平(ㄈㄣˇ ㄕˋ ㄊㄞˋ ㄆㄧㄥˊ)
to whitewash or embellish in order to hide a serious trouble or problem; to pretend that everything is going well

粉身碎骨(ㄈㄣˇ ㄕㄣ ㄙㄨㄟˋ ㄍㄨˇ)
(even) at the cost of one's life; great danger or very risky

粉刷(ㄈㄣˇ ㄕㄨㄚ)
to plaster or whitewash a wall, etc.): 他決定粉刷那道牆。He decided to whitewash the wall.

粉刺(ㄈㄣˇ ㄘˋ)
pimples; acne

粉絲(ㄈㄣˇ ㄙ)
bean flour noodles

粉碎(ㄈㄣˇ ㄙㄨㄟˋ)
①to shatter; to crush up; to smash ②broken into pieces: 茶杯掉下來摔得粉碎。The cup fell and smashed to pieces.

五畫

【粗】 4236
ㄘㄨ tsu cū

1. thick; bulky; big
2. coarse; rough; crude
3. gruff; husky
4. rude; vulgar
5. brief; sketchy

粗脖子(ㄘㄨ ㄅㄛˊ ˙ㄗ)
①an overgrown neck—a symptom of goiter ②to get angry; to get tough or rough

粗暴(ㄘㄨ ㄅㄠˋ)
rude; violent; rough: 他們粗暴地對待囚犯。They treated the prisoners rough.

粗笨(ㄘㄨ ㄅㄣˋ)
awkward; maladroit; clumsy: 他是個粗笨的傢伙。He is a clumsy fellow.

粗鄙(ㄘㄨ ㄅㄧˇ)
vulgar; crude: 他談吐粗鄙。He is vulgar in his speech.

粗布(ㄘㄨ ㄅㄨˋ)
coarse fabric

粗眉大眼(ㄘㄨ ㄇㄟˊ ㄉㄚˋ ㄧㄢˇ)
(literally) thick-eyebrowed and big-eyed — the appearance of a big or rough man

粗米(ㄘㄨ ㄇㄧˇ)
unpolished rice

粗風暴雨(ㄘㄨ ㄈㄥ ㄅㄠˋ ㄩˇ)
a violent storm; strong winds and pouring rain

粗大(ㄘㄨ ㄉㄚˋ)
thick and big: 那次風雨中許多粗大的樹倒了。Many thick and big trees fell in the storm.

粗通(ㄘㄨ ㄊㄨㄥ)
to know a little about (a language, learning, craft, art, etc.)

粗剌剌(ㄘㄨ ㄌㄚˊ ㄌㄚˊ)
coarse; rough

粗陋(ㄘㄨ ㄌㄡˋ)
coarse and crude

粗糲(ㄘㄨ ㄌㄧˋ)
coarse rice

粗劣(ㄘㄨ ㄌㄧㄝˋ)
crude; inferior: 手藝粗劣，工資就少。Crude workmanship deserves poor pay.

粗糧(ㄘㄨ ㄌㄧㄤˊ)or 粗糧食(ㄘㄨ ㄌㄧㄤˊ ㄕˊ)
coarse grain (e.g. corn, sorghum, millet, etc. as distinct from wheat and rice)

粗魯 or 粗鹵(ㄘㄨ ㄌㄨˇ)
rude; impolite; rough

粗略(ㄘㄨ ㄌㄩㄝˋ)
cursory; rough; sketchy

粗獷(ㄘㄨ ㄍㄨㄤˇ)
① rough; rude; boorish ②
bold and unconstrained; rugged

粗工(ㄘㄨ ㄍㄨㄥ)
① crude work ② an unskilled workman; a laborer:
他是個粗工。He was an unskilled workman.

粗豪(ㄘㄨ ㄏㄠˊ)
manly and straightforward; generous but paying no attention to niceties

粗話(ㄘㄨ ㄏㄨㄚˋ)
obscene language; a vulgar expression

粗活(ㄘㄨ ㄏㄨㄛˊ)
work of a laborer or coolie; work which demands little brains but lots of brawn

粗貨(ㄘㄨ ㄏㄨㄛˋ)
coarse commodities; crude products: 這雕刻品是粗貨。This carving is of coarse work.

粗具規模(ㄘㄨ ㄐㄩˋ ㄍㄨㄟ ㄇㄛˊ)
(said of an undertaking) having just laid a foundation; having begun to take shape; having finished the spadework

粗淺(ㄘㄨ ㄑㄧㄢˇ)
superficial; coarse and shallow; simple

粗細(ㄘㄨ ㄒㄧˋ)
① thickness (of the thread, stick, rope, or anything which is long and round) ② roughness ③ thick and thin ④ crudeness or fineness; quality of work

粗線條作風(ㄘㄨ ㄒㄧㄢˋ ㄊㄧㄠˊ ㄗㄨㄛˋ ㄈㄥ)
(said of one's style of conduct) straightforward; having little regard for niceties; frank but without tact

粗心(ㄘㄨ ㄒㄧㄣ)
careless (in work)

粗心浮氣(ㄘㄨ ㄒㄧㄣ ㄈㄨˊ ㄑㄧˋ)
unthoughtful and rash

粗心大意(ㄘㄨ ㄒㄧㄣ ㄉㄚˋ ㄧˋ)
rash and careless; thought-

less; inadvertency: 錯誤有時純粹由於粗心大意而造成。Mistakes are sometimes due to inadvertency.

粗枝大葉(ㄘㄨ ㄓ ㄉㄚˋ ㄧㄝˋ)
sketchy (description); roughly finished; careless

粗製品(ㄘㄨ ㄓˋ ㄆㄧㄣˇ)
① an semi-finished product that requires further processing ② a product of low quality; a crude or coarse product

粗製濫造(ㄘㄨ ㄓˋ ㄌㄢˋ ㄗㄠˋ)
to turn out (products) in large quantities without any regard for quality; to manufacture in a rough and slipshod way

粗拙(ㄘㄨ ㄓㄨㄛˊ)
crude; coarse

粗壯(ㄘㄨ ㄓㄨㄤˋ)
stout; muscular; sturdy; brawny: 他是個粗壯的小孩。He is a sturdy child.

粗重(ㄘㄨ ㄓㄨㄥˋ)
① bulky (products, etc.) of low value ② work (of a coolie or unskilled laborer) that needs more muscles than brains: 他無法勝任這粗重的工作。He is not adequate to the heavy task.

粗茶淡飯(ㄘㄨ ㄔㄚˊ ㄉㄢˋ ㄈㄢˋ)
simple food; plain fare

粗實(ㄘㄨ ㄕˊ)
big and strong; raw and durable

粗手笨腳(ㄘㄨ ㄕㄡˇ ㄅㄣˋ ㄐㄧㄠˇ)
awkward; maladroit; clumsy

粗疏(ㄘㄨ ㄕㄨ)
① careless ② unpolished or unrefined; rough

粗率(ㄘㄨ ㄕㄨㄞˋ)
① crude and coarse ② careless; rash: 你不應該輕率的許下諾言。You should never make rash promises.

粗人(ㄘㄨ ㄖㄣˊ)
① a person of much muscle but little refinement; a person of little education ② a boor; an unrefined person

粗糙(ㄘㄨ ㄘㄠ)
(said of a surface, etc.) coarse; rough; unpolished: 他的皮膚粗糙。He has a rough

skin.

粗俗(ㄘㄨ ㄙㄨˊ)
coarse; vulgar; unrefined:他說話粗俗。He uses vulgar language.

粗野(ㄘㄨ ㄧㄝˇ)
rough; rude; boorish; unrefined or unpolished; rustic and coarse: 他在遊戲中動作粗野。He played rough in games.

【粒】4237
ㄌㄧˋ lih lì
1. a grain (of rice, etc.)
2. rice food; to get grain to eat
3. a pill; a bead

粒粒皆辛苦(ㄌㄧˋ ㄌㄧˋ ㄐㄧㄝ ㄒㄧㄣ ㄎㄨˇ)
Every (rice) grain is the product of toiling.

粒兒(ㄌㄧˋ ㄦ)
① a grain (of rice) ② a pill; a bead

【粕】4238
ㄆㄛˋ poh pò
the lees; dregs; sediment of liquor

【粘】4239
(黏) ㄋㄧㄢˊ nian nián
to paste up; to stick up; to stick up; to glue: 他用膠水將封面粘在書上。He glued the cover to the book.

粘貼(ㄋㄧㄢˊ ㄊㄧㄝ)
to paste; to stick: 我們在牆上粘貼標語。We pasted slogans on the wall.

六畫

【粟】4240
ㄙㄨˋ suh sù
1. grain; paddy
2. millet
3. goose flesh; goose pimples; goose bumps; goose skin
4. a Chinese family name

粟帛(ㄙㄨˋ ㄅㄛˊ)
grain and cloth

粟米(ㄙㄨˋ ㄇㄧˇ)
millet; grain

粟飯(ㄙㄨˋ ㄈㄢˋ)
coarse staple food

粟紅貫朽(ㄙㄨˋ ㄏㄨㄥˊ ㄍㄨㄢˋ ㄒㄧㄡˇ)
in time of great prosperity; in a land of plenty

粟倉(ㄙㄨˋ ㄘㄤ)
a granary; a barn for grain

【米部】

【粢】 4241
1. ㄗ tzy zī
1. the millet to be offered in sacrifice
2. the grain

粢盛(ㄗ ㄔㄥ)
the millet placed in a sacrificial vessel

【粢】 4241
2. ㄘ tsyr cí
rice cakes

【粥】 4242
　　ㄓㄡ juh zhú
（讀音 ㄓㄡ jou zhōu）
congee; rice gruel

粥餳(ㄓㄡ ㄒㄧㄥ)
sweetened congee

粥少僧多(ㄓㄡ ㄕㄠ ㄙㄥ ㄉㄨㄛ)
(literally) The congee is not enough for the many monks. —not enough for circulation or distribution

【粤】 4243
　　ㄩㄝ yueh yuè
1. Kwangtung Province
2. Kwangtung and Kwangsi Provinces
3. an opening particle

粤東(ㄩㄝ ㄉㄨㄥ)
Kwangtung Province

粤海(ㄩㄝ ㄏㄞ)
① the South China Sea ② short for Kwangtung's Customs House

粤漢鐵路(ㄩㄝ ㄏㄢ ㄊㄧㄝ ㄌㄨ)
the Canton-Hankow Railway

粤江(ㄩㄝ ㄐㄧㄤ)
another name of the Pearl River

粤江流域(ㄩㄝ ㄐㄧㄤ ㄌㄧㄡ ㄩ)
the Pearl River Valley

粤劇(ㄩㄝ ㄐㄩ)
Canton opera

粤犬吠雪(ㄩㄝ ㄑㄩㄢ ㄈㄟ ㄒㄩㄝ)
(literally) A Kwangtung dog barks at the snow. (Kwangtung being a subtropical region)—People are startled by an unusual phenomenon.

粤西(ㄩㄝ ㄒㄧ)
the former name of Kwangsi

粤人(ㄩㄝ ㄖㄣ)
a Cantonese

【粧】 4244
　　（妝）ㄓㄨㄤ juang zhuāng

1. toilet; to adorn; to doll up: 她梳粧打扮後就出門了。She went out after dressing her hair and applying makeup.
2. woman's personal adornments
3. a bride's trousseau
4. to disguise or pretend

粧粉(ㄓㄨㄤ ㄈㄣ)
to doll up: 她粧粉得漂漂亮亮的去參加宴會。She was all dolled up for the party.

粧臺(ㄓㄨㄤ ㄊㄞ)
a dressing table

粧奩(ㄓㄨㄤ ㄌㄧㄢ)
a bride's trousseau; a dowry

粧飾(ㄓㄨㄤ ㄕ)
① to adorn; to doll up ② to pretend

七畫

【粲】 4245
　　ㄘㄢ tsann càn
1. bright and clear; radiant
2. beautiful; splendid; excellent
3. smiling; laughing
4. well-polished rice

粲爛(ㄘㄢ ㄌㄢ)
brilliant; sparkling; radiant; bright

粲花(ㄘㄢ ㄏㄨㄚ)
good at speech; skilled in talking

粲者(ㄘㄢ ㄓㄜ)
a beauty; a pretty girl

粲然(ㄘㄢ ㄖㄢ)
① bright and brilliant ② smiling brightly

粲然一笑(ㄘㄢ ㄖㄢ ㄧ ㄒㄧㄠ)
to give a beaming smile

粲煥(ㄘㄢ ㄏㄨㄢ)
(said of dresses, etc.) bright, splendid and eye-catching

【粱】 4246
　　ㄌㄧㄤ liang liáng
maize; grain; sorghums

粱肉(ㄌㄧㄤ ㄖㄡ)
(literally) grain and meat —a sumptuous meal

【糧】 4247
　　（糧）ㄌㄧㄤ liang liáng
provisions; food; grain; rations

4248
【粳】 （秔,稉）《ㄥ geng gēng
（顗音 ㄐㄧㄥ jing jīng）
nonglutinous rice

八畫

【精】 4249
　　ㄐㄧㄥ jing jīng
1. polished rice; unmixed rice
2. the essence; the essentials: 薄荷精 essence of peppermint
3. energy; spirits
4. the male sperm; semen
5. fine and delicate; exquisite
6. dedicated; intensive
7. very; extremely; completely
8. keen; smart; sharp; clever; shrewd: 他太精了，我們不過他。He was too smart for us.
9. skilled; to specialize in: 他於繪畫。He is skilled in painting.
10. a goblin; a spirit; a demon

精白(ㄐㄧㄥ ㄅㄞ)
extremely white; very pure

精兵(ㄐㄧㄥ ㄅㄧㄥ)
crack troops

精疲力竭(ㄐㄧㄥ ㄆㄧ ㄌㄧ ㄐㄧㄝ)
exhausted; dog-tired; worn-out: 長途跋涉後他精疲力竭。He was worn-out after the long hike.

精闢(ㄐㄧㄥ ㄆㄧ)
penetrating; brilliant; incisive: 這是一篇精闢的評論。This is a brilliant comment.

精品(ㄐㄧㄥ ㄆㄧㄣ)
an exquisite article; an article of top quality

精美(ㄐㄧㄥ ㄇㄟ)
exquisite; delicate and beautiful: 這花瓶工藝極精美。This vase is of exquisite workmanship.

精密(ㄐㄧㄥ ㄇㄧ)
minute or detailed; precise; accurate; careful: 科學家對病菌做精密的觀察。Scientists make accurate observations of germs.

精密儀器(ㄐㄧㄥ ㄇㄧ ㄧˊ ㄑㄧ)
precision instruments

精妙(ㄐㄧㄥ ㄇㄧㄠ)
exquisite and delicate; wonderful; ingenious

精敏(ㄐㄧㄥ ㄇㄧㄣ)
keen and active (or energetic)

精明(ㄐㄧㄥ ㄇㄧㄥ)
keen or sharp; clever

精明強幹(ㄐㄧㄥ ㄇㄧㄥ ㄑㄧㄤ ㄍㄢ)
shrewd and capable man

打打細算(ㄐㄧㄥ ㄉㄚ ㄒㄧ ㄙㄨㄢ)
calculate carefully and budget strictly

精到(ㄐㄧㄥ ㄉㄠ)
keen and cautious; sharp and careful to the very last detail

精當(ㄐㄧㄥ ㄉㄤ)
precise and appropriate

精讀(ㄐㄧㄥ ㄉㄨ)
to study or read in minute detail; intensive reading

精挑細選(ㄐㄧㄥ ㄊㄧㄠ ㄒㄧ ㄒㄩㄢ)
very choosy

精通(ㄐㄧㄥ ㄊㄨㄥ)
well versed in; good at; to have an excellent command of; expert at; to master: 他們精通多種語言。They master many languages.

精囊(ㄐㄧㄥ ㄋㄤ)
a spermary

精力(ㄐㄧㄥ ㄌㄧ)
the sum total of a person's mental and physical strength; stamina; vitality; energy: 不要浪費精力。Don't waste your energy.

精力旺盛(ㄐㄧㄥ ㄌㄧ ㄨㄤ ㄕㄥ)
very energetic and vigorous; to be full of vitality: 他是個精力旺盛的工作者。He is an energetic worker.

精練(ㄐㄧㄥ ㄌㄧㄢ)
smart and capable; skillful and experienced

精煉(ㄐㄧㄥ ㄌㄧㄢ)
to rectify; to refine; refined: 油及砂糖是精煉過的。Oil and sugar are refined.

精良(ㄐㄧㄥ ㄌㄧㄤ)
of very high quality; exquisite; fine; excellent

精靈(ㄐㄧㄥ ㄌㄧㄥ)
①an elf; a fairy; goblins, ghosts, spirits, etc. ②(said of children) a very clever and naughty young fellow

精廬(ㄐㄧㄥ ㄌㄨ)
①a house decorated with

very refined tastes ②a study; a reading room

精怪(ㄐㄧㄥ ㄍㄨㄞˋ)
a general name of demons, monsters, etc.

精光(ㄐㄧㄥ ㄍㄨㄤ)
①stark-naked; without a stitch on; completely nude ②nothing left; exhausted; completely gone: 他把積蓄花得精光。He exhausted his savings.

精工(ㄐㄧㄥ ㄍㄨㄥ)
delicate and painstaking work; exquisite craftsmanship

精勘(ㄐㄧㄥ ㄏㄢ)
a careful and intensive examination or survey

精悍(ㄐㄧㄥ ㄏㄢ)
strong and unyielding

精華(ㄐㄧㄥ ㄏㄨㄚ)
the essence; the essentials; the cream or choicest parts: 最好的學生即是全班的精華。The cream of the class is made up of the best students.

精簡(ㄐㄧㄥ ㄐㄧㄢ)
to simplify

精金良玉(ㄐㄧㄥ ㄐㄧㄣ ㄌㄧㄤ ㄩ)
(said of a person's disposition) pure and kind; virtuous and tolerant

精進(ㄐㄧㄥ ㄐㄧㄣ)
①to dedicate oneself to progress; to devote oneself to improvement; to forge ahead vigorously ②(Buddhism) *virya*; courageously progressing in the good and eliminating the evil

精絕(ㄐㄧㄥ ㄐㄩㄝ)
exquisite to the very last detail; perfect

精氣(ㄐㄧㄥ ㄑㄧ)
①(Chinese medicine) vitality; essence and vital energy ②(Buddhism) vitality; virility

精巧(ㄐㄧㄥ ㄑㄧㄠ)
exquisite; fine and delicate (workmanship, etc.): 這是一件精巧的藝術品。This is an exquisite work of art.

精勤(ㄐㄧㄥ ㄑㄧㄣ)
dedicated and diligent; devoted and industrious

精確(ㄐㄧㄥ ㄑㄩㄝ)
precise; accurate; precision; accuracy: 你做算術一定要精確。You must be accurate in arithmetic.

精細(ㄐㄧㄥ ㄒㄧ)
①fine (materials, etc.); delicate and painstaking (workmanship, handicraft, etc.); exquisite ②very careful and attentive; thorough

精心(ㄐㄧㄥ ㄒㄧㄣ)
elaborate; attentive and circumspect; meticulous; to put all one's mind in: 他精心設計一種新型的冰箱。He puts all his mind in designing a new refrigerator.

精心傑作(ㄐㄧㄥ ㄒㄧㄣ ㄐㄧㄝ ㄗㄨㄛ)
a masterpiece; a brainchild

精選(ㄐㄧㄥ ㄒㄩㄢ)
handpicked; choice; to pick the best; to handpick; to select

精緻(ㄐㄧㄥ ㄓ)
(said of materials, etc.) fine; exquisite; delicate: 好精緻的刺繡。What a delicate piece of embroidery!

精製(ㄐㄧㄥ ㄓ)
specially picked and baked (tea, etc.); highly finished; refined; manufactured with special care

精湛(ㄐㄧㄥ ㄓㄢ)
consummate; exquisite; perfect: 這位雕刻家以精湛的技巧聞名。The sculptor is famous for his consummate skill.

精裝本(ㄐㄧㄥ ㄓㄨㄤ ㄅㄣ)
(said of books) a deluxe edition: 這本字典是精裝本。This dictionary is a deluxe edition.

精裝品(ㄐㄧㄥ ㄓㄨㄤ ㄆㄧㄣ)
articles in deluxe packing

精忠報國(ㄐㄧㄥ ㄓㄨㄥ ㄅㄠ ㄍㄨㄛ)
to serve one's fatherland with unreserved loyalty

精巢(ㄐㄧㄥ ㄔㄠ)
a spermary 亦作「精囊」

精誠(ㄐㄧㄥ ㄔㄥ)
purity and sincerity; earnest and sincere

精誠團結(ㄐㄧㄥ ㄔㄥ ㄊㄨㄢ ㄐㄧㄝ)
to unite together with utmost sincerity; gung ho;

esprit de corps

精誠所至，金石爲開（ㄐㄧㄥ ㄔㄥ
ㄙㄨㄛˇ ㄓˋ，ㄐㄧㄣ ㄕˊ ㄨㄟˊ ㄎㄞ）
Where wholehearted dedication is directed, the whole
world will step aside to let
you by.

精純（ㄐㄧㄥ ㄔㄨㄣˊ）
① pure; unalloyed; unmixed
② to refine; refinement

精蟲（ㄐㄧㄥ ㄔㄨㄥˊ）
spermatozoa

精舍（ㄐㄧㄥ ㄕㄜˋ）
① a study ② a pure abode; a
Buddhist temple ③ a villa

精深（ㄐㄧㄥ ㄕㄣ）
profound; profundity

精神（ㄐㄧㄥ ㄕㄣˊ）
① one's spirit: 你今天很沒精
神。You lack spirit today. ②
lively; vigorous ③ mental

精神飽滿（ㄐㄧㄥ ㄕㄣˊ ㄅㄠˇ ㄇㄢˇ）
in high spirits; vigorous and
energetic

精神病（ㄐㄧㄥ ㄕㄣˊ ㄅㄧㄥˋ）
mental illness

精神病學（ㄐㄧㄥ ㄕㄣˊ ㄅㄧㄥˋ ㄒㄩㄝˊ）
psychiatry

精神病院（ㄐㄧㄥ ㄕㄣˊ ㄅㄧㄥˋ ㄩㄢˋ）
a mental hospital or sanitarium; an asylum

精神不死（ㄐㄧㄥ ㄕㄣˊ ㄅㄨˋ ㄙˇ）
The spirit (of martyrs, etc.)
will never die.

精神分裂症（ㄐㄧㄥ ㄕㄣˊ ㄈㄣ ㄌㄧㄝˋ ㄓㄥˋ）
schizophrenia

精神分析（ㄐㄧㄥ ㄕㄣˊ ㄈㄣ ㄒㄧ）
psychoanalysis

精神抖擻（ㄐㄧㄥ ㄕㄣˊ ㄉㄡˇ ㄙㄡˇ）
high-spirited; sprightly; vigorous and energetic; enthusiastic

精神感召（ㄐㄧㄥ ㄕㄣˊ ㄍㄢˇ ㄓㄠˋ）
to be moved to emulate a
noble example; to be inspired
by (a great leader)

精神恍惚（ㄐㄧㄥ ㄕㄣˊ ㄏㄨㄤˇ ㄏㄨ）
absent-minded

精神教育（ㄐㄧㄥ ㄕㄣˊ ㄐㄧㄠˋ ㄩˋ）
moral education

精神狀態（ㄐㄧㄥ ㄕㄣˊ ㄓㄨㄤˋ ㄊㄞˋ）
a state of mind; a mental
condition

精神失常（ㄐㄧㄥ ㄕㄣˊ ㄕ ㄔㄤˊ）

mental disorder; mental
derangement; out of one's
mind

精神生活（ㄐㄧㄥ ㄕㄣˊ ㄕㄥ ㄏㄨㄛˊ）
spiritual life; moral life

精神文明（ㄐㄧㄥ ㄕㄣˊ ㄨㄣˊ ㄇㄧㄥˊ）
spiritual civilization

精銳（ㄐㄧㄥ ㄖㄨㄟˋ）
crack; picked

精銳部隊（ㄐㄧㄥ ㄖㄨㄟˋ ㄅㄨˋ ㄉㄨㄟˋ）
crack troops; picked troops

精子（ㄐㄧㄥ ㄗˇ）
spermatozoa 亦作「精蟲」

精彩（ㄐㄧㄥ ㄘㄞˇ）
① the highlight or climax
(of a play, etc.); the most
attractive or wonderful part
(of something) ② Wonder-
ful! 或 Bravo! 或 Excellent!

精粗（ㄐㄧㄥ ㄘㄨ）
the fineness and coarseness
of things

精萃（ㄐㄧㄥ ㄘㄨㄟˋ）
cream; pick

精粹（ㄐㄧㄥ ㄘㄨㄟˋ）
the essence or essentials;
refined and pure; the cream
—the best part of anything:
這是我國民族文化的精粹。This
is the cream of our national
culture.

精髓（ㄐㄧㄥ ㄙㄨㄟˇ）
the marrow; the pith; the
quintessence; the essence

精一（ㄐㄧㄥ ㄧ）
dedicated; devoted; pure

精義（ㄐㄧㄥ ㄧˋ）
the essential significance;
the profound meaning

精益求精（ㄐㄧㄥ ㄧˋ ㄑㄧㄡˊ ㄐㄧㄥ）
Second best is not good
enough.—to try for the best;
to do still better; 我們凡事精
益求精。We endeavored to do
everything better.

精液（ㄐㄧㄥ ㄧㄝˋ）
sperm; semen

精要（ㄐㄧㄥ ㄧㄠˋ）
the essentials; the fundamentals

精研（ㄐㄧㄥ ㄧㄢˊ）
to study intensively: 她精研
社會學。She studies sociol-
ogy intensively.

精鹽（ㄐㄧㄥ ㄧㄢˊ）
refined salt; purified salt; 請
把精鹽遞給我。Pass me the

refined salt, please.

精微（ㄐㄧㄥ ㄨㄟˊ）
deep; profound; profundity

精衛填海（ㄐㄧㄥ ㄨㄟˋ ㄊㄧㄢˊ ㄏㄞˇ）
Ching-wei, a legendary
small bird, supposed to be
the metamorphosis of the
drowned daughter of Yen Ti
(炎帝), was also known as
寃禽 (the bird of hate), and
as it was often in the habit
of dropping bits of wood
and stone into the ocean, in
the vain hope of filling it, it
was looked upon as a sym-
bol of deep and unsatiable
hatred.

精於此道（ㄐㄧㄥ ㄩˊ ㄘˇ ㄉㄠˋ）
skilled in this field

【粹】 4250
ㄘㄨㄟˋ tsuey cuì
1. pure; unmixed; perfect;
unadulterated
2. the essence; the best

粹白（ㄘㄨㄟˋ ㄅㄞˊ）
pure white

【粺】 4251
ㄅㄞˋ bay bài
polished rice

九畫

【糊】 4252
ㄏㄨˊ hwu hú
1. paste: 請用漿糊把它貼上。
Stick it with paste.
2. to paste
3. scorched
4. not clear; blurred; confused;
ambiguous; unintelligible

糊塗（ㄏㄨˊ ㄊㄨ）
① mixed-up; confused ② stupid; foolish: 別裝糊塗。Do not
play the fool.

糊塗蟲（ㄏㄨˊ ㄊㄨ ㄔㄨㄥˊ）
a blunderer; a bungler

糊裏糊塗（ㄏㄨˊ ㄌㄧˇ ㄏㄨˊ ㄊㄨ）
(to do something) without
thinking; confused or mixed-
up; muddled:他仍然是糊裏糊
塗地混日子。He's still mud-
dling on.

糊口（ㄏㄨˊ ㄎㄡˇ）
to make a living; to make
both ends meet; to live from
hand to mouth亦作「餬口」他
以割草餬口。Mowing lawns is
his livelihood.

糊精（ㄏㄨˊ ㄐㄧㄥ）
(chemistry) dextrine

糊牆（ㄏㄨˊ ㄑㄧㄤˊ）
to wallpaper; to paper a wall; paperhanging

糊窗（ㄏㄨˊ ㄔㄨㄤ）
to paper a window: 他用紙糊窗。He pasted a sheet of paper over a lattice window.

【糉】4253
（粽）ㄗㄨㄥˋ tzong zòng
glutinous rice tamale—made by wrapping the rice in broad leaves of reeds and boiled for a few hours—usually with other ingredients, such as dates, meat, oysters, beans, etc.

糭子 or 粽子（ㄗㄨㄥˋ·ㄗ）
glutinous rice dumplings; rice tamale

【糅】4254
ㄖㄡˊ roou róu
to mix; mixed

糅合（ㄖㄡˊ ㄏㄜˊ）
to mix together; to blend; to form a mixture

糅雜（ㄖㄡˊ ㄗㄚˊ）
mixed; disorderly

十畫

【糗】4255
ㄑㄧㄡˇ cheou qiǔ
parched grain, rice, etc.; dry food; dry rations

【糒】4256
ㄅㄟˋ bey bèi
parched rice—as a dry food for a journey in the days of old

【糕】4257
（餻）ㄍㄠ gau gāo
cakes; pastries; steamed dumpliings

糕餅（ㄍㄠ ㄅㄧㄥˇ）
cakes and biscuits

糕餅店（ㄍㄠ ㄅㄧㄥˇ ㄉㄧㄢˋ）
a pastry shop

糕點（ㄍㄠ ㄉㄧㄢˇ）
cakes and pastries

【糖】4258
ㄊㄤˊ tarng táng
sugar

糖分（ㄊㄤˊ ㄈㄣˋ）
sugar content; the percentage of natural sugar in food items

糖尿病（ㄊㄤˊ ㄋㄧㄠˋ ㄅㄧㄥˋ）
diabetes

糖尿病人（ㄊㄤˊ ㄋㄧㄠˋ ㄅㄧㄥˋ ㄖㄣˊ）
a diabetic

糖類（ㄊㄤˊ ㄌㄟˋ）
(chemistry) carbohydrate

糖蘿蔔（ㄊㄤˊ ㄌㄨㄛˊ·ㄅㄛ）
sugar beets; sweet carrots

糖果（ㄊㄤˊ ㄍㄨㄛˇ）
candy; sweets

糖果店（ㄊㄤˊ ㄍㄨㄛˇ ㄉㄧㄢˋ）
a candy shop

糖果錢（ㄊㄤˊ ㄍㄨㄛˇ ㄑㄧㄢˊ）
a child's candy allowance or pocket money

糖葫蘆（ㄊㄤˊ ㄏㄨˊ·ㄌㄨ）
sweetened fruit on stick handles; sugarcoated haws on a stick

糖漿（ㄊㄤˊ ㄐㄧㄤ）
syrup; molasses

糖精（ㄊㄤˊ ㄐㄧㄥ）
saccharin; gluside

糖廠（ㄊㄤˊ ㄔㄤˇ）
a sugar mill; a sugar refinery

糖食（ㄊㄤˊ ㄕˊ）
sweetmeats; sugar-sweetened edibles

糖商（ㄊㄤˊ ㄕㄤ）
a sugar merchant

糖水（ㄊㄤˊ ㄕㄨㄟˇ）
sweetened water; sugar solution

糖醋排骨（ㄊㄤˊ ㄘㄨˋ ㄆㄞˊ ㄍㄨˇ）
sweet and sour spareribs

糖醋魚（ㄊㄤˊ ㄘㄨˋ ㄩˊ）
fish in sweet and sour sauce

糖衣（ㄊㄤˊ ㄧ）
sugarcoating

糖業（ㄊㄤˊ ㄧㄝˋ）
the sugar industry

十一畫

【糜】4259
ㄇㄧˊ mi mí
1. congee; porridge; rice gruel
2. mashed; rotten; corrupted
3. to waste

糜費（ㄇㄧˊ ㄈㄟˋ）
extravagant or wasteful; to waste

糜爛（ㄇㄧˊ ㄌㄢˋ）
① rotten; corrupt debauchery: 她生活糜爛。She lived a

life of debauchery. ② to oppress and destroy the people (through devious means)

糜粥（ㄇㄧˊ ㄓㄡ）
congee; porridge

【糞】
ㄈㄣˋ ferin fèn
1. night soil; manure; dung: 糞被用做肥料。Dung is used as manure.
2. to fertilize the land
3. to sweep; to wipe out

糞便（ㄈㄣˋ ㄅㄧㄢˋ）
excrement; night soil

糞門（ㄈㄣˋ ㄇㄣˊ）
the anus 亦作「肛門」

糞夫（ㄈㄣˋ ㄈㄨ）
one whose vocation is to collect night soil; a nightman

糞堆（ㄈㄣˋ ㄉㄨㄟ）
a dunghill

糞土（ㄈㄣˋ ㄊㄨˇ）or 糞壤（ㄈㄣˋ ㄖㄤˇ）
(literally) dung and earth—something of little value; dirty earth; refuse: 他視金錢如糞土。He looked upon money as dirt.

糞坑（ㄈㄣˋ ㄎㄥ）
a manure pit; a cesspool

糞箕（ㄈㄣˋ ㄐㄧ）
a dustpan 亦作「畚箕」

糞池（ㄈㄣˋ ㄔˊ）
a manure pit; a septic tank 亦作「化糞池」

【糙】4261
ㄘㄠ tsau cāo
1. coarse or unpolished; rough: 這布料有些粗糙。This cloth feels rough.
2. rough; rude; rash; desultory; careless

糙米（ㄘㄠ ㄇㄧˇ）
unpolished rice

【糝】4262
ㄙㄢˇ saan sǎn
1. a grain of rice
2. mixing rice with broth

【糟】4263
ㄗㄠ tzau zāo
1. sediment or dregs of wine; 酒糟 fermented grain mash
2. to soak food (such as fish, meat, etc.) in wine or wine sediment
3. (said of a plan, arrangement, etc.) to become a mess, or in bad shape: 你已

【米】
部

【米部】

經把這事弄糟了。You've made a mess of the job.

4. decayed; rotten; spoiled: 這桌子糟爛了。This table is rotten.

5. not sturdy or strong

6. lousy; a louse

糟鼻子(ㄗㄠ ㄅㄧˊ ˙ㄗ)
a drunkard's nose

糟粕(ㄗㄠ ㄆㄛˋ)
①dregs or sediment of wine ②something of little value; refuse; dregs: 我們剔除糟粕，吸取精華。We discard the dregs and absorb the essence.

糟蹋(ㄗㄠ ˙ㄊㄚ)
①to waste (talent, great ability, etc. on trifles); to ruin; to degrade or debase: 別裁時要留意，別把布料糟蹋了。Cut the cloth carefully. Don't spoil it.② to insult; to affront: 你說話可不要這樣糟蹋人。Do not affront anyone by talking like this.

糟透了(ㄗㄠ ㄊㄡˋ ˙ㄌㄜ)
Too bad! 或What a mess!

糟了(ㄗㄠ ˙ㄌㄜ)
Too bad! 或Alas!

糟爛(ㄗㄠ ㄌㄢˋ)
spoiled, rotten or decayed

糟糕(ㄗㄠ ㄍㄠ)
Alas! 或What a mess! 或Too bad! 糟糕! 我把車子鑰匙搞丟了! Alas! I've lost the car key.

糠糠(ㄗㄠ ㄎㄤ)
①distillers' grains, husks, chaff, etc.——(figuratively) food of a destitute person ② the wife one married in poverty

糟糠之妻(ㄗㄠ ㄎㄤ ㄓ ㄑㄧ)
the wife one married in poverty (should not be discarded in one's affluence)

糟踐(ㄗㄠ ㄐㄧㄢˋ)
①to waste; to debase or degrade; to ruin ②to insult; to libel

糟心(ㄗㄠ ㄒㄧㄣ)
①unlucky ②(said of plans, arrangements, etc.) to get into a mess: 你把事情搞得糟心透了。You got things into such a mess.

糟魚(ㄗㄠ ㄩˊ)
fish pickled with distillers' grains

【糠】 4264
ㄎㄤ kang kāng
1. husks of rice; rice bran or chaff

2. of inferior quality; not sturdy; empty inside; things of no value

3. spongy

糠秕(ㄎㄤ ㄅㄧˇ)
rice bran 亦作「秕糠」

糠糜(ㄎㄤ ㄇㄧˊ)
coarse food

糠蝦(ㄎㄤ ㄒㄧㄚ)
Mysis opossum shrimp, a variety of greyish freshwater shrimp about one inch long

糠市(ㄎㄤ ㄕˋ)
slums; shantytowns

【糢】 4265
(模) ㄇㄛˊ mo mó
blurred; indistinct

糢糊(ㄇㄛˊ ㄏㄨˊ)
blurred; indistinct; unclear; confused: 眼淚使他的眼睛糢糊。Tears blurred his eyes.

【糨】 4266
(糨) ㄐㄧㄤˋ jiang
jiàng
1. paste; to paste together; starched; to starch

2. thick

糨糊(ㄐㄧㄤˋ ˙ㄏㄨ)or 糨子(ㄐㄧㄤˋ ˙ㄗ)
paste; glue

十二畫

【糧】 4267
(粮) ㄌㄧㄤˊ liang
liáng
1. grain; food; provisions; rations: 敵軍彈盡糧絕。The enemy ran out of ammunition and food.

2. farm or land taxes

糧票(ㄌㄧㄤˊ ㄆㄧㄠˋ)
a food coupon; a grain coupon

糧秣(ㄌㄧㄤˊ ㄇㄛˋ)
military food supplies

糧米(ㄌㄧㄤˊ ㄇㄧˇ)
foodstuffs

糧道(ㄌㄧㄤˊ ㄉㄠˋ)
①a road for transportation of food ②(formerly) an official in charge of land taxes

糧行(ㄌㄧㄤˊ ㄏㄤˊ)
a store selling grain and provisions

糧餉(ㄌㄧㄤˊ ㄒㄧㄤˇ)
army provisions and payroll

糧船(ㄌㄧㄤˊ ㄔㄨㄢˊ)
boats for transporting grain

糧食(ㄌㄧㄤˊ ㄕˊ)
foodstuffs; provisions; grain for human consumption: 穀類及肉類皆係糧食。Grain and meat are foodstuffs.

糧食局(ㄌㄧㄤˊ ㄕˊ ㄐㄩˊ)
a grain bureau

糧草(ㄌㄧㄤˊ ㄘㄠˇ)
provisions (for men) and fodder (for horses); food supplies for an army; rations and forage

糧倉(ㄌㄧㄤˊ ㄘㄤ)
a granary

十三畫

【粺】 4268
ㄅㄛˋ bor bó
half-cooked rice; parboiled rice

十四畫

【糯】 4269
(糯,粳) ㄋㄨㄛˋ nuoh
nuò
glutinous rice

糯米(ㄋㄨㄛˋ ㄇㄧˇ)
polished glutinous rice

糯稻(ㄋㄨㄛˋ ㄉㄠˋ)
unhusked glutinous rice

【糰】 4270
ㄊㄨㄢˊ twan tuán
round dumplings made from wheat or glutinous rice flour

糰子(ㄊㄨㄢˊ ˙ㄗ)
a small dough cake

十五畫

【糲】 4271
ㄌㄧˋ lih lì
1. unpolished rice

2. coarse; rough

糲飯(ㄌㄧˋ ㄈㄢˋ)
cooked unpolished rice

糲粱(ㄌㄧˋ ㄌㄧㄤˊ)
coarse or simple food

十六畫

【糴】4272
ㄉㄧ dyi dí
to buy grain

糴米(ㄉㄧˊ)
to buy rice

十七畫

【糵】4273
(糱) ㄋㄧㄝˋ nieh niè
yeast, leaven or barm for making liquors

十九畫

【糶】4274
ㄊㄧㄠˋ tiaw tiào
to sell grain

糶米(ㄊㄧㄠˋ)
to sell rice

糸 部
ㄇㄧ mih mì

一畫

【系】4275
ㄒㄧˋ shih xì
1. a system; a line; a connecting link; a connection
2. lineage; a genealogy
3. (politics) a clique; a theoretic or party line
4. (in a college or a university) a department or school
5. to relate to; to bear on: 我們成敗系於此舉。We stand or fall by this.
6. to be
7. a Chinese family name

系縛(ㄒㄧˊ ㄅㄛˊ)
to bridle; to tie; to hinder; to fetter; to restrain; to confine

系譜(ㄒㄧˊ ㄆㄨˇ)
a genealogy; lineage; a family tree

系統(ㄒㄧˊ ㄊㄨㄥˇ)
a system; systematic: 這是有系統的計畫。This is a systematic project.

系統分類學(ㄒㄧˊ ㄊㄨㄥˇ ㄈㄣˋ ㄌㄟˋ ㄒㄩㄝˊ)
phylogenetic systematics

系統化(ㄒㄧˊ ㄊㄨㄥˇ ㄏㄨㄚˋ)
to systematize; systematized

系列(ㄒㄧˊ ㄌㄧㄝˋ)
①a line or lineage (of thoughts, theories, etc. arranged chronologically) ②a row; a series

系主任(ㄒㄧˊ ㄓㄨˇ ㄖㄣˋ)
the head or chairman of a department (in a college): 他是系主任。He is chairman of the department.

系出名門(ㄒㄧˊ ㄔㄨ ㄇㄧㄥˊ ㄇㄣˊ)
to come of a noble or reputed family

系族(ㄒㄧˊ ㄗㄨˊ)
the family lineage; a genealogy

系孫(ㄒㄧˊ ㄙㄨㄣ)
a grandson of someone of the same family lineage of one's own generation

【紀】4276
ㄐㄧㄡˇ jeou jiǔ
(又讀 ㄐㄧㄡ jiou jiū)
to collaborate; to band together

二畫

【糾】4277
ㄐㄧㄡ jiou jiū
(又讀ㄐㄧㄡˇ jeou jiǔ)
1. to supervise; to inspect; to investigate
2. to correct; to censure; to impeach; to discipline
3. to collaborate; to band together; to bind together; to entangle; to involve; involved

糾謬(ㄐㄧㄡ ㄇㄧㄡˋ)
to correct a mistake, blunder or evil

糾紛(ㄐㄧㄡ ㄈㄣ)
disputes; quarrels; entanglements: 這事與政治糾紛無關。It is independent of political entanglements.

糾彈(ㄐㄧㄡ ㄊㄢˊ)
to censure and impeach (officials)

糾葛(ㄐㄧㄡ ㄍㄜˊ)
a dispute; an endless involvement: 我們之間有一點糾

葛。There's a dispute between us.

糾合(ㄐㄧㄡ ㄏㄜˊ)
to band together: 他糾合了一夥流氓。He banded together a bunch of rascals.

糾劾(ㄐㄧㄡ ㄏㄜˊ)
to censure and impeach

糾夥行劫(ㄐㄧㄡ ㄏㄨㄛˇ ㄒㄧㄥˊ ㄐㄧㄝˊ)
to band together and commit robbery

糾集(ㄐㄧㄡ ㄐㄧˊ)
to get together; to muster

糾結(ㄐㄧㄡ ㄐㄧㄝˊ)
to collaborate; to band together

糾正(ㄐㄧㄡ ㄓㄥˋ)
to correct; to check; to discipline; to rectify

糾衆(ㄐㄧㄡ ㄓㄨㄥˋ)
to stir up a mob; to gather a crowd

糾察(ㄐㄧㄡ ㄔㄚˊ)
①to discipline; to investigate; to picket ②a disciplinary officer

糾察隊(ㄐㄧㄡ ㄔㄚˊ ㄉㄨㄟˋ)
a disciplinary patrol; pickets

糾察員(ㄐㄧㄡ ㄔㄚˊ ㄩㄢˊ)
a disciplinary officer; an inspector; an officer in charge of maintaining order and discipline

糾纏(ㄐㄧㄡ ㄔㄢˊ)
①to tangle; to involve; entanglement or involvement ②to pester: 她為了錢屢次糾纏他。She repeatedly pestered him for money.

糾繩(ㄐㄧㄡ ㄕㄥˊ)
to correct; to discipline

三畫

【紀】4278
ㄐㄧˋ jih jì
1. a historical record; annals; chronicles
2. a period of 12 years
3. a century
4. to arrange; to put in order
5. institutions; laws and regulations; discipline
6. the age of a person
7. a geological period
8. a Chinese family name

紀年(ㄐㄧˊ ㄋㄧㄢˊ)

（糸部）

〔糸

部〕

annals or chronicles

紀念(ㄐㄧˋ ㄋㄧㄢˋ)
to remember; to commemorate: 那是一個值得紀念的日子。It is a memorable day.

紀念碑(ㄐㄧˋ ㄋㄧㄢˋ ㄅㄟ)
a monument; a memorial

紀念品(ㄐㄧˋ ㄋㄧㄢˋ ㄆㄧㄣˇ)
a souvenir; a keepsake; a memento

紀念館(ㄐㄧˋ ㄋㄧㄢˋ ㄍㄨㄢˇ)
a memorial hall; a museum in memory of somebody

紀念會(ㄐㄧˋ ㄋㄧㄢˋ ㄏㄨㄟˋ)
a commemorative meeting or rally

紀念週(ㄐㄧˋ ㄋㄧㄢˋ ㄓㄡ)
a commemorative meeting on every Monday in memory of Dr. Sun Yat-sen, the founder of the Republic of China

紀念章(ㄐㄧˋ ㄋㄧㄢˋ ㄓㄤ)
a commemoration badge or medal

紀念日(ㄐㄧˋ ㄋㄧㄢˋ ㄖˋ)
a commemoration day; a memorial day; an anniversary: 今天是我們的結婚紀念日。Today is our wedding anniversary.

紀念冊(ㄐㄧˋ ㄋㄧㄢˋ ㄘㄜˋ)
an autograph book

紀念醫院(ㄐㄧˋ ㄋㄧㄢˋ ㄧ ㄩㄢˋ)
a memorial hospital

紀念郵票(ㄐㄧˋ ㄋㄧㄢˋ ㄧㄡˊ ㄆㄧㄠˋ)
a commemorative stamp

紀念郵戳(ㄐㄧˋ ㄋㄧㄢˋ ㄧㄡˊ ㄔㄨㄛ)
a commemoration postmark

紀錄(ㄐㄧˋ ㄌㄨˋ)
①a record; minutes (of a conference); to take notes: 這事載於會議紀錄中。It is on the minutes. ②one who records; a recording clerk; a recorder

紀錄片(ㄐㄧˋ ㄌㄨˋ ㄆㄧㄢˋ)
a documentary film

紀律(ㄐㄧˋ ㄌㄩˋ)
discipline; laws and regulations

紀綱(ㄐㄧˋ ㄍㄤ)
①institutions; rules and regulations②(obsolete) a servant

紀功(ㄐㄧˋ ㄍㄨㄥ)
to record an accomplishment

紀功碑(ㄐㄧˋ ㄍㄨㄥ ㄅㄟ)
a stone tablet erected in memory of a worthy deed

紀限儀(ㄐㄧˋ ㄒㄧㄢˋ ㄧˊ)
a sextant 亦作「大分儀」

紀傳體(ㄐㄧˋ ㄓㄨㄢˋ ㄊㄧˇ)
a form of historical record that centers on individuals and their performances (as opposed to annals or chronicles)

紀實(ㄐㄧˋ ㄕˊ)
①to record the facts; a recording of facts②an on-the-spot report

紀事(ㄐㄧˋ ㄕˋ)
to record a happening, an occurrence or an incident; to chronicle

紀事本末體(ㄐㄧˋ ㄕˋ ㄅㄣˇ ㄇㄛˋ ㄊㄧˇ)
a form of historical writing in which every chapter is devoted to the recording of a particular event of significance

紀述(ㄐㄧˋ ㄕㄨˋ)
the objective reporting or recording of facts and phenomena

紀要(ㄐㄧˋ ㄧㄠˋ)
a recording of important facts; a summary

紀元(ㄐㄧˋ ㄩㄢˊ)
the beginning of a new era

紀元後(ㄐㄧˋ ㄩㄢˊ ㄏㄡˋ)
A.D. (anno Domini)

紀元前(ㄐㄧˋ ㄩㄢˊ ㄑㄧㄢˊ)
B.C. (before Christ)

【紂】4279
ㄓㄡˋ jow zhòu
1. the last emperor of the Yin Dynasty, whose name stands for tyranny
2. the crupper of a saddle

紂王(ㄓㄡˋ ㄨㄤˊ)
see above 1.

【紃】4280
ㄒㄩㄣˊ shyun xún
a cord

【紆】4281
ㄩ iu yū
1. to wind; to spiral; to bend; to twist; to distort; to meander
2. a knot in one's heart; melancholy

紆體(ㄩ ㄊㄧˇ)
to bend one's body; to crouch; to bow down

紆迴(ㄩ ㄏㄨㄟˊ)
winding (roads); circuitous; roundabout 亦作「迂迴」

紆緩(ㄩ ㄏㄨㄢˇ)
slow; dilatory

紆金拖玉(ㄩ ㄐㄧㄣ ㄊㄨㄛ ㄩˋ)
dresses and ornaments of prominent officials

紆謨(ㄩ ㄇㄛˊ)
(said of a story) with many twists and turns

紆青拖紫(ㄩ ㄑㄧㄥ ㄊㄨㄛ ㄗˇ)
the dresses and ornaments of high officials

紆曲(ㄩ ㄑㄩ)
①twists and turns; to wind 我們紆曲行經窄巷。We wound our way through the narrow streets.② insinuating; to insinuate

紆行(ㄩ ㄒㄧㄥˊ)
to proceed through a winding and twisting path

紆徐(ㄩ ㄒㄩˊ)
to walk slowly: 那老人正在紆徐漫步。The old man is walking slowly.

紆軫(ㄩ ㄓㄣˇ)
①(said of a road) winding and twisting; tortuous ②hidden secrets in one's heart; melancholy

紆尊降貴(ㄩ ㄗㄨㄣ ㄐㄧㄤˋ ㄍㄨㄟˋ)
to condescend; to deign to

紆縈(ㄩ ㄧㄥˊ)
winding and twisting

紆鬱(ㄩ ㄩˋ)
sad; melancholy

【約】4282
ㄩㄝ iue yuē
1. an agreement; a covenant; a contract; a treaty
2. brief(ly); simply
3. about; around; approximately; estimated; 現在大約是九點。It is about nine o'clock now.
4. a date; an appointment or engagement; a rendezvous; to make an appointment; to date: 我們約好下星期二碰面。We agreed to meet next Tuesday.
5. poor; poverty; hardship; straitened
6. (mathematics) to reduce

〔糸部〕

7. to bind; to restrain
8. vague(ly)

約莫(ㄩㄝ ㄇㄛˋ)
or so; about; approximately:
這約莫在一天以前發生的. It happened a day or so ago.

約盟(ㄩㄝ ㄇㄥˊ)
a covenant; an agreement; an alliance; a sworn compact

約明(ㄩㄝ ㄇㄧㄥˊ)
to specify in an agreement; with the mutual understanding that...

約法(ㄩㄝ ㄈㄚˋ)
①to bind with rules or regulations ②a provisional constitution

約法三章(ㄩㄝ ㄈㄚˋ ㄙㄢ ㄓㄤ)
①a three-article provisional law promulgated by Emperor Kao Tsu of the Han Dynasty (漢高祖) ②a verbal agreement

約分(ㄩㄝ ㄈㄣ)
(mathematics) reduction; to reduce a fraction

約旦(ㄩㄝ ㄉㄢˋ)
Jordan

約定(ㄩㄝ ㄉㄧㄥˋ)
to agree upon; to agree to: 我們約定會晤地點. We agreed on a meeting place.

約定地點(ㄩㄝ ㄉㄧㄥˋ ㄉㄧˋ ㄉㄧㄢˇ)
an appointed place; a place agreed upon: 我們在約定地點見面. We met at an appointed place.

約定期限(ㄩㄝ ㄉㄧㄥˋ ㄑㄧˊ ㄒㄧㄢˋ)
stipulated duration

約定時間(ㄩㄝ ㄉㄧㄥˋ ㄕˊ ㄐㄧㄢ)
the appointed time; to agree upon a time for doing something: 我們在約定時間內去. We went at the appointed time.

約定俗成(ㄩㄝ ㄉㄧㄥˋ ㄙㄨˊ ㄔㄥˊ)
practices, rules, etc. initiated by a few and later adopted by all as a common practice or recognized precedent

約同(ㄩㄝ ㄊㄨㄥˊ)
to make an appointment; to agree to do something together: 他約同我們去戲院. He agreed to accompany us to the theater.

約略(ㄩㄝ ㄌㄩㄝˋ)
①brief(ly); sketchy ②approximate

約翰(ㄩㄝ ㄏㄢˋ)
a transliteration of John

約翰尼斯堡(ㄩㄝ ㄏㄢˋ ㄋㄧˊ ㄙ ㄅㄠˇ)
Johannesburg, a city in South Africa

約翰孫(ㄩㄝ ㄏㄢˋ ㄙㄨㄣ)
Samuel Johnson, 1709-84, English lexicographer

約會(ㄩㄝ ㄏㄨㄟˋ)
an appointment or engagement; a date: 我明天有個約會. I have an engagement tomorrow.

約計(ㄩㄝ ㄐㄧˋ)
estimated at around...; a rough estimate

約期(ㄩㄝ ㄑㄧˊ)
a date; an appointment or engagement; the appointed time; the term or duration of an agreement; to stipulate a time; to make an appointment

約請(ㄩㄝ ㄑㄧㄥˇ)
to invite: 我們請他到我家裏. I invited him to my house.

約之以禮(ㄩㄝ ㄓ ㄧˇ ㄌㄧˇ)
to control one's conduct in accordance with rites

約章(ㄩㄝ ㄓㄤ)
an international treaty

約束(ㄩㄝ ㄕㄨˋ)
to bind or restrain; restraint; restriction

約數(ㄩㄝ ㄕㄨˋ)
①(mathematics) an exact divisor ②an estimated number

約瑟(ㄩㄝ ㄙㄜˋ)
a transliteration of Joseph

約瑟芬(ㄩㄝ ㄙㄜˋ ㄈㄣ)
a transliteration of Josephine

約言(ㄩㄝ ㄧㄢˊ)
in short; in a word; in brief

4283

【紅】 1. ㄏㄨㄥˊ horng
         hóng

1. red; vermilion; rosy: 他因憤怒而漲紅了臉. He was red in the face with anger.

2. to blush; to redden: 她不禁臉一紅而淺露了真相. She could not help blushing the truth.

3. eminent; influential; (said of players) very popular
4. specially favored; a favorite

紅白事(ㄏㄨㄥˊ ㄅㄞˊ ㄕˋ)
weddings and funerals

紅包(ㄏㄨㄥˊ ㄅㄠ)
①a red paper bag containing money as a gift ②a bribe or kickback

紅寶石(ㄏㄨㄥˊ ㄅㄠˇ ㄕˊ)
a ruby

紅斑(ㄏㄨㄥˊ ㄅㄢ)
①(medicine) erythema ②(marine biology) red-spotted grouper

紅幫(ㄏㄨㄥˊ ㄅㄤ)
name of a secret underworld society 亦作「洪幫」

紅砒(ㄏㄨㄥˊ ㄆㄧ)
sulphurated arsenic

紅皮書(ㄏㄨㄥˊ ㄆㄧˊ ㄕㄨ)
(a diplomatic document) a red book

紅墨(ㄏㄨㄥˊ ㄇㄛˋ)
an ink stick made of vermilion

紅墨水(ㄏㄨㄥˊ ㄇㄛˋ ㄕㄨㄟˇ)
red ink

紅毛(ㄏㄨㄥˊ ㄇㄠˊ)or 紅毛番(ㄏㄨㄥˊ ㄇㄠˊ ㄈㄢ)
(in old China) the redhaired barbarians——Westerns (especially the Dutch)

紅毛丹(ㄏㄨㄥˊ ㄇㄠˊ ㄉㄢ)
a rambutan

紅帽子(ㄏㄨㄥˊ ㄇㄠˋ ˙ㄗ)
①the redcaps—railway porters ②the label of being a Communist (usually a false accusation)

紅模子(ㄏㄨㄥˊ ㄇㄛˊ ˙ㄗ)
a copy book for children in practicing calligraphy in which characters are printed in red to be traced by the pupils

紅木(ㄏㄨㄥˊ ㄇㄨˋ)
a redwood; a padauk

紅番(ㄏㄨㄥˊ ㄈㄢ)
Red Indians

紅粉(ㄏㄨㄥˊ ㄈㄣˇ)
①women; the fair sex ②rouge and powder

紅粉佳人(ㄏㄨㄥˊ ㄈㄣˇ ㄐㄧㄚ ㄖㄣˊ)
a young beauty; a sweet young thing

【糸部】

紅粉知己（ㄏㄨㄥˊ ㄈㄣˇ ㄓ ㄐㄧˇ）
a girlfriend; a mistress

紅得發紫（ㄏㄨㄥˊ ㄉㄜ˙ ㄈㄚ ㄗˇ）
①(said of entertainers) very popular ②(said of a government official) very influential; enjoying complete trust of the boss

紅豆（ㄏㄨㄥˊ ㄉㄡˋ）
① *Abrus precatorius*, the red bean—a token of love and endearment; a love pea 亦作「相思子」②《 Ormosia

紅豆相思（ㄏㄨㄥˊ ㄉㄡˋ ㄒㄧㄤ ㄙ）
red beans that inspire the memory of one's love

紅燈（ㄏㄨㄥˊ ㄉㄥ）
① the red traffic light ② a red light

紅頂子（ㄏㄨㄥˊ ㄉㄧㄥˇ ㄗ˙）
the official hat worn by a high-ranking government official during the Ching Dynasty

紅糖（ㄏㄨㄥˊ ㄊㄤ）
brown sugar: 在水裡加些紅糖。Put some brown sugar into the water.

紅帖(子)（ㄏㄨㄥˊ ㄊㄧㄝˇ ㄗ˙）
a "red card"—a card announcing a happy event (such as a betrothal, a birthday, etc.)

紅鐵礦（ㄏㄨㄥˊ ㄊㄧㄝˇ ㄎㄨㄤˋ）
hematite

紅土（ㄏㄨㄥˊ ㄊㄨˇ）
red clay; red earth

紅通通（ㄏㄨㄥˊ ㄊㄨㄥ ㄊㄨㄥ）
bright red; glowing; aglow 亦作「紅彤彤」：她因爲害羞臉紅紅通通的。Her face is aglow with shame.

紅銅（ㄏㄨㄥˊ ㄊㄨㄥˊ）
copper: 紅銅導電良好。Copper conducts electricity well.

紅銅礦（ㄏㄨㄥˊ ㄊㄨㄥˊ ㄎㄨㄤˋ）
cuprite

紅男綠女（ㄏㄨㄥˊ ㄋㄢˊ ㄌㄩˋ ㄋㄩˇ）
fashionably dressed men and women

紅娘（ㄏㄨㄥˊ ㄋㄧㄤˊ）
name of a maid in *The West Chamber* (西廂記), who helped unite the hero and the heroine—a nonprofit-making woman go-between for lovers

紅辣椒（ㄏㄨㄥˊ ㄌㄚˋ ㄐㄧㄠ）
the pimiento

紅淚（ㄏㄨㄥˊ ㄌㄟˋ）
tears with blood—tears of sadness

紅樓（ㄏㄨㄥˊ ㄌㄡˊ）or 紅閨（ㄏㄨㄥˊ ㄍㄨㄟ）
a boudoir; women's living quarters

紅樓夢（ㄏㄨㄥˊ ㄌㄡˊ ㄇㄥˋ）
The Dream of the Red Chamber—one of the greatest Chinese novels, authored by Tsao Hsüeh-chin（曹雪芹）of the Ching Dynasty

紅利（ㄏㄨㄥˊ ㄌㄧˋ）
dividends for stockholders; a net profit; a bonus: 這一行生意紅利不大。The net profits in this business are not large.

紅痢（ㄏㄨㄥˊ ㄌㄧˋ）
dysentery (characterized by blood in a patient's excrement)

紅臉（ㄏㄨㄥˊ ㄌㄧㄢˇ）
① a red face; a blushed face; shamefaced ② an angry look ③ the red face, face painting in Chinese opera, traditionally for the heroic or the honest

紅磷（ㄏㄨㄥˊ ㄌㄧㄣˊ）
red phosphorus (usually for making safety matches)

紅羅（ㄏㄨㄥˊ ㄌㄨㄛˊ）
red silk

紅蘿蔔（ㄏㄨㄥˊ ㄌㄨㄛˊ ㄅㄛ˙）
a radish

紅鸞星動（ㄏㄨㄥˊ ㄌㄨㄢˊ ㄒㄧㄥ ㄉㄨㄥˋ）or 紅鸞照命（ㄏㄨㄥˊ ㄌㄨㄢˊ ㄓㄠˋ ㄇㄧㄥˋ）
(literally) The propitious star governing marriages is in the ascendant. —a wedding being imminent

紅綠燈（ㄏㄨㄥˊ ㄌㄩˋ ㄉㄥ）
traffic lights; red and green lights

紅股（ㄏㄨㄥˊ ㄍㄨˇ）
bonus; stocks given in return for services rendered

紅果樹（ㄏㄨㄥˊ ㄍㄨㄛˇ ㄕㄨˋ）
holly

紅果兒（ㄏㄨㄥˊ ㄍㄨㄛˇㄦ）
the holly haw

紅光滿面（ㄏㄨㄥˊ ㄍㄨㄤ ㄇㄢˇ ㄇㄧㄢˋ）
a healthy and hearty look; in ruddy health

紅鶴（ㄏㄨㄥˊ ㄏㄜˋ）
the ibis

紅海（ㄏㄨㄥˊ ㄏㄞˇ）
Red Sea

紅鬍子（ㄏㄨㄥˊ ㄏㄨˊ ㄗ˙）
mounted bandits in Manchuria

紅花（ㄏㄨㄥˊ ㄏㄨㄚ）
the safflower

紅花子油（ㄏㄨㄥˊ ㄏㄨㄚ ㄗ˙ ㄧㄡˊ）
safflower oil

紅貨（ㄏㄨㄥˊ ㄏㄨㄛˋ）
jewels, jade, etc.

紅菊花（ㄏㄨㄥˊ ㄐㄩˊ ㄏㄨㄚ）
a red daisy

紅軍（ㄏㄨㄥˊ ㄐㄩㄣ）
Red Army; Communist troops

紅槍會（ㄏㄨㄥˊ ㄑㄧㄤ ㄏㄨㄟˋ）
① Red Spear Society, an outgrowth of the White Lotus Sect, founded in Hunan during the Ching Dynasty ② a name adopted by local militia units in the late 1920's and early 1930's

紅情綠意（ㄏㄨㄥˊ ㄑㄧㄥˊ ㄌㄩˋ ㄧˋ）
tender affections between a couple in love

紅雀（ㄏㄨㄥˊ ㄑㄩㄝˋ）
a linnet; a redbird; a cardinal bird

紅霞（ㄏㄨㄥˊ ㄒㄧㄚˊ）
red clouds; flaming clouds (in the evening)

紅血球（ㄏㄨㄥˊ ㄒㄧㄝˇ ㄑㄧㄡˊ）
red blood cells; erythrocyte; red corpuscles 亦作「紅細胞」

紅繡鞋（ㄏㄨㄥˊ ㄒㄧㄡˋ ㄒㄧㄝˊ）
① an old Chinese torture device—by forcing a criminal to wear red-hot iron shoes ② (in old China) women's embroidered red shoes

紅線（ㄏㄨㄥˊ ㄒㄧㄢˋ）
① name of a heroine in a Tang Dynasty legend ② (in Chinese folklore) the red string that brings a man and his mate together (Cupid's arrow in its Chinese version)

紅心（ㄏㄨㄥˊ ㄒㄧㄣ）

the bull's-eye (of a target): 他用鎗瞄準了紅心。He aimed his gun at the bull's-eye.

紅鋅礦(ㄏㄨㄥˊㄒㄧㄣㄎㄨㄤˋ)
zincite

紅杏出牆(ㄏㄨㄥˊㄒㄧㄥˋㄔㄨㄑㄧㄤˊ)
(said of a married woman) to have a lover; to commit adultery: 他的妻子紅杏出牆。His wife committed adultery.

紅痣(ㄏㄨㄥˊㄓˋ)
a reddish mole

紅疹(ㄏㄨㄥˊㄓㄣˇ)
German measles; rubella

紅燭(ㄏㄨㄥˊㄓㄨˊ)
red candles

紅磚 or 紅甎(ㄏㄨㄥˊㄓㄨㄢ)
red bricks

紅妝(ㄏㄨㄥˊㄓㄨㄤ)
① make-up or ornaments for women ② a young woman

紅腫(ㄏㄨㄥˊㄓㄨㄥˇ)
a red swelling of the skin

紅種人(ㄏㄨㄥˊㄓㄨㄥˇㄖㄣˊ)
the Red Man—the American Indian

紅茶(ㄏㄨㄥˊㄔㄚˊ)
black tea: 我喜歡紅茶甚於咖啡。I like black tea better than coffee.

紅潮(ㄏㄨㄥˊㄔㄠˊ)
① to blush ② the menses

紅塵(ㄏㄨㄥˊㄔㄣˊ)
the mundane world; the world of mortals: 他看破紅塵。He saw through the vanity of the world.

紅場(ㄏㄨㄥˊㄔㄤˇ)or(ㄏㄨㄥˊㄔㄤˋ)
Red Square (in Moscow)

紅十字會(ㄏㄨㄥˊㄕˊㄗˋㄏㄨㄟˋ)
Red Cross Society

紅事(ㄏㄨㄥˊㄕˋ)
auspicious occasions, such as weddings, birthdays, etc.

紅痧(ㄏㄨㄥˊㄕㄚ)
scarlet fever

紅燒肉(ㄏㄨㄥˊㄕㄠㄖㄡˋ)
a Chinese dish prepared by cooking and simmering pork with soybean sauce and sugar

紅杉(ㄏㄨㄥˊㄕㄢ)
① a redwood 參看「紅木」 ② Chinese larch

紅繩繫足(ㄏㄨㄥˊㄕㄥˊㄒㄧˋㄗㄨˊ)

(said of a young couple) to be engaged to each other

紅薯(ㄏㄨㄥˊㄕㄨˇ)
sweet potatoes: 紅薯長在地下。Sweet potatoes grow under the ground.

紅樹(ㄏㄨㄥˊㄕㄨˋ)
a mangrove

紅日(ㄏㄨㄥˊㄖˋ)
the sun: 紅日自東方升起。The sun rises in the east.

紅熱(ㄏㄨㄥˊㄖㄜˋ)
① red heat ② red-hot

紅人(ㄏㄨㄥˊㄖㄣˊ)
① the trusted lieutenant of the boss ② Red Indians

紅潤(ㄏㄨㄥˊㄖㄨㄣˋ)
(said of the skin, cheeks, etc.) glowing, tender and rosy: 她的臉色健康紅潤。There is a glow of health in her face.

紅字(ㄏㄨㄥˊㄗˋ)
① a red mark for failure in an examination ② red entry in budget ③ The Scarlet Letter by Nathaniel Hawthorne

紅棗(ㄏㄨㄥˊㄗㄠˇ)
red dates

紅色(ㄏㄨㄥˊㄙㄜˋ)
red color: 他昨天把大門漆成紅色。He painted the gate red yesterday.

紅松鶴(ㄏㄨㄥˊㄙㄨㄥㄏㄜˋ)
a moorfowl

紅松雞(ㄏㄨㄥˊㄙㄨㄥㄐㄧ)
a moorcock; a moorhen

紅衣主教(ㄏㄨㄥˊㄧㄓㄨˇㄐㄧㄠˋ)
(Roman Catholicism) a cardinal

紅夷(ㄏㄨㄥˊㄧˊ)
the Westerners

紅葉(ㄏㄨㄥˊㄧㄝˋ)
red leaves (of maples, etc.); autumn leaves

紅藥水(ㄏㄨㄥˊㄧㄠˋㄕㄨㄟˇ)
mercurochrome

紅顏(ㄏㄨㄥˊㄧㄢˊ)
① young beauties ② youths ③ rosy cheeks

紅顏薄命(ㄏㄨㄥˊㄧㄢˊㄅㄛˊㄇㄧㄥˋ)
(a popular Chinese saying) Beauties are often ill-fated.

紅顏美少年(ㄏㄨㄥˊㄧㄢˊㄇㄟˇㄕㄠˋㄋㄧㄢˊ)
a handsome young man: 他

是一個紅顏美少年。He's a handsome young fellow.

紅眼鳥(ㄏㄨㄥˊㄧㄢˇㄋㄧㄠˇ)
a chewink

紅羊浩刧(ㄏㄨㄥˊㄧㄤˊㄏㄠˋㄐㄧㄝˊ)
the catastrophe of war and rampage of bandits

紅外線(ㄏㄨㄥˊㄨㄞˋㄒㄧㄢˋ)
infrared rays

紅衛兵(ㄏㄨㄥˊㄨㄟˋㄅㄧㄥ)
Red Guards (created by Mao Tse-tung as a weapon to fight his political opponents)

紅魚(ㄏㄨㄥˊㄩˊ)
the gurnard

紅雨(ㄏㄨㄥˊㄩˇ)
the falling of blossoms (which looks like red raindrops)

紅暈(ㄏㄨㄥˊㄩㄣˋ)
a blush; a flush

紅運(ㄏㄨㄥˊㄩㄣˋ)
good luck; lucky opportunities, etc.

紅運當頭(ㄏㄨㄥˊㄩㄣˋㄉㄤㄊㄡˊ)
Lucky star shines bright.

【紅】 4283
ㄍㄨㄥ gong gòng
work; working

紅女(ㄍㄨㄥㄋㄩˇ)
working girls

【紇】 4284
ㄏㄜˊ her hé
1. silk of an inferior quality
2. name of a barbarian tribe, ancestors of the Huns (匈奴)

【紇】 4284
ㄍㄜˋ ge gé
a knot made of a rope or string

紇縫(ㄍㄜˊ·ㄉㄚ)
a knot made of a rope or string

【紈】 4285
ㄨㄢˊ wan wán
processed fine and light silk

紈袴(ㄨㄢˊㄎㄨˋ)
① expensive dresses of children from wealthy families ② a good-for-nothing young man from a wealthy family

紈袴子弟(ㄨㄢˊㄎㄨˋㄗˇㄉㄧˋ)
a good-for-nothing young man from a wealthy family; a playboy; a dandy; a fop; profligate sons of the rich

【糸部】

納扇 (ㄋㄚˋ ㄕㄢˋ)
　　a round, silk fan

絿素 (ㄒㄩˋ ㄙㄨˋ)
　　fine, white silk

【紉】 4286
　　ㄖㄣˊ renn rén
1. to sew; to stitch
2. to tie; to wear
3. to feel deeply
4. to thread a needle

紉佩 (ㄖㄣˊ ㄆㄟˋ)
　　to be very grateful

紉綴 (ㄖㄣˊ ㄓㄨㄟˋ)
　　to mend; to repair

四畫

【紋】 4287
　　ㄨㄣˊ wen wén
1. stripes; lines; streaks; veins
2. ripples (of water)
3. (finger) prints
4. wrinkles (on the face)
5. to tattoo

紋兒 (ㄨㄣˊ ㄦ)
　　stripes; streaks; lines; grain

紋理 (ㄨㄣˊ ㄌㄧˇ)
　　lines; stripes; veins; grain: 那
　　大理石的紋理很好看。 That
　　marble has a beautiful
　　grain.

紋身 (ㄨㄣˊ ㄕㄣ)
　　tattoo; to tattoo the body

紋絲兒不動 (ㄨㄣˊ ㄙㄦ ㄅㄨˋ ㄉㄨㄥˋ)
　　not to make even the slight
　　est move

紋銀 (ㄨㄣˊ ㄧㄣˊ)
　　a horseshoe-shaped silver
　　ingot with the highest per
　　centage of fineness; fine sil
　　ver

【納】 4288
　　ㄋㄚˋ nah nà
1. to receive; to take; to
　　accept; to admit; to adopt
2. to offer as tribute
3. to enjoy; to feel
4. to repress; to restrain
5. to patch old clothes
6. a Chinese family name

納幣 (ㄋㄚˋ ㄅㄧˋ)
　　to present betrothal gifts to
　　the girl's family

納聘 (ㄋㄚˋ ㄆㄧㄣˋ)
　　to give betrothal money or
　　presents to the girl's family

納悶 (ㄋㄚˋ ㄇㄣˋ) or 納悶兒 (ㄋㄚˋ
　　ㄇㄣˋ)

①to feel depressed ②to
　　feel curious; to wonder

納福 (ㄋㄚˋ ㄈㄨˊ)
　　to have a good time; to
　　enjoy oneself; to live in com
　　fortable circumstances: 他在
　　家納福。 He enjoyed a life of
　　comfort at home.

納涼 (ㄋㄚˋ ㄌㄧㄤˊ)
　　to enjoy the cool air; to
　　enjoy the cool night

納貢 (ㄋㄚˋ ㄍㄨㄥˋ)
　　to offer tribute as a vassal
　　state

納款 (ㄋㄚˋ ㄎㄨㄢˇ)
　　(said of an enemy) to surren
　　der in all sincerity

納罕 (ㄋㄚˋ ㄏㄢˇ)
　　to feel curious; to feel sur
　　prised: 這消息使我們納罕。We
　　are surprised at the news.

納賄 (ㄋㄚˋ ㄏㄨㄟˋ)
　　①to offer bribes ②to re
　　ceive bribes

納吉 (ㄋㄚˋ ㄐㄧˊ)
　　one of the six matrimonial
　　rites in ancient China—to
　　divine the good or bad luck
　　of a marriage in a temple
　　and report back to the
　　bride's family

納節 (ㄋㄚˋ ㄐㄧㄝˊ)
　　(in ancient China) to resign
　　from a government office
　　and return the credentials of
　　the office

納交 (ㄋㄚˋ ㄐㄧㄠ)
　　to make friends with; to
　　befriend

納諫 (ㄋㄚˋ ㄐㄧㄢˋ)
　　to accept an admonition; to
　　receive instruction or ad
　　vice: 他欣然納諫。 He takes
　　our advice quite cheerfully.

納姿 (ㄋㄚˋ ㄑㄩˋ) or 納寵 (ㄋㄚˋ ㄔㄨㄥˇ)
　　to take a concubine

納稅 (ㄋㄚˋ ㄕㄨㄟˋ)
　　to pay duties or taxes

納稅人 (ㄋㄚˋ ㄕㄨㄟˋ ㄖㄣˊ)
　　the taxpayer

納入 (ㄋㄚˋ ㄖㄨˋ)
　　to bring into

納采 (ㄋㄚˋ ㄘㄞˇ)
　　to present betrothal gifts to
　　the girl's family

納粹黨 (ㄋㄚˋ ㄘㄨㄟˋ ㄉㄤˇ)
　　Nazi party (National So

cialist German Workers'
　　Party, NSDAP, 1919-1945) of
　　Germany

納粹主義 (ㄋㄚˋ ㄘㄨㄟˋ ㄓㄨˇ ㄧˋ)
　　Nazism

納粟 (ㄋㄚˋ ㄙㄨˋ)
　　to contribute grain to the
　　government in return for a
　　public post

納爾遜 (ㄋㄚˋ ㄦˇ ㄙㄨㄣˋ)
　　Admiral Horatio Nelson,
　　1758-1805, of the British
　　Navy

【紐】 4289
　　ㄋㄧㄡˇ neou niǔ
1. a knot; a tie; a cord
2. a hold (of a vessel) or han
　　dle
3. a button
4. a Chinese family name

紐襻 (ㄋㄧㄡˇ ㄆㄢˋ)
　　loops for buttons

紐芬蘭 (ㄋㄧㄡˇ ㄈㄣ ㄌㄢˊ)
　　Newfoundland

紐扣 (ㄋㄧㄡˇ ㄎㄡˋ)
　　a button

紐西蘭 (ㄋㄧㄡˇ ㄒㄧ ㄌㄢˊ)
　　New Zealand

紐約 (ㄋㄧㄡˇ ㄩㄝ)
　　New York

【純】 4290
　　ㄔㄨㄣˊ chwen chún
1. pure; net (profits, etc.);
　　unalloyed: 這是一杯純淨的
　　水。 This is a glass of pure
　　water.
2. sincere; honest; simple;
　　faithful
3. completely; purely; entirely
4. (now rare) great; large
5. (now rare) silk; silk strands
　　or threads

純白 (ㄔㄨㄣˊ ㄅㄞˊ)
　　pure white

純品 (ㄔㄨㄣˊ ㄆㄧㄣˇ)
　　of the purest quality; com
　　pletely unmixed

純樸 (ㄔㄨㄣˊ ㄆㄨˊ)
　　simple and sincere

純毛 (ㄔㄨㄣˊ ㄇㄠˊ)
　　all-wool; 100% wool

純理論 (ㄔㄨㄣˊ ㄌㄧˇ ㄌㄨㄣˋ)
　　(philosophy) a theory that
　　recognition comes from
　　instinct instead of senses or
　　experience

純利 (ㄔㄨㄣˊ ㄌㄧˋ)

net profits: 這一行生意純利不
大。The net profits in this
business are not large.

純利潤 (ㄔㄨㄣˊ ㄌㄧˋ ㄖㄨㄣˋ)
  the portion of net profit
  after paying dividends to the
  shareholders, etc.

純良 (ㄔㄨㄣˊ ㄌㄧㄤˊ)
  kind; honest

純潔 (ㄔㄨㄣˊ ㄐㄧㄝˊ)
  innocent; pure and clean;
  honest, sincere and faithful

純金 (ㄔㄨㄣˊ ㄐㄧㄣ)
  pure gold; unalloyed gold

純淨 (ㄔㄨㄣˊ ㄐㄧㄥˋ)
  pure and clean

純真 (ㄔㄨㄣˊ ㄓㄣ)
  pure, sincere and faithful;
  genuine; unsophisticated: 她
  是一個純真無邪的女孩。She is
  a pure and innocent girl.

純正 (ㄔㄨㄣˊ ㄓㄥˋ)
  ① pure and unadulterated;
  pure and genuine ② honest;
  sincere

純種 (ㄔㄨㄣˊ ㄓㄨㄥˇ)
  thoroughbred; purebred

純熟 (ㄔㄨㄣˊ ㄕㄨˊ)
  proficient; very skillful;
  adroit; skill; deft

純屬虛構 (ㄔㄨㄣˊ ㄕㄨˇ ㄒㄩ ㄍㄡˋ)
  The matter is an out-and-
  out fabrication. 或It is a
  sheer fabrication.

純粹 (ㄔㄨㄣˊ ㄘㄨㄟˋ)
  ① pure; genuine; unadulterated: 它純粹是虛造的事實。It
  is a pure fabrication.② completely; entirely

純色 (ㄔㄨㄣˊ ㄙㄜˋ)
  ① of one color (especially
  referring to textiles) ②
  (physics) pure colors

純一 (ㄔㄨㄣˊ ㄧ)
  sincere; simple; unanimous;
  pure; uniform

純文學 (ㄔㄨㄣˊ ㄨㄣˊ ㄒㄩㄝˊ)
  belles-lettres; pure literature
  such as poetry, drama,
  novels, etc., without extraneous implications, political
  or otherwise

【紓】 4291
ㄕㄨ shu shū

1. to relax; to slacken; to slow
   down; to mitigate
2. to free from; to remove

(causes of difficulties, poverty, etc.); to extricate from

紓難 (ㄕㄨ ㄋㄢˊ)
  to extricate from trouble or
  danger; to free from difficulties or straits; to give
  relief in time of distress

紓困 (ㄕㄨ ㄎㄨㄣˋ)
  to provide financial relief

紓禍 (ㄕㄨ ㄏㄨㄛˋ)
  to extricate from the grip of
  misfortune or catastrophe

紓憂 (ㄕㄨ ㄧㄡ)
  to remove worries

【紕】 4292
  1. ㄆㄧ pi pī
1. errors; mistakes; blunders
2. (said of cloth, thread, etc.)
   to become unwoven or un-
   twisted

紕繆 (ㄆㄧ ㄇㄧㄡˋ)
  mistakes or blunders

紕漏 (ㄆㄧ ㄌㄡˋ)
  errors or mistakes; something going wrong: 他出了紕
  漏。He made a small error.

【紕】 4292
  2. ㄆㄧ pyi pí
  hem ornaments

【紘】 4293
ㄏㄨㄥˊ horng hóng
1. a hat string fastened under
   the chin
2. vast; spacious

【紗】 4294
ㄕㄚ sha shā
1. gauze; thin silk or cloth
2. yarn, as cotton yarn: 他們把
   棉花紡成紗。They spin cotton
   into yarn.
3. a thin, netty or meshy sheet
   of any materials—such as
   cotton, silk, nylon, wires
   —that permits the passing
   of air but prevents mosquitoes, insects, etc.

紗包線 (ㄕㄚ ㄅㄠ ㄒㄧㄢˋ)
  cotton-covered wire

紗布 (ㄕㄚ ㄅㄨˋ)
  ① gauze ② a bandage

紗帽 (ㄕㄚ ㄇㄠˋ)
  hats worn by noblemen or
  high officials in former
  times

紗錠 (ㄕㄚ ㄉㄧㄥˋ)
  a spindle

紗籠 (ㄕㄚ ㄌㄨㄥˊ)
  a sarong

紗罩 (ㄕㄚ ㄓㄠˋ)
  ① a gauze cover stretched
  over a frame to keep insects
  away from food items ② a
  gas mantle

紗帳 (ㄕㄚ ㄓㄤˋ)
  a mosquito net

紗廠 (ㄕㄚ ㄔㄤˇ)
  a cotton yarn mill; a cotton
  mill; a textile mill

紗櫥 (ㄕㄚ ㄔㄨˊ)
  ① a gauze cabinet for keeping food items ② a mosquito
  net shaped like a cabin

紗窗 (ㄕㄚ ㄔㄨㄤ)
  a window screen

【紙】 4295
ㄓˇ jyy zhǐ
paper

紙包不住火 (ㄓˇ ㄅㄠ ㄅㄨˋ ㄓㄨˋ ㄏㄨㄛˇ)
  (literally) Paper can never
  wrap up fire.—Plots or evil
  deeds will be exposed sooner or later.

紙版 (ㄓˇ ㄅㄢˇ)
  (printing) paper shells for a
  stereotype; a paper matrix

紙板 (ㄓˇ ㄅㄢˇ)
  cardboard: 這玩具是用硬紙板
  造的。This toy is made of
  cardboard.

紙幣 (ㄓˇ ㄅㄧˋ)
  paper money; bank notes: 把
  這張紙幣換成零錢。Give me
  change for this note.

紙牌 (ㄓˇ ㄆㄞˊ)
  playing cards: 我們來玩紙牌
  吧。Let's play cards.

紙片 (ㄓˇ ㄆㄧㄢˋ)
  scraps of paper

紙媒子 (ㄓˇ ㄇㄟˊ·ㄗ)or 紙捻兒 (ㄓˇ
  ㄋㄧㄢˇㄦ)
  a rolled or twisted strip of
  paper, used to light candles,
  tobacco in a pipe, etc.; a
  paper spill

紙彈 (ㄓˇ ㄉㄢˋ)
  ① psywar leaflets ② a ballot

紙條 (ㄓˇ ㄊㄧㄠˊ)
  a slip of paper

紙老虎 (ㄓˇ ㄌㄠˇ ㄏㄨˇ)or 紙糊老虎
  (ㄓˇ ㄏㄨˊ ㄌㄠˇ ㄏㄨˇ)
  a paper tiger: 我們的敵人不是
  紙老虎。Our enemies are not
  paper tigers.

紙貴洛陽 (ㄓˇ ㄍㄨㄟˋ ㄌㄨㄛˋ ㄧㄤˊ)
  The copying of a literary

【糸部】

masterpiece makes the price of paper soar.—A literary masterpiece becomes a best-seller.

紙盒 (ㄓㄏㄜˊ)
a carton; a paper box

紙婚 (ㄓㄏㄨㄣ)
paper wedding; the first wedding anniversary

紙漿 (ㄓㄐㄧㄤ)
paper pulp: 紙是由紙漿做成的。Paper is made from paper pulp.

紙錢兒 (ㄓㄑㄧㄢˊ)
paper money burnt as offerings to the dead

紙型 (ㄓㄒㄧㄥˊ)
a paper mold; a matrix

紙張 (ㄓㄓㄤ)
paper; sheets of paper; stationery

紙扇 (ㄓㄕㄢˋ)
a paper fan

紙上談兵 (ㄓㄕㄤˋㄊㄢˊㄅㄧㄥ)
impractical schemes; empty talks; academic talks; to be an armchair strategist

紙醉金迷 (ㄓㄗㄨㄟˋㄐㄧㄣㄇㄧˊ)
to indulge in a wanton life

紙業 (ㄓㄧㄝˋ)
the paper industry or enterprise

紙業公司 (ㄓㄧㄝˋㄍㄨㄥㄙ)
a pulp and paper mill

紙煙 (ㄓㄧㄢ)
cigarettes

紙鳶 (ㄓㄩㄢ)
kites (of paper): 他在放紙鳶。He is flying a kite.

【紜】 4296
ㄩㄣˊ yún yún
confusing; disorderly

紜紜 (ㄩㄣˊㄩㄣˊ)
diverse and confused; numerous and disorderly

【紝】 4297
(紉) ㄖㄣˊ reen rén
(又讀) ㄖㄣˋ ren rèn
to lay the warp; to weave

【級】 4298
ㄐㄧˊ jyi jí
1. a grade; a class (at school)
2. a level; a degree; a mark of merit; a rank
3. a step (of a flight of steps)
4. a decapitated head

級別 (ㄐㄧˊㄅㄧㄝˊ)
ranks; levels; grades; scales

級會 (ㄐㄧˊㄏㄨㄟˋ)
a class meeting (at school)

級長 (ㄐㄧˊㄓㄤˇ)
a class leader; a monitor

級數 (ㄐㄧˊㄕㄨˋ)
(mathematics) progression

級任 (ㄐㄧˊㄖㄣˋ)
a class tutor

級任導師 (ㄐㄧˊㄖㄣˋㄉㄠˇㄕ)
a homeroom teacher

【紛】 4299
ㄈㄣ fen fēn
1. confused; disorderly: 桌上紛亂不堪。The table was in great disorder.
2. numerous; many; varied

紛披 (ㄈㄣㄆㄧ)
① to spread out in a disorderly manner ② numerous

紛飛 (ㄈㄣㄈㄟ)
to whirl around in confusion; to fly all over: 大雪紛飛。The snow fell in a whirl.

紛繁 (ㄈㄣㄈㄢˊ)
numerous and complicated: 這案子頭緒紛繁。This case is highly complicated.

紛紛 (ㄈㄣㄈㄣ)
① numerous and disorderly ② (said of people moving) in droves; numerous and in great confusion

紛杳 (ㄈㄣㄠˋ)
in endless succession

紛吵 (ㄈㄣㄔㄠˇ)
noisy and disorderly

紛亂 (ㄈㄣㄌㄨㄢˋ)
confusion; confused or disorderly; chaotic

紛綸 (ㄈㄣㄌㄨㄣˊ)
① (said of knowledge, learning, etc.) vast and profound ② confusion; chaos

紛紅駭綠 (ㄈㄣㄏㄨㄥˊㄏㄞˋㄌㄩˋ)
luxuriant growth of flowers and vegetation swaying (in the wind, etc.)

紛歧 (ㄈㄣㄑㄧˊ)
greatly divided (in opinions); diversified; disharmonious; in disorder or diverging; disunited: 我們的意見紛歧。Our opinions are divided.

紛至沓來 (ㄈㄣㄓˋㄊㄚˋㄌㄞˊ)
to come in continuous suc-

cession; (said of people) to flock in endless waves: 客人紛至沓來。The guests came in succession.

紛爭 (ㄈㄣㄓㄥ)
a dispute; to dispute; to wrangle; to quarrel: 他們對該問題有一場紛爭。They had a dispute over the question.

紛擾 (ㄈㄣㄖㄠˇ)
to confuse; confused or disorderly; turmoil; disturbance; to disturb

紛然 (ㄈㄣㄖㄢˊ)
disorderly; chaotic; confused

紛雜 (ㄈㄣㄗㄚˊ)
numerous and disorderly

紛紜 (ㄈㄣㄩㄣˊ)
① numerous and disorderly ② (said of opinions) widely divided; diverse and confused

紛緼 (ㄈㄣㄩㄣ)
flourishing in a disorderly manner

【紡】 4300
ㄈㄤˇ faang fǎng
1. to reel; to spin: 她把羊毛紡成毛線。She spun wool into thread.
2. reeled pongee (a kind of thin silk)

紡織 (ㄈㄤˇㄓ)
to spin and weave; spinning and weaving

紡織娘 (ㄈㄤˇㄓㄋㄧㄤˊ)
Mecopoda nipponensis, a kind of grasshopper; a katydid; a long-horned grasshopper

紡織工人 (ㄈㄤˇㄓㄍㄨㄥㄖㄣˊ)
a textile factory worker

紡織公司 (ㄈㄤˇㄓㄍㄨㄥㄙ)
a spinning and weaving mill; a textile company

紡織機 (ㄈㄤˇㄓㄐㄧ)
looms; spinning and weaving machines

紡織廠 (ㄈㄤˇㄓㄔㄤˇ)
a (cotton) spinning and weaving mill; a textile mill

紡織業 (ㄈㄤˇㄓㄧㄝˋ)
the textile industry

紡甎 (ㄈㄤˇㄓㄨㄢ)
tiles used in weaving

紡車 (ㄈㄤˇㄔㄜ)
a spinning wheel; a spinning

machine

紡綢 (ㄈㄤˇ ㄔㄡˊ)
reeled pongee

紡錘 (ㄈㄤˇ ㄔㄨㄟˊ)
a spindle

紡紗 (ㄈㄤˇ ㄕㄚ)
to spin cotton, etc. into yarn

紡紗機 (ㄈㄤˇ ㄕㄚ ㄐㄧ)
a jenny; a spinning jenny

紡紗織布 (ㄈㄤˇ ㄕㄚ ㄓ ㄅㄨˋ)
to spin and weave

紡絲 (ㄈㄤˇ ㄙ)
spinning

【紊】 4301
ㄨㄣˇ wenn **wèn**
confused; tangled; involved; disorderly

紊亂 (ㄨㄣˇ ㄌㄨㄢˋ)
confused; tangled; chaotic; chaos; disorder; confusion:她的房間紊亂不堪。Her room was in great disorder.

【素】 4302
ㄙㄨˋ suh **sù**
1. pure white silk
2. white (color)
3. plain; simple
4. mourning
5. vegetable food; a vegetarian diet
6. heretofore; up to the present
7. usually; generally
8. the original constitution of things; matter; elements

素不相識 (ㄙㄨˋ ㄅㄨˋ ㄒㄧㄤ ㄕˋ)
to have never met or seen before; a total stranger: 我們素不相識。We have never met before.

素朴 or 素樸 (ㄙㄨˋ ㄆㄨˇ)
plain and simple (clothing, food, taste, etc.)

素昧平生 (ㄙㄨˋ ㄇㄟˋ ㄆㄧㄥˊㄕㄥ)
to have never known, met or seen before; to be a total stranger

素門 (ㄙㄨˋ ㄇㄣˊ)
a poor family

素描 (ㄙㄨˋ ㄇㄧㄠˊ)
(said of writing or painting) a sketch

素麵 (ㄙㄨˋ ㄇㄧㄢˋ)
a vegetarian preparation of noodles

素面朝天 (ㄙㄨˋ ㄇㄧㄢˋ ㄔㄠˊ ㄊㄧㄢ)
(said of a woman) to wear no make-up during an audi-

ence with the emperor

素髮 (ㄙㄨˋ ㄈㄚˇ)
white hair

素幡 (ㄙㄨˋ ㄈㄢ)
white streamers or flags

素飯 (ㄙㄨˋ ㄈㄢˋ)
a vegetarian diet

素封 (ㄙㄨˋ ㄈㄥ)
to become wealthy without holding a public office

素風 (ㄙㄨˋ ㄈㄥ)
① contemporary customs or practices ② one's usual habits or practices

素服 (ㄙㄨˋ ㄈㄨˊ)
white dresses or clothing (especially mourning dress): 他身著素服。He is clad in white clothing.

素來 (ㄙㄨˋ ㄌㄞˊ)
heretofore; always; up to the present

素練 (ㄙㄨˋ ㄌㄧㄢˋ)
① white silk ② (figuratively) a waterfall; a cascade; a cataract

素履 (ㄙㄨˋ ㄌㄩˇ)
① a simple life ② a common scholar contented with a quiet and simple life

素故 (ㄙㄨˋ ㄍㄨˋ)
an old friend

素官 (ㄙㄨˋ ㄍㄨㄢ)
a poor government official (connoting honesty)

素口罵人 (ㄙㄨˋ ㄎㄡˇ ㄇㄚˋ ㄖㄣˊ)
(literally) to eat vegetables (as a Buddhist) but freely use abusive language—to practice not what one preaches

素火腿 (ㄙㄨˋ ㄏㄨㄛˇ ㄊㄨㄟˇ)
a cold vegetarian dish made of soybean which looks like ham

素懷 (ㄙㄨˋ ㄏㄨㄞˊ)
long-cherished ambitions or hopes

素鷄 (ㄙㄨˋ ㄐㄧ)
a cold vegetarian dish made of soybean which looks like chicken meat

素節 (ㄙㄨˋ ㄐㄧㄝˊ)
① the Moon Festival ② autumn ③ moral fortitude; integrity ④ one's usual behavior or conduct

素交 (ㄙㄨˋ ㄐㄧㄠ)
a true old friend; a long-known friend; an old acquaintance

素舊 (ㄙㄨˋ ㄐㄧㄡˋ)
old friendship

素儉 (ㄙㄨˋ ㄐㄧㄢˇ)
simple and disciplined (life, taste, etc.)

素淨 (ㄙㄨˋ ㄐㄧㄥˋ)
① simple, or plain (clothes) ② simple, or not greasy (food)

素車白馬 (ㄙㄨˋ ㄔㄜ ㄅㄞˊ ㄇㄚˇ)
a funeral procession—white carriages and white horses

素秋 (ㄙㄨˋ ㄑㄧㄡ)
autumn; fall

素琴 (ㄙㄨˋ ㄑㄧㄣˊ)
a harp, guitar, etc. without strings

素昔 (ㄙㄨˋ ㄒㄧˊ)
usually; ordinarily; regularly; so far

素席 (ㄙㄨˋ ㄒㄧˊ)
a vegetarian feast

素心 (ㄙㄨˋ ㄒㄧㄣ)
① simple and honest ② one's true mind or conscience

素心蘭 (ㄙㄨˋ ㄒㄧㄣ ㄌㄢˊ)
a cymbidium

素馨 (ㄙㄨˋ ㄒㄧㄣ)
(botany) a jasmine

素行 (ㄙㄨˋ ㄒㄧㄥˊ)
daily conduct or behavior

素性 (ㄙㄨˋ ㄒㄧㄥˋ)
one's true disposition or temperament

素知 (ㄙㄨˋ ㄓ)
to have known for some time

素質 (ㄙㄨˋ ㄓˊ)
① one's true quality; one's natural talent ② white

素志 (ㄙㄨˋ ㄓˋ)
a long-cherished ambition or aspiration

素常 (ㄙㄨˋ ㄔㄤˊ)
usually; ordinarily; regularly; commonly; so far: 她素常行爲十分良好。Ordinarily she behaved quite well.

素稱 (ㄙㄨˋ ㄔㄥ)
usually called; ordinarily or commonly known as; reputed to be

【糸部】

素食(ㄙㄨ ㄕ)
①vegetables; a vegetarian diet; vegetarian food ②daily diets or food; food one eats on ordinary or usual occasions ③to live like a parasite

素士(ㄙㄨ ㄕ)
a scholar who is not in government service

素事(ㄙㄨ ㄕ)
funeral matters

素室(ㄙㄨ ㄕ)
①a plain and simple family —not well-to-do ②a white-walled chamber

素識(ㄙㄨ ㄕ)
to have known or been familiar with

素手(ㄙㄨ ㄕㄡ)
①fair hands; white and tender hands ②empty hands; empty-handed

素尚(ㄙㄨ ㄕㄤ)
simple and plain virtues; simple aspiration: 謙遜是一種素尚美德。Humility is a simple and plain virtue.

素數(ㄙㄨ ㄕㄨ)
(mathematics) a prime number 亦作「質數」

素日(ㄙㄨ ㄖ)
usually; commonly; daily; regularly; frequently: 她素日喜愛閒談。She is usually very chatty.

素稔(ㄙㄨ ㄖㄣ)
to have known or been familiar with

素族(ㄙㄨ ㄗㄨ)
a commoner

素材(ㄙㄨ ㄘㄞ)
material; themes (of an artistic work) collected through daily experience

素菜(ㄙㄨ ㄘㄞ)
vegetable food; vegetarian dishes

素餐(ㄙㄨ ㄘㄢ)
to eat the bread of idleness

素餐尸位(ㄙㄨ ㄘㄢ ㄕ ㄨㄟ)
to occupy a high position without doing anything; a practically sinecure office

素娥(ㄙㄨ ㄜ)
①(Chinese mythology) the lady of the moon 亦作「嫦娥」

②beauties

素愛(ㄙㄨ ㄞ)
usually (love to do something); commonly (read novels, etc.); regularly (eat certain food, etc.); frequently (fool around the gambling joint, etc.)

素一(ㄙㄨ ㄧ)
simple and honest

素衣(ㄙㄨ ㄧ)
①plain clothes ②white garments—for mourning

素雅(ㄙㄨ ㄧㄚ)
simple but elegant; unadorned and in good taste

素業(ㄙㄨ ㄧㄝ)
a former profession or vocation

素油(ㄙㄨ ㄧㄡ)
vegetable oil: 他們吃素油。They ate vegetable oil.

素友(ㄙㄨ ㄧㄡ)
an old friend

素筵(ㄙㄨ ㄧㄢ)
①a vegetarian feast ②food offerings to Buddha

素因數(ㄙㄨ ㄧㄣ ㄕㄨ)or素因子(ㄙㄨ ㄧㄣ ㄗ)
(mathematics) a prime factor 亦作「質因數」

素仰(ㄙㄨ ㄧㄤ)
to have always looked up to or admired

素養(ㄙㄨ ㄧㄤ)
one's general capacity and disposition as a result of long and regular self-discipline; accomplishments: 她具有音樂素養。She has a musical accomplishment.

素位(ㄙㄨ ㄨㄟ)
one's current position or present circumstances

素聞(ㄙㄨ ㄨㄣ)
to have often heard; to have been frequently told

素望(ㄙㄨ ㄨㄤ)
one's good reputation and prestige: 他是個素望良好的人。He is a man of good reputation and prestige.

素約(ㄙㄨ ㄩㄝ)
an old promise or vow

素月(ㄙㄨ ㄩㄝ)
the brilliant moon; the chaste moon

素願(ㄙㄨ ㄩㄢ)
a long-cherished ambition, aspiration or hope

【索】　4303
1. ㄙㄨㄛ suoo　suǒ
1. a thick rope; a cable
2. alone; lonely; solitary
3. to search or inquire into
4. to exhaust
5. to tighten; to squeeze; to twist
6. laws and regulations; rules
7. to demand; to ask; to exact
8. to need
9. a Chinese family name

索賠(ㄙㄨㄛ ㄆㄟ)
to demand compensation; to claim

索馬利蘭(ㄙㄨㄛ ㄇㄚ ㄌㄧ ㄌㄢ)
Somaliland

索馬利亞(ㄙㄨㄛ ㄇㄚ ㄌㄧ ㄧㄚ)
Somalia

索寞(ㄙㄨㄛ ㄇㄛ)
(said of one's looks) despondent, discouraged or crestfallen

索命(ㄙㄨㄛ ㄇㄧㄥ)
(usually referring to a ghost, a victim of injustice) to demand one's life

索道(ㄙㄨㄛ ㄉㄠ)
a cableway; a ropeway

索價(ㄙㄨㄛ ㄐㄧㄚ)
to demand a price; to state a price; to quote a price

索解(ㄙㄨㄛ ㄐㄧㄝ)
to search for an explanation or solution

索居(ㄙㄨㄛ ㄐㄩ)
to live alone (like a hermit); to go into retreat

索橋(ㄙㄨㄛ ㄑㄧㄠ)
a suspension bridge

索求(ㄙㄨㄛ ㄑㄧㄡ)
to seek (persons, jobs, etc.)

索欠(ㄙㄨㄛ ㄑㄧㄢ)
to demand the repayment of a debt

索取(ㄙㄨㄛ ㄑㄩ)
①to ask for; to demand: 我們索取樣品。We asked for a sample. ②to exact; to extort

索薪(ㄙㄨㄛ ㄒㄧㄣ)
to demand one's wages or salary

索然(ㄙㄨㄛ ㄖㄢ)

insipid; listless: 這個故事索然
寡味。This story was flat and
insipid.

索然無味 (ㄙㄨㄛˇ ㄖㄢˊ ㄨˊ ㄨㄟˋ)
not interesting; tasteless;
listless

索要 (ㄙㄨㄛˇ ㄧㄠˋ)
to demand; to ask for

索引 (ㄙㄨㄛˇ ㄧㄣˇ)
①the index (of a book)②
to bring together

索隱 (ㄙㄨㄛˇ ㄧㄣˇ)
to expose, unearth, or
expound something con-
cealed, hidden or obscure

索閱 (ㄙㄨㄛˇ ㄩㄝˋ)
to ask for (a book, certificate, card, etc.) for reference

【索】 4303
2. ㄙㄨㄛ swo suó
to decide to go ahead and
do something without any
more consideration; may as
well; simply

索性 (ㄙㄨㄛˇ ㄒㄧㄥˋ)
directly; to go all the way;
might as well

五畫

【紮】 4304
1. (紮) ㅂㄚ jar zhá
1. to bind, tie or fasten; to
make a bundle; a bundle
2. to stop; to station; to post

紮裹 (ㅂㄚˊ ㄍㄨㄛˇ)
to mend and tidy up (clothing); to bandage (a wound,
etc.); to pack up (belongings, etc.)

紮寨 (ㅂㄚˊ ㅂㄞˋ)
to establish barracks; to
make camps; to station soldiers

紮營 (ㅂㄚˊ ㄧㄥˊ)
to bivouac; to pitch tents; to
station troops; to encamp

【紮】 4304
2. (紮) ㄗㄚ tza zā
to bind; to tie; to fasten: 她
紮起她的頭髮。She binds her
hair up.

紮帶子 (ㄗㄚ ㄉㄞˋ ˙ㄗ)
to bind with a ribbon; to tie
a string; to tighten the girdle

紮好 (ㄗㄚ ㄏㄠˇ)

to tie up; to bind together:
她用繃帶紮好他的傷。She
bound his wound with a
bandage.

紮緊 (ㄗㄚ ㄐㄧㄣˇ)
to tighten; to fasten securely

紮綵樓 (ㄗㄚ ㄘㄞˇ ㄌㄡˊ)
to pitch up a festooned platform—for a show, exhibi-
tion, contest, etc.

【絇】 4305
ㄑㄩ chyu qú
ornaments for the frontal
part of shoes

【紫】 4306
ㄗˇ tzyy zǐ
1. purple; violet:紫色是高貴的顏
色。Purple is a noble color.
2. a Chinese family name

紫茉莉 (ㄗˇ ㄇㄛˋ ㄌㄧˋ)
(botany) a false jalap; a
four-o'clock

紫丁香花 (ㄗˇ ㄉㄧㄥ ㄒㄧㄤ ㄏㄨㄚ)
a lilac

紫檀 (ㄗˇ ㄊㄢˊ)
(botany) red sandalwood

紫藤 (ㄗˇ ㄊㄥˊ)
(botany) a wistaria, or a
wisteria

紫銅 (ㄗˇ ㄊㄨㄥˊ)
red copper

紫羅蘭 (ㄗˇ ㄌㄨㄛˊ ㄌㄢˊ)
(botany) the violet; the
stock

紫毫 (ㄗˇ ㄏㄠˊ)
a fine writing brush made of
rabbit's hair

紫紅 (ㄗˇ ㄏㄨㄥˊ)
dark red, almost purplish: 我
有一套紫紅色的衣服。I have a
dark red suit.

紫金牛 (ㄗˇ ㄐㄧㄣ ㄋㄧㄡˊ)
(botany) Ardisia japonica;
Japanese ardisia

紫金山 (ㄗˇ ㄐㄧㄣ ㄕㄢ)
name of a hill outside Nanking City

紫禁城 (ㄗˇ ㄐㄧㄣˋ ㄔㄥˊ)
the Forbidden City in Pe-
king with four gates and a
circumference of approxi-
mately four kilometers

紫荊 (ㄗˇ ㄐㄧㄥ)
(botany) Cercis chinensis;
Chinese redbud

紫晶 (ㄗˇ ㄐㄧㄥ) or 紫水晶 (ㄗˇ ㄕㄨㄟˇ
ㄐㄧㄥ)

amethyst: 紫水晶被用來做珠
寶。Amethyst is used for
jewelry.

紫景天 (ㄗˇ ㄐㄧㄥˇ ㄊㄧㄢ)
(botany) live-forever; or-
pine

紫菊 (ㄗˇ ㄐㄩˊ)
China aster

紫闥 (ㄗˇ ㄊㄚˋ)
①elaborate security precautions in an imperial palace
②the abode of immortals

紫虛 (ㄗˇ ㄒㄩ)
the sky; the firmament

紫杉 (ㄗˇ ㄕㄢ)
(botany) yew tree

紫菜 (ㄗˇ ㄘㄞˋ)
(botany) laver

翠翠玉 (ㄗˇ ㄘㄨㄟˋ ㄩˋ)
alexandrite

紫色 (ㄗˇ ㄙㄜˋ)
purple; violet: 他氣得臉色發
紫。His face becomes purple
with rage.

紫衣 (ㄗˇ)
①(botany) purple moss ②
the imperial purple ③ a purple Buddhist gown presented
by the emperor to an accomplished monk ④ official
dress of high officials in
ancient times

紫藥水 (ㄗˇ ㄧㄠˋ ㄕㄨㄟˇ)
gentian violet solution

紫陽花 (ㄗˇ ㄧㄤˊ ㄏㄨㄚ)
(botany) hydrangea

紫陽書院 (ㄗˇ ㄧㄤˊ ㄕㄨ ㄩㄢˋ)
(originally) name of a
study on a hill in Anhwei
built by Chu Sung (朱松)of
the Sung Dynasty, whose
famous son, Chu Hsi (朱熹),
also studied there

紫外線 (ㄗˇ ㄨㄞˋ ㄒㄧㄢˋ)
ultraviolet rays

紫菀 (ㄗˇ ㄨㄢˇ)
(botany) aster

紫雲英 (ㄗˇ ㄩㄣˊ ㄧㄥ)
Astragalus sinicus, a grassy
plant with purple flowers
which are plowed into the
earth as fertilizer

【累】 4307
1. ㄌㄟˇ leii lěi
1. to accumulate through a
length of time
2. to pile up

〔糸
部〕

〔糸部〕

3. to repeat; repeatedly; successively

累犯(ㄌㄟˊ ㄈㄢˋ)
①to offend or violate the law repeatedly; recidivism ② a repeated lawbreaker; a recidivist

累代(ㄌㄟˊ ㄉㄞˋ)
generation after generation; many generations

累牘連篇(ㄌㄟˊ ㄉㄨˊ ㄌㄧㄢˊ ㄆㄧㄢ)
(said of writings) long and tiresome; redundant; verbose

累年(ㄌㄟˊ ㄋㄧㄢˊ)
in consecutive years; year after year 亦作「累歲」

累累(ㄌㄟˊ ㄌㄟˊ)
①repeatedly; successively; consecutively ②piling up ③ innumerable; countless

累卵(ㄌㄟˊ ㄌㄨㄢˇ)
(literally) like a pile of eggs —a very dangerous or precarious situation

累卵之危(ㄌㄟˊ ㄌㄨㄢˇ ㄓ ㄨㄟ)
great, imminent danger

累積(ㄌㄟˊ ㄐㄧ)
accumulation; to accumulate; to pile up

累計(ㄌㄟˊ ㄐㄧˋ)
to include previous figures in the calculation

累加(ㄌㄟˊ ㄐㄧㄚ)
to keep multiplying; to increase; to accumulate

累減(ㄌㄟˊ ㄐㄧㄢˇ)
(law) gradual commutation of sentences

累減稅(ㄌㄟˊ ㄐㄧㄢˇ ㄕㄨㄟˋ)
regressive taxation

累進稅(ㄌㄟˊ ㄐㄧㄣˋ ㄕㄨㄟˋ)
progressive taxation

累遷(ㄌㄟˊ ㄑㄧㄢ)
successive promotion in official position

累行犯(ㄌㄟˊ ㄒㄧㄥˊ ㄈㄢˋ)
a repeated offender (of law); a criminal who has committed offenses many times; a recidivist

累戰(ㄌㄟˊ ㄓㄢˋ)
successive battles; one battle after another

累月(ㄌㄟˊ ㄩㄝˋ)
repeatedly; for a long time

累世(ㄌㄟˊ ㄕˋ)
for successive generations

累日(ㄌㄟˊ ㄖˋ)
for a number of days in succession

累增(ㄌㄟˊ ㄗㄥ)
to increase progressively

累次(ㄌㄟˊ ㄘˋ)
repeatedly; many times: 他累次的努力終於獲得成功. His repeated efforts at last won success.

累月經年(ㄌㄟˊ ㄩㄝˋ ㄐㄧㄥ ㄋㄧㄢˊ)
for months and years; for a long time

【累】 4307
2. ㄌㄟˇ ley lěi

1. to involve; involvement; to implicate
2. to owe; to be in debt
3. tired; weary; fatigue
4. (said of eyes) to strain
5. a family burden

累病了(ㄌㄟˊ ㄅㄧㄥˋ ˙ㄌㄜ)or 累倒了(ㄌㄟˊ ㄉㄠˇ ˙ㄌㄜ)
to become sick owing to hard work

累得慌(ㄌㄟˊ ˙ㄉㄜ ˙ㄏㄨㄤ)
very tired

累了(ㄌㄟˊ ˙ㄌㄜ)
tired: 我累了. I was tired.

累活兒(ㄌㄟˊ ㄏㄨㄛˊ ㄦ)
a backbreaking job; hard work; toil

累壞了(ㄌㄟˊ ㄏㄨㄞˋ ˙ㄌㄜ)
to become ill as a result of backbreaking toil; to be tired out: 你累壞了。You are tired out.

累及他人(ㄌㄟˊ ㄐㄧˊ ㄊㄚ ㄖㄣˊ)
to involve or implicate others

累及無辜(ㄌㄟˊ ㄐㄧˊ ㄨˊ ㄍㄨ)
to involve the innocent

累極了(ㄌㄟˊ ㄐㄧˊ ˙ㄌㄜ)
dog-tired; dead tired: 我們累極了。We were dog-tired.

累心(ㄌㄟˊ ㄒㄧㄣ)
to toil one's mind; to cudgel one's brains

累事(ㄌㄟˊ ㄕˋ)
dependents and property

累事(ㄌㄟˊ ㄕˋ)
drudgery; toil

累人(ㄌㄟˊ ㄖㄣˊ)
to make another tired; to wear down; to be tiring

累坐(ㄌㄟˊ ㄗㄨㄛˋ)
to become involved in a crime and suffer the consequences

累死(ㄌㄟˊ ㄙˇ)
very tired

【累】 4307
3. ㄌㄟˋ lei lèi

1. a nuisance
2. to fasten; to bind

累贅(ㄌㄟˋ ˙ㄓㄨㄟ)
①a nuisance; a burden; a troublesome thing ②wordy; verbose: 這個句子太累贅. This sentence is too wordy.

【紬】 4308
1.(綢) ㄔㄡˊ chóu

a kind of silk fabric

【紬】 4308
2. ㄔㄡ chou chōu

1. to draw out
2. to collect and edit

紬次(ㄔㄡ ㄘˋ)
to collect and arrange in order

紬繹(ㄔㄡ ㄧˋ)
to explain

【細】 4309
ㄒㄧˋ shih xì

1. tiny; small; little
2. thin; slender; tall but lean; slim
3. fine
4. petty; trifling; detailed
5. precise; exquisite; delicate (workmanship, etc.)

細胞(ㄒㄧˋ ㄅㄠ)
a cell

細胞膜(ㄒㄧˋ ㄅㄠ ㄇㄛˊ)
the cell membrane

細胞分裂(ㄒㄧˋ ㄅㄠ ㄈㄣ ㄌㄧㄝˋ)
cell division

細胞體(ㄒㄧˋ ㄅㄠ ㄊㄧˇ)
the cell body

細胞核(ㄒㄧˋ ㄅㄠ ㄏㄜˊ)
the cell nucleus

細胞學(ㄒㄧˋ ㄅㄠ ㄒㄩㄝˊ)
cytology

細胞質(ㄒㄧˋ ㄅㄠ ㄓˊ)
cellularity; cytoplasm

細胞組織(ㄒㄧˋ ㄅㄠ ㄗㄨˇ ㄓ)
cellular tissue

細胞液(ㄒㄧˋ ㄅㄠ ㄧㄝˋ)
cell sap

細布(ㄒㄧˋ ㄅㄨˋ)
fine cloth

細部(ㄒㄧㄅㄨ)
details (of a drawing); minute parts

細密(ㄒㄧㄇㄧ)
①(said of materials) fine and delicate ②careful; cautious; circumspect

細民(ㄒㄧㄇㄧㄣ)
commoners; the people; the masses

細目(ㄒㄧㄇㄨ)
detailed items

細大不捐(ㄒㄧㄉㄚㄅㄨㄐㄩㄢ)
not to cast away anything, big or small

細讀(ㄒㄧㄉㄨ)
to read carefully: 我們細讀這本書。We read this book carefully.

細談(ㄒㄧㄊㄢ)
to talk in detail; to go into every minute point in a conversation: 沒有時間細談。There isn't time to talk in detail.

細條條的(ㄒㄧㄊㄧㄠㄊㄧㄠ˙ㄉㄜ)or
細挑(ㄒㄧㄊㄧㄠ)
(said of one's figure) slender; willowy

細嫩(ㄒㄧㄋㄣ)
(said of the skin) fair and tender; delicate

細膩(ㄒㄧㄋㄧ)
①fine and delicate (in writings, dramas and movie directing) to take care of even the smallest points; not to overlook any details: 這本小說描寫細膩。This novel has a minute description.

細流(ㄒㄧㄌㄧㄡ)
①a small creek ②(said of water) to trickle

細路(ㄒㄧㄌㄨ)
a narrow path

細論(ㄒㄧㄌㄨㄣ)
to discuss in detail; to elaborate

細縷(ㄒㄧㄌㄩ)
a very fine thread or strand

細高挑兒(ㄒㄧㄍㄠㄊㄧㄠㄦ)
a tall person with a slender figure

細故(ㄒㄧㄍㄨ)
trifling matter or cause (which leads to a dispute, etc.)

細工(ㄒㄧㄍㄨㄥ)
fine and delicate work; fine and delicate craftsmanship

細看(ㄒㄧㄎㄢ)
to look at carefully; to examine in detail: 你必須細看一切事實。You must look at all the facts in detail.

細活(ㄒㄧㄏㄨㄛ)
fine and delicate work

細節(ㄒㄧㄐㄧㄝ)
minor points; trifles; detail

細究(ㄒㄧㄐㄧㄡ)
to examine or study into all details

細謹(ㄒㄧㄐㄧㄣ)
to be overcautious about small points in etiquette

細講(ㄒㄧㄐㄧㄤ)
to state in detail

細君(ㄒㄧㄐㄩㄣ)
one's wife

細菌(ㄒㄧㄐㄩㄣ)
bacteria; germs

細菌學(ㄒㄧㄐㄩㄣㄒㄩㄝ)
bacteriology

細菌戰(ㄒㄧㄐㄩㄣㄓㄢ)
bacteriological warfare

細巧(ㄒㄧㄑㄧㄠ)
fine and delicate (work, etc.); delicate and ingenious (articles)

細情(ㄒㄧㄑㄧㄥ)
details of a matter

細細(ㄒㄧㄒㄧ)
①very low (voice) ②very light ③very fine or thin ④fine and delicate

細小(ㄒㄧㄒㄧㄠ)
tiny; little; thin; petty

細心(ㄒㄧㄒㄧㄣ)
careful; attentive; cautious; circumspective; to think of all aspects of something: 他細心從事工作。He is careful at his work.

細想(ㄒㄧㄒㄧㄤ)
to think over carefully; to give careful thought to; to ponder

細行(ㄒㄧㄒㄧㄥ)
one's behavior in trivial matters

細枝(ㄒㄧㄓ)
a slender twig; twiggery

細枝末節(ㄒㄧㄓㄇㄛㄐㄧㄝ)
minor details; nonessentials

細緻(ㄒㄧㄓ)
①fine and delicate; exquisite ②careful and thorough; meticulous; painstaking:她設想細緻周到。She thought it out carefully and thoroughly.

細針密縷(ㄒㄧㄓㄣㄇㄧㄌㄩ)
delicate and fine needlework

細賬(ㄒㄧㄓㄤ)
a detailed account

細究(ㄒㄧㄓㄡ)
to investigate thoroughly

細察(ㄒㄧㄔㄚ)
to observe carefully or in detail; to examine thoroughly

細長(ㄒㄧㄔㄤ)
slender; thin and long

細事(ㄒㄧㄕ)
trifling matters; trifles; matters of little significance

細沙(ㄒㄧㄕㄚ)
fine sand

細紗(ㄒㄧㄕㄚ)
(textile) spun yarn

細聲(ㄒㄧㄕㄥ)
a very low voice

細聲細氣(ㄒㄧㄕㄥㄒㄧㄑㄧ)
in a soft voice; soft-spoken

細說(ㄒㄧㄕㄨㄛ)or 細述(ㄒㄧㄕㄨ)
①to give a detailed account; to state in detail ②a one-sided story from a mean fellow

細水長流(ㄒㄧㄕㄨㄟㄔㄤㄌㄧㄡ)
(literally) Water flowing out in a trickle takes a long time to exhaust.— ①One will not go broke if he is frugal. ②One will finally prevail if he persists.

細人(ㄒㄧㄖㄣ)
①a person of narrow vision ②a person of low social standing ③a concubine

細弱(ㄒㄧㄖㄨㄛ)
①(said of physique) slender and weak ②(said of voice) low and weak: 她的聲音細弱無力。She has a low and weak voice.

細軟(ㄒㄧㄖㄨㄢ)
fine clothes and jewels (of a woman); valuables

細字(ㄒㄧㄗ)

fine print; characters of very small size

細則(ㄒㄧˋ ㄗˊ)
bylaws

細作(ㄒㄧˋ ㄗㄨㄛˋ)
(military) spies; agents; underground workers

細瓷(ㄒㄧˋ ㄘˊ)
fine porcelain

細草(ㄒㄧˋ ㄘㄠˇ)
silky grass; fine grass

細絲(ㄒㄧˋ ㄙ)
a fine thread

細瑣(ㄒㄧˋ ㄙㄨㄛˇ)or 細碎(ㄒㄧˋ ㄙㄨㄟˋ)
petty; trifles

細兒(ㄒㄧˋ ㄦˊ)
a young son

細腰(ㄒㄧˋ ㄧㄠ)
①a slender waist ②a slim-waisted wasp

細微(ㄒㄧˋ ㄨㄟˊ)
tiny; minute

細味(ㄒㄧˋ ㄨㄟˋ)
to reflect, think over, or study carefully

細問(ㄒㄧˋ ㄨㄣˋ)
to question in detail

細雨(ㄒㄧˋ ㄩˇ)
a misty rain; drizzle

細語(ㄒㄧˋ ㄩˇ)
low and tender talk; pillow talk

【紱】 4310 ㄈㄨˊ fwu fú
1. ribbons, strands, or sashes
2. ceremonial dress worn during sacrificial rituals

紱冕(ㄈㄨˊ ㄇㄧㄢˋ)
a high-ranking official

【紳】 4311 ㄕㄣ shan shēn
1. the middle class as a group or individuals; the gentry; a gentleman
2. a sash; a girdle
3. to tie

紳董(ㄕㄣ ㄉㄨㄥˇ)
the local gentry

紳宦(ㄕㄣ ㄏㄨㄢˋ)
retired government officials

紳士(ㄕㄣ ㄕˋ)
a gentleman; an esquire

紳士協定(ㄕㄣ ㄕˋ ㄒㄧㄝˊ ㄉㄧㄥˋ)
a gentlemen's agreement

紳商(ㄕㄣ ㄕㄤ)
the gentry and merchant class

【紹】 4312 ㄕㄠˋ shaw shào
1. to bring together; to connect or join
2. to hand down; to continue

紹介(ㄕㄠˋ ㄐㄧㄝˋ)
to serve as a medium or go-between; to introduce; to recommend

紹興(ㄕㄠˋ ㄒㄧㄥ)
Shaohsing in Chekiang, famous for its Shaohsing wine

紹興酒(ㄕㄠˋ ㄒㄧㄥ ㄐㄧㄡˇ)or 紹酒(ㄕㄠˋ ㄐㄧㄡˇ)
the Shaohsing wine, a mild rice brew of a golden yellow color

紹述(ㄕㄠˋ ㄕㄨˋ)
to continue; to follow

【紼】 4313 ㄈㄨˊ fwu fú
1. a large rope
2. the cord or rope attached to a bier or coffin

【紾】 4314 ㄓㄣˇ jeen zhěn
1. turns or twists; to turn or twist
2. to switch

紾臂(ㄓㄣˇ ㄅㄧˋ)
to twist the arm

【紬】 4315 ㄔㄨ chuh chū
1. to sew
2. to bend
3. to degrade
4. deficient; wanting; insufficient; inadequate
5. red; a deep red color

【紵】 4315 ㄓㄨˋ juh zhù
boehmeria; ramie; linen; sackcloth

【紺】 4317 ㄍㄢˋ gann gàn
a reddish dark color; a deep purple color

紺坊(ㄍㄢˋ ㄈㄤ)or 紺園(ㄍㄢˋ ㄩㄢˊ)
or 紺宇(ㄍㄢˋ ㄩˇ)or 紺殿(ㄍㄢˋ ㄉㄧㄢˋ)
a Buddhist monastery

【絃】 4318 ㄒㄧㄢˊ shyan xián
1. the string of a musical instrument; a cord. 她把小提琴的絃控緊。She tightened the strings of her violin.
2. first and last quarters of the

moon

絃馬(ㄒㄧㄢˊ ㄇㄚˇ)
the bridge of a violin

絃歌不輟(ㄒㄧㄢˊ ㄍㄜ ㄅㄨˋ ㄔㄨㄛˋ)
(literally) The sound of music and singing never ends.—Reading and studying are not interrupted even in times of distress.

絃子(ㄒㄧㄢˊ ˙ㄗ)
a kind of three-stringed musical instrument

絃索(ㄒㄧㄢˊ ㄙㄨㄛˇ)
stringed instruments

絃誦(ㄒㄧㄢˊ ㄙㄨㄥˋ)
the music and sound of reading

絃外之音(ㄒㄧㄢˊ ㄨㄞˋ ㄓ ㄧㄣ)
(literally) sound outside what the string is making—overtones; connotations; suggestion; implied meaning

絃樂(ㄒㄧㄢˊ ㄩㄝˋ)
string music

絃樂隊(ㄒㄧㄢˊ ㄩㄝˋ ㄉㄨㄟˋ)
a string band

絃樂器(ㄒㄧㄢˊ ㄩㄝˋ ㄑㄧˋ)
stringed instruments

【終】 4319 ㄓㄨㄥ jong zhōng
1. the end; to come to the end; the conclusion
2. death; to die or pass away
3. finally; at last; in the end; after all; in the long run
4. whole; all; entire

終篇(ㄓㄨㄥ ㄆㄧㄢ)
to complete writing or finish reading an article

終點(ㄓㄨㄥ ㄉㄧㄢˇ)
①the terminus; the final point; the end; a destination
②(sports)finish

終端(ㄓㄨㄥ ㄉㄨㄢ)
(electricity) a terminal

終端機(ㄓㄨㄥ ㄉㄨㄢ ㄐㄧ)
a teletype machine or similar device for remote input or output of data, as in time-sharing; a terminal

終身(ㄓㄨㄥ ㄕㄣ)
forever: 他抱恨終天。He regrets forever.

終天年(ㄓㄨㄥ ㄊㄧㄢ ㄋㄧㄢˊ)
to live up one's allotted life span

終南捷徑(ㄓㄨㄥ ㄋㄢˊ ㄐㄧㄝˊ ㄐㄧㄥˋ)

a short cut or snap course to officialdom (usually with an implication of sarcasm)

終南山 (ㄓㄨㄥ ㄋㄢˊ ㄕㄢ)
name of a mountain in Shensi Province

終年 (ㄓㄨㄥ ㄋㄧㄢˊ)
①the whole year; throughout the year ②the age at which one dies: 他終年八十歲。He died at the age of eighty.

終老 (ㄓㄨㄥ ㄌㄠˇ)
throughout one's life; until death

終了 (ㄓㄨㄥ ㄌㄧㄠˇ)
to end; to complete; to conclude; to terminate: 我們的交往到此終了。Our intercourse is at an end.

終古 (ㄓㄨㄥ ㄍㄨˇ)
①for a long time; forever ②in ancient times; through all antiquity

終歸 (ㄓㄨㄥ ㄍㄨㄟ)
①the conclusion; to end or conclude ②finally; after all; at last: 她終歸是個孩子。After all she is still a child.

終極 (ㄓㄨㄥ ㄐㄧˊ)
the finality or end

終結 (ㄓㄨㄥ ㄐㄧㄝˊ)
the end, conclusion, termination, etc.: 這件事得到很好的終結。The affair was brought to a happy termination.

終久 (ㄓㄨㄥ ㄐㄧㄡˇ)or終究 (ㄓㄨㄥ ㄐㄧㄡˋ)
after all; in the end; in the long run: 你終究會成功的。In the end you'll succeed.

終竟 (ㄓㄨㄥ ㄐㄧㄥˋ)
①finally; after all; in the end; in the long run ②to end; to come to an end

終局 (ㄓㄨㄥ ㄐㄩˊ)
①(said of a gambling session, chess game, etc.) the conclusion, end, etc. ②(said of a game, contest, etc.) the result, outcome, etc.

終其一生 (ㄓㄨㄥ ㄑㄧˊ ㄧ ㄕㄥ)
throughout one's life

終獻 (ㄓㄨㄥ ㄒㄧㄢˋ)
the third wine offering in a sacrificial ceremony

終須 (ㄓㄨㄥ ㄒㄩ)

to have to...in the end; unavoidable in the long run 或 There is no escaping of it sooner or later.人終須歸土。Man has to go the way of all the earth in the end.

終止 (ㄓㄨㄥ ㄓˇ)
to come to an end or close; to stop; to end: 罷工終止了。The strike is at an end.

終止符 (ㄓㄨㄥ ㄓˇ ㄈㄨˊ)
a full stop; a period

終制 (ㄓㄨㄥ ㄓˋ)
to complete the three-year mourning for one's parents

終朝 (ㄓㄨㄥ ㄓㄠ)
①the whole morning ②the whole day; throughout the day

終站 (ㄓㄨㄥ ㄓㄢˋ)
the terminal stop or station: 我們在終站下車。We got off at the terminal stop.

終場 (ㄓㄨㄥ ㄔㄤˇ)or(ㄓㄨㄥ ㄔㄤˋ)
①the conclusion of any matter; the end of a show, game, etc. ②the last test under the former civil service examination system

終食 (ㄓㄨㄥ ㄕˊ)
the duration of a meal

終始 (ㄓㄨㄥ ㄕˇ)
from beginning to end

終身 (ㄓㄨㄥ ㄕㄣ)
the whole life:我預料將在此地居留終身。I expect to live here all my life.

終身伴侶 (ㄓㄨㄥ ㄕㄣ ㄅㄢˋ ㄌㄩˇ)
a life company—wife or husband

終身不忘 (ㄓㄨㄥ ㄕㄣ ㄅㄨˋ ㄨㄤˋ)
to keep in memory throughout one's life span

終身大事 (ㄓㄨㄥ ㄕㄣ ㄉㄚˋ ㄕˋ)
a great event affecting one's whole life (especially referring to one's marriage): 婚姻乃終身大事。Marriage is an important event in one's life.

終身職 (ㄓㄨㄥ ㄕㄣ ㄓˊ)
an office for life; a lifetime job

終身事業 (ㄓㄨㄥ ㄕㄣ ㄕˋ ㄧㄝˋ)
a lifelong career; a career, endeavor, undertaking, etc. to which one dedicates his whole life: 我以教書爲終身事

業。I take teaching as my life career.

終審 (ㄓㄨㄥ ㄕㄣˇ)
(law) the third, or final trial (which concludes a case once for all)

終審法庭 (ㄓㄨㄥ ㄕㄣˇ ㄈㄚˊ ㄊㄧㄥˊ)
a court of the last resort

終生 (ㄓㄨㄥ ㄕㄥ)
the whole life; throughout one's life: 他終生都住在倫敦。He has lived in London all his life.

終日 (ㄓㄨㄥ ㄖˋ)
from morning till night; throughout the day

終夜 (ㄓㄨㄥ ㄧㄝˋ)
throughout the night; the whole night through: 我們終夜看守了。We watched all night (long).

終養 (ㄓㄨㄥ ㄧㄤˇ)
to resign from one's office to care for one's parents at home

終於 (ㄓㄨㄥ ㄩˊ)
in the end; finally; at last

終譽 (ㄓㄨㄥ ㄩˋ)
an everlasting name; immortality; a long-lasting fame

【組】 ㄗㄨ tzuu zǔ
1. a group; a team; a section; a department; an organization; a union: 每三個人組成一組。Every three persons constitute a group.
2. to organize; to arrange; to unite; to form: 他們組織新的政黨。They organized a new political party.
3. tassels; a fringe; a girdle; a tape

組閣 (ㄗㄨ ㄍㄜˊ)
(government) to form a cabinet

組合 (ㄗㄨ ㄏㄜˊ)
①(mathematics) combinations ②to unite; to make up; to form a partnership ③a company; a corporation; a union

組曲 (ㄗㄨ ㄑㄩˇ)
(music) a suite

組訓 (ㄗㄨ ㄒㄩㄣˋ)
to organize and train (militia units or local self-defense units)

〔糸 部〕

組織（ㄗㄨ ㄓ）
①to organize; to form; to constitute; to found: 那篇小說組織得很好。That novel is well-organized. ②an organization; a formation: 沒有組織的軍隊是無用的。An army without organization would be useless. ③(biology) tissue; texture

組織法（ㄗㄨ ㄓ ㄈㄚ）
organic law

組織化（ㄗㄨ ㄓ ㄏㄨㄚˋ）
to systematize; systematization; organized

組織學（ㄗㄨ ㄓ ㄒㄩㄝˊ）
histology

組長（ㄗㄨ ㄓㄤˇ）
the chief of a department or section in a government agency

組成（ㄗㄨ ㄔㄥˊ）
to form; to compose; to constitute

【絆】 4321
ㄅㄢˋ bann bàn
1. shackles; fetters
2. to stumble; to trip over; to trip: 她被樹根絆了一下。She stumbled over the root of a tree.

絆倒（ㄅㄢˋ ㄉㄠˇ）
to trip over; to trip: 這塊鬆弛的木板把他絆倒。The loose board tripped him.

絆腳（ㄅㄢˋ ㄐㄧㄠ）
fettered; hindered

絆腳石（ㄅㄢˋ ㄐㄧㄠ ㄕˊ）
a stumbling block

絆住（ㄅㄢˋ ㄓㄨˋ）
to be detained, hindered or held back; to be bogged down

絆創膏（ㄅㄢˋ ㄔㄨㄤˋ ㄍㄠ）
an adhesive tape

【綱】 4322
ㄐㄩㄥˇ jeong jiǒng
an overall with no lining; a dust coat

【紽】 4323
ㄊㄨㄛˊ two tuó
a strand of silk; braiding

【紩】 4324
ㄓˋ jyh zhì
to sew

【絁】 4325
ㄕ shy shī
a kind of coarse silk fabric

六畫

【結】 4326
1. ㄐㄧㄝˊ jye jié
1. to tie; to knot; to weave: 那條絲帶沒結好。That ribbon doesn't tie well.
2. a knot: 他在繩上打了一個結。He tied a knot in a rope.
3. to unite; to join; to connect
4. to congeal; coagulation: 水結成冰。Water congeals into ice.
5. to form; to found; to constitute
6. to bear fruit; a result; an outcome: 你的研究會有結果。Your study will bear fruit.
7. to pay; to settle (as an account, etc.)
8. a node: 淋巴結 a lymph node

結疤（ㄐㄧㄝˊ ㄅㄚ）
to heal up; to scar; to form a scab: 她的傷口結疤情形良好。Her wound is scarring well.

結拜（ㄐㄧㄝˊ ㄅㄞˋ）
sworn (brothers, or sisters); to pledge in a sworn brotherhood: 他們是結拜兄弟。They were sworn brothers.

結伴（ㄐㄧㄝˊ ㄅㄢˋ）
to accompany; (to tour, play, take a trip, etc.) together, or in a group: 我們結伴而行。We went in a group.

結冰（ㄐㄧㄝˊ ㄅㄧㄥ）
to freeze; to form ice; to turn to ice

結不解仇（ㄐㄧㄝˊ ㄅㄨˋ ㄐㄧㄝˇ ㄔㄡˊ）
to become a sworn enemy of

結不解緣（ㄐㄧㄝˊ ㄅㄨˋ ㄐㄧㄝˇ ㄩㄢˊ）
(said of marriage, love, close association, etc.) to be united by an ironclad bond

結膜（ㄐㄧㄝˊ ㄇㄛˊ）or **結合膜**（ㄐㄧㄝˊ ㄇㄛˊ）
conjunctiva

結膜炎（ㄐㄧㄝˊ ㄇㄛˊ ㄧㄢˊ）
conjunctivitis

結茅（ㄐㄧㄝˊ ㄇㄠˊ）
to build a cottage

結盟（ㄐㄧㄝˊ ㄇㄥˊ）
to form an alliance; to ally with; to enter into an alliance; alignment

結髮（ㄐㄧㄝˊ ㄈㄚˇ）
to knot the hair upon reaching adulthood in former times

結髮夫妻（ㄐㄧㄝˊ ㄈㄚˇ ㄈㄨ ㄑㄧ）
a legally married couple—the first marriage for both husband and wife

結黨營私（ㄐㄧㄝˊ ㄉㄤˇ ㄧㄥˊ ㄙ）
to gang together for clandestine and illegal activities; to form a clique to pursue selfish interests

結隊成羣（ㄐㄧㄝˊ ㄉㄨㄟˋ ㄔㄥˊ ㄑㄩㄣˊ）
in groups and droves

結同心（ㄐㄧㄝˊ ㄊㄨㄥˊ ㄒㄧㄣ）
to be of one mind

結褵（ㄐㄧㄝˊ ㄌㄧˊ）
to be married

結廬（ㄐㄧㄝˊ ㄌㄨˊ）
①to build a house (or hut)
②(figuratively) retirement

結論（ㄐㄧㄝˊ ㄌㄨㄣˋ）
the conclusion (of a meeting, argument, etc.): 不要忙於下結論。Don't jump to conclusions.

結構（ㄐㄧㄝˊ ㄍㄡˋ）
①structure; structural ②(said of a piece of writing) the arrangement of ideas; presentation; composition: 這篇文章的結構很好。The composition of this article is very good.

結果（ㄐㄧㄝˊ ㄍㄨㄛˇ）
①(said of plants) to bear fruit ②the result, outcome or consequence ③in the end; finally

結合（ㄐㄧㄝˊ ㄏㄜˊ）
①to get united; to combine with; to form an alliance; to associate ②to get married; to marry

結合線（ㄐㄧㄝˊ ㄏㄜˊ ㄒㄧㄢˋ）
(said of a music score) a tie

結核（ㄐㄧㄝˊ ㄏㄜˊ）
(pothology) tubercle

結核病（ㄐㄧㄝˊ ㄏㄜˊ ㄅㄧㄥˋ）
tuberculosis

結核病院（ㄐㄧㄝˊ ㄏㄜˊ ㄅㄧㄥˋ ㄩㄢˋ）
a T.B. hospital

結核防治中心（ㄐㄧㄝˊ ㄏㄜˊ ㄈㄤˊ ㄓˋ ㄓㄨㄥ ㄒㄧㄣ）
a T.B. prevention and treatment center

結核菌（ㄐㄧㄝˊ ㄏㄜˊ ㄐㄩㄣˋ）

tubercle bacilli

結核性的(ㄐㄧㄝˊㄏㄜˊㄒㄧㄥˋ·ㄉㄜ)
tuberculated

結好(ㄐㄧㄝˊㄏㄠˇ)
to befriend; to be intimate with; to collaborate with; to win favor from

結夥(ㄐㄧㄝˊㄏㄨㄛˇ)
to form a band; to gang up; to band together; to collude: 他們結夥抗議。They banded together to protest.

結匯(ㄐㄧㄝˊㄏㄨㄟˋ)
to sell foreign exchange to (or to buy it from) banks; foreign exchange settlement

結歡(ㄐㄧㄝˊㄏㄨㄢ)
to please; to win favor; to associate with another in order to win his or her heart; to have a lover

結婚(ㄐㄧㄝˊㄏㄨㄣ)
marriage; to get married

結婚證書(ㄐㄧㄝˊㄏㄨㄣ ㄓㄥˋㄕㄨ)
a marriage certificate

結集(ㄐㄧㄝˊㄐㄧˊ)
to concentrate (troops, etc.); concentration (of troops, etc.)

結交(ㄐㄧㄝˊㄐㄧㄠ)
to associate with; to befriend; to make friends with

結晶(ㄐㄧㄝˊㄐㄧㄥ)
to crystallize; crystallization; crystal

結晶體(ㄐㄧㄝˊㄐㄧㄥ ㄊㄧˇ)
a crystal; a crystalloid

結晶學(ㄐㄧㄝˊㄐㄧㄥ ㄒㄩㄝˊ)
crystallography

結晶岩(ㄐㄧㄝˊㄐㄧㄥ ㄧㄢˊ)
crystalline rocks

結局(ㄐㄧㄝˊㄐㄩˊ)
the outcome; the result; the end (of an incident, story, etc.); the ending: 這故事有一個快樂的結局。The story has a happy ending.

結契(ㄐㄧㄝˊㄑㄧˋ)
to be on very good or intimate terms with

結欠(ㄐㄧㄝˊㄑㄧㄢˋ)
to owe after the settlement of accounts; to remain or continue in debt; the balance due; the debit balance in the red

結親(ㄐㄧㄝˊㄑㄧㄣ)
to strike up a matrimonial relationship; to unite in marriage

結清(ㄐㄧㄝˊㄑㄧㄥ)
to pay up a bill; to settle a debt; to square accounts; all squared: 我們與他結清賬目。We square accounts with him.

結嫌(ㄐㄧㄝˊㄒㄧㄢˊ)
to develop suspicion or animosity (between two or more parties)

結帳 or 結賬(ㄐㄧㄝˊㄓㄤˋ)
to settle accounts; to pay up; to square accounts

結撰(ㄐㄧㄝˊㄓㄨㄢˋ)
to compose or plan writings, reports, etc.

結軼(ㄐㄧㄝˊㄧˋ)
heavy traffic of carriages

結仇 or 結讎(ㄐㄧㄝˊㄔㄡˊ)
to contract ill will or animus of; to incur hostility or enmity of

結腸(ㄐㄧㄝˊㄔㄤˊ)
colons

結石(ㄐㄧㄝˊㄕˊ)
(pathology) stone; calculus

結實(ㄐㄧㄝˊㄕˊ)
to bear fruit: 這棵梨樹結實纍纍。This pear tree bears fruit in clusters.

結識(ㄐㄧㄝˊㄕˋ)
to know or associate with; to strike up an acquaintance with

結舌(ㄐㄧㄝˊㄕㄜˊ)
to be tongue-tied (as a result of stage fright, etc.): 他結舌緘口。He was tongue-tied and mouth-sealed.

結社(ㄐㄧㄝˊㄕㄜˋ)
to form a union, association, etc.

結繩(ㄐㄧㄝˊㄕㄥˊ)or 結繩記事(ㄐㄧㄝˊㄕㄥˊ ㄐㄧˋㄕˋ)
to tie knots on a string or rope for recording before the invention of written language: 古人結繩記事。The ancients kept records by tying knots.

結束(ㄐㄧㄝˊㄕㄨˋ)
to conclude; to end; to wind up: 代表團結束了對日本的訪問。The delegation has concluded its visit to Japan.

結子(ㄐㄧㄝˊ·ㄗ)
a knot on a string or rope

結紮(ㄐㄧㄝˊㄗㄚ)
(medicine) ligation; ligature; to ligature

結綵(ㄐㄧㄝˊㄘㄞˇ)
to festoon; a festoon (for celebration)

結草銜環(ㄐㄧㄝˊㄘㄠˇ ㄒㄧㄢˊㄏㄨㄢˊ)or 結草(ㄐㄧㄝˊㄘㄠˇ)
to repay favors received even after one's death; most sincere thanks and gratitude

結存(ㄐㄧㄝˊㄘㄨㄣˊ)
the credit balance; (said of government finance) foreign exchange reserves

結駟連騎(ㄐㄧㄝˊㄙˋㄌㄧㄢˊㄐㄧˋ)
a carriage drawn by four horses—pomposity

結算(ㄐㄧㄝˊㄙㄨㄢˋ)
statements of accounts; settlement of accounts; to settle accounts

結案(ㄐㄧㄝˊㄢˋ)
to conclude a case

結義兄弟(ㄐㄧㄝˊㄧˋ ㄒㄩㄥ ㄉㄧˋ)
sworn brothers: 我們是結義兄弟。We are sworn brothers.

結業(ㄐㄧㄝˊㄧㄝˋ)
to graduate; to conclude or complete a training course

結業典禮(ㄐㄧㄝˊㄧㄝˋㄉㄧㄢˇㄌㄧˇ)
a commencement (ceremony); a graduation ceremony

結尾(ㄐㄧㄝˊㄨㄟˇ)
the conclusion; the end; the ending; the final part: 他演說的結尾很有力量。His speech has a forceful ending.

結網(ㄐㄧㄝˊㄨㄤˇ)
to make a net

結餘(ㄐㄧㄝˊㄩˊ)
a cash surplus; a surplus

結約(ㄐㄧㄝˊㄩㄝ)
to conclude a treaty, agreement, etc.

結冤(ㄐㄧㄝˊㄩㄢ)
to contract animus, enmity, hatred, ill will, etc.: 他和鄰人結冤。He was at enmity with his neighbors.

結緣(ㄐㄧㄝˊㄩㄢˊ)
to associate on good terms; to form ties of affection;

〔糸部〕

〔糸部〕

(Buddhism) to form a connection, e.g. for future salvation

結怨(ㄐㄧㄝˊㄩㄢˋ)
to arouse ill will or dislike; to incur hatred: 我從不結怨。I never incurred hatred.

【結】 4326
2. ㄐㄧㄝ jie jiē
1. to stutter; to stammer
2. tough; strong; durable
3. to bear (fruit); to form (seed)

結巴(ㄐㄧㄝ·ㄅㄚ)
to stutter; to stammer

結巴頦子(ㄐㄧㄝ·ㄅㄚ ㄎㄜ·ㄗ)
one who stutters

結結巴巴的(ㄐㄧㄝˊㄐㄧㄝˊㄅㄚ ㄅㄚ ㄉㄜ)
stuttering; stammering: 他結結巴巴的道歉。He stuttered an apology.

結實(ㄐㄧㄝ·ㄕ)
①tough; durable; solid; not easily breakable ②strong; sturdy; muscular and healthy

結子(ㄐㄧㄝ ㄗ)or結子兒(ㄐㄧㄝ ㄗㄦ)
(said of plants, especially flowers, etc.) to produce seeds; to bear fruit: 此樹不結子兒。This tree bears no fruit.

【絓】 4327
《ㄍㄨㄚ guah guā
obstructed; hindered

絓礙(《ㄨㄚˋㄞˋ)
an obstacle

絓誤(《ㄨㄚˋㄨˋ)
①to be reprimanded for a certain involvement in the mistakes of someone else ②to get others involved in criminal acts by lying 亦作「詿誤」or「罣誤」

【絕】 4328
1. ㄐㄩㄝ jyue jué
1. to sever; to break off; to cut
2. to renounce; to decline
3. to run out of; exhausted; used up; finished
4. without match; peerless; unparalleled; the utmost
5. isolated; to get out of circulation; to separate
6. to discontinue; to terminate; to stop; to cease
7. without posterity; heirless

8. extremely; utmost; most; absolutely
9. to destroy
10. leaving no leeway; making no allowance; uncompromising
11. a poem of four lines

絕版(ㄐㄩㄝˊㄅㄢˇ)
out-of-print (books): 這本書絕版了。This book was out-of-print.

絕筆(ㄐㄩㄝˊㄅㄧˇ)
①one's last writing (before death) ②to discontinue writing

絕壁(ㄐㄩㄝˊㄅㄧˋ)
cliffs: 他由絕壁墜崖而死。He died in a fall from a cliff.

絕不(ㄐㄩㄝˊㄅㄨˋ)
never: 她絕不出去。She never goes out.

絕塵(ㄐㄩㄝˊㄔㄣˊ)
①(said of horses) fast ②(said of a person) elegant or stately in a casual manner

絕品(ㄐㄩㄝˊㄆㄧㄣˇ)
second-to-none commodities; goods of the highest quality or value; an exquisite article

絕妙(ㄐㄩㄝˊㄇㄧㄠˋ)
extremely good or wonderful; exquisite

絕妙好辭(ㄐㄩㄝˊㄇㄧㄠˋㄏㄠˇㄘˊ)
quotable quotes; the last say in (wisecracks, quotes, etc.)

絕妙好詞(ㄐㄩㄝˊㄇㄧㄠˋㄏㄠˇㄘˊ)
an anthology edited by Chou Mi (周密) of the Sung Dynasty containing verses and lyrics of 132 contemporary scholars

絕命(ㄐㄩㄝˊㄇㄧㄥˋ)
to die; death

絕命書(ㄐㄩㄝˊㄇㄧㄥˋㄕㄨ)
one's last writing (before death); a suicide note: 他把絕命書留在桌子上。He left a suicide note on the table.

絕命詞(ㄐㄩㄝˊㄇㄧㄥˋㄘˊ)
a poem one writes just before anticipated death

絕目(ㄐㄩㄝˊㄇㄨˋ)
as far as one's eyes can reach

絕乏(ㄐㄩㄝˊㄈㄚˊ)

completely empty; absolutely nothing

絕代(ㄐㄩㄝˊㄉㄞˋ)
①matchless, unsurpassed or peerless in one's generation ②in times immemorial

絕代佳人(ㄐㄩㄝˊㄉㄞˋㄐㄧㄚ ㄖㄣˊ)
a matchless beauty; a beauty of beauties: 她是絕代佳人。She is a beauty of beauties.

絕倒(ㄐㄩㄝˊㄉㄠˇ)
①to bring the house down; to split one's sides with laughter ②to admire exceedingly ③to faint on account of deep grief

絕等(ㄐㄩㄝˊㄉㄥˇ)
peerless; the utmost (in quality, etc.)

絕地(ㄐㄩㄝˊㄉㄧˋ)
①extremely dangerous spots ②a dead end; an impasse; the end of one's rope

絕頂(ㄐㄩㄝˊㄉㄧㄥˇ)
①the top of a mountain peak ②extremely; very (used in the positive sense)

絕頂聰明(ㄐㄩㄝˊㄉㄧㄥˇㄘㄨㄥ ㄇㄧㄥ)
extremely bright, clever or intelligent

絕對(ㄐㄩㄝˊㄉㄨㄟˋ)
absolute(ly); definite(ly); positive; unconditional

絕對服從(ㄐㄩㄝˊㄉㄨㄟˋㄈㄨˊㄘㄨㄥˊ)
absolute obedience; to obey without questioning

絕對單位(ㄐㄩㄝˊㄉㄨㄟˋㄉㄢ ㄨㄟˋ)
an absolute unit

絕對零度(ㄐㄩㄝˊㄉㄨㄟˋㄌㄧㄥˊㄉㄨˋ)
absolute zero—273.16 degrees below zero C.

絕對論(ㄐㄩㄝˊㄉㄨㄟˋㄌㄨㄣˋ)
absolutism

絕對濕度(ㄐㄩㄝˊㄉㄨㄟˋㄕ ㄉㄨˋ)
absolute humidity

絕對溫度(ㄐㄩㄝˊㄉㄨㄟˋㄨㄣ ㄉㄨˋ)
absolute temperature

絕斷(ㄐㄩㄝˊㄉㄨㄢˋ)
to sever or cut off (relationship, etc.)

絕粒(ㄐㄩㄝˊㄌㄧˋ)
①to take no food; to go on a hunger strike ②to eat no grain (in order to attain immortality)

絕流(ㄐㄩㄝˊㄌㄧㄡˊ)

〔糸部〕

to cross a stream or river

絕糧(ㄐㄩㄝ ㄌㄧㄤ)
to run out of food supplies

絕路(ㄐㄩㄝ ㄌㄨ)
a dead end, an impasse; a road of no return (with retreat cut off)

絕倫(ㄐㄩㄝ ㄌㄨㄣ)
without match; peerless; unparalleled

絕港(ㄐㄩㄝ ㄍㄤ)
a seaport which has no river to link with the interior

絕國(ㄐㄩㄝ ㄍㄨㄛ)
an isolated country; a remote country

絕功棄利(ㄐㄩㄝ ㄍㄨㄥ ㄑㄧ ㄌㄧ)
to work for neither money nor prestige

絕口(ㄐㄩㄝ ㄎㄡ)
①never to mention again: 我絕口不談. I never mentioned it again. ② to stop talking about

絕好(ㄐㄩㄝ ㄏㄠ)
extremely good; simply excellent

絕後(ㄐㄩㄝ ㄏㄡ)
①heirless; without posterity ②(said of extremely good writings, paintings, etc.) probably cannot be repeated again

絕戶(ㄐㄩㄝ ㄏㄨ)
①heirless; without posterity ②an heirless person

絕迹(ㄐㄩㄝ ㄐㄧ)
to vanish completely; to be completely wiped out; to be stamped out

絕技(ㄐㄩㄝ ㄐㄧ)
a feat or stunt

絕佳(ㄐㄩㄝ ㄐㄧㄚ)
extremely good; excellent

絕交(ㄐㄩㄝ ㄐㄧㄠ)
to cut off or sever friendship, diplomatic relations, etc.

絕景(ㄐㄩㄝ ㄐㄧㄥ)
an excellent view; extremely beautiful landscapes or scenes

絕境(ㄐㄩㄝ ㄐㄧㄥ)
a desperate spot; the end of one's rope; a helpless situation; an impasse: 我們已瀕於絕境。We have faced an impasse.

絕裾(ㄐㄩㄝ ㄐㄩ)
to go ahead with determination in disregard of any obstruction, unfavorable response, etc.

絕句(ㄐㄩㄝ ㄐㄩ)
a four-line verse with five or seven characters to each line

絕羣(ㄐㄩㄝ ㄑㄩㄣ)
unmatched; peerless

絕響(ㄐㄩㄝ ㄒㄧㄤ)
①lost arts ②(said of a great musician) cannot be heard again

絕緒(ㄐㄩㄝ ㄒㄩ)
heirless; without posterity

絕學(ㄐㄩㄝ ㄒㄩㄝ)
①a lost art ②unique and matchless arts or learning ③to discard conventional or worthless learning

絕招(ㄐㄩㄝ ㄓㄠ)
①unique skill ②an unexpected tricky move (as the last resort) ③a masterstroke

絕症(ㄐㄩㄝ ㄓㄥ)
an incurable disease; a fatal illness

絕種(ㄐㄩㄝ ㄓㄨㄥ)
(said of species of animals, etc.) extinction; extinct: 許多鳥獸現已絕種。Many birds and beasts are now extinct.

絕塵(ㄐㄩㄝ ㄔㄣ)
to move faster than the flying dust—very fast

絕唱(ㄐㄩㄝ ㄔㄤ)
extremely beautiful poems, songs, lyrics, etc.

絕處逢生(ㄐㄩㄝ ㄔㄨ ㄈㄥ ㄕㄥ)
to get saved at a critical moment; to survive a crisis

絕食(ㄐㄩㄝ ㄕ)
to fast; to go on a hunger strike

絕世(ㄐㄩㄝ ㄕ)
①unmatched, unrivaled or unparalleled in one's generation ②without posterity—heirless ③to die

絕世獨立(ㄐㄩㄝ ㄕ ㄉㄨ ㄌㄧ)
to hold on to one's views, stand, etc. in spite of a world of objection

絕世佳人(ㄐㄩㄝ ㄕ ㄐㄧㄚ ㄖㄣ)
an incomparable beauty; a rare beauty

絕世超倫(ㄐㄩㄝ ㄕ ㄔㄠ ㄌㄨㄣ)
absolutely matchless and unparalleled

絕聖棄智(ㄐㄩㄝ ㄕㄥ ㄑㄧ ㄓ)
to prevent enlightenment; to resort to obscurantism

絕早(ㄐㄩㄝ ㄗㄠ)
very early; soonest

絕才(ㄐㄩㄝ ㄘㄞ)
incomparable talent or capability: 他眞是個曠世絕才。He is really an incomparable talent.

絕嗣(ㄐㄩㄝ ㄙ)
without heir or posterity

絕色(ㄐㄩㄝ ㄙㄜ)
a stunning beauty; an incomparably beautiful girl

絕塞(ㄐㄩㄝ ㄙㄞ)
the remote border

絕俗(ㄐㄩㄝ ㄙㄨ)
①above the worldly ways ②to sever oneself from worldly ways or matters

絕詣(ㄐㄩㄝ ㄧ)
profoundly well-versed

絕藝(ㄐㄩㄝ ㄧ)
a unique feat, stunt or performance; consummate skill

絕業(ㄐㄩㄝ ㄧㄝ)
a career or an endeavor, etc. which has been cut short or interrupted

絕垠(ㄐㄩㄝ ㄧㄣ)
remote, outlandish places; very distant land

絕轡而馳(ㄐㄩㄝ ㄧㄣ ㄦ ㄔ)
(said of a talented person) to have a brilliant career after getting a break

絕無(ㄐㄩㄝ ㄨ)
absolutely negative; nothing; never

絕無僅有(ㄐㄩㄝ ㄨ ㄐㄧㄣ ㄧㄡ)
very rare; unique

絕聞(ㄐㄩㄝ ㄨㄣ)
to have no communication with

絕望(ㄐㄩㄝ ㄨㄤ)
hopeless; hopelessness; des-

（糸
部）

perate; desperation; despair;
to give up hope

絕域（ㄐㄩㄝˊ ㄩˋ）
out-of-the-way or inaccessible places; inaccessible
remote areas

絕緣（ㄐㄩㄝˊ ㄩㄢˊ）
to insulate

絕緣體（ㄐㄩㄝˊ ㄩㄢˊ ㄊㄧˇ）
an insulator

【綖】 4329
（綖）ㄒㄧㄝˋ shieh xie
1. reins; ropes for leading animals
2. to bind; fetters; bonds

【絞】 4330
ㄐㄧㄠˇ jeau jiǎo
1. to twist; to twine; to wring
2. to hang (a criminal)
3. rudeness
4. to mix up

絞盤（ㄐㄧㄠˇ ㄆㄢˊ）
a capstan; a windlass

絞痛（ㄐㄧㄠˇ ㄊㄨㄥˋ）
an acute or gripping pain
caused by cholera, appendicitis, etc.

絞臉（ㄐㄧㄠˇ ㄌㄧㄢˇ）
to roll twisted threads over
the face (of a woman) to
root out fine hairs

絞緊（ㄐㄧㄠˇ ㄐㄧㄣˇ）
to twist tight

絞盡腦汁（ㄐㄧㄠˇ ㄐㄧㄣˋ ㄋㄠˇ ㄓ）
to cudgel one's brains: 我絞
盡腦汁想記起她的名字。I cudgeled my brains to recall her
name.

絞決（ㄐㄧㄠˇ ㄐㄩㄝˊ）
the execution of a death
convict by strangulation or
hanging

絞刑（ㄐㄧㄠˇ ㄒㄧㄥˊ）
death by hanging or strangulation

絞車（ㄐㄧㄠˇ ㄔㄜ）
a winch: 他們用絞車舉起車子。
They used a winch to lift
the car.

絞腸痧（ㄐㄧㄠˇ ㄔㄤˊ ㄕㄚ）
acute appendicitis

絞死（ㄐㄧㄠˇ ㄙˇ）
to kill by hanging; death by
hanging

【絡】 4331
1. ㄌㄨㄛˋ luoh luò
1. to wrap around; to encompass

2. a net; a web
3. a cellulose structure in
fruits, as melons
4. to associate; to unite; connected
5. a halter
6. (said of blood vessels) capillaries
7. to unravel silk
8. cotton fiber
9. hemp
10. a Chinese family name

絡頭（ㄌㄨㄛˋ ㄊㄡˊ）
a halter

絡腮鬍子（ㄌㄨㄛˋ ㄙㄞ ㄏㄨˊ·ㄗ）
whiskers

絡繹不絕（ㄌㄨㄛˋ ㄧˋ ㄅㄨˋ ㄐㄩㄝˊ）
(said of people）to come
one after another; in uninterrupted succession; continuous: 參觀美術展覽會的人絡繹
不絕。A continuous stream of
visitors came to the art
exhibition.

絡緯（ㄌㄨㄛˋ ㄨㄟˇ）or 絡絲娘（ㄌㄨㄛˋ ㄙ ㄋㄧㄤˊ）
a cricket—whose nocturnal
buzzing in summer sounds
like unreeled silk

【絡】 2. ㄌㄠˋ law lào
a web or net

絡子（ㄌㄠˋ·ㄗ）
a fine thread basket; a small
net

【絢】 4332
ㄒㄩㄢˋ shiuann xuàn
bright and brilliant; adorned
and stylish

絢爛（ㄒㄩㄢˋ ㄌㄢˋ）
bright and brilliant; glittering; splendid

絢麗（ㄒㄩㄢˋ ㄌㄧˋ）
gorgeous; magnificent

【給】 1. ㄐㄧˇ jii jǐ
1. to provide; provisions; to
supply; supplies
2. to award; to approve; to
grant
3. sufficiency; affluence
4. glib; eloquent

給假（ㄐㄧˇ ㄐㄧㄚˋ）
to grant a leave of absence:
他要求老闆給假一星期。He
asks the boss to grant him a
week's leave.

給諫（ㄐㄧˇ ㄐㄧㄢˋ）or 給事中（ㄐㄧˇ ㄕˋ

ㄓㄨㄥ）
an official rank in ancient
China, roughly equivalent to
a censor

給獎（ㄐㄧˇ ㄐㄧㄤˇ）
to award prizes

給水（ㄐㄧˇ ㄕㄨㄟˇ）
a water supply

給足（ㄐㄧˇ ㄗㄨˊ）
sufficiency; affluence

給養（ㄐㄧˇ ㄧㄤˇ）
military provisions and supplies: 我軍給養充足。Our army
is abundantly provisioned.

給與（ㄐㄧˇ ㄩˇ）or（ㄍㄟˇ ㄩˇ）
to give: 他給叫化一些錢。He
gave the beggar some money.

【給】 2. ㄍㄟˇ geei gěi
1. to give: 給我東西喝好嗎？
Will you give me something
to drink?
2. for; for the benefit of
3. to let; to allow: 給我看看。
Let me have a look.
4. used to indicate a passive
meaning or voice
5. used after a verb to indicate
"giving": 請把奶油遞給我。
Please pass me the butter.

給付（ㄍㄟˇ ㄈㄨˋ）or（ㄐㄧˇ ㄈㄨˋ）
to pay

給臉（ㄍㄟˇ ㄌㄧㄢˇ）
to save (another's) face—so
as not to embarrass him; to
be nice or considerate to
others

給以（ㄍㄟˇ ㄧˇ）
to give; to grant

【絨】 4334
ㄖㄨㄥˊ rong róng
1. fine wool; woolen; velvety;
velvet
2. any kind of woolen goods
or fabric with a felt-like surface
3. fine; furry; flossy

絨布（ㄖㄨㄥˊ ㄅㄨˋ）
flannel; woolen or cotton
piece goods with a felt-like
surface; felt

絨毛（ㄖㄨㄥˊ ㄇㄠˊ）
down

絨毯（ㄖㄨㄥˊ ㄊㄢˇ）
a woolen blanket or carpet:
這小孩被裹在絨毯裡。The
child was wrapped in a
woolen blanket.

絨花(ㄖㄨㄥˊ ㄏㄨㄚ)
artificial flowers made of silk

絨線(ㄖㄨㄥˊ ㄒㄧㄢˋ)
woolen yarn; floss for embroidering; knitting wool

絨繩(ㄖㄨㄥˊ ㄕㄥˊ)
woolen yarn for knitting

【絪】 4335
ㄧㄣ in yin
misty; foggy; cloudy

絪縕(ㄧㄣ ㄩㄣ)
misty; foggy 亦作「氤氳」

【絰】 4336
ㄉㄧㄝˊ dye die
a hemp flax worn in mourning for one's parents

【統】 4337

1. to govern; to rule; to control
2. to unify; to unite
3. wholly; totally; completely; generally; all
4. succession; consecutive generations; from generation to generation

統舖(ㄊㄨㄥˇ ㄆㄨˋ)
a wide bed for a number of people (as in barracks, inns, etc.)

統帶(ㄊㄨㄥˇ ㄉㄞˋ)
(Ching Dynasty) a regiment commander

統統(ㄊㄨㄥˇ ㄊㄨㄥˇ)
wholly; completely; all: 那統統是他的錯。It is completely his fault.

統領(ㄊㄨㄥˇ ㄌㄧㄥˇ)
a commanding officer; a commander of troops

統購統銷(ㄊㄨㄥˇ ㄍㄡˋ ㄊㄨㄥˇ ㄒㄧㄠ)
state purchasing and selling

統括(ㄊㄨㄥˇ ㄍㄨㄚ)
all included; all-encompassing

統共(ㄊㄨㄥˇ ㄍㄨㄥˋ)
all together; total: 旅行的費用共多少？What is the total cost of the trip?

統計(ㄊㄨㄥˇ ㄐㄧˋ)
① statistics ② to count

統計表(ㄊㄨㄥˇ ㄐㄧˋ ㄅㄧㄠˇ)
a statistical table, chart, graph, etc.

統計圖表(ㄊㄨㄥˇ ㄐㄧˋ ㄊㄨˊ ㄅㄧㄠˇ)
a statistical diagram; a pictograph

統計學(ㄊㄨㄥˇ ㄐㄧˋ ㄒㄩㄝˊ)
statistics (as a science)

統計資料(ㄊㄨㄥˇ ㄐㄧˋ ㄗ ㄌㄧㄠˋ)
statistical data

統轄(ㄊㄨㄥˇ ㄒㄧㄚˊ)
to rule; to govern; to control

統銷(ㄊㄨㄥˇ ㄒㄧㄠ)
to sell jointly; joint marketing

統制(ㄊㄨㄥˇ ㄓˋ)
① a former military rank, equivalent to today's division commander ② to control; to govern and regulate; to exercise control (over): 政府嚴格統制軍用物資。The government strictly controls military supplies.

統制經濟(ㄊㄨㄥˇ ㄓˋ ㄐㄧㄥ ㄐㄧˋ)
planned economy

統治(ㄊㄨㄥˇ ㄓˋ)
to reign; to rule; to govern: 這位國王賢明地統治他的國家。The king governs his country wisely.

統治階級(ㄊㄨㄥˇ ㄓˋ ㄐㄧㄝ ㄐㄧˊ)
the ruling class

統治權(ㄊㄨㄥˇ ㄓˋ ㄑㄩㄢˊ)
sovereign power

統治者(ㄊㄨㄥˇ ㄓˋ ㄓㄜˇ)
the ruler

統籌(ㄊㄨㄥˇ ㄔㄡˊ)
to plan as a whole

統籌辦理(ㄊㄨㄥˇ ㄔㄡˊ ㄅㄢˋ ㄌㄧˇ)
(said of several matters) to be dealt with simultaneously by a single government agency

統籌兼顧(ㄊㄨㄥˇ ㄔㄡˊ ㄐㄧㄢ ㄍㄨˋ)
to plan jointly so as to take into consideration every aspect of a matter

統稱(ㄊㄨㄥˇ ㄔㄥ)
known together as

統攝(ㄊㄨㄥˇ ㄕㄜˋ)
to control; to rule

統帥(ㄊㄨㄥˇ ㄕㄨㄞˋ)
the commander in chief

統率(ㄊㄨㄥˇ ㄕㄨㄞˋ)
to lead (troops, a mission, etc.); to rule; to govern

統艙(ㄊㄨㄥˇ ㄘㄤ)
steerage (of a passenger steamer)

統一(ㄊㄨㄥˇ ㄧ)
to unify; uniform; unitary: 中國是統一的多民族國家。China is a unitary multinational state.

統一發票(ㄊㄨㄥˇ ㄧ ㄈㄚ ㄆㄧㄠˋ)
a uniform invoice

統一天下(ㄊㄨㄥˇ ㄧ ㄊㄧㄢ ㄒㄧㄚˋ)
to unify the whole country

統御 or 統馭(ㄊㄨㄥˇ ㄩˋ)
to reign; to rule; to control; reign: 一個賢明治理者的統御對國家有利。The reign of a wise ruler benefits his country.

【絳】 4338
ㄐㄧㄤˋ jiang jiàng
crimson; a deep red color

絳袍(ㄐㄧㄤˋ ㄆㄠˊ)
a red robe

絳頰(ㄐㄧㄤˋ ㄐㄧㄚˊ)
rosy cheeks; a flushed face

絳帳(ㄐㄧㄤˋ ㄓㄤˋ)
the seat of the teacher—formerly with a red curtain behind it

絳脣(ㄐㄧㄤˋ ㄔㄨㄣˊ)
red lips

絳樹(ㄐㄧㄤˋ ㄕㄨˋ)
① coral ② name of an ancient beauty

絳幘(ㄐㄧㄤˋ ㄗㄜˊ)
(in ancient China) the imperial guards who wear red turbans

絳色(ㄐㄧㄤˋ ㄙㄜˋ)
a deep red color; a red color

【絲】 4339
ㄙ sy si

1. silk
2. very fine thread, fiber, etc. as those making a spider's web
3. a general name of silk fabrics or goods
4. strings of musical instruments
5. infinitesimal; a trace; a thread; a tiny bit: 她的臉上露出一絲笑容。There is a trace of a smile on her face.
6. 1/100,000 of a tael

絲布(ㄙ ㄅㄨˋ)
cloth with silk and cotton yarn as the warp and the woof respectively

絲帕(ㄙ ㄆㄚˋ)
a silk handkerchief: 她掉了她的絲帕。She lost her silk

【糸部】

handkerchief.

絲棉 (ㄙ ㄇㄧㄢˊ)
silk batting; silk wadding; silk padding

絲髮 (ㄙ ㄈㄚˇ)
①glossy, silky hair ②the tiniest bit

絲帶 (ㄙ ㄉㄞˋ)
silk ribbons: 她結粉紅色的絲帶在頭髮上。She had a pink ribbon in her hair.

絲桐 (ㄙ ㄊㄨㄥˊ)
a Chinese harp or lute

絲牽線去 (ㄙ ㄌㄨㄢˊ ㄒㄧㄢˋ ㄑㄩˋ)
tangled and involved endlessly

絲淚 (ㄙ ㄌㄟˋ)
little teardrops

絲蘿 (ㄙ ㄌㄨㄛˊ)
marriage

絲瓜 (ㄙ ㄍㄨㄚ)
the sponge gourd (the fruit of a loofah); towel gourds

絲光棉 (ㄙ ㄍㄨㄤ ㄇㄧㄢˊ)
mercerized cotton

絲毫 (ㄙ ㄏㄠˊ)
the tiniest, slightest, or least bit

絲毫不爽 (ㄙ ㄏㄠˊ ㄅㄨˋ ㄕㄨㄤˇ)
perfectly matching; very reliable or accurate

絲線 (ㄙ ㄒㄧㄢˋ)
silk thread

絲織品 (ㄙ ㄓ ㄆㄧㄣˇ)
silk fabrics; silk goods

絲竹 (ㄙ ㄓㄨˊ)
①Chinese musical instruments ②music

絲綢 (ㄙ ㄔㄡˊ)
silk cloth; silk

絲綢之路 (ㄙ ㄔㄡˊ ㄓ ㄌㄨˋ)or 絲路 (ㄙ ㄌㄨˋ)
(history) the Silk Road

絲絨 (ㄙ ㄖㄨㄥˊ)
velvet

絲 (ㄙ)
an expression to describe the fineness or thinness of things

絲絲拉拉 (ㄙ ㄙ ㄌㄚ ㄌㄚ)
endless tangles and involvement

絲絲入扣 (ㄙ ㄙ ㄖㄨˋ ㄎㄡˋ)
ingenious and touching; right on the beat; even the tiniest bits fit (into the whole thing)

絲兒 (ㄙ ㄦ)
tender and delicate things

絲恩髮怨 (ㄙ ㄣ ㄈㄚˇ ㄩㄢˋ)
gratitude for the slightest favor received or a grudge against the slightest wrong done

絲襪 (ㄙ ㄨㄚˋ)
silk stockings; silk socks: 我買了一雙絲襪。I bought a pair of silk stockings.

絲雨 (ㄙ ㄩˇ)
drizzle; misty rain

【絮】 4340
ㄒㄩˋ shiuh xù
1. raw, coarse, old, waste cotton or silk
2. wooly; fluffy
3. catkins and similar blossoms
4. padding; cushioning
5. (said of chatter, writing, etc.) windy
6. to wad with cotton

絮煩 (ㄒㄩˋ ㄈㄢˊ)
①windy; talkative ②tired of; weary; bored

絮叨 (ㄒㄩˋ ㄉㄠ)or 絮叨叨 (ㄒㄩˋ ㄉㄠ ㄉㄠ)or 絮絮叨叨 (ㄒㄩˋ ㄒㄩ ㄉㄠ ㄉㄠ)
nagging; tiresomely talkative; to talk endlessly; to nag: 她絮叨得把他嘮死了。She nagged him to death.

絮羹 (ㄒㄩˋ ㄍㄥ)
to add seasoning into broth

絮聒 (ㄒㄩˋ ㄍㄨㄚ)
①windy and tiresome ②to importune incessantly: 他用問題向我絮聒。He importuned me with questions.

絮絮不休 (ㄒㄩˋ ㄒㄩˋ ㄅㄨˋ ㄒㄧㄡ)
to din; to chatter; annoyingly talkative: 她絮絮不休地談論她的工作。She was chattering over her work.

絮語 (ㄒㄩˋ ㄩˇ)
incessant chatter

【絜】 4341
1. ㄐㄧㄝˊ jye jié
clean; pure

【絜】 4341
2. ㄒㄧㄝˊ shye xié
1. to assess; to ascertain; to measure
2. to restrain; to regulate

絜矩 (ㄒㄧㄝˊ ㄐㄩˇ)

to examine oneself and think of the others so that each will get what he wants

【七畫】

【條】 4342
ㄊㄧㄠˊ tau tiáo
a silk band, sash, or ribbon

條蟲 (ㄊㄧㄠˊ ㄔㄨㄥˊ)
a tapeworm

條子 (ㄊㄧㄠˊ ㄗ)
lace or embroidery used for hemming

【絹】 4343
ㄐㄩㄢˋ jiuann juàn
1. a kind of thick, loosely-woven raw silk fabric
2. a handkerchief

絹布 (ㄐㄩㄢˋ ㄅㄨˋ)
cottonlike lustring

絹畫 (ㄐㄩㄢˋ ㄏㄨㄚˋ)
classical Chinese paintings on silk

絹綢 (ㄐㄩㄢˋ ㄔㄡˊ)
a kind of silk fabric

絹扇 (ㄐㄩㄢˋ ㄕㄢˋ)
a fan made with silk

絹子 (ㄐㄩㄢˋ ㄗ)
a handkerchief

絹絲 (ㄐㄩㄢˋ ㄙ)
spun silk yarn

絹素 (ㄐㄩㄢˋ ㄙㄨˋ)
a kind of white silk for painting or calligraphy

【絺】 4344
ㄔ chy chī
1. a kind of fine hemp cloth; linen
2. a Chinese family name

【綁】 4345
ㄅㄤˇ baang bǎng
to tie; to bind; to fasten: 他們將他的手腳綁起來。They bound him hand and foot.

綁票 (ㄅㄤˇ ㄆㄧㄠˋ)
to kidnap for ransoms; kidnapping

綁匪 (ㄅㄤˇ ㄈㄟˇ)
a kidnaper

綁赴市曹 (ㄅㄤˇ ㄈㄨˋ ㄕˋ ㄘㄠˊ)
to tie the hands of a prisoner behind the back and parade him down the streets to the execution ground

綁腿 (ㄅㄤˇ ㄊㄨㄟˇ)
leggings; gaiters

綁架(ㄅㄤˇ ㄐㄧㄚˋ)
to kidnap for ransoms

綁緊(ㄅㄤˇ ㄐㄧㄣˇ)
to bind or fasten tight

綁起來(ㄅㄤˇ ㄑㄧˇ ˙ㄌㄞ)
to tie up: 小狗被綁起來了。
The dog is tied up.

【綃】 4346
ㄒㄧㄠ shiau xiāo
1. a fabric made of raw silk
2. raw silk

綃頭(ㄒㄧㄠ ㄊㄡˊ)
a silk hood for binding the
hair

【綈】 4347
ㄊㄧˊ tyi tí
a glossy thick silk fabric

綈袍(ㄊㄧˊ ㄆㄠˊ)
a robe made of inferior silk
—(figuratively) old friendship

【綆】 4348
ㄍㄥˇ geeng gěng
a rope for drawing up water
(from a well, stream, etc.)

綆短汲深(ㄍㄥˇ ㄉㄨㄢˇ ㄐㄧˊ ㄕㄣ)
(literally) The rope is short
while the well is deep.—unequal to the job

【綏】 4349
ㄙㄨㄟ suei suí
(又讀 ㄙㄨㄟˊ swei suí)
1. to repose; to pacify; to
appease; to soothe; to tranquilize
2. to retreat
3. a strap to help one mount a
carriage, etc.
4. a banner; a flag

綏服(ㄙㄨㄟ ㄈㄨˊ)
one of the five peace-secur-
ing domains around the
imperial capital in ancient
China

綏撫(ㄙㄨㄟ ㄈㄨˇ)
to pacify; to placate; to
soothe; to tranquilize

綏靖(ㄙㄨㄟ ㄐㄧㄥˋ)
to pacify; pacification; to
restore peace and order

綏靖政策(ㄙㄨㄟ ㄐㄧㄥˋ ㄓㄥˋ ㄘㄜˋ)
an appeasement or pacification policy

綏靖主任(ㄙㄨㄟ ㄐㄧㄥˋ ㄓㄨˇ ㄖㄣˋ)
an official rank established
in the early 1930's responsible for directing and
controlling troops and the

local militia in an area
where the Communist insurgents had just been rooted
out

綏遠(ㄙㄨㄟ ㄩㄢˇ)
Suiyüan Province

【經】 4350
ㄐㄧㄥ jing jīng
1. classic books; religious
scriptures; books of significant value: 他讀佛經。He
reads Buddhist scriptures.
2. the warp of a fabric; things
running lengthwise
3. common or customary ways,
rules, regulations, etc.
4. to plan; to arrange; to regulate; to rule; to manage; to
deal in; to engage in: 她經
商。She engaged in trade.
5. menses
6. human arteries, etc.
7. as a result; after
8. to pass through or by: 你將
經過郵局。You will pass the
post office.
9. to stand; to bear; to endure
10. longitude
11. a Chinese family name

經邦(ㄐㄧㄥ ㄅㄤ)
to rule a nation; to govern a
country

經閉(ㄐㄧㄥ ㄅㄧˋ)
a stoppage of the menses;
amenorrhea

經部(ㄐㄧㄥ ㄅㄨˋ)
the first of the four categories of Chinese classics
〈經史子集〉亦作「甲部」

經脈(ㄐㄧㄥ ㄇㄞˋ)
blood vessels

經費(ㄐㄧㄥ ㄈㄟˋ)
an outlay, or expenditure
(within the budget); a
budget; funds: 此計畫因缺經
費而作罷。The project was
abandoned for want of funds.

經典(ㄐㄧㄥ ㄉㄧㄢˇ)
① religious scriptures ②
Chinese classics

經度(ㄐㄧㄥ ㄉㄨˋ)
degrees of longitude

經天緯地(ㄐㄧㄥ ㄊㄧㄢ ㄨㄟˇ ㄉㄧˋ)
great ability—capable of
governing the universe

經痛(ㄐㄧㄥ ㄊㄨㄥˋ)
dysmenorrhea; painful menstruation

經年(ㄐㄧㄥ ㄋㄧㄢˊ)
① for a whole year ② for
years: 他經年在外。He was
out for years.

經年累月(ㄐㄧㄥ ㄋㄧㄢˊ ㄌㄟˇ ㄩㄝˋ)
for months and years

經理(ㄐㄧㄥ ㄌㄧˇ)
① a manager (of a com-
pany) ② to manage, direct,
regulate, etc.

經歷(ㄐㄧㄥ ㄌㄧˋ)
① one's past experiences ②
to undergo; to go through

經練(ㄐㄧㄥ ㄌㄧㄢˋ)
(said of somebody) experienced; keen and sharp

經絡(ㄐㄧㄥ ㄌㄨㄛˋ)
(blood) the circulation system of the human body

經綸(ㄐㄧㄥ ㄌㄨㄣˊ)
principles and policies in
government administration;
statecraft

經略(ㄐㄧㄥ ㄌㄩㄝˋ)
① to plan and operate ② an
old official rank responsible
for security in border provinces

經過(ㄐㄧㄥ ㄍㄨㄛˋ)
① to pass by or through: 他
的車子從我面前經過。His car
passed in front of me. ② the
ins and outs of an occur-
rence ③ after; through

經過良好(ㄐㄧㄥ ㄍㄨㄛˋ ㄌㄧㄤˊ ㄏㄠˇ)
to have done without a
hitch; to have completed
doing something satisfactorily

經官動詞(ㄐㄧㄥ ㄍㄨㄢ ㄉㄨㄥˋ ㄘˊ)
to get involved in a lawsuit

經管(ㄐㄧㄥ ㄍㄨㄢˇ)
to take charge of; to have
charge of; to be in charge
of: 他經管財務。He took
charge of financial affairs.

經籍(ㄐㄧㄥ ㄐㄧˊ)
classic books; religious
scriptures

經紀人(ㄐㄧㄥ ㄐㄧˋ ㄖㄣˊ)
① a manager (of enter-
tainers, boxers, etc.) ② a
broker; an agent: 他是個房地
產經紀人。He is an estate
agent.

經濟(ㄐㄧㄥ ㄐㄧˋ)
① economy; economic ② eco-

〔糸部〕

nomical; to economize

經濟崩潰(ㄐㄧㄥ ㄐㄧ ㄅㄥ ㄆㄨㄟ)
economic disintegration; economic bankruptcy; economic collapse

經濟部(ㄐㄧㄥ ㄐㄧ ㄅㄨ)
Ministry of Economic Affairs

經濟封鎖(ㄐㄧㄥ ㄐㄧ ㄈㄥ ㄙㄨㄛ)
an economic blockade; to cut off all commercial or financial relations

經濟復甦(ㄐㄧㄥ ㄐㄧ ㄈㄨˋ ㄙㄨ)
economic resurgence

經濟大恐慌(ㄐㄧㄥ ㄐㄧ ㄉㄚˋ ㄎㄨㄥˇ ㄏㄨㄤ)
the Great Depression, the economic crisis and period of low business activity in the U. S. and other countries, beginning in October, 1929, and continuing through the 1930's

經濟利益(ㄐㄧㄥ ㄐㄧ ㄌㄧˋ ㄧˋ)
economic interests

經濟領域(ㄐㄧㄥ ㄐㄧ ㄌㄧㄥˇ ㄩˋ)
an economic sphere

經濟革命(ㄐㄧㄥ ㄐㄧ ㄍㄜˊ ㄇㄧㄥˋ)
an economic revolution

經濟寬裕(ㄐㄧㄥ ㄐㄧ ㄎㄨㄢ ㄩˋ)
well-off; well-to-do

經濟困難(ㄐㄧㄥ ㄐㄧ ㄎㄨㄣˋ ㄋㄢˊ)
financial straits or difficulties

經濟恐慌(ㄐㄧㄥ ㄐㄧ ㄎㄨㄥˇ ㄏㄨㄤ)
financial straits; economic depressions; an economic crisis: 經濟恐慌常使勞工階級受苦. Economic depressions usually cause misery among the working classes.

經濟基礎(ㄐㄧㄥ ㄐㄧ ㄐㄧ ㄔㄨˇ)
an economic base; an economic basis

經濟結構(ㄐㄧㄥ ㄐㄧ ㄐㄧㄝˊ ㄍㄡˋ)
economic structure

經濟建設(ㄐㄧㄥ ㄐㄧ ㄐㄧㄢˋ ㄕㄜˋ)
economic construction

經濟絕交(ㄐㄧㄥ ㄐㄧ ㄐㄩㄝˊ ㄐㄧㄠ)
to break off economic relations; severance of economic ties

經濟起飛(ㄐㄧㄥ ㄐㄧ ㄑㄧˇ ㄈㄟ)
economic takeoff

經濟蕭條(ㄐㄧㄥ ㄐㄧ ㄒㄧㄠ ㄊㄧㄠˊ)
economic stagnation

經濟學(ㄐㄧㄥ ㄐㄧ ㄒㄩㄝˊ)

economics (as a course of study)

經濟學家(ㄐㄧㄥ ㄐㄧ ㄒㄩㄝˊ ㄐㄧㄚ)
an economist

經濟指標(ㄐㄧㄥ ㄐㄧ ㄓˇ ㄅㄧㄠ)
an economic indicator

經濟制度(ㄐㄧㄥ ㄐㄧ ㄓˋ ㄉㄨˋ)
the economic system

經濟制裁(ㄐㄧㄥ ㄐㄧ ㄓˋ ㄘㄞˊ)
economic sanctions

經濟政策(ㄐㄧㄥ ㄐㄧ ㄓㄥˋ ㄘㄜˋ)
an economic policy

經濟成長(ㄐㄧㄥ ㄐㄧ ㄔㄥˊ ㄓㄤˇ)
economic growth

經濟史觀(ㄐㄧㄥ ㄐㄧ ㄕˇ ㄍㄨㄢ)
economic interpretation of history

經濟衰退(ㄐㄧㄥ ㄐㄧ ㄕㄨㄞ ㄊㄨㄟˋ)
the economic recession

經濟作物(ㄐㄧㄥ ㄐㄧ ㄗㄨㄛˋ ㄨˋ)
the industrial crop; the cash crop

經濟危機(ㄐㄧㄥ ㄐㄧ ㄨㄟ ㄐㄧ)
economic Dunkirk

經濟援助(ㄐㄧㄥ ㄐㄧ ㄩㄢˊ ㄓㄨˋ)
economic aid

經解(ㄐㄧㄥ ㄐㄧㄝˇ)
① notations on the classics ② name of a chapter in the Book of Rites

經界(ㄐㄧㄥ ㄐㄧㄝˋ)
boundary markings on the farmland

經久耐用(ㄐㄧㄥ ㄐㄧㄡˇ ㄋㄞˋ ㄩㄥˋ)
(said of goods) durable; sturdy

經期(ㄐㄧㄥ ㄑㄧ)
the woman's period

經銷(ㄐㄧㄥ ㄒㄧㄠ)
to sell as a consignee: 李先生經銷外國書籍. Mr. Lee sells foreign books as a consignee.

經線(ㄐㄧㄥ ㄒㄧㄢˋ)
longitude; the meridian

經線儀(ㄐㄧㄥ ㄒㄧㄢˋ ㄧˊ)
a chronometer (a navigational instrument)

經心(ㄐㄧㄥ ㄒㄧㄣ)
very careful and attentive; painstaking

經學(ㄐㄧㄥ ㄒㄩㄝˊ)
learning devoted to the study of the classics

經訓(ㄐㄧㄥ ㄒㄩㄣˋ)
teachings and instructions

derived from the classics

經之營(ㄐㄧㄥ ㄓ ㄧㄥˊ ㄓ)
to devote painstaking efforts (to an undertaking)

經傳(ㄐㄧㄥ ㄓㄨㄢˋ)
classics and books by lesser authors

經常(ㄐㄧㄥ ㄔㄤˊ)
frequently; often; constantly; regularly: 她經常上學遲到. She is often late for school.

經常費(ㄐㄧㄥ ㄔㄤˊ ㄈㄟˋ)
routine outlays or expenditures, including operational expenses (as opposed to extra or special outlays caused by unexpected happenings, etc.); recurrent appropriation; the overheads

經師(ㄐㄧㄥ ㄕ)
① a teacher of classics ② a teacher whose sole concern is to impart book learning to students(as opposed to 人師)

經師易得, 人師難求(ㄐㄧㄥ ㄕ ㄧˋ ㄉㄜˊ, ㄖㄣˊ ㄕ ㄋㄢˊ ㄑㄧㄡˊ)
(literally) It's easier to get a teacher of classics than a teacher of man.—It's easier to find a learned scholar than an exemplary man of virtue.

經史子集(ㄐㄧㄥ ㄕˇ ㄗˇ ㄐㄧˊ)
an old classification of ancient Chinese books—classics, history, philosophy, and literary works

經世(ㄐㄧㄥ ㄕˋ)
① to manage affairs ② for a generation

經世濟民(ㄐㄧㄥ ㄕˋ ㄐㄧˋ ㄇㄧㄣˊ)
to govern and benefit the people

經世之才(ㄐㄧㄥ ㄕˋ ㄓ ㄘㄞˊ)
great ability; statesmanship

經手(ㄐㄧㄥ ㄕㄡˇ)
to handle; to deal with; to attend to a matter personally: 這件事是她經手的. She is the one who handled this matter.

經手人(ㄐㄧㄥ ㄕㄡˇ ㄖㄣˊ)
one who is responsible for, or personally attends to a matter

經售(ㄐㄧㄥ ㄕㄡˋ)

to sell under a consignment agreement; to sell; to deal in: 這家公司經售棉織品。This firm deals in cotton goods.

經商(ㄐㄧㄥ ㄕㄤ)
to engage in commercial activities; to go into business; to be a businessman: 他離校後要去經商。He will go to business when he leaves school.

經生(ㄐㄧㄥ ㄕㄥ)
a master of the classics

經書(ㄐㄧㄥ ㄕㄨ)
classic books

經笥(ㄐㄧㄥ ㄙ)
erudite; learned

經義(ㄐㄧㄥ ㄧˋ)
①the true meanings of classics ②to take a quotation from the classics as a subject for composition in the civil service examination of former times

經意(ㄐㄧㄥ ㄧˋ)
careful; attentive; advertent

經由(ㄐㄧㄥ ㄧㄡˊ)
by (a person); through or via (a place): 他將經由日本去美國。He will be bound for U.S.A. via Japan.

經驗(ㄐㄧㄥ ㄧㄢˋ)
experience; empirical: 經驗為良師。Experience is a good teacher.

經驗豐富(ㄐㄧㄥ ㄧㄢˋ ㄈㄥ ㄈㄨˋ)
well-experienced

經驗論(ㄐㄧㄥ ㄧㄢˋ ㄌㄨㄣˋ)
empiricism

經驗之談(ㄐㄧㄥ ㄧㄢˋ ㄓ ㄊㄢˊ)
statements based on personal experience

經驗哲學(ㄐㄧㄥ ㄧㄢˋ ㄓㄜˊ ㄒㄩㄝˊ)
empirical philosophy

經驗主義者(ㄐㄧㄥ ㄧㄢˋ ㄓㄨˇ ㄧˋ ㄓㄜˇ)
an empiricist

經營(ㄐㄧㄥ ㄧㄥˊ)
to operate or manage or carry on (a shop, a business, etc.)

經緯(ㄐㄧㄥ ㄨㄟˇ)
①longitude and latitude ②the warp and the woof ③logical planning ④main points of something

經緯儀(ㄐㄧㄥ ㄨㄟˇ ㄧˊ)
a theodolite; a transit instru-ment

經緯萬端(ㄐㄧㄥ ㄨㄟˇ ㄨㄢˋ ㄉㄨㄢ)
very complicated

經文(ㄐㄧㄥ ㄨㄣˊ)
classical text

經緯武(ㄐㄧㄥ ㄨㄣˊ ㄨˇ)
to map and execute government policies and military affairs

【綱】4351
(綱) ㄎㄤ koen kun
1. a bundle; to make a bundle; to tie up; to bundle up
2. to weave

綱綁(ㄎㄨㄣ ㄅㄤˇ)
to bind; to tie up: 他們把他的手足綱綁起來。They bound him hand and foot.

綱好(ㄎㄨㄣ ㄏㄠˇ)
to tie up; to bundle up

綱緊(ㄎㄨㄣ ㄐㄧㄣˇ)
to bind tight; to tighten the rope: 把繩子綱緊些。Tighten the ropes a little.

綱起來(ㄎㄨㄣ ㄑㄧˇ·ㄌㄞ)
to bind; to tie up

【綖】4352
|ㄢˊ yan yán
the hanging flap in front and at the back of a hat in ancient times

八畫

【綜】4353
ㄗㄨㄥˋ tzong zòng
1. to sum up; in a nutshell
2. in view of; to take account of
3. to arrange
4. synthesis; synthetic
5. to inquire or examine into

綜覽(ㄗㄨㄥˋ ㄌㄢˇ)
a general or comprehensive survey; to view generally

綜攬(ㄗㄨㄥˋ ㄌㄢˇ)
to be in overall charge

綜理(ㄗㄨㄥˋ ㄌㄧˇ)
to arrange or manage everything; to be in overall charge

綜括(ㄗㄨㄥˋ ㄍㄨㄚ)
to sum up; to encompass all; to recapitulate

綜觀(ㄗㄨㄥˋ ㄍㄨㄢ)
①a general and comprehensive view ②to view the whole situation

綜管(ㄗㄨㄥˋ ㄍㄨㄢˇ)
to arrange and manage all; to be in overall charge

綜合(ㄗㄨㄥˋ ㄏㄜˊ)
synthesis; to synthesize

綜合報導(ㄗㄨㄥˋ ㄏㄜˊ ㄅㄠˋ ㄉㄠˇ)
a comprehensive dispatch

綜合法(ㄗㄨㄥˋ ㄏㄜˊ ㄈㄚˇ)
a method of synthesis; synthesis

綜合雜誌(ㄗㄨㄥˋ ㄏㄜˊ ㄗㄚˊ ㄓˋ)
a catchall magazine; a magazine of general interest

綜合所得稅(ㄗㄨㄥˋ ㄏㄜˊ ㄙㄨㄛˇ ㄉㄜˊ ㄕㄨㄟˋ)
consolidated income tax

綜合藝術(ㄗㄨㄥˋ ㄏㄜˊ ㄧˋ ㄕㄨˋ)
arts which require both the visual sense and hearing to appreciate, such as performing arts

綜核名實(ㄗㄨㄥˋ ㄏㄜˊ ㄇㄧㄥˊ ㄕˊ)
to check and investigate the actual facts

【綠】4354
1. ㄌㄩˋ liuh lü
1. green(color): 那見有綠油油的秧苗。There are green and lush seedlings.
2. chlorine, which is now written as 氯

綠寶石(ㄌㄩˋ ㄅㄠˇ ㄕˊ)
emerald; beryl: 她戴着綠寶石戒指。She wore an emerald ring.

綠黴素 or 氯黴素(ㄌㄩˋ ㄇㄟˊ ㄙㄨˋ)
chloromycetin

綠帽子(ㄌㄩˋ ㄇㄠˋ·ㄗ)or綠頭巾(ㄌㄩˋ ㄊㄡˊ ㄐㄧㄣ)
(literally) a green hat—the sign of a cuckold

綠肥(ㄌㄩˋ ㄈㄟˊ)
green manure

綠礬(ㄌㄩˋ ㄈㄢˊ)
melanterite, or green vitriol

綠島(ㄌㄩˋ ㄉㄠˇ)
Green Island, off the southeastern Taiwan coast, the site of a reformatory camp

綠豆(ㄌㄩˋ ㄉㄡˋ)
the green beans; green lentils (Phaseolus mungo var. radiatus)

綠豆糕(ㄌㄩˋ ㄉㄡˋ ㄍㄠ)
small cakes made with green-bean flour

綠豆粥(ㄌㄩˋ ㄉㄡˋ ㄓㄡ)or綠豆稀飯

〔糸部〕

〔糸部〕

（ㄌㄩ ㄎㄨㄟ ㄒㄧㄣˊ）
congee or rice porridge cooked with green beans

綠豆芽（ㄌㄩ ㄌㄡ ㄧˊ）
green bean sprouts

綠燈（ㄌㄩ ㄉㄥ）
①(transportation)the green light ② permission to go ahead with some project; the green light

綠地（ㄌㄩ ㄉㄧˋ）
space reserved for parks, trees or meadows in an urban community

綠內障（ㄌㄩ ㄋㄟˋ ㄓㄤ）
glaucoma

綠卡（ㄌㄩ ㄎㄚˇ）
a green card, permanent residence permit issued by the U.S. government

綠化（ㄌㄩ ㄏㄨㄚˋ）
to plant trees, build parks, or lay out lawns in deserts or urban areas; to afforest: 我們綠化安全島。We afforested the safety islands.

綠鉛礦（ㄌㄩ ㄑㄧㄢ ㄎㄨㄤˋ）
pyromorphite

綠洲（ㄌㄩ ㄓㄡ）
an oasis: 沙漠中的旅客時常停宿於綠洲上。Travelers in the desert often stop at an oasis.

綠柱石（ㄌㄩ ㄓㄨˋ ㄕˊ）
(geology) beryl

綠茶（ㄌㄩ ㄔㄚˊ）
green tea

綠藻（ㄌㄩ ㄗㄠˇ）
algae; chlorophyceae; chlorella

綠草如茵（ㄌㄩ ㄘㄠˇ ㄖㄨˊ ㄧㄣ）
The green grass looks like a velvet carpet.

綠野（ㄌㄩ ㄧㄝˇ）
the green field

綠油（ㄌㄩ ㄧㄡˊ）
anthracene oil

綠油腦（ㄌㄩ ㄧㄡˊ ㄋㄠˇ）
anthracene

綠油油（ㄌㄩ ㄧㄡˊ ㄧㄡˊ）
bright green

綠蔭（ㄌㄩ ㄧㄣˋ）
a green shade; the shade of trees

【綠】 4354
2. 讀音 ㄌㄨˋ luh lù

綠肥紅瘦（ㄌㄩ ㄈㄟˊ ㄏㄨㄥˊ ㄕㄡˋ）
① Leaves are growing dark green when flowers are fading in late spring. ② beautiful women of all descriptions

綠林好漢（ㄌㄩ ㄌㄧㄣˊ ㄏㄠˇ ㄏㄢˋ）or 綠林豪傑（ㄌㄩ ㄌㄧㄣˊ ㄏㄠˊ ㄐㄧㄝˊ）
① heroes of the greenwood; outlaws (who live in thick forest as Robin Hood did) ② a band of bandits entrenched in a mountain stronghold; brigands

綠竹（ㄌㄩ ㄓㄨˊ）
green bamboos 亦作「菉竹」

綠水（ㄌㄩ ㄕㄨㄟˇ）or（ㄌㄩ ㄕㄨㄟˇ）
① crystal clear water ② a green river

綠衣使者（ㄌㄩ ㄧ ㄕˇ ㄓㄜˇ）or（ㄌㄩ ㄧ ㄕˇ ㄓㄜˇ）
① a mailman ② another name of parrots

綠衣人（ㄌㄩ ㄧ ㄖㄣˊ）or（ㄌㄩ ㄧ ㄖㄣˊ）
a postman; a mailman (Chinese mailmen wear green uniforms.)

綠葉成蔭（ㄌㄩ ㄧㄝˋ ㄔㄥˊ ㄧㄣ）
(literally) The thick foliage forms a good shade.—She has become a mother of many children.

綠陰（ㄌㄩ ㄧㄣ）
the shade of trees

綠營（ㄌㄩ ㄧㄥˊ）
(in the Ching Dynasty) Chinese troops identified by green banners, as distinct from Manchu troops identified by banners of white, yellow, red and blue

綠玉（ㄌㄩ ㄩˋ）or（ㄌㄩ ㄩˋ）
emerald; green jade

綠雲（ㄌㄩ ㄩㄣˊ）
the hair of a beautiful girl

【綢】 4355
ㄔㄡˊ chour chóu
1. a general name of all silk fabrics
2. fine and delicate
3. (now rarely)to twine and tangle

綢繆（ㄔㄡˊ ㄇㄡˊ）
①to weave (beforehand)—to get prepared ② sentimentally attached; tender love ③ to consolidate; to strengthen, to make strong ④ luxuriant growth of flowers

綢緞（ㄔㄡˊ ㄉㄨㄢˋ）
a general name of silk goods; silks and satins: 她穿着綢緞製的衣服。She was dressed in silks and satins.

綢緞莊（ㄔㄡˊ ㄉㄨㄢˋ ㄓㄨㄤ）
a mercery; a store selling textiles

綢直（ㄔㄡˊ ㄓˊ）
(said of dispositions) careful, considerate and honest

綢子（ㄔㄡˊ ㄗ）
a general name of silk fabrics

綢兒緞兒（ㄔㄡˊ ㄦ ㄉㄨㄢˋ ㄦ）
expensive clothing

【綣】 4356
ㄑㄩㄢˇ chuan quǎn
to make tender love 參看「繾綣③」

【綬】 4357
ㄕㄡˋ show shòu
silk ribbons attached to an official seal or medal—(figuratively) an office seal: 他解綬而去。He returned the office seal and resigned.

綬帶（ㄕㄡˋ ㄉㄞˋ）
a cordon (as a badge of honor)

【維】 4358
ㄨㄟˊ wei wéi
1. to tie; to hold fast; to secure
2. to maintain; to safeguard
3. to unite; to hold together
4. long and slender—as fibers
5. an initial particle — only, but, etc.
6. a pattern or rule

維妙維肖（ㄨㄟˊ ㄇㄧㄠˋ ㄨㄟˊ ㄒㄧㄠˋ）
so skillfully imitated as to be indistinguishable from the original; remarkably true to life

維多利亞（ㄨㄟˊ ㄉㄨㄛ ㄌㄧˋ ㄧㄚ）
a transliteration of Victoria

維他命（ㄨㄟˊ ㄊㄚ ㄇㄧㄥˋ）
vitamins

維那斯（ㄨㄟˊ ㄋㄚˋ ㄙ）or 維納斯（ㄨㄟˊ ㄋㄚˋ ㄙ）
Venus

維恭維謹（ㄨㄟˊ ㄍㄨㄥ ㄨㄟˊ ㄐㄧㄣˇ）
sincere and respectful

維護（ㄨㄟˊ ㄏㄨˋ）
to safeguard; to uphold; to preserve; to protect: 我們必須維護言論自由。We must uphold freedom of speech.

維吉尼亞(ㄨㄟ ㄐㄧ ㄋㄧˊ ㄧㄚ)
the state of Virginia,U.S.A.

維艱(ㄨㄟ ㄐㄧㄢ)
very hard or difficult

維繫(ㄨㄟ ㄒㄧˋ)
to maintain; to keep; to make secure and bind together

維修(ㄨㄟ ㄒㄧㄡ)
to keep in (good) repair; to service; to maintain: 這機器維修得很好。The machine had been kept in good repair.

維新(ㄨㄟ ㄒㄧㄣ)
to make political reforms; to reform (government, etc.)

維新派(ㄨㄟ ㄒㄧㄣ ㄆㄞˋ)
reformers

維新政治(ㄨㄟ ㄒㄧㄣ ㄓㄥˋ ㄓˋ)
to reform politics; political reformation

維繫(ㄨㄟ ㄒㄧˋ)
①to tie and tether　②to detain; to hold back

維舟(ㄨㄟ ㄓㄡ)
to moor a boat

維持(ㄨㄟ ㄔˊ)
to maintain; to keep; to guard and support; to sustain; to preserve: 我們來維持世界和平吧。Let's maintain peace in the world.

維持費(ㄨㄟ ㄔˊ ㄈㄟˋ)
maintenance charges; maintenance costs

維持現狀(ㄨㄟ ㄔˊ ㄒㄧㄢˋ ㄓㄨㄤˋ)
to maintain the status quo; to maintain the present condition

維持秩序(ㄨㄟ ㄔˊ ㄓˋ ㄒㄩˋ)
to maintain order; to keep order

維持治安(ㄨㄟ ㄔˊ ㄓˋ ㄢ)
to maintain public order

維持世界和平(ㄨㄟ ㄔˊ ㄕˋ ㄐㄧㄝˋ ㄏㄜˊ ㄆㄧㄥˊ)
to maintain or preserve world peace

維生素(ㄨㄟ ㄕㄥ ㄙㄨˋ)
vitamins 亦作「維他命」

維斯杜拉河(ㄨㄟ ㄙ ㄉㄨˋ ㄌㄚ ㄏㄜˊ)
the Vistula River in central Europe

維蘇威(ㄨㄟ ㄙㄨ ㄨㄟ)
Vesuvius, a volcanic mountain in southern Italy

維也納(ㄨㄟ ㄧㄝˇ ㄋㄚˋ)
Vienna

維也納會議(ㄨㄟ ㄧㄝˇ ㄋㄚˋ ㄏㄨㄟˋ ㄧˋ)
the Vienna Conference(1814-1815) held after the defeat of Napoleon Bonaparte

維吾爾(ㄨㄟ ㄨˊ ㄦˇ)
the Uigur tribe in Sinkiang

【縮】4359
ㄨㄢ woan wan
to string together; to bind up, as the hair; to coil up: 她把頭髮縮起來。She coiled her hair.

【綱】4360
ㄍㄤ gang gang
1. the large rope of a net, round which it is netted, and by which it is drawn
2. main points; an outline
3. a principle; discipline

綱目(ㄍㄤ ㄇㄨˋ)
①the outline and detailed items　②a form of chronicle

綱理(ㄍㄤ ㄌㄧˇ)
to rule; to govern

綱領(ㄍㄤ ㄌㄧㄥˇ)
an outline

綱紀(ㄍㄤ ㄐㄧˋ)
①a principle; discipline; law; order　②a manager; a magistrate

綱紀廢弛(ㄍㄤ ㄐㄧˋ ㄈㄟˋ ㄔˊ)
Discipline is lax.

綱舉目張(ㄍㄤ ㄐㄩˇ ㄇㄨˋ ㄓㄤ)
There is strict order prevailing.

綱常(ㄍㄤ ㄔㄤˊ)
the three bonds(君臣、父子、夫婦－the relations between ruler and subject, father and son, husband and wife)and the five constant virtues(仁、義、禮、智、信－benevolence, righteousness, propriety, knowledge, and faith)

綱要(ㄍㄤ ㄧㄠˋ)
main points; an outline

【網】4361
ㄨㄤˇ woang wang
1. a net; a network; a web: 他們用網捕魚。They caught fish with a net.
2. (figuratively)the dragnet; the arms of law
3. to bring together; to collect
網膜(ㄨㄤˇ ㄇㄛˊ)
a retina

網目(ㄨㄤˇ ㄇㄨˋ)
meshes 參看「網眼」

網漏吞舟之魚(ㄨㄤˇ ㄌㄡˋ ㄊㄨㄣ ㄓㄡ ㄓ ㄩˊ)
(literally) The net has such wide meshes that even fishes large enough to gulp a boat can escape from it.—The law is so lax that even principal criminals are overlooked.

網籃(ㄨㄤˇ ㄌㄢˊ)
a basket covered with a net; a basket with a net on top

網路(ㄨㄤˇ ㄌㄨˋ)
a network

網羅(ㄨㄤˇ ㄌㄨㄛˊ)
①to bring together; to collect; to assemble②a net (for catching fish or birds)③to recruit; to enlist the services of

網罟(ㄨㄤˇ ㄍㄨˇ)
nets

網開三面(ㄨㄤˇ ㄎㄞ ㄙㄢ ㄇㄧㄢˋ)
(literally) to open the net on three sides—to be lenient with offenders

網開一面(ㄨㄤˇ ㄎㄞ ㄧ ㄇㄧㄢˋ)
to leave one side of the net open--to give a wrongdoer a way out

網球(ㄨㄤˇ ㄑㄧㄡˊ)
tennis: 她喜歡打網球。She likes playing tennis.

網球拍(ㄨㄤˇ ㄑㄧㄡˊ ㄆㄞˊ)
a racket (for playing tennis)

網球場(ㄨㄤˇ ㄑㄧㄡˊ ㄔㄤˇ)
a tennis court

網狀脈(ㄨㄤˇ ㄓㄨㄤˋ ㄇㄞˋ)
(said of tree leaves) net-veined

網狀葉(ㄨㄤˇ ㄓㄨㄤˋ ㄧㄝˋ)
(botany) a reticulate leaf

網子(ㄨㄤˇ ㄗ˙)
a net

網眼(ㄨㄤˇ ㄧㄢˇ)
meshes of a net: 這個網有半英寸見方的網眼。This net has half-inch meshes.

網魚(ㄨㄤˇ ㄩˊ)
to net fish

【綴】4362
ㄓㄨㄟˋ juey zhuì
1. to put together; to combine; to compose
2. to mend clothes; to patch

【糸部】

up; to sew; to stitch
3. to decorate; to stud

綴補 (ㄓㄨㄟˋ ㄅㄨˇ)
to patch up (clothes)

綴法 (ㄓㄨㄟˋ ㄈㄚˇ)
a lesson on sentence construction and composition

綴輯 (ㄓㄨㄟˋ ㄐㄧˊ)
to compile and edit

綴文 (ㄓㄨㄟˋ ㄨㄣˊ)
to write a composition

【綵】 4363
ㄘㄞˇ tsae cǎi

1. varicolored silk; a silk festoon

2. motley; varicolored

綵牌樓 (ㄘㄞˇ ㄆㄞˊ ㄌㄡˊ)
a varicolored celebration arch

綵棚 (ㄘㄞˇ ㄆㄥˊ)
a gaily decorated wooden framework

綵樓 (ㄘㄞˇ ㄌㄡˊ)
a gaily decorated tower or pavilion

綵轎 (ㄘㄞˇ ㄐㄧㄠˋ)
a gaily decorated sedan chair

綵球 (ㄘㄞˇ ㄑㄧㄡˊ)
a ball wound up from varicolored silk

綵綢 (ㄘㄞˇ ㄔㄡˊ)
varicolored silk

綵船 (ㄘㄞˇ ㄔㄨㄢˊ)
a gaily decorated boat

綵衣娛親 (ㄘㄞˇ ㄧ ㄩˊ ㄑㄧㄣ)
to wear a motley to entertain one's parents, a reference about Lao Lai-tzu (老萊子), who at seventy behaved like a child to please his parents—to be a filial son

【綹】 4364
ㄌㄧㄡˇ leou liǔ

a tuft; a lock; a skein (of yarn)

【綸】 4365
1. ㄌㄨㄣˊ luen lún

1. a fishing line
2. a green silk cord

綸繩 (ㄌㄨㄣˊ ㄕㄥˊ)
a fishing line

綸音 (ㄌㄨㄣˊ ㄧㄣ)
an imperial edict or rescript

【綸】
2. 《ㄨㄢ guan guān

a kind of ancient cap

綸巾 (《ㄨㄢ ㄐㄧㄣ)
a kind of ancient cap resembling a ridged roof

【綺】 4366
ㄑㄧˇ chii qǐ

1. beautiful; magnificent; fine; fair; gorgeous; resplendent; elegant

2. twilled silk cloth; figured woven silk material

綺靡 (ㄑㄧˇ ㄇㄧˇ)
① extravagantly beautiful ② (said of a literary style) ornate

綺年 (ㄑㄧˇ ㄋㄧㄢˊ) or 綺歲 (ㄑㄧˇ ㄙㄨㄟˋ)
youthful

綺年玉貌 (ㄑㄧˇ ㄋㄧㄢˊ ㄩˋ ㄇㄠˋ)
(said of a girl) young and beautiful

綺麗 (ㄑㄧˇ ㄌㄧˋ)
beautiful; fair; magnificent; gorgeous; resplendent; enchanting

綺井 (ㄑㄧˇ ㄐㄧㄥˇ)
the ceiling (of a house)

綺情 (ㄑㄧˇ ㄑㄧㄥˊ)
tender feeling

綺想 (ㄑㄧˇ ㄒㄧㄤˇ)
beautiful thoughts

綺室 (ㄑㄧˇ ㄕˋ)
a gorgeous room; a magnificent room

綺襦紈袴 (ㄑㄧˇ ㄖㄨˊ ㄨㄢˊ ㄎㄨˋ)
fops from a good family

綺思 (ㄑㄧˇ ㄙ)
beautiful thoughts (in literature) 亦作「綺想」

綺筵 (ㄑㄧˇ ㄧㄢˊ)
a magnificent feast

綺語 (ㄑㄧˇ ㄩˇ)
① (Buddhism) profane expressions; sexual talks ② literary pieces concerning love and sex

【綻】 4367
ㄓㄢˋ jann zhàn

1. a ripped seam; a crack
2. a flaw or defect (in a scheme, etc.)

綻露 (ㄓㄢˋ ㄌㄨˋ)
to reveal a matter

綻裂 (ㄓㄢˋ ㄌㄧㄝˋ)
ripped; to split; to rip

綻線 (ㄓㄢˋ ㄒㄧㄢˋ)
to have a ripped seam

【綽】 4368
ㄔㄨㄛˋ chuoh chuò

1. spacious; roomy
2. delicate

綽號 (ㄔㄨㄛˋ ㄏㄠˋ) or 綽名 (ㄔㄨㄛˋ ㄇㄧㄥˊ)
a nickname; a sobriquet

綽綽有餘 (ㄔㄨㄛˋ ㄔㄨㄛˋ ㄧㄡˇ ㄩˊ) or 綽有餘裕 (ㄔㄨㄛˋ ㄧㄡˇ ㄩˊ ㄩˋ)
① There is enough room to spare. 或 It's more than enough. ② generous feeling

綽約多姿 (ㄔㄨㄛˋ ㄩㄝ ㄉㄨㄛ ㄗ)
charmingly delicate

【綾】 4369
ㄌㄧㄥˊ ling líng

very fine silk cloth; damask silk

綾羅 (ㄌㄧㄥˊ ㄌㄨㄛˊ)
silk gauze

綾羅錦繡 (ㄌㄧㄥˊ ㄌㄨㄛˊ ㄐㄧㄣˇ ㄒㄧㄡˋ)
expensive clothes; expensive dress materials

【緇】 4370
ㄗ tzy zī

1. black
2. black silk

緇帶 (ㄗ ㄉㄞˋ)
a black belt

緇流 (ㄗ ㄌㄧㄡˊ)
Buddhist monks

緇黃 (ㄗ ㄏㄨㄤˊ)
Buddhist monks and Taoist priests

緇素 (ㄗ ㄙㄨˋ)
Buddhist monks and laymen

緇衣 (ㄗ ㄧ)
① black garments (or robes) worn by courtiers on formal occasions in ancient times ② black garments worn by monks

【緅】 4371
ㄗㄡ tzou zōu

1. bluish red; a puce color
2. light red

【綿】 (縣) 4372
ㄇㄧㄢˊ mian mián

1. cotton
2. everlasting; endless
3. weak

綿薄 (ㄇㄧㄢˊ ㄅㄛˊ)
(a polite expression) my feeble strength, limited power, or poor abilities

綿密 (ㄇㄧㄢˊ ㄇㄧˋ)
paying attention to all

details; circumspect

綿邈(ㄇㄧㄢˊ ㄇㄧㄠˇ)
long (in time)

綿綿(ㄇㄧㄢˊ ㄇㄧㄢˊ)
continuous; everlasting; to go on and on. 春雨綿綿。The spring rain goes on and on.

綿延不絕(ㄇㄧㄢˊ ㄧㄢˊ ㄅㄨˋ ㄐㄩㄝˊ)
to last forever; to keep on endlessly

綿綿絮語(ㄇㄧㄢˊ ㄇㄧㄢˊ ㄒㄩˋ ㄩˇ)
to whisper continually

綿篤(ㄇㄧㄢˊ ㄉㄨˇ)
seriously ill; dangerously ill

綿頓(ㄇㄧㄢˊ ㄉㄨㄣˋ)
seriously ill

綿裏針(ㄇㄧㄢˊ ㄌㄧˇ ㄓㄣ)
(literally) a needle hidden in cotton—cruelty or harshness hidden behind a friendly appearance

綿力(ㄇㄧㄢˊ ㄌㄧˋ)
(a self-depreciatory term) my limited power

綿亙(ㄇㄧㄢˊ ㄍㄣˋ)
to stretch in an unbroken chain: 這森林綿亙數英里之長。The forest stretches for miles.

綿絮(ㄇㄧㄢˊ ㄒㄩˋ)
cotton

綿長(ㄇㄧㄢˊ ㄔㄤˊ)
lasting forever; very long (in time)

綿軟(ㄇㄧㄢˊ ㄖㄨㄢˇ) or 綿弱(ㄇㄧㄢˊ ㄖㄨㄛˋ)
soft; weak: 我覺得兩腿綿軟無力。I feel weak in the legs.

綿延(ㄇㄧㄢˊ ㄧㄢˊ)
to extend very long; to stretch over a long distance; to be continuous; to go on

綿羊(ㄇㄧㄢˊ ㄧㄤˊ)
sheep

【綦】 4373
　　ㄑㄧˊ chyi qí
1. very; exceedingly
2. dark grey
3. shoelaces

綦重(ㄑㄧˊ ㄓㄨㄥˋ)
very heavy

綦嚴(ㄑㄧˊ ㄧㄢˊ)
very stringent; very severe

【綮】 4374
　　1.(綮) ㄑㄧˇ chii qǐ
a sheath for a lanchead

【綮】 4374
　　2. ㄑㄧㄥˋ chinq qìng
as in 肯綮—the main point; the gist

【緊】 4375
　　ㄐㄧㄣˇ jiin jǐn
1. tight; firm; fast; secure; taut; tense; close
2. urgent; critical; pressing: 任務緊切。The task is urgent.

緊繃(ㄐㄧㄣˇ ㄅㄥ)
to stretch taut

緊逼(ㄐㄧㄣˇ ㄅㄧ)
① to press hard; to close in on ② (basketball) press

緊迫(ㄐㄧㄣˇ ㄆㄛˋ)
urgent; pressing: 他有更緊迫的事情要處理。He has more pressing things to deal with.

緊密(ㄐㄧㄣˇ ㄇㄧˋ)
① rigidly precise; rigorous ② compact and orderly ③ to close together ④ rapid and intense

緊防(ㄐㄧㄣˇ ㄈㄤˊ)
to guard closely or tightly; to remain vigilant against

緊鄰(ㄐㄧㄣˇ ㄌㄧㄣˊ)
a close neighbor

緊鑼密鼓(ㄐㄧㄣˇ ㄌㄨㄛˊ ㄇㄧˋ ㄍㄨˇ)
wildly beating gongs and drums—(figuratively) to publicize a campaign urgently in preparation for some undertaking

緊跟著(ㄐㄧㄣˇ ㄍㄣ ˙ㄓㄜ)
on the heels of; close behind; to follow closely or immediately; to keep in step with: 這小孩緊跟著他的母親。This child keeps in step with his mother.

緊急(ㄐㄧㄣˇ ㄐㄧˊ)
urgent; critical; of an emergency; pressing: 外面情況緊急。The outside situation is critical.

緊急命令(ㄐㄧㄣˇ ㄐㄧˊ ㄇㄧㄥˋ ㄌㄧㄥˋ)
emergent orders; urgent orders

緊急動議(ㄐㄧㄣˇ ㄐㄧˊ ㄉㄨㄥˋ ㄧˋ)
an urgent or emergent motion (in a parliament, etc.)

緊急集合(ㄐㄧㄣˇ ㄐㄧˊ ㄐㄧˊ ㄏㄜˊ)
an emergency muster

緊急警報(ㄐㄧㄣˇ ㄐㄧˊ ㄐㄧㄥˇ ㄅㄠˋ)
an air-raid alarm sounded when enemy planes are near or already overhead

緊急起飛(ㄐㄧㄣˇ ㄐㄧˊ ㄑㄧˇ ㄈㄟ)
a scramble

緊急信號(ㄐㄧㄣˇ ㄐㄧˊ ㄒㄧㄣˋ ㄏㄠˋ)
an emergency signal

緊急着陸(ㄐㄧㄣˇ ㄐㄧˊ ㄓㄨㄛˊ ㄌㄨˋ)
emergency landing

緊接(ㄐㄧㄣˇ ㄐㄧㄝ)
to follow close behind; on the heels of; immediately afterward

緊(ㄐㄧㄣˇ)
tightly; firmly; closely: 他緊盯着我。He watched me closely.

緊張(ㄐㄧㄣˇ ㄓㄤ)
tense; nervous; taut; tight; tension; strained: 昨天英文考試時我有些緊張。I got nervous at the English examination yesterday.

緊身兒(ㄐㄧㄣˇ ㄕㄣ ㄦ)
fitting the body closely; tight; close

緊湊(ㄐㄧㄣˇ ㄘㄡˋ)
① closely and firmly packed; compact ② (said of an entertainment program, a show, a composition, etc.) one climax after another; absorbingly interesting throughout; well-knit; well-organized: 這篇文章寫得很緊湊。It was a well-organized composition.

緊促(ㄐㄧㄣˇ ㄘㄨˋ)
pressing; urgent: 這件事很緊促。The matter is pressing.

緊縮(ㄐㄧㄣˇ ㄙㄨㄛˋ)
to retrench; to curtail; to cut down; to reduce: 我們緊縮開支。We cut down expenses.

緊隨(ㄐㄧㄣˇ ㄙㄨㄟˊ)
to follow closely

緊要(ㄐㄧㄣˇ ㄧㄠˋ)
important; urgent; vital; critical: 瞭解自己，對我們很重要。It's important for us to know ourselves.

緊要關頭(ㄐㄧㄣˇ ㄧㄠˋ ㄍㄨㄢ ㄊㄡˊ)
a critical moment

緊握(ㄐㄧㄣˇ ㄨㄛˋ)
to grasp firmly; to take a tight hold of (or over): 緊握繩子。Take a tight hold of the rope.

【緋】 4376
ㄈㄟ fēi fēi
scarlet; crimson

緋紅(ㄈㄟ ㄏㄨㄥˊ)
scarlet; crimson: 羞愧使得她兩頰緋紅。Shame made her cheeks crimson.

緋聞(ㄈㄟ ㄨㄣˊ)
sexy news 亦作「桃色新聞」

【綏】 4377
ㄖㄨㄟˊ ruei ruí
ornamental strings on a hat

【綫】 4378
(線) ㄒㄧㄢˋ shiann xiàn
1. a line
2. threads

綫索(ㄒㄧㄢˋ ㄙㄨㄛˇ)
a clue

九畫

【緒】 4379
ㄒㄩˋ shiuh xù
1. the end of a thread or string
2. a clue: 一點頭緒也沒有。There is no clue at all.
3. a beginning
4. a task; a cause; an enterprise: 他們繼未竟之緒。He continued an unfinished task.
5. a mental or emotional state; mood: 我的情緒不好。I was in a bad mood.
6. remnants; remains; leftovers

緒論(ㄒㄩˋ ㄌㄨㄣˊ)
a preface; a foreword; an introduction

緒戰(ㄒㄩˋ ㄓㄢˋ)
the first battle between two forces

緒業(ㄒㄩˋ ㄧㄝˋ)
business; a calling

緒言(ㄒㄩˋ ㄧㄢˊ)
a preface; a foreword; a preamble; an introduction

緒餘(ㄒㄩˋ ㄩˊ)
the remnants; a surplus

【緘】 4380
ㄐㄧㄢ jian jiān
1. to seal; to close
2. a letter

緘默(ㄐㄧㄢ ㄇㄛˋ)
to keep silence

緘封(ㄐㄧㄢ ㄈㄥ)
to seal

緘口(ㄐㄧㄢ ㄎㄡˇ)
to keep the mouth shut

緘札(ㄐㄧㄢ ㄓㄚˊ)
a letter

緘繩(ㄐㄧㄢ ㄕㄥˊ)
a rope for tying up a coffin

【線】 4381
(綫) ㄒㄧㄢˋ shiann xiàn
1. a line
2. threads
3. wires

線膨脹(ㄒㄧㄢˋ ㄆㄥˊ ㄓㄤˋ)
(physics) linear expansion

線民(ㄒㄧㄢˋ ㄇㄧㄣˊ)
a stool pigeon; an informer

線粉(ㄒㄧㄢˋ ㄈㄣˇ)
noodles made of bean flour

線頭(ㄒㄧㄢˋ ㄊㄡˊ)
①the end of a thread ②a odd piece of thread ③beginnings of things

線條(ㄒㄧㄢˋ ㄊㄧㄠˊ)
lines; streaks

線路(ㄒㄧㄢˋ ㄌㄨˋ)
①(electricity) a circuit ②a narrow path

線縷(ㄒㄧㄢˋ ㄌㄩˇ)
threads

線圈(ㄒㄧㄢˋ ㄑㄩㄢ)
a coil

線膨係數(ㄒㄧㄢˋ ㄆㄥˊ ㄒㄧˋ ㄕㄨˋ)
a coefficient of linear expansion

線裝本(ㄒㄧㄢˋ ㄓㄨㄤ ㄅㄣˇ)or線裝書(ㄒㄧㄢˋ ㄓㄨㄤ ㄕㄨ)
a book bound in the traditional Chinese style

線蟲類(ㄒㄧㄢˋ ㄔㄨㄥˊ ㄌㄟˋ)
Nematoda

線索(ㄒㄧㄢˋ ㄙㄨㄛˇ)
a clue; a lead

【緞】 4382
ㄉㄨㄢˋ duann duàn
satin

緞帶(ㄉㄨㄢˋ ㄉㄞˋ)
a satin ribbon

緞子(ㄉㄨㄢˋ ・ㄗ)
satin

【緝】 4382
ㄑㄧˋ chih qì
1. to order the arrest of; to arrest; to capture
2. to twist and join (cords)
3. to continue
4. to hem clothing

緝辦(ㄑㄧˋ ㄅㄢˋ)
to arrest and punish

緝捕(ㄑㄧˋ ㄅㄨˇ)
to search and arrest; to capture

緝睦(ㄑㄧˋ ㄇㄨˋ)
at peace with each other

緝盜(ㄑㄧˋ ㄉㄠˋ)
to capture thieves

緝拿(ㄑㄧˋ ㄋㄚˊ)
to arrest; to apprehend: 警緝拿凶手。The police apprehended the murderer.

緝理(ㄑㄧˋ ㄌㄧˇ)
to set in order

緝獲(ㄑㄧˋ ㄏㄨㄛˋ)
to arrest; to capture; to seize

緝照(ㄑㄧˋ ㄓㄠˋ)
bright; brilliant

緝私(ㄑㄧˋ ㄙ)
to arrest smugglers

緝私船(ㄑㄧˋ ㄙ ㄔㄨㄢˊ)
a revenue cutter; an anti-smuggling patrol boat

【絹】 4383
ㄐㄩㄢˋ chi qì
to sew in close and straight stitches

【緗】 4384
ㄒㄧㄤ shiang xiāng
light-yellow silk

緗縹(ㄒㄧㄤ ㄆㄧㄠˇ)
simple, light-yellow clothes

緗帙(ㄒㄧㄤ ㄓˋ)
①a light-yellow book jacket ②a book

緗素(ㄒㄧㄤ ㄙㄨˋ)
①light-yellow silk ②a scroll made of the light-yellow silk

【締】 4385
ㄉㄧˋ dìh dì
to connect; to join; to unite

締盟(ㄉㄧˋ ㄇㄥˊ)
to form an alliance

締結(ㄉㄧˋ ㄐㄧㄝˊ)
to conclude (treaties, agreements, etc.): 兩國締結和平條約。Two nations concluded a peace treaty.

締交(ㄉㄧˋ ㄐㄧㄠ)
to establish diplomatic ties or friendship

締造(ㄉㄧˋ ㄗㄠˋ)
to construct; to compose; to build; to found; to create

締姻(ㄉㄧˋ ㄧㄣ)
to be united in wedlock

締約(ㄉㄧˋ ㄩㄝ)
to conclude a treaty

締約國(ㄉㄧˋ ㄩㄝ ㄍㄨㄛˊ)
a treaty power; a signatory power

【緡】 4386
(緡) ㄇㄧㄣˊ min mín
1. a fishing line
2. cords for stringing up coins

【緦】 4387
ㄙ sy sī
1. fine jute cloth
2. to spin jute thread or yarn

緦麻服(ㄙ ㄇㄚˊ ㄈㄨˊ)or 緦服(ㄙ ㄈㄨˊ)
mourning dress of the lowest degree, worn for three months for distant relatives

【緣】 4388
ㄩㄢˊ yuan yuán
1. a cause; a reason; 為何緣故?
For what reason?
2. to go along; to follow
3. a hem; a margin; an edge; a fringe
4. relationship by fate; predestined relationship

緣邊(ㄩㄢˊ ㄅㄧㄢ)
a hem; a margin; an edge; a border

緣簿(ㄩㄢˊ ㄅㄨˋ)
records of contributions kept at a Buddhist temple

緣木求魚(ㄩㄢˊ ㄇㄨˋ ㄑㄧㄡˊ ㄩˊ)
(literally) to climb a tree to get fish—to seek something from a wrong source; impossible to succeed

緣法(ㄩㄢˊ ㄈㄚˇ)
①to copy or follow the old laws ②to follow or abide by the law ③(Buddhism) predestined relationship

緣分(ㄩㄢˊ ㄈㄣˋ)
relationship by fate; predestined relationship; natural affinity among friends; 我們又遇到了，真是緣分。So we meet again. It must be fate.

緣故(ㄩㄢˊ ㄍㄨˋ)
a cause; a reason

緣何(ㄩㄢˊ ㄏㄜˊ)
why

緣起(ㄩㄢˊ ㄑㄧˇ)
①origins ②a preface; a foreword

緣飾(ㄩㄢˊ ㄕˋ)
to embellish with words

緣坐(ㄩㄢˊ ㄗㄨㄛˋ)
to be punished by the law because of one's relationship with the offender 亦作「連坐」

緣由(ㄩㄢˊ ㄧㄡˊ)
a cause; a reason; the whys and wherefores

緣故(ㄩㄢˊ ㄍㄨˋ)
cause 亦作「原故」

【編】 4389
ㄅㄧㄢ bian biān
1. to knit; to weave
2. to put together; to organize; to form; to arrange
3. to fabricate; to make up; to invent
4. to compile; to edit
5. (part of)a book; a volume

編貝(ㄅㄧㄢ ㄅㄟˋ)
(said of teeth) beautiful and sparkling

編班(ㄅㄧㄢ ㄅㄢ)
①formation of classes (at school) ②to assign (students) to various classes

編排(ㄅㄧㄢ ㄆㄞˊ)
①to arrange in order ②to write and present (a play, etc.)

編造(ㄅㄧㄢ ㄆㄞˊ)
to libel; to vilify

編目(ㄅㄧㄢ ㄇㄨˋ)
to prepare or compile a catalogue; to arrange a table of contents; to catalogue: 新到的書迄今尚未編目。The new books are still uncatalogued.

編髮(ㄅㄧㄢ ㄈㄚˇ)
to braid the hair

編導(ㄅㄧㄢ ㄉㄠˇ)
①to write and direct (a play, film, etc.) ②a director

編訂(ㄅㄧㄢ ㄉㄧㄥˋ)
to compile and to revise

編隊(ㄅㄧㄢ ㄉㄨㄟˋ)
①formation (of aircrafts, etc.): 戰鬥機群編隊飛行。The fighters made a formation flight. ②to organize into groups

編年表(ㄅㄧㄢ ㄋㄧㄢˊ ㄅㄧㄠˇ)
to prepare a chronological record; to compile annals

編年體(ㄅㄧㄢ ㄋㄧㄢˊ ㄊㄧˇ)
(said of history) chronological style

編年史(ㄅㄧㄢ ㄋㄧㄢˊ ㄕˇ)
chronicles; annals

編類(ㄅㄧㄢ ㄌㄟˋ)
to arrange into categories

編列(ㄅㄧㄢ ㄌㄧㄝˋ)
to arrange systematically; to list (the expenses for a project in the budget); to compile

編練(ㄅㄧㄢ ㄌㄧㄢˋ)
to organize and train (the militia troops, etc.)

編號(ㄅㄧㄢ ㄏㄠˋ)
①to arrange under numbers; to number ②a serial number

編戶(ㄅㄧㄢ ㄏㄨˋ)
families entered in household registers—common people

編輯(ㄅㄧㄢ ㄐㄧˊ)
①to edit; to compile ②an editor

編輯部(ㄅㄧㄢ ㄐㄧˊ ㄅㄨˋ)
an editorial department; the editorial office

編輯者(ㄅㄧㄢ ㄐㄧˊ ㄓㄜˇ)or 編輯人(ㄅㄧㄢ ㄐㄧˊ ㄖㄣˊ)
an editor

編結(ㄅㄧㄢ ㄐㄧㄝˊ)
to knit; to weave

編劇(ㄅㄧㄢ ㄐㄩˋ)
①to write a play ②a playwright

編遣(ㄅㄧㄢ ㄑㄧㄢˇ)
to lay off or discharge personnel after reorganization

編磬(ㄅㄧㄢ ㄑㄧㄥˋ)
an ancient musical instrument with 16 musical stones

編寫(ㄅㄧㄢ ㄒㄧㄝˇ)
①to compile: 編寫字典 to compile a dictionary ②to write; to compose: 她正在編寫歌劇。She is composing an opera.

編修(ㄅㄧㄢ ㄒㄧㄡ)
①to compile; to edit: 請現在停止編修。Stop editing now, please. ②a government compiler (in ancient times)

編選(ㄅㄧㄢ ㄒㄩㄢˇ)
to select and edit; to compile

編織(ㄅㄧㄢ ㄓ)
to knit: 她正用毛線編織手套。She is knitting wool into

〔糸部〕

（糸部）

gloves.

编织机（ㄅㄧㄢ ㄓ ㄐㄧ）
a knitting machine

编制（ㄅㄧㄢ ㄓ）
① organic structure; organization ② to work out; to draw up

编制人员（ㄅㄧㄢ ㄓ ㄖㄣˊ ㄩㄢˊ）
employees of a government agency specified in its organic law

编者（ㄅㄧㄢ ㄓㄜˇ）
an editor: 他是那份雜誌的運動版編者。He is the sports editor of that magazine.

编著（ㄅㄧㄢ ㄓㄨˋ）or 编撰（ㄅㄧㄢ ㄓㄨㄢˋ）
to edit; to compile: 他父親編著了一冊美語讀本。His father compiled an English reader.

编钟（ㄅㄧㄢ ㄓㄨㄥ）
an ancient musical instrument with 16 bells

编审（ㄅㄧㄢ ㄕㄣˇ）
① to edit and screen (textbooks, etc.) ② a member of the editing and screening committee

编审委员会（ㄅㄧㄢ ㄕㄣˇ ㄨㄟˇ ㄩㄢˊ ㄏㄨㄟˋ）
an editing and screening committee (for textbooks, etc.)

编书（ㄅㄧㄢ ㄕㄨ）
to edit or compile books

编述（ㄅㄧㄢ ㄕㄨˋ）
to arrange and narrate

编入（ㄅㄧㄢ ㄖㄨˋ）
① to include (in a budget) ② to enlist; to recruit

编造（ㄅㄧㄢ ㄗㄠˋ）
① to fabricate ② to form; to prepare (a budget)

编组（ㄅㄧㄢ ㄗㄨˇ）
to organize into groups

编纂（ㄅㄧㄢ ㄗㄨㄢˇ）
to compile

编译（ㄅㄧㄢ ㄧˋ）
① to translate and compile ② a translator; an interpreter

编译馆（ㄅㄧㄢ ㄧˋ ㄍㄨㄢˇ）
an institute for compilation and translation

编舞（ㄅㄧㄢ ㄨˇ）
to choreograph

编舆（ㄅㄧㄢ ㄩˊ）
a bamboo sedan chair

【缓】 4390
　　ㄏㄨㄢˇ hoan huǎn
1. slow; gradual; tardy; leisurely; unhurried
2. to delay; to slacken; to put off; to postpone; to defer
3. to revive; to refresh

缓办（ㄏㄨㄢˇ ㄅㄢˋ）
to delay action; to put off a project

缓兵之计（ㄏㄨㄢˇ ㄅㄧㄥ ㄓ ㄐㄧˋ）
a strategy for gaining time; delaying tactics

缓不济急（ㄏㄨㄢˇ ㄅㄨˋ ㄐㄧˋ ㄐㄧˊ）
too late to be of use in a crisis 或 Slow action cannot save a critical situation.

缓步（ㄏㄨㄢˇ ㄅㄨˋ）
to walk slowly; to stroll; to ramble

缓慢（ㄏㄨㄢˇ ㄇㄢˋ）
slow: 她行動緩慢。She is slow in action.

缓图（ㄏㄨㄢˇ ㄊㄨˊ）
to plan slowly and carefully

缓和（ㄏㄨㄢˇ ㄏㄜˊ）
① to allay; to subside; to moderate; to relax; to alleviate: 熱常常能緩和疼痛。Heat often alleviates pain. ② calm; mild; moderate; detente

缓缓（ㄏㄨㄢˇ ㄏㄨㄢˇ）
slowly; gradually; little by little: 請緩緩地說。Please speak slowly.

缓急（ㄏㄨㄢˇ ㄐㄧˊ）
degrees of urgency

缓颊（ㄏㄨㄢˇ ㄐㄧㄚˊ）
to dissuade someone from taking certain punitive action (usually on behalf of someone else); to intercede: 我們為他緩頰。We interceded for him.

缓决（ㄏㄨㄢˇ ㄐㄩㄝˊ）
to stay the execution (of a death convict)

缓期（ㄏㄨㄢˇ ㄑㄧˊ）
to postpone a deadline; to suspend

缓限（ㄏㄨㄢˇ ㄒㄧㄢˋ）
to put off the deadline; to extend the time limit

缓刑（ㄏㄨㄢˇ ㄒㄧㄥˊ）
to suspend a sentence; to

---

reprieve; a reprieve; probation

缓召（ㄏㄨㄢˇ ㄓㄠˋ）
to defer the draft (of a man for military service)

缓徵（ㄏㄨㄢˇ ㄓㄥ）
① to remit (taxes) ② to defer the draft of (a man for military service)

缓冲（ㄏㄨㄢˇ ㄔㄨㄥ）
to serve as a buffer; to buff

缓冲地带（ㄏㄨㄢˇ ㄔㄨㄥ ㄉㄧˋ ㄉㄞˋ）
a buffer zone; a neutral zone

缓冲国（ㄏㄨㄢˇ ㄔㄨㄥ ㄍㄨㄛˊ）
a buffer state

缓冲区域（ㄏㄨㄢˇ ㄔㄨㄥ ㄑㄩ ㄩˋ）
a buffer zone

缓冲作用（ㄏㄨㄢˇ ㄔㄨㄥ ㄗㄨㄛˋ ㄩㄥˋ）
buffer reaction

缓役（ㄏㄨㄢˇ ㄧˋ）
draft deferment

缓议（ㄏㄨㄢˇ ㄧˋ）
to defer the discussion

缓一口氣（ㄏㄨㄢˇ ㄧ ㄎㄡˇ ㄑㄧˋ）
to get a breathing space

【缈】 4391
　　ㄇㄧㄠˇ meau miǎo
distant; far and dim—unsubstantial

【缅】 4392
　　ㄇㄧㄢˇ mean miǎn.
1. distant; far; remote
2. to think of something or somebody in the past

缅邈（ㄇㄧㄢˇ ㄇㄧㄠˋ）
far and remote

缅甸（ㄇㄧㄢˇ ㄉㄧㄢˋ）
Burma

缅甸人（ㄇㄧㄢˇ ㄉㄧㄢˋ ㄖㄣˊ）
a Burmese; the Burmese

缅腆（ㄇㄧㄢˇ ㄊㄧㄢˇ）
shy; bashful; shamefaced because of a guilty conscience

缅怀（ㄇㄧㄢˇ ㄏㄨㄞˊ）
to think of; to remember; to cherish the memory of; to recall: 地緬懷過去。She recalled her past.

缅想（ㄇㄧㄢˇ ㄒㄧㄤˇ）
to think of fondly; to remember with affection

缅因（ㄇㄧㄢˇ ㄧㄣ）
the state of Maine, U.S.A.

【纬】 4393
　　ㄨㄟˇ woei wěi
1. the woof
2. parallels showing latitude

on a map
3. books about charms, omens, etc. circulated as appendices to the classics

緯度(ㄨㄟ ㄉㄨˋ)
degrees of latitude (in geography)

緯線(ㄨㄟ ㄒㄧㄢˋ)
parallels or latitude on maps

緯書(ㄨㄟ ㄕㄨ)
books about charms, omens, etc. circulated as appendices to the classics in the latter years of the Earlier Han Dynasty

【緱】 4394
《ㄡ gou gōu》
cord binding on the hilt of a sword

【練】 4395
ㄌㄧㄢˋ liann liàn
1. to practice; to train; to exercise: 我每天練習彈鋼琴。I practice on the piano every day.
2. skilled; experienced: 他很老練。He was an experienced man.
3. to soften and whiten raw silk by boiling

練把式(ㄌㄧㄢˋ ㄅㄚ˙ㄕ˙)
to practice Chinese pugilism

練兵(ㄌㄧㄢˋ ㄅㄧㄥ)
to drill troops; to train troops

練達(ㄌㄧㄢˋ ㄉㄚˊ)
experienced; sophisticated: 他是一位練達的學者。He is an experienced scholar.

練功(ㄌㄧㄢˋ ㄍㄨㄥ)
to do exercises in gymnastics, kung fu. etc.; to practice one's skill

練球(ㄌㄧㄢˋ ㄑㄧㄡˊ)
to practice a ball game

練拳(ㄌㄧㄢˋ ㄑㄩㄢˊ)
to practice boxing

練習(ㄌㄧㄢˋ ㄒㄧˊ)
① to train; to practice (so as to gain skill): 我練習造句。I practice making sentences.
② exercises

練習簿(ㄌㄧㄢˋ ㄒㄧˊ ㄅㄨˋ)
an exercise book

練習題(ㄌㄧㄢˋ ㄒㄧˊ ㄊㄧˊ)
exercises

練習艦(ㄌㄧㄢˋ ㄒㄧˊ ㄐㄧㄢˋ)

a training ship

練習生(ㄌㄧㄢˋ ㄒㄧˊ ㄕㄥ)
a trainee; an apprentice

練習所(ㄌㄧㄢˋ ㄒㄧˊ ㄙㄨㄛˇ)
a training school, institute, station, or camp

練武(ㄌㄧㄢˋ ㄨˇ)
to train oneself in martial arts

練勇(ㄌㄧㄢˋ ㄩㄥˇ)
a militiaman

【緹】 4396
ㄊㄧˊ tyi tí
1. reddish yellow silk
2. reddish yellow soil
3. reddish; red

緹騎(ㄊㄧˊ ㄐㄧ)
① cavaliers in reddish yellow— officials sent out to arrest lawbreakers ② the retinue of ranking officials

緹縈救父(ㄊㄧˊ ㄧㄥˊ ㄐㄧㄡˋ ㄈㄨˋ)
the story of Ti Ying (緹縈), a devoted daughter in the Han Dynasty, saving her father from a cruel punishment by offering to serve the Emperor Wen (漢文帝) as a lowly housemaid in an appeal to him

【緻】 4397
ㄓ jyh zhì
fine; close; dense; delicate

緻密(ㄓ ㄇㄧˋ)
① fine; close; dense; minute ② (said of conduct) appropriate; careful; irreproachable

【緶】 4398
ㄅㄧㄢˋ biann biàn
1. a narrow strip of woven material (such as the hem of a straw hat)
2. to sew up a hem

【緯】 4399
ㄎㄜˋ keh kè
the woof of a woven item

緯絲(ㄎㄜˋ ㄙ)
tapestry

【緜】 4400
(綿) ㄇㄧㄢˊ mian miǎn
1. soft; downy
2. enduring

十畫

【縈】 4401
ㄧㄥ yng yíng

1. to coil; to entwine; to wind around and around; to twine; to round
2. to entangle; to preoccupy; to bog: 他有麻煩縈身。He was preoccupied with trouble.

縈帶(ㄧㄥ ㄉㄞˋ)or 縈迴(ㄧㄥ ㄏㄨㄟˊ)
to wind around and around; to coil

縈懷(ㄧㄥ ㄏㄨㄞˊ)
to linger; to be constantly on one's mind

縈繞(ㄧㄥ ㄖㄠˋ)
to linger; to encircle; to wind around: 疑慮仍縈繞在我心中。A doubt still lingers in my mind.

縈紆(ㄧㄥ ㄩ)
to wind around

【縣】 4402
1. ㄒㄧㄢˋ shiann xiàn
a county; a prefecture

縣太爺(ㄒㄧㄢˋ ㄊㄞˋ ㄧㄝˊ)
a reference to a county magistrate among the people in former times

縣立學校(ㄒㄧㄢˋ ㄌㄧˋ ㄒㄩㄝˊ ㄒㄧㄠˋ)
a county-operated school; a county school

縣令(ㄒㄧㄢˋ ㄌㄧㄥˋ)
(an official title in former times) a county magistrate

縣官(ㄒㄧㄢˋ ㄍㄨㄢ)
(a popular term in former times) a county magistrate

縣學(ㄒㄧㄢˋ ㄒㄩㄝˊ)
a county school (in former times)

縣知事(ㄒㄧㄢˋ ㄓ ㄕˋ)
a county magistrate (in the early years of the Republic)

縣志(ㄒㄧㄢˋ ㄓˋ)
general records of a county; county annals

縣治(ㄒㄧㄢˋ ㄓˋ)
the district under the jurisdiction of a county government

縣長(ㄒㄧㄢˋ ㄓㄤˇ)
① the hsien (or county) magistrate (in old China) ② the chief hsien (or county) executive; the head of a county (in modern China)

縣政府(ㄒㄧㄢˋ ㄓㄥˋ ㄈㄨˇ)
a county government

縣城(ㄒㄧㄢˋ ㄔㄥˊ)

【糸部】

the seat of a county government; a county town

縣試 (ㄒㄧㄢˋ ㄕˋ)
the county examination (as distinct from the provincial and the imperial examinations under the former civil examination system)

縣議會 (ㄒㄧㄢˋ ㄧˋ ㄏㄨㄟˋ)
a county council (with members elected periodically by the people)

縣議員 (ㄒㄧㄢˋ ㄧˋ ㄩㄢˊ)
members of a district council

【縣】 4402
2.(縣) ㄒㄩㄢˊ shyuan
xuan
to hang

【縠】 4403
ㄏㄨˊ hwu hú
crepe

【縋】 4404
ㄓㄨㄟˋ juey zhuì
to hang by a rope; to let down by a rope

縋登 (ㄓㄨㄟˋ ㄉㄥ)
to climb down by a rope

縋城 (ㄓㄨㄟˋ ㄔㄥˊ)
to climb down a city wall by a rope

【縐】 4405
ㄓㄡˋ jow zhòu
1. crepe; crape
2. wrinkled; creased; crinkled

縐布 (ㄓㄡˋ ㄅㄨˋ)
crepe; crape

縐補 (ㄓㄡˋ ㄅㄨˇ)
fine linen cloth; crepe linen

縐綢 (ㄓㄡˋ ㄔㄡˊ)
crepe silk

縐紗 (ㄓㄡˋ ㄕㄚ)
crepe silk

縐紋 (ㄓㄡˋ ㄨㄣˊ)
wrinkles; creases; folds 亦作「皺紋」

【縑】 4406
ㄐㄧㄢ jian jiān
a kind of fine silk

縑帛 (ㄐㄧㄢ ㄅㄛˊ)
silk fabric

縑素 (ㄐㄧㄢ ㄙㄨˋ)
silk used for painting and calligraphic works

【縗】 4407
ㄘㄨㄟ tsuei cui
a piece of sackcloth worn on the breast in mourning

【縛】 4408
ㄈㄨˋ fwu fú
to bind; to tie

縛鷄之力 (ㄈㄨˋ ㄐㄧ ㄓ ㄌㄧˋ)
the strength for binding a chicken—very limited strength

縛緊 (ㄈㄨˋ ㄐㄧㄣˇ)
to tie or bind tightly

縛住 (ㄈㄨˋ ㄓㄨˋ)
to tie up; to bind up

縛手縛脚 (ㄈㄨˋ ㄕㄡˇ ㄈㄨˋ ㄐㄧㄠˇ)
with too many constraints; unable to act freely

【縉】 4409
ㄐㄧㄣˋ jinn jìn
red silk

縉紳 (ㄐㄧㄣˋ ㄕㄣ)
a ranking government official; a government official in retirement; the gentry 亦作「搢紳」

【縕】 4410
ㄩㄣˋ yunn yùn
1. loose hemp; old yarn
2. confused; chaotic

縕袍 (ㄩㄣˋ ㄆㄠˊ)
coarse clothing

【縞】 4411
ㄍㄠˇ gao gǎo
plain white raw silk

縞冠 (ㄍㄠˇ ㄍㄨㄢ)
a plain white cap worn in mourning

縞素 (ㄍㄠˇ ㄙㄨˋ)
①plain white clothes worn in mourning ② white silk

縞衣 (ㄍㄠˇ ㄧ)
①plain white clothes worn in mourning ② thin white silks

【縝】 4412
ㄓㄣˇ jeen zhěn
fine; close; minute

縝密 (ㄓㄣˇ ㄇㄧˋ)
fine; minute; well considered and planned in every respect; careful; meticulous; deliberate

【縟】 4413
ㄖㄨˋ ruh rù
1. rich ornament
2. excessive formality or ceremony

縟禮 (ㄖㄨˋ ㄌㄧˇ)
excessive formality or ceremony

縟節 (ㄖㄨˋ ㄐㄧㄝˊ)
excessive formality or ceremony: 我不喜歡繁文縟節。I dislike complex and excessive ceremony.

縟麗 (ㄖㄨˋ ㄌㄧˋ)
resplendent; gorgeous; magnificent

【縢】 4414
ㄊㄥˊ terng téng
1. to bind; to tie; to restrict; to restrain
2. a band

縢履 (ㄊㄥˊ ㄌㄩˇ)
shoes for bound feet

【縊】 4415
ㄧˋ yih yì
to strangle; to hang: 他自縊。He hanged himself.

縊頸 (ㄧˋ ㄐㄧㄥˇ)
to hang oneself

縊殺 (ㄧˋ ㄕㄚ)
to strangle to death; to hang

縊死 (ㄧˋ ㄙˇ)
to hang oneself

十一畫

【縫】 4416
1. ㄈㄥˊ ferng féng
1. to sew; to stitch
2. to suture

縫補 (ㄈㄥˊ ㄅㄨˇ)
to mend (clothes, etc.)

縫工 (ㄈㄥˊ ㄍㄨㄥ)
a sewing worker; a sewer; a seamstress

縫合 (ㄈㄥˊ ㄏㄜˊ)
(medicine) to join by sewing; to suture; to sew up: 醫生將傷口縫合。The doctor sewed up the wound.

縫合線 (ㄈㄥˊ ㄏㄜˊ ㄒㄧㄢˋ)
a suture

縫製 (ㄈㄥˊ ㄓˋ)
to make or manufacture (sewed products)

縫紉 (ㄈㄥˊ ㄖㄣˋ)
to sew

縫紉 (ㄈㄥˊ ㄖㄣˋ)
sewing; needlework

縫紉機 (ㄈㄥˊ ㄖㄣˋ ㄐㄧ)
a sewing machine

縫衣婦 (ㄈㄥˊ ㄧ ㄈㄨˋ)
a seamstress; a needle-woman

縫衣服 (ㄈㄥˊ ㄧ ㄈㄨˊ)
to sew clothes; to do needle-

work

【縫】 4416
2. ㄈㄥˊ feng féng

1. a suture
2. a crack, an opening; a fissure; a cleft; a chink; a crevice: 牆上裂了一條縫兒。There is a crack in the wall.

縫隙(ㄈㄥˊ ㄒㄧˋ)
a chink; a crack; a crevice

縫子(ㄈㄥˊ ˙ㄗ)or 縫兒(ㄈㄥˊ ㄦ)
①a suture ②a crack; an opening; a cleft; a chink

【縭】 4417
ㄌㄧˊ lí

1. a bridal veil; a bride's sash
2. to tie; to bind

【縱】 4418
1. ㄗㄨㄥˇ tzonq zòng

1. to allow to move or work freely; to let go; to let fly
2. to indulge; indulgence
3. even if; although

縱步(ㄗㄨㄥˇ ㄅㄨˋ)
①to stride: 他縱步向前走。He strode forward. ②a jump; a bound: 他一傾縱步跳過了小溪。He crossed the stream in a jump.

縱目(ㄗㄨㄥˇ ㄇㄨˋ)
to look as far as one's eyes can see

縱盜(ㄗㄨㄥˇ ㄉㄠˋ)
to overlook thieves

縱談(ㄗㄨㄥˇ ㄊㄢˊ)
to talk without inhibition; to speak freely: 我們縱談夢想和抱負。We spoke freely about our dreams and ambitions.

縱跳(ㄗㄨㄥˇ ㄊㄧㄠˋ)
to look far and wide

縱脫(ㄗㄨㄥˇ ㄊㄨㄛ)
uninhibited; unrestrained

縱覽(ㄗㄨㄥˇ ㄌㄢˇ)
to look freely and extensively

縱浪(ㄗㄨㄥˇ ㄌㄤˋ)
①uninhibited; unrestrained ②profligate; dissolute

縱令(ㄗㄨㄥˇ ㄌㄧㄥˋ)
even if; even though: 縱令你錯了，你也錯了。Even if I am wrong, you are wrong too.

縱觀(ㄗㄨㄥˇ ㄍㄨㄢ)
to take a free, wide look; to take a sweeping look

縱橫馳騁(ㄗㄨㄥˇ ㄏㄥˊ ㄔˊ ㄔㄥˇ)
to move about freely and

swiftly; to sweep through the length and breadth of

縱虎歸山(ㄗㄨㄥˇ ㄏㄨˇ ㄍㄨㄟ ㄕㄢ)
(literally) to allow the tiger to return to the mountain —to allow an evildoer to escape

縱火(ㄗㄨㄥˇ ㄏㄨㄛˇ)
to commit arson

縱火犯(ㄗㄨㄥˇ ㄏㄨㄛˇ ㄈㄢˋ)
an arsonist: 他是縱火犯。He is an arsonist.

縱酒(ㄗㄨㄥˇ ㄐㄧㄡˇ)
to drink to excess

縱囚(ㄗㄨㄥˇ ㄑㄧㄡˊ)
to release prisoners

縱情(ㄗㄨㄥˇ ㄑㄧㄥˊ)or 縱性(ㄗㄨㄥˇ ㄒㄧㄥˋ)
to do as one pleases; to follow one's inclinations; to act without self-control; to one's heart's content: 我們縱情的舞蹈。We danced to our hearts' content.

縱便(ㄗㄨㄥˇ ㄕˋ)
even if; even though: 縱使他不來, 我也不介意。I shan't mind even if he doesn't come.

縱身(ㄗㄨㄥˇ ㄕㄣ)
to let the body move (upward, forward, etc.) with full force; to jump; to leap: 兵士們縱身上馬。The soldiers leaped onto their horses.

縱聲(ㄗㄨㄥˇ ㄕㄥ)
to shout or laugh at the top of one's voice

縱然(ㄗㄨㄥˇ ㄖㄢˊ)
even if; even though: 縱然成功的希望不大, 我也要試試。I'll try even though there is little hope of success.

縱容(ㄗㄨㄥˇ ㄖㄨㄥˊ)
to pass over indulgently; to connive at: 有些警察縱容賭博。Some policemen connive at gambling.

縱恣(ㄗㄨㄥˇ ㄗˋ)
to give free rein to the passions; to behave without restraint; to indulge; indulgence

縱逸(ㄗㄨㄥˇ ㄧˋ)
unrestrained; uninhibited; dissolute

縱有(ㄗㄨㄥˇ ㄧㄡˇ)

even if there is...; even though there is...

縱淫(ㄗㄨㄥˇ ㄧㄣˊ)or 縱慾(ㄗㄨㄥˇ ㄩˋ)
to abandon oneself to carnal desire; to be dissolute; to be debauched: 他有縱淫的氣色。He had the look of a debauched man.

縱飲(ㄗㄨㄥˇ ㄧㄣˇ)
to indulge in drinking; to drink immoderately: 他縱飲無度。He indulges in drinking.

縱慾無度(ㄗㄨㄥˇ ㄩˋ ㄨˊ ㄉㄨˋ)
to indulge in carnal pleasure without restraint

【縱】 4418
2. ㄗㄨㄥ tzong zōng

vertical; longitudinal

縱波(ㄗㄨㄥ ㄅㄛ)
(physics) longitudinal waves

縱隊(ㄗㄨㄥ ㄉㄨㄟˋ)
column (as opposed to rank) of troops: 一路縱隊行軍。A column of troops marched.

縱斷面(ㄗㄨㄥ ㄉㄨㄢˋ ㄇㄧㄢˋ)
a longitudinal or vertical section; a profile

縱谷(ㄗㄨㄥ ㄍㄨˇ)
a longitudinal valley: 他在縱谷中迷失。He got lost in a longitudinal valley.

縱貫(ㄗㄨㄥ ㄍㄨㄢˋ)
to run lengthwise through

縱貫鐵路(ㄗㄨㄥ ㄍㄨㄢˋ ㄊㄧㄝˇ ㄌㄨˋ)
the main north-south railway of Taiwan

縱海岸(ㄗㄨㄥ ㄏㄞˇ ㄢˋ)
(geology) longitudinal coast

縱橫(ㄗㄨㄥ ㄏㄥˊ)
①the horizontal and the vertical; in length and breadth ②(during the Epoch of Warring States) the two opposing principles of a confederacy against Chin and a federation under Chin ③to roam about without opposition ④with great ease: 他的筆意縱橫。He wrote with great ease.

縱橫捭闔(ㄗㄨㄥ ㄏㄥˊ ㄅㄞˇ ㄏㄜˊ)
to deal with friends and enemies with skill

縱橫家(ㄗㄨㄥ ㄏㄥˊ ㄐㄧㄚ)
the Political Strategists (in the Epoch of Warring

〔糸部〕

〔糸部〕

States)

縱橫交錯（ㄗㄨㄥ ㄏㄥˊ ㄐㄧㄠ ㄘㄨㄛˋ）
arranged in a crisscross pattern

縱橫自如（ㄗㄨㄥ ㄏㄥˊ ㄗˋ ㄖㄨˊ）
capable of moving in any direction

縱橫四海（ㄗㄨㄥ ㄏㄥˊ ㄙˋ ㄏㄞˇ）
to overrun the four seas; to overrun the whole China

縱軸（ㄗㄨㄥˋ ㄓㄡˊ）
the axis of an ordinate

縱深（ㄗㄨㄥˋ ㄕㄣ）
(military) the depth (of defense works)

縱座標（ㄗㄨㄥˋ ㄗㄨㄛˋ ㄅㄧㄠ）
the ordinate (as opposed to the abscissa)

【縮】 4419
ㄙㄨㄛ suo suō
（讀音 ㄙㄨˋ suh sù）
1. to contract; to shorten; to reduce; to decrease; to shrink
2. to draw back; to recoil; to wince
3. to bind

縮本（ㄙㄨㄛ ㄅㄣˇ）
①a pocket size edition (of a book) ②an abridged edition (of a book)

縮地之術（ㄙㄨㄛ ㄉㄧˋ ㄓ ㄕㄨˋ）
technique of contracting space; magic of reducing distance

縮短（ㄙㄨㄛ ㄉㄨㄢˇ）
to shorten; to cut down; to shrink; to reduce in length; to contract: 我把文章縮短成一半。I cut the article to half its length.

縮頭吐舌（ㄙㄨㄛ ㄊㄡˊ ㄊㄨˇ ㄕㄜˊ）
to shrug and stick out the tongue (as a jocular expression of fear)

縮頭縮腦（ㄙㄨㄛ ㄊㄡˊ ㄙㄨㄛ ㄋㄠˇ）
to cower or shrink from fear; to be hesitant; to be timid; to be fainthearted

縮圓器（ㄙㄨㄛ ㄩㄢˊ ㄑㄧˋ）
a reduction machine

縮合（ㄙㄨㄛ ㄏㄜˊ）
(chemistry) condensation; to condense

縮回（ㄙㄨㄛ ㄏㄨㄟˊ）
to draw back; to wince; to flinch; to recoil

縮減（ㄙㄨㄛ ㄐㄧㄢˇ）
to reduce; to lessen; to decrease; to curtail; to cut down: 日本縮減軍費。Japan cut down military expenditure.

縮寫（ㄙㄨㄛ ㄒㄧㄝˇ）
abbreviation; to abbreviate: 基督教青年會縮寫成 Y.M.C.A.。Young Men's Christian Association is commonly abbreviated to Y.M.C.A.

縮小（ㄙㄨㄛ ㄒㄧㄠˇ）
to contract; to lessen; to reduce

縮小範圍（ㄙㄨㄛ ㄒㄧㄠˇ ㄈㄢˋ ㄨㄟˊ）
to reduce the scope

縮尺（ㄙㄨㄛ ㄔˇ）
a scale rule; a tape measure

縮成一團（ㄙㄨㄛ ㄔㄥˊ ㄧˋ ㄊㄨㄢˊ）
to huddle up; to curl up: 我們嚇得縮成一團。We huddled ourselves up with fear.

縮手旁觀（ㄙㄨㄛ ㄕㄡˇ ㄆㄤˊ ㄍㄨㄢ）
to watch from the sideline without interfering; to stand by with folded arms

縮手縮腳（ㄙㄨㄛ ㄕㄡˇ ㄙㄨㄛ ㄐㄧㄠˇ）
①to keep hands and feet drawn (from cold, reluctance to act; etc.) ②timid; overcautious: 不要像隻老鼠縮手縮腳的。Don't be as timid as a rat.

縮水（ㄙㄨㄛ ㄕㄨㄟˇ）
①dehydration ②(said of fabrics) to shrink after washing; shrinkage

縮水劑（ㄙㄨㄛ ㄕㄨㄟˇ ㄐㄧˋ）
a dehydrating agent

縮衣節食（ㄙㄨㄛ ㄧ ㄐㄧㄝˊ ㄕˊ）
to reduce expenses on clothing and food; to practice austerity; to economize: 他爲了出國縮衣節食。He economized on food and clothing in order to go abroad.

縮印（ㄙㄨㄛ ㄧㄣˋ）
to reprint books in a reduced format

縮影（ㄙㄨㄛ ㄧㄥˇ）
a miniature; an epitome

【縵】 4420
ㄇㄢˋ mann màn
1. plain silk
2. plain; unadorned
3. slow

【縲】 4421
ㄌㄟˊ lei léi
black rope (for a criminal)

縲絏（ㄌㄟˊ ㄒㄧㄝˋ）
bonds; rope for binding a criminal—(figuratively) prison

【縴】 4422
ㄑㄧㄢ chiann qiàn
a towrope; a towline

縴夫（ㄑㄧㄢ ㄈㄨ）
a boat tower

縴戶（ㄑㄧㄢ ㄏㄨˋ）
workers who tow boats; boat towers

縴繩（ㄑㄧㄢ ㄕㄥˊ）
a towrope; a towline

【縷】 4423
ㄌㄩˇ leu lǚ
1. a thread; yarn
2. a wisp; a strand; a lock: 一縷頭髮 a lock of hair
3. detailed; in detail

縷縷（ㄌㄩˇ ㄌㄩˇ）
continuous; endlessly: 炊烟縷縷上升。Wisps of smoke rose continuously from the chimneys.

縷解（ㄌㄩˇ ㄐㄧㄝˇ）
to explain in detail

縷析（ㄌㄩˇ ㄒㄧ）
to analyze in detail

縷陳（ㄌㄩˇ ㄔㄣˊ）
to state in detail; to go into details

縷述（ㄌㄩˇ ㄕㄨˋ）
to describe or narrate in detail; to go into particulars: 船長縷述他冒險的故事。The captain narrated his adventures in detail.

【縹】 4424
ㄆㄧㄠ peau piǎo
1. light-blue silk
2. light blue
3. dim; misty; indistinct

縹緲（ㄆㄧㄠ ㄇㄧㄠˇ）
wafting lightly

縹渺（ㄆㄧㄠ ㄇㄧㄠˇ）
distant and dim; far and indistinct; intangible and incorporeal

縹囊（ㄆㄧㄠ ㄋㄤˊ）
a silk bag for holding books

縹緗（ㄆㄧㄠ ㄒㄧㄤ）
valuable books

縹帙（ㄆㄧㄠ ㄓˋ）

books

總瓦(ㄨㄚˇ ㄨㄚˊ)
glossy tiles

【總】 4425
ㄗㄨㄥˇ tzoong zǒng

1. to gather; to collect; to assemble; to unite
2. always
3. all; general; overall; complete; total
4. chief; principal; central
5. at any rate; in any event; anyway; after all; sooner or later: 這個事遲早是要面對的。We will face the facts sooner or later.

總罷工(ㄗㄨㄥˇ ㄅㄚˋ ㄍㄨㄥ)
a general strike

總包寄遞(ㄗㄨㄥˇ ㄅㄠ ㄐㄧˋ ㄉㄧˋ)
mail of printed materials en masse at reduced postage under a contract with the post office

總辦(ㄗㄨㄥˇ ㄅㄢˋ)
managers or directors (especially of some government agencies toward the end of the Ching Dynasty)

總崩潰(ㄗㄨㄥˇ ㄅㄥ ㄎㄨㄟˋ)
total collapse

總編輯(ㄗㄨㄥˇ ㄅㄧㄢ ㄐㄧˊ)
an editor-in-chief; a managing editor: 他是總編輯。He is the chief editor.

總兵(ㄗㄨㄥˇ ㄅㄧㄥ)
one of the titles of a high-ranking military officer in former times

總部(ㄗㄨㄥˇ ㄅㄨˋ)
headquarters

總批發(ㄗㄨㄥˇ ㄆㄧ ㄈㄚ)
general wholesale distribution (of commodities in a given area)

總評(ㄗㄨㄥˇ ㄆㄧㄥˊ)
general comment; overall appraisal: 他對此結果作了總評。He made a general comment on the results.

總平均(ㄗㄨㄥˇ ㄆㄧㄥˊ ㄐㄩㄣ)
an overall average

總目(ㄗㄨㄥˇ ㄇㄨˋ)
a general index

總髮(ㄗㄨㄥˇ ㄈㄚˇ)
childhood

總得(ㄗㄨㄥˇ ㄉㄟˇ)
to have to; somehow: 我總得

設法將其完成。I must get it finished somehow.

總代理(ㄗㄨㄥˇ ㄉㄞˋ ㄌㄧˇ)
(business) a general agent

總督(ㄗㄨㄥˇ ㄉㄨ)
a viceroy; a governor-general

總動員(ㄗㄨㄥˇ ㄉㄨㄥˋ ㄩㄢˊ)
general mobilization

總體戰(ㄗㄨㄥˇ ㄊㄧˇ ㄓㄢˋ)
an all-out war; a total war

總退卻(ㄗㄨㄥˇ ㄊㄨㄟˋ ㄑㄩㄝˋ)
general retreat: 全軍總退卻。The whole army was in full retreat.

總統(ㄗㄨㄥˇ ㄊㄨㄥˇ)
the president (of a state)

總統府(ㄗㄨㄥˇ ㄊㄨㄥˇ ㄈㄨˇ)
the presidential office

總統當選人(ㄗㄨㄥˇ ㄊㄨㄥˇ ㄉㄤ ㄒㄩㄢˇ ㄖㄣˊ)
a president-elect

總統候選人(ㄗㄨㄥˇ ㄊㄨㄥˇ ㄏㄡˋ ㄒㄩㄢˇ ㄖㄣˊ)
a presidential candidate

總統制(ㄗㄨㄥˇ ㄊㄨㄥˇ ㄓˋ)
a political system under which the president is the chief executive

總攬大權(ㄗㄨㄥˇ ㄌㄢˇ ㄉㄚˋ ㄑㄩㄢˊ)
to be in full power; to have full control of the government; to have overall authority

總理(ㄗㄨㄥˇ ㄌㄧˇ)
① a prime minister; a premier ② a president of a political party, etc.) ③ a reference to Dr. Sun Yat-sen among members of the Kuomintang which he founded

總理衙門(ㄗㄨㄥˇ ㄌㄧˇ ㄧㄚˊ ㄇㄣˊ)
the Ministry or Department of Foreign Affairs, set up toward the end of the Ching Dynasty

總量(ㄗㄨㄥˇ ㄌㄧㄤˋ)
a total amount

總領事(ㄗㄨㄥˇ ㄌㄧㄥˇ ㄕˋ)
a consul general

總領事館(ㄗㄨㄥˇ ㄌㄧㄥˇ ㄕˋ ㄍㄨㄢˇ)
a consulate general

總路線(ㄗㄨㄥˇ ㄌㄨˋ ㄒㄧㄢˋ)
a general line (a Chinese Communist terminology)

general discussion; a summary; an introduction: 這本歷史書於每章末均有一總論。The history book has a summary at the end of each chapter.

總綱(ㄗㄨㄥˇ ㄍㄤ)
general principles

總括(ㄗㄨㄥˇ ㄍㄨㄚ)
to sum up; to summarize: 總括之，她是一個可愛的女孩。To sum up, she is a nice girl.

總歸(ㄗㄨㄥˇ ㄍㄨㄟ)
anyhow; eventually; after all: 事實總歸是事實。After all, facts are facts.

總管(ㄗㄨㄥˇ ㄍㄨㄢˇ)
① a superintendent; a supervisor; a director; a manager ② the title of a ranking military officer in ancient times ③ to supervise: 自修室由教師總管。Study halls are supervised by teachers.

總攻擊令(ㄗㄨㄥˇ ㄍㄨㄥ ㄐㄧ ㄌㄧㄥˋ)
orders for the general offensive

總工會(ㄗㄨㄥˇ ㄍㄨㄥ ㄏㄨㄟˋ)
a federation of labor unions

總工程師(ㄗㄨㄥˇ ㄍㄨㄥ ㄔㄥˊ ㄕ)
a chief engineer

總共(ㄗㄨㄥˇ ㄍㄨㄥˋ)
altogether; in all; all told: 總共有五十個客人。There were 50 guests all told.

總合(ㄗㄨㄥˇ ㄏㄜˊ)
an assemblage

總和(ㄗㄨㄥˇ ㄏㄜˊ)
the sum total; the total; the grand total; as a whole

總行(ㄗㄨㄥˇ ㄏㄤˊ)or**總店**(ㄗㄨㄥˇ ㄉㄧㄢˋ)
a head office (of a business firm)

總會(ㄗㄨㄥˇ ㄏㄨㄟˋ)
① a conglomeration; an assemblage; a collection ② central committee or administrative body (of an association, etc.) ③ a club ④ bound to; inevitable; sure to happen

總匯(ㄗㄨㄥˇ ㄏㄨㄟˋ)
① (said of books) an assemblage; a collection ② (said of

（糸部）

糸部

rivers) confluence

總機(ㄗㄨㄥ ㄐㄧ)
a telephone switchboard

總機關(ㄗㄨㄥ ㄐㄧ ㄍㄨㄢ)
①headquarters ②a chief mechanism (of a machine)

總集(ㄗㄨㄥ ㄐㄧ)
the complete works (of one or more writers)

總計(ㄗㄨㄥ ㄐㄧ)
the sum total; the total; the grand total: 他的債務總計達二百萬元。His debts reached a total of two million dollars.

總結(ㄗㄨㄥ ㄐㄧㄝ)
①summation; conclusion; finale ②to sum up: 法官總結證詞。The judge summed up the evidence.

總教練(ㄗㄨㄥ ㄐㄧㄠ ㄌㄧㄢ)
a chief coach (of a sport delegation): 他是我們的足球總教練。He is our chief coach in football.

總教官(ㄗㄨㄥ ㄐㄧㄠ ㄍㄨㄢ)
a chief instructor (of a service school)

總監(ㄗㄨㄥ ㄐㄧㄢ)
an inspector general; a chief inspector

總經理(ㄗㄨㄥ ㄐㄧㄥ ㄌㄧ)
a general manager

總局(ㄗㄨㄥ ㄐㄩ)
the head office; headquarters (of the police in a city or county): 他在總局工作。He works in the head office.

總角(ㄗㄨㄥ ㄐㄩㄝ)
a child's hair bound into a hornlike knot—childhood

總角之交(ㄗㄨㄥ ㄐㄩㄝ ㄓ ㄐㄧㄠ)
a friend since childhood

總選(ㄗㄨㄥ ㄒㄩㄢ)
a general election

總之(ㄗㄨㄥ ㄓ)
in short; in conclusion; in brief; in a word: 總之, 這就是對於辯論的答覆。This, in brief, is the answer to the argument.

總值(ㄗㄨㄥ ㄓ)
total value; a total price

總指揮(ㄗㄨㄥ ㄓ ㄏㄨㄟ)
the commander-in-chief: 他是這征隊的總指揮。He is the commander-in-chief of an

expedition.

總指揮部(ㄗㄨㄥ ㄓ ㄏㄨㄟ ㄅㄨ)
the headquarters of a high command

總鎮(ㄗㄨㄥ ㄓㄣ)
one of the titles of a high-ranking military officer in former times 亦稱「總兵」

總長(ㄗㄨㄥ ㄓㄤ)
①a cabinet minister in the early years of the Republic ②short for chief of the general staff

總帳(ㄗㄨㄥ ㄓㄤ)
(bookkeeping) a general ledger; a ledger: 他要看總帳。He wants to see a ledger.

總主筆(ㄗㄨㄥ ㄓㄨ ㄅㄧ)
a chief editorial writer: 他是紐約客的總主筆。He is the chief editorial writer of New Yorker.

總狀花序(ㄗㄨㄥ ㄓㄨㄤ ㄏㄨㄚ ㄒㄩ)
(botany) raceme

總重量(ㄗㄨㄥ ㄓㄨㄥ ㄌㄧㄤ)
gross weight

總稱(ㄗㄨㄥ ㄔㄥ)
a generic name; a general term

總是(ㄗㄨㄥ ㄕ)
always; without exception: 他們總是星期六來。They always come on Saturday.

總商會(ㄗㄨㄥ ㄕㄤ ㄏㄨㄟ)
the general chamber of commerce

總署(ㄗㄨㄥ ㄕㄨ)
①the Ministry of Foreign Affairs in former times (總理衙門) ②headquarters; the head office

總數(ㄗㄨㄥ ㄕㄨ)
the total amount; the total; the amount: 總數是一百二十。The total is 120.

總人口(ㄗㄨㄥ ㄖㄣ ㄎㄡ)
total population

總則(ㄗㄨㄥ ㄗㄜ)
general principles

(ㄗㄨㄥ ㄗㄚ)
numerous; abundant; teeming

總辭職(ㄗㄨㄥ ㄘ ㄓ)
to resign en bloc (usually referring to a cabinet): 舊內閣已總辭職。The old cabinet has resigned en bloc.

總册(ㄗㄨㄥ ㄘㄜ)
a book of general record (as opposed to one carrying specifics)

總裁(ㄗㄨㄥ ㄘㄞ)
a director general, president or governor (of a bank, political party, etc.): 他是我們銀行的總裁。He is the president of our bank.

總司令(ㄗㄨㄥ ㄙ ㄌㄧㄥ)
the commander-in-chief: 他是陸軍總司令。He is the commander-in-chief of the army.

總司令部(ㄗㄨㄥ ㄙ ㄌㄧㄥ ㄅㄨ)
general headquarters (of the military service)

總數(ㄗㄨㄥ ㄙㄨ)
①on the whole; all things considered; in general ②at long last; finally

總額(ㄗㄨㄥ ㄜ)
the total amount; the sum total

總而言之(ㄗㄨㄥ ㄦ ㄧㄢ ㄓ)
in short; in a word; to sum up: 總而言之, 我們生氣地回家了。In short, we went home angry.

總要(ㄗㄨㄥ ㄧㄠ)
should always; must always

總務(ㄗㄨㄥ ㄨ)
general affairs

總預算(ㄗㄨㄥ ㄩ ㄙㄨㄢ)
a general budget

【縶】 4426
ㄓ jyr zhí
1. to tie; to bind; to connect
2. to imprison
3. a bridle

縶維(ㄓ ㄨㄟ)
to retain (a man of talent)

【縻】 4427
ㄇㄧ mi mí
to tie; to fasten; to connect

【繁】 4428
1.(縏)ㄈㄢ farn fán
1. many; numerous; abundant; prolific
2. complex; complicated; intricate

繁茂(ㄈㄢ ㄇㄠ)
(said of vegetation) lush or luxuriant

繁忙(ㄈㄢ ㄇㄤ)
very busy; hectic: 他們的工作很繁忙。They are very busy

with their work.

繁密(ㄈㄢˊㄇㄧˋ)
dense; thick

繁分數(ㄈㄢˊㄈㄣ ㄕㄨˋ)
a complex fraction

繁富(ㄈㄢˊㄈㄨˋ)
many; numerous; abundant: 美國的天然資源繁富。America is abundant in natural resources.

繁複(ㄈㄢˊㄈㄨˋ)
complex; complicated; intricate

繁多(ㄈㄢˊㄉㄨㄛ)
many; numerous

繁體字(ㄈㄢˊㄊㄧˇㄗˋ)
the original complex form of a simplified Chinese character

繁難(ㄈㄢˊㄋㄢˊ)
complicated and troublesome

繁華(ㄈㄢˊㄏㄨㄚˊ)
① prosperous; flourishing; booming; thriving ② pompous; extravagant

繁華世界(ㄈㄢˊㄏㄨㄚˊㄕˋㄐㄧㄝˋ)
this vain world

繁劇(ㄈㄢˊㄐㄩˋ)
a very heavy work load

繁缺(ㄈㄢˊㄑㄩㄝ)
a post with a very heavy work load

繁細(ㄈㄢˊㄒㄧˋ)
detailed in a complicated way; overloaded with details

繁星(ㄈㄢˊㄒㄧㄥ)
numerous stars: 我們在夜晚可看見繁星。We can see the numerous stars at night.

繁殖(ㄈㄢˊㄓˊ)
to multiply by reproduction; to propagate; to breed: 大多數的鳥在春季繁殖。Most birds breed in the spring.

繁殖力(ㄈㄢˊㄓˊㄌㄧˋ)
procreative power

繁徵博引(ㄈㄢˊㄓㄥ ㄅㄛˊㄧㄣˇ)
to use an abundance of proofs; to quote from many sources

繁重(ㄈㄢˊㄓㄨㄥˋ)
(said of work loads) heavy; arduous; strenuous

繁盛(ㄈㄢˊㄕㄥˋ)
thriving; flourishing; prosperous

繁暑(ㄈㄢˊㄕㄨˇ)
intense heat in summer

繁縟(ㄈㄢˊㄖㄨˋ)
abundant; prolific

繁榮(ㄈㄢˊㄖㄨㄥˊ)
prosperous; flourishing; thriving

繁雜(ㄈㄢˊㄗㄚˊ)
complicated; complex; intricate: 他們的教育制度十分繁雜。Their educational system is very complex.

繁瑣(ㄈㄢˊㄙㄨㄛˇ)
minute and complicated

繁碎(ㄈㄢˊㄙㄨㄟˋ)
detailed in a complicated way

繁衍(ㄈㄢˊㄧㄢˇ)
to proliferate; to teem

繁蕪(ㄈㄢˊㄨˊ)
loaded with unnecessary words; expressed in too many words; verbose

繁文縟節(ㄈㄢˊㄨㄣˊㄖㄨˋㄐㄧㄝˊ)
excessive ceremony

【繁】 4428
2. ㄆㄛˊ por pó
a Chinese family name

【繄】 4429
1. ㄧ i
1. a phrase-initial particle (in archaic Chinese)
2. a verb functioning like the verb "to be" (in archaic Chinese)
3. alas

【繇】 4430
1. ㄧㄡˊ you yóu
1. same as 由—through; via; by way of
2. same as 悠—to be in a leisurely manner and satisfied with oneself

【繇】 4430
2.(傜) ㄧㄠˊ yau yáo
1. labor service
2. luxuriant

繇賦(ㄧㄠˊㄈㄨˋ)
compulsory labor and land tax

【績】 4431
ㄐㄧ ji jī
1. to spin; to twist
2. merit; achievements; exploits; meritorious labor

績麻(ㄐㄧ ㄇㄚˊ)
to spin hemp

績紡(ㄐㄧ ㄈㄤˇ)
to spin

績女(ㄐㄧ ㄋㄩˇ)
a spinster (who spins)

績溪(ㄐㄧ ㄒㄧ)
name of a county in Anhwei

績效(ㄐㄧ ㄒㄧㄠˋ)
results; effects; achievements

績效預算(ㄐㄧ ㄒㄧㄠˋㄩˋㄙㄨㄢˋ)
performance budgeting

績學(ㄐㄧ ㄒㄩㄝˊ)
to pursue knowledge

績成(ㄐㄧ ㄔㄥˊ)
achievements

績用(ㄐㄧ ㄩㄥˋ)
utility; use

【繅】 4432
ㄙㄠ sau sāo
to draw or unwind (silk from cocoons)

繅繭(ㄙㄠ ㄐㄧㄢˇ)or 繅繭出絲(ㄙㄠ ㄐㄧㄢˇㄔㄨ ㄙ)
to draw silk from cocoons

繅絲(ㄙㄠ ㄙ)
to draw silk (from cocoons)

【繃】 4433
1.(綳) ㄅㄥ beng bēng
to bind

繃繃場面(ㄅㄥ ㄅㄥ ㄔㄤˇㄇㄧㄢˋ)
to manage somehow to keep up appearances

繃帶(ㄅㄥ ㄉㄞˋ)
a bandage: 他的頭用繃帶紮起。He has his head in bandages.

繃線(ㄅㄥ ㄒㄧㄢˋ)
bastings

繃子(ㄅㄥ ㄗˇ)
an embroidery frame

【繃】 4433
2.(綳) ㄅㄥˇ beeng běng
1. taut; tense
2. to endure or bear

繃不住(ㄅㄥˇㄅㄨˋㄓㄨˋ)
unable to endure or bear

繃着臉(ㄅㄥˇㄓㄜˊㄌㄧㄢˇ)
to have a taut face; to assume a serious or displeased look; to pull a long face

【繃】 4433
3.(綳) ㄅㄥˋ benq bèng
to break open; to burst open; to split open; to crack

繃斷(ㄅㄥˋㄉㄨㄢˋ)

〔糸部〕

〔糸部〕

a snap from tension

【繆】 4434
1. ㄇㄡˊ mou móu
precautions; preparations

繆篆
one of the six styles of characters begun in the reign of Wang Mang (王莽)

【繆】 4434
2. ㄇㄧㄠˋ miaw miào
a Chinese family name

【繆】 4434
3. ㄇㄧㄡˋ miow miù
erroneous; preposterous; absurd; false; an error; a mistake 亦作「謬」

繆巧(ㄇㄧㄠˇ ㄑㄧㄠˇ)
tricks; wiles; ruses

繆種流傳(ㄇㄧㄠˋ ㄓㄨㄥˇ ㄌㄧㄡˊ ㄔㄨㄢˊ)
People of inability become prosperous while the real talents live in obscurity.

繆誤(ㄇㄧㄡˋ ㄨˋ)
an error; a mistake

【繆】 4434
4. (穆) ㄇㄨˋ muh mù
1. beautiful
2. harmonious
3. silent

【縧】 4435
(絛) ㄊㄠ tau tāo
ribbon; flat silk cord

十二畫

【繒】 4436
1. ㄗㄥ tzeng zēng
silk; silk fabrics

繒綾(ㄗˊ ㄌㄧㄥˊ)
rugged; not smooth

繒繳(ㄗˊ ㄓㄨㄛˊ)
a string made of raw silk fastened to the arrow

【繒】 4436
2. ㄗㄥˋ tzeng zèng
繒絣(ㄗˊ ㄅㄥ)
to fasten tight

【織】 4437
ㄓ jy zhī
to weave; to knit

織補(ㄓ ㄅㄨˇ)
to darn; to mend

織布(ㄓ ㄅㄨˋ)
to weave cloth: 她用織布機織布。She is weaving cloth on the loom.

織布鳥(ㄓ ㄅㄨˋ ㄋㄧㄠˇ)
a Java sparrow

織布娘(ㄓ ㄅㄨˋ ㄋㄧㄤˊ)
Mecopoda nipponensis, a kind of grasshopper

織布機(ㄓ ㄅㄨˋ ㄐㄧ)or 織機(ㄓ ㄐㄧ)
a loom

織布廠(ㄓ ㄅㄨˋ ㄔㄤˇ)
a weaving mill

織女(ㄓ ㄋㄩˇ)
①(Chinese mythology) the three stars representing the three Weaving Sisters, daughters of Celestial Ruler
②a weaving woman

織女星(ㄓ ㄋㄩˇ ㄒㄧㄥ)
the Weaving Damsel--the star Vega in the constellation Lyra

織花(ㄓ ㄏㄨㄚ)
to weave figures into fabrics

織畫(ㄓ ㄏㄨㄚˋ)
woven pictures: 多麼美麗的一幅織畫呀! What a beautiful woven picture!

織錦(ㄓ ㄐㄧㄣˇ)
brocade or silk brocade

織錦迴文(ㄓ ㄐㄧㄣˇ ㄏㄨㄟˊ ㄨㄣˊ)
a palindrome

織席(ㄓ ㄒㄧˊ)
to weave a mat

織造(ㄓ ㄗㄠˋ)
a government agency during the Ming and Ching dynasties, responsible for manufacturing silks for the exclusive use of the royal household and imperial palace

織物(ㄓ ㄨˋ)
fabric; cloth; textiles

織襪(ㄓ ㄨㄚˋ)
to knit socks or stockings: 母親正在織襪。Mother is knitting socks.

織紋(ㄓ ㄨㄣˊ)
a woven pattern

【繕】 4438
ㄕㄢˋ shann shàn
1. to mend; to repair: 他正在修繕房子。He is mending his house.
2. to copy; to transcribe

繕補(ㄕㄢˋ ㄅㄨˇ)
to mend: 他繕補壞了的玩具。He mended the broken toy.

繕錄(ㄕㄢˋ ㄌㄨˋ)
to transcribe

繕就(ㄕㄢˋ ㄐㄧㄡˋ)
to copy; to transcribe; to finish copying or transcribing

繕寫(ㄕㄢˋ ㄒㄧㄝˇ)
to transcribe; to copy neatly: 把這幾句繕寫在你的筆記本上。Copy neatly these sentences in your notebook.

繕修(ㄕㄢˋ ㄒㄧㄡ)
to repair; to mend: 一些人在繕修房屋。Some men were repairing the house.

繕正(ㄕㄢˋ ㄓㄥˋ)
to copy neatly; to write a neat copy

【繚】 4439
ㄌㄧㄠˊ liau liáo
to wind round

繚亂(ㄌㄧㄠˊ ㄌㄨㄢˋ)
intricate; tangled; disorderly; confused

繚繞(ㄌㄧㄠˊ ㄖㄠˋ)
winding round and round (usually referring to musical sound or incense smoke)

【繖】 4440
ㄙㄢˇ saan sǎn
an umbrella; a parasol; a canopy

繖房花序(ㄙㄢˇ ㄈㄤˊ ㄏㄨㄚ ㄒㄩˋ)
(botany) corymb

繖形花序(ㄙㄢˇ ㄒㄧㄥˊ ㄏㄨㄚ ㄒㄩˋ)
(botany) umbel

【繙】 4441
ㄈㄢ fan fān
1. to translate; to interpret
2. (said of a flag, etc.) to flutter; to fly

繙譯(ㄈㄢ ㄧˋ)
to speak an incomprehensible local dialect

繙譯 or 翻譯(ㄈㄢ ㄧˋ)
to translate; to interpret

【繞】 4442
ㄖㄠˋ raw rào
1. to go around; to make a detour
2. to march round; to circle

繞道(ㄖㄠˋ ㄉㄠˋ)or 繞路(ㄖㄠˋ ㄌㄨˋ)
to make a detour; to detour

繞梁三日(ㄖㄠˋ ㄌㄧㄤˊ ㄙㄢ ㄖˋ)
(said of a song, etc.) to linger long in the air

繞過(ㄖㄠˋ ㄍㄨㄛˋ)
to pass over a point by a detour

繞口令兒(ㄖㄠˋ ㄎㄡˇ ㄌㄧㄥˋㄦ)
a tongue twister

繞圈子(ㄖㄠ ㄑㄩㄢ˙ㄗ)or繞圈兒(ㄖㄠ ㄑㄩㄢㄦ)
①to go round and round ②to beat around the bush; to talk in a roundabout way

繞膝承歡(ㄖㄠ ㄒㄧ ㄔㄥˊㄏㄨㄢ)
to stay with one's parents in order to make them happy

繞行(ㄖㄠ ㄒㄧㄥˊ)
①to detour ②to orbit; to revolve around something

繞指柔(ㄖㄠ ㄓˇㄖㄡˊ)
(said of temperaments) very pliable

繞著彎兒(ㄖㄠ ˙ㄓㄜ ㄨㄢㄦ)
①to be circuitous or roundabout ②to make a detour

繞日(ㄖㄠ ㄖˋ)
to revolve around the sun: 地球繞日轉。The earth revolves around the sun.

繞嘴(ㄖㄠ ㄗㄨㄟˇ)
jawbreaking; to be difficult to articulate: 他的名字很繞嘴。His name is really jawbreaking.

繞彎兒(ㄖㄠ ㄨㄢㄦ)
to take a stroll

繞彎子(ㄖㄠ ㄨㄢ˙ㄗ)
①to go round; to make a detour ②to talk in a roundabout way; to beat about the bush

繞遠兒(ㄖㄠ ㄩㄢㄦ)
to take a circuitous road; to go a long way round

繞越(ㄖㄠ ㄩㄝˋ)
to cross or pass by a detour

【繢】4443
　　(繪) ㄏㄨㄟˋ huey huì
to draw; to make a sketch of

【繡】4444
　　ㄒㄧㄡˋ shiow xiù
1. to embroider
2. embroidery

繡被(ㄒㄧㄡˋㄅㄟˋ)
bedding adorned with embroidery; embroidered bedding

繡補(ㄒㄧㄡˋㄅㄨˇ)
to darn

繡佛(ㄒㄧㄡˋㄈㄛˊ)
an embroidered Buddha image

繡房(ㄒㄧㄡˋㄈㄤˊ)or繡閣(ㄒㄧㄡˋㄍㄜˊ)or繡戶(ㄒㄧㄡˋㄏㄨˋ)
a young lady's chamber; a boudoir

繡工(ㄒㄧㄡˋㄍㄨㄥ)or繡活(ㄒㄧㄡˋㄏㄨㄛˊ)
embroidery

繡口(ㄒㄧㄡˋㄎㄡˇ)
talented in literary expressions

繡虎(ㄒㄧㄡˋㄏㄨˇ)
a literary genius (a sobriquet originally bestowed on 曹植)

繡花(ㄒㄧㄡˋㄏㄨㄚ)
embroidery; to embroider: 她在綠巾上繡花。She embroidered flowers on a silk scarf.

繡花鞋(ㄒㄧㄡˋㄏㄨㄚ ㄒㄧㄝˊ)
embroidered shoes

繡花針(ㄒㄧㄡˋㄏㄨㄚ ㄓㄣ)
an embroidery needle

繡花枕頭(ㄒㄧㄡˋㄏㄨㄚ ㄓㄣ˙ㄊㄡ)
(literally) an embroidered pillow—a person impressive in appearance but disappointing in substance

繡畫(ㄒㄧㄡˋㄏㄨㄚˋ)
embroidered pictures or designs

繡球(ㄒㄧㄡˋㄑㄧㄡˊ)
a ball of rolled silk

繡球風(ㄒㄧㄡˋㄑㄧㄡˊㄈㄥ)
a pruritus scrotum

繡球花(ㄒㄧㄡˋㄑㄧㄡˊㄏㄨㄚ)
(botany) hydrangea

繡鞋(ㄒㄧㄡˋㄒㄧㄝˊ)
embroidered shoes

繡線(ㄒㄧㄡˋㄒㄧㄢˋ)
embroidery thread

繡像(ㄒㄧㄡˋㄒㄧㄤˋ)
①embroidered images; to embroider images ②a fine figure painting

繡衣直指(ㄒㄧㄡˋㄧ ㄓˊㄓˇ)
an official post during the Han Dynasty, responsible for censure and justice

十三畫

【繩】4445
　　ㄕㄥˊ sherng shéng
1. a rope; a cord; a line
2. to restrain
3. to rectify; to correct

繩墨(ㄕㄥˊㄇㄛˋ)
①(carpenter's) marking lines ②rules of conduct: 他總是拘守繩墨。He always sticks to the rules of conduct.

繩髮(ㄕㄥˊㄈㄚˇ)
rope-like braids of hair

繩梯(ㄕㄥˊㄊㄧ)
a rope ladder: 一條繩梯懸於船側。A rope ladder hung over the ship's side.

繩妓(ㄕㄥˊㄐㄧˋ)
a female tightrope walker

繩檢(ㄕㄥˊㄐㄧㄢˇ)
to restrain; to exercise self-restraint

繩其祖武(ㄕㄥˊㄑㄧˊㄗㄨˇㄨˇ)
to imitate one's forebears

繩橋(ㄕㄥˊㄑㄧㄠˊ)
a suspension bridge: 繩橋已經拆下。The suspension bridge has been taken down.

繩愆糾繆(ㄕㄥˊㄑㄧㄢ ㄐㄧㄡ ㄇㄧㄡˋ)
to correct mistakes

繩趨尺步(ㄕㄥˊㄑㄩ ㄔˇㄅㄨˋ)
to behave according to decorums

繩戲(ㄕㄥˊㄒㄧˋ)
the stunt of walking on a tightrope

繩之以法(ㄕㄥˊㄓ ㄧˇㄈㄚˇ)
to prosecute according to the law: 他被繩之以法。He was prosecuted according to the law.

繩正(ㄕㄥˊㄓㄥˋ)
to rectify; to correct: 她繩正錯誤。She rectified errors.

繩尺(ㄕㄥˊㄔˇ)
a rule; law; standard; a criterion

繩子(ㄕㄥˊ˙ㄗ)or繩兒(ㄕㄥˊㄦ)
a rope; a line; a cord: 我用繩子包緊盒子。I tied up the box with a cord.

繩索(ㄕㄥˊㄙㄨㄛˇ)
ropes; cords: 抓住繩索。Grasp the ropes.

【繪】4446
　　ㄏㄨㄟˋ huey huì
to draw (pictures)

繪圖(ㄏㄨㄟˋㄊㄨˊ)
①to draw pictures: 她正在繪圖。She is drawing a picture. ②to prepare (engineering) drawings

繪圖員(ㄏㄨㄟˋㄊㄨˊㄩㄢˊ)

（糸部）

〔糸部〕

a draftsman (of an engineering firm)

繪畫（ㄏㄨㄟˋ ㄏㄨㄚˋ）
painting; drawing: 她有繪畫的天才。She has a talent for painting.

繪具（ㄏㄨㄟˋ ㄐㄩˋ）
drawing tools

繪像（ㄏㄨㄟˋ ㄒㄧㄤˋ）
to draw portraits: 他擅長繪像。He is good at drawing portraits.

繪事（ㄏㄨㄟˋ ㄕˋ）
painting; drawing

繪影繪聲（ㄏㄨㄟˋ ㄧㄥˇ ㄏㄨㄟˋ ㄕㄥ）
or 繪聲繪影（ㄏㄨㄟˋ ㄕㄥ ㄏㄨㄟˋ ㄧㄥˇ）
(literally) to portray even shadows and sounds—to give a very vivid description

【繮】 4447   ㄐㄧㄤ jiang jiāng
（又讀《ㄤ gang gāng）
reins; a bridle; a halter

繮繩（ㄐㄧㄤ ㄕㄥˊ）
reins; a bridle; a halter

【繯】 4448   ㄏㄨㄢˊ hwan huán
1. a noose
2. to hang (to death): 她投繯自盡。She hanged herself.

【繳】 4449   1. ㄐㄧㄠˇ jeau jiǎo
1. to surrender (articles); to submit; to lay down: 繳械投降！Lay down your arms!
2. to pay (taxes, tuition, etc.)

繳費（ㄐㄧㄠˇ ㄈㄟˋ）
to pay fees

繳納（ㄐㄧㄠˇ ㄋㄚˋ）
to pay (taxes, tuition, etc.)

繳庫（ㄐㄧㄠˇ ㄎㄨˋ）
to turn (revenues) to the treasury

繳款（ㄐㄧㄠˇ ㄎㄨㄢˇ）
to make payments (to some authorities, etc.)

繳回（ㄐㄧㄠˇ ㄏㄨㄟˊ）
to return (government property issued)

繳交（ㄐㄧㄠˇ ㄐㄧㄠ）
to turn in; to hand over; to surrender; to submit

繳卷（ㄐㄧㄠˇ ㄐㄩㄢˋ）
to hand in examination papers: 他們立刻繳卷。They hand in examination papers

at once.

繳械（ㄐㄧㄠˇ ㄒㄧㄝˋ）or 繳槍（ㄐㄧㄠˇ ㄑㄧㄤ）
to surrender arms; to hand over weapons; to disarm

繳稅（ㄐㄧㄠˇ ㄕㄨㄟˋ）
to pay taxes: 他繳稅五十鎊。He paid £50 in taxes.

繳繞（ㄐㄧㄠˇ ㄖㄠˋ）
to harass

繳存（ㄐㄧㄠˇ ㄘㄨㄣˊ）
to hand in for safekeeping

繳驗（ㄐㄧㄠˇ ㄧㄢˋ）
to hand in for inspection

【繳】 4449   2. ㄓㄨㄛˊ jwo zhuó
a string made of raw silk fastened to the arrow

【繾】 4450   ·ㄉㄚˇ ·da da
（又讀 ㄉㄚˇ dar dǎ）
a knot (of a rope)

【繹】 4451   1. ㄧˋ yih yì
1. to draw silk
2. continuous; uninterrupted
3. to infer; to deduce

繹如（ㄧˋ ㄖㄨˊ）
continuous

【繫】 4452   1. ㄒㄧˋ shih xì
to connect; to link; to join

繫泊（ㄒㄧˋ ㄅㄛˊ）
to moor (a boat)

繫絆（ㄒㄧˋ ㄅㄢˋ）
to bridle; to hinder: 別繫絆我。Don't hinder me.

繫戀（ㄒㄧˋ ㄌㄧㄢˋ）
to be inextricably in love with; to be reluctant to leave

繫懷（ㄒㄧˋ ㄏㄨㄞˊ）
to have one's heart drawn by

繫囚（ㄒㄧˋ ㄑㄧㄡˊ）
to be imprisoned: 他因何罪繫囚？For what offense was he imprisoned?

繫辭（ㄒㄧˋ ㄘˊ）
① the title of a section of the *Book of Changes* ② a copula (in grammar and logic)

繫獄（ㄒㄧˋ ㄩˋ）
to imprison; to be imprisoned

【繫】 4452   2. ㄐㄧˋ jih jì

to bind; to tie; to hang up

繫鞋帶兒（ㄐㄧˋ ㄒㄧㄝˊ ㄉㄞˋ ㄦ）
to tie a shoelace

【繭】 4453   ㄐㄧㄢˇ jean jiǎn
1. cocoons; a chrysalis
2. a callus

繭眉（ㄐㄧㄢˇ ㄇㄟˊ）
beautiful eyebrows

繭栗（ㄐㄧㄢˇ ㄌㄧˋ）
① a calf ② moral uprightness ③ the bulb of flowers ④ young bamboo shoots

繭紙（ㄐㄧㄢˇ ㄓˇ）
silk fabric used as paper for drawing or writing

繭綢（ㄐㄧㄢˇ ㄔㄡˊ）
pongee

繭稅（ㄐㄧㄢˇ ㄕㄨㄟˋ）
taxes; levies

繭衣（ㄐㄧㄢˇ ㄧ）
rough outside of a cocoon

【繰】 4454   1. ㄗㄠˇ tzao zǎo
a kind of silk

【繰】 4454   2. ㄙㄠ sau sāo
to draw silk from cocoons
參見「繅」

十四畫

【辮】 4455   ㄅㄧㄢˋ biann biàn
a braid of hair; a pigtail; a queue

辮髮（ㄅㄧㄢˋ ㄈㄚˇ）
plaited hair

辮子（ㄅㄧㄢˋ ·ㄗ）
a pigtail; a queue; a braid; a plait: 她把她的頭髮梳成辮子。She wears her hair in braids.

【纂】 4456   ㄗㄨㄢˇ tzoan zuǎn
1. a kind of red cloth
2. to compile; to collect

纂輯（ㄗㄨㄢˇ ㄐㄧˊ）
to compile; to collect

纂修（ㄗㄨㄢˇ ㄒㄧㄡ）
to compile; to edit

【繻】 4457   ㄒㄩ shiu xū
1. fine gauze
2. pieces of silk used as credentials

【繽】 4458   ㄅㄧㄣ bin bīn

1. abundant; plentiful; thriving
2. disorderly; confused

繽紛 (ㄅㄧㄣ ㄈㄣ)
(said of flags) fluttering: 旗幟繽紛. Flags are fluttering.

繽紛 (ㄅㄧㄣ ㄈㄣ)
① flourishing; thriving; abundant ② disorderly; chaotic

繽亂 (ㄅㄧㄣ ㄌㄨㄢˋ)
chaotic; disorderly; confused

【繼】 4459
(ㄐㄧˋ jih jì)
1. to continue; to carry on: 本故事下週繼續. The story will be continued next week.
2. then; afterwards: 她初感暈，繼而昏厥. She felt dizzy and then fainted.
3. to follow; to inherit; to succeed to

繼配 (ㄐㄧˋ ㄆㄟˋ)
a new wife (in place of the deceased)

繼母 (ㄐㄧˋ ㄇㄨˇ)
a stepmother

繼父 (ㄐㄧˋ ㄈㄨˋ)
a stepfather: 他告訴他繼父實情. He told his stepfather the truth.

繼電器 (ㄐㄧˋ ㄉㄧㄢˋ ㄑㄧˋ)
a relay (for electricity)亦作「電驛」

繼起 (ㄐㄧˋ ㄑㄧˇ)
to rise as a successor

繼續 (ㄐㄧˋ ㄒㄩˋ)
to continue; to last; to go on: 聚會繼續到午夜. The party went on till midnight.

繼續不斷 (ㄐㄧˋ ㄒㄩˋ ㄅㄨˋ ㄉㄨㄢˋ)
without a break

繼續犯 (ㄐㄧˋ ㄒㄩˋ ㄈㄢˋ)
a continued offense

繼續進行 (ㄐㄧˋ ㄒㄩˋ ㄐㄧㄣˋ ㄒㄧㄥˊ)
to continue the process; to maintain the effort; to go on; keep going

繼志 (ㄐㄧˋ ㄓˋ)
to continue the pursuit of the deceased

繼踵 (ㄐㄧˋ ㄓㄨㄥˇ)
to follow; to shadow

繼承 (ㄐㄧˋ ㄔㄥˊ)
to inherit; to succeed to

繼承權 (ㄐㄧˋ ㄔㄥˊ ㄑㄩㄢˊ)
the right of succession; the right of inheritance

繼承人 (ㄐㄧˋ ㄔㄥˊ ㄖㄣˊ)
a successor; an heir

繼承財產 (ㄐㄧˋ ㄔㄥˊ ㄘㄞˊ ㄔㄢˇ)
to inherit property

繼承遺志 (ㄐㄧˋ ㄔㄥˊ ㄧˊ ㄓˋ)
to carry on the unfinished lifework of the deceased

繼室 (ㄐㄧˋ ㄕˋ)
a new wife (in place of the deceased)

繼任 (ㄐㄧˋ ㄖㄣˋ)
to succeed to an office

繼子 (ㄐㄧˋ ㄗˇ)
an adopted heir: 他是我的繼子. He is my adopted heir.

繼則 (ㄐㄧˋ ㄗㄜˊ)or繼而(ㄐㄧˋ ㄦˊ)
and then; next: 他洗髮澡，繼而刷牙. He had a bath and then brushed his teeth.

繼武 (ㄐㄧˋ ㄨˇ)
to carry on the unfinished task of the deceased

繼位 (ㄐㄧˋ ㄨㄟˋ)
to succeed to the throne

繼開來 (ㄐㄧˋ ㄎㄞ ㄌㄞˊ)
to carry on the heritage so as to pave the way for future generations; to carry forward the past and forge ahead into the future

【繾】 4460
(ㄑㄧㄢˇ chean qiǎn)
entangled

繾綣 (ㄑㄧㄢˇ ㄑㄩㄢˇ)
① entangled; inextricable; inseparable ② (figuratively) a parasite ③ to make tender love

【纁】 4461
(ㄒㄩㄣ shiun xūn)
light red

纁裳 (ㄒㄩㄣ ㄔㄤˊ)
light red dress

十五畫

【纈】 4462
(ㄒㄧㄝˋ shye xié)
1. to tie a knot
2. silk with patterns or designs woven into it

【纊】 4463
(ㄎㄨㄤˋ kuang kuàng)
cotton

【續】 4464
(ㄒㄩˋ shiuh xù)
1. to continue; to extend; to renew
2. to add; to supply more

續版 (ㄒㄩˋ ㄅㄢˇ)
a reprint (of a book)

續篇 (ㄒㄩˋ ㄆㄧㄢ)
a sequel; a continuation of a previous book: 你看了那本小說的續篇嗎? Have you read the sequel of that novel?

續聘 (ㄒㄩˋ ㄆㄧㄣˋ)
to continue to employ (a person); to renew the contract of employment with (an employee)

續鳧 (ㄒㄩˋ ㄈㄨˊ)
(literally) to try to make the legs of a duck longer —to make an absurd and futile effort

續貂 (ㄒㄩˋ ㄉㄧㄠ)
① to appoint incompetent persons to important posts ② (a self-depreciatory expression) to continue another's unfinished job with poor skill

續航力 (ㄒㄩˋ ㄏㄤˊ ㄌㄧˋ)
(said of an airplane or ship) the duration to stay in the air or on the sea without refueling

續集 (ㄒㄩˋ ㄐㄧˊ)
the sequel (of a long movie, etc.)

續假 (ㄒㄩˋ ㄐㄧㄚˋ)
to extend a leave of absence

續借 (ㄒㄩˋ ㄐㄧㄝˋ)
to renew (a library book)

續絃 (ㄒㄩˋ ㄒㄧㄢˊ)or續娶(ㄒㄩˋ ㄑㄩˇ)
(said of a man) to remarry

續約 (ㄒㄩˋ ㄩㄝ)
to renew a contract: 我們必須續約. We must renew our contract.

【纏】 4465
(ㄔㄢˊ charn chán)
1. to wind round; to twine round; to bind; to wrap; to tangle
2. to bother persistently
3. to pester; to worry: 他纏著向我要錢. He pestered me for money.
4. to deal with: 這小孩真難纏. This child is really hard to deal with.

纏門纏戶 (ㄔㄢˊ ㄇㄣˊ ㄔㄢˊ ㄏㄨˋ)
to be a persistent bother at

糸部

the door

纏綿 (ㄔㄢ ㄇㄧㄢ)
tenderly attached to each other; affectionate; inseparable

纏綿病榻 (ㄔㄢ ㄇㄧㄢ ㄅㄧㄥ ㄊㄚˋ)
to be bedridden with a lingering illness

纏綿悱惻 (ㄔㄢ ㄇㄧㄢ ㄈㄟˇ ㄘㄜˋ)
(said of a story or narrative) very pathetic; extremely sad; exceedingly sentimental

纏縛 (ㄔㄢ ㄈㄨˊ)
to bind; to wrap: 他們將他的手足纏縛。 They bound him hand and foot.

纏頭 (ㄔㄢ ㄊㄡˊ)
①a turban ②money and gifts given to a prostitute

纏頭回子 (ㄔㄢ ㄊㄡˊ ㄏㄨㄟˊ ㄗˇ)
a turbaned Islamic tribe living in Kansu and Sinkiang

纏來纏去 (ㄔㄢ ㄌㄞˊ ㄔㄢ ㄑㄩˋ)
to be a persistent bother

纏裹 (ㄔㄢ ㄍㄨㄛˇ)
to wrap up; to cover tightly

纏腳 (ㄔㄢ ㄐㄧㄠˇ) or 纏足 (ㄔㄢ ㄗㄨˊ)
to bind the feet (as was done by women in former times)

纏住 (ㄔㄢ ㄓㄨˋ)
entangled; entwined; to wrap tightly; to wind around: 鬆弛的繩子容易纏住。 Loose string is easily entangled.

纏身 (ㄔㄢ ㄕㄣ)
to be delayed; to be held up by or burdened with something

纏擾 (ㄔㄢ ㄖㄠˇ)
to bother persistently

纏繞 (ㄔㄢ ㄖㄠˋ)
①to wind round; to twine around: 藤蔓纏繞樹身。 The vine twines around the tree. ②to bother persistently

纏繞莖 (ㄔㄢ ㄖㄠˋ ㄐㄧㄥ)
a twining stem

纏訟 (ㄔㄢ ㄙㄨㄥˋ)
to be involved in a tangled lawsuit

【纍】 4466   ㄌㄟˊ léi
1. strung together
2. a heavy rope
3. to tie; to bind; to twine

around; to wind round

纍纍 (ㄌㄟˊ ㄌㄟˊ)
①strung together ②tired; exhausted ③dejected; despondent; frustrated; disappointed

纍囚 (ㄌㄟˊ ㄑㄧㄡˊ)
a prisoner

纍紲 (ㄌㄟˊ ㄒㄧㄝˋ)
rope for tying up a prisoner 亦作「縲絏」

纍臣 (ㄌㄟˊ ㄔㄣˊ)
a vassal or subject in captivity

【纇】 4467   ㄌㄟˋ ley lèi
1. a knot on a thread
2. a flaw

十六畫

【纑】 4468   ㄌㄨˊ lu lú
1. thread
2. to soften hemp, etc., by boiling

十七畫

【纔】 4469   ㄘㄞˊ tsair cái
1. just now; just then
2. only: 這個小女孩纔六歲。 The little girl is only six.
3. not until; for the first time; then and only then

纔明白 (ㄔㄞˊ ㄇㄧㄥˊ ㄅㄞˊ) or 纔知道 (ㄔㄞˊ ㄓ ㄉㄠˋ)
to understand for the first time; not to have understood until then

纔到 (ㄔㄞˊ ㄉㄠˋ)
①just arrived: 我早上纔到台北。 I just arrived at Taipei in the morning. ②to have only reached (after so much time and effort)

纔來 (ㄔㄞˊ ㄌㄞˊ)
to have just come; to have just arrived: 我們纔來。 We have just arrived.

纔好 (ㄔㄞˊ ㄏㄠˇ)
just fine

纔是 (ㄔㄞˊ ㄕˋ)
then and only then is (he, it, etc.)....

【纓】 4470   ㄧㄥ ing yīng

1. chin straps for holding a hat
2. a tassel
3. leaves of turnips

纓帽 (ㄧㄥ ㄇㄠˋ)
a ceremonial hat with red tassels worn during the Ching Dynasty

纓絡 (ㄧㄥ ㄌㄨㄛˋ)
ornamental fringes on a garment

纓冠 (ㄧㄥ ㄍㄨㄢ)
to put on a hat hastily (with the chin strap on the head)

【纕】 4471   1. ㄒㄧㄤ shiang xiōng
to wear

【纕】 4471   2. ㄖㄤˇ rang rǎng
same as 攘—to roll up one's sleeve to show the arm

【纖】 4472   ㄒㄧㄢ shian xiōn
tiny; minute; fine; delicate; slender

纖毛 (ㄒㄧㄢ ㄇㄠˊ)
cilia

纖離 (ㄒㄧㄢ ㄌㄧˊ)
a species of horse produced in an ancient state in northern China

纖毫 (ㄒㄧㄢ ㄏㄠˊ)
tiny; very little; minute; every small detail

纖介 (ㄒㄧㄢ ㄐㄧㄝˋ)
minute; very small

纖鉅 (ㄒㄧㄢ ㄐㄩˋ)
big and small; hefty and minute

纖巧 (ㄒㄧㄢ ㄑㄧㄠˇ)
fine; delicately formed; squeamishly refined

纖悉 (ㄒㄧㄢ ㄒㄧ)
to know thoroughly; to be familiar with every detail of

纖細 (ㄒㄧㄢ ㄒㄧˋ) or 纖小 (ㄒㄧㄢ ㄒㄧㄠˇ)
fine; tiny; minute

纖屑 (ㄒㄧㄢ ㄒㄧㄝˋ)
piddling; trivial; frothy (affairs)

纖纖 (ㄒㄧㄢ ㄒㄧㄢ)
①delicate; fine; minute ②sharp

纖指 (ㄒㄧㄢ ㄓˇ)
slender or delicate fingers (of a woman)

纖手 (ㄒㄧㄢ ㄕㄡˇ)

delicate hands (of a woman)

纖瘦(ㄒㄧㄢ ㄕㄡˋ)
delicate and slender: 她是個身材纖瘦的女孩。She is a delicate and slender girl.

纖柔(ㄒㄧㄢ ㄖㄡˊ)
(said of hands) delicate and soft

纖人(ㄒㄧㄢ ㄖㄣˊ)
a fragile person

纖弱(ㄒㄧㄢ ㄖㄨㄛˋ)
fragile; delicate

纖腰(ㄒㄧㄢ ㄧㄠ)
a slender waist (of a woman)

纖妍(ㄒㄧㄢ ㄧㄢˊ)
slim and pretty

纖微(ㄒㄧㄢ ㄨㄟˊ)
very small; tiny; microscopic; infinitesimal

纖維(ㄒㄧㄢ ㄨㄟˊ)
fiber

纖維工業(ㄒㄧㄢ ㄨㄟˊ ㄍㄨㄥ ㄧㄝˋ)
the textile industry

纖維素(ㄒㄧㄢ ㄨㄟˊ ㄙㄨˋ)
cellulose

纖玉(ㄒㄧㄢ ㄩˋ)
delicate jade—a woman's delicate hands

十八畫

【纛】 4473
ㄉㄠˋ daw dòo
(又讀 ㄉㄨˊ dwu dú)
a banner; a streamer

十九畫

【續】 4474
ㄗㄨㄢˇ tzoan zuǎn
to continue; to carry on; to keep up

續緒(ㄒㄩˋ ㄒㄩˋ)
to continue (especially great enterprises)

二十一畫

【纜】 4475
ㄌㄢˇ laan lǎn
(又讀 ㄌㄢˋ larn làn)
a hawser; a cable

纜車(ㄌㄢˇ ㄔㄜ)
a cable car

纜車道(ㄌㄢˇ ㄔㄜ ㄉㄠˋ)
a cable railroad

纜繩(ㄌㄢˇ ㄕㄥˊ)
cordage; a thick rope

缶 部
ㄈㄡˇ foou fŏu

【缶】 4476
ㄈㄡˇ foou fŏu
a crock with a narrow opening

三畫

【缸】 4477
ㄍㄤ gang gāng
a cistern; a crock

四畫

【缺】 4478
ㄑㄩㄝ chiue quē
1. deficient; lacking; short; incomplete; defective
2. a vacancy; an opening

缺筆(ㄑㄩㄝ ㄅㄧˇ)
a stroke or strokes missing from a written character

缺乏(ㄑㄩㄝ ㄈㄚˊ)
to lack; to be without; to be deficient in; to be short of

缺乏人才(ㄑㄩㄝ ㄈㄚˊ ㄖㄣˊ ㄘㄞˊ)
to be short of talents

缺德(ㄑㄩㄝ ㄉㄜˊ)
deficient in the sense of morality; to have no regard for other members of society; mischievous; wicked: 那人這樣做可真缺德。It's wicked of the fellow to act like that.

缺德鬼(ㄑㄩㄝ ㄉㄜˊ ㄍㄨㄟˇ)
a public nuisance; a mean fellow: 他是缺德鬼。He is a mean fellow.

缺點(ㄑㄩㄝ ㄉㄧㄢˇ)
a defect; a shortcoming; a flaw

缺奶(ㄑㄩㄝ ㄋㄞˇ)
to have dry breasts

缺漏(ㄑㄩㄝ ㄌㄡˋ)
gaps and omissions

缺糧(ㄑㄩㄝ ㄌㄧㄤˊ)
to lack food supplies

缺課(ㄑㄩㄝ ㄎㄜˋ)
to be absent from class

缺刻葉(ㄑㄩㄝ ㄎㄜˋ ㄧㄝˋ)
(botany) dentate leaf; incised leaf

缺口(ㄑㄩㄝ ㄎㄡˇ)
①an indentation; an indenture ②a breach; an opening ③inadequately fed

缺口兒(ㄑㄩㄝ ㄎㄡˇㄦ)or 缺齒兒
an indentation

缺憾(ㄑㄩㄝ ㄏㄢˋ)
a flaw; a shortcoming; a defect

缺貨(ㄑㄩㄝ ㄏㄨㄛˋ)
(merchandise) to run out of stock: 我們缺貨。We've run out of stock.

缺角(ㄑㄩㄝ ㄐㄧㄠˇ)
a knocked-off corner

缺欠(ㄑㄩㄝ ㄑㄧㄢˋ)
a defect; a shortcoming

缺席(ㄑㄩㄝ ㄒㄧˊ)
to be absent (from a meeting, etc.): 他今天缺席。He is absent from the meeting today.

缺陷(ㄑㄩㄝ ㄒㄧㄢˋ)
a defect; a shortcoming; a handicap; inadequacy

缺陷美(ㄑㄩㄝ ㄒㄧㄢˋ ㄇㄟˇ)
attraction of some special characteristic or imperfection

缺吃缺穿(ㄑㄩㄝ ㄔ ㄑㄩㄝ ㄔㄨㄢ)
to have insufficient food and clothing

缺穿缺戴(ㄑㄩㄝ ㄔㄨㄢ ㄑㄩㄝ ㄉㄞˋ)
to have insufficient clothing

缺脣(ㄑㄩㄝ ㄔㄨㄣˊ)
a harelip; a cleft lip

缺食(ㄑㄩㄝ ㄕˊ)
insufficiently fed

缺少(ㄑㄩㄝ ㄕㄠˇ)
to be short of; to lack; to be deficient in: 他缺少勇氣。He is deficient in courage.

缺水(ㄑㄩㄝ ㄕㄨㄟˇ)
inadequately watered or irrigated; to run out of water supply: 我們缺水。We've run out of water supply.

缺字(ㄑㄩㄝ ㄗˋ)
words or characters inadvertently left out

〔缶部〕

缺額（ㄑㄩㄝˉㄜˊ）
vacancies waiting to be filled

缺疑（ㄑㄩㄝˊ ㄧˊ）
a dubious point

缺氧（ㄑㄩㄝˉ）
(sports physiology) oxygen deficit

八畫

【缾】4479
ㄆㄧㄥˊ pyng píng
a bottle; a pitcher, etc. 亦作「瓶」

十畫

【罃】4480
ㄧㄥ ing yīng
a long-necked bottle

十一畫

【罄】4481
ㄑㄧㄥˋ chinq qìng
to exhaust; to use up; to empty

罄筆難書（ㄑㄧˋ ㄅㄧˇ ㄋㄢˊ ㄕㄨ）
(said of atrocities or misdeeds) too numerous to be cited

罄匱（ㄑㄧˋ ㄎㄨㄟˋ）
used up; exhausted

罄竭（ㄑㄧˋ ㄐㄧㄝˊ）
used up; exhausted

罄盡（ㄑㄧˋ ㄐㄧㄣˋ）
to use up; to exhaust: 我的糖已經罄盡。I have used up my sugar.

罄其所有（ㄑㄧˋ ㄑㄧˊ ㄙㄨㄛˇ ㄧㄡˇ）
to use up all that is available

罄竹難書（ㄑㄧˋ ㄓㄨˊ ㄋㄢˊ ㄕㄨ）
(said usually of one's crimes) too numerous to be recorded fully even if all the available bamboos are used up

【罅】4482
ㄒㄧㄚˋ shiah xià
a crack; a rift; cleft; a fissure; a flaw

罅縫（ㄒㄧㄚˋ ㄈㄥˋ）
a fissure; cleft; a crack

罅漏（ㄒㄧㄚˋ ㄌㄡˋ）
a flaw; a fault; a short-coming; a defect; a loophole

罅隙（ㄒㄧㄚˋ ㄒㄧˋ）
a crack; a rift; cleft; a fissure; a flaw

十二畫

【罇】4483
ㄗㄨㄣ tzuen zūn
same as 尊, 樽—a goblet, a bottle

【罈】4484
ㄊㄢˊ tarn tán
same as 罎—an earthenware jar or jug

罈子（ㄊㄢˊˉㄗ）
an earthen jar

十三畫

【罋】4485
ㄨㄥˋ wenq wèng
same as 甕—an earthen jar

十四畫

【罌】4486
ㄧㄥ ing yīng
a jar with a small mouth

罌粟（ㄧㄥ ㄙㄨˋ）or 罌子粟（ㄧㄥ ˉㄗ ㄙㄨˋ）
an opium poppy

十五畫

【罍】4487
ㄌㄟˊ lei léi
an earthenware wine jar

十六畫

【罎】4488
ㄊㄢˊ tarn tán
an earthenware jar or jug for wine

【罏】4489
ㄌㄨˊ lu lú
an earthen stand for wine jars

十八畫

【罐】4490
ㄍㄨㄢˋ guann guàn
a vessel; a container; a jar; a jug; a can

罐頭（ㄍㄨㄢˋˉㄊㄡ）
canned goods

罐頭工廠（ㄍㄨㄢˋ ˉㄊㄡ ㄍㄨㄥ ㄔㄤˇ）
a cannery

罐頭食品（ㄍㄨㄢˋ ˉㄊㄡ ㄕˊ ㄆㄧㄣˇ）
canned food

罐裝（ㄍㄨㄢˋ ㄓㄨㄤ）
canned

罐子（ㄍㄨㄢˋˉㄗ）or 罐兒（ㄍㄨㄢˋㄦ）
a can; a jar; a jug

网 部
ㄨㄤˇ woang wǎng

三畫

【罔】4491
ㄨㄤˇ woang wǎng
1. to libel; to slander; to deceive
2. not straight; crooked
3. not

罔不（ㄨㄤˇ ㄅㄨˋ）
there are none that do not...

罔兩（ㄨㄤˇ ㄌㄧㄤˇ）
①spirits, monsters of the mountain rivers亦作「魍魎」,「蝄蜽」,「罔閬」②the penumbra

罔顧人道（ㄨㄤˇ ㄍㄨˋ ㄖㄣˊ ㄉㄠˋ）
inhuman; against humanity

罔極（ㄨㄤˇ ㄐㄧˊ）
①infinite　②to transgress; to go to the utmost extent of what is not right

罔效（ㄨㄤˇ ㄒㄧㄠˋ）
ineffective; to (or of) no avail; in vain

罔上（ㄨㄤˇ ㄕㄤˋ）
to deceive the emperor

【罕】4492
ㄏㄢˇ haan hǎn
rare; few; seldom

罕譬而喻（ㄏㄢˇ ㄆㄧˋ ㄦˊ ㄩˋ）
to explain clearly with few illustrations; to draw a striking but easily understood analogy

罕覯（ㄏㄢˇ ㄍㄡˋ）or 罕見（ㄏㄢˇ ㄐㄧㄢˋ）
rarely found; rare: 這些郵票罕見。These stamps are rare.

罕事（ㄏㄢˇ ㄕˋ）
a rare thing or event: 這眞是罕事。This is really a rare

event.

罕有(ㄏㄢˇ 一ㄡˇ)
rare: 古騰堡版之聖經爲罕有之書。The Gutenberg Bible is a rare book.

罕匹(ㄏㄢˇ ㄆㄧˇ)
rarely equaled

罕物(ㄏㄢˇ ㄨˋ)
a curiosity; a rare thing: 他買了許多罕物。He bought a lot of curiosities.

罕聞(ㄏㄢˇ ㄨㄣˊ)
seldom heard of

罕用(ㄏㄢˇ ㄩㄥˋ)
seldom used: 他罕用字典。He seldom used the dictionary.

四畫

【罘】 4493
ㄈㄨ fwu fú
(又讀 ㄈㄡˊ four fóu)
a net for catching rabbits or hares

五畫

【罡】 4494
《ㄤ gang gāng
the Taoist name of the Dipper

罡風(《ㄤ ㄈㄥ)
(Taoism) winds blowing over high places

【罟】 4495
《ㄨˇ guu gǔ
a net

【罝】 4496
ㄐㄩ jiu jū
a net for catching rabbits or hares

六畫

【罣】 4497
《ㄨㄚˋ guah guà
1. hindrance; obstruction
2. a sieve
3. to be concerned; to be worried

罣念(《ㄨㄚˋ ㄋㄧㄢˋ)
to be concerned; to be worried: 我罣念你的健康。I am concerned about your health.

罣篩(《ㄨㄚˋ ㄕ)
a sieve

罣礙(《ㄨㄚˋ ㄞˋ)
hindrance; obstruction; to

block; to hinder

罤誤(《ㄨㄚˋ ㄨˋ)
to be remiss; to be at fault

八畫

【罩】 4498
ㄓㄠˋ jaw zhào
1. a bamboo basket for catching fish
2. to coop; to cover; to wrap
3. a cover; a shade
4. a mantle; a cloak

罩不住(ㄓㄠˋ ㄅㄨˋ ㄓㄨˋ)
(informal) unable to control a situation

罩袍(ㄓㄠˋ ㄆㄠˊ)
a dust-robe; a dust-gown; an overall

罩子(ㄓㄠˋ ˙ㄗ)or 罩兒(ㄓㄠˋㄦ)
a cover; a shade

【罪】 4499
ㄗㄨㄟˋ tzuey zuì
1. sin; crime; fault; vice; evil; guilt
2. suffering; pain

罪不容誅(ㄗㄨㄟˋ ㄅㄨˋ ㄖㄨㄥˊ ㄓㄨ)
The crime is so serious that no punishment is adequate for it. 或 to deserve more than death

罪莫大焉(ㄗㄨㄟˋ ㄇㄛˋ ㄉㄚˋ 一ㄢ)
The crime or sin is too serious.

罪名(ㄗㄨㄟˋ ㄇㄧㄥˊ)
a charge (brought against a person)

罪犯(ㄗㄨㄟˋ ㄈㄢˋ)
a criminal; an offender

罪大惡極(ㄗㄨㄟˋ ㄉㄚˋ ㄜˋ ㄐㄧˊ)
a heinous crime; a capital offense; most vicious

罪孽(ㄗㄨㄟˋ ㄋㄧㄝˋ)
sin: 戰爭是違反人道的罪孽。War is a sin against humanity.

罪深重(ㄗㄨㄟˋ 一ㄣ ㄕㄣ ㄓㄨㄥˋ)
The sin is great.

罪戾(ㄗㄨㄟˋ ㄌㄧˋ)
crime; vice; evil

罪該萬死(ㄗㄨㄟˋ 《ㄞ ㄨㄢˋ ㄙˇ)
The crime deserves death for ten thousand times.

罪過(ㄗㄨㄟˋ ㄍㄨㄛˋ)
fault; sin

罪魁(ㄗㄨㄟˋ ㄎㄨㄟˊ)or 罪魁禍首
(ㄗㄨㄟˋ ㄎㄨㄟˊ ㄏㄨㄛˋ ㄕㄡˇ)

a chief offender; a ringleader

罪惡(ㄗㄨㄟˋ ㄜˋ)
wrongdoing; crime; vice; evil

罪行(ㄗㄨㄟˋ ㄒㄧㄥˊ)
criminal acts; atrocities; offenses

罪刑(ㄗㄨㄟˋ ㄒㄧㄥˊ)
punishment; penalty

罪障(ㄗㄨㄟˋ ㄓㄤˋ)
(Buddhism) sin

罪證(ㄗㄨㄟˋ ㄓㄥˋ)
proof of a crime; evidence of one's guilt

罪狀(ㄗㄨㄟˋ ㄓㄨㄤˋ)
the nature of an offense or crime; a charge (brought against a person)

罪上加罪(ㄗㄨㄟˋ ㄕㄤˋ ㄐㄧㄚ ㄗㄨㄟˋ)
to add an offense on top of another

罪人(ㄗㄨㄟˋ ㄖㄣˊ)
① a criminal; a sinner ② to blame others

罪惡(ㄗㄨㄟˋ ㄜˋ)
sin; crime; vice; evil; guilt

罪惡滔天(ㄗㄨㄟˋ ㄜˋ ㄊㄠ 一ㄢ)
The list of crimes committed is long enough to reach the heavens.

罪案(ㄗㄨㄟˋ ㄢˋ)
a criminal case: 他把罪案交法庭。He took the criminal case to court.

罪有應得(ㄗㄨㄟˋ 一ㄡˇ 一ㄥ ㄉㄜˊ)
The punishment is well deserved.

罪因(ㄗㄨㄟˋ 一ㄣ)
the cause of a crime

【置】 4500
ㄓˋ jyh zhì
1. to put; to place
2. to establish; to set
3. to procure; to purchase

置備(ㄓˋ ㄅㄟˋ)
to have (a thing) within convenient reach

置辦(ㄓˋ ㄅㄢˋ)
to procure; to secure

置辯(ㄓˋ ㄅㄧㄢˋ)or 置喙(ㄓˋ ㄏㄨㄟˋ)
to rebut; to refute; to defend (with words); to explain

置酒(ㄓˋ ㄐㄧㄡˇ)
to throw a banquet; to give a feast

置信(ㄓˋ ㄒㄧㄣˋ)

〔网部〕

to believe: 此事令人難以置信。
It is hard to believe.或It is difficult to believe.

置之不理(ㄓˋ ㄅㄨˋ ㄌㄧˇ)
to disregard it totally; to ignore

置之度外(ㄓˋ ㄉㄨˋ ㄨㄞˋ)
to give no thought to; without regard to; to care nothing about; regardless of

置之腦後(ㄓˋ ㄓ ㄋㄠˇ ㄏㄡˋ)
to disregard it; to forget it

置之死地而後生(ㄓˋ ㄓ ㄙˇ ㄉㄧˋ ㄦˊ ㄏㄡˋ ㄕㄥ)
(military strategy) to deploy troops in such a way as to leave no room for a maneuver or a route for escape so that the soldiers will fight for their dear lives out of desperation and eventually win the battle

置產(ㄓˋ ㄔㄢˇ)
to buy an estate: 他在鄉下置產。He bought an estate in the country.

置身度外(ㄓˋ ㄕㄣ ㄉㄨˋ ㄨㄞˋ)
to keep oneself from getting involved; to be indifferent

置身事外(ㄓˋ ㄕㄣ ㄕˋ ㄨㄞˋ)
to stay away from an affair; to keep out of it; to remain aloof: 你怎能置身事外呢? How could you keep yourself out of it?

置若罔聞(ㄓˋ ㄖㄨㄛˋ ㄨㄤˇ ㄨㄣˊ)
to turn a deaf ear to; to disregard completely; to pay no heed to

置辭(ㄓˋ ㄘˊ)
a choice of words; to find words to say

置疑(ㄓˋ ㄧˊ)
doubt: 此案不容置疑。This case allows of no doubt.

九畫

【罰】 4501
ㄈㄚˊ far fá
to punish; to penalize; to fine: 他處事賞罰分明。He is fair in meting out rewards and punishments.

罰立(ㄈㄚˊ ㄌㄧˋ)or罰站(ㄈㄚˊ ㄓㄢˋ)
to make a person stand as punishment

罰跪(ㄈㄚˊ ㄍㄨㄟˋ)
to keep a person kneeling as punishment

罰款(ㄈㄚˊ ㄎㄨㄢˇ)
a fine; to fine

罰鍰(ㄈㄚˊ ㄏㄨㄢˊ)
a fine

罰酒(ㄈㄚˊ ㄐㄧㄡˇ)
to impose a drinking penalty; the wine to be drunk as a penalty

罰金(ㄈㄚˊ ㄐㄧㄣ)
to impose a fine; a fine

罰球(ㄈㄚˊ ㄑㄧㄡˊ)
(basketball) a penalty shot; (football) a penalty kick

罰則(ㄈㄚˊ ㄗㄜˊ)
penal regulations; punitive provisions

【署】 4502
1. ㄕㄨˇ shuu shǔ
a public office

【署】 4502
2. ㄕㄨˋ shuh shù
1. to arrange
2. to write down; to put down
3. to be a deputy

署辦(ㄕㄨˋ ㄅㄢˋ)
to act as a deputy

署名(ㄕㄨˋ ㄇㄧㄥˊ)
to sign one's name: 所有學生都在海報上署了名。The poster was jointly signed by all the students.

署理(ㄕㄨˋ ㄌㄧˇ)
to administer in an acting capacity

署款(ㄕㄨˋ ㄎㄨㄢˇ)
to sign one's name; to put down one's signature

署簽(ㄕㄨˋ ㄑㄧㄢ)
to inscribe a title-label on a book

署事(ㄕㄨˋ ㄕˋ)
①to deal with public affairs ② public affairs

署字(ㄕㄨˋ ㄗˋ)
to sign on a document: 他忘了署字。He's forgotten to sign on a document.

【罳】 4503
ㄙˋ sih sì
a screen with meshes or holes

十畫

【罵】 4504
ㄇㄚˋ mah mà
to call names; to swear; to curse; to revile

罵不回口(ㄇㄚˋ ㄅㄨˋ ㄏㄨㄟˊ ㄎㄡˇ)
to remain silent when verbally abused

罵不絕口(ㄇㄚˋ ㄅㄨˋ ㄐㄩㄝˊ ㄎㄡˇ)
to curse unceasingly

罵大街(ㄇㄚˋ ㄉㄚˋ ㄐㄧㄝ)or罵街(ㄇㄚˋ ㄐㄧㄝ)
to curse without naming names

罵題(ㄇㄚˋ ㄊㄧˊ)
①(said of a piece of writing) contents disagreeing with the topic or title ② acting against what one preaches ③ behavior not matching with one's social standing

罵人(ㄇㄚˋ ㄖㄣˊ)
to call names; to scold

罵座(ㄇㄚˋ ㄗㄨㄛˋ)
to curse fellow guests

【罷】 4505
1. ㄅㄚˋ bah bà
to cease; to stop; to finish; to be done with

罷!罷!(ㄅㄚˋ ㄅㄚˋ)
an interjection of exasperating disappointment

罷兵(ㄅㄚˋ ㄅㄧㄥ)
to suspend hostilities

罷免(ㄅㄚˋ ㄇㄧㄢˇ)
to recall (officials by the people)

罷免權(ㄅㄚˋ ㄇㄧㄢˇ ㄑㄩㄢˊ)
the right of recall; the right of removing a public official from office by a vote of the people, specified in the Three Principles of the People

罷了(ㄅㄚˋ ㄌㄜ)
①(as a sentence-final phrase) merely; only; that's all ② That is enough. 或 Let's have no more of it. 或 Be done with it.

罷論(ㄅㄚˋ ㄌㄨㄣˋ)
①(said of a proposal) shelved; cancelled: 此案已作罷論。The case has already been shelved. ② an abandoned idea

罷官(ㄅㄚˋ ㄍㄨㄢ)

罷工(ㄅㄚˋ ㄍㄨㄥ)
(said of workers) to stage a
strike; to strike; a strike

罷課(ㄅㄚˋ ㄎㄜˋ)
to boycott classes

罷教(ㄅㄚˋ ㄐㄧㄠˋ)
(said of teachers) to stage a
strike; to strike; a teacher
strike

罷休(ㄅㄚˋ ㄒㄧㄡ)
to cease; to stop: 我不達目
的，決不罷休。 I'll not stop
until I reach my goal.

罷相(ㄅㄚˋ ㄒㄧㄤˋ)
the ouster of a prime minister

罷職(ㄅㄚˋ ㄓˊ)
to remove from office

罷斥(ㄅㄚˋ ㄔˋ)
to reject (an official) by
removing him from office

罷黜(ㄅㄚˋ ㄔㄨˋ)
to remove from office; to
fire: 他因行賄而被罷黜。 He
was fired for bribery.

罷市(ㄅㄚˋ ㄕˋ)
to close shops (in protest)

罷手(ㄅㄚˋ ㄕㄡˇ)
to discontinue an action; to
stop; to pause; to give up

罷業(ㄅㄚˋ ㄧㄝˋ)
(said of shopkeepers, workers, etc.) to go on strike;
to strike

【罷】 4505
3. ㄅㄚ ·ba be
same as 吧—a sentence-final
particle

【罷】 4505
3. ㄆㄧˊ pyi pí
tired; exhausted; weary

罷弊(ㄆㄧˊ ㄅㄧˋ)
exhausted; weary

十一畫

【罹】 4506
ㄌㄧˊ lí lí
1. sorrow; grief
2. to meet (disaster, misfortune, etc.); to be stricken by

罹病(ㄌㄧˊ ㄅㄧㄥˋ)
to fall ill; to suffer from disease

罹難(ㄌㄧˊ ㄋㄢˋ)
to fall victim to a disaster

罹禍(ㄌㄧˊ ㄏㄨㄛˋ)
to meet disaster

罹災(ㄌㄧˊ ㄗㄞ)
to meet a disaster; to be
stricken by a calamity

罹殃(ㄌㄧˊ ㄧㄤ)
to be victimized by a calamity; to meet a disaster: 他罹
殃。 He was victimized by a
calamity.

十二畫

【罽】 4507
ㄐㄧˋ jih jì
1. a kind of woolen fabric
2. a fishing net

罽賓(ㄐㄧˋ ㄅㄧㄣ)
the ancient name of Cash-
mere

罽魚(ㄐㄧˋ ㄩˊ)
another name of *siniperca
chuatsi* (鱖魚)

十四畫

【羆】 4508
ㄆㄧˊ pyi pí
a kind of bear (*Ursus arctos*)

羆虎(ㄆㄧˊ ㄏㄨˇ)
fierce animals

【羅】 4509
ㄌㄨㄛˊ luo luó
1. thin, light silk
2. a net; a snare
3. to arrange over a wide
space
4. a Chinese family name

羅賓(ㄌㄨㄛˊ ㄅㄧㄣ)
Robin Hood

羅布(ㄌㄨㄛˊ ㄅㄨˋ)
to arrange or display over a
wide space

羅布泊(ㄌㄨㄛˊ ㄅㄨˋ ㄆㄛ)
Lop Nor, a lake in Sinkiang

羅盤(ㄌㄨㄛˊ ㄆㄢˊ)
a compass

羅馬(ㄌㄨㄛˊ ㄇㄚˇ)
Rome: 條條大路通羅馬。 All
roads lead to Rome.

羅馬不是一天造成的(ㄌㄨㄛˊ
ㄇㄚˇ ㄅㄨˊ ㄕˋ ㄧˋ ㄊㄧㄢ ㄗㄠˋ ㄔㄥˊ ·ㄉㄜ)
Rome was not built in a
day.

羅馬法(ㄌㄨㄛˊ ㄇㄚˇ ㄈㄚˇ)
Roman law

羅馬帝國(ㄌㄨㄛˊ ㄇㄚˇ ㄉㄧˋ ㄍㄨㄛˊ)

the Roman Empire

羅馬尼亞(ㄌㄨㄛˊ ㄇㄚˇ ㄋㄧˊ ㄧㄚˋ)
Romania

羅馬教會(ㄌㄨㄛˊ ㄇㄚˇ ㄐㄧㄠˋ ㄏㄨㄟˋ)
the Roman Catholic Church

羅馬教皇(ㄌㄨㄛˊ ㄇㄚˇ ㄐㄧㄠˋ ㄏㄨㄤˊ)
the Pope

羅馬數字(ㄌㄨㄛˊ ㄇㄚˇ ㄕㄨˋ ㄗˋ)
Roman numerals

羅馬人(ㄌㄨㄛˊ ㄇㄚˇ ㄖㄣˊ)
a Roman; the Romans

羅馬字(ㄌㄨㄛˊ ㄇㄚˇ ㄗˋ)
the Roman alphabet

羅曼蒂克(ㄌㄨㄛˊ ㄇㄢ ㄉㄧˋ ㄎㄜˋ)
romantic (a transliteration):
他過着羅曼蒂克的生活。 He
lived a romantic life.

羅曼諾夫(ㄌㄨㄛˊ ㄇㄢ ㄋㄨㄛˋ ㄈㄨ)
Romanov dynasty of Russia
that ruled from 1613 to 1917

羅曼羅蘭(ㄌㄨㄛˊ ㄇㄢ ㄌㄨㄛˊ ㄌㄢˊ)
Romain Rolland, 1866-1944,
French playwright and nov-
elist

羅曼斯(ㄌㄨㄛˊ ㄇㄢ ㄙ)or 羅曼史
(ㄌㄨㄛˊ ㄇㄢ ㄕˇ)
a romance; a love affair; a
romantic story

羅密歐(ㄌㄨㄛˊ ㄇㄧˋ ㄡ)
Romeo

羅敷有夫(ㄌㄨㄛˊ ㄈㄨˊ ㄧㄡˇ ㄈㄨ)
(literally) Lady Lo Fu (a
beautiful talented woman of
the state of Chao (趙) during the Epoch of Warring
States) was a married
woman.—She is a married
woman.

羅浮宮(ㄌㄨㄛˊ ㄈㄨˊ ㄍㄨㄥ)
Louvre, a national museum
in Paris

羅德島(ㄌㄨㄛˊ ㄉㄜˊ ㄉㄠˇ)
the state of Rhode Island,
U.S.A.

羅德西亞(ㄌㄨㄛˊ ㄉㄜˊ ㄒㄧ ㄧㄚ)
Rhodesia

羅蘭夫人(ㄌㄨㄛˊ ㄌㄢˊ ㄈㄨ ㄖㄣˊ)
Madame Roland — Marie
Jeanne Roland de la Plati-
ère, 1754-1793

羅列(ㄌㄨㄛˊ ㄌㄧㄝˋ)
to arrange for display; to
spread out

羅貫中(ㄌㄨㄛˊ ㄍㄨㄢˋ ㄓㄨㄥ)
Lo Kuan-chung, a novelist
of the Yüan Dynasty, known

for the *Romance of the Three Kingdoms* (三國演義)

羅漢(ㄌㄨㄛˊ ㄏㄢˋ)
(Buddhism) ① *arhat*, a perfect man of Hinayana ② the sixteen, eighteen, or 500 disciples appointed to witness to Buddhist truth and save the world

羅漢身子(ㄌㄨㄛˊ ㄏㄢˋ ㄕㄣ ˙ㄗ)
a woman with no menstruation in her whole lifetime, hence barren

羅雀掘鼠(ㄌㄨㄛˊ ㄑㄩㄝˋ ㄐㄩㄝˊ ㄕㄨˇ)
or 羅掘(ㄌㄨㄛˊ ㄐㄩㄝˊ)
to try very hard to scrape money together

羅裙(ㄌㄨㄛˊ ㄑㄩㄣˊ)
a skirt of thin silk

羅織(ㄌㄨㄛˊ ㄓ)
to bring a false charge against an innocent person; to frame a charge

羅致人才(ㄌㄨㄛˊ ㄓˋ ㄖㄣˊ ㄘㄞˊ)
to recruit talented people

羅帳(ㄌㄨㄛˊ ㄓㄤˋ)
a curtain of thin silk

羅斯福(ㄌㄨㄛˊ ㄙ ㄈㄨˊ)
① Franklin Delano Roosevelt, 1882-1945, 32nd president of the U.S. (1933-1945) ② Theodore Roosevelt, 1858-1919, 26th president of the U.S. (1901-1909)

羅素(ㄌㄨㄛˊ ㄙˋ)
Bertrand Russell, 1872-1970, British philosopher

羅衣(ㄌㄨㄛˊ ㄧ)
a garment of thin silk

羅幃 or 羅帷(ㄌㄨㄛˊ ㄨㄟˊ)
a gauze curtain

羅紋(ㄌㄨㄛˊ ㄨㄣˊ)
① grain (of wood) ② finger prints

羅網(ㄌㄨㄛˊ ㄨㄤˇ)
a net; a snare: 孩子們設羅網捉兔。The boys made snares to catch rabbits.

十七畫

【羈】 4510
(ㄐㄧ ㄐㄧ ㄐㄧˊ)
to lodge at somebody's house

羈旅(ㄐㄧ ㄌㄩˇ)

① a lodger; a traveler ② to be traveling

羈客(ㄐㄧ ㄎㄜˋ)
a lodger; a traveler

羈滯(ㄐㄧ ㄓˋ)
to detain (an offender)

羈愁(ㄐㄧ ㄔㄡˊ)
a traveler's depression or sorrow

十九畫

【韁】 4511
(ㄐㄧ ㄐㄧ ㄐㄧˊ)
1. a bridle
2. to confine; to restrain; to bind
3. to lodge at another's house
參看「羈」

羈泊(ㄐㄧ ㄅㄛˊ)
to wander about; to travel from place to place; to be without a fixed home

羈絆(ㄐㄧ ㄅㄢˋ)
to restrain; to confine; to fetter; to tie; to shackle

羈縻(ㄐㄧ ㄇㄧˊ)
to control; to bridle

羈勒(ㄐㄧ ㄌㄜˋ)
to bridle; to restrain; to control

羈留(ㄐㄧ ㄌㄧㄡˊ)
① to detain (an offender) ② to stop over

羈旅(ㄐㄧ ㄌㄩˇ)
① a traveler ② traveling

羈宦(ㄐㄧ ㄏㄨㄢˋ)
to travel far to enter government service

羈牽(ㄐㄧ ㄑㄧㄢ)
to restrain; to bind

羈繫(ㄐㄧ ㄒㄧˋ)
to restrain; to bind: 他受到契約的羈繫。He is bound by a contract.

羈緤(ㄐㄧ ㄒㄧㄝˋ)
bridles and reins

羈滯(ㄐㄧ ㄓˋ)
① to detain (an offender) ② to delay; to hold up

羈束(ㄐㄧ ㄕㄨˋ)
to restrain; to bind

羈押(ㄐㄧ ㄧㄚ)
to detain (an offender); to take into custody

羊 部
ㄧㄤˊ yang yáng

【羊】 4512
(ㄧㄤˊ yang yáng)
a sheep; a goat

羊白頭 or 楊白頭(ㄧㄤˊ ㄅㄞˊ ㄊㄡˊ)
an albino

羊皮紙(ㄧㄤˊ ㄆㄧˊ ㄓˇ)
parchment or sheepskin

羊皮襖(ㄧㄤˊ ㄆㄧˊ ㄠˇ)
a sheepskin jacket

羊膜(ㄧㄤˊ ㄇㄛˊ)
an amnion

羊毛(ㄧㄤˊ ㄇㄠˊ)
wool: 我的毛衣是羊毛製的。My sweater is made of wool.

羊毛袋(ㄧㄤˊ ㄇㄠˊ ㄉㄞˋ)
a woolsack

羊毛脂(ㄧㄤˊ ㄇㄠˊ ㄓ)
wool oil

羊毛出在羊身上(ㄧㄤˊ ㄇㄠˊ ㄔㄨ ㄗㄞˋ ㄧㄤˊ ㄕㄣ ㄕㄤˋ)
(literally) Without a sheep, there can be no wool.—The benefit comes, after all, from a price one has paid. 或 Whatever is the expense, somebody is going to pay for it. 或 One has to pay for what he gets.

羊毛衫(ㄧㄤˊ ㄇㄠˊ ㄕㄢ)
a woolen sweater

羊毛商(ㄧㄤˊ ㄇㄠˊ ㄕㄤ)
a wool stapler: 他是個羊毛商。He is a wool stapler.

羊毛衣(ㄧㄤˊ ㄇㄠˊ ㄧ)
woolen wear

羊毛襪(ㄧㄤˊ ㄇㄠˊ ㄨㄚˋ)
woolen socks

羊癲風(ㄧㄤˊ ㄉㄧㄢ ㄈㄥ)or 羊角風
(ㄧㄤˊ ㄐㄧㄠˇ ㄈㄥ)or 羊癇風(ㄧㄤˊ ㄒㄧㄢˊ ㄈㄥ)
epilepsy

羊頭(ㄧㄤˊ ㄊㄡˊ)
① a sheep's head ② *Archosargus probatocephalus*, sheephead

羊欄(ㄧㄤˊ ㄌㄢˊ)
a sheepcot(e); a sheepfold: 羊被趕入羊欄。The sheep are

driven into a sheepfold.

羊羔(ㄧㄤ ㄍㄠ)
①a lamb ②a kind of alcoholic beverage

羊羹(ㄧㄤ ㄍㄥ)
a sort of cake

羊毫(ㄧㄤ ㄏㄠˊ)
a writing brush made of wool

羊角(ㄧㄤ ㄐㄧㄠˇ)
①a ram's horns ②a whirlwind; a cyclone

羊叫(ㄧㄤ ㄐㄧㄠˋ)
the bleating of a sheep or goat

羊圈(ㄧㄤ ㄐㄩㄢˋ)
a sheepfold; a sheepcote; a sheep pen

羊群(ㄧㄤ ㄑㄩㄣˊ)
a flock of sheep or goats

羊脂(ㄧㄤ ㄓ)
suet (from a sheep or goat)

羊脂玉(ㄧㄤ ㄓ ㄩˋ)
white jade

羊質虎皮(ㄧㄤ ㄓˊ ㄏㄨˇ ㄆㄧˊ)
(literally) a sheep in a tiger's skin--impressive in appearance but disappointing in substance

羊齒(ㄧㄤ ㄔˇ)
ferns: 地面上佈滿了羊齒。The ground was covered with ferns.

羊齒植物(ㄧㄤ ㄔˇ ㄓˋ ㄨˋ)
ferns; pteridophyte

羊腸小徑(ㄧㄤ ㄔㄤˊ ㄒㄧㄠˇ ㄐㄧㄥˋ)or **羊腸小道**(ㄧㄤ ㄔㄤˊ ㄒㄧㄠˇ ㄉㄠˋ)
a narrow, winding path

羊舍(ㄧㄤ ㄕㄜˋ)
a sheepfold; a sheepcote

羊水(ㄧㄤ ㄕㄨㄟˇ)
amniotic fluid

羊肉(ㄧㄤ ㄖㄡˋ)
mutton

羊入虎口(ㄧㄤ ㄖㄨˋ ㄏㄨˇ ㄎㄡˇ)or **羊落虎口**(ㄧㄤ ㄌㄨㄛˋ ㄏㄨˇ ㄎㄡˇ)
(literally) a sheep in a tiger's mouth--a hopelessly perilous situation

羊胃羊頭(ㄧㄤ ㄨㄟˋ ㄧㄤ ㄊㄡˊ)
the untouchables who hold high government posts

【芈】 4513
ㄇㄧㄝ mhie miĕ
(讀音 ㄇㄧˇ mii mi)
the bleating of a sheep or

goat

二畫

【羌】 4514
(羗,羗) ㄑㄧㄤ chiang qiāng
name of an ancient tribe in West China

羌蠻(ㄑㄧㄤ ㄇㄢˊ)
an ancient barbarian people in West China

羌笛(ㄑㄧㄤ ㄉㄧˊ)
a Tartar pipe; the shepherd's flute

羌胡(ㄑㄧㄤ ㄏㄨˊ)
an ancient tribe in West China

羌活(ㄑㄧㄤ ㄏㄨㄛˊ)
angelica 亦作「白芷」

羌羯(ㄑㄧㄤ ㄐㄧㄝˊ)
an ancient tribe in West China

羌無故實(ㄑㄧㄤ ㄨˊ ㄍㄨˋ ㄕˊ)
a poetic expression containing no allusion whatsoever

三畫

【美】 4515
ㄇㄟˇ meei mei
1. beautiful; pretty; fine; fair: 那女孩多美啊! How beautiful the girl is!
2. good; excellent; exquisite; nice
3. to be pleased with oneself
4. to praise

美(ㄇㄟˇ)
good in all respects; perfect

美不勝收(ㄇㄟˇ ㄅㄨˋ ㄕㄥ ㄕㄡ)
(said of landscape, etc.) too many beautiful or excellent things to be fully appreciated; more beauty than one can take in

美盼(ㄇㄟˇ ㄆㄢˋ)
a charming glance

美貌(ㄇㄟˇ ㄇㄠˋ)
a beautiful face (of a woman); beauty

美滿(ㄇㄟˇ ㄇㄢˇ)
(said of a life, home, etc.) happy; sweet

美滿姻緣(ㄇㄟˇ ㄇㄢˇ ㄧㄣ ㄩㄢˊ)
a happy marriage

美夢(ㄇㄟˇ ㄇㄥˋ)

a fond dream; a beautiful dream

美妙(ㄇㄟˇ ㄇㄧㄠˋ)
exquisite; very pleasant

美眄(ㄇㄟˇ ㄇㄧㄢˋ)
a captivating glance

美名(ㄇㄟˇ ㄇㄧㄥˊ)
an impressive title; fame; high prestige; a good reputation; a good name: 美名勝於財富。A good name is better than riches.

美目(ㄇㄟˇ ㄇㄨˋ)
beautiful(or lovely) eyes

美方(ㄇㄟˇ ㄈㄤ)
the American side; on the part of the Americans

美富(ㄇㄟˇ ㄈㄨˋ)
beautiful and abundant

美婦(ㄇㄟˇ ㄈㄨˋ)
a beautiful woman; a fine woman

美德(ㄇㄟˇ ㄉㄜˊ)
virtue: 節儉是一種美德。Frugality is a virtue.

美談(ㄇㄟˇ ㄊㄢˊ)
an instructive anecdote; a story of an exemplary deed

美男子(ㄇㄟˇ ㄋㄢˊ ㄗˇ)
a handsome man; an Adonis: 他是個美男子。He is a handsome man.

美女(ㄇㄟˇ ㄋㄩˇ)
a beautiful woman; a beauty

美女簪花(ㄇㄟˇ ㄋㄩˇ ㄗㄢ ㄏㄨㄚ)
the graceful strokes of calligraphic works

美拉尼西亞(ㄇㄟˇ ㄌㄚ ㄋㄧˊ ㄒㄧ ㄧㄚˋ)
Melanesia

美麗(ㄇㄟˇ ㄌㄧˋ)
beautiful; pretty; fair

美利堅(ㄇㄟˇ ㄌㄧˋ ㄐㄧㄢ)or **美利堅合衆國**(ㄇㄟˇ ㄌㄧˋ ㄐㄧㄢ ㄏㄜˊ ㄓㄨㄥˋ ㄍㄨㄛˊ)
the United States of America; America

美輪美奐(ㄇㄟˇ ㄌㄨㄣˊ ㄇㄟˇ ㄏㄨㄢˋ)
splendid and magnificent: a phrase commonly used to congratulate a person on the completion of a new house)

美感(ㄇㄟˇ ㄍㄢˇ)
a sense of the beautiful; the sense of beauty; the esthetic sense

〔羊部〕

〔羊部〕

美國(ㄇㄟ ㄍㄨㄛ)
America; the United States; the United States of America

美國的(ㄇㄟ ㄍㄨㄛ˙ㄉㄜ)
American

美國獨立戰爭(ㄇㄟ ㄍㄨㄛ ㄉㄨ ㄌㄧˋ ㄓㄢˋ ㄓㄥ)
the American Revolution; the American Revolutionary War; the War of (American) Independence

美國南北戰爭(ㄇㄟ ㄍㄨㄛ ㄋㄢˊ ㄅㄟˇ ㄓㄢˋ ㄓㄥ)
the American Civil War 1861-1865

美國佬(ㄇㄟ ㄍㄨㄛ ㄌㄠˇ)
a Yankee

美國國會(ㄇㄟ ㄍㄨㄛ ㄍㄨㄛ ㄏㄨㄟˋ)
the American Congress

美國新聞處(ㄇㄟ ㄍㄨㄛ ㄒㄧㄣ ㄨㄣˊ ㄔㄨˋ)
the United States Information Service (USIS)

美國之音(ㄇㄟ ㄍㄨㄛ ㄓ ㄧㄣ)
the Voice of America (VOA)

美國中央情報局(ㄇㄟ ㄍㄨㄛ ㄓㄨㄥ ㄧㄤ ㄑㄧㄥˊ ㄅㄠˋ ㄐㄩˊ)
the Central Intelligence Agency (CIA)

美國人(ㄇㄟ ㄍㄨㄛ ㄖㄣˊ)
an American; the Americans

美官(ㄇㄟ ㄍㄨㄢ)
an impressive government post

美觀(ㄇㄟ ㄍㄨㄢ)
pleasant to the eye; beautiful to look at

美觀大方(ㄇㄟ ㄍㄨㄢ ㄉㄚˋ ㄈㄤ)
beautiful and dignified

美工(ㄇㄟ ㄍㄨㄥ)
① art designing ② an art designer

美好(ㄇㄟ ㄏㄠˇ)
exquisite; fine: 多美好的天氣！ What a fine day!

美化(ㄇㄟ ㄏㄨㄚˋ)
① to beautify; beautification: 花卉美化環境。 Flowers beautify environment. ② Americanized; Americanization

美貨(ㄇㄟ ㄏㄨㄛˋ)
American merchandise; U.S. products

美機(ㄇㄟ ㄐㄧ)
American planes

美籍(ㄇㄟ ㄐㄧˊ)
of American nationality

美酒(ㄇㄟ ㄐㄧㄡˇ)
good wine; delicious wine

美艦(ㄇㄟ ㄐㄧㄢˋ)
an American naval ship: 美艦昨天啟航了。 The American naval ship sailed yesterday.

美金(ㄇㄟ ㄐㄧㄣ)or 美元(ㄇㄟ ㄩㄢˊ)
the (American) dollar

美錦(ㄇㄟ ㄐㄧㄣˇ)
beautiful brocade

美景(ㄇㄟ ㄐㄧㄥˇ)
beautiful scenery; beautiful landscape

美景良辰(ㄇㄟ ㄐㄧㄥˇ ㄌㄧㄤˊ ㄔㄣˊ)
beautiful scenery and a pleasant morning—an enjoyable situation or experience

美舉(ㄇㄟ ㄐㄩˇ)
a praiseworthy deed

美軍(ㄇㄟ ㄐㄩㄣ)
American troops; U.S. forces

美其名曰(ㄇㄟ ㄑㄧˊ ㄇㄧㄥˊ ㄩㄝ)
to give a dignified name to something ugly or condemnable

美妾(ㄇㄟ ㄑㄧㄝˋ)
an attractive concubine

美僑(ㄇㄟ ㄑㄧㄠˊ)
an American living abroad; an American resident in a foreign country

美缺(ㄇㄟ ㄑㄩㄝ)
an attractive opening or vacancy

美秀(ㄇㄟ ㄒㄧㄡˋ)
handsome and brilliant; beautiful and intelligent; handsome and accomplished

美學(ㄇㄟ ㄒㄩㄝˊ)
esthetics; aesthetics: 美學是哲學的分枝。 Esthetics is a branch of philosophy.

美製(ㄇㄟ ㄓˋ)
made in U.S.A.; manufactured in the United States

美洲(ㄇㄟ ㄓㄡ)
the Americas

美洲杉(ㄇㄟ ㄓㄡ ㄕㄢ)
a sequoia

美饌(ㄇㄟ ㄓㄨㄢˋ)
a sumptuous meal

美中不足(ㄇㄟ ㄓㄨㄥ ㄅㄨˋ ㄗㄨˊ)
a flaw that mars perfection; the only drawback

美齒(ㄇㄟ ㄔˇ)
beautiful teeth

美醜(ㄇㄟ ㄔㄡˇ)
beauty and ugliness

美稱(ㄇㄟ ㄔㄥ)
① an honorific term; a title of respect; an honorific ② a good name

美事(ㄇㄟ ㄕˋ)
① a laudable act; a worthy deed ② a happy event

美術(ㄇㄟ ㄕㄨˋ)
the fine arts

美術館(ㄇㄟ ㄕㄨˋ ㄍㄨㄢˇ)
an art museum (or gallery)

美術家(ㄇㄟ ㄕㄨˋ ㄐㄧㄚ)or 畫家(ㄏㄨㄚˋ ㄐㄧㄚ)
an artist; a painter

美術設計(ㄇㄟ ㄕㄨˋ ㄕㄜˋ ㄐㄧˋ)
artistic design

美髯公(ㄇㄟ ㄖㄢˊ ㄍㄨㄥ)
an old gentleman with a flowing beard

美人(ㄇㄟ ㄖㄣˊ)
① a beauty; a belle: 他妹妹是個美人。 His younger sister is a beauty. ②(figuratively) a king ③(figuratively) a man of virtue

美人計(ㄇㄟ ㄖㄣˊ ㄐㄧˋ)
a snare using a beautiful woman as a bait

美人蕉(ㄇㄟ ㄖㄣˊ ㄐㄧㄠ)
a canna

美人遲暮(ㄇㄟ ㄖㄣˊ ㄔˊ ㄇㄨˋ)
(literally) a beauty in her old age—the helpless and frustrating feeling of a has-been

美人魚(ㄇㄟ ㄖㄣˊ ㄩˊ)
a mermaid

美容(ㄇㄟ ㄖㄨㄥˊ)
to apply make-up or undergo plastic surgery

美容師(ㄇㄟ ㄖㄨㄥˊ ㄕ)
a beautician

美容術(ㄇㄟ ㄖㄨㄥˊ ㄕㄨˋ)
the art of make-up; the technology for improving one's appearance

美容院(ㄇㄟ ㄖㄨㄥˊ ㄩㄢˋ)
a beauty parlor

美色(ㄇㄟ ㄙㄜˋ)
① an attractive woman ②(woman's) beauty: 美色只是外表而已。 Beauty is only (or

（羊部）

but) skin-deep.

美索不達米亞(ㄇㄟˇ ㄙㄨㄛˇ ㄅㄨˋ ㄉㄚˊ ㄇㄧˇ ㄧㄚˋ)
Mesopotamia

美惡(ㄇㄟˇ ㄜˋ)
right and wrong; good and bad

美而賢(ㄇㄟˇ ㄦˊ ㄒㄧㄢˊ)
(said of a woman) beautiful and virtuous

美意(ㄇㄟˇ ㄧˋ)
a kind intention; goodwill

美意延年(ㄇㄟˇ ㄧˋ ㄧㄢˊ ㄋㄧㄢˊ)
(a congratulatory expression) A carefree life insures longevity.

美言(ㄇㄟˇ ㄧㄢˊ)
①a fine saying ②commending remarks

美豔(ㄇㄟˇ ㄧㄢˋ)
beautiful and voluptuous; glamorous

美味(ㄇㄟˇ ㄨㄟˋ)
delicious; tasty

美文(ㄇㄟˇ ㄨㄣˊ)
belles-lettres 譯作「純文學」。「美文」一詞來自法文。The term "belles-lettres" comes from French.

美玉(ㄇㄟˇ ㄩˋ)
fine jade: 他喜歡搜集美玉。He likes to collect fine jades.

美育(ㄇㄟˇ ㄩˋ)
esthetic education: 美育是件重要的事。Esthetic education is an important thing.

美譽(ㄇㄟˇ ㄩˋ)
honor; fame; glory: 他的美譽傳布全國。His fame spread all over the country.

美援(ㄇㄟˇ ㄩㄢˋ)
American aid; U.S. aid

美元集團(ㄇㄟˇ ㄩㄢˊ ㄐㄧˊ ㄊㄨㄢˊ)
the dollar bloc

【羑】 4516
ㄧㄡˇ yeou yòu
to guide to goodness

【羌】 4517
ㄑㄧㄤ chiang qiāng
same as 羌—an ancient people in West China

四畫

【羔】 4518
ㄍㄠ gau gāo
a lamb

羔皮(ㄍㄠ ㄆㄧˊ)
lambskin

羔雁(ㄍㄠ ㄧㄢˋ)
lamb and wild goose—presents of ceremony from high officials in ancient times

羔羊(ㄍㄠ ㄧㄤˊ)
a lamb: 她如羔羊般溫柔。She is as gentle as a lamb.

【羖】 4519
ㄍㄨˇ guu gǔ
a black ram

【羓】 4520
ㄅㄚ ba bā
salted meat

【羒】 4521
ㄈㄣˊ fern fén
a white ram

五畫

【羝】 4522
ㄉㄧ di dī
a ram; a he-goat

羝羊(ㄉㄧ ㄧㄤˊ)
a ram; a he-goat

羝羊觸藩(ㄉㄧ ㄧㄤˊ ㄔㄨˋ ㄈㄢˊ)
to be in a dilemma

【羚】 4523
ㄌㄧㄥˊ ling líng
an antelope

羚羊(ㄌㄧㄥˊ ㄧㄤˊ)
an antelope

羚羊掛角(ㄌㄧㄥˊ ㄧㄤˊ ㄍㄨㄚˋ ㄐㄧㄠˇ)
(literally) the antelope sticks its horns among branches at night—(said of poetic works) the excellent quality or transcendental charm

【羞】 4524
ㄒㄧㄡ shiou xiū
1. ashamed; abashed: 他對他所做的事感到羞恥。He is ashamed of what he has done.
2. shy; bashful: 她因太害羞而沒跟他講話。She was too shy to speak to him.
3. to disgrace; to insult; to shame

羞明(ㄒㄧㄡ ㄇㄧㄥˊ)
①allergic to strong light; afraid of strong light ②(medicine) photophobia

羞憤(ㄒㄧㄡ ㄈㄣˋ)
ashamed and angry

羞答答(ㄒㄧㄡ ㄉㄚˊ ㄉㄚˊ)
shy; bashful

羞刀難入鞘(ㄒㄧㄡ ㄉㄠ ㄋㄢˊ ㄖㄨˋ ㄑㄧㄠˋ)
What is done cannot be undone.

羞惱成怒(ㄒㄧㄡ ㄋㄠˇ ㄔㄥˊ ㄋㄨˋ)
to become angry from shame 亦作「惱羞成怒」

羞赧(ㄒㄧㄡ ㄋㄢˇ)
to blush; to redden; blush: 她轉過臉以掩其羞赧。She turned away to hide her blush.

羞愧(ㄒㄧㄡ ㄎㄨㄟˋ)
mortified; disgraced; shamed

羞花閉月(ㄒㄧㄡ ㄏㄨㄚ ㄅㄧˋ ㄩㄝˋ)
(said of a woman) so beautiful as to cause the flowers to blush and the moon to hide 亦作「閉月羞花」

羞怯(ㄒㄧㄡ ㄑㄧㄝˋ)or(ㄒㄧㄡ ㄑㄩㄝˋ)
shy and nervous: 她羞怯得說不出話來。She is too shy and nervous to utter a word.

羞恥(ㄒㄧㄡ ㄔˇ)
a sense of shame

羞手羞腳(ㄒㄧㄡ ㄕㄡˇ ㄒㄧㄡ ㄐㄧㄠˇ)
afraid to go ahead because of shyness; timid

羞人答答(ㄒㄧㄡ ㄖㄣˊ ㄉㄚˊ ㄉㄚˊ)
ashamed; abashed; bashful

羞辱(ㄒㄧㄡ ㄖㄨˋ)
to shame; to insult; to disgrace

羞慚(ㄒㄧㄡ ㄘㄢˊ)
ashamed; abashed; mortified; humiliated: 你應該對自己的行為感到羞慚。You should be ashamed of your conduct.

羞澀(ㄒㄧㄡ ㄙㄜˋ)
①to act awkwardly because of shame ②to be short of

羞澀阮囊(ㄒㄧㄡ ㄙㄜˋ ㄖㄨㄢˇ ㄋㄤˊ)
embarrassed for being short of money; short of cash

羞惡(ㄒㄧㄡ ㄨˋ)
to be ashamed of evil deeds

羞惡之心(ㄒㄧㄡ ㄨˋ ㄓ ㄒㄧㄣ)
the feeling of shame and dislike; the sense of right and wrong

羞於啟齒(ㄒㄧㄡ ㄩˊ ㄑㄧˇ ㄔˇ)
too shy to speak out one's mind

羞與為伍(ㄒㄧㄡ ㄩˇ ㄨㄟˊ ㄨˇ)
ashamed to associate with somebody

六畫

【羢】 4525
ㄖㄨㄥˊ rong róng
fine wool

七畫

【羣】 4526
(群) ㄑㄩㄣˊ chyun qún
a group; a multitude; a host;
a crowd; a swarm; a large
number; a flock; a herd

羣芳 (ㄑㄩㄣˊㄈㄤ)
①a multitude of flowers ②
a multitude of beauties

羣芳爭豔 (ㄑㄩㄣˊㄈㄤㄓㄥㄧㄢˋ)
①Many flowers rival for
gorgeousness ②A host of
beautiful women compete
for attention.

羣島 (ㄑㄩㄣˊㄉㄠˇ)
an archipelago; a group of
islands

羣落 (ㄑㄩㄣˊㄌㄨㄛˋ)
a colony (of corals, etc.)

羣利益 (ㄑㄩㄣˊㄌㄧˋㄧˋ)
group interest

羣聚 (ㄑㄩㄣˊㄐㄩˋ)
the masses; the populace

羣僚 (ㄑㄩㄣˊㄌㄧㄠˊ)
the whole body of courtiers

羣龍無首 (ㄑㄩㄣˊㄌㄨㄥˊㄨˊㄕㄡˇ)
a multitude without a
leader; leaderless

羣集 (ㄑㄩㄣˊㄐㄧˊ)
to swarm; to crowd; to
gather in great numbers

羣籍 (ㄑㄩㄣˊㄐㄧˊ)
a host of books; a multitude
of books

羣經 (ㄑㄩㄣˊㄐㄧㄥ)
all the classics

羣居 (ㄑㄩㄣˊㄐㄩ)
to live as a group; gregarious: 牛羊是羣居的動物。Sheep
and cattles are gregarious.

羣居生活 (ㄑㄩㄣˊㄐㄩㄕㄥㄏㄨㄛˊ)
gregarious life; social life

羣聚 (ㄑㄩㄣˊㄐㄩˋ)
to swarm; to crowd; to
gather in large numbers

羣起而攻之 (ㄑㄩㄣˊㄑㄧˇㄦˊㄍㄨㄥㄓ)
People rise in a mass to
attack it, him, etc.

羣青 (ㄑㄩㄣˊㄑㄧㄥ)
ultramarine 亦作「紺青」

羣輕折軸 (ㄑㄩㄣˊㄑㄧㄥ ㄓㄜˊ ㄓㄡˊ)
A combination of insignificant efforts or resources can
work miracles.

羣情 (ㄑㄩㄣˊㄑㄧㄥˊ)
popular feeling; public sentiment; 羣情激奮。Popular feel-
ing ran high.

羣小 (ㄑㄩㄣˊㄒㄧㄠˇ)
a mob; mean fellows; seamy
characters

羣賢 (ㄑㄩㄣˊㄒㄧㄢˊ)
a host of wise men; all the
wise men: 羣賢畢至。A host
of wise men are all present.

羣星 (ㄑㄩㄣˊㄒㄧㄥ)
①the myriad of stars ②a
galaxy (of movie stars, etc.)

羣性 (ㄑㄩㄣˊㄒㄧㄥˋ)or 羣居性 (ㄑㄩㄣˊㄐㄩㄒㄧㄥˋ)
gregariousness; sociality

羣學 (ㄑㄩㄣˊㄒㄩㄝˊ)
sociology 亦作「社會學」

羣雄割據 (ㄑㄩㄣˊㄒㄩㄥˊㄍㄜ ㄐㄩˋ)
rivalry among local barons;
fragmentation of a country
by rivaling warlords

羣衆 (ㄑㄩㄣˊㄓㄨㄥˋ)
a crowd; a mob: 羣衆聚集在
建築物周圍。Mobs gathered
round the building.

羣衆心理 (ㄑㄩㄣˊㄓㄨㄥˋㄒㄧㄣㄌㄧˇ)
the mental processes, emotions, thoughts, etc. of the
mob

羣衆運動 (ㄑㄩㄣˊㄓㄨㄥˋㄩㄣˋㄉㄨㄥˋ)
(sociology)mass movement

羣臣 (ㄑㄩㄣˊㄔㄣˊ)
the entire body of ministers

羣山 (ㄑㄩㄣˊㄕㄢ)
many mountains

羣山環抱 (ㄑㄩㄣˊㄕㄢㄏㄨㄢˊㄅㄠˋ)
to be surrounded by moun-
tains

羣生 (ㄑㄩㄣˊㄕㄥ)
the people; the masses 亦作
「大衆」

羣從 (ㄑㄩㄣˊㄘㄨㄥˊ)
nephews and nieces collectively

羣策羣力 (ㄑㄩㄣˊㄘㄜˋㄑㄩㄣˊㄌㄧˋ)
to join the force and intelligence of the group; to work
as a team

羣殿 (ㄑㄩㄣˊㄉㄧㄢˋ)

to gather and have a melee

羣蟻附羶 (ㄑㄩㄣˊㄧˇㄈㄨˋㄕㄢ)
(literally) a myriad of ants
swarming about a piece of
meat that smells—a rush (of
people) in search of profit

羣有 (ㄑㄩㄣˊㄧㄡˇ)
all things; all God's creation

羣英 (ㄑㄩㄣˊㄧㄥ)
a large number of brilliant
minds

羣育 (ㄑㄩㄣˊㄩˋ)
(education) training in group
life

【羨】 4527
ㄒㄧㄢˋ shiann xiàn
to envy; to covet

羨慕 (ㄒㄧㄢˋㄇㄨˋ)
to envy; to covet: 他很羨慕我
有這樣的好媽媽。He envies
me my good mother.

羨財 (ㄒㄧㄢˋㄘㄞˊ)
spare money; surplus money

【義】 4528
ㄧˋ yih yì
1. justice; righteousness
2. generosity; charity; philanthropy; chivalry
3. meaning; connotations: 此字
有數種意義。The word has
several meanings.
4. unreal; artificial; false
5. a Chinese family name

義兵 (ㄧˋㄅㄧㄥ)
①troops of justice ②volun-
teers; militiamen

義不容辭 (ㄧˋㄅㄨˋㄖㄨㄥˊㄘˊ)
Moral obligation prohibits
declination of the call. 或
duty-bound

義僕 (ㄧˋㄆㄨˊ)
a faithful servant; a royal
servant: 他是個義僕。He's a
faithful servant.

義賣 (ㄧˋㄇㄞˋ)
a charity sale; a bazaar

義門 (ㄧˋㄇㄣˊ)
a family noted for righteousness

義民 (ㄧˋㄇㄧㄣˊ)
people with a deep sense of
justice

義母 (ㄧˋㄇㄨˇ)
a foster mother

義憤填膺 (ㄧˋㄈㄣˋㄊㄧㄢˊㄧㄥ)or 義憤
填胸 (ㄧˋㄈㄣˋㄊㄧㄢˊㄒㄩㄥ)
to feel indignant at the in-

justice; to be filled with righteous indignation

義方 (ㄧ ㄈㄤ)
the principle of justice

義風 (ㄧ ㄈㄥ)
a prevailing sense of justice

義父 (ㄧ ㄈㄨˋ)
a foster father

義大利 or 意大利 (ㄧˋ ㄉㄚˋ ㄌㄧˋ)
Italy

義大利麵食 (ㄧˋ ㄉㄚˋ ㄌㄧˋ ㄇㄧㄢˋ ㄕˊ)
pasta; spaghetti

義大利脆餅 (ㄧˋ ㄉㄚˋ ㄌㄧˋ ㄘㄨㄟˋ ㄅㄧㄥˇ)
a pizza

義弟 (ㄧˋ ㄉㄧˋ)
a younger foster brother

義田 (ㄧˋ ㄊㄧㄢˊ)
a field leased to others with the rental collected for relief of the needy among one's own clan

義女 (ㄧˋ ㄋㄩˇ)
a foster daughter

義理 (ㄧˋ ㄌㄧˇ)
principles; reason

義例 (ㄧˋ ㄌㄧˋ)
the outline, or scope, of a book

義工 (ㄧˋ ㄍㄨㄥ)
a volunteer worker

義和團 (ㄧˋ ㄏㄜˊ ㄊㄨㄢˊ)
the Boxers (responsible for the Boxer Uprising of 1900)

義警 (ㄧˋ ㄐㄧㄥˇ)
one who volunteers to do police work

義舉 (ㄧˋ ㄐㄩˇ)
an act of charity; a chivalrous deed

義軍 (ㄧˋ ㄐㄩㄣ)
troops of justice

義旗 (ㄧˋ ㄑㄧˊ)
a banner of justice; a flag of the troops of justice

義氣 (ㄧˋ ㄑㄧˋ)
①spirit of justice or righteousness ②loyalty to friends: 他因義氣而受人尊敬。He is respected for his loyalty to friends.

義犬 (ㄧˋ ㄑㄩㄢˇ)
a loyal dog; a faithful dog

義俠 (ㄧˋ ㄒㄧㄚˊ)
a chivalrous person

義形於色 (ㄧˋ ㄒㄧㄥˊ ㄩˊ ㄙㄜˋ)
righteousness manifested in

one's appearance

義行 (ㄧˋ ㄒㄧㄥˊ)
an act of justice; a chivalrous act: 幫助被壓迫者是種義行。Helping the oppressed is an act of justice.

義學 (ㄧˋ ㄒㄩㄝˊ)
①a free private school ②study of philosophic principles (which prevailed in the Sung Dynasty)

義兄 (ㄧˋ ㄒㄩㄥ)
an elder foster brother: 他有三位義兄。He has three elder foster brothers.

義肢 (ㄧˋ ㄓ)
artificial limbs

義戰 (ㄧˋ ㄓㄢˋ)
a war for justice; a holy war

義正辭嚴 (ㄧˋ ㄓㄥˋ ㄘˊ ㄧㄢˊ)
speaking sternly and forcefully in the cause of justice

義莊 (ㄧˋ ㄓㄨㄤ)
a farmstead leased to others with the rental collected for the relief of the needy among one's own clan

義塚 (ㄧˋ ㄓㄨㄥˇ)
a cemetery for burying the remains of unidentified persons

義齒 (ㄧˋ ㄔˇ)
artificial teeth

義師 (ㄧˋ ㄕ)
troops of justice

義士 (ㄧˋ ㄕˋ)
an adherent to justice; a patriot; a freedom-seeker: 他是個義士。He is a patriot.

義手 (ㄧˋ ㄕㄡˇ)
an artificial hand

義塾 (ㄧˋ ㄕㄨˊ)
a free private school

義疏 (ㄧˋ ㄕㄨ)
annotations

義乳 (ㄧˋ ㄖㄨˇ)
falsies

義子 (ㄧˋ ㄗˇ)
a foster son

義足 (ㄧˋ ㄗㄨˊ)
an artificial leg: 他有隻腳是義足。One of his legs is an artificial leg.

義倉 (ㄧˋ ㄘㄤ)
a public granary for storing surplus grains in time of

plenty to be used for the relief of the needy in time of famine

義粟仁漿 (ㄧˋ ㄙㄨˋ ㄖㄣˊ ㄐㄧㄤ)
alms; contributions to charity

義演 (ㄧˋ ㄧㄢˇ)
a charity performance (by entertainers); a charity show

義無反顧 (ㄧˋ ㄨˊ ㄈㄢˇ ㄍㄨˋ)
to pursue justice without ever turning back

義務 (ㄧˋ ㄨˋ)
duty; obligation: 他有義務出席這個會議。He has an obligation to attend the meeting.

義務教育 (ㄧˋ ㄨˋ ㄐㄧㄠˋ ㄩˋ)
compulsory education; mandatory education: 義務教育是免費的。Compulsory education is free.

義勇 (ㄧˋ ㄩㄥˇ)
①righteous and courageous; patriotic: 他乃義勇之人。He is a patriotic man. ②(said of troops, etc.) volunteer

義勇艦隊 (ㄧˋ ㄩㄥˇ ㄐㄧㄢˋ ㄉㄨㄟˋ)
merchant marine reorganized into a navy

義勇軍 (ㄧˋ ㄩㄥˇ ㄐㄩㄣ)
a volunteer army; the militia: 他加入義勇軍。He joined the volunteer army.

九畫

【羯】 4529 ㄐㄧㄝˊ jye jié
1. a castrated ram
2. name of an ancient barbarian people

羯鼓 (ㄐㄧㄝˊ ㄍㄨˇ)
a kind of drum

羯胡 (ㄐㄧㄝˊ ㄏㄨˊ)
an ancient barbarian people

羯雞 (ㄐㄧㄝˊ ㄐㄧ)
a castrated cock; a capon 亦作「閹雞」

十畫

【羲】 4530 ㄒㄧ shi xī
Fu Hsi (伏羲), a legendary ruler who introduced houses

羲農 (ㄒㄧ ㄋㄨㄥˊ)
the legendary rulers Fu Hsi

(伏羲), who introduced
houses, and Shen Nung (神
農), who introduced agriculture

義和 (ㄒㄧˊㄏㄜˊ)
two legendary astronomers
Hsi (羲氏) and Ho (和氏)

義黃 (ㄒㄧˊㄏㄨㄤˊ)
the legendary rulers Fu Hsi
(伏羲) and Huang Ti (黃帝)

義皇上人 (ㄒㄧˊㄏㄨㄤˊㄕㄤˋㄖㄣˊ)
people who lived before the
legendary ruler Fu Hsi (伏
羲); the "noble savage"

十二畫

【羴】 4531
【羴】 ㄕㄢ shan shān
same as 羶—the odor of a
sheep or goat

十三畫

【羶】 4532
ㄕㄢ shan shān
the odor of a sheep or goat

羶氣 (ㄕㄢㄑㄧˋ)
the odor of a sheep or goat

羶腥 (ㄕㄢㄒㄧㄥ)
the odor of mutton

羶味 (ㄕㄢㄨㄟˋ)
the odor of a sheep or goat

【羹】 4533
ㄍㄥ geng gēng
thick soup; broth

羹湯 (ㄍㄥㄊㄤ)
thick soup; broth

羹匙 (ㄍㄥㄔˊ)
a spoon

【羸】 4534
ㄌㄟˊ lei léi
1. lean; emaciated
2. weak; feeble
3. to entangle; to bind

羸憊 (ㄌㄟˊㄅㄟˋ)
very weary; exhausted

羸劣 (ㄌㄟˊㄌㄧㄝˋ)
lean and weak

羸瘠 (ㄌㄟˊㄐㄧˊ)
emaciated; lean

羸師 (ㄌㄟˊㄕ)
a weak army; exhausted
troops

羸瘦 (ㄌㄟˊㄕㄡˋ)
emaciated: 長期臥病道病人
羸瘦了。A long illness had

emaciated the invalid.

羸弱 (ㄌㄟˊㄖㄨㄛˋ)
emaciated and weak

十五畫

【屦】 4535
ㄔㄢ chann chàn
to mix; to interpolate

羽 部
ㄩˇ yeu yǔ

【羽】 4536
ㄩˇ yeu yǔ
1. feathers; plumes
2. wings of a bird
3. one of the five notes in the
Chinese musical scale

羽毛 (ㄩˇㄇㄠˊ)
feathers; plumes; down

羽毛豐滿 (ㄩˇㄇㄠˊㄈㄥㄇㄢˇ)
① having thick feathers ②
experienced; mature; full-
fledged

羽撣 (ㄩˇㄉㄢˇ)
a feather duster

羽毛球 (ㄩˇㄇㄠˊㄑㄧㄡˊ)
badminton: 你打羽毛球嗎?
Do you play badminton?

羽毛球拍 (ㄩˇㄇㄠˊㄑㄧㄡˊㄆㄞ)
a badminton racket

羽毛球場 (ㄩˇㄇㄠˊㄑㄧㄡˊㄔㄤˇ)
a badminton court

羽毛球網 (ㄩˇㄇㄠˊㄑㄧㄡˊㄨㄤˇ)
a badminton net

羽毛未豐 (ㄩˇㄇㄠˊㄨㄟˋㄈㄥ)
still fledgling; inexperienced;
immature

羽獵 (ㄩˇㄌㄧㄝˋ)
to hunt; a hunt

羽林 (ㄩˇㄌㄧㄣˊ)or 羽林軍 (ㄩˇㄌㄧㄣˊ
ㄐㄩㄣ)
imperial guards 亦作「御林」
or「御林軍」

羽量級 (ㄩˇㄌㄧㄤˋㄐㄧˊ)
a bantamweight; feather-
weight: 他是羽量級的冠軍。He
is the bantamweight cham-
pion.

羽葆 (ㄩˇㄅㄠˇ)
a feathered carriage top

羽客 (ㄩˇㄎㄜˋ)
a Taoist priest

羽翮 (ㄩˇㄏㄜˊ)
the shaft of a feather

羽化登仙 (ㄩˇㄏㄨㄚˋㄉㄥㄒㄧㄢ)
① to ascend to heaven and
become a fairy immortal ②
(said of a Taoist) to die ③
(zoology) eclosion

羽化登仙 (ㄩˇㄏㄨㄚˋㄉㄥㄒㄧㄢ)
to take flight to the land of
the immortal

羽檄 (ㄩˇㄒㄧˊ)or 羽書 (ㄩˇㄕㄨ)
an urgent message or dis-
patch (with a feather
attached to indicate the
urgency) calling men to
arms

羽狀脈 (ㄩˇㄓㄨㄤˋㄇㄞˋ)
pinnate veins

羽狀複葉 (ㄩˇㄓㄨㄤˋㄈㄨˋㄧㄝˋ)
(botany) pinnate compound
leaf

羽士 (ㄩˇㄕˋ)
a Taoist priest 參看「羽客」
或「羽人」

羽扇 (ㄩˇㄕㄢˋ)
a feather fan

羽扇綸巾 (ㄩˇㄕㄢˋㄍㄨㄢㄐㄧㄣ)
(said of a military com-
mander) free from anxiety;
calm; composed

羽觴 (ㄩˇㄕㄤ)
the wine cup

羽人 (ㄩˇㄖㄣˊ)
a Taoist priest 參看「羽士」
或「羽客」

羽族 (ㄩˇㄗㄨˊ)
the feathered tribe; birds

羽衣 (ㄩˇㄧ)
a Taoist priest

羽翼 (ㄩˇㄧˋ)
assistants; helpers

三畫

【羿】 4537
ㄧˋ yih yì
Yi, name of a legendary
archer

四畫

【翁】 4538
ㄨㄥ ueng wēng
1. the father
2. the father-in-law
3. an old man
4. a title of respect

5. a Chinese family name

翁同龢 (ㄨㄥ ㄊㄨㄥ ㄏㄜˊ)
Weng Tung-ho, 1830-1904, a Ching Dynasty scholar and the tutor of two successive emperors

翁姑 (ㄨㄥ ㄍㄨ)
a woman's parents-in-law

翁壻 (ㄨㄥ ㄒㄩˋ)
father-in-law and son-in-law

翁仲 (ㄨㄥ ㄓㄨㄥˋ)
stone statues placed in front of tombs

【翅】 4539
ㄔˋ chyh chi
1. wings
2. fins

翅膀 (ㄔˋ ㄅㄤˇ)
wings

【翃】 4540
ㄏㄨㄥˊ horng hóng
(said of insects) flying

五畫

【翊】 4541
ㄧˋ yih yì
1. flying
2. to assist; to help
3. respectful

翊戴 (ㄧˋ ㄉㄞˋ)
to assist and support (a ruler)

翊贊 (ㄧˋ ㄗㄢˋ)
to assist

翊翊 (ㄧˋ ㄧˋ)
respectful

【翎】 4542
ㄌㄧㄥˊ ling líng
feathers; plumes

翎毛 (ㄌㄧㄥˊ ㄇㄠˊ)
① feathers ② birds (a term used in Chinese painting)

【翌】 4543
ㄧˋ yih yì
tomorrow

翌朝 (ㄧˋ ㄓㄠ)
tomorrow morning: 我翌朝將離開此地。I will leave here tomorrow morning.

翌日 (ㄧˋ ㄖˋ)
tomorrow

【習】 4544
ㄒㄧˊ shyi xí
1. to learn; to familiarize oneself with; to receive training in
2. habit; custom; practice

3. to follow; to repeat
4. a Chinese family name

習兵 (ㄒㄧˊ ㄅㄧㄥ)
① to train troops ② versed in the art of war

習非 (ㄒㄧˊ ㄈㄟ)
accustomed to wrongdoing

習非成是 (ㄒㄧˊ ㄈㄟ ㄔㄥˊ ㄕˋ)
Through usage the wrong becomes the right.

習題 (ㄒㄧˊ ㄊㄧˊ)
problems to be worked out in the course of study; exercises

習慣 (ㄒㄧˊ ㄍㄨㄢˋ)
habit; custom; practice; to get used to; to be accustomed to

習慣法 (ㄒㄧˊ ㄍㄨㄢˋ ㄈㄚˇ)
consuetudinary law

習慣性 (ㄒㄧˊ ㄍㄨㄢˋ ㄒㄧㄥˋ)
① inertia ② habitual

習慣成自然 (ㄒㄧˊ ㄍㄨㄢˋ ㄔㄥˊ ㄗˋ ㄖㄢˊ)
Habit is second nature.

習慣語 (ㄒㄧˊ ㄍㄨㄢˋ ㄩˇ)
an idiom

習見 (ㄒㄧˊ ㄐㄧㄢˋ)
often or frequently seen

習氣 (ㄒㄧˊ ㄑㄧˋ)
bad habit or custom

習習 (ㄒㄧˊ ㄒㄧˊ)
① (descriptive of the east wind) blowing gently; breezy; refreshing ② flying; lively

習性 (ㄒㄧˊ ㄒㄧㄥˋ)
temperament; dispositions

習尚 (ㄒㄧˊ ㄕㄤˋ)
① honored practice or custom ② fashion

習熟 (ㄒㄧˊ ㄕㄨˊ)
to be familiar with; to understand

習染 (ㄒㄧˊ ㄖㄢˇ)
to be corrupted by (evil practices)

習字 (ㄒㄧˊ ㄗˋ)
to learn penmanship or calligraphy

習字帖 (ㄒㄧˊ ㄗˋ ㄊㄧㄝˋ)
a copybook

習作 (ㄒㄧˊ ㄗㄨㄛˋ)
to learn to do

習俗 (ㄒㄧˊ ㄙㄨˊ)
custom; practice

習俗移人 (ㄒㄧˊ ㄙㄨˊ ㄧˊ ㄖㄣˊ)
Habit and custom can

change one's nature.

習而不察 (ㄒㄧˊ ㄦˊ ㄅㄨˋ ㄔㄚˊ)
to do something without studying it first after one has become accustomed to it

習以為常 (ㄒㄧˊ ㄧˇ ㄨㄟˊ ㄔㄤˊ)
to have become a force of habit; to fall into a habit; having been accustomed to it: 他說謊已習以為常。He has fallen into the habit of telling lies.

習藝 (ㄒㄧˊ ㄧˋ)
to learn a skill or trade

習藝所 (ㄒㄧˊ ㄧˋ ㄙㄨㄛˇ)
a vocational training institution (for paupers, convicts, etc.)

習與性成 (ㄒㄧˊ ㄩˇ ㄒㄧㄥˋ ㄔㄥˊ)
Habit becomes one's second nature.

習用 (ㄒㄧˊ ㄩㄥˋ)
to use as a habit

六畫

【翔】 4545
ㄒㄧㄤˊ shyang xióng
1. to soar
2. same as 詳—detailed

翔集 (ㄒㄧㄤˊ ㄐㄧˊ)
to gather the essence from many sources

翔盡 (ㄒㄧㄤˊ ㄐㄧㄣˋ)
detailed and complete

翔實 (ㄒㄧㄤˊ ㄕˊ)
detailed and accurate

翔泳 (ㄒㄧㄤˊ ㄩㄥˇ)
birds and fish

【翕】 4546
ㄒㄧˋ shih xì
1. to fold; to close
2. to draw together; to gather

翕赩 (ㄒㄧˋ ㄏㄜˋ)
vigorous; thriving

翕忽 (ㄒㄧˋ ㄏㄨˋ)
swift; agile; nimble

翕闢 (ㄒㄧˋ ㄆㄧˋ)
to open and close alternately

翕張 (ㄒㄧˋ ㄓㄤ)
to open and close alternately

翕然 (ㄒㄧˋ ㄖㄢˊ)
peace and stability

翕翼 (ㄒㄧˋ ㄧˋ)
to fold wings

〔羽部〕

八畫

（羽部）

【翟】 4547
1. ㄓㄞˊ jair zhái （讀音 ㄓㄜˊ jer zhé）
a Chinese family name

【翟】 4547
2. ㄉㄧˊ dyi dí
a kind of pheasant with long tail feathers

翟羽（ㄉㄧˊ ㄩˇ）
pheasant feathers

【翠】 4548
ㄘㄨㄟˋ tsuey cui
1. bluish green
2. green jade
3. a kingfisher

翠波（ㄘㄨㄟˋ ㄅㄛ）
green waves

翠柏（ㄘㄨㄟˋ ㄅㄛˊ）
a bluish green cypress

翠眉（ㄘㄨㄟˋ ㄇㄟˊ）
① blackened eyebrows ② a beauty's eyebrows

翠黛（ㄘㄨㄟˋ ㄉㄞˋ）
① material for blackening eyebrows ② a beauty's eyebrows

翠鳥（ㄘㄨㄟˋ ㄋㄧㄠˇ）
a kingfisher; a halcyon

翠綠（ㄘㄨㄟˋ ㄌㄩˋ）
emerald; bluish green: 那女孩著翠綠色的衣服。The girl dressed in bluish green.

翠亨村（ㄘㄨㄟˋ ㄏㄥ ㄘㄨㄣ）
the village of Tsuiheng in Kwangtung, where Dr. Sun Yat-sen was born

翠華（ㄘㄨㄟˋ ㄏㄨㄚˊ）
an imperial banner adorned with feathers of kingfishers or halcyons

翠鬢（ㄘㄨㄟˋ ㄅㄧㄣˋ）
beautiful dark hair (of a woman)

翠菊（ㄘㄨㄟˋ ㄐㄩˊ）
(botany) a China aster: 翠菊很快就會開了。China asters will come into flower soon.

翠翹（ㄘㄨㄟˋ ㄑㄧㄠˊ）
① feathers of a kingfisher or halcyon ② a kind of ancient headdress for women

翠竹（ㄘㄨㄟˋ ㄓㄨˊ）
green bamboos

翠繞珠圍（ㄘㄨㄟˋ ㄖㄠˋ ㄓㄨ ㄨㄟˊ）
① (said of a woman) to be fully dressed up ② to be surrounded by beauties

翠幃（ㄘㄨㄟˋ ㄨㄟˊ）
a curtain adorned with feathers of kingfishers

翠微（ㄘㄨㄟˋ ㄨㄟˊ）
① the blue-green mountain side ② blue-green mountain vapor

翠羽（ㄘㄨㄟˋ ㄩˇ）
feathers of kingfishers or halcyons

翠玉（ㄘㄨㄟˋ ㄩˋ）
emerald; blue jade: 她喜歡翠玉甚於珍珠。She prefers emerald to pearls.

【翣】 4549
ㄕㄚˋ shah shà
feathers adorning a coffin

【翡】 4550
ㄈㄟˇ feei fěi
1. a kingfisher
2. emerald

翡翠（ㄈㄟˇ ㄘㄨㄟˋ）
① a kingfisher or halcyon ② emerald

九畫

【翦】 4551
ㄐㄧㄢˇ jean jiǎn
same as 剪—to trim; to clip; to cut with scissors

【翥】 4552
ㄓㄨˋ juh zhù
to take off; to soar

【翬】 4553
ㄏㄨㄟ huei huī
1. to fly
2. a multi-colored pheasant

【翩】 4554
ㄆㄧㄢ pian piān
to fly swiftly

翩翩（ㄆㄧㄢ ㄆㄧㄢ）
① to fly swiftly; to flutter: 蝴蝶在花叢中翩翩飛舞。The butterfly fluttered among the flowers. ② (descriptive of movement) lightly and swiftly ③ complacent ④ elegant; stylish

翩翩公子（ㄆㄧㄢ ㄆㄧㄢ ㄍㄨㄥ ㄗˇ）or 翩翩少年（ㄆㄧㄢ ㄆㄧㄢ ㄕㄠˋ ㄋㄧㄢˊ）
a dandy; a beau

翩躚（ㄆㄧㄢ ㄒㄧㄢ）
to flutter about; to fly up and down

翩躚（ㄆㄧㄢ ㄒㄧㄢ）
flying or dancing gracefully

翩然（ㄆㄧㄢ ㄖㄢˊ）
sprightly

翩然而至（ㄆㄧㄢ ㄖㄢˊ ㄦˊ ㄓˋ）
to come trippingly

【翫】 4555
ㄨㄢˋ wann wàn
1. careless or casual due to familiarity
2. to play

翫愒（ㄨㄢˋ ㄎㄞˋ）
to trifle away one's time

翫忽（ㄨㄢˋ ㄏㄨ）
negligent; careless

翫味（ㄨㄢˋ ㄨㄟˋ）
appreciation: 這首詩值得翫味。This poem is worthy of appreciation.

十畫

【翱】 4556
ㄠˊ aur áo
same as 翺—to soar

【翮】 4557
ㄏㄜˊ her hé
the shaft of a feather

【翰】 4558
ㄏㄢˋ hann hàn
1. a white horse
2. a long and hard feather
3. a piece of writing

翰墨（ㄏㄢˋ ㄇㄛˋ）
(literally) quill and ink—literary pursuits

翰林（ㄏㄢˋ ㄌㄧㄣˊ）
① the literary circles ② a high literary degree in the former system ③ a scholar with a high literary degree in old China

翰林院（ㄏㄢˋ ㄌㄧㄣˊ ㄩㄢˋ）
the National Academy (in former times)

翰海 or 翰海（ㄏㄢˋ ㄏㄞˇ）
the Gobi Desert in Mongolia

翰札（ㄏㄢˋ ㄓㄚˊ）
letters

翰池（ㄏㄢˋ ㄔˊ）
an inkstone; an ink slab

翰苑（ㄏㄢˋ ㄩㄢˋ）
the literary circles

十一畫

【翳】 4559
ㄧ yih yì
(又讀 ㄧ yi yì)
1. to screen; to conceal
2. the haziness of objects due to weakened vision
3. the chariot cover made of feathers
4. the film over a diseased eye

翳翳 (ㄧˋ ㄧˋ)
dim; hazy; obscure; vague

【翼】 4560
ㄧˋ yih yì
1. wings
2. fins
3. to assist; to help
4. to protect; to patronize; to harbor

翼蔽 (ㄧˋ ㄅㄧˋ)
to cover

翼戴 (ㄧˋ ㄉㄞˋ)
to assist and support

翼卵 (ㄧˋ ㄌㄨㄢˇ)
to protect; to patronize

翼然 (ㄧˋ ㄖㄢˊ)
(said of architectural features) like extended wings aloft

翼贊 (ㄧˋ ㄗㄢˋ)
to assist and support

翼翼 (ㄧˋ ㄧˋ)
①cautious; careful ②robust; vigorous

十二畫

【翹】 4561
1. ㄑㄧㄠˊ chyau qiáo
1. long tail feathers
2. to raise
3. outstanding

翹企 (ㄑㄧㄠˊ ㄑㄧˇ)
to long eagerly

翹秀 (ㄑㄧㄠˊ ㄒㄧㄡˋ)or 翹楚 (ㄑㄧㄠˊ ㄔㄨˇ)
a man of outstanding ability

翹首 (ㄑㄧㄠˊ ㄕㄡˇ)
(literally) to raise the head —to long eagerly

翹首而望 (ㄑㄧㄠˊ ㄕㄡˇ ㄦˊ ㄨㄤˋ)
to raise one's head in hope

翹足而待 (ㄑㄧㄠˊ ㄗㄨˊ ㄦˊ ㄉㄞˋ)
to wait on tiptoe—to expect something to be soon forthcoming

翹材 (ㄑㄧㄠˊ ㄘㄞˊ)
a man of outstanding ability

亦作「翹秀」

翹望 (ㄑㄧㄠˊ ㄨㄤˋ)
to long eagerly 亦作「翹思」

【翹】 4561
2. ㄑㄧㄠˇ chiaw qiǎo
to project upward; to stick up; to turn upward

翹辮子 (ㄑㄧㄠˇ ㄅㄧㄢˋ ˙ㄗ)
to die; to kick the bucket

翹翹板 (ㄑㄧㄠˇ ㄑㄧㄠˇ ㄅㄢˇ)
seesaw 亦作「蹺蹺板」

【翻】 4562
ㄈㄢ fan fān
1. to fly; to flutter
2. to turn; to upset; to capsize: 車子翻了。The car turned over.
3. to rummage
4. to translate
5. to fall out; to break up: 我們鬧翻了。We quarreled and broke up.

翻版 (ㄈㄢ ㄅㄢˇ)
a reprint of a book (with or without proper permission)

翻本 (ㄈㄢ ㄅㄣˇ)or 翻本兒 (ㄈㄢ ㄅㄣˇ ㄦ)
to recover the money lost (in gambling)

翻覆 (ㄈㄢ ㄈㄨˋ)
unstable; vacillating 亦作「反覆」

翻覆無常 (ㄈㄢ ㄈㄨˋ ㄨˊ ㄔㄤˊ)
vacillating; unstable; capricious; whimsical: 他是個翻覆無常的人。He is a man of capricious temper.

翻騰 (ㄈㄢ ˙ㄊㄥ)
①to throw into disorder ②to turn over and over (as water); to roll about; to toss: 波濤翻騰。The waves tossed.

翻天覆地 (ㄈㄢ ㄊㄧㄢ ㄈㄨˋ ㄉㄧˋ)
to turn everything upside down; world-shaking

翻來覆去 (ㄈㄢ ㄌㄞˊ ㄈㄨˋ ㄑㄩˋ)
①to turn over and over; to roll about; to toss and turn ②to vacillate

翻老帳 (ㄈㄢ ㄌㄠˇ ㄓㄤˋ)
to bring up old scores again

翻臉 (ㄈㄢ ㄌㄧㄢˇ)
to show displeasure; to get angry; to turn hostile

翻臉不認人 (ㄈㄢ ㄌㄧㄢˇ ㄅㄨˋ ㄖㄣˋ ㄖㄣˊ)
to deny a friend; to turn

against an old acquaintance

翻臉無情 (ㄈㄢ ㄌㄧㄢˇ ㄨˊ ㄑㄧㄥˊ)
to turn against a friend and show him no mercy; to be deceptive and ruthless

翻蓋 (ㄈㄢ ㄍㄞˋ)
to rebuild (a house)

翻跟頭 (ㄈㄢ ㄍㄣ ˙ㄊㄡ)or 翻筋斗 (ㄈㄢ ㄐㄧㄣ ㄉㄡˇ)or 翻跟斗 (ㄈㄢ ㄍㄣ ㄉㄡˇ)
①to turn a somersault ②(aeronautic) to loop the loop

翻過兒 (ㄈㄢ ㄍㄨㄛˋ ㄦ)
to turn upside down

翻滾 (ㄈㄢ ㄍㄨㄣˇ)
to roll; to toss; to tumble

翻供 (ㄈㄢ ㄍㄨㄥˋ)
to withdraw a confession; to retract a testimony (at a law court)

翻開 (ㄈㄢ ㄎㄞ)
to turn open

翻悔 (ㄈㄢ ㄏㄨㄟˇ)
to disavow a statement, commitment, promise, act, etc.

翻江倒海 (ㄈㄢ ㄐㄧㄤ ㄉㄠˇ ㄏㄞˇ)
to overturn the river and upset the sea—overwhelming; convulsive; world-shaking

翻切 (ㄈㄢ ㄑㄧㄝˋ)
(in ancient Chinese phonetics) to indicate the pronunciation of a character by quick enunciation of two other characters 亦作「反切」

翻修 (ㄈㄢ ㄒㄧㄡ)
to rebuild; to overhaul; to remodel: 他想翻修那道牆。He wants to rebuild the wall.

翻新 (ㄈㄢ ㄒㄧㄣ)
to overhaul; to rebuild; to recondition; to revamp: 舊房子可以翻新。Old houses can be reconditioned.

翻箱倒櫃 (ㄈㄢ ㄒㄧㄤ ㄉㄠˇ ㄍㄨㄟˋ)
(literally) to overturn every box and basket—to make a thorough search

翻車 (ㄈㄢ ㄔㄜ)
①a scoop wheel ②(said of a vehicle) to overturn; to capsize ③a kind of snare for birds

翻車魚 (ㄈㄢ ㄔㄜ ㄩˊ)
the sunfish

翻船 (ㄈㄢ ㄔㄨㄢˊ)

[羽部]

(said of a boat) to capsize

翻砂 (ㄈㄢ ㄕㄚ)
(machinery) to cast metal forms in earthen moulds; to found; founding

翻山越嶺 (ㄈㄢ ㄕㄢ ㄩㄝ ㄌㄧㄥ)
to travel over mountains and valleys

翻身 (ㄈㄢ ㄕㄣ)
①to turn the body over ②to rise from poverty to affluence; to have a break of fortune: 他沒幾會翻身 He has no chance to rise again.

翻然悔悟 (ㄈㄢ ㄖㄢ ㄏㄨㄟ ㄨ)
quickly wake up to one's mistakes

翻案 (ㄈㄢ ㄢ)
to reverse a previous verdict

翻案文章 (ㄈㄢ ㄢ ㄨㄣ ㄓㄤ)
articles expressing a new point of view about historic incidents

翻譯 (ㄈㄢ ㄧ)
to translate; to interpret

翻譯本 (ㄈㄢ ㄧ ㄅㄣ)
a translation (of a book); a translated version

翻譯官 (ㄈㄢ ㄧ ㄍㄨㄢ)
an officer whose business is to interpret or translate

翻譯權 (ㄈㄢ ㄧ ㄑㄩㄢ)
the translation right (for a book)

翻譯者 (ㄈㄢ ㄧ ㄓㄜ)
a translator

翻印 (ㄈㄢ ㄧㄣ)
to reprint (a book with or without proper permission)

翻印必究 (ㄈㄢ ㄧㄣ ㄅㄧ ㄐㄧㄡ)
(said of a book) all rights reserved

翻胃 (ㄈㄢ ㄨㄟ)
to feel nausea; nauseating

翻閱 (ㄈㄢ ㄩㄝ)
to browse; to look over; to glance over; to leaf through; to thumb through (a book, magazine, etc.)

翻雲覆雨 (ㄈㄢ ㄩㄣ ㄈㄨ ㄩ)
(said of human affections) as changeable as clouds and rain

【翱】 4563
(翱) ㄠ aur áo
1. to soar; to fly
2. to roam; to wander

翶翔 (ㄈㄟ ㄒㄧㄤ)
①to soar; to fly ②to roam

十三畫

【翾】 4564
ㄒㄩㄢ shiuan xuān
to flit

翾翾 (ㄒㄩㄢ ㄒㄩㄢ)
flitting; flying sprightly

【翽】 4565
ㄏㄨㄟ huey huì
sounds of wings flapping

十四畫

【纛】 4566
ㄉㄠ daw dào
(又讀 ㄊㄠ taur táo)
a kind of streamer or screen adorned with feathers carried by dancers

【耀】 4567
ㄧㄠ yaw yào
(又讀 ㄩㄝ yueh yuè)
1. to shine; to dazzle
2. to show off

耀光 (ㄧㄠ ㄍㄨㄤ)
luster (especially of minerals); to sparkle; sparkling

耀耀 (ㄧㄠ ㄧㄠ)
bright

耀眼 (ㄧㄠ ㄧㄢ)
dazzling; to dazzle

耀眼增光 (ㄧㄠ ㄧㄢ ㄗㄥ ㄍㄨㄤ)
dazzling

耀武揚威 (ㄧㄠ ㄨ ㄧㄤ ㄨㄟ)
①to parade military prowess ②to show off one's strength or power; to bluff and bluster

老 部
ㄌㄠ lao lǎo

【老】 4568
ㄌㄠ lao lǎo
1. old; aged; venerable: 活到老學到老. There is still much to learn after one has grown old.
2. always: 他老是遲到. He is always late.
3. the youngest
4. very

---

5. a particle indicating ordinal numbers to designate order of birth
6. parents
7. a particle used before a man's family name to indicate familiarity and friendship
8. (said of meat, etc.) tough; over-cooked: 這塊牛肉太老. The beef is over-cooked.
9. to treat with the reverence to the aged
10. (said of color) dark: 這件外套顏色太老了. This coat is too dark.

老八板兒 (ㄌㄠ ㄅㄚ ㄅㄢ ㄦ)
an ultraconservative

老把戲 (ㄌㄠ ㄅㄚ ㄒㄧ)
an old trick: 他的狗只會玩老把戲. His dog knows only old tricks.

老把勢 (ㄌㄠ ㄅㄚ ㄕ)
an old hand

老伴兒 (ㄌㄠ ㄅㄢ ㄦ)
one's dear old companion—one's spouse in old age

老伯 (ㄌㄠ ㄅㄛ)
(respectful address) uncle; one's father's friend or friend's father

老百姓 (ㄌㄠ ㄅㄞ ㄒㄧㄥ)
the people; the common people

老耄 (ㄌㄠ ㄇㄠ)
in dotage; senile

老輩 (ㄌㄠ ㄅㄟ)
one's senior

老媽 (ㄌㄠ ㄇㄚ)
a procuress

老板 or 老闆 (ㄌㄠ ㄅㄢ)
①a boss; a master or keeper; a proprietor

老板娘 (ㄌㄠ ㄅㄢ ㄋㄧㄤ)
①a proprietress; proprietor's wife ②boss's wife; a mistress

老半天 (ㄌㄠ ㄅㄢ ㄊㄧㄢ)
quite a while

老本 (ㄌㄠ ㄅㄣ) or 老本錢 (ㄌㄠ ㄅㄣ ㄑㄧㄢ)
①a principal; a capital; the original investment ②an old edition

老蚌生珠 (ㄌㄠ ㄅㄤ ㄕㄥ ㄓㄨ)
(literally) a pearl from an old oyster—a son born in

one's old age

老婢(ㄌㄠˇㄅㄧˋ)
an old housemaid

老表(ㄌㄠˇㄅㄧㄠˇ)
①an old (in the sense of "dear") cousin (on the maternal side) ②a common greeting among men in Kiangsi which amounts to something like "old pal" or "buddy"

老兵(ㄌㄠˇㄅㄧㄥ)
an old soldier

老病(ㄌㄠˇㄅㄧㄥˋ)
①old and ailing ②an old ailment; a chronic disease

老病侵尋(ㄌㄠˇㄅㄧㄥˋㄑㄧㄣㄒㄩㄣˊ)
aging and ailing

老不正經(ㄌㄠˇㄅㄨˋㄓㄥˋㄐㄧㄥ)
a gray-haired womanizer; an old philanderer; old but still licentious

老不死的(ㄌㄠˇㄅㄨˋㄙˇ·ㄉㄜ)
an old bastard

老不修(ㄌㄠˇㄅㄨˋㄒㄧㄡ)
an old lecher

老派兒(ㄌㄠˇㄆㄞˋㄦ)
a conservative

老婆婆(ㄌㄠˇㄆㄛˊㄆㄛ)
respectful address for an old woman

老婆子(ㄌㄠˇㄆㄛˊ·ㄗ)or 老婆兒
①an old woman ②an old wife ③an old maid

老婆(ㄌㄠˇ·ㄆㄛ)
(vulgar usage) a wife

老牌(ㄌㄠˇㄆㄞˊ)or 老牌兒(ㄌㄠˇㄆㄞˊ·ㄦ)or 老牌兒(ㄌㄠˇㄆㄞˊㄦ)
①an old brand ②a veteran (actor or actress)

老彭(ㄌㄠˇㄆㄥˊ)
Lao-tzu (老子) and Pengtsu (彭祖)

老朋友(ㄌㄠˇㄆㄥˊ·ㄧㄡ)
an old friend

老僕(ㄌㄠˇㄆㄨˊ)
an old servant

老圃(ㄌㄠˇㄆㄨˇ)
①an old vegetable garden ②an old vegetable gardener

老譜兒(ㄌㄠˇㄆㄨˇㄦ)
old rules

老鋪(ㄌㄠˇㄆㄨˋ)or 老店(ㄌㄠˇㄉㄧㄢˋ)
an old store

老嬤嬤(ㄌㄠˇㄇㄚ·ㄇㄚ)

an old housemaid

老媽媽論(ㄌㄠˇㄇㄚ·ㄇㄚㄌㄨㄣˋ)
a set of mostly superstitious rules handed down from generation to generation in former times

老媽子(ㄌㄠˇㄇㄚ·ㄗ)
a housemaid; an amah

老馬識途(ㄌㄠˇㄇㄚˇㄕˋㄊㄨˊ)
(literally) An old horse knows the way—experienced and capable of leading others wisely

老邁(ㄌㄠˇㄇㄞˋ)
senile and weak

老邁無能(ㄌㄠˇㄇㄞˋㄨˊㄋㄥˊ)
old and powerless, aged and impotent

老妹妹(ㄌㄠˇㄇㄟˋ·ㄇㄟ)
the youngest sister

老毛病(ㄌㄠˇㄇㄠˊㄅㄧㄥˋ)
①an old ailment; an old weakness

老耄(ㄌㄠˇㄇㄠˋ)
①dim sight of the aged ②a person who is more than eighty years old

老耄(ㄌㄠˇㄇㄠˋ)
senile

老謀深算(ㄌㄠˇㄇㄡˊㄕㄣㄙㄨㄢˋ)
scheming and calculating; experienced and astute

老米(ㄌㄠˇㄇㄧˇ)
(during the Ming and Ching dynasties) the rice shipped from the southern provinces to Peking or Tungchow, which ferments and changes into a brownish color after being kept too long in the barns

老面皮(ㄌㄠˇㄇㄧㄢˋㄆㄧˊ)
shameless; brazen

老面子(ㄌㄠˇㄇㄧㄢˋ·ㄗ)
①old friendship ②out of respect for the aged

老命(ㄌㄠˇㄇㄧㄥˋ)
①the life of an old person ②one's dear life

老母(ㄌㄠˇㄇㄨˇ)
one's old mother

老法子(ㄌㄠˇㄈㄚˇ·ㄗ)
an old method

老佛爺(ㄌㄠˇㄈㄛˊㄧㄝˊ)
①Buddha ②a reference to the late emperor or to the empress dowager in the

Ching Dynasty

老廢物(ㄌㄠˇㄈㄟˋㄨˋ)
①waste matter; waste material ②a good-for-nothing

老方子(ㄌㄠˇㄈㄤㄗ·)
an old prescription

老夫(ㄌㄠˇㄈㄨ)
①(used by an old man) I; me ②an old husband

老夫老妻(ㄌㄠˇㄈㄨㄌㄠˇㄑㄧ)
an old couple

老夫少妻(ㄌㄠˇㄈㄨㄕㄠˋㄑㄧ)
an old man with a young wife

老夫子(ㄌㄠˇㄈㄨㄗ·)
①a private school master (in former times) ②a reference to a confidential secretary in former times

老腐敗(ㄌㄠˇㄈㄨˇㄅㄞˋ)
a corrupt old fellow

老婦(ㄌㄠˇㄈㄨˋ)or 老婦人(ㄌㄠˇㄈㄨˋㄖㄣˊ)
an old woman

老父台(ㄌㄠˇㄈㄨˋㄊㄞˊ)
a reference to the local magistrate in old China

老搭檔(ㄌㄠˇㄉㄚㄉㄤˋ)
an old partner; an old workmate

老大(ㄌㄠˇㄉㄚˋ)
①old ②the eldest child; a firstborn ③the leader of a gang ④extremely; exceedingly

老大不小(ㄌㄠˇㄉㄚˋㄅㄨˋㄒㄧㄠˇ)
to have grown up; to have come of age

老大徒傷悲(ㄌㄠˇㄉㄚˋㄊㄨˊㄕㄤㄅㄟ)
to grieve vainly in one's old age

老大哥(ㄌㄠˇㄉㄚˋㄍㄜ)
a reference to one's senior of equal standing; elder brothers

老呆 or 老獃(ㄌㄠˇㄉㄞ)
an old fool

老道(ㄌㄠˇㄉㄠˋ)
a Taoist priest

老到(ㄌㄠˇㄉㄠˋ)
showing much experience; expert; reliable

老豆腐(ㄌㄠˇㄉㄡˋㄈㄨˇ)
hardened bean curd

老聃(ㄌㄠˇㄉㄢ)
another name for Lao-tzu,

【老部】

604-531 B.C.
the role of an old female in Chinese opera

老當益壯（ㄌㄠ ㄉㄤ ㄧ ㄓㄨㄤ）
to gain vigor with age

老等（ㄌㄠ ㄉㄥ）
to wait patiently

老底子（ㄌㄠ ㄉㄧ ˙ㄗ）or 老底兒（ㄌㄠ ㄉㄧ ㄦ）or 老根兒（ㄌㄠ ㄍㄣ）
①an inherited fortune ②ancestry; pedigree ③the unpublicized seamy side of one's life

老弟（ㄌㄠ ㄉㄧ）
①a reference to one's junior of equal standing ②my dear student; my dear disciple

老爹（ㄌㄠ ㄉㄧㄝ）
①one's father ②respectful address for an aged man

老調重彈（ㄌㄠ ㄉㄧㄠ ˙ㄔㄨㄥ ㄊㄢ）
to play the same old tune

老掉牙（ㄌㄠ ㄉㄧㄠ ㄧㄚ）
very old; old-fashioned; outdated; obsolete

老店新開（ㄌㄠ ㄉㄧㄢ ㄒㄧㄣ ㄎㄞ）
①a store reopened after a period of suspension ②the marriage of a couple who have already had sexual intercourse

老杜（ㄌㄠ ㄉㄨ）
Tu Fu（杜甫）, 712-770, a famous poet of the Tang Dynasty

老東西（ㄌㄠ ㄉㄨㄥ ˙ㄒㄧ）
①old stuff; old things ②an abusive reference to an aged person

老態（ㄌㄠ ㄊㄞ）
①one's old way ②the appearance, or manner of the aged

老態龍鍾（ㄌㄠ ㄊㄞ ㄌㄨㄥ ㄓㄨㄥ）
the appearance of senility and dotage of the aged

老太婆（ㄌㄠ ㄊㄞ ㄆㄛ）
an old woman

老太太（ㄌㄠ ㄊㄞ ·ㄊㄞ）
an old lady

老太爺（ㄌㄠ ㄊㄞ ㄧㄝ）
①(in addressing an aged man) venerable sir ②an old gentleman

老饕（ㄌㄠ ㄊㄠ）
a glutton

老頭子（ㄌㄠ ㄊㄡ ·ㄗ）
①an old chap; an old fellow ②one's husband

老頭兒（ㄌㄠ ㄊㄡㄦ）
①an old fellow; an old chap ②one's father

老頭樂（ㄌㄠ ㄊㄡㄌ ㄌㄜ）
①a kind of muskmelon that is soft and mushy ②a kind of cotton shoes

老天（ㄌㄠ ㄊㄧㄢ）
Heaven—divine justice: 看在老天的份上, 原諒我吧! Please forgive me for Heaven's sake.

老天爺（ㄌㄠ ㄊㄧㄢ ㄧㄝ）
Heaven: 老天爺不負苦心人。 Heaven helps those who help themselves.

老禿翁（ㄌㄠ ㄊㄨ ㄨㄥ）
an old baldhead

老童生（ㄌㄠ ㄊㄨㄥ ㄕㄥ）
an old man who had repeatedly flunked the civil service examination in former times

老衲（ㄌㄠ ㄋㄚ）
self-reference of an aged Buddhist monk

老腦筋（ㄌㄠ ㄋㄠ ㄐㄧㄣ）
an old (or outmoded) way of thinking

老牛舐犢（ㄌㄠ ㄋㄧㄡ ㄕ ㄉㄨ）
(literally) the old cow licking her calf—a parent's indulgent love

老年（ㄌㄠ ㄋㄧㄢ）
old age; old life; late years

老年性痴呆症（ㄌㄠ ㄋㄧㄢ ㄒㄧㄥ ㄔ ㄞ ㄓㄥ）
(pathology) senile dementia

老年人（ㄌㄠ ㄋㄧㄢ ㄖㄣ）
the aged; the old people

老娘（ㄌㄠ ㄋㄧㄤ）
①one's old mother ②self-reference of a virago in a quarrel ③a midwife

老奴（ㄌㄠ ㄋㄨ）
①self-reference of an old servant ②an abusive reference to an aged man

老農（ㄌㄠ ㄋㄨㄥ）
an old farmer; a veteran farmer: 這老農經營一個農場。 The old farmer runs a farm.

老辣（ㄌㄠ ㄌㄚ）
①drastic and ruthless ②(said of literary works) incisive; penetrating

老了（ㄌㄠ ·ㄌㄜ）
to have grown old: 他已經老了。 He has grown old.

老來（ㄌㄠ ㄌㄞ）
when one gets old: 他老來富。 He lives in richness in his old age.

老來俏（ㄌㄠ ㄌㄞ ㄑㄧㄠ）
(said of a woman) to become more attractive as she gets older

老來少（ㄌㄠ ㄌㄞ ㄕㄠ）
①old in age but young in spirit ②(botany) Joseph's coat 亦作「老少年」或「雁來紅」

老來子（ㄌㄠ ㄌㄞ ㄗ）
a son born in one's old age

老萊子（ㄌㄠ ㄌㄞ ㄗ）
Lao Lai-tse, who flourished in the Epoch of Spring and Autumn, was famous for his filial piety, for when he was seventy he still behaved like a child, wearing a motley in the presence of his parents, so as to please them.

老羸（ㄌㄠ ㄌㄟ）
old and weak

老淚（ㄌㄠ ㄌㄟ）
tears of an old person

老淚縱橫（ㄌㄠ ㄌㄟ ㄗㄨㄥ ㄏㄥ）
(said of an aged person) tearful

老姥 or 姥姥（ㄌㄠ ·ㄇㄨ）
①one's maternal grandmother ②a midwife

老實實的（ㄌㄠ ㄕ ㄕ ·ㄉㄜ）
conscientiously; honest

老例（ㄌㄠ ㄌㄧ）or 老例兒（ㄌㄠ ㄌㄧㄦ）
old practices

老吏斷獄（ㄌㄠ ㄌㄧ ㄉㄨㄢ ㄩ）
to decide a legal case promptly and correctly

老臉（ㄌㄠ ㄌㄧㄢ）
①shameless; brazen ②an actor wearing a painted face in Peking opera

老練（ㄌㄠ ㄌㄧㄢ）
experienced; skilled; expert; veteran: 他車開得很老練。 He is expert at driving a car.

老哥（ㄌㄠ ㄍㄜ）
my dear friend (used among

males): 老哥，請聽我說。My
dear friend, listen to me,
please.

老狗(ㄌㄠ ㄍㄡ)
an old dog (an abusive term
for an old person)

老幹部(ㄌㄠ ㄍㄢ ㄅㄨ)
a veteran cadre

老姑娘(ㄌㄠ ㄍㄨ ㄋㄧㄤ)
an old spinster; an old maid

老骨頭(ㄌㄠ ㄍㄨ ㄊㄡ)
the life of an old person

老古董(ㄌㄠ ㄍㄨ ㄉㄨㄥ)
①antiques; curios ②an
ultraconservative

老鴰(ㄌㄠ ㄍㄨㄚ)
a crow

老規矩(ㄌㄠ ㄍㄨㄟ ㄐㄩ)
old rules; old practices

老公(ㄌㄠ ㄍㄨㄥ)
①an old man ②one's hus-
band (a vulgar usage)

老公公(ㄌㄠ ㄍㄨㄥ ·ㄍㄨㄥ)
①an old man ②a eunuch

老開(ㄌㄠ ㄎㄞ)
Laokai, a town in the Viet-
namese side of the Sino-
Vietnamese border

老好人(ㄌㄠ ㄏㄠ ㄖㄣ)or老好子
a good-natured person; a
soft-hearted person

老漢(ㄌㄠ ㄏㄢ)
an old man: 那老漢笛子吹得
好。The old man played well
on the flute.

老行家(ㄌㄠ ㄏㄤ ㄐㄧㄚ)
an expert; an old hand

老糊塗(ㄌㄠ ㄏㄨ ·ㄊㄨ)
a dotard: 他不能十分相信那老
糊塗。He can't quite believe
the dotard.

老狐狸(ㄌㄠ ㄏㄨ ·ㄌㄧ)
①an old fox ②a cunning
old man

老虎(ㄌㄠ ㄏㄨ)
a tiger

老虎鉗(ㄌㄠ ㄏㄨ ㄑㄧㄢ)
a vice, or vise

老花子(ㄌㄠ ㄏㄨㄚ ·ㄗ)
a beggar

老花眼(ㄌㄠ ㄏㄨㄚ ㄧㄢ)
presbyopia 亦作「老光」

老花眼鏡(ㄌㄠ ㄏㄨㄚ ㄧㄢ ㄐㄧㄥ)
convex glasses for one suffering from presbyopia

老花樣(ㄌㄠ ㄏㄨㄚ ㄧㄤ)
the same old stuff; the same
old trick

老滑頭(ㄌㄠ ㄍㄨㄚ ㄊㄡ)
a cunning old fellow

老話(ㄌㄠ ㄏㄨㄚ)
①an old saying; a saying;
an adage ②remarks about
the old days

老話兒(ㄌㄠ ㄏㄨㄚ ㄦ)
old remarks; oft-repeated
remarks

老幾(ㄌㄠ ㄐㄧ)
①one's seniority among
brothers or sisters: 你在家中
排行老幾？What's your
seniority in your family? ②
who; a nobody: 他算老幾。He
is a nobody.

老驥伏櫪，志在千里(ㄌㄠ ㄐㄧ ㄈㄨ
ㄌㄧ，ㄓ ㄗㄞ ㄑㄧㄢ ㄌㄧ)
An old steed hidden in the
stable still aspires to gallop
a thousand li. — (figuratively said of people) aged but
still ambitious

老家(ㄌㄠ ㄐㄧㄚ)
①one's original home ②
hell: 我送你回老家。I'll send
you to hell.

老街坊(ㄌㄠ ㄐㄧㄝ ·ㄈㄤ)
a neighbor

老街舊鄰(ㄌㄠ ㄐㄧㄝ ㄐㄧㄡ ㄌㄧㄣ)
an old neighbor

老交情(ㄌㄠ ㄐㄧㄠ ㄑㄧㄥ)
old friendship

老酒(ㄌㄠ ㄐㄧㄡ)
old wine

老舊(ㄌㄠ ㄐㄧㄡ)
old-style; old and worn-out;
old-fashioned

老奸巨猾(ㄌㄠ ㄐㄧㄢ ㄐㄩ ㄏㄨㄚ)
shrewd and crafty; a crafty
old scoundrel

老繭(ㄌㄠ ㄐㄧㄢ)
calluses

老江湖(ㄌㄠ ㄐㄧㄤ ㄏㄨ)
a sophisticated old traveler;
a worldly-wise person

老將(ㄌㄠ ㄐㄧㄤ)
①an old general ②a vet-
eran: 他是沙場老將。He is a
veteran of battlefield.

老景(ㄌㄠ ㄐㄧㄥ)
one's lot in old age

老境(ㄌㄠ ㄐㄧㄥ)

①the late years of one's life
②one's circumstances in old
age

老君(ㄌㄠ ㄐㄩㄣ)
a respectful name for Lao-
tzu(老子), 604-531 B.C.

老氣(ㄌㄠ ㄑㄧ)
①an experienced air or
style ②old-fashioned ③(said
of colors) plain or dark

老氣橫秋(ㄌㄠ ㄑㄧ ㄏㄥ ㄑㄧㄡ)
①to exhibit much sophistication (though young) ②to
be too obtrusively proud
because of one's advanced
age; arrogant on account of
one's seniority

老千(ㄌㄠ ㄑㄧㄢ)
a swindler

老慳(ㄌㄠ ㄑㄧㄢ)
an old miser

老前輩(ㄌㄠ ㄑㄧㄢ ㄅㄟ)
a term used to address one's
senior or an aged person

老親(ㄌㄠ ㄑㄧㄣ)
①parents ②old relatives

老槍(ㄌㄠ ㄑㄧㄤ)
①a heavy smoker; a chain
smoker ②a veteran opium
smoker

老去(ㄌㄠ ㄑㄩ)
to grow old

老拳(ㄌㄠ ㄑㄩㄢ)
the fist

老小(ㄌㄠ ㄒㄧㄠ)
①the old and the young ②
one's dependents

老羞成怒(ㄌㄠ ㄒㄧㄡ ㄔㄥ ㄋㄨ)
to be angry as a result of
embarrassment; to be moved
to anger by the feeling of
shame

老朽(ㄌㄠ ㄒㄧㄡ)
①aged and useless ②a
polite self-reference of an
old man

老先生(ㄌㄠ ㄒㄧㄢ ·ㄕㄥ)
①(in addressing an old gentleman) venerable sir ②an
old gentleman

老鄉(ㄌㄠ ㄒㄧㄤ)
①a fellow villager; a fellow
townsman ②a term used to
address a (male) stranger

老學究(ㄌㄠ ㄒㄩㄝ ㄐㄧㄡ)
an old pedant

老兄(ㄌㄠ ㄒㄩㄥ)

〔老部〕

老 (ㄌㄠˇ ㄓˋ)
my dear friend (a term used among males of equal standing)

老者 (ㄌㄠˇ ㄓˇ)
an old man; the old

老丈 (ㄌㄠˇ ㄓㄤˋ)
an old gentleman

老丈人 (ㄌㄠˇ ㄓㄤˋ ㄖㄣˊ)
a man's father-in-law

老帳 (ㄌㄠˇ ㄓㄤˋ)
① old debts; old bills ② old scores

老主顧 (ㄌㄠˇ ㄓㄨˇ ㄍㄨˋ)
an old customer; an old client

老撾 (ㄌㄠˇ ㄓㄨㄚ)
Laos

老拙 (ㄌㄠˇ ㄓㄨㄛˊ)
old and stupid (depreciatory self-reference of an old person)

老莊 (ㄌㄠˇ ㄓㄨㄤ)
the Taoist philosophers Lao-tzu (老子), 604-531 B.C., and Chuang-tzu (莊子), 369-295 B.C.

老巢 (ㄌㄠˇ ㄔㄠˊ)
a den (of robbers)

老成 (ㄌㄠˇ ㄔㄥˊ)
sophisticated; experienced

老成凋謝 (ㄌㄠˇ ㄔㄥˊ ㄉㄧㄠ ㄒㄧㄝˋ)
(a conventional sentence mourning the death of a respected old person) The experienced and accomplished person has passed away.

老成持重 (ㄌㄠˇ ㄔㄥˊ ㄔˊ ㄓㄨㄥˋ)
experienced and cautious: 他是個老成持重的人。He is an experienced and cautious person.

老處女 (ㄌㄠˇ ㄔㄨˇ ㄋㄩˇ)
an old maid; a spinster

老師 (ㄌㄠˇ ㄕ)
a teacher

老師傅 (ㄌㄠˇ ㄕ ㄈㄨˋ)
an old master (of a trade)

老師宿儒 (ㄌㄠˇ ㄕ ㄙㄨˋ ㄖㄨˊ)
a respectable old scholar

老實 (ㄌㄠˇ ㄕˊ)
honest; truthful

老實頭 (ㄌㄠˇ ㄕˊ ㄊㄡˊ)
an honest, simple-minded person

老式 (ㄌㄠˇ ㄕˋ)
old-fashioned; of an old style

老世交 (ㄌㄠˇ ㄕˋ ㄐㄧㄠ)
families on friendly terms for generations

老少咸宜 (ㄌㄠˇ ㄕㄠˋ ㄒㄧㄢˊ ㄧˊ)
suitable for both the old and the young

老少無欺 (ㄌㄠˇ ㄕㄠˋ ㄨˊ ㄑㄧ)
(literally) to cheat neither the old nor the young—We are honest with our customers.

老手 (ㄌㄠˇ ㄕㄡˇ)
an old hand: 他是開車老手。He is an old hand at driving.

老壽星 (ㄌㄠˇ ㄕㄡˋ ㄒㄧㄥ)
a term of compliment for an aged person

老身 (ㄌㄠˇ ㄕㄣ)
self-reference of an old woman or man

老生 (ㄌㄠˇ ㄕㄥ)
① the role of an old man in Chinese opera ② an aged student or scholar

老聲老氣 (ㄌㄠˇ ㄕㄥ ㄌㄠˇ ㄑㄧˋ)
the sound and look of an old person

老生常談 (ㄌㄠˇ ㄕㄥ ㄔㄤˊ ㄊㄢˊ)
a threadbare argument or talk; a cliché: 他的演講都是老生常談。His speech is full of clichés.

老書 (ㄌㄠˇ ㄕㄨ)
① old books (as distinct from new publications) ② books written by the authors in the past

老鼠 (ㄌㄠˇ ㄕㄨˇ)
a rat; a mouse

老人 (ㄌㄠˇ ㄖㄣˊ)
① an old person ② the original members of an organization; old faces in an organization after a reshuffle

老人家 (ㄌㄠˇ ㄖㄣˊ ㄐㄧㄚ)
① old persons (a term of respect) ② parents: 老人家好嗎? How are your parents?

老弱 (ㄌㄠˇ ㄖㄨㄛˋ)
the old and weak

老弱殘兵 (ㄌㄠˇ ㄖㄨㄛˋ ㄘㄢˊ ㄅㄧㄥ)
① old and weak surviving soldiers ② incompetent workers

老資格 (ㄌㄠˇ ㄗ ㄍㄜˊ)
an old-timer; a veteran

老子 (ㄌㄠˇ ㄗˇ)
① (ㄌㄠˇ ㄗˇ) Lao-tzu (or Lao-tse), 604-531 B.C., a renowned philosopher and founder of Taoism

老早 (ㄌㄠˇ ㄗㄠˇ)
① very early ② long ago: 他老早就死了。He died long ago.

老祖宗 (ㄌㄠˇ ㄗㄨˇ ㄗㄨㄥ)
ancestors; forefathers

老總 (ㄌㄠˇ ㄗㄨㄥˇ)
① a reference to soldiers in former times ② the leader

老顙作嚼 (ㄌㄠˇ ㄗㄨㄥˇ ㄗㄨㄛˋ ㄐㄧㄠˊ)
to toil for a living in one's old age

老殘遊記 (ㄌㄠˇ ㄘㄢˊ ㄧㄡˊ ㄐㄧˋ)
The Travels of Lao Ts'an: A Social Novel—a Ching Dynasty novel by Liu O (劉鶚)

老粗 (ㄌㄠˇ ㄘㄨ)
a rude fellow; a boor; an uneducated person

老蔥 (ㄌㄠˇ ㄘㄨㄥ)
a thick green onion

老死 (ㄌㄠˇ ㄙˇ)
① stubborn; obstinate ② to die of old age

老死不相往來 (ㄌㄠˇ ㄙˇ ㄅㄨˋ ㄒㄧㄤ ㄨㄤˇ ㄌㄞˊ)
to obstinately refuse all social intercourse; to be completely isolated from each other

老死牖下 (ㄌㄠˇ ㄙˇ ㄧㄡˇ ㄒㄧㄚˋ)
to live an insignificant life without any accomplishment

老叟 (ㄌㄠˇ ㄙㄡˇ)
an old man

老僧 (ㄌㄠˇ ㄙㄥ)
an old priest; the aged priest

老僧入定 (ㄌㄠˇ ㄙㄥ ㄖㄨˋ ㄉㄧㄥˋ)
(literally) to sit quietly with eyes closed (like an old Buddhist monk contemplating truth)—very calm and without worldly passions

老蘇 (ㄌㄠˇ ㄙㄨ)
the elder Su—Su Hsün (蘇洵), 1009-1066, father of

Su Shih (蘇軾) and Su Che (蘇轍)

老宿(ㄌㄠˇ ㄙㄨˋ)
① an aged monk or priest
② an aged scholar

老嫗(ㄌㄠˇ ㄩˋ)
an old woman

老兒(ㄌㄠˇ ㄦ)
① a comical reference to an old man ② one's husband

老兒子(ㄌㄠˇ ㄦ ˙ㄗ)
the youngest son

老而不死(ㄌㄠˇ ㄦˊ ㄅㄨˋ ㄙˇ)
(an abusive phrase) old but not dead—The world would be better off without that old bastard.

老一輩(ㄌㄠˇ ㄧ ㄅㄟˋ)
the older generation

老鴉(ㄌㄠˇ ㄧㄚ)
a crow; a raven

老爺(ㄌㄠˇ ㄧㄝˊ)
① sir ② an old man

老爺們(ㄌㄠˇ ㄧㄝˊ ˙ㄇㄣ)
men; gentlemen

老么(ㄌㄠˇ ㄧㄠ)
① the youngest child of a family ② the youngest one in a group

老油條(ㄌㄠˇ ㄧㄡˊ ㄊㄧㄠˊ)
a person who has learned to be sly; a sleeky fellow

老油子(ㄌㄠˇ ㄧㄡˊ ˙ㄗ)
an experienced and cunning person

老友(ㄌㄠˇ ㄧㄡˇ)
an old friend: 他是我父親的老友。He is an old friend of my father's.

老幼(ㄌㄠˇ ㄧㄡˋ)
aged people and young children

老眼昏花(ㄌㄠˇ ㄧㄢˇ ㄏㄨㄣ ㄏㄨㄚ)
the blurred vision of an old person

老樣子(ㄌㄠˇ ㄧㄤˋ ˙ㄗ)or 老樣兒(ㄌㄠˇ ㄧㄤˋ ㄦ)
the way a thing or person used to look

老鷹(ㄌㄠˇ ㄧㄥ)
the eagle

老吾老以及人之老(ㄌㄠˇ ㄨˊ ㄌㄠˇ ㄧˇ ㄐㄧˊ ㄖㄣˊ ㄓ ㄌㄠˇ)
take care of one's own aged parents first and then extend the same care to the

aged people in general

老物(ㄌㄠˇ ㄨˋ)
(an abusive term) an old person

老外(ㄌㄠˇ ㄨㄞˋ)
(slang) a foreigner

老頑固(ㄌㄠˇ ㄨㄢˊ ㄍㄨˋ)
a stubborn person; an old diehard; a stubborn old person

老王賣瓜，自賣自誇(ㄌㄠˇ ㄨㄤˊ ㄇㄞˋ ㄍㄨㄚ，ㄗˋ ㄇㄞˋ ㄗˋ ㄎㄨㄚ)
(literally)Lao Wang selling melons praises his own goods.—(figuratively)One praises one's own work or wares.

老翁(ㄌㄠˇ ㄨㄥ)
① an old man ② one's father

老媼(ㄌㄠˇ ㄠˇ)
an old woman

老媼能解(ㄌㄠˇ ㄠˇ ㄋㄥˊ ㄐㄧㄝˇ)
intelligible even to a senile woman

老玉米(ㄌㄠˇ ㄩˋ ㄇㄧˇ)
(Indian) corn

老遠(ㄌㄠˇ ㄩㄢˇ)
a very long way; a very great distance; very far

老運(ㄌㄠˇ ㄩㄣˋ)
one's lot in old age; good luck in one's old age: 他老運亨通。He has good luck in old age.

【考】4569
(攷)ㄎㄠˇ kao kǎo
1. one's deceased father
2. to test; to examine
3. to check; to investigate; to study

考妣(ㄎㄠˇ ㄅㄧˇ)
one's deceased father and mother

考畢(ㄎㄠˇ ㄅㄧˋ)
to finish an examination

考不取(ㄎㄠˇ ㄅㄨˋ ㄑㄩˇ)or 考不上(ㄎㄠˇ ㄅㄨˋ ㄕㄤˋ)
to fail in an examination (for admission to a school, employment, etc.)

考訂(ㄎㄠˇ ㄉㄧㄥˋ)
to review (a piece of writing) for correction

考題(ㄎㄠˇ ㄊㄧˊ)
questions on examination papers

考慮(ㄎㄠˇ ㄌㄩˋ)

to consider; to weigh; consideration; to think over

考古(ㄎㄠˇ ㄍㄨˇ)
to study the life and culture of ancient people

考古家(ㄎㄠˇ ㄍㄨˇ ㄐㄧㄚ)or 考古學家(ㄎㄠˇ ㄍㄨˇ ㄒㄩㄝˊ ㄐㄧㄚ)
an archeologist

考古學(ㄎㄠˇ ㄍㄨˇ ㄒㄩㄝˊ)
archeology

考官(ㄎㄠˇ ㄍㄨㄢ)
an examiner (especially under the former civil service examination system)

考課(ㄎㄠˇ ㄎㄜˋ)
to grade the service (of an official)

考覈 or 考核(ㄎㄠˇ ㄏㄜˊ)
to review or assess (a plan, proposal, etc.); to evaluate

考績(ㄎㄠˇ ㄐㄧ)
to grade the service (of an employee)

考校(ㄎㄠˇ ㄐㄧㄠˋ)
to examine; to check; to collate

考究(ㄎㄠˇ ㄐㄧㄡˋ)
① to examine and consider ② elaborate; beautiful ③ tasteful; elegant; choosy; particular

考據(ㄎㄠˇ ㄐㄩˋ)
to search for proofs (in textual research)

考據學(ㄎㄠˇ ㄐㄩˋ ㄒㄩㄝˊ)
textual research

考卷(ㄎㄠˇ ㄐㄩㄢˋ)
an examination paper

考求(ㄎㄠˇ ㄑㄧㄡˊ)
to try to find out by investigation

考勤(ㄎㄠˇ ㄑㄧㄣˊ)
to appraise the diligence (of an employee)

考區(ㄎㄠˇ ㄑㄩ)
an examination district

考取(ㄎㄠˇ ㄑㄩˇ)
to pass an examination (for admission to employment, a school, etc.) 亦作「考中」or「考上」

考選(ㄎㄠˇ ㄒㄩㄢˇ)
to select by a competitive examination

考證(ㄎㄠˇ ㄓㄥˋ)
(in textual research) to try

【老
部】

〔而 部〕

to verify a point

考住了 (ㄎㄠˇ ㄓㄨˋ ·ㄌㄜ)
unable to answer a question or solve a problem in an examination; to fail to answer a question asked verbally

考終 (ㄎㄠˇ ㄓㄨㄥ) or 考終命 (ㄎㄠˇ ㄓㄨㄥ ㄇㄧㄥˋ)
to die a natural death in old age

考中 (ㄎㄠˇ ㄓㄨㄥˋ)
to pass an examination (for admission to employment, a school, etc.) 參看「考取」

考查 (ㄎㄠˇ ㄔㄚˊ)
to examine; to check; to investigate

考察 (ㄎㄠˇ ㄔㄚˊ)
to inspect; to examine; to observe; to study

考察團 (ㄎㄠˇ ㄔㄚˊ ㄊㄨㄢˊ)
an investigation team; a fact-finding mission

考場 (ㄎㄠˇ ㄔㄤˇ) or (ㄎㄠˇ ㄔㄤˊ)
an examination hall or site

考成 (ㄎㄠˇ ㄔㄥˊ)
to appraise the service (of an employee)

考試 (ㄎㄠˇ ㄕˋ)
an examination; a test; a quiz

考試不及格 (ㄎㄠˇ ㄕˋ ㄅㄨˋ ㄐㄧˊ ㄍㄜˊ)
to fail in an examination: 這學生考試不及格。The student failed in the examination.

考試題目 (ㄎㄠˇ ㄕˋ ㄊㄧˊ ㄇㄨˋ)
examination questions 亦作「試題」

考試及格 (ㄎㄠˇ ㄕˋ ㄐㄧˊ ㄍㄜˊ)
to pass an examination: 他考試及格了。He passed the examination.

考試卷子 (ㄎㄠˇ ㄕˋ ㄐㄩㄢˋ ·ㄗ)
examination papers 亦作「試卷」

考試院 (ㄎㄠˇ ㄕˋ ㄩㄢˋ)
Examination Yuan (of the Republic of China)

考上 (ㄎㄠˇ ㄕㄤˋ)
to pass an examination (for admission to employment, a school, etc.)

考生 (ㄎㄠˇ ㄕㄥ)
an examinee; an examination candidate: 考生按時到達。The examinees arrived

on time.

考異 (ㄎㄠˇ ㄧˋ)
to collate the variants (in textual research)

考驗 (ㄎㄠˇ ㄧㄢˋ)
① to test; to try ② a test; a trial

考完 (ㄎㄠˇ ㄨㄢˊ)
to finish an examination

考問 (ㄎㄠˇ ㄨㄣˋ)
to examine and question; to examine orally

考語 (ㄎㄠˇ ㄩˇ)
comments made on the result of an inspection or examination

四畫

【耄】 4570
ㄇㄠˋ maw mào
1. in an extremely old age; in one's eighties or nineties
2. confused

耄耋 (ㄇㄠˋ ㄉㄧㄝˊ)
aged

耄齡 (ㄇㄠˋ ㄌㄧㄥˊ)
more than 80 or 70 years old

耄勤 (ㄇㄠˋ ㄑㄧㄣˊ)
to remain diligent in old age

【耆】 4571
ㄑㄧˊ chyi qí
to be in one's sixties; old

耆年碩德 (ㄑㄧˊ ㄋㄧㄢˊ ㄕㄨㄛˋ ㄉㄜˊ)
aged and virtuous

耆闍 (ㄑㄧˊ ㄕㄜˊ)
an aged Buddhist monk

耆老 (ㄑㄧˊ ㄌㄠˇ)
an aged and respected person

耆碩 (ㄑㄧˊ ㄕㄨㄛˋ) or 耆宿 (ㄑㄧˊ ㄙㄨˋ)
a respected old person

耆儒 (ㄑㄧˊ ㄖㄨˊ)
an aged scholar; a learned old person

【耆】 4571
2. ㄓˇ jyy zhǐ
as in 耆定—to bring into effect

【耆】 4571
3. ㄕˋ shyh shì
as in 耆欲—sensory pleasures

五畫

【者】 4572
ㄓㄜˇ jee zhě
1. those who; he who
2. a particle combining with some words to form adverbials

【耇】 4573
(ㄍㄡˇ goou gǒu
old age; the wizened face of age

六畫

【耋】 4574
ㄉㄧㄝˊ dye dié
octogenarians; in one's eighties

而 部
ㄦˊ erl ér

【而】 4575
ㄦˊ erl ér
1. accordingly; otherwise
2. and yet; but; nevertheless
3. you
4. on the condition that; supposing that; if
5. and; also

而立 (ㄦˊ ㄌㄧˋ)
30 years old

而後 (ㄦˊ ㄏㄡˋ)
then; afterwards; later; thenceforward; thenceforth; thereafter: 而後他寫了一封信給我。He wrote me a letter afterwards.

而今 (ㄦˊ ㄐㄧㄣ)
now: 而今他已是位成功的律師了。He is now a successful lawyer.

而且 (ㄦˊ ㄑㄧㄝˇ)
① and: 這房間很寬敞，而且光線充足。The room is spacious and bright. ② moreover; furthermore; besides; in addition: 他很勇敢而且很親切。He is brave; moreover, he is kind.

而已 (ㄦˊ ㄧˇ)
merely; only; and that is all: 這只是個託詞而已。It is merely a pretense.

而外 (ㄦˊ ㄨㄞˋ)
aside from; apart from; with

the exception of; except; exclusive of

三畫

【耐】 4576 （ㄋㄞˋ nay nài）
to bear; to endure; to stand; to resist: 他不耐孤寂。He can't bear living alone.

耐不久（ㄋㄞˋ ㄅㄨˋ ㄐㄧㄡˇ）
unable to last or endure long

耐不住（ㄋㄞˋ ㄅㄨˋ ㄓㄨˋ）
unable to bear, stand, or endure: 他耐不住嘈閒聲。He is unable to bear the noise.

耐磨（ㄋㄞˋ ㄇㄛˊ）
(said of metals) wear-resisting; wearproof

耐煩（ㄋㄞˋ ㄈㄢˊ）
patient

耐冬（ㄋㄞˋ ㄉㄨㄥ）
① able to endure cold ② a kind of evergreen tree

耐勞（ㄋㄞˋ ㄌㄠˊ）
able to endure hard work

耐力（ㄋㄞˋ ㄌㄧˋ）
endurance; staying power; stamina

耐寒（ㄋㄞˋ ㄏㄢˊ）
able to endure cold

耐火（ㄋㄞˋ ㄏㄨㄛˇ）
fireproof

耐火泥（ㄋㄞˋ ㄏㄨㄛˇ ㄋㄧˊ）
fire clay

耐火磚（ㄋㄞˋ ㄏㄨㄛˇ ㄓㄨㄢ）
a firebrick

耐久（ㄋㄞˋ ㄐㄧㄡˇ）
lasting a long time; durable

耐久力（ㄋㄞˋ ㄐㄧㄡˇ ㄌㄧˋ）
durability; endurance

耐心（ㄋㄞˋ ㄒㄧㄣ）
patience; perseverance

耐性（ㄋㄞˋ ㄒㄧㄥˋ）
patience; perseverance

耐熱（ㄋㄞˋ ㄖㄜˋ）
heat-proof

耐人尋味（ㄋㄞˋ ㄖㄣˊ ㄒㄩㄣˊ ㄨㄟˋ）
intriguing; puzzling; perplexing; providing food for thought: 這學者的話很耐人尋味。What the scholar said gives one much food for thought.

耐用（ㄋㄞˋ ㄩㄥˋ）
durable; sturdy; able to stand wear and tear

【耍】 4577 （ㄕㄨㄚˇ shoa shuǎ）
to play; to sport: 男孩們正在公園裏耍玩要。The boys are playing in the park.

耍把戲（ㄕㄨㄚˇ ㄅㄚˇ ㄒㄧˋ）
to juggle; to play tricks: 他以球耍把戲。He juggled with balls.

耍筆桿（ㄕㄨㄚˇ ㄅㄧˇ ㄍㄢˇ）
to be skilled in literary tricks

耍脾氣（ㄕㄨㄚˇ ㄆㄧˊ ㄑㄧˋ）
to lose one's temper; to get angry: 他向他哥哥耍脾氣。He got angry with his elder brother.

耍貧嘴 or 耍頻嘴（ㄕㄨㄚˇ ㄆㄧㄣˊ ㄗㄨㄟˋ）
to joke a great deal

耍大牌（ㄕㄨㄚˇ ㄉㄚˋ ㄆㄞˊ）
to display the temper of or behave like a top-billing actor or actress; to act like a prima donna

耍閒（ㄕㄨㄚˇ ㄒㄧㄢˊ）
to frolic; to sport: 我們在一起耍閒作樂。We met in frolic and in laughter.

耍賴（ㄕㄨㄚˇ ㄌㄞˋ）
to act shamelessly; to be unreasonable 亦作「耍無賴」

耍懶（ㄕㄨㄚˇ ㄌㄢˇ）
to loiter; to loaf

耍流氓（ㄕㄨㄚˇ ㄌㄧㄡˊ ㄇㄤˊ）
to behave like a hooligan; to act rudely

耍弄（ㄕㄨㄚˇ ㄋㄨㄥˋ）
to make a fool of; to deceive

耍猴（ㄕㄨㄚˇ ㄏㄡˊ）
to make a monkey do tricks

耍花槍（ㄕㄨㄚˇ ㄏㄨㄚ ㄑㄧㄤ）
to play sleight of hand; to be dishonest; to cheat

耍花招（ㄕㄨㄚˇ ㄏㄨㄚ ㄓㄠ）
① to show off some special skill ② to play tricks: 別耍花招了！Don't try any tricks!

耍錢（ㄕㄨㄚˇ ㄑㄧㄢˊ）
to gamble

耍笑（ㄕㄨㄚˇ ㄒㄧㄠˋ）
to poke fun at

耍心眼兒（ㄕㄨㄚˇ ㄒㄧㄣ ㄧㄢˇㄦ）
to exercise one's wits for personal gain; to be very

crafty; to pull a shrewd trick: 他老愛耍心眼兒。He is very crafty.

耍手藝（ㄕㄨㄚˇ ㄕㄡˇ ㄧˋ）
to make a living by some special skill

耍子（ㄕㄨㄚˇ ˙ㄗ）
to play; to sport

耍嘴皮子（ㄕㄨㄚˇ ㄗㄨㄟˇ ㄆㄧˊ ˙ㄗ）
to show off one's joking talent; to brag; to talk big

耍威風（ㄕㄨㄚˇ ㄨㄟ ㄈㄥ）
to make a show of authority; to throw one's weight about; to be overbearing

【耑】 4578 （ㄉㄨㄢ duan duǎn）
same as 端—an end; a tip; a point

【耑】 4578 （ㄓㄨㄢ juan zhuān）
same as 專—for a particular person, occasion, purpose, etc.

耒 部

（ㄌㄟˇ leei lěi）

【耒】 4579 （ㄌㄟˇ leei lěi）
the wooden handle of a plough

耒耜（ㄌㄟˇ ㄙˋ）
to till; to plough; to cultivate

耒耝（ㄌㄟˇ ㄙˋ）
ploughs

三畫

【耔】 4580 （ㄗˇ tzyy zǐ）
to hoe up earth around a plant

四畫

【耙】 4581 （ㄆㄚˊ par pá）（又讀 ㄅㄚˋ bah bà）
1. a harrow; a drag
2. to rake: 他把田地耙平。He rakes the field.

耙櫛（ㄆㄚˊ ㄔㄨ）

【耕部】

①a harrow ②to plough with a harrow

耙子(ㄆㄚˊ•ㄗ)
①a harrow; a drag ②a clue (to a matter)

4582

【耕】 《ㄥ geng gēng
(語音ㄐㄧㄥ jīng)
to till; to plough; to cultivate

耕牧(《ㄥ ㄇㄨˋ)
tilling and pasturing

耕地(《ㄥ ㄉㄧˋ)
①cultivated land ②to till land

耕田(《ㄥ ㄊㄧㄢˊ)
to till land

耕牛(《ㄥ ㄋㄧㄡˊ)
an ox used in farming

耕稼(《ㄥ ㄐㄧㄚˋ)
tilling and planting

耕織(《ㄥ ㄓ)
(the men) tilling and (the women) weaving

耕者有其田(《ㄥ ㄓㄜˇ ㄧㄡˇ ㄑㄧˊ ㄊㄧㄢˊ)
land to the tiller (the final phase of the land reform program on Taiwan)

耕種(《ㄥ ㄓㄨㄥˋ)
①to plough and sow; to cultivate ②cultivation

耕事(《ㄥ ㄕˋ)
farm work

耕作(《ㄥ ㄗㄨㄛˋ)
to cultivate land and grow crops

耕鑿(《ㄥ ㄗㄠˊ)
tilling land and drilling wells

耕耘(《ㄥ ㄩㄣˊ)
to till and weed; ploughing and weeding; to cultivate: 一分耕耘，一分收穫。The more ploughing and weeding, the better the crop. 或 As you sow, so shall you reap.

耕耘機(《ㄥ ㄩㄣˊ ㄐㄧ)
a power tiller

4583

【耘】 ㄩㄣˊ yun yún
to weed

耘田(ㄩㄣˊ ㄊㄧㄢˊ)
to weed rice fields

耘人之田(ㄩㄣˊ ㄖㄣˊ ㄓ ㄊㄧㄢˊ)
(literally) to weed the rice fields of others—to manage

a business on behalf of others

耘草(ㄩㄣˊ ㄘㄠˇ)
to remove weeds; to weed:
他正忙着耘草。He is busy weeding.

4584

【耗】 ㄏㄠˋ haw hào
1. to expend; to use up; to waste; to squander; to consume
2. news; a report

耗費(ㄏㄠˋ ㄈㄟˋ)
to expend; to squander

耗電量(ㄏㄠˋ ㄉㄧㄢˋ ㄌㄧㄤˋ)
power consumption

耗體力(ㄏㄠˋ ㄊㄧˇ ㄌㄧˋ)
to expend bodily strength

耗端(ㄏㄠˋ ㄉㄨㄢ)
to exhaust; to use up: 所有材料都耗端了。All the material is used up.

耗減(ㄏㄠˋ ㄐㄧㄢˇ)
to diminish by expending

耗盡(ㄏㄠˋ ㄐㄧㄣˋ)
to exhaust; to use up; to consume entirely: 他耗盡了所有的錢。He exhausted his money.

耗時間(ㄏㄠˋ ㄕˊ ㄐㄧㄢ)
to consume time; time-consuming: 他寫書耗時間又費精力。He consumed time and energy in writing this book.

耗子(ㄏㄠˋ •ㄗ)
a mouse; a rat

耗損(ㄏㄠˋ ㄙㄨㄣˇ)
to diminish by expending

五畫

4585

【耜】 ㄙˋ syh sì
a plough

七畫

4586

【耡】 ㄔㄨˊ chwu chú
same as 鋤—to hoe; a hoe

九畫

4587

【耦】 ㄡˇ oou ǒu
1. to plough side by side
2. even (numbers); in pairs
3. a spouse; a mate

耦耕(ㄡˇ 《ㄥ)
to plough side by side

耦語(ㄡˇ ㄩˇ)
to have a tête-à-tête; to whisper to each other

十畫

4588

【耨】 ㄋㄡˋ now nòu
1. a hoe
2. to weed; to hoe

十五畫

4589

【耰】 ㄧㄡ iou yōu
1. to draw earth over newly-sown grain; to cover the seed
2. a kind of hoe

耳 部
ㄦˇ eel ěr

4590

【耳】 ㄦˇ eel ěr
1. ears
2. (a phrase-final particle) only; merely
3. a Chinese family name

耳鼻科(ㄦˇ ㄅㄧˊ ㄎㄜ)
otorhinology

耳鼻喉科(ㄦˇ ㄅㄧˊ ㄏㄡˊ ㄎㄜ)
otorhinolaryngology; otolaryngology

耳邊風(ㄦˇ ㄅㄧㄢ ㄈㄥ) or 耳旁風(ㄦˇ ㄆㄤˊ ㄈㄥ)
(literally) the wind past the ear—a matter of no concern; to turn a deaf ear to something

耳鬢廝磨(ㄦˇ ㄅㄧㄣˋ ㄙ ㄇㄛˊ)
(literally) ears and side-burns rubbing—(usually said of childhood lovers) very intimate

耳門(ㄦˇ ㄇㄣˊ)
①a side door ②the external ear; the earlap; the auricle; the pinna

耳鳴(ㄦˇ ㄇㄧㄥˊ)
buzzing in the ears; tinnitus aurium

耳目(ㄦ ㄇㄨ)
① ears and eyes ② one's attention or notice ③ an informer

耳目衆多(ㄦ ㄇㄨ ㄓㄨㄥ ㄉㄨㄛ)
There are many spies.

耳目一新(ㄦ ㄇㄨ ㄧ ㄒㄧㄣ)
to have a completely new impression

耳糞(ㄦ ㄈㄣ)or 耳垢(ㄦ ㄍㄡ)or 耳屎(ㄦ ㄕ)
earwax; cerumen

耳朶(ㄦ ㄉㄨㄛ)
ears: 老師扭住學生的耳朶。The teacher seized the student by the ear.

耳朶軟(ㄦ ㄉㄨㄛ ㄖㄨㄢ)
capable of hearing much

耳軟(ㄦ ㄖㄨㄢ)
credulous

耳朶眼兒(ㄦ ㄉㄨㄛ ㄧㄢ)
a hole pierced in the lobe of an ear for earrings

耳提面命(ㄦ ㄊㄧ ㄇㄧㄢ ㄇㄧㄥ)
(literally)to hold one's head by the ears when giving him instructions—to give instructions earnestly; to din into one's ears

耳聽八方(ㄦ ㄊㄧㄥ ㄅㄚ ㄈㄤ)
very alert; extremely vigilant: 他們耳聽八方。They were very alert.

耳痛(ㄦ ㄊㄨㄥ)
otalgia

耳漏(ㄦ ㄌㄡ)
(medicine) the otorrhea

耳力(ㄦ ㄌㄧ)
the power of hearing; the sense of hearing; audition: 她的耳力不太好。Her sense of hearing is not very good.

耳聾(ㄦ ㄌㄨㄥ)
deaf: 他變成耳聾。He became deaf.

耳根(ㄦ ㄍㄣ)
(Buddhism) the organ of hearing

耳根清靜(ㄦ ㄍㄣ ㄑㄧㄥ ㄐㄧㄥ)
peace of mind achieved by staying away from nagging, bickering, etc.

耳鼓(ㄦ ㄍㄨ)
the eardrum; the tympanum

耳刮子(ㄦ ㄍㄨㄚ ·ㄗ)or 耳光(ㄦ ㄍㄨㄤ)or 耳光子(ㄦ ㄍㄨㄤ ·ㄗ)

a box on the ear

耳科(ㄦ ㄎㄜ)
otology

耳科醫生(ㄦ ㄎㄜ ㄧ ㄕㄥ)
an ear specialist; an aurist; an otologist: 你必須去看耳科醫生。You must see an aurist.

耳殼(ㄦ ㄎㄜ)
the concha, or auricle

耳道(ㄦ ㄉㄠ)
an otic channel

耳環(ㄦ ㄏㄨㄢ)
earrings: 她在找她的耳環。She is looking for her earrings.

耳機(ㄦ ㄐㄧ)
an earphone: 他的耳機性能不佳。His earphone does not function very well.

耳下腺(ㄦ ㄒㄧㄚ ㄒㄧㄢ)
a parotid gland

耳下腺炎(ㄦ ㄒㄧㄚ ㄒㄧㄢ ㄧㄢ)
parotitis

耳墜子(ㄦ ㄓㄨㄟ ·ㄗ)
earrings; an eardrop

耳垂(ㄦ ㄔㄨㄟ)
an ear lobe; a lobule

耳食(ㄦ ㄕ)
to taste food with ears—(figuratively) to be apt to believe hearsay because of one's vulgar and superficial knowledge

耳視目食(ㄦ ㄕ ㄇㄨ ㄕ)
very intelligent

耳生(ㄦ ㄕㄥ)
unfamiliar to the ears; rarely heard of: 這首歌聽起來耳生。The song sounds unfamiliar to me.

耳熟(ㄦ ㄕㄡ)
familiar to the ears; much heard of

耳熟能詳(ㄦ ㄕㄡ ㄋㄥ ㄒㄧㄤ)
so frequently heard about that it can be told (in detail or word by word)

耳屬(ㄦ ㄕㄨ)
to eavesdrop; to listen with effort and attention

耳順之年(ㄦ ㄕㄨㄣ ㄓ ㄋㄧㄢ)
(literally)the age when nothing one hears can be objectionable—60 years old(from the phrase "六十而耳順")

耳熱(ㄦ ㄖㄜ)
to have a burning sensation

in the ears; to have burning ears

耳濡目染(ㄦ ㄖㄨ ㄇㄨ ㄖㄢ)
thoroughly imbued with what one frequently hears and sees

耳聰目明(ㄦ ㄘㄨㄥ ㄇㄨ ㄇㄧㄥ)
sharp in hearing and keen in seeing—(figuratively) very clever

耳塞(ㄦ ㄙㄞ)
an earplug

耳耳(ㄦ ㄦ)
① flourishing; thriving; vigorous ② erect; straight ③ an exclamation of discontent

耳炎(ㄦ ㄧㄢ)
inflammation of the ear; otitis

耳挖子(ㄦ ㄨㄚ ·ㄗ)
an ear pick

耳聞(ㄦ ㄨㄣ)
① to hear ② what one hears about; hearsay

耳聞不如目見(ㄦ ㄨㄣ ㄅㄨ ㄖㄨ ㄇㄨ ㄐㄧㄢ)
Seeing for oneself is better than hearing a hundred times. or Seeing is believing.

耳聞目睹(ㄦ ㄨㄣ ㄇㄨ ㄉㄨ)
what one sees and hears—widely known

耳語(ㄦ ㄩ)
to whisper into another's ear; whispers

三畫

【耶】 4591
1. ㄧㄝ ye yē
a phrase-final particle for a question: 是耶? 非耶? Is it or isn't it? or Yes or no?

【耶】 4591
2. ㄧㄝ ie yē
transliteration of English names

耶誕禮物(ㄧㄝ ㄉㄢ ㄌㄧ ㄨ)
Christmas gifts

耶誕卡(ㄧㄝ ㄉㄢ ㄎㄚ)or 耶誕卡片(ㄧㄝ ㄉㄢ ㄎㄚ ㄆㄧㄢ)
a Christmas card

耶誕節(ㄧㄝ ㄉㄢ ㄐㄧㄝ)
Christmas

耶誕樹(ㄧㄝ ㄉㄢ ㄕㄨ)
a Christmas tree

耶拿(ㄧㄝ ㄋㄚ)

【耳部】

Jena, a German city

耶魯大學（一せ カメ カY ㄒㄩㄝˊ）
Yale University: 他畢業於耶魯大學。He graduated from Yale University.

耶路撒冷（一せ ㄌㄨˋ ㄙㄚ ㄌㄥˇ）
Jerusalem

耶和華（一せ ㄏㄜˊ ㄏㄨㄚˊ）
Jehovah

耶穌（一せ ㄙㄨ）
Jesus

耶穌復活日（一せ ㄙㄨ ㄈㄨˋ ㄏㄨㄛˊ ㄖˋ）
Easter

耶穌會（一せ ㄙㄨ ㄏㄨㄟˋ）
the Society of Jesus

耶穌基督（一せ ㄙㄨ ㄐ一 ㄉㄨ）
Jesus Christ

耶穌紀元（一せ ㄙㄨ ㄐ一ˋ ㄩㄢˊ）
the Christian Era 亦作「公元」or「西元」

耶穌教（一せ ㄙㄨ ㄐ一ㄠˋ）
Protestant Christianity (as distinct from Roman Catholicism)

耶穌聖誕（一せ ㄙㄨ ㄕㄥˋ ㄉㄢˋ）
Christmas

【耷】 4592
ㄉㄚ da dā
1. big ears
2. the given name of a famous Ching artist, Chu Ta (朱耷)

耷拉（ㄉㄚ · ㄌㄚ）
to hang down; to droop

四畫

【耽】 4593
ㄉㄢ dan dān
1. to indulge in; to be addicted to
2. delightful and enduring
3. (said of ears) large and drooping
4. negligent

耽美主義（ㄉㄢ ㄇㄟˇ ㄓㄨˇ 一ˋ）
estheticism

耽（ㄉㄢ 一ˇ）
addicted to: 他耽湎於酒。He was addicted to alcohol.

耽耽（ㄉㄢ ㄉㄢ）
(said of a tiger's eyes) glaring covetously; eying greedily

耽讀（ㄉㄢ ㄉㄨˊ）
addicted to reading

耽（ㄉㄢ 一ˋ）
to indulge in (evil ways); un-

able to free oneself from (bad habits): 他耽溺於賭博。He indulges himself in gambling.

耽樂（ㄉㄢ ㄌㄜˋ）
to indulge in pleasure

耽擱（ㄉㄢ ·ㄍㄜ）
① to stay; to stop over; a stopover ② to delay: 別把婚期結耽擱了。Don't delay the date of wedding.

耽習（ㄉㄢ ㄒ一ˊ）
to be absorbed in study

耽心（ㄉㄢ ㄒ一ㄣ）
to be worried 亦作「擔心」

耽思（ㄉㄢ ㄙ）
to think deeply; to ponder

耽憂（ㄉㄢ 一ㄡ）
to worry

耽誤（ㄉㄢ ·ㄨ）
to delay; to hold up: 他們耽誤了整個工程。They held up the whole project.

【耿】 4594
《ㄥ geeng gěng
1. bright
2. upright; incorruptible
3. a Chinese family name

耿耿（《ㄥ 《ㄥ）
① bright; shining ② concerned; anxious; apprehensive; restless

耿耿於懷（《ㄥ 《ㄥ ㄩ ㄏㄨㄞˊ）
to keep something anxiously in one's mind; to take something to heart

耿介（《ㄥ ㄐ一ㄝˋ）
① magnificent ② upright; just; righteous

耿直（《ㄥ ㄓˊ）
honest; upright: 他秉性耿直。He is upright by nature.

【耼】 4595
ㄉㄢ dan dān
1. another name of Lao-tzu (老子)
2. a deformed ear

【耻】 4596
ㄔˇ chyy chǐ
same as 恥—shame

五畫

【聆】 4597
ㄌ一ㄥˊ ling líng
to listen; to hear

聆聽（ㄌ一ㄥˊ ㄊ一ㄥ）
to listen to

聆教（ㄌ一ㄥˊ ㄐ一ㄠˋ）
to listen to someone's instructions

聆悉（ㄌ一ㄥˊ ㄒ一）
to learn; to hear

【聊】 4598
ㄌ一ㄠˊ liao liáo
1. somehow; somewhat; a little
2. to rely; to depend
3. to chat; a chat
4. interest
5. for the time being

聊備一格（ㄌ一ㄠˊ ㄅㄟˋ 一 《ㄜˊ）
may serve as a specimen

聊表寸忱（ㄌ一ㄠˊ ㄅ一ㄠˇ ㄘㄨㄣˋ ㄔㄣˊ）
as a token of respect or good will (an expression often used when presenting somebody with a gift)

聊天（ㄌ一ㄠˊ ㄊ一ㄢ）
to chat; a chat

聊賴（ㄌ一ㄠˊ ㄌㄞˋ）
something to live for; something to rely upon

聊聊（ㄌ一ㄠˊ ㄌ一ㄠˊ）
to have a chat: 我們到咖啡廳聊聊。Let's have a chat in the coffee shop.

聊啾（ㄌ一ㄠˊ ㄐ一ㄡ）
buzzing in the ears

聊且（ㄌ一ㄠˊ ㄑㄧㄝˇ）
for the time being

聊齋誌異（ㄌ一ㄠˊ ㄓㄞ ㄓˋ 一ˋ）
Strange Stories from a Chinese Studio (title of a collection of bizarre stories by Pu Sung-ling (蒲松齡) of the Ching Dynasty)

聊生（ㄌ一ㄠˊ ㄕㄥ）
to make a living

聊勝一籌（ㄌ一ㄠˊ ㄕㄥˋ 一ˋ ㄔㄡˊ）or 聊勝一等（ㄌ一ㄠˊ ㄕㄥˋ 一ˋ ㄉㄥˇ）
to surpass only a little bit

聊勝於無（ㄌ一ㄠˊ ㄕㄥˋ ㄩˊ ㄨˊ）
at least better than nothing 或 It's better than nothing.

聊以解嘲（ㄌ一ㄠˊ 一ˇ ㄐ一ㄝˇ ㄔㄠˊ）
to manage somehow to relieve embarrassment

聊以自慰（ㄌ一ㄠˊ 一ˇ ㄗˋ ㄨㄟˋ）
just to console oneself; to take comfort in

聊以塞責（ㄌ一ㄠˊ 一ˇ ㄙㄜˋ ㄗㄜˊ）
merely to avoid the charge of a dereliction of duty

六畫

【聒】 4599
《ㄍㄨㄚ guā guà
clamorous; uproarious

聒聒(《ㄨㄚ《ㄨㄚ)
uproarious; clamorous; noisy

聒聒叫(《ㄨㄚ《ㄨㄚ ㄐㄧㄠ)
very good; wonderful; excellent: 他的 英文 聒聒叫。His English is excellent.

聒架(《ㄨㄚ ㄐㄧㄚˋ)
to keep talking noisily; 他們 聒架不休。They kept talking noisily.

聒噪(《ㄨㄚ ㄗㄠˋ)
to be uproarious; to be noisy: 這隻鸚鵡十分聒噪。This parrot is very noisy.

聒耳(《ㄨㄚ ㄦˇ)
offensive to the ear

七畫

【聖】 4600
ㄕㄥˋ shèng shèng
1. a sage
2. sacred; holy

聖保羅(ㄕㄥˋ ㄅㄠˇ ㄌㄨㄛˊ)
①St. Paul, U.S.A. ②São Paulo, Brazil

聖彼得(ㄕㄥˋ ㄅㄧˇ ㄉㄜˊ)
St. Peter

聖彼得堡(ㄕㄥˋ ㄅㄧˇ ㄉㄜˊ ㄅㄠˇ)
St. Petersburg, the old name of Leningrad

聖彼得大教堂(ㄕㄥˋ ㄅㄧˇ ㄉㄜˊ ㄉㄚˋ ㄐㄧㄠˋ ㄊㄤˊ)
St. Peter's

聖馬力諾(ㄕㄥˋ ㄇㄚˇ ㄌㄧˋ ㄋㄨㄛˋ)
San Marino

聖廟(ㄕㄥˋ ㄇㄧㄠˋ)
a Confucian temple

聖明(ㄕㄥˋ ㄇㄧㄥˊ)
①His Majesty; His Holiness ②(said of a leader) capable and virtuous

聖母(ㄕㄥˋ ㄇㄨˇ)
①the Virgin Mary; the Holy Mother ②an empress dowager

聖母瑪利亞(ㄕㄥˋ ㄇㄨˇ ㄇㄚˇ ㄌㄧˋ ㄧㄚˇ)
the Virgin Mary

Madonna; an image of the Virgin Mary

聖基(ㄕㄥˋ ㄐㄧ)
the tomb of a sage or saint

聖誕(ㄕㄥˋ ㄉㄢˋ)
Christmas

聖誕老人(ㄕㄥˋ ㄉㄢˋ ㄌㄠˇ ㄖㄣˊ)
Santa Claus

聖誕禮物(ㄕㄥˋ ㄉㄢˋ ㄌㄧˇ ㄨˋ)
a Christmas present; a Christmas gift

聖誕卡(ㄕㄥˋ ㄉㄢˋ ㄎㄚˇ)
a Christmas card

聖誕紅(ㄕㄥˋ ㄉㄢˋ ㄏㄨㄥˊ)
a poinsettia

聖誕節(ㄕㄥˋ ㄉㄢˋ ㄐㄧㄝˊ)
Christmastide; Christmas-time

聖誕前夕(ㄕㄥˋ ㄉㄢˋ ㄑㄧㄢˊ ㄒㄧ)
Christmas Eve

聖誕樹(ㄕㄥˋ ㄉㄢˋ ㄕㄨˋ)
a Christmas tree

聖地(ㄕㄥˋ ㄉㄧˋ)
a holy ground

聖地牙哥(ㄕㄥˋ ㄉㄧˋ ㄧㄚˊ ㄍㄜ)
Santiago, capital of Chile

聖多明哥(ㄕㄥˋ ㄉㄨㄛ ㄇㄧㄥˊ ㄍㄜ)
Santo Domingo, the capital of the Dominican Republic and the republic's old name

聖多斯(ㄕㄥˋ ㄉㄨㄛ ㄙ)
Santos, a harbor in Brazil

聖壇(ㄕㄥˋ ㄊㄢˊ)
an altar

聖堂(ㄕㄥˋ ㄊㄤˊ)
a sanctuary

聖徒(ㄕㄥˋ ㄊㄨˊ)
an apostle; a saint

聖林(ㄕㄥˋ ㄌㄧㄣˊ)
the Confucian tomb 亦作「孔林」

聖靈(ㄕㄥˋ ㄌㄧㄥˊ)
the Holy Ghost; the Holy Spirit

聖路易(ㄕㄥˋ ㄌㄨˋ ㄧˋ)
①St. Louis, U.S.A. ②St. Louis, Senegal

聖公會(ㄕㄥˋ ㄍㄨㄥ ㄏㄨㄟˋ)
the Episcopal Church

聖赫勒拿島(ㄕㄥˋ ㄏㄜˋ ㄌㄜˋ ㄋㄚˊ ㄉㄠˇ)
Saint Helena Island 亦作「聖海倫島」

聖湖(ㄕㄥˋ ㄏㄨˊ)
another name of the West Lake (西湖), Hangchow, Chekiang

聖蹟(ㄕㄥˋ ㄐㄧ)
relics of a sage

聖駕(ㄕㄥˋ ㄐㄧㄚˋ)
His Majesty

聖潔(ㄕㄥˋ ㄐㄧㄝˊ)
holy and immaculate

聖教(ㄕㄥˋ ㄐㄧㄠˋ)
Confucianism

聖經(ㄕㄥˋ ㄐㄧㄥ)
①the Bible ②works of a sage (especially Confucius)

聖經賢傳(ㄕㄥˋ ㄐㄧㄥ ㄒㄧㄢˊ ㄓㄨㄢˋ)
the classics of the sages

聖君(ㄕㄥˋ ㄐㄩㄣ)
①His Majesty ②a reference to General Kuan Yü (關羽)

聖賢(ㄕㄥˋ ㄒㄧㄢˊ)
sages and virtuous men; saints

聖心(ㄕㄥˋ ㄒㄧㄣ)
①His Majesty's heart ②the Sacred Heart

聖像(ㄕㄥˋ ㄒㄧㄤˋ)
①sacred images; idols ②an image of Confucius ③an image of Jesus Christ

聖職(ㄕㄥˋ ㄓˊ)
holy orders; the ministry: 他就任聖職。He takes holy orders.

聖旨(ㄕㄥˋ ㄓˇ)
an imperial decree

聖哲(ㄕㄥˋ ㄓㄜˊ)
①sages and saints ②the wisdom of a sage

聖者(ㄕㄥˋ ㄓㄜˇ)
a sage; a saint

聖戰(ㄕㄥˋ ㄓㄢˋ)
a holy war; a sacred war

聖朝(ㄕㄥˋ ㄔㄠˊ)
the present dynasty

聖城(ㄕㄥˋ ㄔㄥˊ)
the Holy City: 耶路撒冷及麥加是聖城。Jerusalem and Mecca are Holy Cities.

聖詩(ㄕㄥˋ ㄕ)
a psalm

聖手(ㄕㄥˋ ㄕㄡˇ)
a master (of a skill)

聖善(ㄕㄥˋ ㄕㄢˋ)
sacred; holy

聖上(ㄕㄥˋ ㄕㄤˋ)
His Majesty

聖水(ㄕㄥˋ ㄕㄨㄟˇ)
holy water

聖人(ㄕㄥˋ ㄖㄣˊ)
a sage; a saint

聖餐(ㄕㄥˋ ㄘㄢ)

〔耳部〕

the Lord's Supper

聖恩(ㄕㄥ ㄣ)
imperial favor or graciousness

聖裔(ㄕㄥ ㄧˋ)
descendants of a sage (especially of Confucius)

聖域(ㄕㄥ ㄩˋ)
the state of being a sage or saint

聖諭(ㄕㄥ ㄩˋ)
an imperial edict

【聘】 4601
1. ㄆㄧㄣˋ pinn pìn
1. to invite for service; to employ; to engage
2. to be betrothed; to be engaged
3. to pay respect by sending an envoy
4. to ask; to inquire

聘禮(ㄆㄧㄣˋ ㄌㄧˇ)
①a gift for inviting one's service ②presents for betrothal sent to a girl's family

聘金(ㄆㄧㄣˋ ㄐㄧㄣ)
money paid (to the parents of the prospective bride) at a betrothal

聘君(ㄆㄧㄣˋ ㄐㄩㄣ)
a capable scholar recruited by the imperial court for public service

聘妻(ㄆㄧㄣˋ ㄑㄧ)
a fiancée

聘請(ㄆㄧㄣˋ ㄑㄧㄥˇ)
to invite someone for service; to engage; to appoint

聘召(ㄆㄧㄣˋ ㄓㄠˋ)
to invite someone for service (usually with presents)

聘書(ㄆㄧㄣˋ ㄕㄨ)
the formal letter of employment; the letter of appointment

聘任(ㄆㄧㄣˋ ㄖㄣˋ)
to employ or engage for a post

聘物(ㄆㄧㄣˋ ㄨˋ)
presents for betrothal (sent to the parents of the prospective bride)

聘問(ㄆㄧㄣˋ ㄨㄣˋ)
international exchange of visits

聘用(ㄆㄧㄣˋ ㄩㄥˋ)

to employ; to engage

【聘】 4601
2. ㄆㄧㄥ ping pīng
to give (a daughter) in marriage; to marry

聘姑娘(ㄆㄧㄥ ㄍㄨ · ㄋㄧㄤ)
to give a daughter in marriage; to marry a daughter to someone

八畫

【聚】 4602
ㄐㄩˋ jiuh jù
to come or put together; to gather; to assemble; to collect

聚寶盆(ㄐㄩˋ ㄅㄠˇ ㄆㄣˊ)
a legendary earthen pot in which money multiplies

聚賭(ㄐㄩˋ ㄉㄨˇ)
to assemble for gambling

聚斂(ㄐㄩˋ ㄌㄧㄢˋ)
to gather, to collect, or to amass illegally or immorally

聚落(ㄐㄩˋ ㄌㄨㄛˋ)
a place where people live; a village; a town

聚攏(ㄐㄩˋ ㄌㄨㄥˇ)
to gather; to assemble; to come together

聚光鏡(ㄐㄩˋ ㄍㄨㄤ ㄐㄧㄥˋ)
a condensing lens

聚合(ㄐㄩˋ ㄏㄜˊ)
①to gather; to assemble; to come together ②(chemistry) polymerization

聚合體(ㄐㄩˋ ㄏㄜˊ ㄊㄧˇ)
a polymer

聚會(ㄐㄩˋ ㄏㄨㄟˋ)
to assemble; to gather; to meet; to get together: 他們聚會討論問題。They got together to discuss a problem.

聚會所(ㄐㄩˋ ㄏㄨㄟˋ ㄙㄨㄛˇ)
a place for a meeting; a gathering place

聚積(ㄐㄩˋ ㄐㄧ)
to accumulate

聚集(ㄐㄩˋ ㄐㄧˊ)
to gather; to assemble: 學生們在學校禮堂聚集。The students assembled in the school hall.

聚精會神(ㄐㄩˋ ㄐㄧㄥ ㄏㄨㄟˋ ㄕㄣˊ)
to concentrate oneself; with

attention: 你應聚精會神讀書。You should read with attention.

聚居(ㄐㄩˋ ㄐㄩ)
to live together

聚齊(ㄐㄩˋ ㄑㄧˊ)
to be all present at a gathering

聚星(ㄐㄩˋ ㄒㄧㄥ)
multiple stars

聚形(ㄐㄩˋ ㄒㄧㄥˊ)
(mineralogy) combination form

聚眾(ㄐㄩˋ ㄓㄨㄥˋ)
to gather a mob; to assemble a crowd

聚沙成塔(ㄐㄩˋ ㄕㄚ ㄔㄥˊ ㄊㄚˇ)
Accumulation of small amounts results in a huge quantity.

聚首(ㄐㄩˋ ㄕㄡˇ)
to get together; to meet: 我們設法至少每一年聚首一次。We try to get together at least once a year.

聚餐(ㄐㄩˋ ㄘㄢ)
to get together for luncheon or dinner

聚散(ㄐㄩˋ ㄙㄢˋ)
meeting and parting

聚散無常(ㄐㄩˋ ㄙㄢˋ ㄨˊ ㄔㄤˊ)
Meeting and departing are irregular.

聚訟(ㄐㄩˋ ㄙㄨㄥˋ)
to hold different views

聚訟紛紜(ㄐㄩˋ ㄙㄨㄥˋ ㄈㄣ ㄩㄣˊ)
Opinions are divided.

聚乙烯(ㄐㄩˋ ㄧˇ ㄒㄧ)
polyethylene

聚蚊成雷(ㄐㄩˋ ㄨㄣˊ ㄔㄥˊ ㄌㄟˊ)
(literally) A swarm of mosquitos may become a thunder.—United strength can be very great.

【聞】 4603
1. ㄨㄣˊ wen wén
1. to hear; to have heard
2. to learn; learning; to understand
3. to convey, forward or transmit (a message, etc.)
4. to smell
5. to make known
6. a Chinese family name

聞報(ㄨㄣˊ ㄅㄠˋ)
to learn of; to hear it reported

聞不得（ㄨㄣ·ㄅㄨ·ㄉㄜ）
too strong to be smelled

聞不見（ㄨㄣ·ㄅㄨ ㄐㄧㄢ）
cannot sense the smell

聞名（ㄨㄣ ㄇㄧㄥ）
①famous; distinguished: 此地以風景幽美聞名。The place is famous for its scenic beauty.②to hear of someone's name

聞名不如見面（ㄨㄣ ㄇㄧㄥ ㄅㄨˋㄖㄨˊ ㄐㄧㄢˋ ㄇㄧㄢˋ）
Knowing someone by his reputation is not as good as meeting him in person.

聞名天下（ㄨㄣ ㄇㄧㄥ ㄊㄧㄢ ㄒㄧㄚˋ）
world-famous; known far and wide

聞名四方（ㄨㄣ ㄇㄧㄥ ㄙˋ ㄈㄤ）
to become famous throughout the land

聞風逃避（ㄨㄣ ㄈㄥ ㄊㄠˊ ㄅㄧˋ）
to run away or escape upon learning the news

聞風響應（ㄨㄣ ㄈㄥ ㄒㄧㄤˇ ㄧㄥˋ）
to hear the news and rise up in response

聞風喪膽（ㄨㄣ ㄈㄥ ㄙㄤˋ ㄉㄢˇ）
to become terror-stricken at the news

聞而而起（ㄨㄣ ㄈㄥ ㄦˊ ㄑㄧˇ）
to rise up on hearing the news

聞過則喜（ㄨㄣ ㄍㄨㄛˋ ㄗㄜˊ ㄒㄧˇ）
to be pleased upon hearing one's own mistakes (the mark of a true gentleman)

聞鷄起舞（ㄨㄣ ㄐㄧ ㄑㄧˇ ㄨˇ）
(literally) to rise up upon hearing the crow of a rooster—diligent and full of enthusiasm; highly motivated (the reference is to 祖逖)

聞見（ㄨㄣ ㄐㄧㄢˋ）
to have learned (by hearing or seeing)

聞喜宴（ㄨㄣ ㄒㄧˇ ㄧㄢˋ）
banquets given in honor of successful candidates of the civil service examination in the Tang Dynasty and the Sung Dynasty

聞訊（ㄨㄣ ㄒㄩㄣˋ）
to learn of the news; to hear of the message

聞知（ㄨㄣ ㄓ）
to learn; to hear; to know

from others

聞所未聞（ㄨㄣ ㄙㄨㄛˇ ㄨㄟˋ ㄨㄣˊ）
unheard of

聞一知十（ㄨㄣ ㄧ ㄓ ㄕˊ）
(literally) to learn one thing and know ten—a very bright or clever person

聞間（ㄨㄣ ㄐㄧㄢ）
communications or correspondence between two persons

【聞】 4603
2. ㄨㄣˋ wenn wèn

聞達（ㄨㄣ ㄉㄚˊ）
illustrious; eminent; famous and influential

聞人（ㄨㄣ ㄖㄣˊ）
a prominent figure; a famous person

十一畫

【聯】 4604
ㄌㄧㄢˊ lian lián

1. to unite; to ally; to connect; to join; to make an alliance with
2. allied (forces, etc.); joint (effort, etc.); mutual (guaranties, etc.)
3. a couplet

聯播（ㄌㄧㄢˊ ㄅㄛ）
a radio hookup

聯保（ㄌㄧㄢˊ ㄅㄠˇ）
a mutual guarantee (of proper conduct, etc.)

聯邦（ㄌㄧㄢˊ ㄅㄤ）
a federal union; a federal state

聯邦調查局（ㄌㄧㄢˊ ㄅㄤㄉㄧㄠˋㄔㄚˊ ㄐㄩˊㄐㄩˊ）
Federal Bureau of Investigation (FBI) of the United States

聯邦制（ㄌㄧㄢˊ ㄅㄤ ㄓˋ）
the federation system

聯票（ㄌㄧㄢˊ ㄆㄧㄠˋ）
①an interline ticket; a through ticket②bills in set

聯翩（ㄌㄧㄢˊ ㄆㄧㄢ）
①continuously; successively②continuously and quickly; in quick succession

聯袂（ㄌㄧㄢˊ ㄇㄟˋ）
side by side; together; jointly

聯盟（ㄌㄧㄢˊ ㄇㄥˊ）

an alliance; a union; a league (as the League of Nations); to form an alliance, etc.

聯緜（ㄌㄧㄢˊ ㄇㄧㄢˊ）
continuous or incessant; successive(ly)

聯緜字（ㄌㄧㄢˊ ㄇㄧㄢˊ ㄗˋ）
a Chinese phrase consisting of two characters, often alliterated or rhymed (as 徘徊 or 徘徊)

聯名（ㄌㄧㄢˊ ㄇㄧㄥˊ）
to sign together; to put two or more signatures on a document

聯防（ㄌㄧㄢˊ ㄈㄤˊ）
joint defense; mutual defense

聯防協定（ㄌㄧㄢˊ ㄈㄤˊ ㄒㄧㄝˊ ㄉㄧㄥˋ）
a joint defense treaty

聯單（ㄌㄧㄢˊ ㄉㄢ）
a certificate, document, etc. in duplicate, triplicate, etc.

聯隊（ㄌㄧㄢˊ ㄉㄨㄟˋ）
(said of the air force) a wing

聯立方程式（ㄌㄧㄢˊㄌㄧˋㄈㄤ ㄔㄥˊ ㄕˋ）
(mathematics) a simultaneous equation

聯絡（ㄌㄧㄢˊ ㄌㄨㄛˋ）
to keep in contact; to communicate with; to contact

聯絡官（ㄌㄧㄢˊ ㄌㄨㄛˋ ㄍㄨㄢ）
a liaison officer

聯貫（ㄌㄧㄢˊ ㄍㄨㄢˋ）
connection; links; relevance; to link or string together

聯貫性（ㄌㄧㄢˊ ㄍㄨㄢˋ ㄒㄧㄥˋ）
continuity

聯合（ㄌㄧㄢˊ ㄏㄜˊ）
to unite; to form an alliance of some kind; joint (effort, etc.)

聯合內閣（ㄌㄧㄢˊ ㄏㄜˊ ㄋㄟˋ ㄍㄜˊ）
a coalition cabinet

聯合國（ㄌㄧㄢˊ ㄏㄜˊ ㄍㄨㄛˊ）
United Nations

聯合國大會（ㄌㄧㄢˊ ㄏㄜˊ ㄍㄨㄛˊ ㄉㄚˋ ㄏㄨㄟˋ or 聯大（ㄌㄧㄢˊ ㄉㄚˋ）
United Nations General Assembly

聯合國糧農組織（ㄌㄧㄢˊ ㄏㄜˊ ㄍㄨㄛˊ ㄌㄧㄤˊ ㄋㄨㄥˊ ㄗㄨˇ ㄓ）
United Nations Food and Agriculture Organization

聯合國憲章（ㄌㄧㄢˊ ㄏㄜˊ ㄍㄨㄛˊ ㄒㄧㄢˋ ㄓㄤ）

U.N. Charter

聯合國善後救濟總署 (ㄌㄧㄢˊ ㄏㄜˊ 《ㄨㄛˊ ㄕㄢˋ ㄏㄡˋ ㄐㄧˋ ㄐㄧˋ ㄗㄨㄥˇ ㄕㄨˋ)
United Nations Relief and Rehabilitation Administration (UNRRA)

聯合國日 (ㄌㄧㄢˊ ㄏㄜˊ 《ㄨㄛˊ ㄖˋ)
United Nations Day

聯合國安全理事會 (ㄌㄧㄢˊ ㄏㄜˊ 《ㄨㄛˊ ㄢ ㄑㄩㄢˊ ㄌㄧˇ ㄕˋ ㄏㄨㄟˋ)
U.N. Security Council

聯合國文教組織 (ㄌㄧㄢˊ ㄏㄜˊ 《ㄨㄛˊ ㄨㄣˊ ㄐㄧㄠˋ ㄗㄨˇ ㄓ)
United Nations Educational, Scientific, and Cultural Organization (UNESCO)

聯合公報 (ㄌㄧㄢˊ ㄏㄜˊ 《ㄨㄥ ㄅㄠˋ)
a joint communiqué

聯合戰線 (ㄌㄧㄢˊ ㄏㄜˊ ㄓㄢˋ ㄒㄧㄢˋ)
a united front

聯合政府 (ㄌㄧㄢˊ ㄏㄜˊ ㄓㄥˋ ㄈㄨˇ)
a coalition government

聯合聲明 (ㄌㄧㄢˊ ㄏㄜˊ ㄕㄥ ㄇㄧㄥˊ)
a joint statement or declaration: 他們發表聯合聲明。 They made a joint statement.

聯號 (ㄌㄧㄢˊ ㄏㄠˋ)
① (said of banknotes, tickets, etc.) with contiguous numbers ② an allied company

聯歡會 (ㄌㄧㄢˊ ㄏㄨㄢ ㄏㄨㄟˋ)
a get-together; a social gathering; a gay party: 我邀參加他們的聯歡會。 I was invited to their gay party.

聯接 (ㄌㄧㄢˊ ㄐㄧㄝ)
to connect; to join together; contiguous: 這兩個城市由鐵路聯接。The two towns are connected by a railway.

聯接代名詞 (ㄌㄧㄢˊ ㄐㄧㄝ ㄉㄞˋ ㄇㄧㄥˊ ㄘˊ)
a group of characters which are used after a verb to form a noun, such as "的"in 賣花的 or "者"in 捕蛇者

聯盟 (ㄌㄧㄢˊ ㄇㄥˊ)
to form an alliance; to join together or gang up

聯句 (ㄌㄧㄢˊ ㄐㄩˋ)
joint authorship of poems, with one participant chanting one line to be followed by the next until a poem is completed (a literary game among intellectuals of the past)

聯軍 (ㄌㄧㄢˊ ㄐㄩㄣ)
allied forces

聯席會議 (ㄌㄧㄢˊ ㄒㄧˊ ㄏㄨㄟˋ ㄧˋ)
a joint meeting or conference; a joint session: 他出席聯席會議。 He attended the joint conference.

聯絡 (ㄌㄧㄢˊ ㄌㄨㄛˋ)
① to unite; to join together (under a cause, etc.); to link; to relate ② to maintain communications, contact, or liaison; to get in touch with

聯想 (ㄌㄧㄢˊ ㄒㄧㄤˇ)
association of ideas; to associate

聯手 (ㄌㄧㄢˊ ㄕㄡˇ)
to join hands (with someone); to gang up

聯署 (ㄌㄧㄢˊ ㄕㄨˇ)
to sign jointly

聯屬 (ㄌㄧㄢˊ ㄕㄨˇ)
continuous; connected; un-interrupted

聯宗 (ㄌㄧㄢˊ ㄗㄨㄥ)
to join persons of different ancestors and make them bear the same family name

聯誼 (ㄌㄧㄢˊ ㄧˋ) or 聯誼活動 (ㄌㄧㄢˊ ㄧˋ ㄏㄨㄛˊ ㄉㄨㄥˋ)
activities for promoting fellowship

聯姻 (ㄌㄧㄢˊ ㄧㄣ)
connections through marriage; to unite by marriage: 他們兩家聯姻。The two families are united by marriage.

聯營 (ㄌㄧㄢˊ ㄧㄥˊ)
(said of two or more business setups) joint operation; a pool

聯運 (ㄌㄧㄢˊ ㄩㄣˋ)
joint transportation, or through transportation via several railroads

【聰】 4605
ㄘㄨㄥ tsong cong
1. clever; astute; bright; quick of apprehension
2. with a good faculty of hearing

聰敏 (ㄘㄨㄥ ㄇㄧㄣˇ)
clever and intelligent

聰明 (ㄘㄨㄥ ㄇㄧㄥˊ)
① clever; bright; intelligent; quick of comprehension: 聰

明反被聰明誤。Clever people may fall victim to their own cleverness. ② sharp hearing and seeing faculties

聰明絕頂 (ㄘㄨㄥ ㄇㄧㄥˊ ㄐㄩㄝˊ ㄉㄧㄥˇ)
extremely clever or intelligent: 他是個聰明絕頂的學生。 He is an extremely intelligent student.

聰明自誤 (ㄘㄨㄥ ㄇㄧㄥˊ ㄗˋ ㄨˋ)
(literally) ruined by one's own cleverness—too smart

聰明一世，糊塗一時 (ㄘㄨㄥ ㄇㄧㄥˊ ㄧ ㄕˋ ，ㄏㄨˊ ㄊㄨˊ ㄧˋ ㄕˊ)
A lifetime of cleverness can be interrupted by moments of stupidity.

聰了 (ㄘㄨㄥ ㄌㄧㄠˇ)
bright and quick of comprehension; astute; intelligent; clever

聰慧 (ㄘㄨㄥ ㄏㄨㄟˋ)
intelligent; astute; clever: 她是個聰慧的女孩。 She is a clever girl.

聰穎 (ㄘㄨㄥ ㄧㄥˇ)
clever and bright: 她的聰穎超過她的年齡。She is clever and bright beyond her years.

【聲】 4606
ㄕㄥ sheng sheng
1. sound; voice; a tone
2. music
3. language; a tongue
4. reputation; fame
5. to make known

聲波 (ㄕㄥ ㄅㄛ)
sound waves; acoustic waves

聲門 (ㄕㄥ ㄇㄣˊ)
the glottis

聲名 (ㄕㄥ ㄇㄧㄥˊ)
reputation; fame: 他是個聲名很好的人。He is a man of good (or high) fame.

聲名狼藉 (ㄕㄥ ㄇㄧㄥˊ ㄌㄤˊ ㄐㄧˊ)
a notorious reputation

聲明 (ㄕㄥ ㄇㄧㄥˊ)
to announce; to declare; to assert; to make a statement; to clarify publicly: 他聲明他的清白。He asserted his innocence.

聲母 (ㄕㄥ ㄇㄨˇ)
the 21 Chinese phonetic signs equivalent to the consonants in European languages

聲帶(ㄕㄥ ㄉㄞˋ)
the vocal cords

聲調(ㄕㄥ ㄉㄧㄠˋ)
①a tone (of a voice), as a severe tone ②a tone in Chinese phonetics ③a melody in a musical composition

聲調兒(ㄕㄥ ㄉㄧㄠˋㄦ)
① the tone of a human voice ② the sound of a musical instrument

聲東擊西(ㄕㄥ ㄉㄨㄥ ㄐㄧˊ ㄒㄧ)
(literally) to make noise in the east while striking in the west—feigning tactics

聲討(ㄕㄥ ㄊㄠˇ)
to condemn or attack (a rebel, traitor, etc.) by words

聲納(ㄕㄥ ㄋㄚˋ)
(physics) sonar

聲淚俱下(ㄕㄥ ㄌㄟˋ ㄐㄩˋ ㄒㄧㄚˋ)
to cry while speaking

聲浪(ㄕㄥ ㄌㄤˋ)
the sound wave

聲律(ㄕㄥ ㄌㄩˋ)
rules governing rhythm of words

聲光(ㄕㄥ ㄍㄨㄤ)
① fame and conditions (of a person, etc.) ② (said of movies) sound and lighting

聲價(ㄕㄥ ㄐㄧㄚˋ)
fame or popularity of a person

聲敎(ㄕㄥ ㄐㄧㄠˋ)
imperial cultural education for the people

聲氣(ㄕㄥ ㄑㄧˋ)
① information ② to rouse one's spirit; to spur on troop morale

聲氣相求(ㄕㄥ ㄑㄧˋ ㄒㄧ ㄑㄧㄡˊ)
(said of a group of people) to share the same interests and purpose

聲請(ㄕㄥ ㄑㄧㄥˇ)
to make requests with reasons stated

聲息(ㄕㄥ ㄒㄧˊ)
①sound; voices: 屋裏裏一點聲息都沒有。Not a sound was heard in the house. ②news; information

聲響(ㄕㄥ ㄒㄧㄤˇ)
①sound; noise; a tone ② reputation

聲學(ㄕㄥ ㄒㄩㄝˊ)
acoustics

聲張(ㄕㄥ ㄓㄤ)
to make known; to announce or publicize: 不要聲張這件事。Don't make this thing known to anyone.

聲叉(ㄕㄥ ㄔㄚ)
a tuning fork

聲稱(ㄕㄥ ㄔㄥ)
to assert; to declare

聲勢(ㄕㄥ ㄕˋ)
influence; fame; prestige and power

聲勢浩大(ㄕㄥ ㄕˋ ㄏㄠˋ ㄉㄚˋ)
an impressive display of power or influence

聲述(ㄕㄥ ㄕㄨˋ)
to tell; to state or present (reasons); to explain

聲如洪鐘(ㄕㄥ ㄖㄨˊ ㄏㄨㄥˊ ㄓㄨㄥ)
The voice sounds like a roaring bell.

聲嘶力竭(ㄕㄥ ㄙ ㄌㄧˋ ㄐㄧㄝˊ)
The voice is husky as a result of exhaustion.

聲色(ㄕㄥ ㄙㄜˋ)
① music and women ② the voice and the facial expression

聲色俱厲(ㄕㄥ ㄙㄜˋ ㄐㄩˋ ㄌㄧˋ)
to speak in a harsh tone and with a severe expression

聲色犬馬之樂(ㄕㄥ ㄙㄜˋ ㄑㄩㄢˇ ㄇㄚˇ ㄓ ㄌㄜˋ)
carnal pleasure; sensory pleasure

聲速(ㄕㄥ ㄙㄨˋ)
the velocity of sound

聲兒(ㄕㄥㄦ)
sound; voice; a tone

聲言(ㄕㄥ ㄧㄢˊ)
to announce; to profess; to claim; to declare

聲音(ㄕㄥ ㄧㄣ)
a sound; a voice: 我們聽到遠處有奇怪的聲音。We heard strange sounds in the distance.

聲威(ㄕㄥ ㄨㄟ)
fame and the influence that goes with it

聲聞於天(ㄕㄥ ㄨㄣˊ ㄩˊ ㄊㄧㄢ)
The voice is heard by Heaven.

聲聞(ㄕㄥ ㄨㄣˊ)

reputation

聲聞(ㄕㄥ ㄨㄣˋ)
① reputation ② information

聲望(ㄕㄥ ㄨㄤˋ)
fame; reputation; prestige: 他的聲望提高了。His prestige rose.

聲譽(ㄕㄥ ㄩˋ)
reputation; fame: 他是個聲譽很好的老師。He has a good reputation as a teacher.

聲譽卓著(ㄕㄥ ㄩˋ ㄓㄨㄛˊ ㄓㄨˋ)
① famous; widely known ② (said of a business firm) with a good reputation

聲樂(ㄕㄥ ㄩㄝˋ)
vocal music

聲樂家(ㄕㄥ ㄩㄝˋ ㄐㄧㄚ)
a vocalist

聲援(ㄕㄥ ㄩㄢˊ)
to give moral support: 他聲援我們。He gave us moral support.

聲韻(ㄕㄥ ㄩㄣˋ)
rhymes and tones of words 亦作「音韻」

聲韻學(ㄕㄥ ㄩㄣˋ ㄒㄩㄝˊ)
phonology 亦作「音韻學」

【聳】 4607
ㄙㄨㄥˇ soong sŏng
1. to alarm; to alert; to warn; to be sensational
2. to rise up; to stretch up erect or at full length
3. to be born deaf
4. to urge; to egg on

聳動(ㄙㄨㄥˇ ㄉㄨㄥˋ)
① to urge; to egg on ② to be moved or alarmed

聳動視聽(ㄙㄨㄥˇ ㄉㄨㄥˋ ㄕˋ ㄊㄧㄥ)
to create a sensation

聳聽(ㄙㄨㄥˇ ㄊㄧㄥ)
to alarm others with something sensational; to stimulate others

聳立(ㄙㄨㄥˇ ㄌㄧˋ)
to tower aloft; to rise up steeply

聳肩(ㄙㄨㄥˇ ㄐㄧㄢ)
to shrug shoulders

聳峙(ㄙㄨㄥˇ ㄓˋ)
(said of mountains) to rise up high above; to soar skyward; to stab deep into the sky

聳然(ㄙㄨㄥˇ ㄖㄢˊ)
rising in sharp elevation;

【耳部】

〔耳部〕

cliffy

聳人聽聞(ㄙㄨㄥ ㄖㄣ ㄊㄧㄥ ㄨㄣ)
(often said of news-reporting, etc.) sensational; to cause false alarm; alarmist talk

聳恿(ㄙㄨㄥ ㄩㄥˇ)
to urge; to egg on

【聱】 4608
ㄠˊ aur áo
1. hard to read or understand —too many big words and a tortuous style
2. perverse; unruly
3. lying and winding, as snakes, old trees, etc.

聱牙(ㄠˊ ㄧㄚˊ)
(said of writings) full of characters that are difficult to make out and pronounce

十二畫

【職】 4609
ㄓˊ jyr zhí
1. a profession or a vocation; a career
2. a post; a position
3. an office; official duties
4. to govern; to direct; to manage
5. used in place of "I" in documents to a superior
6. only; particularly

職別(ㄓˊ ㄅㄧㄝˊ)
official rank

職分(ㄓˊ ㄈㄣˋ)
official duties; duty

職蜂(ㄓˊ ㄈㄥ)
a worker bee 亦作「工蜂」

職等(ㄓˊ ㄉㄥˇ)
official rank; grade of position

職官(ㄓˊ ㄍㄨㄢ)
① one's official position and duties; profession ② presidents over the different departments of office

職工(ㄓˊ ㄍㄨㄥ)
① officers and workers (in a plant, company, etc.) ② workers with permanent jobs

職工保險基金(ㄓˊ ㄍㄨㄥ ㄅㄠˇ ㄒㄧㄢˇ ㄐㄧ ㄐㄧㄣ)
the employees' insurance funds

職工福利(ㄓˊ ㄍㄨㄥ ㄈㄨˊ ㄌㄧˋ)

employee benefits

職貢(ㄓˊ ㄍㄨㄥˋ)
tributes paid by a vassal state

職前教育(ㄓˊ ㄑㄧㄢˊ ㄐㄧㄠˋ ㄩˋ)
pre-vocational education

職權(ㄓˊ ㄑㄩㄢˊ)
authority for exercising or discharging one's duties

職權範圍(ㄓˊ ㄑㄩㄢˊ ㄈㄢˋ ㄨㄟˊ)
limits or scope of one's functions and powers

職銜(ㄓˊ ㄒㄧㄢˊ)
the official title of a person: 他的職銜是總經理。His official title is general manager.

職志(ㄓˊ ㄓˋ)
① a flag officer in ancient China ② aspiration; long cherished wish or hope ③ a mission; a lifework: 他以興辦教育爲職志。He takes establishment of education as his lifework.

職掌(ㄓˊ ㄓㄤˇ)
① to have charge of; to direct, manage or supervise, etc. as part of one's official duties ② (said of an organization or official post) functions and duties

職稱(ㄓˊ ㄔㄥ)
the name of a position one holds; the title of a technical or professional post (such as engineer, professor, lecturer, academician, etc.)

職是(ㄓˊ ㄕˋ)
It is for (this reason) that....

職守(ㄓˊ ㄕㄡˇ)
one's official duties, office, etc.: 他因擅離職守而被免職。He was dismissed from office because he left his duties without permission.

職任(ㄓˊ ㄖㄣˋ)
one's position or duties in an office

職責(ㄓˊ ㄗㄜˊ)
one's position and responsibility; charge: 逮捕罪犯是警方的職責。Arresting criminals is the charge of the police.

職責所在(ㄓˊ ㄗㄜˊ ㄙㄨㄛˇ ㄗㄞˋ)
duty-bound

職司(ㄓˊ ㄙ)
one's official duties, charge,

etc.

職業(ㄓˊ ㄧㄝˋ)
a profession; a vocation; an occupation

職業病(ㄓˊ ㄧㄝˋ ㄅㄧㄥˋ)
the occupational disease

職業婦女(ㄓˊ ㄧㄝˋ ㄈㄨˋ ㄋㄩˇ)
career women; working girls

職業介紹所(ㄓˊ ㄧㄝˋ ㄐㄧㄝˋ ㄕㄠˋ ㄙㄨㄛˇ)
an employment agency

職業教育(ㄓˊ ㄧㄝˋ ㄐㄧㄠˋ ㄩˋ)
vocational education

職業學校(ㄓˊ ㄧㄝˋ ㄒㄩㄝˊ ㄒㄧㄠˋ)
a vocational school

職業學生(ㄓˊ ㄧㄝˋ ㄒㄩㄝˊ ㄕㄥ)
① political underlings who pose as students in a college for stirring up troubles ② athletes admitted to a school with fat scholarships in return for their services in school teams

職業訓練(ㄓˊ ㄧㄝˋ ㄒㄩㄣˋ ㄌㄧㄢˋ)
vocational training

職業專科學校(ㄓˊ ㄧㄝˋ ㄓㄨㄢ ㄎㄜ ㄒㄩㄝˊ ㄒㄧㄠˋ)
a vocational junior college

職業外交官(ㄓˊ ㄧㄝˋ ㄨㄞˋ ㄐㄧㄠ ㄍㄨㄢ)
a career diplomat

職務(ㄓˊ ㄨˋ)
one's official duties or obligations

職位(ㄓˊ ㄨㄟˋ)
one's office; one's position in an office: 他在政府中擔任高職位。He has a high office in the government.

職員(ㄓˊ ㄩㄢˊ)
staff members or employees of a company, office, etc.: 他是這家公司的正式職員。He is a regular employee of the company.

職員錄(ㄓˊ ㄩㄢˊ ㄌㄨˋ)
a roster of staff members

職員宿舍(ㄓˊ ㄩㄢˊ ㄙㄨˋ ㄕㄜˋ)
company officers' dormitory; apartments or housing units built for employees

【聵】 4610
ㄎㄨㄟˋ kuey kuì
1. deaf; hard of hearing
2. stupid and unreasonable

【聶】 4611
ㄋㄧㄝˋ nieh niè
1. to whisper into another's ear

2. a Chinese family name

十六畫

【聽】 4612

1. 去l∠ ting ting
1. to hear; to listen
2. to obey; to follow
3. to wait for
4. a hall

聽不明白(去l∠ ㄅㄨ ㄇl∠ ㄅㄞ)
cannot understand (what the other is talking about); can not hear well or comprehend

聽不得(去l∠ ㄅㄨ˙ㄉㄜ)
should not be heard; should not listen to

聽不見(去l∠ ㄅㄨ ㄐl马)
cannot hear (because voice, or sound is too low or far away)

聽不清(去l∠ ㄅㄨ ㄑl∠)
unable to hear distinctly or clearly

聽命(去l∠ ㄇl∠)
to follow orders

聽得入神(去l∠ ㄉㄜ ㄖㄨ ㄕㄣˊ)
completely absorbed (in music, lectures, etc.)

聽頭(去l∠ ˙ㄊㄡ)
worth listening to: 這音樂很有聽頭。The music is worth listening to.

聽筒(去l∠ ㄊㄨㄥˇ)
a telephone receiver

聽膩(去l∠ ㄋlˋ˙ㄌㄜ)
bored with listening to (music or words repeated too often)

聽力(去l∠ ㄌlˋ)
① the sense of hearing ② aural comprehension (in language teaching)

聽力試驗(去l∠ ㄌlˋ ㄕˋ lㄢˋ)
audiometry; an audiometric test

聽骨(去l∠ ㄍㄨˇ)
ossicula auditus

聽管(去l∠ ㄍㄨㄢˇ)
the auditory canal

聽慣(去l∠ ㄍㄨㄢˋ)
to get used to hearing (such foul language, etc.)

聽課(去l∠ ㄎㄜˋ)
to attend class teaching or lectures

聽候(去l∠ ㄏㄡˋ)
to wait for (instructions, orders, etc.): 他聽候你的命令。He is waiting for your orders.

聽話(去l∠ ㄏㄨㄚˋ)
① to obey; obedient ② to wait for word or a reply

聽見(去l∠ ㄐlㄢˋ)
to hear

聽講(去l∠ ㄐlㄤˇ)
to listen to a lecture, speech, etc.

聽覺(去l∠ ㄐㄩㄝˊ)
hearing; the sense of hearing

聽起來(去l∠ ㄑlˇ ㄌㄞˊ)
to sound; to ring

聽取(去l∠ ㄑㄩˇ)
to listen (with due attention); to hear (a report)

聽勸告(去l∠ ㄑㄩㄢˋ ㄍㄠˋ)
to accept or listen to another's advice

聽戲(去l∠ ㄒlˋ)
to see an operatic show (especially referring to an experienced theatergoer who is more interested in the singing than in the spectacles on the stage)

聽寫(去l∠ ㄒlㄝˇ)
dictation; to dictate: 老師考學生聽寫。The teacher gave the pupils dictation.

聽信(去l∠ ㄒlㄣˋ)
① to listen to and believe (what others said): 不要聽信謠言, Don't believe rumors. ② to wait for news, messages, information, etc.

聽著(去l∠ ˙ㄓㄜ)
to listen 或 Listen!

聽診器(去l∠ ㄓㄣˇ ㄑlˋ)
a stethoscope

聽眾(去l∠ ㄓㄨㄥˋ)
an audience; listeners: 聽眾感動淚下。The audience were moved to tears.

聽差(去l∠ ㄔㄞ)
a factotum; a servant; an errand man: 他是個好聽差。He is a good servant.

聽事(去l∠ ㄕˋ)
a hall

聽事(去l∠ ㄕˋ˙ㄉㄜ)
a servant

聽神經(去l∠ ㄕㄣˊ ㄐl∠)
the auditory nerve

聽審(去l∠ ㄕㄣˇ)
to stand trial; to be tried

聽說(去l∠ ㄕㄨㄛ)
① It is reported that.... 或 It is said that.... 或 according to unconfirmed reports; to hear of ② to obey; obedient

聽錯(去l∠ ㄘㄨㄛˋ)
to hear incorrectly; to misunderstand what someone has said

聽從(去l∠ ㄘㄨㄥˊ)
to listen to (another's advice, etc.); to listen and follow

聽而不聞(去l∠ ㄦˊ ㄅㄨˋ ㄨㄣˊ)
to turn a deaf ear to; to hear without understanding

聽膩了(去l∠ ㄋlˋ˙ㄌㄜ)
to be tired of hearing something repeated too often

聽聞(去l∠ ㄨㄣˊ)
what one has heard

【聽】 4612
2. 去l∠ ting ting
1. to let
2. to comply with; to submit to
3. to manage; to govern; to rule
4. to judge and decide

聽便(去l∠ ㄅlㄢˋ)
to suit one's convenience; to leave it to one's own discretion; to have no fixed opinion and act according to the circumstances

聽憑(去l∠ ㄆl∠) or 聽任(去l∠ ㄖㄣˋ)
to let someone do whatever he likes; to do nothing to stop or reverse a situation; to sit tight and let it happen

聽命(去l∠ ㄇl∠)
to submit oneself to the will of Heaven; to be resigned to one's fate

聽斷(去l∠ ㄉㄨㄢˋ)
to pass judgment or verdict after hearing the case

聽天由命(去l∠ ㄊlㄢ lㄡˊ ㄇl∠)
to submit to the will of Heaven and one's fate; resign oneself to fate

聽其自然(去l∠ ㄑlˊ ㄗˋ ㄖㄢˊ)
to let things take their course

聽政(去l∠ ㄓㄥˋ)

（耳部）

【隸】部

to administer; to govern; to rule

聽使(ㄊㄧㄥˇㄕˇ)
①convenient; suitable for use ②to await instructions or orders and be ready for errands

聽訟(ㄊㄧㄥ ㄙㄨㄥˋ)
to serve as a judge in a lawsuit

【聾】 4613 ㄌㄨㄥˊ long lóng
1. deaf; hard of hearing
2. deaf—stupid and ignorant

聾聵(ㄌㄨㄥˊ ㄎㄨㄟˋ)
①deaf ②ignorant and stupid

聾子(ㄌㄨㄥˊ ㄗˇ)
a deaf person

聾啞(ㄌㄨㄥˊ ㄧㄚˇ)
deaf-and-dumb; a deaf-mute

聾啞學校(ㄌㄨㄥˊ ㄧㄚˇ ㄒㄩㄝˊ ㄒㄧㄠˋ)
a school for deaf-mutes; a deaf-and-dumb school

聿 部
ㄩ yuh yù

【聿】 4614 ㄩˋ yuh yù
1. a writing instrument—a pen, a writing brush, etc.
2. a particle, used in introducing a phrase or sentence
3. agile and quick; nimble

七畫

【肄】 4615 ㄧˋ yih yì
1. to study; to learn; to practice
2. to toil; to work hard
3. remnants; leftovers
4. fresh twigs

肄習(ㄧˋ ㄒㄧˊ)
to practice

肄業(ㄧˋ ㄧㄝˋ)
to learn; to study (at a certain school)

【肆】 4616 ㄙˋ syh sì
1. to let loose; to indulge in; to behave without restraint
2. a marketplace; a shop; a

place to display goods: 茶肆 a teahouse 酒肆 a wineshop
3. to exhibit; to display
4. to execute a criminal and expose his corpse in the market
5. to extend; to expand
6. to assault; to attack suddenly
7. to use to the utmost; to exhaust
8. an elaborate form of 四 (four) to prevent forgery

肆目(ㄙˋ ㄇㄨˋ)
to stretch one's eyes as far as one can see

肆虐(ㄙˋ ㄋㄩㄝˋ)
①to indulge in atrocities; to do damage unhinderedly ②reckless and oppressive; rampant: 霍亂肆虐此城。Cholera was rampant in this town.

肆力(ㄙˋ ㄌㄧˋ)
to do one's best or utmost: 我必須肆力幫他的忙。I must do my best to help him.

肆掠(ㄙˋ ㄌㄩㄝˋ)
to indulge in looting, robbery, without restraint; rapine

肆口大罵(ㄙˋ ㄎㄡˇ ㄉㄚˋ ㄇㄚˋ)
to abuse someone outrageously and without any restraint

肆劫(ㄙˋ ㄐㄧㄝˊ)or 肆劫無忌(ㄙˋ ㄐㄧㄝˊ ㄨˊ ㄐㄧˋ)
to loot, or rob freely and without any restraint; rapine

肆行(ㄙˋ ㄒㄧㄥˊ)
to act at the dictate of one's own will without any thought for others; to indulge

肆肆(ㄙˋ ㄕˋ)
shops; stores

肆縱(ㄙˋ ㄗㄨㄥˋ)
indulgent and without restraint

肆意(ㄙˋ ㄧˋ)
at will; without any restraint; indulgently; recklessly

肆飲(ㄙˋ ㄧㄣˇ)
to indulge in drinking

肆應(ㄙˋ ㄧㄥˋ)
to be good at dealing with varied matters properly

肆無忌憚(ㄙˋ ㄨˊ ㄐㄧˋ ㄉㄢˋ)
indulgent and reckless; without restraint of any kind; unscrupulous

【肅】 4617 ㄙㄨˋ suh sù
1. respectful; reverential; to pay respects; to salute
2. solemn; serious; majestic; awe-inspiring
3. to usher in
4. neat and quiet
5. to withdraw; to shrink (as in cold weather, etc.)
6. a Chinese family name

肅穆(ㄙㄨˋ ㄇㄨˋ)
①solemn: 他們注視著肅穆的典禮。They watched the solemn ceremony. ②peaceful

肅立(ㄙㄨˋ ㄌㄧˋ)
to stand upright as a mark of respect

肅客(ㄙㄨˋ ㄎㄜˋ)
to receive a guest

肅函(ㄙㄨˋ ㄏㄢˊ)
to write to you in great reverence

肅敬(ㄙㄨˋ ㄐㄧㄥˋ)
respectful

肅靜(ㄙㄨˋ ㄐㄧㄥˋ)
①a solemn silence: 禮堂內肅靜無聲。A solemn silence reigned in the auditorium. ②peaceful

肅靜無譁(ㄙㄨˋ ㄐㄧㄥˋ ㄨˊ ㄏㄨㄚˊ)
strict silence

肅清(ㄙㄨˋ ㄑㄧㄥ)
①to wipe out or eliminate (rebels, enemy troops, etc.): 他們肅清叛徒。They wiped out the rebels. ②cold and solemn—as a winter night

肅殺(ㄙㄨˋ ㄕㄚ)
①an awe-inspiring, stern, forbidding look ②a lonesome scene of late autumn

肅然(ㄙㄨˋ ㄖㄢˊ)
respectful; reverently

肅然起敬(ㄙㄨˋ ㄖㄢˊ ㄑㄧˇ ㄐㄧㄥˋ)
great respect rising in one's heart

肅坐(ㄙㄨˋ ㄗㄨㄛˋ)
to sit erect and in silence

八畫

【肇】 4618 ㄓㄠˋ jaw zhào

1. to begin; to start; to commence
2. to found; to devise
3. to incur (misfortune, etc.)
4. to adjust; to make right

肇端 (ㄓㄨ ㄎㄢ)
the beginning; the start; to originate or initiate

肇亂 (ㄓㄨ ㄌㄨㄢ)
to create upheaval or trouble; to start the whole confusion, uprising, etc.

肇國 (ㄓㄨ ㄍㄨㄜ)
to found a nation or state

肇禍 (ㄓㄨ ㄏㄨㄛ)
to incur or court misfortune; to start or stir up trouble: 他肇禍了。 He incurred misfortune.

肇基 (ㄓㄨ ㄐㄧ)
to lay the foundation; to do the spadework; to pave the way

肇建 (ㄓㄨ ㄐㄧㄢ)
to found

肇釁 (ㄓㄨ ㄒㄧㄣ)
to stir up an incident or trouble

肇始 (ㄓㄨ ㄕ)
to begin

肇事 (ㄓㄨ ㄕ)
to stir up trouble or disturbances

肇造 (ㄓㄨ ㄗㄠ)
to found; to first establish

肉 部
ㄖㄨ ruh rù

【肉】   4619
ㄖㄨ row ròu
〔讀音 ㄖㄨ ruh rù〕

1. flesh
2. physical; carnal
3. meat of animals; meat or pulp of fruits, etc.
4. flesh and blood — dearest, as one's children
5. slow-motion

肉搏 (ㄖㄨ ㄅㄛ) or 肉搏戰 (ㄖㄨ ㄅㄛ ㄓㄢ)
hand-to-hand combat

肉包子 (ㄖㄨ ㄅㄠ·ㄗ) or 肉包兒 (ㄖㄨ ㄅㄠ ㄦ)
meat dumplings; steamed dumplings stuffed with meat

肉餅 (ㄖㄨ ㄅㄧㄥ)
meat cake: 這是自製的肉餅。 This is a homemade meat cake.

肉片兒 (ㄖㄨ ㄆㄧㄢ ㄦ)
slices of meat; sliced meat

肉票 (ㄖㄨ ㄆㄧㄠ)
a hostage kidnapped for a ransom

肉鋪 (ㄖㄨ ㄆㄨ)
a butcher's shop

肉麻 (ㄖㄨ ㄇㄚ)
a creepy feeling; disgusting; revolting; something that gives one goose pimples

肉饅頭 (ㄖㄨ ㄇㄢ·ㄊㄡ)
steamed dumplings with meat stuffing

肉脯 (ㄖㄨ ㄈㄨ)
dried meat in threads or sliced form

肉彈 (ㄖㄨ ㄉㄢ)
a buxom beauty; a woman with an hourglass figure; a siren

肉店 (ㄖㄨ ㄉㄧㄢ)
a butcher's shop

肉釘兒 (ㄖㄨ ㄉㄧㄥ ㄦ) or 肉丁 (ㄖㄨ ㄉㄧㄥ)
diced meat

肉胎 (ㄖㄨ ㄊㄞ)
to make a statue (for worshiping, etc.) by applying layers of lacquer to the body of the deceased

肉袒 (ㄖㄨ ㄊㄢ) or 肉袒負荆 (ㄖㄨ ㄊㄢ ㄈㄨ ㄐㄧㄥ) or 肉袒謝罪 (ㄖㄨ ㄊㄢ ㄒㄧㄝ ㄗㄨㄟ)
(according to an old Chinese story) to strip off the upper garment as a token of sincere apology—ready to submit to any punishment the other party may give

肉體 (ㄖㄨ ㄊㄧ)
flesh and blood; the human body; physical; carnal; sensory

肉跳 (ㄖㄨ ㄊㄧㄠ)
frightening; awesome; apprehensive

肉泥爛醬 (ㄖㄨ ㄋㄧ ㄌㄢ ㄐㄧㄤ)
the chilling sight of dismembered bodies and mashed flesh

肉類 (ㄖㄨ ㄌㄟ)
meats

肉瘤 (ㄖㄨ ㄌㄧㄡ)
a fleshy tumor

肉林 (ㄖㄨ ㄌㄧㄣ)
vast quantities of meat (stored in palaces)

肉感 (ㄖㄨ ㄍㄢ)
voluptuous; buxom; sexy

肉桂 (ㄖㄨ ㄍㄨㄟ)
cinnamon

肉冠 (ㄖㄨ ㄍㄨㄢ)
the comb (of a bird)

肉塊 (ㄖㄨ ㄎㄨㄞ)
chopped meat; meat chops

肉醬 (ㄖㄨ ㄐㄧㄤ)
meat pulp; mashed meat cooked with soybean sauce

肉餡 (ㄖㄨ ㄒㄧㄢ)
meat stuffing; chopped or ground meat

肉星兒 (ㄖㄨ ㄒㄧㄥ ㄦ)
tiniest bits of meat (along with a good deal of vegetables)—a poor man's diet

肉刑 (ㄖㄨ ㄒㄧㄥ)
corporeal punishment, including mutilation, etc.

肉芝 (ㄖㄨ ㄓ)
thousand-year-old toads, bats, or swallows which are supposed to make the eater immortal

肉汁 (ㄖㄨ ㄓ)
meat juice; meat broth; meat extract

肉食 (ㄖㄨ ㄕ)
to eat meat; meat-eating; carnivorous

肉食動物 (ㄖㄨ ㄕ ㄉㄨㄥ ㄨ)
carnivorous animals

肉食者鄙 (ㄖㄨ ㄕ ㄓㄜ ㄅㄧ)
(literally) The meat-eaters are vulgar.—High-ranking government officials are mostly stupid and inefficient.

肉食獸 (ㄖㄨ ㄕ ㄕㄡ) or 肉食動物 (ㄖㄨ ㄕ ㄉㄨㄥ ㄨ)
meat-eating animals; carnivorous animals

肉身 (ㄖㄨ ㄕㄣ)
the physical body; the flesh

肉絲麵 (ㄖㄨ ㄙ ㄇㄧㄢ)
noodles with shredded meat

（肉部）

肉絲兒（ㄖㄡˋㄙㄦ）
shredded meat

肉色（ㄖㄡˋㄙㄜˋ）
yellowish pink; flesh-colored

肉鬆（ㄖㄡˋㄙㄨㄥ）
fried shredded meat; meat fluff

肉眼（ㄖㄡˋㄧㄢˇ）
① a layman's eyes; vulgar eyes ② the naked eye

肉眼凡胎（ㄖㄡˋㄧㄢˇㄈㄢˊㄊㄞ）
① a layman—without an immortal bone in him ② vulgar and stupid

肉眼無珠（ㄖㄡˋㄧㄢˇㄨˊㄓㄨ）
(literally) eyes without pupils—stupid; shallow

肉丸子（ㄖㄡˋㄨㄢˊ˙ㄗ）
meatballs

肉慾（ㄖㄡˋㄩˋ）
carnal desire; sexual desire

一畫

【肐】 ⁴⁶²⁰ ㄧˋ yih yì
1. breastbone
2. same as 臆 — one's mind, heart, disposition, feelings, or views

二畫

【肋】 ⁴⁶²¹ ㄌㄟˋ ley lèi
(讀音 ㄌㄜˋ leh lè)
the ribs; the sides

肋膜（ㄌㄟˋㄇㄛˊ）
the pleura

肋膜炎（ㄌㄟˋㄇㄛˊㄧㄢˊ）
pleurisy

肋條（ㄌㄟˋㄊㄧㄠˊ）
the ribs

肋骨（ㄌㄟˋㄍㄨˇ）
the ribs; 他跌了一跤摔斷了三根肋骨。He fell and broke three ribs.

【肌】 ⁴⁶²² ㄐㄧ ji jī
1. tissue; muscles; flesh
2. the skin

肌膚（ㄐㄧㄈㄨ）
① the skin and flesh ② the intimate relation between man and woman

肌膚之親（ㄐㄧㄈㄨㄓㄑㄧㄣ）
intimacy arising from sexual

intercourse

肌體（ㄐㄧˉㄊㄧˇ）
the body

肌理（ㄐㄧㄌㄧˇ）
the texture of the skin (as coarse, tender, or delicate)

肌骨（ㄐㄧㄍㄨˇ）
muscles and bones

肌肉（ㄐㄧㄖㄡˋ）
muscles

三畫

【肖】 ⁴⁶²³ ㄒㄧㄠˋ shiaw xiào
to resemble; to be like; alike; similar: 她酷肖其母。She strongly resembles her mother.

肖像（ㄒㄧㄠˋㄒㄧㄤˋ）
a portrait; a likeness, either painted or carved, of a person: 這幅肖像看起來很真實。This portrait looks real.

肖子（ㄒㄧㄠˋ˙ㄗ）
a good (filial) son

肖似（ㄒㄧㄠˋㄙˋ）
to look very much alike; to be like(another)

【肘】 ⁴⁶²⁴ ㄓㄡˇ joou zhǒu
1. the elbow
2. to catch one by the elbow

肘關節（ㄓㄡˇㄍㄨㄢㄐㄧㄝˊ）
the elbow joint

肘子（ㄓㄡˇ˙ㄗ）or 肘兒（ㄓㄡˇㄦ）
① the upper part of a leg of pork ② the elbow

肘腋（ㄓㄡˇㄧㄝˋ）
close by; near at hand

【肓】 ⁴⁶²⁵ ㄏㄨㄤ huang huāng
the vitals; the region between the heart and the diaphragm

【肚】 ⁴⁶²⁶ ㄉㄨˋ duh dù
1. the belly; the abdomen; the bowels

肚皮（ㄉㄨˋㄆㄧˊ）
the abdomen; the belly

肚皮舞（ㄉㄨˋㄆㄧˊㄨˇ）
a belly dance

肚裏明白（ㄉㄨˋㄌㄧˇㄇㄧㄥˊㄅㄞˊ）
to know in one's heart; clear to oneself; a tacit understanding

肚量（ㄉㄨˋㄌㄧㄤˋ）
capacity for tolerance and forgiveness

肚臍眼（ㄉㄨˋㄑㄧˊㄧㄢˇ）or 肚臍（ㄉㄨˋㄑㄧˊ）
the navel; the belly button

肚腸（ㄉㄨˋㄔㄤˊ）
the bowels

肚子（ㄉㄨˋ˙ㄗ）
the belly; the abdomen: 我們肚子餓了。Our bellies are empty.

肚子疼（ㄉㄨˋ˙ㄗㄊㄥˊ）
bellyache; celialgia; to suffer from abdominal pain: 他鬧肚子疼。He suffers from abdominal pain.

【肚】 ⁴⁶²⁶ ㄉㄨˇ duu dǔ
the stomach: 我肚子痛。I have a pain in my stomach.

肚子（ㄉㄨˇ˙ㄗ）or 肚兒（ㄉㄨˇㄦ）
tripe

【肛】 ⁴⁶²⁷ ㄍㄤ gang gāng
the anus

肛門（ㄍㄤㄇㄣˊ）
the anus

【肝】 ⁴⁶²⁸ ㄍㄢ gan gān
the liver: 他患有肝病。He has liver trouble.

肝病（ㄍㄢㄅㄧㄥˋ）or 肝疾（ㄍㄢㄐㄧˊ）
a liver ailment

肝膽（ㄍㄢㄉㄢˇ）
① intimate; intimacy ② sincere; sincerity ③ courage; courageous

肝膽俱裂（ㄍㄢㄉㄢˇㄐㄩˋㄌㄧㄝˋ）
extremely frightened; terror-stricken

肝膽相照（ㄍㄢㄉㄢˇㄒㄧㄤㄓㄠˋ）or 肝膽照人（ㄍㄢㄉㄢˇㄓㄠˋㄖㄣˊ）
to show the deepest sincerity

肝膽之交（ㄍㄢㄉㄢˇㄓㄐㄧㄠ）
sincere friendship

肝動脈（ㄍㄢㄉㄨㄥˋㄇㄞˋ）
a hepatic artery

肝糖（ㄍㄢㄊㄤˊ）
glycogen; hepatin

肝腦塗地（ㄍㄢㄋㄠˇㄊㄨˊㄉㄧˋ）
to try one's very best to serve someone, even at the expense of one's own life

肝膈（ㄍㄢㄍㄜˊ）

intimate; sincere

肝火旺（ㄍㄢ ㄏㄨㄛˇ ㄨㄤˋ）
irritable and unpredictable;
irascible

肝靜脈（ㄍㄢ ㄐㄧㄥˋ ㄇㄞˋ）
a hepatic vein

肝氣（ㄍㄢ ㄑㄧˋ）
①（Chinese medicine) a
depressed feeling or pain in
the general area of the chest
②irritable and unpredict-
able dispositions

肝蛭（ㄍㄢ ㄓˋ）
Fasciola hepatica, a kind of
parasites found in the livers
of human beings and some
animals

肝腸寸斷（ㄍㄢ ㄔㄤˊ ㄘㄨㄣˋ ㄉㄨㄢˋ）
greatly afflicted; heart-
broken; deep sorrow

肝臟（ㄍㄢ ㄗㄤˋ）
the liver

肝臟脫出（ㄍㄢ ㄗㄤˋ ㄊㄨㄛ ㄔㄨ）
hepatocele

肝臟硬化（ㄍㄢ ㄗㄤˋ ㄧㄥˋ ㄏㄨㄚˋ）or 肝
硬化（ㄍㄢ ㄧㄥˋ ㄏㄨㄚˋ）
cirrhosis of liver

肝炎（ㄍㄢ ㄧㄢˊ）
hepatitis

肝癌（ㄍㄢ ㄞˊ）
cancer of the liver

【肱】 4629
（胳）《ㄍ ㄜ ge gē
the arm—from the armpit to
the wrist

肱膊（ㄍㄜ ㄅㄛˊ）
the arm

肱膊肘子（ㄍㄜ ㄅㄛˊ ㄓㄡˇ ㄗ）or 肱膊
肘兒（ㄍㄜ ㄅㄛˊ ㄓㄡˇㄦ）
the elbow

肱膊腕兒（ㄍㄜ ㄅㄛˊ ㄨㄢˋ ㄦ）or 肱膊
腕子（ㄍㄜ ㄅㄛˊ ㄨㄢˋ ㄗ）
the wrist

肱臂（ㄍㄜ ㄅㄟˋ）
the arm

肱窩（ㄍㄜ ㄨ ㄨㄛ）
the armpit

【肜】 4630
ㄖㄨㄥˊ rong róng
an ancient sacrificial ritual
lasting two successive days

四畫

【股】 4631
《ㄨ guu gǔ

1. the thigh; the haunches; the
hips
2. a department; a section
3. shares; stock
4. a puff; a blast (of hot air)
5. a bunch or band (of bandits)

股本（ㄍㄨ ㄅㄣˇ）
subscribed capital (of a business firm)

股票（ㄍㄨ ㄆㄧㄠˋ）
a share or stock certificate;
stocks: 股票上漲。Stock is
going up.

股票交易（ㄍㄨ ㄆㄧㄠˋ ㄐㄧㄠ ㄧˋ）
stock deals

股票交易所（ㄍㄨ ㄆㄧㄠˋ ㄐㄧㄠ ㄧˋ ㄙㄨㄛˇ）
a stock exchange

股票掮客（ㄍㄨ ㄆㄧㄠˋ ㄑㄧㄢˊ ㄎㄜˋ）
a stockbroker

股票市場（ㄍㄨ ㄆㄧㄠˋ ㄕˋ ㄔㄤˇ）
the stock market: 股票市場蕭
條。The stock market is dull.

股份 or 股分（ㄍㄨ ㄈㄣˋ）
shares or stock (in a business concern): 他擁有這公司
的一千股份。He owns one
thousand shares of the company.

股份有限公司（ㄍㄨ ㄈㄣˋ ㄧㄡˇ ㄒㄧㄢˋ
ㄍㄨㄥ ㄙ）
a limited liability company

股東（ㄍㄨ ㄉㄨㄥ）
a shareholder or stockholder

股東大會（ㄍㄨ ㄉㄨㄥ ㄉㄚˋ ㄏㄨㄟˋ）
a shareholders' meeting; a
stockholders' conference

股東權益（ㄍㄨ ㄉㄨㄥ ㄑㄩㄢˊ ㄧˋ）
stockholders' equity

股利（ㄍㄨ ㄌㄧˋ）
interest on shares 參看「股息」

股慄（ㄍㄨ ㄌㄧˋ）
trembling with fear

股關節（ㄍㄨ ㄍㄨㄢ ㄐㄧㄝˊ）
the hip joint

股肱（ㄍㄨ ㄍㄨㄥ）
top aides; a right-hand man

股肱之臣（ㄍㄨ ㄍㄨㄥ ㄓ ㄔㄣˊ）
top ministers

股金（ㄍㄨ ㄐㄧㄣ）
capitalization (of a company,
or corporation); share capital

股權（ㄍㄨ ㄑㄩㄢˊ）
the ownership of a share or
stock

股券（ㄍㄨ ㄑㄩㄢˋ）
a share or stock certificate

股息（ㄍㄨ ㄒㄧˊ）
dividends: 該公司去年付出一
成股息。The company paid a
10% dividend last year.

股戰（ㄍㄨ ㄓㄢˋ）
trembling with fear

股長（ㄍㄨ ㄓㄤˇ）
a section chief; the head of
a subdivision

股市（ㄍㄨ ㄕˋ）
the stock market

股子（ㄍㄨ ㄗˇ）or 股兒（ㄍㄨ ㄦ）
①a share ②a strand or
bundle (of hair, thread, etc.)

股員（ㄍㄨ ㄩㄢˊ）
a junior office clerk

【肢】 4632
ㄓ jy zhī

1. the four limbs of a person
2. the legs of an animal
3. the wings or feet of a bird

肢體（ㄓ ㄊㄧˇ）
the body

肢骨（ㄓ ㄍㄨˇ）
the bones of one's limbs

肢解（ㄓ ㄐㄧㄝˇ）
to dismember; dismember-
ment

【肥】 4633
ㄈㄟˊ feir féi

1. fat; plump; portly; obese;
corpulent: 你太肥了。You are
too fat.
2. fat (of meat)
3. sufficiency; affluence; plenty
4. fertile
5. to fertilize (land)
6. fertilizers
7. baggy

肥胖（ㄈㄟˊ ㄆㄤˋ）
fat; obese: 你變得太肥胖了。
You are getting too fat.

肥胖症（ㄈㄟˊ ㄆㄤˋ ㄓㄥˋ）
obesity

肥美（ㄈㄟˊ ㄇㄟˇ）
plump and pretty

肥大（ㄈㄟˊ ㄉㄚˋ）
fat and big; large and wide

肥地（ㄈㄟˊ ㄉㄧˋ）
①to fertilize the land ②a
fat land

肥頭胖耳（ㄈㄟˊ ㄊㄡˊ ㄆㄤˋ ㄦˇ）or 肥頭
大耳（ㄈㄟˊ ㄊㄡˊ ㄉㄚˋ ㄦˇ）
(said of a person) fat; portly

〔肉部〕

〔肉部〕

肥田(ㄈㄟˊ ㄊㄧㄢˊ)
①a piece of fertile land ②
to fertilize the land: 人造肥
料可以肥田。Artificial ma-
nures can fertilize the land.

肥田粉(ㄈㄟˊ ㄊㄧㄢˊ ㄈㄣˇ)
chemical fertilizers

肥嫩(ㄈㄟˊ ㄋㄣˋ)
meaty and tender; fleshy
and delicate

肥膩(ㄈㄟˊ ㄋㄧˋ)
fatty; greasy

肥料(ㄈㄟˊ ㄌㄧㄠˋ)
fertilizers; manure: 糞被用做
肥料。Dung is used as
manure.

肥料廠(ㄈㄟˊ ㄌㄧㄠˋ ㄔㄤˇ)
a fertilizer plant

肥甘(ㄈㄟˊ ㄍㄢ)
tasty; palatable

肥厚(ㄈㄟˊ ㄏㄡˋ)
plump; fleshy: 這果肉肥厚美
味。The pulp is fleshy and
tasty.

肥己(ㄈㄟˊ ㄐㄧˇ)
to enrich oneself

肥瘠(ㄈㄟˊ ㄐㄧˊ)
the fat and the thin; the rich
and the poor; the fertile and
the barren (fields)

肥缺(ㄈㄟˊ ㄑㄩㄝ)or 肥差(ㄈㄟˊ ㄔㄞ)
a lucrative post; a job which
offers many sources of income on the side; a fat job:
這肥缺待遇優厚。The fat job
pays well.

肥鮮(ㄈㄟˊ ㄒㄧㄢ)
rich and fresh foods (usually referring to meat)

肥壯(ㄈㄟˊ ㄓㄨㄤˋ)
husky

肥碩(ㄈㄟˊ ㄕㄨㄛˋ)
big and corpulent (persons)

肥瘦(ㄈㄟˊ ㄕㄡˋ)or 肥瘦兒(
ㄕㄡˋㄦ)
①the fat and the thin; the rich
and poor, etc. ②the sizes of
clothing

肥饒(ㄈㄟˊ ㄖㄠˊ)
fertile (land)

肥肉(ㄈㄟˊ ㄖㄡˋ)
fat meat: 你吃太多肥肉。You
eat too much fat meat.

肥皂(ㄈㄟˊ ㄗㄠˋ)
soap: 他買了一塊肥皂。He
bought a cake of soap.

肥皂泡(ㄈㄟˊ ㄗㄠˋ ㄆㄠˋ)
soap bubbles; suds

肥皂沫(ㄈㄟˊ ㄗㄠˋ ㄇㄛˋ)
suds; lather

肥皂粉(ㄈㄟˊ ㄗㄠˋ ㄈㄣˇ)
detergent powder

肥皂盒(ㄈㄟˊ ㄗㄠˋ ㄏㄜˊ)
a soap container; a soap
box

肥皂水(ㄈㄟˊ ㄗㄠˋ ㄕㄨㄟˇ)
suds; soapsuds

肥沃(ㄈㄟˊ ㄨㄛˋ)
fertile (land): 這塊地很肥沃。
The land is fertile.

【肩】 4634
ㄐㄧㄢ jian jiān
1. shoulders
2. to shoulder (responsibility,
etc.)
3. to employ; to appoint
①the shoulder: 他讓小孩子騎
在他肩膀上。He gave the
child a ride on his shoulders.
②a sense of responsibility

肩摩轂擊(ㄐㄧㄢ ㄇㄛˊ ㄍㄨˇ ㄐㄧˊ)
(literally) shoulders rubbing
and carriages knocking at
each other—busy traffic

肩負(ㄐㄧㄢ ㄈㄨˋ)
to take on; to undertake; to
shoulder; to bear: 我們肩負著
光榮的任務。We are undertak-
ing a glorious task.

肩負重任(ㄐㄧㄢ ㄈㄨˋ ㄓㄨㄥˋ ㄖㄣˋ)
to shoulder heavy responsibilities

肩挑背負(ㄐㄧㄢ ㄊㄧㄠ ㄅㄟˋ ㄈㄨˋ)
to carry on the shoulder and
back—the work of coolies
or peddlers

肩胛(ㄐㄧㄢ ㄐㄧㄚˊ)
the shoulder

肩胛骨(ㄐㄧㄢ ㄐㄧㄚˊ ㄍㄨˇ)
the shoulder blade; the scap-
ula

肩臼(ㄐㄧㄢ ㄐㄧㄡˋ)
a glenoid cavity

肩起(ㄐㄧㄢ ㄑㄧˇ)
to shoulder or take up (the
responsibility, etc.): 他應肩起
責任。He should shoulder his
responsibility.

肩章(ㄐㄧㄢ ㄓㄤ)
an epaulet; a shoulder badge:
學童常帶肩章。School boys
usually have shoulder badges.

肩輿(ㄐㄧㄢ ㄩˊ)
a sedan chair 亦作「轎」

【肪】 4635
ㄈㄤ farng fáng
(又讀 ㄈㄤ fang fāng)
fat

【腖】 4636
ㄓㄨㄣ juen zhūn
1. sincere; earnest
2. the gizzard of a fowl

【肯】 4637
(肎，肎) ㄎㄣˇ keen
ken
(又讀 ㄎㄥˇ keeng
keng)
to be willing; to approve of;
to consent to; to permit; to
agree

肯不肯(ㄎㄣˇ ㄅㄨˋ ㄎㄣˇ)or 肯否(ㄎㄣˇ
ㄈㄡˇ)
Are you willing (to do something) or not? 或Do you approve of it or not?

肯定(ㄎㄣˇ ㄉㄧㄥˋ)
affirmative; positive; sure;
definite: 我不能肯定他是否生
病了。I'm not sure whether
he is ill.

肯堂肯構(ㄎㄣˇ ㄊㄤˊ ㄎㄣˇ ㄍㄡˋ)
The deceased father started
and the son would complete
the endeavor.

肯幹(ㄎㄣˇ ㄍㄢˋ)
willing to put in hard work;
indefatigable

肯綮(ㄎㄣˇ ㄑㄧˋ)
the main point; the gist

肯亞(ㄎㄣˇ ㄧㄚˇ)
Kenya

【肱】 4638
ㄍㄨㄥ gong gōng
the forearm

肱骨(ㄍㄨㄥ ㄍㄨˇ)
a humerus

【育】 4639
ㄩˋ yuh yù
1. to produce; to give birth to;
to breed
2. to raise; to bring up; to
nourish; to nurse
3. to educate

育苗(ㄩˋ ㄇㄧㄠˊ)
to cultivate seedlings; seeding: 他正在育苗。He is cul-
tivating seedlings.

育民(ㄩˋ ㄇㄧㄣˊ)
to educate the people

育德(ㄩˋ ㄉㄜˊ)

to cultivate one's virtue

育種(ⅱ ㄓㄨㄥˇ)
breeding

育才(ⅱ ㄘㄞˊ)
to cultivate talents; to educate men of ability

育蠶(ⅱ ㄘㄢˊ)
to raise silkworms

育兒法(ⅱ ㄦˊ ㄈㄚˇ)
proper care and feeding of children or babies

育幼院(ⅱ ㄧㄡˋ ㄩㄢˋ)
a nursery school

育嬰堂(ⅱ ㄧㄥ ㄊㄤˊ)
a nursery for foundlings; a foundling hospital; an orphanage; child care

【肴】 4640
ㄧㄠˊ yau yáo
cooked food, especially meat and fish; dishes

肴饌(ㄧㄠˊ ㄓㄨㄢˋ)
rich food; sumptuous dishes

【肸】 4641
ㄒㄧ shih xī
1. to spread out; dispersed
2. diligent

五畫

【肺】 4642
ㄈㄟˋ fey fèi
the lungs

肺胞(ㄈㄟˋ ㄅㄠ)
a pulmonary vesicle

肺部(ㄈㄟˋ ㄅㄨˋ)
lungs

肺病(ㄈㄟˋ ㄅㄧㄥˋ)
tuberculosis; a lung ailment

肺膜(ㄈㄟˋ ㄇㄛˋ)
a pleura

肺膜炎(ㄈㄟˋ ㄇㄛˋ ㄧㄢˊ)
pulmonary pleurisy

肺腑(ㄈㄟˋ ㄈㄨˇ)
①close or intimate ②from the bottom of one's heart

肺腑之言(ㄈㄟˋ ㄈㄨˇ ㄓ ㄧㄢˊ)
words from the bottom of one's heart

肺動脈(ㄈㄟˋ ㄉㄨㄥˋ ㄇㄞˋ)
a pulmonary artery

肺癆(ㄈㄟˋ ㄌㄠˊ)
tuberculosis; consumption: 她死於肺癆. She died of (or from) consumption.

肺肝(ㄈㄟˋ ㄍㄢ)
(literally) the lungs and liver—the inner thoughts of a person

肺活量(ㄈㄟˋ ㄏㄨㄛˊ ㄌㄧㄤˋ)
vital capacity; lung capacity

肺活量計(ㄈㄟˋ ㄏㄨㄛˊ ㄌㄧㄤˋ ㄐㄧˋ)
a spirometer

肺結核(ㄈㄟˋ ㄐㄧㄝˊ ㄏㄜˊ)
tuberculosis; pulmonary phthisis; consumption: 他罹患肺結核. He suffered from tuberculosis of the lungs.

肺結核防治中心(ㄈㄟˋ ㄐㄧㄝˊ ㄏㄜˊ ㄈㄤˊ ㄓˋ ㄓㄨㄥ ㄒㄧㄣ)
TB Prevention and Treatment Center

肺靜脈(ㄈㄟˋ ㄐㄧㄥˋ ㄇㄞˋ)
a pulmonary vein

肺循環(ㄈㄟˋ ㄒㄩㄣˊ ㄏㄨㄢˊ)
pulmonary circulation

肺出血(ㄈㄟˋ ㄔㄨ ㄒㄧㄝˇ)
pneumonorrhagia

肺葉(ㄈㄟˋ ㄧㄝˋ)
the lobes of the lungs

肺炎(ㄈㄟˋ ㄧㄢˊ)
pneumonia: 醫生診斷出此病爲肺炎. The doctor diagnosed the illness as pneumonia.

肺癌(ㄈㄟˋ ㄞˊ)
carcinomas of the lungs; lung cancer

【胥】 4643
ㄒㄩ shiu xū
1. all; together
2. to wait for
3. to assist; to serve as an advisory role
4. to survey; to inspect
5. to keep away from; separated
6. a final particle
7. mutual
8. a variety of official ranks through ancient dynasties
9. a Chinese family name

【胃】 4644
ㄨㄟˋ wey wèi
the stomach; the gizzard (of birds and fowls)

胃病(ㄨㄟˋ ㄅㄧㄥˋ)
a stomach ailment or complaint

胃疼(ㄨㄟˋ ㄊㄥˊ)or 胃痛(ㄨㄟˋ ㄊㄨㄥˋ)
a stomach pain or ache: 他胃痛. He has a stomach ache.

胃口(ㄨㄟˋ ㄎㄡˇ)
appetite: 他的胃口好. He has a good appetite.

胃潰瘍(ㄨㄟˋ ㄎㄨㄟˋ ㄧㄤˊ)or 胃瘍(ㄨㄟˋ ㄩㄥˊ)
a gastric ulcer

胃加答兒(ㄨㄟˋ ㄐㄧㄚ ㄉㄚˊ ㄦˊ)or 胃炎(ㄨㄟˋ ㄧㄢˊ)
inflammation of the stomach; catarrh of the stomach

胃鏡(ㄨㄟˋ ㄐㄧㄥˋ)
a gastroscope

胃下垂(ㄨㄟˋ ㄒㄧㄚˋ ㄔㄨㄟˊ)
gastroptosis

胃腺(ㄨㄟˋ ㄒㄧㄢˋ)
gastric glands

胃腸(ㄨㄟˋ ㄔㄤˊ)
the stomach and intestines

胃出血(ㄨㄟˋ ㄔㄨ ㄒㄧㄝˇ)
gastrorrhagia

胃臟(ㄨㄟˋ ㄗㄤˋ)
the stomach

胃酸過多(ㄨㄟˋ ㄙㄨㄢ ㄍㄨㄛˋ ㄉㄨㄛ)
hyperacidity of the gastric juice; superacidity

胃液(ㄨㄟˋ ㄧㄝˋ)
gastric juice

胃液素(ㄨㄟˋ ㄧㄝˋ ㄙㄨˋ)
pepsin

胃炎(ㄨㄟˋ ㄧㄢˊ)
gastritis

胃癌(ㄨㄟˋ ㄞˊ)
a gastric carcinoma: 那老人死於胃癌. The old man died of gastric carcinoma.

【胄】 4645
ㄓㄡˋ jow zhòu
1. descendants; posterity; offspring
2. the eldest (son, etc.) 參看門部「胄」

【背】 4646
1. ㄅㄟˋ bey bèi
1. the back: 他背脊痛. He has a terrible pain in the back.
2. the reverse side; the back side
3. to cast away; to turn one's back on; to give up
4. to go against; to rebel: 這與我的原則相背. It goes against my principles.
5. to remember by rote; to commit to memory in detail
6. (now rarely) to faint; to lapse into a coma

背包(ㄅㄟ ㄅㄠ)

【肉部】

背部(ㄅㄟ ㄅㄨˋ)
the back (of a man or an animal, etc.): 他背部受傷。He was hurt on the back.

背叛(ㄅㄟ ㄆㄢˋ)
to rebel; to betray; to defect; to apostatize: 他們背叛自己的國家。They betrayed their country.

背盟(ㄅㄟ ㄇㄥˊ)
to break a promise, agreement, or treaty; a breach of contract or agreement

背謬(ㄅㄟ ㄇㄧㄡˋ)
to go against all good reasons; errors

背面(ㄅㄟ ㄇㄧㄢˋ)or背面兒(ㄅㄟ ㄇㄧㄢˋㄦ)
the reverse side; the back side

背風(ㄅㄟ ㄈㄥ)
on the lee side; leeward

背負(ㄅㄟ ㄈㄨˋ)
to carry on the back

背道而馳(ㄅㄟ ㄉㄠˋ ㄦˊ ㄔˊ)
to proceed in opposite directions; to be diametrically opposed to; to run counter to: 他的計劃與我的計劃背道而馳。His plans run counter to mine.

背地裏(ㄅㄟ ㄉㄧˋ·ㄌㄧ)
behind one's back; secretly

背地性(ㄅㄟ ㄉㄧˋ ㄒㄧㄥˋ)
(botany) negative geotropism

背對背(ㄅㄟ ㄉㄨㄟˋ ㄅㄟ)
back to back

背累(ㄅㄟ ·ㄌㄟ)
(said of a family, etc.) a burden: 她是家族的背累。She is a burden on (or to) her family.

背離(ㄅㄟ ㄌㄧˊ)
to deviate from; to depart from: 他們背離了正道。They deviated from the right path.

背理(ㄅㄟ ㄌㄧˇ)
to go against good reason or conscience

背光(ㄅㄟ ㄍㄨㄤ)
to be in a poor light; to do something with one's back to the light

背後(ㄅㄟ ㄏㄡˋ)
behind one's back; on the back side (of one's body); the rear in secret: 他們在背後批評他。They criticized him behind his back.

背脊骨(ㄅㄟ ㄐㄧˇ ㄍㄨˇ)
the backbone; the spine; the spinal column

背教(ㄅㄟ ㄐㄧㄠˋ)
to go against what one is taught; to renege; to apostatize

背景(ㄅㄟ ㄐㄧㄥˇ)
background: 我們要知道他的家庭背景。We want to know his family background.

背井離鄉(ㄅㄟ ㄐㄧㄥˇ ㄌㄧˊ ㄒㄧㄤ)
to leave one's hometown; to stay on a strange land

背棄(ㄅㄟ ㄑㄧˋ)
to turn one's back on; to renounce; to betray

背心(ㄅㄟ ㄒㄧㄣ)or背心兒(ㄅㄟ ㄒㄧㄣㄦ)
a vest; a waistcoat; a sleeveless jacket

背信(ㄅㄟ ㄒㄧㄣˋ)
to break one's word or promise; to be faithless; a breach of faith

背著(ㄅㄟ ·ㄓㄜ)
in secret; to avoid others

背著手(兒)(ㄅㄟ ·ㄓㄜ ㄕㄡˇ(ㄦ))or背手(ㄅㄟ ㄕㄡˇ(ㄦ))
with one's hands clasped behind one's back

背人(ㄅㄟ ㄖㄣˊ)
behind other's back; in secret: 他背著人告訴我此事。He told me about the matter in secret.

背馳(ㄅㄟ ㄔˊ)
to proceed in opposite directions

背城借一(ㄅㄟ ㄔㄥˊ ㄐㄧㄝˋ ㄧ)
to engage in a last-ditch battle; to fight with one's back to the wall

背時(ㄅㄟ ㄕˊ)
to be out of luck; unlucky

背山面水(ㄅㄟ ㄕㄢ ㄇㄧㄢˋ ㄕㄨㄟˇ)
(literally) with hills at the back and water in front —beautiful scenes or views (usually referring to a building)

背上(ㄅㄟ ·ㄕㄤ)
on the back

背書(ㄅㄟ ㄕㄨ)
① to recite a lesson; to commit a lesson to memory: 輪到你背書了。It's your turn to recite. ② to endorse a check ③ endorsement

背水一戰(ㄅㄟ ㄕㄨㄟˇ ㄧ ㄓㄢˋ)
(literally) to fight with one's back to the river—to fight to the last ditch

背日性(ㄅㄟ ㄖˋ ㄒㄧㄥˋ)
(botany) negative heliotropism

背誦(ㄅㄟ ㄙㄨㄥˋ)
to recite

背陰(ㄅㄟ ㄧㄣ)
in the shade; obscurity

背影(ㄅㄟ ㄧㄥˇ)
the sight of one's back

背約(ㄅㄟ ㄩㄝ)
a breach of promise or agreement; to break one's promise

背運(ㄅㄟ ㄩㄣˋ)
to be out of luck; to be in one's unlucky day, month, year, etc.

【背】 4646
2. ㄅㄟ bei bēi
to bear or shoulder (a load, burden, etc.); to carry on the back

背包袱(ㄅㄟ ㄅㄠ ·ㄈㄨ)
to have a weight on one's mind; to take on a mental burden

背榜(ㄅㄟ ㄅㄤˇ)
the last on the list of successful candidates of the civil service examination in former times

背不動(ㄅㄟ ·ㄅㄨ ㄉㄨㄥˋ)
unable to bear it on the back—too heavy

背帶(ㄅㄟ ㄉㄞˋ)
suspenders

背黑鍋(ㄅㄟ ㄏㄟ ㄍㄨㄛ)
to take the blame for another person

背著(ㄅㄟ ·ㄓㄜ)
to carry on the back

背債(ㄅㄟ ㄓㄞˋ)
to be in debt; to be burdened with debts

背上(ㄅㄟ ·ㄕㄤ)
to put on the back for carry-

ing

背子(ㄅㄟ ·ㄗ)
a device for carrying something on the back

【胎】 4647
　　ㄊㄞ tāi tōi
1. a fetus; an embryo
2. an unpolished, semiprocessed molding of something

胎盤(ㄊㄞ ㄆㄢ)or 胎衣(ㄊㄞ ㄧ)or 胎胞(ㄊㄞ ㄅㄠ)
the placenta

胎髮(ㄊㄞ ㄈㄚˇ)
the hair of a newborn baby

胎毒(ㄊㄞ ㄉㄨˊ)
(Chinese medicine) fetal toxins (toxic materials causing infantile infectious diseases)

胎動(ㄊㄞ ㄉㄨㄥˋ)
the quickening of the womb; fetal movement

胎記(ㄊㄞ ㄐㄧˋ)
a birthmark

胎教(ㄊㄞ ㄐㄧㄠˋ)
prenatal education or influences (An expectant mother's conduct is believed to influence the unborn baby.)

胎氣(ㄊㄞ ㄑㄧˋ)
①fetus-energy ②nausea, vomiting and edema of legs during pregnancy

胎生(ㄊㄞ ㄕㄥ)
viviparous

胎生學(ㄊㄞ ㄕㄥ ㄒㄩㄝˊ)
embryology

胎生魚(ㄊㄞ ㄕㄥ ㄩˊ)
viviparous fish, as whales or certain sharks

胎座(ㄊㄞ ㄗㄨㄛˋ)
(botany) placentas (of flowers)

胎死腹中(ㄊㄞ ㄙˇ ㄈㄨˋ ㄓㄨㄥ)
(literally) death in the womb—(said of a plan, or operation) to fail or be discarded before it gets started; abortive

胎兒(ㄊㄞ ㄦˊ)
a fetus; an unborn baby; an embryo

胎位(ㄊㄞ ㄨㄟˋ)
the position of a fetus

【胖】 4648
　　1. ㄆㄤˋ pang pàng
obese; fat; corpulent

胖病(ㄆㄤˋ ㄅㄧㄥˋ)
obesity

胖腫(ㄆㄤˋ ㄓㄨㄥˇ)
general swelling over the body

胖子(ㄆㄤˋ ·ㄗ)
a fat or corpulent person; a fatty

【胖】 4648
　　2. ㄆㄢˊ parn pán
comfortable

【胙】 4649
　　ㄗㄨㄛˋ tzuoh zuò
1. flesh, meat offered in sacrifices
2. blessings from Heaven
3. (now rarely) to report

【胛】 4650
　　ㄐㄧㄚˇ jea jiǎ
the shoulder; the shoulder blade

【胚】 4651
　　ㄆㄟ pei pēi
1. a three-month-old fetus; three months of pregnancy
2. things in the embryonic stage; unfinished moldings
3. the tender sprouts of plants

胚盤(ㄆㄟ ㄆㄢˊ)
a germinal disk, or blastoderm

胚胎(ㄆㄟ ㄊㄞ)
①the origination or beginning of things ②an embryo

胚胎學(ㄆㄟ ㄊㄞ ㄒㄩㄝˊ)
embryology

胚囊(ㄆㄟ ㄋㄤˊ)
an embryo sac; a gastrula

胚軸(ㄆㄟ ㄓㄡˊ)
(botany) a hypocotyl

胚珠(ㄆㄟ ㄓㄨ)
an ovule

胚乳(ㄆㄟ ㄖㄨˇ)
albumen (in seeds)

胚子(ㄆㄟ ·ㄗ)
① seeds ② things in their embryonic stage; an unpolished and unfinished molding

胚芽(ㄆㄟ ㄧㄚˊ)
to germinate; to cause to sprout; a sprout

胚芽米(ㄆㄟ ㄧㄚˊ ㄇㄧˇ)
germinated rice

【胞】 4652
　　ㄅㄠ bau bāo
1. the placenta
2. children of the same parents

胞妹(ㄅㄠ ㄇㄟˋ)
my younger sister; one's own younger sister

胞弟(ㄅㄠ ㄉㄧˋ)
my kid brother; one's own younger brother

胞姊(ㄅㄠ ㄐㄧˇ)
my elder sister; one's own elder sister

胞兄弟(ㄅㄠ ㄒㄩㄥ ㄉㄧˋ)
brothers by the same parents

胞子(ㄅㄠ ㄗˇ)
(botany) spores

胞子囊(ㄅㄠ ㄗˇ ㄋㄤˊ)
a sporangium

胞衣(ㄅㄠ ㄧ)
the placenta

胞與為懷(ㄅㄠ ㄩˇ ㄨㄟˊ ㄏㄨㄞˊ)
fraternity; to treat all creatures like one's brothers

【胠】 4653
　　ㄑㄩ chiu qū
1. to open
2. the armpit
3. (in ancient warfare) the right flank of an army

胠篋(ㄑㄩ ㄑㄧㄝˋ)
①to open a chest and steal
②name of a chapter in Chuangtze (莊子)

【胡】 4654
　　ㄏㄨˊ hwu hú
1. to blunder; reckless; wildly; disorderly
2. stupidly; blindly; confusedly
3. (in ancient China) a general name of the northern tribes (北狄)
4. (an interrogative particle) How? 或 Why? 或 When?
5. (now rarely) long and lasting
6. a Chinese family name

胡餅(ㄏㄨˊ ㄅㄧㄥˇ)
a baked cake of wheat flour usually topped with sesame 亦作「燒餅」

胡麻(ㄏㄨˊ ㄇㄚˊ)
linseed; sesame

胡母(ㄏㄨˊ ㄇㄨˇ)
①(now very rarely) a Chinese family name ②the mother of anyone whose family name is 胡

胡佛(ㄏㄨˊ ㄈㄛˊ)
Hoover, Herbert Clark,

（肉
部）

（肉部）

1874-1964, the 31st American president (1929-33)

胡服（ㄏㄨ ㄈㄨˊ）
the clothing of the northern barbarians

胡豆（ㄏㄨ ㄉㄡˋ）
lima beans

胡蝶（ㄏㄨ ㄉㄧㄝˊ）
a butterfly 亦作「蝴蝶」

胡蝶蘭（ㄏㄨ ㄉㄧㄝˊ ㄌㄢˊ）
phalaenopsis 亦作「蝴蝶蘭」

胡桃（ㄏㄨ ㄊㄠˊ）
walnuts

胡塗（ㄏㄨ ㄊㄨˊ）
confused; muddleheaded; stupid

胡同兒（ㄏㄨ ㄊㄨㄥˋ ㄦ）
a lane 亦作「衚衕兒」

胡鬧（ㄏㄨ ㄋㄠˋ）
to make a row or cause a disturbance without obvious reasons; reckless, irresponsible words or actions

胡來（ㄏㄨ ㄌㄞˊ）
to proceed (with a matter, etc.) recklessly and without thought

胡虜（ㄏㄨ ㄌㄨˇ）
the northern barbarians (北狄), who used to invade China from time to time through the dynasties

胡蘿蔔（ㄏㄨ ㄌㄨㄛˊ ㄅㄛ˙）
the carrot

胡亂（ㄏㄨ ㄌㄨㄢˋ）
①at will; at random; recklessly ②without being particular; not choosy

胡攪（ㄏㄨ ㄍㄠˇ）
①ⓐto behave at will or at random—without either objective or cause ⓑ to mess things up; to meddle with something 亦作「胡搞」②（ㄏㄨ ㄍㄠˇ）to cause confusion or a disturbance recklessly

胡瓜（ㄏㄨ ㄍㄨㄚ）
a cucumber

胡漢民（ㄏㄨ ㄏㄢˋ ㄇㄧㄣˊ）
Hu Han-min, 1879-1936, a follower of Dr. Sun Yat-sen

胡花亂用（ㄏㄨ ㄏㄨㄚ ㄌㄨㄢˋ ㄩㄥˋ）
to spend money extravagantly and recklessly

胡混（ㄏㄨ ㄏㄨㄣˋ）
to loaf around; to fool

around

胡騎（ㄏㄨ ㄐㄧˋ）
mounted northern barbarian troops

胡笳（ㄏㄨ ㄐㄧㄚ）
a reed pipe, a musical instrument of the Tartars in ancient times

胡椒（ㄏㄨ ㄐㄧㄠ）
pepper

胡琴（ㄏㄨ ㄑㄧㄣˊ）
the two-stringed violin (a major Chinese musical instrument today, used especially in Peking opera)

胡扯（ㄏㄨ ㄔㄜˇ）
①random talk; aimless conversation ②wild talk; lies

胡纏（ㄏㄨ ㄔㄢˊ）
endless (and usually aimless) bothering of another person; to harass

胡牀（ㄏㄨ ㄔㄨㄤˊ）
a lightweight rope chair which can be readily folded

胡適（ㄏㄨ ㄕˋ）
Hu Shih (1891-1962), educator and philosopher, pioneering a new literary movement which made the vernacular the dominating medium in modern Chinese literature

胡哨（ㄏㄨ ㄕㄠˋ）
a whistle made by the mouth

胡說（ㄏㄨ ㄕㄨㄛ）
Nonsense! 或 wild talk; to talk nonsense

胡說八道（ㄏㄨ ㄕㄨㄛ ㄅㄚ ㄉㄠˋ）
to talk nonsense; wild talk; lies

胡人（ㄏㄨ ㄖㄣˊ）
the northern barbarian tribes in ancient China

胡謅（ㄏㄨ ㄗㄡ）
wild talk; nonsensical talk; to invent (something false); to lie: 你胡謅! You're lying!

胡作非爲（ㄏㄨ ㄗㄨㄛˋ ㄈㄟ ㄨㄟˊ）
to bully others as if the law were non-existent; to do as one pleases

胡思亂想（ㄏㄨ ㄙ ㄌㄨㄢˋ ㄒㄧㄤˇ）
to daydream; to give one's thoughts free rein

胡亂（ㄏㄨ ㄌㄨㄢˋ）
northern barbarians in

ancient China

胡言亂語（ㄏㄨ ㄧㄢˊ ㄌㄨㄢˋ ㄩˇ）
to talk nonsense; to gibber; to talk incoherently or unintelligibly; lies or wild talk

胡爲（ㄏㄨ ㄨㄟˊ）
①why; how ②to act like a bully; to act recklessly

【胤】 ㄧㄣˋ　yinn; yin
long successions of descendants; posterity

胤嗣（ㄧㄣˋ ㄙ）
descendants

【胊】 4656　ㄑㄩ chyu qú
1. dried meat strips
2. far; faraway

【胗】 4657　ㄓㄣ jen zhēn
the gizzard of a fowl 亦作「肫」

胗肝（ㄓㄣ ㄍㄢ）
the gizzard of a fowl

【胗】 4657　ㄓㄣˇ jeen zhěn
pustules; a rash; measles 亦作「疹」

【胝】 4658　ㄓ jy zhī
calluses on hands or feet

六畫

【胭】 4659
（臙）ㄧㄢ ian yān
1. cosmetics, especially referring to rouge and face powder
2. the throat 亦作「咽」

胭粉（ㄧㄢ ㄈㄣˇ）
rouge and face powder

胭粉小說（ㄧㄢ ㄈㄣˇ ㄒㄧㄠˇ ㄕㄨㄛ）
novels featuring love or romantic plots

胭脂（ㄧㄢ ㄓ）
rouge

胭脂虎（ㄧㄢ ㄓ ㄏㄨˇ）
a shrew; a virago; a Circe

【胯】 4660　ㄎㄨㄚ kuah kuà
space between the legs; the groin

胯部（ㄎㄨㄚˋ ㄅㄨˋ）
the crotch

胯下辱（ㄎㄨㄚˋ ㄒㄧㄚˋ ㄖㄨˋ）
submitting the disgrace of crawling under another's

legs—said of Han Hsin (韓信), a famous general, who helped found the Han Dynasty

【胰】 4661 ㄧˊ yí yì
the pancreas

胰島素 (ㄧˊ ㄉㄠˇ ㄙㄨˋ)
(medicine) insulin; pancreatin

胰子 (ㄧˊ ˙ㄗ)
soap

胰臟 (ㄧˊ ㄗㄤˋ)
the pancreas

胰液素 (ㄧˊ ㄧㄝˋ ㄙㄨˋ)
pancreatin; insulin

【胱】 4662 ㄍㄨㄤ guang guāng
the bladder

【胴】 4663 ㄉㄨㄥˋ dong dòng
1. the large intestine
2. the trunk; the body

胴體 (ㄉㄨㄥˋ ㄊㄧˇ)
the trunk; the body

【胸】 4664 (舊) ㄒㄩㄥ shiong xiōng
1. the chest; the breast; the bosom; the bust; the thorax
2. one's ambition or aspiration
3. the mind (as narrow-minded, etc.); one's capacity

胸部 (ㄒㄩㄥ ㄅㄨˋ)
the chest

胸脯兒 (ㄒㄩㄥ ㄆㄨˊ ㄦ)
the breast, or bosom

胸腹 (ㄒㄩㄥ ㄈㄨˋ)
the chest and belly—vital points

胸膛 (ㄒㄩㄥ ㄊㄤˊ)
the breast or bosom; the thorax

胸肋膜 (ㄒㄩㄥ ㄌㄜˋ ㄇㄛˊ)
pleura costalis

胸膈 (ㄒㄩㄥ ㄍㄜˊ)
① the diaphragm ② feelings

胸骨 (ㄒㄩㄥ ㄍㄨˇ)
the breastbone; the sternum

胸管 (ㄒㄩㄥ ㄍㄨㄢˇ)
ductus thoracicus

胸口 (ㄒㄩㄥ ㄎㄡˇ)
the middle of the chest; the pit in the upper part of the stomach

the thorax

胸廓橫肌 (ㄒㄩㄥ ㄎㄨㄛˋ ㄏㄥˊ ㄐㄧ)
a transversal muscle of the thorax

胸花 (ㄒㄩㄥ ㄏㄨㄚ)
a corsage

胸懷 (ㄒㄩㄥ ㄏㄨㄞˊ) or 胸襟 (ㄒㄩㄥ ㄐㄧㄣ) or 胸次 (ㄒㄩㄥ ㄘˋ)
ambition or aspiration; mind

胸懷磊落 (ㄒㄩㄥ ㄏㄨㄞˊ ㄌㄟˇ ㄌㄨㄛˋ)
frank; honest; harboring no evil thought

胸肌 (ㄒㄩㄥ ㄐㄧ)
muscles in the general area of one's chest, as those between one's ribs

胸脊 (ㄒㄩㄥ ㄐㄧˊ)
the thoracic vertebrae

胸襟開闊 (ㄒㄩㄥ ㄐㄧㄣ ㄎㄞ ㄎㄨㄛˋ)
broad-minded; large-minded

胸前 (ㄒㄩㄥ ㄑㄧㄢˊ)
on one's chest or breast; right in front

胸腔 (ㄒㄩㄥ ㄑㄧㄤ)
the thoracic cavity

胸針 (ㄒㄩㄥ ㄓㄣ)
a brooch

胸章 (ㄒㄩㄥ ㄓㄤ)
a badge or a medal worn on the breast

胸中鱗甲 (ㄒㄩㄥ ㄓㄨㄥ ㄌㄧㄣˊ ㄐㄧㄚˇ)
treachery and murder in one's mind; treacherous; vicious; mean

胸中甲兵 (ㄒㄩㄥ ㄓㄨㄥ ㄐㄧㄚˇ ㄅㄧㄥ)
well-versed in military strategy and tactics

胸衣 (ㄒㄩㄥ ㄧ)
corsets

胸臆 (ㄒㄩㄥ ㄧˋ)
① the chest ② thoughts; feelings

胸有城府 (ㄒㄩㄥ ㄧㄡˇ ㄔㄥˊ ㄈㄨˇ)
scheming; calculating

胸有成竹 (ㄒㄩㄥ ㄧㄡˇ ㄔㄥˊ ㄓㄨˊ)
to have had ready or well-thought-out plans or designs in one's mind (in coping with a matter, situation, etc.)

胸無點墨 (ㄒㄩㄥ ㄨˊ ㄉㄧㄢˇ ㄇㄛˋ)
unlearned; ignorant; illiterate

胸無城府 (ㄒㄩㄥ ㄨˊ ㄔㄥˊ ㄈㄨˇ)
honest; frank; having nothing hidden in the mind

胸無宿物 (ㄒㄩㄥ ㄨˊ ㄙㄨˋ ㄨˋ)
frank; straightforward; outspoken

胸圍 (ㄒㄩㄥ ㄨㄟˊ)
the measurement around the bust; the first of the vital statistics of a woman

胸字 (ㄒㄩㄥ ㄗˋ)
one's ambition or aspiration

【胱】 4665 ㄊㄧㄠˋ tiaw tiào
sacrificial rites

【能】 4666 ㄋㄥˊ neng néng
1. can; to be able to 你明天能來嗎? Will you be able to come tomorrow?
2. capability; talent; competence
3. energy, as atomic energy

能不 (ㄋㄥˊ ㄅㄨˋ)
can't help but; how can one not: 對她你能不切切思念嗎? Can you not help thinking of her?

能不能 (ㄋㄥˊ ㄅㄨˋ ㄋㄥˊ)
can or can't; may or may not

能名 (ㄋㄥˊ ㄇㄧㄥˊ)
famed for great capability

能否 (ㄋㄥˊ ㄈㄡˇ)
can or cannot; may or may not

能耐 (ㄋㄥˊ ㄋㄞˋ)
skill; capability; ability; resourcefulness

能力 (ㄋㄥˊ ㄌㄧˋ)
① power, as the power of the Almighty, etc. ② a faculty; ability; capability

能吏 (ㄋㄥˊ ㄌㄧˋ)
a capable official

能量 (ㄋㄥˊ ㄌㄧㄤˋ)
① (physics) energy ② capabilities

能量不滅定律 (ㄋㄥˊ ㄌㄧㄤˋ ㄅㄨˋ ㄇㄧㄝˋ ㄉㄧㄥˋ ㄌㄩˋ)
the law of conservation of energy

能率 (ㄋㄥˊ ㄌㄩˋ)
the rate of work efficiency

能歌善舞 (ㄋㄥˊ ㄍㄜ ㄕㄢˋ ㄨˇ)
(usually said of a woman) skilled in both singing and dancing

能夠 or 能彀 (ㄋㄥˊ ㄍㄡˋ)
able to; capable of; can;

能幹 (ㄋㄥ ㄍㄢ)
capable; able; very competent and efficient: 他是一位能幹的律師。He is an able lawyer.

能見度 (ㄋㄥ ㄐㄧㄢ ㄉㄨ)
visibility: 在霧中能見度很低。In a fog the visibility is very poor.

(肉部)

能屈能伸 (ㄋㄥ ㄑㄩ ㄋㄥ ㄕㄣ)
adaptable; flexible: 他是個能屈能伸的人。He is an adaptable man.

能之變化 (ㄋㄥ ㄓ ㄅㄧㄢ ㄏㄨㄚˋ)
transformation of energy

能者多勞 (ㄋㄥ ㄓㄜ ㄉㄨㄛ ㄌㄠ)
The capable are usually the busy ones. (a compliment to a busy person)

能臣 (ㄋㄥ ㄔㄣ)
a capable minister or high official

能士 (ㄋㄥ ㄕ)
capable or talented persons

能事 (ㄋㄥ ㄕ)
①that which is within one's ability to do ②one's specialty, or special skill

能手 (ㄋㄥ ㄕㄡ)
a capable or competent person; an expert; a good hand: 她是桌球能手。She is a good hand at table tennis.

能說會道 (ㄋㄥ ㄕㄨㄛ ㄏㄨㄟ ㄉㄠ)
very eloquent

能人 (ㄋㄥ ㄖㄣ)
a capable or talented person

能忍自安 (ㄋㄥ ㄖㄣ ㄗ ㄢ)
Patience brings peace of mind.

能做 (ㄋㄥ ㄗㄨㄛ)
able to do; capable of doing: 他同時能做很多事。He is able to do lots of things at the same time.

能言快語 (ㄋㄥ ㄧㄢ ㄎㄨㄞ ㄩ)
eloquent and frank (in speaking)

能言善辯 (ㄋㄥ ㄧㄢ ㄕㄢ ㄅㄧㄢ)
eloquent and glib in argument

能為 (ㄋㄥ ㄨㄟ)
①capable of doing ②capability; ability; talent; re-

sourcefulness

能文能武 (ㄋㄥ ㄨㄣ ㄋㄥ ㄨ)
gifted in both intellectual and martial arts; efficient in both brainy and brawny activities

能源 (ㄋㄥ ㄩㄢ)
the sources of energy; energy resources; energy

能源計劃 (ㄋㄥ ㄩㄢ ㄐㄧ ㄏㄨㄚ)
an energy program

能源需求 (ㄋㄥ ㄩㄢ ㄒㄩ ㄑㄧㄡ)
energy needs

能源危機 (ㄋㄥ ㄩㄢ ㄨㄟ ㄐㄧ)
the energy crisis: 我們必須面對能源危機。We must face the energy crisis.

【胾】 4667
ㄗ tzyh zì
meat cuts; minced meat

【脂】 4668
ㄓ jy zhī
1. the fat of animals; grease; lard; tallow
2. the gum or sap of trees; resin
3. to anoint; to grease; to lubricate
4. cosmetics
5. a Chinese family name

脂麻 (ㄓ ˙ㄇㄚ)
sesame

脂粉 (ㄓ ㄈㄣ)
rouge and face powder—cosmetics

脂粉氣 (ㄓ ㄈㄣ ㄑㄧ)
feminine; sissy

脂肪 (ㄓ ㄈㄤ)
the fat of animals or plants

脂肪腺 (ㄓ ㄈㄤ ㄒㄧㄢ)
sebaceous glands

脂肪組織 (ㄓ ㄈㄤ ㄗㄨ ㄓ)
adipose tissue; fatty tissue

脂肪酸 (ㄓ ㄈㄤ ㄙㄨㄢ)
fatty acid

脂膏 (ㄓ ㄍㄠ)
①fat, grease, etc. ②wealth; affluence ③hard toil; sweat and blood (of the people)

脂光石 (ㄓ ㄍㄨㄤ ㄕ)
elaeolite

脂澤 (ㄓ ㄗㄜ)
well-oiled and glossy

脂油 (ㄓ ㄧㄡ)
lard

【脆】 4669
(脆) ㄘㄨㄟˋ tsuey cuì

1. brittle; fragile; hard but easily broken (as glass, porcelain, etc.): 這紙太脆。The kind of paper is too fragile.
2. crisp: 她的聲音很清脆。Her voice is clear and crisp.
3. light; shallow; thin
4. (said of the operation, etc. of something) easy, quick and convenient; neat: 她回答得很乾脆。She gave a neat answer.

脆薄 (ㄘㄨㄟ ㄅㄛ)
①thin and brittle: 這玻璃是脆薄的。The glass is thin and brittle. ②shallow

脆皮鴨 (ㄘㄨㄟ ㄆㄧ ㄧㄚ)
roasted Peking duck

脆骨 (ㄘㄨㄟ ㄍㄨ)
a cartilage; gristle

脆怯 (ㄘㄨㄟ ㄑㄧㄝ)
timid; cowardly; weak

脆性 (ㄘㄨㄟ ㄒㄧㄥ)
brittleness

脆弱 (ㄘㄨㄟ ㄖㄨㄛ)
weak; fragile; delicate: 他病後覺得很脆弱。He felt very weak after illness.

脆銀鑛 (ㄘㄨㄟ ㄧㄣ ㄎㄨㄤ)
stephanite

【脅】 4670
ㄒㄧㄝ shye xié

1. the sides of the trunk from armpits to ribs; the flank
2. to threaten with force; to force
3. to shrug (shoulders); to shrink

脅迫 (ㄒㄧㄝ ㄆㄛ)
to threaten with force; to coerce; coercion

脅肩 (ㄒㄧㄝ ㄐㄧㄢ)
to shrug the shoulders

脅肩累足 (ㄒㄧㄝ ㄐㄧㄢ ㄌㄟ ㄗㄨ)
frightened; apprehensive and nervous; jittery

脅肩諂笑 (ㄒㄧㄝ ㄐㄧㄢ ㄔㄢ ㄒㄧㄠ)
to be sycophantic; to act obsequiously

脅息 (ㄒㄧㄝ ㄒㄧ)
trembling and breathing heavily—very afraid or scared; in trepidation or great fright

脅制 (ㄒㄧㄝ ㄓ)
to control with threat of force, etc.; to coerce

脅持 (ㄒㄧㄝ ㄔ)

①to take somebody on both sides by the arms ②to hold somebody by violence

脅從(ㄒㄧㄝ ㄗㄨㄥˊ)
to be forced to join (rebellion, banditry, etc.)

脅從罔治(ㄒㄧㄝ ㄗㄨㄥˊ ㄨㄤˇ ㄓ)
Those who are forced to follow or take part are not to be punished.

【脈】 4671
(脤・脉)ㄇㄛˋ moh mò
(又讀 ㄇㄞˋ may mài)

1. the blood vessels; the veins or arteries; the circulation system
2. the pulse
3. a mountain range
4. things that are related and form a system of some kind
5. stipules or stems of a leaf

脈搏(ㄇㄛˋ ㄅㄛˊ)
the pulse; pulsation

脈搏停止(ㄇㄛˋ ㄅㄛˊ ㄊㄧㄥˊ ㄓˇ)
the cessation or stoppage of pulsation

脈脈(ㄇㄛˋ ㄇㄛˋ)
affectionately; lovingly; amorously

脈脈含情(ㄇㄛˋ ㄇㄛˋ ㄏㄢˊ ㄑㄧㄥˊ)
(said of eyes) quietly sending the message of love 亦作「脈眽含情」

脈理(ㄇㄛˋ ㄌㄧˇ)
the relationship between a patient's pulse and his illness

脈絡(ㄇㄛˋ ㄌㄨㄛˋ)
things that are related and form a system of their own (as veins and arteries forming the circulation system)

脈絡膜(ㄇㄛˋ ㄌㄨㄛˋ ㄇㄛˊ)
(anatomy) choroid

脈管(ㄇㄛˋ ㄍㄨㄢˇ)
the artery

脈縫(ㄇㄛˋ ㄈㄥˋ)
a fissure filling

脈息(ㄇㄛˋ ㄒㄧˊ)
the pulse; pulsation

脈石(ㄇㄛˋ ㄕˊ)
gangue, or vein stuff

脈岩(ㄇㄛˋ ㄧㄢˊ)
a vein rock

【脊】 4672
ㄐㄧˇ jii jǐ
(又讀 ㄐㄧˊ jyi jí)

1. the spine; spinal column
2. the ridge

脊梁(ㄐㄧ ㄌㄧㄤ)
①the back 亦作「脊背」②(construction) a ridgepole 亦作「桁木」或「棟梁」

脊柱(ㄐㄧ ㄓㄨˋ)
the vertebral column

脊椎(ㄐㄧˇ ㄓㄨㄟ)
the vertebrae

脊椎動物(ㄐㄧˇ ㄓㄨㄟ ㄉㄨㄥˋ ㄨˋ)
the vertebrates

脊椎骨(ㄐㄧˇ ㄓㄨㄟ ㄍㄨˇ)
a vertebra; the spine

脊髓(ㄐㄧˇ ㄙㄨㄟˇ)
the spinal cord

脊髓神經(ㄐㄧˇ ㄙㄨㄟˇ ㄕㄣˊ ㄐㄧㄥ)
the spinal nerves

脊髓炎(ㄐㄧˇ ㄙㄨㄟˇ ㄧㄢˊ)
myelitis

【肺】 4673
ㄦˊ erl ér
cooked; well-done

【胳】 4674
ㄍㄜ ge gē
the arms; the armpits 亦作「肐」

胳臂(ㄍㄜ·ㄅㄟ)or(ㄍㄜ ㄅㄟˋ)
the upper arm

胳肢窩(ㄍㄜ ㄓ ㄨㄛ)
the armpit

七畫

【脘】 4675
ㄨㄢˇ goan guǎn
the inside of the stomach —the gastric cavity; a duct in the body

【脛】 4676
ㄐㄧㄥˋ jing jìng
the calf; the part of a leg between the knee and ankle; the shank

脛骨(ㄐㄧㄥˋ ㄍㄨˇ)
the shinbone, or tibia

脛衣(ㄐㄧㄥˋ ㄧ)
trousers with the seat and upper part missing, worn by old folks in former times 亦作「套褲」

【唇】 4677
(脣)ㄔㄨㄣˊ chwen chún
the lips; the labia

唇兒(ㄔㄨㄛˊㄦ)
the lips

唇膏(ㄔㄨㄣˊ ㄍㄠ)
lipstick

唇紅齒白(ㄔㄨㄣˊ ㄏㄨㄥˊ ㄔˇ ㄅㄞˊ)
red lips and white teeth —very handsome or beautiful

唇槍舌劍(ㄔㄨㄣˊ ㄑㄧㄤ ㄕㄜˊ ㄐㄧㄢˋ)
a heated verbal exchange or debate; 雙方唇槍舌劍。There is an exchange of heated words between the two.

唇形花冠(ㄔㄨㄣˊ ㄒㄧㄥˊ ㄏㄨㄚ ㄍㄨㄢ)
a labiate corolla

唇脂(ㄔㄨㄣˊ ㄓ)
lipstick

唇齒(ㄔㄨㄣˊ ㄔˇ)
the lips and teeth—very close neighbors (implying a sense of interdependency)

唇齒相依(ㄔㄨㄣˊ ㄔˇ ㄒㄧㄤ ㄧ)
closely related and mutually dependent like the lips and teeth

唇齒音(ㄔㄨㄣˊ ㄔˇ ㄧㄣ)
(linguistics) labiodental consonants

唇舌(ㄔㄨㄣˊ ㄕㄜˊ)
①eloquence②spoken words; explanation

唇亡齒寒(ㄔㄨㄣˊ ㄨㄤˊ ㄔˇ ㄏㄢˊ)
(literally) When the lips are gone, the teeth will feel the chill.—mutual dependency of neighboring countries (usually small ones) when confronted with a powerful and aggressive enemy

【脩】 4678
ㄒㄧㄡ shiou xiū
1. to do, act, restore, regulate, cultivate, etc. 亦作「修」
2. dried meat
3. salary for a teacher in ancient times
4. a Chinese family name

脩脯(ㄒㄧㄡ ㄈㄨˇ)
dried meat

脩金(ㄒㄧㄡ ㄐㄧㄣ)or 脩敬(ㄒㄧㄡ ㄐㄧㄥˋ)
salary presented to a tutor or teacher

【脫】 4679
ㄊㄨㄛ tuo tuō
1. to strip; to undress; to take off
2. to abandon; to renounce; to cast off
3. to leave; to escape from; to

〔肉部〕

〔肉部〕

get out of
4. to omit; omission; to miss
out
5. to slip off
6. if; in case; perhaps

脱膊(ㄊㄨㄛ ㄅㄛ)
to slip to the waist; to be
bare from the waist up

脱班(ㄊㄨㄛ ㄅㄢ)
(said of scheduled trains,
buses, and airplanes) to be
late; to be behind schedule:
火車脱班了。The train was
behind schedule.

脱皮(ㄊㄨㄛ ㄆㄧ)
①(said of some kinds of reptiles or insects) ecdyses; to
molt ②to cast off the skin;
to peel

脱毛(ㄊㄨㄛ ㄇㄠ)
(said of animals) the falloff
of old hair; to molt; to shed

脱帽(ㄊㄨㄛ ㄇㄠ)
to take off one's hat—an
ancient way of admitting
defeat, now a gesture of
respect

脱黨(ㄊㄨㄛ ㄉㄤ)
to renounce one's party affiliation; to break off from
one's party

脱掉(ㄊㄨㄛ ㄉㄧㄠ)
to take off (one's garment,
etc.)

脱胎換骨(ㄊㄨㄛ ㄊㄞ ㄏㄨㄢ ㄍㄨ)
①to disembody (and become
immortal) ② to change oneself inside out

脱逃(ㄊㄨㄛ ㄊㄠ)
to escape from; to withdraw
or run away: 犯人從獄中脱
逃。The prisoner escaped
from the jail.

脱套(ㄊㄨㄛ ㄊㄠ)
to drop ceremony or formalities

脱體(ㄊㄨㄛ ㄊㄧ)
①(said of illness) to leave
one's body ②(Buddhism) to
get rid of the body

脱兔(ㄊㄨㄛ ㄊㄨ)
speedily; very quickly; in a
flash

脱漏(ㄊㄨㄛ ㄌㄡ)
to omit; omission; to miss

脱離(ㄊㄨㄛ ㄌㄧ)
①to sever one's relation

with; to break away ②not
within; away from; out of

脱離關係(ㄊㄨㄛ ㄌㄧ ㄍㄨㄢ ㄒㄧ)
to sever relations; to
divorce; to disown

脱離現實(ㄊㄨㄛ ㄌㄧ ㄒㄧㄢ ㄕ)
to be divorced from reality

脱落(ㄊㄨㄛ ㄌㄨㄛ)
to drop; to come off; to fall
off; to peel off: 牆上油漆逐漸
脱落。The paint is peeling off
the walls.

脱稿(ㄊㄨㄛ ㄍㄠ)
to complete a piece of writing

脱肛 or 脱肛(ㄊㄨㄛ ㄍㄤ)
prolapse of the rectum;
proctocele; (said of piles) to
slip out of the anus

脱軌(ㄊㄨㄛ ㄍㄨㄟ)
to derail: 火車脱軌了。The
train was derailed.

脱光(ㄊㄨㄛ ㄍㄨㄤ)
to strip nude: 他上半身衣服被
脱光了。He was stripped to
the waist.

脱殼(ㄊㄨㄛ ㄎㄜ)
① to cast the shell, as
insects ② to make an escape
(usually with a coup)

脱開(ㄊㄨㄛ ㄎㄞ)
to escape; to withdraw; to
untie or extricate (oneself,
etc. from bondage, troubles,
etc.)

脱口成章(ㄊㄨㄛ ㄎㄡ ㄔㄥ ㄓㄤ)
to speak beautifully

脱口而出(ㄊㄨㄛ ㄎㄡ ㄦ ㄔㄨ)
to slip out of one's lips; to
speak without thinking of
the consequence

脱空(ㄊㄨㄛ ㄎㄨㄥ)
①to work hard without any
success ②to lie

脱籍(ㄊㄨㄛ ㄐㄧ)
①(said of licensed prostitutes in former times) to get
married ②to drop party
membership or nationality

脱節(ㄊㄨㄛ ㄐㄧㄝ)
① disconnected; irrelevant
or incoherent; to come
apart; to lose contact ②dis-
location; luxation; to dislocate

脱臼(ㄊㄨㄛ ㄐㄧㄡ)
to luxate; luxation; disloca-

tion (of the joints)

脱肩(ㄊㄨㄛ ㄐㄧㄢ)
to relinquish or shirk one's
responsibility

脱韁野馬(ㄊㄨㄛ ㄐㄧㄤ ㄧㄝ ㄇㄚ) or
脱韁之馬(ㄊㄨㄛ ㄐㄧㄤ ㄓ ㄇㄚ)
(literally) an unbridled wild
horse--(usually said of a
person's disposition, a piece
of writing, etc.) wild and
unconventional collapse syndrome; forceful and unre-
strained

脱去(ㄊㄨㄛ ㄑㄩ)
① to take off or strip (one's
clothing, etc.); to throw off:
他脱去外套。He took off his
coat.② to vindicate (one's
bad reputation, etc.)

脱下(ㄊㄨㄛ ㄒㄧㄚ)
to take off; to shed or drop
(one's clothing, etc.)

脱鞋(ㄊㄨㄛ ㄒㄧㄝ)
to remove shoes; to take off
shoes

脱卸(ㄊㄨㄛ ㄒㄧㄝ)
to relinquish or shirk (one's
responsibility)亦作「脱肩」

脱孝(ㄊㄨㄛ ㄒㄧㄠ)
(literally) to take off one's
mourning clothes—The
mourning period is over.

脱險(ㄊㄨㄛ ㄒㄧㄢ)
to escape from danger; to be
out of danger

脱星(ㄊㄨㄛ ㄒㄧㄥ)
(informal) an actress who
dresses scantily on screen

脱序(ㄊㄨㄛ ㄒㄩ)
disorderliness; breakdown of
discipline

脱靴(ㄊㄨㄛ ㄒㄩㄝ)
①to pull off one's boots ②
to keep the boots of a
retired or transferred official at the city gate for
memory

脱脂棉(ㄊㄨㄛ ㄓ ㄇㄧㄢ)
defatted cotton; medicinal
cotton; absorbent cotton

脱脂奶(ㄊㄨㄛ ㄓ ㄋㄞ)
skim milk

脱脂奶粉(ㄊㄨㄛ ㄓ ㄋㄞ ㄈㄣ)
nonfat dried milk; defatted
milk powder

脱手(ㄊㄨㄛ ㄕㄡ)
①(said of goods or stock at

hand) to sell out; to dispose of: 這些貨不好脫手。 These goods are difficult to sell out. ②to slip off one's hands

脫售(ㄊㄨㄛ ㄕㄡˋ)
to sell out

脫身(ㄊㄨㄛ ㄕㄣ)
to leave; to get away from; to shake off; to escape

脫水(ㄊㄨㄛ ㄕㄨㄟˇ)
to dehydrate; dehydrated; dehydration

脫水機(ㄊㄨㄛ ㄕㄨㄟˇ ㄐㄧ)
a hydroextractor; a whizzer

脫水劑(ㄊㄨㄛ ㄕㄨㄟˇ ㄐㄧˋ)
a dehydrating agent

脫然無累(ㄊㄨㄛ ㄖㄢˊ ㄨˊ ㄌㄟˋ)
without a worry or care in the world

脫罪(ㄊㄨㄛ ㄗㄨㄟˋ)
to exonerate someone from a charge

脫色(ㄊㄨㄛ ㄙㄜˋ)
①to decolor; to decolorize ②to fade: 這張畫很快就脫色了。 This painting fades fast.

脫俗(ㄊㄨㄛ ㄙㄨˊ)
to free oneself from worldly ways; to drop formalities or ceremony; original; free from vulgarity

脫素(ㄊㄨㄛ ㄙㄨˋ)
to live a simple and frugal life

脫粟(ㄊㄨㄛ ㄙㄨˋ)
to unhusk (rice)

脫衣服(ㄊㄨㄛ ㄧ ㄈㄨˊ)
to remove one's clothing

脫衣舞(ㄊㄨㄛ ㄧ ㄨˇ)
a striptease

脫陽(ㄊㄨㄛ ㄧㄤˊ)
a kind of shock which a male may suffer during orgasm

脫穎而出(ㄊㄨㄛ ㄧㄥˇ ㄦˊ ㄔㄨ)
to pale others by showing one's ability and talents; (in a race, competition, etc.) to overtake others or outscore rival teams; to come to the fore: 那位藝術家脫穎而出。 The Artist has come to the fore.

脫誤(ㄊㄨㄛ ㄨˋ)
omissions and errors

【脯】 4680
1. ㄈㄨ fuu fú
1. dried and seasoned meat
2. preserved fruits

【脯】 4680
2. ㄆㄨˇ pwu pǔ
flesh or meat in the general area of the chest or breast

【脬】 4681
ㄆㄠ pau pāo
the bladder

【脰】 4682
ㄉㄡ dow dòu
the neck

【脞】 4683
ㄘㄨㄛˇ tsuoo cuǒ
tiny; petty; little pieces

【脤】 4684
ㄕㄣ shenn shèn
1. raw meat for a sacrifice
2. the buttocks; the bottom

【脖】 4685
ㄅㄛˊ bor bó
the neck

脖領兒(ㄅㄛˊ ㄌㄧㄥˇ ㄦ)
the neck or collar of a garment

脖頸子(ㄅㄛˊ ㄐㄧㄥˇ ㄗ)or 脖頸兒
(ㄅㄛˊ ㄐㄧㄥˇ ㄦ)
the neck.

脖子(ㄅㄛˊ ㄗ)
the neck: 他抓住我的脖子。 He caught me by the neck.

【脗】 4686
ㄨㄣˇ woen wěn
1. to kiss; a kiss 亦作「吻」
2. to join together; to match; to tally
3. the lips

脗合(ㄨㄣˇ ㄏㄜˊ)
to match; to tally; to be identical: 這兩人所說的相脗合。 The stories of the two men tallied.

【腳】 4687
(脚)ㄐㄧㄠˇ jeau jiǎo
1. the foot or feet
2. the base or foundation of anything

八畫

【脹】 4688
ㄓㄤ jang zhāng
1. full-stomached; glutted
2. swelling of the skin, etc.
3. to expand; expansion

脹滿(ㄓㄤ ㄇㄢˇ)
full; inflated; glutted

脹率(ㄓㄤ ㄌㄩˋ)
the rate of expansion

脹氣(ㄓㄤ ㄑㄧˋ)
①inflated with air ②(medicine) flatulence

【胼】 4689
(胼)ㄆㄧㄢˊ pyan pián
calluses

胼胝(ㄆㄧㄢˊ ㄓ)or 胼手胝足(ㄆㄧㄢˊ ㄕㄡˇ ㄓ ㄗㄨˊ)
calluses on the hands and feet—to toil or work hard

【腆】 4690
ㄊㄧㄢˇ tean tiǎn
1. prosperous; affluence
2. good; virtuous
3. protruding (as the belly, etc.)
4. bashful; to blush

腆默(ㄊㄧㄢˇ ㄇㄛˋ)
to blush and keep silence

腆贈(ㄊㄧㄢˇ ㄗㄥˋ)
rich gifts; costly presents

【腋】 4691
(讀音「 」 yih yì)
ㄧㄝˋ yeh yè
the armpits; the part under the forelegs of animals

腋毛(ㄧㄝˋ ㄇㄠˊ)
armpit hair

腋氣(ㄧㄝˋ ㄑㄧˋ)
the odor emanating from under the arms; a body odor

腋(ㄧㄝˋ ㄒㄧㄚˋ)
under the arms; the armpits

腋臭(ㄧㄝˋ ㄔㄡˋ)
the odor emanating from the armpits; a body odor 亦作「腋氣」or「狐臭」

腋芽(ㄧㄝˋ ㄧㄚˊ)
(plants) an axillary bud

腋窩(ㄧㄝˋ ㄨㄛ)
the armpits

【腌】 4692
1. ㄤ ang āng
(又讀ㄚ a à)
unclean; filthy

腌臢(ㄤ ㄗㄚ)or(ㄚ ㄗㄚ)
unclean; dirty; filthy: 他衣服腌臢。 His clothes are filthy.

腌臢貨(ㄤ ㄗㄚ ㄏㄨㄛˋ)
a filthy person; a lousy or vicious fellow: 他是個腌臢貨。 He is a filthy person.

【腌】 4692
2.(醃)ㄧㄢ ian yān
to salt; to pickle

〔肉
部〕

【膵】 4693
(膵) ㄘㄨㄟˋ tsuey cuì
the pancreas

【腎】 4694
ㄕㄣˋ shenn shèn
1. the kidneys
2. the testicles

腎門(ㄕㄣˋ ㄇㄣˊ)
a hilum renalis

腎動脈(ㄕㄣˋ ㄉㄨㄥˋ ㄇㄞˋ)
a renal artery

腎痛(ㄕㄣˋ ㄊㄨㄥˋ)
nephralgia

腎囊(ㄕㄣˋ ㄋㄤˊ)
the scrotum

腎虧(ㄕㄣˋ ㄎㄨㄟ)
impotence; a general weakness of the male sexual
prowess 亦作「腎虛」

腎靜脈(ㄕㄣˋ ㄐㄧㄥˋ ㄇㄞˋ)
a renal vein

腎虛(ㄕㄣˋ ㄒㄩ)
a general weakness of the
male sexual prowess

腎上腺(ㄕㄣˋ ㄕㄤˋ ㄒㄧㄢˋ)
adrenals; the adrenal glands

腎臟(ㄕㄣˋ ㄗㄤˋ)
the kidneys

腎臟病(ㄕㄣˋ ㄗㄤˋ ㄅㄧㄥˋ)
a kidney ailment or disease

腎臟結石(ㄕㄣˋ ㄗㄤˋ ㄐㄧㄝˊ ㄕˊ)or 腎結
石(ㄕㄣˋ ㄐㄧㄝˊ ㄕˊ)
(pathology) nephrolithia-
sis; renal calculus; kidney
stone

腎臟炎(ㄕㄣˋ ㄗㄤˋ ㄧㄢˊ)
inflammation of the kidneys;
nephritis

腎髓(ㄕㄣˋ ㄙㄨㄟˇ)
the purplish tissue that constitutes the inner part of the
kidneys

腎盂(ㄕㄣˋ ㄩˊ)
a pelvis

【腐】 4695
ㄈㄨˇ fuu fǔ
1. to decay; to rot; rotten;
putrid; to disintegrate; stale
2. corrupt; evil; worthless
3. old; worn-out; useless or
worthless
4. to castrate; castration (as a
punishment in ancient China)
5. short for 豆腐—bean curd

腐敗(ㄈㄨˇ ㄅㄞˋ)
①corrupt and rotten (practice, administration, etc.) ②

putrid; decayed; to decay; to
decompose

腐爛(ㄈㄨˇ ㄌㄢˋ)
to rot or decay; to disintegrate or decompose

腐化(ㄈㄨˇ ㄏㄨㄚˋ)
corrupt or rotten; decadent

腐化分子(ㄈㄨˇ ㄏㄨㄚˋ ㄈㄣ ㄗˇ)
corrupt or rotten elements; a
depraved person

腐舊(ㄈㄨˇ ㄐㄧㄡˋ)
old and worn-out; worthless
or useless

腐臭(ㄈㄨˇ ㄔㄡˋ)
①an odor or stench of
decaying (foods, etc.) ②pedantic; pigheaded

腐朽(ㄈㄨˇ ㄒㄧㄡˇ)
decayed; rotten

腐心(ㄈㄨˇ ㄒㄧㄣ)
①extreme hatred ②extreme-
ly worried or anxious

腐刑(ㄈㄨˇ ㄒㄧㄥˊ)
(in ancient China) punishment by castration

腐植土(ㄈㄨˇ ㄓˊ ㄊㄨˇ)
humic soil; humus soil

腐臭(ㄈㄨˇ ㄔㄡˋ)
decaying and with a bad
odor or stench

腐腸之藥(ㄈㄨˇ ㄔㄤˊ ㄓ ㄧㄠˋ)
(figuratively) rich foods

腐蝕(ㄈㄨˇ ㄕˊ)
①to erode; erosion; to corrode; corrosion: 金屬爲酸所腐
蝕. Metals are eroded by
acids. ②(chemistry) to etch;
etching

腐蝕劑(ㄈㄨˇ ㄕˊ ㄐㄧˋ)
a corrodent

腐鼠(ㄈㄨˇ ㄕㄨˇ)
cheap or worthless things
but highly treasured by the
vulgar

腐肉(ㄈㄨˇ ㄖㄡˋ)
①rotten flesh or meat ②
(medicine) slough

腐儒(ㄈㄨˇ ㄖㄨˊ)
pedants; worthless and
narrow-minded scholars

腐乳(ㄈㄨˇ ㄖㄨˇ)
bean cheese

【腑】 4696
ㄈㄨˇ fuu fǔ
the bowels; the entrails; the
viscera

腑臟(ㄈㄨˇ ㄗㄤˋ)

the bowels; the entrails; the
viscera

【腔】 4697
ㄑㄧㄤ chiang qiāng
1. the cavity—especially referring to the chest and belly
2. a cavity in any vessel
3. an accent of one's pronunciation; a tone of one's voice
4. a manner

腔調(ㄑㄧㄤ ㄉㄧㄠˋ)
①a tune; the melody of a
tune ②an accent ③a man-
ner or style of behavior

腔兒(ㄑㄧㄤ)
①a cavity in any vessel ②
a tune

【腕】 4698
ㄨㄢˋ wann wàn
the wrist

腕法(ㄨㄢˋ ㄈㄚˇ)
the three positions of the
wrist 枕腕, 提腕, 懸腕 in writ-
ing Chinese characters

腕力(ㄨㄢˋ ㄌㄧˋ)
the strength of the wrist
which is the key factor in
forceful penmanship

腕骨(ㄨㄢˋ ㄍㄨˇ)
the wrist bones; the carpus:
他折斷了腕骨。He broke his
wrist bones.

腕子(ㄨㄢˋ ·ㄗ)
the wrist: 我捉住他的腕子。I
took him by the wrist.

【脾】 4699
ㄆㄧˊ pyi pí
1. the spleen
2. a temper; a disposition

脾氣(ㄆㄧˊ ·ㄑㄧ)
a temper or disposition: 他脾
氣暴躁。He has a quick tem-
per.

脾臟(ㄆㄧˊ ㄗㄤˋ)
the spleen

脾胃(ㄆㄧˊ ㄨㄟˋ)
①the stomach ②appetite ③
one's temperament or natural inclination

【腊】 4700
1. ㄒㄧˊ shyi xí
1. dried meat
2. very; extremely

【臘】 4700
2. ㄌㄚˋ lah là
an abbreviated form of 臘

腊梅(ㄌㄚˋ ㄇㄟˊ)

plum flowers

腊肉(ㄌㄚˊ ㄖㄡˋ)
salted and dried meat

腊月(ㄌㄚˊ ㄩㄝˋ)
the twelfth month of the lunar year

【腓】 4701 ㄈㄟˊ feir féi
1. the calf (of the leg)
2. (now rarely) sick; ill
3. (now rarely) to avoid
4. (now rarely) to decay

腓特力大帝(ㄈㄟˊ ㄊㄜˋ ㄌㄧˋ ㄉㄚˋ ㄉㄧˋ)
Frederick the Great, 1712-1786, king of Prussia

腓尼基(ㄈㄟˊ ㄋㄧˊ ㄐㄧ)
Phenicia, or Phoenicia

腓骨(ㄈㄟˊ ㄍㄨˇ)
the fibula

九畫

【腠】 4702 ㄘㄡˋ tsow còu
the texture of muscle

【腥】 4703 ㄒㄧㄥ shing xīng
1. raw, undressed meat
2. an offensive smell, especially of fish or blood

腥風血雨(ㄒㄧㄥ ㄈㄥ ㄒㄩㄝˋ ㄩˇ)
(literally) winds carrying an offensive smell of flesh and rain of blood; the carnage of war

腥行(ㄒㄧㄥ ㄒㄧㄥˊ)
evil conduct; debauchery; dissipated ways

腥穢(ㄒㄧㄥ ㄏㄨㄟˋ)or腥污(ㄒㄧㄥ ㄨ)
smelly and dirty

腥臊(ㄒㄧㄥ ㄙㄠ)
smelly; an offensive smell of meat, fish, blood, etc.

腥臭(ㄒㄧㄥ ㄔㄡˋ)
an offensive smell of fish, meat, blood, etc.

腥羶(ㄒㄧㄥ ㄕㄢ)
the smell of sheep or goats

腥膻(ㄒㄧㄥ ㄕㄢ)
①a bad smell of fish or meat; a stench ②evil (administration, etc.)

腥味兒(ㄒㄧㄥ ㄨㄟˋㄦ)
an offensive smell of fish, etc.

腥聞(ㄒㄧㄥ ㄨㄣˊ)
a malodorous reputation

---

known far and wide; scandalous acts; notoriety; rank odor

【腦】 4704 ㄋㄠˇ nao nǎo
the brain

腦瓢兒(ㄋㄠˇ ㄆㄧㄠˊㄦ)
the top of the head; the plate of the head

腦貧血(ㄋㄠˇ ㄆㄧㄣˊ ㄒㄧㄝˇ)
cerebral anemia

腦膜(ㄋㄠˇ ㄇㄛˊ)
meninges

腦膜炎(ㄋㄠˇ ㄇㄛˊ ㄧㄢˊ)
meningitis

腦滿腸肥(ㄋㄠˇ ㄇㄢˇ ㄔㄤˊ ㄈㄟˊ)
①a fool or stupid fellow —one who gluts his stomach but never uses his brains ②fat like a pig

腦門子(ㄋㄠˇ ㄇㄣˊ ˙ㄗ)or腦門兒(ㄋㄠˇ ㄇㄣˊㄦ)
the forehead

腦袋(ㄋㄠˇ ㄉㄞˋ)or腦袋瓜子(ㄋㄠˇ ㄉㄞˋ ㄍㄨㄚ ˙ㄗ)or腦袋瓜兒(ㄋㄠˇ ㄉㄞˋ ㄍㄨㄚㄦ)
the head: 他把他的腦袋伸出窗外。He put his head out of the window.

腦電波圖(ㄋㄠˇ ㄉㄧㄢˋ ㄅㄛ ㄊㄨˊ)
an electroencephalogram

腦力(ㄋㄠˇ ㄌㄧˋ)
brains; mental capability; mental exertion

腦蓋(ㄋㄠˇ ㄍㄞˋ)
the top of the skull

腦蓋骨(ㄋㄠˇ ㄍㄞˋ ㄍㄨˇ)
the cranium

腦瓜頂(ㄋㄠˇ ㄍㄨㄚ ㄉㄧㄥˇ)
the top of the head

腦殼(ㄋㄠˇ ㄎㄜˊ)
①the head ②a jocular reference to one's general appearance

腦海(ㄋㄠˇ ㄏㄞˇ)
the mind

腦後(ㄋㄠˇ ㄏㄡˋ)
disregard; to disregard: 他把我的警告抛在腦後。He disregarded my warnings.

腦筋(ㄋㄠˇ ㄐㄧㄣ)
brains; mentality; mental capacity: 她腦筋很好。She has a good brain.

腦筋靈敏(ㄋㄠˇ ㄐㄧㄣ ㄌㄧㄥˊ ㄇㄧㄣˇ)
keen and sharp in thinking; brainy; bright

腦漿(ㄋㄠˇ ㄐㄧㄤ)
the cerebrum, the cerebellum and the medulla oblongata collectively when they are exposed after the skull is crushed

腦汁(ㄋㄠˇ ㄓ)
mental effort or exertion —(figuratively) brains: 他為了答案絞盡腦汁。He racked his brains for the answer.

腦震盪(ㄋㄠˇ ㄓㄣˋ ㄉㄤˋ)
brain concussion

腦脹(ㄋㄠˇ ㄓㄤˋ)
heavy feeling in the brain

腦中風(ㄋㄠˇ ㄓㄨㄥ ㄈㄥ)
(pathology) stroke

腦出血(ㄋㄠˇ ㄔㄨ ㄒㄧㄝˇ)
cerebral hemorrhage; an apoplectic stroke; cerebral apoplexy

腦充血(ㄋㄠˇ ㄔㄨㄥ ㄒㄧㄝˇ)
congestion of the brain

腦杓子(ㄋㄠˇ ㄕㄠˊ ˙ㄗ)
the back of the head

腦神經(ㄋㄠˇ ㄕㄣˊ ㄐㄧㄥ)
cranial nerves

腦子(ㄋㄠˇ ˙ㄗ)
①the brain ②brains; mental capability; the faculty of memory

腦髓(ㄋㄠˇ ㄙㄨㄟˇ)
a general name of the brain —including cerebrum, cerebellum and medulla oblongata

腦兒(ㄋㄠˇㄦ)
①the brains of animals (for food) ②any greyish white substance resembling the brain, as soft bean curd, etc.

腦溢血(ㄋㄠˇ ㄧˋ ㄒㄧㄝˇ)
cerebral hemorrhage; a stroke; apoplexy

腦炎(ㄋㄠˇ ㄧㄢˊ)
encephalitis

【腫】 4705 ㄓㄨㄥˇ joong zhǒng
to swell; a swelling; a boil: 她受傷的指頭腫起來了。Her injured finger swelled.

腫皰(ㄓㄨㄥˇ ㄆㄠˋ)
a pimple; acne

腫大(ㄓㄨㄥˇ ㄉㄚˋ)
to swell up

腫毒(ㄓㄨㄥˇ ㄉㄨˊ)
a swelling; a tumor

【肉部】

腫瘤(ㄓㄨㄥ ㄌㄧㄡ)
(medicine) a tumor: 良(惡)性腫瘤a benign (malignant) tumor

腫起來(ㄓㄨㄥ ㄑㄧ ㄌㄞ)
to swell up: 他的臉孔開始腫起來。His face began to swell up.

腫脹(ㄓㄨㄥ ㄓㄤ)
to swell; swelling

【腰】 4706 ㄧㄠ iau yāo
1. the midriff; the waist: 她的腰很細。She has a small waist.
2. the kidneys
3. the middle of something; the waist portion of a region

腰板兒(ㄧㄠ ㄅㄢ ㄦ)
the back of the midriff; the waist and the back

腰包(ㄧㄠ ㄅㄠ)
a purse; a billfold; a wallet; a girdle with a built-in pocket worn by farmers in former times ②one's money

腰脖硬(ㄧㄠ ㄅㄛ ㄧㄥ)
stiff or rigid in movements

腰部(ㄧㄠ ㄅㄨ)
the waist; the small part of the body between the thorax and hips

腰帶(ㄧㄠ ㄉㄞ)
①a girdle; a waistband ②(anatomy) a pelvic girdle

腰刀(ㄧㄠ ㄉㄠ)
a saberlike knife carried at the waist in former times

腰疼(ㄧㄠ ㄊㄥ)
lumbago

腰腿(ㄧㄠ ㄊㄨㄟ)
nimbleness of one's waist and legs

腰痛(ㄧㄠ ㄊㄨㄥ)
lumbago; a muscular pain in the lumbar regions

腰骨(ㄧㄠ ㄍㄨ)
the five lowest pieces of bone of the spinal column

腰鼓(ㄧㄠ ㄍㄨ)
a kind of drum, having a large end stretched over with skin and a slender hollow cylinder

腰果(ㄧㄠ ㄍㄨㄛ)
a cashew nut

腰花(ㄧㄠ ㄏㄨㄚ)
hog kidneys cut lightly which will blossom like flowers when cooked

腰肢(ㄧㄠ ㄓ)
the waistline; the circumference of the body at the waist

腰舟(ㄧㄠ ㄓㄡ)
an empty gourd tied to the waist as a kind of life jacket in former times

腰斬(ㄧㄠ ㄓㄢ)
(an ancient Chinese punishment) to chop in two at the waist

腰纏(ㄧㄠ ㄔㄢ)
money one carries when traveling

腰纏萬貫(ㄧㄠ ㄔㄢ ㄨㄢ ㄍㄨㄢ)
very rich; loaded

腰身(ㄧㄠ ㄕㄣ)
the waist; the waistline (in dress-making); the size of the midriff: 這條裙子腰身太大。The skirt is too big in the waist.

腰子(ㄧㄠ ˙ㄗ)
the kidneys

腰酸背痛(ㄧㄠ ㄙㄨㄢ ㄅㄟ ㄊㄨㄥ)
a sore waist and an aching back

腰兒(ㄧㄠ ㄦ)
the waist

腰窩兒(ㄧㄠ ㄨㄛ ㄦ)
mutton cut from the side of sheep

腰圍(ㄧㄠ ㄨㄟ)
①the waist; the waistline; the second of a girl's vital statistics ②a girdle

【腳】 4707
(脚) ㄐㄧㄠ jeau jiǎo
(讀音 ㄐㄩㄝ jyue jué)
1. the feet
2. the leg or base of something

腳本(ㄐㄧㄠ ㄅㄣ)
the script of a play, an opera, etc.

腳步(ㄐㄧㄠ ㄅㄨ)
steps; paces; strides; footfalls; footsteps

腳盆(ㄐㄧㄠ ㄆㄣ)
a foot tub

腳面(ㄐㄧㄠ ㄇㄧㄢ)
the instep; the back of a foot

腳夫(ㄐㄧㄠ ㄈㄨ)
a porter or coolie

腳燈(ㄐㄧㄠ ㄉㄥ)
footlights on a stage

腳凳(ㄐㄧㄠ ㄉㄥ)
a footstool; a footrest

腳底板兒(ㄐㄧㄠ ㄉㄧ ㄅㄢ ㄦ)
the sole of the foot

腳底下(ㄐㄧㄠ ㄉㄧˇ˙ㄒㄧㄚ)
①under the feet ②feet

腳踏板(ㄐㄧㄠ ㄊㄚ ㄅㄢ)
①a footboard ②a pedal

腳踏兩隻船(ㄐㄧㄠ ㄊㄚ ㄌㄧㄤ ㄓ ㄔㄨㄢ)
to straddle the fence; to be undecided

腳踏車(ㄐㄧㄠ ㄊㄚ ㄔㄜ)
a bicycle: 你騎腳踏車嗎? Do you ride a bicycle?

腳踏實地(ㄐㄧㄠ ㄊㄚ ㄕ ㄉㄧ)
(literally) to plant one's feet on solid ground—to do a job honestly and with dedication

腳踢(ㄐㄧㄠ ㄊㄧ)
to kick

腳力(ㄐㄧㄠ ㄌㄧ)
①a messenger; an errandboy ②carriage charges; porterage ③ strength of one's legs

腳鐐(ㄐㄧㄠ ㄌㄧㄠ)
foot shackles or fetters

腳爐(ㄐㄧㄠ ㄌㄨ)
a charcoal foot warmer made of metal

腳後跟(ㄐㄧㄠ ㄏㄡ ㄍㄣ)or 腳跟(ㄐㄧㄠ ㄍㄣ)
①the heel of the foot ②(figuratively) foothold

腳行(ㄐㄧㄠ ㄏㄤ)
(formerly) a transportation company which employed coolies to do the carrying

腳印(ㄐㄧㄠ ㄧㄣ)
footprints; footmarks; footsteps

腳尖兒(ㄐㄧㄠ ㄐㄧㄢ ㄦ)
the point of the foot; tiptoe: 她踮著腳尖兒走。She walks on tiptoe.

腳氣病(ㄐㄧㄠ ㄑㄧ ㄅㄧㄥ)or 腳氣(ㄐㄧㄠ ㄑㄧ)
beriberi

腳錢(ㄐㄧㄠ ㄑㄧㄢ)
a fee for the delivery man of a store

腳下(ㄐㄧㄠ ㄒㄧㄚ)

① under one's feet ② the foot ③ now; presently

腳心(ㄐㄧㄠˇ ㄒㄧㄣ)
the foot arch; the arch of the foot

腳指頭(ㄐㄧㄠˇ ㄓˇ·ㄊㄡ)or **腳趾**(ㄐㄧㄠˇ ㄓˇ)
toes: 我的腳趾很痛。 My toe is very sore.

腳指甲(ㄐㄧㄠˇ ㄓˇ·ㄐㄧㄚˇ)
toenails

腳掌(ㄐㄧㄠˇ ㄓㄤˇ)
the sole (of the foot)

腳註(ㄐㄧㄠˇ ㄓㄨˋ)
a footnote: 他忘了打上腳註。 He forgot to type the footnotes.

腳踩(ㄐㄧㄠˇ ㄘㄞˇ)
to pedal; to trample; to stamp with the feet

腳色(ㄐㄧㄠˇ ㄙㄜˋ)
① a character; a role: 他扮演哈姆雷特的腳色。 He played the role of Hamlet. ② personal background of examinees under the old civil service examination system ③ a talented or resourceful person

腳丫縫兒(ㄐㄧㄠˇ ㄧㄚ ㄈㄥˋ儿)
space between the toes

腳鴨子(ㄐㄧㄠˇ ㄧㄚ·ㄗ)or **腳鴨兒**(ㄐㄧㄠˇ ㄧㄚ·儿)
the foot

腳印兒(ㄐㄧㄠˇ ㄧㄣˋ儿)
footprints; footmarks; footsteps

腳腕子(ㄐㄧㄠˇ ㄨㄢˋ·ㄗ)
the ankle

【腱】 4708
ㄐㄧㄢˋ jiann jiàn
(anatomy)tendon

腱子(ㄐㄧㄢˋ·ㄗ)
tendons (of meat animals)

【腴】 4709
ㄩˊ yu yú
1. fat
2. plump and soft
3. fertile
4. intestines of dogs and hogs
5. rich

【腸】 4710
ㄔㄤˊ charng cháng
the intestines; the bowels

腸肚(ㄔㄤˊ ㄉㄨˇ)
the intestines and the belly —one's heart (good, evil, etc.)

腸斷(ㄔㄤˊ ㄉㄨㄢˋ)
heartbroken; deeply grieved

腸潰瘍(ㄔㄤˊ ㄎㄨㄟˋ ㄧㄤˊ)
an intestinal ulcer

腸子(ㄔㄤˊ·ㄗ)
the intestines

腸炎(ㄔㄤˊ ㄧㄢˊ)
intestinal or bowel catarrh; enteritis

腸癌(ㄔㄤˊ ㄞˊ)
bowel cancer

腸胃(ㄔㄤˊ ㄨㄟˋ)
intestines and the stomach

腸胃病(ㄔㄤˊ ㄨㄟˋ ㄅㄧㄥˋ)
a digestive ailment; the disease of stomach and bowels

【腹】 4711
ㄈㄨˋ fuh fù
1. the belly; under the chest; the abdomen
2. the front part
3. the inside; inner

腹背(ㄈㄨˋ ㄅㄟˋ)
① in front and behind ② close

腹背之毛(ㄈㄨˋ ㄅㄟˋ ㄓ ㄇㄠˊ)
(literally) feathers on the back and underside (of a bird)—unimportant

腹背受敵(ㄈㄨˋ ㄅㄟˋ ㄕㄡˋ ㄉㄧˊ)
to be attacked from front and rear

腹部(ㄈㄨˋ ㄅㄨˋ)
the abdominal region; the abdomen; the belly

腹部運動(ㄈㄨˋ ㄅㄨˋ ㄩㄣˋ ㄉㄨㄥˋ)
physical exercise for the abdominal region

腹膜(ㄈㄨˋ ㄇㄛˊ)
the peritoneum

腹膜炎(ㄈㄨˋ ㄇㄛˊ ㄧㄢˊ)
peritonitis

腹誹(ㄈㄨˋ ㄈㄟ)or **腹非**(ㄈㄨˋ ㄈㄟ)
silent curses or disagreement; to criticize in one's mind

腹地(ㄈㄨˋ ㄉㄧˋ)
a hinterland; the interior

腹痛(ㄈㄨˋ ㄊㄨㄥˋ)
bellyache

腹稿(ㄈㄨˋ ㄍㄠˇ)
(literally) a manuscript in the mind—a rough plan or sketch not yet put down in black and white

腹呼吸(ㄈㄨˋ ㄏㄨ ㄒㄧ)
abdominal respiration

腹瀉(ㄈㄨˋ ㄒㄧㄝˋ)
diarrhea

腹心(ㄈㄨˋ ㄒㄧㄣ)
the belly and the heart — (figuratively)① true thoughts and feelings ② trusted subordinates③ a close friend

腹心之患(ㄈㄨˋ ㄒㄧㄣ ㄓ ㄏㄨㄢˋ)
danger from within; danger posed by an enemy lurking nearby

覆式呼吸(ㄈㄨˋ ㄕˋ ㄏㄨ ㄒㄧ)or **腹部呼吸**(ㄈㄨˋ ㄅㄨˋ ㄏㄨ ㄒㄧ)
deep or abdominal breathing

腹熱心煎(ㄈㄨˋ ㄖㄜˋ ㄒㄧㄣ ㄐㄧㄢ)
to hope anxiously; to look forward to something very eagerly

腹足類動物(ㄈㄨˋ ㄗㄨˊ ㄌㄟˋ ㄉㄨㄥˋ ㄨˋ)
the gastropod

腹誹(ㄈㄨˋ ㄈㄟ)
a silent censure; to criticize in one's mind

腹有鱗甲(ㄈㄨˋ ㄧㄡˇ ㄌㄧㄣˊ ㄐㄧㄚˇ)
vicious; treacherous

腹語(ㄈㄨˋ ㄩˇ)
ventriloquy, or ventriloquism

【腩】 4712
ㄋㄢˇ naan nǎn
tender beef

【腺】 4713
ㄒㄧㄢˋ shiann xiàn
a gland

腺體(ㄒㄧㄢˋ ㄊㄧˇ)
a gland

【腼】 4714
ㄇㄧㄢˇ mean miǎn
1. shy; bashful
2. (said of girls) quiet and graceful

腼腆(ㄇㄧㄢˇ ㄊㄧㄢˇ)
bashful; shy: 這孩子見了生人有點腼腆。 The child is shy with strangers.

【腭】 4715
(齶)ㄜˋ eh è
the roof of the mouth; the palate

【腮】 4716
(顋)ㄙㄞ sai sāi
the cheeks: 這小孩腮頰緋紅。 The boy has rosy cheeks.

腮幫子(ㄙㄞ ㄅㄤ·ㄗ)
(colloquial) the cheek

〔肉部〕

十畫

【腿】 4717
（ㄊㄨㄟˇ toei tuǐ）
the legs and the thighs
腿肚子（ㄊㄨㄟˇ ㄉㄨˋ ㄗ）
the calf of the leg
腿腳兒（ㄊㄨㄟˇ ㄐㄧㄠˇ）
steps; gaits; strides

【膀】 4718 1.
（ㄅㄤˇ baang bǎng）
the upper arms
膀臂（ㄅㄤˇ ㄅㄧˋ）
① the arms ② capable aides
膀子（ㄅㄤˇ ㄗ）
① the shoulder ② the upper arm

【膀】 4718 2.
（ㄆㄤ parng pāng）
the bladder
膀胱（ㄆㄤ ㄍㄨㄤ）
the bladder
膀胱結石（ㄆㄤ ㄍㄨㄤ ㄐㄧㄝˊ ㄕˊ）
a calculus of the bladder; a bladder stone
膀胱炎（ㄆㄤ ㄍㄨㄤ ㄧㄢ）
cystitis; inflammation of the bladder
膀胱癌（ㄆㄤ ㄍㄨㄤ ㄞˊ）
bladder cancer

【膀】 4718 3.
（ㄅㄤˋ banq bàng）
to make passes at (used in the phrase 弔膀子)

【膂】 4719
（ㄌㄩˇ leu lǚ）
1. the spinal column; the backbone
2. one's physical strength
膂力（ㄌㄩˇ ㄌㄧˋ）
one's physical strength

【膈】 4720
（ㄍㄜˊ ger gé）
the diaphragm

【膏】 4721 1.
（ㄍㄠ gau gāo）
1. fat; grease
2. ointment
3. fertile
4. the region just below the heart
5. grace; favors
6. sweet
7. (Chinese medicine) a paste-like preparation for external use
8. plaster
9. (food and fruit) cooked to a very thick or pasty form
膏沐（ㄍㄠ ㄇㄨˋ）
oil or grease women used to render their hair glossy in former days
膏粱子弟（ㄍㄠ ㄌㄧㄤˊ ㄗˇ ㄉㄧˋ）
piggish and ignorant offspring of the rich families; fops
膏油（ㄍㄠ ㄧㄡˊ）
lamp oil
膏肓（ㄍㄠ ㄏㄨㄤ）
the vital region between the heart and diaphragm
膏壤（ㄍㄠ ㄖㄤˇ）
fertile land
膏澤（ㄍㄠ ㄗㄜˊ）
good grace; great favors; the blessings
膏藥（ㄍㄠ ㄧㄠˋ）
① medicated plaster attached to pieces of cloth or paper
② propaganda; boastful claims
膏油（ㄍㄠ ㄧㄡˊ）
grease; lard
膏腴之地（ㄍㄠ ㄩˊ ㄓ ㄉㄧˋ）
fertile land
膏雨（ㄍㄠ ㄩˇ）
a timely rain

【膏】 4721 2.
（ㄍㄠˋ gaw gào）
1. to lubricate; to grease; to make smooth or glossy
2. to enrich; to freshen
膏油（ㄍㄠˋ ㄧㄡˊ）
to add lubricating oil

【膆】 4722
（ㄙㄨˋ suh sù）
1. the crop of a bird or fowl
2. fat
膆囊（ㄙㄨˋ ㄋㄤˊ）
the crop of a fowl

【膊】 4723
（ㄅㄛˊ bor bó）
the shoulders; the upper arms

十一畫

【膚】 4724
（ㄈㄨ fu fū）
1. the skin; the surface: 他的皮膚是棕色的。He has a brown skin.
2. skin-deep; shallow; superficial
3. (now rare) great, as achieve-ments or merit
膚皮（ㄈㄨ ㄆㄧˊ）
dry, dandruff-like scales of the dead skin on the body
膚泛（ㄈㄨ ㄈㄢˋ）
(said of a piece of writing, a speech, etc.) shallow and way off the mark; superficial and off the beam
膚覺（ㄈㄨ ㄐㄩㄝˊ）
cutaneous sensation
膚淺（ㄈㄨ ㄑㄧㄢˇ）
shallow or superficial (views, etc.); skin-deep
膚如凝脂（ㄈㄨ ㄖㄨˊ ㄋㄧㄥˊ ㄓ）
a creamy skin
膚色（ㄈㄨ ㄙㄜˋ）
color of the skin
膚色歧視（ㄈㄨ ㄙㄜˋ ㄑㄧˊ ㄕˋ）
racial discrimination

【膜】 4725 1.
（又讀 ㄇㄛˊ mo mó）
1. membrane: 細胞膜 cell membrane
2. a film; a thin coating
膜翅目（ㄇㄛˊ ㄔˋ ㄇㄨˋ）
(zoology) Hymenoptera
膜外（ㄇㄛˊ ㄨㄞˋ）
outside of one's attention, consideration, etc.

【膜】 4725 2.
（ㄇㄛˊ mo mó）
to kneel and worship
膜拜（ㄇㄛˊ ㄅㄞˋ）
to kneel and worship

【膝】 4726
（ㄒㄧ shi xī）
the knee
膝步（ㄒㄧ ㄅㄨˋ）or 膝行（ㄒㄧ ㄒㄧㄥˊ）
to walk on knees (a gesture of submission)
膝袒（ㄒㄧ ㄊㄢˇ）
to walk on knees and bare one's breast—a gesture of the deepest apology
膝蓋（ㄒㄧ ㄍㄞˋ）
a knee
膝蓋骨（ㄒㄧ ㄍㄞˋ ㄍㄨˇ）
the kneecap; the patella
膝關節（ㄒㄧ ㄍㄨㄢ ㄐㄧㄝˊ）
a knee joint
膝席（ㄒㄧ ㄒㄧˊ）
to kneel on a mat which was used as a substitute for a table in ancient times
膝下（ㄒㄧ ㄒㄧㄚˋ）

respectful address for one's parents in letters

膝下承歡(ㄒㄧ ㄒㄧㄚˋ ㄔㄥˊ ㄏㄨㄢ)
to please one's parents by living with them

膝癢搔背(ㄒㄧ ㄧㄤˇ ㄙㄠ ㄅㄟˋ)
(literally) to scratch the back while the knee is itching—entirely missing the point; irrelevant

【縢】 4727 ㄊㄥˊ terng téng
1. name of a state in the Epoch of Spring and Autumn in today's Shantung Province
2. a Chinese family name

縢王閣(ㄊㄥˊ ㄨㄤˊ ㄍㄜˊ)
a famous resort in Kiangsi Province, where Wang Po (王勃) composed his famous verse of dedication in his teens

【膠】 4728 ㄐㄧㄠ jiau jiāo
1. glue; gum
2. resin; sap
3. anything sticky
4. rubber; plastics
5. to stick on or together; to adhere
6. stubborn; obstinate
7. a Chinese family name

膠版(ㄐㄧㄠ ㄅㄢˇ)
an offset plate

膠布(ㄐㄧㄠ ㄅㄨˋ)
rubber cloth; plastic cloth

膠片(ㄐㄧㄠ ㄆㄧㄢˋ)
film

膠棉(ㄐㄧㄠ ㄇㄧㄢˊ)
collodion

膠附(ㄐㄧㄠ ㄈㄨˋ)
to adhere to; to stick together tightly

膠帶(ㄐㄧㄠ ㄉㄞˋ)
an adhesive tape

膠體物(ㄐㄧㄠ ㄊㄧˇ ㄨˋ)
a colloid

膠囊(ㄐㄧㄠ ㄋㄤˊ)
a medical capsule

膠固(ㄐㄧㄠ ㄍㄨˋ)
①sturdy; strong ②obstinate; stubborn

膠合板(ㄐㄧㄠ ㄏㄜˊ ㄅㄢˇ)
plywood

膠濟鐵路(ㄐㄧㄠ ㄐㄧˋ ㄊㄧㄝˇ ㄌㄨˋ)
the Tsingtao-Tsinan Rail-

way in Shantung Province

膠捲兒(ㄐㄧㄠ ㄐㄩㄢˇ)
unexposed film: 我找到一卷膠捲兒. I found a roll of unexposed film.

膠讒(ㄐㄧㄠ ㄔㄢˊ)
to cheat; to swindle

膠漆(ㄐㄧㄠ ㄑㄧ)
close and intimate; very much in love

膠漆相投(ㄐㄧㄠ ㄑㄧ ㄒㄧㄤ ㄊㄡˊ)
the intimate and complete meeting of minds

膠鞋(ㄐㄧㄠ ㄒㄧㄝˊ)
rubber shoes; galoshes; 我們在下雨天穿膠鞋. We wear galoshes in wet weather.

膠質(ㄐㄧㄠ ㄓˊ)
①gluey; glue ②gelatinous; gelatin

膠州灣(ㄐㄧㄠ ㄓㄡ ㄨㄢ)
the Chaochow Gulf in the Yellow Sea

膠柱鼓瑟(ㄐㄧㄠ ㄓㄨˋ ㄍㄨˇ ㄙㄜˋ)
obstinate; inflexible; very conservative

膠著(ㄐㄧㄠ ㄓㄨㄛˊ)
stalemated; at a stalemate; a standstill: 戰爭情勢已成膠著狀態. The warfare was at a stalemate.

膠語(ㄐㄧㄠ ㄩˇ)
an agglutinative language

膠水(ㄐㄧㄠ ㄕㄨㄟˇ)
glue; size: 請用膠水粘. Please stick it with glue.

【膛】 4729 ㄊㄤˊ tarng táng
1. the breast; the chest
2. a cavity
3. the chamber of a firearm

【膣】 4730 ㄓ jyh zhí
the vagina

十二畫

【膨】 4731 ㄆㄥˊ perng péng
to expand; to swell; to inflate

膨脝(ㄆㄥˊ ㄏㄥ)
(said of the stomach) full; loaded

膨脹(ㄆㄥˊ ㄓㄤˋ)
expansion; swelling; inflation; bloated; to expand; to

swell: 熱使金屬膨脹. Heat expands metals.

膨脹係數(ㄆㄥˊ ㄓㄤˋ ㄒㄧˋ ㄕㄨˋ)
coefficient of expansion

【膩】 4732 ㄋㄧˋ nih nì
1. fatty or greasy (food)
2. smooth
3. dirty
4. bored; tired; weary
5. intimate (friends)

膩煩(ㄋㄧˋ ㄈㄢˊ)
①bored; tired; to be fed up ②to loathe; to hate

膩得慌(ㄋㄧˋ ㄉㄜ˙ ㄏㄨㄤ)
very depressed and listless

膩人(ㄋㄧˋ ㄖㄣˊ)
①boring; tiresome ②too greasy

膩友(ㄋㄧˋ ㄧㄡˇ)
bosom friends

膩胃(ㄋㄧˋ ㄨㄟˋ)
(said of rich, greasy food) to kill one's appetite

【膳】 4733 ㄕㄢˋ shann shàn
meals; food; provisions

膳費(ㄕㄢˋ ㄈㄟˋ)
charges for board

膳房(ㄕㄢˋ ㄈㄤˊ)
①the imperial kitchen 亦作「御膳房」②a kitchen

膳夫(ㄕㄢˋ ㄈㄨ)
①the chief cook in charge of the royal family's victuals ②a cook

膳廳(ㄕㄢˋ ㄊㄧㄥ)or膳堂(ㄕㄢˋ ㄊㄤˊ)
a mess hall; a dining hall

膳食(ㄕㄢˋ ㄕˊ)
meat; victuals

膳宿(ㄕㄢˋ ㄙㄨˋ)
food and lodging

膳宿費(ㄕㄢˋ ㄙㄨˋ ㄈㄟˋ)
charges for board and lodging; boarding charges

膳宿生(ㄕㄢˋ ㄙㄨˋ ㄕㄥ)
a boarding student

【膰】 4734 ㄈㄢˊ farn fán
cooked meat for sacrifice or offering

十三畫

【膿】 4735 ㄋㄨㄥˊ nong nóng
pus or purulent matter

〔肉部〕

【肉部】

膿包(ㄋㄨㄥ ㄅㄠ)
①a pustule; an abscess ② a good-for-nothing; a useless person

膿血(ㄋㄨㄥ ㄒㄧㄝˇ)
pus and blood

膿腫(ㄋㄨㄥ ㄓㄨㄥˇ)
purulence

膿腫(ㄋㄨㄥ ㄓㄨㄥˇ)
purulent swellings

膿瘡(ㄋㄨㄥ ㄔㄨㄤ)
an abscess; a boil

膿水(ㄋㄨㄥ ㄕㄨㄟˇ)
pus

【膽】 4736

(胆) ㄉㄢˇ daan dǎn

1. the gall
2. courage; bravery; audacity: 他是個有膽量的人。He is a man of courage.
3. the internal parts, etc. of a vessel
4. the tube of a tire, basketball, etc.

膽破(ㄉㄢˇ ㄆㄛˋ)
to be frightened or scared to death

膽瓶(ㄉㄢˇ ㄆㄧㄥˊ)
a hanging-gall-shaped bottle

膽礬(ㄉㄢˇ ㄈㄢˊ)
chalcanthite

膽大(ㄉㄢˇ ㄉㄚˋ)
bold; audacious 亦作「大膽」

膽大包天(ㄉㄢˇ ㄉㄚˋ ㄅㄠ ㄊㄧㄢ)
extremely audacious; recklessly bold

膽大心細(ㄉㄢˇ ㄉㄚˋ ㄒㄧㄣ ㄒㄧˋ)
brave but cautious; courageous but careful or circumspective

膽大妄為(ㄉㄢˇ ㄉㄚˋ ㄨㄤˋ ㄨㄟˊ)
audacious and reckless

膽囊(ㄉㄢˇ ㄋㄤˊ)
(anatomy)the gall bladder

膽囊炎(ㄉㄢˇ ㄋㄤˊ ㄧㄢˊ)
cholecystitis

膽力(ㄉㄢˇ ㄌㄧˋ)
courage; bravery

膽裂(ㄉㄢˇ ㄌㄧㄝˋ)
scared to death

膽量(ㄉㄢˇ ㄌㄧㄤˋ)
courage; bravery; guts

膽落(ㄉㄢˇ ㄌㄨㄛˋ)
extremely frightened

膽略(ㄉㄢˇ ㄌㄩㄝˋ)
courage and resourcefulness

so audacious as to; reckless to the extent of; to dare

膽固醇(ㄉㄢˇ ㄍㄨˋ ㄔㄨㄣˊ)
cholesterol; cholesterin

膽怯(ㄉㄢˇ ㄑㄧㄝ)
scared; to lose one's nerve

膽怯(ㄉㄢˇ ㄑㄧㄝˋ)
frightened; afraid; fainthearted

膽小(ㄉㄢˇ ㄒㄧㄠˇ)
timid; cowardly

膽小鬼(ㄉㄢˇ ㄒㄧㄠˇ ㄍㄨㄟˇ)
a coward: 沒有人願意被認為是膽小鬼。No one wants to be thought a coward.

膽小如鼠(ㄉㄢˇ ㄒㄧㄠˇ ㄖㄨˊ ㄕㄨˇ)
as scared as a mouse; as timid as a mouse: 她膽小如鼠。She is as timid as a mouse.

膽虛(ㄉㄢˇ ㄒㄩ)
nervous; jittery; scared

膽汁(ㄉㄢˇ ㄓ)
bile

膽汁質(ㄉㄢˇ ㄓ ㄓˋ)or膽液質(ㄉㄢˇ ㄧㄝˋ)
choleric temperament

膽戰心驚(ㄉㄢˇ ㄓㄢˋ ㄒㄧㄣ ㄐㄧㄥ)
scared and jittery; nervous and jumpy; to tremble with fear

膽壯(ㄉㄢˇ ㄓㄨㄤˋ)
to be full of courage; fearless

膽石(ㄉㄢˇ ㄕˊ)or膽石症(ㄉㄢˇ ㄕˊ ㄓㄥˋ)
a gallstone

膽識(ㄉㄢˇ ㄕˋ)
courage and wisdom

膽子(ㄉㄢˇ ˙ㄗ)or膽兒(ㄉㄢˇㄦ)
courage; bravery; audacity; nerve

【膾】 4737

ㄎㄨㄞˋ kuay kuài

minced meat

膾炙(ㄎㄨㄞˋ ㄓˋ)
minced and roasted—very tasty

膾炙人口(ㄎㄨㄞˋ ㄓˋ ㄖㄣˊ ㄎㄡˇ)
(said of interesting things, good writings, etc.) to be on everybody's lips; to be talked about by everyone: 他的英勇事蹟膾炙人口。His heroic deeds are on everybody's lips.

【膺】 4738

ㄧㄥ ing yīng

1. the breast of a person
2. (now rarely) a belt across the breast of a horse
3. to receive; to be given (a responsibility, etc.); to undertake; to shoulder; to bear; to sustain
4. (now rarely) to punish (the enemy, etc.) by war

膺期(ㄧㄥ ㄑㄧˊ)
to receive or inherit (a title, the throne, etc.)

膺選(ㄧㄥ ㄒㄩㄢˇ)
to be elected

膺任(ㄧㄥ ㄖㄣˋ)
to be appointed to or given (an office, etc.)

【臀】 4739

ㄊㄨㄣˊ twen tún

1. the buttocks; the behind; the bottom; the rump
2. (now rarely) the bottom of a ware or vessel

臀部(ㄊㄨㄣˊ ㄅㄨˋ)
the buttocks; the bottom; the rump

【臂】 4740

ㄅㄧˋ bih bì
(又讀 ㄅㄟ bey bèi)

the arms (of a human being or a tool, machine, etc.)

臂膊(ㄅㄧˋ ㄅㄛˊ)
the two arms (of a person)

臂膀(ㄅㄧˋ ㄅㄤˇ)
the arm (usually indicating the upper arm and part of the shoulder)

臂環(ㄅㄧˋ ㄏㄨㄢˊ)
bracelets

臂節(ㄅㄧˋ ㄐㄧㄝˊ)
the elbow (of a piece of machinery)

臂章(ㄅㄧˋ ㄓㄤ)
an arm badge; a brassard: 軍人通常帶著臂章。Soldiers usually have arm badges on.

臂助(ㄅㄧˋ ㄓㄨˋ)
a helping hand; help

【臃】 4741

ㄩㄥ yeong yōng
(又讀 ㄩㄥ iong yǒng)

1. to swell; a swelling
2. fat and clumsy

臃腫(ㄩㄥ ㄓㄨㄥˇ)
fat and clumsy

【臆】 4742 （ㄧ` yìh yì）
1. one's breast, heart, thoughts, etc.
2. one's personal views or feelings

臆度（ㄉㄨㄛˋ）or 臆測（ㄘㄜˋ）
to guess or conjecture; speculation

臆斷 to draw a conclusion from conjecture; an arbitrary judgment

臆說（ㄕㄨㄛ）
one's personal assumption or conjecture; a hypothesis

臆造（ㄗㄠˋ）
to fabricate (a story, reason, etc.); to concoct; to make up

【臉】 4743 （ㄌㄧㄢˇ lean liǎn）
the face (used both in its physical and figurative senses)

臉蛋兒（ㄌㄧㄢˇ ㄉㄢˋ ˙ㄦ）or 臉盤兒（ㄌㄧㄢˇ ㄆㄢˊㄦ）
the shape of one's face; a facial configuration 亦作「臉龐」

臉盆（ㄌㄧㄢˇ ㄆㄣˊ）
a washing basin

臉皮（ㄌㄧㄢˇ ㄆㄧˊ）
the cheek; one's face (in its figurative sense)

臉皮薄（ㄌㄧㄢˇ ㄆㄧˊ ㄅㄛˊ）
very sensitive; easily getting embarrassed or bashful

臉皮厚（ㄌㄧㄢˇ ㄆㄧˊ ㄏㄡˋ）
thick-skinned; brazen; shameless

臉譜（ㄌㄧㄢˇ ㄆㄨˇ）
(Chinese opera) face paintings indicating the personality, dispositions, etc. of the characters

臉面（ㄌㄧㄢˇ ㄇㄧㄢˋ）
face—(figuratively) sake

臉大（ㄌㄧㄢˇ ㄉㄚˋ）
①a big face—rather influential ②(usually said of women) unabashed

臉蛋兒（ㄌㄧㄢˇ ㄉㄢˋㄦ）or 臉蛋子（ㄌㄧㄢˇ ㄉㄢˋ ˙ㄗ）
the shape of a woman's face

臉嫩（ㄌㄧㄢˇ ㄋㄨㄣˋ）
bashful; shy; timid

臉孔（ㄌㄧㄢˇ ㄎㄨㄥˇ）
the face: 這次聚會我看到幾張新臉孔。I saw some new faces at the party.

臉皮厚（ㄌㄧㄢˇ ㄆㄧˊ ㄏㄡˋ）
brazen; shameless

臉紅（ㄌㄧㄢˇ ㄏㄨㄥˊ）
blushing because of embarrassment, anger or shame; a blush; to blush

臉紅脖子粗（ㄌㄧㄢˇ ㄏㄨㄥˊ ㄅㄛˊ ˙ㄗ ㄘㄨ）
furious; mad

臉頰（ㄌㄧㄢˇ ㄐㄧㄚˊ）
cheeks

臉上（ㄌㄧㄢˇ ㄕㄤˋ）
①in (or on) the face: 陽光直射在我們的臉上。The sun was shining in our faces. ②face (in its figurative sense)

臉水（ㄌㄧㄢˇ ㄕㄨㄟˇ）
water for washing one's face

臉軟（ㄌㄧㄢˇ ㄖㄨㄢˇ）
kindhearted; good-natured; unable to hurt others' feelings

臉色（ㄌㄧㄢˇ ㄙㄜˋ）
①facial expression ②a complexion

臉硬（ㄌㄧㄢˇ ㄧㄥˋ）
flinty; devoid of emotion or compassion; ruthless

【臊】 4744 1. （ㄙㄠ sau sāo）
a bad odor or smell, as that of decaying fish, meat, fox, sheep, etc.

臊韃子（ㄙㄠ ㄉㄚˊ ˙ㄗ）
(an abusive expression for) Mongols

臊根（ㄙㄠ ㄍㄣ）
the penis

臊氣（ㄙㄠ ㄑㄧˋ）
a bad odor or smell; a stench

臊聲（ㄙㄠ ㄕㄥ）or 臊聞（ㄙㄠ ㄨㄣˊ）
notoriety; a scandalous reputation

【臊】 4744 2. （ㄙㄠˋ saw sào）
1. ashamed; bashful
2. minced meat

臊得慌（ㄙㄠˋ ˙ㄉㄜ ㄏㄨㄤ）
very much ashamed

【臌】 4745 （ㄍㄨˇ guu gǔ）
to expand; to swell; swollen

臌脹（ㄍㄨˇ ㄓㄤˋ）
①expansion; to expand; to swell ②dropsy; edema

【膽】 4746 （ㄕㄥˋ sheng shèng）
See「脹 5805」under the radical「貝」.

【膻】 4747 （羶）（ㄕㄢ shan shān）
the bad odor of sheep, deer, etc.

十四畫

【臏】 4748 （髕）（ㄅㄧㄣˋ binn bìn）
1. the kneecap
2. the punishment of removing kneecaps in ancient times

臏骨（ㄅㄧㄣˋ ㄍㄨˇ）
the kneecap

【臍】 4749 （ㄑㄧˊ chyi qí）
1. the navel; the umbilicus
2. the underside of a crab

臍帶（ㄑㄧˊ ㄉㄞˋ）
the umbilical cord: 臍帶未脫。The umbilical cord is still on.

十五畫

【臘】 4750 （ㄌㄚˋ lah là）
1. sacrifice at the end of the lunar year
2. the end of the lunar year
3. salted and smoked meat, fish, chicken, etc.
4. the age of a Buddhist monk

臘八（ㄌㄚˋ ㄅㄚ）or 臘八日（ㄌㄚˋ ㄅㄚ ㄖˋ）
the 8th day of the 12th moon in the lunar calendar when Buddha found the truth of life

臘八米（ㄌㄚˋ ㄅㄚ ㄇㄧˇ）
glutinous rice, mixed grains and cereals and dried fruit for cooking 臘八粥

臘八粥（ㄌㄚˋ ㄅㄚ ㄓㄡ）
congee or porridge of glutinous rice, mixed grains and cereals and dried fruit, eaten on the 8th day of the 12th moon, originally in memory of the Buddhist Festival

臘梅（ㄌㄚˋ ㄇㄟˊ）
plum flowers

臘丁（ㄌㄚˋ ㄉㄧㄥ）

Latin 亦作「拉丁」

臘鼓 (ㄌㄚˋ ㄍㄨˇ)
drumbeat on the eighth day of the twelfth month by the ancient calendar (for driving off devils causing pestilence)

臘祭 (ㄌㄚˋ ㄐㄧˋ)
the ancient winter sacrificial ceremony held three days after the winter solstice (冬至)

臘盡多殘 (ㄌㄚˋ ㄐㄧㄣˋ ㄉㄨㄛ ㄘㄢˊ)
The (lunar) year and the winter are ending.

臘腸 (ㄌㄚˋ ㄔㄤˊ)
Chinese sausage made by stuffing salted meat, liver, etc. in casings

臘腸狗 (ㄌㄚˋ ㄔㄤˊ ㄍㄡˇ)
a dachshund

臘肉 (ㄌㄚˋ ㄖㄡˋ)
salted and dried meat

臘鴨 (ㄌㄚˋ ㄧㄚ)
salted and dried duck

臘味 (ㄌㄚˋ ㄨㄟˋ)
preserved meat; cured meat, fish, etc.

臘味飯 (ㄌㄚˋ ㄨㄟˋ ㄈㄢˋ)
a Cantonese dish consisting of steamed rice and salted meat, sausage, etc.

臘魚 (ㄌㄚˋ ㄩˊ)
salted and dried fish

臘月 (ㄌㄚˋ ㄩㄝˋ)
the 12th moon of the lunar year

【膘】 4751
(膔) ㄅㄧㄠ biau
biāo
fat

十六畫

【臚】 4752
ㄌㄨˊ lu lú
1. to display; to exhibit; to arrange in order
2. the belly
3. the skin
4. to forward; to convey; to announce

臚列 (ㄌㄨˊ ㄌㄧㄝˋ)
to display; to arrange in order for exhibit

臚歡 (ㄌㄨˊ ㄏㄨㄢ)
to convey one's pleasure; to express one's joy

臚情 (ㄌㄨˊ ㄑㄧㄥˊ)
to state one's case, situation, predicament; to report on such

【臙】 4753
(臙) ㄧㄢ ian yān
rouge, face powder or cosmetics

十七畫

【臝】 4754
ㄌㄨㄛˇ luoo luǒ
to bare; nude

十八畫

【臟】 4755
ㄗㄤˋ tzanq zàng
a general name of all the internal organs in the chest and abdomen; the viscera

臟腑 (ㄗㄤˋ ㄈㄨˇ)
① viscera; entrails ② one's integrity, aspirations, etc.

十九畫

【臠】 4756
ㄌㄨㄢˊ luan luán
1. meat chops or cuts
2. lean; thin

【臢】 4757
ㄗㄤ tzang zāng
(又讀 ㄗㄚ tza zā)
dirty; filthy

【臡】 4758
ㄋㄧˊ ni ní
pickled, minced meat

臣 部
彳ㄣˊ chern chén

【臣】 4759
彳ㄣˊ chern chén
1. a subject; a vassal
2. to subjugate; to conquer
3. a term for "I" used by officials when addressing the king or emperor
4. (in ancient China) a polite term for "I"
5. a minister; an official; a statesman

臣僕 (彳ㄣˊ ㄆㄨˊ)
officials (who serve the king or nation) and servants (who serve the household)

臣民 (彳ㄣˊ ㄇㄧㄣˊ)
subjects of a kingdom; subjects of a feudal ruler

臣服 (彳ㄣˊ ㄈㄨˊ)
① to be subjugated or conquered; to be made a subject ② to serve a king or emperor as his minister

臣妾 (彳ㄣˊ ㄑㄧㄝˋ)
(in ancient China) a self-reference of a prince born by an imperial concubine in speaking to the monarch

臣僚 (彳ㄣˊ ㄌㄧㄠˊ)
officials in a kingdom or monarchy

臣工 (彳ㄣˊ ㄍㄨㄥ)
ministers and officials

臣妾 (彳ㄣˊ ㄑㄧㄝˋ)
slaves; concubines; humble people; female attendants

臣下 (彳ㄣˊ ㄒㄧㄚˋ)
① a term for "I" used by an official when addressing a king or emperor ② ministers

臣事 (彳ㄣˊ ㄕˋ)
to serve a ruler as his minister

臣庶 (彳ㄣˊ ㄕㄨˋ)
subjects

臣子 (彳ㄣˊ ㄗˇ)
a minister of state; officials in ancient China

臣一主二 (彳ㄣˊ ㄧ ㄓㄨˇ ㄦˋ)
One has the right of choosing the ruler he serves.

一畫

【臣】 4760
(臣) ㄧˋ yi yì
the cheeks

二畫

【臥】 4761
ㄨㄛˋ woh wò
1. to lie down; to rest; to sleep

2. to lay or place across; to lie across

臥冰(ㄨㄛˋ ㄅㄧㄥ)
to lie on ice (in order to melt it and catch fish to feed one's parents)—the highest show of filial piety

臥病(ㄨㄛˋ ㄅㄧㄥˋ)
bedridden on account of illness

臥鋪(ㄨㄛˋ ㄆㄨˋ)
a sleeping berth on a train or ship

臥佛(ㄨㄛˋ ㄈㄛˊ)
a statue of Buddha in a lying position

臥房(ㄨㄛˋ ㄈㄤˊ)or臥屋(ㄨㄛˋ ㄨ)
a bedroom

臥倒(ㄨㄛˋ ㄉㄠˇ)
to lie down (on the ground to escape enemy fire or detection)

臥底(ㄨㄛˋ ㄉㄧˇ)
(said of thieves, etc.) to act from inside, or do an inside job; to act as a stool pigeon

臥榻(ㄨㄛˋ ㄊㄚˋ)or臥牀(ㄨㄛˋ ㄔㄨㄤˊ)
a bed

臥內(ㄨㄛˋ ㄋㄟˋ)
a bedroom

臥龍(ㄨㄛˋ ㄌㄨㄥˊ)
the sleeping dragon—a remarkable talent who has not been discovered

臥龍岡(ㄨㄛˋ ㄌㄨㄥˊ ㄍㄤ)
the Sleeping Dragon Hill, in Honan Province—where Chu-Ko Kung-ming (諸葛孔明), a brilliant military strategist in the Epoch of the Three Kingdoms, was supposed to have lived before he was recruited by Liu Pei (劉備), the ruler of Shu (蜀)

臥軌自殺(ㄨㄛˋ ㄍㄨㄟˇ ㄗˋ ㄕㄚ)
to commit suicide by throwing oneself on a railroad

臥虎(ㄨㄛˋ ㄏㄨˇ)
①a severe law-enforcing official ②a tyrannical official ③the awe inspired by a high government official ④a brave general

臥具(ㄨㄛˋ ㄐㄩˋ)
bedding

臥起(ㄨㄛˋ ㄑㄧˇ)
to sleep and get up—things

pertaining to daily life

臥薪嘗膽(ㄨㄛˋ ㄒㄧㄣ ㄔㄤˊ ㄉㄢˇ)
(literally) to lie on faggots and taste gall—to goad oneself ahead by depriving oneself of all daily comforts and subjecting oneself to life's bitterness (a reference to Kou Chien (勾踐)when he was nursing vengeance)

臥雪(ㄨㄛˋ ㄒㄩㄝˇ)
(literally) to stay at home without bothering others when it snows heavily—the behavior of a man of integrity and superiority

臥治(ㄨㄛˋ ㄓˋ)
to govern without interfering with the people

臥車(ㄨㄛˋ ㄔㄜ)
a railway sleeping car, or sleeper

臥床(ㄨㄛˋ ㄔㄨㄤˊ)
to lie in bed

臥室(ㄨㄛˋ ㄕˋ)
a bedroom

臥姿(ㄨㄛˋ ㄗ)
a prone position; a lying position

臥遊(ㄨㄛˋ ㄧㄡˊ)
to make a vicarious sightseeing tour by viewing landscape paintings or by reading travelogues, etc.

臥雲(ㄨㄛˋ ㄩㄣˊ)
to make clouds one's bed—the life of a hermit

八畫

【臧】 ⁴⁷⁶²
ㄗㄤ tzang zōng
1. good; right; generous
2. a slave; a servant
3. stolen goods or loots 亦作「贓」
4. a Chinese family name

臧否(ㄗㄤ ㄆㄧˇ)
①right or wrong; gain or loss ②to evaluate; to criticize; to pass judgment

臧獲(ㄗㄤ ㄏㄨㄛˋ)
slaves

十一畫

【臨】 ⁴⁷⁶³
ㄌㄧㄣˊ lin lín

1. to look down from above —preside over
2. to approach; to descend; to come to; to reach; to visit: 聖誕節即將來臨。Christmas is approaching.
3. on the point of; near to; during; at; whilst; while
4. to copy; to imitate
5. temporary; provisional
6. a Chinese family name

〔臣部〕

臨別(ㄌㄧㄣˊ ㄅㄧㄝˊ)
at the time of parting; on departure: 她在臨別時哭了。She cried at the time of parting.

臨別贈言(ㄌㄧㄣˊ ㄅㄧㄝˊ ㄗㄥˋ ㄧㄢˊ)
advice given by one just before parting

臨盆(ㄌㄧㄣˊ ㄆㄣˊ)
parturition; childbirth

臨摹(ㄌㄧㄣˊ ㄇㄛˊ)
to copy or imitate (paintings or calligraphy)

臨命(ㄌㄧㄣˊ ㄇㄧㄥˋ)
on the point of breathing one's last; before death

臨到(ㄌㄧㄣˊ ㄉㄠˋ)
to approach; to come to; to reach; to happen to

臨難(ㄌㄧㄣˊ ㄋㄢˊ)
(said of disasters) descending; imminent; hovering over the head: 大難臨頭。A great calamity is imminent.

臨帖(ㄌㄧㄣˊ ㄊㄧㄝˋ)
to copy or imitate calligraphy as a way of practice

臨眺(ㄌㄧㄣˊ ㄊㄧㄠˋ)
to view from a high point

臨難(ㄌㄧㄣˊ ㄋㄢˊ)
beset by disasters or troubles; at difficult times

臨年(ㄌㄧㄣˊ ㄋㄧㄢˊ)
at an advanced age

臨了(ㄌㄧㄣˊ ㄌㄧㄠˇ)or臨了兒(ㄌㄧㄣˊ ㄌㄧㄠˇ ㄦ)
in the end; at last

臨渴掘井(ㄌㄧㄣˊ ㄎㄜˇ ㄐㄩㄝˊ ㄐㄧㄥˇ)
(literally) to dig a well when one feels thirsty—to do something too late and without preparations; to make no timely preparations

臨畫(ㄌㄧㄣˊ ㄏㄨㄚˋ)
to copy a painting

臨機應變(ㄌㄧㄣˊ ㄐㄧ ㄧㄥˋ ㄅㄧㄢˋ)

〔臣部〕

to make changes or adjustments as the situation demands; to act according to what the circumstances dictate

臨急 (ㄌㄧㄣˊ ㄐㄧˊ)
in time of emergency

臨街 (ㄌㄧㄣˊ ㄐㄧㄝ)
facing the street

臨界點 (ㄌㄧㄣˊ ㄐㄧㄝˋ ㄉㄧㄢˇ)
(physics) a critical point

臨界角 (ㄌㄧㄣˊ ㄐㄧㄝˋ ㄐㄧㄠˇ)
(physics) a critical angle

臨界溫度 (ㄌㄧㄣˊ ㄐㄧㄝˋ ㄨㄣ ㄉㄨˋ)
(physics) critical temperature

臨近 (ㄌㄧㄣˊ ㄐㄧㄣˋ)
close by; close to; close on

臨期 (ㄌㄧㄣˊ ㄑㄧˊ)
to come to the moment; to approach the right time; to mature: 票據本日臨期。The bill matures today.

臨歧 (ㄌㄧㄣˊ ㄑㄧˊ)
to accompany another to where the road branches out

臨去秋波 (ㄌㄧㄣˊ ㄑㄩˋ ㄑㄧㄡ ㄅㄛ)
(literally) to cast a bewitching look on departing—a parting favor; to give others something to remember by before parting

臨行 (ㄌㄧㄣˊ ㄒㄧㄥˊ) or 臨走 (ㄌㄧㄣˊ ㄗㄡˇ)
on the point of departure; just before parting

臨幸 (ㄌㄧㄣˊ ㄒㄧㄥˋ)
a personal visit by the emperor (regarded as a great honor)

臨軒 (ㄌㄧㄣˊ ㄒㄩㄢ)
when the emperor was not taking his seat on the throne

臨陣磨鎗 (ㄌㄧㄣˊ ㄓㄣˋ ㄇㄛˊ ㄑㄧㄤ) or 臨陣磨槍 (ㄌㄧㄣˊ ㄓㄣˋ ㄇㄛˊ ㄑㄧㄤ)
(literally) to grind the spear just before battle—to make preparations at the last moment

臨陣脫逃 (ㄌㄧㄣˊ ㄓㄣˋ ㄊㄨㄛ ㄊㄠˊ)
to escape just before engaging the enemy; to absent oneself when one's presence counts

臨終 (ㄌㄧㄣˊ ㄓㄨㄥ) or 臨死 (ㄌㄧㄣˊ ㄙˇ)
at one's deathbed; just before dying; about to

breathe one's last

臨池 (ㄌㄧㄣˊ ㄔˊ)
to diligently practice calligraphy (a reference to Wang Hsi-chih (王羲之), China's greatest calligrapher who was said to have blackened the water in a pond in practicing calligraphy)

臨朝 (ㄌㄧㄣˊ ㄔㄠˊ)
①to sit on the throne and govern the nation ②(said of an empress dowager) to govern the nation as regent

臨產 (ㄌㄧㄣˊ ㄔㄢˇ)
in childbirth; about to give birth to a child

臨牀 (ㄌㄧㄣˊ ㄔㄨㄤˊ)
clinical

臨牀經驗 (ㄌㄧㄣˊ ㄔㄨㄤˊ ㄐㄧㄥ ㄧㄢˋ): 他有豐富的臨床經驗。He has rich clinical experience.

臨時 (ㄌㄧㄣˊ ㄕˊ)
for the time being; temporary; provisional

臨時抱佛腳 (ㄌㄧㄣˊ ㄕˊ ㄅㄠˋ ㄈㄛˊ ㄐㄧㄠˇ)
(literally) to embrace Buddha's feet and pray for help in time of emergency—to do something too late and without preparation

臨時大總統 (ㄌㄧㄣˊ ㄕˊ ㄉㄚˋ ㄗㄨㄥˇ ㄊㄨㄥˇ)
the president of a provisional government; a provisional president

臨時代辦 (ㄌㄧㄣˊ ㄕˊ ㄉㄞˋ ㄅㄢˋ)
chargé d'affaires ad interim

臨時動議 (ㄌㄧㄣˊ ㄕˊ ㄉㄨㄥˋ ㄧˋ)
an extraordinary motion

臨時工 (ㄌㄧㄣˊ ㄕˊ ㄍㄨㄥ)
a short-term worker; a rush-season worker; an odd-job worker

臨時會 (ㄌㄧㄣˊ ㄕˊ ㄏㄨㄟˋ)
an extraordinary meeting; an unscheduled meeting: 俱樂部召開一次臨時會。The club held an unscheduled meeting.

臨時執照 (ㄌㄧㄣˊ ㄕˊ ㄓˊ ㄓㄠˋ)
a temporary or provisional license

臨時執政 (ㄌㄧㄣˊ ㄕˊ ㄓˊ ㄓㄥˋ)
to govern (the nation) provisionally; a provisional

government

臨時政府 (ㄌㄧㄣˊ ㄕˊ ㄓㄥˋ ㄈㄨˇ)
a provisional government

臨時事故 (ㄌㄧㄣˊ ㄕˊ ㄕˋ ㄍㄨˋ)
an unforeseen matter; an incident; an accident: 這是一樁臨時事故。It was quite an accident.

臨時議會 (ㄌㄧㄣˊ ㄕˊ ㄧˋ ㄏㄨㄟˋ)
a provisional assembly

臨時演員 (ㄌㄧㄣˊ ㄕˊ ㄧㄢˇ ㄩㄢˊ)
an extra

臨時約法 (ㄌㄧㄣˊ ㄕˊ ㄩㄝ ㄈㄚˇ)
the provisional constitution of the Republic of China in the early years of the Republic

臨視 (ㄌㄧㄣˊ ㄕˋ)
(usually said of a bigwig) to investigate something in person; to inspect

臨深履薄 (ㄌㄧㄣˊ ㄕㄣ ㄌㄩˇ ㄅㄛˊ)
wading in deep water and treading on thin ice—very cautious or careful

臨睡 (ㄌㄧㄣˊ ㄕㄨㄟˋ)
before sleep

臨蓐 (ㄌㄧㄣˊ ㄖㄨˋ)
in childbirth; childbirth; lying-in: 她在臨蓐時神經緊張。She got nervous in childbirth.

臨財母苟得，臨難母苟免 (ㄌㄧㄣˊ ㄘㄞˊ ㄇㄨˊ ㄍㄡˇ ㄉㄜˊ, ㄌㄧㄣˊ ㄋㄢˋ ㄇㄨˊ ㄍㄡˇ ㄇㄧㄢˇ)
Don't be unscrupulous in money matters; don't shrink in face of disaster. (from the Book of Rites)

臨安 (ㄌㄧㄣˊ ㄢ)
old name of Hangchow (杭州), capital of the Southern Sung Dynasty

臨崖勒馬 (ㄌㄧㄣˊ ㄧㄞˊ ㄌㄜˋ ㄇㄚˇ)
(literally) to rein in the horse at the edge of a cliff—to practice self-restraint at a crucial moment

臨危 (ㄌㄧㄣˊ ㄨㄟˊ)
①in face of great danger or emergency ②at one's deathbed; just before dying

臨危授命 (ㄌㄧㄣˊ ㄨㄟˊ ㄕㄡˋ ㄇㄧㄥˋ)
to give a very important assignment in time of a national emergency

臨文 (ㄌㄧㄣˊ ㄨㄣˊ)

when one is writing or composing (an article, etc.): 他在臨文時常抽煙。He used to smoke when he was writing.

臨問(ㄌㄧㄣ ㄨㄣˋ)
(said of a dignitary) to visit, cheer up or comfort in person

臨月(ㄌㄧㄣ ㄩㄝˋ)
the month when the childbirth is due

臨淵羨魚(ㄌㄧㄣ ㄩㄢ ㄒㄧㄢˋ ㄩˊ)
(literally) to covet the fish by merely staring into the water—to envy the store of great wealth (but never plan a way to get it)

自 部
ㄗˋ tzyh zì

【自】 4764
ㄗˋ tzyh zì
1. self; personal; private; in person; personally
2. from
3. natural; naturally
4. a Chinese family name

自拔(ㄗˋ ㄅㄚˊ)
to free oneself (from pain or evildoing); to extricate oneself

自白(ㄗˋ ㄅㄞˊ)or(ㄗˋ ㄅㄛˊ)
confession; to make a personal statement

自白書(ㄗˋ ㄅㄞˊ ㄕㄨ)
an affidavit; a written confession

自卑(ㄗˋ ㄅㄟ)
to slight oneself, to despise oneself; to underestimate oneself

自卑感(ㄗˋ ㄅㄟ ㄍㄢˇ)or 自卑情結 (ㄗˋ ㄅㄟ ㄑㄧㄥˊ ㄐㄧㄝˊ)
inferiority complex; a sense of inferiority

自備(ㄗˋ ㄅㄟˋ)
self-provided; to provide oneself

自暴自棄(ㄗˋ ㄅㄠˋ ㄗˋ ㄑㄧˋ)
to abandon oneself to a dissipated life; to have no ambition at all

自本自力(ㄗˋ ㄅㄣˇ ㄗˋ ㄌㄧˋ)

with one's own capital and effort; to do something alone

自必(ㄗˋ ㄅㄧˋ)
naturally; unavoidably; certainly, surely; 我們的球隊自必獲勝。Certainly our team will win the game.

自斃(ㄗˋ ㄅㄧˋ)
to destroy oneself; self-destruction

自閉症(ㄗˋ ㄅㄧˋ ㄓㄥˋ)
(psychiatry) autism

自便(ㄗˋ ㄅㄧㄢˋ)
as one wishes: 聽其自便。Let her do as she wishes.

自不量力(ㄗˋ ㄅㄨˋ ㄌㄧㄤˋ ㄌㄧˋ)
not to recognize one's own limited strength or resources; to do something beyond one's ability

自賣自誇(ㄗˋ ㄇㄞˋ ㄗˋ ㄎㄨㄚ)
to praise the goods one sells; to blow one's own trumpet

自滿(ㄗˋ ㄇㄢˇ)
complacency; to be satisfied with oneself

自民黨(ㄗˋ ㄇㄧㄣˊ ㄉㄤˇ)
Liberal Democratic Party in Japan

自鳴得意(ㄗˋ ㄇㄧㄥˊ ㄉㄜˊ ㄧˋ)
to be very much pleased with what one has done or what one has achieved; smug

自鳴清高(ㄗˋ ㄇㄧㄥˊ ㄑㄧㄥ ㄍㄠ)
to consider oneself morally superior to others; to look down on all others as vulgar or dishonest

自鳴鐘(ㄗˋ ㄇㄧㄥˊ ㄓㄨㄥ)
a striking clock

自命不凡(ㄗˋ ㄇㄧㄥˋ ㄅㄨˋ ㄈㄢˊ)
conceited; to have a very high opinion of oneself

自發(ㄗˋ ㄈㄚ)
to work without being prodded; to take the initiative; spontaneous

自伐(ㄗˋ ㄈㄚˊ)
①to abuse oneself ②to be conceited

自肥(ㄗˋ ㄈㄟˊ)
to fatten oneself; to enrich oneself

自費(ㄗˋ ㄈㄟˋ)

to pay one's own expenses; self-provided: 他這次是自費旅行。This time he traveled at his own expense.

自反(ㄗˋ ㄈㄢˇ)
to introspect; introspection; to examine one's own conduct; self-examination

自焚(ㄗˋ ㄈㄣˊ)
to burn oneself to death—self-immolation

自分(ㄗˋ ㄈㄣˋ)
to anticipate; to think or believe; to figure

自封(ㄗˋ ㄈㄥ)
①to be conservative ②to enrich oneself without regard for others

自奉(ㄗˋ ㄈㄥˋ)
to treat oneself (especially in material matter as food, etc.)

自負(ㄗˋ ㄈㄨˋ)
to have a very high opinion of oneself; conceited: 他極其自負。He's full of conceit.

自負盈虧(ㄗˋ ㄈㄨˋ ㄧㄥˊ ㄎㄨㄟ)
(said of an enterprise) to assume sole responsibility for its profits or losses

自達達人(ㄗˋ ㄉㄚˊ ㄉㄚˊ ㄖㄣˊ)
One must be enlightened oneself before one can enlighten others.

自大(ㄗˋ ㄉㄚˋ)
conceited; egomaniacal; egotistic

自得(ㄗˋ ㄉㄜˊ)
①conceited; complacent; to feel satisfied with oneself ②to find joy in one's life

自得其樂(ㄗˋ ㄉㄜˊ ㄑㄧˊ ㄌㄜˋ)
to find joy in one's own way (no matter what others may think)

自蹈法網(ㄗˋ ㄉㄠˋ ㄈㄚˇ ㄨㄤˇ)
to break the law out of free will

自當(ㄗˋ ㄉㄤ)
should naturally: 兒童自當服從他們的父母。Children should naturally obey their parents.

自頂至踵(ㄗˋ ㄉㄧㄥˇ ㄓˋ ㄓㄨㄥˇ)
from head to foot

自瀆(ㄗˋ ㄉㄨˊ)
self-abuse; masturbation

〔自部〕

自度曲 (ㄗ ㄉㄨˋ ㄑㄩˇ)
a self-composed musical piece; a musical composition which does not follow the old rules or scores

自動 (ㄗ ㄉㄨㄥˋ)
① voluntary; of one's own free will ② automatic

自動步槍 (ㄗ ㄉㄨㄥˋ ㄅㄨˋ ㄑㄧㄤˇ)
an automatic rifle

自動販賣機 (ㄗ ㄉㄨㄥˋ ㄈㄢˋ ㄇㄞˋ ㄐㄧ)
a vending machine: 她從自動販賣機買了一罐可口可樂。 She bought a can of Coca-Cola from a vending machine

自動電話 (ㄗ ㄉㄨㄥˋ ㄉㄧㄢˋ ㄏㄨㄚˋ)
a dial telephone; an automatic telephone

自動電信機 (ㄗ ㄉㄨㄥˋ ㄉㄧㄢˋ ㄒㄧㄣˋ ㄐㄧ)
an autokinetic telegraph

自動提款機 (ㄗ ㄉㄨㄥˋ ㄊㄧˊ ㄎㄨㄢˇ ㄐㄧ)
a cashomat 參看「自動櫃員機」

自動櫃員機 (ㄗ ㄉㄨㄥˋ 《ㄨㄟˋ ㄩㄢˊ ㄐㄧ)
an automated-teller machine

自動開關 (ㄗ ㄉㄨㄥˋ ㄎㄞ ㄍㄨㄢ)
an automatic switch

自動化 (ㄗ ㄉㄨㄥˋ ㄏㄨㄚˋ)
automation; to automate

自動檢波器 (ㄗ ㄉㄨㄥˋ ㄐㄧㄢˇ ㄅㄛ ㄑㄧˋ)
an autocoherer

自動鉛筆 (ㄗ ㄉㄨㄥˋ ㄑㄧㄢ ㄅㄧˇ)
a mechanical pencil

自動車 (ㄗ ㄉㄨㄥˋ ㄔㄜ)
automotive vehicles

自動售貨機 (ㄗ ㄉㄨㄥˋ ㄕㄡˋ ㄏㄨㄛˋ ㄐㄧ)
a vending machine

自討沒趣 (ㄗ ㄊㄠˇ ㄇㄟˊ ㄑㄩˋ)
"You ask for it!"—to get an insult unnecessarily

自討苦吃 (ㄗ ㄊㄠˇ ㄎㄨˇ ㄔ)
to ask for trouble

自投羅網 (ㄗ ㄊㄡˊ ㄌㄨㄛˊ ㄨㄤˇ)
to walk right into a trap

自歎 (ㄗ ㄊㄢˋ)
to pity oneself; to regret; to sigh to oneself

自歎不如 (ㄗ ㄊㄢˋ ㄅㄨˋ ㄖㄨˊ)
to admit with regret that one is not as good; to concede that the other fellow is better qualified

自餒 (ㄗ ㄋㄟˇ)
to hold defeatist views; to think that one cannot do the job without even trying; to

lack confidence: 怯懦者自餒。 A coward lacks confidence.

自拉自唱 (ㄗ ㄌㄚ ㄗ ㄔㄤˋ)
(literally) to sing while playing the two-stringed violin as an accompaniment all by oneself—①to praise one's own effort or achievement ②to do something all by oneself

自來火 (ㄗ ㄌㄞˊ ㄏㄨㄛˇ)
① a safety match ② a gaslight ③ a cigarette lighter

自來水 (ㄗ ㄌㄞˊ ㄕㄨㄟˇ)
running water; tap water

自來水筆 (ㄗ ㄌㄞˊ ㄕㄨㄟˇ ㄅㄧˇ)
a fountain pen

自來水錶 (ㄗ ㄌㄞˊ ㄕㄨㄟˇ ㄅㄧㄠˇ)
a water meter

自來水龍頭 (ㄗ ㄌㄞˊ ㄕㄨㄟˇ ㄌㄨㄥˊ ㄊㄡˊ)
a faucet

自來水管 (ㄗ ㄌㄞˊ ㄕㄨㄟˇ ㄍㄨㄢˇ)
water pipes

自來水廠 (ㄗ ㄌㄞˊ ㄕㄨㄟˇ ㄔㄤˇ)
a waterworks

自立 (ㄗ ㄌㄧˋ)
independent; self-supporting

自立門戶 (ㄗ ㄌㄧˋ ㄇㄣˊ ㄏㄨˋ)
to establish one's own school of thought or clique

自利 (ㄗ ㄌㄧˋ)
① to think of nothing but one's own gain ② (Buddhism) atmahitam, self-profit; beneficial to oneself

自力更生 (ㄗ ㄌㄧˋ ㄍㄥ ㄕㄥ)
to achieve self-renewal with one's own effort; self-reliance

自力救濟 (ㄗ ㄌㄧˋ ㄐㄧㄡˋ ㄐㄧˋ)
to redress a perceived wrong by taking the law into one's own hands

自了 (ㄗ ㄌㄧㄠˇ)
to be able to conclude or complete something all by oneself

自了漢 (ㄗ ㄌㄧㄠˇ ㄏㄢˋ)
a selfish person

自料 (ㄗ ㄌㄧㄠˋ)
to figure; to anticipate; to think or believe

自流井 (ㄗ ㄌㄧㄡˊ ㄐㄧㄥˇ)
① name of a district of Tzu-kung (自貢) in Szechwan, a site of more than 4,000 wells of high salt contents ②an

artesian well

自戀 (ㄗ ㄌㄧㄢˋ)
narcissism

自量 (ㄗ ㄌㄧㄤˊ)
to measure oneself; to have a general idea of one's own abilities or resources; to make a self-assessment

自律 (ㄗ ㄌㄩˋ)
①to control oneself; to exercise self-restraint or self-control; self-discipline: 她不能自律。 She has no control of herself. ②(ethics) autonomy

自個兒 (ㄗ ㄍㄜˋ ㄦ)
oneself: 人不應該專爲自個兒而活。 One should not live for oneself alone.

自告奮勇 (ㄗ ㄍㄠˋ ㄈㄣˋ ㄩㄥˇ)
to volunteer

自甘墮落 (ㄗ ㄍㄢ ㄉㄨㄛˋ ㄌㄨㄛˋ)
to abandon oneself to wanton ways; to indulge in debauchery out of one's own free will

自感應 (ㄗ ㄍㄢˇ ㄧㄥˋ)
self-induction

自耕農 (ㄗ ㄍㄥ ㄋㄨㄥˊ)
farmers who till the land they own; owner-farmers

自古及今 (ㄗ ㄍㄨˇ ㄐㄧˊ ㄐㄧㄣ)
from ancient times till the present; since time immemorial

自古如此 (ㄗ ㄍㄨˇ ㄖㄨˊ ㄘˇ)
It has been this way since the beginning of time.

自古以來 (ㄗ ㄍㄨˇ ㄧˇ ㄌㄞˊ)
since ancient times; since time immemorial; down through the ages

自顧不暇 (ㄗ ㄍㄨˋ ㄅㄨˋ ㄒㄧㄚˊ)
to have trouble even in taking care of oneself

自顧自 (ㄗ ㄍㄨˋ ㄗ)
① selfish ②to mind one's business ③everyone for himself

自苦 (ㄗ ㄎㄨˇ)
to look for trouble; to give oneself unnecessary pains

自誇 (ㄗ ㄎㄨㄚ)
to brag; to boast

自郐以下 (ㄗ ㄎㄨㄞˋ ㄧˇ ㄒㄧㄚˋ)
Except so-and-so, none of them was worth a dime. (an

〔自部〕

expression used in commenting on historic personalities)

自寬 (ㄗ ㄎㄨㄢ)
to comfort oneself; self-consolation

自況 (ㄗ ㄎㄨㄤ)
to compare oneself with another person

自豪 (ㄗ ㄏㄠ)
to feel proud of; to pride oneself on; to take pride in

自好 (ㄗ ㄏㄠ)
self-respect; self-esteem

自後 (ㄗ ㄏㄡ)
from now on; henceforth: 我許諾自後不再喝酒。I promise never to get drunk henceforth.

自花受精 (ㄗ ㄏㄨㄚ ㄕㄡ ㄐㄧㄥ)
self-fertilization

自畫像 (ㄗ ㄏㄨㄚˋ ㄒㄧㄤ)
a self-portrait

自毀長城 (ㄗ ㄏㄨㄟˇ ㄔㄤˊ ㄔㄥˊ) or **自壞長城** (ㄗ ㄏㄨㄞ ㄔㄤˊ ㄔㄥˊ)
to get rid of a capable lieutenant

自己 (ㄗ ㄐㄧ)
self; oneself; one's person: 讓我們爲自己乾一杯。Let us drink a toast to ourselves.

自己人 (ㄗ ㄐㄧ ㄖㄣ)
persons within the same circle; persons closely related with each other

自給自足 (ㄗ ㄐㄧ ㄗ ㄗㄨ)
self-sufficient; self-supporting; self-sufficiency: 他們的糧食自給自足。They are self-sufficient in grain.

自家 (ㄗ ㄐㄧㄚ)
(colloquial) oneself

自家人 (ㄗ ㄐㄧㄚ ㄖㄣ)
persons within the same circle or closely related with each other in some way

自解 (ㄗ ㄐㄧㄝ)
①to explain to oneself; self-explanation ②to extricate oneself (from certain bondage, etc.)

自救 (ㄗ ㄐㄧㄡ)
self-salvation; to rescue oneself (from evil ways): 讓我們團結自救。Let us get united for our own salvation.

自薦 (ㄗ ㄐㄧㄢ)
to introduce or recommend oneself; to volunteer

自今 (ㄗ ㄐㄧㄣ)
from now on; henceforth: 自今以後他將在另一處工作。From now on he will work in another office.

自矜 (ㄗ ㄐㄧㄣ)
to brag: 他自矜其財富。He bragged his wealth.

自盡 (ㄗ ㄐㄧㄣˋ)
to commit suicide; to kill oneself

自經 (ㄗ ㄐㄧㄥ)
①to hang oneself ②to commit suicide

自剄 (ㄗ ㄐㄧㄥˇ)
to commit suicide by cutting the throat

自居 (ㄗ ㄐㄩ)
to consider oneself to be (a genius, VIP, famous figure, etc.)

自決 (ㄗ ㄐㄩㄝ)
to decide or solve (a problem, etc.) by oneself; self-determination

自絕 (ㄗ ㄐㄩㄝ)
①to isolate oneself ②to seek self-destruction

自覺 (ㄗ ㄐㄩㄝ)
①self-consciousness; self-realization ②to feel something concerning oneself; aware

自覺運動 (ㄗ ㄐㄩㄝ ㄩㄣ ㄉㄨㄥ)
a self-renewal movement; a drive to promote dedication to the nation

自掘墳墓 (ㄗ ㄐㄩㄝ ㄈㄣ ㄇㄨ)
to dig one's own grave

自欺 (ㄗ ㄑㄧ)
to deceive oneself; self-deceit

自欺欺人 (ㄗ ㄑㄧ ㄑㄧ ㄖㄣ)
to deceive oneself and others as well

自謙 (ㄗ ㄑㄧㄢ)
self-debasement (as a gesture of politeness); to be modest: 那英雄對他的豐功偉業很自謙。The hero was very modest about his great deeds.

自遣 (ㄗ ㄑㄧㄢˇ)
to comfort, console or cheer oneself; to amuse oneself: 我讀偵探小說自遣。I amused myself by reading detective stories.

自戕 (ㄗ ㄑㄧㄤ)
to harm or abuse oneself; to inflict injuries on oneself

自強 (ㄗ ㄑㄧㄤ)
to goad oneself; to drive oneself hard; to strive for improvement or progress

自強不息 (ㄗ ㄑㄧㄤ ㄅㄨ ㄒㄧ)
to exert and strive hard without stop; continuous self-renewal

自強運動 (ㄗ ㄑㄧㄤ ㄩㄣ ㄉㄨㄥ)
a movement of self-improvement, self-strengthening and self-renewal

自取 (ㄗ ㄑㄩ)
of one's own doing

自取滅亡 (ㄗ ㄑㄩ ㄇㄧㄝ ㄨㄤ)
to court destruction upon oneself; to take the road to one's doom

自取其咎 (ㄗ ㄑㄩ ㄑㄧ ㄐㄧㄡ)
to receive punishment, censure, etc. through one's own fault

自取其辱 (ㄗ ㄑㄩ ㄑㄧ ㄖㄨ)
to ask for an insult; to invite humiliation

自習 (ㄗ ㄒㄧ)
to learn and practice by oneself

自修 (ㄗ ㄒㄧㄡ)
to learn and practice by oneself; to educate oneself; to discipline oneself

自新 (ㄗ ㄒㄧㄣ)
to make a new person out of oneself; self-renewal

自信 (ㄗ ㄒㄧㄣ)
self-confidence

自相矛盾 (ㄗ ㄒㄧㄤ ㄇㄠ ㄉㄨㄣˋ)
inconsistent; inconsistency; self-contradictory

自相殘殺 (ㄗ ㄒㄧㄤ ㄘㄢ ㄕㄚ)
to engage in an intramural fight

自行 (ㄗ ㄒㄧㄥ)
individually; personally; by oneself

自行辦理 (ㄗ ㄒㄧㄥ ㄅㄢ ㄌㄧ)
to manage something individually

自行其是 (ㄗ ㄒㄧㄥ ㄑㄧ ㄕ)
to act as one thinks proper; to go one's own way

自行車 (ㄗ ㄒㄧㄥ ㄔㄜ)

〔自部〕

a bicycle; a bike

自省 (ㄗ ㄒㄧㄥˇ)
to examine oneself; self-examination; introspection

自詡 (ㄗ ㄒㄩˇ)
to brag; to boast

自許 (ㄗ ㄒㄩˇ)
to regard oneself as; conceited; pretentious: 他以聰明自許。He is wise in his own conceit.

自序 (ㄗ ㄒㄩˋ)
the author's preface or foreword

自衒 (ㄗ ㄒㄩㄢˋ)
to show off

自尋煩惱 (ㄗ ㄒㄩㄣˊ ㄈㄢˊ ㄋㄠˇ)
to look for trouble

自知理缺 (ㄗ ㄓ ㄌㄧˇ ㄑㄩㄝ)
to realize that one is on the wrong side

自知之明 (ㄗ ㄓ ㄓ ㄇㄧㄥˊ)
to know oneself; a correct self-assessment

自制 (ㄗ ㄓˋ)
self-restraint; self-discipline

自製 (ㄗ ㄓˋ)
self-made; self-manufactured; to manufacture locally or by the plant concerned

自治 (ㄗ ㄓˋ)
① self-government; autonomy ② self-discipline

自治領 (ㄗ ㄓˋ ㄌㄧㄥˇ)
a dominion; an autonomous region

自治會 (ㄗ ㄓˋ ㄏㄨㄟˋ)
① the student government of a school ② a public welfare organization operated by the citizens of a community

自治區 (ㄗ ㄓˋ ㄑㄩ)
an autonomous region

自治行政 (ㄗ ㄓˋ ㄒㄧㄥˊ ㄓㄥˋ)
(said of villages, counties, cities, etc.) self-government

自招 (ㄗ ㄓㄠ)
to confess; confession: 我自招做了這件事。I confess to doing it.

自找麻煩 (ㄗ ㄓㄠˇ ㄇㄚˊ ·ㄈㄢ)
to look for trouble

自主 (ㄗ ㄓㄨˇ)
independent; independence; autonomy

自主權 (ㄗ ㄓㄨˇ ㄑㄩㄢˊ)

sovereignty (of a state)

自助 (ㄗ ㄓㄨˋ)
self-help; to help oneself

自助洗衣店 (ㄗ ㄓㄨˋ ㄒㄧˇ ㄧ ㄉㄧㄢˋ)
a launderette

自助人助 (ㄗ ㄓㄨˋ ㄖㄣˊ ㄓㄨˋ)
People help those who help themselves.

自助餐 (ㄗ ㄓㄨˋ ㄘㄢ)
a buffet lunch or supper

自助餐廳 (ㄗ ㄓㄨˋ ㄘㄢ ㄊㄧㄥ)
a cafeteria

自專 (ㄗ ㄓㄨㄢ)
dictatorial; arbitrary; having implicit faith in oneself

自轉 (ㄗ ㄓㄨㄢˇ) or (ㄗ ㄓㄨㄢˋ)
(astronomy) rotation; to revolve on its own axis

自轉週期 (ㄗ ㄓㄨㄢˇ ㄓㄡ ㄑㄧ)
a period of rotation

自傳 (ㄗ ㄓㄨㄢˋ)
an autobiography

自重 (ㄗ ㄓㄨㄥˋ)
self-respect; self-discipline; self-esteem

自持 (ㄗ ㄔˊ)
① to restrain or discipline oneself; self-discipline ② to keep oneself arrogantly aloof

自察 (ㄗ ㄔㄚˊ)
to make self-examination; to be aware of one's own behavior

自陳 (ㄗ ㄔㄣˊ)
to state personally

自稱 (ㄗ ㄔㄥ)
to call oneself; to style oneself; to claim

自乘 (ㄗ ㄔㄥˊ)
(said of a figure) to multiply itself

自成一家 (ㄗ ㄔㄥˊ ㄧ ㄐㄧㄚ)
(said of a creative writer, painter, etc.) to create a school or style of one's own

自出機杼 (ㄗ ㄔㄨ ㄐㄧ ㄓㄨˋ)
to be original in writing

自處 (ㄗ ㄔㄨˇ)
one's own position, situation or predicament; where to place oneself

自吹自擂 (ㄗ ㄔㄨㄟ ㄗ ㄌㄟˊ)
to brag; to boast

自食其力 (ㄗ ㄕˊ ㄑㄧˊ ㄌㄧˋ)
to live by one's own exer-

tion: 他以自食其力為榮。He takes pride in living by his own exertion.

自食其果 (ㄗ ㄕˊ ㄑㄧˊ ㄍㄨㄛˇ)
to reap the fruit of what one has sown; to suffer the consequences of one's own doing

自始至終 (ㄗ ㄕˇ ㄓˋ ㄓㄨㄥ)
from beginning to end; all the way through: 他們自始至終友善。They were on good terms from beginning to end.

自是 (ㄗ ㄕˋ)
① to consider oneself as right ② from then on, since then

自恃 (ㄗ ㄕˋ)
to presume on one's (talent, wealth, influential connections, etc.)

自視 (ㄗ ㄕˋ)
to consider, to think or to imagine oneself: 其人自視甚高。That person thinks highly of himself.

自視歉然 (ㄗ ㄕˋ ㄑㄧㄢˋ ㄖㄢˊ)
to be dissatisfied with oneself

自殺 (ㄗ ㄕㄚ)
to commit suicide; suicide

自殺未遂 (ㄗ ㄕㄚ ㄨㄟˋ ㄙㄨㄟˋ)
an attempted suicide

自首 (ㄗ ㄕㄡˇ)
to give oneself up to the law; to surrender oneself to the authorities

自身 (ㄗ ㄕㄣ)
oneself: 人將後此種方法而自身受害。One hurts oneself by such methods.

自身難保 (ㄗ ㄕㄣ ㄋㄢˊ ㄅㄠˇ)
unable even to protect oneself

自傷 (ㄗ ㄕㄤ)
① (law) to inflict injury on oneself ② to feel sorrow for oneself; to pity oneself: 他因失敗而自傷。He felt much sorrow for his failure.

自生自滅 (ㄗ ㄕㄥ ㄗ ㄇㄧㄝˋ)
to grow and die without outside interference

自贖 (ㄗ ㄕㄨˊ)
to redeem oneself; to atone for one's crime

自述(ㄗ ㄕㄨ)
to narrate one's own story or experience

自署(ㄗ ㄕㄨˇ)
to sign one's name

自說自話(ㄗ ㄕㄨㄛ ㄗ ㄏㄨㄚˋ)
to make an arrangement without consulting those who are involved and who are in a position to disagree

自然(ㄗ ㄖㄢˊ)
(chemistry) spontaneous combustion (or ignition)

自然(ㄗ ㄖㄢˊ)
①nature; natural world ②at ease; natural; naturally:這次演出很自然。It was a very natural piece of acting. ③a matter of course; certainly; surely; of course: 他自然會失敗。Of course he will fail. ④(in primary school) a subject or course of study concerning natural sciences

自然美(ㄗ ㄖㄢˊ ㄇㄟˇ)
natural beauty; beauty of nature

自然法(ㄗ ㄖㄢˊ ㄈㄚˇ)
natural law

自然淘汰(ㄗ ㄖㄢˊ ㄊㄠˊ ㄊㄞˋ)
evolution; the survival of the fittest; natural selection

自然力(ㄗ ㄖㄢˊ ㄌㄧˋ)
the forces of nature

自然療法(ㄗ ㄖㄢˊ ㄌㄧㄠˊ ㄈㄚˇ)
naturopathy; natural ways of healing—without drugs

自然律(ㄗ ㄖㄢˊ ㄌㄩˋ)
the laws of nature; natural law

自然科學(ㄗ ㄖㄢˊ ㄎㄜ ㄒㄩㄝˊ)
natural sciences: 他決定研究自然科學。He decided to study natural sciences.

自然界(ㄗ ㄖㄢˊ ㄐㄧㄝˋ)
the natural world, including animals, plants and minerals

自然趨勢(ㄗ ㄖㄢˊ ㄑㄩ ㄕˋ)
the natural trend

自然現象(ㄗ ㄖㄢˊ ㄒㄧㄢˋ ㄒㄧㄤˋ)
a natural phenomenon

自然主義(ㄗ ㄖㄢˊ ㄓㄨˇ ㄧˋ)
naturalism

自然人(ㄗ ㄖㄢˊ ㄖㄣˊ)
(law) a natural person

自然而然(ㄗ ㄖㄢˊ ㄦˊ ㄖㄢˊ)
a matter of course; natural

---

consequences

自任(ㄗ ㄖㄣˋ)
to appoint oneself to the key post; to take personal command; to assume control personally; to assume responsibility voluntarily

自認(ㄗ ㄖㄣˋ)
①to believe: 他自認他是對的。He believed that he was right. ②to accept adversity with resignation

自如(ㄗ ㄖㄨˊ)or自若(ㄗ ㄖㄨㄛˋ)
①unperturbed ②freely; unhindered

自茲(ㄗ ㄗ)
①from now on; henceforth ②from here

自責(ㄗ ㄗㄜˊ)
to blame oneself; self-reproach

自在(ㄗ ㄗㄞˋ)
①comfortable; at ease (with oneself and the world): 她過着自在的生活。She lives a comfortable life. ②freely; at will ③(Buddhism) free from resistance; the mind free from delusion; independent

自誇(ㄗ ㄎㄨㄚ)
①to praise oneself: 大多數人喜歡自誇。Most people like to praise themselves. ②to introduce or recommend oneself

自足(ㄗ ㄗㄨˊ)
self-sufficient

自足經濟(ㄗ ㄗㄨˊ ㄐㄧㄥ ㄐㄧˋ)
self-sufficient or self-sustaining economy within a family, clan, etc.

自足社會(ㄗ ㄗㄨˊ ㄕㄜˋ ㄏㄨㄟˋ)
society with self-sufficient or self-sustaining economy

自作多情(ㄗ ㄗㄨㄛˋ ㄉㄨㄛ ㄑㄧㄥˊ)
to imagine oneself as the favorite of one of the opposite sex; to be under the hallucination that the other party is willing

自作孽(ㄗ ㄗㄨㄛˋ ㄋㄧㄝˋ)
to bring disaster to oneself

自作主張(ㄗ ㄗㄨㄛˋ ㄓㄨˇ ㄓㄤ)
to reach a decision one is not in a position to make; to take liberties; to decide for

---

oneself

自作自受(ㄗ ㄗㄨㄛˋ ㄗ ㄕㄡˋ)
One reaps what he sows. 或to suffer the consequences of one's own doing

自作聰明(ㄗ ㄗㄨㄛˋ ㄘㄨㄥ ㄇㄧㄥˊ)
to act as if one were an expert; presumptuous; pretentious

自尊(ㄗ ㄗㄨㄣ)
①self-respect; self-esteem ②egotistic

自尊心(ㄗ ㄗㄨㄣ ㄒㄧㄣ)
a sense of self-respect; one's feelings; self-esteem

自此(ㄗ ㄘˇ)
from then on; henceforth

自裁(ㄗ ㄘㄞˊ)
to commit suicide

自慚鳩拙(ㄗ ㄘㄢˊ ㄐㄧㄡ ㄓㄨㄛˊ)
to feel ashamed of one's lack of creative talent

自慚形穢(ㄗ ㄘㄢˊ ㄒㄧㄥˊ ㄏㄨㄟˋ)
to feel inferior to others

自從(ㄗ ㄘㄨㄥˊ)
from (a certain period of time); since then; ever since

自私(ㄗ ㄙ)or自私自利(ㄗ ㄙ ㄗ ㄌㄧˋ)
selfish; selfishness: 他相當自私。He is rather selfish.

自訴(ㄗ ㄙㄨˋ)
private prosecution

自訴人(ㄗ ㄙㄨˋ ㄖㄣˊ)
a self-complainant

自訟(ㄗ ㄙㄨㄥˋ)
to blame oneself; self-censure

自愛(ㄗ ㄞˋ)
self-respect; to behave like a gentleman: 他雖窮但很自愛。He is poor but has self-respect.

自以為是(ㄗ ㄧˇ ㄨㄟˊ ㄕˋ)
to regard oneself as correct or right, in total disregard of others' or public opinion; self-approbation

自縊(ㄗ ㄧˋ)
to hang oneself

自由(ㄗ ㄧㄡˊ)
①freedom; liberty; free: 言論自由 freedom of speech ②at ease; (to feel) at home of one's own free will

自由貿易(ㄗ ㄧㄡˊ ㄇㄠˋ ㄧˋ)

〔自部〕

free trade
自由黨 (ㄗ ㄧㄡ ㄉㄤˇ)
British Liberal Party
自由女神像 (ㄗ ㄧㄡ ㄋㄩˇ ㄕㄣˊ ㄒㄧㄤˋ)
the Statue of Liberty in
New York harbor
自由戀愛 (ㄗ ㄧㄡ ㄌㄧㄢˋ ㄞˋ)
free love (between a man
and a woman) as distinct
from the old-fashioned idea
of marriage
自由港 (ㄗ ㄧㄡ ㄍㄤˇ)
a free port
自由教育 (ㄗ ㄧㄡ ㄐㄧㄠˋ ㄩˋ)
liberal education, whose
objective is the seeking of
knowledge, not preparation
for jobs or occupations
自由競爭 (ㄗ ㄧㄡ ㄐㄧㄥˋ ㄓㄥ)
free competition
自由權 (ㄗ ㄧㄡ ㄑㄩㄢˊ)
rights of freedom of the people guaranteed by the constitution
自由行動 (ㄗ ㄧㄡ ㄒㄧㄥˊ ㄉㄨㄥˋ)
free movements; a free hand;
free action
自由職業 (ㄗ ㄧㄡ ㄓˊ ㄧㄝˋ)
professions that do not
require fixed office hours,
such as doctors, writers,
lawyers, etc.
自由主義 (ㄗ ㄧㄡ ㄓㄨˇ ㄧˋ)
liberalism; the principle of
liberty 參看〔放任政策〕
自由鐘 (ㄗ ㄧㄡ ㄓㄨㄥ)
the Liberty Bell
自由城 (ㄗ ㄧㄡ ㄔㄥˊ)
Freetown, the capital of
Sierra Leone in W Africa
自由城市 (ㄗ ㄧㄡ ㄔㄥˊ ㄕˋ)
(in Europe, after the Industrial Revolution) a self-
governing free city after
shaking off the bondage of
feudalism
自由詩 (ㄗ ㄧㄡ ㄕ)
free verse; vers libre; 他擅於
寫自由詩。He is good at writ-
ing free verse.
自由式 (ㄗ ㄧㄡ ㄕˋ)
(swimming) freestyle
自由自在 (ㄗ ㄧㄡ ㄗˋ ㄗㄞˋ)
comfortable and at ease;
carefree
自由思想 (ㄗ ㄧㄡ ㄙ ㄒㄧㄤˇ)
liberal ideas or thoughts

自由意志 (ㄗ ㄧㄡ ㄧˋ ㄓˋ)
free will
自有道理 (ㄗ ㄧㄡˇ ㄉㄠˋ ㄌㄧˇ)
There must be a reason (for
it).
自有公論 (ㄗ ㄧㄡˇ ㄍㄨㄥ ㄌㄨㄣˋ)
There is always (fair) public opinion.
自幼 (ㄗ ㄧㄡˋ)
since childhood: 他們自幼即
爲好友。They have been good
friends since childhood.
自言自語 (ㄗ ㄧㄢˊ ㄗˋ ㄩˇ)
to talk to oneself
自應 (ㄗ ㄧㄥ)
ought to; to be obliged to;
should: 你自應服從你的父母。
You ought to obey your parents.
自侮 (ㄗ ㄨˇ)
to insult oneself (through
scandalous acts, shady practices, etc.)
自誤 (ㄗ ㄨˋ)
to forfeit one's own chances;
to cause damage to one's
own interest
自誤誤人 (ㄗ ㄨˋ ㄨˋ ㄖㄣˊ)
to compromise the interest
of oneself and those of
others
自我 (ㄗ ㄨㄛˇ)
self; ego
自我批評 (ㄗ ㄨㄛˇ ㄆㄧ ㄆㄧㄥˊ)
self-criticism; to criticize
oneself
自我陶醉 (ㄗ ㄨㄛˇ ㄊㄠˊ ㄗㄨㄟˋ)
to indulge in daydreaming;
to be intoxicated by the joy
of one's imaginary successes
自我檢討 (ㄗ ㄨㄛˇ ㄐㄧㄢˇ ㄊㄠˇ)
self-examination; to review
one's conduct, achievements,
etc. objectively
自我犧牲 (ㄗ ㄨㄛˇ ㄒㄧ ㄕㄥ)
to sacrifice oneself (for the
sake of others, nation, etc.);
self-sacrifice
自我作古 (ㄗ ㄨㄛˇ ㄗㄨㄛˋ ㄍㄨˇ)
to be a pioneer or trail-
blazer (instead of a tradition-
bound copycat)
自外生成 (ㄗ ㄨㄞˋ ㄕㄥ ㄔㄥˊ)
to shut oneself from civilized ways
自慰 (ㄗ ㄨㄟˋ)
① to comfort oneself; self-

consolation ② onanism
自衛 (ㄗ ㄨㄟˋ)
self-defense; to defend oneself
自衛隊 (ㄗ ㄨㄟˋ ㄉㄨㄟˋ)
militia corps; a team of
citizen-soldiers for local
self-defense
自衛權 (ㄗ ㄨㄟˋ ㄑㄩㄢˊ)
the right of self-defense
自刎 (ㄗ ㄨㄣˇ)
to commit suicide by cutting
one's own throat
自問 (ㄗ ㄨㄣˋ)
to ask oneself; to search
one's own soul
自娛 (ㄗ ㄩˊ)
to amuse oneself
自圓其說 (ㄗ ㄩㄢˊ ㄑㄧˊ ㄕㄨㄛ)
to explain oneself away; to
make one's story sound
plausible
自願 (ㄗ ㄩㄢˋ)
voluntary; of one's own
accord; of one's own free
will
自怨自艾 (ㄗ ㄩㄢˋ ㄗˋ ㄞˋ)
to blame and censure one-
self; to complain about oneself
自用 (ㄗ ㄩㄥˋ)
① to do something without
consulting others; to have
morbid faith in one's talent
and capability ② personal
or private (property); for
personal or private use

四畫

【臬】 4765
　　ㄋㄧㄝˋ nieh niè
1. a rule; a law; an institution
2. another name of 按察使 —
the provincial judge in ancient China
3. a doorpost
臬司 (ㄋㄧㄝˋ ㄙ)
the provincial judge in old
China

【臭】 4766
　　1. ㄔㄡˋ chow chòu
1. stinking; smelly
2. notorious; flagrant; disreputable
3. very; much; soundly; sternly
4. (said of friendship, love,
etc.) to cool off

5. foul and petty; worthless
6. an odor; a stench

臭皮囊 (彳又 ㄆ丨 ㄋㄤ)
the human body

臭罵 (彳又 ㄇㄚ)
a stern scolding; to scold soundly

臭美 (彳又 ㄇㄟ)
presumptuous; smug

臭名 (彳又 ㄇㄧㄥ)
a notorious reputation

臭腐 (彳又 ㄈㄨ)
stinking and rotten

臭打 (彳又 ㄉㄚ)
a sound thrashing or beating

臭豆腐 (彳又 ㄉㄡ ㄈㄨ)
the fermented bean curd (a popular Chinese food item)

臭東西 (彳又 ㄉㄨㄥ ㄒㄧ)
a stinking slut; a good-for-nothing

臭蹄子 (彳又 ㄊㄧ˙ㄗ)
a stinking whore or slut

臭爛 (彳又 ㄌㄢ)
rotten and stinking

臭溝 (彳又 ㄍㄡ)
a stinking ditch; a gutter

臭烘烘 (彳又 ㄏㄨㄥ ㄏㄨㄥ)
to stink; stinking

臭街爛巷 (彳又 ㄐㄧㄝ ㄌㄢ ㄒㄧㄤ)
(said of goods or commodities) plentiful and cheap

臭嘴 (彳又 ㄗㄨㄟ)
to keep on jawing nonsense; to chatter on and on meaninglessly

臭氣冲天 (彳又 ㄑㄧ ㄔㄨㄥ ㄊㄧㄢ)
a stinking smell assaulting one's nostrils

臭錢 (彳又 ㄑㄧㄢ)
stinking money; the money of a rich miser

臭小子 (彳又 ㄒㄧㄠ˙ㄗ)
a bum; a tramp

臭喫臭喝 (彳又 ㄔ 彳又 ㄏㄜ)
to drink like a fish and eat like a pig

臭蟲 (彳又 ㄔㄨㄥ)
the bedbug

臭事 (彳又 ㄕ)
a scandal

臭揍 (彳又 ㄗㄡ)
a sound thrashing; a good beating

臭鼬 (彳又 ㄧㄡ)
a skunk

臭氧 (彳又 ㄧㄤ)
ozone

臭氧層 (彳又 ㄧㄤ ㄘㄥ)
the ozonosphere

臭味相投 (彳又 ㄨㄟ ㄒㄧㄤ ㄊㄡ) or
(ㄒㄧㄡ ㄨㄟ ㄒㄧㄤ ㄊㄡ)
to share the same rotten tastes, habits, etc.; to be two of a kind; birds of the same feather; persons of similar (atrocious) tastes; a meeting of (dirty) minds

【臭】 4766
2. (嗅) ㄒㄧㄡ　shiow xiù

1. scent; smells; odors
2. to smell

六畫

【皋】 4767
(皐, 皞) 《ㄍㄠ　gau gāo

1. a lake or pool
2. the bank or shore
3. to utter a long, wailing sound
4. a Chinese family name

十畫

【臲】 4768
ㄋㄧㄝ　nieh niè

jumpy; jittery; worried

臲硊 (ㄋㄧㄝ)
jumpy; jittery; worried; anxious

至 部
ㄓ jyh zhì

【至】 4769
ㄓ jyh zhì

1. to arrive at; to reach (a destination)
2. very; extremely; to indicate the superlative degree—the most

至寶 (ㄓ ㄅㄠ)
the most precious treasure

至大 (ㄓ ㄉㄚ)
the greatest; extremely large

至大至剛 (ㄓ ㄉㄚ ㄓ ㄍㄤ)
the greatest and most unbending

至德 (ㄓ ㄉㄜ)
the highest virtue

至當不移 (ㄓ ㄉㄤ ㄅㄨ ㄧ)
most suitable and not subject to change

至多 (ㄓ ㄉㄨㄛ)
at (the) most

至樂 (ㄓ ㄌㄜ)
extremely happy and jubilant

至理名言 (ㄓ ㄌㄧ ㄇㄧㄥ ㄧㄢ)
a proverb of lasting value; a truthful remark; a quotable quote

至高無上 (ㄓ ㄍㄠ ㄨˊ ㄕㄤ)
the highest; the most exalted; above everything else; the supreme

至關緊要 (ㄓ ㄍㄨㄢ ㄐㄧㄣ ㄧㄠ)
of utmost importance

至公 (ㄓ ㄍㄨㄥ)
absolutely just or unbiased:
這法官至公無私。The judge was absolutely just.

至靠 (ㄓ ㄎㄠ)
a most dependable or faithful (friend)

至好 (ㄓ ㄏㄠ)
①the best; simply wonderful and fabulous ②the closest friend; a great friend: 我們是至好。We are great friends.

至急 (ㄓ ㄐㄧ)
most or extremely urgent

至極 (ㄓ ㄐㄧ)
extremely; the most; to the utmost degree

至交 (ㄓ ㄐㄧㄠ)
one's closest friend

至今 (ㄓ ㄐㄧㄣ)
until now; so far; up to the present time

至親 (ㄓ ㄑㄧㄣ)
the closest relative

至親好友 (ㄓ ㄑㄧㄣ ㄏㄠ ㄧㄡ)
close relatives and dear friends

至親無文 (ㄓ ㄑㄧㄣ ㄨˊ ㄨㄣ)
One does not have to stand on ceremony in dealing with close relatives and friends.

至情 (ㄓ ㄑㄧㄥ)
(said of friendship, kinship, etc.) the most genuine feeling

至孝 (ㄓ ㄒㄧㄠ)

【至部】

extremely filial

至心 (垚 ㄒㄧㄣ)
①the most sincere heart or thought ②(Buddhism) with the utmost mind, or a perfect mind

至行 (垚 ㄒㄧㄥ)
the most virtuous conduct

至性 (垚 ㄒㄧㄥ)
the natural disposition to love one's parents, brothers and sisters; a great capacity for love

至囑 (垚 ㄓㄨ)
instructions of the utmost importance or urgency; to instruct or exhort most earnestly

至誠 (垚 ㄔㄥ)
sincere; the greatest sincerity

至誠感神 (垚 ㄔㄥ ㄍㄢ ㄕㄣ)
Utmost sincerity can move even gods.

至少 (垚 ㄕㄠ)
at least; the least

至善 (垚 ㄕㄢ)
the highest level of virtue; the supreme good

至上 (垚 ㄕㄤ)
the most revered

至聖 (垚 ㄕㄥ)
the greatest sage—Confucius

至聖先師 (垚 ㄕㄥ ㄒㄧㄢ ㄕ)
the greatest sage and teacher—Confucius

至日 (垚 ㄖ)
the winter and the summer solstices

至仁 (垚 ㄖㄣ)
the highest degree of kindness and magnanimity

至人 (垚 ㄖㄣ)
①a saint; a sage; a man of virtue ②(Buddhism) the perfect man, i.e. Sakyamuni

至人無夢 (垚 ㄖㄣ ㄨ ㄇㄥ)
A virtuous man seldom has dreams.

至人無己 (垚 ㄖㄣ ㄨ ㄐㄧ)
A sage is selfless.

至如 (垚 ㄖㄨ)
as to; with regard to

至若 (垚 ㄖㄨㄛ)
to come to (that degree, etc.); as to; with regard to

至再至三 (垚 ㄗㄞ 垚 ㄙㄢ)
twice and thrice; repeatedly: 我曾至再至三地警告他。 I've given him repeated warnings.

至尊 (垚 ㄗㄨㄣ)
①the most august—the emperor ②(Buddhism) Sakyamuni

至此 (垚 ㄘ)
①to come here; to arrive here ②to have come this far; to have developed to this point

至材 (垚 ㄘㄞ)
extremely gifted or talented; extremely capable men

至死 (垚 ㄙ)
till death; to the last; to death: 他們將奮戰至死。 They will fight to the death.

至死不變 (垚 ㄙ ㄅㄨ ㄅㄧㄢ)
unswerving till death; consistent or unswerving (love, faith, etc.)

至死不屈 (垚 ㄙ ㄅㄨ ㄑㄩ)
to stick to one's principle, faith, etc. till one breathes his last

至死不渝 (垚 ㄙ ㄅㄨ ㄩ)
to remain faithful until death

至矣盡矣 (垚 ㄧ ㄐㄧㄣ ㄧ)
to have done everything possible (to help, encourage, etc.)

至意 (垚 ㄧ)
the best and sincerest intention

至要 (垚 ㄧㄠ)
the most important; imperative

至友 (垚 ㄧㄡ)
the closest friend; a close friend: 他是我的至友。 He is my close friend.

至言 (垚 ㄧㄢ)
①words of the utmost importance or significance ②the most virtuous or proper utterances ③(Buddhism) words of complete explanation

至於 (垚 ㄩ)
①as to; with regard to ②to the extent of

三畫

【致】 4770
(致) (垚 ㄓ) jyh zhì

1. to send; to present; to convey; to transmit; to extend (thanks, etc.)

2. to cause to come; to cause (injury, death, etc.)

3. to achieve; to attain; to amass (fortune)

4. one's principle, interest, hobby, etc.

5. to bring about; to occasion or result in

6. to retire; to resign

致命 (垚 ㄇㄧㄥ)
①to sacrifice one's life ②fatal; fatality

致命處 (垚 ㄇㄧㄥ ㄔㄨ)
①spots in the human body where injury can easily cause death ②key points in a plan, etc.

致命傷 (垚 ㄇㄧㄥ ㄕㄤ)
①a mortal wound ②vulnerability; the weak point; the major cause that makes failure inevitable

致富 (垚 ㄈㄨ)
to become rich; to acquire wealth: 他以勤儉致富。 He became rich because of diligence and frugality.

致奠 (垚 ㄉㄧㄢ)
(in old China, especially Ching Dynasty) the offering of personal condolences or sacrifices to the family of a deceased high official by a representative of the emperor; to offer sacrifices at the funeral service by the representative

致電 (垚 ㄉㄧㄢ)
to send a telegram or cable

致力 (垚 ㄌㄧ)
to devote or dedicate oneself to: 他畢生致力幫助盲人。 He has devoted his life to helping blind people.

致果 (垚 ㄍㄨㄛ)
to achieve victory; to attain result

致賀 (垚 ㄏㄜ)
to extend or offer congratulations: 他的成功值得致賀。

His success deserves congratulation.

致敬(ㄓ ㄐㄧㄥˋ)
to pay respects or homage; to salute

致謝(ㄓ ㄒㄧㄝˋ)
to offer thanks; to thank

致知(ㄓ ㄓ)
to extend one's knowledge; to pursue knowledge to the utmost

致政(ㄓ ㄓㄥˋ)
(said of a regent) to return the governing power to the throne; to retire from official life; to resign (from office) 參看「致仕」

致仕 or 致事(ㄓ ㄕˋ)
to resign from office; to retire from official life

致身(ㄓ ㄕㄣ)
to dedicate or give one's life to (a cause, etc.)

致書(ㄓ ㄕㄨ)
to send a letter: 余將致書令兄。 I'll send a letter to your elder brother.

致辭(ㄓ ㄘˊ)
to address; to deliver a speech

致死(ㄓ ㄙˇ)
to cause death; to result in death

致意(ㄓ ㄧˋ)
to convey one's best wishes or regards

致癌物質(ㄓ ㄞˊ ㄨˋ ㄓˋ)
(medicine) carcinogen; a carcinogenic substance

致用(ㄓ ㄩㄥˋ)
to attain practical use; for practical purposes

八畫

【臺】 4771
(台) ㄊㄞˊ tair tái
1. a lookout; a tower; an observatory
2. a terrace; an elevated platform; a stage; a stand
3. a title of respect
4. short for Taiwan
5. a Chinese family name

臺北市(ㄊㄞˊ ㄅㄟˇ ㄕˋ)

Taipei Special Municipality, provisional capital of the Republic of China

臺幣(ㄊㄞˊ ㄅㄧˋ)
Taiwan currency

臺風(ㄊㄞˊ ㄈㄥ)
the deportment of an actor or actress on stage

臺地(ㄊㄞˊ ㄉㄧˋ)
a tableland; a plateau

臺東(ㄊㄞˊ ㄉㄨㄥ)
① Taitung County ② Taitung City

臺南縣(ㄊㄞˊ ㄋㄢˊ ㄒㄧㄢˋ)
Tainan County

臺南市(ㄊㄞˊ ㄋㄢˊ ㄕˋ)
Tainan City: 臺南市以古蹟著名。 Tainan City is noted for its historic relics.

臺閣(ㄊㄞˊ ㄍㄜˊ)
(in former times) a cabinet minister

臺階(ㄊㄞˊ ㄐㄧㄝ)
① brick or stone steps ② a means to save face or resolve a dispute

臺諫(ㄊㄞˊ ㄐㄧㄢˋ)
(in ancient China) a censor

臺下(ㄊㄞˊ ㄒㄧㄚˋ)
off the stage

臺榭(ㄊㄞˊ ㄒㄧㄝˋ)
terraces and pavilions in a garden or park

臺柱子(ㄊㄞˊ ㄓㄨˋ ˙ㄗ)
(colloquial) the most important person in an organization or a group; the leading light; a pillar; a mainstay

臺中縣(ㄊㄞˊ ㄓㄨㄥ ㄒㄧㄢˋ)
Taichung County

臺中市(ㄊㄞˊ ㄓㄨㄥ ㄕˋ)
Taichung City

臺秤(ㄊㄞˊ ㄔㄥˋ)
① a platform scale ② the Taiwan standard of weight measure

臺上(ㄊㄞˊ ㄕㄤˋ)
on the stage

臺子(ㄊㄞˊ ˙ㄗ)
① (colloquial) a platform; a stage; a terrace ② (dialect) a table; a desk

臺詞(ㄊㄞˊ ㄘˊ)
lines in a play a player is supposed to memorize; actor's lines

臺兒莊(ㄊㄞˊ ㄦˊ ㄓㄨㄤ)
name of a town near the Kiangsu (江蘇) and Shantung (山東) border, where one of the bloodiest battles in the eight-year Sino-Japanese War (1938-1945) was fought and won

臺灣(ㄊㄞˊ ㄨㄢ)
Taiwan (Formosa)

臺灣肥料公司(ㄊㄞˊ ㄨㄢ ㄈㄟˊ ㄌㄧㄠˋ ㄍㄨㄥ ㄙ) or 臺肥(ㄊㄞˊ ㄈㄟˊ)
Taiwan Fertilizer Company

臺灣大學(ㄊㄞˊ ㄨㄢ ㄉㄚˋ ㄒㄩㄝˊ) or 臺大(ㄊㄞˊ ㄉㄚˋ)
National Taiwan University

臺灣電力公司(ㄊㄞˊ ㄨㄢ ㄉㄧㄢˋ ㄌㄧˋ ㄍㄨㄥ ㄙ) or 臺電(ㄊㄞˊ ㄉㄧㄢˋ)
Taiwan Power Company

臺灣糖業公司(ㄊㄞˊ ㄨㄢ ㄊㄤˊ ㄧㄝˋ ㄍㄨㄥ ㄙ) or 臺糖(ㄊㄞˊ ㄊㄤˊ)
Taiwan Sugar Corporation

臺灣光復節(ㄊㄞˊ ㄨㄢ ㄍㄨㄤ ㄈㄨˋ ㄐㄧㄝˊ)
Restoration Day of Taiwan (on October 25) commemorating the restoration of the island province to Chinese sovereignty in 1945 亦作「光復節」

臺灣海峽(ㄊㄞˊ ㄨㄢ ㄏㄞˇ ㄒㄧㄚˊ)
Taiwan Strait

臺灣省(ㄊㄞˊ ㄨㄢ ㄕㄥˇ)
the province of Taiwan

臺灣省政府(ㄊㄞˊ ㄨㄢ ㄕㄥˇ ㄓㄥˋ ㄈㄨˇ)
Taiwan Provincial Government

臺灣省議會(ㄊㄞˊ ㄨㄢ ㄕㄥˇ ㄧˋ ㄏㄨㄟˋ)
Taiwan Provincial Assembly

臺灣省菸酒公賣局(ㄊㄞˊ ㄨㄢ ㄕㄥˇ ㄧㄢ ㄐㄧㄡˇ ㄍㄨㄥ ㄇㄞˋ ㄐㄩˊ)
Taiwan Tobacco and Wine Monopoly Bureau

臺灣省物資局(ㄊㄞˊ ㄨㄢ ㄕㄥˇ ㄨˋ ㄗ ㄐㄩˊ)
Taiwan Supply Bureau

臺灣水泥公司(ㄊㄞˊ ㄨㄢ ㄕㄨㄟˇ ㄋㄧˊ ㄍㄨㄥ ㄙ) or 臺泥(ㄊㄞˊ ㄋㄧˊ)

〔至部〕

Taiwan Cement Corporation

臺灣造船公司 (ㄊㄞˊ ㄨㄢˊ ㄗㄠˋ ㄔㄨㄢˊ ㄍㄨㄥ ㄙ)
Taiwan Shipbuilding Corporation

臺灣銀行 (ㄊㄞˊ ㄨㄢˊ ㄧㄣˊ ㄏㄤˊ)
Bank of Taiwan

十畫

【臻】 4772 ㄓㄣ jen zhēn
1. the utmost; the best
2. to arrive at; to reach

臼 部
ㄐㄧㄡˋ jiow jiù

【臼】 4773 ㄐㄧㄡˋ jiow jiù
1. a mortar for unhusking rice
2. a socket at a bone joint
3. a Chinese family name

臼砲 (ㄐㄧㄡˋ ㄆㄠˋ)
(weaponry) a mortar

臼齒 (ㄐㄧㄡˋ ㄔˇ)
the molars

一畫

【臼】 4774 (㊣) ㄐㄩ jyu jū
to hold or take in both hands

二畫

【臾】 4775 ㄩˊ yu yú
1. a moment; an instant; a little while; a short time
2. a Chinese family name

三畫

【臿】 4776 ㄔㄚ cha chā
1. a kind of farming instrument
2. same as 插—to insert; to drive in

四畫

【舁】 4777 ㄩˊ yu yú
to lift; to raise; to carry

【舀】 4778 ㄧㄠˇ yeau yǎo
(讀音 ㄎㄞˇ koai kuài)
to ladle out (water): 她舀出
一碗湯來. She ladled out a bowl of soup.

五畫

【舂】 4779 ㄔㄨㄥ chong chōng
1. to thresh (grain in order to remove the husk)
2. to pound

舂米 (ㄔㄨㄥ ㄇㄧˇ)
to pound rice to remove the husk; to husk rice by pounding

舂碓 (ㄔㄨㄥ ㄉㄨㄟˋ)
a pestle (for husking grain)

六畫

【舄】 4780 (舄) ㄒㄧˋ shih xì
shoes; slippers

七畫

【舅】 4781 ㄐㄧㄡˋ jiow jiù
1. a maternal uncle (one's mother's brother)
2. a brother-in-law (one's wife's brother)
3. a woman's father-in-law
4. a man's father-in-law

舅媽 (ㄐㄧㄡˋ ㄇㄚ) or 舅母 (ㄐㄧㄡˋ ㄇㄨˇ)
a maternal aunt (one's mother's brother's wife)

舅父 (ㄐㄧㄡˋ ㄈㄨˋ) or 舅舅 (ㄐㄧㄡˋ
·ㄐㄧ)
a maternal uncle (one's mother's brother)

舅姑 (ㄐㄧㄡˋ ㄍㄨ)
a woman's parents-in-law

舅公 (ㄐㄧㄡˋ ㄍㄨㄥ)
one's father's maternal uncle

舅甥 (ㄐㄧㄡˋ ㄕㄥ)
the child of one's mother's brother or sister; a cousin on the mother's side

舅子 (ㄐㄧㄡˋ ㄗ)
a brother-in-law (one's wife's

brother)

舅祖 (ㄐㄧㄡˋ ㄗㄨˇ)
the brother of one's paternal grandmother; a granduncle; a great-uncle

舅嫂 (ㄐㄧㄡˋ ㄙㄠˇ)
a sister-in-law (the wife of one's wife's brother)

舅爺 (ㄐㄧㄡˋ ·ㄧㄝ)
a maternal uncle (one's mother's brother)

【與】 4782 ㄩˇ yeu yǔ
1. and; with; together with
2. to give; to impart

與民更始 (ㄩˇ ㄇㄧㄣˊ ㄍㄥ ㄕˇ)
(said of a ruler) to initiate political reforms and make a fresh start with the people

與黨 (ㄩˇ ㄉㄤˇ)
a political party as an ally of another political party; a friendly party

與奪 (ㄩˇ ㄉㄨㄛˊ)
giving and taking 亦作「予奪」

與他何干 (ㄩˇ ㄊㄚ ㄏㄜˊ ㄍㄢ)
What does it have to do with him? 或 What has it to do with him?

與古為徒 (ㄩˇ ㄍㄨˇ ㄨㄟˊ ㄊㄨˊ)
to imitate ancient ways

與國 (ㄩˇ ㄍㄨㄛˊ)
a state as an ally of another state; a friendly nation; an ally

與鬼為鄰 (ㄩˇ ㄍㄨㄟˇ ㄨㄟˊ ㄌㄧㄣˊ)
(literally) to be a next-door neighbor of ghosts—to be near one's death; dying

與共 (ㄩˇ ㄍㄨㄥˋ)
to share...with...: 他們甘苦與
共. They shared their joys and sorrows.

與儈為伍 (ㄩˇ ㄎㄨㄞˋ ㄨㄟˊ ㄨˇ)
to associate with vulgar people

與虎謀皮 (ㄩˇ ㄏㄨˇ ㄇㄡˊ ㄆㄧˊ) or 與狐
謀皮 (ㄩˇ ㄏㄨˊ ㄇㄡˊ ㄆㄧˊ)
(literally) to negotiate with a tiger (fox) for its hide—to try to persuade someone to do what is against his interest

與其…不如 (ㄩˇ ㄑㄧˊ ㄅㄨ ㄖㄨˊ)
It's better to...than... 或 rather...than...; ...rather than...

與衆不同(ㄩ ㄓㄨㄥ ㄅㄨ ㄊㄨㄥ)
　different from other people;
　extraordinary; uncommon;
　unlike others

與世浮沉(ㄩ ㄕ ㄈㄨ ㄔㄣ)
　to rise and sink with the
　rest of the world—to have
　no independent course of
　one's own

與世推移(ㄩ ㄕ ㄊㄨㄟ ㄧ)
　to change with the times

與世長辭(ㄩ ㄕ ㄔㄤ ㄘ)
　to depart from the world for
　good; to pass away

與世偃仰(ㄩ ㄕ ㄧㄢˇ ㄧㄤˇ)
　to rise and fall with the
　world—to have no independ-
　ent thinking or action of
　one's own

與世無爭(ㄩ ㄕ ㄨˊ ㄓㄥ)
　to be in harmony with the
　rest of the world—to stand
　aloof from worldly success

與日俱增(ㄩ ㄖˋ ㄐㄩˋ ㄗㄥ)
　to grow with each passing
　day; to be on the increase;
　ever increasing

與日月爭光(ㄩ ㄖˋ ㄩㄝˋ ㄓㄥ ㄍㄨㄤ)
　(literally) to equal the sun
　and the moon in glory—to
　achieve glorious success; to
　die heroically for a just
　cause

與人方便(ㄩ ㄖㄣˊ ㄈㄤ ㄅㄧㄢˋ)
　to give people convenience;
　to accommodate others

與人無忤(ㄩ ㄖㄣˊ ㄨˊ)
　to have no discord with
　others; to live in harmony
　with other people; to be at
　peace with others

與人爲善(ㄩ ㄖㄣˊ ㄨㄟˊ ㄕㄢˋ)
　to help others

與物無忤(ㄩ ㄨˋ ㄨˊ)
　to have offended no one; to
　be at peace with the world

與我無涉(ㄩ ㄨㄛˇ ㄨˊ ㄕㄜˋ)
　none of my business; having
　nothing to do with me

【與】 4782
　2. ㄩ yùh yù
　to take part in; to partici-
　pate in

與聞(ㄩ ㄨㄣˊ)
　to participate in the affair

【與】 4782
　3. ㄩ yu yú

same as 歟—one of the interrogative particles

九畫

【興】 4783
　1. ㄒㄧㄥ shing xīng
1. to rise; to thrive; to prosper;
　to flourish
2. to happen; to take place; to
　occur
3. to start; to begin; to launch;
　to initiate; to establish; to
　found; to open

興辦(ㄒㄧㄥ ㄅㄢˋ)
　to establish; to found

興邦(ㄒㄧㄥ ㄅㄤ)
　to rejuvenate a country

興兵(ㄒㄧㄥ ㄅㄧㄥ)
　to mobilize troops; to open
　hostilities

興不起來(ㄒㄧㄥ ㄅㄨˋ ㄑㄧˇ ㄌㄞˊ)
　unable to rise

興滅繼絕(ㄒㄧㄥ ㄇㄧㄝˋ ㄐㄧˋ ㄐㄩㄝˊ)
　to restore a fallen state or
　dynasty

興廢(ㄒㄧㄥ ㄈㄟˋ)
　rise or fall

興奮(ㄒㄧㄥ ㄈㄣˋ)
　excited; stimulated; excite-
　ment: 人人爲此勝利的消息而
　興奮。Everybody was excited
　by the news of the victory.

興奮劑(ㄒㄧㄥ ㄈㄣˋ ㄐㄧˋ)
　a stimulant

興風作浪(ㄒㄧㄥ ㄈㄥ ㄗㄨㄛˋ ㄌㄤˋ)
　to cause unrest; to stir up
　trouble

興復(ㄒㄧㄥ ㄈㄨˋ)
　to revive; to restore

興得起來(ㄒㄧㄥ ˙ㄉㄜ ㄑㄧˇ ㄌㄞˊ)
　able to rise

興騰(ㄒㄧㄥ ㄊㄥ)
　to gain vigor; to become
　increasingly prosperous; to
　rise

興替(ㄒㄧㄥ ㄊㄧˋ)
　rise and fall; waxing and
　waning; ups and downs;
　vicissitudes

興利除弊(ㄒㄧㄥ ㄌㄧˋ ㄔㄨˊ ㄅㄧˋ)
　to initiate the useful and
　abolish the harmful

興隆(ㄒㄧㄥ ㄌㄨㄥˊ)
　prosperous; thriving; vigor-
　ous

興革(ㄒㄧㄥ ㄍㄜˊ)

to initiate what is good to
the people and get rid of
what is harmful; to reform

興工(ㄒㄧㄥ ㄍㄨㄥ)
　to start construction

興開了(ㄒㄧㄥ ㄎㄞ ˙ㄌㄜ)
　to have become popular

興化灣(ㄒㄧㄥ ㄏㄨㄚˋ ㄨㄢ)
　a bay in the East China Sea,
　to the east of Fukien

興建(ㄒㄧㄥ ㄐㄧㄢˋ)
　to establish; to build; to con-
　struct

興居(ㄒㄧㄥ ㄐㄩ)
　one's daily life 亦作「起居」

興起(ㄒㄧㄥ ㄑㄧˇ)
　to gain power; to rise

興修(ㄒㄧㄥ ㄒㄧㄡ)
　to start reconstruction

興學(ㄒㄧㄥ ㄒㄩㄝˊ)
　to promote learning; to build
　schools

興中會(ㄒㄧㄥ ㄓㄨㄥ ㄏㄨㄟˋ)
　Hsing Chung Hui, the prede-
　cessor of the Kuomintang,
　founded by Dr. Sun Yat-sen
　at Honolulu in 1894

興師動衆(ㄒㄧㄥ ㄕ ㄉㄨㄥˋ ㄓㄨㄥˋ)
　to mobilize troops and stir
　up the people

興師問罪(ㄒㄧㄥ ㄕ ㄨㄣˋ ㄗㄨㄟˋ)
　to mobilize troops to chas-
　tise rebels

興盛(ㄒㄧㄥ ㄕㄥˋ)
　prosperous; thriving; vigor-
　ous; flourishing: 他們的生意
　似乎很興盛。Their business
　seemed to flourish.

興衰(ㄒㄧㄥ ㄕㄨㄞ)
　rise and fall; vicissitudes

興戎(ㄒㄧㄥ ㄖㄨㄥˊ)
　to mobilize troops; to open
　hostilities

興作(ㄒㄧㄥ ㄗㄨㄛˋ)
　① to gain power; to rise ②
　to build; to construct; to
　establish; to found

興訟(ㄒㄧㄥ ㄙㄨㄥˋ)
　to start a lawsuit; to com-
　mence litigation

興安(ㄒㄧㄥ ㄢ)
　Hsingan Province

興亡(ㄒㄧㄥ ㄨㄤˊ)
　rise and fall; prosperity and
　adversity: 國家興亡，匹夫有
　責。All men share a common

responsibility for the rise and fall of their nation.

興旺 (ㄒㄧㄥ ㄨㄤˋ)
prosperous; flourishing; thriving

〔白部〕

【興】 4783
2. ㄒㄧㄥˋ shìng xìng

1. cheerful; happy; gay; merry
2. interest; enthusiasm; eagerness; willingness

興頭上 (ㄒㄧㄥˋ ㄊㄡ ㄕㄤˋ)
at the height of one's enthusiasm or interest; to be carried away with something

興頭兒 (ㄒㄧㄥˋ ㄊㄡ ㄦ)
the height of one's eagerness or interest

興高采烈 (ㄒㄧㄥˋ ㄍㄠ ㄘㄞˇ ㄌㄧㄝˋ)
cheerful; in high spirits; elated; jubilant

興會 (ㄒㄧㄥˋ ㄏㄨㄟˋ)
a fit of enthusiasm

興會淋漓 (ㄒㄧㄥˋ ㄏㄨㄟˋ ㄌㄧㄣˊ ㄌㄧˊ)
showing much interest and enthusiasm

興起 (ㄒㄧㄥˋ ㄑㄧˇ)
aroused; excited

興趣 (ㄒㄧㄥˋ ㄑㄩˋ)
① interest; eagerness; enthusiasm; willingness ② enjoyability

興致 (ㄒㄧㄥˋ ㄓˋ)
interest; eagerness; enthusiasm; willingness

興致勃勃 (ㄒㄧㄥˋ ㄓˋ ㄅㄛˊ ㄅㄛˊ)
very much interested; full of enthusiasm

興匆匆 (ㄒㄧㄥˋ ㄘㄨㄥ ㄘㄨㄥ) or 興冲冲 (ㄒㄧㄥˋ ㄔㄨㄥ ㄔㄨㄥ)
cheerful; sprightly; gay; excitedly

興味 (ㄒㄧㄥˋ ㄨㄟˋ)
enjoyability; interest

十畫

【舉】 4784
ㄐㄩˇ jeu jǔ

1. to lift; to raise: 舉起你的右手。Raise your right hand.
2. to recommend; to commend; to praise
3. entire; whole; all
4. manner; deportment: 我不喜歡他的舉止。I don't like his manner.
5. to give birth to a child

舉杯 (ㄐㄩˇ ㄅㄟ)
to lift the cup; to propose a toast

舉辦 (ㄐㄩˇ ㄅㄢˋ)
to sponsor, organize, or initiate

舉兵 (ㄐㄩˇ ㄅㄧㄥ)
to mobilize troops; to start hostilities

舉步 (ㄐㄩˇ ㄅㄨˋ)
to take strides

舉目無親 (ㄐㄩˇ ㄇㄨˋ ㄨˊ ㄑㄧㄣ)
There is not a single friend or relative around.—to have no one to turn to (for help)

舉發 (ㄐㄩˇ ㄈㄚ)
to expose (a secret or conspiracy)

舉凡 (ㄐㄩˇ ㄈㄢˊ)
generally speaking

舉鼎絕臏 (ㄐㄩˇ ㄉㄧㄥˇ ㄐㄩㄝˊ ㄅㄧㄣˋ)
(literally) to hurt the kneecap in trying to carry a caldron—to shoulder a heavy responsibility with limited strength

舉動 (ㄐㄩˇ ㄉㄨㄥˋ)
① deportment; conduct; manner; behavior ② act; movement

舉頭三尺有神明 (ㄐㄩˇ ㄊㄡˊ ㄙㄢ ㄔˇ ㄧㄡˇ ㄕㄣˊ ㄇㄧㄥˊ)
There is a witness everywhere.

舉例 (ㄐㄩˇ ㄌㄧˋ)
to give examples

舉例說明 (ㄐㄩˇ ㄌㄧˋ ㄕㄨㄛ ㄇㄧㄥˊ)
to illustrate; to cite an example by way of explanation

舉國 (ㄐㄩˇ ㄍㄨㄛˊ)
the entire nation

舉國上下 (ㄐㄩˇ ㄍㄨㄛˊ ㄕㄤˋ ㄒㄧㄚˋ)
the entire nation regardless of classes; the ruler and the ruled alike

舉劾 (ㄐㄩˇ ㄏㄜˊ)
① to name and impeach ② recommendation and impeachment

舉火 (ㄐㄩˇ ㄏㄨㄛˇ)
to cook

舉家 (ㄐㄩˇ ㄐㄧㄚ)
the whole family

舉薦 (ㄐㄩˇ ㄐㄧㄢˋ)
to recommend (a person)

舉進士 (ㄐㄩˇ ㄐㄧㄣˋ ㄕˋ)
to become a successful candidate at the imperial examination

舉棋不定 (ㄐㄩˇ ㄑㄧˊ ㄅㄨˋ ㄉㄧㄥˋ)
(literally) unable to decide about a move in playing chess—indecisive; irresolute

舉起 (ㄐㄩˇ ㄑㄧˇ)
to lift; to raise: 把石塊舉起來。Lift up the stone.

舉鎗 (ㄐㄩˇ ㄑㄧㄤ)
to present arms in salute

舉行 (ㄐㄩˇ ㄒㄧㄥˊ)
to hold (examinations, rallies, parties, etc.); to take place: 宴會何時舉行? When will the party take place?

舉行典禮 (ㄐㄩˇ ㄒㄧㄥˊ ㄉㄧㄢˇ ㄌㄧˇ)
to hold a ceremony

舉止 (ㄐㄩˇ ㄓˇ)
deportment; conduct; manner; behavior

舉止大方 (ㄐㄩˇ ㄓˇ ㄉㄚˋ ㄈㄤ)
to have a dignified air; to have poise

舉止行動 (ㄐㄩˇ ㄓˇ ㄒㄧㄥˊ ㄉㄨㄥˋ)
deportment; conduct; manner

舉證 (ㄐㄩˇ ㄓㄥˋ)
to give proof or evidence

舉箸 (ㄐㄩˇ ㄓㄨˋ)
to raise chopsticks to eat

舉踵 (ㄐㄩˇ ㄓㄨㄥˇ)
to be on tiptoe (with eager expectation)

舉重 (ㄐㄩˇ ㄓㄨㄥˋ)
weightlifting

舉翅 (ㄐㄩˇ ㄔˋ)
to wing; to fly

舉出 (ㄐㄩˇ ㄔㄨ)
to enumerate; to itemize; to cite (as an example)

舉士 (ㄐㄩˇ ㄕˋ)
to recommend learned men for public service

舉事 (ㄐㄩˇ ㄕˋ)
to rise up; to start an uprising

舉世 (ㄐㄩˇ ㄕˋ)
all the world

舉世風從 (ㄐㄩˇ ㄕˋ ㄈㄥ ㄘㄨㄥˊ)
The whole world follows the example.

舉世無匹 (ㄐㄩˇ ㄕˋ ㄨˊ ㄆㄧˇ) or 舉世無雙 (ㄐㄩˇ ㄕˋ ㄨˊ ㄕㄨㄤ)
without a match in the

world—unique; peerless

舉世聞名(ㄐㄩˇ ㄕˋ ㄨㄣˊ ㄇㄧㄥˊ)
to be known to the whole
world; world-renowned

舉首(ㄐㄩˇ ㄕㄡˇ)
to raise one's head

舉手(ㄐㄩˇ ㄕㄡˇ)
to raise one's hand

舉手表決(ㄐㄩˇ ㄕㄡˇ ㄅㄧㄠˇ ㄐㄩㄝˊ)
to vote by raising hands

舉手之勞(ㄐㄩˇ ㄕㄡˇ ㄓ ㄌㄠˊ)
(literally) the trouble
involved in raising a hand
—little effort

舉人(ㄐㄩˇ ㄖㄣˊ)
(in the former civil service
examination system) a successful candidate in the provincial examination

舉子(ㄐㄩˇ ㄗˇ)
① to give birth to a son ② a
candidate in the provincial
civil service examination in
former times

舉足輕重(ㄐㄩˇ ㄗㄨˊ ㄑㄧㄥ ㄓㄨㄥˋ)
so important is the role one
plays in a matter that each
step one takes may affect it
in a significant way; capable
of tipping the scale because
of the sensitive post one
holds

舉座(ㄐㄩˇ ㄗㄨㄛˋ)
all those present

舉措(ㄐㄩˇ ㄘㄨㄛˋ)
deportment; conduct; man-
ner

舉哀(ㄐㄩˇ ㄞ)
to weep in mourning; to go
into mourning

舉案齊眉(ㄐㄩˇ ㄢˋ ㄑㄧˊ ㄇㄟˊ)
(literally) to raise the tray
to the height of one's eyebrows, a reference to Liang
Hung (梁鴻) and Meng
Kuang (孟光)—to show
respect to one's spouse

舉一反三(ㄐㄩˇ ㄧ ㄈㄢˇ ㄙㄢ)
(literally) to be able to infer
three from only one that has
been told—to infer the rest
from what is already known

舉義(ㄐㄩˇ ㄧˋ)
to take up arms in the cause
of justice

舉業(ㄐㄩˇ ㄧㄝˋ)
(in the former civil service

examination system) compositions of examinees

十二畫

【舊】 4785
ㄐㄧㄡˋ jiow jiù
1. old; past; former
2. ancient; antique
3. longstanding

舊邦(ㄐㄧㄡˋ ㄅㄤ)
① an ancient kingdom ②
name of a tune in Wei (魏)

舊病復發(ㄐㄧㄡˋ ㄅㄧㄥˋ ㄈㄨˋ ㄈㄚ)
to have a relapse of an old
ailment

舊部(ㄐㄧㄡˋ ㄅㄨˋ)
soldiers or men who used to
be under one's command;
former subordinates

舊瓶裝新酒(ㄐㄧㄡˋ ㄆㄧㄥˊ ㄓㄨㄤ ㄒㄧㄣ ㄐㄧㄡˇ)
(literally) new wine in an
old bottle—new concepts in
an old framework

舊夢重溫(ㄐㄧㄡˋ ㄇㄥˋ ㄔㄨㄥˊ ㄨㄣ)
to renew a sweet experience
of bygone days

舊大陸(ㄐㄧㄡˋ ㄉㄚˋ ㄌㄨˋ)
the Old World (as distinct
from the New World, Amer-
ica) 亦作「舊世界」

舊道德(ㄐㄧㄡˋ ㄉㄠˋ ㄉㄜˊ) or 舊德
(ㄐㄧㄡˋ ㄉㄜˊ)
virtues of the forefathers

舊地(ㄐㄧㄡˋ ㄉㄧˋ)
a once visited place

舊地重遊(ㄐㄧㄡˋ ㄉㄧˋ ㄔㄨㄥˊ ㄧㄡˊ)
to revisit a place

舊調重彈(ㄐㄧㄡˋ ㄉㄧㄠˋ ㄔㄨㄥˊ ㄊㄢˊ)
(literally) to play an old
tune again—to repeat an old
argument or sermon

舊都(ㄐㄧㄡˋ ㄉㄨ)
a former capital; an ancient
capital

舊套(ㄐㄧㄡˋ ㄊㄠˋ)
old stuff; a threadbare plan,
suggestion, etc.

舊唐書(ㄐㄧㄡˋ ㄊㄤˊ ㄕㄨ)
The Old Tang History, by
Liu Hsü (劉昫), etc.—one of
the Twenty-Four Histories

舊筋(ㄐㄧㄡˋ ㄋㄠˇ ㄐㄧㄣ)
conservative-minded

舊年(ㄐㄧㄡˋ ㄋㄧㄢˊ)
① last year; yesteryear ②

the Lunar New Year

舊禮教(ㄐㄧㄡˋ ㄌㄧˇ ㄐㄧㄠˋ)
the old concepts of propriety

舊曆(ㄐㄧㄡˋ ㄌㄧˋ)
the lunar calendar

舊曆年(ㄐㄧㄡˋ ㄌㄧˋ ㄋㄧㄢˊ)
the Lunar New Year; the
Chinese New Year; the
Spring Festival

舊稿(ㄐㄧㄡˋ ㄍㄠˇ)
an old manuscript draft

舊故(ㄐㄧㄡˋ ㄍㄨˋ)
an old friend

舊觀(ㄐㄧㄡˋ ㄍㄨㄢ)
the former appearance; the
previous look; the former
condition

舊觀念(ㄐㄧㄡˋ ㄍㄨㄢ ㄋㄧㄢˋ)
old ideas

舊管(ㄐㄧㄡˋ ㄍㄨㄢˇ)
what one used to be in
charge of

舊貫(ㄐㄧㄡˋ ㄍㄨㄢˋ)
a former system

舊好(ㄐㄧㄡˋ ㄏㄠˇ)
an old friend; old friendship

舊恨新愁(ㄐㄧㄡˋ ㄏㄣˋ ㄒㄧㄣ ㄔㄡˊ)
sorrows old and new; new
sorrows piled on old hatred

舊貨(ㄐㄧㄡˋ ㄏㄨㄛˋ)
secondhand goods; junk

舊貨攤(ㄐㄧㄡˋ ㄏㄨㄛˋ ㄊㄢ)
a stall selling used articles;
a junk store

舊歡(ㄐㄧㄡˋ ㄏㄨㄢ)
a former sweetheart; an ex-
lover; an old flame

舊籍(ㄐㄧㄡˋ ㄐㄧˊ)
old books

舊交(ㄐㄧㄡˋ ㄐㄧㄠ)
an old friend

舊金山(ㄐㄧㄡˋ ㄐㄧㄣ ㄕㄢ)
San Francisco

舊居(ㄐㄧㄡˋ ㄐㄩ)
a former residence

舊情(ㄐㄧㄡˋ ㄑㄧㄥˊ)
former friendship or affection

舊戲(ㄐㄧㄡˋ ㄒㄧˋ)
an old-style drama

舊鄉(ㄐㄧㄡˋ ㄒㄧㄤ)
one's native town

舊學(ㄐㄧㄡˋ ㄒㄩㄝˊ)
① what one learned in by-
gone days ② classic learning

舊址(ㄐㄧㄡˋ ㄓˇ)

〔舊部〕

a former site; a former address

舊制(ㄐㄧㄡˋ ㄓˋ)
a former system; an old system

舊債(ㄐㄧㄡˋ ㄓㄞˋ)
an old debt; an old loan

舊章(ㄐㄧㄡˋ ㄓㄤ)
old regulations

舊賬(ㄐㄧㄡˋ ㄓㄤˋ)
old debts; old bills

舊主(ㄐㄧㄡˋ ㄓㄨˇ)
one's former master

舊著(ㄐㄧㄡˋ ㄓㄨˋ)
an old work (of a writer)

舊稱(ㄐㄧㄡˋ ㄔㄥ)
a former name or designation; known formerly as …

舊詩(ㄐㄧㄡˋ ㄕ)
old-style poetry; classical Chinese poetry: 他喜歡研究舊詩。 He enjoys studying old-style poetry.

舊石器時代(ㄐㄧㄡˋ ㄕˊ ㄑㄧˋ ㄉㄞˋ)
(archeology) the Old Stone Age; the Paleolithic Age

舊式(ㄐㄧㄡˋ ㄕˋ)
old-style; old-type; old-fashioned; out-of-date; obsolescent

舊式婚姻(ㄐㄧㄡˋ ㄕˋ ㄏㄨㄣ ㄧㄣ)
an old-style marriage; an old-fashioned wedding

舊式家庭(ㄐㄧㄡˋ ㄕˋ ㄐㄧㄚ ㄊㄧㄥˊ)
an old-fashioned household; an old-style family

舊事(ㄐㄧㄡˋ ㄕˋ)
an old affair

舊事重提(ㄐㄧㄡˋ ㄕˋ ㄔㄨㄥˊ ㄊㄧˊ)
to refer again to something discussed before or that happened in the past

舊書(ㄐㄧㄡˋ ㄕㄨ)
①a used book: 舊書通常很便宜。 Used books are usually very cheap. ②ancient books; antique books: 這本舊書已絕版。 The ancient book is out of print.

舊書店(ㄐㄧㄡˋ ㄕㄨ ㄉㄧㄢˋ)
a secondhand bookstore

舊書攤(ㄐㄧㄡˋ ㄕㄨ ㄊㄢ)
a secondhand bookstand

舊屬(ㄐㄧㄡˋ ㄕㄨˇ)
former subordinates 參看「舊部」

舊日(ㄐㄧㄡˋ ㄖˋ)
bygone days; former times

舊族(ㄐㄧㄡˋ ㄗㄨˊ)
an ancient family or clan

舊思想(ㄐㄧㄡˋ ㄙ ㄒㄧㄤˇ)
old-fashioned ideas; archaic thinking

舊俗(ㄐㄧㄡˋ ㄙㄨˊ)
old custom; custom or practice no longer prevalent; traditional custom; tradition

舊惡(ㄐㄧㄡˋ ㄜˋ)
①a past feud; an old grudge ②past mistakes; former wickednesses

舊案(ㄐㄧㄡˋ ㄢˋ)
an old case

舊恩(ㄐㄧㄡˋ ㄣ)
a past kindness or favor: 他對我有舊恩。 He has done me many kindnesses in the past.

舊衣服(ㄐㄧㄡˋ ㄧ ㄈㄨˊ)
used clothes; old clothes

舊業(ㄐㄧㄡˋ ㄧㄝˋ)
①a former profession ②estates inherited from ancestors

舊友(ㄐㄧㄡˋ ㄧㄡˇ)
an old friend

舊五代史(ㄐㄧㄡˋ ㄨˇ ㄉㄞˋ ㄕˇ)
The Old History of the Five Dynasties, by Hsüeh Chücheng (薛居正), etc.—one of the Twenty-Four Histories

舊雨新知(ㄐㄧㄡˋ ㄩˇ ㄒㄧㄣ ㄓ)
old friends and new acquaintances

舊約全書(ㄐㄧㄡˋ ㄩㄝ ㄑㄩㄢˊ ㄕㄨ)
the Old Testament

舌 部
ㄕㄜˊ sher shé

【舌】 4786
ㄕㄜˊ sher shé
the tongue

舌本(ㄕㄜˊ ㄅㄣˇ)
the root of the tongue; the back of the tongue

舌敝脣焦(ㄕㄜˊ ㄅㄧˋ ㄔㄨㄣˊ ㄐㄧㄠ)
The tongue is weary and the lips are dry (from talking too much). 或 to talk oneself hoarse

舌鋒(ㄕㄜˊ ㄈㄥ)
eloquence: 她是一個舌鋒銳利的女人。 She is an eloquent woman.

舌苔(ㄕㄜˊ ㄊㄞ)
(Chinese medicine) fur on the tongue; coating on the tongue

舌頭(ㄕㄜˊ ㄊㄡˊ)
the tongue

舌疳(ㄕㄜˊ ㄍㄢ)
(Chinese medicine) an ulcer on the tongue 亦作「舌菌」

舌根(ㄕㄜˊ ㄍㄣ)
the root of the tongue

舌根音(ㄕㄜˊ ㄍㄣ ㄧㄣ)
(phonetics) a dorsal sound

舌耕(ㄕㄜˊ ㄍㄥ)
(literally) to plow with the tongue—to teach for a living

舌骨(ㄕㄜˊ ㄍㄨˇ)
(anatomy) a hyoid bone

舌管(ㄕㄜˊ ㄍㄨㄢˇ)
①reeds (of certain wind instruments) ②reed pipes

舌尖(ㄕㄜˊ ㄐㄧㄢ)
the tip of the tongue

舌尖音(ㄕㄜˊ ㄐㄧㄢ ㄧㄣ)
(phonetics) an apical sound

舌劍脣槍(ㄕㄜˊ ㄐㄧㄢˋ ㄔㄨㄣˊ ㄑㄧㄤ)
acrimonious words used in a quarrel or debate

舌戰(ㄕㄜˊ ㄓㄢˋ)
to debate with verbal confrontation

舌狀花冠(ㄕㄜˊ ㄓㄨㄤˋ ㄏㄨㄚ ㄍㄨㄢ)
a ligulate corolla

舌人(ㄕㄜˊ ㄖㄣˊ)
an interpreter

舌葉(ㄕㄜˊ ㄧㄝˋ)
the tongue blade

舌音(ㄕㄜˊ ㄧㄣ)
(phonetics) lingual sounds

二畫

【舍】 4787
ㄕㄜˋ sheh shè
1. a house
2. an inn
3. to halt; to stop; to rest
4. a self-depreciatory possessive pronoun for the first person singular in formal speech

舍妹(ㄕㄜ ㄇㄟ)
(a self-depreciatory term)
my younger sister

舍弟(ㄕㄜ ㄉㄧ)
(a self-depreciatory term)
my younger brother

舍匿(ㄕㄜ ㄋㄧ)
to hide (a person); to harbor (a criminal)

舍利(ㄕㄜ ㄌㄧ)
①(Buddhism) relics or ashes left after the cremation of a Buddha or saint, placed in stupas and worshiped ② a mynah

舍利塔(ㄕㄜ ㄌㄧ ㄊㄚˇ)
(Buddhism) a tower serving as a depository of holy relics

舍利鹽(ㄕㄜ ㄌㄧ ㄧㄢˊ)
Epsom salt; magnesium sulfate

舍間(ㄕㄜ ㄐㄧㄢ)or 舍下(ㄕㄜ ㄒㄧㄚˋ)
my humble house; my home

舍監(ㄕㄜ ㄐㄧㄢ)
a dormitory superintendent

舍親(ㄕㄜ ㄑㄧㄣ)
(a self-depreciatory term)
my relatives

舍姪(ㄕㄜ ㄓˊ)
(a self-depreciatory term)
my niece or nephew

舍人(ㄕㄜ ㄖㄣˊ)
a kind of palace secretary in the Chou (周)and some later dynasties

【舍】 4787
2. ㄕㄜˋ shee she*
same as 捨—to throw away

四畫

【舐】 4788
ㄕˋ shyh shì
to lick

舐犢情深(ㄕˋ ㄉㄨˊ ㄑㄧㄥˊ ㄕㄣ)
very affectionate toward one's children (like a cow caressing her calves with the tongue)

舐糠(ㄕˋ ㄎㄤ ㄐㄧˊ ㄇㄧˇ)
(literally) to lick the bran until the tongue finally

touches the rice—A country finally falls after its territory is nibbled away.

舐痔吮癰(ㄕˋ ㄓˋ ㄕㄨㄣˇ ㄩㄥ)
(literally) to lick piles and suck tumors (of VIPs)—to show sycophancy; obsequious

舐窗以覘(ㄕˋ ㄔㄨㄤ ㄧˇ ㄔㄢ)
(literally) to lick a hole in a paper window and peep through it—to look stealthily

六畫

【舒】 4789
ㄕㄨ shu shū
1. to unfold; to stretch; to open; to relax
2. slow; unhurried; leisurely
3. a Chinese family name

舒勃(ㄕㄨ ㄅㄛˊ)
to expand; to grow; to develop

舒眉(ㄕㄨ ㄇㄟˊ)
(literally) to relax the brows—to show pleasure

舒眉展眼(ㄕㄨ ㄇㄟˊ ㄓㄢˇ ㄧㄢˇ)
(literally) to relax the brows and stretch the eyes—to show pleasure

舒服(ㄕㄨ ㄈㄨˊ)or 舒適(ㄕㄨ ㄕˋ)
comfortable; cosy; comfort:
他過著舒適的生活。He lives in comfort.

舒泰(ㄕㄨ ㄊㄞˋ)
happy and healthy; well

舒坦(ㄕㄨ ㄊㄢˇ)
in good health; happy; comfortable

舒懷(ㄕㄨ ㄏㄨㄞˊ)
to free the mind from tension; to set the mind at rest

舒緩(ㄕㄨ ㄏㄨㄢˇ)
leisurely; relaxed; to relax

舒筋活血(ㄕㄨ ㄐㄧㄣ ㄏㄨㄛˊ ㄒㄩㄝˋ)
to relax the muscles and enliven the blood

舒卷(ㄕㄨ ㄐㄩㄢˇ)or 舒捲(ㄕㄨ ㄐㄩㄢˇ)
to roll back and forth; to fold or unfold

舒卷自如(ㄕㄨ ㄐㄩㄢˇ ㄗˋ ㄖㄨˊ)or 舒捲自如(ㄕㄨ ㄐㄩㄢˇ ㄗˋ ㄖㄨˊ)
to fold or unfold at will; to do as one pleases

舒心(ㄕㄨ ㄒㄧㄣ)

pleasant; agreeable

舒展(ㄕㄨ ㄓㄢˇ)
to limber up; to unfold; to relax; to stretch

舒張壓(ㄕㄨ ㄓㄤ ㄧㄚ)
(medicine) diastolic pressure

舒暢(ㄕㄨ ㄔㄤˋ)
①pleasant; comfortable: We spent a pleasant vacation. ② leisurely and harmonious

舒適(ㄕㄨ ㄕˋ)
comfortable; cosy; snug 參看〔舒服〕

舒散(ㄕㄨ ㄙㄢˋ)
relaxed; leisurely: 看一場電影舒散一下吧。Take a show and relax.

八畫

【舔】 4790
ㄊㄧㄢˇ tean tiǎn
to lick; to taste: 貓在舔牛奶。
The cat was licking milk.

舔乾淨(ㄊㄧㄢˇ ㄍㄢ ㄐㄧㄥ)
to lick clean

舔一舔(ㄊㄧㄢˇ ㄧˋ ㄊㄧㄢˇ)
to taste by licking

九畫

【舖】 4791
(舗) ㄆㄨˋ puh pù
a shop; a store

十畫

【舘】 4792
(館) ㄍㄨㄢˇ goan guǎn
a mansion; a building

舛 部
ㄔㄨㄢ choan chuān

〔舛 部〕

【舛】 4793
ㄔㄨㄢˇ choan chuǎn
1. chaotic; disorderly; messy; confused; mixed up
2. to run counter to; to disobey; to oppose; to deviate from
3. mishap sufferings; setbacks;

【舟 部】

我的命運多舛。I suffered many a setback during my life.

舛駁(ㄔㄨㄢ ㄅㄛ)
incongruous; contradictory; 這是一個前後舛駁的故事。This is an incongruous story.

舛逆(ㄔㄨㄢ ㄋㄧ)
contrary to reason; absurd

舛互(ㄔㄨㄢ ㄏㄨ)
to interlace; to intermingle; to interlock

舛馳(ㄔㄨㄢ ㄔ)
to go in the opposite direction

舛雜(ㄔㄨㄢ ㄗㄚ)
all mixed up; chaotic

舛辭(ㄔㄨㄢ ㄘ)
irony

舛錯(ㄔㄨㄢ ㄘㄨㄛ)
①erroneous; inexact ②untidy; disorderly; unsystematic

舛午(ㄔㄨㄢ ㄨ)
to oppose each other; to bicker

舛誤(ㄔㄨㄢ ㄨ)
a mistake; an error

六畫

【舜】 4794 ㄕㄨㄣ shuenn shùn
Shun, a legendary ruler said to have ruled ancient China around 2200 B.C.

舜江(ㄕㄨㄣ ㄐㄧㄤ)or 舜水(ㄕㄨㄣ ㄕㄨㄟ)
name of a river in Chekiang

舜日堯年(ㄕㄨㄣ ㄖ ㄧㄠ ㄋㄧㄢ)
(literally) the reign of the legendary emperors Yao(堯) and Shun(舜), supposedly noted for peace and order —the golden age

七畫

【舝】 4795 (精) ㄒㄧㄚ shya xiá
a linchpin

八畫

【舞】 4796 ㄨ wuu wǔ
1. to dance; to prance

2. to brandish; to wave
3. to stir up; to agitate

舞伴(ㄨ ㄅㄢ)
a dancing partner

舞弊(ㄨ ㄅㄧ)
misconduct, malpractice or irregularities (of an official); to bribe; to indulge in corruption

舞抃(ㄨ ㄅㄧㄢ)
to dance for joy

舞步(ㄨ ㄅㄨ)
a dance step

舞票(ㄨ ㄆㄧㄠ)
a dance hall ticket

舞刀(ㄨ ㄉㄠ)
to brandish a knife or sword; to perform swordplay

舞蹈(ㄨ ㄉㄠ)
①dancing ②a dance

舞蹈指揮(ㄨ ㄉㄠ ㄓ ㄏㄨㄟ)
a choreographer

舞動(ㄨ ㄉㄨㄥ)
①to dance; to prance ②to brandish

舞臺(ㄨ ㄊㄞ)
a stage (in a theater)

舞臺監督(ㄨ ㄊㄞ ㄐㄧㄢ ㄉㄨ)
a stage manager

舞臺劇(ㄨ ㄊㄞ ㄐㄩ)
a stage play

舞臺效果(ㄨ ㄊㄞ ㄒㄧㄠ ㄍㄨㄛ)
stage effects

舞臺照明(ㄨ ㄊㄞ ㄓㄠ ㄇㄧㄥ)
stage lighting

舞臺裝置(ㄨ ㄊㄞ ㄓㄨㄤ ㄓ)
a stage setting

舞臺設計(ㄨ ㄊㄞ ㄕㄜ ㄐㄧ)
a stage set

舞臺藝術(ㄨ ㄊㄞ ㄧ ㄕㄨ)
theatrical art; theatricalism

舞廳(ㄨ ㄊㄧㄥ)
a dance hall

舞孃(ㄨ ㄋㄧㄤ)
a taxi dancer

舞女(ㄨ ㄋㄩ)
a taxi dancer; a dancing girl

舞龍(ㄨ ㄌㄨㄥ)
a dragon dance (a team of men dancing with a cloth-made dragon on Chinese festivals)

舞弄(ㄨ ㄌㄨㄥ)
①to wave; to wield; to brandish ②to make fun of

(a person)

舞弄文墨(ㄨ ㄌㄨㄥ ㄨㄣ ㄇㄛ)or 舞文弄墨(ㄨ ㄨㄣ ㄌㄨㄥ ㄇㄛ)
①to amuse oneself with writing ②to tamper with documents (for fraudulent purposes); to pervert the law by playing with legal phraseology

舞客(ㄨ ㄎㄜ)
a dance hall customer

舞會(ㄨ ㄏㄨㄟ)
a dancing party; a dance; a ball

舞技(ㄨ ㄐㄧ)
dancing skills

舞劍(ㄨ ㄐㄧㄢ)
to brandish a sword; to perform swordplay

舞劇(ㄨ ㄐㄩ)
ballet

舞曲(ㄨ ㄑㄩ)
dance music; a dance tune

舞榭歌臺(ㄨ ㄒㄧㄝ ㄍㄜ ㄊㄞ)
a place for dancing and singing; entertainment set-ups

舞池(ㄨ ㄔ)
a dance floor

舞場(ㄨ ㄔㄤ)or(ㄨ ㄔㄤ)
a dance house; a dance hall

舞師(ㄨ ㄕ)
a dancing master or mistress

舞獅(ㄨ ㄕ)
a lion dance (a two-man team dancing inside a cloth-made lion on Chinese festivals)

舞文弄法(ㄨ ㄨㄣ ㄌㄨㄥ ㄈㄚ)
to tamper with the language of documents or laws for illicit purposes

舟 部
ㄓㄡ jou zhōu

【舟】 4797 ㄓㄡ jou zhōu
a boat; a ship; a vessel

舟楫(ㄓㄡ ㄐㄧ)
①ships; vessels ②a capable assistant

舟中敵國 (ㄓㄡ ㄓㄨㄥ ㄉㄧˊ ㄍㄨㄛˊ)
(literally) the enemy in the same boat—treacherous close friends

舟車勞頓 (ㄓㄡ ㄔㄜ ㄌㄠˊ ㄉㄨㄣˋ)
exhausted from a long travel

舟師 (ㄓㄡ ㄕ)
the navy (in ancient times)

舟山羣島 (ㄓㄡ ㄕㄢ ㄑㄩㄣˊ ㄉㄠˇ)
the Choushan Islands (off the Chekiang coast)

舟人 (ㄓㄡ ㄖㄣˊ) or 舟子 (ㄓㄡ ㄗ)
a boatman

舟次 (ㄓㄡ ㄘˋ)
① to moor a boat ② in the way of a boat trip

二畫

【舠】 4798 ㄉㄠ dau dāo
a knife-shaped boat

三畫

【舢】 4799 ㄕㄢ shan shān
a sampan

舢板 or 舢舨 (ㄕㄢ ㄅㄢˇ)
a sampan

【舡】 4800 ㄒㄧㄤ shiang xiāng
a ship; a boat

四畫

【航】 4801 ㄏㄤˊ harng háng
1. a ship; a boat; a vessel
2. to navigate

航道 (ㄏㄤˊ ㄉㄠˋ)
a navigation route

航路 (ㄏㄤˊ ㄌㄨˋ)
a route (of a ship or airplane)

航路標記 (ㄏㄤˊ ㄌㄨˋ ㄅㄧㄠ ㄐㄧˋ)
route markers (for ships, etc.)

航空 (ㄏㄤˊ ㄎㄨㄥ)
aviation; aeronautics

航空母艦 (ㄏㄤˊ ㄎㄨㄥ ㄇㄨˇ ㄐㄧㄢˋ)
an aircraft carrier; a flattop

航空掛號 (ㄏㄤˊ ㄎㄨㄥ ㄍㄨㄚˋ ㄏㄠˋ)
registered airmail

航空工程學 (ㄏㄤˊ ㄎㄨㄥ ㄍㄨㄥ ㄔㄥˊ ㄒㄩㄝˊ)

aeronautical engineering

航空公司 (ㄏㄤˊ ㄎㄨㄥ ㄍㄨㄥ ㄙ)
an airline

航空信 (ㄏㄤˊ ㄎㄨㄥ ㄒㄧㄣˋ)
airmail; an airmail letter: 我寄給她一封航空信。I sent her a letter by airmail.

航空學校 (ㄏㄤˊ ㄎㄨㄥ ㄒㄩㄝˊ ㄒㄧㄠˋ)
an aviation school

航空站 (ㄏㄤˊ ㄎㄨㄥ ㄓㄢˋ)
an air station; an airfield

航空署 (ㄏㄤˊ ㄎㄨㄥ ㄕㄨˇ)
the aviation department or bureau; the aeronautical bureau or department

航空郵件 (ㄏㄤˊ ㄎㄨㄥ ㄧㄡˊ ㄐㄧㄢˋ)
airmail: 今早有航空郵件嗎? Is there any airmail this morning?

航空網 (ㄏㄤˊ ㄎㄨㄥ ㄨㄤˇ)
a network of air routes

航空員 (ㄏㄤˊ ㄎㄨㄥ ㄩㄢˊ)
an airman; an aviator: 那位航空員駕駛他的飛機。The aviator pilots his airplane.

航海 (ㄏㄤˊ ㄏㄞˇ)
maritime navigation; a voyage; to sail on the seas

航海曆書 (ㄏㄤˊ ㄏㄞˇ ㄌㄧˋ ㄕㄨ)
nautical almanacs

航海家 (ㄏㄤˊ ㄏㄞˇ ㄐㄧㄚ)
a navigator; a seafarer

航海節 (ㄏㄤˊ ㄏㄞˇ ㄐㄧㄝˊ)
Navigation Day (falling on July 11)

航海學 (ㄏㄤˊ ㄏㄞˇ ㄒㄩㄝˊ)
maritime navigation

航海術 (ㄏㄤˊ ㄏㄞˇ ㄕㄨˋ)
the art of (sea) navigation

航海日誌 (ㄏㄤˊ ㄏㄞˇ ㄖˋ ㄓˋ)
a log (of a ship)

航權 (ㄏㄤˊ ㄑㄩㄢˊ)
the right of navigation

航線 (ㄏㄤˊ ㄒㄧㄢˋ)
routes (of an airline or shipping company)

航向 (ㄏㄤˊ ㄒㄧㄤˋ)
a course (of a ship or plane)

航行 (ㄏㄤˊ ㄒㄧㄥˊ)
① to sail ② to fly

航政 (ㄏㄤˊ ㄓㄥˋ)
shipping administration

航程 (ㄏㄤˊ ㄔㄥˊ)
the distance of an air or a sea trip; sail: 此處距香港有兩

日之航程。It is two days' sail from Hongkong.

航船 (ㄏㄤˊ ㄔㄨㄢˊ)
a liner

航業 (ㄏㄤˊ ㄧㄝˋ)
shipping business

航業公司 (ㄏㄤˊ ㄧㄝˋ ㄍㄨㄥ ㄙ)
a shipping company

航運 (ㄏㄤˊ ㄩㄣˋ)
shipping: 他們從事航運業。They engage in shipping business.

【般】 4802 ㄅㄢ ban bān
1. kind; sort; class
2. same as 搬—to carry; to move
3. same as 班—to return; to call back

般般 (ㄅㄢ ㄅㄢ)
① colorful; gorgeous 亦作「斑斑」② all kinds; every sort

般配 (ㄅㄢ ㄆㄟˋ)
to match: 他的服飾與年齡般配。His clothes match his age.

般師 (ㄅㄢ ㄕ)
to call back troops; to withdraw troops after a victorious campaign

【般】 4802 ㄆㄢˊ parn pán
1. to linger
2. comfort
3. a leather bag

般樂 (ㄆㄢˊ ㄌㄜˋ)
to have fun without being conscious of time; pleasure

般遊 (ㄆㄢˊ ㄧㄡˊ)
to play without being conscious of time

【般】 4802 3. ㄅㄛ bo bō
(Buddhism) intelligence

般若 (ㄅㄛ ㄖㄜˋ)
(Buddhism) *prajna*, wisdom

【舫】 4803 ㄈㄤ faang fāng
1. two boats lashed side by side
2. boats; ships

【舨】 4804 ㄅㄢˇ baan bǎn
as in 舢舨—a sampan

五畫

（舟部）

【舲】 4805
ㄌㄧㄥˊ ling líng
a small boat with portholes

【舳】 4806
ㄓㄨˊ jwu zhú
（又讀 ㄓㄡ jour zhóu）
the stern (of a ship)

舳艫（ㄓㄨˊ ㄌㄨˊ）
a rectangular boat

舳艫千里（ㄓㄨˊ ㄌㄨˊ ㄑㄧㄢ ㄌㄧˇ）
(literally) formation of ships extending over a thousand miles—a very large flotilla

【舴】 4807
ㄗㄜˊ tzer zé
a small boat

舴艋（ㄇㄥˇ měng）
a small boat

【舵】 4808
ㄉㄨㄛˋ duoh duò
a rudder; a helm

舵手（ㄉㄨㄛˋ ㄕㄡˇ）
a helmsman; a steersman: 首相是國家的舵手。 The Prime Minister is the helmsman of the state.

【舶】 4809
ㄅㄛˊ bor bó
an ocean-going ship

舶來品（ㄅㄛˊ ㄌㄞˊ ㄆㄧㄣˇ）
imported goods; foreign goods

【舷】 4810
ㄒㄧㄢˊ shyan xián
bulwarks (of a ship); the gunwale or gunnel

【舸】 4811
《ㄜˇ gee gě
a large boat

【船】 4812
ㄔㄨㄢˊ chwan chuán
a ship; a boat; a vessel; a craft

船舶（ㄔㄨㄢˊ ㄅㄛˊ）
ships; vessels; boats; crafts

船板（ㄔㄨㄢˊ ㄅㄢˇ）
the deck (of a ship)

船幫（ㄔㄨㄢˊ ㄅㄤ）
sides of a ship

船埠（ㄔㄨㄢˊ ㄅㄨˋ）
a port; a harbor; a wharf

船破又遇打頭風（ㄔㄨㄢˊ ㄆㄛˋ ㄧㄡˋ ㄩˋ ㄉㄚˇ ㄊㄡˊ ㄈㄥ）
(literally) to meet unfavorable winds when the boat is broken—to meet additional difficulty

船篷（ㄔㄨㄢˊ ㄆㄥˊ）
coverings of a boat

船票（ㄔㄨㄢˊ ㄆㄧㄠˋ）
a ticket for passage by sea

船面（ㄔㄨㄢˊ ㄇㄧㄢˋ）
the deck (of a ship): 我們去船面上散步吧。 Let's have a walk round the deck.

船費（ㄔㄨㄢˊ ㄈㄟˋ）
a fare for a voyage

船夫（ㄔㄨㄢˊ ㄈㄨ）
a sailor; a boatman

船到江心補漏遲（ㄔㄨㄢˊ ㄉㄠˋ ㄐㄧㄤ ㄒㄧㄣ ㄅㄨˇ ㄌㄡˋ ㄔˊ）
(literally) It will be too late to mend a boat when it has reached the middle of the river.—It's too late to take corrective measures when a crisis has already developed.

船到橋頭自然直（ㄔㄨㄢˊ ㄉㄠˋ ㄑㄧㄠˊ ㄊㄡˊ ㄗˋ ㄖㄢˊ ㄓˊ）
It will take care of itself when the time comes.或 Everything will be all right when the time comes.

船多不礙江（ㄔㄨㄢˊ ㄉㄨㄛ ㄅㄨˋ ㄞˋ ㄐㄧㄤ）
(literally) There is no harm to the river when there are many boats sailing on it.—Competition among businessmen does no harm to business prosperity.

船隊（ㄔㄨㄢˊ ㄉㄨㄟˋ）
a fleet; a flotilla

船東（ㄔㄨㄢˊ ㄉㄨㄥ）
a shipowner

船頭（ㄔㄨㄢˊ ㄊㄡˊ）
the bow or prow (of a boat)

船齡（ㄔㄨㄢˊ ㄌㄧㄥˊ）
the age of a ship

船客（ㄔㄨㄢˊ ㄎㄜˋ）
the passengers of a ship

船客名單（ㄔㄨㄢˊ ㄎㄜˋ ㄇㄧㄥˊ ㄉㄢ）
the passenger list (of a boat)

船戶（ㄔㄨㄢˊ ㄏㄨˋ）
a boatman's family

船貨（ㄔㄨㄢˊ ㄏㄨㄛˋ）
cargo

船籍（ㄔㄨㄢˊ ㄐㄧˊ）
nationality of a ship

船家（ㄔㄨㄢˊ ㄐㄧㄚ）
a boatman

船腳（ㄔㄨㄢˊ ㄐㄧㄠˇ）

①a boatman ②shipping freight

船期（ㄔㄨㄢˊ ㄑㄧ）
a shipping schedule

船舷（ㄔㄨㄢˊ ㄒㄧㄢˊ）
bulwarks (of a boat); the gunwale or gunnel

船隻（ㄔㄨㄢˊ ㄓ）
ships; boats; crafts; vessels

船長（ㄔㄨㄢˊ ㄓㄤˇ）
the captain or skipper (of a boat)

船主（ㄔㄨㄢˊ ㄓㄨˇ）
①the captain or skipper (of a boat) ②the owner (of a boat)

船廠（ㄔㄨㄢˊ ㄔㄤˇ）
a shipyard; a dockyard

船槍（ㄔㄨㄢˊ ㄔㄤˊ）
the bow or prow (of a boat)

船身（ㄔㄨㄢˊ ㄕㄣ）
a ship's hull

船身傾斜（ㄔㄨㄢˊ ㄕㄣ ㄑㄧㄥ ㄒㄧㄝˊ）
(said of a ship) listing; to list

船深（ㄔㄨㄢˊ ㄕㄣ）
draft (of a ship): 這船船深十英呎。 This is a ship of 10 feet draft.

船上交貨價（ㄔㄨㄢˊ ㄕㄤˋ ㄐㄧㄠ ㄏㄨㄛˋ ㄐㄧㄚˋ）
free on board (F.O.B.)

船艙（ㄔㄨㄢˊ ㄘㄤ）
the hold or cabin (of a boat)

船塢 or 船澳（ㄔㄨㄢˊ ㄨˋ）
a dock (in a shipyard)

船桅（ㄔㄨㄢˊ ㄨㄟˊ）
the mast (of a ship)

船尾（ㄔㄨㄢˊ ㄨㄟˇ）
the stern (of a ship)

船位（ㄔㄨㄢˊ ㄨㄟˋ）
①accommodation (on a ship) ②a ship's position

船員（ㄔㄨㄢˊ ㄩㄢˊ）
the crew (of a ship)

船運（ㄔㄨㄢˊ ㄩㄣˋ）
to transport by ship

七畫

【艇】 4813
ㄊㄧㄥˇ tǐng tǐng
a long, narrow boat

艇長（ㄊㄧㄥˇ ㄓㄤˇ）
the skipper of a naval boat

【艄】 4814
ㄕㄠ shau shāo
1. the stern (of a boat)
2. a rudder; a helm: 誰在掌艄? Who is at the helm?

艄婆(ㄕㄠ ㄆㄛˊ)
a boatwoman

艄公(ㄕㄠ ㄍㄨㄥ)
a helmsman; a boatman 亦作「船夫」

八畫

【艋】 4815
ㄇㄥˇ meeng měng
a small boat

十畫

【艘】 4816
ㄙㄠ sau sōu
a numerary adjunct for ships

【艙】 4817
ㄘㄤ tsang cāng
the hold or cabin (of a ship)

艙房(ㄘㄤ ㄈㄤˊ)
cabins (of a ship)

艙底(ㄘㄤ ㄉㄧˇ)
the bottom of a ship's hold

艙位(ㄘㄤ ㄨㄟˋ)
space for passengers (in a liner); a berth

十二畫

【艟】 4818
ㄔㄨㄥˊ torng tóng
as in 艨艟—an ancient warship

十三畫

【艤】 4819
ㄧˇ yii yǐ
to moor (a boat) to the bank

十四畫

【艦】 4820
ㄐㄧㄢˋ jiann jiàn
a warship; a man-of-war; a naval vessel

艦隊(ㄐㄧㄢˋ ㄉㄨㄟˋ)
a fleet; a naval task force

艦隊司令(ㄐㄧㄢˋ ㄉㄨㄟˋ ㄙ ㄌㄧㄥˋ)
a fleet commander

艦艇(ㄐㄧㄢˋ ㄊㄧㄥˇ)
naval vessels

艦橋(ㄐㄧㄢˋ ㄑㄧㄠˊ)
the bridge (of a naval ship)

艦隻(ㄐㄧㄢˋ ㄓ)
naval vessels

艦長(ㄐㄧㄢˋ ㄓㄤˇ)
the captain or skipper of a naval vessel

【艨】 4821
ㄇㄥˊ meng méng
as in 艨艟—an ancient warship

十六畫

【艫】 4822
ㄌㄨˊ lu lú
the bow or prow (of a boat)

艮 部
ㄍㄣ genn gèn

【艮】 4823
1. ㄍㄣˋ genn gèn
one of the Eight Diagrams for divination

艮苦冰涼(ㄍㄣˇ ㄎㄨˇ ㄅㄧㄥ ㄌㄧㄤˊ)
①stark poverty; great misery ②ruthless; relentless; merciless; cold

【艮】 4823
2. ㄍㄣ geen gén
1. (said of food) tough; leathery
2. straightforward; outspoken; blunt
3. (said of clothing) simple
4. (said of one's personality) honest; upright

一畫

【良】 4824
ㄌㄧㄤˊ liang liáng
1. good; fine; desirable: 她出身良好。 She has a good background.
2. very
3. instinctive; inborn; innate

良伴(ㄌㄧㄤˊ ㄅㄢˋ)
a good companion

良弼(ㄌㄧㄤˊ ㄅㄧˋ)
a good assistant

良兵(ㄌㄧㄤˊ ㄅㄧㄥ)
good troops

良庖(ㄌㄧㄤˊ ㄆㄠˊ)
a good cook; a fine chef

良朋(ㄌㄧㄤˊ ㄆㄥˊ)or良友(ㄌㄧㄤˊ ㄧㄡˇ)or良朋益友(ㄌㄧㄤˊ ㄆㄥˊ ㄧˋ ㄧㄡˇ)
worthy friends; good friends; beneficial friends

良平之智(ㄌㄧㄤˊ ㄆㄧㄥˊ ㄓ ㄓˋ)
(literally) the wisdom of Chang Liang (張良) and Chen Ping(陳平)(who helped Liu Pang(劉邦) found the Han Dynasty)—great political sagacity

良馬(ㄌㄧㄤˊ ㄇㄚˇ)
a fine horse

良媒(ㄌㄧㄤˊ ㄇㄟˊ)
an able matchmaker

良民(ㄌㄧㄤˊ ㄇㄧㄣˊ)
law-abiding people; loyal subjects

良方(ㄌㄧㄤˊ ㄈㄤ)
①a good remedy; a good prescription: 這是治咳嗽的良方。 This is a good prescription for a cough. ②a good course of action

良導體(ㄌㄧㄤˊ ㄉㄠˇ ㄊㄧˇ)
a good conductor (of heat or electricity)

良多(ㄌㄧㄤˊ ㄉㄨㄛ)
very much; numerous; a great deal

良田(ㄌㄧㄤˊ ㄊㄧㄢˊ)
fertile fields; good land

良圖(ㄌㄧㄤˊ ㄊㄨˊ)
a good plan or scheme

良能(ㄌㄧㄤˊ ㄋㄥˊ)
inborn ability; intuitive ability; instinct

良吏(ㄌㄧㄤˊ ㄌㄧˋ)
a good official; a virtuous public servant

良港(ㄌㄧㄤˊ ㄍㄤˇ)
a good harbor

良弓(ㄌㄧㄤˊ ㄍㄨㄥ)
①a good bowmaker ②a fine bow

良工心苦(ㄌㄧㄤˊ ㄍㄨㄥ ㄒㄧㄣ ㄎㄨˇ)
Expert craftsmanship is the result of long practice and hard work.

良好(ㄌㄧㄤˊ ㄏㄠˇ)
good; fine; desirable

良機(ㄌㄧㄤˊ ㄐㄧ)
a good chance

〔色部〕

良機勿失(ㄌㄧㄤˊ ㄐㄧ ㄨˋ ㄕ)
Don't let the good chance slip.

良計(ㄌㄧㄤˊ ㄐㄧˋ)
a good plan, scheme, or strategy

良家(ㄌㄧㄤˊ ㄐㄧㄚ)
a good family; a respectable family

良家子女(ㄌㄧㄤˊ ㄐㄧㄚ ㄗˇ ㄋㄩˇ)
children of good parentage

良久(ㄌㄧㄤˊ ㄐㄧㄡˇ)
for a very long time: 我們在那邊停留良久。We stayed there for a very long time.

良賤(ㄌㄧㄤˊ ㄐㄧㄢˋ)
the different social classes; high and low

良金美玉(ㄌㄧㄤˊ ㄐㄧㄣ ㄇㄟˇ ㄩˋ)
(said of character, writing, etc.) like fine gold and fair jade

良將(ㄌㄧㄤˊ ㄐㄧㄤˋ)
a brilliant general

良禽擇木而棲(ㄌㄧㄤˊ ㄑㄧㄣˊ ㄗㄜˊ ㄇㄨˋ ㄦˊ ㄑㄧ)
(literally) Clever birds choose their trees when they nest.—Capable men choose the right leader to serve.

良宵(ㄌㄧㄤˊ ㄒㄧㄠ)
an enjoyable night: 那是一個滿天星斗的良宵。It was a starry enjoyable night.

良心(ㄌㄧㄤˊ ㄒㄧㄣ)
conscience

良心發現(ㄌㄧㄤˊ ㄒㄧㄣ ㄈㄚ ㄒㄧㄢˋ)
The conscience is moved.

良心譴責(ㄌㄧㄤˊ ㄒㄧㄣ ㄑㄧㄢˇ ㄗㄜˊ)
to feel the pricks of conscience; to have a guilty conscience

良心喪盡(ㄌㄧㄤˊ ㄒㄧㄣ ㄙㄤˋ ㄐㄧㄣˋ)
utterly conscienceless: 他已良心喪盡。He is utterly conscienceless.

良相(ㄌㄧㄤˊ ㄒㄧㄤˋ)
a wise prime minister

良知(ㄌㄧㄤˊ ㄓ)
①instinct; innate knowledge
②understanding friend

良知良能(ㄌㄧㄤˊ ㄓ ㄌㄧㄤˊ ㄋㄥˊ)
innate knowledge and ability; instinct

良緣(ㄌㄧㄤˊ ㄩㄢˊ)
a peaceful death

良辰(ㄌㄧㄤˊ ㄔㄣˊ)or 良日(ㄌㄧㄤˊ ㄖˋ)
a pleasant day

良辰美景(ㄌㄧㄤˊ ㄔㄣˊ ㄇㄟˇ ㄐㄧㄥˇ)
a pleasant day coupled with a fine landscape

良師(ㄌㄧㄤˊ ㄕ)
a good teacher: 大自然是我們的良師。Nature is our good teacher.

良師興國(ㄌㄧㄤˊ ㄕ ㄒㄧㄥ ㄍㄨㄛˊ)
Good teachers can help bring a nation to power.

良師益友(ㄌㄧㄤˊ ㄕ ㄧˋ ㄧㄡˇ)
good teachers and helpful friends

良史(ㄌㄧㄤˊ ㄕˇ)
①a good history book ②a good historian

良士(ㄌㄧㄤˊ ㄕˋ)
a person of high moral standing

良善(ㄌㄧㄤˊ ㄕㄢˋ)
good; fine

良風俗(ㄌㄧㄤˊ ㄈㄥ ㄙㄨˊ)
good custom or practice

良深(ㄌㄧㄤˊ ㄕㄣ)
deeply; very: 他感動良深。He was deeply moved.

良人(ㄌㄧㄤˊ ㄖㄣˊ)
①a good person ②one's husband

良策(ㄌㄧㄤˊ ㄘㄜˋ)
a good policy, scheme, or strategy

良材(ㄌㄧㄤˊ ㄘㄞˊ)
an able person

良死(ㄌㄧㄤˊ ㄙˇ)
to die a natural death

良醫(ㄌㄧㄤˊ ㄧ)
an able physician; a good doctor

良冶(ㄌㄧㄤˊ ㄧㄝˇ)
a fine metalist

良夜(ㄌㄧㄤˊ ㄧㄝˋ)
a pleasant night

良藥苦口(ㄌㄧㄤˊ ㄧㄠˋ ㄎㄨˇ ㄎㄡˇ)
(literally) Good medicine tastes bitter.—Good advice is never pleasant to the ear.

良莠不齊(ㄌㄧㄤˊ ㄧㄡˇ ㄅㄨˋ ㄑㄧˊ)
some good, some bad (especially said of a crowd of people)

良月(ㄌㄧㄤˊ ㄩㄝˋ)
the tenth month of the lunar calendar

良緣(ㄌㄧㄤˊ ㄩㄢˊ)
a harmonious union; a happy match

十一畫

【艱】 4825 ㄐㄧㄢ jiān jiān
1. difficult; hard; trying
2. mourning for one's parents

艱難(ㄐㄧㄢ ㄋㄢˊ)
difficulty; distress; hardship

艱難困苦(ㄐㄧㄢ ㄋㄢˊ ㄎㄨㄣˋ ㄎㄨˇ)
great difficulties or hardships

艱苦(ㄐㄧㄢ ㄎㄨˇ)
trying; hard; privation

艱苦備嘗(ㄐㄧㄢ ㄎㄨˇ ㄅㄟˋ ㄔㄤˊ)
to have experienced all sorts of hardships

艱困(ㄐㄧㄢ ㄎㄨㄣˋ)
difficult

艱鉅(ㄐㄧㄢ ㄐㄩˋ)
hard; difficult; arduous; laborious; formidable

艱險(ㄐㄧㄢ ㄒㄧㄢˇ)or 艱危(ㄐㄧㄢ ㄨㄟˊ)
difficult and dangerous

艱辛(ㄐㄧㄢ ㄒㄧㄣ)
arduous; laborious; hard; difficult

艱貞(ㄐㄧㄢ ㄓㄣ)
fortitude under trying conditions

艱深(ㄐㄧㄢ ㄕㄣ)
abstruse; difficult: 這是一個艱深的問題。This is an abstruse question.

艱阻(ㄐㄧㄢ ㄗㄨˇ)
troublesome obstacles

艱澀(ㄐㄧㄢ ㄙㄜˋ)
abstruse; difficult

色 部
ㄙㄜˋ seh sè

【色】 4826
ㄙㄜˋ seh sè
(語音 ㄕㄞˇ shae shai)

1. a color; a tinge; a tint; a hue

2. facial expression; a look; an appearance

3. sensuality; lust; lewdness; carnal pleasure

4. worldly things

5. a kind; a sort

色玻璃（ㄙㄜ ㄅㄛ‧ㄌㄧ）
stained glass; colored glass

色盲（ㄙㄜ ㄇㄤ）
color blindness; color-blind; achromatopsy

色迷（ㄙㄜ ㄇㄧ）
a sensualist; a Don Juan

色目（ㄙㄜ ㄇㄨ）
social status (as distinguished from the colors of clothing)

色膽包天（ㄙㄜ ㄉㄢ ㄅㄠ ㄊㄧㄢ）
extremely daring in lewdness

色調（ㄙㄜ ㄉㄧㄠ）
a shade of color; a tone

色狼（ㄙㄜ ㄌㄤ）
(slang) a wolf—a lecherous person 參看「色鬼」

色属內荏（ㄙㄜ ㄍㄚ ㄋㄟ ㄖㄣˇ）
looking tough but scared at heart; fierce of mien but faint of heart

色鬼（ㄙㄜ ㄍㄨㄟ）
a satyr; a lecher: 他 是 個 色鬼。He is a satyr.

色荒（ㄙㄜ ㄏㄨㄤ）
unrestrained indulgence in lust

色卽是空（ㄙㄜ ㄐㄧ ㄕ ㄎㄨㄥ）
(a Buddhist concept) Everything visible is empty.

色覺（ㄙㄜ ㄐㄩㄝ）
sensation of color

色情（ㄙㄜ ㄑㄧㄥ）
sexual passion; lust

色情狂（ㄙㄜ ㄑㄧㄥ ㄎㄨㄤ）
① sexual insanity; satyriasis ② erotomania; nymphomania ③ an erotomaniac; a nymphomaniac

色喜（ㄙㄜ ㄒㄧˇ）
showing pleasure; looking pleased

色笑（ㄙㄜ ㄒㄧㄠ）
a benign look

色相（ㄙㄜ ㄒㄧㄤ）
①(Buddhism) the outward appearance of a thing ② feminine charm

色紙（ㄙㄜ ㄓˇ）
colored paper

色智（ㄙㄜ ㄓ）
looking arrogant in the belief that one is superior to others

色中餓鬼（ㄙㄜ ㄓㄨㄥ ㄜ《ㄨㄟˇ）
a satyr; an erotomaniac

色授神與（ㄙㄜ ㄕㄡ ㄕㄣ ㄩˇ）
communication between minds without use of words

色身（ㄙㄜ ㄕㄣ）
①(Buddhism) the physical body ② outward charm of a woman

色衰愛弛（ㄙㄜ ㄕㄨㄞ ㄞ ㄔ）
to lose beauty as well as affection

色澤（ㄙㄜ ㄗㄜˊ）
a tinge; a color; a hue; a tint

色彩（ㄙㄜ ㄘㄞˇ）
a color; a hue; a tint; a tinge: 紅、藍 和 黃 都 是 色彩。Red, blue and yellow are colors.

色彩鮮明（ㄙㄜ ㄘㄞ ㄒㄧㄢ ㄇㄧㄥ）
bright-colored

色色俱全（ㄙㄜ ㄙㄜ ㄐㄩˋ ㄑㄩㄢˊ）
complete with all sorts of things

色素（ㄙㄜ ㄙㄨˋ）
pigment

色素細胞（ㄙㄜ ㄙㄨ ㄒㄧˋ ㄅㄠ）
a chromatophore

色藝（ㄙㄜ ㄧˋ）
beauty and accomplishments (of a woman)

色艷桃李（ㄙㄜ ㄧㄢ ㄊㄠ ㄌㄧˇ）
(said of a woman) as beautiful as a flower

色慾（ㄙㄜ ㄩˋ）
sexual desire; sexual passion; lust: 他縱情色慾。He indulged himself in lust.

五畫

【觓】 4827
（ㄈㄨ ㄈㄨˊ）fwu fwu
to look angry

觓然（ㄈㄨ ㄖㄢˊ）
to look angry; an angry look

十八畫

【艷】 4828
（艷）ㄢˋ yann yàn
beautiful; 她 是 一個 艷婦。She

is a beautiful woman.

艸 部
ㄘㄠˇ tsao cáo

【艸】 4829
ㄘㄠˇ tsao cǎo
grass; straw; weeds

二畫

【艾】 4830
ㄞˋ ay ài
1. moxa
2. fine; fair; beautiful; good
3. old
4. to end; to cease; to stop; to discontinue
5. a Chinese family name

艾老（ㄞ ㄌㄠˇ）
over 50 years old

艾酒（ㄞ ㄐㄧㄡˇ）
moxa wine

艾灸（ㄞ ㄐㄧㄡ）or 艾炷灸（ㄞ ㄓㄨ ㄐㄧㄡ）
moxibustion

艾森豪（ㄞ ㄙㄣ ㄏㄠˊ）
Dwight David Eisenhower, 1890-1969, 34th president of the United States

艾艾（ㄞ ㄞ）
stammering; stuttering

【芀】 4831
ㄋㄞˇ nae nǎi
a kind of vegetable

三畫

【芃】 4832
ㄆㄥˊ perng péng
growing luxuriantly; lush

【芄】 4833
ㄨㄢˊ wan wán
Metaplexis japonica

【芊】 4834
ㄑㄧㄢ chian qiān
(said of grass) lush; green

【芋】 4835
ㄩˋ yuh yù
a taro

芋頭（ㄩ ‧ㄊㄡ）or 芋芍（ㄩ ㄋㄞˇ）
(botany) a taro

【芍】
4836
ㄕㄠ shaur　shǎo
（讀音 ㄕㄨㄛ shuoh　shuò）

Paeonia; a peony

芍藥（ㄕㄠ ㄧㄠˋ）
a Chinese herbaceous peony

【芎】
4837
ㄒㄩㄥ chiong　qióng
（讀音 ㄑㄩㄥˊ chyong　qióng）

a kind of herb (*Cnidium officinale*)

【芒】
4838
ㄇㄤ mang　máng

1. *Miscanthus sinensis*, a kind of grass whose leaves can be used to make sandals
2. a sharp point
3. (botany) an awn; an arista; beards of wheat
4. rays (of stars)
5. a Chinese family name

芒芒（ㄇㄤ ㄇㄤ）
①tired；weary②vast；extensive 亦作「茫茫」③abundant

芒果（ㄇㄤ ㄍㄨㄛˇ）
a mango

芒鞋（ㄇㄤ ㄒㄧㄝˊ）
straw sandals：僧人穿芒鞋。
Monks wear straw sandals.

芒種（ㄇㄤ ㄓㄨㄥˇ）
one of the 24 seasonal periods into which the year is divided (occurring about June 5-7)

芒刃（ㄇㄤ ㄖㄣˋ）
a sharp blade

芒刺在背（ㄇㄤ ㄘˋ ㄗㄞˋ ㄅㄟˋ）
(literally) having prickles down the back—ill at ease；deeply worried

四畫

【芙】
4839
ㄈㄨˊ fwu　fú

a hibiscus

芙蕖（ㄈㄨˊ ㄑㄩˊ）
lotus flowers

芙蓉（ㄈㄨˊ ㄖㄨㄥˊ）
a hibiscus

芙蓉面（ㄈㄨˊ ㄖㄨㄥˊ ㄇㄧㄢˋ）
a face fair as a hibiscus；a pretty face

芙蓉鳥（ㄈㄨˊ ㄖㄨㄥˊ ㄋㄧㄠˇ）
Serinus cannaria, a kind of singing bird

芙蓉帳（ㄈㄨˊ ㄖㄨㄥˊ ㄓㄤˋ）
a mosquito net dyed with the juice of hibiscus flowers

芙蓉出水（ㄈㄨˊ ㄖㄨㄥˊ ㄔㄨ ㄕㄨㄟˇ）
a hibiscus rising out of water (descriptive of the gracefulness of a piece of writing, a woman, etc.)

【芝】
4840
ㄓ jy　zhī

1. a kind of purplish fungus symbolizing nobility
2. a kind of fragrant herb
3. a Chinese family name

芝麻（ㄓ ㄇㄚˊ）
sesame

芝麻楷（ㄓ ㄇㄚˊ ㄐㄧㄝˊ）
sesame stalks and husks after its seeds have been collected

芝麻醬（ㄓ ㄇㄚˊ ㄐㄧㄤˋ）
a pasty preparation from sesame；sesame butter

芝麻油（ㄓ ㄇㄚˊ ㄧㄡˊ）
sesame oil

芝眉（ㄓ ㄇㄟˊ）
dignified eyebrows

芝罘條約（ㄓ ㄈㄨˊ ㄊㄧㄠˊ ㄩㄝ）
a treaty signed with Great Britain in 1876, under which China opened five ports and paid 200,000 taels of silver as compensation for the death of a British citizen killed in Yunnan 亦作「煙臺條約」

芝焚蕙歎（ㄓ ㄈㄣˊ ㄏㄨㄟˋ ㄊㄢˋ）
One is saddened over the fall of a kindred spirit.

芝泥（ㄓ ㄋㄧˊ）
stamp ink 亦作「印泥」

芝蘭（ㄓ ㄌㄢˊ）
①the glossy ganoderma and the fragrant thoroughwort—both of them are fragrant herbs ②(figuratively) a virtuous behavior

芝蘭臭味（ㄓ ㄌㄢˊ ㄔㄡˋ ㄨㄟˋ）
noble friendship

芝蘭室（ㄓ ㄌㄢˊ ㄕˋ）
a morally fine environment

芝蘭玉樹（ㄓ ㄌㄢˊ ㄩˋ ㄕㄨˋ）
worthy followers or disciples

芝加哥（ㄓ ㄐㄧㄚ ㄍㄜ）
Chicago, Illinois

芝草（ㄓ ㄘㄠˇ）
a kind of parasitic fungus

芝艾俱焚（ㄓ ㄞˋ ㄐㄩˋ ㄈㄣˊ）
The noble and the lowly alike met their fate.

芝儀（ㄓ ㄧˊ）or 芝顏（ㄓ ㄧㄢˊ）or 芝宇（ㄓ ㄩˇ）
your noble face

【芟】
4841
ㄕㄢ shan　shān

1. to mow；to cut down
2. to eliminate；to exterminate
3. a scythe

芟薙（ㄕㄢ ㄏㄨㄛˋ）
to weed out causes of harm

芟除（ㄕㄢ ㄔㄨˊ）
to weed out；to eliminate；to exterminate；to eradicate

芟草除根（ㄕㄢ ㄘㄠˇ ㄔㄨˊ ㄍㄣ）
to clear the ground of weeds and roots

芟夷（ㄕㄢ ㄧˊ）
to exterminate；to eliminate；to weed out

【芡】
4842
ㄑㄧㄢˋ chiann　qiàn

(botany) Gorgon euryale (*Euryale ferox*)

芡粉（ㄑㄧㄢˋ ㄈㄣˇ）
a kind of starch

芡實（ㄑㄧㄢˋ ㄕˊ）
Gorgon fruit 亦作「雞頭米」

【芣】
4843
ㄈㄡ four　fóu

a plantain

芣苢 or 芣苡（ㄈㄡ ㄧˇ）
a plantain

【芥】
4844
ㄐㄧㄝ jieh　jiè

1. a mustard plant
2. tiny

芥末（ㄐㄧㄝ ·ㄇㄛ）
ground mustard

芥蒂 or 芥蔕（ㄐㄧㄝ ㄉㄧˋ）
①remorse；a grudge ②a barrier which mars friendship

芥藍菜（ㄐㄧㄝ ㄌㄢˊ ㄘㄞˋ）
a kind of green vegetable

芥子（ㄐㄧㄝ ㄗˇ）
①mustard seed ②a tiny thing

芥子瓦斯（ㄐㄧㄝ ㄗˇ ㄨㄚˇ ㄙ）or 芥子氣（ㄐㄧㄝ ㄗˇ ㄑㄧˋ）
(chemistry) mustard gas

芥菜（ㄐㄧㄝ ㄘㄞˋ）

a mustard plant; leaf mustard

【芧】 4845
ㄒㄩ shiuh xù
a kind of chestnut oak

芧栗(ㄒㄩ ㄌㄧ)
a small chestnut

【芩】 4846
ㄑㄧㄣ chyn qín
Phragmites japonica, a kind of herb whose root is medicinal

【芫】 4847
ㄩㄢ yuán yuán
Daphne genkwa, a kind of poisonous plant

芫荽(ㄩㄢ ㄙㄨㄟ)
parsley

【芬】 4848
ㄈㄣ fen fēn
fragrance; aroma; a sweet smell; perfume

芬菲(ㄈㄣ ㄈㄟ)
fragrance of flowers

芬芬(ㄈㄣ ㄈㄣ)
a sweet smell; fragrance; aroma

芬芳(ㄈㄣ ㄈㄤ)
fragrant; aromatic: 花園中的玫瑰很芬芳。The roses in the garden were fragrant.

芬馥(ㄈㄣ ㄈㄨ)
fragrant

芬蘭(ㄈㄣ ㄌㄢ)
Finland

芬蘭人(ㄈㄣ ㄌㄢ ㄖㄣ)
the Finns; a Finlander

芬蘭語(ㄈㄣ ㄌㄢ ㄩ)
the Finnish language; Finnish

芬烈(ㄈㄣ ㄌㄧㄝ)
exceedingly fragrant

芬華(ㄈㄣ ㄏㄨㄚ)
①glory; pomp ②luxuriant beauty

芬郁(ㄈㄣ ㄩ)
intense fragrance

【芚】 4849
ㄊㄨㄣ twen tǔn
a kind of vegetable

【芭】 4850
ㄅㄚ ba bā
1. a fragrant plant
2. a plantain; a palmetto

芭棚(ㄅㄚ ㄆㄥ)
a screen of straw, leaves, or grass for barring wind

芭蕾舞(ㄅㄚ ㄌㄟ ㄨ)
ballet

芭蕾舞迷(ㄅㄚ ㄌㄟ ㄨ ㄇㄧ)
a balletomane

芭蕾舞女(ㄅㄚ ㄌㄟ ㄨ ㄋㄩ)
a ballerina

芭蕾舞裙(ㄅㄚ ㄌㄟ ㄨ ㄑㄩㄣ)
a tutu

芭蕉(ㄅㄚ ㄐㄧㄠ)
a plantain

芭蕉布(ㄅㄚ ㄐㄧㄠ ㄅㄨ)
cloth woven from plantain fiber

芭蕉扇(ㄅㄚ ㄐㄧㄠ ㄕㄢ)
a palm-leaf fan

【芯】 4851
1. ㄒㄧㄣ shinn xīn
pith of rushes

【芯】 4851
2. ㄒㄧㄣ shinn xìn
the central part of an object

【芮】 4852
ㄖㄨㄟ ruey ruì
1. small; tiny
2. name of an ancient state in what is Shansi today
3. a Chinese family name

【芰】 4853
ㄐㄧ jyi jì
a water caltrop

芰實(ㄐㄧ ㄕ)
a water caltrop

【花】 4854
ㄏㄨㄚ hua huā
1. a flower; a blossom
2. a flowering plant
3. a prostitute; prostitution
4. as in 天花—smallpox
5. varicolored
6. fireworks
7. to spend; to expend

花白(ㄏㄨㄚ ㄅㄞ)
(said of hair) white with black spots; gray; graying

花被(ㄏㄨㄚ ㄅㄟ)
a floral envelope; a perianth

花萼(ㄏㄨㄚ ㄜ)
a calyx

花瓣(ㄏㄨㄚ ㄅㄢ)
the petal (of a flower or blossom)

花邊(ㄏㄨㄚ ㄅㄧㄢ)
①lace; an embroidered hem (of a garment)②fancy borders (in printing)

花邊新聞(ㄏㄨㄚ ㄅㄧㄢ ㄒㄧㄣ ㄨㄣ)
a sidebar

花布(ㄏㄨㄚ ㄅㄨ)
calico; printed cotton

花炮(ㄏㄨㄚ ㄆㄠ)
fireworks and firecrackers

花盤(ㄏㄨㄚ ㄆㄢ)
(botany) a disk

花盆(ㄏㄨㄚ ㄆㄣ)
a flower pot

花棚(ㄏㄨㄚ ㄆㄥ)or 花架(ㄏㄨㄚ ㄐㄧㄚ)
an arbor; a flower stand; a pergola

花片(ㄏㄨㄚ ㄆㄧㄢ)
fallen petals

花品(ㄏㄨㄚ ㄆㄧㄣ)
a flower's grade of excellence

花瓶(ㄏㄨㄚ ㄆㄧㄥ)
a vase

花圃(ㄏㄨㄚ ㄆㄨ)
a flower bed

花蜜(ㄏㄨㄚ ㄇㄧ)
(botany) nectar

花面(ㄏㄨㄚ ㄇㄧㄢ)
(Chinese opera) an actor with a painted face

花名(ㄏㄨㄚ ㄇㄧㄥ)
one's official name(as given in the census register)

花名冊(ㄏㄨㄚ ㄇㄧㄥ ㄘㄜ)
a list of names; a roster

花名兒(ㄏㄨㄚ ㄇㄧㄥ ㄦ)
①names of flowers ② names of prostitutes

花木(ㄏㄨㄚ ㄇㄨ)
vegetation; flowers and trees (in parks or gardens)

花木蘭(ㄏㄨㄚ ㄇㄨ ㄌㄢ)
Hua Mu-lan, a well-known female character who went to war in place of her father

花費(ㄏㄨㄚ ㄈㄟ)
to spend; to expend

花販(ㄏㄨㄚ ㄈㄢ)
a florist

花粉(ㄏㄨㄚ ㄈㄣ)
pollen

花房(ㄏㄨㄚ ㄈㄤ)
①a greenhouse; a hothouse ②a corolla

花旦(ㄏㄨㄚ ㄉㄢ)
the vivacious female role in Chinese opera

花燈(ㄏㄨㄚ ㄉㄥ)
a fancy lantern (made for the Lantern Festival on the

【艸 部】

15th of the first moon)

花彫 or 花雕(ㄏㄨㄚ ㄉㄧㄠ)
rice wine of the best quality from Shaohsing (紹興)

花店(ㄏㄨㄚ ㄉㄧㄢˋ)
a flower shop; a florist's shop

花鈿(ㄏㄨㄚ ㄉㄧㄢˋ)
women's head ornaments in ancient times

花朵(ㄏㄨㄚ ㄉㄨㄛˇ)
flowers: 你喜歡這些花朵嗎? Do you like these flowers?

花緞(ㄏㄨㄚ ㄉㄨㄢˋ)
brocade; flowered satin: 她穿着花緞製的衣服。She was dressed in flowered satin.

花頭(ㄏㄨㄚ ㄊㄡˊ)
a trick; a ruse; an artifice; a stratagem

花壇(ㄏㄨㄚ ㄊㄢˊ)
a flower bed (especially a raised one)

花壜(ㄏㄨㄚ ㄊㄢˊ)
the juggling of an earthen jar by an acrobat

花天酒地(ㄏㄨㄚ ㄊㄧㄢ ㄐㄧㄡˇ ㄉㄧˋ)
to lead a life of debauchery

花廳(ㄏㄨㄚ ㄊㄧㄥ)
a reception room; a parlor

花托(ㄏㄨㄚ ㄊㄨㄛ)
(botany) a receptacle; a torus

花團錦簇(ㄏㄨㄚ ㄊㄨㄢˊ ㄐㄧㄣˇ ㄘㄨˋ)
① a conglomeration of splendid and beautiful things ② a group of richly attired women

花童(ㄏㄨㄚ ㄊㄨㄥˊ)
a bridal page

花鳥畫(ㄏㄨㄚ ㄋㄧㄠˇ ㄏㄨㄚˋ)
paintings of flowers and birds

花娘(ㄏㄨㄚ ㄋㄧㄤˊ)
a prostitute

花農(ㄏㄨㄚ ㄋㄨㄥˊ)
a flower grower

花刺子模(ㄏㄨㄚ ㄘˋ ㄗˇ ㄇㄛˊ)
Khorasm, or Khwarism, a state in the Middle East exterminated by the Mongols

花蕾(ㄏㄨㄚ ㄌㄟˇ)or 花咕朵(ㄏㄨㄚ ㄍㄨ ㄉㄨㄛˇ)
a flower bud

花籃(ㄏㄨㄚ ㄌㄢˊ)or 花籃兒(ㄏㄨㄚ ㄌㄢˊㄦ)
a basket of flowers; a flower basket

花郎(ㄏㄨㄚ ㄌㄤˊ)
a male beggar

花柳(ㄏㄨㄚ ㄌㄧㄡˇ)
① brothels ② prostitutes

花柳病(ㄏㄨㄚ ㄌㄧㄡˇ ㄅㄧㄥˋ)
a venereal disease; V.D.

花蓮縣(ㄏㄨㄚ ㄌㄧㄢˊ ㄒㄧㄢˋ)
Hualien County, Taiwan Province

花臉(ㄏㄨㄚ ㄌㄧㄢˇ)
(Chinese opera) a male role in Chinese opera with heavily painted face 亦作「淨」or「花面」

花露(ㄏㄨㄚ ㄌㄨˋ)
dew on flowers

花露水(ㄏㄨㄚ ㄌㄨˋ ㄕㄨㄟˇ)
Cologne water—a mildly perfumed toilet water

花蓋(ㄏㄨㄚ ㄍㄞˋ)
a perianth

花岡岩(ㄏㄨㄚ ㄍㄤ ㄧㄢˊ)or 花岡石(ㄏㄨㄚ ㄍㄤ ㄕˊ)
granite

花梗(ㄏㄨㄚ ㄍㄥˇ)
a flower stalk; a peduncle

花鼓戲(ㄏㄨㄚ ㄍㄨˇ ㄒㄧˋ)
the flower-drum opera, a kind of stage show featuring obscene singing to the accompaniment of drum beats

花國(ㄏㄨㄚ ㄍㄨㄛˊ)
① the world of flowers ② the world of prostitutes

花冠(ㄏㄨㄚ ㄍㄨㄢ)
① a corolla ② a gaily decorated hat or cap

花光(ㄏㄨㄚ ㄍㄨㄤ)
to spend all the money

花魁(ㄏㄨㄚ ㄎㄨㄟˊ)
① the plum flower ② a famous prostitute

花好月圓(ㄏㄨㄚ ㄏㄠˇ ㄩㄝˋ ㄩㄢˊ)
(literally) The flowers are in full bloom, and the moon is full.—perfect conjugal bliss

花花綠綠(ㄏㄨㄚ ㄏㄨㄚ ㄌㄩˋ ㄌㄩˋ)
varicolored; brightly colored; colorful

花花公子(ㄏㄨㄚ ㄏㄨㄚ ㄍㄨㄥ ㄗˇ)
a beau; a fop; a playboy

花花絮絮(ㄏㄨㄚ ㄏㄨㄚ ㄒㄩˋ ㄒㄩˋ)
variegated

花花世界(ㄏㄨㄚ ㄏㄨㄚ ㄕˋ ㄐㄧㄝˋ)
the gay and material world; the dazzling human world with its myriad temptations

花卉(ㄏㄨㄚ ㄏㄨㄟˋ)
flowering plants

花環(ㄏㄨㄚ ㄏㄨㄢˊ)
a flower wreath; a lei

花黃(ㄏㄨㄚ ㄏㄨㄤˊ)
yellow petals worn on the forehead by women for ornament in ancient times

花黃素(ㄏㄨㄚ ㄏㄨㄤˊ ㄙㄨˋ)
lipochrome

花紅(ㄏㄨㄚ ㄏㄨㄥˊ)
① a kind of apple, Malus asiatica ② a dividend

花紅柳綠(ㄏㄨㄚ ㄏㄨㄥˊ ㄌㄧㄡˇ ㄌㄩˋ)
(said of vegetation and other things) luxuriant and colorful

花雞(ㄏㄨㄚ ㄐㄧ)
a brambling 亦作「燕雀」

花甲(ㄏㄨㄚ ㄐㄧㄚˇ)
(said of a person) 60 years old

花街柳巷(ㄏㄨㄚ ㄐㄧㄝ ㄌㄧㄡˇ ㄒㄧㄤˋ)
streets of ill fame

花界(ㄏㄨㄚ ㄐㄧㄝˋ)
① the world of prostitution ② the Buddhist temple

花根(ㄏㄨㄚ ㄍㄣ)
Xanthoxylum, a kind of wild pepper

花嬌柳媚(ㄏㄨㄚ ㄐㄧㄠ ㄌㄧㄡˇ ㄇㄟˋ)
Flowers are charming and willows are fascinating.(a conventional phrase for describing spring landscapes)

花轎(ㄏㄨㄚ ㄐㄧㄠˋ)
a bridal sedan chair

花酒(ㄏㄨㄚ ㄐㄧㄡˇ)
a drinking party with prostitutes attending

花箋(ㄏㄨㄚ ㄐㄧㄢ)
fancy stationery

花匠(ㄏㄨㄚ ㄐㄧㄤˋ)
a gardener; a horticulturist: 那花匠以種植花木爲樂。The gardener gardens for pleasure.

花莖(ㄏㄨㄚ ㄐㄧㄥ)or 花軸(ㄏㄨㄚ ㄓㄡˊ)
a floral axis

花鏡(ㄏㄨㄚ ㄐㄧㄥˋ)

spectacles, or glasses, for the aged 亦作「老花眼鏡」

花捲兒(ㄏㄨㄚ ㄐㄩㄢˇ ㄦ)
a steamed roll

花捐(ㄏㄨㄚ ㄐㄩㄢ)
taxes levied on a house of ill fame

花期(ㄏㄨㄚ ㄑㄧ)
the flower season

花旗(ㄏㄨㄚ ㄑㄧˊ)
the Stars and Stripes; the Star-Spangled Banner

花旗國(ㄏㄨㄚ ㄑㄧˊ ㄍㄨㄛˊ)
the United States of America

花旗銀行(ㄏㄨㄚ ㄑㄧˊ ㄧㄣˊ ㄏㄤˊ)
National City Bank of New York

花錢(ㄏㄨㄚ ㄑㄧㄢˊ)
to spend money: 花錢之前必須先賺錢。Earn before you spend.

花前月下(ㄏㄨㄚ ㄑㄧㄢˊ ㄩㄝˋ ㄒㄧㄚˋ)
before flowers and in the moonlight--an ideal setting for a couple in love

花槍(ㄏㄨㄚ ㄑㄧㄤ)
①a kind of spear ②a trick

花腔(ㄏㄨㄚ ㄑㄧㄤ)
fancy vocalism; fioritura; coloratura

花腔女高音(ㄏㄨㄚ ㄑㄧㄤ ㄋㄩˇ ㄍㄠ ㄧㄣ)
a coloratura soprano

花圈(ㄏㄨㄚ ㄑㄩㄢ)
a garland; a wreath; a lei

花拳(ㄏㄨㄚ ㄑㄩㄢˊ)
exhibition boxing

花拳繡腿(ㄏㄨㄚ ㄑㄩㄢˊ ㄒㄧㄡˋ ㄊㄨㄟˇ)
fancy boxing, dazzling to the eye but hardly devastating in combat

花信(ㄏㄨㄚ ㄒㄧㄣˋ)
①news of flowers blooming ②(said of a woman) 24 years old

花香(ㄏㄨㄚ ㄒㄧㄤ)
fragrance of a flower: 空氣中有花香。There is fragrance of flowers in the air.

花絮(ㄏㄨㄚ ㄒㄩˋ)
small episodes of human interest

花序(ㄏㄨㄚ ㄒㄩˋ)
the arrangement of flowers on a stem or axis; inflorescence

花枝(ㄏㄨㄚ ㄓ)
a flowering branch

花枝招展(ㄏㄨㄚ ㄓ ㄓㄠ ㄓㄢˇ)
(said of beautifully dressed women) like a flowering branch attracting people's attention

花枝兒(ㄏㄨㄚ ㄓ ㄦ)
a flowering branch (a metaphor for a pretty woman)

花招兒(ㄏㄨㄚ ㄓㄠ ㄦ)
a sly trick: 這個老人會很多花招兒。The old fellow knows many sly tricks.

花朝(ㄏㄨㄚ ㄓㄠ)
the birthday of flowers (the 12th of the second lunar month)

花朝月夕(ㄏㄨㄚ ㄓㄠ ㄩㄝˋ ㄒㄧˋ)
a flowering morning and a moonlight evening— (figuratively) delightful circumstances or occasions

花帳(ㄏㄨㄚ ㄓㄤˋ)
padded accounts or bills; false accounts

花障(ㄏㄨㄚ ㄓㄤˋ)
a bamboo fence with flowering vines

花燭(ㄏㄨㄚ ㄓㄨˊ)
painted candles as the symbol of a wedding—(metaphorically) a wedding or honeymoon

花燭夫妻(ㄏㄨㄚ ㄓㄨˊ ㄈㄨ ㄑㄧ)
a formally married couple

花燭之夜(ㄏㄨㄚ ㄓㄨˊ ㄓ ㄧㄝˋ)
the wedding night

花柱(ㄏㄨㄚ ㄓㄨˋ)
(botany) a style

花磚(ㄏㄨㄚ ㄓㄨㄢ)
an ornamental brick

花種(ㄏㄨㄚ ㄓㄨㄥˇ)
seeds of flowering plants

花癡(ㄏㄨㄚ ㄔ)or 花顛(ㄏㄨㄚ ㄉㄧㄢ)
a nymphomaniac

花茶(ㄏㄨㄚ ㄔㄚˊ)
jasmine tea; flower-scented tea

花車(ㄏㄨㄚ ㄔㄜ)
a float; a decorated vehicle in parade

花釵(ㄏㄨㄚ ㄔㄞ)
hair ornaments for women

花船(ㄏㄨㄚ ㄔㄨㄢˊ)
①a gaily decorated boat ②

---

a boat carrying prostitutes to attract passengers

花市(ㄏㄨㄚ ㄕ)
a flower market

花事(ㄏㄨㄚ ㄕˋ)
a spring outing; a spring excursion

花式溜冰(ㄏㄨㄚ ㄕˋ ㄌㄧㄡ ㄅㄧㄥ)
figure skating

花神(ㄏㄨㄚ ㄕㄣˊ)
①Flora; deity of flowers ②the soul or spirit of a flower as captured in a painting

花生(ㄏㄨㄚ ㄕㄥ)
a peanut plant

花生米(ㄏㄨㄚ ㄕㄥ ㄇㄧˇ)or 花生仁兒(ㄏㄨㄚ ㄕㄥ ㄖㄣˊ ㄦ)
a peanut

花生糖(ㄏㄨㄚ ㄕㄥ ㄊㄤˊ)
peanut brittle; peanut candy

花生醬(ㄏㄨㄚ ㄕㄥ ㄐㄧㄤˋ)
peanut butter

花生油(ㄏㄨㄚ ㄕㄥ ㄧㄡˊ)
peanut oil

花束(ㄏㄨㄚ ㄕㄨˋ)
a bouquet; a bunch of flowers

花蕊(ㄏㄨㄚ ㄖㄨㄟˇ)
(botany) pistils and stamens

花容月貌(ㄏㄨㄚ ㄖㄨㄥˊ ㄩㄝˋ ㄇㄠˋ)
(said of a woman) fair as a flower and the moon

花子(ㄏㄨㄚ ˙ㄗ)
a beggar 亦作「叫化子」

花草(ㄏㄨㄚ ㄘㄠˇ)
flowers and grass

花叢(ㄏㄨㄚ ㄘㄨㄥˊ)
①flowering bushes ②the world of prostitution

花色(ㄏㄨㄚ ㄙㄜˋ)
varieties; kinds; sorts: 你沒有別的花色了嗎？Haven't you any other kind?

花案(ㄏㄨㄚ ㄢˋ)
cases of sex crimes

花萼(ㄏㄨㄚ ㄜˋ)
(botany) a calyx

花兒(ㄏㄨㄚ ㄦ)
①a flower; a blossom ②a flowering plant ③smallpox

花兒針(ㄏㄨㄚ ㄦ ㄓㄣ)
a fine needle for embroidery

花押(ㄏㄨㄚ ㄧㄚ)
a signature (on a document)

花椰菜(ㄏㄨㄚ 丨ㄝ ㄘㄞ)
a cauliflower

花煙館(ㄏㄨㄚ 丨ㄢ ㄍㄨㄢ)
a girlie opium den

花言巧語(ㄏㄨㄚ 丨ㄢ ㄑ丨ㄠ ㄩ)
honeyed words

花眼(ㄏㄨㄚ 丨ㄢˇ)
farsightedness after middle age; presbyopia 亦作「老花眼」

花樣(ㄏㄨㄚ 丨ㄤˋ)or 花樣兒(ㄏㄨㄚ 丨ㄤˋ)
a pattern; a style; a model

花樣翻新(ㄏㄨㄚ 丨ㄤˋ ㄈㄢ ㄒ丨ㄣ)
to play new tricks

花影(ㄏㄨㄚ 丨ㄥˇ)
the shadow of flowers

花無百日紅(ㄏㄨㄚ ㄨˊ ㄅㄞˇ ㄖˋ ㄏㄨㄥˊ)
(literally) No flower can bloom for a hundred days. —An ideal state cannot last long.

花紋(ㄏㄨㄚ ㄨㄣˊ)
a decorative design or pattern

花王(ㄏㄨㄚ ㄨㄤˊ)
the king of flowers—the peony: 牡丹被稱爲花王。The peony is called the king of flowers.

花兔枉錢(ㄏㄨㄚ ㄨㄢˇ ·ㄨㄤˇ ㄑㄧㄢˊ)
to spend money to no avail; to throw money away

花園(ㄏㄨㄚ ㄩㄢˊ)or 花園兒(ㄏㄨㄚ ㄩㄢˊ)
a flower garden; a garden

【芳】 4855
ㄈㄤ fang fāng
1. sweet-smelling; fragrant; aromatic
2. your (used commonly in addressing a young lady)
3. virtuous; honorable; good; respectable: 孔子百世流芳。Confucius left a good name to posterity.

芳名(ㄈㄤ ㄇ丨ㄥˊ)
①your name (used especially in speaking to a woman)②a good reputation

芳名錄(ㄈㄤ ㄇ丨ㄥˊ ㄌㄨˋ)
a roster of names (a euphemistic expression)

芳菲(ㄈㄤ ㄈㄟ)
①fragrance and beauty (of flowers) ②flowers

芳馥(ㄈㄤ ㄈㄨˋ)
fragrant

芳蘭(ㄈㄤ ㄌㄢˊ)
a fragrant orchid—(figuratively) a gentleman

芳醴(ㄈㄤ ㄌ丨ˇ)
fragrant wine; excellent wine

芳林(ㄈㄤ ㄌ丨ㄣˊ)
trees in spring

芳鄰(ㄈㄤ ㄌ丨ㄣˊ)
one's neighbor (a polite expression): 她是我們的芳鄰。She is our neighbor.

芳齡(ㄈㄤ ㄌ丨ㄥˊ)
age (of a young lady): 她芳齡二十。She is twenty years of age.

芳汗(ㄈㄤ ㄏㄢˋ)
perspiration (of a young woman)

芳華(ㄈㄤ ㄏㄨㄚˊ)
①the beautiful season or time②youth: 她善於保養芳華。She keeps her youth well.

芳魂(ㄈㄤ ㄏㄨㄣˊ)
the spirit, or soul (of a young lady)

芳卿(ㄈㄤ ㄑ丨ㄥ)
a lover; a sweetheart

芳心(ㄈㄤ ㄒ丨ㄣ)
the affection, or heart (of a young lady): 這小姐的芳心已碎。This lady's heart is broken.

芳心無主(ㄈㄤ ㄒ丨ㄣ ㄨˊ ㄓㄨˇ)
(said of a lady) not knowing what to do

芳香(ㄈㄤ ㄒ丨ㄤ)
fragrance; aroma

芳香族化合物(ㄈㄤ ㄒ丨ㄤ ㄗㄨˊ ㄏㄨㄚˋ ㄏㄜˊ ㄨˋ)
aromatic compounds 亦作「芳族化合物」

芳訊(ㄈㄤ ㄒㄩㄣˋ)
①your esteemed letter ②news of flowers coming into bloom

芳旨(ㄈㄤ ㄓˇ)
fragrance; aroma

芳躅(ㄈㄤ ㄓㄨˊ)
tracks of a famous person of former times

芳辰(ㄈㄤ ㄔㄣˊ)or 芳序(ㄈㄤ ㄒㄩˋ)
a beautiful morning in spring

芳塵(ㄈㄤ ㄔㄣˊ)
a good reputation

芳澤(ㄈㄤ ㄗㄜˊ)
perfumed ointment (especially for the hair of a young lady)

芳蹤(ㄈㄤ ㄗㄨㄥ)
your whereabouts (a respectful expression)

芳草(ㄈㄤ ㄘㄠˇ)or 芳芷(ㄈㄤ ㄓˇ)
a fragrant plant

【芷】 4856
ㄓˇ jyy zhǐ
angelica

芷若(ㄓˇ ㄖㄨㄛˋ)
angelica

【芸】 4857
ㄩㄣˊ yun yún
1. a strong-scented herb; rue
2. same as 耘—to weed

芸編(ㄩㄣˊ ㄅ丨ㄢ)
books

芸臺(ㄩㄣˊ ㄊㄞˊ)or 芸閣(ㄩㄣˊ ㄍㄜˊ)
the imperial library

芸簽縹帶(ㄩㄣˊ ㄑ丨ㄢ ㄆ丨ㄠˇ ㄉㄞˋ)
(literally) perfumed book markers and silken laces —books

芸香(ㄩㄣˊ ㄒ丨ㄤ)
a strong-scented herb; rue

芸香科(ㄩㄣˊ ㄒ丨ㄤ ㄎㄜ)
Rutaceae

芸帙(ㄩㄣˊ ㄓˋ)
books

芸窗(ㄩㄣˊ ㄔㄨㄤ)
a study

芸省(ㄩㄣˊ ㄕㄥˇ)or 芸署(ㄩㄣˊ ㄕㄨˇ)
the imperial library

芸草(ㄩㄣˊ ㄘㄠˇ)
a strong-scented herb; rue

芸芸(ㄩㄣˊ ㄩㄣˊ)
many; numerous

芸芸衆生(ㄩㄣˊ ㄩㄣˊ ㄓㄨㄥˋ ㄕㄥ)
①people of the world ②all living things

【芹】 4858
ㄑ丨ㄣˊ chyn qín
celery

芹獻(ㄑ丨ㄣˊ ㄒ丨ㄢˋ)
a humble gift (a self-depreciatory term referring to a gift one is presenting to another)

芹菜(ㄑ丨ㄣˊ ㄘㄞˋ)
celery

【芼】 4859
ㄇㄠˋ maw mào
1. to choose; to select
2. green vegetables; greens

莩藿(ㄆㄧㄠ ㄍㄨㄥ)
the stew of meat and greens

【芽】 4860
  ㄧㄚ ya yá
a sprout; a shoot; a bud: 芽
在春天萌發。Buds sprout in
the spring.

芽胞(ㄧㄚ ㄅㄠ)
(botany) spores

芽韮(ㄧㄚ ㄐㄧㄡ)
leek shoots

芽茶(ㄧㄚ ㄔㄚ)
bud tea

芽菜(ㄧㄚ ㄘㄞ)
bean sprouts 亦作「豆芽菜」

芽兒(ㄧㄚ)
a shoot; a sprout; a bud: 樹
在發芽兒。The trees are un-
folding their buds.

【芾】 4861
  ㄈㄟ fey fèi
small; little; tiny

【芾】 4861
  ㄈㄨ fwu fú
lush; luxuriant

【芻】 4862
  ㄔㄨ chwu chú
1. to cut grass; to mow
2. hay; fodder
3. to feed (livestock)
4. animals that feed on grass

芻秣(ㄔㄨ ㄇㄛ)
fodder; provender

芻牧(ㄔㄨ ㄇㄨ)
to pasture or graze livestock

芻糧(ㄔㄨ ㄌㄧㄤ)
fodder for horses and food
for men

芻靈(ㄔㄨ ㄌㄧㄥ)
effigies burned with or for
the deceased in ancient
times

芻蕘(ㄔㄨ ㄖㄠ)
hay

芻狗(ㄔㄨ ㄍㄡ)
straw dogs for sacrifice
—things thrown away after
use

芻豢(ㄔㄨ ㄏㄨㄢ)
animals that feed on grass
or grain—cattle, sheep, dogs,
etc.

芻菽(ㄔㄨ ㄕㄨ)
grass and beans

芻蕘之言(ㄔㄨ ㄖㄠ ㄓ ㄧㄢ)
(literally) the opinion of a
woodcutter—my humble

opinion or view: 請聽芻蕘之
見。Please listen to my humble opinion.

芻議(ㄔㄨ ㄧˋ)or 芻言(ㄔㄨ ㄧㄢ)
my humble views or opin-
ions

五畫

【苑】 4863
  1. ㄩㄢ yuann yuàn
1. a garden; a park
2. a gathering place

苑囿(ㄩㄢ ㄧㄡ)
a park; a garden

【苑】 4863
  2. ㄩㄢ yuan yuán
a Chinese family name

【苒】 4864
  ㄖㄢ raan rǎn
(said of flowers and grass)
lush or delicate

苒苒(ㄖㄢ ㄖㄢ)
(said of flowers and grass)
luxuriant, lush or delicate

苒荏(ㄖㄢ ㄖㄣ)
time passing gradually 亦作
「荏苒」：時光苒苒。Time
passes gradually.

苒弱(ㄖㄢ ㄖㄨㄛ)
drooping

【苓】 4865
  ㄌㄧㄥ ling líng
1. a variety of fungus
2. tuckahoe
3. licorice, or liquorice 亦作「甘
草」

【苔】 4866
  1. ㄊㄞ tair tái
moss; lichen: 滾石不生苔。A
rolling stone gathers no
moss.

苔砌(ㄊㄞ ㄑㄧ)
mossy steps

苔錢(ㄊㄞ ㄑㄧㄢ)
coin-shaped lichen

苔蘚(ㄊㄞ ㄒㄧㄢ)
moss and lichen

苔蘚(ㄊㄞ ㄒㄧㄢ)
lichen (a skin disease)

苔衣(ㄊㄞ ㄧ)
moss: 石頭生滿了苔衣。The
stones are covered with
moss.

【苔】 4866
  2. ㄊㄞ tai tāi
as in 舌苔—fur (on the
tongue)

【苕】 4867
  ㄊㄧㄠ tyau tiáo
a plant much used for making brooms

苕帚(ㄊㄧㄠ ㄓㄡ)
a broom

【苗】 4868
  ㄇㄧㄠ miau miáo
1. a sprout
2. descendants; posterity
3. (said of children) peevish or
disobedient
4. the Miao tribe in southwestern China
5. summer hunting
6. a Chinese family name
7. a beginning or omen

苗圃(ㄇㄧㄠ ㄆㄨ)
a seedbed; a nursery

苗頭(ㄇㄧㄠ ㄊㄡ)
the first sign of success

苗條(ㄇㄧㄠ ㄊㄧㄠ)
(said of a woman) slim

苗栗(ㄇㄧㄠ ㄌㄧ)
Miaoli, a county in central
Taiwan

苗戶(ㄇㄧㄠ ㄏㄨ)
naturalized Miao (苗) people

苗牀(ㄇㄧㄠ ㄔㄨㄤ)
a seedbed; a nursery

苗子(ㄇㄧㄠ ㄗ)or苗族(ㄇㄧㄠ ㄗㄨ)
the Miao (苗) people (in
southwestern China)

苗兒(ㄇㄧㄠ)
a sprout; a shoot; a seedling

苗而不秀(ㄇㄧㄠ ㄦ ㄅㄨ ㄒㄧㄡ)
(literally) to sprout but
never to flower—to fail to
fulfill one's potentialities

苗裔(ㄇㄧㄠ ㄧˋ)or 苗胤(ㄇㄧㄠ ㄧㄣ)
or 苗嗣(ㄇㄧㄠ ㄙ)
descendants; posterity

【苛】 4869
  ㄎㄜ ke kē
harsh; severe; rigorous; caustic

苛法(ㄎㄜ ㄈㄚ)
a harsh law; a severe law

苛待(ㄎㄜ ㄉㄞ)
to treat harshly or severely

苛虐(ㄎㄜ ㄋㄩㄝ)
to treat cruelly; to maltreat

苛濫(ㄎㄜ ㄌㄢ)
improperly severe or lenient

苛儀(ㄎㄜ ㄧˊ)
excessive ceremony or formality

（艸部）

〔艸部〕

苛吏(ㄎㄜ ㄌㄧˋ)
a cruel official

苛令(ㄎㄜ ㄌㄧㄥˋ)
harsh orders and regulations

苛刻(ㄎㄜ ㄎㄜˋ)
harsh; pitiless; relentless;
merciless; unkind; cold-
hearted

苛捐雜稅(ㄎㄜ ㄐㄩㄢ ㄗㄚˊ ㄕㄨㄟˋ)
extortive levies and miscellaneous taxes

苛求(ㄎㄜ ㄑㄧㄡˊ)
to be very exacting

苛細(ㄎㄜ ㄒㄧˋ)
(said of regulations, etc.)
severe and exacting

苛性(ㄎㄜ ㄒㄧㄥˋ)
(chemistry) caustic

苛性鈉(ㄎㄜ ㄒㄧㄥˋ ㄋㄚˋ)
(chemistry) sodium hydroxide; caustic soda

苛性鉀(ㄎㄜ ㄒㄧㄥˋ ㄐㄧㄚˇ)
(chemistry) caustic potash;
potassium hydroxide

苛性鹼(ㄎㄜ ㄒㄧㄥˋ ㄐㄧㄢˇ)
(chemistry) caustic alkali

苛性蘇達(ㄎㄜ ㄒㄧㄥˋ ㄙㄨ ㄉㄚˊ)
(chemistry) caustic soda;
sodium hydroxide

苛性鹽(ㄎㄜ ㄒㄧㄥˋ ㄧㄢˊ)
(chemistry) caustic salt

苛政(ㄎㄜ ㄓㄥˋ)
despotic rule; despotism; tyranny

苛政猛於虎(ㄎㄜ ㄓㄥˋ ㄇㄥˇ ㄩˊ ㄏㄨˇ)
A tyrannical government is
worse than a tiger.

苛察(ㄎㄜ ㄔㄚˊ)
relentless faultfinding

苛責(ㄎㄜ ㄗㄜˊ)
to criticize severely; to
rebuke; to excoriate

苛俗(ㄎㄜ ㄙㄨˊ)
tasking customs

苛碎(ㄎㄜ ㄙㄨㄟˋ)
(said of regulations, etc.)
rigorous and troublesome

【苜】 4870
ㄇㄨˋ muh mù

clover

苜蓿(ㄇㄨˋ ㄒㄩˋ)
Medicago hispida, clover,
often grown as food for cattle

【苞】 4871
ㄅㄠ bau bāo

1. a variety of rush
2. a bract
3. to wrap
4. profuse; thick
5. seeds with the germ ready
to burst; seeds bursting up

苞苴(ㄅㄠ ㄐㄩ)
①a bribe ②a gift ③a par-
cel

苞筍(ㄅㄠ ㄙㄨㄣˇ)
tender bamboo shoots in
winter 亦作「苞筍」

苞葉(ㄅㄠ ㄧㄝˋ)
a bract

【苡】 4872
ㄧˇ yii yǐ
Coix lacryma-jobi, a kind of
plant whose grains are used
as food or medicine

【若】 4873
1. ㄖㄨㄛˋ ruoh ruò
1. if; suppose; supposing;
assuming; provided that
2. you
3. similar to; like

若輩(ㄖㄨㄛˋ ㄅㄟˋ)
you all; ye 亦作「若曹」

若不然(ㄖㄨㄛˋ ㄅㄨˋ ㄖㄢˊ)
if not; otherwise

若非(ㄖㄨㄛˋ ㄈㄟ)
unless; if not: 若非疲倦了這
嬰兒很少哭。 This baby sel-
dom cries unless he is tired.

若夫(ㄖㄨㄛˋ ㄈㄨ)
a connective often used to
introduce a new passage in
archaic Chinese

若大旱望雲霓(ㄖㄨㄛˋ ㄉㄚˋ ㄏㄢˋ ㄨㄤˋ
ㄩㄣˊ ㄋㄧˊ)
It is like longing for clouds
during a serious drought.

若干(ㄖㄨㄛˋ ㄍㄢ)
some; a few; several: 我看見
若干認識的人。 I saw some
people I knew.

若果(ㄖㄨㄛˋ ㄍㄨㄛˇ)
if; provided that: 若果他來
了,我一定告訴他。 If he comes,
I will tell him.

若何(ㄖㄨㄛˋ ㄏㄜˊ)
how; what now

若合符節(ㄖㄨㄛˋ ㄏㄜˊ ㄈㄨˊ ㄐㄧㄝˊ)
as similar as the two halves
of a tally—to match com-
pletely; to tally perfectly; to
fit exactly

若即若離(ㄖㄨㄛˋ ㄐㄧˊ ㄖㄨㄛˋ ㄌㄧˊ)
to appear to come together
sometimes and apart at
other times; to keep at arm's
length

若許(ㄖㄨㄛˋ ㄒㄩˇ)
thus; like this

若使(ㄖㄨㄛˋ ㄕˇ)
assuming that...; supposing
that...; if

若是(ㄖㄨㄛˋ ㄕˋ)
if; suppose: 若是我錯了, 你也
錯了。 If I am wrong, you are
wrong too.

若曹(ㄖㄨㄛˋ ㄘㄠˊ)
you all; ye

若要(ㄖㄨㄛˋ ㄧㄠˋ)
if...has (have) to...: 你若要做
這件事, 便早些做。 If you have
to do this, then do it earlier.

若要人不知, 除非己莫為(ㄖㄨㄛˋ
ㄧㄠˋ ㄖㄣˊ ㄅㄨˋ ㄓ, ㄔㄨˊ ㄈㄟ ㄐㄧˇ ㄇㄛˋ
ㄨㄟˊ)
The best way to hide a misdeed is not to commit it.

若有若無(ㄖㄨㄛˋ ㄧㄡˇ ㄖㄨㄛˋ ㄨˊ)
vague; intangible

若隱若現(ㄖㄨㄛˋ ㄧㄣˇ ㄖㄨㄛˋ ㄒㄧㄢˋ)
half-hidden; discernible at
one moment and gone the
next (like a will-o'-the-wisp)

若無其事(ㄖㄨㄛˋ ㄨˊ ㄑㄧˊ ㄕˋ)
as if nothing had happened;
to remain calm; with perfect
composure: 他雖面臨危機, 卻
能若無其事。 He faced a crisis
with perfect composure.

【若】 4873
2. ㄖㄜˇ ree rě
as in 般若(ㄅㄛ ㄖㄜˇ)—a trans-
literation of a Sanskrit word

【苦】 4874
ㄎㄨˇ kuu kǔ
1. bitter: 良藥苦口。 Good medicines taste bitter.
2. painful; hard; difficult; laborious; miserable
3. strenuous; earnest; diligent
4. to abhor
5. to feel miserable about

苦不堪言(ㄎㄨˇ ㄅㄨˋ ㄎㄢ ㄧㄢˊ)
painful or miserable beyond
description

苦生意(ㄎㄨˇ ㄕㄥ ㄧˋ)
a hard business

苦悶(ㄎㄨˇ ㄇㄣˋ)
boredom; bored; distressed;
low-spirited; depressed;

dejected

苦命(ㄎㄨ ㄇ一ㄥ)
a hard lot

苦命人(ㄎㄨ ㄇ一ㄥ ㄖㄣ)
a luckless person

苦鬥(ㄎㄨ ㄉㄡ)
①a hard fight or struggle
②to fight desperately

苦頭兒(ㄎㄨ ㄊㄡ ㄦ)
hardship(s)

苦土(ㄎㄨ ㄊㄨ)
magnesia

苦痛(ㄎㄨ ㄊㄨㄥ)
pain; suffering; discomfort;
misery. I dreaded the pain of
separation from them.

苦惱(ㄎㄨ ㄋㄠ)
misery; distress; trouble. 他
因胃痛而苦惱。He is in misery
with a stomachache.

苦難(ㄎㄨ ㄋㄢ)
privation; suffering; hardship; trials; adversity

苦樂(ㄎㄨ ㄌㄜ)
comfort and discomfort; joys
and sorrows

苦累(ㄎㄨ ㄌㄟ)
toil; hardship; privation;
trials; adversity

苦力(ㄎㄨ ㄌ一)
①strenuous efforts; hard
work ②a coolie; a laborer

苦戀(ㄎㄨ ㄌ一ㄢ)
unrequited love 亦作「單戀」

苦楝子(ㄎㄨ ㄌ一ㄢ ㄗ)
Melia azedarach, the seeds of
which are used as medicine

苦幹(ㄎㄨ ㄍㄢ)
①to make a strenuous
effort ②to do something
against great odds

苦瓜(ㄎㄨ ㄍㄨㄚ)
a bitter gourd (*Momordica
charantia*)

苦功(ㄎㄨ ㄍㄨㄥ)
hard work; painstaking
effort 亦作「苦工夫」

苦工(ㄎㄨ ㄍㄨㄥ)
toil; hard labor

苦工夫(ㄎㄨ ㄍㄨㄥ ㄈㄨ)
painstaking effort 參看「苦功」

苦口(ㄎㄨ ㄎㄡ)
①bitter to the taste ②to
exhort or admonish earnestly

苦口婆心(ㄎㄨ ㄎㄡ ㄆㄛ ㄒ一ㄣ)
to exhort or remonstrate
with earnest words prompt-
ed by a kind heart

苦苦(ㄎㄨ ㄎㄨ)
strenuously; hard; arduously;
persistently

苦況(ㄎㄨ ㄎㄨㄤ)
miserable conditions; hardship. 那些孤兒生活在苦況中。
The orphans live in miserable conditions.

苦海(ㄎㄨ ㄏㄞ)
(literally) a sea of hardship
—boundless hardship; a sea
of bitterness

苦海無邊(ㄎㄨ ㄏㄞ ㄨ ㄅㄧㄢ)
(literally) a boundless sea
of hardship—boundless hardship. 苦海無邊，回頭是岸。The
sea of bitterness is boundless; if you repent, you will
be saved.

苦活兒(ㄎㄨ ㄏㄨㄛ ㄦ)
jobs requiring much work
but paying little; profitless
jobs 亦作「苦差事」

苦節(ㄎㄨ ㄐ一ㄝ)
integrity maintained through
hardships

苦酒(ㄎㄨ ㄐ一ㄡ)
bitter wine

苦諫(ㄎㄨ ㄐ一ㄢ)
an earnest admonition; to
admonish earnestly

苦盡甘來(ㄎㄨ ㄐ一ㄣ ㄍㄢ ㄌㄞ)
The happy sunny days are
coming after all the hardships endured

苦勸(ㄎㄨ ㄑㄩㄢ)
earnest exhortation; to
exhort or advise earnestly

苦戲(ㄎㄨ ㄒ一)
(Chinese opera) a tragedy; a
tearjerker

苦笑(ㄎㄨ ㄒ一ㄠ)
to force a smile; a forced
smile

苦辛(ㄎㄨ ㄒ一ㄣ)
hardship; suffering; adversity

苦心(ㄎㄨ ㄒ一ㄣ)
great pains taken for something

苦心孤詣(ㄎㄨ ㄒ一ㄣ ㄍㄨ 一)
①to achieve a deep under-
standing through diligent

studies ②to manage a
business with great efforts

苦刑(ㄎㄨ ㄒ一ㄥ)
torture

苦行(ㄎㄨ ㄒ一ㄥ)
①to make strenuous effort
②to lead an ascetic life;
self-mortification

苦行者(ㄎㄨ ㄒ一ㄥ ㄓㄜ)
an ascetic

苦學(ㄎㄨ ㄒㄩㄝ)
to study or learn under
adversity

苦汁(ㄎㄨ ㄓ)
(chemistry) bittern

苦戰(ㄎㄨ ㄓㄢ)
to fight against heavy odds;
to have a tough game or bitter struggle

苦竹(ㄎㄨ ㄓㄨ)
Phyllostachys bambusoides, a
variety of bamboo

苦主(ㄎㄨ ㄓㄨ)
①a victim of robbery or
theft ②the bereaved family
of a murdered person

苦衷(ㄎㄨ ㄓㄨㄥ)
a reason for doing some-
thing not easily understood
by others

苦中作樂(ㄎㄨ ㄓㄨㄥ ㄗㄨㄛ ㄌㄜ)
to find joy amid hardship; to
enjoy in adversity

苦差事(ㄎㄨ ㄔㄞ ㄕ)
①an unpleasant task ②a
profitless assignment 參看「苦
活兒」

苦楚(ㄎㄨ ㄔㄨ)
pain; suffering

苦處(ㄎㄨ ㄔㄨ)
the cause of pain; difficulty

苦上加苦(ㄎㄨ ㄕㄤ ㄐ一ㄚ ㄎㄨ)
to bring additional pain

苦水(ㄎㄨ ㄕㄨㄟ)
①bitter water ②gastric
secretion, etc. rising to the
mouth ③sufferings; griev-
ances

苦日子(ㄎㄨ ㄖ ㄗ)
days of hardship

苦肉計(ㄎㄨ ㄖㄡ ㄐ一)
a trick of securing another's
faith by intentionally injur-
ing oneself; acting the under-
dog to win sympathy

苦子(ㄎㄨ ㄗ)

〔艸
部〕

【艸部】

misery or loss

苦思（ㄎㄨˇ ㄙ）
to think hard; to cudgel one's brains

苦死（ㄎㄨˇ ㄙˇ）
extremely painful; extremely hard to bear.

苦澀（ㄎㄨˇ ㄙㄜˋ）
①bitter and astringent ②pained; agonized; anguished

苦艾（ㄎㄨˇ ㄞ）
absinth(e)

苦艾酒（ㄎㄨˇ ㄞ ㄐㄧㄡˇ）
absinth(e)

苦役（ㄎㄨˇ ㄧ）
hard labor; drudgery

苦顏（ㄎㄨˇ ㄧㄢˊ）
a look of distress; a distressful expression

苦味（ㄎㄨˇ ㄨㄟ）
a bitter taste

苦味酸（ㄎㄨˇ ㄨㄟ ㄙㄨㄢ）
picric acid

苦於（ㄎㄨˇ ㄩˊ）
to suffer from (a disadvantage); to be handicapped: 他苦於貧窮。He is handicapped by poverty.

苦雨（ㄎㄨˇ ㄩˇ）
a distressing rain; an incessant rain

苦雨淒風（ㄎㄨˇ ㄩˇ ㄑㄧ ㄈㄥ）
distressing rains and depressing winds

【苧】 4875
ㄓㄨˋ jùh zhù
ramie; China grass

苧麻（ㄓㄨˋ ㄇㄚˊ）
ramie

【苫】 4876
ㄕㄢ shàn shān
to thatch

苫塊（ㄕㄢ ㄎㄨㄞˋ）
(literally) to sleep on a mat of straw and a pillow of earth—to mourn for a parent

苫次（ㄕㄢ ㄘ）
in mourning for one's parents

【英】 4877
ㄧㄥ ing yīng
1. a flower; a leaf; a petal
2. surpassing; outstanding; prominent; distinguished
3. fine; handsome: 他是一個英俊的男子。He is a handsome

fellow.
4. English; British
5. a hero; an outstanding person
6. a Chinese family name

英拔（ㄧㄥ ㄅㄚˊ）
outstanding; distinguished; surpassing; prominent

英鎊（ㄧㄥ ㄅㄤˋ）
the pound sterling 亦作「英磅」

英鎊集團（ㄧㄥ ㄅㄤˋ ㄐㄧˊ ㄊㄨㄢˊ）
the sterling bloc

英布（ㄧㄥ ㄅㄨˋ）
General Ying Pu (?-195 B.C.), who played an important role in the fall of the Chin Dynasty and the rise of the Han Dynasty

英美（ㄧㄥ ㄇㄟˇ）
Britain and America; Anglo-American

英髦（ㄧㄥ ㄇㄠˊ）
men of ability 亦作「英旄」

英明（ㄧㄥ ㄇㄧㄥˊ）
(said of leaders) intelligent; sagacious; perspicacious

英名（ㄧㄥ ㄇㄧㄥˊ）
fame; glory; renown: 他的英名傳遍全國。His fame spread all over the country.

英名掃地（ㄧㄥ ㄇㄧㄥˊ ㄙㄠˇ ㄉㄧˋ）
to have one's great fame tarnished or soiled

英畝（ㄧㄥ ㄇㄨˇ）
(square measure) acre

英發（ㄧㄥ ㄈㄚ）
intelligent and energetic

英法聯軍（ㄧㄥ ㄈㄚˇ ㄌㄧㄢˊ ㄐㄩㄣ）
the allied troops of Britain and France that invaded Canton (廣州), Tientsin (天津) and Peking (北京) in 1856-60

英德（ㄧㄥ ㄉㄜˊ）
①name of a county in Kwangtung (廣東) ②England and Germany

英斷（ㄧㄥ ㄉㄨㄢˋ）
intelligent decision

英噸（ㄧㄥ ㄉㄨㄣ）
a long ton; a gross ton

英挺（ㄧㄥ ㄊㄧㄥˇ）
outstanding; prominent; distinguished 亦作「英特」

英年（ㄧㄥ ㄋㄧㄢˊ）
years of youthful vigor

英里（ㄧㄥ ㄌㄧˇ）
(linear measure) mile

英烈（ㄧㄥ ㄌㄧㄝˋ）
①heroic deeds ②a person of great achievements

英靈（ㄧㄥ ㄌㄧㄥˊ）
①noble spirit ②souls or spirits of the dead

英倫三島（ㄧㄥ ㄌㄨㄣˊ ㄙㄢ ㄉㄠˇ）
British Isles

英格蘭（ㄧㄥ ㄍㄜˊ ㄌㄢˊ）
England

英國（ㄧㄥ ㄍㄨㄛˊ）
Great Britain; Britain; the United Kingdom; England: 倫敦是英國的首都。London is the capital of England.

英國的（ㄧㄥ ㄍㄨㄛˊ ·ㄉㄜ）
British; English: 他們居住在英國的鄉村中。They live in an English village.

英國人（ㄧㄥ ㄍㄨㄛˊ ㄖㄣˊ）
an Englishman; a Briton; English; the British

英國文學（ㄧㄥ ㄍㄨㄛˊ ㄨㄣˊ ㄒㄩㄝˊ）
English literature

英國文學系（ㄧㄥ ㄍㄨㄛˊ ㄨㄣˊ ㄒㄩㄝˊ ㄒㄧˋ）
the department of English literature

英國文學史（ㄧㄥ ㄍㄨㄛˊ ㄨㄣˊ ㄒㄩㄝˊ ㄕˇ）
the history of English literature

英豪（ㄧㄥ ㄏㄠˊ）
heroes; outstanding persons 亦作「英傑」

英漢辭典（ㄧㄥ ㄏㄢˋ ㄘˊ ㄉㄧㄢˇ）
an English-Chinese dictionary

英華（ㄧㄥ ㄏㄨㄚˊ）
①luxuriant beauty ②honor; glory; fame

英魂（ㄧㄥ ㄏㄨㄣˊ）
(honorable) spirits, or souls, of the war dead

英吉利（ㄧㄥ ㄐㄧ ㄌㄧˋ）
Great Britain; Britain; the United Kingdom; the British Commonwealth; England

英吉利病（ㄧㄥ ㄐㄧ ㄌㄧˋ ㄅㄧㄥˋ）
rickets

英吉利海峽（ㄧㄥ ㄐㄧ ㄌㄧˋ ㄏㄞˇ ㄒㄧㄚˊ）
the English Channel

英傑（ㄧㄥ ㄐㄧㄝˊ）
a great man; a hero

英軍(ㄧㄥ ㄐㄩㄣ)
British troops; British forces

英俊(ㄧㄥ ㄐㄩㄣˋ)
(said of a man) handsome

英氣(ㄧㄥ ㄑㄧˋ)
noble spirit; bravery

英雄(ㄧㄥ ㄒㄩㄥˊ)
a hero; a great man

英雄末路(ㄧㄥ ㄒㄩㄥˊ ㄇㄛˋ ㄌㄨˋ)
the end of a hero

英雄美人(ㄧㄥ ㄒㄩㄥˊ ㄇㄟˇ ㄖㄣˊ)
an ideal combination of a
hero and a beauty

英雄氣短(ㄧㄥ ㄒㄩㄥˊ ㄑㄧˋ ㄉㄨㄢˇ)
A hero has lost his might.

英雄主義(ㄧㄥ ㄒㄩㄥˊ ㄓㄨˇ ㄧˋ)
obsession with idea of making oneself a hero

英雄崇拜(ㄧㄥ ㄒㄩㄥˊ ㄔㄨㄥˊ ㄅㄞˋ)
hero worship

英雄無用武之地(ㄧㄥ ㄒㄩㄥˊ ㄨˊ ㄩㄥˋ ㄨˇ ㄓ ㄉㄧˋ)
A hero has no chance of
using his might.

英制(ㄧㄥ ㄓˋ)
the British system (of measurement)

英尺(ㄧㄥ ㄔˇ)
foot (as a measure of
length)

英屬(ㄧㄥ ㄕㄨˇ)
(said of a colony) administered by the British; under
British administration

英姿(ㄧㄥ ㄗ)
a dashing appearance

英才(ㄧㄥ ㄘㄞˊ)
a person of outstanding ability or talent

英寸(ㄧㄥ ㄘㄨㄣˋ)
(linear measure) inch: 去年
的雨量有多少英寸? How
many inches of rain fell last
year?

英俄(ㄧㄥ ㄜˊ)or 英蘇(ㄧㄥ ㄙㄨ)
Britain and Russia; Anglo-
Russian

英武(ㄧㄥ ㄨˇ)
brave and strong; gallant;
valiant; valorous

英偉(ㄧㄥ ㄨㄟˇ)
great

英文(ㄧㄥ ㄨㄣˊ)
the (written) English language; English

英文文法(ㄧㄥ ㄨㄣˊ ㄨㄣˊ ㄈㄚˇ)
English grammar

英語(ㄧㄥ ㄩˇ)
the (spoken) English lan-
guage; English: 你會說英語
嗎? Do you speak English?

英勇(ㄧㄥ ㄩㄥˇ)
brave; courageous; heroic;
gallant; valiant; valorous: 他
是一個英勇的士兵。He is a
brave soldier.

【苴】4878
1. ㄐㄩ jiu jū
1. to pack
2. a female plant of common
hemp

苴布(ㄐㄩ ㄅㄨˋ)
sackcloth

苴麻(ㄐㄩ ㄇㄚˊ)
a female plant of common
hemp

苴絰(ㄐㄩ ㄉㄧㄝˊ)
hemp for the heaviest
mourning (for a parent)

苴稭(ㄐㄩ ㄐㄧㄝ)
a straw mat

苴杖(ㄐㄩ ㄓㄤˋ)
a mourner's staff

【苴】4878
2. ㄔㄚˊ char chá
1. grass floating in the water;
water plants
2. withered grass

【茶】4879
2. ㄐㄧㄝˊ nie nié
exhausting; tired

【苯】4880
ㄅㄣˇ been běn
benzene

苯胺(ㄅㄣˇ ㄢ)
aniline, or phenylamine

【苹】4881
ㄆㄧㄥˊ pyng píng
1. a kind of herb
2. same as 萍—duckweed
3. celery

苹苹(ㄆㄧㄥˊ ㄆㄧㄥˊ)
(said of grass) luxuriant;
lush

苹縈(ㄆㄧㄥˊ ㄧㄥˊ)
circling; revolving

【茈】4882
1. ㄗˇ tzyy zǐ
a kind of herb

【茈】4882
2. ㄔㄞˊ chair chái
Bupleurum, a kind of herb
medicine 亦作「柴胡」

茈胡(ㄔㄞˊ ㄏㄨˊ)

Bupleurum, a kind of herb
medicine 亦作「柴胡」

【苻】4883
ㄈㄨˊ fwu fú
a kind of herb

苻堅(ㄈㄨˊ ㄐㄧㄢ)
Fu Chien, 338-385 A.D., the
founder of 前秦 (one of the
16 kingdoms formed in
North China by barbarian
invaders during the Tsin
Dynasty), who tried in vain
to invade the south

苻秦(ㄈㄨˊ ㄑㄧㄣˊ)
same as 前秦, 351-394 A. D.,
one of the 16 barbarian
kingdoms in North China
that existed concurrently
with the Tsin (晉) Dynasty

【苾】4884
ㄅㄧˋ bih bì
fragrant

苾勃(ㄅㄧˋ ㄅㄛˊ)
fragrant

苾芬(ㄅㄧˋ ㄈㄣ)
fragrant

苾芻(ㄅㄧˋ ㄔㄨˊ)
bhiksu, a Buddhist monk 亦
作「比丘」

苾芻尼(ㄅㄧˋ ㄔㄨˊ ㄋㄧˊ)
bhiksuni, a nun 亦作「比丘尼」

【茁】4885
ㄓㄨㄛˊ jwo zhuó
1. sprouting; growing
2. vigorous; strong; sturdy

茁茁(ㄓㄨㄛˊ ㄓㄨㄛˊ)
sprouting

茁壯(ㄓㄨㄛˊ ㄓㄨㄤˋ)
vigorous; strong

茁芽(ㄓㄨㄛˊ ㄧㄚˊ)
to sprout

【茂】4886
ㄇㄠˋ maw mào
(又讀) ㄇㄡˋ mow mòu)
1. exuberant; lush; luxuriant;
flourishing; healthy; vigorous; strong
2. fine; fair; excellent

茂密(ㄇㄠˋ ㄇㄧˋ)
growing densely

茂年(ㄇㄠˋ ㄋㄧㄢˊ)
youth; the prime of life

茂林修竹(ㄇㄠˋ ㄌㄧㄣˊ ㄒㄧㄡ ㄓㄨˊ)
an exuberant growth of
trees and bamboos

茂齒(ㄇㄠˋ ㄔˇ)
the prime of life

〔艸
部〕

茂士(ㄇㄠˋ ㄕˋ)
a virtuous and capable man

茂盛(ㄇㄠˋ ㄕㄥˋ)
luxuriant; exuberant; lush; flourishing

茂才(ㄇㄠˋ ㄘㄞˊ)
①a talented person ②same as 秀才

【范】 4887
ㄈㄢˋ fann fàn
1. the bee
2. a Chinese family name

范蠡(ㄈㄢˋ ㄌㄧˇ)
Fan Li, a statesman in the Epoch of Spring and Autumn, who helped the state of Yüeh(越) to conquer the state of Wu(吳)

范仲淹(ㄈㄢˋ ㄓㄨㄥˋ ㄧㄢ)
Fan Chung-yen, 989-1052, a famed statesman of the Sung (宋) Dynasty

范增(ㄈㄢˋ ㄗㄥ)
Fan Tseng, 275-204 B.C., a strategist who helped Hsiang Yu (項羽) in his rise to power

【茄】 4888
ㄑㄧㄝˊ chye qié
an eggplant; an aubergine

茄袋(ㄑㄧㄝˊ ㄉㄞˋ)
an eggplant-shaped bag or pouch for cash

茄科(ㄑㄧㄝˊ ㄎㄜ)
Solanaceae

茄子(ㄑㄧㄝˊ ˙ㄗ)
an eggplant

茄子茸(ㄑㄧㄝˊ ˙ㄗ ㄖㄨㄥˊ)
purple-colored soft cores of the young antlers of the deer

【茅】 4889
ㄇㄠˊ mau máo
1. couch grass
2. a Chinese family name

茅棚(ㄇㄠˊ ㄆㄥˊ)
a thatched shed

茅房(ㄇㄠˊ ㄈㄤˊ)
①a thatched house ②a latrine

茅店(ㄇㄠˊ ㄉㄧㄢˋ)
a thatched shop or store

茅台酒(ㄇㄠˊ ㄊㄞˊ ㄐㄧㄡˇ)
Maotai—a strong, colorless liquor produced in Maotai, Kweichow

茅土(ㄇㄠˊ ㄊㄨˇ)

to confer land to vassals

茅利塔尼亞(ㄇㄠˊ ㄌㄧˋ ㄊㄚˇ ㄋㄧˊ ㄧㄚˇ)
Mauritania

茅廬(ㄇㄠˊ ㄌㄨˊ)
a simple dwelling: 我的茅廬
在那邊 I have my simple dwelling there.

茅坑(ㄇㄠˊ ㄎㄥ)
a latrine

茅坤(ㄇㄠˊ ㄎㄨㄣ)
Mao Kun, 1512-1601, a statesman and man of letters of the Ming Dynasty

茅蕈(ㄇㄠˊ ㄒㄩㄣˋ)
(botany) a kind of edible mushroom

茅舍(ㄇㄠˊ ㄕㄜˋ)
①a straw hut; a thatched house ②my humble cottage: 歡迎光臨茅舍。Welcome to my humble cottage.

茅茨土階(ㄇㄠˊ ㄘˊ ㄊㄨˇ ㄐㄧㄝ)
a simple building

茅草(ㄇㄠˊ ㄘㄠˇ)
thatch; straw; couch grass

茅司(ㄇㄠˊ ㄙ)
a privy; a toilet; a water closet

茅廁(ㄇㄠˊ ㄘˋ)
a latrine; a lavatory; a water closet

茅塞(ㄇㄠˊ ㄙㄜˋ)
an obstacle in the mind to understanding

茅塞頓開(ㄇㄠˊ ㄙㄜˋ ㄉㄨㄣˋ ㄎㄞ)
to come to an understanding all of a sudden

茅簷(ㄇㄠˊ ㄧㄢˊ)
straw eaves

茅屋(ㄇㄠˊ ㄨ)
a thatched house; a straw hut: 他在鄉間有一幢茅屋。He has a thatched house in the country.

【茆】 4890
ㄇㄠˊ mau máo
1. Brasenia schreberi
2. same as 茅—couch grass
3. a Chinese family name

【茌】 4891
ㄔˊ chyr chí
as in 茌平—name of a county in Shantung

【茊】 4892
ㄐㄧ ji
1. a pigsty; a pigpen
2. a kind of medicinal herb

【苣】 4893
ㄐㄧㄡˇ ㄐㄩˋ jiuh jù
as in 萵苣—lettuce

【苺】 4894
(苺) ㄇㄟˊ mei méi
berries 參看「莓」

【茀】 4895
ㄈㄨˊ fwu fú
1. weedy
2. a rank growth of weeds obstructing the way—a hindrance; an obstacle
3. luck; fortune

茀茀(ㄈㄨˊ ㄈㄨˊ)
①(said of plants) luxuriant; exuberant; lush ②vigorous

【茇】 4896
ㄅㄚˊ bar bá
1. a grass root
2. to halt in the open country, amid the grass

【茉】 4897
ㄇㄛˋ moh mò
white jasmine

茉莉(ㄇㄛˋ ㄌㄧˋ)
white jasmine

【苟】 4898
ㄍㄡˇ goou gǒu
1. against principle; illicit; improper
2. careless
3. if

苟免(ㄍㄡˇ ㄇㄧㄢˇ)
①to shirk; to avoid ②to escape (a disaster) luckily

苟非(ㄍㄡˇ ㄈㄟ)
had it not been

苟得(ㄍㄡˇ ㄉㄜˊ)
to acquire illicitly; to possess something by improper ways

苟同(ㄍㄡˇ ㄊㄨㄥˊ)
to agree without giving serious thought; to agree with somebody against principle

苟能(ㄍㄡˇ ㄋㄥˊ)
if possible; if... can

苟合(ㄍㄡˇ ㄏㄜˊ)
①to join or associate against one's principle ②an illicit sexual act

苟活(ㄍㄡˇ ㄏㄨㄛˊ)
to live at the expense of one's principle or honor

苟簡(ㄍㄡˇ ㄐㄧㄢˇ)
unduly brief or simple

苟進(ㄍㄡˇ ㄐㄧㄣˋ)
to get promoted against

(艸部)

【艸部】

one's principle

苟且 (《ㄍㄡˇ ㄑㄧㄝˇ)
①against one's principle ②
perfunctory ③illicit (sexual
relations)

苟且偷生 (《ㄍㄡˇ ㄑㄧㄝˇ ㄊㄡ ㄕㄥ)
to drag out an ignominious
existence

苟且偷安 (《ㄍㄡˇ ㄑㄧㄝˇ ㄊㄡ ㄢ)
to enjoy ease against one's
principle or with a false
sense of security

苟全 (《ㄍㄡˇ ㄑㄩㄢˊ)
to manage barely to survive

苟全性命 (《ㄍㄡˇ ㄑㄩㄢˊ ㄒㄧㄥˋ ㄇㄧㄥˋ)
to manage to survive in
times of hardship or unrest
at all costs

苟安 (《ㄍㄡˇ ㄢ)
to live in precarious peace
without doing anything to
avert the looming danger
ahead; to live with a false
sense of security

苟言 (《ㄍㄡˇ ㄧㄢˊ)
careless speech; rash re-
marks

苟延殘喘 (《ㄍㄡˇ ㄧㄢˊ ㄘㄢˊ ㄔㄨㄢˇ)
to prolong one's life only
temporarily; to be on one's
last legs; to linger on in a
steadily deteriorating condition

【苤】 4899
ㄆㄧㄝˇ piee piě
(讀音 ㄆㄧˇ pii pǐ)
1. a kind of plant
2. luxuriant flora or vegetation

苤藍 (ㄆㄧㄝˇ ㄌㄢˊ)
a kohlrabi

【菰】 4900
(菰) 《ㄨ gu gū
Zizania latifolia

【苢】 4901
(苡) ㄧˇ yii yǐ
Coix agrestis

六畫

【茗】 4902
ㄇㄧㄥˊ ming míng
(又讀 ㄇㄧㄥˊ miíng
míng)
tea; a tea plant

茗圃 (ㄇㄧㄥˊ ㄆㄨˇ)
a tea plantation

茗坊 (ㄇㄧㄥˊ ㄈㄤˊ)or 茗肆 (ㄇㄧㄥˊ ㄙˋ)
a tea shop; a teahouse

茗具 (ㄇㄧㄥˊ ㄐㄩˋ)
a tea set

【荔】 4903
ㄌㄧˋ lih lì
a lichee

荔枝 (ㄌㄧˋ ㄓ)
a lichee

【茼】 4904
ㄊㄨㄥˊ torng tóng
a kind of green vegetable

茼蒿 (ㄊㄨㄥˊ ㄏㄠ)
Chrysanthemum coronarium,
a kind of green vegetable

【茨】 4905
ㄘˊ tsyr cí
1. to thatch; a thatched house
2. Tribulus terrestris, a kind of
thorny plant
3. to fill with earth

茨菰 or 慈姑 (ㄘˊ ㄍㄨ)
(botany) an arrowhead

【茫】 4906
ㄇㄤˊ mang máng
1. vast; boundless
2. vague; uncertain

茫昧 (ㄇㄤˊ ㄇㄟˋ)
unfathomably dark

茫茫 (ㄇㄤˊ ㄇㄤˊ)
vast; boundless

茫茫大海 (ㄇㄤˊ ㄇㄤˊ ㄉㄚˋ ㄏㄞˇ)
the boundless ocean

茫然 (ㄇㄤˊ ㄖㄢˊ)
vague; uncertain; ignorant;
blank

茫然不知 (ㄇㄤˊ ㄖㄢˊ ㄅㄨˋ ㄓ)
helplessly ignorant; com-
pletely in the dark; com-
pletely at a loss

茫然自失 (ㄇㄤˊ ㄖㄢˊ ㄗˋ ㄕ)
stupefied; dazed; bewildered;
to be in bewilderment: 他茫
然自失。He was in great
bewilderment.

茫無頭緒 (ㄇㄤˊ ㄨˊ ㄊㄡˊ ㄒㄩˋ)
①(said of things) to be all
in a jumble ②not knowing
where or how to start

【茯】 4907
ㄈㄨˊ fwu fú
tuckahoe

茯苓 (ㄈㄨˊ ㄌㄧㄥˊ)
tuckahoe

【茱】 4908
ㄓㄨ ju zhū
a dogwood

茱萸 (ㄓㄨ ㄩˊ)

a dogwood

茱萸囊 (ㄓㄨ ㄩˊ ㄋㄤˊ)
a bag filled with dogwoods
to be carried at a drinking
party on the Double-Nine
Festival (9th day of the 9th
lunar month) to ward off
disaster

茱萸會 (ㄓㄨ ㄩˊ ㄏㄨㄟˋ)
a drinking party on the
Double-Nine Festival (9th
day of the 9th lunar month)

【茲】 4909
1. ㄗ tzy zī
1. this
2. now; here; at present
3. year: 今茲 this year

茲定 (ㄗ ㄉㄧㄥˋ)
It is hereby decided....

茲令 (ㄗ ㄌㄧㄥˋ) is hereby sent
to....
(So-and-so) is hereby sent
to....

茲者 (ㄗ ㄓㄜˇ)
now

茲查 (ㄗ ㄔㄚˊ)
(a documentary usage) It
has been found that....

茲事體大 (ㄗ ㄕˋ ㄊㄧˇ ㄉㄚˋ)
This is a big problem. 或
This is a serious matter.

茲有 (ㄗ ㄧㄡˇ)
Now here is....

茲因 (ㄗ ㄧㄣ)
now because...

【茲】 4909
2. ㄘˊ tsyr cí
a form used in "龜茲"(ㄑㄧㄡ ㄘˊ)

【茴】 4910
ㄏㄨㄟˊ hwei huí
fennel; aniseed

茴香 (ㄏㄨㄟˊ ㄒㄧㄤ)
fennel; aniseed

茴香菜 (ㄏㄨㄟˊ ㄒㄧㄤ ㄘㄞˋ)
fennel stalks and leaves (as
a kind of vegetable)

【茵】 4911
ㄧㄣ yin yīn
a cushion; a mat; a carpet

茵席 (ㄧㄣ ㄒㄧˊ)
a cushion; a mat

茵陳 or 茵蔯 (ㄧㄣ ㄔㄣˊ) or 茵陳蒿
(ㄧㄣ ㄔㄣˊ ㄏㄠ)
(botany) Artemisia capillaris,
a kind of medicinal herb

茵蓐 or 茵褥 (ㄧㄣ ㄖㄨˋ) or 茵鞾
a mat; a cushion

【茶】 4912
ㄔㄚ char chá

茶
tea

茶博士(ㄔㄚ ㄅㄛˊ ㄕ)
a tearoom keeper

茶杯(ㄔㄚ ㄅㄟ)
a teacup; a cup

茶焙(ㄔㄚ ㄅㄟˋ)
a bamboo tray used in baking tea

茶餅(ㄔㄚ ㄅㄧㄥˇ)
brick tea

茶盤兒(ㄔㄚ ㄆㄢˊ ㄦ)
a tea tray

茶棚(ㄔㄚ ㄆㄥˊ)
a tea booth

茶末(ㄔㄚ ㄇㄛˋ)
refuse tea; tea dust

茶飯(ㄔㄚ ㄈㄢˋ)
meals

茶飯無心(ㄔㄚ ㄈㄢˋ ㄨˊ ㄒㄧㄣ)
to have no appetite

茶坊(ㄔㄚ ㄈㄤ)
a tearoom; a teahouse; a tea shop

茶房(ㄔㄚ ㄈㄤˊ)
a waiter; an attendant

茶袋(ㄔㄚ ㄉㄞˋ)
a tea bag

茶道(ㄔㄚ ㄉㄠˋ)
the tea ceremony

茶顛(ㄔㄚ ㄉㄧㄢ)
"Tea Maniac," the nickname of 陸羽, a Tang Dynasty man of letters who was extremely fond of tea

茶點(ㄔㄚ ㄉㄧㄢˇ)
refreshments

茶點招待(ㄔㄚ ㄉㄧㄢˇ ㄓㄠ ㄉㄞˋ)
to entertain with refreshments

茶攤兒(ㄔㄚ ㄊㄢ ㄦ)
a tea stand (on the roadside)

茶托(ㄔㄚ ㄊㄨㄛ)
a tea tray

茶筒(ㄔㄚ ㄊㄨㄥˇ)
a tea caddy

茶農(ㄔㄚ ㄋㄨㄥˊ)
a tea grower (or planter)

茶樓(ㄔㄚ ㄌㄡˊ)
a tearoom; a teahouse

茶樓酒肆(ㄔㄚ ㄌㄡˊ ㄐㄧㄡˇ ㄙˋ)
tearooms and taverns

茶果(ㄔㄚ ㄍㄨㄛˇ)
tea and fruits

茶館(ㄔㄚ ㄍㄨㄢˇ)
a tearoom; a teahouse

茶罐(ㄔㄚ ㄍㄨㄢˋ)
a tea caddy

茶褐色(ㄔㄚ ㄏㄜˊ ㄙㄜˋ)
tea-brown

茶壺(ㄔㄚ ㄏㄨˊ)
a teapot

茶戶(ㄔㄚ ㄏㄨˋ)
① a tea merchant; a tea dealer ② a tea grower

茶花(ㄔㄚ ㄏㄨㄚ)
a camellia

茶花女(ㄔㄚ ㄏㄨㄚ ㄋㄩˇ)
La Dame Aux Camelias, a romantic drama by Alexandre Dumas (1824-1895)

茶話會(ㄔㄚ ㄏㄨㄚˋ ㄏㄨㄟˋ) or 茶會
(ㄔㄚ ㄏㄨㄟˋ)
a tea party; a tea reception

茶几(ㄔㄚ ㄐㄧ) or 茶几兒(ㄔㄚ ㄐㄧ ㄦ)
① a teapoy ② a small table

茶具(ㄔㄚ ㄐㄩˋ)
tea utensils; tea-things: 她把茶具放在桌上。 She put the tea-things on the table.

茶錢(ㄔㄚ ㄑㄧㄢˊ)
① tea bills ② tips (for attendants, waiters, etc.): 他給侍者茶錢。 He gave the waiter a tip.

茶青(ㄔㄚ ㄑㄧㄥ)
dark green

茶箱(ㄔㄚ ㄒㄧㄤ)
a tea chest

茶磚(ㄔㄚ ㄓㄨㄢ)
brick tea

茶莊(ㄔㄚ ㄓㄨㄤ)
a tea dealer's shop

茶盅(ㄔㄚ ㄓㄨㄥ)
a teacup

茶匙(ㄔㄚ ㄔˊ)
a teaspoon

茶食(ㄔㄚ ㄕˊ)
cookies, cakes, etc.; tea pastry

茶市(ㄔㄚ ㄕˋ)
the tea market

茶室(ㄔㄚ ㄕˋ)
① a tearoom ② a brothel

茶商(ㄔㄚ ㄕㄤ)
a tea dealer; a tea merchant

茶樹(ㄔㄚ ㄕㄨˋ)
a tea tree

茶水(ㄔㄚ ㄕㄨㄟˇ)
tea or boiled water (furnished to walkers, trippers, etc.)

茶水錢(ㄔㄚ ㄕㄨㄟˇ ㄑㄧㄢˊ)
tips given to hotel attendants

茶座(ㄔㄚ ㄗㄨㄛˋ)
seats in a tearoom

茶肆(ㄔㄚ ㄙˋ)
a tearoom; a teahouse

茶色(ㄔㄚ ㄙㄜˋ)
dark brown

茶素(ㄔㄚ ㄙㄨˋ)
theine

茶葉(ㄔㄚ ㄧㄝˋ)
tea leaves

茶業(ㄔㄚ ㄧㄝˋ)
the tea industry

茶油(ㄔㄚ ㄧㄡˊ)
tea oil

茶舞(ㄔㄚ ㄨˇ)
a tea dance

茶碗(ㄔㄚ ㄨㄢˇ)
a teacup; a tea bowl

茶園(ㄔㄚ ㄩㄢˊ)
① a tea plantation ② formerly, an opera theater

【茸】 4913
ㄖㄨㄥˊ rong róng

1. soft, fine hair; down
2. soft; downy; fluffy
3. untidy; messy; confused; disorderly
4. luxuriant; lush

茸茸(ㄖㄨㄥˊ ㄖㄨㄥˊ)
(said of grass, hair, etc.) fine, soft and thick; luxuriant; lush: 兩岸青草茸茸. Lush grass grows along the river banks.

【茹】 4914
ㄖㄨˊ ru rú
(又讀 ㄖㄨˇ ruh rǔ)

1. entangled roots
2. to eat; to taste; to mouth
3. (figuratively) to experience
4. stinking

茹筆(ㄖㄨˊ ㄅㄧˇ)
to make writing brushes

茹毛飲血(ㄖㄨˊ ㄇㄠˊ ㄧㄣˇ ㄒㄧㄝˇ) or 茹毛飲血(ㄖㄨˊ ㄇㄠˊ ㄧㄣˇ ㄒㄩㄝˋ)
(said of primitive people) to eat birds and beasts uncooked

茹苦(ㄖㄨˊ ㄎㄨˇ)
to undergo hardships; to suf-

fer

茹苦含辛 (ㄖㄨˊ ㄎㄨˇ ㄏㄢˊ ㄒㄧㄣ)
to undergo all possible hardships

茹柔吐剛 (ㄖㄨˊ ㄖㄡˊ ㄊㄨˇ ㄍㄤ)
(literally) to eat the soft and spit the hard—to bully the good-natured and fear the atrocious

茹素 (ㄖㄨˊ ㄙㄨˋ)
to abstain from meat; to be a vegetarian

【荀】 *4915*
ㄒㄩㄣˊ shyun xún
1. name of an ancient state
2. a kind of herb
3. a Chinese family name

荀況 (ㄒㄩㄣˊ ㄎㄨㄤˋ)
Hsün Kuang, a contemporary of Mencius, known for his doctrine of man's natural wickedness

荀子 (ㄒㄩㄣˊ ㄗˇ)
① Hsün-tzu or Hsün Kuang
② the works of Hsün-tzu

【荄】 *4916*
《ㄞ gai gāi
roots of grass

【草】 *4917*
ㄘㄠˇ tsao cǎo
1. grass; straw; a herb; a weed
2. coarse; crude
3. a draft (of writing); to draft
4. the script type of Chinese calligraphy

草包 (ㄘㄠˇ ㄅㄠ)
a grass bag—a crude fellow; a good-for-nothing; a simpleton

草本 (ㄘㄠˇ ㄅㄣˇ)
① a manuscript: 著作的草本已完成, The work is already complete in manuscript. ② herbaceous

草本植物 (ㄘㄠˇ ㄅㄣˇ ㄓˊ ㄨˋ)
herbage

草鄙 (ㄘㄠˇ ㄅㄧˇ)
unlearned; uncultured; crude

草標 (ㄘㄠˇ ㄅㄧㄠ)
a straw attached to an article to indicate that it is on sale

草棚 (ㄘㄠˇ ㄆㄥˊ)
a thatched shanty; a straw shed

草皮 (ㄘㄠˇ ㄆㄧˊ)
a young grass cover

草坪 (ㄘㄠˇ ㄆㄧㄥˊ)
a lawn; meadow; pasture

草莓 (ㄘㄠˇ ㄇㄟˊ)
a strawberry

草昧 (ㄘㄠˇ ㄇㄟˋ)
the chaos at the beginning of the world

草芥 (ㄘㄠˇ ㄇㄠˊ)
① thatch; straw; grass ② the common people (as distinct from those in the imperial service)

草帽 (ㄘㄠˇ ㄇㄠˋ)
a straw hat

草辮 or 草帽纏 (ㄘㄠˇ ㄇㄠˋ ㄅㄧㄢˋ)
straw braids for making hats

草莽 (ㄘㄠˇ ㄇㄤˇ)
the wilderness; thickets

草莽流寇 (ㄘㄠˇ ㄇㄤˇ ㄌㄧㄡˊ ㄎㄡˋ)
bandits of the wilderness; bandits

草棉 (ㄘㄠˇ ㄇㄧㄢˊ)
a cotton plant

草木 (ㄘㄠˇ ㄇㄨˋ)
grass and trees; vegetation; flora

草木皆兵 (ㄘㄠˇ ㄇㄨˋ ㄐㄧㄝ ㄅㄧㄥ)
All grass and trees are mistaken for enemy troops. (descriptive of the imaginary fears of a routed army)

草房 (ㄘㄠˇ ㄈㄤˊ)
a thatched cottage

草地 (ㄘㄠˇ ㄉㄧˋ)
meadow; pasture; a lawn: 我們要把草地上的草割去。We are going to mow the meadow.

草堆 (ㄘㄠˇ ㄉㄨㄟ)
a haystack

草頭露 (ㄘㄠˇ ㄊㄡˊ ㄌㄨˋ)
(literally) dew on the grass —ephemeral; fleeting

草堂 (ㄘㄠˇ ㄊㄤˊ) or 草廬 (ㄘㄠˇ ㄌㄨˊ)
a humble cottage (used by a hermit in reference to his simple dwelling)

草圖 (ㄘㄠˇ ㄊㄨˊ)
a sketch map; a draft

草擬 (ㄘㄠˇ ㄋㄧˇ)
to draft (documents): 他們正在草擬一份法案。They are drafting a bill.

草萊 (ㄘㄠˇ ㄌㄞˊ)
① the wilderness ② fields

草蘭 (ㄘㄠˇ ㄌㄢˊ)
Cymbidium virens

草料 (ㄘㄠˇ ㄌㄧㄠˋ)
fodder; hay: 馬以草料為食。The horses feed on fodder.

草履蟲 (ㄘㄠˇ ㄌㄩˇ ㄔㄨㄥˊ)
a paramecium

草綠 (ㄘㄠˇ ㄌㄩˋ)
green

草稿 or 草藁 (ㄘㄠˇ ㄍㄠˇ)
a rough draft

草根大使 (ㄘㄠˇ ㄍㄣ ㄉㄚˋ ㄕˇ)
a grass-roots ambassador; a trainee under the 4-H Club exchange program

草根樹皮 (ㄘㄠˇ ㄍㄣ ㄕㄨˋ ㄆㄧˊ)
roots of grass and bark of trees (which one may eat when starving)

草菇 (ㄘㄠˇ ㄍㄨ)
a mushroom

草寇 (ㄘㄠˇ ㄎㄡˋ)
a bandit

草夾竹桃 (ㄘㄠˇ ㄐㄧㄚ ㄓㄨˊ ㄊㄠˊ)
phlox

草芥 (ㄘㄠˇ ㄐㄧㄝ)
a bundle of grass—valueless things; insignificant things

草芥小民 (ㄘㄠˇ ㄐㄧㄝˋ ㄒㄧㄠˇ ㄇㄧㄣˊ)
an unimportant member of a community; the humble people

草菅人命 (ㄘㄠˇ ㄐㄧㄢ ㄖㄣˊ ㄇㄧㄥˋ)
to treat human life as grass; to attach no importance to human life

草裙舞 (ㄘㄠˇ ㄑㄩㄣˊ ㄨˇ)
a Hawaiian dance; a hula-hula: 夏威夷以草裙舞聞名。Hawaii is famous for its Hawaiian dance.

草席 (ㄘㄠˇ ㄒㄧˊ)
a straw mat

草檄 (ㄘㄠˇ ㄒㄧˊ)
to draft a call to arms

草蝦 (ㄘㄠˇ ㄒㄧㄚ)
a prawn

草鞋 (ㄘㄠˇ ㄒㄧㄝˊ)
straw sandals

草寫 (ㄘㄠˇ ㄒㄧㄝˇ)
the script type of calligraphy

草紙 (ㄘㄠˇ ㄓˇ)
coarse paper; toilet paper

草詔 (ㄘㄠˇ ㄓㄠˋ)
to draft an imperial edict

(艸
部)

（艸部）

草長鶯飛(ㄘㄠˇ ㄓㄤˇ ㄧㄥ ㄈㄟ)
The grasses are tall and the nightingales are in the air. (descriptive of landscapes in late spring)

草創(ㄘㄠˇ ㄔㄨㄤˋ)or 草制(ㄘㄠˇ ㄓˋ)
① the beginning or initial period (of a project) ② to make the rough copy

草食獸(ㄘㄠˇ ㄕˊ ㄕㄡˋ)or 草食動物
(ㄘㄠˇ ㄕˊ ㄉㄨㄥˋ ㄨˋ)
herbivorous animals: 牛是草食動物。Cattle are herbivorous animals.

草繩(ㄘㄠˇ ㄕㄥˊ)
a straw rope; a grass rope: 擲給他一條草繩。Throw him a straw rope.

草聖(ㄘㄠˇ ㄕㄥˋ)
prodigies of the script type of calligraphy—referring to Chang Chih (張芝) of the Han Dynasty and Chang Hsü (張旭) of the Tang Dynasty

草書(ㄘㄠˇ ㄕㄨ)or 草字(ㄘㄠˇ ㄗˋ)
the script type of calligraphy

草率(ㄘㄠˇ ㄕㄨㄞˋ)
careless; perfunctory

草率從事(ㄘㄠˇ ㄕㄨㄞˋ ㄘㄨㄥˊ ㄕˋ)
to do a job carelessly or perfunctorily

草人(ㄘㄠˇ ㄖㄣˊ)
a scarecrow 亦作「稻草人」

草字(ㄘㄠˇ ㄗˋ)
① characters written in the script type ② my humble style (name)

草賊(ㄘㄠˇ ㄗㄟˊ)
bandits; outlaws

草澤(ㄘㄠˇ ㄗㄜˊ)
① the wilderness; thickets ② the common people (as distinct from the governing class)

草澤英雄(ㄘㄠˇ ㄗㄜˊ ㄧㄥ ㄒㄩㄥˊ)
heroes of the common people

草草(ㄘㄠˇ ㄘㄠˇ)
① roughly; carelessly; hastily 亦作「草艸」 ② in sorrow ③ (said of trees, etc.) lush; exuberant; luxuriant

草草了事(ㄘㄠˇ ㄘㄠˇ ㄌㄧㄠˇ ㄕˋ)
to dispose of a thing carelessly or hastily

草叢(ㄘㄠˇ ㄘㄨㄥˊ)
a thick growth of grass

草酸(ㄘㄠˇ ㄙㄨㄢ)
oxalic acid

草案(ㄘㄠˇ ㄢˋ)
a draft plan; a proposed plan: 草案已修訂完成。The draft has been amended.

草野(ㄘㄠˇ ㄧㄝˇ)
① the common people ② fields ③ lowly; base

草藥(ㄘㄠˇ ㄧㄠˋ)
herb medicine

草藥商(ㄘㄠˇ ㄧㄠˋ ㄕㄤ)
a herbalist

草魚(ㄘㄠˇ ㄩˊ)
a grass carp

草約(ㄘㄠˇ ㄩㄝ)
a draft agreement or contract

草原(ㄘㄠˇ ㄩㄢˊ)
a prairie; grassland; a steppe

【荏】 4918 ㄖㄣˇ reen rěn
1. Perilla frutescens, whose seeds are birds' feed
2. soft; weak; fragile

荏苒(ㄖㄣˇ ㄖㄢˇ)
(said of time) to elapse imperceptibly; to slip by 亦作「荏苒」: 光陰荏苒，轉瞬又是一年。Time slipped by and the year was soon over.

荏弱(ㄖㄣˇ ㄖㄨㄛˋ)
soft; weak; fragile: 她愈來愈荏弱。She grew weaker and weaker.

【荑】 4919 1. ㄊㄧˊ tyi tí
sprouts

【荑】 4919 2. ㄧˊ yi yí
to weed; to mow

【荒】 4920 ㄏㄨㄤ huang huāng
1. uncultivated; desolate; wild; deserted; barren; waste
2. absurd; ridiculous
3. famine; scarcity; deficiency
4. to neglect
5. a Chinese family name

荒僻(ㄏㄨㄤ ㄆㄧˋ)
desolate and remote

荒謬(ㄏㄨㄤ ㄇㄧㄡˋ)
grossly absurd; ridiculous; preposterous: 那真是荒謬至極! That is ridiculous!

荒謬絕倫(ㄏㄨㄤ ㄇㄧㄡˋ ㄐㄩㄝˊ ㄌㄨㄣˊ)
absurd in the extreme

荒湎(ㄏㄨㄤ ㄇㄧㄢˇ)
to abandon oneself to (drinking, etc.)

荒廢(ㄏㄨㄤ ㄈㄟˋ)
to neglect; to leave completely unattended to

荒怠(ㄏㄨㄤ ㄉㄞˋ)
negligent; neglectful

荒島(ㄏㄨㄤ ㄉㄠˇ)
an uninhabited island; a barren island

荒誕(ㄏㄨㄤ ㄉㄢˋ)
absurd; nonsensical; wild

荒誕不經(ㄏㄨㄤ ㄉㄢˋ ㄅㄨˋ ㄐㄧㄥ)
absurd and unthinkable

荒地(ㄏㄨㄤ ㄉㄧˋ)
the wilderness; waste land

荒唐(ㄏㄨㄤ ㄊㄤˊ)
absurd; wild; nonsensical; preposterous

荒唐無稽(ㄏㄨㄤ ㄊㄤˊ ㄨˊ ㄐㄧ)
flagrantly absurd or ridiculous; preposterous

荒田(ㄏㄨㄤ ㄊㄧㄢˊ)
fields left uncultivated; desolate fields

荒酖(ㄏㄨㄤ ㄊㄢ)
addicted to alcoholic drinks

荒土(ㄏㄨㄤ ㄊㄨˇ)
uncultivated land; the wilderness; waste land

荒年(ㄏㄨㄤ ㄋㄧㄢˊ)
a year of bad crops; a year of famine

荒涼(ㄏㄨㄤ ㄌㄧㄤˊ)
desolate; deserted; wild

荒忽(ㄏㄨㄤ ㄏㄨ)
dim; vague; indistinct

荒瘠(ㄏㄨㄤ ㄐㄧˊ)
barren land

荒郊(ㄏㄨㄤ ㄐㄧㄠ)
the wilderness; a desolate area

荒饉(ㄏㄨㄤ ㄐㄧㄣˇ)
famine 亦作「飢荒」

荒歉(ㄏㄨㄤ ㄑㄧㄢˋ)
famine; deficiency

荒腔走調(ㄏㄨㄤ ㄑㄧㄤ ㄗㄡˇ ㄉㄧㄠˋ)

out of tune

荒政（ㄏㄨㄤ ㄓㄥ）
①measures for relief of a famine ②to neglect affairs of the state

荒塚（ㄏㄨㄤ ㄓㄨㄥ）
an abandoned grave; an uncared-for grave

荒山（ㄏㄨㄤ ㄕㄢ）
a desolate mountain; a lone hill

荒疏（ㄏㄨㄤ ㄕㄨ）
to neglect practice (of some skill)

荒草（ㄏㄨㄤ ㄘㄠ）
weeds

荒村（ㄏㄨㄤ ㄘㄨㄣ）
a deserted village

荒野（ㄏㄨㄤ ㄧㄝ）
the wilderness

荒煙蔓草（ㄏㄨㄤ ㄧㄢ ㄇㄢ ㄘㄠ）
deserted by men and infested with weeds

荒淫（ㄏㄨㄤ ㄧㄣ）
dissipated; dissolute; profligate

荒淫無度（ㄏㄨㄤ ㄧㄣ ㄨ ㄉㄨ）
immeasurably dissolute

荒蕪（ㄏㄨㄤ ㄨ）
deserted and desolate; desolation

荒外（ㄏㄨㄤ ㄨㄞ）
very remote

荒原（ㄏㄨㄤ ㄩㄢ）
wasteland; the wilderness

【菮】 4921
（ㄍㄣ） genn gèn
Rhus toxicodendron, a kind of poisonous vine

【茜】 4922
（ㄑㄧㄢ） chiann qiàn
madder

茜草（ㄑㄧㄢ ㄘㄠ）
madder

茜素（ㄑㄧㄢ ㄙㄨ）
alizarin

【茭】 4923
（ㄐㄧㄠ） jiau jiāo
Zizania latifolia, a kind of edible aquatic grass

茭白（ㄐㄧㄠ ㄅㄞˊ）or 茭白筍（ㄐㄧㄠ ㄅㄞˊ ㄙㄨㄣ）
Zizania latifolia, water oats

【荃】 4924
（ㄑㄩㄢ） chyuan quán
1. a fragrant herb
2. fine cloth

【荇】 4925
（ㄒㄧㄥ） shing xìng
Nymphoides peltatum, a kind of vegetable

荇菜（ㄒㄧㄥ ㄘㄞ）
Nymphoides peltatum, a kind of vegetable; duckweed

【荐】 4926
（薦） ㄐㄧㄢ jiann jiàn
1. repeatedly; again and again
2. to offer; to recommend
3. a straw mattress

七畫

【荷】 4927
1. （ㄏㄜˊ） her hé
a lotus; a water lily

荷包（ㄏㄜˊ ㄅㄠ）
a pouch (carried with oneself); a purse

荷包蛋（ㄏㄜˊ ㄅㄠ ㄉㄢ）
fried eggs

荷馬（ㄏㄜˊ ㄇㄚ）
Homer, Greek poet

荷蘭（ㄏㄜˊ ㄌㄢˊ）
Holland; the Netherlands

荷蘭話（ㄏㄜˊ ㄌㄢˊ ㄏㄨㄚ）or 荷蘭語（ㄏㄜˊ ㄌㄢˊ ㄩ）
the Dutch language; Dutch

荷蘭豬（ㄏㄜˊ ㄌㄢˊ ㄓㄨ）
a guinea pig

荷蘭水（ㄏㄜˊ ㄌㄢˊ ㄕㄨㄟ）
aerated water; soda water

荷蘭人（ㄏㄜˊ ㄌㄢˊ ㄖㄣˊ）
a Dutchman; the Dutch people; the Dutch

荷花（ㄏㄜˊ ㄏㄨㄚ）or 荷華（ㄏㄜˊ ㄏㄨㄚ）
a lotus flower

荷錢（ㄏㄜˊ ㄑㄧㄢˊ）
sprouting lotus leaves

荷爾蒙（ㄏㄜˊ ㄦ ㄇㄥ）
hormone

荷葉（ㄏㄜˊ ㄧㄝ）
lotus leaves

荷葉肉（ㄏㄜˊ ㄧㄝ ㄖㄡ）
slices of pork seasoned and wrapped in lotus leaves and then steamed

荷月（ㄏㄜˊ ㄩㄝ）
the month of the lotus—the 6th lunar month

【荷】 4927
1. a load; a burden
2. to bear; to carry; to shoulder

3. to receive

荷蒙（ㄏㄜˊ ㄇㄥˊ）
to receive (favor, etc.)

荷負（ㄏㄜˊ ㄈㄨ）
to carry; to bear

荷戴（ㄏㄜˊ ㄉㄞ）
to carry; to bear

荷鎗實彈（ㄏㄜˊ ㄑㄧㄤ ㄕˊ ㄉㄢ）
to carry loaded rifles—ready for emergencies

【荽】 4928
（ㄙㄨㄟ） suei suī
as in 芫荽—parsley

【莅】 4929
（蒞） ㄌㄧ lih lì
to arrive; to be present

莅臨（ㄌㄧ ㄌㄧㄣˊ）
to arrive; to be present

【荻】 4930
（ㄉㄧ） dyi dí
1. *Anaphalis yedoensis*
2. *Miscanthus sacchariflorus*, a kind of reed

荻筆（ㄉㄧ ㄅㄧ）
to learn to write on ash with reed stems

荻花（ㄉㄧ ㄏㄨㄚ）
a reed flower

荻畫（ㄉㄧ ㄏㄨㄚ）
to learn by writing on the ground with a reed stem, as Ou-Yang Hsiu（歐陽修）did in his childhood

【茶】 4931
（ㄊㄨ） twu tú
1. *Sonchus oleraceus*, a kind of bitter-tasting vegetable; sow thistle 亦作「苦荼」
2. to harm; to poison

荼毗（ㄊㄨ ㄆㄧˊ）
to cremate a body (transliteration from Sanskrit)

荼蘼 or 荼縻（ㄊㄨ ㄇㄧˊ）
brambles, a kind of shrub

荼毒（ㄊㄨ ㄉㄨˊ）
harm; poison; to cause injury or disaster

荼毒生靈（ㄊㄨ ㄉㄨˊ ㄕㄥ ㄌㄧㄥˊ）
to injure the people

荼炭（ㄊㄨ ㄊㄢ）
suffering of the common people 亦作「塗炭」

荼蓼（ㄊㄨ ㄌㄧㄠˇ）
①a kind of bitter weed ②(figuratively) hardship; privation

（艸
部）

【苬】 ⁴⁹³²
ㄒㄧㄥˊ shíng xíng
Nymphoides peltatum, a kind
of water plant

苬菜（ㄒㄧㄥˊ ㄘㄞˋ）
Nymphoides peltatum, a kind
of water plant

【莊】 ⁴⁹³³
ㄓㄨㄤ juang zhuāng
1. solemn; dignified; stately;
august; sober; gravity
2. a large farmhouse; a manor
house
3. a village; a hamlet
4. a market; a shop; a store; a
bank
5. a Chinese family name

莊票（ㄓㄨㄤ ㄆㄧㄠˋ）
a note issued by a local
bank

莊頭（ㄓㄨㄤ ㄊㄡˊ）
a supervisor of tenant
farmers

莊田（ㄓㄨㄤ ㄊㄧㄢˊ）
①fields tilled by tenants ②
(Ching Dynasty) fields near
the capital with the levy
turned to the imperial coffer
directly

莊奴（ㄓㄨㄤ ㄋㄨˊ）
a tenant farmer

莊列（ㄓㄨㄤ ㄌㄧㄝˋ）
Chuang-tzu (莊子) and Lieh-
tzu (列子), who preached
Taoism after Lao-tzu (老子)

莊論（ㄓㄨㄤ ㄌㄨㄣˋ）or 莊語（ㄓㄨㄤ ㄩˇ）
a dignified statement

莊客（ㄓㄨㄤ ㄎㄜˋ）
tenant farmers

莊口（ㄓㄨㄤ ㄎㄡˇ）
a market

莊款（ㄓㄨㄤ ㄎㄨㄢˇ）
money exchanged between
banks

莊戶（ㄓㄨㄤ ㄏㄨˋ）
a farmer

莊家（ㄓㄨㄤ ㄐㄧㄚ）
①a farmhouse ②the banker
(in gambling games)

莊稼（ㄓㄨㄤ ㄐㄧㄚˋ）
①farming ②crops; harvests

莊稼地（ㄓㄨㄤ ㄐㄧㄚˋ ㄉㄧˋ）
a farm; a field

莊稼老兒（ㄓㄨㄤ ㄐㄧㄚˋ ㄌㄠˇ ㄦ）or 莊
稼漢（ㄓㄨㄤ ㄐㄧㄚˋ ㄏㄢˋ）or 莊稼人
（ㄓㄨㄤ ㄐㄧㄚˋ ㄖㄣˊ）
a farmer

莊稼活（ㄓㄨㄤ ㄐㄧㄚˋ ㄏㄨㄛˊ）
farming; farm chores

莊諧並作（ㄓㄨㄤ ㄒㄧㄝˊ ㄅㄧㄥˋ ㄗㄨㄛˋ）
to combine sobriety with
humor

莊周（ㄓㄨㄤ ㄓㄡ）
Chuang Chou, a contempo-
rary of Mencius who advo-
cated Taoism 亦作「莊子」

莊重（ㄓㄨㄤ ㄓㄨㄥˋ）
dignified; solemn: 他看起來很
莊重。He looks very solemn.

莊子（ㄓㄨㄤ ㄗˇ）
①（ㄓㄨㄤ ㄗˇ）ⓐ Chuang Chou
參看「莊周」ⓑ the works of
Chuang Chou
②（ㄓㄨㄤ ˙ㄗ）the landlord's
mansion; a manor house; a
farm village

莊驤（ㄓㄨㄤ ㄙㄠˋ）
the works of the philosopher
Chuang-tzu (莊子) and the
poet Chü Yüan (屈原), regarded as representatives of
southern literature in the
Epoch of Warring States

莊嚴（ㄓㄨㄤ ㄧㄢˊ）
①dignified; solemn; stately;
august ②to adorn; to make
solemn

莊園（ㄓㄨㄤ ㄩㄢˊ）
a manor

【莒】 ⁴⁹³⁴
ㄐㄩˇ jeu jǔ
1. taros
2. name of an ancient state
3. name of a county in Shantung

【莓】 ⁴⁹³⁵
ㄇㄟˊ mei méi
1. berries
2. moss; lichen

【莖】 ⁴⁹³⁶
ㄐㄧㄥ jing jīng
a stalk; a stem

莖菜類（ㄐㄧㄥ ㄘㄞˋ ㄌㄟˋ）
stem vegetables

【莘】 ⁴⁹³⁷
ㄕㄣ shen shēn
（又讀 ㄒㄧㄣ shin xīn）
1. long
2. numerous
3. *Asarum sieboldi*
4. a Chinese family name

莘莘（ㄕㄣ ㄕㄣ）or（ㄙㄢ ㄙㄢ）
numerous; many

莘莘學子（ㄒㄧㄣ ㄒㄧㄣ ㄒㄩㄝˊ ㄗˇ）or
（ㄙㄢ ㄙㄢ ㄒㄩㄝˊ ㄗˇ）

students in large numbers

【莞】 ⁴⁹³⁸
1. ㄨㄢˇ woan wǎn
smiling

莞爾（ㄨㄢˇ ㄦˇ）
smiling

【莞】 ⁴⁹³⁸
2. 《ㄨㄢ guan guān
as in 東莞—a county in
Kwangtung

【莞】 ⁴⁹³⁸
3. 《ㄨㄢ guan guān
Scirpus lacustris, a kind of
aquatic herb

【莠】 ⁴⁹³⁹
ㄧㄡˇ yeou yǒu
（又讀 ㄧˇ yow yǒu）
1. foxtail (a kind of weed) 亦
作「狗尾草」
2. bad; ugly; undesirable;
detestable; vicious: 良莠不齊。
The good and the bad are
intermingled.

莠民（ㄧㄡˇ ㄇㄧㄣˊ）
wicked people; villains; outlaws

莠言（ㄧㄡˇ ㄧㄢˊ）
dirty words; bad words: 莠言
不聽。Do not listen to bad
words.

【莢】 ⁴⁹⁴⁰
ㄐㄧㄚˊ jya jiá
a pod—the shell or case in
which plants like beans and
peas grow their seed

莢果（ㄐㄧㄚˊ ㄍㄨㄛˇ）
(botany) a pod

莢錢（ㄐㄧㄚˊ ㄑㄧㄢˊ）
a small light coin

【莧】 ⁴⁹⁴¹
ㄒㄧㄢˋ shiann xiàn
an amaranth

莧科（ㄒㄧㄢˋ ㄎㄜ）
Amaranthaceae, the ama-
ranth family

莧菜（ㄒㄧㄢˋ ㄘㄞˋ）
an amaranth

【莩】 ⁴⁹⁴²
1. ㄈㄨˊ fwu fú
membrane in stems of
rushes or reeds

【莩】 ⁴⁹⁴²
2. (殍) ㄆㄧㄠˇ peau
piǎo
the corpse of a person who
was starved to death

【莪】 ⁴⁹⁴³
ㄜˊ er é

（艸部）

Artemisia, a kind of plant;
the aster-southernwood

莪蒿(ㄜˊ ㄏㄠ)
Artemisia, a kind of plant
with edible leaves

【莫】 4944
1. not: 莫蹉跎光陰。Don't waste
time.
2. a Chinese family name

莫泊桑(ㄇㄜˋ ㄆㄛ ㄙㄤ)
Guy de Maupassant, 1850-
1893, French novelist

莫不(ㄇㄜˋ ㄅㄨˋ)
there is no one that does
not; there is no one that is
not: 莫不為之歡欣鼓舞。There
was no one who was not
very pleased.

莫不成(ㄇㄜˋ ㄅㄨˋ ㄔㄥˊ)
Can it be that…? 亦作「莫不
是」

莫名(ㄇㄜˋ ㄇㄧㄥˊ)
inexpressible; indescribable

莫名其妙(ㄇㄜˋ ㄇㄧㄥˊ ㄑㄧˊ ㄇㄧㄠˋ)
①incomprehensible; mysterious; baffling ②impossible
(as in "an impossible person")

莫非(ㄇㄜˋ ㄈㄟ)
①certainly; surely ②all;
all-inclusive; the whole
amount, quantity or extent
of ③Can it be that…?

莫大(ㄇㄜˋ ㄉㄚˋ)
greatest; utmost

莫道(ㄇㄜˋ ㄉㄠˋ)
Do not say…

莫逆之交(ㄇㄜˋ ㄋㄧˋ ㄓ ㄐㄧㄠ)
close friendship; bosom
friends

莫干山(ㄇㄜˋ ㄍㄢ ㄕㄢ)
a mountain in Chekiang,
known as a summer resort

莫過于(ㄇㄜˋ ㄍㄨㄛˋ)or 莫過於(ㄇㄜˋ
ㄍㄨㄛˋ ㄩˊ)
Nothing (or no one) is
more…than…看信之樂,莫過於
此。Of the pleasures of letter
reading, none is more than
this.

莫怪(ㄇㄜˋ ㄍㄨㄞˋ)
①No wonder that… ②
Please excuse…

莫管(ㄇㄜˋ ㄍㄨㄢˇ)
do not meddle with

莫可言狀(ㄇㄜˋ ㄎㄜˇ ㄧㄢˊ ㄓㄨㄤˋ)

indescribable; unspeakable;
inexpressible

莫須有(ㄇㄜˋ ㄒㄩ ㄧㄡˇ)
(literally) Though not certain, it's likely to be true. (a
phrase used by the traitorous minister Chin Kuei (秦
檜)as a charge against the
loyal general Yüeh Fei(岳
飛) in the Southern Sung
Dynasty)—a trumped-up
charge; false accusation

莫札特(ㄇㄜˋ ㄓㄚˊ ㄊㄜˋ)
Wolfgang Amadeus Mozart,
1756-1791, Austrian com-
poser

莫衷一是(ㄇㄜˋ ㄓㄨㄥ ㄧ ㄕˋ)
There is no agreement of
opinion at all.

莫愁湖(ㄇㄜˋ ㄔㄡˊ ㄏㄨˊ)
a lake outside Nanking(南
京), named after Lu Mo-
chou(盧莫愁), a famed girl
in the Six Dynasties

莫是(ㄇㄜˋ ㄕˋ)
①Can it be that…? ②no
longer

莫說(ㄇㄜˋ ㄕㄨㄛ)
Do not say…or not to men-
tion

莫如(ㄇㄜˋ ㄖㄨˊ)or 莫若(ㄇㄜˋ ㄖㄨㄛˋ)
①had better ②Nothing is
better than…或would be
better

莫此為甚(ㄇㄜˋ ㄘˇ ㄨㄟˊ ㄕㄣˋ)
There is nothing worse than
this.

莫測高深(ㄇㄜˋ ㄘㄜˋ ㄍㄠ ㄕㄣ)
unfathomable; inscrutable

莫斯科(ㄇㄜˋ ㄙ ㄎㄜ)
Moscow

莫三比克(ㄇㄜˋ ㄙㄢ ㄅㄧˇ ㄎㄜˋ)
Mozambique, a republic in
SE Africa

莫索里尼(ㄇㄜˋ ㄙㄨㄛˇ ㄌㄧˇ ㄋㄧˊ)
Benito Mussolini, 1883-1945,
Italian dictator

莫邪(ㄇㄜˋ ㄧㄝ)
name of a legendary sword

莫臥兒帝國(ㄇㄜˋ ㄨㄛˋ ㄦˊ ㄉㄧˋ ㄍㄨㄜˊ)
the Mogul Empire, 1526-1857
亦作「蒙兀兒帝國」

【莫】 4944
2.(暮)ㄇㄨˋ muh mù
evening; dusk

【莆】 4945
1. ㄈㄨˇ fuu fŭ

a kind of legendary tree
with small leaves

【莆】 4945
2. ㄆㄨˊ pwu pú
as in 莆田—a county in Fu-
kien(福建)

【莉】 4946
ㄌㄧˋ lih lì
as in 茉莉—white jasmine

【莽】 4947
1.(蟒)ㄇㄤˇ maang mǎng
1. bushy; weedy
2. *Illicium anisatum*, a poisonous bushy plant
3. rude; uncultured; impolite;
reckless

莽莽(ㄇㄤˇ ㄇㄤˇ)
①weedy; bushy ②bound-
less; endless

莽夫(ㄇㄤˇ ㄈㄨ)
a rude fellow

莽蕩(ㄇㄤˇ ㄉㄤˋ)
vast and wild; extensive and
undeveloped

莽漢(ㄇㄤˇ ㄏㄢˋ)
a rude fellow; a rough

莽撞(ㄇㄤˇ ㄓㄨㄤˋ)
rude; rough; uncultured: 他的
行為莽撞。He has rude man-
ners.

莽草(ㄇㄤˇ ㄘㄠˇ)
Illicium anisatum; a kind of
poisonous shrub

莽蒼(ㄇㄤˇ ㄘㄤ)
verdure of the countryside

【莎】 4948
1. ㄙㄨㄛ suo suō
Cyperus rotundus, a kind of
medicinal herb

莎草(ㄇㄤˇ ㄘㄠˇ)
Cyperus rotundus, a kind of
medicinal herb

【莎】 4948
2. ㄕㄚ sha shā
a kind of insect

莎士比亞(ㄕㄚ ㄕˋ ㄅㄧˇ ㄧㄚˋ)or 莎翁
(ㄕㄚ ㄨㄥ)
William Shakespeare, 1564-
1616, British poet and playwright

【挲】 4949
ㄙㄨㄛ suo suō
(讀音 ㄘㄨㄛ tsuo
cuō)
to rub hands together

【荸】 4950
ㄅㄧˊ byi bí
(又讀 ㄅㄛˊ bor bó)

【艸
部】

a water chestnut

荸薺 (ㄅㄧˊ ㄑㄧˊ)
a water chestnut

【茝】 4951
ㄔㄞˇ chae chǎi
angelica 亦作「白芷」

【莝】 4952
ㄘㄨㄛˋ tsuoh cuò
1. to chop straw or hay for animals
2. chopped straw or hay

【莨】 4953
ㄌㄤˊ lang láng
Scopolia japonica, a kind of herb

莨草 (ㄌㄤˊ ㄘㄠˇ)
Chinese pennisetum, a kind of herb 亦作「狼尾草」

【荳】 4954
(豆) ㄉㄡˋ dow dòu
beans, peas, etc.; legumes

荳蔻 (ㄉㄡˋ ㄎㄡˋ)
①a nutmeg 亦作「豆蔻」②a virgin

荳蔻年華 (ㄉㄡˋ ㄎㄡˋ ㄋㄧㄢˊ ㄏㄨㄚˊ)
(said of girls) the age of 13 or 14 in ancient China; marriageable age

八畫

【菟】 4955
ㄊㄨˊ tuh tú
(botany) a dodder

菟葵 (ㄊㄨˊ ㄎㄨㄟˊ)
① Eranthis pinnatifida, a kind of mallow ② sea anemone, a kind of coral insect 亦作「海葵」

菟絲子 (ㄊㄨˊ ㄙ ㄗˇ)
(botany) a dodder

【菀】 4956
ㄨㄢˇ woan wǎn
1. exuberant; luxuriant; lush
2. clogged; stagnant

【菅】 4957
ㄐㄧㄢ jian jiān
Themeda triandra, a coarse grass (used for making brushes, brooms, etc.)

【菊】 4958
ㄐㄩˊ jyu jú
a chrysanthemum

菊科 (ㄐㄩˊ ㄎㄜ)
Compositae, the chrysanthemum family

菊花 (ㄐㄩˊ ㄏㄨㄚ)
a chrysanthemum

菊花酒 (ㄐㄩˊ ㄏㄨㄚ ㄐㄧㄡˇ)
chrysanthemum wine

菊花茶 (ㄐㄩˊ ㄏㄨㄚ ㄔㄚˊ)
an infusion made from dried chrysanthemums

菊枕 (ㄐㄩˊ ㄓㄣˇ)
a pillow stuffed with dried chrysanthemums

菊月 (ㄐㄩˊ ㄩㄝˋ)
the month of the chrysanthemum—the 9th lunar month

【菌】 4959
ㄐㄩㄣˋ jiunn jùn
1. fungi; mushrooms
2. bacteria
3. a bamboo shoot

菌柄 (ㄐㄩㄣˋ ㄅㄧㄥˇ)
mushroom stalks

菌類 (ㄐㄩㄣˋ ㄌㄟˋ)
fungi

菌藻植物 (ㄐㄩㄣˋ ㄗㄠˇ ㄓˊ ㄨˋ)
a thallophyte

菌傘 (ㄐㄩㄣˋ ㄙㄢˇ)
a mushroom top

【菜】 4960
ㄈㄣ fen fēn
a kind of wood burnt for perfume

【菑】 4961
1.(畬) ㄗ tzy zī
1. land under cultivation for one year
2. to weed grass

菑畬 (ㄗ ㄩˊ)
farming; husbandry

【菑】 4961
2.(甾,災) ㄗㄞ tzai zāi
misfortune; disaster; calamity

【菔】 4962
ㄈㄨˊ fwu fú
(botany) turnip

【菖】 4963
ㄔㄤ chang chāng
a sweet flag; a calamus

菖蒲 (ㄔㄤ ㄆㄨˊ)
a sweet flag; a calamus

菖蒲酒 (ㄔㄤ ㄆㄨˊ ㄐㄧㄡˇ)
calamus wine (served on the 5th of the 5th lunar month, the Dragon-Boat Festival)

【菜】 4964
ㄘㄞˋ tsay cài
1. vegetables; greens
2. food eaten with rice or alcoholic drinks
3. a dish; a course

菜包子 (ㄘㄞˋ ㄅㄠ ˙ㄗ)
① vegetable dumpling ② (abusive) an idiot

菜園 (ㄘㄞˋ ㄩㄢˊ)
a vegetable garden (or field)

菜刀 (ㄘㄞˋ ㄉㄠ)
a kitchen knife

菜豆 (ㄘㄞˋ ㄉㄡˋ)
kidney beans; string beans

菜單兒 (ㄘㄞˋ ㄉㄢ ㄦ) or 菜單子 (ㄘㄞˋ ㄉㄢ ˙ㄗ)
a bill of fare; a menu: 請拿菜單給我看。Shew me the menu, please.

菜墩子 (ㄘㄞˋ ㄉㄨㄣ ˙ㄗ)
a chopping board

菜攤兒 (ㄘㄞˋ ㄊㄢ ㄦ) or 菜攤子 (ㄘㄞˋ ㄊㄢ ˙ㄗ)
a vegetable vendor's stall

菜牛 (ㄘㄞˋ ㄋㄧㄡˊ)
beef cattle

菜農 (ㄘㄞˋ ㄋㄨㄥˊ)
a vegetable grower

菜籃 (ㄘㄞˋ ㄌㄢˊ)
a basket for carrying vegetables and other food items

菜根 (ㄘㄞˋ ㄍㄣ)
the inedible root of a vegetable, cabbage stalks

菜瓜 (ㄘㄞˋ ㄍㄨㄚ)
cucumber

菜館 (ㄘㄞˋ ㄍㄨㄢˇ)
a restaurant 亦作「餐館」: 我們在菜館吃晚飯。We had dinner at a restaurant.

菜花 (ㄘㄞˋ ㄏㄨㄚ)
① a cauliflower ② a rape flower

菜貨 (ㄘㄞˋ ㄏㄨㄛˋ)
a person of little use

菜心 (ㄘㄞˋ ㄒㄧㄣ)
young leaves of a vegetable

菜畦 (ㄘㄞˋ ㄑㄧˊ)
a vegetable garden

菜市場 (ㄘㄞˋ ㄕˋ ㄔㄤˇ)
a grocery market; a vegetable market; a food market

菜蔬 (ㄘㄞˋ ㄕㄨ)
vegetables 亦作「蔬菜」

菜籽 (ㄘㄞˋ ㄗˇ) or 菜子 (ㄘㄞˋ ˙ㄗ)
① vegetable seeds ② rapeseed

菜籽油 (ㄘㄞˋ ㄗˇ ㄧㄡˊ) or 菜子油 (ㄘㄞˋ ˙ㄗ ㄧㄡˊ)
rapeseed oil; rape oil; colza oil

茶色(ㄘㄞ ㄙㄜˋ)
　　pallor due to hunger; a famished or emaciated look

茶肴(ㄘㄞ ㄧㄠˊ)
　　food eaten with rice or alcoholic drinks

茶油(ㄘㄞ ㄧㄡˊ)
　　vegetable oil 亦作「植物油」

茶園(ㄘㄞ ㄩㄢˊ)
　　a vegetable garden

【菠】 4965
　　　　ㄅㄛ bo bō
　　spinach

菠薐菜(ㄅㄛ ㄌㄥ ㄘㄞˋ)or 菠菜(ㄅㄛ ㄘㄞˋ)
　　spinach

菠蘿(ㄅㄛ ㄌㄨㄛˊ)
　　a pineapple 亦作「鳳梨」

菠次坦宣言(ㄅㄛ ㄘˋ ㄊㄢˇ ㄒㄩㄢ ㄧㄢˊ)
　　the Potsdam Declaration in July, 1945, calling on Japan to surrender to the Allies unconditionally

【華】 4966
　　　　1. ㄏㄨㄚˊ hwa huá
1. Cathay; China
2. splendid; majestic; gorgeous; colorful; brilliant; bright; fine; beautiful; luxurious
3. prosperous; thriving

華北(ㄏㄨㄚˊ ㄅㄟˇ)
　　North China

華表(ㄏㄨㄚˊ ㄅㄧㄠˇ)
　　a monument formerly erected on the roadside as a guidepost

華美(ㄏㄨㄚˊ ㄇㄟˇ)
　　beautiful; splendid; luxurious 參看「華麗」

華美協進會(ㄏㄨㄚˊ ㄇㄟˇ ㄒㄧㄝˊ ㄐㄧㄣˋ ㄏㄨㄟˋ)
　　China Institute in the United States

華髮(ㄏㄨㄚˊ ㄈㄚˇ)
　　gray hair; white hair

華服(ㄏㄨㄚˊ ㄈㄨˊ)
　　fine clothes

華府(ㄏㄨㄚˊ ㄈㄨˇ)
　　Washington D.C.

華麗(ㄏㄨㄚˊ ㄌㄧˋ)
　　birthday (usually of an honored person)

華燈(ㄏㄨㄚˊ ㄉㄥ)
　　a colorful lantern

華燈初上(ㄏㄨㄚˊ ㄉㄥ ㄔㄨ ㄕㄤˋ)
　　(descriptive of urban scenes at dusk) Colorful lamps are

beginning to light up.

華顛(ㄏㄨㄚˊ ㄉㄧㄢ)
　　gray hair; white hair

華甸(ㄏㄨㄚˊ ㄉㄧㄢˋ)
　　the capital (of a state)

華殿(ㄏㄨㄚˊ ㄉㄧㄢˋ)
　　a palace

華東(ㄏㄨㄚˊ ㄉㄨㄥ)
　　East China

華南(ㄏㄨㄚˊ ㄋㄢˊ)
　　South China

華年(ㄏㄨㄚˊ ㄋㄧㄢˊ)
　　youth

華麗(ㄏㄨㄚˊ ㄌㄧˋ)
　　magnificent; resplendent; gorgeous

華格納(ㄏㄨㄚˊ ㄍㄜˊ ㄋㄚˋ)
　　Wilhelm Richard Wagner, 1813-1883, German composer

華蓋(ㄏㄨㄚˊ ㄍㄞˋ)
　　a canopy over a carriage

華貴(ㄏㄨㄚˊ ㄍㄨㄟˋ)
　　luxurious; sumptuous; costly

華工(ㄏㄨㄚˊ ㄍㄨㄥ)
　　Chinese laborers abroad

華翰(ㄏㄨㄚˊ ㄏㄢˋ)or 華緘(ㄏㄨㄚˊ ㄐㄧㄢ)or 華札(ㄏㄨㄚˊ ㄓㄚˊ)
　　your esteemed letter

華界(ㄏㄨㄚˊ ㄐㄧㄝˋ)
　　the Chinese district (in Shanghai before World War II)

華僑(ㄏㄨㄚˊ ㄑㄧㄠˊ)
　　overseas Chinese

華僑節(ㄏㄨㄚˊ ㄑㄧㄠˊ ㄐㄧㄝˊ)
　　Overseas Chinese Day (falling on December 21)

華僑學校(ㄏㄨㄚˊ ㄑㄧㄠˊ ㄒㄩㄝˊ ㄒㄧㄠˋ)
　　a Chinese school abroad

華清宮(ㄏㄨㄚˊ ㄑㄧㄥ ㄍㄨㄥ)
　　name of a palace with a mineral spring in the Tang Dynasty (in today's Shensi)

華清池(ㄏㄨㄚˊ ㄑㄧㄥ ㄔˊ)
　　Hua Ching Pool, name of a mineral spring where 楊貴妃, a concubine of Emperor Hsüan (玄宗) of the Tang Dynasty, once bathed

華夏(ㄏㄨㄚˊ ㄒㄧㄚˋ)
　　Cathay

華軒(ㄏㄨㄚˊ ㄒㄩㄢ)
　　①the magnificent carriage of a high official ②(figuratively) worldly splendors

華胄(ㄏㄨㄚˊ ㄓㄡˋ)

①descendants of a nobleman ②Chinese people; people of Chinese ancestry

華燭(ㄏㄨㄚˊ ㄓㄨˊ)
　　painted candles—the symbol of a wedding

華中(ㄏㄨㄚˊ ㄓㄨㄥ)
　　Central China

華飾(ㄏㄨㄚˊ ㄕˋ)
　　beautiful decorations

華氏寒暑表(ㄏㄨㄚˊ ㄕˋ ㄏㄢˊ ㄕㄨˇ ㄅㄧㄠˇ)or 華氏溫度計(ㄏㄨㄚˊ ㄕˋ ㄨㄣ ㄉㄨˋ ㄐㄧˋ)
　　a Fahrenheit thermometer

華沙(ㄏㄨㄚˊ ㄕㄚ)
　　Warsaw

華首(ㄏㄨㄚˊ ㄕㄡˇ)
　　①gray hair; white hair ②a beauty's hair

華商(ㄏㄨㄚˊ ㄕㄤ)
　　businessmen of Chinese ancestry

華盛頓(ㄏㄨㄚˊ ㄕㄥˋ ㄉㄨㄣˋ)
　　①George Washington, 1732-1799, founder of the U.S.A. ②Washington D.C., capital of the U.S.A. ③the state of Washington, U.S.A.

華人(ㄏㄨㄚˊ ㄖㄣˊ)
　　Chinese people (especially those living abroad)

華滋華斯(ㄏㄨㄚˊ ㄗ ㄏㄨㄚˊ ㄙ)
　　William Wordsworth, 1770-1850, English poet

華簪(ㄏㄨㄚˊ ㄗㄢ)
　　high officials

華族(ㄏㄨㄚˊ ㄗㄨˊ)
　　①the peerage; the aristocracy; the nobility ②Chinese people

華宗(ㄏㄨㄚˊ ㄗㄨㄥ)
　　of one's own clan

華辭(ㄏㄨㄚˊ ㄘˊ)
　　impressive but insincere words

華而不實(ㄏㄨㄚˊ ㄦˊ ㄅㄨˋ ㄕˊ)
　　(literally) to flower without bearing fruit—impressive merely in appearance

華爾街(ㄏㄨㄚˊ ㄦˇ ㄐㄧㄝ)
　　Wall Street, New York City

華爾姿舞 or 華爾茲舞(ㄏㄨㄚˊ ㄦˇ ㄗ ㄨˇ)
　　waltz

華裔(ㄏㄨㄚˊ ㄧˋ)
　　foreign citizens of Chinese

〔艸部〕

origin

華言 (ㄏㄨㄚˊ 一ㄢˊ)
impressive but insincere words

華嚴經 (ㄏㄨㄚˊ 一ㄢˊ ㄐㄧㄥ)
the Avatamsaka Sutra (a Buddhist scripture)

華洋雜處 (ㄏㄨㄚˊ 一ㄤˊ ㄗㄚˊ ㄔㄨˇ)
Chinese and foreigners live together.

華屋山丘 (ㄏㄨㄚˊ ㄨ ㄕㄢ ㄑㄧㄡ)
(literally) A magnificent house has become a mound of earth.—(figuratively) vicissitudes; ups and downs

華文 (ㄏㄨㄚˊ ㄨㄣˊ)
the Chinese language; Chinese 亦作「中文」

華文學校 (ㄏㄨㄚˊ ㄨㄣˊ ㄒㄩㄝˊ ㄒㄧㄠˋ)
a Chinese school (usually run by foreigners for teaching Chinese to foreigners)

華腴 (ㄏㄨㄚˊ ㄩˊ)
① food and clothing in abundance; a luxurious life ② the nobility; the peerage; the aristocracy

華語 (ㄏㄨㄚˊ ㄩˇ)
the Chinese language; Chinese 亦作「中文」

華譽 (ㄏㄨㄚˊ ㄩˋ)
insincere compliments; flattery

【華】 4966
2.(花) ㄏㄨㄚ hua huā
flowers

【華】 4966
3. ㄏㄨㄚˋ huah huà
1. luster; brilliancy; glory; splendor
2. a Chinese family name

華陀 (ㄏㄨㄚˊ ㄊㄨㄛˊ)
Hua To, a legendary surgeon at the end of the Han Dynasty

華山 (ㄏㄨㄚˋ ㄕㄢ)
Mountain Hua, a sacred mountain in Shensi Province

華陰 (ㄏㄨㄚˋ 一ㄣˊ)
name of a county in Shensi Province, north of Mountain Hua

【菇】 4967
ㄍㄨ gu gū
mushrooms; a fungus

【菰】 4968
1. Zizania latifolia, an aquatic grass, the stalk of which is eaten as vegetable 亦作「茭白」
2. same as 菇—mushrooms

【菁】 4969
ㄐㄧㄥ jing jīng
1. the flower of the leek
2. the rape turnip
3. luxuriant; lush

菁華 (ㄐㄧㄥ ㄏㄨㄚˊ)
essence 亦作「精華」

菁菁 (ㄐㄧㄥ ㄐㄧㄥ)
a lush or rich growth (of vegetation); of luxuriant growth

菁莪 (ㄐㄧㄥ ㄜˊ)
to educate promising talents

【菲】 4970
1. ㄈㄟˇ feei fěi
1. an edible vegetable—a kind of radish
2. thin; trifling; meager
3. frugal; sparing

菲薄 (ㄈㄟˇ ㄅㄛˊ)
① to slight; to belittle; to underestimate: 你不可妄自菲薄, You should not underestimate yourself. ② thin; humble; poor ③ frugal; thrifty

菲敬 (ㄈㄟˇ ㄐㄧㄥˋ)
(a polite expression) a trifling gift given as a token of my respect

菲酌 (ㄈㄟˇ ㄓㄨㄛˊ)
(a polite expression) my poor feast

菲材 (ㄈㄟˇ ㄘㄞˊ)
(a polite expression) my meager talent

菲儀 (ㄈㄟˇ 一ˊ) or 菲禮 (ㄈㄟˇ ㄌㄧˇ)
(a polite expression) my meager gift

【菲】 4970
2. ㄈㄟ fei fēi
1. fragrant
2. the Philippines
3. luxuriant

菲菲 (ㄈㄟ ㄈㄟ)
① fragrant ② (said of flowers) beautiful ③ mixed; confused ④ unstable

菲律賓 (ㄈㄟ ㄌㄩˋ ㄅㄧㄣ)
the Philippines

菲律賓群島 (ㄈㄟ ㄌㄩˋ ㄅㄧㄣ ㄑㄩㄣˊ ㄉㄠˇ)
the Philippine Islands

菲律賓人 (ㄈㄟ ㄌㄩˋ ㄅㄧㄣ ㄖㄣˊ)
Filipinos

菲律賓語 (ㄈㄟ ㄌㄩˋ ㄅㄧㄣ ㄩˇ)
Tagalog

菲僑 (ㄈㄟ ㄑㄧㄠˊ)
overseas Chinese in the Philippines

【菸】 4971
一ㄢ ian yān
a tobacco leaf

菸酒 (一ㄢ ㄐㄧㄡˇ)
tobacco and alcoholic drinks

菸酒稅 (一ㄢ ㄐㄧㄡˇ ㄕㄨㄟˋ)
duties or taxes on tobacco and alcoholic drinks

菸鹼 (一ㄢ ㄐㄧㄢˇ)
nicotine 亦作「尼古丁」

菸草 (一ㄢ ㄘㄠˇ) or 菸絲 (一ㄢ ㄙ)
tobacco

菸萎 (一ㄢ ㄨㄟˇ)
to wither

菸葉 (一ㄢ 一ㄝˋ)
tobacco leaves

【菹】 4972
ㄐㄩ ju jū
1. salted or pickled vegetables
2. a pond or lake with a lot of weeds; grassy marshes
3. to mince human flesh and bones (a form of capital punishment in ancient times)

菹醢 (ㄐㄩ ㄏㄞˇ)
to kill a person and mince his flesh and bones (a form of capital punishment in ancient times)

【菽】 4973
ㄕㄨ shwu shú
the general term for beans, peas, etc.

菽麥 (ㄕㄨ ㄇㄞˋ)
(literally) beans and wheat—easily distinguishable; distinctly different

菽水承歡 (ㄕㄨ ㄕㄨㄟˇ ㄔㄥˊ ㄏㄨㄢ)
to practice great filial piety even in poverty

菽粟 (ㄕㄨ ㄙㄨˋ)
beans and grains; pulse and grain

【萁】 4974
ㄑㄧˊ chyi qí
the stalks of beans

【萃】 4975
ㄘㄨㄟˋ tsuey cuì
1. a thick or dense growth of grass
2. a group; a set
3. to gather; to meet; to con-

gregate

萃取(ㄘㄨㄟ ㄑㄩ)
(chemistry) extraction

【萄】 4976
　　ㄊㄠ taur táo
as in 葡萄—grapes

【莨】 4977
　　ㄔㄤ charng cháng
the fruit of *Averrhoa carambola*

莨楚(ㄔㄤ ㄔㄨ)
Averrhoa carambola

【荺】 4978
　　ㄉㄠ daw dào
tall grass

【萊】 4979
　　ㄌㄞ lai lái
1. fields lying fallow
2. wild weeds
3. to weed
4. a Chinese family name

萊菔(ㄌㄞ ㄈㄨ)
turnips 亦作「蘿蔔」

萊因河(ㄌㄞ ㄧㄣ ㄏㄜ)
the Rhine River

萊蕪(ㄌㄞ ㄨ)
①a field with a dense
growth of wild weeds ②
name of a county in Shan-
tung Province

【萋】 4980
　　ㄑㄧ chi qī
1. luxuriant foliage; a dense
growth of grass
2. many; crowded

萋萋(ㄑㄧ ㄑㄧ)
①a luxuriant growth of
grass ②massing of clouds

【萌】 4981
　　ㄇㄥ meng méng
1. to bud; to sprout; to germinate; to shoot forth
2. to harbor (a thought)
3. the beginning; initiation; initial

萌動(ㄇㄥ ㄉㄨㄥ)
①to sprout; to bud ②to
begin or start an action; to
initiate

萌黎(ㄇㄥ ㄌㄧ)or萌氓(ㄇㄥ ㄇㄤ)
the people; the masses

萌兆(ㄇㄥ ㄓㄠ)
an omen; a warning of a
coming event 亦作「預兆」

萌芽(ㄇㄥ ㄧㄚ)
to sprout; to bud

萌生(ㄇㄥ ㄕㄥ)
①to produce; to conceive (a

view, idea, etc.) ②numerous

萌芽 or 萌芽(ㄇㄥ ㄧㄚ)
①the initial stage of something ②to sprout; to be in
bud: 雨水使種子萌芽。Rain
sprouts the seed.

【萍】 4982
　　ㄆㄧㄥ pyng píng
1. duckweed
2. moving about rootlessly;
traveling or wandering

萍泊(ㄆㄧㄥ ㄅㄛˊ)
to wander about rootlessly
like duckweed

萍蓬(草)(ㄆㄧㄥ ㄆㄥˊ (ㄘㄠˇ))
(botany) *Nuphar japonicum*,
related with the lotus

萍浮(ㄆㄧㄥ ㄈㄨˊ)
to wander about like duckweed

萍梗(ㄆㄧㄥ ㄍㄥˇ)
to have no permanent ad-
dress because of constant
traveling

萍跡(ㄆㄧㄥ ㄐㄧ)
the whereabouts of a con-
stant traveler

萍寄(ㄆㄧㄥ ㄐㄧ)
to stay in a place only briefly like someone constantly
traveling

萍鄉(ㄆㄧㄥ ㄒㄧㄤ)
Pinghsiang, a county rich in
coal in Kiangsi Province

萍水相逢(ㄆㄧㄥ ㄕㄨㄟˇ ㄒㄧㄤ ㄈㄥˊ)
to meet by accident

萍蹤(ㄆㄧㄥ ㄗㄨㄥ)
the whereabouts of a con-
stant traveler

萍蹤無定(ㄆㄧㄥ ㄗㄨㄥ ㄨ ㄉㄧㄥˋ)or
萍蹤浪跡(ㄆㄧㄥ ㄗㄨㄥ ㄌㄤˋ ㄐㄧ)
to have no fixed abode because of constant traveling

【萎】 4983
　　ㄨㄟ uei wěi
1. to wither
2. ill; sick
3. to fall; to decline; to
weaken

萎靡(ㄨㄟ ㄇㄧˇ)
listless; dispirited

萎靡不振(ㄨㄟ ㄇㄧˇ ㄅㄨˋ ㄓㄣˋ)
unable to pick oneself up;
despondent; lethargic

萎落(ㄨㄟ ㄌㄨㄛˋ)
to wither and fall; to
weaken and decline

萎黃病(ㄨㄟ ㄏㄨㄤˊ ㄅㄧㄥˋ)
chlorosis

萎絕(ㄨㄟ ㄐㄩㄝˊ)
to wither

萎謝(ㄨㄟ ㄒㄧㄝˋ)
(said of flowers) to wither;
to fade

萎縮(ㄨㄟ ㄙㄨㄛ)
①to dry up and shrink; to
shrink back ②to atrophy

萎縮症(ㄨㄟ ㄙㄨㄛ ㄓㄥˋ)
atrophy

【菡】 4984
　　ㄏㄢ hann hàn
another name of water lily
or lotus flower

菡萏(ㄏㄢ ㄉㄢˋ)
a water lily, or a lotus
flower

【萏】 4985
　　ㄉㄢ dann dàn
as in 菡萏—another name of
water lily

【菩】 4986
　　ㄆㄨ pwu pú
1. a fragrant herb
2. the sacred tree of the Buddhists

菩提(ㄆㄨ ㄊㄧˊ)
bodhi—knowledge ; under-
standing ; perfect wisdom;
the illuminated or enlightened mind

菩提樹(ㄆㄨ ㄊㄧˊ ㄕㄨˋ)
①a peepul tree ② (Bud-
dhism) a bo tree; *Ficus
religiosa*; a bodhi tree— the
wisdom tree under which
Sakyamuni attained his
enlightenment and became
Buddha

菩薩(ㄆㄨ ㄙㄚˋ)
① Bodhisattva ②Buddha

菩薩低語(ㄆㄨ ㄙㄚˋ ㄉㄧ ㄩˇ)
kind, gentle or soothing
words

菩薩心腸(ㄆㄨ ㄙㄚˋ ㄒㄧㄣ ㄔㄤˊ)
kind-hearted; compassionate

【菱】 4987
　　ㄌㄧㄥ ling líng
a water chestnut

菱錳礦(ㄌㄧㄥ ㄇㄥˇ ㄎㄨㄤˋ)
rhodochrosite

菱面體(ㄌㄧㄥ ㄇㄧㄢ ㄊㄧˇ)
a rhombohedron

菱鐵礦(ㄌㄧㄥ ㄊㄧㄝˇ ㄎㄨㄤˋ)
siderite

〔艸部〕

〔艸部〕

菱歌（カ | ㄥ 《ㄜ）
songs of the water-caltrop pickers

菱苦土礦（カ | ㄥ ㄎㄨ ㄊㄨˇ ㄎㄨㄤˋ）
magnesite

菱角（カ | ㄥ 4 | ㄠ）
a water chestnut

菱鋅礦（カ | ㄥ T | ㄣ ㄎㄨㄤˋ）
smithsonite

菱形（カ | ㄥ T | ㄥˊ）
a rhomb or rhombus; rhombic

【菴】 4988
1.（庵）ㄢ an an

1. a small round hut
2. a small Buddhist nunnery or monastery; a temple

菴婪（ㄢ ㄌㄢˊ）
greedy; avaricious

菴廬（ㄢ ㄌㄨˊ）
a hut

【菴】 4988
2. ㄢˇ ann ǎn

luxuriant; prosperous

菴藹（ㄢˇ ㄞˇ）
luxuriant

【萆】 4989
ㄅ | ˋ bih bì

a herb with long hard roots

【菉】 4990
ㄌㄩˋ liuh lǜ
（又讀 ㄌㄨˋ luh lù）

1. a kind of grass
2. green

菉竹（ㄌㄨˋ ㄓㄨˊ）
the green bamboo 亦作「綠竹」

菉筍（ㄌㄨˋ ㄙㄨㄣˇ）
greenish bamboo shoots

菉豆（ㄌㄨˋ ㄉㄡˋ）
the green beans; lentils 亦作「綠豆」

【菢】 4991
ㄅㄠˋ baw bào

to hatch (eggs); to incubate

菢蛋（ㄅㄠˋ ㄉㄢˋ）
to hatch eggs

菢小雞（ㄅㄠˋ T | ㄠˇ 4 | ）
(said of a hen) to hatch eggs

菢窩（ㄅㄠˋ ㄨㄛ）
to sit on the nest to hatch eggs

【菏】 4992
《ㄜ ge gē

name of a tributary of the Chi River in ancient times

菏澤（《ㄜ ㄗˊ）

①name of a county in Shantung Province ②name of a lake in Shantung Province

【菫】 4993
4 | ㄣˇ jiin jǐn
Viola verecunda, a violet

【荊】 4994
（荆）4 | ㄥ jing jīng

1. a kind of bramble; a thorn
2. a cane for punishment used in ancient China
3. (a polite expression) my wife
4. (in ancient China) name of one of the nine political regions
5. a Chinese family name

荊布（4 | ㄥ ㄅㄨˋ）
(said of women) simply adorned; in coarse clothing

荊璞（4 | ㄥ ㄆㄨˊ）or 荊玉（4 | ㄥ ㄩˋ）
unpolished precious jade

荊釵（4 | ㄥ ㄔㄞ）
①a collective name of four ancient counties in Hunan Province ②rough and primitive places

荊婦（4 | ㄥ ㄈㄨˋ）or 荊人（4 | ㄥ ㄖㄣˊ）
my wife (a polite expression)

荊桃（4 | ㄥ ㄊㄠˊ）
a cherry

荊條（4 | ㄥ ㄊ | ㄠˊ）
stems of a bramble which can be made into baskets, etc.

荊軻（4 | ㄥ ㄎㄜ）
Ching Ko, a brave man of the State of Wei (衛) in the Epoch of Warring States, who was asked by the prince of Yen (燕) to assassinate the king of Chin (秦) but failed

荊棘（4 | ㄥ 4 | ˊ）
①thorns; thorny ②a difficult situation

荊卿（4 | ㄥ ㄑ | ㄥ）
another way of calling Ching Ko (荊軻)

荊州（4 | ㄥ ㄓㄡ）
①Kingchow (name of one of the nine political regions in ancient China, including Hunan, Hupeh and part of today's Szechwan) ② an ancient name of Hupeh Province

荊釵布裙（4 | ㄥ ㄔㄞ ㄅㄨˋ ㄑㄩㄣˊ）
thorns as hairpins and cotton cloth for skirts—a poor woman's wear

荊柴（4 | ㄥ ㄔㄞˊ）
a poor family; a destitute household

荊楚（4 | ㄥ ㄔㄨˇ）
the state of Chu which occupied Kingchow (荊州) in ancient China

荊室（4 | ㄥ ㄕˋ）
(a polite expression) my wife

【菓】 4995
《ㄨㄛˇ guoo guǒ
fruits and nuts

九畫

【萬】 4996
（万）ㄨㄢˋ wann wàn

1. ten thousand
2. all; omni-
3. a very great number; myriad
4. very; extremely; absolutely
5. name of an ancient dance
6. a Chinese family name

萬把（ㄨㄢˋ ㄅㄚˇ）
a little more than 10,000

萬倍（ㄨㄢˋ ㄅㄟˋ）
ten thousandfold

萬般（ㄨㄢˋ ㄅㄢ）
①all; every; various; in many different ways ②extremely

萬般皆下品，惟有讀書高（ㄨㄢˋ ㄅㄢ 4 | ㄝ T | ㄚˋ ㄆ | ㄣˇ ㄨㄟˊ | ㄡˇ ㄉㄨˊ ㄕㄨ 《ㄠ）
(a Chinese saying) Learning is the noblest of human pursuits.

萬邦（ㄨㄢˋ ㄅㄤ）
all nations; nations all over the world; the myriad states

萬變不離其宗（ㄨㄢˋ ㄅ | ㄢˋ ㄅㄨˋ ㄌ | ˊ ㄑ | ˊ ㄗㄨㄥ）
The methods used may vary, but the principle is the same. 或 to undergo numerous changes without abandoning the basic position

萬不得已（ㄨㄢˋ ㄅㄨˋ ㄉㄜˊ | ˇ）
①if the worst comes to happen; as a last resort ②to

have no alternative; to have to do it; to be forced to do it; very reluctantly

萬馬奔騰 (ㄨㄢˋ ㄇㄚˇ ㄅㄣ ㄊㄥˊ)
①(literally) ten thousand horses stampeding—a thunderous or roaring sound ②(figuratively) whirling wildly

萬民 (ㄨㄢˋ ㄇㄧㄣˊ)
all the people

萬目睽睽 (ㄨㄢˋ ㄇㄨˋ ㄎㄨㄟˊ ㄎㄨㄟˊ)
right before 10,000 eyes — under the glare of the public

萬分 (ㄨㄢˋ ㄈㄣ)
very; extremely

萬方 (ㄨㄢˋ ㄈㄤ)
①all nations; the myriad regions ②all sides ③(of manners) graceful ④all and every way

萬方多難 (ㄨㄢˋ ㄈㄤ ㄉㄨㄛ ㄋㄢˋ)
natural disasters and man-made calamities everywhere

萬夫不當 (ㄨㄢˋ ㄈㄨ ㄅㄨˋ ㄉㄤ)
(literally) Even 10,000 men are not his match.—very brave

萬福 (ㄨㄢˋ ㄈㄨˊ)
①boundless blessings; all blessings ②(said of women) a gesture to show politeness equivalent to a curtsy in the Western world

萬代 (ㄨㄢˋ ㄉㄞˋ)
endless generations afterward; eternity

萬端 (ㄨㄢˋ ㄉㄨㄢ)
very complicated; numerous leads (not knowing which one to follow)

萬難 (ㄨㄢˋ ㄋㄢˊ)
extremely difficult; well-nigh impossible

萬能 (ㄨㄢˋ ㄋㄥˊ)
omnipotent; almighty

萬能博士 (ㄨㄢˋ ㄋㄥˊ ㄅㄛˊ ㄕˋ)
a jack-of-all-trades; a Mr. Know-all

萬年 (ㄨㄢˋ ㄋㄧㄢˊ)
10,000 years—a very long time

萬年曆 (ㄨㄢˋ ㄋㄧㄢˊ ㄌㄧˋ)
①a calendar system adopted briefly during the Yüan Dynasty ②a calendar designed for use in many

years

萬年青 (ㄨㄢˋ ㄋㄧㄢˊ ㄑㄧㄥ)
a Chinese evergreen

萬年枝 (ㄨㄢˋ ㄋㄧㄢˊ ㄓ)
an ilex 亦作「冬青」

萬念俱灰 (ㄨㄢˋ ㄋㄧㄢˋ ㄐㄩˋ ㄏㄨㄟ)
completely discouraged; extremely pessimistic; totally devoid of ambition and hope

萬籟俱寂 (ㄨㄢˋ ㄌㄞˋ ㄐㄩˋ ㄐㄧˊ)
All is still. 或 All sounds are hushed (in the dead of the night).

萬里鵬程 (ㄨㄢˋ ㄌㄧˇ ㄆㄥˊ ㄔㄥˊ)
(a congratulatory term) very promising; an unlimited future

萬里侯 (ㄨㄢˋ ㄌㄧˇ ㄏㄡˊ)
a marquis with an extensive fief bestowed by the emperor in recognition of extremely meritorious services

萬里長征 (ㄨㄢˋ ㄌㄧˇ ㄔㄤˊ ㄓㄥ)
①to launch a military expedition very far away; to embark on a long journey; mile after mile to battle ②(in Chinese Communist terminology) the Long March to Yenan after they were routed by government troops in the early 1930's

萬里長城 (ㄨㄢˋ ㄌㄧˇ ㄔㄤˊ ㄔㄥˊ)
the Great Wall (of China)

萬里無雲 (ㄨㄢˋ ㄌㄧˇ ㄨˊ ㄩㄣˊ)
cloudless

萬流赴壑 (ㄨㄢˋ ㄌㄧㄡˊ ㄈㄨˋ ㄏㄨㄛˋ)
countless things converging on the same spot

萬靈藥 (ㄨㄢˋ ㄌㄧㄥˊ ㄧㄠˋ) or 萬應藥
a panacea; a cure-all; a wonder drug: 這並不是萬靈藥。 This is not a cure-all.

萬隆 (ㄨㄢˋ ㄌㄨㄥˊ)
Bandung, Indonesia

萬綠叢中一點紅 (ㄨㄢˋ ㄌㄩˋ ㄘㄨㄥˊ ㄓㄨㄥ ㄧ ㄉㄧㄢˇ ㄏㄨㄥˊ)
(literally) a single red flower in the midst of thick foliage—very outstanding or eye-catching

萬古 (ㄨㄢˋ ㄍㄨˇ)
for a long, long time; immortal

萬古流芳 (ㄨㄢˋ ㄍㄨˇ ㄌㄧㄡˊ ㄈㄤ)

a good name that will last forever (now often used in eulogizing a dead person at the funeral)

萬古流傳 (ㄨㄢˋ ㄍㄨˇ ㄌㄧㄡˊ ㄔㄨㄢˊ)
(said of a legend, achievement, etc.) to be remembered forever

萬古長青 (ㄨㄢˋ ㄍㄨˇ ㄔㄤˊ ㄑㄧㄥ)
to remain fresh forever; to be everlasting

萬國 (ㄨㄢˋ ㄍㄨㄛˊ)
all nations; countless states; all over the world; international

萬國公法 (ㄨㄢˋ ㄍㄨㄛˊ ㄍㄨㄥ ㄈㄚˇ)
international law

萬國音標 (ㄨㄢˋ ㄍㄨㄛˊ ㄧㄣ ㄅㄧㄠ)
International Phonetic Alphabet (IPA) 亦作「國際音標」

萬國語 (ㄨㄢˋ ㄍㄨㄛˊ ㄩˇ)
a lingua franca

萬國語音協會 (ㄨㄢˋ ㄍㄨㄛˊ ㄩˇ ㄧㄣ ㄒㄧㄝˊ ㄏㄨㄟˋ)
International Phonetic Association, founded in 1886 亦作「國際語音協會」

萬貫 (ㄨㄢˋ ㄍㄨㄢˋ)
very rich or wealthy: 他家財萬貫。 He is very rich.

萬貫家私 (ㄨㄢˋ ㄍㄨㄢˋ ㄐㄧㄚ ㄙ)
very wealthy; very rich

萬斛源泉 (ㄨㄢˋ ㄏㄨˊ ㄩㄢˊ ㄑㄩㄢˊ)
full of inspirations in writing

萬戶侯 (ㄨㄢˋ ㄏㄨˋ ㄏㄡˊ)
(Han Dynasty) a marquis with a fief of 10,000 families

萬花筒 (ㄨㄢˋ ㄏㄨㄚ ㄊㄨㄥˇ)
a kaleidoscope: 人生猶如萬花筒。 Life is like a kaleidoscope.

萬花爭艷 (ㄨㄢˋ ㄏㄨㄚ ㄓㄥ ㄧㄢˋ)
all kinds of flowers in full bloom

萬化 (ㄨㄢˋ ㄏㄨㄚˋ)
①all matters; all things ②too many variations or changes to recount

萬機 (ㄨㄢˋ ㄐㄧ) or 萬幾
(said of an emperor or president) 10,000 matters to be managed (in a single day) —a heavy work load

萬急 (ㄨㄢˋ ㄐㄧˊ)
extremely or most urgent

萬家燈火 (ㄨㄢˋ ㄐㄧㄚ ㄉㄥ ㄏㄨㄛˇ)

（艸
部）

萬家生佛(ㄨㄢ ㄐㄧㄚ ㄕㄥ ㄈㄛˊ)
(literally) a living Buddha to 10,000 families—a benefactor to all

萬劫(ㄨㄢ ㄐㄧㄝˊ)
countless generations or ages

萬劫不復(ㄨㄢ ㄐㄧㄝˊ ㄅㄨˋ ㄈㄨˋ)
never to be recovered or restored

萬金油(ㄨㄢ ㄐㄧㄣ ㄧㄡˊ)
the Tiger Balm, a very popular Chinese ointment (with soothing effect derived mainly from its menthol or peppermint contents)

萬卷(ㄨㄢ ㄐㄩㄢˋ)
10,000 volumes; a countless number of books; mountains of printed matter

萬鈞(ㄨㄢ ㄐㄩㄣ)
300,000 catties—very heavy; very powerful; overwhelming

萬鈞之力(ㄨㄢ ㄐㄩㄣ ㄓ ㄌㄧˋ)
extremely powerful; great strength; overwhelming force

萬千(ㄨㄢ ㄑㄧㄢ)
numerous; myriads: 星辰萬千。There are myriads of stars.

萬籤挿架(ㄨㄢ ㄑㄧㄢ ㄔㄚ ㄐㄧㄚˋ)
overflowing (book) shelves —a countless number of books

萬頃(ㄨㄢ ㄑㄧㄥˇ)
10,000 hectares (of land); large landholding; a vast space

萬頃碧波(ㄨㄢ ㄑㄧㄥˇ ㄅㄧˋ ㄅㄛ)
a vast expanse of water—as a big lake

萬全(ㄨㄢ ㄑㄩㄢˊ)
extremely safe or sound; failure-proof

萬全之計(ㄨㄢ ㄑㄩㄢˊ ㄓ ㄐㄧˋ)
an absolutely safe measure, plan, device, etc.

萬象(ㄨㄢ ㄒㄧㄤˋ)
the countless aspects, forms, etc. of the world and natural phenomena

萬象更新(ㄨㄢ ㄒㄧㄤˋ ㄍㄥ ㄒㄧㄣ)
a new year—as all things change from old to new

萬姓(ㄨㄢ ㄒㄧㄥˋ)
the people

萬幸(ㄨㄢ ㄒㄧㄥˋ)
extremely lucky; very fortunate indeed

萬丈深淵(ㄨㄢ ㄓㄤˋ ㄕㄣ ㄩㄢ)
an abyss of 100,000 feet—a bottomless abyss

萬狀(ㄨㄢ ㄓㄨㄤˋ)
①all possible shapes and forms; myriad forms ② extremely (frightened)

萬鍾(ㄨㄢ ㄓㄨㄥ)
rich reward or high salary for a government official

萬衆一心(ㄨㄢ ㄓㄨㄥˋ ㄧ ㄒㄧㄣ)
all for one and one for all; with one aspiration in their hearts; solidarity

萬世之後(ㄨㄢ ㄕˋ ㄓ ㄏㄡˋ)
down to endless posterity; after countless generations

萬世師表(ㄨㄢ ㄕˋ ㄕ ㄅㄧㄠˇ)
(literally) a paragon for all generations—Confucius

萬事通(ㄨㄢ ㄕˋ ㄊㄨㄥ)
a jack-of-all-trades

萬事休(ㄨㄢ ㄕˋ ㄒㄧㄡ)
All is lost.

萬事足(ㄨㄢ ㄕˋ ㄗㄨˊ)
well satisfied (usually referring to a man with a new born heir)

萬壽(ㄨㄢ ㄕㄡˋ)
①(in ancient China) the birthday of the emperor ② (modern usage) a congratulatory term wishing a person on his birthday many, many happy returns

萬壽山(ㄨㄢ ㄕㄡˋ ㄕㄢ)
name of a hill in Peking's old imperial park Yi-ho Garden (頤和園)

萬壽無疆(ㄨㄢ ㄕㄡˋ ㄨˊ ㄐㄧㄤ)
May you attain boundless longevity!

萬牲園(ㄨㄢ ㄕㄥ ㄩㄢˊ)
a zoo; a zoological garden

萬聖節(ㄨㄢ ㄕㄥˋ ㄐㄧㄝˊ)
All Saints' Day

萬乘之國(ㄨㄢ ㄕㄥˋ ㄓ ㄍㄨㄛˊ)
an empire; a big country

萬乘之尊(ㄨㄢ ㄕㄥˋ ㄓ ㄗㄨㄣ)
the emperor—with ten thousand chariots at his command

萬殊(ㄨㄢ ㄕㄨ)
all different; myriads of variations

萬人敵(ㄨㄢ ㄖㄣˊ ㄉㄧˊ)
the art of war which a field commander must master

萬人坑(ㄨㄢ ㄖㄣˊ ㄎㄥ)
a mass grave

萬人空巷(ㄨㄢ ㄖㄣˊ ㄎㄨㄥ ㄒㄧㄤˋ)
Everyone (in a city) turns out (to watch a spectacle, to welcome a hero, etc.)

萬人塚(ㄨㄢ ㄖㄣˊ ㄓㄨㄥˇ)
a mass burial ground; a mass grave

萬仞(ㄨㄢ ㄖㄣˋ)
very high and steep (hills or mountains)

萬紫千紅(ㄨㄢ ㄗˇ ㄑㄧㄢ ㄏㄨㄥˊ)
(said of flowers) a vast display of dazzling colors

萬死一生(ㄨㄢ ㄙˇ ㄧ ㄕㄥ)
a very slim chance of keeping oneself alive; very risky; very lucky for escaping death

萬歲(ㄨㄢ ㄙㄨㄟˋ)
①the emperor; Your Majesty; His Majesty ②(a slogan) Long live the....

萬歲爺(ㄨㄢ ㄙㄨㄟˋ ㄧㄝ˙)
the emperor

萬惡(ㄨㄢ ㄜˋ)
all the evils; extremely evil

萬惡淫為首(ㄨㄢ ㄜˋ ㄧㄣˊ ㄨㄟˊ ㄕㄡˇ)
Lewdness is the worst of all sins.

萬一(ㄨㄢ ㄧ)
①one ten thousandth—a very tiny fraction ②just in case that; if by any chance ③something not anticipated or happening accidentally

萬有(ㄨㄢ ㄧㄡˇ)
all matters in the world; all things under the sun; all creation

萬有引力(ㄨㄢ ㄧㄡˇ ㄧㄣˇ ㄌㄧˋ)
gravitation

萬言書(ㄨㄢ ㄧㄢˊ ㄕㄨ)
a long report, statement of views, etc. prepared by a subject for the emperor's

perusal

萬無(ㄨㄢˋ ㄨˊ)
never; not the least; absolutely not

萬無一失(ㄨㄢˋ ㄨˊ ㄧ ㄕ)
not the least mishap or mistake; absolutely safe or sure; certain to succeed

萬物(ㄨㄢˋ ㄨˋ)
all things under the sun; all God's creation

萬物之靈(ㄨㄢˋ ㄨˋ ㄓ ㄌㄧㄥˊ)
man—the wisest of all creatures

萬萬(ㄨㄢˋ ㄨㄢˋ)
①a great many ②(used in the negative sense) extremely; absolutely ③100 million

萬萬不可(ㄨㄢˋ ㄨㄢˋ ㄅㄨˋ ㄎㄜˇ)
absolutely forbidden; not by any means; under no circumstances; in no event

萬歲(ㄨㄢˋ ㄨㄢˋ ㄙㄨㄟˋ)
Long live (the emperor).

萬愚節(ㄨㄢˋ ㄩˊ ㄐㄧㄝˊ)
All Fools' Day

【萱】 4997
ㄒㄩㄢ shiuan xuān
a daylily (*Hemerocallis fulva*) whose edible dried flowers are known as 金針菜

萱堂(ㄒㄩㄢ ㄊㄤˊ)
one's mother

萱草(ㄒㄩㄢ ㄘㄠˇ)
the daylily 亦作「忘憂草」

【萵】 4998
ㄨㄛ uo wō
a lettuce

萵苣(ㄨㄛ ㄐㄩˋ)
a lettuce

萵筍(ㄨㄛ ㄙㄨㄣˇ)
a lettuce

【蕚】 4999
ㄜˋ eh è
the calyx

蕚片(ㄜˋ ㄆㄧㄢˋ)
(botany) sepal

【落】 5000
1. ㄌㄨㄛˋ luoh luò
1. to fall; to decline; to wither; weakened; fallen
2. to lose
3. few and far-spaced; to stand apart; loose and scattered
4. a village; a hamlet
5. to put (pen to paper)
6. to settle down

---

7. a pile; a heap

落泊(ㄌㄨㄛˋ ㄅㄛˊ)or **落魄**(ㄌㄨㄛˋ ㄆㄛˋ)
jobless and listless; down in one's luck; out of luck

落榜(ㄌㄨㄛˋ ㄅㄤˇ)
to flunk a competitive examination for a job or school admission

落筆(ㄌㄨㄛˋ ㄅㄧˇ)
①to start writing ②a pen mark

落寞or **落莫**(ㄌㄨㄛˋ ㄇㄛˋ)
desolate and scattered; lonely; left alone

落脈(ㄌㄨㄛˋ ㄇㄞˋ)
(geomancy) the "lode" of a dragon descending from the heights

落墨(ㄌㄨㄛˋ ㄇㄛˋ)
to start writing or painting

落髮(ㄌㄨㄛˋ ㄈㄚˇ)
to shave off one's hair; to tonsure—to become a monk or nun

落得(ㄌㄨㄛˋ ㄌㄜˊ)
to result in; as a result; to end in: 偽君子必然要落得可恥的下場。 Hypocrites come to no good end.

落膽(ㄌㄨㄛˋ ㄉㄢˇ)
to be frightened out of one's wits; very scared

落彈(ㄌㄨㄛˋ ㄉㄢˋ)
(said of bullets or artillery shells) to land at a place; to hit an area

落第(ㄌㄨㄛˋ ㄉㄧˋ)
to fail in a competitive examination for a job or school admission

落地(ㄌㄨㄛˋ ㄉㄧˋ)
①to be born. ②to fall to the ground

落地燈(ㄌㄨㄛˋ ㄉㄧˋ ㄉㄥ)
a floor lamp

落地電扇(ㄌㄨㄛˋ ㄉㄧˋ ㄉㄧㄢˋ ㄕㄢˋ)
an electric fan with an adjustable stand

落地窗(ㄌㄨㄛˋ ㄉㄧˋ ㄔㄨㄤ)
a French window

落地生根(ㄌㄨㄛˋ ㄉㄧˋ ㄕㄥ ㄍㄣ)
①(botany) an air plant; a life plant ②to have one's abode in a strange place

落點(ㄌㄨㄛˋ ㄉㄧㄢˇ)

---

①(in tennis, badminton, handball, etc.) placement ②(military) the point of a fall

落胎(ㄌㄨㄛˋ ㄊㄞ)
to abort; to effect an abortion

落湯螃蟹(ㄌㄨㄛˋ ㄊㄤ ㄆㄤˊ ㄒㄧㄝˋ)
at a loss as to what to do (like a crab in hot water)

落湯雞(ㄌㄨㄛˋ ㄊㄤ ㄐㄧ)
(said of a person) drenched and bedraggled; soaked in rainwater; dripping wet

落體(ㄌㄨㄛˋ ㄊㄧˇ)
a falling body

落拓(ㄌㄨㄛˋ ㄊㄨㄛˋ)or **落托**(ㄌㄨㄛˋ ㄊㄨㄛˋ)
unrestrained and unhampered; uninhibited; not to stick to conventions; Bohemian

落難(ㄌㄨㄛˋ ㄋㄢˊ)
to encounter difficulty, disaster, calamity, etc.; to suffer a misfortune; to be out of luck

落淚(ㄌㄨㄛˋ ㄌㄟˋ)
to cry or weep; to shed tears

落落穆穆(ㄌㄨㄛˋ ㄌㄨㄛˋ ㄇㄨˋ ㄇㄨˋ)
a reserved person who does not show much outside; an introvert

落落大方(ㄌㄨㄛˋ ㄌㄨㄛˋ ㄉㄚˋ ㄈㄤ)
(said of manner) natural; unaffected; easy

落落寡合(ㄌㄨㄛˋ ㄌㄨㄛˋ ㄍㄨㄚˇ ㄏㄜˊ)
aloofness that keeps others at a distance; unsociable; standoffish

落款(ㄌㄨㄛˋ ㄎㄨㄢˇ)
a calligrapher's or painter's signature, seal, dedicatory notes, etc. on a painting, etc.

落空(ㄌㄨㄛˋ ㄎㄨㄥ)
to fail in an attempt; to come to nothing

落後(ㄌㄨㄛˋ ㄏㄡˋ)
to fall behind; to lag behind

落後地區(ㄌㄨㄛˋ ㄏㄡˋ ㄉㄧˋ ㄑㄩ)
underdeveloped areas

落戶(ㄌㄨㄛˋ ㄏㄨˋ)
to take up one's residence in a place away from one's hometown; to settle down

落花(ㄌㄨㄛˋ ㄏㄨㄚ)
falling flowers; fallen petals

落花流水(ㄌㄨㄛˋ ㄏㄨㄚ ㄌㄧㄡˊ ㄕㄨㄟˇ)

（艸部）

【艸部】

①like flowers scattered in a flowing stream—the saddening state of a fallen family or country ②(said of a fight) to turn everything topsy-turvy; to be utterly routed

落花生(ㄌㄨㄛˋ ㄏㄨㄚ ㄕㄥ)
a groundnut, or peanut

落花有意，流水無情(ㄌㄨㄛˋ ㄏㄨㄚ ㄧㄡˇ ㄧˋ，ㄌㄧㄡˊ ㄕㄨㄟˇ ㄨˊ ㄑㄧㄥˊ)
(said of a man and a woman) a one-sided love; only one party willing; an unrequited love

落暉(ㄌㄨㄛˋ ㄏㄨㄟ)
the setting sun

落荒(ㄌㄨㄛˋ ㄏㄨㄤ)
to escape in a hurry after defeat

落荒而逃(ㄌㄨㄛˋ ㄏㄨㄤ ㄦˊ ㄊㄠˊ)
to take to the wilds—to be defeated and run away the battlefield; to turn tail

落紅(ㄌㄨㄛˋ ㄏㄨㄥˊ)
(said of a virgin) to bleed during the first sexual intercourse

落籍(ㄌㄨㄛˋ ㄐㄧˊ)
①to be discharged from military service ②(said of a prostitute in old China) to get married

落腳(ㄌㄨㄛˋ ㄐㄧㄠˇ)
to stay at; to stop at; to put up at: 我們在旅館落腳。We put up at an inn.

落井下石 or 落穽下石(ㄌㄨㄛˋ ㄐㄧㄥˇ ㄒㄧㄚˋ ㄕˊ)
(literally) to drop stones on a person who has fallen into a well—to beat a person when he's already down; to injure a person already in great difficulty

落圈套(ㄌㄨㄛˋ ㄑㄩㄢ ㄊㄠˋ)
to be trapped or swindled

落霞(ㄌㄨㄛˋ ㄒㄧㄚˊ)
colorful clouds at sunset

落下(ㄌㄨㄛˋ ㄒㄧㄚˋ)
to fall down; to descend; to drop

落雪(ㄌㄨㄛˋ ㄒㄩㄝˇ)
snowing: 我們預料在天明之前會落雪。We expect snow before morning.

落選(ㄌㄨㄛˋ ㄒㄩㄢˇ)

---

unable to make the list; to fail in an election

落照(ㄌㄨㄛˋ ㄓㄠˋ)
the setting sun; sunset

落差(ㄌㄨㄛˋ ㄔㄚ)
the drop in elevation (usually referring to the difference in elevation between two points along a stream, etc.)

落潮(ㄌㄨㄛˋ ㄔㄠˊ)
the ebb tide; a low tide

落塵(ㄌㄨㄛˋ ㄔㄣˊ)
①falling dust ②fallout

落成(ㄌㄨㄛˋ ㄔㄥˊ)
completion (of a new building, etc.)

落成典禮(ㄌㄨㄛˋ ㄔㄥˊ ㄉㄧㄢˇ ㄌㄧˇ)
the dedication ceremony of a new building or construction project

落實(ㄌㄨㄛˋ ㄕˊ)
①practicable; workable ② to fix (or to decide) in advance; to make sure ③ to carry out; to fulfill; to translate into reality; to implement; to put into effect ④ (dialect) to feel at ease: 我心裡總是不落實。I just can not set my mind at ease.

落水(ㄌㄨㄛˋ ㄕㄨㄟˇ)
to fall into water; to duck;to fall overboard

落水狗(ㄌㄨㄛˋ ㄕㄨㄟˇ ㄍㄡˇ)
a dog in the water—(figuratively) a person who is down

落日(ㄌㄨㄛˋ ㄖˋ)
the setting sun

落日餘暉(ㄌㄨㄛˋ ㄖˋ ㄩˊ ㄏㄨㄟ)
the last light of the day; the lingering light of the setting sun

落子(ㄌㄨㄛˋ ㄗˇ)
(in go game) to place a stone on the chessboard; to make a move

落草(ㄌㄨㄛˋ ㄘㄠˇ)
to become a bandit

落索(ㄌㄨㄛˋ ㄙㄨㄛˇ)
desolate and lonely; spiritless and discouraged

落葉(ㄌㄨㄛˋ ㄧㄝˋ)
fallen leaves

落葉樹(ㄌㄨㄛˋ ㄧㄝˋ ㄕㄨˋ)
a deciduous tree; trees that

---

change foliage every year

落葉松(ㄌㄨㄛˋ ㄧㄝˋ ㄙㄨㄥ)
Larix leptolepis, a variety of deciduous pine tree with very tough timber good for building purposes

落雁(ㄌㄨㄛˋ ㄧㄢˋ)
a kind of medicinal plant

落英繽紛(ㄌㄨㄛˋ ㄧㄥ ㄅㄧㄣ ㄈㄣ)
fallen flowers scattering and flying around like snow flakes

落伍(ㄌㄨㄛˋ ㄨˇ)
backward; overconservative; anachronistic; to be behind the times; outmoded; to outdate; outdated

落伍思想(ㄌㄨㄛˋ ㄨˇ ㄙ ㄒㄧㄤˇ)
backward or anachronistic thinking or ideas

落網(ㄌㄨㄛˋ ㄨㄤˇ)
(said of a criminal) to be caught in the meshes of the law—to be caught; to be captured

落雨(ㄌㄨㄛˋ ㄩˇ)
to rain; raining: 此地六月間常落雨。It often rains here in June.

落雨天(ㄌㄨㄛˋ ㄩˇ ㄊㄧㄢ)
a rainy day: 落雨天，路很滑。In a rainy day, the road is slippery.

落月(ㄌㄨㄛˋ ㄩㄝˋ)
the setting moon

【落】 5000
②.ㄌㄚˋ　*law　lɑo*
1. to fall or drop (in prices, etc.)
2. (said of a bird, etc.) to land; to perch
3. to get
4. a net income; a surplus
5. to place

落價(ㄌㄚˋ ㄐㄧㄚˋ)
to come down in prices: 電視機落價了。The price of television sets has come down.

落棧(ㄌㄚˋ ㄓㄢˋ)
to take up one's lodgings in an inn or a tavern

落枕(ㄌㄚˋ ㄓㄣˇ)
①to drop the head on the pillow—to go to sleep ② (Chinese medicine) stiff neck

落子(ㄌㄚˋ ㄗ˙)
①a way to make a living; a

means of living ② a kind of singing in parts of North China 亦作「蓮花落」

【落】 5000
　　　3. カY lah là
1. to leave behind
2. to fall behind
3. to miss; to omit

落了(カY ·カ亡)
to lose, to miss, or omit unintentionally: 這裡落了一段文字。A paragraph is missing here.

落下(カY ·TIY)
① to leave behind ② to fall behind

【葉】 5001
　　　1.Iせ yeh yè
1. a leaf; a petal (of a flower)
2. a leaf or two pages (of a book)
3. a period; an era or epoch
4. something light and tiny —as a small boat in a lake
5. a Chinese family name

葉柄(Iせ クIㄥ)
(botany) the petiole; the leafstalk

葉片(Iせ タIㄢ)
(botany) the leaf blade 亦作「葉身」

葉脈(Iせ ㄇㄞ)or葉筋(Iせ ㄐIㄣ)
the veins (of a leaf)

葉茂(Iせ ㄇㄠ)
leafy

葉門(Iせ ㄇㄣ)
Yemen

葉落歸根(Iせ カㄨㄛ ㄍㄨㄟ ㄍㄣ)
(literally) The leaves always fall toward the root. —When a person gets old, he thinks of going back home.

葉落知秋(Iせ カㄨㄛ ㄓ くIㄡ)
(literally) The failing leaves annouce the approach of autumn.—Revealing signs foretell things to come.

葉綠素(Iせ カㄩˋ ㄙㄨˋ)or(Iせ カㄨㄛ ㄙㄨˋ)
(biochemistry) chlorophyll

葉黃素(Iせ ㄏㄨㄤˊ ㄙㄨˋ)
(biochemistry) xanthophyll

葉尖(Iせ ㄐIㄢ)
the apex (of a leaf)

葉鞘(Iせ くIㄠ)
the sheath (of a leaf)

葉序(Iせ Tㄩ)
(botany) a cycle

葉針(Iせ ㄓㄣ)
(botany) leaf thorns

葉肉(Iせ ㄖㄡ)
(botany) mesophyll

葉子(Iせ ·ㄗ)or葉兒(Iせ ㄦ)
leaves: 他被葉子遮住。He was hidden by the leaves.

葉慈
William Butler Yeats, 1865-1939, Irish poet and dramatist

葉芽(Iせ IY)
(botany) a leaf bud

葉緣(Iせ ㄩㄢ)
the margin (of a leaf)

【葉】 5001
　　　2.ㄕˊ sheh shè
used in names of places

葉公好龍(ㄕˊ ㄍㄨㄥ ㄏㄠˊ ㄌㄨㄥ)
One is not sure what he really likes (like 葉公 who was very fond of dragons in painting but was scared when a real dragon appeared). 或 One does not like what he pretends to like.

葉縣(ㄕˊ TIㄢ)
name of a county in Honan Province

【葑】 5002
　　　ㄈㄥ feng fēng
same as 蕪菁, the rape-turnip

葑菲(ㄈㄥ ㄈㄟ)
the mustard plant and earth melons — One has his good points as well as shortcomings. 或 Don't take part for all.

【著】 5003
　　　1. ㄓㄨˋ juh zhù
1. apparent; obvious; famous: 這是相當顯著的。It is quite obvious.
2. to write; to author
3. writings; a literary work; books
4. to set forth; to manifest; to make known

著名(ㄓㄨˋ ㄇIㄥˊ)
famous; renowned

著績(ㄓㄨˋ ㄐI)
well-known achievements (especially administrative)

著稱(ㄓㄨˋ ㄔㄥ)
celebrated; famous

著書(ㄓㄨˋ ㄕㄨ)
to author or compile a book

著書立說(ㄓㄨˋ ㄕㄨ カI ㄕㄨㄛ)
to write books and establish one's theory

著述(ㄓㄨˋ ㄕㄨˋ)
① to write ② writings; a literary work

著作(ㄓㄨˋ ㄗㄨㄛˋ)
① to write ② writings; a literary work

著作等身(ㄓㄨˋ ㄗㄨㄛˋ ㄉㄥˇ ㄕㄣ)
(said of an author) with many works to his credit

著作郎(ㄓㄨˋ ㄗㄨㄛˋ ㄌㄤˊ)
(in old China) an official in charge of compiling and editing national history

著作權(ㄓㄨˋ ㄗㄨㄛˋ くㄩㄢˊ)
copyright

著作者(ㄓㄨˋ ㄗㄨㄛˋ ㄓㄜˇ)or 著者(ㄓㄨˋ ㄓㄜˇ)
the writer or author

【著】 5003
　　　2.(音) ㄓㄨㄛˊ jwo zhuó
1. to wear (garments, etc.): 她著新衣。She is wearing a new dress.
2. a move (on the chessboard, in action, plans, etc.)
3. to apply (color, etc.); to start (an assignment, investigation, etc.)

著筆(ㄓㄨㄛˊ ㄅIˇ)
to put (or to set) pen to paper; to begin to write or paint

著地(ㄓㄨㄛˊ ㄉI)
to reach the ground; to touch the ground

著力(ㄓㄨㄛˊ カI)
to apply force; to exert

著陸(ㄓㄨㄛˊ ㄌㄨˋ)
(said of an airplane) to land; to alight; to descend to the ground

著落(ㄓㄨㄛˊ ㄌㄨㄛˋ)or(ㄓㄨㄛˊ ·ㄌㄠ)
whereabouts; results

著花(ㄓㄨㄛˊ ㄏㄨㄚ)
to blossom; to flower

著棋(ㄓㄨㄛˊ くI)
to play chess

著先鞭(ㄓㄨㄛˊ TIㄢ ㄅIㄢ)
to make a head start; to be the first to move

著想(ㄓㄨㄛˊ TIㄤ)
for the sake of

〔艸 部〕

（艸部）

著著進逼(ㄓㄨㄛ ㄓㄨㄛ ㄐㄧㄣ ㄅㄧ)
to close in step by step

著著失敗(ㄓㄨㄛ ㄓㄨㄛ ㄕ ㄅㄞ)
to fail in every move

著重(ㄓㄨㄛ ㄓㄨㄥ)
to emphasize; emphasis

著實(ㄓㄨㄛ ㄕ)
①concrete and substantial;
dependable ②really

著手(ㄓㄨㄛ ㄕㄡ)
to start doing something; to
put or set one's hand to

著手成春(ㄓㄨㄛ ㄕㄡ ㄔㄥ ㄔㄨㄣ)
(said of a good physician)
to cure every patient he
treats

著色(ㄓㄨㄛ ㄙㄜ)
to apply coloring; to color:
他著色於圖畫。He colors a
picture.

著衣(ㄓㄨㄛ ㄧ)
to wear clothing; to put on
garments

著衣鏡(ㄓㄨㄛ ㄧ ㄐㄧㄥ)
a full-length dressing mirror;
a cheval glass

著意(ㄓㄨㄛ ㄧ)
to pay attention to

【著】 5003
　　　③(著)ㄓㄠ jaur zhāo
1. to hit the bull's-eye; right to
the point; very worthwhile
2. to catch (fire, cold, etc.): 紙
易著火。Paper catches fire
easily.
3. to make a move or take
action; to use

著魔(ㄓㄠ ㄇㄛ)
to be bewitched; to be possessed

著迷(ㄓㄠ ㄇㄧ)
to be fascinated; to be
captivated: 這齣劇使觀眾著
迷。The opera has captivated
the audience.

著火(ㄓㄠ ㄏㄨㄛ)
to catch fire

著眼(ㄓㄠ ㄧㄢ)
to watch; to eye with attention; to direct one's attention to; to have something in
mind; to see from the angle
of; to aim at

著眼點(ㄓㄠ ㄧㄢ ㄉㄧㄢ)
the point to watch; the point
of emphasis; a starting point

useful; applicable

【著】 5003
　　　4.(著)ㄓㄠ jau zhāo
1. to bear; to take
2. a plan; a method

著忙(ㄓㄠ ㄇㄤ)
anxious or nervous; panicky

著風(ㄓㄠ ㄈㄥ)
to expose to wind

著涼(ㄓㄠ ㄌㄧㄤ)
to catch cold: 我昨夜著涼了。
I caught cold last night.

著慌(ㄓㄠ ㄏㄨㄤ)
anxious or worried; jittery:
他們對她的延遲著慌。They
became anxious at her
delay.

著急(ㄓㄠ ㄐㄧ)
anxious or worried: 他們爲後
果著急。They were worried
about the results.

著雨(ㄓㄠ ㄩ)
to get wet in the rain; to be
drenched by rain

【著】 5003
　　　5.(著)ㄓㄜ •je zhe
an adverbial particle

【葚】 5004
　　　ㄕㄣ shenn shèn
the mulberry

【葛】 5005
　　　1.(ㄜ) ger gé
dolichos (Pueraria thunbergiana), a creeping, edible
bean whose fibers can be
made into linen-like cloth
and whose roots are used in
herbal medicine

葛布(ㄍㄜ ㄅㄨ)
cloth made with the fiber of
Pueraria thunbergiana; linen

葛粉(ㄍㄜ ㄈㄣ)
edible starch obtained by
grinding the roots of Pueraria thunbergiana

葛藤(ㄍㄜ ㄊㄥ)
①(botany) Pueraria lobata
②(Buddhism) tangled and
involved; complications or
difficulty

葛巾(ㄍㄜ ㄐㄧㄣ)
a scarf or kerchief made
with kudzu

葛騰腹霜(ㄍㄜ ㄒㄩ ㄍㄨ ㄕㄨㄤ)
improper thrift; thrift at the
expense of propriety

葛紗(ㄍㄜ ㄕㄚ)
fine linen cloth made with

the fiber of Pueraria thunbergiana

葛衣(ㄍㄜ ㄧ)
clothing made with 葛布

【葛】 5005
　　　2.《ㄜ gee gě
a Chinese family name

葛天氏(ㄍㄜ ㄊㄧㄢ ㄕ)
name of a legendary emperor
in ancient times who gov-
erned with few words and
less orders

葛天氏之民(ㄍㄜ ㄊㄧㄢ ㄕ ㄓ ㄇㄧㄣ)
subjects of 葛天氏—people
with great freedom and joy

葛洪(ㄍㄜ ㄏㄨㄥ)
Ko Hung, a minister in the
reign of Emperor Yüan (元
帝) of Tsin (晉), c.290-c.370

【葡】 5006
　　　ㄆㄨ pwu pú
1. a grape; a vine
2. short for Portugal

葡萄(ㄆㄨ ㄊㄠ)or(ㄆㄨ •ㄊㄠ)
grapes

葡萄糖(ㄆㄨ ㄊㄠ ㄊㄤ)
glucose

葡萄藤(ㄆㄨ ㄊㄠ ㄊㄥ)
a grapevine

葡萄乾(ㄆㄨ ㄊㄠ ㄍㄢ)
raisins

葡萄架(ㄆㄨ ㄊㄠ ㄐㄧㄚ)
a grapevine trellis

葡萄酒(ㄆㄨ ㄊㄠ ㄐㄧㄡ)
wine; grape wine; port wine;
a vintage

葡萄球菌(ㄆㄨ ㄊㄠ ㄑㄧㄡ ㄐㄩㄣ)
(microbiology) a staphy-
lococcus

葡萄汁(ㄆㄨ ㄊㄠ ㄓ)
grape juice

葡萄牙(ㄆㄨ ㄊㄠ ㄧㄚ)
Portugal

葡萄牙人(ㄆㄨ ㄊㄠ ㄧㄚ ㄖㄣ)
the Portuguese

葡萄牙語(ㄆㄨ ㄊㄠ ㄧㄚ ㄩ)
Portuguese (language)

葡萄柚(ㄆㄨ ㄊㄠ ㄧㄡ)
a grapefruit

葡萄園(ㄆㄨ ㄊㄠ ㄩㄢ)
a grapevine orchard or
yard; a vine garden

【葠】 5007
　　　(蔘,參) ㄕㄣ shen
　　　　　　　shēn
1. ginseng
2. one of the 28 constellations

【董】 5008
ㄉㄨㄥ doong dǒng
1. to supervise; to oversee; to rectify; to correct
2. short for directors (as a board of directors, etc.)
3. a Chinese family name

董狐
Tung Hu, an official-historian of Chin (秦) in the Epoch of Spring and Autumn

董其昌(ㄉㄨㄥ ㄑㄧ ㄔㄤ)
Tung Chi-chang (1555-1636), a famous painter and calligrapher of the Ming Dynasty

董小宛(ㄉㄨㄥ ㄒㄧㄠ ㄨㄢˇ)
name of a very famous and talented courtesan toward the end of the Ming Dynasty

董卓(ㄉㄨㄥ ㄓㄨㄛˊ)
Tung Cho, a prime minister at the end of the Han Dynasty

董仲舒(ㄉㄨㄥ ㄓㄨㄥˋ ㄕㄨ)
Tung Chung-shu, a famous scholar in the Han Dynasty

董事(ㄉㄨㄥ ㄕˋ)
a director (on the board of a school, company, etc.); a director

董事會(ㄉㄨㄥ ㄕˋ ㄏㄨㄟˋ)
a meeting of board of directors; the board of directors

董事長(ㄉㄨㄥ ㄕˋ ㄓㄤˇ)
a board director; the chairman of the board of directors or of the board of trustees

【葦】 5009
ㄨㄟˇ woei wěi
a reed

葦箔(ㄨㄟˇ ㄅㄛˊ)
a reed screen

葦塘(ㄨㄟˇ ㄊㄤˊ)
a swampy or marshy ground covered with reeds

葦簾子(ㄨㄟˇ ㄌㄧㄢˊ ˙ㄗ)
screens or curtains woven with reeds

葦杖(ㄨㄟˇ ㄓㄤˋ)
a birch or whip of reeds

【葼】 5010
ㄗㄨㄥ tzong zōng
1. small twigs
2. a kind of grass

【葩】 5011
ㄆㄚ pa pā
1. flowers
2. as in 奇葩—a wonderful work

【葫】 5012
ㄏㄨˊ hwu hú
the calabash or bottle gourd

葫蘆(ㄏㄨˊ ㄌㄨˊ)or(ㄏㄨˊ ˙ㄌㄨ)
a bottle gourd; a calabash

葫蘆島(ㄏㄨˊ ㄌㄨˊ ㄉㄠˇ)
name of a peninsula in Liaoning Province, so called because it's shaped like a bottle gourd

【葬】 5013
ㄗㄤˋ tzang zàng
to bury, inter or consign to a grave: 他昨天下葬。He was buried yesterday.

葬埋(ㄗㄤˋ ㄇㄞˊ)
to bury (the dead) 亦作「埋葬」

葬地(ㄗㄤˋ ㄉㄧˋ)
the site of burial; a burial ground; a grave

葬禮(ㄗㄤˋ ㄌㄧˇ)
a funeral or burial service

葬身之地(ㄗㄤˋ ㄕㄣ ㄓ ㄉㄧˋ)
a burial ground

葬身魚腹(ㄗㄤˋ ㄕㄣ ㄩˊ ㄈㄨˋ)
to be drowned in a river or sea, thus to become food for fish

葬送(ㄗㄤˋ ㄙㄨㄥˋ)
to bury or waste (one's talent, future, hopes, etc.)

葬儀(ㄗㄤˋ ㄧˊ)
burial or funeral rites

葬玉埋香(ㄗㄤˋ ㄩˋ ㄇㄞˊ ㄒㄧㄤ)
①to bury a beauty ②the untimely death of a beauty

【葭】 5014
ㄐㄧㄚ jia jiā
1. a reed; a bulrush
2. a flute

葭莩(ㄐㄧㄚ ㄈㄨˊ)
distant relatives

【萑】 5015
ㄔㄨㄟˊ chwei chuí
a bramble; a thorn

【葳】 5016
ㄨㄟ uei wēi
1. luxuriant; flourishing
2. used for various plants

葳蕤(ㄨㄟ ㄖㄨㄟˊ)
①*Polygonatum cyrtonema*, a kind of herb ②luxuriant; lush

【葵】 5017
ㄎㄨㄟˊ kwei kuí
1. a sunflower (*Althaea rosea*)

葵笠(ㄎㄨㄟˊ ㄌㄧˋ)
a crude palm-leaf hat

葵花(ㄎㄨㄟˊ ㄏㄨㄚ)
a sunflower

葵花(ㄎㄨㄟˊ ㄏㄨㄚ ㄒㄧㄤˋ ㄖˋ)
(literally) The sunflower always turns to the sun.—The loyal always look to their master.

葵花子(ㄎㄨㄟˊ ㄏㄨㄚ ˙ㄗ)or葵瓜子(ㄎㄨㄟˊ ㄍㄨㄚ ˙ㄗ)
sunflower seeds

葵花油(ㄎㄨㄟˊ ㄏㄨㄚ ㄧㄡˊ)
sunflower oil

葵傾(ㄎㄨㄟˊ ㄑㄧㄥ)or葵向(ㄎㄨㄟˊ ㄒㄧㄤˋ)
to look to; to admire; to lean toward

葵扇(ㄎㄨㄟˊ ㄕㄢˋ)
a palm-leaf fan

【葷】 5018
1. ㄏㄨㄣ huen hūn
1. a meat and fish diet; meat-eating (as opposed to what vegetarians are practicing)
2. strong smelling foods or spices—such as onions, leeks, garlic, etc.
3. obscene or dirty language, narration, films, etc.

葷辛(ㄏㄨㄣ ㄒㄧㄣ)
strong smelling foods or spices

葷腥(ㄏㄨㄣ ㄒㄧㄥ)
a meat and fish diet

葷菜(ㄏㄨㄣ ㄘㄞˋ)
dishes containing meat or fish

葷油(ㄏㄨㄣ ㄧㄡˊ)
animal fat

【葷】 5018
2. ㄒㄩㄣ shiun xūn
name of a barbaric tribe in ancient China

葷粥(ㄒㄩㄣ ㄩˋ)or獯鬻(ㄒㄩㄣ ㄩˋ) or 獯尤(ㄒㄩㄣ ㄧㄡˊ)
name of a barbaric tribe in ancient China

【葸】 5019
ㄒㄧˇ shii xǐ
1. scared; timid
2. not pleasant; a displeased look

【萋】 5020
ㄑㄧ chih qī

〔艸部〕

1. to repair; to have something put in repair
2. thatched
3. to pile up; to heap together

葺補〔くⁱ ㄅㄨˇ〕
to repair and mend

葺覆〔くⁱ ㄈㄨˋ〕
to cover or roof in

葺牆〔くⁱ くⁱㄤˊ〕
to repair a wall

葺屋〔くⁱ ㄨ〕
a thatched house; to thatch a house

【蕘】 5021　ㄧㄠˊ iau yáo
1. *Polygala japonica*, a variety of grass
2. a dense or luxuriant growth of grass or weeds

【葆】 5022　ㄅㄠˇ bao bǎo
1. reserved; hidden; not easily revealed
2. a dense or luxuriant growth of vegetation
3. to protect; protection

葆葆〔ㄅㄠˇ ㄅㄠˇ〕
a lush and luxuriant growth

葆光〔ㄅㄠˇ ㄍㄨㄤ〕
the shaded light; the precious light—(figuratively) one's wisdom; one's profound knowledge

葆真 or 保眞〔ㄅㄠˇ ㄓㄣ〕
to safeguard one's divine nature—untarnished by all desires, etc.

【葒】 5023　ㄏㄨㄥˊ horng hóng
Polygonum orientale

【萸】 5024　ㄩˊ yu yú
dogwood

【萹】 5025　1. ㄆㄧㄢ piān
a variety of weed or grass with narrow thick blades

【萹】 5025　2.（稨）ㄅㄧㄢˇ bean biǎn
a kind of bean

【葖】 5026　ㄊㄨˊ twu tú
(botany) a turnip

【葱】 5027　（蔥）ㄘㄨㄥ tsong cōng
1. scallions; onions
2. bright green

葱白〔ㄘㄨㄥ ㄅㄞˊ〕
①pale green ②the white-colored section near the root of a scallion

葱頭〔ㄘㄨㄥ ㄊㄡˊ〕
onions 亦作「洋葱」

葱嶺〔ㄘㄨㄥ ㄌㄧㄥˇ〕
a mountain range in south-western Sinkiang Province, known as the ridge of Asia

葱蒨〔ㄘㄨㄥ 〕
a luxuriant growth of green vegetation

葱綠〔ㄘㄨㄥ ㄌㄩˋ〕
a fresh, bright green: 稻苗一片葱綠 The rice shoots are a lush green.

葱髯子〔ㄘㄨㄥ ㄖㄢˊ ㄗ〕
the tiny roots of a scallion which look like a beard

葱花〔ㄘㄨㄥ ㄏㄨㄚ〕
scallions cut into tiny pieces for seasoning or dressing

葱黃〔ㄘㄨㄥ ㄏㄨㄤˊ〕
greenish yellow

葱心綠〔ㄘㄨㄥ ㄒㄧㄣ ㄌㄩˋ〕
light bright green

葱翠〔ㄘㄨㄥ ㄘㄨㄟˋ〕
fresh green; luxuriantly green

【蒂】 5028　（蔕）ㄉㄧˋ dih dì
1. a peduncle or footstalk of a flower or fruit; a stem; a base
2. a (cigaret) butt

蒂芥〔ㄉㄧˋ ㄐㄧㄝˋ〕
resentment; ill will or un-friendly feeling

【蓋】 5029　（蓋）ㄍㄞˋ gay gài
to cover, build, etc.

【葯】 5030　ㄧㄠˋ yaw yào（讀音 ㄩㄝˋ yueh yuè）
1. (botany) an angelica
2. to wrap up 亦作「約」
3. a simplified form as 藥—medicine

葯胞〔ㄧㄠˋ ㄅㄠ〕
(botany) a loculus

【菹】 5031　（菹）ㄐㄩ jiu jū
1. salted or pickled vegetable or meat
2. a marshland covered with reeds

【韭】 5032　（韮）ㄐㄧㄡˇ jeou jiǔ
fragrant-flowered garlic; (Chinese) chives

韭黃〔ㄐㄧㄡˇ ㄏㄨㄤˊ〕
tender chives (which are yellow in color)

韭菜〔ㄐㄧㄡˇ ㄘㄞˋ〕
fragrant-flowered garlic; (Chinese) chives

十畫

【蒐】 5033　ㄙㄡ sou sōu
1. to gather; to collect
2. to hunt or search for; hunting
3. (botany) *Rubia cordifolia*, madder

蒐羅〔ㄙㄡ ㄌㄨㄛˊ〕
to search and collect

蒐集〔ㄙㄡ ㄐㄧˊ〕
to collect or gather 亦作「搜集」: 我的嗜好是蒐集郵票。My hobby is collecting stamps.

蒐索〔ㄙㄡ ㄙㄨㄛˇ〕
to search

【蒙】 5034　ㄇㄥˊ meng méng
1. to cover; to cover up; to wrap
2. naive; childish
3. ignorant; gullible; stupid
4. to cheat; to deceive; to fool
5. to bear; to take; to suffer
6. short for Mongolia
7. a Chinese family name

蒙蔽〔ㄇㄥˊ ㄅㄧˋ〕
to deceive; to swindle; to fool

蒙騙〔ㄇㄥˊ ㄆㄧㄢˋ〕
to fool with the intention to cheat

蒙昧〔ㄇㄥˊ ㄇㄟˋ〕
ignorant and stupid

蒙昧時代〔ㄇㄥˊ ㄇㄟˋ ㄕˊ ㄉㄞˋ〕
the period of ignorance; the primitive age

蒙昧無知〔ㄇㄥˊ ㄇㄟˋ ㄨˊ ㄓ〕
stupid and ignorant

蒙面盜〔ㄇㄥˊ ㄇㄧㄢˋ ㄉㄠˋ〕
a masked bandit, robber or burglar

蒙大拿〔ㄇㄥˊ ㄉㄚˋ ㄋㄚˊ〕
the state of Montana, U.S.A.

蒙特卡羅〔ㄇㄥˊ ㄊㄜˋ ㄎㄚˇ ㄌㄨㄛˊ〕

蒙太奇(ㄇㄥ ㄊㄞ ㄑㄧ)
(movie) montage

蒙頭蓋臉(ㄇㄥ ㄊㄡ ㄍㄞ ㄌㄧㄢˇ)
to cover one's head and face

蒙恬(ㄇㄥ ㄊㄧㄢˊ)
Meng Tien, a famous general in the Chin (秦) Dynasty, who supervised the building of the Great Wall and was credited with the invention of the writing brush

蒙童(ㄇㄥ ㄊㄨㄥˊ)
innocent or ignorant children

蒙難(ㄇㄥ ㄋㄢˊ)
to suffer disaster; to be in distress

蒙茸(ㄇㄥ ㄖㄨㄥˊ)
①nebulous ②(said of plants) luxuriant

蒙古(ㄇㄥ ㄍㄨˇ)
Mongolia; Mongolian

蒙古包(ㄇㄥ ㄍㄨˇ ㄅㄠ)
a yurt (a portable, tentlike dwelling used by nomadic Mongols)

蒙古大夫(ㄇㄥ ㄍㄨˇ ㄉㄚ ˙ㄈㄨ)or
(ㄇㄥ ㄍㄨˇ ㄉㄞˋ ˙ㄈㄨ)
a medical quack

蒙古利亞(ㄇㄥ ㄍㄨˇ ㄌㄧˋ ㄧㄚˇ)
Mongolia

蒙古症(ㄇㄥ ㄍㄨˇ ㄓㄥˋ)
(medicine) mongolism

蒙古人(ㄇㄥ ㄍㄨˇ ㄖㄣˊ)
the Mongols; the Mongolians

蒙古人種(ㄇㄥ ㄍㄨˇ ㄖㄣˊ ㄓㄨㄥˇ)
(anthropology) Mongolian stock

蒙古文(ㄇㄥ ㄍㄨˇ ㄨㄣˊ)
the Mongolian language

蒙館(ㄇㄥ ㄍㄨㄢˇ)
a village school for children

蒙汗藥(ㄇㄥ ㄏㄢˋ ㄧㄠˋ)
any drug or concoction used as an anesthetic; knockout drops

蒙混(ㄇㄥ ㄏㄨㄣˋ)
to use a fake in place of a genuine article; to hoodwink; to deceive and swindle

蒙羞(ㄇㄥ ㄒㄧㄡ)
to suffer shame or insult; (said of a state) to be conquered by foreigners

蒙稚(ㄇㄥ ㄓˋ)
childish; naive; ignorant: 他不是愚笨，是蒙稚。He's not stupid, merely ignorant.

蒙塵(ㄇㄥ ㄔㄣˊ)
(said of the emperor) to flee the capital, or to be taken prisoner

蒙師(ㄇㄥ ㄕ)
a village school teacher

蒙受(ㄇㄥ ㄕㄡˋ)
to suffer; to sustain

蒙上(ㄇㄥ ˙ㄕㄤˋ)
to deceive one's elders; to hide the truth from superiors

蒙在鼓裡(ㄇㄥ ㄗㄞˋ ㄍㄨˇ ㄌㄧˇ)
to be deceived; to be kept completely in the dark

蒙藏委員會(ㄇㄥ ㄗㄤˋ ㄨㄟˇ ㄩㄢˊ ㄏㄨㄟˋ)
Mongolian-Tibetan Affairs Commission (of the Executive Yüan)

蒙恩(ㄇㄥ ㄣ)
to receive favors; to be indebted for favors granted

【蒜】 5035
ㄙㄨㄢˋ suann suàn
garlic

蒜瓣(ㄙㄨㄢˋ ㄅㄢˋ)
the quarters of a head of garlic

蒜苗(ㄙㄨㄢˋ ㄇㄧㄠˊ)
garlic sprouts (used as food)

蒜髮(ㄙㄨㄢˋ ㄈㄚˇ)
the premature white hair of a young person

蒜頭兒(ㄙㄨㄢˋ ㄊㄡˊ ㄦ)
the garlic head

蒜泥(ㄙㄨㄢˋ ㄋㄧˊ)
mashed garlic

【蒯】 5036
ㄎㄨㄞˇ koai kuǎi
(又讀 ㄎㄨㄞˊ kuay
kuái)
1. Scirpus cyperinus Kunth var. concolor Makino, a rush, from which many things are weaved
2. a Chinese family name

【蒲】 5037
ㄅㄨˊ pwu pú
an ancient dice game

蒲戲(ㄅㄨˊ ㄒㄧˋ)
an ancient dice game

【蒲】 5038
ㄆㄨˊ pwu pú

1. various kinds of rush from which mats, bags, etc. are made; vines of the rushes
2. a Chinese family name

蒲包(ㄆㄨˊ ㄅㄠ)
a rushbag (for packing)

蒲鞭(ㄆㄨˊ ㄅㄧㄢ)
(literally) a birch or whip made of rush for punishment
—leniency

蒲團(ㄆㄨˊ ㄊㄨㄢˊ)
a rushy mat for kneeling (used especially in Buddhist temples)

蒲柳(ㄆㄨˊ ㄌㄧㄡˇ)
①(botany) Salix gracilistyla ②(said of a physical constitution) feeble; weak ③(said of a social position) humble; lowly

蒲隆地(ㄆㄨˊ ㄌㄨㄥˊ ㄉㄧˋ)
Burundi

蒲公英(ㄆㄨˊ ㄍㄨㄥ ㄧㄥ)
the dandelion

蒲葵(ㄆㄨˊ ㄎㄨㄟˊ)
the Chinese fan palm

蒲節(ㄆㄨˊ ㄐㄧㄝˊ)
the Dragon Boat Festival on the fifth day of the fifth lunar month

蒲劍(ㄆㄨˊ ㄐㄧㄢˋ)
the rush sword, hung in the doorway on the Dragon Boat Festival to ward off evil spirits

蒲式耳(ㄆㄨˊ ㄕˋ ㄦˇ)
a bushel

蒲扇(ㄆㄨˊ ㄕㄢˋ)
a rush-leaf fan

蒲草(ㄆㄨˊ ㄘㄠˇ)
the stem or leaf of a cattail

蒲松齡(ㄆㄨˊ ㄙㄨㄥ ㄌㄧㄥˊ)
Pu Sung-ling, 1640-1715, the author of Strange Stories from a Chinese Studio (聊齋誌異), a collection of ghost stories

蒲月(ㄆㄨˊ ㄩㄝˋ)
the fifth month in the lunar calendar

【蒸】 5039
ㄓㄥ jeng zhēng
1. steam; to steam; to cook by steaming
2. to evaporate
3. twigs or slender branches as fuel

【艸 部】

4. crowded; crowds; the masses

蒸餅（ㄓㄥ ㄅㄧㄥˇ）
steamed cake

蒸木油（ㄓㄥ ㄇㄨˋ ㄧㄡˊ）
creosote

蒸發（ㄓㄥ ㄈㄚ）
evaporation; to evaporate

蒸發熱（ㄓㄥ ㄈㄚ ㄖㄜˋ）
evaporation heat

蒸發作用（ㄓㄥ ㄈㄚ ㄗㄨㄛˋ ㄩㄥˋ）
evaporation; transpiration

蒸騰（ㄓㄥ ㄊㄥˊ）
rising vapor or steam

蒸餾（ㄓㄥ ㄌㄧㄡˊ）
distillation; to distill

蒸餾器（ㄓㄥ ㄌㄧㄡˊ ㄑㄧˋ）
a still; a distiller

蒸餾水（ㄓㄥ ㄌㄧㄡˊ ㄕㄨㄟˇ）
distilled water

蒸籠（ㄓㄥ ㄌㄨㄥˊ）
a tight basket and sieve of bamboo for steaming food

蒸餃（ㄓㄥ ㄐㄧㄠˇ）
steamed ravioli

蒸汽 or 蒸氣（ㄓㄥ ㄑㄧˋ）
steam; vapor: 蒸汽轉動機器。
Steam drives machinery.

蒸汽鍋爐（ㄓㄥ ㄑㄧˋ ㄍㄨㄛ ㄌㄨˊ）
a steam boiler

蒸汽機（ㄓㄥ ㄑㄧˋ ㄐㄧ）
a steam engine

蒸汽浴（ㄓㄥ ㄑㄧˋ ㄩˋ）
a steam bath; a vapor bath; a Turkish bath

蒸蒸日上（ㄓㄥ ㄓㄥ ㄖˋ ㄕㄤˋ）
(usually said of business, etc.) rising and ascending; getting more and more prosperous

蒸食（ㄓㄥ ㄕˊ）
a general name of various kinds of steamed dumplings

蒸沙成飯（ㄓㄥ ㄕㄚ ㄔㄥˊ ㄈㄢˋ）
(literally) to cook sand with the hope of turning it into rice—a hopeless task

蒸暑（ㄓㄥ ㄕㄨˇ）
steaming heat (of summer); sultry 亦作「酷熱」

蒸溽（ㄓㄥ ㄖㄨˋ）
steaming heat of summer; sultry

蒸靈（ㄓㄥ ㄌㄧˊ）
the rising of steam or vapor

【蒹】 5040
ㄐㄧㄢ jian jiān

a kind of reed with a pithy stem

【蒺】 5041
ㄐㄧˊ jyi jí
the caltrop, or caltrap

蒺藜（ㄐㄧˊ ㄌㄧˊ）
the caltrop, or caltrap

【蒼】 ㄘㄤ tsang cāng
1. green; deep green or blue
2. gray (hair); hoary: 他頭髮漸蒼白。His hair (or He) is growing gray.
3. old
4. the masses
5. a Chinese family name

蒼白（ㄘㄤ ㄅㄞˊ）
pale; pallid: 她臉色蒼白而且面露倦容。She is pale and tired-looking.

蒼茫（ㄘㄤ ㄇㄤˊ）
a vast expanse without a boundary

蒼民（ㄘㄤ ㄇㄧㄣˊ）
the masses; the ordinary people

蒼苔（ㄘㄤ ㄊㄞˊ）
deep green moss; dark moss

蒼頭（ㄘㄤ ㄊㄡˊ）(or ㄘㄤ ㄊㄡ˙)
①(in old China) servants (with green turbans) ②(in ancient China) green-turbaned soldiers

蒼天（ㄘㄤ ㄊㄧㄢ）
①the heavens; the sky ②springtime

蒼老（ㄘㄤ ㄌㄠˇ）
(said of people) hoary and old: 他顯得蒼老。He looks old.

蒼涼（ㄘㄤ ㄌㄧㄤˊ）
desolate; bleak

蒼狗白雲（ㄘㄤ ㄍㄡˇ ㄅㄞˊ ㄩㄣˊ）
the ephemeral world; ever-changing ways of a man

蒼黃（ㄘㄤ ㄏㄨㄤˊ）
①greenish yellow ②hurriedly; hastily

蒼頡（ㄘㄤ ㄐㄧㄝˊ）
Tsang Chieh, a legendary figure, who was supposed to be the inventor of Chinese characters

蒼勁（ㄘㄤ ㄐㄧㄥˋ）
①old and strong ②(said of calligraphy or painting) vigorous; bold

蒼穹（ㄘㄤ ㄑㄩㄥˊ）
the sky; the vault of heaven; the firmament

蒼朮（ㄘㄤ ㄓㄨˊ）
Atractylis lancea, a medicinal herb

蒼生（ㄘㄤ ㄕㄥ）
the ordinary people; the masses

蒼蒼（ㄘㄤ ㄘㄤ）
①deep green; blue ②old and hoary ③gray-headed

蒼翠（ㄘㄤ ㄘㄨㄟˋ）
green and bright—like leaves after a spring shower; emerald

蒼鷹（ㄘㄤ ㄧㄥ）
the eagle; the falcon

蒼蠅（ㄘㄤ ㄧˊ）
the fly: 蒼蠅嗡嗡作響。The flies are buzzing.

蒼蠅拍子（ㄘㄤ ㄧˊ ㄆㄞ ˙ㄗ）
a flyswatter; a flyflap

蒼蠅紙（ㄘㄤ ㄧˊ ㄓˇ）
flypaper

【蒿】 5043
ㄏㄠ hau hāo
1. the southernwood; plants of the mugwort or artemisia family
2. rising vapor

蒿目（ㄏㄠ ㄇㄨˋ）
①to look far ②to close one's eyes and worry about worldly affairs

蒿萊（ㄏㄠ ㄌㄞˊ）
①to live in the jungle ②the jungle

蒿里（ㄏㄠ ㄌㄧˇ）
①a tomb ②an elegiac song in ancient times

蒿廬（ㄏㄠ ㄌㄨˊ）
a hut

蒿子（ㄏㄠ ˙ㄗ）
(botany) the mugwort or artemisia

蒿子稈兒（ㄏㄠ ˙ㄗ ㄍㄢˇ）
the stem of the mugwort or artemisia

【蓀】 5044
ㄙㄨㄣ suen sūn
a kind of aromatic grass

【蓁】 5045
ㄓㄣ jen zhēn
1. luxuriant
2. a wild pepper

蓁蓁（ㄓㄣ ㄓㄣ）

luxuriant (vegetation)

【蓄】 5046
ㄒㄩ shiuh xù
1. to collect; to store; to save up; to reserve
2. to cultivate (long hair or a beard); to grow
3. to raise; to rear; to breed
4. to wait; to expect

蓄謀（ㄒㄩ ㄇㄡˊ）
a plan which is being considered but not revealed; a secret scheme

蓄髮（ㄒㄩ ㄈㄚˇ）
to grow or cultivate long hair

蓄電量（ㄒㄩ ㄉㄧㄢˋ ㄌㄧㄤˋ）
the capacity of storing electricity; the capacity of a storage battery

蓄電池（ㄒㄩ ㄉㄧㄢˋ ㄔˊ）
a storage battery, cell, or accumulator

蓄念（ㄒㄩ ㄋㄧㄢˋ）
a long-conceived idea, plan, intention, etc.

蓄恨（ㄒㄩ ㄏㄣˋ）
a long pent-up hatred

蓄火（ㄒㄩ ㄏㄨㄛˇ）
(in ancient times) a fire in reserve

蓄洪（ㄒㄩ ㄏㄨㄥˊ）
to store floodwater

蓄積（ㄒㄩ ㄐㄧ）
to store or save up; storage or savings

蓄志（ㄒㄩ ㄓˋ）
a long-conceived hope, wish or aspiration; to harbor such hope, etc.

蓄水池（ㄒㄩ ㄕㄨㄟˇ ㄔˊ）
a reservoir

蓄銳（ㄒㄩ ㄖㄨㄟˋ）
to husband one's strength and store up energy (for a big undertaking)—as soldiers before a decisive engagement or a prize fighter before a bout

蓄財（ㄒㄩ ㄘㄞˊ）
to store up money or wealth

蓄意（ㄒㄩ ㄧˋ）
to harbor certain intentions or ideas; premeditated (murder, etc.): 這兇殺是蓄意的。The murder was premeditated.

蓄音器（ㄒㄩ ㄧㄣ ㄑㄧˋ）
a phonograph; a gramophone 亦作「留聲機」

蓄養（ㄒㄩ ㄧㄤˇ）
to raise (ducks, etc.)

蓄怨（ㄒㄩ ㄩㄢˋ）
to harbor animosity or ill will

【蓆】 5047
ㄒㄧˊ shyi xí
a mat, especially a straw mat

蓆子（ㄒㄧˊ ˙ㄗ）
a mat, especially a straw mat: 我們重新舖了蓆子。We had the mats recovered.

【蓉】 5048
ㄖㄨㄥˊ rong róng
as in 芙蓉—the hibiscus

【蓋】 1.（蓋,蓋）ㄍㄞˋ gay gài
1. to cover; to hide
2. a lid; a covering
3. to build; to construct; to erect
4. to affix (a seal)
5. (an initial particle) now; then; but; because
6. (a particle indicating doubt) for; perhaps; possibly; about
7. to surpass; to excel
8. to brag; to boast

蓋被窩（ㄍㄞˋ ㄅㄟˋ ㄨㄛ）
to cover with a quilt

蓋房子（ㄍㄞˋ ㄈㄤˊ ˙ㄗ）
to build a house

蓋頭（ㄍㄞˋ ˙ㄊㄡ）or 蓋巾（ㄍㄞˋ ㄐㄧㄣ）
(formerly) the head-cover or veil for the bride at a wedding

蓋圖章（ㄍㄞˋ ㄊㄨˊ ㄓㄤ）or 蓋章（ㄍㄞˋ ㄓㄤ）or 蓋印（ㄍㄞˋ ㄧㄣˋ）
to affix the seal

蓋關防（ㄍㄞˋ ㄍㄨㄢ ㄈㄤˊ）
to affix an official seal

蓋棺論定（ㄍㄞˋ ㄍㄨㄢ ㄌㄨㄣˋ ㄉㄧㄥˋ）
When one's coffin is covered, one's deserts can be properly judged.

蓋仙（ㄍㄞˋ ㄒㄧㄢ）
a brag: 他是個蓋仙。He is a brag.

蓋戳（ㄍㄞˋ ㄔㄨㄛˋ）
to stamp (postmarks, etc.); to affix a seal; to chop

蓋世（ㄍㄞˋ ㄕˋ）or 蓋代（ㄍㄞˋ ㄉㄞˋ）
surpassing one's generation;

without a match; to rank supreme in one's time

蓋世太保（ㄍㄞˋ ㄕˋ ㄊㄞˋ ㄅㄠˇ）
the Gestapo

蓋世之才（ㄍㄞˋ ㄕˋ ㄓ ㄘㄞˊ）
talent or capability unsurpassed or unmatched in one's generation

蓋世英雄（ㄍㄞˋ ㄕˋ ㄧㄥ ㄒㄩㄥˊ）
a hero among heroes: 他是一位蓋世英雄。He was a hero among heroes.

蓋世無雙（ㄍㄞˋ ㄕˋ ㄨˊ ㄕㄨㄤ）
unrivaled; matchless; peerless: 他是蓋世無雙的拳擊手。He is a peerless boxer.

蓋氏計算器（ㄍㄞˋ ㄕˋ ㄐㄧˋ ㄙㄨㄢˋ ㄑㄧˋ）or 蓋革計數器（ㄍㄞˋ ㄍㄜˊ ㄐㄧˋ ㄕㄨˋ ㄑㄧˋ）
a Geiger counter

蓋上（ㄍㄞˋ ˙ㄕㄤ）
to cover: 母親幫他蓋上毯子。Mother covered him with a blanket.

蓋然率（ㄍㄞˋ ㄖㄢˊ ㄌㄩˋ）or 蓋然性（ㄍㄞˋ ㄖㄢˊ ㄒㄧㄥˋ）
probability; the rate of probability

蓋子（ㄍㄞˋ ˙ㄗ）or 蓋兒（ㄍㄞˋ ㄦ）
①a lid; a cover: 請打開蓋子。Take off the lid, please. ②a shell (of a tortoise, etc.)

蓋藏（ㄍㄞˋ ㄘㄤˊ）
wealth or commodities stored away

蓋亞那（ㄍㄞˋ ㄧˇ ㄋㄚˋ）
Guyana

【蓋】 2.（ㄍㄜˇ） gee gě
a Chinese family name

【蓋】 5049
（蓋）ㄏㄜˊ her hé
Why not? 或 Would it not be better to...?

【蓐】 5050
ㄖㄨˋ ruh rù
matting; a bed mat

蓐母（ㄖㄨˋ ㄇㄨˇ）or 蓐婦（ㄖㄨˋ ㄈㄨˋ）
a midwife

蓐食（ㄖㄨˋ ㄕˊ）
①to breakfast in bed; to take meals in bed ②rich food

【蓑】 5051
ㄙㄨㄛ suo suō
1. a raincoat or cloak of straw, rushes, coir. etc.

〔艸部〕

【艸部】

2. (now rarely) to cover with grass

蓑笠 (ㄙㄨㄛ ㄌㄧ)
a coir raincoat and leaf hat; a bamboo cape and hat

蓑草 (ㄙㄨㄛ ㄘㄠ)
sedge (of which a raincoat can be made)

蓑衣 (ㄙㄨㄛ ㄧ)
a coir raincoat

【蓓】 5052
ㄅㄟ bey bèi
a flower bud; a bud

蓓蕾 (ㄅㄟ ㄌㄟ)
a flower bud

【蒔】 5053
ㄕ shyr shí
1. to plant; to cultivate; to transplant
2. *Anethum graveolens*, a kind of spice

蒔花 (ㄕ ㄏㄨㄚ)
to grow flowers

【蒨】 5054
ㄑㄧㄢ chiann qiàn
1. a luxuriant growth (of grass or vegetation)
2. red; crimson

蒨蒨 (ㄑㄧㄢ ㄑㄧㄢ)
①bright and clear ②a luxuriant growth

【蒻】 5055
ㄖㄨㄛ ruoh ruò
1. a water plant; a wild arum
2. a rush mat

蒻席 (ㄖㄨㄛ ㄒㄧ)
a rush mat made of arum

【蓊】 5056
ㄨㄥ woeng wěng
(said of vegetation) luxuriant; flourishing; lush

蓊勃 (ㄨㄥ ㄅㄛ)
(said of vegetation) luxuriant; lush

蓊茸 (ㄨㄥ ㄖㄨㄥ)
luxuriant; lush

蓊蔚 (ㄨㄥ ㄨㄟ)
the luxuriant growth of vegetation

蓊蓊 (ㄨㄥ ㄨㄥ)
the lush or luxuriant growth of vegetation

蓊鬱 (ㄨㄥ ㄩ)
the lush or luxuriant growth of vegetation

【蓍】 5057
ㄕ shy shī
milfoil, the stalks of which

were used in divination in ancient times

蓍龜 (ㄕ ㄍㄨㄟ) or 蓍蔡 (ㄕ ㄘㄞ)
① milfoil and tortoise divination ② foresight

蓍簪 (ㄕ ㄗㄣ)
to treasure old things of little value for sentimental reasons

蓍草 (ㄕ ㄘㄠ)
milfoil (used in divination in ancient times)

【蓇】 5058
ㄍㄨ guu gǔ
a follicle

蓇葖 (ㄍㄨ ㄊㄨ)
a follicle

【蒓】 5059
(專) ㄔㄨㄣ chwen chún
Brasenia schreberi, water shield

【蒞】 5060
(涖) ㄌㄧ lih lì
to arrive

【蓖】 5061
ㄅㄧ bih bì
(botany) the castor-oil plant

蓖麻 (ㄅㄧ ㄇㄚ)
(botany) the castor-oil plant

蓖麻油 (ㄅㄧ ㄇㄚ ㄧㄡ)
castor oil

【蒭】 5062
(芻) ㄔㄨ chwu chú
1. to cut grass
2. hay; fodder

十一畫

【蓬】 5063
ㄆㄥ perng péng
1. *Erigeron acer*, a species of raspberry
2. tangled
3. disheveled (hair)
4. flourishing; prospering
5. a Chinese family name

蓬勃 (ㄆㄥ ㄅㄛ)
rising and flourishing; booming; vigorously

蓬蓽 (ㄆㄥ ㄅㄧ)
①houses of the destitute ② my humble house

蓬蓽生輝 (ㄆㄥ ㄅㄧ ㄕㄥ ㄏㄨㄟ)
(Your gracious presence) has added glitter to my humble house.

蓬勃勃 (ㄆㄥ ㄅㄛ ㄅㄛ)
flourishing and prospering; booming

蓬飄萍轉 (ㄆㄥ ㄆㄧㄠ ㄆㄧㄥ ㄓㄨㄢ)
wandering about; having no fixed address

蓬門 (ㄆㄥ ㄇㄣ) or 蓬門蓽戶 (ㄆㄥ ㄇㄣ ㄅㄧ ㄏㄨ)
①houses of the poor ② my humble house; my thorn-wood gate

蓬髮 (ㄆㄥ ㄈㄚ)
disheveled hair

蓬島 (ㄆㄥ ㄉㄠ)
(Chinese legends) a fairy-tale island in the Yellow Sea

蓬頭垢面 (ㄆㄥ ㄊㄡ ㄍㄡ ㄇㄧㄢ)
disheveled hair and a dirty face—very untidy in appearance

蓬萊 (ㄆㄥ ㄌㄞ)
①a fairy-tale island in the Yellow Sea or name of an enchanted hill on such an island

蓬萊仙境 (ㄆㄥ ㄌㄞ ㄒㄧㄢ ㄐㄧㄥ)
a fairyland; a paradise

蓬蒿 (ㄆㄥ ㄏㄠ)
①a garland chrysanthemum 亦作「茼蒿」② the wilderness ③ weeds and thistles

蓬戶甕牖 (ㄆㄥ ㄏㄨ ㄨㄥ ㄧㄡ)
houses of the destitute

蓬轉 (ㄆㄥ ㄓㄨㄢ)
①quickly; rapidly ②to go adrift

蓬折 (ㄆㄥ ㄓㄜ)
①the beat of dance music ②to dance

蓬首 (ㄆㄥ ㄕㄡ)
disheveled hair

蓬生麻中，不扶自直 (ㄆㄥ ㄕㄥ ㄇㄚ ㄓㄨㄥ，ㄅㄨ ㄈㄨ ㄗˋ ㄓˊ)
(literally) When a raspberry grows among hemp, it stands erect without support.—When one is surrounded by the virtuous, he'll be assimilated.

蓬茸 (ㄆㄥ ㄖㄨㄥ)
a luxuriant growth (of grass); lush

蓬鬆 (ㄆㄥ ㄙㄨㄥ)
disheveled; very loose

蓬瀛 (ㄆㄥ ㄧㄥ)
蓬萊 and 瀛洲, both legendary fairylands

【蓮】 5064 ㄌㄧㄢ lian lián
1. the lotus, or water lily
2. (Buddhism) the "clean" land
—Buddhist Paradise

蓮邦(ㄌㄧㄢ ㄅㄤ)
(Buddhism) the Lotus Land,
or the Pure Land, of
Amitabha

蓮步(ㄌㄧㄢ ㄅㄨˋ)
steps of a beautiful woman;
ladylike steps

蓮蓬(ㄌㄧㄢˊ·ㄆㄥ)or 蓮房(ㄌㄧㄢ ㄈㄤˊ)
the cupule of a lotus

蓮蓬頭(ㄌㄧㄢˊ·ㄆㄥ ㄊㄡˊ)
a finely perforated nozzle
for a shower bath

蓮蓬子兒(ㄌㄧㄢ·ㄆㄥ ㄗㄦˋ)
lotus seeds

蓮斷絲牽(ㄌㄧㄢ ㄉㄨㄢˋ ㄙ ㄑㄧㄢ)
lingering affection or friendship after a formal break
(as in the case of a divorced
couple)

蓮塘(ㄌㄧㄢ ㄊㄤˊ)
a lotus pond

蓮鉤(ㄌㄧㄢ ㄍㄡ)
slender feet of a woman
(especially referring to the
bound feet of former days)

蓮龕(ㄌㄧㄢ ㄎㄢ)
a niche for the statue of
Buddha

蓮花 or 蓮華(ㄌㄧㄢ ㄏㄨㄚˊ)
lotus blossoms or water
lilies

蓮花燈(ㄌㄧㄢ ㄏㄨㄚ ㄉㄥ)
a lantern shaped like a lotus
blossom

蓮花落(ㄌㄧㄢ ㄏㄨㄚ ㄌㄠˋ)
a kind of folk song often
sung by beggars

蓮花池(ㄌㄧㄢ ㄏㄨㄚ ㄔˊ)
a lotus pond

蓮經(ㄌㄧㄢ ㄐㄧㄥ)
(Buddhism) the Lotus Sutra
亦作「法華經」

蓮炬(ㄌㄧㄢ ㄐㄩˋ)
ornamental candles in the
shape of lotus flowers

蓮心(ㄌㄧㄢ ㄒㄧㄣ)
the heart of a lotus seed
—my bitter heart

蓮船(ㄌㄧㄢ ㄔㄨㄢˊ)
①tiny boats for collecting
lotus seeds ②large feet of
women(an expression of sarcasm)

蓮實(ㄌㄧㄢ ㄕˊ)
lotus seeds

蓮社(ㄌㄧㄢ ㄕㄜˋ)
①a gathering of scholars
—usually for extemporizing
poems, etc. ②a gathering of
Buddhists ③the White
Lotus sect, a quasi-religious
secret society in the Yüan
Dynasty

蓮子(ㄌㄧㄢ ㄗˇ)
lotus seeds

蓮座(ㄌㄧㄢ ㄗㄨㄛˋ)
the pedestal of a Buddha
statue; a Buddha's seat in
the form of a lotus flower

蓮宗(ㄌㄧㄢ ㄗㄨㄥ)
name of a Buddhist sect,
founded in the Tsin (晉)
Dynasty by Hui Yüan (慧遠)
circa A.D. 390 亦作「淨土宗」

蓮藕(ㄌㄧㄢ ㄡˇ)
the lotus root

蓮霧(ㄌㄧㄢ ㄨˋ)
the wax apple

蓮輿(ㄌㄧㄢ ㄩˊ)
a sedan chair for a woman
in ancient times

【蔻】 5065 ㄎㄡ kow kòu
cardamom seeds 參看「豆蔻」

蔻丹(ㄎㄡ ㄉㄢ)
red nail polish (a transliteration of the trade name
"Cutex")

【蓼】 5066 1. ㄌㄧㄠˇ leau liǎo
1. the smartweed
2. name of a state in today's
Honan Province in the
Epoch of Spring and Au-
tumn
3. a Chinese family name

蓼花(ㄌㄧㄠ ㄏㄨㄚ)
the smartweed

【蓼】 5066 2. ㄌㄨˋ luh lù
(said of vegetation) luxuriant; high

蓼蓼(ㄌㄨˋ ㄌㄨˋ)
(said of vegetation) luxuriant; long and large

蓼莪(ㄌㄨˋ ㄜˊ)
a poem in the *Book of Odes*
(《詩經》) in memory of one's
parents

【蓿】 5067 ㄙㄨ suh sù
(又讀 ㄒㄩ shiu xù)
clover; lucerne

【蔑】 5068
(蔑) ㄇㄧㄝˋ mieh miè
1. to disdain; to slight; to
despise; to neglect; to disregard; to feel contempt for
2. without; none; no
3. to cast away
4. tiny; small

蔑飛(ㄇㄧㄝˋ ㄈㄟ)
to fly past rapidly; to hurtle
or catapult

蔑賤(ㄇㄧㄝˋ ㄐㄧㄢˋ)
humble; lowly

蔑棄(ㄇㄧㄝˋ ㄑㄧˋ)
to despise and cast away

蔑視(ㄇㄧㄝˋ ㄕˋ)
to disdain; to slight; to flout
or disregard (rules, etc.); to
defy (orders, etc.)

蔑如(ㄇㄧㄝˋ ㄖㄨˊ)
to slight; to belittle

【蔓】 5069
1. ㄇㄢˋ mann màn
plants with creeping tendrils
or vines

蔓生植物(ㄇㄢ ㄕㄥ ㄓ ㄨˋ)
creeping plants

蔓說(ㄇㄢˋ ㄕㄨㄛ)
a windy talk

蔓草(ㄇㄢˋ ㄘㄠˇ)
grass that creeps and
spreads fast and luxuriantly;
creeping weeds

蔓延(ㄇㄢˋ ㄧㄢˊ)
to spread; to creep: 葡萄藤沿
牆蔓延. The grapevine creeps
along the wall.

蔓衍(ㄇㄢˋ ㄧㄢˇ)
to spread out far and wide

【蔓】 5069
2. ㄨㄢˊ wann wàn
a tendril; a creeper

【蔓】 5069
3. ㄇㄢˊ man mán
the rape turnip

蔓菁(ㄇㄢˊ ㄐㄧㄥ)
the rape turnip 亦作「蕪菁」

【蒂】 5070
(蔕) ㄉㄧˋ dih dì
a peduncle or footstalk of a
flower or fruit

【蔗】 5071 ㄓㄜˋ jeh zhè
sugarcane

（艸部）

【艸 部】

蔗糖(业さ 去尤)
sugar from sugarcane; cane sugar

蔗酒(业さ り｜ㄡˇ)
an alcoholic drink made with sugarcane juice; rum

蔗漿(业さ り｜ㄤ)
sugarcane pulp

蔗境(业さ り｜ㄥˋ)
(said of circumstances) improving; getting better and better (like eating sugarcane from the stem downward)

蔗汁(业さ 业)
sugarcane juice

【蔚】 5072
1. ㄨㄟˋ wey wèi
1. (said of vegetation) luxuriant; ornamental and colorful
2. Artemisia japonica

蔚藍(ㄨㄟˋ ㄌㄢˊ)
sky-blue

蔚然成風(ㄨㄟˋ ㄖㄢˊ ㄔㄥˊ ㄈㄥ)
to become common practice; to become the order of the day

蔚爲奇觀(ㄨㄟˋ ㄨㄟˊ ㄑ｜ˊ ㄍㄨㄢ)
to present a magnificent sight; to offer a thrilling view

【蔚】 5072
2. ㄩˋ yuh yù
1. a Chinese family name
2. name of a county in Hopeh Province

【蔡】 5073
ㄘㄞˋ tsay cài
1. a large turtle or tortoise (whose shell was used in divination in ancient China)
2. name of an ancient state in the Epoch of Spring and Autumn
3. a Chinese family name

蔡倫(ㄘㄞˋ ㄌㄨㄣˊ)
Tsai Lun, an official in the Eastern Han Dynasty, credited with the invention of paper with bark and rag pulp

蔡襄(ㄘㄞˋ ㄒ｜ㄤ)
Tsai Hsiang, a famed calligrapher of the Sung Dynasty

蔡鍔(ㄘㄞˋ さˋ)
Tsai O, 1882-1916, a general who was the first to rise against Yüan Shih-kai's (袁世凱) plan to become an emperor

蔡文姬(ㄘㄞˋ ㄨㄣˊ ㄐ｜)
Tsai Wen-chi, a talented woman at the end of the Han Dynasty, kidnapped by the northern barbarians for 12 years before she was ransomed

蔡元培(ㄘㄞˋ ㄩㄢˊ ㄆㄟˊ)
Tsai Yüan-pei (1867-1940), a scholar and the first president of the Academia Sinica

蔡邕(ㄘㄞˋ ㄩㄥ)
Tsai Yung, a famous scholar and father of Tsai Wen-chi (蔡文姬)

【蔣】 5074
ㄐ｜ㄤˇ jeang jiǎng
a Chinese family name

蔣中正(ㄐ｜ㄤˇ ㄓㄨㄥ ㄓㄥˋ)or 蔣介石
(ㄐ｜ㄤˇ ㄐ｜ㄝˋ ㄕˊ)
Chiang Kai-shek,1887-1975, late President of the Republic of China (1948-1975)

蔣山(ㄐ｜ㄤˇ ㄕㄢ)
name of a mountain outside Nanking 亦作「紫金山」

【蔥】 5075
(蔥) ㄘㄨㄥ tsong cōng
scallions; onions

【蔦】 5076
ㄋ｜ㄠˇ neau niǎo
Ribes ambiguum, a kind of creeping plant; mistletoe

蔦蘿(ㄋ｜ㄠˇ ㄌㄨㄛˊ)
①ivy ②dependent relatives

【蔬】 5077
ㄕㄨ shu shū
1. vegetables; greens
2. a vegetarian diet; vegetable food

蔬圃(ㄕㄨ ㄆㄨˇ)
a vegetable garden

蔬飯(ㄕㄨ ㄈㄢˋ)
vegetables and rice

蔬糲(ㄕㄨ ㄌ｜ˋ)
wild vegetables and coarse rice—food of the destitute

蔬果(ㄕㄨ ㄍㄨㄛˇ)
vegetables and fruit

蔬食(ㄕㄨ ㄕˊ)
①a vegetarian diet ② simple or coarse food

蔬食主義(ㄕㄨ ㄕˊ ㄓㄨˇ ｜ˋ)
vegetarianism

蔬菜(ㄕㄨ ㄘㄞˋ)
vegetables; greens

【蓴】 5078
(蓴) ㄔㄨㄢˊ chwen chún
Brasenia schreberi, water shield

蓴鱸(ㄔㄨㄢˊ ㄌㄨˊ)
retirement from government office (蓴 and 鱸 being delicacies of a particular locality, which seekers of fortune must deny themselves)

蓴鱸之思(ㄔㄨㄢˊ ㄌㄨˊ ㄓ ㄙ)
homesickness; intention of retiring from office and going back home

蓴羹鱸膾(ㄔㄨㄢˊ ㄍㄥ ㄌㄨˊ ㄎㄨㄞˋ)
delicacies that make one think of retirement from government office in order to return home

蓴菜(ㄔㄨㄢˊ ㄘㄞˋ)
Brasenia schreberi, water shield

【蓽】 5079
(蓽) ㄅ｜ˋ bih bì
1. bamboo or wicker for making baskets, etc.
2. Piper longum, a kind of herb growing among bamboos, used in Chinese medicine

蓽茇(ㄅ｜ˋ ㄅㄚˊ)or 蓽撥(ㄅ｜ˋ ㄅㄛˊ)
(botany) Piper longum, long pepper

蓽門圭竇(ㄅ｜ˋ ㄇㄣˊ ㄍㄨㄟ ㄉㄡˋ)
a small door of bamboo—a house of a poor man

蓽路藍縷 or 蓽路藍褸(ㄅ｜ˋ ㄌㄨˋ ㄌㄢˊ ㄌㄩˇ)
firewood carts and rags—the hard life of pioneers

【蔌】 5080
ㄙㄨˋ suh sù
vegetables

蔌蔌(ㄙㄨˋ ㄙㄨˋ)
①crude and coarse ②the heaving of high winds ③streams or fountains flowing ④flowers falling ⑤descriptive of mean, abject creatures

【蔔】 5081
ㄅㄛˊ bor bó
as in 蘿蔔→a common name for such edible roots as turnips, carrots, radishes

【蔞】 5082 ㄌㄡ lou lóu
a kind of artemisia whose tender leaves are edible

蔞藤 (ㄌㄡ ㄊㄥ)
a kind of vine

蔞蒿 (ㄌㄡ ㄏㄠ)
Artemisia vulgaris, an edible water plant

【蔫】 5083 1. ㄋ1ㄢ nhian nián
1. (said of plants) fading or withering
2. spiritless; ennui; listless
3. calm and quiet; expressionless

蔫了 (ㄋ1ㄢ ·ㄌㄜ)
withered; finished

【蔫】 5083 2. 1ㄢ ian yān
stale; rotting or decaying

【蔭】 5084 1ㄣ yinn yìn
1. the shade of trees; shade
2. to shelter; to protect
3. (with) the support or blessing of

蔭蔽 (1ㄣ ㄅ1)
to shelter; to hide in the shade: 小木屋蔭蔽在樹林中。The log cabin lies hidden among the trees.

蔭庇 (1ㄣ ㄅ1)
to protect; to patronize

蔭涼 (1ㄣ ㄌ1ㄤ)
shady and cool

蔭生 (1ㄣ ㄕㄥ)
(formerly) a student admitted to the Imperial Academy (國子監) because of the meritorious services rendered by his forefathers 亦作「廕生」

蔭翳 (1ㄣ 1)
in the shade of a luxuriant growth of trees or vegetation

【蔯】 5085 ㄔㄣ chern chén
a variety of artemisia

【蔟】 5086 ㄘㄨ tsuh cù
1. a cluster 亦作「簇」
2. a frame on which silkworms spin

蔟聚 (ㄘㄨ ㄐㄩ)
to be crowded together

【莏】 5087 ㄒ1 shii xī
1. a variety of grass
2. five times of anything

【蔴】 5088 (麻) ㄇㄚ ma má
1. hemp
2. sesame; sesamum

十二畫

【蔽】 5089 ㄅ1 bih bì
1. to cover; to cover up
2. to hide; to conceal; to shelter
3. to screen; to separate

蔽目 (ㄅ1 ㄇㄨ)
to cover the eyes; to blindfold

蔽芾 (ㄅ1 ㄈㄟ) or 蔽茀 (ㄅ1 ㄈㄨ)
①tiny; petite ②to be umbrageous

蔽風雨 (ㄅ1 ㄈㄥ ㄩ)
to shelter from the wind and rain

蔽體 (ㄅ1 ㄊ1)
to cover the body

蔽匿 (ㄅ1 ㄋ1)
to hide; to conceal; to lie low

蔽護 (ㄅ1 ㄏㄨ)
to shelter; to take cover; to protect

蔽賢 (ㄅ1 ㄒ1ㄢ)
to keep the capable or virtuous from attaining fame or eminence

蔽形術 (ㄅ1 ㄒ1ㄥ ㄕㄨ)
(Taoism, etc.) a form of witchcraft supposedly capable of making a person invisible

蔽日 (ㄅ1 ㄖ)
to cover the sun from view; to dull the sunlight

蔽塞 (ㄅ1 ㄙㄜ)
①to block up ②stupid or dull; ignorance

蔽野 (ㄅ1 1ㄝ)
(descriptive of numerous banners or exuberant trees) to cover the whole field

蔽月羞花 or 閉月羞花 (ㄅ1 ㄩㄝ ㄒ1ㄡ ㄏㄨㄚ)
(said of a stunning beauty) that outshines the moon and puts flowers to shame

【蕃】 5090 1. ㄈㄢ farn fán
1. (said of vegetation) luxuriant; flourishing
2. to increase; to multiply; to propagate
3. numerous; plentiful

蕃茂 (ㄈㄢ ㄇㄠ)
flourishing and booming; thriving

蕃變 (ㄈㄢ ㄅ1ㄢ)
fabulous; splendid; exceedingly pretty or charming

蕃息 (ㄈㄢ ㄒ1)
to increase and multiply; to propagate in great numbers

蕃殖 (ㄈㄢ ㄓ)
to breed; to multiply; to reproduce; to propagate

蕃昌 (ㄈㄢ ㄔㄤ)
thriving and prosperous; flourishing and booming

蕃庶 (ㄈㄢ ㄕㄨ)
numerous

蕃滋 or 蕃孳 (ㄈㄢ ㄗ)
to multiply or increase in large numbers; to reproduce rapidly

蕃衍 (ㄈㄢ 1ㄢ)
①to increase or multiply in large numbers; to propagate rapidly ②large and luxuriant

蕃蕪 (ㄈㄢ ㄨ)
flourishing and thriving

蕃育 (ㄈㄢ ㄩ)
to increase and multiply in great numbers

【蕃】 5090 2. ㄈㄢ fan fān
barbarians (as opposed to native Chinese); foreign; uncivilized

蕃舶 (ㄈㄢ ㄅㄛ)
(Tang Dynasty) a foreign boat; a boat from a distant land

蕃坊 (ㄈㄢ ㄈㄤ)
(Sung Dynasty) a reservation or settlement for foreigners

蕃椒 (ㄈㄢ ㄐ1ㄠ)
capsicum

蕃茄 (ㄈㄢ ㄑ1ㄝ)
a. tomato: 蕃茄可以生吃。Tomatoes can be eaten uncooked.

〔艸 部〕

（艸部）

番茄醬(ㄈㄢˉㄑㄧㄝˊㄐㄧㄤ)
tomato catsup; tomato paste

番茄汁(ㄈㄢˉㄑㄧㄝˊㄓ)
tomato juice

蕃薯(ㄈㄢˊㄕㄨˇ)
a sweet potato

番人(ㄈㄢ ㄖㄣˊ)
barbarians; uncivilized people

【蕆】 5091
ㄔㄢˇ chaan chǎn
to complete; to finish

【蕉】 5092
ㄐㄧㄠ jiau jiāo
1. the banana
2. the plantain

蕉布(ㄐㄧㄠ ㄅㄨˋ)
cloth made from the fibers of the plantain

蕉風椰雨(ㄐㄧㄠ ㄈㄥ ㄧㄝˊ ㄩˇ)
(literally)banana winds and cocoanut rains—tropical sights

蕉農(ㄐㄧㄠ ㄋㄨㄥˊ)
banana growers

蕉葛(ㄐㄧㄠ ㄍㄜˊ)
linen made from the fibers of the plantain

蕉扇(ㄐㄧㄠ ㄕㄢˋ)
a palm-leaf fan

蕉葉(ㄐㄧㄠ ㄧㄝˋ)
①the leaf of a banana plant
②a very shallow wine-cup

蕉園(ㄐㄧㄠ ㄩㄢˊ)
a banana plantation

【蕊】 5093
ㄖㄨㄟˇ roei ruǐ
1. a flower bud; an unopened flower
2. the stamens or pistils of a flower

【蕎】 5094
ㄑㄧㄠˊ chyau qiáo
buckwheat

蕎麥(ㄑㄧㄠˊ ㄇㄞˋ)
buckwheat

蕎麥麵(ㄑㄧㄠˊ ㄇㄞˋ ㄇㄧㄢˋ)
buckwheat flour ②noodles or vermicelli made with buckwheat flour

【蕕】 5095
ㄧㄡˊ you yóu
Caryopteris divaricata, a water plant with a foul smell that lasts very long —usually used figuratively to indicate an evil person

【蕘】 5096
ㄖㄠˊ rau ráo
1. grass or rushes, etc. used for fuel
2. *Wikstroemia japonica*, a kind of shrub about three feet tall with yellow flowers, whose bark is used for making paper
3. the turnip
4. firewood-gatherers

【蕙】 5097
ㄏㄨㄟˋ huey huì
1. a species of fragrant grass with red flowers and black seeds in early fall
2. a species of fragrant orchid

蕙蘭(ㄏㄨㄟˋ ㄌㄢˊ)
a species of fragrant orchid having seven to eight flowers to one stalk

蕙心(ㄏㄨㄟˋ ㄒㄧㄣ)
a pure heart

蕙質(ㄏㄨㄟˋ ㄓˊ)
a good and pure quality(of a person)

蕙蘭闌心(ㄏㄨㄟˋ ㄓ ㄌㄢˊ ㄒㄧㄣ)
(said of a lady) beautiful and intelligent

蕙折蘭摧(ㄏㄨㄟˋ ㄓㄜˊ ㄌㄢˊ ㄘㄨㄟ)
The good and pure are destroyed.

蕙若(ㄏㄨㄟˋ ㄖㄨㄛˋ)
two species of fragrant grass, used figuratively in reference to good people

【蕡】 5098
ㄈㄣˊ fern fén
1. the seeds of hemp
2. (said of fruit) large and abundant
3. a Chinese family name

【蕞】 5099
ㄗㄨㄟˋ tzuey zuì
very small; tiny

蕞爾小國(ㄗㄨㄟˋ ㄦˇ ㄒㄧㄠˇ ㄍㄨㄛˊ)
a very small state

【蕢】 5100
ㄎㄨㄟˊ kuey kuí
1. a straw basket
2. a vegetable with a red stalk
3. a Chinese family name

【蕨】 5101
ㄐㄩㄝˊ jyue jué
the bracken

【蕭】 5102
ㄒㄧㄠ shiau xiāo
1. a common variety of artemisia; oxtail-southernwood

2. reverent; respectful
3. quiet; lonely; desolate
4. a Chinese family name

蕭伯納(ㄒㄧㄠ ㄅㄛˊ ㄋㄚˋ)
George Bernard Shaw (1856-1950), Irish dramatist and critic

蕭邦(ㄒㄧㄠ ㄅㄤ)
Frederic Francois Chopin (1810-1849), famous Polish pianist and composer

蕭條(ㄒㄧㄠ ㄊㄧㄠˊ)
①(said of a place or situation) deserted; desolate ②(said of business) sluggish; depressed; slack

蕭統(ㄒㄧㄠ ㄊㄨㄥˇ)
Hsiao Tung (501-531), also known as Prince Chao-ming (昭明太子), the compiler of 昭明文選, a 60-volume collection of literary works from the Chin Dynasty down to his era

蕭娘(ㄒㄧㄠ ㄋㄧㄤˊ)
a reference to girls in the poems of the Tang Dynasty

蕭郎(ㄒㄧㄠ ㄌㄤˊ)
a reference to a male-lover in the poems of the Tang Dynasty

蕭梁(ㄒㄧㄠ ㄌㄧㄤˊ)
the Liang Dynasty (502 557) founded by Hsiao Yen(蕭衍), during the South and North Dynasties(南北朝), as distinguished from the Liang Dynasty (後梁, 907-923) of the Five Dynasties(五代)

蕭規曹隨(ㄒㄧㄠ ㄍㄨㄟ ㄘㄠˊ ㄙㄨㄟˊ)
(literally) Hsiao Ho (蕭何) laid down the rules and Tsao Shen (曹參) followed them.—to follow the rules. methods, etc. of one's predecessor; to move in a rut; to follow suit

蕭何(ㄒㄧㄠ ㄏㄜˊ)
Hsiao Ho (? -193), who helped the first emperor of the Han Dynasty unify the whole nation and who authored many laws and regulations observed during the Han Dynasty

蕭牆之禍(ㄒㄧㄠ ㄑㄧㄤˊ ㄓ ㄏㄨㄛˋ)
a civil strife, disaster or trouble within

蕭蕭（ㄒ丨ㄠ ㄒ丨ㄠ）
①the whistling of strong winds ②the rustling sound of falling leaves ③the neighing of a horse

蕭齋（ㄒ丨ㄠ ㄓ）
①a humble house ②a Buddhist temple

蕭晨（ㄒ丨ㄠ ㄔㄣ）
the autumn morning

蕭疏（ㄒ丨ㄠ ㄕㄨ）
(said of leaves) scattered and bleak

蕭然（ㄒ丨ㄠ ㄖㄢˊ）
①desolate; deserted ②in commotion; disorderly

蕭寺（ㄒ丨ㄠ ㄙˋ）
monasteries in the Liang Dynasty, A.D. 502-557, because Liang Wu Ti (梁武帝) built so many that they were called after his surname Hsiao (蕭)

蕭灑（ㄒ丨ㄠ ㄙˇ）
elegant; stately and easy (in one's appearance and manner)

蕭颯（ㄒ丨ㄠ ㄙㄚˋ）
cool and soothing winds of autumn

蕭瑟（ㄒ丨ㄠ ㄙㄜˋ）
①rough and stormy; chilly, desolate, deserted, lonely, etc ②rustle in the air; to rustle; to sough: 秋風蕭瑟。 The autumn wind is soughing.

蕭騷（ㄒ丨ㄠ ㄙㄠ）
desolate; lonely

蕭散（ㄒ丨ㄠ ㄙㄢˇ）
uninhibited and carefree

蕭寥（ㄒ丨ㄠ ㄌ一ㄠˊ）
desolate; lonely

蕭索（ㄒ丨ㄠ ㄙㄨㄛˇ）
deserted; chilly; lonely

蕭艾（ㄒ丨ㄠ ㄞˋ）
the worst variety of grass—evil elements

【蕤】 5103
ㄖㄨㄟˊ ruei ruí
1. drooping leaves, flowers or fruits
2. a shrub about three feet tall with narrow leaves and white flowers

蕤賓（ㄖㄨㄟˊ ㄅ一ㄣ）
a musical pitch roughly equivalent to an F-sharp

【蕩】 5104
ㄉㄤˋ dang dàng
1. a pond; a pool
2. to cleanse; to wash away
3. to shake; to oscillate; to move to and fro; unsettled; vagrant; to loaf about
4. dissipated; wanton; debauched; licentious; of loose morals
5. agitated; disturbed
6. vast; large; magnificent

蕩平（ㄉㄤˋ ㄆ一ㄥˊ）
to quell (a rebellion); to wipe out

蕩婦（ㄉㄤˋ ㄈㄨˋ）
a woman of loose morals; a dissolute woman

蕩蕩（ㄉㄤˋ ㄉㄤˋ）
①vast; large ②to be satisfied and composed ③spoilt or ruined

蕩漾悠悠（ㄉㄤˋ ㄉㄤˋ 一ㄡ 一ㄡ）
swinging; moving to and fro; to shake and move

蕩滌（ㄉㄤˋ ㄉ一ˊ）
to cleanse; to wash out; to clean up: 他們蕩滌水溝。 They cleaned up the ditch.

蕩寇（ㄉㄤˋ ㄎㄡˋ）
to eliminate bandits

蕩檢逾閑（ㄉㄤˋ ㄐ一ㄢˇ ㄩˊ ㄒ一ㄢˊ）
not restrained by propriety or rules; wanton

蕩氣迴腸（ㄉㄤˋ ㄑ一ˋ ㄏㄨㄟˊ ㄔㄤˊ）
(said of music or writing) very touching; pathetic

蕩鞦韆（ㄉㄤˋ ㄑ一ㄡ ㄑ一ㄢ）
to swing on a swing

蕩析（ㄉㄤˋ ㄒ一）
(said of the people in troubled times) dispersed or separated

蕩產（ㄉㄤˋ ㄔㄢˇ）
to bankrupt; to be bankrupt; to go bankrupt

蕩產傾家（ㄉㄤˋ ㄔㄢˇ ㄑ一ㄥ ㄐ一ㄚ）
to squander inherited property and ruin the family

蕩船（ㄉㄤˋ ㄔㄨㄢˊ）
to row a boat; boating

蕩然（ㄉㄤˋ ㄖㄢˊ）
all gone; entirely wasted or spent

蕩然無存（ㄉㄤˋ ㄖㄢˊ ㄨˊ ㄘㄨㄣˊ）
to have nothing left; everything ruined; completely gone; wiped out

蕩子（ㄉㄤˋ ㄗˇ）
①a vagrant; a jobless and dissipated person ②a traveler to a distant land having no thought of returning home

蕩漾（ㄉㄤˋ 一ㄤˋ）
①moving, as in ripples: 湖水蕩漾。 There were ripples on the lake. ②agitated or excited ③to rise and fall like waves; to ripple: 金黃色的稻子在微風中蕩漾。 The golden rice rippled in the breeze.

〔艸 部〕

【蕁】 5105
ㄒㄩㄣˊ shyun xún
as in 蕁麻—an urtica

蕁麻（ㄒㄩㄣˊ ㄇㄚˊ）
an urtica; a nettle

蕁麻疹（ㄒㄩㄣˊ ㄇㄚˊ ㄓㄣˇ）
(pathology) nettle rash; urticaria 亦作「風疹」

【蕈】 5106
ㄒㄩㄣˋ shiunn xùn
1. a mushroom; fungus
2. mold, or mildew

【蕪】 5107
ㄨˊ wu wú
1. a luxuriant growth of weeds
2. decayed or rotten vegetation
3. confused; mixed-up; in disorder
4. waste; neglected, as land

蕪駁（ㄨˊ ㄅㄛˊ）
disorderly or mixed-up; confused

蕪累（ㄨˊ ㄌㄟˇ）
mixed-up and superfluous

蕪俚（ㄨˊ ㄌ一ˇ）
coarse and vulgar

蕪湖（ㄨˊ ㄏㄨˊ）
Wuhu, name of a lake and a county in Anhwei Province

蕪穢（ㄨˊ ㄏㄨㄟˋ）
the luxuriant growth of weeds in deserted fields

蕪菁（ㄨˊ ㄐ一ㄥ）
the turnip

蕪雜（ㄨˊ ㄗㄚˊ）
(usually referring to a piece of writing) disorderly and confusing; mixed-up and illogical

（艸部）

【藘】 5108
ㄑㄩ chyu qū

1. a taro
2. as in 芙蕖 —a lotus flower

【藈】 5109
ㄐㄩㄝ jyue jué

as in 茅蕝 —to designate an assigned position in practicing a court ceremony

【蕓】 5110
ㄩㄣ yun yún

蕓薹（ㄩㄣ ㄊㄞˊ）
rape 亦作「油菜」

十三畫

【薄】 5111
1. ㄅㄛˊ bor bó
（語音 ㄅㄠˊ baur báo）

1. thin; light; slight: 這是一張薄紙。This is a thin sheet of paper.
2. to despise; to slight; to disdain: 他薄此薄彼。He favored this and slighted that.
3. barren; not fertile
4. to cover; to hide or conceal; to shut
5. a screen
6. a patch of grass
7. to close in; to press near: 日薄西山。The sun is near the western hills.
8. an initial particle—ah; so; now
9. frivolous: 它是輕薄的話。It is a frivolous remark.
10. a Chinese family name

薄餅（ㄅㄛˊ ㄅㄧㄥˇ）
thin pancakes for wrapping up meat, vegetables, etc.

薄片（ㄅㄛˊ ㄆㄧㄢˋ）
a thin slice; a thin section: 他把檸檬切成薄片。He cut a lemon into thin slices.

薄嫵（ㄅㄛˊ ㄇㄛˇ）
very light make-up—that adds more to her charms

薄命（ㄅㄛˊ ㄇㄧㄥˋ）
①star-crossed; ill-fated; born unlucky (usually referring to young and beautiful girls) ②short-lived: 她是個薄命佳人。She was a short-lived beauty.

薄命女子負心漢（ㄅㄛˊ ㄇㄧㄥˋ ㄋㄩˇ ㄗˇ ㄈㄨˋ ㄒㄧㄣ ㄏㄢˋ）
an unfortunate girl and a heartless man

薄暮（ㄅㄛˊ ㄇㄨˋ）
around sunset; dusk

薄暮之年（ㄅㄛˊ ㄇㄨˋ ㄓ ㄋㄧㄢˊ）
old age; approaching one's grave; the sunset of life

薄夫（ㄅㄛˊ ㄈㄨ）
a person with little sentiment or affection

薄福（ㄅㄛˊ ㄈㄨˊ）
(a life) with little joy, happiness or bliss

薄待（ㄅㄛˊ ㄉㄞˋ）
to treat (a person) rather badly: 她一向薄待他人。She always treats others badly.

薄田（ㄅㄛˊ ㄊㄧㄢˊ）
barren or unfertile land

薄陋（ㄅㄛˊ ㄌㄡˋ）
without talent or ability

薄禮（ㄅㄛˊ ㄌㄧˇ）
a meager present; my humble gift (as a polite usage)

薄利多銷（ㄅㄛˊ ㄌㄧˋ ㄉㄨㄛ ㄒㄧㄠ）
small profits but a quick turnover; small profits and quick returns; to cut down the profit margin in order to sell more—commercial tactics

薄海騰歡（ㄅㄛˊ ㄏㄞˇ ㄊㄥˊ ㄏㄨㄢ）
cheers from all over the country

薄宦（ㄅㄛˊ ㄏㄨㄢˋ）
a low-ranking official position

薄技（ㄅㄛˊ ㄐㄧˋ）
meager skills or feats not worth mentioning; my poor skill (a polite usage)

薄酒（ㄅㄛˊ ㄐㄧㄡˇ）
(a polite expression) dilute wine

薄具（ㄅㄛˊ ㄐㄩˋ）
(a polite expression) coarse food

薄情（ㄅㄛˊ ㄑㄧㄥˊ）
heartless; ungrateful

薄情郎（ㄅㄛˊ ㄑㄧㄥˊ ㄌㄤˊ）
a heartless lover; an unfaithful husband

薄曉（ㄅㄛˊ ㄒㄧㄠˇ）
around sunrise; dawn

薄行（ㄅㄛˊ ㄒㄧㄥˊ）
unscrupulous conduct; immoral behavior

薄倖（ㄅㄛˊ ㄒㄧㄥˋ）
heartlessness (especially concerning love)

薄懲（ㄅㄛˊ ㄔㄥˊ）
a light punishment

薄生生的（ㄅㄛˊ ㄕㄥ ㄕㄥ ㄉㄜ˙）
thin and easily breakable

薄弱（ㄅㄛˊ ㄖㄨㄛˋ）
weak; fragile: 他是個意志薄弱之人。He is a man of weak character.

薄脆（ㄅㄛˊ ㄘㄨㄟˋ）
thin and brittle (biscuits)

薄俗（ㄅㄛˊ ㄙㄨˊ）
very practical customs that reflect no sense of hospitality, love, etc.

薄物細故（ㄅㄛˊ ㄨˋ ㄒㄧˋ ㄍㄨˋ）
trifles; trivial matters

【薄】 5111
2. ㄅㄛˊ boh bò

薄荷（ㄅㄛˊ ㄏㄜˊ）
peppermint

薄荷（ㄅㄛˊ ㄏㄜˊ）
peppermint

薄荷精（ㄅㄛˊ ㄏㄜˊ ㄐㄧㄥ）or 薄荷腦（ㄅㄛˊ ㄏㄜˊ ㄋㄠˇ）
menthol

薄荷油（ㄅㄛˊ ㄏㄜˊ ㄧㄡˊ）
peppermint oil

【薅】 5112
ㄏㄠ hau hāo

1. to weed (rice fields, etc.); to root out; to pick off; to clear away

【薯】 5113
ㄩˋ yuh yù

as in 薯蕷—the Chinese yam

【蕾】 5114
ㄌㄟˇ leei lěi

as in 蓓蕾—a flower bud; an unopened flower

【薆】 5115
ㄞˋ ay ài

1. a luxuriant growth of vegetation
2. to cover; to hide; to conceal; to be under cover

【薇】 5116
ㄨㄟˊ wei wéi

1. Osmunda regalis, a kind of fern; thorn-ferns
2. used with other characters for a variety of plants

【薈】 5117
ㄏㄨㄟˋ huey huì

1. a luxuriant growth of vegetation
2. to cover or conceal

薈萃（ㄏㄨㄟˋ ㄘㄨㄟˋ）
①flourishing or thriving ②

(said of distinguished people) to gather; to assemble

薈蔚（ㄏㄨㄟˋ ㄨㄟˋ）
a dense and luxuriant growth of vegetation

【薊】 5118
ㄐㄧˋ jih jì
1. *Cirsium*, a family of thorny plants
2. a Chinese family name

【薌】 5119
ㄒㄧㄤ shiang xiāng
1. the smell of rice grains
2. aromatic; spicy; a pleasant smell
3. incense used for fumigation

【薏】 5120
ㄧˋ yih yì
1. the heart of a lotus seed
2. the seeds of Job's tears; pearl barley, used for cooking congee with rice in herbal medicine

薏米（ㄧˋ ㄇㄧˇ）
(Chinese medicine) the seed of Job's tears 亦作「薏仁米」

【薐】 5121
ㄌㄥˊ leng léng
old name of spinach

【薑】 5122
ㄐㄧㄤ jiang jiāng
ginger

薑餅（ㄐㄧㄤ ㄅㄧㄥˇ）
gingerbread; gingersnaps: 他喜歡吃薑餅。 He likes gingerbread.

薑片蟲（ㄐㄧㄤ ㄆㄧㄢˋ ㄔㄨㄥˊ）
Fasciolopsis buski, an intestinal parasite

薑桂（ㄐㄧㄤ ㄍㄨㄟˋ）
①ginger and cinnamon ②stubborn; unyielding; unshakable

薑黃（ㄐㄧㄤ ㄏㄨㄤˊ）
curcuma; turmeric

薑紙（ㄐㄧㄤ ㄓˇ）
curcuma paper; turmeric paper

薑酒（ㄐㄧㄤ ㄐㄧㄡˇ）
ginger wine

薑汁（ㄐㄧㄤ ㄓ）
ginger juice

薑汁汽水（ㄐㄧㄤ ㄓ ㄑㄧˋ ㄕㄨㄟˇ）
ginger ale

【薔】 5123
ㄑㄧㄤˊ chyang qiáng
the roses

薔薇（ㄑㄧㄤˊ ㄨㄟˊ）
the roses

薔薇科（ㄑㄧㄤˊ ㄨㄟˊ ㄎㄜ）
Rosaceae, the rose family

薔薇戰爭（ㄑㄧㄤˊ ㄨㄟˊ ㄓㄢˋ ㄓㄥ）
Britain's "War of the Roses" (1455-1485)

【薙】 5124
ㄊㄧˋ tih tì
1. to weed
2. to cut (hair); to shave (hair)

薙髮（ㄊㄧˋ ㄈㄚˇ）
to cut hair; a haircut; to shave hair

薙刀（ㄊㄧˋ ㄉㄠ）
a shaving knife or razor

【薛】 5125
ㄒㄩㄝ shiue xué
1. a kind of marsh grass
2. name of an ancient state in today's Shantung Province
3. a Chinese family name

【薤】 5126
ㄒㄧㄝˋ shieh xiè
Allium bakeri, a vegetable roughly resembling a leek with tiny purple flowers in summer whose scaly stalks are edible when tender

薤露（ㄒㄧㄝˋ ㄌㄨˋ）
name of an ancient funeral song

【薦】 5127
ㄐㄧㄢˋ jiann jiàn
1. to recommend; to offer; to present
2. fodder for animals; grass
3. a straw mat; a mat, especially for sleeping
4. food and dishes
5. to repeat; repeatedly

薦拔（ㄐㄧㄢˋ ㄅㄚˊ）
to recommend and promote

薦酒（ㄐㄧㄢˋ ㄐㄧㄡˇ）
to offer wine

薦舉（ㄐㄧㄢˋ ㄐㄩˇ）or 薦引（ㄐㄧㄢˋ ㄧㄣˇ）
to propose; to introduce; to recommend (a competent person for a post): 他薦引同志。 He introduced a comrade.

薦賢（ㄐㄧㄢˋ ㄒㄧㄢˊ）
to recommend, introduce or present a good and capable person

薦賢自代（ㄐㄧㄢˋ ㄒㄧㄢˊ ㄗˋ ㄉㄞˋ）
to recommend one's own

successor upon leaving a post; to recommend a good man in place of oneself

薦枕席（ㄐㄧㄢˋ ㄓㄣˇ ㄒㄧˊ）
(said of a woman) to volunteer to sleep with a man

薦擢（ㄐㄧㄢˋ ㄓㄨㄛˊ）
to recommend and employ

薦任（ㄐㄧㄢˋ ㄖㄣˋ）
recommended appointment rank, the second of the three grades in the civil service of modern China

薦任官（ㄐㄧㄢˋ ㄖㄣˋ ㄍㄨㄢ）
an official of recommended appointment rank

薦材（ㄐㄧㄢˋ ㄘㄞˊ）
to recommend or present a talented person

【薨】 5128
ㄏㄨㄥ hong hōng
1. the death of a feudal lord
2. the loud buzzing of insects in flight

薨薨（ㄏㄨㄥ ㄏㄨㄥ）
①the loud buzzing of insects in flight ②the chattering and shouting of the people ③numerous

【薪】 5129
ㄒㄧㄣ shin xīn
1. firewood; fuel; faggots
2. salary; pay

薪俸（ㄒㄧㄣ ㄈㄥˋ）or 薪金（ㄒㄧㄣ ㄐㄧㄣ）or 薪水（ㄒㄧㄣ ㄕㄨㄟˇ）
one's salary or pay; wages

薪桂米珠（ㄒㄧㄣ ㄍㄨㄟˋ ㄇㄧˇ ㄓㄨ）
the high cost of living (with firewood bought at the price of cinnamon and rice at the price of pearls)

薪工（ㄒㄧㄣ ㄍㄨㄥ）
wages; pay

薪火（ㄒㄧㄣ ㄏㄨㄛˇ）
①a torch ②the torch of learning passed from master to pupil

薪盡火傳（ㄒㄧㄣ ㄐㄧㄣˋ ㄏㄨㄛˇ ㄔㄨㄢˊ）or 薪傳（ㄒㄧㄣ ㄔㄨㄢˊ）
a learning, skill, etc. passing from master to pupil in endless succession

薪水階級（ㄒㄧㄣ ㄕㄨㄟˇ ㄐㄧㄝ ㄐㄧˊ）
the white-collar workers

【蕺】 5130
ㄐㄧˊ jyi jí
Houttuynia cordata, a smelly

（艸部）

but edible vegetable with light yellow flowers in summer 亦作「藊菜」

【薜】 5131
1. ㄅㄛ boh bò
Chinese angelica; angelica radix 亦作「當歸」

【薜】 5131
2. ㄅㄧˋ bih bì
Ficus pumila, a climbing fig 參看「薜荔」

薜荔（ㄅㄧˋ ㄌㄧˋ）
Ficus pumila; a climbing fig

薜蘿（ㄅㄧˋ ㄌㄨㄛˊ）
the clothing of a hermit

十四畫

【薩】 5132
1. ㄙㄚˋ sah sà
1. a general name of Buddhist gods or immortals; Buddha
2. a Chinese family name

薩摩亞（ㄙㄚˋ ㄇㄛˊ ㄧㄚˋ）
Samoa

薩克遜人（ㄙㄚˋ ㄎㄜˋ ㄒㄩㄣˋ ㄖㄣˊ）
the Saxons

薩爾瓦多（ㄙㄚˋ ㄦˇ ㄨㄚˇ ㄉㄨㄛ）
El Salvador

薩伊（ㄙㄚˋ ㄧ）
Republic of Zaire

【薯】 5133
ㄕㄨˇ shuu shǔ
a yam; a potato

薯條（ㄕㄨˇ ㄊㄧㄠˊ）
French fries: 他喜歡吃薯條。
He likes French fries.

薯蕷（ㄕㄨˇ ㄩˋ）
a yam 亦作「山藥」

【薰】 5134
ㄒㄩㄣ shiun xūn
1. to cauterize
2. to perfume; to embalm
3. to smoke; to fumigate
4. warm
5. Coumarouna odorata, a medical herb with a strong smell

薰沐（ㄒㄩㄣ ㄇㄨˋ）
to burn incense and take a bath—a gesture of great respect

薰風（ㄒㄩㄣ ㄈㄥ）
a warm wind from the south

薰腐（ㄒㄩㄣ ㄈㄨˇ）
the punishment of castration in ancient China

薰陶（ㄒㄩㄣ ㄊㄠˊ）
to mold a person's character, etc. through the influence of education, proper discipline, good examples, etc.; to edify

薰爐（ㄒㄩㄣ ㄌㄨˊ）
a brazier

薰心（ㄒㄩㄣ ㄒㄧㄣ）
to becloud the mind (with lust, greed, sexual desire, etc.): 他遭人利慾薰心。His mind is beclouded by greed.

薰香（ㄒㄩㄣ ㄒㄧㄤ）
perfume; fragrance

薰蒸（ㄒㄩㄣ ㄓㄥ）
(said of the sultry heat in summer) to swelter and steam

薰薰（ㄒㄩㄣ ㄖㄣˊ）
gently; amiably; warmly

薰染（ㄒㄩㄣ ㄖㄢˇ）
to be influenced and contaminated by one's surroundings

薰蕕（ㄒㄩㄣ ㄧˊ）
fragrant and noisome grasses —good and evil people

【薺】 5135
1. ㄐㄧˋ jih jì
Capsella bursa-pastoris, a kind of vegetable; shepherd's-purse

薺菜（ㄐㄧˋ ㄘㄞˋ）
shepherd's-purse (Capsella bursa-pastoris)

【薺】 5135
2. ㄑㄧˊ chyi qí
1. the caltrop 亦作「茨藜」
2. a water chestnut 亦作「荸薺」

【藉】 5136
1. ㄐㄧㄝˋ jieh jiè
1. a mat, pad, or cushion of grass (or straw)
2. to rely on; to lean on; on the strength of; to avail oneself of; by means of: 憑藉你自己的努力。Rely on your own efforts.
3. on the excuse or pretext of

藉端（ㄐㄧㄝˋ ㄉㄨㄢ）
on the excuse or pretext of

藉端敲詐（ㄐㄧㄝˋ ㄉㄨㄢ ㄑㄧ ㄓㄚˋ）
to blackmail by taking advantage of a certain occasion or occurrence

藉端生事（ㄐㄧㄝˋ ㄉㄨㄢ ㄕㄥ ㄕˋ）
to stir up trouble on the pretext or excuse of something

藉故（ㄐㄧㄝˋ ㄍㄨˋ）
to avail oneself of a certain excuse or pretext

藉故推辭（ㄐㄧㄝˋ ㄍㄨˋ ㄊㄨㄟ ㄘˊ）
to decline or reject with an excuse or pretext

藉口（ㄐㄧㄝˋ ㄎㄡˇ）
an excuse; a pretext; to seize an excuse or pretext: 那不是一個好藉口。It is not a good excuse

藉重（ㄐㄧㄝˋ ㄓㄨㄥˋ）
(a polite expression) to rely on (your, his or her) capability

藉手（ㄐㄧㄝˋ ㄕㄡˇ）
by means of; by (another's) hand, as a murder, etc.

藉甚（ㄐㄧㄝˋ ㄕㄣˋ）
(said of reputation) exalted; great

藉以（ㄐㄧㄝˋ ㄧˇ）
to avail oneself of something in order to

藉詞（ㄐㄧㄝˋ ㄘˊ）
to make excuses; on the pretext of 參看「藉口」: 他藉詞卸責。He shirked his responsibility by making an excuse.

藉此（ㄐㄧㄝˋ ㄘˇ）
in order to; by means of; to take advantage of: 我們並未好好藉此機會發揮。We're not taking proper advantage of this opportunity.

【藉】 5136
2. ㄐㄧˊ jyi jí
disorder; confusion

藉藉（ㄐㄧˊ ㄐㄧˊ）
(in) disorder or confusion

【藍】 5137
ㄌㄢˊ lan lán
1. blue; indigo: 他打著一條藍領帶。He wears a blue necktie.
2. an indigo plant
3. a Chinese family name

藍寶石（ㄌㄢˊ ㄅㄠˇ ㄕˊ）
sapphire

藍本（ㄌㄢˊ ㄅㄣˇ）
the original; a blueprint

藍布（ㄌㄢˊ ㄅㄨˋ）
blue cloth

藍布大掛（ㄌㄢˊ ㄅㄨˋ ㄉㄚˋ ㄍㄚˋ ㄨㄞˋ）
the long blue-cloth gown worn by men

藍皮書（ㄌㄢˊ ㄆㄧˊ ㄕㄨ）
the blue book

藍方石(ㄌㄢ ㄈㄤ ㄕˊ)
haüynite

藍靛(ㄌㄢ ㄉㄧㄢˋ)
indigo

藍銅鑛(ㄌㄢ ㄊㄨㄥˊ ㄎㄨㄤˋ)
vivianite

藍田(ㄌㄢ ㄊㄧㄢˊ)
name of a county and a hill
in Shensi Province, famous
for producing precious jade

藍田種玉(ㄌㄢ ㄊㄧㄢˊ ㄓㄨㄥˇ ㄩˋ)
to make a girl or woman
impregnated

藍田生玉(ㄌㄢ ㄊㄧㄢˊ ㄕㄥ ㄩˋ)
A good and capable father
begets good and capable
sons.

藍鑛(ㄌㄢ ㄎㄨㄤˋ)
a blueprint; an outline of a
project

藍銅鑛(ㄌㄢ ㄊㄨㄥˊ ㄎㄨㄤˋ)
azurite

藍領階級(ㄌㄢ ㄌㄧㄥˇ ㄐㄧㄝ ㄐㄧˊ)
blue-collar

藍晶石(ㄌㄢ ㄐㄧㄥ ㄕˊ)
cyanite

藍青(ㄌㄢ ㄑㄧㄥ)
①indigo blue; a color that
combines blue and green ②
mixed (especially referring
to a form of spoken Mandarin)

藍青官話(ㄌㄢ ㄑㄧㄥ ㄍㄨㄢ ㄏㄨㄚˋ)
spoken Mandarin with a
local accent

藍試紙(ㄌㄢ ㄕˋ ㄓˇ)
litmus paper

藍色申報(ㄌㄢ ㄙㄜˋ ㄕㄣ ㄅㄠˋ)
a blue return

【藎】 5138
ㄐㄧㄣˋ jinn jìn
1. Arthraxon hispidus, a kind
of weed whose stalk is used
as a yellow dye
2. faithfulness; great loyalty
and love

藎臣(ㄐㄧㄣˋ ㄔㄣˊ)
a loyal official; a loyal minister

【藏】 5139
1. ㄘㄤˊ tsarng cáng
1. to hide; to conceal
2. to store; to save; to hoard:
松鼠蓄藏堅果過冬。A squirrel
hoards nuts for the winter.
3. a Chinese family name

藏不住(ㄘㄤˊ ㄅㄨˋ ㄓㄨˋ)

cannot be hidden ((any
longer); (said of a talkative
person) cannot keep a
secret: 他藏不住秘密。He can
not keep a secret.

藏鋒(ㄘㄤˊ ㄈㄥ)
①hidden talent or ability
(which one doesn't want to
reveal unless absolutely necessary)②a style of calligraphy

藏伏(ㄘㄤˊ ㄈㄨˊ)
to hide or conceal; to lie low

藏頭露尾(ㄘㄤˊ ㄊㄡˊ ㄌㄨˋ ㄨㄟˇ)
(literally) to hide the head
but show the tail—① to try
to hide something without
success ② to reveal part of
the truth and conceal the
rest

藏匿(ㄘㄤˊ ㄋㄧˋ)
to hide; to conceal; to harbor (criminals)

藏怒(ㄘㄤˊ ㄋㄨˋ)
to harbor wrath in one's
mind; to lay up anger

藏垢納污(ㄘㄤˊ ㄍㄡˋ ㄋㄚˋ ㄨ)
(said of disreputable places)
to receive evil people; to
harbor criminals

藏度(ㄘㄤˊ ㄉㄨˋ)
to store or hoard

藏嬌(ㄘㄤˊ ㄐㄧㄠ)
to keep one's mistress at a
secret residence; to marry a
concubine

藏奸(ㄘㄤˊ ㄐㄧㄢ)
①to harbor treachery or
guilt ②unwilling to help
another though one has
power to spare

藏器待時(ㄘㄤˊ ㄑㄧˋ ㄉㄞˋ ㄕˊ)
to wait for the right mo-
ment to demonstrate one's
ability; to use one's talent
or ability when the time
comes

藏拙(ㄘㄤˊ ㄓㄨㄛˊ)
to hide one's weak points; to
keep one's weaknesses unexposed

藏室史(ㄘㄤˊ ㄕˋ ㄕˇ)
an official librarian in
ancient China

藏身(ㄘㄤˊ ㄕㄣ)
to hide oneself; to go into
hiding; to conceal: 他無處藏

身。He has no place to hide.

藏身之地(ㄘㄤˊ ㄕㄣ ㄓ ㄉㄧˋ)
a hiding place; a place to
hide oneself; a hideout; a
place to keep oneself out of
sight

藏書(ㄘㄤˊ ㄕㄨ)
①to collect books ②a book
collection

藏書目錄(ㄘㄤˊ ㄕㄨ ㄇㄨˋ ㄌㄨˋ)
a library catalogue

藏書樓(ㄘㄤˊ ㄕㄨ ㄌㄡˊ)
a library

藏書家(ㄘㄤˊ ㄕㄨ ㄐㄧㄚ)
a book collector; a bibliophile: 他是個藏書家。He is a
bibliophile.

藏躲躲(ㄘㄤˊ ㄘㄤˇ ㄉㄨㄛˇ ㄉㄨㄛˇ)
unwilling to appear before
others because of social
timidity, bashfulness or a
secret

藏私(ㄘㄤˊ ㄙ)
to hide part of a full
account of something; un-
willing to reveal all

藏掖(ㄘㄤˊ ㄧㄝ)
①a hiding place; a hideout
②to conceal or hide a dishonest act, etc.

【藏】 5139
2. ㄗㄤˋ tzanq zàng
1. Tibet; Tibetans
2. a storage; a warehouse; a
depository
3. a collective name for the
Buddhist and Taoist scriptures

藏胞(ㄗㄤˋ ㄅㄠ)
the Tibetans (used in the
sense that they form part of
the Chinese race)

藏府(ㄗㄤˋ ㄈㄨˇ)
a storage; a warehouse; government coffers

藏紅(ㄗㄤˋ ㄏㄨㄥˊ)
a reddish-blue color

藏青(ㄗㄤˋ ㄑㄧㄥ)
indigo blue

藏族(ㄗㄤˋ ㄗㄨˊ)
the Tibetans; the Tibetan
people

藏文(ㄗㄤˋ ㄨㄣˊ)
the Tibetan language

【藐】 5140
ㄇㄧㄠˇ meau miǎo
1. to slight; to despise; to belit-

艸部

tle; to treat with disdain
2. small, petite; petty; insignificant

蔑蔑(ㄇㄧㄝˋ ㄇㄧㄝˋ)
①descriptive of a contemptuous manner ② (said of Heaven) high and distant—mysterious ③ grand; magnificent

蔑法(ㄇㄧㄝˋ ㄈㄚˇ)
to disregard the law; to treat the law with contempt

蔑孤(ㄇㄧㄝˋ ㄍㄨ)
a small orphan

蔑小(ㄇㄧㄝˋ ㄒㄧㄠˇ)
small; petty; insignificant

蔑視(ㄇㄧㄝˋ ㄕˋ)
to treat with contempt or disdain; to disdain; to slight; to look down upon; to despise; to belittle

蔑視一切(ㄇㄧㄝˋ ㄕˋ ㄧ ㄑㄧㄝˋ)
to treat everything lightly or carelessly; to look down upon everything; to despise everything

【蒐】 5141
ㄨㄟ wei1 wei3
1. polygala, a herb
2. a Chinese family name

十五畫

【藕】 5142
ㄡˇ oou3 ou3
rhizomes, or rootstocks of the lotus
① rootstocks of the lotus
②(figuratively) woman's or child's white and fat arms

藕粉(ㄡˇ ㄈㄣˇ)
starch extracted from the rhizomes of lotuses

藕斷絲連(ㄡˇ ㄉㄨㄢˋ ㄙ ㄌㄧㄢˊ)
The rootstock is split but the fibers are still joined. —The ties are severed but not completely.

藕花(ㄡˇ ㄏㄨㄚ)
a lotus flower

藕灰(ㄡˇ ㄏㄨㄟ)
light grayish red

藕節(ㄡˇ ㄐㄧㄝˊ)or 藕節兒(ㄡˇ ㄐㄧㄝˊㄦ)
joints of the rhizome of a lotus

藕絲(ㄡˇ ㄙ)
the fibers of the rhizome of

a lotus

藕色(ㄡˇ ㄙㄜˋ)
light grayish red; pale purple

【藜】 5143
ㄌㄧˊ lii2 li2
pigweeds; lamb's-quarters

藜藿(ㄌㄧˊ ㄏㄨㄛˋ)
coarse food

藜藿(ㄌㄧˊ ㄏㄨㄛˋ)
coarse food (of commoners in ancient times)

藜蕨不采(ㄌㄧˊ ㄏㄨㄛˋ ㄅㄨˋ ㄘㄞˇ)
not daring to go to the hills to pick edible grass

藜蕨(ㄌㄧˊ ㄐㄩㄝˊ)
coarse food

藜杖(ㄌㄧˊ ㄓㄤˋ)
a pigweed staff

藜林(ㄌㄧˊ ㄌㄧㄣˊ)
a pigweed bed

【藝】 5144
ㄧˋ yih4 yi4
art; skill; talent; craft; dexterity: 她繪畫的技藝很高。 She has great skill in painting.

藝名(ㄧˋ ㄇㄧㄥˊ)
a stage name, or a screen name (of an entertainer)

藝徒(ㄧˋ ㄊㄨˊ)
an apprentice

藝能(ㄧˋ ㄋㄥˊ)
artistic skill; art; skill

藝林(ㄧˋ ㄌㄧㄣˊ)
①an artistic or literary salon ② the world of art; the artistic circles

藝林瓌寶(ㄧˋ ㄌㄧㄣˊ ㄍㄨㄟ ㄅㄠˇ)
a collection of art treasures

藝高膽大(ㄧˋ ㄍㄠ ㄉㄢˇ ㄉㄚˋ)
The talented or skilled are generally bold. 或 Boldness of execution stems from superb skill.

藝妓(ㄧˋ ㄐㄧˋ)
a geisha girl; a geisha

藝術(ㄧˋ ㄕㄨˋ)
art

藝術品(ㄧˋ ㄕㄨˋ ㄆㄧㄣˇ)
a work of art; an objet d'art

藝術天才(ㄧˋ ㄕㄨˋ ㄊㄧㄢ ㄘㄞˊ)
a gift for art; an artistic talent

藝術家(ㄧˋ ㄕㄨˋ ㄐㄧㄚ)
an artist: 他是個大藝術家。He is a great artist.

藝術界(ㄧˋ ㄕㄨˋ ㄐㄧㄝˋ)
the world of art; the artistic circles

藝術教育(ㄧˋ ㄕㄨˋ ㄐㄧㄠˋ ㄩˋ)
art education

藝術學系(ㄧˋ ㄕㄨˋ ㄒㄩㄝˊ ㄒㄧˋ)
the department of fine arts (in a college or university)

藝術之宮(ㄧˋ ㄕㄨˋ ㄓ ㄍㄨㄥ)
the Palace of Art (as coined by the poet Tennyson)

藝術至上主義(ㄧˋ ㄕㄨˋ ㄓˋ ㄕㄤˋ ㄓㄨˇ ㄧˋ)
art for art's sake

藝術字(ㄧˋ ㄕㄨˋ ㄗˋ)
(printed or written) characters in a fancy style

藝術無國境(ㄧˋ ㄕㄨˋ ㄨˊ ㄍㄨㄛˊ ㄐㄧㄥˋ)
Art knows no national boundary.

藝人(ㄧˋ ㄖㄣˊ)
an entertainer; a performing artist: 她是個出名的藝人。She is a famous entertainer.

藝文(ㄧˋ ㄨㄣˊ)
literature and fine arts

藝文志(ㄧˋ ㄨㄣˊ ㄓˋ)
a bibliographical sketch (of the kind as contained in old history books)

藝苑(ㄧˋ ㄩㄢˋ)
① places where works of art are collected; an artistic or literary salon; an art gallery ② the art and literary circles

【藟】 5145
ㄌㄟˇ leei3 lei3
1. a variety of climbing plant
2. to wind; to entwine
3. same as 蕾—a flower bud

【藻】 5146
ㄊㄢˇ tarn3 tan3
algae 亦作「石衣」or「水苔」

【藤】 5147
ㄊㄥˊ terng2 teng2
a rattan; a vine

藤鞭(ㄊㄥˊ ㄅㄧㄢ)
a rattan whip

藤牌(ㄊㄥˊ ㄆㄞˊ)
a rattan shield

藤條(ㄊㄥˊ ㄊㄧㄠˊ)
a rattan

藤蘿(ㄊㄥˊ ㄌㄨㄛˊ)
(botany) wisteria

藤黃(ㄊㄥˊ ㄏㄨㄤˊ)
gamboge

藤子(ㄊㄥˊ ˙ㄗ)

a rattan

藤椅(ㄊㄥˊ ㄧˇ)
a rattan chair; a cane chair

【藥】 5148 ㄧㄠˋ yaw yào
(讀音 ㄩㄝˋ yueh yuè)
1. medicine; remedy; a drug;
pharmaceuticals: 良藥苦口。A
good medicine tastes bitter.
2. to kill with poison; to poison: 他們在藥老鼠。They are
poisoning rats.

藥片(ㄧㄠˋ ㄆㄧㄢˋ)
a tablet of medicine

藥品(ㄧㄠˋ ㄆㄧㄣˇ)
pharmaceutical products;
drugs

藥瓶(ㄧㄠˋ ㄆㄧㄥˊ)
a medicine bottle

藥舖(ㄧㄠˋ ㄆㄨˋ)or 藥店(ㄧㄠˋ ㄉㄧㄢˋ)
a druggist's store; a dispensary

藥劑兒(ㄧㄠˋ ㄇㄧㄢˊ)
medicine in powder form

藥棉(ㄧㄠˋ ㄇㄧㄢˊ)
absorbent cotton; medically
decontaminated cotton

藥粉(ㄧㄠˋ ㄈㄣˇ)
medicinal powder

藥方(ㄧㄠˋ ㄈㄤ)
a (medicinal) prescription

藥房(ㄧㄠˋ ㄈㄤˊ)
a druggist's shop; a dispensary; a pharmacy

藥單(ㄧㄠˋ ㄉㄢ)
a (medicinal) prescription

藥碾子(ㄧㄠˋ ㄋㄧㄢˇ•ㄗ)
a medicine mortar

藥理學(ㄧㄠˋ ㄌㄧˇ ㄒㄩㄝˊ)
pharmacology

藥力(ㄧㄠˋ ㄌㄧˋ)
the potency or effect of a
drug: 藥力發作了。The medicine is taking effect.

藥料(ㄧㄠˋ ㄌㄧㄠˋ)
medicinal substance; material for a drug; material for
a decoction

藥量(ㄧㄠˋ ㄌㄧㄤˋ)
dosage

藥膏(ㄧㄠˋ ㄍㄠ)
ointment; salve

藥罐子(ㄧㄠˋ ㄍㄨㄢˋ•ㄗ)
①a pottery jar for cooking
medicinal decoctions; a drug
boiler ② one who is perenni-

ally ill; a chronic invalid

藥劑(ㄧㄠˋ ㄐㄧˋ)
medicine; remedy; a drug

藥劑師(ㄧㄠˋ ㄐㄧˋ ㄕ)
a pharmacist; a druggist; a
chemist; an apothecary

藥酒(ㄧㄠˋ ㄐㄧㄡˇ)
medicinal wine or liquor;
medicated wine or liquor

藥局(ㄧㄠˋ ㄐㄩˊ)
a druggist's store; a dispensary 參看「藥房」: 他去藥局了。
He went to the dispensary.

藥線(ㄧㄠˋ ㄒㄧㄢˋ)
①a fuse②a medicated
thread

藥箱(ㄧㄠˋ ㄒㄧㄤ)
a medicine chest; a medical
kit

藥性(ㄧㄠˋ ㄒㄧㄥˋ)
the nature of a drug: 此藥
性溫和。The nature of the
drug is gentle.

藥學(ㄧㄠˋ ㄒㄩㄝˊ)
pharmacology: 她專攻藥學。
She majors in pharmacology.

藥渣(ㄧㄠˋ ㄓㄚ)
dregs left after preparing a
decoction

藥針(ㄧㄠˋ ㄓㄣ)
an injection syringe

藥廠(ㄧㄠˋ ㄔㄤˇ)
a pharmaceutical factory

藥師(ㄧㄠˋ ㄕ)
a pharmacist; a druggist; a
chemist; an apothecary;
pharmaceutist

藥石(ㄧㄠˋ ㄕˊ)
① medicines ② sincere admonitions

藥石之言(ㄧㄠˋ ㄕˊ ㄓ ㄧㄢˊ)
sincere admonitions; exhortations

藥罔效(ㄧㄠˋ ㄕ ㄨㄤˊ ㄒㄧㄠˋ)
All medicines have failed to
effect a cure.

藥商(ㄧㄠˋ ㄕㄤ)
a drug dealer; a chemist

藥水(ㄧㄠˋ ㄕㄨㄟˇ)
liquid medicine

藥皂(ㄧㄠˋ ㄗㄠˋ)
medicated soap

藥材(ㄧㄠˋ ㄘㄞˊ)
medicinal substance; material for a drug; material for
a decoction; medicine; a

drug; medicinal herbs

藥草(ㄧㄠˋ ㄘㄠˇ)
medicinal herbs

藥死(ㄧㄠˋ ㄙˇ)
to poison to death

藥餌(ㄧㄠˋ ㄦˇ)
a medicine to give strength;
tonics

藥衣子(ㄧㄠˋ ㄧ•ㄗ)
the coat of a pill medicine

藥引子(ㄧㄠˋ ㄧㄣˇ•ㄗ)
an auxiliary remedy or medicine; a helping ingredient
added to enhance the efficacy of a medicine

藥物(ㄧㄠˋ ㄨˋ)
drug; medicine

藥物過敏(ㄧㄠˋ ㄨˋ ㄍㄨㄛˋ ㄇㄧㄣˇ)
drug allergy

藥物學(ㄧㄠˋ ㄨˋ ㄒㄩㄝˊ)
pharmacology

藥味(ㄧㄠˋ ㄨㄟˋ)
①medicine ②the taste of a
drug ③a medicine-like taste
亦作「藥味兒」

藥丸(ㄧㄠˋ ㄨㄢˊ)
a pill medicine; a pill

藥用(ㄧㄠˋ ㄩㄥˋ)
for medical use

【藩】 5149 ㄈㄢ farn fān
a fence; a hedge; a boundary; a frontier; a barrier

藩蔽(ㄈㄢ ㄅㄧˋ)
a barrier

藩屏(ㄈㄢ ㄆㄧㄥˊ)
a protective barrier; a line
of defense 亦作「屏藩」

藩附(ㄈㄢ ㄈㄨˋ)
a protectorate; a vassal
state

藩籬(ㄈㄢ ㄌㄧˊ)
①a fence; a hedge: 此馬跳過
了藩籬。This horse jumped
over the fence. ②anything
acting as a hedge ③a line
of defense; a barrier

藩國(ㄈㄢ ㄍㄨㄛˊ)
a vassal state; a feudatory
state

藩庫(ㄈㄢ ㄎㄨˋ)
a provincial treasury (in
former times)

藩鎮(ㄈㄢ ㄓㄣˋ)
(Tang Dynasty)the governor of a frontier province in
charge of both civil and mil-

艸
部

**艸
部**

itary affairs

藩臣(ㄈㄢˊ ㄔㄣˊ)
a vassal

藩屬(ㄈㄢˊ ㄕㄨˇ)
a vassal state; a protectorate

藩司(ㄈㄢˊ ㄙ)
a provincial governor (in ancient times)

藩維(ㄈㄢˊ ㄨㄟˊ)
vassal states and frontier posts

【藪】 5150 　ㄙㄡˇ soou sǒu
1. a shallow lake overgrown with wild plants
2. an assembling place
3. same as 搜—to search

藪澤(ㄙㄡˇ ㄗㄜˊ)
a shallow lake

【藭】 5151 　ㄑㄩㄥˊ chyong qióng
as in 芎藭—*Cnidium officinale*, a kind of medicinal herb

十六畫

【藺】 5152 　ㄌㄧㄣˋ linn lìn
1. a variety of rush used in making mats
2. a Chinese family name

藺相如(ㄌㄧㄣˋ ㄒㄧㄤ ㄖㄨˊ)
Lin Hsiang-ju, a prime minister of the state of Chao (趙) during the Epoch of Warring States

藺石(ㄌㄧㄣˋ ㄕˊ)
rocks used as artillery shells in ancient warfare

【蘑】 5153 　ㄇㄛˊ mo mó
a variety of edible mushroom

蘑菇or **蘑菰**(ㄇㄛˊ ㄍㄨ)
①a variety of edible mushrooms ②to dawdle; to dilly-dally ③to pester; to worry

【蕲】 5154 　ㄑㄧˊ chyi qí
1. ligusticum; levisticum 亦 作「當歸」or「山蕲」
2. same as 祈—to beg; to seek

蕲竹(ㄑㄧˊ ㄓㄨˊ)
①bamboos produced in Chichow (蕲州), Hupeh Province ②bamboo mats

蕲水(ㄑㄧˊ ㄕㄨㄟˇ)
name of a tributary of the Yangtze River originating in Hupeh

蕲艾(ㄑㄧˊ ㄞˋ)
moxa from the Chi (蕲) area in Hupeh

【藹】 5155 　ㄞˇ ae ǎi
1. exuberant; luxuriant; lush
2. gentle; kind; amiable; affable; friendly
3. gloomy; dim

藹然(ㄞˇ ㄖㄢˊ)
①glossy; lustrous ②amiable; affable; friendly; gentle; kind

藹然可親(ㄞˇ ㄖㄢˊ ㄎㄜˇ ㄑㄧㄣ)
kind and gentle; affable and friendly

藹彩(ㄞˇ ㄘㄞˇ)
a fresh look

藹藹(ㄞˇ ㄞˇ)
①exuberant; luxuriant; lush ②abundant; much; many ③(said of moonlight) gloomy; dim ④(said of the wood) shady

【藻】 5156 　ㄗㄠˇ tzao zǎo
1. algae; pondweeds
2. diction; wording; language

藻類(ㄗㄠˇ ㄌㄟˋ)or **藻類植物**(ㄗㄠˇ ㄌㄟˋ ㄓˊ ㄨˋ)
algae

藻麗(ㄗㄠˇ ㄌㄧˋ)
beautiful; splendid

藻翰(ㄗㄠˇ ㄏㄢˋ)
①a beautiful feather ②(figuratively) elegant writing

藻繪(ㄗㄠˇ ㄏㄨㄟˋ)
magnificence; splendor; elegance

藻井(ㄗㄠˇ ㄐㄧㄥˇ)
a plafond

藻飾(ㄗㄠˇ ㄕˋ)
①literary decorativeness; embellishment in writing ②to polish writings

藻思(ㄗㄠˇ ㄙ)
a fine or elegant inspiration (in writing)

藻雅(ㄗㄠˇ ㄧㄚˇ)
elegant; graceful; fine

藻玉(ㄗㄠˇ ㄩˋ)
multicolored jade

【藿】 5157 　ㄏㄨㄛˋ huoh huò
1. leaves of a legume; bean sprouts
2. *Agastache rugosa*, a kind of medicinal herb 參看「藿香」

藿羹(ㄏㄨㄛˋ ㄍㄥ)
coarse food

藿香(ㄏㄨㄛˋ ㄒㄧㄤ)
Agastache rugosa, wrinkled gianthyssop

藿食(ㄏㄨㄛˋ ㄕˊ)
coarse food

【蘀】 5158 　ㄊㄨㄛˋ tuoh tuò
fallen leaves and barks; withered leaves

【蘅】 5159 　ㄏㄥˊ herng héng
Asarum blumei, a fragrant plant

蘅芷(ㄏㄥˊ ㄓˇ)
a fragrant plant

蘅蕪(ㄏㄥˊ ㄨˊ)
a kind of incense

【蘆】 5160 　ㄌㄨˊ lu lú
1. reeds; rushes
2. gourds 參看「葫蘆」

蘆藩(ㄌㄨˊ ㄈㄢ)
a reed fence; a reed hedge

蘆荻(ㄌㄨˊ ㄉㄧˊ)
a variety of reed

蘆田(ㄌㄨˊ ㄊㄧㄢˊ)
sandy fields where reeds grow

蘆溝橋(ㄌㄨˊ ㄍㄡ ㄑㄧㄠˊ)
the Marco Polo Bridge (in Hopeh, where the first shot of the Sino-Japanese War, 1937-1945, was fired)

蘆溝橋事變(ㄌㄨˊ ㄍㄡ ㄑㄧㄠˊ ㄕˋ ㄅㄧㄢˋ)
The Marco Polo Bridge Incident (on July 7, 1937, which triggered the Sino-Japanese War)

蘆管(ㄌㄨˊ ㄍㄨㄢˇ)
a reed pipe

蘆花(ㄌㄨˊ ㄏㄨㄚ)or **蘆絮**(ㄌㄨˊ ㄒㄩˋ)
reed flowers; reed catkins; rush flowers

蘆薈(ㄌㄨˊ ㄏㄨㄟˋ)
aloes: 蘆薈可作藥。 Aloes can be used in medicine.

蘆席(ㄌㄨˊ ㄒㄧˊ)
a rush mat

蘆竹(ㄌㄨˊ ㄓㄨˊ)

①a variety of edible bamboo ② *Arundo donax*

蘆筍(ㄌㄨˊ ㄙㄨㄣˇ)
(botany) asparagus

蘆葦(ㄌㄨˊ ㄨㄟˇ)
reeds

【孽】 5161
(孽) ㄋㄧㄝˋ nieh niè
1. the son of a concubine
2. sin; evil
3. calamity

孽黨(ㄋㄧㄝˋ ㄉㄤˇ)
a traitorous faction; dissenters

孽障(ㄋㄧㄝˋ ㄓㄤˋ)
retribution for past evil

孽子(ㄋㄧㄝˋ ㄗˇ)
the son of a concubine

孽孫(ㄋㄧㄝˋ ㄙㄨㄣ)
the grandson of a concubine

【蘇】 5162
ㄙㄨ su sū
1. purple perilla 亦作「紫蘇」
2. to come back to life; to revive; to resurrect
3. to awake
4. to rest
5. short for Soviet Russia
6. short for Kiangsu Province or Soochow
7. a Chinese family name

蘇白(ㄙㄨ ㄅㄞˊ)
the Soochow dialect

蘇必略湖(ㄙㄨ ㄅㄧˋ ㄌㄩㄝˋ ㄏㄨˊ)
Lake Superior

蘇曼殊(ㄙㄨ ㄇㄢˊ ㄕㄨ)
Su Man-shu, 1884-1918, a writer, translator and artist

蘇門答臘(ㄙㄨ ㄇㄣˊ ㄉㄚˊ ㄌㄚˋ)
Sumatra

蘇打(ㄙㄨ ㄉㄚˇ)
soda 亦作「蘇達」

蘇打餅乾(ㄙㄨ ㄉㄚˇ ㄅㄧㄥˇ ㄍㄢ)
a soda biscuit; a soda cracker

蘇丹(ㄙㄨ ㄉㄢ)
Sudan

蘇隄(ㄙㄨ ㄊㄧˊ)or(ㄙㄨ ㄉㄧ)
either of two dikes in the West Lake, Hangchow, built by the Sung Dynasty poet Su Tung-po (蘇東坡)

蘇鐵(ㄙㄨ ㄊㄧㄝˇ)
(botany) a cycad 亦作「鳳尾蕉」

蘇黎世(ㄙㄨ ㄌㄧˊ ㄕˋ)
Zurich, Switzerland

蘇利南(ㄙㄨ ㄌㄧˋ ㄋㄢˊ)
Surinam

蘇格拉底(ㄙㄨ ㄍㄜˊ ㄌㄚ ㄉㄧˇ)
Socrates, 469?-399B.C., Athenian philosopher and teacher

蘇格蘭(ㄙㄨ ㄍㄜˊ ㄌㄢˊ)
Scotland

蘇杭(ㄙㄨ ㄏㄤˊ)
Soochow and Hangchow

蘇黃米蔡(ㄙㄨ ㄏㄨㄤˊ ㄇㄧˇ ㄘㄞˋ)
the four great calligraphic masters of the North Sung Dynasty—Su Shih (蘇軾), Huang Ting-chien (黃庭堅), Mi Fei (米芾), and Tsai Hsiang (蔡襄)

蘇秦(ㄙㄨ ㄑㄧㄣˊ)
Su Chin, a strategist in the Epoch of Warring States

蘇息(ㄙㄨ ㄒㄧˊ)
①to rest ②to come back to life; to revive

蘇小妹(ㄙㄨ ㄒㄧㄠˇ ㄇㄟˋ)
Su Hsiao-mei, talented daughter of Su Hsün (蘇洵)

蘇小小(ㄙㄨ ㄒㄧㄠˇ ㄒㄧㄠˇ)
a famed 6th century courtesan whose grave is one of the tourist attractions of the West Lake in Hangchow

蘇醒(ㄙㄨ ㄒㄧㄥˇ)
to regain consciousness; to come to; to awaken; to revive: 他使那個暈厥的人蘇醒。He revived that man who had fainted.

蘇洵(ㄙㄨ ㄒㄩㄣˊ)
Su Hsün, 1009-1066, renowned man of letters in the Sung Dynasty, father of Su Shih (蘇軾), Su Che(蘇轍), and Su Hsiao-mei (蘇小妹)

蘇州(ㄙㄨ ㄓㄡ)
Soochow, Kiangsu Province

蘇轍(ㄙㄨ ㄔㄜˋ)
Su Che, 1039-1112, renowned man of letters in the Sung Dynasty, 2nd son of Su Hsün (蘇洵) and brother of Su Shih (蘇軾)

蘇軾(ㄙㄨ ㄕˋ)
Su Shih, 1036-1101, renowned man of letters in the Sung Dynasty, also known as Su Tung-po (蘇東坡), eldest son of Su Hsün (蘇洵) and

brother of Su Che (蘇轍)

蘇俄(ㄙㄨ ㄜˊ)
Soviet Russia

蘇伊士運河(ㄙㄨ ㄧ ㄕˋ ㄩㄣˋ ㄏㄜˊ)
the Suez Canal

蘇武(ㄙㄨ ㄨˇ)
Su Wu, (c.143-60 B.C.), an emissary who spent 19 years in captivity among the Huns during the Han Dynasty

蘇維埃(ㄙㄨ ㄨㄟˊ ㄞ)
Soviet

蘇維埃聯邦(ㄙㄨ ㄨㄟˊ ㄞ ㄌㄧㄢˊ ㄈㄤ)
or 蘇聯(ㄙㄨ ㄌㄧㄢˊ)
the Soviet Union; the Union of Soviet Socialist Republics; U.S.S.R.

【蘊】 5163
(蘊) ㄩㄣˋ yunn yùn
1. to collect; to gather
2. to store; to have in store
3. deep; profound
4. sweltering; sultry

蘊釀(ㄩㄣˋ ㄋㄧㄤˋ)
(said of a storm, trouble, etc.)to brew; to foment

蘊涵(ㄩㄣˋ ㄏㄢˊ)
①to contain ②(logics)implication

蘊結(ㄩㄣˋ ㄐㄧㄝˊ)
(said of feelings) pent-up; restrained

蘊藉(ㄩㄣˋ ㄐㄧㄝˋ)
refined and cultivated; urbanely charming

蘊蓄(ㄩㄣˋ ㄒㄩˋ)
to hold, or contain, beneath the surface; to have in store

蘊藏(ㄩㄣˋ ㄘㄤˊ)
to have in store; to be rich in: 該國蘊藏豐富的石油和煤礦。The country is rich in oil and coal.

蘊藏量(ㄩㄣˋ ㄘㄤˊ ㄌㄧㄤˋ)
(said of minerals) deposit

蘊蒻(ㄩㄣˋ ㄖˋ)
exuberant; luxuriant

蘊隆(ㄩㄣˋ ㄌㄨㄥˊ)
sweltering; sultry

【蘋】 5164
ㄆㄧㄣˊ pyn pín
duckweeds

【蘋】 5164
2. ㄆㄧㄥˊ pyng píng
an apple

蘋果(ㄆㄧㄥˊ ㄍㄨㄛˇ)
an apple

【艸部】

蘋果綠（ㄆㄧㄥˊ ㄍㄨㄛˇ ㄌㄩˋ）
a kind of ancient porcelain with a light-green color

蘋果酒（ㄆㄧㄥˊ ㄍㄨㄛˇ ㄐㄧㄡˇ）
hard cider; applejack

蘋果汁（ㄆㄧㄥˊ ㄍㄨㄛˇ ㄓ）
apple juice

蘋果酸（ㄆㄧㄥˊ ㄍㄨㄛˇ ㄙㄨㄢ）
malic acid

蘋果臉兒（ㄆㄧㄥˊ ㄍㄨㄛˇ ㄌㄧㄢˇㄦ）
rosy cheeks

【藷】 （藷）ㄕㄨ shuu shú
a sweet potato

【蘢】 5166
ㄌㄨㄥˊ long lóng
a kind of tall grass

蘢蔥（ㄌㄨㄥˊ ㄘㄨㄥ）
(said of vegetation) luxuriant and beautiful; verdant

十七畫

【蘧】 5167
ㄑㄩˊ chyu qú
1. pleasantly surprised
2. a Chinese family name

【蘗】 5168
ㄅㄛˋ boh bò
a cork tree (Phellodendron)

【蘖】 5169
（蘖）ㄋㄧㄝˋ nieh niè
sprouts and shoots from the stump of a felled tree

【蘚】 5170
ㄒㄧㄢˇ shean xiǎn
(botany) moss; lichen

蘚苔（ㄒㄧㄢˇ ㄊㄞˊ）
moss; lichen

蘚痕（ㄒㄧㄢˇ ㄏㄣˊ）
a moss scar; marks made by moss on rocks or steps

蘚徑（ㄒㄧㄢˇ ㄐㄧㄥˋ）
a mossy path

【蘩】 5171
ㄈㄢˊ farn fán
Artemisia stelleriana, a kind of herb; white southernwood 亦作「白蒿」

【蘭】 5172
ㄌㄢˊ lan lán
an orchid

蘭盆（ㄌㄢˊ ㄆㄣˊ）or 蘭盆會（ㄌㄢˊ ㄆㄣˊ ㄏㄨㄟˋ）
(Buddhism) Ullambana, the festival of masses for destitute ghosts, a Buddhist service on the 15th of the sev-

---

enth lunar month 亦作「盂蘭盆會」

蘭譜（ㄌㄢˊ ㄆㄨˇ）
a testimonial of sworn brothers

蘭臺（ㄌㄢˊ ㄊㄞˊ）
① an alternative title by which the official historian was referred to in the Han Dynasty ② name of a county in Hupeh Province

蘭亭帖（ㄌㄢˊ ㄊㄧㄥˊ ㄊㄧㄝˇ）
a handwritten copy of 蘭亭序, by Wang Hsi-chih（王羲之）, a 4th century writer and calligraphic master

蘭亭序（ㄌㄢˊ ㄊㄧㄥˊ ㄒㄩˋ）
the title of a literary piece by Wang Hsi-chih（王羲之）, whose literary worth is dwarfed by its artistic value as a calligraphic masterpiece

蘭閨（ㄌㄢˊ ㄍㄨㄟ）
a boudoir

蘭科（ㄌㄢˊ ㄎㄜ）
the orchid family

蘭客（ㄌㄢˊ ㄎㄜˋ）
a good friend

蘭花（ㄌㄢˊ ㄏㄨㄚ）
an orchid; a cymbidium

蘭交（ㄌㄢˊ ㄐㄧㄠ）
a harmonious friendship

蘭藏桂馥（ㄌㄢˊ ㄘㄤˊ ㄍㄨㄟˋ ㄈㄨˋ）
the fragrance of orchids and the scent of cinnamon—① prosperous descendants ② a lasting moral influence

蘭訊（ㄌㄢˊ ㄒㄩㄣˋ）
your letters

蘭芝（ㄌㄢˊ ㄓ）
① the fragrant thoroughwort and the glossy ganoderma—both of them are fragrant herbs ② (figuratively) virtue

蘭芷（ㄌㄢˊ ㄓˇ）
the fragrant thoroughwort and the angelica—both of them are fragrant herbs

蘭州（ㄌㄢˊ ㄓㄡ）
Lanchow, capital city of Kansu Province

蘭章（ㄌㄢˊ ㄓㄤ）
① beautiful writings ② (a polite expression) your letters

蘭室（ㄌㄢˊ ㄕˋ）
a Buddhist temple

蘭蕙（ㄌㄢˊ ㄏㄨㄟˋ）
① the fragrant thoroughwort and the musk—both of them are fragrant herbs ② fragrance; scent

蘭若（ㄌㄢˊ ㄖㄨㄛˋ）
① （ㄌㄢˊ ㄖㄨㄛˋ）(botany) Chinese and Japanese thoroughwort
② （ㄌㄢˊ ㄖㄜˇ）Aranyaka, a Buddhist monastery 亦作「阿蘭若」

蘭藻（ㄌㄢˊ ㄗㄠˇ）
literary beauty

蘭摧玉折（ㄌㄢˊ ㄘㄨㄟ ㄩˋ ㄓㄜˊ）
(literally) The orchid has withered and the jade is broken.—The man of virtue is dead while still young.

蘭孫（ㄌㄢˊ ㄙㄨㄣ）
your fine grandchildren

蘭艾同焚（ㄌㄢˊ ㄞˋ ㄊㄨㄥˊ ㄈㄣˊ）
(literally) to burn the orchid and the moxa together—to impose the same destiny upon the noble and the mean alike

蘭因絮果（ㄌㄢˊ ㄧㄣ ㄒㄩˋ ㄍㄨㄛˇ）
(said of a man and a woman) well-predestined relationship and ill fated end, usually referring to the break-up of a marriage

蘭嶼（ㄌㄢˊ ㄩˇ）
Lanyü, an islet off the coast of Southeastern Taiwan

蘭月（ㄌㄢˊ ㄩㄝˋ）
the month of the orchid—the seventh lunar month

【蘞】 5173
ㄌㄧㄢˊ lian lián
a variety of vine; a convolvulus

十九畫

【蘸】 5174
ㄓㄢˋ jann zhàn
to dip

蘸筆（ㄓㄢˋ ㄅㄧˇ）
to dip a writing brush in ink

蘸濕（ㄓㄢˋ ㄕ）
to dip.

【蘺】 5175
ㄌㄧˊ li lí
a kind of fragrant herb 亦作

【江蘺】

【蘼】 5176
ㄇㄧ mi. mí
a kind of fragrant herb 參看
【蘼蕪】

蘼蕪（ㄇㄧ ㄨˊ）
coarse vegetable

蘼蕪（ㄇㄧ ㄨˊ）
Gracilaria confervoides, a kind of fragrant herb

【蘿】 5177
ㄌㄨㄛˊ luo luo
1. a kind of creeping plant; a wistaria
2. a radish; a turnip

蘿蔔（ㄌㄨㄛˊ·ㄅㄛ）
a radish; a turnip

蘿蔔乾（ㄌㄨㄛˊ·ㄅㄛ ㄍㄢ）
a dried radish or turnip

蘿蔔糕（ㄌㄨㄛˊ·ㄅㄛ ㄍㄠ）
turnip pudding

【虀】 5178
ㄐㄧ jī
minced pickles

二十一畫

【蘽】 5179
ㄌㄟˇ lei lei
1. grass that creeps and spread fast and luxuriantly
2. a basket for carrying earth

虍 部
ㄏㄨ hu hū

二畫

【虎】 5180
ㄏㄨˇ huu hǔ
1. a tiger;
2. fierce; savage; brave; vigorous

虎背熊腰（ㄏㄨˇ ㄅㄟ ㄒㄩㄥˊ ㄧㄠ）
the back of a tiger and the waist of a bear—heavy and muscular build of the body

虎斑草（ㄏㄨˇ ㄅㄢ ㄘㄠˇ）
a tigerflower

虎賁（ㄏㄨˇ ㄅㄣ）
a warrior; a lifeguard—(figuratively) intrepid

虎榜（ㄏㄨˇ ㄅㄤˇ）
a bulletin announcing successful candidates in the examination for military officers in ancient times

虎步（ㄏㄨˇ ㄅㄨˋ）
a strutting gait

虎皮（ㄏㄨˇ ㄆㄧˊ）
① a tiger skin ② seeming bravery

虎符（ㄏㄨˇ ㄈㄨˊ）
a tiger-shaped tally used in wartime in ancient times

虎父無犬子（ㄏㄨˇ ㄈㄨˋ ㄨˊ ㄑㄩㄢˇ ㄗˇ）
(literally) A tiger father will not beget a dog son.—There will be no laggard among the children of a brave or talented man.

虎毒不食兒（ㄏㄨˇ ㄉㄨˊ ㄅㄨˋ ㄕˊ ㄦˊ）
(literally) Even a vicious tigress will not eat its cubs.—No one is capable of hurting his own children.

虎蹲砲（ㄏㄨˇ ㄉㄨㄣ ㄆㄠˋ）
a short-barreled artillery piece

虎頭牌（ㄏㄨˇ ㄊㄡˊ ㄆㄞˊ）
a tiger-headed tablet outside a public office warning against disorder

虎頭虎腦（ㄏㄨˇ ㄊㄡˊ ㄈㄨˇ ㄋㄠˇ）
looking dignified and strong

虎頭蛇尾（ㄏㄨˇ ㄊㄡˊ ㄕㄜˊ ㄨㄟˇ）
to start doing something with vigor but fail to see it through; impressive in the beginning but disappointing in the end

虎狼之年（ㄏㄨˇ ㄌㄤˊ ㄓ ㄋㄧㄢˊ）
the wolfish years of a woman from the early thirties to early forties when her sexual desire is the strongest

虎狼之國（ㄏㄨˇ ㄌㄤˊ ㄓ ㄍㄨㄛˊ）
a nation of greed and violence

虎列拉（ㄏㄨˇ ㄌㄧㄝˋ ㄌㄚ）亦作「霍亂」
cholera

虎落平陽被犬欺（ㄏㄨˇ ㄌㄨㄛˋ ㄆㄧㄥˊ ㄧㄤˊ ㄅㄟˋ ㄑㄩㄢˇ ㄑㄧ）
(literally) The tiger, once out of his natural environment, may be bullied even by a dog.—A hero or brave man is bullied by a bunch of weaklings when he is down

in his luck.

虎克黨（ㄏㄨˇ ㄎㄜˋ ㄉㄤˇ）
the Huks in the Philippines

虎口（ㄏㄨˇ ㄎㄡˇ）
① a tiger's mouth—a dangerous place; the jaws of death ② the part of a hand between the thumb and the index finger

虎口餘生（ㄏㄨˇ ㄎㄡˇ ㄩˊ ㄕㄥ）
(literally) to escape from the tiger's mouth—to survive a dangerous experience; to have a narrow escape

虎虎有生氣（ㄏㄨˇ ㄏㄨˇ ㄧㄡˇ ㄕㄥ ㄑㄧˋ）
lively; vigorous

虎將（ㄏㄨˇ ㄐㄧㄤˋ）
a brave general

虎踞龍蟠（ㄏㄨˇ ㄐㄩ ㄌㄨㄥˊ ㄆㄢˊ）
(literally) like a tiger crouching or a dragon curling—located in a strategic place

虎圈（ㄏㄨˇ ㄐㄩㄢˋ）
a tiger's cage or pen

虎嘯風生（ㄏㄨˇ ㄒㄧㄠˋ ㄈㄥ ㄕㄥ）
(literally) Tigers howl with the rise of winds.—Great men appear in response to the call of the times.

虎穴（ㄏㄨˇ ㄒㄩㄝˋ）
a tiger's cave—a dangerous place; a hazardous spot: 不入虎穴, 焉得虎子. The only way to catch tiger cubs is to go into the tiger's cave.

虎賁（ㄏㄨˇ ㄅㄣ）
brave warriors

虎掌（ㄏㄨˇ ㄓㄤˇ）
(botany) a poisonous plant (*Arisaema ambiguum*)

虎帳（ㄏㄨˇ ㄓㄤˋ）
a military camp

虎政（ㄏㄨˇ ㄓㄥˋ）
tyrannical administration; misrule

虎倀（ㄏㄨˇ ㄔㄤ）
a spirit believed to lead a tiger to its human victims—a man who encourages or helps in sinful acts; an accomplice

虎士（ㄏㄨˇ ㄕˋ）
a brave warrior; a brave fighter

虎視眈眈（ㄏㄨˇ ㄕˋ ㄉㄢ ㄉㄢ）
to gaze with the cruel greed

of a tiger

虎入羊群(ㄏㄨ ㄖㄨˋ ㄧㄤˊ ㄑㄩㄣˊ)
a tiger among a flock of
sheep— (figuratively) With
irresistable power, one does
as one pleases.

虎子(ㄏㄨˇ ㄗˇ)
the cub of a tiger

虎殘(ㄏㄨˇ ㄘㄢˊ)
remains of a tiger's prey
—(figuratively)to have a
narrow escape

虎威(ㄏㄨˇ ㄨㄟ)
the frightful appearance of a
tiger (assumed to scare
others)

（庄部）

三畫

【虐】 5181
　　　ㄋㄩㄝˋ nüeh nüè
1. cruel; ferocious; atrocious
2. to tyrannize over; to
oppress

虐待(ㄋㄩㄝˋ ㄉㄞˋ)
to maltreat; to abuse; to torture; to ill-treat

虐待狂(ㄋㄩㄝˋ ㄉㄞˋ ㄎㄨㄤˊ)
①sadism ②a sadist

虐政(ㄋㄩㄝˋ ㄓㄥˋ)
tyrannical rule; tyranny

四畫

【虔】 5182
　　　ㄑㄧㄢˊ chyan qián
reverence; reverent; respectful; pious

虔婆(ㄑㄧㄢˊ ㄆㄛˊ)
①a low woman ②a procur-
ess

虔心(ㄑㄧㄢˊ ㄒㄧㄣ)
sincere reverence; piety

虔誠(ㄑㄧㄢˊ ㄔㄥˊ)
devout; piety; sincerity;
pious: 他是個虔誠的基督徒。
He is a devout Christian.

五畫

【處】 5183
　　　1. ㄔㄨˇ chuh chǔ
1. a place; a spot; a location; a
locality: 他的住處在台北。His
dwelling place is in Taipei.
2. a department in a government agency

3. a special quality; a distin-
guishing mark; a point: 烹飪
是她的長處。Cooking is her
strong point.

處長(ㄔㄨˇ ㄓㄤˇ)
the head of a department in
a government agency

處處(ㄔㄨˇ ㄔㄨˇ)
①everywhere: 他們處處都去。
They go everywhere. ②in
all respects

處所(ㄔㄨˇ ㄙㄨㄛˇ)
a place; a locality

【處】 5183
　　　2. ㄔㄨˋ chuu chù
1. to place oneself in; to be
faced with; to live in
2. to get along: 他們不好相處。
They are hard to get along
with.
3. to dispose of; to deal with;
to manage; to handle
4. to sentence; to punish: 他被
判處死刑。He was sentenced
to death.
5. to dwell; to live

處罰(ㄔㄨˇ ㄈㄚˊ)
to punish

處分(ㄔㄨˇ ㄈㄣˋ)
①to take action against; to
take disciplinary action
against; to punish: 學校給他
警告處分。The school gave
him disciplinary warning. ②
to deal with (a matter)

處方(ㄔㄨˇ ㄈㄤ)
to write out a medical prescription; to prescribe

處斷(ㄔㄨˇ ㄉㄨㄢˋ)
to decide; to determine; to
resolve

處女(ㄔㄨˇ ㄋㄩˇ)
a virgin

處女膜(ㄔㄨˇ ㄋㄩˇ ㄇㄛˊ)
the hymen; the maidenhead

處女地(ㄔㄨˇ ㄋㄩˇ ㄉㄧˋ)
virgin land; maiden ground

處女航(ㄔㄨˇ ㄋㄩˇ ㄏㄤˊ)
a maiden voyage of a ship;
a maiden flight of a plane

處女作(ㄔㄨˇ ㄋㄩˇ ㄗㄨㄛˋ)
a maiden work

處理(ㄔㄨˇ ㄌㄧˇ)
①to dispose of; to handle;
to deal with: 事務處理得很成
功。The business has been
disposed of successfully.②to

treat by a special process

處境(ㄔㄨˇ ㄐㄧㄥˋ)
the position or situation one
is in; the circumstances one
faces

處決(ㄔㄨˇ ㄐㄩㄝˊ)
①to decide; to resolve ②to
execute (an offender); to
put to death: 他們處決一名兇
手。They executed a mur-
derer.

處心積慮(ㄔㄨˇ ㄒㄧㄣ ㄐㄧ ㄌㄩˋ)
to have in mind for a long
time; deliberately; to be bent
on: 他處心積慮想當政治家。He
is bent on becoming a
statesman.

處刑(ㄔㄨˇ ㄒㄧㄥˊ)
to inflict punishment; to punish; to execute; to mete out
a sentence

處之泰然(ㄔㄨˇ ㄓ ㄊㄞˋ ㄖㄢˊ)
to keep one's head; to be unmoved; to maintain compo-
sure

處置 or 處治(ㄔㄨˇ ㄓˋ)
①to dispose of; to deal
with; to handle 亦作「處理」;
此事必須嚴加處置。The mat-
ter should be dealt with
sternly.② to punish

處斬(ㄔㄨˇ ㄓㄢˇ)
to behead; to decapitate

處士(ㄔㄨˇ ㄕˋ)
a scholar in retirement; a
recluse

處世(ㄔㄨˇ ㄕˋ)
to conduct oneself in life: 他
處世正直。He conducts him-
self honestly in life.

處事(ㄔㄨˇ ㄕˋ)
to deal with affairs; to manage business

處身(ㄔㄨˇ ㄕㄣ)
to conduct oneself in life

處暑(ㄔㄨˇ ㄕㄨˇ)
one of the 24 climatic
periods of a year, falling on
August 23 or 24

處子(ㄔㄨˇ ㄗˇ)
①a virgin; a young lady ②
a scholar in retirement; a
recluse

處死(ㄔㄨˇ ㄙˇ)
to punish with death; to put
to death

處約(ㄔㄨˇ ㄩㄝ)

to be in adversity; to suffer privation; to be in a condition of poverty and hardship

【虖】 5184 ㄏㄨ hu hū
to cry; to shout; to howl; to roar

六畫

【虛】 5185 ㄒㄩ shiu xū
1. empty; hollow; void; unoccupied: 座無虛席。 There was no empty seat.
2. unreal; false; deceptive; unfounded; groundless
3. weak; feeble: 他病後體虛。 He weakened after his illness.
4. abstract; shapeless

虛薄 (ㄒㄩ ㄅㄛˊ)
to be poor in ability

虛報 (ㄒㄩ ㄅㄠˋ)
to report untruthfully

虛誣 (ㄒㄩ ㄨ)
to accuse groundlessly

虛麼 (ㄒㄩ ㄇㄧˊ) or 虛費 (ㄒㄩ ㄈㄟˋ)
to spend to no avail; to waste: 他虛麼光陰。 He wasted his time.

虛名 (ㄒㄩ ㄇㄧㄥˊ) or 虛譽 (ㄒㄩ ㄩˋ)
a reputation unsupported by facts; an empty reputation; a false reputation; an undeserved reputation

虛發 (ㄒㄩ ㄈㄚ)
to shoot without hitting the target

虛浮 (ㄒㄩ ㄈㄨˊ)
impractical; unsubstantial; vain; empty: 那是個虛浮的計畫。 That's an impractical plan.

虛誕 (ㄒㄩ ㄉㄢˋ)
unreal; fantastic; preposterous

虛度 (ㄒㄩ ㄉㄨˋ)
to pass (time) fruitlessly; to fritter away; to dream away: 切勿讓青春虛度。 Don't let your youth slip by.

虛頭 (ㄒㄩ ㄊㄡˊ)
a false statement; a lie

虛談 (ㄒㄩ ㄊㄢˊ)
an empty talk; impractical suggestions

虛脫 (ㄒㄩ ㄊㄨㄛ)
(medicine) collapse; prostration

虛擬 (ㄒㄩ ㄋㄧˇ)
to suppose; to assume; to imagine; fictitious: 那是個虛擬的故事。 That's a fictitious story.

虛構 (ㄒㄩ ㄍㄡˋ)
made-up; fictitious; to trump up; to invent; to frame: 他虛構一篇故事。 He trumped up a story.

虛誇 (ㄒㄩ ㄎㄨㄚ)
to boast; to brag

虛空 (ㄒㄩ ㄎㄨㄥ)
empty; hollow; void: 那是場虛空的勝利。 It's a hollow victory.

虛喝 (ㄒㄩ ㄏㄜˋ)
to give an empty scare; to intimidate by an empty scare

虛耗 (ㄒㄩ ㄏㄠˋ)
to expend to no avail; to waste; to fritter away

虛話 (ㄒㄩ ㄏㄨㄚˋ)
an empty talk; an unfounded statement; a lie

虛懷 (ㄒㄩ ㄏㄨㄞˊ)
to be humble or openminded (in accepting advice, instructions, etc.)

虛懷若谷 (ㄒㄩ ㄏㄨㄞˊ ㄖㄨㄛˋ ㄍㄨˇ)
(literally) to open the mind wide as a valley—to be open-minded

虛幻 (ㄒㄩ ㄏㄨㄢˋ)
illusory; visionary; unreal: 這只是一場虛幻的情景。 It's a mere illusion.

虛己 (ㄒㄩ ㄐㄧˇ)
open-minded; humble

虛假 (ㄒㄩ ㄐㄧㄚˇ)
false; unreal; dishonest: 我們認為那個人待人有點虛假。 We think that man is quite dishonest with people.

虛價 (ㄒㄩ ㄐㄧㄚˋ)
overcharge; a nominal price

虛竭 (ㄒㄩ ㄐㄧㄝˊ)
empty; exhausted

虛驕 (ㄒㄩ ㄐㄧㄠ)
unfounded pride

虛驚 (ㄒㄩ ㄐㄧㄥ)
a false alarm; a nervous fear: 我們飽受虛驚。 We suffered from nervous fears.

虛靜 (ㄒㄩ ㄐㄧㄥˋ)
having an open and peaceful mind

虛情假意 (ㄒㄩ ㄑㄧㄥˊ ㄐㄧㄚˇ ㄧˋ)
hypocrisy; insincerity; hypocritical; insincere; pretended friendship or affection

虛線 (ㄒㄩ ㄒㄧㄢˋ)
① a dotted line ② an imaginary line

虛心 (ㄒㄩ ㄒㄧㄣ)
open-minded (for advice, instructions, etc.); modesty: 虛心使人進步。 Modesty helps one to go forward.

虛心下氣 (ㄒㄩ ㄒㄧㄣ ㄒㄧㄚˋ ㄑㄧˋ)
humble and meek

虛像 (ㄒㄩ ㄒㄧㄤˋ)
(physics) a virtual image

虛實實 (ㄒㄩ ㄕˊ ㄕˊ)
(said of military strategy, tactics, etc.) seemingly false and real at the same time; feints and ambushes

虛詐 (ㄒㄩ ㄓㄚˋ)
falsehood and trickery

虛張聲勢 (ㄒㄩ ㄓㄤ ㄕㄥ ㄕˋ)
to make a deceptive show of power; to bluff: 整個會議中他都是在虛張聲勢。 He bluffed all through the conference.

虛牟 (ㄒㄩ ㄇㄨˊ)
modest; unassuming

虛實 (ㄒㄩ ㄕˊ)
① true or false; falsehood versus reality; abstractness versus concreteness: 他不知虛實。 He did not know whether it is true or false. ② the actual situation

虛室 (ㄒㄩ ㄕˋ)
an unfurnished room; an empty room

虛設 (ㄒㄩ ㄕㄜˋ)
to exist in name only

虛聲 (ㄒㄩ ㄕㄥ)
① to make a deceptive show of power; to bluff ② empty reputation; undeserved reputation

虛聲恫喝 (ㄒㄩ ㄕㄥ ㄉㄨㄥˋ ㄏㄜˋ)
to scare others by an empty threat

虛數 (ㄒㄩ ㄕㄨˋ)
(mathematics) an imaginary number

虛弱 (ㄒㄩ ㄖㄨㄛˋ)

〔虍部〕

〔庀部〕

debility; weak; feeble; 她愈來
愈虛弱了。She grew weaker
and weaker.

虛榮(ㄒㄩ ㄖㄨㄥˊ)
vanity; empty glory; vainglorious; 她愛慕虛榮。She was
affected by vanity.

虛榮心(ㄒㄩ ㄖㄨㄥˊ ㄒㄧㄣ)
vainglory; vanity

虛字(ㄒㄩ ㄗˋ)
grammatical particles; grammatical formatives; function
words; form words

虛造(ㄒㄩ ㄗㄠˋ)
to fabricate; to invent: 我們
能虛造出什麼理由呢? What
excuse can we invent?

虛左以待(ㄒㄩ ㄗㄨㄛˇ ㄧˇ ㄉㄞˋ)
to leave the seat of honor
open (for a wise man)

虛歲(ㄒㄩ ㄙㄨㄟˋ)
age according to Chinese
calculation (i.e. a person is
one year old at birth)

虛有其表(ㄒㄩ ㄧㄡˇ ㄑㄧˊ ㄅㄧㄠˇ)
impressive only in appearance; to appear better than
it is

虛言(ㄒㄩ ㄧㄢˊ)
① unfounded statements;
false remarks ② an empty
talk; meaningless words; a
platitude

虛掩(ㄒㄩ ㄧㄢˇ)
(said of a door) half open,
half closed; with the door
left unlocked or unlatched

虛應故事(ㄒㄩ ㄧㄥˋ ㄍㄨˋ ㄕˋ)
to do a thing in a perfunctory manner; to go through
the motions of doing something

虛無(ㄒㄩ ㄨˊ)
nothingness; emptiness; void;
nil

虛無飄渺(ㄒㄩ ㄨˊ ㄆㄧㄠ ㄇㄧㄠˇ)
shapeless and elusive; floating and intangible; purely
imaginary

虛無黨(ㄒㄩ ㄨˊ ㄉㄤˇ)
the Nihilists

虛無主義(ㄒㄩ ㄨˊ ㄓㄨˇ ㄧˋ)
nihilism

虛誣(ㄒㄩ ㄨ)
to accuse groundlessly

虛偽(ㄒㄩ ㄨㄟˇ)
false; spurious; hypocritical;

insincere; hypocrisy

虛位以待(ㄒㄩ ㄨㄟˋ ㄧˇ ㄉㄞˋ)
to leave a position open to
await (a wise man to fill it)

虛文(ㄒㄩ ㄨㄣˊ)
impractical formality or ceremony

虛文褥節(ㄒㄩ ㄨㄣˊ ㄖㄨˋ ㄐㄧㄝˊ)
empty forms or rituals

虛妄(ㄒㄩ ㄨㄤˋ)
showing wild imagination;
preposterously fantastic

虛與委蛇(ㄒㄩ ㄩˇ ㄨㄟˇ ㄧˊ)
to pretend kindness; to feign
civility

七畫

【虞】 5186
(ㄩˊ yu yú)

1. anxieties ; worries
2. to expect; to anticipate
3. to deceive; to cheat
4. name of a legendary dynasty
5. name of a state in the
Epoch of Spring and Au-
tumn
6. a Chinese family name

虞美人(ㄩˊ ㄇㄟˇ ㄖㄣˊ)
① a corn poppy ② the mis-
tress of Hsiang Yü (項羽),
also known as 虞姬

虞姬(ㄩˊ ㄐㄧ)
the mistress of Hsiang Yü
(項羽), who ended the Chin
(秦) Dynasty by defeating
its army

虞舜(ㄩˊ ㄕㄨㄣˋ)
a legendary emperor of
great wisdom, believed to
have ruled around 2,200 B.C.

虞人(ㄩˊ ㄖㄣˊ)
an official in charge of forests, lakes, and imperial gardens in ancient times

【虜】 5187
(ㄌㄨˇ luu lǔ)
(又讀 ㄌㄨㄛˇ luoo luo)

1. a captive; a prisoner
2. to take prisoner; to capture
alive

虜獲(ㄌㄨˇ ㄏㄨㄛˋ)
① to capture ② men and
arms captured

【號】 5188
1. ㄏㄠˋ haw hào
1. a designation; a title

2. sizes
3. orders; a command; a call
4. number (for identification
or classification)
5. a mark; a sign; a signal: 語
言是思想的符號。Words are
the signs of ideas.
6. a store; a shop
7. a bugle
8. date: 今天幾號? What is the
date today?

號兵(ㄏㄠˋ ㄅㄧㄥ)
a bugler in the army

號礮(ㄏㄠˋ ㄆㄠˋ)
artillery fire as a signal

號碼(ㄏㄠˋ ㄇㄚˇ)
a number (for identifica-
tion): 你的電話號碼幾號?
What's your telephone number?

號脈(ㄏㄠˋ ㄇㄞˋ)or(ㄏㄠˋ ㄇㄛˋ)
to feel the pulse

號房(ㄏㄠˋ ㄈㄤˊ)
① a janitor; a messenger ②
the dormitory for candidates
in civil service examination
in the Ming Dynasty

號燈(ㄏㄠˋ ㄉㄥ)
a signal lamp

號頭(ㄏㄠˋ ㄊㄡˊ)
① a mark or number (for
classification) ② a head
workman; a foreman

號筒(ㄏㄠˋ ㄊㄨㄥˇ)
a bugle

號令(ㄏㄠˋ ㄌㄧㄥˋ)
a command; an order

號令如山(ㄏㄠˋ ㄌㄧㄥˋ ㄖㄨˊ ㄕㄢ)
Orders (in the army, etc.)
are as inviolable as a mountain.

號角(ㄏㄠˋ ㄐㄧㄠˇ)
a bugle; a horn

號金(ㄏㄠˋ ㄐㄧㄣ)
registration fees

號旗(ㄏㄠˋ ㄑㄧˊ)
a signal flag

號誌(ㄏㄠˋ ㄓˋ)
a signal; a sign

號召(ㄏㄠˋ ㄓㄠˋ)
a call (to the public for an
action); to summon (the
public for a cause)

號稱(ㄏㄠˋ ㄔㄥ)
① to claim; to profess ② to
be known as

號手(ㄏㄠˋ ㄕㄡˇ)

a bugler (in the army, etc.)

號聲 (ㄏㄠˋ ㄕㄥ)
the sound of a bugle call

號數 (ㄏㄠˋ ㄕㄨˋ)
number (for identification or classification)

號子 (ㄏㄠˋ ˙ㄗ)
①a work song sung to synchronize movements, with one person leading ②(slang) a stock exchange

號衣 (ㄏㄠˋ ㄧ)
military uniforms

號外 (ㄏㄠˋ ㄨㄞˋ)
an extra (issue of a newspaper)

【號】 5188
　　ㄏㄠˊ haur háo
to cry; to shout; to howl; to wail

號咷 or 號啕 (ㄏㄠˊ ㄊㄠˊ)
to burst out crying; to weep aloud; to wail

號哭 (ㄏㄠˊ ㄎㄨ)
to weep aloud; to wail

號寒啼飢 (ㄏㄠˊ ㄏㄢˊ ㄊㄧˊ ㄐㄧ)
to cry and moan for cold and hunger

號叫 (ㄏㄠˊ ㄐㄧㄠˋ)
to shout; to yell

八畫

【虡】 5189
　　ㄐㄩˋ jiuh jù
1. a post in the framework for a bell
2. a small table with long legs placed beside a bed

九畫

【號】 5190
　　ㄍㄨㄛˊ gwo guó
name of an ancient feudal state

虢國夫人 (ㄍㄨㄛˊ ㄍㄨㄛˊ ㄈㄨ ㄖㄣˊ)
Lady of Kuo—the title given to the elder sister of Yang Yü-huan (楊玉環), a famed beauty and concubine of Emperor Hsüan Tsung (玄宗) of the Tang Dynasty

十一畫

【虧】 5191
　　ㄎㄨㄟ kuei kuī
1. to lose; to damage; to have a deficit
2. to lack; to want; short; deficient
3. to treat unfairly; to be unfair to: 我們不會虧待你的。We won't treat you unfairly.
4. fortunately; luckily; thanks to
5. used in a mocking sense: 虧他做得出來! He had the nerve to do so.
6. the waning of the moon; to wane: 月亮漸虧。The moon is waning.

虧本 (ㄎㄨㄟ ㄅㄣˇ) or 虧本兒 (ㄎㄨㄟ ㄅㄦˇ)
to suffer losses in business; to suffer a deficit

虧負 (ㄎㄨㄟ ㄈㄨˋ)
①to be deficient ②to be negligent of an obligation; to fail

虧得 (ㄎㄨㄟ ˙ㄉㄜ)
①fortunately; luckily; thanks to ②a term used in a mocking sense: 虧得你說得出口! You had the nerve to say it.

虧待 (ㄎㄨㄟ ㄉㄞˋ)
to treat (someone) shabbily; to maltreat

虧短 (ㄎㄨㄟ ㄉㄨㄢˇ)
deficient; insufficient

虧累 (ㄎㄨㄟ ㄌㄟˇ)
unable to make both ends meet; to spend more than one makes; to be in debt

虧空 (ㄎㄨㄟ ˙ㄎㄨㄥ)
①to spend more than one makes; to be in the red ②a loss; a deficit

虧耗 (ㄎㄨㄟ ㄏㄠˋ)
to lose money; loss by a natural process

虧欠 (ㄎㄨㄟ ㄑㄧㄢˋ)
①a deficit ②deficiency; insufficiency ③to owe

虧心 (ㄎㄨㄟ ㄒㄧㄣ)
to go against one's conscience; ungrateful; discreditable

虧心事 (ㄎㄨㄟ ㄒㄧㄣ ㄕˋ)
a matter for remorse; something which gives one a guilty conscience

虧折 (ㄎㄨㄟ ㄓㄜˊ)
①to lose ②a deficit

虧蝕 (ㄎㄨㄟ ㄕˊ)
①an eclipse of the sun or moon ②a deficit

虧殺 (ㄎㄨㄟ ㄕㄚ)
fortunately; luckily

虧損 (ㄎㄨㄟ ㄙㄨㄣˇ)
①a deficit; a loss; to deplete: 我的虧損很大。My losses have been great. ②enfeebled or weakened by illness

虫部
ㄏㄨㄟˇ hoei huǐ

一畫

【虬】 5192
　　(虯) ㄑㄧㄡˊ chyou qiú
a young dragon

二畫

【虯】 5193
　　(虬) ㄑㄧㄡˊ chyou qiú
a young dragon

虯蟠 (ㄑㄧㄡˊ ㄆㄢˊ)
curled up like a dragon

虯龍 (ㄑㄧㄡˊ ㄌㄨㄥˊ)
a young dragon

虯髯 (ㄑㄧㄡˊ ㄖㄢˊ) or 虯須 (ㄑㄧㄡˊ ㄒㄩ)
whiskers twisted like the barbels of a dragon; curly whiskers

虯髯客 (ㄑㄧㄡˊ ㄖㄢˊ ㄎㄜˋ)
the hero of a romance by Chang Yüeh (張說) of the Tang Dynasty

【虱】 5194
　　(蝨) ㄕ shy shī
a louse

虱目魚 (ㄕ ㄇㄨˋ ㄩˊ)
milkfish

虱子 (ㄕ ˙ㄗ)
a louse

三畫

【虹】 5195
　　ㄏㄨㄥˊ horng hóng
(翻音 《ㄤˋ ganq gàng)

【虫部】

a rainbow: 一道彩虹出現了。A rainbow appeared.

虹霓（ㄏㄨㄥˊ ㄋㄧˊ）
a rainbow and its reflection

虹橋（ㄏㄨㄥˊ ㄑㄧㄠˊ）
a rainbow-shaped bridge

虹吸管（ㄏㄨㄥˊ ㄒㄧ ㄍㄨㄢˇ）
a siphon

虹采（ㄏㄨㄥˊ ㄘㄞˇ）
banners; flags

虹彩（ㄏㄨㄥˊ ㄘㄞˇ）
①colors of a rainbow ②(anatomy) the iris

虹彩膜（ㄏㄨㄥˊ ㄘㄞˇ ㄇㄛˊ）
(anatomy) the iris

【虺】5196 1. ㄏㄨㄟˇ hoei huǐ
a species of venomous snake

虺虺（ㄏㄨㄟˇ ㄏㄨㄟˇ）
(said of thunder)to rumble; rumbling

虺蜮（ㄏㄨㄟˇ ㄩˋ）
mean and vicious people

【虺】5196 2. ㄏㄨㄟˊ huei huí
1. diseased; sick; ill
2. discouraged

虺隤（ㄏㄨㄟˊ ㄊㄨㄟˊ）
①diseased; ill; sick ②discouraged ③tired

【虼】5197 《ㄜ geh gè
a flea

虼蚤（《ㄜˋ ㄗㄠˇ）
a flea

【虻】5198 ㄇㄥˊ meng méng
a gadfly

四畫

【蚌】5199 ㄅㄤˋ bang bàng
an oyster

蚌埠（ㄅㄢˋ ㄅㄨˋ）
Pangfou, a city in Anhwei

蚌胎（ㄅㄤˋ ㄊㄞ）
the conception of an oyster —a pearl

蚌殼（ㄅㄤˋ ㄎㄜˊ）
an oyster shell

蚌線（ㄅㄤˋ ㄒㄧㄢˋ）
(mathematics) conchoid

蚌珠（ㄅㄤˋ ㄓㄨ）
a pearl

【蚊】5200 (蟁) ㄨㄣˊ wen wén

a mosquito; a gnat

蚊負蟻運（ㄨㄣˊ ㄈㄨˋ ㄧˇ ㄩㄣˋ）
(literally) mosquitoes carry and ants transport—to bear a heavy load with little strength

蚊雷（ㄨㄣˊ ㄌㄟˊ）
the buzz of a swarm of mosquitoes

蚊力（ㄨㄣˊ ㄌㄧˋ）
the strength of a mosquito —limited strength

蚊睫（ㄨㄣˊ ㄐㄧㄝˊ）
a mosquito's eyelash—a very tiny thing

蚊香（ㄨㄣˊ ㄒㄧㄤ）or蚊煙（ㄨㄣˊ ㄧㄢ）
a mosquito coil; mosquito incense

蚊陣（ㄨㄣˊ ㄓㄣˋ）
swarms of mosquitoes

蚊幮（ㄨㄣˊ ㄔㄨˊ）
a mosquito net; a mosquito-curtain; a mosquito bar

蚊蟲（ㄨㄣˊ ㄔㄨㄥˊ）
mosquitoes; gnats

蚊市（ㄨㄣˊ ㄕˋ）
swarms of mosquitoes found at dusk

蚊蚋（ㄨㄣˊ ㄖㄨㄟˋ）
mosquitoes and gnats

蚊子（ㄨㄣˊ ˙ㄗ）
a mosquito; a gnat: 蚊子會咬人。Mosquitoes bite.

蚊子香（ㄨㄣˊ ˙ㄗ ㄒㄧㄤ）
a mosquito coil; a mosquito stick

【蚪】5201 ㄉㄡˇ doou dǒu
as in 蝌蚪—a tadpole

【蚋】5202 (蜹) ㄖㄨㄟˋ ruey ruì
a gnat

蚋翼（ㄖㄨㄟˋ ㄧˋ）
wings of a gnat—very tiny things

【蚍】5203 ㄆㄧˊ pyi pí
a large ant; a species of big ant

蚍蜉（ㄆㄧˊ ㄈㄨˊ）
Camponotus liquiperdus, a kind of black ant living on pines

蚍蜉撼大樹（ㄆㄧˊ ㄈㄨˊ ㄏㄢˋ ㄉㄚˋ ㄕㄨˋ）
(literally) an ant trying to shake a large tree—an attempt to do what is far

beyond one's power

【蚓】5204 ㄧㄣˇ yiin yǐn
as in 蚯蚓—an earthworm

【蚜】5205 ㄧㄚ ya yā
a plant louse; an aphid

蚜蟲（ㄧㄚˊ ㄔㄨㄥˊ）
a plant louse; an aphid

【蚣】5206 《ㄨㄥ gong gōng
as in 蜈蚣—a centipede

【蚤】5207 ㄗㄠˇ tzao zǎo
a flea

【蚨】5208 ㄈㄨˊ fwu fú
1. a kind of water beetle
2. as in 青蚨—another name of money or cash

【蚩】5209 ㄔ chy chī
1. a kind of worm
2. ignorant; stupid
3. to laugh
4. ugly

蚩拙（ㄔ ㄓㄨㄛˊ）
stupid; ignorant

蚩蚩（ㄔ ㄔ）
ignorant; simple-looking

蚩尤（ㄔ ㄧㄡˊ）
Chih Yu, name of a legendary rebel overcome by Huang Ti(黃帝)

【蚇】5210 ㄔ chyy chǐ
an inchworm; a measuring worm; a looper

蚇蠖 or 尺蠖（ㄔˇ ㄏㄨㄛˋ）
an inchworm; a measuring worm; a looper

五畫

【蚯】5211 ㄑㄧㄡ chiou qiū
an earthworm

蚯蚓（ㄑㄧㄡ ㄧㄣˇ）
an earthworm

【蚰】5212 ㄧㄡˊ you yóu
a millipede; a milleped

蚰蜒（ㄧㄡˊ ㄧㄢˊ）
①a millipede; a common house centipede ②(said of a road) winding; zigzag

【蚱】5213 ㄓㄚˋ jah zhà

a locust; a grasshopper

蚱蜢(ㄓㄚˋ ㄇㄥˇ)
a grasshopper

蚱蟬(ㄓㄚˋ ㄔㄢˊ)
a variety of cicada

【蚶】5214 ㄏㄢ han hān
Arca inflata, a kind of clam

蚶子(ㄏㄢ ˙ㄗ)
(animal) a blood clam

【蛀】5215 ㄓㄨˋ juh zhù
1: worms that eat into wood or books
2. (said of worms) to eat into; to bore: 這些書給蟲子蛀了。The books are moth-eaten.

蛀洞(ㄓㄨˋ ㄉㄨㄥˋ)
a cavity (in a decayed tooth)

蛀齒(ㄓㄨˋ ㄔˇ)or 蛀牙(ㄓㄨˋ ㄧㄚˊ)
decayed teeth; dental caries: 他常受蛀齒之苦。He often suffers from dental caries.

蛀蟲(ㄓㄨˋ ㄔㄨㄥˊ)
worms that eat into wood, books, etc.; a moth

【蛄】5216 ㄍㄨ gu gū
a mole cricket 參見「螻蛄」

【蛆】5217 ㄑㄩ chiu qū
a maggot

【蛇】5218 ㄕㄜˊ sher shé
1. (虵)ㄕㄜˊ a snake; a serpent

蛇皮(ㄕㄜˊ ㄆㄧˊ)
a snake's skin

蛇皮癬(ㄕㄜˊ ㄆㄧˊ ㄒㄧㄢˇ)
(pathology)pityriasis, a skin disease marked by the shedding of branlike scales of epidermis

蛇蛻(ㄕㄜˊ ㄊㄨㄟˋ)
the slough of a snake

蛇吞象(ㄕㄜˊ ㄊㄨㄣ ㄒㄧㄤˋ)
very greedy (like a snake attempting to swallow an elephant)

蛇類(ㄕㄜˊ ㄌㄟˋ)
ophidia; snakes

蛇弓(ㄕㄜˊ ㄍㄨㄥ)
a kind of bow

蛇口蜂針(ㄕㄜˊ ㄎㄡˇ ㄈㄥ ㄓㄣ)
(literally) a snake's bite and a bee's sting—a very injurious thing or person

蛇蠍(ㄕㄜˊ ㄒㄧㄝ)
snakes and scorpions—things to be dreaded; vicious people: 此人毒如蛇蠍。This man was as vicious as a viper.

蛇行(ㄕㄜˊ ㄒㄧㄥˊ)
①to move like a snake; to take a zigzag course ②to creep along; to crawl

蛇神(ㄕㄜˊ ㄕㄣˊ)
①a deity in the form of a snake ②bizarre

蛇鼠橫行(ㄕㄜˊ ㄕㄨˇ ㄏㄥˊ ㄒㄧㄥˊ)
(literally) Snakes and rats are rampant.—Wicked people are rampant.

蛇足(ㄕㄜˊ ㄗㄨˊ)
feet for a snake—superfluity

蛇影杯弓(ㄕㄜˊ ㄧㄥˇ ㄅㄟ ㄍㄨㄥ)
illusion caused by suspicion

蛇無頭不行(ㄕㄜˊ ㄨˊ ㄊㄡˊ ㄅㄨˋ ㄒㄧㄥˊ)
(literally) A snake cannot move without a head.—A group of people can accomplish little without a leader.

蛇紋石(ㄕㄜˊ ㄨㄣˊ ㄕˊ)
(mining) serpentine (a dull-greenish rock)

【蛇】5218 2. (她)ㄧˊ yi yí
1. complacent
2. to pretend cordiality

【蛉】5219 ㄌㄧㄥˊ ling líng
1. as in 蜻蛉—*Libellulidae*, a variety of dragonfly
2. as in 螟蛉—the larva of *Chilo simplex*, a kind of harmful insect; the mulberry insect

【蛋】5220 ㄉㄢˋ dann dàn
1. an egg
2. a fellow

蛋白(ㄉㄢˋ ㄅㄞˊ)or 蛋清(ㄉㄢˋ ㄑㄧㄥ)
the white of an egg; egg white; albumen

蛋白質(ㄉㄢˋ ㄅㄞˊ ㄓˊ)
protein; albumen

蛋白石(ㄉㄢˋ ㄅㄞˊ ㄕˊ)
opal

蛋粉(ㄉㄢˋ ㄈㄣˇ)
powdered eggs

蛋糕(ㄉㄢˋ ㄍㄠ)
cake: 吃點蛋糕吧! Have some cake.

蛋殼(ㄉㄢˋ ㄎㄜˊ)
the eggshell

蛋戶 or 蜑戶(ㄉㄢˋ ㄏㄨˋ)
the boat people of Kwang-tung (廣東)

蛋黃(ㄉㄢˋ ㄏㄨㄤˊ)
yolk

蛋酒(ㄉㄢˋ ㄐㄧㄡˇ)
egg flip; eggnog

蛋捲(ㄉㄢˋ ㄐㄩㄢˇ)
an egg roll

蛋捲冰淇淋(ㄉㄢˋ ㄐㄩㄢˇ ㄅㄧㄥ ㄑㄧˊ ㄌㄧㄣˊ)
an ice-cream cone

蛋形(ㄉㄢˋ ㄒㄧㄥˊ); oval
egg-shaped; oval

六畫

【蛙】5221 ㄨㄚ ua wā
a frog

蛙鳴(ㄨㄚ ㄇㄧㄥˊ)
croaks of frogs

蛙鳴蟬噪(ㄨㄚ ㄇㄧㄥˊ ㄔㄢˊ ㄗㄠˋ)
(literally) croaks of frogs and chirps of cicadas —meaningless argument or debate

蛙生(ㄨㄚ ㄕㄥ)
the noise of frogs in the evening

蛙人(ㄨㄚ ㄖㄣˊ)
a frogman

蛙泳(ㄨㄚ ㄩㄥˇ)
(swimming) the breaststroke

【蛔】5222 ㄏㄨㄟˊ hwei huí
an ascarid; a roundworm

蛔蟲(ㄏㄨㄟˊ ㄔㄨㄥˊ)
an ascarid; a roundworm

【蛛】5223 ㄓㄨ ju zhū
a spider

蛛絲(ㄓㄨ ㄙ)
gossamer; the thread spun by a spider

蛛絲馬跡(ㄓㄨ ㄙ ㄇㄚˇ ㄐㄧ)
①subtle organization (of a composition, etc.) ②clues; leads

蛛網(ㄓㄨ ㄨㄤˇ)
a spider's web; a cobweb

【蛟】5224 ㄐㄧㄠ jiau jiāo
1. flood dragon, a mythical creature capable of invoking storms and floods

〔虫部〕

【虫部】

2. a shark

蛟龍(ㄐㄧㄠ ㄌㄨㄥˊ)
a flood dragon

蛟龍得水(ㄐㄧㄠ ㄌㄨㄥˊ ㄉㄜˊ ㄕㄨㄟˇ)
(literally) water for the flood dragon—opportunity for a great man to fulfill his ambition

蚓蚰(ㄐㄧㄠ ㄧㄡˊ)
curled up like a dragon

蛟篆(ㄐㄧㄠ ㄓㄨㄢˋ)
wriggly-shaped seal-type characters on bells, tripods, etc.

【蛤】 5225
1.《ㄜˊ ger gé
a clam

蛤蚌(《ㄜˊ ㄅㄤˋ)or 蛤蜊(《ㄜˊ ㄌㄧˊ)
or 蛤蠣(《ㄜˊ ㄌㄧˋ)
Mactra veneriformis, a kind of bivalve

蛤灰(《ㄜˊ ㄏㄨㄟ)
lime obtained by burning sea shells

【蛤】 5225
2. ㄏㄚˊ har há
a toad

蛤蟆(ㄏㄚˊ ·ㄇㄚ)or 蝦蟆(ㄒㄧㄚˊ ·ㄇㄚ)
a toad

【蛩】 5226
ㄑㄩㄥˊ chyong qióng
1. a locust
2. a cricket

蛩鳴(ㄑㄩˊ ㄇㄧㄥˊ)
the chirps of crickets

蛩蟬(ㄑㄩˊ ㄔㄢˊ)
crickets and cicadas

蛩蛩(ㄑㄩˊ ㄑㄩˊ)
anxious; apprehensive

蛩鳴(ㄑㄩˊ ㄇㄧㄥˊ)
the chirps of crickets

蛩吟(ㄑㄩˊ ㄧㄣˊ)
the chirps of crickets

【蛭】 5227
ㄓ jyh zhì
a leech

蛭石(ㄓ ㄕˊ)
(mining) vermiculite

【蛆】 5228
ㄑㄩ chiu qū
a cricket

蛐蛐兒(ㄑㄩ ·ㄑㄩㄦ)
a cricket

【蛐】 5228
ㄑㄩ chyu qú
an earthworm

蛐蟮(ㄑㄩ ·ㄕㄢˋ)
an earthworm

【蚰】 5229
ㄎㄨㄣ kuen kūn
insects

七畫

【蛺】 5230
ㄐㄧㄚˊ jya jiá
butterflies

蛺蝶(ㄐㄧㄚˊ ㄉㄧㄝˊ)
butterflies (harmful to crop plants); a vanessa

【蛸】 5231
ㄒㄧㄠ shiau xiāo
as in 螵蛸—mantis's egg capsule

【蛸】 5231
ㄕㄠ shau shāo
a variety of spider

【蛹】 5232
ㄩㄥˇ yeong yǒng
a chrysalis; a pupa

蛹化(ㄩㄥˇ ㄏㄨㄚˋ)
pupation

蛹臥(ㄩㄥˇ ㄨㄛˋ)
to live in seclusion (like a chrysalis in its cocoon)

【蛻】 5233
ㄕㄨㄟˋ shuey shuì
(又讀 ㄊㄨㄟˋ tuey tuì)
1. to slough; to exuviate
2. exuviae; a slough
①to undergo transformation ②decay

蛻皮(ㄕㄨㄟˋ ㄆㄧˊ)
to exuviate; to slough

蛻蛻(ㄕㄨㄟˋ ㄕㄨㄟˋ)
exuviae; to exuviate

【蛾】 5234
ㄜˊ er é
a moth

蛾眉(ㄜˊ ㄇㄟˊ)
long, slender eyebrows arched like the antennae of a moth; beautiful eyebrows of a woman

蛾眉月(ㄜˊ ㄇㄟˊ ㄩㄝˋ)
the crescent moon

蛾綠(ㄜˊ ㄌㄩˋ)or 蛾翠(ㄜˊ ㄘㄨㄟˋ)
dark-green coloring material for eyebrows formerly used by women

【蜀】 5235
ㄕㄨˇ shuu shǔ
1. Shu, an ancient kingdom in

what is Szechwan today
2. an alternative name of Szechwan (四川)

蜀道難(ㄕㄨˇ ㄉㄠˋ ㄋㄢˊ)
The roads in Szechwan are difficult to walk.

蜀葵(ㄕㄨˇ ㄎㄨㄟˊ)
a hollyhock (Althaea rosea)

蜀漢(ㄕㄨˇ ㄏㄢˋ)
the Kingdom of Shu (221-263) established by Liu Pei (劉備), one of the Three Kingdoms that followed the Han Dynasty

蜀雞(ㄕㄨˇ ㄐㄧ)
a variety of large chicken (believed to originate in Szechwan)

蜀錦(ㄕㄨˇ ㄐㄧㄣˇ)
tapestry from Szechwan

蜀犬吠日(ㄕㄨˇ ㄑㄩㄢˇ ㄈㄟˋ ㄖˋ)
(literally) Szechwan dogs barking at the sun (which they see very rarely)—an inexperienced person feeling curious at or getting excited over something new to him

蜀窯(ㄕㄨˇ ㄧㄠˊ)
name of an ancient porcelain kiln in Szechwan

【蜂】 5236
ㄈㄥ feng fēng
a bee; a wasp: 蜜蜂釀蜜。The bee makes honey.

蜂蜜(ㄈㄥ ㄇㄧˋ)
honey: 這果汁像蜂蜜一樣的甜。The juice is (as) sweet as honey.

蜂目豺聲(ㄈㄥ ㄇㄨˋ ㄔㄞˊ ㄕㄥ)
with the eyes of a wasp and the voice of a wolf—very fierce; very cruel

蜂房(ㄈㄥ ㄈㄤˊ)or 蜂窩(ㄈㄥ ㄨㄛ)or 蜂巢(ㄈㄥ ㄔㄠˊ)
a beehive; a honeycomb

蜂鳥(ㄈㄥ ㄋㄧㄠˇ)
hermit, Oreatus underwoodi, a tiny tropical hummingbird

蜂蠟(ㄈㄥ ㄌㄚˋ)
beeswax

蜂聚(ㄈㄥ ㄐㄩˋ)
to swarm to a place

蜂起(ㄈㄥ ㄑㄧˇ)
to rise in a swarm

蜂餳(ㄈㄥ ㄒㄧㄥˊ)
honey 亦作「蜂蜜」

蜂準(ㄈㄥ ㄓㄨㄣˇ)

a high nose

蜂巢胃(ㄈㄥ ㄔㄠˊ ㄨㄟˋ)or 蜂窩胃
(ㄈㄥ ㄨㄛ ㄨㄟˋ)
the reticulum (a digestive organ of animals); the honeycomb stomach

蜂出(ㄈㄥ ㄔㄨ)
numerous and confusing (like bees flying about in a swarm)

蜂乳(ㄈㄥ ㄖㄨˇ)
royal jelly

蜂刺(ㄈㄥ ㄘˋ)
the sting of a bee or wasp

蜂腰(ㄈㄥ ㄧㄠ)
①a slim waist (like that of a wasp) ②an error in versification, one of the eight faults in writing a poem

蜂午(ㄈㄥ ㄨˇ)
crowded and confusing

蜂王(ㄈㄥ ㄨㄤˊ)
a queen bee; a queen wasp

蜂擁(ㄈㄥ ㄩㄥ)
in a swarm; to swarm

蜂擁而上(ㄈㄥ ㄩㄥˊ ㄦˊ ㄕㄤˋ)
to close in a swarm

【蜃】 5237　ㄕㄣˋ　shenn　shèn
clams

蜃樓(ㄕㄣˋ ㄌㄡˊ)
as in 海市蜃樓—a mirage

蜃蛤(ㄕㄣˋ ㄍㄜˊ)
a clam

蜃氣(ㄕㄣˋ ㄑㄧˋ)or 蜃市(ㄕㄣˋ ㄕˋ)
a mirage

蜃車(ㄕㄣˋ ㄔㄜ)
a hearse

【蜆】 5238　ㄒㄧㄢˇ　shean　xiǎn
Corbicula leana, a variety of bivalve

【蜇】 5239　ㄓㄜˊ　jer　zhé
1. as in 海蜇—jellyfish
2. to sting

【蜊】 5240　ㄌㄧˊ　li　lí
as in 蛤蜊—a kind of bivalve

【蜓】 5241　ㄊㄧㄥˊ　tyng　tíng
as in 蜻蜓—a dragonfly

【蜒】 5242　ㄧㄢˊ　yan　yán
1. as in 蜒蚰—a millipede
2. as in 蜿蜒—to stretch for

miles

【蜈】 5243　ㄨˊ　wu　wú
a centipede

蜈蚣(ㄨˊ ㄍㄨㄥ)
a centipede

【蜉】 5244　ㄈㄨˊ　fwu　fú
an ephemera; an ephemerid; a mayfly

蜉蝣(ㄈㄨˊ ㄧㄡˊ)
an ephemera; an ephemerid; a mayfly

【蜍】 5245　ㄔㄨˊ　chwu　chú
as in 蟾蜍—a toad

【蜋】 5246
1. as in 螳蜋 or 螗蜋—a mantis
2. a cicada

蜋蜩(ㄌㄤˊ ㄊㄧㄠˊ)
a cicada

【蜋】 5246
2. ㄌㄧㄤˊ　liang　liáng
as in 蜣蜋—the dung beetle (*Geotrupes laevistriatus*)

【蜑】 5247　ㄉㄢˋ　dann　dàn
the boat people in the coastal areas of Fukien (福建) and Kwangtung (廣東)

蜑戶(ㄉㄢˋ ㄏㄨˋ)or 蜑人(ㄉㄢˋ ㄖㄣˊ)
the boat people in the coastal areas of Fukien (福建) and Kwangtung (廣東)

蜑家(ㄉㄢˋ ㄐㄧㄚ)
boat houses of the boat people

八畫

【蜥】 5248　ㄒㄧ　shi　xī
a lizard

蜥蜴(ㄒㄧ ㄧˋ)
a lizard

蜥蜴類(ㄒㄧ ㄧˋ ㄌㄟˋ)
saurians

【蜘】 5249　ㄓ　jy　zhī
a spider

蜘蛛(ㄓ ㄓㄨ)
a spider: 蜘蛛織網。A spider weaves a web.

蜘蛛絲(ㄓ ㄓㄨ ㄙ)
gossamer; the thread spun by a spider

蜘蛛網(ㄓ ㄓㄨ ㄨㄤˇ)

a spider's web; a cobweb

【蜚】 5250　ㄈㄟˇ　feei　fěi
a cockroach

蜚蠊(ㄈㄟˇ ㄌㄧㄢˊ)
a cockroach 亦作「蜚蠊」

【蜚】 5250
2.(飛)ㄈㄟ　fei　fēi
to fly

蜚短流長(ㄈㄟ ㄉㄨㄢˇ ㄌㄧㄡˊ ㄔㄤˊ)
to spread rumors; to gossip; rumors; gossips 亦作「飛短流長」

蜚聲(ㄈㄟ ㄕㄥ)
spreading fame; to make a name; to become famous

蜚聲國際(ㄈㄟ ㄕㄥ ㄍㄨㄛˊ ㄐㄧˋ)
world-renowned; internationally famous

蜚語(ㄈㄟ ㄩˇ)
rumors: 是誰散佈了流言蜚語？Who spread the rumors?

【蜜】 5251　ㄇㄧˋ　mih　mì
1. honey; nectar (in a flower)
2. sweet; syrupy; honeyed

蜜蜂(ㄇㄧˋ ㄈㄥ)
a honeybee; a bee: 他們像蜜蜂一樣忙。They are as busy as bees.

蜜蠟(ㄇㄧˋ ㄌㄚˋ)
beeswax

蜜裏調油(ㄇㄧˋ ㄌㄧˇ ㄊㄧㄠˊ ㄧㄡˊ)
on intimate terms

蜜柑(ㄇㄧˋ ㄍㄢ)or 蜜橘(ㄇㄧˋ ㄐㄩˊ)
a variety of sweet tangerine from South China

蜜供(ㄇㄧˋ ㄍㄨㄥˋ)
narrow strips of dough fried and sweetened (used as a sacrifice)

蜜酒(ㄇㄧˋ ㄐㄧㄡˇ)
sweetened wine or liquor

蜜餞(ㄇㄧˋ ㄐㄧㄢˋ)
preserves; sweetmeats; candied fruit

蜜餞砒霜(ㄇㄧˋ ㄐㄧㄢˋ ㄆㄧ ㄕㄨㄤ)
sweetmeats made with arsenic—sugarcoated poison

蜜漬(ㄇㄧˋ ㄗˋ)
preserves

蜜棗(ㄇㄧˋ ㄗㄠˇ)
date preserves

蜜語(ㄇㄧˋ ㄩˇ)
honeyed words; sweet talk

蜜月(ㄇㄧˋ ㄩㄝˋ)
a honeymoon: 他們在鄉間度

〔虫部〕

〔虫部〕

蜜月：They spent their honeymoon in the country.
蜜月旅行（ㄇㄧˋ ㄩㄝˋ ㄌㄩˇ ㄒㄧㄥˊ）
a honeymoon tour

【蜡】 5252 ㄓㄚˋ jah zhà
year-end sacrifice of the Chou Dynasty
蜡祭（ㄓㄚˋ ㄐㄧˋ）
year-end sacrifice
蜡月（ㄓㄚˋ ㄩㄝˋ）
the 12th lunar month

【蝂】 5253 ㄅㄢˇ baan bǎn
as in 蟲蝂—a kind of small insect which can move things many times its weight

【蜢】 5254 ㄇㄥˇ meeng měng
as in 蚱蜢—a grasshopper

【蜣】 5255 ㄑㄧㄤ chiang qiāng
a dung beetle
蜣螂（ㄑㄧㄤ ㄌㄤˊ）or 蜣蜋（ㄑㄧㄤ ㄌㄧㄤˊ）
a dung beetle

【蝄】 5256 ㄨㄤˇ woang wǎng
a kind of monster
蝄蜽（ㄨㄤˇ ㄌㄧㄤˇ）
a kind of monster

【蜩】 5257 ㄊㄧㄠˊ tyau tiáo
cicadas
蜩螗沸羹（ㄊㄧㄠˊ ㄊㄤˊ ㄈㄟˋ ㄍㄥ）
very noisy
蜩甲（ㄊㄧㄠˊ ㄐㄧㄚˇ）
a cicada's exuviae; the shell of the cicada

【蜮】 5258 ㄩˋ yuh yù
a fabulous tortoise-like creature, the sand cast out of whose mouth is believed deadly to humans

【蜴】 5259 ㄧˋ yih yì
as in 蜥蜴—a lizard

【蜷】 5260 ㄑㄩㄢˊ chyuan quán
to wriggle; to be coiled; to be curled up
蜷伏（ㄑㄩㄢˊ ㄈㄨˊ）
to curl up; to huddle up; to lie with the knees drawn up
蜷局 or 蜷跼 or 踡跼（ㄑㄩㄢˊ ㄐㄩˊ）
curled up
蜷曲（ㄑㄩㄢˊ ㄑㄩ）

wriggly; twisted
蜷縮（ㄑㄩㄢˊ ㄙㄨˋ）
not stretched; twisted; wriggly
蜷蜿（ㄑㄩㄢˊ ㄨㄢ）
to wind round and round

【蜻】 5261 ㄑㄧㄥ ching qīng
a dragonfly
蜻蜓（ㄑㄧㄥ ㄊㄧㄥˊ）
a dragonfly
蜻蜓點水（ㄑㄧㄥ ㄊㄧㄥˊ ㄉㄧㄢˇ ㄕㄨㄟˇ）
a delicate touch (like that of a dragonfly upon the water surface)—to touch on something without going into it deeply
蜻蛉（ㄑㄧㄥ ㄌㄧㄥˊ）
Libellulidae, a species of dragonfly
蜻蜻（ㄑㄧㄥ ㄑㄧㄥ）
an insect resembling a cicada

【蜾】 5262 ㄍㄨㄛˇ guoo guǒ
a kind of wasp; the sphex
蜾蠃（ㄍㄨㄛˇ ㄌㄨㄛˇ）
Eumenes pomiformis, a kind of wasp; the sphex

【蜿】 5263 ㄨㄢ uan wān
to creep; to wriggle; to wind up: 道路蜿蜒到山丘上。 The road winds up the hill.
蜿蜒（ㄨㄢ ㄧㄢˊ）
①creeping; snaky ②wriggly ③to wriggle; to snake; to meander

【蝀】 5264 ㄉㄨㄥ dong dōng
（又讀 ㄉㄨㄥˋ donq dòng）
as in 螮蝀—a rainbow

【蜨】 5265 ㄉㄧㄝˊ dye dié
a butterfly

【蜺】 5266 ㄋㄧˊ ni ní
the reflection of a rainbow

【蜹】 5267 ㄖㄨㄟˋ ruey ruì
a gnat

九畫

【蝙】 5268 ㄅㄧㄢ bian biān
（又讀 ㄅㄧㄢ bean biān）
a bat
蝙蝠（ㄅㄧㄢ ㄈㄨˊ）
a bat
蝙蝠類（ㄅㄧㄢ ㄈㄨˊ ㄌㄟˋ）
Chiroptera

【蝌】 5269 ㄎㄜ ke kē
a tadpole
蝌蚪（ㄎㄜ ㄉㄡˇ）
a tadpole
蝌蚪文（ㄎㄜ ㄉㄡˇ ㄨㄣˊ）
tadpole characters (of the Chou Dynasty, with strokes of characters shaped like tadpoles)

【蝕】 5270 ㄕˊ shyr shí
1. to eclipse; an eclipse: 日蝕 a solar eclipse 月蝕 a lunar eclipse
2. to erode; to eat up slowly: 金屬為酸所腐蝕。 Metals are eroded by acids.
蝕本（ㄕˊ ㄅㄣˇ）
to suffer losses in business; to lose money; to lose one's capital
蝕損（ㄕˊ ㄙㄨㄣˇ）
to suffer losses in (funds, capital, etc.)

【蝗】 5271 ㄏㄨㄤˊ hwang huáng
a locust
蝗蟲（ㄏㄨㄤˊ ㄔㄨㄥˊ）
a locust

【蝘】 5272 ㄧㄢˇ yean yǎn
1. a variety of cicada
2. a gecko
蝘蜓（ㄧㄢˇ ㄊㄧㄥˊ）
a gecko 亦作「壁虎」

【蝎】 5273 ㄒㄧㄝ shie xiē
a scorpion
蝎毒（ㄒㄧㄝ ㄉㄨˊ）
scorpion venom

【蝟】 5274 ㄨㄟˋ wey wèi
a hedgehog
蝟毛（ㄨㄟˋ ㄇㄠˊ）
the spines of a hedgehog—crowded and complicated
蝟集（ㄨㄟˋ ㄐㄧˊ）
to be crowded and compli-

cated (like the spines of a hedgehog)

蝟起(ㄨㄟ ㄑㄧˇ)
(said of troubles, etc.) to arise in large numbers (like the spines of a hedgehog)

蝟鼠(ㄨㄟ ㄕㄨˇ)
a hedgehog 亦作「刺蝟」

蝟縮(ㄨㄟ ㄙㄨ)
to curl up like a hedgehog; to recoil; to wince; to shrink; scared

【蝠】5275
ㄈㄨˊ fwu fú
as in 蝙蝠—a bat

【蜵】5276
ㄖㄨㄢˇ roan ruǎn
to wriggle

【蝣】5277
ㄧㄡˊ you yóu
as in 蜉蝣—an ephemera; a mayfly

【蝤】5278
ㄑㄧㄡˊ chyou qiú
1. the chrysalis of a kind of beetle
2. an ephemera; a mayfly

蝤蠐(ㄑㄧㄡˊ ㄑㄧˊ)
the chrysalis of a kind of beetle; a tree-grub (to which a woman's neck was likened in ancient times)

【蝥】5279
ㄇㄠˊ mau máo
a kind of noxious insect that feeds on the roots of rice plants

【蝦】5280
1. ㄒㄧㄚ shia xiā
a shrimp

蝦米(ㄒㄧㄚ ㄇㄧˇ)
dried shrimps

蝦荒蟹亂(ㄒㄧㄚ ㄏㄨㄤ ㄒㄧㄝˋ ㄌㄨㄢˋ)
panic among shrimps and crabs—an omen of war

蝦醬(ㄒㄧㄚ ㄐㄧㄤˋ)
salty shrimp paste

蝦簾(ㄒㄧㄚ ㄌㄧㄢˊ)
①barbels of a shrimp ②a bamboo curtain

蝦仁(ㄒㄧㄚ ㄖㄣˊ)or 蝦仁兒(ㄒㄧㄚ ㄖㄜˊㄦ)
a shrimp with its shell removed

蝦夷(ㄒㄧㄚ ㄧˊ)
①a people who in ancient times inhabited northern Japan; Aino (or Ainu)②old

name of Hokkaido 亦作「北海道」

【蝦】5280
2. ㄏㄚˊ har há
as in 蝦蟆—a toad

蝦蟆(ㄏㄚˊ ㄇㄚ)
a toad

【蝮】5281
ㄈㄨˊ fuh fú
a kind of small insect which can move things many times its weight

蝮蜪(ㄈㄨˊ ㄘㄢˊ)
a kind of small insect which can move things many times its weight

【蝨】5282
(虱) ㄕ shy shī
a louse

蝨目魚(ㄕ ㄇㄨˋ ㄩˊ)
a milkfish

蝨官(ㄕ ㄍㄨㄢ)
a corrupt official; a wicked official

蝨處褌中(ㄕ ㄔㄨˇ ㄎㄨㄣ ㄓㄨㄥ)
a louse inside the pants —lacking vision; mentally nearsighted

蝨子(ㄕ ˙ㄗ)
a louse

【蝮】5283
ㄈㄨˊ fuh fú
a viper

蝮蛇(ㄈㄨˊ ㄕㄜˊ)
a viper

【蝱】5284
(虻) ㄇㄥˊ meng méng
a gadfly

【蝴】5285
ㄏㄨˊ hwu hú
a butterfly

蝴蝶(ㄏㄨˊ ㄉㄧㄝˊ)
a butterfly

蝴蝶夢(ㄏㄨˊ ㄉㄧㄝˊ ㄇㄥˋ)
①a drama, by Kuan Han-ching (關漢卿) ②a play about Chuang-tzu's testing the chastity of his wife, by an anonymous author in the Ching Dynasty

蝴蝶骨(ㄏㄨˊ ㄉㄧㄝˊ ㄍㄨˇ)
(anatomy) the sphenoid bone 亦作「蝶骨」

蝴蝶花(ㄏㄨˊ ㄉㄧㄝˊ ㄏㄨㄚ)
a fringed iris; a fleur-de-lis

蝴蝶結(ㄏㄨˊ ㄉㄧㄝˊ ㄐㄧㄝˊ)
a rosette; a bow tie

蝴蝶裝(ㄏㄨˊ ㄉㄧㄝˊ ㄓㄨㄤ)
a way of binding books in former times somewhat similar to today's Western-style binding

【蝶】5286
(蜨) ㄉㄧㄝˊ dye dié
a butterfly

蝶夢(ㄉㄧㄝˊ ㄇㄥˋ)
to dream in sleep (from the story of Chuang-tzu's once dreaming that he was a butterfly)

蝶粉(ㄉㄧㄝˊ ㄈㄣˇ)
powdery substance on the wings of a butterfly

蝶粉蜂黃(ㄉㄧㄝˊ ㄈㄣˇ ㄈㄥ ㄏㄨㄤˊ)
woman's virginity (from the observation that the color of a butterfly or a bee fade after mating)

蝶衣(ㄉㄧㄝˊ ㄧ)
wings of a butterfly

蝶泳(ㄉㄧㄝˊ ㄩㄥˇ)
(swimming) butterfly stroke

【蝸】5287
ㄍㄨㄚ gua guā
a snail

蝸髻(ㄍㄨㄚ ㄐㄧˋ)
snaillike hair style of a child (in former times)

蝸牛(ㄍㄨㄚ ㄋㄧㄡˊ)
a snail: 車子像蝸牛似的前進。
The cars moved at a snail's pace.

蝸廬(ㄍㄨㄚ ㄌㄨˊ)or 蝸舍(ㄍㄨㄚ ㄕㄜˋ)
a cottage; a simple dwelling

蝸角(ㄍㄨㄚ ㄐㄧㄠˇ)
a snail's tentacles—very tiny things

蝸居(ㄍㄨㄚ ㄐㄩ)
(my) humble house

蝸跡(ㄍㄨㄚ ㄐㄧˋ)
the track of a snail

【蜠】5288
ㄐㄧㄝˊ jye jié
1. a cricket
2. a centipede
3. a dragonfly

蜠蛉(ㄐㄧㄝˊ ㄌㄧㄥˊ)
a dragonfly

蜠蛆(ㄐㄧㄝˊ ㄐㄩ)
①a centipede ②a cricket

【蝯】5289
(猿) ㄩㄢˊ yuan yuán
a monkey

部
虫

十　畫

【蟷】 5290
ㄊㄤˊ tarng táng
蟷蜋(ㄊㄤ ㄌㄤˊ)
a kind of cicada
蟷蜋(ㄊㄤ ㄌㄤˊ)
a kind of cicada

【螃】 5291
ㄆㄤˊ parng páng
a crab
螃蜞(ㄆㄤˊ ㄑㄧˊ)
Grapsus sp., a kind of crab
螃蟹(ㄆㄤˊ ㄒㄧㄝˋ)
Grapsus nankin, a kind of crab

【蝴】 5292
ㄙ sy sī
a kind of mollusk with spiral shell

【螈】 5293
ㄩㄢˊ yuan yuán
1. Diemyctylus pyrrhogaster, a kind of amphibious reptile; a salamander
2. a kind of silkworm

【融】 5294
ㄖㄨㄥˊ rong róng
1. very bright; glowing; burning
2. to melt
3. to melt into; to blend; to harmonize: 油和水不相融。 Oil and water don't blend.
4. cheerful; happy; joyful
5. a Chinese family name

融風(ㄖㄨㄥˊ ㄈㄥ)
spring breeze
融通(ㄖㄨㄥˊ ㄊㄨㄥ)
to comprehend; to bring together and understand thoroughly
融合 or 融和(ㄖㄨㄥˊ ㄏㄜˊ)
to blend; to fuse
融化(ㄖㄨㄥˊ ㄏㄨㄚˋ)
to melt; to fuse; to thaw
融會(ㄖㄨㄥˊ ㄏㄨㄟˋ)
to blend harmoniously
融會貫通(ㄖㄨㄥˊ ㄏㄨㄟˋ ㄍㄨㄢˋ ㄊㄨㄥ)
to blend harmoniously and grasp thoroughly; well digested and completely understood
融解(ㄖㄨㄥˊ ㄐㄧㄝˇ)
to melt; to thaw
融解點(ㄖㄨㄥˊ ㄐㄧㄝˇ ㄉㄧㄢˇ)
the melting point; the point of fusion

融解熱(ㄖㄨㄥˊ ㄐㄧㄝˇ ㄖㄜˋ)
the heat of fusion
融洽(ㄖㄨㄥˊ ㄒㄧㄚˋ)or(ㄖㄨㄥˊ ㄑㄧㄚˋ)
(said especially of human relations) harmonious
融融(ㄖㄨㄥˊ ㄖㄨㄥˊ)
①merry; happy; gay; joyful; cheerful ② warm; mild
融液(ㄖㄨㄥˊ ㄧㄝˋ)
a solid in a molten state

【螓】 5295
ㄑㄧㄣˊ chyn qín
a kind of small cicada
螓首蛾眉(ㄑㄧㄣˊ ㄕㄡˇ ㄜˊ ㄇㄟˊ)
the beautiful look of a woman 參看「蛾眉」

【螞】 5296
ㄇㄚˇ maa mǎ
1. an ant
2. a kind of leech
螞蟥(ㄇㄚˇ ㄏㄨㄤˊ)
a kind of leech
螞蟻(ㄇㄚˇ ㄧˇ)
an ant

【螟】 5297
ㄇㄧㄥˊ ming míng
the larva of Chilo simplex, a kind of moth
螟蛉(ㄇㄧㄥˊ ㄌㄧㄥˊ)
the larva of Chilo simplex
螟蛉子(ㄇㄧㄥˊ ㄌㄧㄥˊ ˙ㄗ)
an adopted son
螟蛉蛾(ㄇㄧㄥˊ ㄌㄧㄥˊ ㄜˊ)
Heliothis armigera, a kind of moth
螟蟲(ㄇㄧㄥˊ ㄔㄨㄥˊ)
the larva of Chilo simplex, a kind of moth
螟蛾(ㄇㄧㄥˊ ㄜˊ)
Chilo simplex, a kind of moth

【螢】 5298
ㄧㄥˊ yng yíng
a luminous insect; a firefly; a glowworm
螢光(ㄧㄥˊ ㄍㄨㄤ)
fluorescence
螢光板(ㄧㄥˊ ㄍㄨㄤ ㄅㄢˇ)
a fluorescent screen
螢光幕(ㄧㄥˊ ㄍㄨㄤ ㄇㄨˋ)
a screen
螢光燈(ㄧㄥˊ ㄍㄨㄤ ㄉㄥ)
a fluorescent lamp 亦作「日光燈」
螢火蟲(ㄧㄥˊ ㄏㄨㄛˇ ㄔㄨㄥˊ)
a firefly; a glowworm
螢窗(ㄧㄥˊ ㄔㄨㄤ)

to study by the light of glowworms
螢石(ㄧㄥˊ ㄕˊ)
fluorite

【蚉】 5299
(蚊) ㄨㄣˊ wen wén
a mosquito

【螂】 5300
(蜋) ㄌㄤˊ lang láng
same as 蜋

十一畫

【蜇】 5301
ㄓㄜ je zhē
(又讀ㄕˋ shyh shì)
1. a poisonous insect; a scorpion
2. to sting

【螬】 5302
ㄘㄠˊ tsaur cáo
a grub (the larva of a beetle)

【螭】 5303
ㄔ chy chī
a hornless dragon (usually represented in engravings adorning palaces, etc.)
螭陛(ㄔ ㄅㄧˋ)
steps of the imperial palace
螭魅 or 螭魅(ㄔ ㄇㄟˋ)
a man-eating goblin
螭魅罔兩(ㄔ ㄇㄟˋ ㄨㄤˇ ㄌㄧㄤˇ)
monsters and devils 亦作「魑魅魍魎」
螭首(ㄔ ㄕㄡˇ)or 螭頭(ㄔ ㄊㄡˊ)
the top of various structures adorned with a representation of the hornless dragon

【螮】 5304
(蝃) ㄉㄧˋ dih dì
a rainbow
螮蝀(ㄉㄧˋ ㄉㄨㄥ)
a rainbow

【螯】 5305
ㄠˊ aur áo
nippers (of crabs, etc.)

【螳】 5306
ㄊㄤˊ tarng táng
a mantis
螳臂當車(ㄊㄤˊ ㄅㄧˋ ㄉㄤ ㄐㄩ)
(literally) a mantis trying to stop a cart with its arms—brave but rash attempts to do what is far beyond one's ability
螳斧(ㄊㄤˊ ㄈㄨˇ)
ax-shaped forelegs of a man-

〔虫部〕

tis

螗螂(ㄊㄤ ㄌㄤ)

a mantis

螗螂捕蟬，黃雀在後(ㄊㄤ ㄌㄤ
ㄅㄨˇ ㄔㄢˊ ㄏㄨㄤˊ ㄑㄩㄝˋ ㄗㄞˋ ㄏㄡˋ)

(literally) the mantis seizing
the cicada not knowing the
oriole was just behind
—recklessness of one blinded by greed; to covet gains
ahead without knowing the
danger behind

【螺】 5307
ㄌㄨㄛˊ luo luó

1. a spiral shell; a conch
2. an alias of wine cups
3. a spiral

螺杯(ㄌㄨㄛˊ ㄅㄟ)

a cup made of a spiral shell

螺貝(ㄌㄨㄛˊ ㄅㄟˋ)

a spiral shell

螺黛(ㄌㄨㄛˊ ㄉㄞˋ)

coloring material for the
eyebrows used in former
times

螺鈿(ㄌㄨㄛˊ ㄉㄧㄢˋ)

①inlay of polished conchs
(on wares) ②mother-of-
pearl inlay

螺髻(ㄌㄨㄛˊ ㄐㄧˋ)

a spiral headdress

螺階(ㄌㄨㄛˊ ㄐㄧㄝ)

a spiral staircase

螺距(ㄌㄨㄛˊ ㄐㄩˋ)

pitch

螺旋(ㄌㄨㄛˊ ㄒㄩㄢˊ)

(mathematics) spiral

螺線管(ㄌㄨㄛˊ ㄒㄧㄢˋ ㄍㄨㄢˇ)

(physics) a solenoid

螺旋(ㄌㄨㄛˊ ㄒㄩㄢˊ)

a screw; a spiral

螺旋扳手(ㄌㄨㄛˊ ㄒㄩㄢˊ ㄅㄢ ㄕㄡˇ)or
螺旋起子(ㄌㄨㄛˊ ㄒㄩㄢˊ ㄑㄧˇ˙)

a spanner

螺旋推進機(ㄌㄨㄛˊ ㄒㄩㄢˊ ㄊㄨㄟ
ㄐㄧㄣ ㄐㄧ)

a screw propeller; a propeller; a screw

螺旋槳(ㄌㄨㄛˊ ㄒㄩㄢˊ ㄐㄧㄤˇ)

a propeller; a screw

螺旋菌(ㄌㄨㄛˊ ㄒㄩㄢˊ ㄐㄩㄣˋ)

spirillum

螺絲(ㄌㄨㄛˊ ㄙ)

a male screw; an external
screw; a screw

螺絲母(ㄌㄨㄛˊ ㄙ ㄇㄨˇ)

a nut (to go with a screw)

螺絲刀(ㄌㄨㄛˊ ㄙ ㄉㄠ)

a screwdriver

螺絲釘(ㄌㄨㄛˊ ㄙ ㄉㄧㄥ)

a male screw; an external
screw; a screw

螺絲起子(ㄌㄨㄛˊ ㄙ ㄑㄧˇ˙)

a screwdriver

螺絲鉗(ㄌㄨㄛˊ ㄙ ㄑㄧㄢˊ)

a wrench

螺螄(ㄌㄨㄛˊ ㄙ)

a kind of mollusk with a
spiral shell; a snail

螺壓機(ㄌㄨㄛˊ ㄧㄚ ㄐㄧ)

a screw press

螺縈(ㄌㄨㄛˊ ㄧㄥˊ)

rayon

螺紋(ㄌㄨㄛˊ ㄨㄣˊ)

①the spiral (at the tip of a
finger, etc.)②the screw
thread

【螻】 5308
ㄌㄡ lou lóu

a mole cricket

螻蛄(ㄌㄡ ㄍㄨ)or 螻蟈(ㄌㄡ ㄍㄨㄛˊ)

a mole cricket

螻蟈(ㄌㄡ ㄍㄨㄛˊ)

another name of the frog

螻蟻(ㄌㄡ ㄧˇ)

mole crickets and ants—insignificant creatures

【螽】 5309
ㄓㄨㄥ jong zhōng

a katydid; a long-horned
grasshopper; a locust

螽花(ㄓㄨㄥ ㄏㄨㄚ)

a spikelet 亦作「小穗」

螽斯(ㄓㄨㄥ ㄙ)

katydid (Gompsocleis mikado)
a variety of the locust

螽斯衍慶(ㄓㄨㄥ ㄙ ㄧㄢˇ ㄑㄧㄥˋ)

May your offsprings be as
numerous as a katydid's. (a
congratulatory expression
used when a son is born to
a friend)

【螿】 5310
ㄐㄧㄤ jiang jiāng

a kind of cicada

【蟀】 5311
ㄕㄨㄞˋ shuay shuài
(讀音 ㄕㄨㄛ shuoh)

as in 蟋蟀—a cricket

【蟄】 5312
ㄓˊ jyr zhí
(語音 ㄓㄜˊ jer zhé)

to hibernate; hibernation

蟄伏(ㄓˊ ㄈㄨˊ)

①to hibernate ②to lie low

蟄雷(ㄓˊ ㄌㄟˊ)

the first spring thunder
(that awakes insects from
dormancy)

蟄居(ㄓˊ ㄐㄩ)

to live in seclusion; to cloister (oneself in)

蟄蟲(ㄓˊ ㄔㄨㄥˊ)

torpid insects; dormant
insects; hibernating insects

蟄獸(ㄓˊ ㄕㄡˋ)

a hibernating animal or
beast

【蟆】 5313
ㄇㄚˊ ma má
(語音 ㄇㄚˊ ·ma ma)

as in 蝦蟆—a toad

【蟈】 5314
ㄍㄨㄛ guo guō

1. a frog
2. a mole cricket

蟈蟈兒(ㄍㄨㄛ ㄍㄨㄛ ㄦ)

a large kind of green
cricket; a katydid

【蟋】 5315
ㄒㄧ shi xī

a cricket (insect)

蟋蟀(ㄒㄧ ㄕㄨㄞˋ)

a cricket

【蟑】 5316
ㄓㄤ jang zhāng

a cockroach; a roach

蟑螂(ㄓㄤ ㄌㄤ)

a cockroach

【蟊】 5317
ㄇㄠˊ mau máo

insects that are injurious to
crops—devourers of the
grain

蟊賊(ㄇㄠˊ ㄗㄟˊ)

①insects that eat the roots
of grain plants ②persons
that are injurious to society;
vermin

十二畫

【蟥】 5318
ㄏㄨㄤˊ hwang huáng

as in 螞蟥—a horseleech

【蟒】 5319
ㄇㄤˇ maang mǎng

1. a python; a boa
2. ceremonial robes worn by
mandarins, or the embroi-

〔虫部〕

dered patterns on such robes

鷩袍 (ㄅㄧˋ ㄆㄠˊ)
ceremonial robes worn by mandarins

鷩蛇 (ㄅㄧˋ ㄕㄜˊ)
a python; a boa

鷩衣 (ㄅㄧˋ ㄧ)
ceremonial robes worn by mandarins

【蟠】 5320
ㄆㄢˊ parn pán
1. to coil; to curl up
2. to occupy

蟠木 (ㄆㄢˊ ㄇㄨˋ)
a twisted tree

蟠桃 (ㄆㄢˊ ㄊㄠˊ)
①the flat peach; the saucer peach ②a legendary peach which enables the eater to live forever

蟠桃會 (ㄆㄢˊ ㄊㄠˊ ㄏㄨㄟˋ)
the festival held on the 3rd day of the 3rd lunar month in honor of the Grand Old Lady of the West Heaven (西天王母)

蟠龍 (ㄆㄢˊ ㄌㄨㄥˊ)
a curled-up dragon

蟠踞 (ㄆㄢˊ ㄐㄩˋ)
to occupy

蟠虺紋 (ㄆㄢˊ ㄏㄨㄟˇ ㄨㄣˊ)
the dragon patterns on the surface of pillars, bronzes, etc.

【蟢】 5321
ㄒㄧˇ shii xǐ
a kind of long-bodied and long-legged spider

【蟣】 5322
ㄐㄧˇ jii jǐ
1. larvae of lice
2. leeches

【蟪】 5323
ㄏㄨㄟˋ huey huì
Platypleura kaempferi, a kind of bright-colored cicada

蟪蛄 (ㄏㄨㄟˋ ㄍㄨ)
Platypleura kaempferi, a kind of bright-colored cicada 亦作「寒蟬」

蟪蛄不知春秋 (ㄏㄨㄟˋ ㄍㄨ ㄅㄨˋ ㄓ ㄔㄨㄣ ㄑㄧㄡ)
limited in experience or vision (like a cicada that is ignorant of spring and autumn)

【蟬】 5324
ㄔㄢˊ charn chán

1. a cicada
2. continuous; uninterrupted

蟬鬢 (ㄔㄢˊ ㄅㄧㄣˋ)
the attractive hair on the temples (of a woman)

蟬不知雪 (ㄔㄢˊ ㄅㄨˋ ㄓ ㄒㄩㄝˇ)
ignorant or inexperienced (like a cicada ignorant of snow)

蟬冕 (ㄔㄢˊ ㄇㄧㄢˇ)or**蟬冠** (ㄔㄢˊ ㄍㄨㄢ)
a kind of beautifully adorned cap worn by nobles in ancient times

蟬蛻 (ㄔㄢˊ ㄊㄨㄟˋ)
①exuviae of the cicada ②to commit suicide in order to escape this dirty world

蟬聯 (ㄔㄢˊ ㄌㄧㄢˊ)
①to keep on without interruption ②to stay on a position for another term; to continue to hold a post or title

蟬綃 (ㄔㄢˊ ㄒㄧㄠ)
a kind of very thin silk

蟬嘶 (ㄔㄢˊ ㄙ)
the shrill sound of a cicada

蟬翼 (ㄔㄢˊ ㄧˋ)
①wings of the cicada—very light things ②a kind of very thin silk

蟬吟 (ㄔㄢˊ ㄧㄣˊ)
the shrill sound of the cicada

蟬紋 (ㄔㄢˊ ㄨㄣˊ)
engraved cicada patterns

【蟲】 5325
ㄔㄨㄥˊ chorng chóng
insects; worms: 蠅、蚊、蛹皆是蟲, 蟲. Flies, mosquitoes and gnats are insects.

蟲媒花 (ㄔㄨㄥˊ ㄇㄟˊ ㄏㄨㄚ)
entomophilous flowers

蟲害 (ㄔㄨㄥˊ ㄏㄞˋ)
damage to farm crops caused by pests; insect pest

蟲聚 (ㄔㄨㄥˊ ㄐㄩˋ)
to swarm

蟲豸 (ㄔㄨㄥˊ ㄓˋ)
insects and reptiles

蟲篆 (ㄔㄨㄥˊ ㄓㄨㄢˋ)
a wriggly form of written characters (found on ancient bronzes, etc.)

蟲蟲蟻蟻 (ㄔㄨㄥˊ ㄔㄨㄥˊ ㄧˇ ㄧˇ)
infested with insects and worms

蟲蝕 (ㄔㄨㄥˊ ㄕˊ)
worm-eaten

蟲書 (ㄔㄨㄥˊ ㄕㄨ)
①a wriggly form of characters (found usually on ancient bronzes) ②marks on worm-eaten objects (which look like the seal type character)

蟲霜水旱 (ㄔㄨㄥˊ ㄕㄨㄤ ㄕㄨㄟˇ ㄏㄢˋ)
insects, frost, floods, and droughts—the four major terrors of farmers

蟲子 (ㄔㄨㄥˊ ˙ㄗ)
①eggs of insects ②worms; insects

蟲災 (ㄔㄨㄥˊ ㄗㄞ)
a plague of insects

蟲兒 (ㄔㄨㄥˊ ㄦˊ)
insects; worms

蟲兒眼 (ㄔㄨㄥˊ ㄦˊ ㄧㄢˇ)
a worm-eaten cavity (in fruit)

蟲牙 (ㄔㄨㄥˊ ㄧㄚˊ)
a decayed tooth; a carious tooth; dental caries

蟲癭 (ㄔㄨㄥˊ ㄧㄥˇ)
galls—gnarls on plants caused by injurious insects 亦作「五倍子」or「沒食子」

蟲魚之學 (ㄔㄨㄥˊ ㄩˊ ㄓ ㄒㄩㄝˊ)
textual research of little value

【蟟】 5326
ㄌㄧㄠˊ leau liáo
as in 蛁蟟—Pomponia maculaticollis, a kind of cicada

【蟮】 5327
ㄕㄢˋ shann shàn
an earthworm

十三畫

【蟹】 5328
(蠏) ㄒㄧㄝˋ shieh xiè
a crab

蟹杯 (ㄒㄧㄝˋ ㄅㄟ)
a crab shell used as a wine cup

蟹殼黃 (ㄒㄧㄝˋ ㄎㄜˊ ㄏㄨㄤˊ)
a crisp roll with sesame on the upper crust

蟹黃 (ㄒㄧㄝˋ ㄏㄨㄤˊ)
crab spawn

蟹臍 (ㄒㄧㄝˋ ㄑㄧˊ)
the underside of a crab

蟹箝 (ㄒㄧㄝˋ ㄑㄧㄢ)
nippers, or pincers, of a crab

蟹行 (ㄒㄧㄝˋ ㄒㄧㄥˊ)
to go sideways; to move laterally

蟹行文字 (ㄒㄧㄝˋ ㄒㄧㄥˊ ㄨㄣˊ ㄗˋ)
the lateral writing system of European languages, such as English, Latin, etc.

蟹螯 (ㄒㄧㄝˋ ㄠˊ)
nippers, or pincers, of a crab

【蟶】 5329
ㄔㄥ　cheng chēng
a razor clam; a razor shell

蟶田 (ㄔㄥ ㄊㄧㄢˊ) or 蟶埕 (ㄔㄥ ㄔㄥˊ)
fields on the seashore where razor shells are cultivated

蟶乾 (ㄔㄥ ㄍㄢ)
a dried razor clam

蟶子 (ㄔㄥ ㄗˇ)
a razor clam; a razor shell

【蟺】 5330
(蟺) ㄕㄢˇ shann shàn
an earthworm

【蟻】 5331
ㄧˇ　ㄇㄧˇ yii yǐ
an ant

蟻民 (ㄧˇ ㄇㄧㄣˊ)
we (a term used in petitions to the government by the people in former times)

蟻慕 (ㄧˇ ㄇㄨˋ)
to yearn for; to long for

蟻封 (ㄧˇ ㄈㄥ)
an ant hill; a formicary

蟻附 (ㄧˇ ㄈㄨˋ)
to swarm over (as ants swarm over their prey)

蟻垤 (ㄧˇ ㄉㄧㄝˊ) or 蟻冢 (ㄧˇ ㄓㄨㄥˇ)
an ant hill; a formicary

蟻動 (ㄧˇ ㄉㄨㄥˋ)
to swarm or move like ants; to formicate

蟻寇 (ㄧˇ ㄎㄡˋ)
a petty robber

蟻潰 (ㄧˇ ㄎㄨㄟˋ)
to disperse like ants

蟻合 (ㄧˇ ㄏㄜˊ)
to swarm to a place from all sides

蟻結 (ㄧˇ ㄐㄧㄝˊ)
to band together

蟻聚 (ㄧˇ ㄐㄩˋ)
to swarm to a place from

all sides

蟻丘 (ㄧˇ ㄑㄧㄡ)
an ant hill

蟻醛 (ㄧˇ ㄑㄩㄢˊ)
formaldehyde

蟻穴 (ㄧˇ ㄒㄩㄝˋ)
①an ants' nest ②small losses or nibblings which should be stopped in time to prevent a major disaster

蟻視 (ㄧˇ ㄕˋ)
to despise: 不要蟻視窮人。
Don't despise the poor.

蟻術 (ㄧˇ ㄕㄨˋ)
the technique, or art, of the ant—diligence or industry

蟻壤 (ㄧˇ ㄖㄤˇ)
an ants' nest

蟻酸 (ㄧˇ ㄙㄨㄢ)
formic acid

【蟾】 5332
ㄔㄢˊ charn chán
a toad (especially the one supposed to live on the moon)

蟾晄 (ㄔㄢˊ ㄉㄜˋ)
the moon

蟾兔 (ㄔㄢˊ ㄊㄨˋ)
the hare supposed to live on the moon

蟾輪 (ㄔㄢˊ ㄌㄨㄣˊ)
the moon

蟾桂 (ㄔㄢˊ ㄍㄨㄟˋ)
the shades on the moon

蟾光 (ㄔㄢˊ ㄍㄨㄤ)
moonlight

蟾宮 (ㄔㄢˊ ㄍㄨㄥ)
the moon

蟾宮折桂 (ㄔㄢˊ ㄍㄨㄥ ㄓㄜˊ ㄍㄨㄟˋ)
to emerge in success from a civil service examination

蟾蜍 (ㄔㄢˊ ㄔㄨˊ)
a toad (especially in reference to the one supposed to live on the moon)

蟾彩 (ㄔㄢˊ ㄘㄞˇ)
moonlight

【蠅】 5333
ㄧㄥˊ yng yíng
a fly

蠅拂 (ㄧㄥˊ ㄈㄨˊ)
a fly brush; a swatter

蠅頭小楷 (ㄧㄥˊ ㄊㄡˊ ㄒㄧㄠˇ ㄎㄞˇ) or 蠅頭小字 (ㄧㄥˊ ㄊㄡˊ ㄒㄧㄠˇ ㄗˋ)
letters or characters as small as the head of a fly;

very small (handwritten) characters

蠅頭微利 (ㄧㄥˊ ㄊㄡˊ ㄨㄟˊ ㄌㄧˋ) or 蠅頭小利 (ㄧㄥˊ ㄊㄡˊ ㄒㄧㄠˇ ㄌㄧˋ)
petty profits

蠅蠅 (ㄧㄥˊ ㄧㄥˊ)
wriggling; crawling

蠅營狗苟 (ㄧㄥˊ ㄧㄥˊ ㄍㄡˇ ㄍㄡˇ)
corrupt and servile practices; to seek advantage meanly

【蠆】 5334
ㄔㄞˋ chay chài
a kind of scorpion

蠆尾 (ㄔㄞˋ ㄨㄟˇ)
the poisonous tail of a scorpion—a harmful thing or person

【蠍】 5335
ㄒㄧㄝˇ shie xiě
a scorpion

蠍虎 (ㄒㄧㄝˇ ㄏㄨˇ)
a gecko; a house lizard

蠍子 (ㄒㄧㄝˇ ㄗˇ)
a scorpion

【蠃】 5336
ㄌㄨㄛˇ luoo luǒ
the solitary wasp

十四畫

【蠐】 5337
ㄑㄧˊ chyi qí
a grub (a kind of larva)

蠐螬 (ㄑㄧˊ ㄘㄠˊ)
a grub (a kind of larva)

【蠑】 5338
ㄖㄨㄥˊ rong róng
1. a kind of mollusk
2. a kind of reptile

【蠓】 5339
ㄇㄥˇ meeng měng
a kind of gnat; a midge; a biting midge

蠓蟲 (ㄇㄥˇ ㄔㄨㄥˊ)
a kind of gnat

【蠔】 5340
ㄏㄠˊ haur háo
an oyster 亦作「牡蠣」

蠔白 (ㄏㄠˊ ㄅㄞˊ)
the edible part of an oyster

蠔油 (ㄏㄠˊ ㄧㄡˊ)
oyster sauce

【蠕】 5341
ㄖㄨㄢˇ roan ruǎn
to wriggle; to squirm

蠕動 (ㄖㄨㄢˇ ㄉㄨㄥˋ)

〔虫部〕

〔虫部〕

第一欄

to wriggle; to squirm

蠕形動物(ㄖㄨㄢ ㄒㄧㄥˊ ㄉㄨㄥˋ ㄨˋ)
vermicular animals; Vermes

蠕蠕(ㄖㄨㄢˊ ㄖㄨㄢˊ)
①wriggling; wriggly; vermicular ②name of an ancient Chinese tribe in the north

【蠖】 5342 ㄏㄨㄛˋ huoh huò
a measuring worm; a looper

蠖屈(ㄏㄨㄛˋ ㄑㄩ)
to humble oneself temporarily (as a looper loops itself momentarily)

十五畫

【蠟】 5343 ㄌㄚˋ lah là
1. wax
2. a candle

蠟板(ㄌㄚˋ ㄅㄢˇ)
a stencil plate

蠟筆(ㄌㄚˋ ㄅㄧˇ)
a crayon: 他用蠟筆畫肖像。He drew a portrait with crayons.

蠟梅(ㄌㄚˋ ㄇㄟˊ)
Calycanthus praecox, a kind of plum blooming in winter

蠟淚(ㄌㄚˋ ㄌㄟˋ)
wax guttering; drips from a burning candle

蠟炬(ㄌㄚˋ ㄐㄩˋ)
a candle

蠟扦(ㄌㄚˋ ㄑㄧㄢ)or 蠟扦兒(ㄌㄚˋ ㄑㄧㄚㄦ)
the top of a candlestick

蠟芯兒(ㄌㄚˋ ㄒㄧㄣㄦ)
a candlewick

蠟像(ㄌㄚˋ ㄒㄧㄤˋ)
a wax figure; a waxwork

蠟像館(ㄌㄚˋ ㄒㄧㄤˋ ㄍㄨㄢˇ)
a waxworks hall; a wax museum

蠟紙(ㄌㄚˋ ㄓˇ)
①wax paper; waxed paper ②stencil paper: 她正在刻蠟紙。She's cutting a stencil.

蠟燭(ㄌㄚˋ ㄓㄨˊ)
①a candle: 他正點着一支蠟燭。He is lighting a candle. ②(Shanghai dialect) one who bullies the weak and is easily bullied by the strong

蠟蟲(ㄌㄚˋ ㄔㄨㄥˊ)

第二欄

a wax insect

蠟染(ㄌㄚˋ ㄖㄢˇ)
batik, or battik

蠟人(ㄌㄚˋ ㄖㄣˊ)
a wax figure 亦作「蠟像」

蠟油(ㄌㄚˋ ㄧㄡˊ)
melted wax

蠟丸(ㄌㄚˋ ㄨㄢˊ)
a wax-coated pill; a wax ball

【蠹】 5344 ㄉㄨˋ liì
1. a wood-boring insect
2. (said of insects) to bore or eat wood
3. worm-eaten

【蠡】 5344 ㄌㄧˊ lií
1. a calabash
2. a calabash shell serving as a dipper; a dipper

蠡測(ㄌㄧˊ ㄘㄜˋ)
to be very naive (like one trying to measure the ocean with a calabash)

【蠢】 5345 (蠢) ㄔㄨㄣˇ choen chün
1. to wriggle; to squirm
2. stupid; foolish; dull; silly

蠢笨(ㄔㄨㄣˇ ㄅㄣˋ)
stupid; foolish: 他犯了蠢笨的錯誤。He made a stupid mistake.

蠢笨愚頑(ㄔㄨㄣˇ ㄅㄣˋ ㄩˊ ㄨㄢˊ)
stupid and stubborn

蠢動(ㄔㄨㄣˇ ㄉㄨㄥˋ)
①to wriggle; to squirm ②(said of enemy troops, etc.) to move busily in preparation for action 參看「蠢蠢欲動」

蠢陋(ㄔㄨㄣˇ ㄌㄡˋ)
stupid and uncultured

蠢貨(ㄔㄨㄣˇ ㄏㄨㄛˋ)
a simpleton; a fool; an idiot; a blockhead; a dunce

蠢蠢欲動(ㄔㄨㄣˇ ㄔㄨㄣˇ ㄩˋ ㄉㄨㄥˋ)
(said of enemy troops, etc.) moving busily in preparation for action

蠢才 or 蠢材(ㄔㄨㄣˇ ㄘㄞˊ)
a simpleton; a fool; an idiot

【蠣】 5346 ㄌㄧˋ liì
an oyster 亦作「牡蠣」

蠣粉(ㄌㄧˋ ㄈㄣˇ)
lime obtained by burning

第三欄

oyster shells

蠣房(ㄌㄧˋ ㄈㄤˊ)
oyster shells

蠣黃(ㄌㄧˋ ㄏㄨㄤˊ)
the edible part of an oyster

十六畫

【蟏】 5347 ㄒㄧㄠ shiau xiāo
Teragnatha, a kind of spider with long legs 亦作「喜蛛」

十七畫

【蠱】 5348 ㄍㄨˇ guu gǔ
1. poison; venom; harm
2. to bewitch; to enchant

蠱惑(ㄍㄨˇ ㄏㄨㄛˋ)
ills; evils

蠱媚(ㄍㄨˇ ㄇㄟˋ)
to bewitch or charm by sensual appeal

蠱毒(ㄍㄨˇ ㄉㄨˊ)
①to enchant and injure; to cast a harmful spell over ②to poison

蠱惑(ㄍㄨˇ ㄏㄨㄛˋ)
to confuse by magic or witchcraft; to put under a spell; to enchant

蠱疾(ㄍㄨˇ ㄐㄧˊ)
insanity; derangement

【蠲】 5349 ㄐㄩㄢ jiuan juān
1. a millipede
2. clean; pure; bright
3. to clean; to wash; to cleanse
4. to remit or remove (taxes, sentences, etc.)

蠲免(ㄐㄩㄢ ㄇㄧㄢˇ)
to remit (taxes, etc.)

蠲賦(ㄐㄩㄢ ㄈㄨˋ)
to remit levies

蠲滌(ㄐㄩㄢ ㄉㄧˊ)
to wash; to cleanse

蠲體(ㄐㄩㄢ ㄊㄧˇ)
to cleanse the body; to clean oneself

蠲苛(ㄐㄩㄢ ㄎㄜ)
to remove oppressive laws or taxes

蠲潔(ㄐㄩㄢ ㄐㄧㄝˊ)
to cleanse; to clean; to purify

蠲減(ㄐㄩㄢ ㄐㄧㄢˇ)

to remove or lighten (taxes, sentences, etc.)

蠲除 (ㄐㄩㄢ ㄔㄨˊ)
to remove (oppressive laws, levies, etc.); to exempt

蠲租 (ㄐㄩㄢ ㄗㄨ)
to remit rentals or taxes

【蠭】 5350
蠭 (ㄈㄥ) feng fēng
a bee; a wasp

十八畫

【蠶】 5351
蠶 (ㄘㄢˊ) tsarn cán
a silkworm

蠶箔 or 蠶薄 (ㄘㄢˊ ㄅㄛˊ)
an apparatus made of reeds for raising silkworms

蠶眠 (ㄘㄢˊ ㄇㄧㄢˊ)
torpidity of a silkworm before casting its skin

蠶豆 (ㄘㄢˊ ㄉㄡˋ)
a horse bean; a fava bean

蠶女 (ㄘㄢˊ ㄋㄩˇ) or 蠶姑 (ㄘㄢˊ ㄍㄨ)
a silkworm-raising woman

蠶工 (ㄘㄢˊ ㄍㄨㄥ)
silkworm culture; sericulture

蠶繭 (ㄘㄢˊ ㄐㄧㄢˇ)
the cocoon of the silkworm

蠶師 (ㄘㄢˊ ㄕ)
a sericulturist

蠶食鯨吞 (ㄘㄢˊ ㄕˊ ㄐㄧㄥ ㄊㄨㄣ)
now nibbling like a silkworm, now engulfing like a whale (said of the aggressive expansion of a nation)

蠶室 (ㄘㄢˊ ㄕˋ)
① a silkworm nursery ② a prison where the punishment of castration was inflicted in ancient times

蠶事 (ㄘㄢˊ ㄕˋ)
silkworm culture; sericulture

蠶沙 (ㄘㄢˊ ㄕㄚ)
the black excretion of silkworms

蠶子 (ㄘㄢˊ ㄗˇ)
the eggs of silkworms

蠶絲 (ㄘㄢˊ ㄙ)
natural silk; silk: 這條領帶是蠶絲製成的。This tie is made of silk.

蠶桑 (ㄘㄢˊ ㄙㄤ)
a silkworm mulberry

蠶蛾 (ㄘㄢˊ ㄜˊ)
a silkworm moth

蠶衣 (ㄘㄢˊ ㄧ)
① the cocoon of the silkworm ② silk dress ③ the dress of a woman who raises silkworms

蠶蟻 (ㄘㄢˊ ㄧˇ)
newly-hatched silkworms

蠶月 (ㄘㄢˊ ㄩㄝˋ)
the third lunar month; the silkworm month

蠶蛹 (ㄘㄢˊ ㄩㄥˇ)
a silkworm chrysalis or pupa

【�】 5352
蠵 (ㄒㄧ) shi xī
a kind of large-sized turtle

【蠹】 5353
蠹 (蠧) (ㄉㄨˋ) duh dù
1. a moth; a kind of insect that eats into books or clothing: 書蠹 a bookworm
2. moth-eaten; worm-eaten
3. an insect that eats up the resources—(figuratively) an embezzler

蠹國害民 (ㄉㄨˋ ㄍㄨㄛˊ ㄏㄞˋ ㄇㄧㄣˊ)
to rob the state and hurt the people; to eat up public funds and prey upon the people

蠹簡 (ㄉㄨˋ ㄐㄧㄢˇ)
old worm-eaten books

蠹蟲 (ㄉㄨˋ ㄔㄨㄥˊ)
① a moth ② a harmful person; vermin

蠹魚 (ㄉㄨˋ ㄩˊ)
Lepisma saccharina, a kind of silvery worm that eats clothes, books, etc.; silverfish: 蠹魚蝕書 Silverfish eat away books.

十九畫

【蠻】 5354
蠻 (ㄇㄢˊ) man mán
1. barbarous; savage; barbarians in the south
2. quite; pretty; very; fairly: 這本書還不錯的。This is quite a good book.

蠻不講理 (ㄇㄢˊ ㄅㄨˋ ㄐㄧㄤˇ ㄌㄧˇ)
savage; rude; impervious to reason; brutal; unreasonable

蠻不錯 (ㄇㄢˊ ㄅㄨˋ ㄘㄨㄛˋ)
not bad at all

蠻貊 (ㄇㄢˊ ㄇㄛˋ)

barbarian tribes

蠻力氣 (ㄇㄢˊ ㄌㄧˋ ㄑㄧˋ)
great strength

蠻幹 (ㄇㄢˊ ㄍㄢˋ)
to go ahead without considering the consequences

蠻好 (ㄇㄢˊ ㄏㄠˇ)
very good; fairly good

蠻橫 (ㄇㄢˊ ㄏㄥˋ)
barbarous; savage; arbitrary; peremptory; unreasonable; arbitrarily: 他那蠻橫無理的要求很荒謬。His unreasonable demands are ridiculous.

蠻子 (ㄇㄢˊ ㄗˇ)
barbarians (a contemptuous term applied to southerners by northerners in ancient times)

蠻族 (ㄇㄢˊ ㄗㄨˊ)
barbarian tribes; savage tribes; primitive people

蠻夷戎狄 (ㄇㄢˊ ㄧˊ ㄖㄨㄥˊ ㄉㄧˊ)
(collectively) the barbarians

蠻有道理 (ㄇㄢˊ ㄧㄡˇ ㄉㄠ˙ㄌㄧ)
It sounds reasonable.

蠻有意思 (ㄇㄢˊ ㄧㄡˇ ㄧˋ˙ㄙ)
very interesting; quite interesting 亦作「蠻有趣」

二十畫

【蠼】 5355
蠼 (ㄐㄩㄝˊ) jyue jué
1. a female monkey 亦作「玃」
2. a black insect with six legs, capable of ejecting poison for self-defense

血 部
(ㄒㄩㄝˋ) shiueh xuè

【血】 5356
血 (ㄒㄩㄝˋ) shiueh xuè
(語音 ㄒㄧㄝˇ shiee xiě)
1. blood; blood relationship
2. the menses

血泊 (ㄒㄧㄝˇ ㄆㄛˊ)
a pool of blood

血本 (ㄒㄧㄝˇ ㄅㄣˇ)
the net cost; the rock-bottom cost; the original capital

〔血 部〕

【血部】

血本無歸(ㄒㄧㄝˇ ㄅㄣˇ ㄨˊ ㄍㄨㄟ)
no return of hard-earned capital

血崩(ㄒㄧㄝˇ ㄅㄥ)
menorrhagia

血餅(ㄒㄧㄝˇ ㄅㄧㄥˇ)or血塊(ㄒㄧㄝˇ ㄎㄨㄞˋ)
a cake of blood; coagulated blood

血珀(ㄒㄧㄝˇ ㄆㄛˋ)
crimson amber

血盆大口(ㄒㄧㄝˇ ㄆㄣˊ ㄉㄚˋ ㄎㄡˇ)
a large and fierce-looking mouth

血沫子(ㄒㄧㄝˇ ㄇㄛˋ ˙ㄗ)
blood foam formed on the surface of a pool of blood

血脈(ㄒㄧㄝˇ ㄇㄞˋ)
①large and small blood vessels ②blood relationship; a strain

血點(ㄒㄧㄝˇ ㄉㄧㄢˇ)or血滴(ㄒㄧㄝˇ ㄉㄧ)
bloody spots; drops of blood; blood splashes

血糖(ㄒㄧㄝˇ ㄊㄤˊ)
blood sugar; blood glucose

血統(ㄒㄧㄝˇ ㄊㄨㄥˇ)
blood relationship; a strain; lineage; consanguinity; pedigree

血統證明書(ㄒㄧㄝˇ ㄊㄨㄥˇ ㄓㄥˋ ㄇㄧㄥˊ ㄕㄨ)
the pedigree certificate (of a pet)

血濃於水(ㄒㄧㄝˇ ㄋㄨㄥˊ ㄩˊ ㄕㄨㄟˇ)
Blood is thicker than water.

血淚(ㄒㄧㄝˇ ㄌㄟˋ)
tears and blood—extreme sorrow

血淚史(ㄒㄧㄝˇ ㄌㄟˋ ㄕˇ)
a story written in tears and blood—a very sad story; a heart-rending story

血流漂杵(ㄒㄧㄝˇ ㄌㄧㄡˊ ㄆㄧㄠ ㄔㄨˇ)
so much blood being shed as to float the pestles—descriptive of a fierce battle or a scene of big carnage

血流成河(ㄒㄧㄝˇ ㄌㄧㄡˊ ㄔㄥˊ ㄏㄜˊ)
People are bleeding so much on the battlefield that their blood flows as a river.

血流如注(ㄒㄧㄝˇ ㄌㄧㄡˊ ㄖㄨˊ ㄓㄨˋ)
blood cascading down without stop

血淋淋(ㄒㄧㄝˇ ㄌㄧㄣˊ ㄌㄧㄣˊ)
①sanguinary; blood-dripping; bloody ②the down-to-earth (truth); naked (facts)

血量(ㄒㄧㄝˇ ㄌㄧㄤˋ)
the total amount of blood in a human body; blood volume

血路(ㄒㄧㄝˇ ㄌㄨˋ)
a blood vessel

血淥淥(ㄒㄧㄝˇ ㄌㄨˋ ㄌㄨˋ)
blood dripping all around; sanguinary

血管(ㄒㄧㄝˇ ㄍㄨㄢˇ)
blood vessels

血管硬化(ㄒㄧㄝˇ ㄍㄨㄢˇ ㄧㄥˋ ㄏㄨㄚˋ)
sclerosis vascularis, the hardening or sclerosis of blood vessels

血口噴人(ㄒㄧㄝˇ ㄎㄡˇ ㄆㄣ ㄖㄣˊ)
to curse and slander; to make false accusations against others

血庫(ㄒㄧㄝˇ ㄎㄨˋ)
a blood bank

血塊子(ㄒㄧㄝˇ ㄎㄨㄞˋ ˙ㄗ)
clotted blood; a clot of blood; blood clots

血虧(ㄒㄩㄝˋ ㄎㄨㄟ)
anemia or anaemia 參看「血虛」

血海深仇(ㄒㄧㄝˇ ㄏㄞˇ ㄕㄣ ㄔㄡˊ)
a blood feud; intense and deep-seated hatred

血汗(ㄒㄧㄝˇ ㄏㄢˋ)
blood and sweat—hard toil

血汗錢(ㄒㄧㄝˇ ㄏㄢˋ ㄑㄧㄢˊ)
money earned by very hard work or toil; hard-earned money

血花(ㄒㄧㄝˇ ㄏㄨㄚ)
blood splashes; bloodstains

血紅(ㄒㄧㄝˇ ㄏㄨㄥˊ)
as red as blood; scarlet

血跡(ㄒㄧㄝˇ ㄐㄧ)
bloodstained; bloodstains

血跡斑斑(ㄒㄧㄝˇ ㄐㄧ ㄅㄢ ㄅㄢ)
all covered with bloodstains; bloodstains everywhere; sanguinary

血祭(ㄒㄧㄝˇ ㄐㄧˋ)
a blood sacrifice or offering

血漿(ㄒㄧㄝˇ ㄐㄧㄤ)
blood plasma

血氣(ㄒㄧㄝˇ ㄑㄧˋ)
①one's temperament, disposition, etc. ②vigor; animal spirits or powers ③courageous and upright: 他是個有血氣的青年。He is a courageous and upright young man. ④blood and breath —human beings

血氣方剛(ㄒㄩㄝˋ ㄑㄧˋ ㄈㄤ ㄍㄤ)
(said of youths) hot-tempered; easily excited; full of vigor

血氣之勇(ㄒㄧㄝˇ ㄑㄧˋ ㄓ ㄩㄥˇ)
foolhardiness; courage or bravery emanating from one's emotional outbursts, not from cool judgment or the sense of righteousness; brute courage

血球(ㄒㄧㄝˇ ㄑㄧㄡˊ)or血輪(ㄒㄧㄝˇ ㄌㄨㄣˊ)
blood corpuscles; blood cells: 紅血球 the red corpuscles

血球素(ㄒㄧㄝˇ ㄑㄧㄡˊ ㄙㄨˋ)
globin

血親(ㄒㄧㄝˇ ㄑㄧㄣ)
blood relatives; blood relation

血清(ㄒㄧㄝˇ ㄑㄧㄥ)
serum

血清療法(ㄒㄧㄝˇ ㄑㄧㄥ ㄌㄧㄠˊ ㄈㄚˇ)
serotherapy

血清學(ㄒㄧㄝˇ ㄑㄧㄥ ㄒㄩㄝˊ)
serology

血吸蟲(ㄒㄧㄝˇ ㄒㄧ ㄔㄨㄥˊ)
a blood fluke

血小板(ㄒㄧㄝˇ ㄒㄧㄠˇ ㄅㄢˇ)
blood platelets; thrombocyte

血腥(ㄒㄧㄝˇ ㄒㄧㄥ)
reeking of blood; bloody; sanguinary

血腥氣(ㄒㄧㄝˇ ㄒㄧㄥ ㄑㄧˋ)
the smell of raw flesh and blood

血型(ㄒㄧㄝˇ ㄒㄧㄥˊ)
a blood type; a blood group

血型鑑定(ㄒㄧㄝˇ ㄒㄧㄥˊ ㄐㄧㄢˋ ㄉㄧㄥˋ)
blood grouping

血性(ㄒㄧㄝˇ ㄒㄧㄥˋ)
a strong sense of righteousness

血虛(ㄒㄧㄝˇ ㄒㄩ)
anemia; blood deficiency 參看「血虧」

血債(ㄒㄧㄝˇ ㄓㄞˋ)
a blood debt; a heinous crime: 侵略者在中國血債累累。

The invaders had heavy blood debts in China.

血債血還(ㄒㄧㄝˋ ㄓㄞˋ ㄒㄧㄝˋ ㄏㄨㄢˊ)
Debts of blood must be paid in blood.

血詔(ㄒㄧㄝˋ ㄓㄠˋ)
an imperial decree written in the monarch's own blood

血戰(ㄒㄧㄝˋ ㄓㄢˋ)
a fierce or bloody battle

血赤素(ㄒㄧㄝˋ ㄔˋ ㄙㄨˋ)
hemoglobin

血仇(ㄒㄧㄝˋ ㄔㄡˊ)
a blood feud

血石(ㄒㄧㄝˋ ㄕˊ)or 血石髓(ㄒㄧㄝˋ ㄕˊ ㄙㄨㄟˇ)
(mineral) bloodstone

血書(ㄒㄧㄝˋ ㄕㄨ)
① to write in blood—in great desperation or extreme indignation ② a petition, letter, etc. written in blood

血屬(ㄒㄧㄝˋ ㄕㄨˇ)
blood relatives

血水(ㄒㄧㄝˋ ㄕㄨㄟˇ)
① blood ② bloodstained water

血栓症(ㄒㄧㄝˋ ㄕㄨㄢ ㄓㄥˋ)or 血塞(ㄒㄧㄝˋ ㄙㄜˋ)
thrombosis

血肉模糊(ㄒㄧㄝˋ ㄖㄡˋ ㄇㄛˊ ㄏㄨˊ)
(said of human bodies) badly mutilated; mutilated beyond recognition

血肉橫飛(ㄒㄧㄝˋ ㄖㄡˋ ㄏㄥˊ ㄈㄟ)
flesh and blood flying in all directions—descriptive of a fierce battle or carnage

血肉之軀(ㄒㄧㄝˋ ㄖㄡˋ ㄓ ㄑㄩ)
the human body; flesh and blood

血染沙場(ㄒㄧㄝˋ ㄖㄢˇ ㄕㄚ ㄔㄤˊ)
The battlefield is stained with blood.

血刃(ㄒㄧㄝˋ ㄖㄣˋ)
to bloody one's blade—to kill

血族(ㄒㄧㄝˋ ㄗㄨˊ)
a clan with blood relationship

血絲蟲(ㄒㄧㄝˋ ㄙ ㄔㄨㄥˊ)
filaria

血絲兒(ㄒㄧㄝˋ ㄙ ㄦ)
detectable traces of blood (in sputum, etc.) in silky or fibrous form

血祀(ㄒㄧㄝˋ ㄙˋ)
a blood sacrifice or offering 亦作「血祭」

血嗣(ㄒㄧㄝˋ ㄙˋ)or 血胤(ㄒㄧㄝˋ ㄧㄣˋ)
one's offspring or descendants

血色(ㄒㄧㄝˋ ㄙㄜˋ)
① scarlet; red ② one's complexion (rosy or pale)

血色素(ㄒㄧㄝˋ ㄙㄜˋ ㄙㄨˋ)
hematin

血案(ㄒㄧㄝˋ ㄢˋ)
a bloody incident; a murder case

血衣(ㄒㄧㄝˋ ㄧ)
bloodstained garments, dresses, etc.

血壓(ㄒㄧㄝˋ ㄧㄚ)
blood pressure

血壓低(ㄒㄧㄝˋ ㄧㄚ ㄉㄧ)
low blood pressure; hypotension 亦作「低血壓」

血壓高(ㄒㄧㄝˋ ㄧㄚ ㄍㄠ)
high blood pressure or hypertension 亦作「高血壓」

血壓計(ㄒㄧㄝˋ ㄧㄚ ㄐㄧˋ)
a sphygmomanometer; a hemadynamometer

血液(ㄒㄧㄝˋ ㄧㄝˋ)
the blood: 新鮮的血液 fresh blood

血液學(ㄒㄧㄝˋ ㄧㄝˋ ㄒㄩㄝˊ)
hematology

血液循環(ㄒㄧㄝˋ ㄧㄝˋ ㄒㄩㄣˊ ㄏㄨㄢˊ)
blood circulation

血友症(ㄒㄧㄝˋ ㄧㄡˇ ㄓㄥˋ)or 血友病(ㄒㄧㄝˋ ㄧㄡˇ ㄅㄧㄥˋ)
hemophilia, or haemophilia

血癌(ㄒㄧㄝˋ ㄧㄢˊ)
leukemia 亦作「白血病」

血印(ㄒㄧㄝˋ ㄧㄣˋ)
marks made with blood (as footprints, etc.)

血污(ㄒㄧㄝˋ ㄨ)
bloodstained; blood-smeared

血雨腥風(ㄒㄧㄝˋ ㄩˇ ㄒㄧㄥ ㄈㄥ)
the scene of a field where a fierce battle has just been fought

血緣(ㄒㄧㄝˋ ㄩㄢˊ)
blood; blood relationship; a strain

血暈(ㄒㄧㄝˋ ㄩㄣˋ)
a coma after childbirth for the excessive loss of blood

四畫

【衄】 5357
ㄋㄩˋ niuh nǜ
(又讀) ㄋㄧㄡˋ niow niù

1. nose bleeding; a bleeding nose
2. to be defeated or given a bloody nose

衄血(ㄋㄩˋ ㄒㄧㄝˋ)
nose bleeding; epistaxis

六畫

【眾】 5358
(原) ㄓㄨㄥˋ jonq zhòng

1. a multitude; the crowd; the people
2. many; numerous
3. all

眾生(ㄓㄨㄥˋ ㄕㄥ)
all living creatures

十五畫

【衊】 5359
ㄇㄧㄝˋ mieh miè

1. to stain with blood
2. to slander; to trump up a charge; to smear

行 部
ㄒㄧㄥˊ shyng xíng

【行】 5360
1. ㄒㄧㄥˊ shyng xíng

1. to walk; to go on foot: 我有時步行上學。I sometimes walk to school.
2. to move; to go; to travel
3. to act; to do; to work: 他照別人的忠告行事。He acted upon another's advice.
4. to publish
5. to be current; to prevail: 此種款式曾風行一時。The style prevailed for a time.
6. able; capable:他雖老但還很行。He is old but still quite able.
7. all right; O.K.; enough: 行了，我吃不下了。That's enough. I can't eat any more.

（行

部）

8.baggage for travel: 我倘未打
開行李。I have not unpacked
my baggage yet.

9.a road; a path

10.ready to...; immediately;
soon: 他行將出國留學。He will
study abroad soon.

行百里者半九十(ㄒㄧㄥ ㄅㄞ ㄌㄧ ㄓㄜ
ㄅㄢ ㄐㄧㄡ ㄕ)
(literally) To cover 90 per
cent of one's destined distance brings one no farther
than the midway point.
—The last part of an
endeavor is the hardest to
finish (for one may lose
one's patience and give up).

行不得也哥哥(ㄒㄧㄥ ㄅㄨ ㄉㄜ ㄧㄝ ㄍㄜ
ㄍㄜ)
sounds imitating the cry of
a partridge—(figuratively)
The road is rough; we can
not go ahead.

行不得(ㄒㄧㄥ ㄅㄨ ㄉㄜ)
①cannot or should not be
done ②cannot or should not
go

行不通(ㄒㄧㄥ ㄅㄨ ㄊㄨㄥ)
①to block; unable to pass
②won't do (or work); to get
nowhere: 這個構想行不通。
This idea won't work.③im-
practicable; not feasible

行不開(ㄒㄧㄥ ㄅㄨ ㄎㄞ)
confined or restricted; unable to act freely or as one
sees fit

行不行(ㄒㄧㄥ ㄅㄨ ㄒㄧㄥ)
(a term used in requesting
permission) can; may 或
Will it do? 或 Is it all right?

行不由徑(ㄒㄧㄥ ㄅㄨ ㄧㄡ ㄐㄧㄥ)
do not take shortcuts—(figuratively) to follow the
proper rules

行騙(ㄒㄧㄥ ㄆㄧㄢ)
to cheat; to deceive; to swindle

行聘(ㄒㄧㄥ ㄆㄧㄣ)
to send betrothal presents to
the girl's family

行販(ㄒㄧㄥ ㄈㄢ)
a vender; a hawker; a peddler; a traveling salesman

行房(ㄒㄧㄥ ㄈㄤ)
to have sexual relations
with one's legal spouse

行大禮(ㄒㄧㄥ ㄉㄚ ㄌㄧ)

to pay the highest respect
by kowtowing

行道(ㄒㄧㄥ ㄉㄠ)
①to practice what one has
learned, as a doctor ②to
preach or propagate one's
theory, belief, etc.

行動(ㄒㄧㄥ ㄉㄨㄥ)
①to act; to move; to make
a move ②to get about; to
proceed ③conduct; behavior;
acts; movements; actions

行動電話(ㄒㄧㄥ ㄉㄨㄥ ㄉㄧㄢ ㄏㄨㄚ)
the cellular telephone

行動自如(ㄒㄧㄥ ㄉㄨㄥ ㄗ ㄖㄨ)
to move freely or without
impairment

行動自由(ㄒㄧㄥ ㄉㄨㄥ ㄗ ㄧㄡ)
freedom of movements

行動坐臥(ㄒㄧㄥ ㄉㄨㄥ ㄗㄨㄛ ㄨㄛ)
behavior; conduct

行踏(ㄒㄧㄥ ㄊㄚˋ)
to walk; to frequent

行臺(ㄒㄧㄥ ㄊㄞˊ)
①an ancient official post in
the border regions ②a temporary residence of a high-
ranking official ③a make-
shift stage

行頭(ㄒㄧㄥ ㄊㄡˊ)
costumes, etc. for the stage

行同狗彘(ㄒㄧㄥ ㄊㄨㄥ ㄍㄡ ㄓ)
mean; bestial

行囊(ㄒㄧㄥ ㄋㄤ)
one's baggage and money
for travel

行年(ㄒㄧㄥ ㄋㄧㄢ)
to be at the age of: 他行年五
十。He is at the age of fifty.

行樂(ㄒㄧㄥ ㄌㄜ)
to play; to make merry

行樂須及時(ㄒㄧㄥ ㄌㄜ ㄒㄩ ㄐㄧˊ ㄕ)
Enjoy life before it's too
late! 或 Carpe diem.

行禮(ㄒㄧㄥ ㄌㄧ)
①to salute; to bow curtsey
or kowtow to show respect:
他向軍官行禮。He saluted an
officer. ②to undergo a ceremony

行李(ㄒㄧㄥ ㄌㄧ)
baggage; luggage: 他們有五
件行李。They have five
pieces of luggage.

行李票(ㄒㄧㄥ ㄌㄧ ㄆㄧㄠ)
the ticket for baggage transportation; baggage checks

行李房(ㄒㄧㄥ ㄌㄧ ㄈㄤ)
a baggage room (or office)

行李車(ㄒㄧㄥ ㄌㄧ ㄔㄜ)
a baggage car on a train; a
luggage van

行獵(ㄒㄧㄥ ㄌㄧㄝ)
to hunt; to go hunting

行令(ㄒㄧㄥ ㄌㄧㄥ)
to play wine-drinking games

行露(ㄒㄧㄥ ㄌㄨ)
the dew on the path—(fig-
uratively) exposure of a
lady's chastity to danger

行路(ㄒㄧㄥ ㄌㄨ)
to travel; to walk on the
road

行路人(ㄒㄧㄥ ㄌㄨ ㄖㄣ)
①passers-by ②totally dis-
interested parties

行侶(ㄒㄧㄥ ㄌㄩ)
traveling companions

行旅(ㄒㄧㄥ ㄌㄩ)
travelers: 此地交通良好，行旅
稱便。Traffic here is good
and travelers find it convenient

行賈(ㄒㄧㄥ ㄍㄨ)
a traveling businessman

行館(ㄒㄧㄥ ㄍㄨㄢ)
a temporary dwelling place
of a high official

行宮(ㄒㄧㄥ ㄍㄨㄥ)
the abode of an emperor on
a tour

行客(ㄒㄧㄥ ㄎㄜ)
travelers

行好(ㄒㄧㄥ ㄏㄠ)
to do good; to practice charitable deeds

行賄(ㄒㄧㄥ ㄏㄨㄟ)
to bribe; to offer a bribe: 行
賄者可鄙。He who bribes is
to be despised

行劫(ㄒㄧㄥ ㄐㄧㄝ)
to loot or rob

行腳(ㄒㄧㄥ ㄐㄧㄠ)
(said of a Buddhist monk)
to travel far and wide on
foot in order to attain understanding of the essence
of Buddhist teachings

行酒(ㄒㄧㄥ ㄐㄧㄡ)
to pour wine for a guest

行姦(ㄒㄧㄥ ㄐㄧㄢ)
to commit adultery

行檢(ㄒㄧㄥ ㄐㄧㄢ)

the code of conducts

行進(ㄒㄧㄥㄐㄧㄣˋ)
- (military) to move forward; to march

行將(ㄒㄧㄥㄐㄧㄤ)
imminent; just going to; about to; on the verge of

行將就木(ㄒㄧㄥㄐㄧㄤㄐㄧㄡˋㄇㄨˋ)
dying; nearing death

行經(ㄒㄧㄥㄐㄧㄥ)
① to pass (a place, store, etc.); to pass through ② (said of women) in the period

行徑(ㄒㄧㄥㄐㄧㄥˋ)
① one's conduct or behavior; actions: 那眞是殘忍的行徑。 That's really cruel conduct. ② a path; a trail

行軍(ㄒㄧㄥㄐㄩㄣ)
① the movement of an army; a march ② the deployment of military forces

行軍牀(ㄒㄧㄥㄐㄩㄣㄔㄨㄤˊ)
a cot (for sleeping)

行期(ㄒㄧㄥㄑㄧˊ)
the date of departure

行乞(ㄒㄧㄥㄑㄧˇ)
to beg; to be a beggar

行篋(ㄒㄧㄥㄑㄧㄝˋ)
a traveler's box for holding clothes, money, etc.

行竊(ㄒㄧㄥㄑㄧㄝˋ)
to steal: 此賊在行竊時被捕。 The thief was caught in the act of stealing.

行銷(ㄒㄧㄥㄒㄧㄠ)
to sell; to effect sales; to be on sale: 此書行銷各地。 The book sells everywhere.

行險(ㄒㄧㄥㄒㄧㄢˇ)
to take great risks; to embark on a dangerous task

行香(ㄒㄧㄥㄒㄧㄤ)
the burning and offering of incense at Buddhist temples on special national occasions by officials in ancient times

行星(ㄒㄧㄥㄒㄧㄥ)
the planets

行刑(ㄒㄧㄥㄒㄧㄥˊ)
① to execute (criminals); execution ② to torture (prisoners)

行刑場(ㄒㄧㄥㄒㄧㄥˊㄔㄤˇ)
an execution ground

行幸(ㄒㄧㄥㄒㄧㄥˋ)
the imperial tour away from the capital

行兇(ㄒㄧㄥㄒㄩㄥ)
to commit killing or murder

行止(ㄒㄧㄥㄓˇ)
① whereabouts of a person ② ways or methods of doing things ③ personal conduct or behavior

行詐(ㄒㄧㄥㄓㄚˋ)
to cheat, deceive or swindle

行者(ㄒㄧㄥㄓㄜˇ)
① a Buddhist monk ② a servant of a Buddhist abbot

行政(ㄒㄧㄥㄓㄥˋ)
① government; administration of public affairs ② the executive branch of a government

行政法(ㄒㄧㄥㄓㄥˋㄈㄚˇ)
administrative law

行政機關(ㄒㄧㄥㄓㄥˋㄐㄧㄍㄨㄢ)
administrative organizations

行政區畫(ㄒㄧㄥㄓㄥˋㄑㄩㄏㄨㄚˋ)
the political division of an area for administrative purposes

行政區域(ㄒㄧㄥㄓㄥˋㄑㄩㄩˋ)
an administrative district

行政權(ㄒㄧㄥㄓㄥˋㄑㄩㄢˊ)
administrative power; executive authority

行政長官(ㄒㄧㄥㄓㄥˋㄓㄤˇㄍㄨㄢ)
the top administrator (in an area, or region)

行政處分(ㄒㄧㄥㄓㄥˋㄔㄨˇㄈㄣˋ)
disciplinary measures taken against an official guilty of abuse of administrative powers (as opposed to punishment meted out by a court of law)

行政人員(ㄒㄧㄥㄓㄥˋㄖㄣˊㄩㄢˊ)
an administrator

行政院(ㄒㄧㄥㄓㄥˋㄩㄢˋ)
Executive Yuan

行裝(ㄒㄧㄥㄓㄨㄤ)
baggage or luggage

行裝甫卸(ㄒㄧㄥㄓㄨㄤㄈㄨˇㄒㄧㄝˋ)
to have just concluded a homeward journey

行車(ㄒㄧㄥㄔㄜ)
① the movement of vehicles ② to drive a vehicle

行車執照(ㄒㄧㄥㄔㄜㄓˊㄓㄠˋ)

a driver's license; a driving license

行車時間表(ㄒㄧㄥㄔㄜㄕˊㄐㄧㄢㄅㄧㄠˇ)
schedules or timetables of trains

行常(ㄒㄧㄥㄔㄤˊ)
ordinary; usual; common

行成(ㄒㄧㄥㄔㄥˊ)
to hold peace talks; to obtain peace

行程(ㄒㄧㄥㄔㄥˊ)
① a traveler's route or itinerary ② to embark on a journey ③ a march; a journey: 二十哩的行程。 It's a march of twenty miles.

行船(ㄒㄧㄥㄔㄨㄢˊ)
① to sail or steer a boat ② the passing of boats

行尸走肉(ㄒㄧㄥㄕ ㄗㄡˇㄖㄡˋ)
a walking corpse--an absolutely useless person

行使(ㄒㄧㄥㄕˇ)
to exercise (powers, etc.); to employ: 他行使自己的權利。 He exercised his rights.

行使權(ㄒㄧㄥㄕˇㄑㄩㄢˊ)
the right to exercise powers inherent in one's office

行駛(ㄒㄧㄥㄕˇ)
to drive (cars); to sail or steer (boats); to ride (bicycles or pedicabs); to fly (planes)

行事(ㄒㄧㄥㄕˋ)
① to proceed; to execute (usually a clandestine mission); to do something planned: 我們按計畫行事。 We proceeded according to plan. ② conduct or behavior ③ to deal with people

行事曆(ㄒㄧㄥㄕˋㄌㄧˋ)
a calendar

行善(ㄒㄧㄥㄕㄢˋ)
to do good deeds; to do charitable work

行商(ㄒㄧㄥㄕㄤ)
a traveling salesman

行觴(ㄒㄧㄥㄕㄤ)
to pour wine for guests

行賞(ㄒㄧㄥㄕㄤˇ)
to reward (the meritorious)

行省(ㄒㄧㄥㄕㄥˇ)
a province (a political division in the Republic of

〔行部〕

〔行
部〕

China)

行書(ㄒㄧㄥˊ ㄕㄨ)
the running style of Chinese calligraphy

行水(ㄒㄧㄥˊ ㄕㄨㄟˇ)
①flowing water ②to travel by water, as on boats, to inspect flood ③to convey away the waters

行人(ㄒㄧㄥˊ ㄖㄣˊ)
pedestrians; passers-by

行人道(ㄒㄧㄥˊ ㄖㄣˊ ㄉㄠˋ)
sidewalks of a street

行人穿越道(ㄒㄧㄥˊ ㄖㄣˊ ㄔㄨㄢ ㄩㄝˋ ㄉㄠˋ)
a pedestrian crossing

行在(ㄒㄧㄥˊ ㄗㄞˋ)
the temporary palace of the emperor on a tour

行走(ㄒㄧㄥˊ ㄗㄡˇ)
①to walk ②a part-time worker in a government office in ancient times ③to have some connection

行蹤 or 行踪(ㄒㄧㄥˊ ㄗㄨㄥ)
tracks or whereabouts of a person;敵軍企圖隱匿他們的行踪。The enemy tried to cover their whereabouts.

行蹤不明 or 行踪不明(ㄒㄧㄥˊ ㄗㄨㄥ ㄅㄨˋ ㄇㄧㄥˊ)
whereabouts unknown: 她現在行蹤不明。Her present whereabouts is (or are) unknown.

行蹤飄忽(ㄒㄧㄥˊ ㄗㄨㄥ ㄆㄧㄠ ㄏㄨ)or
行踪飄忽(ㄒㄧㄥˊ ㄐㄩ ㄆㄧㄠ ㄈㄨˊ)
to travel here and there without a fixed itinerary; to have no fixed whereabouts

行蹤無定 or 行踪無定(ㄒㄧㄥˊ ㄗㄨㄥ ㄨˊ ㄉㄧㄥˋ)
to have no fixed abode; to have an uncertain place of lodging; to have no fixed itinerary in traveling

行刺(ㄒㄧㄥˊ ㄘˋ)
to assassinate: 他們計劃行刺暴君。They planned to assassinate the tyrant.

行藏(ㄒㄧㄥˊ ㄘㄤˊ)
one's behavior and background

行色(ㄒㄧㄥˊ ㄙㄜˋ)
scenes, conditions, display, etc. at one's departure for a journey

行色匆匆(ㄒㄧㄥˊ ㄙㄜˋ ㄘㄨㄥ ㄘㄨㄥ)
in a hurry to leave; in a hurry to go on a trip

行所無事(ㄒㄧㄥˊ ㄙㄨㄛˇ ㄨˊ ㄕˋ)
to maintain perfect composure; to be unruffled

行醫(ㄒㄧㄥˊ ㄧ)
to practice medicine: 他已行醫多年。He has practiced medicine for many years.

行易知難(ㄒㄧㄥˊ ㄧˋ ㄓ ㄋㄢˊ)
To do is easier than to know. 或To know how is easier than to know why.

行有餘力(ㄒㄧㄥˊ ㄧㄡˇ ㄩˊ ㄌㄧˋ)
to have extra resources (besides those needed to take care of oneself and his family)

行吟(ㄒㄧㄥˊ ㄧㄣˊ)
to wander while reciting or composing poems

行吟詩人(ㄒㄧㄥˊ ㄧㄣˊ ㄕ ㄖㄣˊ)
a minstrel

行營(ㄒㄧㄥˊ ㄧㄥˊ)
military headquarters set up at various strategic places

行為(ㄒㄧㄥˊ ㄨㄟˊ)
①behavior; conduct ②(law) acts

行為犯(ㄒㄧㄥˊ ㄨㄟˊ ㄈㄢˋ)
a criminal caught in the act; flagrante delicto

行文(ㄒㄧㄥˊ ㄨㄣˊ)
①to send a despatch (to another government office) ②the style or manner of writing

行轅(ㄒㄧㄥˊ ㄩㄢˊ)
the temporary residence of a high official on a tour

行遠自邇(ㄒㄧㄥˊ ㄩㄢˇ ㄗˋ ㄦˇ)
(literally) To go far, one must start from near.—One must start with the easy or basic things before one proceeds to deal with the difficult or profound subjects.

行雲流水(ㄒㄧㄥˊ ㄩㄣˊ ㄌㄧㄡˊ ㄕㄨㄟˇ)
(literally) moving clouds and flowing water—a natural and flowing style of writing, etc.: 她的詩有如行雲流水。She writes verses with natural and flowing style.

行運(ㄒㄧㄥˊ ㄩㄣˋ)
to be favored by good luck;

to have everything going one's way

【行】5360
2. ㄒㄧㄥˋ shinq xinq
one's conduct or behavior

行狀(ㄒㄧㄥˋ ㄓㄨㄤˋ)or 行述(ㄒㄧㄥˋ ㄕㄨˋ)
a brief biography of the deceased (usually accompanying an obituary notice)

行誼(ㄒㄧㄥˋ ㄧˋ)
conduct and virtues

【行】5360
1. ㄏㄤˊ harng hang
1. a row; a line; a series:該詩每節有六行。There are six lines in each stanza of the poem.
2. a business firm; a company
3. a trade; a line; a profession: 那不是我的本行。That's not my line.
4. order of brothers (and sisters) according to seniority
5. a generation

行輩(ㄏㄤˊ ㄅㄟˋ)
sequence of seniority in a clan

行道(ㄏㄤˊ ㄉㄠˋ)
(dialect) a trade; a profession; an occupation

行東(ㄏㄤˊ ㄉㄨㄥ)
a shopkeeper

行頭(ㄏㄤˊ ㄊㄡˊ)
①(in ancient China) a team leader ②(Han Dynasty) a shopkeeper

行列(ㄏㄤˊ ㄌㄧㄝˋ)
the rank and file; rows and columns: 他們排成整齊的行列。They are drawn up in orderly ranks.

行列式(ㄏㄤˊ ㄌㄧㄝˋ ㄕˋ)
(mathematics) a determinant

行規(ㄏㄤˊ ㄍㄨㄟ)
guild regulations; rules obeyed among members of a profession

行號(ㄏㄤˊ ㄏㄠˋ)
shops; stores; business establishments

行行出狀元(ㄏㄤˊ ㄏㄤˊ ㄔㄨ ㄓㄨㄤˋ ㄩㄢˊ)
Every trade has its master. 或One may distinguish himself in any trade.

行話(ㄏㄤˊ ㄏㄨㄚˋ)
the professional jargon of a

trade

行會 (ㄒㄧㄥˊ ㄏㄨㄟˋ)
trade unions; guilds

行家 (ㄒㄧㄥˊ ˙ㄐㄧㄚ)
a professional; an expert

行間 (ㄒㄧㄥˊ ㄐㄧㄢ)
①in the army ②between the lines of a piece of writing

行情 (ㄒㄧㄥˊ ㄑㄧㄥˊ)
①market prices of certain commodities; a quotation; market: 行情上漲了。The market has risen. ②general standing of a person in terms of finance, influence, popularity, etc.

行棧 (ㄒㄧㄥˊ ㄓㄢˋ)
a warehouse, godown or depot

行市 (ㄒㄧㄥˊ ㄕˋ)
market quotations

行業 (ㄒㄧㄥˊ ㄧㄝˋ)
a trade; an occupation

行伍 (ㄒㄧㄥˊ ㄨˇ)
the army

行伍出身 (ㄒㄧㄥˊ ㄨˇ ㄔㄨ ㄕㄣ)
①to rise from the ranks (of the army): 他是行伍出身。He rose from the ranks. ②to have a regular military background

行員 (ㄒㄧㄥˊ ㄩㄢˊ)
a clerk (especially referring to one in the bank)

三畫

【衍】 5361 ㄧㄢˇ yean yǎn
1. to overflow; to spread out
2. plenty and abundant; ample
3. (said of fields or plains) level; plane and even
4. a lake; a marsh
5. a slope
6. superfluous
7. a bamboo box or chest
8. a Chinese family name

衍變 (ㄧㄢˇ ㄅㄧㄢˋ)
to develop and change; to evolve

衍生 (ㄧㄢˇ ㄕㄥ)
to derive from

衍聖公 (ㄧㄢˇ ㄕㄥˋ ㄍㄨㄥ)
Duke of Yen, a hereditary title of the eldest male

among the lineal descendants of Confucius (from 1055 A.D. until 1935), now known as 奉祀官

衍繹 (ㄧㄢˇ ㄧˋ)
to expound or elaborate

衍衍 (ㄧㄢˇ ㄧㄢˇ)
to walk fast

衍沃 (ㄧㄢˇ ㄨㄛˋ)
fertile plains

衍文 (ㄧㄢˇ ㄨㄣˊ)
interpolations; redundancies owing to misprinting or miscopying

五畫

【衒】 5362 ㄒㄩㄢˋ shiuann xuàn
1. to brag; to boast; to show off
2. to recommend oneself

衒賣 (ㄒㄩㄢˋ ㄇㄞˋ) or 衒鬻 (ㄒㄩㄢˋ ㄩˋ)
(said of a peddler, etc.) to brag about the high quality of his goods

衒女 (ㄒㄩㄢˋ ㄋㄩˇ)
a girl who flaunts her beauty all around

衒露 (ㄒㄩㄢˋ ㄌㄨˋ)
to show off one's talent

衒俏 (ㄒㄩㄢˋ ㄑㄧㄠˋ)
to show off one's charms; to try to be cute

衒士 (ㄒㄩㄢˋ ㄕˋ)
a boastful scholar; one who always tries to show off his learning

衒異 (ㄒㄩㄢˋ ㄧˋ)
to show off one's talents

衒耀 (ㄒㄩㄢˋ ㄧㄠˋ)
to show off; to flaunt; to brag or boast

衒玉賈石 (ㄒㄩㄢˋ ㄩˋ ㄍㄨˇ ㄕˊ)
(literally) to advertise jade but sell rock—to preach like a saint but act like a crook

衒玉求售 (ㄒㄩㄢˋ ㄩˋ ㄑㄧㄡˊ ㄕㄡˋ)
to recommend oneself to a position; to brag about one's own talent with a view to getting a job

【術】 5363 ㄕㄨˋ shuh shù
1. a skill; a feat
2. a way or method to do something

術科 (ㄕㄨˋ ㄎㄜ)
courses offered in school for vocational training or learning of skills, as practical mechanics, etc.

術愧長房 (ㄕㄨˋ ㄎㄨㄟˋ ㄓㄤˇ ㄈㄤˊ)
to regret that one cannot make the space shrink so as to meet a dear friend faraway

術智 (ㄕㄨˋ ㄓˋ)
clever and skillful

術士 (ㄕㄨˋ ㄕˋ)
①one who practices occult arts ②scholars

術數 (ㄕㄨˋ ㄕㄨˋ)
①ways of administering or governing a nation ②magical calculation or fortune-telling

術語 (ㄕㄨˋ ㄩˇ)
professional jargon terminology; technical terms

術語學 (ㄕㄨˋ ㄩˇ ㄒㄩㄝˊ)
terminology

【術】 5363 ㄙㄨㄟˋ suey suì
2. an administrative district in ancient China in the suburbs of a city

六畫

【衕】 5364 ㄊㄨㄥˊ tonq tóng
a lane; an alley

【衖】 5365 ㄌㄨㄥˋ lonq lòng
a lane; an alley

衖堂 (ㄌㄨㄥˋ ㄊㄤˊ)
a lane; an alley

【街】 5366 ㄐㄧㄝ jie jiē
a street; a road in a city; a thoroughfare

街門 (ㄐㄧㄝ ㄇㄣˊ)
the front gate facing the street; a street entrance

街面兒 (ㄐㄧㄝ ㄇㄧㄢˋ ㄦ)
market or street conditions

街坊 (ㄐㄧㄝ ˙ㄈㄤ)
①neighbors; the neighborhood ②neighborhood

街道 (ㄐㄧㄝ ㄉㄠˋ)
streets; roads in a city or town

街燈 (ㄐㄧㄝ ㄉㄥ)

〔行
部〕
一

street lights; street lamps

街頭(ㄐㄧㄝ ㄊㄡˊ)
street corners; streets

街頭巷尾(ㄐㄧㄝ ㄊㄡˊ ㄒㄧㄤˋ ㄨㄟˇ)
throughout the city; in every
nook and corner of the city

街談巷議(ㄐㄧㄝ ㄊㄢˊ ㄒㄧㄤˋ ㄧˋ)
the talk of the town; street
rumors

街里街坊(ㄐㄧㄝ ㄌㄧˇ ㄐㄧㄝ ㄈㄤ)
neighborliness; friendship
among neighbors

街官(ㄐㄧㄝ ㄍㄨㄢ)
a police officer on the beat;
a police patrolman

街衢(ㄐㄧㄝ ㄑㄩˊ)
streets, roads or lanes in a
city or town

街巷(ㄐㄧㄝ ㄒㄧㄤˋ)
streets and lanes

街市(ㄐㄧㄝ ㄕˋ)
shopping streets; the downtown area

街衢戰(ㄐㄧㄝ ㄕˋ ㄓㄢˋ)
street fighting

街上(ㄐㄧㄝ ㄕㄤˋ)
on or in the street: 我碰巧在
街上遇見他。I happened to
meet him on the street.

街卒(ㄐㄧㄝ ㄗㄨˊ)
(in ancient China) scaven-
gers

七畫

【衙】 5367
ㄧˊ ya yá
1. a government office
2. to meet; to gather; to congregate
3. (Tang Dynasty) a front hall
of the palace
4. a Chinese family name

衙門(ㄧˊ ㄇㄣˊ)
"yamen"—a government
office in feudal China

衙內(ㄧˊ ㄋㄟˋ)
a reference to the sons of a
high official in the Sung (宋)
and Yüan (元) dynasties

衙署(ㄧˊ ㄕㄨˇ)
a government office

衙役(ㄧˊ ㄧˋ)
errand men in a government
office; an office boy; a public office runner

九畫

【衝】 5368
1. ㄔㄨㄥ chong
chóng
1. to rush; to thrust; to forge
ahead; to dash
2. to charge forward; to hit
with force
3. a thoroughfare; a hub; a
strategic place
4. to offend

衝破(ㄔㄨㄥ ㄆㄛˋ)
to break through; to breach;
to smash

衝鋒(ㄔㄨㄥ ㄈㄥ)
(military) to charge; a
charge; an assault

衝鋒隊(ㄔㄨㄥ ㄈㄥ ㄉㄨㄟˋ)
storm troops

衝鋒鎗(ㄔㄨㄥ ㄈㄥ ㄑㄧㄤ)
a Tommy gun, or a tommy
gun

衝鋒陷陣(ㄔㄨㄥ ㄈㄥ ㄒㄧㄢˋ ㄓㄣˋ)
to charge ahead and take
enemy positions; to charge
the enemy lines; to charge
forward

衝倒(ㄔㄨㄥ ㄉㄠˇ)
to knock down by the
impact of a collision, etc.

衝動(ㄔㄨㄥ ㄉㄨㄥˋ)
①an impulse; a sudden urge
②to be excited; to get
excited: 不要太衝動! 冷靜些!
Don't get excited! Keep
cool!

衝突(ㄔㄨㄥ ㄊㄨˊ)
a conflict; a fight; a clash

衝浪(ㄔㄨㄥ ㄌㄤˋ)
to surf

衝力(ㄔㄨㄥ ㄌㄧˋ)
impulsive forces; momentum

衝冠(ㄔㄨㄥ ㄍㄨㄢ)
extreme anger that makes
the hair stand on end and
raise one's own cap

衝剋(ㄔㄨㄥ ㄎㄜˋ)
(a Chinese superstition) the
contradicting and conflicting
forces of nature

衝口而出(ㄔㄨㄥ ㄎㄡˇ ㄦˊ ㄔㄨ)
to blurt out without thinking

衝激(ㄔㄨㄥ ㄐㄧ)
①a fierce conflict; a powerful collision ②to offend

衝擊(ㄔㄨㄥ ㄐㄧ)
to strike against; to pound
against; to charge

衝擊力(ㄔㄨㄥ ㄐㄧ ㄌㄧˋ)
the force of thrust or impact

衝勁(ㄔㄨㄥ ㄐㄧㄥˋ)
aggressiveness; enterprising
spirit; drive: 她做任何事情總
有一股衝勁。She is always
full of enterprising spirit in
doing everything.

衝進(ㄔㄨㄥ ㄐㄧㄣˋ)
to burst in; to rush in: 兵
士們向前衝進。The soldiers
rushed forward.

衝決(ㄔㄨㄥ ㄐㄩㄝˊ)or 衝潰(ㄔㄨㄥ
ㄎㄨㄟˋ)
to burst open (an enemy
siege, dike, etc.): 江水衝潰堤
岸。The river burst its banks

衢(ㄔㄨㄥ ㄑㄩˊ)
a thoroughfare

衝霄(ㄔㄨㄥ ㄒㄧㄠ)
to shoot up to the sky, as
smoke, fire, etc.

衝陷(ㄔㄨㄥ ㄒㄧㄢˋ)
to charge and take (enemy
positions)

衝撞(ㄔㄨㄥ ㄓㄨㄤˋ)
①to collide; to ram: 汽車遭
到一輛卡車的衝撞。The car
was rammed by a truck. ②
to offend; to treat impolitely: 我有沒有什麼地方衝撞了
你? Have I done anything to
offend you?

衝出(ㄔㄨㄥ ㄔㄨ)
to rush out; to dash out; to
fight a way out: 他們從屋裏
衝出去。They rushed out of
the room.

衝殺(ㄔㄨㄥ ㄕㄚ)
to charge; to rush ahead

衝刺(ㄔㄨㄥ ㄘˋ)
a spurt; a sprint; a burst of
speed: 這跑者向終點線做最後
衝刺。The runner put on a
spurt toward the tape.

衝散(ㄔㄨㄥ ㄙㄢˋ)
to break up; to scatter; to
disperse: 警察衝散群眾。The
police dispersed the crowd.

衝要(ㄔㄨㄥ ㄧㄠˋ)
a strategic point; an important junction 亦作「要衝」

【衝】 5368
2. ㄔㄨㄥˋ chòng chǒng

1. to head or go (south, north, etc.): 衝前走。Go straight up. 衝北走。Go north.
2. strong (smell): 這煙味很濃。This smoke has a strong smell.
3. brave and fierce
4. to take a nap
5. for (your, his, etc.) sake
6. to direct (one's attack, etc.) toward

衝盹兒(ㄔㄨㄥ ㄉㄨㄣˇㄦ)
to take a nap

衝著(ㄔㄨㄥˋ·ㄓㄜ)
①for (your, his, etc.) sake
②to direct (one's attack, etc.) toward

【衚】 5369
　　ㄏㄨˊ hwu hú
a lane; a sub-lane; a side street

衚衕(ㄏㄨˊ ㄊㄨㄥˋ)
a lane; an alley

【衛】 5370 ㄨㄟˋ wey wèi
to guard or protect; to stand guard over

十畫

【衛】 5371
　　(衞) ㄨㄟˋ wey wèi
1. to guard; to protect; to defend: 保衛國家是軍人的責任。The duty of a soldier is to defend his country.
2. a keeper; a bodyguard; a guard; a person having charge of guarding or protecting something or somebody
3. name of an ancient state in the Chou Dynasty
4. a Chinese family name

衛兵(ㄨㄟˋ ㄅㄧㄥ)
(military) guard; sentry

衛冕(ㄨㄟˋ ㄇㄧㄢˇ)
to defend a title

衛道(ㄨㄟˋ ㄉㄠˋ)
to protect or guard traditional cultural heritage, especially the code of ethics attributed to Confucius

衛隊(ㄨㄟˋ ㄉㄨㄟˋ)
bodyguards; guard units

衛國(ㄨㄟˋ ㄍㄨㄛˊ)
to defend one's country

衛國衛民(ㄨㄟˋ ㄍㄨㄛˊ ㄨㄟˋ ㄇㄧㄣˊ)
to defend the country and protect the people

衛青(ㄨㄟˋ ㄑㄧㄥ)
Wei Ching, one of the greatest generals during the reign of Emperor Wu of the Han Dynasty (漢武帝)

衛星(ㄨㄟˋ ㄒㄧㄥ)
satellites

衛星通訊(ㄨㄟˋ ㄒㄧㄥ ㄊㄨㄥ ㄒㄩㄣˋ)
communication by satellite

衛星國家(ㄨㄟˋ ㄒㄧㄥ ㄍㄨㄛˊ ㄐㄧㄚ)
satellite nations

衛星轉播站(ㄨㄟˋ ㄒㄧㄥ ㄓㄨㄢˇ ㄅㄛ ㄓㄢˋ)
a satellite earth station

衛士(ㄨㄟˋ ㄕˋ)
①a guard; a bodyguard ②a protector or guardian of (morality, etc.)

衛生(ㄨㄟˋ ㄕㄥ)
sanitation; sanitary; public health

衛生棉(ㄨㄟˋ ㄕㄥ ㄇㄧㄢˊ)
a sanitary napkin

衛生節(ㄨㄟˋ ㄕㄥ ㄐㄧㄝˊ)
Sanitation Day (on April 7)

衛生局(ㄨㄟˋ ㄕㄥ ㄐㄩˊ)
the bureau of public health; the bureau of sanitation

衛生學(ㄨㄟˋ ㄕㄥ ㄒㄩㄝˊ)
hygiene; hygienics

衛生知識(ㄨㄟˋ ㄕㄥ ㄓ ㄕˋ)
knowledge pertaining to sanitation or health

衛生紙(ㄨㄟˋ ㄕㄥ ㄓˇ)
tissue paper; toilet paper

衛生處(ㄨㄟˋ ㄕㄥ ㄔㄨˋ)
the department of public health; the department of sanitation

衛生設備(ㄨㄟˋ ㄕㄥ ㄕㄜˋ ㄅㄟˋ)
sanitary facilities; sanitary ware

衛生所(ㄨㄟˋ ㄕㄥ ㄙㄨㄛˇ)
a public health clinic

衛生衣(ㄨㄟˋ ㄕㄥ ㄧ)
a kind of tight cotton underwear

衛生院(ㄨㄟˋ ㄕㄥ ㄩㄢˋ)
a public health clinic; a hospital

衛戍(ㄨㄟˋ ㄕㄨˋ)
to garrison

衛戍部隊(ㄨㄟˋ ㄕㄨˋ ㄅㄨˋ ㄉㄨㄟˋ)
garrison troops

衛戍司令部(ㄨㄟˋ ㄕㄨˋ ㄙ ㄌㄧㄥˋ ㄅㄨˋ)
garrison headquarters

【衡】 5372
　　ㄏㄥˊ herng héng
1. to weigh; to measure; to assess; to consider
2. horizontal
3. railings
4. a beam
5. the beam of a steelyard
6. a Chinese family name

衡平(ㄏㄥˊ ㄆㄧㄥˊ)
to weigh and consider in order to uphold justice

衡量(ㄏㄥˊ ㄌㄧㄤˊ)
to weigh; to measure; to consider; to judge; to estimate; to assess: 勿用一般標準來衡量它。Don't measure it by common criteria.

衡廬(ㄏㄥˊ ㄌㄨˊ)
names of two famous mountains, Mt. Heng and Mt. Lu, in China

衡鑑(ㄏㄥˊ ㄐㄧㄢˋ)
a yardstick to tell right from wrong

衡情(ㄏㄥˊ ㄑㄧㄥˊ)
to consider the actual conditions or situations; to judge the circumstances of a case

衡視(ㄏㄥˊ ㄕˋ)
to look horizontally

衡山(ㄏㄥˊ ㄕㄢ) or 衡嶽(ㄏㄥˊ ㄩㄝˋ)
Mountain Heng, one of the Five Sacred Mountains

衡陽(ㄏㄥˊ ㄧㄤˊ)
Hengyang, a city in Hunan Province

衡宇(ㄏㄥˊ ㄩˇ)
the roof of a house

十八畫

【衢】 5373
　　ㄑㄩˊ chyu qú
a thoroughfare; a highway junction

衢道(ㄑㄩˊ ㄉㄠˋ)
a side street; crossroads

衢塗(ㄑㄩˊ ㄊㄨˊ)
a side street; crossroads

衢路(ㄑㄩˊ ㄌㄨˋ)
a thoroughfare

衢肆(ㄑㄩˊ ㄙˋ)
a store beside a thoroughfare

〔行部〕

衣 部

〔衣 部〕

丨 i yī

【衣】 5374
丨 i yī

1. clothing; dress; apparel; garments; attire
2. a coating; a covering
3. skin or peel of fruits
4. a Chinese family name

衣鉢(丨 ㄅㄛ)
teaching, skill, etc. handed down from a master to his pupil

衣包(丨 ㄅㄠ)
a canvas bag, usually for traveling

衣胞(丨 ㄅㄠ)
the placenta; the human afterbirth 亦作「胞衣」

衣不蔽體(丨 ㄅㄨ ㄅㄧ ㄊㄧ)
to wear rags, shabby clothes, or tatters

衣帽架(丨 ㄇㄠ ㄐㄧㄚ)
a hat tree; a hall tree

衣帽間(丨 ㄇㄠ ㄐㄧㄢ)
a cloakroom (in restaurants, theaters, etc.); a checkroom

衣服(丨 ㄈㄨ)
clothes; clothing; dress

衣帶詔(丨 ㄉㄞ ㄓㄠ)
an imperial decree smuggled out of the palace by sewing it into robes or girdles (when the emperor was a prisoner of a powerful minister)

衣帶水(丨 ㄉㄞ ㄕㄨㄟ)
a narrow strip of water (such as a narrow channel)

衣來伸手，飯來張口(丨 ㄌㄞ ㄕㄣ ㄕㄡ，ㄈㄢ ㄌㄞ ㄓㄤ ㄎㄡ)
to live on the labor of others; to lead the life of a parasite

衣料(丨 ㄌㄧㄠ)
clothing material

衣領(丨 ㄌㄧㄥ)
a collar

衣履敝穿(丨 ㄌㄩ ㄅㄧ ㄔㄨㄢ)
in rags; ragged clothing

衣鉤(丨 ㄍㄡ)
a hook for hanging clothes

衣櫃(丨 ㄍㄨㄟ)
a wardrobe; a chest of drawers for clothing

衣冠(丨 ㄍㄨㄢ)
① clothes and caps—dress ② the appearance of a gentleman; the gentry

衣冠不整(丨 ㄍㄨㄢ ㄅㄨ ㄓㄥ)
sloppily dressed

衣冠禽獸(丨 ㄍㄨㄢ ㄑㄧㄣ ㄕㄡ)
a gentleman in appearance but a beast in conduct; a beast in human clothing; a wolf in sheep's clothing

衣冠中人(丨 ㄍㄨㄢ ㄓㄨㄥ ㄖㄣ)
the gentry

衣冠塚(丨 ㄍㄨㄢ ㄓㄨㄥ)
the grave of a hero whose body cannot be found (so called because only his clothes and hat are buried in place of his remains)

衣冠楚楚(丨 ㄍㄨㄢ ㄔㄨ ㄔㄨ)
in immaculate attire; dressed like a gentleman

衣冠文物(丨 ㄍㄨㄢ ㄨㄣ ㄨ)
civilization and culture

衣架(丨 ㄐㄧㄚ)
a rack for clothes; a clothes-horse; a coat hanger

衣襟(丨 ㄐㄧㄣ)
lapels of a garment

衣衾(丨 ㄑㄧㄣ)
the clothes and coverlet on the deceased in the coffin

衣取蔽寒(丨 ㄑㄩ ㄅㄧ ㄏㄢ)
Clothing is for keeping one warm.

衣箱(丨 ㄒㄧㄤ)
a box or chest for storing clothes

衣香鬢影(丨 ㄒㄧㄤ ㄅㄧㄣ ㄧㄥ)
women in rich attire

衣著(丨 ㄓㄨㄛ)
clothing; attire; apparel; dress

衣裝(丨 ㄓㄨㄤ)
clothes and traveling baggage

衣櫥(丨 ㄔㄨ)
a wardrobe; a clothespress

衣食(丨 ㄕ)
food and clothing; what one lives on

衣食不周(丨 ㄕ ㄅㄨ ㄓㄡ)
to be wanting in food and

---

clothing—very poor

衣食父母(丨 ㄕ ㄈㄨ ㄇㄨ)
those, on whom one's livelihood depends (like customers to businessmen)

衣食住行(丨 ㄕ ㄓㄨ ㄒㄧㄥ)
food, clothing, housing and transportation—the four essential requirements of the people

衣食足然後知榮辱(丨 ㄕ ㄗㄨ ㄖㄢ ㄏㄡ ㄓ ㄖㄨㄥ ㄖㄨ)
One has a sense of shame and honor only when his livelihood is assured. 或 Human dignity is not the offspring of an empty stomach. 或 Well fed, well bred.

衣衫(丨 ㄕㄢ)
dress (and general appearance)

衣衫襤褸(丨 ㄕㄢ ㄌㄢ ㄌㄩ)
in rags; ragged clothing

衣裳(丨 ㄕㄤ)
clothes; garments; clothing: 她有很多漂亮的衣裳。 She has many beautiful clothes.

衣幘(丨 ㄗㄜ)
clothes and turbans

衣索比亞(丨 ㄙㄨㄛ ㄅㄧ ㄧㄚ)
Ethiopia, a kingdom in Africa

衣阿華(丨 ㄧ ㄏㄨㄚ)
the state of Iowa, U.S.A. 亦作「愛阿華」

衣魚(丨 ㄩ)
lepisma

【衣】 5374
丨 yih yì

to clothe; to wear; to dress

衣被(丨 ㄅㄟ)
to cover (with blankets, etc.)—(figuratively) to do someone a favor

衣錦還鄉(丨 ㄐㄧㄣ ㄏㄨㄢ ㄒㄧㄤ)
to return home in glory

衣錦夜行(丨 ㄐㄧㄣ ㄧㄝ ㄒㄧㄥ)
(literally) to travel at night in rich garments—glory unknown to others 亦作「衣繡夜行」

三畫

【表】 5375
ㄅㄧㄠ beau biǎo

1. outside; external; apparent;

appearance; exteriors; superficial

2. to announce; to manifest; to show;

3. relatives on the side of one's mother's sisters or brothers; relatives on the side of one's father's sisters

4. a report to the emperor

5. a table; a schedule; a chart; a form

表白(ㄅㄧㄠˇ ㄅㄞˊ)
to express or state clearly; to explain; to clear up; to defend (one's position, etc.); to bare one's heart; to bare: 他表白了誠意。He expressed his sincerity.

表報(ㄅㄧㄠˇ ㄅㄠˋ)
tables, charts, reports, etc. of an office

表皮(ㄅㄧㄠˇ ㄆㄧˊ)
① the epidermis ② the cuticle (of plants)

表妹(ㄅㄧㄠˇ ㄇㄟˋ)
a cousin (a daughter of one's father's sister or of one's mother's brother or sister, who is younger than oneself): 這位是我的表妹。This is my cousin.

表面(ㄅㄧㄠˇ ㄇㄧㄢˋ)
on the surface; externally; outwardly; superficial: 他的聰明僅僅是表面的。His cleverness is only on the surface.

表面化(ㄅㄧㄠˇ ㄇㄧㄢˋ ㄏㄨㄚˋ)
(said of a relationship, dispute, secret, etc.) to come to the surface; to become apparent

表面張力(ㄅㄧㄠˇ ㄇㄧㄢˋ ㄓㄤ ㄌㄧˋ)
(physics) surface tension

表面上(ㄅㄧㄠˇ ㄇㄧㄢˋ ㄕㄤˋ)
on the surface; externally; outwardly

表明(ㄅㄧㄠˇ ㄇㄧㄥˊ)
to indicate or state clearly or plainly

表達(ㄅㄧㄠˇ ㄉㄚˊ)
to convey or transmit (one's feelings, meaning, etc.); to present; to express; to make known; to voice: 我無法適當地把它表達出來。I can't express it properly.

表弟(ㄅㄧㄠˇ ㄉㄧˋ)
a cousin (a son of one's

father's sister or of one's mother's brother or sister, who is younger than oneself)

表態(ㄅㄧㄠˇ ㄊㄞˋ)
to make known one's position towards an issue; to declare where one stands: 他已作明確表態。He has taken a clear-cut stand.

表土(ㄅㄧㄠˇ ㄊㄨˇ)
surface soil; topsoil

表同情(ㄅㄧㄠˇ ㄊㄨㄥˊ ㄑㄧㄥˊ)
to express one's sympathy; to commiserate

表裏(ㄅㄧㄠˇ ㄌㄧˇ)
① both sides—inside and outside; in front and behind ②(Chinese medicine) exterior and interior

表裏不一(ㄅㄧㄠˇ ㄌㄧˇ ㄅㄨˋ ㄧ)
to think in one way and behave in another

表裏受敵(ㄅㄧㄠˇ ㄌㄧˇ ㄕㄡˋ ㄉㄧˊ)
to encounter the enemy in front and behind

表裏一致(ㄅㄧㄠˇ ㄌㄧˇ ㄧ ㄓˋ)or 表裏如一(ㄅㄧㄠˇ ㄌㄧˇ ㄖㄨˊ ㄧ)
honest and sincere

表列(ㄅㄧㄠˇ ㄌㄧㄝˋ)
to catalogue; to list

表露(ㄅㄧㄠˇ ㄌㄨˋ)
to make plain; to express or expose; to voice: 他們表露了憤怒。They gave voice to their indignation.

表哥(ㄅㄧㄠˇ ㄍㄜ)
a cousin (a son of one's father's sister or of one's mother's brother or sister, who is older than oneself)

表格(ㄅㄧㄠˇ ㄍㄜˊ)
a form or blank (for filling); a table or chart

表記(ㄅㄧㄠˇ ㄐㄧˋ)
① a mark; a sign ② a souvenir

表姊(ㄅㄧㄠˇ ㄐㄧㄝˇ)
a cousin (a daughter of one's father's sister or of one's mother's brother or sister, who is older than oneself)

表姊妹(ㄅㄧㄠˇ ㄐㄧㄝˇ ㄇㄟˋ)
female first cousins (daughters of one's maternal uncles and aunts and of one's

father's sisters)

表決(ㄅㄧㄠˇ ㄐㄩㄝˊ)
to vote; to put to the vote: 投票表決吧。Let's decide by vote.

表決權(ㄅㄧㄠˇ ㄐㄩㄝˊ ㄑㄩㄢˊ)
the right of voting: 他們行使表決權。They exercised the right of voting.

表親(ㄅㄧㄠˇ ㄑㄧㄣ)
relatives on the side of one's parents' sisters or of one's mother's brothers

表情(ㄅㄧㄠˇ ㄑㄧㄥˊ)
facial expression: 她的表情不自然。She wore an unnatural expression.

表情達意(ㄅㄧㄠˇ ㄑㄧㄥˊ ㄉㄚˊ ㄧˋ)
to communicate views; to convey one's ideas or feelings

表顯(ㄅㄧㄠˇ ㄒㄧㄢˇ)
to express; to display

表現(ㄅㄧㄠˇ ㄒㄧㄢˋ)
① to appear ② to behave ③ to distinguish oneself ④ to perform (a task); the way one does something: 他表現良好。He performs well.

表象(ㄅㄧㄠˇ ㄒㄧㄤˋ)
(psychology) presentation; idea

表兄(ㄅㄧㄠˇ ㄒㄩㄥ)
a cousin (a son of one's father's sister or of one's mother's brother or sister, who is older than oneself): 他是我的表兄。He is my cousin.

表兄弟(ㄅㄧㄠˇ ㄒㄩㄥ ㄉㄧˋ)
male first cousins (sons of one's maternal uncles and aunts and of one's father's sisters)

表姪(ㄅㄧㄠˇ ㄓˊ)
grandsons of one's paternal aunts

表章(ㄅㄧㄠˇ ㄓㄤ)
① a report to the emperor ② to honor 亦作「表彰」

表彰(ㄅㄧㄠˇ ㄓㄤ)
to honor; to cite; citation

表示(ㄅㄧㄠˇ ㄕˋ)
to express; to show; to indicate; expression; reaction: 他們對我表示厚意。They showed me great kindness.

〔衣部〕

表示滿意(ㄅㄧㄠˇ ㄕˋ ㄇㄢˇ ㄧˋ)
to express or indicate satisfaction

表示反對(ㄅㄧㄠˇ ㄕˋ ㄈㄢˇ ㄉㄨㄟˋ)
to express or indicate one's opposition

表示同意(ㄅㄧㄠˇ ㄕˋ ㄊㄨㄥˊ ㄧˋ)
to indicate or show one's concurrence or approval

表示敬意(ㄅㄧㄠˇ ㄕˋ ㄐㄧㄥˋ ㄧˋ)
to show or pay respect

表示慶賀(ㄅㄧㄠˇ ㄕˋ ㄑㄧㄥˋ ㄏㄜˋ)
to show or express one's congratulations

表示謝意(ㄅㄧㄠˇ ㄕˋ ㄒㄧㄝˋ ㄧˋ)
to express one's thanks or appreciation; to express one's gratitude

表叔(ㄅㄧㄠˇ ㄕㄨˊ)
an uncle (a son of one's grandfather's sister, or a son of one's grandmother's sister or brother)

表率(ㄅㄧㄠˇ ㄕㄨㄞˋ)
an example; a paragon: 她為朋友們樹立了好表率。She set a good example to her friends.

表字(ㄅㄧㄠˇ ㄗˋ)
a courtesy name; a second name; an alias 亦作「別號」

表子(ㄅㄧㄠˇ ㄗˊ)
a prostitute 亦作「婊子」

表冊(ㄅㄧㄠˇ ㄘㄜˋ)
tables, indexes, files, etc.

表層(ㄅㄧㄠˇ ㄘㄥˊ)
a surface layer

表示親情(ㄅㄧㄠˇ ㄕˋ ㄑㄧㄣ ㄑㄧㄥˊ)
to show friendliness to or express support for someone who does not appreciate it

表儀(ㄅㄧㄠˇ ㄧˊ)
one's majestic appearance

表演(ㄅㄧㄠˇ ㄧㄢˇ)
to perform; to demonstrate; demonstration; a performance; a show: 你表演得很不錯。You performed very well.

表揚(ㄅㄧㄠˇ ㄧㄤˊ)
to praise in public; to cite for all to know: 他因那研究而受表揚。He was cited for his research work.

【衫】5376
ㄕㄢ shan shān
a shirt; a garment; a gown

【衩】5377
ㄔㄚˋ chah chà

slits on the lower part of a gown for freedom of movement

衩衣(ㄔㄚˋ ㄧ)
a woman's gown with slits on the sides

衩襪(ㄔㄚˋ ㄨㄚˋ)
stockings without bands

四畫

【衰】5378
1. ㄕㄨㄞ shuai shuāi
1. to decline; weakening; failing (health, etc.); debility: 懶惰則體衰。Laziness leads to debility.
2. declining or falling (nations, etc.)

衰敗(ㄕㄨㄞ ㄅㄞˋ)
to decline and disintegrate

衰弊(ㄕㄨㄞ ㄅㄧˋ)
decadent and corrupt

衰邁(ㄕㄨㄞ ㄇㄞˋ) or 衰暮(ㄕㄨㄞ ㄇㄨˋ)
old and weak

衰頹(ㄕㄨㄞ ㄊㄨㄟˊ)
discouraged and despondent

衰退(ㄕㄨㄞ ㄊㄨㄟˋ)
failing (energy, strength, memory, etc.); weakening (as a result of old age, poor health, etc.); decline: 他的健康衰退了。He failed in his health.

衰老(ㄕㄨㄞ ㄌㄠˇ)
senile; senility: 他已相當衰老了。He has become perfectly senile.

衰陵(ㄕㄨㄞ ㄌㄧㄥˊ)
the decline and fall (of a nation, dynasty, etc.)

衰落(ㄕㄨㄞ ㄌㄨㄛˋ)
the decline and fall (of a nation, family fortune, etc.); to go into oblivion

衰耗(ㄕㄨㄞ ㄏㄠˋ)
to weaken and deteriorate

衰疾(ㄕㄨㄞ ㄐㄧˊ)
decrepit and beset by illness

衰竭(ㄕㄨㄞ ㄐㄧㄝˊ)
exhaustion; prostration

衰倦(ㄕㄨㄞ ㄐㄩㄢˋ)
enfeebled and tired

衰缺(ㄕㄨㄞ ㄑㄩㄝ)
declining and full of defects

衰息(ㄕㄨㄞ ㄒㄧˊ)
to come to a halt or stop

(as a lawsuit, etc.)

衰謝(ㄕㄨㄞ ㄒㄧㄝˋ)
① old and desolate ②(said of hair) sparse

衰朽(ㄕㄨㄞ ㄒㄧㄡˇ)
old and useless

衰世(ㄕㄨㄞ ㄕˋ)
an age of decline and tumult

衰弱(ㄕㄨㄞ ㄖㄨㄛˋ)
to debilitate; weak; sickly; not healthy

衰弱症(ㄕㄨㄞ ㄖㄨㄛˋ ㄓㄥˋ)
a wasting disease

衰容(ㄕㄨㄞ ㄖㄨㄥˊ)
the face of an old person

衰草寒煙(ㄕㄨㄞ ㄘㄠˇ ㄏㄢˊ ㄧㄢ)
withering grass and chilly mists (descriptive of a desolate scene)

衰顏(ㄕㄨㄞ ㄧㄢˊ)
the face of an old person

衰微(ㄕㄨㄞ ㄨㄟˊ)
to decline; to wane; declining

衰亡(ㄕㄨㄞ ㄨㄤˊ)
the decline and fall

【衰】5378
2. ㄘㄨㄟ tsuei cui
1. order or series—from the top downward
2. mourning garments (of hemp, etc.)

【袂】5379
ㄇㄟˋ mey mèi
sleeves

【衲】5380
1. to sew; to mend; to patch
2. the robe of a monk
3. a monk

衲被(ㄋㄚˋ ㄅㄟˋ)
① a quilt with patches on it ② a collection of cards on which literary allusions are copied and explained and then arranged and made use of in a piece of composition —a reference to the practice of Yang Yi (楊億) of the Sung Dynasty

衲頭(ㄋㄚˋ ㄊㄡˊ)
a monk's clothes made of rags

衲子(ㄋㄚˋ ㄗˇ)
a polite self-reference of a Buddhist monk

【袍】5381
ㄋㄧˊ nih ní

a woman's underwear

衵（ㄖˋ ㄈㄨˊ）
women's underwear

【衷】 5382
　　　　　　ㄓㄨㄥ jong zhōng
. the bottom of one's heart;
honest; sincere
. good and virtuous; goodness
. proper; appropriate; befit-
ting; propriety
. undergarments
. a Chinese family name

衷款（ㄓㄨㄥ ㄎㄨㄢˇ）
sincerity

衷情（ㄓㄨㄥ ㄑㄧㄥˊ）
the feelings or affection in
one's heart

衷曲（ㄓㄨㄥ ㄑㄩ）
words from the bottom of
one's heart; the voice of one's
heart; inner feelings

衷心（ㄓㄨㄥ ㄒㄧㄣ）
heartfelt; wholehearted; cordial

衷心感謝（ㄓㄨㄥ ㄒㄧㄣ ㄍㄢˇ ㄒㄧㄝˋ）
to thank sincerely; to thank
from the bottom of one's
heart

衷腸（ㄓㄨㄥ ㄔㄤˊ）or衷懷（ㄓㄨㄥ
ㄏㄨㄞˊ）
innermost feelings; sincere
words

衷衣（ㄓㄨㄥ ㄧ）
underwear

【衺】 5383
　　（邪）ㄒㄧㄝˊ shye xié
evil

【衽】 5384
　　（袵）ㄖㄣˋ renn rèn
. the lapel or collar of a garment
. sleeves
. to arrange (one's lapel, etc.)
. a sleeping mat

衽席（ㄖㄣˋ ㄒㄧˊ）
a sleeping mat

【衾】 5385
　　　　　　ㄑㄧㄣ chin qīn
　　（又讀）ㄑㄧㄣˊ chyn
　　　　　　　　　　qín
. a large coverlet or quilt
. garments or dress for the
deceased

衾單（ㄑㄧㄣ ㄉㄢ）
①clothes, etc. for the deceased ②sheets

衾枕（ㄑㄧㄣ ㄓㄣˇ）
quilts and pillows

衾衽（ㄑㄧㄣ ㄖㄣˋ）
in bed; between the sheets

衾影無慚（ㄑㄧㄣ ㄧㄥˇ ㄨˊ ㄘㄢˊ）
to do nothing that one can
be ashamed of even if there
is no one watching

【衿】 5386
　　　　　　ㄐㄧㄣ jin jīn
1. the front of a Chinese gown
2. the lapel of a Chinese dress
—worn by the literati in former days

衿契（ㄐㄧㄣ ㄑㄧˋ）
a good friend, with whom
one sees eye to eye about
everything

【袁】 5387
　　　　　　ㄩㄢˊ yuan yuán
1. the graceful look of a flowing robe
2. a Chinese family name

袁大頭（ㄩㄢˊ ㄉㄚˋ ㄊㄡˊ）
silver coins minted in the
early years of the Republic
of China with the head of
Yüan Shih-kai（袁世凱）on
the obverse side

袁枚（ㄩㄢˊ ㄇㄟˊ）
Yüan Mei, a man of letters
in the Ching Dynasty

袁世凱（ㄩㄢˊ ㄕˋ ㄎㄞˇ）
Yüan Shih-kai（1859-1916）,
the first President of the
Republic of China, who died
shortly after he proclaimed
himself an emperor

袁紹（ㄩㄢˊ ㄕㄠˋ）
Yüan Shao（?-202）, a war-
lord toward the end of the
Han Dynasty

【袞】 5388
　　（兗）ㄍㄨㄣˇ goen
　　　　　　　　　gǔn
1. the imperial robe with embroidered dragons
2. robes of very high officials

袞冕（ㄍㄨㄣˇ ㄇㄧㄢˇ）
a robe embroidered with
dragons and a crown worn
by the emperor in sacrificial
ceremonies

袞命（ㄍㄨㄣˇ ㄇㄧㄥˋ）
the office or appointment of
the three highest officials（三
公）in ancient China

袞服（ㄍㄨㄣˇ ㄈㄨˊ）
ceremonial dress or robe in
ancient China

袞龍袍（ㄍㄨㄣˇ ㄌㄨㄥˊ ㄆㄠˊ）
the imperial robe embroi-
dered with coiled dragons

袞袞諸公（ㄍㄨㄣˇ ㄍㄨㄣˇ ㄓㄨ ㄍㄨㄥ）
many eminent personalities;
many VIPs; high-ranking
officials

袞闕（ㄍㄨㄣˇ ㄑㄩㄝ）
the faults of the emperor

袞職（ㄍㄨㄣˇ ㄓˊ）
①the throne; the responsibility of an emperor ②the
office of the three highest
officials（三公）in ancient
China

袞司（ㄍㄨㄣˇ ㄙ）
the three highest-ranking
officials in the imperial
court of ancient China 亦作
「三公」

袞衣（ㄍㄨㄣˇ ㄧ）
robes embroidered with
dragons worn only by the
emperor

五畫

【袈】 5389
　　　　　　ㄐㄧㄚ jia jiā
the cassock or robe of a
Buddhist monk

袈裟（ㄐㄧㄚ ㄕㄚ）
a kasaya or cassock, the
robe of a Buddhist monk

【袖】 5390
　　　　　　ㄒㄧㄡˋ shiow xiù
1. the sleeve
2. to hide or put things in
sleeves

袖頭兒（ㄒㄧㄡˋ ㄊㄡˊㄦ）
the cuff

袖筒兒（ㄒㄧㄡˋ ㄊㄨㄥˊㄦ）
the sleeve

袖口（兒）（ㄒㄧㄡˋ ㄎㄡˇㄦ）
the cuff (of a sleeve); the
far ends of sleeves; a wrist-
band

袖扣（ㄒㄧㄡˋ ㄎㄡˋ）
cuff links

袖箭（ㄒㄧㄡˋ ㄐㄧㄢˋ）
a cylindrical device hidden
in the sleeve, which can
launch small darts with its
spring catapult

袖珍（ㄒㄧㄡˋ ㄓㄣ）
pocket-size; pocket

袖珍本（ㄒㄧㄡˋ ㄓㄣ ㄅㄣˇ）

〔衣部〕

a pocket edition; a pocket book

袖珍戰艦(ㄒㄧㄡ ㄓㄣ ㄓㄢ ㄐㄧㄢˋ)
a pocket battleship

袖珍字典(ㄒㄧㄡ ㄓㄣ ㄗˋ ㄉㄧㄢˇ)
a pocket dictionary

袖手旁觀(ㄒㄧㄡ ㄕㄡˇ ㄆㄤˊ ㄍㄨㄢ)
to look on without even lifting a finger (to help, etc.); to watch with folded arms

袖刃(ㄒㄧㄡ ㄖㄣˋ)
to hide a dagger or knife in a sleeve

袖子(ㄒㄧㄡ ˙ㄗ)or 袖兒(ㄒㄧㄡㄦ)
the sleeve: 她拉著她的袖子。He pulled her by the sleeve.

袖刺(ㄒㄧㄡ ㄘˋ)
to put one's visiting cards in the sleeve

【袋】 5391
ㄉㄞˋ day dài
a bag, a sack; a pocket; a pouch

袋兒(ㄉㄞˋㄦ)
a purse; a pocket

袋鼠(ㄉㄞˋ ㄕㄨˇ)
the kangaroo

袋子(ㄉㄞˋ ˙ㄗ)
a bag; a sack; a pocket: 他買了一個購物袋子。He bought a shopping bag.

【袍】 5392
ㄆㄠˊ paur páo
a long gown; a robe

袍掛(ㄆㄠˊ ㄍㄨㄚˋ)
a long gown topped off with a jacket, the ceremonial robe in the Ching Dynasty and among old-fashioned Chinese gentlemen of modern times, also worn as ceremonial dress

袍笏(ㄆㄠˊ ㄏㄨˋ)
an official robe and tablet, formal dress in audience with the emperor

袍笏登場(ㄆㄠˊ ㄏㄨˋ ㄉㄥ ㄔㄤˇ)
①(Chinese opera) to go on stage and perform ②(said of rebels or traitors) to establish a bogus government and claim legality

袍子(ㄆㄠˊ ˙ㄗ)
a robe; a long gown: 他穿了一襲袍子。He wears a robe.

袍澤(ㄆㄠˊ ㄗㄜˊ)
one's buddies in the army;
comrades in arms

【祖】 5393
ㄊㄢˇ taan tǎn
1. to bare; to strip; bared
2. to protect or screen (with an implication of prejudice); to be partial: 勿偏袒她。Do not be partial to her.

袒胸(ㄊㄢˇ ㄒㄩㄥ)
to strip to the waist; bared to the waist

袒免(ㄊㄢˇ ㄇㄧㄢˇ)
to bare one's left arm and take off one's cap—a gesture of great sorrow in ancient times

袒縛(ㄊㄢˇ ㄈㄨˋ)
to bare oneself to the waist and bind one's hands at the back—an act of surrendering or submitting in ancient times; an expression used to show a submission

袒露(ㄊㄢˇ ㄌㄨˋ)
to expose

袒護(ㄊㄢˇ ㄏㄨˋ)
to shield; to protect; to screen; to side with; to be partial: 他公然袒護一方。He was partial to one side publicly.

袒裼(ㄊㄢˇ ㄒㄧˊ)
to bare one's breast and arms; with one's breast and arms bare

袒胸露臂(ㄊㄢˇ ㄒㄩㄥ ㄌㄨˋ ㄅㄧˋ)
to bare the chest and expose the arms

祖衣(ㄊㄢˇ ㄧ)
to dress in a hurry with part of flesh showing

【袜】 5394
1. ㄇㄛˋ moh mò
a stomacher

袜腹(ㄇㄛˋ ㄈㄨˋ)
a stomacher

袜肚(ㄇㄛˋ ㄉㄨˋ)
①a waistband ②a saddle girth

袜胸(ㄇㄛˋ ㄒㄩㄥ)
a stomacher

【袜】 5394
2. ㄨㄚˋ wah wà
a simplified form of 襪—stockings; socks

【袤】 5395
ㄇㄠˋ maw mào
(又讀 ㄇㄡˋ mow mòu)
length; lengthwise—from north to south (as opposed to 廣)

【袪】 5396
ㄑㄩ chiu qū
1. cuffs; sleeves
2. to raise the sleeves; to lift up one's arms
3. to relieve

【被】 5397
1. ㄅㄟˋ bey bèi
1. bedding; a coverlet; a quilt
2. to cover; to shroud
3. to spread; to reach
4. placed before verbs to show a passive voice
5. because of; due to
6. a Chinese family name

被保護國(ㄅㄟˋ ㄅㄠˇ ㄏㄨˋ ㄍㄨㄛˊ)
a protectorate

被綁架(ㄅㄟˋ ㄅㄤˇ ㄐㄧㄚˋ)
to be kidnaped: 一個男孩被綁架。A boy was kidnaped.

被謗(ㄅㄟˋ ㄅㄤˋ)
to be slandered

被迫(ㄅㄟˋ ㄆㄛˋ)or 被逼(ㄅㄟˋ ㄅㄧ)
to be compelled or forced to

被迫降落(ㄅㄟˋ ㄆㄛˋ ㄐㄧㄤˋ ㄌㄨㄛˋ)
a forced landing; to be forced to land

被騙(ㄅㄟˋ ㄆㄧㄢˋ)
to be swindled; to be fooled

被面(ㄅㄟˋ ㄇㄧㄢˋ)
the cover side of a comforter

被俘(ㄅㄟˋ ㄈㄨˊ)
to be captured; to be taken prisoner

被服(ㄅㄟˋ ㄈㄨˊ)
①coverlets and clothes ②(figuratively) to receive; to benefit

被服廠(ㄅㄟˋ ㄈㄨˊ ㄔㄤˇ)
a factory that makes uniforms, tents and other textile goods for military use; a clothing factory

被單兒(ㄅㄟˋ ㄉㄢ ㄦ)or 被單子(ㄅㄟˋ ㄉㄢ ˙ㄗ)
a bedsheet; a bedspread; bed cover; bed linens

被底鴛鴦(ㄅㄟˋ ㄉㄧˇ ㄩㄢ ㄧㄤ)
(literally) mandarin duck under the quilt—a devoted couple

被動(ㄅㄟˋ ㄉㄨㄥˋ)
passive; to act on order

被動式(ㄅㄟˋ ㄉㄨㄥˋ ㄕˋ)
(grammar) the passive voice

被套(ㄅㄟˋ ㄊㄠˋ)
ticking

被虐待狂(ㄅㄟˋ ㄋㄩㄝˋ ㄉㄞˋ ㄎㄨㄤˊ)
masochism

被裏(ㄅㄟˋ ㄌㄧˇ)or 被裏子(ㄅㄟˋ ㄌㄧˇ ㄗ˙)
the underneath side of a quilt; the lining of a comforter

被告(ㄅㄟˋ ㄍㄠˋ)
the accused; the defendant

被害(ㄅㄟˋ ㄏㄞˋ)
to be killed or murdered

被害者(ㄅㄟˋ ㄏㄞˋ ㄓㄜˇ)
the injured or wronged party; a victim; an injured person

被加數(ㄅㄟˋ ㄐㄧㄚ ㄕㄨˋ)
a summand

被刦(ㄅㄟˋ ㄐㄧㄝˊ)
to be robbed; 我鄰居於上週被刦。The house next to mine was robbed last week.

被刦持(ㄅㄟˋ ㄐㄧㄝˊ ㄔˊ)
to be held as a hostage

被減數(ㄅㄟˋ ㄐㄧㄢˇ ㄕㄨˋ)
a minuend

被竊(ㄅㄟˋ ㄑㄧㄝˋ)
to be victimized by burglary

被擒(ㄅㄟˋ ㄑㄧㄣˊ)
to be captured alive; to be taken prisoner

被搶(ㄅㄟˋ ㄑㄧㄤˇ)
to be robbed; 我的錶被搶了。I was robbed of my watch.

被選舉權(ㄅㄟˋ ㄒㄩㄢˇ ㄐㄩˇ ㄑㄩㄢˊ)
the right of being elected; eligibility for election

被選舉人(ㄅㄟˋ ㄒㄩㄢˇ ㄐㄩˇ ㄖㄣˊ)
the person to be elected; a candidate of an election

被乘數(ㄅㄟˋ ㄔㄥˊ ㄕㄨˋ)
a multiplicand

被除數(ㄅㄟˋ ㄔㄨˊ ㄕㄨˋ)
a dividend

被殺(ㄅㄟˋ ㄕㄚ)
to be killed or assassinated; 這熊昨天被殺了。The bear was killed yesterday.

被辱(ㄅㄟˋ ㄖㄨˇ)
to be insulted or humiliated

被褥(ㄅㄟˋ ㄖㄨˋ)
coverlets and mattresses;

---

bedding

被子植物(ㄅㄟˋ ㄗ˙ ㄓˊ ㄨˋ)
(botany) angiosperm

被子(ㄅㄟˋ ㄗ˙)
a quilt

被刺(ㄅㄟˋ ㄘˋ)
to be assassinated

被誣(ㄅㄟˋ ㄨ)
to be falsely accused

被窩兒(ㄅㄟˋ ㄨㄛ ㄦ)或 被窩子(ㄅㄟˋ ㄨㄛ ㄗ˙)
a quilt folded like a sleeve for sleeping

【被】 5397
2.(ㄆㄧ) ㄆㄧ pi pī
1. to put on or throw on(garments, etc.)without buttoning up
2. to open
3. to disperse or spread out
4. to read desultory or to thumb through

被髮入山(ㄆㄧ ㄈㄚˇ ㄖㄨˋ ㄕㄢ)
to go and live in the mountains with hair disheveled —to become a hermit

被髮左衽(ㄆㄧ ㄈㄚˇ ㄗㄨㄛˇ ㄖㄣˋ)
hair unbound and coats buttoned on the left side—to become a barbarian

被髮佯狂(ㄆㄧ ㄈㄚˇ ㄧㄤˊ ㄎㄨㄤˊ)
With hair disheveled, one pretends to be a lunatic.

被髮文身(ㄆㄧ ㄈㄚˇ ㄨㄣˊ ㄕㄣ)
(said of a barbarian) hair disheveled and the body tattooed

被褐懷玉(ㄆㄧ ㄏㄜˋ ㄏㄨㄞˊ ㄩˋ)
(said of a hermit)to dress shabbily in order to hide one's real worth

被堅執銳(ㄆㄧ ㄐㄧㄢ ㄓˊ ㄖㄨㄟˋ)or 披堅執銳(ㄆㄧ ㄐㄧㄢ ㄓˊ ㄖㄨㄟˋ)
to wear armor and hold sharp weapons—ready to defend the country

【袞】 5398
(ㄍㄨㄣˇ) goen gǔn
the ceremonial dress of the emperor or very high officials

六畫

【袴】 5399
(袴、褲)ㄎㄨˋ kuh kù
trousers; drawers; breeches; pants; panties 參看「褲」

〔衣部〕

袴襠(ㄎㄨˋ ㄉㄤ)
the crotch (of trousers)

袴腿(ㄎㄨˋ ㄊㄨㄟˇ)
legs of trousers

袴脚(ㄎㄨˋ ㄐㄧㄠˇ)
the part of trousers near or around the ankles

袴叉兒(ㄎㄨˋ ㄔㄚ ㄦ)
pants or trousers reaching just above the knees; short pants; shorts

袴子(ㄎㄨˋ ㄗ˙)
trousers; breeches; pants

袴腰(ㄎㄨˋ ㄧㄠ)or 褲腰(ㄎㄨˋ ㄧㄠ)
the waist of trousers

袴腰帶(ㄎㄨˋ ㄧㄠ ㄉㄞˋ)
a waist belt or rope for fastening the trousers

【袱】 5400
ㄈㄨˊ fwu fú
as in包袱—a bundle wrapped in cloth

【袷】 5401
1. ㄐㄧㄚˊ jya jiá
garments with linings

【袷】 5401
2. ㄐㄧㄝˊ jye jié
the lapel or collar of robes, or, in former times, of ceremonial dress in imperial audience

【裁】 5402
ㄘㄞˊ tsair cói
1. to cut paper, cloth, etc. with a knife and scissors; to cut out or cut off
2. to diminish; to reduce
3. to delete
4. to consider; to discern; to decide; to judge
5. a form; a style
6. sanctions
7. to weight; to measure
8. to kill

裁兵(ㄘㄞˊ ㄅㄧㄥ)
to reduce the number of troops; disarmament

裁併(ㄘㄞˊ ㄅㄧㄥˋ)
(said of organizations)to cut down in size and merge into one

裁判(ㄘㄞˊ ㄆㄢˋ)
①a judge; a referee; an umpire②a verdict or judgment by law

裁判書(ㄘㄞˊ ㄆㄢˋ ㄕㄨ)
a written court verdict

裁判委員(ㄘㄞˊ ㄆㄢˋ ㄨㄟˇ ㄩㄢˊ)

a member of a panel of
judges, or referees

裁縫
①(ㄘㄞ ㄈㄥ)to tailor; to make
dress
②(ㄘㄞ ·ㄈㄥ)a tailor; a dress-
maker 亦作「裁縫師」

裁縫補習班(ㄘㄞ ㄈㄥ ㄅㄨˇ ㄒㄧˊ ㄅㄢ)
a training class for tailoring

裁縫鋪(ㄘㄞ ㄈㄥ ㄆㄨˋ)
a tailor shop

裁答(ㄘㄞ ㄉㄚˊ)
to reply to a letter

裁定(ㄘㄞ ㄉㄧㄥˋ)
(law) a court decision on
the legality of a case, or
the propriety or appropriate-
ness of a verdict

裁奪(ㄘㄞ ㄉㄨㄛˊ)
to decide; decision

裁度(ㄘㄞ ㄉㄨㄛˋ)
to weigh, consider and
decide

裁斷(ㄘㄞ ㄉㄨㄢˋ)
to decide; decision

裁汰(ㄘㄞ ㄊㄞˋ)
to reduce or eliminate (the
superfluous) staff, etc.

裁量(ㄘㄞ ㄌㄧㄤˋ)
to consider and decide; to
measure

裁可(ㄘㄞ ㄎㄜˇ)
to approve; to sign a bill
into law

裁開(ㄘㄞ ㄎㄞ)
to cut apart with a knife or
scissors

裁剪(ㄘㄞ ㄐㄧㄢˇ)
①to tailor; to cut out(a
dress): 她正在裁剪衣服。 She's
cutting out garments. ②to
delete the unimportant or
superfluous part (of a piece
of writing, etc.)

裁減(ㄘㄞ ㄐㄧㄢˇ)
①to reduce (personnel, the
staff, etc.)②reduction

裁決(ㄘㄞ ㄐㄩㄝˊ)
①to judge and decide ②a
ruling; a judgment; a decision

裁軍(ㄘㄞ ㄐㄩㄣ)
disarmament

裁紙(ㄘㄞ ㄓˇ)
to cut paper into portions
with a knife

裁制(ㄘㄞ ㄓˋ)

---

to restrain; to restrict; to
limit

裁尺(ㄘㄞ ㄔˇ)
a tailor's measure

裁撤(ㄘㄞ ㄔㄜˋ)
to abolish (an organization)

裁成(ㄘㄞ ㄔㄥˊ)
to regulate and bring to
completion; accomplishment

裁處(ㄘㄞ ㄔㄨˇ)
to make an arrangement or
decision after due consideration

裁衣(ㄘㄞ ㄧ)
to cut cloth for making
dress

裁彎取直(ㄘㄞ ㄨㄢ ㄑㄩˇ ㄓˊ)
to get rid of the unnecessary
and take the most appropriate

裁員(ㄘㄞ ㄩㄢˊ)
to eliminate unnecessary
personnel; to lay off workers

【裂】 5403
(ㄌㄧㄝˋ lieh liè)
1. to crack; to break; a crack:
杯上有一裂痕。There was a
crack in the cup.
2. to split or divide up
(profits, etc.); to rend; to
sever; to rip open: 我頭痛欲
裂。My head is splitting.

裂帛(ㄌㄧㄝˋ ㄅㄛˊ)
①a very crisp sound—like
splitting silk ②ancient books
③ to cut silk into pieces
for writing letters in ancient times

裂縫(ㄌㄧㄝˋ ㄈㄥˋ)
a crack or cleavage; a split;
a breach; a crevice; a fissure

裂膚(ㄌㄧㄝˋ ㄈㄨ)
(literally) to crack up the
skin—extreme cold

裂膽(ㄌㄧㄝˋ ㄉㄢˇ)
extremely scared or frightened

裂果(ㄌㄧㄝˋ ㄍㄨㄛˇ)
dehiscent fruits

裂開(ㄌㄧㄝˋ ㄎㄞ)
to split, rip or break apart:
衣縫裂開了。A seam rips.

裂口(ㄌㄧㄝˋ ㄎㄡˇ)
a crack; a chink

裂紋(ㄌㄧㄝˋ ㄨㄣˊ)
①a chasm (in friendship,

---

etc.)②a fissure; a split; a
crack: 木頭上有一大裂痕。
There was a big split in the
wood.

裂罅(ㄌㄧㄝˋ ㄒㄧㄚˋ)
a crack; a crevice

裂眦(ㄌㄧㄝˋ ㄗˋ)
to open one's eyes wide in
extreme anger

裂眼(ㄌㄧㄝˋ ㄧㄢˇ)
an angry look

裂紋(ㄌㄧㄝˋ ㄨㄣˊ)
a line of cleavage; crackle

【裉】 5404
ㄎㄣˇ kenn kèn
the seams below the sleeves
in a garment

【衽】 5405
(ㄖㄣˋ) ㄖㄣˇ renn rèn
1. lapels; collars
2. sleeves
3. bedding

七畫

【裊】 5406
ㄋㄧㄠˇ neau niǎo
1. curling up (as smoke, etc.);
wavering gently
2. around; all around, as sound
of music or voices of spring

裊裊(ㄋㄧㄠˇ ㄋㄧㄠˇ)
①curling up ②continuous
(sound of music, etc.)

裊娜婷婷 or 婷婷裊娜(ㄋㄧㄠˇ
ㄋㄨㄛ ㄊㄧㄥˊ ㄊㄧㄥˊ)
(said of the charming figure
and poise of a woman) curvaceous and soft

裊娜 or 娜裊(ㄋㄧㄠˇ ㄋㄨㄛˋ)
①soft and slender ②charm-
ing figure and poise of a
woman

【裋】 5407
ㄕㄨˋ shuh shù
cotton clothes of a boy servant

裋褐(ㄕㄨˋ ㄏㄜˊ)
the short, coarse garment of
a boy servant

【裙】 5408
ㄑㄩㄣˊ chyun qún
a skirt; a petticoat; an apron

裙帶(ㄑㄩㄣˊ ㄉㄞˋ)
①connected through one's
female relatives; apron
strings (used figuratively in
most cases) ②a girdle

裙帶官（くﾝ ㄉㄞ 《メㄢ）
an official appointment obtained through the influence of one's wife or her family

裙帶關係（くﾝ ㄉㄞ 《メㄢ Tㄧ）
apron-string influence or relationship; petticoat influence

裙帶親（くﾝ ㄉㄞ くㄧㄣ）
(said of a man) relatives by marriage (sometimes also used figuratively and sarcastically)

裙屐少年（くﾝ ㄐㄧ ㄕㄠ ㄋㄧㄢ）
fops; dandies; coxcombs

裙襇（くﾝ ㄐㄧㄢ）
plaits on the sides of a petticoat

裙釵（くﾝ ㄔㄞ）
petticoats and hairpins —women

裙子（くﾝ ˙ㄗ）
a woman's skirt; a petticoat

【裎】 5409
　（裎）　ㄔㄥˊ　cherng chéng
bare or nude; naked; to bare

【裏】 5410
　（裡）　ㄌㄧˇ　lǐ lì

1. within; inside
2. used to indicate time of day, night, a season, etc.
3. the lining of a dress or clothes

裏邊（ㄌㄧ ㄅㄧㄢ）or 裏邊兒（ㄌㄧ ·ㄅㄧㄚㄦ）
inside: 我們到裏邊(兒)去好嗎? Shall we go inside?

裏面兒（ㄌㄧ ㄇㄧㄢㄦ）
inside; within: 廚房裏面很清潔。It's very clean inside the kitchen.

裏封（ㄌㄧ ㄈㄥ）
a title page

裏胎（ㄌㄧ ㄊㄞ）
(colloquial) an inner tube (of a tire)

裏頭（ㄌㄧ ·ㄊㄡ）
inside: 他走進裏頭。He went inside.

裏外外（ㄌㄧ ㄨㄞˋ ㄨㄞˋ）
inside and out

裏勾外聯（ㄌㄧ 《ㄡ ㄨㄞˋ ㄌㄧㄢˊ）
collusion of forces within and without; to be in collusion with the enemy

裏海（ㄌㄧ ㄏㄞˇ）
the Caspian Sea

裏脊肉（ㄌㄧ ㄐㄧ ㄖㄡˋ）or 裏脊（ㄌㄧ ㄐㄧ）
lean pork taken from under the spinal column of a hog; tenderloin

裏間兒（ㄌㄧ ㄐㄧㄚㄦ）
an inner room

裏出外進（ㄌㄧ ㄔㄨ ㄨㄞˋ ㄐㄧㄣ）
① uneven; not neat ② a motley of people coming and going

裏子（ㄌㄧ ˙ㄗ）or 裏兒（ㄌㄧ ㄦ）
the lining of a garment, a hat or shoes

裏衣（ㄌㄧ ㄧ）
underwear

裏應外合（ㄌㄧ ㄧㄥ ㄨㄞ ㄏㄜˊ）
the joining of forces within and without; to enter into conspiracy with the dissidents within the enemy camp

裏外受敵（ㄌㄧ ㄨㄞˋ ㄕㄡˋ ㄉㄧˊ）
to encounter the enemy within and without; to face opposition inside and out

【裡】 5410
　2 ·ㄌㄧ　·li lì
used after 這 and 那 to mean "here" and "there" respectively: 把它放在這裏。Place it here.

【裒】 5411
　ㄆㄡˊ　pour póu

1. to collect; to gather; to scrape together
2. to reduce; to deduct

裒多益寡（ㄆㄡ ㄉㄨㄜ ㄧˋ 《ㄨㄚˇ）
to collect from the rich and benefit the poor

裒斂（ㄆㄡ ㄌㄧㄢˇ）
to exploit (the people); to amass (a fortune)

裒輯（ㄆㄡ ㄐㄧˊ）
to collect and edit

【裔】 5412
　ㄧˊ　yih yì

1. descendants; posterity
2. the hem of a garment, robe, etc.
3. remote or border regions
4. (now rarely) a general name of northern barbarians
5. a Chinese family name

裔胄（ㄧˋ ㄓㄡˋ）or 裔孫（ㄧˋ ㄙㄨㄣ）
remote descendants or posterity

裔夷（ㄧˊ）
frontier tribes

裔裔（ㄧˋ）
① walking ② cascading down (as rain, etc.)

【裕】 5413
　ㄩˋ　yuh yù

1. abundance; affluent; plenty; to be abundant: 他生活得很富裕。He lived in plenty.
2. tolerant (administration, etc.); lenient (punishment, etc.)
3. generous; magnanimous
4. slowly; to take time

裕國（ㄩˋ 《ㄨㄛˊ）
to enrich the nation

裕後光前（ㄩˋ ㄏㄡˋ 《ㄨㄤ くㄧㄢˊ）
to enrich one's posterity and honor one's ancestors

裕如（ㄩˋ ㄖㄨˊ）
① affluent; rich; well-to-do; in good circumstances; ample ② to take it easy; without hurry; with ease: 對於此事，他應付裕如。He handled it with ease.

裕裕（ㄩˋ ㄩˋ）
to take it easy; to be at peace with the world

【裘】 5414
　くㄧㄡˊ　chyou qiú

1. furs; any garments, robes, etc. of fur
2. a Chinese family name

裘弊金盡（くㄧㄡˊ ㄅㄧˋ ㄐㄧㄣ ㄐㄧㄣˋ）
destitute; to have exhausted one's means; to go broke

裘馬（くㄧㄡˊ ㄇㄚˇ）
furs and horses—the rich

裘馬輕肥（くㄧㄡˊ ㄇㄚˇ くㄧㄥ ㄈㄟˊ）
wealthy; affluent; well-to-do; in good circumstances

裘葛屢更（くㄧㄡˊ 《ㄜˊ ㄌㄩˇ 《ㄥ）
(literally) many changes from furs (winter) to hemp (summer)—the lapse of many years

裘褐（くㄧㄡˊ ㄏㄜˊ）
to dress economically or simply

【補】 5415
　ㄅㄨˇ　buu bǔ

1. to repair; to patch; to mend; to fill
2. to add to; to supplement; to supply
3. addenda; supplements; replen-

〔衣
部〕

ishments; complements
4. nutritious; nutrient
5. rich foods; tonics
6. to nourish
7. to make up; to help(finance, etc.); to subsidize
8. to appoint to or fill a post
9. to be of help; benefit; use

〔衣部〕

補白(ㄅㄨ ㄅㄞ)
to fill a vacant space with a short piece of writing; a filler

補報(ㄅㄨ ㄅㄠ)
①to repay favors granted ②an additional statement, report, account, etc. to supplement the one submitted previously

補票(ㄅㄨ ㄆㄧㄠ)
to buy one's ticket after one gets on a bus, a train ,etc.

補偏救弊(ㄅㄨ ㄆㄧㄢ ㄐㄧㄡ ㄅㄧ)
to repair or correct defects, flaws, etc.

補品(ㄅㄨ ㄆㄧㄣ)
foods or medicines of highly nutritious value; tonics

補發(ㄅㄨ ㄈㄚ)
to issue or distribute behind schedule; to issue or distribute the balance, remaining portion, etc.; to reissue: 裝備丟失，不補發。 The equipment will not be reissued if lost.

補付(ㄅㄨ ㄈㄨ)
to supplement a deficit; to pay arrears

補釘 or **補釘**(ㄅㄨ ㄉㄧㄥ)
patches (of a garment, etc.): 船帆上有一個補釘。 There is a patch on the sail.

補短(ㄅㄨ ㄉㄨㄢ)
①to supplement a deficit ②to make up for a shortcoming or flaw

補貼(ㄅㄨ ㄊㄧㄝ)
to subsidize; a subsidy; an allowance

補天(ㄅㄨ ㄊㄧㄢ)
(a reference to the goddess 女媧氏 in Chinese mythology) to patch up or mend the sky

補天浴日(ㄅㄨ ㄊㄧㄢ ㄩˋ ㄖ)
(literally) to mend the sky and wash the sun—a peerless achievement; a great accomplishment

補鍋(ㄅㄨ ㄍㄨㄛ)
to tinker a pan

補過(ㄅㄨ ㄍㄨㄛ)
to make up for a mistake, fault, etc.

補課(ㄅㄨ ㄎㄜ)
(said of students or teachers) a private tutoring to supplement regular schooling; to make up for classes one missed

補考(ㄅㄨ ㄎㄠ)
a make-up test; an examination held for students who fail to take part in the regular one for legitimate reasons: 他上週參加補考。 He took the make-up exam last week.

補空(ㄅㄨ ㄎㄨㄥ)
to fill up an empty space

補弧(ㄅㄨ ㄏㄨˊ)
(mathematics) a supplementary arc

補給(ㄅㄨ ㄐㄧˇ)
(military) provisions; supplies; to supply

補給品(ㄅㄨ ㄐㄧˇ ㄆㄧㄣˇ)
supplies

補給線(ㄅㄨ ㄐㄧˇ ㄒㄧㄢˋ)
a line of logistic support; a supply line

補給站(ㄅㄨ ㄐㄧˇ ㄓㄢˋ)
a supply depot

補角(ㄅㄨ ㄐㄧㄠˇ)
(mathematics) a supplementary angle

補救(ㄅㄨ ㄐㄧㄡˋ)
to save the situation; to rectify shortcomings ; to repair; to redress abuses; redress: 他們正在補救一項錯誤。They are repairing a mistake.

補救辦法(ㄅㄨ ㄐㄧㄡˋ ㄅㄢˋ ㄈㄚˇ)
means to save the situation; corrective measures; remedy

補苴(ㄅㄨ ㄐㄩ) or **補苴罅漏**(ㄅㄨ ㄐㄩ ㄒㄧㄚˋ ㄌㄡˋ)
to make up for a deficiency or defect

補不足(ㄅㄨ ㄅㄨˋ ㄗㄨˊ)
to make up a deficit or deficiency

補其所短(ㄅㄨ ㄑㄧˊ ㄙㄨㄛˇ ㄉㄨㄢˇ)
①to make up for one's shortcomings or defects ②to make up for a deficiency

補氣(ㄅㄨ ㄑㄧˋ)
to nourish or conserve one's vitality

補葺(ㄅㄨ ㄑㄧˋ)
to repair; to mend

補情(ㄅㄨ ㄑㄧㄥˊ)
to repay a favor; to repay hospitality

補缺(ㄅㄨ ㄑㄩㄝ)
to fill a vacancy; to fill an official post

補習(ㄅㄨ ㄒㄧˊ)
private tutoring to supplement regular schooling; to tutor

補習班(ㄅㄨ ㄒㄧˊ ㄅㄢ)
a class for supplementary schooling; a supplementary school to take care of drop-outs or those who have failed in the entrance exams of regular schools; an extension school

補習教育(ㄅㄨ ㄒㄧˊ ㄐㄧㄠˋ ㄩˋ)
supplementary education —for preparing the students for jobs

補習學校(ㄅㄨ ㄒㄧˊ ㄒㄩㄝˊ ㄒㄧㄠˋ)
extension schools; continuation schools

補鞋匠(ㄅㄨ ㄒㄧㄝˊ ㄐㄧㄤˋ)
a cobbler

補血(ㄅㄨ ㄒㄧㄝˇ)
to nourish the blood; to increase the blood

補修(ㄅㄨ ㄒㄧㄡ)
(said of college students) to study for a second time courses one has flunked; to make up

補修學分(ㄅㄨ ㄒㄧㄡ ㄒㄩㄝˊ ㄈㄣ)
(said of college students)to catch up with the credit requirement; to study courses in order to get the minimum credits required for graduation

補絃 or **補弦**(ㄅㄨ ㄒㄧㄢˊ)
(mathematics) a supplementary chord

補選(ㄅㄨ ㄒㄩㄢˇ)
by-election

補正(ㄅㄨ ㄓㄥˋ)
(said of printed materials) additions and corrections

補助(ㄅㄨ ㄓㄨˋ)

to subsidize; to help (finance, etc.)

補助費 (ㄅㄨ ㄓㄨ ㄈㄟ) or 補助金 (ㄅㄨ ㄓㄨ ㄐㄧㄣ)
a subsidy; subsidiary payments

補助角 (ㄅㄨ ㄓㄨ ㄐㄧㄠ)
(mathematics) an auxiliary angle

補助金 (ㄅㄨ ㄓㄨ ㄐㄧㄣ)
a grant

補助圓 (ㄅㄨ ㄓㄨ ㄩㄢ)
(mathematics) an auxiliary circle

補注 or 補註 (ㄅㄨ ㄓㄨ)
supplementary notes; to make supplementary notes

補拙 (ㄅㄨ ㄓㄨㄛ)
to offset or make up for one's lack of acumen: 勤能補拙。Hard work can often make up for a lack of intelligence.

補綴 (ㄅㄨ ㄓㄨㄟ)
to patch or mend (a garment, etc.); to darn: 他的襪子一再補綴。His socks have been darned again and again.

補償 (ㄅㄨ ㄔㄤ)
to compensate; to make up; compensation: 他們補償她所受的損失。They compensated her for a loss.

補償損失 (ㄅㄨ ㄔㄤ ㄙㄨㄣ ㄕ)
to compensate for damage, loss, etc.

補充 (ㄅㄨ ㄔㄨㄥ)
to add; to supplement; to make up for a deficiency; to replenish; a supplement; supplementary: 我補充兩點意見。I have two points to add.

補充兵 (ㄅㄨ ㄔㄨㄥ ㄅㄧㄥ)
(military) replacements

補足 (ㄅㄨ ㄗㄨ)
to make up a deficit; to make complete or whole

補足語 (ㄅㄨ ㄗㄨ ㄩ)
a complement; a supplementary clause 亦作「補語」

補色 (ㄅㄨ ㄙㄜ)
complementary colors

補衣服 (ㄅㄨ ㄧ ㄈㄨ)
to patch or mend a garment, dress, etc.: 她在補衣服。She is mending clothes now.

補遺 (ㄅㄨ ㄧ)

---

addenda or appendixes to take care of omissions in a book, etc.

補益 (ㄅㄨ ㄧ)
benefit; help

補牙 (ㄅㄨ ㄧㄚ)
to fill a tooth cavity; to have a tooth stopped

補藥 (ㄅㄨ ㄧㄠ)
tonics

【裝】   5416   ㄓㄨㄤ juang zhuāng
1. to fill in or up; to pack; to load: 裝好你的箱子。Pack your trunk.
2. to pretend; to feign: 她假裝自己是無辜的。She pretended innocence.
3. to adorn; to dress or make up; ornamental dressing; to decorate (a room, etc.)
4. to disguise
5. to store; to keep
6. to install (machines, equipment, etc.)
7. clothes and personal effects; an outfit: 全套新娘裝 an outfit for a bride

裝備 (ㄓㄨㄤ ㄅㄟ)
equipment or an outfit (especially for a soldier, or armed forces): 這軍隊裝備很差。The army was poorly equipped.

裝扮 (ㄓㄨㄤ ㄅㄢ)
①adornment; make-up; to dress or doll up; attire ②to disguise

裝裱 (ㄓㄨㄤ ㄅㄧㄠ)
to mount a piece of calligraphy or a painting

裝病 (ㄓㄨㄤ ㄅㄧㄥ)
to feign illness; to pretend illness; to malinger

裝病者 (ㄓㄨㄤ ㄅㄧㄥ ㄓㄜ)
a malingerer

裝不下 (ㄓㄨㄤ ㄅㄨ ㄒㄧㄚ)
no more space to cram in; cannot hold any more

裝配 (ㄓㄨㄤ ㄆㄟ)
to assemble (a machine): 他裝配了一隻手錶。He assembled a watch.

裝配線 (ㄓㄨㄤ ㄆㄟ ㄒㄧㄢ)
the assembly line (of a factory)

裝滿 (ㄓㄨㄤ ㄇㄢ)
to fill up; to pack until no

---

space is left

裝門面 (ㄓㄨㄤ ㄇㄣ ㄇㄧㄢ)
to put up a front; to adorn or embellish for the sake of face

裝模作樣 (ㄓㄨㄤ ㄇㄛ ㄗㄨㄛ ㄧㄤ)
to act affectedly; to be pretentious; to act with affected manners; to strike a pose

裝瘋賣傻 (ㄓㄨㄤ ㄈㄥ ㄇㄞ ㄕㄚ)
to pretend to be crazy and stupid; to play the fool

裝點 (ㄓㄨㄤ ㄉㄧㄢ)
to decorate; to dress; to deck: 大廳裏裝點着花燈。The hall was decorated with fancy lanterns.

裝訂 (ㄓㄨㄤ ㄉㄧㄥ)
to bind pages into a volume or book; binding: 他裝訂報紙。He binds the papers together.

裝訂廠 (ㄓㄨㄤ ㄉㄧㄥ ㄔㄤ)
a plant for binding books

裝老 (ㄓㄨㄤ ㄌㄠ)
(euphemism) clothes for the dead in preparation for burial

裝殮 (ㄓㄨㄤ ㄌㄧㄢ)
to dress up the deceased and put him into the coffin

裝聾作啞 (ㄓㄨㄤ ㄌㄨㄥ ㄗㄨㄛ ㄧㄚ)
to pretend to hear and know nothing; to pretend ignorance; to pretend to be deaf and dumb; to play deaf

裝裹 (ㄓㄨㄤ ㄍㄨㄛ)
to put on clothes for the dead

裝糊塗 (ㄓㄨㄤ ㄏㄨ ㄊㄨ)
to pretend not to know; to feign ignorance 亦作「裝憨兒」

裝貨 (ㄓㄨㄤ ㄏㄨㄛ)
to load or pack goods: 他裝貨於車上。He loaded the cart.

裝潢 (ㄓㄨㄤ ㄏㄨㄤ)
①to mount a painting or a piece of calligraphy ②to decorate (a room, shop, etc.); decoration: 他花了很多錢裝潢房子。He spent quite a large sum of money for the decoration of his house. 亦作「裝璜」

裝幌子 (ㄓㄨㄤ ㄏㄨㄤ ˙ㄗ)
to put up a (false) front with a view to impressing

【衣部】

others

裝甲 (ㄓㄨㄤ ㄐㄧㄚˇ)
①plate armor ②armored

裝甲兵團 (ㄓㄨㄤ ㄐㄧㄚˇ ㄅㄧㄥ ㄊㄨㄢˊ)
an armored corps; a panzer corps

裝甲部隊 (ㄓㄨㄤ ㄐㄧㄚˇ ㄅㄨˋ ㄉㄨㄟˋ)
armored troops or units

裝甲車 (ㄓㄨㄤ ㄐㄧㄚˇ ㄔㄜ)
an armored vehicle; a tank

裝甲師 (ㄓㄨㄤ ㄐㄧㄚˇ ㄕ)
an armored division

裝腔作勢 (ㄓㄨㄤ ㄑㄧㄤ ㄗㄨㄛˋ ㄕˋ)
affected; pretentious; to strike an attitude; to affect manners; to put on airs: 他裝腔作勢令人難以忍受。His affectations are insufferable.

裝卸 (ㄓㄨㄤ ㄒㄧㄝˋ)
to load and unload

裝修 (ㄓㄨㄤ ㄒㄧㄡ)
to decorate and repair; to equip; to refurbish; to fit up (a house, etc.): 他們裝修一間舊房子。They refurbished an old house.

裝箱 (ㄓㄨㄤ ㄒㄧㄤ)
to pack in a box or chest; to box: 他將衣服裝箱。He packed clothes into a trunk.

裝置 (ㄓㄨㄤ ㄓˋ)
①to install (equipment, etc.) ②an installation; a (mechanical) device; a unit; a plant

裝池 (ㄓㄨㄤ ㄔˊ)
to mount a painting or calligraphic work

裝車 (ㄓㄨㄤ ㄔㄜ)
to load on a truck, vehicle, etc.

裝船 (ㄓㄨㄤ ㄔㄨㄢˊ)
to load cargoes aboard a freighter

裝飾 (ㄓㄨㄤ ㄕˋ)
①to doll up; to deck; to make up ②to decorate; to adorn; to embellish: 她以花裝飾頭髮。She adorned her hair with flowers.

裝飾品 (ㄓㄨㄤ ㄕˋ ㄆㄧㄣˇ)
an ornamental item; an ornament; an adornment; a decorative article

裝傻 (ㄓㄨㄤ ㄕㄚˇ)
to feign stupidity or ignorance

裝設 (ㄓㄨㄤ ㄕㄜˋ)
to be equipped with; to install; to equip

裝束 (ㄓㄨㄤ ㄕㄨˋ)
①to pack up; to do packing and get ready for travel ②to dress up; clothing or attire; dress

裝束入時 (ㄓㄨㄤ ㄕㄨˋ ㄖㄨˋ ㄕˊ)
in fashionable dress or attire

裝睡 (ㄓㄨㄤ ㄕㄨㄟˋ)
to feign sleep; to pretend to be asleep

裝子彈 (ㄓㄨㄤ ㄗˇ ㄉㄢˋ)
to load a gun, or pistol: 裝子彈! Load your gun!

裝載 (ㄓㄨㄤ ㄗㄞˋ)
(said of a truck, car, vessel, etc.) loaded with; to pack; to stow

裝醉 (ㄓㄨㄤ ㄗㄨㄟˋ)
to pretend to be drunk

裝死 (ㄓㄨㄤ ㄙˇ)
to play dead; to feign death; to sham death

裝蒜 (ㄓㄨㄤ ㄙㄨㄢˋ)
to be pretentious or affected

裝樣子 (ㄓㄨㄤ ㄧㄤˋ ㄇ)
to put on an act; to do something for appearance sake

裝運 (ㄓㄨㄤ ㄩㄣˋ)
to pack and transport; to load and ship

【裟】 5417
ㄕㄚ sha shā
a cassock or robe of a Buddhist monk 參看「袈裟」

【裛】 5418
ㄧˋ yih yì
1. to wrap and bind
2. damp; dripping; wet
3. a book bag

【袷】 5419
(袷) ㄐㄧㄚ jya jiā
a lined garment or dress

八畫

【裸】 5420
ㄎㄨㄛˇ luoo luǒ
bare; nude; naked

裸袒 (ㄎㄨㄛˇ ㄊㄢˇ)
bare or naked

裸體 (ㄎㄨㄛˇ ㄊㄧˇ) or 裸形 (ㄎㄨㄛˇ ㄒㄧㄥˊ)
nude; naked; without a stitch on; in the altogether

裸體畫 (ㄎㄨㄛˇ ㄊㄧˇ ㄏㄨㄚˋ)
a nude; a painting of a nude human figure (especially woman)

裸體像 (ㄎㄨㄛˇ ㄊㄧˇ ㄒㄧㄤˋ)
a nude; a nude figure or statue

裸露 (ㄎㄨㄛˇ ㄌㄨˋ)
uncovered; exposed

裸跣 (ㄎㄨㄛˇ ㄒㄧㄢˇ)
(said of poor people) naked body and naked feet

裸線 (ㄎㄨㄛˇ ㄒㄧㄢˋ)
(electricity) an uninsulated wire; a bare wire

裸裎 (ㄎㄨㄛˇ ㄔㄥˊ)
naked; undressed

裸子植物 (ㄎㄨㄛˇ ㄗˇ ㄓˊ ㄨˋ)
a gymnosperm, a plant with exposed seeds, e.g. a pine

【裰】 5421
ㄉㄨㄛ dwo duó
to darn; to mend; to patch (clothing): 她補裰他的襪子。She darned his socks.

【裨】 5422
ㄅㄧˋ bih bì
1. to aid; to supplement
2. to benefit; to help: 無補於事。It will not help matters.

裨補 (ㄅㄧˋ ㄅㄨˇ)
to supplement; to aid; to support

裨益 (ㄅㄧˋ ㄧˋ)
to benefit; benefit: 運動裨益我們的健康。Exercise benefits our health.

【裨】 5422
ㄆㄧˊ pyi pí
1. small; petty
2. subordinate
3. a Chinese family name

裨販 (ㄆㄧˊ ㄈㄢˋ)
a hawker or peddler

裨海 (ㄆㄧˊ ㄏㄞˇ)
a small sea

裨將 (ㄆㄧˊ ㄐㄧㄤˋ)
a deputy commander

【裯】 5423
ㄔㄡˊ chour chóu
a bed sheet

【裱】 5424
ㄅㄧㄠˇ beau biǎo
1. to mount (paintings, calligraphy, etc.)
2. a scarf

裱褙(ㄅㄧㄠˇ ㄅㄟˋ)
to mount (paintings, etc.): 他懂得裱褙國畫。He knows how to mount Chinese paintings.

裱店(ㄅㄧㄠˇ ㄉㄧㄢˋ)
a shop specialized in mounting paintings, calligraphy, etc.

裱工(ㄅㄧㄠˇ ㄍㄨㄥ)
① the work of mounting ② expenses for mounting ③ one who mounts paintings or calligraphic works

　　　　　　5425

裱糊(ㄅㄧㄠˇ ㄏㄨˊ)
to paste; to paper (a wall, ceiling, etc.)

裱糊匠(ㄅㄧㄠˇ ㄏㄨˊ ㄐㄧㄤˋ)
a mounting craftsman; a paper hanger

【裳】 ㄔㄤˊ charng cháng
(語音·ㄕㄤ·shang shang as in衣裳)
1. a skirt (worn in ancient China); the lower garments
2. dress; garments; clothing

【裴】 5426　ㄆㄟˊ peir péi
1. the look of a flowing gown
2. a Chinese family name

【裹】 5427
ㄍㄨㄛˇ guoo guǒ
1. to tie up; to wrap or bind: 她頭上裹著帕巾。She had her head wrapped in a towel.
2. things wrapped, as a parcel
3. to surround; to encompass
4. to close in and force obedience

裹肚(ㄍㄨㄛˇ ㄉㄨˋ)
a cloth band worn around the midriff in ancient China

裹腿(ㄍㄨㄛˇ ㄊㄨㄟˇ)
leggings; puttees (usually used by soldiers in former days)

裹糧(ㄍㄨㄛˇ ㄌㄧㄤˊ)
bags of provisions for traveling

裹脚(ㄍㄨㄛˇ ㄐㄧㄠˇ)or 裹足(ㄍㄨㄛˇ ㄗㄨˊ)
(said of women in former times) to bind the feet

裹脚布(ㄍㄨㄛˇ ㄐㄧㄠˇ ㄅㄨˋ)or 裹脚條子(ㄍㄨㄛˇ ㄐㄧㄠˇ ㄊㄧㄠˊ·ㄗ)
bandages for binding women's feet in old times

裹脅(ㄍㄨㄛˇ ㄒㄧㄝˊ)
duress; to force to join; to coerce

裹創(ㄍㄨㄛˇ ㄔㄨㄤ)
to dress a wound; to bind up a wound

裹尸 or 裹屍(ㄍㄨㄛˇ ㄕ)
to wrap up a corpse

裹足不前(ㄍㄨㄛˇ ㄗㄨˊ ㄅㄨˋ ㄑㄧㄢˊ)
to be afraid to move ahead; to be reluctant to go forward; to hesitate to move forward: 做那件事我可別裹足不前。Don't hesitate about doing that.

【裼】 5428
ㄒㄧˊ shyi xí
1. to take off one's top garment
2. (in ancient China) a wrapper or outer garment worn over a fur

【製】 5429
ㄓˋ jyh zhì
1. to produce; to make; to manufacture; to create: 這個娃娃是布製的。The doll is made of cloth.
2. to compose (writings, literature, etc.); literary works
3. to cut out garments and make them
4. a model; a fashion; a pattern

製版(ㄓˋ ㄅㄢˇ)
to make a printing plate

製片(ㄓˋ ㄆㄧㄢˋ)or 製片人(ㄓˋ ㄆㄧㄢˋ ㄖㄣˊ)
(movie) a producer

製片廠(ㄓˋ ㄆㄧㄢˋ ㄔㄤˇ)
a movie studio

製品(ㄓˋ ㄆㄧㄣˇ)
products; manufactured items; manufactures

製法(ㄓˋ ㄈㄚˇ)
a formula, process, way or method of making something

製圖(ㄓˋ ㄊㄨˊ)
to make (or draw) maps, charts, etc.

製圖室(ㄓˋ ㄊㄨˊ ㄕˋ)
a draft or drawing room

製圖員(ㄓˋ ㄊㄨˊ ㄩㄢˊ)
a draughtsman; a draftsman; a cartographer

製革(ㄓˋ ㄍㄜˊ)

---

tanning

製革工廠(ㄓˋ ㄍㄜˊ ㄍㄨㄥ ㄔㄤˇ)
a tannery

製成(ㄓˋ ㄔㄥˊ)
to have completed production or making; to have produced or manufactured

製成品(ㄓˋ ㄔㄥˊ ㄆㄧㄣˇ)
finished products; manufactured goods; manufactures

製造(ㄓˋ ㄗㄠˋ)
to make; to produce; to manufacture; to create: 不要製造麻煩。Do not create a disturbance.

製造品(ㄓˋ ㄗㄠˋ ㄆㄧㄣˇ)
manufactured goods

製造過程(ㄓˋ ㄗㄠˋ ㄍㄨㄛ ㄔㄥˊ)
manufacturing process

製造技術(ㄓˋ ㄗㄠˋ ㄐㄧˋ ㄕㄨˋ)
manufacturing technology

製造廠(ㄓˋ ㄗㄠˋ ㄔㄤˇ)
a factory, plant or manufactory

製造商(ㄓˋ ㄗㄠˋ ㄕㄤ)
a manufacturer

製造業(ㄓˋ ㄗㄠˋ ㄧㄝˋ)
the manufacturing industry

製作(ㄓˋ ㄗㄨㄛˋ)
to make; to produce; to manufacture

製作人(ㄓˋ ㄗㄨㄛˋ ㄖㄣˊ)
a producer

【裾】 5430
ㄐㄩ jiu jū
the overlap of a robe; the hinder part of a garment; the lapei of a coat

【褂】 5431
ㄍㄨㄚˋ guah guà
an overcoat; a robe or gown; a jacket

褂子(ㄍㄨㄚˋ·ㄗ)or 褂兒(ㄍㄨㄚˋㄦ)
an overcoat; a gown or robe

九畫

【複】 5432
ㄈㄨˋ fuh fù
1. double; overlapping
2. complex (concepts, etc.); compound (interest, etc.)
3. to repeat; to reiterate
4. a lined garment, dress, etc.

複本(ㄈㄨˋ ㄅㄣˇ)
a duplicate: 我們寄出了信，但留了複本。We mailed the let-

〔衣部〕

複比(ㄈㄨˋㄅㄧˇ)
compound ratio

複比例(ㄈㄨˋㄅㄧˇㄌㄧˋ)
compound proportion

複壁(ㄈㄨˋㄅㄧˋ)
double partition walls with secret hiding space in-between

複名數(ㄈㄨˋㄇㄧㄥˊㄕㄨˋ)
compound number

複利(ㄈㄨˋㄌㄧˋ)
compound interest

複合(ㄈㄨˋㄏㄜˊ)
compound; complex; composite

複合句(ㄈㄨˋㄏㄜˊㄐㄩˋ)
(linguistics) a compound sentence

複合詞(ㄈㄨˋㄏㄜˊㄘˊ)
nouns, phrases or idioms formed by two or more characters 亦作「複詞」

複基(ㄈㄨˋㄐㄧ)
(chemistry) a compound radical

複句(ㄈㄨˋㄐㄩˋ)or 複雜句(ㄈㄨˋㄗㄚˊㄐㄩˋ)
a complex sentence

複決權(ㄈㄨˋㄐㄩㄝˊㄑㄩㄢˊ)
a referendum

複習(ㄈㄨˋㄒㄧˊ)
to review; to revise 亦作「復習」: 我們在考試前複習所學過的功課。Before the examinations we reviewed the lessons we had learned.

複寫(ㄈㄨˋㄒㄧㄝˇ)
to duplicate or produce copies of a piece of writing, etc. with carbon paper, etc.: 他複寫了一份公文。He duplicated a document.

複寫紙(ㄈㄨˋㄒㄧㄝˇㄓˇ)
carbon paper

複姓(ㄈㄨˋㄒㄧㄥˋ)
a compound surname; a surname which comprises two characters, as 司馬, 歐陽, etc.

複選(ㄈㄨˋㄒㄩㄢˇ)
①an election by delegates; an indirect election ② a run-off (election) ③ (in beauty contests, etc.) a semi-final

複製(ㄈㄨˋㄓˋ)
to make a reproduction; to reproduce; to duplicate: 那幅畫複製得很好。The painting reproduced well.

複製品(ㄈㄨˋㄓˋㄆㄧㄣˇ)
a reproduction (of the original article); a replica: 這幅人像是原畫的複製品。This portrait is a replica of the original.

複查(ㄈㄨˋㄔㄚˊ)
to reinvestigate; to check again

複式學級(ㄈㄨˋㄕˋㄒㄩㄝˊㄐㄧˊ)
a class in which more than two grades of school children are taught at the same time

複數(ㄈㄨˋㄕㄨˋ)
the plural number (of a noun or pronoun)

複雜(ㄈㄨˋㄗㄚˊ)
complex; complicated (matters, etc.): 這是個複雜的觀念。It's a complex idea.

複色(ㄈㄨˋㄙㄜˋ)
compound colors

複色光(ㄈㄨˋㄙㄜˋㄍㄨㄤ)
polychromatic light

複賽(ㄈㄨˋㄙㄞˋ)
(sports) a semifinal; a play-off; intermediary heat

複葉(ㄈㄨˋㄧㄝˋ)
a compound leaf

複眼(ㄈㄨˋㄧㄢˇ)
(biology) a compound eye

複印(ㄈㄨˋㄧㄣˋ)
the reproduction of the original copy by a copying machine; duplication

複印機(ㄈㄨˋㄧㄣˋㄐㄧ)
a copying machine; a duplicator; a duplicating machine

【褊】 5433 ㄅㄧㄢˇ bean biǎn
1. narrow; small; petty
2. small size clothes
3. narrow minded

褊能(ㄅㄧㄢˇㄋㄥˊ)
of little ability (sometimes used as a polite and self-depreciative expression)

褊陋(ㄅㄧㄢˇㄌㄡˋ)
cramped and crude; narrow-minded and ignorant

褊急(ㄅㄧㄢˇㄐㄧˊ)
easily irritated; lacking patience; short-tempered

褊淺(ㄅㄧㄢˇㄑㄧㄢˇ)
narrow-minded and shallow

褊狹(ㄅㄧㄢˇㄒㄧㄚˊ)
①small (piece of land) ② narrow(-minded)

褊小(ㄅㄧㄢˇㄒㄧㄠˇ)
petty; small; narrow

褊心(ㄅㄧㄢˇㄒㄧㄣ)
narrow-minded and impatient

褊隘(ㄅㄧㄢˇㄞˋ)
narrow-minded and impatient

【褌】 5434 ㄎㄨㄣ kuen kūn
trousers; drawers; short pants

【褐】 5435 ㄏㄜˋ her hè
1. coarse woolen cloth; coarse cloth; haircloth; rough cloth
2. the poor or destitute
3. brown: 這餅變成褐色了。The pie has become brown.

褐鋁礦(ㄏㄜˋㄌㄩˇㄎㄨㄤˋ)
braunite

褐夫(ㄏㄜˋㄈㄨ)
a person dressed in cloth of hair—a person of little means; a humble person

褐炭(ㄏㄜˋㄊㄢˋ)
brown coal, or lignite

褐鐵礦(ㄏㄜˋㄊㄧㄝˇㄎㄨㄤˋ)
limonite; brown iron ore

褐色(ㄏㄜˋㄙㄜˋ)
(color) brown

【褓】 5436 ㄅㄠˇ bao bǎo
1. swaddling bands; swaddling clothes
2. as in 襁褓—infancy

褓母(ㄅㄠˇㄇㄨˇ)
a nurse; a baby-sitter; 她是個好褓母。She is a good nurse.

【褘】 5437 ㄏㄨㄟ huei huī
ceremonial gowns of a queen

褘衣(ㄏㄨㄟㄧ)
ceremonial dress of a queen

【褙】 5438 ㄅㄟˋ bey bèi
to mount (paintings, or calligraphic works)

【褚】 5439 ㄔㄨˇ chuu chǔ
1. a bag
2. to stuff a lined garment with cotton
3. to reserve; to save

4. a Chinese family name

褚幕 (ㄔㄨ ㄇㄨˋ)
a piece of red cloth for covering the coffin

褚遂良 (ㄔㄨ ㄙㄨㄟˋ ㄌㄧㄤˊ)
Chu Sui-liang (596-658), a famous scholar-calligrapher in the Tang Dynasty

【褕】 5440
　　 ㄩˊ yu yú
1. beautiful or pretty (dresses, etc.)
2. a loose garment or cloak

【襃】 5441
　　 (襃) ㄅㄠ bau bāo
1. to praise; to cite
2. big; great

十畫

【褥】 5442
　　 ㄖㄨˋ ruh rù
bedding; quilts or coverlets; a mattress; cushion; bed-clothes

褥單兒 (ㄖㄨˋ ㄉㄢ ㄦ)
a bed sheet

褥套 (ㄖㄨˋ ㄊㄠˋ)
a large bag holding cotton or other fibers used as a quilt or a mattress; ticking

褥子 (ㄖㄨˋ ˙ㄗ)
bedding; coverlets or quilts; a mattress

褥瘡 (ㄖㄨˋ ㄔㄨㄤ)
(medicine) bedsores

【褦】 5443
　　 1. ㄋㄞˋ nay nài
1. ignorant; stupid; naive
2. a palm-leaf hat worn in summer for shading the sun or rain

褦襶 (ㄋㄞˋ ㄉㄞˋ)
①a light-weight hat of palm leaves or bamboo for shading the sun or rain ②ignorant; naive; unsophisticated

【褦】 5443
　　 2. ㄌㄜ le lē
untidily dressed

褦襶 (ㄋㄞˋ ㄉㄞˋ)
untidily dressed

褦襶兵 (ㄋㄞˋ ㄉㄞˋ ㄅㄧㄥ)
a person in untidy or ill-fitting dress or over-burdened with accessories

【褪】 5444
　　 ㄊㄨㄣˋ tuenn tùn

1. to take off one's clothing; to strip; to slip out of something
2. to fall off; to fade, as color; 襯衫的顏色褪了。The color of the shirt has faded.
3. to retreat; to move backward

褪手 (ㄊㄨㄣˋ ㄕㄡˇ)
to hide one's hands in sleeves

褪色 (ㄊㄨㄣˋ ㄙㄜˋ)
color fading

【褫】 5445
　　 ㄔˇ chyy chǐ
1. to strip off; to deprive of
2. to undress forcibly

褫魄 (ㄔˇ ㄆㄛˋ)
to be scared out of one's wits; to be extremely frightened

褫奪 (ㄔˇ ㄉㄨㄛˊ)
to deprive of; to strip off

褫奪公權 (ㄔˇ ㄉㄨㄛˊ ㄍㄨㄥ ㄑㄩㄢˊ)
to strip or deprive one of one's civil rights; deprivation of civil rights

褫革 (ㄔˇ ㄍㄜˊ)
to strip one of one's uniform, insignia, etc.—to strip one of one's office; to dismiss

褫職 (ㄔˇ ㄓˊ)
to dismiss one from office; a dishonorable discharge

【褰】 5446
　　 ㄑㄧㄢ chian qiān
1. to lift or raise (one's dress, skirt, etc.)
2. trousers; drawers; pants
3. to shrink

【褡】 5447
　　 ㄉㄚ da dā
1. a kerchief hung at the waist
2. a purse; a tiny sack
3. worn clothes

褡褳 (ㄉㄚ ㄌㄧㄢˊ)
a pouch worn at the girdle

【褟】 5448
　　 ㄊㄚ ta tā
1. the lace-trimmed hem of a dress; lace of a dress
2. a singlet; a thin T-shirt as underwear

【褲】 5449
　　 (褲) ㄎㄨˋ kuh kù
drawers; trousers; pants

褲帶 (ㄎㄨˋ ㄉㄞˋ)
a trousers belt

褲襠 (ㄎㄨˋ ㄉㄤ)
the crotch of a pair of trousers

褲管 (ㄎㄨˋ ㄍㄨㄢˇ)
the legs of a pair of trousers

褲襪 (ㄎㄨˋ ㄨㄚˋ)
pantyhose

十一畫

【襦】 5450
　　 (襦) ㄌㄧˊ li lí
a bridal veil

【褶】 5451
　　 ㄌㄧㄝˊ dye dié
a lined garment or dress

【褶】 5451
　　 ㄓㄜˇ jer zhě
1. to fold; pleated

褶曲 (ㄓㄜˇ ㄑㄩ)
(geology) folds

褶裙 (ㄓㄜˇ ㄑㄩㄣˊ)
a pleated skirt

褶子 (ㄓㄜˇ ˙ㄗ)
①pleats ②folds ③wrinkles (on the face)

【褸】 5452
　　 ㄌㄩˇ leu lǚ
1. the collar or lapel of a garment
2. (said of clothes) tattered; in rags 參見「襤褸」

【襃】 5453
　　 (襃) ㄅㄠ bau bāo
1. to praise; to cite; to commend; a citation
2. big; great
3. name of an ancient state in today's Shensi Province
4. a Chinese family name

襃貶 (ㄅㄠ ㄅㄧㄢˇ)
①to praise and disparage; criticism ②to disparage; unfavorable criticisms

襃美 (ㄅㄠ ㄇㄟˇ)
to praise and cite

襃賞 (ㄅㄠ ㄕㄤˇ)
to commend and reward

襃錄 (ㄅㄠ ㄌㄨˋ)
to recommend (talented scholars) for government appointments

襃獎 (ㄅㄠ ㄐㄧㄤˇ)
to praise and cite; to commend and award: 他襃獎你的工作嗎? Did he praise your work?

〔衣部〕

褒章（ㄅㄠ ㄓㄤ）
a medal of commendation

褒狀（ㄅㄠ ㄓㄨㄤˋ）
a citation (of a good deed, great achievement, etc.)

褒獎（ㄅㄠ ㄐㄧㄤˇ）
a reward (for a praiseworthy act, etc.); to reward

褒贊（ㄅㄠ ㄗㄢˋ）
to praise; to commend; to extol; to acclaim

褒賜（ㄅㄠ ㄘˋ）
to reward; a reward for a praiseworthy deed, etc.

褒姒（ㄅㄠ ㄙˋ）
name of a favorite concubine of Emperor Yu (幽王) of the Chou Dynasty, who cost him his empire

褒衣（ㄅㄠ ㄧ）
to give dresses to officials or their wives as a token of imperial favor

褒衣博帶（ㄅㄠ ㄧ ㄅㄛˊ ㄉㄞˋ）
a robe with large sleeves and a broad waist band—the dress of an ancient scholar

褒揚（ㄅㄠ ㄧㄤˊ）
to cite; to commend; a citation

【褓】 5454
（褓）ㄅㄠˇ cheang qiang
swaddling clothes for infant; a broad bandage for carrying an infant on the back

褓褓（ㄅㄠˇ ㄌㄧㄤˊ）
①swaddling clothes or carrying band for an infant ②infancy: 還小孩仍在褓褓中. The baby is still in its infancy.

褓負（ㄑㄧ ㄈㄨˋ）
①infancy ②to carry an infant on the back with a broad bandage

【襄】 5455
ㄒㄧㄤ shiang xiāng
1. to help; to assist
2. to achieve; to accomplish; to complete
3. to rise; to raise
4. high
5. to remove
6. a Chinese family name

襄辦（ㄒㄧㄤ ㄅㄢˋ）
to help manage, arrange,

etc.

襄理（ㄒㄧㄤ ㄌㄧˇ）
①to help manage, arrange, etc. ②an assistant manager (of a bank)

襄助（ㄒㄧㄤ ㄓㄨˋ）
to help; to assist

襄贊（ㄒㄧㄤ ㄗㄢˋ）
to assist and support

襄陽（ㄒㄧㄤ ㄧㄤˊ）
Hsiangyang, a county in Hupeh Province

【褻】 5456
（褻）ㄒㄧㄝˋ shieh xiè
1. underwear; clothes worn in one's bedroom or house
2. dirty; filthy
3. intimate (sometimes denoting a degree of indecency)
4. to slight; to look down upon
5. to be familiar or acquainted with

褻服（ㄒㄧㄝˋㄈㄨˊ）
clothes worn at home; underclothing

褻瀆（ㄒㄧㄝˋㄉㄨˊ）
①to slight; to abuse; to insult; to blaspheme; to desecrate ②(a polite expression) to bother others with trifles, etc.

褻瀆神明（ㄒㄧㄝˋㄉㄨˊㄕㄣˊㄇㄧㄥˊ）
blasphemy; to blaspheme the gods

褻狎（ㄒㄧㄝˋㄒㄧㄚˊ）
to be close and unduly intimate

褻臣（ㄒㄧㄝˋㄔㄣˊ）
an intimate courtier

褻尊（ㄒㄧㄝˋㄗㄨㄣ）
to condescend; to deign to

褻玩（ㄒㄧㄝˋㄨㄢˊ）
to treat with disrespect because of over-intimacy

褻衣（ㄒㄧㄝˋㄧ）
undies; underwear

【褳】 5457
ㄌㄧㄢˊ lian lián
used in the phrase 褡褳—a pouch worn at the girdle

十二畫

【裥】 5458
ㄐㄧㄢˇ jean jiǎn
the pleats of a skirt

十三畫

【襞】 5459
ㄅㄧˋ bih bì
to fold clothes

襞積（ㄅㄧˋ ㄐㄧ）
pleats (in a skirt, etc.)

襞褶（ㄅㄧˋ ㄒㄧㄝˊ）
lines or pleats on clothes as a result of folding

【襠】 5460
ㄉㄤ dang dāng
the crotch or bottom of a pair of trousers, drawers or panties 「裤襠」

【襟】 5461
ㄐㄧㄣ jin jīn
1. the lapel or collar of a garment or robe
2. aspiration; ambition; the mental outlook
3. (said of waters) to converge
4. the husbands of one's sisters

襟抱（ㄐㄧㄣ ㄅㄠˋ）
ambition; aspiration

襟帶（ㄐㄧㄣ ㄉㄞˋ）
strategic points; a place of strategic significance

襟弟（ㄐㄧㄣ ㄉㄧˋ）
the husband of one's wife's younger sister

襟度（ㄐㄧㄣ ㄉㄨˋ）
the mental outlook and capacity for tolerance

襟喉（ㄐㄧㄣ ㄏㄡˊ）
(literally) the collar and throat—very vital or strategic points

襟懷（ㄐㄧㄣ ㄏㄨㄞˊ）or 襟期（ㄐㄧㄣ ㄑㄧˊ）
one's feelings, ambitions, aspirations, bosom, (breadth of) mind, etc.

襟契（ㄐㄧㄣ ㄑㄧˋ）
one's bosom friends

襟情（ㄐㄧㄣ ㄑㄧㄥˊ）
feelings or emotions buried deep in one's heart

襟曲（ㄐㄧㄣ ㄑㄩ）
the true feelings, hopes, aspirations, etc. deep in one's heart

襟兄（ㄐㄧㄣ ㄒㄩㄥ）
the husband of one's wife's elder sister

襟山帶河（ㄐㄧㄣ ㄕㄢ ㄉㄞˋ ㄏㄜˊ）

cloaked by mountains and girded by rivers

襟韻（ㄐㄧㄣ ㄩㄣˋ）
one's aspirations and manners

【襖】 5462　ㄠˇ ao ǎo
a coat; a jacket or top garment padded with cotton or lined with fur

【襜】 5463　ㄔㄢ chan chān
1. the lower front of a robe, gown, etc.
2. (said of appearances) clean and neat
3. shaking or vibrating; flapping, as of curtains

十四畫

【襤】 5464　ㄌㄢˊ lan lán
1. ragged garments; clothes without a hem
2. shabbily dressed

襤褸（ㄌㄢˊ ㄌㄩˇ）
(said of clothes) tattered; in rags; ragged; shabby: 她衣衫襤褸。She was shabbily dressed.

【襦】 5465　ㄖㄨˊ ru rú
1. a short coat; a short top garment
2. the neckwear for babies
3. very fine silk fabric

十五畫

【襪】 5466　（袜）ㄨㄚˋ wah wà
stockings; socks

襪帶（ㄨㄚˋ ㄉㄞˋ）
garters

襪底兒（ㄨㄚˋ ㄉㄧˇ ㄦ）
the soles of stockings or socks

襪套（ㄨㄚˋ ㄊㄠˋ）
wrappers either worn outside stockings or worn bare-footed as a protection from chafing with shoes

襪頭兒（ㄨㄚˋ ㄊㄡˊ ㄦ）
socks

襪子（ㄨㄚˋ ㄗˇ）

stockings; socks

【襬】 5467　ㄅㄞˇ bae bǎi
the lower part of a Chinese long gown: 下襬 the hem of a long gown

十六畫

【襯】 5468　ㄔㄣˋ chenn chèn
1. inner garments; underwear
2. to provide a background; to bring to the fore; to supplement
3. a lining; a liner
4. to line; to place something underneath
5. to give alms (as to Buddhist monks, etc.)

襯托（ㄔㄣˋ ㄊㄨㄛ）
to bring into relief; to set off; to supplement; to embellish; to provide a contrast; a foil

襯裏（兒）（ㄔㄣˋ ㄌㄧˇ ㄦ）
a lining

襯裙（ㄔㄣˋ ㄑㄩㄣˊ）
a petticoat; an underskirt

襯衫（ㄔㄣˋ ㄕㄢ）
a shirt

襯字（ㄔㄣˋ ㄗˋ）
words added to a Chinese poem（詞 or 曲）over and above the minimum number required

襯衣（ㄔㄣˋ ㄧ）
undergarments

【襲】 5469　ㄒㄧˊ shyi xí
1. to put on; to clothe in; to wear
2. a suit (of clothes); a set (of dress)
3. repeated; double
4. hereditary; to inherit
5. to attack or take by surprise; to raid; to assail
6. to plagiarize; to appropriate
7. to enter (a town, etc.)
8. to unite; to accord with
9. to conform to
10. a Chinese family name

襲封（ㄒㄧˊ ㄈㄥ）
to inherit a title from one's forefathers

襲奪（ㄒㄧˊ ㄉㄨㄛˊ）
to take or attack by sur-

prise

襲迹（ㄒㄧˊ ㄐㄧ）
to follow in the footsteps of the predecessors

襲擊（ㄒㄧˊ ㄐㄧˊ）
a surprise attack; to attack by surprise; to make a raid

襲爵（ㄒㄧˊ ㄐㄩㄝˊ）
to inherit a hereditary title

襲人故智（ㄒㄧˊ ㄖㄣˊ ㄍㄨˋ ㄓˋ）
to copy an old trick

襲用（ㄒㄧˊ ㄩㄥˋ）
to take over (something that has long been used in the past)

十七畫

【襴】 5470　ㄌㄢˊ lan lán
a one-piece garment

襴裙（ㄌㄢˊ ㄑㄩㄣˊ）
an apron (used by women in the kitchen)

十八畫

【襶】 5471　1. ㄉㄞˋ day dài
as in 襶襶（ㄉㄞˋ ㄉㄞˋ）

【襶】 5471　2. ˙ㄉㄜ de de
as in 襶襶（ㄉㄞˋ ˙ㄉㄜ）

十九畫

【襻】 5472　ㄆㄢˋ pann pàn
1. a loop for a button
2. to tie or fasten with a rope, string, etc.

西 部
ㄧㄚˋ yah yà

【西】 5473　ㄒㄧ shi xī
1. west; the west; western
2. Western; the West; European; American; Occidental; foreign
3. a Chinese family name

西伯（ㄒㄧ ㄅㄛˊ）
the feudal title of King Wen before he rose in arms

（右側：西 部）

（ㄒㄧ部）

against Chou（紂）the tyrant

西伯利亞（ㄒㄧ ㄅㄛ ㄌㄧˋ ㄧㄚˇ）
Siberia

西伯利亞鐵路（ㄒㄧ ㄅㄛ ㄌㄧˋ ㄧㄚˇ
ㄊㄧㄝˇ ㄌㄨˋ）
the Siberia Railway

西柏林（ㄒㄧ ㄅㄛˊ ㄌㄧㄣˊ）
West Berlin

西北（ㄒㄧ ㄅㄟˇ）
northwest

西北航空公司（ㄒㄧ ㄅㄟˇ ㄏㄤˊ ㄎㄨㄥ
ㄍㄨㄥ ㄙ）
the Northwest Airlines

西北西（ㄒㄧ ㄅㄟˇ ㄒㄧ）
northwest-by-west; north-
west by west

西班牙（ㄒㄧ ㄅㄢ ㄧㄚˊ）
Spain

西班牙人（ㄒㄧ ㄅㄢ ㄧㄚˊ ㄖㄣˊ）
a Spaniard; the Spanish

西班牙語（ㄒㄧ ㄅㄢ ㄧㄚˊ ㄩˇ）
Spanish (language): 你會說
西班牙語嗎? Do you speak
Spanish?

西半球（ㄒㄧ ㄅㄢˋ ㄑㄧㄡˊ）
the Western Hemisphere

西賓（ㄒㄧ ㄅㄧㄣ）
a private tutor who lodges
in the house of the employer

西部（ㄒㄧ ㄅㄨˋ）
the western part (of a territory); the West

西部武打片（ㄒㄧ ㄅㄨˋ ㄨˇ ㄉㄚˇ ㄆㄧㄢˋ）
or 西部片（ㄒㄧ ㄅㄨˋ ㄆㄧㄢˋ）
cowboy pictures; a Western:
這是一部西部片。 The picture
is a Western.

西皮（ㄒㄧ ㄆㄧˊ）
name of a popular tune in
Peking opera

西門（ㄒㄧ ㄇㄣˊ）
①the west gate in a city
wall ②a Chinese double surname

西門豹（ㄒㄧ ㄇㄣˊ ㄅㄠˋ）
Hsi-Men Pao, a famous
magistrate in the Epoch of
Warring States, who did
away with the evil custom
of marrying maidens to the
river god and who intro-
duced an irrigation system

西門子（ㄒㄧ ㄇㄣˊ ㄗˇ）
Ernst Werner von Siemens
(1816-1892), a famous German electrical engineer and

industrialist

西米（ㄒㄧ ㄇㄧˇ）
sago 亦作「西穀米」

西法（ㄒㄧ ㄈㄚˇ）
European and American
methods; Western or Oc-
cidental methods

西番蓮（ㄒㄧ ㄈㄢ ㄌㄧㄢˊ）
①a passionflower ②a
dahlia

西方（ㄒㄧ ㄈㄤ）
①west; the West or West-
ern: 日落於西方。 The sun sets
in the west. ②a Buddhist
paradise ③a Chinese double
surname

西方極樂世界（ㄒㄧ ㄈㄤ ㄐㄧˊ ㄌㄜˋ ㄕˋ
ㄐㄧㄝˋ）or 西方淨土（ㄒㄧ ㄈㄤ ㄐㄧㄥˋ
ㄊㄨˇ）
a Buddhist paradise, or
heaven

西風（ㄒㄧ ㄈㄥ）
①a west wind; a wester; a
westerly ②influences, customs, ways, etc. of the West

西風東漸（ㄒㄧ ㄈㄥ ㄉㄨㄥ ㄐㄧㄢˋ）
the spread of Western influences to the East

西服（ㄒㄧ ㄈㄨˊ）or 西裝（ㄒㄧ ㄓㄨㄤ）
Western clothes; European
or American attire

西德（ㄒㄧ ㄉㄜˊ）
West Germany (East Ger-
many and West Germany
were united in 1990.)

西點（ㄒㄧ ㄉㄧㄢˇ）
①western-style dessert ②
West Point

西太后（ㄒㄧ ㄊㄞˋ ㄏㄡˋ）
Empress Dowager Tzu Hsi
(慈禧), who ruled China as
a regent toward the end of
the 19th century

西天（ㄒㄧ ㄊㄧㄢ）
①the Buddhist paradise or
heaven; Western Paradise ②
India, as known to ancient
Chinese Buddhists

西土（ㄒㄧ ㄊㄨˇ）
①the Western lands ②the
Buddhist paradise or heaven
③India ④an old name of
Changan, capital city of
Shensi Province

西奈半島（ㄒㄧ ㄋㄞˋ ㄅㄢˋ ㄉㄠˇ）
Sinai Peninsula

西南（ㄒㄧ ㄋㄢˊ）

southwest

西南非（ㄒㄧ ㄋㄢˊ ㄈㄟ）
South West Africa

西南西（ㄒㄧ ㄋㄢˊ ㄒㄧ）
southwest-by-west; south-
west by west

西南夷（ㄒㄧ ㄋㄢˊ ㄧˊ）
(Han Dynasty) a general
name of the tribes in the
southwestern Chinese provinces of Kweichow, Yunnan,
Vietnam, Burma, etc.

西里伯島（ㄒㄧ ㄌㄧˇ ㄅㄛˊ ㄉㄠˇ）
Celebes, former name of Su-
lawesi, an island in central
Indonesia

西曆（ㄒㄧ ㄌㄧˋ）
the Gregorian calendar

西涼（ㄒㄧ ㄌㄧㄤˊ）
one of the 16 tribal states in
China during the Tsin (晉)
Dynasty

西陵峽（ㄒㄧ ㄌㄧㄥˊ ㄒㄧㄚˊ）
one of the Three Gorges (三
峽) on the upper Yangtze
River, near Yichang (宜昌) in
Hupeh Province

西羅馬帝國（ㄒㄧ ㄌㄨㄛˊ ㄇㄚˇ ㄉㄧˋ ㄍㄨㄛˊ）
the Western (Roman)
Empire

西螺大橋（ㄒㄧ ㄌㄨㄛˊ ㄉㄚˋ ㄑㄧㄠˊ）
the Silo Bridge, the longest
highway bridge in Taiwan

西穀椰子（ㄒㄧ ㄍㄨˇ ㄧㄝˊ ˙ㄗ）
sago palms

西瓜（ㄒㄧ ㄍㄨㄚ）
watermelons

西瓜子兒（ㄒㄧ ㄍㄨㄚ ㄗˇㄦ）or 西瓜
子（ㄒㄧ ㄍㄨㄚ ㄗˇ）
watermelon seeds

西宮（ㄒㄧ ㄍㄨㄥ）or 西宮娘娘
（ㄒㄧ ㄍㄨㄥ ㄋㄧㄤˊ ㄋㄧㄤˊ）
the concubines of the king
or emperor; the imperial
concubines

西貢（ㄒㄧ ㄍㄨㄥˋ）
Saigon, the capital of former South Vietnam

西康（ㄒㄧ ㄎㄤ）
Sikang, a province on the
southwest border of China

西崑體（ㄒㄧ ㄎㄨㄣ ㄊㄧˇ）
a style of Chinese poetry,
deriving its name from 西崑
酬唱集, authored by Yang Yi

（楊億）and others of the Sung Dynasty, featuring ornate diction and jingling rhythm

西河之痛（ㄒㄧ ㄏㄜˊ ㄓ ㄊㄨㄥˋ）
a reference to Pu Tzu-hsia（卜子夏）who lived in Hsi Ho（西河）and became blind in lamenting the loss of a son—now a condolatory expression used when a friend loses a son

西海岸（ㄒㄧ ㄏㄞˇ ㄢˋ）
① the western coast ② the West Coast of the United States

西漢（ㄒㄧ ㄏㄢˋ）
the Western Han or Earlier Han Dynasty, which lasted for 231 years from 206 B.C. to A.D. 24

西湖（ㄒㄧ ㄏㄨˊ）or **西子湖**（ㄒㄧ ㄗˇ ㄏㄨˊ）
the West Lake, name of various lakes in a number of provinces, the most famous one is at Hangchow（杭州）

西紅柿（ㄒㄧ ㄏㄨㄥˊ ㄕˋ）
tomatoes 亦作「番茄」

西極（ㄒㄧ ㄐㄧˊ）
the remote regions in the west as known to ancient Chinese

西晉（ㄒㄧ ㄐㄧㄣˋ）
the Earlier Tsin Dynasty（265-316 A.D.）with capital at Loyang（洛陽）

西進（ㄒㄧ ㄐㄧㄣˋ）
(said of troops) to march westward

西江（ㄒㄧ ㄐㄧㄤ）
the West River, a tributary of the Pearl River（珠江）

西京（ㄒㄧ ㄐㄧㄥ）
the western capital (referring to different cities in different dynasties, particularly 長安 and 洛陽）

西經（ㄒㄧ ㄐㄧㄥ）
① west longitude ② to go through or past a certain place to the west

西秦（ㄒㄧ ㄑㄧㄣˊ）
one of the 16 states in China founded by northern tribes during the Tsin（晉）Dynasty

西里（ㄒㄧ ㄌㄧˇ）

Sicily, Italy

西席（ㄒㄧ ㄒㄧˊ）
a private tutor; a teacher 參看「西賓」

西夏（ㄒㄧ ㄒㄧㄚˋ）
Hsi Hsia（1032-1227）, a state in the Sung Dynasty, which occupied today's Inner Mongolia（內蒙）and Kansu（甘肅）

西廂記（ㄒㄧ ㄒㄧㄤ ㄐㄧˋ）
The West Chamber, one of the most famous Chinese dramas, authored by Wang Shih-fu（王實甫）in the Yüan Dynasty

西行（ㄒㄧ ㄒㄧㄥˊ）
to go west; to travel westward

西學（ㄒㄧ ㄒㄩㄝˊ）
Western learning (a late Ching Dynasty term for Western natural sciences)

西哲（ㄒㄧ ㄓㄜˊ）
European or American sages

西周（ㄒㄧ ㄓㄡ）
① the Earlier Chou Dynasty（1111-771 B.C.）② name of a state in ancient China

西裝（ㄒㄧ ㄓㄨㄤ）
Western-style clothes; a Western suit

西川（ㄒㄧ ㄔㄨㄢ）
the western part of the Szechwan Province

西窗剪燭（ㄒㄧ ㄔㄨㄤ ㄐㄧㄢˇ ㄓㄨˊ）
(literally) to cut the candle wick under the western window—the happy reunion of friends chatting together late into the night

西施（ㄒㄧ ㄕ）or **西子**（ㄒㄧ ㄗˇ）
Hsi Shih, a famed beauty in the Period of Spring and Autumn, who was offered to Fu Chai（夫差）, King of Wu（吳）, by Kou Chien（句踐）, King of Yüeh（越）

西式（ㄒㄧ ㄕˋ）
Western-style; European or American style; Occidental style

西沙群島（ㄒㄧ ㄕㄚ ㄑㄩㄣˊ ㄉㄠˇ）
Hsisha Chuntao (the Paracel Islands)

西曬（ㄒㄧ ㄕㄞˋ）
(said of houses, rooms, etc.)

exposed to the intensive heat of the afternoon sun

西山（ㄒㄧ ㄕㄢ）
① western hills or mountains ② name of various scenic resorts, the most famous one being in Peking（北京）

西人（ㄒㄧ ㄖㄣˊ）
Westerners; Europeans or Americans; Occidentals

西戎（ㄒㄧ ㄖㄨㄥˊ）
tribesmen in the western borders in the Chou Dynasty

西崽（ㄒㄧ ㄗㄞˇ）
waiters in cabarets, nightclubs, restaurants, etc. owned by foreigners

西藏（ㄒㄧ ㄗㄤˋ）
① Tibet ② Tibetan

西餐（ㄒㄧ ㄘㄢ）
Western food; European or American meals

西薩摩亞（ㄒㄧ ㄙㄚˋ ㄇㄛˊ ㄧㄚˇ）
Western Samoa

西歐（ㄒㄧ ㄡ）
Western Europe

西安（ㄒㄧ ㄢ）
Sian, in Shensi Province 參看「長安」

西醫（ㄒㄧ ㄧ）
Western medicine; doctors practicing Western medicine (as distinct from Chinese herb doctors)

西雅圖（ㄒㄧ ㄧㄚˇ ㄊㄨˊ）
Seattle, an American port city

西藥（ㄒㄧ ㄧㄠˋ）
Western medicines or pharmaceuticals (as distinct from medical herbs)

西遊記（ㄒㄧ ㄧㄡˊ ㄐㄧˋ）
Pilgrimage to the West, one of the most popular novels, telling the adventures of a Buddhist monk and his three disciples on their way to India

西燕（ㄒㄧ ㄧㄢˋ）
one of the 16 tribal states in China during the Tsin Dynasty

西諺（ㄒㄧ ㄧㄢˋ）
a Western proverb; European or American aphorisms:「天助自助者」是一句西諺。"God helps those who

（西部）

（西部）

help themselves" is a Western proverb.

西印度羣島 (ㄒㄧ ㄧㄣ ㄉㄨˋ ㄑㄩㄣˊ ㄉㄠˇ)
the West Indies

西洋 (ㄒㄧ ㄧㄤˊ)
the West; Western; European or American nations

西洋景 (ㄒㄧ ㄧㄤˊ ㄐㄧㄥˇ) or 西洋鏡 (ㄒㄧ ㄧㄤˊ ㄐㄧㄥˋ)
①a peep show ②trickery; tricks; hanky-panky: 她拆穿了他的西洋鏡。She exposed his tricks.

西洋史 (ㄒㄧ ㄧㄤˊ ㄕˇ)
history of Europe and America

西洋參 (ㄒㄧ ㄧㄤˊ ㄕㄣ)
ginsengs produced in America

西洋人 (ㄒㄧ ㄧㄤˊ ㄖㄣˊ)
Westerners

西洋菜 (ㄒㄧ ㄧㄤˊ ㄘㄞˋ)
water cress

西魏 (ㄒㄧ ㄨㄟˋ)
the Western Wei Dynasty (535-556), one of the Northern Dynasties

西王母 (ㄒㄧ ㄨㄤˊ ㄇㄨˇ)
①name of an ancient state ②(name of a goddess) the Grand Old Lady of the West

西域 (ㄒㄧ ㄩˋ)
a general name of regions west of Tunhwang (敦煌) in the Han Dynasty

西樂 (ㄒㄧ ㄩㄝˋ)
Western music; European or American music: 他主修西樂。He majors in Western music.

西嶽 (ㄒㄧ ㄩㄝˋ)
another name of Mountain Hua (華山) in Shensi Province, one of the Five Sacred Mountains in China

西元 (ㄒㄧ ㄩㄢˊ)
the Gregorian calendar, which begins with the year in which Christ was supposedly born; A.D. 亦作「公元」

三畫

【要】 5474
1. ㄧㄠ yaw yāo
1. necessary; important; essential; necessity: 睡眠對健康是必要的。Sleep is necessary to health.
2. must; should; ought to: 我想要早點動身。I should like to start early.
3. to want; to demand; to need; to require; to desire; to take: 我想要一輛新車。I want a new car.
4. to summarize; a summary; a generalization; a synopsis
5. will; shall—to indicate the future tense: 天快要黑了。It's going to be dark.
6. brief
7. if; in case

要不 (ㄧㄠˋ ㄅㄨˋ) or 要不然 (ㄧㄠˋ ㄅㄨˋ ㄖㄢˊ)
if not; otherwise; the other alternative being...; or

要不得 (ㄧㄠˋ ㄅㄨˋ ㄉㄜˊ)
①(said of things) unusable, useless; extremely bad ②(said of people or acts) very bad; inappropriate; condemnable; intolerable: 這種墮落的行爲要不得。Such depraved acts are intolerable.

要不是 (ㄧㄠˋ ㄅㄨˋ ㄕˋ)
If it were not for...或But for.... 要不是你相助，我早已失敗。But for your help, I should have failed.

要不要 (ㄧㄠˋ ㄅㄨˋ ㄧㄠˋ)
Do you want it? 或Do I have to...? 或Shall (I, he, etc.)...? 或Do you want (me, him, etc.)...?

要麼 (ㄧㄠˋ ㄇㄜ˙)
or; either...or...

要面子 (ㄧㄠˋ ㄇㄧㄢˋ ㄗˇ)
to be keen on face-saving; to be anxious to keep up honor

要命 (ㄧㄠˋ ㄇㄧㄥˋ)
①very; extremely; awfully: 冷得要命。It's awfully cold. ②impossible: 你真是要命！You are really impossible! ③too much to endure; an awful nuisance

要命鬼 (ㄧㄠˋ ㄇㄧㄥˋ ㄍㄨㄟˇ)
①(an expression referring to one's children) the devils who make one work to death ②a person who imperils another

要目 (ㄧㄠˋ ㄇㄨˋ)

要件 (ㄧㄠˋ ㄐㄧㄢˋ)
①main items; main topics or subjects: 要目繁多。Main items are multifarious. ②(archaic) statistics

要犯 (ㄧㄠˋ ㄈㄢˋ)
an important or dangerous criminal; a most-wanted criminal

要飯的 (ㄧㄠˋ ㄈㄢˋ ㄉㄜ˙)
a beggar

要得 (ㄧㄠˋ ㄉㄜˊ)
①good; well done; bravo: 這個辦法真是要得！That's indeed a good idea! ②acceptable; okay

要道 (ㄧㄠˋ ㄉㄠˋ)
①an important road or passage; a main route; a highway; an important line ②the essential points of what is good and appropriate

要地 (ㄧㄠˋ ㄉㄧˋ)
an important or strategic place

要點 (ㄧㄠˋ ㄉㄧㄢˇ)
the important or main points; the gist; the essential points (in an article, book, etc.): 告訴我他所說的要點。Tell me the gist of what he said.

要圖 (ㄧㄠˋ ㄊㄨˊ)
an important plan or scheme; an urgent program or task

要臉 (ㄧㄠˋ ㄌㄧㄢˇ) or 要臉面 (ㄧㄠˋ ㄌㄧㄢˇ ㄇㄧㄢˋ)
to be concerned with one's face or honor; to be highly sensitive about what others may think of oneself

要領 (ㄧㄠˋ ㄌㄧㄥˇ)
essential points; important points; essentials

要路 (ㄧㄠˋ ㄌㄨˋ)
①a thoroughfare; a main route ②eminent position

要略 (ㄧㄠˋ ㄌㄩㄝˋ)
①an important plan or scheme ②a synopsis: 一週新聞要略 the synopsis of the week's news

要港 (ㄧㄠˋ ㄍㄤˇ)
an important port; a key port: 高雄是一要港。Kaohsiung is an important port.

要公 (ㄧㄠˋ ㄍㄨㄥ)
an urgent official business

要口(ㄧㄠ ㄎㄡ)
an important checkpoint

要害(ㄧㄠ ㄏㄞ)
①fatal points in a human body; a vital part; a crucial point ②strategic locations or points

要好(ㄧㄠ ㄏㄠ)
①to desire to excel ②to befriend; to be on good terms; to be close friends: 他們倆很要好。They are very good to each other. ③to be in love with

要(我, 你, 他…)好看兒(ㄧㄠ (ㄨㄛˇ·ㄋㄧˇ·ㄊㄚ) ㄏㄠˇ ㄎㄢˋㄦ)
to want to embarrass (me, you, him, etc.); to want to make (me, you, him, etc.) suffer

要價兒(ㄧㄠ ㄐㄧㄚˋㄦ)
a price demanded by the seller; to quote a price which may be slashed by haggling

要件(ㄧㄠ ㄐㄧㄢˋ)
①an important document; an urgent or confidential matter, etc. ②a prerequisite; a necessary condition

要津(ㄧㄠ ㄐㄧㄣ)
①an important passage; a key road ②a key position; a sensitive post; an influential post ③(Buddhism) an important turning point

要緊(ㄧㄠ ㄐㄧㄣˇ)
①important and urgent ②to be serious; to matter

要訣(ㄧㄠ ㄐㄩㄝˊ)
the secret of doing something; the key to doing something successfully

要強(ㄧㄠ ㄑㄧㄤˊ)
to strive to excel; aggressive; desiring to accept no second spot; eager to be at the top

要項(ㄧㄠ ㄒㄧㄤˋ)
key points or items

要之(ㄧㄠ ㄓ)
in a nutshell; in short; to sum up

要職(ㄧㄠ ㄓˊ)
an important post: 他曾身居要職。He used to hold an important post.

要旨(ㄧㄠ ㄓˇ)
key points; themes; epitomes; essential ideas: 要旨甚多。The essential ideas are numerous.

要賬(ㄧㄠ ㄓㄤˋ)
to demand payment of a debt, bill, etc.

要著(ㄧㄠ ㄓㄨㄛˊ)
an effective step; an important move; a timely measure

要衝(ㄧㄠ ㄔㄨㄥ)
a strategic position; a key place; a communication hub

要事(ㄧㄠ ㄕˋ)
an important matter; an urgent business: 它是件要事。It is an important matter.

要是(ㄧㄠ ㄕˋ)
if; in case: 要是下雨, 怎麼辦? What if it rains?

要甚麼(ㄧㄠ ㄕㄣˊ·ㄇㄜ)
What do you want? 或 What does he (or she) want?

要人(ㄧㄠ ㄖㄣˊ)
a VIP; a person in the Who's Who; a prominent figure: 要人善忘。A person of importance is forgetful of thing.

要死要活的(ㄧㄠ ㄙˇ ㄧㄠ ㄏㄨㄛˊ·ㄉㄜ)
to importune desperately

要塞(ㄧㄠ ㄙㄞˋ)
a fortress; a strategic point

要素(ㄧㄠ ㄙㄨˋ)
essentials; chief ingredients or elements or factors

要隘(ㄧㄠ ㄞˋ)
a strategic pass; a key point; a fortress 參看「要塞」

要義(ㄧㄠ ㄧˋ)
key points; main themes; essentials

要言不煩(ㄧㄠ ㄧㄢˊ ㄅㄨˋ ㄈㄢˊ)
brief and to the point

要務(ㄧㄠ ㄨˋ)
an important or urgent business, matter, task, etc.

要聞(ㄧㄠ ㄨㄣˊ)
important news items; headlines

要員(ㄧㄠ ㄩㄢˊ)
important officials; high-ranking officials; VIPs

【要】 5474
ㄧㄠ iau yāo
1. to invite; to request the presence of

2. to engage; to date; to make an agreement

3. to ask for; to demand; to claim; to make a claim; to request; requests: 她要求我留下。She requested me to stay.

4. to coerce; to force; to blackmail; to threaten

5. to stop

6. to censure; to investigate; to examine

7. the waist or midriff 亦作「腰」

8. a Chinese family name

要買人心(ㄧㄠ ㄇㄞˇ ㄖㄣˊ ㄒㄧㄣ)
to win people's hearts by statecraft

要盟(ㄧㄠ ㄇㄥˊ)
to impose an alliance, agreement, etc. on another (state, etc.) by threat of force

要擊(ㄧㄠ ㄐㄧˊ)
to ambush midway; to intercept (an enemy)

要求(ㄧㄠ ㄑㄧㄡˊ)
to demand; to request; a demand; a request: 我應他的要求而來。I came at his request.

要挾(ㄧㄠ ㄒㄧㄝˊ)
to blackmail; to put pressure on; to coerce; to threaten: 他們要挾對方。They put pressure on the other party.

要斬 or 腰斬(ㄧㄠ ㄓㄢˇ)
(an ancient punishment) to cut a criminal in half at the waist

要束(ㄧㄠ ㄕㄨˋ)
restriction or restraint; to restrain

要約(ㄧㄠ ㄩㄝ)
to enter into an agreement or a contract

六畫

【罩】 5475
ㄊㄢˊ tarn tán
1. to spread to; to involve
2. deep and vast; profound

罩第(ㄊㄢˊ ㄉㄧˋ)
①a vast or an extensive residence ②your house

罩思(ㄊㄢˊ ㄙ)
deep or profound thought; deep in thought; meditation

罩恩(ㄊㄢˊ ㄣ)
grace, favor or benefits for

（西部）

all

【覃】 5475
1. ㄊㄢˊ tarn
2. ㄑㄧㄣˊ chyn qín
a Chinese family name

十二畫

【覆】 5476
ㄈㄨˋ fuh fù
1. to pour out
2. to overturn; to topple; to upset; to capsize; to put something upside down
3. a reply; to reply; to respond: 她沒有答覆。She made no reply.
4. to defeat; to destroy; to conquer
5. to investigate; to examine carefully
6. to cover; to screen
7. to repeat; a second time; again: 他反覆地勸告他。He warned her again and again.
8. to hide; to conceal

覆敗(ㄈㄨˋ ㄅㄞˋ)
to be beaten and destroyed; to topple

覆杯(ㄈㄨˋ ㄅㄟ)
①to put a wine-cup upside down—to decline to drink ②to drink to one's heart's content

覆蔽(ㄈㄨˋ ㄅㄧˋ)
to hide; to conceal; to cover up

覆瓿(ㄈㄨˋ ㄅㄡˋ)
(literally) to be used as a covering to a jar—worthless (a polite reference to one's own writing)

覆盆(ㄈㄨˋ ㄆㄣˊ)
①within the overturned bowl—dark and without justice ②a raspberry

覆盆之冤(ㄈㄨˋ ㄆㄣˊ ㄓ ㄩㄢ)
a wrong that cannot be redressed

覆盆子(ㄈㄨˋ ㄆㄣˊ ˙ㄗ)
(Chinese medicine) a raspberry

覆沒(ㄈㄨˋ ㄇㄛˋ)
①(said of a boat) to wreck and sink ②(said of an army) routed; wiped out; destroyed

覆冒(ㄈㄨˋ ㄇㄠˋ)
to cover up; to hide or conceal

覆幬(ㄈㄨˋ ㄉㄠˋ)
to overshadow and curtain

覆蓋(ㄈㄨˋ ㄍㄞˋ)
to cover; to put a cover over something

覆核(ㄈㄨˋ ㄏㄜˊ)
to reexamine; to restudy

覆校(ㄈㄨˋ ㄐㄧㄠˋ)
to proofread again; the second proofreading: 他將該書覆校一遍。He proofread the book again.

覆車之戒(ㄈㄨˋ ㄔㄜ ㄓ ㄐㄧㄝˋ)
the lesson of a failure

覆軍(ㄈㄨˋ ㄐㄩㄣ)
to cause the whole army to be wiped out; to destroy the whole army

覆信(ㄈㄨˋ ㄒㄧㄣˋ)
①a letter in reply ②to reply a letter

覆選(ㄈㄨˋ ㄒㄩㄢˇ)
①an election by delegates; an indirect election ②a run-off (election)

覆舟(ㄈㄨˋ ㄓㄡ)
①to capsize ②a capsized boat

覆轍(ㄈㄨˋ ㄔㄜˋ)
(literally) the rut of an overturned cart—the lesson of a failure

覆巢之下無完卵(ㄈㄨˋ ㄔㄠˊ ㄓ ㄒㄧㄚˋ ㄨˊ ㄨㄢˊ ㄌㄨㄢˇ)
(literally) If the nest is overturned there won't be whole eggs left.—If a city falls, none of the residents will be safe. 或 If a country is beaten, all its people will suffer.

覆試(ㄈㄨˋ ㄕˋ)
①to test again ②a second test or examination

覆手(ㄈㄨˋ ㄕㄡˇ)
to turn one's palm—an easy task

覆審(ㄈㄨˋ ㄕㄣˇ)
a retrial of a case

覆書(ㄈㄨˋ ㄕㄨ)
①to reply a letter ②a letter in reply

覆水難收(ㄈㄨˋ ㄕㄨㄟˇ ㄋㄢˊ ㄕㄡ)
(literally) Spilt water can't be recovered.—①A divorced woman cannot hope to re-unite with her former husband. ②There is no use crying over spilt milk. 或What is done can't be undone.

覆染(ㄈㄨˋ ㄖㄢˇ)
to dye old clothes

覆載(ㄈㄨˋ ㄗㄞˋ)
the heaven and the earth

覆思(ㄈㄨˋ ㄙ)
a carved screen in a palace 亦作「罘罳」

覆餗(ㄈㄨˋ ㄙㄨˋ)
to fail owing to incompetence

覆按(ㄈㄨˋ ㄢˋ)
to reexamine; to reinvestigate

覆議(ㄈㄨˋ ㄧˋ)
①to discuss again ②a renewed discussion

覆文(ㄈㄨˋ ㄨㄣˊ)
an official reply in written form

覆亡(ㄈㄨˋ ㄨㄤˊ)
the downfall (of a nation, dynasty, or family); decline and fall

覆育(ㄈㄨˋ ㄩˋ)
protected by heaven and nourished by the earth

十三畫

【覈】 5477
(核) ㄏㄜˊ her hé
1. to test; to examine; to investigate
2. deep; deeply
3. the stone (of a fruit)

覈實(ㄏㄜˊ ㄕˊ)
to examine or investigate the fact or truth

覈物(ㄏㄜˊ ㄨˋ)
fruits that have stones

【覇】 5478
ㄅㄚˋ bah bà
1. the strong; the fierce ones
2. the dean or head of nobility
3. to stand out; outstanding; superior
4. hegemony

十七畫

【覊】 5479
(羈) ㄐㄧ ji jī
to travel; to be on a tour or trip

羈旅（ㄐㄧ ㄌㄩˇ）
a traveler 亦作「覊旅」

十九畫

【羈】 5480
（羈）ㄐㄧ ㄐㄧˊ
1. a halter
2. restriction; restraint
3. to live in another house; to stay in a place other than one's hometown

見 部
ㄐㄧㄢˋ jiann jiàn

【見】 5481
ㄐㄧㄢˋ jiann jiàn
1. to see; to catch sight of; to perceive; to understand; to observe or examine: 百聞不如一見。Seeing is believing.
2. to visit; to see; to call on or at; to meet
3. to receive (visitors, etc.); to come face to face with
4. vide; see: 詳見註釋。For further information, see the footnotes.
5. to be used roughly as a verb to be in the passive voice: 即希告知。I hope to be informed immediately.
6. (said of a situation, condition, etc.) to move toward a certain direction, as getting worse, better, slimmer, etc.

見背（ㄐㄧㄢˋ ㄅㄟˋ）
(especially referring to parents) to turn their backs —dead; to pass away

見報（ㄐㄧㄢˋ ㄅㄠˋ）
to appear in the newspapers

見不得（ㄐㄧㄢˋ ㄅㄨˋ ㄉㄜˊ）
① not to be exposed to ② not fit to be seen or revealed

見不得人（ㄐㄧㄢˋ ㄅㄨˋ ㄉㄜˊ ㄖㄣˊ）
too ashamed to show up in public

見不及此（ㄐㄧㄢˋ ㄅㄨˋ ㄐㄧˊ ㄘˇ）
to have not considered this point; to have not observed or examined to such (depth, details, etc.); to fail to see

this point
見不著（ㄐㄧㄢˋ ㄅㄨˋ ㄓㄠˊ）
cannot see; unable to meet

見票即付（ㄐㄧㄢˋ ㄆㄧㄠˋ ㄐㄧˊ ㄈㄨˋ）
payable at sight; payable to the bearer

見面（ㄐㄧㄢˋ ㄇㄧㄢˋ）or 見面兒（ㄐㄧㄢˋ ㄇㄧㄢˋㄦ）
to come face to face; to see; to meet

見面禮（ㄐㄧㄢˋ ㄇㄧㄢˋ ㄌㄧˇ）
gift(s) given at one's first meeting, especially with a relative of a junior generation

見分曉（ㄐㄧㄢˋ ㄈㄣ ㄒㄧㄠˇ）
(said of results) to become known; to manifest; to tell

見方（ㄐㄧㄢˋ ㄈㄤ）
square, as a foot square

見風轉舵（ㄐㄧㄢˋ ㄈㄥ ㄓㄨㄢˇ ㄉㄨㄛˋ）
to steer by the wind—to see how the wind blows; to go with the tide

見風使船（ㄐㄧㄢˋ ㄈㄥ ㄕˇ ㄔㄨㄢˊ）or 見風使帆（ㄐㄧㄢˋ ㄈㄥ ㄕˇ ㄈㄢˊ）
to trim one's sails—to act as the occasion dictates

見復 or 見覆（ㄐㄧㄢˋ ㄈㄨˋ）
to receive a reply

見到（ㄐㄧㄢˋ ㄉㄠˋ）
① to meet; to see: 很高興見到你。I'm glad to meet you. ② to perceive or think of

見地（ㄐㄧㄢˋ ㄉㄧˋ）
one's views, beliefs or ideas; insight: 他很有見地。He has keen insight.

見多識廣（ㄐㄧㄢˋ ㄉㄨㄛ ㄕˋ ㄍㄨㄤˇ）
experienced and knowledgeable

見天日（ㄐㄧㄢˋ ㄊㄧㄢ ㄖˋ）
(literally) to see the heaven and the sun—① to see justice prevail ② to emerge from misery

見兔顧犬（ㄐㄧㄢˋ ㄊㄨˋ ㄍㄨˋ ㄑㄩㄢˇ）
(literally) to signal to the hunting dog upon seeing a rabbit—to do the right thing to cope with a sudden new situation

見禮（ㄐㄧㄢˋ ㄌㄧˇ）
to salute or greet another upon meeting him

見利忘義（ㄐㄧㄢˋ ㄌㄧˋ ㄨㄤˋ ㄧˋ）
to forget one's integrity

under the temptation of personal gain; to be blinded by the lust for gain

見獵心喜（ㄐㄧㄢˋ ㄌㄧㄝˋ ㄒㄧㄣ ㄒㄧˇ）
to have one's interest in an old hobby revived upon seeing someone else doing it; to thrill to see one's favorite sport and itch to have a go

見諒（ㄐㄧㄢˋ ㄌㄧㄤˋ）or 見原（ㄐㄧㄢˋ ㄩㄢˊ）
to pardon me; to forgive me; to excuse me

見高低（ㄐㄧㄢˋ ㄍㄠ ㄉㄧ）
to see who's the better one; to compete or fight it out

見告（ㄐㄧㄢˋ ㄍㄠˋ）
to tell; to inform; to notify

見過（ㄐㄧㄢˋ ㄍㄨㄛˋ）
to have seen; to have met

見過世面（ㄐㄧㄢˋ ㄍㄨㄛˋ ㄕˋ ㄇㄧㄢˋ）
to have seen much of the world; experienced; sophisticated

見怪（ㄐㄧㄢˋ ㄍㄨㄞˋ）
to take offense; to blame; to mind: 招待不周，請勿見怪。I hope you won't mind my poor reception.

見怪不怪，其怪自敗（ㄐㄧㄢˋ ㄍㄨㄞˋ ㄅㄨˋ ㄍㄨㄞˋ，ㄑㄧˊ ㄍㄨㄞˋ ㄗˋ ㄅㄞˋ）
If one remains calm upon seeing strange things, the strangeness will do no harm.

見鬼（ㄐㄧㄢˋ ㄍㄨㄟˇ）
(literally) to see the devil —Nonsense! 或 absurd: 活見鬼！Nonsense! You're daydreaming.

見慣（ㄐㄧㄢˋ ㄍㄨㄢˋ）
to be accustomed to seeing something

見客（ㄐㄧㄢˋ ㄎㄜˋ）
to receive guests

見好（ㄐㄧㄢˋ ㄏㄠˇ）
① to get better (especially said of illness); mend ② to be appreciated; to curry favor

見惠（ㄐㄧㄢˋ ㄏㄨㄟˋ）
to favor with

見幾 or 見機（ㄐㄧㄢˋ ㄐㄧ）
to perceive what is yet to take place; provident; farsighted

見機行事（ㄐㄧㄢˋ ㄐㄧ ㄒㄧㄥˊ ㄕˋ）
to act as the circumstances

〔見部〕

【見部】

見解(ㄐㄧㄢˋ ㄐㄧㄝˇ)
one's views, ideas or observations or opinions about something: 這只是他個人的見解。This is just his own opinion.

見教(ㄐㄧㄢˋ ㄐㄧㄠˋ)
(a polite expression) your teachings or exhortations; to favor me with your advice; to instruct me: 有何見教? Is there something you want to instruct me?

見景生情(ㄐㄧㄢˋ ㄐㄧㄥˇ ㄕㄥ ㄑㄧㄥˊ)
to be touched by the scene; to have one's old emotion aroused by a sight

見棄(ㄐㄧㄢˋ ㄑㄧˋ)
to be cast away or rejected

見錢眼開(ㄐㄧㄢˋ ㄑㄧㄢˊ ㄧㄢˇ ㄎㄞ)
(literally) to keep one's eyes wide open upon seeing money—greedy; avaricious

見習(ㄐㄧㄢˋ ㄒㄧˊ)
apprenticeship; in-service training; probation

見習生(ㄐㄧㄢˋ ㄒㄧˊ ㄕㄥ)
an apprentice; an in-service trainee; a probationer

見習醫生(ㄐㄧㄢˋ ㄒㄧˊ ㄧ ㄕㄥ)
an intern

見小(ㄐㄧㄢˋ ㄒㄧㄠˇ)
①the ability to see what others are apt to neglect ② to see only the details

見效(ㄐㄧㄢˋ ㄒㄧㄠˋ)
effective; efficacious

見笑(ㄐㄧㄢˋ ㄒㄧㄠˋ)
①to be laughed at ②to incur ridicule (by one's poor performance)

見笑於大方之家(ㄐㄧㄢˋ ㄒㄧㄠˋ ㄩˊ ㄉㄚˋ ㄈㄤ ㄓ ㄐㄧㄚ)
to become a laughingstock of the learned people

見賢思齊(ㄐㄧㄢˋ ㄒㄧㄢˊ ㄙ ㄑㄧˊ)
to see the virtuous and think of equaling or emulating them

見信(ㄐㄧㄢˋ ㄒㄧㄣˋ)
upon reading the letter

見證(ㄐㄧㄢˋ ㄓㄥˋ)
①to bear witness ②(in a criminal case) an eyewitness

見黜(ㄐㄧㄢˋ ㄔㄨˋ)

to be rejected or dismissed; to be discharged or degraded

見世面(ㄐㄧㄢˋ ㄕˋ ㄇㄧㄢˋ)
to see the world; to enrich one's experience

見識(ㄐㄧㄢˋ ㄕˋ)
① knowledge and experience; scope; sense: 他富有見識。 He has plenty of sense. ②to experience (something new)

見識識(ㄐㄧㄢˋ ㄕˋ ㄐㄧㄢˋ ㄕˋ)
to experience or see (something new)

見殺(ㄐㄧㄢˋ ㄕㄚ)
to be killed or murdered

見說(ㄐㄧㄢˋ ㄕㄨㄛ)
It is learned…. 或 It is heard…. 或 It is said,…

見人(ㄐㄧㄢˋ ㄖㄣˊ)
to meet people; to appear in public

見字(ㄐㄧㄢˋ ㄗˋ)
upon reading this letter

見責(ㄐㄧㄢˋ ㄗㄜˊ)
to be blamed; to be reprimanded

見罪(ㄐㄧㄢˋ ㄗㄨㄟˋ)
to get the blame

見財起意(ㄐㄧㄢˋ ㄘㄞˊ ㄑㄧˇ ㄧˋ)
to have evil thoughts at the sight of riches

見死不救(ㄐㄧㄢˋ ㄙˇ ㄅㄨˋ ㄐㄧㄡˋ)
to see someone in mortal danger without lifting a finger to save him

見色不亂(ㄐㄧㄢˋ ㄙㄜˋ ㄅㄨˋ ㄌㄨㄢˋ)
to harbor no lustful thought in the presence of a beauty

見異思遷(ㄐㄧㄢˋ ㄧˋ ㄙ ㄑㄧㄢ)
easily moved by what one sees or hears; easily swinged by changing conditions; unstable; unfaithful

見義勇為(ㄐㄧㄢˋ ㄧˋ ㄩㄥˇ ㄨㄟˊ)
to have the courage to do what is right regardless of consequences; to act heroically

見外(ㄐㄧㄢˋ ㄨㄞˋ)
to treat as an outsider

見危致命(ㄐㄧㄢˋ ㄨㄟ ㄓˋ ㄇㄧㄥˋ)or 見

危授命(ㄐㄧㄢˋ ㄨㄟ ㄕㄡˋ ㄇㄧㄥˋ)
to be ready to die for one's country in times of a national crisis

見聞(ㄐㄧㄢˋ ㄨㄣˊ)
what one has seen and heard—experience; knowledge; information: 他見聞不廣。He has only limited knowledge.

見聞廣博(ㄐㄧㄢˋ ㄨㄣˊ ㄍㄨㄤˇ ㄅㄛˊ)
experienced and knowledge-able; to have seen much of the world and heard of a lot of things

見聞有限(ㄐㄧㄢˋ ㄨㄣˊ ㄧㄡˇ ㄒㄧㄢˋ)
to have limited experience and knowledge

【見】 5481
2.(現) ㄒㄧㄢˋ shiann
xiàn

1. to appear; to be visible
2. to introduce

四畫

【規】 5482
《ㄍㄨㄟ guei guī

1. regulations; laws; rules; customs or usages: 你須遵守規規。You must obey the rules of the school.
2. a pair of compasses
3. to plan; to scheme
4. to advise so as to correct; to admonish
5. (now rarely) to copy; to imitate

規避(《ㄍㄨㄟ ㄅㄧˋ)
to evade (obligations or duties); to shun or avoid: 不可規避問題的實質。Don't evade the substance of the issue.

規模(《ㄍㄨㄟ ㄇㄛˊ)
①patterns; formulas ②scale; magnitude; scope; extent

規模宏大(《ㄍㄨㄟ ㄇㄛˊ ㄏㄨㄥˊ ㄉㄚˋ)
on a large scale

規範(《ㄍㄨㄟ ㄈㄢˋ)
a norm; a standard: 他的行為合乎規範。His behavior conforms to the standard.

規費(《ㄍㄨㄟ ㄈㄟˋ)
fees paid to government agencies or court

規復(《ㄍㄨㄟ ㄈㄨˋ)

to return to normalcy or former conditions

規定《ㄍㄨㄟ ㄉㄧㄥ》
to rule; to specify; to stipulate; to prescribe; to regulate; rules or regulations: 他以規定的速度駕駛。He drove at the regulation speed.

規條《ㄍㄨㄟ ㄊㄧㄠ》
items of regulation; rules

規律《ㄍㄨㄟ ㄌㄩ》
① laws, rules or regulations; discipline ② regular; regularity

規律性《ㄍㄨㄟ ㄌㄩ ㄒㄧㄥ》
regularity: 季節變換具規律性。The seasons come and go with regularity.

規略《ㄍㄨㄟ ㄌㄩㄝ》
to plan and operate

規格《ㄍㄨㄟ ㄍㄜ》
specifications (of a manufactured item); standards; gauges: 這些產品不合規格。These products fell short of specifications.

規矩矩矩《ㄍㄨㄟ ㄍㄨㄟ ㄐㄩ ㄐㄩ》
① gentlemanlike; honest; polite ② well-behaved ③ orderly

規畫《ㄍㄨㄟ ㄏㄨㄚ》
① to map out or draw up (a plan) ② a plan or scheme: 他有一個長遠的規畫。He has a long-term scheme.

規誡《ㄍㄨㄟ ㄐㄧㄝ》
to admonish

規諫《ㄍㄨㄟ ㄐㄧㄢ》
to advise or admonish: 他規諫我說那是違法的事。He advised me that it was illegal.

規矩《ㄍㄨㄟ ㄐㄩ》
① rules; practices ② gentlemanlike; honest ③ well-behaved; well-disciplined ④ the compass and square

規矩準繩《ㄍㄨㄟ ㄐㄩ ㄓㄨㄣˇ ㄕㄥˊ》
a fixed rule or way

規求《ㄍㄨㄟ ㄑㄧㄡˊ》
greedy; avaricious

規勸《ㄍㄨㄟ ㄑㄩㄢˋ》
to admonish; to give friendly advice

規行矩步《ㄍㄨㄟ ㄒㄧㄥˊ ㄐㄩˇ ㄅㄨˋ》
to act strictly according to rules or accepted practices;

to follow the beaten track

規箴《ㄍㄨㄟ ㄓㄣ》
admonitions

規章《ㄍㄨㄟ ㄓㄤ》
rules; regulations

規正《ㄍㄨㄟ ㄓㄥˋ》
to advise so as to correct a mistake

規程《ㄍㄨㄟ ㄔㄥˊ》
regulations and rules

規則《ㄍㄨㄟ ㄗㄜˊ》
① a rule or regulation ② regular; fixed; inflexible

規則動詞《ㄍㄨㄟ ㄗㄜˊ ㄉㄨㄥˋ ㄘˊ》
(grammar) regular verbs

規約《ㄍㄨㄟ ㄩㄝ》
a covenant or an agreement among members of an organization

規圓矩方《ㄍㄨㄟ ㄩㄢˊ ㄐㄩˇ ㄈㄤ》
to adhere to rules strictly

【覓】 5483
（覓）ㄇㄧˋ　mih. mî
to seek; to search or look for

覓保《ㄇㄧˋ ㄅㄠˇ》
to find a guarantor

覓得《ㄇㄧˋ ㄉㄜˊ》
to find what one has been looking for

覓句《ㄇㄧˋ ㄐㄩˋ》
to find a good line (for a poem)

覓索《ㄇㄧˋ ㄙㄨㄛˇ》
to seek or search for

五畫

【覘】 5484
ㄓㄢ　jan zhān
to spy on; to see; to observe; to inspect; to investigate secretly

覘國《ㄓㄢ ㄍㄨㄛˊ》
to inspect and survey conditions within a nation

覘候《ㄓㄢ ㄏㄡˋ》
to spy on; to look out for

【視】 5485
ㄕˋ　shyh shì
1. to look at; to observe; to inspect; to see; to watch
2. to consider or regard as; to take it for; to look upon as: 他視她如仇敵。He looks upon her as his enemy.
3. to compare; to be equivalent

to
4. (now rarely) to show 亦作「示」
5. (now rarely) to receive (a present, etc.)
6. to take as a model; to imitate

視半徑《ㄕˋ ㄅㄢˋ ㄐㄧㄥˋ》
(astronomy) an apparent semidiameter

視民如傷《ㄕˋ ㄇㄧㄣˊ ㄖㄨˊ ㄕㄤ》
to take good care of the people as if they were patients

視端容寂《ㄕˋ ㄉㄨㄢ ㄖㄨㄥˊ ㄐㄧˊ》
to look serious and quiet

視聽《ㄕˋ ㄊㄧㄥ》
① what one saw and heard; knowledge and experience ② public opinion ③ audio-visual

視聽教具《ㄕˋ ㄊㄧㄥ ㄐㄧㄠˋ ㄐㄩˋ》
audio-visual aids

視聽教育《ㄕˋ ㄊㄧㄥ ㄐㄧㄠˋ ㄩˋ》
audio-visual education

視聽言動《ㄕˋ ㄊㄧㄥ ㄧㄢˊ ㄉㄨㄥˋ》
to see, hear, talk and move

視同路人《ㄕˋ ㄊㄨㄥˊ ㄌㄨˋ ㄖㄣˊ》
to treat as outsiders or strangers

視同具文《ㄕˋ ㄊㄨㄥˊ ㄐㄩˋ ㄨㄣˊ》
to regard as mere empty words

視同兒戲《ㄕˋ ㄊㄨㄥˊ ㄦˊ ㄒㄧˋ》
to take it lightly; to regard it as unimportant; to trifle; to treat (a serious matter) as a trifle: 你不應該把你的健康視同兒戲。You should not trifle with your health.

視同一體《ㄕˋ ㄊㄨㄥˊ ㄧˋ ㄊㄧˇ》
to make no distinction; to accord the same treatment to all; to be impartial

視力《ㄕˋ ㄌㄧˋ》
the visual faculty; eyesight; the power of vision: 他視力差。His vision is poor.

視力表《ㄕˋ ㄌㄧˋ ㄅㄧㄠˇ》
an eye chart

視力計《ㄕˋ ㄌㄧˋ ㄐㄧˋ》
an optometer

視官《ㄕˋ ㄍㄨㄢ》
the organ of vision

視界《ㄕˋ ㄐㄧㄝˋ》
the field or range of vision

視角《ㄕˋ ㄐㄧㄠˇ》

〔見部〕

（見部）

視覺(ㄕ ㄐㄩㄝˊ)
(physics) the visual angle

視覺(ㄕ ㄐㄩㄝˊ)
the sense of sight; visual sensation; vision: 他有很敏銳的視覺。 He has a keen sense of sight.

視覺器(ㄕ ㄐㄩㄝˊ ㄑ`ㄧ)
an organ of sight

視覺型(ㄕ ㄐㄩㄝˊ ㄒㄧㄥˊ)
(psychology) the visual type

視覺暫留(ㄕ ㄐㄩㄝˊ ㄓㄢˋ ㄌㄧㄡˊ)
persistence of vision

視線(ㄕ ㄒㄧㄢˋ)
①the line of vision or sight —the straight line between an object and one's eyes ② eyesight: 這房子在視線以內。 The house is within eye-sight.

視差(ㄕ ㄔㄚ)
(astronomy) the parallax

視察(ㄕ ㄔㄚˊ)
to inspect; to observe; to see or examine: 他們在視察公共工程。 They were inspecting public works.

視察團(ㄕ ㄔㄚˊ ㄊㄨㄢˊ)
an inspection team; a study group

視事(ㄕ ㄕˋ)
①to administer; to govern or rule ②to be installed or inaugurated; to be sworn in

視神經(ㄕ ㄕㄣˊ ㄐㄧㄥ)
the optic nerve

視如敝屣(ㄕ ㄖㄨˊ ㄅㄧˋ ㄒㄧˇ)
to regard as worn-out shoes; to throw away as worthless

視如己出(ㄕ ㄖㄨˊ ㄐㄧˇ ㄔㄨ)
to treat a child as if he (she) were one's own

視如草芥(ㄕ ㄖㄨˊ ㄘㄠˇ ㄐㄧㄝˋ)
to regard as worthless

視若無睹(ㄕ ㄖㄨㄛˋ ㄨˊ ㄉㄨˇ)
to be undisturbed by what one has seen

視死如歸(ㄕ ㄙˇ ㄖㄨˊ ㄍㄨㄟ)
to look upon death as going home—fearless and daunt-less

視而不見(ㄕ ㄦˊ ㄅㄨˋ ㄐㄧㄢˋ)
(literally) to look but see nothing—absent-minded; to ignore

視野(ㄕ ㄧㄝˇ)
the field of vision; visual field

視為(ㄕ ㄨㄟˊ)
to regard or consider as: 她把他視為傻瓜。 She regarded him as a fool.

視網膜炎(ㄕ ㄨㄤˇ ㄇㄛˊ ㄧㄢˊ)
retinitis

七畫

【覡】 5486
ㄒㄧˊ　shyi　xí
a wizard

八畫

【覥】 5487
(覥) ㄊㄧㄢˇ　tean　tiǎn
ashamed 參看「覥覥」

九畫

【覦】 5488
ㄩˊ　yu　yú
a strong desire for possession; to covet 參看「覬覦」

【覩】 5489
(睹) ㄉㄨˇ　duu　dǔ
to see; to gaze at; to observe; to witness

覩物思人(ㄉㄨˇ ㄨˋ ㄙ ㄖㄣˊ)
to think of someone who is dead or far away upon seeing something he left behind

【親】 5490
1. ㄑㄧㄣ　chin　qīn
1. parents: 他的雙親都很健康。 His parents are quite well.
2. relatives: 我們有很多親戚。 We have many relatives.
3. to love; intimate; near to; dear
4. personally; personal; in person; self
5. to kiss: 她親這小男孩一下。 She kissed the little boy.

親筆(ㄑㄧㄣ ㄅㄧˇ)
one's own handwriting; to write personally

親筆信(ㄑㄧㄣ ㄅㄧˇ ㄒㄧㄣˋ)
a letter in one's own hand-writing; an autograph letter

親兵(ㄑㄧㄣ ㄅㄧㄥ)
bodyguards

親朋(ㄑㄧㄣ ㄆㄥˊ)
relatives and friends

親密(ㄑㄧㄣ ㄇㄧˋ)
intimate; intimacy; close: 我和他是極為親密的朋友。 I am

on intimate terms with him.

親母(ㄑㄧㄣ ㄇㄨˇ)
①one's own mother, who is a concubine ②one's own mother (as distinct from a foster mother or step-mother)

親夫(ㄑㄧㄣ ㄈㄨ)
one's own husband

親父(ㄑㄧㄣ ㄈㄨˋ)
one's own father (as distinct from a foster father or step-father)

親等(ㄑㄧㄣ ㄉㄥˇ)
(law) the degree of kinship

親爹(ㄑㄧㄣ ㄉㄧㄝ)
one's own father (as distinct from a stepfather)

親痛仇快(ㄑㄧㄣ ㄊㄨㄥˋ ㄔㄡˊ ㄎㄨㄞˋ)
(said of a mistake, blunder, etc.) to pain one's friends and please one's enemies

親暱(ㄑㄧㄣ ㄋㄧˋ)
intimate; very dear to; affec-tionate: 這是個親暱的稱呼。 This is an affectionate form of address.

親娘(ㄑㄧㄣ ㄋㄧㄤˊ)
one's own mother (as dis-tinct from a foster mother or stepmother)

親歷其境(ㄑㄧㄣ ㄌㄧˋ ㄑㄧˊ ㄐㄧㄥˋ)
to go through the whole thing personally; to be on the spot or scene in person; to experience personally

親臨(ㄑㄧㄣ ㄌㄧㄣˊ)
(said of a superior or elder) to arrive personally

親告罪(ㄑㄧㄣ ㄍㄠˋ ㄗㄨㄟˋ)
offenses that can be prose-cuted only upon the complaint of the aggrieved party

親骨肉(ㄑㄧㄣ ㄍㄨˇ ㄖㄡˋ)
(literally) one's own flesh and blood—the ties between parents and children

親故(ㄑㄧㄣ ㄍㄨˋ) or 親舊(ㄑㄧㄣ ㄐㄧㄡˋ)
relatives and old friends

親供(ㄑㄧㄣ ㄍㄨㄥˋ)
to confess in person; a per-sonal confession

親口(ㄑㄧㄣ ㄎㄡˇ)
(said of words, etc.) right from one's own mouth; to state or tell personally

親和力(くｌㄣㄏㄜˊㄌㄧˋ)
①(chemistry) affinity ②
affability; amiability

親姊妹(くｌㄣㄐㄧㄝˇㄇㄟˋ)
sisters born of the same parents

親交(くｌㄣㄐㄧㄠ)
①to deliver (a letter, etc.)
personally ②intimate friendship

親見(くｌㄣㄐㄧㄢˋ)
to have seen in person

親近(くｌㄣㄐㄧㄣˋ)
to be near to or intimate
with; to be close to

親眷(くｌㄣㄐㄩㄢˋ)
family members

親啓(くｌㄣㄑㄧˇ)
(said of a letter) to be
opened personally; confidential

親戚(くｌㄣ‧ㄑㄧ)
relatives: 他們是我的親戚。
They are my relatives.

親切(くｌㄣㄑㄧㄝˋ)
intimately; cordially; kind:
她對我親切。 She was kind to
me.

親權(くｌㄣㄑㄩㄢˊ)
the right to assume guardianship for one's own children before they come of
age; parental authority

親狎(くｌㄣㄒㄧㄚˊ)
close and intimate

親信(くｌㄣㄒㄧㄣˋ)
a confidant; an intimate; a
trusted subordinate, etc.

親兄弟(くｌㄣㄒㄩㄥㄉㄧˋ)
brothers born of the same
parents

親兄弟明算賬(くｌㄣㄒㄩㄥㄉㄧˋㄇㄧㄥˊㄙㄨㄢˋㄓㄤˋ)
Financial matters should be
settled clearly even between
brothers.

親炙(くｌㄣㄓˋ)
(a polite expression) personally receive your admonishment, instructions, etc.

親展(くｌㄣㄓㄢˇ)
①to meet in person ②(a
confidential letter, etc.) to
be opened by the recipient
personally

親征(くｌㄣㄓㄥ)
(said of a king or an emper-or) to lead an army personally to war

親政(くｌㄣㄓㄥˋ)
(said of a young king) to
take over the administration
or government from a regent upon coming of age

親事(くｌㄣㄕˋ)
①(くｌㄣㄕˋ) to attend to personally
②(くｌㄣ‧ㄕ) marriage

親手(くｌㄣㄕㄡˇ)
personally; with one's own
hands

親善(くｌㄣㄕㄢˋ)
friendship or goodwill

親身(くｌㄣㄕㄣ)
personally; in person

親上加親(くｌㄣㄕㄤˋㄐㄧㄚㄑㄧㄣ)
to cement old ties by marriage, as a marriage between
cousins, etc.

親生父母(くｌㄣㄕㄥㄈㄨˋㄇㄨˇ)
one's own parents (as distinct from foster parents or
stepparents)

親生子女(くｌㄣㄕㄥㄗˇㄋㄩˇ)
one's own children (as distinct from adopted children)

親疎(くｌㄣㄕㄨ)
dear ones and indifferent
persons; intimacy and remoteness

親屬(くｌㄣㄕㄨˇ)
relatives; family members

親率(くｌㄣㄕㄨㄞˋ)
to lead personally (an army,
a group of welcomers, a
troupe, etc.)

親熱(くｌㄣㄖㄜˋ)
very dear; very intimate;
very much in love

親人(くｌㄣㄖㄣˊ)
close relatives—as one's parents, brothers, spouse, children, etc.

親任(くｌㄣㄖㄣˋ)
one's confidants

親子(くｌㄣㄗˇ)
one's own son (as distinct
from an adopted son)

親自(くｌㄣㄗˋ)
personally; in person: 他親自
拜訪。 He made a personal
call.

親自出馬(くｌㄣㄗˋㄔㄨㄇㄚˇ)
to go out and take care of

something in person; to confront (the enemy, etc.) personally

親族(くｌㄣㄗㄨˊ)
one's kinsmen; members of
the same clan

親嘴(くｌㄣㄗㄨㄟˇ)
to kiss

親裁(くｌㄣㄘㄞˊ)
to decide personally

親隨(くｌㄣㄙㄨㄟˊ)
aides; entourages

親愛(くｌㄣㄞˋ)
love; affection; dear

親愛的(くｌㄣㄞˋ‧ㄉㄜ)
my dear; my darling

親愛精誠(くｌㄣㄞˋㄐㄧㄥㄔㄥˊ)
camaraderie; *esprit de corps*

親友(くｌㄣㄧㄡˇ)
friends and relatives: 他有許
多親友。 He has many relatives and friends.

親眼看見(くｌㄣㄧㄢˇㄎㄢˋㄐㄧㄢˋ)
to witness; to see with one's
own eyes: 他親眼看見那意外
事件。 He witnessed the accident.

親迎(くｌㄣㄧㄥˊ)
to receive or welcome (a
visitor, etc.) personally

親吻(くｌㄣㄨㄣˇ)
to kiss

親王(くｌㄣㄨㄤˊ)
① members of the royal
family who were conferred
dukedom or dubbed in ancient
times ② (a modern sense)
a prince

【親】 5490
2. くｌㄥˋ　chinq qing
relatives by marriage

親爹(くｌㄥˋㄉㄧㄝ)
a term of address by the
junior members of one of
the two families related by
marriage for a senior male
member of the other family

親家(くｌㄥˋㄐㄧㄚ)
①relatives as a result of
marriage ②parents of the
married couple

親家母(くｌㄥˋㄐㄧㄚㄇㄨˇ)
mother of one's daughter-in-
law or son-in-law

親家女兒(くｌㄥˋㄐㄧㄚㄋㄩˇㄦˊ)
a term of address for sisters
of one's daughter-in-law or

【見
‧
部】

son-in-law

親家老爺(ㄑㄧㄜ‧ㄐㄧㄚ ㄌㄠˇ ㄧㄝˊ)
a term of address for male
parents of the married couple

親家公(ㄑㄧㄜ‧ㄐㄧㄚ ㄍㄨㄥ)
father of one's daughter-in-
law or son-in-law

親家兒子(ㄑㄧㄜ‧ㄐㄧㄚ ㄦˊ‧ㄗ)
brothers of one's daughter-
in-law or son-in-law

十畫

【覬】 5491
ㄐㄧ ㄐㄧˋ
to covet; to desire for something belonging to others

覬覦
to covet, to desire something
belonging to others

【覯】 5492
ㄍㄡˋ gow gòu
to meet

十一畫

【覝】 5493
ㄐㄧㄢˇ jiin jǐn
（又讀 ㄐㄧㄣˋ jinn jìn）
to have an audience with a
chief of state

覝禮(ㄐㄧㄢˇ ㄌㄧˇ)
rituals performed during
audience

覝見(ㄐㄧㄢˇ ㄐㄧㄢˋ)
to have an audience with a
chief of state

【覷】 5494
（覰‧覻）ㄑㄩ chiuh qù
to spy on; to watch; to look;
to gaze

覷步(ㄑㄩˋ ㄅㄨˋ)
to spy on

覷著眼(ㄑㄩˋ ‧ㄓㄜ ㄧㄢˇ)
to narrow one's eyes and
gaze at something with great
attention

十二畫

【覶】 5495
（覶）ㄌㄨㄛˊ luo luó
to see carefully

覶縷(ㄌㄨㄛˊ ㄌㄩˇ)
to present (a case, etc.) in a
detailed and systematic way

十三畫

【覺】 5496
1. ㄐㄩㄝˊ jyue jué
1. to wake up from sleep
2. senses: 他有敏銳的嗅覺。He
has a keen sense of smell.
3. to be conscious of; to sense
4. to awaken; to realize; to discover: 他察覺到自己的危險。
He awoke to his danger.
5. to tell; to sense: 我感覺冷得很。
I feel so cold.
6. high, large, and straight

覺得(ㄐㄩㄝˊ‧ㄉㄜ)
①to be conscious of; to
realize; to sense ②to feel ③
to think; to be of the opinion

覺痛(ㄐㄩㄝˊ ㄊㄨㄥˋ)
to feel the sensation of pain

覺冷(ㄐㄩㄝˊ ㄌㄥˇ)
to feel cold

覺醒(ㄐㄩㄝˊ ㄒㄧㄥˇ)
to wake up

覺察(ㄐㄩㄝˊ ㄔㄚˊ)
to discover; to realize; to
detect; to be aware; to sense

覺書(ㄐㄩㄝˊ ㄕㄨ)
(diplomacy) a memorandum

覺熱(ㄐㄩㄝˊ ㄖㄜˋ)
to feel hot

覺癢(ㄐㄩㄝˊ ㄧㄤˇ)
to feel itchy

覺悟(ㄐㄩㄝˊ ㄨˋ)
to become aware; to realize;
to awake

【覺】 5496
2. ㄐㄧㄠˋ jiaw jiào
a sleep; a nap: 他熟睡了一覺。
He slept a sound sleep.

十四畫

【覽】 5497
ㄌㄢˇ laan lǎn
1. to look at; to sightsee
2. to read: 他博覽群書。He reads
widely.
3. to listen to (what others
say)
4. a Chinese family name

覽古(ㄌㄢˇ ㄍㄨˇ)
to tour ancient relics

覽揆(ㄌㄢˇ ㄎㄨㄟˊ)
one's birthday

覽勝(ㄌㄢˇ ㄕㄥˋ)
to tour a resort; to see or
visit a scenic spot

十五畫

【覿】 5498
ㄉㄧˊ dyi dí
to meet; to see each other

覿面(ㄉㄧˊ ㄇㄧㄢˋ)
to see each other; to meet

覿儀(ㄉㄧˊ ㄧˊ)
presents offered at a meeting

十八畫

【觀】 5499
1. ㄍㄨㄢ guan guān
1. to see; to observe; to behold;
to view; to take a view of;
to look; to inspect: 我們參觀
了世界博覽會。We saw the
World's Fair.
2. sights; views
3. to display
4. a point of view; a conception: 他的人生觀是錯誤的。He
has a wrong conception of
life.

觀兵(ㄍㄨㄢ ㄅㄧㄥ)
to review troops; to display
military might

觀摩(ㄍㄨㄢ ㄇㄛˊ)
to emulate the good points
of others; to compare notes

觀風(ㄍㄨㄢ ㄈㄥ)
①to look for opportunities
②to observe local customs
③to keep watch when a
robbery or larceny is being
committed by a confederate
or confederates

觀點(ㄍㄨㄢ ㄉㄧㄢˇ)
a point of view; one's view
on a certain matter; one's
ideas or opinions concerning
something

觀鼎(ㄍㄨㄢ ㄉㄧㄥˇ)
to covet the throne

觀臺(ㄍㄨㄢ ㄊㄞˊ)
an elevated stand or platform on which one can see
far and wide

觀念(ㄍㄨㄢ ㄋㄧㄢˋ)
a conception; an idea; a
view

觀念論(ㄍㄨㄢ ㄋㄧㄢˋ ㄌㄨㄣˋ)

idealism

觀禮（ㄍㄨㄢ ㄌㄧˇ）
to attend a celebration or ceremony

觀感（ㄍㄨㄢ ㄍㄢˇ）
one's feelings or emotional reactions after seeing or reading something

觀過知仁（ㄍㄨㄢ ㄍㄨㄛˋ ㄓ ㄖㄣˊ）
(originally from the *Analects*) After observing a person's faults and failings, one will understand what he really is.

觀光（ㄍㄨㄢ ㄍㄨㄤ）
sightseeing; to see the sights: 我喜歡觀光。I am fond of sightseeing.

觀光團（ㄍㄨㄢ ㄍㄨㄤ ㄊㄨㄢˊ）
a tour group; a tourist group

觀光旅館（ㄍㄨㄢ ㄍㄨㄤ ㄌㄩˇ ㄍㄨㄢˇ）
a tourist hotel

觀光客（ㄍㄨㄢ ㄍㄨㄤ ㄎㄜˋ）
a tourist

觀光事業（ㄍㄨㄢ ㄍㄨㄤ ㄕˋ ㄧㄝˋ）
tourism; the tourist industry

觀看（ㄍㄨㄢ ㄎㄢˋ）
to look at; to observe or inspect; to see

觀火（ㄍㄨㄢ ㄏㄨㄛˇ）
to see the fire—to view clearly

觀劇（ㄍㄨㄢ ㄐㄩˋ）
to see an opera; to watch a stage show

觀棋不語真君子（ㄍㄨㄢ ㄑㄧˊ ㄅㄨˋ ㄩˇ ㄓㄣ ㄐㄩㄣ ㄗˇ）
He is truly a gentleman who watches in silence a game of chess.

觀心術（ㄍㄨㄢ ㄒㄧㄣ ㄕㄨˋ）
the art of mind reading

觀釁（ㄍㄨㄢ ㄒㄧㄣˋ）
to look for an opportunity (to take action or start something)

觀象（ㄍㄨㄢ ㄒㄧㄤˋ）
to observe heavenly bodies; to watch celestial phenomena

觀象臺（ㄍㄨㄢ ㄒㄧㄤˋ ㄊㄞˊ）
an observatory

觀相知人（ㄍㄨㄢ ㄒㄧㄤˋ ㄓ ㄖㄣˊ）
to study a man's physiognomy and know his character

觀止（ㄍㄨㄢ ㄓˇ）
(literally) What one has seen is perfect.—good beyond comparison: 觀止! What perfection! 或 What an unrivaled sight!

觀者如堵（ㄍㄨㄢ ㄓㄜˇ ㄖㄨˊ ㄉㄨˇ）
The spectators formed a solid wall of humanity.

觀瞻（ㄍㄨㄢ ㄓㄢ）
①the appearance or outward look of something ②to look at; to see; to view

觀戰（ㄍㄨㄢ ㄓㄢˋ）
to witness a battle; to observe a military operation

觀眾（ㄍㄨㄢ ㄓㄨㄥˋ）
the audience or spectators: 這場球賽有很多觀眾。There were many spectators at the football match.

觀察（ㄍㄨㄢ ㄔㄚˊ）
to observe; to watch; to inspect; observation: 小心觀察你可以學到很多事。You can learn many things by careful observation.

觀察家（ㄍㄨㄢ ㄔㄚˊ ㄐㄧㄚ）
an observer; one who observes and makes comments on current events

觀潮（ㄍㄨㄢ ㄔㄠˊ）
to view a tide

觀賞（ㄍㄨㄢ ㄕㄤˇ）
to see and enjoy

觀賞植物（ㄍㄨㄢ ㄕㄤˇ ㄓˊ ㄨˋ）
garden plants; ornamental (or decorative) plants

觀測（ㄍㄨㄢ ㄘㄜˋ）
to observe and survey

觀測站（ㄍㄨㄢ ㄘㄜˋ ㄓㄢˋ）
an observation post

觀測員（ㄍㄨㄢ ㄘㄜˋ ㄩㄢˊ）
an observer (aboard an airplane or in an artillery unit)

觀音（ㄍㄨㄢ ㄧㄣ）or 觀世音（ㄍㄨㄢ ㄕˋ ㄧㄣ）or 觀音大士（ㄍㄨㄢ ㄧㄣ ㄉㄚˋ ㄕˋ）or 觀自在（ㄍㄨㄢ ㄗˋ ㄗㄞˋ）
the Goddess of Mercy; the feminine form of *Avalokitesvara Bodhisattva*

觀往知來（ㄍㄨㄢ ㄨㄤˇ ㄓ ㄌㄞˊ）
To review the past will enable one to predict the future.

觀望（ㄍㄨㄢ ㄨㄤˋ）
a wait-and-see attitude; to wait and see; to hesitate: 不要採取觀望態度。Don't take a wait-and-see attitude.

觀望不前（ㄍㄨㄢ ㄨㄤˋ ㄅㄨˋ ㄑㄧㄢˊ）
to hesitate and make no move

【觀】 5499
（ㄍㄨㄢ guann guàn）
a Taoist temple or shrine

角 部
ㄐㄩㄝˊ jyue · jué

【角】 5500
1. （ㄐㄧㄠˇ jeau jiǎo）
1. the horn of an animal
2. a direction; a corner
3. an angle
4. a tenth of a dollar; a 10-cent piece
5. something in the shape of a horn
6. a cape; a promontory

角皮（ㄐㄧㄠˇ ㄆㄧˊ）or 角質層（ㄐㄧㄠˇ ㄓˊ ㄘㄥˊ）or 角質膜（ㄐㄧㄠˇ ㄓˊ ㄇㄛˊ）
(botany) cuticle; cutin

角膜（ㄐㄧㄠˇ ㄇㄛˊ）
(anatomy) cornea

角膜炎（ㄐㄧㄠˇ ㄇㄛˊ ㄧㄢˊ）
keratitis

角度（ㄐㄧㄠˇ ㄉㄨˋ）
①an angle ②angular measure

角立（ㄐㄧㄠˇ ㄌㄧˋ）
①to stand out (without a peer) ②to become stalemated

角鋼（ㄐㄧㄠˇ ㄍㄤ）
(metallurgy) angle steel

角距（ㄐㄧㄠˇ ㄐㄩˋ）
(astronomy) an angular distance

角質（ㄐㄧㄠˇ ㄓˊ）
horny; corneous

角柱（ㄐㄧㄠˇ ㄓㄨˋ）
(mathematics) a prism

角錐體（ㄐㄧㄠˇ ㄓㄨㄟ ㄊㄧˇ）
(mathematics) a pyramid

角兒（ㄐㄧㄠˇ ㄦ）
①a corner ②a direction

角岩（ㄐㄧㄠˇ ㄧㄢˊ）
hornstone

〔角部〕

【角】 5500
2. 讀音ㄐㄩㄝ jyue jué

1. to compete; to contest; to wrestle
2. a corner
3. an ancient, three-legged wine-cup
4. a dramatic role; a character
5. one of the five musical notes in ancient Chinese music

角觝 or 角抵(ㄐㄩㄝ ㄉㄧˇ)
to wrestle or wrestling—as a sport

角樓(ㄐㄩㄝ ㄌㄡˊ)
an attic

角力(ㄐㄩㄝ ㄌㄧˋ)
a contest in strength; to wrestle; wrestling

角力者(ㄐㄩㄝ ㄌㄧˋ ㄓㄜˇ)
a wrestler

角力場(ㄐㄩㄝ ㄌㄧˋ ㄔㄤˇ)
a palaestra; a ring for wrestling

角落(ㄐㄩㄝ ㄌㄨㄛˋ)or(ㄐㄩㄝ ㄌㄚˋ)
a corner; a nook: 喜訊傳遍全國各個角落。The good news spread to every corner of the country.

角巾(ㄐㄩㄝ ㄐㄧㄣ)
clothing for the retired or hermits in ancient times

角巾私第(ㄐㄩㄝ ㄐㄧㄣ ㄙ ㄉㄧˋ)
to live in retirement; to lead a hermit's life

角逐(ㄐㄩㄝ ㄓㄨˊ)
to contest (for a post, etc.); to jockey (for position); to struggle for hegemony

角試(ㄐㄩㄝ ㄕˋ)
(in old China) a contest in martial arts

角色(ㄐㄩㄝ ㄙㄜˋ)
a role; a character

角兒(ㄐㄩㄝ ㄦˊ)
(Chinese Opera) a player

【角】 3.ㄌㄨˋ luh lù
參見「角里」

角里(ㄌㄨˋ ㄌㄧˇ)
① name of a place southwest of Soochow, Kiangsu Province ② a Chinese family name

二畫

【觔】 5501 ㄐㄧㄣ jin jīn

1. sinews or muscular strength 亦作「筋」
2. a catty, equivalent to 1.10231 pounds

觔斗(ㄐㄧㄣ ㄉㄡˇ)
a somersault: 我在草地上翻觔斗。I turned a somersault on the lawn.

四畫

【觖】 5502 ㄐㄩㄝ jyue jué
dissatisfied; discontented; not satisfactory

觖望(ㄐㄩㄝ ㄨㄤˋ)
to bear animus as a result of dissatisfaction; to harbor (or nurse) a grudge

五畫

【觚】 5503 ㄍㄨ gu gū

1. an ancient wine vessel; a beaker or goblet
2. a corner; an angle; angular
3. a rule
4. a square
5. correspondence or a file, etc.

觚牘(ㄍㄨ ㄉㄨˊ)
correspondence

觚稜(ㄍㄨ ㄌㄥˊ)
the tile ridge at the corner of a roof

【觝】 5504 ㄉㄧˇ dii dǐ
to butt; to resist; to push

觝排(ㄉㄧˇ ㄆㄞˊ)
to reject; to get rid of

六畫

【解】 5505 1.ㄐㄧㄝˇ jiee jiě

1. to unfasten; to untie; to loosen; to undo
2. to solve (difficult problems, etc.)
3. to explain; to clarify; to interpret; explanation; interpretation
4. to understand
5. ideas; views
6. to break up, separate or disperse
7. to take off; to strip; to remove (clothing, etc.); to get rid of
8. to relieve; to alleviate (pain, etc.)
9. to cut apart; to dissect
10. to dissolve
11. to discharge (water, etc.); to defecate

解剖(ㄐㄧㄝˇ ㄆㄡ)
① to dissect; dissection; anatomization ② to analyze; analysis

解剖刀(ㄐㄧㄝˇ ㄆㄡ ㄉㄠ)
a scalpel; a dissecting knife

解剖學(ㄐㄧㄝˇ ㄆㄡ ㄒㄩㄝˊ)
anatomy: 他在醫學院研究解剖學。He studied anatomy in medical school.

解剖室(ㄐㄧㄝˇ ㄆㄡ ㄕˋ)
a dissecting room

解聘(ㄐㄧㄝˇ ㄆㄧㄣˋ)
to relieve one of his duties; to dismiss or discharge a person from his post

解悶兒(ㄐㄧㄝˇ ㄇㄣˋㄦ)
to kill time; to dispel loneliness; to get rid of boredom

解民倒懸(ㄐㄧㄝˇ ㄇㄧㄣˊ ㄉㄠˇ ㄒㄩㄢˊ)
to liberate the people from tyranny

解紛(ㄐㄧㄝˇ ㄈㄣ)
to resolve a dispute; to disentangle

解放(ㄐㄧㄝˇ ㄈㄤˋ)
to untie or set free; to liberate; liberation

解放區(ㄐㄧㄝˇ ㄈㄤˋ ㄑㄩ)
a liberated area; an area liberated from enemy occupation

解答(ㄐㄧㄝˇ ㄉㄚˊ)
explanations or answers to certain questions; to answer or explain

解毒(ㄐㄧㄝˇ ㄉㄨˊ)
to detoxify; to neutralize poison; to antidote; detoxication

解毒劑(ㄐㄧㄝˇ ㄉㄨˊ ㄐㄧˋ)or解毒藥(ㄐㄧㄝˇ ㄉㄨˊ ㄧㄠˋ)
an antidote

解凍(ㄐㄧㄝˇ ㄉㄨㄥˋ)
① to thaw: 魚已解凍了。The fish has thawed. ② to unfreeze (funds, assets, etc.)

解題(ㄐㄧㄝˇㄊㄧˊ)
explanation or answer to a problem or subject

解體(ㄐㄧㄝˇㄊㄧˇ)
disintegration; dissolution; to disintegrate; to fall apart; to take apart; to dismember

解脫(ㄐㄧㄝˇㄊㄨㄛ)
to free oneself from worldly worries; to get rid of shackles; to extricate

解囊(ㄐㄧㄝˇㄋㄤˊ)
to untie one's purse strings —to contribute money to charities

解纜(ㄐㄧㄝˇㄌㄢˋ)or 解維(ㄐㄧㄝˇㄨㄟˊ)
to weigh anchor; to leave port or set sail

解鈴繫鈴(ㄐㄧㄝˇㄌㄧㄥˊㄒㄧˋㄌㄧㄥˊ)
(literally) He who tied the bell on the tiger's neck is the only one to untie it.—He who caused the dispute is the only one to resolve it.

解詁(ㄐㄧㄝˇㄍㄨˋ)
explanatory notes for ancient classics; to explain ancient classics in modern language

解故(ㄐㄧㄝˇㄍㄨˋ)
①explanatory notes for ancient classics; to explain ancient classics in modern language ②to explain one's conduct, etc.

解雇(ㄐㄧㄝˇㄍㄨˋ)
to get fired; to fire; to dismiss; to discharge

解渴(ㄐㄧㄝˇㄎㄜˇ)
to quench thirst; to allay thirst

解開(ㄐㄧㄝˇㄎㄞ)
to untie; to unbind; to loosen; to undo

解扣兒(ㄐㄧㄝˇㄎㄡˋㄦ)
①to unbutton ②to resolve a dispute

解和(ㄐㄧㄝˇㄏㄜˊ)
to resolve a dispute; to mediate

解恨(ㄐㄧㄝˇㄏㄣˋ)
to feel satisfied or avenged; to slake one's hatred

解惑(ㄐㄧㄝˇㄏㄨㄛˋ)
to remove doubts

解甲歸田(ㄐㄧㄝˇㄐㄧㄚˇㄍㄨㄟㄊㄧㄢˊ)
(literally) to take off the armor and return to the farm—to quit military service and resume civilian life; to be demobilized

解酒(ㄐㄧㄝˇㄐㄧㄡˇ)
to neutralize the effect of alcoholic drinks; to alleviate a hangover

解救(ㄐㄧㄝˇㄐㄧㄡˋ)
to deliver (the people from tyranny, etc.); to rescue

解決(ㄐㄧㄝˇㄐㄩㄝˊ)
①to settle (a dispute, fight, etc.); to solve (a problem) ②to dispose of; to finish off

解決辦法(ㄐㄧㄝˇㄐㄩㄝˊㄅㄢˋㄈㄚˇ)
a solution (of a problem)

解氣(ㄐㄧㄝˇㄑㄧˋ)
to pacify; to placate; to ease anger

解勸(ㄐㄧㄝˇㄑㄩㄢˋ)
to pacify; to appease (an angry person, etc.); to mediate (a dispute, etc.); to patch up

解析(ㄐㄧㄝˇㄒㄧ)
to analyze; analysis

解析幾何(ㄐㄧㄝˇㄒㄧㄐㄧˇㄏㄜˊ)
analytic geometry

解職(ㄐㄧㄝˇㄓˊ)
to relieve someone of his duties; to dismiss or fire from office

解裝(ㄐㄧㄝˇㄓㄨㄤ)
(literally) to take off one's traveling clothes—to take a rest

解嘲(ㄐㄧㄝˇㄔㄠˊ)
to offer an explanation to save one's own face

解饞(ㄐㄧㄝˇㄔㄢˊ)
to satisfy a desire for delicious food

解酲(ㄐㄧㄝˇㄔㄥˊ)
to alleviate a hangover

解除(ㄐㄧㄝˇㄔㄨˊ)
①to annul or cancel (a contract, agreement, etc.) ②(law) to restore to the original status ③to fire (a person); to relieve (a person of his duties, etc.) ④to remove (restrictions); to get rid of

解除婚約(ㄐㄧㄝˇㄔㄨˊㄏㄨㄣㄩㄝ)
to renounce an engagement

解除警報(ㄐㄧㄝˇㄔㄨˊㄐㄧㄥˇㄅㄠˋ)
a siren signaling "all clear"

解除武裝(ㄐㄧㄝˇㄔㄨˊㄨˇㄓㄨㄤ)
to disarm

解釋(ㄐㄧㄝˇㄕˋ)
to explain; explanation; to analyze; to expound; to interpret; to account for

解事(ㄐㄧㄝˇㄕˋ)
clever and understanding

解手(ㄐㄧㄝˇㄕㄡˇ)
①to separate ②to relieve nature; to relieve oneself ③to let go; to loosen one's grip on something

解手兒(ㄐㄧㄝˇㄕㄡˇㄦ)or 解溲(ㄐㄧㄝˇㄙㄡ)
to urinate or empty the bowels

解綬(ㄐㄧㄝˇㄕㄡˋ)
to resign from public office

解說(ㄐㄧㄝˇㄕㄨㄛ)
①to explain ②to appease; to resolve (a dispute, etc.)

解熱劑(ㄐㄧㄝˇㄖㄜˋㄐㄧˋ)
antipyretic; antipyrin(e)

解人(ㄐㄧㄝˇㄖㄣˊ)
a clever and understanding person; an intelligent person

解葷(ㄐㄧㄝˇㄏㄨㄣ)
to resume eating animal food after a period of a vegetarian diet

解散(ㄐㄧㄝˇㄙㄢˋ)
①to dismiss (a group of soldiers in drill) ②to dissolve (a parliament, etc.); to disband (an organization, a gang, etc.)

解衣(ㄐㄧㄝˇㄧ)
to disrobe; to strip; to remove one's clothes; to undress

解衣推食(ㄐㄧㄝˇㄧㄊㄨㄟ ㄕˊ)
(literally) to give one's own clothes and food to others —compassionate; to treat others with friendship and sincerity

解顏(ㄐㄧㄝˇㄧㄢˊ)or 解顏(ㄐㄧㄝˇㄧㄢˊ)
to laugh; to smile

解憂(ㄐㄧㄝˇㄧㄡ)
to alleviate sorrow; to relieve worries

解嚴(ㄐㄧㄝˇㄧㄢˊ)
to announce martial law ended

解悟(ㄐㄧㄝˇㄨˋ)

〔角部〕

〔角部〕

to realize; to understand

解危（ㄐㄧㄝˇ ㄨㄟ）
to head off danger

解圍（ㄐㄧㄝˇ ㄨㄟˊ）
① to resolve difficulties for others; to save others from embarrassment, etc. ② to force an enemy to raise a siege

解網（ㄐㄧㄝˇ ㄨㄤˇ）
to let loose one end of the net—merciful or lenient

解語花（ㄐㄧㄝˇ ㄩˇ ㄏㄨㄚ）
a beautiful woman

解約（ㄐㄧㄝˇ ㄩㄝ）
① to annul a contract or agreement ② to annul a marital engagement

【解】 5505
2. ㄐㄧㄝ jieh jiè
to escort (prisoners, goods, etc.) from one place to another; to forward; to send someone in custody to; to dispatch

解差（ㄐㄧㄝ ㄔㄞ）
① to send prisoners from one place to another under escort ② guardsmen escorting prisoners from one place to another

解送（ㄐㄧㄝ ㄙㄨㄥ）
to transfer (a prisoner) under escort; to send (a criminal) under guard

解元（ㄐㄧㄝˇ ㄩㄢˊ）
the top candidate of the former civil service examination held on the provincial level

【解】 5505
3. ㄒㄧㄝˋ shieh xiè
a Chinese family name

【觥】 5506
《ㄨㄥ gong gòng
1. a wine vessel made of horn in ancient times
2. big; great

觥觥（《ㄨㄥ 《ㄨㄥ）
straightforward; honest; upright

觥籌交錯（《ㄨㄥ ㄔㄡ ㄐㄧㄠ ㄘㄨㄛˋ）
to drink together noisily in a large party: 賓客觥籌交錯。The guests drank together noisily in the party.

觥船（《ㄨㄥ ㄔㄨㄢˊ）
a big wine vessel

觟羊（ㄒㄩㄝˋ ㄧㄤˊ）
a large sheep

七畫

【觫】 5507
ㄙㄨˋ suh sù
to shrink and tremble in fear

八畫

【觭】 5508
ㄐㄧ ji jī
1. (said of horns of an animal) one turning up and one turning down
2. to obtain; to get
3. odd (as contrasted to even) 亦作「奇」

觭夢（ㄐㄧ ㄇㄥˋ）
a strange dream; what one gets in a dream

觭輪（ㄐㄧ ㄌㄨㄣˊ）
a single wheel

觭偶（ㄐㄧ ㄡˇ）
odd and even 亦作「奇偶」

九畫

【觱】 5509
ㄅㄧˋ bih bì
1. a chilly wind
2. water emerging from ground

觱發（ㄅㄧˋ ㄈㄚ）
a chilly wind

觱沸（ㄅㄧˋ ㄈㄟˋ）
spring water bubbling

觱篥 or 觱栗（ㄅㄧˋ ㄌㄧˋ）
an ancient windpipe musical instrument, shaped roughly like a trumpet

十畫

【觳】 5510
1. ㄏㄨˊ hwu hú
1. a measure for volume in ancient times
2. to shrink and tremble in fear

觳觫（ㄏㄨˊ ㄙㄨˋ）
shrinking and trembling in fear; the appearance of fearing death

【觳】 5510
2. ㄐㄩㄝˊ chiueh guè

1. barren, unproductive (land
2. simple and crude

觳土（ㄐㄩㄝˊ ㄊㄨˇ）
barren land

十一畫

【觴】 5511
ㄕㄤ shang shāng
1. a general name of all sor of wine vessels
2. to offer drinks to others

觴豆（ㄕㄤ ㄉㄡˋ）
wine vessels and food containers—wine and food

觴令（ㄕㄤ ㄌㄧㄥˋ）or 觴政（ㄕㄤ ㄓㄥˋ）
wine-drinking games conducted by an elected leader

觴詠（ㄕㄤ ㄩㄥˋ）
to compose or chant poem while drinking

十三畫

【觸】 5512
ㄔㄨˋ chuh chù
1. to touch; to contact: 油漆乾, 請勿觸摸。Don't touch th paint; it's wet.
2. (said of an animal) to ra with the horn; to ram; to butt
3. to move or touch emotion ally
4. to offend; to infuriate

觸媒（ㄔㄨˋ ㄇㄟˊ）
a catalyst; a catalyzer; catalytic agent

觸媒作用（ㄔㄨˋ ㄇㄟˊ ㄗㄨㄛˋ ㄩㄥˋ）
catalysis

觸霉頭（ㄔㄨˋ ㄇㄟˊ ㄊㄡˊ）
to have a stroke of ba luck; to be unfortunate

觸目皆是（ㄔㄨˋ ㄇㄨˋ ㄐㄧㄝ ㄕˋ）
can be seen everywhere very common

觸目驚心（ㄔㄨˋ ㄇㄨˋ ㄐㄧㄥ ㄒㄧㄣ）
frightening; bloodcurdling; shocking; emotionally dis turbed (by a sight)

觸發（ㄔㄨˋ ㄈㄚ）
① to touch off (a war, dis pute, etc.) ② to move o touch (one's feelings)

觸犯（ㄔㄨˋ ㄈㄢˋ）
① to offend; to incur the dis pleasure of ② to violate o

infringe (regulations, rules, etc.)

觸電(ㄔㄨ ㄉㄧㄢ)
an electric shock; to get an electric shock

觸動(ㄔㄨ ㄉㄨㄥ)
① to touch something, and move it slightly ② to move one's heart

觸怒(ㄔㄨ ㄋㄨˋ)
to infuriate; to offend and cause anger

觸雷(ㄔㄨ ㄌㄟˊ)
(said of ships) to hit a floating mine; (said of foot soldiers) to step on a land mine

觸類旁通(ㄔㄨ ㄌㄟˋ ㄆㄤˊ ㄊㄨㄥ)
to draw an analogy; to understand by means of inference processes

觸感(ㄔㄨ ㄍㄢˇ)
the tactile impression

觸官(ㄔㄨ ㄍㄨㄢ)
the organ of touch or feeling

觸機(ㄔㄨ ㄐㄧ)
to inspire a stroke of genius; to have a brainstorm

觸擊(ㄔㄨ ㄐㄧ)
(baseball) a bunt

觸礁(ㄔㄨ ㄐㄧㄠ)
① to strike a submerged reef; to run aground ② to hit a snag; to meet unexpected difficulty; 我們的計畫已經觸礁。Our plans have hit a snag.

觸角(ㄔㄨ ㄐㄧㄠˇ)
feelers; tentacles; antennae

觸景生情(ㄔㄨ ㄐㄧㄥˇ ㄕㄥ ㄑㄧㄥˊ)
The scene or circumstance arouses a sense (of joy, sorrow, etc.).

觸覺(ㄔㄨ ㄐㄩㄝˊ)
the sense of touch

觸興(ㄔㄨ ㄒㄧㄥˋ)
to arouse enthusiasm or interest

觸鬚(ㄔㄨ ㄒㄩ)
a palpus; feelers; antennae; tentacles

觸處(ㄔㄨ ㄔㄨˋ)
everywhere; all over

觸腎(ㄔㄨ ㄕㄣˊ)
the organ of touch in molluscs

觸殺(ㄔㄨ ㄕㄚ)
(baseball) to tag; tag

觸手(ㄔㄨ ㄕㄡˇ)
tentacles

觸眼(ㄔㄨ ㄧㄢˇ)
to strike the eye; eye-catching

觸網(ㄔㄨ ㄨㄤˇ)
to commit an offense against the law

十八畫

【觿】 5513
ㄒㄧ　shi xī
a bodkin made of ivory, horn, etc. used for undoing knots

觿年(ㄒㄧ ㄋㄧㄢˊ)
childhood years

言部
ㄧㄢˊ　yan yán

【言】 5514
ㄧㄢˊ　yan yán
1. speech; words
2. to say; to talk; to speak; to mean; to express: 他常常自言自語。He often talks to himself.
3. a language; a dialect; a tongue
4. a Chinese family name
5. (now rarely) used as a particle, adverb, etc. in various ancient expressions without meaning

言必信,行必果(ㄧㄢˊ ㄅㄧˋ ㄒㄧㄣ, ㄒㄧㄥˊ ㄅㄧˋ ㄍㄨㄛˇ)
Promises must be kept and action must be resolute.

言必有中(ㄧㄢˊ ㄅㄧˋ ㄧㄡˇ ㄓㄨㄥˋ)
Whenever he (or she) speaks, his (or her) words sound convincing.

言不及義(ㄧㄢˊ ㄅㄨˋ ㄐㄧˊ ㄧˋ)
to make idle talks; to talk frivolously

言不盡意(ㄧㄢˊ ㄅㄨˋ ㄐㄧㄣˋ ㄧˋ)
(often used at the end of letters) What I have said or written does not convey all in my mind.

言不出衆,貌不驚人(ㄧㄢˊ ㄅㄨˋ ㄔㄨ ㄓㄨㄥˋ, ㄇㄠˋ ㄅㄨˋ ㄐㄧㄥ ㄖㄣˊ)
neither outstanding in speech nor impressive in appearance—a mediocre person

言不由衷(ㄧㄢˊ ㄅㄨˋ ㄧㄡˊ ㄓㄨㄥ)
not speaking one's mind; not to talk from the bottom of one's heart

言而無信(ㄧㄢˊ ㄦˊ ㄨˊ ㄒㄧㄣˋ)
to give one's word which one does not keep; to break one's word

言明(ㄧㄢˊ ㄇㄧㄥˊ)
to state clearly; to make a statement; to declare

言多必失(ㄧㄢˊ ㄉㄨㄛ ㄅㄧˋ ㄕ)
One is bound to have a slip of the tongue if he talks too much.

言對(ㄧㄢˊ ㄉㄨㄟˋ)
① to meet and talk; to converse ② coupling of words

言動(ㄧㄢˊ ㄉㄨㄥˋ)
words and conduct; speech and behavior

言談(ㄧㄢˊ ㄊㄢˊ)
words and speech; conversation

言談林藪(ㄧㄢˊ ㄊㄢˊ ㄌㄧㄣˊ ㄙㄡˇ)
one gifted with a glib tongue; a good talker

言聽計從(ㄧㄢˊ ㄊㄧㄥ ㄐㄧˋ ㄘㄨㄥˊ)
to have full confidence in someone; to trust someone completely; to listen to every word someone says

言路(ㄧㄢˊ ㄌㄨˋ)
the channel by which one's words can reach the government

言論(ㄧㄢˊ ㄌㄨㄣˋ)
① open discussion ② speech

言論自由(ㄧㄢˊ ㄌㄨㄣˋ ㄗˋ ㄧㄡˊ)
freedom of speech

言過其實(ㄧㄢˊ ㄍㄨㄛˋ ㄑㄧˊ ㄕˊ)
to exaggerate; to boast or brag; to overstate

言歸正傳(ㄧㄢˊ ㄍㄨㄟ ㄓㄥˋ ㄓㄨㄢˋ)
Let's resume the narration. 或 Let's go back to the main topic.

言歸於好 or 言歸于好(ㄧㄢˊ ㄍㄨㄟ ㄩˊ ㄏㄠˇ)
to resume friendship; to be on good terms again; to reconcile; to be reconciled; to

〔言部〕

---

maintain amicable relations hereafter

言官(1ㄢˊ ㄍㄨㄢ)
imperial censors

言和(1ㄢˊ ㄏㄜˊ)
to make peace; to become reconciled; to bury the hatchet (or tomahawk); to make it up: 我希望你們握手言和。I hope you shake hands and make it up.

言及(1ㄢˊ ㄐㄧˊ)
to talk about; to touch on; to mention

言教(1ㄢˊ ㄐㄧㄠˋ)
to teach by words, as distinct from by setting an example; to give verbal directions

言簡意賅(1ㄢˊ ㄐㄧㄢˇ 1ˋ ㄍㄞ)
Few words were spoken, but none of the major points was missing. or brief and to the point; terse but comprehensive

言近指遠(1ㄢˊ ㄐㄧㄣˋ ㄓˇ ㄩㄢˇ)
words that carry a deeper meaning but are easily understood; to speak in plain language about something very profound in meaning

言盡於此(1ㄢˊ ㄐㄧㄣˋ ㄩˊ ㄘˇ)
to have said all; to have nothing more to say

言泉(1ㄢˊ ㄑㄩㄢˊ)
(literally) the spring of words—glib and talkative

言笑(1ㄢˊ ㄒㄧㄠˋ)
to talk and laugh

言行(1ㄢˊ ㄒㄧㄥˊ)
words and deeds; statements and actions

言行錄(1ㄢˊ ㄒㄧㄥˊ ㄌㄨˋ)
a book recording the words and deeds of a sage

言行相悖(1ㄢˊ ㄒㄧㄥˊ ㄒㄧㄤ ㄅㄟˋ)or
言行不符(1ㄢˊ ㄒㄧㄥˊ ㄅㄨˋ ㄈㄨˊ)
to practice against what one preaches

言行相顧(1ㄢˊ ㄒㄧㄥˊ ㄒㄧㄤ ㄍㄨˋ)or
言行一致(1ㄢˊ ㄒㄧㄥˊ 1 ㄓˋ)
words conforming to actions; to practice what one preaches

言之過早(1ㄢˊ ㄓ ㄍㄨㄛˋ ㄗㄠˇ)
still too early to say; premature to say

言之成理(1ㄢˊ ㄓ ㄔㄥˊ ㄌㄧˇ)
to present in a reasonable way; to talk sense; to speak on the strength of reason; to sound reasonable

言之有物(1ㄢˊ ㄓ 1ㄡˇ ㄨˋ)
(said of a speech or writing) having substance; convincing

言者諄諄, 聽者藐藐(1ㄢˊ ㄓㄜˇ ㄓㄨㄣ ㄓㄨㄣ, ㄊㄧㄥ ㄓㄜˇ ㄇㄧㄠˇ ㄇㄧㄠˇ)
The speaker talked with great earnestness, but the audience paid little attention.

言狀(1ㄢˊ ㄓㄨㄤˋ)
to describe; description

言重(1ㄢˊ ㄓㄨㄥˋ)
① to speak sincerely and carefully ② to use laudatory words that are unduly strong

言重九鼎(1ㄢˊ ㄓㄨㄥˋ ㄐㄧㄡˇ ㄉㄧㄥˇ)
One's word carries weight of nine tripods.—One's opinions are of great importance.

言差語錯(1ㄢˊ ㄔㄚ ㄩˇ ㄘㄨㄛˋ)
erroneous utterances; misunderstanding in verbal exchanges

言出法隨(1ㄢˊ ㄔㄨ ㄈㄚˇ ㄙㄨㄟˊ)
(said of a ruler) The orders, once given, will be strictly enforced.

言出如山(1ㄢˊ ㄔㄨ ㄖㄨˊ ㄕㄢ)
A promise is a promise.

言傳(1ㄢˊ ㄔㄨㄢˊ)
to explain in words

言人人殊(1ㄢˊ ㄖㄣˊ ㄖㄣˊ ㄕㄨ)
Everybody has a different story. or Everyone gives a different version.

言責(1ㄢˊ ㄗㄜˊ)
responsibility of offering advice or speaking honestly about public affairs

言詞 or **言辭**(1ㄢˊ ㄘˊ)
words or expressions; statements; wording; diction

言詞辯論(1ㄢˊ ㄘˊ ㄅㄧㄢˋ ㄌㄨㄣˋ)
oral statements, verbal argument, or confrontation of litigants at a court of law

言三語四(1ㄢˊ ㄙㄢ ㄩˇ ㄙˋ)
to criticize without much thinking

言而有信(1ㄢˊ ㄦˊ 1ㄡˇ ㄒㄧㄣˋ)

---

to be as good as one's wo

言猶在耳(1ㄢˊ 1ㄡˊ ㄗㄞˋ ㄦˇ)
The words are still ringin in the ear.

言偃(1ㄢˊ 1ㄢˇ)
name of a disciple of Co fucius 亦作「子游」

言外(1ㄢˊ ㄨㄞˋ)
beyond the words spoke between the lines: 意在言外
The meaning is beyond th words spoken.

言外之意(1ㄢˊ ㄨㄞˋ ㄓ 1ˋ)
hidden meaning between the lines; overtones

言為心聲(1ㄢˊ ㄨㄟˊ ㄒㄧㄣ ㄕㄥ)
(literally) Speech is the voice of one's heart.—Yo know someone's real inten tion by his words.

言文對照(1ㄢˊ ㄨㄣˊ ㄉㄨㄟˋ ㄓㄠˋ)
writings in archaic Chines printed side by side with th vernacular version for th benefit of modern readers

言文一致(1ㄢˊ ㄨㄣˊ 1 ㄓˋ)
the unification of spoke language and written la guage

言語(1ㄢˊ ㄩˇ)
① (1ㄢˊ ㄩˇ) spoken language words; speech
② (1ㄢˊ ㆍㄩ) to report; to tal to tell; to speak

言語妙天下(1ㄢˊ ㄩˇ ㄇㄧㄠˋ ㄊㄧㄢ ㄒㄧㄚˋ)
to have no peer in wise cracking

言語道斷(1ㄢˊ ㄩˇ ㄉㄠˋ ㄉㄨㄢˋ)
the highest principle o essence (appearing mostl in Buddhist scriptures which can not be explaine in words

言語學(1ㄢˊ ㄩˇ ㄒㄩㄝˊ)
philology; linguistics 亦作「言語學」

言語支吾(1ㄢˊ ㄩˇ ㄓ ㄨˊ)
to mince words; to mumbl or stammer in an attempt t hide something; to prevar cate

言語無味(1ㄢˊ ㄩˇ ㄨˊ ㄨㄟˋ)
insipid talk; to keep on jaw ing

二畫

計 ⁵⁵¹⁵
ㄐㄧˋ jìh jì

a scheme; a plot; a trick; a
coup; a trap; a ruse
a plan; a program; to discuss or plan
to calculate; to count
a mechanical measuring
device
a Chinese family name

不得售(ㄅㄨˋ ㄉㄜˊ ㄕㄡˋ)
to fail to attain the objective one has schemed for

不出此(ㄅㄨˋ ㄔㄨ ㄘˇ)
to fail to adopt the plan just
described

謀(ㄇㄡˊ)
a scheme; to scheme; a contrivance or device

分(ㄈㄣ)
①to count scores or points
②divided or classified as
follows

吏(ㄌㄧˋ)
an official in charge of
accounts in a feudal principality during the Han
Dynasty

量(ㄌㄧㄤˋ)
to calculate; to weigh; to
estimate

略(ㄌㄩㄝˋ)
to scheme; to deliberate; a
scheme

開(ㄎㄞ)
to list item by item as follows

畫 or 計劃(ㄏㄨㄚˋ)
a plan; a program; to plan;
to devise

畫經濟 or 計劃經濟(ㄏㄨㄚˋ
ㄐㄧㄥ ㄐㄧˋ)
planned economy

畫中 or 計劃中(ㄏㄨㄚˋ
ㄓㄨㄥ)
under consideration or
contemplation

畫生產 or 計劃生產(ㄏㄨㄚˋ
ㄕㄥ ㄔㄢˇ)
planned production; production according to plan

畫書 or 計劃書(ㄏㄨㄚˋ ㄕㄨ)
a prospectus (of a business
setup or factory)

較(ㄐㄧˋ ㄐㄧㄠˋ)or(ㄐㄧˋ ㄐㄧㄠˇ)
①to dispute; to haggle; to

fuss about ②to discuss; to
talk it over; to negotiate ③
to mind; to care ④to plan

計件(ㄐㄧˋ ㄐㄧㄢˋ)
to reckon by the piece

計件工資(ㄐㄧˋ ㄐㄧㄢˋ《ㄨㄥ ㄗ》)
wages paid on a piecework
basis

計窮(ㄐㄧˋ ㄑㄩㄥˊ)
to be at the end of one's
wits; to be at the end of
one's rope

計程(ㄐㄧˋ ㄔㄥˊ)
to calculate according to
mileage

計程車(ㄐㄧˋ ㄔㄥˊ ㄔㄜ)
a taxi

計出萬全(ㄐㄧˋ ㄔㄨ ㄨㄢˋ ㄑㄩㄢˊ)
a foolproof plan or scheme

計時(ㄐㄧˋ ㄕˊ)
to count time to see how
long something lasts

計時表(ㄐㄧˋ ㄕˊ ㄅㄧㄠˇ)
a chronometer

計時工資(ㄐㄧˋ ㄕˊ《ㄨㄥ ㄗ》)
wages paid on a time basis;
time wages

計上心來(ㄐㄧˋ ㄕㄤˋ ㄒㄧㄣ ㄌㄞˊ)
to come across a scheme; to
hit upon an idea

計定(ㄐㄧˋ ㄉㄧㄥˋ)
to count

計數(ㄐㄧˋ ㄕㄨˋ)
to count

計策(ㄐㄧˋ ㄘㄜˋ)
a scheme; a device; a trick
or trap

計算(ㄐㄧˋ ㄙㄨㄢˋ)
①to calculate; calculation;
to count; to weigh: 他正在計
算出席人數。He is counting
the number of people present. ②to consider

計算機(ㄐㄧˋ ㄙㄨㄢˋ ㄐㄧ)
an adding machine; a calculating machine; a computer

計算器(ㄐㄧˋ ㄙㄨㄢˋ ㄑㄧˋ)
a calculating device (such
as an abacus, a slide rule,
etc.)

計算尺(ㄐㄧˋ ㄙㄨㄢˋ ㄔˇ)
a slide rule

計議(ㄐㄧˋ ㄧˋ)
to negotiate; to discuss; to
talk it over; to consider; to
deliberate; to consult: 這件事
我們要從長計議。We'll discuss
this matter in detail.

計無所出(ㄐㄧˋ ㄨˊ ㄙㄨㄛˇ ㄔㄨ)

unable to think of a way (to
cope with a situation, etc.);
to be at the end of one's
rope

【訂】 ⁵⁵¹⁶
ㄉㄧㄥˋ dìng dǐng

1. to draw up or conclude (a
contract, treaty, agreement,
etc.)
2. to subscribe to (a magazine,
newspaper, etc.)
3. to edit; to collate; to revise;
to make corrections
4. to arrange; to settle; to fix
5. to make reservations (in a
hotel, restaurant, etc.)

訂報(ㄉㄧㄥˋ ㄅㄠˋ)
to subscribe to a newspaper

訂盟(ㄉㄧㄥˋ ㄇㄥˊ)
to conclude or sign a treaty
of alliance

訂明(ㄉㄧㄥˋ ㄇㄧㄥˊ)
to specify clearly in a contract or agreement

訂房間(ㄉㄧㄥˋ ㄈㄤˊ ㄐㄧㄢ)
to make room reservations:
你訂房間沒有? Have you made
your room reservations?

訂定(ㄉㄧㄥˋ ㄉㄧㄥˋ)
①to fix or arrange beforehand ②(law) specified in a
contract or agreement
between the two parties concerned

訂條約(ㄉㄧㄥˋ ㄊㄧㄠˊ ㄩㄝ)
to sign a treaty; to conclude

訂立(ㄉㄧㄥˋ ㄌㄧˋ)
to conclude or sign (a contract, agreement, treaty,
etc.)

訂購(ㄉㄧㄥˋ 《ㄡˋ)
to place a mail order for; to
order (a product) in advance:
她訂購了一些新衣。She has
ordered some new clothes.

訂戶(ㄉㄧㄥˋ ㄏㄨˋ)
①a subscriber (to a news-
paper, etc.)②a person with
a standing order for milk,
etc.

訂貨(ㄉㄧㄥˋ ㄏㄨㄛˋ)
to place an order for goods

訂貨單(ㄉㄧㄥˋ ㄏㄨㄛˋ ㄉㄢ)or 訂單
(ㄉㄧㄥˋ ㄉㄢ)
an order form (or blank); a
list of goods ordered

［言部］

〔言 部〕

訂婚（ㄉㄧㄥˋ ㄏㄨㄣ）
to engage or betroth; an
engagement; a betrothal

訂機票（ㄉㄧㄥˋ ㄐㄧ ㄆㄧㄠˋ）
to book for a seat aboard a
passenger liner

訂交（ㄉㄧㄥˋ ㄐㄧㄠ）
to establish friendly relations with...

訂正（ㄉㄧㄥˋ ㄓㄥˋ）
to revise; to correct: 如有錯
誤，請予以訂正. Correct er-
rors, if any.

訂車票（ㄉㄧㄥˋ ㄔㄜ ㄆㄧㄠˋ）
to book for a seat aboard a
bus or train

訂書（ㄉㄧㄥˋ ㄕㄨ）
to order books

訂雜誌（ㄉㄧㄥˋ ㄗㄚˊ ㄓˋ）
to subscribe to a magazine

訂座（ㄉㄧㄥˋ ㄗㄨㄛˋ）
to make reservations for
seats in theaters, restaurants, etc.

訂約（ㄉㄧㄥˋ ㄩㄝ）
to conclude or sign a contract, agreement or treaty

訂閱（ㄉㄧㄥˋ ㄩㄝˋ）
to subscribe to (a publication); subscription

【訕】5517 ㄕㄢˋ jiaw jiào
1. to call in a loud voice; to
yell or scream
2. to tell a falsehood; to talk
wildly

【訃】5518 ㄈㄨˋ fuh fù
a notice announcing the
death of a person; an obituary

訃告（ㄈㄨˋ ㄍㄠˋ）or 訃聞（ㄈㄨˋ ㄨㄣˊ）
an obituary notice

【訇】5519 ㄏㄨㄥ hong hōng
1. loudly; stentorian
2. a Chinese family name

訇訇（ㄏㄨㄥ ㄏㄨㄥ）
loud(ly); stentorian

訇嘩（ㄏㄨㄥ ㄒㄧㄠˋ）
roaring (winds)

訇然（ㄏㄨㄥ ㄖㄢˊ）
loudly; stentorian

三畫

【討】5520 ㄊㄠˇ tao tǎo
1. to quell (an uprising, or
rebellion); to punish; to suppress; to put down
2. to denounce; to condemn
3. to marry (a wife or concubine)
4. to demand; to beg for; to
get
5. to study; to examine into; to
research
6. (now rarely) to govern; to
administer

討便宜（ㄊㄠˇ ㄆㄧㄢˊ ˙ㄧ）
to seek profit or benefit in
an improper way; to seek
undue advantage: 不要讓他討
(了)便宜. Don't let him seek
undue advantage.

討沒趣（ㄊㄠˇ ㄇㄟˊ ㄑㄩˋ）
to ask for an insult; to make
a request which is most likely to be rejected; to offer
advice or service when it is
not needed

討伐（ㄊㄠˇ ㄈㄚˊ）
to quell (an uprising, a
rebellion, etc.); to punish
(another nation, etc.) by
force of arms

討飯（ㄊㄠˇ ㄈㄢˋ）
to beg for food; to be a beggar

討飯的（ㄊㄠˇ ㄈㄢˋ ˙ㄉㄜ）
a beggar

討亂（ㄊㄠˇ ㄌㄨㄢˋ）
to quell an uprising or a
rebellion; to launch a punitive campaign against rebels

討論（ㄊㄠˇ ㄌㄨㄣˋ）
to discuss; discussion

討論會（ㄊㄠˇ ㄌㄨㄣˋ ㄏㄨㄟˋ）
a discussion meeting; a
forum; a symposium

討個吉利（ㄊㄠˇ ˙ㄍㄜ ㄐㄧˊ ㄌㄧˋ）
to ask for something as a
token of good omen

討愧（ㄊㄠˇ ㄎㄨㄟˋ）
to be ashamed

討海人（ㄊㄠˇ ㄏㄞˇ ㄖㄣˊ）
a fisherman

討好（ㄊㄠˇ ㄏㄠˇ）
①to curry favor; to please;
to fawn on ②to be reward-
ed with a fruitful result

討價還價（ㄊㄠˇ ㄐㄧㄚˋ ㄏㄨㄢˊ ㄐㄧㄚˋ）
to haggle over prices;
bargain

討教（ㄊㄠˇ ㄐㄧㄠˋ）
(a polite expression) May
ask for your advice (
esteemed view)? 我來討教，
是求爭論。I come to ask f
advice, not to argue.

討究（ㄊㄠˇ ㄐㄧㄡˋ）
to study and find the truth

討救兵（ㄊㄠˇ ㄐㄧㄡˋ ㄅㄧㄥ）
①to ask for relieving troo
to request for reinforceme
②to seek help

討賤（ㄊㄠˇ ㄐㄧㄢˋ）
to ask for insult, belitt
ment, etc. through lack
self-respect or self-restrain

討巧（ㄊㄠˇ ㄑㄧㄠˇ）
to try to gain advantag
benefit, etc. with little effo
to try to use finesse or ta
a snap course to attain the
end

討錢（ㄊㄠˇ ㄑㄧㄢˊ）
to ask for money; to ask f
repayment

討親（ㄊㄠˇ ㄑㄧㄣ）
to take a wife

討情（ㄊㄠˇ ㄑㄧㄥˊ）
to ask for forgiveness;
plead for leniency

討取（ㄊㄠˇ ㄑㄩˇ）
to ask for something;
demand

討媳婦（ㄊㄠˇ ㄒㄧˊ ˙ㄈㄨ）
to get a wife for one's so

討嫌（ㄊㄠˇ ㄒㄧㄢˊ）
to incur dislike or disgu
disgusting; repulsive; revo
ing

討債（ㄊㄠˇ ㄓㄞˋ）
to demand repayment of
loan

討債鬼（ㄊㄠˇ ㄓㄞˋ ㄍㄨㄟˇ）
①(literally) devils aski
for repayment—one's ov
children who died young
an importunate or insiste
person whom one finds
difficult to deal with

討賬（ㄊㄠˇ ㄓㄤˋ）or 討帳（ㄊㄠˇ ㄓㄤˋ）
to ask for repayment of
loan; to collect bills overdu
to demand the payment of
debt

討賫（ㄊㄠˇ ㄓˋ）

to ask for a reward or gratuity

†生活(ㄕㄥ ㄏㄨㄛˊ)
to make a living: 為了討生活, 他不得不辛苦工作。He had to work hard to make a living.

†聽(ㄊㄧㄥ ㄖˋ)
to ask for mercy; to ask for leniency

†人喜歡(ㄖㄣˊ ㄒㄧˇ ㄏㄨㄢ)
likable; cute; pretty; charming; delightful: 她是個非常討人喜歡的小女孩。She's a very likable little girl.

†人嫌(ㄖㄣˊ ㄒㄧㄢˊ)
to incur dislike or disgust; annoying: 你真討人嫌。How annoying you are!

†賊(ㄗㄟˊ)
to punish the rebels by force

†厭(ㄧㄢˋ)
troublesome; disgusting; nasty; to dislike; to incur dislike or disgust

【訐】 5521   ㄐㄧㄝˊ jye jié
. to pry into or expose another's secret
. to accuse or charge; to defame; to malign (a person)

訐直(ㄐㄧㄝˊ ㄓˊ)
to blame someone bluntly for his faults

訐揚(ㄐㄧㄝˊ ㄧㄤˊ)
to expose or reveal the faults of another

【訊】 5522   ㄒㄩㄣˋ shiunn xùn
. to ask; to inquire; to question
. information; news
. to put on trial; to question in court; to interrogate; interrogation

訊辦(ㄒㄩㄣˋ ㄅㄢˋ)
to put on trial and convict; to prosecute

訊斷(ㄒㄩㄣˋ ㄉㄨㄢˋ)
to hand down a judgment or verdict

訊聽(ㄒㄩㄣˋ ㄊㄧㄥ)
to make inquiries 亦作「打聽」

訊供(ㄒㄩㄣˋ ㄍㄨㄥ)
interrogations and confessions in a court of law

---

to hold a trial

訊息(ㄒㄩㄣˋ ㄒㄧˊ)
news; information; tidings; messages 亦作「音訊」

訊問(ㄒㄩㄣˋ ㄨㄣˋ)
①to cross-examine; to interrogate ② correspondence

【訌】 5523   ㄏㄨㄥˊ horng hóng
confusion; discord; strife; a quarrel

【訓】 5524   ㄒㄩㄣˋ shiunn xùn
1. to lecture; to instruct; to teach; to exhort; to admonish; a lecture; a scolding: 我被他教訓了一番。I received a scolding from him.
2. (to serve as) a lesson; a model: 那不足為訓。It is not fit to serve as a model.
3. an old proverb, motto, etc.

訓蒙(ㄒㄩㄣˋ ㄇㄥˊ)
to tutor children; to teach young boys and girls

訓勉(ㄒㄩㄣˋ ㄇㄧㄢˇ)
to exhort and encourage

訓導(ㄒㄩㄣˋ ㄉㄠˇ)
to teach and guide

訓導長(ㄒㄩㄣˋ ㄉㄠˇ ㄓㄤˇ)
the dean of students (at a university)

訓導主任(ㄒㄩㄣˋ ㄉㄠˇ ㄓㄨˇ ㄖㄣˋ)
the dean of students (at a primary school or high school)

訓導處(ㄒㄩㄣˋ ㄉㄠˇ ㄔㄨˋ)
an office of the dean of students

訓迪(ㄒㄩㄣˋ ㄉㄧˊ)
to teach and enlighten (the young)

訓典(ㄒㄩㄣˋ ㄉㄧㄢˇ)
books authored by sages and good emperors of ancient times

訓練(ㄒㄩㄣˋ ㄌㄧㄢˋ)
to drill; to train; training

訓練班(ㄒㄩㄣˋ ㄌㄧㄢˋ ㄅㄢ)
a training class

訓練所(ㄒㄩㄣˋ ㄌㄧㄢˋ ㄙㄨㄛˇ)
a training institute

訓令(ㄒㄩㄣˋ ㄌㄧㄥˋ)
instructions from a superior office

訓詁(ㄒㄩㄣˋ ㄍㄨˇ)
explanatory notes in ancient

---

books

訓詁學(ㄒㄩㄣˋ ㄍㄨˇ ㄒㄩㄝˊ)
scholium

訓詁學者(ㄒㄩㄣˋ ㄍㄨˇ ㄒㄩㄝˊ ㄓㄜˇ)
a scholiast

訓話(ㄒㄩㄣˋ ㄏㄨㄚˋ)
a speech of exhortation; to lecture; to exhort

訓誨(ㄒㄩㄣˋ ㄏㄨㄟˋ)
to teach and exhort the younger generation; to instruct

訓誡(ㄒㄩㄣˋ ㄐㄧㄝˋ)
to exhort and warn; to admonish; exhortation and warning

訓政(ㄒㄩㄣˋ ㄓㄥˋ)
①political tutelage ②(Ching Dynasty) participation in political affairs by the abdicated emperor or the empress dowager

訓政時期(ㄒㄩㄣˋ ㄓㄥˋ ㄕˊ ㄑㄧ)
the period of political tutelage (in the early years of the Chinese Republic before the adoption of the Constitution in 1946)

訓斥(ㄒㄩㄣˋ ㄔˋ)
to scold a junior or subordinate severely; to reprimand; to rebuke; to dress down

訓飭(ㄒㄩㄣˋ ㄔˋ)
to admonish and censure a junior or subordinate severely

訓示(ㄒㄩㄣˋ ㄕˋ)
instructions; to admonish

訓人(ㄒㄩㄣˋ ㄖㄣˊ)
①(an old usage) the teacher, tutor or master ②to exhort people

訓詞(ㄒㄩㄣˋ ㄘˊ)
a speech of exhortation or admonition; instructions

訓誘(ㄒㄩㄣˋ ㄧㄡˋ)
to teach and lead on

訓育(ㄒㄩㄣˋ ㄩˋ)
to educate and train

訓諭(ㄒㄩㄣˋ ㄩˋ)
to instruct; instructions from a superior or elder

【訕】 5525   ㄕㄢ shann shàn
1. to laugh at; to sneer
2. to slander; to abuse
3. embarrassed; awkward; shame-

〔言
部〕

faced

訕謗(ㄕㄢ ㄅㄤˋ)
to slander; to libel; to back-bite

訕臉(ㄕㄢ ㄌㄧㄢˇ)
brazen; shameless

訕笑(ㄕㄢ ㄒㄧㄠˋ)
to laugh or sneer at; to ridicule; to mock; to deride

訕上(ㄕㄢ ㄕㄤˋ)
to slander one's superiors

【訖】 5526　ㄑㄧˋ chih qì
1. to come to an end; to conclude; cleared or settled
2. until; up to 亦作「迄」

訖了(ㄑㄧˋ ㄌㄧㄠˇ)
to end; to conclude

【託】 5527　ㄊㄨㄛ tuo tuō
1. to commission; to entrust to; to charge with; to rely on
2. to ask; to request
3. to consign; consignment
4. to use as an excuse or pretext
5. (said of a dead person, etc.) to appear (in a dream)
6. to send (messages, etc.) indirectly

託辦(ㄊㄨㄛ ㄅㄢˋ)
to consign; to do something entrusted by others

託庇(ㄊㄨㄛ ㄅㄧˋ)
①to seek protection ②(a polite expression) Thanks for your protection.

託病(ㄊㄨㄛ ㄅㄧㄥˋ)
on the pretext of being ill; to use illness as an excuse: 他託病不去學校。 He used his illness as an excuse for not going to school.

託夢(ㄊㄨㄛ ㄇㄥˋ)
(said of a dead person) to appear in one's dream

託名(ㄊㄨㄛ ㄇㄧㄥˊ)
①to acquire influence by making use of the name of a more prestigious person ② to assume another's name

託辭(ㄊㄨㄛ ㄘˊ)
to seek escape in doing something which has nothing to do with one's regular duties or career 亦作「託迹」

託諷(ㄊㄨㄛ ㄈㄥˋ)
to give vent to one's feelings

in writing

託福(ㄊㄨㄛ ㄈㄨˊ)
(a polite expression) Thank you.

託福考試(ㄊㄨㄛ ㄈㄨˊ ㄎㄠˇ ㄕˋ)
TOEFL (Test of English as a Foreign Language) administered by the Educational Testing Service for foreign students who wish to pursue advanced studies in the U.S.亦作「托福測驗」

託付(ㄊㄨㄛ ㄈㄨˋ)
to entrust to; to commission

託大(ㄊㄨㄛ ㄉㄚˋ)
self-important; conceited; to act arrogantly

託辣斯(ㄊㄨㄛ ㄌㄚˋ ㄙ)
(business) a trust 亦作「托辣斯」

託孤(ㄊㄨㄛ ㄍㄨ)or託孤寄命(ㄊㄨㄛ ㄍㄨ ㄐㄧˋ ㄇㄧㄥˋ)
to entrust an orphan to the care of a guardian

託故(ㄊㄨㄛ ㄍㄨˋ)
to make an excuse; to find a pretext: 他託故不來。 He did not come under some pretexts.

託管(ㄊㄨㄛ ㄍㄨㄢˇ)
trusteeship; a mandate; to trust; to mandate

託管理事會(ㄊㄨㄛ ㄍㄨㄢˇ ㄌㄧˇ ㄕˋ ㄏㄨㄟˋ)
Trusteeship Council (of the United Nations)

託管領土(ㄊㄨㄛ ㄍㄨㄢˇ ㄌㄧㄥˇ ㄊㄨˇ)
trust territories; mandatory territories

託管權(ㄊㄨㄛ ㄍㄨㄢˇ ㄑㄩㄢˊ)
mandatory powers

託迹(ㄊㄨㄛ ㄐㄧˋ)
to seek escape in doing something which has nothing to do with one's regular duties or career

託疾(ㄊㄨㄛ ㄐㄧˊ)
to use poor health as an excuse

託交(ㄊㄨㄛ ㄐㄧㄠ)
①c/o; to deliver (something) in care of somebody ②to befriend; to make friends with

託情(ㄊㄨㄛ ㄑㄧㄥˊ)
to take advantage of personal friendship to gain a

special privilege or favor

託之空言(ㄊㄨㄛ ㄓ ㄎㄨㄥ ㄧㄢˊ)
to give empty promises; pay lip service

託處(ㄊㄨㄛ ㄔㄨˋ)
to lodge at places other than one's own home

託食(ㄊㄨㄛ ㄕˊ)
to eat meals at a friend's or relative's home

託賞(ㄊㄨㄛ ㄕˇ)
to receive gifts or presents and take it for granted

託始(ㄊㄨㄛ ㄕˇ)
the beginning; the origin

託身(ㄊㄨㄛ ㄕㄣ)
to entrust oneself to; to live at a friend's or relative's place

託生(ㄊㄨㄛ ㄕㄥ)
(Chinese mythology) re-incarnation of ghosts

託人(ㄊㄨㄛ ㄖㄣˊ)
to ask somebody to do something for oneself; to entrust to someone

託足(ㄊㄨㄛ ㄗㄨˊ)
to lodge at places other than one's home

託辭(ㄊㄨㄛ ㄘˊ)
to make excuses; pretexts or excuses: 他說有事，不過是託辭。He said he was busy, but that was just an excuse.

託兒所(ㄊㄨㄛ ㄦˊ ㄙㄨㄛˇ)
a public nursery

託言(ㄊㄨㄛ ㄧㄢˊ)
to make excuses

託運(ㄊㄨㄛ ㄩㄣˋ)
to consign for shipment; to check: 他將行李託運至台中。He checked his baggage to Taichung.

【記】 5528　ㄐㄧˋ jih jì
1. to remember; to call to mind; to bear or keep in mind
2. to record; to register
3. a book recording persons or things, anecdotes, etc.
4. seals or chops; a sign; a mark

記不得(ㄐㄧˋ ㄅㄨˋ ㄉㄜˊ)
unable to remember or recall

記不清(ㄐㄧˋ ㄅㄨˋ ㄑㄧㄥ)

〔言部〕

unable to remember exactly

記名(ㄐㄧˋㄇㄧㄥˊ)
①to record the name; to sign ②registered (stock, bonds, etc.)

記名投票(ㄐㄧˋㄇㄧㄥˊㄊㄡˊㄆㄧㄠˋ)
to vote with signed ballot; open ballot 參看「無記名投票」

記分(ㄐㄧˋㄈㄣ)
①to record scores or points ②to register a student's mark

記分員(ㄐㄧˋㄈㄣㄩㄢˊ)
a scorekeeper; a scorer; a marker

記得(ㄐㄧˋ˙ㄉㄜ)
to remember; to have not forgotten: 我還記得他的模樣兒。I still remember what he looked like.

記念(ㄐㄧˋㄋㄧㄢˋ)
to remember or commemorate 亦作「紀念」

記牢(ㄐㄧˋㄌㄠˊ)
to commit to memory firmly

記錄(ㄐㄧˋㄌㄨˋ)
①to record; to put on record; to note down ②a note-taker ③minutes of a meeting; a record 亦作「紀錄」

記錄片(ㄐㄧˋㄌㄨˋㄆㄧㄢˋ)
a documentary film; a documentary

記掛(ㄐㄧˋㄍㄨㄚˋ)
to remember and be anxious about; to be constantly on one's mind; to miss

記過(ㄐㄧˋㄍㄨㄛˋ)
to record a demerit

記功(ㄐㄧˋㄍㄨㄥ)
to record a merit

記功碑(ㄐㄧˋㄍㄨㄥㄅㄟ)
a tablet on which the merits of a person or persons are recorded

記號(ㄐㄧˋㄏㄠˋ)
a mark; a sign; a symbol

記恨(ㄐㄧˋㄏㄣˋ)
to bear a grudge: 他對我記恨。He bears me a grudge.

記取(ㄐㄧˋㄑㄩˇ)
to remember or bear in mind (this lesson, defeat, etc.): 你須將欲速則不達一語記取在心。You must bear in mind that haste makes waste.

記下來(ㄐㄧˋㄒㄧㄚˋㄌㄞˊ)
to take down (dictation, etc.); to make a note of

記性(ㄐㄧˋㄒㄧㄥˋ)
memory; the power of recollection

記性好(ㄐㄧˋㄒㄧㄥˋㄏㄠˇ)
a powerful memory: 他的記性好。He has a powerful memory.

記性壞(ㄐㄧˋㄒㄧㄥˋㄏㄨㄞˋ)
a poor memory

記敘文(ㄐㄧˋㄒㄩˋㄨㄣˊ)
a written narration; narrative writing

記者(ㄐㄧˋㄓㄜˇ)
a reporter; a newsman; a journalist: 一位地方記者報導這個故事。A local reporter covered the story.

記者公會(ㄐㄧˋㄓㄜˇㄍㄨㄥㄏㄨㄟˋ)
a newsmen's association, federation or league

記者節(ㄐㄧˋㄓㄜˇㄐㄧㄝˊ)
Journalist's Day (on September 1)

記者席(ㄐㄧˋㄓㄜˇㄒㄧˊ)
seats reserved for the press; a press gallery; a press box; a press stand

記者招待會(ㄐㄧˋㄓㄜˇㄓㄠㄉㄞˋㄏㄨㄟˋ)
a press conference

記賬(ㄐㄧˋㄓㄤˋ)
①to buy or sell on credit; to charge to an account ②to record buying, selling, etc. in books

記賬員(ㄐㄧˋㄓㄤˋㄩㄢˊ)
a bookkeeper

記住(ㄐㄧˋ˙ㄓㄨ)
Remember! 或to bear in mind: 記住我告訴你的話。Remember what I told you.

記傳體(ㄐㄧˋㄓㄨㄢˋㄊㄧˇ)
the style of writing recording historical facts

記仇(ㄐㄧˋㄔㄡˊ)
to bear a grudge; to harbor or nourish hatred

記室(ㄐㄧˋㄕˋ)
a secretary or clerk

記事(ㄐㄧˋㄕˋ)
to record facts; to make a memorandum of events

記事簿(ㄐㄧˋㄕˋㄅㄨˋ)
a notebook

記事牌(ㄐㄧˋㄕˋㄆㄞˊ)
a blackboard recording things to be done on certain days

記述(ㄐㄧˋㄕㄨˋ)
to record and narrate

記述體(ㄐㄧˋㄕㄨˋㄊㄧˇ)
the narrative style of writing

記入(ㄐㄧˋㄖㄨˋ)
to enter… in; to make an entry

記載(ㄐㄧˋㄗㄞˋ)
to record; an account: 警察詳細記載事情經過。The policeman recorded the incident in detail.

記錯(ㄐㄧˋㄘㄨㄛˋ)
①to remember incorrectly ②to make an incorrect entry in a book; to record or list something erroneously

記誦(ㄐㄧˋㄙㄨㄥˋ)
to recite; to commit to memory (by rote)

記憶(ㄐㄧˋㄧˋ)
memory or recollection: 這是我記憶中最熱的夏季。This is the hottest summer in my recollection.

記憶力(ㄐㄧˋㄧˋㄌㄧˋ)
the faculty of memory or recollection; a retentive faculty

記憶畫(ㄐㄧˋㄧˋㄏㄨㄚˋ)
memory drawing

記憶猶新(ㄐㄧˋㄧˋㄧㄡˊㄒㄧㄣ)
The memory is still fresh.

記誦(ㄐㄧˋㄙㄨㄥˋ)
a record of lectures, sayings, verbal teachings in writing

記問之學(ㄐㄧˋㄨㄣˋㄓㄒㄩㄝˊ)
learning that consists in repeating to students what one has read from ancient classics without proper reorganization or digestion

【訑】5529
ㄧ yí yí
overbearing; assuming; self-satisfaction

【訑】5529
2.ㄊㄨㄛˊ two tuó
to cheat

【訒】5530
ㄖㄣˋ renn rèn
difficult to speak out; cau-

（言部）

tious in speech

【訏】 5531
ㄒㄩ shiu xū
1. boasts; braggings
2. big; great
3. to sigh

四畫

【訟】 5532
ㄙㄨㄥˋ song sòng
1. a lawsuit; litigation; to bring a dispute to court
2. to argue over the right and wrong of something; to dispute; to demand justice
3. publicly; in public
4. (now rarely) to accuse; to regret; to repent; to blame

訟費（ㄙㄨㄥˋ ㄈㄟˋ）
　fees entailed in a lawsuit

訟牒（ㄙㄨㄥˋ ㄉㄧㄝˊ）
　the plaintiff's written complaint

訟庭（ㄙㄨㄥˋ ㄊㄧㄥˊ）
　a court of law

訟棍（ㄙㄨㄥˋ ㄍㄨㄣˋ）
　pettifoggers; those who foment litigation; shysters: 他為訟棍所害。He was the victim of a pettifogger.

訟案（ㄙㄨㄥˋ ㄢˋ）
　a lawsuit; litigation

訟案 a case at law: 政府贏得那件訟案。The government won that case.

訟言（ㄙㄨㄥˋ ㄧㄢˊ）
　to speak in public; to announce or declare

訟獄（ㄙㄨㄥˋ ㄩˋ）
　litigation; lawsuits

【訛】 5533
ㄜˊ er é
1. rumors
2. errors; erroneous; wrong
3. to extort; to swindle; to deceive; to bluff
4. to move about
5. to change or transform
6. a Chinese family name

訛奪（ㄜˊ ㄉㄨㄛˊ）
　errors or omissions in writing

訛詐（ㄜˊ ㄓㄚˋ）
　to extort; to blackmail; to swindle: 他訛詐她的錢。He extorted money from her.

訛傳（ㄜˊ ㄔㄨㄢˊ）
　false rumors; wrong information; erroneously reported

訛舛（ㄜˊ ㄔㄨㄢˇ）
　mistakes; errors

訛字（ㄜˊ ㄗˋ）
　the corrupted form of a character

訛音（ㄜˊ ㄧㄣ）
　inaccurate or improper pronunciation

訛誤（ㄜˊ ㄨˋ）
　errors; mistakes; inaccurate or wrong

【訝】 5534
ㄧㄚˋ yah yà
1. surprised to or to express surprise; to wonder: 你的行為使我驚訝。I'm surprised at you.
2. (now rarely) to welcome or receive 亦作「迓」

【訢】 5535
ㄒㄧㄣ shin xīn
joy; delight; happy

訢訢（ㄒㄧㄣ ㄒㄧㄣ）
　joyfully

訢然（ㄒㄧㄣ ㄖㄢˊ）
　very pleasant; happy

【訣】 5536
ㄐㄩㄝˊ jyue jué
1. to part; to separate
2. sorcery; an esoteric or occult art
3. a way or formula of doing something; the secret or knack of doing things

訣別（ㄐㄩㄝˊ ㄅㄧㄝˊ）
　①to say good-bye; to bid farewell ②to part forever

訣竅（ㄐㄩㄝˊ ㄑㄧㄠˋ）
　the secret or knack of doing something: 老實說, 我不懂其中之訣竅。To tell the truth, I can't get the knack of it.

訣要（ㄐㄩㄝˊ ㄧㄠˋ）
　①a secret, occult art or way ②the secret or knack of doing something

【訥】 5537
ㄋㄜˋ neh nè
　（又讀 ㄋㄚˋ nah nà）
slow of speech; to stammer

訥口（ㄋㄜˋ ㄎㄡˇ）
　slow of speech

訥澀（ㄋㄜˋ ㄙㄜˋ）
　slow of speech; to stammer

【訩】 5538
ㄒㄩㄥ shiong xiōng

1. (said of a crowd) noisy; loudly arguing
2. litigation; to be engaged in a lawsuit
3. disorders; miseries

訩訩（ㄒㄩㄥ ㄒㄩㄥ）
　(said of a crowd) noisy; loudly arguing

【訪】 5539
ㄈㄤˇ faang fǎng
1. to visit; to call on
2. to inquire of or to look for; to find out
3. a Chinese family name

訪古（ㄈㄤˇ ㄍㄨˇ）
　to search for ancient relics

訪客（ㄈㄤˇ ㄎㄜˋ）
　a visitor; a caller: 訪客只留下了名片。The caller merely left her card.

訪求（ㄈㄤˇ ㄑㄧㄡˊ）
　to seek; to look for; to search for

訪親（ㄈㄤˇ ㄑㄧㄣ）
　①to look for a relative ②to visit a kinsman

訪賢（ㄈㄤˇ ㄒㄧㄢˊ）
　to search for or call upon men of virtue and ability; to inquire and search for worthies

訪查（ㄈㄤˇ ㄔㄚˊ）
　to inquire about and investigate

訪友（ㄈㄤˇ ㄧㄡˇ）
　to visit friends; to call on friends

訪問（ㄈㄤˇ ㄨㄣˋ）
　to visit; visiting (missions); to call upon; to interview

訪問團（ㄈㄤˇ ㄨㄣˋ ㄊㄨㄢˊ）
　a visiting mission

訪員（ㄈㄤˇ ㄩㄢˊ）
　a reporter or correspondent sent by a press agency

【設】 5540
ㄕㄜˋ sheh shè
1. to lay out; to display
2. to establish; to set up; to found
3. to furnish; to provide
4. to arrange; to plan or devise
5. supposing that; what if; in case of

設備（ㄕㄜˋ ㄅㄟˋ）
　①equipment; installations; facilities: 設備簡陋。Equip-

ment is simple and common.
②to get prepared militarily;
defense works

設法(ㄕㄜˋㄈㄚˇ)
to think up a method; to
devise a way; to try: 那個樂
團正設法找個大提琴手。That
orchestra is trying to find a
cellist.

設防(ㄕㄜˋㄈㄤˊ)
to fortify; to set up defense
installations; to garrison: 他
們在該城設防抗敵。They for-
tify the town against the
enemy.

設防城市(ㄕㄜˋㄈㄤˊㄔㄥˊㄕˋ)
a fortified city

設伏(ㄕㄜˋㄈㄨˊ)
to lay an ambush: 我們設伏
待敵。We laid an ambush for
the enemy.

設奠(ㄕㄜˋㄉㄧㄢˋ)
to offer sacrifices to the
newly dead

設定(ㄕㄜˋㄉㄧㄥˋ)
(law) to establish legal relationship

設立(ㄕㄜˋㄌㄧˋ)
to establish; to set up: 我們
將在此地設立一所學校。We'll
set up a school here.

設或(ㄕㄜˋㄏㄨㄛˋ)
supposing that; what if; in
case of

設計(ㄕㄜˋㄐㄧˋ)
①to map out a plan,
scheme or coup ②to devise;
to plan; to design; a design:
他正在設計一部新機器。He is
designing a new machine.

設計教學法(ㄕㄜˋㄐㄧˋㄐㄧㄠˋㄒㄩㄝˊㄈㄚˇ)
the project method of teaching

設計者(ㄕㄜˋㄐㄧˋㄓㄜˇ)
the designer

設教(ㄕㄜˋㄐㄧㄠˋ)
to exert cultural influence;
to teach

設穽(ㄕㄜˋㄐㄧㄥˇ)
to set a trap or pitfall

設局(ㄕㄜˋㄐㄩˊ)
①to set a trap (usually
gambling, etc.) ②to establish a board or bureau

設下圈套(ㄕㄜˋㄒㄧㄚˋㄑㄩㄢ ㄊㄠˋ)
to set a snare

設險(ㄕㄜˋㄒㄧㄢˇ)
to fortify strategic points

設想(ㄕㄜˋㄒㄧㄤˇ)
①an idea; a rough plan; a
scheme; a tentative plan or
idea ②to think; to imagine;
to have consideration for: 設
想看看我當時的感受如何。Just
imagine how I felt then.

設置(ㄕㄜˋㄓˋ)
①to establish; to set up; to
found ②establishment; in-
stallations

設帳(ㄕㄜˋㄓㄤˋ)
①to pitch a tent ②to set
up a school

設帳授徒(ㄕㄜˋㄓㄤˋㄕㄡˋㄊㄨˊ)
to set up a school and
instruct students

設施(ㄕㄜˋㄕ)
①to plan and execute ②
(administrative) measures;
installations; facilities

設使(ㄕㄜˋㄕˇ)
if; what if; supposing that

設身處地(ㄕㄜˋㄕㄣ ㄔㄨˇㄉㄧˋ)
to put oneself in another's
position; to be considerate:
請你設身處地為我想。Put
yourself in my position.

設若(ㄕㄜˋㄖㄨㄛˋ)
if; suppose; provided: 設若有
病，你必須請醫生診治。You
must consult a doctor if you
get ill.

設座(ㄕㄜˋㄗㄨㄛˋ)
to install seats

設辭(ㄕㄜˋㄘˊ)
an excuse or pretext; a subterfuge

設色(ㄕㄜˋㄙㄜˋ)
to apply color in painting

設宴(ㄕㄜˋㄧㄢˋ)
to give a dinner party; to
throw a banquet

【許】 5541
ㄒㄩˇ sheu xǔ
1. to promise; to approve; to
permit
2. to praise; to commend
3. (said of a young girl) to be
betrothed; to promise to
marry
4. to expect
5. perhaps; maybe
6. (said of a person's age)
about; a little more than

7. a place
8. a final particle
9. so; this
10.a Chinese family name

許配(ㄒㄩˇㄆㄟˋ)或**許聘**(ㄒㄩˇㄆㄧㄣˋ)
(said of a girl) to betroth;
to affiance

許多(ㄒㄩˇㄉㄨㄛ)
many; numerous; much; a
great deal of; a lot of: 屋子
裏有許多人。There are many
people in the room.

許諾(ㄒㄩˇㄋㄨㄛˋ)
to promise; a promise

許可(ㄒㄩˇㄎㄜˇ)
to approve; to permit or
allow; approval

許可證(ㄒㄩˇㄎㄜˇㄓㄥˋ)
a permit; a license

許婚(ㄒㄩˇㄏㄨㄣ)
(said of a girl) to betroth

許嫁(ㄒㄩˇㄐㄧㄚˋ)
to betroth a daughter

許久(ㄒㄩˇㄐㄧㄡˇ)
for quite some time; for a
long time; for ages: 我們許久
沒有看到他了。We have not
seen him for ages.

許是(ㄒㄩˇㄕˋ)
perhaps; maybe

許慎(ㄒㄩˇㄕㄣˋ)
Hsü Shen, a high official in
the Eastern Han Dynasty
and author of 說文解字

許字(ㄒㄩˇㄗˋ)
(said of a girl) to betroth; to
affiance

許由(ㄒㄩˇㄧㄡˊ)
Hsü Yu, a legendary figure,
who supposedly turned down
offers to become emperor

許願(ㄒㄩˇㄩㄢˋ)
①to promise to a deity certain offerings in exchange
for divine blessings; to make
a vow (to a god) ②to promise somebody a reward

五畫

【訴】 5542
ㄙㄨˋ suh sù
1. to tell; to inform
2. to accuse; to file a complaint; to charge
3. to appeal; to petition
4. to resort to

〔言 部〕

〔言部〕

訴苦(ㄙㄨ ㄎㄨˇ)
to complain about one's grievances; to air complaints; to vent one's grievances; to pour out one's woes

訴苦窮兒(ㄙㄨ ㄎㄨˇ ㄑㄩㄥˊㄦ)
to tell others of one's state of poverty or destitution

訴之武力(ㄙㄨ ㄓ ㄨˇㄌㄧˋ)or訴諸武力(ㄙㄨ ㄓㄨ ㄨˇ ㄌㄧˋ)
to resort to force; to resort to violence: 如果其他手段都失敗，我們將訴諸武力。If other means fail, we shall resort to force.

訴諸公論(ㄙㄨ ㄓㄨ ㄍㄨㄥ ㄌㄨㄣˋ)
to appeal to public opinion

訴狀(ㄙㄨ ㄓㄨㄤˋ)
a plaint; a written complaint; a petition: 他向法院提出訴狀。He filed a plaint at court.

訴說(ㄙㄨ ㄕㄨㄛ)
to tell; to complain; to air grievances; to relate; to recount

訴訟(ㄙㄨ ㄙㄨㄥˋ)
a lawsuit; to go to law; litigation

訴訟法(ㄙㄨ ㄙㄨㄥˋ ㄈㄚˇ)
legal procedures involved in a lawsuit

訴訟費用(ㄙㄨ ㄙㄨㄥˋ ㄈㄟˋ ㄩㄥˋ)
fees entailed in a lawsuit; the cost of a civil action

訴訟代理人(ㄙㄨ ㄙㄨㄥˋ ㄉㄞˋ ㄌㄧˇ ㄖㄣˊ)
a legal counsel; an attorney; a legal representative

訴冤(ㄙㄨ ㄩㄢ)
to complain about grievances; to state injustice

訴願(ㄙㄨ ㄩㄢˋ)
to petition to a higher government agency against a decision of a lower office

【訶】5543
ㄏㄜ he hē
to scold or blame in a loud voice

訶護(ㄏㄜ ㄏㄨˋ)
divine protection

訶求(ㄏㄜ ㄑㄧㄡˊ)
to find fault; to make a stiff demand

訶譴(ㄏㄜ ㄑㄧㄢˇ)
to scold; to blame; to repri-

mand; to censure

訶叱(ㄏㄜ ㄔ)
to scold in a loud voice; to upbraid or revile: 不要老是訶叱。Don't scold so much.

訶責(ㄏㄜ ㄗㄜˊ)
to scold; to berate; to vituperate; scoldings: 我們當時的訶責已經習慣了。We were used to our mother's scoldings.

【診】5544
ㄓㄣ jeen zhěn
(又讀 ㄓㄣ jen zhěn)
1. to examine (diseases, ailments, etc.); to diagnose
2. to tell; to report

診病(ㄓㄣ ㄅㄧㄥˋ)
to examine a patient: 醫生替你診病了沒？Did the doctor examine you?

診脈(ㄓㄣ ㄇㄞˋ)or(ㄓㄣ ㄇㄛˋ)
to feel the pulse

診斷(ㄓㄣ ㄉㄨㄢˋ)
to diagnose(a disease); a diagnosis

診斷書(ㄓㄣ ㄉㄨㄢˋ ㄕㄨ)
a written diagnosis; a medical certificate

診療(ㄓㄣ ㄌㄧㄠˊ)
to diagnose and treat

診療室(ㄓㄣ ㄌㄧㄠˊ ㄕˋ)
a doctor's consultation room

診候(ㄓㄣ ㄏㄡˋ)
to examine and diagnose; to treat(a patient)

診治(ㄓㄣ ㄓˋ)
to diagnose and treat

診察(ㄓㄣ ㄔㄚˊ)
to examine and observe(the progress of a disease)

診視(ㄓㄣ ㄕˋ)
to examine(a patient): 醫生仔細診視她。The doctor examined her carefully.

診所(ㄓㄣ ㄙㄨㄛˇ)
a clinic; a dispensary

【註】5545
ㄓㄨˋ juh zhù
1. an explanatory note; a footnote; a commentary or remark; annotations
2. to register; to record or list

註明(ㄓㄨˋ ㄇㄧㄥˊ)
to explain or state clearly in writing; to explain the clear indication of: 引文要註明出

處。You must explain the sources of quotations clearly.

註定(ㄓㄨˋ ㄉㄧㄥˋ)
destined; predestined; doomed. 那是命中註定的。It is destined by fate.

註解(ㄓㄨˋ ㄐㄧㄝˇ)
explanatory notes or commentaries; definition; to define; to explain 亦作「注解」

註腳(ㄓㄨˋ ㄐㄧㄠˇ)
explanatory notes; footnotes

註銷(ㄓㄨˋ ㄒㄧㄠ)
to cancel; to nullify; to annul; to revoke; to write off

註失(ㄓㄨˋ ㄕ)
to report loss of documents, etc. to the authorities concerned

註釋(ㄓㄨˋ ㄕˋ)
explanatory notes

註疏(ㄓㄨˋ ㄕㄨ)or(ㄓㄨˋ ㄕㄨ)
① to explain ② explanatory notes or commentaries 亦作「注疏」

註冊(ㄓㄨˋ ㄘㄜˋ)
to register(with authorities concerned, etc.); registration

註冊費(ㄓㄨˋ ㄘㄜˋ ㄈㄟˋ)
registration fees

註冊主任(ㄓㄨˋ ㄘㄜˋ ㄓㄨˇ ㄖㄣˋ)
(in schools)the chief registrar; the registrar

註冊處(ㄓㄨˋ ㄘㄜˋ ㄔㄨˋ)
the register office

註冊手續(ㄓㄨˋ ㄘㄜˋ ㄕㄡˇ ㄒㄩˋ)
registration procedures

註冊商標(ㄓㄨˋ ㄘㄜˋ ㄕㄤ ㄅㄧㄠ)
a registered trademark; a registered brand

註冊組(ㄓㄨˋ ㄘㄜˋ ㄗㄨˇ)
the registration section

【訾】5546
(訿) ㄗˇ tzyy zǐ
1. to slander; to traduce; to attack
2. faults; blemishes
3. to measure
4. to consider
5. to estimate
6. poor(food); meager

訾病(ㄗˇ ㄅㄧㄥˋ)
to find fault with

訾屬(ㄗˇ ㄓㄨ)
illness; disease

訾紫（ｐˊ ｐˇ）
to slander; to defame

訾議（ｐˊ ｙˋ）
unfavorable criticism; to criticize; to impeach

【詁】 5547
《ㄍㄨ guu guˇ》
1. explanatory notes or commentaries
2. to transcribe the classics in everyday language

詁訓（ｃㄨˋ ㄒㄩㄣˋ）
to explain classics in everyday language 參看「訓詁」

【訛】 5548
ㄗ（ ｄㄧˇ dii diˇ）
to censure; to slander; to defame

訛謾（ｐˇ ㄇㄢˊ）
to slander and insult

訛諱（ｐˇ ㄏㄨㄟˋ）
to cover up with lies

訛詞（ｐˇ ㄏㄜˊ）
to slander; to defame; to disparage

訛毀（ｐˇ ㄏㄨㄟˇ）
to defame; to slander

訛謗（ｐˇ ㄅㄤˋ）
to slander or defame

【詈】 5549
ㄌㄧ（ ㄌㄧˋ lih liˋ）
to scold; to berate; to upbraid; to revile; to vituperate

詈罵（ㄌㄧˋ ㄇㄚˋ）
to scold; to abuse; to revile

詈辱（ㄌㄧˋ ㄖㄨˇ）
to scold and insult

【詠】 5550
（詠）ㄩㄥˇ yeong yongˇ
1. to sing; to chant; to hum
2. the chirping of birds

詠歎（ㄩㄥˇ ㄊㄢˋ）
to sigh (usually in admiration)

詠歎曲（ㄩㄥˇ ㄊㄢˋ ㄑㄩˇ）or 詠歎調
（ㄩㄥˇ ㄊㄢˋ ㄉㄧㄠˋ）
(opera) arias

詠古（ㄩㄥˇ ㄍㄨˇ）
to write poems on ancient subjects

詠絮之才（ㄩㄥˇ ㄒㄩˋ ㄓ ㄘㄞˊ）
a female who has a ready talent in composing verses

詠詩（ㄩㄥˇ ㄕ）
to chant poems

【詎】 5551
ㄐㄩˋ jiuh juˋ
an interjection indicating surprise

詎非所料（ㄐㄩˋ ㄈㄟ ㄙㄨㄛˇ ㄌㄧㄠˋ）
unexpectedly; nobody has expected that...

詎料（ㄐㄩˋ ㄌㄧㄠˋ）
who could have expected that...; unexpectedly

詎知（ㄐㄩˋ ㄓ）
who could have expected that...; unexpectedly

詎意（ㄐㄩˋ ㄧˋ）
who could have expected that...; unexpectedly

【詐】 5552
ㄓㄚˋ jah zhàˋ
1. deceitful; false; fake; fraudulent; crafty; artful; cunning
2. to deceive; to cheat; to lie; to swindle; to pretend; to feign
3. to trick into; to bluff somebody into giving information
4. sudden(ly); unexpected(ly)
亦作「乍」

詐敗（ㄓㄚˋ ㄅㄞˋ）
to feign defeat: 他常常詐敗誘敵。He often feigns defeat in order to lead on the enemy.

詐病（ㄓㄚˋ ㄅㄧㄥˋ）
to pretend to be ill

詐騙（ㄓㄚˋ ㄆㄧㄢˋ）
to swindle

詐婚（ㄓㄚˋ ㄏㄨㄣ）
to cheat by using marriage as a bait

詐欺（ㄓㄚˋ ㄑㄧ）
fraud; imposture; cheating

詐欺罪（ㄓㄚˋ ㄑㄧ ㄗㄨㄟˋ）
fraud (as a legal offense): 法官判定這人有詐欺罪。The judge found the man guilty of fraud.

詐降（ㄓㄚˋ ㄒㄧㄤˊ）
to fake surrender

詐譎（ㄓㄚˋ ㄒㄩㄝˊ）
dishonest; unfaithful; artful and crafty

詐稱（ㄓㄚˋ ㄔㄥ）
to tell a lie; to state falsely

詐術（ㄓㄚˋ ㄕㄨˋ）
fraud; cheating; chicanery; guile

詐財（ㄓㄚˋ ㄘㄞˊ）
to cheat for money

詐死（ㄓㄚˋ ㄙˇ）
to fake death; to feign death; to pretend to be dead; to play dead

詐偽（ㄓㄚˋ ㄨㄟˋ）
falsehood; deceitful; cunning; artful

【詒】 5553
ㄧˊ yi yíˊ
1. words as a gift usually given on parting
2. to hand down to posterity

【詔】 5554
ㄓㄠˋ jaw zhàoˇ
1. to proclaim; to announce
2. to instruct; to teach and direct; to coach
3. an imperial decree or mandate; an edict

詔命（ㄓㄠˋ ㄇㄧㄥˋ）
an imperial decree or edict

詔令（ㄓㄠˋ ㄌㄧㄥˋ）
an imperial decree or edict

詔告（ㄓㄠˋ ㄍㄠˋ）
(said of the emperor)to proclaim

詔敕（ㄓㄠˋ ㄔˋ）
an imperial rescript

詔書（ㄓㄠˋ ㄕㄨ）
a proclamation by the emperor; an imperial decree or edict

詔諭（ㄓㄠˋ ㄩˋ）
imperial instructions

【評】 5555
ㄆㄧㄥˊ pyng píng
1. to comment; to criticize; to review
2. comments; reviews
3. to judge; a decision after comparison, etc. by a group, as judges in a beauty contest
4. a Chinese family name

評判（ㄆㄧㄥˊ ㄆㄢˋ）
to criticize; to judge or decide, as in a beauty contest, etc.

評判員（ㄆㄧㄥˊ ㄆㄢˋ ㄩㄢˊ）
a judge; an umpire; a juror

評分（ㄆㄧㄥˊ ㄈㄣ）
marks or points given by a judge

評點（ㄆㄧㄥˊ ㄉㄧㄢˇ）
to superscribe punctuation marks and running commentaries on a well-known book

評定（ㄆㄧㄥˊ ㄉㄧㄥˋ）

〔言部〕

【言部】

to examine, judge and decide; to evaluate

評斷 (ㄆㄧㄥˊ ㄉㄨㄢˋ)
to decide; to arbitrate

評頭論足 (literally) to comment from head to feet—to make critical comments on the appearance of a woman

評理 (ㄆㄧㄥˊ ㄌㄧˇ)
to ask a third party to judge which side is right

評量 (ㄆㄧㄥˊ ㄌㄧㄤˊ)
to weigh; to evaluate

評論 (ㄆㄧㄥˊ ㄌㄨㄣˋ)
to comment; to review; comments; commentary: 他在閒暇時寫評論文章。He reviews in his spare time.

評論家 (ㄆㄧㄥˊ ㄌㄨㄣˋ ㄐㄧㄚ)
a commentator; a critic

評話 (ㄆㄧㄥˊ ㄏㄨㄚˋ)
① professional storytelling 亦作「說書」② novels or anecdotes written in plain language 亦作「平話」

評價 (ㄆㄧㄥˊ ㄐㄧㄚˋ)
① to estimate; to appraise; to assess: 他們對你的人格評價很高。They estimate your character highly. ② an objective assessment of the worth or merit of a person, a piece of writing, etc.

評註 (ㄆㄧㄥˊ ㄓㄨˋ)
critical notes; commentaries; annotations

評註者 (ㄆㄧㄥˊ ㄓㄨˋ ㄓㄜˇ)
a person who writes critical notes for an old book; an annotator

評傳 (ㄆㄧㄥˊ ㄓㄨㄢˋ)
a critical biography

評議 (ㄆㄧㄥˊ ㄧˋ)
to discuss or judge the right or wrong of something; to arbitrate

評議會 (ㄆㄧㄥˊ ㄧˋ ㄏㄨㄟˋ)
an advisory or policy-making council; an arbitration board

評議員 (ㄆㄧㄥˊ ㄧˋ ㄩㄢˊ)
① a member of 評議會 ② officers in an organization responsible for discussing and drafting the rules and operation of the organiza-

tion

評語 (ㄆㄧㄥˊ ㄩˇ)
comments; criticism

評閱 (ㄆㄧㄥˊ ㄩㄝˋ)
to read and grade (student papers, etc.)

【詖】 5556
ㄅㄧ bih bì

1. unfair; erroneous; wrong
2. to argue; to debate

詖論 (ㄅㄧ ㄌㄨㄣˋ)
erroneous statements in which the speaker is unable to see the error

詖行 (ㄅㄧˋ ㄒㄧㄥˊ)
evil and one-sided conduct (or actions)

詖辭 (ㄅㄧ ㄘˊ)
one-sided words; biased remarks; partial statements

【詛】 5557
ㄗㄨˇ tzuu zǔ

1. to curse; to imprecate
2. to vow; to pledge; to take an oath

詛罵 (ㄗㄨˇ ㄇㄚˋ)
to curse and berate

詛盟 (ㄗㄨˇ ㄇㄥˊ)
a vow; an oath

詛祝 (ㄗㄨˇ ㄓㄨˋ)
to pray to a deity that the enemy be brought down by divine wrath

詛咒 (ㄗㄨˇ ㄓㄡˋ)
to curse; to imprecate; to wish someone evil

【詞】 5558
ㄘˊ tsyr cí

1. words; phrases; expressions; speech; statements: 雙方各執一詞。Each sticks to his own words.
2. a part of speech in grammar
3. to talk, speak or tell
4. (Chinese literature) tzu, a form of poetry characterized by lines of irregular length

詞不達意 (ㄘˊ ㄅㄨˋ ㄉㄚˊ ㄧˋ)
The language cannot convey the ideas intended.

詞牌 (ㄘˊ ㄆㄞˊ)
the verse form of tzu (詞)

詞譜 (ㄘˊ ㄆㄨˇ)
① a collection of tzu (詞) ② name of a book edited by Wang Yi-ching (王奕清), etc. in the Ching Dynasty, includ-

ing 2,300 tzu (詞)

詞鋒 (ㄘˊ ㄈㄥ)
① the sharpness of one's tongue ② incisiveness of a piece of writing: 他的詞鋒銳利。His writings are sharp and incisive.

詞典 (ㄘˊ ㄉㄧㄢˇ)
a dictionary 亦作「辭典」; 詞典是他的常伴。A dictionary is his frequent companion.

詞頭 (ㄘˊ ㄊㄡˊ)
a prefix

詞類 (ㄘˊ ㄌㄟˋ)
the parts of speech: 英文有八大詞類。There are eight parts of speech in English.

詞林 (ㄘˊ ㄌㄧㄣˊ)
① (in old China) the Hanlin Academy (翰林院) ② a place where men of letters congregate

詞律 (ㄘˊ ㄌㄩˋ)
rules of prosody

詞根 (ㄘˊ ㄍㄣ)
a word root; a stem

詞翰 (ㄘˊ ㄏㄢˋ)
① literary works, as poems, proses, etc. ② letters; correspondence

詞華 (ㄘˊ ㄏㄨㄚˊ)
poetic diction

詞話 (ㄘˊ ㄏㄨㄚˋ)
a book dealing with forms, styles or authors of tzu (詞)

詞彙 (ㄘˊ ㄏㄨㄟˋ)
① a dictionary ② a vocabulary

詞句 (ㄘˊ ㄐㄩˋ)
wording; text of a piece of writing; expressions; words and phrases

詞曲 (ㄘˊ ㄑㄩ)
poems and songs

詞窮 (ㄘˊ ㄑㄩㄥˊ)
(literally) to run short of words—unable to put up a riposte in an argument; unable to give an answer when confronted with overwhelming evidence of guilt, etc.

詞性 (ㄘˊ ㄒㄧㄥˋ)
the characteristic or property of a word, by which one can determine which part of speech the word belongs to

詞章(ㄘ ㄓㄤ)
literary works

詞臣(ㄘ ㄔㄣ)
a court official who specializes in literature

詞書(ㄘ ㄕㄨ)
dictionaries

詞人(ㄘ ㄖㄣ)
① men of letters ② one who is well versed in *tzu* (詞)

詞藻(ㄘ ㄗㄠ)
ornamentation in the use of words; ornate terms or expressions; flowery language

詞宗(ㄘ ㄗㄨㄥ)
a great man of letters; a literary lion

詞意(ㄘ ㄧ)
meanings of phrases; the gist of a piece of writing; the drift

詞尾(ㄘ ㄨㄟ)
a suffix

詞語(ㄘ ㄩ)
words and expressions; terms

【詘】 5559
　 ㄑㄩ chiu qū
1. to bend; to crouch
2. to yield (to another's views, etc.); to submit
3. short
4. a Chinese family name

【訿】 5560
（訾）ㄗ tzyy zǐ
to defame or slander, etc.

【証】 5561
（證）ㄓㄥ jenq zhèng
evidence; proof; a certificate; to certify

六畫

【詣】 5562
　 ㄧ yih yì
1. to go (to a place); to arrive
2. to visit; to call on
3. achievements; attainments

詣門(ㄧ ㄇㄣ)
to visit someone

詣闕(ㄧ ㄑㄩㄝ)
to go to the palace—to see the emperor

詣謁(ㄧ ㄧㄝ)
to pay a visit to

【訹】 5563
　 ㄒㄩ sheu xū

1. to boast; to brag; to exaggerate
2. popular; to make widely known; common
3. (now rarely) clever and brave
4. (now rarely) harmonious

翻詡(ㄒㄩ ㄒㄩ)
① vivid; lively ② to boast; to brag ③ harmonious

【詢】 5564
　 ㄒㄩㄣ shyun xún
1. to inquire; to ask: 我探詢他來此的原因。I inquired his reason for coming.
2. to deliberate and plan
3. truely; honesty

詢察(ㄒㄩㄣ ㄔㄚˊ)
to investigate and inquire

詢問(ㄒㄩㄣ ㄨㄣ)
to inquire; to ask; to make inquiries

詢問處(ㄒㄩㄣ ㄨㄣˋ ㄔㄨ)
an information desk: 你可到詢問處詢問。Ask at the information office.

【試】 5565
　 ㄕ shyh shì
1. to try; to test; to experiment; a trial; a test
2. to use
3. to examine; examination
4. to sound out; to put up a trial balloon
5. to compare
6. a Chinese family name

試辦(ㄕ ㄅㄢ)
to do something on an experimental basis; to implement a pilot project

試飛(ㄕ ㄈㄟ)
to test a new airplane in flight; a test flight; a trial flight

試飛員(ㄕ ㄈㄟ ㄩㄢ)
a test pilot

試探(ㄕ ㄊㄢ)
to test; to sound out; to put up a trial balloon; to probe; to explore: 試探一下他對這個問題的看法。Try to sound him out about the question

試題(ㄕ ㄊㄧ)
questions in a test or examination

試帖(ㄕ ㄊㄧㄝ)
① the composition of poetry-writing in the civil service

examination in the olden days ② a test in classics in the civil service examination during the Tang Dynasty

試試(ㄕ ㄕ)
to attempt; to try

試官(ㄕ ㄍㄨㄢ)
① the official in charge of an examination ② officials appointed on a probational basis

試管(ㄕ ㄍㄨㄢ)
a test tube

試管嬰兒(ㄕ ㄍㄨㄢˇ ㄧ ㄦ)
a test-tube baby; a human embryo in the laboratory

試航(ㄕ ㄏㄤ)
① the trial run of a new ship ② the test flight of a new plane ③ a test sail or flight along a new route

試婚(ㄕ ㄏㄨㄣ)
trial marriage

試教(ㄕ ㄐㄧㄠ)or(ㄕ ㄐㄧㄠ)
to practise teaching

試劍(ㄕ ㄐㄧㄢ)
to test the sharpness of a newly made sword or blade; to try out a new sword

試金石(ㄕ ㄐㄧㄣ ㄕ)
① Lydian stone ② something which can make a person reveal his true character

試金術(ㄕ ㄐㄧㄣ ㄕㄨ)
assaying

試鏡(ㄕ ㄐㄧㄥ)
to undergo a screen test

試卷(ㄕ ㄐㄩㄢ)
a test paper; an examination paper

試銷(ㄕ ㄒㄧㄠ)
to put a new product on sale or to sell something in a new market on a limited scale in order to see the result; to sell a product on a trial basis; trial sale

試新(ㄕ ㄒㄧㄣ)
① name of a kind of tea ② to try the newly harvested rice ③ to try a new product

試想(ㄕ ㄒㄧㄤ)
to think it over; considering that...; just think

試行(ㄕ ㄒㄧㄥ)
to try out something

試紙(ㄕ ㄓ)

①(chemistry) test paper: 石蕊試紙 lttmus test paper ②
an examination paper

試裝(ㄕ ㄓㄨㄤ)
to try a new suit

試車(ㄕ ㄔㄜ)
① a trial run of a vehicle ②
a trial run of machinery in
a new factory

試場(ㄕ ㄔㄤ)or 試驗場
an examination place; a test
ground: 你知道你的試場在那
裏嗎? Do you know where
your examination place is?

試穿(ㄕ ㄔㄨㄢ)
to try on (a garment, shoes,
etc.)

試晬(ㄕ ㄓㄨㄟ)
to try to find out a baby's
likely career in the future
by placing before him an
assortment of articles on his
first birthday and letting
him pick one of them which
may provide a clue to the
observers

試思(ㄕ ㄙ)
just think; to think it over;
considering that...

試藝(ㄕ ㄧˋ)
writing or composition in
the civil service examination
of former times

試一試(ㄕ ㄧ· ㄕ)or 試試(ㄕ·ㄕ)
to try 或 Let's give it a try
(and see what happens). 來
試試看。Come on; give it a
try.

試藥(ㄕ ㄧㄠˋ)
a reagent

試演(ㄕ ㄧㄢˇ)
a dress rehearsal; a preview;
to make a dress rehearsal; a
trial performance

試驗(ㄕ ㄧㄢ)
an experiment; to experi-
ment; to try, test or examine

試驗管(ㄕ ㄧㄢ ㄍㄨㄢˇ)
a test tube

試驗紙(ㄕ ㄧㄢ ㄓˇ)
test paper; litmus paper

試驗場(ㄕ ㄧㄢ ㄔㄤ)or 試驗場
an experimental station or
ground

試驗室(ㄕ ㄧㄢ ㄕˋ)
a laboratory 亦作「實驗室」

試映(ㄕ ㄧㄥ)

a preview (of a movie); to
give a preview

試問(ㄕ ㄨㄣˋ)
Let me ask....或 Let's post
this question.... 或 May we
ask...?

試用(ㄕ ㄩㄥ)
to use on a trial basis; to
employ on a probational
basis

試用人員(ㄕ ㄩㄥ ㄖㄣˊ ㄩㄢˊ)
probational personnel; pro-
bationers

【詩】 5566
ㄕ shy shī
1. poetry; poems; poetic
2. anything or quality as an
offspring of pure imagination
3. short for *The Book of Odes*
edited by Confucius

詩伯(ㄕ ㄅㄛˊ)or 詩豪(ㄕ ㄏㄠˊ)
a master in poetry; a great
poet

詩派(ㄕ ㄆㄞ)
the different schools of
poetry-writing

詩癖(ㄕ ㄆㄧˇ)
a deep love for poetry

詩篇(ㄕ ㄆㄧㄢ)
① poems ② the *Book of
Psalms* in the *Old Testament*

詩品(ㄕ ㄆㄧㄣˇ)
the title of a book by Chung
Jung (鍾嶸) of the Liang
Dynasty and Ssu-Kung Tu
(司空圖) of Tang Dynasty
respectively

詩魔(ㄕ ㄇㄛˊ)
① an unorthodox style of
poetry-writing ② one who
has an obsessive love for
poetry

詩謎(ㄕ ㄇㄧˊ)
① a riddle in the form of a
poem ② a kind of gambling
featuring the use of ancient
poems

詩壇(ㄕ ㄊㄢˊ)
the circle of poets

詩體(ㄕ ㄊㄧˇ)
the style or form of poetry

詩奴(ㄕ ㄋㄨˊ)
inferior poets; poetasters

詩禮傳家(ㄕ ㄌㄧˇ ㄔㄨㄢˊ ㄐㄧㄚ)
a family of scholars

詩料(ㄕ ㄌㄧㄠˋ)

materials that inspire the
composition of poems

詩律(ㄕ ㄌㄩˋ)
rules of prosody; restrictions
of verse form

詩歌(ㄕ ㄍㄜ)
① poems and songs collec-
tively ② poetry

詩格(ㄕ ㄍㄜˊ)
a style of poetry

詩稿(ㄕ ㄍㄠˇ)or 詩草(ㄕ ㄘㄠˇ)
scripts of poems; draft
poems

詩虎(ㄕ ㄏㄨˇ)
riddles in poetry form

詩話(ㄕ ㄏㄨㄚˋ)
① a book containing com-
ments on poetry or poets ②
narratives written in the
Sung Dynasty

詩集(ㄕ ㄐㄧˊ)
a collection of poems

詩箋(ㄕ ㄐㄧㄢ)
paper for writing poems

詩經(ㄕ ㄐㄧㄥ)
The Book of Odes or *The
Book of Poetry*, one of the
Chinese classics compiled
and edited by Confucius

詩句(ㄕ ㄐㄩˋ)
a stanza or line in a poem

詩情畫意(ㄕ ㄑㄧㄥˊ ㄏㄨㄚˋ ㄧˋ)
(said of a landscape) idyllic

詩窮而後工(ㄕ ㄑㄩㄥˊ ㄦˊ ㄏㄡˋ ㄍㄨㄥ)
In writing poems one gains
depth after suffering poverty.

詩仙(ㄕ ㄒㄧㄢ)
the Poetic God—Li Po (李白)

詩興(ㄕ ㄒㄧㄥˋ)
an urge to compose poems,
in the mood or having a
sudden inspiration for writing poems

詩興大發(ㄕ ㄒㄧㄥˋ ㄉㄚˋ ㄈㄚ)
to feel a strong urge to compose poems; to be in the
mood for writing poems

詩序(ㄕ ㄒㄩˋ)
the forewords before every
chapter of *The Book of Odes*,
supposedly written by Tzu-
hsia (子夏), one of Confucian
disciples

詩學(ㄕ ㄒㄩㄝˊ)
poetics

詩選(ㄕ ㄒㄩㄢˇ)
a selection of poems

詩債(ㄕ ㄓㄞˋ)
(literally) a poetic debt—an unfulfilled promise to respond with a poem

詩鐘(ㄕ ㄓㄨㄥ)
a game in poem-composition—within a limited period of time poems are written on two different topics with unlikely associations

詩中有畫，畫中有詩(ㄕ ㄓㄨㄥ ㄧㄡˇ ㄏㄨㄚˋ, ㄏㄨㄚˋ ㄓㄨㄥ ㄧㄡˇ ㄕ)
(literally) There's a picture in the poem and a poem in the picture.—a poem replete with graphic descriptions or picture images and a painting having the quality of a good poem

詩讖(ㄕ ㄔㄣˋ)
a poem which portends what will happen to the poet

詩史(ㄕ ㄕˇ)
poems reflecting the troubles of the time, to which the-works of Tu Fu (杜甫) of the Tang Dynasty is often referred

詩社(ㄕ ㄕㄜˋ)
a site of regular meetings of poets

詩聖(ㄕ ㄕㄥˋ)
the Poetic Sage—Tu Fu (杜甫)

詩書(ㄕ ㄕㄨ)
① *The Book of Odes* and *The Book of History* ② classics in general

詩書門第(ㄕ ㄕㄨ ㄇㄣˊ ㄉㄧˋ)
a scholarly family; a family of high academic standing: 他出身於詩書門第。He was brought up in a scholarly family.

詩人(ㄕ ㄖㄣˊ)
a poet

詩人節(ㄕ ㄖㄣˊ ㄐㄧㄝˊ)
Poets' Day, on the fifth day of the fifth month in the lunar calendar

詩詞歌賦(ㄕ ㄘˊ ㄍㄜ ㄈㄨˋ)
the four forms of Chinese poetry

詩思(ㄕ ㄙ)
poetic inspiration; poetical

---

thoughts

詩以言志(ㄕ ㄧˇ ㄧㄢˊ ㄓˋ)
Poetry serves as a medium to convey one's aspiration or ambition.

詩意(ㄕ ㄧˋ)
the poetic quality; the romantic atmosphere

詩妖(ㄕ ㄧㄠ)
perversive poems and songs which are usually the harbinger of social unrest or moral degeneracy

詩友(ㄕ ㄧㄡˇ)
a friend in poetry

詩文(ㄕ ㄨㄣˊ)
literary works in general: 他晚年以詩文自娛。He amused himself by reading literary works in his old age.

詩翁(ㄕ ㄨㄥ)
a renowned poet at his advanced age

詩餘(ㄕ ㄩˊ)
another name of a form of 詞(a form of poetry)

詩韻(ㄕ ㄩㄣˋ)
① rhyme of verses ② a rhyme book

【詫】 5567
　　ㄔㄚˋ chah chà
1. surprised; to wonder
2. to brag; to boast
3. to cheat; to deceive
4. to inform

詫異(ㄔㄚˋ ㄧˋ)
to be surprised

【詬】 5568
　　ㄍㄡˋ gow gòu
1. to insult; to shame
2. to berate; to vituperate; to abuse
3. a Chinese family name

詬病(ㄍㄡˋ ㄅㄧㄥˋ)
to insult; to criticize; to blame: 它將爲世人所詬病。It will become an object that the public blame.

詬罵(ㄍㄡˋ ㄇㄚˋ)
to berate; to abuse

詬厲(ㄍㄡˋ ㄌㄧˋ)
to shame; ashamed

詬詈(ㄍㄡˋ ㄌㄧˋ)
to berate; to vituperate

詬辱(ㄍㄡˋ ㄖㄨˇ)
to insult; to shame; to mortify; mortification; an in-

---

sult

【詭】 5569
　　ㄍㄨㄟˇ goei guǐ
1. to cheat; to deceive; to feign; to defraud
2. strange; rare; odd; peculiar; uncanny; weird
3. cunning; shrewd; stealthy
4. to urge oneself; to consider as one's responsibility
5. to go against; to defy; to contradict

詭辯(ㄍㄨㄟˇ ㄅㄧㄢˋ)
sophistry; sophistication; to argue one's point in a subtle, artful, clever, and sophisticated way

詭辯家(ㄍㄨㄟˇ ㄅㄧㄢˋ ㄐㄧㄚ)
a sophist or sophister

詭辯學派(ㄍㄨㄟˇ ㄅㄧㄢˋ ㄒㄩㄝˊ ㄆㄞˋ)
the sophistic school; the sophists

詭秘(ㄍㄨㄟˇ ㄇㄧˋ)
stealthy; clandestine; secret; surreptitious: 他的行蹤詭秘。He is surreptitious in his movements.

詭道(ㄍㄨㄟˇ ㄉㄠˋ)
perverse ways; ways which are not normally or ordinarily followed

詭特(ㄍㄨㄟˇ ㄊㄜˋ)
strange; odd; peculiar

詭計(ㄍㄨㄟˇ ㄐㄧˋ)
a trick; an artful device or trap

詭計多端(ㄍㄨㄟˇ ㄐㄧˋ ㄉㄨㄛ ㄉㄨㄢ)
to have many tricks up one's sleeves; very tricky or crafty; cunning

詭譎(ㄍㄨㄟˇ ㄐㄩㄝˊ)
① changing; cunning; crafty; treacherous ② strange; odd; weird

詭詐(ㄍㄨㄟˇ ㄓㄚˋ)
tricky; deceptive; deceit; cunningness

詭辭(ㄍㄨㄟˇ ㄘˊ)
lies or deceptive words to cover up the truth

詭隨(ㄍㄨㄟˇ ㄙㄨㄟˊ)
the wily and obsequious persons

詭異(ㄍㄨㄟˇ ㄧˋ)
strange; odd; abnormal; weird; uncanny

【詮】 5570
　　ㄑㄩㄢˊ chyuan quán

［言部］

〔言部〕

1. to explain; to expound; to illustrate. 你的論論正確。You explain accurately.
2. the truth or core of something
3. to weigh; to assess; to rate; to appraise

詮釋 (ㄑㄩㄢ ㄕ)
to interpret; to explain; to expound; interpretation; explanation; annotations; explanatory notes

詮次 (ㄑㄩㄢ ㄘ)
to arrange in order

【詰】 5571
ㄐㄧㄝ jye jié

1. to question; to interrogate; to ask
2. to punish
3. to prohibit; to restrain

詰屈 or 詰詘 (ㄐㄧㄝ ㄑㄩ)
bent and twisting

詰屈聱牙 (ㄐㄧㄝ ㄑㄩ ㄠ ㄧㄚ)
(said of writings) hard and difficult to read. 他的散文讀起來詰屈聱牙。His essays are difficult to read.

詰責 (ㄐㄧㄝ ㄗㄜ)
to berate; to censure; to rebuke; to denounce

詰問 (ㄐㄧㄝ ㄨㄣ) or (ㄑㄧ ㄨㄣ)
to demand an explanation angrily; to question closely; to cross-examine

【話】 5572
ㄏㄨㄚ huah huà

1. a speech, talk or conversation; words; sayings
2. to speak; to talk; to converse; to say
3. language

話靶 (ㄏㄨㄚ ㄅㄚ) or 話把兒 (ㄏㄨㄚ ㄅㄚ ㄦ)
one's words or conduct which become material for gossip by others; cause for talk

話本 (ㄏㄨㄚ ㄅㄣ)
the plain-language version of an original work written in archaic language; the text of a story

話別 (ㄏㄨㄚ ㄅㄧㄝ)
to bid farewell; to say good-bye

話柄 (ㄏㄨㄚ ㄅㄧㄥ)
①words or behavior as material for others' gossip; the subject of ridicule: 不要留下話柄。Don't leave any subject of ridicule. ②a promise, remark, etc. made casually which is subsequently used by others as a weapon against the speaker

話不投機 (ㄏㄨㄚ ㄅㄨ ㄊㄡ ㄐㄧ)
not seeing eye to eye in conversation or talk; remarks not appealing to the other side

話不投機半句多 (ㄏㄨㄚ ㄅㄨ ㄊㄡ ㄐㄧ ㄅㄢ ㄐㄩ ㄉㄨㄛ)
When the conversation gets disagreeable, to say one word more is a waste of breath.

話頭兒 (ㄏㄨㄚ ㄊㄡ ㄦ) or 話頭 (ㄏㄨㄚ ㄊㄡ)
something to talk about; something to open a conversation

話題 (ㄏㄨㄚ ㄊㄧ)
the topic of conversation or discussion

話題一轉 (ㄏㄨㄚ ㄊㄧ ㄧ ㄓㄨㄢ)
to change the topic of conversation

話筒 (ㄏㄨㄚ ㄊㄨㄥ)
①a microphone ②a telephone transmitter ③a megaphone

話裏套話 (ㄏㄨㄚ ㄌㄧ ㄊㄠ ㄏㄨㄚ)
①to try to pry into or obtain the secret of the other party through apparently innocent conversation ②to touch upon other matters when a discussion is centered on one topic

話料兒 (ㄏㄨㄚ ㄌㄧㄠ ㄦ)
material for talk, conversation or gossip

話舊 (ㄏㄨㄚ ㄐㄧㄡ)
to talk over old times with a friend

話家常 (ㄏㄨㄚ ㄐㄧㄚ ㄔㄤ)
to chitchat; to exchange small talk

話劇 (ㄏㄨㄚ ㄐㄩ)
a play or drama (as distinct from opera); modern drama

話匣子 (ㄏㄨㄚ ㄒㄧㄚ ㄗ)
①a phonograph ②a chatterbox: 那女人是個話匣子。That woman is a chatter-box.

話中有話 (ㄏㄨㄚ ㄓㄨㄥ ㄧㄡ ㄏㄨㄚ) or 話裏有話 (ㄏㄨㄚ ㄌㄧ ㄧㄡ ㄏㄨㄚ)
something more (implied) in what is said; overtones in conversation

話中有刺 (ㄏㄨㄚ ㄓㄨㄥ ㄧㄡ ㄘ)
hidden barbs in one's words

話鋒兒 (ㄏㄨㄚ ㄈㄥ ㄦ)
①implication or real meaning in what is said ②the thread of discourse

話說 (ㄏㄨㄚ ㄕㄨㄛ)
an expression introducing an episode in old novels

話音 (ㄏㄨㄚ ㄧㄣ) or 話音兒 (ㄏㄨㄚ ㄧㄣ ㄦ)
a hint in conversation; a tone: 聽他的話音兒，他想當科學家。His tone suggests that he wishes to be a scientist.

【該】 5573
《ㄍㄞ gai gōi

1. should; ought to; obliged to: 他不該如此。He should not do this.
2. fated to; preordained
3. to owe
4. that; the said (person, place, matter, etc.)
5. to be somebody's turn to do something
6. to deserve: 他該受到懲罰。He deserves to be punished.
7. inclusive; complete

該博 (《ㄞ ㄅㄛ)
erudite and well-experienced

該備 (《ㄞ ㄅㄟ)
complete; nothing lacking

該班 (《ㄞ ㄅㄢ)
①to be on duty by rotation ②that class or squad

該罵 (《ㄞ ㄇㄚ)
to deserve a scolding

該犯 (《ㄞ ㄈㄢ)
the said prisoner: 該犯已遭處決。The said prisoner has been executed.

該打 (《ㄞ ㄉㄚ)
to deserve a flogging or spanking: 你真該打。You deserve a spanking.

該當 (《ㄞ ㄉㄤ)
①ought to; should; proper to ②to deserve

該地 (《ㄞ ㄉㄧ)
that place; the said place

該管（《ㄞ《ㄨㄢ）
①the competent authorities; the official in charge ②ought to exercise control or assume responsibility; should be disciplined

該員（《ㄞ《ㄨㄢ）
erudite; learned

該項（《ㄞ ㄒㄧㄤ）
that item; that matter

該眼（《ㄞ 业ㄥ）
to owe debt or money

該處（《ㄞ ㄔㄨ）
①that place ②that department

該死（《ㄞ ㄙ）
to deserve death 或 Confounded! 或 Go to hell!

該員（《ㄞ ㄩㄢ）
the said so-and-so (a documentary expression referring to a subordinate)

【詳】 5574 ㄒㄧㄤ shyang xiáng
1. complete; detailed; details; particulars; minute
2. to know; to know the details
3. please see ... for details
4. to explain; to interpret

詳夢（ㄒㄧㄤ ㄇㄥ）
to interpret dreams

詳密（ㄒㄧㄤ ㄇㄧ）
detailed and comprehensive

詳明（ㄒㄧㄤ ㄇㄧㄥ）
detailed and very clear: 這本書有詳明的註解。The book has full and clear annotations.

詳談（ㄒㄧㄤ ㄊㄢ）
to speak in detail; to go into details

詳略（ㄒㄧㄤ ㄌㄩㄝ）
detailed or brief; complete or sketchy

詳解（ㄒㄧㄤ ㄐㄧㄝ）
to explain in detail

詳盡（ㄒㄧㄤ ㄐㄧㄣ）
detailed and complete

詳情（ㄒㄧㄤ ㄑㄧㄥ）
details of an event, incident, etc.: 詳情請至辦事處詢問。Please apply to the office for details.

詳細（ㄒㄧㄤ ㄒㄧ）or 詳細細（ㄒㄧㄤ ㄒㄧ ㄒㄧ）
in every detail and particu-lar; detailed; minute; nothing omitted: 請說詳細一點。Please explain in greater detail.

詳細審計（ㄒㄧㄤ ㄒㄧ ㄕㄣˇ ㄐㄧ）
a detailed audit

詳徵博引（ㄒㄧㄤ ㄓㄥ ㄅㄛ ㄧㄣˇ）
to quote extensively and in detail (in order to support one's view or prove one's point)

詳註（ㄒㄧㄤ 业ㄨ）
copious (explanatory) notes; to annotate fully

詳查（ㄒㄧㄤ ㄔㄚ）
to investigate fully; to examine every detail

詳實（ㄒㄧㄤ ㄕ）
(said of a report) detailed and accurate

詳審（ㄒㄧㄤ ㄕㄣˇ）
to think, consider or examine carefully; to go into details

詳述（ㄒㄧㄤ ㄕㄨ）
to narrate in complete detail; detailed narration

詳言之（ㄒㄧㄤ ㄧㄢ 业）
to state in detail and particular

詳閱（ㄒㄧㄤ ㄩㄝ）
to read carefully: 請詳閱他的計畫。Please read his plan carefully.

【詹】 5575 业ㄢ jan zhān
1. to talk too much; verbosity
2. to reach
3. a Chinese family name
4. (now rarely) to divine
5. to look up 亦作「瞻」

詹天佑（业ㄢ ㄊㄧㄢ ㄧㄡˋ）
Chan Tien-yu (1861-1919), a railroad engineer who invented a type of rail-car coupler still in use today

詹森（业ㄢ ㄙㄣ）
Lyndon B. Johnson, 1908-1973, the 36th president of the United States

詹尹（业ㄢ ㄧㄣˇ）
(in ancient China) an official in charge of divination

【詼】 5576 ㄏㄨㄟ huei huī
1. funny; humorous
2. to ridicule; to joke

詼誹（ㄏㄨㄟ ㄈㄟ）
to joke or jest; to ridicule

詼諧（ㄏㄨㄟ ㄒㄧㄝ）
to joke or jest; to ridicule

詼詭（ㄏㄨㄟ 《ㄨㄟˇ）
grotesquely funny or hilarious

詼諧（ㄏㄨㄟ ㄒㄧㄝ）
funny; humorous; comical; to tell jokes; to make humorous remarks

【誄】 5577 ㄌㄟˇ leei lěi
1. writings eulogizing a dead person; a speech, an ode, etc. in praise of the dead
2. to eulogize in prayer
3. to confer a posthumous title
4. to pray for the dead

【誅】 5578 业ㄨ ju zhū
1. to kill; to execute; execution; to put to death
2. to punish
3. to weed out; to exterminate

誅滅（业ㄨ ㄇㄧㄝˋ）
to eliminate; to eradicate

誅戮（业ㄨ ㄌㄨ）
to kill; to slaughter

誅奸（业ㄨ ㄐㄧㄢ）
to punish the traitorous

誅求（业ㄨ ㄑㄧㄡ）
to exact; to exploit; to demand greedily

誅心之論（业ㄨ ㄒㄧㄣ 业 ㄌㄨㄣˋ）
a statement condemning someone not because of what he did but because of his motive for doing it

誅除（业ㄨ ㄔㄨˊ）
to eliminate; to root out

誅夷（业ㄨ ㄧˊ）
to launch a punitive campaign against barbarians

誅意（业ㄨ ㄧˋ）
to criticize someone not because of what he has done but because of his motive for doing it

【誇】 5579 ㄎㄨㄚ kua kuā
1. to exaggerate; to boast; to brag
2. big; great
3. to show off; to flaunt
4. to praise

誇大（ㄎㄨㄚ ㄉㄚˋ）
①to exaggerate; exaggeration; to overstate; to magnify: 這分報告有點誇大。This

〔言部〕

report is somewhat exaggerated. ② arrogant

誇大狂(ㄎㄨㄚ ㄉㄚ ㄎㄨㄤ)
　①megalomania ②a megalomaniac

誇大其詞(ㄎㄨㄚ ㄉㄚ ㄑㄧ ㄘ)
　to make an overstatement; to exaggerate

誇誕(ㄎㄨㄚ ㄉㄢ)
　exaggerating to an incredible extent

誇多鬥靡(ㄎㄨㄚ ㄉㄨㄛ ㄉㄡ ㄇㄧ)
　to show off one's learning

誇功(ㄎㄨㄚ ㄍㄨㄥ)
　to boast of one's contribution or achievement

誇口(ㄎㄨㄚ ㄎㄡ)
　to boast; to brag; to talk big

誇獎(ㄎㄨㄚ ㄐㄧㄤ)
　to praise; to extol; to acclaim; to commend

誇下海口(ㄎㄨㄚ ㄒㄧㄚ ㄏㄞ ㄎㄡ)
　to have boasted; to have made the boast that...

誇詡(ㄎㄨㄚ ㄒㄩ)
　to boast; to exaggerate

誇張(ㄎㄨㄚ ㄓㄤ)
　to exaggerate; exaggeration; to overstate

誇張的語言(ㄎㄨㄚ ㄓㄤ ㄉㄜ ㄩ ㄧㄢ)
　inflated language; exaggerations

誇張法(ㄎㄨㄚ ㄓㄤ ㄈㄚ)
　hyperbole

誇示(ㄎㄨㄚ ㄕ)
　to show off; to flaunt

誇飾(ㄎㄨㄚ ㄕ)
　to exaggerate

誇讚(ㄎㄨㄚ ㄗㄢ)
　to praise; to extol

誇嘴(ㄎㄨㄚ ㄗㄨㄟ)
　to brag; to boast

誇耀(ㄎㄨㄚ ㄧㄠ)
　to flaunt; to show off

【詵】 ㄕㄣ　shen　shēn
1. to ask; to question
2. to address; to speak to
3. numerous; many; swarming

詵詵(ㄕㄣ ㄕㄣ)
　①numerous ②collecting harmoniously

【誆】 5581 ㄎㄨㄤ　kuang　kuǎng
　to lie; to cheat; to deceive; to hoax

誆騙(ㄎㄨㄤ ㄆㄧㄢ)

to cheat; to swindle; to hoax; to dupe

誆哄(ㄎㄨㄤ ㄏㄨㄥ)
　to lie; to cheat; to deceive

【詿】 5582 ㄍㄨㄚ　guah　guà
1. an error; a mistake
2. to cheat; to deceive

詿誤(ㄍㄨㄚ ㄨ)
　to be punished for a mistake made by someone else 亦作「罣誤」

七畫

【認】 5583 ㄖㄣ　renn　rèn
1. to recognize; to understand; to know; to make out; to identify
2. to admit; to acknowledge; to own
3. to accept; to resign oneself to
4. to enter into a certain relationship with; to adopt
5. to promise to do something; to subscribe

認不得(ㄖㄣ ㄅㄨ ㄉㄜ)
　unable to recognize; unrecognizable; not familiar

認不清(ㄖㄣ ㄅㄨ ㄑㄧㄥ)
　unable to identify

認不出來(ㄖㄣ ㄅㄨ ㄔㄨ ㄌㄞ)
　to fail to recognize; unable to recognize

認賠(ㄖㄣ ㄆㄟ)
　to admit an obligation to pay (for damage, etc.)

認票不認人(ㄖㄣ ㄆㄧㄠ ㄅㄨ ㄖㄣ ㄖㄣ)
　to consider the validity of a note, ticket, check, etc. independently of its bearer; payable to the bearer

認明(ㄖㄣ ㄇㄧㄥ)
　to see clearly; to recognize: 他們認明他是合法的繼承人。 They recognized him as the lawful heir.

認命(ㄖㄣ ㄇㄧㄥ)
　to accept fate; to resign oneself to destiny

認罰(ㄖㄣ ㄈㄚ)
　to admit that one deserves punishment

認得(ㄖㄣ ㄉㄜ)
　to recognize; to know

認定(ㄖㄣ ㄉㄧㄥ)

①to conclude or decide (with or without adequate proof); to believe firmly ②to set one's mind on

認同(ㄖㄣ ㄊㄨㄥ)
　to identify; identification

認了(ㄖㄣ ㄌㄜ)
　①to accept; to tolerate; to resign oneself to what is inevitable ②to admit

認領(ㄖㄣ ㄌㄧㄥ)
　①to identify and claim (a child, a lost article, etc.) ②(said of a man) to adopt a child born out of wedlock

認購公債(ㄖㄣ ㄍㄡ ㄍㄨㄥ ㄓㄞ)
　to subscribe for bonds

認股(ㄖㄣ ㄍㄨ)
　to become a shareholder; to subscribe to shares

認可(ㄖㄣ ㄎㄜ)
　to sanction; to approve

認捐(ㄖㄣ ㄐㄩㄢ)
　to subscribe; to donate

認親(ㄖㄣ ㄑㄧㄣ)
　to acknowledge relationship (as the families of the bride and the bridegroom do at a wedding)

認清(ㄖㄣ ㄑㄧㄥ)
　to see or know clearly (which is which); to identify clearly

認知(ㄖㄣ ㄓ)
　cognition

認真(ㄖㄣ ㄓㄣ)
　to be serious; to be earnest

認賬 或 認帳(ㄖㄣ ㄓㄤ)
　①to acknowledge a debt ②to admit a mistake; to accept responsibility for a failure; to admit what one has said or done: 他自己說的話,怎能不認賬? How can he refuse to admit what he has said?

認屍(ㄖㄣ ㄕ)
　to identify (dead) bodies

認識(ㄖㄣ ㄕ)
　①to recognize; to know ②to understand; to comprehend; to realize; understanding; knowledge ③(psychology) cognition

認識論(ㄖㄣ ㄕ ㄌㄨㄣ)
　epistemology

認生(ㄖㄣ ㄕㄥ)

(said of children or pets) to be scared of strangers; to be shy in the presence of strangers

認輸(ㄖㄣˋ ㄕㄨ)
to concede defeat; to throw in the towel; to give up

認字(ㄖㄣˋ ㄗˋ)
① able to read; literate ② to learn to read individual characters

認賊作父(ㄖㄣˋ ㄗㄟˊ ㄗㄨㄛˋ ㄈㄨˋ)
(literally) to treat a thief as one's father—to give allegiance to an usurper or invader; to mistake an enemy for one's friend

認罪(ㄖㄣˋ ㄗㄨㄟˋ)
to acknowledge a fault; to plead guilty

認錯(ㄖㄣˋ ㄘㄨㄛˋ)
① to admit a fault or mistake ② to make identification incorrectly

認為(ㄖㄣˋ ㄨㄟˊ)
to be of the opinion that...; to think that...; to consider that...; to hold; to deem: 這件事我們認為有必要跟他說清楚。We deem it necessary to make this clear to him.

【誌】 5584　ㄓˋ jyh zhì
1. to write down; to put down; to record
2. a record

誌銘(ㄓˋ ㄇㄧㄥˊ)
an epitaph 亦作「墓誌銘」

誌悼(ㄓˋ ㄉㄠˋ)
to condole

誌慶(ㄓˋ ㄑㄧㄥˋ)
to offer congratulations

誌喜(ㄓˋ ㄒㄧˇ)
to offer congratulations

誌哀(ㄓˋ ㄞ)
to condole

【誆】 5585　ㄎㄨㄤ kwang kuāng
(又讀《ㄨㄤ guang guāng)
to deceive; to delude: 你別誆我。Don't try to deceive me.

誆騙(ㄎㄨㄤ ㄆㄧㄢˋ)
to deceive; to cheat; to swindle; to defraud

誆誕(ㄎㄨㄤ ㄉㄢˋ)
to deceive; to delude

誆言(ㄎㄨㄤ ㄧㄢˊ)or **誆語**(ㄎㄨㄤ ㄩˇ)
a lie; wild talk; a falsehood: 他常口出誆語。He often utters falsehoods.

【誓】 5586　ㄕˋ shyh shì
1. to pledge; to vow; to swear; a vow; an oath
2. to take an oath (of allegiance, office, etc.)

誓不兩立(ㄕˋ ㄅㄨˋ ㄌㄧㄤˇ ㄌㄧˋ)
to vow to fight till oneself or the other party falls

誓不甘休(ㄕˋ ㄅㄨˋ ㄍㄢ ㄒㄧㄡ)
to vow never to let the offender get away with it

誓師(ㄕˋ ㄕ)
to brief and rouse the troops before a military action; to give a pep talk to the troops at the start of a military expedition

誓詞(ㄕˋ ㄘˊ)
an oath; a pledge

誓死不屈(ㄕˋ ㄙˇ ㄅㄨˋ ㄑㄩ)
to vow that one would rather die than yield

誓言(ㄕˋ ㄧㄢˊ)
a solemn pledge; a vow; an oath

誓約(ㄕˋ ㄩㄝ)
a solemn pledge; a vow; an oath

誓願(ㄕˋ ㄩㄢˋ)
a vow or pledge (especially one made to oneself)

【誕】 5587　ㄉㄢˋ dann dàn
1. birth
2. preposterous; absurd
3. an initial particle

誕辰(ㄉㄢˋ ㄔㄣˊ)
birthday

誕生(ㄉㄢˋ ㄕㄥ)
birth

誕生地(ㄉㄢˋ ㄕㄥ ㄉㄧˋ)
birthplace: 新竹是我的誕生地。Hsinchu is my birthplace.

誕辰(ㄉㄢˋ ㄔㄣˊ)or **誕日**(ㄉㄢˋ ㄖˋ)
birthday

誕妄(ㄉㄢˋ ㄨㄤˋ)
to cheat with lies

【誘】 5588　ㄧㄡˋ yow yòu
1. to guide; to lead
2. to decoy; to tempt; to allure; to lure; to captivate; to entice

誘兵(ㄧㄡˋ ㄅㄧㄥ)
to pretend to flee in order to lead the enemy into an ambush: 誘兵不追。Do not press the troops that pretend to flee.

誘捕(ㄧㄡˋ ㄅㄨˇ)
to lure a criminal out of hiding and arrest him

誘騙(ㄧㄡˋ ㄆㄧㄢˋ)
to induce by deceit; to beguile; to cajole; to inveigle: 他誘騙我簽這合同。He beguiled me into signing this contract.

誘導(ㄧㄡˋ ㄉㄠˇ)
to guide; to lead to the right path; to induce; induction

誘導反應(ㄧㄡˋ ㄉㄠˇ ㄈㄢˇ ㄧㄥˋ)
(chemistry) an induced reaction

誘導圈(ㄧㄡˋ ㄉㄠˇ ㄑㄩㄢ)
(chemistry)an induction coil

誘敵(ㄧㄡˋ ㄉㄧˊ)
to induce the enemy (to make a wrong move)

誘逃(ㄧㄡˋ ㄊㄠˊ)
to induce someone to run away from home or abscond

誘良為娼(ㄧㄡˋ ㄌㄧㄤˊ ㄨㄟˊ ㄔㄤ)
to induce innocent girls into prostitution

誘拐(ㄧㄡˋ ㄍㄨㄞˇ)
to seduce; to entice; to abduct; to kidnap: 那孩子昨天被誘拐。The child was abducted yesterday.

誘惑(ㄧㄡˋ ㄏㄨㄛˋ)
① to entice; to lure; to allure; to tempt; to beguile ② to attract; attractive: 窗外景色誘惑人。The view outside the window is attractive.

誘惑色(ㄧㄡˋ ㄏㄨㄛˋ ㄙㄜˋ)
alluring colors (of animals or insects)

誘姦(ㄧㄡˋ ㄐㄧㄢ)
to seduce (a girl, especially a minor); to entice into unlawful sexual intercourse; statutory rape

誘脅(ㄧㄡˋ ㄒㄧㄝˊ)
to tempt and threaten; to cajole and coerce alternatively

誘致(ㄧㄡˋ ㄓˋ)

〔言部〕

〔言

部〕

to attain an objective by
means of temptation

誘殺(1ㄨ ㄕㄚ)
to trap and kill; to lure to
destruction

誘人犯罪(1ㄨ ㄖㄣˊ ㄈㄢˋ ㄗㄨㄟˋ)
to induce others to break
the law

誘餌(1ㄨ ㄦˇ)
① a bait ② a shill

誘掖(1ㄨ 1ㄝˋ)
to guide and encourage; to
lead and help

誘因(1ㄨ 1ㄣ)
an incentive; an inducement

【誚】5589
　　ㄑ1ㄠˋ chiaw qiào
to blame; to reproach; to
censure

誚讓(ㄑ1ㄠˋ ㄖㄤˋ)
to blame; to reproach

【誡】5590
　　ㄐ1ㄝˋ jieh jiè
1. to warn; to admonish
2. a commandment

【語】5591
　　1. ㄩˇ yeu yǔ
1. language; speech
2. a word; a sentence; an expression
3. a saying; a proverb
4. a sign; a signal
5. to speak; to say; to talk

語病(ㄩˇ ㄅ1ㄥˋ)
① illogical use of words;
faulty wording or formulation ② difficulty in speaking
caused by vocal defects

語妙天下(ㄩˇ ㄇ1ㄠˋ ㄊ1ㄢ ㄒ1ㄚˋ)
unequaled in making wise-
cracks

語法(ㄩˇ ㄈㄚˇ)
wording; grammar; syntax

語法學(ㄩˇ ㄈㄚˇ ㄒㄩㄝˊ)
syntax

語調(ㄩˇ ㄉ1ㄠˋ)
the tone of one's speech;
intonation

語態(ㄩˇ ㄊㄞˋ)
(grammar) voice: 主動語態
the active voice 被動語態 the
passive voice

語體文(ㄩˇ ㄊ1ˇ ㄨㄣˊ)
writings in the spoken style

語能喪失症(ㄩˇ ㄋㄥˊ ㄙㄤˋ ㄕ ㄓㄥˋ)
(pathology) aphasia

語錄(ㄩˇ ㄌㄨˋ)

written records of lectures
(especially of the Sung
Dynasty Confucian scholars);
quotations

語錄體(ㄩˇ ㄌㄨˋ ㄊ1ˇ)
the lecture style of writing

語感(ㄩˇ ㄍㄢˇ)
the linguistic sense, feel, or
intuition

語根(ㄩˇ ㄍㄣ)
an etymology: 幫我查查這幾
個字的語根. Just look up the
etymologies of these words
for me.

語彙(ㄩˇ ㄏㄨㄟˋ)
vocabulary

語驚四座(ㄩˇ ㄐ1ㄥ ㄙˋ ㄗㄨㄛˋ)
The statement was received
with raised eyebrows.

語句(ㄩˇ ㄐㄩˋ)
sentences; phrases: 這篇文章
的語句冗長. The phrases of
this article are miscellaneous and long.

語氣(ㄩˇ ㄑ1ˋ)
① (grammar) mood ② the
tone (of one's speech); the
manner of speaking

語系(ㄩˇ ㄒ1ˋ)
a family of languages; a language family; a linguistic
family

語學(ㄩˇ ㄒㄩㄝˊ)
linguistics 參看「語言學」

語助詞(ㄩˇ ㄓㄨˋ ㄘˊ)
a grammatical particle; an
auxiliary

語重心長(ㄩˇ ㄓㄨㄥˋ ㄒ1ㄣ ㄔㄤˊ)
One's words are serious and
(one's) heart is thoughtful.

語勢(ㄩˇ ㄕˋ)
the force of an utterance or
statement

語族(ㄩˇ ㄗㄨˊ)
a language family

語詞(ㄩˇ ㄘˊ)
words; phrases

語塞(ㄩˇ ㄙㄜˋ)
unable to utter a word in
self-defense (when confronted with unfavorable evidence)

語意(ㄩˇ 1ˋ)
the meaning (of a word,
phrase, sentence, etc.): 這句
子的語意清楚. The meaning
of the sentence is clear.

語意學(ㄩˇ 1ˋ ㄒㄩㄝˊ)

semantics

語焉不詳(ㄩˇ 1ㄢ ㄅㄨˋ ㄒ1ㄤˊ)
The statement is too brief
to be clear. 或 very sketchy;
too generalized

語言(ㄩˇ 1ㄢˊ)
a language; speech: 拉丁文是
一種死語言. Latin is a dead
language.

語言教學法(ㄩˇ 1ㄢˊ ㄐ1ㄠˋ ㄒㄩㄝˊ ㄈㄚˇ)
language teaching methods

語言教室(ㄩˇ 1ㄢˊ ㄐ1ㄠˋ ㄕˋ)
a language class

語言心理學(ㄩˇ 1ㄢˊ ㄒ1ㄣ ㄌ1ˇ ㄒㄩㄝˊ)
linguistic psychology

語言學(ㄩˇ 1ㄢˊ ㄒㄩㄝˊ)
linguistics; philology

語言學家(ㄩˇ 1ㄢˊ ㄒㄩㄝˊ ㄐ1ㄚ)
a linguist; a linguistic scientist; a philologist

語言實驗室(ㄩˇ 1ㄢˊ ㄕˊ 1ㄢˋ ㄕˋ)
a language laboratory; a
language lab

語音(ㄩˇ 1ㄣ)
① a speech sound; a phone
② pronunciation

語音學(ㄩˇ 1ㄣ ㄒㄩㄝˊ)
phonetics 參看「聲韻學」

語無倫次(ㄩˇ ㄨˊ ㄌㄨㄣˊ ㄘˋ)
to talk incoherently

語尾(ㄩˇ ㄨㄟˇ)
(grammar) a suffix

語文(ㄩˇ ㄨㄣˊ)
① Chinese (as a subject of
study or a means of communication) ② language and
literature

語文學(ㄩˇ ㄨㄣˊ ㄒㄩㄝˊ)
the study of written lan-
guage

語源學(ㄩˇ ㄩㄢˊ ㄒㄩㄝˊ)
etymology

語云(ㄩˇ ㄩㄣˊ)
as the saying goes

【語】5591
　　2. ㄩˋ yuh yù
to tell; to inform; to admonish

語人(ㄩˋ ㄖㄣˊ)
to tell others

【誠】5592
　　ㄔㄥˊ cherng chéng
1. sincere; honest; cordial; sincerity
2. true; real; truly; indeed;
actually

誠樸(ㄔㄥˊ ㄆㄨˊ)

honest and simple

誠非所料(ㄔㄥˊ ㄈㄟ ㄙㄨㄛˇ ㄌㄧㄠˋ)
It is really unexpected.

誠服(ㄔㄥˊ ㄈㄨˊ)
to obey willingly; to submit willingly

誠篤(ㄔㄥˊ ㄉㄨˊ)
honest

誠懇(ㄔㄥˊ ㄎㄣˇ)
sincere; true-hearted; cordial

誠惶誠恐(ㄔㄥˊ ㄏㄨㄤˊ ㄔㄥˊ ㄎㄨㄥˇ)
extremely afraid; very fearful (an expression usually used in a memorial to the emperor)

誠敬(ㄔㄥˊ ㄐㄧㄥˋ)
sincere and respectful

誠心(ㄔㄥˊ ㄒㄧㄣ)
sincerity; wholeheartedness

誠心誠意(ㄔㄥˊ ㄒㄧㄣ ㄔㄥˊ ㄧˋ)
earnestly and sincerely

誠摯(ㄔㄥˊ ㄓˋ)
sincere; true-hearted; cordial

誠實(ㄔㄥˊ ㄕˊ)
honest; upright; trustworthy; honesty: 誠實為上策. Honesty is the best policy.

誠實可靠(ㄔㄥˊ ㄕˊ ㄎㄜˇ ㄎㄠˋ)
honest and reliable; trustworthy

誠屬(ㄔㄥˊ ㄕㄨˇ)
It is certainly....或 They are certainly....

誠然(ㄔㄥˊ ㄖㄢˊ)
certainly; surely; indeed; to be sure

誠如所言(ㄔㄥˊ ㄖㄨˊ ㄙㄨㄛˇ ㄧㄢˊ)
①It is exactly as you said.
②if it is exactly as you say

誠壹(ㄔㄥˊ ㄧ)
single-minded; single-hearted

誠意(ㄔㄥˊ ㄧˋ)
sincerity; good faith

【誣】 5593
　　ㄨ wu wū
　　(讀音 ㄨ ㄨ wǔ)
to accuse falsely; to bring a false charge against

誣謗(ㄨ ㄅㄤˇ)
to slander; to libel

誣衊(ㄨ ㄇㄧㄝˋ)
to slander; to libel; to vilify; to calumniate; to smear

誣服(ㄨ ㄈㄨˊ)
to plead guilty when one is not (usually as a result of torture)

誣捏事實(ㄨ ㄋㄧㄝ ㄕˋ ㄕˊ)
to fabricate a false story

誣賴(ㄨ ㄌㄞˋ)
to slander; to accuse falsely; to incriminate falsely

誣良為盜(ㄨ ㄌㄧㄤˊ ㄨㄟˊ ㄉㄠˋ)
to bring a false charge of theft against an upright man; to charge an innocent man with robbery

誣告(ㄨ ㄍㄠˋ)or誣控(ㄨ ㄎㄨㄥˋ)
to bring a false charge against; to accuse falsely

誣告反坐(ㄨ ㄍㄠˋ ㄈㄢˇ ㄗㄨㄛˋ)
False charges will bring upon the accuser the same punishment which he intends to inflict upon the accused.

誣告罪(ㄨ ㄍㄠˋ ㄗㄨㄟˋ)
an offense of malicious accusation

誣書(ㄨ ㄕㄨ)
to accuse falsely

誣陷(ㄨ ㄒㄧㄢˋ)
to incriminate falsely; to frame somebody

誣證(ㄨ ㄓㄥˋ)
a perjury; to give false testimony

誣染(ㄨ ㄖㄢˇ)
to slander; to libel

誣罔(ㄨ ㄨㄤˇ)
to accuse falsely; to bring a false charge against: 切勿誣罔善人. Never accuse an innocent person.

【誤】 5594
　　ㄨ wuh wù
1. to err; a mistake; an error
2. to harm; to suffer; to injure
3. to delay
4. to miss
5. by mistake; by accident

誤報(ㄨ ㄅㄠˋ)
to report incorrectly

誤筆(ㄨ ㄅㄧˇ)
a slip of the pen 亦作「筆誤」

誤卯(ㄨ ㄇㄠˇ)
to fail to show up at the roll call

誤謬(ㄨ ㄇㄧㄡˋ)
a mistake; an error: 那是愚蠢的誤謬. That was a foolish mistake.

誤犯(ㄨ ㄈㄢˋ)
to offend or violate unintentionally

誤服(ㄨ ㄈㄨˊ)
to take the wrong (medicine); to take (medicine) by mistake

誤導(ㄨ ㄉㄠˇ)
to mislead: 有些報紙誤導輿論. Some newspapers mislead public opinion.

誤點(ㄨ ㄉㄧㄢˇ)
(said of trains, etc.) to be behind time; late; overdue: 火車誤點半小時. The train was half an hour late.

誤了(ㄨ ㄌㄜˋ)
①to have caused an undue delay in ②to have mismanaged

誤國(ㄨ ㄍㄨㄛˊ)
to mismanage national affairs; to cause harm to national causes; to damage national interests

誤刊(ㄨ ㄎㄢ)
to publish something incorrectly

誤會(ㄨ ㄏㄨㄟˋ)
to misunderstand; to misinterpret; to misconstrue; a misunderstanding

誤記(ㄨ ㄐㄧˋ)
to record incorrectly

誤解(ㄨ ㄐㄧㄝˇ)
to misunderstand; to misinterpret; to misconstrue; a misunderstanding

誤盡蒼生(ㄨ ㄐㄧㄣˋ ㄘㄤ ㄕㄥ)
to bring calamity to humanity; to lead the masses to the road of disaster

誤期(ㄨ ㄑㄧˊ)
to fail to meet the deadline; to be behind schedule

誤信(ㄨ ㄒㄧㄣˋ)
to misplace one's confidence; to believe what is unreliable

誤差(ㄨ ㄔㄚ)
(mathematics) an error

誤傳(ㄨ ㄔㄨㄢˊ)
to transmit (facts) incorrectly

誤時(ㄨ ㄕˊ)
to be behind time

誤食(ㄨ ㄕˊ)
to eat (something poisonous or inedible) by mistake

誤事(ㄨ ㄕˋ)

〔言部〕

〔言部〕

to ruin a plan through mis-management, negligence, etc.; to bungle matters

誤殺(ㄨ ㄕㄚ)
① unintentional homicide; manslaughter ② to kill or murder a person mistaken for the intended victim

誤傷(ㄨ ㄕㄤ)
to hurt by mistake

誤人子弟(ㄨ ㄖㄣˊ ㄗˇ ㄉㄧˋ)
(usually said of a poor teacher) to mislead the children of others

誤人誤己(ㄨ ㄖㄣˊ ㄨ ㄐㄧˇ)
to harm both others and oneself

誤認(ㄨ ㄖㄣˋ)
to identify incorrectly

誤入歧途(ㄨ ㄖㄨˋ ㄑㄧˊ ㄊㄨˊ)
to go astray (morally)

誤算(ㄨ ㄙㄨㄢˋ)
to miscalculate; to miscount

誤譯(ㄨ ㄧˋ)
to translate incorrectly

誤爲(ㄨ ㄨㄟˊ)
to mistake one thing for another

【誥】 5595
《ㄍ gaw gào

1. to grant; to confer; to bestow
2. to admonish
3. a written admonition; an imperial mandate

誥命(ㄍㄠˋ ㄇㄧㄥˋ)
a monarch's orders of conferment of titles; an imperial mandate

誥封(ㄍㄠˋ ㄈㄥ)
to bestow (a title upon the wife, living parents, etc. of an official); the conferment of honorary titles by an imperial mandate

誥誡(ㄍㄠˋ ㄐㄧㄝˋ)
an injunction of exhortation

誥敕(ㄍㄠˋ ㄔˋ)
a decree of conferment of titles upon officials in the Ming and Ching dynasties

誥授(ㄍㄠˋ ㄕㄡˋ)
to bestow (titles upon officials)

誥贈(ㄍㄠˋ ㄗㄥˋ)
to bestow (titles upon officials posthumously)

【誦】 5596
ㄙㄨㄥˋ sonq sòng

1. to recite; to intone; to chant
2. poetry; poems; songs

誦讀(ㄙㄨㄥˋ ㄉㄨˊ)
to read aloud; to recite; to intone

誦經(ㄙㄨㄥˋ ㄐㄧㄥ)
to recite passages from scriptures

誦習(ㄙㄨㄥˋ ㄒㄧˊ)
to learn by recitation

誦詩(ㄙㄨㄥˋ ㄕ)
to recite or intone a verse

【誨】 5597
ㄏㄨㄟˋ huey huì
(又讀 ㄏㄨㄟˊ hoei huí)

1. to teach; to instruct
2. instructions
3. to admonish
4. to induce

誨盗誨淫(ㄏㄨㄟˋ ㄉㄠˋ ㄏㄨㄟˋ ㄧㄣˊ)
to encourage theft by being careless about one's valuables and incite lust by displaying one's physical charms

誨人不倦(ㄏㄨㄟˋ ㄖㄣˊ ㄅㄨˋ ㄐㄩㄢˋ)
to teach without weariness (often used as a complimentary expression in citation of teachers)

【說】 5598
1. ㄕㄨㄛ shuo shuō

1. to speak; to talk; to utter; to say
2. to explain; to clarify
3. a description; a narration; a statement
4. a theory
5. to scold; to talk to; a talking-to; a scolding

說白(ㄕㄨㄛ ㄅㄞˊ)
(Chinese opera) the spoken part (as distinct from the part that is sung)

說白道綠(ㄕㄨㄛ ㄅㄞˊ ㄉㄠˋ ㄌㄩˋ)
to comment on various things without restraint

說白了(ㄕㄨㄛ ㄅㄞˊ ·ㄌㄜ)
to put in plain language

說不得(ㄕㄨㄛ ·ㄅㄨ ㄉㄜˊ)
① unspeakable; indescribable ② unfit for mention; scandalous ③ unavailable

說不定(ㄕㄨㄛ ·ㄅㄨ ㄉㄧㄥˋ)
maybe; perhaps; probably:

說不定那船已經入港了。Maybe the ship has already arrived in harbor.

說不來(ㄕㄨㄛ ·ㄅㄨ ㄌㄞˊ)
① unable to speak; unable to utter ② not on friendly terms; unable to get along with each other

說不過(ㄕㄨㄛ ·ㄅㄨ ㄍㄨㄛˋ)
unable to outspeak or outdebate

說不過去(ㄕㄨㄛ ·ㄅㄨ ㄍㄨㄛˋ ·ㄑㄩ)
unacceptable to one's sense of propriety or justice; cannot be justified or explained away

說不開(ㄕㄨㄛ ·ㄅㄨ ㄎㄞ)
unable to reach a mutual understanding

說不清(ㄕㄨㄛ ·ㄅㄨ ㄑㄧㄥ)
unable to explain clearly

說不下去(ㄕㄨㄛ ·ㄅㄨ ㄒㄧㄚˋ ·ㄑㄩ)
① unable to continue one's speech ② not acceptable to one's sense of propriety

說不出口(ㄕㄨㄛ ·ㄅㄨ ㄔㄨ ㄎㄡˇ)
unutterable; unable to speak out

說不上(ㄕㄨㄛ ·ㄅㄨ ㄕㄤˋ)
① do not deserve mention; do not fit the description ② cannot say or tell

說不上來(ㄕㄨㄛ ·ㄅㄨ ㄕㄤˋ ㄌㄞˊ)
unable to get the words out

說破(ㄕㄨㄛ ㄆㄛˋ)
to unravel or expose by some remarks

說媒(ㄕㄨㄛ ㄇㄟˊ)
to propose a marriage as a matchmaker

說夢(ㄕㄨㄛ ㄇㄥˋ)
to talk nonsense

說夢話(ㄕㄨㄛ ㄇㄥˋ ㄏㄨㄚˋ)
① to talk in one's sleep ② to talk nonsense

說明(ㄕㄨㄛ ㄇㄧㄥˊ)
① to explain; to clarify; to expound ② expository writing; exposition; caption

說明書(ㄕㄨㄛ ㄇㄧㄥˊ ㄕㄨ)
a written explanation; written instructions attached to merchandise

說法(ㄕㄨㄛ ㄈㄚˇ)
① to preach Buddhism ② the way of reasoning; an argument; interpretation; a state-

ment; a version; wording;
這意思可以有數種說法。This
idea can be formulated in
different ways.

說風涼話(ㄕㄨㄛ ㄈㄥ ㄌㄧㄤ ㄏㄨㄚˋ)
to talk like an unconcerned
person; to make nonchalant
statements

說大話(ㄕㄨㄛ ㄉㄚˋ ㄏㄨㄚˋ)
to brag; to boast; to talk
big; to talk through one's
hat

說得來(ㄕㄨㄛ ㄉㄜˊ ㄌㄞˊ)
(said of two or more peo-
ple) able to get along; to be
on good terms: 他們很說得
來。They are on good terms.

說得過去(ㄕㄨㄛ ㄉㄜˊ ㄍㄨㄛˋ ㄑㄩˋ)
acceptable; passable; excusable; pardonable

說得好(ㄕㄨㄛ ㄉㄜˊ ㄏㄠˇ)
well said

說得好聽(ㄕㄨㄛ ㄉㄜˊ ㄏㄠˇ ㄊㄧㄥ)
to make an unpleasant fact
sound attractive

說得下去(ㄕㄨㄛ ㄉㄜˊ ㄒㄧˋ ㄑㄩˋ)
passable

說得上(ㄕㄨㄛ ㄉㄜˊ ㄕㄤˋ)
to deserve mention

說得有理(ㄕㄨㄛ ㄉㄜˊ ㄧㄡˇ ㄌㄧˇ)
to sound reasonable

說到(ㄕㄨㄛ ㄉㄠˋ)
to speak of; to mention; to
refer to; as to: 我希望你沒有
向她說到我。I hope you did
not mention my name to
her.

說到做到(ㄕㄨㄛ ㄉㄠˋ ㄗㄨㄛˋ ㄉㄠˋ)
to do what one says; to live
up to one's word: 我會說到做
到的。I'll live up to my word.

說道(ㄕㄨㄛ ㄉㄠˋ)
to say

說地談天(ㄕㄨㄛ ㄉㄧˋ ㄊㄢˊ ㄊㄧㄢ)
①to talk about everything
under the sun ②skilled in
speech; eloquent 亦作「談天
說地」

說定(ㄕㄨㄛ ㄉㄧㄥˋ)
to settle; to agree on: 關於價
格我們尚未說定。We haven't
agreed on the price yet.

說短論長(ㄕㄨㄛ ㄉㄨㄢˇ ㄌㄨㄣˋ ㄔㄤˊ)
to gossip; to criticize others

說東道西(ㄕㄨㄛ ㄉㄨㄥ ㄉㄠˋ ㄒㄧ)
to talk about all sorts of
subjects without restraint

說頭兒(ㄕㄨㄛ·ㄊㄡ ㄦˇ)
①something worth talking
about ②an excuse

說天說地(ㄕㄨㄛ ㄊㄧㄢ ㄕㄨㄛ ㄉㄧˋ)
①to brag; to boast ②
skilled in speech; eloquent

說通(ㄕㄨㄛ ㄊㄨㄥ)
to succeed in reaching an
understanding

說了不算(ㄕㄨㄛ·ㄌㄜ ㄅㄨˋ ㄙㄨㄢˋ)
to fail to keep a promise; to
go back on one's word

說了算數(ㄕㄨㄛ·ㄌㄜ ㄙㄨㄢˋ ㄕㄨˋ)
I mean what I say.

說來話長(ㄕㄨㄛ ㄌㄞˊ ㄏㄨㄚˋ ㄔㄤˊ)
It is a long story....

說來說去(ㄕㄨㄛ ㄌㄞˊ ㄕㄨㄛ ㄑㄩˋ)
to say the same thing over
and over again

說理(ㄕㄨㄛ ㄌㄧˇ)
①to give a sermon; to
preach ②to be reasonable;
to argue; to reason things
out

說溜了嘴(ㄕㄨㄛ ㄌㄧㄡ·ㄌㄜ ㄗㄨㄟˇ)
to have a slip of the tongue;
to blurt out something

說高道低(ㄕㄨㄛ ㄍㄠ ㄉㄠˋ ㄉㄧ)
to criticize others thought-
lessly

說古(ㄕㄨㄛ ㄍㄨˇ)
(a derisive expression) to
talk about one's pet subject

說鼓書(ㄕㄨㄛ ㄍㄨˇ ㄕㄨ)
the accompaniment of a
drum when narrating stories
in metrical form

說過(ㄕㄨㄛ ㄍㄨㄛˋ)
to have said or mentioned

說鬼話(ㄕㄨㄛ ㄍㄨㄟˇ ㄏㄨㄚˋ)
to tell a lie; to lie

說客(ㄕㄨㄛ ㄎㄜˋ)
one who tries to persuade or
convince somebody on
behalf of another

說開(ㄕㄨㄛ ㄎㄞ)
to explain

說合(ㄕㄨㄛ ㄏㄜˊ)
to help arrange a union

說和(ㄕㄨㄛ·ㄏㄜ)
to act as a mediator; to
mediate: 我去給他們說和。I'll
try to mediate between
them.

說黑道白(ㄕㄨㄛ ㄏㄟ ㄉㄠˋ ㄅㄞˊ)
to criticize others thought-

lessly

說好(ㄕㄨㄛ ㄏㄠˇ)
to complete negotiations; to
come to an agreement

說好說歹(ㄕㄨㄛ ㄏㄠˇ ㄕㄨㄛ ㄉㄞˇ)
to speak both well and ill in
an attempt to influence or
induce

說話(ㄕㄨㄛ ㄏㄨㄚˋ)
①to speak; to talk; to say
②to tell stories ③to have a
talk ④gossip; talk ⑤(colloquial) in a minute; in a
moment; in a jiffy; right
away

說話不當話(ㄕㄨㄛ ㄏㄨㄚˋ ㄅㄨˋ ㄉㄤˋ
ㄏㄨㄚˋ)
to fail to keep a promise; to
break one's word

說三道四(ㄕㄨㄛ ㄙㄢ ㄉㄠˋ ㄙˋ)
to criticize others

說謊(ㄕㄨㄛ ㄏㄨㄤˇ)
to tell a lie; to lie

說謊者(ㄕㄨㄛ ㄏㄨㄤˇ ㄓㄜˇ)
a liar

說教(ㄕㄨㄛ ㄐㄧㄠˋ)
to preach; to deliver a sermon

說起(ㄕㄨㄛ ㄑㄧˇ)
①to start talking about; to
bring up (a subject) ②with
reference to; as for

說起來(ㄕㄨㄛ ㄑㄧˇ·ㄌㄞ)
①as a matter of fact; in
fact: 說起來我們還是同學。In
fact, we were in the same
school. ②to mention

說千道萬(ㄕㄨㄛ ㄑㄧㄢ ㄉㄠˋ ㄨㄢˋ)
to speak thousands of times;
to speak again and again

說親(ㄕㄨㄛ ㄑㄧㄣ)
to propose a marriage as a
matchmaker

說親道熱(ㄕㄨㄛ ㄑㄧㄣ ㄉㄠˋ ㄖㄜˋ)
to say friendly things; to
sound very friendly

說清道白(ㄕㄨㄛ ㄑㄧㄥ ㄉㄠˋ ㄅㄞˊ)
to talk clearly

說情(ㄕㄨㄛ ㄑㄧㄥˊ)
to solicit a favor or to ask
for mercy on behalf of
others; to intercede

說笑笑(ㄕㄨㄛ ㄒㄧㄠˋ ㄒㄧㄠˋ)
(ㄕㄨㄛ ㄒㄧㄠˋ ㄒㄧㄠˋ)
to joke; to talk and laugh

說笑話(ㄕㄨㄛ ㄒㄧㄠˋ ㄏㄨㄚˋ)

〔言
部〕

〔言部〕

to tell jokes

說閒話（ㄕㄨㄛ ㄒㄧㄢ ㄏㄨㄚˋ）
to gossip; to criticize; to make unfavorable comments; a gossip: 她太喜歡說閒話。She is too fond of gossip.

說現成話（ㄕㄨㄛ ㄒㄧㄢˋ ㄔㄥˊ ㄏㄨㄚˋ）
to make comments like an after-the-event prophet

說項（ㄕㄨㄛ ㄒㄧㄤˋ）
to speak favorably of another; to say a good word for another; to intercede for somebody 參看「說情」

說相聲（ㄕㄨㄛ ㄒㄧㄤˋ ㄕㄥ）
a kind of comic dialogue for entertainment

說著玩兒（ㄕㄨㄛ ㄓㄜ˙ ㄨㄢˊㄦ）
to say something without seriously meaning it; to joke

說眞話（ㄕㄨㄛ ㄓㄣ ㄏㄨㄚˋ）
to tell the truth

說叉了（ㄕㄨㄛ ㄔㄚ ㄌㄜ˙）
to start quarreling (while having a conversation)

說長道短（ㄕㄨㄛ ㄔㄤˊ ㄉㄠˋ ㄉㄨㄢˇ）
to criticize others

說唱（ㄕㄨㄛ ㄔㄤˋ）
a kind of performance consisting mainly of talking and singing

說出（ㄕㄨㄛ ㄔㄨ）
to speak out; to reveal; to utter

說穿（ㄕㄨㄛ ㄔㄨㄢ）
to unravel or expose by some remarks; to tell what something really is; to reveal

說時容易做時難（ㄕㄨㄛ ㄕˊㄖㄨㄥˊ ㄧˋ ㄗㄨㄛˋ ㄕˊ ㄋㄢˊ）
Easier said than done.

說是一回事，做是另一回事
（ㄕㄨㄛ ㄕˋ ㄧˋ ㄏㄨㄟˊ ㄕˋ，ㄗㄨㄛˋ ㄕˋㄌㄧㄥˋ ㄧˋ ㄏㄨㄟˊ ㄕˋ）
To say is one thing; to practice is another.

說書（ㄕㄨㄛ ㄕㄨ）
to tell stories (as professional storytellers do)

說書的（ㄕㄨㄛ ㄕㄨ ˙ㄉㄜ）
a professional storyteller

說走就走（ㄕㄨㄛ ㄗㄡˇ ㄐㄧㄡˋ ㄗㄡˇ）
to announce the intention to leave and really mean it

說嘴（ㄕㄨㄛ ㄨㄟˇ）
① to brag; to boast: 我們誰也別說嘴。Let's not make any boast. ② to argue; to quarrel: 他常常和人說嘴。He often quarrels with people.

說辭（ㄕㄨㄛ ㄘˊ）
excuses; pretexts: 我不相信他缺席的說辭。I don't believe his excuse for absence.

說曹操，曹操就到（ㄕㄨㄛ ㄘㄠˊ ㄘㄠ，ㄘㄠˊ ㄘㄠ ㄐㄧㄡˋ ㄉㄠˋ）
Talk of the devil and the devil appears.

說錯（ㄕㄨㄛ ㄘㄨㄛˋ）
to speak incorrectly

說錯了話（ㄕㄨㄛ ㄘㄨㄛˋ ˙ㄌㄜ ㄏㄨㄚˋ）
to speak what shouldn't have been uttered

說三不接兩（ㄕㄨㄛ ㄙㄢ ㄅㄨˋ ㄐㄧㄝ ㄌㄧㄤˇ）
to talk incoherently

說三道四（ㄕㄨㄛ ㄙㄢ ㄉㄠˋ ㄙˋ）
to make thoughtless comments

說一不二（ㄕㄨㄛ ㄧ ㄅㄨˋ ㄦˋ）or 說一是一（ㄕㄨㄛ ㄧ ㄕˋ ㄧ）
to be a man of his word; to keep one's promise; to stand by one's word

說也奇怪（ㄕㄨㄛ ㄧㄝˇ ㄑㄧˊ ㄍㄨㄞˋ）
for a wonder

說五道六（ㄕㄨㄛ ㄨˇ ㄉㄠˋ ㄌㄧㄡˋ）
to make thoughtless comments

說完（ㄕㄨㄛ ㄨㄢˊ）
to finish speaking: 他說完話就走出去。He went out after he finished speaking.

說文解字（ㄕㄨㄛ ㄨㄣˊ ㄐㄧㄝˇ ㄗˋ）or 說文（ㄕㄨㄛ ㄨㄣˊ）
the title of an etymological dictionary authored by Hsü Shen (許愼) of the Han Dynasty

【說】 5598
2. ㄕㄨㄟˋ shuey shuì
to persuade; to influence

說服（ㄕㄨㄟˋ ㄈㄨˊ）or（ㄕㄨㄛ ㄈㄨˊ）
to persuade; to convince; to bring around (or round); to prevail on: 她的演講很有說服力。Her speech is very convincing.

說客（ㄕㄨㄟˋ ㄎㄜˋ）
a professional commissary in ancient times sent by one

monarch to another with a view to convincing him 亦作「說士」

【說】 5598
3.（悅）ㄩㄝˋ yueh yuè
to delight; to please

【詤】 5599
an exclamation of affirmation

八畫

【課】 5600
ㄎㄜˋ keh kè
1. a class meeting
2. a course (of study)
3. a lesson
4. to impose; to levy; tax
5. a session at divination
6. a suboffice or bureau
7. to supervise

課本（ㄎㄜˋ ㄅㄣˇ）
a textbook

課表（ㄎㄜˋ ㄅㄧㄠˇ）
school timetable 亦作「功課表」

課目（ㄎㄜˋ ㄇㄨˋ）
a topic or subject of study

課堂（ㄎㄜˋ ㄊㄤˊ）
a classroom

課題（ㄎㄜˋ ㄊㄧˊ）
① a task or problem (for students) ② a theme; a question for study or discussion: 我們下次討論的課題是什麼？What's the theme of our discussion next time?

課卷（ㄎㄜˋ ㄐㄩㄢˋ）
students' papers

課長（ㄎㄜˋ ㄓㄤˇ）
a section chief (in an office)

課桌（ㄎㄜˋ ㄓㄨㄛ）
a classroom desk

課程（ㄎㄜˋ ㄔㄥˊ）
a curriculum: 這學期課程排得太多了。The curriculum is overloaded this semester.

課程表（ㄎㄜˋ ㄔㄥˊ ㄅㄧㄠˇ）
a school schedule; a class schedule; a school timetable

課室（ㄎㄜˋ ㄕˋ）
a classroom

課稅（ㄎㄜˋ ㄕㄨㄟˋ）
to levy taxes; to impose taxes: 政府爲了國家的開支而課稅。The government levies

taxes for national expenses.

課業 (ㄎㄜ˙ㄧㄝˋ)
schoolwork; lessons

課外 (ㄎㄜˋ ㄨㄞˋ)
extracurricular; outside class; after school

課外活動 (ㄎㄜˋ ㄨㄞˋ ㄏㄨㄛˊ ㄉㄨㄥˋ)
extracurricular activities

課外作業 (ㄎㄜˋ ㄨㄞˋ ㄗㄨㄛˋ ㄧㄝˋ)
homework (for a student); 我作完課外作業了。I have finished my homework.

課文 (ㄎㄜˋ ㄨㄣˊ)
the text or contents of a lesson

課餘 (ㄎㄜˋ ㄩˊ)或課後 (ㄎㄜˋ ㄏㄡˋ)
after school or class: 課後到我辦公室來。Come to my office after school.

5601
【誰】ㄕㄟˊ sheir shéi
（讀音 ㄕㄨㄟˊ shwei shuí)

1. who
2. anyone; someone

誰的 (ㄕㄟˊ ˙ㄉㄜ)
Whose? 這是誰的意見? Whose idea is it?

誰能 (ㄕㄟˊ ㄋㄥˊ)
Who can? 或 Who could? 誰能幫助他? Who can help him?

誰料 (ㄕㄟˊ ㄌㄧㄠˋ)
Who could have known? 或 Who could have expected? 或 Who would have thought?

誰敢 (ㄕㄟˊ ㄍㄢˇ)
Who dares?

誰肯 (ㄕㄟˊ ㄎㄣˇ)
Who is willing? 誰肯付出他所要的價錢? Who is willing to pay the price he asked?

誰何 (ㄕㄟˊ ㄏㄜˊ)
① Who? ② Who can do anything about it?

誰家 (ㄕㄟˊ ㄐㄧㄚ)
① Whose home (or house)? 那是誰家? Whose house is that? ② Who?

誰想到 (ㄕㄟˊ ㄒㄧㄤˇ ㄉㄠˋ)
Who would have thought?

誰知道 (ㄕㄟˊ ㄓ ㄉㄠˋ)或誰知 (ㄕㄟˊ ㄓ)
① Who knows? ② Who would have thought?

誰承望 (ㄕㄟˊ ㄔㄥˊ ㄨㄤˋ)
Who would have expected?

誰是誰非 (ㄕㄟˊ ㄕˋ ㄕㄟˊ ㄈㄟ)

Who is right and who is wrong?

誰人 (ㄕㄟˊ ㄖㄣˊ)
Who?

5602
【誶】ㄙㄨㄟˋ suey suì
to reproach; to scold; to upbraid

誶罵 (ㄙㄨㄟˋ ㄇㄚˋ)
to scold; to reproach; to upbraid

5603
【誹】ㄈㄟˇ feei fěi
to attack; to condemn; to slander

誹謗 (ㄈㄟˇ ㄅㄤˋ)
to libel; to slander; to calumniate: 他似乎以誹謗我為樂。He seems to enjoy libeling me.

誹謗行為 (ㄈㄟˇ ㄅㄤˋ ㄒㄧㄥˊ ㄨㄟˊ)
an act of libel or slander; libel; slander

誹謗者 (ㄈㄟˇ ㄅㄤˋ ㄓㄜˇ)
a libeler; a slanderer

誹謗罪 (ㄈㄟˇ ㄅㄤˋ ㄗㄨㄟˋ)
libel (as a criminal offense)

5604
【誼】ㄧˋ yih yì
（又讀 ㄧˊ yí yí)

1. friendship
2. same as 義—justice; righteousness

5605
【調】ㄊㄧㄠˊ tyau tiáo
1. to mix; to blend
2. to regulate; to adjust
3. balance; regular
4. to make fun of; to tease
5. to mediate

調配 (ㄊㄧㄠˊ ㄆㄟˋ)
① to prepare (a concoction); to mix; to blend ② to coordinate; to arrange

調皮 (ㄊㄧㄠˊ ㄆㄧˊ)或 (ㄉㄧㄠˋ ㄆㄧˊ)
① naughty ② sly; treacherous; cunning; unruly; tricky

調皮搗蛋 (ㄊㄧㄠˊ ㄆㄧˊ ㄉㄠˇ ㄉㄢˋ)
ungovernable; making troubles; mischievous

調頻 (ㄊㄧㄠˊ ㄆㄧㄣˊ)
(electricity) frequency modulation (FM)

調幅 (ㄊㄧㄠˊ ㄈㄨˊ)
(radio) amplitude modulation (AM)

調停 (ㄊㄧㄠˊ ㄊㄧㄥˊ)
to mediate

調弄 (ㄊㄧㄠˊ ㄋㄨㄥˋ)
① to make fun of; to tease ② to arrange; to adjust ③ to instigate; to stir up ④ to play musical instruments

調理 (ㄊㄧㄠˊ ㄌㄧˇ)
① to train; to teach ② to nurse impaired health; to recuperate ③ to take care of; to look after

調料 (ㄊㄧㄠˊ ㄌㄧㄠˋ)
condiment; seasoning; flavoring

調羹 (ㄊㄧㄠˊ ㄍㄥ)
a spoon

調侃 (ㄊㄧㄠˊ ㄎㄢˇ)
to scoff; to mock; to jeer: 不要介意別人的調侃。Don't take to heart what was said in mock.

調和 (ㄊㄧㄠˊ ㄏㄜˊ)
① to mix; to blend: 這兩種顏色不能調和。The two colors don't mix well. ② to harmonize; to bring into agreement ③ to adjust; to tune; to put in tune ④ to mediate; to reconcile

調和比例 (ㄊㄧㄠˊ ㄏㄜˊ ㄅㄧˇ ㄌㄧˋ)
harmonic proportion

調和級數 (ㄊㄧㄠˊ ㄏㄜˊ ㄐㄧˊ ㄕㄨˋ)
a harmonic progression

調和中項 (ㄊㄧㄠˊ ㄏㄜˊ ㄓㄨㄥ ㄒㄧㄤˋ)
a harmonic mean

調護 (ㄊㄧㄠˊ ㄏㄨˋ)
to attend to and protect; to take care of; to nurse

調劑 (ㄊㄧㄠˊ ㄐㄧˋ)
① to prepare drugs or medicines ② to adjust; to make adjustments

調劑師 (ㄊㄧㄠˊ ㄐㄧˋ ㄕ)
a druggist; a chemist; an apothecary; a pharmacist

調劑身心 (ㄊㄧㄠˊ ㄐㄧˋ ㄕㄣ ㄒㄧㄣ)
to provide physical and mental relaxation

調節 (ㄊㄧㄠˊ ㄐㄧㄝˊ)
① to regulate; to adjust ② to moderate

調解 (ㄊㄧㄠˊ ㄐㄧㄝˇ)
to mediate; to patch up: 只有你才能調解他們的家庭糾紛。Only you can patch up their family quarrels.

調經 (ㄊㄧㄠˊ ㄐㄧㄥ)
to regulate menstruation

〔言部〕

according to the normal cycle by medical means

調情(ㄊㄧㄠˊㄑㄧㄥˊ)
to flirt; to play at love

調戲(ㄊㄧㄠˊㄒㄧˋ)
to flirt with (women); to assail (a woman) with obscenities

調笑(ㄊㄧㄠˊㄒㄧㄠˋ)
to poke fun at; to make fun of; to tease

調製(ㄊㄧㄠˊㄓˋ)
to prepare or concoct (drugs, etc.): 她喜歡調製外國菜。 She enjoyed concocting foreign dishes.

調治(ㄊㄧㄠˊㄓˋ)
to undergo medical treatment and recuperation

調整(ㄊㄧㄠˊㄓㄥˇ)
to adjust; to tune up; to regulate

調處(ㄊㄧㄠˊㄔㄨˇ)
to mediate and settle (disputes, quarrels, etc.); to arbitrate

調攝(ㄊㄧㄠˊㄕㄜˋ)
to nurse impaired health

調人(ㄊㄧㄠˊㄖㄣˊ)
a mediator; an arbitrator: 這調人過於偏袒。 The arbitrator is biased.

調色(ㄊㄧㄠˊㄙㄜˋ)
to mix colors; to mix paints

調色板(ㄊㄧㄠˊㄙㄜˋㄅㄢˇ)
a palette

調三幹四(ㄊㄧㄠˊㄙㄢㄍㄢˋㄙˋ)
to sow the seeds of discord everywhere

調音(ㄊㄧㄠˊㄧㄣ)
(music) tuning

調養(ㄊㄧㄠˊㄧㄤˇ)
to nurse one's health; to take care of oneself

調味(ㄊㄧㄠˊㄨㄟˋ)
to season foods; to mix flavors

調味品(ㄊㄧㄠˊㄨㄟˋㄆㄧㄣˇ)
seasoning; spice; dressing material; condiment: 鹽和胡椒是調味品。 Salt and pepper are seasonings.

調勻(ㄊㄧㄠˊㄩㄣˊ)
to mix evenly

【調】 5605 2. ㄉㄧㄠˋ diàw diào
1. to transfer; to move; to

shift; to change
2. to collect; to mobilize
3. a tune; a melody; an accent; a tone

調包(ㄉㄧㄠˋㄅㄠ)
to substitute an inferior thing in secret

調兵遣將(ㄉㄧㄠˋㄅㄧㄥㄑㄧㄢˇㄐㄧㄤˋ)
(literally) to move troops and despatch generals—to prepare for war; to deploy forces

調派(ㄉㄧㄠˋㄆㄞˋ)
to assign: 他被調派到第七艦隊服務。 He is assigned to the Seventh Fleet.

調門兒(ㄉㄧㄠˋㄇㄣˊㄦˊ)
a melody; a tune; a pitch: 她說話調門兒高。 She speaks in a high pitch.

調兒(ㄉㄧㄠˋㄦˊ)
one's peculiar hobby, preference, fancy, etc.

調度(ㄉㄧㄠˋㄉㄨˋ)
①to move (available equipment or manpower) about according to needs; to dispatch; to manage; to control
②a dispatcher: 他是該運輸公司的調度。 He is a dispatcher at the transportation company.

調動(ㄉㄧㄠˋㄉㄨㄥˋ)
to transfer; to shift; to move (troops)

調頭寸(ㄉㄧㄠˋㄊㄡˊㄘㄨㄣˋ)
to scrape up enough cash; to raise money for an immediate expenditure

調虎離山(ㄉㄧㄠˋㄏㄨˇㄌㄧˊㄕㄢ)
(literally) to induce the tiger out of the mountain—to use the stratagem of luring the opponent out of his citadel

調換(ㄉㄧㄠˋㄏㄨㄢˋ)
to exchange; to swap; to replace

調集(ㄉㄧㄠˋㄐㄧˊ)
to concentrate (troops, etc.) in a place: 敵人調集了六個師。 Our enemy concentrated six divisions.

調遣(ㄉㄧㄠˋㄑㄧㄢˇ)
to transfer (officials, troops, etc.)

調職(ㄉㄧㄠˋㄓˊ)

to transfer to a new post

調查(ㄉㄧㄠˋㄔㄚˊ)
to investigate; to study; to probe; to survey; investigation; a survey

調查表(ㄉㄧㄠˋㄔㄚˊㄅㄧㄠˇ)
a questionnaire

調查法(ㄉㄧㄠˋㄔㄚˊㄈㄚˇ)
the survey method

調查戶口(ㄉㄧㄠˋㄔㄚˊㄏㄨˋㄎㄡˇ)
to take the census

調查員(ㄉㄧㄠˋㄔㄚˊㄩㄢˊ)
an investigator

調車場(ㄉㄧㄠˋㄔㄜㄔㄤˇ)
a marshaling yard; a switch yard

調差(ㄉㄧㄠˋㄔㄞ)
to transfer to a new assignment

調任(ㄉㄧㄠˋㄖㄣˋ)
to transfer to a new post

調子(ㄉㄧㄠˋ˙ㄗ)or 調兒(ㄉㄧㄠˋㄦˊ)
a tune; a melody; a tone: 她哼的這個調子倒是挺動聽的。 The tune she is humming is quite familiar.

調走(ㄉㄧㄠˋㄗㄡˇ)
to send away; to banish

調用(ㄉㄧㄠˋㄩㄥˋ)
to transfer (an official) for temporary assignment in another organization

【諂】 5606 ㄔㄢˇ chǎan chǎn
to flatter; to cringe; to fawn

諂媚(ㄔㄢˇㄇㄟˋ)
to flatter; to toady; flattery

諂佞(ㄔㄢˇㄋㄧㄥˋ)
to flatter; to toady

諂笑(ㄔㄢˇㄒㄧㄠˋ)
a fawning smile

諂諛(ㄔㄢˇㄩˊ)
to flatter; to curry favor

【諄】 5607 ㄓㄨㄣ juen zhūn
patient or earnest (in explaining, teaching, etc.)

諄諄(ㄓㄨㄣㄓㄨㄣ)
patient or earnest (in explaining, teaching, etc.)

諄諄教誨(ㄓㄨㄣㄓㄨㄣㄐㄧㄠˋㄏㄨㄟˋ)or 諄諄教導(ㄓㄨㄣㄓㄨㄣㄐㄧㄠˋㄉㄠˇ)
to teach and admonish with patience

【談】 5608
ㄊㄢˊ tarn tán

1. to talk; to converse; to chat:
我們明天好好談一談。Let's
have a good chat tomorrow.
2. what is said or talked
about; a talk; gossip
3. a Chinese family name

談柄(ㄊㄢˊ ㄅㄧㄥˇ)
an incident, etc. that makes
an interesting topic of conversation

談判(ㄊㄢˊ ㄆㄢˋ)
negotiation; to negotiate;
talks: 雙方談判中斷。The
talks between two sides
broke down.

談鋒(ㄊㄢˊ ㄈㄥ)
incisiveness of speech

談到(ㄊㄢˊ ㄉㄠˋ)
to speak of; to talk about;
to refer to: 這是不是幾天前你
談到的那本書？ Is this the
book you spoke of the other
day?

談天(ㄊㄢˊ ㄊㄧㄢ)
to chat idly

談天說地(ㄊㄢˊ ㄊㄧㄢ ㄕㄨㄛ ㄉㄧˋ)
to chat about all sorts of
subjects

談吐(ㄊㄢˊ ㄊㄨˇ)
the way a person talks; the
manner of speaking: 他的談
吐風雅。His talk is elegant.

談吐風生(ㄊㄢˊ ㄊㄨˇ ㄈㄥ ㄕㄥ)
fascinatingly voluble; eloquent and humorous

談論(ㄊㄢˊ ㄌㄨㄣˋ)
to discuss; to talk about

談客(ㄊㄢˊ ㄎㄜˋ)
an able talker

談空說有(ㄊㄢˊ ㄎㄨㄥ ㄕㄨㄛ ㄧㄡˇ)
to get together and chat

談何容易(ㄊㄢˊ ㄏㄜˊ ㄖㄨㄥˊ ㄧˋ)
How easy it is just to talk
about it! (But it is easier
said than done.) 或 by no
means easy: 一天完成工作，
豈是談何容易。It's by no means
easy to finish the work in
one day.

談虎色變(ㄊㄢˊ ㄏㄨˇ ㄙㄜˋ ㄅㄧㄢˋ)
(literally) to turn pale at
the mention of a tiger--to
turn pale when something
horrible is mentioned

談話(ㄊㄢˊ ㄏㄨㄚˋ)
a statement; conversation; a
talk; a chat; to talk; to converse

談話會(ㄊㄢˊ ㄏㄨㄚˋ ㄏㄨㄟˋ)
an informal meeting for conversation; a symposium

談起(ㄊㄢˊ ㄑㄧˇ)
to mention; to speak of

談情說愛(ㄊㄢˊ ㄑㄧㄥˊ ㄕㄨㄛ ㄞˋ)
(said of a couple in love) to
chat intimately

談笑封侯(ㄊㄢˊ ㄒㄧㄠˋ ㄈㄥ ㄏㄡˊ)
(literally) to be ennobled
while talking and laughing
--to rise in the world with
great ease

談笑風生(ㄊㄢˊ ㄒㄧㄠˋ ㄈㄥ ㄕㄥ)
to talk cheerfully and
humorously

談笑自若(ㄊㄢˊ ㄒㄧㄠˋ ㄗ˙ ㄖㄨㄛˋ)
cheerful and composed (in
the face of great dangers,
imminent disaster, etc.); 他
們面對危機還談笑自若。They
are cheerful and composed
in the face of great dangers.

談心(ㄊㄢˊ ㄒㄧㄣ)
to have a tête-à-tête: 他們昨
天在公園談心。They had a
tête-à-tête in the park yesterday.

談玄(ㄊㄢˊ ㄒㄩㄢˊ)
to discuss metaphysics

談塵(ㄊㄢˊ ㄔㄣˊ)
a hair duster which ancient
scholars held while they
were talking

談助(ㄊㄢˊ ㄓㄨˋ)
a matter for conversation:
足資談助。It serves as a good
topic of conversation.

談宗(ㄊㄢˊ ㄗㄨㄥ)
one who is universally admired as a great talker

談叢(ㄊㄢˊ ㄘㄨㄥˊ) 或談藪
a collection of conversations

談言微中(ㄊㄢˊ ㄧㄢˊ ㄨㄟ ㄓㄨㄥˋ)
able to satirize aptly

【諉】 5609
ㄨㄟˇ woei wěi
to shirk; to evade; to pass
the buck

諉過(ㄨㄟˇ ㄍㄨㄛˋ)
to lay the blame upon
others: 不要諉過他人。Don't
lay the blame on others.

諉為不知(ㄨㄟˇ ㄨㄟˊ ㄅㄨˋ ㄓ)
to pretend not to know

【請】 5610
ㄑㄧㄥˇ chiing qǐng

1. to request; to ask; to beg; to
beseech; to entreat: 敬請指
教。I humbly request your
advice.
2. please: 請坐。Please be seated.
3. to hire; to seek the service
of; to engage: 她請了個新傭
人。She engaged a new ser-
vant.

請便(ㄑㄧㄥˇ ㄅㄧㄢˋ)
as you please: 你想那樣就請
便。You can go ahead if you
want to.

請不動(ㄑㄧㄥˇ ㄅㄨˋ ㄉㄨㄥˋ)或請不到
(ㄑㄧㄥˇ ㄅㄨˋ ㄉㄠˋ)
unable to make someone
come by an invitation

請不起(ㄑㄧㄥˇ ㄅㄨˋ ㄑㄧˇ)
cannot afford to hire

請命(ㄑㄧㄥˇ ㄇㄧㄥˋ)
①to beg for life; to ask for
clemency ②to request for
instructions or orders

請大夫(ㄑㄧㄥˇ ㄉㄞˋ ㄈㄨ)
to send for a doctor

請帖(ㄑㄧㄥˇ ㄊㄧㄝˇ)或請柬(ㄑㄧㄥˇ ㄐㄧㄢˇ)
a printed invitation; an invitation card: 他已發出宴客請
帖。He has sent out invita-
tions to a dinner party.

請託(ㄑㄧㄥˇ ㄊㄨㄛ)
to ask for a favor

請客(ㄑㄧㄥˇ ㄎㄜˋ)
to invite guests; to give a
party; to stand treat

請款(ㄑㄧㄥˇ ㄎㄨㄢˇ)
to request for funds or
appropriation

請假(ㄑㄧㄥˇ ㄐㄧㄚˋ)
to ask for leave of absence

請教(ㄑㄧㄥˇ ㄐㄧㄠˋ)
to request instructions or
advice; to consult

請求兵(ㄑㄧㄥˇ ㄐㄧㄡˋ ㄅㄧㄥ)
to ask for reinforcements

請見(ㄑㄧㄥˇ ㄐㄧㄢˋ)
to request an audience or
interview

請君入甕(ㄑㄧㄥˇ ㄐㄩㄣ ㄖㄨˋ ㄨㄥˋ)
to make a person suffer
from his own scheme (from
the story of a man who,

【言部】

after suggesting the placing of a jar in burning coals and standing prisoners in it, was made to step therein himself)

請求(ㄑㄧㄥˇ ㄑㄧㄡˊ)
to request; to ask; to beg; to entreat: 他請求她一同去。He requested her to go with him.

請求乃論(ㄑㄧㄥˇ ㄑㄧㄡˊ ㄋㄞˇ ㄌㄨㄣˋ)
(said of cases of civil offense, etc.) to consider only upon request

請示(ㄑㄧㄥˇ ㄕˋ)
to ask for instructions

請入席(ㄑㄧㄥˇ ㄖㄨˋ ㄒㄧˊ)
Please be seated at table.

請坐(ㄑㄧㄥˇ ㄗㄨㄛˋ)
Please have a seat. 或 Please take your seat. 或 Please sit down. 或 Please be seated.

請罪(ㄑㄧㄥˇ ㄗㄨㄟˋ)
①to ask for punishment ②to appeal for leniency

請辭(ㄑㄧㄥˇ ㄘˊ)
to request permission to resign; to tender one's resignation

請安(ㄑㄧㄥˇ ㄢ)
to pay respects; to inquire after (an elder)

請益(ㄑㄧㄥˇ ㄧˋ)
to ask for advice or instructions

請謁(ㄑㄧㄥˇ ㄧㄝˋ)
to ask for an audience

請纓(ㄑㄧㄥˇ ㄧㄥ)
to submit a request for a military assignment; to volunteer for military service

請勿(ㄑㄧㄥˇ ㄨˋ)
please don't: 請勿吸煙。No smoking.

請勿動手(ㄑㄧㄥˇ ㄨˋ ㄉㄨㄥˋ ㄕㄡˇ)
Do not touch. 或 Keep your hands off.

請問(ㄑㄧㄥˇ ㄨㄣˋ)
May I ask you...? 或 Please tell me...: 請問，到博物館怎麼走？ Excuse me, but could you tell me the way to the museum?

請願(ㄑㄧㄥˇ ㄩㄢˋ)
to petition

請願書(ㄑㄧㄥˇ ㄩㄢˋ ㄕㄨ)
a written petition

【諍】 5611
ㄓㄥˋ　jeng zheng
1.to expostulate; to remonstrate; to criticize somebody's faults frankly; to admonish
2.to dispute; to compete; to vie 亦作「爭」

諍訟(ㄓㄥˋ ㄙㄨㄥˋ)
to fight a legal battle; a lawsuit

諍友(ㄓㄥˋ ㄧㄡˇ)
a friend who does not hesitate to remonstrate

諍言(ㄓㄥˋ ㄧㄢˊ)
a remonstrance; an expostulation; forthright admonition: 我的諍言無效。My expostulations had no result.

【諏】 5612
ㄗㄡ　tzou zou
1.to confer
2.to consult; to seek the advice of

諏訪(ㄗㄡ ㄈㄤˇ)
to consult; to seek the advice of

諏吉(ㄗㄡ ㄐㄧˊ)
to pick an auspicious day

【諑】 5613
ㄓㄨㄛˊ　jwo zhuo
rumors

【諒】 5614
1.honest; sincere
2.to forgive; to excuse; to understand: 原諒我來遲了。Excuse me for coming late.
3.to conjecture; to guess; to infer; to assume; to presume; to think; to expect; to suppose: 諒必如此。I think it must be so.
4.stubborn

諒必(ㄌㄧㄤˋ ㄅㄧˋ)
most likely; probably; in all probability

諒可(ㄌㄧㄤˋ ㄎㄜˇ)
to assume that something is possible

諒解(ㄌㄧㄤˋ ㄐㄧㄝˇ)
to forgive; to be understanding

諒已(ㄌㄧㄤˋ ㄧˇ)
I presume you (he, she, they) must have.... 或 Presumably it must have been....

【諒】 5614
2.ㄌㄧㄤˊ liang liáng

參見「諒陰」

諒陰(ㄌㄧㄤˊ ㄧㄣ)
①imperial mourning ②a mourning shed 亦作「諒闇」or 「涼陰」

【論】 5615
1.ㄌㄨㄣˊ　luenn lun
1.to discuss; to comment on; to appraise; to evaluate; to talk about; to discourse
2.to debate; to dispute; to argue
3.a theory; a system of thoughts; a dissertation; an essay
4.to mention; to regard; to consider
5.by; in terms of

論辨(ㄌㄨㄣˋ ㄅㄧㄢˋ)
argumentation (as distinct from "description," "narration," and "exposition")

論評(ㄌㄨㄣˋ ㄆㄧㄥˊ)
to comment; a commentary

論調(ㄌㄨㄣˋ ㄉㄧㄠˋ)
the tone or argument (of a speech, writing, etc.); views: 這種論調簡直可笑。Such views are simply ridiculous.

論點(ㄌㄨㄣˋ ㄉㄧㄢˇ)
the point at issue; an issue; the point of discussion; an argument; a thesis

論斷(ㄌㄨㄣˋ ㄉㄨㄢˋ)
to discuss and judge

論壇(ㄌㄨㄣˋ ㄊㄢˊ)
the world of criticism; a tribune of opinions; a forum

論難(ㄌㄨㄣˋ ㄋㄢˊ)
to harass by arguing; to thrash out

論理(ㄌㄨㄣˋ ㄌㄧˇ)
①to reason ②logic: 他的說辭頗合乎論理。There is much logic in his argument. ③normally; as things should be

論理學(ㄌㄨㄣˋ ㄌㄧˇ ㄒㄩㄝˊ)
logic

論理學家(ㄌㄨㄣˋ ㄌㄧˇ ㄒㄩㄝˊ ㄐㄧㄚ)
a logician

論列(ㄌㄨㄣˋ ㄌㄧㄝˋ)
to discuss and point out the favorable and unfavorable aspects of a matter

論功行賞(ㄌㄨㄣˋ ㄍㄨㄥ ㄒㄧㄥˊ ㄕㄤˇ)
to evaluate services and

grant rewards accordingly;
to award people according
to their contribution

論及(ㄌㄨㄣˊ ㄐㄧˊ)
to touch upon (in an exposition or argumentation)

論價(ㄌㄨㄣˊ ㄐㄧㄚˋ)
to negotiate prices

論件計酬(ㄌㄨㄣˊ ㄐㄧㄢˋ ㄐㄧˋ ㄔㄡˊ)
payment by the piece

論據(ㄌㄨㄣˊ ㄐㄩˋ)
grounds or bases (of an argument)

論者(ㄌㄨㄣˊ ㄓㄜˇ)
those who hold different opinions

論戰(ㄌㄨㄣˊ ㄓㄢˋ)
controversy; debate; argument; a battle of words; polemics: 他們曾激烈論戰。They had a bitter controversy.

論爭(ㄌㄨㄣˊ ㄓㄥ)
argument; debate; controversy

論政(ㄌㄨㄣˊ ㄓㄥˋ)
to discuss politics; to make comments on politics

論證(ㄌㄨㄣˊ ㄓㄥˋ)
proof; demonstration; to expound and prove: 這是無可辯駁的論證。This is irrefutable proof.

論著(ㄌㄨㄣˊ ㄓㄨˋ)
a treatise; a discourse; a work; a book

論述(ㄌㄨㄣˊ ㄕㄨˋ)
to discuss; to expound

論說(ㄌㄨㄣˊ ㄕㄨㄛ)
a theory, or thoughts (advanced in a treatise); exposition and argumentation

論說文(ㄌㄨㄣˊ ㄕㄨㄛ ㄨㄣˊ)
an argumentative treatise

論贊(ㄌㄨㄣˊ ㄗㄢˋ)
appraising remarks conventionally placed at the end of a biography in history books

論罪(ㄌㄨㄣˊ ㄗㄨㄟˋ)
to be considered as an offense: 這人以行賄論罪。The man was found guilty of bribery.

論次(ㄌㄨㄣˊ ㄘˋ)
to settle the order of priority, seniority, etc.

論文(ㄌㄨㄣˊ ㄨㄣˊ)
a treatise; a thesis; a dissertation; an essay; a discourse

【論】 5615
2. ㄌㄨㄣˊ luen lún
1. an alternative of 論 for some phrases
2. a Chinese family name

論語(ㄌㄨㄣˊ ㄩˇ)
The Analects of Confucius, one of the *Four Books*

【諗】 5616
ㄕㄣˇ sheen shěn
1. to think of
2. to let know; to tell; to announce
3. to remonstrate
4. to hide; to conceal

【諆】 5617
ㄑㄧ chi qī
to cheat

九畫

【諡】 5618
(謚) ㄕˋ shyh shì
a posthumous title

諡法(ㄕˋ ㄈㄚˇ)
the system of conferring posthumous titles

【諭】 5619
1. ㄩˋ yuh yù
1. to notify or inform by a directive, edict, etc.; to instruct; to tell
2. a decree; an edict; an instruction; a command

諭知(ㄩˋ ㄓ)
to notify or inform by a directive, edict, etc.

諭旨(ㄩˋ ㄓˇ)
an imperial edict

諭示(ㄩˋ ㄕˋ)
to notify or announce by an edict or decree: 諭示百姓 to notify the masses by proclamation

【諼】 5620
ㄒㄩㄢ shiuan xuān
1. to deceive; to fail in promise or appointment
2. to forget

諼草(ㄒㄩㄢ ㄘㄠˇ)
a day lily 亦作「萱草」

【諵】 5621
ㄋㄢˊ nan nán
to chatter; to gabble

【諛】 5622
ㄩˊ yu yú
to flatter; to toady

諛墓(ㄩˊ ㄇㄨˋ)
a flattering epitaph; to flatter the dead

諛辭 or **諛詞**(ㄩˊ ㄘˊ)
flattering words; flattery

諛言(ㄩˊ ㄧㄢˊ)
flattering words; flattery: 諛言可憎。Flattering words are detestable.

【諜】 5623
ㄉㄧㄝˊ dye dié
1. glib; garrulous; voluble 亦作「喋」
2. spying; espionage

諜報(ㄉㄧㄝˊ ㄅㄠˋ)
a spy's report; information obtained through espionage

諜員(ㄉㄧㄝˊ ㄩㄢˊ)
an intelligence agent; a spy

【諞】 5624
1. ㄆㄧㄢˊ pyan pián
to quibble

諞(ㄆㄧㄢˊ)
to quibble

【諞】 5624
2. ㄆㄧㄢˇ pean piǎn
to boast; to show off

諞闊(ㄆㄧㄢˇ ㄎㄨㄛˋ)
to show off; to be boastful

【諠】 5625
(喧) ㄒㄩㄢ shiuan xuān
to bawl; to shout

諠呶(ㄒㄩㄢ ㄋㄠˊ)
an uproar; tumult

諠譁(ㄒㄩㄢ ㄏㄨㄚˊ)
turmoil; a hubbub; tumult; an uproar: 會議在諠譁中結束。The meeting ended in (an) uproar.

【諢】 5626
ㄏㄨㄣˋ huenn hùn
ridicule; derision; a joke; a jest

諢名(ㄏㄨㄣˋ ㄇㄧㄥˊ)
a nickname; a sobriquet

【諤】 5627
ㄜˋ eh è
honest speech; frank comments

諤諤(ㄜˋ ㄜˋ)
① outspoken; honest ②(said of a procession) magnificent

【諦】 5628
ㄉㄧˋ dih dì
1. attentive; careful
2. (Buddhism) truth; true

meaning

諦聽 (ㄉㄧˋ ㄊㄧㄥ)
to listen attentively

諦視 (ㄉㄧˋ ㄕˋ)
to look attentively; to scrutinize

【諧】 5629 ㄒㄧㄝˊ shye xié

1. harmonious; congruous; in harmony; in accord
2. to come to an agreement; to settle
3. to joke; to jest; funny; humorous

諧比 (ㄒㄧㄝˊ ㄅㄧˇ)
improperly familiar or intimate

諧附 (ㄒㄧㄝˊ ㄈㄨˋ)
to compromise and follow

諧謔 (ㄒㄧㄝˊ ㄒㄩㄝˋ)
to wisecrack, joke or jest; pleasantry; banter: 他說話時語多諧謔。He speaks somewhat jokingly.

諧和 (ㄒㄧㄝˊ ㄏㄜˊ)
harmony; accord; agreement; harmonious; concordant

諧價 (ㄒㄧㄝˊ ㄐㄧㄚˋ)
to negotiate the price

諧劇 (ㄒㄧㄝˊ ㄐㄩˋ)
a farce

諧趣 (ㄒㄧㄝˊ ㄑㄩˋ)
fun; pleasantry; humor

諧戲 (ㄒㄧㄝˊ ㄒㄧˋ)
to jest; to joke

諧星 (ㄒㄧㄝˊ ㄒㄧㄥ)
a comedian

諧臣 (ㄒㄧㄝˊ ㄔㄣˊ)
court players; court jesters

諧聲 (ㄒㄧㄝˊ ㄕㄥ)
one of the six groups of Chinese characters (in which the radical gives the meaning and the other part gives the sound) 亦作「形聲」

諧暢 (ㄒㄧㄝˊ ㄔㄤˋ)
humorous and easygoing

諧音 (ㄒㄧㄝˊ ㄧㄣ)
①(said of characters) representing sound ②(physics) harmonics

【諫】 5630 ㄐㄧㄢˋ jiann jiàn
to admonish; to remonstrate

諫果 (ㄐㄧㄢˋ ㄍㄨㄛˇ)
an olive 亦作「橄欖」

諫官 (ㄐㄧㄢˋ ㄍㄨㄢ)
officials in charge of admonishing the emperor; imperial censors

諫諍 (ㄐㄧㄢˋ ㄓㄥˋ)
to admonish or remonstrate (a superior)

諫書 (ㄐㄧㄢˋ ㄕㄨ)
a written admonition to the emperor: 大臣已呈上諫書。The minister has submitted a written admonition.

諫議大夫 (ㄐㄧㄢˋ ㄧˋ ㄉㄚˋ ㄈㄨ)
an official in charge of admonition and arbitration

諫言 (ㄐㄧㄢˋ ㄧㄢˊ)
admonition

諫院 (ㄐㄧㄢˋ ㄩㄢˋ)
the office of imperial censors

【諮】 5631 ㄗ tzy zī

1. to inquire; to confer; to consult
2. an official communication between offices of the same level

諮詢 (ㄗ ㄒㄩㄣˊ)
to inquire and consult; to seek advice

諮商 (ㄗ ㄕㄤ)
(psychology) counseling

諮詢 (ㄗ ㄐㄩㄝˊ)
to consult (especially on affairs of the state)

諮議 (ㄗ ㄧˋ)
①to confer; to discuss ②government consultants or counselors

諮文 (ㄗ ㄨㄣˊ)
an official communication between equals

【諱】 5632 ㄏㄨㄟˋ huey huì

1. to conceal; to hide
2. to shun; to avoid; to regard as taboo; taboo
3. name of a deceased elder member of the family

諱莫如深 (ㄏㄨㄟˋ ㄇㄛˋ ㄖㄨˊ ㄕㄣ)
kept as a top secret; to avoid mentioning something completely

諱疾忌醫 (ㄏㄨㄟˋ ㄐㄧˊ ㄐㄧˋ ㄧ)
(literally) to conceal one's ailment and refuse to consult the doctor—to refuse to face a harsh reality; to hide one's troubles and take no

remedial measures

諱飾 (ㄏㄨㄟˋ ㄕˋ)
to conceal the truth

諱言 (ㄏㄨㄟˋ ㄧㄢˊ)
to avoid mentioning something; to conceal: 她毫不諱言。She makes no attempt to conceal the truth.

【諳】 5633 ㄢ an ān
familiar with; skilled in; versed in

諳練 (ㄢ ㄌㄧㄢˋ)
skilled in, familiar with; versed in: 他諳練馬術。He is skilled in horsemanship.

諳習 (ㄢ ㄒㄧˊ)
skilled in; familiar with; versed in

諳算 (ㄢ ㄙㄨㄢˋ)
to calculate mentally

諳誦 (ㄢ ㄙㄨㄥˋ)
to recite from memory

【諝】 5634 ㄒㄩ sheu xū

1. wisdom; sagacity
2. a clever idea; a stratagem

【諶】 5635 ㄔㄣˊ chern chén

1. sincere; honest; candid
2. a Chinese family name

【諷】 5636 ㄈㄥ feng fēng

1. to recite; to chant
2. to satirize; to mock; to ridicule
3. to admonish in a round-about way

諷諫 (ㄈㄥ ㄐㄧㄢˋ)
to admonish or remonstrate in a roundabout way

諷示 (ㄈㄥ ㄕˋ)
to admonish in a roundabout way

諷刺 (ㄈㄥ ㄘˋ)
①to satirize; to mock ②irony

諷喻畫 (ㄈㄥ ㄏㄨㄚˋ)
a caricature; a cartoon

諷誦 (ㄈㄥ ㄙㄨㄥˋ)
to recite; to chant; to intone

諷一勸百 (ㄈㄥ ㄧˋ ㄑㄩㄢˋ ㄅㄞˇ)
to satirize one in order to admonish a hundred

諷味 (ㄈㄥ ㄨㄟˋ)
to recite and enjoy (a verse, etc.); to repeat a remark and ponder its hidden mean-

ing

諷喩(ㄈㄥ ㄩ)
a parable; an allegory

【諸】5637
ㄓㄨ ju zhū
1. all; various
2. a contraction of 之乎 or 之於 (as prepositions—in, to, from, etc.)
3. a Chinese family name

諸般(ㄓㄨ ㄅㄢ)
all sorts; all kinds

諸母(ㄓㄨ ㄇㄨ)
one's father's concubine

諸父(ㄓㄨ ㄈㄨ)
one's father's brothers; paternal uncles

諸姑(ㄓㄨ ㄍㄨ)
all the concubines

諸多(ㄓㄨ ㄉㄨㄛ)
many; numerous; a lot of: 很抱歉給你帶來諸多不便。I am sorry that I put you to a lot of inconvenience.

諸葛(ㄓㄨ ㄍㄜ)
a Chinese family name

諸葛亮(ㄓㄨ ㄍㄜ ㄌㄧㄤ)
Chu-Ko Liang, 181-234 A.D., prime minister of the Kingdom of Shu (蜀) during the Epoch of the Three Kingdoms, noted for great wisdom 亦作「孔明」

諸姑(ㄓㄨ ㄍㄨ)
one's father's sisters

諸姑姊妹(ㄓㄨ ㄍㄨ ㄗ ㄇㄟ)
all the ladies

諸公(ㄓㄨ ㄍㄨㄥ)
all the gentlemen

諸宮調(ㄓㄨ ㄍㄨㄥ ㄉㄧㄠ)
a style of songs prevalent in the 11th century

諸侯(ㄓㄨ ㄏㄡ)
the feudal princes; dukes or princes under an emperor

諸季(ㄓㄨ ㄐㄧ)
all the younger brothers

諸暨(ㄓㄨ ㄐㄧ)
Chuchi, a county in Che-kiang (浙江)

諸舅(ㄓㄨ ㄐㄧㄡ)
all the maternal uncles

諸君(ㄓㄨ ㄐㄩㄣ)
you gentlemen

諸國(ㄓㄨ ㄍㄨㄛ)
the various Chinese kingdoms

諸行無常(ㄓㄨ ㄒㄧㄥ ㄨ ㄔㄤ)
(Buddhism) Whatever is phenomenal is ephemeral.

諸生(ㄓㄨ ㄕㄥ)
① a successful candidate in the lowest level of civil service examination under the former system 亦作「秀才」② all the students

諸如(ㄓㄨ ㄖㄨ)
such as

諸如此類(ㄓㄨ ㄖㄨ ㄘ ㄌㄟ)
various things like this; such; and so on; and so forth: 諸如此類,不勝枚舉。Such instances are too numerous to mention.

諸子(ㄓㄨ ㄗ)
① the various schools of thinkers or their works in the late Chou Dynasty ② an official in charge of education and discipline in ancient times

諸子百家(ㄓㄨ ㄗ ㄅㄞ ㄐㄧㄚ)
the numerous schools of thinkers or their works in the late Chou Dynasty

諸位(ㄓㄨ ㄨㄟ)
Ladies and Gentlemen

【諺】5638
ㄧㄢˋ yann yàn
a proverb; an aphorism; a saying; a saw; an adage

諺文(ㄧㄢˋ ㄨㄣˊ)
the Korean alphabet

諺語(ㄧㄢˋ ㄩˇ)
a proverb; an aphorism; a saying; a saw; an adage

諺云(ㄧㄢˋ ㄩㄣˊ)
as the proverb says; as the saying goes: 諺云:「無風不起浪。」As the saying goes, "There is no smoke without fire."

【諾】5639
ㄋㄨㄛˋ nuoh nuò
1. to assent
2. to promise; to pledge

諾貝爾(ㄋㄨㄛˋ ㄅㄟ ㄦ)
Alfred Bernhard Nobel, 1833-1896, Swedish chemist

諾貝爾獎(ㄋㄨㄛˋ ㄅㄟ ㄦ ㄐㄧㄤ)
Nobel prizes

諾曼(ㄋㄨㄛˋ ㄇㄢˋ)
Norman

諾曼第(ㄋㄨㄛˋ ㄇㄢˋ ㄉㄧ)
Normandy, France

諾諾(ㄋㄨㄛˋ ㄋㄨㄛˋ)
Yes, yes.

諾魯(ㄋㄨㄛˋ ㄌㄨˇ)
Nauru, a small island state in the Pacific

諾已(ㄋㄨㄛˋ ㄧˇ)
an interjection of disappointment

諾亞方舟(ㄋㄨㄛˋ ㄧㄚ ㄈㄤ ㄓㄡ)
Noah's Ark

諾言(ㄋㄨㄛˋ ㄧㄢˊ)
a promise; a pledge: 他從不守諾言。He never keeps his promises.

【謀】5640
ㄇㄡˊ mou móu
1. to scheme; to plan; to plot; to design; to devise
2. a scheme; a stratagem, a plan; a conspiracy
3. resourceful; astute
4. to consult
5. to seek; to try to get

謀叛(ㄇㄡˊ ㄅㄢˋ)
to plot a revolt

謀面(ㄇㄡˊ ㄇㄧㄢˋ)
to meet each other; to see each other

謀反(ㄇㄡˊ ㄈㄢˇ)
to plot a revolt; to conspire against the state

謀利(ㄇㄡˊ ㄌㄧˋ)
to seek profit

謀略(ㄇㄡˊ ㄌㄩㄝˋ) or 謀策
① a strategy; a scheme; a plot ② (said of a person) resourceful; astute: 他頗有謀略。He is a man of resource and astuteness.

謀和(ㄇㄡˊ ㄏㄜˊ)
to sue for peace

謀害(ㄇㄡˊ ㄏㄞˋ)
① to plot against someone ② to murder

謀畫(ㄇㄡˊ ㄏㄨㄚˋ)
to scheme; to plot; to plan; to design; to devise

謀救(ㄇㄡˊ ㄐㄧㄡˋ)
to plan the deliverance, rescue or relief of

謀求(ㄇㄡˊ ㄑㄧㄡˊ)
to try to get; to seek: 我們正在謀求解決方法。We are trying to find a solution.

謀取(ㄇㄡˊ ㄑㄩˇ)
to try to gain; to seek; to

〔言部〕

〔言部〕

obtain
謀職（ㄇㄡ ㄓˊ）
to try to find employment;
to hunt for a job
謀主（ㄇㄡ ㄓㄨˇ）
a planner; a designer; a plotter; a conspirator
謀臣（ㄇㄡ ㄔㄣˊ）
a brain truster or clever minister of the emperor or the king
謀食（ㄇㄡ ㄕˊ）
to seek food; to make a living
謀士（ㄇㄡ ㄕˋ）
a strategist; a man of ideas; a resourceful man; an adviser; a counselor
謀事（ㄇㄡ ㄕˋ）
①to manage business ②to scheme or plan for an affair ③to look for a job
謀事在人，成事在天（ㄇㄡ ㄕˋ ㄗㄞˋ ㄖㄣˊ，ㄔㄥˊ ㄕˋ ㄗㄞˋ ㄊㄧㄢ）
Man proposes, but God disposes.
謀殺（ㄇㄡ ㄕㄚ）
to murder
謀殺案（ㄇㄡ ㄕㄚ ㄢˋ）
a murder case
謀生（ㄇㄡ ㄕㄥ）
to make a living; to get a livelihood
謀財害命（ㄇㄡ ㄘㄞˊ ㄏㄞˋ ㄇㄧㄥˋ）
to commit murder out of greed; to murder somebody for his money
謀議（ㄇㄡ ㄧˋ）
to meet and plan; to confer
謀猷 or 謀猶（ㄇㄡ ㄧㄡˊ）
a strategy; a scheme; a plot

【謁】 5641
（ㄧㄝˋ yeh yè）
to have an audience with; to see a superior
謁陵（ㄧㄝˋ ㄌㄧㄥˊ）
to pay homage to a great leader by visiting his tomb or mausoleum
謁告（ㄧㄝˋ ㄍㄠˋ）
to ask for leave of absence
謁歸（ㄧㄝˋ ㄍㄨㄟ）
to go home on leave
謁見（ㄧㄝˋ ㄐㄧㄢˋ）
to have an audience with; to see a superior
謁禁（ㄧㄝˋ ㄐㄧㄣˋ）

a ban on visitors; a ban on audiences
謁者（ㄧㄝˋ ㄓㄜˇ）
an official in charge of receptions, etc. (prior to the Tang Dynasty)
謁舍（ㄧㄝˋ ㄕㄜˋ）
a hostel; a guest house
謁刺（ㄧㄝˋ ㄘˋ）
a visiting card; a calling card

【謂】 5642
（ㄨㄟˋ wey wèi）
1. to tell; to say
2. to name; to call; to designate
3. to think; to be of the opinion; to assume
4. meaning; sense
謂何（ㄨㄟˋ ㄏㄜˊ）
What can be done about...?
亦作「奈何」

【諲】 5643
（ㄧㄣ in yīn）
to respect; to venerate

【諰】 5644
（ㄒㄧ shii xǐ）
1. to speak frankly
2. apprehensive
諰諰（ㄒㄧ，ㄒㄧ）
apprehensive

【諴】 5645
（ㄒㄧㄢˊ shyan xián）
1. in harmony
2. sincerity; honesty

【諟】 5646
（ㄕˋ shyh shì）
1. yes; to be 亦作「是」
2. to examine and correct

【謔】 5647
（ㄋㄩㄝˋ niueh nüè）
1. to jest; to joke; to banter; to tease
2. to ridicule; to satirize
謔謔（ㄋㄩㄝˋ ㄋㄩㄝˋ）
cheerful; happy
謔浪（ㄋㄩㄝˋ ㄌㄤˋ）
to make fun without restraint
謔而不虐（ㄋㄩㄝˋ ㄦˊ ㄅㄨˋ ㄋㄩㄝˋ）
to joke without hurting anyone

十畫

【謎】 5648
（ㄇㄧˊ mi mí）
（又讀 ㄇㄟˋ mey mèi）

a riddle; a puzzle; a conundrum; an enigma; a mystery
謎面（ㄇㄧˊ ㄇㄧㄢˋ）
the verbal version of a riddle
謎底（ㄇㄧˊ ㄉㄧˇ）
an answer to a riddle; a truth
謎兒（ㄇㄧˊ ㄦˊ）
a riddle; a conundrum
謎語（ㄇㄧˊ ㄩˇ）
a riddle; a conundrum: 他出個謎語給我們猜。He asked us a riddle.

【謄】 5649
（ㄊㄥˊ terng téng）
to transcribe; to copy
謄本（ㄊㄥˊ ㄅㄣˇ）
a transcript; a copy
謄錄（ㄊㄥˊ ㄌㄨˋ）
①to copy; to transcribe ②to copy the examination papers of participants of the civil service examination of the old system before sending them to officials in charge with a view to preventing favoritism
謄清（ㄊㄥˊ ㄑㄧㄥ）
to make a clean copy: 我想謄清我的手稿。I wish to make a clean copy of my manuscript.
謄清賬（ㄊㄥˊ ㄑㄧㄥ ㄓㄤˋ）
a ledger
謄寫（ㄊㄥˊ ㄒㄧㄝˇ）
to copy; to transcribe
謄寫員（ㄊㄥˊ ㄒㄧㄝˇ ㄩㄢˊ）
a scribe
謄正（ㄊㄥˊ ㄓㄥˋ）
to make a clean copy

【謊】 5650
（ㄏㄨㄤˇ hoang huǎng）
a lie; to lie: 不許說謊。Do not lie.
謊報（ㄏㄨㄤˇ ㄅㄠˋ）
to report a falsehood; to lie about something; to give false information: 她謊報年齡。She lied about her age.
謊騙（ㄏㄨㄤˇ ㄆㄧㄢˋ）
to cheat; to deceive; to hoax
謊花兒（ㄏㄨㄤˇ ㄏㄨㄚ ㄦ）
sterile flowers
謊話（ㄏㄨㄤˇ ㄏㄨㄚˋ）
a lie
謊言（ㄏㄨㄤˇ ㄧㄢˊ）

a lie: 那都是謊言，別聽他的。
It's all lies; don't believe
him.

【諏】5651
ㄗㄡ tzou zōu
to talk nonsense: 別胡諏了。
Stop talking nonsense.

【謇】5652
ㄐㄧㄢ jean jiǎn
1. to stutter; to stammer
2. to speak out boldly

謇謇(ㄐㄧㄢˇㄐㄧㄢˇ)
faithful; loyal

謇諤(ㄐㄧㄢˇㄜˋ)
outspoken; frank; candid

【謏】5653
ㄒㄧㄠˇ sheau xiǎo
1. small; little
2. to induce

謏才(ㄒㄧㄠˇㄘㄞˊ)
a limited talent

謏聞(ㄒㄧㄠˇㄨㄣˊ)
known only to a small circle

【謐】5654
ㄇㄧˋ mih mì
silent; quiet; serene; still

謐謐(ㄇㄧˋㄇㄧˋ)
silent; quiet; serene; still

謐靜(ㄇㄧˋㄐㄧㄥˋ)
quiet; tranquil; serene; silent;
calm

【謗】5655
ㄅㄤˋ banq bàng
to slander; to libel; to condemn

謗木(ㄅㄤˋㄇㄨˋ)
a board set up on roadside
for the people to record the
errors in the public administration

謗書(ㄅㄤˋㄕㄨ)
defamatory writing

謗議(ㄅㄤˋㄧˋ)
to slander; to criticize; to
libel

謗讟(ㄅㄤˋㄉㄨˊ)
a libel; a slander; defamatory remarks

【謙】5656
ㄑㄧㄢ chian qiān
modest; humble; retiring;
self-effacing

謙卑(ㄑㄧㄢㄅㄟ)
humble; self-deprecating;
modest: 挫折與失敗使人謙卑。
Defeat and failure make
people humble.

謙退(ㄑㄧㄢㄊㄨㄟˋ)

modest and retiring; re-
served

謙光(ㄑㄧㄢㄍㄨㄤ)
shining modesty

謙恭(ㄑㄧㄢㄍㄨㄥ)
respectful; unassuming; modest and courteous: 他的兒子
謙恭有禮。His son is respect-
ful and polite.

謙克(ㄑㄧㄢㄎㄜˋ)
humble and self-controlled

謙和(ㄑㄧㄢㄏㄜˊ)
modest and good-natured

謙謙君子(ㄑㄧㄢㄑㄧㄢㄐㄩㄣㄗˇ)
a modest gentleman

謙虛(ㄑㄧㄢㄒㄩ)
①modest; unassuming; self-
effacing ②to make modest
remarks

謙遜 or 謙巽(ㄑㄧㄢㄒㄩㄣˋ)
humble; modest; lowly; unassuming

謙冲(ㄑㄧㄢㄔㄨㄥ)
modest; unassuming

謙讓(ㄑㄧㄢㄖㄤˋ)
to yield from modesty

謙辭(ㄑㄧㄢㄘˊ)
①modest speech; a humble
remark ②to decline out of
humbleness

謙受益，滿招損(ㄑㄧㄢㄕㄡˋㄧˋ，ㄇㄢˇ
ㄓㄠㄙㄨㄣˇ)
Benefit goes to the humble,
while failure awaits the
arrogant. 或 The modest
receive benefit, while the
conceited reap failure.

【講】5657
ㄐㄧㄤˇ jeang jiǎng
1. to speak; to talk; to say
2. to pay particular attention
to; to be particular about; to
be elaborate about
3. to explain; to explicate
4. as far as something is concerned; when it comes to; as
to; as regards
5. to have recourse to

講排場(ㄐㄧㄤˇㄆㄞˊㄔㄤˇ)
to impress others by extravagance; to display riches

講評(ㄐㄧㄤˇㄆㄧㄥˊ)
to review (a literary work,
a game, etc., especially in
speech); to make critical
comments on some perform-
ance

講面子(ㄐㄧㄤˇㄇㄧㄢˋ·ㄗ)
to care about reputation or
face

講明(ㄐㄧㄤˇㄇㄧㄥˊ)
to explain; to make (a
point) clear by explanation:
我們先講明我們的立場。We'll
explain our stand first.

講法(ㄐㄧㄤˇㄈㄚˇ)
①a way of stating ideas or
facts ②interpretation (of a
theory, phenomenon, etc.)

講道(ㄐㄧㄤˇㄉㄠˋ)
to preach; to give sermons

講臺(ㄐㄧㄤˇㄊㄞˊ)or 講壇
a platform; a dais; a po-
dium; a rostrum

講堂(ㄐㄧㄤˇㄊㄤˊ)
a lecture hall; a lecture
room; a classroom

講題(ㄐㄧㄤˇㄊㄧˊ)
the topic (of a speech or lecture)

講來講去(ㄐㄧㄤˇㄌㄞˊㄐㄧㄤˇㄑㄩˋ)
to talk repeatedly

講理(ㄐㄧㄤˇㄌㄧˇ)
①to have regard for reason;
reasonable 亦作「講情理」②
to argue with someone in
order to convince him that
he is wrong; to reason; to
settle a dispute

講論(ㄐㄧㄤˇㄌㄨㄣˋ)
to discuss; to expound

講稿(ㄐㄧㄤˇㄍㄠˇ)
the manuscript of a pre-
pared speech; lecture notes

講古(ㄐㄧㄤˇㄍㄨˇ)
to recount ancient tales; to
tell stories of the past

講故事(ㄐㄧㄤˇㄍㄨˋ·ㄕ)
to tell stories

講課(ㄐㄧㄤˇㄎㄜˋ)
to teach; to lecture

講和(ㄐㄧㄤˇㄏㄜˊ)
to make peace; to conclude
peace; to settle a dispute; to
become reconciled

講話(ㄐㄧㄤˇㄏㄨㄚˋ)
to talk; to speak; to address;
a speech; a talk

講價(ㄐㄧㄤˇㄐㄧㄚˋ)
to haggle over prices; to
bargain

講解(ㄐㄧㄤˇㄐㄧㄝˇ)
to discuss and explain (diffi-

【言部】

cult ideas, problems, etc.)

講交情(ㄐㄧㄤˇ ㄐㄧㄠ ㄑㄧㄥˊ)
to care about friendship

講究(ㄐㄧㄤˇ ㄐㄧㄡˋ)
① to be particular or elaborate (about something); to stress; to have regard for ② (said of dress, buildings, furniture, etc.) tasteful

講經(ㄐㄧㄤˇ ㄐㄧㄥ)
to expound Buddhist sutras

講求(ㄐㄧㄤˇ ㄑㄧㄡˊ)
① to investigate; to study ② to strive for; to be particular or elaborate about

講情(ㄐㄧㄤˇ ㄑㄧㄥˊ)
to ask for leniency for someone else; to intercede; to plead for somebody

講席(ㄐㄧㄤˇ ㄒㄧˊ)
the position of a lecturer

講習(ㄐㄧㄤˇ ㄒㄧˊ)
short-term training or instruction (usually for adults)

講習班(ㄐㄧㄤˇ ㄒㄧˊ ㄅㄢ)
a short-term course of training or instruction; a seminar

講習會(ㄐㄧㄤˇ ㄒㄧˊ ㄏㄨㄟˋ)
a session (usually one of a brief series) for receiving instruction; a seminar

講習所(ㄐㄧㄤˇ ㄒㄧˊ ㄙㄨㄛˇ)
a school for short-term training or instruction

講笑話(ㄐㄧㄤˇ ㄒㄧㄠˋ ㄏㄨㄚˋ)
to tell jokes; to crack jokes: 她講了一些很有趣的笑話。She told some very funny jokes.

講信修睦(ㄐㄧㄤˇ ㄒㄧㄣˋ ㄒㄧㄡ ㄇㄨˋ)
to cement peaceful relations by upholding good faith

講學(ㄐㄧㄤˇ ㄒㄩㄝˊ)
to lecture; to discourse on an academic subject

講師(ㄐㄧㄤˇ ㄕ)
a lecturer; an instructor

講授(ㄐㄧㄤˇ ㄕㄡˋ)
to teach; to lecture; to instruct

講書(ㄐㄧㄤˇ ㄕㄨ)
(said of a teacher in the classroom) to explain and discuss the content of the textbook

講疏(ㄐㄧㄤˇ ㄕㄨ)
to explain or explicate (something obscure)

講述(ㄐㄧㄤˇ ㄕㄨˋ)
to explain and discuss (subjects, problems, etc.); to tell about; to give an account of; to narrate; to relate

講座(ㄐㄧㄤˇ ㄗㄨㄛˋ)
a lectureship; a professorship; a chair

講詞(ㄐㄧㄤˇ ㄘˊ)
the text of a speech (delivered before an audience)

講兒(ㄐㄧㄤˇ ㄦ)
① meaning; the import ② reason

講義(ㄐㄧㄤˇ ㄧˋ)
① teacher's handouts at school; (mimeographed or printed) teaching materials ② commentaries on classics

講筵(ㄐㄧㄤˇ ㄧㄢˊ)
the teacher's seat

講演(ㄐㄧㄤˇ ㄧㄢˇ)
to speak or lecture; a speech

講武(ㄐㄧㄤˇ ㄨˇ)
to train in martial arts

【謝】　　5658

謝 ㄒㄧㄝˋ shieh xiè

1. to thank: 無需向我道謝。There's no need to thank me.

2. to decline

3. to fade; to wither: 花很快就凋謝了。The flowers soon withered.

4. a Chinese family name

謝表(ㄒㄧㄝˋ ㄅㄧㄠˇ)or**謝章**(ㄒㄧㄝˋ ㄓㄤ)
a letter of thanks to one's lord; a letter of thanks to the emperor for some appointment or other favor

謝病(ㄒㄧㄝˋ ㄅㄧㄥˋ)
to decline office on account of ill health

謝媒(ㄒㄧㄝˋ ㄇㄟˊ)
to reward a matchmaker

謝幕(ㄒㄧㄝˋ ㄇㄨˋ)
a curtain call; to bow to the audience on stage at the end of the show

謝道韞(ㄒㄧㄝˋ ㄉㄠˋ ㄩㄣˋ)
Hsieh Tao-yün (circa 376), a niece of Hsieh An (謝安), and a famed female talent

謝帖(ㄒㄧㄝˋ ㄊㄧㄝˇ)
a letter of thanks; a thank-you note

謝天謝地(ㄒㄧㄝˋ ㄊㄧㄢ ㄒㄧㄝˋ ㄉㄧˋ)
Thank God! 或 Thank Heaven!

謝禮(ㄒㄧㄝˋ ㄌㄧˇ)
① a gift sent as a token of gratitude; a return present ② an honorarium

謝靈運(ㄒㄧㄝˋ ㄌㄧㄥˊ ㄩㄣˋ)
Hsieh Ling-yün, 385-433, a renowned man of letters

謝領(ㄒㄧㄝˋ ㄌㄧㄥˇ)
to accept with thanks

謝客(ㄒㄧㄝˋ ㄎㄜˋ)
to decline to see visitors

謝函(ㄒㄧㄝˋ ㄏㄢˊ)
a thank-you letter

謝惠連(ㄒㄧㄝˋ ㄏㄨㄟˋ ㄌㄧㄢˊ)
Hsieh Hui-lien, 394-430, a talented man of letters and cousin of Hsieh Ling-yün (謝靈運)

謝絕(ㄒㄧㄝˋ ㄐㄩㄝˊ)
to decline (an offer, a request, etc.)

謝絕參觀(ㄒㄧㄝˋ ㄐㄩㄝˊ ㄘㄢ ㄍㄨㄢ)
No visitors allowed. 或 Not open to visitors.

謝啓(ㄒㄧㄝˋ ㄑㄧˇ)
a thank-you notice in the ad column of a newspaper

謝謝(ㄒㄧㄝˋ ㄒㄧㄝ˙)
Thank you. 或 Thanks.

謝忱(ㄒㄧㄝˋ ㄔㄣˊ)
sincere gratitude; thankfulness

謝師宴(ㄒㄧㄝˋ ㄕ ㄧㄢˋ)
a dinner party given by graduating students in honor of their teachers

謝世(ㄒㄧㄝˋ ㄕˋ)
to pass away; to leave the world; to die: 此人已謝世經年。The man passed away a year ago.

謝神(ㄒㄧㄝˋ ㄕㄣˊ)
to thank the gods by offering sacrifices

謝罪(ㄒㄧㄝˋ ㄗㄨㄟˋ)
to apologize

謝詞(ㄒㄧㄝˋ ㄘˊ)
a thank-you speech

謝安(ㄒㄧㄝˋ ㄢ)
Hsieh An, 320-385, a general of Tsin (晉), who repulsed northern invaders in a major battle

謝恩 (ㄒㄧㄝˋ ㄣ)
to express thanks for great favors

謝儀 (ㄒㄧㄝˋ ㄧˊ)
a present sent as a token of gratitude; a return present

謝意 (ㄒㄧㄝˋ ㄧˋ)
gratitude; appreciation

【謠】 5659 ㄧㄠˊ yau yáo
1. rumor
2. a ballad; a folk song; a song

謠諑 (ㄧㄠˊ ㄓㄨㄛˊ)
rumor

謠諑紛紜 (ㄧㄠˊ ㄓㄨㄛˊ ㄈㄣ ㄩㄣˊ)
There are many rumors going the rounds.

謠傳 (ㄧㄠˊ ㄔㄨㄢˊ)
①unfounded report, rumor; hearsay②according to rumor; it is rumored; rumor has it that...

謠俗 (ㄧㄠˊ ㄙㄨˊ)
folklore

謠言 (ㄧㄠˊ ㄧㄢˊ)
unfounded report; rumor

謠言滿天飛 (ㄧㄠˊ ㄧㄢˊ ㄇㄢˇ ㄊㄧㄢ ㄈㄟ)
All sorts of rumors are going the rounds.

謠惑眾 (ㄧㄠˊ ㄧㄢˊ ㄏㄨㄛˋ ㄓㄨㄥˋ)
to delude the people with rumors

【譖】 5660 ㄗㄨˊ suh sù
1. folded; closed
2. to rise; to raise

【謟】 5661 ㄊㄠ tau tāo
confusing; uncertain

【諡】 5662 ㄕˋ shyh shì
to confer posthumous titles
亦作「謚」

十一畫

【謾】 5663 ㄇㄢˊ mann mǎn
1. to scorn; to disdain
2. disrespectful; rude

謾罵 (ㄇㄢˊ ㄇㄚˋ)
to revile scornfully; to fling abuse; to rail

【謾】 5663 ㄇㄢˊ man mǎn
2. to deceive

謾天謾地 (ㄇㄢˊ ㄊㄧㄢ ㄇㄢˊ ㄉㄧˋ)
to deceive everybody

【譬】 5664 ㄠˋ aur ào
1. to slander; to revile; to abuse
2. massive and great

謷醜 (ㄠˋ ㄔㄡˇ)
to slander; to abuse

謷謷 (ㄠˋ ㄠˋ)
①slanderous; abusive ② sound of a mourning crowd

【謦】 5665 ㄑㄧㄥˇ chinq qǐng
to cough slightly

謦欬 (ㄑㄧㄥˇ ㄎㄞˋ)
talking and laughing

【謨】 5666 ㄇㄛˊ mo mó
1. a plan; a course of action
2. to have no; without; to lack

謨罕驀德 (ㄇㄛˊ ㄏㄢˇ ㄇㄛˋ ㄉㄜˊ)
Mohammed (or Mahomet or Muhammad), 570-632, founder of the Moslem religion 亦作「穆罕默德」

謨信 (ㄇㄛˊ ㄒㄧㄣˋ)
treacherous; not to be trusted

【謫】 5667 ㄓㄜˊ jer zhé
1. to censure; to reproach
2. to punish; to penalize
3. one's fault
4. to exile; to banish(an official) to a distant place

謫奸 (ㄓㄜˊ ㄐㄧㄢ)
to punish the wicked

謫降 (ㄓㄜˊ ㄐㄧㄤˋ)
①to demote and exile (an official) to the frontier: 他被謫降. He was degraded from his high rank. ②(said of immortals) to descend to the earth

謫居 (ㄓㄜˊ ㄐㄩ)
to live in exile

謫仙 (ㄓㄜˊ ㄒㄧㄢ)
an immortal living among mortals—a genius; a prodigy

謫戍 (ㄓㄜˊ ㄕㄨˋ)
(said of officials) to be exiled to the border

【謬】 5668 ㄇㄧㄡˋ miow miù
(又讀 ㄋㄧㄡˋ niow niù)
1. incorrect; wrong; erroneous; mistaken

2. absurd; unreasonable

謬耄 (ㄇㄧㄡˋ ㄇㄠˋ)
feeble-minded and senile

謬戾 (ㄇㄧㄡˋ ㄌㄧˋ)
stubbornly unreasonable

謬論 (ㄇㄧㄡˋ ㄌㄨㄣˋ)
an absurd statement; a fallacious argument: 謬論不足以服人. The absurd statement convince nobody.

謬見 (ㄇㄧㄡˋ ㄐㄧㄢˋ)
①a fallacious opinion ②(in self-depreciation) my absurd opinion

謬種流傳 (ㄇㄧㄡˋ ㄓㄨㄥˇ ㄌㄧㄡˊ ㄔㄨㄢˊ)
to transmit falsehood or inaccuracies from one generation to another; the dissemination of error or fallacy

謬悠 (ㄇㄧㄡˋ ㄧㄡ)
absurd and inaccurate

謬誤 (ㄇㄧㄡˋ ㄨˋ)
an error; inaccuracy; fallacy: 謬誤百出. There are hundreds of errors.

謬妄 (ㄇㄧㄡˋ ㄨㄤˋ)
absurd and reckless

【謳】 5669 ㄡ ou ōu
to sing; to chant

謳歌 (ㄡ ㄍㄜ)
to sing in praise; to glorify; to eulogize

【謹】 5670 ㄐㄧㄣˇ jiin jǐn
1. cautious; prudent; careful; attentive
2. respectful; reverent; deferential; sincerely; 謹致謝意. Please accept my sincere thanks.

謹備菲酌 (ㄐㄧㄣˇ ㄅㄟˋ ㄈㄟ ㄓㄨㄛˊ)
to provide some light wine respectfully (a conventional phrase on an invitation card for a dinner party or luncheon)

謹稟 (ㄐㄧㄣˇ ㄅㄧㄥˇ)
reported respectfully by...(a conventional phrase in formal letters addressed to seniors or superiors)

謹防 (ㄐㄧㄣˇ ㄈㄤˊ)
to guard carefully against; to take precautions against; to beware of

謹防扒手 (ㄐㄧㄣˇ ㄈㄤˊ ㄆㄚˊ ㄕㄡˇ)

〔言部〕

Beware of pickpockets!
謹防假冒(ㄐㄧㄣˇ ㄈㄤˊ ㄐㄧㄚˇ ㄇㄠˋ)
Beware of imitations! 或
Beware of fakes!
謹聽(ㄐㄧㄣˇ ㄊㄧㄥ)
to listen attentively
謹領(ㄐㄧㄣˇ ㄌㄧㄥˇ)
to receive with respect
謹記(ㄐㄧㄣˇ ㄐㄧˋ)
to remember with reverence
謹具(ㄐㄧㄣˇ ㄐㄩˋ)
①respectfully prepared by...
②respectfully signed by...
謹啟(ㄐㄧㄣˇ ㄑㄧˇ)
written respectfully by... (a
conventional phrase placed
after the writer's signature
in a formal letter); humbly
yours
謹誌 or 謹識(ㄐㄧㄣˇ ㄓˋ)
written respectfully by... (a
conventional phrase placed
after the writer's signature
in a preface, commentary,
etc.)
謹飭 or 謹飭(ㄐㄧㄣˇ ㄔˋ)
conducting oneself with prudence
謹呈(ㄐㄧㄣˇ ㄔㄥˊ)
presented respectfully by...
(a conventional phrase
placed after the writer's signature in a formal letter);
respectfully yours
謹守(ㄐㄧㄣˇ ㄕㄡˇ)
①to guard with care ②to
follow faithfully; strictly
comply with
謹慎(ㄐㄧㄣˇ ㄕㄣˋ)
prudent; cautious
謹上(ㄐㄧㄣˇ ㄕㄤˋ)
presented respectfully by...
(a conventional phrase
placed after the writer's signature in a formal letter);
humbly yours
謹嚴(ㄐㄧㄣˇ ㄧㄢˊ)
strict; rigorous; careful and
precise: 他治學嚴謹。He is
careful and precise in studying.
謹言慎行(ㄐㄧㄣˇ ㄧㄢˊ ㄕㄣˋ ㄒㄧㄥˊ)
to be prudent in making
statements and careful in
personal conduct
謹愿(ㄐㄧㄣˇ ㄩㄢˋ)
sincere; honest

【謰】 5671
ㄌㄧㄢˊ lian lián
1. to talk vaguely
2. the combination of two
closely related characters
which forms an inseparable
thought unit
謰謱(ㄌㄧㄢˊ ㄌㄡˊ)
to talk vaguely and aimlessly
謰語(ㄌㄧㄢˊ ㄩˇ)
the combination of two
characters closely related in
pronunciation and meaning
which forms an inseparable
thought unit, as澎湃, 崔嵬,
etc.

十二畫

【譏】 5672
ㄐㄧ ji jī
1. to ridicule; to jeer; to sneer
2. to inspect
譏評(ㄐㄧ ㄆㄧㄥˊ)
to make jeering comments
譏誚(ㄐㄧ ㄑㄧㄠˋ)
to ridicule; to deride; to satirize
譏諷(ㄐㄧ ㄈㄥˇ)
to taunt; to mock; to jeer; to
sneer at; to deride: 他常常譏
諷同僚。He often jeers at his
colleagues.
譏笑(ㄐㄧ ㄒㄧㄠˋ)
to laugh at; to make fun of;
to deride; to ridicule; taunts;
sneers
譏刺(ㄐㄧ ㄘˋ)
to taunt; to satirize

【譁】 5673
ㄏㄨㄚˊ hwa huá
noise; tumult; hubbub; clamor;
uproar
譁變(ㄏㄨㄚˊ ㄅㄧㄢˋ)
tumultuous mutiny; to mutiny
譁囂(ㄏㄨㄚˊ ㄒㄧㄠ)
noisy commotion; tumult;
uproar
譁笑(ㄏㄨㄚˊ ㄒㄧㄠˋ)
noisy laughter
譁眾取寵(ㄏㄨㄚˊ ㄓㄨㄥˋ ㄑㄩˇ ㄔㄨㄥˇ)
to practice demagogy; to
make seditious speeches; to
try to win popularity by
shocking words; to please
the public with claptrap

譁然(ㄏㄨㄚˊ ㄖㄢˊ)
uproarious; boisterous; tumultuous: 舉座譁然。The au-
dience burst into an tumult.
譁噪(ㄏㄨㄚˊ ㄗㄠˋ)
noisy; hubbub

【證】 5674
ㄓㄥˋ jeng zhèng
1. to give evidence; to bear
testimony; to bear witness;
to prove; to testify; to confirm; to corroborate; to
attest to; to certify
2. evidence; proof; testimony
3. a certificate; a card
4. a symptom; indication
證明(ㄓㄥˋ ㄇㄧㄥˊ)
to prove; to testify; to certify; to attest to; to confirm;
to corroborate; evi-
dence; testimony: 我可以證明
他的無事。I can testify to his
innocence.
證明書(ㄓㄥˋ ㄇㄧㄥˊ ㄕㄨ)
a certificate; a voucher
證明文件(ㄓㄥˋ ㄇㄧㄥˊ ㄨㄣˊ ㄐㄧㄢˋ)
supporting documents or
papers; a certificate; a testimonial 亦作「證件」
證道(ㄓㄥˋ ㄉㄠˋ)
(Christianity) to give a testimonial; a testimonial
證果(ㄓㄥˋ ㄍㄨㄛˇ)
(Buddhism) the fruits or
rewards of the various
stages of attainment
證候(ㄓㄥˋ ㄏㄡˋ)
a symptom; indication; a
sign: 發熱是許多疾病的證候。
Fever is a symptom of many
diseases.
證婚人(ㄓㄥˋ ㄏㄨㄣ ㄖㄣˊ)
a witness at a wedding
證件(ㄓㄥˋ ㄐㄧㄢˋ)
papers or documents sup-
porting a claim; documen-
tary proof; credentials; a
certificate: 請出示證件。
Please show your credentials
(or papers).
證見(ㄓㄥˋ ㄐㄧㄢˋ)
evidence
證據(ㄓㄥˋ ㄐㄩˋ)
testimony; evidence; witness;
proof
證券(ㄓㄥˋ ㄑㄩㄢˋ)
securities (bills, bonds, etc.)

stocks and bonds

證券交易所 (ㄓㄥˋ ㄑㄩㄢˊ ㄐㄧㄠˊ ㄧˋ ㄙㄨㄛˇ)
the stock exchange

證券市場 (ㄓㄥˋ ㄑㄩㄢˊ ㄕˋ ㄔㄤˇ)
the stock market

證章 (ㄓㄥˋ ㄓㄤ)
a badge

證實 (ㄓㄥˋ ㄕˊ)
to confirm; to corroborate;
to prove; to verify

證書 (ㄓㄥˋ ㄕㄨ)
a certificate; a diploma;
credentials

證人 (ㄓㄥˋ ㄖㄣˊ) or 證左 (ㄓㄥˋ ㄗㄨㄛˇ)
a witness

證言 (ㄓㄥˋ ㄧㄢˊ)
testimony given at a court
of law

證言 (ㄓㄥˋ ㄧㄢˊ)
testimony: 那證人的證言不實。
The witness's testimony is
false.

證驗 (ㄓㄥˋ ㄧㄢˋ)
① to verify; to bear out ②
real results; efficacy

證物 (ㄓㄥˋ ㄨˋ)
physical evidence; an exhibit

【譎】 5675
　ㄐㄩㄝˊ jyue jué
1. to cheat; to deceive; to swindle
2. wily; artful; crafty; cunning;
tricky

譎詭 (ㄐㄩㄝˊ ㄍㄨㄟˇ)
unpredictable; changing constantly

譎諫 (ㄐㄩㄝˊ ㄐㄧㄢˋ)
to admonish by hints; to
remonstrate with somebody
in indirect ways

【譖】 5676
　ㄗㄣˋ tzenn zèn
to slander; to charge falsely

譖人 (ㄗㄣˋ ㄖㄣˊ)
to slander others

譖言 (ㄗㄣˋ ㄧㄢˊ)
slanderous remarks; slanders

【識】 5677
　ㄕˋ shyh shì
1. to know; to recognize; to
discern
2. an opinion; a view
3. knowledge

識拔 (ㄕˋ ㄅㄚˊ)
to appreciate and promote

(an employee or subordi-
nate)

識別 (ㄕˋ ㄅㄧㄝˊ)
① to discern; to distinguish;
to identify ② identification

識別力 (ㄕˋ ㄅㄧㄝˊ ㄌㄧˋ)
the power of discernment

識別證 (ㄕˋ ㄅㄧㄝˊ ㄓㄥˋ)
an I.D. card

識破 (ㄕˋ ㄆㄛˋ)
to see through: 你能識破他的
騙局嗎？ Can you see through
his fraud?

識多見廣 (ㄕˋ ㄉㄨㄛ ㄐㄧㄢˋ ㄍㄨㄤˇ)
learned and experienced

識途老馬 (ㄕˋ ㄊㄨˊ ㄌㄠˇ ㄇㄚˇ)
an old horse which knows
the way—an experienced
person

識貨 (ㄕˋ ㄏㄨㄛˋ)
to appreciate; able to evaluate wares correctly; able to
judge the worth of an artistic work; able to tell good
from bad

識見 (ㄕˋ ㄐㄧㄢˋ)
knowledge; experience; insight; understanding

識荊 (ㄕˋ ㄐㄧㄥ)
(a polite expression) one's
first acquaintance with a
person ; to have the honor
of knowing you in person

識鑒 (ㄕˋ ㄐㄧㄢˋ)
to know how to ride the
political tide; to be able to
see which way the stream of
time runs

識趣 (ㄕˋ ㄑㄩˋ)
to have tact; tactful; to
know how to behave in a
delicate situation

識相 (ㄕˋ ㄒㄧㄤˋ)
to know one's own limita-
tions; to know when to yield
with grace; to know how to
avoid embarrassment; tactful

識者 (ㄕˋ ㄓㄜˇ)
the knowledgeable; those in
the know; an expert

識時務者為俊傑 (ㄕˋ ㄕˊ ㄨˋ ㄓㄜˇ ㄨㄟˊ ㄐㄩㄣˋ ㄐㄧㄝˊ)
A great man knows how to
ride the tide of his times.

識人 (ㄕˋ ㄖㄣˊ)
able to appraise a person's

ability and character correctly

識字 (ㄕˋ ㄗˋ)
able to read; literate

識字教育 (ㄕˋ ㄗˋ ㄐㄧㄠˋ ㄩˋ)
education for literacy

識字運動 (ㄕˋ ㄗˋ ㄩㄣˋ ㄉㄨㄥˋ)
a literacy campaign or
movement

【識】 5677
　2.(識) ㄓˋ jyh zhì
1. to record; to remember,
etc.
2. a mark; a sign

【譙】 5678
　1. ㄑㄧㄠˊ chyau qiáo
1. a tower
2. a Chinese family name

譙門 (ㄑㄧㄠˊ ㄇㄣˊ) or 譙樓 (ㄑㄧㄠˊ ㄌㄡˊ)
a watchtower over the city
gate

譙樓 (ㄑㄧㄠˊ ㄌㄡˊ)
a donjon; a tower built on
the wall of a city for
defense

【譙】 5678
　2.(誚) ㄑㄧㄠˋ chiaw
　　　　　　　　qiào
to scold; to blame

【譚】 5679
　ㄊㄢˊ tarn tán
1. same as 談—to talk
2. a Chinese family name

譚嗣同 (ㄊㄢˊ ㄙˋ ㄊㄨㄥˊ)
Tan Szu-tung, 1865-1898, a
late Ching Dynasty reform-
er, executed by Empress
Dowager Tzu Hsi (慈禧太后)

【譊】 5680
　ㄋㄠˊ nau náo
to argue; to dispute; to
wrangle; to clamor

譊譊 (ㄋㄠˊ ㄋㄠˊ)
arguing voices

【譜】 5681
　ㄆㄨˇ puu pǔ
1. a register; a record; a table;
a list
2. (music)a score
3. to compose (a song)
4. a general idea; a rough picture; something to count on
5. a collection of examples for
reference purpose; a manual;
a guide

譜表 (ㄆㄨˇ ㄅㄧㄠˇ)
(music) a score; a staff

譜第 (ㄆㄨˇ ㄉㄧˋ)

〔言部〕

a genealogy
譜牒(ㄆㄨ ㄉㄧㄝˊ)or 譜錄(ㄆㄨ ㄌㄨˋ)
a genealogy
譜號(ㄆㄨ ㄏㄠˋ)
① musical notes ② a clef
譜曲(ㄆㄨ ㄑㄩˇ)
to compose a song; to write
a musical composition
譜系(ㄆㄨ ㄒㄧˋ)
a genealogy; a family tree:
他追溯譜系到十七世紀。He
traced his family tree back
to the 17th century.
譜新聲(ㄆㄨ ㄒㄧㄣ ㄕㄥ)
to compose a new song
譜兄弟(ㄆㄨ ㄒㄩㄥ ㄉㄧˋ)
sworn brothers
譜子(ㄆㄨ ˙ㄗ)or 譜兒(ㄆㄨˊㄦ)
① a list (of formulas, rules,
procedures, etc.) ② a musical score

【譌】 5682
(訛) ㄜˊ er é
false; erroneous

十三畫

【議】 5683
ㄧˋ yih yì
1. to discuss; to argue; to
debate; to negotiate; to talk
over
2. an opinion; a view
3. to criticize; to comment;
criticism; comment
3. argumentative writing; argumentation; an essay; a treatise
議定(ㄧˋ ㄉㄧㄥˋ)
to arrive at a decision after
discussion or negotiation
議定書(ㄧˋ ㄉㄧㄥˋ ㄕㄨ)
a protocol: 他們簽訂貿易議定
書。They signed a trade protocol.
議題(ㄧˋ ㄊㄧˊ)
a topic for discussion; a subject of debate
議論(ㄧˋ ㄌㄨㄣˋ)
① argument; debate ② com-
ments ③ to discuss; discussion; to talk
議論風生(ㄧˋ ㄌㄨㄣˋ ㄈㄥ ㄕㄥ)
to create a lively atmos-
phere by one's talk
議論文(ㄧˋ ㄌㄨㄣˋ ㄨㄣˊ)
argumentative writing, argu-

mentation
議和(ㄧˋ ㄏㄜˊ)
to negotiate peace
議會(ㄧˋ ㄏㄨㄟˋ)
a parliament; an assembly; a
council: 召開議會 to convene
(or summon) a parliament
議會政治(ㄧˋ ㄏㄨㄟˋ ㄓㄥˋ ㄓˋ)
parliamentary politics; parliamentary government
議價(ㄧˋ ㄐㄧㄚˋ)
① to negotiate over the
price ② the negotiated price;
the price agreed upon
議決(ㄧˋ ㄐㄩㄝˊ)
to decide or resolve (at a
meeting); to pass a resolution
議決案(ㄧˋ ㄐㄩㄝˊ ㄢˋ)
a resolution (at a meeting)
議親(ㄧˋ ㄑㄧㄣ)
to negotiate a marriage
議長(ㄧˋ ㄓㄤˇ)
the speaker, president, or
chairman of an assembly,
parliament, etc.
議場(ㄧˋ ㄔㄤˇ)or(ㄧˋ ㄔㄤ)
an assembly hall
議程(ㄧˋ ㄔㄥˊ)
agenda
議處(ㄧˋ ㄔㄨˇ)
to take disciplinary action
against (derelict officials,
etc.)
議事(ㄧˋ ㄕˋ)
to discuss official business
議事廳(ㄧˋ ㄕˋ ㄊㄧㄥ)
an assembly hall
議事規則(ㄧˋ ㄕˋ ㄍㄨㄟ ㄗㄜˊ)
rules of procedure; rules of
debate
議事槌(ㄧˋ ㄕˋ ㄔㄨㄟˊ)
a gavel (used by the
speaker of a legislature)
議事日程(ㄧˋ ㄕˋ ㄖˋ ㄔㄥˊ)
agenda; order of the day
議案(ㄧˋ ㄢˋ)
a bill, a proposal (for a legislative body); a motion
議而不決，決而不行(ㄧˋ ㄦˊ ㄅㄨˋ
ㄐㄩㄝˊ ㄐㄩㄝˊ ㄦˊ ㄅㄨˋ ㄒㄧㄥˊ)
Meetings produce no deci-
sions and decisions produce
no actions.
議員(ㄧˋ ㄩㄢˊ)
an assemblyman; a council-

man; a councilor; a parliamentarian; a congressman
議院(ㄧˋ ㄩㄢˋ)
parliament; a legislature; a
legislative assembly; congress

【譟】 5684
ㄗˋ tzaw zào
1. noise of a crowd; (said of a
crowd) to shout noisily
2. to slander; to abuse

【警】 5685
ㄐㄧㄥ jiing jǐng
1. to guard; to keep watch
2. to warn; to alert
3. an alarm: 火警的警報器響了。
The fire alarm sounded.
4. quick; alert; agile: 他很機警。
He has an alert mind.
5. the police
警戒(ㄐㄧㄥˇ ㄐㄧㄝˋ)
to be on one's guard to keep
watch
警備司令部(ㄐㄧㄥˇ ㄅㄟˋ ㄙ ㄌㄧㄥˋ ㄅㄨˋ)
garrison headquarters
警報(ㄐㄧㄥˇ ㄅㄠˋ)
an alert; an alarm; a warning
警報器(ㄐㄧㄥˇ ㄅㄠˋ ㄑㄧˋ)
a siren
警蹕(ㄐㄧㄥˇ ㄅㄧˋ)
a herald who clears the
emperor's road
警笛(ㄐㄧㄥˇ ㄉㄧˊ)
a police whistle; an alarm
siren
警探(ㄐㄧㄥˇ ㄊㄢˋ)
a police detective
警惕(ㄐㄧㄥˇ ㄊㄧˋ)
① to be vigilant; to be wary;
to be alert; to be watchful ②
a warning
警廳(ㄐㄧㄥˇ ㄊㄧㄥ)
police headquarters
警鈴(ㄐㄧㄥˇ ㄌㄧㄥˊ)
a warning bell; an alarm
bell
警告(ㄐㄧㄥˇ ㄍㄠˋ)
① to warn; to caution; to
admonish ② a warning
警鼓(ㄐㄧㄥˇ ㄍㄨˇ)
a warning drum; an alarm
drum
警官(ㄐㄧㄥˇ ㄍㄨㄢ)
a police officer
警官學校(ㄐㄧㄥˇ ㄍㄨㄢ ㄒㄩㄝˊ ㄒㄧㄠˋ)
a police academy

警棍(ㄐㄧㄥ ㄍㄨㄣ)
a policeman's baton or trun cheon

警號(ㄐㄧㄥ ㄏㄠ)
a warning signal

警徽(ㄐㄧㄥ ㄏㄨㄟ)
a police insignia; a police badge

警誡(ㄐㄧㄥ ㄐㄧㄝ)
to warn and admonish

警戒(ㄐㄧㄥ ㄐㄧㄝ)
①to be on the alert; to be on one's guard; to be vigilant; to stand guard ②to warn and admonish

警戒部隊(ㄐㄧㄥ ㄐㄧㄝ ㄅㄨ ㄉㄨㄟ)
guarding troops; troops on alert; outpost troops

警戒線(ㄐㄧㄥ ㄐㄧㄝ ㄒㄧㄢ)
①a cordon (of sentinels, forts, etc.) ②a danger line or mark (on a riverbank, etc. for warning of floods)

警戒色(ㄐㄧㄥ ㄐㄧㄝ ㄙㄜ)
(biology) warning color

警句(ㄐㄧㄥ ㄐㄩ)or 警語(ㄐㄧㄥ ㄩ)
an epigram

警覺(ㄐㄧㄥ ㄐㄩㄝ)
vigilant; alert; watchful

警覺性(ㄐㄧㄥ ㄐㄩㄝ ㄒㄧㄥ)
vigilance; alertness

警犬(ㄐㄧㄥ ㄑㄩㄢ)
a police dog

警醒(ㄐㄧㄥ ㄒㄧㄥ)
①easily awakened from sleep; quick to awake ②vigilant

警長(ㄐㄧㄥ ㄓㄤ)
a police chief

警政(ㄐㄧㄥ ㄓㄥ)
police administration

警鐘(ㄐㄧㄥ ㄓㄨㄥ)
an alarm bell; a tocsin

警衆(ㄐㄧㄥ ㄓㄨㄥ)
to warn the people; to alert the public

警察(ㄐㄧㄥ ㄔㄚ)
cops; the police

警察派出所(ㄐㄧㄥ ㄔㄚ ㄆㄞ ㄔㄨ ㄙㄨㄛ)
a police substation; a station house

警察分局(ㄐㄧㄥ ㄔㄚ ㄈㄣ ㄐㄩ)
police precinct headquarters

警察局(ㄐㄧㄥ ㄔㄚ ㄐㄩ)
county (or city) police head-

quarters

警察學校(ㄐㄧㄥ ㄔㄚ ㄒㄩㄝ ㄒㄧㄠ)
a police school; a police academy

警車(ㄐㄧㄥ ㄔㄜ)
a squad car; a police patrol car; a police car

警世(ㄐㄧㄥ ㄕ)
to warn or caution mankind against impending disasters

警世通言(ㄐㄧㄥ ㄕ ㄊㄨㄥ ㄧㄢ)
the title of a forty-volume novel by Feng Meng-lung (馮夢龍) of the Ming Dynasty

警策(ㄐㄧㄥ ㄘㄜ)
a key phrase, sentence or passage in a piece of writing (which enlivens the writing as a whip enlivens a horse)

警悟(ㄐㄧㄥ ㄨ)
quick to realize or understand

警務(ㄐㄧㄥ ㄨ)
police affairs

警務處(ㄐㄧㄥ ㄨ ㄔㄨ)
a provincial department of the police

警衛(ㄐㄧㄥ ㄨㄟ)
①to guard ②a guard

警員(ㄐㄧㄥ ㄩㄢ)
a policeman; a cop

【譬】 5686　ㄆㄧˋ pih pì
1. to liken; to compare
2. a simile; an example
3. to tell
4. to understand

譬如(ㄆㄧˋ ㄖㄨˊ)or 譬若(ㄆㄧˋ ㄖㄨㄛˋ)
suppose; for instance; for example

譬喻(ㄆㄧˋ ㄩˋ)
a simile or metaphor

【譯】 5687　ㄧˋ yih yì
to translate; translation

譯本(ㄧˋ ㄅㄣˇ)
a translated version (of a book); a translation

譯筆(ㄧˋ ㄅㄧˇ)
(literally) a translator's pen—a translator's skill; the quality or style of a translation

譯名(ㄧˋ ㄇㄧㄥˊ)
a translated name

譯電(ㄧˋ ㄉㄧㄢˋ)

to decode, or encode, a telegram

譯學館(ㄧˋ ㄒㄩㄝˊ ㄍㄨㄢˇ)
the school for training students in foreign languages set up toward the end of the Ching Dynasty

譯者(ㄧˋ ㄓㄜˇ)
a translator

譯注(ㄧˋ ㄓㄨˋ)
to translate and annotate

譯述(ㄧˋ ㄕㄨˋ)
to translate freely

譯述者(ㄧˋ ㄕㄨˋ ㄓㄜˇ)
a translator who does not claim literal accuracy

譯意風(ㄧˋ ㄧˋ ㄈㄥ)
earphones (provided at each seat in a movie house whereby the spectator can hear the dialogues of foreign movies interpreted into Chinese); a simultaneous interpretation installation

譯音(ㄧˋ ㄧㄣ)
a transliteration; sound transcription

譯音符號(ㄧˋ ㄧㄣ ㄈㄨˊ ㄏㄠˋ)
the National Romanization, or Gwoyeu Romatzyh, for Mandarin Chinese 亦作「國語羅馬字」

譯文(ㄧˋ ㄨㄣˊ)
translated texts; a translation: 譯文不雅。The translation is not elegant.

譯員(ㄧˋ ㄩㄢˊ)
an interpreter; a translator

十四畫

【護】 5688　ㄏㄨˋ huh hù
1. to protect; to guard; to defend; to shield
2. to take sides; to be partial to

護庇(ㄏㄨˋ ㄅㄧˋ)
to shelter; to cover up

護兵(ㄏㄨˋ ㄅㄧㄥ)
military guards

護民官(ㄏㄨˋ ㄇㄧㄣˊ ㄍㄨㄢ)
(in ancient Rome) a tribune

護法(ㄏㄨˋ ㄈㄚˇ)
①to protect or maintain the Buddha-truth ②to uphold the constitution

〔言部〕

（言部）

護法運動 (ㄏㄨㄈㄚˇㄩㄣˋㄉㄨㄥˋ)
the movement to defend the Constitution led by Dr. Sun Yat-sen when the warlord Tuan Chi-jui (段祺瑞) dissolved the parliament in 1917

護符 (ㄏㄨˋㄈㄨˊ)
an amulet; a charm for self-protection

護短 (ㄏㄨˋㄉㄨㄢˇ)
①to conceal one's faults ② to side with a disputant who is in the wrong

護理 (ㄏㄨˋㄌㄧˇ)
①to act for a senior official ②nursing

護理專科學校 (ㄏㄨˋㄌㄧˇㄓㄨㄢㄎㄜ ㄒㄩㄝˊㄒㄧㄠˋ)
a junior college of nursing

護國軍 (ㄏㄨˋㄍㄨㄛˊㄐㄩㄣ)
the troops that rallied against Yüan Shih-kai (袁世凱) when he attempted to restore monarchy in 1916

護航 (ㄏㄨˋㄏㄤˊ)
a guardrail

護航 (ㄏㄨˋㄏㄤˊ)
①to escort another vessel ② to help another illicitly during an examination

護花 (ㄏㄨˋㄏㄨㄚ)
to protect women

護花使者 (ㄏㄨˋㄏㄨㄚㄕˇㄓㄜˇ)
a protector of women; a woman's escort

護駕 (ㄏㄨˋㄐㄧㄚˋ)
to guard the emperor; to escort the emperor

護照 (ㄏㄨˋㄓㄠˋ)
a passport

護持 (ㄏㄨˋㄔˊ)
to protect and maintain

護城河 (ㄏㄨˋㄔㄥˊㄏㄜˊ)
a city moat

護士 (ㄏㄨˋㄕˋ)
a nurse

護士節 (ㄏㄨˋㄕˋㄐㄧㄝˊ)
Nurses' Day (May 12)

護手 (ㄏㄨˋㄕㄡˇ)
the guard (of a sword or knife)

護身符 (ㄏㄨˋㄕㄣㄈㄨˊ)
①an amulet; a charm for self-protection ② anything which one uses as a protec-

tive shield

護喪 (ㄏㄨˋㄙㄤ)
one who presides over a funeral service (usually an elder of the clan)

護送 (ㄏㄨˋㄙㄨㄥˋ)
to escort; to convoy

護岸 (ㄏㄨˋㄢˋ)
a dike; a levee; an embankment

護衛 (ㄏㄨˋㄨㄟˋ)
to guard; to escort; to convoy

護運 (ㄏㄨˋㄩㄣˋ)
to ship or transport something under guard

【譴】 5689
〈ㄑㄧㄢˇ chean qiǎn
1. to reproach; to reprimand; to upbraid
2. punishment

譴訶 (ㄑㄧㄢˇㄏㄜ)
to scold; to reproach

譴責 (ㄑㄧㄢˇㄗㄜˊ)
to reprimand; to reproach; to upbraid; to blame

【譽】 5690
ㄩˋ yuh yù
1. fame; honor; glory
2. to praise; to eulogize

譽滿全球 (ㄩˋㄇㄢˇㄑㄩㄢˊㄑㄧㄡˊ)
to achieve global fame; world-famous: 她是譽滿全球的鋼琴家。 She is a world-famous pianist.

十五畫

【譾】 5691
ㄐㄧㄢˇ jean jiǎn
1. (mentally) shallow

譾陋 (ㄐㄧㄢˇㄌㄡˋ)
(mentally) shallow

【讀】 5692
1. ㄉㄨˊ dwu dú
1. to read
2. to attend school; to go to school, college, etc.
3. to study

讀本 (ㄉㄨˊㄅㄣˇ)
a reader (for a language course, etc.); a textbook: 讀本緊俏。 Textbooks are great in number.

讀畢 (ㄉㄨˊㄅㄧˋ)
to finish reading

讀秒 (ㄉㄨˊㄇㄧㄠˇ)
to remind a player in a

chess game of how much time left when he has almost used up his alloted time

讀法 (ㄉㄨˊㄈㄚˇ)
pronunciation (of a word)

讀卡機 (ㄉㄨˊㄎㄚˇㄐㄧ)
(computers) a card reader

讀畫 (ㄉㄨˊㄏㄨㄚˋ)
to appraise a painting

讀寫算 (ㄉㄨˊㄒㄧㄝˇㄙㄨㄢˋ)
reading, writing, and arithmetic

讀者 (ㄉㄨˊㄓㄜˇ)
the reader (as opposed to the writer): 希望讀者能原諒我。 I hope my readers will excuse me.

讀者文摘 (ㄉㄨˊㄓㄜˇㄨㄣˊㄓㄞ)
The Reader's Digest

讀書 (ㄉㄨˊㄕㄨ)
①to read books ② to study; to receive education

讀書不求甚解 (ㄉㄨˊㄕㄨㄅㄨˋㄑㄧㄡˊㄕㄣˋㄐㄧㄝˇ)
In reading a book, one does not care about the details too much.

讀書界 (ㄉㄨˊㄕㄨㄐㄧㄝˋ)
the reading public

讀書種子 (ㄉㄨˊㄕㄨㄓㄨㄥˇㄗˇ)
the seed of learning — the continuity of the scholarly tradition

讀書人 (ㄉㄨˊㄕㄨㄖㄣˊ)
a scholar; an intellectual: 他可說是個讀書人。 He is something of a scholar.

讀書三到 (ㄉㄨˊㄕㄨㄙㄢㄉㄠˋ)
the three things to be used in reading a book—the eye, the mouth, and the mind

讀書五車 (ㄉㄨˊㄕㄨㄨˇㄔㄜ)
having read five cartloads of books—learned; erudite; well-read

讀熟 (ㄉㄨˊㄕㄡˊ)
to read until one can recite out of memory

讀錯 (ㄉㄨˊㄘㄨㄛˋ)
to mispronounce (a word): 他將此字讀錯了。 He mispronounced this word.

讀音 (ㄉㄨˊㄧㄣ)
pronunciation (of a word)

讀物 (ㄉㄨˊㄨˋ)
reading matter; reading: 課

外讀物 outside reading

讀完(ㄉㄨ ㄨㄢˊ)
①to finish reading (an article or a book) ②to finish studying (at a school)

【讀】 5692
2. ㄉㄡˋ dow dou
pauses in a sentence

【諗】 5693
ㄕㄣˇ sheen shen
to know; to be aware

【讁】 5694
(讁) ㄓㄜˊ jer zhe
to punish; to blame

十六畫

【變】 5695
ㄅㄧㄢˋ biann bian
1. to change; to alter
2. to change; to become different
3. to turn into; to become
4. extraordinary; uncommon
5. an accident; misfortune; tragedy; upheaval; disturbance; an unexpected turn of events
6. changeable

變本加厲(ㄅㄧㄢˋ ㄅㄣˇ ㄐㄧ ㄌㄧˋ)
(said of tyranny, personal conduct, etc.) to get worse; worsening; to intensify one's effort to do something wrong

變賣(ㄅㄧㄢˋ ㄇㄞˋ)
to sell (possessions) to meet an immediate financial need

變法兒(ㄅㄧㄢˋ ㄈㄚˇㄦ)
by various ways; to try different ways

變法(ㄅㄧㄢˋ ㄈㄚˇ)
to revise the law; to initiate political reform

變法自強(ㄅㄧㄢˋ ㄈㄚˇ ㄗˋ ㄑㄧㄤˊ)
to initiate political reform in quest for national strength

變法維新(ㄅㄧㄢˋ ㄈㄚˇ ㄨㄟˊ ㄒㄧㄣ)
the Constitutional Reform and Modernization (1898)

變得(ㄅㄧㄢˋ ˙ㄉㄜ)
to become

變調(ㄅㄧㄢˋ ㄉㄧㄠˋ)
to change a tune or melody; to change the key (of a tune); variations

變電所(ㄅㄧㄢˋ ㄉㄧㄢˋ ㄙㄨㄛˇ)
a power substation

變動(ㄅㄧㄢˋ ㄉㄨㄥˋ)

①(said of organizations, arrangements, etc.) to change; to reshuffle; to reorganize ②a change; alteration ③variation

變態(ㄅㄧㄢˋ ㄊㄞˋ)
①abnormality ②(zoology) metamorphosis

變態心理學(ㄅㄧㄢˋ ㄊㄞˋ ㄒㄧㄣ ㄌㄧˇ ㄒㄩㄝˊ)
abnormal psychology

變體(ㄅㄧㄢˋ ㄊㄧˇ)
a new style derived from the original

變天(ㄅㄧㄢˋ ㄊㄧㄢ)
①a change of weather (usually from fine to bad) ②the changes of political situations

變通(ㄅㄧㄢˋ ㄊㄨㄥ)
to adapt oneself to circumstances; to be flexible

變通辦理(ㄅㄧㄢˋ ㄊㄨㄥ ㄅㄢˋ ㄌㄧˇ)
to handle something without the rigid application of rules

變弄(ㄅㄧㄢˋ ㄋㄨㄥˋ)
to get (money, articles, etc.) in some uncommon way

變了(ㄅㄧㄢˋ ˙ㄌㄜ)
to have changed

變臉(ㄅㄧㄢˋ ㄌㄧㄢˇ)
to turn hostile; to get angry

變亂(ㄅㄧㄢˋ ㄌㄨㄢˋ)
rebellion; revolt; upheaval; chaos; turmoil

變革(ㄅㄧㄢˋ ㄍㄜˊ)
(said of an institution, a system, etc.) to change or reform

變更(ㄅㄧㄢˋ ㄍㄥ)
to change (plans, methods, etc.); to alter; to modify: 我們的計畫稍有變更。We have modified our plan.

變故(ㄅㄧㄢˋ ㄍㄨˋ)
an accident; misfortune; mishap: 發生了變故。An accident has happened.

變卦(ㄅㄧㄢˋ ㄍㄨㄚˋ)
to change one's mind; to go back on one's words; to break an agreement: 你怎麼變卦了? What made you change your mind?

變好(ㄅㄧㄢˋ ㄏㄠˇ)
①(said of weather) to become fine; to clear up ②

(said of a person) to reform; to become good

變化(ㄅㄧㄢˋ ㄏㄨㄚˋ)
①to transform; to metamorphose; to transmute ②to change ③a change; changeable

變化多端(ㄅㄧㄢˋ ㄏㄨㄚˋ ㄉㄨㄛ ㄉㄨㄢ)
changeable

變化氣質(ㄅㄧㄢˋ ㄏㄨㄚˋ ㄑㄧˋ ㄓˊ)
to change one's temperament: 教育可以變化氣質。Education can change one's temperament.

變化語(ㄅㄧㄢˋ ㄏㄨㄚˋ ㄩˇ)
an inflective language

變壞(ㄅㄧㄢˋ ㄏㄨㄞˋ)
①(said of illness) to get worse ②(said of weather or a person) to become bad

變換(ㄅㄧㄢˋ ㄏㄨㄢˋ)
①to convert (foreign money, etc.) ②to change; to vary; to switch

變幻(ㄅㄧㄢˋ ㄏㄨㄢˋ)
①to change; to metamorphose; to fluctuate irregularly

變幻莫測(ㄅㄧㄢˋ ㄏㄨㄢˋ ㄇㄛˋ ㄘㄜˋ)
to metamorphose in an unpredictable way

變價(ㄅㄧㄢˋ ㄐㄧㄚˋ)
to appraise at the current price

變節(ㄅㄧㄢˋ ㄐㄧㄝˊ)
①to desert a cause or principle; to defect; to make a political recantation; to turn one's coat ②to reform; to abandon evil ways and return to the right path

變局(ㄅㄧㄢˋ ㄐㄩˊ)
a critical situation; a crisis

變遷(ㄅㄧㄢˋ ㄑㄧㄢ)
evolution; change; vicissitudes

變戲法兒(ㄅㄧㄢˋ ㄒㄧˋ ㄈㄚˇㄦ)
to perform sleight of hand; to manipulate by trickery; to conjure; to juggle

變心(ㄅㄧㄢˋ ㄒㄧㄣ)
①to change in faith or loyalty; to turn a traitor ②to jilt a lover; to cease to love one's spouse

變相(ㄅㄧㄢˋ ㄒㄧㄤˋ)
changed only in appearance; disguised; in disguise

〔言部〕

變相津貼(ㄅㄧㄢ ㄒㄧㄤ ㄐㄧㄣ ㄊㄧㄝ)
money paid legitimately; but not as a straightforward allowance, to an employee who is underpaid according to the official pay scale

變星(ㄅㄧㄢ ㄒㄧㄥ)
a variable star

變形(ㄅㄧㄢ ㄒㄧㄥ)
to transfigure; to transform; to change shape; to be out of shape

變形蟲(ㄅㄧㄢ ㄒㄧㄥ ㄔㄨㄥˊ)
an amoeba

變性(ㄅㄧㄢ ㄒㄧㄥ)
①to change sex by surgical means ②denaturation

變性酒精(ㄅㄧㄢ ㄒㄧㄥ ㄐㄧㄡˇ ㄐㄧㄥ)
denatured alcohol

變質(ㄅㄧㄢ ㄓˊ)
①to change in quality or objectives ②to deteriorate; to go bad: 這魚肉已經變質了。 The fish has gone bad ③to degenerate

變種(ㄅㄧㄢ ㄓㄨㄥˇ)
an extraordinary variety (of something), a mutant; mutation

變成(ㄅㄧㄢ ㄔㄥˊ)
to become; to convert into; to change into: 毛毛蟲會變成蝴蝶。 Caterpillars change into butterflies.

變聲(ㄅㄧㄢ ㄕㄥ)
(said of a person at puberty) change of voice

變數(ㄅㄧㄢ ㄕㄨˋ)
(mathematics) a variable

變造(ㄅㄧㄢ ㄗㄠˋ)
(law) to make changes in value of property (checks) owing to alterations

變奏曲(ㄅㄧㄢ ㄗㄡˋ ㄑㄩˇ)
variations

變阻器(ㄅㄧㄢ ㄗㄨˇ ㄑㄧˋ)
a rheostat

變色(ㄅㄧㄢ ㄙㄜˋ)
①(said of a person) to turn white (from fear) or red (from anger); to change color; to change countenance ②to change in color, to stain; to fade, to discolor; to change the color of

變速(ㄅㄧㄢ ㄙㄨˋ)
to change in speed; gearshift

變異(ㄅㄧㄢ ㄧˋ)
(biology) variation; mutation

變易(ㄅㄧㄢ ㄧˋ)
to alter; to change

變壓器(ㄅㄧㄢ ㄧㄚ ㄑㄧˋ)
a transformer

變電站(ㄅㄧㄢ ㄧㄚˋ ㄓㄢˋ)
a power substation

變音(ㄅㄧㄢ ㄧㄣ)
(phonetics) umlaut

變樣(ㄅㄧㄢ ㄧㄤˋ)
to change in design, patterns, style, appearance, etc.

變爲(ㄅㄧㄢ ㄨㄟˊ)
to become; to be converted or transformed into: 那習俗現已變爲成規。 The custom has now become a rule.

變味(ㄅㄧㄢ ㄨㄟˋ)
(said of stale food or drink) to taste unpleasant to the palate

【讌】5696
(ㄧㄢˋ yann yàn)
a feast; a banquet

讌服(ㄧㄢ ㄈㄨˊ)
everyday dress; informal dress

讌會(ㄧㄢ ㄏㄨㄟˋ)
a feast; a banquet

讌飲(ㄧㄢ ㄧㄣˇ)
a feast; a banquet

【讎】5697
(讐)(ㄔㄡˊ chour chóu)
1. an enemy; a rival; a foe
2. to collate; to compare
3. to toast
4. an answer

讎敵(ㄔㄡˊ ㄉㄧˊ)
an enemy; a foe

讎定(ㄔㄡˊ ㄉㄧㄥˋ)
to correct or revise while proofreading

讎家(ㄔㄡˊ ㄐㄧㄚ)
a rival; an enemy; a foe

讎校(ㄔㄡˊ ㄐㄧㄠˋ)
to collate; to proofread

讎視(ㄔㄡˊ ㄕˋ)
to regard with hostility; to be hostile to

讎殺(ㄔㄡˊ ㄕㄚ)
to kill from hatred; murder committed out of a grudge

讎問(ㄔㄡˊ ㄨㄣˋ)
to ask difficult questions

十七畫

【讕】5698
(ㄌㄢˊ lan lán)
to abuse; to revile; to slander; to libel

讕言(ㄌㄢˊ ㄧㄢˊ)
abusive words; slanderous remarks; calumny

【讒】5699
(ㄔㄢˊ charn chán)
to misrepresent; to slander; to calumniate; to defame

讒謗(ㄔㄢˊ ㄅㄤˋ)
to defame; to slander; to calumniate

讒口交加(ㄔㄢˊ ㄎㄡˇ ㄐㄧㄠ ㄐㄧㄚ)
Slanders come from all quarters. 或 beset by slanders

讒害(ㄔㄢˊ ㄏㄞˋ)或讒陷(ㄔㄢˊ ㄒㄧㄢˋ)
to incriminate by false charges

讒言(ㄔㄢˊ ㄧㄢˊ)
malicious, slanderous talk

讒言惹禍(ㄔㄢˊ ㄧㄢˊ ㄖㄜˇ ㄏㄨㄛˋ)
Calumny brings disaster.

【讓】5700
(ㄖㄤˋ rang ràng)
1. to give way; to make concession; to back down; to yield; to give ground
2. to allow; to let; to permit
3. to turn over; to transfer; to surrender; to cede
4. by: 我的眼鏡讓他打破了。 My glasses have been broken by him.
5. to step aside; to make way; to let by: 請讓一讓。 Please step aside. 或 Let me by, please.

讓步(ㄖㄤˋ ㄅㄨˋ)
to make a concession; to give way; to back down; to yield

讓畔(ㄖㄤˋ ㄆㄢˋ)
to be conciliatory in fixing the boundary of one's field

讓渡(ㄖㄤˋ ㄉㄨˋ)
to turn over; to transfer; to cede

讓梨(ㄖㄤˋ ㄌㄧˊ)
a reference to the story of Kung Jung (孔融), who yielded the bigger pear to his elder brother—to be con-

cessive to one's sibling; to
show brotherly love

讓路(ㄖㄤ ㄌㄨˋ)
to make way; to get out of
the way

讓開(ㄖㄤ ㄎㄞ)
to make way; to step aside;
to get out of the way 參看
「讓路」

讓價(ㄖㄤ ㄐㄧㄚˋ)
the reduced price after haggling

讓賢(ㄖㄤ ㄒㄧㄢˊ)
to yield one's position to a
more talented person or a
better qualified person

讓受(ㄖㄤ ㄕㄡˋ)
to take another's property or
right through due process of
law; acquisition

讓人(ㄖㄤ ㄖㄣˊ)
to yield to others; to be
concessive

讓棗推梨(ㄖㄤ ㄗㄠˇ ㄊㄨㄟ ㄌㄧˊ)
to show brotherly love

讓座(ㄖㄤ ㄗㄨㄛˋ)
to yield a seat: 他讓座給一位
老人。He yielded his bus seat
to an old man.

讓位(ㄖㄤ ㄨㄟˋ)
①to yield the throne; to
abdicate the throne ② to
yield to; to give way to

讓王(ㄖㄤ ㄨㄤˊ)or 讓國(ㄖㄤ ㄍㄨㄛˊ)
to yield the throne to
another

讓與(ㄖㄤ ㄩˇ)
to cede or surrender (titles,
privileges, etc.)

【讖】 5701
ㄔㄣ chenn chèn
1. a prophecy; an omen
2. books about omens

讖緯(ㄔㄣ ㄨㄟˇ)
books about the occult

讖語(ㄔㄣ ㄩˇ)
a prophetic remark made
casually which later comes
true; a prophecy: 讖語靈驗。
The prophecy is efficacious.

十八畫

【讙】 5702
ㄏㄨㄢ huan huān
1. to be noisy; to clamor
2. same as 歡—to rejoice

讙呼(ㄏㄨㄢ ㄏㄨ)
to give a cheer; to cheer: 萬
衆讙呼。The crowd cheered
uproariously.

十九畫

【讚】 5703
ㄗㄢ tzann zàn
1. to commend; to eulogize; to
praise; to applaud; to laud
2. same as 贊

讚佩(ㄗㄢ ㄆㄟˋ)
to think highly of; to
esteem; to admire

讚美(ㄗㄢ ㄇㄟˇ)
①to praise; to eulogize; to
glorify; to extol; to laud ②
laud; praise; eulogy

讚美詩(ㄗㄢ ㄇㄟˇ ㄕ)
hymns; psalms

讚歌(ㄗㄢ ㄍㄜ)
to sing the praises of; to
gasp in admiration

讚賞(ㄗㄢ ㄕㄤˇ)
to praise; to commend; to
extol; to laud; to appreciate

讚詞(ㄗㄢ ㄘˊ)or 讚辭(ㄗㄢ ㄘˊ)
words of praise; an en-
comium; phrases of eulogy:
讚詞甚美。Phrases of eulogy
are extremely beautiful.

讚頌(ㄗㄢ ㄙㄨㄥˋ)
to eulogize; to extol; to
praise

讚揚(ㄗㄢ ㄧㄤˊ)
①to glorify; to exalt; to uphold ②commendation; glorification

讚仰(ㄗㄢ ㄧㄤˇ)
to regard with admiration
and respect

二十畫

【讞】 5704
ㄧㄢˋ yann yàn
to judge at a court of law

【讜】 5705
ㄉㄤˇ daang dǎng
to speak out boldly; (said of
advice or comment) honest;
unbiased; straightforward

讜言(ㄉㄤˇ ㄧㄢˊ)
outspoken statements

讜辭(ㄉㄤˇ ㄘˊ)
outspoken words

讜議(ㄉㄤˇ ㄧˋ)
outspoken remarks

谷 部
《ㄨˇ guu gǔ

【谷】 5706
1. 《ㄨˇ guu gǔ
1. a valley; a waterway between
two mountains; a ravine
2. a hollow; a pit
3. a dilemma; a difficult situation; a predicament
4. a Chinese family name

谷盆地(《ㄨˇ ㄆㄣˊ ㄉㄧˋ)
a basin

谷風(《ㄨˇ ㄈㄥ)
①an east wind ②an up-
draft in a valley

谷底(《ㄨˇ ㄉㄧˇ)
the bottom of a valley

谷飲(《ㄨˇ ㄧㄣˇ)
to live like a hermit

【谷】 5706
2. ㄩˋ yuh yù
a Chinese family name

谷渾(ㄩˋ ㄏㄨㄣˊ)
a Chinese double-name

十畫

【豁】 5707
1. ㄏㄨㄛ huo huō
1. a crack; a break; a breach
2. to crack; to break open; to
split
3. to give up; to sacrifice; to
risk one's life for

豁命(ㄏㄨㄛ ㄇㄧㄥˋ)
at the expense of one's life;
to risk one's life

豁口子(ㄏㄨㄛ ㄎㄡˇ ˙ㄗ)or 豁口兒
(ㄏㄨㄛ ㄎㄡˇㄦ)or 豁子(ㄏㄨㄛ ˙ㄗ)
a crack of a vessel

豁出去(ㄏㄨㄛ ˙ㄔㄨ ㄑㄩˋ)
to forge ahead in disregard
of the consequence

豁唇子(ㄏㄨㄛ ㄔㄨㄣˊ ˙ㄗ)or 豁唇
(ㄏㄨㄛ ㄔㄨㄣˊ)or 豁嘴(ㄏㄨㄛ ㄗㄨㄟˇ)
a person with a harelip

【豁】 5707
2. ㄏㄨㄛˋ huoh huò
1. to open up; clear

2. to exempt from (duties, etc.)

谿免（ㄏㄨㄟ ㄇㄧㄢˇ）
to exempt from (taxes, military service, etc.); exemption; immunity

谿達（ㄏㄨㄛ ㄉㄚˊ）
①open and clear ②generous or magnanimous; open-minded

谿達大度（ㄏㄨㄛ ㄉㄚˊ ㄉㄚˋ ㄉㄨˋ）
generous; open-minded and magnanimous

谿瀟（ㄏㄨㄛ ㄒㄧㄠ）
unrestrained; carefree

谿然（ㄏㄨㄛ ㄖㄢˊ）
open and clear

谿然貫通（ㄏㄨㄛ ㄖㄢˊ 《ㄨㄢˋ ㄊㄨㄥ）
to dawn upon one suddenly; to understand all of a sudden

谿然開朗（ㄏㄨㄛ ㄖㄢˊ ㄎㄞ ㄌㄤ）
①to become clear or visible all of a sudden ②(said of space) to become extensive all of a sudden

谿如（ㄏㄨㄛ ㄖㄨˊ）
open and clear; thoroughly clear

【谿】 5707 3. ㄏㄜ heh hé
bright and spacious

谿亮（ㄏㄜˋ ㄌㄧㄤ）
bright and spacious

【谿】 5707 4. ㄏㄨㄚˊ hwa huá
to play a finger-guessing game

谿拳（ㄏㄨㄚˊ ㄑㄩㄢˊ）
finger-guessing game—a drinking game at feasts

【豀】 5708 ㄒㄧ shi xī
to squabble; to quarrel; to brawl

【谿】 5709 ㄒㄧ shi xī
1. a valley; a gorge
2. a stream; a creek; a brook 亦作「溪」

谿谷（ㄒㄧ ㄍㄨˇ）
a valley

谿壑（ㄒㄧ ㄏㄨㄛˋ）
a ravine

豆 部
ㄉㄡ dow dòu

【豆】 5710 ㄉㄡ dow dòu
1. beans and peas collectively；豆富於蛋白質。Beans are rich in protein.
2. a vessel of wood for containing flesh, sauces, etc. at sacrifices and feasts
3. a Chinese family name

豆瓣醬（ㄉㄡˋ ㄅㄢˋ ㄐㄧㄤ）
thick broad bean sauce

豆餅（ㄉㄡˋ ㄅㄧㄥˇ）
soybean cake (a kind of animal feed)

豆剖瓜分（ㄉㄡˋ ㄆㄡˇ 《ㄨㄚ ㄈㄣ）
to divide up the territory (of a nation); to partition (land)

豆苗（ㄉㄡˋ ㄇㄧㄠˊ）
tender stalks and leaves of peas as a vegetable

豆腐（ㄉㄡˋ ㄈㄨˇ）
bean curd; tofu

豆腐皮（ㄉㄡˋ ㄈㄨˇ ㄆㄧˊ）or **豆腐皮兒**（ㄉㄡˋ ㄈㄨˇ ㄆㄧˊ ㄦˊ）
a semitransparent film formed on the surface of soybean milk

豆腐店（ㄉㄡˋ ㄈㄨˇ ㄉㄧㄢˋ）
a store where bean curd is made for sale

豆腐乾（ㄉㄡˋ ㄈㄨˇ 《ㄢ）or **豆腐乾兒**（ㄉㄡˋ ㄈㄨˇ 《ㄚㄦ）
spiced and dried bean curd

豆腐乳（ㄉㄡˋ ㄈㄨˇ ㄖㄨˇ）
soybean cheese; fermented bean curd

豆綠（ㄉㄡˋ ㄌㄩˋ）
the green (color) of peas

豆科植物（ㄉㄡˋ ㄎㄜ ㄓˊ ㄨˋ）
legume; the pulse family; bean or pea family

豆蔻（ㄉㄡˋ ㄎㄡˋ）or **荳蔻**（ㄉㄡˋ ㄎㄡˋ）
①a cardamom; a nutmeg ②a virgin or maiden; young girls

豆蔻年華（ㄉㄡˋ ㄎㄡˋ ㄋㄧㄢˊ ㄏㄨㄚˊ）or **荳蔻年華**（ㄉㄡˋ ㄎㄡˋ ㄋㄧㄢˊ ㄏㄨㄚˊ）
(said of girls) in their teens

豆莢（ㄉㄡˋ ㄐㄧㄚˊ）
the pods of beans or peas

豆角（ㄉㄡˋ ㄐㄧㄠˇ）
string beans

豆漿（ㄉㄡˋ ㄐㄧㄤ）
soybean milk

豆醬（ㄉㄡˋ ㄐㄧㄤˋ）
fermented beans in paste form

豆萁（ㄉㄡˋ ㄑㄧˊ）
the stalks of beans

豆汁（ㄉㄡˋ ㄓ）
a beverage made from fermented mung beans

豆渣（ㄉㄡˋ ㄓㄚ）
the residue of soybeans in making bean curd

豆豉（ㄉㄡˋ ㄔˇ）or（ㄉㄡˋ ㄕˇ）
fermented and seasoned soy beans

豆石（ㄉㄡˋ ㄕˊ）
pisolite

豆沙（ㄉㄡˋ ㄕㄚ）
mashed beans (usually used as stuffing for dumplings)

豆子（ㄉㄡˋ ㄗ˙）
beans or peas

豆素（ㄉㄡˋ ㄙㄨˋ）
legumin

豆芽（ㄉㄡˋ ㄧㄚˊ）
bean sprouts as a vegetable

豆芽菜（ㄉㄡˋ ㄧㄚˊ ㄘㄞˋ）
mung bean sprouts as a vegetable dish

豆油（ㄉㄡˋ ㄧㄡˊ）
soybean oil

三畫

【豇】 5711 ㄐㄧㄤ jiang jiāng
a cowpea

豇豆（ㄐㄧㄤ ㄉㄡˋ）
cowpea, an asparagus bean

【豈】 5712 1. ㄑㄧˇ chii qǐ
an interrogative particle implying a conflicting or dissenting view or answer —how; what

豈有此理（ㄑㄧˇ ㄧㄡˇ）or **豈非**（ㄑㄧˇ ㄈㄟ）
Wouldn't it result in..? or Isn't that..? 或 Wouldn't it be...? 豈不困難? Wouldn't it be difficult?

豈但（ㄑㄧˇ ㄉㄢˋ）

not only

豈能（ㄑ一ˇ ㄋㄥˊ）
How can...? 我豈能留下你孤單一人？ How can I leave you alone?

豈敢（ㄑ一ˇ ㄍㄢˇ）
(a term implying humbleness or sarcasm) How dare I...? 或 would not dare...

豈可（ㄑ一ˇ ㄎㄜˇ）
How can...?

豈止（ㄑ一ˇ ㄓˇ）
not at all limited to...; much more than...

豈只（ㄑ一ˇ ㄓˇ）
not only that... (but)

豈有此理（ㄑ一ˇ 一ㄡˇ ㄘˇ ㄌ一ˇ）
totally unreasonable 或 What kind of reasoning is that? 或 How absurd!

【豈】 5712
2. ㄎㄞˇ kae kǎi
happy; delighted; jubilant; harmonious

豈弟 or 愷悌（ㄎㄞˇ ㄊ一ˋ）
happy and courteous; easy to get along with

四畫

【豉】 5713
ㄔˋ chyy chì
（讀音 ㄕˋ shyh shì）
fermented beans; pickled black beans 亦作「豆豉」

六畫

【登】 5714
ㄉㄥ deng dēng
vessels for food used in ancient times

【豊】 5715
ㄌ一ˇ lii lǐ
a kind of ritual vessel in ancient times

八畫

【豌】 5716
ㄨㄢ uan wān
peas; garden peas

豌豆（ㄨㄢ ㄉㄡˋ）
garden peas (*Pisum sativum*)

豌豆泥（ㄨㄢ ㄉㄡˋ ㄋ一ˊ）
mashed peas (served as a dessert)

豌豆糕（ㄨㄢ ㄉㄡˋ ㄍㄠ）
a small sweetened cake made of mashed peas

豌豆黄兒（ㄨㄢ ㄉㄡˋ ㄏㄨㄤˊ儿）
a cake made of garden-pea flour and sugar

【豎】 5717
ㄕㄨˋ shuh shù
1. to erect; to set up; to stand
2. upright; perpendicular; vertical
3. boys who have not come of age; a young servant
4. petty officers in the palace
5. a downward, perpendicular stroke in calligraphy

豎毛（ㄕㄨˋ ㄇㄠˊ）
the hair standing on end (for trepidation or as a response to some creeping expressions)

豎夫（ㄕㄨˋ ㄈㄨ）
a coolie; a servant

豎笛（ㄕㄨˋ ㄉ一ˊ）
a clarinet

豎立（ㄕㄨˋ ㄌ一ˋ）
to erect

豎箜篌（ㄕㄨˋ ㄎㄨㄥ ㄏㄡˊ）
an ancient musical instrument with 23 strings

豎褐（ㄕㄨˋ ㄏㄜˊ）
short garments worn by coolies

豎官（ㄕㄨˋ ㄍㄨㄢ）
eunuchs

豎起大拇指（ㄕㄨˋ ㄑ一ˇ ㄉㄚˋ ㄇㄨˇ ㄓˇ）
to hold up one's thumb in approval; thumbs up

豎起脊梁（ㄕㄨˋ ㄑ一ˇ ㄐ一ˇ ㄌ一ㄤˊ）
to straighten up one's back —to get set for action, or to pull oneself together

豎琴（ㄕㄨˋ ㄑ一ㄣˊ）
the harp

豎蜻蜓（ㄕㄨˋ ㄑ一ㄥ ㄊ一ㄥˊ）
to stand erect on one's hands

豎直立（ㄕㄨˋ ㄓˊ ㄌ一ˋ）
to stand erect on one's hands

豎柱（ㄕㄨˋ ㄓㄨˋ）
to erect the pillars (of a house, etc.)

豎臣（ㄕㄨˋ ㄔㄣˊ）
(an abusive expression) a low-ranking court official

豎儒（ㄕㄨˋ ㄖㄨˊ）
①(an abusive expression used mostly in the Han Dynasty) petty pedants ② a fool

豎子（ㄕㄨˋ ㄗˇ）
① a boy; a youngster ② a good-for-nothing

豎劃（ㄕㄨˋ ㄏㄨㄚˋ）
(Chinese calligraphy) a downward, perpendicular stroke

豎眼（ㄕㄨˋ 一ㄢˇ）
angry looks

十畫

【豏】 5718
ㄒ一ㄢˋ shiann xiàn
half-grown beans

十一畫

【豐】 5719
ㄈㄥ feng fēng
1. abundant; luxuriant; copious; fruitful; plentiful; plenty; thick; big
2. a crop; a harvest
3. a Chinese family name

豐沛（ㄈㄥ ㄆㄟˋ）
copious or plentiful (rainfall, etc.): 今年雨水豐沛。We have plenty of rain this year.

豐茂（ㄈㄥ ㄇㄠˋ）
luxuriant (growth, etc.); plentiful

豐滿（ㄈㄥ ㄇㄢˇ）
① rich; affluence; plentiful: 五穀豐滿。All food crops are plentiful. ② full-fledged ③ (said of a woman's figure) very full and voluptuous; plump; buxom

豐富（ㄈㄥ ㄈㄨˋ）
① abundant; copious or plentiful; rich ② to enrich

豐登（ㄈㄥ ㄉㄥ）
a bumper crop

豐年（ㄈㄥ ㄋ一ㄢˊ）
a plentiful year; a year of a good harvest

豐功偉績（ㄈㄥ ㄍㄨㄥ ㄨㄟˇ ㄐ一）
great achievements; significant contribution

豐鎬（ㄈㄥ ㄏㄠˋ）

【豕部】

the capital of the Chou people before they overthrew the Hsia Dynasty

豐厚(ㄈㄥ ㄏㄡˋ)
handsome (pay, gifts, etc.); plentiful or rich

豐肌(ㄈㄥ ㄐㄧ)
plump; fleshy

豐歉(ㄈㄥ ㄑㄧㄢˋ)
plenty and deficiency; a year of a bumper crop or famine

豐取刻與(ㄈㄥ ㄑㄩˇ ㄎㄜˋ ㄩˇ)
(literally) to take a lot and give away little—very greedy

豐熾(ㄈㄥ ㄔ)
rich or affluent; abundant; abundance; prosperous

豐實(ㄈㄥ ㄕˊ)
abundant; plentiful; rich

豐碩(ㄈㄥ ㄕㄨㄛˋ)
rich; plenty

豐殺(ㄈㄥ ㄕㄚˋ)
to increase or decrease

豐收(ㄈㄥ ㄕㄡ)
a rich harvest; a bumper crop: 今年豐收在望。 A good harvest is in sight this year

豐贍(ㄈㄥ ㄕㄢˋ)
prosperous; abundant; rich; plentiful

豐上銳下(ㄈㄥ ㄕㄤˋ ㄖㄨㄟˋ ㄒㄧㄚˋ)
(said of a face) plump in the upper part but sharp toward the chin

豐茂(ㄈㄥ ㄇㄠˋ)
flourishing; luxuriant; prosperous or abundant; sumptuous

豐饒(ㄈㄥ ㄖㄠˊ)
plentiful; abundant; abundance; fertile

豐稔(ㄈㄥ ㄖㄣˇ)
a rich harvest; a bumper crop

豐穰(ㄈㄥ ㄖㄤˊ)
a bumper crop

豐壤(ㄈㄥ ㄖㄤˇ)
fertile soil; rich earth

豐潤(ㄈㄥ ㄖㄨㄣˋ)
①abundant; affluent ②name of a county in Hopeh Province

豐融(ㄈㄥ ㄖㄨㄥˊ)
(said of a woman) regal and beautiful

豐足(ㄈㄥ ㄗㄨˊ)
affluent, wealthy; abundant

豐衣足食(ㄈㄥ ㄧ ㄗㄨˊ ㄕˊ)
good clothes and rich food; well-fed and well-clad; to eat and dress well; to live in affluence: 我們都過着豐衣足食的生活。 We all live in affluence.

豐衍(ㄈㄥ ㄧㄢˇ)
plentiful; abundant

豐盈(ㄈㄥ ㄧㄥˊ)
①rich and full (figure, etc.); plump: 她有豐盈的身材。 She has a rich and full figure. ②rich or wealthy ③a good harvest

豐偉(ㄈㄥ ㄨㄟˇ)
tall and stout

豐腴(ㄈㄥ ㄩˊ)
plump; buxom and fair; fertile: 臺灣是塊豐腴之地。 Taiwan is a fertile piece of land.

豐裕(ㄈㄥ ㄩˋ)
abundance; plentiful; high (pay, etc.): 他的生活豐裕。 He lives in plenty. 或 He is comfortably off.

十七畫

【艷】 5720 (ㄧㄢˋ yann yàn)
same as 豔

二十一畫

【豔】 5721 (艷) (ㄧㄢˋ yann yàn)
1. plump; voluptuous
2. beautiful and captivating (literary writings, etc.)
3. gorgeous; colorful; gaudy
4. anything pertaining to love, as a love story, love song, etc.; amorous
5. a beauty
6. radiant
7. to admire or envy

豔婢(ㄧㄢˋ ㄅㄧˋ)
a beautiful maidservant

豔福(ㄧㄢˋ ㄈㄨˊ)
(said of a man) good fortune or success in love affairs

豔福不淺(ㄧㄢˋ ㄈㄨˊ ㄅㄨˋ ㄑㄧㄢˇ)
(said of a man) to have a

lot of good fortune or success in love affairs; to have a beautiful girl friend or wife

豔麗(ㄧㄢˋ ㄌㄧˋ)
radiantly beautiful; magnificent; charming; captivating; gorgeous

豔歌(ㄧㄢˋ ㄍㄜ)
love songs

豔(ㄧㄢˋ)
extremely or stunningly beautiful

豔羨(ㄧㄢˋ ㄒㄧㄢˋ)
to admire; to long for

豔稱(ㄧㄢˋ ㄔㄥ)
famed for her beauty

豔詩(ㄧㄢˋ ㄕ)
love poems

豔史(ㄧㄢˋ ㄕˇ)
one's love affairs; romantic adventures; amorous adventures

豔事(ㄧㄢˋ ㄕˋ)
erotic affairs; romantic adventures

豔姿(ㄧㄢˋ ㄗ)
a beautiful appearance; charming or enticing looks

豔色(ㄧㄢˋ ㄙㄜˋ)
the beauty of a woman

豔陽(ㄧㄢˋ ㄧㄤˊ)
sunny spring weather

豔陽天(ㄧㄢˋ ㄧㄤˊ ㄊㄧㄢ)
charming, bright springtime; bright sunny skies

豔舞(ㄧㄢˋ ㄨˇ)
striptease; voluptuous, enticing dances

豔遇(ㄧㄢˋ ㄩˋ)
an encounter with a beautiful woman

豕 部
ㄕˇ shyy shǐ

【豕】 5722 (ㄕˇ shyy shǐ)
a swine; a pig; a hog

豕突(ㄕˇ ㄊㄨˊ)
to run wild

豕奴(ㄕˇ ㄋㄨˊ)
a swineherd

豬喙（ㄓㄨˋㄏㄨㄟˋ）
(said of a person's mouth)
shaped like that of a pig

豕交獸畜（ㄕˋㄐㄧㄠ ㄕㄡˋㄒㄩˋ）
to treat people like beasts

豕心（ㄕˋㄒㄧㄣ）
greedy; avaricious

四畫

【豚】 5723
ㄊㄨㄣˊ twen tún
1. a small pig
2. a Chinese family name

豚犢（ㄊㄨㄣˊㄉㄨˋ）
bad sons—like pigs

豚蹄穰田（ㄊㄨㄣˊㄊㄧˊㄖㄤˊㄊㄧㄢˊ）
to expect a tremendous
return from a meager investment

豚肩（ㄊㄨㄣˊㄐㄧㄢ）
the pig's shoulder

豚犬（ㄊㄨㄣˊㄑㄩㄢˇ）
①pigs and dogs ②(self-
depreciatory term) one's
own sons

豚兒（ㄊㄨㄣˊㄦˊ）
(a self-derogative expression
in polite society) my son

【豝】 5724
ㄅㄚ ba bā
a female pig; a sow

五畫

【象】 5725
ㄒㄧㄤˋ shianq xiàng
1. an elephant
2. a portrait; an image snapshot
3. a phenomenon; the outward
appearance or expression of
anything—especially weather,
heavenly bodies, etc.; shape;
an image
4. ivory

象鼻（ㄒㄧㄤˋㄅㄧˊ）
an elephant's trunk; a pro-
boscis

象鼻蟲（ㄒㄧㄤˋㄅㄧˊㄔㄨㄥˊ）
a curculio; a weevil; a snout
beetle

象皮病（ㄒㄧㄤˋㄆㄧˊㄅㄧㄥˋ）
elephantiasis

象皮紙（ㄒㄧㄤˋㄆㄧˊㄓˇ）
a kind of thick and strong
paper for drawing

象奴（ㄒㄧㄤˋㄋㄨˊ）or象夫（ㄒㄧㄤˋㄈㄨ）
a mahout

象管（ㄒㄧㄤˋㄍㄨㄢˇ）
an ivory tube for holding
the Chinese writing brush

象笏（ㄒㄧㄤˋㄏㄨˋ）
an ivory tablet held before
the breast in ceremony or
audience 亦作「象簡」

象環（ㄒㄧㄤˋㄏㄨㄢˊ）
an ivory ring

象櫛（ㄒㄧㄤˋㄐㄧㄝˊ）
an ivory comb

象教（ㄒㄧㄤˋㄐㄧㄠˋ）
Buddhism

象棋（ㄒㄧㄤˋㄑㄧˊ）
Chinese chess

象限（ㄒㄧㄤˋㄒㄧㄢˋ）
a quadrant

象形（ㄒㄧㄤˋㄒㄧㄥˊ）
image shapes, or picto-
graphs—one of the six
groups into which Chinese
characters are divided,
which consists of greatly
simplified drawings of
objects the characters
denote

象形文字（ㄒㄧㄤˋㄒㄧㄥˊㄨㄣˊㄗˋ）
hieroglyphics; a pictograph;
a hieroglyph

象徵（ㄒㄧㄤˋㄓㄥ）
①to symbolize ②a symbol

象徵性（ㄒㄧㄤˋㄓㄥ ㄒㄧㄥˋ）
as a token, a token (gift,
etc.); symbolic

象箸（ㄒㄧㄤˋㄓㄨˋ）
ivory chopsticks

象齒焚身（ㄒㄧㄤˋㄔˇㄈㄣˊㄕㄣ）
The elephant is killed
because of its tusks.

象牀（ㄒㄧㄤˋㄔㄨㄤˊ）
a bed adorned with ivory

象人（ㄒㄧㄤˋㄖㄣˊ）
the semblances of men buried with the dead in ancient
times

象牙（ㄒㄧㄤˋㄧㄚˊ）
ivory; elephant tusks

象牙塔（ㄒㄧㄤˋㄧㄚˊㄊㄚˇ）
the ivory tower

象牙海岸（ㄒㄧㄤˋㄧㄚˊㄏㄞˇㄢˋ）
the Ivory Coast

象牙婚（ㄒㄧㄤˋㄧㄚˊㄏㄨㄣ）
Ivory Wedding, the 14th
wedding anniversary

象牙質（ㄒㄧㄤˋㄧㄚˊㄓˊ）
(physiology) dentine

象魏（ㄒㄧㄤˋㄨㄟˋ）
the palace door 亦作「象闕」

【豨】 5726
（音）日ㄨㄟˋ ruei ruì

1. hat sashes hanging down
2. luxuriant vegetation

六畫

【豢】 5727
ㄏㄨㄢˋ huann huàn
1. to feed animals with grains
2. to tempt or entice people
with profit or gains
3. domesticated animals

豢養（ㄏㄨㄢˋㄧㄤˇ）
to feed; to rear; to raise; to
keep

豢圈（ㄏㄨㄢˋㄐㄩㄢ）
a pen for animals; an animal barn or stable

七畫

【豪】 5728
ㄏㄠˊ haur háo
1. a person outstanding in
intelligence or talent; a
heroic person
2. a leader; a ringleader
3. a proclivity to the use of
force, bullying ways, etc.
4. tiny; fine hair 亦作「毫」

豪邁（ㄏㄠˊㄇㄞˋ）
straightforward and care-
free; generous and open-
minded; heroic

豪門（ㄏㄠˊㄇㄣˊ）
a rich and powerful family;
a wealthy and highly influential family

豪放（ㄏㄠˊㄈㄤˋ）
vigorous and unrestrained;
virile; careless about details

豪放不羈（ㄏㄠˊㄈㄤˋㄅㄨˋㄐㄧ）
vigorous and unrestrained;
virile and unconventional

豪富（ㄏㄠˊㄈㄨˋ）
millionaires

豪強（ㄏㄠˊㄑㄧㄤˊ）
a group of the influential
local gentry who take law
in their own hands

豪邁（ㄏㄠˊㄇㄞˋ）
gallant, chivalrous but not
behaving very properly

〔豕
部〕

【豸部】

豪賭 (ㄏㄠˊ ㄉㄨˇ)
to gamble with big stakes

豪奪 (ㄏㄠˊ ㄉㄨㄛˊ)
to rob; to take by force

豪奴 (ㄏㄠˊ ㄋㄨˊ)
a servant of a powerful family who bullies around

豪光 (ㄏㄠˊ ㄍㄨㄤ)
a dazzling ray; flashing light

豪客 (ㄏㄠˊ ㄎㄜˋ)
① robbers; burglars ② persons who spend money like water, especially in entertainment and gambling

豪橫 (ㄏㄠˊ ㄏㄥˋ)
overbearing and bullying; despotic

豪華 (ㄏㄠˊ ㄏㄨㄚˊ)
luxurious (hotels, theaters, etc.); swanky; plush: 他們過着豪華的生活。They led a luxurious life.

豪傑 (ㄏㄠˊ ㄐㄧㄝˊ)
a man of outstanding talent, intelligence and courage; a scholar of heroism

豪舉 (ㄏㄠˊ ㄐㄩˇ)
a gallant or chivalrous act; a surprisingly generous act or undertaking

豪氣 (ㄏㄠˊ ㄑㄧˋ)
undaunted spirit; heroism

豪強 (ㄏㄠˊ ㄑㄧㄤˊ)
bullies; those who throw their weight around

豪情 (ㄏㄠˊ ㄑㄧㄥˊ)
lofty sentiments

豪俠 (ㄏㄠˊ ㄒㄧㄚˊ)
a hero; chivalry; a champion of justice

豪性 (ㄏㄠˊ ㄒㄧㄥˋ)
chivalry; gallantry

豪豬 (ㄏㄠˊ ㄓㄨ)
a porcupine

豪士 (ㄏㄠˊ ㄕˋ)
one who excels in intellectual capacity

豪爽 (ㄏㄠˊ ㄕㄨㄤˇ)
bold and generous; chivalrous; straightforward

豪飲 (ㄏㄠˊ ㄧㄣˇ)
to drink like a fish: 他每回豪飲必醉。Whenever he drinks like a fish, he gets drunk.

豪雨 (ㄏㄠˊ ㄩˇ)
to rain cats and dogs; pouring rain; a downpour

豪語 (ㄏㄠˊ ㄩˇ)
big talk; a bold promise

【豨】 5729
ㄒㄧ　shi xī
a pig; a hog

九畫

【豫】 5730
ㄩˋ　yuh yù
1. comfort; to be at ease
2. same as 預— to get ready or prepared; beforehand
3. to travel; to make an excursion or a trip
4. to cheat; to lie
5. one of the nine political divisions in ancient China
6. to hesitate
7. short for Honan (河南)
8. happy; delighted; pleased
9. a Chinese family name

【豭】 5731
ㄐㄧㄚ　jia jiā
a male pig; a boar

【豬】 5732
ㄓㄨ　ju zhū
1. a pig; a hog; a swine
2. a pigheaded person

豬八戒 (ㄓㄨ ㄅㄚ ㄐㄧㄝˋ)
one of the chief characters in *Pilgrimage to the West* (西遊記), who was supposedly incarnated through the spirit of a pig, a symbol of man's cupidity

豬排 (ㄓㄨ ㄆㄞˊ)
a pork chop

豬肚 (ㄓㄨ ㄉㄨˋ)
pig's tripe

豬頭 (ㄓㄨ ㄊㄡˊ)
pig's head (a favorite dish for drinking)

豬蹄 (ㄓㄨ ㄊㄧˊ)
pigs' feet

豬腿 (ㄓㄨ ㄊㄨㄟˇ)
① pig's legs ② ham; leg-meat of the hog

豬欄 (ㄓㄨ ㄌㄢˊ)
a pigpen; a pigsty

豬苓 (ㄓㄨ ㄌㄧㄥˊ)
a kind of fungus grown on maple trees, used in herbal medicine

豬玀 (ㄓㄨ ㄌㄨㄛˊ)
(a term used in reviling in Shanghai) Swine!

豬肝 (ㄓㄨ ㄍㄢ)
pig's liver

豬肝麵 (ㄓㄨ ㄍㄢ ㄇㄧㄢˋ)
noodles prepared with pig's liver

豬肝湯 (ㄓㄨ ㄍㄢ ㄊㄤ)
pig's liver broth or soup

豬肝色 (ㄓㄨ ㄍㄢ ㄙㄜˋ)
liver-colored

豬叫 (ㄓㄨ ㄐㄧㄠˋ)
grunting of hogs

豬圈 (ㄓㄨ ㄐㄩㄢˋ)
a pigsty; a pigpen; a hogpen

豬血 (ㄓㄨ ㄒㄧㄝˇ)
coagulated pig blood used as a food item

豬肉 (ㄓㄨ ㄖㄡˋ)
pork

豬仔 (ㄓㄨ ㄗˇ)
young pigs

豬鬃 (ㄓㄨ ㄗㄨㄥ)
hog's bristles

豬腰子 (ㄓㄨ ㄧㄠ ㄗ)
pig kidneys

豬油 (ㄓㄨ ㄧㄡˊ)
lard: 她總是用豬油炒菜。She always cooks in lard.

十畫

【豳】 5733
ㄅㄧㄣ　bin bīn
1. Pin, name of a state in the Chou Dynasty
2. name of a mountain in Shensi

<big>豸 部</big>
ㄓ　jyh zhī

【豸】 5734
ㄓ　jyh zhì
insects without feet or legs

三畫

【豹】 5735
ㄅㄠˋ　baw bào
1. a leopard; a panther
2. a Chinese family name

豹略 (ㄅㄠˋ ㄐㄩㄝˋ)
① a military commander ② generalship; military strategy and tactics

豹子 (ㄅㄠˋ ˙ㄗ)
a leopard; a panther; a kind of wildcat

豹死留皮 (ㄅㄠˋ ㄙˇ ㄌㄧㄡˊ ㄆㄧˊ)
(literally) A leopard leaves behind its skin when it dies. — A man has a reputation to leave to posterity when he dies.

豹隱 (ㄅㄠˋ ㄧㄣˇ)
to live in retirement; to lead the life of a hermit

【豺】 5736
ㄔㄞˊ chair chái
1. Canis hodophilax, a raven-ous beast, akin to the wolf
2. wickedly cunning; cruel

豺狼 (ㄔㄞˊ ㄌㄤˊ)
ravenous and cruel beasts —mean and wicked persons

豺狼當道 (ㄔㄞˊ ㄌㄤˊ ㄉㄤ ㄉㄠˋ)
jackals and wolves on the road—(figuratively) wicked persons in power

豺虎 (ㄔㄞˊ ㄏㄨˇ)
①cruel bandits ②jackals and tigers

豺聲 (ㄔㄞˊ ㄕㄥ)
to roar as fiercely as a wild beast

【豻】 5737
ㄏㄢˋ hann hàn
1. a kind of wild dog
2. a lockup

五畫

【貂】 5738
ㄉㄧㄠ diau diāo
the sable; the marten; the mink

貂皮 (ㄉㄧㄠ ㄆㄧˊ)
sable skin or fur; mink

貂皮大衣 (ㄉㄧㄠ ㄆㄧˊ ㄉㄚˋ ㄧ)
a mink (coat)

貂璫 (ㄉㄧㄠ ㄉㄤ)
a eunuch

貂裘換酒 (ㄉㄧㄠ ㄑㄧㄡˊ ㄏㄨㄢˋ ㄐㄧㄡˇ)
(literally) to trade a mink coat for wine—extravagance of the rich

貂蟬 (ㄉㄧㄠ ㄔㄢˊ)
①hat ornaments of an army officer in ancient China ②Tiao Chan, wife of General Lü Pu (呂布) in the Period of Three Kingdoms

貂扇 (ㄉㄧㄠ ㄕㄢˋ)
a fan made of sable tails

貂寺 (ㄉㄧㄠ ㄙˋ)
a eunuch

貂羽 (ㄉㄧㄠ ㄩˇ)
the fur of a sable

六畫

【貅】 5739
ㄒㄧㄡ shiou xiū
1. a kind of animal like a tiger
2. a fierce and courageous sol-dier

【貉】 5740
1. ㄏㄠˊ haur háo
(又讀 ㄏㄜˊ her hé)
a badger; a racoon dog; a foxlike animal nocturnal in habit

貉絨 (ㄏㄠˊ ㄖㄨㄥˊ)
badger skin or fur

貉子 (ㄏㄠˊ ˙ㄗ)
a young badger

【貉】 5740
2.(貊) ㄇㄛˋ moh mò
1. (in ancient China) the name of a northern barbarian tribe
2. quiet

七畫

【貌】 5741
ㄇㄠˋ maw mào
1. a facial appearance; fea-tures
2. a general appearance; a manner; form; bearing
3. to appear or pretend to be like
4. a ceremonious manner

貌不驚人 (ㄇㄠˋ ㄅㄨˋ ㄐㄧㄥ ㄖㄣˊ)
to look mediocre

貌美 (ㄇㄠˋ ㄇㄟˇ)
(said of a woman) beautiful

貌合神離 (ㄇㄠˋ ㄏㄜˊ ㄕㄣˊ ㄌㄧˊ)
to appear united outwardly but divided at heart

貌寢 (ㄇㄠˋ ㄑㄧㄣˇ)or 貌寢 (ㄇㄠˋ ㄑㄧㄣˇ)
ugly; homely

貌相 (ㄇㄠˋ ㄒㄧㄤˋ)
to judge someone by his appearance only

貌醜 (ㄇㄠˋ ㄔㄡˇ)
ugly; ill-looking

貌似 (ㄇㄠˋ ㄙˋ)
(said of a person) to look like: 他貌似忠厚。He looks like an honest man.

【貍】 5742
ㄌㄧˊ líi
Nyctereutus procynoides, a foxlike animal

貍貓 (ㄌㄧˊ ㄇㄠ)
Paradoxurus sp., a catlike animal

貍奴 (ㄌㄧˊ ㄋㄨˊ)
a cat

貍鼪 (ㄌㄧˊ ㄕㄥ)
two animals which prey on rats

九畫

【貓】 5743
(貓) ㄇㄠ mhau māo
the cat

貓頭鷹 (ㄇㄠ ㄊㄡˊ ㄧㄥ)
the owl

貓哭老鼠—假慈悲 (ㄇㄠ ㄎㄨ ㄌㄠˇ ㄕㄨˇ ㄐㄧㄚˇ ㄘˊ ㄅㄟ)
to shed crocodile tears (as a cat crying over the death of a rat)

貓叫 (ㄇㄠ ㄐㄧㄠˋ)
the meowing of a cat

貓熊 (ㄇㄠ ㄒㄩㄥˊ)
(animal) a panda

貓鼠同眠 (ㄇㄠ ㄕㄨˇ ㄊㄨㄥˊ ㄇㄧㄢˊ)
(literally) The cat and the rat sleep together.—Corrupt officials collude with rascals exploiting common people.

貓眼石 (ㄇㄠ ㄧㄢˇ ㄕˊ)or 貓兒眼 (ㄇㄠ ㄦˊ ㄧㄢˇ)
(mineral) cat's-eye; cymo-phane

十畫

【貔】 5744
ㄆㄧˊ pyi pí
a fierce animal of the pan-ther family

貔虎 (ㄆㄧˊ ㄏㄨˇ)
fierce and courageous sol-diers

貔貅 (ㄆㄧˊ ㄒㄧㄡ)
①fierce and courageous sol-diers ②a kind of fierce wild beast

〔豸部〕

十一畫

【貘】 5745
ㄇㄛˋ moh mò
1. the panther; the leopard
2. the tapir

十八畫

【貛】 (獾) ㄏㄨㄢ huan uān 5746
1. a he-wolf
2. a wild boar
3. a badger

貝 部
ㄅㄟˋ bey bèi

【貝】 5747
ㄅㄟˋ bey bèi
1. shells; cowries (used in ancient China as currency)
2. precious; treasure; valuable
3. (physics) bel
4. a Chinese family name

貝幣(ㄅㄟˋ ㄅㄧˋ)
shells used as money in ancient times

貝編(ㄅㄟˋ ㄅㄧㄢ)
Buddhist sutras

貝母(ㄅㄟˋ ㄇㄨˇ)
(botany) fritillary, used as herbal medicine

貝多芬(ㄅㄟˋ ㄉㄨㄛ ㄈㄣ)
Ludwig van Beethoven (1770-1827), German composer

貝南(ㄅㄟˋ ㄋㄢˊ)
Benin

貝勒(ㄅㄟˋ ㄌㄜˋ)
①a rank of the Manchu nobility below that of the Prince (親王) ②shell decorations on a bridle

貝類(ㄅㄟˋ ㄌㄟˋ)
shellfish; molluscs

貝殼(ㄅㄟˋ ㄎㄜˊ)
seashells; shells; 海岸有很多貝殼。The seashore was covered with shells.

貝殼學(ㄅㄟˋ ㄎㄜˊ ㄒㄩㄝˊ)
conchology

貝殼學家(ㄅㄟˋ ㄎㄜˊ ㄒㄩㄝˊ ㄐㄧㄚ)
a conchologist

貝魯特(ㄅㄟˋ ㄌㄨˊ ㄊㄜˋ)
Beirut, the capital of Lebanon

貝貨(ㄅㄟˋ ㄏㄨㄛˋ)
cowries used as currency in ancient times

貝加爾湖(ㄅㄟˋ ㄐㄧㄚ ㄦˇ ㄏㄨˊ)
the Baikal Lake in southern Siberia

貝子(ㄅㄟˋ ˙ㄗ)
a rank of the Manchu nobility below that of 貝勒

貝葉(ㄅㄟˋ ㄧㄝˋ)
①palm leaves from the *Borassus flabelliformis* ② Buddhist sutras written on such leaves

二畫

【負】 5748
ㄈㄨˋ fuh fù
1. defeated; beaten; to lose; to fail; defeat
2. to bear; to sustain; to carry on the back; to shoulder
3. to take refuge in
4. to be proud and complacent
5. to owe
6. negative, minus
7. to turn one's back on; ungrateful
8. to let (someone) down; to disappoint
9. a Chinese family name

負負(ㄈㄨˋ ㄈㄨˋ)
ashamed or embarrassed

負德(ㄈㄨˋ ㄉㄜˊ)
against virtuous practice or morality

負戴(ㄈㄨˋ ㄉㄞˋ)
to bear and sustain (loads, etc.); the work of a laborer

負擔(ㄈㄨˋ ㄉㄢ)
①an obligation; a burden; a load; an encumbrance ②to support (a family, etc.) or pay the expenses ③liability

負電(ㄈㄨˋ ㄉㄧㄢˋ)
negative electricity

負笈前驅(ㄈㄨˋ ㄐㄧˊ ㄑㄧㄢˊ ㄑㄩ)
①to join the army and fight at the front ②to show respect to a ranking official

負累(ㄈㄨˋ ㄌㄟˇ)
①to be defamed without

grounds ②to be dragged into trouble

負固(ㄈㄨˋ ㄍㄨˋ)
to hold a strategic position

負荷(ㄈㄨˋ ㄏㄜˋ)
①to bear or sustain ②the load (of electricity, etc.)

負號(ㄈㄨˋ ㄏㄠˋ)
the negative sign (-)

負笈從師(ㄈㄨˋ ㄐㄧˊ ㄘㄨㄥˊ ㄕ)
to leave one's home in search of learned masters

負疚(ㄈㄨˋ ㄐㄧㄡˋ)
to regret; uneasy in heart; to have a guilty conscience

負荊(ㄈㄨˋ ㄐㄧㄥ)or 負荊請罪(ㄈㄨˋ ㄐㄧㄥ ㄑㄧㄥˇ ㄗㄨㄟˋ)
to proffer a birch and ask for a whipping—to offer a modest apology; to apologize

負氣(ㄈㄨˋ ㄑㄧˋ)
sullen; morose; ill-humored; stubbornly; unyielding; to do something in a fit of pique: 她負氣而去。She went off in a fit of pique.

負險(ㄈㄨˋ ㄒㄧㄢˇ)
to hold a key position

負心(ㄈㄨˋ ㄒㄧㄣ)
ungrateful; heartless

負薪救火(ㄈㄨˋ ㄒㄧㄣ ㄐㄧㄡˋ ㄏㄨㄛˇ)
(literally) to carry firewood to put out a fire—to make things worse

負債(ㄈㄨˋ ㄓㄞˋ)
to be in debt; to owe; to incur debts; 他已負債累累。He is heavily in debt.

負重致遠(ㄈㄨˋ ㄓㄨㄥˋ ㄓˋ ㄩㄢˇ)
to bear a heavy burden and cover a long distance—to put in hard work and achieve one's goal

負重忍辱(ㄈㄨˋ ㄓㄨㄥˋ ㄖㄣˇ ㄖㄨˋ)
to bear a heavy burden and suffer disgrace with patience

負手(ㄈㄨˋ ㄕㄡˇ)
to cross one's hands behind the back

負傷(ㄈㄨˋ ㄕㄤ)
to be wounded; to sustain injuries

負數(ㄈㄨˋ ㄕㄨˋ)
a negative number

負責(ㄈㄨˋ ㄗㄜˊ)or 負責任(ㄈㄨˋ ㄗㄜˊ ㄖㄣˋ)

to be responsible; to bear the responsibility; to be in charge of; conscientious: 他工作很負責。He is very conscientious in his work.

負罪(ㄈㄨˋ ㄗㄨㄟˋ)
to bear the blame

負恩(ㄈㄨˋ ㄣ)
ungrateful for favor received

負義忘恩(ㄈㄨˋ ㄧˋ ㄨㄤˋ ㄣ)
ungrateful; ingrate

負嵎頑抗(ㄈㄨˋ ㄩˊ ㄨㄢˊ ㄎㄤˋ)
to put up a stubborn resistance at a strategic position; to fight obstinately with one's back to the wall; to make a desperate struggle

負約(ㄈㄨˋ ㄩㄝ)
to break a contract, agreement, promise, etc.; to go back on one's word (or promises)

【貞】 5749
ㄓㄣ jen zhēn
(又讀 ㄓㄥ jeng zhēng)

1. chastity of a woman
2. pure; virtuous
3. to be incorruptible; to be correctly firm
4. devotion; dedication
5. to divine; to inquire by divination

貞白(ㄓㄣ ㄅㄞˊ)
chastity; integrity

貞卜文字(ㄓㄣ ㄅㄨˇ ㄨㄣˊ ㄗˋ)
(in ancient China) oracle-bone characters

貞婦(ㄓㄣ ㄈㄨˋ)
a chaste woman: 她是位年輕貞婦。She was a chaste young woman.

貞德(ㄓㄣ ㄉㄜˊ)
Saint Joan of Arc (French, Jeanne d'Arc, 1412-1431), French heroine, also called the Maid of Orleans

貞女(ㄓㄣ ㄋㄩˇ)
a chaste girl; a virgin

貞女不更二夫(ㄓㄣ ㄋㄩˇ ㄅㄨˋ ㄍㄥ ㄦˋ ㄈㄨ)or貞女不事二夫(ㄓㄣ ㄋㄩˇ ㄅㄨˋ ㄕˋ ㄦˋ ㄈㄨ)
A chaste woman never remarries.

貞烈(ㄓㄣ ㄌㄧㄝˋ)

honesty, straightforwardness, courage and virtue—which enable a person to look death in the eye without fear

貞固(ㄓㄣ ㄍㄨˋ)
to stick to righteousness and virtue

貞觀之治(ㄓㄣ ㄍㄨㄢˋ ㄓ ㄓˋ)
the enlightened administration of Emperor Tai Tsung of the Tang Dynasty, whose reign lasted from 627 to 649

貞潔(ㄓㄣ ㄐㄧㄝˊ)
chaste and pure; virtuous

貞節(ㄓㄣ ㄐㄧㄝˊ)
①tenacity to hold on to one's virtuous way or integrity ②(said of a woman) chastity; purity; virtue

貞節牌坊(ㄓㄣ ㄐㄧㄝˊ ㄆㄞˊ ㄈㄤ)
a stone arch erected by the government of former times in honor of a chaste woman widowed at a young age

貞士(ㄓㄣ ㄕˋ)
a man of virtue or integrity

貞淑(ㄓㄣ ㄕㄨˊ)
(said of women) pure and chaste

貞人(ㄓㄣ ㄖㄣˊ)
a person of high moral standing and integrity

貞操(ㄓㄣ ㄘㄠ)
①purity and chastity in one's conduct ②a woman's chastity or virginity

三畫

【貢】 5750
ㄍㄨㄥˋ gonq gòng

1. the tribute from a vassal state; to offer tribute
2. to recommend (a person to an office, etc.); to submit
3. (in ancient China) land tax
4. to contribute; to offer
5. a Chinese family name

貢品(ㄍㄨㄥˋ ㄆㄧㄣˇ)
items offered as tribute

貢奉(ㄍㄨㄥˋ ㄈㄥˋ)
to offer as tribute to the court

貢獻(ㄍㄨㄥˋ ㄒㄧㄢˋ)
to offer or contribute (oneself to the national cause,

etc.); contribution

貢燭(ㄍㄨㄥˋ ㄓㄨˊ)
candles of the best quality

貢生(ㄍㄨㄥˋ ㄕㄥ)
(formerly) scholars recommended by local governments on the basis of their scholastic accomplishments and virtue

【財】 5751
ㄘㄞˊ tsair cái
wealth; riches; money

財帛(ㄘㄞˊ ㄅㄛˊ)
wealth; riches; valuables

財寶(ㄘㄞˊ ㄅㄠˇ)
money and jewels; valuables

財不露眼(ㄘㄞˊ ㄅㄨˋ ㄌㄡˋ ㄧㄢˇ)or財不露白(ㄘㄞˊ ㄅㄨˋ ㄌㄡˋ ㄅㄞˊ)
Let not your wealth be exposed.

財迷(ㄘㄞˊ ㄇㄧˊ)
a person who craves for money; a moneygrubber; a miser

財迷心竅(ㄘㄞˊ ㄇㄧˊ ㄒㄧㄣ ㄑㄧㄠˋ)
to have one's head turned by greed

財命(ㄘㄞˊ ㄇㄧㄥˋ)
luck in making money

財閥(ㄘㄞˊ ㄈㄚˊ)
a financial tycoon; a plutocrat; a financier

財富(ㄘㄞˊ ㄈㄨˋ)
wealth or fortune; riches: 自然財富不同於精神財富。Natural wealth is different from spiritual wealth.

財大氣粗(ㄘㄞˊ ㄉㄚˋ ㄑㄧˋ ㄘㄨ)
(literally) He who has wealth speaks louder than others.—to presume on one's wealth and exercise undue power or authority

財團(ㄘㄞˊ ㄊㄨㄢˊ)
a consortium; a financial syndicate

財團法人(ㄘㄞˊ ㄊㄨㄢˊ ㄈㄚˇ ㄖㄣˊ)
a juridical person; a corporate body

財力(ㄘㄞˊ ㄌㄧˋ)
financial resources: 他的財力不缺。His financial resources are never exhausted.

財可通神(ㄘㄞˊ ㄎㄜˇ ㄊㄨㄥ ㄕㄣˊ)
(literally) With money one can make contacts even with gods.—(figuratively)

〔貝部〕

Money is all-powerful

財貨(ちゅう ㄏㄨㄜˋ)
money, currency and finances

財賄(ちゅう ㄏㄨㄟˋ)
(in ancient China) money and grains

財盡(ちゅう ㄐㄧㄣˋ)
money exhausted; broke

財經(ちゅう ㄐㄧㄥ)
finance and economy

財氣(ちゅう ㄑㄧˋ)
luck in making big money

財權(ちゅう ㄑㄩㄢˊ)
(law) ownership of movable property

財政(ちゅう ㄓㄥˋ)
finance; financial administration

財政部(ちゅう ㄓㄥˋ ㄅㄨˋ)
Ministry of Finance

財政部長(ちゅう ㄓㄥˋ ㄅㄨˋ ㄓㄤˇ)
the Minister of Finance

財政廳(ちゅう ㄓㄥˋ ㄊㄧㄥ)
Provincial Department of Finance

財政廳長(ちゅう ㄓㄥˋ ㄊㄧㄥ ㄓㄤˇ)
the director of the Department of Finance

財政年度(ちゅう ㄓㄥˋ ㄋㄧㄢˊ ㄉㄨˋ)
the fiscal year

財政關稅(ちゅう ㄓㄥˋ ㄍㄨㄢ ㄕㄨㄟˋ)
financial customs

財政困難(ちゅう ㄓㄥˋ ㄎㄨㄣˋ ㄋㄢˊ)
financial straits or difficulties: 該項計畫有財政上的困難。The project is in financial difficulties.

財政局(ちゅう ㄓㄥˋ ㄐㄩˊ)
Bureau of Finance

財政局長(ちゅう ㄓㄥˋ ㄐㄩˊ ㄓㄤˇ)
the director of the Bureau of Finance

財政學(ちゅう ㄓㄥˋ ㄒㄩㄝˊ)
the science of finance

財主(ちゅう ㄓㄨˇ)
a wealthy man; a capitalist; a millionaire; a moneybags

財產(ちゅう ㄔㄢˇ)
property

財產目錄(ちゅう ㄔㄢˇ ㄇㄨˋ ㄌㄨˋ)
an inventory of property

財產權(ちゅう ㄔㄢˇ ㄑㄩㄢˊ)
ownership of property; property right

財產稅(ちゅう ㄔㄢˇ ㄕㄨㄟˋ)
property tax

財神(ちゅう ㄕㄣˊ)or**財神爺**(ちゅう ㄕㄣˊ 1ㄝˊ)
① the God of Wealth; Mammon ② a very wealthy man

財色(ちゅう ㄙㄜˋ)
money and women: 很多人為財色而活。Many people live for money and women.

財物(ちゅう ㄨˋ)
property; belongings

財務(ちゅう ㄨˋ)
finance; financial affairs

財務報告(ちゅう ㄨˋ ㄅㄠˋ ㄍㄠˋ)
a financial report

財務地位(ちゅう ㄨˋ ㄉㄧˋ ㄨㄟˋ)
financial position

財務管理(ちゅう ㄨˋ ㄍㄨㄢˇ ㄌㄧˇ)
financial management

財運兒(ちゅう ㄩㄣˊ ㄦ)
opportunity of making big money

財源(ちゅう ㄩㄢˊ)
a source of finances; financial resources

財源滾滾(ちゅう ㄩㄢˊ ㄍㄨㄣˇ ㄍㄨㄣˇ)
profits pouring in from all sides

財運(ちゅう ㄩㄣˋ)
luck in making money

財用(ちゅう ㄩㄥˋ)
finances

【扡】 5752
1. 1. yih yí
1. to pile one upon another; to superimpose
2. to extend; to prolong

【扡】 5752
2. 1. yǐ yí
to move; to remove; to turn

扡封
(Ching Dynasty) a request to the throne to transfer a title one was conferred upon to the most senior member of one's family

扡贈(1 ㄗㄥˋ)
a request to the throne to transfer a title one was conferred upon to a senior member of one's family who is already dead

四畫

【貧】 5753
ㄆ1ㄣˊ pyn pín

1. poverty; poor; destitute; impoverished
2. deficiency; deficient; lack
3. (now rarely) stingy; tightfisted
4. long, repetitious or superfluous
5. garrulous

貧病(ㄆ1ㄣˊ ㄅ1ㄥˋ)
impoverished and in poor health

貧病交迫(ㄆ1ㄣˊ ㄅ1ㄥˋ ㄐ1ㄠ ㄆㄛˋ)or**貧病交加**(ㄆ1ㄣˊ ㄅ1ㄥˋ ㄐ1ㄠ ㄐ1ㄚ)
to be beset by poverty and illness

貧婆(ㄆ1ㄣˊ ㄆㄛˊ)
① a poor woman ② a nagging, old, female busybody

貧民(ㄆ1ㄣˊ ㄇ1ㄣˊ)
destitute or impoverished people; poor people; a pauper

貧民窟(ㄆ1ㄣˊ ㄇ1ㄣˊ ㄎㄨ)
a slum area; a shantytown: 他在不健全的貧民窟長大。He was brought up in an unwholesome slum.

貧民區(ㄆ1ㄣˊ ㄇ1ㄣˊ ㄑㄩ)
a slum area; a slum district

貧民學校(ㄆ1ㄣˊ ㄇ1ㄣˊ ㄒㄩㄝˊ ㄒ1ㄠˋ)
a school run by the government, charity organization, etc. for the poor with tuition and all other expenses exempted

貧民住宅(ㄆ1ㄣˊ ㄇ1ㄣˊ ㄓㄨˋ ㄓㄞˊ)
housing for poor family

貧民施醫(ㄆ1ㄣˊ ㄇ1ㄣˊ ㄕ 1)
medical care for the poor

貧乏(ㄆ1ㄣˊ ㄈㄚˊ)
wanting; destitute; insufficient; deficient

貧富不均(ㄆ1ㄣˊ ㄈㄨˋ ㄅㄨˋ ㄐㄩㄣ)
the disparity between the rich and the poor; unequal distribution of wealth

貧富懸殊(ㄆ1ㄣˊ ㄈㄨˋ ㄒㄩㄢˊ ㄕㄨ)
extreme disparity between the rich and the poor

貧道(ㄆ1ㄣˊ ㄉㄠˋ)
a humble self-reference of a Taoist priest

貧農(ㄆ1ㄣˊ ㄋㄨㄥˊ)
poor peasants

貧骨頭(ㄆ1ㄣˊ ㄍㄨˇ ㄊㄡˊ)
① a nagging and talkative person ② a stingy or tightfisted person; a miser

貧苦(ㄆㄧㄣ ㄎㄨˇ)
poverty and hardship; poor; destitute; poverty-stricken

貧困(ㄆㄧㄣ ㄎㄨㄣˋ)
impoverished; poor; in straitened circumstances

貧寒(ㄆㄧㄣ ㄏㄢˊ)
poor; destitute: 他出身貧寒之家。He was born in a poor family.

貧戶(ㄆㄧㄣ ㄏㄨˋ)
a destitute household or family

貧瘠(ㄆㄧㄣ ㄐㄧˊ)
(said of land)poor and barren; wanting in natural resources

貧賤(ㄆㄧㄣ ㄐㄧㄢˋ)
in humble and destitute circumstances

貧賤不能移(ㄆㄧㄣ ㄐㄧㄢˋ ㄅㄨˋ ㄋㄥˊ ㄧˊ)
(said of one's determination, integrity, etc.) not to be shaken or modified by one's poverty or destitution

貧賤夫妻百事哀(ㄆㄧㄣ ㄐㄧㄢˋ ㄈㄨ ㄑㄧ ㄅㄞˇ ㄕˋ ㄞ)
To a destitute couple nothing goes well.

貧賤驕人(ㄆㄧㄣ ㄐㄧㄢˋ ㄐㄧㄠ ㄖㄣˊ)
Poor as one is, one does not flatter the rich.

貧賤之交(ㄆㄧㄣ ㄐㄧㄢˋ ㄓ ㄐㄧㄠ)
a friend of one's humble days

貧窮(ㄆㄧㄣ ㄑㄩㄥˊ)
poverty; impoverishment; destitution; penury; poor; needy; impoverished

貧血(ㄆㄧㄣ ㄒㄩㄝˋ)
anaemia; anaemic

貧血症(ㄆㄧㄣ ㄒㄩㄝˋ ㄓㄥˋ)
anaemia

貧相(ㄆㄧㄣ ㄒㄧㄤˋ)
manners of the poor

貧齒類動物(ㄆㄧㄣ ㄔˇ ㄌㄟˋ ㄉㄨㄥˋ ㄨˋ)
an edentate

貧士(ㄆㄧㄣ ㄕˋ)
a scholar with very limited means

貧嘴(ㄆㄧㄣ ㄗㄨㄟˇ)
talkative; garrulous

貧僧(ㄆㄧㄣ ㄙㄥ)
a term of self-address of a Buddhist monk

貧無所有(ㄆㄧㄣ ㄨˊ ㄙㄨㄛˇ ㄧㄡˇ)
abject poverty; to be as poor as a church mouse: 我年輕時貧無所有。I was as poor as a church mouse when I was young.

【貨】 5754 ㄏㄨㄛˋ huoh huò

1. commodities; goods; products; freight; cargo: 他賣賣皮貨。He buys and sells leather goods.
2. money; currency; property
3. to bribe; bribery
4. to sell
5. used as a term of reviling with an abusive suffix: 我看他不是好貨。I think he is not a decent person.

貨幣(ㄏㄨㄛˋ ㄅㄧˋ)
currency; money

貨布(ㄏㄨㄛˋ ㄅㄨˋ)
the name of an ancient currency introduced by Wang Mang (王莽)

貨品(ㄏㄨㄛˋ ㄆㄧㄣˇ)
commodities; goods

貨到付款(ㄏㄨㄛˋ ㄉㄠˋ ㄈㄨˋ ㄎㄨㄢˇ)
cash on delivery (C.O.D.)

貨單(ㄏㄨㄛˋ ㄉㄢ)
a manifest; a list of goods; an invoice

貨輪(ㄏㄨㄛˋ ㄌㄨㄣˊ)
cargo tanker; cargo vessel

貨櫃(ㄏㄨㄛˋ ㄍㄨㄟˋ)
a container 亦作「貨箱」

貨櫃運輸(ㄏㄨㄛˋ ㄍㄨㄟˋ ㄩㄣˋ ㄕㄨ)
container shipment; container transport

貨款(ㄏㄨㄛˋ ㄎㄨㄢˇ)
money for buying or selling goods; payment for goods

貨價(ㄏㄨㄛˋ ㄐㄧㄚˋ)
the price of a commodity or goods

貨泉(ㄏㄨㄛˋ ㄑㄩㄢˊ)
the name of a currency introduced by Wang Mang (王莽)

貨殖(ㄏㄨㄛˋ ㄓˊ)
(in ancient China) to hoard commodities to make profit; to accumulate money in order to generate interest; to increase in wealth

貨真價實(ㄏㄨㄛˋ ㄓㄣ ㄐㄧㄚˋ ㄕˊ)
①(a commercial slogan) goods of high quality sold at reasonable prices ②through and through; out-and-out

貨主(ㄏㄨㄛˋ ㄓㄨˇ)
the owner of a batch of commodities or goods

貨車(ㄏㄨㄛˋ ㄔㄜ)
a freight car; a cargo truck; a lorry: 我把貨物交由貨車運上。I am sending my goods by truck.

貨暢其流(ㄏㄨㄛˋ ㄔㄤˋ ㄑㄧˊ ㄌㄧㄡˊ)
to have the goods freely distributed among the consumers

貨船(ㄏㄨㄛˋ ㄔㄨㄢˊ)
a freighter; a cargo boat; a cargo vessel

貨倉(ㄏㄨㄛˋ ㄘㄤ)
a warehouse; a storehouse

貨艙(ㄏㄨㄛˋ ㄘㄤ)
the hold of a freighter; the cargo bay (of a plane)

貨色(ㄏㄨㄛˋ ㄙㄜˋ)
kinds, material or quality of goods; stock in trade; stuff: 那家商店貨色繁多。The store was rich in its variety of goods.

貨腰(ㄏㄨㄛˋ ㄧㄠ)
to work as a taxi dancer

貨腰女郎(ㄏㄨㄛˋ ㄧㄠ ㄋㄩˇ ㄌㄤˊ)
a taxi dancer

貨樣(ㄏㄨㄛˋ ㄧㄤˋ)
samples of goods

貨物(ㄏㄨㄛˋ ㄨˋ)
commodities; goods; cargo; merchandise

貨源(ㄏㄨㄛˋ ㄩㄢˊ)
the source of goods; the supply of goods

貨運(ㄏㄨㄛˋ ㄩㄣˋ)
shipment of commodities; transportation service

【販】 5755 ㄈㄢˋ fann fàn

1. to buy and sell; to deal in; to trade in
2. to carry about for sale; to peddle
3. a seller of goods; a peddler; a monger

販賣(ㄈㄢˋ ㄇㄞˋ)
to deal in; to sell; to peddle

販賣部(ㄈㄢˋ ㄇㄞˋ ㄅㄨˋ)
a commissary (in schools, barracks, etc.) ; a store

販賣人口(ㄈㄢˋ ㄇㄞˋ ㄖㄣˊ ㄎㄡˇ)

to deal in human beings;
white slavery

販夫(ㄈㄢˋ ㄈㄨ)
a peddler; a hawker

〔貝部〕

販夫走卒(ㄈㄢˋ ㄈㄨ ㄗㄡˇ ㄗㄨˊ)
people of the lower class

販婦(ㄈㄢˋ ㄈㄨˋ)
a female peddler or hawker

販毒(ㄈㄢˋ ㄉㄨˊ)
to deal in narcotics

販土(ㄈㄢˋ ㄊㄨˇ)
to sell opium

販子(ㄈㄢˋ ˙ㄗ)
a seller; a peddler; a dealer;
他是個毛皮販子。He is a
dealer in furs.

販運(ㄈㄢˋ ㄩㄣˋ)
to ship goods from one
place to another for sale

【貪】 5756
ㄊㄢ tan tān
1. to desire for more than
one's rightful share; to
covet; greedy: 貪多則無得。
All covet all lose.
2. to hope or wish for; to
probe or search for

貪杯(ㄊㄢ ㄅㄟ)
to indulge in drinking

貪便宜(ㄊㄢ ㄅㄧㄢˊ ˙ㄧ)
to have a strong desire for
(usually very small) gains
(often at the expense of
quality or at the price of big
losses); to gain petty advantages

貪夫殉財(ㄊㄢ ㄈㄨ ㄒㄩㄣˋ ㄘㄞˊ)
The greedy die in search of
wealth.

貪得無饜(ㄊㄢ ㄉㄜˊ ㄨˊ ㄧㄢˋ)
never satisfied with what
one has got; to have an
unlimited desire for more; insatiable covetousness

貪多嚼不爛(ㄊㄢ ㄉㄨㄛ ㄐㄧㄠˊ ㄅㄨˋ
ㄌㄢˋ)
(literally)to bite more than
one can chew—(figurative-
ly) to want more than one
can effectively use

貪多務得(ㄊㄢ ㄉㄨㄛ ㄨˋ ㄉㄜˊ)
insatiable covetousness

貪天之功(ㄊㄢ ㄊㄧㄢ ㄓ ㄍㄨㄥ)
to take credit for what is
accomplished naturally

貪圖(ㄊㄢ ㄊㄨˊ)
to hope, wish, desire or long

for; to hanker after; to
covet: 他常常貪圖小利。He
often covets small advan-
tages.

貪念(ㄊㄢ ㄋㄧㄢˋ)
covetous thoughts

貪婪(ㄊㄢ ㄌㄢˊ)
covetousness; greed; cupidity; avarice: 他已經貪婪成性。
His avarice has become his
second nature.

貪狼(ㄊㄢ ㄌㄤˊ)
(literally) as greedy as a
wolf—a very greedy person

貪戀(ㄊㄢ ㄌㄧㄢˋ)
to desire or long for
(women); to hanker after;
unwilling to part with something one loves

貪吝(ㄊㄢ ㄌㄧㄣˋ)
avaricious and miserly

貪官汙吏(ㄊㄢ ㄍㄨㄢ ㄨ ㄌㄧˋ)or**貪官
墨吏**(ㄊㄢ ㄍㄨㄢ ㄇㄛˋ ㄌㄧˋ)or**貪墨
官吏**(ㄊㄢ ㄇㄛˋ ㄍㄨㄢ ㄌㄧˋ)
corrupt officials; venal officials

貪花(ㄊㄢ ㄏㄨㄚ)
to indulge in carnal passion

貪求(ㄊㄢ ㄑㄧㄡˊ)
to desire or long for(usually
more than one's rightful
share)

貪小失大(ㄊㄢ ㄒㄧㄠˇ ㄕ ㄉㄚˋ)
to be tempted by small
gains and suffer a big loss;
to win battles but lose the
war

貪心(ㄊㄢ ㄒㄧㄣ)
greed; cupidity; avarice;
greedy; avaricious; in-
satiable; voracious

貪心不足(ㄊㄢ ㄒㄧㄣ ㄅㄨˋ ㄗㄨˊ)
insatiable greed or covetousness: 他這個人貪心不足。He is
insatiably greedy.

貪吃(ㄊㄢ ㄔ)
gluttonous; to eat piggishly

貪生怕死(ㄊㄢ ㄕㄥ ㄆㄚˋ ㄙˇ)
cowardly; cowardice; to care
for nothing but saving one's
skin; to be mortally afraid
of death

貪睡(ㄊㄢ ㄕㄨㄟˋ)
to be fond of sleep; lazy

貪贓(ㄊㄢ ㄗㄤ)
to take bribes; to practice
graft

貪贓枉法(ㄊㄢ ㄗㄤ ㄨㄤˇ ㄈㄚˇ)
to twist the law in order to
obtain bribes; corrupt

貪嘴(ㄊㄢ ㄗㄨㄟˇ)
gluttonous; piggish

貪財害命(ㄊㄢ ㄘㄞˊ ㄏㄞˋ ㄇㄧㄥˋ)
to kill for money; to commit
murder for money

貪色(ㄊㄢ ㄙㄜˋ)
to have a weakness for
women

貪汙(ㄊㄢ ㄨ)
corruption; graft

貪汙瀆職(ㄊㄢ ㄨ ㄉㄨˊ ㄓˊ)
(said of officials) corrupt
and negligent of one's duties

貪玩(ㄊㄢ ㄨㄢˊ)
to be fond of playing or
fooling around

貪慾(ㄊㄢ ㄩˋ)
greed; avarice

【貫】 5757
ㄍㄨㄢˋ guann guàn
1. a thread for stringing holed
copper coins; to string on a
thread
2. a string of 1,000 holed copper coins
3. to pierce through; to pass
through; to see through;
throughout; thorough
4. to be linked together; to follow in a continuous line
5. to hit the target
6. one's native place
7. (in Japanese) a weight measure equivalent to about 7
pounds
8. a Chinese family name

貫通(ㄍㄨㄢˋ ㄊㄨㄥ)
①to have a thorough understanding; to be well versed
in ②to link up; to thread
together

貫錢(ㄍㄨㄢˋ ㄑㄧㄢˊ)
to string holed copper coins

貫珠(ㄍㄨㄢˋ ㄓㄨ)
a string of pearls

貫注(ㄍㄨㄢˋ ㄓㄨˋ)
①to concentrate one's attention on; to be absorbed in:
他全神貫注於他的學業。He
was absorbed in his studies.
②to be connected in mean-
ing or feeling

貫徹(ㄍㄨㄢˋ ㄔㄜˋ)
thoroughly; from beginning

to end; to adhere to; to carry out

徹始終(ㄔㄜˋ ㄕˇ ㄓㄨㄥ)
to remain consistent from the start to the very end

貫穿(ㄍㄨㄢˋ ㄔㄨㄢ)
①to penetrate or pierce through ②to run through ③ to understand thoroughly

貫串(ㄍㄨㄢˋ ㄔㄨㄢˋ)
①to string or thread together; to connect ②to run through; to permeate

貫耳(ㄍㄨㄢˋ ㄦˇ)
①to hear; to have heard: 掌聲如雷貫耳 The applause was like a thunderclap piercing through the ear. ② (in ancient China) a punishment in the military camp —to pierce the ear with an arrow

貫盈(ㄍㄨㄢˋ ㄧㄥ)
a long list of criminal acts; (said of iniquity) to be full

【責】5758
ㄗㄜˊ tzer zé

1. one's duty, responsibility, obligation, etc.
2. to demand; to be strict with
3. to punish; punishment
4. to upbraid; to censure; to reprimand; to blame

責備(ㄗㄜˊ ㄅㄟˋ)
to upbraid; to reprimand; to reproach

責罵(ㄗㄜˊ ㄇㄚˋ)
to upbraid; to blame; to scold. 別老是責罵人。Don't scold so much.

責罰(ㄗㄜˊ ㄈㄚˊ)
to punish; a punishment; a penalty

責分(ㄗㄜˊ ㄈㄣ)
one's duty; one's share of responsibility

責打(ㄗㄜˊ ㄉㄚˇ)
to punish by beating

責難(ㄗㄜˊ ㄋㄢˊ)
①(ㄗㄜˊ ㄋㄢˊ) to urge someone to a difficult task; to hold high expectations for another person
②(ㄗㄜˊ ㄋㄢˋ) to demand an explanation; to upbraid; to censure

責怪(ㄗㄜˊ ㄍㄨㄞˋ)
to blame

責己(ㄗㄜˊ ㄐㄧˇ)
to blame oneself; to hold oneself responsible

責全(ㄗㄜˊ ㄑㄩㄢˊ)
to demand perfection in others; to expect others to do a flawless job

責成(ㄗㄜˊ ㄔㄥˊ)
to hold one responsible for accomplishing a task; to charge one with a duty

責善(ㄗㄜˊ ㄕㄢˋ)
to exhort or admonish someone to practice good deeds; to urge someone to virtuous deeds

責人(ㄗㄜˊ ㄖㄣˊ)
to blame others

責任(ㄗㄜˊ ㄖㄣˋ)
①duty; responsibility; an obligation ②responsibility for a fault; blame

責任保險(ㄗㄜˊ ㄖㄣˋ ㄅㄠˇ ㄒㄧㄢˇ)
liability insurance

責任內閣(ㄗㄜˊ ㄖㄣˋ ㄋㄟˋ ㄍㄜˊ)
a cabinet which is responsible to the parliament for its administrative measures

責任感(ㄗㄜˊ ㄖㄣˋ ㄍㄢˇ)or責任心(ㄗㄜˊ ㄖㄣˋ ㄒㄧㄣ)
a sense of responsibility

責讓(ㄗㄜˊ ㄖㄤˋ)
to upbraid

責無旁貸(ㄗㄜˊ ㄨˊ ㄆㄤˊ ㄉㄞˋ)
duty-bound 或 There is no passing the buck. 或 There's no shirking the responsibility.

責問(ㄗㄜˊ ㄨㄣˋ)
to blame and demand an explanation; to call (or bring) somebody to account

責望(ㄗㄜˊ ㄨㄤˋ)
to blame and complain when someone fails to accomplish a difficult task

五畫

【貯】5759
ㄓㄨˋ juu zhù

to store up; to hoard; to save up; to deposit

貯備(ㄓㄨˋ ㄅㄟˋ)
to store up or hoard for future needs

貯備金(ㄓㄨˋ ㄅㄟˋ ㄐㄧㄣ)
reserve funds

貯積(ㄓㄨˋ ㄐㄧ)
to store up; to accumulate

貯蓄(ㄓㄨˋ ㄒㄩˋ)
to store up; to hoard

貯水(ㄓㄨˋ ㄕㄨㄟˇ)
to store water

貯水池(ㄓㄨˋ ㄕㄨㄟˇ ㄔˊ)
a pond for storing water; a reservoir

貯水組織(ㄓㄨˋ ㄕㄨㄟˇ ㄗㄨˇ ㄓ)
(botany) aqueous tissue

貯藏(ㄓㄨˋ ㄘㄤˊ)
①to store up; to hoard ② (mineral) deposits

貯藏根(ㄓㄨˋ ㄘㄤˊ ㄍㄣ)
storage roots

貯藏室(ㄓㄨˋ ㄘㄤˊ ㄕˋ)
a storage room

貯存(ㄓㄨˋ ㄘㄨㄣˊ)
to store up; to stockpile; to deposit

【貰】5760
ㄕˋ shyh shì

1. to lend or loan; to lease
2. pardon; to pardon; to forgive
3. to sell (or buy) on credit

貰酒(ㄕˋ ㄐㄧㄡˇ)
to buy wine on credit

貰赦(ㄕˋ ㄕㄜˋ)
to pardon a criminal offense

【貲】5761
ㄗ tzy zī

1. property; wealth; riches; money
2. to count; to measure; to estimate
3. a fine

貲郎(ㄗ ㄌㄤˊ)
one who purchases a public post

貲財(ㄗ ㄘㄞˊ)
wealth; money; valuables

【貳】5762
ㄦˋ ell èr

1. (in ancient China) a deputy; to serve as a deputy
2. to suspect; to doubt; to distrust
3. changeable
4. an elaborate form of "two" (used in writing checks, etc. to prevent forgery)
5. to repeat
6. doubleness
7. a Chinese family name

[貝 部]

貳車《ㄦˋㄐㄩ》
a carriage for a deputy or top aide

貳心《ㄦˋㄒㄧㄣ》
a rebellious mind

貳志《ㄦˋㄓˋ》
disloyalty

貳臣《ㄦˋㄔㄣˊ》
an official who serves under two dynasties; a turncoat official

貳室《ㄦˋㄕˋ》
a second palace of the emperor

貳言《ㄦˋㄧㄢˊ》
a different view; objection

【貴】 5763
《ㄍㄨㄟˋ guey guì》
1. high-placed; high-ranking; honorable; distinguished
2. expensive; costly; high-priced
3. to esteem; to treat with respect
4. to treasure; to value highly; to prize
5. valuable; precious
6. a polite expression referring to another person—you or your
7. a Chinese family name
8. short for Kweichow Province (貴州省)

貴賓《ㄍㄨㄟˋㄅㄧㄣ》
distinguished guests; honored guests; a VIP (a very important person)

貴賓席《ㄍㄨㄟˋㄅㄧㄣㄒㄧˊ》
seats reserved for distinguished guests

貴賓室《ㄍㄨㄟˋㄅㄧㄣㄕˋ》
a VIP room; a VIP lounge

貴嬪《ㄍㄨㄟˋㄆㄧㄣˊ》
women officials in the ancient Chinese court

貴妃《ㄍㄨㄟˋㄈㄟ》
highly honored women officials or imperial concubines in ancient China

貴府《ㄍㄨㄟˋㄈㄨˇ》
(a polite expression) your home; your house: 改日再到貴府拜訪，I'll call at your house some other day.

貴婦《ㄍㄨㄟˋㄈㄨˋ》
a noblewoman; a woman of rank

貴德《ㄍㄨㄟˋㄉㄜˊ》
① a distinguished and virtuous person ② to treasure virtue ③ name of a county in Tsinghai Province (青海省)

貴幹《ㄍㄨㄟˋㄍㄢˋ》
What can I do for you? 或 May I help you?

貴庚《ㄍㄨㄟˋㄍㄥ》
(a polite expression) How old are you?

貴國《ㄍㄨㄟˋㄍㄨㄛˊ》
(a polite expression) your country

貴官《ㄍㄨㄟˋㄍㄨㄢ》
honored or distinguished officials

貴客《ㄍㄨㄟˋㄎㄜˋ》
honored or distinguished guests; the guest of honor

貴行《ㄍㄨㄟˋㄏㄤˊ》
(a polite expression) your company

貴家子《ㄍㄨㄟˋㄐㄧㄚㄗ˙》
a scion of a noble family

貴介《ㄍㄨㄟˋㄐㄧㄝˋ》
a noble

貴价《ㄍㄨㄟˋㄐㄧㄝˋ》
(a polite expression) your servant

貴賤《ㄍㄨㄟˋㄐㄧㄢˋ》
① the eminent and the humble ② the expensive and the cheap

貴金屬《ㄍㄨㄟˋㄐㄧㄣㄕㄨˇ》
precious metals; noble metals

貴戚《ㄍㄨㄟˋㄑㄧ》
relatives of the emperor

貴妾《ㄍㄨㄟˋㄑㄧㄝˋ》
① a concubine who has given birth to a son ② the senior concubine

貴顯《ㄍㄨㄟˋㄒㄧㄢˇ》
highly-placed and eminent (people, etc.)

貴幸《ㄍㄨㄟˋㄒㄧㄥˋ》
to earn the emperor's favor and a high position in court

貴姓《ㄍㄨㄟˋㄒㄧㄥˋ》
(a polite expression) May I know your distinguished name? 或 Your name, please.

貴州《ㄍㄨㄟˋㄓㄡ》
Kweichow, a province in Southwest China

貴胄《ㄍㄨㄟˋㄓㄡˋ》
offspring of the nobility

貴主《ㄍㄨㄟˋㄓㄨˇ》
a princess

貴重《ㄍㄨㄟˋㄓㄨㄥˋ》
precious; expensive; rare valuable; highly treasured

貴處《ㄍㄨㄟˋㄔㄨˋ》
(a polite expression) What's your native place? 或 Where are you from?

貴寵《ㄍㄨㄟˋㄔㄨㄥˇ》
① to be esteemed and favored ② a favorite of the emperor

貴人《ㄍㄨㄟˋㄖㄣˊ》
① a distinguished, high ranking person ② a court lady second to the queen in rank

貴人多忘事《ㄍㄨㄟˋㄖㄣˊㄉㄨㄛ ㄨㄤˋㄕˋ》
A highly-placed person is apt to be forgetful (because he has too many things drawing his attention).

貴族《ㄍㄨㄟˋㄗㄨˊ》
the nobility; the blue blood an aristocrat

貴族政治《ㄍㄨㄟˋㄗㄨˊㄓㄥˋㄓˋ》
aristocracy

貴族文學《ㄍㄨㄟˋㄗㄨˊㄨㄣˊㄒㄩㄝˊ》
aristocratic literature (as distinct from popular literature)

貴族院《ㄍㄨㄟˋㄗㄨˊㄩㄢˋ》
the House of Lords; the House of Peers; the Upper House; the Senate

貴耳賤目《ㄍㄨㄟˋㄦˇㄐㄧㄢˋㄇㄨˋ》
to trust what one hears more than what one sees

貴要《ㄍㄨㄟˋㄧㄠˋ》
powerful and influential officials

貴陽《ㄍㄨㄟˋㄧㄤˊ》
Kweiyang, capital city of Kweichow Province (貴州省)

貴恙《ㄍㄨㄟˋㄧㄤˋ》
(a polite expression) your illness

貴為天子《ㄍㄨㄟˋㄨㄟˊㄊㄧㄢㄗˇ》
as highly-placed as an emperor

【貶】 5764
ㄅㄧㄢˇ bean biǎn
1. to reduce or lower (prices, etc.); to devalue

2. to degrade; to reduce; to demote: 他被貶爲平民。He was reduced to a commoner.

3. to disparage; to condemn; to censure

4. to dismiss; to send away

貶低(ㄅㄧㄢˇㄉㄧ)
to belittle; to depreciate; to play down: 他貶低運動的重要性。He depreciated the importance of exercise.

貶官(ㄅㄧㄢˇㄍㄨㄢ)
to demote an official

貶價(ㄅㄧㄢˇㄐㄧㄚˋ)
to reduce the price

貶值(ㄅㄧㄢˇㄓˊ)
to devalue or debase (especially referring to a currency); devaluation; depreciation

貶謫(ㄅㄧㄢˇㄓㄜˊ)
to demote and exile an official; to relegate; to banish from the court

貶斥(ㄅㄧㄢˇㄔˋ)
①to demote ②to denounce

貶黜(ㄅㄧㄢˇㄔㄨˋ)
to dismiss an official

貶黜官職(ㄅㄧㄢˇㄔㄨˋㄍㄨㄢㄓˊ)
to dismiss an official from office

貶詞(ㄅㄧㄢˇㄘˊ)
criticism; unfavorable comments; derogatory remarks

貶損(ㄅㄧㄢˇㄙㄨㄣˇ)
①to criticize; to speak of something unfavorably ②to derogate

貶抑(ㄅㄧㄢˇㄧˋ)
to debase; to devalue; to belittle; to depreciate

【買】 5765
　　　　ㄇㄞˇ mae măi

1. to buy; to purchase

2. to win over (usually with a promise of favors in return)

買辦(ㄇㄞˇㄅㄢˋ)
①a person responsible for making purchases ②a compradore (in the early days of the Republic)

買不來(ㄇㄞˇ·ㄅㄨㄞㄌㄞˊ)or 買不了
(ㄇㄞˇ·ㄅㄨㄌㄧㄠˇ)
cannot be bought with money: 金錢買不來幸福。Happiness cannot be bought with money.

買不起(ㄇㄞˇ·ㄅㄨㄑㄧˇ)
cannot afford it—too expensive

買不著(ㄇㄞˇ·ㄅㄨㄓㄠˊ)or 買不到
(ㄇㄞˇ·ㄅㄨㄉㄠˋ)
cannot buy it—do not know where to buy it; sold out

買賣
①(ㄇㄞˇㄇㄞˋ) to buy and sell
②(ㄇㄞˇ·ㄇㄞ) a line of business; trade; a business transaction; a deal: 他今天做成一筆買賣。He made a deal today.

買賣人口(ㄇㄞˇㄇㄞˋㄖㄣˊㄎㄡˇ)
to deal in human beings; white slavery

買方(ㄇㄞˇㄈㄤ)
the buyer; the buying party

買得起(ㄇㄞˇ·ㄉㄜㄑㄧˇ)
able to afford it: 她買得起貂皮大衣嗎? Is she able to afford a mink?

買定(ㄇㄞˇㄉㄧㄥˋ)
to settle a purchase (usually with a deposit or down payment)

買櫝還珠(ㄇㄞˇㄉㄨˊㄏㄨㄢˊㄓㄨ)
(literally) to buy a loaded jewelry box and return its contents—to choose the wrong thing; to show lack of judgment 亦作「得匣還珠」

買斷(ㄇㄞˇㄉㄨㄢˋ)
to buy completely; to buy out

買通(ㄇㄞˇㄊㄨㄥ)
to offer bribes to facilitate one's operations; to obtain the collusion of officials with bribes; to buy off

買樂(ㄇㄞˇㄌㄜˋ)
to buy amusement; to spend money for entertainment

買鄰(ㄇㄞˇㄌㄧㄣˊ)
to select neighbors before moving to a new place

買路錢(ㄇㄞˇㄌㄨˋㄑㄧㄢˊ)
money, etc. paid to bandits for passage

買官(ㄇㄞˇㄍㄨㄢ)
to buy an official title with money

買客(ㄇㄞˇㄎㄜˋ)
a buyer; a customer

買空賣空(ㄇㄞˇㄎㄨㄥㄇㄞˋㄎㄨㄥ)
to speculate (on the stock, etc. markets); to buy long

and sell short; speculation

買好兒(ㄇㄞˇㄏㄠˇㄦ)
to please; to flatter; to try to win somebody's favor; to ingratiate oneself with; to play up to

買回(ㄇㄞˇㄏㄨㄟˊ)
(dealing in futures) to buy a contracted commodity which one has already sold; to buy back

買價(ㄇㄞˇㄐㄧㄚˋ)
the buying price; the purchase price: 買價多少? What was the purchase price?

買進(ㄇㄞˇㄐㄧㄣˋ)
to buy

買爵(ㄇㄞˇㄐㄩㄝˊ)
to buy an official or a nobility title

買下來(ㄇㄞˇ·ㄒㄧㄚㄌㄞˊ)
to settle a purchase; to contract a purchase

買笑(ㄇㄞˇㄒㄧㄠˋ)
to visit a whorehouse

買舟(ㄇㄞˇㄓㄡ)or 買棹(ㄇㄞˇㄓㄠˋ)
to hire a boat (for a trip)

買主(ㄇㄞˇㄓㄨˇ)
the buyer: 誰是這幅畫的買主? Who was the buyer of this picture?

買囑(ㄇㄞˇㄓㄨˇ)
to bribe another to perform something on one's behalf

買春(ㄇㄞˇㄔㄨㄣ)
to buy drinks

買山(ㄇㄞˇㄕㄢ)
to retire from public life

買入(ㄇㄞˇㄖㄨˋ)
to buy: 他以每個十元的價錢買入。He bought them for ten dollars each.

買醉(ㄇㄞˇㄗㄨㄟˋ)
to buy drinks

買一送一(ㄇㄞˇㄧㄙㄨㄥˋㄧ)
to buy one item with another similar item presented free (a marketing gimmick)

買宴(ㄇㄞˇㄧㄢˋ)
(said of an emperor) to throw a banquet and ask the guests to contribute money

【貸】 5766
　　　　ㄉㄞˋ day dài

1. to loan; to lend or borrow; a loan

〔貝部〕

2. the credit side in book keeping
3. to pardon; to be lenient
4. to shift (responsibility); to shirk

貸方(ㄉㄞˋ ㄈㄤ)
the credit (or creditor side) in bookkeeping or an account

貸給(ㄉㄞˋ ㄍㄟˇ)
to loan to; to lend to

貸款(ㄉㄞˋ ㄎㄨㄢˇ)
a loan (of money); credit; to provide(or grant) a loan; to extend credit to

貸借(ㄉㄞˋ ㄐㄧㄝˋ)
①credit and debit sides in bookkeeping ②to borrow

貸借對照表(ㄉㄞˋ ㄐㄧㄝˋ ㄉㄨㄟˋ ㄓㄠˋ ㄅㄧㄠˇ)
(accounting) a balance sheet; a statement of assets and liabilities

貸金(ㄉㄞˋ ㄐㄧㄣ)
money borrowed or lent

貸出(ㄉㄞˋ ㄔㄨ)
to loan to; to lend: 有些人既不貸出，亦不貸入。Some people neither borrow nor lend.

貸入(ㄉㄞˋ ㄖㄨˋ)
to borrow; to get a loan: 他向銀行貸入一筆大款。He borrowed a large sum from the bank.

貸餘(ㄉㄞˋ ㄩˊ)
credit balance

〔貺〕 5767
ㄎㄨㄤˋ kuang kuàng

1. to give or bestow; to confer
2. (a polite expression) to be favored with
3. a Chinese family name

脫貺(ㄊㄨㄛ ㄎㄨㄤˋ)
to be honored by your presence

貺我多珍(ㄎㄨㄤˋ ㄨㄛˇ ㄉㄨㄛ ㄓㄣ)
your handsome gift

〔費〕 5768
1. ㄈㄟˋ fey fèi

1. expenditure; expenses; fees; dues; charges
2. to waste; to use more than is needed; wasteful; consuming too much
3. to consume; to use; to spend; to cost; to expend
4. a Chinese family name

費邊協會(ㄈㄟˋ ㄅㄧㄢ ㄒㄧㄝˊ ㄏㄨㄟˋ)

Fabian Society

費電(ㄈㄟˋ ㄉㄧㄢˋ)
to consume a lot of electricity; power-consuming

費拉得爾費亞(ㄈㄟˋ ㄌㄚ ㄉㄜˊ ㄦˇ ㄈㄟˋ ㄧㄚˇ)or 費城(ㄈㄟˋ ㄔㄥˊ)
Philadelphia, U. S. A.

費力(ㄈㄟˋ ㄌㄧˋ)
①taking a lot of exertion; to need or use great effort ②difficult (tasks)

費力不討好(ㄈㄟˋ ㄌㄧˋ ㄅㄨˋ ㄊㄠˇ ㄏㄠˇ)
to put in a lot of work without pleasing anybody; to work hard without accomplishing any good; to waste energy and come to nothing

費工(ㄈㄟˋ ㄍㄨㄥ)or 費工夫(ㄈㄟˋ ㄍㄨㄥ·ㄈㄨ)
to take a lot of time or work; labor-consuming

費解(ㄈㄟˋ ㄐㄧㄝˇ)
difficult to understand: 他的話真在令人費解。His words are really difficult to understand.

費勁(ㄈㄟˋ ㄐㄧㄣˋ)
①labor-consuming; strenuous ②difficult (work, matters, etc.): 他毫不費勁地做完了那工作。He did the work without any difficulty.

費盡心機(ㄈㄟˋ ㄐㄧㄣˋ ㄒㄧㄣ ㄐㄧ)
to exhaust all mental efforts; to rack one's brains in scheming

費盡唇舌(ㄈㄟˋ ㄐㄧㄣˋ ㄔㄨㄣˊ ㄕㄜˊ)
to have wasted all one's breath

費錢(ㄈㄟˋ ㄑㄧㄢˊ)
to cost a great deal of money

費心(ㄈㄟˋ ㄒㄧㄣ)or 費神(ㄈㄟˋ ㄕㄣˊ)
①requiring mental exertion; to give a lot of care: 她爲她的家可費心不少。She devoted a lot of care to her family. ②Please be kind enough to.... 或 Many thanks (for doing this for me). 或 Would you mind (doing something)?

費周折(ㄈㄟˋ ㄓㄡ ㄓㄜˊ)
to take a good deal of planning, work, physical or mental exertion, etc.

費唇舌(ㄈㄟˋ ㄔㄨㄣˊ ㄕㄜˊ)

to have a lot of explaining to do; requiring a lot of talking

費時(ㄈㄟˋ ㄕˊ)
to take, need or waste a lot of time; time-consuming

費事(ㄈㄟˋ ㄕˋ)
requiring a lot of trouble to accomplish; difficult

費手腳(ㄈㄟˋ ㄕㄡˇ ㄐㄧㄠˇ)
time-consuming or troublesome; difficult

費商量(ㄈㄟˋ ㄕㄤ ·ㄌㄧㄤ)
to need a good deal of talking or negotiation

費材料(ㄈㄟˋ ㄘㄞˊ ㄌㄧㄠˋ)
to require a large quantity of material

費眼(ㄈㄟˋ ㄧㄢˇ)
to strain the eye; to waste eyesight

費用(ㄈㄟˋ ㄩㄥˋ)
expenditure; expenses; costs

〔費〕 5768
2. ㄅㄧˋ bih bì
name of a town in the Period of Spring and Autumn in today's 費縣, Shantung Province(山東省)

〔貼〕 5769
ㄊㄧㄝ tie tiē

1. to paste; to stick; to glue
2. to keep close to; to nestle closely to
3. to make up the deficiency to subsidize; subsidies; an allowance
4. proper; appropriate; comfortable
5. attached to

貼邊(ㄊㄧㄝ ㄅㄧㄢ)
a hem; edging; trimming; lacing

貼補(ㄊㄧㄝ ㄅㄨˇ)
to make up a deficiency; to supplement; to help (out) financially; to subsidize

貼膏藥(ㄊㄧㄝ ㄍㄠ ㄧㄠˋ)
to stick on a medicated plaster

貼廣告(ㄊㄧㄝ ㄍㄨㄤˇ ㄍㄠˋ)
to paste up promotion posters; to post bills

貼己(ㄊㄧㄝ ㄐㄧˇ)
intimate; close

貼金(ㄊㄧㄝ ㄐㄧㄣ)
①to boast or brag about

oneself ② to gild; to cover with gold leaf (or gold foil)

貼近(ㄊㄧㄝ ㄐㄧㄣ)
nearby; close to; to press close to; to nestle up against

貼切(ㄊㄧㄝ ㄑㄧㄝ)
proper or appropriate; apt; suitable; very much to the point

貼錢(ㄊㄧㄝ ㄑㄧㄢ)
to pay out of one's own pocket—especially when one is not supposed to, as in performing an official duty

貼現(ㄊㄧㄝ ㄒㄧㄢ)
(banking) discount

貼現率(ㄊㄧㄝ ㄒㄧㄢ ㄌㄩ)
the discount rate 亦作「貼現利率」

貼心(ㄊㄧㄝ ㄒㄧㄣ)
intimate; close: 他對大家都很客氣，但貼心好友無幾。He was courteous to all, but intimate with few.

貼心貼意(ㄊㄧㄝ ㄒㄧㄣ ㄊㄧㄝ ㄧ)
① docile; amiable ② satisfying

貼身(ㄊㄧㄝ ㄕㄣ)
① personal servants ② closely attached, as children, undergarments, concubines, etc.

貼水(ㄊㄧㄝ ㄕㄨㄟ)
payment for the difference in changing silver dollars of lower fineness for those of higher fineness; an agio

貼耳(ㄊㄧㄝ ㄦ)
to be ready to listen

【貽】 5770 ㄧ yí
1. to give to; to present to
2. to hand down; to transmit; to pass on to; to bequeath; to leave behind

貽累(ㄧ ㄌㄟ)
to involve or implicate another

貽害(ㄧ ㄏㄞ)or **貽禍**(ㄧ ㄏㄨㄛ)
to bring trouble or harm to another

貽笑大方(ㄧ ㄒㄧㄠ ㄉㄚ ㄈㄤ)
to become a laughingstock (by showing one's ignorance, etc.); to be laughed at by experts

貽羞(ㄧ ㄒㄧㄡ)
to cause shame or scandal

貽人口實(ㄧ ㄖㄣ ㄎㄡ ㄕ)
to give an occasion for scandal or gossip

貽贈(ㄧ ㄗㄥ)
① to present (a gift) ② to leave something to posterity

貽誤(ㄧ ㄨ)
to cause delay or hindrance; to bungle

貽誤戎機(ㄧ ㄨ ㄖㄨㄥ ㄐㄧ)
to hinder military operations; to cause damage to military operations; to forfeit or bungle a chance for combat

【賀】 5771 ㄏㄜˋ heh hè
1. to congratulate; to send a present in congratulation: 他的成功值得慶賀。His success deserves congratulation.
2. a Chinese family name

賀表(ㄏㄜ ㄅㄧㄠ)
a letter of congratulation and praise presented to the subjects to a king or emperor on special occasions

賀電(ㄏㄜ ㄉㄧㄢ)
a congratulatory cable or telegram

賀帖(ㄏㄜ ㄊㄧㄝ)
congratulatory cards

賀年(ㄏㄜ ㄋㄧㄢ)or **賀歲**(ㄏㄜ ㄙㄨㄟ)
New Year's greetings; to offer congratulations on New Year's Day

賀年片(ㄏㄜ ㄋㄧㄢ ㄆㄧㄢ)
New Year's greeting cards

賀蘭山(ㄏㄜ ㄌㄢ ㄕㄢ)
Holan Shan, a mountain range in Ningsia Province

賀禮(ㄏㄜ ㄌㄧ)
a congratulatory present; a present given as a token of congratulation

賀盈門(ㄏㄜ ㄧㄥ ㄇㄣ)
The house is crowded with well-wishers (on a happy occasion).

賀函(ㄏㄜ ㄏㄢ)or **賀柬**(ㄏㄜ ㄐㄧㄢ)
a letter of congratulation; a congratulatory message

賀節(ㄏㄜ ㄐㄧㄝ)
to offer congratulations on festivals

賀喜(ㄏㄜ ㄒㄧ)
to congratulate; to felicitate: 朋友們爲他的成功賀喜。Friends congratulated him on his success.

賀正(ㄏㄜ ㄓㄥ)
to offer congratulations on New Year's Day 亦作「賀年」

賀忱(ㄏㄜ ㄔㄣ)or **賀悃**(ㄏㄜ ㄎㄨㄣ)
sincerity in offering congratulations

賀詞(ㄏㄜ ㄘ)
messages of congratulation; congratulations; greetings

賀儀(ㄏㄜ ㄧ)
money, etc. sent as a token of one's congratulation

賀爾蒙(ㄏㄜ ㄦ ㄇㄥ)
hormones 亦作「荷爾蒙」

【貿】 5772 ㄇㄠˋ maw mào
1. to trade; to barter; to exchange
2. mixed
3. rashly

貿然(ㄇㄠ ㄖㄢ)
rashly; without forethought or consideration

貿名(ㄇㄠ ㄇㄧㄥ)
to purchase fame

貿然(ㄇㄠ ㄖㄢ)
rashly; blindly: 你不可貿然許諾。You should never make a rash promise. 訛作「冒然」

貿易(ㄇㄠ ㄧ)
trade; to trade: 年貿易良好。Trade was good last year.

貿易平衡(ㄇㄠ ㄧ ㄆㄧㄥ ㄏㄥ)
the balance of trade

貿易風(ㄇㄠ ㄧ ㄈㄥ)
the trade wind

貿易逆差(ㄇㄠ ㄧ ㄋㄧ ㄔㄚ)
trade deficit

貿易港(ㄇㄠ ㄧ ㄍㄤ)
a trading port; a commercial port: 香港是一貿易港。Hong Kong is a trading port.

貿易公司(ㄇㄠ ㄧ ㄍㄨㄥ ㄙ)
a trading company or firm: 這家貿易公司專門進口玩具。The trading company imports toys exclusively.

貿易區(ㄇㄠ ㄧ ㄑㄩ)
a trade area

貿易協定(ㄇㄠ ㄧ ㄒㄧㄝ ㄉㄧㄥ)
a trade agreement

貿易中心(ㄇㄠ ㄧ ㄓㄨㄥ ㄒㄧㄣ)
a trading center

〔貝 部〕

〔貝部〕

貿易商 (ㄇㄠˋ ㄧˋ ㄕㄤ)
a trader; an importer; an exporter: 他是國際貿易商。He is an international trader.

貿易順差 (ㄇㄠˋ ㄧˋ ㄕㄨㄣˋ ㄔㄚ)
a favorable balance of trade

貿易自由化 (ㄇㄠˋ ㄧˋ ㄗˋ ㄧㄡˊ ㄏㄨㄚˋ)
liberalization of trade

貿易額 (ㄇㄠˋ ㄧˋ ㄜˊ)
a volume of trade

【賁】 5773
ㄅㄧˋ bih bì
1. to adorn; ornamental
2. bright; luminous

賁臨 (ㄅㄧˋ ㄌㄧㄣˊ)
(a polite expression) your illustrious presence

賁然 (ㄅㄧˋ ㄖㄢˊ)
bright and brilliant

賁如 (ㄅㄧˋ ㄖㄨˊ)
richly adorned; brightly ornamental

【賁】 5773
ㄅㄣ ben bēn
1. to forge ahead
2. energetic; strenuous
3. a Chinese family name

【賁】 5773
ㄈㄣˊ fern fén
large; great

六畫

【賃】 5774
ㄌㄧㄣˋ linn lìn
1. to rent; to hire
2. a hireling

賃借 (ㄌㄧㄣˋ ㄐㄧㄝˋ)
to hire; to borrow

賃金 (ㄌㄧㄣˋ ㄐㄧㄣ)
①rent of a house ②wages of a hired hand

賃書 (ㄌㄧㄣˋ ㄕㄨ)
①one who is hired to write ②to borrow books (with rental) for reading

賃租 (ㄌㄧㄣˋ ㄗㄨ)
to rent

賃屋 (ㄌㄧㄣˋ ㄨ)
to rent a house

【賂】 5775
ㄌㄨˋ luh lù
1. to send a gift
2. to bribe

【賄】 5776
ㄏㄨㄟˋ huey huì
(又讀 ㄏㄨㄟˇ hoei huǐ)

1. to bribe; bribery: 他被控受賄。He is charged with bribery.
2. money; wealth

賄賂 (ㄏㄨㄟˋ ㄌㄨˋ)
to bribe; bribery: 他們用貴重的禮物賄賂他。They bribed him with costly presents.

賄選 (ㄏㄨㄟˋ ㄒㄩㄢˇ)
to try to win in an election by means of bribery; to get elected by bribery

【資】 5777
ㄗ tzy zī
1. money; wealth; property; means; capital
2. expenses; fees; charges
3. natural endowments or gifts; one's disposition
4. to avail of
5. to aid or help; to assist; to subsidize; to support
6. to supply; to provide
7. one's qualifications, position, or record of service
8. to trust to

資本 (ㄗ ㄅㄣˇ)
capital

資本逃避 (ㄗ ㄅㄣˇ ㄊㄠˊ ㄅㄧˋ)
flight of capital

資本論 (ㄗ ㄅㄣˇ ㄌㄨㄣˋ)
Capital (Das Kapital) by Karl Marx

資本集中 (ㄗ ㄅㄣˇ ㄐㄧˊ ㄓㄨㄥ)
centralization of capital

資本家 (ㄗ ㄅㄣˇ ㄐㄧㄚ)
a capitalist: 多餘的錢叫做資本,其所有人叫資本家。Spare money is called capital; its owner is called a capitalist.

資稟 (ㄗ ㄅㄧㄥˇ)
one's natural endowments or gifts: 他兒子資稟過人。His son's natural gifts excel others.

資方 (ㄗ ㄈㄤ)
the management (of a shop, factory, etc.); capital

資俸 (ㄗ ㄈㄥˋ)
qualifications and duration of service of an official

資斧 (ㄗ ㄈㄨˇ)
traveling expenses

資敵 (ㄗ ㄉㄧˊ)
to assist the enemy; treason

資歷 (ㄗ ㄌㄧˋ)
qualifications and experiences (of an applicant, etc.); professional background: 他的資歷不夠。His qualification and experience are insufficient.

資料 (ㄗ ㄌㄧㄠˋ)
data: 資料已齊備,等待處理。The data is ready for processing.

資料庫 (ㄗ ㄌㄧㄠˋ ㄎㄨˋ)
(computers) data base

資料處理 (ㄗ ㄌㄧㄠˋ ㄔㄨˇ ㄌㄧˇ)
information processing

資格 (ㄗ ㄍㄜˊ)
qualifications, requirements, or seniority of a person: 我具有必要的資格。I have the requisite qualifications.

資金 (ㄗ ㄐㄧㄣ)
funds; capital

資金凍結 (ㄗ ㄐㄧㄣ ㄉㄨㄥˋ ㄐㄧㄝˊ)
freezing of funds or capital

資遣 (ㄗ ㄑㄧㄢˇ)
to dismiss (employees) with severance pay: 他去年被資遣。He was dismissed with severance pay last year.

資性 (ㄗ ㄒㄧㄥˋ)
one's disposition; one's natural endowments: 這位學生資性忠厚。The student's natural disposition is honest.

資訊 (ㄗ ㄒㄩㄣˋ)
information

資質 (ㄗ ㄓˊ)
one's natural gifts or endowments; one's natural disposition: 他具有藝術方面的資質。He has a gift for art.

資治通鑑 (ㄗ ㄓˋ ㄊㄨㄥ ㄐㄧㄢˋ)
the title of a 294-volume chronicle by Ssu-Ma Kuang (司馬光), covering a period of 1,362 years down to the Epoch of the Five Dynasties

資政 (ㄗ ㄓㄥˋ)
a political advisor to the President of the Republic of China

資政院 (ㄗ ㄓㄥˋ ㄩㄢˋ)
a nominated advisory council established toward the close of the Ching Dynasty

資助 (ㄗ ㄓㄨˋ)
to help another with money to provide financial assistance: 這位老人常常資助窮人

The old man often helps the poor with money.

資產(ㄗ ㄔㄢˇ)
① property; real estate ②(accounting) assets

資產負債表(ㄗ ㄔㄢˇ ㄈㄨˋ ㄓㄞ ㄅㄧㄠˇ)
a statement of assets and liabilities; a balance sheet

資產階級(ㄗ ㄔㄢˇ ㄐㄧㄝ ㄐㄧˊ)
the bourgeoisie; the middle class 亦作「中產階級」

資深(ㄗ ㄕㄣ)
senior; seniority

資水
Tsu-shui, name of a river in Hunan Province

資財(ㄗ ㄘㄞˊ)
wealth; riches; assets

資送(ㄗ ㄙㄨㄥˋ)
① to send away with money provided ② to give a dowry to a daughter on her marriage

資優生(ㄗ ㄧㄡ ㄕㄥ)
a bright student; a student with a high IQ

資望(ㄗ ㄨㄤˋ)
qualification and prestige

資源(ㄗ ㄩㄢˊ)
resources; natural resources: 中國是資源豐富的國家。China is a resourceful country.

【賅】 5778
《ㄍㄞ gai gāi》
provided for; included in; all-inclusive; nothing left out

【賈】 1. ㄐㄧㄚˇ jea jiǎ
a Chinese family name

賈島(ㄐㄧㄚˇ ㄉㄠˇ)
Chia Tao (779-843), a poet of the Tang Dynasty

賈誼(ㄐㄧㄚˇ ㄧˋ)
Chia Yi (200-168B.C.), a writer and political commentator of the Western Han Dynasty

【賈】 5779
2. ㄍㄨˇ guu gǔ
1. a merchant; a businessman
2. to buy; to trade

賈舶(ㄍㄨˇ ㄅㄛˊ)
merchant marine; trading vessels

賈利(ㄍㄨˇ ㄌㄧˋ)
to make a profit

賈儈(ㄍㄨˇ ㄎㄨㄞˋ)

merchants

賈禍(ㄍㄨˇ ㄏㄨㄛˋ)
to invite or bring on calamity or misfortune

賈人(ㄍㄨˇ ㄖㄣˊ)
merchants; businessmen

賈餘(ㄍㄨˇ ㄩˊ)
with courage to spare

賈怨(ㄍㄨˇ ㄩㄢˋ)
to invite complaints or grudges

賈勇(ㄍㄨˇ ㄩㄥˇ)
with courage to spare

【賊】 5780
ㄗㄟˊ tzeir zéi
(讀音 ㄗㄜˊ tzer zé)
1. a thief; a burglar; a robber; a bandit
2. rebels; traitors
3. to harm
4. to kill
5. pests on the farm
6. a term of reviling
7. clever; cunning; crafty

賊兵(ㄗㄟˊ ㄅㄧㄥ)
rebel soldiers; enemy troops

賊頭鼠腦(ㄗㄟˊ ㄊㄡˊ ㄕㄨˇ ㄋㄠˇ)
the appearance of a low, cunning person; a mean look

賊眉鼠眼(ㄗㄟˊ ㄇㄟˊ ㄕㄨˇ ㄧㄢˇ)
roguish looks

賊匪(ㄗㄟˊ ㄈㄟˇ)
rebels; bandits: 這鎮為賊匪所擾害。The town is infested with bandits.

賊黨(ㄗㄟˊ ㄉㄤˇ)
the rebel faction; a gang of bandits or rebels; a group of traitors: 賊黨已分裂為兩派。The rebel faction has split into two factions.

賊店(ㄗㄟˊ ㄉㄧㄢˋ)
an inn operated by an evil person or persons who kill the lodgers for money, jewels, etc.

賊頭(ㄗㄟˊ ㄊㄡˊ) or **賊首**(ㄗㄟˊ ㄕㄡˇ)
the leader of a band of thieves; the chief robber; a bandit leader

賊頭賊腦(ㄗㄟˊ ㄊㄡˊ ㄗㄟˊ ㄋㄠˇ)
to act suspiciously; thief-like; a mean look; acting stealthily

賊禿(ㄗㄟˊ ㄊㄨ)
an abusive term for Buddhist monks

賊徒(ㄗㄟˊ ㄊㄨˊ)
thieves

賊骨頭(ㄗㄟˊ ㄍㄨˇ ㄊㄡˊ)
depravity; meanness; wickedness

賊鬼(ㄗㄟˊ ㄍㄨㄟˇ)
cunning and crafty

賊鬼溜滑(ㄗㄟˊ ㄍㄨㄟˇ ㄌㄧㄡ ㄏㄨㄚˊ)
dishonest; crafty: 他賊鬼溜滑如狐狸。He is as crafty as a fox.

賊寇(ㄗㄟˊ ㄎㄡˋ)
rebels; bandits

賊害(ㄗㄟˊ ㄏㄞˋ)
to cause harm or injury to another

賊將(ㄗㄟˊ ㄐㄧㄤˋ)
a rebel general; a general of the enemy troops

賊心(ㄗㄟˊ ㄒㄧㄣ)
a crooked mind; a wicked and suspicious mind; evil designs

賊相(ㄗㄟˊ ㄒㄧㄤˋ)
criminal looks

賊星發旺(ㄗㄟˊ ㄒㄧㄥ ㄈㄚ ㄨㄤˋ)
(a sarcastical expression) a small-time operator hitting the jackpot

賊性(ㄗㄟˊ ㄒㄧㄥˋ)
① a crafty or cunning disposition ② an evil mind

賊性難改(ㄗㄟˊ ㄒㄧㄥˋ ㄋㄢˊ ㄍㄞˇ)
The habitual criminal is incorrigible.

賊巢(ㄗㄟˊ ㄔㄠˊ)
a den or hideout of thieves and bandits

賊出關門(ㄗㄟˊ ㄔㄨ ㄍㄨㄢ ㄇㄣˊ)
(literally) to close the door after the thieves are gone —too late

賊船(ㄗㄟˊ ㄔㄨㄢˊ)
a pirate ship; a ship owned by bandits or rebels: 賊船被燒。The pirate ship was burned.

賊人(ㄗㄟˊ ㄖㄣˊ)
a thief or robber

賊贓(ㄗㄟˊ ㄗㄤ)
stolen goods or property; loot: 賊贓起回。Stolen goods were recovered.

賊眼(ㄗㄟˊ ㄧㄢˇ)
eyes with evil twinkle; shifty eyes; a furtive glance

〔貝部〕

【貝部】

賊營(ㄗㄟˊ ㄧㄥˊ)
the camp of rebels, bandits, etc.: 賊營着火了。The camp of bandits caught (on) fire.

賊窩子(ㄗㄟˊ ㄨㄛ ˙ㄗ)
a den or hideout of thieves or bandits

【賉】 5781
ㄒㄩˋ shiuh syù
1. sympathy; pity
2. to give alms or compensation

【賍】 5782
ㄗㄤ tzang zāng
stolen goods or property; loot

七畫

【賑】 5783
ㄓㄣˋ jenn zhèn
1. to relieve or give aid to the distressed; to support
2. rich; wealthy; prosperous

賑田(ㄓㄣˋ ㄊㄧㄢˊ)
farmland, whose produce is used for relief or charity

賑糧(ㄓㄣˋ ㄌㄧㄤˊ)
relief food or grain

賑款(ㄓㄣˋ ㄎㄨㄢˇ)
relief funds

賑饑(ㄓㄣˋ ㄐㄧ)
to feed the hungry (refugees); to relieve famine

賑濟(ㄓㄣˋ ㄐㄧˋ) or 賑瞻(ㄓㄣˋ ㄕㄢˋ)
to relieve or give aid to the distressed; to provide relief for: 政府賑濟難民。The government provided relief for refugees.

賑捐(ㄓㄣˋ ㄐㄩㄢ)
to contribute to relief funds

賑恤(ㄓㄣˋ ㄒㄩˋ)
to relieve the distressed: 這基金用於賑恤。The fund is for relieving the distressed.

賑災(ㄓㄣˋ ㄗㄞ)
to relieve the afflicted area; to relieve victims of a natural disaster

【賒】 5784
ㄕㄜ she shē
1. to buy or sell on credit
2. distant; faraway
3. slow; slowly
4. to put off or postpone
5. luxurious or extravagant

賒貸(ㄕㄜ ㄉㄞˋ)
credit

賒貨(ㄕㄜ ㄏㄨㄛˋ)
to get goods on credit

賒欠(ㄕㄜ ㄑㄧㄢˋ)
to buy on credit; such credit which has not been settled

賒賬(ㄕㄜ ㄓㄤˋ)
to buy on account or credit

賒售(ㄕㄜ ㄕㄡˋ)
sales on account

【賓】 5785
(賔)ㄅㄧㄣ bin bīn
1. a guest; a visitor
2. to treat as a guest
3. to obey; to follow instructions; to submit
4. a Chinese family name

賓白(ㄅㄧㄣ ㄅㄞˊ)
dialogue in Chinese opera

賓朋(ㄅㄧㄣ ㄆㄥˊ)
friends and guests

賓服(ㄅㄧㄣ ㄈㄨˊ)
①(said of feudal lords)to have an audience with the emperor and present him with tribute ②to pay homage

賓待(ㄅㄧㄣ ㄉㄞˋ)
to receive someone as a guest

賓禮(ㄅㄧㄣ ㄌㄧˇ)
①the courtesy or etiquette on the part of a guest ②international courtesy

賓格(ㄅㄧㄣ ㄍㄜˊ)
(grammar)the objective case

賓果(ㄅㄧㄣ ㄍㄨㄛˇ)
bingo

賓館(ㄅㄧㄣ ㄍㄨㄢˇ)
a guesthouse

賓貢(ㄅㄧㄣ ㄍㄨㄥˋ)
①(an ancient practice) to treat capable and virtuous persons in a locality as guests and recommend them to the imperial court ②(said of a small country) to pledge allegiance and offer tributes to a strong country

賓客(ㄅㄧㄣ ㄎㄜˋ)
guests and visitors

賓夕法尼亞(ㄅㄧㄣ ㄒㄧ ㄈㄚˇ ㄋㄧˊ ㄧㄚˋ) or 賓州(ㄅㄧㄣ ㄓㄡ)
the state of Pennsylvania, U.S.A.

賓至如歸(ㄅㄧㄣ ㄓˋ ㄖㄨˊ ㄍㄨㄟ)
Guests flock to the place like returning home.—to feel at home in a place: 在這一流的旅館，我們覺得賓至如歸。We feel at home in this first-class hotel.

賓主(ㄅㄧㄣ ㄓㄨˇ)
①the guest and the host ②secondary and principal

賓主盡歡(ㄅㄧㄣ ㄓㄨˇ ㄐㄧㄣˋ ㄏㄨㄢ)
Both the guests and the host are having a great time.

賓師(ㄅㄧㄣ ㄕ)
one who does not hold a public post but is highly respected

賓從(ㄅㄧㄣ ㄘㄨㄥˊ)
servants or retinue of a guest

賓位(ㄅㄧㄣ ㄨㄟˋ)
(grammar) the objective case

賓語(ㄅㄧㄣ ㄩˇ)
(grammar) the object of a transitive verb 亦作「受詞」

【賕】 5786
ㄑㄧㄡˊ chyou qiú
to bribe

八畫

【賚】 5787
ㄌㄞˋ lay lài
to bestow; to confer

賚品(ㄌㄞˋ ㄆㄧㄣˇ)
an article, item, gift, etc. bestowed by a superior

【賙】 5788
ㄓㄡ jou zhōu
to give; to aid; to relieve

賙濟(ㄓㄡ ㄐㄧˋ)
to relieve the needy: 我們必須賙濟貧困的家庭。We have to relieve needy families.

【賜】 5789
ㄙˋ syh sì
(語音 ㄘˋ tsyh cì)
1. to bestow or confer on an inferior; to grant
2. favors; benefits
3. to order; to appoint

賜帛(ㄙˋ ㄅㄛˊ)
(in ancient China) to be bestowed silk by the emperor for hanging oneself

賜福(ㄙˋ ㄈㄨˊ)
to bless; to give blessings

賜覆(ㄙˋ ㄈㄨˋ)
Please reply. 或 to favor

with a reply: 請即賜覆。
Please favor me with an
early reply.

賜 (ㄌㄐㄧㄣˋ)
(said of the emperor, especially in the Ching Dynasty)
to personally offer condolences or pay last tribute to
the deceased

賜給 (ㄙˋ ㄍㄟˇ)
to grant; to bestow

賜告 (ㄙˋ ㄍㄠˋ)
to be given official leave by
the emperor

賜顧 (ㄙˋ ㄍㄨˋ)
(a polite business expression) your patronage

賜函 (ㄙˋ ㄏㄢˊ)
Please write me.

賜環 (ㄙˋ ㄏㄨㄢˊ)
(said of an official exiled to
the frontier) to be forgiven
and recalled to the capital

賜假 (ㄙˋ ㄐㄧㄚˋ)
to be granted a leave of
absence

賜教 (ㄙˋ ㄐㄧㄠˋ)
(a polite expression) your
instructions; your advice: 敬
請多多賜教。Please favor me
with your advice.

賜爵 (ㄙˋ ㄐㄩㄝˊ)
to confer titles of nobility
upon the meritorious

賜姓 (ㄙˋ ㄒㄧㄥˋ)
to be given the emperor's
family name (in recognition
of one's meritorious service)

賜示 (ㄙˋ ㄕˋ)
(a polite expression) Please
tell me....

賜諡 (ㄙˋ ㄕˋ)
(said of a high minister) to
have an honorary title conferred posthumously

賜書 (ㄙˋ ㄕㄨ)
letters received from a superior or client

賜死 (ㄙˋ ㄙˇ)
to be ordered by the emperor
to commit suicide

賜宴 (ㄙˋ ㄧㄢˋ)
to be invited to dine with
the emperor

賜予 or 賜與 (ㄙˋ ㄩˇ)
to bestow or confer upon; to
grant (approval, etc.)

【賞】 5790
ㄕㄤˇ shaang shǎng
1. to reward; to award; to
bestow; to grant; to give to
an inferior
2. a reward; an award
3. to appreciate; to enjoy; to
admire
4. (now rarely) to respect
5. (a polite expression) to be
given the honor of...

賞罰 (ㄕㄤˇ ㄈㄚˊ)
to reward and punish; reward
and punishment

賞罰分明 (ㄕㄤˇ ㄈㄚˊ ㄈㄣ ㄇㄧㄥˊ)
to confer reward and inflict
punishment impartially

賞田 (ㄕㄤˇ ㄊㄧㄢˊ)
(Chou Dynasty) land be-
stowed by the government

賞臉 (ㄕㄤˇ ㄌㄧㄢˇ)
①to favor me with your
presence or company ②to
condescend to receive my
humble gifts ③to do me a
favor

賞格 (ㄕㄤˇ ㄍㄜˊ)
the amount of cash reward
offered (for locating a person or an object)

賞光 (ㄕㄤˇ ㄍㄨㄤ)
(a polite expression) to hon-
or me with your gracious
presence or company

賞花 (ㄕㄤˇ ㄏㄨㄚ)
to enjoy the sight of flowers

賞金 (ㄕㄤˇ ㄐㄧㄣ)
reward money; a bonus

賞錢 (ㄕㄤˇ ㄑㄧㄢˊ)
tips (for waiters, servants,
etc.): 他給侍者賞錢。He gave
the waiter a tip.

賞心 (ㄕㄤˇ ㄒㄧㄣ)
to please the heart, as a
beautiful sight, etc.

賞心樂事 (ㄕㄤˇ ㄒㄧㄣ ㄌㄜˋ ㄕˋ)
pleasant things that one enjoys doing

賞心悅目 (ㄕㄤˇ ㄒㄧㄣ ㄩㄝˋ ㄇㄨˋ)
to flatter the heart and
please the eye—beautiful
and restful

賞雪 (ㄕㄤˇ ㄒㄩㄝˇ)
to enjoy snow scenes

賞識 (ㄕㄤˇ ㄕˋ)
to appreciate the virtues in
a person or thing: to recog-

nize the worth of a person:
他的辛勞獲得賞識。His serv-
ices were appreciated.

賞音 (ㄕㄤˇ ㄙㄥ)
the third tone in Chinese
phonetics 亦作「上聲」

賞賜 (ㄕㄤˇ ㄙˋ) or (ㄕㄤˇ ㄘˋ)
to bestow money or presents
on an inferior or junior;
gifts or money given as a
reward; to award; to grant a
reward

賞音 (ㄕㄤˇ ㄧㄣ)
to appreciate music

賞玩 (ㄕㄤˇ ㄨㄢˊ)
to enjoy or appreciate the
sight of; to delight in

賞雨 (ㄕㄤˇ ㄩˇ)
to enjoy rainy scenes

賞月 (ㄕㄤˇ ㄩㄝˋ)
to enjoy moonlight: 他們正在
賞月。They are enjoying
moonlight.

【賠】 5791
ㄆㄟˊ peir péi
1. to compensate or indemnify;
to make up for a loss due to
one's fault; to pay for
2. to offer (an apology)
3. to lose money

賠本 (ㄆㄟˊ ㄅㄣˇ)
to lose money in business; to
sell at a loss: 他的貨物均賠本
出售。All his goods sell at a
loss.

賠本生意沒人做 (ㄆㄟˊ ㄅㄣˇ ㄕㄥ ㄧˋ
ㄇㄟˊ ㄖㄣˊ ㄗㄨㄛˋ)
No one will be interested in
doing a losing business.

賠不是 (ㄆㄟˊ ㄅㄨˋ ㄕˋ)
to apologize

賠補 (ㄆㄟˊ ㄅㄨˇ)
to compensate and make up
for the deficiency

賠不起 (ㄆㄟˊ ㄅㄨˋ ㄑㄧˇ)
cannot afford to pay (for the
loss); unable to pay for compensation

賠墊 (ㄆㄟˊ ㄉㄧㄢˋ)
to advance money (for
another) in making payment

賠了夫人又折兵 (ㄆㄟˊ ㄌㄜ˙ ㄈㄨ ㄖㄣˊ
ㄧㄡˋ ㄓㄜˊ ㄅㄧㄥ)
to suffer a double loss; to
throw the helve after the
hatchet

賠累 (ㄆㄟˊ ㄌㄟˇ)

貝
部

〔貝部〕

賠禮(ㄆㄟˊ ㄌㄧˇ)
to offer an apology; to apologize

賠光(ㄆㄟˊ ㄍㄨㄤ)
to lose all the capital in a business adventure

賠款(ㄆㄟˊ ㄎㄨㄢˇ)
an indemnity; a compensation; reparations

賠還(ㄆㄟˊ ㄏㄨㄢˊ)
to repay: 他賠還了借款。He repaid the money he had borrowed.

賠錢(ㄆㄟˊ ㄑㄧㄢˊ)
①to make a pecuniary compensation ②to lose money in business 參看「賠本」

賠錢貨(ㄆㄟˊ ㄑㄧㄢˊ ㄏㄨㄛˋ)
daughters(who need dowries but will not bear the family name after marriage)

賠小心(ㄆㄟˊ ㄒㄧㄠˇ ㄒㄧㄣ)
to make apologies; to apologize

賠笑(ㄆㄟˊ ㄒㄧㄠˋ)
to smile obsequiously or apologetically

賠償(ㄆㄟˊ ㄔㄤˊ)
reparation; compensation; indemnity; to recompense; to compensate; to indemnify; to make reparation for; to make amends for; to make good a loss due to one's own fault: 他答應賠償我的損失。He promised to indemnify me for my losses.

賠償費(ㄆㄟˊ ㄔㄤˊ ㄈㄟˋ)
damages

賠償協定(ㄆㄟˊ ㄔㄤˊ ㄒㄧㄝˊ ㄉㄧㄥˋ)
a reparations agreement

賠償損失(ㄆㄟˊ ㄔㄤˊ ㄙㄨㄣˇ ㄕ)
to indemnify; to make good a loss due to one's own fault

賠罪(ㄆㄟˊ ㄗㄨㄟˋ)
to apologize

【賡】 5792
ㄍㄥ gēng
to continue; to carry on

賡續(ㄍㄥ ㄒㄩˋ)
to continue

賡酬(ㄍㄥ ㄔㄡˊ)
to write poems to each other as a means of communication

賡颺 or 賡揚(ㄍㄥ ㄧㄤˊ)
to carry on; to continue

賡韻(ㄍㄥ ㄩㄣˋ)
to write a poem in response, using the same rhyme as the one received

【賢】 5793
ㄒㄧㄢˊ shyan xián
1. capable; able; versatile; talented
2. good; worthy; virtuous
3. to admire; to praise; to esteem
4. a term of respectful address to another

賢明(ㄒㄧㄢˊ ㄇㄧㄥˊ)
capable and virtuous: 他是個賢明的君主。He was a capable and virtuous king.

賢達(ㄒㄧㄢˊ ㄉㄚˊ)
wise and virtuous; the social élite

賢德(ㄒㄧㄢˊ ㄉㄜˊ)
good conduct; virtuous

賢弟(ㄒㄧㄢˊ ㄉㄧˋ)
my dear brother(a term of address to a male friend who is younger than oneself)

賢內助(ㄒㄧㄢˊ ㄋㄟˋ ㄓㄨˋ)
a good wife

賢能(ㄒㄧㄢˊ ㄋㄥˊ)
talented and virtuous

賢良(ㄒㄧㄢˊ ㄌㄧㄤˊ)
virtuous; the virtuous

賢良方正(ㄒㄧㄢˊ ㄌㄧㄤˊ ㄈㄤ ㄓㄥˋ)
the selection of proficient literary scholars from the various districts to be presented to the central government——a system started in the Han Dynasty

賢路(ㄒㄧㄢˊ ㄌㄨˋ)
a channel through which worthy men of ability can attain officialdom

賢昆仲(ㄒㄧㄢˊ ㄎㄨㄣ ㄓㄨㄥˋ)
(a polite expression)you and your brother

賢惠 or 賢慧(ㄒㄧㄢˊ ㄏㄨㄟˋ)
(usually said of women) virtuous and intelligent; good and wise

賢妻(ㄒㄧㄢˊ ㄑㄧ)
①a good wife ②my dear wife

賢妻良母(ㄒㄧㄢˊ ㄑㄧ ㄌㄧㄤˊ ㄇㄨˇ)
a dutiful wife and loving mother

賢契(ㄒㄧㄢˊ ㄑㄧˋ)
a polite term of address to one's pupils or children of one's friends

賢倩(ㄒㄧㄢˊ ㄑㄧㄢˋ)
my dear son-in-law

賢相(ㄒㄧㄢˊ ㄒㄧㄤˋ)
a capable and upright prime minister

賢哲(ㄒㄧㄢˊ ㄓㄜˊ)
a person outstanding in virtue and learning

賢者(ㄒㄧㄢˊ ㄓㄜˇ)
men of talents and virtue; the good; the virtuous

賢士(ㄒㄧㄢˊ ㄕˋ)
a person of high moral standing

賢甥(ㄒㄧㄢˊ ㄕㄥ)
my dear nephew

賢淑(ㄒㄧㄢˊ ㄕㄨˊ)
(usually said of women) virtuous and understanding

賢人(ㄒㄧㄢˊ ㄖㄣˊ)
a person of virtue and talents; a worthy man; a worthy person

賢才(ㄒㄧㄢˊ ㄘㄞˊ)
a capable and virtuous person

賢達(ㄒㄧㄢˊ ㄉㄚˊ)
a virtuous person

賢愚(ㄒㄧㄢˊ ㄩˊ)
the wise and the stupid

【賣】 5794
ㄇㄞˋ may mài
1. to sell
2. to betray; to harm another in order to benefit oneself
3. to show off; to flaunt

賣本事(ㄇㄞˋ ㄅㄣˇ ㄕ)
to show off one's feat, skill, etc.

賣卜(ㄇㄞˋ ㄅㄨˇ)
to make a living as a fortuneteller

賣不了(ㄇㄞˋ ㄅㄨˋ ㄌㄧㄠˇ)or 賣不出去(ㄇㄞˋ ㄅㄨˋ ㄔ ㄑㄩˋ)
cannot be sold

賣面子(ㄇㄞˋ ㄇㄧㄢˋ ㄗ)
to do somebody a favor for the sake of one's friendship with a third party, with whom the former is closely related or associated

賣名(ㄇㄞˋ ㄇㄧㄥˊ)or 賣名氣(ㄇㄞˋ ㄇㄧㄥˊ ㄑㄧˋ)
to capitalize on one's reputation or prestige

賣命(ㄇㄞˋ ㄇㄧㄥˋ)
①to work oneself to the bone for somebody ②to die (unworthily) for

賣主(ㄇㄞˋ ㄓㄨˇ)
the seller

賣風流(ㄇㄞˋ ㄈㄥ ㄌㄧㄡˊ)
to flirt; to act coquettishly

賣獃 or 賣呆(ㄇㄞˋ ㄉㄞ)or 賣傻(ㄇㄞˋ ㄕㄚˇ)
to feign stupidity; to pretend to know nothing

賣力(ㄇㄞˋ ㄌㄧˋ)or 賣力氣(ㄇㄞˋ ㄌㄧˋ ㄑㄧˋ)
①to work as a laborer ②to work hard willingly

賣臉(ㄇㄞˋ ㄌㄧㄢˇ)
①to try to please someone obsequiously ②(said of a girl) to sell her company but not her body

賣弄(ㄇㄞˋ ㄋㄨㄥˋ)
to flaunt; to show off

賣弄風情(ㄇㄞˋ ㄋㄨㄥˋ ㄈㄥ ㄑㄧㄥˊ)
to flirt and coquet

賣弄口齒(ㄇㄞˋ ㄋㄨㄥˋ ㄎㄡˇ ㄔˇ)
to show off one's glibness in speech or wits

賣膏藥(ㄇㄞˋ ㄍㄠ ㄧㄠˋ)
(literally) to be a mountebank—to make high-sounding statements without sincerity; to make propaganda 亦作「賣狗皮膏藥」

賣國(ㄇㄞˋ ㄍㄨㄛˊ)
to betray one's country; sedition or treason

賣國求榮(ㄇㄞˋ ㄍㄨㄛˊ ㄑㄧㄡˊ ㄖㄨㄥˊ)
to betray one's country in exchange for a high position

賣國賊(ㄇㄞˋ ㄍㄨㄛˊ ㄗㄟˊ)
a traitor; one who collaborates with an enemy country

賣乖(ㄇㄞˋ ㄍㄨㄞ)
to show off one's cleverness

賣關子(ㄇㄞˋ ㄍㄨㄢ ˙ㄗ)
(in storytelling) to create suspense by stopping narration when it comes to the most interesting part; to withhold information that the listeners are most eager to know

賣官鬻爵(ㄇㄞˋ ㄍㄨㄢ ㄩˋ ㄐㄩㄝˊ)
to accept bribery and confer official ranks for money

賣空買空(ㄇㄞˋ ㄎㄨㄥ ㄇㄞˇ ㄎㄨㄥ)
to speculate on the stock market; speculation on the stock market

賣價(ㄇㄞˋ ㄐㄧㄚˋ)
the selling price

賣劍買牛(ㄇㄞˋ ㄐㄧㄢˋ ㄇㄞˇ ㄋㄧㄡˊ)or 賣刀買犢(ㄇㄞˋ ㄉㄠ ㄇㄞˇ ㄉㄨˊ)
(said of an official) to bring peace and diligence to a lawless area

賣勁(ㄇㄞˋ ㄐㄧㄣˋ)or 賣勁兒(ㄇㄞˋ ㄐㄧㄦ)
to do one's utmost without complaining; to exert all one's strength

賣絕(ㄇㄞˋ ㄐㄩㄝˊ)or 賣斷(ㄇㄞˋ ㄉㄨㄢˋ)
to sell outright—without any chance of buying back

賣妻鬻子(ㄇㄞˋ ㄑㄧ ㄩˋ ㄗˇ)
to sell one's wife and sons (as in time of famine)

賣契(ㄇㄞˋ ㄑㄧˋ)
a contract for selling something; a contract of sale

賣俏(ㄇㄞˋ ㄑㄧㄠˋ)
to flirt or coquet

賣錢(ㄇㄞˋ ㄑㄧㄢˊ)
to sell for money

賣笑(ㄇㄞˋ ㄒㄧㄠˋ)
to work as a prostitute

賣招牌(ㄇㄞˋ ㄓㄠ ㄆㄞˊ)
to sell some merchandise on the strength of its well-known brand name

賣主(ㄇㄞˋ ㄓㄨˇ)
the seller

賣唱(ㄇㄞˋ ㄔㄤˋ)
to live on singing

賣春(ㄇㄞˋ ㄔㄨㄣ)
prostitution

賣舌(ㄇㄞˋ ㄕㄜˊ)
to make sensational statements for the sake of publicity

賣身(ㄇㄞˋ ㄕㄣ)
①to sell oneself as a slave ②to become a prostitute; to prostitute

賣身投靠(ㄇㄞˋ ㄕㄣ ㄊㄡˊ ㄎㄠˋ)
to join the enemy camp for sheer profit

賣身契(ㄇㄞˋ ㄕㄣ ㄑㄧˋ)
a written contract by which one sells oneself or a member of one's family

賣人情(ㄇㄞˋ ㄖㄣˊ ㄑㄧㄥˊ)
to do someone a favor for personal consideration

賣座(ㄇㄞˋ ㄗㄨㄛˋ)
①(said of a theater, etc.) to draw large audiences ②(said of a restaurant, etc.) to attract large numbers of customers

賣恩(ㄇㄞˋ ㄣ)
to do someone a favor with a view to earning his gratitude

賣藝(ㄇㄞˋ ㄧˋ)
to earn a living by entertaining others with one's skills or stunts

賣藝人(ㄇㄞˋ ㄧˋ ㄖㄣˊ)
acrobats, jugglers, etc.

賣人頭(ㄇㄞˋ ㄖㄣˊ ㄊㄡˊ)
(Shanghai dialect) to exaggerate

賣友(ㄇㄞˋ ㄧㄡˇ)
to betray a friend: 吾人不能賣友。We shouldn't betray our friends.

賣淫(ㄇㄞˋ ㄧㄣˊ)
to earn a living as a prostitute

賣盡(ㄇㄞˋ ㄒㄧㄥ)or 賣光(ㄇㄞˋ ㄍㄨㄤ)
sold out: 我們大號的貨品完全賣完了。We are sold out of large sizes.

賣文(ㄇㄞˋ ㄒㄧㄣˊ)or 賣文爲生(ㄇㄞˋ ㄒㄣˊ ㄨㄟˊ ㄕㄥ)
to make a living by writing; to make a living from literary work

【賤】 5795 ㄐㄧㄢˋ jiann jiàn
1. cheap; inexpensive; low cost
2. lowly; humble; inferior in position
3. low-down; base; ignoble; despicable
4. to slight; to look down on
5. my, a self-derogatory expression
6. a Chinese family name

賤買貴賣(ㄐㄧㄢˋ ㄇㄞˇ ㄍㄨㄟˋ ㄇㄞˋ)
to buy cheap and sell high

賤買賤賣(ㄐㄧㄢˋ ㄇㄞˇ ㄐㄧㄢˋ ㄇㄞˋ)
to buy and sell at low prices

賤內(ㄐㄧㄢˋ ㄋㄟˋ)

〔貝部〕

〔貝部〕

my humble wife

賤骨頭(ㄐㄧㄢˋㄍㄨˇㄊㄡ˙)
a despicable fellow; a good-for-nothing

賤貨(ㄐㄧㄢˋㄏㄨㄛˋ)
①(a term of revile) a tramp; a slut ②worthless goods

賤伎(ㄐㄧㄢˋㄐㄧˋ)
inferior arts; lowly arts

賤價(ㄐㄧㄢˋㄐㄧㄚˋ)
a low price; low-priced

賤荆(ㄐㄧㄢˋㄐㄧㄥ)
my humble wife

賤妾(ㄐㄧㄢˋㄑㄧㄝˋ)
a self-reference among women of ancient times

賤軀(ㄐㄧㄢˋㄑㄩ)
my body; my health condition

賤息(ㄐㄧㄢˋㄒㄧˊ)
my humble son

賤行(ㄐㄧㄢˋㄒㄧㄥˊ)
evil conduct or ways

賤室(ㄐㄧㄢˋㄕˋ)
my humble wife

賤人(ㄐㄧㄢˋㄖㄣˊ)
(a term of revile used in old novels) a slut or tramp

賤儒(ㄐㄧㄢˋㄖㄨˊ)
a pedant

賤子(ㄐㄧㄢˋㄗˇ)
(archaic) a polite way of referring to oneself

賤族(ㄐㄧㄢˋㄗㄨˊ)
an inferior race or tribe

賤業(ㄐㄧㄢˋㄧㄝˋ)
a lowly or mean occupation; a low-down business (now usually referring to prostitution)

賤恙(ㄐㄧㄢˋㄧㄤˋ)
(a polite expression) my illness

賤物(ㄐㄧㄢˋㄨˋ)
a cheap and worthless thing

【賦】 5796
ㄈㄨˋ fuh fù

1. a tax; revenue
2. troops; the army; military levies
3. to bestow; to give
4. natural endowments or gifts
5. to spread; to diffuse
6. to compose or sing (especially poems)
7. one of the Chinese literary

forms akin to poetry

賦稟(ㄈㄨˋㄅㄧㄥˇ)
natural endowments or gifts

賦(ㄈㄨˋㄎㄞ)
to levy taxes

賦歸(ㄈㄨˋㄍㄨㄟ)
to return home

賦貢(ㄈㄨˋㄍㄨㄥˋ)
to pay tribute or levy

賦課(ㄈㄨˋㄎㄜˋ)
land tax, farm tax, excise tax, etc.

賦閒(ㄈㄨˋㄒㄧㄢˊ)
to be out of employment; jobless

賦性(ㄈㄨˋㄒㄧㄥˋ)
one's natural disposition or temperament

賦詩(ㄈㄨˋㄕ)
to compose or sing poems

賦稅(ㄈㄨˋㄕㄨㄟˋ)
farm tax and excise tax

賦額(ㄈㄨˋㄜˊ)
the prescribed amount of farm revenue

賦役(ㄈㄨˋㄧˋ)
a general name of all national taxes, revenues, levies, compulsory service, etc.

賦(ㄈㄨˋㄩˇ)
endowed or gifted with

賦予 or 賦與(ㄈㄨˋㄩˇ)
to give; to bestow; to endow

【質】 5797
1. ㄓˋ jyr zhí

1. matters; substances; elements
2. one's disposition or temperament; qualities
3. simple; plain
4. to question
5. to confront

質朴 or 質樸(ㄓˋㄆㄨˇ)
simple and unadorned

質地(ㄓˋㄉㄧˋ)
① quality of something ② one's disposition or endowments ③ material of piece goods

質點(ㄓˋㄉㄧㄢˇ)
(physics) a particle

質料(ㄓˋㄌㄧㄠˋ)
quality; raw materials: 這套衣服的質料很好。This suit is made of very good material.

質量(ㄓˋㄌㄧㄤˋ)

① (physics) mass ② quality

質量不滅律(ㄓˋㄌㄧㄤˋㄅㄨˋㄇㄧㄝˋㄌㄩˋ)
the law of conservation of mass

質詢(ㄓˋㄒㄩㄣˊ)
to interpellate; interpellation; to ask for an explanation

質直(ㄓˋㄓˊ)
simple and honest; solid and straightforward

質成(ㄓˋㄔㄥˊ)
to ask a third party to arbitrate a dispute, etc.

質數(ㄓˋㄕㄨˋ)
a prime number 亦作「素數」

質讓(ㄓˋㄖㄤˋ)
to admonish bluntly

質子(ㄓˋㄗˇ)
(physics) a proton

質疑(ㄓˋㄧˊ)
to ask questions about something with which one is not familiar; to question; to query

質言(ㄓˋㄧㄢˊ)
an honest talk; a plain talk

質言之(ㄓˋㄧㄢˊㄓ)
to put it in plain language; in short; in other words

質問(ㄓˋㄨㄣˋ)
① to interrogate ② to raise questions in order to resolve one's doubt

【質】 5797
2. ㄓˋ jyh zhì

1. to pawn
2. a pledge; a hostage

質押(ㄓˋㄧㄚ)
to assign something as security under an arrangement; to mortgage

【賬】 5798
(賬) ㄓㄤˋ jang zhàng

1. accounts
2. debts
3. credits; loans; bills

賬簿(ㄓㄤˋㄅㄨˋ)
accounts; account books

賬目(ㄓㄤˋㄇㄨˋ)
accounts; details or items of accounts: 這賬目有條不紊。The accounts were perfectly in order.

賬房(ㄓㄤˋㄈㄤˊ)
① a cashier's office ② a cashier; a teller; a treasurer

賬單 (ㄓㄤ ㄉㄢ)
bills; invoices: 我有許多賬單
需要付款。I have many bills
to pay.

賬籍 (ㄓㄤ ㄐㄧˊ)
accounts; books

賬務 (ㄓㄤ ㄨˋ)
affairs concerning accounts

九畫

【賭】 5799
ㄉㄨˇ　duu dǔ
1. to gamble; to bet; to wager
2. to compete
3. to swear

賭博 (ㄉㄨˇ ㄅㄛˊ)
to gamble; gambling: 他賭博
輸去了一半財產。He has gam-
bled away his wealth.

賭本 (ㄉㄨˇ ㄅㄣˇ)
money to gamble with

賭品 (ㄉㄨˇ ㄆㄧㄣˇ)
one's manners, conduct and
honesty, or the absence of it,
manifested in gambling

賭命 (ㄉㄨˇ ㄇㄧㄥˋ)
to gamble on one's life—to
do something extremely dangerous

賭犯 (ㄉㄨˇ ㄈㄢˋ)
a person guilty of gambling

賭束注 (ㄉㄨˇ ㄉㄨㄥˋ)
to bet on something in
which a loser has to pay a
wager

賭徒 (ㄉㄨˇ ㄊㄨˊ)
a gambler: 那賭徒賭掉家產。
That gambler gambled away
his fortune.

賭個輸贏 (ㄉㄨˇ ˙ㄍㄜ ㄕㄨ ㄧㄥˊ)
to bet or wager

賭鬼 (ㄉㄨˇ ㄍㄨㄟˇ)
a congenital gambler

賭棍 (ㄉㄨˇ ㄍㄨㄣˋ)
a person who makes a liv-
ing as a gambler

賭局 (ㄉㄨˇ ㄐㄩˊ)
a gambling game; a gam-
bling gathering

賭具 (ㄉㄨˇ ㄐㄩˋ)
things used in gambling—as
cards, dice, mah-jong, etc.

賭氣 (ㄉㄨˇ ㄑㄧˋ)
to do something out of spite
(or in a rage)

賭錢 (ㄉㄨˇ ㄑㄧㄢˊ)

to gamble (for money)

賭債 (ㄉㄨˇ ㄓㄞˋ) or 賭眼 (ㄉㄨˇ ㄓㄞˋ)
a gambling debt; a debt of
honor

賭咒 (ㄉㄨˇ ㄓㄡˋ)
to make an oath; to swear:
他賭咒。He swore an oath.

賭注 (ㄉㄨˇ ㄓㄨˋ)
stakes: 他下很大的賭注。He
played for high stakes.

賭場 (ㄉㄨˇ ㄔㄤˇ)
a gambling joint; a gam-
bling den or house

賭誓 (ㄉㄨˇ ㄕˋ)
to make an oath; to vow: 他
賭誓絕不再還家。He vowed
never to leave home again.

賭輸 (ㄉㄨˇ ㄕㄨ)
to lose in gambling; to lose
a wager

賭賽 (ㄉㄨˇ ㄙㄞˋ)
to compete or contest in order to determine the winner

賭友 (ㄉㄨˇ ㄧㄡˇ)
gambling companions; gam-
bling company

【賴】 5800
ㄌㄞˋ　lay lài
1. to rely on; to depend on
2. to accuse without grounds
or evidence; to put the
blame on somebody else
3. to repudiate (a debt); to disavow; to deny something
which one has said or done
4. to postpone or procrastinate
intentionally
5. no good; poor; bad
6. lazy
7. a Chinese family name

賴比瑞亞 (ㄌㄞˋ ㄅㄧˇ ㄖㄨㄟˋ ㄧㄚˋ)
Liberia

賴不掉 (ㄌㄞˋ ㄅㄨˋ ㄉㄧㄠˋ)
cannot be denied or re-
pudiated

賴皮 (ㄌㄞˋ ㄆㄧˊ)
① a person without any
sense of shame; a rogue ②
shameless: 這男孩真賴皮。
The boy is thoroughly shameless.

賴得一乾二淨 (ㄌㄞˋ ˙ㄉㄜ ㄧ ㄍㄢ ㄦˋ
ㄐㄧㄥ)
to deny or repudiate com-
pletely

賴婚 (ㄌㄞˋ ㄏㄨㄣ)
to break or repudiate a marriage contract

賴學 (ㄌㄞˋ ㄒㄩㄝˊ)
to play truant; to evade
study at school: 他又賴學了。
He played truant again.

賴債 (ㄌㄞˋ ㄓㄞˋ)
to repudiate a debt: 那商人賴
債。The merchant repudiated
a debt.

賴眼 (ㄌㄞˋ ㄓㄤˋ)
① to repudiate accounts ②
to go back on one's word: 他
老是賴賬。He goes back on
his word all the time.

賴人 (ㄌㄞˋ ㄖㄣˊ)
① to impute (a fault, etc.)
to another ② to rely on
somebody

賴子 (ㄌㄞˋ ˙ㄗ)
a rogue 亦作「無賴」

賴索托王國 (ㄌㄞˋ ㄙㄨㄛˇ ㄊㄨㄛ ㄨㄤˊ
ㄍㄨㄛˊ)
the Kingdom of Lesotho

賴以為生 (ㄌㄞˋ ㄧˇ ㄨㄟˊ ㄕㄥ)
to rely on something or
someone for a living

十畫

【賺】 5801
ㄓㄨㄢˋ　juann zhuàn
1. to earn; to make money; to
gain
2. to cheat; to deceive

賺頭 (兒) (ㄓㄨㄢˋ ˙ㄊㄡ—ㄦˋ)
something to gain; a profit:
這一行生意賺頭不大。The
profits in this business are
not large.

賺錢 (ㄓㄨㄢˋ ㄑㄧㄢˊ)
to earn money; to make a
profit: 他一天賺錢五千元。He
earns 5,000 dollars a day.

【賻】 5802
ㄈㄨˋ　fuh fù
to help another with money
in financing a funeral

賻錢 (ㄈㄨˋ ㄑㄧㄢˊ)
money for helping another
finance a funeral

賻贈 (ㄈㄨˋ ㄗㄥˋ)
donations to another for
financing a funeral

賻贈香儀 (ㄈㄨˋ ㄗㄥˋ ㄒㄧㄤ ㄧˊ)
to give incense money for
funeral expenses

賻儀 (ㄈㄨˋ ㄧˊ)
money presented to another

〔貝
部〕

〔貝部〕

for financing a funeral

【購】 5803
《ㄍㄡ gow gòu
to buy; to purchase

購備《ㄍㄡ ㄅㄟˋ
to purchase or buy before-hand (or in preparation)

購辦《ㄍㄡ ㄅㄢˋ
to purchase; to buy

購買《ㄍㄡ ㄇㄞˇ
to buy: 我為她購買一頂新帽子。I bought her a new hat.

購買力《ㄍㄡ ㄇㄞˇ ㄌㄧˋ
purchasing power

購買慾《ㄍㄡ ㄇㄞˇ ㄩˋ
the desire to buy

購料《ㄍㄡ ㄌㄧㄠˋ
to buy materials or supplies

購求《ㄍㄡ ㄑㄧㄡˊ
①to offer a reward for the arrest of a person ②to offer money for something which cannot be readily bought on the market, as antiques, rare objects, etc.

購置《ㄍㄡ ㄓˋ
to purchase; to buy

購物《ㄍㄡ ㄨˋ
to do one's shopping; to go shopping: 他和他太太出去購物。He went out shopping with his wife.

購用《ㄍㄡ ㄩˋ
to buy for use

【賽】 5804
ㄙㄞˋ say sài
1. to compete; to contest; to rival; to contend for superiority
2. a race; a tournament; a match; a game
3. to surpass
4. (now rarely) an ancient sacrifice
5. a Chinese family name

賽跑《ㄙㄞˋ ㄆㄠˇ
to run a race on foot; a foot race: 誰贏了賽跑? Who won the foot race?

賽普勒斯《ㄙㄞˋ ㄆㄨˇ ㄌㄜ ㄙ
Cyprus, an island republic in the Mediterranean

賽馬《ㄙㄞˋ ㄇㄚˇ
to race horses; a horse race

賽馬場《ㄙㄞˋ ㄇㄚˇ ㄔㄤˇ
a race course (or ground)

賽璐珞《ㄙㄞˋ ㄌㄨˋ ㄌㄨㄛˋ
celluloid

賽龍船《ㄙㄞˋ ㄌㄨㄥˊ ㄔㄨㄢˊ
a dragon-boat regatta (on Poets' Day)

賽狗《ㄙㄞˋ ㄍㄡˇ
to race dogs; a dog race

賽過《ㄙㄞˋ ㄍㄨㄛˋ
to surpass; to be better than

賽會《ㄙㄞˋ ㄏㄨㄟˋ
①a procession on a religious festival; a carnival ②an exhibition; a display; an exposition

賽金花《ㄙㄞˋ ㄐㄧㄣ ㄏㄨㄚ
Sai Chin-hua, a famous patriotic courtesan (1875-1937) who allegedly saved many civilian lives when China was invaded by eight powers in the wake of the Boxer Rebellion

賽球《ㄙㄞˋ ㄑㄧㄡˊ
a ball game

賽夏族《ㄙㄞˋ ㄒㄧㄚˋ ㄗㄨˊ
the Saishet tribe (one of the aborigine tribes in Taiwan)

賽珍珠《ㄙㄞˋ ㄓㄣ ㄓㄨ
Mrs. Pearl S. Buck (1892-1973), American authoress

賽車《ㄙㄞˋ ㄔㄜ
a car race; to race cars

賽神《ㄙㄞˋ ㄕㄣˊ
to offer sacrifices to thank gods

【膡】 5805
(剩) ㄕㄥˋ shenq shèng
1. a surplus; an overplus
2. remnants; remains; residues
3. superfluous

膡下《ㄕㄥˋ ㄒㄧㄚˋ
to leave behind; to be left over

膡餘《ㄕㄥˋ ㄩˊ
to leave in surplus; remnants

膡餘價值《ㄕㄥˋ ㄩˊ ㄐㄧㄚˋ ㄓˊ
surplus value

膡餘物資《ㄕㄥˋ ㄩˊ ㄨˋ ㄗ
a surplus; surplus goods

膡語《ㄕㄥˋ ㄩˇ
superfluous words

十一畫

【贄】 5806
ㄓˋ jyh zhì
1. presents given at the first meeting

2. gifts to a superior

贄見《ㄓˋ ㄐㄧㄢˋ
to bring gifts along and request an audience

贄禮《ㄓˋ ㄌㄧˇ
presents offered at calling on someone

贄敬《ㄓˋ ㄐㄧㄥˋ
money offered to a teacher or tutor

贄儀《ㄓˋ ㄧˊ
ceremonial presents; presents of homage

【贅】 5807
ㄓㄨㄟˋ juey zhuì
1. useless; superfluous; redundant
2. repetition; to repeat; repetitious
3. to follow around, as children
4. to be burdensome
5. to pawn things for money
6. to meet; to congregate
7. a son-in-law who takes the place of a son in his wife's parental family which is lacking for an heir

贅筆《ㄓㄨㄟˋ ㄅㄧˇ
a superfluous touch or stroke

贅瘤《ㄓㄨㄟˋ ㄌㄧㄡˊ
①a wen; an excrescence ②something useless or superfluous

贅及《ㄓㄨㄟˋ ㄐㄧˊ
①to add to ②to append to

贅婿 or 贅壻《ㄓㄨㄟˋ ㄒㄩˋ
a son-in-law who takes the place of a son and lives in his wife's home, usually an heirless family

贅述《ㄓㄨㄟˋ ㄕㄨˋ
a repetitious or superfluous statement; verbosity; redundance: 不必贅述。It's unnecessary to make a superfluous statement.

贅子《ㄓㄨㄟˋ ㄗˇ
(in ancient China) to sell one's son to another as a slave

贅詞《ㄓㄨㄟˋ ㄘˊ
repetitious or superfluous words; redundance

贅疣《ㄓㄨㄟˋ ㄧㄡˊ
a wen; an excrescence: 這只

是贅疣而已。This is merely a wen.

贅言（ㄓㄨㄟˋ　ㄧㄢˊ）
verbosity; repetitious or superfluous statements, words, etc.

十二畫

【贋】 5808
（贗）ㄧㄢˋ yann yàn
a counterfeit; a sham; a fake; bogus; spurious; forged

贋本（ㄧㄢˋㄅㄣˇ）
(said of paintings, rare editions of a book, etc.) an imitation; a phony; a sham; a fake: 牆上的畫是贋本。The painting on the wall is an imitation.

贋品（ㄧㄢˋㄆㄧㄣˇ）
a counterfeit; an imitation; a phony; a sham; a fake; a forgery

贋鼎（ㄧㄢˋㄉㄧㄥˇ）
a counterfeit; an imitation; a sham; a phony; a fake—from the story of a fake tripod sent by a kingdom as a tribute to another kingdom

【贈】 5809
ㄗㄥˋ tzenq zèng
to send (gifts); to confer or bestow (titles); to give

贈別（ㄗㄥˋㄅㄧㄝˊ）
to wish (a leaving person) well with gifts or writings

贈品（ㄗㄥˋㄆㄧㄣˇ）
a gift; a present

贈賻（ㄗㄥˋㄈㄨˋ）
to contribute to funeral expenses

贈答（ㄗㄥˋㄉㄚˊ）
to present each other with gifts, poems, etc.

贈給（ㄗㄥˋㄍㄟˇ）
to present; to confer; to bestow; to give; to donate: 我贈給她一本金集郵冊。I presented an album to her.

贈款（ㄗㄥˋㄎㄨㄢˇ）
to present money as a gift; a grant

贈金（ㄗㄥˋㄐㄧㄣ）
to give a cash gift; a cash gift

贈券（ㄗㄥˋㄑㄩㄢˋ）
a gift coupon

贈序（ㄗㄥˋㄒㄩˋ）
a farewell message for a departing person

贈送（ㄗㄥˋㄙㄨㄥˋ）
to present; to give; to donate

贈言（ㄗㄥˋㄧㄢˊ）
words of advice

贈遺（ㄗㄥˋㄨㄟˊ）
to present; to give; to donate; to bequeath

贈與（ㄗㄥˋㄩˇ）
to present; to give; to donate

贈閱（ㄗㄥˋㄩㄝˋ）
(said of publications) given free of charge; given as a compliment of the publisher or author

【賾】 5810
ㄗㄜˊ tzer zé
deep; profound; abstruse

【贊】 5811
ㄗㄢˋ tzann zàn
1. to assist; to aid; to help; to support; to back
2. to praise; to commend; to exalt; to glorify; to extol; to eulogize

贊不絕口（ㄗㄢˋㄅㄨˋㄐㄩㄝˊㄎㄡˇ）
to praise profusely; to heap praises on...

贊美（ㄗㄢˋㄇㄟˇ）
to praise; to extol; to exalt; to glorify

贊歎（ㄗㄢˋㄊㄢˋ）
to exclaim in praise; to gasp with admiration

贊同（ㄗㄢˋㄊㄨㄥˊ）
to consent to; to approve of; to agree; to endorse: 我贊同你的看法。I agree with you.

贊理（ㄗㄢˋㄌㄧˇ）
to help manage

贊禮（ㄗㄢˋㄌㄧˇ）
①to direct the proceeding (as the master of ceremonies) ②the master of ceremonies (a government post in ancient times)

贊襄（ㄗㄢˋㄒㄧㄤ）
to assist; to aid: 我以金錢贊襄他。I aid him with money.

贊贊（ㄗㄢˋㄗㄢˋ）
a message dedicated to a deity

贊許（ㄗㄢˋㄒㄩˇ）
to approve of: 新歌劇大受贊

許。The new opera is highly approved of.

贊助（ㄗㄢˋㄓㄨˋ）
to sponsor; to patronize; support

贊助人（ㄗㄢˋㄓㄨˋㄖㄣˊ）
a patron; a sponsor

贊成（ㄗㄢˋㄔㄥˊ）
to agree to; to be in favor of; to approve; to support: 他立刻贊成這計劃。He agreed to this plan immediately.

贊賞（ㄗㄢˋㄕㄤˇ）
to commend; to praise; to extol; to admire

贊襄（ㄗㄢˋㄒㄧㄤ）
to assist; to aid

贊揚（ㄗㄢˋㄧㄤˊ）
to exalt; to glorify; to extol; to praise; to commend; commendation: 他們贊揚他的勇敢。They exalted his bravery.

【贇】 5812
ㄩㄣ iun yūn
fine; pleasant; agreeable

十三畫

【贍】 5813
ㄕㄢˋ shann shàn
1. to provide; to supply
2. abundance; plenty; adequate

贍恤（ㄕㄢˋㄒㄩˋ）
to contribute money to charity

贍足（ㄕㄢˋㄗㄨˊ）
abundant; plenty

贍養（ㄕㄢˋㄧㄤˇ）
to provide with means of support; to support: 他工作以贍養家小。He is working to support his family.

贍養費（ㄕㄢˋㄧㄤˇㄈㄟˋ）
alimony

贍養父母（ㄕㄢˋㄧㄤˇㄈㄨˋㄇㄨˇ）
to support one's parents

【贏】 5814
ㄧㄥˊ yng yíng
1. to win; to beat
2. profits

贏得（ㄧㄥˊㄉㄜˊ）
to win (honor, a privilege, etc.)

贏利（ㄧㄥˊㄌㄧˋ）
profits; gains: 這一行贏利不大。The profits in this busi-

〔貝部〕

〔赤
部〕

ness are not large.
贏家（ㄌㄧㄥˊㄐㄧㄚ）
the winner
贏錢（ㄌㄧㄥˊㄑㄧㄢˊ）
to win money by gambling

十四畫

【贓】 5815
ㄗㄤ tzang zāng
1. bribes; to bribe
2. stolen goods; loot; booty;
plunder; spoils
贓品（ㄗㄤ ㄆㄧㄣˇ）
stolen goods; plunder; loot;
booty: 強盜在分配贓品。The
robbers share the plunder.
贓官（ㄗㄤ ㄍㄨㄢ）
a corrupt official
贓款（ㄗㄤ ㄎㄨㄢˇ）
money acquired illicitly
贓證（ㄗㄤ ㄓㄥˋ）
plunder as evidence of theft
or graft
贓物（ㄗㄤ ㄨˋ）
stolen goods; plunder; booty;
loot; spoils; goods obtained
illicitly

【贐】 5816
ㄐㄧㄣˋ jinn jìn
a farewell present
贐儀（ㄐㄧㄣˋ ㄧˊ）
a farewell present

【賢】 5817
（賢）ㄒㄧㄢˊ shyan xián
wise; sagacious

十五畫

【贖】 5818
ㄕㄨˊ shwu shú
1. to redeem; to ransom
2. (now rarely) to buy
3. to atone for; to expiate
贖命（ㄕㄨˊ ㄇㄧㄥˋ）
to save one from death penalty by a payment
贖當（ㄕㄨˊ ㄉㄤ）
to redeem pawned articles
贖款（ㄕㄨˊ ㄎㄨㄢˇ）
a ransom
贖回（ㄕㄨˊ ㄏㄨㄟˊ）
to recover by paying money;
to redeem; to ransom: 他贖回
抵押品。He redeemed his
mortgage.
贖金（ㄕㄨˊ ㄐㄧㄣ）or 贖價（ㄕㄨˊ ㄐㄧㄚˋ）

a ransom
贖刑（ㄕㄨˊ ㄒㄧㄥˊ）
to buy freedom from punishment
贖出（ㄕㄨˊ ㄔㄨ）
to get back from pawn; to
redeem
贖身（ㄕㄨˊ ㄕㄣ）
to buy freedom (from slavery, prostitution, captivity,
etc.)
贖罪（ㄕㄨˊ ㄗㄨㄟˋ）
① to atone for a sin; to
expiate a sin② to buy freedom from punishment ③
(Christianity) redemption
贖罪券（ㄕㄨˊ ㄗㄨㄟˋ ㄑㄩㄢˋ）
papal indulgence (proclaimed
by Pope Leo X)

【贗】 5819
（贗）ㄧㄢˋ yann yàn
counterfeit; bogus

十七畫

【贛】 5820
《ㄢˋ gann gàn
1. an alternative name of
Kiangsi Province
2. a river in Kiangsi Province
3. a county in Kiangsi Province
贛江（《ㄢˋ ㄐㄧㄤ）
Kan River in Kiangsi
Province
贛縣（《ㄢˋ ㄒㄧㄢˋ）
name of a county in Kiangsi Province

赤 部
ㄔˋ chyh chì

【赤】 5821
ㄔˋ chyh chì
1. red
2. bare; naked
3. sincere; loyal; single-hearted
赤膊（ㄔˋㄅㄛˊ）or 赤背（ㄔˋㄅㄟˋ）
with the upper half of the
body bared; naked to the
waist
赤壁（ㄔˋㄅㄧˋ）
the Red Cliff (name of a
cliff in Hupeh over the Yang-

tze River made famous by a
major battle during the
Epoch of the Three King-
doms, and by a number of
literary works)
赤壁之戰（ㄔˋㄅㄧˋㄓ ㄓㄢˋ）
a major battle fought at the
Red Cliff (赤壁) during the
Epoch of the Three King-
doms
赤貧（ㄔˋ ㄆㄧㄣˊ）
extreme poverty; abject poverty; utterly destitute
赤貧如洗（ㄔˋㄆㄧㄣˊ ㄖㄨˊ ㄒㄧˇ）
in extreme poverty
赤眉（ㄔˋ ㄇㄟˊ）
a party of bandits rampant
toward the end of the Western Han Dynasty (206 B.C.—
8 A.D.)
赤道（ㄔˋ ㄉㄠˋ）
① the equator ②(astron-
omy) the celestial equator
赤道儀（ㄔˋ ㄉㄠˋ ㄧˊ）
an equatorial
赤膽（ㄔˋ ㄉㄢˇ）
sincere loyalty
赤膽忠心（ㄔˋ ㄉㄢˇ ㄓㄨㄥ ㄒㄧㄣ）
utter devotion
赤黨（ㄔˋ ㄉㄤˇ）
the Communist Party 亦作
「共產黨」
赤帝（ㄔˋ ㄉㄧˋ）
the god of the south
赤地千里（ㄔˋㄉㄧˋ ㄑㄧㄢ ㄌㄧˇ）
barren land extending over
thousands of miles
赤塔（ㄔˋ ㄊㄚˇ）
Chita, a city in Siberia
赤鐵礦（ㄔˋ ㄊㄧㄝˇ ㄎㄨㄤˋ）
hematite
赤條條（ㄔˋ ㄊㄧㄠˊ ㄊㄧㄠˊ）
stark naked
赤條精光（ㄔˋ ㄊㄧㄠˊ ㄐㄧㄥ 《ㄨㄤ）
stark naked
赤土（ㄔˋ ㄊㄨˇ）
land made barren by severe
drought
赤兔（ㄔˋ ㄊㄨˋ）
name of a renowned swift
horse
赤銅（ㄔˋ ㄊㄨㄥˊ）
the alloy of copper and gold
赤銅礦（ㄔˋ ㄊㄨㄥˊ ㄎㄨㄤˋ）
cuprite
赤銅器時代（ㄔˋ ㄊㄨㄥˊ ㄑㄧˋ ㄕˊ ㄉㄞˋ）

the Bronze Age

赤痢 (ㄔˋ ㄌ丨ˋ)
dysentery characterized by blood in the stool

赤燐 (ㄔˋ ㄌ丨ㄣˊ)
red phosphorus

赤裸裸 (ㄔˋ ㄌㄨㄛˇ ㄌㄨㄛˇ)
① stark naked; naked ② frank; plain; unadorned: 這事件是個赤裸裸的事實。The matter is a plain truth.

赤口白舌 (ㄔˋ ㄎㄡˇ ㄅㄞˊ ㄕˊ)
inauspicious remarks; unlucky words

赤口毒舌 (ㄔˋ ㄎㄡˇ ㄉㄨˊ ㄕˊ)
① a sharp tongue ② to slander venomously

赤崁樓 (ㄔˋ ㄎㄢˇ ㄌㄡˊ)
Fort Providentia (at Tainan, Taiwan, from which the Dutch ruled Taiwan till they were ousted by Koxinga, 國姓爺 or 鄭成功, in the 17th century)

赤化 (ㄔˋ ㄏㄨㄚˋ)
to sovietize; to communize: 越南被赤化了。Vietnam was communized.

赤禍 (ㄔˋ ㄏㄨㄛˋ)
the calamities brought about by Communism

赤腳 (ㄔˋ ㄐ丨ㄠˇ)
① bare feet ② barefooted

赤腳大仙 (ㄔˋ ㄐ丨ㄠˇ ㄉㄚˋ ㄒ丨ㄢ)
the barefooted immortal, a reference to Emperor Jen Tzung (仁宗) of the Northern Sung Dynasty

赤金 (ㄔˋ ㄐ丨ㄣ)
① deep-colored gold ② copper

赤經 (ㄔˋ ㄐ丨ㄥ)
(astronomy) right ascension

赤鉛礦 (ㄔˋ ㄑ丨ㄢ ㄎㄨㄤˋ)
crocoite

赤血球 (ㄔˋ ㄒ丨ㄝˋ ㄑ丨ㄡˊ)
red blood cells; red blood corpuscles; erythrocytes

赤縣神州 (ㄔˋ ㄒ丨ㄢˋ ㄕㄣˊ ㄓㄡ)
China (an ancient name)

赤心 (ㄔˋ ㄒ丨ㄣ)
sincere loyalty

赤墀 (ㄔˋ ㄔˊ)
(in a Chinese palace-style building) the yard between the main hall and the steps

赤城 (ㄔˋ ㄔㄥˊ)

name of a county in Chahar Province

赤誠 (ㄔˋ ㄔㄥˊ)
sincerity; loyal; upright

赤誠待人 (ㄔˋ ㄔㄥˊ ㄉㄞˋ ㄖㄣˊ)
to treat people with absolute sincerity

赤舌燒城 (ㄔˋ ㄕˊ ㄕㄠ ㄔㄥˊ)
A slanderous tongue can burn up a city.

赤手 (ㄔˋ ㄕㄡˇ) or 赤手空拳 (ㄔˋ ㄕㄡˇ)
① bare hands ② barehanded

赤身露體 (ㄔˋ ㄕㄣ ㄌㄨˋ ㄊ丨ˇ)
stark naked

赤繩繫足 (ㄔˋ ㄕㄥˊ ㄒ丨ˋ ㄗㄨˊ)
to bind the feet with a red rope—to be united in wedlock

赤日 (ㄔˋ ㄖˋ)
the burning sun; the scorching sun

赤子 (ㄔˋ ㄗˇ)
① a newborn baby; an infant ② (figuratively) a ruler's subjects

赤子之心 (ㄔˋ ㄗˇ ㄓ ㄒ丨ㄣ)
(literally) a child's heart—man's natural kindness

赤字 (ㄔˋ ㄗˋ)
the red (in bookkeeping); a deficit; a loss

赤幘 (ㄔˋ ㄗㄜˊ)
cloth for binding the hair used by military officers in ancient times

赤足 (ㄔˋ ㄗㄨˊ)
① barefooted ② bare feet 參看「赤腳」: 我看到他赤足跑步。I saw him running with bare feet.

赤色 (ㄔˋ ㄙㄜˋ)
Red; Communist; Bolshevist

赤色分子 (ㄔˋ ㄙㄜˋ ㄈㄣ ㄗˇ)
Communists; Radicals

赤色國際 (ㄔˋ ㄙㄜˋ ㄍㄨㄛˊ ㄐ丨ˋ)
the Third International

赤素馨 (ㄔˋ ㄙㄨˋ ㄒ丨ㄣ)
frangipani

赤俄 (ㄔˋ ㄜˊ) or 赤(ㄔˋ)
Soviet Russia

赤楊 (ㄔˋ 丨ㄤˊ)
an alder

赤外線 (ㄔˋ ㄨㄞˋ ㄒ丨ㄢˋ)
infrared rays

赤緯 (ㄔˋ ㄨㄟˇ)

(astronomy) declination

四畫

【赦】 5822
ㄕㄜˋ sheh shè
to pardon; to excuse; to forgive; to amnesty; an amnesty

赦免 (ㄕㄜˋ ㄇ丨ㄢˇ)
to pardon (an offender)

赦過 (ㄕㄜˋ ㄍㄨㄛˋ)
to pardon a fault

赦書 (ㄕㄜˋ ㄕㄨ)
(written) orders of pardon or amnesty

赦罪 (ㄕㄜˋ ㄗㄨㄟˋ)
to pardon (a criminal); to forgive (an offender)

赦宥 (ㄕㄜˋ 丨ㄡˋ)
to pardon; pardon

五畫

【赧】 5823
ㄋㄢˇ naan nǎn
to turn red from shame or embarrassment; to blush

赧愧 (ㄋㄢˇ ㄎㄨㄟˋ)
to blush; to be ashamed: 我深感慚愧。I feel deeply ashamed.

赧然 (ㄋㄢˇ ㄖㄢˊ)
ashamed; blushing

赧顏 (ㄋㄢˇ 丨ㄢˊ)
blushing; shamefaced

七畫

【赫】 5824
ㄏㄜˋ heh hè
1. bright; glowing
2. brilliant; glorious
3. angry; indignant
4. a Chinese family name

赫怒 (ㄏㄜˋ ㄋㄨˋ)
angry; furious

赫赫 (ㄏㄜˋ ㄏㄜˋ)
① brilliant; bright; glorious ② arid; dry ③ awe-inspiring

赫赫有名 (ㄏㄜˋ ㄏㄜˋ 丨ㄡˇ ㄇ丨ㄥˊ)
illustrious; far-famed

赫胥黎 (ㄏㄜˋ ㄒㄩ ㄌ丨ˊ)
Thomas Henry Huxley, 1825-1895, British biologist-philosopher

赫咺 (ㄏㄜˋ ㄒㄩㄢ) or 赫烜 (ㄏㄜˋ ㄒㄩㄢ)

【走部】

brilliant and distinguished

赫咤（ㄏㄜˋ ㄓㄚˋ）
angry; indignant

赫哲（ㄏㄜˋ ㄓㄜˊ）or 赫哲族（ㄏㄜˋ ㄓㄜˊ ㄗㄨˊ）
name of a border tribe in Manchuria

赫然（ㄏㄜˋ ㄖㄢˊ）
① looking angry; in flaming anger: 他勃然震怒。He is in flaming anger. ② astonishing; shocking; consternation

赫爾辛基（ㄏㄜˋ ㄦˇ ㄒㄧㄣ ㄐㄧ）
Helsinki, capital of Finland

赫奕（ㄏㄜˋ ㄧˋ）
bright; glorious; magnificent

九畫

【赭】 5825
ㄓㄜˇ jee zhě
1. red
2. ocher

赭面（ㄓㄜˇ ㄇㄧㄢˋ）
to dye the face red

赭黃（ㄓㄜˇ ㄏㄨㄤˊ）
yellow ocher

赭石（ㄓㄜˇ ㄕˊ）
(mineral) ocher

赭衣（ㄓㄜˇ ㄧ）
red dress worn by convicts in ancient times

【赬】 5826
ㄔㄥ cheng chēng

赬尾（ㄔㄥ ㄨㄟˇ）
the toils of a gentleman

走 部
ㄗㄡˇ tzoou zǒu

【走】 5827
ㄗㄡˇ tzoou zǒu
1. to walk; to go on foot
2. to run; to go swiftly
3. to go; to travel
4. to leave; to go away; to depart
5. to let out or lose (unintentionally); to leak out
6. to visit

走背運（ㄗㄡˇ ㄅㄟˋ ㄩㄣˋ）
to suffer from a spell of bad

luck

走板（ㄗㄡˇ ㄅㄢˇ）
to sing out of rhythm

走筆疾書（ㄗㄡˇ ㄅㄧˇ ㄐㄧˊ ㄕㄨ）
to write swiftly

走避（ㄗㄡˇ ㄅㄧˋ）
to run away from; to evade; to shun

走邊（ㄗㄡˇ ㄅㄧㄢ）
(Peking opera) to move in supposed darkness such as stealing, peeping, etc.

走遍（ㄗㄡˇ ㄅㄧㄢˋ）
to travel all over (an area)

走不得（ㄗㄡˇ ㄅㄨˋ ㄉㄜˊ）
①(said of a way, road, path, etc.) unfit to travel; not safe to travel ②(said of a person) not entitled to leave; not allowed to leave; should not leave—indispensable

走不到（ㄗㄡˇ ㄅㄨˋ ㄉㄠˋ）
unable to walk as far as; unable to travel as far as; unable to go as far as

走不動（ㄗㄡˇ ㄅㄨˋ ㄉㄨㄥˋ）
too tired to walk

走不了（ㄗㄡˇ ㄅㄨˋ ㄌㄧㄠˇ）
not likely to leave; not able to leave

走不過去（ㄗㄡˇ ㄅㄨˋ ㄍㄨㄛˋ ㄑㄩˋ）
not able to go over

走不開（ㄗㄡˇ ㄅㄨˋ ㄎㄞ）
not able to leave; not able to get away

走馬（ㄗㄡˇ ㄇㄚˇ）
① to go swiftly on horseback; to ride swiftly ② an ambling horse

走馬燈（ㄗㄡˇ ㄇㄚˇ ㄉㄥ）
a lantern adorned with a revolving circle of paper horses

走馬看花（ㄗㄡˇ ㄇㄚˇ ㄎㄢˋ ㄏㄨㄚ）
(literally) to view flowers from the back of a galloping horse—to examine a thing hurriedly

走馬上任（ㄗㄡˇ ㄇㄚˇ ㄕㄤˋ ㄖㄣˋ）
to travel to a place for a new post

走門路（ㄗㄡˇ ㄇㄣˊ ㄌㄨˋ）
to approach men of influence in seeking an objective

走方步（ㄗㄡˇ ㄈㄤ ㄅㄨˋ）
to exercise caution; to be prudent

走訪（ㄗㄡˇ ㄈㄤˇ）
① to interview; to have an interview with ② to visit; to go and see

走風（ㄗㄡˇ ㄈㄥ）
(said of a secret plan, etc.) to leak out; to become known

走得慢（ㄗㄡˇ ㄉㄜˊ ㄇㄢˋ）
to walk slowly; to go slowly

走得快（ㄗㄡˇ ㄉㄜˊ ㄎㄨㄞˋ）
to walk fast; to go fast

走道（ㄗㄡˇ ㄉㄠˋ）
① a pavement; a sidewalk ② a path; a footpath ③ an aisle

走調兒（ㄗㄡˇ ㄉㄧㄠˋ ㄦ）
out of tune

走電（ㄗㄡˇ ㄉㄧㄢˋ）
electric power leakage

走讀（ㄗㄡˇ ㄉㄨˊ）
to live outside the school that one attends

走讀生（ㄗㄡˇ ㄉㄨˊ ㄕㄥ）
nonresident students (as distinct from boarding students)

走動（ㄗㄡˇ ㄉㄨㄥˋ）or 走動走動（ㄗㄡˇ ㄉㄨㄥˋ ㄗㄡˇ ㄉㄨㄥˋ）
① to take a walk; to go for a stroll ② to have intercourse; to visit

走投無路（ㄗㄡˇ ㄊㄡˊ ㄨˊ ㄌㄨˋ）
to have no one to turn to; to have no way out; to drive to the wall; in a tight corner: 他被逼得走投無路。He was driven to the wall

走堂（ㄗㄡˇ ㄊㄤˊ）
a waiter

走內線（ㄗㄡˇ ㄋㄟˋ ㄒㄧㄢˋ）
to go through the back door (to achieve one's own goal); to curry favor with the wife of one's boss

走南闖北（ㄗㄡˇ ㄋㄢˊ ㄔㄨㄤˇ ㄅㄟˇ）
to travel everywhere

走來走去（ㄗㄡˇ ㄌㄞˊ ㄗㄡˇ ㄑㄩˋ）
to walk back and forth; to pace in anxiety

走漏（ㄗㄡˇ ㄌㄡˋ）
(said of secrets, plots, etc.) to leak

走漏消息（ㄗㄡˇ ㄌㄡˋ ㄒㄧㄠ ㄒㄧ）
to divulge secrets

走廊（ㄗㄡˇ ㄌㄤˊ）
a corridor; a hall; a veran-

da

走路(ㄗㄡ ㄌㄨˋ)
to walk; to go on foot: 我寧
可走路而不搭公車。I would
rather go on foot than by
bus.

走狗(ㄗㄡ ㄍㄡˇ)
a lackey; a tool

走光(ㄗㄡ ㄍㄨㄤ)
①(said of a place) to be
completely deserted; everyone walking away ②(said
of photographic film) ex-
posed accidentally

走開(ㄗㄡ ㄎㄞ)
Beat it! 或 Get out of the
way!

走好運(ㄗㄡ ㄏㄠˇ ㄩㄣˋ)
to enjoy a spell of good luck

走候(ㄗㄡ ㄏㄡˋ)
to call at a person's house
and inquire after him

走後門(ㄗㄡ ㄏㄡˋ ㄇㄣˊ)
to get in by the back door;
to secure advantages through
pull or influence

走話(ㄗㄡ ㄏㄨㄚˋ)
to divulge secrets

走火(ㄗㄡ ㄏㄨㄛˇ)
①(said of firearms) to go
off accidentally; 槍走火
火。The gun went off ac-
cidentally. ②(electricity) a
short circuit ③to go too
far in what one says; to put
something too strongly; to
overstate

走火入魔(ㄗㄡ ㄏㄨㄛˇ ㄖㄨˋ ㄇㄛˊ)
to be obsessed with some-
thing

走紅運(ㄗㄡ ㄏㄨㄥˊ ㄩㄣˋ)
to enjoy a spell of good luck
亦作「走好運」

走江湖
①(ㄗㄡ ㄐㄧㄤ ㄏㄨˊ) to live in
seclusion
②(ㄗㄡ ㄐㄧㄤ ·ㄏㄨ) to wander
from place to place to make
a living by performing acro-
batics

走氣(ㄗㄡ ㄑㄧˋ)
(said of spirits, perfume,
etc.) to lose flavor, fragrance, etc.

走向(ㄗㄡ ㄒㄧㄤˋ)
①the run; the trend ②(geology) strike ③to move

toward; to head for; to be
on the way to

走著瞧(ㄗㄡ ·ㄓㄜ ㄑㄧㄠˊ)
to wait and see

走失(ㄗㄡ ㄕ)
(said of persons, animals,
etc.) to get lost; to be
missing; to wander away

走獸(ㄗㄡ ㄕㄡˋ)
beasts; quadrupeds

走走(ㄗㄡ ·ㄗㄡ)
to take a walk; to take an
airing: 我們到公園走走。Let's
take a walk in the park.

走卒(ㄗㄡ ㄗㄨˊ)
a servant assigned exclusively to run errands

走嘴(ㄗㄡ ㄗㄨㄟˇ)
to let out a secret by careless speech; to make a slip
of the tongue

走私(ㄗㄡ ㄙ)
to engage in smuggling; to
smuggle; smuggling

走散(ㄗㄡ ㄙㄢˋ)
①to walk away in different
directions ②to get separated
from other travelers

走索(ㄗㄡ ㄙㄨㄛˇ)
to walk the rope

走一步看一步(ㄗㄡ ㄧˋ ㄅㄨˋ ㄎㄢˋ ㄧˋ ㄅㄨˋ)
to take one step and look
around before taking another
—to proceed without a plan,
or with caution

走樣(ㄗㄡ ㄧㄤˋ)
①to get out of shape; to
lose shape; to deviate from
the original ②to be different from what is expected
or intended

走味兒(ㄗㄡ ㄨㄟˋㄦ)
to turn stale; to lose flavor:
烟草已經走味兒了。The to-
bacco has lost its flavor.

走運(ㄗㄡ ㄩㄣˋ)
to be enjoying good luck; to
be in luck; to have good
luck

二畫

【赳】　5828
ㄐㄧㄡˇ jeou jiu
(又讀 ㄐㄧㄡ jiou
jiū)

valiant; gallant

赳赳(ㄐㄧㄡˇ ㄐㄧㄡˇ)
valiant; gallant; stalwart

【赴】　5829
ㄈㄨˋ fuh fù
to go to; to proceed to

赴敵(ㄈㄨˋ ㄉㄧˊ)
to go forward to fight the
enemy

赴湯蹈火(ㄈㄨˋ ㄊㄤ ㄉㄠˋ ㄏㄨㄛˇ)
to go through fire and
water; to defy all difficulties
and dangers

赴難(ㄈㄨˋ ㄋㄢˋ)
to serve the nation in a crisis

赴考(ㄈㄨˋ ㄎㄠˇ)or 赴試(ㄈㄨˋ ㄕˋ)
to proceed to take an examination; to leave for an
examination

赴會(ㄈㄨˋ ㄏㄨㄟˋ)
to go to a meeting

赴席(ㄈㄨˋ ㄒㄧˊ)
to go to a banquet

赴任(ㄈㄨˋ ㄖㄣˋ)
to proceed to one's new post

赴宴(ㄈㄨˋ ㄧㄢˋ)
to go to a banquet; to attend
a banquet

赴約(ㄈㄨˋ ㄩㄝ)
to leave for an engagement

三畫

【起】　5830
ㄑㄧˇ chii qǐ
1. to begin; to start
2. to rise; to get up; to stand
up; to go up
3. to happen; to take place
4. to unfold; to uncover
5. to build; to establish
6. a numeracy adjunct for incidents

起兵(ㄑㄧˇ ㄅㄧㄥ)
to rise in arms; to start a
military action

起不來(ㄑㄧˇ ·ㄅㄨ ㄌㄞˊ)
unable to get up; unable to
stand up; unable to rise

起泡(ㄑㄧˇ ㄆㄠˋ)
①to get blisters ②to form
bubbles

起碼(ㄑㄧˇ ㄇㄚˇ)
at least

起錨(ㄑㄧˇ ㄇㄠˊ)
to weigh anchor

〔走
部〕

〔走部〕

起錨機(ㄑㄧˇ ㄇㄠˊ ㄐㄧ)
a windlass; a capstan

起名字(ㄑㄧˇ ㄇㄧㄥˊ ㄗˋ)or 起名兒(ㄑㄧˇ ㄇㄧㄥˊ ㄦ)
to name; to give a name

起飛(ㄑㄧˇ ㄈㄟ)
to take off; a takeoff

起風(ㄑㄧˇ ㄈㄥ)
to get windy

起伏(ㄑㄧˇ ㄈㄨˊ)
① to undulate; undulation；ups and downs; the rise and fall: 人生起伏良多。Life is full of ups and downs.

起點(ㄑㄧˇ ㄉㄧㄢˇ)
a starting point

起電盤(ㄑㄧˇ ㄉㄧㄢˋ ㄆㄢˊ)
an electrophorus

起電機(ㄑㄧˇ ㄉㄧㄢˋ ㄐㄧ)
an electric machine

起端(ㄑㄧˇ ㄉㄨㄢ)
the origin; the beginning; the genesis

起動(ㄑㄧˇ ㄉㄨㄥˋ)
to start (a machine, etc.): 那引擎終於起動了。The engine started at last.

起頭(ㄑㄧˇ ㄊㄡˊ)or 起頭兒(ㄑㄧˇ ㄊㄡˊ ㄦ)
① the origin; the beginning ② at first; in the beginning: 萬事起頭難。Everything is difficult in the beginning.

起跳(ㄑㄧˇ ㄊㄧㄠˋ)
(sports) to take off

起來
①(ㄑㄧˇ ㄌㄞ) ⓐ to stand up; to sit up; to rise: 她從椅子站起來。She rose from her chair. ⓑ to get up
②(ㄑㄧˇ ·ㄌㄞ) an adverbial phrase used after a verb denoting that an action is taking place: 天氣漸漸暖和起來了。The weather is getting warm.

起立(ㄑㄧˇ ㄌㄧˋ)
to stand up

起落(ㄑㄧˇ ㄌㄨㄛˋ)
rising and falling

起稿(ㄑㄧˇ ㄍㄠˇ)
to prepare a draft

起工(ㄑㄧˇ ㄍㄨㄥ)
to start work

起火(ㄑㄧˇ ㄏㄨㄛˇ)
① to catch fire; to be on fire

② to lose one's temper ③ to cook meals

起貨(ㄑㄧˇ ㄏㄨㄛˋ)
to take goods (from a warehouse)

起閧 or 起鬨(ㄑㄧˇ ㄏㄨㄥˋ)
to create disturbances; to boo; to hoot: 聽衆起閧把演講者轟下台。The audience hooted the speaker down.

起家(ㄑㄧˇ ㄐㄧㄚ)
① the early background of a successful person ② to establish oneself in the world; to carve out a career

起價(ㄑㄧˇ ㄐㄧㄚˋ)
to raise the price; price soaring

起解(ㄑㄧˇ ㄐㄧㄝˋ)
to pack off (a captive); to transfer (a prisoner) under escort

起轎(ㄑㄧˇ ㄐㄧㄠˋ)
to set out in a sedan chair

起見(ㄑㄧˇ ㄐㄧㄢˋ)
in view of; with a view to; with the view of; for the sake of; for the purpose of; in order to

起勁(ㄑㄧˇ ㄐㄧㄣˋ)
(said of actions, performances, etc.) showing much zeal; eager; energetic; vigorous; enthusiastic; with gusto

起講(ㄑㄧˇ ㄐㄧㄤˇ)
(in the stereotyped style of compositions written in civil service examinations under the former system) the introductory passage

起敬(ㄑㄧˇ ㄐㄧㄥˋ)
to show respect

起居(ㄑㄧˇ ㄐㄩ)
rising up and sitting down—one's everyday life at home

起居注(ㄑㄧˇ ㄐㄩ ㄓㄨˋ)
① an official in charge of the emperor's daily life ② the record of the emperor's daily activities

起句(ㄑㄧˇ ㄐㄩˋ)
the opening line (of a poem)

起訖(ㄑㄧˇ ㄑㄧˋ)
the beginning and the end

起息(ㄑㄧˇ ㄒㄧˊ)
① to get up (in the morn-

ing) and retire (in the night) ② to start bearing interest

起先(ㄑㄧˇ ㄒㄧㄢ)
at first; in the beginning 參看起初]: 起先沒人相信我。No one believe me at first.

起釁(ㄑㄧˇ ㄒㄧㄣˋ)
to start a feud; to provoke a fight

起行(ㄑㄧˇ ㄒㄧㄥˊ)
to set out; to start on a journey

起止(ㄑㄧˇ ㄓˇ)
the beginning and the end

起縐(ㄑㄧˇ ㄓㄡˋ)
to wrinkle; to crumple: 這種布容易起縐。This cloth crumples easily.

起重螺旋(ㄑㄧˇ ㄓㄨㄥˋ ㄌㄨㄛˊ ㄒㄩㄢˊ)
a jackscrew

起重機(ㄑㄧˇ ㄓㄨㄥˋ ㄐㄧ)
a crane (for lifting or moving heavy objects); a derrick

起程(ㄑㄧˇ ㄔㄥˊ)
to start on a journey; to set out

起承轉合(ㄑㄧˇ ㄔㄥˊ ㄓㄨㄢˇ ㄏㄜˊ)
the introduction, the follow-up, the transition and the conclusion (formerly accepted as the four cardinal steps of composition)

起初(ㄑㄧˇ ㄔㄨ)
at first; in the beginning; originally 參看「起先」: 那個花園起初很小。That garden was originally very small.

起牀(ㄑㄧˇ ㄔㄨㄤˊ)
to get out of bed; to get up; to rise

起牀號(ㄑㄧˇ ㄔㄨㄤˊ ㄏㄠˋ)
the reveille

起始(ㄑㄧˇ ㄕˇ)
the beginning; the start; the outset

起誓(ㄑㄧˇ ㄕˋ)
to take an oath; to swear

起事(ㄑㄧˇ ㄕˋ)
to rise in arms; to rise in revolt

起手(ㄑㄧˇ ㄕㄡˇ)
to start an action

起首(ㄑㄧˇ ㄕㄡˇ)
the beginning

起身(ㄑㄧˇ ㄕㄣ)
① to start on a journey; to

set out; to leave; to get off
②to get out of bed; to get
up

起身炮(ㄑㄧˇ ㄕㄣ ㄆㄠˋ)
appointments or promotions
made (by a ranking official)
right before leaving a post

起子(ㄑㄧˇ ˙ㄗ)
①(dialect) baking powder;
leaven ②(dialect) a screwdriver ③a bottle opener

起早睡晚(ㄑㄧˇ ㄗㄠˇ ㄈㄨㄟˋ ㄨㄢˇ)
to get up early and to go to
bed late

起贓(ㄑㄧˇ ㄗㄤ)
to recover stolen articles

起租(ㄑㄧˇ ㄗㄨ)
(said of a lease contract) to
enter into force; to start
paying rent (from a date)

起坐(兒)(ㄑㄧˇ ㄗㄨㄛˋㄦ)
to rise from one's seat as
form of respect

起作用(ㄑㄧˇ ㄗㄨㄛˋ ㄩㄥˋ)
(said of an effect) to tell; to
show effect

起草(ㄑㄧˇ ㄘㄠˇ)
to prepare a draft; to draft:
他起草議院的議案。He drafts
a parliamentary bill.

起死回生(ㄑㄧˇ ㄙˇ ㄏㄨㄟˊ ㄕㄥ)
to revive the dead; to come
back to life

起色(ㄑㄧˇ ㄙㄜˋ)
①a sign of improvement ②
a sign of recovery; to make
a quick recovery

起訴(ㄑㄧˇ ㄙㄨˋ)
(said of a prosecutor) to file
a formal indictment; to indict; to sue; to prosecute

起訴人(ㄑㄧˇ ㄙㄨˋ ㄖㄣˊ)
a prosecutor

起算(ㄑㄧˇ ㄙㄨㄢˋ)
to start counting (the number of days, hours, etc., in a
period or term) from a
given point

起疑(ㄑㄧˇ ㄧˊ)or 起疑心(ㄑㄧˇ ㄧˊ
ㄒㄧㄣ)
to begin to suspect; to
become suspicious

起意(ㄑㄧˇ ㄧˋ)
to conceive a design; to
have an idea (of doing
something)

起義(ㄑㄧˇ ㄧˋ)

to start an uprising (in a
righteous revolution); to
revolt

起油(ㄑㄧˇ ㄧㄡˊ)
to remove greasy stains
(from clothing, etc.)

起眼(ㄑㄧˇ ㄧㄢˇ)
to attract attention: 這些衣服
不起眼。The clothes do not
attract attention.

起因(ㄑㄧˇ ㄧㄣ)
a cause

起舞(ㄑㄧˇ ㄨˇ)
①to rise and dance ②to be
excited with joy

起臥(ㄑㄧˇ ㄨㄛˋ)
to get up and to sleep

起源(ㄑㄧˇ ㄩㄢˊ)
the origin; the source; the
beginning; the genesis

起運(ㄑㄧˇ ㄩㄣˋ)
to start shipping; to be
under way

起用(ㄑㄧˇ ㄩㄥˋ)
to employ (officials previously dismissed or in retirement)

【赸】 5831
ㄕㄢˋ shann shàn
to try to conceal embarrassment

五畫

【趁】 5832
(趂) ㄔㄣˋ chenn
chèn

1. to take advantage of; to
avail oneself of
2. while

趁便(ㄔㄣˋ ㄅㄧㄢˋ)
to take advantage of a convenient occasion; at one's
convenience: 你趁便爲我寄封
信好嗎？Would you mail a
letter for me at your convenience?

趁風揚帆(ㄔㄣˋ ㄈㄥ ㄧㄤˊ ㄈㄢˊ)
Hoist the sail when there is
wind.

趁空(ㄔㄣˋ ㄎㄨㄥˋ)
to avail oneself of leisure

趁火打劫(ㄔㄣˋ ㄏㄨㄛˇ ㄉㄚˇ ㄐㄧㄝˊ)
(literally) to plunder a
house when it is on fire—to
try to profit from another's
misfortune; to fish in trou-

bled waters

趁機會(ㄔㄣˋ ㄐㄧ ㄏㄨㄟˋ)
to take advantage of an
opportunity

趁心(ㄔㄣˋ ㄒㄧㄣ)
to have as one wishes; very
gratifying and satisfactory
亦作「稱心如意」

趁虛(ㄔㄣˋ ㄒㄩ)
to take advantage of another's unwariness or absence

趁時候(ㄔㄣˋ ㄕˊ ㄏㄡˋ)
to take advantage of the
chance; to act before it is
too late

趁勢(ㄔㄣˋ ㄕˋ)
to take advantage of the
prevailing circumstances

趁熱(ㄔㄣˋ ㄖㄜˋ)
①while it is still hot: 趁熱把
這麵輪吃了吧。Eat the noodles
while they are hot. ②to act
before it is too late

趁熱打鐵(ㄔㄣˋ ㄖㄜˋ ㄉㄚˇ ㄊㄧㄝˇ)
to strike while the iron is
hot

趁人之危(ㄔㄣˋ ㄖㄣˊ ㄓ ㄨㄟˊ)
to take advantage of others'
perilous states; to take
advantage of others' weakness

趁早(ㄔㄣˋ ㄗㄠˇ)
as early as possible; to act
before it is too late

趁願(ㄔㄣˋ ㄩㄢˋ)
to feel satisfaction

【趄】 5833
ㄐㄩ jiu jū
as in 趑趄——to falter

【超】 5834
ㄔㄠ chau chāo
1. to jump over; to leap over;
to fly across
2. to be more than; to exceed
3. to be better than; to excel;
to surpass
4. to rise above; to transcend
5. to overtake

超拔(ㄔㄠ ㄅㄚˊ)
outstanding; surpassing

超凡入聖(ㄔㄠ ㄈㄢˊ ㄖㄨˋ ㄕㄥˋ)
to transcend worldliness and
attain holiness

超等(ㄔㄠ ㄉㄥˇ)or 超級(ㄔㄠ ㄐㄧˊ)
of a special grade; of a special class

超度(ㄔㄠ ㄉㄨˋ)

①to transcend; to rise above ②(Buddhism) to raise the soul from suffering in the next world

超短裙 (彳ㄠ ㄉㄨㄢˇ ㄑㄩㄣˊ)
a miniskirt 亦作「迷你裙」

超脫 (彳ㄠ ㄊㄨㄛ)
to transcend worldliness; to be detached; to detach oneself from

超齡 (彳ㄠ ㄌㄧㄥˊ)
to be over the specified age

超倫 (彳ㄠ ㄌㄨㄣˊ)
surpassing; outstanding

超格 (彳ㄠ ㄍㄜˊ)
surpassing the average; surpassing

超過 (彳ㄠ ㄍㄨㄛˋ)
①to exceed; to be more than ②to excel; to surpass; to outweigh

超級 (彳ㄠ ㄐㄧˊ)
super

超級明星 (彳ㄠ ㄐㄧˊ ㄇㄧㄥˊ ㄒㄧㄥ)
a superstar 亦作「超級巨星」

超級間諜 (彳ㄠ ㄐㄧˊ ㄐㄧㄢ ㄉㄧㄝˊ)
a superspy

超級強國 (彳ㄠ ㄐㄧˊ ㄑㄧㄤˊ ㄍㄨㄛˊ)
a superpower; a superstate

超級市場 (彳ㄠ ㄐㄧˊ ㄕˋ ㄔㄤˇ)
a supermarket

超絕 (彳ㄠ ㄐㄩㄝˊ)
incomparable; unsurpassed; unequaled; transcendent

超遷 (彳ㄠ ㄑㄧㄢ)
to promote, or get promoted, past one or more grades

超前 (彳ㄠ ㄑㄧㄢˊ)
①(electricity) lead ②to overtake

超群 (彳ㄠ ㄑㄩㄣˊ)
head and shoulders above all others; preeminent; surpassing: 她的美貌超群。She was of surpassing beauty.

超慕絕倫 (彳ㄠ ㄇㄨˋ ㄐㄩㄝˊ ㄌㄨㄣˊ)
surpassing all others; incomparably above everything

超現實主義 (彳ㄠ ㄒㄧㄢˋ ㄕˊ ㄓㄨˇ ㄧˋ)
surrealism

超支 (彳ㄠ ㄓ)
to overspend; to overdraw

超卓 (彳ㄠ ㄓㄨㄛˊ)
transcendent; surpassing

超重 (彳ㄠ ㄓㄨㄥˋ)
①an overload ②overweight;

excess

超車 (彳ㄠ ㄔㄜ)
to overtake a car: 不准超車。No overtaking!

超拔拔俗 (彳ㄠ ㄅㄚˊ ㄙㄨˊ)
to transcend the worldly

超出 (彳ㄠ ㄔㄨ)
to exceed; to surpass; to overtake: 他們的成功超出我們的預料之外。Their success exceeded our expectations.

超視綜合體 (彳ㄠ ㄕˋ ㄗㄨㄥˋ ㄏㄜˊ ㄊㄧˇ)
a Cinerama

超收 (彳ㄠ ㄕㄡ)
to receive more (funds) than needed; to collect more (tax) revenues) than expected

超升 (彳ㄠ ㄕㄥ)
①to get promoted past one (or more) grades ②(said of the soul) to rise to Heaven upon death

超生 (彳ㄠ ㄕㄥ)
to excuse from death

超然 (彳ㄠ ㄖㄢˊ)
①transcendent ②detached; unprejudiced

超然物外 (彳ㄠ ㄖㄢˊ ㄨˋ ㄨㄞˋ)
to be above all material desires

超人 (彳ㄠ ㄖㄣˊ)
a superman

超自然 (彳ㄠ ㄗˋ ㄖㄢˊ)
supernatural: 天使和魔鬼都是超自然的存在物。Angels and devils are supernatural beings.

超載 (彳ㄠ ㄗㄞˋ)
overloading; to overload

超速 (彳ㄠ ㄙㄨˋ)
speeding

超額 (彳ㄠ ㄜˊ)
to exceed a quota or target amount

超逸 (彳ㄠ ㄧˋ)
above worldly desires; free from material desires

超音波 (彳ㄠ ㄧㄣ ㄅㄛ)
supersonic waves

超音速 (彳ㄠ ㄧㄣ ㄙㄨˋ)
supersonic speed

超越 (彳ㄠ ㄩㄝˋ)
①to excel; to surpass; to rise above; to transcend ②to fly across; to jump over

【越】 5835
ㄩㄝˋ yueh yuè

1. to go beyond; to transgress
2. to skip; to climb over; to cross over; to go across
3. even more; the more
4. name of an ancient state
5. a Chinese family name

越描越黑 (ㄩㄝˋ ㄇㄧㄠˊ ㄩㄝˋ ㄏㄟ)
(informal) The more one tries to cover up a scandal, the more it stinks.

越發 (ㄩㄝˋ ㄈㄚ)
even more; the more

越島進攻 (ㄩㄝˋ ㄉㄠˇ ㄐㄧㄣˋ ㄍㄨㄥ)
to take enemy-held islands in a leapfrog fashion as Gen. MacArthur did in the Pacific)

越多越好 (ㄩㄝˋ ㄉㄨㄛ ㄩㄝˋ ㄏㄠˇ)
The more, the better.

越南 (ㄩㄝˋ ㄋㄢˊ)
Vietnam

越年 (ㄩㄝˋ ㄋㄧㄢˊ)
the following year

越來越… (ㄩㄝˋ ㄌㄞˊ ㄩㄝˋ)
more and more; increasingly more; steadily more

越雷池一步 (ㄩㄝˋ ㄌㄟˊ ㄔˊ ㄧ ㄅㄨˋ)
to transgress the bounds

越禮 (ㄩㄝˋ ㄌㄧˇ)
to go beyond the bounds of propriety

越過 (ㄩㄝˋ ㄍㄨㄛˋ)
①to exceed; to overstep ②to go across; to cross

越軌 (ㄩㄝˋ ㄍㄨㄟˇ)
to go beyond what is proper

越軌行為 (ㄩㄝˋ ㄍㄨㄟˇ ㄒㄧㄥˊ ㄨㄟˊ)
impermissible behavior

越級 (ㄩㄝˋ ㄐㄧˊ)
to skip grades in promotion, etc.

越界 (ㄩㄝˋ ㄐㄧㄝˋ)
to go beyond the boundary; to transgress the bounds; to encroach; to trespass; to intrude

越境 (ㄩㄝˋ ㄐㄧㄥˋ)
to encroach upon the territory of an adjacent country; to go beyond the national border

越劇 (ㄩㄝˋ ㄐㄩˋ)
Shaohsing opera, prevalent in Chekiang (浙江) and Shanghai (上海)

越牆 (ㄩㄝˋ ㄑㄧㄤˊ)
to climb over a wall;

scale a wall: 小偷越牆而逃.
The thief scaled the wall
and escaped.

越權(ㄩㄝˋ ㄑㄩㄢˊ)
to act without authorization

越限(ㄩㄝˋ ㄒㄧㄢˋ)
to exceed the time limit

越日(ㄩㄝˋ ㄖˋ)
the following day

越俎代庖(ㄩㄝˋ ㄗㄨˇ ㄉㄞˋ ㄆㄠˊ)
to go beyond one's duties;
to meddle with another's
affairs

越次(ㄩㄝˋ ㄘˋ)
to disregard the proper
order or sequence

越野賽跑(ㄩㄝˋ ㄧㄝˇ ㄙㄞˋ ㄆㄠˇ)
a cross-country race

越獄(ㄩㄝˋ ㄩˋ)
to break jail; a jailbreak: 兩
名犯人越獄了. Two prisoners
broke jail.

越…越好(ㄩㄝˋ…ㄩㄝˋ ㄏㄠˇ)
The..., the better. 越多越好.
The more, the better.

六畫

【赼】 5836
　ㄗ tzy zî
to falter

赼趄(ㄗ ㄐㄩ)
to falter; to hesitate to proceed

【趔】 5837
　ㄌㄧㄝˋ lieh liè
1. falling behind; not progressing
2. unskillful; awkward

趔趄(ㄌㄧㄝˋ ㄐㄩ)
①falling behind; not pro-
gressing ②awkward; un-
skillful ③to stagger; to reel;
to stumble

七畫

【趙】 5838
　ㄓㄠˋ jaw zhào
1. name of an ancient feudal
state
2. a Chinese family name

和璧(ㄓㄠˋ ㄅㄧˋ)
a famous precious stone
belonging to the state of
Chao (趙) during the Epoch
of Warring States

趙孟頫(ㄓㄠˋ ㄇㄥˋ ㄈㄨˇ)
Chao Meng-fu, 1254-1322, a
painter and calligrapher

趙飛燕(ㄓㄠˋ ㄈㄟ ㄧㄢˋ)
Chao Fei-yen, a favorite
concubine of Emperor Cheng
(成帝) of the Han Dynasty

趙盾(ㄓㄠˋ ㄉㄨㄣˇ)
Chao Tun, son of Chao Tsui
(趙衰), a statesman of the
state of Tsin (晉) during the
Epoch of Spring and Au-
tumn

趙高(ㄓㄠˋ ㄍㄠ)
Chao Kao, a powerful eu-
nuch during the Chin (秦)
Dynasty (221-206 B.C.)

趙匡胤(ㄓㄠˋ ㄎㄨㄤ ㄧㄣˋ)
Chao Kuang-yin, 927-976,
founder of the Sung (宋)
Dynasty (960-1279)

趙衰(ㄓㄠˋ ㄘㄨㄟ)
Chao Tsui, father of Chao
Tun (趙盾), a statesman of
the state of Tsin (晉) during
the Epoch of Spring and
Autumn

趙宋(ㄓㄠˋ ㄙㄨㄥˋ)
the Sung Dynasty (960-1279,
of the House of Chao, as
distinct from the Sung of
the House of Liu in the 5th
century A.D.)

趙雲(ㄓㄠˋ ㄩㄣˊ)
Chao Yün, ? -229, a general
of the Kingdom of Shu (蜀)
during the Epoch of the
Three Kingdoms

【趕】 5839
　ㄍㄢˇ gaan gǎn
1. to pursue; to catch up with;
to overtake; to keep up with
2. to drive; to expel
3. to hurry; to rush; to hasten
4. to try to catch; to make a
dash for; to rush for

趕辦(ㄍㄢˇ ㄅㄢˋ)
to hurry (work)

趕不及(ㄍㄢˇ ㄅㄨˋ ㄐㄧˊ)
unable to manage to be on
time

趕不上(ㄍㄢˇ ㄅㄨˋ ㄕㄤˋ)
①unable to catch up with
②inferior to ③to be too
late for (the train, etc.) ④
to miss; unable to chance
upon

趕忙(ㄍㄢˇ ㄇㄤˊ)
with haste; hurriedly

趕明兒(ㄍㄢˇ ㄇㄧㄥˊ ㄦ)
some other day; later: 我們趕
明兒再討論它吧. Let's discuss
it some other day.

趕得上(ㄍㄢˇ ㄉㄜˊ ㄕㄤˋ)
①able to be in time for ②
able to catch up with ③able
to chance upon

趕到(ㄍㄢˇ ㄉㄠˋ)
①to arrive in haste; to
come hurriedly ②by the
time when...

趕牛(ㄍㄢˇ ㄋㄧㄡˊ)
to herd cattle

趕路(ㄍㄢˇ ㄌㄨˋ)
to walk hurriedly; to travel
in haste; to hurry on with
one's journey; to push on
with one's journey

趕開(ㄍㄢˇ ㄎㄞ)
to drive away

趕考(ㄍㄢˇ ㄎㄠˇ)
to go to an examination

趕快(ㄍㄢˇ ㄎㄨㄞˋ)
to make haste; to hurry;
quickly; at once

趕活(ㄍㄢˇ ㄏㄨㄛˊ)
to hurry work

趕會(ㄍㄢˇ ㄏㄨㄟˋ)
to go to a temple fair

趕回來(ㄍㄢˇ ㄏㄨㄟˊ ㄌㄞˊ)
①to come back hurriedly;
to hurry back ②to chase
after someone and force him
to come back

趕集(ㄍㄢˇ ㄐㄧˊ)
to go to market 亦作「趁墟」

趕緊(ㄍㄢˇ ㄐㄧㄣˇ)
to hurry; quickly; with no
loss of time

趕盡殺絕(ㄍㄢˇ ㄐㄧㄣˋ ㄕㄚ ㄐㄩㄝˊ)
to injure and oppress to the
extreme

趕製(ㄍㄢˇ ㄓˋ)
to rush the manufacture of

趕著(ㄍㄢˇ ㄓㄜ)
①hurrying ②catching up;
pursuing ③to chance upon

趕車(ㄍㄢˇ ㄔㄜ)
①to drive a cart or car-
riage ②to catch a bus or
train

趕場(ㄍㄢˇ ㄔㄤˊ)
(said of actors) after finishing a performance, to hurry

〔走部〕

【足部】

趕出去(《ㄢˇ ㄔㄨ ·ㄑㄩ)
to drive out; to expel

趕時髦(《ㄢˇ ㄕˊ ㄇㄠˊ)
to follow the fashion; to try to be in the swim

趕上(《ㄢˇ ·ㄕㄤ)
① to catch up with; to overtake; to keep pace with ② to be in time for ③ to chance upon

趕早兒(《ㄢˇ ㄗㄠˇ ㄦ)
to act before it is too late

趕三關(《ㄢˇ ㄙㄢ ㄍㄨㄢ)
to be in a great hurry to do one thing after another

趕鴨子上架(《ㄢˇ ㄧㄚ ·ㄗ ㄕㄤ ㄐㄧㄚˋ)
to drive a duck onto a perch —to force someone to do something against his will

趕羊(《ㄢˇ ㄧㄤˊ)
to herd sheep

趕羊的(《ㄢˇ ㄧㄤˊ ·ㄉㄜ)
a shepherd

八畫

【趣】   5840
1. ㄑㄩˋ chiuh qù
interest; fun; interesting; funny

趣話(ㄑㄩˋ ㄏㄨㄚˋ)
an amusing story; a funny story; a joke

趣向(ㄑㄩˋ ㄒㄧㄤˋ)
a personal inclination; aptitude

趣事(ㄑㄩˋ ㄕˋ)
an amusing incident; an interesting episode

趣兒(ㄑㄩˋ ㄦ)
fun; interest

趣味(ㄑㄩˋ ㄨㄟˋ)
fun; interest; taste: 懸疑可增加故事的趣味。Suspense can add interest to a story.

趣聞(ㄑㄩˋ ㄨㄣˊ)
an amusing report; interesting news

【趣】   5840
2.(促) ㄘㄨˋ tsuh cù
to hasten

【趟】   5841
ㄊㄤ tanq tǎng
an auxiliary noun for verbs meaning "to walk," "to jour-

ney," etc.

趟子(ㄊㄤˋ ·ㄗ)
a round trip between two localities; commutation

十畫

【趨】   5842
ㄑㄩ chiu qū
1. to go quickly; to hasten; to hurry
2. to be inclined; to tend; to follow

趨拜(ㄑㄩ ㄅㄞˋ)
to hurry on to pay respects to

趨奉(ㄑㄩ ㄈㄥˋ)
to try to please (a notable, etc.); to hasten to please; to fawn on

趨附(ㄑㄩ ㄈㄨˋ)
to hang on (men of influence)

趨庭(ㄑㄩ ㄊㄧㄥˊ)
to receive the teachings of one's father

趨利(ㄑㄩ ㄌㄧˋ)
to go after material gain

趨候(ㄑㄩ ㄏㄡˋ)
to go to a place to pay respects to someone

趨吉避凶(ㄑㄩ ㄐㄧˊ ㄅㄧˋ ㄒㄩㄥ)
to pursue good fortune and shun the course of calamity

趨向(ㄑㄩ ㄒㄧㄤˋ)
① a tendency; a trend; a direction ② to tend to; to incline to

趨之若鶩(ㄑㄩ ㄓ ㄖㄨㄛˋ ㄨˋ)
to go after in a swarm

趨戰(ㄑㄩ ㄓㄢˋ)
to fight an enemy already firmly entrenched

趨承(ㄑㄩ ㄔㄥˊ)
to cater to someone

趨時(ㄑㄩ ㄕˊ)
to follow the trend of the times

趨勢(ㄑㄩ ㄕˋ)
① a trend; a tendency ② to go after men of power

趨走(ㄑㄩ ㄗㄡˇ)
to go in haste; to run away

趨義(ㄑㄩ ㄧˋ)
to see right and act quickly to follow it

趨謁(ㄑㄩ ㄧㄝˋ)

to go and see (a senior)

趨炎附勢(ㄑㄩ ㄧㄢˊ ㄈㄨˋ ㄕˋ)or趨炎附熱(ㄑㄩ ㄧㄢˊ ㄈㄨˋ ㄖㄜˋ)
to hang on men of influence

趨迎(ㄑㄩ ㄧㄥˊ)or趨而迎之(ㄑㄩ ㄦˊ
to hasten to greet or receive (a visitor)

十九畫

【趲】   5843
ㄗㄢˇ tzaan zǎn
1. to hurry; to hasten; to rush through
2. to urge
3. to save (money)

趲路(ㄗㄢˇ ㄌㄨˋ)
to hurry in a journey; to journey hurriedly

趲行(ㄗㄢˇ ㄒㄧㄥˊ)
to travel hurriedly; to hurry in a journey

趲程(ㄗㄢˇ ㄔㄥˊ)
to hurry in a journey; to journey hurriedly

足 部

ㄗㄨˊ tzwu zú

【足】   5844
1. ㄗㄨˊ tzwu zú
1. the foot; the leg
2. the base (of an object)
3. sufficient; enough; adequate full

足本(ㄗㄨˊ ㄅㄣˇ)
(said of a novel, etc.) un-abridged

足不出戶(ㄗㄨˊ ㄅㄨˋ ㄔㄨ ㄏㄨˋ)
to refrain from stepping out side the house

足智謀斷(ㄗㄨˊ ㄓˋ ㄇㄡˊ ㄉㄨㄢˋ)
resourceful but irresolute

足敷(ㄗㄨˊ ㄈㄨ)
enough for

足跗骨(ㄗㄨˊ ㄈㄨ ㄍㄨˇ)
the tarsal bone; the tarsus

足夠(ㄗㄨˊ ㄍㄡˋ)
enough; sufficient; full ample

足跟(ㄗㄨˊ ㄍㄣ)
the heel: 他跌倒的時候，傷了足

跟。He hurt his heel when he
fell.

足迹(ㄗㄨˊㄐㄧˋ)
① footprints; footmarks;
tracks ② whereabouts

足繭(ㄗㄨˊㄐㄧㄢˇ)
the callous skin on the feet

足見(ㄗㄨˊㄐㄧㄢˋ)
from this it is clear that; it
serves to show

足金(ㄗㄨˊㄐㄧㄣ)
pure gold 亦作「足赤」

足球(ㄗㄨˊㄑㄧㄡˊ)
football; soccer; 你喜歡踢足
球嗎? Do you like playing
soccer?

足球隊(ㄗㄨˊㄑㄧㄡˊㄉㄨㄟˋ)
a football team; a soccer
team

足球賽(ㄗㄨˊㄑㄧㄡˊㄙㄞˋ)
a football game; a soccer
game

足球員(ㄗㄨˊㄑㄧㄡˊㄩㄢˊ)
a football player; a footballer; a soccer player

足下(ㄗㄨˊㄒㄧㄚˋ)
① terms of respect placed
after the name when addressing another (found usually
in letters): 足下意見如何?
What is your opinion? ②
under one's feet—a footing;
a foothold

足智多謀(ㄗㄨˊㄓˋㄉㄨㄛ ㄇㄡˊ)
wise and resourceful

足吃足喝(ㄗㄨˊㄔ ㄗㄨˊㄏㄜ)
to eat and drink to one's
heart's content

足赤(ㄗㄨˊㄔˋ)
pure gold

足食足兵(ㄗㄨˊㄕˊㄗㄨˊㄅㄧㄥ)
adequacy in the supply of
foodstuffs and the means of
defense

足資借鑑(ㄗㄨˊㄗ ㄐㄧㄝˋ ㄐㄧㄢˋ)
to be an object lesson

足足(ㄗㄨˊㄗㄨˊ)
full; no less than; as much
as: 行程足足花費四小時。
The journey took fully four
hours.

足色(ㄗㄨˊㄙㄜˋ)
(said of gold, silver, etc.) of
standard purity; sterling

足歲(ㄗㄨˊㄙㄨㄟˋ)
to have actually reached a
certain age (as distinct from

the Chinese way of counting
age, which makes a person
one year old at the time of
birth)

足額(ㄗㄨˊㄜˊ)
to have reached the quota
or required number

足衣足食(ㄗㄨˊㄧ ㄗㄨˊㄕˊ)
to have no shortage of food
and clothing

足以(ㄗㄨˊㄧˇ)
sufficient to; enough to: 他
的話不足以影響我。What he
says isn't enough to affect
me.

足以自豪(ㄗㄨˊㄧˇ ㄗˋ ㄏㄠˊ)
enough for one to be proud
of

足音跫然(ㄗㄨˊㄧㄣ ㄑㄩㄥˊ ㄖㄢˊ)
(literally) excited to hear
footsteps—longing to have
visitors

足銀(ㄗㄨˊㄧㄣˊ)
sterling silver

足紋(ㄗㄨˊㄨㄣˊ)
sterling silver

【足】 5844
　　　 2. ㄐㄩˋ jiuh jǔ
overly modest or humble

足恭(ㄐㄩˋㄍㄨㄥ)
overly modest; too humble;
obsequious

二畫

【趴】 5845
　　　 ㄆㄚ pa pā
1. to prostrate oneself; to lie
face downwards
2. to bend over

趴下(ㄆㄚ·ㄒㄧㄚ)
① to prostrate oneself; to lie
face downwards ② to fall
flat on the ground

趴著(ㄆㄚ·ㄓㄜ)
lying flat on the ground;
prostrate

三畫

【趵】 5846
　　　 ㄅㄠ baw bào
to jump; to leap

趵突泉(ㄅㄠ ㄊㄨˊ ㄑㄩㄢˊ)
a renowned spring at Tsinan,
Shantung

四畫

【趾】 5847
　　　 ㄓˇ jyy zhǐ
1. a toe
2. a foot
3. footprints; tracks

趾高氣揚(ㄓˇ ㄍㄠ ㄑㄧˋ ㄧㄤˊ)
(literally) to walk in a vain,
swaggering manner—elated
and proud; smug; to hold
one's head high: 那影后趾高
氣揚。The movie queen holds
her head high.

趾骨(ㄓˇㄍㄨˇ)
the phalanx (of the foot)

趾甲(ㄓˇㄐㄧㄚˇ)
a toenail

【趺】 5848
　　　 ㄈㄨ fu fū
1. the back of the foot
2. to sit cross-legged (as a
Buddhist monk does)

趺骨(ㄈㄨㄍㄨˇ)
the tarsal bone; the tarsus

趺坐(ㄈㄨ ㄗㄨㄛˋ)
to sit cross-legged (as a
Buddhist monk does)

【跂】 5849
　　　 1. ㄑㄧˊ chyi qí
1. an extra toe
2. (said of insects) crawling

【跂】 5849
　　　 2. ㄑㄧˋ chih qì
to stand on tiptoe

跂想(ㄑㄧˋㄒㄧㄤˇ)
to expect anxiously

跂踵(ㄑㄧˋ ㄓㄨㄥˇ)
to wait expectantly; to look
forward anxiously

跂望 or 企望(ㄑㄧˋ ㄨㄤˋ)
to wait on tiptoe—to look
forward with eagerness

【跋】 5850
　　　 1. ㄙㄚˊ sah sà
to pick up with the foot

【跋】 5850
　　　 2. ㄊㄚˋ ta tà
to wear (shoes) in a casual
way

跋拉(ㄊㄚˋ·ㄌㄚ)
to wear (shoes) in a casual
way; to wear shoes with the
backs turned in

五畫

（足部）

足

部

【跋】 5851
ㄅㄚˊ bar bá

1. to travel
2. a postscript
3. to trample

跋剌 (ㄅㄚˊ ㄌㄚˋ)
the sound of fish jumping or birds flying up

跋扈 (ㄅㄚˊ ㄏㄨˋ)
to be rampant in defiance of authority

跋前疐後 (ㄅㄚˊ ㄑㄧㄢˊ ㄓˋ ㄏㄡˋ)
allowed to move neither forward nor backward

跋涉 (ㄅㄚˊ ㄕㄜˋ)
to travel over land and water; to trudge; to trek; to wade

跋山涉水 (ㄅㄚˊ ㄕㄢ ㄕㄜˋ ㄕㄨㄟˇ)
to scale mountains and ford streams; to travel across mountains and rivers

【跌】 5852
ㄉㄧㄝˊ dye dié

1. to fall; to drop
2. to stamp
3. a fall

跌打損傷 (ㄉㄧㄝˊ ㄉㄚˇ ㄙㄨㄣˇ ㄕㄤ)
(literally) injuries caused by a fall or beating—Chinese osteopathy

跌得倒爬得起 (ㄉㄧㄝˊ ㄉㄜˊ ㄉㄠˇ ㄆㄚˊ ㄉㄜˊ ㄑㄧˇ)
able to rise after a fall —capable of adapting oneself to circumstances

跌倒 (ㄉㄧㄝˊ ㄉㄠˇ)
to stumble and fall; to fall down

跌蕩 or 跌宕 (ㄉㄧㄝˊ ㄉㄤˋ)
to behave without decorum; to act without restraint

跌跌撞撞 (ㄉㄧㄝˊ ㄉㄧㄝˊ ㄓㄨㄤˋ ㄓㄨㄤˋ)
to walk unsteadily; to stagger forward

跌停板 (ㄉㄧㄝˊ ㄊㄧㄥˊ ㄅㄢˇ)
(stock trading) to fall to the lowest price allowed for a single trading day; to hit the rock bottom

跌落 (ㄉㄧㄝˊ ㄌㄨㄛˋ)
to go down; to fall; to drop

跌價 (ㄉㄧㄝˊ ㄐㄧㄚˋ)
to cut a price; a price drop; to go down in price: 雞蛋跌價了。The price of eggs has gone down.

跌跤 (ㄉㄧㄝˊ ㄐㄧㄠ)
① to have a fall; to stumble and fall; a fall: 他因跌跤而傷了。He had been hurt by a fall. ② to make a mistake

跌進 (ㄉㄧㄝˊ ㄐㄧㄣˋ)
① to fall into ② (said of a price) to fall below a certain level

跌傷 (ㄉㄧㄝˊ ㄕㄤ)
to get injured by a fall; to fall and get hurt

跌足 (ㄉㄧㄝˊ ㄗㄨˊ)
to stamp the feet

跌死 (ㄉㄧㄝˊ ㄙˇ)
to be killed by a fall: 他跌死了。He was killed by a fall.

跌碎 (ㄉㄧㄝˊ ㄙㄨㄟˋ)
to break into pieces upon falling on the ground

【跎】 5853
ㄊㄨㄛˊ two tuó

1. to miss one's footing; to stumble
2. to miss the opportunity; to waste time

【跑】 5854
ㄆㄠˇ pao pǎo

1. to run
2. to run away; to flee

跑冰 (ㄆㄠˇ ㄅㄧㄥ)
to ice-skate; to skate on ice

跑步 (ㄆㄠˇ ㄅㄨˋ)
to run; on the double

跑不掉 (ㄆㄠˇ ㄅㄨˋ ㄉㄧㄠˋ)
unable to run away

跑不動 (ㄆㄠˇ ㄅㄨˋ ㄉㄨㄥˋ)
too tired to run away: 他疲倦得跑不動。He is too tired to run.

跑不了 (ㄆㄠˇ ㄅㄨˋ ㄌㄧㄠˇ)
not likely to run away

跑跑顛顛 (ㄆㄠˇ ㄆㄠˇ ㄉㄧㄢ ㄉㄧㄢ)
working in a hectic manner; to bustle about

跑馬 (ㄆㄠˇ ㄇㄚˇ)
① horse racing ② to go swiftly on horseback ③ to have an involuntary emission of semen

跑馬錶 (ㄆㄠˇ ㄇㄚˇ ㄅㄧㄠˇ)
a stopwatch 亦作「跑錶」

跑馬場 (ㄆㄠˇ ㄇㄚˇ ㄔㄤˇ)
a racecourse (for horse racing); a racetrack

跑道 (ㄆㄠˇ ㄉㄠˋ)
① a track (in a racecourse, stadium, etc.) ② a runway (in an airfield): 飛機離開跑道。The plane left the runway.

跑單幫 (ㄆㄠˇ ㄉㄢ ㄅㄤ)
to smuggle goods on a small scale by a single individual

跑肚 (ㄆㄠˇ ㄉㄨˋ)
to have diarrhea

跑櫃檯 (ㄆㄠˇ ㄍㄨㄟˋ ㄊㄞˊ)
to steal money from the counter of a shop or bank during business hours

跑堂 (ㄆㄠˇ ㄊㄤˊ)
a waiter

跑廳的 (ㄆㄠˇ ㄊㄧㄥ ㄉㄜ)
a servant in a brothel

跑腿 (ㄆㄠˇ ㄊㄨㄟˇ)
to run errands

跑來跑去 (ㄆㄠˇ ㄌㄞˊ ㄆㄠˇ ㄑㄩˋ)
to run back and forth

跑壘 (ㄆㄠˇ ㄌㄟˇ)
(baseball) base running

跑壘員 (ㄆㄠˇ ㄌㄟˇ ㄩㄢˊ)
(baseball) a base runner

跑路 (ㄆㄠˇ ㄌㄨˋ)
to travel on foot

跑龍套 (ㄆㄠˇ ㄌㄨㄥˊ ㄊㄠˋ)
to play an insignificant role

跑開 (ㄆㄠˇ ㄎㄞ)
① to get out of the way ② to leave; to go away; to run away

跑街 (ㄆㄠˇ ㄐㄧㄝ)
to act as a traveling salesman

跑江湖 (ㄆㄠˇ ㄐㄧㄤ ㄏㄨˊ)
to wander from place to place, making a living as a predictor, fortuneteller, acrobat, etc.

跑鞋 (ㄆㄠˇ ㄒㄧㄝˊ)
spiked shoes (of a sprinter)

跑車 (ㄆㄠˇ ㄔㄜ)
a car, bicycle, etc. for races; a racer; a sports car

【跖】 5855
ㄓˊ jyr zhí

1. the sole (of the foot)
2. name of a notorious robber

跖犬吠堯 (ㄓˊ ㄑㄩㄢˇ ㄈㄟˋ ㄧㄠˊ)
to side with the wicked and hate the wise

【跗】 5856
ㄈㄨ fu fū
the instep

跗骨 (ㄈㄨ ㄍㄨˇ)

the tarsus; the tarsal bone

胕蹠（ㄈㄨ ㄓ）
tarsi and metatarsi

【跚】 5857
ㄕㄢ shan shān
to walk unsteadily; to stagger

【跛】 5858
1. ㄅㄛ boo bǒ
lame; crippled

跛躄（ㄅㄛ ㄅㄧˋ）
lame; crippled

跛鱉千里（ㄅㄛ ㄅㄧˋ ㄑㄧㄢ ㄌㄧˇ）
(literally) Even a lame turtle can travel a thousand miles.—Persistence insures success.

跛脚（ㄅㄛ ㄐㄧㄠˇ）
lame; crippled

跛蹇（ㄅㄛ ㄐㄧㄢˇ）
lame; crippled

跛蹶（ㄅㄛ ㄐㄩㄝˊ）
to stumble and fall

跛躓（ㄅㄛ ㄓˋ）
to stumble and fall

跛子（ㄅㄛ ˙ㄗ）
a cripple

跛足（ㄅㄛ ㄗㄨˊ）
lame; crippled

【跛】 5858
2. ㄅㄧˋ bih bì
to lean; to be partial

跛倚（ㄅㄧˋ ㄧˇ）
partial; biased; prejudiced

【距】 5859
ㄐㄩˋ jiuh jù
1. a bird's spur
2. distance

距離（ㄐㄩˋ ㄌㄧˊ）
distance

距今（ㄐㄩˋ ㄐㄧㄣ）
ago: 距今已有二十年。That was twenty years ago.

六畫

【跨】 5860
ㄎㄨㄚˋ kuah kuà
1. to take a stride; to stride
2. to sit astride on; to straddle; to ride
3. to cross; to go beyond; to extend across

跨馬（ㄎㄨㄚˋ ㄇㄚˇ）
to sit astride on a horse; to mount a horse

跨黨（ㄎㄨㄚˋ ㄉㄤˇ）
to be a member of two political parties at the same time

跨年度（ㄎㄨㄚˋ ㄋㄧㄢˊ ㄉㄨˋ）
to go beyond the year

跨鶴（ㄎㄨㄚˋ ㄏㄜˋ）
to ride the crane—to become an immortal 亦作「跨鶴西歸」

跨海（ㄎㄨㄚˋ ㄏㄞˇ）
to cross the sea; to sail across the ocean

跨竈（ㄎㄨㄚˋ ㄗㄠˋ）
to excel one's own father

跨越（ㄎㄨㄚˋ ㄩㄝˋ）
to stride over (a ditch, etc.); to leap over; to cut across: 他跨越小河。He strode over the brook.

【跰】 5861
（跰）ㄐㄧㄢˇ jean jiǎn
the callous skin or blisters on hands or feet

【跟】 5862
ㄍㄣ gen gēn
1. the heel
2. to follow
3. to attend upon
4. and

跟包（ㄍㄣ ㄅㄠ ˙ㄅㄜ）
the attendant of an entertainer

跟班（ㄍㄣ ㄅㄢ）
an attendant (especially of an official)

跟不上（ㄍㄣ ㄅㄨˋ ㄕㄤˋ）
unable to keep pace with; unable to catch up with

跟定（ㄍㄣ ㄉㄧㄥˋ）
to decide to follow (a leader) for good

跟頭（ㄍㄣ ˙ㄊㄡ）
①a somersault ②failure; a frustration 亦作「栽跟頭」

跟官（ㄍㄣ ㄍㄨㄢ ˙ㄍㄜ）
an attendant of an official

跟進（ㄍㄣ ㄐㄧㄣˋ）
to follow suit

跟前
①（ㄍㄣ ㄑㄧㄢˊ）the front, side, or presence (of a person): 在她跟前別說大話。Don't talk big in her presence.
②（ㄍㄣ ㄑㄧㄢˊ）used with reference to children in the presence of their parents 亦作「膝下」: 您跟前有幾位公子？How many sons do you have?

跟著（ㄍㄣ ˙ㄓㄜ）
①going after; following ②soon after that

跟主兒（ㄍㄣ ㄓㄨˇ ㄦ）
to be a servant

跟人（ㄍㄣ ㄖㄣˊ）
an attendant; a retainer

跟蹤（ㄍㄣ ㄗㄨㄥ）
to follow other's tracks or footsteps; to pursue 參看「跟蹤」

跟蹤（ㄍㄣ ㄗㄨㄥ）
to keep track of; to shadow; to tail 亦作「跟踪」: 小偷被警察跟蹤了。The thief was tailed by a policeman.

跟隨（ㄍㄣ ㄙㄨㄟˊ）
①to go closely behind; to follow: 她跟隨他進入房間。She followed him into the room.
②a retainer; an attendant

跟兒（ㄍㄣ ㄦ）
the heel

【跡】 5863
（跡）ㄐㄧ jiji jī
traces; tracks; relics; a print

【踅】 5864
ㄔˊ chyh chí
to walk back and forth

踅蹀（ㄔˊ ㄉㄨㄛˊ）
to walk or move back and forth

【踩】 5865
（踹）ㄘㄞˇ tsae cǎi
1. to trample; to tread on
2. to chase; to pursue

踩扁（ㄘㄞˇ ㄅㄧㄢˇ）
to trample (an object) flat

踩壞（ㄘㄞˇ ㄏㄨㄞˋ）
to break or damage by trampling; to trample and break

踩著（ㄘㄞˇ ˙ㄓㄜ）
treading on; trampling

踩住（ㄘㄞˇ ㄓㄨˋ）
to keep the feet upon

踩水（ㄘㄞˇ ㄕㄨㄟˇ）
(sports) to tread water

踩三輪車（ㄘㄞˇ ㄙㄢ ㄌㄨㄣˊ ㄔㄜ）
to pedal a pedicab; to work as a pedicab driver

【跣】 5866
ㄒㄧㄢˇ shean xiǎn
barefooted

跣子（ㄒㄧㄢˇ ˙ㄗ）
slippers

跣足（ㄒㄧㄢˇ ㄗㄨˊ）
barefooted

〔足部〕

【跪】 5867 《ㄨㄟ guey guì
to kneel

跪拜《ㄨㄟ ㄅㄞˋ
to kowtow

跪稟《ㄨㄟ ㄅㄧㄥˇ
to report in a kneeling position

跪門《ㄨㄟ ㄇㄣˊ
to kneel at another's door (and beg for forgiveness)

跪倒《ㄨㄟ ㄉㄠˇ
to go on one's knees; to kneel down; to prostrate oneself; to grovel

跪倒俯起《ㄨㄟ ㄉㄠˇ ㄈㄨˇ ㄑㄧˇ
to kowtow again and again

跪地《ㄨㄟ ㄉㄧˋ
to kneel on the ground

跪下《ㄨㄟ ㄒㄧㄚˋ
to go on one's knees; to kneel down

跪謝《ㄨㄟ ㄒㄧㄝˋ
to express thanks on one's knees

跪乳《ㄨㄟ ㄖㄨˇ
(literally) to kneel to suck (as a lamb does)—to show filial piety

跪乳之恩《ㄨㄟ ㄖㄨˇ ㄓ ㄣ
filial piety

跪姿《ㄨㄟ ㄗ
a kneeling position

跪送《ㄨㄟ ㄙㄨㄥˋ
to bid goodbye in a kneeling position

跪迎《ㄨㄟ ㄧㄥˊ
to greet or receive in a kneeling position

【跫】 5868 ㄑㄩㄥˊ chyong qióng
the sound of steps; footsteps

跫然《ㄑㄩㄥˊ ㄖㄢˊ
the sound of footsteps

跫音《ㄑㄩㄥˊ ㄧㄣ
the sound of steps; footsteps: 我聽到跫音。I hear footsteps.

【跬】 5869 ㄎㄨㄟˇ koei kuǐ
half a pace

跬步《ㄎㄨㄟˇ ㄅㄨˋ
half a pace

跬步千里《ㄎㄨㄟˇ ㄅㄨˋ ㄑㄧㄢ ㄌㄧˇ
Even small steps may carry one a thousand miles.—If you try hard, you will succeed.

跬譽《ㄎㄨㄟˇ ㄩˋ
short-lived glory or honor

【跲】 5870 ㄐㄧㄚˊ jya jiá
to stumble

【路】 5871 ㄌㄨˋ luh lù
1. a way; a road; a path
2. a sort; a kind; a gang
3. a way; means
4. directions; courses
5. province (an administrative division during the Sung Dynasty)
6. a Chinese family name

路斃《ㄌㄨˋ ㄅㄧˋ
to die on the roadside

路標《ㄌㄨˋ ㄅㄧㄠ
a road sign; a signpost

路不拾遺《ㄌㄨˋ ㄅㄨˋ ㄕˊ ㄧˊ
People do not pick up what others have left on the roadside.—efficient government administration

路旁《ㄌㄨˋ ㄆㄤˊ
the roadside: 我們在路旁用餐。We ate our meal by the roadside.

路面《ㄌㄨˋ ㄇㄧㄢˋ
a road surface

路費《ㄌㄨˋ ㄈㄟˋ
traveling expenses

路德會《ㄌㄨˋ ㄉㄜˊ ㄏㄨㄟˋ
the Lutheran Church

路道《ㄌㄨˋ ㄉㄠˋ
①a way; a method ②a faction; a type

路燈《ㄌㄨˋ ㄉㄥ
a street lamp

路段《ㄌㄨˋ ㄉㄨㄢˋ
a section of a highway or railway

路透電《ㄌㄨˋ ㄊㄡˋ ㄉㄧㄢˋ
(news) a Reuters report

路透社《ㄌㄨˋ ㄊㄡˋ ㄕㄜˋ
Reuters; Reuter's News Agency

路條《ㄌㄨˋ ㄊㄧㄠˊ
(communist terminology) a traveling passport; a safe-conduct

路途《ㄌㄨˋ ㄊㄨˊ
way; a road

路柳牆花《ㄌㄨˋ ㄌㄧㄡˇ ㄑㄧㄤˊ ㄏㄨㄚ
(euphemism) prostitutes

路路通《ㄌㄨˋ ㄌㄨˋ ㄊㄨㄥ
(said of a person) versed in everything

路過《ㄌㄨˋ ㄍㄨㄛˋ
to pass by or through (a place)

路軌《ㄌㄨˋ ㄍㄨㄟˇ
railway tracks

路口《ㄌㄨˋ ㄎㄡˇ
an entrance to a road or street; a street intersection; a street crossing

路基《ㄌㄨˋ ㄐㄧ
a road base

路祭《ㄌㄨˋ ㄐㄧˋ
the offering of sacrifices by friends or admirers on the roadside along the way of a funeral procession

路劫《ㄌㄨˋ ㄐㄧㄝˊ
to commit robbery on highways; to waylay travelers

路警《ㄌㄨˋ ㄐㄧㄥˇ
policemen patrolling railways or highways

路徑《ㄌㄨˋ ㄐㄧㄥˋ
a way; a road; a route

路線《ㄌㄨˋ ㄒㄧㄢˋ
a route; a road; a course; a line: 這是到歐洲最快的路線。It's the quickest route to Europe.

路障《ㄌㄨˋ ㄓㄤˋ
a roadblock

路政《ㄌㄨˋ ㄓㄥˋ
the administration of land transportation

路中《ㄌㄨˋ ㄓㄨㄥ
①on the way; along the way; en route: 我在回家的路中看見他。I saw him on the way home. ②a Chinese family name

路程《ㄌㄨˋ ㄔㄥˊ
distance to be traveled; a journey; traveling distance: 這路程是很艱苦的。The journey was long and difficult.

路上《ㄌㄨˋ ㄕㄤˋ
on the way; along the way; en route: 回家路上不要耽擱。Don't waste any time on the way home.

路人《ㄌㄨˋ ㄖㄣˊ
a method; a process; the way of doing things that is peculiar to a certain sect or group

①a wayfarer ②a stranger:
一個路人對我說話。A stranger
spoke to me.

路子(ㄌㄨˋ˙ㄗ)
a way; a method; means; an
approach: 路子不對等於白費
時間。A wrong method
means a waste of time.

路次(ㄌㄨˋㄘˋ)
en route; on the way; along
the way: 他路次香港。He is
en route to Hong Kong.

路易十六(ㄌㄨˋㄧˋㄕˊㄌㄧㄡˋ)
Louis XVI, 1754-1793

路易十四(ㄌㄨˋㄧˋㄕˊㄙˋ)
Louis XIV, 1638-1715

路易斯安那(ㄌㄨˋㄧˋㄙㄢㄋㄚˋ)
the state of Louisiana, U.S.

路遙知馬力(ㄌㄨˋㄧㄠˊㄓㄇㄚˇㄌㄧˋ)
(literally) a horse's strength
is to be known only when
the road is long.—A person's
true color is revealed only
in the long run.

路遠(ㄌㄨˋㄩㄢˇ)
great distance

【跳】 5872　ㄊㄧㄠˋ tiaw tiào

1. to jump; to leap; to bounce;
to spring: 他跳過泥坑。He
jumped the puddle.

2. to throb; to pulsate; to beat:
我的脈搏跳動得很快。My pulse
is beating fast.

3. to skip (over); to jump; to
make omissions.

跳白(ㄊㄧㄠˋㄅㄞˊ)
(Kwangtung dialect) a small
fishing boat

跳班(ㄊㄧㄠˋㄅㄢ)
(education) to skip a grade;
to be advanced two or more
classes or grades at once

跳板(ㄊㄧㄠˋㄅㄢˇ)
①a gangplank ②a diving
board; a springboard ③a
steppingstone; a staging
area

跳票(ㄊㄧㄠˋㄆㄧㄠˋ)
a bounced check; a check
that bounced 參看「空頭支票」

跳動(ㄊㄧㄠˋㄉㄨㄥˋ)
to throb; to pulsate; to beat

跳踉頓躠(ㄊㄧㄠˋㄌㄧㄤˊㄉㄨㄣˋㄘㄨˊ)
to jump and skip; to gambol;
to caper; to trip

跳兔(ㄊㄧㄠˋㄊㄨˋ)

a hare; a rabbit; a jumping
hare

跳脫(ㄊㄧㄠˋㄊㄨㄛ)
a bracelet

跳樓自殺(ㄊㄧㄠˋㄌㄡˊㄗˋㄕㄚ)
to jump to death from a
building

跳欄(ㄊㄧㄠˋㄌㄢˊ)
(sports) hurdle race; the
hurdles

跳踉(ㄊㄧㄠˋㄌㄧㄤˊ)
to jump about; to hop about

跳梁(ㄊㄧㄠˋㄌㄧㄤˊ)
①to revolt; to rebel; to defy
the authorities ②to leap

跳梁小醜(ㄊㄧㄠˋㄌㄧㄤˊㄒㄧㄠˇㄔㄡˇ)
petty thieves; mischief-
makers

跳高(ㄊㄧㄠˋㄍㄠ)
(sports) high jump (in track
and field)

跳過(ㄊㄧㄠˋㄍㄨㄛˋ)
to jump over or across; to
succeed in jumping over or
across; to clear

跳河(ㄊㄧㄠˋㄏㄜˊ)
to jump into the river to
drown oneself

跳海(ㄊㄧㄠˋㄏㄞˇ)
to jump into the sea to
drown oneself

跳行(ㄊㄧㄠˋㄒㄧㄥˊ)
①to skip lines in reading or
copying ②to change to a
new occupation

跳火坑(ㄊㄧㄠˋㄏㄨㄛˇㄎㄥ)
to plunge into a life of
infamy, danger, etc.

跳級(ㄊㄧㄠˋㄐㄧˊ)
(education) to skip a grade;
to be advanced two or more
classes or grades at once

跳加官(ㄊㄧㄠˋㄐㄧㄚㄍㄨㄢ)
a ceremonial dance performed
by a masked actor before
the start of a Peking opera
show

跳腳(ㄊㄧㄠˋㄐㄧㄠˇ)
to stamp one's foot: 他氣得直
跳腳。He stamped his foot
with rage.

跳棋(ㄊㄧㄠˋㄑㄧˊ)
Chinese checkers

跳牆(ㄊㄧㄠˋㄑㄧㄤˊ)
to jump over a fence; to
jump down from a wall in
desperation

跳下去(ㄊㄧㄠˋㄒㄧㄚˋㄑㄩˋ)
to jump down; to leap down:
他從岸上跳下去。He jumped
down from the bank.

跳出(ㄊㄧㄠˋㄔㄨ)
to jump out; to leap out

跳出牢籠(ㄊㄧㄠˋㄔㄨㄌㄠˊㄎㄨㄥˊ)
to jump out of the cage—to
gain freedom

跳出火坑(ㄊㄧㄠˋㄔㄨㄏㄨㄛˇㄎㄥ)
①to free oneself from a life
of torture ②to free oneself
from white slavery

跳神(ㄊㄧㄠˋㄕㄣˊ)
ceremonial dances performed
by the Manchus, Tibetans
and Mongolians in exorcism

跳繩(ㄊㄧㄠˋㄕㄥˊ)
rope skipping; rope jumping:
女孩子喜歡玩跳繩。Girls like
to play rope jumping.

跳水(ㄊㄧㄠˋㄕㄨㄟˇ)
to dive; to jump into the
water; to dive from a diving
board (or a springboard)

跳水自殺(ㄊㄧㄠˋㄕㄨㄟˇㄗˋㄕㄚ)
to jump into the water and
drown oneself

跳蚤(ㄊㄧㄠˋㄗㄠˇ)or 跳蝨(ㄊㄧㄠˋㄕ)
a flea: 小心別被跳蚤咬了。
Take care not to be bitten
by the fleas.

跳槽(ㄊㄧㄠˋㄘㄠˊ)
to abandon one occupation
in favor of another; to get
new employment

跳傘(ㄊㄧㄠˋㄙㄢˇ)
to parachute

跳舞(ㄊㄧㄠˋㄨˇ)
to dance; dancing

跳舞會(ㄊㄧㄠˋㄨˇㄏㄨㄟˋ)
a dancing party; a ball 亦作
「舞會」

跳月(ㄊㄧㄠˋㄩㄝˋ)
(by the custom of the Miao
people) an outdoor dancing
party on a spring night at
which unmarried youths
select their future spouses

跳躍(ㄊㄧㄠˋㄩㄝˋ)
to jump; to leap; to hop: 麻
雀在草地上到處跳躍。Spar-
rows were hopping about on
the lawn.

跳遠(ㄊㄧㄠˋㄩㄢˇ)
(sports) the broad jump; the
long jump

【跥】5873 ㄉㄨㄛˊ duoh duó
to stamp the feet
跥脚 (ㄉㄨㄛˊ ㄐㄧㄠˇ)
to stamp one's foot

【跩】ㄓㄨㄞˇ joai zhuǎi
waddling

【跤】5875 ㄐㄧㄠ jiau jiāo
a stumble; a fall

七畫

【跔】5876 ㄐㄩˊ jyu jú
1. bent
2. contracted; cramped; confined
跔天蹐地 (ㄐㄩˊ ㄊㄧㄢ ㄐㄧˊ ㄉㄧˋ)
not stretched; confined; restricted
跔跔 (ㄐㄩˊ ㄐㄩˊ)
not stretched; confined
跔跔 (ㄐㄩˊ ㄓㄨˋ)
halting; faltering
跔促 or 侷促 (ㄐㄩˊ ㄘㄨˋ)
①narrow-minded　②ill at ease; uneasy

【跽】5877 ㄐㄧˋ jih jí
to kneel for a long time

【踉】5878 ㄌㄤˊ lang láng
(又讀 ㄌㄧㄤˊ liang liáng)
to jump about; to hop about

【踉】5878 ㄌㄧㄤˋ liang liàng
to walk unsteadily; to limp
踉蹌 or 踉蹡 (ㄌㄧㄤˋ ㄑㄧㄤ)〔ㄌㄧㄤˋ ㄑㄧㄤ〕 or 踉蹡
踉蹡 (ㄌㄧㄤ ㄑㄧㄤ〔ㄌㄧㄤˋ ㄑㄧㄤˋ〕)
limping; walking unsteadily

【踅】5879 1. ㄔˊ chyh chí
to go on one leg

【踅】5879 2. ㄒㄩㄝˊ shyue xué
to loiter around; to hang around
踅門瞭戶 (ㄒㄩㄝˊ ㄇㄣˊ ㄌㄧㄠˊ ㄏㄨˋ)
to loiter and chat at friends' houses
踅探 (ㄒㄩㄝˊ ㄊㄢˋ)
to spy; to peep; to watch and investigate stealthily
踅溜風 (ㄒㄩㄝˊ ㄌㄧㄡˋ ㄈㄥ)
a whirlwind; a cyclone

【踅轉】(ㄒㄩㄝˊ ㄓㄨㄢˇ)
to whirl; to turn; to rotate

【踊】5880 ㄩㄥˇ yeong yǒng
1. to jump; to leap
2. to rise
3. the shoes worn by the person whose feet were cut off as a form of punishment
踊貴 (ㄩㄥˇ ㄍㄨㄟˋ)
the rise of a price
踊躍 or 踴躍 (ㄩㄥˇ ㄩㄝˋ)
①joyful; happy　②glad to do something; eagerly

八畫

【踐】5881 ㄐㄧㄢˋ jiann jiàn
1. to tread upon; to trample
2. to fulfill; to carry out; to perform
3. to ascend; to occupy
踐冰 (ㄐㄧㄢˋ ㄅㄧㄥ)
(literally) to tread on ice—to run a risk
踐踏 (ㄐㄧㄢˋ ㄊㄚˋ)
①to trample; to tread on: 不要踐踏踏花圃。 Don't tread on the flower bed. ②to abuse
踐諾 (ㄐㄧㄢˋ ㄋㄨㄛˋ)
to keep a promise; to fulfill a pledge
踐履 (ㄐㄧㄢˋ ㄌㄩˇ)
①to trample　②to fulfill (pledge, etc.)
踐極 (ㄐㄧㄢˋ ㄐㄧˊ)
to ascend the throne
踐阼 (ㄐㄧㄢˋ ㄗㄨㄛˋ)
to succeed to the throne
踐言 (ㄐㄧㄢˋ ㄧㄢˊ)
to fulfill a promise
踐位 (ㄐㄧㄢˋ ㄨㄟˋ)
to ascend the throne
踐約 (ㄐㄧㄢˋ ㄩㄝ)
to honor an agreement; to fulfill a promise

【踠】5882 ㄨㄢˇ woan wǎn
a crooked leg

【踏】5883 ㄊㄚˋ tah tà
1. to step upon; to tread upon; to trample
2. to go to the spot (to make an investigation or survey)
踏板 (ㄊㄚˋ ㄅㄢˇ)
①a footboard; a footrest; foothold; a footstool　②a treadle
踏遍 (ㄊㄚˋ ㄅㄧㄢˋ)
to traverse the length and breadth of (some place)
踏破鐵鞋 (ㄊㄚˋ ㄆㄛˋ ㄊㄧㄝˇ ㄒㄧㄝˊ)
(literally) to wear out the iron shoes—to search painstakingly everywhere
踏破鐵鞋無覓處，得來全不費功夫 (ㄊㄚˋ ㄆㄛˋ ㄊㄧㄝˇ ㄒㄧㄝˊ ㄨˊ ㄇㄧˋ ㄔㄨˋ，ㄉㄜˊ ㄌㄞˊ ㄑㄩㄢˊ ㄅㄨˋ ㄈㄟˋ ㄍㄨㄥ ㄈㄨ)
to find something or somebody by chance after a painstaking search
踏伏 (ㄊㄚˋ ㄈㄨˊ)
to search out hidden enemy soldiers and wipe them out
踏歌 (ㄊㄚˋ ㄍㄜ)
to beat time to a song with the feet
踏看 or 踏勘 (ㄊㄚˋ ㄎㄢ)
to make a field investigation over (an area); to survey (a construction site)
踏脚板 (ㄊㄚˋ ㄐㄧㄠˇ ㄅㄢˇ)
a footboard; a footrest; a foothold
踏脚石 (ㄊㄚˋ ㄐㄧㄠˇ ㄕˊ)
a steppingstone
踏蹻 (ㄊㄚˋ ㄑㄧㄠ)
to walk on stilts
踏青 (ㄊㄚˋ ㄑㄧㄥ)
to go hiking on a spring day; a spring outing
踏雪尋梅 (ㄊㄚˋ ㄒㄩㄝˇ ㄒㄩㄣˊ ㄇㄟˊ)
(literally) to look for plum flowers on a snowy day—the behavior of a poet
踏實 (ㄊㄚˋ ㄕˊ)
(said of actions, etc.) practical; realistic: 他是個踏實的人。 He is a practical man.
踏月 (ㄊㄚˋ ㄩㄝˋ)
to walk in the moonlight

【踝】5884 ㄏㄨㄞˊ hwai huái
an ankle
踝子骨 (ㄏㄨㄞˊ ·ㄗ ㄍㄨˇ)
an anklebone; a talus; an astragalus

【踞】5885 ㄐㄩˋ jiuh jù
1. to squat; to crouch
2. to occupy

【跙】5886
彳 chyr chí
to hesitate
唎踟 or 踟躕(彳彳ㄨ)
①to hesitate ②linked together ③a comb ④to be in perplexity

【踡】5887
ㄑㄩㄢ chyuan quán
coiled; curled; drawn together; not stretched
踡伏(ㄑㄩㄢ ㄈㄨˊ)
(said of a snake, etc.) to coil up: 那蛇踡伏在樹枝上。The snake coiled itself up round the branch.
踡跼(ㄑㄩㄢˊ ㄐㄩˊ)
contracted; not stretched
踡屈(ㄑㄩㄢˊ ㄑㄩ)
curled up; not stretched

【踢】5888
ㄊㄧ ti tī
1. to kick
2. to play (football)
踢皮球(ㄊㄧ ㄆㄧˊ ㄑㄧㄡˊ)
①to kick a ball ②to kick something back and forth like a ball—(figuratively) to shirk (responsibility, etc.)
踢飛脚(ㄊㄧ ㄈㄟ ㄐㄧㄠˇ)
a kind of acrobatic stunt involving successive kicking motions
踢躂(ㄊㄧ ㄉㄚ)
pitapat—a succession of light, rapid pats (as of footfalls)
踢開(ㄊㄧ ㄎㄞ)
①to kick open (a door) ②to kick (something) out of the way
踢毽子(ㄊㄧ ㄐㄧㄢˋ ˙ㄗ)
the game of repeatedly bouncing a shuttlecock off a foot
踢球(ㄊㄧ ㄑㄧㄡˊ)
①to kick a ball ②to play football: 他 很 會 踢球。He plays football well.
踢正步(ㄊㄧ ㄓㄥˋ ㄅㄨˋ)
to march in goose steps
踢出去(ㄊㄧ ㄔㄨ ㄑㄩˋ)
to kick out
踢死(ㄊㄧ ㄙˇ)
to kick to death

【踣】5889
ㄅㄛˊ bor bó
1. to stumble and fall

2. dead; stiff

【蹀】5890
ㄑㄧㄝˋ chieh qiè
to walk; to be in motion
蹀躞(ㄑㄧㄝˋ ㄒㄧㄝˋ)
walking; in motion
蹀蹀(ㄑㄧㄝˋ ㄑㄧㄝˋ)
moving back and forth

【踧】5891
ㄘㄨˋ tsuh cù
reverent and nervous
踧踖(ㄘㄨˋ ㄐㄧˊ)
reverent and nervous
踧爾(ㄘㄨˋ ㄦˇ)
surprised

【踧】5891
ㄉㄧˋ dyi dì
level and easy
踧踧(ㄉㄧˋ ㄉㄧˋ)
(said of roads, etc.) level and easy

【踏】5892
ㄐㄧˊ jyi jí
to trample; to tread upon

【踔】5893
ㄓㄨㄛˊ jwo zhuó
1. to go across; to go beyond
2. very high; very far
踔厲風發(ㄓㄨㄛˊ ㄌㄧˋ ㄈㄥ ㄈㄚ)
to talk eloquently and knowledgeably
踔絕(ㄓㄨㄛˊ ㄐㄩㄝˊ)
①very high ②prominent
踔遠(ㄓㄨㄛˊ ㄩㄢˇ)
very high; very far

【踩】5894
ㄘㄞˇ tsae cǎi
to tread upon; to trample; to step upon
踩高蹺(ㄘㄞˇ ㄍㄠ ㄑㄧㄠ)
to walk on stilts
踩蹺(ㄘㄞˇ ㄑㄧㄠ)
(said of a vivacious lady role in Peking opera) to walk on small, artificial wooden feet tied to the ankles so that the actress sways while walking
踩三輪車(ㄘㄞˇ ㄙㄢ ㄌㄨㄣˊ ㄔㄜ)
to paddle a pedicab

【踦】5895
ㄐㄧ jii jī
1. the shin
2. to lean against

【踦】5895
ㄧˋ yi yì
to touch; to pierce

【踪】5896
(蹤) ㄗㄨㄥ tzong zōng
a footprint; traces; tracks

九畫

【踰】5897
ㄩ yu yú
1. same as 逾—to pass over; to cross; to go beyond; to transgress; to exceed
2. excessive; overly
踰分(ㄩ ㄈㄣˋ)
to go beyond one's proper function or position
踰年(ㄩ ㄋㄧㄢˊ)
the following year
踰矩(ㄩ ㄐㄩˇ)
to transgress the bounds of correctness
踰閑(ㄩ ㄒㄧㄢˊ)
to break moral conventions; to break decorum
踰侈(ㄩ ㄔˇ)
too extravagant; too luxurious
踰越(ㄩ ㄩㄝˋ)
to go beyond; to transgress
踰垣(ㄩ ㄩㄢˊ)
to go over a wall—to run away; to escape

【踱】5898
ㄉㄨㄛˊ duoh duó
to stroll; to walk slowly
踱步(ㄉㄨㄛˊ ㄅㄨˋ)
to pace; to walk slowly
踱來踱去(ㄉㄨㄛˊ ㄌㄞˊ ㄉㄨㄛˊ ㄑㄩˋ)
to stroll to and fro; to pace to and fro; to pace up and down

【踵】5899
ㄓㄨㄥˇ joong zhǒng
1. the heel
2. to follow
3. to call personally at; to go personally to; to call in person
踵門(ㄓㄨㄥˇ ㄇㄣˊ)
to call at another's house in person
踵接(ㄓㄨㄥˇ ㄐㄧㄝ)
so crowded that the people move with their toes on the heels of others
踵見(ㄓㄨㄥˇ ㄐㄧㄢˋ)
to call repeatedly in person

足部

【足部】

踶決肘見（ㄓㄨㄝˊ ㄐㄩㄝˊ ㄓㄡˇ ㄐㄧㄢˋ）
(literally) out at heels and elbows—tattered dress

踶謝（ㄓㄨˋ ㄒㄧㄝˋ）
to thank in person

踵至（ㄓㄨˇ ㄓˋ）
to arrive upon the heels of another; to arrive just behind

踵事增華（ㄓㄨˇ ㄕˋ ㄗㄥ ㄏㄨㄚˊ）
to follow a precedent and add to its excellence

踵武（ㄓㄨˇ ㄨˇ）
to carry on the work of one's predecessors

【踽】 5900 ㄐㄩˇ jeu juˇ
to walk alone

踽踽（ㄐㄩˇ ㄐㄩˇ）
walking alone

【踤】 5901 ㄉㄧㄝˊ dye dieˊ
to stamp one's foot

踤躞（ㄉㄧㄝˊ ㄒㄧㄝˋ）
①ambling: 我看到他踤躞而行。I saw him ambling along the road. ②going back and forth

踤足（ㄉㄧㄝˊ ㄗㄨˊ）
to stamp one's foot

【踼】 5902 ㄆㄧㄢ pyan pi¯an
walking unsteadily; limping

踼踼（ㄆㄧㄢ ㄆㄧㄢ）
①to walk unsteadily ②to walk with a dancing gait

【蹂】 5903 ㄖㄡˊ rou rouˊ
1. to tread upon; to trample
2. to tread out grain

蹂躪（ㄖㄡˊ ㄌㄧㄣˋ）
①to trample ②to devastate; rapacious acts

蹂踐（ㄖㄡˊ ㄐㄧㄢˋ）
to trample

【蹄】 5904 （蹏）ㄊㄧˊ tyi tiˊ
1. (zoology) a hoof
2. the feet of beasts

蹄膀（ㄊㄧˊ ㄆㄤˇ）
(dialect) the uppermost part of legs of pork

蹄筋（ㄊㄧˊ ㄐㄧㄣ）
the tendon of Achilles

蹄筌（ㄊㄧˊ ㄑㄩㄢˊ）
a kind of snare for game or fish

蹄形磁石（ㄊㄧˊ ㄒㄧㄥˊ ㄘˊ ㄕˊ）
a horseshoe magnet

蹄子（ㄊㄧˊ ˙ㄗ）
①hoofs ②(derogatory use) a wench

【踹】 5905 ㄔㄨㄞˋ chuay chua¯i
1. to kick
2. to tread; to trample; to stamp: 他一腳踹進水溝裏。He stamped into a ditch.
3. to spoil: 那項計劃被人踹了。Somebody spoiled that plan.

踹路（ㄔㄨㄞˋ ㄌㄨˋ）
to trample; to tread

【踳】 5906 ㄔㄨㄣˇ choen chunˇ
incongruous; disorderly

踳駮（ㄔㄨㄣˇ ㄅㄛˊ）
incongruous; disorderly

踳踳（ㄔㄨㄣˇ ㄔㄨㄣˇ）
disappointed; frustrated; unhappy

十畫

【蹈】 5907 ㄉㄠˋ daw da¯o
1. to tread; to step; to stamp one's foot
2. to follow; to pursue

蹈覆轍（ㄉㄠˋ ㄈㄨˋ ㄓㄜˊ）
to repeat a mistake someone has previously made

蹈歌（ㄉㄠˋ ㄍㄜ）
to beat time to a song with the feet

蹈海（ㄉㄠˋ ㄏㄞˇ）or 蹈海而死（ㄉㄠˋ ㄏㄞˇ ㄦˊ ㄙˇ）
to kill oneself by jumping into the sea

蹈虎尾（ㄉㄠˋ ㄏㄨˇ ㄨㄟˇ）
(literally) to tread on a tiger's tail—to run a great risk

蹈火赴湯（ㄉㄠˋ ㄏㄨㄛˇ ㄈㄨˋ ㄊㄤ）
to go through fire and water; to brave all possible difficulties 亦作「赴湯蹈火」

蹈襲（ㄉㄠˋ ㄒㄧˊ）
to copy or imitate (style, practice, etc.) slavishly

蹈常襲故（ㄉㄠˋ ㄔㄤˊ ㄒㄧˊ ㄍㄨˋ）
to follow conventions blindly; to follow the beaten track

蹈義（ㄉㄠˋ ㄧˋ）
to die for a cause; to be martyr to a cause

【蹇】 5908 ㄐㄧㄢˇ jean jianˇ
1. lame; crippled
2. slow
3. difficult; hard
4. haughty

蹇剝（ㄐㄧㄢˇ ㄅㄛˊ）
suffering from unfavorable times or bad luck

蹇兔（ㄐㄧㄢˇ ㄊㄨˋ）
a slow hare

蹇連（ㄐㄧㄢˇ ㄌㄧㄢˊ）
difficult to travel

蹇驢（ㄐㄧㄢˇ ㄌㄩˊ）
a lame donkey

蹇吃（ㄐㄧㄢˇ ㄔ）
to speak indistinctly

蹇澀（ㄐㄧㄢˇ ㄙㄜˋ）
difficult; hard

蹇修（ㄐㄧㄢˇ ㄒㄧㄡ）
a matchmaker 參見「媒人」

蹇滯（ㄐㄧㄢˇ ㄓˋ）
not proceeding smoothly

蹇澀（ㄐㄧㄢˇ ㄙㄜˋ）
difficult; hard

蹇諤（ㄐㄧㄢˇ ㄜˋ）
honest; upright

【蹉】 5909 ㄘㄨㄛ tsuo cuo¯
a failure; a miss

蹉跌（ㄘㄨㄛ ㄉㄧㄝˊ）
a failure; a slip; a mistake

蹉跎（ㄘㄨㄛ ㄊㄨㄛˊ）
①to slip and fall ②to miss a chance; to waste time: 他一再蹉跎。He lets one opportunity after another slip away.

【蹊】 5910 ㄒㄧ shi xi¯
1. a path; a footpath
2. to trample; to tread

蹊徑（ㄒㄧ ㄐㄧㄥˋ）
a narrow path

蹊蹺（ㄒㄧ ㄑㄧㄠ）
extraordinary; strange; queer: 那舊閣樓有點蹊蹺。There's something strange in the old attic.

【蹋】 5911 ㄊㄚˋ tah ta¯
to tread on

蹋地（ㄊㄚˋ ㄉㄧˋ）
to beat time to a song with the feet 亦作「踏歌」

【蹌】5912
1. ㄑㄧㄤ chiang qiāng
walking rapidly
蹌踉(ㄑㄧㄤ ㄌㄧㄤ)
①walking rapidly ②dancing

【蹌】5912
2. ㄑㄧㄤ chianq qiàng
walking unsteadily; limping

【蹎】5913
ㄐㄧ jyi jí
to walk daintily; to walk with small steps

【跳】5914
ㄊㄧ tyi tí
same as 蹄—hoofs

十一畫

【蹣】5915
ㄇㄢ man mǎn
1. to jump over
2. to limp
蹣跚(ㄇㄢ ㄕㄢ)
limping; to walk haltingly; to hobble

【蹕】5916
ㄅㄧ bih bì
1. to clear (the emperor's route) of traffic
2. an imperial carriage
蹕路(ㄅㄧ ㄌㄨ)
to clear the emperor's route of traffic

【蹙】5917
(蹵) ㄘㄨ tsuh cù
1. to contract; to draw together
2. urgent; imminent
3. sad; sorrowful; discomposed
蹙眉(ㄘㄨ ㄇㄟ)
to knit the brows; to frown
蹙頓(ㄘㄨ ㄐㄧˊ)
to hesitate to advance
蹙金(ㄘㄨ ㄐㄧㄣ)
a kind of embroidery worked with golden threads
蹙蹙(ㄘㄨ ㄘㄨ)
①drawn together; wrinkled ②descriptive of general distress
蹙蹜(ㄘㄨ ㄙㄨㄛ)
frightened; horrified; scared
蹙頞(ㄘㄨ ㄜ)
to knit the brows; to look distressed; to have a worried look

【蹚】5918
ㄊㄤ tang tāng
1. to tread on; to tread
2. to walk through mud or water; to wade; to ford
蹚渾水(ㄊㄤ ㄏㄨㄣ ㄕㄨㄟ)
(literally) to tread on muddy water — to associate with wicked people
蹚水(ㄊㄤ ㄕㄨㄟ)
to tread or wade water

【蹤】5919
(踪) ㄗㄨㄥ tzong zōng
1. a footprint; a track; traces; a vestige: 我找不到她的行蹤. I found no vestiges of her presence.
2. to follow the tracks of; to keep track of: 警方追蹤罪犯. The police trailed the criminal.
蹤跡(ㄗㄨㄥ ㄐㄧ)
①a track; traces; a vestige ②to keep track; to follow up clues
蹤由(ㄗㄨㄥ ㄧㄡ)
origin and development
蹤影(ㄗㄨㄥ ㄧㄥ)
traces; a vestige

【蹠】5920
ㄓ jyr zhí
1. to tread on; to step on
2. the sole (of the foot)
蹠骨(ㄓ ㄍㄨ)
(anatomy) the metatarsus; metatarsal bones

【蹡】5921
1. ㄑㄧㄤ chiang qiāng
walking; in motion
蹡蹡(ㄑㄧㄤ ㄑㄧㄤ)
walking

【蹡】5921
2. ㄑㄧㄤ chianq qiàng
to limp

【蹢】5922
1. ㄓ jyr zhí
to falter; to hesitate
蹢躅 or 蹢蠋(ㄓ ㄓㄨ)
①faltering; hesitant ②(botany) an azalea 亦作「山躑躅」or「羊躑躅」

【蹢】5922
2. ㄉㄧ dyi dí
a hoof

【蹦】5923
ㄅㄥ benq bèng
to skip; to caper; to trip; to

jump; to leap
蹦蹦跳跳(ㄅㄥ ㄅㄥ ㄊㄧㄠ ㄊㄧㄠ)
skipping; capering; tripping; romping; frolicsome
蹦蹦兒戲(ㄅㄥ ㄅㄥ ㄦ ㄒㄧ)
a form of Chinese opera enjoyed by the lower classes of Hopei Province 亦作「評戲」

【蹧】5924
ㄗㄠ tzau zāo
to spoil; to ruin
蹧踏 or 蹧蹋(ㄗㄠ ㄊㄚ)
to spoil; to ruin
蹧蹚 or 蹧踐(ㄗㄠ ㄐㄧㄢ)
to spoil; to ruin

【蹟】5925
ㄐㄧ ji jí
footprints; traces

【蹔】5926
ㄓㄢ jann zhǎn
same as 暫—temporary; fleeting; ephemeral

【蹴】5927
ㄘㄨ tsuh cù
same as 蹙—to contract or draw together

十二畫

【蹲】5928
ㄉㄨㄣ duen dūn
(讀音 ㄘㄨㄣ tswen cún)
1. to squat; to crouch: 他蹲了下來. He squatted (himself) down.
2. to stay
蹲不下去(ㄉㄨㄣ ㄅㄨ ㄒㄧㄚ ㄑㄩ)
unable to squat or crouch
蹲伏(ㄉㄨㄣ ㄈㄨ)
to squat; to crouch
蹲踞(ㄉㄨㄣ ㄐㄩ)
to squat; to crouch
蹲下去(ㄉㄨㄣ ㄒㄧㄚ ㄑㄩ) or 蹲下(ㄉㄨㄣ ㄒㄧㄚ)
to squat
蹲著(ㄉㄨㄣ ㄓㄜ)
squatting; crouching

【蹩】5929
(蹩) ㄅㄧㄝ bye bié
to limp
蹩腳(ㄅㄧㄝ ㄐㄧㄠ)
①lame ②inferior in quality; poor ③dejected

【蹬】5930
ㄉㄥ denq dèng
1. to tread on; to step on

【足部】

2. deprived of power or influence

【蹭】 5931
ㄘㄥ tseng cèng
1. deprived of power
2. to stroll
3. to protract

蹭蹬 (ㄘㄥ ㄉㄥ)
deprived of power or influence; to meet with setbacks; to be down on one's luck

【蹯】 5932
ㄈㄢ farn fán
paws

【蹙】 5933
(蹵) ㄘㄨ tsuh cù
1. to tread on
2. to kick
3. respectful

蹙然
①respectful ②uneasy; nervous; worried

【蹶】 5934
1. ㄐㄩㄝ jyue jué
1. to tread
2. to stumble and fall
3. to overturn; an overthrow
4. to daunt; to frustrate; to suffer a setback

蹶躓 (ㄐㄩㄝ ㄓˋ)
to stumble and fall

蹶然 (ㄐㄩㄝ ㄖㄢˊ)
standing up from fright; rising suddenly from fear

【蹶】 5934
2. ㄐㄩㄝ jyue jué
to kick backward

蹶子 (ㄐㄩㄝ ˙ㄗ)
a horse's backward kick with its hind hoof

【蹺】 5935
ㄑㄧㄠ chiau qiāo
1. same as 蹻—to raise the feet
2. on tiptoe: 那舞者蹺著脚走路。
The dancer walks on tiptoe.
3. stilts

蹺辮子 (ㄑㄧㄠ ㄅㄧㄢˋ ˙ㄗ)
to die

蹺課 (ㄑㄧㄠ ㄎㄜˋ)
(slang) to avoid attending classes

蹺家 (ㄑㄧㄠ ㄐㄧㄚ)
(slang) to run away from home

蹺捷 (ㄑㄧㄠ ㄐㄧㄝˊ)
able to move quickly and easily; agile

蹺敲 (ㄑㄧㄠ ㄑㄧ)

extraordinary; unusual

蹺蹺板 (ㄑㄧㄠ ㄑㄧㄠ ㄅㄢˇ)
a seesaw; a teeterboard

蹊蹺 (ㄑㄧ ㄒㄧ)
extraordinary; queer; strange
亦作【蹺蹊】

【蹻】 5936
1. ㄑㄧㄠ chiau qiāo
1. same as 蹺—to raise feet
2. stilts (高蹻)

蹻足 (ㄑㄧㄠ ㄗㄨˊ)
①to raise a foot (ready to go) ②a very brief period

【蹻】 5936
2. ㄐㄩㄠ jeau jiǎo
1. strong; brave
2. haughty; overbearing

蹻蹻 (ㄐㄩㄠ ㄐㄩㄠ)
①strong; brave ②haughty; overbearing; to be full of pride

蹻勇 (ㄐㄩㄠ ㄩㄥˇ)
(said of a man) strong

【蹼】 5937
ㄆㄨ pwu pú
webs on the feet of water fowls

【蹴】 5938
(蹵) ㄘㄨ tsuh cù
1. to tread
2. to kick

【蹩】 5939
ㄅㄧㄝˊ bye bié
same as 蹩—to limp

【蹰】 5940
ㄔㄨˊ chwu chú
same as 躕—to hesitate to advance

十三畫

【躄】 5941
(躃) ㄅㄧˋ bih bì
having both legs disabled; crippled in both legs

躄踊 (ㄅㄧˋ ㄩㄥˇ)
to stamp with grief

【躁】 5942
ㄗㄠˋ tzaw zào
1. irritable; hot-tempered
2. restless; uneasy
3. rashness

躁佻 (ㄗㄠˋ ㄊㄧㄠ)
frivolous; rash

躁戾 (ㄗㄠˋ ㄌㄧˋ)
irritable and cruel

躁狂 (ㄗㄠˋ ㄎㄨㄤˊ)
irritable and unrestrained

躁急 (ㄗㄠˋ ㄐㄧˊ)
impatient; uneasy

躁進 (ㄗㄠˋ ㄐㄧㄣˋ)
impatient to rise in the world

躁競 (ㄗㄠˋ ㄐㄧㄥˋ)
impatient to excel others; eager to grab power from others

躁切 (ㄗㄠˋ ㄑㄧㄝˋ)
anxious or impatient

躁率 (ㄗㄠˋ ㄕㄨㄞˋ)
impatient and careless

【躅】 5943
ㄓㄨˊ jwu zhú
to falter; to hesitate

【躇】 5944
ㄔㄨˊ chwu chú
to hesitate

【躉】 5945
ㄉㄨㄣˇ doen dǔn
1. a whole batch or amount
2. to buy or sell wholesale

躉批 (ㄉㄨㄣˇ ㄆㄧ)
by wholesale

躉賣 (ㄉㄨㄣˇ ㄇㄞˋ)
to sell wholesale

躉購 (ㄉㄨㄣˇ ㄍㄡˋ)
to buy wholesale: 我們係大批躉購。We buy goods wholesale.

躉船 (ㄉㄨㄣˇ ㄔㄨㄢˊ)
a lighter (for loading or unloading larger ships)

躉售 (ㄉㄨㄣˇ ㄕㄡˋ)
to sell wholesale

【躂】 5946
ㄊㄚˇ tah tǎ
to stumble; to slip

【躃】 5947
ㄅㄧˋ bih bì
same as 躄—crippled in both legs

十四畫

【躊】 5948
ㄔㄡˊ chour chóu
1. hesitant
2. complacent; confident

躊行 (ㄔㄡˊ ㄓㄨˊ)
to falter; to hesitate

躊躇 (ㄔㄡˊ ㄔㄨˊ)
①to hesitate; to waver; to falter; to vacillate; shilly-shally ②complacent; confident

【躋】 5949
ㄐㄧ jī jī
to go up; to rise; to ascend

【躍】 5950
ㄩㄝˋ yueh yuè
(舊音 ㄧㄠˋ yaw yào)
to jump; to leap; to bound; to spring

躍馬(ㄩㄝˋ ㄇㄚˇ)
to give the horse his head; to let a horse gallop

躍馬橫戈(ㄩㄝˋ ㄇㄚˇ ㄏㄥˊ ㄍㄜ)
to spur the horse and level the spear—to take a challenging position

躍動(ㄩㄝˋ ㄉㄨㄥˋ)
to move actively; to be in lively motion

躍進(ㄩㄝˋ ㄐㄧㄣˋ)or(ㄧㄠˋ ㄐㄧㄣˋ)
①to leap forward ②to make rapid progress: 他的功課躍進神速. He is making rapid progress in his studies.

躍起(ㄩㄝˋ ㄑㄧˇ)
to leap up; to jump up

躍然紙上(ㄩㄝˋ ㄖㄢˊ ㄓˇ ㄕㄤˋ)
(said of things portrayed in literature or paintings) full of life; vivid

躍躍欲試(ㄩㄝˋ ㄩㄝˋ ㄩˋ ㄕˋ)
impatient to have a try; eager to do something

十五畫

【躐】 5951
ㄌㄧㄝˋ lieh liè
to transgress; to overstep

躐等(ㄌㄧㄝˋ ㄉㄥˇ)
to skip steps; to fail to follow proper order

躐席(ㄌㄧㄝˋ ㄒㄧˊ)
to take a seat which one is not entitled to

【躓】 5952
ㄓˇ jyr zhǐ
to falter; to hesitate

躑躅(ㄓˊ ㄓㄨˊ)
①to falter; to hesitate; to loiter around ②(botany) an azalea

【躓】 5953
ㄓˋ jyh zhì
1. to stumble; to trip
2. to be frustrated; to suffer a setback

躓頓(ㄓˋ ㄉㄨㄣˋ)
to stumble and stop

【躕】 5954
ㄔㄨˊ chwu chú
to falter; to hesitate

十六畫

【躚】 5955
ㄒㄧㄢ shian xiān
to turn round and round

躚躚(ㄒㄧㄢ ㄒㄧㄢ)
turning round and round; twirling; dancing

十七畫

【躞】 5956
ㄒㄧㄝˋ shieh xiè
1. walking; proceeding
2. a pin or rod for rolling a scroll; an axis

躞蹀(ㄒㄧㄝˋ ㄉㄧㄝˊ)
walking; proceeding

十八畫

【躡】 5957
ㄋㄧㄝˋ nieh niè
1. to tread on; to step over
2. to follow; to pursue
3. to walk lightly; to tiptoe: 她躡著腳走出書房. She tiptoed out of the study.

躡步(ㄋㄧㄝˋ ㄅㄨˋ)
walking with mincing steps

躡跟(ㄋㄧㄝˋ ㄍㄣ)
(said of shoes) too large or too small for the feet

躡手躡腳(ㄋㄧㄝˋ ㄕㄡˇ ㄋㄧㄝˋ ㄐㄧㄠˇ)
walking with light steps; walking stealthily: 他躡手躡腳走下樓梯. He walked downstairs stealthily.

躡足(ㄋㄧㄝˋ ㄗㄨˊ)
to step upon another's foot

躡足潛蹤(ㄋㄧㄝˋ ㄗㄨˊ ㄑㄧㄢˊ ㄗㄨㄥ)
walking with light steps; walking stealthily

躡影追蹤(ㄋㄧㄝˋ ㄧㄥˇ ㄓㄨㄟ ㄗㄨㄥ)
to trace; to look for; to locate

【躥】 5958
ㄘㄨㄢ tsuan cuān
1. to jump
2. (said of someone) to get promoted
3. to spurt out

躥房越脊(ㄘㄨㄢ ㄈㄤˊ ㄩㄝˋ ㄐㄧˊ)
to rush about on the roofs

(as housebreakers)

二十畫

【躪】 5959
ㄌㄧㄣˋ linn lìn
to trample; to devastate; to overrun; to lay a place waste

身 部
ㄕㄣ shen shēn

【身】 5960
1. ㄕㄣ shen shēn
1. a body; a trunk
2. one's own person; oneself
3. a child in the womb
4. in person; personally

身敗名裂(ㄕㄣ ㄅㄞˋ ㄇㄧㄥˊ ㄌㄧㄝˋ)
to lose both one's fortune and honor

身邊(ㄕㄣ ㄅㄧㄢ) or 身畔(ㄕㄣ ㄆㄢˋ)
one's vicinity; one's side; one's immediate surroundings: 她坐在我身邊. She sat at my side.

身邊人(ㄕㄣ ㄅㄧㄢ ㄖㄣˊ)
①an attendant ②a concubine

身不動勝不搖(ㄕㄣ ㄅㄨˋ ㄉㄨㄥˋ ㄕㄥˋ ㄅㄨˋ ㄧㄠˊ)
not to move even the body or the arms—not to labor at all

身不由主(ㄕㄣ ㄅㄨˋ ㄧㄡˊ ㄓㄨˇ) or 身不由己(ㄕㄣ ㄅㄨˋ ㄧㄡˊ ㄐㄧˇ)
unable to act according to one's own will; involuntarily

身法(ㄕㄣ ㄈㄚˇ)
techniques or arts of maneuvering the body in self-defense

身分證(ㄕㄣ ㄈㄣˋ ㄓㄥˋ) or 身份證(ㄕㄣ ㄈㄣˋ ㄓㄥˋ)
a citizenship card; an identity card; an ID card

身分(ㄕㄣ ㄈㄣˋ)
one's status or position

身底下(ㄕㄣ ㄉㄧˇ ㄒㄧㄚˋ)
①under the body ②the place where one is living

身段(ㄕㄣ ㄉㄨㄢˋ)
①physique; a figure ②postures (of a dancer, etc.)

〔身部〕

身體(ㄕㄣ ㄊㄧˇ)
①the body ②health: 他一向身體俱健康。He has always had good health.

身體力行(ㄕㄣ ㄊㄧˇ ㄌㄧˋ ㄒㄧㄥˊ)
to carry out by actual efforts; to practice personally (what one preaches)

身體檢查(ㄕㄣ ㄊㄧˇ ㄐㄧㄢˇ ㄔㄚˊ)
a physical examination; a physical checkup

身歷聲(ㄕㄣ ㄌㄧˋ ㄕㄥ)
stereophonic; high fidelity 亦作「高度傳真」

身臨其境(ㄕㄣ ㄌㄧㄣˊ ㄑㄧˊ ㄐㄧㄥˋ)
to experience personally; to be personally on the scene

身量(ㄕㄣ ㄌㄧㄤˋ)
one's height; one's physical dimensions: 她身量不高。She is not tall.

身高(ㄕㄣ ㄍㄠ)
stature; height

身故(ㄕㄣ ㄍㄨˋ)
to die: 張先生去年身故。Mr. Chang died last year.

身後(ㄕㄣ ㄏㄡˋ)
after one's death

身後名(ㄕㄣ ㄏㄡˋ ㄇㄧㄥˊ)
posthumous fame

身後蕭條(ㄕㄣ ㄏㄡˋ ㄒㄧㄠ ㄊㄧㄠˊ)
to die without leaving property or progeny behind

身火(ㄕㄣ ㄏㄨㄛˇ)
(Buddhism) desires

身懷六甲(ㄕㄣ ㄏㄨㄞˊ ㄌㄧㄡˋ ㄐㄧㄚˇ)
to be pregnant: 她身懷六甲。She is pregnant.

身己(ㄕㄣ ㄐㄧˇ)
oneself

身家(ㄕㄣ ㄐㄧㄚ)
family background; ancestry; pedigree

身家不清(ㄕㄣ ㄐㄧㄚ ㄅㄨˋ ㄑㄧㄥ)
of mean descent or parentage (formerly said of the offspring of prostitutes, entertainers, servants, and foot soldiers, who were barred from civil service examinations)

身家調查(ㄕㄣ ㄐㄧㄚ ㄉㄧㄠˋ ㄔㄚˊ)
the investigation of one's family background

身家難保(ㄕㄣ ㄐㄧㄚ ㄋㄢˊ ㄅㄠˇ)
to live in great danger; having no safety for oneself and

one's dependents

身家清白(ㄕㄣ ㄐㄧㄚ ㄑㄧㄥ ㄅㄞˊ)
of respectable descent or parentage

身家性命(ㄕㄣ ㄐㄧㄚ ㄒㄧㄥˋ ㄇㄧㄥˋ)
one's personal safety as well as that of one's family

身價(ㄕㄣ ㄐㄧㄚˋ)
one's social position or prestige

身價百倍(ㄕㄣ ㄐㄧㄚˋ ㄅㄞˇ ㄅㄟˋ)
to receive a tremendous boost in one's social position or prestige

身教(ㄕㄣ ㄐㄧㄠˋ)
to teach by personal example: 身教勝於言教。Example is better than precept.

身經百戰(ㄕㄣ ㄐㄧㄥ ㄅㄞˇ ㄓㄢˋ)
to have gone through numerous battles

身輕言微(ㄕㄣ ㄑㄧㄥ ㄧㄢˊ ㄨㄟˊ)
When one's position is low, one's words carry little weight.

身軀(ㄕㄣ ㄑㄩ)
one's body; one's person

身心(ㄕㄣ ㄒㄧㄣ)
body and mind: 他有健全的身心。He has a sound body and mind.

身心健康(ㄕㄣ ㄒㄧㄣ ㄐㄧㄢˋ ㄎㄤ)
sound in body and mind; physically and mentally healthy

身心愉快(ㄕㄣ ㄒㄧㄣ ㄩˊ ㄎㄨㄞˋ)
feeling well both physically and mentally

身正不怕影兒斜(ㄕㄣ ㄓㄥˋ ㄅㄨˋ ㄆㄚˋ ㄧㄥˇ ㄦˊ ㄒㄧㄝˊ)
A righteous man fears no criticisms.

身長(ㄕㄣ ㄓㄤˇ)
①the stature or height (of a person) ②the body length (of an animal)

身世(ㄕㄣ ㄕˋ)
experiences in one's lifetime; one's life

身手(ㄕㄣ ㄕㄡˇ)
agility; dexterity; artistic skill

身首(ㄕㄣ ㄕㄡˇ)
the trunk and the head

身首異處(ㄕㄣ ㄕㄡˇ ㄧˋ ㄔㄨˋ)
to be beheaded

身受(ㄕㄣ ㄕㄡˋ)

①to accept personally; to receive in person ②to experience or endure personally

身上(ㄕㄣ ㄕㄤˋ)
①on one's body: 我身上不舒服。I'm not feeling well. ②(to have something) with one: 我身上沒帶錢。I haven't got money with me.

身子(ㄕㄣ ˙ㄗ)
①the body; the trunk ②a child in the womb; pregnancy

身在福中不知福(ㄕㄣ ㄗㄞˋ ㄈㄨˊ ㄓㄨㄥ ㄅㄨˋ ㄓ ㄈㄨˊ)
Living in happiness, one often fails to appreciate what happiness really means.

身材(ㄕㄣ ㄘㄞˊ)
physique; physical build; figure: 她身材很好。She has a nice figure.

身兒(ㄕㄣ ㄦ)
①a suit (of clothes) ②physical build

身影(ㄕㄣ ㄧㄥˇ)
a person's silhouette; a form; a figure

身無長物(ㄕㄣ ㄨˊ ㄓㄤˇ ㄨˋ)
to have nothing; penniless

身外之物(ㄕㄣ ㄨㄞˋ ㄓ ㄨˋ)
(literally) things that are not part of one's body; money; material wealth

身孕(ㄕㄣ ㄩㄣˋ)
a child in the womb; pregnancy

【身】 5960
②(ㄐㄩㄢ) jiuan juǎn
參看「身毒」

身毒(ㄐㄩㄢ ㄉㄨˊ)
an ancient name of India

三畫

【躬】 5961
(ㄍㄨㄥ) gong gōng
1. the body; the person
2. in person; personally
3. to bend (the body)

躬逢其盛(ㄍㄨㄥ ㄈㄥˊ ㄑㄧˊ ㄕㄥˋ)
to be personally present at the gala occasion

躬臨(ㄍㄨㄥ ㄌㄧㄣˊ)
to be present personally; to attend in person

躬耕(ㄍㄨㄥ ㄍㄥ)

躬耕《《ㄍㄨㄥ ㄐ|ㄥ》
to plough in person (especially said of an emperor)

躬稼《《ㄍㄨㄥ ㄐ|Ｙ》
to work on the farm personally

躬行《《ㄍㄨㄥ ㄒ|ㄥ》
in person; personally

躬行《《ㄍㄨㄥ ㄒ|ㄥ》
to take action personally; to practice a thing personally

躬身《《ㄍㄨㄥ ㄕㄣ》
to bend the body in respect; to bow

躬詣《《ㄍㄨㄥ |》
to call at (another's house) personally

四畫

【軑】 5962
(軑) ㄉㄢ dan dàn
to delay (unintentionally)

軑擱《ㄉㄢ ㄍㄜ》
to delay (unintentionally); to fail to complete in time

軑心《ㄉㄢ ㄒ|ㄣ》or 軑憂《ㄉㄢ |ㄨ》
to be worried; to be apprehensive

軑誤《ㄉㄢ ㄨ》
①to mismanage (a thing) by an improper delay ②to take more (time) than justified; to delay

六畫

【躱】 5963
ㄉㄨㄛ duoo duǒ
1. to dodge; to shun; to avoid; to escape
2. to hide

躲避《ㄉㄨㄛ ㄅ|》
to dodge; to ward off; to shun: 她在人群中躲避他。She dodged him in the crowd.

躲避球《ㄉㄨㄛ ㄅ| ㄑ|ㄡ》
dodge ball (a kind of ball game played by children)

躲不了《ㄉㄨㄛ ·ㄅㄨㄜ ·ㄌ|ㄠ》
unavoidable, inescapable

躲不開《ㄉㄨㄛ ·ㄅㄨㄜ ㄎㄞ》
unable to dodge; unable to shun

躲躲閃閃《ㄉㄨㄛ ㄉㄨㄛ ㄕㄢ ㄕㄢ》
①moving carefully so as to avoid danger ②bashful, timid; shy

躲匿《ㄉㄨㄛ ㄋ|》
to hide oneself

躲懶《ㄉㄨㄛ ㄌㄢ》
to shun work; to shy away from work

躲開《ㄉㄨㄛ ·ㄎㄞ》
①to ward off; to dodge: 他躲開了這個球。He dodged the ball. ②to run away from; to shirk: 他總是躲開責任。He always shirks his duty.

躲債《ㄉㄨㄛ ㄓㄞ》
to run away from one's creditor; to avoid a creditor

躲閃《ㄉㄨㄛ ㄕㄢ》
to dodge; to ward off

躲藏《ㄉㄨㄛ ㄘㄤ》
to hide oneself; to hide: 你最好躲藏起來。You had better hide.

躲雨《ㄉㄨㄛ ㄩ》
to take shelter from the rain

八畫

【躺】 5964
ㄊㄤ taang tǎng
to be in a lying position; to lie down

躺下《ㄊㄤ ·ㄒ|Ｙ》
to lie down

躺著《ㄊㄤ ·ㄓㄜ》
to be in a lying position

躺椅《ㄊㄤ |》
a couch; a deck chair; a divan; a reclining chair: 坐在躺椅上。Sit on the couch.

十一畫

【軀】 5965
ㄑㄩ chiu qū
1. the body; the trunk
2. a child in the womb

軀體《ㄑㄩ ㄊ|》
the body

軀幹《ㄑㄩ ㄍㄢ》
①(anatomy) the trunk ②the body; the physical build

軀幹骨《ㄑㄩ ㄍㄢ ㄍㄨ》
the bones of the trunk

軀殼《ㄑㄩ ㄑ|ㄠ》or《ㄑㄩ ㄎㄜ》or《ㄑㄩ ㄎㄨㄞ》
the body (conceived as the shell of the soul)

車 部
ㄐ|ㄡ jiu jū

【車】 5966
ㄐ|ㄡ jiu jū
name of a chessman in a kind of Chinese chess known as 象棋

【車】 5366
(語音 ㄔㄜ che chē)
1. a vehicle
2. a wheeled machine
3. to carry in a cart
4. to shape (things) on a lathe; to lathe; to turn
5. to lift water by a water-wheel

車僕《ㄐ|ㄡ ㄆㄨ》
an official in charge of vehicles in ancient times

車馬《ㄐ|ㄡ ㄇㄚ》or《ㄐ|ㄡ ㄇㄚ》
vehicles and horses

車馬喧闐《ㄐ|ㄡ ㄇㄚ ㄒㄩㄢ ㄊ|ㄢ》
the hustle and bustle of a city

車馬殷闐《ㄐ|ㄡ ㄇㄚ |ㄣ ㄊ|ㄢ》
crowded with carriages and horses

車服《ㄐ|ㄡ ㄈㄨ》
chariots and robes (commonly used in feudal times to reward vassals)

車殆馬煩 or 車怠馬煩《ㄐ|ㄡ ㄉㄞ ㄇㄚ ㄈㄢ》
(literally) The vehicle is worn down and the horse is weary.—the hardships of long travel

車徒《ㄐ|ㄡ ㄊㄨ》
chariots and foot soldiers

車同軌《ㄐ|ㄡ ㄊㄨㄥ ㄍㄨㄟ》
(literally) All vehicles have the same gauge.—The country is unified.

車笠之盟《ㄐ|ㄡ ㄌ| ㄓ ㄇㄥ》
close friendship

車騎《ㄐ|ㄡ ㄐ|》
groups of vehicles and horses

車騎將軍《ㄐ|ㄡ ㄐ| ㄐ|ㄤ ㄐㄩㄣ》
an ancient title of a commanding general

（車部）

車駕(ㄔㄜ ㄐㄧㄚˋ)
the Emperor; His Majesty

車轍(ㄔㄜ ㄓㄜˊ)or(ㄔㄜ ㄔㄜˋ)
ruts (of vehicles)

車師(ㄔㄜ ㄕ)
name of an ancient country in what is Chinese Turkestan today

車在馬前(ㄔㄜ ㄗㄞˋ ㄇㄚˇ ㄑㄧㄢˊ)
to put the cart before the horse—preposterous

車載斗量(ㄔㄜ ㄗㄞˋ ㄉㄡˇ ㄌㄧㄤˊ)
by cartloads and bushelfuls—a great deal; available in great quantity

車右(ㄔㄜ ㄧㄡˋ)
an armed escort who proceeds on the right of the escorted carriage

車把(ㄔㄜ ㄅㄚˇ)
handle bars (on bicycles or other vehicles); the shaft (of a wheelbarrow, etc.)

車把式 or 車把勢(ㄔㄜ ㄅㄚˇ ˙ㄕ)
a carrier; a carter

車牌(ㄔㄜ ㄆㄞˊ)
the license plate (on a vehicle)

車篷子(ㄔㄜ ㄆㄥˊ ˙ㄗ)
the canvas tops on vehicles

車票(ㄔㄜ ㄆㄧㄠˋ)
a train or bus ticket

車馬費(ㄔㄜ ㄇㄚˇ ㄈㄟˋ)
transportation allowances

車幔(ㄔㄜ ㄇㄢˋ)
curtains on a carriage

車門(ㄔㄜ ㄇㄣˊ)
doors of a vehicle

車費(ㄔㄜ ㄈㄟˋ)
a fare

車房(ㄔㄜ ˙ㄈㄤ)
a garage

車夫(ㄔㄜ ˙ㄈㄨ)
a cabman; a carter; a driver; a rickshaw man; a chauffeur

車道(ㄔㄜ ㄉㄠˋ)
roads or lanes for vehicular traffic

車燈(ㄔㄜ ㄉㄥ)
the headlight (or headlamp) of an automobile or a motorcycle or bicycle

車墊子(ㄔㄜ ㄉㄧㄢˋ ˙ㄗ)
a cushioned seat on a vehicle

車胎(ㄔㄜ ㄊㄞ)
tires (on vehicle wheels)

車頭(ㄔㄜ ㄊㄡˊ)
the engine or locomotive of a train

車僮(ㄔㄜ ㄊㄨㄥˊ)
boys serving passengers (on a train)

車輛(ㄔㄜ ㄌㄧㄤˋ)
vehicles; rolling stock

車輪(ㄔㄜ ㄌㄨㄣˊ)
wheels of a vehicle: 脚踏車有兩個車輪。A bicycle has two wheels.

車輪戰(ㄔㄜ ㄌㄨㄣˊ ㄓㄢˋ)
to fight an enemy by turns in order to wear him down

車轂(ㄔㄜ ㄍㄨˇ)
wheels of a vehicle

車軲轆話(ㄔㄜ ㄍㄨ ˙ㄌㄨ ㄏㄨㄚˋ)
to keep saying the same thing

車攻(ㄔㄜ ㄍㄨㄥ)
to attack by chariots

車庫(ㄔㄜ ㄎㄨˋ)
a garage; a vehicle barn

車行(ㄔㄜ ㄏㄤˊ)
①a vehicle dealer's shop ②a taxi company

車禍(ㄔㄜ ㄏㄨㄛˋ)
an automobile or a train accident; a traffic accident: 昨天有一椿車禍。There was a motorcar accident yesterday.

車匠(ㄔㄜ ㄐㄧㄤˋ)
a wheelwright

車前子(ㄔㄜ ㄑㄧㄢˊ ˙ㄗ)
(botany) plantago seeds (used as medicine)

車前草(ㄔㄜ ㄑㄧㄢˊ ㄘㄠˇ)
(botany) the plantain

車錢(ㄔㄜ ˙ㄑㄧㄢ)
a taxi fare; a pedicab or rickshaw fare; a fare: 下個月車錢要漲了。Fares will be raised next month.

車繡(ㄔㄜ ㄒㄧㄡˋ)
embroidery done on a sewing machine

車廂(ㄔㄜ ㄒㄧㄤ)
cars (of a train); railway carriages; compartments

車照(ㄔㄜ ㄓㄠˋ)
the license (of a car, motorcycle, etc.)

車軸(ㄔㄜ ㄓㄡˊ)
an axle

車軸關節(ㄔㄜ ㄓㄡˊ ㄍㄨㄢ ㄐㄧㄝˊ)
a pivot joint

車站(ㄔㄜ ㄓㄢˋ)
①a railway station ②a bus station; a bus stop; a bus terminal

車長(ㄔㄜ ㄓㄤˇ)
a train master

車長室(ㄔㄜ ㄓㄤˇ ㄕˋ)
the train master's compartment

車掌(ㄔㄜ ㄓㄤˇ)
a bus conductress or conductor

車廠(ㄔㄜ ㄔㄤˇ)
a shop in which motorcars are repaired or serviced

車窗(ㄔㄜ ㄔㄨㄤ)
car windows; train windows: 誰打破車窗呢? Who broke the car window?

車牀(ㄔㄜ ㄔㄨㄤˊ)
a lathe

車身(ㄔㄜ ㄕㄣ)
the car body; the vehicle body; the automobile body

車水(ㄔㄜ ㄕㄨㄟˇ)
to lift water by means of a scoop wheel

車水馬龍(ㄔㄜ ㄕㄨㄟˇ ㄇㄚˇ ㄌㄨㄥˊ)or(ㄐㄩ ㄕㄨㄟˇ ㄇㄚˇ ㄌㄨㄥˊ)
(literally) Carts flow like a stream and horses move like a dragon.—Traffic is heavy.

車資(ㄔㄜ ㄗ)
a fare for a vehicle ride

車子(ㄔㄜ ˙ㄗ)
a vehicle

車次(ㄔㄜ ㄘˋ)
①the train number ②the motor coach number (designating a schedule of departure)

車速(ㄔㄜ ㄙㄨˋ)
the speed of a motor vehicle

車帷(ㄔㄜ ㄨㄟˊ)
curtains on a carriage or car

【車】5966
3. ㄔㄜ che chē
a Chinese family name

車胤(ㄔㄜ ㄧㄣˋ)
Che Yin, a 4th century scholar who studied under the light of glowworms in his youth

車螢孫雪(ㄔㄜˊ ㄧㄥˊ ㄙㄨㄣ ㄒㄩㄝˇ)
(literally) Che Yin (車胤) studied by the light of glow-worms and Sun Kang (孫康) studied by the light of snow. —to study very diligently

一畫

【軋】 5967
1. ㄧㄚˋ yah yà
to crush; to grind

軋布機(ㄧㄚˋ ㄅㄨˋ ㄐㄧ)
a mangle; a calender 亦作「軋光機」

軋花機(ㄧㄚˋ ㄏㄨㄚ ㄐㄧ)or 軋棉機(ㄧㄚˋ ㄇㄧㄢˊ ㄐㄧ)
a cotton gin

軋傷(ㄧㄚˋ ㄕㄤ)
to run over and injure

軋死(ㄧㄚˋ ㄙˇ)or 軋斃(ㄧㄚˋ ㄅㄧˋ)
to run over and kill: 他被火車軋死。He was run over and killed by the train.

軋碎(ㄧㄚˋ ㄙㄨㄟˋ)
to crush to pieces

軋軋(ㄧㄚˋ ㄧㄚˋ)
the creaking sound of a machine in operation

【軋】 5967
2. ㄍㄚˊ gar gá
1. (in the Wu dialect) to crowd
2. (in the Wu dialect) to make friends
3. (in the Wu dialect) to check

軋姘頭(ㄍㄚˊ ㄆㄧㄣ ㄊㄡˊ)
(in the Wu dialect) to commit adultery

軋頭寸(ㄍㄚˊ ㄊㄡˊ ㄘㄨㄣˋ)
(informal) to scramble for cash to meet a payment 參看「調頭寸」

二畫

【軌】 5968
1. ㄍㄨㄟˇ goei guǐ
1. the space between the right and the left wheels of a vehicle
2. a rut; a track; a path
3. an orbit
4. a rule; a regulation
5. to follow; to comply with; to obey

軌模(ㄍㄨㄟˇ ㄇㄛˊ)
a pattern; a rule: 他是所有美德之軌模。He is a pattern of all the virtues.

軌範(ㄍㄨㄟˇ ㄈㄢˋ)
a pattern; a model; a rule

軌道(ㄍㄨㄟˇ ㄉㄠˋ)
① a railway track ② an orbit ③laws and conventions ④ a course; a track

軌度(ㄍㄨㄟˇ ㄉㄨˋ)
a rule; a regulation

軌跡(ㄍㄨㄟˇ ㄐㄧ)
①(mathematics) a locus ② (astronomy) an orbit

軌距(ㄍㄨㄟˇ ㄐㄩˋ)
(said of railroad tracks) the gauge

軌制(ㄍㄨㄟˇ ㄓˋ)
a system; a rule

軌轍(ㄍㄨㄟˇ ㄓㄜˊ)or(ㄍㄨㄟˇ ㄔㄜˋ)
a rut

軌則(ㄍㄨㄟˇ ㄗㄜˊ)
a rule; a regulation: 軌則甚嚴。The regulations are strict.

軌外行為(ㄍㄨㄟˇ ㄨㄞˋ ㄒㄧㄥˊ ㄨㄟˊ)
transgression of rules or regulations

【軍】 5969
ㄐㄩㄣ jiun jūn
1. the military; forces; of national defense
2. corps (as a military unit)
3. an armed service

軍備(ㄐㄩㄣ ㄅㄟˋ)
armaments; arms

軍部(ㄐㄩㄣ ㄅㄨˋ)
the war ministry; the defense department

軍票(ㄐㄩㄣ ㄆㄧㄠˋ)
bank notes used by military personnel in war zones

軍帽(ㄐㄩㄣ ㄇㄠˋ)
a military cap or hat

軍門(ㄐㄩㄣ ㄇㄣˊ)
①the entrance to a military camp, fort, etc. ② (Ching Dynasty) a commander in chief

軍民(ㄐㄩㄣ ㄇㄧㄣˊ)
soldiers and civilians

軍民合作(ㄐㄩㄣ ㄇㄧㄣˊ ㄏㄜˊ ㄗㄨㄛˋ)
cooperation between soldiers and civilians

軍閥(ㄐㄩㄣ ㄈㄚˊ)
① a military clique ② the militarists ③a warlord

軍閥割據(ㄐㄩㄣ ㄈㄚˊ ㄍㄜˋ ㄐㄩˋ)
the rampancy of warlords; the segmentation of a country by warlords

軍法(ㄐㄩㄣ ㄈㄚˇ)
military law

軍法官(ㄐㄩㄣ ㄈㄚˇ ㄍㄨㄢ)
a judge advocate

軍法會審(ㄐㄩㄣ ㄈㄚˇ ㄏㄨㄟˋ ㄕㄣˇ)or 軍法審判(ㄐㄩㄣ ㄈㄚˇ ㄕㄣˇ ㄆㄢˋ)
courts-martial

軍法會議(ㄐㄩㄣ ㄈㄚˇ ㄏㄨㄟˋ ㄧˋ)
a court-martial sitting or session; a court-martial

軍法局長(ㄐㄩㄣ ㄈㄚˇ ㄐㄩˊ ㄓㄤˇ)
the judge advocate general

軍法裁判所(ㄐㄩㄣ ㄈㄚˇ ㄘㄞˊ ㄆㄢˋ ㄙㄨㄛˇ)
a military court; a court-martial 參看「軍事法庭」

軍法從事(ㄐㄩㄣ ㄈㄚˇ ㄘㄨㄥˊ ㄕˋ)
to be dealt with according to martial law

軍費(ㄐㄩㄣ ㄈㄟˋ)
military expenses; a defense budget: 軍費被縮減了。Military expenses were cut down.

軍方(ㄐㄩㄣ ㄈㄤ)
the military authorities

軍服(ㄐㄩㄣ ㄈㄨˊ)
(military) uniform

軍刀(ㄐㄩㄣ ㄉㄠ)
a saber

軍刀機(ㄐㄩㄣ ㄉㄠ ㄐㄧ)
Saberjet (of the U.S. Air Force in the 1950's)

軍隊(ㄐㄩㄣ ㄉㄨㄟˋ)
troops; the armed forces

軍帖(ㄐㄩㄣ ㄊㄧㄝˇ)
a military proclamation

軍團(ㄐㄩㄣ ㄊㄨㄢˊ)
①an army (a unit consisting of a number of corps) ② any large unit of troops; a legion

軍壘(ㄐㄩㄣ ㄌㄟˇ)
barriers around a fort; a fort 亦作「軍壁」

軍禮(ㄐㄩㄣ ㄌㄧˇ)
military rites; a military salute: 軍官回了一個軍禮。The officer returned the military salute.

軍力(ㄐㄩㄣ ㄌㄧˋ)
military strength (or power)

軍糧(ㄐㄩㄣ ㄌㄧㄤˊ)

〔軍部〕

〔軍部〕

food supplies for military units

軍令(ㄐㄩㄣ ㄌㄧㄥˋ)
military orders

軍令狀(ㄐㄩㄣ ㄌㄧㄥˋ ㄓㄨㄤˋ)
a written pledge to do something, the failing of which would subject one to military punishment

軍令如山(ㄐㄩㄣ ㄌㄧㄥˋ ㄖㄨˊ ㄕㄢ)
Military orders cannot be disobeyed or revoked.

軍旅(ㄐㄩㄣ ㄌㄩˇ)
troops; armies

軍律(ㄐㄩㄣ ㄌㄩˋ)
military discipline; military laws: 軍律嚴明。Military laws are peremptory.

軍略(ㄐㄩㄣ ㄌㄩㄝˋ)
military strategy

軍歌(ㄐㄩㄣ ㄍㄜ)
a war song; a martial chant: 她唱了一首軍歌。She sang a war song.

軍港(ㄐㄩㄣ ㄍㄤˇ)
a naval harbor; a naval port

軍國民教育(ㄐㄩㄣ ㄍㄨㄛˊ ㄇㄧㄣˊ ㄐㄧㄠˋ ㄩˋ)
national military education

軍國大事(ㄐㄩㄣ ㄍㄨㄛˊ ㄉㄚˋ ㄕˋ)
affairs of national defense and administration

軍國主義(ㄐㄩㄣ ㄍㄨㄛˊ ㄓㄨˇ ㄧˋ)
militarism

軍規(ㄐㄩㄣ ㄍㄨㄟ)
military discipline

軍官(ㄐㄩㄣ ㄍㄨㄢ)
(military) an officer: 他希望當軍官。He wished to be an officer.

軍官學校(ㄐㄩㄣ ㄍㄨㄢ ㄒㄩㄝˊ ㄒㄧㄠˋ)
an academy for the training of officers, such as the military academy, naval academy and air force academy

軍管區(ㄐㄩㄣ ㄍㄨㄢˇ ㄑㄩ)
a military organization on the provincial level in charge of conscription, training and mobilization of recruits and reservists, etc.

軍功(ㄐㄩㄣ ㄍㄨㄥ)
military achievements; meritorious military services; military exploits

軍號(ㄐㄩㄣ ㄏㄠˋ)
a bugle

軍火(ㄐㄩㄣ ㄏㄨㄛˇ)
arms; munitions

軍火庫(ㄐㄩㄣ ㄏㄨㄛˇ ㄎㄨˋ)
an arsenal

軍機(ㄐㄩㄣ ㄐㄧ)
① a military secret: 軍機洩漏出去了。The military secret has leaked out. ② a military aircraft: 他搭軍機到高雄。He went to Kaohsiung by military aircraft.

軍機大臣(ㄐㄩㄣ ㄐㄧ ㄉㄚˋ ㄔㄣˊ)
the minister of defense (prior to the Republic)

軍機處(ㄐㄩㄣ ㄐㄧ ㄔㄨˋ)
the ministry of defense (but later expanded to deal with other affairs as well) under the Manchu government

軍籍(ㄐㄩㄣ ㄐㄧˊ)
① a military register ② military status

軍妓(ㄐㄩㄣ ㄐㄧˋ)
a military prostitute

軍紀(ㄐㄩㄣ ㄐㄧˋ)
military discipline

軍階(ㄐㄩㄣ ㄐㄧㄝ)
(military) a rank; a grade

軍界(ㄐㄩㄣ ㄐㄧㄝˋ)
the military circles; the military

軍艦(ㄐㄩㄣ ㄐㄧㄢˋ)
a war vessel; a warship; a man-of-war

軍警(ㄐㄩㄣ ㄐㄧㄥˇ)
the military and the police

軍旗(ㄐㄩㄣ ㄑㄧˊ)
military banners, colors or flags

軍器(ㄐㄩㄣ ㄑㄧˋ)
military equipment

軍情(ㄐㄩㄣ ㄑㄧㄥˊ)
a military (or war) situation

軍權(ㄐㄩㄣ ㄑㄩㄢˊ)
the power over military or national defense matters

軍犬(ㄐㄩㄣ ㄑㄩㄢˇ)
police dogs used for military purposes

軍械(ㄐㄩㄣ ㄒㄧㄝˋ)
military equipment; ordnance; armaments

軍校(ㄐㄩㄣ ㄒㄧㄠˋ)
a military school

軍校學生(ㄐㄩㄣ ㄒㄧㄠˋ ㄒㄩㄝˊ ㄕㄥ)

a military cadet

軍校高年級生(ㄐㄩㄣ ㄒㄧㄠˋ ㄍㄠ ㄋㄧㄢˊ ㄐㄧˊ ㄕㄥ)
the upperclassmen of a military academy

軍校一年級生(ㄐㄩㄣ ㄒㄧㄠˋ ㄧ ㄋㄧㄢˊ ㄐㄧˊ ㄕㄥ)
a plebe

軍心(ㄐㄩㄣ ㄒㄧㄣ)
the morale of the troops: 軍心消沈。The morale of the troops is low.

軍餉(ㄐㄩㄣ ㄒㄧㄤˇ)
pay and allowances for soldiers; military payroll

軍興(ㄐㄩㄣ ㄒㄧㄥ)
① to requisition property for the army in ancient times ② the outbreak of hostilities

軍需(ㄐㄩㄣ ㄒㄩ)
① military supplies and equipment; war materials; materiel ② short for 軍需官

軍需品(ㄐㄩㄣ ㄒㄩ ㄆㄧㄣˇ)
military supplies and equipment; war materials; materiel

軍需官(ㄐㄩㄣ ㄒㄩ ㄍㄨㄢ)
an officer in charge of military supplies

軍需處(ㄐㄩㄣ ㄒㄩ ㄔㄨˋ)
the department of war materials

軍靴(ㄐㄩㄣ ㄒㄩㄝ)
combat boots

軍訓(ㄐㄩㄣ ㄒㄩㄣˋ)
military training

軍職(ㄐㄩㄣ ㄒㄩㄣˊ)
a military (as opposed to civilian) office or post; a military appointment

軍制(ㄐㄩㄣ ㄓˋ)
the military system

軍長(ㄐㄩㄣ ㄓㄤˇ)
a corps commander

軍政(ㄐㄩㄣ ㄓㄥˋ)
① a military government ② the administration of the armed forces

軍政部(ㄐㄩㄣ ㄓㄥˋ ㄅㄨˋ)
Ministry of War (in the early years of the Republic)

軍政部長(ㄐㄩㄣ ㄓㄥˋ ㄅㄨˋ ㄓㄤˇ)
Minister of War (in the early years of the Republic)

軍政府(ㄐㄩㄣ ㄓㄥˋ ㄈㄨˇ)

a military government

軍政大權集於一身(ㄐㄩㄣ ㄓㄥ ㄉㄚˋ ㄑㄩㄢˊ ㄐㄧˊ ㄩˊ ㄧ ㄕㄣ)
to have both civil and military powers held in the hands of a single individual

軍政權(ㄐㄩㄣ ㄓㄥˋ ㄑㄩㄢˊ)
powers for military administration

軍政時期(ㄐㄩㄣ ㄓㄥˋ ㄕˊ ㄑㄧ)
the Period of Military Administration (first of the three steps of growth envisaged by Dr. Sun Yat-sen for the Republic)

軍裝(ㄐㄩㄣ ㄓㄨㄤ)
a soldier's outfit; military uniform

軍中(ㄐㄩㄣ ㄓㄨㄥ)
in the army; in the armed forces

軍中服務(ㄐㄩㄣ ㄓㄨㄥ ㄈㄨˊ ㄨˋ)
service in the army (rendered by civilians); troop-scheering activities

軍中無戲言(ㄐㄩㄣ ㄓㄨㄥ ㄨˊ ㄒㄧˋ ㄧㄢˊ)
(literally) There are no jokes in the armed forces. —A military pledge or order must be carried out.

軍種(ㄐㄩㄣ ㄓㄨㄥˇ)
the armed services; branches of the armed forces

軍車(ㄐㄩㄣ ㄔㄜ)
a military vehicle or conveyance

軍師(ㄐㄩㄣ ㄕ)
①a strategist; a tactician (a military post in ancient times roughly equivalent to the modern chief of a staff)
②an adviser; a consultant

軍使(ㄐㄩㄣ ㄕˇ)
a military envoy

軍士(ㄐㄩㄣ ㄕˋ)
a noncommissioned officer; a noncom 參看「軍曹」

軍事(ㄐㄩㄣ ㄕˋ)
military affairs

軍事犯(ㄐㄩㄣ ㄕˋ ㄈㄢˋ)
a military offender

軍事地理(ㄐㄩㄣ ㄕˋ ㄉㄧˋ ㄌㄧˇ)
military geography

軍事地區(ㄐㄩㄣ ㄕˋ ㄉㄧˋ ㄑㄩ)or軍區(ㄐㄩㄣ ㄑㄩ)
a military area; a military scope; a military district

軍事顧問團(ㄐㄩㄣ ㄕˋ ㄍㄨˋ ㄨㄣˋ ㄊㄨㄢˊ)
a military assistance and advisory group

軍事化(ㄐㄩㄣ ㄕˋ ㄏㄨㄚˋ)
to militarize; militarization

軍事基地(ㄐㄩㄣ ㄕˋ ㄐㄧ ㄉㄧˋ)
a military base

軍事教育(ㄐㄩㄣ ㄕˋ ㄐㄧㄠˋ ㄩˋ)
military education

軍事行動(ㄐㄩㄣ ㄕˋ ㄒㄧㄥˊ ㄉㄨㄥˋ)
military action

軍事學(ㄐㄩㄣ ㄕˋ ㄒㄩㄝˊ)
military science

軍事學校(ㄐㄩㄣ ㄕˋ ㄒㄩㄝˊ ㄒㄧㄠˋ)
a military school

軍事訓練(ㄐㄩㄣ ㄕˋ ㄒㄩㄣˋ ㄌㄧㄢˋ)
military training

軍事制裁(ㄐㄩㄣ ㄕˋ ㄓˋ ㄘㄞˊ)
military sanctions

軍事占領(ㄐㄩㄣ ㄕˋ ㄓㄢˋ ㄌㄧㄥˇ)
military occupation

軍事政變(ㄐㄩㄣ ㄕˋ ㄓㄥˋ ㄅㄧㄢˋ)
a coup d'état

軍事裝備(ㄐㄩㄣ ㄕˋ ㄓㄨㄤ ㄅㄟˋ)
military equipment

軍事要塞(ㄐㄩㄣ ㄕˋ ㄧㄠˋ ㄙㄞ)
a military stronghold; a fortress

軍事演習(ㄐㄩㄣ ㄕˋ ㄧㄢˇ ㄒㄧˊ)
military maneuvers; military exercises; war games (or exercises)

軍事委員會(ㄐㄩㄣ ㄕˋ ㄨㄟˇ ㄩㄢˊ ㄏㄨㄟˋ)
Military Council (before and during the Second World War)

軍事委員會委員長(ㄐㄩㄣ ㄕˋ ㄨㄟˇ ㄩㄢˊ ㄏㄨㄟˋ ㄨㄟˇ ㄩㄢˊ ㄓㄤˇ)
the chairman of the Military Council; a generalissimo

軍書(ㄐㄩㄣ ㄕㄨ)
military letters; military correspondence

軍事旁午(ㄐㄩㄣ ㄕˋ ㄆㄤˊ ㄨˇ)
(said of military commanders) very busy with directing military operations

軍人(ㄐㄩㄣ ㄖㄣˊ)
a soldier; a serviceman

軍人魂(ㄐㄩㄣ ㄖㄣˊ ㄏㄨㄣˊ)
a soldier's willingness to die for his country instead of surrendering to the enemy

軍人家屬(ㄐㄩㄣ ㄖㄣˊ ㄐㄧㄚ ㄕㄨˇ)or軍眷(ㄐㄩㄣ ㄐㄩㄢˋ)
a soldier's dependants

軍人節(ㄐㄩㄣ ㄖㄣˊ ㄐㄧㄝˊ)
Armed Forces Day (falling on September 3)

軍容(ㄐㄩㄣ ㄖㄨㄥˊ)
the impression which a military unit gives to a beholder; the general appearance of a military force

軍佐(ㄐㄩㄣ ㄗㄨㄛˇ)
a noncombatant member of a military unit with officer rank

軍曹(ㄐㄩㄣ ㄘㄠˊ)
a sergeant; a noncom 參看「軍士」

軍醫(ㄐㄩㄣ ㄧ)
(military) a surgeon; a medic

軍醫署長(ㄐㄩㄣ ㄧ ㄕㄨˇ ㄓㄤˇ)or軍醫總監(ㄐㄩㄣ ㄧ ㄗㄨㄥˇ ㄐㄧㄢ)
a surgeon general

軍油(ㄐㄩㄣ ㄧㄡˊ)
military gasoline

軍郵(ㄐㄩㄣ ㄧㄡˊ)
Army Post Office (A.P.O.); military mail service

軍營(ㄐㄩㄣ ㄧㄥˊ)
a military camp

軍務(ㄐㄩㄣ ㄨˋ)
administrative matters of the armed forces

軍威(ㄐㄩㄣ ㄨㄟ)
military prestige; military prowess

軍文(ㄐㄩㄣ ㄨㄣˊ)
civilian employees in the armed forces

軍語(ㄐㄩㄣ ㄩˇ)
military terms

軍樂(ㄐㄩㄣ ㄩㄝˋ)
a martial tune

軍樂隊(ㄐㄩㄣ ㄩㄝˋ ㄉㄨㄟˋ)
a military band

軍用(ㄐㄩㄣ ㄩㄥˋ)
for military use; military

軍用品(ㄐㄩㄣ ㄩㄥˋ ㄆㄧㄣˇ)
military supplies and equipment; war materials; materiel

軍用飛機場(ㄐㄩㄣ ㄩㄥˋ ㄈㄟ ㄐㄧ ㄔㄤˇ)or軍用機場(ㄐㄩㄣ ㄩㄥˋ ㄐㄧ ㄔㄤˇ)
a military airfield

軍用電話(ㄐㄩㄣ ㄩㄥˋ ㄉㄧㄢˋ ㄏㄨㄚˋ)

〔軍部〕

a military telephone

軍用車(ㄐㄩㄣ ㄩㄥ ㄔㄜ)
a military vehicle

軍用物資(ㄐㄩㄣ ㄩㄥ ㄨ ㄗ)
military supplies; materiel;
war materials

三畫

【軒】 5970 ㄒㄩㄢ shiuan xuān
1. a carriage formerly used by
high officials
2. the high front of a chariot
or carriage
3. a balcony; a porch
4. a window
5. open; wide
6. high; lofty
7. smiling; laughing; delighted
8. a studio; a room

軒冕(ㄒㄩㄢ ㄇㄧㄢ)
①carriages and garments
for high officials in former
times ②eminent personages
and high officials

軒朗(ㄒㄩㄢ ㄌㄤ)
open; wide

軒豁(ㄒㄩㄢ ㄏㄨㄛ)
open; wide

軒駕(ㄒㄩㄢ ㄐㄧㄚ)
①the emperor's carriage ②
Hsüan-yüan (軒轅), a legendary ruler of virtue 亦作「黃
帝」

軒檻(ㄒㄩㄢ ㄐㄧㄢ)
railings of a balcony

軒軒(ㄒㄩㄢ ㄒㄩㄢ)
①smug; complacent ②out-
standing

軒輊(ㄒㄩㄢ ㄓ)
the high front and the low
rear of a chariot—difference
in height, rank, excellence,
etc.

軒敞(ㄒㄩㄢ ㄔㄤ)
open; wide

軒然(ㄒㄩㄢ ㄖㄢ)
①smiling; delighted ②very
high; towering; lofty

軒然大波(ㄒㄩㄢ ㄖㄢ ㄉㄚ ㄅㄛ)
(literally) towering waves
—great repercussions; violent reactions; a great stir

軒昂(ㄒㄩㄢ ㄤ)
high; lofty; dignified

軒轅(ㄒㄩㄢ ㄩㄢ)

an alternative name of
Huang Ti (黃帝), regarded
as the first great ruler of
China

【軔】 5971 ㄖㄣˋ renn rèn
1. a skid (for checking the
motion of a vehicle)
2. to block; to obstruct
3. soft
4. idle
5. a measure of length equaling to 8 cubits

【軛】 5972 ㄩㄝˋ yueh yuè
a crossbar at the end of the
poles of a cart, etc.; an
arrangement for yoking the
horses in a light carriage

四畫

【軶】 5973 ㄜˋ eh è
a yoke

【軟】 5974 ㄖㄨㄢˇ roan ruǎn
(輭)
1. soft; pliable; tender; plastic;
flexible; supple: 松木比橡木軟
些。Pine wood is softer than
oak.
2. soft; gentle; mild
3. weak; feeble; effeminate;
cowardly
4. poor in quality, ability, etc.
5. easily moved or influenced

軟皮塞兒(ㄖㄨㄢ ㄆㄧ ㄙㄞ ㄦ)
a cork stopper; a cork

軟片(ㄖㄨㄢ ㄆㄧㄢ)
(photographic) film: 他需要
一卷軟片。He needed a roll
of film.

軟錳鑛(ㄖㄨㄢ ㄇㄥ ㄎㄨㄤ)
pyrolusite

軟綿綿(ㄖㄨㄢ ㄇㄧㄢ ㄇㄧㄢ)
①soft ② (said of songs)
sentimental ③weak

軟木塞兒(ㄖㄨㄢ ㄇㄨ ㄙㄞ ㄦ)
a cork stopper; a cork

軟風(ㄖㄨㄢ ㄈㄥ)
a light wind; a gentle
breeze; a zephyr

軟墊(ㄖㄨㄢ ㄉㄧㄢ)
(machinery) packing

軟糖(ㄖㄨㄢ ㄊㄤ)
a fondant; fudge

軟梯(ㄖㄨㄢ ㄊㄧ)
a rope ladder

軟體(ㄖㄨㄢ ㄊㄧˇ)
software 參看「硬體」

軟體動物(ㄖㄨㄢ ㄊㄧ ㄉㄨㄥ ㄨ)
molluscs; mollusks

軟鐵(ㄖㄨㄢ ㄊㄧㄝ)
wrought iron; soft iron

軟蛋包(ㄖㄨㄢ ㄉㄢ ㄅㄠ)
a coward: 他是個軟蛋包。He
is a coward.

軟膏(ㄖㄨㄢ ㄍㄠ)
ointment: 冷霜是一種軟膏。
Cold cream is an ointment.

軟骨(ㄖㄨㄢ ㄍㄨ)
(anatomy) a cartilage

軟骨病(ㄖㄨㄢ ㄍㄨ ㄅㄧㄥ)
(medicine) rickets; rachitis
亦作「佝僂症」

軟骨組織(ㄖㄨㄢ ㄍㄨ ㄗ ㄓ)
(anatomy) cartilaginous tissue

軟管(ㄖㄨㄢ ㄍㄨㄢ)
hose

軟工夫(ㄖㄨㄢ ㄍㄨㄥ ˙ㄈㄨ)
stunts performed by virtue
of nimbleness or agility
instead of physical strength

軟口蓋(ㄖㄨㄢ ㄎㄡ ㄍㄞ)
(anatomy) the soft palate;
the velum

軟化(ㄖㄨㄢ ㄏㄨㄚ)
①to soften; to conciliate ②
to soften: 鐵受熱即軟化。Iron
softens with heat.

軟和(ㄖㄨㄢ ˙ㄏㄨㄛ)
①soft ②gentle; kind

軟腳病(ㄖㄨㄢ ㄐㄧㄠ ㄅㄧㄥ)
(medicine) beriberi 亦作「腳
氣病」

軟禁(ㄖㄨㄢ ㄐㄧㄣ)or軟監(ㄖㄨㄢ
ㄐㄧㄢ)
to put under house arrest; to
confine informally

軟席(ㄖㄨㄢ ㄒㄧ)
a soft seat or berth

軟席車廂(ㄖㄨㄢ ㄒㄧ ㄔㄜ ㄒㄧㄤ)
a railway coach with soft
seats or berths

軟心腸(ㄖㄨㄢ ㄒㄧㄣ ㄔㄤ)
soft-hearted: 她是個軟心腸的
女人。She is a soft-hearted
woman.

軟刑(ㄖㄨㄢ ㄒㄧㄥ)
to torment or torture mentally

軟性(ㄖㄨㄢ ㄒㄧㄥ)
soft; mild; bland; gentle;

light

軟性下疳(ㄖㄨㄢˇ ㄒㄧㄥˋ ㄒㄧㄚˋ ㄍㄢ)
or 軟下疳(ㄖㄨㄢˇ ㄒㄧㄚˋ ㄍㄢ)
(medicine) soft chancre;
chancroid

軟性新聞(ㄖㄨㄢˇ ㄒㄧㄥˋ ㄒㄧㄣ ㄨㄣˊ)
light news; light stories;
human-interest stories

軟脂(ㄖㄨㄢˇ ㄓ)
palmitin

軟脂酸(ㄖㄨㄢˇ ㄓ ㄙㄨㄢ)
(chemistry) palmitic acid

軟牀(ㄖㄨㄢˇ ㄔㄨㄤˊ)
a stretcher; a litter

軟水(ㄖㄨㄢˇ ㄕㄨㄟˇ)
(chemistry) soft water;
water free from mineral contents

軟弱(ㄖㄨㄢˇ ㄖㄨㄛˋ)
①weak; feeble: 他因病而身體
軟弱。 He is weak from ill-
ness. ②(said of character,
etc.) flabby; weak: 我不喜歡
他軟弱的性格。 I don't like his
flabby character.

軟硬不喫(ㄖㄨㄢˇ ㄧㄥˋ ㄅㄨˋ ㄔ)
to yield to neither the carrot
nor the stick; to stand pat

軟硬兼施(ㄖㄨㄢˇ ㄧㄥˋ ㄐㄧㄢ ㄕ)
to use both hard and soft
tactics; to use the carrot and
the stick

軟文學(ㄖㄨㄢˇ ㄨㄣˊ ㄒㄩㄝˊ)
light literature

軟語(ㄖㄨㄢˇ ㄩˇ)
gentle words

軟玉(ㄖㄨㄢˇ ㄩˋ)
①nephrite ②bean curd

軟玉溫香(ㄖㄨㄢˇ ㄩˋ ㄨㄣ ㄒㄧㄤ)
(said of a beauty's skin) as
fair as jade

五畫

【軫】 5975 ㄓㄣˇ jeen zhen
1. the wooden bumper at the
rear of a cart or carriage
2. a Chinese family name

軫恤(ㄓㄣˇ ㄒㄩˋ)
to remember with deep emotion

軫悼(ㄓㄣˇ ㄉㄠˋ)
to mourn deeply

軫念(ㄓㄣˇ ㄋㄧㄢˋ)
to remember with deep emotion

軫懷(ㄓㄣˇ ㄏㄨㄞˊ)
to remember with deep emotion 亦作「軫念」

軫惜(ㄓㄣˇ ㄒㄧˊ)
to mourn with deep regret;
to have pity on

軫恤(ㄓㄣˇ ㄒㄩˋ)
to pity deeply

【軨】 5976 ㄌㄧㄥˊ ling líng
1. the framework on a carriage
2. the wheels of a carriage

【軸】 5977 ㄓㄡˊ jour zhóu
(讀音 ㄓㄡˋ jou zhú)
1. an axis; a pivot; an axle: 地
球繞軸自轉。 The earth
rotates on its own axis.
2. (said of mounted paintings
or calligraphic works) a
scroll
軸(ㄓㄡˊ)
(geology) pinacoidal faces

軸對稱(ㄓㄡˊ ㄉㄨㄟˋ ㄔㄥ)
(mathematics) axial symmetry

軸心(ㄓㄡˊ ㄒㄧㄣ)
an axis

軸心國(ㄓㄡˊ ㄒㄧㄣ ㄍㄨㄛˊ)
the Axis (in World War II)

軸承(ㄓㄡˊ ㄔㄥˊ)
bearings

軸子(ㄓㄡˊ ˙ㄗ)or 軸兒(ㄓㄡˊㄦ)
an axis; a pivot; an axle

【軺】 5978 ㄧㄠˊ yau yáo
a kind of light carriage

【軹】 5979 ㄓˇ jyy zhǐ
the ends of an axle

軹道(ㄓˇ ㄉㄠˋ)
name of an ancient place

【軻】 5980 ㄎㄜ ke kē
1. a kind of ancient carts
2. name of Mencius

軻峨(ㄎㄜ ㄜˊ)
lofty

【軼】 5981 ㄧˋ yih yì
1. to excel; to surpass
2. to be scattered; to go loose

軼蕩(ㄧˋ ㄉㄤˋ)
unrestrained

軼倫(ㄧˋ ㄌㄨㄣˊ)or 軼群(ㄧˋ ㄑㄩㄣˊ)
to surpass one's contemporaries; to be outstanding

軼詩(ㄧˋ ㄕ)
poems not included in
anthologies; scattered poems

軼事(ㄧˋ ㄕˋ)
an anecdote (not included in
history)

軼材(ㄧˋ ㄘㄞˊ)
outstanding talents

軼聞(ㄧˋ ㄨㄣˊ)
an anecdote: 有很多關於他的
軼聞。 Many anecdotes are
told about him.

【軱】 5982 ㄍㄨ gu gū
1. a wheel
2. to turn; to revolve; to rotate

軲轆(ㄍㄨ ㄌㄨ)
①a wheel ②to turn; to
revolve

六畫

【較】 5983 ㄐㄧㄠˋ jiaw jiào
(又讀 ㄐㄧㄠˇ jeau jiǎo)
1. to compare
2. in a greater or lesser
degree; more or less; earlier
or later
3. clear; conspicuous; obvious;
marked
4. to compete; to dispute
5. fairly; quite; relatively

較柄(ㄐㄧㄠˋ ㄅㄧㄥˇ)
clear; obvious; conspicuous

較量(ㄐㄧㄠˋ ㄌㄧㄤˋ)
to compare (strength, etc.)
in a contest; to contest; to
have a trial (or test) of
strength: 他們兩人較量高下。
They contest and see who is
the better (or the stronger).

較略(ㄐㄧㄠˋ ㄌㄩㄝˋ)
generally speaking; in general

較勁兒(ㄐㄧㄠˋ ㄐㄧㄥˋㄦ)
①to have a trial of strength
②to get worse; to become
worse

較著(ㄐㄧㄠˋ ㄓㄨˋ)
conspicuous; obvious

較勝一籌(ㄐㄧㄠˋ ㄕㄥˋ ㄧˋ ㄔㄡˊ)
better by one degree; a little
better

【軾】 5984 ㄕˋ shyh shì
the horizontal front bar on
a cart or carriage

【車部】

[軍部]

【輅】5985
ㄌㄨˋ luh lù
1. a heavy carriage
2. the horizontal front bar on a cart or carriage
3. a state carriage

【輈】5986
ㄓㄡ jou zhōu
the shaft or pole (of a cart or carriage)

【載】5987　ㄗㄞˋ tzay zài
1. (said of vehicles, vessels, etc.) to carry (loads); to load
2. to record; to publish
3. to fill

載滿 (ㄗㄞˋㄇㄢˇ)
to carry a full load; to be fully laden

載明 (ㄗㄞˋㄇㄧㄥˊ)
to record clearly

載福 (ㄗㄞˋㄈㄨˊ)
to receive blessings; to enjoy happiness

載道 (ㄗㄞˋㄉㄠˋ)
①to fill the streets (as complaints); (said of voices) to be heard all over: 怨聲載道 Voices of complaint can be heard all over. ②(said of writings) to convey philosophical principles

載歌載舞 (ㄗㄞˋㄍㄜㄗㄞˋㄨˇ)
to sing and dance at the same time

載客 (ㄗㄞˋㄎㄜˋ)
to carry passengers

載貨 (ㄗㄞˋㄏㄨㄛˋ)
to carry cargo; to carry goods: 火車及船舶可用來載貨。 Trains and ships can carry goods.

載籍 (ㄗㄞˋㄐㄧˊ)
books

載記 (ㄗㄞˋㄐㄧˋ)
chronicles or narratives about the vicissitudes of various feudal lords (as distinct from regular dynastic histories)

載酒問字 (ㄗㄞˋㄐㄧㄡˇㄨㄣˋㄗˋ)
studious and inquisitive

載重 (ㄗㄞˋㄓㄨㄥˋ)
①to carry heavy loads; heavily loaded ②carrying capacity

載重量 (ㄗㄞˋㄓㄨㄥˋㄌㄧㄤˋ)
loading capacity; dead-weight capacity

載運 (ㄗㄞˋㄩㄣˋ)
to transport; to carry

【載】5987　ㄗㄞˇ tzae zǎi
a year

【輊】5988
ㄓˋ jyh zhì
the low rear of a chariot, etc.

七畫

【輒】5989
（輒）ㄓㄜˊ jer zhé
1. sides of a chariot, etc., that point downward at the front
2. arbitrary; dictatorial
3. then; in that case
4. every time; always

【輓】5990
ㄨㄢˇ woan wǎn
1. to draw or pull (a cart)
2. to mourn
3. late 亦作「晚」

輓聯 (ㄨㄢˇㄌㄧㄢˊ)
funeral scrolls

輓歌 (ㄨㄢˇㄍㄜ)
a funeral hymn; a dirge; an elegy

輓近 or 晚近 (ㄨㄢˇㄐㄧㄣˋ)
of late; lately; recently

輓詩 (ㄨㄢˇㄕ)
a funeral ode; an elegy

【輔】5991
ㄈㄨˇ fuu fǔ
1. human cheeks
2. protective bars on both sides of a cart or carriage
3. to assist; to help; to complement

輔弼 (ㄈㄨˇㄅㄧˋ)
①to assist ②a prime minister

輔幣 (ㄈㄨˇㄅㄧˋ)
coins of small denominations

輔導 (ㄈㄨˇㄉㄠˇ) or (ㄈㄨˇㄉㄠˋ)
①to assist and guide ②guidance

輔導員 (ㄈㄨˇㄉㄠˇㄩㄢˊ)
an assistant; an instructor

輔車相依 (ㄈㄨˇㄐㄩㄒㄧㄤ一)
to depend upon each other

輔相 (ㄈㄨˇㄒㄧㄤˋ)
to assist ②a prime minister

輔助 (ㄈㄨˇㄓㄨˋ)
to assist; assistance: 她輔助我工作。 She assisted me in my work.

輔佐 (ㄈㄨˇㄗㄨㄛˇ)
to assist

輔翼 (ㄈㄨˇ一ˋ)
to assist

輔音 (ㄈㄨˇ一ㄣ)
(phonetics) a consonant

【輕】5992
（輕）ㄑㄧㄥ ching qīng
1. light: 油比水輕。 Oil is lighter than water.
2. simple; easy; facile
3. mild; gentle; soft; tender; lightly; gently; softly
4. mean; base; lowly; unimportant
5. frivolous; flippant; fickle; rash; reckless
6. to slight; to neglect; to ignore; to underestimate; to disparage: 文人相輕。 Scholars disparage one another.

輕薄 (ㄑㄧㄥㄅㄛˊ)
①frivolous; flippant ②disrespectful; irreverent ③to insult

輕薄少年 (ㄑㄧㄥㄅㄛˊㄕㄠˋㄋㄧㄢˊ)
a frivolous youngster; a coxcomb

輕薄子 (ㄑㄧㄥㄅㄛˊㄗˇ) or 輕薄兒 (ㄑㄧㄥㄅㄛˊㄦˊ)
a frivolous youth; a fickle, callous fellow

輕便 (ㄑㄧㄥㄅㄧㄢˋ)
handy; convenient; light; portable

輕便鐵路 (ㄑㄧㄥㄅㄧㄢˋㄊㄧㄝˇㄌㄨˋ)
a light railway

輕拍 (ㄑㄧㄥㄆㄞ)
to pat; to tap: 他輕拍她的肩膀。 He patted her shoulder.

輕飄飄 (ㄑㄧㄥㄆㄧㄠㄆㄧㄠ)
very light; lightly

輕慢 (ㄑㄧㄥㄇㄢˋ)
disrespectful; irreverent

輕蔑 (ㄑㄧㄥㄇㄧㄝˋ)
to despise; to disdain; to contemn; to slight: 一個偉人應該輕蔑諂媚者。 A great man should disdain flatterers.

輕描淡寫 (ㄑㄧㄥㄇㄧㄠˊㄉㄢˋㄒㄧㄝˇ)
to describe in a light, moderate tone; to play down (the importance or seriousness of

something); to water down;
to touch on lightly

輕裘(くＩ∠ くＩㄡ)
those who have light clothes
and fat horses—the wealthy

輕放(くＩ∠ ㄈㄤ)
to put down gently

輕風(くＩ∠ ㄈ∠)
a light wind; a breeze

輕浮(くＩ∠ ㄈㄨ)
flippant; frivolous; playful;
她是個輕浮的漂女孩。She is a
frivolous, empty-headed girl.

輕敵(くＩ∠ ㄉＩ)
to underestimate the enemy.
不要輕敵。Don't underesti-
mate the enemy.

輕佻(くＩ∠ ㄊＩㄠ)or輕窕(くＩ∠
ㄊＩㄠ)
frivolous; flippant; capricious; playful; sportive; skit-
tish; giddy

輕脫(くＩ∠ ㄊㄨㄛ)
frivolous; playful

輕諾寡信(くＩ∠ ㄋㄨㄛ ㄍㄨㄚˇ ㄒＩㄣˋ)
to give a promise easily and
break it easily

輕利(くＩ∠ ㄌＩˋ)
①to think little of material
gain ② light and sharp

輕憐蜜愛(くＩ∠ ㄌＩㄢˊ ㄇＩ ㄞˋ)
tender affection between a
couple in love

輕量級(くＩ∠ ㄌＩㄤˋ ㄐＩˊ)
(boxing) a lightweight, a
boxer weighing between 126
and 135 pounds

輕歌曼舞(くＩ∠ ㄍㄜ ㄇㄢˋ ㄨˇ)
to sing cheerfully and dance
gracefully

輕骨頭(くＩ∠ ㄍㄨˇ ㄊㄡ)
①mean; base; lowly ② frivolous

輕工業(くＩ∠ ㄍㄨ∠ Ｉㄝˋ)
light industry

輕口薄舌(くＩ∠ ㄎㄡˇ ㄅㄛˊ ㄕㄜˊ)
to speak impolitely or rudely

輕快(くＩ∠ ㄎㄨㄞˋ)
①agile; sprightly; nimble;
brisk; spry; 他走路輕快。He is
a brisk walker. ②light-
hearted ③lively; 她正在唱一
首輕快的歌。She is singing a
lively song.

輕狂(くＩ∠ ㄎㄨㄤˊ)
very frivolous

輕忽(くＩ∠ ㄏㄨ)
to neglect; to slight; to
ignore; 他輕忽了他的健康。He
neglected his health.

輕機槍(くＩ∠ ㄐＩ くＩㄤ)
a light machine gun

輕騎(くＩ∠ くＩˊ)
①a light cavalryman; light
cavalry ②a sprightly horse

輕捷(くＩ∠ ㄐＩㄝˊ)
agile; nimble

輕賤(くＩ∠ ㄐＩㄢˋ)
mean; base

輕金屬(くＩ∠ ㄐＩㄣ ㄕㄨˇ)
light metals

輕車簡從(くＩ∠ ㄔㄜ ㄐＩㄢˇ ㄗㄨㄥˋ)
(said of a high official, etc.)
to travel with a minimum of
pomp

輕車熟路(くＩ∠ ㄔㄜ ㄕㄨˊ ㄌㄨˋ)
as facile as traveling along
a familiar road in a light
carriage

輕舉妄動(くＩ∠ ㄐㄩˇ ㄨㄤˋ ㄉㄨㄥˋ)
to act rashly and blindly; to
do something foolish

輕氣 or 氫氣(くＩ∠ くＩˋ)
hydrogen

輕氣球(くＩ∠ くＩˋ くＩㄡˊ)
a balloon

輕趫(くＩ∠ くＩㄠ)
agile

輕巧(くＩ∠ くＩㄠˇ)
①light and efficient; handy
②dexterous(ly)

輕裘緩帶(くＩ∠ くＩㄡˊ ㄏㄨㄢˇ ㄉㄞˋ)
(said of a general in former
times) reposeful and scholarly

輕輕的(くＩ∠ くＩ∠ ˙ㄉㄜ)
lightly; gently; softly; 風從西
方輕輕的吹來。The wind was
blowing lightly from the
west.

輕取(くＩ∠ くㄩˇ)
to beat easily; to win an
easy victory

輕信(くＩ∠ ㄒＩㄣˋ)
gullible; credulous; to
believe lightly; 與其猜疑, 不如
輕信。Better be too credulous
than too skeptical.

輕刑(くＩ∠ ㄒＩ∠ˊ)
light punishment

輕巡洋艦(くＩ∠ ㄒㄩㄣˊ Ｉㄤˊ ㄐＩㄢˋ)
a light cruiser

輕舟(くＩ∠ ㄓㄡ)
a light boat; a small boat

輕裝(くＩ∠ ㄓㄨㄤ)
light and simple luggage

輕重(くＩ∠ ㄓㄨㄥˋ)
①weight; light and heavy.
這兩個包裹輕重不一樣。The
two packages do not weigh
the same. ②degree of seriousness; of relative importance: 事情應分輕重緩急。
Things should be done in
order of importance and
urgency. ③propriety

輕重倒置(くＩ∠ ㄓㄨㄥˋ ㄉㄠˋ ㄓˋ)
to neglect the important and
emphasize the unimportant;
to put the cart before the
horse

輕脣音(くＩ∠ ㄔㄨㄣˊ Ｉㄣ)
(traditional Chinese phonology) labiodentals

輕視(くＩ∠ ㄕˋ)or輕看(くＩ∠ ㄎㄢˋ)
to think little of; to slight;
to make light of; to look
down upon; to despise: 只因
他家貧她便輕視他。She looks
down upon him just because
his family is poor.

輕手輕腳(くＩ∠ ㄕㄡˇ くＩ∠ ㄐＩㄠˇ)
gently; softly

輕身(くＩ∠ ㄕㄣ)
①to make light of one's life
②without a burden; unmar-
ried

輕傷(くＩ∠ ㄕㄤ)
a slight injury; a minor
wound: 他的頭部受了輕傷。He
received a slight injury to
his head.

輕生(くＩ∠ ㄕ∠)
to commit suicide

輕聲(くＩ∠ ㄕ∠)
①(phonetics of Mandarin
and many other Chinese dialects) a neutral tone ② in a
soft voice; softly

輕聲細語(くＩ∠ ㄕ∠ ㄒＩˋ ㄩˇ)
to speak softly; to whisper

輕率(くＩ∠ ㄕㄨㄞˋ)
①to make light of; to ne-
glect; to slight; to ignore ②
careless; reckless; rash; indiscreet; hardy: 這樣安排太輕
率。It was indiscreet of you
to arrange it that way.

輕爽(くＩ∠ ㄕㄨㄤˇ)

【車部】

【車 部】

relaxed; easy; comfortable

輕柔（くﾘㄥ ㄖㄡˊ）
soft; gentle: 她以輕柔的聲調回答我。She answered me in a gentle tone.

輕銳（くﾘㄥ ㄖㄨㄟˋ）
light and sharp

輕財好義（くﾘㄥ ㄘㄞˊ ㄏㄠˋ ㄧˋ）
generous and philanthropic

輕脆（くﾘㄥ ㄘㄨㄟˋ）
light and fragile; flimsy; frail

輕鬆（くﾘㄥ ㄙㄨㄥ）
① to lighten; to relax: 音樂使我們輕鬆。Music relaxes us.
② light; easy; comfortable

輕而易舉（くﾘㄥ ㄦˊ ㄧˋ ㄐㄩˇ）
easy to accomplish; easy to do; to do without making an effort: 這是輕而易舉的工作。This job is easy to accomplish.

輕易（くﾘㄥ ㄧˋ）
① easy; facile; effortless ② reckless; rash: 我不輕易發表意見。I do not express my viewpoint rashly.

輕油（くﾘㄥ ㄧㄡˊ）
naphtha 亦作「石油精」

輕言（くﾘㄥ ㄧㄢˊ）
to speak lightly; to speak without thinking

輕言細語（くﾘㄥ ㄧㄢˊ ㄒㄧˋ ㄩˇ）
to speak softly; to talk in a soft voice

輕音樂（くﾘㄥ ㄧㄣ ㄩㄝˋ）
light music

輕盈（くﾘㄥ ㄧㄥˊ）
(said of a woman) nimble and shapely; lithe

輕侮（くﾘㄥ ㄨˇ）
to insult; to contemn: 惡人輕侮上帝。The wicked contemn God.

輕微（くﾘㄥ ㄨㄟˊ）
light; slight; little; unimportant; trivial; insignificant

輕微警告（くﾘㄥ ㄨㄟˊ ㄐㄧㄥˇ ㄍㄠˋ）
a slap on the wrist

輕文重武（くﾘㄥ ㄨㄣˊ ㄓㄨㄥˋ ㄨˇ）
to emphasize physical training at the expense of humanities; to put the sword above the pen

輕於鴻毛（くﾘㄥ ㄩˊ ㄏㄨㄥˊ ㄇㄠˊ）
(literally) lighter than a feather; more trivial than a

feather—without the least significance

八畫

【輜】 5993
ㄗ tzy zī
1. a curtained carriage
2. a wagon for supplies

輜重（ㄗ ㄓㄨㄥˋ）
① luggage ② military supplies

輜重兵（ㄗ ㄓㄨㄥˋ ㄅㄧㄥ）
transportation corps (as a branch of the army)

輜重隊（ㄗ ㄓㄨㄥˋ ㄉㄨㄟˋ）
transport troops; transport units; convoys of military supplies

輜重車（ㄗ ㄓㄨㄥˋ ㄔㄜ）
(military) transport vehicles

【輗】 5994
ㄋㄧˊ ni ní
the crossbar at the ends of carriage poles

【輘】 5995
ㄌㄧㄥˊ líng líng
run over by a vehicle

輘輷（ㄌㄧㄥˊ ㄏㄨㄥ）
① to conflict ② to oppress

【輛】 5996
ㄌㄧㄤˋ liang liàng
a numeracy adjunct for vehicles: 我有一輛汽車。I have a car.

【輝】 5997
ㄏㄨㄟ huei huī
brightness; splendor; light; luster; luminosity; brilliance

輝沸石（ㄏㄨㄟ ㄈㄟˋ ㄕˊ）
heulandite

輝鐵礦（ㄏㄨㄟ ㄊㄧㄝˇ ㄎㄨㄤˋ）
specular iron

輝銅礦（ㄏㄨㄟ ㄊㄨㄥˊ ㄎㄨㄤˋ）
chalcocite

輝綠岩（ㄏㄨㄟ ㄌㄩˋ ㄧㄢˊ）
diabase

輝光（ㄏㄨㄟ ㄍㄨㄤ）
brightness; luminosity; brilliance

輝光燈（ㄏㄨㄟ ㄍㄨㄤ ㄉㄥ）
(physics) a glow lamp

輝赫（ㄏㄨㄟ ㄏㄜˋ）
shining; brilliant; bright; luminous

輝煌（ㄏㄨㄟ ㄏㄨㄤˊ）
magnificent; splendid; glori-

ous; brilliant

輝石（ㄏㄨㄟ ㄕˊ）
(geology) pyroxene; augite

輝石岩（ㄏㄨㄟ ㄕˊ ㄧㄢˊ）
(geology) pyroxenite

輝耀（ㄏㄨㄟ ㄧㄠˋ）
shining; brilliant; bright; luminous

輝銀礦（ㄏㄨㄟ ㄧㄣˊ ㄎㄨㄤˋ）
argentite

輝映（ㄏㄨㄟ ㄧㄥˋ）
to emit and reflect light

【輞】 5998
ㄨㄤˇ woang wǎng
the rim of a wheel; a felly; a felloe

輞川（ㄨㄤˇ ㄔㄨㄢ）
name of a river in Shensi Province

【輟】 5999
ㄔㄨㄛˋ chuoh chuò
to stop; to halt; to suspend; to cease

輟水（ㄔㄨㄛˋ ㄕㄨㄟˇ）
to stop in the middle of writing or painting

輟耕（ㄔㄨㄛˋ ㄍㄥ）
to stop plowing

輟學（ㄔㄨㄛˋ ㄒㄩㄝˊ）
to drop out of school

輟朝（ㄔㄨㄛˋ ㄔㄠˊ）
to suspend business at the imperial court on account of a misfortune

【輦】 6000
ㄋㄧㄢˇ nean niǎn
1. a handcart
2. the king's carriage; the imperial carriage

輦夫（ㄋㄧㄢˇ ㄈㄨ）
a porter

輦道（ㄋㄧㄢˇ ㄉㄠˋ）or 輦路（ㄋㄧㄢˇ ㄌㄨˋ）
the emperor's road

輦轂下（ㄋㄧㄢˇ ㄍㄨˇ ㄒㄧㄚˋ）
the imperial capital

輦下（ㄋㄧㄢˇ ㄒㄧㄚˋ）
the imperial capital

【輧】 6001
ㄆㄧㄥˊ pyng píng
a curtained carriage (for women)

輧輅（ㄆㄧㄥˊ ㄌㄨˋ）
a curtained carriage for princesses

輧車（ㄆㄧㄥˊ ㄔㄜ）
a curtained carriage

【輩】 6002 ㄅㄟˋ bey bèi
1. rank; a grade
2. a generation

輩輩兒(ㄅㄟˋ ㄅㄟˊ)
generation after generation;
for generations

輩分(ㄅㄟˋ ㄈㄣˋ)
difference in seniority;
seniority (among relatives)

輩流(ㄅㄟˋ ㄌㄧㄡˊ)
people of one's generation

輩行(ㄅㄟˋ ㄒㄧㄥˊ)
order of seniority (among
relatives, etc.)

輩出(ㄅㄟˋ ㄔㄨ)
to appear one after another;
to come out in succession

輩數兒(ㄅㄟˋ ㄕㄨˋ ㄦ)
seniority (among relatives)

輩子(ㄅㄟˋ ˙ㄗ)
① all one's life; a lifetime ②
a generation

輩兒(ㄅㄟˋ ㄦ)
a generation

【輪】 6003 ㄌㄨㄣˊ luen lún
1. a wheel
2. to recur; to alternate
3. majestic; stately
4. to take turns; by turns; in
relays

輪撥兒(ㄌㄨㄣˊ ㄅㄛㄦ)
by turns

輪暴(ㄌㄨㄣˊ ㄅㄠˋ)
to gang-rape; gang rape

輪班(ㄌㄨㄣˊ ㄅㄢ)or 輪班兒(ㄌㄨㄣˊ
ㄅㄢㄦ)
to go on duty by rotation; to
take turns; in shifts; in
relays; in rotation

輪盤睹(ㄌㄨㄣˊ ㄆㄢˊ ㄉㄨˇ)
roulette

輪番(ㄌㄨㄣˊ ㄈㄢ)
to assume duties in turn; to
take turns; in relays: 我們輪
番上陣。We took turns going
to battle.

輪輻(ㄌㄨㄣˊ ㄈㄨˊ)
the spokes of a wheel

輪調(ㄌㄨㄣˊ ㄉㄧㄠˋ)
to serve at a post or place
for a fixed period by turns

輪渡(ㄌㄨㄣˊ ㄉㄨˋ)
a ferryboat; a steam ferry 亦
作「渡輪」

輪胎(ㄌㄨㄣˊ ㄊㄞ)

the tire (of a wheel): 請給這
個胎打氣。Please pump up
this tire.

輪流(ㄌㄨㄣˊ ㄌㄧㄡˊ)
to take turns; by turns: 他們
輪流划船。They rowed by
turns.

輪廓(ㄌㄨㄣˊ ㄎㄨㄛˋ)
an outline; a silhouette

輪迴(ㄌㄨㄣˊ ㄏㄨㄟˊ)
①to recur successively; to
move in a cycle ②trans-
migration (of the soul);
metempsychosis (Buddhism)
samsara—the process of coming into existence as a dif-
ferentiated, mortal creature

輪奐(ㄌㄨㄣˊ ㄏㄨㄢˋ)
(said of a building) stately;
majestic

輪換(ㄌㄨㄣˊ ㄏㄨㄢˋ)
to alternate

輪機(ㄌㄨㄣˊ ㄐㄧ)
①a turbine ②a motorship
engine; an engine

輪機長(ㄌㄨㄣˊ ㄐㄧ ㄓㄤˇ)
a chief engineer

輪姦(ㄌㄨㄣˊ ㄐㄧㄢ)
to gang-rape 參看「輪暴」

輪下冤鬼(ㄌㄨㄣˊ ㄒㄧㄚˋ ㄩㄢ ㄍㄨㄟˇ)
the victim of a traffic accident run over by a vehicle

輪休(ㄌㄨㄣˊ ㄒㄧㄡ)
to rest by turns; to take a
day off by turns

輪形(ㄌㄨㄣˊ ㄒㄧㄥˊ)
wheel-shaped

輪軒(ㄌㄨㄣˊ ㄒㄩㄢ)
carriages of noblemen

輪值(ㄌㄨㄣˊ ㄓˊ)
to go on duty in turn; to
take turns

輪軸(ㄌㄨㄣˊ ㄓㄡˊ)
wheels and axles; wheel
shafts

輪轉(ㄌㄨㄣˊ ㄓㄨㄢˇ)
①to turn round; to revolve;
to rotate ②to recur successively; to move in a cycle

輪轉機(ㄌㄨㄣˊ ㄓㄨㄢˇ ㄐㄧ)
(printing) a rotary press

輪種(ㄌㄨㄣˊ ㄓㄨㄥˇ)
to rotate crops; the rotation
of crops

輪齒(ㄌㄨㄣˊ ㄔˇ)
gear teeth

輪擊(ㄌㄨㄣˊ ㄐㄧˊ)
brakes (of wheels)

輪唱(ㄌㄨㄣˊ ㄔㄤˋ)
①to chant Buddhist prayers
②(singing) to troll ③a
canon (a form of musical
composition)

輪船(ㄌㄨㄣˊ ㄔㄨㄢˊ)
a steamship; a steamer

輪充(ㄌㄨㄣˊ ㄔㄨㄥ)
to undertake a task in turn;
to take turns

輪生葉(ㄌㄨㄣˊ ㄕㄥ ㄧㄝˋ)
(botany) verticillate leaves;
whorled leaves

輪子(ㄌㄨㄣˊ ˙ㄗ)or 輪兒(ㄌㄨㄣˊ ㄦ)
a wheel

輪栽法(ㄌㄨㄣˊ ㄗㄞ ㄈㄚˇ)or 輪作法
(ㄌㄨㄣˊ ㄗㄨㄛˋ ㄈㄚˇ)
crop rotation

輪繖花序(ㄌㄨㄣˊ ㄙㄢˇ ㄏㄨㄚ ㄒㄩˋ)
verticillaster

輪椅(ㄌㄨㄣˊ ㄧˇ)
a wheelchair

輪輿(ㄌㄨㄣˊ ㄩˊ)or 輪人(ㄌㄨㄣˊ ㄖㄣˊ)
a wheelwright; a carriage-
maker

【輬】 6004 ㄌㄧㄤˊ liang liáng
1. a hearse
2. a sleeping carriage

【輒】 6005 ㄓㄜˊ jer zhé
same as 輙—then; in that
case

九畫

【輯】 6006 ㄐㄧˊ jyi jí
1. friendly
2. to collect; to gather; to compile

輯睦 or 輯穆(ㄐㄧˊ ㄇㄨˋ)
friendliness

輯錄(ㄐㄧˊ ㄌㄨˋ)
to gather and record; to
compile; to edit

輯略(ㄐㄧˊ ㄌㄩㄝˋ)
name of a bibliographical
work by Liu Hsin (劉歆,
?-23 A.D.)

輯佚(ㄐㄧˊ ㄧˋ)
to gather rare and scattered
writings or books

輯要(ㄐㄧˊ ㄧㄠˋ)
an outline; a summary: 他說

〔車
部〕

明了那計劃的輪要。He gave an outline of the plan.

〔車部〕

【轃】 6007
ㄗㄡ tsow cōu
to converge (as spokes of a wheel do at the hub)

【輶】 6008
ㄧㄡ you yóu
1. light.
2. a light carriage

輶車(ㄧㄡ ㄔㄜ)
a light carriage

輶軒(ㄧㄡ ㄒㄩㄢ)
a light carriage for an imperial emissary

【輸】 6009
ㄕㄨ shu shū
1. to transport; to convey; to haul
2. to hand in; to contribute; to donate; to submit
3. to be beaten; to lose (a game, contest, etc.): 我們比賽輸了。We lost the game.

輸不起(ㄕㄨ ㄅㄨˋ ㄑㄧˇ)
①to display ill humor after losing a game, etc.; to lack sportsmanship: 他輸不起。He is a bad loser. ②cannot afford to lose

輸東道(ㄕㄨ ㄉㄨㄥ ㄉㄠˋ)or 輸東兒
(ㄕㄨ ㄉㄨㄥ ㄦ)
the penalty (imposed upon the loser in a bet or gamble) of treating others to a dinner

輸納(ㄕㄨ ㄋㄚˋ)
to pay or submit (money, goods, etc.) to the authorities

輸尿管(ㄕㄨ ㄋㄧㄠˋ ㄍㄨㄢˇ)
(anatomy) the ureter

輸了(ㄕㄨ ㄌㄜ)
to be the loser; to have lost (a game, bet, etc.): 我們這隊輸了。Our team lost.

輸糧(ㄕㄨ ㄌㄧㄤˊ)
①to submit or hand in grain (as tax) ②to transport grain

輸卵管(ㄕㄨ ㄌㄨㄢˇ ㄍㄨㄢˇ)
(anatomy) the oviduct; fallopian tubes

輸攻墨守(ㄕㄨ ㄍㄨㄥ ㄇㄛˋ ㄕㄡˇ)
(literally) Kung-Shu Pan (公輸班) attacked the state of Sung (宋) with his new offensive devices but was repeatedly repelled by Mo-tze (墨子) with his counter-devices.—Each displayed his special ability. 或 Each does his own best.

輸家(ㄕㄨ ㄐㄧㄚ)
the loser: 輸家必須付款。The loser must pay.

輸將(ㄕㄨ ㄐㄧㄤ)
①to transport; to haul ②to pay taxes or contributions to the government

輸精管(ㄕㄨ ㄐㄧㄥ ㄍㄨㄢˇ)
the deferent duct; the spermaduct

輸錢(ㄕㄨ ㄑㄧㄢˊ)
to lose money in gambling

輸情(ㄕㄨ ㄑㄧㄥˊ)
to supply secret information

輸血(ㄕㄨ ㄒㄧㄝˇ)
①(medicine) blood transfusion ②to give aid and support; to give somebody a shot in the arm

輸心服罪(ㄕㄨ ㄒㄧㄣ ㄈㄨˊ ㄗㄨㄟˋ)
to follow or obey with sincere willingness

輸著兒(ㄕㄨ ㄓㄠˊ ㄦ)
a wrong move (in planning something)

輸誠(ㄕㄨ ㄔㄥˊ)
①to show sincerity ②to surrender: 該上尉不得不向敵人輸誠。The captain had to surrender to the enemy.

輸出(ㄕㄨ ㄔㄨ)
①export (of goods); to export: 中國輸出茶、絲到外國。China exported tea and silk to foreign countries. ②(computers) output

輸出指令(ㄕㄨ ㄔㄨ ㄓˇ ㄌㄧㄥˋ)
(computers) an output statement

輸出稅(ㄕㄨ ㄔㄨ ㄕㄨㄟˋ)
export duties

輸出額(ㄕㄨ ㄔㄨ ㄜˊ)
the amount of exports; the value of exports: 今年輸出額不如去年。The amount of exports this year is less than that of last year.

輸入(ㄕㄨ ㄖㄨˋ)
①import (of goods); to import: 美國自日本輸入生絲。America imports raw silk from Japan. ②(computers) input

輸入稅(ㄕㄨ ㄖㄨˋ ㄕㄨㄟˋ)
import duties

輸入額(ㄕㄨ ㄖㄨˋ ㄜˊ)
the amount of imports; the value of imports

輸誠(ㄕㄨ ㄖㄨˋ)
①to fail to keep promises ②to admit a mistake

輸財(ㄕㄨ ㄘㄞˊ)
to give cash donations or contributions

輸送(ㄕㄨ ㄙㄨㄥˋ)
to transport; to convey

輸送系統(ㄕㄨ ㄙㄨㄥˋ ㄒㄧˋ ㄊㄨㄥˇ)
a conveyer system

輸油管(ㄕㄨ ㄧㄡˊ ㄍㄨㄢˇ)
a pipeline (for transporting petroleum)

輸氧(ㄕㄨ ㄧㄤˇ)
(medicine) oxygen therapy

輸贏(ㄕㄨ ㄧㄥˊ)
losses and gains (in gambling, etc.); defeat or victory (in a game, etc.)

【輻】 6010
ㄈㄨˊ fwu fú
spokes (of a wheel)

輻輳(ㄈㄨˊ ㄘㄡˋ)
to gather, or converge, like spokes of a wheel

輻狀花冠(ㄈㄨˊ ㄓㄨㄤˋ ㄏㄨㄚ ㄍㄨㄢ)
the rotate corolla

輻射(ㄈㄨˊ ㄕㄜˋ)
to radiate; radiation: 這儀器產生有害的輻射。This apparatus produces harmful radiation.

輻射體(ㄈㄨˊ ㄕㄜˋ ㄊㄧˇ)
a radiant body; a radiator

輻射能(ㄈㄨˊ ㄕㄜˋ ㄋㄥˊ)
radiant energy

輻射計(ㄈㄨˊ ㄕㄜˋ ㄐㄧˋ)
a radiometer

輻射線(ㄈㄨˊ ㄕㄜˋ ㄒㄧㄢˋ)
radiant rays

輻射塵(ㄈㄨˊ ㄕㄜˋ ㄔㄣˊ)
radioactive dust; atomic fallout

輻射熱(ㄈㄨˊ ㄕㄜˋ ㄖㄜˋ)
(physics) radiant heat

輻輳 or 輻湊(ㄈㄨˊ ㄘㄡˋ)
to converge (as the spokes of a wheel do at the hub)

【輮】 6011
ㄖㄡˊ rou róu

1. the rim (of a wheel); a felly; a felloe
2. to trample

輳轢(ㄖㄨㄥ ㄌㄧˋ)
trace of a wheel; a rut

【輭】 6012
ㄖㄨㄢˇ roan ruǎn
same as 軟—soft; mild; gentle

【輹】 6013
ㄈㄨˊ fuh fú
pieces of wood holding the axle underneath a cart

十畫

【輾】 6014
1. ㄓㄢˇ jaan zhǎn
to turn over; to roll over

輾轉(ㄓㄢˇ ㄓㄨㄢˇ)
①to roll about; to toss ②to take a roundabout course; to pass through many places

輾轉反側(ㄓㄢˇ ㄓㄨㄢˇ ㄈㄢˇ ㄘㄜˋ)
to toss about in bed; to turn around in bed and cannot get a sound sleep; to be sleepless

【輾】 6014
2. ㄋㄧㄢˇ nean niǎn
same as 碾—to grind; to crush; to run over

輾斃(ㄋㄧㄢˇ ㄅㄧˋ)
to be run over by a vehicle and got killed

輾鐵工場(ㄋㄧㄢˇ ㄊㄧㄝˇ ㄍㄨㄥ ㄔㄤˇ)
a rolling mill

【輿】 6015
ㄩˊ yu yú
1. a carriage; a vehicle
2. a sedan chair
3. the land; the earth
4. all; general
5. to carry; to transport

輿夫(ㄩˊ ㄈㄨ)
sedan chair bearers

輿服(ㄩˊ ㄈㄨˊ)
one's carriage and garments

輿地(ㄩˊ ㄉㄧˋ)
the land; the earth

輿臺(ㄩˊ ㄊㄞˊ)
coolies; mean laborers

輿圖(ㄩˊ ㄊㄨˊ)
①a map ②territory (of a nation)

輿論(ㄩˊ ㄌㄨㄣˋ)
public opinion: 輿論贊成這個計劃。Public opinion is in favor of the plan.

輿論譁然(ㄩˊ ㄌㄨㄣˋ ㄏㄨㄚˊ ㄖㄢˊ)
Public opinion is seething with indignation.

輿論界(ㄩˊ ㄌㄨㄣˋ ㄐㄧㄝˋ)
the media; press circles

輿情(ㄩˊ ㄑㄧㄥˊ)
public sentiment; public feeling: 輿情激憤。Public feeling is in fury.

輿薪(ㄩˊ ㄒㄧㄣ)
a cartload of firewood — something very obvious

輿櫬(ㄩˊ ㄔㄣˋ)
to show one's determination to succeed or die by loading a coffin on one's carriage

輿師(ㄩˊ ㄕ)
a host; an army

輿人(ㄩˊ ㄖㄣˊ)
①a wheelwright ②a lowly official ③the masses; the people

輿皂(ㄩˊ ㄗㄠˋ)
a mean servant; a menial

【轂】 6016
1. ㄍㄨˇ guu gǔ
the hub (of a wheel)

轂擊肩摩(ㄍㄨˇ ㄐㄧˊ ㄐㄧㄢ ㄇㄛ)
(literally) Hubs hit hubs and shoulders rub shoulders. —(figuratively) a scene of a booming city

轂下(ㄍㄨˇ ㄒㄧㄚˋ)
the capital (of the empire)

【轂】 6016
2. ㄍㄨ gu gū
a wheel

轂輠(ㄍㄨ ㄏㄨㄛˇ)
a wheel

轂轆兒(ㄍㄨ ㄌㄨˋ ㄦ)
①a small wheel ②a section of anything cylindric in shape (as sausage, etc.)

【轄】 6017
ㄒㄧㄚˊ shya xiá
1. a linchpin
2. to govern; to administer; administration; to manage
3. the noise of wheels

轄境(ㄒㄧㄚˊ ㄐㄧㄥˋ)or 轄境(ㄒㄧㄚˊ ㄏㄨㄢˋ)or 轄區(ㄒㄧㄚˊ ㄑㄩ)
an area under the jurisdiction (of a magistrate, etc.); magistracy

轄下(ㄒㄧㄚˊ ㄒㄧㄚˋ)
under the command or jurisdiction of

轄治(ㄒㄧㄚˊ ㄓˋ)
to govern; to rule; to administer

【轅】 6018
ㄩㄢˊ yuan yuán
1. shafts (of a cart or carriage)
2. the magistrate's office or residence; the yamen
3. a Chinese family name

轅門(ㄩㄢˊ ㄇㄣˊ)
①an outer gate of the yamen ②an outer gate (of a commander's or an emperor's temporary residence) formed by two carriages

轅下駒(ㄩㄢˊ ㄒㄧㄚˋ ㄐㄩ)
(literally) a horse between the shafts—to be under restraint

【輼】 6019
ㄨㄣ uen wēn
1. a hearse
2. a sleeping carriage

輼輬(ㄨㄣ ㄌㄧㄤˊ)
①a hearse ②a sleeping carriage

十一畫

【轉】 6020
1. ㄓㄨㄢˇ joan zhuǎn
1. to turn: 他將車子向左轉。He turned the car to the left.
2. to take a turn; to shift; to change: 這病人的情形好轉。The sick man has taken a turn for the better.
3. to transport; to convey; to transfer; to pass on
4. indirect; roundabout
5. to roll
6. to migrate; to move

轉播(ㄓㄨㄢˇ ㄅㄛˋ)or(ㄓㄨㄢˇ ㄆㄛˋ)
to relay a broadcast or telecast: 這場比賽將有電視現場轉播。The race will be telecast live.

轉播站(ㄓㄨㄢˇ ㄅㄛˋ ㄓㄢˋ)
a relay station

轉敗為勝(ㄓㄨㄢˇ ㄅㄞˋ ㄨㄟˊ ㄕㄥˋ)
to turn a defeat into a victory; to turn the tables (on someone)

〔車部〕

轉變(ㄓㄨㄢˇ ㄅㄧㄢˋ)
①to undergo changes; to change: 熱把水轉變成蒸氣。Heat changes water into steam。②a change or shift (of attitude, thinking, etc.)

轉盼(ㄓㄨㄢˇ ㄆㄢˋ)
to turn the eyes

轉蓬(ㄓㄨㄢˇ ㄆㄥˊ)
to wander about like stray weeds in the wind

轉賣(ㄓㄨㄢˇ ㄇㄞˋ)
to resell

轉面子(ㄓㄨㄢˇ ㄇㄧㄢˋ˙ㄗ)
to regain lost face

轉發(ㄓㄨㄢˇ ㄈㄚ)
to send (or distribute) through another person or office

轉達(ㄓㄨㄢˇ ㄉㄚˊ)
to transmit through another person or office; to convey: 請轉達我對她的問候。Please convey to her my best regards。

轉道(ㄓㄨㄢˇ ㄉㄠˋ)
①to make a detour; to go by way of ②(in ancient China) an official route of the shipping of food

轉遞(ㄓㄨㄢˇ ㄉㄧˋ)
to send through another person

轉地療養(ㄓㄨㄢˇ ㄉㄧˋ ㄌㄧㄠˊ ㄧㄤˇ)
a change of air for one's health

轉調(ㄓㄨㄢˇ ㄉㄧㄠˋ)
(music) modulation

轉動(ㄓㄨㄢˇ ㄉㄨㄥˋ)or(ㄓㄨㄢˇ ㄉㄨㄥˋ)
①to turn; to revolve; to rotate ②to budge; to move

轉頭(ㄓㄨㄢˇ ㄊㄡˊ)
to turn one's head

轉託(ㄓㄨㄢˇ ㄊㄨㄛ)
to request or entrust through another person

轉念(ㄓㄨㄢˇ ㄋㄧㄢˋ)
to change one's mind; to have second thoughts

轉振點(ㄓㄨㄢˇ ㄓㄣˋ ㄉㄧㄢˇ)
a turning point

轉令(ㄓㄨㄢˇ ㄌㄧㄥˋ)
to request a higher office to order another agency to do something

轉告(ㄓㄨㄢˇ ㄍㄠˋ)
to pass on (words); to communicate; to transmit

轉轂(ㄓㄨㄢˇ ㄍㄨˇ)
to transport by carts

轉攻為守(ㄓㄨㄢˇ ㄍㄨㄥ ㄨㄟˊ ㄕㄡˇ)
to change from the offensive to the defensive

轉口(ㄓㄨㄢˇ ㄎㄡˇ)
transit

轉化(ㄓㄨㄢˇ ㄏㄨㄚˋ)
①to change; to transform ②to react chemically

轉禍為福(ㄓㄨㄢˇ ㄏㄨㄛˋ ㄨㄟˊ ㄈㄨˊ)
to turn a disaster into a blessing

轉回(ㄓㄨㄢˇ ㄏㄨㄟˊ)
to turn back; to return

轉回記錄(ㄓㄨㄢˇ ㄏㄨㄟˊ ㄐㄧˋ ㄌㄨˋ)
(accounting) reversing entries

轉週(ㄓㄨㄢˇ ㄓㄡ)
the transmigration of souls; a metempsychosis 亦作「輪廻」

轉圜(ㄓㄨㄢˇ ㄏㄨㄢˊ)
①to intercede; to retrieve or revert an undesirable development ②to listen to counsel or advice readily

轉換(ㄓㄨㄢˇ ㄏㄨㄢˋ)
transition; to change; to switch: 我們轉換話題。We changed the topic of conversation.

轉換期(ㄓㄨㄢˇ ㄏㄨㄢˋ ㄑㄧ)
a transition period

轉機(ㄓㄨㄢˇ ㄐㄧ)
a turning point (usually from bad to good); a favorable turn; a turn for the better: 那女孩的病情已有了轉機。The sick girl has taken a turn for the better.

轉嫁(ㄓㄨㄢˇ ㄐㄧㄚˋ)
①(said of a woman) to remarry ②to transfer (a tax burden upon consumers, etc.); to pass (the blame, responsibility, etc. to someone else)

轉借(ㄓㄨㄢˇ ㄐㄧㄝˋ)
to lend (what has been borrowed)

轉交(ㄓㄨㄢˇ ㄐㄧㄠ)
to send or deliver through or in care of another person; to pass on to; to forward

轉角(ㄓㄨㄢˇ ㄐㄧㄠˇ)
a corner of a building; a corner of the street: 轉角處會我。Meet me at the corner of the street.

轉進(ㄓㄨㄢˇ ㄐㄧㄣˋ)
(literally) to advance backward — (euphemism) to retreat

轉去(ㄓㄨㄢˇ ㄑㄩˋ)
to turn and go; to go back

轉徙(ㄓㄨㄢˇ ㄒㄧˇ)
to migrate from place to place

轉向(ㄓㄨㄢˇ ㄒㄧㄤˋ)
(said of wind) to change directions; to turn in the direction of; to shift: 風轉向北吹。The wind shifted to the north.

轉學(ㄓㄨㄢˇ ㄒㄩㄝˊ)
to transfer to another school: 那男孩轉學到另一所學校。The boy transferred to another school.

轉學生(ㄓㄨㄢˇ ㄒㄩㄝˊ ㄕㄥ)
a transfer student: 他是個轉學生。He is a transfer student.

轉致(ㄓㄨㄢˇ ㄓˋ)
to convey or send (messages) through another person

轉折(ㄓㄨㄢˇ ㄓㄜˊ)
complications; twists and turns

轉戰(ㄓㄨㄢˇ ㄓㄢˋ)
to fight in one place after another

轉賬(ㄓㄨㄢˇ ㄓㄤˋ)
to transfer accounts (in banking)

轉注(ㄓㄨㄢˇ ㄓㄨˋ)
mutually interpretative symbols, one of the six classes of Chinese characters

轉飭(ㄓㄨㄢˇ ㄔˋ)
to order or instruct (subordinates) in accordance with orders or instructions received from one's superior

轉車(ㄓㄨㄢˇ ㄔㄜ)
to change trains or buses; to transfer to another train or bus: 我們必須在台中轉車。We have to change trains at Taichung.

轉世(ㄓㄨㄢˇ ㄕˋ)
(said of the soul) to trans-

migrate into another body; reincarnation; transmigration

轉手(ㄓㄨㄢ ㄕㄡˇ)
① to fall into another's hands; to change hands ② a very brief period of time

轉守為攻(ㄓㄨㄢ ㄕㄡˇ ㄨㄟˊ ㄍㄨㄥ)
to change from the defensive to the offensive

轉身(ㄓㄨㄢ ㄕㄣ)
to turn the body; to turn around

轉眼(ㄓㄨㄢ ㄧㄢˇ)
① to turn the eyes ② a trice; a very brief period of time; an instant; a moment

轉讓(ㄓㄨㄢ ㄖㄤˋ)
to transfer (ownership, title, etc.): 這座農場已經轉讓給他了。This farm has been transferred to him.

轉入(ㄓㄨㄢ ㄖㄨˋ)
to change over to; to shift to; to switch over to

轉載(ㄓㄨㄢ ㄗㄞˇ)
to reprint (articles published in another publication)

轉側(ㄓㄨㄢ ㄘㄜˋ)
① to toss oneself in bed ② to shift positions; to move about

轉漕(ㄓㄨㄢ ㄘㄠˊ)
to transport by land and water

轉移(ㄓㄨㄢ ㄧˊ)
to change in position or direction; to divert; to shift; to turn; to transfer: 那狗已把它的感情轉移給新主人。The dog has transferred its affection to its new master.

轉移陣地(ㄓㄨㄢ ㄧˊ ㄓㄣˋ ㄉㄧˋ)
to evacuate position (in military action)

轉移視線(ㄓㄨㄢ ㄧˊ ㄕˋ ㄒㄧㄢˋ)
① to turn the gaze ② to divert public attention; to draw attention to some other matter

轉頁(ㄓㄨㄢ ㄧㄝˋ)
to turn over the leaf (in reading)

轉業(ㄓㄨㄢ ㄧㄝˋ)
to change one's trade; to change one's career

轉眼(ㄓㄨㄢ ㄧㄢˇ)or **轉眼間**(ㄓㄨㄢ ㄧㄢˇ ㄐㄧㄢ)

(ㄐㄧㄢ)
a very brief period of time; in the twinkling of an eye; an instant; a moment: 小偷一轉眼就不見了。The thief disappeared in the twinkling of an eye.

轉危為安(ㄓㄨㄢ ㄨㄟˊ ㄨㄟˊ ㄢ)
① to become safe; to avert a danger; to turn the corner ② (said of a gravely ill patient) out of danger

轉彎(ㄓㄨㄢ ㄨㄢ)
to take a turn; to turn in another direction; to make a turn: 道卸踏車向右轉彎兒。The bicycle made a turn to the right.

轉彎抹角(ㄓㄨㄢ ㄨㄢ ㄇㄛˇ ㄐㄧㄠˇ)
① to go along a zigzag course ② to talk in a roundabout way; to beat around the bush; to mince

轉彎子(ㄓㄨㄢ ㄨㄢ ˙ㄗ)
to be roundabout (in speech)

轉文(ㄓㄨㄢ ㄨㄣˊ)
to quote from the classics with a view to showing off one's erudition

轉韻(ㄓㄨㄢ ㄩㄣˋ)
to shift to a new rhyme

轉運(ㄓㄨㄢ ㄩㄣˋ)
① to transport; to convey; to forward ② to be in a constant cyclic motion ③ to have a turn of luck (for the better)

轉運港(ㄓㄨㄢ ㄩㄣˋ ㄍㄤˇ)
a transit port

轉運公司(ㄓㄨㄢ ㄩㄣˋ ㄍㄨㄥ ㄙ)
a forwarding company; a transportation company

轉運使(ㄓㄨㄢ ㄩㄣˋ ㄕˇ)
an official in charge of transportation (during the Tang and Sung Dynasties)

【轉】6020
2. ㄓㄨㄢˋ juann zhuàn
to turn round and round; to rotate; to revolve; to gyrate: 陀螺以軸為中心旋轉。A top rotates on its axis.

轉磨(ㄓㄨㄢˋ ㄇㄛˊ)
to be at a loss in the face of a difficulty

轉門(ㄓㄨㄢˋ ㄇㄣˊ)
a turnstile; a revolving door

轉檯(ㄓㄨㄢˋ ㄊㄞˊ)
a turntable

轉臺(ㄓㄨㄢˋ ㄊㄞˊ)
a revolving stage

轉來轉去(ㄓㄨㄢˋ ㄌㄞˊ ㄓㄨㄢˋ ㄑㄩˋ)
to walk back and forth; to hang around

轉向(ㄓㄨㄢˋ ㄒㄧㄤˋ)
① to lose one's bearings; to lose one's way ② a change in one's philosophy, beliefs, etc.

轉椅(ㄓㄨㄢˋ ㄧˇ)
a swivel chair: 我為他買了一把轉椅。I bought him a swivel chair.

轉一轉(ㄓㄨㄢˋ ㄧˋ ㄓㄨㄢˋ)or **轉轉**(ㄓㄨㄢˋ ㄓㄨㄢˋ)
to take a short walk or ride (for exercise, etc.); to take a turn

【輥】6021
ㄍㄨˇ luh lǔ
1. a wheel
2. a capstan

輥軸(ㄍㄨˇ ㄓㄡˊ)
① a capstan; a windlass ② a pulley for drawing water from a well

【摎】6022
ㄐㄧㄡ jiou jiū
1. a dispute
2. deep and vast
3. disorder

摎轕or **摎葛**(ㄐㄧㄡ ㄍㄜˊ)
① a dispute; an endless involvement亦作「糾葛」: 他們對該問題有一場摎轕。They had a dispute over the question. ② deep and vast ③ disorder

十二畫

【轍】6023
彳ㄜˊ cheh ㄔㄜ che(語音 ㄐㄧㄜˇ jer zhé)
ruts; wheel tracks

轍鮒(ㄔㄜˋ ㄈㄨˋ)
(literally) a fish in a rut—in dire straits

轍亂旗靡(ㄔㄜˋ ㄌㄨㄢˋ ㄑㄧˊ ㄇㄧˇ)
(literally) chariots in disorder and banners dropping —(said of an army) completely routed

轍環天下(ㄔㄜˋ ㄏㄨㄢˊ ㄊㄧㄢ ㄒㄧㄚˋ)
to leave one's footprints all

〔車部〕

over the country (or the world)

轍迹(ㄔㄜˋ ㄐㄧ)
wheel tracks; ruts

【轎】 6024   ㄐㄧㄠˋ jiaw jiào
a chair; a sedan chair; a palankeen or a pa!anquin

轎夫(ㄐㄧㄠˋ ㄈㄨ)
sedan chair bearers

轎車(ㄐㄧㄠˋ ㄔㄜ)
a sedan (a kind of automobile)

轎子(ㄐㄧㄠˋ ·ㄗ)
a chair; a sedan chair; a palankeen or palanquin

【轔】 6025   ㄌㄧㄣˊ lín lín
1. noise of wheels; the rumble of vehicles
2. the threshold
3. wheels

轔轢(ㄌㄧㄣˊ ㄌㄧˋ)
①to be run over under wheels ②to oppress

轔轔(ㄌㄧㄣˊ ㄌㄧㄣˊ)
the rumble of vehicles; to rattle

十三畫

【轘】 6026   ㄏㄨㄢˋ huann huàn
to tear (an offender) asunder between vehicles (a form of ancient punishment)

轘裂(ㄏㄨㄢˋ ㄌㄧㄝˋ)
to tear (an offender) asunder between vehicles (a form of ancient punishment)

轘磔(ㄏㄨㄢˋ ㄓㄜˊ)
to tear (an offender) asunder between vehicles (a form of punishment)

轘轅(ㄏㄨㄢˋ ㄩㄢˊ)
①a topographically inaccessible place ②name of a mountain in Honan (河南)

【轕】 6027   ㄍㄜˊ ger gé
1. a dispute
2. deep and vast
3. disorder

【轙】 6028   ㄧˇ yii yǐ
1. rings on the yokes
2. to wait

【轏】 6029   ㄓㄢˋ kaan kàn
(said of vehicles) to proceed with difficulty

轗軻(ㄓㄢˋ ㄎㄜ)
①(said of vehicles) to move with difficulty ②down in luck; frustrated; disappointed

十四畫

【轟】 6030   ㄏㄨㄥ hong hōng
1. noise of a number of vehicles
2. noise; an uproar
3. grand; magnificent
4. to bombard; to blast

轟倒(ㄏㄨㄥ ㄉㄠˇ)
to knock down by bombardment

轟動(ㄏㄨㄥ ㄉㄨㄥˋ)
①to cause an uproar; to create a sensation ②to excite (the public)

轟動一時(ㄏㄨㄥ ㄉㄨㄥˋ ㄧ ㄕˊ)
to create a sensation: 他們兩人的結婚轟動一時。 Their marriage created a sensation.

轟隆(ㄏㄨㄥ ㄌㄨㄥˊ)
a thundering sound

轟轟(ㄏㄨㄥ ㄏㄨㄥ)
①a booming sound; a roaring sound ②in a grand fashion; with grandeur

轟轟烈烈(ㄏㄨㄥ ㄏㄨㄥ ㄌㄧㄝˋ ㄌㄧㄝˋ)
in a grand fashion; with grandeur; on a grand and spectacular scale

轟擊(ㄏㄨㄥ ㄐㄧ)
to bombard; to fire on (with artillery or rockets): 此城被敵人轟擊。 The city was bombarded by the enemy.

轟炸(ㄏㄨㄥ ㄓㄚˋ)
to bomb (from an airplane)

轟炸機(ㄏㄨㄥ ㄓㄚˋ ㄐㄧ)
a bomber

轟沉(ㄏㄨㄥ ㄔㄣˊ)
to sink (a vessel) by bombardment

轟然(ㄏㄨㄥ ㄖㄢˊ)
with a deafening sound

轟走(ㄏㄨㄥ ㄗㄡˇ)
to send away unceremoniously

【轝】 6031   ㄩ yu yú
same as 輿—a carriage; a sedan chair

【轞】 6032   ㄒㄧㄢˋ shiann xiàn
1. noise of wheels
2. sealed carts for transporting criminals

檻車(ㄒㄧㄢˋ ㄔㄜ)
a sealed cart for transporting criminals

十五畫

【轢】 6033   ㄌㄧˋ lih lì
1. (said of a wheel) to run over
2. to oppress; to bully

【轡】 6034   ㄆㄟˋ pey pèi
reins; a bridle

轡勒(ㄆㄟˋ ㄌㄜˋ)
reins and bits

十六畫

【轤】 6035   ㄌㄨˊ lu lú
1. a pulley for drawing water
2. a windlass; a capstan

【轆】 6036   ㄌㄧˋ lih lì
1. a pulley for drawing water
2. rails for vehicles

轆轤(ㄌㄧˋ ㄌㄨˊ)
①a pulley for drawing water ②rails for vehicles

辛 部
ㄒㄧㄣ shin xīn

【辛】 6037   ㄒㄧㄣ shin xīn
1. the eighth of the ten celestial stems
2. bitter; acrid
3. hard; toilsome; laborious
4. a Chinese family name

辛辣(ㄒㄧㄣ ㄌㄚˋ)
pungent; hot; bitter; peppery and acrid

辛勞(ㄒㄧㄣ ㄌㄠˊ)
great care or effort; pains

辛苦(ㄒㄧㄣ ㄎㄨˇ)

① laborious; toilsome: 捕魚
這工作很辛苦, Fishing is a
laborious task. ②to work
hard; to go through hard-
ships

辛亥革命(ㄒㄧㄣ ㄏㄞˋ ㄍㄜˋ ㄇㄧㄥˋ)
the Revolution of 1911 (the
year of 辛亥), which led to
the overthrow of the Ching
Dynasty

辛棄疾(ㄒㄧㄣ ㄑㄧˋ ㄐㄧˊ)
Hsin Chi-chi, 1140-1207, Sung
Dynasty poet

辛勤(ㄒㄧㄣ ㄑㄧㄣˊ)
hard-working; diligent;
industrious: 他是我們班上最辛
勤的學生, He is the most
diligent student in our class.

辛那堤(ㄒㄧㄣ ㄋㄚˋ ㄉㄧ)
Cincinnati, U.S.A.

辛苦苦(ㄒㄧㄣ ㄒㄧㄣ ㄎㄨˇ ㄎㄨˇ)
laboriously; with great
efforts; to take great pains

辛丑和約(ㄒㄧㄣ ㄔㄡˇ ㄏㄜˊ ㄩㄝ)
the Peace Treaty of 1901
(the year of 辛丑), signed
between China and ten foreign powers in the wake of
the Boxer Uprising

辛臭(ㄒㄧㄣ ㄔㄡˋ)
acrid and stinking

辛酸(ㄒㄧㄣ ㄙㄨㄢ)
hardships; the bitters of life:
他受盡各種辛酸, He suffered
all kinds of hardships.

辛味(ㄒㄧㄣ ㄨㄟˋ)
an acrid taste

五畫

辜 6038
ㄍㄨ gu gū
sin; crime; guilt
to be negligent in an obligation or expectation; to fail
a Chinese family name

辜負(ㄍㄨ ㄈㄨˋ)
to fail to live up to (another's expectation, etc.);
to let someone down: 我們決
不辜負老師的期望, We will
never let our teachers down.

辜鴻銘(ㄍㄨ ㄏㄨㄥˊ ㄇㄧㄥˊ)
Ku Hung-ming, 1847-1928,
an eccentric conservative
scholar who translated a
number of Chinese classics
into English

辜人(《ㄨ ㄖㄣˊ)
an executed criminal

辜月(《ㄨ ㄩㄝˋ)
the eleventh month of the
lunar year

六畫

【辟】 6039
1.(避) ㄅㄧˋ bih bì
1. a monarch
2. to summon; to call
3. to govern; to take the law
(to people)
4. to avoid; to escape

辟邪(ㄅㄧˋ ㄒㄧㄝˊ)
① to ward off evils ② a fabulous animal with two horns

辟世(ㄅㄧˋ ㄕˋ)
to withdraw (or retire) from
the world; to live in seclusion

辟易(ㄅㄧˋ ㄧˋ)
to retreat or recoil (in
fright)

辟言(ㄅㄧˋ ㄧㄢˊ)
① to go away because of an
offensive statement ② the
justest words

辟引(ㄅㄧˋ ㄧㄣˇ)
to summon to court; to
appoint to office

【辟】 6039
2. ㄆㄧˋ pih pì
same as 僻—remote; inaccessible

辟匿(ㄆㄧˋ ㄋㄧˋ)
remote; out-of-the-way

辟陋(ㄆㄧˋ ㄌㄡˋ)
(said of a house) remote
and crude

辟穀(ㄆㄧˋ ㄍㄨˇ)
to avoid eating cereals in
order to gain immortality

辟踊(ㄆㄧˋ ㄩㄥˇ)
in extreme grief; grief-
stricken

【皋】 6040
ㄗㄨㄟˋ tzuey zuì
same as 罪—sin; crime; guilt

七畫

【辣】 6041
ㄌㄚˋ lah là
1. pungent; hot
2. (said of smell or taste) to
burn; to bite

---

3. vicious; ruthless

辣醬兒醬(ㄌㄚˋ ㄐㄧㄤˋ ㄦˊ ㄐㄧㄤˋ)
pungent bean paste

辣撻(ㄌㄚˋ ㄊㄚˋ)
untidy; not neat 亦作「邋遢」

辣湯(ㄌㄚˋ ㄊㄤ)
peppered soup

辣椒(ㄌㄚˋ ㄐㄧㄠ)
capsicum

辣醬(ㄌㄚˋ ㄐㄧㄤˋ)
paste of pungent condiment
(especially one prepared
from capsicum)

辣手(ㄌㄚˋ ㄕㄡˇ)
① cruel means; drastic
means ② a ruthless person
③ difficult to handle; causing much headache; a hot
potato; a knotty problem (a
corrupt form of 棘手 which
has gained currency): 那件事
真辣手。That's really a
knotty problem.

辣子(ㄌㄚˋ ˙ㄗ)
capsicum

辣味(ㄌㄚˋ ㄨㄟˋ)
piquancy; pungency; peppery
taste

九畫

【辦】 6042
ㄅㄢˋ bann bàn
1. to manage; to handle; to
transact; to deal with; to
attend to
2. to try and punish
3. to purchase

辦報(ㄅㄢˋ ㄅㄠˋ)
to publish a newspaper; to
run a newspaper

辦不到(ㄅㄢˋ ㄅㄨˋ ㄉㄠˋ)
unable to accomplish or
manage; impossible to
accomplish or manage

辦不來(ㄅㄢˋ ㄅㄨˋ ㄌㄞˊ)
too much for one to handle

辦不了(ㄅㄢˋ ㄅㄨˋ ㄌㄧㄠˇ)
too much for one to accomplish or finish

辦不成(ㄅㄢˋ ㄅㄨˋ ㄔㄥˊ)
unable to be accomplished

辦不完(ㄅㄢˋ ㄅㄨˋ ㄨㄢˊ)
(said of work) too much for
one to finish

辦法(ㄅㄢˋ ㄈㄚˇ)
means; schemes; ways;

resources: 我總有辦法說服他。
I will persuade him by some
ways or other.

（辛
部）

辦得不好(ㄅㄢ˙ㄉㄜ ㄅㄨ ㄏㄠˇ)
badly managed; poorly handled; mismanaged; bungled:
他事情辦得不好。He bungled
the job.

辦得好(ㄅㄢ˙ㄉㄜ ㄏㄠˇ)
well-handled; well-managed;
well-done

辦到(ㄅㄢˋ ㄉㄠˋ)
to get something done; to
accomplish

辦妥(ㄅㄢˋ ㄊㄨㄛˇ)
to complete (procedures); to
finish doing something properly

辦理(ㄅㄢˋ ㄌㄧˇ)
to take care of (some business); to handle; to:
這件事情你斟酌辦理。You han-
dle this matter as you see
fit.

辦理公使(ㄅㄢˋ ㄌㄧˇ ㄍㄨㄥ ㄕˇ)
a minister resident

辦稿(ㄅㄢˋ ㄍㄠˇ)
to draft a document

辦公(ㄅㄢˋ ㄍㄨㄥ)
to attend to business; to do
office work

辦公費(ㄅㄢˋ ㄍㄨㄥ ㄈㄟˋ)
special administration allowances (paid to the head of
an office in addition to the
regular salary)

辦公廳(ㄅㄢˋ ㄍㄨㄥ ㄊㄧㄥ)
①an office building; an
office: 我到他的辦公廳去訪
他。I called on him at his
office. ②the secretariat（of
an official agency

辦公時間(ㄅㄢˋ ㄍㄨㄥ ㄕˊ ㄐㄧㄢ)
office hours

辦公室(ㄅㄢˋ ㄍㄨㄥ ㄕˋ)
an office space; an office: 他
的辦公室在市中心。He has his
office in the center of the
city.

辦後事(ㄅㄢˋ ㄏㄡˋ ㄕˋ)
to arrange matters for the
deceased

辦貨(ㄅㄢˋ ㄏㄨㄛˋ)
to handle the purchase of
goods

辦酒席(ㄅㄢˋ ㄐㄧㄡˇ ㄒㄧˊ)
to prepare a banquet; to

host a feast

辦交涉(ㄅㄢˋ ㄐㄧㄠ ㄕㄜˋ)
to negotiate

辦喜事(ㄅㄢˋ ㄒㄧˇ ㄕˋ)
to host a party on a joyous
occasion (especially a wedding); to organize a wed-
ding: 他們正忙著辦喜事。They
were busy organizing a wedding.

辦事(ㄅㄢˋ ㄕˋ)
to handle business; to manage an affair

辦事處(ㄅㄢˋ ㄕˋ ㄔㄨˋ)
a branch office (of an organization)

辦事員(ㄅㄢˋ ㄕˋ ㄩㄢˊ)
a low-ranking staff member;
a staffer

辦賊(ㄅㄢˋ ㄗㄟˊ)
to try and punish thieves or
rebels

辦罪(ㄅㄢˋ ㄗㄨㄟˋ)
to try and punish an
offender

辦喪事(ㄅㄢˋ ㄙㄤ ㄕˋ)
to arrange or handle funeral
matters

辦案(ㄅㄢˋ ㄢˋ)
to handle a (legal or business) case

【辨】 6043
ㄅㄧㄢˋ　biann　biàn
1. to distinguish; to discern
2. to identify; to recognize

辨白(ㄅㄧㄢˋ ㄅㄞˊ)or 辨明(ㄅㄧㄢˋ
ㄇㄧㄥˊ)
①to distinguish clearly; to
identify clearly ② to ac-
count for

辨別(ㄅㄧㄢˋ ㄅㄧㄝˊ)
to distinguish between; to
see the difference between;
to identify

辨明是非(ㄅㄧㄢˋ ㄇㄧㄥˊ ㄕˋ ㄈㄟ)
to distinguish right from
wrong; to distinguish between
right and wrong: 我們應該知
道如何辨明是非。We should
know how to distinguish
right from wrong.

辨識(ㄅㄧㄢˋ ㄕˋ)
to distinguish and evaluate

辨惑(ㄅㄧㄢˋ ㄏㄨㄛˋ)
to straighten out confusing
points

辨析(ㄅㄧㄢˋ ㄒㄧ)

to analyze and distinguish

辨志(ㄅㄧㄢˋ ㄓˋ)
to analyze and identify one's
intentions

辨正(ㄅㄧㄢˋ ㄓㄥˋ)
to identify and correct
(errors)

辨士(ㄅㄧㄢˋ ㄕˋ)
pence

辨識(ㄅㄧㄢˋ ㄕˋ)
to recognize; to identify; recognition

辨認(ㄅㄧㄢˋ ㄖㄣˋ)
to identify; to recognize

辨色(ㄅㄧㄢˋ ㄙㄜˋ)
①to read another's facial
expressions ②to distinguish
colors ③twilight

十二畫

【辭】 6044
ㄘˊ　tsyr　cí
1. language; words; a phrase;
an expression
2. to decline; to refuse
3. to leave; to part from; to
depart; to bid adieu
4. to resign; to dismiss

辭別(ㄘˊ ㄅㄧㄝˊ)
to bid farewell; to say
good-bye; to take one's
leave; to make one's adieus

辭不達意(ㄘˊ ㄅㄨˋ ㄉㄚˊ ㄧˋ)
The words fail to express
what is meant.

辭不獲命(ㄘˊ ㄅㄨˋ ㄏㄨㄛˊ ㄇㄧㄥˋ)
to have one's resignation or
declination rejected

辭費(ㄘˊ ㄈㄟˋ)
verbose; wordy

辭賦(ㄘˊ ㄈㄨˋ)
an ancient style of metrical
composition

辭典(ㄘˊ ㄉㄧㄢˇ)
a dictionary; a lexicon;
thesaurus: 辭典是他的常伴。A
dictionary is his frequent
companion.

辭謝(ㄘˊ ㄒㄧㄝˋ)
to decline (offers)

辭退(ㄘˊ ㄊㄨㄟˋ)
①to remove from office; to
dismiss: 他被辭退了。He was
dismissed (from) the service. ②to resign from office

辭令(ㄘˊ ㄌㄧㄥˋ)

diction appropriate to the occasion

辭工 (ㄘˊ ㄍㄨㄥ)
to resign from manual work

辭海 (ㄘˊ ㄏㄞˇ)
a collection of words

辭彙 (ㄘˊ ㄏㄨㄟˋ)
vocabulary: 他的辭彙有限。
His vocabulary is limited.
亦作「詞彙」

辭去 (ㄘˊ ㄑㄩˋ)
to resign from (a post)

辭卻 (ㄘˊ ㄑㄩㄝˋ)
to decline (offers)

辭謝 (ㄘˊ ㄒㄧㄝˋ)
to decline with thanks; to
ask to be excused: 他辭謝邀
請。He declined the invita-
tion with thanks.

辭行 (ㄘˊ ㄒㄧㄥˊ)
to take leave of; to say
good-bye to

辭職 (ㄘˊ ㄓˊ)
to resign from one's post;
resignation

辭章 or 詞章 (ㄘˊ ㄓㄤ)
① literary compositions;
poetry and prose ② the art
of writing; rhetoric

辭呈 (ㄘˊ ㄔㄥˊ)
a formal notice of resignation; a resignation: 他的辭呈
照准了。His resignation is
accepted.

辭世 (ㄘˊ ㄕˋ)
to depart from the world; to
die; to pass away: 他父親昨
晚辭世。His father died last
night.

辭讓 (ㄘˊ ㄖㄤˋ)
to decline (offers)

辭藻 or 詞藻 (ㄘˊ ㄗㄠˇ)
expressions in literary compositions

辭宗 (ㄘˊ ㄗㄨㄥ)
a master of words; a master
writer

辭色 (ㄘˊ ㄙㄜˋ)
utterances and facial expressions; speech and counte-
nance

辭歲 (ㄘˊ ㄙㄨㄟˋ)
a family gathering on the
Lunar New Year's Eve

辭意已決 (ㄘˊ ㄧˋ ㄐㄩㄝˊ)
The decision to resign has
been made.

辭嚴義正 (ㄘˊ ㄧㄢˊ ㄧˋ ㄓㄥˋ)
The language is stern and
the reason for it is justifiable.

辭源 (ㄘˊ ㄩㄢˊ)
the origin of a phrase or
expression

十三畫

【辮】 6045
ㄅㄧㄢˋ biann biàn
1. to plait; to braid
2. a queue; a pigtail; a braid

辮髮 (ㄅㄧㄢˋ ㄈㄚˇ)
① to braid the hair ② wearing a queue

辮子 (ㄅㄧㄢˋ ㄗ)
① a queue; a pigtail; a
braid; a plait ② a mistake
or defect that may be ex-
ploited by an opponent

十四畫

【辯】 6046
ㄅㄧㄢˋ biann biàn
1. to debate; to argue; to dispute
2. to use specious arguments

辯駁 (ㄅㄧㄢˋ ㄅㄛˊ)
to defend and refute; to
debate

辯白 (ㄅㄧㄢˋ ㄅㄞˊ)
to defend oneself verbally;
to justify

辯難 (ㄅㄧㄢˋ ㄋㄢˊ)
to defend and question; to
debate

辯論 (ㄅㄧㄢˋ ㄌㄨㄣˋ)
to debate; a debate

辯口 (ㄅㄧㄢˋ ㄎㄡˇ)
skill as a debater; eloquence

辯護 (ㄅㄧㄢˋ ㄏㄨˋ)
① to speak in defense of; to
defend verbally; to defend ②
(law) to plead; to defend;
defense: 被告人未作辯護。The
accused man made no
defense.

辯護士 (ㄅㄧㄢˋ ㄏㄨˋ ㄕˋ)
a lawyer; a barrister 亦作「律
師」

辯護人 (ㄅㄧㄢˋ ㄏㄨˋ ㄖㄣˊ)
defense counsel; an advocate

辯解 (ㄅㄧㄢˋ ㄐㄧㄝˇ)
to provide an explanation;

to try to defend oneself

辯證法 (ㄅㄧㄢˋ ㄓㄥˋ ㄈㄚˇ)
dialectic

辯士 (ㄅㄧㄢˋ ㄕˋ)
① an able speaker; a gifted
debater ② a sophist

辯才 (ㄅㄧㄢˋ ㄘㄞˊ)
ability as a debater; eloquence

辯才無礙 (ㄅㄧㄢˋ ㄘㄞˊ ㄨˊ ㄞˋ)
very eloquent

辯誣 (ㄅㄧㄢˋ ㄨ)
to defend oneself or someone falsely accused

辰 部
ㄔㄣˊ chern chén
〔辰部〕

【辰】 6047
ㄔㄣˊ chern chén
1. the fifth of the twelve Terrestrial Branches (地支)
2. 7:00-9:00 in the morning;
early morning
3. a time
4. fortune; luck
5. a heavenly body—the sun,
the moon and stars

辰駕 (ㄔㄣˊ ㄐㄧㄚˋ)
an imperial carriage

辰星 (ㄔㄣˊ ㄒㄧㄥ)
① a morning star ② the
planet Mercury 亦作「水星」

辰時 (ㄔㄣˊ ㄕˊ)
the period of a day from 7
a.m. to 9 a.m.

辰砂 (ㄔㄣˊ ㄕㄚ)
cinnabar 亦作「朱砂」

三畫

【辱】 6048
ㄖㄨˇ ruh rǔ
(又讀 ㄖㄨˊ ruu rǔ)
1. disgrace: 他說他寧死不受辱。
He says he will choose
death before disgrace.
2. to disgrace; to insult; to dishonor: 他常每辱別人。He al-
ways insults people.
3. to condescend; to deign
4. undeservingly

辱罵 (ㄖㄨˇ ㄇㄚˋ)
to abuse and insult

辱没 (ㄖㄨˇ ㄇㄛˋ)
to insult; to disgrace

辱命 (ㄖㄨˇ ㄇㄧㄥˋ)
to fail to live up to the expectation of one's superior; to dishonor one's commission; to fail to accomplish a mission

辱臨 (ㄖㄨˇ ㄌㄧㄣˊ)
to condescend to come to such a humble place (a self-depreciatory expression in addressing a guest)

辱國 (ㄖㄨˇ ㄍㄨㄛˊ)
to bring shame upon the fatherland; to disgrace the mother country

辱荷 (ㄖㄨˇ ㄏㄜˋ)
(a self-depreciatory expression) to receive (a favor) undeservingly

辱教 (ㄖㄨˇ ㄐㄧㄠˋ)
thanks for your instructions

辱承 (ㄖㄨˇ ㄔㄥˊ)
(a self-depreciatory expression) to receive (a favor) undeservingly

辱賜 (ㄖㄨˇ ㄘˋ)
thanks for your gifts

辱愛 (ㄖㄨˇ ㄞˋ)
(a self-depreciatory expression) to receive a favor undeservingly

六畫

【農】 6049 ㄋㄨㄥˊ nong nǒng
1. agriculture; farming
2. to farm
3. a farmer; a peasant; a husbandman

農忙 (ㄋㄨㄥˊ ㄇㄤˊ)
the busy season for farmers

農民 (ㄋㄨㄥˊ ㄇㄧㄣˊ)
farmers; peasants; the farming population

農民節 (ㄋㄨㄥˊ ㄇㄧㄣˊ ㄐㄧㄝˊ)
Farmer's Day on February 4th

農民協會 (ㄋㄨㄥˊ ㄇㄧㄣˊ ㄒㄧㄝˊ ㄏㄨㄟˋ)
a farmers' association; a farmers' cooperative

農民意識 (ㄋㄨㄥˊ ㄇㄧㄣˊ ㄧˋ ㄕˋ)
peasant consciousness

農民運動 (ㄋㄨㄥˊ ㄇㄧㄣˊ ㄩㄣˋ ㄉㄨㄥˋ)
a peasants' movement

農夫 (ㄋㄨㄥˊ ㄈㄨ)
a farmer; a husbandman

農婦 (ㄋㄨㄥˊ ㄈㄨˋ)
a farm woman

農地 (ㄋㄨㄥˊ ㄉㄧˋ)
farmland, agricultural land; 他擁有很多農地。 He owns a lot of farmland.

農地重劃 (ㄋㄨㄥˊ ㄉㄧˋ ㄔㄨㄥˊ ㄏㄨㄚˋ)
farmland consolidation

農田 (ㄋㄨㄥˊ ㄊㄧㄢˊ)
agricultural fields; farmland; agricultural land; cultivated land

農奴 (ㄋㄨㄥˊ ㄋㄨˊ)
a serf

農奴制度 (ㄋㄨㄥˊ ㄋㄨˊ ㄓˋ ㄉㄨˋ)
the serf system

農曆 (ㄋㄨㄥˊ ㄌㄧˋ)
the traditional Chinese calendar; the lunar calendar

農林 (ㄋㄨㄥˊ ㄌㄧㄣˊ)
agriculture and forestry

農林廳 (ㄋㄨㄥˊ ㄌㄧㄣˊ ㄊㄧㄥ)
Department of Agriculture and Forestry (under a provincial government); 他在農林廳服務。 He serves in the Department of Agriculture and Forestry.

農耕隊 (ㄋㄨㄥˊ ㄍㄥ ㄉㄨㄟˋ)
an agricultural demonstration team, particularly referring to those teams dispatched to work abroad

農工 (ㄋㄨㄥˊ ㄍㄨㄥ)
① agriculture and industry
② a hired farm worker

農科 (ㄋㄨㄥˊ ㄎㄜ)
the department of agriculture (in college)

農戶 (ㄋㄨㄥˊ ㄏㄨˋ)
a peasant family

農會 (ㄋㄨㄥˊ ㄏㄨㄟˋ)
a farmers' association; a farmers' cooperative

農家 (ㄋㄨㄥˊ ㄐㄧㄚ)
a farming family

農家子 (ㄋㄨㄥˊ ㄐㄧㄚ ㄗˇ)
one who is brought up in a peasant family

農郊 (ㄋㄨㄥˊ ㄐㄧㄠ)
countryside; the cultivated suburbs

農具 (ㄋㄨㄥˊ ㄐㄩˋ)
agricultural implements; farm tools: 農夫需要農具。 Farmers need farm tools.

農隙 (ㄋㄨㄥˊ ㄒㄧˋ) or 農閒 (ㄋㄨㄥˊ ㄒㄧㄢˊ)
the slack season for farmer

農學 (ㄋㄨㄥˊ ㄒㄩㄝˊ)
science of agriculture

農學家 (ㄋㄨㄥˊ ㄒㄩㄝˊ ㄐㄧㄚ)
an agriculturist

農學院 (ㄋㄨㄥˊ ㄒㄩㄝˊ ㄩㄢˋ)
the faculty of agriculture

農產物 (ㄋㄨㄥˊ ㄔㄢˇ ㄨˋ) or 農產品 (ㄋㄨㄥˊ ㄔㄢˇ ㄆㄧㄣˇ)
farm products; agricultural products: 它主要的農產物是棉花。 Its chief farm product is cotton.

農場 (ㄋㄨㄥˊ ㄔㄤˇ) or 農庄 (ㄋㄨㄥˊ ㄓㄨㄤ)
a farm: 他在農場工作。 He worked on a farm.

農時 (ㄋㄨㄥˊ ㄕˊ)
the seasons for farming —spring for plowing, summer for weeding, and autumn for reaping

農事 (ㄋㄨㄥˊ ㄕˋ)
farming; agricultural operations

農舍 (ㄋㄨㄥˊ ㄕㄜˋ)
a farmhouse

農神火箭 (ㄋㄨㄥˊ ㄕㄣˊ ㄏㄨㄛˇ ㄐㄧㄢˋ)
the Saturn rocket

農人 (ㄋㄨㄥˊ ㄖㄣˊ)
a farmer; a husbandman; 農人在農田工作。 Farmers work on the land.

農作物 (ㄋㄨㄥˊ ㄗㄨㄛˋ ㄨˋ)
farm products; crops

農村 (ㄋㄨㄥˊ ㄘㄨㄣ)
a rural community; a farm village: 他住在農村。 He lives in a farm village.

農村電氣化 (ㄋㄨㄥˊ ㄘㄨㄣ ㄉㄧㄢˋ ㄑㄧˋ ㄏㄨㄚˋ)
rural electrification

農桑 (ㄋㄨㄥˊ ㄙㄤ)
agriculture and sericulture

農藝 (ㄋㄨㄥˊ ㄧˋ ㄩㄝˋ)
agronomy: 他對農藝學感興趣。 He is interested in agronomy.

農藝學家 (ㄋㄨㄥˊ ㄧˋ ㄒㄩㄝˊ ㄐㄧㄚ)
農藝師 (ㄋㄨㄥˊ ㄧˋ ㄕ)
an agronomist

農業 (ㄋㄨㄥˊ ㄧㄝˋ)
agriculture; farming: 農業是生產性的勞動。 Farming

productive labor.

農業土壤學（ㄋㄨㄥˊ ㄧㄝˋ ㄊㄨˇ ㄖㄤˇ ㄒㄩㄝˊ）
agrology: 他教農業土壤學。He teaches agrology.

農業國（ㄋㄨㄥˊ ㄧㄝˋ ㄍㄨㄛˊ）
an agricultural nation

農業化學（ㄋㄨㄥˊ ㄧㄝˋ ㄏㄨㄚˋ ㄒㄩㄝˊ）
agricultural chemistry

農業機械（ㄋㄨㄥˊ ㄧㄝˋ ㄐㄧ ㄒㄧㄝˋ）
farm machinery

農業學校（ㄋㄨㄥˊ ㄧㄝˋ ㄒㄩㄝˊ ㄒㄧㄠˋ）or
農校（ㄋㄨㄥˊ ㄒㄧㄠˋ）
a vocational school of agriculture

農業時代（ㄋㄨㄥˊ ㄧㄝˋ ㄕˊ ㄉㄞˋ）
the age of agriculture

農業試驗所（ㄋㄨㄥˊ ㄧㄝˋ ㄕˋ ㄧㄢˋ ㄙㄨㄛˇ）
an agricultural laboratory; an experimental farm

農業社會（ㄋㄨㄥˊ ㄧㄝˋ ㄕㄜˋ ㄏㄨㄟˋ）
agricultural society

農業生物學（ㄋㄨㄥˊ ㄧㄝˋ ㄕㄥ ㄨˋ ㄒㄩㄝˊ）
agrobiology

農藥（ㄋㄨㄥˊ ㄧㄠˋ）
pesticide; agricultural chemicals

辵 部
ㄔㄨㄛˋ chuoh chuò

三畫

【迂】 6050
ㄩ　iu yū
impractical; unrealistic; old-fashioned; trite; hackneyed; stale; pedantic

roundabout; indirect; circuitous; winding: 這是條迂迴小徑。It's a winding path.

迂道（ㄩ ㄉㄠˋ）
. to make a detour

迂曲（ㄩ ㄑㄩ）
. absurd; preposterous

迂夫子（ㄩ ㄈㄨ ㄗˇ）
an impractical scholar; a pedant

迂腐（ㄩ ㄈㄨˇ）
trite; stale; hackneyed; pedantic: 不要那麼迂腐。Don't be so pedantic.

迂道（ㄩ ㄉㄠˋ）or 迂路（ㄩ ㄌㄨˋ）
to detour

迂誕（ㄩ ㄉㄢˋ）
preposterous; absurd: 多麼迂誕的建議啊! What an absurd suggestion!

迂陋（ㄩ ㄌㄡˋ）
stale; hackneyed

迂論（ㄩ ㄌㄨㄣˋ）or 迂闊之論（ㄩ ㄎㄨㄛˋ ㄓ ㄌㄨㄣˋ）
an impractical argument; an unrealistic statement; a pedantic talk

迂闊（ㄩ ㄎㄨㄛˋ）
impractical; unrealistic

迂迴（ㄩ ㄏㄨㄟˊ）
① twisty; circuitous (road)
② (military) detouring tactics; flanking tactics

迂迴曲折（ㄩ ㄏㄨㄟˊ ㄑㄩ ㄓㄜˊ）
having many turns and curves; not straightforward; circuitous; in zigzags and by roundabout ways

迂迴戰術（ㄩ ㄏㄨㄟˊ ㄓㄢˋ ㄕㄨˋ）
flanking tactics

迂緩（ㄩ ㄏㄨㄢˇ）
slow; slothful; sluggish

迂久（ㄩ ㄐㄧㄡˇ）
for a long time

迂見（ㄩ ㄐㄧㄢˋ）
an absurd view; an impractical opinion

迂氣（ㄩ ㄑㄧˋ）
indifference to reality or practicality; stubborn adherence to the absurd or the impractical; spirit of the old-fashioned

迂曲（ㄩ ㄑㄩ）
zigzag; winding; twisted: 這條小路迂曲地通往山上。The path ran zigzag up the hill.

迂直（ㄩ ㄓˊ）
impractical and artless

迂滯（ㄩ ㄓˋ）
dull; clumsy; slow

迂拙（ㄩ ㄓㄨㄛˊ）
impractical and clumsy

迂儒（ㄩ ㄖㄨˊ）
an impractical scholar; a pedant

迂叟（ㄩ ㄙㄡˇ）
an impractical old man

迂言（ㄩ ㄧㄢˊ）
an absurd statement; impractical remarks

迂遠（ㄩ ㄩㄢˇ）

① impractical; unrealistic ② long and twisty (road)

【迄】 6051
ㄑㄧˋ chih qì
up to; down to; so far; till

迄今（ㄑㄧˋ ㄐㄧㄣ）
up to now; until now; so far; to this day: 他迄今還不知道事實真象。He doesn't know the fact up to now.

迄未（ㄑㄧˋ ㄨㄟˋ）
not until now; not yet: 這工作迄未完成。The work is not yet finished.

【迅】 6052
ㄒㄩㄣˋ　shiunn xùn
swift; rapid; sudden

迅風（ㄒㄩㄣˋ ㄈㄥ）
a gale

迅雷（ㄒㄩㄣˋ ㄌㄟˊ）
a sudden clap of thunder

迅雷不及掩耳（ㄒㄩㄣˋ ㄌㄟˊ ㄅㄨˋ ㄐㄧˊ ㄧㄢˇ ㄦˇ）
as swift as a sudden clap of thunder which leaves no time for covering the ears; out of the blue

迅流（ㄒㄩㄣˋ ㄌㄧㄡˊ）
a rapid stream

迅疾（ㄒㄩㄣˋ ㄐㄧˊ）
swift; rapid; quick; speedy

迅捷（ㄒㄩㄣˋ ㄐㄧㄝˊ）
swift; quick; rapid; speedy

迅走（ㄒㄩㄣˋ ㄗㄡˇ）
to go fast; to hurry on

迅速（ㄒㄩㄣˋ ㄙㄨˋ）
by leaps and bounds; quick; swift; rapid

【巡】 6053
ㄒㄩㄣˊ　shyun xún
參看「巡」，under the radical《 P.401

【迤】 6054
1.(迆) ㄧˇ yii yǐ
1. to extend obliquely or along a zigzag course; to proceed in a winding way
2. connected; joined

迤麗（ㄧˇ ㄌㄧˋ）
joined; connected

迤邐（ㄧˇ ㄌㄧˇ）
① joined together ② winding; meandering

迤邐（ㄧˇ ㄌㄧˇ）
to extend continuously

【迤】 6054
2.ㄧˊ yi yí

辵
部

meandering; winding

四畫

【辵部】

【迎】 6055

1. ㄧㄥˊ yíng
to receive; to greet; to meet;
to welcome

迎面 (ㄧㄥˊ ㄇㄧㄢˋ)
right against one's face in
the opposite direction; in
one's face: 微風迎面向我吹來。
A breeze was blowing in my
face.

迎風 (ㄧㄥˊ ㄈㄥ)
① facing the wind; against
the wind: 小鳥迎風飛翔。The
birds fly against the wind.
② down the wind; with the
wind

迎風招展 (ㄧㄥˊ ㄈㄥ ㄓㄠ ㄓㄢˇ)
to flutter in the wind

迎敵 (ㄧㄥˊ ㄉㄧˊ)
to meet the enemy in battle;
to engage the enemy forces:
士兵們開始迎敵作戰。Soldiers
began to meet the enemy in
battle.

迎眸 (ㄧㄥˊ ㄇㄡˊ)
to meet with the eye

迎頭痛擊 (ㄧㄥˊ ㄊㄡˊ ㄊㄨㄥˋ ㄐㄧˊ)
to make a frontal attack; to
deal the enemy troops a
stunning blow by a frontal
attack; to deal a head-on
blow: 他給予敵人迎頭痛擊。He
dealt the enemy head-on
blows.

迎趕裡上 (ㄧㄥˊ ㄊㄡˊ ㄍㄢˇ ㄕㄤˋ)
to try hard to catch up

迎駕 (ㄧㄥˊ ㄐㄧㄚˋ)
to greet the imperial carriage

迎合 (ㄧㄥˊ ㄏㄜˊ)
① to cater to ② to make an
appointment to meet each
other in the future

迎候 (ㄧㄥˊ ㄏㄡˋ)
to go out to await (a visitor)

迎擊 (ㄧㄥˊ ㄐㄧˊ)
to meet and attack (an advancing enemy); to inter-
cept

迎接 (ㄧㄥˊ ㄐㄧㄝ)
to receive; to greet; to welcome: 他走到門前迎接客人。

He went to the door to
receive his visitors.

迎親 (ㄧㄥˊ ㄑㄧㄣ)
to go to meet one's bride at
her home before escorting
her back to one's own home
for the wedding

迎新 (ㄧㄥˊ ㄒㄧㄣ)
① to see the New Year in
② to welcome new arrivals

迎新送舊 (ㄧㄥˊ ㄒㄧㄣ ㄙㄨㄥˋ ㄐㄧㄡˋ)
to usher in the new and send
off the old; (a dinner party
held) to greet a new boss,
fellow students, etc. and bid
good-bye to a departing
boss, graduates, etc.

迎戰 (ㄧㄥˊ ㄓㄢˋ)
to meet (an approaching
enemy) head-on

迎娶 (ㄧㄥˊ ㄑㄩˇ)
to receive the dowry (on the
eve of the wedding) by the
bridegroom's family and
friends

迎晨 (ㄧㄥˊ ㄔㄣˊ)
at dawn or daybreak

迎春 (ㄧㄥˊ ㄔㄨㄣ) or 迎年 (ㄧㄥˊ ㄋㄧㄢˊ)
the ceremony of greeting the
New Year; to greet the New
Year

迎春典禮 (ㄧㄥˊ ㄔㄨㄣ ㄉㄧㄢˇ ㄌㄧˇ)
the ceremony of welcoming
spring

迎春花 (ㄧㄥˊ ㄔㄨㄣ ㄏㄨㄚ)
a winter jasmine (*Jasminum
nudiflorum*)

迎神賽會 (ㄧㄥˊ ㄕㄣˊ ㄙㄞˋ ㄏㄨㄟˋ)
noisy processions and festivals held in honor of local
deities

迎上來來 (ㄧㄥˊ ㄕㄤˋ ㄌㄞˊ)
to come onward

迎刃而解 (ㄧㄥˊ ㄖㄣˋ ㄦˊ ㄐㄧㄝˇ)
(literally) to meet the edge
of the knife blade and split
in two—(said of a difficult
problem) to be solved neatly; to solve itself

迎送 (ㄧㄥˊ ㄙㄨㄥˋ)
to greet (new arrivals) and
see off (those who are departing)

迎阿 (ㄧㄥˊ ㄜ)
to flatter; to act like a sycophant

迎逛 (ㄧㄥˊ ㄧㄚˊ)

to receive; to greet; to welcome

迎養 (ㄧㄥˊ ㄧㄤˇ)
to support one's parents or
benefactors by taking them
to one's own home

【迎】 6055

2. ㄧㄥˋ yìng
to go out in person to meet
(a visitor)

【近】 6056

ㄐㄧㄣˋ jìnn jìn

1. near or close (in space): 郵
局距離這兒很近。The post
office is quite near.
2. near or close (in time);
immediate; recent
3. near or close (in abstract
relation); intimate
4. to approach; to approx-
mate: 這作品幾近完美。This
work approximates to per-
fection.

近便 (ㄐㄧㄣˋ ㄅㄧㄢˋ)
at a conveniently little distance; close and convenient

近傍 (ㄐㄧㄣˋ ㄅㄤˋ)
adjacent to; nearby

近代 (ㄐㄧㄣˋ ㄉㄞˋ)
modern times; recent times

近代史 (ㄐㄧㄣˋ ㄉㄞˋ ㄕˇ)
modern history

近代思想 (ㄐㄧㄣˋ ㄉㄞˋ ㄙㄨ ㄒㄧㄤˇ)
modern thought

近地點 (ㄐㄧㄣˋ ㄉㄧˋ ㄉㄧㄢˇ)
(astronomy) perigee

近東 (ㄐㄧㄣˋ ㄉㄨㄥ)
the Near East

近體詩 (ㄐㄧㄣˋ ㄊㄧˇ ㄕ)
"modern style" poetry, including the "regulated
verse" (律詩) and "cut-short
verse" (絕句), the innova-
tions in classical poetry during the Tang Dynasty (618-
907)

近年 (ㄐㄧㄣˋ ㄋㄧㄢˊ)
in recent years

近來 (ㄐㄧㄣˋ ㄌㄞˊ)
recently; lately: 我近來一直很
累。I have been very tired
recently.

近利 (ㄐㄧㄣˋ ㄌㄧˋ)
immediate gain

近鄰 (ㄐㄧㄣˋ ㄌㄧㄣˊ)
a close neighbor: 他是我們的
近鄰。He is a close neighbor

of ours.

近路(ㄐㄧㄣ ㄌㄨˋ)
a shortcut

近古(ㄐㄧㄣ ㄍㄨˇ)
the period between now and the Middle Ages

近況(ㄐㄧㄣ ㄎㄨㄤˋ)
a recent situation; how things stand

近海(ㄐㄧㄣ ㄏㄞˇ)
(said of land) near the sea; coastal; offshore

近海漁業(ㄐㄧㄣ ㄏㄞˇ ㄩˊ ㄧㄝˋ)
inshore fishery

近乎(ㄐㄧㄣ ·ㄏㄨ)
close to; almost; nearly

近畿(ㄐㄧㄣ ㄐㄧ)
the outskirts of the national capital; areas around the capital

近郊(ㄐㄧㄣ ㄐㄧㄠ)
suburbs; outskirts: 他住在近郊。He lives in the suburbs.

近距離(ㄐㄧㄣ ㄐㄩˋ ㄌㄧˊ)
a little distance; a short distance; at close range

近期(ㄐㄧㄣ ㄑㄧ)
in the near future

近親(ㄐㄧㄣ ㄑㄧㄣ)
close relatives: 我們有很多近親。We have many close relatives.

近情(ㄐㄧㄣ ㄑㄧㄥˊ)or 近情近理(ㄐㄧㄣ ㄑㄧㄥˊ ㄐㄧㄣ ㄌㄧˇ)
acceptable to reason; reasonable; sensible

近頃(ㄐㄧㄣ ㄑㄧㄥˇ)
recently; of late

近幸(ㄐㄧㄣ ㄒㄧㄥˋ)
favorites at imperial court

近支(ㄐㄧㄣ ㄓ)
related families of clans

近戰(ㄐㄧㄣ ㄓㄢˋ)
a close-quarter combat; a hand-to-hand combat

近朱者赤，近墨者黑(ㄐㄧㄣ ㄓㄨ ㄓㄜˇ ㄔˋ，ㄐㄧㄣ ㄇㄛˋ ㄓㄜˇ ㄏㄟ)
(literally) He who nears vermilion becomes red; he who nears ink becomes black.—Good companions have good influence while bad ones have bad influence.

近臣(ㄐㄧㄣ ㄔㄣˊ)
courtiers close to the monarch; trusted courtiers;

favorite courtiers; ministers belonging to a court

近程(ㄐㄧㄣ ㄔㄥˊ)
a short range

近處(ㄐㄧㄣ ㄔㄨˋ)
places nearby

近世(ㄐㄧㄣ ㄕˋ)
①the present era; in modern times②the period between now and the Middle Ages

近視(ㄐㄧㄣ ㄕˋ)or 近視眼(ㄐㄧㄣ ㄕˋ ㄧㄢˇ)
nearsightedness; myopia

近視眼鏡(ㄐㄧㄣ ㄕˋ ㄧㄢˇ ㄐㄧㄥˋ)
glasses for myopia

近侍(ㄐㄧㄣ ㄕˋ)
a personal attendant

近水樓臺(ㄐㄧㄣ ㄕㄨㄟˇ ㄌㄡˊ ㄊㄞˊ)
a point of vantage

近水樓臺先得月(ㄐㄧㄣ ㄕㄨㄟˇ ㄌㄡˊ ㄊㄞˊ ㄒㄧㄢ ㄉㄜˊ ㄩㄝˋ)
A waterfront pavilion gets the moonlight first.—the advantage of being in a favorable position

近日(ㄐㄧㄣ ㄖˋ)
recently; lately: 我近日未曾見到他。I haven't seen him lately.

近日點(ㄐㄧㄣ ㄖˋ ㄉㄧㄢˇ)
(astronomy) perihelion

近在眉睫(ㄐㄧㄣ ㄗㄞˋ ㄇㄟˊ ㄐㄧㄝˊ)
very near as if located right before one's eyelashes

近在咫尺(ㄐㄧㄣ ㄗㄞˋ ㄓˇ ㄔˇ)
very near as if just a few feet away

近在眼前(ㄐㄧㄣ ㄗㄞˋ ㄧㄢˇ ㄑㄧㄢˊ)
very near as if located right before one's eyes; right under one's nose

近作(ㄐㄧㄣ ㄗㄨㄛˋ)
recent works (of a writer, an artist, etc.): 我讀過你的近作。I have read your recent works.

近村(ㄐㄧㄣ ㄘㄨㄣ)
a village nearby

近似(ㄐㄧㄣ ㄙˋ)
similar to; resembling

近似值(ㄐㄧㄣ ㄙˋ ㄓˊ)
(mathematics) approximate value

近歲(ㄐㄧㄣ ㄙㄨㄟˋ)
in recent years

近憂(ㄐㄧㄣ ㄧㄡ)

sorrow near at hand; an immediate cause of worry

近因(ㄐㄧㄣ ㄧㄣ)
an immediate cause

近悅遠來(ㄐㄧㄣ ㄩㄝˋ ㄩㄢˇ ㄌㄞˊ)
(said of a good government) Those who are near are made happy, and those who are far off are attracted.

【迕】　6057
ㄨˋ yah yù
to go out to meet or receive

【返】　6058
ㄈㄢˇ faan fǎn

1. to go back; to come back; to return

2. to send back; to give back; to return

返轡(ㄈㄢˇ ㄆㄟˋ)
(said of a rider) to turn the horse back

返防(ㄈㄢˇ ㄈㄤˊ)
(said of a serviceman) to return to his unit on garrison duty

返老還童(ㄈㄢˇ ㄌㄠˇ ㄏㄨㄢˊ ㄊㄨㄥˊ)
to regain youth; to rejuvenate oneself

返里(ㄈㄢˇ ㄌㄧˇ)
to go home (after an extended stay elsewhere)

返國(ㄈㄢˇ ㄍㄨㄛˊ)
to return from abroad

返航(ㄈㄢˇ ㄏㄤˊ)
to return to a base or port

返回(ㄈㄢˇ ㄏㄨㄟˊ)
to return; to come or go back: 他離開辦公室，又立刻返回。He left the office and soon returned.

返魂(ㄈㄢˇ ㄏㄨㄣˊ)
to come back to life; to resurrect; to revive 亦作「復活」

返校(ㄈㄢˇ ㄒㄧㄠˋ)
to return to school; to go back to school: 他昨天返校。He returned to school yesterday.

返棹(ㄈㄢˇ ㄓㄠˋ)
(said of a boat) to take a return trip

返照(ㄈㄢˇ ㄓㄠˋ)
(said of light) to be reflected

返潮(ㄈㄢˇ ㄔㄠˊ)
to get moist; to get clammy; to get damp

〔走部〕

（走部）

返程（ㄷㄢˇ ㄔㄥˊ）
a return trip

【迕】6059
ㄨˇ wuh wù
1. to meet
2. to oppose; to disobey
迕逆（ㄨˇ ㄋㄧˋ）
①to go against one's superiors ②delinquent in filial piety

【迍】6060
ㄓㄨㄣ juen zhūn
a difficult position
迍邅（ㄓㄨㄣ ㄓㄢ）
to be in a difficult position
亦作「屯邅」

【远】6061
ㄏㄤˊ harng háng
1. animal tracks
2. a path; a way; a road

五畫

【迢】6062
ㄊㄧㄠˊ tyau tiáo
far; distant; remote
迢遰（ㄊㄧㄠˊ ㄉㄧˋ）
far-off; faraway
迢迢（ㄊㄧㄠˊ ㄊㄧㄠˊ）
faraway; far and remote
迢递（ㄊㄧㄠˊ ㄉㄧˋ）or 迢逺（ㄊㄧㄠˊ ㄩㄢˇ）
far; distant

【迆】6063
ㄧˇ yii yǐ
same as 迤—connected; to proceed in a winding way

【泂】6064
（迥）ㄐㄩㄥˇ jeong jiǒng
1. faraway
2. widely different
泂拔（ㄐㄩㄥˇ ㄅㄚˊ）
standing erect and high
泂别（ㄐㄩㄥˇ ㄅㄧㄝˊ）
a great difference; vastly different
泂非昔比（ㄐㄩㄥˇ ㄈㄟ ㄒㄧˊ ㄅㄧˇ）
so different that there is no way of comparing it with what it used to be
泂泂（ㄐㄩㄥˇ ㄐㄩㄥˇ）
faraway
泂殊（ㄐㄩㄥˇ ㄕㄨ）
vastly different; not similar at all
泂然不同（ㄐㄩㄥˇ ㄖㄢˊ ㄅㄨˋ ㄊㄨㄥˊ）
not in the least alike; diametrically different; poles

apart in (nature or appearance, etc.)
泂異（ㄐㄩㄥˇ ㄧˋ）
a great difference; vastly different
泂遠（ㄐㄩㄥˇ ㄩㄢˇ）
faraway; remote

【迦】6065
ㄐㄧㄚ jia jiā
a character used in transliterating foreign (especially Sanskrit) sounds
迦太基（ㄐㄧㄚ ㄊㄞˋ ㄐㄧ）
Carthage
迦納（ㄐㄧㄚ ㄋㄚˋ）
Ghana

【迨】6066
ㄉㄞˋ day dài
until; up until; by the time when; to wait till

【迪】6067
（廸）ㄉㄧˊ dyi dí
1. to advance; to progress
2. to enlighten; to teach
迪克推多（ㄉㄧˊ ㄎㄜˋ ㄊㄨㄟ ㄉㄨㄛ）
a dictator 亦作「獨裁者」
迪化（ㄉㄧˊ ㄏㄨㄚˋ）
Urumchi (or Tihwa), capital of Sinkiang Province
迪吉（ㄉㄧˊ ㄐㄧˊ）
lucky; prosperous; going well; blessed
迪斯可（ㄉㄧˊ ㄙ ㄎㄜˇ）
disco

【迫】6068
（廹）ㄆㄛˋ poh pò
1. to press; to force; to compel; to stress: 我强迫他做此事。I forced him to do it.
2. pressing; urgent; imminent
迫不得已（ㄆㄛˋ ㄅㄨˋ ㄉㄜˊ ㄧˇ）
to have no alternative (but to); compelled by circumstances
迫不及待（ㄆㄛˋ ㄅㄨˋ ㄐㄧˊ ㄉㄞˋ）
so urgent that there is no time for waiting; too impatient to wait
迫令（ㄆㄛˋ ㄌㄧㄥˋ）
to order or demand forcibly
迫害（ㄆㄛˋ ㄏㄞˋ）
to persecute; to oppress cruelly: 基督徒受到最嚴重迫害。Christians were terribly persecuted.
迫擊砲（ㄆㄛˋ ㄐㄧˊ ㄆㄠˋ）
a mortar (a shortbarreled

cannon)
迫近（ㄆㄛˋ ㄐㄧㄣˋ）
①to press near; to close in
②to draw near: 婚期迫近。The date of wedding is drawing near. ②imminent
迫降（ㄆㄛˋ ㄐㄧㄤˋ）
a forced landing; a distress landing
迫切（ㄆㄛˋ ㄑㄧㄝˋ）
pressing; urgent: 他迫切需要錢。He is urgent for money.
迫切需要（ㄆㄛˋ ㄑㄧㄝˋ ㄒㄩ ㄧㄠˋ）
an urgent need
迫脅（ㄆㄛˋ ㄒㄧㄝˊ）
to force; to coerce
迫使（ㄆㄛˋ ㄕˇ）
to force or compel (one to do a thing): 環境迫使他不得不—切。Circumstances compelled him to be desperat
迫在眉睫（ㄆㄛˋ ㄗㄞˋ ㄇㄟˊ ㄐㄧㄝˊ）
①extremely urgent and nea
②imminent
迫促（ㄆㄛˋ ㄘㄨˋ）
urgent; pressed for time
迫從（ㄆㄛˋ ㄘㄨㄥˊ）
to force to comply; to compel to submit
迫於（ㄆㄛˋ ㄩˊ）
to have no other alternativ because of...

【迭】6069
ㄉㄧㄝˊ dye dié
1. to alternate
2. repeatedly; frequently
3. as in 不迭—to stop; to ceas
迭斯（ㄉㄧㄝˊ ㄙ）《ㄙㄥ》
Charles Dickens, 1812-187 English novelist
迭擊（ㄉㄧㄝˊ ㄐㄧˊ）
to attack by turns
迭興（ㄉㄧㄝˊ ㄒㄧㄥ）
to rise one after another
迭次（ㄉㄧㄝˊ ㄘˋ）
again and again; repeatedl 我迭次警告他。I warned hi again and again.
迭用（ㄉㄧㄝˊ ㄩㄥˋ）
to use alternately

【述】6070
ㄕㄨˋ shuh shù
1. to give an account of; explain; to expound
2. to follow (precedents); carry forward; to continu (another's work)

祝職(ㄓㄨˋ ㄓˊ)
to report in person the performance of one's official duties; to report on one's work

祝聖
an honorary title for Tzu Szu(子思), Confucius' grandson

祝說(ㄓㄨˋ ㄕㄨㄛ)
to give an account of; to narrate

祝作(ㄓㄨˋ ㄗㄨㄛ)
to compose and create; to write; writings: 他的述作包括詩和散文。His writings include poetry and prose.

述而不作(ㄓㄨˋ ㄦˊ ㄅㄨˋ ㄗㄨㄛˋ)
to expound the theories or writings of ancient people without producing original writings oneself

祝語(ㄓㄨˋ ㄩˇ)
the predicate (as distinct from the subject)

【迍】 6071
ㄓㄨ ㄣ tzer zé
1. pressing; urgent
2. hurried; helter-skelter

六畫

【迴】 6072
(廻) ㄏㄨㄟˊ hwei húi
1. to turn; to rotate; to revolve
2. to zigzag; to wind: 峰迴路轉。The path winds along mountain ridges.
3. same as 回—to return

迴避(ㄏㄨㄟˊ ㄅㄧˋ)
①to avoid meeting (another person) ②(law) to withdraw, withdrawal ③to decline an offer, or resign from a job, in order to avoid likely suspicion of favoritism

迴風(ㄏㄨㄟˊ ㄈㄥ)
a whirlwind 亦作「旋風」

迴廊(ㄏㄨㄟˊ ㄌㄤˊ)
a winding corridor: 我走出房間到這條迴廊。I went out of the room into the winding corridor.

迴鑾(ㄏㄨㄟˊ ㄌㄨㄢˊ)
the return of the emperor to the capital

迴環(ㄏㄨㄟˊ ㄏㄨㄢˊ)
to recur in a cycle

迴環測試(ㄏㄨㄟˊ ㄏㄨㄢˊ ㄘㄜˋ ㄕˋ)
(computers) loop testing

迴翔(ㄏㄨㄟˊ ㄒㄧㄤˊ)
to soar round and round; to circle in the air

迴響(ㄏㄨㄟˊ ㄒㄧㄤˇ)
to echo; to resound; to reverberate

迴旋(ㄏㄨㄟˊ ㄒㄩㄢˊ)
to turn round and round; to circle

迴旋曲(ㄏㄨㄟˊ ㄒㄩㄢˊ ㄑㄩˇ)
(music) a rondo

迴轉(ㄏㄨㄟˊ ㄓㄨㄢˇ)
to turn round

迴轉爐(ㄏㄨㄟˊ ㄓㄨㄢˇ ㄌㄨˊ)
(metallurgy) a rotary furnace; a converter (for refining steel)

迴轉器(ㄏㄨㄟˊ ㄓㄨㄢˇ ㄑㄧˋ)or 迴轉儀(ㄏㄨㄟˊ ㄓㄨㄢˇ ㄧˊ)
(astronomy) a gyroscope; a gyro

迴腸(ㄏㄨㄟˊ ㄔㄤˊ)
(anatomy) the ileum

迴腸盪氣(ㄏㄨㄟˊ ㄔㄤˊ ㄉㄤˋ ㄑㄧˋ)
(said of music, poetry, etc.) to deeply affect one's emotions; very touching

迴誦(ㄏㄨㄟˊ ㄙㄨㄥˋ)
to recite, or chant repeatedly

迴文(ㄏㄨㄟˊ ㄨㄣˊ)
a palindrome

迴文錦(ㄏㄨㄟˊ ㄨㄣˊ ㄐㄧㄣˇ)
a kind of elaborately woven silk

迴紋針(ㄏㄨㄟˊ ㄨㄣˊ ㄓㄣ)or 迴形針(ㄏㄨㄟˊ ㄒㄧㄥˊ ㄓㄣ)
a paper clip

迴文詩(ㄏㄨㄟˊ ㄨㄣˊ ㄕ)
palindromic verses

【迷】 6073
ㄇㄧˊ mi mí
1. indistinct; vague; dim
2. to bewitch; to enchant; to be crazy about; to charm; to fascinate; to infatuate: 她對游泳着迷了。She was crazy about swimming.
3. a fan; a fiend: 他是個棒球迷。He is a baseball fan.

迷茫(ㄇㄧˊ ㄇㄤˊ)
vague; hazy; indistinct

迷茫(ㄇㄧˊ ㄇㄤˊ)
①vast and hazy ②confused; perplexed; dazed

迷蒙精(ㄇㄧˊ ㄇㄥˊ ㄐㄧㄥ)
(medicine) chloroform 亦作「哥羅芳」

迷蒙藥(ㄇㄧˊ ㄇㄥˊ ㄧㄠˋ)
anesthetics

迷夢(ㄇㄧˊ ㄇㄥˋ)
a delusive dream; an illusion; a delusion

迷湯(ㄇㄧˊ ㄊㄤ)
flatteries; honey words

迷途(ㄇㄧˊ ㄊㄨˊ)
①to go astray; to get lost ②a wrong path

迷途知返(ㄇㄧˊ ㄊㄨˊ ㄓ ㄈㄢˇ)
able to return to the proper path after going astray; able to correct one's own mistake

迷你(ㄇㄧˊ ㄋㄧˇ)
mini

迷你電腦(ㄇㄧˊ ㄋㄧˇ ㄉㄧㄢˋ ㄋㄠˇ)
a minicomputer

迷你裙(ㄇㄧˊ ㄋㄧˇ ㄑㄩㄣˊ)
a miniskirt

迷離(ㄇㄧˊ ㄌㄧˊ)
indistinct; vague

迷戀(ㄇㄧˊ ㄌㄧㄢˋ)
to be in blind love with; to be infatuated with; to be a slave of: 他迷戀着那個女孩。He's infatuated with that girl.

迷路(ㄇㄧˊ ㄌㄨˋ)
to go astray; to get lost: 她迷路了。She lost her way.

迷亂(ㄇㄧˊ ㄌㄨㄢˋ)
to derange; to confuse

迷宮(ㄇㄧˊ ㄍㄨㄥ)
a labyrinth; a maze

迷航(ㄇㄧˊ ㄏㄤˊ)
(said of a plane, ship, etc.) to drift off course; to lose one's course

迷忽忽(ㄇㄧˊ ㄏㄨ ㄏㄨ)
①having a confused mind; muddleheaded ②unconscious

迷糊(ㄇㄧˊ ·ㄏㄨ)or 迷迷糊糊(ㄇㄧˊ··ㄇㄧ·ㄏㄨ·ㄏㄨ)
①vague; dim; indistinct ②unconscious; half awake and half asleep ③dazzled ④muddleheaded: 她這個人有點迷糊。She's somewhat muddleheaded.

迷惑(ㄇㄧˊ ㄏㄨㄛˋ)
①to misguide; to delude; to confuse; to mislead ②confused; puzzled; bewildered

〔辵部〕

〔辵部〕

迷幻藥(ㄇㄧˊㄏㄨㄢˋㄧㄠˋ)
a hallucinogenic

迷魂湯(ㄇㄧˊㄏㄨㄣˊㄊㄤ)
①the soup of infatuation; the water of oblivion ②(figuratively) flattering words

迷魂陣(ㄇㄧˊㄏㄨㄣˊㄓㄣˋ)
the charming company of beautiful women (which makes one forget everything)

迷津(ㄇㄧˊㄐㄧㄣ)
①a labyrinth; confusion; a puzzle ②to lose one's way ③(Buddhism) the ford of delusion, i.e. mortality

迷信(ㄇㄧˊㄒㄧㄣˋ)
superstition; to believe blindly

迷住(ㄇㄧˊ‧ㄓㄨ)
to bewitch; to infatuate; to charm; to captivate; to enchant; to spellbind

迷失(ㄇㄧˊㄕ)
to get lost; to lose (one's way, etc.)

迷人(ㄇㄧˊㄖㄣˊ)
charming; fascinating; enchanting; bewitching; 她是個迷人的女孩。 She is a charming girl.

迷藏(ㄇㄧˊㄘㄤˊ)
hide-and-seek

迷岸(ㄇㄧˊㄢˋ)
(Buddhism) the shore of delusion

迷藥(ㄇㄧˊㄧㄠˋ)
knockout drops

迷霧(ㄇㄧˊㄨˋ)
①a dense fog ②anything that misguides people

迷惘 or 迷惆(ㄇㄧˊㄨㄤˇ)
bemused

迷雲(ㄇㄧˊㄩㄣˊ)
clouds of confusion (over the mind)

【迹】 6074
(跡) ㄐㄧˊ ji jí
footprints; traces; tracks

迹象(ㄐㄧˋㄒㄧㄤˋ)
signs; marks; indications: 那是一種奇怪的迹象。 That is a strange indication.

【追】 6075
ㄓㄨㄟ juei zhuī
1. to chase; to pursue; to follow; to trace
2. to drive; to expel

3. to demand insistently; to dun for
4. to try to recover (stolen goods, etc.); to retrieve

追奔逐北(ㄓㄨㄟㄅㄣㄓㄨˊㄅㄛˋ)
to chase an enemy force in full retreat

追本溯源(ㄓㄨㄟㄅㄣˇㄙㄨˋㄩㄢˊ)
to trace to the very source of something; to get at the root of the matter

追兵(ㄓㄨㄟㄅㄧㄥ)
troops in pursuit; pursuing troops

追捕(ㄓㄨㄟㄅㄨˇ)
to pursue and apprehend; to chase

追不到(ㄓㄨㄟ‧ㄅㄨㄉㄠˇ)
unable to catch up with; unable to overtake

追放(ㄓㄨㄟㄈㄤˋ)
to banish 亦作「放逐」

追封(ㄓㄨㄟㄈㄥ)
to ennoble posthumously

追到(ㄓㄨㄟㄉㄠˋ)
to catch up with

追悼(ㄓㄨㄟㄉㄠˋ)
to commemorate (the dead)

追悼會(ㄓㄨㄟㄉㄠˋㄏㄨㄟˋ)
a memorial service

追討(ㄓㄨㄟㄊㄠˇ)
①to dun for (debt) ②to pursue and subdue (rebels)

追念(ㄓㄨㄟㄋㄧㄢˋ)
to remember with nostalgia or gratitude

追趕(ㄓㄨㄟㄍㄢˇ)
to pursue; to chase; to try to catch up with or overtake: 獵人追趕狐狸。 The hunter chased a fox.

追根問底(ㄓㄨㄟㄍㄣㄨㄣˋㄉㄧˇ)or 追根究底(ㄓㄨㄟㄍㄣㄐㄧㄡˋㄉㄧˇ)
to raise one question after another (in order to reach the bottom of a matter)

追回(ㄓㄨㄟㄏㄨㄟˊ)
①to recover (what has been taken away illicitly) ②to catch up with someone on the way and make him come back

追悔(ㄓㄨㄟㄏㄨㄟˇ)
to regret afterward; to repent

追歡(ㄓㄨㄟㄏㄨㄢ)
to pursue pleasure

追還(ㄓㄨㄟㄏㄨㄢˊ)
to recover (what has bee taken away illicitly)

追擊(ㄓㄨㄟㄐㄧˊ)
to chase and attack; to giv chase

追記(ㄓㄨㄟㄐㄧˋ)
a postscript; to record after ward

追加(ㄓㄨㄟㄐㄧㄚ)
to make an addition (to a document, etc.)

追加預算(ㄓㄨㄟㄐㄧㄚㄩˋㄙㄨㄢˋ)
an additional budget; a sup plementary budget

追剿(ㄓㄨㄟㄐㄧㄠˇ)
to chase and attack retreat ing enemy troops

追繳(ㄓㄨㄟㄐㄧㄠˇ)
to demand the payment (o tax arrears, debts, etc.)

追究(ㄓㄨㄟㄐㄧㄡˋ)
①to try insistently to find out (the ultimate cause etc.) ②to investigate (a fault, mistake, etc.) and pun ish (the guilty)

追薦(ㄓㄨㄟㄐㄧㄢˋ)
to seek blessings for the dead; to pray for the dead

追求(ㄓㄨㄟㄑㄧㄡˊ)
①to seek; to pursue; to go after: 他一生都在追求真理。 He sought after the truth throughout his life. ②to court (a woman); courtship

追想(ㄓㄨㄟㄒㄧㄤˇ)
to remember nostalgically

追尋(ㄓㄨㄟㄒㄩㄣˊ)
to seek; to pursue

追逐(ㄓㄨㄟㄓㄨˊ)
to chase; to pursue

追查(ㄓㄨㄟㄔㄚˊ)
to investigate; to trace (by observing marks, tracks, bits of evidence)

追諡(ㄓㄨㄟㄕˋ)
to confer a posthumous title upon

追認(ㄓㄨㄟㄖㄣˋ)
to confirm; to ratify; to approve afterward

追贓(ㄓㄨㄟㄗㄤ)
to try to recover stolen articles

追贈(ㄓㄨㄟㄗㄥˋ)
to confer (titles or ranks)

追尊(ㄓㄨㄟ ㄗㄨㄣ)
to bestow posthumous honors upon

追蹤(ㄓㄨㄟ ㄗㄨㄥ)
①to follow the examples of the predecessors ②to trace; to trail: 警察循跡追蹤罪犯。The police are tracing the criminal.

追思彌撒(ㄓㄨㄟ ㄙ ㄇㄧˊ ㄙㄚ)
(Catholics) Requiem Mass

追思禮拜(ㄓㄨㄟ ㄙ ㄌㄧˇ ㄅㄞˋ)
(Protestants) Requiem Service

追溯(ㄓㄨㄟ ㄙㄨˋ)
to trace the origin of; to trace back 亦作「溯源」

追訴權(ㄓㄨㄟ ㄙㄨˋ ㄑㄩㄢˊ)
the right of prosecution; the right to prosecute someone for an offense committed long ago

追訴權時效法(ㄓㄨㄟ ㄙㄨˋ ㄑㄩㄢˊ ㄕˊ ㄒㄧㄠˋ ㄈㄚˇ)
(law) the statute of limitations

追訴時效(ㄓㄨㄟ ㄙㄨˋ ㄕˊ ㄒㄧㄠˋ)
the period within which a legal action may be taken; the period stipulated in a statute of limitations

追索(ㄓㄨㄟ ㄙㄨㄛˇ)
to make insistent demands for (payment)

追隨(ㄓㄨㄟ ㄙㄨㄟˊ)
to follow (a leader)

追憶(ㄓㄨㄟ ㄧˋ)
to call to memory; to remember; to look back: 事隔很久，難以追憶。It happened years ago and I can't call it to memory.

追影(ㄓㄨㄟ ㄧㄥˇ)
to paint somebody's likeness after his death

追問(ㄓㄨㄟ ㄨㄣˋ)
to question insistently

追遠(ㄓㄨㄟ ㄩㄢˇ)
to honor ancestors with sacrifices

【退】 6076
ㄊㄨㄟˋ tuey tuì
1. to retreat; to withdraw; to recede; to regress; to retrogress: 敵人已經撤退了。The enemy has retreated.

2. to recoil; to shrink

3. to bow out; to retire: 他六十歲退休。He retired at the age of sixty.

4. to send back; to give back; to return

退保(ㄊㄨㄟˋ ㄅㄠˇ)
①to return a bond; to cease to be a guarantor ②to return an insurance policy

退避(ㄊㄨㄟˋ ㄅㄧˋ)
to withdraw and avoid; to keep out of the way

退避三舍(ㄊㄨㄟˋ ㄅㄧˋ ㄙㄢ ㄕㄜˋ)
(literally) to retreat ninety li(里)—to retreat as far as possible in the face of a strong adversary or contestant

退兵(ㄊㄨㄟˋ ㄅㄧㄥ)
①to withdraw troops; to sound a retreat: 擊鼓退兵。The drums sounded a retreat. ②to repel enemy troops

退步(ㄊㄨㄟˋ ㄅㄨˋ)
①to fall off; to regress; to retrogress; to fall backwards; to suffer a relapse ②to retreat

退票(ㄊㄨㄟˋ ㄆㄧㄠˋ)
①(said of theaters, music halls, etc.) to refund; to return the ticket and get the money back ②(said of checks) to be dishonored; to bounce

退黨(ㄊㄨㄟˋ ㄉㄤˇ)
to withdraw from a political party

退敵(ㄊㄨㄟˋ ㄉㄧˊ)
to repel the enemy

退庭(ㄊㄨㄟˋ ㄊㄧㄥˊ) or 退堂(ㄊㄨㄟˋ ㄊㄤˊ)
to retire from the courtroom

退老(ㄊㄨㄟˋ ㄌㄠˇ)
to retire (from public life) due to old age

退路(ㄊㄨㄟˋ ㄌㄨˋ)
①a retreat ②something to fall back on

退股(ㄊㄨㄟˋ ㄍㄨˇ)
to withdraw investment in a company

退歸林下(ㄊㄨㄟˋ ㄍㄨㄟ ㄌㄧㄣˊ ㄒㄧㄚˋ)
to retire from public life

退款(ㄊㄨㄟˋ ㄎㄨㄢˇ)

to reimburse

退後(ㄊㄨㄟˋ ㄏㄡˋ)
to fall backward; to move backward

退化(ㄊㄨㄟˋ ㄏㄨㄚˋ)
to degenerate; to atrophy

退火(ㄊㄨㄟˋ ㄏㄨㄛˇ)
(metallurgy) annealing

退伙(ㄊㄨㄟˋ ㄏㄨㄛˇ)
to stop joining public mess

退貨(ㄊㄨㄟˋ ㄏㄨㄛˋ)
to return goods already purchased

退回(ㄊㄨㄟˋ ㄏㄨㄟˊ)
①to return (a gift, defective merchandise, etc.); to send back: 她的稿子已經被退回。Her manuscript has been sent back. ②to retreat; to turn back

退還(ㄊㄨㄟˋ ㄏㄨㄢˊ)
to return (a gift, defective merchandise, etc.)

退換(ㄊㄨㄟˋ ㄏㄨㄢˋ)
to return (merchandise) in exchange for another; to exchange a purchase

退婚(ㄊㄨㄟˋ ㄏㄨㄣ)
to break off a marital engagement

退居(ㄊㄨㄟˋ ㄐㄩ)
①to occupy a position less important or influential than the one held previously ②to live a retired life

退錢(ㄊㄨㄟˋ ㄑㄧㄢˊ)
to reimburse; to refund

退親(ㄊㄨㄟˋ ㄑㄧㄣ)
to break off a marital engagement

退卻(ㄊㄨㄟˋ ㄑㄩㄝˋ)
①to retreat: 敵人不得不退卻。The enemy had to retreat. ②to decline

退席(ㄊㄨㄟˋ ㄒㄧˊ)
to withdraw (from the presence of others); to retire from a banquet before it is finished; to walk out (of a meeting in protest): 他退席以示抗議。He walked out in protest.

退休(ㄊㄨㄟˋ ㄒㄧㄡ)
to retire from active life: 他自公職退休。He retired from public life.

退休年齡(ㄊㄨㄟˋ ㄒㄧㄡ ㄋㄧㄢˊ ㄌㄧㄥˊ)

〔辵部〕

retirement age

退休基金(ㄊㄨㄟˋㄒㄧㄡㄐㄧㄐㄧㄣ)
a superannuation fund

退休金(ㄊㄨㄟˋㄒㄧㄡㄐㄧㄣ)
a retiring allowance; a pension

退休制度(ㄊㄨㄟˋㄒㄧㄡㄓˋㄉㄨˋ)
a retirement system

退間(ㄊㄨㄟˋㄐㄧㄢ)
to retire (to a life of leisure)

退省(ㄊㄨㄟˋㄒㄧㄥˇ)
to pause for reflection or self-examination

退學(ㄊㄨㄟˋㄒㄩㄝˊ)
to withdraw from a school; to drop out of a school

退職(ㄊㄨㄟˋㄓˊ)
to resign from office; to retire: 他退職了。He resigned from office.

退志(ㄊㄨㄟˋㄓˋ)
the intention to resign or retire

退朝(ㄊㄨㄟˋㄔㄠˊ)
to retire from the (emperor's) court

退潮(ㄊㄨㄟˋㄔㄠˊ)
(said of the tide) to ebb

退場(ㄊㄨㄟˋㄔㄤˇ)
to leave the stage; an exit

退出(ㄊㄨㄟˋㄔㄨ)
to withdraw or retreat (from a city or position); to renounce (membership in an organization); to step out; to bow out

退出去(ㄊㄨㄟˋㄔㄨˋㄑㄩˋ)
to withdraw; to bow out

退食(ㄊㄨㄟˋㄕˊ)
to retire or rest for a meal

退士(ㄊㄨㄟˋㄕˋ)
①a recluse ②a retired official

退燒(ㄊㄨㄟˋㄕㄠ)or退熱(ㄊㄨㄟˋㄖㄜˋ)
to reduce or remove fever; (said of a person's temperature) to come down

退燒藥(ㄊㄨㄟˋㄕㄠㄧㄠˋ)
febrifuges; antipyretics

退守(ㄊㄨㄟˋㄕㄡˇ)
to retreat (to a city, position, etc.) and defend it

退稅(ㄊㄨㄟˋㄕㄨㄟˋ)
(economics) a tax rebate

退讓(ㄊㄨㄟˋㄖㄤˋ)
to yield (a position, etc., especially in one's modesty); to make a concession

退走(ㄊㄨㄟˋㄗㄡˇ)
to retreat; to withdraw

退租(ㄊㄨㄟˋㄗㄨ)
to terminate a lease contract

退縮(ㄊㄨㄟˋㄙㄨㄛ)
to shrink; to recoil; to flinch

退而求其次(ㄊㄨㄟˋㄦˊㄑㄧㄡˊㄑㄧˊㄘˋ)
to seek what is less attractive than one's original objective

退一步想(ㄊㄨㄟˋㄧˊㄅㄨˋㄒㄧㄤˇ)
to consider a matter in a concessive way; to view a matter in a less favorable light; to remind oneself that things might have been worse

退役(ㄊㄨㄟˋㄧˋ)
to be discharged from military service

退隱(ㄊㄨㄟˋㄧㄣˇ)
to go into retirement; to retire from public life

退伍(ㄊㄨㄟˋㄨˇ)
to retire or to be discharged from military service; to leave the army

退伍軍人(ㄊㄨㄟˋㄨˇㄐㄩㄣㄖㄣˊ)
a retired soldier; a discharged serviceman; veterans

退位(ㄊㄨㄟˋㄨㄟˋ)
to abdicate the throne. 國王退位了。The king abdicated.

退約(ㄊㄨㄟˋㄩㄝ)
to break off a contract or agreement

【送】6077.
ㄙㄨㄥˋ　sòng　sòng

1. to send; to despatch; to deliver; to convey

2. to present; to give: 父親送我一本書。My father gave me a book.

3. to see someone off; to send off; to wish Godspeed to; to send away in a complimentary manner

送報(ㄙㄨㄥˋㄅㄠˋ)
to deliver newspapers

送報生(ㄙㄨㄥˋㄅㄠˋㄕㄥ)
a newsboy

送別(ㄙㄨㄥˋㄅㄧㄝˊ)
to see (a person) off; to

give a send-off; to wish Godspeed to

送別會(ㄙㄨㄥˋㄅㄧㄝˊㄏㄨㄟˋ)
a farewell party; a send-off

送殯(ㄙㄨㄥˋㄅㄧㄣˋ)or送喪(ㄙㄨㄥˋㄙㄤ)
to attend a funeral

送命(ㄙㄨㄥˋㄇㄧㄥˋ)
to bring death upon oneself; to lose one's life; to go to one's doom

送飯(ㄙㄨㄥˋㄈㄢˋ)
to bring meals (for a person)

送達(ㄙㄨㄥˋㄉㄚˊ)
①to deliver to; to despatch to; to send to ②(law) to serve a writ on a person)

送到(ㄙㄨㄥˋㄉㄠˋ)
to send to; to deliver to

送暖偷寒(ㄙㄨㄥˋㄋㄨㄢˇㄊㄡㄏㄢˊ)
(said of young lovers) to have affectionate concern for each other

送老(ㄙㄨㄥˋㄌㄠˇ)
①to pass one's later years ②to prepare the dead for burial (especially one's parents)

送禮(ㄙㄨㄥˋㄌㄧˇ)
to give presents; to send gifts: 他送禮給我。He sent me gifts.

送故迎新(ㄙㄨㄥˋㄍㄨˋㄧㄥˊㄒㄧㄣ)
to bid farewell to those departing and greet the arrival of new comers ②to send off the old year and usher in the new year

送鬼(ㄙㄨㄥˋㄍㄨㄟˇ)
to exorcise evil spirits

送官(ㄙㄨㄥˋㄍㄨㄢ)
(in former times) to deliver a criminal to the yamen for punishment

送客(ㄙㄨㄥˋㄎㄜˋ)
①to escort a visitor on his way out ②to speed a parting guest

送寒衣(ㄙㄨㄥˋㄏㄢˊㄧ)
the ceremony of burning paper garments before a tomb on the first of the 10th lunar month

送話器(ㄙㄨㄥˋㄏㄨㄚˋㄑㄧˋ)
the transmitter (of a tele-

〔辵部〕

phone)

送貨(ㄙㄨㄥ ㄏㄨㄛˋ)
to deliver goods

送貨員(ㄙㄨㄥ ㄏㄨㄛˋ ㄩㄢˊ)
a deliveryman

送回(ㄙㄨㄥ ㄏㄨㄟˊ)or 送還(ㄙㄨㄥ
ㄏㄨㄢˊ)
to send back; to return

送交(ㄙㄨㄥ ㄐㄧㄠ)
to hand over to; to deliver
to: 請把這封信送交費老板。
Please hand over this letter
to your boss.

送餞(ㄙㄨㄥ ㄐㄧㄢˋ)
to give a send-off party

送秋波(ㄙㄨㄥ ㄑㄧㄡ ㄅㄛ)
to cast an amorous glance;
to make eyes at

送情(ㄙㄨㄥ ㄑㄧㄥˊ)
to convey one's feelings

送窮(ㄙㄨㄥ ㄑㄩㄥˊ)
to drive away poverty (a
ceremony held on the last
day of the first lunar month
in the Tang Dynasty)

送信(ㄙㄨㄥ ㄒㄧㄣˋ)or 送信兒(ㄙㄨㄥ
ㄒㄧㄦˋ)
to carry letters, to deliver
letters; to deliver a message

送香火光兒的(ㄙㄨㄥ ㄒㄧㄤ ㄏㄨㄛˇㄦ
·ㄉㄜ)
(in Peking in former times)
beggars who light pipes for
smokers and get paid in
return

送行(ㄙㄨㄥ ㄒㄧㄥˊ)
to give a send-off; to see
someone off; to wish God-
speed: 我到車站去為他送行。
I went to the station to see
him off.

送粧(ㄙㄨㄥ ㄓㄨㄤ)
to deliver the dowry to the
bridegroom's house

送終(ㄙㄨㄥ ㄓㄨㄥ)
to prepare for the burial of
one's parents

送神(ㄙㄨㄥ ㄕㄣˊ)
to send off the gods after
the offering of sacrifices

送上(ㄙㄨㄥ ·ㄕㄤ)
(a polite expression) to send
or deliver

送人(ㄙㄨㄥ ㄖㄣˊ)
①to send gifts; to give presents　②to see off a person;
to see someone off

送人情(ㄙㄨㄥ ㄖㄣˊ ㄑㄧㄥˊ)
to do another person a
favor at no great cost to
oneself

送子(ㄙㄨㄥ ㄗˇ)
(said of a goddess) to make
a woman give birth to a
child

送灶(ㄙㄨㄥ ㄗㄠˋ)
the ceremony (on the 23rd
of the 12th lunar month) of
sending off the kitchen god
on his annual trip to
Heaven with foods, drinks,
etc., offered as sacrifices

送葬(ㄙㄨㄥ ㄗㄤˋ)
to attend a funeral; to take
part in a funeral procession

送做堆(ㄙㄨㄥ ㄗㄨㄛˋ ㄉㄨㄟ)
(slang) to arrange a wed-
ding for a young couple who
have already lived under the
same roof since their childhood

送死(ㄙㄨㄥ ㄙˇ)
①to prepare for the burial
of one's parents　②to bring
death upon oneself

送往事居(ㄙㄨㄥ ㄨㄤˋ ㄕˋ ㄐㄩ)
to bury the dead and sup-
port the living

送往迎來(ㄙㄨㄥ ㄨㄤˋ ㄧㄥˊ ㄌㄞˊ)
to escort the parting and
welcome the coming—to be
busy entertaining guests
from afar

【适】6078
《ㄍㄨㄚ　gua guà
quick; fast; swift

【逃】6079
　ㄊㄠˊ　taur táo
1. to run away; to flee; to fly;
to abscond; to escape: 軍隊潰
逃.The troops fled in dis-
order.
2. to dodge; to evade; to avoid;
to shirk: 他逃避我的質問。He
evaded my question.

逃奔(ㄊㄠˊ ㄅㄣ)
to run away; to flee

逃避(ㄊㄠˊ ㄅㄧˋ)
to run away from; to shirk;
to evade; to dodge

逃避兵役(ㄊㄠˊ ㄅㄧˋ ㄅㄧㄥ ㄧˋ)
to dodge the draft; to evade
or shirk military service

逃避責任(ㄊㄠˊ ㄅㄧˋ ㄗㄜˊ ㄖㄣˋ)
to evade or shirk a responsi-

bility

逃兵(ㄊㄠˊ ㄅㄧㄥ)
a deserter; a fugitive soldier

逃不了(ㄊㄠˊ ·ㄅㄨ ㄌㄧㄠˇ)
inescapable from; unable to
escape

逃跑(ㄊㄠˊ ㄆㄠˇ)
to run away; to escape; to
flee

逃名(ㄊㄠˊ ㄇㄧㄥˊ)
to avoid fame; to shun publicity

逃命(ㄊㄠˊ ㄇㄧㄥˋ)
to flee for one's life

逃反(ㄊㄠˊ ㄈㄢˇ)
to seek refuge from social
unrest

逃犯(ㄊㄠˊ ㄈㄢˋ)
a fugitive from the law; a
jailbreaker; a wanted criminal

逃遁(ㄊㄠˊ ㄉㄨㄣˋ)
to run away; to flee; to
escape; to evade: 他受驚而逃
遁。He was frightened and
ran away.

逃脫(ㄊㄠˊ ㄊㄨㄛ)
to escape from; to free oneself from; to succeed in escaping from

逃難(ㄊㄠˊ ㄋㄢˋ)
to seek refuge from calamities: 難民逃難。Refugees seek
refuge from calamities.

逃匿(ㄊㄠˊ ㄋㄧˋ)
to flee to a hiding place

逃藏(ㄊㄠˊ ㄘㄤˊ)
to avoid employment

逃歸(ㄊㄠˊ ㄍㄨㄟ)or 逃回(ㄊㄠˊ ㄏㄨㄟˊ)
to escape from (a dangerous
place, etc.) and return home

逃婚(ㄊㄠˊ ㄏㄨㄣ)
to run away so as to avoid
a marriage

逃荒(ㄊㄠˊ ㄏㄨㄤ)
to flee from a famine

逃家(ㄊㄠˊ ㄐㄧㄚ)
to run away from home

逃嫁(ㄊㄠˊ ㄐㄧㄚˋ)
①to desert a husband and
remarry　②(said of a girl) to
run away when reluctant to
marry

逃軍(ㄊㄠˊ ㄐㄩㄣ)
①(said of a commander) to
desert the troops　②a de-

serter

逃席(ㄊㄠ ㄒㄧˊ)
to leave a feast, etc., without permission

逃刑(ㄊㄠ ㄒㄧㄥˊ)
(said of a convict) to escape the sentence or punishment

逃學(ㄊㄠ ㄒㄩㄝˊ)
to play truant; to cut class; to truant

逃之夭夭(ㄊㄠ ㄓ ㄧㄠ ㄧㄠ)
to escape without leaving a single trace behind; to slip away: 他一聽到這消息就逃之夭夭。 He slipped away on hearing the news.

逃債(ㄊㄠ ㄓㄞˋ)
to run away from the creditor

逃出虎口(ㄊㄠ ㄔㄨ ㄏㄨˇ ㄎㄡˇ)
(literally) to escape from a tiger's mouth—to escape from a very dangerous situation

逃出重圍(ㄊㄠ ㄔㄨ ㄔㄨㄥˊ ㄨㄟˊ)
to break out from a heavy siege

逃世(ㄊㄠ ㄕˋ)
to run away from the world; to go into seclusion

逃生(ㄊㄠ ㄕㄥ)
to flee for one's life

逃稅(ㄊㄠ ㄕㄨㄟˋ)
to avoid tax payment; tax evasion

逃走(ㄊㄠ ㄗㄡˇ)
to run away; to escape; to flee; to fly: 他已逃走。 He has flown.

逃罪(ㄊㄠ ㄗㄨㄟˋ)
to escape punishment

逃竄(ㄊㄠ ㄘㄨㄢˋ)
to disperse and flee; to run away: 他們狼狽逃竄。 They dispersed and fled helter-skelter.

逃散(ㄊㄠ ㄙㄢˋ)
to flee in all directions; to be separated in flight

逃逸(ㄊㄠ ㄧˋ)
to break loose and get away; to escape

逃隱(ㄊㄠ ㄧㄣˇ)
to flee into seclusion

逃亡(ㄊㄠ ㄨㄤˊ)
to run away; to escape; to flee; to fly; to abscond

逃亡者(ㄊㄠ ㄨㄤˊ ㄓㄜˇ)
a fugitive

逃往(ㄊㄠ ㄨㄤˇ)
to flee toward

6080
【逅】ㄏㄡˋ how hòu
(又讀《ㄡˋ gow gòu)
to meet unexpectedly; to come across; to run into

6081
【逆】ㄋㄧˋ nìh nì
1. to meet; to welcome
2. to oppose; to go against
3. beforehand; in advance
4. inverse; converse; adverse; contrary

逆叛(ㄋㄧˋ ㄆㄢˋ)
to rebel; to revolt

逆反應(ㄋㄧˋ ㄈㄢˇ ㄧㄥˋ)
an inverse reaction

逆風(ㄋㄧˋ ㄈㄥ)
①a head wind ②against the wind

逆黨(ㄋㄧˋ ㄉㄤˇ)
the rebel faction; a group of traitors

逆定理(ㄋㄧˋ ㄉㄧㄥˋ ㄌㄧˇ)
a converse theorem

逆覩(ㄋㄧˋ ㄉㄨˇ)
to see beforehand; to foresee: 我們無法逆覩未來。 We cannot foresee the future.

逆來順受(ㄋㄧˋ ㄌㄞˊ ㄕㄨㄣˋ ㄕㄡˋ)
to accept adversity philosophically; to be resigned to one's fate

逆料(ㄋㄧˋ ㄌㄧㄠˋ)
to conjecture beforehand; to predict; to anticipate; to foresee

逆流(ㄋㄧˋ ㄌㄧㄡˊ)
①an adverse current ②against the stream; up the stream: 他逆流游泳。 He swam against the current.

逆倫(ㄋㄧˋ ㄌㄨㄣˊ)
violation of primary relations among relatives or family members (especially referring to crimes committed against one's elders)

逆旅(ㄋㄧˋ ㄌㄩˇ)
an inn

逆跡昭彰(ㄋㄧˋ ㄐㄧ ㄓㄠ ㄓㄤ)
Signs of rebellion are evident.

逆計(ㄋㄧˋ ㄐㄧˋ)
to reckon or conjecture beforehand

逆境(ㄋㄧˋ ㄐㄧㄥˋ)
adverse circumstances; adversity

逆取順守(ㄋㄧˋ ㄑㄩˇ ㄕㄨㄣˋ ㄕㄡˇ)
to rule a country peacefully after obtaining the throne by violence

逆襲(ㄋㄧˋ ㄒㄧˊ)
a counterattack; to counterattack

逆向(ㄋㄧˋ ㄒㄧㄤˋ)
in the opposite direction

逆行(ㄋㄧˋ ㄒㄧㄥˊ)
①to proceed in the opposite direction; to go against the general trend ②(astronomy) retrograde motion

逆知(ㄋㄧˋ ㄓ)
to know beforehand; to foresee

逆折(ㄋㄧˋ ㄓㄜˊ)
to turn backward halfway

逆轉(ㄋㄧˋ ㄓㄨㄢˇ)
①to deteriorate; to turn to the worse ②a reversal

逆差(ㄋㄧˋ ㄔㄚ)
(commerce) an adverse balance of trade; a deficit

逆產(ㄋㄧˋ ㄔㄢˇ)
①(obstetrics) breech presentation, as opposed to face presentation ②the estate of a traitor

逆臣(ㄋㄧˋ ㄔㄣˊ)
a traitorous vassal; a traitor

逆事(ㄋㄧˋ ㄕˋ)
adverse affairs; misfortunes; mishaps: 他平靜地忍受逆事。 He bears misfortunes calmly.

逆數(ㄋㄧˋ ㄕㄨˋ)
①(mathematics) reciprocal; a reciprocal number ②unseasonable weather

逆水行舟(ㄋㄧˋ ㄕㄨㄟˇ ㄒㄧㄥˊ ㄓㄡ)
a boat going against the stream; to sail a boat against the current: 逆水行舟,不進則退。 A boat sailing against the stream must forge ahead or it will be driven back.

逆子(ㄋㄧˋ ㄗˇ)
an undutiful son; an unfilial

son

逆賊（ㄋ丨ˋ ㄗㄟˊ）
a rebellious bandit; a rebel;
a traitor

逆耳（ㄋ丨ˋ ㄦˇ）
(said of statements) to grate
on the ear; to be unpleasant
to the ear: 忠言逆耳。Good
advice is often grating on
the ear.

逆溫層（ㄋ丨ˋ ㄨㄣ ㄘㄥˊ）
(meteorology) the inversion
layer

【迻】 6082
丨ˊ yi i
to transfer; to translate

迻譯（丨ˊ 丨ˋ）
to translate: 這本書迻譯得很
好。The book translates well.

【逢】 6083
ㄆㄥˊ parng póng
a Chinese family name

【逈】 6084
（逈）ㄐㄩㄥˇ jeong
jiong
far

【迺】 6085
（乃）ㄋㄞˇ nae nǎi
a conjunctive and disjunc-
tive particle with a variety
of meanings

七畫

【逍】 6086
ㄒ丨ㄠ shiau xiāo
1. to wander in a leisurely
manner; to saunter; to loiter
2. free and unfettered; to be
leisurely and carefree; to
take one's ease; at ease

逍遙（ㄒ丨ㄠ 丨ㄠˊ）
to loiter about; to saunter
about

逍遙法外（ㄒ丨ㄠ 丨ㄠˊ ㄈㄚˇ ㄨㄞˋ）
to remain out of the law's
reach; to get off scot-free

逍遙學派（ㄒ丨ㄠ 丨ㄠˊ ㄒㄩㄝˊ ㄆㄞˋ）
the Peripatetics

逍遙自在（ㄒ丨ㄠ 丨ㄠˊ ㄗ ㄗㄞˋ）
to enjoy leisure without
restraint; to enjoy a free and
leisurely life; carefree

【逝】 6087
ㄕˋ shyh shì
1. to pass; to be gone; to
depart
2. to pass on; to die

逝去（ㄕˋ ㄑㄩˋ）
to pass; to be gone; to
depart

逝世（ㄕˋ ㄕˋ）
going and staying

逝止（ㄕˋ ㄓˇ）
going and staying

逝世（ㄕˋ ㄕˋ）
to pass away; to die

【逋】 6088
ㄅㄨ bu bū
1. to flee; to abscond
2. to neglect

逋慢（ㄅㄨ ㄇㄢˋ）
heedless of regulations or
orders

逋負（ㄅㄨ ㄈㄨˋ）
to neglect to pay debts

逋蕩（ㄅㄨ ㄉㄤˋ）
to neglect one's duty and
loaf

逋逃（ㄅㄨ ㄊㄠˊ）
to abscond; to flee (from justice)

逋留（ㄅㄨ ㄌ丨ㄡˊ）
to stay; to remain; to linger:
我很匆忙，沒有時間逋留。I'm
in a hurry; I've no time to
stay.

逋客（ㄅㄨ ㄎㄜˋ）
①a recluse ②a fugitive

逋峭（ㄅㄨ ㄑ丨ㄠˋ）
(said of a writing) containing many surprising turns;
not monotonous

逋懸（ㄅㄨ ㄒㄩㄢˊ）
a long overdue rent; arrears

逋租（ㄅㄨ ㄗㄨ）
to neglect the payment of
rent

逋亡（ㄅㄨ ㄨㄤˊ）
to flee; to escape; to abscond 亦作「逋逃」

【透】 6089
ㄊㄡˋ tow tòu
1. to pass through; to penetrate
2. to let out; to let through
3. thorough; quite; complete:
蘋果熟透了。The apples are
quite ripe.
4. to appear; to show

透闢（ㄊㄡˋ ㄆ丨ˋ）
(said of statements, reasoning, etc.) revealing; penetrating

透明（ㄊㄡˋ ㄇ丨ㄥˊ）
transparent: 窗戶的玻璃是透
明的。Window glass is trans-

parent.

透明體（ㄊㄡˋ ㄇ丨ㄥˊ ㄊ丨ˇ）
a transparent body

透風（ㄊㄡˋ ㄈㄥ）
①to let the wind through ②
to divulge a secret; to let
out a secret

透頂（ㄊㄡˋ ㄉ丨ㄥˇ）
①in the extreme; to the
utmost ②(said of syphilitic
symptoms) to reach the
head

透漏（ㄊㄡˋ ㄌㄡˋ）
to let out; to leak; to
divulge; to reveal (secrets or
news)

透亮（ㄊㄡˋ ㄌ丨ㄤˋ）
①(ㄊㄡˋ ㄌ丨ㄤˋ) ⓐ letting light
through; transparent; ⓑ
perfectly clear
②(ㄊㄡˋ・ㄌ丨ㄤ˙) ⓐ (said of precious stones, etc.) brilliant;
shiny ⓑ (said of statements)
penetrating; incisive

透露（ㄊㄡˋ ㄌㄨˋ）
(said of something) to come
to light; to divulge; to
reveal; to let out: 誰透露了這
個消息? Who let the news
out?

透骨（ㄊㄡˋ ㄍㄨˇ）
(said of the cold) piercing;
chilled to the bone

透過（ㄊㄡˋ ㄍㄨㄛˋ）
①to pass through; to penetrate ②through the intermediary of

透光（ㄊㄡˋ ㄍㄨㄤ）
①diaphaneity ②to let the
light pass through

透光鏡（ㄊㄡˋ ㄍㄨㄤ ㄐ丨ㄥˋ）
lenses 亦作「透鑑」

透汗（ㄊㄡˋ ㄏㄢˋ）
to perspire all over

透鏡（ㄊㄡˋ ㄐ丨ㄥˋ）
lenses

透氣（ㄊㄡˋ ㄑ丨ˋ）
①to let air through ②to
give vent to a pent-up feeling of discontent ③to relax
from strain

透消息（ㄊㄡˋ ㄒ丨ㄠ ㄒ丨ˊ）
to reveal news; to let out a
secret

透心涼（ㄊㄡˋ ㄒ丨ㄣ ㄌ丨ㄤˊ）
①penetrating coolness ②
utterly disappointing

辵部

[走 部]

透支 (ㄊㄡˋ ㄓ)
to overdraw; to spend more than the budgeted fund

透著 (ㄊㄡˋ ˙ㄓㄜ)
to appear to be; to seem to be

透徹 (ㄊㄡˋ ㄔㄜˋ)
thorough; thoroughly; penetrating

透澈 (ㄊㄡˋ ㄔㄜˋ)
clear; transparent; lucid

透濕 (ㄊㄡˋ ㄕ)
dripping wet; wet through 亦作「濕透」: 我身上透濕了。I got wet to the skin.

透視 (ㄊㄡˋ ㄕˋ)
①to see through; to penetrate ②to observe what is behind a solid covering (by X-ray, etc.) ③ to gain a perspective of; perspective

透視畫 (ㄊㄡˋ ㄕˋ ㄏㄨㄚˋ)
a perspective drawing

透一口氣 (ㄊㄡˋ ㄧ ㄎㄡˇ ㄑㄧˋ)
to catch a breath; to have a breathing spell

透味 (ㄊㄡˋ ㄨㄟˋ)
(said of cooked meat, etc.) thoroughly flavored

【逐】 6090 ㄓㄨˊ jwu zhú
1. to chase; to pursue; to follow
2. to drive off; to banish; to exile; to expel: 他被放逐終身。He was exiled for life.
3. little by little; gradually

逐波而去 (ㄓㄨˊ ㄅㄛ ㄦˊ ㄑㄩˋ)
to be carried away by waves; to go over the waves

逐步 (ㄓㄨˊ ㄅㄨˋ)
step by step; to proceed orderly: 逐步加以解決 to settle something step by step

逐末 (ㄓㄨˊ ㄇㄛˋ)
to pursue trivial things

逐條 (ㄓㄨˊ ㄊㄧㄠˊ)
item by item; article by article; point by point

逐退 (ㄓㄨˊ ㄊㄨㄟˋ)
to drive back; to repulse

逐年 (ㄓㄨˊ ㄋㄧㄢˊ)
year by year; year after year; annually: 人口逐年增加。Population has been increasing year after year.

逐利 (ㄓㄨˊ ㄌㄧˋ)
to pursue material gains

逐鹿 (ㄓㄨˊ ㄌㄨˋ)
(literally)to chase the deer —to vie for the throne; to vie for power; to seek an office

逐箇 or 逐個 (ㄓㄨˊ ㄍㄜ˙)
one by one: 他們逐箇調查這些問題。They investigate these questions one by one.

逐客令 (ㄓㄨˊ ㄎㄜˋ ㄌㄧㄥˋ)
an annoucement to a visitor that he is unwelcome

逐漸 (ㄓㄨˊ ㄐㄧㄢˋ)
little by little; gradually; by degrees

逐臣 (ㄓㄨˊ ㄔㄣˊ)
a banished subject; a vassal in exile

逐出 (ㄓㄨˊ ㄔㄨ)
to drive out; to expel; to eject; to kick out; to oust; to chase someone (or something) out of: 他們把他逐出屋外。They chased him out of the house.

逐水 (ㄓㄨˊ ㄕㄨㄟˇ)
(Chinese medicine) to eliminate the retention of fluid with powerful purgatives

逐日 (ㄓㄨˊ ㄖˋ)
①day by day; day after day; daily ②(said of a horse) galloping very fast

逐字 (ㄓㄨˊ ㄗˋ)
word by word; word for word: 請將此規則逐字解釋給我聽。Please explain this rule to me word by word.

逐次 (ㄓㄨˊ ㄘˋ)
on each of the occasions; in succession

逐一 (ㄓㄨˊ ㄧ)
one by one: 讓我們逐一上車吧。Let's get on the bus one by one.

逐月 (ㄓㄨˊ ㄩㄝˋ)
month by month; monthly: 他逐月來此。He comes here monthly.

【逑】 6091 ㄑㄧㄡˊ chyou qiú
1. to pair; to match; to marry
2. to collect; to draw together; to gather together
3. a mate

【逕】 6092 ㄐㄧㄥˋ jing jìng

1. a path
2. direct

逕庭 (ㄐㄧㄥˋ ㄊㄧㄥˊ)
very unlike; quite different; poles apart

逕寄 (ㄐㄧㄥˋ ㄐㄧˋ)
to mail directly to

逕啓者 (ㄐㄧㄥˋ ㄑㄧˇ ㄓㄜˇ)
(a salutation in letters)Dear Sir

逕行 (ㄐㄧㄥˋ ㄒㄧㄥˊ)
to do something directly; to do something on one's own initiative

【途】 6093 ㄊㄨˊ twu tú
a way; a road

途經 (ㄊㄨˊ ㄐㄧㄥ)
to pass through(a place); to go by way of: 他途經上海。He came by way of Shanghai.

途徑 (ㄊㄨˊ ㄐㄧㄥˋ)
a way; a road

途窮 (ㄊㄨˊ ㄑㄩㄥˊ)
to come to the end of a road —at the end of one's resources

途中 (ㄊㄨˊ ㄓㄨㄥ)
on the way; en route: 他在往義大利的途中。He was en route to Italy.

途遇 (ㄊㄨˊ ㄩˋ)
to encounter on the way; to meet en route

【逖】 6094 ㄊㄧˋ tih tì
far; distant

【逗】 6095 ㄉㄡˋ dow dòu
1. to stay; to linger; to remain to pause
2. to stir; to rouse; to tickle
3. funny: 這故事真逗! What a funny story!
4. a slight pause in reading

逗點 (ㄉㄡˋ ㄉㄧㄢˇ)
a comma(,)亦作「逗號」

逗弄 (ㄉㄡˋ ㄋㄨㄥˋ ·ㄋㄥˊ)
to make fun of; to sport with; to tease; to kid: 他在逗弄那嬰兒。He's kidding that baby.

逗樂 (ㄉㄡˋ ㄌㄜˋ)
to cause mirth; to rouse gaiety

逗留 (ㄉㄡˋ ㄌㄧㄡˊ)
to stay; to stop over; to lin

ger; to loiter

逗哯(ㄌㄡˋ ㄏㄠˇ)
- a comma(,)

逗趣(ㄌㄡˋ ㄑㄩˋ)
to amuse; to entertain(with
jokes, etc.)

逗笑兒(ㄌㄡˋ ㄒㄧㄠˋ ㄦ)
to rouse laughter; to cause
mirth

逗人(ㄌㄡˋ ㄖㄣˊ)
to tease; to tickle; to amuse

逗人喜愛(ㄌㄡˋ ㄖㄣˊ ㄒㄧˇ ㄞˋ)
(said of a child) to arouse
the affection of adults

【這】 6096
　　　　ㄓㄜˋ jeh zhè
1. this (a pronoun)
2. this (a demonstrative adjective); such

這般
　such; like this

這般光景(ㄓㄜˋ ㄅㄢ ㄍㄨㄤ ㄐㄧㄥˇ)or
這般地步(ㄓㄜˋ ㄅㄢ ㄉㄧˋ ㄅㄨˋ)
such a sad condition; such a
pitiable state of affairs

這邊(ㄓㄜˋ ㄅㄧㄢ)
①this side; here: 請到這邊來。
Please come over here. ②
this side; our side: 勝利在我
們這邊。Victory is on our
side.

這步田地(ㄓㄜˋ ㄅㄨˋ ㄊㄧㄢˊ ㄉㄧˋ)
(to) such a pass; (to) such a
deplorable situation

這麼(ㄓㄜˋ ㄇㄜ˙)
so; thus; (in) this way; like
this: 大家都這麼說。So they
say.

這麼點兒(ㄓㄜˋ ㄇㄜ˙ ㄉㄧㄢˇㄦ)
such a little bit

這麼個(ㄓㄜˋ ㄇㄜ˙ ㄍㄜ˙)
such a one as this

這麼著(ㄓㄜˋ ㄇㄜ˙ ㄓㄜ˙)
this way (an expression to
introduce a suggestion; an
instruction of how to do
something, etc.); like this; so

這麼一來(ㄓㄜˋ ㄇㄜ˙ ㄧ ㄌㄞˊ)
as a result of this; that as a
result; in this way; consequently

這麼說(ㄓㄜˋ ㄇㄜ˙ ㄕㄨㄛ)
so; thus; (in) this way; like
this

這番(ㄓㄜˋ ㄈㄢ)
all this

這等(ㄓㄜˋ ㄉㄥˇ)

such; like this

這裏(ㄓㄜˋ ㄌㄧˇ)or 這兒(ㄓㄜˋㄦ)
here; this place; where we
are: 她不在這裡。She is not
here.

這個(ㄓㄜˋ ㄍㄜ˙)
① this; this one ② h'm, hem,
or hum(an interjection indicating indecision when the
sound ·ㄍㄜ is dragged too
long)

這個那個的(ㄓㄜˋ ㄍㄜ˙ ㄋㄚˋ ㄍㄜ˙ ㄉㄜ˙)
wavering; irresolute; hesitant; to hem and haw

這還了得(ㄓㄜˋ ㄏㄞˊ ㄌㄧㄠˇ ㄉㄜˊ)
How dare! or How can such
a thing be tolerated!

這會兒(ㄓㄜˋ ㄏㄨㄟˋㄦ)or 這會子
(ㄓㄜˋ ㄏㄨㄟˋ ㄗ˙)
now; at the moment; at present: 他這會兒很忙。He is busy
at the moment.

這就(ㄓㄜˋ ㄐㄧㄡˋ)
① at once; right away ② If
this happens, then....或 If that
is the case, then....

這其間(ㄓㄜˋ ㄑㄧˊ ㄐㄧㄢ)
meanwhile; in the meantime

這些(ㄓㄜˋ ㄒㄧㄝ)
these

這種(ㄓㄜˋ ㄓㄨㄥˇ)
this kind; such kind; this
type; such type

這程子(ㄓㄜˋ ㄔㄥˊ ㄗ˙)
recent; recently

這山望着那山高(ㄓㄜˋ ㄕㄢ ㄨㄤˋ ㄓㄜ˙
ㄋㄚˋ ㄕㄢ ㄍㄠ)
It's always the other mountain that looks higher.—(figuratively) One is never
satisfied with one's own
present circumstance, position, etc.

這早晚兒(ㄓㄜˋ ㄗㄠˇ ㄨㄢˇㄦ)
as late as this; so late: 她怎
麼這早晚兒才來? Why does
she come so late?

這次(ㄓㄜˋ ㄘˋ)
this time; present; current

這廝(ㄓㄜˋ ㄙ)
this fellow; this guy

這兒(ㄓㄜˋㄦ)
①here: 我住在這兒。I live
here. ②now; then

這一向(ㄓㄜˋ ㄧ ㄒㄧㄤˋ)
recently

這一陣子(ㄓㄜˋ ㄧ ㄓㄣˋ ·ㄗ)
recent; recently

這一回(ㄓㄜˋ ㄧ ㄏㄨㄟˊ)
this time

這樣那樣(ㄓㄜˋ ㄧㄤˋ ㄋㄚˋ ㄧㄤˋ)
this and that

這樣(ㄓㄜˋ ㄧㄤˋ)or 這樣子(ㄓㄜˋ
ㄧㄤˋ ·ㄗ)
so; thus; (in) this way: 別跑
這樣快。Don't run so fast.

【這】 6096
　　2. ㄓㄟˋ jey zhèi
this or that (an emphatic
demonstrative adjective)

這邊(ㄓㄟˋ ㄅㄧㄢ)
over here; on this side: 到我
這邊來。Come over here.

這天(ㄓㄟˋ ㄊㄧㄢ)
(on) this (particular) day;
(on) that (particular) day

這年(ㄓㄟˋ ㄋㄧㄢˊ)
(in) this (particular) year;
(in) that (particular) year

這溜兒(ㄓㄟˋ ㄌㄧㄡ ㄦ)
this (particular) area; this
(particular) district; this
(particular) neighborhood

這個(ㄓㄟˋ ㄍㄜ˙)
this one

這塊兒(ㄓㄟˋ ㄎㄨㄞˋㄦ)
①this area; this neighborhood ②this lump

這陣兒(ㄓㄟˋ ㄓㄣˋㄦ)
this (very) moment

【通】 6097
　　　　ㄊㄨㄥ tong tōng
1. to go, move, or flow unobstructed
2. to communicate; to interchange
3. to lead to; to reach: 條條大
路通羅馬。All roads lead to
Rome.
4. to understand thoroughly; to
be versed in
5. to let through; through
6. smooth; fluent
7. open; passable
8. all; general; overall;
throughout
9. thorough
10. common; popular
11. (said of a sentence) well-
constructed; containing no
fallacy

通寳(ㄊㄨㄥ ㄅㄠˇ)

〔走
部〕

〔走部〕

通報(ㄊㄨㄥ ㄅㄠ)
to notify

通便(ㄊㄨㄥ ㄅㄧㄢ)
to facilitate bowels movement

通便劑(ㄊㄨㄥ ㄅㄧㄢ ㄐㄧ)
a laxative

通病(ㄊㄨㄥ ㄅㄧㄥ)
common ills; common deficiencies; common faults

通不過(ㄊㄨㄥ ㄅㄨˋ ㄍㄨㄛˋ)
(said of a motion, law, bill, etc.) cannot be passed; cannot get the approval or consent of

通盤(ㄊㄨㄥ ㄆㄢ)
overall; all-round; entire

通盤考慮(ㄊㄨㄥ ㄆㄢ ㄎㄠˇ ㄌㄩˋ)
to consider from every possible angle; to take into consideration every aspect of a matter

通盤計畫(ㄊㄨㄥ ㄆㄢ ㄐㄧˋ ㄏㄨㄚˋ)
an overall plan

通判(ㄊㄨㄥ ㄆㄢˋ)
an assistant prefectural magistrate (in former times)

通票(ㄊㄨㄥ ㄆㄧㄠˋ)
a through ticket

通謀(ㄊㄨㄥ ㄇㄡˊ)
to conspire

通名(ㄊㄨㄥ ㄇㄧㄥˊ)
to introduce to each other; to identify oneself

通分(ㄊㄨㄥ ㄈㄣ)
reduction of fractions to a common denominator

通風(ㄊㄨㄥ ㄈㄥ)
① to let the wind through; ventilation：這教室不通風。 This classroom is badly ventilated. ② to let out news or secrets

通風口(ㄊㄨㄥ ㄈㄥ ㄎㄡˇ)
an opening for ventilation

通達(ㄊㄨㄥ ㄉㄚˊ)
① to understand clearly ② open to traffic; unobstructed ③ (said of a road) to lead to

通達事理(ㄊㄨㄥ ㄉㄚˊ ㄕˋ ㄌㄧˇ)
to understand ways of doing business

通道(ㄊㄨㄥ ㄉㄠˋ)
a passage; a way

通敵(ㄊㄨㄥ ㄉㄧˊ)
to collaborate with the enemy secretly

通牒(ㄊㄨㄥ ㄉㄧㄝˊ)
diplomatic communications or messages

通電(ㄊㄨㄥ ㄉㄧㄢˋ)
① to cable all concerned ② to supply electricity to; to link with the source of an electric current

通都大邑(ㄊㄨㄥ ㄉㄨ ㄉㄚˋ ㄧˋ)
a metropolis with roads leading everywhere

通透(ㄊㄨㄥ ㄊㄡˋ)
to understand thoroughly

通體(ㄊㄨㄥ ㄊㄧˇ)
① the whole ② to merge; to unite ③ sexual intercourse

通條(ㄊㄨㄥ ㄊㄧㄠˊ)
a thick iron wire used to clear blocked pipes, tubes or other small-bore objects

通天(ㄊㄨㄥ ㄊㄧㄢ)
(literally) great or high enough to reach heaven—① (said of one's abilities) the greatest; surpassing ② to have access to top leaders

通通(ㄊㄨㄥ ㄊㄨㄥ)
wholly; altogether; without exception; all：我把所有的錢通通給他，I gave him all the money I had.

通同(ㄊㄨㄥ ㄊㄨㄥˊ)
① in common ② to maintain secret contact with (bandits, etc.)

通同作弊(ㄊㄨㄥ ㄊㄨㄥˊ ㄗㄨㄛˋ ㄅㄧˋ)
to collude in cheating or illegal activities

通例(ㄊㄨㄥ ㄌㄧˋ)
a common practice; a general rule

通力合作(ㄊㄨㄥ ㄌㄧˋ ㄏㄜˊ ㄗㄨㄛˋ)
to make a concerted effort; to join forces with; to cooperate for a common cause; to work in concert：他們通力合作。 They worked in concert.

通靈(ㄊㄨㄥ ㄌㄧㄥˊ)
(said of animals, inanimate objects, etc.) to possess supernatural powers; to have human intelligence

通令(ㄊㄨㄥ ㄌㄧㄥˋ)

to issue circular orders

通路(ㄊㄨㄥ ㄌㄨˋ)
a thoroughfare; a passageway; a route

通論(ㄊㄨㄥ ㄌㄨㄣˋ)
① a clear and logical argument ② a general discussion or exposition

通告(ㄊㄨㄥ ㄍㄠˋ)
① to notify ② an announcement; a public notice

通古斯族(ㄊㄨㄥ ㄍㄨˇ ㄙ ㄗㄨˊ)
the Tunguses

通古斯語(ㄊㄨㄥ ㄍㄨˇ ㄙ ㄩˇ)
the Tungusic; the Tungusic language

通過(ㄊㄨㄥ ㄍㄨㄛˋ)
① to pass through ② (said of a motion or bill) to be passed ③ (said of a nomination or appointment) to be confirmed or approved

通過稅(ㄊㄨㄥ ㄍㄨㄛˋ ㄕㄨㄟˋ)
a transit tax

通關(ㄊㄨㄥ ㄍㄨㄢ)
① (while drinking in a group) engaging everyone else at the table in turn in a finger game 參看「打通關」 ② customs clearance ③ to clear goods with the customs; to complete formalities at an immigration or customs check point at an airport or seaport

通共(ㄊㄨㄥ ㄍㄨㄥˋ)
all put together; in sum; altogether

通款曲(ㄊㄨㄥ ㄎㄨㄢˇ ㄑㄩ)
to socialize with each other; to make friendly contacts

通好(ㄊㄨㄥ ㄏㄠˇ)
(said of nations, races, etc.) to establish friendly relations

通航(ㄊㄨㄥ ㄏㄤˊ)
air or sea navigation; (said of a river) navigable, or negotiable

通話(ㄊㄨㄥ ㄏㄨㄚˋ)
to communicate by telephone or radio

通貨(ㄊㄨㄥ ㄏㄨㄛˋ)
currency 亦作「貨幣」：這個國家的通貨穩定。 The currency of this country is sound.

通貨膨脹(ㄊㄨㄥ ㄏㄨㄛˋ ㄆㄤˊ ㄓㄤˋ)

（economics）inflation

通婚(ㄊㄨㄥ ㄏㄨㄣ)
to marry (said of members
of two families, tribes, etc.);
to intermarry

通紅(ㄊㄨㄥ ㄏㄨㄥ)
red through and through;
aglow; flaming red

通家之好(ㄊㄨㄥ ㄐㄧㄚ ㄓ ㄏㄠˇ)
friendship between two families which has existed for
several generations

通假(ㄊㄨㄥ ㄐㄧㄚˇ)
interchangeability of words
or characters

通解(ㄊㄨㄥ ㄐㄧㄝˇ)
(mathematics) a general
solution

通姦(ㄊㄨㄥ ㄐㄧㄢ)
adultery; illicit intercourse;
fornication

通鑑(ㄊㄨㄥ ㄐㄧㄢˋ)or 資治通鑑(ㄗ
ㄓ ㄊㄨㄥ ㄐㄧㄢˋ)
the title of a chronological
history of China, covering
1,362 years from the Epoch
of Warring States to the
author's time, by Ssu-Ma
Kuang (司馬光) of the Sung
Dynasty

通氣(ㄊㄨㄥ ㄑㄧˋ)
①sympathetic to each other
②breathing freely ③not
airtight; to aerate

通氣孔(ㄊㄨㄥ ㄑㄧˋ ㄎㄨㄥˇ)
air vents

通緝(ㄊㄨㄥ ㄑㄧ)
to order the arrest(of a
criminal) by circular orders

通緝犯(ㄊㄨㄥ ㄑㄧ ㄈㄢˋ)
a criminal wanted by the
law

通緝令(ㄊㄨㄥ ㄑㄧ ㄌㄧㄥˋ)
circular orders for the arrest
of a criminal

通竅(ㄊㄨㄥ ㄑㄧㄠˋ)
to get the knack of it; to
understand things

通情達理(ㄊㄨㄥ ㄑㄧㄥˊ ㄉㄚˊ ㄌㄧˇ)
sensible; reasonable: 他們是
通情達理的人。They are sen-
sible people.

通衢(ㄊㄨㄥ ㄑㄩˊ)
a highway; a thoroughfare

通權達變(ㄊㄨㄥ ㄑㄩㄢˊ ㄉㄚˊ ㄅㄧㄢˋ)
to be flexible; to act according to changes in circum-

stances; to exercise one's
discretion: 偉大的思想家有通
權達變的頭腦。Great thinkers
have flexible minds.

通宵(ㄊㄨㄥ ㄒㄧㄠ)
all night; the whole night;
throughout the night

通宵達旦(ㄊㄨㄥ ㄒㄧㄠ ㄉㄚˊ ㄉㄢˋ)
all night long; till daybreak

通宵值班(ㄊㄨㄥ ㄒㄧㄠ ㄓˊ ㄅㄢ)
on duty all night

通宵商店(ㄊㄨㄥ ㄒㄧㄠ ㄕㄤ ㄉㄧㄢˋ)
a shop that is open all night

通曉(ㄊㄨㄥ ㄒㄧㄠˇ)
to be familiar with; to
understand

通宿(ㄊㄨㄥ ㄒㄧㄡˋ)
all night long: 我們通宵看守。
We watch all night (long).

通顯(ㄊㄨㄥ ㄒㄧㄢˇ)
to achieve prominence in
officialdom

通心(ㄊㄨㄥ ㄒㄧㄣ)
(said of a cylinder)hollow;
tubular

通心粉(ㄊㄨㄥ ㄒㄧㄣ ㄈㄣˇ)
macaroni

通信(ㄊㄨㄥ ㄒㄧㄣˋ)
in correspondence with;
communication

通信兵(ㄊㄨㄥ ㄒㄧㄣˋ ㄅㄧㄥ)
a member of the signal
corps

通信鴿(ㄊㄨㄥ ㄒㄧㄣˋ ㄍㄜ)
a homing pigeon; a carrier
pigeon

通信處(ㄊㄨㄥ ㄒㄧㄣˋ ㄔㄨˋ)
a mailing address: 他變更了
通信處。He changed his mail-
ing address.

通信網(ㄊㄨㄥ ㄒㄧㄣˋ ㄨㄤˇ)
a communication network

通行(ㄊㄨㄥ ㄒㄧㄥˊ)
①to travel through(a road,
etc.) ②common practice

通行權(ㄊㄨㄥ ㄒㄧㄥˊ ㄑㄩㄢˊ)
the right of way

通行證(ㄊㄨㄥ ㄒㄧㄥˊ ㄓㄥˋ)
a safe-conduct; a pass

通行無阻(ㄊㄨㄥ ㄒㄧㄥˊ ㄨˊ ㄗㄨˇ)
to travel everywhere without obstruction

通性(ㄊㄨㄥ ㄒㄧㄥˋ)
common characteristics

通學(ㄊㄨㄥ ㄒㄩㄝˊ)
to attend a school by taking

daily trips; to commute

通學生(ㄊㄨㄥ ㄒㄩㄝˊ ㄕㄥ)
students living outside the
school (as distinct from
those living in school dormi-
tories); day students; com-
muters

通訊(ㄊㄨㄥ ㄒㄩㄣˋ)
correspondence; communication

通訊錄(ㄊㄨㄥ ㄒㄩㄣˋ ㄌㄨˋ)
an address book

通訊社(ㄊㄨㄥ ㄒㄩㄣˋ ㄕㄜˋ)
a news agency; a news service

通訊員(ㄊㄨㄥ ㄒㄩㄣˋ ㄩㄢˊ)or 通訊記
者(ㄊㄨㄥ ㄒㄩㄣˋ ㄐㄧˋ ㄓㄜˇ)
a (press) correspondent; a
reporter

通知(ㄊㄨㄥ ㄓ)
to inform; to notify; a notification

通知單(ㄊㄨㄥ ㄓ ㄉㄢ)or 通知書
(ㄊㄨㄥ ㄓ ㄕㄨ)
a notification

通飭(ㄊㄨㄥ ㄔˋ)
to order or instruct (all subordinate agencies concerned)

通車(ㄊㄨㄥ ㄔㄜ)
(said of roads, etc.) to be
open (to vehicular traffic)

通徹(ㄊㄨㄥ ㄔㄜˋ)
having a thorough under-
standing

通常(ㄊㄨㄥ ㄔㄤˊ)
normally; usually; generally;
as a rule; ordinarily: 你通常
在什麼地方度暑夏？Where do
you usually spend the summer?

通暢(ㄊㄨㄥ ㄔㄤˋ)
①(said of writings) smooth;
easy to read; highly read-
able: 他的文章通暢。His writ-
ing is smooth. ②passing
freely or smoothly

通稱(ㄊㄨㄥ ㄔㄥ)
a popular name; popularly
(or generally) known as...:
汞通稱水銀。Mercury is popu-
larly known as quicksilver.

通史(ㄊㄨㄥ ㄕˇ)
general history: 他研究中國通
史。He studies general
Chinese history.

通市(ㄊㄨㄥ ㄕˋ)
to have commercial rela-

〔走
部〕

tions 亦作「通商」

通事 (ㄊㄨㄥ ㄕˋ)
①an interpreter ②official intercourse between two states; diplomatic affairs

通身 (ㄊㄨㄥ ㄕㄣ)
all over the body

通神 (ㄊㄨㄥ ㄕㄣˊ)
①(said of ability, etc.) superhuman: 他有通神的智慧。He has superhuman wisdom. ②(said of money) capable of buying even the gods

通商 (ㄊㄨㄥ ㄕㄤ)
to have commercial intercourse; to trade

通商條約 (ㄊㄨㄥ ㄕㄤ ㄊㄧㄠˊ ㄩㄝ)
a trade pact or treaty

通商口岸 (ㄊㄨㄥ ㄕㄤ ㄎㄡˇ ㄢˋ)or 通商港
a trading port; a commercial port

通書 (ㄊㄨㄥ ㄕㄨ)
an almanac; a calendar

通順 (ㄊㄨㄥ ㄕㄨㄣˋ)
(said of writings) fluent; smooth: 這篇文章不通順。This article doesn't read smoothly.

通人 (ㄊㄨㄥ ㄖㄣˊ)
a well-read, much experienced person

通曉 (ㄊㄨㄥ ㄖㄨˋ)
a man of great learning and practical sense; an erudite scholar: 他是通儒。He is a man of great learning.

通融 (ㄊㄨㄥ ㄖㄨㄥˊ)
①departure from principles for convenience; compromise; to accommodate ② to accommodate somebody with a short-term loan

通則 (ㄊㄨㄥ ㄗㄜˊ)
a general principle

通才 (ㄊㄨㄥ ㄘㄞˊ)
an all-round talent; a versatile scholar

通才教育 (ㄊㄨㄥ ㄘㄞˊ ㄐㄧㄠˋ ㄩˋ)
liberal education

通財 (ㄊㄨㄥ ㄘㄞˊ)
to establish monetary relations

通草紙 (ㄊㄨㄥ ㄘㄠˇ ㄓˇ)
rice paper

通塞 (ㄊㄨㄥ ㄙㄜ)

①openness and cloggedness ②success and failure; satisfaction and frustration

通俗 (ㄊㄨㄥ ㄙㄨˊ)
popular; common; capable of being understood or appreciated by the less educated: 這部小說通俗易懂。This novel is easy to understand.

通俗化 (ㄊㄨㄥ ㄙㄨˊ ㄏㄨㄚˋ)
to popularize; popularization

通俗小說 (ㄊㄨㄥ ㄙㄨˊ ㄒㄧㄠˇ ㄕㄨㄛ)
popular fiction

通俗文學 (ㄊㄨㄥ ㄙㄨˊ ㄨㄣˊ ㄒㄩㄝˊ)
popular literature

通義 (ㄊㄨㄥ ㄧˋ)
a constant rule or principle

通譯 (ㄊㄨㄥ ㄧˋ)
①to translate ②a translator; an interpreter

通夜 (ㄊㄨㄥ ㄧㄝˋ)
all night long: 他通夜不眠。He lay awake all night.

通郵 (ㄊㄨㄥ ㄧㄡˊ)
postal communication

通韻 (ㄊㄨㄥ ㄩㄣˋ)
interchangeable rhyme

通運 (ㄊㄨㄥ ㄩㄣˋ)
to transport; to ship

通運公司 (ㄊㄨㄥ ㄩㄣˋ ㄍㄨㄥ ㄙ)
a forwarding company

通用 (ㄊㄨㄥ ㄩㄥˋ)
①(said of words or characters) interchangeable ②in common use ③practicable; usable ④(said of currency) in circulation

【逛】 6098
《ㄨㄤ guang guàng
to stroll; to roam; to ramble; to wander about

逛燈 (ㄍㄨㄤˋ ㄉㄥ)
to look at the lanterns on display on the streets (on the Lantern Festival, the 15th day of the first month in the lunar calendar)

逛街 (ㄍㄨㄤˋ ㄐㄧㄝ)
to stroll down the street; to go window-shopping: 我們昨天去逛街。We strolled down the streets yesterday.

逛一逛 (ㄍㄨㄤˋ ·ㄧ ·ㄍㄨㄤˋ)or 逛逛
《ㄨㄤˋ ·ㄍㄨㄤˋ》
to take a stroll; to go for a walk

【逞】 6099
ㄔㄥˇ cheng chěng
1. to indulge in (pleasures, etc.)
2. to use up; to exhaust
3. to display; to show off; to pose; to put up a false front: 別逞英雄。Don't pose as a hero.
4. fast; speedy
5. to presume on; presumptuous

逞能 (ㄔㄥˇ ㄋㄥˊ)
to display or show off one's ability, feat, etc.; boastful

逞快一時 (ㄔㄥˇ ㄎㄨㄞˋ ㄧ ㄕˊ)
to indulge in a moment of pleasure (implying that one is going to pay dearly for it)

逞強 (ㄔㄥˇ ㄑㄧㄤˊ)
to parade one's superiority; to bully; to throw one's weight around

逞兇 (ㄔㄥˇ ㄒㄩㄥ)
to resort to violence; to act like a brute

逞志 (ㄔㄥˇ ㄓˋ)
to satisfy oneself; to indulge oneself

逞惡 (ㄔㄥˇ ㄜˋ)
to presume on powerful connections or one's strength in doing evil

逞意 (ㄔㄥˇ ㄧˋ)
to act as one pleases

逞威 (ㄔㄥˇ ㄨㄟ)
to behave like a tyrant

逞勇 (ㄔㄥˇ ㄩㄥˇ)
to display one's bravery

【速】 6100
ㄙㄨˋ suh sù
1. quick; speed; speedy; prompt
2. to invite: 他是不速之客。He was an uninvited guest.

速答 (ㄙㄨˋ ㄉㄚˊ)
to reply promptly

速讀 (ㄙㄨˋ ㄉㄨˊ)
speed-reading

速度 (ㄙㄨˋ ㄉㄨˋ)
①velocity; speed ②(music) a tempo

速度計 (ㄙㄨˋ ㄉㄨˋ ㄐㄧˋ)
a speedometer; a speed indicator

速度限制 (ㄙㄨˋ ㄉㄨˋ ㄒㄧㄢˋ ㄓˋ)
the speed limit

速率(ㄙㄨˋ ㄌㄩˋ)
speed

速記(ㄙㄨˋ ㄐㄧˋ)
speedwriting; shorthand; stenography; to write in shorthand

速記學(ㄙㄨˋ ㄐㄧˋ ㄒㄩㄝˊ)or 速記術
(ㄙㄨˋ ㄐㄧˋ ㄕㄨˋ)
stenography

速記員(ㄙㄨˋ ㄐㄧˋ ㄩㄢˊ)
a stenographer

速駕(ㄙㄨˋ ㄐㄧㄚˋ)
to request the pleasure of your early company

速寫(ㄙㄨˋ ㄒㄧㄝˇ)
(painting) to sketch; a sketch: 他畫了一張塔的速寫。He made a sketch of the tower.

速效(ㄙㄨˋ ㄒㄧㄠˋ)
speedy relief (of suffering, disease, etc.); immediate efficacy or efficiency

速戰速決(ㄙㄨˋ ㄓㄢˋ ㄙㄨˋ ㄐㄩㄝˊ)
a blitzkrieg strategy; a military strategy, that calls for speedy decision by applying overwhelming forces against the enemy

速成(ㄙㄨˋ ㄔㄥˊ)
to attain goals within a short time; to complete rapidly

速成班(ㄙㄨˋ ㄔㄥˊ ㄅㄢ)
a training class for quick mastery of a subject, course; a rash course; an intensive course

速食(ㄙㄨˋ ㄕˊ)
fast food

速食麵(ㄙㄨˋ ㄕˊ ㄇㄧㄢˋ)
instant noodles

速食店(ㄙㄨˋ ㄕˊ ㄉㄧㄢˋ)
a fast food restaurant

速射炮(ㄙㄨˋ ㄕㄜˋ ㄆㄠˋ)
a rapid-fire gun; a case gun

速死(ㄙㄨˋ ㄙˇ)
to hasten one's death; to die quickly

速賜康(ㄙㄨˋ ㄘˋ ㄎㄤ)
pentazocine

造 6101
ㄗㄠˋ tzaw zào

1. to create; to make: 上帝創造世界。God created the world.
2. to manufacture; to make; to produce

3. to make up; to invent; to manufacture: 他捏造謠言。He invents rumors.
4. to build: 我們造房子。We built a house.
5. to arrive at; to reach
6. (law) a party concerned in the suit
7. an era; a period
8. to institute

造報表(ㄗㄠˋ ㄅㄠˋ ㄅㄧㄠˇ)
to prepare a financial report or statement

造幣權(ㄗㄠˋ ㄅㄧˋ ㄑㄩㄢˊ)
coinage (as a right)

造幣廠(ㄗㄠˋ ㄅㄧˋ ㄔㄤˇ)
a mint

造反(ㄗㄠˋ ㄈㄢˇ)
to rebel; to rise up against; revolt; uprising

造訪(ㄗㄠˋ ㄈㄤˇ)
to pay a visit to; to call on

造福(ㄗㄠˋ ㄈㄨˊ)
to bring benefit to; benefit

造福人羣(ㄗㄠˋ ㄈㄨˊ ㄖㄣˊ ㄑㄩㄣˊ)
to do good deeds to benefit mankind (as building a road, bridge, school, orphanage, etc.)

造府(ㄗㄠˋ ㄈㄨˇ)
(a polite expression) to call on someone at his home

造孽(ㄗㄠˋ ㄋㄧㄝˋ)
to do evil things

造林(ㄗㄠˋ ㄌㄧㄣˊ)
afforestation; reforestation

造花(ㄗㄠˋ ㄏㄨㄚ)
to make artificial (permanent) flowers

造化(ㄗㄠˋ ㄏㄨㄚˋ)
①(ㄗㄠˋ ㄏㄨㄚˋ) Heaven; Mother Nature; the Creator
②(ㄗㄠˋ ㄏㄨㄚ˙) one's luck or fortune: 他沒有這麼好的造化。He has no such good fortune.

造化弄人(ㄗㄠˋ ㄏㄨㄚˋ ㄋㄨㄥˋ ㄖㄣˊ)or
造物弄人(ㄗㄠˋ ㄨˋ ㄋㄨㄥˋ ㄖㄣˊ)
to be a sport of fate

造價(ㄗㄠˋ ㄐㄧㄚˋ)
building cost; manufacturing cost: 這種廠房造價比較低。It costs less to build this kind of building.

造酒(ㄗㄠˋ ㄐㄧㄡˇ)
to brew alcoholic beverages: 他造酒自用。He brewed wine

for home use.

造酒廠(ㄗㄠˋ ㄐㄧㄡˇ ㄔㄤˇ)
a brewery

造就(ㄗㄠˋ ㄐㄧㄡˋ)
①to educate; to bring up: 教育造就一代新人。Education brings up a new generation.
②one's achievement or accomplishment

造就人才(ㄗㄠˋ ㄐㄧㄡˋ ㄖㄣˊ ㄘㄞˊ)
to make useful citizens through education

造句(ㄗㄠˋ ㄐㄩˋ)
to make a sentence

造具(ㄗㄠˋ ㄐㄩˋ)
to prepare; to get ready (a report, etc.)

造像(ㄗㄠˋ ㄒㄧㄤˋ)
to make a statue; to make an image or a portrait

造型(ㄗㄠˋ ㄒㄧㄥˊ)
①modeling; mold-making ②a model; a mold ③(machinery) molding

造形藝術(ㄗㄠˋ ㄒㄧㄥˊ ㄧˋ ㄕㄨˋ)
formative arts; plastic arts

造紙(ㄗㄠˋ ㄓˇ)
to make paper

造紙廠(ㄗㄠˋ ㄓˇ ㄔㄤˇ)
a paper mill

造成(ㄗㄠˋ ㄔㄥˊ)
①to complete; to build up; to compose ②to result in; to cause to happen; to bring about: 火災造成重大的損害。The fire caused much damage.

造船(ㄗㄠˋ ㄔㄨㄢˊ)
to build a ship

造船公司(ㄗㄠˋ ㄔㄨㄢˊ ㄍㄨㄥ ㄙ)
a shipbuilding company

造船廠(ㄗㄠˋ ㄔㄨㄢˊ ㄔㄤˇ)
a shipbuilding yard; a dockyard

造始(ㄗㄠˋ ㄕˇ)
the beginning: 智慧造始於謙遜。Humility is the beginning of wisdom.

造絲(ㄗㄠˋ ㄙ)
to spin

造字(ㄗㄠˋ ㄗˋ)
to coin words

造作(ㄗㄠˋ ㄗㄨㄛˋ)
①to make ②affectations; pretentious; artificial; unnatural

[走部]

〔走 部〕

造次 (ㄗㄠˋ ㄘˋ)
in a hurry; rashly; in urgency and haste; rashness

造册子 (ㄗㄠˋ ㄘㄜˋ ˙ㄗ)
to make an overall report; to compile a register

造詣 (ㄗㄠˋ ㄧˋ)
①one's scholastic attainment, depth or profundity ②to call on; to visit

造意犯 (ㄗㄠˋ ㄧˋ ㄈㄢˋ)
(law) an instigator

造謠 (ㄗㄠˋ ㄧㄠˊ)or 造謠言 (ㄗㄠˋ ㄧㄠˊ ㄧㄢˊ)
to start a rumor

造謠惑衆 (ㄗㄠˋ ㄧㄠˊ ㄏㄨㄛˋ ㄓㄨㄥˋ)
to cheat, swindle or mislead the people with lies or rumors of one's own creation

造謠生事 (ㄗㄠˋ ㄧㄠˊ ㄕㄥ ㄕˋ)
to start rumors and incite incidents; to spread rumors to cause trouble

造物 (ㄗㄠˋ ㄨˋ)
Heaven; the Creator

造物主 (ㄗㄠˋ ㄨˋ ㄓㄨˇ)
the Creator

造獄 (ㄗㄠˋ ㄩˋ)
①to start litigation ②the extraordinary criminal code

【逡】 6102 (ㄑㄩㄣ chiun ㄑㄩㄣ)
to withdraw; to retreat; to move backward

逡巡 or 逡循 (ㄑㄩㄣ ㄒㄩㄣˊ)
to hesitate; to waver; to shrink back

逡巡不前 (ㄑㄩㄣ ㄒㄩㄣˊ ㄅㄨˋ ㄑㄧㄢˊ)
to hesitate; to waver; to be reluctant to move ahead

【逢】 6103 (ㄈㄥˊ ferng feng)
1. to meet; to come across: 我們久別重逢。 We met again after a long separation.
2. to happen; to fall in with
3. to talk or act in order to please (a superior, etc.)
4. a Chinese family name

逢年過節 (ㄈㄥˊ ㄋㄧㄢˊ ㄍㄨㄛˋ ㄐㄧㄝˊ)
on New Year's Day or other festivals

逢凶化吉 (ㄈㄥˊ ㄒㄩㄥ ㄏㄨㄚˋ ㄐㄧˊ)
to turn bad luck into good fortune: 你會逢凶化吉的。 You may turn ill luck into good fortune.

逢場作戲 (ㄈㄥˊ ㄔㄤˇ ㄗㄨㄛˋ ㄒㄧˋ)
to participate in pleasure-seeking as a social activity without being a slave to it; to engage in merry-making occasionally; to fool around with women; to make love to a woman just for the fun of it

逢山開路 (ㄈㄥˊ ㄕㄢ ㄎㄞ ㄌㄨˋ)
(literally) to open a path when faced with a mountain —to overcome a difficulty whenever it arises

逢人說項 (ㄈㄥˊ ㄖㄣˊ ㄕㄨㄛ ㄒㄧㄤˋ)
to praise someone's virtue everywhere

逢迎 (ㄈㄥˊ ㄧㄥˊ)
①to receive (guests, visitors, etc.) ②to talk and act in order to please; to ingratiate; to flatter: 他是在逢迎你。 He is flattering you.

【連】 6104 (ㄌㄧㄢˊ lian lian)
1. to connect; to join; to unite: 我們的田沿河毗連。 Our farms join along the river.
2. in succession
3. a company (of soldiers)
4. together with
5. even; and; including
6. a Chinese family name

連敗 (ㄌㄧㄢˊ ㄅㄞˋ)
①to defeat repeatedly ②repeated defeats; to be defeated repeatedly

連本帶利 (ㄌㄧㄢˊ ㄅㄣˇ ㄉㄞˋ ㄌㄧˋ)
both capital and interest

連比 (ㄌㄧㄢˊ ㄅㄧˇ)
(mathematics) continued proportion

連轂並轸 (ㄌㄧㄢˊ ㄍㄨˇ ㄅㄧㄥˋ ㄓㄣˇ)
matching; shoulder to shoulder

連不上 (ㄌㄧㄢˊ ㄅㄨˋ ㄕㄤˋ)
to lack sequence—cannot be put or connected together (usually referring to two paragraphs in a piece of writing, etc.)

連篇累牘 (ㄌㄧㄢˊ ㄆㄧㄢ ㄌㄟˇ ㄉㄨˊ)
(said of a piece of writing) long and repetitious; redundant; lengthy and tedious

連袂 (ㄌㄧㄢˊ ㄇㄟˋ)
①(to go, visit, etc.) together

②husbands of sisters

連忙 (ㄌㄧㄢˊ ㄇㄤˊ)
promptly; quickly; immediately; at once

連綿 or 連緜 (ㄌㄧㄢˊ ㄇㄧㄢˊ)
continuous; unbroken; uninterrupted: 陰雨連綿。 There was a continuous rain.

連縣不絕 (ㄌㄧㄢˊ ㄇㄧㄢˊ ㄅㄨˋ ㄐㄩㄝˊ)
in endless succession; continuously

連名 (ㄌㄧㄢˊ ㄇㄧㄥˊ)
(said of a petition, document, etc.) jointly signed

連發 (ㄌㄧㄢˊ ㄈㄚ)
to fire in rapid succession

連發槍 (ㄌㄧㄢˊ ㄈㄚ ㄑㄧㄤ)
a repeating rifle; a machine gun

連番 (ㄌㄧㄢˊ ㄈㄢ)
repeatedly

連分數 (ㄌㄧㄢˊ ㄈㄣ ㄕㄨˋ)
(mathematics) a continued fraction

連帶 (ㄌㄧㄢˊ ㄉㄞˋ)
joint (responsibility, obligation, etc.); to involve; to be related: 他的行動和思想是有連帶關係的。 His movement is related to his ideology.

連帶責任 (ㄌㄧㄢˊ ㄉㄞˋ ㄗㄜˊ ㄖㄣˋ)
joint responsibility; responsibility incurred as a result of personal or official involvement

連…都 (ㄌㄧㄢˊ …ㄉㄡ)or 連…也 (ㄌㄧㄢˊ …ㄧㄝˇ)
even…can (or cannot)…: 她甚至連看也沒看他一眼。 She never even took a look at him.

連偷帶扒 (ㄌㄧㄢˊ ㄊㄡ ㄉㄞˋ ㄆㄚˊ)
to steal or cheat by all the means at one's command

連踢帶打 (ㄌㄧㄢˊ ㄊㄧ ㄉㄞˋ ㄉㄚˇ)
to knock and kick; to beat severely with both hands and feet

連體雙生 (ㄌㄧㄢˊ ㄊㄧˇ ㄕㄨㄤ ㄕㄥ)
Siamese twins

連天 (ㄌㄧㄢˊ ㄊㄧㄢ)
①(said of high mountains, etc.) to stab deep into the sky ②incessantly; continuously (especially said of complaining) ③to shake the sky (as the sound of fight-

ing in battle ④for several
days in a row ⑤(said of the
distant horizon) to merge
with the sky

連同(ㄌㄧㄢˊㄊㄨㄥˊ)
together with; in addition to;
along with

連年(ㄌㄧㄢˊㄋㄧㄢˊ)
for successive years; for
years in a row; year after
year: 人口連年上升。Popula-
tion increases year after
year.

連弩(ㄌㄧㄢˊㄋㄨˇ)
a kind of crossbow which
can shoot in quick succession by means of a mechanical device

連累(ㄌㄧㄢˊㄌㄟˋ)
to involve; to get someone
into trouble: 我連累了你們。I
got you into trouble.

連理(ㄌㄧㄢˊㄌㄧˇ)
①trees whose branches
interlock or join together ②
a couple very much in love

連連(ㄌㄧㄢˊㄌㄧㄢˊ)
①continuously; unceasingly;
again and again: 小女孩連連
點頭。The little girl nods
again and again. ②one
after another

連絡(ㄌㄧㄢˊㄌㄨㄛˋ)
liaison; to make contact with

連絡官(ㄌㄧㄢˊㄌㄨㄛˋㄍㄨㄢ)
a liaison officer

連絡站(ㄌㄧㄢˊㄌㄨㄛˋㄓㄢˋ)
a liaison office or station

連貫(ㄌㄧㄢˊㄍㄨㄢˋ)
①to link up; to piece
together; to hang together ②
coherent; consistent: 這個故
事情節不連貫。The plot of the
story is incoherent.

連貫性(ㄌㄧㄢˊㄍㄨㄢˋㄒㄧㄥˋ)
continuity; coherence: 字典的
主題是沒有連貫性的。There is
no continuity of subjects in
a dictionary.

連合(ㄌㄧㄢˊㄏㄜˊ)
to connect or join together;
to unite together

連號(ㄌㄧㄢˊㄏㄠˋ)
a consecutive serial number
(on banknotes, tickets, etc.)

連衡 or 連橫(ㄌㄧㄢˊㄏㄥˊ)
a proposal advanced by

Chang Yi (張儀)in the Epoch
of Warring States, which
called for the six other
states to serve Chin

連環(ㄌㄧㄢˊㄏㄨㄢˊ)
interlocked rings (like those
of a chain)

連環保(ㄌㄧㄢˊㄏㄨㄢˊㄅㄠˇ)
a mutual guarantee

連環圖畫(ㄌㄧㄢˊㄏㄨㄢˊㄊㄨˊㄏㄨㄚˋ)
a pictorial story in series;
comics; a comic strip

連環計(ㄌㄧㄢˊㄏㄨㄢˊㄐㄧˋ)
a coup with coup(s) in it; a
set of interlocking stratagems

連枷(ㄌㄧㄢˊㄐㄧㄚ)
a flail

連假帶真(ㄌㄧㄢˊㄐㄧㄚˇㄉㄞˋㄓㄣ)
altogether, fake and genuine

連接(ㄌㄧㄢˊㄐㄧㄝ)
①continuously ②to adjoin;
adjoining: 這兩幢房屋連接在
一起。The two houses adjoin.

連接不斷(ㄌㄧㄢˊㄐㄧㄝ ㄅㄨˋㄉㄨㄢˋ)
successively; continuously

連接桿(ㄌㄧㄢˊㄐㄧㄝ ㄍㄢˇ)or 連桿
(ㄌㄧㄢˊㄍㄢˇ)
(machinery) a connecting rod

連接詞(ㄌㄧㄢˊㄐㄧㄝ ㄘˊ)
(grammar) a conjunction

連結(ㄌㄧㄢˊㄐㄧㄝˊ)
to connect; to join: 這兩部分
連結得不好。The two parts
do not connect properly.

連結線(ㄌㄧㄢˊㄐㄧㄝˊㄒㄧㄢˋ)
(mathematics) a connecting
line

連襟 or 連衿(ㄌㄧㄢˊㄐㄧㄣ)
a mutual reference among
husbands of sisters

連翹(ㄌㄧㄢˊㄑㄧㄠˊ)
(botany) forsythia

連雀(ㄌㄧㄢˊㄑㄩㄝˋ)
a waxwing

連繫(ㄌㄧㄢˊㄒㄧˋ)
to keep in contact; contact;
to keep in touch with

連線(ㄌㄧㄢˊㄒㄧㄢˋ)
unbroken; continuous

連心(ㄌㄧㄢˊㄒㄧㄣ)
the meeting of minds; bosom
(friends); deeply attached to
each other: 我們父子連心。
We, father and son, are
deeply attached to each

other.

連續(ㄌㄧㄢˊㄒㄩˋ)
successive; continuous; incessantly

連續犯(ㄌㄧㄢˊㄒㄩˋㄈㄢˋ)
①(law) repeated offenses of
the same kind ②an old (or
repeated) offender

連續劇(ㄌㄧㄢˊㄒㄩˋㄐㄩˋ)
(television) a soap opera; a
drama series

連選連任(ㄌㄧㄢˊㄒㄩㄢˇㄌㄧㄢˊㄖㄣˋ)
to hold a post for another
term after being reelected

連枝(ㄌㄧㄢˊㄓ)
brothers; close relatives (of
the same family tree)

連戰皆北(ㄌㄧㄢˊㄓㄢˋㄐㄧㄝ ㄅㄟˇ)
to suffer one defeat after
another

連戰皆捷(ㄌㄧㄢˊㄓㄢˋㄐㄧㄝ ㄐㄧㄝˊ)
to win one victory after
another: 我們的棒球隊連戰皆
捷。Our baseball team won
one victory after another.

連長(ㄌㄧㄢˊㄓㄤˇ)
a company commander

連珠(ㄌㄧㄢˊㄓㄨ)
continuous, in quick succession: 我們聽到連珠似的機槍
聲。We heard a continuous
rattle of machine gun fire.

連珠炮(ㄌㄧㄢˊㄓㄨㄅㄠˋ)
①a rapid-fire gun ②continuous firing; drumfire

連綴(ㄌㄧㄢˊㄓㄨㄟˋ)
joined or linked together

連乘積(ㄌㄧㄢˊㄔㄥˊㄐㄧ)
(mathematics) a continued
product

連串(ㄌㄧㄢˊㄔㄨㄢˋ)
to string together; a string
(of events, etc.); a series

連史紙(ㄌㄧㄢˊㄕˇㄓˇ)
a kind of high-grade bam-
boo paper made in Fukien
and Kiangsi provinces

連手(ㄌㄧㄢˊㄕㄡˇ)
①to take concerted action
②(gambling) to gang up on
cheating

連聲道謝(ㄌㄧㄢˊㄕㄥㄉㄠˋㄒㄧㄝˋ)
to say "Thanks." repeatedly

連勝(ㄌㄧㄢˊㄕㄥˋ)
to win repeatedly; to score
one victory after another

連署(ㄌㄧㄢˊㄕㄨˋ)

〔走
部〕

to sign jointly; joint signatures

連署人(ㄌㄧㄢˊ ㄕㄨˇ ㄖㄣˊ)
a joint signer

連說對不起(ㄌㄧㄢˊ ㄕㄨㄛ ㄉㄨㄟˋ ㄅㄨˋ ㄑㄧˇ)
to say "I'm sorry." time and again

連日(ㄌㄧㄢˊ ㄖˋ)
for consecutive days; for days in a row; day after day: 連日下大雪。It snowed hard for several days running.

連任(ㄌㄧㄢˊ ㄖㄣˋ)
to continue in one's office for another term; to be reappointed or reelected: 教育部長連任。The Minister of Education was reappointed.

連字號(ㄌㄧㄢˊ ㄗˋ ㄏㄠˋ)
a hyphen "-"

連載(ㄌㄧㄢˊ ㄗㄞˋ)
to publish serially in a newspaper or magazine; to serialize: 他的小說曾在報上連載。His novel was serialized in the newspaper.

連遭敗績(ㄌㄧㄢˊ ㄗㄠ ㄅㄞˋ ㄐㄧ)
to suffer one defeat after another: 他連遭敗績。Defeats have befallen him in succession.

連坐(ㄌㄧㄢˊ ㄗㄨㄛˋ)
to share the criminal responsibility of another person without being actually guilty oneself

連詞(ㄌㄧㄢˊ ㄘˊ)
(grammar) a conjunction 亦作「連接詞」

連三帶四(ㄌㄧㄢˊ ㄙㄢ ㄉㄞˋ ㄙˋ) or 連三併四(ㄌㄧㄢˊ ㄙㄢ ㄅㄧㄥˋ ㄙˋ)
time and again; repeatedly: 我曾連三帶四地警告他。I've given him repeated warnings.

連鎖反應(ㄌㄧㄢˊ ㄙㄨㄛˇ ㄈㄢˇ ㄧㄥˋ)
a chain reaction

連鎖店(ㄌㄧㄢˊ ㄙㄨㄛˇ ㄉㄧㄢˋ)
a chain store

連夜(ㄌㄧㄢˊ ㄧㄝˋ)
all through the night

連姻(ㄌㄧㄢˊ ㄧㄣ)
(said of two families) to have a matrimonial tie

連陰雨(ㄌㄧㄢˊ ㄧㄣ ㄩˇ)
rainy days in a row

連用(ㄌㄧㄢˊ ㄩㄥˋ)
to use consecutively; to use together

【逌】 6105
ㄧㄡˊ you yóu
pleased; smiling; complacent

八畫

【迸】 6106
(迸) ㄅㄥˋ benq bèng
1. to scatter; to explode: 煙火亂迸。Fireworks explode in all directions.
2. to crack; to spit out; to burst forth: 你怎麼突然迸出這句話來？What made you burst out such a remark?

迸淚(ㄅㄥˋ ㄌㄟˋ)
tears pouring out

迸裂(ㄅㄥˋ ㄌㄧㄝˋ)
to crack; to split; to dash out: 他的腦漿迸裂。He has his brains dashed out

迸流(ㄅㄥˋ ㄌㄧㄡˊ)
(said of fluid under pressure) to spit out in all directions

迸出來(ㄅㄥˋ ㄔㄨ ㄌㄞˊ)
to squeeze out; to spit out

迸脆(ㄅㄥˋ ㄘㄨㄟˋ)
(usually said of food, etc.) crisp

【逮】 6107
1. ㄉㄞˋ day dài
1. to reach; to come up to: 我力有未逮。It was beyond my reach.
2. to be after; to hunt; to chase and make arrest

逮捕(ㄉㄞˋ ㄅㄨˇ)
to make arrest: 警察逮捕那些歹徒了。The policeman arrested the evil fellows.

逮繫(ㄉㄞˋ ㄒㄧˋ)
to arrest and detain

【逮】 6107
2. ㄉㄞˇ dae dǎi
to capture; to catch: 警察已逮到兇手。The policeman has caught the murderer.

逮住(ㄉㄞˇ ㄓㄨˋ)
to catch (a thief, a ball, etc.)：我們逮住那個賊。We caught the thief.

【週】 6108
ㄓㄡ jou zhōu

1. a week; a period: 上週我很忙。I was busy last week.
2. a cycle; a revolution; to revolve

週報(ㄓㄡ ㄅㄠˋ)
a weekly paper

週末(ㄓㄡ ㄇㄛˋ)
a weekend: 我們每個週末都去釣魚。We go fishing weekends.

週末旅行(ㄓㄡ ㄇㄛˋ ㄌㄩˇ ㄒㄧㄥˊ)
a weekend trip

週到(ㄓㄡ ㄉㄠˋ)
(often said of service, etc.) thoughtful; considerate

週年(ㄓㄡ ㄋㄧㄢˊ)
a full year; an anniversary

週年紀念(ㄓㄡ ㄋㄧㄢˊ ㄐㄧˋ ㄋㄧㄢˋ)
commemoration of an anniversary: 今天是我們的結婚一週年紀念日。Today is our first wedding anniversary.

週率(ㄓㄡ ㄌㄩˋ)
a frequency

週刊(ㄓㄡ ㄎㄢ)
a weekly periodical; a weekly: 你讀什麼週刊？What weeklies do you read?

週會(ㄓㄡ ㄏㄨㄟˋ)
a weekly meeting

週期(ㄓㄡ ㄑㄧ)
a period; a cycle; time of a revolution or rotation

週期表(ㄓㄡ ㄑㄧ ㄅㄧㄠˇ)
(chemistry) a periodic table; a table of periodic law

週期律(ㄓㄡ ㄑㄧ ㄌㄩˋ)
(chemistry) periodic law

週期性(ㄓㄡ ㄑㄧ ㄒㄧㄥˋ)
periodicity; periodic; cyclic

週全(ㄓㄡ ㄑㄩㄢˊ)
①complete and perfect; nothing left out ②to help; assistance; help

週薪(ㄓㄡ ㄒㄧㄣ)
a weekly salary: 他的週薪是三千元。His weekly salary is $3,000.

週知(ㄓㄡ ㄓ)
to make known to all; known to all

週轉(ㄓㄡ ㄓㄨㄢˇ)
①circulating or revolving (funds) ②to have enough to meet the need

週歲(ㄓㄡ ㄙㄨㄟˋ)
a full year (especially said

of a child's age)

週而復始 (ㄓㄡ ㄦˊ ㄈㄨˋ ㄕˇ)
to repeat the cycle all over again

遇遊世界 (ㄓㄡ ㄧㄡˊ ㄕˋ ㄐㄧㄝˋ)
to go around the world; to travel all over the world

【進】 6109
ㄐㄧㄣˋ jinn jìn

1. to go ahead; to move forward; to proceed; to progress; to advance
2. to improve; improvement; progress
3. to recommend; to introduce
4. to offer (advice, presents, etc.)
5. a generation
6. income
7. rooms in a house divided by a courtyard; a courtyard
8. to enter
9. to eat; to take; to have
10. a Chinese family name

進逼 (ㄐㄧㄣˋ ㄅㄧ)
to close in; to press upon: 我軍步步進逼。Our army steadily closed in.

進兵 (ㄐㄧㄣˋ ㄅㄧㄥ)
to march troops forward; to lead troops onward

進步 (ㄐㄧㄣˋ ㄅㄨˋ)
to improve; to progress; improvement; progress; progressive; advance: 她的發音很有進步。Her pronunciation has greatly improved.

進門 (ㄐㄧㄣˋ ㄇㄣˊ)
① to enter a door ② to master the ABCs of a subject

進犯 (ㄐㄧㄣˋ ㄈㄢˋ)
to intrude into; to invade: 我們打敗進犯的敵人。We beat back the invading enemy.

進度 (ㄐㄧㄣˋ ㄉㄨˋ)
(said of work) degree of progress

進度表 (ㄐㄧㄣˋ ㄉㄨˋ ㄅㄧㄠˇ)
a work schedule

進退 (ㄐㄧㄣˋ ㄊㄨㄟˋ)
① to advance or retreat ② to stay or quit a job ③ to employ or fire a person ④ a sense of propriety: 這年青人不知進退。The young man has no sense of propriety.

進退莫決 (ㄐㄧㄣˋ ㄊㄨㄟˋ ㄇㄛˋ ㄐㄩㄝˊ)
not knowing what course of

action to take

進退兩難 (ㄐㄧㄣˋ ㄊㄨㄟˋ ㄌㄧㄤˇ ㄋㄢˊ)
difficult either to proceed or retreat; in a dilemma; in a jam or spot; in a (tight) box

進退失據 (ㄐㄧㄣˋ ㄊㄨㄟˋ ㄕ ㄐㄩˋ)
in a dilemma; in a jam or spot

進退維谷 (ㄐㄧㄣˋ ㄊㄨㄟˋ ㄨㄟˊ ㄍㄨˇ)
in a dilemma; in an awkward situation

進與共 (ㄐㄧㄣˋ ㄩˇ ㄍㄨㄥˋ)
to cast one's lot with another person

進來 (ㄐㄧㄣˋ ㄌㄞˊ)
Come in. 或 to come in; to enter

進港 (ㄐㄧㄣˋ ㄍㄤˇ)
to make port; to enter a harbor

進攻 (ㄐㄧㄣˋ ㄍㄨㄥ)
to attack; attack; offensive

進貢 (ㄐㄧㄣˋ ㄍㄨㄥˋ)
(said of a vassal state) to offer tribute

進口 (ㄐㄧㄣˋ ㄎㄡˇ)
to import; importation ② an intake (for liquid or gaseous matters)

進口貿易 (ㄐㄧㄣˋ ㄎㄡˇ ㄇㄠˋ ㄧˋ)
import trade

進口港 (ㄐㄧㄣˋ ㄎㄡˇ ㄍㄤˇ)
a port of entry

進口貨 (ㄐㄧㄣˋ ㄎㄡˇ ㄏㄨㄛˋ)
imported goods; imports

進口限額 (ㄐㄧㄣˋ ㄎㄡˇ ㄒㄧㄢˋ ㄜˊ)
import quotas

進口許可證 (ㄐㄧㄣˋ ㄎㄡˇ ㄒㄩˇ ㄎㄜˇ ㄓㄥˋ)
an import license

進口商 (ㄐㄧㄣˋ ㄎㄡˇ ㄕㄤ)
an importer

進口稅 (ㄐㄧㄣˋ ㄎㄡˇ ㄕㄨㄟˋ)
an import duty

進口稅率 (ㄐㄧㄣˋ ㄎㄡˇ ㄕㄨㄟˋ ㄌㄩˋ)
an import tariff

進款 (ㄐㄧㄣˋ ㄎㄨㄢˇ) or 進錢 (ㄐㄧㄣˋ ㄑㄧㄢˊ)
income; proceeds

進化 (ㄐㄧㄣˋ ㄏㄨㄚˋ)
to evolve; evolution; to progress culturally: 人是由類人猿進化而來的。Man evolved from the anthropoid ape.

進化論 (ㄐㄧㄣˋ ㄏㄨㄚˋ ㄌㄨㄣˋ)
the theory of evolution

進貨 (ㄐㄧㄣˋ ㄏㄨㄛˋ)

(said of a shop) to replenish the stock of merchandise

進擊 (ㄐㄧㄣˋ ㄐㄧ)
to advance and attack: 他們進擊敵人。They advanced and attacked the enemy.

進級 (ㄐㄧㄣˋ ㄐㄧˊ)
to get promoted (in ranks, grades, etc.)

進剿 (ㄐㄧㄣˋ ㄐㄧㄠˇ)
to attack rebels or bandits

進酒 (ㄐㄧㄣˋ ㄐㄧㄡˇ)
to fill the winecup for a guest and urge him to drink it up

進見 (ㄐㄧㄣˋ ㄐㄧㄢˋ)
to call on (a superior) 亦作「晉見」

進京 (ㄐㄧㄣˋ ㄐㄧㄥ)
to go to the capital 亦作「晉京」

進爵 (ㄐㄧㄣˋ ㄐㄩㄝˊ)
to be promoted to the rank of nobility 亦作「晉爵」

進軍 (ㄐㄧㄣˋ ㄐㄩㄣ)
to march (troops to war); to advance (with armed forces): 我們吹響了進軍的號角。We sounded the bugle to advance.

進取 (ㄐㄧㄣˋ ㄑㄩˇ)
① to be aggressive, as in jockeying for position, etc. ② to forge ahead with effort; to advance: 我們應當永遠保持謙虛和進取的精神。We should always remain modest and keep forging ahead.

進取心 (ㄐㄧㄣˋ ㄑㄩˇ ㄒㄧㄣ)
aggressiveness; the desire to get ahead; enterprising spirit; initiative

進去 (ㄐㄧㄣˋ ㄑㄩˋ)
to get in; to enter; to go in

進修 (ㄐㄧㄣˋ ㄒㄧㄡ)
to advance in study; to engage in advanced studies

進賢 (ㄐㄧㄣˋ ㄒㄧㄢˊ)
to employ the virtuous and capable

進獻 (ㄐㄧㄣˋ ㄒㄧㄢˋ)
to offer as tribute; to present something (to a superior)

進香 (ㄐㄧㄣˋ ㄒㄧㄤ)
to go to a Buddhist temple and offer incense to the

〔走部〕

〔辵
部〕

Buddha

進香客(ㄐㄧㄣ ㄒㄧㄤ ㄎㄜ)
a Buddhist pilgrim

進項(ㄐㄧㄣ ㄒㄧㄤ)
income; earnings; revenue

進行(ㄐㄧㄣ ㄒㄧㄥ)
① to advance; to march forward ② to proceed (with one's business, plan, etc.); to carry on; to carry out; to engage; to conduct: 我們進行科學試驗. We engage in scientific experiment.

進行曲(ㄐㄧㄣ ㄒㄧㄥ ㄑㄩ)
(music) a march

進行式(ㄐㄧㄣ ㄒㄧㄥ ㄕ)
(grammar) the progressive tense

進學(ㄐㄧㄣ ㄒㄩㄝ)
① to show marked progress in one's study or learning ② to pass the lowest level of civil service examinations of former times

進止(ㄐㄧㄣ ㄓ)
to proceed or stop; a course of action

進展(ㄐㄧㄣ ㄓㄢ)
progress; headway: 計畫進展很順利. The plan is making good progress.

進佔(ㄐㄧㄣ ㄓㄢ)
to enter and occupy (a city, position, etc.)

進賬(ㄐㄧㄣ ㄓㄤ)
income; receipts; earnings

進帳(ㄐㄧㄣ ㄓㄤ)
① to enter a tent ② income 參見「進賬」

進駐(ㄐㄧㄣ ㄓㄨ)
to march troops to a place and garrison it: 部隊已進駐該村. Troops have been garrisoned in the village.

進場(ㄐㄧㄣ ㄔㄤ)
① to get into an examination room, a theater, a sports arena, etc. ② (navigation) an approach 亦作「進近」: 飛機進場失敗. The plane missed approach.

進呈(ㄐㄧㄣ ㄔㄥ)
to offer or present (something to a superior or an elder)

進城(ㄐㄧㄣ ㄔㄥ)
to go to town; to enter a

city

進程(ㄐㄧㄣ ㄔㄥ)
progress in a course of action

進出(ㄐㄧㄣ ㄔㄨ) or 進進出出(ㄐㄧㄣ ㄔㄨ ㄐㄧㄣ ㄔㄨ)
① to get in and out; incoming and outgoing ② (business) a turnover

進出口(ㄐㄧㄣ ㄔㄨ ㄎㄡ)
① imports and exports ② exits and entrances

進出口貿易(ㄐㄧㄣ ㄔㄨ ㄎㄡ ㄇㄠ ㄧ)
import and export trade; foreign trade

進出口商行(ㄐㄧㄣ ㄔㄨ ㄎㄡ ㄕㄤ ㄏㄤ)
a trading company engaged in import-export business

進出口商(ㄐㄧㄣ ㄔㄨ ㄎㄡ ㄕㄤ)
an importer-exporter

進食(ㄐㄧㄣ ㄕ)
to eat; to take food: 這病人不能進食. The patient can't take food.

進士(ㄐㄧㄣ ㄕ)
a successful candidate of the national civil service examination held at the imperial capital in former times

進身之階(ㄐㄧㄣ ㄕㄣ ㄓ ㄐㄧㄝ)
a steppingstone for getting a post or promotion

進水(ㄐㄧㄣ ㄕㄨㄟ)
(said of a house) to get flooded; water flowing in

進水閘(ㄐㄧㄣ ㄕㄨㄟ ㄓㄚ)
an entry lock

進入(ㄐㄧㄣ ㄖㄨ)
to enter; to get in; to reach: 火車進入隧道. The train entered a tunnel.

進寸退尺(ㄐㄧㄣ ㄘㄨㄣ ㄊㄨㄟ ㄔ)
(literally) to advance by one inch but to retreat by a foot—to lose much more than what one gets

進而(ㄐㄧㄣ ㄦ)
to proceed to the next step

進一步(ㄐㄧㄣ ㄧ ㄅㄨ)
to take one step ahead; to move further ahead

進益(ㄐㄧㄣ ㄧ)
progress

進謁(ㄐㄧㄣ ㄧㄝ)
to call on (a superior)

進言(ㄐㄧㄣ ㄧㄢ)
to offer advice

進位(ㄐㄧㄣ ㄨㄟ)
(mathematics) to carry (a number, as in adding)

進用(ㄐㄧㄣ ㄩㄥ)
wealth; fortune; money

【逵】 6110
ㄎㄨㄟ kwei kuí
a thoroughfare; where many ways meet

【透】 6111
ㄨㄟ uei wéi
winding; curved; tortuous (road, way)

逶迤(ㄨㄟ ㄧ)
① to wind; winding (river, road, etc.) ② long; distant

【逸】 6112
ㄧ yih yì
1. to flee; to escape; to run away
2. to go beyond; to exceed; to go to excess
3. to rusticate; to live in retirement
4. ease; idleness; leisure
5. to let loose; to let go
6. a fault; an error; a mistake
7. quick; rapid
8. lost
9. superior; outstanding

逸品(ㄧ ㄆㄧㄣ)
a superior piece of artistic work

逸民(ㄧ ㄇㄧㄣ)
a hermit; a person of virtue and ability who leads a private life

逸度(ㄧ ㄉㄨ)
an elegant air; a refined manner

逸樂(ㄧ ㄌㄜ)
enjoyment of an easy life

逸口(ㄧ ㄎㄡ)
to make an indiscreet remark

逸經(ㄧ ㄐㄧㄥ)
classical learning which did not originate from the orthodox classics

逸居(ㄧ ㄐㄩ)
to live in retirement or idleness; to be comfortably lodged

逸氣(ㄧ ㄑㄧ)
an outstanding or out-of-this-world air or disposition

逸趣橫生(ㄧ ㄑㄩ ㄏㄥ ㄕㄥ)
replete with humor or refined interest

逸羣(ㄧ ㄑㄩㄣˊ)
outstanding; head and shoulders above others

逸暇(ㄧ ㄒㄧㄚˊ)
leisure; spare time

逸想(ㄧ ㄒㄧㄤˇ)
thoughts that are not worldly; idealistic thoughts

逸興(ㄧ ㄒㄧㄥˋ)
refined interest or taste

逸出常軌(ㄧ ㄔㄨ ㄔㄤˊ ㄍㄨㄟˇ)
to run off the track; not regular or common; against the regular practice

逸詩(ㄧ ㄕ)
ancient poems which were not collected in the *Book of Odes* (詩經)

逸事 or 軼事(ㄧ ㄕˋ)
an anecdote; an episode

逸樂(ㄧ ㄌㄜˋ)
decadent music

逸書(ㄧ ㄕㄨ)
ancient books which have been partly lost or in private collection

逸則淫(ㄧ ㄗㄜˊ ㄧㄣˊ)
Ease leads to vice.

逸足(ㄧ ㄗㄨˊ)
walking or running very fast; fleet-footed

逸材 or 逸才(ㄧ ㄘㄞˊ)
outstanding talent

逸豫(ㄧ ㄩˋ)
to live in idleness

【逭】 6113 ㄏㄨㄢˋ huann huàn
to run away or escape from; to flee; to avoid; to evade

【逯】 6114 ㄌㄨˋ luh lù
1. to go away suddenly for no particular reason
2. a Chinese family name

九畫

【逾】 6115 ㄩˊ yú
1. to exceed; to pass over; more than; over: 這位老人逾年高九十。 The old man is over ninety.
2. to transgress
3. added; even more: 他疼痛逾甚。 His pain became even more acute.

逾邁(ㄩˊ ㄇㄞˋ)
to pass away (as time or years)

逾分(ㄩˊ ㄈㄣˋ)
① to exceed propriety; to overdo something; to transgress ② exorbitant: 他沒有逾分的要求。 He has no exorbitant demands.

逾格(ㄩˊ ㄍㄜˊ)
(to do something, grant a favor, etc.) as an exception

逾恆(ㄩˊ ㄏㄥˊ)
to go beyond the common or regular practice; more than usual; excessive

逾矩(ㄩˊ ㄐㄩˇ)
to transgress what is right

逾期(ㄩˊ ㄑㄧˊ)
to exceed a time limit

逾限(ㄩˊ ㄒㄧㄢˋ)
to go beyond the limits or bounds; to exceed the limit

逾越(ㄩˊ ㄩㄝˋ)
① to pass over; to scale (a wall, etc.) ② to do what one is not supposed to do; to overstep one's position; to transgress; to exceed: 你逾越權限。 You exceeded your powers.

【逼】 6116 ㄅㄧ bi bī
(又讀 ㄅㄧˊ bíh bí)
1. to press; to compel; to pressure; to force; to coerce
2. to close in; to draw near; to press up to: 敵軍直逼城下。 The enemy pressed up to the city wall.
3. to importune; to harass; to annoy
4. narrow; strait

逼不得已(ㄅㄧ ㄅㄨˋ ㄉㄜˊ ㄧˇ)
to be compelled or forced to; can't help but; to have no alternative

逼迫(ㄅㄧ ㄆㄛˋ)
to compel; to force: 沒有任何人可以逼迫我做這件事。 Nobody can compel me to do such a thing.

逼勒(ㄅㄧ ㄌㄜˋ)
to force or compel; to blackmail

逼供(ㄅㄧ ㄍㄨㄥ)
to force a confession; to exact confessions by means

of torture; to obtain confessions by compulsion

逼嫁(ㄅㄧ ㄐㄧㄚˋ)
to force a woman to marry

逼姦(ㄅㄧ ㄐㄧㄢ)
to rape

逼近(ㄅㄧ ㄐㄧㄣˋ)
to close in; to draw near; to press: 敵軍逼近運河。 The enemy was pressing on towards the canal.

逼取(ㄅㄧ ㄑㄩˇ)
to extort; to blackmail; to take or get by forcible means

逼肖(ㄅㄧ ㄒㄧㄠˋ)
(said of a portrait, twins, etc.) with striking resemblance; very much alike

逼窄(ㄅㄧ ㄓㄞˇ)
very narrow; cramped

逼債(ㄅㄧ ㄓㄞˋ)
to press for payment of debts

逼真(ㄅㄧ ㄓㄣ)
(said of acting, performances, etc.) lifelike; almost real; verisimilitude

逼視(ㄅㄧ ㄕˋ)
to stare at sternly

逼上梁山(ㄅㄧ ㄕㄤˋ ㄌㄧㄤˊ ㄕㄢ)
to be forced to do something, especially to break the law; to be forced to go to extremities

逼人(ㄅㄧ ㄖㄣˊ)
pressing; threatening: 暑氣逼人。 The summer heat is very oppressive.

逼人太甚(ㄅㄧ ㄖㄣˊ ㄊㄞˋ ㄕㄣˋ)
to push someone too hard

逼走(ㄅㄧ ㄗㄡˇ)
to force to leave: 他們被逼走了。 They were forced to leave.

逼死(ㄅㄧ ㄙˇ)
to be hard-pressed so that one has to commit suicide as an escape

逼問(ㄅㄧ ㄨㄣˋ)
to question closely

【遁】 6117 ㄉㄨㄣˋ duenn dùn
1. to run away; to escape
2. to conceal oneself; to retire

遁北(ㄉㄨㄣˋ ㄅㄟˇ)
to be defeated and escape

〔走部〕

【辵
部】

遁化(ㄉㄨㄣˋㄏㄨㄚˋ)
(said of a Taoist) to die

遁跡(ㄉㄨㄣˋㄐㄧ)
to rusticate; to retire from
public life; to live like a hermit

遁跡山林(ㄉㄨㄣˋㄐㄧㄕㄢㄌㄧㄣˊ)
to retire to the mountains;
to retire from official life:
那老人遁跡山林。The old man
retired to the mountains.

遁甲(ㄉㄨㄣˋㄐㄧㄚˇ)
a school of ancient Chinese
sorcery, supposedly based
on some principles from The
Book of Changes (易經)

遁去(ㄉㄨㄣˋㄑㄩˋ)
to take to one's heels; to run
away: 土匪很快地遁去。Soon
the bandit ran away.

遁形(ㄉㄨㄣˋㄒㄧㄥˊ)
to become invisible; to vanish

遁世(ㄉㄨㄣˋㄕˋ)
(said of a man of ability
and virtue) to live incognito;
to lead the life of a recluse

遁走(ㄉㄨㄣˋㄗㄡˇ)
to flee; to take to one's heels

遁辭(ㄉㄨㄣˋㄘˊ)
an excuse; a pretext; a subterfuge; a quibble; evasive
words

遁藏(ㄉㄨㄣˋㄘㄤˊ)
to conceal oneself

【遂】 6118
ㄙㄨㄟˋ suey suì
(又讀 ㄙㄨㄟˋ swei suì)
1. to have one's will; to satisfy; to fulfill
2. successful; to succeed
3. to proceed to; to reach
4. then; consequently; thereupon
5. to flee; to escape

遂令(ㄙㄨㄟˋㄌㄧㄥˋ)
①to order thereupon ②to
result in

遂即(ㄙㄨㄟˋㄐㄧˊ)
thereupon; forthwith; then

遂心(ㄙㄨㄟˋㄒㄧㄣ)
to have one's will; to have
one's own way; to satisfy: 眾
人皆遂心如意。All were per-
fectly satisfied.

遂致(ㄙㄨㄟˋㄓˋ)
consequently; thereupon;

subsequently

遂初(ㄙㄨㄟˋㄔㄨ)
to retire from official life as
one originally wished

遂意(ㄙㄨㄟˋㄧˋ)
to have everything going
one's way

遂願(ㄙㄨㄟˋㄩㄢˋ)
to have one's wish fulfilled

【遄】 6119
ㄔㄨㄢˊ chwan chuán
1. swiftly; quickly; to hurry
2. coming and going frequently and swiftly; to and fro

遄返(ㄔㄨㄢˊㄈㄢˇ)
to hurry back

遄死(ㄔㄨㄢˊㄙˇ)
to die very quickly

【遇】 6120
ㄩˋ yuh yù
1. to meet; to run into; to
come across; to encounter
2. to treat; treatment
3. opportunity; luck
4. meeting of minds; to win
confidence (of a superior,
king, etc.)
5. to rival; to match with
6. a Chinese family name

遇便(ㄩˋㄅㄧㄢˋ)
at one's convenience

遇到(ㄩˋㄉㄠˋ)
to run into; to meet with; to
encounter; to come across:
探險隊遇到強烈的暴風雨。The
expedition met with a violent storm.

遇敵(ㄩˋㄉㄧˊ)
to encounter the enemy

遇難(ㄩˋㄋㄢˋ)
①to get killed in an accident ②to be murdered by
enemy troops, rebels, etc.

遇合(ㄩˋㄏㄜˊ)
①meeting of minds ②to
enjoy the emperor's com-
plete confidence

遇害(ㄩˋㄏㄞˋ)
to be murdered or assas-
sinated

遇救(ㄩˋㄐㄧㄡˋ)
to be rescued; to be saved

遇見(ㄩˋㄐㄧㄢˋ)
to meet with; to run into; to
come across; to bump into

遇險(ㄩˋㄒㄧㄢˇ)
to meet with danger; to be

in danger; to be in distress:
海岸外有船遇險。There was a
ship in distress off the
shore.

遇著(ㄩˋ·ㄓㄜˋ)
to meet; to encounter

遇時(ㄩˋㄕˊ)
to ride the crest of one's
fortune; to catch the right
opportunity

遇事生風(ㄩˋㄕˋㄕㄥㄈㄥ)
to make a mountain out of
a molehill; to stir up trouble

遇人不淑(ㄩˋㄖㄣˊㄅㄨˋㄕㄨˊ)
to marry the wrong guy; to
have married a bad husband

遇刺(ㄩˋㄘˋ)
to be attacked by an assassin; to be assassinated: 總統
遇刺身亡。The president was
assassinated.

遇雨(ㄩˋㄩˇ)
in the event of; in case of

遇雨(ㄩˋㄩˇ)
to be caught in the rain

【遊】 6121
ㄧㄡˊ you yóu
1. to travel; to go to a distance
2. to roam; to saunter
3. to befriend; to make friends
4. freely while (a sword),
move (one's eyes), stretch
(one's sight), etc.

遊伴(ㄧㄡˊㄅㄢˋ)
a travel companion

遊兵(ㄧㄡˊㄅㄧㄥ)
militiamen; soldiers who are
not listed as regulars

遊民(ㄧㄡˊㄇㄧㄣˊ)
a vagrant; a vagabond; an
idle wanderer 亦作「無業遊民」

遊牧(ㄧㄡˊㄇㄨˋ)
to move about to search for
pasture; to rove around as a
nomad

遊牧民族(ㄧㄡˊㄇㄨˋㄇㄧㄣˊㄗㄨˊ)
a nomadic people or tribe

遊牧時代(ㄧㄡˊㄇㄨˋㄕˊㄉㄞˋ)
the nomadic period or era

遊牧生活(ㄧㄡˊㄇㄨˋㄕㄥㄏㄨㄛˊ)
nomadic life; nomadism

遊目騁懷(ㄧㄡˊㄇㄨˋㄔㄥˇㄏㄨㄞˊ)
to stretch one's sight and let
one's mind roam freely

遊方(ㄧㄡˊㄈㄤ)
(usually referring to Bud-

dhist or Taoist monks and nuns) to roam around all corners of the world

遊蕩(ㄧㄡ ㄉㄤ)
to fool around; to act like a bum or vagrant

遊惰(ㄧㄡ ㄉㄨㄛˋ)
to fool around and do nothing productive

遊動(ㄧㄡ ㄉㄨㄥˋ)
to go from place to place; to move about

遊艇(ㄧㄡ ㄊㄧㄥˇ)
a yacht; a pleasure boat

遊樂(ㄧㄡ ㄌㄜˋ)or遊豫(ㄧㄡ ㄩˋ)
to make merry; to seek pleasure; entertainment

遊樂場(ㄧㄡ ㄌㄜˋ ㄔㄤˇ)
an amusement park; a ground where all sorts of vaudeville shows are given; a kiddie land

遊覽(ㄧㄡ ㄌㄢˇ)
① to visit; to tour; sightseeing: 我們大部分的時間都花在遊覽上。 Most of our time was spent in sightseeing. ② to read extensively

遊覽車(ㄧㄡ ㄌㄢˇ ㄔㄜ)
a bus or train for tourists or sightseers; a tourist coach; a sightseeing bus

遊廊(ㄧㄡ ㄌㄤˊ)
corridors, etc. between pavilions, etc. in a garden; a veranda

遊歷(ㄧㄡ ㄌㄧˋ)
to travel abroad for study, research, inspection, etc.

遊獵(ㄧㄡ ㄌㄧㄝˋ)
① to travel here and there for hunting ② to dabble in (certain reading, etc.)

遊觀(ㄧㄡ ㄍㄨㄢ)
to travel and see the sights

遊逛(ㄧㄡ ㄍㄨㄤˋ)
to stroll; to roam about: 這對夫婦手牽著手遊逛。 The couple strolled hand in hand.

遊客(ㄧㄡ ㄎㄜˋ)
a traveler; a tourist

遊客止步(ㄧㄡ ㄎㄜˋ ㄓˇ ㄅㄨˋ)
No trespassing.

遊魂(ㄧㄡ ㄏㄨㄣˊ)
(literally) a homeless spirit —somebody or something which cannot remain long in a place

遊記(ㄧㄡ ㄐㄧˋ)
a travelogue (in writing); a writing about one's travels; a travel sketch

遊騎(ㄧㄡ ㄐㄧˊ)
mounted troopers

遊騎兵(ㄧㄡ ㄐㄧˊ ㄅㄧㄥ)
a ranger

遊騎無歸(ㄧㄡ ㄐㄧˊ ㄨˊ ㄍㄨㄟ)
rootless or homeless; no place to go back to

遊街(ㄧㄡ ㄐㄧㄝ)
to parade a prisoner down the street as a warning to would-be offenders

遊氣(ㄧㄡ ㄑㄧˋ)
① fleeting clouds ② feeble breathing

遊息(ㄧㄡ ㄒㄧˊ)
to play and rest

遊戲(ㄧㄡ ㄒㄧˋ)
to play; play: 孩子們在院子裡遊戲。 The children are playing in the yard.

遊戲場(ㄧㄡ ㄒㄧˋ ㄔㄤˇ)
a public amusement park or ground

遊戲人間(ㄧㄡ ㄒㄧˋ ㄖㄣˊ ㄐㄧㄢ)
to take nothing serious in life; to live for fun

遊狎(ㄧㄡ ㄒㄧㄚˊ)
to befriend and be intimate with

遊俠(ㄧㄡ ㄒㄧㄚˊ)
a cavalier who moves about to help the poor and weak; any person who acts in this manner without asking for reward either in money or fame; a roving gallant

遊仙(ㄧㄡ ㄒㄧㄢ)
(said of one's mind) to roam in a fairyland and forget all worldly affairs

遊心(ㄧㄡ ㄒㄧㄣ)
to think deep into something

遊行(ㄧㄡ ㄒㄧㄥˊ)
① to parade; a parade ② to demonstrate (in protest); demonstration

遊行示威(ㄧㄡ ㄒㄧㄥˊ ㄕˋ ㄨㄟ)
to demonstrate (in protest); demonstration: 學生舉行遊行示威。 The students held a demonstration.

遊興(ㄧㄡ ㄒㄧㄥˋ)
enthusiasm in merry-making, touring or sightseeing; wanderlust

遊學(ㄧㄡ ㄒㄩㄝˊ)
to study abroad; to pursue advanced study far away from home

遊塵(ㄧㄡ ㄔㄣˊ)
fine dust floating in the air

遊春(ㄧㄡ ㄔㄨㄣ)
a spring outing; to roam about and enjoy the sights of spring

遊食(ㄧㄡ ㄕˊ)
to fool around without doing anything productive; to be a bum

遊手好閒(ㄧㄡ ㄕㄡˇ ㄏㄠˋ ㄒㄧㄢˊ)
to be a lazy good-for-nothing; to lead a parasitic life; to idle about: 他兒子遊手好閒, 不務正業。 His son idles about and does no decent work.

遊山玩水(ㄧㄡ ㄕㄢ ㄨㄢˊ ㄕㄨㄟˇ)
to travel high and low and enjoy the sights of mountains and rivers

遊說(ㄧㄡ ㄕㄨㄟˋ)
to travel around and try to talk people into accepting one's views; to lobby; to canvass 亦作「游說」: 這團體試圖遊說說法案通過。 The group tried to lobby the bill through.

遊人(ㄧㄡ ㄖㄣˊ)
a sightseer; a tourist; a visitor

遊刃有餘(ㄧㄡ ㄖㄣˋ ㄧㄡˇ ㄩˊ)
to handle a difficult task with great ease

遊資(ㄧㄡ ㄗ)
idle funds; idle money; floating capital; floating assets

遊子(ㄧㄡ ㄗˇ)
a traveler; a wanderer

遊蹤(ㄧㄡ ㄗㄨㄥ)
the whereabouts of a traveler

遊絲(ㄧㄡ ㄙ)
gossamer

遊藝會(ㄧㄡ ㄧˋ ㄏㄨㄟˋ)
public entertainment; a gathering where variety

〔走部〕

〔走
部〕

shows are staged by sponsoring organizations and by the participants too

遊冶 (ㄧㄡˊ ㄧㄝˇ)
to indulge in the pursuit of pleasure

遊玩 (ㄧㄡˊ ㄨㄢˊ)
to play; to recreate; to go for a ramble: 他們經常去郊外遊玩。 They often go to the suburbs to play.

遊園會 (ㄧㄡˊ ㄩㄢˊ ㄏㄨㄟˋ)
a carnival; a garden party

【運】 6122
ㄩㄣˋ yunn yùn

1. to move; to revolve: 地球繞太陽運轉。 The earth revolves round the sun.
2. to transport; to ship
3. to utilize; to make use of
4. one's luck or fortune: 我這個星期運氣不錯。 I have had good luck this week.
5. a Chinese family name

運搬 (ㄩㄣˋ ㄅㄢ)
to transport; to move

運筆 (ㄩㄣˋ ㄅㄧˇ)
to wield the brush (pen) in writing or painting

運命 (ㄩㄣˋ ㄇㄧㄥˋ)
fate; destiny; fortune

運費 (ㄩㄣˋ ㄈㄟˋ)
a freight charge; freight

運道 (ㄩㄣˋ ㄉㄠˋ)
①fortune or luck: 他的運道不佳。 His fortune is not good, 或 He is out of luck. ②a road for grain transportation

運動 (ㄩㄣˋ ㄉㄨㄥˋ)
①sports; physical exercises ②motion; movement ③a social movement; a campaign; a drive ④to lobby

運動定律 (ㄩㄣˋ ㄉㄨㄥˋ ㄉㄧㄥˋ ㄌㄩˋ)
(Sir Isaac Newton's) law of motion

運動體型 (ㄩㄣˋ ㄉㄨㄥˋ ㄊㄧˇ ㄒㄧㄥˊ)
sportsman's somatotype

運動力學 (ㄩㄣˋ ㄉㄨㄥˋ ㄌㄧˋ ㄒㄩㄝˊ)
(physics) kinetics

運動規範 (ㄩㄣˋ ㄉㄨㄥˋ ㄍㄨㄟ ㄈㄢˋ)
sports norms

運動科學 (ㄩㄣˋ ㄉㄨㄥˋ ㄎㄜ ㄒㄩㄝˊ)
sports science

運動會 (ㄩㄣˋ ㄉㄨㄥˋ ㄏㄨㄟˋ)
an athletic meet; a sports

meeting; games: 我們今天下午開運動會。 We had a sports meeting this afternoon.

運動家 (ㄩㄣˋ ㄉㄨㄥˋ ㄐㄧㄚ)
a sportsman; an athlete

運動精神 (ㄩㄣˋ ㄉㄨㄥˋ ㄐㄧㄥ ㄕㄣˊ)
sportsmanship: 他稱讚你的運動精神嗎? Did he praise your sportsmanship?

運動器官 (ㄩㄣˋ ㄉㄨㄥˋ ㄑㄧˋ ㄍㄨㄢ)
organs of locomotion

運動器材 (ㄩㄣˋ ㄉㄨㄥˋ ㄑㄧˋ ㄘㄞˊ)
sports supplies; sports equipment; sporting goods

運動信條 (ㄩㄣˋ ㄉㄨㄥˋ ㄒㄧㄣˋ ㄊㄧㄠˊ)
the sports creed

運動學 (ㄩㄣˋ ㄉㄨㄥˋ ㄒㄩㄝˊ)
(physics) kinematics

運動場 (ㄩㄣˋ ㄉㄨㄥˋ ㄔㄤˇ)or(ㄩㄣˋ ㄉㄨㄥˋ ㄔㄤˊ)
a playground; a stadium; a gymnasium; a sports arena

運動神經 (ㄩㄣˋ ㄉㄨㄥˋ ㄕㄣˊ ㄐㄧㄥ)
motor nerves

運動傷害 (ㄩㄣˋ ㄉㄨㄥˋ ㄕㄤ ㄏㄞˋ)
sports injuries

運動人口 (ㄩㄣˋ ㄉㄨㄥˋ ㄖㄣˊ ㄎㄡˇ)
sports population

運動資訊 (ㄩㄣˋ ㄉㄨㄥˋ ㄗ ㄒㄩㄣˋ)
sports information

運動員 (ㄩㄣˋ ㄉㄨㄥˋ ㄩㄢˊ)
①an athlete; a sportsman: 他是熱心的運動員。 He is a keen sportsman. ②a lobbyist

運糧 (ㄩㄣˋ ㄌㄧㄤˊ)
to transport food (or provisions)

運河 (ㄩㄣˋ ㄏㄜˊ)
①a canal ②the Grand Canal in China

運貨 (ㄩㄣˋ ㄏㄨㄛˋ)
to transport goods

運會 (ㄩㄣˋ ㄏㄨㄟˋ)
trends of the time; international mathematics

運斤成風 (ㄩㄣˋ ㄐㄧㄣ ㄔㄥˊ ㄈㄥ)
(literally) to create a gust by wielding the ax—an uncanny feat

運氣 (ㄩㄣˋ ㄑㄧˋ)
①(Chinese pugilism) dynamic tension of muscles ②luck or fortune

運球 (ㄩㄣˋ ㄑㄧㄡˊ)

to dribble balls; dribbling

運銷 (ㄩㄣˋ ㄒㄧㄠ)
to ship (goods) for sales; shipping and marketing

運行 (ㄩㄣˋ ㄒㄧㄥˊ)
to move in an orbit, as a planet or satellite

運轉 (ㄩㄣˋ ㄓㄨㄢˇ)
①to revolve; revolution; to set in motion around a circular orbit: 地球繞着太陽運轉。 The earth revolves round the sun. ②to work; to operate; to run: 機器運轉正常。 The machine is working (or running) well.

運籌 (ㄩㄣˋ ㄔㄡˊ)
to plan; to map out strategy

運籌帷幄 (ㄩㄣˋ ㄔㄡˊ ㄨㄟˊ ㄨㄛˋ)
to map out or devise strategy in the command tent

運輸 (ㄩㄣˋ ㄕㄨ)
transportation; to transport; conveyance; to convey: 該公司負責運輸。 Transportation was supplied by the company.

運輸工具 (ㄩㄣˋ ㄕㄨ ㄍㄨㄥ ㄐㄩˋ)
means of transportation; means of delivery

運輸機 (ㄩㄣˋ ㄕㄨ ㄐㄧ)
a military transport; a cargo plane

運輸艦 (ㄩㄣˋ ㄕㄨ ㄐㄧㄢˋ)
a naval supply ship; a navy transport

運數 (ㄩㄣˋ ㄕㄨˋ)
fortune; fate; luck: 他不相信運數之說。 He doesn't believe in fate.

運祚 (ㄩㄣˋ ㄗㄨㄛˋ)
the national fortune; the fate of the world

運漕 (ㄩㄣˋ ㄘㄠˊ)
to convey food by water

運算 (ㄩㄣˋ ㄙㄨㄢˋ)
(mathematics) an operation

運送 (ㄩㄣˋ ㄙㄨㄥˋ)
to convey; to transport; to deliver; to ship: 他用快車還是用貨車運送? Did he ship it by express or by freight?

運用 (ㄩㄣˋ ㄩㄥˋ)
to employ; to make use of; to exercise

運用資本 (ㄩㄣˋ ㄩㄥˋ ㄗ ㄅㄣˇ)
working capital

【遍】 6123
ㄅㄧㄢˋ biàn biàn
(語音 ㄆㄧㄢ piann piàn)

1. a time
2. everywhere; throughout; all over

遍布(ㄅㄧㄢˋ ㄅㄨˋ)
all over; everywhere

遍地(ㄅㄧㄢˋ ㄉㄧˋ)
everywhere; throughout the land

遍體(ㄅㄧㄢˋ ㄊㄧˇ)
all over the body

遍體鱗傷(ㄅㄧㄢˋ ㄊㄧˇ ㄌㄧㄣˊ ㄕㄤ)
with wounds all over the body

遍歷(ㄅㄧㄢˋ ㄌㄧˋ)
to have experienced all sorts of...; to have traveled all (the places)

遍告(ㄅㄧㄢˋ ㄍㄠˋ)
to announce to all; to tell everyone

遍及(ㄅㄧㄢˋ ㄐㄧˊ)
to spread throughout (the world, nation, etc.); 謠言已遍及全島。The rumor has spread throughout the whole island.

遍身(ㄅㄧㄢˋ ㄕㄣ)
all over the body: 這件羊毛衫使我遍身發癢。This wool shirt itches me all over the body.

【過】 6124
1. 《ㄍㄨㄛˋ guòh guò》
(又讀 《ㄍㄨㄛ guo guō》)

1. to pass; to pass through or by; to ford
2. across; past; through; over: 有一條近路橫過這片原野。There is a short cut across the field.
3. to spend or pass (time): 你的春假是怎麼過的？How did you pass the spring holidays?
4. after; past: 那個老人超過九十歲了。That old man is past ninety.
5. to go beyond the ordinary or proper limits; to surpass
6. too much; excessive
7. a mistake; a demerit; a fault; a sin: 他勇於改過。He was bold in correcting his mistakes.
8. a particle indicating the past perfect tense: 他說他曾見過她。He said that he had once met her.
9. contagious
10. to visit
11. to transfer
12. to die; death
13. to arrive; to get to

過飽和《ㄍㄨㄛˋ ㄅㄠˇ ㄏㄜˊ》
(said of a solution) supersaturated; supersaturation

過飽和溶液《ㄍㄨㄛˋ ㄅㄠˇ ㄏㄜˊ ㄖㄨㄥˊ 一ㄝˋ》
supersaturated solution

過半《ㄍㄨㄛˋ ㄅㄢˋ》
more than half

過半數《ㄍㄨㄛˋ ㄅㄢˋ ㄕㄨˋ》
over half of the number; the majority

過磅《ㄍㄨㄛˋ ㄅㄤˋ》or《ㄍㄨㄛˋ ㄅㄥˋ》
to weigh

過不來《ㄍㄨㄛˋ ㄅㄨˋ ㄌㄞˊ》
unable to come over

過不去《ㄍㄨㄛˋ ㄅㄨˋ ㄑㄩˋ》
① unable to get through ② to feel sorry for ③ intentionally to make it difficult for somebody; to have a grudge against; to give someone a hard time; to be hard on

過不下去《ㄍㄨㄛˋ ㄅㄨˋ ㄒㄧㄚˋ ㄑㄩˋ》
unable to live on

過門兒《ㄍㄨㄛˋ ㄇㄣˊ ㄦ》
(Chinese opera) the musical interlude between singing parts when the string accompaniment plays alone 亦作「過板兒」

過門《ㄍㄨㄛˋ ㄇㄣˊ》
① to pass the door ②(said of girls) to get married

過門不入《ㄍㄨㄛˋ ㄇㄣˊ ㄅㄨˋ ㄖㄨˋ》
(literally) to pass one's own door without entering (because of urgent official duties)—to act beyond the call of duty

過敏《ㄍㄨㄛˋ ㄇㄧㄣˇ》
(medicine) allergy

過目《ㄍㄨㄛˋ ㄇㄨˋ》
to give a glance; to take a look; to read; to go over

過目不忘《ㄍㄨㄛˋ ㄇㄨˋ ㄅㄨˋ ㄨㄤˋ》
to have a photographic memory

過目成誦《ㄍㄨㄛˋ ㄇㄨˋ ㄔㄥˊ ㄙㄨㄥˋ》
able to recite what one has casually read only once

過分《ㄍㄨㄛˋ ㄈㄣˋ》
to go beyond the normal or proper limits; to overdo; to go too far; excessive: 不要過分謙虛。Don't carry your modesty too far.

過房《ㄍㄨㄛˋ ㄈㄤˊ》
(said of an heirless person) to adopt a son of one's brother as one's own

過訪《ㄍㄨㄛˋ ㄈㄤˇ》
to come for a visit: 今承過訪，無任感謝。Thank you for your visit today.

過得去《ㄍㄨㄛˋ ㄉㄜˊ ㄑㄩˋ》
① passable; not too bad; so-so; fair: 我還算過得去。I'm just so-so. ② not to embarrass another ③ to be at peace with oneself ④ passable; able to get through: 卡車從這條路過得去嗎？Can the truck get through the road?

過道兒《ㄍㄨㄛˋ ㄉㄠˋ ㄦ》
a narrow corridor or passageway between houses

過當《ㄍㄨㄛˋ ㄉㄤ》
beyond the proper limits; improper; inappropriate

過度《ㄍㄨㄛˋ ㄉㄨˋ》
① to go beyond the normal limits; to overdo ② excessive; too much: 抽煙過度對身體有害。Excessive smoking is harmful to the health.

過渡《ㄍㄨㄛˋ ㄉㄨˋ》
①(an) intermediate (state, stage, etc.); (a) transitional (period) ② to cross a river, stream, etc. by ferry

過渡時期《ㄍㄨㄛˋ ㄉㄨˋ ㄕˊ ㄑㄧˊ》
a period or stage of transition; a transitional stage or period

過多《ㄍㄨㄛˋ ㄉㄨㄛ》
too many or much; more than enough; excessive: 雨量過多引起了洪水。The excessive rainfall caused floods.

過冬《ㄍㄨㄛˋ ㄉㄨㄥ》
to pass the winter; to winter: 我們計畫到義大利過冬。We plan to winter in Italy.

過頭《ㄍㄨㄛˋ ㄊㄡˊ》
to go beyond the norm or

〔走部〕

the set goal; to overdo; too much: 飯煮過頭了。The meal is overcooked.

過堂《ㄍㄨㄛ ㄊㄤ》
①to stand a trial in court ②(said of successful candidates of the national civil service examination in the Tang Dynasty) to call on the prime minister

過屠門而大嚼《ㄍㄨㄛ ㄊㄨ ㄇㄣˊ ㄦˊ ㄉㄚˋ ㄐㄩㄝˊ》
(literally) to do chewing actions energetically while passing by the door of a butcher—to hanker for things one cannot get

過年《ㄍㄨㄛ ㄋㄧㄢˊ》
①to pass the New Year: 我今年在國外過年。I'll pass the New Year holiday abroad. ②next year

過勞《ㄍㄨㄛ ㄌㄠˊ》
to work too hard; to overwork

過來人《ㄍㄨㄛ ㄌㄞˊ ㄖㄣˊ》
a person who has had the experience of something in question

過來《ㄍㄨㄛ ㄌㄞˊ》
Come here. 或 Come on. 或 to come up; to come over: 過來這裏你可以看得更清楚些。Come over here, you will see better.

過磷酸鈣《ㄍㄨㄛ ㄌㄧㄣˊ ㄙㄨㄢ ㄍㄞˇ》
calcium superphosphate

過兩天《ㄍㄨㄛ ㄌㄧㄤˇ ㄊㄧㄢ》
in the near future; in a few days, in a couple of days: 過兩天我將去拜訪你。I'll visit you in a few days.

過量《ㄍㄨㄛ ㄌㄧㄤˋ》
an overdose; to go beyond the limits (usually referring to drinking); to overdo: 他死於服用過量嗎啡。He died of an overdose of morphine.

過路《ㄍㄨㄛ ㄌㄨˋ》
to pass by; in transit

過慮《ㄍㄨㄛ ㄌㄩˋ》
to be worrying too much or overanxious

過濾《ㄍㄨㄛ ㄌㄩˋ》
to filter; to filtrate

過濾器《ㄍㄨㄛ ㄌㄩˋ ㄑㄧˋ》
a filter

過濾設備《ㄍㄨㄛ ㄌㄩˋ ㄕㄜˋ ㄅㄟˋ》
filtrating equipment

過關《ㄍㄨㄛ ㄍㄨㄢ》
①to go through a checkpoint ②to pass a critical test; to go through an ordeal; to weather a crisis with success ③to come up to the standard; to reach a standard

過客《ㄍㄨㄛ ㄎㄜˋ》
a traveler; a sojourner; a passerby

過河拆橋《ㄍㄨㄛ ㄏㄜˊ ㄔㄞ ㄑㄧㄠˊ》
(literally) to destroy the bridge after one has crossed the river—very ungrateful; to discard a person after he has outlasted his usefulness

過後《ㄍㄨㄛ ㄏㄡˋ》
later; afterward: 我們過後再討論這項計畫。Let's discuss the plan later on.

過戶《ㄍㄨㄛ ㄏㄨˋ》
to transfer the ownership (of bonds, stocks, or property) from one person to another: 這間公寓不能過戶。This apartment couldn't transfer ownership.

過活《ㄍㄨㄛ ㄏㄨㄛˊ》
to make a living: 她父親靠捕魚過活。Her father makes a living by fishing.

過火《ㄍㄨㄛ ㄏㄨㄛˇ》
to go beyond the proper limits; to overdo; to go to extremes; to go too far: 別把玩笑開得太過火。Don't carry the joke too far.

過激《ㄍㄨㄛ ㄐㄧ》
too violent, radical or outspoken: 他的言論過激。His opinions are too radical.

過激派《ㄍㄨㄛ ㄐㄧ ㄆㄞˋ》
the radical faction; the radicals

過激分子《ㄍㄨㄛ ㄐㄧ ㄈㄣ ㄗˇ》
radicals; extremists

過激思想《ㄍㄨㄛ ㄐㄧ ㄙ ㄒㄧㄤˇ》
dangerously extreme views or thoughts

過急《ㄍㄨㄛ ㄐㄧˊ》
too hasty; to make haste: 勿操之過急。Don't make haste.

過繼《ㄍㄨㄛ ㄐㄧˋ》
①(said of an heirless person) to adopt a son of one's brother or relative as one's own ②to have one's own child adopted by a male relative as his heir: 他把兒子過繼給親戚。He has his son adopted by a relative.

過街《ㄍㄨㄛ ㄐㄧㄝ》
to cross the street

過節《ㄍㄨㄛ ㄐㄧㄝˊ》
①to pass a festival; to celebrate a festival ②a grudge: 他們之間有過節。They bear grudges against each other.

過江之鯽《ㄍㄨㄛ ㄐㄧㄤ ㄓ ㄐㄧˋ》
as numerous as a large school of fish migrating to a river

過獎《ㄍㄨㄛ ㄐㄧㄤˇ》
①to overpraise; to flatter: 你過獎了。You flatter me. ②(a polite expression) I don't deserve your praise.

過境《ㄍㄨㄛ ㄐㄧㄥˋ》
(said of airplanes, ships, etc.) to pass through; in transit

過境旅客《ㄍㄨㄛ ㄐㄧㄥˋ ㄌㄩˇ ㄎㄜˋ》
a transit visitor

過境簽證《ㄍㄨㄛ ㄐㄧㄥˋ ㄑㄧㄢ ㄓㄥˋ》
a transit visa

過期《ㄍㄨㄛ ㄑㄧˊ》
to have passed the deadline; (said of permits, etc.) to have passed the date of expiration; overdue

過期支票《ㄍㄨㄛ ㄑㄧˊ ㄓ ㄆㄧㄠˋ》
an out-of-date check; an overdue check

過謙《ㄍㄨㄛ ㄑㄧㄢ》
to be too modest: 你得獎是應該的，不必過謙了。You really deserve the prize. Don't be so modest.

過去《ㄍㄨㄛ ㄑㄩˋ》
①in the past; formerly; once: 她過去住在法國。She formerly lived in France. ②to go over: 我們過去對街購物吧。Let's go over to the other side of the street to go shopping. ③to pass; to pass by: 火車剛過去。The train has just passed by. ④to die; to pass away

過去分詞《ㄍㄨㄛ ㄑㄩˋ ㄈㄣ ㄘˊ》
(grammar) the past participle

過去了《ㄍㄨㄛ ㄑㄩˋ ·ㄌㄜ》
to pass away; to die: 她母親昨晚過去了。Her mother passed away last night.

過去式《ㄍㄨㄛ ㄑㄩˋ ㄕˋ》
(grammar) the past tense

過去完成式《ㄍㄨㄛ ㄑㄩˋ ㄨㄢˊ ㄔㄥˊ ㄕˋ》
(grammar) the past perfect tense

過細《ㄍㄨㄛ ㄒㄧˋ》
very careful or cautious; squeamish

過招《ㄍㄨㄛ ㄓㄠ》
(informal) to have an encounter in combat; to exchange blows

過帳《ㄍㄨㄛ ㄓㄤˋ》
to transfer accounts or items (from a daybook to a ledger); to post

過程《ㄍㄨㄛ ㄔㄥˊ》
(in) the process; (in) the course (of)

過秤《ㄍㄨㄛ ㄔㄥˋ》
to weigh

過處《ㄍㄨㄛ ㄔㄨˋ》
mistakes; errors; faults

過失《ㄍㄨㄛ ㄕ》
errors committed unintentionally; faults: 他懺悔過去生活中的過失。He repented of a past life.

過失殺人罪《ㄍㄨㄛ ㄕ ㄕㄚ ㄖㄣˊ ㄗㄨㄟˋ》
manslaughter

過失傷害罪《ㄍㄨㄛ ㄕ ㄕㄤ ㄏㄞˋ ㄗㄨㄟˋ》
bodily injury done to others owing to negligence

過時《ㄍㄨㄛ ㄕˊ》
old-fashioned; anachronistic; outdated; to outdate

過時不候《ㄍㄨㄛ ㄕˊ ㄅㄨˋ ㄏㄡˋ》
The deadline (appointed time, or specified date) will not be extended.

過少《ㄍㄨㄛ ㄕㄠˇ》
too little; too few; far from enough: 他的薪水過少，無法維生。His salary was too little to live on.

過山砲《ㄍㄨㄛ ㄕㄢ ㄆㄠˋ》
a light field piece which can be easily hauled across a hill; a mountain howitzer

過生日《ㄍㄨㄛ ㄕㄥ ㄖˋ》
to celebrate a birthday: 他過生日請我吃飯。He celebrated his birthday by inviting us to a dinner.

過剩《ㄍㄨㄛ ㄕㄥˋ》
a surplus: 巴西有很多過剩的咖啡。Brazil has a big surplus of coffee.

過剩人口《ㄍㄨㄛ ㄕㄥˋ ㄖㄣˊ ㄎㄡˇ》
surplus population

過水麵《ㄍㄨㄛ ㄕㄨㄟˇ ㄇㄧㄢˋ》
cooked noodles which have been cooled with water

過日子《ㄍㄨㄛ ㄖˋ ·ㄗ》
① to practice economy ② to live: 我們勤儉過日子。We lived industriously and frugally.

過人《ㄍㄨㄛ ㄖㄣˊ》
to surpass others (in intelligence, bravery and other attributes): 他有過人的記憶力。He surpasses others in memory.

過載《ㄍㄨㄛ ㄗㄞˋ》
(said of a car, ship, etc.) overloaded

過錯《ㄍㄨㄛ ㄘㄨㄛˋ》
mistakes; faults

過存《ㄍㄨㄛ ㄘㄨㄣˊ》
to give one's regards to

過從《ㄍㄨㄛ ㄘㄨㄥˊ》
frequency of communication or mutual visits between friends; to be associated with: 我和他們過從甚密。I am in close association with them.

過意不去《ㄍㄨㄛ ㄧˋ ㄅㄨˋ ㄑㄩˋ》
① very much obliged; unable to express one's thanks adequately ② to feel sorry; not knowing how to express one's regrets

過夜《ㄍㄨㄛ ㄧㄝˋ》
① to pass the night; to overnight ② to spend a whole night with a prostitute (as distinct from "short-time quickies")

過猶不及《ㄍㄨㄛ ㄧㄡˊ ㄅㄨˋ ㄐㄧˊ》
Too much is as bad as not enough.

過眼《ㄍㄨㄛ ㄧㄢˇ》
① to pass before the eyes ② to take a glance

過眼煙雲《ㄍㄨㄛ ㄧㄢˇ ㄧㄢ ㄩㄣˊ》
(literally) smoke and clouds passing before the eyes—transient; ephemeral

過癮《ㄍㄨㄛ ㄧㄣˇ》
① to do something to one's heart's content ② to satisfy the urge of an addiction

過氧化鈉《ㄍㄨㄛ ㄧㄤˋ ㄏㄨㄚˋ ㄋㄚˋ》
sodium peroxide

過氧化鉀《ㄍㄨㄛ ㄧㄤˋ ㄏㄨㄚˋ ㄐㄧㄚˇ》
potassium peroxide

過氧化物《ㄍㄨㄛ ㄧㄤˋ ㄏㄨㄚˋ ㄨˋ》
peroxide

過午《ㄍㄨㄛ ㄨˇ》
afternoon

過午不食《ㄍㄨㄛ ㄨˇ ㄅㄨˋ ㄕˊ》
(a rule for the monks) not to eat after noontime

過五關《ㄍㄨㄛ ㄨˇ ㄍㄨㄢ》
a kind of solitaire, played with dominoes

過問《ㄍㄨㄛ ㄨㄣˋ》
① to make inquiry about; to ask about. 我從不過問他們的政治活動。I never asked about their political activities. ② to interfere with: 不要過問他人的事。Don't interfere with others. ③ to care; to show concern

過往《ㄍㄨㄛ ㄨㄤˇ》
① comings and goings: 旅客的過往 the comings and goings of tourists ② social contacts; mutual visits

過望《ㄍㄨㄛ ㄨㄤˋ》
beyond one's hope or expectations

過於《ㄍㄨㄛ ㄩˊ》
too much; excessive; over

過譽《ㄍㄨㄛ ㄩˋ》
excessive praise; to acclaim excessively

【過】6124
2.《ㄍㄨㄛ guō guǒ》
a Chinese family name

【遏】6125
ㄜˋ eh è
1. to curb; to stop; to restrain; to prevent
2. to cause one's own extinction; to extinguish; to ruin

遏捺《ㄜˋ ㄋㄚˋ》
to suppress (one's anger, etc.); to restrain

遏止《ㄜˋ ㄓˇ》

〔辵部〕

〔辵部〕

to check; to hold back; to stop

遏制(ㄜˋ)
to restrain; to check; to stop; to curb

遏阻(ㄜˋ)
to curb; to arrest; to stop

遏惡揚善(ㄜˋㄜˋ一ㄤˊㄕㄢˋ)
to refrain from talking about another's evildoing but cite his good points

遏抑(ㄜˋ)
to suppress; to restrain; to curb; to check

【遑】 6126
ㄏㄨㄤˊ hwang huáng
1. hurry; to hurry
2. anxious; disturbed
3. leisurely
4. not to

遑論其他(ㄏㄨㄤˊㄌㄨㄣˋ〈ㄧˊㄊㄚ)
not to mention the others; let alone the other points

遑遽(ㄏㄨㄤˊㄐㄩˋ)
disturbed; jittery; scared

遑急(ㄏㄨㄤˊㄐㄧˊ)
scared and in a hurry: 他遑急萬狀。He was in a great hurry.

遑遽(ㄏㄨㄤˊㄐㄩˋ)
jittery and anxious; frightened

【退】 6127
ㄒㄧㄚˊ shya xiá
1. distant; far
2. a long time
3. advanced in years
4. to die down; to vanish
5. to abandon; to cast off
6. Why not? 或 How? 或 What?

退布(ㄒㄧㄚˊㄅㄨˋ)
to spread far and wide

退方(ㄒㄧㄚˊㄈㄤ)
distant places

退福(ㄒㄧㄚˊㄈㄨˊ)
great happiness; lasting blessings or happiness

退眺(ㄒㄧㄚˊㄊㄧㄠˋ)
to stretch one's sight as far as it can reach

退齡(ㄒㄧㄚˊㄌㄧㄥˊ)
longevity; a long life; an advanced age

退荒(ㄒㄧㄚˊㄏㄨㄤ)
distant and out-of-the-way places

退迹(ㄒㄧㄚˊㄐㄧ)

matters and stories of ancient people

退舉(ㄒㄧㄚˊㄐㄩˇ)
to go on a distant journey

退棄(ㄒㄧㄚˊㄑㄧˋ)
①to cast away; to reject; to shun ②to desert one's post

退心(ㄒㄧㄚˊㄒㄧㄣ)
①the thought of keeping aloof ②the wish to abandon ③the desire to live in retirement

退想(ㄒㄧㄚˊㄒㄧㄤˇ)
wild and fanciful thoughts; reverie; a daydream

退祉(ㄒㄧㄚˊㄓˇ)
lasting blessings or happiness

退志(ㄒㄧㄚˊㄓˋ)
lofty ambition or aspiration

退胄(ㄒㄧㄚˊㄓㄡˋ)
distant descendants

退思(ㄒㄧㄚˊㄙ)
wild and fanciful thoughts

退邇(ㄒㄧㄚˊㄦˇ)
far and near (usually said of one's reputation): 他退邇聞名。He was well-known far and near.

退邇一體(ㄒㄧㄚˊㄦˇㄧˋㄊㄧˇ)
Both the near and the distant are treated alike.

【遒】 6128
〈ㄧㄡˊ chyou qiú
1. strong; forceful; powerful; vigorous; sturdy
2. to come to an end; to close
3. to gather; to concentrate

遒美(〈ㄧㄡˊㄇㄟˇ)
(said of the style of calligraphy) forceful and graceful

遒健(〈ㄧㄡˊㄐㄧㄢˋ)
strong; vigorous

遒勁(〈ㄧㄡˊㄐㄧㄥˋ)
①(said of calligraphy) forceful; vigorous ②strong; sturdy

遒逸(〈ㄧㄡˊㄧˋ)
(said of a piece of writing) forceful and flowing

【道】 6129
ㄉㄠˋ daw dào
1. a road; a path; a street
2. the "way" (in the metaphysical sense)
3. a way; a method: 致富沒有簡易之道。There is no easy way

to wealth.
4. Taoism; a Taoist
5. to say; to speak
6. an administrative district in old China
7. a theory; a doctrine
8. to govern; to lead
9. to think; to suppose
10. a skill; an art; a craft
11. a Chinese family name

道白(ㄉㄠˋㄅㄞˊ)
spoken lines in Chinese opera (as distinct from the singing parts)

道不同不相為謀(ㄉㄠˋㄅㄨˋㄊㄨㄥˊㄅㄨˋㄒㄧㄤ ㄨㄟˊㄇㄡˊ)
People adhering to different principles will not map their plan together. 或 Birds of different feathers will no flock together. 或 There i little common ground fo understanding between per sons of differing principles.

道不拾遺(ㄉㄠˋㄅㄨˋㄕˊㄧˊ)
(said of an orderly society) No one will pick up any thing dropped by others on the road.—Honesty prevail throughout society.

道破(ㄉㄠˋㄆㄛˋ)
to expose or reveal som secret in utterance: 他一語道破其中奧秘。He exposed its secret with one remark.

道袍(ㄉㄠˋㄆㄠˊ)
a Taoist robe

道貌岸然(ㄉㄠˋㄇㄠˋㄢˋㄖㄢˊ)
①to maintain a serene loo or dignified appearance ②to pretend to be a moralis to look gentlemanly (bu with a dirty mind)

道謀(ㄉㄠˋㄇㄡˊ)
to consult passers-by — their views will certainly b different and even contradic tory)

道乏(ㄉㄠˋㄈㄚˊ)
to thank someone for hi attendance at a wedding funeral, etc.

道德(ㄉㄠˋㄉㄜˊ)
morality; morals; ethics: 我 們應該遵守公共道德。W should keep public morality

道德觀念(ㄉㄠˋㄉㄜˊㄍㄨㄢㄋㄧㄢˋ)
moral concepts

道德經(ㄉㄠˋ ㄉㄜˊ ㄐㄧㄥ)
Tao Te Ching, another title of Lao-tzu (老子)

道德心(ㄉㄠˋ ㄉㄜˊ ㄒㄧㄣ)
a sense of morality

道德哲學(ㄉㄠˋ ㄉㄜˊ ㄓㄜˊ ㄒㄩㄝˊ)
moral philosophy

道德問題(ㄉㄠˋ ㄉㄜˊ ㄨㄣˋ ㄊㄧˊ)
a question of morality or ethics

道地(ㄉㄠˋ ㄉㄧˋ)
genuine; real

道(ㄉㄠˋ)
the magistrate of a *tao*, an ancient administrative district

道體(ㄉㄠˋ ㄊㄧˇ)
①(a polite expression) your health ②the essence of the "Way"

道聽塗說(ㄉㄠˋ ㄊㄧㄥ ㄊㄨˊ ㄕㄨㄛ)
rumor; hearsay; groundless talk

道統(ㄉㄠˋ ㄊㄨㄥˇ)
orthodoxy of teachings or precepts

道里(ㄉㄠˋ ㄌㄧˇ)
①the common standard for measuring distance ②a journey

道理(ㄉㄠˋ ㄌㄧˇ)
①reason; rationality; 你的話很有道理。There is reason in what you say. ②the right way; the proper way

道林紙(ㄉㄠˋ ㄌㄧㄣˊ ㄓˇ)
Dowling paper; wood-free printing paper

道路(ㄉㄠˋ ㄌㄨˋ)
a road; 道路泥濘。The road is muddy.

道路傳聞(ㄉㄠˋ ㄌㄨˋ ㄔㄨㄢˊ ㄨㄣˊ)
news spread on roads—inaccurate and unreliable rumors

道路以目(ㄉㄠˋ ㄌㄨˋ ㄧˇ ㄇㄨˋ)
(said of the people) to be frightened (by a tyrant or ruffian) to complete silence but exchange their hatred with eyes

道籙(ㄉㄠˋ ㄌㄨˋ)
the diagrams and scriptures of Taoism

道高一尺，魔高一丈(ㄉㄠˋ ㄍㄠ ㄧ ㄔˇ，ㄇㄛˊ ㄍㄠ ㄧ ㄓㄤˋ)
(literally) If righteousness grows by a foot, the devil will grow by ten times as much. The force of evil always manages to beat the force of law.

道姑(ㄉㄠˋ ㄍㄨ)
a woman Taoist

道故(ㄉㄠˋ ㄍㄨˋ)
to talk about old times

道觀(ㄉㄠˋ ㄍㄨㄢˋ)
a Taoist temple or shrine

道光(ㄉㄠˋ ㄍㄨㄤ)
①the glory of morality ②the reigning title of the sixth emperor, Hsüan Tzung (宣宗, 1821-1850), in the Ching Dynasty

道賀(ㄉㄠˋ ㄏㄜˋ)
to congratulate; to offer congratulations; 請接受我們的道賀。Please accept our congratulations.

道候(ㄉㄠˋ ㄏㄡˋ)
to convey one's regards to somebody

道濟(ㄉㄠˋ ㄐㄧˋ)
①name of a Buddhist monk in the Sung Dynasty 亦作「濟顚」②name of a Buddhist monk in the Ching Dynasty noted for his paintings 亦作「石濤」

道家(ㄉㄠˋ ㄐㄧㄚ)
the Taoist school

道教(ㄉㄠˋ ㄐㄧㄠˋ)
(religion) Taoism

道具(ㄉㄠˋ ㄐㄩˋ)
stage properties

道歉(ㄉㄠˋ ㄑㄧㄢˋ)
to apologize; to make an apology

道喜(ㄉㄠˋ ㄒㄧˇ)
to congratulate; to offer congratulations

道謝(ㄉㄠˋ ㄒㄧㄝˋ)
to thank; to express thanks; 無須向我道謝。There is no need to thank me.

道行(ㄉㄠˋ ㄒㄧㄥˊ)or(ㄉㄠˋ ㄏㄥˊ)
the attainment of a Taoist

道學(ㄉㄠˋ ㄒㄩㄝˊ)
①the emphasis on rationality in learning as advocated by the Sung scholars ②the teachings of Taoism

道學先生(ㄉㄠˋ ㄒㄩㄝˊ ㄒㄧㄢ ˙ㄕㄥ)
a scholar rigidly adhering to principles; a conservative scholar

道場(ㄉㄠˋ ㄔㄤˇ)
①sites of Taoist or Buddhist rituals ②a Buddhist temple

道士(ㄉㄠˋ ㄕˋ)
a Taoist priest

道是(ㄉㄠˋ ㄕˋ)
to say so; to appear as if: 道是無情却有情。You might say someone is cold, but he isn't.

道山(ㄉㄠˋ ㄕㄢ)
①a paradise where the souls of good people dwell after death ②a cultural center

道上(ㄉㄠˋ ㄕㄤˋ)
on the way

道術(ㄉㄠˋ ㄕㄨˋ)
Taoist magic or sorcery

道人(ㄉㄠˋ ㄖㄣˊ)
①a Buddhist ②a Taoist priest

道子(ㄉㄠˋ ㄗˇ)
lines on the surface of something, as a piece of furniture

道藏(ㄉㄠˋ ㄗㄤˋ)
Taoist books, scriptures, etc.

道次(ㄉㄠˋ ㄘˋ)
on the way

道兒(ㄉㄠˋ ㄦ)
①a road; a street ②a coup; a trick; a trap

道義(ㄉㄠˋ ㄧˋ)
morals; morality; a sense of righteousness; honor

道義力量(ㄉㄠˋ ㄧˋ ㄌㄧˋ ˙ㄌㄧㄤ)
the moral force

道義之交(ㄉㄠˋ ㄧˋ ㄓ ㄐㄧㄠ)
a friendship cemented by common belief in principles or adherence to righteousness

道友(ㄉㄠˋ ㄧㄡˋ)
①friends of the same religion or belief ②friends sharing the same hobby

道院(ㄉㄠˋ ㄩㄢˋ)
a Taoist monastery

【達】6130
1. ㄉㄚˊ *dar dá*

1. intelligent; smart; understanding; reasonable; 他通情達理。He is understanding and reasonable.

2. prominent; successful

〔走部〕

3. to reach; to arrive at
4. to inform; to tell
5. open-minded
6. a Chinese family name

達摩 (ㄉㄚˊ ㄇㄛˊ)
Bodhidharma, who introduced the Zen (禪) sect into China in the 6th century

達姆彈 (ㄉㄚˊ ㄇㄨˇ ㄉㄢˋ)
a dumdum bullet

達達派 (ㄉㄚˊ ㄉㄚˊ ㄆㄞˋ) or 達達主義 (ㄉㄚˊ ㄉㄚˊ ㄓㄨˇ ㄧˋ)
Dada, or Dadaism

達達尼爾海峽 (ㄉㄚˊ ㄉㄚˊ ㄋㄧˊ ㄦˇ ㄏㄞˇ ㄒㄧㄚˊ)
Dardanelles

達德 (ㄉㄚˊ ㄉㄜˊ)
a virtue of all times

達到 (ㄉㄚˊ ㄉㄠˋ)
to reach (a decision, or conclusion); to achieve or attain (a goal, etc.): 我希望你會達到目的. I hope you will attain your object.

達道 (ㄉㄚˊ ㄉㄠˋ)
the universal path; the way everyone follows

達旦 (ㄉㄚˊ ㄉㄢˋ)
(to work) until dawn or throughout the night: 我們通宵達旦地工作. We worked all through the night.

達賴喇嘛 (ㄉㄚˊ ㄌㄞˋ ㄌㄚˇ ㄇㄚˊ)
Dalai Lama, the ruler and chief monk of Tibet, believed to be a reincarnation of Avalokitesvara and sought for among children after the death of the preceding Dalai Lama

達觀 (ㄉㄚˊ ㄍㄨㄢ)
a kind of wisdom which enables a person to be oblivious of emotions and adversity; to take things philosophically

達官貴人 (ㄉㄚˊ ㄍㄨㄢ ㄍㄨㄟˋ ㄖㄣˊ)
prominent officials and eminent personages

達卡爾 (ㄉㄚˊ ㄎㄚˇ ㄦˇ)
Dakar, capital of Senegal

達荷美 (ㄉㄚˊ ㄏㄜˊ ㄇㄟˇ)
Dahomey

達成 (ㄉㄚˊ ㄔㄥˊ)
to succeed in (a mission, etc.); to accomplish; to reach (an agreement)

達士 (ㄉㄚˊ ㄕˋ)
① a highly intelligent person; a wise man ② a reasonable and understanding man

達識 (ㄉㄚˊ ㄕˋ)
intelligent, knowledgeable and well-informed

達人 (ㄉㄚˊ ㄖㄣˊ)
① a very wise man ② to enlarge other's mind, knowledge, etc.

達人知命 (ㄉㄚˊ ㄖㄣˊ ㄓ ㄇㄧㄥˋ)
A wise person understands the will of Heaven.

達尊 (ㄉㄚˊ ㄗㄨㄣ)
the thing which is revered by all

達爾文 (ㄉㄚˊ ㄦˇ ㄨㄣˊ)
Charles Robert Darwin (1809-1882), English naturalist and author

達意 (ㄉㄚˊ ㄧˋ)
to make one's meaning clear

達因 (ㄉㄚˊ ㄧㄣ)
(physics) dyne

【達】 6130
2. ㄊㄚˋ tah tà
loose and impudent

【違】 6131
ㄨㄟˊ wéi wéi
1 to go against; to defy; to disobey; to disregard: 士兵不可違令. Soldiers must not disobey orders.
2. to be separated
3. to avoid
4. evil; fault

違背 (ㄨㄟˊ ㄅㄟˋ)
to defy; to disobey; to disregard; to be contrary to

違法 (ㄨㄟˊ ㄈㄚˇ)
to be against the law; to be unlawful; to violate the law; to be illegal

違法行為 (ㄨㄟˊ ㄈㄚˇ ㄒㄧㄥˊ ㄨㄟˊ)
an unlawful act

違反 (ㄨㄟˊ ㄈㄢˇ)
to contradict; to disregard (the rules, etc.); to violate; to run counter to: 你違反交通規則. You violated traffic regulations.

違犯 (ㄨㄟˊ ㄈㄢˋ)
to violate (a rule or law): 我並沒有違犯法律. I didn't violate the law.

違理 (ㄨㄟˊ ㄌㄧˇ)
to defy good reasoning; unreasonable

違禮 (ㄨㄟˊ ㄌㄧˇ)
to disregard proper rules of behavior or conduct; to go against accepted etiquette

違例 (ㄨㄟˊ ㄌㄧˋ)
contrary to precedents or practices

違令 (ㄨㄟˊ ㄌㄧㄥˋ)
to disobey orders

違規 (ㄨㄟˊ ㄍㄨㄟ)
to be against regulations: 他違規停車. His parking was against regulations.

違抗 (ㄨㄟˊ ㄎㄤˋ)
to defy and oppose; to disobey: 小孩不應違抗他的父母. No child should ever defy his parents.

違命令 (ㄨㄟˊ ㄇㄧㄥˋ ㄌㄧㄥˋ)
to disobey orders

違和 (ㄨㄟˊ ㄏㄜˊ)
to be indisposed; ill (a polite expression)

違禁 (ㄨㄟˊ ㄐㄧㄣˋ)
to defy a prohibition

違禁品 (ㄨㄟˊ ㄐㄧㄣˋ ㄆㄧㄣˇ) or 違禁物品 (ㄨㄟˊ ㄐㄧㄣˋ ㄨˋ ㄆㄧㄣˇ)
forbidden goods and articles; goods prohibited by law from being imported or exported

違警 (ㄨㄟˊ ㄐㄧㄥˇ)
to break a police regulation; a breach of police regulations; violation of police regulations

違警罰法 (ㄨㄟˊ ㄐㄧㄥˇ ㄈㄚˊ ㄈㄚˇ)
The Law for the Punishment of Police Offenses

違警行為 (ㄨㄟˊ ㄐㄧㄥˇ ㄒㄧㄥˊ ㄨㄟˊ)
a police offense

違憲 (ㄨㄟˊ ㄒㄧㄢˋ)
unconstitutional; violation of the Constitution; to violate the Constitution

違心之論 (ㄨㄟˊ ㄒㄧㄣ ㄓ ㄌㄨㄣˋ)
insincere utterances, comments

違章建築 (ㄨㄟˊ ㄓㄤ ㄐㄧㄢˋ ㄓㄨˊ) or (ㄨㄟˊ ㄓㄤ)
buildings erected without license or against the provisions of the building code

違失 (ㄨㄟˊ ㄕ)

faults; errors; misconduct: 他因違失而被開除。 She was dismissed because of misconduct.

遜擬(ㄒㄩㄣ ㄋㄧˇ)
defying (orders) and going against (traditions or customs)

遜拗(ㄒㄩㄣ ㄠˋ)
to defy; to disobey; defiance; disobedience: 恕我違拗。 Pardon me for my defying you.

遜貳(ㄒㄩㄣ ㄦˋ)
to harbor disloyalty

遜言(ㄒㄩㄣ ㄧㄢˊ)
① to be on bad terms as a result of dispute ② unreasonable talk; nonsense

遜忤(ㄒㄩㄣ ㄨˇ)
disobedient and unruly

遜誤(ㄒㄩㄣ ㄨˋ)
to disobey orders and cause delay

遜約(ㄒㄩㄣ ㄩㄝ)
a breach of contract; to break a contract or agreement

遜約金(ㄒㄩㄣ ㄩㄝ ㄐㄧㄣ)
a forfeit or penalty (imposed on for a breach of contract or agreement)

十畫

【遜】 6132

ㄒㄩㄣˋ shiunn xùn
(又讀 ㄙㄨㄣˋ suenn sùn)

respectful and compliant; obedient
to bow; resigning; to surrender; to abdicate; yielding
humble; modest
not as good as; inferior to
a Chinese family name

遜(ㄒㄩㄣˋ ㄧㄤ̄)
① humble and resigning ② to shirk; to shun; to be cowardly

遜國(ㄒㄩㄣˋ ㄍㄨㄛˊ)
to surrender the reign of a state to another; to abdicate

遜謝(ㄒㄩㄣˋ ㄒㄧㄝˋ)
to decline humbly and modestly

遜順(ㄒㄩㄣˋ ㄕㄨㄣˋ)
respectfully obedient; hum-

ble and yielding

遜讓(ㄒㄩㄣˋ ㄖㄤˋ)
to surrender (a position) to another; to yield

遜色(ㄒㄩㄣˋ ㄙㄜˋ)
inferior to; not as good as: 這布料較眞絲遜色。 This cloth is inferior to real silk.

遜位(ㄒㄩㄣˋ ㄨㄟˋ)
to abdicate; abdication

遜王(ㄒㄩㄣˋ ㄨㄤˊ)
an abdicated king

【遘】 6133
《ㄡˋ gow gòu
to meet; to come across; to encounter

遘閔(《ㄡˋ ㄇㄧㄣ̌)
① to meet with distress; to suffer malicious accusations from hidden enemies ② to suffer bereavement of a parent or parents

遘患(《ㄡˋ ㄏㄨㄢˋ)
to meet with misfortune or bad luck; to meet with trouble

【遙】 6134
ㄧㄠˊ yau yáo
distant; far; remote

遙臨(ㄧㄠˊ ㄌㄧㄣˊ)
to approach from afar

遙領(ㄧㄠˊ ㄌㄧㄥˇ)
to accept a position far away on a concurrent basis without attending to the day-to-day operations of that office in person

遙控(ㄧㄠˊ ㄎㄨㄥˋ)
remote control; telecontrol

遙控飛機(ㄧㄠˊ ㄎㄨㄥˋ ㄈㄟ ㄐㄧ)
a remote control aircraft; a telecontrolled airplane

遙控無人機(ㄧㄠˊ ㄎㄨㄥˋ ㄨˊ ㄖㄣˊ ㄐㄧ)
remotely piloted vehicle (RPV)

遙祭(ㄧㄠˊ ㄐㄧˋ)
to offer sacrifice to the dead whose remains are buried far away

遙見(ㄧㄠˊ ㄐㄧㄢˋ)
to see at a distance

遙夜(ㄧㄠˊ ㄧㄝˋ)
a long night

遙遙領先(ㄧㄠˊ ㄧㄠˊ ㄌㄧㄥˇ ㄒㄧㄢ)
to be far ahead; to enjoy a

commanding lead

遙遙相對(ㄧㄠˊ ㄧㄠˊ ㄒㄧㄤ ㄉㄨㄟˋ)
facing one another at a distance: 他們倆遙遙相對。 They faced each other across a great distance.

遙遙無期(ㄧㄠˊ ㄧㄠˊ ㄨˊ ㄑㄧˊ)
in the indefinite future

遙望(ㄧㄠˊ ㄨㄤˋ)
to take a distant look; to look at a distant place

遙遠(ㄧㄠˊ ㄩㄢˇ)
far and remote: 這趟途遙遠且難行。 The journey was long and difficult.

【遛】 6135
1. ㄌㄧㄡˊ liou liú
to hang around ; to linger at a place

【遛】 6135
2. ㄌㄧㄡˋ liow liù
to stroll; to walk slowly; to roam: 我想出去遛遛。 I want to go for a stroll.

遛馬(ㄌㄧㄡˋ ㄇㄚˇ)
to walk a horse

遛達(ㄌㄧㄡˋ ㄉㄚˊ)
to take a walk; to stroll as an exercise 亦作「溜達」

遛彎(ㄌㄧㄡˋ ㄨㄢ)
to take a walk

遛彎兒(ㄌㄧㄡˋ ㄨㄢㄦ)
to take a walk; to stroll

【遴】 6136
ㄌㄧㄣˊ tah ㄌㄧˊ
numerous; many; a large number of

【遞】 6137
ㄉㄧˋ dih dì
1. to forward; to transmit; to hand or pass over to: 請把報紙遞給我。 Hand me the paper, please.
2. to substitute; to alternate

遞補(ㄉㄧˋ ㄅㄨˇ)
to fill a vacancy: 空缺已遞補了。 The vacancy has already been filled.

遞代(ㄉㄧˋ ㄉㄞˋ)
to substitute for each other; to take the place of each other

遞給(ㄉㄧˋ ㄍㄟˇ)
to hand over; to pass on: 請把牛油遞給我。 Pass (me) the butter, please.

遞過來(ㄉㄧˋ ㄍㄨㄛˋ ㄌㄞˊ)
to pass (it) over here: 請把

（辵

部）

胡椒遞過來。Pass the pepper over here, please.

遞過去（ㄉ一 ㄍㄨㄛˋ ㄑㄩˋ）
to pass (it) over there

遞加（ㄉ一 ㄐ一Y）
progressive increase; to increase gradually

遞解（ㄉ一 ㄐ一ㄝˇ）
to escort a prisoner over a long distance while the guards are changed at each stop

遞解出境（ㄉ一ㄐ一ㄝˇ ㄔㄨ ㄐ一ㄥˋ）
to deport; deportation

遞交（ㄉ一 ㄐ一ㄠ）
to hand over; to deliver

遞減（ㄉ一 ㄐ一ㄢˇ）
to decrease or reduce progressively

遞進（ㄉ一 ㄐ一ㄣˋ）
to go forward one by one

遞降（ㄉ一 ㄐ一ㄤˋ）
to decrease or reduce gradually; progressive decrease

遞降函數（ㄉ一ㄐ一ㄤˋ ㄏㄢˊ ㄕㄨˋ）
(mathematics) a descending function

遞信（ㄉ一 ㄒ一ㄣˋ）
to deliver a letter

遞傳（ㄉ一 ㄔㄨㄢˊ）
to hand over; to pass on

遞上（ㄉ一 ㄕㄤˋ）
to forward; to present

遞昇（ㄉ一 ㄕㄥ）
to rise or increase progressively

遞昇函數（ㄉ一 ㄕㄥ ㄏㄢˊ ㄕㄨˋ）
(mathematics) an ascending function

遞增（ㄉ一 ㄗㄥ）
to increase progressively: 汽車的數量在迅速遞增中。The number of cars is increasing rapidly.

遞送（ㄉ一 ㄙㄨㄥˋ）
to deliver (a letter, etc.): 郵差是遞送信件和郵包的人。A postman is a man who delivers letters and parcels.

遞眼色（ㄉ一 一ㄢˇ ㄙㄜˋ）
to give a signal with the eyes; to signal with the eyes; to tip somebody the wink: 我向她遞眼色。I tipped her the wink.

【遠】 6138
1. ㄩㄢˇ yeuan yuan

1. far; distant; remote: 石門水庫離這裏有多遠？ How far is the Shih-men Reservoir from here?

2. deep; profound

3. to keep at a distance; to keep away

遠播（ㄩㄢˇ ㄅㄛ）
to spread far and wide (as fame, etc.)

遠避（ㄩㄢˇ ㄅ一ˋ）
to keep far away from; to keep at a distance

遠別（ㄩㄢˇ ㄅ一ㄝˊ）
①to separate for a journey to a distant land ②to part for a long time

遠謀（ㄩㄢˇ ㄇㄡˊ）
to plan far ahead

遠方（ㄩㄢˇ ㄈㄤ）
a distant place; remote places

遠房（ㄩㄢˇ ㄈㄤˊ）
related through remote ancestry; distantly related: 他是我的遠房親戚。He is my distant relative.

遠大（ㄩㄢˇ ㄉㄚˋ）
very promising (person, etc.); (to look) far ahead; not to be limited or confined by the present

遠道（ㄩㄢˇ ㄉㄠˋ）or 遠路（ㄩㄢˇ ㄌㄨˋ）
faraway; distant; afar: 他遠道而來。He came a long way.

遠地點（ㄩㄢˇ ㄉ一ˋ ㄉ一ㄢˇ）
(astronomy) an apogee

遠遁（ㄩㄢˇ ㄉㄨㄣˋ）
to escape to a faraway place; to flee to distant places

遠東（ㄩㄢˇ ㄉㄨㄥ）
the Far East

遠眺（ㄩㄢˇ ㄊ一ㄠˋ）
to take a distant look; to view distant places: 他遠眺海洋。He took a distant view of the ocean.

遠圖（ㄩㄢˇ ㄊㄨˊ）
to plan far ahead; a plan for the future

遠念（ㄩㄢˇ ㄋ一ㄢˋ）
to show concern for a dear one during separation

遠來的和向會念經（ㄩㄢˇ ㄌㄞˊ ˙ㄉㄜ ㄏㄜˊ ˙ㄕㄤ ㄏㄨㄟˋ ㄋ一ㄢˋ ㄐ一ㄥ）
(literally) Buddhist monks

who come from afar are always better at reciting the scriptures.—(used sarcastically) Persons who come from distant lands are always better than local talents.

遠離（ㄩㄢˇ ㄌ一ˊ）
①to depart for a distant place ②to keep away at great distance

遠離塵囂（ㄩㄢˇ ㄌ一ˊ ㄔㄣˊ ㄒ一ㄠ）
far from the madding crowd

遠慮（ㄩㄢˇ ㄌㄩˋ）
to worry and plan far ahead; advance planning

遠略（ㄩㄢˇ ㄌㄩㄝˋ）
①a great plan or strategy for the future ②to accomplish great achievements in a distant place

遠隔（ㄩㄢˇ ㄍㄜˊ）
far; remote; distant (in places or time)

遠古（ㄩㄢˇ ㄍㄨˇ）
ancient times; remote antiquity

遠客（ㄩㄢˇ ㄎㄜˋ）
persons coming from a distant place; a stranger; traveler; a visitor or guest from a distant place

遠航（ㄩㄢˇ ㄏㄤˊ）
to sail to distant places

遠嫁（ㄩㄢˇ ㄐ一ㄚˋ）
(said of a girl) to marry a man who lives in a distant place

遠交近攻（ㄩㄢˇ ㄐ一ㄠ ㄐ一ㄣˋ ㄍㄨㄥ）
to make friends with distant countries and attack the neighboring ones (a strategem adopted by the state of Chin during the Epoch of Warring States）或 Make war on that which is near and cultivate friendship with that which is remote.

遠見（ㄩㄢˇ ㄐ一ㄢˋ）
foresight; a farsighted view; prescience

遠近（ㄩㄢˇ ㄐ一ㄣˋ）
①far and near; remote and close (relatives, etc.) ②distance

遠景（ㄩㄢˇ ㄐ一ㄥˇ）
①a vista; a distant view;

long-range perspective ②
(movies) a long shot

鏡(ㄩㄢˇㄐㄧㄥˋ)
a telescope

期(ㄩㄢˇㄑㄧ)
at a specified future date;
forward

親(ㄩㄢˇㄑㄧㄣ)
① distant relatives ② relatives who live far away

遠親不如近鄰(ㄩㄢˇㄑㄧㄣㄅㄨˋㄖㄨˊㄐㄧㄣˋㄌㄧㄣˊ)
Distant relatives (or relatives who live in a distant place) are not as helpful as close neighbors. 常言說，遠親不如近鄰。As the saying goes, "Neighbors are dearer than distant relatives."

心力(ㄒㄧㄣㄌㄧˋ)
centrifugal force 亦作「離心力」

心花序(ㄒㄧㄣㄏㄨㄚㄒㄩˋ)
centrifugal inflorescence

行(ㄒㄧㄥˊ)
to travel to a distant place;
a journey to a distant place:
他遠行在即。He will take a
long journey at once.

支(ㄓ)
a remote branch of one's relatives

志(ㄓˋ)
①(a medical herb) polygala
②great ambition

征(ㄓㄥ)
to do battle in a distant
land; an expedition

征軍(ㄓㄥㄐㄩㄣ)
an expeditionary force

矚(ㄓㄨˇ)
to look far ahead; to take a
look at faraway places

臣(ㄔㄣˊ)
①officials who had very
remote connection with the
capital or throne ②officials
from distant districts

程(ㄔㄥˊ)
long range

處(ㄔㄨˋ)
distant; distant places; located far away: 遠光由遠處射
來。The light came from
afar.

識(ㄕˋ)
farsightedness (as a product

of wisdom); forward-looking

遠視(ㄩㄢˇㄕˋ)
① farsightedness (as a physical defect); hypermetropia
② to look from a distance

遠視眼(ㄩㄢˇㄕˋㄧㄢˇ)
farsighted (in eye vision);
hypermetropia; hyperopia

遠視眼鏡(ㄩㄢˇㄕˋㄧㄢˇㄐㄧㄥˋ)
spectacles for long sight

遠射(ㄩㄢˇㄕㄜˋ)
①to fire over a long range
②(ball games) a long shot

遠涉重洋(ㄩㄢˇㄕㄜˋㄔㄨㄥˊㄧㄤˊ)
to cross many seas—to go
abroad

遠山近水(ㄩㄢˇㄕㄢㄐㄧㄣˋㄕㄨㄟˇ)
(literally) the faraway
mountains and the nearby
waters—beautiful scenery

遠水不救近火(ㄩㄢˇㄕㄨㄟˇㄅㄨˋㄐㄧㄡˋㄐㄧㄣˋㄏㄨㄛˇ)
Water from afar cannot
quench a nearby fire. 或 Distant water cannot quench a
fire nearby.

遠日點(ㄩㄢˇㄖˋㄉㄧㄢˇ)
(astronomy) aphelion

遠走高飛(ㄩㄢˇㄗㄡˇㄍㄠㄈㄟ)
to go (or flee) far away

遠足(ㄩㄢˇㄗㄨˊ)
an excursion; an outing: 我
們星期天全班到日月潭去遠足。Our
class went on an excursion
to the Sun Moon Lake.

遠族(ㄩㄢˇㄗㄨˊ)
a remote clan; one's distant
relatives

遠祖(ㄩㄢˇㄗㄨˇ)
one's distant ancestors

遠裔(ㄩㄢˇㄧˋ)
distant descendants 亦作「遠胄」

遊(ㄩㄢˇㄧㄡˊ)
to travel far away

遠因(ㄩㄢˇㄧㄣ)
remote causes (of a war,
etc.)

遠揚(ㄩㄢˇㄧㄤˊ)
(said of fame) to be known
far and wide

遠颺(ㄩㄢˇㄧㄤˊ)
to escape or flee far away

遠洋(ㄩㄢˇㄧㄤˊ)
①an ocean ②of the open
sea beyond the littoral zone;

oceanic

遠洋航行(ㄩㄢˇㄧㄤˊㄏㄤˊㄒㄧㄥˊ)
an oceangoing voyage

遠洋貨輪(ㄩㄢˇㄧㄤˊㄏㄨㄛˋㄌㄨㄣˊ)
an oceangoing freighter

遠洋漁業(ㄩㄢˇㄧㄤˊㄩˊㄧㄝˋ)
deep-sea fishery; pelagic
fishery

遠味(ㄩㄢˇㄨㄟˋ)
rare and delicious foods
from distant places

遠遠兒(ㄩㄢˇㄩㄢˇㄦ)
from afar; a great distance
away

【遠】6138
2. ㄩㄢˋ yuann yuàn
to keep at a distance; to
keep away from; to avoid;
to shun

遠庖廚(ㄩㄢˋㄆㄠˊㄔㄨˊ)
to keep away from the
kitchen (said of gentlemen)

遠小人(ㄩㄢˋㄒㄧㄠˇㄖㄣˊ)
to keep away from mean
persons

【溯】6139
(溯) ㄙㄨˋ suh sù
1. to trace back to a source
2. to go against a stream

溯游(ㄙㄨˋㄧㄡˊ)
to go down the stream; to go
downstream 亦作「溯游」or「泝
游」

【遢】6140
ㄊㄚˋ tah tà
untidy; slipshod; careless or
negligent

【遣】6141
ㄑㄧㄢˇ chean qiǎn
1. to dispatch; to send: 誰遣你
到我這裏來的? Who sent you
to me?
2. to kill (time); to forget
(one's sorrow); to divert
3. to banish; to drive away
4. to release

遣悶(ㄑㄧㄢˇㄇㄣˋ)
to drive away melancholy;
to kill time

遣返(ㄑㄧㄢˇㄈㄢˇ)
to send back; to send home;
to deport; to repatriate;
repatriation

遣歸(ㄑㄧㄢˇㄍㄨㄟ)
to send (a prisoner) home;
to repatriate

遣懷(ㄑㄧㄢˇㄏㄨㄞˊ)
to dispel one's sorrow in

〔走部〕

【走部】

writing on the spur of the moment

遣仆(くㄧㄢ ㄆㄨˊ)
to send a servant on an errand

遣將(くㄧㄢ ㄐㄧㄤˋ)
to send generals or officers (to a battle, etc.)

遣刑(くㄧㄢ ㄒㄧㄥˊ)
banishment or exile (as a form of punishment in the Ching Dynasty)

遣興(くㄧㄢ ㄒㄧㄥˋ)
to dispel one's sad thoughts in writing on the spur of the moment 參看「遣懷」

遣使(くㄧㄢ ㄕˇ)
to dispatch or send an envoy

遣戍(くㄧㄢ ㄕㄨˋ)
to exile or banish prisoners to the frontier

遣詞造句(くㄧㄢ ㄘˊ ㄗㄠˋ ㄐㄩˋ)
the choice of words and building of sentences

遣散(くㄧㄢ ㄙㄢˋ)
to disband; to dissolve and send away; to lay off (employees)

遣散費(くㄧㄢ ㄙㄢˋ ㄈㄟˋ)
severance pay

遣送(くㄧㄢ ㄙㄨㄥˋ)
to send away; to deport

遣憂(くㄧㄢ ㄧㄡ)
to dispel sadness

十一畫

【遭】 6142
　ㄗㄠ tzau zāo
1. to meet with; to incur; to be victimized; to suffer: 他遭了幾次挫折。 He met with several setbacks.
2. times of binding or turning around, as with a rope
3. a time; a turn

遭變(ㄗㄠ ㄅㄧㄢˋ)
to have an accident; to be hit by a great misfortune

遭逢(ㄗㄠ ㄈㄥˊ)
①to meet with: 他的家道逢不幸。 His family met with misfortune. ②vicissitudes in one's life

遭到(ㄗㄠ ㄉㄠˋ)
to suffer; to meet with; to

encounter

遭難(ㄗㄠ ㄋㄢˊ)
to meet with difficulty, misfortune, or death

遭害(ㄗㄠ ㄏㄞˋ)
to be murdered or assassinated

遭際(ㄗㄠ ㄐㄧˋ)
one's lot in life; what one has experienced in life

遭家不造(ㄗㄠ ㄐㄧㄚ ㄅㄨˋ ㄗㄠˋ)
to be bereaved of a parent or parents

遭�близ(ㄗㄠ ㄐㄧㄝˋ)
to meet with disaster

遭受(ㄗㄠ ㄕㄡˋ)
to incur (losses, etc.); to be subjected to: 無禮的行爲使自己遭受同樣的對待。 Rudeness subjects one to retorts in kind.

遭災(ㄗㄠ ㄗㄞ)
to encounter disaster

遭殃(ㄗㄠ ㄧㄤ)
to meet with misfortune or disaster

遭瘟(ㄗㄠ ㄨㄣ)
to meet with disaster, calamity or misfortune

遭遇(ㄗㄠ ㄩˋ)
①to meet with; to encounter: 游擊隊與敵人遭遇了。 The guerilla encountered the enemy. ②vicissitudes in one's life; what one has encountered in life

遭遇戰(ㄗㄠ ㄩˋ ㄓㄢˋ)
an encounter (between opposing military forces)

【遨】 6143
　ㄠ aur áo
to travel for pleasure; to ramble

遨嬉(ㄠ ㄒㄧ)
to ramble; to travel for pleasure; to make merry

遨遊(ㄠ ㄧㄡˊ)
to ramble; to travel: 他總是夢想遨遊太空。 He always dreams of traveling through space.

【適】 6144
1. ㄕˋ shyh shì
1. to go; to arrive at; to reach
2. just right; exactly; appropriate; fit; just
3. comfortable; at ease with

oneself: 我感到不適。 I didn't feel comfortable.
4. (said of a girl) to marry
5. to follow; to be faithful to 我無所適從。 I don't know what course to follow.
6. only
7. by chance; accidentally
8. just now

適逢其會(ㄕˋ ㄈㄥˊ ㄑㄧˊ ㄏㄨㄟˋ)
to happen to be present at the right moment

適得其反(ㄕˋ ㄉㄜˊ ㄑㄧˊ ㄈㄢˇ)
to get exactly the opposite

適當(ㄕˋ ㄉㄤ)
proper; appropriate; fit: 晚上是睡眠的適當時間。 Night is the proper time to sleep.

適度(ㄕˋ ㄉㄨˋ)
appropriate; within limits; a moderate degree: 適度的運動有益健康。 A moderate amount of physical exercise will benefit one's health.

適度人口(ㄕˋ ㄉㄨˋ ㄖㄣˊ ㄎㄡˇ)
optimal population

適來(ㄕˋ ㄌㄞˊ)
just now

適齡(ㄕˋ ㄌㄧㄥˊ)
suitable or right age; the required age (for schooling, military service, etc.)

適可而止(ㄕˋ ㄎㄜˇ ㄦˊ ㄓˇ)
to stop at the right moment or point; to exercise moderation or restraint

適口(ㄕˋ ㄎㄡˇ)
pleasant to the palate; tasty

適合(ㄕˋ ㄏㄜˊ)
suitable or suitable for; fit; to suit

適值(ㄕˋ ㄓˊ)
to happen exactly when; to incidentally; to happen by coincidence

適者生存(ㄕˋ ㄓㄜˇ ㄕㄥ ㄘㄨㄣˊ)
the survival of the fittest

適中(ㄕˋ ㄓㄨㄥ)
proper; adequate; appropriate; propriety; just right

適時(ㄕˋ ㄕˊ)
at the right time; in the nick of time

適然(ㄕˋ ㄖㄢˊ)
①accidentally; by chance ②a matter of course

適人(ㄕˋ ㄖㄣˊ)

(said of a woman) to marry

織 (ㄕㄞ)
just now

從 (ㄕ ㄘㄨㄥ)
to follow; to head in a direction

宜 (ㄕ ㄧˊ)
fit; suitable; proper

意 (ㄕ ㄧˋ)
comfortable; agreeable; as desired

有 (ㄕ ㄧㄡˇ)
there happened to be; it just happened that; coincidentally; to happen by coincidence

因 (ㄕ ㄧㄣ)
because just now

應 (ㄕ ㄧㄥ)
to adapt; adaptation (to environment, etc.); to adjust; to make an adjustment: 你能適應新的工作嗎? Can you adapt yourself to a new job?
應環境 (ㄕ ㄧㄥ ㄏㄨㄢˊ ㄐㄧㄥˋ)
adaptation to environment; to adapt to circumstances
應性 (ㄕ ㄧㄥ ㄒㄧㄥˋ)
adaptability

於 (ㄕ ㄩˊ)
suitable for; fitting for

用 (ㄕ ㄩㄥˋ)
fit or suitable for use; (said of a law, rule, etc.) to apply; applicable

【適】 6144
2. (姓) ㄎㄨㄞˋ dyi dí
legal (wife, as opposed to concubines, etc.); sons born of one's legal wife

【遮】 6145
ㄓㄜ je zhē
1. to hide; to cover; to screen; to shade; to shield; to conceal; to shut out: 雪遮蓋著大地. Snow covered the ground.
2. to intercept; to block

蔽 (ㄓㄜ ㄅㄧˋ)
to cover; to screen

蔽物 (ㄓㄜ ㄅㄧˋ ㄨˋ)
a cover; a shelter

不了 (ㄓㄜ ˙ㄅㄨ ㄌㄧㄠˇ)
cannot be covered or concealed

不住 (ㄓㄜ ˙ㄅㄨ ㄓㄨˋ)
unable to cover up; cannot be concealed

瞞 (ㄓㄜ ㄇㄢˊ)
to hide the truth; to lie in order to conceal the truth

面 (ㄓㄜ ㄇㄧㄢˋ)
to cover the face

風 (ㄓㄜ ㄈㄥ)
to shield from wind

擋 (ㄓㄜ ㄉㄤˇ)
to fend

斷 (ㄓㄜ ㄉㄨㄢˋ)
to block from view; to block off; to obstruct

頭蓋面 (ㄓㄜ ㄊㄡˊ 《ㄞˋ ㄇㄧㄢˋ)
(literally) to cover one's head and face—to act stealthily; to be bashful

攔 (ㄓㄜ ㄌㄢˊ)
to fend off; to cover or screen

蓋 (ㄓㄜ ㄍㄞˋ)
to cover; to cover up: 你的謊言遮蓋不住事實的. Your lie cannot cover up the fact.

光 (ㄓㄜ ㄍㄨㄤ)
to block light

擊 (ㄓㄜ ㄐㄧ)
to intercept; to ambush

架 (ㄓㄜ ㄐㄧㄚˋ)
to defend; to fend off

截 (ㄓㄜ ㄐㄧㄝˊ)
to stop; to block; to shut off

羞 (ㄓㄜ ㄒㄧㄡ)
to hush up a scandal; to cover up one's embarrassment

遮羞費 (ㄓㄜ ㄒㄧㄡ ㄈㄟˋ)
a compensation paid by a man to a woman or her family for violating her chastity with or without her consent

遮羞臉 (ㄓㄜ ㄒㄧㄡ ㄌㄧㄢˇ)
(a polite expression in sending a gift) a token of one's gratitude

住 (ㄓㄜ ㄓㄨˋ)
to cover; to block; to obstruct

醜 (ㄓㄜ ㄔㄡˇ)
① to hide one's shame ② 亦作「遮羞臉」

掩 (ㄓㄜ ㄧㄢˇ)
① to hide; to cover up; to conceal: 不要遮掩你的錯誤. Don't try to cover your mistakes up. ② to cover; to envelop: 太陽被雲遮掩著. The sun was enveloped in clouds.

蔭 (ㄓㄜ ㄧㄣˋ)
to shade

陽 (ㄓㄜ ㄧㄤˊ)
to protect from the sunlight

遮陽傘 (ㄓㄜ ㄧㄤˊ ㄙㄢˇ)
a parasol

【遯】 6146
ㄉㄨㄣˋ duenn dùn
1. to escape; to run off
2. to cheat

遯世 (ㄉㄨㄣˋ ㄕˋ)
to escape from the world —to retire

十二畫

【運】 6147
1. ㄔ chyr chí
1. late: 現在去太遲了. It's too late to go now.
2. slow; dilatory; tardy
3. to delay
4. (said of a person) dull; stupid
5. a Chinese family name

遲暮 (ㄔ ㄇㄨˋ)
① to be advanced in years
② slowly and unhurriedly

遲到 (ㄔ ㄉㄠˋ)
to come or arrive late; to be late: 他去年上學遲到四次. He was late for school four times last year.

遲鈍 (ㄔ ㄉㄨㄣˋ)
①stupid ②awkward; clumsy; ponderous; slow (in thought or action): 他反應遲鈍. He is slow in reacting.

遲留 (ㄔ ㄌㄧㄡˊ)
to linger on; to stay

遲緩 (ㄔ ㄏㄨㄢˇ) or 遲慢 (ㄔ ㄇㄢˋ)
slow; tardy; tardiness

遲滯 (ㄔ ㄓˋ)
① slow; dilatory; sluggish ② late; behindhand

遲遲不進 (ㄔ ㄔ ˙ㄅㄨ ㄐㄧㄣˋ)
to hesitate; to be reluctant to advance; to hesitate to push forward

遲早 (ㄔ ㄗㄠˇ)
sooner or later: 你遲早會後悔. You will repent it sooner or later.

遲疑 (ㄔ ㄧˊ)
to hesitate; hesitancy

遲疑不決 (ㄔ ㄧˊ ˙ㄅㄨ ㄐㄩㄝˊ)

【走部】

〔走部〕

cannot make up one's mind; to hesitate to make a decision; to be irresolute: 我對於接受那職位還疑不決。 I hesitated about taking the position.

遲延(彳ㄧㄢˊ)
to delay; to procrastinate; delay

遲誤(彳ㄨˋ)
to spoil a matter because of procrastination: 此事不得遲誤。 This matter admitted of no procrastination.

【遲】 6147
2. 业 jyh zhì
to wait

遲明(彳ㄇㄧㄥˊ)
dawn; daybreak 亦作「遲旦」

【遴】 6148
ㄌㄧㄣˊ lin lín
to choose or select carefully

遴派(ㄌㄧㄣˊ ㄆㄞˋ)
to dispatch or appoint a person after careful selection

遴集(ㄌㄧㄣˊ ㄐㄧˊ)
to gather together; to flock together

遴選(ㄌㄧㄣˊ ㄒㄩㄢˇ)or遴柬(ㄌㄧㄣˊ ㄐㄧㄢˇ)
to choose or pick (a person); to select

【遵】 6149
ㄗㄨㄣ tzuen zūn
1. to follow: 病人遵醫囑。 The patients follow the doctor's advice.
2. to observe (rules, regulations, etc.); to abide by (laws, etc.): 士兵們遵紀愛民。 Soldiers observed discipline and cherished the people.

遵辦(ㄗㄨㄣ ㄅㄢˋ)or遵照辦理(ㄗㄨㄣ 业ㄠˋ ㄅㄢˋ ㄌㄧˇ)
to execute or manage according to instructions

遵命(ㄗㄨㄣ ㄇㄧㄥˋ)or遵令(ㄗㄨㄣ ㄌㄧㄥˋ)
to obey orders; to observe instructions

遵奉(ㄗㄨㄣ ㄈㄥˋ)
to observe; to obey

遵行(ㄗㄨㄣ ㄒㄧㄥˊ)
to act in accordance with (a principle, etc.); to put into practice (an idea, or a principle)

遵循(ㄗㄨㄣ ㄒㄩㄣˊ)
①to follow; to accord with; to obey; to go by ②to hesitate 亦作「遊巡」

遵旨(ㄗㄨㄣ 业ˇ)
to follow imperial orders or decrees

遵照(ㄗㄨㄣ 业ㄠˋ)
to follow; to observe; to accord with; to obey

遵守(ㄗㄨㄣ ㄕㄡˇ)
to observe; to abide by; to keep (a promise): 人人遵守公共秩序。 Every one observes public order.

遵從(ㄗㄨㄣ ㄘㄨㄥˊ)
to follow; to comply with; to obey (orders, etc.): 學生遵從老師的教導。 Students follow the teacher's advice.

遵依(ㄗㄨㄣ ㄧ)
to follow; to comply with

遵義(ㄗㄨㄣ ㄧˋ)
①to guard or stand up for righteousness or justice ②name of a county in Kweichow Province

遵養時晦(ㄗㄨㄣ ㄧㄤˊ ㄕˊ ㄏㄨㄟˋ)or遵時養晦(ㄗㄨㄣ ㄕˊ ㄧㄤˊ ㄏㄨㄟˋ)
to live in retirement and wait for the right time for a comeback in public life

【遶】 6150
ㄖㄠˋ raw ráo
to surround

【遷】 6151
ㄑㄧㄢ chian qiān
1. to move; to remove: 他家遷往他處。 His family moved to another place.
2. to change: 這件事情已經事過境遷。 This matter is all over, and the situation has changed.
3. (said of officials, etc.) to get transferred
4. to be banished

遷地為良(ㄑㄧㄢ ㄉㄧˋ ㄨㄟˊ ㄌㄧㄤˊ)
It's better to move to another place. 或A change of place is advisable.

遷調(ㄑㄧㄢ ㄉㄧㄠˋ)
to get transferred to another post

遷都(ㄑㄧㄢ ㄉㄨ)
to move the national capital

遷怒(ㄑㄧㄢ ㄋㄨˋ)
①to blame a person for one's own blunder, failure etc. ②to shift or transfer one's anger from one person to another; to vent one's anger on (someone else): 遷怒於他的孩子。 He vented his anger on his child who was not to blame.

遷客(ㄑㄧㄢ ㄎㄜˋ)
an official banished to minor post

遷換(ㄑㄧㄢ ㄏㄨㄢˋ)
to change

遷就(ㄑㄧㄢ ㄐㄧㄡˋ)
to compromise; to meet halfway; to accommodate: 他不能遷就於環境。 He cannot accommodate himself to the circumstances.

遷居(ㄑㄧㄢ ㄐㄩ)
to move into a new residence or to a new place: 他遷居到另一個城市去了。 He moved to another town.

遷徙(ㄑㄧㄢ ㄒㄧˇ)
to move; to remove: 他們遷徙鄉下。 They moved to the country.

遷徙流離(ㄑㄧㄢ ㄒㄧˇ ㄌㄧㄡˊ ㄌㄧˊ)
(said of refugees) homeless and wandering from place to place

遷謫(ㄑㄧㄢ 业ㄜˊ)
to be demoted and banished to distant places; banishment

遷善(ㄑㄧㄢ ㄕㄢˋ)
to reform one's ways

遷善改過(ㄑㄧㄢ ㄕㄢˋ ㄍㄞˇ ㄍㄨㄛˋ)
to change one's evil ways and reform

遷染(ㄑㄧㄢ ㄖㄢˇ)
to be corrupted by evil surroundings

遷移(ㄑㄧㄢ ㄧˊ)
to move (to a new address): 許多農民從農村遷移到城市。 Many farmers moved from rural areas to urban areas.

遷移推理(ㄑㄧㄢ ㄧˊ ㄊㄨㄟ ㄌㄧˇ)
transfereutial inference

遷延(ㄑㄧㄢ ㄧㄢˊ)
to procrastinate; to delay: 他把宴會遷延一個星期。 He delayed the party for a week.

【選】6152
ㄒㄩㄢ sheuan xuǎn
to select; to choose; choice:
慎選你的朋友。Choose your
friend carefully.
to elect; elections

選拔(ㄒㄩㄢ ㄅㄚˊ)
to select; to pick the better
ones from a group of people

選拔賽(ㄒㄩㄢ ㄅㄚˊ ㄙㄞˋ)
a selective trial; a tryout
(for athletes, etc.)

選派(ㄒㄩㄢ ㄆㄞˋ)
to nominate; to designate

選票(ㄒㄩㄢ ㄆㄧㄠˋ)or 選舉票(ㄒㄩㄢ
ㄐㄩˇ ㄆㄧㄠˋ)
a ballot

選美(ㄒㄩㄢ ㄇㄟˇ)
a beauty contest: 他姐姐參加
選美。His sister took part in
a beauty contest.

選美大會(ㄒㄩㄢ ㄇㄟˇ ㄉㄚˋ ㄏㄨㄟˋ)
a beauty pageant

選民(ㄒㄩㄢ ㄇㄧㄣˊ)
the eligible voters among
the citizenry; constituency

選定(ㄒㄩㄢ ㄉㄧㄥˋ)
to decide on a selection

選讀(ㄒㄩㄢ ㄉㄨˊ)
①to take an elective course
in a college ②selected readings: 文學選讀 selected read-
ings in literature

選體(ㄒㄩㄢ ㄊㄧˇ)
the style of poems and
prose, included in the literary collection 昭明文選

選購(ㄒㄩㄢ ㄍㄡˋ)
to select and make purchase

選科(ㄒㄩㄢ ㄎㄜ)or 選修科(ㄒㄩㄢ
ㄒㄧㄡ ㄎㄜ)
an elective course (as distinct from a required
course)

選課(ㄒㄩㄢ ㄎㄜˋ)
to take courses in a college

選課表(ㄒㄩㄢ ㄎㄜˋ ㄅㄧㄠˇ)
a table of elective courses
for the reference of college
students

選礦(ㄒㄩㄢ ㄎㄨㄤˋ)
to separate the usable and
unusable components of mineral or ore by mechanical
means

選集(ㄒㄩㄢ ㄐㄧˊ)
a collection of literary

works

選家(ㄒㄩㄢ ㄐㄧㄚ)
a collector of "eight-legged"
compositions for the reference of participants in the
civil service examination in
former times

選舉(ㄒㄩㄢ ㄐㄩˇ)
to elect; to vote; elections:
人民選他當總統。The people
elected him President.

選舉法(ㄒㄩㄢ ㄐㄩˇ ㄈㄚˇ)
laws governing elections

選舉區(ㄒㄩㄢ ㄐㄩˇ ㄑㄩ)or 選區
(ㄒㄩㄢ ㄑㄩ)
an electoral district; a constituency

選舉權(ㄒㄩㄢ ㄐㄩˇ ㄑㄩㄢˊ)
the right to vote; the elective franchise; suffrage: 他
有選舉權。He has the right
to vote.

選人(ㄒㄩㄢ ㄐㄩˇ ㄖㄣˊ)
a voter

選舉訴訟(ㄒㄩㄢ ㄐㄩˇ ㄙㄨˋ ㄙㄨㄥˋ)
lawsuits pertaining to election

選曲(ㄒㄩㄢ ㄑㄩˇ)
selected songs (or tunes)

選取(ㄒㄩㄢ ㄑㄩˇ)
to select; to choose

選修(ㄒㄩㄢ ㄒㄧㄡ)
to take as an elective
course

選賢舉能(ㄒㄩㄢ ㄒㄧˊ ㄐㄩˇ ㄋㄥˊ)or
選賢與能(ㄒㄩㄢ ㄒㄧˊ ㄩˇ ㄋㄥˊ)
to pick the good and select
the capable for public posts

選學(ㄒㄩㄢ ㄒㄩㄝˊ)
the critical study of 昭明文選

選種(ㄒㄩㄢ ㄓㄨㄥˇ)
seed selection

選中(ㄒㄩㄢ ㄓㄨㄥˋ)
①to pick out (a man) by
choice or competitive examinations ②to be selected in
such examinations

選出(ㄒㄩㄢ ㄔㄨ)
to pick out; to select; to
elect

選侍(ㄒㄩㄢ ㄕˋ)
to select girls as maids in
the imperial palace

選手(ㄒㄩㄢ ㄕㄡˇ)
a member of a sports team
or delegation representing a

school, an area or a country; a contestant

選任(ㄒㄩㄢ ㄖㄣˋ)
to appoint; to designate

選擇(ㄒㄩㄢ ㄗㄜˊ)
a choice; to choose: 我沒有選
擇的餘地。I have no choice at
all.

選擇題(ㄒㄩㄢ ㄗㄜˊ ㄊㄧˊ)
a multiple-choice question

選材(ㄒㄩㄢ ㄘㄞˊ)
to select the right materi-
al(s)

選樣(ㄒㄩㄢ ㄧㄤˋ)
sampling; a sample

選用(ㄒㄩㄢ ㄩㄥˋ)
to select and appoint to a
post

【遹】6153
ㄩˋ yuh yù
1. to follow; to comply with
2. to avoid; to shun
3. to be perverse; to be bad
4. a Chinese family name

【遺】6154
1. ㄧˊ yi yí
1. to lose; lost
2. things lost: 路不拾遺。Peo-
ple do not pick up what
others have left on the roadside.
3. to miss; an omission due to
negligence
4. to forget: 我遺忘了我的帽子。
I've forgotten my hat.
5. to leave over
6. remnants; leftovers
7. to abandon; to desert
8. anything left behind by the
deceased; to bequeath; to
hand down; a legacy
9. to urinate
10. short for nocturnal emission

遺筆(ㄧˊ ㄅㄧˇ)
writings of a deceased person

遺墨(ㄧˊ ㄇㄛˋ)
the calligraphy or paintings
by a dead person

遺民(ㄧˊ ㄇㄧㄣˊ)
①people who refuse to take
official jobs in a new
dynasty ②descendants

遺命(ㄧˊ ㄇㄧㄥˋ)
the injunctions of a dead
person

遺風(ㄧˊ ㄈㄥ)

（辵
部）

〔辵部〕

a custom left by a preceding generation or dynasty: 昔日榮華之遺風消失了。The remains of the former glory disappeared.

遺腹子(ㄧ ㄈㄨˋ ˙ㄗ)
an infant born after the death of its father; a posthumous child

遺大投艱(ㄧ ㄉㄚˋ ㄊㄡˊ ㄐㄧㄢ)
to shoulder a heavy and difficult responsibility

遺毒(ㄧ ㄉㄨˊ)
the evil influence or poison of some old theory, practice, etc.

遺體(ㄧ ㄊㄧˇ)
① the remains (of a deceased person); the corpse: 他的遺體被埋於此。His remains are buried here. ② one's body (handed down by one's parents)

遺尿(ㄧ ㄋㄧㄠˋ)
bed-wetting; the incontinence of urine

遺念(ㄧ ㄋㄧㄢˋ)
souvenirs or things left by a dead person; a legacy

遺老(ㄧ ㄌㄠˇ)
① ministers of the preceding emperor (father of the current emperor) ② ministers of the preceding dynasty ③ old, experienced men in the country

遺漏(ㄧ ㄌㄡˋ)
to omit or miss; an omission; an oversight: 我遺漏了一個字。I left out a word.

遺烈(ㄧ ㄌㄧㄝˋ)
the achievements of forefathers

遺留(ㄧ ㄌㄧㄡˊ)
to leave behind either intentionally or unintentionally: 他遺留下五千鎊。He left £5,000.

遺落(ㄧ ㄌㄨㄛˋ)
① to lose; lost: 我遺落了房門的鑰匙。I've lost the key of the house. ② carefree; indifferent to what's happening around

遺稿(ㄧ ㄍㄠˇ)
manuscripts or writings left behind by a dead person

遺孤(ㄧ ㄍㄨ)
orphans

遺骸(ㄧ ㄏㄞˊ)
one's remains; one's corpse

遺憾(ㄧ ㄏㄢˋ)
to regret; to feel sorry; regrettable: 我很遺憾不能幫助你。I regret that I cannot help you.

遺恨(ㄧ ㄏㄣˋ)
to regret; regret; to feel sorry; regrettable

遺跡(ㄧ ㄐㄧ)
relics; vestiges; traces: 那裡是古城的遺跡。There are vestiges of ancient cities.

遺漏(ㄧ ㄐㄧ)
a mistake; a loophole; a drawback

遺教(ㄧ ㄐㄧㄠˋ)
① exhortation of a dying person ② teachings of a dead person

遺精(ㄧ ㄐㄧㄥ)
nocturnal emission; spermatorrhea

遺棄(ㄧ ㄑㄧˋ)
①(law) to desert, or to fail to support one's legal dependents: 他遺棄他的妻子。He deserted his wife. ②to cast away; to abandon: 我永遠不會遺棄我的朋友。I would never abandon my friends.

遺棄罪(ㄧ ㄑㄧˋ ㄗㄨㄟˋ)
the offense of abandonment

遺下(ㄧ ㄒㄧㄚˋ)
to leave behind: 他遺下一妻六子。He left a wife and six children.

遺像(ㄧ ㄒㄧㄤˋ)
the portrait of a dead person

遺訓(ㄧ ㄒㄩㄣˋ)
instructions or teachings of a dead person

遺缺(ㄧ ㄑㄩㄝ)
①a vacated position ②a position made vacant by the departure or death of the original holder

遺址(ㄧ ㄓˇ)
the old site of some building or a city which no longer exists

遺志(ㄧ ㄓˋ)
the ideal or wish not carried

out before one's death; the behest of a dying person

遺詔(ㄧ ㄓㄠˋ)
instructions or decrees of dying emperor

遺珠(ㄧ ㄓㄨ)
a talented person out of employment

遺囑(ㄧ ㄓㄨˇ)
① the will of a dead person ② instructions of a dying person

遺囑執行人(ㄧ ㄓㄨˇ ㄓˊ ㄒㄧㄥˊ ㄖㄣˊ)
an executor

遺囑人(ㄧ ㄓㄨˇ ㄖㄣˊ)
a testator

遺著(ㄧ ㄓㄨˋ)
a posthumous book

遺臭萬年(ㄧ ㄔㄡˋ ㄨㄢˋ ㄋㄧㄢˊ)
(literally) The stench will persist for 10,000 years.— bad reputation that will be long remembered

遺產(ㄧ ㄔㄢˇ)
① property left behind by deceased person ② a bequest; a legacy

遺產稅(ㄧ ㄔㄢˇ ㄕㄨㄟˋ)
legacy tax; inheritance tax

遺臣(ㄧ ㄔㄣˊ)
surviving officials of a previous dynasty

遺傳(ㄧ ㄔㄨㄢˊ)
to inherit; hereditary; heredity

遺傳病(ㄧ ㄔㄨㄢˊ ㄅㄧㄥˋ)
a hereditary disease

遺傳論(ㄧ ㄔㄨㄢˊ ㄌㄨㄣˋ)
hereditism

遺傳性(ㄧ ㄔㄨㄢˊ ㄒㄧㄥˋ)
heredity; hereditary

遺傳學(ㄧ ㄔㄨㄢˊ ㄒㄩㄝˊ)
genetics

遺失(ㄧ ㄕ)
to lose; lost: 我的汽車鑰匙遺失了。I have lost the keys of my car.

遺失啓事(ㄧ ㄕ ㄑㄧˇ ㄕˋ)
a classified ad announcing the annulment of a lost season ID card, check, etc.

遺失招領(ㄧ ㄕ ㄓㄠ ㄌㄧㄥˇ)
lost and found

遺失通知(ㄧ ㄕ ㄊㄨㄥ ㄓ)
a lost property notice

遺世獨立(ㄧ ㄕˋ ㄉㄨˊ ㄌㄧˋ)

to forget all about worldly affairs

少(ㄕㄠˋ)
youths who stick to old customs; young conservatives

書(ㄕㄨ)
①letters written by a suicide ②ancient books scattered or lost ③manuscripts published posthumously

孀(ㄕㄨㄤ)
a widow

容(ㄖㄨㄥˊ)
①the portrait of a dead person ②remains (of the deceased): 我們瞻仰市長的遺容。We paid our respects to the remains of the mayor.

澤(ㄗㄜˊ)
the benevolence left behind by a dead person

贈(ㄗㄥˋ)
a legacy; bequest; to bequeath

族(ㄗㄨˊ)
survivors of a deceased person's family

著(ㄓㄨˋ)
①a mistake; a wrong move ②a plan left behind by the dead

才(ㄘㄞˊ)
talents who failed in the civil service examinations

俗(ㄙㄨˊ)
an old custom; traditional practices: 這是唐朝的遺俗嗎？Is this the old custom of the Tang Dynasty?

愛(ㄞˋ)
the love or benevolence left behind by a dead person

業(ㄧㄝˋ)
the business or career left behind by one's ancestors

言(ㄧㄢˊ)
instructions, words, etc. of a dying person; a will; (a person's) last words: 老人大死時未留遺言。That old man died without last words.

物(ㄨˋ)
things left behind by a dead person; relics of the deceased; personal belongings of a dead person

忘(ㄨㄤˋ)

to forget; to neglect: 我們不應遺忘了我們的責任。We should not be forgetful of our responsibilities.

【遺】 6154
ㄨㄟˊ wey wéi
1. to send or present as a gift
2. to be left to; to be laid upon
遺書(ㄨㄟˊ ㄕㄨ)
to send a letter

【遼】 6155
ㄌㄧㄠˊ liau liáo
1. distant; far
2. the Liao River in Manchuria
3. the Liao Dynasty (916-1125) founded by the Kitan Tartars in the greater part of northern China

遼北(ㄌㄧㄠˊ ㄅㄟˇ)
①Liaopei, a province in Manchuria ②name of an ancient political division, the northern part of the old Liaoning Province in Northeast China

遼東半島(ㄌㄧㄠˊ ㄉㄨㄥ ㄅㄢˋ ㄉㄠˇ)
the Liaotung Peninsula

遼東灣(ㄌㄧㄠˊ ㄉㄨㄥ ㄨㄢ)
the Liaotung Bay

遼寧(ㄌㄧㄠˊ ㄋㄧㄥˊ)
Liaoning Province

遼遠(ㄌㄧㄠˊ ㄩㄢˇ)
distant

遼闊(ㄌㄧㄠˊ ㄎㄨㄛˋ)
open and spacious

遼隔(ㄌㄧㄠˊ ㄍㄜˊ)
distantly apart

遼闊 or 遼廓(ㄌㄧㄠˊ ㄎㄨㄛˋ)
vast; distant: 沙哈拉沙漠面積遼闊。The Sahara covers a vast area.

遼河(ㄌㄧㄠˊ ㄏㄜˊ)
the Liao River in Manchuria

十三畫

【避】 6156
ㄅㄧˋ bih bì
1. to avoid; to shun; to evade; to hide: 我們盡力避免危險。We try to avoid danger.
2. to prevent; to keep away; to repel

避不見面(ㄅㄧˋ ㄅㄨˋ ㄐㄧㄢˋ ㄇㄧㄢˋ)
to avoid meeting someone

避不作答(ㄅㄧˋ ㄅㄨˋ ㄗㄨㄛˋ ㄉㄚˊ)
to parry a question; to

decline answering a question

避免(ㄅㄧˋ ㄇㄧㄢˇ)
to avoid; to forestall; to prevent something from happening; to avert

避面(ㄅㄧˋ ㄇㄧㄢˋ)
to avoid meeting a person

避風(ㄅㄧˋ ㄈㄥ)
①to lie low; to hide from trouble ②to seek shelter against a strong wind

避災(ㄅㄧˋ ㄗㄞ)
to escape a calamity; to avoid disaster; to take refuge

避難港(ㄅㄧˋ ㄋㄢˋ ㄍㄤˇ)
a harbor or port of refuge; a haven

避難所(ㄅㄧˋ ㄋㄢˋ ㄙㄨㄛˇ)
a refuge; a haven; a sanctuary

避匿(ㄅㄧˋ ㄋㄧˋ)
to lie in hiding; to hide or conceal

避瘧(ㄅㄧˋ ㄩㄝˋ)
to escape from malaria by hiding oneself at someone else's home during the interval of recurrent fevers (a superstitious practice dating back to the Tang Dynasty)

避雷針(ㄅㄧˋ ㄌㄟˊ ㄓㄣ)
a needle gap arrester; a lightning arrester; a lightning rod 亦作「避雷器」

避亂(ㄅㄧˋ ㄌㄨㄢˋ)
to run away from social upheavals; to find shelter against anarchy

避開(ㄅㄧˋ ㄎㄞ)
to get out of the way; to keep away from; to dodge

避坑落井(ㄅㄧˋ ㄎㄥ ㄌㄨㄛˋ ㄐㄧㄥˇ)
(literally) to avoid the pit only to fall into the well —to succeed in escaping one disaster but is caught in the next

避害(ㄅㄧˋ ㄏㄞˋ) or避禍(ㄅㄧˋ ㄏㄨㄛˋ)
to run away from a calamity; to escape disaster

避寒(ㄅㄧˋ ㄏㄢˊ)
to go to a winter resort; to winter; to escape the cold: 他在南方避寒。He wintered in the south.

避諱(ㄅㄧˋ ㄏㄨㄟˋ)

〔辵部〕

【走 部】

①(an old Chinese custom) to avoid mentioning the emperor or one's ancestors by name or using any character of it in writing except the family name ② to evade

避秦
(literally) to seek refuge from the tyranny of Chin—to find a shelter in time of unrest

避席
(in ancient times) to stand up from the floor mattress to show respect

避邪(ㄅㄧˋ ㄒㄧㄝˊ)
to avoid evil spirits or influences

避嫌(ㄅㄧˋ ㄒㄧㄢˊ)
to avoid suspicion

避賢讓路(ㄅㄧˋ ㄒㄧㄢˊ ㄖㄤˋ ㄌㄨˋ)
(literally) to make room for the virtuous—to resign from a public post

避債(ㄅㄧˋ ㄓㄞˋ)
to avoid creditors

避重就輕(ㄅㄧˋ ㄓㄨㄥˋ ㄐㄧㄡˋ ㄑㄧㄥ)
①to take the easier way out; to choose the easier of the two alternatives ② to dwell on the minor points but avoid touching the core of a matter

避世
to retire or withdraw from worldly affairs—to live as a recluse

避暑(ㄅㄧˋ ㄕㄨˇ)
to run away from summer heat; to take a summer vacation

避暑勝地(ㄅㄧˋ ㄕㄨˇ ㄕㄥˋ ㄉㄧˋ)
a summer resort

避稅(ㄅㄧˋ ㄕㄨㄟˋ)
to evade a tax or duty

避姙(ㄅㄧˋ ㄖㄣˋ)or 避孕(ㄅㄧˋ ㄩㄣˋ)
contraception; to avoid pregnancy

避疫(ㄅㄧˋ ㄧˋ)
to escape from epidemics

避役(ㄅㄧˋ ㄧˋ)
a chameleon (a lizard-like reptile)

避雨(ㄅㄧˋ ㄩˇ)
to find shelter against rain: 我們在一個穀倉裡避雨。We found shelter against rain in

a barn.

避孕套(ㄅㄧˋ ㄩㄣˋ ㄊㄠˋ)
a condom

避孕器(ㄅㄧˋ ㄩㄣˋ ㄑㄧˋ)
contraceptive devices

避孕藥(ㄅㄧˋ ㄩㄣˋ ㄧㄠˋ)
contraceptives

避孕藥丸(ㄅㄧˋ ㄩㄣˋ ㄧㄠˋ ㄨㄢˊ)
the pill

【遽】 6157 ㄐㄩˋ jiuh jù
1. suddenly; abruptly; hastily; hurriedly: 別遽下結論。Don't pass judgment hastily.
2. scared; frightened; agitated; agitation
3. a stagecoach

遽步(ㄐㄩˋ ㄅㄨˋ)
to walk hastily or hurriedly

遽返道山(ㄐㄩˋ ㄈㄢˇ ㄉㄠˋ ㄕㄢ)
to die suddenly or unexpectedly (an expression used in condolences)

遽然(ㄐㄩˋ ㄖㄢˊ)
suddenly: 那頭牛遽然地向他衝來。Suddenly the bull rushed at him.

遽色(ㄐㄩˋ ㄙㄜˋ)
a hurried look

遽爾(ㄐㄩˋ ㄦˇ)
suddenly; unexpectedly

【邀】 6158 ㄧㄠ iau yāo
1. to invite; to ask; to request
2. to intercept
3. (now rarely) to weigh or measure

邀買人心(ㄧㄠ ㄇㄞˇ ㄖㄣˊ ㄒㄧㄣ)
to dispense favors in order to win popularity

邀天之倖(ㄧㄠ ㄊㄧㄢ ㄓ ㄒㄧㄥˋ)
to be very lucky or fortunate

邀功(ㄧㄠ ㄍㄨㄥ)
to take credit for the deeds achieved by someone else

邀功圖賞(ㄧㄠ ㄍㄨㄥ ㄊㄨˊ ㄕㄤˇ)
to strive for achievements for the sake of a reward; to seek credit for something done

邀喝 or 吆喝(ㄧㄠ・ㄏㄜ)
to warn people to get out the way when a ranking official of former days was passing by

邀集(ㄧㄠ ㄐㄧˊ)

to invite to a gathering

邀擊(ㄧㄠ ㄐㄧ)
to intercept and attack; to waylay and attack

邀截(ㄧㄠ ㄐㄧㄝˊ)
to intercept (enemy troops)

邀請(ㄧㄠ ㄑㄧㄥˇ)
to invite; invitation

邀寵(ㄧㄠ ㄔㄨㄥˇ)
①to make oneself liked by a superior ②(said of concubines) to try to win the husband's love

邀遊(ㄧㄠ ㄧㄡˊ)
to invite someone for an outing

邀宴(ㄧㄠ ㄧㄢˋ)
①to invite to a feast ②an invitation to a luncheon or dinner party

邀約(ㄧㄠ ㄩㄝ)
①an engagement; an invitation ②to invite; to make an appointment or engagement

【邁】 6159 ㄇㄞˋ may mài
1. to surpass or exceed
2. to stride; to step: 他邁着大步在街上走。He strides along the street.
3. to go on a long journey
4. old (age)
5. to pass

邁步(ㄇㄞˋ ㄅㄨˋ)
to stride; to take a step; to make a step

邁方步(ㄇㄞˋ ㄈㄤ ㄅㄨˋ)
to walk slowly

邁達(ㄇㄞˋ ㄉㄚˊ)
open-minded

邁立開江(ㄇㄞˋ ㄌㄧˋ ㄎㄞ ㄐㄧㄤ)
the Malikha River in Sikang Province

邁過去(ㄇㄞˋ ㄍㄨㄛˋ ・ㄑㄩ)
to pass over; to stride

邁跡(ㄇㄞˋ ㄐㄧ)
to follow the examples of ancient sages

邁進(ㄇㄞˋ ㄐㄧㄣˋ)
to forge ahead

邁向(ㄇㄞˋ ㄒㄧㄤˋ)
to march toward: 軍隊邁向柏林。The soldiers marched toward Berlin.

邁往(ㄇㄞˋ ㄨㄤˇ)
to forge ahead dauntlessly

【邂】 6160

ㄒㄧㄝˋ shieh xìe

to meet without a prior engagement; to meet by chance

邂逅(ㄒㄧㄝˋ《ㄡˋ or (ㄒㄧㄝ ㄏㄡˋ))
to meet by chance; to meet accidentally; to meet (a relative, friend, etc.) unexpectedly: 我們邂逅相遇。We met by chance.

【還】 6161

1. ㄏㄨㄢˊ hwan huán

1. to return; to come back; return: 把那本書還給圖書館。Return that book to the library.

2. to repay; to pay back; to restore; to give back: 下星期你要還我錢。You'll pay me back next week.

3. a Chinese family name

還報(ㄏㄨㄢˊ ㄅㄠˋ)
to repay; to pay back; repayment

還本(ㄏㄨㄢˊ ㄅㄣˇ)
to pay the principal (as upon the maturity of bonds, loans, etc.)

還目(ㄏㄨㄢˊ ㄇㄨˋ)
afraid to look at someone straight in the face on account of fear or respect

還禮(ㄏㄨㄢˊ ㄌㄧˇ)
①to return a salute: 他沒有還禮。He didn't return my salute. ②to send a present in return

還口(ㄏㄨㄢˊ ㄎㄡˇ)
to retort; to talk back

還魂(ㄏㄨㄢˊ ㄏㄨㄣˊ)
to come to life again; to come round

還擊(ㄏㄨㄢˊ ㄐㄧ)
①to fight back; to return fire; to hit back; to counterattack: 我們向敵人還擊。We hit back at the enemy. ②(fencing) a riposte

還價(ㄏㄨㄢˊ ㄐㄧㄚˋ)
to haggle over a price

還錢(ㄏㄨㄢˊ ㄑㄧㄢˊ)
to return money; to pay back a debt

還清(ㄏㄨㄢˊ ㄑㄧㄥ)
to settle an account; all paid—as an account or debt: 他還清債款。He paid off his loans.

還情(ㄏㄨㄢˊ ㄑㄧㄥˊ)
to repay a favor

還席(ㄏㄨㄢˊ ㄒㄧˊ)
①to return a dinner ②(comically) to vomit after heavy drinking at a feast

還鄉(ㄏㄨㄢˊ ㄒㄧㄤ)
to return to one's hometown: 我的還鄉使他們驚奇。My return to the hometown surprised them.

還債(ㄏㄨㄢˊ ㄓㄞˋ)
to repay a debt; to get out of debt: 負債容易還債難。It is easier to get into debt than to get out of it.

還賬(ㄏㄨㄢˊ ㄓㄤˋ)
to pay in order to settle an account; to pay a bill or debt

還政於民(ㄏㄨㄢˊ ㄓㄥˋ ㄩˊ ㄇㄧㄣˊ)
to return the power of government to the hands of the people; to return to parliamentary rule

還手(ㄏㄨㄢˊ ㄕㄡˇ)
to hit back; to strike back; to retaliate: 他打我，因此我還手打他。He hit me, so I struck back.

還嘴(ㄏㄨㄢˊ ㄗㄨㄟˇ)
to answer (or talk) back; to retort; to answer back in abuse or self-defense

還俗(ㄏㄨㄢˊ ㄙㄨˊ)
(said of a monk or nun) to return to the laity, to return to secular life: 那和尚還俗。That Buddhist monk returned to the laity.

還言(ㄏㄨㄢˊ ㄧㄢˊ)
to retort; to swear at someone in return: 他還言說：「那不關你的事。」"It's none of your business," he retorted.

還陽(ㄏㄨㄢˊ ㄧㄤˊ)
to return to life; to come back from death

還我河山(ㄏㄨㄢˊ ㄨㄛˇ ㄏㄜˊ ㄕㄢ)
(a slogan) Let's restore our lost land!

還味(ㄏㄨㄢˊ ㄨㄟˋ)
to ponder or muse over what someone has said

還原(ㄏㄨㄢˊ ㄩㄢˊ)
①to return to normal or original status ②(chemistry) reduction

還原劑(ㄏㄨㄢˊ ㄩㄢˊ ㄐㄧˋ)
(chemistry) a reducing agent

還原作用(ㄏㄨㄢˊ ㄩㄢˊ ㄗㄨㄛˋ ㄩㄥˋ)
a reducing process

還願(ㄏㄨㄢˊ ㄩㄢˋ)
to fulfill a vow—to thank god for answering one's prayers

【還】 6161

2.(旋) ㄒㄩㄢˊ shyuan xuán

to revolve; to turn back

還踵 or 旋踵(ㄒㄩㄢˊ ㄓㄨㄥˇ)
(literally) a turn of the heels—a brief moment

【還】 6161

3. ㄏㄞˊ hair hái

1. yet; still: 他還沒有來。He has not come yet.

2. passably; fairly; quite

3. also

4. even

5. at the same time

6. or

7. had better: 還是你自己走一趟。You'd better go yourself.

還不夠(ㄏㄞˊ ㄅㄨˋ ㄍㄡˋ)
not enough yet; still not enough

還不錯(ㄏㄞˊ ㄅㄨˋ ㄘㄨㄛˋ)
not bad; passable; so-so

還多(ㄏㄞˊ ㄉㄨㄛ)
①still many or much left ②even more than...

還能(ㄏㄞˊ ㄋㄥˊ)
still able to

還冷(ㄏㄞˊ ㄌㄥˇ)
still cold

還好(ㄏㄞˊ ㄏㄠˇ)
①passable; so-so; not bad ②fortunately

還是(ㄏㄞˊ ㄕˋ)
①still; nevertheless: 你還是最好的。You are still the best. ②again ③had better ④or (showing doubt): 你去還是我去? Are you going or am I?

還熱(ㄏㄞˊ ㄖㄜˋ)
still hot

還在(ㄏㄞˊ ㄗㄞˋ)
①still here ②still (working, gambling, etc.)

還早(ㄏㄞˊ ㄗㄠˇ)

〔走部〕

【遄】 6162 ㄓㄨㄢ jan zhān

very difficult to proceed

十四畫

【邇】 6163 ㄦ eel ěr

1. lately; recently
2. near or close to

邇來(ㄦ ㄌㄞ)

lately; recently

【邃】 6164 ㄙㄨㄟˋ suey suì

1. deep; far
2. profound; depth (of learning); abyss (of one's mind)

邃密(ㄙㄨㄟˋ ㄇㄧˋ)

abstruse and full (as thought)

邃古(ㄙㄨㄟˋ ㄍㄨˇ)

the remote past; time immemorial

邃戶(ㄙㄨㄟˋ ㄏㄨˋ)

an abysmal entrance to a large, quiet house

邃宇(ㄙㄨㄟˋ ㄩˇ)

a large house that is labyrinthic and dark

【邈】 6165 ㄇㄧㄠˇ meau miǎo

1. distant; remote
2. same as 藐 — to slight; to look down upon; to show a low opinion of

邈遠(ㄇㄧㄠˇ ㄩㄢˇ)

distant; remote

邈視(ㄇㄧㄠˇ ㄕˋ)

to despise; to look down upon; to underestimate

邈然(ㄇㄧㄠˇ ㄖㄢˊ)

distant; remote

十五畫

【邊】 6166 ㄅㄧㄢ bian biān

1. an edge; the end of something; a verge; a margin
2. a side
3. a hem; a decorative border
4. the border of a nation's territory; a boundary

---

5. limits; bounds
6. nearby; near to
7. a Chinese family name

邊鄙(ㄅㄧㄢ ㄅㄧˇ)

places near the border; borderlands

邊…邊…(ㄅㄧㄢ…ㄅㄧㄢ…)

a speech pattern indicating two actions taking place simultaneously

邊旁(ㄅㄧㄢ ㄆㄤˊ)

①nearby; close by; adjacent to ②the radical on either side of a character

邊防(ㄅㄧㄢ ㄈㄤˊ)

border defense; frontier defense

邊幅(ㄅㄧㄢ ㄈㄨˊ)

①the appearance of a person; attire: 他不修邊幅。He was careless about his attire. ②the margin (of a piece of cloth, etc.)

邊地(ㄅㄧㄢ ㄉㄧˋ)

a borderland; a frontier

邊頭風(ㄅㄧㄢ ㄊㄡˊ ㄈㄥ)

(Chinese medicine) name of an ailment roughly similar to migraine, sometimes accompanied by a swelling on either side of the head

邊防(ㄅㄧㄢ ㄍㄨㄢ)

strategic positions on the border

邊框(ㄅㄧㄢ ㄎㄨㄤ)

a frame; a rim: 她戴沒邊框的眼鏡。She wore rimless glasses.

邊患(ㄅㄧㄢ ㄏㄨㄢˋ)

trouble along the national border or frontier, as caused by foreign invasion, etc.

邊際(ㄅㄧㄢ ㄐㄧˋ)

①a boundary ②(Buddhism) the extremity of things ③the substance of one's speech or writing: 他說話不着邊際。He talked far off the substance.

邊際利潤(ㄅㄧㄢ ㄐㄧˋ ㄌㄧˋ ㄖㄨㄣˋ)

(accounting) marginal profit

邊際效用(ㄅㄧㄢ ㄐㄧˋ ㄒㄧㄠˋ ㄩㄥˋ)

(economics) marginal utility

邊際收入(ㄅㄧㄢ ㄐㄧˋ ㄕㄡ ㄖㄨˋ)

marginal revenue

邊界(ㄅㄧㄢ ㄐㄧㄝˋ)

---

the national boundary: 我們政府標定邊界。Our government demarcated boundaries.

邊疆(ㄅㄧㄢ ㄐㄧㄤ)

a borderland; a frontier: 我們支援邊疆建設。We supported the construction of the borderlands.

邊疆民族(ㄅㄧㄢ ㄐㄧㄤ ㄇㄧㄣˊ ㄗㄨˊ)

tribes living on the border land (particularly referring to the Mongolians, Tibetans and other ethnic minorities on China's borders)

邊境(ㄅㄧㄢ ㄐㄧㄥˋ)

the national boundary or border; the frontier. 我們封閉邊境。We closed the frontiers.

邊境貿易(ㄅㄧㄢ ㄐㄧㄥˋ ㄇㄠˋ ㄧˋ)

frontier trade

邊沁(ㄅㄧㄢ ㄑㄧㄣˋ)

Jeremy Bentham (1748 1832), British philosopher and political scientist

邊沁主義(ㄅㄧㄢ ㄑㄧㄣˋ ㄓㄨˇ ㄧˋ)

Benthamism, the utilitarian philosophy of Jeremy Bentham

邊區(ㄅㄧㄢ ㄑㄩ)

a border district; the frontier

邊政(ㄅㄧㄢ ㄓㄥˋ)

frontier administration: 他主修邊政學。He majored in frontier administration.

邊陲(ㄅㄧㄢ ㄔㄨㄟˊ)

a border; a borderland; a frontier

邊塞(ㄅㄧㄢ ㄙㄞ)

strategic positions along the border; a border pass; a frontier fortress

邊燧(ㄅㄧㄢ ㄙㄨㄟˋ)

fire and smoke signals made by frontier guards to warn the approach of invading forces

邊障(ㄅㄧㄢ ㄓㄤˋ)

strategic positions along the border

邊兒(ㄅㄧㄢㄦ)

①the hem of a dress; the brim ②the edge: 一古廟聳立在崖邊兒邊。An old temple stood on the edge of a preci-

邊沿(ㄅㄧㄢ ㄧㄢˊ)
the edge; the fringe: 不要太走近懸崖邊沿。Don't walk too near the edge of the cliff.

邊外(ㄅㄧㄢ ㄨㄞˋ)
outside the border defense line

邊緣(ㄅㄧㄢ ㄩㄢˊ)
the edge; the verge: 他瀕於餓死之邊緣。He is on the edge of starvation.

邊遠(ㄅㄧㄢ ㄩㄢˇ)
a remote frontier or borderland

邊遠地區(ㄅㄧㄢ ㄩㄢˇ ㄉㄧˋ ㄑㄩ)
an outlying district

十九畫

【邏】 6167
ㄌㄨㄛˊ luo luó
to patrol; to inspect: 警察正在街上巡邏。The policemen are patrolling the street.

邏輯(ㄌㄨㄛˊ ㄐㄧˊ)
logic: 他的辯論既有學問又合邏輯。He argues with learning and logic.

邏輯分析(ㄌㄨㄛˊ ㄐㄧˊ ㄈㄣ ㄒㄧ)
logical analysis

邏輯符號(ㄌㄨㄛˊ ㄐㄧˊ ㄈㄨˊ ㄏㄠˋ)
a logical symbol

邏輯學(ㄌㄨㄛˊ ㄐㄧˊ ㄒㄩㄝˊ)
logic

邏輯學家(ㄌㄨㄛˊ ㄐㄧˊ ㄒㄩㄝˊ ㄐㄧㄚ)
a logician

邏卒(ㄌㄨㄛˊ ㄗㄨˊ)
a patrolman

【邐】 6168
ㄌㄧˇ lii lǐ
continuous and meandering (as mountains, roads, etc.)

邑 部
ㄧˋ yih yì

【邑】 6169
ㄧˋ yih yì
1. a town
2. a political district in ancient China
3. a county
4. a state

pice.

5. a capital city
6. same as 悒—sad or melancholy

邑庠(ㄧˋ ㄒㄧㄤˊ)
a county school or its graduate in former times

邑紳(ㄧˋ ㄕㄣ)
the gentry

邑人(ㄧˋ ㄖㄣˊ)
people of the same county or district

邑宰(ㄧˋ ㄗㄞˇ)
a county magistrate (in ancient times)亦作「邑侯」

三畫

【邙】 6170
ㄇㄤˊ mang máng
name of a hill near Loyang in Honan Province

【邛】 6171
ㄑㄩㄥˊ chyong qióng
1. name of a county in the Han Dynasty in today's Shantung Province
2. a hill; the heights
3. illness; an ailment
4. a Chinese family name

邛州(ㄑㄩㄥˊ ㄓㄡ)
name of a former political division in today's Szechwan Province

邛水(ㄑㄩㄥˊ ㄕㄨㄟˇ)
①name of a county in Kweichow Province ②name of a river in Szechwan Province

【邕】 6172
ㄩㄥ iong yōng
1. harmony; peaceful; harmonious
2. (now rarely) to cultivate (plants)
3. short for 邕寧, a county in Kwangsi Province

邕江(ㄩㄥ ㄐㄧㄤ)
name of a river in Kwangsi Province

邕邕(ㄩㄥ ㄩㄥ)
harmonious; peaceful

四畫

【邠】 6173
ㄅㄧㄣ bin bīn
name of an ancient state in today's Shensi Province

邠如(ㄅㄧㄣ ㄖㄨˊ)
flourishing or booming, culturally

【那】 6174
1. ㄋㄚˋ nah nà
1. that; those: 那些書是我的。Those books are mine.
2. then; in that case: 那我就不再等了。In that case, I won't wait any longer.

那般(ㄋㄚˋ ㄅㄢ)
that way

那班人(ㄋㄚˋ ㄅㄢ ㄖㄣˊ)
those people

那不勒斯(ㄋㄚˋ ㄅㄨˋ ㄌㄜˋ ㄙ)
Naples, Italy

那麼(ㄋㄚˋ ㄇㄜˊ)
①so; that; in that way: 我們不該那麼說。We shouldn't have said that.②then; such being the case: 那麼，我必須懲罰他。Then I've to punish him. ③about; or so

那麼點兒(ㄋㄚˋ ㄇㄜˊ ㄉㄧㄢˇ ㄦ)
so little; so few

那麼著(ㄋㄚˋ ㄇㄜˊ ㄓㄜ)or(ㄋㄚˋ ㄇㄜˊ ㄓㄠˇ)
①to do that; to do so; in that way or manner ②then

那麼樣(ㄋㄚˋ ㄇㄜˊ ㄧㄤˋ)or(ㄋㄜˋ ㄇㄜˊ ㄧㄤˋ)
that way; in that case

那裏(ㄋㄚˋ ㄌㄧˇ)
that place; at that place; there; over there: 馬上到那裏去。Go there at once.

那個(ㄋㄚˋ ㄍㄜ)
①that one ②embarrassing ③ funny ④ too much, too far, too hot, etc.

那就(ㄋㄚˋ ㄐㄧㄡˋ)
in that case; if that is the case

那其間(ㄋㄚˋ ㄑㄧˊ ㄐㄧㄢ)
at that time or moment

那些(ㄋㄚˋ ㄒㄧㄝ)
those: 那些是我的鉛筆。Those are my pencils.

那時(ㄋㄚˋ ㄕˊ)
at that time or moment; then: 到那時我會告訴你這件事。I'll tell you about it then.

那是(ㄋㄚˋ ㄕˋ)
of course: 那是他對了！Of course he's right!

那廂(ㄋㄚˋ ㄒㄧㄤ)

that fellow; that s. o. b.

那樣(ㄋㄚˋ 一ㄤˋ)
①that case or manner ②
that (indicating degree)

【那】 6174
2. ㄋㄟˋ ney nèi
combined form of 那一
(that+one), often used to
indicate emphasis or con-
tempt

那邊(ㄋㄟˋ ㄅ一ㄢ)or 那邊兒(ㄋㄟˋ
ㄅ一ㄚㄦ)
that way or side; over there;
there (often emphasizing
"not here")

那步田地(ㄋㄟˋ ㄅㄨˋ ㄊ一ㄢˊ ㄉ一ˋ)
that predicament; such a
pass

那批傢伙(ㄋㄟˋ ㄆ一 ㄐ一ㄚ ˙ㄏㄨㄛ)
those guys; those rascals

那天(ㄋㄟˋ ㄊ一ㄢ)
that day

那溜兒(ㄋㄟˋ ㄌ一ㄡㄦ)
that region or area: 孩子們常
在那溜兒玩. The children
often play in that region.

那個(ㄋㄟˋ ˙ㄍㄜ)
①that one (sometimes em-
phasizing "not this one"):這
個總比那個好. This is better
than that. ② embarrassing
③funny ④too much; too
far

那塊兒(ㄋㄟˋ ㄎㄨㄞㄦ)
①that place; that region 亦
作「那溜兒」②that piece of
land, etc., often emphasizing
"not this piece": 他擁有那塊
兒地. He owns that piece of
land.

那回(ㄋㄟˋ ㄏㄨㄟˊ)
that time; that occasion

那陣兒(ㄋㄟˋ ㄓㄣˋㄦ)
that period; that moment

那種(ㄋㄟˋ ㄓㄨㄥˇ)
that kind (often emphasizing "not this kind")

那宗(ㄋㄟˋ ㄗㄨㄥ)
that case

那位(ㄋㄟˋ ㄨㄟˋ)
that gentleman or lady
(often emphasizing "not this
gentleman or lady")

【那】 6174
3.(哪) ㄋㄚˇ naa nǎ
an interrogative particle
—Who? Which? What?

Where?

那般(ㄋㄚˋ ㄅㄢ)
as in 烏那般—Why?

那怕(ㄋㄚˇ ㄆㄚˋ)
①what to be afraid of ②
even if

那能(ㄋㄚˇ ㄋㄥˊ)
How can one...? 或 How
could one...?

那裏(ㄋㄚˇ ˙ㄌ一)or 那兒(ㄋㄚˇㄦ)
①Where? ② a negative par-
ticle—how can: 我那裏能吃得
下這麼多? How can I eat so
much? ③You're being too
modest, polite, etc.

那裏話(ㄋㄚˇ ˙ㄌ一 ㄏㄨㄚˋ)
You're being too modest.

那個(ㄋㄚˇ ˙ㄍㄜ)
①Which one?或 Which?②
Who?

那堪(ㄋㄚˇ ㄎㄢ)
How can one stand or suf-
fer...?

那知(ㄋㄚˇ ㄓ)
Who could have known...?

那有(ㄋㄚˇ 一ㄡˇ)
How can there be...?

【那】 6174
4. ㄋㄟˇ neei něi
an interrogative particle
—which+one

那邊(ㄋㄟˇ ㄅ一ㄢ)or 那邊兒(ㄋㄟˇ
ㄅ一ㄚㄦ)
which way or direction

那年(ㄋㄟˇ ㄋ一ㄢˊ)
what year; which year

那個(ㄋㄟˇ ˙ㄍㄜ)
which one

那回(ㄋㄟˇ ㄏㄨㄟˊ)
which time or occasion

【那】 6174
5. ㄋㄚˋ nha nà
a Chinese family name

那霸(ㄋㄚˋ ㄅㄚˋ)
Naha, capital of the Ryu-
kyus

【邦】 6175
ㄅㄤ bang bāng
1. a state; a country; a nation
2. a manor given to a nobleman by the emperor in feudal China

邦本(ㄅㄤ ㄅㄣˇ)
the very foundation of a
nation

邦土(ㄅㄤ ㄊㄨˇ)
a nation's territory; land of

a country

邦國(ㄅㄤ ㄍㄨㄛˊ)
a nation; a country; a state

邦畿(ㄅㄤ ㄐ一)
the territory of a nation

邦家(ㄅㄤ ㄐ一ㄚ)
one's nation; one's state
one's fatherland

邦家之光(ㄅㄤ ㄐ一ㄚ ㄓ ㄍㄨㄤ)
the glory of one's country or
fatherland

邦交(ㄅㄤ ㄐ一ㄠ)
international relations; diplomatic relations or ties: 兩
國建立邦交關係. Two nations
established diplomatic relations.

邦禁(ㄅㄤ ㄐ一ㄣˋ)
prohibitions of a nation

邦人(ㄅㄤ ㄖㄣˊ)
fellow countrymen; compa-
triots; people of a nation

邦彥(ㄅㄤ 一ㄢ)
capable or virtuous persons
in a country

邦域(ㄅㄤ ㄩˋ)
national territory

邦媛(ㄅㄤ ㄩㄢˊ)
girls of a nation

【邪】 6176
1. ㄒ一ㄝˊ shye xié
1. evil; depraved; wicked
mean; vicious
2. pertaining to sorcery or
demonism; abnormal

邪不勝正(ㄒ一ㄝˊ ˙ㄅㄨ ㄕㄥˋ ㄓㄥˋ)or 邪
不敵正(ㄒ一ㄝˊ ˙ㄅㄨ ㄉ一ˊ ㄓㄥˋ)
The evil will not triumph
over the virtuous.

邪僻(ㄒ一ㄝˊ ㄆ一ˋ)
heterodox; perverse; abnormal

邪魔(ㄒ一ㄝˊ ㄇㄛˊ)
demons; devils

邪魔外道(ㄒ一ㄝˊ ㄇㄛˊ ㄨㄞˋ ㄉㄠˋ)
①(Buddhism) demons and
heretics ②unorthodox; evil
and wicked

邪媚(ㄒ一ㄝˊ ㄇㄟˋ)
obsequiousness; fawning

邪謀(ㄒ一ㄝˊ ㄇㄡˊ)
an evil scheme; conspiracy

邪門兒(ㄒ一ㄝˊ ㄇㄣˊㄦ)
beyond expectation or comprehension; strange; abnormal

邪道(ㄒ一ㄝˊ ㄉㄠˋ)

evil ways; heterodoxy: 他们
走邪道。They abandoned
themselves to evil ways.

邪念(ㄒㄧㄝˊㄋㄧㄢˋ)
evil thoughts or intentions;
wicked ideas: 她起了邪念。A
wicked idea came into her
mind.

邪佞(ㄒㄧㄝˊㄋㄧㄥˋ)
evil persons; mean persons

邪路(ㄒㄧㄝˊㄌㄨˋ)
debauchery; a wrong path;
evil ways

邪計(ㄒㄧㄝˊㄐㄧˋ)
evil schemes; conspiracy

邪教(ㄒㄧㄝˊㄐㄧㄠˋ)
paganism; heathendom; perverse religious sects

邪譎(ㄒㄧㄝˊㄐㄩㄝˊ)
wicked and crafty; evil and
dishonest

邪氣(ㄒㄧㄝˊㄑㄧˋ)
① an evil look; perversity ②
evil influence; a perverse
trend

邪曲(ㄒㄧㄝˊㄑㄩ)
crooked; wicked

邪心(ㄒㄧㄝˊㄒㄧㄣ)
evil thoughts; bad intentions

邪行
①(ㄒㄧㄝˊㄒㄧㄥˊ) evil ways; wicked
conduct
②(ㄒㄧㄝˊㄒㄧㄥˋ) very strange

邪臣(ㄒㄧㄝˊㄔㄣˊ)
evil or wicked officials

邪術(ㄒㄧㄝˊㄕㄨˋ)
sorcery; voodooism; demonic
magic

邪說(ㄒㄧㄝˊㄕㄨㄛ)
heresy; perverted views; a
heretic theory: 他陷入邪說中。
He fell into heresy.

邪惡(ㄒㄧㄝˊㄜˋ)
evil and wicked; debauchery;
wickedly

邪淫(ㄒㄧㄝˊㄧㄣˊ)
licentiousness; lewdness;
lustful

邪 6176
2. ㄧㄝˊ ye yé
1. to answer in unison
2. same as 耶—an ending particle

邪呼(ㄧㄝˊㄏㄨ)
to answer in unison

邪許(ㄧㄝˊㄏㄨˇ)
to yell in unison; to call out

in one voice

邪 6177
(邪) ㄒㄧㄥˊ shyng xíng
1. name of an ancient state
(during the Epoch of Spring
and Autumn)
2. a Chinese family name

邨 6178
ㄘㄨㄣ tsuen cūn
1. same as 村—a village; the
countryside
2. coarse; vulgar
3. name-calling; abusive language
4. to scold
5. to embarrass

五畫

邵 6179
ㄕㄠˋ shaw shào
1. advanced, as age
2. a Chinese family name

邯 6180
ㄏㄢˊ harn hán
1. name of a county in Hopeh
Province
2. name of a river in Chinghai
3. a hill in Hopeh

邯鄲(ㄏㄢˊㄉㄢ)
① Hantan, name of a county
in Hopeh Province ② a
Chinese family name

邯鄲學步(ㄏㄢˊㄉㄢㄒㄩㄝˊㄅㄨˋ)
to imitate another without
success and lose what used
to be one's own (referring
to an anecdote related by
Chuang-tzu)

邰 6181
ㄊㄞˊ tair tái
1. name of an ancient state in
today's Shensi Province
2. a Chinese family name

邱 6182
ㄑㄧㄡ chiou qiū
1. same as 丘—a hill
2. name of a county in
Shantung Province
3. a Chinese family name

邱比特(ㄑㄧㄡㄅㄧˇㄊㄜˋ)
Cupid

邱吉爾(ㄑㄧㄡㄐㄧˊㄦˇ)
Winston Churchill (Sir Winston Leonard Spencer
Churchill, 1874-1965), British statesman

邲 6183
ㄅㄧˋ bih bì

1. good-looking
2. name of an ancient place in
today's Honan Province

邳 6184
ㄆㄟ peir péi
1. joyful; jubilant
2. name of an ancient place in
today's Shantung Province
3. a Chinese family name

邶 6185
ㄅㄟˋ bey bèi
name of an ancient state in
today's Honan Province

邴 6186
ㄅㄧㄥˇ biing bǐng
1. joyful; jubilant
2. name of a place in ancient
China in today's Shantung
Province
3. a Chinese family name

邸 6187
ㄉㄧˇ dii dǐ
1. the residence of a prince or
the nobility; the residence of
a high official
2. princes and noblemen
3. (now rarely) a screen
4. the bottom of something
5. a Chinese family name

邸報(ㄉㄧˇㄅㄠˋ)
official gazettes in ancient
China

邸第(ㄉㄧˇㄉㄧˋ)
residences of lords and the
nobility

邸舍(ㄉㄧˇㄕㄜˋ)
①residences of the nobility
②a shop or store ③an inn
or a tavern

六畫

郁 6188
ㄩˋ yuh yù
1. adorned; colorfully ornamented; beautiful; refined
2. a Chinese family name

郁穆(ㄩˋㄇㄨˋ)
harmonious and refined

郁馥(ㄩˋㄈㄨˋ)
fragrant; aromatic

郁烈(ㄩˋㄌㄧㄝˋ)
permeated with strong
aroma

郁郁(ㄩˋㄩˋ)
①beautifully adorned; or-
namented ②diffusing of
aroma ③flourishing; luxuriant ④elegant; refined

邑部

【邢】⁶¹⁸⁹ （邢）ㄒㄧㄥˊ shyng xing
1. name of an ancient state in China
2. a Chinese family name

【郅】⁶¹⁹⁰ ㄓˋ jyh zhi
1. very; extremely
2. a Chinese family name

郅隆（ㄓˋ ㄌㄨㄥˊ）
extremely flourishing or prosperous

郅治（ㄓˋ ㄓˋ）
extremely well-governed (nation, world, etc.)

【郇】⁶¹⁹¹ ㄒㄩㄣˊ shyun xún
1. name of an ancient state in today's Shansi Province
2. a Chinese family name

郇厨（ㄒㄩㄣˊ ㄔㄨ）
(literally) the cuisine of Duke Hsün 韋陟 of the Tang Dynasty—a sumptuous feast

【郊】⁶¹⁹² ㄐㄧㄠ jiau jiāo
1. suburbs of a city
2. a ceremony for offering sacrifices to Heaven and Earth

郊甸（ㄐㄧㄠ ㄉㄧㄢˋ）
suburbs and the regions beyond the city

郊坰（ㄐㄧㄠ）
countryside; a field; open spaces

郊區（ㄐㄧㄠ ㄑㄩ）
suburban districts; suburbs; outskirts; a suburban area

郊社（ㄐㄧㄠ ㄕㄜˋ）
a sacrifice for Heaven in winter (郊) and a sacrifice for Earth in summer (社)

郊祀（ㄐㄧㄠ ㄙˋ）
to offer a sacrifice to Heaven and Earth

郊野（ㄐㄧㄠ ㄧㄝˇ）
open spaces beyond the city

郊遊（ㄐㄧㄠ ㄧㄡˊ）
an outing; an excursion

郊迎（ㄐㄧㄠ ㄧㄥˊ）
to welcome (a guest) beyond the city limit—as a gesture of profound respect

郊外（ㄐㄧㄠ ㄨㄞˋ）
suburbs

郊原（ㄐㄧㄠ ㄩㄢˊ）
plains beyond the city

【郃】⁶¹⁹³ ㄍㄜˊ ger gé
1. name of a county in Shensi Province
2. a Chinese family name

【邽】⁶¹⁹⁴ ㄍㄨㄟ guei guī
1. name of a county in the Han Dynasty, in today's Kansu Province
2. a Chinese family name

【邾】⁶¹⁹⁵ ㄓㄨ ju zhū
name of an ancient state in today's Shantung Province

七畫

【郛】⁶¹⁹⁶ ㄈㄨˊ fwu fú
the outer city; the suburbs

郛郭（ㄈㄨˊ ㄍㄨㄛ）
① the booming suburbs outside a city; a sturdy outer city wall ② (figuratively) shelter; a shield; protection

【郜】⁶¹⁹⁷ ㄍㄠˋ gaw gào
1. name of an ancient state in today's Shantung Province
2. name of a place in the state of Tsin (晉) in the Epoch of Spring and Autumn, in today's Shansi Province
3. a Chinese family name

【郝】⁶¹⁹⁸ ㄏㄠˇ hao hao
（讀音 ㄏㄜˋ heh hè）
1. name of an ancient place in today's Shensi Province
2. a Chinese family name

【郎】⁶¹⁹⁹ （郞）ㄌㄤˊ lang láng
1. an official rank in ancient times
2. a man
3. the husband; the beau
4. the master (as opposite to servants)
5. a Chinese family name

郎當（ㄌㄤˊ ㄉㄤ）
① (said of clothing) loose ② discouraged; dejected ③ shackles for prisoners

郎官（ㄌㄤˊ ㄍㄨㄢ）
an official rank in the Han Dynasty

郎舅（ㄌㄤˊ ㄐㄧㄡˋ）
brothers-in-law

郎君（ㄌㄤˊ ㄐㄩㄣ）
① a term of address for a man ② your son (a polite expression) ③ the husband

郎中（ㄌㄤˊ ㄓㄨㄥ）
① an official rank in ancient China ② a physician ③ a card shark

郎世寧（ㄌㄤˊ ㄕˋ ㄋㄧㄥˊ）
Guiseppe Castiglione (1698-1768), a naturalized Italian painter, who came to China during the early years of the Ching Dynasty

郎才女貌（ㄌㄤˊ ㄘㄞˊ ㄋㄩˇ ㄇㄠˋ）
a perfect match between a man and a woman

【郏】⁶²⁰⁰ ㄐㄧㄚ jya jiā
1. name of various places in China
2. a Chinese family name

【郡】⁶²⁰¹ ㄐㄩㄣˋ jiunn jùn
a political division in ancient China; a prefecture; a county

郡國（ㄐㄩㄣˋ ㄍㄨㄛˊ）
a system of political zoning adopted by Liu Pang (劉邦), founder of the Han Dynasty, whereby he divided the empire into many prefectures under the direct jurisdiction of the throne and a number of principalities governed by the imperial princes

郡下（ㄐㄩㄣˋ ㄒㄧㄚˋ）
the capital city of a prefecture where the magistrate resides

郡縣（ㄐㄩㄣˋ ㄒㄧㄢˋ）
prefectures and counties; administrative districts smaller than a province

郡主（ㄐㄩㄣˋ ㄓㄨˇ）
a princess

郡丞（ㄐㄩㄣˋ ㄔㄥˊ）
an assistant or a deputy to the chief of a prefecture

郡城（ㄐㄩㄣˋ ㄔㄥˊ）
a prefectural city; a town

郡守（ㄐㄩㄣˋ ㄕㄡˇ）
the magistrate of a prefecture

郡王（ㄐㄩㄣˋ ㄨㄤˊ）
a rank of the nobility next

to prince

【郢】 6202
ㄧㄥˇ yǐng yǐng
name of the capital of the state of Chu (楚), during the Epoch of Spring and Autumn, in today's Hupeh Province

郢書燕說(ㄧㄥˇ ㄕㄨ ㄧㄢ ㄕㄨㄛ)
distorted interpretation; to distort the meaning in order to fit one's idea

【郗】 6203
ㄔ chy chī
1. name of a town in the Chou Dynasty
2. a Chinese family name

【郤】 6204
ㄒㄧˋ shìh xì
1. name of an area in the ancient state of Tsin(晉)
2. a crack
3. a Chinese family name

【郕】 6205
ㄔㄥˊ cherng chéng
name of an ancient state in today's Shantung Province

八畫

【部】 6206
ㄅㄨˋ buh bù
1. a department; a section; a division; a class; a sort; a genus
2. a cabinet ministry
3. a volume; a complete work, novel, writing, etc.
4. to lead; to head

部門(ㄅㄨˋ ㄇㄣˊ)
a class; a section; a department

部分(ㄅㄨˋ ㄈㄣ˙)
a portion; a part; partial; party

部隊(ㄅㄨˋ ㄉㄨㄟˋ)
troops; a military unit: 郡是一支野戰部隊。That is a field military unit.

部隊長(ㄅㄨˋ ㄉㄨㄟˋ ㄓㄤˇ)
the commanding officer; the C.O.

部落(ㄅㄨˋ ㄌㄨㄛˋ)
①　a tribe which has not formed a nation ②　the self-sustaining community of a tribe or clan; a tribal settlement

部落社會(ㄅㄨˋ ㄌㄨㄛˋ ㄕㄜˋ ㄏㄨㄟˋ)
tribal society

部會(ㄅㄨˋ ㄏㄨㄟˋ)
the ministries and commissions under the Executive Yuan of the Chinese government

部將(ㄅㄨˋ ㄐㄧㄤˋ)
military officers under one's command

部首(ㄅㄨˋ ㄕㄡˇ)
classification of words, etc.

部下(ㄅㄨˋ ㄒㄧㄚˋ)
subordinates: 他從不信任他的部下。He never trusts his subordinates.

部長(ㄅㄨˋ ㄓㄤˇ)
①　a cabinet minister ②　(in U.S.) the Secretary (of the army, the navy, the air force, the Defense Department, the Agriculture Department, etc.)

部首(ㄅㄨˋ ㄕㄡˇ)
radicals of Chinese characters

部屬(ㄅㄨˋ ㄕㄨˇ)
subordinates

部署(ㄅㄨˋ ㄕㄨˇ)
to make preparations or arrangements; to make military deployment

部位(ㄅㄨˋ ㄨㄟˋ)
location (of an injury, etc.)

部員(ㄅㄨˋ ㄩㄢˊ)
clerks or staff members in a department, section or ministry

【郫】 6207
ㄆㄧˊ pyi pí
1. name of a town in the Epoch of Spring and Autumn, in today's Honan Province
2. name of a county in Szechwan

郫筒(ㄆㄧˊ ㄊㄨㄥˊ)
a section of huge bamboo produced in Pi Hsien (郫縣), Szechwan, formerly used as a liquor container

【郭】 6208
ㄍㄨㄛ guo guō
1. as in 城郭—a town
2. the outer wall of a city
3. the outer part of anything
4. a Chinese family name

郭瑾(ㄍㄨㄛ ㄊㄨˇ)

Kuo Pu (276-324), a writer of the Tsin Dynasty

郭先生(ㄍㄨㄛ ㄒㄧㄢ ˙ㄕㄥ)
(slang) a dildo

郭子儀(ㄍㄨㄛ ㄗˇ ㄧ)
Kuo Tzu-yi (697-781), a famous general of the Tang Dynasty

郭外(ㄍㄨㄛ ㄨㄞˋ)
beyond the outer city wall; outside the city

【郯】 6209
ㄊㄢˊ tarn tán
1. name of an ancient state in today's Shantung Province
2. a Chinese family name

【郴】 6210
ㄔㄣ chen chēn
1. name of a county in Hunan Province

【郪】 6211
ㄑㄧ chi qī
name of a stream in Szechwan Province

【郲】 6212
ㄌㄞˊ lai lái
1. name of a place in Honan Province
2. a Chinese family name

【郵】 6213
ㄧㄡˊ you yóu
1. a post office
2. postal
3. to deliver mails, letters, etc.
4. a wayside station where couriers on government service change horses
5. a hut; a lodge in the field

郵包(ㄧㄡˊ ㄅㄠ)
a postal parcel

郵票(ㄧㄡˊ ㄆㄧㄠˋ)
postal stamps: 這是一套紀念郵票。This is a set of commemorative stamps.

郵費(ㄧㄡˊ ㄈㄟˋ)
postal charges; postage

郵費不足(ㄧㄡˊ ㄈㄟˋ ㄅㄨˋ ㄗㄨˊ)
insufficient (or short) postage

郵費免付(ㄧㄡˊ ㄈㄟˋ ㄇㄧㄢˇ ㄈㄨˋ)
post-free

郵費已付(ㄧㄡˊ ㄈㄟˋ ㄧˇ ㄈㄨˋ)
postpaid

郵費未付(ㄧㄡˊ ㄈㄟˋ ㄨㄟˋ ㄈㄨˋ)
postage unpaid

郵袋(ㄧㄡˊ ㄉㄞˋ)
a mailbag

〔邑部〕

郵遞(ㄧㄡ ㄉㄧ)
to send by mail; to deliver through postal service; mail service

郵遞區號(ㄧㄡ ㄉㄧ ㄑㄩ ㄏㄠ)
zip code

郵電(ㄧㄡ ㄉㄧㄢ)
postal and cable service

郵亭(ㄧㄡ ㄊㄧㄥ)
①a postal kiosk ②(in ancient China) a lodge for couriers

郵筒(ㄧㄡ ㄊㄨㄥ)
a pillar box; a postbox; a mail drop; a mailbox: 我把信投入郵筒。I took the letter to the postbox.

郵購(ㄧㄡ ㄍㄡ)
①mail order ②to buy by mail order

郵匯(ㄧㄡ ㄏㄨㄟ)
to send money by mail; to remit by post; a postal money order

郵寄(ㄧㄡ ㄐㄧ)
to send by mail; to mail: 他昨天郵寄了遺封信。He mailed the letter yesterday.

郵寄名單(ㄧㄡ ㄐㄧ ㄇㄧㄥ ㄉㄢ)
a mailing list

郵簡(ㄧㄡ ㄐㄧㄢ)
an air letter

郵件(ㄧㄡ ㄐㄧㄢ)
mail matter; postal items; the post; mail: 郵件今早來遲了。The post came late this morning.

郵件補償(ㄧㄡ ㄐㄧㄢ ㄅㄨ ㄔㄤ)
indemnity for mail matter

郵件收集截止日(ㄧㄡ ㄐㄧㄢ ㄕㄡ ㄐㄧ ㄐㄧㄝ ㄓ ㄖ)
a mail-day

郵局(ㄧㄡ ㄐㄩ)or郵政局(ㄧㄡ ㄓㄥ ㄐㄩ)
a post office

郵區(ㄧㄡ ㄑㄩ)
a postal district

郵箱(ㄧㄡ ㄒㄧㄤ)
a postbox; a mailbox; a letter box

郵政(ㄧㄡ ㄓㄥ)
postal affairs; postal system; postal administration

郵政代辦所(ㄧㄡ ㄓㄥ ㄉㄞ ㄅㄢ ㄙㄨㄛ)
a postal agency

郵政滙票(ㄧㄡ ㄓㄥ ㄏㄨㄟ ㄆㄧㄠ)
a postal order

郵政滙款(ㄧㄡ ㄓㄥ ㄏㄨㄟ ㄎㄨㄢ)
postal remittance

郵政局長(ㄧㄡ ㄓㄥ ㄐㄩ ㄓㄤ)
the chief of a post office; the postmaster or postmistress

郵政信箱(ㄧㄡ ㄓㄥ ㄒㄧㄣ ㄒㄧㄤ)
a post-office box (P.O.B.)

郵政支局(ㄧㄡ ㄓㄥ ㄓ ㄐㄩ)
a (postal) suboffice

郵政儲金(ㄧㄡ ㄓㄥ ㄔㄨ ㄐㄧㄣ)
savings deposits in a department of the post office

郵政儲金薄(ㄧㄡ ㄓㄥ ㄔㄨ ㄐㄧㄣ ㄅㄛ)
a post savings book

郵政儲蓄存款(ㄧㄡ ㄓㄥ ㄔㄨ ㄒㄩ ㄘㄨㄣ ㄎㄨㄢ)
post office savings deposits

郵政總局(ㄧㄡ ㄓㄥ ㄗㄨㄥ ㄐㄩ)
the Directorate General of Posts (under the Ministry of Communications)

郵差(ㄧㄡ ㄔㄞ)
a mailman; a postman

郵車(ㄧㄡ ㄔㄜ)
a mail cart; a postal truck or van; postal vehicles

郵戳兒(ㄧㄡ ㄔㄨㄛ ㄦ)
a postmark; a postal dater

郵船(ㄧㄡ ㄔㄨㄢ)
①a luxurious passenger liner ②a mailboat

郵傳部(ㄧㄡ ㄔㄨㄢ ㄅㄨ)
the Ministry of Communications in the Ching Dynasty

郵資(ㄧㄡ ㄗ)
postage

郵資不足(ㄧㄡ ㄗ ㄅㄨ ㄗㄨ)
postage underpaid

郵資免付(ㄧㄡ ㄗ ㄇㄧㄢ ㄈㄨ)
post-free

郵資已付(ㄧㄡ ㄗ ㄧ ㄈㄨ)
postage paid

郵艙(ㄧㄡ ㄘㄤ)
a mail room (aboard a ship)

郵務(ㄧㄡ ㄨ)
postal administration; postal service; postal affairs

郵務生(ㄧㄡ ㄨ ㄕㄥ)
an assistant clerk in a post office

郵務佐(ㄧㄡ ㄨ ㄗㄨㄛ)
a junior clerk in a post office

郵務員(ㄧㄡ ㄨ ㄩㄢ)
a senior clerk in a post

office

郵運(ㄧㄡ ㄩㄣ)
①to deliver by mail ②mail transportation

九畫

【都】　6214
　1. ㄉㄨ　du dū
1. a large town; a city; a metropolis
2. the capital of a nation; to make a city the national capital
3. beautiful; elegant; fine
4. (now rarely) to live or stay in
5. a Chinese family name

都伯林(ㄉㄨ ㄅㄛ ㄌㄧㄣ)
Dublin, Ireland

都鄙(ㄉㄨ ㄅㄧ)
manors of noblemen in ancient China

都門(ㄉㄨ ㄇㄣ)
the national capital

都督(ㄉㄨ ㄉㄨ)
①a big city ②an official rank in the Tang Dynasty

都督(ㄉㄨ ㄉㄨ)
①an army commander in ancient China ②(in the early days of the Chinese Republic) the top commanding officer in a province in charge of both military and civil administration

都會(ㄉㄨ ㄏㄨㄟ)
a big city; a metropolis: 他住在大都會。He lives in the metropolis.

都察院(ㄉㄨ ㄔㄚ ㄩㄢ)
the Court of Censors (in the Ming and Ching dynasties)

都城(ㄉㄨ ㄔㄥ)
①the national capital ②the manor for a minister in ancient China

都市(ㄉㄨ ㄕ)
a city; a metropolis: 台北是個繁忙的大都市。Taipei is a busy city.

都市病(ㄉㄨ ㄕ ㄅㄧㄥ)
endemic diseases among city dwellers

都市更新(ㄉㄨ ㄕ ㄍㄥ ㄒㄧㄣ)
urban renewal

都市規劃(カメ ア 《メへ 厂メY)
urban planning

都市工業區(カメ ア 《メム 一せ ㄑㄩ)
an urban industrial area

都市化(カメ ア 厂メY)
to urbanize; urbanization: 這個小鎮已經都市化了。 The little town has been urbanized.

都市計畫(カメ ア ㄐㄧ 厂メY)
an urban development plan; an urban renewal plan

都市設計(カメ ア アさ ㄐㄧ)
an urban design

都邑(カメ ㄧ)
a metropolitan city; the national capital

【都】 6214
2. カメ dou dōu
1. all; altogether
2. even
3. already

都不對(カメ ㄅメ カメへ)
Nobody is right. 或 Everyone is wrong.

都來了(カメ ㄌㄞ ·ㄌㄜ)
All have come. 或 Everyone is present.

都可以(カメ ㄎㄜ ·ㄧ)
Any one of them will do. 或 Either of them will do.

都是(カメ ア)
all; no exception

都有(カメ ㄧㄡ)
all have...; to include all kinds or varieties

【郿】 6215
ㄇㄟ mei méi
1. Mei, a county in Shensi
2. name of a town of Lu in the Epoch of Spring and Autumn

【鄂】 6216
ㄜ eh è
1. the edge; the verge; the brink; the brim
2. short for Hupeh Province
3. startled; surprised
4. blunt; honest
5. a Chinese family name

鄂木斯克(ㄜ ㄇㄨ ㄙ ㄎㄜ)
Omsk, a Siberian city

鄂霍次克海(ㄜ 厂メㄛ ㄘ ㄎㄜ 厂ㄞ)
the Okhotsk Sea

鄂省(ㄜ ㄕㄥ)
Hupeh Province

【鄲】 6217
ㄉㄢ yunn yùn
1. name of an ancient town in

Shantung Province
2. a Chinese family name

【鄢】 6218
ㄧㄢ yean yān
name of a county in Honan Province

鄢城(ㄧㄢ ㄔㄥ)
name of a county in Honan Province

【鄆】 6219
ㄐㄩㄢˋ jiuann juàn
name of a county in Shantung Province

十畫

【鄗】 6220
厂ㄠˋ haw hào
name of a town in ancient China in today's Hupeh Province

【鄉】 6221
1. ㄒㄧㄤ shiang xiāng
1. a village; the country, as contrasted with a city or town
2. rural
3. a small administrative unit comprising several villages
4. one's native place or birthplace; one's village; one's country: 我回到自己的家鄉。 I returned to my country.

鄉巴佬(ㄒㄧㄤ ㄅㄚ ㄌㄠ)
a country bumpkin; a hillbilly; an unsophisticated villager

鄉兵(ㄒㄧㄤ ㄅㄧㄥ)
the village militia

鄉末(ㄒㄧㄤ ㄇㄛ)
a modest term of self-address when talking to elders of one's own native place

鄉民(ㄒㄧㄤ ㄇㄧㄣ)
villagers; countryfolk

鄉黨(ㄒㄧㄤ ㄉㄤ)
local communities

鄉談(ㄒㄧㄤ ㄊㄢ)
local dialects; native dialects

鄉土(ㄒㄧㄤ ㄊㄨ)
① one's hometown or native place ② local geography and history

鄉土觀念(ㄒㄧㄤ ㄊㄨ 《メㄢ ㄋㄧㄢ)
provincialism; narrow-minded loyalty to one's hometown

鄉土藝術(ㄒㄧㄤ ㄊㄨ ㄧˋ ㄕㄨ)

local art; native art or handicraft

鄉老(ㄒㄧㄤ ㄌㄠ)
① country or village elders ② an official rank in the Chou and Han dynasties

鄉里(ㄒㄧㄤ ㄌㄧ)
① the village where one resides or grew up ② people from the same hometown ③ (now rarely) my wife

鄉裏鄉氣的(ㄒㄧㄤ ㄌㄧ ㄒㄧㄤ ㄑㄧ ·ㄉㄜ)
stupid-looking; foolish and clumsy

鄉鄰(ㄒㄧㄤ ㄌㄧㄣ)
persons from the same rural neighborhood

鄉國(ㄒㄧㄤ 《メㄛ)
one's native place or fatherland

鄉關(ㄒㄧㄤ 《メㄢ)
one's native place or hometown

鄉公所(ㄒㄧㄤ 《メㄥ ㄙㄨㄛ)
a public office in charge of the administration of a group of villages

鄉豪劣紳(ㄒㄧㄤ 厂ㄠ ㄌㄧㄝ ㄕㄣ)
village bullies and local tyrants

鄉間(ㄒㄧㄤ ㄐㄧㄢ)
in the countryside; in the rural area

鄉井(ㄒㄧㄤ ㄐㄧㄥ)
one's native place or hometown

鄉居(ㄒㄧㄤ ㄐㄩ)
to live in the countryside

鄉親(ㄒㄧㄤ ㄑㄧㄣ)
① people hailing from the same area ② local people; villagers

鄉曲(ㄒㄧㄤ ㄑㄩ)
remote and out-of-the-way rural areas

鄉下(ㄒㄧㄤ ·ㄒㄧㄚ)
countryside; a rural area

鄉下老兒(ㄒㄧㄤ ·ㄒㄧㄚ ㄌㄠ ㄦ)
villagers; country bumpkins

鄉下人(ㄒㄧㄤ ·ㄒㄧㄚ ㄖㄣ)
villagers; countryfolk; the country people; rustics

鄉校(ㄒㄧㄤ ㄒㄧㄠ)
a village school

鄉先達(ㄒㄧㄤ ㄒㄧㄢ ㄉㄚ)

（邑部）

〔邑部〕

leaders of a rural community

鄉賢(ㄒㄧㄤ ㄒㄧㄢˊ)
respected village scholars

鄉學(ㄒㄧㄤ ㄒㄩㄝˊ)
a village school

鄉鎮(ㄒㄧㄤ ㄓㄣˋ)
a small town which is essentially a rural village

鄉長(ㄒㄧㄤ ㄓㄤˇ)
①elders in a village ②the chief of a group of villages

鄉愁(ㄒㄧㄤ ㄔㄡˊ)or 鄉思(ㄒㄧㄤ ㄙ)
homesickness; nostalgia

鄉試(ㄒㄧㄤ ㄕˋ)
the civil service examination held once every three years in a provincial capital in ancient times

鄉射(ㄒㄧㄤ ㄕㄜˋ)
an archery contest in villages for choosing the best archers in ancient times

鄉紳(ㄒㄧㄤ ㄕㄣ)
the country gentry; country gentlemen; squires

鄉塾(ㄒㄧㄤ ㄕㄨˊ)
a private village school

鄉人(ㄒㄧㄤ ㄖㄣˊ)
①the villagers ②persons from the same village or rural area

鄉村(ㄒㄧㄤ ㄘㄨㄣ)
a village; a country; a rural area: 他喜歡鄉村的寧靜。He likes the tranquility in the country.

鄉村教育(ㄒㄧㄤ ㄘㄨㄣ ㄐㄧㄠˋ ㄩˋ)
rural education

鄉村音樂(ㄒㄧㄤ ㄘㄨㄣ ㄧㄣ ㄩㄝˋ)
country music

鄉俗(ㄒㄧㄤ ㄙㄨˊ)
local customs of one's native place

鄉誼(ㄒㄧㄤ ㄧˊ)
friendship among people from the same area

鄉野(ㄒㄧㄤ ㄧㄝˇ)
rural; pastoral

鄉友(ㄒㄧㄤ ㄧㄡˇ)
friends from the same area

鄉音(ㄒㄧㄤ ㄧㄣ)
one's native accent; a local accent; a brogue

鄉味(ㄒㄧㄤ ㄨㄟˋ)
①food from one's native

place ②a way of cooking in one's native place

鄉望(ㄒㄧㄤ ㄨㄤˋ)
one's reputation or prestige in one's own town or village

鄉愚(ㄒㄧㄤ ㄩˊ)
stupid rustics

鄉愿(ㄒㄧㄤ ㄩㄢˋ)
a hypocrite or an impostor in the countryside

鄉勇(ㄒㄧㄤ ㄩㄥˇ)
village militiamen; the local militia

【鄉】 6221
2.(舊) ㄒㄧㄤ shianq
xiāng
1. to incline toward; to direct to
2. to guide; to approach
3. (now rarely) to advise

鄉壁虛造(ㄒㄧㄤ ㄅㄧˋ ㄒㄩ ㄗㄠˋ)or 向壁虛造(ㄒㄧㄤˋ ㄅㄧˋ ㄒㄩ ㄗㄠˋ)
to fabricate; to invent

鄉使 or 向使(ㄒㄧㄤ ㄕˇ)
if; had it been

【鄒】 6222
ㄗㄡ tzou zōu
1. name of a state in the Epoch of Warring States
2. a Chinese family name

鄒魯(ㄗㄡ ㄌㄨˇ)
native places of Mencius and Confucius respectively —where culture flourishes; a cultural center

【郞】 6223
ㄨ u wū
1. name of various places in ancient times
2. a Chinese family name

十一畫

【鄙】 6224
ㄅㄧˇ bii bǐ
(又讀ㄅㄧˋ bih bì)
1. mean; base; lowly; despicable
2. superficial; shallow
3. remote; out-of-the-way
4. to despise; to scorn

鄙薄(ㄅㄧˇ ㄅㄛˊ)
①mean; base ②superficial; shallow ③to despise; to loathe: 你不應該鄙薄技術工作。You should not despise technical work.

鄙倍(ㄅㄧˇ ㄅㄟˋ)

despicably unreasonable

鄙夫(ㄅㄧˇ ㄈㄨ)
①a mean fellow; an ignorant fellow ②I (self depreciatory)

鄙陋(ㄅㄧˇ ㄌㄡˋ)
①mean; base ②shallow (views): 他鄙陋無知。He is shallow and ignorant.

鄙俚(ㄅㄧˇ ㄌㄧˇ)
crude; coarse; vulgar

鄙吝(ㄅㄧˇ ㄌㄧㄣˋ)
stingy; niggardly; miserly

鄙賤(ㄅㄧˇ ㄐㄧㄢˋ)
lowly; mean; base

鄙棄(ㄅㄧˇ ㄑㄧˋ)
to despise; to scorn

鄙笑(ㄅㄧˇ ㄒㄧㄠˋ)
to jeer; to ridicule; to mock to taunt

鄙詐(ㄅㄧˇ ㄓㄚˋ)
despicably untruthful; deceitful

鄙事(ㄅㄧˇ ㄕˋ)
trifles; mean matters

鄙視(ㄅㄧˇ ㄕˋ)
to despise; to disdain; to slight; to look down upon

鄙人(ㄅㄧˇ ㄖㄣˊ)
①I (a self-depreciatory way of referring to oneself); your humble servant ②a hillbilly

鄙吝(ㄅㄧˇ ㄌㄧㄣˋ)
①narrow-minded ②miserly niggardly; stingy

鄙俗(ㄅㄧˇ ㄙㄨˊ)
vulgar; philistine

鄙夷(ㄅㄧˇ ㄧˊ)
to despise; to scorn

鄙意(ㄅㄧˇ ㄧˋ)or 鄙見(ㄅㄧˇ ㄐㄧㄢˋ)
my humble opinion

鄙諺(ㄅㄧˇ ㄧㄢˋ)or 鄙語(ㄅㄧˇ ㄩˇ)
a common saying; a proverb

【鄢】 6225
ㄧㄢ ian yān
1. name of an ancient state in what is today's Honan
2. a Chinese family name

【鄘】 6226
ㄩㄥˊ iong yóng
name of an ancient state in what is today's Honan

【鄜】 6227
ㄈㄨ fu fū
name of a county in Shensi

【鄞】 6228
ㄧㄣˊ in yín

name of a county in Che-
kiang

【郸】 6229 业ㄤ jang zhǎng
name of an ancient state in
what is today's Shantung

十二畫

【鄧】 6230 ㄉㄥ deng dèng
1. a Chinese family name
2. name of an ancient state in
what is today's Honan

鄧通(ㄉㄥ ㄊㄨㄥ)
Teng Tung, the favorite
courtier of Emperor Wen of
the Han Dynasty(漢文帝),
famous for his fabulous
wealth

鄧石如(ㄉㄥ ㄕ ㄖㄨˊ)
Teng Shih-ju (1743-1805), a
famous calligrapher

鄧艾(ㄉㄥ ㄞ)
Teng Ai (197-264), a general
of the state of Wei (魏)
during the Epoch of the
Three Kingdoms

鄧尉(ㄉㄥ ㄨㄟˋ)
Tengwei, a hill near Soo-
chow (蘇州), famous for its
plum flowers

【鄭】 6231 业ㄥ jenq zhèng
1. solemn; formal; serious
2. a Chinese family name
3. name of an ancient state in
what is today's Honan

鄭和(业ㄥ ㄏㄜˊ)
Cheng Ho, a powerful
eunuch in the early Ming
Dynasty, who sailed as far
as the east coast of Africa
with a large fleet in a number of expeditions

鄭箋(业ㄥ ㄐㄧㄢ)
a commentary by the Han
Dynasty scholar Cheng Hsüan
(鄭玄) on one version of the
Book of Odes

鄭玄(业ㄥ ㄒㄩㄢˊ)
Cheng Hsüan (127-200), a
Han Dynasty scholar

鄭莊公(业ㄥ 业ㄨㄤ ㄍㄨㄥ)
a ruler of the state of Cheng
(鄭) during the Epoch of
Spring and Autumn

鄭重(业ㄥ 业ㄨㄥˋ)

① cautious; careful ② solemn; serious

鄭重其事(业ㄥ 业ㄨㄥˋ ㄑㄧˊ ㄕˋ)
① to treat it with seriousness ② very careful or cautious

鄭成功(业ㄥ ㄔㄥˊ ㄍㄨㄥ)
Koxinga, or Cheng Cheng-
kung (1624-1662), leader of
an anti-Manchu resistance
after the fall of the Ming
Dynasty, who ousted the
Dutch from Taiwan

鄭聲(业ㄥ ㄕㄥ)
the music of the state of
Cheng (鄭) —decadent music

鄭衛之音(业ㄥ ㄨㄟˋ 业 ㄧㄣ)
the music of the states of
Cheng (鄭) and Wei (衛) —decadent music

【鄯】 6232 ㄕㄢˋ shann shàn
name of a region in Chinese
Turkestan

【鄰】 6233 ㄌㄧㄣˊ lin lín
1. neighboring; adjacent; adjoining; contiguous
2. neighborhood; a community
3. a neighbor
4. a basic community unit
which consists of a number
of families in the same
neighborhood

鄰邦(ㄌㄧㄣˊ ㄅㄤ)
a neighboring state; a neighboring country

鄰比(ㄌㄧㄣˊ ㄅㄧˋ)
neighbors

鄰邊(ㄌㄧㄣˊ ㄅㄧㄢ)
adjacent sides (of a polygon)

鄰睦(ㄌㄧㄣˊ ㄇㄨˋ)
on friendly terms

鄰封(ㄌㄧㄣˊ ㄈㄥ)
a neighboring district

鄰敵(ㄌㄧㄣˊ ㄉㄧˊ)
a hostile neighboring country

鄰里(ㄌㄧㄣˊ ㄌㄧˇ)
neighborhood; a community

鄰里鄉黨(ㄌㄧㄣˊ ㄌㄧˇ ㄒㄧㄤ ㄉㄤˇ)
one's neighborhood and
associates

鄰國(ㄌㄧㄣˊ ㄍㄨㄛˊ)
a neighboring country

鄰家(ㄌㄧㄣˊ ㄐㄧㄚ)

a close neighbor; a next-
door family

鄰近(ㄌㄧㄣˊ ㄐㄧㄣˋ)
① located nearby; located in
the vicinity ② neighborhood:
鄰近沒有銀行。There's no
bank in the neighborhood.

鄰境(ㄌㄧㄣˊ ㄐㄧㄥˋ)
the vicinity; the neighborhood; a surrounding region

鄰居(ㄌㄧㄣˊ ㄐㄩ)
neighbors; people next-door

鄰長(ㄌㄧㄣˊ 业ㄤˇ)
the head of a basic community unit 參看「鄰4.」

鄰舍(ㄌㄧㄣˊ ㄕㄜˋ)
a neighboring family; neighbors

鄰人(ㄌㄧㄣˊ ㄖㄣˊ)
neighbors

鄰右(ㄌㄧㄣˊ ㄧㄡˋ)
neighbors

鄰伍(ㄌㄧㄣˊ ㄨˇ)
next-door neighbors

【鄱】 6234 ㄆㄛˊ por pó
Poyang, name of a county in
Kiangsi

鄱陽湖(ㄆㄛˊ ㄧㄤˊ ㄏㄨˊ)
the Poyang Lake in Kiangsi
Province

【鄲】 6235 ㄉㄢ dan dān
used in Hantan (邯鄲)—①
name of a county in Hopeh
② a Chinese family name

【鄦】 6236 ㄒㄩˇ sheu xǔ
name of an ancient state in
what is today's Honan

十三畫

【鄴】 6237 ㄧㄝˋ yeh yè
1. an ancient name for a part
of what is today's Honan
2. a Chinese family name

【鄶】 6238 ㄎㄨㄞˋ kuay kuài
name of an ancient state in
what is today's Honan

十四畫

【鄒】 6239 ㄗㄡ tzou zōu
name of the birthplace of

Confucius in what is today's
Chūfu (曲阜), Shantung

十五畫

【鄺】 ⁶²⁴⁰ ㄎㄨㄤˋ kuang kuàng
a Chinese family name

十七畫

【酃】 ⁶²⁴¹ ㄌㄧㄥˊ ling líng
1. name of a lake in Hunan
whose water is used to brew
wine
2. name of a county in Hunan

十八畫

【酆】 ⁶²⁴² ㄈㄥ feng fēng
1. the capital of the Chou
Dynasty under King Wen (文
王)
2. a Chinese family name
酆都 (ㄈㄥ ㄉㄨ)
① name of a county in Szechwan ② Hades

十九畫

【酈】 ⁶²⁴³ ㄌㄧ lih lì
1. an ancient name for a part
of what is Honan today
2. a Chinese family name

【酇】 ⁶²⁴⁴ ㄗㄢˇ tzann zǎn
1. a community of a hundred
families during the Chou
Dynasty
2. name of a feudal state in
the Han Dynasty

西 部
ㄧㄡˇ yeou yǒu

【酉】 ⁶²⁴⁵ ㄧㄡˇ yeou yǒu
1. the tenth of the Twelve
Terrestrial Branches
2. 5:00-7:00 p.m.
酉時 (ㄧㄡˇ ㄕˊ)
the period of the day from 5
p.m. to 7 p.m.

二畫

【酊】 ⁶²⁴⁶ ㄉㄧㄥˇ diing dǐng
intoxicated; drunk

【酋】 ⁶²⁴⁷ ㄑㄧㄡˊ chyou qiú
1. the chief of a clan or tribe;
a chieftain
2. to end
酋矛 (ㄑㄧㄡˊ ㄇㄠˊ)
a kind of long spear
酋長 (ㄑㄧㄡˊ ㄓㄤˇ)
① a chieftain; the chief of a
tribe ② a sheik(h); an emir

三畫

【酌】 ⁶²⁴⁸ ㄓㄨㄛˊ jwo zhuó
1. to drink
2. to pour (wine)
3. to weigh and consider
酌辦 (ㄓㄨㄛˊ ㄅㄢˋ)
to handle by taking actual
circumstances into consideration
酌定 (ㄓㄨㄛˊ ㄉㄧㄥˋ)
to decide by taking circumstances into consideration;
to make a considered decision
酌奪 (ㄓㄨㄛˊ ㄉㄨㄛˊ)
to make a considered decision
酌量 (ㄓㄨㄛˊ ㄌㄧㄤˊ)
to weigh and consider
酌加 (ㄓㄨㄛˊ ㄐㄧㄚ)
to make considered addi-
tions
酌酒 (ㄓㄨㄛˊ ㄐㄧㄡˇ)
to pour wine
酌減 (ㄓㄨㄛˊ ㄐㄧㄢˇ)
to make considered reduc-
tions
酌情 (ㄓㄨㄛˊ ㄑㄧㄥˊ)
to take circumstances into
consideration; to make
allowance
酌獻 (ㄓㄨㄛˊ ㄒㄧㄢˋ)
to honor a deity with wine
酌議 (ㄓㄨㄛˊ ㄧˋ)
to consider and discuss

【配】 ⁶²⁴⁹ ㄆㄟˋ pey pèi
1. to join in marriage

2. to mate
3. to pair; to match: 顏色配得
很好. The colors match well.
4. to fit; to suit; to be a match
for; to match; to equal: 我配
把鑰匙. I have a key made to
fit a lock.
5. to dispense (medicines); to
prepare (according to a
demand); to distribute
(according to a plan)
6. to exile
7. a spouse; a partner
8. subordinate; supplementary;
supporting; attached
9. to deserve; to be worthy of;
to be qualified: 他不配當一名
領導者. He is not qualified to
be a leader.
配備 (ㄆㄟˋ ㄅㄟˋ)
① an outfit; equipment ② to
provide; to fit out
配不上 (ㄆㄟˋ ㄅㄨˋ ㄕㄤˋ)
to be no match for
配發 (ㄆㄟˋ ㄈㄚ)
to distribute
配方 (ㄆㄟˋ ㄈㄤ)
to dispense prescriptions
配房 (ㄆㄟˋ ㄈㄤˊ)
(said of a building) a wing
配搭 (ㄆㄟˋ ㄉㄚ)
to accompany in a supporting position; to match
配殿 (ㄆㄟˋ ㄉㄧㄢˋ)
(said of a palace building) a
wing
配對 (ㄆㄟˋ ㄉㄨㄟˋ)
to pair; to be a pair; to
mate; to match: 那兩隻鞋子
不配對. Those two shoes
don't match.
配隸 (ㄆㄟˋ ㄌㄧˋ)
to place in subordination to
配偶 (ㄆㄟˋ ㄡˇ)
a spouse
配料 (ㄆㄟˋ ㄌㄧㄠˋ)
(metallurgy) burden
配合 (ㄆㄟˋ ㄏㄜˊ)
to be in tune with; to be
adapted to; to match; to fit;
to coordinate with; to cooperate with; to synchronize
with: 襯衫的顏色與上衣的顏色
不配合. The color of the
shirt does not match that
of the coat.
配貨 (ㄆㄟˋ ㄏㄨㄛˋ)

to prepare goods for delivery according to an order

配給(ㄆㄟˋ ㄍㄟˇ)
①to distribute in rations; to ration; to allocate ②allocation

配給品(ㄆㄟˋ ㄐㄧˇ ㄆㄧㄣˇ)
rationed goods; an allocation

配給證(ㄆㄟˋ ㄐㄧˇ ㄓㄥˋ)
ration cards; ration coupons

配件(ㄆㄟˋ ㄐㄧㄢˋ)
accessories; 這些是不可缺少的配件。These are indispensable accessories.

配角(ㄆㄟˋ ㄐㄩㄝˊ)
①to appear with another leading player; to costar ②a supporting role; a minor role; a supporting actor or actress

配戴(ㄆㄟˋ ㄉㄞˋ)
to play a supporting role in a play

配享(ㄆㄟˋ ㄒㄧㄤˇ)
(said of courtiers, wise men, etc.) to have the honor of being enshrined in a Confucian temple, the ancestral temple of the emperor, etc.

配享千秋(ㄆㄟˋ ㄒㄧㄤˇ ㄑㄧㄢ ㄑㄧㄡ)
to be honored in a sacred shrine for endless ages

配置(ㄆㄟˋ ㄓˋ)
to station (troops); to equip (troops with weapons); to dispose (troops); to deploy: 哨兵配置在山上站崗。The sentinel was stationed on a hill.

配製(ㄆㄟˋ ㄓˋ)
to prepare or concoct according to a recipe or prescription

配種(ㄆㄟˋ ㄓㄨㄥˇ)
(animal husbandry) breeding

配售(ㄆㄟˋ ㄕㄡˋ)
to ration merchandise for sale

配生式(ㄆㄟˋ ㄕㄥ ㄕˋ)
a transliteration of 'per cent'

配色(ㄆㄟˋ ㄙㄜˋ)
to blend colors; to match colors

配所(ㄆㄟˋ ㄙㄨㄛˇ)
a place of exile

配偶(ㄆㄟˋ ㄡˇ)
a spouse; a mate

配貳(ㄆㄟˋ ㄦˋ)
a deputy; an assistant

配藥(ㄆㄟˋ ㄧㄠˋ)
to dispense medicines; to fill a prescription: 藥劑師照藥方配藥。The druggist filled a prescription.

配鑰匙(ㄆㄟˋ ㄧㄠˋ ˙ㄕ)
to duplicate keys

配眼鏡(ㄆㄟˋ ㄧㄢˇ ㄐㄧㄥˋ)
to get the right lenses for one's eyeglasses

配音(ㄆㄟˋ ㄧㄣ)
(movies) to dub; dubbing; to synchronize; synchronization: 我們爲外國影片配音。We dubbed foreign films in Chinese.

配樂(ㄆㄟˋ ㄩㄝˋ)
to dub in background music; incidental music

【酒】 6250
ㄐㄧㄡˇ jeou jiu
alcoholic drinks (brewed or distilled); wine; liquor; spirits: 酒後是眞情。In wine there is truth.

酒吧(ㄐㄧㄡˇ ㄅㄚ)
a bar (for alcoholic drinks)

酒吧女(ㄐㄧㄡˇ ㄅㄚ ㄋㄩˇ)
a bar girl; a barmaid

酒杯(ㄐㄧㄡˇ ㄅㄟ)
winecups

酒保(ㄐㄧㄡˇ ㄅㄠˇ)
a bartender; a waiter

酒癖(ㄐㄧㄡˇ ㄆㄧˇ)
dipsomania

酒瓶(ㄐㄧㄡˇ ㄆㄧㄥˊ)
a bottle for alcoholic drinks

酒鋪(ㄐㄧㄡˇ ㄆㄨˋ)or 酒店(ㄐㄧㄡˇ ㄉㄧㄢˋ)
a tavern; a saloon; a bar

酒鬼(ㄐㄧㄡˇ ㄇㄛˊ)
an alcoholic; a drunkard

酒母(ㄐㄧㄡˇ ㄇㄨˇ)
distiller's grains or yeast: 酒母開始發酵。The yeast began to work.

酒坊(ㄐㄧㄡˇ ㄈㄤˊ)
a tavern; a bar

酒瘋(ㄐㄧㄡˇ ㄈㄥ)
the silly behavior of a drunkard; temporary mental disorder after drinking too much

酒逢知己千杯少(ㄐㄧㄡˇ ㄈㄥˊ ㄓ ㄐㄧˇ ㄑㄧㄢ ㄅㄟ ㄕㄠˇ)
(literally) When drinking with a bosom friend, a thousand cups will still be too little.—One can drink far more than usual with a bosom friend.

酒德(ㄐㄧㄡˇ ㄉㄜˊ)or 酒品(ㄐㄧㄡˇ ㄆㄧㄣˇ)
decorum in drinking

酒罈(ㄐㄧㄡˇ ㄊㄢˊ)
a large jar for wine or liquor

酒徒(ㄐㄧㄡˇ ㄊㄨˊ)
an alcoholic; a drunkard

酒桶(ㄐㄧㄡˇ ㄊㄨㄥˇ)
a wine barrel or cask

酒囊飯袋(ㄐㄧㄡˇ ㄋㄤˊ ㄈㄢˋ ㄉㄞˋ)
(literally) wine sack and rice bag—a man who can do nothing but drink and eat; a good-for-nothing

酒釀(ㄐㄧㄡˇ ㄋㄧㄤˋ)
fermented rice, barley, etc. for brewing wine or liquor

酒樓(ㄐㄧㄡˇ ㄌㄡˊ)
a tavern; a bar; a saloon; a restaurant

酒闌人散(ㄐㄧㄡˇ ㄌㄢˊ ㄖㄣˊ ㄙㄢˋ)
The wine is running out and the guests are departing.

酒力(ㄐㄧㄡˇ ㄌㄧˋ)
①the strength of an alcoholic drink ②one's capacity for drinking

酒帘(ㄐㄧㄡˇ ㄌㄧㄢˊ)
a tavern sign in the form of a streamer

酒量(ㄐㄧㄡˇ ㄌㄧㄤˋ)
one's capacity for drinking

酒令(ㄐㄧㄡˇ ㄌㄧㄥˋ)
a drinking game conducted by an elected leader

酒缸(ㄐㄧㄡˇ ㄍㄤ)
①a large jar for wine or liquor ②a tavern

酒過三巡(ㄐㄧㄡˇ ㄍㄨㄛˋ ㄙㄢ ㄒㄩㄣˊ)
after the drinking has gone through three rounds

酒鬼(ㄐㄧㄡˇ ㄍㄨㄟˇ)
①a drunkard; a sot ②a toper; a wine bibber

酒館(ㄐㄧㄡˇ ㄍㄨㄢˇ)
a tavern; a pub; a bar: 我們到酒館喝酒。We went round

【酉部】

to the pub for a drink.

酒客(ㄐㄧㄡˇㄎㄜˋ)
a drinker

酒庫(ㄐㄧㄡˇㄎㄨˋ)
a cellar for wine; a wine cellar

酒狂(ㄐㄧㄡˇㄎㄨㄤˊ)
① temporary madness caused by alcoholic intoxication ② a drunken man

酒後失態(ㄐㄧㄡˇㄏㄡˋㄕㄊㄞˋ)
to act ludicrously when drunk

酒後失言(ㄐㄧㄡˇㄏㄡˋㄕㄧㄢˊ)
to say something wrong when drunk

酒酣耳熱(ㄐㄧㄡˇㄏㄢㄦˇㄖㄜˋ)
The enlivening effect of alcohol is just at its height.

酒壺(ㄐㄧㄡˇㄏㄨˊ)
a wine pot or jar

酒話(ㄐㄧㄡˇㄏㄨㄚˋ)
utterances of a drunkard

酒會(ㄐㄧㄡˇㄏㄨㄟˋ)
a cocktail party; a cocktail reception 亦作「鷄尾酒會」

酒荒(ㄐㄧㄡˇㄏㄨㄤ)
① alcoholic addiction ② a shortage of alcoholic drinks

酒家(ㄐㄧㄡˇㄐㄧㄚ)
① a tavern; a bar; a wine-shop ② the Chinese version of the geisha house in Japan; a girlie restaurant

酒家女(ㄐㄧㄡˇㄐㄧㄚㄋㄩˇ)or 酒女
(ㄐㄧㄡˇㄋㄩˇ)
① a barmaid; a bar girl ② the Chinese counterpart of a Japanese geisha

酒窖(ㄐㄧㄡˇㄐㄧㄠˋ)
a wine cellar

酒禁(ㄐㄧㄡˇㄐㄧㄣˋ)
prohibition of alcoholic drinks

酒漿(ㄐㄧㄡˇㄐㄧㄤ)
wine

酒經(ㄐㄧㄡˇㄐㄧㄥ)
books about alcoholic drinks

酒精(ㄐㄧㄡˇㄐㄧㄥ)
alcohol

酒精燈(ㄐㄧㄡˇㄐㄧㄥㄉㄥ)
an alcohol burner

酒精中毒(ㄐㄧㄡˇㄐㄧㄥㄓㄨㄥㄉㄨˊ)
chronic alcoholism; alcoholism; alcohol poisoning; 酒精

中毒會導致死亡。Alcoholism may result in death.

酒旗(ㄐㄧㄡˇㄑㄧˊ)
a tavern sign in the form of a streamer 亦作「酒帘」

酒氣噴噴(ㄐㄧㄡˇㄑㄧˋㄆㄣㄆㄣ)
(said of a drunkard) to smell heavily of alcohol

酒錢(ㄐㄧㄡˇㄑㄧㄢˊ)
tips

酒席(ㄐㄧㄡˇㄒㄧˊ)
a banquet; a feast

酒仙(ㄐㄧㄡˇㄒㄧㄢ)
"An Immortal with the Bottle"—a nickname of Li Po (李白), the famed Tang Dynasty poet, who was said to be at his inspired best in a state of drunkenness

酒興(ㄐㄧㄡˇㄒㄧㄥˋ)
elation from drinking

酒盅(ㄐㄧㄡˇㄓㄨㄥ)
winecups (especially small ones)

酒池肉林(ㄐㄧㄡˇㄔㄖㄡˋㄌㄧㄣˊ)
(literally) ponds of wine and woods of meat—debauchery on a magnificent scale; unprecedented luxury or wealth

酒廠(ㄐㄧㄡˇㄔㄤˇ)
a brewery; a winery; a distillery

酒食(ㄐㄧㄡˇㄕˊ)
food and drink

酒石(ㄐㄧㄡˇㄕˊ)
tartar or argol

酒石酸(ㄐㄧㄡˇㄕˊㄙㄨㄢ)
tartaric acid

酒聖(ㄐㄧㄡˇㄕㄥˋ)
a very strong drinker; a prodigious drinker

酒肉朋友(ㄐㄧㄡˇㄖㄡˋㄆㄥˊㄧㄡˇ)
friends in one's revels (not in one's need); fair-weather friends

酒肉和尚(ㄐㄧㄡˇㄖㄡˋㄏㄜˊㄕㄤˋ)
a drinking and nonvegetarian Buddhist monk

酒資(ㄐㄧㄡˇㄗ)
charges for drinks

酒滓(ㄐㄧㄡˇㄗˇ)or 酒糟(ㄐㄧㄡˇㄗㄠ)
the residue of fermented grain after the alcoholic contents have been distilled

酒糟鼻(ㄐㄧㄡˇㄗㄠㄅㄧˊ)or 酒渣鼻

(ㄐㄧㄡˇㄓㄚㄅㄧˊ)
acne rosacea

酒醉(ㄐㄧㄡˇㄗㄨㄟˋ)
drunk; intoxicated; tipsy

酒醉飯飽(ㄐㄧㄡˇㄗㄨㄟˋㄈㄢˋㄅㄠˇ)
having drunk and eaten to one's heart's content

酒菜(ㄐㄧㄡˇㄘㄞˋ)
① relishes taken with wine ② wine and delicacies

酒肆(ㄐㄧㄡˇㄙˋ)
a tavern; a bar; a saloon

酒色(ㄐㄧㄡˇㄙㄜˋ)
wine and women—sensual pleasures

酒色過度(ㄐㄧㄡˇㄙㄜˋㄍㄨㄛˋㄉㄨˋ)
excessive indulgence in sensual pleasures; debauchery

酒色之徒(ㄐㄧㄡˇㄙㄜˋㄓㄊㄨˊ)
a libertine; a debauchee

酒色財氣(ㄐㄧㄡˇㄙㄜˋㄘㄞˊㄑㄧˋ)
wine, women, wealth, and power—four main temptations to a man

酒意(ㄐㄧㄡˇㄧˋ)
a sign of drunkenness; a tipsy feeling

酒肴(ㄐㄧㄡˇㄧㄠˊ)
wine and delicacies

酒友(ㄐㄧㄡˇㄧㄡˇ)
a bottle companion: 他被酒友引入歧途。He was led away by bottle companions.

酒言酒語(ㄐㄧㄡˇㄧㄢˊㄐㄧㄡˇㄩˇ)
to talk incoherently when drunk; to be unable to speak clearly when drunk

酒宴(ㄐㄧㄡˇㄧㄢˋ)
a feast; a banquet

酒癮(ㄐㄧㄡˇㄧㄣˇ)
addiction to alcohol

酒窩兒(ㄐㄧㄡˇㄨㄛㄦ)
dimples on one's cheeks

酒翁(ㄐㄧㄡˇㄨㄥ)
a brewer

酒暈(ㄐㄧㄡˇㄩㄣˋ)
a flush on the face as a result of drinking

四畫

【酖】6251
1. ㄉㄢ dan dān
addicted to alcoholic drinks

酖酖(ㄉㄢㄉㄢ)
enjoying comfort

【酖】 6251
2. 业ㄣ jenn zhèn
poisonous wine

酖毒（ㄓㄣ ㄉㄨˊ）
poison

【酗】 6252
ㄒㄩ shiuh xù
to lose one's temper when drunk

酗酒（ㄒㄩˋ ㄐㄧㄡˇ）
to indulge in excessive drinking; to take to drinking: 他們酗酒滋事。They indulged in excessive drinking and created a disturbance.

酗訟（ㄒㄩˋ ㄙㄨㄥˋ）
to accuse each other because people got drunk

五畫

【酢】 6253
ㄗㄨㄛˋ tzuoh zuò
(said of a guest)to toast the host

酢漿草（ㄗㄨㄛˋ ㄐㄧ尢 ㄘㄠˇ）
(botany) the creeping oxalis
(*Oxalis corniculata*)

【酣】 6254
ㄏㄢ han hān
1. to enjoy intoxicants; to drink wine
2. to one's heart's content; as much as one wants; without inhibition

酣眠（ㄏㄢ ㄇㄧㄢˊ）
to sleep soundly

酣放（ㄏㄢ ㄈㄤˋ）
①(said of writing) unrestrained ②to indulge in excessive drinking; to drink without restraint

酣謔（ㄏㄢ ㄒㄩㄝˋ）
drinking and joking

酣樂（ㄏㄢ ㄌㄜˋ）
unrestrained pleasure

酣歌（ㄏㄢ ㄍㄜ）
to sing in exhilaration from drinking

酣呼（ㄏㄢ ㄏㄨ）
to yell or shout without restraint

酣興（ㄏㄢ ㄒㄧㄥˋ）
elation or exhilaration from liquor

酣戰（ㄏㄢ ㄓㄢˋ）
① to fight a fierce battle: 兩軍正酣戰。Two armies are fighting a fierce battle. ② the fierceness of a battle

酣中客（ㄏㄢ ㄓㄨㄥ ㄎㄜˋ）
an intoxicated person

酣暢（ㄏㄢ ㄔ尢ˋ）
①to drink to one's heart's content; to drink as much as one can ②with ease and verve; fully

酣賞（ㄏㄢ ㄕ尢ˇ）
to enjoy without restraint

酣睡（ㄏㄢ ㄕㄨㄟˋ）
to sleep soundly

酣醉（ㄏㄢ ㄗㄨㄟˋ）
deeply intoxicated by alcoholic beverages

酣縱（ㄏㄢ ㄗㄨㄥˋ）
to indulge in excessive drinking

酣飲（ㄏㄢ ㄧㄣˇ）
to drink as much as one can; to drink like a fish

酣娛（ㄏㄢ ㄩˊ）
to enjoy oneself to one's heart's content

intoxicated and satiated

【酤】 6255
ㄍㄨ gu gū
to sell or buy alcoholic drinks; to sell or buy spirits

酤酒（ㄍㄨ ㄐㄧㄡˇ）
to sell or buy alcoholic drinks

【酥】 6256
ㄙㄨ su sū
1. brittle; frail; fragile
2. crisp; crunchy
3. lustrous

酥餅（ㄙㄨ ㄅㄧㄥˇ）
a kind of crisp biscuit; shortcake

酥麻（ㄙㄨ ㄇㄚˊ）
frail and numb

酥髮（ㄙㄨ ㄈㄚˇ）
lustrous hair

酥糖（ㄙㄨ ㄊ尢ˊ）
crunchy candy; sugar cakes

酥酪（ㄙㄨ ㄌㄠˋ）
kumiss

酥胸（ㄙㄨ ㄒㄩㄥ）
the soft and smooth skin of a woman's bosom

酥軟（ㄙㄨ ㄖㄨㄢˇ）
lacking strength; feeble

酥脆（ㄙㄨ ㄘㄨㄟˋ）
crisp

酥脆花生（ㄙㄨ ㄘㄨㄟˋ ㄏㄨㄚ ㄕㄥ）
crisp peanuts

酥油（ㄙㄨ ㄧㄡˊ）
butter

六畫

【酩】 6257
ㄇㄧㄥˇ miing mǐng
（又讀 ㄇㄧㄥˊ ming
míng）
drunk; intoxicated; inebriate; inebriety; tipsy

酩酊（ㄇㄧㄥˇ ㄉㄧㄥˇ）
intoxicated; drunk; tipsy; dead drunk

酩酊大醉（ㄇㄧㄥˇ ㄉㄧㄥˇ ㄉㄚˋ ㄗㄨㄟˋ）
dead drunk

【酪】 6258
ㄌㄠˋ iaw lào
（讀音 ㄌㄨㄛˋ luoh luò）
1. alcoholic drinks
2. animal milk
3. cheese
4. fruit jam
5. junket
6. thick fruit juice; fruit jelly

酪餅（ㄌㄠˋ ㄅㄧㄥˇ）
cheese

酪酥（ㄌㄠˋ ㄙㄨ）
cream cheese

酪酸（ㄌㄠˋ ㄙㄨㄢ）
butyric acid

【酯】 6259
ㄓˇ jyy zhǐ
esters

【酬】 6260
ㄔㄡˊ chour chóu
1. to toast; to offer or present a cup of spirits, as in 獻酬
2. to reward; to requite; to reciprocate; reward
3. to fulfill; to realize

酬報（ㄔㄡˊ ㄅㄠˋ）
to reward; to requite

酬答（ㄔㄡˊ ㄉㄚˊ）
to reward; to requite

酬對（ㄔㄡˊ ㄉㄨㄟˋ）
to deal with (guests)

酬勞（ㄔㄡˊ ㄌㄠˊ）
to reward services

酬和（ㄔㄡˊ ㄏㄜˋ）
to exchange literary works as presents

酬金（ㄔㄡˊ ㄐㄧㄣ）

（酉部）

a cash reward; a bounty

酬謝(ㄔㄡ ㄒㄧㄝ)
to thank or reward(with money or gifts)

酬志(ㄔㄡ ㄓ)
to fulfill one's ambition

酬唱(ㄔㄡ ㄔㄤ)
to exchange poems, etc., as presents

酬神(ㄔㄡ ㄕㄣ)
to thank the gods with sacrifices

酬酢(ㄔㄡ ㄗㄨㄛ)
① social intercourse ② to exchange toasts

酬賽(ㄔㄡ ㄙㄞ)
to thank the gods with sacrifices

酬應(ㄔㄡ ㄧㄥ)
① to deal with (guests or visitors) ② social intercourse

酬庸(ㄔㄡ ㄩㄥ)
to reward services

【酮】 6261　ㄊㄨㄥ torng tóng
ketones

七畫

【醒】 6262　ㄔㄥ cherng chéng
hangover after heavy drinking; to be intoxicated, stupefied by drinking

【酵】 6263　ㄒㄧㄠ shiaw xiǎo
yeast; leaven

酵母(ㄒㄧㄠ ㄇㄨ)
yeast; leaven

酵母菌(ㄒㄧㄠ ㄇㄨ ㄐㄩㄣ)
a yeast fungus (Saccharomycetes)

酵素(ㄒㄧㄠ ㄙㄨ)
an enzyme

【酷】 6264　ㄎㄨ kuh kù
1. (said of intoxicants) strong
2. (said of fragrance) very stimulating
3. cruel; relentless; ruthless; brutal; severe; harsh
4. exceedingly

酷吏(ㄎㄨ ㄌㄧ)
a cruel official

酷烈(ㄎㄨ ㄌㄧㄝ)
cruel; brutal; atrocious;

---

harsh; severe

酷好(ㄎㄨ ㄏㄠ)
to be very fond of (a thing); to have a yen for

酷寒(ㄎㄨ ㄏㄢ)
severe cold

酷肖(ㄎㄨ ㄒㄧㄠ)
to resemble very closely

酷刑(ㄎㄨ ㄒㄧㄥ)
to torture; torture

酷暑(ㄎㄨ ㄕㄨ)
very hot weather

酷熱(ㄎㄨ ㄖㄜ)
torturing heat; extremely hot (weather)

酷似(ㄎㄨ ㄙ)
to resemble very closely: 她酷似她的母親。 She strongly resembles her mother.

酷愛(ㄎㄨ ㄞ)
to be very fond of (a thing) 牽看「酷好」; 他酷愛美術和古典音樂。 He was very fond of the fine arts and classical music.

【酸】 6265　ㄙㄨㄢ suan suān
1. sour; acid; tart
2. stale; spoiled
3. sad; grieved; sorrowful
4. aching; a tingle; an ache
5. jealous; envious
6. stingy
7. (chemistry)acid

酸鼻(ㄙㄨㄢ ㄅㄧ)
to have an irritated sensation in the nose; to feel like crying; to be grieved

酸葡萄(ㄙㄨㄢ ㄆㄨ ㄊㄠ)
sour grapes—something scorned because it cannot be had

酸梅(ㄙㄨㄢ ㄇㄟ)
sour plums

酸梅湯(ㄙㄨㄢ ㄇㄟ ㄊㄤ)
a decoction of sour plums used as a summer drink

酸腐(ㄙㄨㄢ ㄈㄨ)
① stale; hackneyed; trite ② erosion caused by acid

酸然(ㄙㄨㄢ ㄖㄢ)or 酸痛(ㄙㄨㄢ ㄊㄨㄥ)
(said of muscles) to ache from overexertion

酸甜苦辣(ㄙㄨㄢ ㄊㄧㄢ ㄎㄨ ㄌㄚ)
sour, sweet, bitter, and hot —the sweets and bitters (of

---

life)

酸奶(ㄙㄨㄢ ㄋㄞ)or 酸牛奶(ㄙㄨㄢ ㄋㄧㄡ ㄋㄞ)
yoghurt; sour milk

酸辣湯(ㄙㄨㄢ ㄌㄚ ㄊㄤ)
a kind of soup seasoned with vinegar and pepper

酸類(ㄙㄨㄢ ㄌㄟ)
acids

酸懶(ㄙㄨㄢ ㄌㄢ)
indolent with aching muscles

酸梨(ㄙㄨㄢ ㄌㄧ)
a variety of pear (with a sour taste)

酸溜溜(ㄙㄨㄢ ㄌㄧㄡ ㄌㄧㄡ)
① sour ② sad; grievous ③ jealous; envious ④ to ache

酸根(ㄙㄨㄢ ㄍㄣ)
acid radicals

酸梗(ㄙㄨㄢ ㄍㄥ)
an aching void in the heart; sorrow

酸懷(ㄙㄨㄢ ㄏㄨㄞ)
sorrow; grief

酸基(ㄙㄨㄢ ㄐㄧ)
acid radicals 參看「酸根」

酸秀才(ㄙㄨㄢ ㄒㄧㄡ ㄘㄞ)
a pedantic scholar

酸辛(ㄙㄨㄢ ㄒㄧㄣ)
hardship; 他受盡各種艱難酸辛。 He suffered all kinds of hardships.

酸心(ㄙㄨㄢ ㄒㄧㄣ)
① heartbroken; sad; grieved ② heartburn

酸性(ㄙㄨㄢ ㄒㄧㄥ)
acidity

酸性廢物(ㄙㄨㄢ ㄒㄧㄥ ㄈㄟ ㄨ)
acid waste

酸性鹽(ㄙㄨㄢ ㄒㄧㄥ ㄧㄢ)
acid salt

酸性雨(ㄙㄨㄢ ㄒㄧㄥ ㄩ)
acid rain 亦作「酸雨」

酸削(ㄙㄨㄢ ㄒㄩㄝ)
to ache

酸楚(ㄙㄨㄢ ㄔㄨ)
hardship

酸愴(ㄙㄨㄢ ㄔㄨㄤ)
grief; sorrow

酸軟(ㄙㄨㄢ ㄖㄨㄢ)
(said of muscles, limbs, etc.) aching and lacking strength: 他四肢酸軟無力。 His limbs are aching and limp.

酸棗子(ㄙㄨㄢ ㄗㄠ ˙ㄗ)or 酸棗兒(ㄙㄨㄢ ㄗㄠ ㄦ)or 酸棗(ㄙㄨㄢ ㄗㄠ)

a kind of date (with a sour taste)

酸菜（ムメ乃 ち历）
pickled cabbage (which tastes sour); pickled vegetables

酸筍（ムメ乃 ㄙㄨㄣˇ）
a kind of edible bamboo shoot

酸噎（ムメ乃 ㄧㄝ）
sad; grieved; heartbroken

酸味（ムメ乃 ㄨㄟˋ）
acid; a sour taste

【酹】 6266 ㄌㄟˋ ley lèi
to make a libation

酹地（ㄌㄟˋ ㄉㄧˋ）
to make a libation; to pour wine in a libation

【酺】 6267 ㄆㄨˊ pwu pú
to drink in company

酺燕（ㄆㄨˊ ㄧㄢ）
to drink with one's subjects or vassals

【酴】 6268 ㄊㄨˊ twu tú
1. a distiller's grain or yeast
2. wine brewed for the second time

酴醿（ㄊㄨˊ ㄇㄧˊ）
① wine brewed for the second time ② a kind of shrub 亦作「荼蘼」

酴醿酒（ㄊㄨˊ ㄇㄧˊ ㄐㄧㄡˇ）or 酴酒（ㄊㄨˊ ㄐㄧㄡˇ）
wine brewed for the second time

酴蘇（ㄊㄨˊ ㄙㄨ）
a kind of medicated wine 亦作「屠蘇酒」

八畫

【醃】 6269 ㄧㄢ ian yān
to pickle; to salt

醃肉（ㄧㄢ ㄖㄡˋ）
salted pork; salted meat

醃菜（ㄧㄢ ㄘㄞˋ）
pickled vegetables

醃魚（ㄧㄢ ㄩˊ）
salted fish

【醅】 6270 ㄆㄟ pei pēi
unstrained wine

【醇】 6271 ㄔㄨㄣˊ chwen chún
1. rich wine; strong wine
2. pure; unadulterated
3. gentle; gracious; judicious
4. ethyl alcohol

醇備（ㄔㄨㄣˊ ㄅㄟˋ）
pure and perfect

醇朴（ㄔㄨㄣˊ ㄆㄨˊ）
gentle and honest

醇美（ㄔㄨㄣˊ ㄇㄟˇ）
pure and fair

醇醲（ㄔㄨㄣˊ ㄋㄨㄥˊ）
rich wine; strong wine

醇釃（ㄔㄨㄣˊ ㄕ）
rich wine; strong wine

醇醨（ㄔㄨㄣˊ ㄌㄧˊ）
strong wines and light wines

醇厚（ㄔㄨㄣˊ ㄏㄡˋ）
① mellow: 這種酒酒味醇厚。This kind of wine is mellow. ② gentle and kind

醇化（ㄔㄨㄣˊ ㄏㄨㄚˋ）
①(Aristotelian) catharsis ② to purify; to idealize

醇美人（ㄔㄨㄣˊ ㄇㄟˇ ㄖㄣˊ）or 醇醾婦人（ㄔㄨㄣˊ ㄐㄧㄡˋ ㄈㄨˋ ㄖㄣˊ）
indulgence in wine and women—sensual pleasures

醇謹（ㄔㄨㄣˊ ㄐㄧㄣˇ）
gentle and judicious

醇精（ㄔㄨㄣˊ ㄐㄧㄥ）
diethyl ether or ethyl ether

醇儒（ㄔㄨㄣˊ ㄖㄨˊ）
a pure-minded scholar; an honest scholar

醇粹（ㄔㄨㄣˊ ㄘㄨㄟˋ）
pure; unadulterated

【醉】 6272 ㄗㄨㄟˋ tzuey zuì
1. drunk; intoxicated; tipsy
2. infatuated; charmed

醉墨（ㄗㄨㄟˋ ㄇㄛˋ）
drawings or writings done when one is drunk

醉倒（ㄗㄨㄟˋ ㄉㄠˇ）
to succumb to the effect of alcohol

醉態（ㄗㄨㄟˋ ㄊㄞˋ）
the state of being drunk

醉鬼（ㄗㄨㄟˋ ㄍㄨㄟˇ）
a drunkard: 醉鬼揚亂。A drunkard caused a disturbance.

醉客（ㄗㄨㄟˋ ㄎㄜˋ）
a drunken man

醉漢（ㄗㄨㄟˋ ㄏㄢˋ）
a drunkard; a drunken person

醉酒飽德（ㄗㄨㄟˋ ㄐㄧㄡˇ ㄅㄠˇ ㄉㄜˊ）
I am drunk with your wine and filled with your virtues. (a conventional phrase for thanking the host at the end of a banquet)

醉蟹（ㄗㄨㄟˋ ㄒㄧㄝˋ）
crabs steeped in wine (considered as a delicacy)

醉心（ㄗㄨㄟˋ ㄒㄧㄣ）
infatuated with (a pursuit); to be engrossed in; to be intoxicated with: 他醉心名譽。He was intoxicated with fame.

醉鄉（ㄗㄨㄟˋ ㄒㄧㄤ）
a paradise or utopia of drunkenness

醉醒（ㄗㄨㄟˋ ㄒㄧㄥˇ）
to regain presence of mind after getting drunk; to sober up

醉醺醺（ㄗㄨㄟˋ ㄒㄩㄣ ㄒㄩㄣ）
inebriated; sottish; drunk; tipsy; under the influence of liquor 亦作「醉薰薰」

醉生夢死（ㄗㄨㄟˋ ㄕㄥ ㄇㄥˋ ㄙˇ）
to live a befuddled life

醉聖（ㄗㄨㄟˋ ㄕㄥˋ）
① a great drinker; a prodigious drinker ② "A Sage with a Bottle"—a nickname of Li Po (李白), a famed Tang Dynasty poet who was said to write best while drinking

醉如泥（ㄗㄨㄟˋ ㄖㄨˊ ㄋㄧˊ）
dead drunk; drunk as a lord

醉意（ㄗㄨㄟˋ ㄧˋ）
slightly drunk; symptoms of drunkenness; tipsy: 你已經有幾分醉意了。You are a bit tipsy.

醉眼惺忪（ㄗㄨㄟˋ ㄧㄢˇ ㄒㄧㄥ ㄙㄨㄥ）
to have one's eyes blurred with drinking

醉臥（ㄗㄨㄟˋ ㄨㄛˋ）
to lie in a drunken stupor: 他醉臥地板上。He lay on the floor in a drunken stupor.

醉翁（ㄗㄨㄟˋ ㄨㄥ）
an old drunkard: 幾個醉翁倒在地上。Several old drunkards lay on the floor.

〔酉 部〕

醉翁亭 (ㄗㄨㄟˋ ㄨㄥ ㄊㄧㄥˊ)
the Pavilion of the Old Drunkard, in Anhwei, built during the Sung Dynasty and named by poet Ou-Yang Hsiu (歐陽修), who called himself the Drunken Lord

醉翁之意不在酒 (ㄗㄨㄟˋ ㄨㄥ ㄓ ㄧˋ ㄅㄨˋ ㄗㄞˋ ㄐㄧㄡˇ)
(literally) The drunkard is not really interested in wine.
—to be secretly interested in something while pretending to show interest in another

【醊】 6273
ㄔㄨㄛˋ chuoh chuò
to pour wine in a libation

【醋】 6274
ㄘㄨˋ tsuh cù
vinegar

醋壜子 (ㄘㄨˋ ㄊㄢˊ ·ㄗ) or 醋罐子 (ㄘㄨˋ ㄍㄨㄢˋ ·ㄗ)
a jealous person, especially a woman

醋海生波 (ㄘㄨˋ ㄏㄞˇ ㄕㄥ ㄅㄛ) or 醋海興波 (ㄘㄨˋ ㄏㄞˇ ㄒㄧㄥˋ ㄅㄛ)
disturbance due to jealousy; marital trouble arising from infidelity

醋勁兒 (ㄘㄨˋ ㄐㄧㄥˋㄦ)
jealousy

醋酸 (ㄘㄨˋ ㄙㄨㄢ)
acetic acid

醋意 (ㄘㄨˋ ㄧˋ)
jealousy: 她的醋意熾熱。She is burning with jealousy.

【醁】 6275
ㄌㄨˋ luh lù
a kind of green-colored wine

九畫

【醒】 6276
ㄒㄧㄥˇ shiing xǐng
1. to recover from (drunkenness, a stupor, etc.); to sober up; to come to: 病人醒過來了。The patient has come to.
2. to awake; to wake up; to be roused: 我醒得很早。I woke up early.
3. to be clear or cool in mind: 他的頭腦清醒。He keeps a cool head.

醒脾 (ㄒㄧㄥˇ ㄆㄧˊ)
①(said of plays, novels, etc.) entertaining ②to make fun of

醒木 (ㄒㄧㄥˇ ㄇㄨˋ)
storyteller's wooden clappers

醒目 (ㄒㄧㄥˇ ㄇㄨˋ)
①to catch the eye; eye-catching; to attract attention; refreshing ②awake; not asleep

醒來 (ㄒㄧㄥˇ ㄌㄞˊ)
to wake up: 你通常在什麼時間醒來？ What time do you usually wake up?

醒狂 (ㄒㄧㄥˇ ㄎㄨㄤˊ)
a wild or an unrestrained person who romps without being drunk

醒豁 (ㄒㄧㄥˇ ㄏㄨㄛˋ)
conspicuous; remarkable; clear; explicit: 那道理說得很豁。That reason is clearly presented.

醒酒 (ㄒㄧㄥˇ ㄐㄧㄡˇ)
to sober up from drunkenness; to dispel the effects of alcohol

醒覺 (ㄒㄧㄥˇ ㄐㄩㄝˊ)
to awake; to wake

醒獅 (ㄒㄧㄥˇ ㄕ)
the awakened lion

醒世 (ㄒㄧㄥˇ ㄕˋ)
to rouse the public from mental slumber

醒眼 (ㄒㄧㄥˇ ㄧㄢˇ)
to attract attention; to catch the eye; refreshing

醒悟 (ㄒㄧㄥˇ ㄨˋ)
to awake (from errors, illusions, etc.); to come to one's senses; to come to realize: 他已醒悟了。He's come to realize the truth.

【醍】 6277
ㄊㄧˊ tyi tí
1. cream (of milk)
2. a kind of reddish wine

醍醐 (ㄊㄧˊ ㄏㄨˊ)
①clarified butter (regarded as a symbol of Buddhist wisdom or truth) ②purity of a man's character

醍醐灌頂 (ㄊㄧˊ ㄏㄨˊ ㄍㄨㄢˋ ㄉㄧㄥˇ)
①(Buddhism) to impart wisdom to one's mind ②to make one comfortable

【醐】 6278
ㄏㄨˊ hwu hú
as in 醍醐—clarified butter

(a symbol of Buddhist truth or wisdom)

十畫

【醜】 6279
ㄔㄡˇ choou chǒu
1. ugly; homely; bad-looking: 她長得不醜。She is not bad-looking.
2. abominable; vile; bad
3. shameful; disgraceful; infamous
4. to compare

醜八怪 (ㄔㄡˇ ㄅㄚ ㄍㄨㄞˋ)
a very ugly fellow; a monstrous fellow; an ugly woman 亦作「醜巴怪」

醜名 (ㄔㄡˇ ㄇㄧㄥˊ)
bad reputation; dishonor; infamy; ill fame; notoriety

醜詆 (ㄔㄡˇ ㄉㄧˇ)
to abuse; to revile

醜態 (ㄔㄡˇ ㄊㄞˋ)
scandalous behavior; an unseemly sight; a disgraceful manner

醜態百出 (ㄔㄡˇ ㄊㄞˋ ㄅㄞˇ ㄔㄨ)
to show all sorts of disgraceful behavior; to act like a buffoon

醜類 (ㄔㄡˇ ㄌㄟˋ)
①the bad kind; rascals; villains ②to compare things of the same kind

醜陋 (ㄔㄡˇ ㄌㄡˋ)
ugly; bad-looking

醜虜 (ㄔㄡˇ ㄌㄨˇ)
(a disparaging term) the enemy

醜化 (ㄔㄡˇ ㄏㄨㄚˋ)
to smear; to uglify; to defame; to vilify: 這齣戲醜化我們的形象。This play vilifies us.

醜極了 (ㄔㄡˇ ㄐㄧˊ ·ㄌㄜ)
extremely ugly; monstrous; abominable

醜行 (ㄔㄡˇ ㄒㄧㄥˊ)
disgraceful behavior; shameful conduct

醜事 (ㄔㄡˇ ㄕˋ)
a disgraceful affair; a scandal

醜聞四溢 (ㄔㄡˇ ㄨㄣˊ ㄙˋ ㄧˋ)
notorious 或 The ill fame has spread far and wide.

魏死了(メㄨㄙ・ㄌㄜ)
abominable; monstrous; extremely ugly

魏惡(メㄨˋㄜˋ)
ulgy; repulsive; hideous

魏樣(メㄨˋ ㄧㄤˋ)
ugly looks

魏聞(メㄨˋ)
scandal

魏語(メㄨˋ ㄩˇ)
abusive words; vile language

醞 6280
ㄩㄣ yunn yùn
1. to brew; to ferment
2. preliminary informal discussion; to deliberate on; deliberation
3. wine

醞釀(ㄩㄣ ㄋㄧㄤˋ)
①to brew(wine or liquor)
②(said of a storm, disturbance, etc.)to begin to form; to brew

醞藉(ㄩㄣ ㄐㄧㄝˋ)
cultivated and refined 亦作「蘊藉」

醚 6281
ㄇㄧ mi mí
ether

醛 6282
ㄑㄩㄢ chyuan quán
aldehyde

醣 6283
ㄊㄤ tarng táng
carbohydrate

醢 6284
ㄏㄞ hae hǎi
1. minced and hashed meat
2. to mince a criminal as a punishment in ancient China

十一畫

醫 6285
ㄧ i yī
to cure or treat (diseases)
a doctor; a physician; a surgeon
medical science; medical service; medicine

醫病(ㄧ ㄅㄧㄥˋ)
to treat a patient; to cure a disease: 醫病是醫生的職責。The business of doctors is to cure diseases.

醫卜星相(ㄧ ㄅㄨˇ ㄒㄧㄥ ㄒㄧㄤˋ)
medicine, prophecy, astrology and physiognomy—the

occult sciences or the practitioners of such

醫方(ㄧ ㄈㄤ)
a medical prescription

醫德(ㄧ ㄉㄜˊ)
medical ethics

醫道(ㄧ ㄉㄠˋ)
medical skill; medical science

醫療(ㄧ ㄌㄧㄠˊ)
to cure or treat (a disease); medical treatment

醫療用具(ㄧ ㄌㄧㄠˊ ㄩㄥˋ ㄐㄩˋ)
medical instruments

醫國(ㄧ ㄍㄨㄛˊ)
to regulate the state; to cure a country of its ills

醫科(ㄧ ㄎㄜ)
the department of medicine (at a university): 他在大學讀醫科。He is studying medicine at the university.

醫家(ㄧ ㄐㄧㄚ)
a skilled doctor

醫界(ㄧ ㄐㄧㄝˋ)
the medical circles; the medical world

醫學(ㄧ ㄒㄩㄝˊ)
medical science

醫學博士(ㄧ ㄒㄩㄝˊ ㄅㄛˊ ㄕˋ)
Doctor of Medicine; M.D.

醫學士(ㄧ ㄒㄩㄝˊ ㄕˋ)
Bachelor of Medicine; M.B.

醫學院(ㄧ ㄒㄩㄝˊ ㄩㄢˋ)
a college of medicine

醫治(ㄧ ㄓˋ)
to cure (a disease); medical treatment; to doctor: 他醫治了那老人的疔。He doctored the old man's boil.

醫師(ㄧ ㄕ)
a physician; a surgeon; a doctor: 哪位醫師替你治病？Which doctor is treating you for this trouble?

醫師公會(ㄧ ㄕ ㄍㄨㄥ ㄏㄨㄟˋ)
medical association

醫師節(ㄧ ㄕ ㄐㄧㄝˊ)
Medical Day (November 12)

醫士(ㄧ ㄕˋ)
a herb doctor; a doctor practicing Chinese herb medicine

醫生(ㄧ ㄕㄥ)
a doctor; a physician; a surgeon

醫術(ㄧ ㄕㄨˋ)
medical skill; the art of healing

醫藥(ㄧ ㄧㄠˋ)
healing drugs; medicines

醫藥保險(ㄧ ㄧㄠˋ ㄅㄠˇ ㄒㄧㄢˇ)
medical insurance

醫藥費(ㄧ ㄧㄠˋ ㄈㄟˋ)
a hospital bill; a doctor's fee; medical expenses; my bill: 我有醫藥費需要付。I have the medical bill to pay.

醫藥顧問(ㄧ ㄧㄠˋ ㄍㄨˋ ㄨㄣˋ)
a medical adviser

醫藥罔效(ㄧ ㄧㄠˋ ㄨㄤˇ ㄒㄧㄠˋ)
incurable with medicine 或 Medical science has failed (to save the patient).

醫務(ㄧ ㄨˋ)
medical matters

醫院(ㄧ ㄩㄢˋ)
a hospital: 他的妹妹是醫院的護士。His younger sister is a hospital nurse.

醨 6286
ㄌㄧ li lí
1. weak wine or liquor
2. light or weak (wine, tea, etc.)

醪 6287
ㄌㄠˊ lau láo
1. unstrained wine or liquor
2. mellow wine

醪糟(ㄌㄠˊ ㄗㄠ)
unstrained wine

醬 6288
ㄐㄧㄤˋ jiang jiàng
1. soybean sauce; soy
2. food in the form of paste; jam

醬瓜(ㄐㄧㄤˋ ㄍㄨㄚ)
cucumbers, etc. pickled in soybean sauce

醬肉(ㄐㄧㄤˋ ㄖㄡˋ)
pork cooked in soy sauce; braised pork seasoned with soy sauce

醬菜(ㄐㄧㄤˋ ㄘㄞˋ)
cabbages, etc. pickled in soybean sauce

醬色(ㄐㄧㄤˋ ㄙㄜˋ)
a dark brownish color

醬油(ㄐㄧㄤˋ ㄧㄡˊ)
soybean sauce; soy; soy sauce

醯 6289
ㄒㄧ shi xī

(酉部)

vinegar; pickle; acid

十二畫

〔采
部〕

6290
【醭】ㄅㄨ bwu bú
(又讀 ㄆㄨ pwu pú)
white specks of mildew

6291
【醮】ㄐㄧㄠ jiaw jiào
1. religious service
2. wedding; marriage
醮壇 (ㄐㄧㄠ ㄊㄢˊ)
an altar for service of offering sacrifices to gods or the deceased

6292
【醱】ㄆㄛ poh pò
to brew for the second time
醱酵 (ㄆㄛ ㄒㄧㄠˋ)
to ferment

十三畫

6293
【醴】ㄌㄧ lii lǐ
1. sweet wine
2. the sweet water from a spring
醴泉 (ㄌㄧ ㄑㄩㄢˊ)
①a sweet spring or fountain ②name of a county in Shensi (陝西省)

6294
【醲】ㄋㄨㄥ nong nóng
1. strong wine; rich wine
2. thick; dense; saturated 亦作「濃」
醲郁 (ㄋㄨㄥ ㄩˋ)
(said of wine) rich; having more body

6295
【醵】ㄐㄩ jiuh jù
to pool money (for a feast, etc.)
醵金 (ㄐㄩ ㄐㄧㄣ)or 醵資 (ㄐㄩ ㄗ)
to pool money

十四畫

6296
【醺】ㄒㄩㄣ shiun xūn
drunk; intoxicated; tipsy
醺酣 (ㄒㄩㄣ ㄏㄢ)
(said of weather) warm; balmy
醺醺 (ㄒㄩㄣ ㄒㄩㄣ)
inebriated; under the influ-

ence of liquor; tipsy

十七畫

6297
【醸】ㄋㄧㄤ niang niàng
1. to brew; to ferment
2. to take shape or form slowly
3. wine
醸蜜 (ㄋㄧㄤ ㄇㄧˋ)
(said of bees) to make honey
醸禍 (ㄋㄧㄤ ㄏㄨㄛˋ)
to brew mischief
醸酒 (ㄋㄧㄤ ㄐㄧㄡ)
to brew wine
醸成 (ㄋㄧㄤ ㄔㄥˊ)
to bring about slowly; to breed; to lead slowly to; to form gradually
醸造 (ㄋㄧㄤ ㄗㄠˋ)
to brew: 這酒是用米醸造的。
This wine is brewed from rice.

6298
【醽】ㄌㄧㄥ ling líng
a kind of wine
醽醁 (ㄌㄧㄥ ㄌㄨˋ)
a kind of green-colored wine

6299
【醾】ㄇㄧ mi mí
as in 酴醾—wine brewed for the second time

十八畫

6300
【釁】ㄒㄧㄣ shinn xìn
1. to anoint (drums, bells, etc.) with blood in worship
2. to anoint (the body)
3. a rift (between people)
釁端 (ㄒㄧㄣ ㄉㄨㄢ)
the cause of a fight
釁鼓 (ㄒㄧㄣ ㄍㄨ)
to consecrate a drum by rubbing on it the blood of a slaughtered animal (before going to a battle in ancient times)
釁隙 (ㄒㄧㄣ ㄒㄧ)
a rift (between groups of people)
釁鐘 (ㄒㄧㄣ ㄓㄨㄥ)
to consecrate a bell by rubbing on it the blood of a slaughtered animal
釁浴 (ㄒㄧㄣ ㄩˋ)

fragrant wine for anointing a dead body
釁浴 (ㄒㄧㄣ ㄩˋ)
to bathe and anoint with fragrant essences (before worship)

二十畫

6301
【釅】ㄧㄢˋ yann yàn
strong (beverages)

采 部

ㄅㄧㄢˋ biann biàn

一畫

6302
【采】 1. ㄘㄞ tsae cǎi
1. to gather; to collect
2. to pick; to select
3. bright colors
采辦 (ㄘㄞ ㄅㄢˋ)
to select and purchase 亦作「采辦」
采集 (ㄘㄞ ㄐㄧ)
to gather or collect (materials, etc.) 亦作「采集」
采芹 (ㄘㄞ ㄑㄧㄣˊ)
(in former times)to pass the civil service examination or the county level 亦作「采芹」
采戲 (ㄘㄞ ㄒㄧˋ)
a kind of game played with dice
采薪之憂 (ㄘㄞ ㄒㄧㄣ ㄓ ㄧㄡ)
(literally) to worry about gathering firewood—illhealth
采摭 (ㄘㄞ ㄓˊ)
to pick up; to collect 亦作「采摭」
采詩 (ㄘㄞ ㄕ)
to collect popular songs (as was done by the emperor's officials in ancient times) 办作「采詩」
采聲 (ㄘㄞ ㄕㄥ)
applause; cheers; shouts of "Bravo!"
采衣 (ㄘㄞ ㄧ)
colorful garments; bright

garments 亦作「彩衣」

【采】 6302
2. ㄘㄞˇ tsay cǎi
a fief; vassalage

采地(ㄘㄞˇ ㄉㄧˋ)
a fief; vassalage

采邑(ㄘㄞˇ ㄧˋ)
a fief; vassalage

五畫

【釉】 6303
ㄧㄡˋ yow yòu
glaze (on pottery, etc.)

釉子(ㄧㄡˋ ㄗ˙)or 釉兒(ㄧㄡˋ)
glaze (on pottery, etc.)

釉藥(ㄧㄡˋ ㄧㄠˋ)or 釉灰(ㄧㄡˋ ㄏㄨㄟ)
substance used to produce glaze for pottery; glaze

十三畫

【釋】 6304
ㄕˋ shyh shì
1. to explain; to interpret
2. to set free
3. to relieve
4. to disperse; to dispel
5. of Buddha or Buddhism

釋門(ㄕˋ ㄇㄣˊ)
a gate to Buddhism — Buddhism

釋悶(ㄕˋ ㄇㄣˋ)
to disperse melancholy; to chase away gloom

釋放(ㄕˋ ㄈㄤˋ)
to set free; to release

釋道(ㄕˋ ㄉㄠˋ)or 釋老(ㄕˋ ㄌㄠˇ)
Buddhism and Taoism

釋典(ㄕˋ ㄉㄧㄢˇ)
the Buddhist scriptures

釋奠(ㄕˋ ㄉㄧㄢˋ)
to honor gods or ancestors with sacrifices of wine and foods

釋例(ㄕˋ ㄌㄧˋ)
explanatory specimens

釋憾(ㄕˋ ㄏㄢˋ)
to dispel hatred or a grudge

釋迦(ㄕˋ ㄐㄧㄚ)
Sakya, the clan or family of Buddha

釋迦牟尼(ㄕˋ ㄐㄧㄚ ㄇㄡˊ ㄋㄧˊ)
Sakyamuni (563-483 B.C.)

釋教(ㄕˋ ㄐㄧㄠˋ)
Buddhism

釋去重負(ㄕˋ ㄑㄩˋ ㄓㄨㄥˋ ㄈㄨˋ)
to be relieved of a heavy responsibility

釋嫌(ㄕˋ ㄒㄧㄢˊ)
① to dispel suspicion ② to dispel ill feeling

釋氏(ㄕˋ ㄕˋ)
① Buddha ② a follower of Buddha

釋手(ㄕˋ ㄕㄡˇ)
to relax the hold; to loosen one's grip

釋然(ㄕˋ ㄖㄢˊ)
① at ease; relaxed ② having all the misunderstandings cleared up

釋子(ㄕˋ ㄗ˙)
Buddhist priests

釋疑(ㄕˋ ㄧˊ)
to dispel doubt; to settle uncertainties

釋義(ㄕˋ ㄧˋ)
expatiation; interpretation; to explain

里 部
ㄌㄧˇ lii lǐ

【里】 6305
ㄌㄧˇ liii lǐ
1. a neighborhood, or community, of 25 families (in ancient times); a neighborhood; a village
2. li (a unit of linear measure about one third of a mile)

里保(ㄌㄧˇ ㄅㄠˇ)
(in ancient times) the head of a neighborhood consisting of 25 families

里門(ㄌㄧˇ ㄇㄣˊ)or 里閈(ㄌㄧˇ ㄏㄢˋ)
① a village gate ② villages; rural communities

里拉(ㄌㄧˇ ㄌㄚ)
a lira

里豪(ㄌㄧˇ ㄏㄠˊ)
a village bully

里居(ㄌㄧˇ ㄐㄩ)
① to live in the country; to live in retirement ② one's address

里巷(ㄌㄧˇ ㄒㄧㄤˋ)
streets

里巷之談(ㄌㄧˇ ㄒㄧㄤˋ ㄓ ㄊㄢˊ)
idle talk in the street; gossip

里胥(ㄌㄧˇ ㄒㄩ)
the village head

里長(ㄌㄧˇ ㄓㄤˇ)
① (in ancient times) the head of a neighborhood of 25 families ② the head of a subdivision of the district, or borough, in a city or county

里程(ㄌㄧˇ ㄔㄥˊ)
① mileage ② the course of development; course

里程碑(ㄌㄧˇ ㄔㄥˊ ㄅㄟ)
a milestone; a milepost 亦作「里程標」

里程表(ㄌㄧˇ ㄔㄥˊ ㄅㄧㄠˇ)
a table of distances

里程錶(ㄌㄧˇ ㄔㄥˊ ㄅㄧㄠˇ)
an odometer; a hodometer

里社(ㄌㄧˇ ㄕㄜˋ)
a village shrine, temple, etc.

里舍(ㄌㄧˇ ㄕㄜˋ)
a residence

里斯本(ㄌㄧˇ ㄙ ㄅㄣˇ)
Lisbon, the capital of Portugal

里昂(ㄌㄧˇ ㄤˊ)
Lyons (or Lyon), a city and industrial center of east France

里諺(ㄌㄧˇ ㄧㄢˋ)
proverbs

里約熱內廬(ㄌㄧˇ ㄩㄝ ㄖㄜˋ ㄋㄟˋ ㄌㄨˊ)
Rio de Janeiro, the former capital of Brazil

二畫

【重】 6306
1. ㄓㄨㄥˋ jonq zhòng
1. heavy; weighty; much: 我的工作很重。I have a heavy work load.
2. to weigh; weight
3. difficult
4. serious; grave
5. severe
6. important; significant
7. to value; to emphasize

重寶(ㄓㄨㄥˋ ㄅㄠˇ)
treasure of much value

重辦(ㄓㄨㄥˋ ㄅㄢˋ)
to take severe action against; to punish severely

重兵(ㄓㄨㄥˋ ㄅㄧㄥ)

〔里部〕

a large force (for military operations); massive forces

重病(ㄓㄨㄥˋ ㄅㄧㄥˋ)
a serious illness

重砲(ㄓㄨㄥˋ ㄆㄠˋ)
heavy artillery; heavy guns

重錳酸鉀(ㄓㄨㄥˋ ㄇㄥˇ ㄙㄨㄢ ㄐㄧㄚˇ)
potassium permanganate

重名(ㄓㄨㄥˋ ㄇㄧㄥˊ)
①fame ②to value fame; to attach importance to fame

重罰(ㄓㄨㄥˋ ㄈㄚˊ)
to fine heavily; to punish severely; heavy fine; severe punishment

重犯(ㄓㄨㄥˋ ㄈㄢˋ)
an important criminal; a criminal who is guilty of a serious crime

重負(ㄓㄨㄥˋ ㄈㄨˋ)
a heavy burden; a heavy load; a heavy responsibility: 他覺得如釋重負。He feels as if relieved of a heavy load.

重大(ㄓㄨㄥˋ ㄉㄚˋ)
①important; of great consequence; significant ②serious; grave

重擔(ㄓㄨㄥˋ ㄉㄢˋ)
a heavy burden; a heavy responsibility

重地(ㄓㄨㄥˋ ㄉㄧˋ)
an important place; a restricted area: 施工重地, 閒人莫進。Construction Site. No Admittance.

重典(ㄓㄨㄥˋ ㄉㄧㄢˇ)
severe provisions (in the law)

重點(ㄓㄨㄥˋ ㄉㄧㄢˇ)
the point or center of emphasis

重讀(ㄓㄨㄥˋ ㄉㄨˊ)
to stress: 重讀音節 a stressed syllable

重頭戲(ㄓㄨㄥˋ ㄊㄡˊ ㄒㄧˋ)
①a play involving much singing and action: 他演重頭戲。He performed a play involving much singing and action. ②a role involving much singing and action

重碳酸鈉(ㄓㄨㄥˋ ㄊㄢˋ ㄙㄨㄢ ㄋㄚˋ)
sodium bicarbonate

重聽(ㄓㄨㄥˋ ㄊㄧㄥ)
weak in hearing; hard of hearing: 她的祖母重聽。Her grandma is hard of hearing.

重農主義(ㄓㄨㄥˋ ㄋㄨㄥˊ ㄓㄨ ㄧˋ)
physiocracy; the advocacy that agriculture is all important

重利(ㄓㄨㄥˋ ㄌㄧˋ)
①a high interest rate (in money lending) ②to value material gain; huge profit

重力(ㄓㄨㄥˋ ㄌㄧˋ)
gravity

重力擺(ㄓㄨㄥˋ ㄌㄧˋ ㄅㄞˇ)
pendulum

重利盤剝(ㄓㄨㄥˋ ㄌㄧˋ ㄆㄢˊ ㄅㄛ)
to lend money at usury; to be a loan shark

重量(ㄓㄨㄥˋ ㄌㄧㄤˋ)
weight

重量級(ㄓㄨㄥˋ ㄌㄧㄤˋ ㄐㄧˊ)
(boxing) heavyweight

重工業(ㄓㄨㄥˋ ㄍㄨㄥ ㄧㄝˋ)
heavy industry

重活(ㄓㄨㄥˋ ㄏㄨㄛˊ)
heavy work

重轟炸機(ㄓㄨㄥˋ ㄏㄨㄥ ㄓㄚˋ ㄐㄧ)
a heavy bomber

重機槍(ㄓㄨㄥˋ ㄐㄧ ㄑㄧㄤ)
a heavy machine gun

重金禮聘(ㄓㄨㄥˋ ㄐㄧㄣ ㄌㄧˇ ㄆㄧㄣˋ)
to employ with good pay

重金屬(ㄓㄨㄥˋ ㄐㄧㄣ ㄕㄨˇ)
heavy metals

重晶石(ㄓㄨㄥˋ ㄐㄧㄥ ㄕˊ)
(mineral) barite

重器(ㄓㄨㄥˋ ㄑㄧˋ)
treasured wares

重遷(ㄓㄨㄥˋ ㄑㄧㄢ)
unwilling to be moved from where one lives

重情(ㄓㄨㄥˋ ㄑㄧㄥˊ)
to attach importance to matters of emotion or affection

重心(ㄓㄨㄥˋ ㄒㄧㄣ)
the center of gravity

重刑(ㄓㄨㄥˋ ㄒㄧㄥˊ)
severe punishment; heavy penalty: 殺人的重刑是死刑。The severe punishment for murder is death.

重型(ㄓㄨㄥˋ ㄒㄧㄥˊ)
heavy-duty

重鎮(ㄓㄨㄥˋ ㄓㄣˋ)
①key positions (in military operations); an important city ②a key figure

重杖(ㄓㄨㄥˋ ㄓㄤˋ)
to flog severely

重重的(ㄓㄨㄥˋ ㄓㄨㄥˋ ·ㄉㄜ)
heavily; severely; seriously

重酬(ㄓㄨㄥˋ ㄔㄡˊ)
a substantial reward; a handsome reward

重臣(ㄓㄨㄥˋ ㄔㄣˊ)
an important official of the emperor

重懲(ㄓㄨㄥˋ ㄔㄥˊ)
to chastise or punish severely

重脣音(ㄓㄨㄥˋ ㄔㄨㄣˊ ㄧㄣ)
(in traditional Chinese phonetics) bilabial sounds; bilabials

重創(ㄓㄨㄥˋ ㄔㄨㄤˋ)
①(ㄓㄨㄥˋ ㄔㄨㄤ) a serious wound ②(ㄓㄨㄥˋ ㄔㄨㄤˋ) to inflict a severe blow on (the enemy)

重視(ㄓㄨㄥˋ ㄕˋ)
to pay much attention to; to consider important; to take matters seriously: 我們重視這件事。We take the matter seriously.

重傷(ㄓㄨㄥˋ ㄕㄤ)
a serious injury; a severe injury

重傷風(ㄓㄨㄥˋ ㄕㄤ ㄈㄥ)
a severe cold

重商主義(ㄓㄨㄥˋ ㄕㄤ ㄓㄨ ㄧˋ)
mercantilism

重賞(ㄓㄨㄥˋ ㄕㄤˇ)
to reward generously

重賞之下, 必有勇夫(ㄓㄨㄥˋ ㄕㄤˇ ㄓ ㄒㄧㄚˋ, ㄅㄧˋ ㄧㄡˇ ㄩㄥˇ ㄈㄨ)
Generous rewards rouse one to heroism.

重水(ㄓㄨㄥˋ ㄕㄨㄟˇ)
heavy water

重諾(ㄓㄨㄥˋ ㄋㄨㄛˋ)
judicious about giving promises; to make promises only after careful consideration

重任(ㄓㄨㄥˋ ㄖㄣˋ)
an important mission; an important office or post

重責(ㄓㄨㄥˋ ㄗㄜˊ)
①important responsibility ②to scold or flog severely

重罪(ㄓㄨㄥˋ ㄗㄨㄟˋ)
a serious offense or crime; felony

重義氣(ㄓㄨㄥˋ ㄧˋ ㄑㄧˋ)

particular about loyalty to friends

重義輕利(ㄓㄨㄥˋ ㄧˋ ㄑㄧㄥ ㄌㄧˋ)
to value justice above material gains

重壓(ㄓㄨㄥˋ ㄧㄚ)
great pressure; a heavy load

重要(ㄓㄨㄥˋ ㄧㄠˋ)
important; significant; vital

重要關鍵(ㄓㄨㄥˋ ㄧㄠˋ ㄍㄨㄢ ㄐㄧㄢˋ)
a key (to a problem); a crucial point

重要人物(ㄓㄨㄥˋ ㄧㄠˋ ㄖㄣˊ ㄨˋ)
an important or great figure

重要問題(ㄓㄨㄥˋ ㄧㄠˋ ㄨㄣˋ ㄊㄧˊ)
an important question; an important issue

重油(ㄓㄨㄥˋ ㄧㄡˊ)
heavy oil

重音(ㄓㄨㄥˋ ㄧㄣ)
(phonetics) accent; stress

重文輕武(ㄓㄨㄥˋ ㄨㄣˊ ㄑㄧㄥ ㄨˇ)
to put mental or intellectual pursuits above martial arts; to put mental training above physical training; to emphasize civil administration at the expense of national defense

重於泰山(ㄓㄨㄥˋ ㄩˊ ㄊㄞˋ ㄕㄢ)
(literally) heavier than Mount Tai—very weighty; very important

重用(ㄓㄨㄥˋ ㄩㄥˋ)
to give (someone) an important assignment

重 6306
2. ㄔㄨㄥˊ chóng chóng

1. to pile one upon another
2. to repeat; to duplicate
3. layers
4. double; manifold
5. numerous; countless

重名兒(ㄔㄨㄥˊ ㄇㄧㄥˊ ㄦ)
a namesake

重返(ㄔㄨㄥˊ ㄈㄢˇ)
to go back; to return: 我們重返家園。We returned to our homeland.

重犯(ㄔㄨㄥˊ ㄈㄢˋ)
to repeat (an error or offense): 我們應避免重犯錯誤。We should avoid repeating past errors.

重逢(ㄔㄨㄥˊ ㄈㄥˊ)
to meet again; to have a reunion: 他們久別重逢。They

meet again after a long separation.

重複(ㄔㄨㄥˊ ㄈㄨˋ)
①to repeat; repetition ②to duplicate

重蹈覆轍(ㄔㄨㄥˊ ㄉㄠˇ ㄈㄨˋ ㄔㄜˋ)
to follow the same old disastrous road; to fall into the same trap

重疊(ㄔㄨㄥˊ ㄉㄧㄝˊ)
to pile one upon another; to superimpose

重提(ㄔㄨㄥˊ ㄊㄧˊ)
to mention again; to bring up (a subject) again

重瞳(ㄔㄨㄥˊ ㄊㄨㄥˊ)
an eye with double pupils

重來(ㄔㄨㄥˊ ㄌㄞˊ)
to do a thing over again; to repeat from the start; to return

重卵(ㄔㄨㄥˊ ㄌㄨㄢˇ)
(literally) eggs piled up in a heap—a dangerous situation

重閨(ㄔㄨㄥˊ ㄍㄨㄟ)
chamber (of a lady) deep inside the mansion

重規疊矩(ㄔㄨㄥˊ ㄍㄨㄟ ㄉㄧㄝˊ ㄐㄩˇ)
to duplicate precedents; repetitions

重光(ㄔㄨㄥˊ ㄍㄨㄤ)
①to return to light from darkness ②(said of once lost territory, etc.) to be recovered

重婚(ㄔㄨㄥˊ ㄏㄨㄣ)
bigamy; to commit bigamy

重婚罪(ㄔㄨㄥˊ ㄏㄨㄣ ㄗㄨㄟˋ)
bigamy: 他犯重婚罪。He committed bigamy.

重九(ㄔㄨㄥˊ ㄐㄧㄡˇ)
the Double Ninth Festival (on the 9th of the 9th lunar month)

重九登高(ㄔㄨㄥˊ ㄐㄧㄡˇ ㄉㄥ ㄍㄠ)
the custom of climbing to a high place to celebrate the Double Ninth Festival (on the 9th of the 9th lunar month)

重繭(ㄔㄨㄥˊ ㄐㄧㄢˇ)
to have blistered and callous feet (from walking)

重建(ㄔㄨㄥˊ ㄐㄧㄢˋ)
to rebuild; to reconstruct; to rehabilitate

重見天日(ㄔㄨㄥˊ ㄐㄧㄢˋ ㄊㄧㄢ ㄖˋ)

to see daylight again—to regain freedom; to be liberated or emancipated

重起爐灶(ㄔㄨㄥˊ ㄑㄧˇ ㄌㄨˊ ㄗㄠˋ)
to begin all over again

重慶(ㄔㄨㄥˊ ㄑㄧㄥˋ)
Chungking, Szechwan

重修(ㄔㄨㄥˊ ㄒㄧㄡ)
①to repair again ②to take (a course at school) for the second time (because of flunking)

重修舊好(ㄔㄨㄥˊ ㄒㄧㄡ ㄐㄧㄡˋ ㄏㄠˇ)
to renew friendly relations; to patch up; to reconcile: 我倆重修舊好。We renewed our friendly relations.

重現(ㄔㄨㄥˊ ㄒㄧㄢˋ)
to appear again; to reappear

重新(ㄔㄨㄥˊ ㄒㄧㄣ)
anew; afresh

重新部署(ㄔㄨㄥˊ ㄒㄧㄣ ㄅㄨˋ ㄕㄨˇ)
redeployment

重新分配(ㄔㄨㄥˊ ㄒㄧㄣ ㄈㄣ ㄆㄟˋ)
to distribute anew; to reallocate

重新組織(ㄔㄨㄥˊ ㄒㄧㄣ ㄗㄨˇ ㄓ)or重組(ㄔㄨㄥˊ ㄗㄨˇ)
to reorganize

重振軍威(ㄔㄨㄥˊ ㄓㄣˋ ㄐㄩㄣ ㄨㄟ)
to restore the prestige of an army

重整(ㄔㄨㄥˊ ㄓㄥˇ)
to readjust (debts or credit)

重整旗鼓(ㄔㄨㄥˊ ㄓㄥˇ ㄑㄧˊ ㄍㄨˇ)
to rearm; to make preparations for a comeback; to rally one's forces

重抄(ㄔㄨㄥˊ ㄔㄠ)
to copy again: 他把書中的一頁重抄。He copied a page of a book again.

重唱(ㄔㄨㄥˊ ㄔㄤˋ)
an ensemble of two or more singers, each singing one part

重出(ㄔㄨㄥˊ ㄔㄨ)
to appear again

重創(ㄔㄨㄥˊ ㄔㄨㄤˋ)
to injure again

重重(ㄔㄨㄥˊ ㄔㄨㄥˊ)
ring upon ring; one after another: 我們克服重重困難。We overcame one difficulty after another.

重重疊疊(ㄔㄨㄥˊ ㄔㄨㄥˊ ㄉㄧㄝˊ ㄉㄧㄝˊ)

〔里部〕

〔里部〕

to pile one upon another

重施故技(ㄔㄨㄥ ㄕ ㄍㄨ ㄐㄧ)
to play the same old trick

重申(ㄔㄨㄥ ㄕㄣ)
to reaffirm; to reiterate; to restate

重奏(ㄔㄨㄥ ㄗㄡ)
an ensemble of two or more instrumentalists, each playing one part

重足側目(ㄔㄨㄥ ㄗㄨ ㄘㄜ ㄇㄨ)
very much scared

重作馮婦(ㄔㄨㄥ ㄗㄨㄛ ㄈㄥ ㄈㄨ)
to do something which one has done before

重操舊業(ㄔㄨㄥ ㄘㄠ ㄐㄧㄡ ㄧㄝ)
to return to one's old trade

重孫(ㄔㄨㄥ ㄙㄨㄣ)
a great-grandchild

重譯(ㄔㄨㄥ ㄧ)
to retranslate

重遊(ㄔㄨㄥ ㄧㄡ)
to revisit: 我重遊該地, I revisited that place.

重演(ㄔㄨㄥ ㄧㄢ)
to repeat the performance of; to repeat: 歷史的錯誤不許重演, Historical mistakes should not be repeated.

重印(ㄔㄨㄥ ㄧㄣ)
to reprint

重洋(ㄔㄨㄥ ㄧㄤ)
the ocean: 她遠渡重洋, She traveled across the oceans.

重圍(ㄔㄨㄥ ㄨㄟ)
a many-layered siege; a tight encirclement: 士兵們殺出重圍, The soldiers broke through a tight encirclement.

重溫舊夢(ㄔㄨㄥ ㄨㄣ ㄐㄧㄡ ㄇㄥ)
to revive an old dream; to reproduce the good old days; to rekindle the old flame of love

重文(ㄔㄨㄥ ㄨㄣ)
graphic variance of a word in Chinese

重淵(ㄔㄨㄥ ㄩㄢ)
deep water; the deepest part of a body of water

四畫

〔野〕 6307 (ㄧㄝ yee yě)

1. the countryside; fields; the wilderness

2. the people (as opposed to the government)

3. wild; uncultured; undomesticated; coarse; barbarous; rude

野百合(ㄧㄝ ㄅㄞ ㄏㄜ)
a kind of lily (Crotalaria sessiliflora)

野堡(ㄧㄝ ㄅㄠ)
a fieldwork

野砲(ㄧㄝ ㄆㄠ)
a field gun; a fieldpiece; field artillery

野葡萄(ㄧㄝ ㄆㄨ ㄊㄠ)
a kind of bryony

野馬(ㄧㄝ ㄇㄚ)
①a wild horse; a mustang ②floating mist

野貓(ㄧㄝ ㄇㄠ)
①a wild cat; a serval; a badger ③(dialect) a hare

野蠻(ㄧㄝ ㄇㄢ)
①barbarous; savage; uncivilized ②unreasonable; rude; brutal

野蠻人(ㄧㄝ ㄇㄢ ㄖㄣ)
barbarians; savages

野牡丹(ㄧㄝ ㄇㄨ ㄉㄢ)
a kind of peony (Melastoma candidum)

野地(ㄧㄝ ㄉㄧ)
①the countryside ②the wilderness

野兔(ㄧㄝ ㄊㄨ)
a hare: 野兔跑得很快, Hares can run very fast.

野牛(ㄧㄝ ㄋㄧㄡ)
a wild ox; a bison; a buffalo: 野牛有大角, Wild buffaloes have big horns.

野老(ㄧㄝ ㄌㄠ)
an aged rustic; an old peasant; an old man

野驢(ㄧㄝ ㄌㄩ)
an onager

野狗(ㄧㄝ ㄍㄡ)
a wild dog; a stray dog; a dog without an owner

野果(ㄧㄝ ㄍㄨㄛ)
wild fruit

野合(ㄧㄝ ㄏㄜ)
illicit copulation or connection

野鶴(ㄧㄝ ㄏㄜ)
a wild crane—a recluse

an urchin; a street urchin

野海棠(ㄧㄝ ㄏㄞ ㄊㄤ)
a begonia

野漢子(ㄧㄝ ㄏㄢ ㄗ)
(a woman's) paramour

野狐禪(ㄧㄝ ㄏㄨ ㄔㄢ)
(Buddhism) wild-fox meditators, i.e. non-Buddhist ascetics; heterodoxy in general

野花(ㄧㄝ ㄏㄨㄚ)
①a wild flower ②a harlot

野火(ㄧㄝ ㄏㄨㄛ)
①will-o'-the-wisp ②prairie fire; bushfire; wildfire ③farm fire (for clearing the field)

野雞(ㄧㄝ ㄐㄧ)
①a pheasant ②a street walker; an unlicensed prostitute ③unlicensed taxicabs

野雞大學(ㄧㄝ ㄐㄧ ㄉㄚ ㄒㄩㄝ)
a university which is not accredited by the authorities and whose major purpose is to make money instead of educating the students

野菊花(ㄧㄝ ㄐㄩ ㄏㄨㄚ)
(botany) mother chrysanthemum

野禽(ㄧㄝ ㄑㄧㄣ)
a wild fowl

野薔薇(ㄧㄝ ㄑㄧㄤ ㄨㄟ)
a wild rose

野小子(ㄧㄝ ㄒㄧㄠ ㄗ)
a boor (an abusive term applied to an ill-mannered stranger)

野蒿菜(ㄧㄝ ㄒㄧㄠ ㄘㄞ)
tumbleweed

野心(ㄧㄝ ㄒㄧㄣ)
①ambition; careerism (especially of the objectionable kind) ②greediness

野心勃勃(ㄧㄝ ㄒㄧㄣ ㄅㄛ ㄅㄛ)
full of ambition: 他野心勃勃, He was over-ambitious.

野心家(ㄧㄝ ㄒㄧㄣ ㄐㄧㄚ)
a man of ambition (especially referring to the ambition one is not supposed to have); a careerist

野性(ㄧㄝ ㄒㄧㄥ)
jungle instincts; ungovernableness; untamedness; unruliness; wild nature

野性難馴(ㄧㄝ ㄒㄧㄥ ㄋㄢ ㄒㄩㄣ)

野戰(ㄧㄝˇ ㄓㄢˋ)
(military) field operations

野戰部隊(ㄧㄝˇ ㄓㄢˋ ㄅㄨˋ ㄉㄨㄟˋ)
(military) combat troops

野戰砲(ㄧㄝˇ ㄓㄢˋ ㄆㄠˋ)
(military) a field gun; a fieldpiece; field artillery

野戰醫院(ㄧㄝˇ ㄓㄢˋ ㄧ ㄩㄢˋ)
(military) field hospitals

野豬(ㄧㄝˇ ㄓㄨ)
a boar: 這些野豬已被閹割。These boars have been castrated.

野種(ㄧㄝˇ ㄓㄨㄥˇ)
a term of abuse applied to an adopted heir, meaning "a man of wild origin"

野史(ㄧㄝˇ ㄕˇ)or 野乘(ㄧㄝˇ ㄕㄥˋ)
unofficial history

野獸(ㄧㄝˇ ㄕㄡˋ)
a wild beast; a brute

野山羊(ㄧㄝˇ ㄕㄢ ㄧㄤˊ)
a markhor

野生(ㄧㄝˇ ㄕㄥ)
wild; undomesticated: 這種玫瑰是野生的。This kind of rose grows wild.

野生動物(ㄧㄝˇ ㄕㄥ ㄉㄨㄥˋ ㄨˋ)
wildlife; undomesticated animals

野生植物(ㄧㄝˇ ㄕㄥ ㄓˊ ㄨˋ)
wild plants; undomesticated plants

野人(ㄧㄝˇ ㄖㄣˊ)
①a rustic ②a barbarian; a savage

野人獻曝(ㄧㄝˇ ㄖㄣˊ ㄒㄧㄢˋ ㄆㄨˋ)or 野人獻日(ㄧㄝˇ ㄖㄣˊ ㄒㄧㄢˋ ㄖˋ)
(literally) a rustic offering sunshine (an expression of self-depreciation)

野菜(ㄧㄝˇ ㄘㄞˋ)
edible wild vegetables

野草(ㄧㄝˇ ㄘㄠˇ)
a weed: 花園中佈滿了野草。The garden was covered with weeds.

野餐(ㄧㄝˇ ㄘㄢ)
a picnic; a barbecue: 我們到山上野餐。We went on a picnic to the hill.

野鴨子(ㄧㄝˇ ㄧㄚ ˙ㄗ)
a wild duck; a mallard

untamable: 他的孩子野性難馴。His son was untamable.

野宴(ㄧㄝˇ ㄧㄢˋ)
a picnic; a barbecue

野營(ㄧㄝˇ ㄧㄥˊ)
outdoor camping: 他外出野營。He went camping.

野外(ㄧㄝˇ ㄨㄞˋ)
the outdoors; the open

野外旅行(ㄧㄝˇ ㄨㄞˋ ㄌㄩˇ ㄒㄧㄥˊ)
an outing; an excursion: 我們去野外旅行。We went for an outing.

野味(ㄧㄝˇ ㄨㄟˋ)
game as food

野鴛鴦(ㄧㄝˇ ㄩㄢ ㄧㄤ)
a couple living as husband and wife without being legally married; illicit lovers

野雲雀(ㄧㄝˇ ㄩㄣˊ ㄑㄩㄝˋ)
a meadow lark

五畫

【量】 6308
1. ㄌㄧㄤˊ liáng
to measure: 我們量這室子。We measured the room.

量杯(ㄌㄧㄤˊ ㄅㄟ)
a graduated cylinder; a measuring glass or cup

量肺器(ㄌㄧㄤˊ ㄈㄟˋ ㄑㄧˋ)
a spirometer

度量(ㄌㄧㄤˊ ㄉㄨˋ)
to measure; to estimate

量角規(ㄌㄧㄤˊ ㄐㄧㄠˇ ㄍㄨㄟ)
a graduator; a protractor

量角器(ㄌㄧㄤˊ ㄐㄧㄠˇ ㄑㄧˋ)
a protractor

量熱器(ㄌㄧㄤˊ ㄖㄜˋ ㄑㄧˋ)
a calorimeter

量一量(ㄌㄧㄤ ˙ㄧ ㄌㄧㄤˊ)or 量量(ㄌㄧㄤˊ ˙ㄌㄧㄤ)
to take a measurement; to measure: 讓我來量量他的身高。Let me measure his height.

量雨表(ㄌㄧㄤˊ ㄩˇ ㄅㄧㄠˇ)
a rain gauge

【量】 6308
2. ㄌㄧㄤˋ liàng liàng
1. quantity
2. capacity
3. to estimate

量力(ㄌㄧㄤˋ ㄌㄧˋ)
to estimate one's strength, resources or ability: 他不自量力。He overrated his abil-

ity.

量力而爲(ㄌㄧㄤˋ ㄌㄧˋ ㄦˊ ㄨㄟˋ)
to estimate one's strength or resources before acting

量入爲出(ㄌㄧㄤˋ ㄖㄨˋ ㄨㄟˊ ㄔㄨ)
to regulate one's expenses according to one's income

量子(ㄌㄧㄤˋ ㄗˇ)
(physics) quantum

量子論(ㄌㄧㄤˋ ㄗˇ ㄌㄨㄣˋ)
the quantum theory

量詞(ㄌㄧㄤˋ ㄘˊ)
a classifier (as 個, 隻, 次)

量才取用(ㄌㄧㄤˋ ㄘㄞˊ ㄑㄩˇ ㄩㄥˋ)
to employ a person on the basis of his merits

十一畫

【釐】 6309
1. ㄌㄧˊ lí
1. a unit of linear measure equal to one thousandth of the Chinese foot
2. a unit of weight equal to one thousandth of the tael
3. to manage; to administer; to arrange
4. to revise; to reform; to correct
5. same as 嫠—a widow

釐米(ㄌㄧˊ ㄇㄧˇ)
centimeter

釐婦(ㄌㄧˊ ㄈㄨˋ)
a widow

釐定(ㄌㄧˊ ㄉㄧㄥˋ)
to formulate (rules, etc.)

釐革(ㄌㄧˊ ㄍㄜˊ)
to revise; to reform

釐金(ㄌㄧˊ ㄐㄧㄣ)
likin, transportation tax levied on traders before the Republic

釐捐(ㄌㄧˊ ㄐㄩㄢ)
transportation tax levied on traders before the Republic

釐正(ㄌㄧˊ ㄓㄥˋ)
to correct; to rectify; to reform

【釐】 6309
2. ㄒㄧ shī xī
a blessing; happiness; bliss

金 部

ㄐㄧㄣ jīn

〔金部〕

【金】 ㄐㄧㄣ jīn 6310

1. gold
2. metal
3. money; wealth
4. weapons; arms
5. precious; excellent; fine
6. golden
7. durable
8. name of the Tungusic Dynasty (1115-1234), which dominated Manchuria and North China
9. a Chinese family name

金波 (ㄐㄧㄣ ㄅㄛ)
golden waves—the moonlight

金箔 (ㄐㄧㄣ ㄅㄛˊ)
gold foil; gold leaf; gilt

金本位制 (ㄐㄧㄣ ㄅㄣˇ ㄨㄟˋ ㄓˋ)
gold monometallism

金榜 (ㄐㄧㄣ ㄅㄤˇ)
(under the former civil service examination system) the billboard announcing the names of successful candidates

金榜題名 (ㄐㄧㄣ ㄅㄤˇ ㄊㄧˊ ㄇㄧㄥˊ)
to emerge successful from a competitive examination

金鎊 (ㄐㄧㄣ ㄅㄤˋ)
pound sterling

金筆 (ㄐㄧㄣ ㄅㄧˇ)
a (quality) fountain pen

金幣 (ㄐㄧㄣ ㄅㄧˋ)
gold coins

金碧輝煌 (ㄐㄧㄣ ㄅㄧˋ ㄏㄨㄟ ㄏㄨㄤˊ)
(said of a building) resplendent; gorgeous; grand; splendid; magnificent

金邊眼鏡 (ㄐㄧㄣ ㄅㄧㄢ ㄧㄢˇ ㄐㄧㄥˋ)
gold-rimmed spectacles

金兵 (ㄐㄧㄣ ㄅㄧㄥ)
troops of the Tungusic Dynasty of Chin (金) (1115-1234) who often invaded China

金不換 (ㄐㄧㄣ ㄅㄨˋ ㄏㄨㄢˋ)
① something not to be exchanged for gold—a very

precious thing ② Chinese ink ③ a Chinese medicinal herb, also known as 三七草 (Gynura pinnatifida)

金牌 (ㄐㄧㄣ ㄆㄞˊ)
a gold medal

金瓶梅 (ㄐㄧㄣ ㄆㄧㄥˊ ㄇㄟˊ)
The Golden Lotus, a title of a novel written by an anonymous author in the Ming Dynasty, commonly regarded as an obscene book

金馬 (ㄐㄧㄣ ㄇㄚˇ) or 金門馬祖 (ㄐㄧㄣ ㄇㄣˊ ㄇㄚˇ ㄗㄨˇ)
Kinmen (or Quemoy) and Matsu, two groups of islands off the Fukien coast remaining free from Communism

金黴素 (ㄐㄧㄣ ㄇㄟˊ ㄙㄨˋ)
Aureomycin

金門 (ㄐㄧㄣ ㄇㄣˊ)
① Kinmen (or Quemoy), an island opposite Amoy in Fukien ② the Gate of Gold—(figuratively) the gate of the palace

金迷紙醉 (ㄐㄧㄣ ㄇㄧˊ ㄓˇ ㄗㄨㄟˋ)
a luxurious life; an extravagant life

金木水火土 (ㄐㄧㄣ ㄇㄨˋ ㄕㄨㄟˇ ㄏㄨㄛˇ ㄊㄨˇ)
metal, wood, water, fire and earth—the five elements in ancient Chinese philosophy and fortunetelling

金髮女郎 (ㄐㄧㄣ ㄈㄚˇ ㄋㄩˇ ㄌㄤˊ)
a blonde

金粉 (ㄐㄧㄣ ㄈㄣˇ)
① women's face powder ② gold dust

金風 (ㄐㄧㄣ ㄈㄥ)
an autumn breeze

金鳳花 (ㄐㄧㄣ ㄈㄥˋ ㄏㄨㄚ)
the buttercup

金丹 (ㄐㄧㄣ ㄉㄢ)
a pill of immortality

金貂 (ㄐㄧㄣ ㄉㄧㄠ)
attendants or retainers (who in ancient times used to wear caps trimmed with golden-colored sable)

金店 (ㄐㄧㄣ ㄉㄧㄢˋ)
a jeweler's shop; a goldsmith's shop

金殿 (ㄐㄧㄣ ㄉㄧㄢˋ)
a magnificent palace

金鈿 (ㄐㄧㄣ ㄉㄧㄢˋ)
a golden hairpin

金太祖 (ㄐㄧㄣ ㄊㄞˋ ㄗㄨˇ)
the founder of the Tungusic Dynasty of Chin (金), which dominated Manchuria and much of North China during 1115-1234 A.D.

金湯 (ㄐㄧㄣ ㄊㄤ)
an impregnable fortress

金條 (ㄐㄧㄣ ㄊㄧㄠˊ)
a gold bar

金柝 (ㄐㄧㄣ ㄊㄨㄛˋ)
a night watchman's bell

金童玉女 (ㄐㄧㄣ ㄊㄨㄥˊ ㄩˋ ㄋㄩˇ)
young boys and girls attending upon an immortal

金猊 (ㄐㄧㄣ ㄋㄧˊ)
an incense burner shaped like a lion's head

金牛宮 (ㄐㄧㄣ ㄋㄧㄡˊ ㄍㄨㄥ) or 金牛座 (ㄐㄧㄣ ㄋㄧㄡˊ ㄗㄨㄛˋ)
Taurus

金諾 (ㄐㄧㄣ ㄋㄨㄛˋ)
your esteemed pledge

金蘭 (ㄐㄧㄣ ㄌㄢˊ)
harmonious friendship; sworn brotherhood

金蓮 (ㄐㄧㄣ ㄌㄧㄢˊ)
(euphemism) bound feet of a woman

金蓮花 (ㄐㄧㄣ ㄌㄧㄢˊ ㄏㄨㄚ)
(botany) a canary-creeper

金陵 (ㄐㄧㄣ ㄌㄧㄥˊ)
Nanking (a former name)

金鈴子 (ㄐㄧㄣ ㄌㄧㄥˊ ˙ㄗ)
① a kind of insect, like a cricket but smaller ② fruit of Melia azedarach (楝樹)

金靈殿 (ㄐㄧㄣ ㄌㄧㄥˊ ㄉㄧㄢˋ)
the main building of the imperial palace

金輪 (ㄐㄧㄣ ㄌㄨㄣˊ)
the golden disk—the moon

金縷衣 (ㄐㄧㄣ ㄌㄩˇ ㄧ)
a gold-threaded robe

金戈鐵馬 (ㄐㄧㄣ ㄍㄜ ㄊㄧㄝˇ ㄇㄚˇ)
① weapons; arms; military hardware ② warfare

金革 (ㄐㄧㄣ ㄍㄜˊ)
military hardware; arms

金剛 (ㄐㄧㄣ ㄍㄤ)
① hard metal ② a Buddhist god sometimes identified with Indra

金剛怒目 (ㄐㄧㄣ ㄍㄤ ㄋㄨˋ ㄇㄨˋ)

〔金部〕

an awful look

金剛經(ㄐㄧㄣ《ㄤ ㄐㄧㄥ)
The Diamond Sutra, also known as *Prajna-Paramita Sutra* (般若波羅密經)

金剛石(ㄐㄧㄣ《ㄤ ㄕ)
diamond

金剛砂(ㄐㄧㄣ《ㄤ ㄕㄚ)
emery

金剛鑽(ㄐㄧㄣ《ㄤ ㄗㄨㄢ)
a diamond drill

金箍棒(ㄐㄧㄣ《ㄨ ㄅㄤ)
a magic cudgel—a weapon used by the Monkey King in the novel *Pilgrimage to the West* (西遊記)

金瓜(ㄐㄧㄣ《ㄨㄚ)
pumpkin

金閨(ㄐㄧㄣ《ㄨㄟ)
①a boudoir ②the imperial court

金魚(ㄐㄧㄣ ㄩˊ)
emblems worn by officials during the Tang Dynasty

金龜壻(ㄐㄧㄣ《ㄨㄟ ㄒㄩˋ)
a fine son-in-law; a rich son-in-law

金龜子(ㄐㄧㄣ《ㄨㄟ ˙ㄗ)
a tumblebug

金匱(ㄐㄧㄣ ㄎㄨㄟˋ)
a metal bookcase

金櫃(ㄐㄧㄣ《ㄨㄟˋ)
a strongbox; a safe

金棺(ㄐㄧㄣ《ㄨㄢ)
①a gilded coffin ②(euphemism) a coffin; a casket

金光黨(ㄐㄧㄣ《ㄨㄤ ㄉㄤ)
swindlers; racketeers

金光閃閃(ㄐㄧㄣ《ㄨㄤ ㄕㄢˇ ㄕㄢˇ)
glittering; glistening

金工(ㄐㄧㄣ《ㄨㄥ)
①metalwork ②a metal craftsman

金科玉律(ㄐㄧㄣ ㄎㄜ ㄩˋ ㄌㄩˋ)
the golden rule; an immutable law

金口(ㄐㄧㄣ ㄎㄡˇ)
①the Buddha's mouth ②utterances that carry weight

金口木舌(ㄐㄧㄣ ㄎㄡˇ ㄇㄨˋ ㄕㄜˊ)
a metal bell with a wooden clapper 亦作「木鐸」

金庫(ㄐㄧㄣ ㄎㄨˋ)
coffers; a treasury

金塊(ㄐㄧㄣ ㄎㄨㄞˋ)
gold bullion; a gold ingot

金鑛(ㄐㄧㄣ ㄎㄨㄤˋ)
a gold mine

金華火腿(ㄐㄧㄣ ㄏㄨㄚˊ ㄏㄨㄛˇ ㄊㄨㄟˇ)
(a noted product) salted ham from Chinhua (金華), Chekiang 亦作「金腿」

金環蝕(ㄐㄧㄣ ㄏㄨㄢˊ ㄕ)
an annular eclipse of the sun

金婚(ㄐㄧㄣ ㄏㄨㄣ)
a golden wedding; the 50th wedding anniversary

金黃色(ㄐㄧㄣ ㄏㄨㄤˊ ㄙㄜˋ)
bright yellow; golden

金紅(色)(ㄐㄧㄣ ㄏㄨㄥˊ(ㄙㄜˋ))
reddish yellow; orange; golden-red

金紅石(ㄐㄧㄣ ㄏㄨㄥˊ ㄕ)
(mineral) rutile

金雞納(ㄐㄧㄣ ㄐㄧ ㄋㄚˋ)
(botany) cinchona

金雞納霜(ㄐㄧㄣ ㄐㄧ ㄋㄚˋ ㄕㄨㄤ)
quinine

金甲(ㄐㄧㄣ ㄐㄧㄚˇ)
armor (worn by a warrior)

金甲蟲(ㄐㄧㄣ ㄐㄧㄚˇ ㄔㄨㄥˊ)
a golden beetle

金價(ㄐㄧㄣ ㄐㄧㄚˋ)
the price of gold: 金價多少? What is the price of gold?

金盡交絕(ㄐㄧㄣ ㄐㄧㄣˋ ㄐㄧㄠ ㄐㄩㄝˊ)
Friendship lasts as long as money does.

金漿玉醴(ㄐㄧㄣ ㄐㄧㄤ ㄩˋ ㄌㄧˇ)
①good wine ②marvelous medicine; a panacea

金匠(ㄐㄧㄣ ㄐㄧㄤˋ)
a goldsmith

金橘(ㄐㄧㄣ ㄐㄩˊ)
(botany) a cumquat

金橘餅(ㄐㄧㄣ ㄐㄩˊ ㄅㄧㄥˇ)
a crushed cumquat preserved with sugar

金器(ㄐㄧㄣ ㄑㄧˋ)
a gold vessel

金錢(ㄐㄧㄣ ㄑㄧㄢˊ)
money; cash; riches; wealth: 時間即是金錢. Time is money.

金錢豹(ㄐㄧㄣ ㄑㄧㄢˊ ㄅㄠˋ)
a spotted leopard

金錢花(ㄐㄧㄣ ㄑㄧㄢˊ ㄏㄨㄚ)
Pentapetes phoenicea

金錢主義(ㄐㄧㄣ ㄑㄧㄢˊ ㄓㄨˇ ㄧˋ)
mercenariness

金錢萬能(ㄐㄧㄣ ㄑㄧㄢˊ ㄨㄢˋ ㄋㄥˊ)
Money is almighty.

金闕(ㄐㄧㄣ ㄑㄩㄝˋ)
an imperial palace; an imperial abode

金雀花(ㄐㄧㄣ ㄑㄩㄝˋ ㄏㄨㄚ)
the furze

金像獎(ㄐㄧㄣ ㄒㄧㄤˋ ㄐㄧㄤˇ)
an Oscar award

金相玉質(ㄐㄧㄣ ㄒㄧㄤˋ ㄩˋ ㄓˊ)
①of very fine and durable material ②immortal literary works

金星(ㄐㄧㄣ ㄒㄧㄥ)
(astronomy) Venus

金枝玉葉(ㄐㄧㄣ ㄓ ㄩˋ ㄧㄝˋ)
a term referring to the members of the royal family

金針度人(ㄐㄧㄣ ㄓㄣ ㄉㄨˋ ㄖㄣˊ)
to teach others a knack of the trade

金針菜(ㄐㄧㄣ ㄓㄣ ㄘㄞˋ)
a day lily

金鐲(ㄐㄧㄣ ㄓㄨㄛˊ)
a gold bracelet

金鐘罩(ㄐㄧㄣ ㄓㄨㄥ ㄓㄠˋ)
(Chinese pugilism) the ability to sustain the thrusts of sharp weapons on one's bare skin

金翅雀(ㄐㄧㄣ ㄔˋ ㄑㄩㄝˋ)
a goldfinch

金釵(ㄐㄧㄣ ㄔㄞ)
a gold hairpin

金釵十二(ㄐㄧㄣ ㄔㄞ ㄕˊ ㄦˋ)
having many concubines

金蟬脫殼(ㄐㄧㄣ ㄔㄢˊ ㄊㄨㄛ ㄎㄜˊ)
to break loose and get away; to escape by a cunning maneuver

金城湯池(ㄐㄧㄣ ㄔㄥˊ ㄊㄤ ㄔˊ)
(literally) a city wall built with gold and a moat filled with boiling water—an impregnable fortress

金創 or 金瘡(ㄐㄧㄣ ㄔㄨㄤ)
wounds inflicted by sharp weapons; knife wounds 亦作「金瘡」

金石(ㄐㄧㄣ ㄕˊ)
①metal and stone—a symbol of durability ②gold and precious stones ③weapons; arms ④bronze and stone inscriptions

〔金部〕

金石交(ㄐㄧㄣ ㄕ ㄐㄧㄠ)
durable friendship

金石學(ㄐㄧㄣ ㄕ ㄒㄩㄝ)
the study of bronze and stone inscriptions

金石聲(ㄐㄧㄣ ㄕ ㄕㄥ)
the sound of metal and stone (said of a piece of good writing)

金石絲竹(ㄐㄧㄣ ㄕ ㄙ ㄓㄨˊ)
various musical instruments made of metals, stone, strings, and bamboo

金石為開(ㄐㄧㄣ ㄕ ㄨㄟˊ ㄎㄞ)
Sincerity can make metal and stone crack.

金史(ㄐㄧㄣ ㄕ)
History of the Chin Dynasty (a Tungusic Dynasty 1115-1234), one of the *Twenty-Four Histories*

金沙江(ㄐㄧㄣ ㄕㄚ ㄐㄧㄤ)
the Kinsha River, the headwaters of the Yangtze

金身(ㄐㄧㄣ ㄕㄣ)
the Buddha's gilded image

金聲玉振(ㄐㄧㄣ ㄕㄥ ㄩˋ ㄓㄣˋ)
(literally) ringing the bells as an overture and striking the stone chimes at the close; making use of various instruments in one musical performance—to gather the best of various schools of thought and form a complete whole

金屬(ㄐㄧㄣ ㄕㄨˇ)
metals

金屬器皿(ㄐㄧㄣ ㄕㄨˇ ㄑㄧˋ ㄇㄧㄣˇ)
metalware

金屬原素(ㄐㄧㄣ ㄕㄨˇ ㄩㄢˊ ㄙㄨˋ)
metallic elements

金人(ㄐㄧㄣ ㄖㄣˊ)
a metal image

金人三緘其口(ㄐㄧㄣ ㄖㄣˊ ㄙㄢ ㄐㄧㄢ ㄑㄧˊ ㄎㄡˇ)
to remain tight-lipped; to say nothing

金融(ㄐㄧㄣ ㄖㄨㄥˊ)
finance; banking, a monetary situation

金融卡(ㄐㄧㄣ ㄖㄨㄥˊ ㄎㄚˇ)
a fiscard

金融恐慌(ㄐㄧㄣ ㄖㄨㄥˊ ㄎㄨㄥˇ ㄏㄨㄤ)
a monetary crisis; a financial panic

金融機關(ㄐㄧㄣ ㄖㄨㄥˊ ㄐㄧ ㄍㄨㄢ)
a financial organization; banking agency

金融界(ㄐㄧㄣ ㄖㄨㄥˊ ㄐㄧㄝˋ)
the financial world; financial circles

金融中心(ㄐㄧㄣ ㄖㄨㄥˊ ㄓㄨㄥ ㄒㄧㄣ)
a financial center

金融市場(ㄐㄧㄣ ㄖㄨㄥˊ ㄕ ㄔㄤˇ)
the money market

金融資本(ㄐㄧㄣ ㄖㄨㄥˊ ㄗ ㄅㄣˇ)
financial capital

金字塔(ㄐㄧㄣ ㄗˋ ㄊㄚˇ)
a pyramid

金字招牌(ㄐㄧㄣ ㄗˋ ㄓㄠ ㄆㄞˊ)
(literally) a signboard with gilded inscriptions—a good reputation; high prestige

金子(ㄐㄧㄣ ˙ㄗ)
gold: 在岩石及溪流中發現金子 Gold is found in rock and streams.

金絲雀(ㄐㄧㄣ ㄙ ㄑㄩㄝˋ)
a canary bird; a canary: 她有一隻金絲雀。 She has a canary.

金絲燕(ㄐㄧㄣ ㄙ ㄧㄢˋ)
Collocalia esculenta

金色(ㄐㄧㄣ ㄙㄜˋ)
golden

金額(ㄐㄧㄣ ㄜˊ)
the amount of money

金甌無缺(ㄐㄧㄣ ㄡ ㄨˊ ㄑㄩㄝ)
(literally) The golden goblet is intact.—The integrity of the national territory is unaffected.

金牙(ㄐㄧㄣ ㄧㄚˊ)
gold-capped teeth

金曜日(ㄐㄧㄣ ㄧㄠˋ ㄖˋ)
Friday

金言(ㄐㄧㄣ ㄧㄢˊ)
a maxim; an adage; a wise saying; sage advice: 「三思而後行」是一句金言, "Look before you leap" is a maxim.

金銀花(ㄐㄧㄣ ㄧㄣˊ ㄏㄨㄚ)
the flower of honeysuckle; honeysuckle

金銀財寶(ㄐㄧㄣ ㄧㄣˊ ㄘㄞˊ ㄅㄠˇ)
treasures; wealth; riches

金印紫綬(ㄐㄧㄣ ㄧㄣˋ ㄗˇ ㄕㄡˋ)
the gold seal and the purple sash—high government posts 亦作「金紫」

金鶯(ㄐㄧㄣ ㄧㄥ)
an oriole

金烏(ㄐㄧㄣ ㄨ)
(literally) the golden crow —the sun: 金烏西墜。 The sun is sinking in the west.

金烏玉兔(ㄐㄧㄣ ㄨ ㄩˋ ㄊㄨˋ)
(literally) the crow of gold and the hare of jade—the sun and the moon

金屋藏嬌(ㄐㄧㄣ ㄨ ㄘㄤˊ ㄐㄧㄠ)
to build a magnificent house for a beloved woman (especially a concubine or mistress)

金文(ㄐㄧㄣ ㄨㄣˊ)
ancient inscriptions on bronze

金魚(ㄐㄧㄣ ㄩˊ)
goldfish

金魚缸(ㄐㄧㄣ ㄩˊ ㄍㄤ)
a goldfish basin; a globe

金魚藻(ㄐㄧㄣ ㄩˊ ㄗㄠˇ)
(botany) hornwort

金魚草(ㄐㄧㄣ ㄩˊ ㄘㄠˇ)
(botany) snapdragon

金玉滿堂(ㄐㄧㄣ ㄩˋ ㄇㄢˇ ㄊㄤˊ)
to have one's house filled with riches

金玉良言(ㄐㄧㄣ ㄩˋ ㄌㄧㄤˊ ㄧㄢˊ)
a wise saying; good counsel: 對於這事, 他給我金玉良言。 He gave me good counsel on this matter.

金玉其外, 敗絮其中(ㄐㄧㄣ ㄩˋ ㄑㄧˊ ㄨㄞˋ, ㄅㄞˋ ㄒㄩˋ ㄑㄧˊ ㄓㄨㄥ)
a rotten interior beneath a fine exterior

金元外交(ㄐㄧㄣ ㄩㄢˊ ㄨㄞˋ ㄐㄧㄠ)
checkbook diplomacy; diplomacy of bribery

金元王國(ㄐㄧㄣ ㄩㄢˊ ㄨㄤˊ ㄍㄨㄛˊ)
(literally) the kingdom of golden dollars—the United States

一畫

【釔】 6311 ㄧˇ yii yǐ
yttrium

【釓】 6312 �《ㄚˊ gar gá
gadolinium

二畫

【釘】 6313
1. ㄉㄧㄥ ding dīng

nails (for fastening things): 這只釘已鬆動了。The nail has started.
3. to look steadily

釘鞋(カl∠ Tlせ)
boots with nailed soles (for wet weather); track shoes; shoes with spikes

釘錘(カl∠ 犭ㄨㄟ)
a hammer

釘梢(カl∠ ㄕㄠ)
to tail; to shadow; to trail: 賊被警察釘梢了。The thief was tailed by a policeman.

釘子(カl∠ ·ㄗ)
nail (for fastening): 只一下他就把釘子釘進去了。With one blow he drove the nail home.

釘問(カl∠ ㄨㄣ)
to question persistently

【釘】 6313
2. カl∠ ding dìng
to fasten (with nails, etc.)

釘馬掌(カl∠ ㄇㄚˇ ㄓㄤˇ)
to shoe a horse; to nail on horseshoes

釘釘子(カl∠ カl∠ ·ㄗ)
to drive a nail

釘鈕扣(カl∠ ㄋlㄡˇㄎㄡˋ)
to sew buttons on: 她在我的外套上釘鈕扣。She sewed buttons on my coat.

釘住(カl∠ ㄓㄨˋ)
to nail securely

釘書(カl∠ ㄕㄨ)
to bind books

釘書機(カl∠ ㄕㄨ ㄐl)
a stapler

釘死(カl∠ ㄙˇ)
①to nail securely; to nail up: 他把窗子釘死。He nailed up a window. ②to nail to death; to crucify

【釜】 6314
ㄈㄨˇ fuu fǔ
1. a cauldron; a kettle
2. an ancient unit of capacity

釜底抽薪(ㄈㄨˇ ㄉlˇ ㄔㄡ Tlㄣ)
(literally) to make water stop boiling by pulling firewood from under the kettle —to remove the ultimate cause of trouble

釜中魚(ㄈㄨˇ ㄓㄨㄥ ㄩˊ)
fish in a kettle—doomed

釜山(ㄈㄨˇ ㄕㄢ)
Pusan, Korea

【釗】 6315
ㄓㄠ jau zhāo
to encourage

【針】 6316
（鍼）ㄓㄣ jen zhēn
1. a needle; a pin; a probe: 針是用來縫紉的。Needles are used for sewing.
2. a stitch

針鼻兒(ㄓㄣ ㄅlˋㄦ)
the eye of a needle

針砭(ㄓㄣ ㄅlㄢ)
①acupuncture ②remonstrance; to point out someone's errors and offer salutary advice; admonition

針鋒(ㄓㄣ ㄈㄥ)or針芒(ㄓㄣ ㄇㄤˊ)
the point of a needle

針鋒相對(ㄓㄣ ㄈㄥ Tlㄤ ㄉㄨㄟˋ)
(literally) two needles pointed against each other —to oppose each other with equal harshness; to attack each other in equally sharp language; to match point by point: 兩邊針鋒相對。Two sides of the argument match point by point.

針對(ㄓㄣ ㄉㄨㄟˋ)
①to aim directly at; to focus on ②in accordance with

針頭(ㄓㄣ ㄊㄡˊ)
(medicine) a syringe needle

針盒(ㄓㄣ ㄏㄜˊ)
a sewing kit

針腳(ㄓㄣ ㄐlㄠˇ)
stitches

針灸(ㄓㄣ ㄐlㄡˇ)
acupuncture and moxibustion; acupuncture and cauterization

針灸麻醉(ㄓㄣ ㄐlㄡˇ ㄇㄚˊ ㄓㄨㄟˋ)
acupuncture anesthesia

針線(ㄓㄣ Tlㄢˋ)
①a needle and thread ②needlework

針線包(ㄓㄣ Tlㄢˋ ㄅㄠ)
a sewing kit

針織(ㄓㄣ ㄓ)
knitting

針織品(ㄓㄣ ㄓ ㄆlㄣˇ)
knit goods; knitwear; knitting

針織廠(ㄓㄣ ㄓ ㄔㄤˇ)
a knitting mill

針黹(ㄓㄣ ㄓˇ)
fine needlework; embroidery

針車(ㄓㄣ ㄔㄜ)
a sewing machine

針樅(ㄓㄣ ㄘㄨㄥ)
(botany) a spruce

針葉樹(ㄓㄣ lㄝˋ ㄕㄨˋ)
conifers; coniferous trees: 松樹和檜樹是針葉樹。The pine and fir are conifers.

針眼(ㄓㄣ lㄢˇ)
①(pathology) hordeolum; sty(e) ②perforation made with a needle

針魚(ㄓㄣ ㄩˊ)
the saury

【釙】 6317
ㄆㄨ pwu pū

polonium

【釕】 6318
カlㄠˇ leau liǎo

ruthenium

三畫

【釩】 6319
ㄈㄢˊ farn fán
vanadium

【釣】 6320
カlㄠˋ diaw diào
1. to fish (with a hook and line); to angle
2. to lure; to tempt
3. a fishhook

釣名(カlㄠˋ ㄇlㄥˊ)or釣譽(カlㄠˋ ㄩˋ)
to angle for fame; to seek publicity

釣臺(カlㄠˋ ㄊㄞˊ)
a platform to fish from

釣鉤(カlㄠˋ ㄍㄡ)
a fishhook

釣竿(カlㄠˋ ㄍㄢ)
a fishing rod; a fish pole

釣線(カlㄠˋ Tlㄢˋ)
a fish twine; a fishing line

釣餌(カlㄠˋ ㄦˇ)
a bait

釣魚(カlㄠˋ ㄩˊ)
to fish; to angle: 我到河中釣魚。I went fishing in the river.

釣魚用具(カlㄠˋ ㄩˊ ㄩㄥˋ ㄐㄩˋ)
fishing gear

【釷】 6321
ㄊㄨˇ tuu tǔ
thorium

釷石(ㄊㄨˇ ㄕˊ)

(mineral) thorite

【釹】 6322
ㄋㄩ neu nǚ
neodymium, a rare-earth metallic chemical element found in cerite and various other rare minerals

【釦】 6323
ㄎㄡ kow kòu
buttons (on garments)

釦子(ㄎㄡ·ㄗ)or 釦兒(ㄎㄡㄦ)
buttons (on garments)

【釧】 6324
ㄔㄨㄢ chuann chuàn
a bracelet; an armlet

【釵】 6325
ㄔㄞ chai chāi
a kind of hairpin

釵光鬢影(ㄔㄞ ㄍㄨㄤ ㄅㄧㄣ ㄧㄥˇ)
gathering of richly dressed women

釵橫鬢亂(ㄔㄞ ㄏㄥˊ ㄅㄧㄣ ㄌㄨㄢˋ)
pins awry and hair in disorder

【釤】 6326
ㄕㄢ shan shān
samarium

四畫

【鈧】 6327
ㄎㄤ kang kàng
scandium

【鈥】 6328
ㄏㄨㄛˇ huoo huǒ
holmium

【鈀】 6329
ㄅㄚ baa bǎ
palladium

【鈦】 6330
ㄊㄞˋ tay tài
titanium

【鈔】 6331
ㄔㄠ chau chāo
("鈔票"又讀 ㄔㄠˋ chaw chào)
1. to copy; to transcribe
2. bank notes

鈔票(ㄔㄠ ㄆㄧㄠˋ)or(ㄔㄠˋ ㄆㄧㄠˋ)
bank notes; paper money; a bill

鈔錄 or 抄錄(ㄔㄠ ㄌㄨˋ)
to copy; to transcribe

鈔寫 or 抄寫(ㄔㄠ ㄒㄧㄝˇ)
to copy or transcribe by hand: 鈔寫這一頁。Copy this page.

【鈇】 6332
ㄈㄨ fu fū
an ax; a hatchet

鈇鑕(ㄈㄨ ㄓˋ)
a kind of ax (for chopping the body of a convict in two)

鈇鉞(ㄈㄨ ㄩㄝˋ)
punishment of crimes

【鈉】 6333
ㄋㄚˋ nah nà
sodium; natrium: 鹽和汔水含有鈉。Salt and soda contain sodium.

鈉玻璃(ㄋㄚˋ ㄅㄛ·ㄌㄧ)
soda glass

【鈍】 6334
ㄉㄨㄣˋ duenn dùn
1. blunt; dull; obtuse: 這把刀鈍了。This knife is blunt.
2. dull; obtuse

鈍兵(ㄉㄨㄣˋ ㄅㄧㄥ)
①blunt weapons ②soldiers low in morale

鈍根(ㄉㄨㄣˋ ㄍㄣ)
(Buddhism) of dull capacity, unable to receive Buddha's truth

鈍漢(ㄉㄨㄣˋ ㄏㄢˋ)
a stupid fellow; a dullard

鈍角(ㄉㄨㄣˋ ㄐㄧㄝˇ)
an obtuse angle

鈍角三角形(ㄉㄨㄣˋ ㄐㄧㄝˇ ㄙㄢ ㄐㄧㄝˇ ㄒㄧㄥˊ)
an obtuse-angled triangle

鈍舌(ㄉㄨㄣˋ ㄕㄜˊ)
ineloquence

【鈐】 6335
ㄑㄧㄢˊ chyan qián
1. a latch; a lock
2. a seal; a stamp; a chop

鈐記(ㄑㄧㄢˊ ㄐㄧˋ)
an official seal; a chop

鈐鍵(ㄑㄧㄢˊ ㄐㄧㄢˋ)
the key; the crucial point

鈐印(ㄑㄧㄢˊ ㄧㄣˋ)
to put a stamp

【鈕】 6336
ㄋㄧㄡˇ neou niǔ
1. buttons: 我按鈕等電梯。I pushed the button for the elevator.
2. a Chinese family name

鈕扣(ㄋㄧㄡˇ ㄎㄡˋ)
buttons: 有一個鈕釦脫落了。One of the buttons is missing.

鈕孔(ㄋㄧㄡˇ ㄎㄨㄥˇ)
a buttonhole

鈕子(ㄋㄧㄡˇ·ㄗ)
buttons

【鈞】 6337
ㄐㄩㄣ jiun jūn
1. a unit of weight (equal to 30 catties) in former times
2. (in addressing a superior in a letter) you; your

鈞命(ㄐㄩㄣ ㄇㄧㄥˋ)
your esteemed instructions (used in formally addressing a superior)

鈞衡(ㄐㄩㄣ ㄏㄥˊ)
to evaluate a person's abilities

鈞鑒(ㄐㄩㄣ ㄐㄧㄢˋ)
a conventional phrase used in the salutation in formal letters addressed to a superior

鈞啟(ㄐㄩㄣ ㄑㄧˇ)
a conventional phrase used in the envelope address of a letter to a superior

鈞座(ㄐㄩㄣ ㄗㄨㄛˋ)
your good self; your excellency; your honor

鈞安(ㄐㄩㄣ ㄢ)
May you enjoy peace. —a form of complimentary close in a letter to a superior

鈞諭(ㄐㄩㄣ ㄩˋ)
your esteemed instructions (used in formally addressing a superior)

【鈣】 6338
ㄍㄞˋ gay gài
calcium

鈣片(ㄍㄞˋ ㄆㄧㄢˋ)
a calcium tablet

鈣質(ㄍㄞˋ ㄓˊ)
calcium content

【鈎】 6339
(鉤)ㄍㄡ gou gōu
a hook; to hook: 請將我的衣服掛到鈎上。Please hook my dress for me.

五畫

【鈸】 6340
ㄅㄚˊ bar bá
(又讀 ㄅㄛˊ bor bó)
cymbals

【鈴】 6341
ㄌㄧㄥˊ ling líng

(jingling) bells: 小鈴叮噹地響。The small bell sounded with a jingle.

鈴鐸(ㄌㄧㄥˊ ㄉㄨㄛˊ)
(jingling) bells

鈴鐸(ㄌㄧㄥˊ ㄉㄨㄛˊ)
bells under palace eaves; wind bells

鈴下(ㄌㄧㄥˊ ㄒㄧㄚˋ)
a general's abode

鈴下(ㄌㄧㄥˊ ㄒㄧㄚˋ)
① sir (in addressing a general) ② bodyguards

鈴聲(ㄌㄧㄥˊ ㄕㄥ)
the tinkle of bells

【鈿】 6342
ㄉㄧㄢˋ diann diàn
(又讀 ㄊㄧㄢˊ tyan tián)
filigree

鈿盒(ㄉㄧㄢˋ ㄏㄜˊ)
a filigree case

【鉀】 6343
ㄐㄧㄚˇ jea jiǎ
potassium

鉀肥(ㄐㄧㄚˇ ㄈㄟˊ)
potash fertilizer

鉀鹽(ㄐㄧㄚˇ ㄧㄢˊ)
sylvite

【鉧】 6344
ㄇㄨˇ muu mǔ
an iron

【鉅】 6345
ㄐㄩˋ jiuh jù
1. great 亦作「巨」
2. steel

鉅公(ㄐㄩˋ ㄍㄨㄥ)
a very rich man; a millionaire; a plutocrat

鉅公(ㄐㄩˋ ㄍㄨㄥ)
① the Emperor; His Majesty ② venerable sir; sir

鉅款(ㄐㄩˋ ㄎㄨㄢˇ)
a large sum of money

鉅子(ㄐㄩˋ ㄗˇ)
a great man; a tycoon; a magnate: 他是化學工業界的鉅子。He is a tycoon of the chemical industry.

鉅萬(ㄐㄩˋ ㄨㄢˋ)
great wealth

【鉉】 6346
ㄒㄩㄢˋ shiuann xuàn
a device for carrying a tripod

【鉋】 6347
(鑤) ㄅㄠˋ baw bào

1. to plane (wood)
2. a plane (for carpentry)

鉋凳(ㄅㄠˋ ㄉㄥˋ)
a stool on which the carpenter sits as he planes wood

鉋花(ㄅㄠˋ ㄏㄨㄚ)
shavings

鉋牀(ㄅㄠˋ ㄔㄨㄤˊ)
a lathe for planing; a planing machine

鉋子(ㄅㄠˋ ㄗˇ)
a plane (for carpentry): 他用鉋子把木頭鉋平。He smoothed the wood with a plane.

【鉏】 6348
1. ㄔㄨˊ chwu chú

1. a hoe
2. to hoe
3. to eliminate; to uproot
4. a Chinese family name

【鉏】 6348
2. ㄐㄩˇ jeu jǔ
discordant; disharmonious

鉏鋙(ㄐㄩˇ ㄩˇ) or **鉏鋙**(ㄐㄩˇ ㄩˇ)
discordant; disharmonious

【鉑】 6349
ㄅㄛˊ bor bó

1. a thin sheet of metal; foil 亦作「箔」
2. platinum

【鉗】 6350
ㄑㄧㄢˊ chyan qián

1. pincers; forceps; tweezers; tongs; pliers; clamps
2. chains put around a prisoner's neck
3. to hold with tongs, etc.

鉗徒(ㄑㄧㄢˊ ㄊㄨˊ)
a pilloried prisoner

鉗工(ㄑㄧㄢˊ ㄍㄨㄥ)
① bench work ② a fitter

鉗口結舌(ㄑㄧㄢˊ ㄎㄡˇ ㄐㄧㄝˊ ㄕㄜˊ)
① to silence a person with a gag; to silence a person with threats ② to remain silent; to keep one's mouth shut

鉗嘴(ㄑㄧㄢˊ ㄗㄨㄟˇ)
to keep one's mouth shut; keep quiet

鉗形攻勢(ㄑㄧㄢˊ ㄒㄧㄥˊ ㄍㄨㄥ ㄕˋ)
a two-pronged offensive; a pincers movement

鉗制 or **拑制**(ㄑㄧㄢˊ ㄓˋ)
to keep under control with force; to tie down or pin down (enemy forces)

鉗制輿論(ㄑㄧㄢˊ ㄓˋ ㄩˊ ㄌㄨㄣˋ)
to muzzle public opinion

鉗子(ㄑㄧㄢˊ ㄗ˙)
① tongs; pincers; forceps; tweezers ② a convict; a prisoner ③ earrings

【鉛】 6351
ㄑㄧㄢ chian qiān
lead (a metal): 鉛是重金屬。Lead is a heavy metal.

鉛板(ㄑㄧㄢ ㄅㄢˇ)
① sheet iron ② a lead plate (in printing)

鉛版(ㄑㄧㄢ ㄅㄢˇ)
a lead plate (in printing)

鉛筆(ㄑㄧㄢ ㄅㄧˇ)
a pencil; a lead pencil

鉛筆畫(ㄑㄧㄢ ㄅㄧˇ ㄏㄨㄚˋ)
pencil drawings

鉛粉(ㄑㄧㄢ ㄈㄣˇ) or **鉛白**(ㄑㄧㄢ ㄅㄞˊ)
① white lead; ceruse ② cosmetic powder; face powder: 她買了些鉛粉。She bought some face powder.

鉛黛(ㄑㄧㄢ ㄉㄞˋ)
face powder and eyebrow paint; cosmetics

鉛刀駑馬(ㄑㄧㄢ ㄉㄠ ㄋㄨˊ ㄇㄚˇ) or **鉛駑**(ㄑㄧㄢ ㄋㄨˊ)
(literally) a lead knife and old horse—a man of little use

鉛丹(ㄑㄧㄢ ㄉㄢ)
red lead; minium

鉛彈(ㄑㄧㄢ ㄉㄢˋ)
a lead bullet; a dumdum bullet

鉛毒(ㄑㄧㄢ ㄉㄨˊ)
lead poisoning; plumbism

鉛條(ㄑㄧㄢ ㄊㄧㄠˊ)
① the graphite stick of a pencil ② slender pieces of lead ③ wire

鉛管(ㄑㄧㄢ ㄍㄨㄢˇ)
a lead pipe; a leaden pipe

鉛塊(ㄑㄧㄢ ㄎㄨㄞˋ)
a block of lead; a piece of lead

鉛礦(ㄑㄧㄢ ㄎㄨㄤˋ)
lead ore

鉛華(ㄑㄧㄢ ㄏㄨㄚˊ)
cosmetics; face powder

鉛黃(ㄑㄧㄢ ㄏㄨㄤˊ)
① proofreading ② lead oxide; litharge

鉛球(ㄑㄧㄢ ㄑㄧㄡˊ)
a shot (thrown in the shotput)

〔金部〕

鉛槧(ㄑㄧㄢ ㄑㄧㄢˋ)
lead and tablets—materials used in recording and printing

鉛字(ㄑㄧㄢ ㄗˋ)
lead type (in printing)

鉛絲(ㄑㄧㄢ ㄙ)
zinc-coated wire

鉛印(ㄑㄧㄢ ㄧㄣˋ)
printing by lead plates

【鉞】 6352
ㄩㄝˋ yueh yuè
a large ax

【鉢】 6353
(鈢·盋) ㄅㄛ bō bō
1. an earthenware basin or bowl
2. a Buddhist priest's rice bowl

鉢盂(ㄅㄛ ㄩˊ)
an earthenware basin or bowl

【鉤】 6354
(鈎) ㄍㄡ gou gōu
1. a hook
2. to hook
3. to probe; to investigate
4. to entice; to lure

鉤毛衣(ㄍㄡ ㄇㄠˊ ㄧ)
to crochet a wool sweater

鉤搭 or 勾搭(ㄍㄡ ㄉㄚ)
① to seduce; to inveigle ② to make a secret alliance; a secret alliance

鉤黨(ㄍㄡ ㄉㄤˇ)
to draw one another to form a clique

鉤梯(ㄍㄡ ㄊㄧ)
a scaling ladder 亦作「雲梯」

鉤勒法 or 勾勒法(ㄍㄡ ㄌㄜˋ ㄈㄚˇ)
drawing or writing in outline

鉤稽(ㄍㄡ ㄐㄧ)
to audit (accounts)

鉤肩搭背(ㄍㄡ ㄐㄧㄢ ㄉㄚˊ ㄅㄟˋ)
to hold each other's arms while walking side by side

鉤距(ㄍㄡ ㄐㄩˋ)
to probe or investigate in a circuitous manner

鉤心鬥角(ㄍㄡ ㄒㄧㄣ ㄉㄡˋ ㄐㄩㄝˊ)
to strain the wits of each other (in a contest, etc.); to engage in a battle of wits; to intrigue against each other: 他們鉤心鬥角。 They in-trigued against each

other.

鉤玄(ㄍㄡ ㄒㄩㄢ)
to probe the depth of something abstract

鉤摭(ㄍㄡ ㄓˊ)
to audit (accounts)

鉤爪(ㄍㄡ ㄓㄠˇ)
talons

鉤針(ㄍㄡ ㄓㄣ)
a crochet hook; a crochet needle

鉤章棘句(ㄍㄡ ㄓㄤ ㄐㄧˊ ㄐㄩˋ)
difficult sentences and phrases (in a piece of writing); abstruse language

鉤住(ㄍㄡ ㄓㄨˋ)
to hold on a hook; to seize with a hook; to hook

鉤出來(ㄍㄡ ㄔㄨ ㄌㄞˊ)
to pull out with a hook; to hook out

鉤蟲(ㄍㄡ ㄔㄨㄥˊ)
a hookworm

鉤繩(ㄍㄡ ㄕㄥˊ)
a straightened line or string used as a marker in construction

鉤子(ㄍㄡ ㄗˇ or 鉤兒(ㄍㄡㄦ)
a hook: 把衣服掛在鉤子上。 Hang your coat on the hook.

鉤引 or 勾引(ㄍㄡ ㄧㄣˇ)
to entice; to ensnare; to lure

【鉦】 6355
ㄓㄥ jeng zhēng
a kind of gong (used by marching troops in ancient times)

【鈺】 6356
ㄩˋ yuh yù
a hard variety of gold

【鈾】 6357
ㄧㄡˊ you yóu
uranium

【鈷】 6358
1. ㄍㄨ gu gū
cobalt

【鈷】 6358
2. ㄍㄨˇ guu gǔ
an iron

【鉈】 6359
ㄊㄚ ta tā
thallium

【鈰】 6360
ㄕˋ shyh shì
cerium

【鉍】 6361
ㄅㄧˋ bih bì

bismuth

【鈹】 6362
ㄆㄧˊ pyi pí
beryllium

【鉬】 6363
ㄇㄨˋ muh mù
molybdenum

【鉭】 6364
ㄉㄢˋ dann dàn
tantalum

【鈳】 6365
ㄎㄜ ke kē
columbium

【鈏】 6366
ㄧˋ yii yì
illinium

【鉮】 6367
ㄕㄣ shen shēn
arsonium

六畫

【銀】 6368
ㄧㄣˊ yn yín
1. silver: 言語似銀，沉默似金。 Speech is silver, but silence is golden.
2. money; wealth
3. silvery

銀杯(ㄧㄣˊ ㄅㄟ)
a silver cup (especially one used as a trophy)

銀本位(ㄧㄣˊ ㄅㄣˇ ㄨㄟˋ)
the silver standard (a monetary standard)

銀幣(ㄧㄣˊ ㄅㄧˋ)
a silver coin; silver

銀牌(ㄧㄣˊ ㄆㄞˊ)
a silver medal

銀票(ㄧㄣˊ ㄆㄧㄠˋ)
a bank note (in former times)

銀瓶(ㄧㄣˊ ㄆㄧㄥˊ)
a silver pot; a silver vase

銀幕(ㄧㄣˊ ㄇㄨˋ)
① screen (for motion pictures) ② the screen

銀粉(ㄧㄣˊ ㄈㄣˇ)
silvery powder

銀錠(ㄧㄣˊ ㄉㄧㄥˋ)
silver ingots

銀盾(ㄧㄣˊ ㄉㄨㄣˋ)
a silver plaque

銀條(ㄧㄣˊ ㄊㄧㄠˊ)
a silver bar

銀樓(ㄧㄣˊ ㄌㄡˊ)
a jeweler's shop

銀兩(ㄧㄣˊ ㄌㄧㄤˇ)

銀鉤(ㄧㄣ ㄍㄡ)
silver (as one of valuables)

銀鉤(ㄧㄣ ㄍㄡ)
①a fine stroke (in calligraphy) ②hooks for bamboo blinds, etc.

銀根(ㄧㄣ ㄍㄣ)
money supply; the money market; money

銀櫃(ㄧㄣ ㄍㄨㄟˋ)
a safe

銀庫(ㄧㄣ ㄎㄨˋ)
a treasury

銀礦(ㄧㄣ ㄎㄨㄤˋ)
silver ore; silver mine

銀河(ㄧㄣ ㄏㄜˊ)or 銀漢(ㄧㄣ ㄏㄢˋ)or 銀潢(ㄧㄣ ㄏㄨㄤˊ)
the Milky Way

銀河倒瀉(ㄧㄣ ㄏㄜˊ ㄉㄠˋ ㄒㄧㄝˋ)
a silvery stream cascading downward (descriptive of a waterfall)

銀河系(ㄧㄣ ㄏㄜˊ ㄒㄧˋ)
the Galaxy

銀海(ㄧㄣ ㄏㄞˇ)
moviedom; filmdom

銀號(ㄧㄣ ㄏㄠˋ)
a banking house

銀行(ㄧㄣ ㄏㄤˊ)
a bank

銀行本票(ㄧㄣ ㄏㄤˊ ㄅㄣˇ ㄆㄧㄠˋ)
promissory notes

銀行電匯(ㄧㄣ ㄏㄤˊ ㄉㄧㄢˋ ㄏㄨㄟˋ)
bank cable transfer

銀行透支(ㄧㄣ ㄏㄤˊ ㄊㄡˋ ㄓ)
bank overdraft

銀行團(ㄧㄣ ㄏㄤˊ ㄊㄨㄢˊ)
a banking consortium; a consortium

銀行利率(ㄧㄣ ㄏㄤˊ ㄌㄧˋ ㄌㄩˋ)
the bank rate

銀行利息(ㄧㄣ ㄏㄤˊ ㄌㄧˋ ㄒㄧˊ)
bank interest

銀行公會(ㄧㄣ ㄏㄤˊ ㄍㄨㄥ ㄏㄨㄟˋ)
a banker's association

銀行行員(ㄧㄣ ㄏㄤˊ ㄒㄧㄥˊ ㄩㄢˊ)
a bank employee

銀行匯票(ㄧㄣ ㄏㄤˊ ㄏㄨㄟˋ ㄆㄧㄠˋ)
a bank draft; a bank bill

銀行家(ㄧㄣ ㄏㄤˊ ㄐㄧㄚ)
a banker

銀行界(ㄧㄣ ㄏㄤˊ ㄐㄧㄝˋ)
the banking circle

銀行借款(ㄧㄣ ㄏㄤˊ ㄐㄧㄝˋ ㄎㄨㄢˇ)
bank loans

銀行經理(ㄧㄣ ㄏㄤˊ ㄐㄧㄥ ㄌㄧˇ)

the manager of a bank

銀行支票(ㄧㄣ ㄏㄤˊ ㄓ ㄆㄧㄠˋ)
a bank check; 請給我這個數額的銀行支票。Please give me a bank check for this amount.

銀行手續費(ㄧㄣ ㄏㄤˊ ㄕㄡˇ ㄒㄩˋ ㄈㄟˋ)
bank charges

銀行存款(ㄧㄣ ㄏㄤˊ ㄘㄨㄣˊ ㄎㄨㄢˇ)
a bank deposit

銀行存摺(ㄧㄣ ㄏㄤˊ ㄘㄨㄣˊ ㄓㄜˊ)
a bankbook; a passbook

銀貨兩清(ㄧㄣ ㄏㄨㄛˋ ㄌㄧㄤˇ ㄑㄧㄥ)
completion of a business transaction with goods delivered and payment made

銀灰色(ㄧㄣ ㄏㄨㄟ ㄙㄜˋ)
silver-gray

銀婚(ㄧㄣ ㄏㄨㄣ)
a silver wedding; the 25th wedding anniversary

銀價(ㄧㄣ ㄐㄧㄚˋ)
the price of silver

銀角(ㄧㄣ ㄐㄧㄠˇ)
silver coins of small denominations

銀匠(ㄧㄣ ㄐㄧㄤˋ)
a silversmith

銀器(ㄧㄣ ㄑㄧˋ)
silverware

銀錢(ㄧㄣ ㄑㄧㄢˊ)
money; wealth

銀杏(ㄧㄣ ㄒㄧㄥˋ)
(botany) gingko; ginkgo

銀朱 or 銀硃(ㄧㄣ ㄓㄨ)
vermilion

銀鼠(ㄧㄣ ㄕㄨˇ)
an ermine; a snow weasel

銀座(ㄧㄣ ㄗㄨㄛˋ)
Ginza (a shopping center of Tokyo)

銀子(ㄧㄣ ㄗˇ)
silver (as one of valuables): 我付他五千兩銀子。I paid him 5,000 taels of silver.

銀色(ㄧㄣ ㄙㄜˋ)
silvery

銀筍 or 銀笋(ㄧㄣ ㄙㄨㄣˇ)
icicles

銀耳(ㄧㄣ ㄦˇ)
a kind of semitransparent white fungus (*Tremella fuciformis*) believed to be highly nutritious

銀洋(ㄧㄣ ㄧㄤˊ)
silver dollar (a major silver

coin in circulation formerly)

銀魚(ㄧㄣ ㄩˊ)
silverfish 亦作「鱠魚」

銀元 or 銀圓(ㄧㄣ ㄩㄢˊ)
①silver dollar (a major silver coin formerly in circulation) ②*yuan*, an arbitrarily fixed monetary unit worth NT$3 now used as a standard in fines only

【鉸】 ㄐㄧㄠ jeau jiao 6369
1. scissors; shears
2. hinges
3. to shear

鉸刀(ㄐㄧㄠ ㄉㄠ)
scissors; shears

鉸鏈(ㄐㄧㄠ ㄌㄧㄢˋ)
hinges

【銃】 ㄔㄨㄥˋ chong chòng 6370
1. firearms
2. a joint of the metal head to the handle of an ax

【銅】 ㄊㄨㄥˊ torng tóng 6371
copper; bronze; brass: 銅是一種甚爲有用的金屬。Copper is a very useful metal.

銅板(ㄊㄨㄥˊ ㄅㄢˇ)
a copper coin 參看「銅幣」

銅版(ㄊㄨㄥˊ ㄅㄢˇ)
copperplate (in printing)

銅版畫(ㄊㄨㄥˊ ㄅㄢˇ ㄏㄨㄚˋ)
copperplate etching (or engraving)

銅版紙(ㄊㄨㄥˊ ㄅㄢˇ ㄓˇ)
art printing paper

銅幣(ㄊㄨㄥˊ ㄅㄧˋ)
a copper coin

銅琶鐵板(ㄊㄨㄥˊ ㄆㄚˊ ㄊㄧㄝˇ ㄅㄢˇ)
bold and vehement language (in writing)

銅牌(ㄊㄨㄥˊ ㄆㄞˊ)
a bronze medal

銅模(ㄊㄨㄥˊ ㄇㄛˊ)
a copper mold

銅頭鐵額(ㄊㄨㄥˊ ㄊㄡˊ ㄊㄧㄝˇ ㄜˊ)
audacious; fearless; intrepid

銅駝荊棘(ㄊㄨㄥˊ ㄊㄨㄛˊ ㄐㄧㄥ ㄐㄧˊ)
devastation of palaces as a result of war

銅鑼(ㄊㄨㄥˊ ㄌㄨㄛˊ)
a copper gong 參看「銅鉦」

銅綠(ㄊㄨㄥˊ ㄌㄩˋ)or 銅青(ㄊㄨㄥˊ ㄑㄧㄥ)
patina; verdigris

〔金 部〕

【金部】

銅礦(ㄊㄨㄥˊ ㄎㄨㄤˋ)
① copper ore ② copper mine

銅壺(ㄊㄨㄥˊ ㄏㄨˊ)
①a copper pot; a copper urn ②a clepsydra; a water clock

銅壺滴漏(ㄊㄨㄥˊ ㄏㄨˊ ㄉㄧ ㄌㄡˋ)
a clepsydra; a water clock

銅筋鐵骨(ㄊㄨㄥˊ ㄐㄧㄣ ㄊㄧㄝˇ ㄍㄨˇ)
(said of a man's physique) strongly built; sturdy

銅匠(ㄊㄨㄥˊ ㄐㄧㄤˋ)
a coppersmith

銅鏡(ㄊㄨㄥˊ ㄐㄧㄥˋ)
a copper mirror

銅器(ㄊㄨㄥˊ ㄑㄧˋ)
bronze utensils

銅器時代(ㄊㄨㄥˊ ㄑㄧˋ ㄕˊ ㄉㄞˋ)
the Copper Age

銅錢(ㄊㄨㄥˊ ㄑㄧㄢˊ)
copper coins

銅牆鐵壁(ㄊㄨㄥˊ ㄑㄧㄤˊ ㄊㄧㄝˇ ㄅㄧˋ)
an extremely sturdy structure; tight (siege); strong (fortress, defense, etc.); impregnable like walls of brass and iron

銅雀臺(ㄊㄨㄥˊ ㄑㄩㄝ ㄊㄞˊ)
a tower built by Tsao Tsao (曹操) in what is Honan today

銅像(ㄊㄨㄥˊ ㄒㄧㄤˋ)
a bronze image; a bronze statue

銅鉦(ㄊㄨㄥˊ ㄓㄥ)
a brass gong

銅臭(ㄊㄨㄥˊ ㄒㄧㄡˋ)
a smell of copper (a term of derision applied to wealthy but mean people); the stink of money, stinking with money: 他滿身銅臭。He was stinking with money.

銅人(ㄊㄨㄥˊ ㄖㄣˊ)
a bronze image; a bronze statue 亦作「銅狄」

銅子兒(ㄊㄨㄥˊ ㄗˇㄦ)
(colloquial) copper coins; coppers

銅絲(ㄊㄨㄥˊ ㄙ)
copper wire

銅印(ㄊㄨㄥˊ ㄧㄣˋ)
a copper seal

銅元(ㄊㄨㄥˊ ㄩㄢˊ)
copper coins

【銑】 6372
ㄒㄧㄢˇ shean xiǎn
1. shiny metal
2. pig iron

銑鐵(ㄒㄧㄢˇ ㄊㄧㄝˇ)
pig iron; cast iron

【銓】 6373
ㄑㄩㄢˊ chyuan quán
1. to weigh
2. to evaluate qualifications in selecting officials
3. a Chinese family name

銓衡(ㄑㄩㄢˊ ㄏㄥˊ)
to measure and select talents

銓敍 or 銓序(ㄑㄩㄢˊ ㄒㄩˋ)
to select and appoint officials

銓敍部(ㄑㄩㄢˊ ㄒㄩˋ ㄅㄨˋ)
Ministry of Personnel (under the Examination Yuan)

銓選(ㄑㄩㄢˊ ㄒㄩㄢˇ)
to select (officials) after evaluating qualifications

銓擇(ㄑㄩㄢˊ ㄗㄜˊ)
to evaluate and select

銓次(ㄑㄩㄢˊ ㄘˋ)
procedures for selecting officials

【銖】 6374
ㄓㄨ ju zhū
1. an ancient unit of weight (equal to 1/48th, or by other interpretations 1/24th, of a tael); the ancient coinage of Han
2. blunt; dull; obtuse
3. a Chinese family name

銖鈍(ㄓㄨ ㄉㄨㄣˋ)
dull knives and spears

銖兩(ㄓㄨ ㄌㄧㄤˇ)
very small; tiny; minute

銖兩悉稱(ㄓㄨ ㄌㄧㄤˇ ㄒㄧ ㄔㄥˋ)
to match in every small detail, to have the same weight

銖積寸累(ㄓㄨ ㄐㄧ ㄘㄨㄣˋ ㄌㄟˇ)
Trifles amount to much when accumulated. 或 to build up bit by bit

銖衣(ㄓㄨ ㄧ)
an extremely light-weight garment

【銘】 6375
ㄇㄧㄥˊ ming míng
1. to engrave; to inscribe; to imprint
2. inscriptions

銘佩(ㄇㄧㄥˊ ㄆㄟˋ)
to remember with admiration

銘感(ㄇㄧㄥˊ ㄍㄢˇ)
to remember with gratitude

銘刻(ㄇㄧㄥˊ ㄎㄜˋ)
to engrave; to imprint

銘肌鏤骨(ㄇㄧㄥˊ ㄐㄧ ㄌㄡˋ ㄍㄨˇ)
to feel deep gratitude

銘記在心(ㄇㄧㄥˊ ㄐㄧˋ ㄗㄞˋ ㄒㄧㄣ)
to imprint on one's mind

銘旌 or 明旌(ㄇㄧㄥˊ ㄐㄧㄥ)
a funeral streamer bearing the titles of the deceased

銘謝(ㄇㄧㄥˊ ㄒㄧㄝˋ)
to show gratefulness

銘心(ㄇㄧㄥˊ ㄒㄧㄣ)
to imprint on one's mind

銘誌(ㄇㄧㄥˊ ㄓˋ)
to record, or commemorate with an engraved inscription

銘篆(ㄇㄧㄥˊ ㄓㄨㄢˋ)
to remember with deep gratitude

銘文(ㄇㄧㄥˊ ㄨㄣˊ)
an inscription; an epigraph

【銚】 6376
1. ㄧㄠˊ yau yáo
1. a kind of farm tool
2. a Chinese family name

【銚】 6376
2. ㄉㄧㄠˋ diaw diào
1. a small pot with a handle
2. a brass cymbal

【銛】 6377
ㄒㄧㄢ shian xiān
sharp; keen-edged

銛利(ㄒㄧㄢ ㄌㄧˋ)
sharp; keen-edged

【銜】 6378
ㄒㄧㄢˊ shyan xián
1. a bit (in a horse's mouth)
2. the title (of an official)
3. to hold in the mouth
4. to harbor; to cherish
5. to follow (orders)

銜璧(ㄒㄧㄢˊ ㄅㄧˋ)
to surrender with one's hands bound and with a piece of jade held in one's mouth

銜鐶(ㄒㄧㄢˊ ㄏㄨㄢˊ)
a bit (in a horse's mouth)

銜枚疾走(ㄒㄧㄢˊ ㄇㄟˊ ㄐㄧˊ ㄗㄡˇ)
to march swiftly with a gag in the mouth (to prevent unnecessary noise which may

alert the enemy)

銜命(ㄒㄧㄢˊㄇㄧㄥˋ)or 銜令(ㄒㄧㄢˊ
ㄌㄧㄥˋ)
to follow an order; to act
according to a directive

銜勒(ㄒㄧㄢˊㄌㄜˋ)
a bit (in a horse's mouth)

銜恨(ㄒㄧㄢˊㄏㄣˋ)
to harbor grudges: 他銜恨以
終。He harbored grudges for
the rest of his life.

銜華佩實(ㄒㄧㄢˊㄏㄨㄚˊㄆㄟˋㄕˊ)
(said of a piece of writing)
rich in substance and graceful in style

銜環(ㄒㄧㄢˊㄏㄨㄢˊ)
A bird returns with rings in
its mouth thanking its
owner for freedom.—to
repay with gratitude

銜環結草(ㄒㄧㄢˊㄏㄨㄢˊㄐㄧㄝˊㄘㄠˇ)
to repay a kindness 參看「衛
環」

銜接(ㄒㄧㄢˊㄐㄧㄝ)
to adjoin; to lie next to; to
connect; to dovetail; to link
up: 這運河把兩城鎮銜接起來。
This canal links up the two
towns.

銜尾相隨(ㄒㄧㄢˊㄨㄟˇㄒㄧㄤㄙㄨㄟˊ)
one close behind another

銜冤(ㄒㄧㄢˊㄩㄢ)
to have no chance of airing
one's grievances; to have a
simmering sense of injustice

【銍】6379
ㄓˋ jyh zhì
a sickle

【銬】6380
ㄎㄠˋ kaw kào
manacles; handcuffs

【銥】6381
ㄧ yii yì
iridium

【鉬】6382
ㄦˇ eel ěr
erbium

【銠】6383
ㄌㄠˇ lao lǎo
rhodium

【銪】6384
ㄧㄡˇ yeou yǒu
europium

【鉿】6385
ㄏㄜˊ her hé
hafnium

【銦】6386
ㄧㄣ in yín
indium

【銫】6387
ㄙㄜˋ seh sè
caesium

【銩】6388
ㄉㄧㄡ diou diū
thulium

【鉻】6389
ㄍㄜˋ geh gè
chromium

【銣】6390
ㄖㄨˊ ruh rú
rubidium

七畫

【銳】6391
ㄖㄨㄟˋ ruey ruì
1. sharp; acute; keen
2. quick-witted; intelligent;
clever
3. energetic; vigorous

銳不可當(ㄖㄨㄟˋㄅㄨˋㄎㄜˇㄉㄤ)
too sharp to resist; too
powerful to stop

銳敏(ㄖㄨㄟˋㄇㄧㄣˇ)
quick-witted; acute; keen;
sharp: 狗的嗅覺銳敏。Dogs
have a keen sense of smell.

銳髮(ㄖㄨㄟˋㄈㄚˇ)
stray hair before the ear

銳利(ㄖㄨㄟˋㄌㄧˋ)
sharp; pointed: 他用銳利的刀
子切斷繩子。He cut the rope
with a sharp knife.

銳角(ㄖㄨㄟˋㄐㄧㄠˇ)
an acute angle

銳角三角形(ㄖㄨㄟˋㄐㄧㄠˇㄙㄢㄐㄧㄠˇ
ㄒㄧㄥˊ)
an acute-angled triangle

銳減(ㄖㄨㄟˋㄐㄧㄢˇ)
to decline sharply; to drop
markedly

銳氣(ㄖㄨㄟˋㄑㄧˋ)
dash; mettle; vigor; virility;
aggressiveness

銳志(ㄖㄨㄟˋㄓˋ)
sharp will; earnest intention;
determination; spirit of
enterprise

銳士(ㄖㄨㄟˋㄕˋ)
①a man of intelligence; a
man of energy ②brave sol-
diers of the state of Chin
(秦)during the Epoch of
Warring States

銳意(ㄖㄨㄟˋㄧˋ)
sharp will; eager intention;
determination 參看「銳志」

銳眼(ㄖㄨㄟˋㄧㄢˇ)
sharp eyes; vision; insight

【銷】6392
ㄒㄧㄠ shiau xiāo
1. to melt
2. to be marketed; to be circulated; to sell
3. to vanish; to dispel; to cancel 亦作「消」
4. pig iron; crude iron

銷路(ㄒㄧㄠㄌㄨˋ)
a sale; a market; a circulation (of publications, commodities, etc.); a market
demand: 這本書銷路很廣。The
book has a large circulation.

銷耗(ㄒㄧㄠㄏㄠˋ)
①expenditure ②to spend;
to cost: 我們爲它銷耗很多勞
力。We spent so much labor
on it.

銷貨部(ㄒㄧㄠㄏㄨㄛˋㄅㄨˋ)
a sales department

銷貨發票(ㄒㄧㄠㄏㄨㄛˋㄈㄚㄆㄧㄠˋ)
(accounting) the invoice for
sales; a sales invoice; sales
tickets

銷貨點(ㄒㄧㄠㄏㄨㄛˋㄉㄧㄢˇ)
points of sale

銷貨折扣(ㄒㄧㄠㄏㄨㄛˋㄓㄜˊㄎㄡˋ)
(accounting) sales discount

銷毀(ㄒㄧㄠㄏㄨㄟˇ)
to destroy: 這嫌疑犯銷毀罪
證。The suspect destroyed
incriminating evidence.

銷魂(ㄒㄧㄠㄏㄨㄣˊ)
enraptured; transported; carried away

銷假(ㄒㄧㄠㄐㄧㄚˋ)
to begin work anew after a
leave of absence or vaca-
tion: 他銷假了。He reported
back after leave of absence.

銷金(ㄒㄧㄠㄐㄧㄣ)
①to lavish wealth ②deco-
rated with gold; gilt

銷金窟(ㄒㄧㄠㄐㄧㄣㄎㄨˋ)
a brothel

銷金紙(ㄒㄧㄠㄐㄧㄣㄓˇ)
gilt paper

銷金帳(ㄒㄧㄠㄐㄧㄣㄓㄤˋ)
a gilt curtain

銷行(ㄒㄧㄠㄒㄧㄥˊ)
(said of goods) to be marketed; to be sold; to sell

〔金部〕

【金部】

銷賬(ㄒㄧㄠ ㄓㄤˋ)
to cancel debts

銷差(ㄒㄧㄠ ㄔㄞ)
to report mission accomplished

銷場(ㄒㄧㄠ ㄔㄤˇ)
demand (for goods, services, etc.)

銷售(ㄒㄧㄠ ㄕㄡˋ)
to sell (goods); 這書銷售得非常久。 The book is selling remarkably well.

銷售部門(ㄒㄧㄠ ㄕㄡˋ ㄅㄨˋ ㄇㄣˊ)
a marketing department

銷售方法(ㄒㄧㄠ ㄕㄡˋ ㄈㄤ ㄈㄚˇ)
the marketing method

銷售服務(ㄒㄧㄠ ㄕㄡˋ ㄈㄨˊ ㄨˋ)
marketing service

銷售地區(ㄒㄧㄠ ㄕㄡˋ ㄉㄧˋ ㄑㄩ)
sales territory

銷售量(ㄒㄧㄠ ㄕㄡˋ ㄌㄧㄤˋ)
sales volume

銷售活動(ㄒㄧㄠ ㄕㄡˋ ㄏㄨㄛˊ ㄉㄨㄥˋ)
marketing activity

銷售計劃(ㄒㄧㄠ ㄕㄡˋ ㄐㄧˋ ㄏㄨㄚˋ)
a marketing plan

銷售折扣(ㄒㄧㄠ ㄕㄡˋ ㄓㄜˊ ㄎㄡˋ)
(accounting) discount on sales

銷售狀況(ㄒㄧㄠ ㄕㄡˋ ㄓㄨㄤˋ ㄎㄨㄤˋ)
sales status

銷聲匿跡(ㄒㄧㄠ ㄕㄥ ㄋㄧˋ ㄐㄧ)
to vanish without leaving any trace behind; to go into hiding

銷鎔(ㄒㄧㄠ ㄖㄨㄥˊ)
to melt

銷贓(ㄒㄧㄠ ㄗㄤ)
(law) the disposal of stolen goods

銷案(ㄒㄧㄠ ㄢˋ)
to close a case

【錦】6393
ㄊㄧˋ tih tì
antimony

【鋱】6394
ㄊㄜˋ teh tè
terbium

【鋇】6395
ㄅㄟˋ bey bèi
barium

【鋰】6396
ㄌㄧˇ lii lǐ
lithium

【鋯】6397
《ㄠˋ gaw gào
zirconium

【鋨】6398
ㄜˊ er é
osmium

【鋁】6399
ㄌㄩˇ leu lǚ
aluminium; aluminum

鋁箔(ㄌㄩˇ ㄅㄛˊ)
aluminium foil

鋁錠(ㄌㄩˇ ㄉㄧㄥˋ)
aluminium ingot

鋁合金(ㄌㄩˇ ㄏㄜˊ ㄐㄧㄣ)
aluminium alloy

鋁廠(ㄌㄩˇ ㄔㄤˇ)
an aluminium plant

【鋃】6400
ㄌㄤˊ lang láng
1. chains for prisoners
2. the tolling of a bell

鋃鐺(ㄌㄤˊ ㄉㄤ)
chains for prisoners

鋃鐺入獄(ㄌㄤˊ ㄉㄤ ㄖㄨˋ ㄩˋ)
to be shackled and imprisoned; to be jailed

【鋅】6401
ㄒㄧㄣ shin xin
zinc

鋅版(ㄒㄧㄣ ㄅㄢˇ)
zincotype; zincograph

鋅鐵礦(ㄒㄧㄣ ㄊㄧㄝˇ ㄎㄨㄤˋ)
franklinite

鋅華(ㄒㄧㄣ ㄏㄨㄚˊ)or 鋅白(ㄒㄧㄣ ㄅㄞˊ)
zinc white

【鋌】6402
ㄊㄧㄥˇ tiing tǐng
to rush

鋌而走險(ㄊㄧㄥˇ ㄦˊ ㄗㄡˇ ㄒㄧㄢˇ)
to be forced to break the law; to risk danger in desperation; 他鋌而走險。 He risked danger in desperation.

【鋏】6403
ㄐㄧㄚˊ jya jiá
1. pincers; tongs
2. a sword
3. a hilt

【鋒】6404
ㄈㄥ feng fēng
1. sharp point (as the tip of a lance, pencil, etc.)
2. the vanguard; the van

鋒芒(ㄈㄥ ㄇㄤˊ)
①sharp point (as of a lance, etc.) ②dash; mettle; vigor

鋒芒畢露(ㄈㄥ ㄇㄤˊ ㄅㄧˋ ㄌㄨˋ)
to show one's intelligence, ability, knowledge, etc. to

the full extent

鋒面(ㄈㄥ ㄇㄧㄢˋ)
(meteorology) frontal surface; a front

鋒發韻流(ㄈㄥ ㄈㄚ ㄩㄣˋ ㄌㄧㄡˊ)
fluent and overpowering (said of a literary style)

鋒鏑(ㄈㄥ ㄉㄧˊ)
sharp-pointed weapons

鋒利(ㄈㄥ ㄌㄧˋ)
①sharp-pointed; sharp: 用一把鋒利的小刀吧。Use a sharp knife. ②vigorous; energetic; keen; sharp; incisive: 他的文章富有鋒利尖銳的筆調。His essay has a sharp and pungent style.

鋒起(ㄈㄥ ㄑㄧˇ)
to rise with irresistible force or suddenness

鋒出(ㄈㄥ ㄔㄨ)
to occur suddenly; to come as a surprise

鋒刃(ㄈㄥ ㄖㄣˋ)
sharp points and edges of weapons

鋒銳(ㄈㄥ ㄖㄨㄟˋ)
sharp; keen; acute; spirited; vigorous

鋒鍔(ㄈㄥ ㄜˋ)
the point and edge of a knife

【銅】6405
ㄐㄩ jiu jù
1. a kind of nail for mending crockery
2. curium 亦作「錒」

銅碗(ㄐㄩ ㄨㄢˇ)
to mend crockery

【鋙】6406
ㄩˇ yeu yǔ
1. discordant; disharmonious
2. a kind of musical instrument

【鋤】6407
ㄔㄨˊ chwu chú
1. a hoe 亦作「鉏」
2. to hoe: 他正在鋤田。He is hoeing the fields.

鋤頭(ㄔㄨˊ ㄊㄡ)
a hoe

鋤奸(ㄔㄨˊ ㄍㄢ)
the vomer bone 亦作「犂骨」

鋤奸(ㄔㄨˊ ㄐㄧㄢ)
to wipe out the wicked elements

鋤強扶弱(ㄔㄨˊ ㄑㄧㄤˊ ㄈㄨˊ ㄖㄨㄛˋ)

to eliminate the bullies and help the downtrodden

【鋩】 6408
ㄇㄤ mang máng
the point of a knife

【錯】 6409
ㄘㄨㄛˋ tsuoh cuò
1. a kind of widemouthed cauldron used in ancient China
2. a file (a steel tool)
3. to make smooth with a file; to file
銼刀 (ㄘㄨㄛˋ ㄉㄠ)
a file (a steel tool)

【鋪】 1. ㄆㄨ pu pū
to lay in order; to spread; to arrange; to pave: 這條路鋪上了瀝青。 The street is paved with asphalt.
鋪排 (ㄆㄨ ㄆㄞˊ)
①to arrange; to lay in order; arrangement ②to handle things with pomp; pomp
鋪平 (ㄆㄨ ㄆㄧㄥˊ)
to smooth out; to spread out and make smooth
鋪地磚 (ㄆㄨ ㄉㄧˋ ㄓㄨㄢ)
a floor tile; a paving tile
鋪墊 (ㄆㄨ ㄉㄧㄢˋ)
①a cushion ②to spread a cushion ③to foreshadow
鋪路 (ㄆㄨ ㄌㄨˋ)
to surface a road; to pave a road; to pave the way: 他小心地工作以便替我鋪路。 He paved the way for me by doing careful work.
鋪蓋 (ㄆㄨ ㄍㄞˋ)
bedding
鋪蓋捲兒 (ㄆㄨ ㄍㄞˋ ㄐㄩㄢˇ)
bedding rolled up for transportation during travel
鋪敘 (ㄆㄨ ㄒㄩˋ)
to state in detail; to give a detailed account of
鋪展 (ㄆㄨ ㄓㄢˇ)
①to arrange; to lay in order: 把報紙鋪展在桌面上。 Arrange the papers on the table. ②to handle things with pomp
鋪張 (ㄆㄨ ㄓㄤ)
①to arrange; to lay in order ②to make an ostentatious or vain show; to be pompous

鋪張浪費 (ㄆㄨ ㄓㄤ ㄌㄤˋ ㄈㄟˋ)
extravagant and wasteful
鋪張揚厲 (ㄆㄨ ㄓㄤ ㄧㄤˊ ㄌㄧˋ)
①to praise profusely; to eulogize ②to exaggerate; to make a big show
鋪陳 (ㄆㄨ ㄔㄣˊ)
①to state in detail; to elaborate ②to arrange for display
鋪牀 (ㄆㄨ ㄔㄨㄤˊ)
to make the bed
鋪設 (ㄆㄨ ㄕㄜˋ)
to lay in order; to arrange

【鋪】 2. (舖) ㄆㄨˋ puh pù
a store; a shop; a grocery: 我在雜貨鋪購買砂糖。 I bought sugar at the grocery.
鋪保 (ㄆㄨˋ ㄅㄠˇ)
a guarantee (for a person's reliability) given by a shopkeeper
鋪面 (ㄆㄨˋ ㄇㄧㄢˋ)
the store front; the facade of a store: 這鋪面面向公園。 The front of this shop faces the park.
鋪房 (ㄆㄨˋ ㄇㄧㄥˊ)
a shop building
鋪底 (ㄆㄨˋ ㄉㄧˇ)
shop fixtures
鋪規 (ㄆㄨˋ ㄍㄨㄟ)
rules of a shop or store
鋪戶 (ㄆㄨˋ ㄏㄨˋ)
shops; stores
鋪子 (ㄆㄨˋ ˙ㄗ)
shops; stores: 她去鋪子買包。 She went to the store to buy bread.

【銲】 6411
(釺) ㄏㄢˋ hann hàn
to solder; to weld
銲工 (ㄏㄢˋ ㄍㄨㄥ)
①welding; soldering ②a welder; a solderer
銲接 (ㄏㄢˋ ㄐㄧㄝ)
to join with solder; to weld; to solder: 這接頭處易於銲接。 The joint solders easily.
銲錫 (ㄏㄢˋ ㄒㄧˊ)
solder
銲住 (ㄏㄢˋ ㄓㄨˋ)
to fix with solder

【銹】 6412
(鏽) ㄒㄧㄡˋ shiow xiù
rust

銹斑 (ㄒㄧㄡˋ ㄅㄢ)
rust stains

八畫

【鋸】 6413
1. ㄐㄩ jiuh jú
1. a saw
2. to saw; to cut with a saw: 軟質的木材容易鋸。 Soft wood saws easily.
3. to amputate: 醫生鋸掉這士兵的腿。 The doctor amputated the soldier's leg.
鋸木 (ㄐㄩ ㄇㄨˋ)
to saw wood
鋸木廠 (ㄐㄩ ㄇㄨˋ ㄔㄤˇ)
a sawmill
鋸腿 (ㄐㄩ ㄊㄨㄟˇ)
to amputate a leg
鋸開 (ㄐㄩ ㄎㄞ)
to saw asunder
鋸屑 (ㄐㄩ ㄒㄧㄝˋ)
sawdust
鋸齒 (ㄐㄩ ㄔˇ)or 鋸牙 (ㄐㄩ ㄧㄚˊ)
teeth of a saw
鋸齒狀 (ㄐㄩ ㄔˇ ㄓㄨㄤˋ)
serrated
鋸子 (ㄐㄩ ˙ㄗ)
a saw: 我用鋸子鋸開木頭。 I cut through the wood with a saw.

【鋸】 2. ㄐㄩ jiu jù
1. a kind of nail for mending crockery
2. to mend (crockery)
3. curium 「鋦」
鋸碗 (ㄐㄩ ㄨㄢˇ)
to mend crockery

【鋼】 6414
《ㄤ gang gāng
steel: 許多工具是鋼製的。 Many tools are made of steel.
鋼板 (《ㄤ ㄅㄢˇ)
a steel plate
鋼筆 (《ㄤ ㄅㄧˇ)
a fountain pen: 用鋼筆和墨水寫。 Write with a fountain pen and ink.
鋼筆頭兒 (《ㄤ ㄅㄧˇ ㄊㄡˊㄦ)
the point of a fountain pen
鋼鐵 (《ㄤ ㄊㄧˇ)
steel; steel and iron: 我有鋼鐵般的意志。 I have an iron will.

〔金部〕

【金部】

鋼鐵公司 (《ㄈㄤ ㄊㄧㄝˇ ㄍㄨㄥ ㄙ)
a steel company: 他在鋼鐵公司上班。He is working in a steel company.

鋼鐵廠 (《ㄈㄤ ㄊㄧㄝˇ ㄔㄤˇ)
a steelworks; a steel mill

鋼條 (《ㄈㄤ ㄊㄧㄠˊ)
a steel wire

鋼骨混凝土 (《ㄈㄤ ㄍㄨˇ ㄏㄨㄣˊ ㄋㄧㄥˊ ㄊㄨˇ)
reinforced concrete 亦作「鋼骨水泥」or「鋼筋水泥」

鋼管 (《ㄈㄤ ㄍㄨㄢˇ)
a steel pipe

鋼盔 (《ㄈㄤ ㄎㄨㄟ)
a steel helmet; a helmet

鋼筋 (《ㄈㄤ ㄐㄧㄣ)
steel bars; steel rods; wire mesh

鋼筋水泥 (《ㄈㄤ ㄐㄧㄣ ㄕㄨㄟˇ ㄋㄧˊ)
reinforced concrete

鋼琴 (《ㄈㄤ ㄑㄧㄣˊ)
a piano: 她鋼琴彈得很好。She plays the piano very well.

鋼琴伴奏 (《ㄈㄤ ㄑㄧㄣˊ ㄅㄢˋ ㄗㄡˋ)
the piano accompaniment

鋼琴家 (《ㄈㄤ ㄑㄧㄣˊ ㄐㄧㄚ)
a pianist

鋼琴協奏曲 (《ㄈㄤ ㄑㄧㄣˊ ㄒㄧㄝˊ ㄗㄡˋ ㄑㄩˇ)
a piano concerto

鋼琴演奏會 (《ㄈㄤ ㄑㄧㄣˊ ㄧㄢˇ ㄗㄡˋ ㄏㄨㄟˋ)
a piano concert; a piano recital

鋼珠 (《ㄈㄤ ㄓㄨ) or 鋼球 (《ㄈㄤ ㄑㄧㄡˊ)
a steel ball (in a ball bearing)

鋼尺 (《ㄈㄤ ㄔˇ)
a steel ruler

鋼絲 (《ㄈㄤ ㄙ)
steel wire: 這條鋼絲太長。This steel wire is too long.

鋼絲絨 (《ㄈㄤ ㄙ ㄖㄨㄥˊ)
steel wool

鋼玉 (《ㄈㄤ ㄩˋ)
corundum; corundumite

【鉲】 6415
《ㄚ   gar gá
gadolinium

【錸】 6416
ㄌㄞˊ lai lái
rhenium

【錒】 6417
ㄚ ah ā
actinium

【錄】 6418
ㄌㄨˋ luh lù
1. to take down; to copy; to record
2. to accept (applicants)
3. a record: 他保持跳高的最高紀錄。He holds the record for the high jump.

錄放影機 (ㄌㄨˋ ㄈㄤˋ ㄧㄥˇ ㄐㄧ)
a videocassette recorder (VCR)

錄供 (ㄌㄨˋ ㄍㄨㄥ)
to take down testimony

錄取 (ㄌㄨˋ ㄑㄩˇ)
to accept (applicants after screening, examinations, etc.)

錄下 (ㄌㄨˋ ㄒㄧㄚˋ)
to record

錄製 (ㄌㄨˋ ㄓˋ)
to record

錄事 (ㄌㄨˋ ㄕˋ)
a clerk whose job is to record or copy documents

錄音 (ㄌㄨˋ ㄧㄣ)
① to record (songs, music, etc.) ②(songs, music, etc.) recording

錄音帶 (ㄌㄨˋ ㄧㄣ ㄉㄞˋ)
a recording tape

錄音機 (ㄌㄨˋ ㄧㄣ ㄐㄧ)
a tape recorder; a recorder

錄音室 (ㄌㄨˋ ㄧㄣ ㄕˋ)
a recording room

錄影帶 (ㄌㄨˋ ㄧㄥˇ ㄉㄞˋ)
a videotape

錄影機 (ㄌㄨˋ ㄧㄥˇ ㄐㄧ)
a videorecorder

錄用 (ㄌㄨˋ ㄩㄥˋ)
to accept for employment

【鉶】 6419
ㄒㄧㄥˊ shyng xíng
a kind of receptacle for food in ancient times

【錐】 6420
ㄓㄨㄟ juei zhuī
1. an awl
2. to pierce; to bore; to drill; to make a hole
3. conical

錐面 (ㄓㄨㄟ ㄇㄧㄢˋ)
①(mathematics) conical surface ②(mineralogy) pyramidal faces

錐刀之末 (ㄓㄨㄟ ㄉㄠ ㄓ ㄇㄛˋ)
small gains; negligible profits

錐股 (ㄓㄨㄟ ㄍㄨˇ)
(literally) to prick the thigh with an awl (as 蘇秦 did in order to stay awake when studying)—to study with great determination and diligence

錐形 (ㄓㄨㄟ ㄒㄧㄥˊ)
a taper; a cone: 鋸屑堆成大錐形狀。Sawdust piled up in a great cone.

錐指 (ㄓㄨㄟ ㄓˇ)
a very limited outlook

錐處囊中 (ㄓㄨㄟ ㄔㄨˇ ㄋㄤˊ ㄓㄨㄥ)
(literally) an awl in a bag (which may be temporarily hidden but will eventually pierce the bag and show itself)—A talented person will sooner or later distinguish himself despite temporary adversity. 或 Real talent will be discovered.

錐子 (ㄓㄨㄟ ˙ㄗ)
an awl

【錘】 6421
ㄔㄨㄟˊ chwei chuí
1. a weight on a steelyard: 平衡錘 a balance weight
2. an ancient unit of weight
3. a kind of ancient weapon
4. to hammer; to pound
5. a hammer

錘鍊 (ㄔㄨㄟˊ ㄌㄧㄢˋ)
①to forge (metal); to temper ②to polish

錘子 (ㄔㄨㄟˊ ˙ㄗ)
a hammer

【錙】 6422
ㄗ tzy zī
an ancient unit of weight (said to equal 8 taels)

錙銖 (ㄗ ㄓㄨ)
a very small quantity; a trifle

錙銖必較 (ㄗ ㄓㄨ ㄅㄧˋ ㄐㄧㄠˋ)
to be particular even about a trifling amount

【錚】 6423
ㄓㄥ jeng zhēng
1. a clang of metal
2. gongs

錚錚 (ㄓㄥ ㄓㄥ)
①a clang of metal ②righteous; incorruptible; upright

錚鏦 (ㄓㄥ ㄘㄨㄥˊ)
a clang of metal; to clang

【錠】 6424
ㄉㄧㄥ ding ding
1. a kind of ancient utensil
2. ingots of gold or silver
3. a spindle
4. a (medical) tablet
定劑(ㄉㄧㄥ ㄐㄧ)
medicine in tablet form

【錡】 6425
ㄑㄧ chyi qi
1. a tripod
2. a kind of chisel

【錢】 6426
ㄑㄧㄢˊ chyan qián
1. money; cash: 時間即是錢。
Time is money.
2. a unit of weight (equal to 1/10th of a tael)
3. a Chinese family name
錢包(ㄑㄧㄢˊ ㄅㄠ)
a wallet; a purse
錢幣(ㄑㄧㄢˊ ㄅㄧˋ)
① coin ② currency; money
錢癖(ㄑㄧㄢˊ ㄆㄧˇ)
inveterate love of money
錢票(ㄑㄧㄢˊ ㄆㄧㄠˋ)
paper money; bank notes
錢舖(ㄑㄧㄢˊ ㄆㄨˋ)
a banking house (in former times)
錢褡褳(ㄑㄧㄢˊ ㄉㄚ·ㄌㄧㄢ)or 錢褡子
(ㄑㄧㄢˊ ㄉㄚ ·ㄗ)
a moneybag
錢袋(ㄑㄧㄢˊ ㄉㄞˋ)
a moneybag; a money purse:
你看到我的小錢袋嗎? Have you seen my little money purse?
錢塘江(ㄑㄧㄢˊ ㄊㄤˊ ㄐㄧㄤ)
the Chientang River, in Che-kiang
錢糧(ㄑㄧㄢˊ ㄌㄧㄤˊ)
taxes on farmland
錢穀(ㄑㄧㄢˊ ㄍㄨˇ)
taxes on farmland
錢櫃(ㄑㄧㄢˊ ㄍㄨㄟˋ)
a cash box
錢滾錢(ㄑㄧㄢˊ ㄍㄨㄣˇ ㄑㄧㄢˊ)
Money begets money.
錢可通神(ㄑㄧㄢˊ ㄎㄜˇ ㄊㄨㄥ ㄕㄣˊ)or
錢能通神(ㄑㄧㄢˊ ㄋㄥˊ ㄊㄨㄥ ㄕㄣˊ)
Money can move the gods. 或 Money makes the mare go. 或 Money talks.
錢可使鬼(ㄑㄧㄢˊ ㄎㄜˇ ㄕˇ ㄍㄨㄟˇ)
Money can make the devil work for you. 或 Money

makes the mare go. 亦作「有錢能使鬼推磨」
錢荒(ㄑㄧㄢˊ ㄏㄨㄤ)
scarcity of money
錢債(ㄑㄧㄢˊ ㄓㄞˋ)
debts
錢莊(ㄑㄧㄢˊ ㄓㄨㄤ)
a banking house (in former times)
錢財(ㄑㄧㄢˊ ㄘㄞˊ)
wealth; riches
錢財身外物(ㄑㄧㄢˊ ㄘㄞˊ ㄕㄣ ㄨㄞˋ ㄨˋ)
Money is not an inherent part of the human being (and therefore is not worth so much of one's efforts to get and to keep it).

【錦】 6427
ㄐㄧㄣˇ jiin jǐn
1. brocade; tapestry
2. brilliant and beautiful
3. glorious
錦標(ㄐㄧㄣˇ ㄅㄧㄠ)
① a championship (in a tournament) ② a trophy (for a sports champion); a cup: 他贏得錦標。He won the cup.
錦標賽(ㄐㄧㄣˇ ㄅㄧㄠ ㄙㄞˋ)
a sports tournament; championship contests; championships: 世界田徑錦標賽 the World Track and Field Championships
錦緞(ㄐㄧㄣˇ ㄉㄨㄢˋ)
brocade
錦堂(ㄐㄧㄣˇ ㄊㄤˊ)
a richly decorated hall
錦囊(ㄐㄧㄣˇ ㄋㄤˊ)
a bag made of brocade (used to hold manuscripts for poetry in ancient times)
錦囊妙計(ㄐㄧㄣˇ ㄋㄤˊ ㄇㄧㄠˋ ㄐㄧˋ)
a clever scheme yet to be revealed
錦葵(ㄐㄧㄣˇ ㄎㄨㄟˊ)
(botany) a mallow
錦還(ㄐㄧㄣˇ ㄏㄨㄢˊ)
to return home with glory
錦雞(ㄐㄧㄣˇ ㄐㄧ)
Phasianus pictus, a golden pheasant
錦箋(ㄐㄧㄣˇ ㄐㄧㄢ)
fancy stationery
錦旗(ㄐㄧㄣˇ ㄑㄧˊ)
an embroidered flag; a pennant; a silk banner (as an

award or a gift)
錦繡河山(ㄐㄧㄣˇ ㄒㄧㄡˋ ㄏㄜˊ ㄕㄢ)
land of splendor—one's fatherland
錦繡前程(ㄐㄧㄣˇ ㄒㄧㄡˋ ㄑㄧㄢˊ ㄔㄥˊ)
a glorious or promising future; a bright or rosy future: 他有着錦繡前程。He has a bright future ahead.
錦心繡口(ㄐㄧㄣˇ ㄒㄧㄣ ㄒㄧㄡˋ ㄎㄡˇ)
exquisite thoughts and elegant language (said of a piece of writing)
錦注(ㄐㄧㄣˇ ㄓㄨˋ)
(a polite expression) your concern, or the interest you have shown (in the matter, etc.) 亦作「錦念」
錦上添花(ㄐㄧㄣˇ ㄕㄤˋ ㄊㄧㄢ ㄏㄨㄚ)
to give something or someone additional splendor; to cap it all
錦字(ㄐㄧㄣˇ ㄗˋ)
characters embroidered on brocade or tapestry
錦瑟(ㄐㄧㄣˇ ㄙㄜˋ)
a kind of Chinese musical instrument with 50 strings
錦衣衛(ㄐㄧㄣˇ ㄧ ㄨㄟˋ)
imperial guards of the Ming Dynasty which eventually became a sort of SS Troops
錦衣玉食(ㄐㄧㄣˇ ㄧ ㄩˋ ㄕˊ)
to lead a luxurious life; to live in luxury

【錫】 6428
ㄒㄧ shyi xi
1. tin
2. to bestow...on; to confer... on
錫箔(ㄒㄧ ㄅㄛˊ)
tinfoil; tinfoil paper
錫命(ㄒㄧ ㄇㄧㄥˋ)
the emperor's edict conferring the degree of nobility on his feudal princes
錫福(ㄒㄧ ㄈㄨˊ)
to bestow happiness; to bless
錫鑞(ㄒㄧ ㄌㄚˋ)
pewter; solder; tin
錫蘭(ㄒㄧ ㄌㄢˊ)
Ceylon, former name of Sri Lanka (亦作「錫蘭卡」)
錫蘭人(ㄒㄧ ㄌㄢˊ ㄖㄣˊ)
a Ceylonese; the Ceylonese
錫蘭語(ㄒㄧ ㄌㄢˊ ㄩˇ)
the Ceylonese language;

〔金
部〕

Ceylonese

錫礦（ㄒㄧ ㄨㄤ）
a can; a tin; a tin can

錫礦（ㄒㄧ ㄨㄤˋ）
① tin ore ② tin mine

錫金（ㄒㄧ ㄐㄧㄣ）
Sikkim

錫匠（ㄒㄧ ㄐㄧㄤˋ）
a tinsmith

錫器（ㄒㄧ ㄑㄧˋ）
tinware

錫紙（ㄒㄧ ㄓˇ）
silver paper; tinfoil

錫杖（ㄒㄧ ㄓㄤˋ）
a Buddhist monk's walking stick 亦作「禪杖」

錫石（ㄒㄧ ㄕˊ）
cassiterite; tinstone

錫砂（ㄒㄧ ㄕㄚ）
stream tin

錫人（ㄒㄧ ㄖㄣˊ）
a tin figure buried together with a dead person

錫酸（ㄒㄧ ㄙㄨㄢ）
stannic acid

錫恩（ㄒㄧ ㄣ）
to do a favor

【錕】 6429
ㄎㄨㄣ kuen kūn
used in "錕鋙", name of a precious sword

【錮】 6430
ㄍㄨ guh gù
1. to run metal into cracks
2. to confine; to keep in custody; to imprison; 禁錮 to throw into a prison
3. sturdy; secure

錮蔽（ㄍㄨˋ ㄅㄧˋ）
stopped up; clogged

錮疾（ㄍㄨˋ ㄐㄧˊ）或稱痼疾
a chronic complaint, disease or ailment

錮寢（ㄍㄨˋ ㄑㄧㄣˇ）
(said of members of an imperial harem) to have the emperor's exclusive affection

錮身（ㄍㄨˋ ㄕㄣ）
to fetter a person

【錯】 6431
ㄘㄨㄛˋ tsuoh cuò
1. wrong; mistaken; erroneous; 你答錯了。You answered wrong.
2. a mistake; an error; a fault; 絕對沒錯。There's no mistake

about it.
3. disorderly; untidy; irregular; uneven; complicated; intricate
4. a grindstone
5. prudent; cautious

錯別字（ㄘㄨㄛˋ ㄅㄧㄝˊ ㄗˋ）
characters wrongly written or mispronounced

錯不了（ㄘㄨㄛˋ ㄅㄨˋ·ㄌㄧㄠˇ）
unlikely to go wrong; to be good: 今年小麥的收成錯不了。This year's wheat harvest is sure to be good.

錯翻眼皮（ㄘㄨㄛˋ ㄈㄢ ㄧㄢˇ ㄆㄧˊ）
to turn a wrong eyelid—to misjudge a person

錯刀（ㄘㄨㄛˋ ㄉㄠ）
① the knife for dressing and polishing jade ② a kind of coin introduced by 王莽

錯落（ㄘㄨㄛˋ ㄌㄨㄛˋ）
disorderly; untidy; irregular; uneven

錯亂（ㄘㄨㄛˋ ㄌㄨㄢˋ）
disorderly; confused; abnormal; deranged: 他有點兒精神錯亂。He is somewhat mentally deranged.

錯過（ㄘㄨㄛˋ ㄍㄨㄛˋ）
to let (a chance) slip by; to miss: 你錯過了大好機會。You missed out on a great chance.

錯過機會（ㄘㄨㄛˋ ㄍㄨㄛˋ ㄐㄧ ㄏㄨㄟˋ）
loss of opportunity

錯怪（ㄘㄨㄛˋ ㄍㄨㄞˋ）
to blame unjustly or wrongly

錯開（ㄘㄨㄛˋ ㄎㄞ）
to stagger: 他們把交通的擁擠時間錯開了。They staggered the rush hour.

錯話（ㄘㄨㄛˋ ㄏㄨㄚˋ）
improper remarks

錯角（ㄘㄨㄛˋ ㄐㄧㄠˇ）
(mathematics) an alternate angle

錯簡（ㄘㄨㄛˋ ㄐㄧㄢˇ）
misplaced leaves, phrases, etc. in a book

錯覺（ㄘㄨㄛˋ ㄐㄩㄝˊ）
hallucination; illusion; a false impression: 這會給我們造成錯覺。This will give us a false impression.

錯處（ㄘㄨㄛˋ ㄔㄨˋ）

an error; a mistake; a fault; 你的報告上有許多錯處。There are a lot of faults in your paper.

錯失（ㄘㄨㄛˋ ㄕ）
an error; a mistake; a fault; 我知道是我的錯失。I know am at fault.

錯認（ㄘㄨㄛˋ ㄖㄣˋ）
to misidentify

錯字（ㄘㄨㄛˋ ㄗˋ）
misspelling; a misprint

錯雜（ㄘㄨㄛˋ ㄗㄚˊ）
intermixed; confused; irregular; intricate

錯綜（ㄘㄨㄛˋ ㄗㄨㄥ）
intermixed; confused; irregular; intricate

錯綜複雜（ㄘㄨㄛˋ ㄗㄨㄥ ㄈㄨˋ ㄗㄚˊ）
very complicated; intricate

錯彩鏤金（ㄘㄨㄛˋ ㄘㄞˇ ㄌㄡˋ ㄐㄧㄣ）
gorgeously wrought; colorfully and dazzlingly embellished

錯愕（ㄘㄨㄛˋ ㄜˋ）
startled; astonished

錯愛（ㄘㄨㄛˋ ㄞˋ）
your misplaced favor; your favor which I do not deserve

錯兒（ㄘㄨㄛˋ ㄦ）
an error; a mistake; a fault; 那是我的錯兒。It was my fault.

錯誤（ㄘㄨㄛˋ ㄨˋ）
① an error; a mistake; a fault: 這書中有許多錯誤。There are many faults in the book. ② erroneous; wrong: 它是個錯誤的答案。is a wrong answer.

錯誤百出（ㄘㄨㄛˋ ㄨˋ ㄅㄞˇ ㄔㄨ）
full of mistakes; riddled with errors

【錳】 6432
ㄇㄥˇ meeng měng
manganese

【錶】 6433
ㄅㄧㄠˇ beau biǎo
a watch (a timepiece): 他錶時撥準。He set his watch.

錶帶（ㄅㄧㄠˇ ㄉㄞˋ）
the band of a wrist watch; watchband

錶鏈（ㄅㄧㄠˇ ㄌㄧㄢˋ）
a watch chain

錶殼（ㄅㄧㄠˇ ㄎㄜˊ）

a watchcase

【錛】 6434
ㄅㄣ ben bēn
an adz; an adze

錛子(ㄅㄣ‧ㄗ)
an adz; an adze

九畫

【鍊】 6435
ㄌㄧㄢ liann liàn
1. to smelt; to refine; to forge; to temper
2. to polish: 他的文詞缺乏洗鍊。His speech needs polishing.
3. a chain 參看「鏈」

鍊丹(ㄌㄧㄢ ㄉㄢ)
to make pills of wonder; to practice alchemy 亦作「煉丹」

鍊丹家(ㄌㄧㄢ ㄉㄢ ㄐㄧㄚ)
an alchemist

鍊鐵(ㄌㄧㄢ ㄊㄧㄝ)
to smelt iron; to refine iron

鍊鋼(ㄌㄧㄢ ㄍㄤ)
to refine steel

鍊鋼廠(ㄌㄧㄢ ㄍㄤ ㄔㄤ)
a steel mill; a steelworks

鍊金術(ㄌㄧㄢ ㄐㄧㄣ ㄕㄨˋ)
alchemy 亦作「煉金術」

鍊句(ㄌㄧㄢ ㄐㄩ)
to remove the superfluous words and reduce the sentence to its simplest and most effective form; to polish and repolish a sentence

鍊石補天(ㄌㄧㄢ ㄕˊ ㄅㄨˇ ㄊㄧㄢ)
to smelt stone to mend the sky (a feat performed by 女媧氏, a mythological character)

鍊乳(ㄌㄧㄢ ㄖㄨˋ)
condensed milk

鍊字(ㄌㄧㄢ ㄗˋ)
to try hard to find the fittest words or expressions (to be used in a composition)

鍊子(ㄌㄧㄢ‧ㄗ) or 鍊兒(ㄌㄧㄚ ㄦ) or 鍊條(ㄌㄧㄢ ㄊㄧㄠˊ)
a chain

【錨】 6436
ㄇㄠˊ mau máo
to anchor; an anchor: 拋錨 to cast(or drop) anchor 起錨 to weigh anchor

【鍋】 6437
ㄍㄨㄛ guo guō
a cooking pot; a pan; a boiler; a caldron: 火鍋 a chafing dish 飯鍋 a rice pot
2.(said of a pipe, etc.) a bowl: 煙袋鍋兒 the bowl of a pipe

鍋巴(ㄍㄨㄛ ㄅㄚ)
burnt rice that sticks to the bottom and sides of the cooking pot

鍋餅(ㄍㄨㄛ ㄅㄧㄥˇ)
a kind of large cake made of dough

鍋貼兒(ㄍㄨㄛ ㄊㄧㄝ ㄦ)
a common Chinese delicacy in the form of minced meat wrapped in a skin of dough and lightly fried; lightly fried dumpling

鍋爐(ㄍㄨㄛ ㄌㄨˊ)
a boiler (especially of a steam engine)

鍋蓋(ㄍㄨㄛ ㄍㄞˋ)
the cover of a cooking pot; a pot cover

鍋戶(ㄍㄨㄛ ㄏㄨˋ)
families which make a living by evaporating seawater to make salt

鍋子(ㄍㄨㄛ‧ㄗ) or 鍋兒(ㄍㄨㄛ ㄦ)
a cooking pot; a pan: 他昨晚買了一口鍋子。He bought a cooking pot yesterday.

鍋煙子(ㄍㄨㄛ ㄧㄢ‧ㄗ)
soot on the underside of a cooking pot, pan, etc.

【鍍】 6438
ㄉㄨˋ duh dù
to plate; to gilt: 電鍍 electroplating

鍍銅(ㄉㄨ ㄊㄨㄥˊ)
plated copper

鍍金(ㄉㄨ ㄐㄧㄣ)
①to plate with gold ②to spend some time abroad to add to the impressiveness of one's background

鍍銀(ㄉㄨ ㄧㄣˊ)
to plate with silver; silver-plating

【鍔】 6439
ㄜ eh è
1. the edge of a knife
2. lofty; towering

鍔鍔(ㄜ ㄜ)
towering; lofty

【鍘】 6440
ㄓㄚˊ jar zhá
1. a long knife hinged at one end for cutting hay
2. to cut up with a hay cutter

鍘刀(ㄓㄚˊ ㄉㄠ)
a long knife hinged at one end for cutting hay; a fodder chopper

鍘刀開關(ㄓㄚˊ ㄉㄠ ㄎㄞ ㄍㄨㄢ)
a knife switch

【鍛】 6441
(煅) ㄉㄨㄢˋ duann duàn
1. to smelt; to refine
2. to forge (iron, etc.)

鍛鐵(ㄉㄨㄢˋ ㄊㄧㄝˇ)
wrought iron

鍛鐵爐(ㄉㄨㄢˋ ㄊㄧㄝˇ ㄌㄨ)
a forge

鍛鍊(ㄉㄨㄢˋ ㄌㄧㄢˋ)
①to forge (metal); to temper ②to train (oneself); to discipline; to (take) exercise

鍛工(ㄉㄨㄢˋ ㄍㄨㄥ)
a smith; a metal worker

【鍥】 6442
ㄑㄧㄝˋ chieh qiè
to carve

鍥薄(ㄑㄧㄝ ㄅㄛˊ)
merciless; unsympathetic; pitiless

鍥而不舍(ㄑㄧㄝˋ ㄦˊ ㄅㄨˋ ㄕㄜˇ)
to carve without rest—to make steady efforts

【鍪】 6443
ㄇㄡˊ mou móu
1. a kind of cooking pot
2. a kind of metal helmet: 兜鍪 a helmet

【鍫】 6444
(鍬) ㄑㄧㄠ chiau qiāo
a shovel; a spade

【鍰】 6445
ㄏㄨㄢˊ hwan huán
1. an ancient unit of weight
2. money; cash: 罰鍰 to fine or be fined cash

【鍵】 6446
ㄐㄧㄢˋ jiann jiàn
key (to a door on a musical instrument, etc.): 關鍵 key to situation

鍵盤(ㄐㄧㄢˋ ㄆㄢˊ)
a keyboard (on a piano, typewriter, etc.)

鍵盤樂器(ㄐㄧㄢˋ ㄆㄢˊ ㄩㄝˋ ㄑㄧˋ)
a keyed instrument

【鍼】 6447
ㄓㄣ jen zhēn
a needle; a pin; a probe 亦作

〔金部〕

「針」

鍼言 or 箴言 (ㄓㄣ ㄧㄢ)
① maxims ② *Proverbs* (a book of the Bible)

【鍾】 6448
ㄓㄨㄥ jong zhōng
1. a kind of wine container
2. to concentrate; to accumulate
3. a Chinese family name

鍾靈毓秀 (ㄓㄨㄥ ㄌㄧㄥ ㄩˋ ㄒㄧㄡˋ)
The subtle spirit of Nature converges to nurture geniuses.

鍾馗 (ㄓㄨㄥ ㄎㄨㄟˊ)
a deity who supposedly protects man from evil spirits

鍾情 (ㄓㄨㄥ ㄑㄧㄥˊ)
to fall in love: 我對她一見鍾情. I fell in love with her at first sight.

鍾嶸 (ㄓㄨㄥ ㄖㄨㄥˊ)
Chung Jung, a sixth century literary critic

鍾子期 (ㄓㄨㄥ ㄗˇ ㄑㄧ)
Chung Tzu-chi, a musician of the state of 楚 during the Epoch of Spring and Autumn

鍾愛 (ㄓㄨㄥ ㄞˋ)
to cherish; to dote on; to love deeply (especially children)

【鎂】 6449
ㄇㄟˇ meei mei
magnesium: 硫酸鎂 magnesium sulphate

鎂光燈 (ㄇㄟˇ ㄍㄨㄤ ㄉㄥ)
a magnesium light

【鍺】 6450
ㄓㄜˇ jee zhě
germanium

【鍶】 6451
ㄙ sy sī
strontium

【鏷】 6452
ㄆㄞˋ pay pài
protactinium

【鍇】 6453
ㄎㄞˇ kae kǎi
refined iron

【鍬】 6454
ㄑㄧㄠ chiau qiāo
a spade; a shovel 亦作「鋅」

十畫

【鎖】 6455
(鎻) ㄙㄨㄛˇ suoo suǒ
1. a lock: 她用鑰匙把鎖打開. She opened the lock with a key.
2. fetters; chains
3. to lock
4. to confine
5. to lockstitch

鎖不住 (ㄙㄨㄛˇ ·ㄅㄨ ㄓㄨˋ)
(said of a captive) cannot be locked up or kept in confinement

鎖不上 (ㄙㄨㄛˇ ·ㄅㄨ ㄕㄤˋ)
(said of a door, etc.) incapable of locking; failing to become locked; failing to lock

鎖眉 (ㄙㄨㄛˇ ㄇㄟˊ)
to knit one's brows; to frown

鎖門 (ㄙㄨㄛˇ ㄇㄣˊ)
to lock a door; to lock a gate

鎖頭 (ㄙㄨㄛˇ ·ㄊㄡ)
a lock

鎖吶 (ㄙㄨㄛˇ ㄋㄚˋ)
a Turkish flute 亦作「嗩吶」

鎖鐐 (ㄙㄨㄛˇ ㄌㄧㄠˊ)
fetters; manacles

鎖鏈 (ㄙㄨㄛˇ ㄌㄧㄢˋ)
chains

鎖骨 (ㄙㄨㄛˇ ㄍㄨˇ)
(anatomy) the collarbone

鎖簧 (ㄙㄨㄛˇ ㄏㄨㄤˊ)
the spring of a lock

鎖匠 (ㄙㄨㄛˇ ㄐㄧㄤˋ)
a locksmith

鎖起來 (ㄙㄨㄛˇ ㄑㄧˇ ·ㄌㄞ)
to lock or lock up (a house, a door, a person or an animal): 請將房子鎖起來好嗎? Will you lock up the house, please?

鎖住 (ㄙㄨㄛˇ ·ㄓㄨ)
to lock up (a captive)

鎖上 (ㄙㄨㄛˇ ·ㄕㄤ)
to lock (a door, etc.)

鎖鑰 (ㄙㄨㄛˇ ㄧㄠˋ)
a key (to a door)

鎖陰 (ㄙㄨㄛˇ ㄧㄣ)
gynatresia, a physical defect characterized by vaginal constriction, which makes sexual intercourse impossible

【鎡】 6456
ㄗ tzy zī
a hoe; a mattock

【鎊】 6457
ㄅㄤˋ bang bàng
pound sterling: 英幣五鎊 five pounds sterling

【鎋】 6458
(轄) ㄒㄧㄚˊ shya xiá
a linchpin

【鎔】 6459
(熔) ㄖㄨㄥˊ rong róng
1. to melt; to smelt; to fuse
2. a mold
3. a kind of spear

鎔點 (ㄖㄨㄥˊ ㄉㄧㄢˇ)
the melting point

鎔度 (ㄖㄨㄥˊ ㄉㄨˋ)
fusibility (of a mineral, etc.)

鎔爐 (ㄖㄨㄥˊ ㄌㄨˊ)
a smelting furnace; a cupola

鎔化 (ㄖㄨㄥˊ ㄏㄨㄚˋ)
to melt; to fuse: 熱使鐵鎔化. Heat will melt iron.

鎔化爐 (ㄖㄨㄥˊ ㄏㄨㄚˋ ㄌㄨˊ)
a melting furnace

鎔劑 (ㄖㄨㄥˊ ㄐㄧˋ)
fusing mixture; flux

鎔解 (ㄖㄨㄥˊ ㄐㄧㄝˇ)
to melt; to fuse: 鐵在高溫下鎔解. The iron was melted by great heat.

鎔解熱 (ㄖㄨㄥˊ ㄐㄧㄝˇ ㄖㄜˋ)
heat of fusion

鎔銷 (ㄖㄨㄥˊ ㄒㄧㄠ)
to melt; to smelt

鎔鑄 (ㄖㄨㄥˊ ㄓㄨˋ)
to cast (metal)

鎔融 (ㄖㄨㄥˊ ㄖㄨㄥˊ)
to melt; to fuse

鎔冶 (ㄖㄨㄥˊ ㄧㄝˇ)
to smelt

鎔岩 (ㄖㄨㄥˊ ㄧㄢˊ)
molten rock; lava; magma

【鎗】 6460
(槍) ㄑㄧㄤ chiang qiāng
firearms; small arms; guns; pistols; rifles: 那強盜持有手鎗. The robber had a pistol.

鎗把 (ㄑㄧㄤ ㄅㄚˇ)
a rifle butt

鎗靶 (ㄑㄧㄤ ㄅㄚˇ)
the target for shooting

鎗斃 (ㄑㄧㄤ ㄅㄧˋ)
execution by a firing squad; execution by shooting

鎗砲 (ㄑㄧㄤ ㄆㄠˋ)
rifles and artillery pieces

鎗彈 (ㄑㄧㄤ ㄉㄢˋ)

bullets

鎗膛(ㄑㄧㄤ ㄊㄤ)
the barrel (of a rifle, pistol,
etc.)亦作「鎗身」或「鎗管」

鎗托(ㄑㄧㄤ ㄊㄨㄛ)
a gunstock; a rifle butt

鎗筒(ㄑㄧㄤ ㄊㄨㄥ)
the barrel (of a rifle, etc.)

鎗林彈雨(ㄑㄧㄤ ㄌㄧㄣ ㄉㄢ ㄩ)
a hail of bullets; heavy gunfire

鎗桿(ㄑㄧㄤ ㄍㄢ)or 鎗桿兒(ㄑㄧㄤ
ㄍㄢㄦ)
rifles; firearms

鎗口(ㄑㄧㄤ ㄎㄡ)
the muzzle of a gun

鎗架(ㄑㄧㄤ ㄐㄧㄚˋ)
a rifle rack

鎗決(ㄑㄧㄤ ㄐㄩㄝ)
to execute by shooting

鎗戰(ㄑㄧㄤ ㄓㄢˋ)
gun battle; exchange of rifle
or pistol fire

鎗手(ㄑㄧㄤ ㄕㄡˇ)
①a gunman ②a substitute
writer in an examination

鎗眼(ㄑㄧㄤ ㄧㄢˇ)
an embrasure (in a para-
pet); a crenel

【鎚】6461
ㄔㄨㄟ chwei chuí
1. to hammer: 我把釘子鎚入木
板中。I hammered a nail into
the board.
2. a hammer
3. an ancient weapon

錘子(ㄔㄨㄟ˙ㄗ)or 錘兒(ㄔㄨㄟㄦ)
a hammer

【鎛】6462
ㄅㄛ bor bó
1. a kind of ancient bell
2. a variety of hoe

【鎧】6463
ㄎㄞˇ kae kǎi
armor (worn by a warrior)

鎧馬(ㄎㄞˇ ㄇㄚˇ)
①armor and war-horses ②
a horse protected by a coat
of mail

鎧甲(ㄎㄞˇ ㄐㄧㄚˇ)
armor; a coat of mail

【鎬】6464
1. ㄏㄠˇ haw hǎo
1. bright
2. an ancient place name (the
first capital of the Chou
Dynasty)

鎬鎬(ㄏㄠˇ ㄏㄠˇ)
bright; brilliant

鎬京(ㄏㄠˇ ㄐㄧㄥ)
the first capital of the Chou
Dynasty (in what is Shensi
today)

【鎬】6464
2. 《ㄠˇ gao gǎo
a kind of hoe

【鎮】6465
ㄓㄣˋ jenn zhèn
1. to subdue; to suppress; to
quell; to put down
2. to cool with water or ice
3. weight (for pressing down)
4. whole
5. a town; a township: 我住在
小鎮上。I live in a small
town.
6. a garrison post

鎮暴(ㄓㄣˋ ㄅㄠˋ)
riot control

鎮服(ㄓㄣˋ ㄈㄨˊ)
to subdue; to conquer: 他終
於鎮服敵人。He finally sub-
dued his enemies.

鎮撫(ㄓㄣˋ ㄈㄨˇ)
to suppress and pacify

鎮定(ㄓㄣˋ ㄉㄧㄥˋ)
self-composed; calm; cool: 你
應保持鎮定。You should keep
cool.

鎮痛劑(ㄓㄣˋ ㄊㄨㄥˋ ㄐㄧ)
an anodyne; a painkiller

鎮南關(ㄓㄣˋ ㄋㄢˊ 《ㄨㄢ)
name of a place in Kwangsi
(the location of a former
border checkpoint)

鎮公所(ㄓㄣˋ 《ㄨㄥ ㄙㄨㄛˇ)
a town hall; a townhouse

鎮江(ㄓㄣˋ ㄐㄧㄤ)
Chenchiang, capital city of
Kiangsu Province

鎮靜(ㄓㄣˋ ㄐㄧㄥˋ)
self-composed; calm; cool: 他
故作鎮靜地如此說。He said so
with forced calm.

鎮靜劑(ㄓㄣˋ ㄐㄧㄥˋ ㄐㄧ)or 鎮定劑
(ㄓㄣˋ ㄉㄧㄥˋ ㄐㄧ)
a sedative; a tranquilizer

鎮紙(ㄓㄣˋ ㄓˇ)
a paperweight

鎮長(ㄓㄣˋ ㄓㄤˇ)
the town master; the head of
a town

鎮守(ㄓㄣˋ ㄕㄡˇ)
to garrison: 他令軍隊鎮守此

城。He garrisoned troops in
the city.

鎮守使(ㄓㄣˋ ㄕㄡˇ ㄕˇ)
a provincial garrison commander (in the early years
of the Republic)

鎮日(ㄓㄣˋ ㄖˋ)
the whole day; all day long:
他鎮日無所事事。He does
nothing the whole day.

鎮遏(ㄓㄣˋ ㄜˋ)
to curb; to quell

鎮壓(ㄓㄣˋ ㄧㄚ)
to suppress; to put down;
suppression: 他們採取鎮壓政
策。They took a policy of
suppression.

【鎰】6466
ㄧˋ yih yì
an ancient unit of weight

【鎳】6467
ㄋㄧㄝˋ nieh niè
nickel

鎳幣(ㄋㄧㄝˋ ㄅㄧˋ)
nickel coins

【鎢】6468
ㄨ wuh wū
tungsten; wolfram

鎢錳鐵礦(ㄨ ㄇㄥˇ ㄊㄧㄝˇ ㄎㄨㄤˋ)
wolframite

鎢鋼(ㄨ 《ㄤ)
wolfram steel; tungsten steel

鎢絲(ㄨ ㄙ)
a tungsten filament

【鎵】6469
ㄊㄚ tah tā
thallium

【鎌】6470
(鐮)ㄌㄧㄢˊ lian lián
a sickle

鎌倉(ㄌㄧㄢˊ ㄘㄤ)
Kamakura, Japan

【鎷】6471
ㄇㄚˇ maa mǎ
masurium

【鎶】6472
《ㄜˊ ger gé
cadmium

【鎵】6473
ㄐㄧㄚ jia jiā
gallium

【鏃】6474
ㄗㄨˊ tzwu zú
as in 箭鏃—an arrowhead

〔金部〕

【鏇】6475 ㄒㄩㄢˋ shiuann xuàn
1. a kind of wine heater
2. a kind of metal tray
3. to pare with a knife

鏇牀（ㄒㄩㄢˋ ㄔㄨㄤˊ）
　a lathe

【鎩】6476 ㄕㄚ sha shò
1. a lance
2. to shed (feathers)

鎩羽（ㄕㄚ ㄩˇ）
　① having shed feathers ②
　discouraged; crestfallen; dis-
　heartened; defeated

【鏦】6477 ㄘㄨㄥ tsong cong
1. a spear
2. to pierce with a spear
3. the clang of metal

鏦鏦（ㄘㄨㄥ ㄘㄨㄥ）
　the clang of metal

【鏈】6478 ㄌㄧㄢˊ liann liàn
　a chain: 他將狗用鏈繫住。He
　fastened the dog with a
　chain.

鏈黴素（ㄌㄧㄢˊ ㄇㄟˊ ㄙㄨˋ）
　streptomycin

鏈條（ㄌㄧㄢˊ ㄊㄧㄠˊ）
　a chain

鏈螺菌素（ㄌㄧㄢˊ ㄌㄨㄛˊ ㄐㄩㄣˋ ㄙㄨˋ）
　streptospirillum

鏈球（ㄌㄧㄢˊ ㄑㄧㄡˊ）
　(sports) ① a hammer ② ham-
　mer throw

鏈球菌（ㄌㄧㄢˊ ㄑㄧㄡˊ ㄐㄩㄣˋ）
　streptococcus

鏈著（ㄌㄧㄢˊ ·ㄓㄜ）
　chained; in chains

鏈子（ㄌㄧㄢˊ ·ㄗ）or 鏈兒（ㄌㄧㄠˋ）
　a chain: 用鏈子將那隻狗拴起
　來。Keep the dog on a chain.

鏈絲菌黴（ㄌㄧㄢˊ ㄙ ㄐㄩㄣˋ ㄇㄟˊ）
　streptomyces

鏈鎖反應（ㄌㄧㄢˊ ㄙㄨㄛˇ ㄈㄢˇ ㄧㄥˋ）
　a chain reaction

【鏊】6479 ㄠˋ aur ào
　a kind of round, flat plate
　for baking; a griddle

【鏑】6480 ㄉㄧˊ dyi dí
1. an arrowhead
2. dysprosium

【鏖】6481 ㄠˋ aur ào
　to fight hard

鏖兵（ㄠˋ ㄅㄧㄥ）
　to engage in hard fighting

鏖戰（ㄠˋ ㄓㄢˋ）
　to engage in hard fighting
　(or a bloody battle)

鏖糟（ㄠˋ ㄗㄠ）
　① to fight a fierce battle ②
　filthy; dirty ③ to be stub-
　born and unpleasant

【鏗】6482 ㄎㄥ keng kēng
1. the clang of metal; clatter
2. the twang of a string
3. to strike; to smash

鏗鏘（ㄎㄥ ㄑㄧㄤ）
　a tinkle; a clang; clatter

鏗鏘（ㄎㄥ ㄑㄧㄤ）
　① a tinkle; a clang ② (fig-
　uratively) sonorous and force-
　ful: 這首詩讀起來鏗鏘有力。
　This poem is sonorous and
　forceful.

【鏘】6483 ㄑㄧㄤ chiang qiāng
　a tinkle; a clang

鏘鏘（ㄑㄧㄤ ㄑㄧㄤ）
　① a tinkle; a clang ② lofty;
　high

【鏹】6484 1. ㄑㄧㄤˇ cheang qiǎng
　money; wealth

【鏹】6484 2. ㄑㄧㄤ chiang qiāng
　corrosive

鏹水（ㄑㄧㄤ ㄕㄨㄟˇ）
　corrosive acid (such as sul-
　furic acid) 亦作「硫酸」

【鏜】6485 1. ㄊㄤ tang tāng
1. the noise of drums or gongs
2. a small gong

【鏜】6485 2. ㄊㄤˊ tarng táng
　(machinery) boring

【鏝】6486 （邊）ㄇㄢˋ mann màn
　a trowel

【鏟】6487 ㄔㄢˇ chaan chǎn
1. a shovel; a scoop
2. to shovel; to scoop

鏟幣（ㄔㄢˇ ㄅㄧˋ）
　a shovel-shaped coin minted
　before the time of Confucius

鏟除（ㄔㄢˇ ㄔㄨˊ）
　to eliminate; to uproot; to
　clear off

鏟子（ㄔㄢˇ ·ㄗ）or 鏟兒（ㄔㄢˇ）
　a shovel; a scoop

【鏡】6488 ㄐㄧㄥˋ jinq jìng
1. a mirror
2. lenses; spectacles; glasses:
　他有兩副眼鏡。He has two
　pairs of glasses.
3. to mirror
4. to take warning (from a
　past failure)

鏡片（ㄐㄧㄥˋ ㄆㄧㄢˋ）
　a lens

鏡臺（ㄐㄧㄥˋ ㄊㄞˊ）
　a mirror stand; a dressing
　stand

鏡頭（ㄐㄧㄥˋ ㄊㄡˊ）
　① the lens of a camera ② a
　scene captured by the cam-
　era

鏡寡（ㄐㄧㄥˋ ㄍㄨㄚˇ）
　to lose one's spouse

鏡框（ㄐㄧㄥˋ ㄎㄨㄤˋ）
　a picture frame

鏡花水月（ㄐㄧㄥˋ ㄏㄨㄚ ㄕㄨㄟˇ ㄩㄝˋ）
　(literally) flowers in a mir-
　ror and the moon in water
　—things appealing but un-
　real

鏡花緣（ㄐㄧㄥˋ ㄏㄨㄚ ㄩㄢˊ）
　the title of a Ching Dynasty
　novel by Li Ju-chen (李汝珍)

鏡戒（ㄐㄧㄥˋ ㄐㄧㄝˋ）or 鏡鑒（ㄐㄧㄥˋ
　ㄐㄧㄢˋ）
　a lesson; a warning

鏡匣（ㄐㄧㄥˋ ㄒㄧㄚˊ）
　a vanity case; a vanity box;
　a dressing case

鏡子（ㄐㄧㄥˋ ·ㄗ）or 鏡兒（ㄐㄧㄥˋㄦ）
　① a mirror ② a mirror (in
　non-material sense): 小說是
　反映時代的一面鏡子。Novels
　are a mirror of the times. ③
　a lens; glasses

【鏢】6489 ㄅㄧㄠ biau biāo
1. a javelin; a dart; a harpoon
　a dartlike weapon
2. an escort; a guard; a body-
　guard

鏢客（ㄅㄧㄠ ㄎㄜˋ）
　(in former times) hired
　escorts for traveling mer-
　chants, etc.

鏢局（ㄅㄧㄠ ㄐㄩˊ）
　(in former times) an estab-
　lishment which provided
　escorts or bodyguards for

【鏤】 6490
ㄌㄡˊ low lòu
to engrave; to carve

鏤版(ㄌㄡˊ ㄅㄢˇ)
an engraved plate

鏤冰(ㄌㄡˊ ㄅㄧㄥ)
(literally) to carve on ice —(figuratively) to labor in vain

鏤骨銘心(ㄌㄡˊ ㄍㄨˇ ㄇㄧㄥˊ ㄒㄧㄣ)
(literally) to engrave on the bones and imprint on the heart—the memory of a favor received; to remember forever with gratitude

鏤刻(ㄌㄡˊ ㄎㄜˋ)
to engrave; to carve

鏤空(ㄌㄡˊ ㄎㄨㄥ)
to hollow out; hollowed-out

鏤花(ㄌㄡˊ ㄏㄨㄚ)
① to engrave a design of flowers ② ornamental engraving

鏤金錯彩(ㄌㄡˊ ㄐㄧㄣ ㄘㄨㄛˋ ㄘㄞˇ)
(said of works of art) exquisitely wrought

鏤塵吹影(ㄌㄡˊ ㄔㄣˊ ㄔㄨㄟ ㄧㄥˇ)
(literally) to carve dust and blow shadows—to make futile efforts

鏤身(ㄌㄡˊ ㄕㄣ)
to tattoo the body 亦作「紋身」

鏤月裁雲(ㄌㄡˊ ㄩㄝˋ ㄘㄞˊ ㄩㄣˊ)
(said of works of art) ingeniously wrought

【鏨】 6491
ㄗㄢˋ tzann zàn
1. a chisel
2. to chisel; to engrave; to carve

鏨刀(ㄗㄢˋ ㄉㄠ)
a chisel; a graver

鏨子(ㄗㄢˋ ˙ㄗ)
a chisel

【鎖】 6492
(鎖) ㄙㄨㄛˇ suoo suǒ
a lock; to lock

十二畫

【鐘】 6493
ㄓㄨㄥ jong zhōng
1. a bell (which tolls as distinct from that which jingles)
2. a clock: 這鐘走得太快了。The clock gains.
3. time as measured in hours and minutes: 現在正好兩點鐘。It's exactly two o'clock.
4. a Chinese family name

鐘擺(ㄓㄨㄥ ㄅㄞˇ)
a pendulum

鐘錶 or 鐘表(ㄓㄨㄥ ㄅㄧㄠˇ)
timepieces; clocks and watches

鐘錶鋪(ㄓㄨㄥ ㄅㄧㄠˇ ㄆㄨˋ)or 鐘錶店(ㄓㄨㄥ ㄅㄧㄠˇ ㄉㄧㄢˋ)or 鐘錶行(ㄓㄨㄥ ㄅㄧㄠˇ ㄏㄤˊ)
a watchmaker's shop

鐘鳴鼎食(ㄓㄨㄥ ㄇㄧㄥˊ ㄉㄧㄥˇ ㄕˊ)
to enjoy affluence

鐘鳴鼎食之家(ㄓㄨㄥ ㄇㄧㄥˊ ㄉㄧㄥˇ ㄕˊ ㄓ ㄐㄧㄚ)
a family of great wealth

鐘鳴漏盡(ㄓㄨㄥ ㄇㄧㄥˊ ㄌㄡˋ ㄐㄧㄣˋ)
to be in one's declining years

鐘點(ㄓㄨㄥ ㄉㄧㄢˇ)
① hours ② a time for something to be done or to happen: 到鐘點兒了，我們快走吧！It's time; let's go.

鐘點費(ㄓㄨㄥ ㄉㄧㄢˇ ㄈㄟˋ)
remuneration for teaching paid by the hour

鐘鼎文(ㄓㄨㄥ ㄉㄧㄥˇ ㄨㄣˊ)
ancient inscriptions on bronzes; bronze inscriptions

鐘頭(ㄓㄨㄥ ㄊㄡˊ)
an hour

鐘樓(ㄓㄨㄥ ㄌㄡˊ)
a bell tower; a belfry

鐘形花植物(ㄓㄨㄥ ㄒㄧㄥˊ ㄏㄨㄚ ㄓˋ ㄨˋ)
(botany) bluebells

鐘狀花冠(ㄓㄨㄥ ㄓㄨㄤˋ ㄏㄨㄚ ㄍㄨㄢ)
(botany) campanulate corolla

鐘聲(ㄓㄨㄥ ㄕㄥ)
the toll of a bell

鐘乳石(ㄓㄨㄥ ㄖㄨˇ ㄕˊ)
a stalactite

鐘兒(ㄓㄨㄥㄦ)
a bell: 教堂的鐘兒正在響。The church bells are ringing.

【鐃】 6494
ㄋㄠˊ nau náo
1. a kind of bell used in the army in ancient times
2. cymbals

鐃鈸(ㄋㄠˊ ㄅㄚˊ)
cymbals

鐃歌(ㄋㄠˊ ㄍㄜ)or 鐃吹(ㄋㄠˊ ㄔㄨㄟˋ)
military music; martial strains

鐃鼓(ㄋㄠˊ ㄍㄨˇ)
a kind of drum

【鐐】 6495
ㄌㄧㄠˊ liau liáo
(又讀 ㄌㄧㄠˇ liaw liǎo)
shackles; fetters

鐐銬(ㄌㄧㄠˊ ㄎㄠˋ)
fetters; manacles: 囚犯上了鐐銬。The prisoners are in fetters.

【鐙】 6496
1. ㄉㄥ deng dēng
a stirrup

鐙骨(ㄉㄥ ㄍㄨˇ)
(anatomy) stapes

【鐙】 6496
2. ㄉㄥ deng dēng
1. same as 燈—a lamp
2. a kind of cooking vessel in ancient times

【鏽】 6497
(銹) ㄒㄧㄡˋ shiow xiù
rust; to rust

【鐗】 6498
1. ㄐㄧㄢˇ jean jiǎn
a kind of ancient weapon; a mace

【鐗】 6498
2. ㄐㄧㄢˋ jiann jiàn
protective metal on the axis of a wheel

【鐠】 6499
ㄆㄨˇ puu pǔ
praseodymium

【鑥】 6500
ㄌㄧㄡˇ liou liǔ
lutecium

十三畫

【鐲】 6501
ㄓㄨㄛˊ jwo zhuó
1. a kind of bell used in the army in ancient times
2. a bracelet; an armlet

鐲子(ㄓㄨㄛˊ ˙ㄗ)
a bracelet; an armlet: 她買了一個金鐲子。She bought a gold bracelet.

【鐫】 6502
ㄐㄩㄢ juan juān
1. to carve; to engrave

〔金部〕

2. (said of an official) to be demoted

鋼刻 (ㄐㄩ ㄎㄜˋ)
to engrave; to carve: 他用石頭鋼刻了一個人像。He carved a figure in stone.

【鐮】 6503
ㄌㄧㄢˊ lian lián
a sickle

鐮刀 (ㄌㄧㄢˊ ㄉㄠ)
a sickle

【鐵】 6504
ㄊㄧㄝˇ tie tiě
1. iron: 這東西堅硬似鐵。This is as hard as iron.
2. firm; indisputable; unyielding (like iron)
3. cruel; merciless; unfeeling
4. arms; weapons

鐵板 (ㄊㄧㄝˇ ㄅㄢˇ)
①an iron plate; sheet iron ②a kind of percussion instrument

鐵板大鼓 (ㄊㄧㄝˇ ㄅㄢˇ ㄉㄚˋ ㄍㄨˇ)
a kind of singing performance in which the singer beats time with a drum on the right and with semicircular metal pieces on the left

鐵板牛扒 (ㄊㄧㄝˇ ㄅㄢˇ ㄋㄧㄡˊ ㄆㄚˊ)
broiled steak

鐵棒 (ㄊㄧㄝˇ ㄅㄤˋ)
an iron club

鐵筆 (ㄊㄧㄝˇ ㄅㄧˇ)
①a burin ②a stylus

鐵餅 (ㄊㄧㄝˇ ㄅㄧㄥˇ)
a discus

鐵布衫 (ㄊㄧㄝˇ ㄅㄨˋ ㄕㄢ)
(Chinese pugilism) the ability to sustain the thrusts of sharp weapons on one's bare skin

鐵皮 (ㄊㄧㄝˇ ㄆㄧˊ)
iron sheet

鐵馬 (ㄊㄧㄝˇ ㄇㄚˇ)
①strong cavalry ②(colloquial) a bicycle ③armored horses

鐵門 (ㄊㄧㄝˇ ㄇㄣˊ)
①a metal security door ②name of a county in Honan

鐵面無私 (ㄊㄧㄝˇ ㄇㄧㄢˋ ㄨˊ ㄙ)
inflexibly just and fair; Rhadamanthine; 他是個鐵面無私的判官。He was a just judge.

鐵幕 (ㄊㄧㄝˇ ㄇㄨˋ)
the Iron Curtain

鐵木真 (ㄊㄧㄝˇ ㄇㄨˋ ㄓㄣ)
name of Genghis Khan,1162-1227, Mongol conqueror of central Asia

鐵肺 (ㄊㄧㄝˇ ㄈㄟˋ)
an iron lung

鐵礬土 (ㄊㄧㄝˇ ㄈㄢˊ ㄊㄨˇ)
bauxite

鐵飯碗 (ㄊㄧㄝˇ ㄈㄢˋ ㄨㄢˇ)
(literally) an iron rice bowl —a very secure job

鐵道 (ㄊㄧㄝˇ ㄉㄠˋ) or 鐵路 (ㄊㄧㄝˇ ㄌㄨˋ)
a railway; a railroad

鐵釘 (ㄊㄧㄝˇ ㄉㄧㄥ)
iron nails

鐵定 (ㄊㄧㄝˇ ㄉㄧㄥˋ)
definitely; ironclad; unalterable; not subject to change

鐵塔 (ㄊㄧㄝˇ ㄊㄚˇ)
an iron or steel tower

鐵蹄 (ㄊㄧㄝˇ ㄊㄧˊ)
①(literally) iron hoofs —(figuratively) devastation by invading troops ②fine horses

鐵桶 (ㄊㄧㄝˇ ㄊㄨㄥˇ)
(literally) an iron bucket —(figuratively) impregnable defense

鐵牛 (ㄊㄧㄝˇ ㄋㄧㄡˊ)
an iron ox (thrown into rivers in ancient times as a ritual for warding off floods)

鐵欄 (ㄊㄧㄝˇ ㄌㄢˊ)
an iron barrier

鐵鏈 (ㄊㄧㄝˇ ㄌㄧㄢˋ)
an iron chain

鐵路 (ㄊㄧㄝˇ ㄌㄨˋ)
a railroad; a railway

鐵路局 (ㄊㄧㄝˇ ㄌㄨˋ ㄐㄩˊ)
Railway Administration

鐵路局長 (ㄊㄧㄝˇ ㄌㄨˋ ㄐㄩˊ ㄓㄤˇ)
the director of the Railway Administration

鐵路網 (ㄊㄧㄝˇ ㄌㄨˋ ㄨㄤˇ)
a railway network; a network of railroads

鐵籠子 (ㄊㄧㄝˇ ㄌㄨㄥˊ ˙ㄗ)
an iron cage

鐵拐李 (ㄊㄧㄝˇ ㄍㄨㄞˇ ㄌㄧˇ)
one of the Eight Immortals of Taoism who limps with an iron walking stick

鐵軌 (ㄊㄧㄝˇ ㄍㄨㄟˇ)

iron rails (of a railway): 火車出了鐵軌。The train went off the rails.

鐵櫃 (ㄊㄧㄝˇ ㄍㄨㄟˋ)
a safe

鐵觀音 (ㄊㄧㄝˇ ㄍㄨㄢ ㄧㄣ)
a variety of oolong tea

鐵棍 (ㄊㄧㄝˇ ㄍㄨㄣˋ)
an iron club

鐵工 (ㄊㄧㄝˇ ㄍㄨㄥ)
①ironwork ②an iron worker; a blacksmith

鐵工場 (ㄊㄧㄝˇ ㄍㄨㄥ ㄔㄤˇ) or 鐵工廠 (ㄊㄧㄝˇ ㄍㄨㄥ ㄔㄤˇ)
ironworks

鐵公鷄 (ㄊㄧㄝˇ ㄍㄨㄥ ㄐㄧ)
an iron cock—a stingy person

鐵礦 (ㄊㄧㄝˇ ㄎㄨㄤˋ)
①iron ore ②an iron mine

鐵漢 (ㄊㄧㄝˇ ㄏㄢˋ)
①a strong fellow ②a man of firm principle; a strong determined person

鐵畫銀鉤 (ㄊㄧㄝˇ ㄏㄨㄚˋ ㄧㄣˊ ㄍㄡ)
vigorous touches and fine strokes (in calligraphy)

鐵蒺藜 (ㄊㄧㄝˇ ㄐㄧˊ ㄌㄧˊ)
barbed-wire barricades; caltrop

鐵騎 (ㄊㄧㄝˇ ㄐㄧˋ)
strong cavalry

鐵甲 (ㄊㄧㄝˇ ㄐㄧㄚˇ)
steel armor

鐵甲車 (ㄊㄧㄝˇ ㄐㄧㄚˇ ㄔㄜ)
an armored car; an armored vehicle

鐵甲船 (ㄊㄧㄝˇ ㄐㄧㄚˇ ㄔㄨㄢˊ)
an ironclad

鐵匠 (ㄊㄧㄝˇ ㄐㄧㄤˋ)
an ironsmith; a blacksmith

鐵軍 (ㄊㄧㄝˇ ㄐㄩㄣ)
①an invincible army ②the Ironsides of Oliver Cromwell, 1599-1658

鐵器 (ㄊㄧㄝˇ ㄑㄧˋ)
ironware

鐵器時代 (ㄊㄧㄝˇ ㄑㄧˋ ㄕˊ ㄉㄞˋ)
the Iron Age

鐵鍬 (ㄊㄧㄝˇ ㄑㄧㄠ)
an iron spade; a spade

鐵橋 (ㄊㄧㄝˇ ㄑㄧㄠˊ)
①an iron bridge ②a railway bridge

鐵球 (ㄊㄧㄝˇ ㄑㄧㄡˊ)
a shot (thrown in shot put)

鐵青(ㄊㄧㄝˇㄑㄧㄥ)
livid; bluish black: 他氣得臉色鐵青 His face was livid with anger.

鐵血主義(ㄊㄧㄝˇㄒㄧㄝˇㄓㄨˇㄧˋ)
blood and iron policy

鐵血宰相(ㄊㄧㄝˇㄒㄧㄝˇㄗㄞˇㄒㄧㄤ)
the Iron Chancellor (Otto von Bismarck, 1815-1898)

鐵銹(ㄊㄧㄝˇㄒㄧㄡˋ)
rust: 這把刀長滿了鐵銹。The knife was covered with rust.

鐵鍬(ㄊㄧㄝˇㄑㄧㄠ)
a shovel; a spade

鐵線蓮(ㄊㄧㄝˇㄒㄧㄢˋㄌㄧㄢˊ)
(botany) cream clematis

鐵線草(ㄊㄧㄝˇㄒㄧㄢˋㄘㄠˇ)
(botany) adiantum

鐵心(ㄊㄧㄝˇㄒㄧㄣ)
①an iron heart; ruthlessness ②a strong will; firm determination ③(iron) core

鐵箱(ㄊㄧㄝˇㄒㄧㄤ)
a safe

鐵柵(ㄊㄧㄝˇㄓㄚˋ)
an iron fence; an iron barrier

鐵證(ㄊㄧㄝˇㄓㄥˋ)
proof strong as iron; irrefutable evidence; ironclad evidence

鐵證如山(ㄊㄧㄝˇㄓㄥˋㄖㄨˊㄕㄢ)
irrefutable, decisive evidence

鐵尺(ㄊㄧㄝˇㄔˇ)
①a short iron staff (used as a weapon)②an iron ruler

鐵廠(ㄊㄧㄝˇㄔㄤˇ)
ironworks

鐵杵磨針(ㄊㄧㄝˇㄔㄨˇㄇㄛˊㄓㄣ)
(literally) An iron pestle can be ground into a needle. —Steady efforts can work miracles.

鐵鎚(ㄊㄧㄝˇㄔㄨㄟˊ)
an iron hammer; a hammer

鐵窗(ㄊㄧㄝˇㄔㄨㄤ)
①a window with metal gratings ②a prison

鐵窗風味(ㄊㄧㄝˇㄔㄨㄤㄈㄥㄨㄟˋ)
(literally) the flavor of iron-barred windows—life in prison of a convict

鐵牀(ㄊㄧㄝˇㄔㄨㄤˊ)
steel beds

鐵石骨子(ㄊㄧㄝˇㄕˊㄍㄨˇ·ㄗ)
a very strong body; great physical strength

鐵石心腸(ㄊㄧㄝˇㄕˊㄒㄧㄣㄔㄤˊ)
a cold heart; an unfeeling heart; iron-hearted; hard-hearted

鐵石人(ㄊㄧㄝˇㄕˊㄖㄣˊ)
an iron-hearted person; an unfeeling person; a cruel person

鐵石英(ㄊㄧㄝˇㄕˊㄧㄥ)
ferruginous quartz

鐵砂(ㄊㄧㄝˇㄕㄚ)
iron ore; iron sand

鐵沙掌(ㄊㄧㄝˇㄕㄚㄓㄤˇ)
a Chinese version of karate

鐵杉(ㄊㄧㄝˇㄕㄢ)
hemlock spruces

鐵樹(ㄊㄧㄝˇㄕㄨˋ)
a cycad 亦作「鳳尾蕉」

鐵樹開花(ㄊㄧㄝˇㄕㄨˋㄎㄞㄏㄨㄚ)
(literally) the blooming of an iron tree—an impossibility; something that very rarely happens

鐵人(ㄊㄧㄝˇㄖㄣˊ)
(literally) an iron man—(figuratively) a man of great physical strength

鐵則(ㄊㄧㄝˇㄗㄜˊ)
unalterable rules; iron rules

鐵嘴(ㄊㄧㄝˇㄗㄨㄟˇ)
accurate judgment or prediction

鐵絲(ㄊㄧㄝˇㄙ)or 鐵線(ㄊㄧㄝˇㄒㄧㄢˋ)
iron wire

鐵絲網(ㄊㄧㄝˇㄙㄨㄤˇ)
①barbed-wire entanglements ②wire netting; wire meshes

鐵索(ㄊㄧㄝˇㄙㄨㄛˇ)
iron cable; cable

鐵算盤(ㄊㄧㄝˇㄙㄨㄢˋㄆㄢˊ)
the iron abacus—the trick, or spell, by which wandering sorcerers were believed to swindle people out of their money.

鐵案如山(ㄊㄧㄝˇㄢˋㄖㄨˊㄕㄢ)
facts as irrevocable as a mountain

鐵衣(ㄊㄧㄝˇㄧ)
①armor ②iron rust

鐵硯磨穿(ㄊㄧㄝˇㄧㄢˋㄇㄛˊㄔㄨㄢ)
to rub through an iron ink slab—to study with uncommon diligence

鐵腕(ㄊㄧㄝˇㄨㄢˋ)
iron hand; iron fist

【鍰】 6505
ㄏㄨㄢˊ hwan huán
a ring

【鐸】 6506
ㄉㄨㄛˊ dwo duó
1. a large bell
2. a Chinese family name

【鐺】 6507
1. ㄉㄤ dang dāng
1. the sound of striking a gong
2. shackles 參看「鋃鐺」

鐺鐺(ㄉㄤㄉㄤ)
the sound of striking a gong

【鐺】 6507
2. ㄔㄥ cheng chēng
1. a kind of wine heater
2. a cauldron-like vessel with legs
3. a pan for frying; a shallow pot

【鐳】 6508
ㄌㄟˊ lei léi
1. radium
2. a pot; a jar

鐳錠(ㄌㄟˊㄉㄧㄥˋ)
radium (Ra)

【鐿】 6509
ㄧˋ yih yì
ytterbium

十四畫

【鑊】 6510
ㄏㄨㄛˋ huoh huò
a cauldron for cooking (used mostly in ancient times)

鑊烹(ㄏㄨㄛˋㄆㄥ)
(an ancient punishment) to cook a criminal in a cauldron

【鑄】 6511
ㄓㄨˋ juh zhù
1. to melt or cast metal; to coin; to mint
2. to make or commit (blunders, etc.)
3. to educate and influence (a person)
4. a Chinese family name

鑄幣(ㄓㄨˋㄅㄧˋ)
to mint (coins)

鑄幣廠(ㄓㄨˋㄅㄧˋㄔㄤˇ)
a mint

鑄鐵(ㄓㄨˋㄊㄧㄝˇ)
①cast iron ②iron casting

鑄像(ㄓㄨˋㄒㄧㄤˋ)

【金部】

to erect a metal statue

鑄成大錯(ㄓㄨˋ ㄔㄥˊ ㄉㄚˋ ㄘㄨㄛˋ)
to commit a serious mistake;
to make a gross error

鑿山煮海(ㄗㄠˊ ㄕㄢ ㄓㄨˇ ㄏㄞˇ)
(literally) to excavate copper from mountain mine for
coining and cook seawater
for salt—to develop natural
resources

鑄人(ㄓㄨˋ ㄖㄣˊ)
to educate and influence
people

鑄字(ㄓㄨˋ ㄗˋ)
type founding; typecasting

鑄造(ㄓㄨˋ ㄗㄠˋ)
①to educate ②to melt or
cast (metal) ③to mint
(coins)

鑄錯(ㄓㄨˋ ㄘㄨㄛˋ)
to commit blunders

【鑑】 6512
ㄐㄧㄢˋ jiann jiàn
1. a mirror
2. to mirror; to reflect; to
shine
3. to study or examine; to
scrutinize
4. an example serving as a
rule or warning

鑑別(ㄐㄧㄢˋ ㄅㄧㄝˊ)
to distinguish (the genuine
from an imitation); to judge
or identify something by
carefully examining it; to
discriminate; to make an
appraisal of something: 她善
於鑑別文物。 She is good at
making an appraisal of a
cultural relic.

鑑定(ㄐㄧㄢˋ ㄉㄧㄥˋ)
to examine and determine;
to judge; to make an
appraisal

鑑定書(ㄐㄧㄢˋ ㄉㄧㄥˋ ㄕㄨ)
the appraisal of an expert in
written form

鑑定人(ㄐㄧㄢˋ ㄉㄧㄥˋ ㄖㄣˊ)
(law) an appraiser; an expert examiner

鑑戒(ㄐㄧㄢˋ ㄐㄧㄝˋ)
a warning example; to take
warning from a past failure

鑑識(ㄐㄧㄢˋ ㄕˋ)
to tell; to judge; to distinguish; to discern

鑑賞(ㄐㄧㄢˋ ㄕㄤˋ)
to examine and appreciate:
她具有鑑賞音樂的能力。 She
has the ability to appreciate
music.

鑑賞家(ㄐㄧㄢˋ ㄕㄤˋ ㄐㄧㄚ)
a connoisseur

鑑往知來(ㄐㄧㄢˋ ㄨㄤˇ ㄓ ㄌㄞˊ)
to foresee the future by reviewing the past

【鑒】 6513
(鑑) ㄐㄧㄢˋ jiann jiàn
to examine, etc.

鑒諒(ㄐㄧㄢˋ ㄌㄧㄤˋ)
to study and forgive (my
fault, etc.)

鑒核(ㄐㄧㄢˋ ㄏㄜˊ)
to examine (a case, etc.)
and make a decision: 請鑒
核。 Please examine.

鑒察(ㄐㄧㄢˋ ㄔㄚˊ)
to examine and study

十五畫

【鑠】 6514
ㄕㄨㄛˋ shuoh shuò
1. to melt metals with fire or
heat; to smelt
2. to wear off
3. shining; lustrous
4. powerful

鑠石流金(ㄕㄨㄛˋ ㄕˊ ㄌㄧㄡˊ ㄐㄧㄣ)
(literally) to melt stone and
turn metal into fluid
—extreme heat

鑠鑠(ㄕㄨㄛˋ ㄕㄨㄛˋ)
brilliant; lustrous

【鑕】 6515
ㄓˋ jyh zhì
an ancient Chinese version
of a guillotine

【鑛】 6516
(礦) ㄎㄨㄤˋ kuang
kuàng
a mine or mineral

鑛山(ㄎㄨㄤˋ ㄕㄢ)
a mine

【鑞】 6517
ㄌㄚˋ lah là
an alloy of tin and lead for
welding

【鑣】 6518
ㄅㄧㄠ biau biāo
1. a bit for a horse
2. said of a horse
3. a dart-like projectile thrown
by hand as a weapon 亦作
「鏢」

十六畫

【鑪】 6519
ㄌㄨˊ lu lú
1. a stove, an oven, a furnace,
etc. 亦作「爐」
2. (chemistry) rutherfordium

【鑫】 6520
ㄒㄧㄣ shin xīn
a word of no definite meaning, used only in names,
with a connotation of prosperity or good profit

十七畫

【鑰】 6521
ㄧㄠˋ yaw yào
(讀音 ㄩㄝˋ yueh yuè)
1. a key
2. a lock

鑰匙(ㄧㄠˋ ㄕˊ)
a key: 他轉動鑰匙。 He turned
the key in the lock.

鑰匙圈(ㄧㄠˋ ㄕˊ ㄑㄩㄢ)
a key ring

鑰匙兒(ㄧㄠˋ ㄕˊ ㄦˊ)
a latchkey child

【鑲】 6522
ㄒㄧㄤ shiang xiāng
1. to fill in (a tooth, etc.); to
mount; to inlay; to set
(jewels, etc.)
2. to edge; to border; to hem;
bordered
3. name of an ancient weapon

鑲邊(ㄒㄧㄤ ㄅㄧㄢ)
to edge or hem (handker-
chief, dress, etc.)

鑲嵌(ㄒㄧㄤ ㄑㄧㄢˋ)
to inlay; to set (jewels, etc.)

鑲住了(ㄒㄧㄤ ㄓㄨˋ ㄌㄜ)
to be constrained by com-
mon practice, courtesy, etc.
so that one can not do anything otherwise

鑲牙(ㄒㄧㄤ ㄧㄚˊ)
to fill in an artificial tooth;
to crown a tooth

十八畫

【鑷】 6523
ㄋㄧㄝˋ nieh niè
1. tweezers; pincers; forceps
2. to pull out; to nip

鑷子(ㄋㄧㄝˋ ㄗˇ)

a pair of tweezers

十九畫

【鑼】 6524
カメで luo luó
a gong. 他正在那兒敲鑼。He is striking a gong there.

鑼鼓(カメで ㄍㄨˇ)
①gongs and drums ②traditional percussion instruments ③ensemble of such instruments with gongs and drums playing the main part

鑼鼓喧天(カメで ㄍㄨ ㄒㄩㄢ ㄊㄧㄢ)
(literally) the sound of gongs and drums shakes the sky—noisy celebration of a festival or carnival

【鑽】 6525
1. ㄗㄨㄢ tzuan zuān
1. to pierce; to drill; to bore; to dig through; to penetrate: 這木頭不容易鑽。The wood bores hard.
2. to go through; to make one's way into
3. to gain (profit, a position, etc.) through special favor, contact, relations, etc.
4. to study intensively; to dig into; to bury oneself in

鑽門子(ㄗㄨㄢ ㄇㄣˊ ㄗ˙)
to try to gain profit, a position, etc. by exploiting personal connections in a devious way

鑽營覓縫兒(ㄗㄨㄢ ㄧㄥˊ ㄇㄧˋ ㄈㄥˋ ㄦ)
or 鑽天入地(ㄗㄨㄢ ㄊㄧㄢ ㄖㄨˋ ㄉㄧˋ)
to look for profit, a position by hook or by crook

鑽探(ㄗㄨㄢ ㄊㄢˋ)
to prospect; to investigate; to explore; (exploration) drilling

鑽牛犄角(ㄗㄨㄢ ㄋㄧㄡˊ ㄐㄧ ㄐㄧㄠˇ) or 鑽牛角尖(ㄗㄨㄢ ㄋㄧㄡˊ ㄐㄧㄠˇ ㄐㄧㄢ)
(literally) to worm oneself into the horn's point—to get oneself into a dead-end alley through sheer stubbornness

鑽狗洞(ㄗㄨㄢ ㄍㄡˇ ㄉㄨㄥˋ)
to do evil

鑽故紙(ㄗㄨㄢ ㄍㄨˋ ㄓˇ)
to be wrapped up in the study of ancient books, like

a pedant

鑽過去(ㄗㄨㄢ ㄍㄨㄛˋ ㄑㄩˋ)
①to bore through ②to squeeze through: 他從人叢中鑽過去。He squeezed through the crowd.

鑽研(ㄗㄨㄢ ㄧㄢˊ)
to study or scrutinize thoroughly; to dig into

鑽營(ㄗㄨㄢ ㄧㄥˊ)
①to seek advantage for oneself by all means ②to study and scrutinize thoroughly

【鑽】 6525
2. ㄗㄨㄢ tzoan zuǎn
(又讀ㄗㄨㄢ tzuan zuān)
to bore or pierce a hole

鑽木取火(ㄗㄨㄢ ㄇㄨˋ ㄑㄩˇ ㄏㄨㄛˇ)
to bore wood and get fire by friction

鑽孔(ㄗㄨㄢ ㄎㄨㄥˇ)
to make a hole; to perforate

鑽孔機(ㄗㄨㄢ ㄎㄨㄥˇ ㄐㄧ)
a drilling machine 亦作「鑽探機」

鑽井(ㄗㄨㄢ ㄐㄧㄥˇ)
①to drill a well ②well drilling

鑽牀(ㄗㄨㄢ ㄔㄨㄤˊ)
a drill; a drilling machine

【鑽】 6525
3. ㄗㄨㄢ tzuann zuàn
1. a gimlet; an awl or auger; a borer; a drill
2. a diamond; a jewel

鑽頭(ㄗㄨㄢ ㄊㄡˊ)
(geophysical exploration) the point of an awl; a bit of a drill

鑽戒(ㄗㄨㄢ ㄐㄧㄝˋ)
a diamond ring: 她戴着一顆鑽戒。She wears a diamond ring.

鑽石(ㄗㄨㄢ ㄉㄢˊ)
a diamond: 她有一顆10克拉的鑽石。She has a diamond of 10 carats.

鑽石婚(ㄗㄨㄢ ㄉㄢˊ ㄏㄨㄣ)
diamond wedding

鑽子(ㄗㄨㄢ ㄗ˙)
an awl; an auger; a drill, etc.

【鑾】 6526
カメㄢ luan luán
1. bells around the neck of a horse; bells hung on the imperial chariot

2. the imperial carriage

鑾鈴(カメㄢ カㄧㄥ)
bells hung on the imperial chariot or carriage

鑾駕(カメㄢ ㄐㄧㄚ)
①carriages or chariots used by the emperor ②the emperor

鑾輿(カメㄢ ㄩˊ)
①the imperial carriage ②the emperor

二十畫

【鑿】 6527
1. ㄗㄨㄛˊ tzuoh zuó
1. an instrument for boring wood
2. to bore or pierce through; to chisel
3. real; true; actual; indisputable; conclusive
4. to polish rice
5. to make a forced interpretation of text

鑿壁偷光(ㄗㄨㄛˊ ㄅㄧˋ ㄊㄡ ㄍㄨㄤ)
(literally) to bore a hole on the wall in order to get some light from the neighbor's house—very studious

鑿枘(ㄗㄨㄛˊ ㄖㄨㄟˋ)
(literally) a square peg for a round hole—not at all fit or suitable

鑿鑿(ㄗㄨㄛˊ ㄗㄨㄛˊ)
①real; indisputable ②with certainty

鑿鑿可據(ㄗㄨㄛˊ ㄗㄨㄛˊ ㄎㄜˇ ㄐㄩˋ)
certain and reliable

【鑿】 6527
2. ㄗㄠˋ tzaur zǎo
1. to chisel or dig; to bore or pierce through
2. to scuttle
3. a chisel

鑿洞(ㄗㄠˋ ㄉㄨㄥˋ)
to bore or drill a hole

鑿開(ㄗㄠˋ ㄎㄞ)
to bore through; to cut open

鑿井(ㄗㄠˋ ㄐㄧㄥˇ)
①to dig or drill a well ②(mining) shaft sinking; pit sinking

鑿子(ㄗㄠˋ ㄗ˙)
a chisel

（金部）

長 部
ㄔㄤ charng cháng

〔長部〕

【長】 6528
1. ㄔㄤ charng cháng

1. long; length: 她有一頭長髮。
She has long hair.

2. a forte; strong points: 舞蹈是她的特長。Dancing is her forte.

3. to be good at; to excel: 他長於數字計算。He is good at figures.

4. a Chinese family name

長波 (ㄔㄤ ㄅㄛ)
long wave

長白山 (ㄔㄤ ㄅㄞ ㄕㄢ)
Chang Pai Shan, a mountain range in Manchuria

長鼻類 (ㄔㄤ ㄅㄧ ㄌㄟˋ)
(zoology) proboscidian

長臂猿 (ㄔㄤ ㄅㄧˋ ㄩㄢˊ)
the gibbon: 動物園裡有兩隻長臂猿。There are two gibbons in the zoo.

長編 (ㄔㄤ ㄅㄧㄢ)
(said of a history, biography, etc.) the collection of data, materials arranged in chronological order

長袍 (ㄔㄤ ㄆㄠˊ)
a long gown; a robe

長袍馬短掛兒 (ㄔㄤ ㄆㄠˊ ㄇㄚˇ ㄉㄨㄢˇ 《ㄨㄚˋㄦ)
long gown and short jacket, the ceremonial dress of a Chinese gentleman

長跑 (ㄔㄤ ㄆㄠˇ)
a long-distance foot race

長篇 (ㄔㄤ ㄆㄧㄢ)
a long (literary) piece

長篇大論 (ㄔㄤ ㄆㄧㄢ ㄉㄚˋ ㄌㄨㄣˋ)
a harangue or tirade; a lengthy comment; a ponderous talk; a long speech

長篇小說 (ㄔㄤ ㄆㄧㄢ ㄒㄧㄠˇ ㄕㄨㄛ)
a novel: 這部長篇小說充滿了冒險的故事。This novel is full of adventures.

長才 (ㄔㄤ ㄘㄞˊ)
a long spear

長毛 (ㄔㄤ ㄇㄠˊ)
the Taiping rebel troops in the mid-19th century

長眠不醒 (ㄔㄤ ㄇㄧㄢˊ ㄅㄨˋ ㄒㄧㄥˇ)
to die

長明燈 (ㄔㄤ ㄇㄧㄥˊ ㄉㄥ)
an oil lamp lit day and night before a Buddha statue

長命 (ㄔㄤ ㄇㄧㄥˋ)
a long life; longevity: 長命者少欲交。To live long is to outlive many.

長命百歲 (ㄔㄤ ㄇㄧㄥˋ ㄅㄞˇ ㄙㄨㄟˋ)
May you live a hundred years! (an expression of congratulations for a month-old baby)

長命富貴 (ㄔㄤ ㄇㄧㄥˋ ㄈㄨˋ 《ㄨㄟˋ)
May you live long and be successful! (a congratulatory expression in celebrating a baby's first month)

長方體 (ㄔㄤ ㄈㄤ ㄊㄧˇ)
a cuboid; a rectangular parallelepiped

長方形 (ㄔㄤ ㄈㄤ ㄒㄧㄥˊ)
a rectangle; an oblong

長島 (ㄔㄤ ㄉㄠˇ)
the Long Island, an island in SE New York

長等短等 (ㄔㄤ ㄉㄥˇ ㄉㄨㄢˇ ㄉㄥˇ)
to wait for a long time

長櫈 (ㄔㄤ ㄉㄥˋ)
a bench

長笛 (ㄔㄤ ㄉㄧˊ)
a flute: 他吹長笛。He plays (on) the flute.

長調 (ㄔㄤ ㄉㄧㄠˋ)
① a Chinese poem of irregular lines, which exceeds 91 characters in length ② (music) major

長短 (ㄔㄤ ㄉㄨㄢˇ)
length: 他們在量田的長度。They were measuring the length of a field.

長短 (ㄔㄤ ㄉㄨㄢˇ)
① long or short ② length ③ mishaps or accidents which may endanger one's life ④ good or bad; malicious criticism

長短不齊 (ㄔㄤ ㄉㄨㄢˇ ㄅㄨˋ ㄑㄧˊ)
not uniform in length

長短句 (ㄔㄤ ㄉㄨㄢˇ ㄐㄩˋ)
another name of tsu (詞)

長談 (ㄔㄤ ㄊㄢˊ)
a long talk or chat; a long

conversation or discussion

長歎 (ㄔㄤ ㄊㄢˋ)
to sigh deeply

長堤 (ㄔㄤ ㄊㄧˊ)
① a long dike ② Long Beach, U.S.A.

長堤選美 (ㄔㄤ ㄊㄧˊ ㄒㄩㄢˇ ㄇㄟˇ)
Miss International Contest at Long Beach

長條兒 (ㄔㄤ ㄊㄧㄠˊㄦ)
a long and narrow strip

長亭 (ㄔㄤ ㄊㄧㄥˊ)
a small pavilion to rest a traveler's weary feet (in ancient China, one was built every 10 li)

長途 (ㄔㄤ ㄊㄨˊ)
a long distance; a long journey

長途跋涉 (ㄔㄤ ㄊㄨˊ ㄅㄚˊ ㄕㄜˋ)
to travel a long distance; to make a long, arduous journey

長途飛行 (ㄔㄤ ㄊㄨˊ ㄈㄟ ㄒㄧㄥˊ)
a long-distance flight

長途電話 (ㄔㄤ ㄊㄨˊ ㄉㄧㄢˋ ㄏㄨㄚˋ)
a long-distance (telephone) call

長途旅行 (ㄔㄤ ㄊㄨˊ ㄌㄩˇ ㄒㄧㄥˊ)
a long journey; a long-distance travel: 他們上個月作了一次長途旅行。They made a long journey last month.

長途汽車 (ㄔㄤ ㄊㄨˊ ㄑㄧˋ ㄔㄜ)
a long-distance bus; a coach

長途運輸 (ㄔㄤ ㄊㄨˊ ㄩㄣˋ ㄕㄨ)
long-distance transport

長統靴 (ㄔㄤ ㄊㄨㄥˇ ㄒㄩㄝ)
jackboots

長統襪 (ㄔㄤ ㄊㄨㄥˇ ㄨㄚˋ)
stockings

長年 (ㄔㄤ ㄋㄧㄢˊ)
yearlong; all the year round

長年累月 (ㄔㄤ ㄋㄧㄢˊ ㄌㄟˇ ㄩㄝˋ)
year in, year out; over the years

長廊 (ㄔㄤ ㄌㄤˊ)
① a roofed corridor or passage; a gallery ② the Long Corridor (of the Summer Palace in Peking)

長林豐草 (ㄔㄤ ㄌㄧㄣˊ ㄈㄥ ㄘㄠˇ)
a field with luxuriant vege-

tation—a seclusion for a hermit to live in

長龍(ㄔㄤ ㄌㄨㄥˊ)
a long line; a long queue

長庚(ㄔㄤ ㄍㄥ)or 長庚星(ㄔㄤ ㄍㄥ ㄒㄧㄥ)
(astronomy) Hesperus; an ancient Chinese name for Venus

長跪(ㄔㄤ ㄍㄨㄟˋ)
to kneel upright

長工(ㄔㄤ ㄍㄨㄥ)
a regular laborer on a farm; a farm hand; a long-term hired hand

長褲(ㄔㄤ ㄎㄨˋ)
a pair of trousers (as distinct from panties or shorts)

長號(ㄔㄤ ㄏㄠˋ)
①(ㄔㄤ ㄏㄠˊ) to cry aloud
②(ㄔㄤ ㄏㄠˋ) (music) a trombone

長恨歌(ㄔㄤ ㄏㄣˋ ㄍㄜ)
the "Song of Eternal Sorrow," by the poet Pai Chü-i (白居易), a long poem describing the rise and downfall of the famed beauty Yang Kuei-fei (楊貴妃)

長話短說(ㄔㄤ ㄏㄨㄚˋ ㄉㄨㄢˇ ㄕㄨㄛ)
to make a long story short

長假(ㄔㄤ ㄐㄧㄚˋ)
①to retire or resign from office ②a long leave of absence

長久(ㄔㄤ ㄐㄧㄡˇ)
permanent; a very long time: 這不是個長久之計。This is not a permanent solution.

長江(ㄔㄤ ㄐㄧㄤ)
the Yangtze River

長江天塹(ㄔㄤ ㄐㄧㄤ ㄊㄧㄢ ㄑㄧㄢˋ)
The Yangtze River is a natural barrier (to invaders).

長頸鹿(ㄔㄤ ㄐㄧㄥˇ ㄌㄨˋ)
a giraffe

長頸烏喙(ㄔㄤ ㄐㄧㄥˇ ㄨ ㄏㄨㄟˋ)
the look of a mean fellow

長徑(ㄔㄤ ㄐㄧㄥˋ)
(mathematics) major axis

長局(ㄔㄤ ㄐㄩˊ)
a permanent or long-term arrangement

長崎(ㄔㄤ ㄑㄧˊ)
Nagasaki, Japan

長期(ㄔㄤ ㄑㄧ)
①a long time ②long-term;

long-range; long-standing: 他們作了長期打算。They made long-term plans.

長期目標(ㄔㄤ ㄑㄧ ㄇㄨˋ ㄅㄧㄠ)
long-term objectives

長期貸款(ㄔㄤ ㄑㄧ ㄉㄞˋ ㄎㄨㄢˇ)
long-term loans

長期抗戰(ㄔㄤ ㄑㄧ ㄎㄤˋ ㄓㄢˋ)
a long-term war of resistance, as the Sino-Japanese War of 1937-1945

長期合同(ㄔㄤ ㄑㄧ ㄏㄜˊ ㄊㄨㄥˊ)
a long-term contract

長期計劃(ㄔㄤ ㄑㄧ ㄐㄧˋ ㄏㄨㄚˋ)
a long-term plan

長期證券(ㄔㄤ ㄑㄧ ㄓㄥˋ ㄑㄩㄢˋ)
long-term securities

長期資本(ㄔㄤ ㄑㄧ ㄗ ㄅㄣˇ)
(accounting) a long-term capital

長期租賃(ㄔㄤ ㄑㄧ ㄗㄨ ㄌㄧㄣˋ)
a long-term lease

長槍(ㄔㄤ ㄑㄧㄤ)
①a spear ②a long-barreled gun

長驅直入(ㄔㄤ ㄑㄩ ㄓˊ ㄖㄨˋ)
(said of an advancing army) to march in without opposition

長嘯(ㄔㄤ ㄒㄧㄠˋ)
to cry or yell loud and long; a long and loud cry

長袖善舞(ㄔㄤ ㄒㄧㄡˋ ㄕㄢˋ ㄨˇ)
①(literally) One who has long sleeves dances best.—One will succeed much easier if he has something to rely upon. ②to be resourceful, especially in a dishonest way

長相廝守(ㄔㄤ ㄒㄧㄤˋ ㄙ ㄕㄡˇ)
to stay married forever; to keep each other company for life

長吁(ㄔㄤ ㄒㄩ)
to heave a deep sigh

長吁短歎(ㄔㄤ ㄒㄩ ㄉㄨㄢˇ ㄊㄢˋ)
to sigh incessantly; to sigh and groan

長支(ㄔㄤ ㄓ)
to overdraw; to spend more than the budgeted fund

長治久安(ㄔㄤ ㄓˋ ㄐㄧㄡˇ ㄢ)
a lengthy peaceful reign

長齋(ㄔㄤ ㄓㄞ)
(said of a Buddhist in secular life) to be a vegetarian

throughout the year

長針(ㄔㄤ ㄓㄣ)
the minute hand; the long hand

長枕大被(ㄔㄤ ㄓㄣˇ ㄉㄚˋ ㄅㄟˋ)
(literally) to share a long pillow and a large bed cover—brotherly love or fraternity

長征(ㄔㄤ ㄓㄥ)
an expedition (usually military); to take a long journey to a distant place

長住(ㄔㄤ ㄓㄨˋ)
to stay long; to live at a place for a long time

長長短短(ㄔㄤ ㄔㄤ ㄉㄨㄢˇ ㄉㄨㄢˇ)
not uniform in length

長城(ㄔㄤ ㄔㄥˊ)
①the Great Wall ②someone who can be trusted

長程(ㄔㄤ ㄔㄥˊ)
long-range; long-distance

長處(ㄔㄤ ㄔㄨˋ)
merits; good points; advantages: 她有許多長處。She has many merits.

長川(ㄔㄤ ㄔㄨㄢ)
①continuous or incessant ②a long river

長春(ㄔㄤ ㄔㄨㄣ)
①Changchun, a city in Kirin Province ②ilex ③the monthly rose

長蟲(ㄔㄤ ㄔㄨㄥˊ)
the long worm—the snake

長石(ㄔㄤ ㄕˊ)
feldspar

長時間(ㄔㄤ ㄕˊ ㄐㄧㄢ)
a long time

長逝(ㄔㄤ ㄕˋ)
to die

長沙(ㄔㄤ ㄕㄚ)
Changsha, capital city of Hunan Province

長舌(ㄔㄤ ㄕㄜˊ)
to be fond of gossip; long-tongued

長舌婦(ㄔㄤ ㄕㄜˊ ㄈㄨˋ)
a loquacious woman of the vicious type

長蛇陣(ㄔㄤ ㄕㄜˊ ㄓㄣˋ)
military formations in a row like a long snake

長射程(ㄔㄤ ㄕㄜˋ ㄔㄥˊ)
(said of artillery pieces)

【長 部】

長-range

長壽(彳尢 ㄕㄡˋ)
longevity; a long life

長壽麵(彳尢 ㄕㄡˋ ㄇ一ㄢˋ)
noodles eaten on one's birthday

長衫(彳尢 ㄕㄢ)
a Chinese long gown for man

長生(彳尢 ㄕㄥ)
to live long; a long life; longevity

長生不老(彳尢 ㄕㄥ ㄅㄨˋ ㄌㄠˇ)
(especially in Taoism) immortality

長生不老藥(彳尢 ㄕㄥ ㄅㄨˋ ㄌㄠˇ 一ㄠˋ)
an elixir to prolong life indefinitely; the elixir of life

長生殿(彳尢 ㄕㄥ ㄉ一ㄢˋ)
name of a palace in the Tang Dynasty, which was made the subject of a drama about Emperor Hsüan Tsung (唐玄宗) and his favorite concubine Lady Yang (楊貴妃)

長生果(彳尢 ㄕㄥ ㄍㄨㄛˇ)
a groundnut, or a peanut

長人(彳尢 ㄖㄣˊ)
an extremely tall man

長足進步(彳尢 ㄗㄨˊ ㄐ一ㄣˋ ㄅㄨˋ)
marked progress; a long way

長此以往(彳尢 ㄘˇ 一ˇ ㄨㄤˇ)
continuously for a long time hence

長策(彳尢 ㄘㄜˋ)
a sound plan; a good scheme

長存(彳尢 ㄘㄨㄣˊ)
to exist forever; to last forever

長安(彳尢 ㄢ)
Changan, an ancient name of Sian (西安), capital of the Chinese empire during several dynasties

長安道上(彳尢 ㄢ ㄉㄠˋ ㄕㄤˋ)
(literally) the road to Changan—an arena where people struggle for fame or wealth

長揖(彳尢 一)
to fold one's hands and make a deep bow

長揖不拜(彳尢 一 ㄅㄨˋ ㄅㄞˋ)
to make a deep bow but refuse to kneel down

長夜(彳尢 一ㄝˋ)

①the long night ②the grave

長夜漫漫(彳尢 一ㄝˋ ㄇㄢˋ ㄇㄢˋ)
the long, long night

長音(彳尢 一ㄣ)
a prolonged sound; a long vowel

長音階(彳尢 一ㄣ ㄐ一ㄝ)
(music) a major scale

長音程(彳尢 一ㄣ ㄔㄥˊ)
(music) a major interval

長襪(彳尢 ㄨㄚˋ)
stockings

長尾雞(彳尢 ㄨㄟˇ ㄐ一)
a phoenix cock; a paradise flycatcher

長尾猴(彳尢 ㄨㄟˇ ㄏㄡˊ)or 長尾猿
a kind of long-tailed monkey in Africa (*Cercopithecus aethiops*)

長圓(彳尢 ㄩㄢˊ)
an ellipse; a regular oval

長遠(彳尢 ㄩㄢˇ)
for a long time; long-range; long-term

長遠之計(彳尢 ㄩㄢˇ ㄓ ㄐ一ˋ)
a long-range plan (for the future)

【長】 6528
②。ㄓㄤˇ jaang zhang

1. senior; old: 他比我年長。She is older than I.

2. the eldest: 他是張先生的長子。He is Mr. Chang's eldest son.

3. a head; a chief; a leader; a commander; a chairman: 他是警察局長。He is the chief of a police station.

4. to grow: 這城市快速成長。The city is growing rapidly.

5. to increase; to advance: 旅行增長了他的知識。Traveling increases his knowledge.

6. to look; to appear; to become

長輩(ㄓㄤˇ ㄅㄟˋ)
the senior generation; the older member of a family; an elder

長胖(ㄓㄤˇ ㄆㄤˋ)
to become fat; to gain weight

長黴(ㄓㄤˇ ㄇㄟˊ)
to mildew; to become mildewy

長毛(ㄓㄤˇ ㄇㄠˊ)
to grow hair; to get hairy; to grow feather

長房(ㄓㄤˇ ㄈㄤˊ)
the branch of the family tree from the first-born male

長大(ㄓㄤˇ ㄉㄚˋ)
to grow up; to attain manhood; to mature

長得(ㄓㄤˇ ㄉㄜˊ)
to look (beautiful, handsome, etc.): 她長得真漂亮。She looks very pretty.

長男(ㄓㄤˇ ㄋㄢˊ)
the eldest son

長女(ㄓㄤˇ ㄋㄩˇ)
the eldest daughter

長老(ㄓㄤˇ ㄌㄠˇ)
①seniors or oldsters ②a presbyter ③reverent address for a monk

長老會(ㄓㄤˇ ㄌㄠˇ ㄏㄨㄟˋ)
the Presbyterian Church

長吏(ㄓㄤˇ ㄌ一ˋ)
①officials of higher seniority ②superiors

長瘤(ㄓㄤˇ ㄌ一ㄡˊ)
to have a tumor

長官(ㄓㄤˇ ㄍㄨㄢ)
one's superior in office, etc. (a polite expression) officers or officials; a commanding officer

長公主(ㄓㄤˇ ㄍㄨㄥ ㄓㄨˇ)
sisters of the emperor

長行市(ㄓㄤˇ ㄏㄤˊ ㄕˋ)
to hike prices

長機(ㄓㄤˇ ㄐ一)
the command plane; the plane piloted by the commanding officer in a group of attacking aircraft; the leading aircraft

長見識(ㄓㄤˇ ㄐ一ㄢˋ ㄕ˙)
to increase one's knowledge or to gain experience

長進(ㄓㄤˇ ㄐ一ㄣˋ)
to make progress (especially in scholastic pursuit, etc.)

長媳(ㄓㄤˇ ㄒ一ˊ)
the wife of one's eldest son

長相(ㄓㄤˇ ㄒ一ㄤˋ)
one's looks or appearances: 她長相兒好。She is good looking.

長兄(ㄓㄤˇ ㄒㄩㄥ)

one's eldest brother

長者(出ˋ 出ˇ)
a senior; an elder; a person of virtue

長成
①to grow to manhood ②to grow into: 她已長成漂亮的女孩。She has grown into a pretty girl.

長瘡(出ˋ ㄔㄨㄤ)
to be affected by scabies; to ulcerate

長上
elders and superiors

長子(出ˇ ㄗˇ)
the eldest son: 他是林先生的長子。He is Mr. Lin's eldest son.

長子繼承權(出ˇ ㄗˇ ㄐㄧ ㄔㄥˊ ㄑㄩㄢˊ)
the right of primogeniture

長子繼承制(出ˇ ㄗˇ ㄐㄧ ㄔㄥˊ ㄓˋ)
primogeniture

長嫂比母(出ˇ ㄙㄠˇ ㄅㄧˇ ㄇㄨˇ)
One should treat his eldest brother's wife with the same respect as that accorded to his mother.

長孫(出ˇ ㄙㄨㄣ)
①the eldest of one's grandsons ②a Chinese double-name

長牙(出ˇ ㄧㄚˊ)
(said of babies or young animals) to grow teeth

長幼(出ˇ ㄧㄡˋ)
young and old; seniority among family members

長幼有序(出ˇ ㄧㄡˋ ㄧㄡˇ ㄒㄩˋ)
respect for seniority; an order, system, institution, etc. arranged according to seniority in age or generation; precedence maintained between seniors and juniors

【長】 6528
3. 出ˋ janq zhòng
a surplus; a remainder

長物(出ˋ ㄨˋ)
property; belongings

門 部
ㄇㄣˊ men mén

【門】 6529
ㄇㄣˊ men mén

1. a door; a gateway; an opening: 門口有人。There is someone at the door.
2. a family; a clan
3. a sect; a school; a gang
4. a class; a category
5. the key; the turning point
6. a piece of (artillery); a (cannon)
7. gate-keeping
8. a Chinese family name

門兒(ㄇㄣˊㄦ)
①the door ②the family ③a branch of study: 你專攻那一門兒? What branch of study do you major in?

門把(ㄇㄣˊㄅㄚˇ)
a doorknob; a door handle

門板(ㄇㄣˊㄅㄢˇ)
the plank(s) of a door

門牓 or 門榜(ㄇㄣˊㄅㄤˇ)
a notice hung at the gateway

門牌(ㄇㄣˊㄆㄞˊ)
a doorplate, indicating the exact address of a residence

門派(ㄇㄣˊㄆㄞˋ)
a sect

門票(ㄇㄣˊㄆㄧㄠˋ)
an admission ticket; an entrance ticket

門脈(ㄇㄣˊㄇㄞˋ)
①the portal system; the portal vein 亦作「門靜脈」②outpatient service

門楣(ㄇㄣˊㄇㄟˊ)
①a beam over a doorway ②family standing

門面(ㄇㄣˊㄇㄧㄢˋ)
①the front of a store ②the outward appearance; a facade

門面話(ㄇㄣˊㄇㄧㄢˋㄏㄨㄚˋ)
insincere talk; lip service; formal and insincere remarks

門閥(ㄇㄣˊㄈㄚˊ)
high family standing

門法(ㄇㄣˊㄈㄚˇ)
a family code of conduct

門房(ㄇㄣˊㄈㄤˊ)
①a gatekeeper; a janitor; a doorman ②a room for a janitor or doorman; a gatehouse ③distant relatives of the same clan

---

門風(ㄇㄣˊㄈㄥ)
moral standing of a family; family reputation

門縫(ㄇㄣˊㄈㄥˋ)
crevices or cracks in the door

門道
①(ㄇㄣˊ・ㄉㄠ) means of approach, influence or contacts; intellectual resources 亦作「門路」
②(ㄇㄣˊㄉㄠˋ) a doorway; a gateway 亦作「門洞兒」

門當戶對(ㄇㄣˊㄉㄤ ㄏㄨˋㄉㄨㄟˋ)
families of equal standing (usually referring to those of a married couple); well matched

門第(ㄇㄣˊㄉㄧˋ)
family standing or reputation; family status: 這兩家門第相稱。The two families are equal in social status.

門丁(ㄇㄣˊㄉㄧㄥ)
a doorkeeper; a janitor

門庭若市(ㄇㄣˊㄊㄧㄥˊㄖㄨㄛˋㄕˋ)
①(said of a store, etc.) doing booming business ②(said of a household) swarmed with visitors; much visited

門徒(ㄇㄣˊㄊㄨˊ)
one's students, pupils, followers, or disciples

門類(ㄇㄣˊㄌㄟˋ)
a category, division, or classification

門樓(ㄇㄣˊㄌㄡˊ)
①the tower above a gate (usually a city gate) ②an arch over a gateway

門吏(ㄇㄣˊㄌㄧˋ)
①a gatekeeper ②a person working for a large family, as a secretary, etc.

門聯(ㄇㄣˊㄌㄧㄢˊ)or 門對(ㄇㄣˊㄉㄨㄟˋ)
couplets pasted on doors or doorposts (usually at the lunar new year)

門簾 or 門帘(ㄇㄣˊㄌㄧㄢˊ)
a door curtain or screen

門鈴
the doorbell: 請按門鈴。Ring the doorbell, please.

門路(ㄇㄣˊㄌㄨˋ)
①one's means of approach, contacts, connections, etc. ②a key or tip to a beginner in

---

the pursuit of a certain skill; a knack

門羅主義(ㄇㄣˊ ㄌㄨㄛˊ ㄓㄨˇ ㄧˋ)
the Monroe Doctrine

門崗(ㄇㄣˊ ㄍㄤ)
guards posted at the door or gateway

門可羅雀(ㄇㄣˊ ㄎㄜˇ ㄌㄨㄛˊ ㄑㄩㄝˋ)
You can catch sparrows on the doorstep.—(said of a store, fallen family, etc.) where visitors are few and far between; deserted

門客(ㄇㄣˊ ㄎㄜˋ)
①(in ancient China) mentor-advisors fed by an influential person at his residence ②(Sung Dynasty) a family tutor

門口(ㄇㄣˊ ㄎㄡˇ)
a gate; a doorway; an entrance

門檻(ㄇㄣˊ ㄎㄢˇ)or 門限(ㄇㄣˊ ㄒㄧㄢˋ)
a threshold; a doorsill

門框(ㄇㄣˊ ㄎㄨㄤˋ)
a doorframe; a doorcase

門戶(ㄇㄣˊ ㄏㄨˋ)
①a family ②a strategic position ③a sect; a bloc; a gang ④a door

門戶開放(ㄇㄣˊ ㄏㄨˋ ㄎㄞ ㄈㄤˋ)
an open-door policy

門戶之見(ㄇㄣˊ ㄏㄨˋ ㄓ ㄐㄧㄢˋ)
prejudiced or biased views of a particular sect, bloc, gang, etc.; factional views; sectarianism

門環(ㄇㄣˊ ㄏㄨㄢˊ)
rings on the doors used as knockers

門戟(ㄇㄣˊ ㄐㄧˇ)
spears displayed at the door of a powerful family in ancient China

門階(ㄇㄣˊ ㄐㄧㄝ)
a doorstep

門臼(ㄇㄣˊ ㄐㄧㄡˋ)
a door socket

門禁(ㄇㄣˊ ㄐㄧㄣˋ)
a checkpoint at the gate

門禁森嚴(ㄇㄣˊ ㄐㄧㄣˋ ㄙㄣ ㄧㄢˊ)
The gate is strictly guarded.

門警(ㄇㄣˊ ㄐㄧㄥˇ)
a police guard at an entrance

門牆(ㄇㄣˊ ㄑㄧㄤˊ)

the invisible boundaries of a school or sect founded by the master

門下(ㄇㄣˊ ㄒㄧㄚˋ)
pupils or disciples

門診(ㄇㄣˊ ㄓㄣˇ)
to treat patients at the OPD; the outpatient service

門診部(ㄇㄣˊ ㄓㄣˇ ㄅㄨˋ)
the outpatient department (OPD)

門齒(ㄇㄣˊ ㄔˇ)or 門牙(ㄇㄣˊ ㄧˊ)
front teeth; incisors

門窗(ㄇㄣˊ ㄔㄨㄤ)
doors and windows: 將門窗關上。Latch the doors and windows.

門市(ㄇㄣˊ ㄕˋ)
to sell by retail; to sell over the counter

門市部(ㄇㄣˊ ㄕˋ ㄅㄨˋ)
a retail department; a sales department

門首(ㄇㄣˊ ㄕㄡˇ)
in front of the door

門扇(ㄇㄣˊ ㄕㄢˋ)
the wing of a door; a door leaf

門神(ㄇㄣˊ ㄕㄣˊ)
the door-god—said to guard the household against evil spirits

門生(ㄇㄣˊ ㄕㄥ)
pupils or disciples

門生故吏(ㄇㄣˊ ㄕㄥ ㄍㄨˋ ㄌㄧˋ)
pupils and former subordinates

門塾(ㄇㄣˊ ㄕㄨˊ)
a family school

門閂(ㄇㄣˊ ㄕㄨㄢ)or 門栓(ㄇㄣˊ ㄕㄨㄢ)or 門插管兒(ㄇㄣˊ ㄔㄚ ㄍㄨㄢˇㄦ)
a latch; a door bolt

門人(ㄇㄣˊ ㄖㄣˊ)
①pupils or disciples ②doorkeepers ③advisors and protégés of a family

門司(ㄇㄣˊ ㄙ)
Moji, a port city in Japan

門鎖(ㄇㄣˊ ㄙㄨㄛˇ)
a door catch; a door lock; a door latch

門外(ㄇㄣˊ ㄨㄞˋ)
outside the door: 他正站在門外。He was standing just outside the door.

門外漢(ㄇㄣˊ ㄨㄞˋ ㄏㄢˋ)

an outsider; the laity; a lay man

門衛(ㄇㄣˊ ㄨㄟˋ)
guards posted at the door or gateway

門望(ㄇㄣˊ ㄨㄤˋ)
family reputation or prestige

一畫

【閂】 6530
ㄕㄨㄢ   *shuān*   shuʌn
1. to fasten with a bolt or latch: 請把門閂好。Please bolt the door.
2. the latch of a door: 此門已上了門閂。The door is on the latch.

二畫

【閃】 6531
ㄕㄢˇ   *shǎn*   shʌn
1. to flash; a flash, as of lightning; a very brief glimpse: 閃電閃過天空。The lightning flashed across the sky.
2. to dodge; to evade; to avoid
3. to twist, strain or sprain (one's back, etc.): 他閃了腰。He sprained his back.
4. to cast away; to leave behind

閃避(ㄕㄢˇ ㄅㄧˋ)
to dodge quickly: 他很靈巧地閃避車子。He dodged the car cleverly.

閃電(ㄕㄢˇ ㄉㄧㄢˋ)
①to lighten: 遠方閃電又打雷。It thundered and lightened in the distance. ②lightning: 閃電之後常有雷聲。Lightning is usually followed by thunder. ③with lightning speed

閃電攻擊(ㄕㄢˇ ㄉㄧㄢˋ ㄍㄨㄥ ㄐㄧˊ)
a lightning attack

閃電戰(ㄕㄢˇ ㄉㄧㄢˋ ㄓㄢˋ)
a blitzkrieg; a blitz; a lightning war

閃躲(ㄕㄢˇ ㄉㄨㄛˇ)
to dodge; to evade

閃動(ㄕㄢˇ ㄉㄨㄥˋ)
to move fast; to shine or and on; to scintillate; to flash; to twinkle; to glisten: 他們的眼裏閃動着興奮的光芒 Their eyes glistened with

excitement.

閃亮兒 (ㄕㄢ ㄌㄧㄤ ㄦ)
(dialect) dawn

閃光 《ㄨㄤ》
①sparks; a flash ②to flash; to sparkle

閃光燈 (ㄕㄢ 《ㄨㄤ ㄉㄥ)
a flashlight; a blinker

閃開 (ㄎㄞ)
to dodge quickly; to avoid (a hit, collision, etc.)

閃景 (ㄕㄢ ㄐㄧㄥ)
(movie) a flash

閃現 (ㄕㄢ ㄒㄧㄢ)
a flicker; a flash; to flash before one: 我突然間靈感忽現。Suddenly I felt a flash of inspiration.

閃失
①errors or mistakes ②an accident

閃爍 (ㄕㄢ)
flickering; scintillating; to glint; to flash: 天空中電光閃閃。Lightning flashed in the sky.

閃閃發光 (ㄕㄢ ㄕㄢ ㄈㄚ 《ㄨㄤ)
sparkling; twinkling; scintillating

閃身 (ㄕㄢ ㄕㄣ)
①to dodge ②sideways: 他閃身進門。He walked sideways through the door.

閃爍
①to twinkle; twinkling; to scintillate: 燦爛的星斗在天空中閃爍。Brilliant stars glitter in the sky. ②vague; evasive

閃爍其詞 (ㄕㄢ ㄕㄨㄛ ㄑㄧ ㄘ)
to speak evasively; to use many evasions in one's speech; to make an ambiguous speech

閃族
the Semites, any of a group of peoples of southern Asia chiefly represented now by the Jews and the Arabs

閃腰 (ㄕㄢ ㄧㄠ)
to strain a muscle on the waist

閃耀 (ㄕㄢ ㄧㄠ)
to glint; to twinkle; to sparkle: 他的眼睛閃耀著光采。His eyes twinkled.

三畫

【閉】 6532
ㄅㄧ bih bì
1. to close; to shut: 他閉上眼睛。He closed his eyes.
2. (said of a conference, etc.) to conclude; to end
3. to block up; to stop; to obstruct: 他突然閉住氣。He suddenly stopped his breath.
4. to restrain

閉門不納 (ㄅㄧ ㄇㄣˊ ㄅㄨˋ ㄋㄚˋ)
to refuse to admit a caller

閉門天子 (ㄅㄧ ㄇㄣˊ ㄊㄧㄢ ㄗˇ)
(literally) a monarch behind closed doors—authority narrowly confined

閉門羹 (ㄅㄧ ㄇㄣˊ 《ㄥ)
to treat someone to a closed door; to close the door on; to turn a cold shoulder on; to refuse to see (a visitor): 她當面把他閉門羹。She shut the door in his face.

閉門却掃 (ㄅㄧ ㄇㄣˊ ㄑㄩㄝ ㄙㄠ)
to cut off communication with the outside world

閉門謝客 (ㄅㄧ ㄇㄣˊ ㄒㄧㄝˋ ㄎㄜˋ)
to refuse visitors; to lead a retiring life

閉門造車 (ㄅㄧ ㄇㄣˊ ㄗㄠˋ ㄔㄜ)
(literally) to make a cart in one's room (that won't go on the road)—to do something impractical, useless, or out of one's pure imagination

閉門思過 (ㄅㄧ ㄇㄣˊ ㄙㄨ 《ㄨㄛˋ)
to reflect on one's faults or misdeeds in private

閉門塞竇 (ㄅㄧ ㄇㄣˊ ㄙㄜˋ ㄉㄡˋ)
strongly guarded

閉幕 (ㄅㄧˋ)
(said of shows, meetings, etc.) to close or conclude: 大會已順利閉幕。The conference has closed successfully.

閉目養神 (ㄅㄧ ㄇㄨˋ ㄧㄤˇ ㄕㄣ)
to close the eyes and give the mind a brief rest

閉路電視 (ㄅㄧ ㄌㄨˋ ㄉㄧㄢˋ ㄕ)
closed-circuit television

閉果 (ㄅㄧ ㄍㄨㄛˇ)
indehiscent fruit

閉關時代 (ㄅㄧ 《ㄨㄢ ㄕ ㄉㄞˋ)
the period of isolationism

閉關自守 (ㄅㄧ 《ㄨㄢ ㄗ ㄕㄡˇ)

---

to adopt a policy of exclusion or isolation

閉口無言 (ㄅㄧ ㄎㄡˇ ㄨˊ ㄧㄢˊ)
to remain silent (in the face of overwhelming evidence pointing to one's guilt): 人臓俱獲使他閉口無言。He was caught together with the loot so he remained silent.

閉會 (ㄅㄧ ㄏㄨㄟˋ)
to close a meeting: 大會將在下月閉會。The conference will be closed next month.

閉結 (ㄅㄧ ㄐㄧㄝˊ)
constipation 亦作「便秘」: 此類食物會引起閉結。This kind of food is constipating.

閉經 (ㄅㄧ ㄐㄧㄥ)
an irregular stoppage of menses; amenorrhea

閉氣 (ㄅㄧ ㄑㄧˋ)
①to feel suffocated; unable to breathe ②to stop breathing—to die

閉歇 (ㄅㄧ ㄒㄧㄝ)
to close shop

閉蟄 (ㄅㄧ ㄓˊ)
the hibernation of animals or insects

閉塞 (ㄅㄧ ㄙㄜˋ)
①to block up; to obstruct ②backward ③hard to get to; inaccessible: 那個地區交通閉塞。That district was very hard to get to.

閉厄 (ㄅㄧˋ)
in a fix or spot; in a difficult position; in straits

閉月羞花 (ㄅㄧ ㄩㄝ ㄒㄧㄡ ㄏㄨㄚ)
(descriptive of a woman's beauty)that causes the moon to hide and put the blossoms to shame

四畫

【開】 6533
ㄎㄞ kai kāi
1. to open: 門打不開。The door won't open.
2. to drive: 他在學開車。He is learning to drive.
3. to begin; to start: 火車準時開了。The train started on time.
4. to reveal; to disclose
5. to state; to explain
6. to found; to expand

門
部

7. to eliminate
8. to divide into
9. to write down; to list
10. to undo; to unfold; to wind off: 張開你的雙臂。Unfold your arms.
11. a carat: 二十四開金 24-carat gold
12. to run (a shop or business)

開拔(ㄎㄞ ㄅㄚˊ)
(troops) to move; to set out

開包 or 開苞(ㄎㄞ ㄅㄠ)
(slang) to have sexual intercourse with a virgin

開辦(ㄎㄞ ㄅㄢˋ)
to start or open (a shop, school, business, etc.)

開辦費(ㄎㄞ ㄅㄢˋ ㄈㄟˋ)
funds needed for starting a school, new organization, etc.; organization cost

開本(ㄎㄞ ㄅㄣˇ)
a format; a book size: 四開本 a quarto 八開本 an octavo

開筆(ㄎㄞ ㄅㄧˇ)
(said of a learner) to begin to write the first composition, poem, etc.

開標(ㄎㄞ ㄅㄧㄠ)
to announce the result of bidding in an open tender; to open sealed tenders

開埠(ㄎㄞ ㄅㄨˋ)
to build a city; the founding of a city

開步走(ㄎㄞ ㄅㄨˋ ㄗㄡˇ)
Forward march!

開不動(ㄎㄞ ㄅㄨˋ ㄉㄨㄥˋ)
①(said of a door, lock, etc.) cannot be opened ②(said of a machine, car, etc.) cannot be started

開不開(ㄎㄞ ㄅㄨˋ ㄎㄞ)
①cannot be opened: 我開不開這扇門。I cannot open the door. ②Will you open it or not?

開砲(ㄎㄞ ㄆㄠˋ)
①(said of a fieldpiece, battery, or artillery) to open fire ②to launch a verbal attack

開盤(ㄎㄞ ㄆㄢˊ)
(said of a market) the opening quotation

開關(ㄎㄞ ㄍㄨㄢ)
to open up or develop (a new market, farm plot, etc.); to start: 他們開闢了一條航線。They opened an air route.

開闢市場(ㄎㄞ ㄆㄧˋ ㄕˋ ㄔㄤˇ)
to open up or develop a market

開票(ㄎㄞ ㄆㄧㄠˋ)
①to count ballots or votes ②to make out an invoice

開票所(ㄎㄞ ㄆㄧㄠˋ ㄙㄨㄛˇ)
a place for counting ballots

開瓶(ㄎㄞ ㄆㄧㄥˊ)
to open or uncork a bottle

開平方(ㄎㄞ ㄆㄧㄥˊ ㄈㄤ)
extraction of the square root

開普敦(ㄎㄞ ㄆㄨˇ ㄉㄨㄣ)
Capetown, South Africa

開麥拉(ㄎㄞ ㄇㄞˋ ㄌㄚ)
①a camera ②(a movie director's command) Camera!

開門(ㄎㄞ ㄇㄣˊ)
to open the door

開門見山(ㄎㄞ ㄇㄣˊ ㄐㄧㄢˋ ㄕㄢ)
to talk or write right to the point; to come straight to the point

開門七件事(ㄎㄞ ㄇㄣˊ ㄑㄧ ㄐㄧㄢˋ ㄕˋ)
daily necessities—fuel, rice, oil or fat, salt, sauce, vinegar, and tea

開門揖盜(ㄎㄞ ㄇㄣˊ ㄧ ㄉㄠˋ)
(literally) to open the door to a thief—to befriend a bad fellow and suffer the consequences

開蒙(ㄎㄞ ㄇㄥˊ)
to teach the beginner

開廟(ㄎㄞ ㄇㄧㄠˋ)
the date of a fair held in a Buddhist temple

開明(ㄎㄞ ㄇㄧㄥˊ)
enlightened; enlightenment; open-minded: 他是個思想開明的人。He is an open-minded man.

開幕(ㄎㄞ ㄇㄨˋ)
①to raise the curtain: 這齣戲已經開幕了。The curtain rose on the play. ②to open; to begin a meeting: 展覽會將於星期天開幕。The exhibition will open on Sunday.

開幕典禮(ㄎㄞ ㄇㄨˋ ㄉㄧㄢˇ ㄌㄧˇ)
inauguration; the opening ceremony 亦作「開幕式」

開發(ㄎㄞ ㄈㄚ)
to develop; developed; development (of natural resources, industry, etc.)

開發票(ㄎㄞ ㄈㄚ ㄆㄧㄠˋ)
to write an invoice

開發條(ㄎㄞ ㄈㄚ ㄊㄧㄠˊ)
to wind a spring

開發中國家(ㄎㄞ ㄈㄚ ㄓㄨㄥ ㄍㄨㄛˊ ㄐㄧㄚ)
a developing country

開飛機(ㄎㄞ ㄈㄟ ㄐㄧ)
to pilot a plane

開飯(ㄎㄞ ㄈㄢˋ)
to prepare food for a meal; to serve a meal: 開飯了！The meal's ready!

開方(ㄎㄞ ㄈㄤ)
①(mathematics) evolution ②name of a prince in the Epoch of Spring and Autumn

開方子(ㄎㄞ ㄈㄤ ㄗ)
to write a prescription; to prescribe for

開放(ㄎㄞ ㄈㄤˋ)
①to open (to trade, traffic, etc.); to be open ②to liberalize or hand over a government monopoly to private operations ③to lift a ban ④to come into bloom: 花都開放了。The flowers were all open.

開封(ㄎㄞ ㄈㄥ)
①Kaifeng, capital city of Honan Province ②to break or open a seal

開赴(ㄎㄞ ㄈㄨˋ)
to march to; to be bound for

開刀(ㄎㄞ ㄉㄠ)
①to operate (on a patient); an operation 亦作「手術」: 醫生爲傷者開刀。The doctor operated on the injured man. ②to punish: 先拿他開刀。He is the first to be punished. ③to behead

開導(ㄎㄞ ㄉㄠˇ)
to educate and enlighten; to explain and make (someone) understand

開道(ㄎㄞ ㄉㄠˋ)
(in ancient China) to clear the way for an important official

開倒車(ㄎㄞ ㄉㄠˋ ㄔㄜ)
①to back a car, train, etc.

②to be old-fashioned or anachronistic; to turn back the clock; to retrograde

開單子(ㄎㄞ ㄉㄢ ˙ㄗ)
①to write a bill, etc. ②to list expenditures or items needed

開襠褲(ㄎㄞ ㄉㄤ ㄎㄨˋ)
a pair of bottomless trousers for babies; a pair of open-bottomed pants for children

開燈(ㄎㄞ ㄉㄥ)
to turn on the light

開弔(ㄎㄞ ㄉㄧㄠˋ)
to hold a memorial service or funeral rites

開店(ㄎㄞ ㄉㄧㄢˋ)
to open a shop; to run a store

開端(ㄎㄞ ㄉㄨㄢ)
the beginning or start: 萬物皆有開端。 Everything has a beginning.

開冬(ㄎㄞ ㄉㄨㄥ)
early winter

開動(ㄎㄞ ㄉㄨㄥˋ)
①to start; to set in motion: 他開動引擎。 He started the engine. ②to be on the move

開頭(ㄎㄞ ㄊㄡˊ)
in the beginning; from the start

開談判(ㄎㄞ ㄊㄢˊ ㄆㄢˋ)
to negotiate; to start negotiations

開天闢地(ㄎㄞ ㄊㄧㄢ ㄆㄧˋ ㄉㄧˋ)
①creation of the world ②to open or develop

開天窗(ㄎㄞ ㄊㄧㄢ ㄔㄨㄤ)
①to open up a skylight ②open space in a newspaper (as when the original story has been censored by the authorities) ③(comically) inflammation or erosion of the nosebone due to syphilitic infection

開庭(ㄎㄞ ㄊㄧㄥˊ)
to start a court trial; to hold a court session

開脫(ㄎㄞ ㄊㄨㄛ)
to extricate a person from certain involvements (usually criminal); to vindicate

開拓(ㄎㄞ ㄊㄨㄛˋ)
to open up, enlarge or expand (new frontiers, territory, etc.): 他們為定居開拓新土地。 They opened new land for settlement.

開通(ㄎㄞ ㄊㄨㄥ)
①open-minded; modern-minded; liberal; enlightened; progressive ②to do away with all obstructions; to be opened; to be dredged

開年(ㄎㄞ ㄋㄧㄢˊ)or開歲(ㄎㄞ ㄙㄨㄟˋ)
at the beginning of a year

開朗(ㄎㄞ ㄌㄤˇ)
①to clear up, as weather ②open and clear; broad-minded and outspoken: 她的性情開朗。 She is of a broad-minded and outspoken disposition.

開例(ㄎㄞ ㄌㄧˋ)
to set a precedent

開立方(ㄎㄞ ㄌㄧˋ ㄈㄤ)
extraction of a cubic root

開列(ㄎㄞ ㄌㄧㄝˋ)
to list; to make a list of

開臉(ㄎㄞ ㄌㄧㄢˇ)
(said of a girl on the eve of marriage) to remove the fine hair on the face and neck

開路(ㄎㄞ ㄌㄨˋ)
to pioneer; to cut the way, as in a jungle

開路先鋒(ㄎㄞ ㄌㄨˋ ㄒㄧㄢ ㄈㄥ)
a pioneer; a trailblazer; to blaze a trail

開鑼(ㄎㄞ ㄌㄨㄛˊ)
(in Chinese opera) to begin a performance

開羅(ㄎㄞ ㄌㄨㄛˊ)
Cairo, capital of Egypt

開羅宣言(ㄎㄞ ㄌㄨㄛˊ ㄒㄩㄢ ㄧㄢˊ)
the Cairo Declaration, signed by China, Great Britain and the United States in 1943

開革(ㄎㄞ ㄍㄜˊ)
to dismiss; to fire; dismissal

開國(ㄎㄞ ㄍㄨㄛˊ)
to found a country or state

開國紀念日(ㄎㄞ ㄍㄨㄛˊ ㄐㄧˋ ㄋㄧㄢˋ ㄖˋ)
the founding anniversary of a nation; the national day

開國元勳(ㄎㄞ ㄍㄨㄛˊ ㄩㄢˊ ㄒㄩㄣ)
elder statesmen or generals who participated in the founding of a new nation or dynasty

開關(ㄎㄞ ㄍㄨㄢ)
①a switch or similar device to put on or shut off an electric current, etc. ②to open the city gate ③to open and close

開棺驗屍(ㄎㄞ ㄍㄨㄢ ㄧㄢˋ ㄕ)
to open the coffin and examine the corpse therein

開館子(ㄎㄞ ㄍㄨㄢˇ ˙ㄗ)
to run a restaurant

開罐器(ㄎㄞ ㄍㄨㄢˋ ㄑㄧˋ)
a can opener

開光(ㄎㄞ ㄍㄨㄤ)
to enshrine a Buddha statue

開弓(ㄎㄞ ㄍㄨㄥ)
to pull or draw a bow

開工(ㄎㄞ ㄍㄨㄥ)
to go into operation; to start work; to begin a building project

開科取士(ㄎㄞ ㄎㄜ ㄑㄩˇ ㄕˋ)
to enlist talents through the old civil service examination system

開課(ㄎㄞ ㄎㄜˋ)
①to lecture on a new subject in the curriculum ②to start a class at the beginning of a new semester

開開玩笑(ㄎㄞ ㄎㄞ ㄨㄢˊ ㄒㄧㄠˋ)
to have a little fun at someone; to make fun of

開口(ㄎㄞ ㄎㄡˇ)
①to open one's mouth; to speak: 他覺得此事難以開口。 He found it difficult to speak of the matter. ②to laugh ③to sharpen the edge of a new blade—to get it ready for cutting ④to cut an opening

開口閉口(ㄎㄞ ㄎㄡˇ ㄅㄧˋ ㄎㄡˇ)
to say the same thing again and again

開墾(ㄎㄞ ㄎㄣˇ)
to open up wasteland for farming

開闊(ㄎㄞ ㄎㄨㄛˋ)
①spacious; open; wide ②tolerant; broad-minded: 他的心胸開闊。 He is broad-minded. ③to widen; to broaden: 旅行開闊了他的眼界。 Travel broadened his outlook.

開快車(ㄎㄞ ㄎㄨㄞˋ ㄔㄜ)

門
部

（門部）

①(said of a car, etc.) to speed; speeding; 他因開快車而被捕。He was arrested for speeding. ②to hasten up with one's work; to catch up with one's working schedule

開礦(ㄎㄞ ㄎㄨㄤ)
to mine; to excavate a mine

開航(ㄎㄞ ㄏㄤ)
①to open up for navigation: 這條運河已經開航了。The canal is open for navigation. ②to set sail

開戶(ㄎㄞ ㄏㄨ)
to open a bank account

開花(ㄎㄞ ㄏㄨㄚ)
①to flower; to blossom: 有些玫瑰早開花。Some roses flower early. ②(said of shells) to burst: 炸彈開花。The bomb burst.

開花彈(ㄎㄞ ㄏㄨㄚ ㄉㄢ)
a fragmentation shell; an artillery shell

開花結果(ㄎㄞ ㄏㄨㄚ ㄐㄧㄝ ㄍㄨㄛ)
to blossom and bear fruit —to yield positive results

開花賬(ㄎㄞ ㄏㄨㄚ ㄓㄤ)
to make a false report or (an) expenditure

開化(ㄎㄞ ㄏㄨㄚ)
civilized

開化史(ㄎㄞ ㄏㄨㄚ ㄕ)
a history recording the development of human civilization in its proper sequence

開話匣子(ㄎㄞ ㄏㄨㄚ ㄒㄧㄚ˙ㄗ)
to keep on talking without stop, like starting a talking machine

開火(ㄎㄞ ㄏㄨㄛ)
to open fire; to engage in battle

開伙(ㄎㄞ ㄏㄨㄛ)
to cook a meal

開豁(ㄎㄞ ㄏㄨㄛ)
①carefree; without a worry ②straightforward; frank

開懷(ㄎㄞ ㄏㄨㄞ)
joyful; jubilant; happy; to one's heart's content: 他開懷暢飲。He drinks to his heart's content.

開會(ㄎㄞ ㄏㄨㄟ)
to hold a meeting; to attend a meeting or conference: 他在開會嗎? Is he at the meet-

ing?

開葷(ㄎㄞ ㄏㄨㄣ)
(said of vegetarians or people fasting) to shift to meat-eating

開荒(ㄎㄞ ㄏㄨㄤ)
to cultivate virgin land

開黃腔(ㄎㄞ ㄏㄨㄤ ㄑㄧㄤ)
(informal) to lace one's utterance with reference to sex; to make lewd utterances

開架(ㄎㄞ ㄐㄧㄚ)
open-shelf

開價(ㄎㄞ ㄐㄧㄚ)
to ask for a price; to quote; the price quoted

開解(ㄎㄞ ㄐㄧㄝ)
to advise and persuade; to explain and make (someone) understand

開戒(ㄎㄞ ㄐㄧㄝ)
to break one's resolution; to break one's abstinence (from smoking, drinking, etc.)

開交(ㄎㄞ ㄐㄧㄠ)
an end or solution; to settle dispute: 他們開得不可開交。They got into a hot dispute.

開禁(ㄎㄞ ㄐㄧㄣ)
to rescind a prohibition

開疆(ㄎㄞ ㄐㄧㄤ)
to expand national boundaries

開獎(ㄎㄞ ㄐㄧㄤ)
to draw the winning numbers of a lottery

開講(ㄎㄞ ㄐㄧㄤ)
to begin a speech or lecture; to begin telling a story

開井(ㄎㄞ ㄐㄧㄥ)
to dig or drill a well

開卷有益(ㄎㄞ ㄐㄩㄢ ㄧㄡˇ ㄧˋ)
(literally) Whenever you open a book, you'll be benefited.—Reading is always beneficial (or profitable).

開濬(ㄎㄞ ㄐㄩㄣ)
to open up, dig or dredge a waterway

開啟(ㄎㄞ ㄑㄧˇ)
to open: 這門可以自動開啟。This door can open automatically.

開竅(ㄎㄞ ㄑㄧㄠ)

①to open one's eyes to; to have one's ideas straightened out; to understand ②(said of a girl) to start getting sex-conscious; to reach puberty

開球(ㄎㄞ ㄑㄧㄡ)
to kick, throw or toss the ball to start a game

開腔(ㄎㄞ ㄑㄧㄤ)
to talk; to speak out; to open one's mouth

開槍(ㄎㄞ ㄑㄧㄤ)
to shoot; to fire: 他朝著目標開槍射擊。He shot at a target.

開缺(ㄎㄞ ㄑㄩㄝ)
to suspend an official from his post because of his faults or death, etc.

開小差(ㄎㄞ ㄒㄧㄠˇ ㄔㄞ)
to desert one's unit or post; desertion

開銷 or 開消(ㄎㄞ ㄒㄧㄠ)
①expenses; (an) expenditure; an account of expenses: 你必須節省開銷。You must cut down your expenses. ②to pay expenses

開心(ㄎㄞ ㄒㄧㄣ)
①happy; to have a grand time ②to play a joke on; to amuse oneself at somebody's expense; to make fun of someone: 別尋他開心了。Do not amuse yourself at his expense. ③to be sincere to others ④to enlighten

開心果(ㄎㄞ ㄒㄧㄣ ㄍㄨㄛˇ)
a pistachio

開釁(ㄎㄞ ㄒㄧㄣˋ)
to start a trouble; to provoke

開學(ㄎㄞ ㄒㄩㄝ)
The school starts. 學校甚麼時候開學? When does the school start?

開學典禮(ㄎㄞ ㄒㄩㄝ ㄉㄧㄢˇ ㄌㄧˇ)
a ceremony held to signal the beginning of a school semester

開支(ㄎㄞ ㄓ)
expenses; (an) expenditure: 他們節省開支。They retrench their expenses.

開支票(ㄎㄞ ㄓ ㄆㄧㄠˋ)
to write a check

開齋(ㄎㄞ ㄓㄞ)
(said of a Buddhist follower) to discontinue a vegetarian diet; to break the fast

開展(ㄎㄞ ㄓㄢ)
to expand; to spread out; to develop: 他正努力開展業務。 He is trying to expand his business.

開戰(ㄎㄞ ㄓㄢ)
to declare war; to do battle

開張(ㄎㄞ ㄓㄤ)
①(said of a store) to open a shop; to start doing a business ②to expand, spread out or develop

開張大吉(ㄎㄞ ㄓㄤ ㄉㄚ ㄐㄧ)
the auspicious beginning of a new enterprise (an expression used when one opens a new shop or factory)

開眼(ㄎㄞ)
to bill (one) for things purchased.

開徵 or 開徵(ㄎㄞ ㄓㄥ)
to start collecting taxes

開茶館(ㄎㄞ ㄔㄚ ㄍㄨㄢ)
to run a tea shop

開衩(ㄎㄞ ㄔㄚ)
to open a slit in a dress

開車(ㄎㄞ ㄔㄜ)
to drive a car, or start a train: 我開車送你去車站。 I drive you to the station.

開場(ㄎㄞ ㄔㄤ)
the beginning of a show or anything

開場白(ㄎㄞ ㄔㄤ ㄅㄞ)
a prologue; a speech that opens a show or a meeting; the opening words; a preface, foreword, preamble in the first issue of a magazine, paper, report, etc.

開城(ㄎㄞ ㄔㄥ)
to open the city gates

開誠布公(ㄎㄞ ㄔㄥ ㄅㄨ ㄍㄨㄥ)
to wear one's heart on one's sleeve; to be honest, frank, sincere and just; to speak frankly and sincerely

開除(ㄎㄞ ㄔㄨ)
to dismiss; to fire; to expel; dishonorable discharge: 他被學校開除了。 He was expelled from school.

開船(ㄎㄞ ㄔㄨㄢ)

to set sail; to weigh anchor

開春(ㄎㄞ ㄔㄨㄣ)
in early spring

開創(ㄎㄞ ㄔㄨㄤ)
to found (a nation, big business, etc.); to start; to initiate: 他們開創一項新事業。 They founded a new business.

開始(ㄎㄞ ㄕ)
to begin; to commence; to start; the beginning; the outset; the start: 學校九點開始上課。 School begins (or starts) at nine.

開市(ㄎㄞ ㄕ)
to start trading; to open the market

開釋(ㄎㄞ ㄕ)
to release (a prisoner, etc.); to set free

開設(ㄎㄞ ㄕㄜ)
to establish; to set up: 他最近開設了一家新店舖。 He has set up a new store recently.

開山祖師(ㄎㄞ ㄕㄢ ㄗㄨ ㄕ)
the founder of a religion or a sect of religion (now used figuratively in most cases)

開曙(ㄎㄞ ㄕㄨ)
to dawn; the beginning of a new day

開水(ㄎㄞ ㄕㄨㄟ)
boiled water

開鑿(ㄎㄞ ㄗㄠ)
to dig (a well, canal, etc.); to drill

開足馬力(ㄎㄞ ㄗㄨ ㄇㄚ ㄌㄧ)
to put into high gear; to go full steam ahead; to go forward at full speed; to open the throttle

開罪(ㄎㄞ ㄗㄨㄟ)
to offend another with what one says, writes or does: 我又怎麼開罪人了？ In what way have I offended?

開宗明義(ㄎㄞ ㄗㄨㄥ ㄇㄧㄥ ㄧ)
an outline delineating the purpose, objectives, means of achievement, etc. of an undertaking or an endeavor (originally, the title of the first chapter of the Canon of Filial Piety 孝經)

開採(ㄎㄞ ㄘㄞ)
to excavate; to mine

開鎖(ㄎㄞ ㄙㄨㄛ)
to pick a lock; to unlock

開恩(ㄎㄞ ㄣ)
to have mercy on; to grant special favor to

開業(ㄎㄞ ㄧㄝ)
to start doing business; to start practicing (law, medicine, etc.): 他已經開業行醫了。 He has practiced medicine.

開夜車(ㄎㄞ ㄧㄝ ㄔㄜ)
to burn the midnight oil; to work late into the night; to sit up late at night

開誘(ㄎㄞ ㄧㄡ)
to teach step by step; to teach by stimulating the learner's interest in the subject taught

開言(ㄎㄞ ㄧㄢ)
to speak; to talk

開筵(ㄎㄞ ㄧㄢ)
to give a feast; to throw a banquet

開顏(ㄎㄞ ㄧㄢ)
to smile; to laugh; to beam

開演(ㄎㄞ ㄧㄢ)
to start showing (a picture, etc.);(said of a play, movie, etc.)to begin; to start performing

開眼(ㄎㄞ ㄧㄢ)
to add to one's experience; to see new things; to extend the mental horizon

開眼界(ㄎㄞ ㄧㄢ ㄐㄧㄝ)
to expand one's experience and horizon

開印(ㄎㄞ ㄧㄣ)
(Ching Dynasty) to resume using the official seal after the New Year holidays (around the 15th of the first month)

開陽(ㄎㄞ ㄧㄤ)
①dried shrimp meat ②(astronomy) Mizar

開洋葷(ㄎㄞ ㄧㄤ ㄏㄨㄣ)
(informal) to have a delightful new experience; to see, eat or do something delightful for the first time

開映(ㄎㄞ ㄧㄥ)
to show motion pictures

開挖(ㄎㄞ ㄨㄚ)
to excavate

開外(ㄎㄞ ㄨㄞ)

（門部）

【門部】

upwards of; over or more than: 她看起來四十開外。She looks over forty.

開胃 (ㄎㄞ ㄨㄟˋ)
① appetizing; to whet or stimulate one's appetite ② to make fun of; to tease: 別拿他開胃。Do not make fun of him.

開玩笑 (ㄎㄞ ㄨㄢˊ ㄒㄧㄠˋ)
to play a joke; to joke: 你一定是開玩笑的。You must be joking (or kidding).

開往 (ㄎㄞ ㄨㄤˇ)
① (said of a train, ship, etc.) to leave for; to be bound for ② (said of troops, etc.) to move; to set out

開源節流 (ㄎㄞ ㄩㄢˊ ㄐㄧㄝˊ ㄌㄧㄡˊ)
to open more sources of income and cut down expenses

開雲見日 (ㄎㄞ ㄩㄣˊ ㄐㄧㄢˋ ㄖˋ)
from dark to light; from obscurity to clarity

【間】 6534
1. ㄐㄧㄢ jiān
1. between two things; the space between; among
2. a numerical adjunct for rooms
3. within a definite time or space

間關 (ㄐㄧㄢ ㄍㄨㄢ)
① the sound of rolling carts ② the sound of birds chirping ③ (said of roads or writings) full of twists and turns

間架 (ㄐㄧㄢ ㄐㄧㄚˋ)
the framework of a house

【間】 6534
2. (閒) ㄐㄧㄢˋ jiann jiàn
1. a crevice; a leak; space in between
2. to divide; a division of a house; to separate
3. to put a space between; to drive a wedge between; to part friends
4. to change; to substitute
5. to block up
6. (said of illness) to get a little better
7. occasionally

間壁 (ㄐㄧㄢˋ ㄅㄧˋ)
on the other side of the wall; next door; the neighbor

間不容髮 (ㄐㄧㄢˋ ㄅㄨˋ ㄖㄨㄥˊ ㄈㄚˇ)
① very close; imminent ② precarious; by a hair's breadth; not a hair's breadth in between—The situation is extremely critical.

間不容息 (ㄐㄧㄢˋ ㄅㄨˋ ㄖㄨㄥˊ ㄒㄧˊ)
a very short while; imminent

間道 (ㄐㄧㄢˋ ㄉㄠˋ)
a trail; an out-of-the-way path; a short cut

間諜 (ㄐㄧㄢˋ ㄉㄧㄝˊ)
a spy; a secret agent

間斷 (ㄐㄧㄢˋ ㄉㄨㄢˋ)
suspended; interrupted

間隔 (ㄐㄧㄢˋ ㄍㄜˊ)
① separated; spaced at intervals ② distance; intervals; space in between: 這一行字間隔勻整。The words on this line are evenly spaced.

間闊 (ㄐㄧㄢˋ ㄎㄨㄛˋ)
to have been separated for a long time

間或 (ㄐㄧㄢˋ ㄏㄨㄛˋ)
occasional(ly): 他間或寫寫信。He writes occasionally.

間接 (ㄐㄧㄢˋ ㄐㄧㄝˊ)
indirect; indirectly; vicariously: 那是間接答覆。It's an indirect answer.

間接貿易 (ㄐㄧㄢˋ ㄐㄧㄝˊ ㄇㄠˋ ㄧˋ)
indirect trade

間接民權 (ㄐㄧㄢˋ ㄐㄧㄝˊ ㄇㄧㄣˊ ㄑㄩㄢˊ)
civil rights that are exercised through representatives

間接滙兌 (ㄐㄧㄢˋ ㄐㄧㄝˊ ㄏㄨㄟˊ ㄉㄨㄟˋ)
(accounting) indirect exchange

間接侵略 (ㄐㄧㄢˋ ㄐㄧㄝˊ ㄑㄧㄣ ㄌㄩㄝˋ)
indirect aggression

間接行動 (ㄐㄧㄢˋ ㄐㄧㄝˊ ㄒㄧㄥˊ ㄉㄨㄥˋ)
indirect action

間接選舉 (ㄐㄧㄢˋ ㄐㄧㄝˊ ㄒㄩㄢˇ ㄐㄩˇ)
indirect election; election by delegates

間接證據 (ㄐㄧㄢˋ ㄐㄧㄝˊ ㄓㄥˋ ㄐㄩˋ)
indirect evidence

間接稅 (ㄐㄧㄢˋ ㄐㄧㄝˊ ㄕㄨㄟˋ)
indirect tax or taxation (as commodity tax)

間隙 (ㄐㄧㄢˋ ㄒㄧˋ)
① a crevice; a space between; an interval ② animosity; a grudge; discord ③ (machinery) clearance

間歇 (ㄐㄧㄢˋ ㄒㄧㄝˊ)
① intermittent; sporadic; intermittently; sporadically: 熱病間歇地發生。The fever intermits. ② short intervals or stops, a pause

間歇泉 (ㄐㄧㄢˋ ㄒㄧㄝˊ ㄑㄩㄢˊ)
an intermittent spring; a geyser

間歇熱 (ㄐㄧㄢˋ ㄒㄧㄝˊ ㄖㄜˋ)
intermittent fever, as in the case of malaria

間歇遺傳 (ㄐㄧㄢˋ ㄒㄧㄝˊ ㄒㄧ ㄔㄨㄢˊ)
heredity occurring in every other generation; atavism

間出 (ㄐㄧㄢˋ ㄔㄨ)
to find time for a private visit; to take a personal tour

間日 (ㄐㄧㄢˋ ㄖˋ)
every other day

間雜 (ㄐㄧㄢˋ ㄗㄚˊ)
to mix; not continuous

間奏曲 (ㄐㄧㄢˋ ㄗㄡˋ ㄑㄩˇ)
(music) an intermezzo

間作 (ㄐㄧㄢˋ ㄗㄨㄛˋ)
intercropping

間色 (ㄐㄧㄢˋ ㄙㄜˋ)
assorted colors; multicolored

【閎】 6535
ㄏㄨㄥˊ horng hóng
1. a gate or barrier across a lane
2. big; large
3. spacious inside
4. a Chinese family name

閎達 or 宏達 (ㄏㄨㄥˊ ㄉㄚˊ)
intelligent and broad-minded

閎中肆外 (ㄏㄨㄥˊ ㄓㄨㄥ ㄙˋ ㄨㄞˋ)
(said of a piece of writing) rich in substance and graceful in style

閎澤 (ㄏㄨㄥˊ ㄗㄜˊ)
a big lake

閎衍 (ㄏㄨㄥˊ ㄧㄢˇ)
a beautiful writing style

【閏】 6536
ㄖㄨㄣˋ ruenn rùn
1. with surplus or leftover
2. usurped; deputy or substitute
3. extra, inserted between others, as a day, or a month; to intercalate

閏年 (ㄖㄨㄣˋ ㄋㄧㄢˊ)
a leap year; an intercalary year: 一九八四年是個閏年。

1984 was a leap year.

閏日(ㄖㄨㄣˋ ㄖ˙)
February 29, the intercalary day; the leap day

閏音(ㄖㄨㄣˋ ㄧㄣ)
sounds in local dialects not found in the Mandarin pronunciation

閏音字母(ㄖㄨㄣˋ ㄧㄣ ㄗˋㄇㄨˇ)
a vowel used in pronouncing certain words peculiar to a local dialect

閏位(ㄖㄨㄣˋ ㄨㄟˋ)
an imperial reign not in the direct or conventional line of succession, as in the case of usurpation

閏月(ㄖㄨㄣˋ ㄩㄝˋ)
an intercalary moon or month—an extra month inserted seven times in 19 years to make for the difference between the solar and the lunar years

【閑】 6537
ㄒㄧㄢˊ shyan xián

1. a fence; a bar; a barrier
2. to defend
3. big
4. familiar with; accustomed to; well-versed in
5. same as 閒—leisure
6. laws or regulations
7. a stable

閑媚(ㄒㄧㄢˊ ㄇㄟˋ)
(said of a woman) quiet and charming

閑話牙(ㄒㄧㄢˊ ㄏㄨㄚ ㄧˊ)
leisure talks or conversation about nothing in particular

閑漢 or 閒漢(ㄒㄧㄢˊ ㄏㄢˋ)
a bum; a vagrant; an idler

閑花野草(ㄒㄧㄢˊ ㄏㄨㄚ ㄧㄝˇ ㄘㄠˇ)
disreputable women; promiscuous women

閑靜(ㄒㄧㄢˊ ㄐㄧㄥˋ)
peaceful and calm in mind —without desires

閑居(ㄒㄧㄢˊ ㄐㄩ)
to lead a quiet life; to lead a retired life

閑習(ㄒㄧㄢˊ ㄒㄧˊ)
to be well versed in or familiar with

閑暇 or 閒暇(ㄒㄧㄢˊ ㄒㄧㄚˊ)
leisure; spare time

閑常(ㄒㄧㄢˊ ㄔㄤˊ)

ordinary; usually

閒書 or 閑書(ㄒㄧㄢˊ ㄕㄨ)
books for killing time, as novels, etc.

閑宴(ㄒㄧㄢˊ ㄧㄢˋ)or 閑玩(ㄒㄧㄢˊ ㄨㄢˊ)
to kill time; to amuse oneself

【閒】 6538
1. ㄒㄧˊ shyan
xián
1. quiet; tranquil; calm; placid
2. leisure; spare time

閒步(ㄒㄧㄢˊ ㄅㄨˋ)
to stroll without a destination; to roam at leisure: 他在街上閒步。He was roaming about the streets.

閒不住(ㄒㄧㄢˊ ㄅㄨˋ ㄓㄨˋ)
①to have to keep oneself busy; unable to remain idle: 我閒不住. I always kept myself busy. ②to have no worry about unemployment

閒篇兒(ㄒㄧㄢˊ ㄆㄧㄢ ㄦ)
random talk or conversation; idle talk

閒民(ㄒㄧㄢˊ ㄇㄧㄣˊ)
the unemployed

閒房(ㄒㄧㄢˊ ㄈㄤˊ)
a vacant house or room

閒蕩(ㄒㄧㄢˊ ㄉㄤˋ)
to saunter; to stroll; to loaf

閒地(ㄒㄧㄢˊ ㄉㄧˋ)
①retirement; a position without responsibility; a sinecure ②vacant land; idle land

閒談(ㄒㄧㄢˊ ㄊㄢˊ)
idle talk; to chat: 他與父親閒談。He chatted with his father.

閒聊(ㄒㄧㄢˊ ㄌㄧㄠˊ)
①to chat; to gossip ②a gossip; a chat

閒官(ㄒㄧㄢˊ ㄍㄨㄢ)
an official with very light duties; one who holds a sinecure position

閒逛(ㄒㄧㄢˊ ㄍㄨㄤˋ)
to saunter; to stroll: 他在市街上閒逛. He strolled about the streets.

閒工夫(ㄒㄧㄢˊ ㄍㄨㄥ·ㄈㄨ)
leisure; spare time

閒磕打牙(ㄒㄧㄢˊ ㄎㄜ ㄉㄚˇ ㄧˊ)or 閒磕牙(ㄒㄧㄢˊ ㄎㄜ ㄧˊ)

to chat without a purpose

閒空兒(ㄒㄧㄢˊ ㄎㄨㄥˋㄦ)
spare time; leisure: 我閒空兒時作畫。I paint at my leisure.

閒漢(ㄒㄧㄢˊ ㄏㄢˋ)
a bum; a vagrant; a jobless person

閒話(ㄒㄧㄢˊ ㄏㄨㄚˋ)
①random or idle talk; gossip:他愛說人閒話。He's fond of gossip. ②complaint ③to talk casually about; to chat about

閒居(ㄒㄧㄢˊ ㄐㄩ)
to lead an idle, leisure, quiet or placid life: 她喜歡閒居獨處。She enjoys living idly and alone.

閒氣(ㄒㄧㄢˊ ㄑㄧˋ)
anger caused by something insignificant; needless anger

閒錢(ㄒㄧㄢˊ ㄑㄧㄢˊ)
spare money; idle money

閒情逸致(ㄒㄧㄢˊ ㄑㄧㄥˊ ㄧˋ ㄓˋ)
a peaceful and comfortable mood

閒暇(ㄒㄧㄢˊ ㄒㄧㄚˊ)
unoccupied; leisure

閒心(ㄒㄧㄢˊ ㄒㄧㄣ)
a peaceful or easy mood

閒置(ㄒㄧㄢˊ ㄓˋ)
to leave unused; to let something lie idle; to set aside

閒扯(ㄒㄧㄢˊ ㄔㄜˇ)
to chat; to engage in chit-chat

閒時(ㄒㄧㄢˊ ㄕˊ)
spare time; leisure

閒事(ㄒㄧㄢˊ ㄕˋ)
matters not of one's concern; others' business; matters one has nothing to do with: 別管閒事! Mind your own business.

閒書(ㄒㄧㄢˊ ㄕㄨ)
books for killing time, as novels

閒人(ㄒㄧㄢˊ ㄖㄣˊ)
①idlers; persons with nothing to do ②persons not concerned

閒人免進(ㄒㄧㄢˊ ㄖㄣˊ ㄇㄧㄢˇ ㄐㄧㄣˋ)
Out of bounds to non-authorized personnel! 或 No admittance! 或 Admittance

（門部）

（門部）

to staff only.

閒冗（ㄒㄧㄢ ㄖㄨㄥˇ）
officials with light duties; supernumeraries

閒雜（ㄒㄧㄢ ㄗㄚˊ）
without fixed duties

閒雜人等（ㄒㄧㄢ ㄗㄚˊ ㄖㄣˊ ㄉㄥˇ）
①loafers; idlers ②unconcerned persons

閒在（ㄒㄧㄢ ㄗㄞˋ）
quiet and comfortable; idle

閒坐（ㄒㄧㄢ ㄗㄨㄛˋ）
to sit idle: 他閒坐在椅子上。
He sat idle on a chair.

閒散（ㄒㄧㄢ ㄙㄢˇ）
with no important tasks or duties at hand; with nothing to do; unoccupied

閒言（ㄒㄧㄢ ㄧㄢˊ）
①gossip; idle talk ②balderdash

閒言閒語（ㄒㄧㄢ ㄧㄢˊ ㄒㄧㄢ ㄩˇ）
sarcastic remarks or complaints; gossips

閒言少敍（ㄒㄧㄢ ㄧㄢˊ ㄕㄠˇ ㄒㄩˋ）
to leave out the nonessentials in narration; to make a long story short

閒宴 or 閒燕（ㄒㄧㄢ ㄧㄢˋ）
peace and quiet

閒屋子（ㄒㄧㄢ ㄨ ˙ㄗ）
an unoccupied house

閒語（ㄒㄧㄢ ㄩˇ）
①a personal or confidential talk ②sarcastic remarks or complaints; gossips

閒月（ㄒㄧㄢ ㄩㄝˋ）
(in a rural community) the leisure months; the time when farmers have little to do; the period between harvest and sowing

閒雲野鶴（ㄒㄧㄢ ㄩㄣˊ ㄧㄝˇ ㄏㄜˋ）
①as free as a bird; carefree ②the quietness and comfortableness of a secluded life

【聞】 6538
2. ㄐㄧㄢ jian jiān
same as 間（ㄐㄧㄢ）

【聞】 6538
3. ㄐㄧㄢˋ jiann jiàn
same as 間（ㄐㄧㄢˋ）—to separate

閒隔（ㄐㄧㄢˋ ㄍㄜˊ）
to be separated in time and space

【閔】 6539
ㄇㄧㄣˇ miin mǐn
1. to mourn; to pity; to commiserate with; to condole with
2. to urge; to encourage
3. trouble; distress
4. to be grieved
5. a Chinese family name

閔閔（ㄇㄧㄣˇ ㄇㄧㄣˇ）
①worried and scared ②grieved; sad

閔凶（ㄇㄧㄣˇ ㄒㄩㄥ）
①sorrow; affliction ②the death of one's parents

五畫

【閘】 6540
ㄓㄚˊ jar zhá
1. a floodgate; a lock; a sluice
2. a brake; a device on a vehicle for halting its motion
3. a switch or similar devices

閘北（ㄓㄚˊ ㄅㄟˇ）
the northwest portion of Shanghai, bordering on the former international settlement

閘板（ㄓㄚˊ ㄅㄢˇ）
a sluice

閘門（ㄓㄚˊ ㄇㄣˊ）
a floodgate

閘口（ㄓㄚˊ ㄎㄡˇ）
a floodgate; a sluice

【閟】 6541
ㄅㄧˋ bih bì
1. to close the door
2. to shut; to repress
3. deep; obscure; solemn

六畫

【閣】 6542
ㄍㄜˊ ger gé
1. a room; a chamber; a pavilion
2. an attic; a place for storing something not frequently in use
3. a cabinet: 他們正在組閣當中。They're forming a cabinet.
4. a boudoir
5. a Chinese family name

閣道（ㄍㄜˊ ㄉㄠˋ）
①a path paved with timber or planks on which vehicles can move smoothly ②name

---

of a constellation

閣老（ㄍㄜˊ ㄌㄠˇ）
elder officials of different ranks in various dynasties

閣樓（ㄍㄜˊ ㄌㄡˊ）
an attic; a garret

閣置（ㄍㄜˊ ㄓˋ）
neat and properly placed

閣揆（ㄍㄜˊ ㄎㄨㄟˊ）
the premier; the prime minister

閣下（ㄍㄜˊ ㄒㄧㄚˋ）
Your Excellency; you (a polite expression)

閣臣（ㄍㄜˊ ㄔㄣˊ）
a deputy premier in the Ming and Ching dynasties

閣子（ㄍㄜˊ ˙ㄗ）or 閣兒（ㄍㄜˊㄦ）
a cabin; a small room

閣議（ㄍㄜˊ ㄧˋ）
a cabinet meeting or conference

閣員（ㄍㄜˊ ㄩㄢˊ）
cabinet ministers; members of the cabinet

【閡】 6543
ㄏㄜˊ her hé
1. to block or separate; to obstruct
2. to prevent; to shut out

【閤】 6544
1. ㄍㄜˊ ger gé
1. a small side door
2. same as 閣—a chamber, pavilion, etc.

閤中（ㄍㄜˊ ㄓㄨㄥ）
your wife (a polite expression)

【閤】 6544
2.(閤) ㄏㄜˊ her hé
1. to close (doors)
2. whole; all

閤第（ㄏㄜˊ ㄉㄧˋ）or 閤府（ㄏㄜˊ ㄈㄨˇ）
your whole family

【閥】 6545
ㄈㄚˊ far fá
1. a threshold; a doorsill
2. an influential person, family, or clique; a bloc: 門閥 a powerful family
3. a valve: 安全閥 a safty valve

閥閱之家（ㄈㄚˊ ㄩㄝˋ ㄓ ㄐㄧㄚ）
an influential or powerful family

【閨】 6546
ㄍㄨㄟ guei guī
1. a small door
2. the women's apartment

. feminine

閨 《ㄍㄨㄟ 门ㄣˊ》
①the door of an inner chamber ②a small door or gate in a palace or city wall

閨範《ㄍㄨㄟ ㄈㄢˋ》
①the code of conduct for women ②a paragon of feminine virtue

閨房《ㄍㄨㄟ ㄈㄤˊ》
the private quarters of a house where women live; a boudoir

閨房之樂《ㄍㄨㄟ ㄈㄤˊ ㄓ ㄌㄜˋ》
marital bliss; the happiness of a married couple

閨闈《ㄍㄨㄟ ㄨㄟˊ》
①apartments for ladies ②a small palace door

閨女《ㄍㄨㄟ ㄋㄩˇ》
a maiden; a virgin; an unmarried girl

閨閣《ㄍㄨㄟ ㄍㄜˊ》
women's quarters

閨闥《ㄍㄨㄟ ㄊㄚˋ》
women's quarters

閨秀《ㄍㄨㄟ ㄒㄧㄡˋ》
a well-educated girl brought up in a good family: 她們是大家閨秀。They are girls from respectable families.

閨怨《ㄍㄨㄟ ㄩㄢˋ》
writings, or verses that reflect and reveal sorrow and woe in a girl's heart

閩 6547 ㄇㄧㄣˊ
（又讀 ㄇㄧㄣ min min）
1. another name for Fukien Province
2. name of a river and an ancient tribe in today's Fukien Province
3. a Chinese family name

閩南《ㄇㄧㄣˊ ㄋㄢˊ》
the southern part of Fukien Province

閩南語《ㄇㄧㄣˊ ㄋㄢˊ ㄩˇ》or 閩南話《ㄇㄧㄣˊ ㄋㄢˊ ㄏㄨㄚˋ》
the southern Fukien dialect

閩江《ㄇㄧㄣˊ ㄐㄧㄤ》
the Min River in Fukien Province

七畫

閫 6548 ㄎㄨㄣˇ koen kun
1. same as 梱—a threshold
2. apartments or quarters for ladies
3. feminine

閫範《ㄎㄨㄣˇ ㄈㄢˋ》
①a paragon of feminine virtue ②the code of conduct for women

閫德《ㄎㄨㄣˇ ㄉㄜˊ》
feminine virtues

閫令《ㄎㄨㄣˇ ㄌㄧㄥˋ》
a woman's orders to her henpecked husband; one's wife's commands

閫寄《ㄎㄨㄣˇ ㄐㄧˋ》
to appoint a commanding officer with full authority to act according to his discretion

閫奧《ㄎㄨㄣˇ ㄠˋ》
①the inner part of a large building ②the essence of learning

閫外之任《ㄎㄨㄣˇ ㄨㄞˋ ㄓ ㄖㄣˋ》
the full authority given to a commanding general

閫威《ㄎㄨㄣˇ ㄨㄟ》
the overwhelming authority of a henpecked man's wife

閫闈《ㄎㄨㄣˇ ㄨㄟˊ》
a boudoir; women's quarters

閬 6549 ㄌㄤˋ laang làng
（又讀 ㄌㄤˊ lang láng）
1. a high door
2. high; tall; big
3. clear; lucid; bright
4. open and spacious

閬中《ㄌㄤˋ ㄓㄨㄥ》
name of a county and a mountain in Szechwan Province

閬苑《ㄌㄤˋ ㄩㄢˋ》
land where immortals dwell; a paradise

閭 6550 ㄌㄩˊ liu lǘ
1. a community of 25 families in ancient China—a community or neighborhood
2. the gate of a village
3. to meet; to gather together
4. a Chinese family name

閭里《ㄌㄩˊ ㄌㄧˇ》or 閭巷《ㄌㄩˊ ㄒㄧㄤˋ》
alleys or lanes—①one's neighbors; one's neighbor-

---

hood ②one's native village; one's hometown

閭丘《ㄌㄩˊ ㄑㄧㄡ》
①name of an ancient county in today's Shantung Province ②a Chinese compound surname

閭閻《ㄌㄩˊ ㄧㄢˊ》
①the gate of a village ②the people; the rural community

閭伍《ㄌㄩˊ ㄨˇ》
neighbors; neighborhood

閱 6551 ㄩㄝˋ yueh yuè
1. to read; to go over (examination papers)
2. to review; to inspect; to examine; to observe
3. to experience
4. to pass
5. (now rarely) to gather; to collect
6. (now rarely) appearance; looks

閱報《ㄩㄝˋ ㄅㄠˋ》
to read newspapers

閱報室《ㄩㄝˋ ㄅㄠˋ ㄕˋ》
a room for reading newspapers and magazines, etc.

閱兵《ㄩㄝˋ ㄅㄧㄥ》
to inspect or review troops

閱兵臺《ㄩㄝˋ ㄅㄧㄥ ㄊㄞˊ》
a stand for reviewing troops

閱兵式《ㄩㄝˋ ㄅㄧㄥ ㄕˋ》
a military parade before the commander in chief or commanding officer; a military review

閱讀《ㄩㄝˋ ㄉㄨˊ》
to read

閱覽《ㄩㄝˋ ㄌㄢˇ》
to read

閱覽室《ㄩㄝˋ ㄌㄢˇ ㄕˋ》
a reading room

閱歷《ㄩㄝˋ ㄌㄧˋ》
①to see, hear, or do for oneself: 他已閱歷過許多事。He has seen much of the world. ②experience; background: 她的閱歷頗淺。She has little experience.

閱卷《ㄩㄝˋ ㄐㄩㄢˋ》
to grade examination papers; to go over examination papers

閱時《ㄩㄝˋ ㄕˊ》

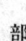

門部

【門部】

to last a period of time

閱世（ㄩㄝˋ ㄕˋ）
to experience the ways of life; one's experience

閱人多矣（ㄩㄝˋ ㄖㄣˊ ㄉㄨㄛ ㄧˇ）
to have a great deal of experience about men

閱操（ㄩㄝˋ ㄘㄠ）
to watch a military drill

八畫

【閻】 6552
（一ㄢˊ yan yán）
1. a village gate; the gate of a lane
2. a Chinese family name

閻羅王（一ㄢˊ ㄌㄨㄛˊ ㄨㄤˊ）or 閻王（一ㄢˊ ㄨㄤˊ）or 閻王爺（一ㄢˊ ㄨㄤˊ 一ㄝˊ）
① the Ruler of Hades; the King of Hell; the Chinese Pluto ② one who is feared by all others; a tyrant

閻王賬（一ㄢˊ ㄨㄤˊ ㄓㄤˋ）
a loan with exorbitantly high interest rate; a usurious loan; a shark's loan

【閶】 6553
（ㄔㄤ chang chāng）
1. the gate of heaven
2. the front gate of a palace

閶風（ㄔㄤ ㄈㄥ）
autumn winds

閶闔（ㄔㄤ ㄏㄜˊ）
① the gate of heaven ② the front gate of a palace

【閼】 6554
（ㄜˋ eh è）
1. to block up; to stop up
2. anything used to block up a flow

閼塞（ㄜˋ ㄙㄜˋ）
to block up; to stop up

【閼】 6554.2
（一ㄢ ian yān）
the formal wife of the chieftain of the Huns （匈奴） in the Han Dynasty

閼氏（一ㄢ ㄓ）
參看「閼2.」

【閹】 6555
（一ㄢ ian yān）
1. to castrate
2. a eunuch

閹黨（一ㄢ ㄉㄤˇ）
the clique faithful to the powerful eunuch, Wei Chung-hsien （魏忠賢）, in the

closing years of the Ming Dynasty

閹割（一ㄢ ㄍㄜˊ）
① to castrate or spay; to emasculate ② to deprive theory, etc. of its essence

閹雞（一ㄢ ㄐㄧ）
a capon

閹人（一ㄢ ㄖㄣˊ）
a castrated person; a eunuch

閹寺（一ㄢ ㄙˋ）
a eunuch

【閽】 6556
（ㄏㄨㄣ huen hūn）
1. a door or gate; a palace gate
2. a gatekeeper

閽人（ㄏㄨㄣ ㄖㄣˊ）
a doorman; a gatekeeper

【閾】 6557
（ㄩˋ yuh yù）
1. a doorsill; a threshold
2. separated
3. confined

九畫

【闃】 6558
（ㄑㄩˋ chiuh qù）
quiet; without people around

闃寂（ㄑㄩˋ ㄐㄧˊ）
still; quiet

闃然（ㄑㄩˋ ㄖㄢˊ）
quiet

【闇】 6559
（ㄢˋ ann àn）
1. to shut the door
2. dark; obscure; obscurity
3. evening; night
4. lunar or solar eclipses
5. stupid and dull; ignorant and foolish

闇昧（ㄢˋ ㄇㄟˋ）
① ignorant and stupid ② clandestine dealings

闇暝（ㄢˋ ㄇㄧㄥˊ）
getting dark

闇劣（ㄢˋ ㄌㄧㄝˋ）
stupid and incompetent

闇練（ㄢˋ ㄌㄧㄢˋ）
to be familiar with; to be proficient in 亦作「諳練」

闇淺（ㄢˋ ㄑㄧㄢˇ）
shallow, ignorant and stupid

闇室（ㄢˋ ㄕˋ）
a dark room 亦作「暗室」

闇然（ㄢˋ ㄖㄢˊ）

obscure; concealed

闇弱（ㄢˋ ㄖㄨㄛˋ）
ignorant, stupid and cowardly; irresolute

闇誦（ㄢˋ ㄙㄨㄥˋ）
to commit to memory; t recite in silence

闇藹（ㄢˋ ㄞˇ）
luxuriant; numerous; flourishing 亦作「暗藹」

闇闇（ㄢˋ ㄢˋ）
dark and obscure 亦作「暗暗」

【闈】 6560
（ㄨㄟˊ wei wéi）
1. the side doors of a palace
2. the living quarters of th queen and the imperial cor cubines
3. ladies' living quarters; pr vate quarters
4. (formerly) a hall where th civil service examination took place

闈墨（ㄨㄟˊ ㄇㄛˋ）
compositions of the success ful candidates in the civi service examination in an cient China

【闉】 6561
（一ㄣ in yīn）
1. curved; bent
2. the gate of the city wall

【闊】 6562
（ㄎㄨㄛˋ kuoh kuò）
1. broad; wide; width
2. separated; widely apart
3. rich; wealthy; extravagant loaded
4. (now rarely) to ease

闊別（ㄎㄨㄛˋ ㄅㄧㄝˊ）
separated for a long time: 我 們是闊別多年的友人。We are long-separated friends.

闊步（ㄎㄨㄛˋ ㄅㄨˋ）
to walk with big strides; t stride: 他在街上闊步行走。H strode along the street.

闊達（ㄎㄨㄛˋ ㄉㄚˊ）
broad-minded; not caring fo trifles

闊大（ㄎㄨㄛˋ ㄉㄚˋ）
capacious; spacious

闊大爺（ㄎㄨㄛˋ ㄉㄚˋ 一ㄝˊ）
a wealthy man who lives a very luxurious life

闊得狠（ㄎㄨㄛˋ ㄉㄜˊ ㄏㄣˇ）
loaded; very rich

闊老 or 闊佬（ㄎㄨㄛˋ ㄌㄠˇ）

a rich man: 他是個闊佬。He's
a rich man.

闊落 (� ㄨㄛ ㄌㄨㄛ)
not fine

闊綽 (ㄎㄨㄛ ˙ㄔ)
extravagant in spending; lavish

闊綽 (ㄎㄨㄛ ㄔ ㄨㄛ)
extravagant; throwing money
around; lavish

闊少 (ㄎㄨㄛ ㄕㄠ)
sons of a wealthy family

闊人 (ㄎㄨㄛ ㄖㄣ)
the rich

闊葉樹 (ㄎㄨㄛ ㄧㄝ ㄕㄨ)
broad-leaved trees

【闋】 6563
　　　ㄑㄩㄝ chiueh què
1. to close or shut the door
after finishing something
2. to be at rest
3. to end
4. the expiry of the period of
mourning
5. a numerical adjunct for
songs
6. empty; blank

【闌】 6564
　　　ㄌㄢ lan lán
1. a door curtain or screen
2. a fence
3. to block up; to cut off
4. the end (of a year, etc.);
late (in the night, etc.): 夜闌
人靜, All is quiet in the dead
of night
5. weakened; withered

闌風 (ㄌㄢ ㄈㄥ)
the continuous blowing of
wind

闌珊 (ㄌㄢ ㄕㄢ)
tired and exhausted

闌干 (ㄌㄢ ㄍㄢ)
①a fence; banisters; a balustrade; railings ②the eye
sockets ③a crisscross

闌檻 (ㄌㄢ ㄐㄧㄢ)
railings or fences

闌出 (ㄌㄢ ㄔㄨ)
to go out wantonly

闌珊 (ㄌㄢ ㄕㄢ)
withered; declining; waning:
春意闌珊, The spring is wan-
ing.

闌入 (ㄌㄢ ㄖㄨ)
①to barge in; to intrude; to
trespass ②to put in some-

thing where it does not
belong

闌尾 (ㄌㄢ ㄨㄟ)
(anatomy) the appendix 亦
作「盲腸」

闌尾炎 (ㄌㄢ ㄨㄟ ㄧㄢ)
appendicitis 亦作「盲腸炎」

【闆】 6565
　　　ㄅㄢ baan bǎn
the boss; the owner: 他被老
闆開除。He is fired by his
boss.

【闍】 6566
　　　1. ㄉㄨ du dú
a tower over a city wall

【闍】 6566
　　　2. ㄕㄜ sher shé
as in 阿闍梨—a Buddhist
high priest

十畫

【闐】 6567
　　　ㄊㄧㄢ tyan tián
to fill; to fill to the brim; to
be full of

闐闐 (ㄊㄧㄢ ㄊㄧㄢ)
①brimming; full; flourishing
②the sound of drums

闐池 (ㄊㄧㄢ ㄔ)
Issyk Köl, or Issyk-Kui, a
lake in Soviet Central Asia

闐溢 (ㄊㄧㄢ ㄧ)
to fill to the brim

【闑】 6568
　　　ㄋㄧㄝ nieh niè
the wood bars on both sides
of the central door

【闒】 6569
　　　ㄊㄚ tah tà
1. the upstairs door
2. the sound of bells and
drums
3. mean

【闓】 6570
　　　ㄎㄞ kae kǎi
1. to open
2. peaceful; harmonious

【闔】 6571
　　　ㄏㄜ her hé
1. a leaf of a door
2. to shut or close
3. all; the whole
4. Why? 或 Why not?

闔府 (ㄏㄜ ㄈㄨ)
your whole family

闔府平安 (ㄏㄜ ㄈㄨ ㄆㄧㄥ ㄢ)
Hope your whole family is

doing well.

闔第光臨 (ㄏㄜ ㄉㄧ ㄍㄨㄤ ㄌㄧㄣ)
(a conventional term used in
Chinese invitation cards)
Please come with your
whole family. 或 The whole
family is invited.

闔廬 (ㄏㄜ ㄌㄨ)or闔閭(ㄏㄜ ㄌㄩ)
①one's house ②name of
the king of Wu in the Epoch
of Spring and Autumn

闔國 (ㄏㄜ ㄍㄨㄛ)
the whole country

闔家 (ㄏㄜ ㄐㄧㄚ)
the whole family

闔城 (ㄏㄜ ㄔㄥ)
the whole city; the whole
town

闔扇 (ㄏㄜ ㄕㄢ)
a door panel; a wing of a
door

【闕】 6572
　　　1. ㄑㄩㄝ chiueh
　　　　　què
1. a watchtower outside the
palace gate in ancient China
2. a palace: 宮闕 the imperial
palace
3. a Chinese family name

闕下 (ㄑㄩㄝ ㄒㄧㄚ)
①the imperial palace ②
Your (or His) Majesty

【闕】 6572
　　　2. ㄑㄩㄝ chiue què
1. faults; errors; mistakes;
defects
2. to lack; deficient, deficiency

闕失 (ㄑㄩㄝ ㄕ)
a mistake; an error

闕如 (ㄑㄩㄝ ㄖㄨ)
lacking; wanting; deficient

闕字 (ㄑㄩㄝ ㄗ)
an omission in an article,
writing, etc.; a hiatus

闕疑 (ㄑㄩㄝ ㄧ)
to lay aside something
doubtful and try to verify
later; to leave the question
open; an unsettled point

闕文 (ㄑㄩㄝ ㄨㄣ)
omissions or missing parts
in writings or books; a hiatus in the text

【闖】 6573
　　　1. ㄔㄨㄤ choang
　　　　　chuǎng
1. to rush in all of a sudden;
to intrude into: 他闖了進來。

【門
部】

He rushed in.
2. to be trained by experience; to hew out one's way
3. to cause (a disaster, etc.)

闖大運《ㄔㄨㄤˋ ㄌㄩㄣˋ》
to rush ahead for a try without much planning beforehand

闖關《ㄔㄨㄤˋ ㄍㄨㄢ》
to run a blockade; to try to break into a guarded point

闖空門《ㄔㄨㄤˋ ㄎㄨㄥ ㄇㄣˊ》
to break into a home or building when the occupants are absent

闖禍《ㄔㄨㄤˋ ㄏㄨㄛˋ》
to cause a disaster or misfortune; to get into trouble

闖紅燈《ㄔㄨㄤˋ ㄏㄨㄥˊ ㄉㄥ》
to continue walking or driving when the red light is on; to run through a red light

闖江湖《ㄔㄨㄤˋ ㄐㄧㄤ ·ㄏㄨˊ》
to roam about to make a living

闖將《ㄔㄨㄤˋ ㄐㄧㄤˋ》
① the title that the rebel leader Li Tzu-cheng (李自成) gave himself in the closing years of the Ming Dynasty ② a rogue; a rascal ③ a pathbreaker

闖子《ㄔㄨㄤˋ ·ㄗ》
a rash and bold person; a fearless and rude person

闖座《ㄔㄨㄤˋ ㄗㄨㄛˋ》or 闖席《ㄔㄨㄤˋ ㄒㄧˊ》
to attend a feast without being invited

闖王《ㄔㄨㄤˋ ㄨㄤˊ》
the title assumed by the rebel leader Kao Ying-hsiang (高迎祥) and later passed to Li Tzu-cheng (李自成) in their uprisings during the closing years of the Ming Dynasty

6573
【闖】 2. ㄔㄨㄤˋ chuanq
     chuǎng
1. to cause (a disaster)
2. to hit

十一畫

6574
【關】 《ㄍㄨㄢ guan guān
1. to shut; to close: 請將門關

上。Will you shut the door?
2. a frontier pass or checkpoint: 我們今晚把關。We guard the pass tonight.
3. the bar across the door
4. a customs house; a customs barrier
5. a key point; a turning point
6. related; relationship; to involve; to concern
7. to negotiate; to go between
8. to draw (money, or pay)
9. a Chinese family name

關閉《ㄍㄨㄢ ㄅㄧˋ》
① to close ② to close down; to shut down (a store, plant, etc.): 該公司因財務困難而關閉工廠。The company shut down the factory because of financial difficulties.

關不住《ㄍㄨㄢ·ㄅㄨ ㄓㄨˋ》
cannot be shut out, as the charming sight of spring; cannot be shut in, as the restless spirit of a child

關門《ㄍㄨㄢ ㄇㄣˊ》
① to close the door ② to close a shop ③ to close its door—to go bankrupt

關門大吉《ㄍㄨㄢ ㄇㄣˊ ㄉㄚˋ ㄐㄧˊ》
to close down for good

關防《ㄍㄨㄢ ㄈㄤˊ》
① the seal of a government agency ② a military position at a strategic point on the border

關夫子《ㄍㄨㄢ ㄈㄨ ·ㄗ》or 關羽《ㄍㄨㄢ ㄩˇ》or 關帝《ㄍㄨㄢ ㄉㄧˋ》or 關公《ㄍㄨㄢ ㄍㄨㄥ》
Kuan Yü (關羽, ?—219), a general in the Epoch of the Three Kingdoms, deified in later generations as China's god of war

關刀《ㄍㄨㄢ ㄉㄠ》
a knife with a long handle for fighting on horseback, so called for it's believed to be the weapon used by Kuan Yü (關羽)

關島《ㄍㄨㄢ ㄉㄠˇ》
Guam

關帝廟《ㄍㄨㄢ ㄉㄧˋ ㄇㄧㄠˋ》
a shrine dedicated to General Kuan Yü (關羽)

關東《ㄍㄨㄢ ㄉㄨㄥ》
① the old name for the area east of the Han Ku Pass (函

谷關), including today' Honan and Shantung Provinces ② the land east of the Shan Hai Pass (山海關) northeast China

關頭《ㄍㄨㄢ ㄊㄡˊ》
a key point; a crucial period; a crux

關內《ㄍㄨㄢ ㄋㄟˋ》or 關裏《ㄍㄨㄢ ㄌㄧˇ》
within the Han Ku Pass (函谷關) or Shan Hai Pass (山海關)

關聯《ㄍㄨㄢ ㄌㄧㄢˊ》
related; connected; involved involvement; connection

關籟《ㄍㄨㄢ ㄌㄞˋ》
the sound of birds chirping

關卡《ㄍㄨㄢ ㄎㄚˇ》
a customs station or barrier

關口《ㄍㄨㄢ ㄎㄡˇ》
① a checkpoint; a strategic point ② a key point; a turning point

關懷《ㄍㄨㄢ ㄏㄨㄞˊ》
to be concerned about; to show concern; concern: 我們十分關懷父母的健康。We pay great attention to our parents' health.

關節《ㄍㄨㄢ ㄐㄧㄝˊ》
① joints in the human body ② to bribe; a bribe ③ illegal transactions between the examiner and the examinee ④ key links; crucial links

關節炎《ㄍㄨㄢ ㄐㄧㄝˊ ㄧㄢˊ》
(pathology) arthritis

關鍵《ㄍㄨㄢ ㄐㄧㄢˋ》
a key point; a key (to a problem); an important turning point; a hinge; a pivotal point; a crux: 它是個關鍵字。It's a key word.

關鍵字《ㄍㄨㄢ ㄐㄧㄢˋ ㄗˋ》
a key word

關津《ㄍㄨㄢ ㄐㄧㄣ》
a hub or key point for both land and water transportation

關禁閉《ㄍㄨㄢ ㄐㄧㄣˋ ㄅㄧˋ》
(military) to be put in a dark cell as a form of punishment

關起來《ㄍㄨㄢ ㄑㄧˇ·ㄌㄞ》
① to close; to shut ② to imprison

關切《ㄍㄨㄢ ㄑㄧㄝˋ》

to be concerned about; to show concern; concern: 他們極為關切此一消息。They are deeply concerned at the news.

關西 (《ㄨㄢ ㄒㄧ)
the land west of the Han Ku Pass (函谷關), including Shensi and Kansu provinces

關係 (《ㄨㄢ ㄒㄧˋ)
① relation; relationship; connection; ties: 她跟你是什麼關係? What relation is she to you? ② to matter: 有何關係? What does it matter?

關係密切 (《ㄨㄢ ㄒㄧˋ ㄇㄧˋ ㄑㄧㄝˋ)
close relationship; intimate contact or connection: 他與那件事關係密切。He had a close relationship to the incident.

關係代名詞 (《ㄨㄢ ㄒㄧˋ ㄉㄞˋ ㄇㄧㄥˊ ㄘˊ)
relative pronouns

關係斷絕 (《ㄨㄢ ㄒㄧˋ ㄉㄨㄢˋ ㄐㄩㄝˊ)
(diplomacy, etc.) severance of relations; relations severed

關係人 (《ㄨㄢ ㄒㄧˋ ㄖㄣˊ)
(law) persons or parties concerned

關係詞 (《ㄨㄢ ㄒㄧˋ ㄘˊ)
(English grammar) a relative pronoun, adverb, etc. (such as who, which, what, ect.)

關心 (《ㄨㄢ ㄒㄧㄣ)
to be concerned about; to show concern; concern: 我很關心她。I was much concerned about her.

關心民瘼 (《ㄨㄢ ㄒㄧㄣ ㄇㄧㄣˊ ㄇㄛˋ)
to be concerned about the afflictions of the people

關照 (《ㄨㄢ ㄓㄠˋ)
① to notify; to inform: 他來的話，請關照一聲。Please inform me if he comes. ② to take care of; to look after: 這裡的工作請多關照了。Please look after the work here.

關注 (《ㄨㄢ ㄓㄨˋ)
to be concerned about; to show concern

關中 (《ㄨㄢ ㄓㄨㄥ)
① the old name of Shensi Province ② the central

Shensi plain

關窗 (《ㄨㄢ ㄔㄨㄤ)
to close the window: 晚上要關窗。Close the windows at night.

關涉 (《ㄨㄢ ㄕㄜˋ)
to involve; to concern; to be related to; relations

關山迢遞 (《ㄨㄢ ㄕㄢ ㄊㄧㄠˊ ㄉㄧˋ)
to be separated far apart

關說 (《ㄨㄢ ㄕㄨㄛ)
to lobby illegally, usually by pedaling one's influence: to ask a favor of someone for a friend

關稅 (《ㄨㄢ ㄕㄨㄟˋ)
customs duty

關稅率 (《ㄨㄢ ㄕㄨㄟˋ ㄌㄩˋ)
customs tariffs

關稅及貿易總協定 (《ㄨㄢ ㄕㄨㄟˋ ㄐㄧˊ ㄇㄠˋ ㄧˋ ㄗㄨㄥˇ ㄒㄧㄝˊ ㄉㄧㄥˋ)
the General Agreement on Tariffs and Trade (GATT)

關稅自主 (《ㄨㄢ ㄕㄨㄟˋ ㄗˋ ㄓㄨˇ)
tariff autonomy

關稅優惠 (《ㄨㄢ ㄕㄨㄟˋ ㄧㄡ ㄏㄨㄟˋ)
tariff preference

關塞 (《ㄨㄢ ㄙㄞˋ)
strategic positions or passes on the border

關隘 (《ㄨㄢ ㄞˋ)
strategic positions or passes on the border

關愛 (《ㄨㄢ ㄞˋ)
to express solicitude for the well-being of someone

關礙 (《ㄨㄢ ㄞˋ)
to hinder; to obstruct

關外 (《ㄨㄢ ㄨㄞˋ)
outside the Han Ku Pass (函谷關) or the Shan Hai Pass (山海關)

關於 (《ㄨㄢ ㄩ)
concerning; with regard to; regarding: 那末關於錢的方面，怎麼辦呢? Now, regarding money, what is to be done?

【闚】 6575
ㄎㄨㄟ kuei kui
1. same as 窺—to steal a glance; to peep; to spy: 他從牆頭闚視。He peeped over a wall.
2. to tempt with material gain

十二畫

【闞】 6576
1. ㄎㄢˋ kann kàn (又讀 ㄎㄢ kaan kān)
1. to steal a glance; to peep; to spy; to watch secretly
2. a Chinese family name

【闞】 6576
2. ㄏㄢˋ haan hòn
1. roaring (of a tiger); growling
2. brave

【闠】 6577
ㄏㄨㄟˋ huey hui
the gate of a market

【闡】 6578
ㄔㄢˇ chaan chǎn
1. to make clear; to elaborate; to elucidate; to expound
2. evident; clear

闡明 (ㄔㄢˇ ㄇㄧㄥˊ)
to elucidate; to clarify; to make clear: 他闡明了自己的理念。He clarified his own concept.

闡發 (ㄔㄢˇ ㄈㄚ)
to expound and promote

闡究 (ㄔㄢˇ ㄐㄧㄡˋ)
to study and expound

闡士 (ㄔㄢˇ ㄕˋ)
a learned monk; a Buddhist high priest

闡釋 (ㄔㄢˇ ㄕˋ)
to explain; to expound; to interpret

闡述 (ㄔㄢˇ ㄕㄨˋ)
to expound; to elaborate; to set forth: 他對浪漫主義作了系統的闡述。He made a systematic exposition of romanticism.

闡幽 (ㄔㄢˇ ㄧㄡ)
to expound the hidden points or meanings

闡揚 (ㄔㄢˇ ㄧㄤˊ)
to expound and propagate; to expound and advocate (an ideology, theory, principle, etc.)

十三畫

【闢】 6579
ㄆㄧˋ pih pì
1. to open up; to develop
2. to rid; to do away with
3. to refute

闢謬 (ㄆㄧˋ ㄇㄧㄡˋ)
to refute absurdities

（門部）

闢佛 (ㄆㄧˋ ㄈㄛˊ)
to argue against Buddhism

闢地 (ㄆㄧˋ ㄉㄧˋ)
to open up land for cultivation

闢田 (ㄆㄧˋ ㄊㄧˊ)
to open up land for farming;
to develop farmland

闢墾 (ㄆㄧˋ ㄎㄣˇ)
to open up land for farming

闢邪 (ㄆㄧˋ ㄒㄧㄝˊ)
to refute heresy

闢謠 (ㄆㄧˋ ㄧㄠˊ)
to refute rumors; to clarify
rumored reports

【闤】 6580
ㄏㄨㄢˊ hwan huán
a wall around a marketplace

【闥】 6581
ㄊㄚˋ tah tà
1. a door; a small door; a
   wicket gate
2. the space between the door
   and the screen; inside the
   door
3. fast

阜 部
ㄈㄨˋ fuh fù

【阜】 6582
ㄈㄨˋ fuh fù
1. a mound; a small hill
2. the continent; the mainland
3. abundant; flourishing; numerous: 物阜民豐. Products
   abound and the people live
   in plenty.

阜陵 (ㄈㄨˋ ㄌㄧㄥˊ)
a mound; a small hill

三畫

【阡】 6583
ㄑㄧㄢ chian qiān
1. paths on farms; a footpath
   between fields, running north
   and south
2. the path leading to a grave

阡表 (ㄑㄧㄢ ㄅㄧㄠˇ)
a tomb tablet; a grave stone

阡陌 (ㄑㄧㄢ ㄇㄛˋ)
paths on farmland; criss-
cross footpaths between

fields

阡陌縱橫 (ㄑㄧㄢ ㄇㄛˋ ㄗㄨㄥˋ ㄏㄥˊ)
crisscross paths on farmland

【阢】 6584
ㄨˋ wuh wù
uneasy; apprehensive

阢陧 (ㄨˋ ㄋㄧㄝˋ)
uneasy; jittery

四畫

【阬】 6585
ㄎㄥ keng kēng
a pit; a shaft

【阨】 6586
ㄜˋ eh è
1. a strategic position
2. a precarious position
3. to block up or obstruct
4. destitute; poverty-stricken;
   difficulty

阨窮 (ㄜˋ ㄑㄩㄥˊ)
destitute; difficulty; poverty-
stricken

阨塞 (ㄜˋ ㄙㄜˋ)
a strategic place or position

【阪】 6587
ㄅㄢˇ baan bǎn
1. the slope of a hill; a hillside
2. a hillside farm field

阪田 (ㄅㄢˇ ㄊㄧㄢˊ)
①a hillside farm field ②a
rugged and stony field

阪上走丸 (ㄅㄢˇ ㄕㄤˋ ㄗㄡˇ ㄨㄢˊ)
(literally) to roll a ball
down the slope—to become
irresistible because of natural advantages

【阮】 6588
ㄖㄨㄢˇ roan ruǎn
1. name of an ancient state in
   today's Kansu Province
2. an ancient musical instrument
3. a Chinese family name

阮囊羞澀 (ㄖㄨㄢˇ ㄋㄤˊ ㄒㄧㄡ ㄙㄜˋ)
having an empty pocket;
short of cash; poor

阮籍 (ㄖㄨㄢˇ ㄐㄧˊ)
Juan Chi (210-263), an eccentric scholar in the Epoch
of the Three Kingdoms

阮咸 (ㄖㄨㄢˇ ㄒㄧㄢˊ)
①Juan Hsien, nephew of
Juan Chi (阮籍), who was
well versed in music ②
name of an ancient Chinese
guitar; a plucked stringed

instrument 亦作「阮」

【阱】 6589
ㄐㄧㄥˇ jiing jǐng
a trap; a snare

【防】 6590
ㄈㄤˊ farng fáng
1. to defend; defense
2. to prepare for; to take precautions; to prevent; prevention: 預防勝於治療. Preven-
   tion is better than cure.
3. a Chinese family name

防波堤 (ㄈㄤˊ ㄅㄛ ㄉㄧ)
a breakwater; a mole

防備 (ㄈㄤˊ ㄅㄟˋ)
to get ready or prepared
(for an incident, etc.); to
guard against

防不勝防 (ㄈㄤˊ ㄅㄨˋ ㄕㄥ ㄈㄤˊ)
There's no way of preventing it. 或It's impossible to
guard against (such things)

防範 (ㄈㄤˊ ㄈㄢˋ)
to be alert against; to take
precautions; to guard against

防風 (ㄈㄤˊ ㄈㄥ)
① Siler divaricatum, a
herbal weed ②protection
against wind

防風林 (ㄈㄤˊ ㄈㄥ ㄌㄧㄣˊ)
a windbreak; a forest shelter
belt

防腐 (ㄈㄤˊ ㄈㄨˇ)
to preserve (food, timber,
etc.) from chemical decomposition; to prevent decay

防腐劑 (ㄈㄤˊ ㄈㄨˇ ㄐㄧˋ)
antiseptic; preservative

防盜 (ㄈㄤˊ ㄉㄠˋ)
prevention of burglary; to
guard against burglary

防彈 (ㄈㄤˊ ㄉㄢˋ)
bulletproof; to protect
against bullets

防彈玻璃 (ㄈㄤˊ ㄉㄢˋ ㄅㄛ ㄌㄧˊ)
bulletproof glass

防彈背心 (ㄈㄤˊ ㄉㄢˋ ㄅㄟˋ ㄒㄧㄣ)
a bulletproof vest; a flak
jacket

防地 (ㄈㄤˊ ㄉㄧˋ)
an area where troops are
stationed for defense

防諜 (ㄈㄤˊ ㄉㄧㄝˊ)
anti-espionage; to prevent
espionage

防毒 (ㄈㄤˊ ㄉㄨˊ)
anti-poison; gas defense

防毒面具(ㄈㄤ ㄉㄨ ㄇㄧㄢˋ ㄐㄩˋ)
a gas mask; a protective mask

防癆(ㄈㄤ ㄌㄠˊ)
tuberculosis prevention; TB control

防老(ㄈㄤ ㄌㄠˇ)
to make provision for one's old age

防空(ㄈㄤ ㄎㄨㄥ)
air defense; antiaircraft

防空洞(ㄈㄤ ㄎㄨㄥ ㄉㄨㄥˋ)
an air-raid or bomb shelter

防空壕(ㄈㄤ ㄎㄨㄥ ㄏㄠˊ)
a ditch serving as an air-raid shelter

防空警報(ㄈㄤ ㄎㄨㄥ ㄐㄧㄥˇ ㄅㄠˋ)
an air defense warning

防空演習(ㄈㄤ ㄎㄨㄥ ㄧㄢˇ ㄒㄧˊ)
air defense exercises; an air-raid drill

防旱(ㄈㄤ ㄏㄢˋ)
prevention of drought

防護(ㄈㄤ ㄏㄨˋ)
① to protect or safeguard ② first aid

防護團(ㄈㄤ ㄏㄨˋ ㄊㄨㄢˊ)
civil defense corps

防護林(ㄈㄤ ㄏㄨˋ ㄌㄧㄣˊ)
a shelter forest

防護裝備(ㄈㄤ ㄏㄨˋ ㄓㄨㄤ ㄅㄟˋ)
protective equipment

防護油(ㄈㄤ ㄏㄨˋ ㄧㄡˊ)
preservative oil

防火(ㄈㄤ ㄏㄨㄛˇ)
to guard against fire hazards; fire prevention; fireproof

防火板(ㄈㄤ ㄏㄨㄛˇ ㄅㄢˇ)
an anti-firing plate

防火牆(ㄈㄤ ㄏㄨㄛˇ ㄑㄧㄤˊ)
a fire wall

防火設備(ㄈㄤ ㄏㄨㄛˇ ㄕㄜˋ ㄅㄟˋ)
fire-fighting facilities; facilities to guard against fire hazards

防患未然(ㄈㄤ ㄏㄨㄢˋ ㄨㄟˋ ㄖㄢˊ)
to take precautions against a calamity

防洪(ㄈㄤ ㄏㄨㄥˊ)
flood control

防洪措施(ㄈㄤ ㄏㄨㄥˊ ㄘㄨㄛˋ ㄕ)
flood control measures

防飢(ㄈㄤ ㄐㄧ)
to guard against famine or hunger

防銹(ㄈㄤ ㄒㄧㄡˋ)
antirust

防線(ㄈㄤ ㄒㄧㄢˋ)
a line of defense

防止(ㄈㄤ ㄓˇ)
to prevent; to guard against; to prohibit: 他們竭力防止戰爭。They tried hard to prevent the war.

防治(ㄈㄤ ㄓˋ)
prevention and treatment (of diseases)

防震(ㄈㄤ ㄓㄣˋ)
shock-resistant; quakeproof

防潮(ㄈㄤ ㄔㄠˊ)
① dampproof; moistureproof ② protection against the tide

防臭劑(ㄈㄤ ㄔㄡˋ ㄐㄧˋ)
a deodorizer; a deodorant

防塵(ㄈㄤ ㄔㄣˊ)
dustproof

防蟲(ㄈㄤ ㄔㄨㄥˊ)
pest control; pest prevention; to guard against harmful insects

防蝕劑(ㄈㄤ ㄕˊ ㄐㄧˋ)
an anticorrosive

防守(ㄈㄤ ㄕㄡˇ)
to defend; to guard: 他們防守此城以禦敵。They defended the city against the enemy.

防身(ㄈㄤ ㄕㄣ)
to guard personal safety; self-protection

防身術(ㄈㄤ ㄕㄣ ㄕㄨˋ)
the science (or art) of self-defense

防水(ㄈㄤ ㄕㄨㄟˇ)
① waterproof; watertight ② to guard against flood; antiflood

防水布(ㄈㄤ ㄕㄨㄟˇ ㄅㄨˋ)
mackintosh; waterproof canvas

防水劑(ㄈㄤ ㄕㄨㄟˇ ㄐㄧˋ)
a waterproofing agent

防水水泥(ㄈㄤ ㄕㄨㄟˇ ㄕㄨㄟˇ ㄋㄧˊ)
waterproof cement

防災(ㄈㄤ ㄗㄞ)
to take precautions against natural calamities

防疫(ㄈㄤ ㄧˋ)
to guard against or prevent an epidemic

防疫所(ㄈㄤ ㄧˋ ㄙㄨㄛˇ)
a quarantine office

防意如城(ㄈㄤ ㄧˋ ㄖㄨˊ ㄔㄥˊ)
to guard against one's desire as if to guard a city against the enemy

防務(ㄈㄤ ㄨˋ)
defense; defense measures

防微杜漸(ㄈㄤ ㄨㄟˊ ㄉㄨˋ ㄐㄧㄢˋ)
to take every precaution at the beginning; to nip trouble in the bud

防衛(ㄈㄤ ㄨㄟˋ)or 防禦(ㄈㄤ ㄩˋ)
to defend; to guard; defense

防雨布(ㄈㄤ ㄩˇ ㄅㄨˋ)
waterproof cloth; tarpaulin

防禦力(ㄈㄤ ㄩˋ ㄌㄧˋ)
the defensive force or strength

防禦工事(ㄈㄤ ㄩˋ ㄍㄨㄥ ㄕˋ)
defense works

防禦戰(ㄈㄤ ㄩˋ ㄓㄢˋ)
the defensive war

〔阜部〕

【址】 6591
(址)　ㄓˇ　jyy　zhǐ
a site; an address

五畫

【阻】 6592
ㄗㄨˇ　tzuu　zǔ
1. to prevent; to stop; to prohibit or proscribe
2. to separate; separated
3. to hinder; to obstruct; to oppose; to impede; to detain; to blockade
4. difficulty; to suffer
5. to rely on
6. a strategic pass

阻擋(ㄗㄨˇ ㄉㄤˇ)
to stop; to be in the way; to block the way; to hinder: 任何事也阻擋不了我們到那裏去。Nothing will stop us from going there.

阻斷交通(ㄗㄨˇ ㄉㄨㄢˋ ㄐㄧㄠ ㄊㄨㄥ)
to obstruct traffic

阻撓(ㄗㄨˇ ㄋㄠˊ)
to obstruct; to thwart; obstruction: 他們設法阻撓敵人的計畫。They tried to thwart the enemy's plans.

阻難(ㄗㄨˇ ㄋㄢˊ)
to obstruct; to make it difficult

阻攔(ㄗㄨˇ ㄌㄢˊ)
to stop; to prevent; to retard

〔阜部〕

阻力(ㄗㄨ ㄌㄧˋ)
the force of resistance

阻隔(ㄗㄨˇ ㄍㄜˊ)
① to be separated; to be isolated ②to cut off: 濃霧阻隔了我們的視線。A thick fog cut off our view.

阻隔活門(ㄗㄨˇ ㄍㄜˊ ㄏㄨㄛˊ ㄇㄣˊ)
a check valve

阻梗(ㄗㄨˇ ㄍㄥˇ)
to obstruct or hinder; to impede

阻擊(ㄗㄨˇ ㄐㄧˊ)
to block; to check

阻絕(ㄗㄨˇ ㄐㄩㄝˊ)
to stop up; to obstruct, hinder or impede

阻修(ㄗㄨˇ ㄒㄧㄡ)
(referring to a road) obstructed and distant

阻止(ㄗㄨˇ ㄓˇ)
to stop or prevent; to prohibit or proscribe; to block: 他們想阻止事態惡化。They tried to prevent the situation from getting worse.

阻滯(ㄗㄨˇ ㄓˋ)
impeded; obstructed; blocked

阻深(ㄗㄨˇ ㄕㄣ)
(said of a place) far away beyond many mountains and streams

阻塞(ㄗㄨˇ ㄙㄜˋ)
①to block up; to clog; to obstruct: 落石阻塞了交通。Fallen rocks obstructed the traffic. ②a jam; a block: 交通阻塞迫使車輛無法通行。A block in the traffic keeps cars from moving on.

阻遏(ㄗㄨˇ ㄜˋ)
to stop; to hinder; to check

阻礙(ㄗㄨˇ ㄞˋ)
an obstacle or hindrance; obstruction; to obstruct; to impede; to prevent; to bar; to retard: 健康不佳阻礙了他成功的機會。Poor health barred his chances of success.

〔阼〕 6593 ㄗㄨㄛˋ tzuoh zuò

1. the main steps
2. the throne

阼階(ㄗㄨㄛˋ ㄐㄧㄝ)
the eastern steps where the host stood to welcome his guests in old and ancient China

〔阿〕 6594 1. ㄜ e e

1. to favor; to toady; to assent; to pander to; to play up to
2. to rely on
3. a riverbank
4. the corner or edge
5. a pillar
6. slender and beautiful
7. to discharge (night soil, urine, etc.)
8. a Chinese family name

阿媚(ㄜ ㄇㄟˋ)
to flatter or toady

阿彌陀佛(ㄜ ㄇㄧˊ ㄊㄨㄛˊ ㄈㄛˊ)
Amitabha, the Buddha of infinite qualities (an imaginary being unknown to ancient Buddhism, possibly of Persian or Iranian origin, who has eclipsed the historical Buddha in becoming the most popular divinity in the Mahayana Pantheon)

阿房宮(ㄜ ㄈㄤˊ ㄍㄨㄥ)
name of a fabulous palace in the Chin Dynasty, which was later destroyed by Hsiang Yü (項羽)

阿芙蓉(ㄜ ㄈㄨˊ ㄖㄨㄥˊ)
a poppy; opium

阿附(ㄜ ㄈㄨˋ)
to toady and support; to flock to; to curry favor with; to jump on the bandwagon (of someone in power)

阿黨(ㄜ ㄉㄤˇ)
to twist law for private purposes

阿尿(ㄜ ㄋㄧㄠˋ)
to urinate

阿羅漢(ㄜ ㄌㄨㄛˊ ㄏㄢˋ)
Arhat or Lohan (羅漢) (from Sanskrit arhat)

阿好(ㄜ ㄏㄠˇ)or 阿其所好(ㄜ ㄑㄧˊ ㄙㄨㄛˇ ㄏㄠˇ)
to flatter whom one likes; to practice favoritism

阿修羅(ㄜ ㄒㄧㄡ ㄌㄨㄛˊ)
(Buddhism) a frightful demon (from Sanskrit asura)

阿諂(ㄜ ㄔㄢˇ)
to flatter; to toady; to fawn upon: 許多親戚阿諂那位老富翁。Many relatives fawned on the rich old man.

阿屎(ㄜ ㄕˇ)
to move the bowels

阿順(ㄜ ㄕㄨㄣˋ)
to flatter and be obsequious

阿私(ㄜ ㄙ)
to be biased or partial

阿諛(ㄜ ㄩˊ)
to flatter

〔阿〕 6594 2. ㄚˇ ah ā

1. an initial particle; a prefix to a name or a term of address
2. a word often used in transliterations; an exclamation of unpleasant surprise

阿比西尼亞(ㄚˇ ㄅㄧˇ ㄒㄧ ㄋㄧˊ ㄧㄚˋ)
Abyssinia; Ethiopia

阿波羅(ㄚˇ ㄅㄛ ㄌㄨㄛˊ)
Apollo 亦作「阿波羅」

阿片(ㄚˇ ㄆㄧㄢˋ)
opium 亦作「鴉片」

阿摩尼亞(ㄚˇ ㄇㄛˊ ㄋㄧˊ ㄧㄚˋ)
ammonia

阿眉(ㄚˇ ㄇㄟˊ)or 阿美族(ㄚˇ ㄇㄟˇ ㄗㄨˊ)
the Ami tribe among the aborigines in Taiwan

阿曼(ㄚˇ ㄇㄢˋ)
①Amman, capital of Jordan ② Oman

阿們(ㄚˇ ㄇㄣˊ)
Amen

阿米巴(ㄚˇ ㄇㄧˇ ㄅㄚ)
ameba, or amoeba 亦作「變形蟲」

阿姆斯特丹(ㄚˇ ㄇㄨˇ ㄙ ㄊㄜˋ ㄉㄢ)
Amsterdam, Holland

阿飛(ㄚˇ ㄈㄟ)
a young man who combines the characteristics of a hippie and a juvenile delinquent; a Teddy boy

阿非利加(ㄚˇ ㄈㄟ ㄌㄧˋ ㄐㄧㄚ)
Africa 亦作「非洲」

阿富汗(ㄚˇ ㄈㄨˋ ㄏㄢˋ)
Afghanistan

阿富汗人(ㄚˇ ㄈㄨˋ ㄏㄢˋ ㄖㄣˊ)
an Afghan

阿斗(ㄚˇ ㄉㄡˇ)
①the pet name of Liu Chan (劉禪), lackluster son of Liu Pei (劉備) in the Epoch of the Three Kingdoms ② a name that has become a synonym of a good-for-nothing

他真是個扶不起的阿斗。He is indeed a good-for-nothing person.

可堵('ㄎㄜˇㄉㄨˇ)
money (used in a contemptuous sense); pelf; wealth

阿拉('ㄚㄌㄚ)
①(Mohammedan) Allah ②(Ningbo dialect) me; I

阿拉巴馬('ㄚㄌㄚㄅㄚㄇㄚˇ)
the state of Alabama, U. S. A.

阿拉斯加('ㄚㄌㄚㄙㄐㄧㄚ)
the state of Alaska, U. S. A.

刺伯('ㄚㄌㄚㄅㄛˊ)
①Arabia ②Arab 亦作「阿拉伯」

刺伯半島('ㄚㄌㄚㄅㄛˊㄅㄢˋㄉㄠˇ)
the Arabian Peninsula 亦作「阿拉伯半島」

刺伯聯合大公國('ㄚㄌㄚㄅㄛˊㄌㄧㄢˊㄏㄜˊㄉㄚˋㄍㄨㄥㄍㄨㄛˊ)
United Arab Emirates (UAE) 亦作「阿拉伯聯合大公國」

刺伯聯合共和國('ㄚㄌㄚㄅㄛˊㄌㄧㄢˊㄏㄜˊㄍㄨㄥˋㄏㄜˊㄍㄨㄛˊ)
the United Arab Republic (UAR) 亦作「阿拉伯聯合共和國」

刺伯數字('ㄚㄌㄚㄅㄛˊㄕㄨˋㄗˋ)
Arabic numerals 亦作「阿拉伯數字」

刺伯人('ㄚㄌㄚㄅㄛˊㄖㄣˊ)
an Arab 亦作「阿拉伯人」

刺伯文('ㄚㄌㄚㄅㄛˊㄨㄣˊ)
Arabic (language) 亦作「阿拉伯文」

里山('ㄚˇㄌㄧˇㄕㄢ)
Mt. Ali, Taiwan

留申群島('ㄚㄌㄧㄡˊㄕㄣㄑㄩㄣˊㄉㄠˇ)
the Aleutian Islands

聯('ㄚㄌㄧㄢˊ)
short for the United Arab Republic (UAR)

根廷('ㄚㄍㄣㄊㄧㄥˊ)
Argentina; the Argentine

肯色('ㄚˇㄎㄣˇㄙㄜˋ)
the state of Arkansas, U. S. A.

基米德('ㄚㄐㄧㄇㄧˇㄉㄜˊ)
Archimedes (287-212 B.C.), Greek physicist, mathematician and inventor

基米德原理('ㄚㄐㄧㄇㄧˇㄉㄜˊㄩㄢˊㄌㄧˇ)

---

the Archimedean principle (of the lever and of specific gravity)

阿司匹靈or阿斯匹靈('ㄚㄙ ㄆㄧ ㄌㄧㄥˊ)
aspirin

阿薩姆('ㄚㄙㄚˇㄇㄨˇ)
Assam, India

阿爾巴尼亞('ㄚˇㄦˇㄅㄚ ㄋㄧˊ ㄧˋ)
Albania

阿爾卑斯山('ㄚˇㄦˇㄅㄟㄙ ㄕㄢ)
the Alps

阿爾泰山('ㄚˇㄦˇㄊㄞˋㄕㄢ)
the Altai Mountains

阿爾及利亞('ㄚˇㄦˇㄐㄧˊㄌㄧˋ ㄧˋ)
Algeria

阿爾薩斯('ㄚˇㄦˇㄙㄚˋㄙ)
Alsace

阿姨('ㄚ ㄧˊ)
①an aunt, one's mother's sister: 這位是我阿姨。This is my aunt. ②one's wife's sister ③a stepmother

【陀】 6595
ㄊㄨㄛˊ two tuó
craggy; rugged terrain

陀螺(ㄊㄨㄛˊㄌㄨㄛˊ)
a top: 我小時候喜歡玩陀螺。I liked to spin (or whip) a top in my boyhood.

陀羅尼(ㄊㄨㄛˊㄌㄨㄛˊㄋㄧˊ)
(Buddhism) *Dharani*, complete in all virtues; able to lay hold of the good so that it cannot be lost, and likewise of the evil so that it cannot arise; magical formulas, or mystic forms of prayer, or spells of the Tantric Order, often in Sanskrit, found in China as early as the third century A. D.

【陂】 6596
1. ㄆㄧˊ pyi pí
1. a reservoir; a water pond
2. a hillside

陂塘(ㄆㄧˊㄊㄤˊ)
a pond; a small lake

陂池(ㄆㄧˊㄔˊ)
a pond; a small lake; a reservoir

【陂】 6596
2. ㄆㄛˇ po pǒ
steep and craggy

陂陀(ㄆㄛˇㄊㄨㄛˊ)
(said of dikes, hill lines,

---

etc.) craggy; steep; winding; with ups and downs

【附】 6597
ㄈㄨˋ fuh fù
1. to rely on; to be dependent on; to attach to; to adhere to
2. to attach; to enclose; to send along with; to append; enclosed
3. near or close to
4. to add to; to increase
5. (said of an evil spirit) to be possessed by; to possess

附表(ㄈㄨˋㄅㄧㄠˇ)
supporting schedules (or statements)

附匪(ㄈㄨˋㄈㄟˇ)
to adhere to the bandits

附帶(ㄈㄨˋㄉㄞˋ)
①supplementary ②to attach ③in passing

附帶民事訴訟(ㄈㄨˋㄉㄞˋㄇㄧㄣˊㄕˋㄙㄨˋㄙㄨㄥˋ)
a supplementary civil action (in a criminal lawsuit)

附帶條件(ㄈㄨˋㄉㄞˋㄊㄧㄠˊㄐㄧㄢˋ)
conditions attached to a pledge, promise, etc.

附圖(ㄈㄨˋㄊㄨˊ)
an attached map or drawing; a figure

附驥(ㄈㄨˋㄐㄧˋ)
to adhere to; to submit to; to follow 亦作「附驥」

附錄(ㄈㄨˋㄌㄨˋ)
an appendix or annex

附郭(ㄈㄨˋㄍㄨㄛ)
near the outer wall of a city

附款(ㄈㄨˋㄎㄨㄢˇ)
appendant provisions in a legal document

附和(ㄈㄨˋㄏㄜˋ)
to agree without conviction; to repeat what others say; to echo; to chime in: 他附和我的意見。He echoed my views.

附化(ㄈㄨˋㄏㄨㄚˋ)
to be assimilated or naturalized

附會(ㄈㄨˋㄏㄨㄟˋ)
to twist in making an explanation; to make a forced interpretation; to make a far-fetched comparison

附記(ㄈㄨˋㄐㄧˋ)

〔阜部〕

附驥（ㄈㄨˋ ㄐㄧˋ）
(a modest expression) to ride on the coattails of a famed person to success

附加（ㄈㄨˋ ㄐㄧㄚ）
①to add to; to add...to...; to append...to; to attach...to...; 這個合約附加了一項說明。The contract has an explanatory note attached to it. ②supplementary

附加稅（ㄈㄨˋ ㄐㄧㄚ ㄕㄨㄟˋ）
a surtax; additional tax

附加語（ㄈㄨˋ ㄐㄧㄚ ㄩˇ）
an adjunct

附交（ㄈㄨˋ ㄐㄧㄠ）
to hand in or deliver as an attachment

附件（ㄈㄨˋ ㄐㄧㄢˋ）
an enclosure; an accessory; an attachment (of a letter, etc.): 這些是不可缺少的附件。These are indispensable accessories.

附近（ㄈㄨˋ ㄐㄧㄣˋ）
around; nearby; the vicinity: 他來自附近的鄉村。He came from a nearby village.

附註（ㄈㄨˋ ㄓㄨˋ）
remarks; notes

附著（ㄈㄨˋ ㄓㄨˋ）
to adhere to; to stick together: 整日下雨，我們的鞋子附著了污泥。It had rained all day and the mud adhered to our shoes.

附著力（ㄈㄨˋ ㄓㄨˋ ㄌㄧˋ）
adhesion; adhesive force

附贅懸疣（ㄈㄨˋ ㄓㄨㄟˋ ㄒㄩㄢˊ ㄧㄡˊ）
a superfluity

附設（ㄈㄨˋ ㄕㄜˋ）
to have as an attached institution: 這個大學附設一所中學。There is a middle school attached to the university.

附上（ㄈㄨˋ ㄕㄤˋ）
enclosed herewith: 隨信附上相片一張。A photograph is enclosed herewith.

附屬（ㄈㄨˋ ㄕㄨˇ）
accessory; subordinate; to affiliate with; to be attached to: 這是個附屬子句。It is a subordinate clause.

附屬品（ㄈㄨˋ ㄕㄨˇ ㄆㄧㄣˇ）
accessory items or articles; an adjunct; an accompaniment

附屬公司（ㄈㄨˋ ㄕㄨˇ ㄍㄨㄥ ㄙ）
a sub-company; a subsidiary company

附屬小學（ㄈㄨˋ ㄕㄨˇ ㄒㄧㄠˇ ㄒㄩㄝˊ）or 附小（ㄈㄨˋ ㄒㄧㄠˇ）
a primary school affiliated with an educational institution of higher level; an affiliated elementary school

附屬中學（ㄈㄨˋ ㄕㄨˇ ㄓㄨㄥ ㄒㄩㄝˊ）or 附中（ㄈㄨˋ ㄓㄨㄥ）
a middle (or high) school affiliated with a college or university; an affiliated middle school

附屬幼稚園（ㄈㄨˋ ㄕㄨˇ ㄧㄡˋ ㄓˋ ㄩㄢˊ）
a kindergarten attached to a primary school

附則（ㄈㄨˋ ㄗㄜˊ）
supplementary or additional rules

附耳（ㄈㄨˋ ㄦˇ）
to whisper: 她對我附耳說了些話。She whispered something in my ear.

附益（ㄈㄨˋ ㄧˋ）
added benefit

附議（ㄈㄨˋ ㄧˋ）
to second a motion; to support a proposal

附言（ㄈㄨˋ ㄧㄢˊ）
a postscript (P.S.)

附庸（ㄈㄨˋ ㄩㄥˊ）
a vassal state; subordinate; a puppet

附庸風雅（ㄈㄨˋ ㄩㄥˊ ㄈㄥ ㄧㄚˇ）
to try to act or speak like a refined, elegant or sophisticated person when one is not

附庸國（ㄈㄨˋ ㄩㄥˊ ㄍㄨㄛˊ）
a satellite state; a vassal state or dependant state

〔阸〕 6598
（阨）ㄜˋ eh ê
difficulty

六畫

〔陋〕 6599
ㄌㄡˋ low lòu
1. narrow and small
2. ugly

3. vile; low; mean; humble
4. ignorant; crude; simple minded
5. poor (performances, knowledge, etc.); inferior; superficial; shallow
6. stingy; tight-fisted

陋規（ㄌㄡˋ ㄍㄨㄟ）
bad practices

陋見（ㄌㄡˋ ㄐㄧㄢˋ）
vulgar views; shallow views

陋習（ㄌㄡˋ ㄒㄧˊ）
bad habits; corrupt practices

陋巷（ㄌㄡˋ ㄒㄧㄤˋ）
a narrow, dirty alley; slums

陋室（ㄌㄡˋ ㄕˋ）
a crude abode; a humble room; a room totally without decoration

陋儒（ㄌㄡˋ ㄖㄨˊ）
an ignorant scholar; a scholar with little learning

陋俗（ㄌㄡˋ ㄙㄨˊ）
vile customs; vulgar custom

〔陌〕 6600
ㄇㄛˋ moh mò
1. paths in the rice field: 阡陌縱橫。The paths crisscrossed on a farmland.
2. a road; a street

陌頭（ㄇㄛˋ ㄊㄡˊ）
①a handkerchief used to tie a man's hair in ancient China ②the roadside

陌路（ㄇㄛˋ ㄌㄨˋ）
①paths in the rice field ②stranger: 我們對他視如陌路。We treat him as a stranger.

陌生（ㄇㄛˋ ㄕㄥ）
unfamiliar; strange; inexperienced

陌生人（ㄇㄛˋ ㄕㄥ ㄖㄣˊ）
a stranger

〔降〕 6601
1. ㄐㄧㄤˋ jiang jiàng
1. to descend
2. to lower
3. to condescend; to deign
4. to drop; to decline
5. to surrender

降凡（ㄐㄧㄤˋ ㄈㄢˊ）
to come into the world; a in the incarnation of th divine

降福（ㄐㄧㄤˋ ㄈㄨˊ）
to bless; blessings fron Heaven: 願上帝降福於你。May bless you!

降低(ㄐㄧㄤ ㄉㄧ)
to lower; to fall; to drop: 他
降低了聲音說話。He lowered
his voice.

降低價格(ㄐㄧㄤ ㄉㄧ ㄐㄧㄚˋ ㄍㄜˊ)
marking down prices

降低身分(ㄐㄧㄤ ㄉㄧ ㄕㄣ ㄈㄣ)
to lower one's social status
or standing

降低生產成本(ㄐㄧㄤ ㄉㄧ ㄕㄥ ㄔㄢˇ ㄔㄥˊ ㄅㄣˇ)
to reduce the production
costs

降臨(ㄐㄧㄤ ㄌㄧㄣˊ)
①to come down; to fall: 黑
夜漸漸降臨。Night is falling.
②to condescend (to visit)

降落(ㄐㄧㄤ ㄌㄨㄛˋ)
①to land; landing; descent;
to descend: 該飛機安全降落
了。The airplane made a safe
landing. ②to drop; to rain
down③as in 跳傘降落—to
parachute

降落傘(ㄐㄧㄤ ㄌㄨㄛˋ ㄙㄢˇ)
a parachute

降落傘部隊(ㄐㄧㄤ ㄌㄨㄛˋ ㄙㄢˇ ㄅㄨˋ ㄉㄨㄟˋ)
paratroopers; paratroop
units

降格(ㄐㄧㄤ ㄍㄜˊ)
to lower the scale, standard,
standing or status

降格以求(ㄐㄧㄤ ㄍㄜˊ ㄧˇ ㄑㄧㄡˊ)
to lower the standard and to
be satisfied with the next
best or less qualified

降級(ㄐㄧㄤ ㄐㄧˊ)
to degrade; to demote; to
downgrade

降級數(ㄐㄧㄤ ㄐㄧˊ ㄕㄨˋ)
a descending series

降價銷售(ㄐㄧㄤ ㄐㄧㄚˋ ㄒㄧㄠ ㄕㄡˋ)
mark-down sale

降咎(ㄐㄧㄤ ㄐㄧㄡˋ)
to send down disaster or
calamity from Heaven

降旗(ㄐㄧㄤ ㄑㄧˊ)
to lower the flag

降心相就(ㄐㄧㄤ ㄒㄧㄣ ㄒㄧㄤ ㄐㄧㄡˋ)
to subject one's own will to
the dictates of others

降祥(ㄐㄧㄤ ㄒㄧㄤˊ)
to send down blessings from
Heaven; a godsend

降旨(ㄐㄧㄤ ㄓˇ)
to issue an imperial decree

降志辱身(ㄐㄧㄤ ㄓˋ ㄖㄨˋ ㄕㄣ)
to lower one's aspiration
and denigrate oneself

降世(ㄐㄧㄤ ㄕˋ)
to come down to the world,
as Jesus Christ

降神(ㄐㄧㄤ ㄕㄣˊ)
to invite the visit of spirits

降生(ㄐㄧㄤ ㄕㄥ)
to be born into the world

降溫(ㄐㄧㄤ ㄨㄣ)
①to lower the temperature
(as in a workshop) ②to
drop in temperature

降雨量(ㄐㄧㄤ ㄩˇ ㄌㄧㄤˋ)
rainfall

【降】 6601
2. ㄒㄧㄤˊ shyang
xiáng

1. to surrender; to submit to
2. to bring to terms; to conquer; to subjugate

降表(ㄒㄧㄤˊ ㄅㄧㄠˇ)
a letter of surrender or
capitulation

降伏(ㄒㄧㄤˊ ㄈㄨˊ)
①to bring to terms; to
conquer; to subjugate ②to
break in; to tame: 他降伏了
一頭野牛。He broke in a wild
ox.

降服(ㄒㄧㄤˊ ㄈㄨˊ)or降附(ㄒㄧㄤˊ ㄈㄨˋ)
① to surrender and give
allegiance to the new master
②to bring to terms; to subdue: 他降服了敵人。He sub-
dued his enemies.

降龍伏虎(ㄒㄧㄤˊ ㄌㄨㄥˊ ㄈㄨˊ ㄏㄨˇ)
①to subjugate dragons and
tigers with magic—to overcome powerful adversaries
②(Taoism) to conquer one's
passions

降將(ㄒㄧㄤˊ ㄐㄧㄤˋ)
a general who has come
over from the enemy camp;
a general who has surren-
dered

降旗(ㄒㄧㄤˊ ㄑㄧˊ)
the white flag signifying surrender

降妖(ㄒㄧㄤˊ ㄧㄠ)
to subjugate evil spirits

【限】 6602
ㄒㄧㄢˋ shiann xiàn

1. a boundary; a line

2. a doorsill or threshold
3. limits; restriction; to limit
or restrict: 我的能力有限。My
powers are limited.
4. to specify; to fix

限定(ㄒㄧㄢˋ ㄉㄧㄥˋ)
to fix (a deadline, time
limit, etc.); to specify (qualifications of a person or merchandise); to limit

限度(ㄒㄧㄢˋ ㄉㄨˋ)
limits; limitation; degree (of
what one can take): 一個人
的忍耐是有限度的。There is a
limit to one's patience.

限量(ㄒㄧㄢˋ ㄌㄧㄤˋ)
limits; limitation; a boundary; to restrict or measure

限令(ㄒㄧㄢˋ ㄌㄧㄥˋ)
to order somebody to do
something within a certain
time

限價(ㄒㄧㄢˋ ㄐㄧㄚˋ)
price control; a price fixed
under a government speci-
fied ceiling

限交本人(ㄒㄧㄢˋ ㄐㄧㄠ ㄅㄣˇ ㄖㄣˊ)
delivery to the addressee in
person

限期(ㄒㄧㄢˋ ㄑㄧˊ)
① a time limit; a deadline:
限期已屆。The time limit has
been reached. ② within a
definite time

限制(ㄒㄧㄢˋ ㄓˋ)
limits; limitations; to
restrict; restrictions; to confine something within certain limits: 車子進口有限
制。There is a limitation on
car imports.

限制行為能力人(ㄒㄧㄢˋ ㄓˋ ㄒㄧㄥˊ ㄨㄟˊ ㄋㄥˊ ㄌㄧˋ ㄖㄣˊ)
(law) a person with a lim-
ited disposing capacity

限制性(ㄒㄧㄢˋ ㄓˋ ㄒㄧㄥˋ)
restricted; restrictive

限制生產(ㄒㄧㄢˋ ㄓˋ ㄕㄥ ㄔㄢˇ)
to control production; controlled production

限時(ㄒㄧㄢˋ ㄕˊ)
to fix or set the time; to set
a time limit or deadline

限時專送(ㄒㄧㄢˋ ㄕˊ ㄓㄨㄢ ㄙㄨㄥˋ)
(Chinese postal service)
prompt delivery

限額(ㄒㄧㄢˋ ㄜˊ)

〔阜部〕

【阜部】

a quota; the maximum number or amount allowed

限外 (ㄒㄧㄢ ㄨㄞ)
beyond the specified limit (as the issuance of bank notes, etc.)

限於 (ㄒㄧㄢ ㄩ)
(in writing, etc.) owing to the limitation of; due to (regulations, etc.): 他的活動限於教育界。 He confined his activities in educational circles.

【陔】 6603
《ㄞ gai gāi
1. steps; grades
2. ridges between plots of farm land

七畫

【陘】 6604
ㄒㄧㄥ shyng xíng
a defile; a gorge; a deep valley

【陛】 6605
ㄅㄧ bih bì
wide and high steps in the palace; the steps to the throne

陛戟 (ㄅㄧ ㄐㄧ)
imperial guards armed with spears

陛見 (ㄅㄧ ㄐㄧㄢ)
to have an audience with the emperor

陛下 (ㄅㄧ ㄒㄧㄚ)
Your Majesty; His or Her Majesty

陛辭 (ㄅㄧ ㄘ)
to leave the capital after bidding the emperor goodbye in audience

陛衞 (ㄅㄧ ㄨㄟ)
the imperial guard

【陞】 6606
ㄕㄥ sheng shēng
1. to ascend; to promote; to hoist; to rise; to elevate
2. a Chinese family name

【陟】 6607
ㄓ jyh zhì
1. to mount; to ascend
2. to advance; to elevate; to promote

陟罰 (ㄓ ㄈㄚ)
to promote and demote; to reward and punish

陟降 (ㄓ ㄐㄧㄤ)
to promote and demote

陟黜 (ㄓ ㄔㄨ)
to promote or demote; to promote or dismiss

【陡】 6608
ㄉㄡ doou dǒu
1. suddenly; abruptly
2. steep; precipitous: 這坡很陡。 The slope is very steep.

陡壁 (ㄉㄡ ㄅㄧ)
a steep bank; a precipitous cliff

陡坡 (ㄉㄡ ㄆㄛ)
a steep slope

陡頓 (ㄉㄡ ㄉㄨㄣ)
suddenly; abruptly

陡覺 (ㄉㄡ ㄐㄩㄝ)
to feel all of a sudden

陡峭 (ㄉㄡ ㄑㄧㄠ)
steep; precipitous

陡然 (ㄉㄡ ㄖㄢ)
suddenly; abruptly: 橋陡然塌下。 The bridge fell suddenly.

【院】 6609
ㄩㄢ yuann yuàn
1. a courtyard; a yard
2. a designation for certain government offices and public places
3. short for the Executive Yuan, Legislative Yuan, Examination Yuan, Judicial Yuan, or Control Yuan

院本 (ㄩㄢ ㄅㄣ)
the plays staged at brothels during the Mongol and Tungusic era

院落 (ㄩㄢ ㄌㄨㄛ)
a courtyard; a compound

院際比賽 (ㄩㄢ ㄐㄧ ㄅㄧ ㄙㄞ)
a competition between colleges; an intercollegiate competition

院牆 (ㄩㄢ ㄑㄧㄤ)
the wall that surrounds a house

院轄市 (ㄩㄢ ㄒㄧㄚ ㄕ)
a municipality under the direct jurisdiction of the Executive Yuan; a special municipality

院長 (ㄩㄢ ㄓㄤ)
the dean of a college or court of law; the director of a hospital, museum, etc.; the president of Academia

Sinica or one of the five Yuan under the Chinese government system (including the premier)

院士 (ㄩㄢ ㄕ)
a member of Academia Sinica, or an academician

院子 (ㄩㄢ ㄗ˙) or 院兒 (ㄩㄢㄦ)
a yard; a courtyard: 院子裡種了一些玫瑰。 There are some roses in the courtyard

院宇 (ㄩㄢ ㄩ)
the house and the yard

【陣】 6610
ㄓㄣ jenn zhèn
1. a column or row of troops in the army; the rank and file
2. to battle; to go to war; to fight at the front; the battle field; battle array (or formation)
3. anything that occurs in a certain duration or spell of time (as rain, wind, business, etc.): 他感到一陣劇痛。 He felt a gust of pain.

陣殁 (ㄓㄣ ㄇㄛ)
to die on the battlefield; to be killed in action 亦作「陣亡」

陣法 (ㄓㄣ ㄈㄚ)
tactical deployment of troops; the plan of a campaign

陣地 (ㄓㄣ ㄉㄧ)
a (military) position: 他們溜入陣地。 They slipped into the position.

陣地戰 (ㄓㄣ ㄉㄧ ㄓㄢ)
trench warfare; position warfare

陣圖 (ㄓㄣ ㄊㄨ)
a map showing the deployment of troops

陣痛 (ㄓㄣ ㄊㄨㄥ)
labor pangs; pangs of childbirth; throes; pains that occur at intervals

陣腳 (ㄓㄣ ㄐㄧㄠ)
① a front line ② position, situation; circumstances: 我們必須穩住陣腳。 We have to secure our position.

陣前 (ㄓㄣ ㄑㄧㄢ)
on the battlefield: 他死在陣前。 He died on the battle field.

陣前起義 (ㄓㄣ ㄑㄧㄢ ㄑㄧ ㄧ)

(said of enemy troops) to defect in the course of a battle

陣線 (ㄓㄣˋ ㄒㄧㄢˋ)
line of battle

陣陣 (ㄓㄣˋ ㄓㄣˋ)
intermittently; intermittent (rains, winds, pain, etc.); now and again; at intervals; repeatedly; by fits and starts; gusts: 風陣陣吹。The wind blew in gusts.

陣勢 (ㄓㄣˋ ㄕˋ)
order of battle; battle array (or formation)

陣首 (ㄓㄣˋ ㄕㄡˇ)
the forward echelons of combat troops in battle

陣容 (ㄓㄣˋ ㄖㄨㄥˊ)
①the appearance of 2 military deployment; the layout of troops ②the lineup of a cabinet; the composition of a sports team, an organization, etc. ③the cast of a movie

陣容整齊 (ㄓㄣˋ ㄖㄨㄥˊ ㄓㄥˇ ㄑㄧˊ)
①a neat or appropriate layout of troops; a flawless deployment ②(said of a movie cast, sports team,) Everyone is a top choice. 或 There is no second-rater among them.

陣子 (ㄓㄣˋ ˙ㄗ)
a spell of

陣營 (ㄓㄣˋ ㄧㄥˊ)
a camp; an encampment; a barracks

陣亡 (ㄓㄣˋ ㄨㄤˊ)
to be killed in action

陣亡將士紀念碑 (ㄓㄣˋ ㄨㄤˊ ㄐㄧㄤˋ ㄕˋ ㄐㄧˋ ㄋㄧㄢˋ ㄅㄟ)
a monument in honor of servicemen killed in action

陣雨 (ㄓㄣˋ ㄩˇ)
occasional drizzle; showers (especially in summer)

陣雲 (ㄓㄣˋ ㄩㄣˊ)
dense clouds

【除】 6611
ㄔㄨˊ chwu chú

1. (mathematics) to divide; division; divisible
2. to remove; to rid of; to wipe out: 他們消除了疑慮。They removed all doubts.

3. to be appointed to an official rank or office
4. to subtract; to deduct
5. aside from; besides; except; unless: 除了李小姐，我們都去了。We all went except Miss Lee.
6. to change or turn, as a new year

除拜 (ㄔㄨˊ ㄅㄞˋ)
to be appointed to an office

除暴安良 (ㄔㄨˊ ㄅㄠˋ ㄢ ㄌㄧㄤˊ)
to get rid of lawless elements and protect the good

除弊 (ㄔㄨˊ ㄅㄧˋ)
to remove evil practices or abuses

除病 (ㄔㄨˊ ㄅㄧㄥˋ)
①to get rid of a disease ②to get rid of a bad habit, practice, etc.

除不盡 (ㄔㄨˊ ㄅㄨˋ ㄐㄧㄣˋ)
indivisible

除剷淨剩 (ㄔㄨˊ ㄔㄢˇ ㄐㄧㄥˋ ㄕㄥˋ)
leftovers; remnants

除貧 (ㄔㄨˊ ㄆㄧㄣˊ)
to save the poor; to get rid of poverty

除名 (ㄔㄨˊ ㄇㄧㄥˊ)
to dismiss; to strike one's name off the list; to expel

除法 (ㄔㄨˊ ㄈㄚˇ)
(mathematics) division

除非 (ㄔㄨˊ ㄈㄟ)
unless: 若欲人不知，除非己莫為。If you don't want people to know, you'd better not do it.

除服 (ㄔㄨˊ ㄈㄨˊ)
to take off the mourning garment at the end of the mourning period

除道 (ㄔㄨˊ ㄉㄠˋ)
to start building a road

除掉 (ㄔㄨˊ ㄉㄧㄠˋ)
to remove; to get rid of (prejudices, obstacles, etc.)

除汰 (ㄔㄨˊ ㄊㄞˋ)
to remove; to get rid of

除了 (ㄔㄨˊ ˙ㄌㄜ)
①except that; except ②aside from; besides

除靈 (ㄔㄨˊ ㄌㄧㄥˊ)
to burn the spirit tablet

after completing the mass for the deceased

除根 (ㄔㄨˊ ㄍㄣ)
to root out; to uproot; to dig up the roots; to cure once and for all

除官 (ㄔㄨˊ ㄍㄨㄢ)
to be formally appointed to an office

除害 (ㄔㄨˊ ㄏㄞˋ)
to get rid of evils, bad habits or practices or evil persons

除號 (ㄔㄨˊ ㄏㄠˋ)
(mathematics) the sign of division "÷"

除籍 (ㄔㄨˊ ㄐㄧˊ)
to strike one's name off the list; to disenroll; to dismiss; to expel

除舊布新 (ㄔㄨˊ ㄐㄧㄡˋ ㄅㄨˋ ㄒㄧㄣ)
to remove the old and introduce the new; to replace the old with the new

除菊 (ㄔㄨˊ ㄐㄩˊ)
the pyrethrum

除清 (ㄔㄨˊ ㄑㄧㄥ)
to clear up

除去 (ㄔㄨˊ ㄑㄩˋ)
to remove; to get rid of; to except: 他們將他從名單上除去。They excepted him from the list.

除却 (ㄔㄨˊ ㄑㄩㄝˋ)
①to remove or root out ②unless

除夕 (ㄔㄨˊ ㄒㄧˋ) or 除夜 (ㄔㄨˊ ㄧㄝˋ)
Lunar New Year's Eve

除邪 (ㄔㄨˊ ㄒㄧㄝˊ)
to do away with evil (spirits, or influences); to exorcise

除臭劑 (ㄔㄨˊ ㄔㄡˋ ㄐㄧˋ)
deodorants

除塵器 (ㄔㄨˊ ㄔㄣˊ ㄑㄧˋ)
a dust remover

除濕機 (ㄔㄨˊ ㄕ ㄐㄧ)
a dehumidifier

除數 (ㄔㄨˊ ㄕㄨˋ)
a divisor

除災 (ㄔㄨˊ ㄗㄞ)
to save from misfortune or disaster

除罪 (ㄔㄨˊ ㄗㄨㄟˋ)
to remit sin or punishment

除此之外 (ㄔㄨˊ ㄘˇ ㄓ ㄨㄞˋ)

〔阜部〕

besides this (or these); in addition: 除此之外，我什麼都不要。I want nothing besides this.

除草(ㄔㄨ ㄘㄠˇ)
to weed (in farming); to mow grass or cut weeds: 他用除草機除草。He mowed the grass with the lawn mower.

除喪(ㄔㄨ ㄙㄤ)
to remove the mourning garments at the end of the mourning period

除惡務盡(ㄔㄨ ㄜˋ ㄨˋ ㄐㄧㄣˋ)
Evil must be completely eradicated. 或One must be thorough in exterminating an evil.

除以(ㄔㄨ ㄧˇ)
(a number) to be divided by

除役(ㄔㄨ ㄧˋ)
to have one's name struck off the reserve list when he reaches the specified age

除外(ㄔㄨ ㄨㄞˋ)
except; to except: 我當然把你除外。Of course I except you.

除月(ㄔㄨ ㄩㄝˋ)
the last (12th) moon of the lunar year

【陝】 6612
ㄕㄢˇ shaan shǎn
1. short for Shensi Province
2. a Chinese family name

陝西(ㄕㄢˇ ㄒㄧ)
Shensi Province

八畫

【陪】 6613
ㄆㄟˊ peir péi
1. to accompany; to keep company: 請陪我散步。Please accompany me on my walk.
2. same as 賠—to make up for; to compensate
3. to assist

陪拜(ㄆㄟˊ ㄅㄞˋ)
to accompany or follow another in making bows or kneeling

陪伴(ㄆㄟˊ ㄅㄢˋ)
to keep company; to accompany: 他陪伴我。He kept me company.

陪不是(ㄆㄟˊ ㄅㄨˋ •ㄕ)
to apologize; to ask forgiveness

陪房(ㄆㄟˊ ㄈㄤˊ)
(in former times) maids that accompanied the bride to her husband's house and stayed there to serve her

陪都(ㄆㄟˊ ㄉㄨ)
an alternate capital; a secondary capital; a provisional capital 亦作「陪京」

陪同(ㄆㄟˊ ㄊㄨㄥˊ)
to accompany

陪禮(ㄆㄟˊ ㄌㄧˇ)
to ask forgiveness; to apologize

陪客(ㄆㄟˊ •ㄎㄜ)
① guests invited to keep the guest of honor company
② (ㄆㄟˊ ㄎㄜˋ) ⓐ to receive guests; to keep guests company ⓑ (said of girls in gay establishments) to attend on patrons

陪話(ㄆㄟˊ ㄏㄨㄚˋ)
to apologize

陪嫁(ㄆㄟˊ ㄐㄧㄚˋ)
the dowry given to a daughter on her marriage

陪酒(ㄆㄟˊ ㄐㄧㄡˇ)
(said of a bar girl, etc.) to accompany a patron in drinking

陪京(ㄆㄟˊ ㄐㄧㄥ)
a secondary capital; a provisional capital; an alternate capital 亦作「陪都」

陪小心(ㄆㄟˊ ㄒㄧㄠˇ ㄒㄧㄣ)
to talk and act obsequiously in order to placate or please another

陪笑(ㄆㄟˊ ㄒㄧㄠˋ) or 陪笑臉(ㄆㄟˊ ㄒㄧㄠˋ ㄌㄧㄢˇ)
to put up a smiling face in order to please or placate someone

陪襯(ㄆㄟˊ ㄔㄣˋ)
to serve as a background in order to bring out the subject with greater brilliance; to serve as a prop (as in photography)

陪侍(ㄆㄟˊ ㄕˋ)
to assist in attendance

陪審(ㄆㄟˊ ㄕㄣˇ)
① to act (or serve) as an assessor (in a law case) ② to serve on a jury

陪審團(ㄆㄟˊ ㄕㄣˇ ㄊㄨㄢˊ)
the jury

陪審制度(ㄆㄟˊ ㄕㄣˇ ㄓˋ ㄉㄨˋ)
the jury system

陪審員(ㄆㄟˊ ㄕㄣˇ ㄩㄢˊ)
a juror member of the jury; a juror; a juryman; a jurywoman

陪葬(ㄆㄟˊ ㄗㄤˋ)
to bury (a person or things) along with the deceased

陪罪(ㄆㄟˊ ㄗㄨㄟˋ)
to ask forgiveness; to apologize

陪送(ㄆㄟˊ ㄙㄨㄥˋ)
the dowry given to a daughter on her marriage

陪位(ㄆㄟˊ ㄨㄟˋ)
to be seated beside the emperor

【阪】 6614
ㄗㄡˇ tzou zǒu
1. a corner; a nook
2. foothills
3. a frontier village where people live together
4. the first month of the lunar year

阪落(ㄗㄡˇ ㄌㄨㄛˋ)
a frontier village where people live together

阪月(ㄗㄡˇ ㄩㄝˋ)
the first month of the lunar year

【陰】 6615
1. ㄧㄣ in yīn
1. negative (as opposite to positive, as electricity)
2. feminine; female
3. cloudy; dark
4. shady
5. secret
6. the back side
7. the north side of a mountain
8. the south side of a stream
9. reproductive organs of both sexes
10. Hades; hell
11. cunning and crafty
12. to injure another in a clandestine manner
13. time
14. a Chinese family name

陰部(ㄧㄣ ㄅㄨˋ)
(said of the human body) the private part

陰平(ㄧㄣ ㄆㄧㄥ)
①(Chinese phonetics) the first tone ② name of an ancient place in Kansu Province (甘肅省)

陰霾(ㄧㄣ ㄇㄞˊ)
haze; thin mist

陰毛(ㄧㄣ ㄇㄠˊ)
the hair at the private part; pubes

陰謀(ㄧㄣ ㄇㄡˊ)
a conspiracy; a plot; a secret scheme

陰謀詭計(ㄧㄣ ㄇㄡˊ ㄍㄨㄟˇ ㄐㄧˋ)
dark schemes and tricks; schemes and intrigues

陰風(ㄧㄣ ㄈㄥ)
① chilly winds ② winds that often precede the appearance of a ghost

陰伏(ㄧㄣ ㄈㄨˊ)
① one's sins unknown to others ② to ambush secretly

陰府(ㄧㄣ ㄈㄨˇ)
the nether world; Hades

陰阜(ㄧㄣ ㄈㄨˋ)
the mound of the vulva

陰德(ㄧㄣ ㄉㄜˊ)
one's unpublicized good deeds

陰道(ㄧㄣ ㄉㄠˋ)
① the vagina ② a shaded road ③ the "subordinate ways"—the ways of subjects to the king, of children to parents and of wife to husband

陰地(ㄧㄣ ㄉㄧˋ)
① a graveyard ② a place where sunshine cannot reach

陰電(ㄧㄣ ㄉㄧㄢˋ)
negative electricity

陰毒(ㄧㄣ ㄉㄨˊ)
mean, cunning, etc. in a clandestine way

陰天(ㄧㄣ ㄊㄧㄢ)
a cloudy day

陰囊(ㄧㄣ ㄋㄤˊ)
the scrotum

陰冷(ㄧㄣ ㄌㄥˇ)
①(said of weather) gloomy and cold; raw ②(said of a person's look) somber; glum

陰離子(ㄧㄣ ㄌㄧˊ ˙ㄗ)
a negative ion

陰曆(ㄧㄣ ㄌㄧˋ)
the lunar calendar

陰涼處(ㄧㄣ ㄌㄧㄤˊ ㄔㄨˋ)
a shaded, cool place: 我們找個陰涼處歇歇吧! Let's have a rest in the shade.

陰靈(ㄧㄣ ㄌㄧㄥˊ)
the spirits of the deceased

陰溝(ㄧㄣ ㄍㄡ)
① a covered drain; a sewer ② the vagina

陰乾(ㄧㄣ ㄍㄢ)
to be placed in the shade to dry; to dry in the shade

陰官(ㄧㄣ ㄍㄨㄢ)
① reigning authorities in Hades ② the rain god

陰功(ㄧㄣ ㄍㄨㄥ)
one's unpublicized good deeds or virtues

陰核(ㄧㄣ ㄏㄜˊ)
the clitoris

陰戶(ㄧㄣ ㄏㄨˋ)
the female reproductive organ; the vagina

陰晦(ㄧㄣ ㄏㄨㄟˋ)
shady; dark; dismal

陰魂(ㄧㄣ ㄏㄨㄣˊ)
the spirits of the dead

陰魂不散(ㄧㄣ ㄏㄨㄣˊ ㄅㄨˋ ㄙㄢˋ)
The soul (or spirit) refuses to leave.

陰極(ㄧㄣ ㄐㄧˊ)
the cathode; the negative pole

陰間(ㄧㄣ ㄐㄧㄢ)
Hades; the shades; the underworld

陰莖(ㄧㄣ ㄐㄧㄥ)
the penis

陰譴(ㄧㄣ ㄑㄧㄢˇ)
punishment meted out by the hands of God

陰險(ㄧㄣ ㄒㄧㄢˇ)
cunning; crafty; deceitful; sinister: 他為人陰險毒辣。He was sinister and ruthless.

陰性(ㄧㄣ ㄒㄧㄥˋ)
① negative ② female

陰性反應(ㄧㄣ ㄒㄧㄥˋ ㄈㄢˇ ㄧㄥˋ)
negative reaction

陰宅(ㄧㄣ ㄓㄞˊ)
a graveyard 參看「陽宅」

陰著兒(ㄧㄣ ㄓㄠˋ ㄦˊ)
a clandestine and vicious move

陰沈(ㄧㄣ ㄔㄣˊ)

①gloomy (sky); overcast; somber; cloudy; clouded: 整個下午天都是陰沈的。The sky was cloudy all afternoon. ② quiet and designing (persons)

陰唇(ㄧㄣ ㄔㄨㄣˊ)
the labia

陰事(ㄧㄣ ㄕˋ)
① secrets ② the affairs between the emperor and his concubines

陰室(ㄧㄣ ㄕˋ)
① one's private quarter; one's bedroom ② an underground cellar for storage of ice

陰山(ㄧㄣ ㄕㄢ)
the Yin Mountains

陰曹地府(ㄧㄣ ㄘㄠˊ ㄉㄧˋ ㄈㄨˇ)
Hades

陰錯陽差(ㄧㄣ ㄘㄨㄛˋ ㄧㄤˊ ㄔㄞ)
due to all sorts of accidental mishaps

陰司(ㄧㄣ ㄙ)
officials in Hades

陰私(ㄧㄣ ㄙ)
personal secrets

陰森(ㄧㄣ ㄙㄣ)
gloomy; gruesome; ghastly: 那是個陰森的樹林。That is a gloomy forest.

陰森森(ㄧㄣ ㄙㄣ ㄙㄣ)
gloomy; weird; ominous

陰惡(ㄧㄣ ㄜˋ)
undiscovered evil deeds

陰暗(ㄧㄣ ㄢˋ)
dim; dark; gloomy; overcast

陰翳(ㄧㄣ ㄧˋ)
shady; dark; gloomy

陰陰沈沈(ㄧㄣ ㄧㄣ ㄔㄣˊ ㄔㄣˊ)
gloomy; dusky; dreary: 天空陰陰沈沈地。It's a gloomy sky.

陰陽(ㄧㄣ ㄧㄤˊ)
(Chinese philosophy, medicine, etc.) yin (shade) and yang (light), the two opposing principles in nature, the former feminine and negative, the latter masculine and positive

陰陽怪氣(ㄧㄣ ㄧㄤˊ ㄍㄨㄞˋ ㄑㄧˋ)
① to act or speak in an odd or queer manner ② eccentric; queer

陰陽家(ㄧㄣ ㄧㄤˊ ㄐㄧㄚ)
① a geomancer; a sorcerer; an astrologer ② the Yin

〔阜

部〕

〔阜 部〕

Yang School (in the Epoch of Warring States, 475-221B.C.)

陰陽人〔一ㄣ 一ㄤ ㄖㄣˊ〕
a hermaphrodite

陰影〔一ㄣ 一ㄥˇ〕
shades; shadows

陰文〔一ㄣ ㄨㄣˊ〕
incised inscriptions 亦作「陰識」

陰紋〔一ㄣ ㄨㄣˊ〕
an internal or female screw

陰雨〔一ㄣ ㄩˇ〕
cloudy and rainy; overcast and rainy: 連日陰雨不斷 It has been cloudy and drizzly day after day.

陰鬱〔一ㄣ ㄩˋ〕
gloomy; dismal; depressed: 他心情陰鬱 He felt depressed.

陰雲〔一ㄣ ㄩㄣˊ〕
dark clouds; rain clouds

【陰】 6615
2.(蔭) 一ˋ yinn yin
shaded by trees

【陲】 6616
ㄔㄨㄟˊ chwei chui
a border; a frontier

【陳】 6617
1. ㄔㄣˊ chern chen
1. a Chinese family name
2. to arrange; to display; to spread out
3. to tell, state, or narrate; to explain
4. old; stale; preserved for a long time
5. name of a state in the Epoch of Spring and Autumn
6. name of a dynasty (557-589)
7. to make public

陳編〔ㄔㄣˊ ㄅㄧㄢ〕
books authored by ancient writers

陳兵〔ㄔㄣˊ ㄅㄧㄥ〕
to mass troops; to deploy troops: 他們陳兵邊境。They are massing troops along the border.

陳病〔ㄔㄣˊ ㄅㄧㄥˋ〕
an old or chronic disease

陳皮梅〔ㄔㄣˊ ㄆㄧˊ ㄇㄟˊ〕
sugar preserved prunes

陳平〔ㄔㄣˊ ㄆㄧㄥˊ〕
Chen Ping, a strategist who helped Liu Pang (劉邦) found the Han Dynasty

陳墨〔ㄔㄣˊ ㄇㄜˋ〕
an old inkstick—considered to be precious

陳米〔ㄔㄣˊ ㄇㄧˇ〕
old rice

陳明〔ㄔㄣˊ ㄇㄧㄥˊ〕
to state clearly: 證人將事實陳明了。The witness stated the facts very clearly.

陳腐〔ㄔㄣˊ ㄈㄨˇ〕
old or hackneyed (expressions, etc.); stale (food or fruit): 「潔白как雪」是個陳腐的比喻。"White as snow" is a hackneyed comparison.

陳那〔ㄔㄣˊ ㄋㄚˋ〕
Dignaga, circa A. D. 500 or 550, a great Buddhist logician and founder of the new logic

陳年〔ㄔㄣˊ ㄋㄧㄢˊ〕
(wine, etc.) of many years' standing

陳年老酒〔ㄔㄣˊ ㄋㄧㄢˊ ㄌㄠˇ ㄐㄧㄡˇ〕
alcoholic drinks that have been preserved for a long time; aged wine

陳列〔ㄔㄣˊ ㄌㄧㄝˋ〕
to arrange and display; to set out; to exhibit: 她們在陳列出售的貨物。They're displaying goods for sale.

陳列品〔ㄔㄣˊ ㄌㄧㄝˋ ㄆㄧㄣˇ〕
articles on display; exhibits

陳列所〔ㄔㄣˊ ㄌㄧㄝˋ ㄙㄨㄛˇ〕
an exhibition hall; a display room

陳琳〔ㄔㄣˊ ㄌㄧㄣˊ〕
Chen Lin, a writer of the Eastern Han Dynasty

陳糧〔ㄔㄣˊ ㄌㄧㄤˊ〕
old grain

陳穀〔ㄔㄣˊ ㄍㄨˇ〕
rice harvested in the previous year

陳穀子爛芝蔴〔ㄔㄣˊ ㄍㄨˇ ˙ㄗ ㄌㄢˋ ㄓ ㄇㄚˊ〕
(figuratively) petty and stale gossip

陳規〔ㄔㄣˊ ㄍㄨㄟ〕
out-of-date conventions

陳後主〔ㄔㄣˊ ㄏㄡˋ ㄓㄨˇ〕
Chen Shu-pao (陳叔寶), 553-604, the last monarch of the Chen Dynasty, noted for his poems and debauchery

陳貨〔ㄔㄣˊ ㄏㄨㄛˋ〕
old goods; goods from old stock

陳迹〔ㄔㄣˊ ㄐㄧ〕
relics; vestiges; things of the past; an old trace

陳酒〔ㄔㄣˊ ㄐㄧㄡˇ〕
old wine: 陳酒香醇。Old wine is fragrant and good.

陳舊〔ㄔㄣˊ ㄐㄧㄡˋ〕
old; worn-out; outmoded; obsolete; shabby: 它是個陳舊的觀念。It is an outmoded idea.

陳腔濫調〔ㄔㄣˊ ㄑㄧㄤ ㄌㄢˋ ㄉㄧㄠˋ〕
hackneyed expressions; cliches; corny statements

陳情〔ㄔㄣˊ ㄑㄧㄥˊ〕
to give a full statement or account of a situation, etc.

陳請〔ㄔㄣˊ ㄑㄧㄥˇ〕
to state and plead

陳寫〔ㄔㄣˊ ㄒㄧㄝˇ〕
to narrate; to describe

陳陳相因〔ㄔㄣˊ ㄔㄣˊ ㄒㄧㄤ ㄧㄣ〕
writing without new ideas; to copy or follow precedents, old practices, etc.

陳誠〔ㄔㄣˊ ㄔㄥˊ〕
Chen Cheng, 1897-1965, architect of land reform in Taiwan

陳屍〔ㄔㄣˊ ㄕ〕
to exhibit or expose a corpse

陳事〔ㄔㄣˊ ㄕˋ〕
things or happenings of the past; old affairs

陳設〔ㄔㄣˊ ㄕㄜˋ〕
to display; to decorate; to exhibit; to set out; to furnish (especially interior)

陳紹〔ㄔㄣˊ ㄕㄠˋ〕
the old Shaohsing wine (紹興酒)

陳壽〔ㄔㄣˊ ㄕㄡˋ〕
Chen Shou, a scholar of the Tsin Dynasty and author of The History of the Three Kingdoms (三國志)

陳述〔ㄔㄣˊ ㄕㄨˋ〕
to tell; to narrate; to state: 請陳述你的見解。Please state your views.

陳說〔ㄔㄣˊ ㄕㄨㄛ or 陳詞〔ㄔㄣˊ ㄘˊ〕
to state; to explain

陳訴〔ㄔㄣˊ ㄙㄨˋ〕
to state; to plead

陳義甚高(ㄔㄣ ㄧˋ ㄕㄣˋ ㄍㄠ)
with lofty ideals

陳言(ㄔㄣˊ ㄧㄢˊ)
hackneyed or stale expressions

陳圓圓(ㄔㄣˊ ㄩㄢˊ ㄩㄢˊ)
a concubine of General Wu San-kuei (吳三桂) of the Ming Dynasty, popularly considered a traitor who asked for military assistance from Ching troops to fight rebel troops

【陳】 6617
2. (陣) ㄓㄣˋ jenn jhen
tactical deployment of troops

【陴】 6618
ㄆㄧˊ pyi pí
a parapet on a city wall

【陵】 6619
ㄌㄧㄥˊ ling líng
1. a high mound
2. the tomb of an emperor; a mausoleum
3. to offend; to insult; to outrage; to abuse
4. to usurp
5. to climb; to scale
6. a Chinese family name

陵廟(ㄌㄧㄥˊ ㄇㄧㄠˋ)
the tomb and ancestral shrine

陵墓(ㄌㄧㄥˊ ㄇㄨˋ)
a tomb; a grave; a mausoleum

陵替(ㄌㄧㄥˊ ㄊㄧˋ)
to deteriorate; to fall into decadence (usually said of law and order, or moral standards)

陵轢(ㄌㄧㄥˊ ㄌㄧˋ)
①to encroach upon each other; to infringe ②to jockey for position

陵谷(ㄌㄧㄥˊ ㄍㄨˇ)
high banks and deep valleys—changes of worldly affairs; ups and downs; vicissitudes

陵居(ㄌㄧㄥˊ ㄐㄩ)
to live on the highland

陵丘(ㄌㄧㄥˊ ㄑㄧㄡ)
a grave or tomb as big as a high mound

陵寢(ㄌㄧㄥˊ ㄑㄧㄣˇ)
the tomb of an emperor or king; a mausoleum

陵遲(ㄌㄧㄥˊ ㄔˊ) 或 凌遲(ㄌㄧㄥˊ ㄔˊ)
①to deteriorate; to fall into decadence ②(in ancient China) to execute a criminal after cutting off his limbs

陵夷(ㄌㄧㄥˊ ㄧˊ)
to deteriorate; to decay

陵雨(ㄌㄧㄥˊ ㄩˇ)
storms; torrential rains

陵園(ㄌㄧㄥˊ ㄩㄢˊ)
the tomb of an emperor; an imperial mausoleum; a tomb surrounded by a park; a cemetery

【陶】 6620
1. ㄊㄠˊ taur táo
1. to make pottery or earthenware; pottery or earthenware
2. happy; joyful
3. to move and influence a person
4. a Chinese family name

陶唐氏(ㄊㄠˊ ㄊㄤˊ ㄕˋ)
another name of Yao the Great (堯)

陶土(ㄊㄠˊ ㄊㄨˇ)
pot earth; pottery clay; potter's clay; kaolin

陶侃(ㄊㄠˊ ㄎㄢˇ)
Tao Kan (259-334), a great minister of the Tsin Dynasty

陶化(ㄊㄠˊ ㄏㄨㄚˋ)
to move, influence and mold (a person)

陶匠(ㄊㄠˊ ㄐㄧㄤˋ)
a pottery maker; a potter 亦作「陶人」

陶器(ㄊㄠˊ ㄑㄧˋ)
pottery; earthenware

陶潛(ㄊㄠˊ ㄑㄧㄢˊ)
Tao Chien (365-427), one of China's great poets 亦作「陶令」or「陶淵明」

陶情(ㄊㄠˊ ㄑㄧㄥˊ)
to feel pleased and at ease with the world

陶犬瓦雞(ㄊㄠˊ ㄑㄩㄢˇ ㄨㄚˇ ㄐㄧ)
(literally) pottery dogs and chickens—useless things

陶朱公(ㄊㄠˊ ㄓㄨ ㄍㄨㄥ)
another name of Fan Li (范蠡), one of the richest men in Chinese history

陶鑄(ㄊㄠˊ ㄓㄨˋ)
to educate and mold persons of talent 亦作「陶甄」or「陶鎔」

陶然(ㄊㄠˊ ㄖㄢˊ)
happy; cheerful; joyous

陶染(ㄊㄠˊ ㄖㄢˇ)
to move, influence and mold (people)

陶醉(ㄊㄠˊ ㄗㄨㄟˋ)
to be intoxicated (with success, etc.); very happy; highly gratified; greatly pleased

陶瓷(ㄊㄠˊ ㄘˊ)
pottery and porcelain

陶瓷業(ㄊㄠˊ ㄘˊ ㄧㄝˋ)
ceramics; the ceramic industry

陶猗(ㄊㄠˊ ㄧ)
rich men

陶冶(ㄊㄠˊ ㄧㄝˇ)
①to mold (pottery) and smelt (metals) ②to cultivate or shape (taste, character, etc.)

陶冶性情(ㄊㄠˊ ㄧㄝˇ ㄒㄧㄥˋ ㄑㄧㄥˊ)
to shape or cleanse one's spirit

陶硯(ㄊㄠˊ ㄧㄢˋ)
an inkstone made of pottery

【陶】 6620
2. ㄧㄠˊ yau yáo
as in 皋陶—name of a person in ancient China

【陷】 6621
ㄒㄧㄢˋ shiann xiàn
1. to sink; to fall; to submerge; to stick; to bog: 我們的車子陷在泥裏。Our car stuck in the mud.
2. to frame (up); to harm another with trumped-up charges
3. to entrap; to beguile: 他陷她於絕境。He was entrapped her to destruction.
4. to crush (the enemy position); to fall; to capture (a city, etc.): 他死於城陷之日。He died on the day the city fell.
5. a defect; a deficiency

陷沒(ㄒㄧㄢˋ ㄇㄛˋ)
①to sink; to submerge ②to be captured by the enemy

陷敵(ㄒㄧㄢˋ ㄉㄧˊ)
①to crash into the enemy position (and take it) ②to fall into the enemy's hands; to be captured by the enemy

陷溺(ㄒㄧㄢˋ ㄋㄧˋ)
to sink; to submerge; to be drowned

〔阜　部〕

〔阜部〕

陷落(ㄒㄧㄢˋ ㄌㄨㄛˋ)
①to sink; to submerge ②(said of a city, position, etc.) to be lost to the enemy

陷坑(ㄒㄧㄢˋ ㄎㄥ)
①a trap; a snare ②a hollow; a cave

陷害(ㄒㄧㄢˋ ㄏㄞˋ)
to frame; to snare; to harm another with a trumped-up charge, slander, etc.

陷阱(ㄒㄧㄢˋ ㄐㄧㄥˇ)
a trap; a snare; a booby trap

陷陣(ㄒㄧㄢˋ ㄓㄣˋ)
to take an enemy position

陷入(ㄒㄧㄢˋ ㄖㄨˋ)
to sink into; to fall into; to be entrapped: 他陷入沈睡中。 He sank into a deep sleep.

陷入絕境(ㄒㄧㄢˋ ㄖㄨˋ ㄐㄩㄝˊ ㄐㄧㄥˋ)
to get into extreme difficulty; to be drawn into a hopeless situation

【陸】 6622
ㄌㄨˋ luh lù

1. land; the shore; a continent: 我們看見遠處的陸地了。We sighted land in the distance.
2. by way of land; land transportation: 水陸交通 land and water communications
3. an elaborate form of 六 (six) used in documents or checks to prevent forgery
4. a Chinese family name

陸半球(ㄌㄨˋ ㄅㄢˋ ㄑㄧㄡˊ)
(geography) the Northern Hemisphere, where land constitutes a greater proportion than that of the Southern Hemisphere

陸稻(ㄌㄨˋ ㄉㄠˋ)
(botany) upland rice; dryland rice 亦作「旱稻」or「旱禾」

陸地(ㄌㄨˋ ㄉㄧˋ)
land (as distinct from the water of oceans and seas): 我們望見了陸地。We came in sight of land.

陸田(ㄌㄨˋ ㄊㄧㄢˊ)
dry field (as distinct from the rice field which is submerged in water during a large part of the rice growing period) 亦作「旱田」

陸離(ㄌㄨˋ ㄌㄧˊ)
①varied and numerous ②a

kind of fine jade

陸路(ㄌㄨˋ ㄌㄨˋ)
by land; a highway or railway; by way of land: 他們走陸路。They traveled by land.

陸海空(ㄌㄨˋ ㄏㄞˇ ㄎㄨㄥ)
land, sea and air

陸海空三軍(ㄌㄨˋ ㄏㄞˇ ㄎㄨㄥ ㄙㄢ ㄐㄩㄣ)
the army, navy and air force; the armed forces

陸九淵(ㄌㄨˋ ㄐㄧㄡˇ ㄩㄢ)
Lu Chiu-yüan (1139-1192), one of the leading philosophers of the Sung Dynasty 亦稱「象山先生」

陸軍(ㄌㄨˋ ㄐㄩㄣ)
the army; the land force

陸軍大學(ㄌㄨˋ ㄐㄩㄣ ㄉㄚˋ ㄒㄩㄝˊ)
Army Command and Staff College

陸軍軍官學校(ㄌㄨˋ ㄐㄩㄣ ㄐㄩㄣ ㄍㄨㄢ ㄒㄩㄝˊ ㄒㄧㄠˋ)
Military Academy

陸軍中將(ㄌㄨˋ ㄐㄩㄣ ㄓㄨㄥ ㄐㄧㄤˋ)
lieutenant general

陸軍中校(ㄌㄨˋ ㄐㄩㄣ ㄓㄨㄥ ㄒㄧㄠˋ)
lieutenant colonel

陸軍中尉(ㄌㄨˋ ㄐㄩㄣ ㄓㄨㄥ ㄨㄟˋ)
first lieutenant

陸軍少將(ㄌㄨˋ ㄐㄩㄣ ㄕㄠˇ ㄐㄧㄤˋ)
major general

陸軍少校(ㄌㄨˋ ㄐㄩㄣ ㄕㄠˇ ㄒㄧㄠˋ)
major

陸軍少尉(ㄌㄨˋ ㄐㄩㄣ ㄕㄠˇ ㄨㄟˋ)
second lieutenant

陸軍上將(ㄌㄨˋ ㄐㄩㄣ ㄕㄤˋ ㄐㄧㄤˋ)
(full) general

陸軍上校(ㄌㄨˋ ㄐㄩㄣ ㄕㄤˋ ㄒㄧㄠˋ)
colonel

陸軍上尉(ㄌㄨˋ ㄐㄩㄣ ㄕㄤˋ ㄨㄟˋ)
captain

陸軍總司令(ㄌㄨˋ ㄐㄩㄣ ㄗㄨㄥˇ ㄙ ㄌㄧㄥˋ)
the commander in chief of the army; (in the U. S. Army) the Chief of Staff

陸橋(ㄌㄨˋ ㄑㄧㄠˊ)
①an overpass 亦作「天橋」②a land bridge

陸續(ㄌㄨˋ ㄒㄩˋ)
continuous; one by one; one after another: 賓客陸續到來。The guests arrived one after another.

陸贄(ㄌㄨˋ ㄓˋ)

Lu Chih, a courtier in the Tang Dynasty, famous for his literary prowess

陸戰隊(ㄌㄨˋ ㄓㄢˋ ㄉㄨㄟˋ)
the marines; the Marine Corps

陸戰隊司令(ㄌㄨˋ ㄓㄢˋ ㄉㄨㄟˋ ㄙ ㄌㄧㄥˋ)
the commandant of the Marine Corps; the marine commandant

陸沈(ㄌㄨˋ ㄔㄣˊ)
①sinking of land ②upheavals; social chaos

陸上(ㄌㄨˋ ㄕㄤˋ)
on land

陸游(ㄌㄨˋ ㄧㄡˊ)
Lu Yu (1125-1210), a prominent poet in the Sung Dynasty 亦作「陸放翁」

陸運(ㄌㄨˋ ㄩㄣˋ)
land transportation

九畫

【陽】 6623
丨ㄤˊ yang yáng

1. positive (electricity, etc.)
2. male; masculine
3. the sun; solar; sunlight
4. the north of a stream
5. the south of a hill
6. bright; brilliant
7. the male genitals
8. pertaining to this world, as opposed to Hades
9. a Chinese family name

陽平(丨ㄤˊ ㄆㄧㄥˊ)
(Chinese phonetics) the second tone

陽明學派(丨ㄤˊ ㄇㄧㄥˊ ㄒㄩㄝˊ ㄆㄞˋ)
the School of Wang Yangming which centers on identity of reason and mind and the theory that action must go hand in hand with knowledge

陽明山(丨ㄤˊ ㄇㄧㄥˊ ㄕㄢ)
Yangmingshan, a mountain resort in suburban Taipei, Taiwan

陽明山管理局(丨ㄤˊ ㄇㄧㄥˊ ㄕㄢ ㄍㄨㄢˇ ㄌㄧˇ ㄐㄩˊ)
the Yangmingshan Administration, a special district in the Taipei Special Municipality

陽奉陰違(一ㄤ ㄈㄥ 一ㄣ ㄨㄟ)
to observe rules or obey orders ostensibly; to pretend to obey

陽道(一ㄤ ㄉㄠˋ)
①the ways or virtues of man ②external affairs (outside the household) ③the male reproductive organ

陽電(一ㄤ ㄉㄧㄢˋ)
positive electricity

陽臺(一ㄤ ㄊㄞˊ)
①a veranda or balcony ②a trysting place; a tryst

陽離子(一ㄤ ㄌㄧˊ ㄗˇ)
a positive ion; a cation

陽曆(一ㄤ ㄌㄧˋ)
the solar calendar; the Gregorian calendar

陽線(一ㄤ ㄒㄧㄢˋ)
a bolt (as distinct from a nut)

陽溝(一ㄤ ㄍㄡ)
an open ditch or drainage 亦作「羊溝」

陽剛(一ㄤ ㄍㄤ)
tough, strong, positive, stern, etc. in character

陽關(一ㄤ ㄍㄨㄢ)
Yang Pass, name of a border gate in the Han Dynasty in Kansu (甘肅)

陽關大道(一ㄤ ㄍㄨㄢ ㄉㄚˋ ㄉㄠˋ)
a wide street, especially a thoroughfare

陽關三疊(一ㄤ ㄍㄨㄢ ㄙㄢ ㄉㄧㄝˊ)
a parting tune with a thrice repeated refrain

陽光(一ㄤ ㄍㄨㄤ)
sunshine; sunlight; sunbeams

陽和(一ㄤ ㄏㄜˊ)
warm; balmy

陽極(一ㄤ ㄐㄧˊ)
the anode; the positive pole

陽間(一ㄤ ㄐㄧㄢ)
the world of the living (as distinct from Hades)

陽具(一ㄤ ㄐㄩˋ)
the male reproductive organ

陽起石(一ㄤ ㄑㄧˇ ㄕˊ)
actinolite

陽性(一ㄤ ㄒㄧㄥˋ)
①positive (electricity, etc.) ②the male sex; masculinity

陽性反應(一ㄤ ㄒㄧㄥˋ ㄈㄢˇ 一ㄥ)
positive reaction

陽宅(一ㄤ ㄓㄞˊ)
a human habitation; a house; the residence of the living

陽春(一ㄤ ㄔㄨㄣ)
①springtime ②the title of an ancient tune ③enlightened rule—as peaceful and delightful as springtime ④name of a county in Kwangtung Province(廣東省)

陽春白雪(一ㄤ ㄔㄨㄣ ㄅㄞˊ ㄒㄩㄝˋ)
songs that appeal to the highbrows only

陽春麪(一ㄤ ㄔㄨㄣ ㄇㄧㄢˋ)
cooked noodles without any dressing

陽世(一ㄤ ㄕˋ)
the world of the living

陽壽(一ㄤ ㄕㄡˋ)
one's predestined life span

陽傘(一ㄤ ㄙㄢˇ)
a parasol; an umbrella

陽物(一ㄤ ㄨˋ)
the penis

陽痿(一ㄤ ㄨㄟˇ)
impotence

陽文(一ㄤ ㄨㄣˊ)
characters cut in relief 亦作「陽識」

陽螺(一ㄤ ㄌㄨㄛˊ)
the external screw; the male screw 亦作「外螺紋」

陽月(一ㄤ ㄩㄝˋ)
the 10th month in the lunar calendar

【陻】 6624
(堙) 一ㄣ in yin
1. a mound
2. to bury
3. to dam (a stream); to block up

【隃】 6625
ㄩˊ yu yú
1. to exceed 亦作「逾」
2. name of a county in Shensi (陝西) Province during the Han Dynasty, famous for producing ink-sticks

【隄】 6626
(堤) ㄊㄧˊ tyi tí
a dike, levee or embankment

隄壩(ㄊㄧˊ ㄅㄚˋ)
dikes and dams

隄邊(ㄊㄧˊ ㄅㄧㄢ)
the side of a dike; by the side of a levee

隄防(ㄊㄧˊ ㄈㄤˊ)
①a dike or levee ②to remain alert; to be watchful 亦作「提防」

隄岸(ㄊㄧˊ ㄢˋ)
a dike, levee or embankment

隄堰(ㄊㄧˊ 一ㄢˋ)
an embankment, dike or levee

【隅】 6627
ㄩˊ yu yú
1. a corner; a nook
2. an angle
3. an out-of-the-way place; a recess

隅目(ㄩˊ ㄇㄨˋ)
①angry eyes ②furious

隅反(ㄩˊ ㄈㄢˇ)
to assess, understand or visualize by inference

隅角(ㄩˊ ㄐㄩㄝˊ)
(geometry) a solid angle

隅中(ㄩˊ ㄓㄨㄥ)
approaching noontime

【隆】 6628
ㄌㄨㄥˊ long lóng
1. prosperous; flourishing; brisk (business, etc.); booming
2. lofty; eminent; glorious
3. abundant; ample; generous
4. the rumble (of thunder, vehicles, artillery fire, etc.)
5. a Chinese family name

隆冬(ㄌㄨㄥˊ ㄉㄨㄥ)
(in) the depth of winter; winter at its coldest

隆替(ㄌㄨㄥˊ ㄊㄧˋ)
the rise and fall (of a reign, regime, nation, etc.)

隆顙(ㄌㄨㄥˊ ㄙㄤˇ)
craggy; not even

隆隆(ㄌㄨㄥˊ ㄌㄨㄥˊ)
①flourishing; booming ②(said of sound) roaring, booming or rumbling

隆古(ㄌㄨㄥˊ ㄍㄨˇ)
prosperous reign in ancient times

隆貴(ㄌㄨㄥˊ ㄍㄨㄟˋ)
very noble; lofty in position

隆厚(ㄌㄨㄥˊ ㄏㄡˋ)
(said of friendship or sentiments) profound; deep; generous

隆塞(ㄌㄨㄥˊ ㄙㄞˋ)

〔阜部〕

winter at its coldest; the severe cold

隆極(ㄌㄨㄥˊ ㄐㄧˊ)
the highest position or status

隆起(ㄌㄨㄥˊ ㄑㄧˇ)
to rise up; to swell up; to bulge: 山漸漸從平原隆起。 Hills swell gradually from the plain.

隆情厚誼(ㄌㄨㄥˊ ㄑㄧㄥˊ ㄏㄡˋ ㄧˋ)
great kindness, hospitality and friendship; profound sentiments of friendship

隆穹(ㄌㄨㄥˊ ㄑㄩㄥˊ)
①high; soaring ②canvas top on a vehicle

隆刑(ㄌㄨㄥˊ ㄒㄧㄥˊ)
strict or severe punishment

隆準(ㄌㄨㄥˊ ㄓㄨㄣˇ)
a prominent nose

隆重(ㄌㄨㄥˊ ㄓㄨㄥˋ)
(said of ceremony, rites, etc.) impressive, grand and solemn: 他受到隆重的接待。He was accorded a grand reception.

隆盛(ㄌㄨㄥˊ ㄕㄥˋ)
abundant; booming; flourishing; prosperous

隆暑(ㄌㄨㄥˊ ㄕㄨˇ)
summer at its hottest

隆胸(ㄌㄨㄥˊ ㄒㄩㄥ)
to raise the breasts of a flat-chested woman by means of plastic surgery

隆恩(ㄌㄨㄥˊ ㄣ)
great kindness, favor or grace

隆顏(ㄌㄨㄥˊ ㄧㄢˊ)
the imperial countenance

【限】 6629
   ㄒㄧㄢˋ uei wei
1. a river bend
2. a mountain recess

【陧】 6630
   ㄋㄧㄝˋ nieh nie
as in 阢隉—precarious; dangerous

【隋】 6631
   ㄙㄨㄟˊ swei sui
1. name of a dynasty (581-618)
2. a Chinese family name

隋隄(ㄙㄨㄟˊ ㄉㄧˊ)
embankments along the Grand Canal dug by order of Emperor Yang (煬帝) of the

Sui Dynasty

隋書(ㄙㄨㄟˊ ㄕㄨ)
a history of the Sui Dynasty

隋煬帝(ㄙㄨㄟˊ ㄧㄤˊ ㄉㄧˋ)
Emperor Yang (580-618), one of the most debauched and vainglorious rulers in ancient China

隋文帝(ㄙㄨㄟˊ ㄨㄣˊ ㄉㄧˋ)
Emperor Wen (541-604), father of Emperor Yang (隋煬帝), the founding monarch of the Sui Dynasty

【隊】 6632
   ㄉㄨㄟˋ duey dui
1. a group; a team; a batch
2. the troops

隊旗(ㄉㄨㄟˋ ㄑㄧˊ)
the flag of a team; the team pennant: 他們互贈隊旗。They exchanged team pennants.

隊形(ㄉㄨㄟˋ ㄒㄧㄥˊ)
formation (of airplanes in flight or soldiers drilling)

隊長(ㄉㄨㄟˋ ㄓㄤˇ)
the team leader; the captain of a sports team; the commanding officer of a small military unit

隊伍(ㄉㄨㄟˋ ㄨˇ)
①troops in ranks and files ②a line of (people)

隊員(ㄉㄨㄟˋ ㄩㄢˊ)
members of a team or group: 我不是任何隊的隊員。I am not on (or in) any team.

【階】 6633
   ㄐㄧㄝ jie jie
1. a way leading to the main hall
2. a flight of steps or stairs
3. a grade or a rank
4. to rely on

階陛(ㄐㄧㄝ ㄅㄧˋ)
a flight of steps leading to the throne 亦作「階墀」

階段(ㄐㄧㄝ ㄉㄨㄢˋ)
a stage or phase (in a development process)

階梯(ㄐㄧㄝ ㄊㄧ)
①a flight of stairs or steps ②(figuratively) a way, ladder or step leading to success

階級(ㄐㄧㄝ ㄐㄧˊ)
a rank; a class (of people): 他們屬於中等階級。They belong to the middle class(es).

階級偏見(ㄐㄧㄝ ㄐㄧˊ ㄆㄧㄢ ㄐㄧㄢˋ)
(sociology) class bias

階級鬥爭(ㄐㄧㄝ ㄐㄧˊ ㄉㄡˋ ㄓㄥ)
a class struggle

階級利益(ㄐㄧㄝ ㄐㄧˊ ㄌㄧˋ ㄧˋ)
class interests

階級衝突(ㄐㄧㄝ ㄐㄧˊ ㄔㄨㄥ ㄊㄨˊ)
(sociology) a class conflict

階級意識(ㄐㄧㄝ ㄐㄧˊ ㄧˋ ㄕˋ)
(sociology) class consciousness

階前萬里(ㄐㄧㄝ ㄑㄧㄢˊ ㄨㄢˋ ㄌㄧˇ)
It's 10,000 miles away, and it's near at hand as well.

階下漢(ㄐㄧㄝ ㄒㄧㄚˋ ㄏㄢˋ)
a beginner; an apprentice; a novice

階下囚(ㄐㄧㄝ ㄒㄧㄚˋ ㄑㄧㄡˊ)
a prisoner; a captive: 他後來成了階下囚。He finally became a prisoner.

階墀(ㄐㄧㄝ ㄔˊ)
a flight of steps leading to the throne

階除(ㄐㄧㄝ ㄔㄨˊ)
steps in the yard

階次(ㄐㄧㄝ ㄘˋ)
grades or ranks in officialdom

階層(ㄐㄧㄝ ㄘㄥˊ)
subdivisions within a class of people; a class of people; a social stratum; a walk of life

階緣(ㄐㄧㄝ ㄩㄢˊ)
to climb by riding on the coattails of a powerful person

十畫

【隔】 6634
   ㄍㄜˊ ger ge
1. to separate; to divide; to partition
2. blocked; to obstruct; to be veiled
3. at a distance from; at an interval of

隔壁(ㄍㄜˊ ㄅㄧˋ)
next door: 她住在隔壁。She lives next door now.

隔別(ㄍㄜˊ ㄅㄧㄝˊ)
separated (for a long time, etc.)

隔膜(ㄍㄜˊ ㄇㄛˊ)
①the diaphragm ②to have

no communication or contact with; to be out of touch with; not familiar with ③ the absence of the meeting of minds; to be estranged

膈膜炎《ㄍㄜˊㄇㄛˋㄧㄢˊ》
diaphragmatitis

隔代遺傳《ㄍㄜˊㄉㄞˋㄧˊㄔㄨㄢˊ》
atavism

隔開《ㄍㄜˊㄎㄞ》
blocked or obstructed; to separate; to cut off: 我們被潮水所隔斷。We were cut off by the tide.

隔年《ㄍㄜˊㄋㄧㄢˊ》
in the following year; in the year following

隔離《ㄍㄜˊㄌㄧˊ》
to separate; to isolate; to segregate; to quarantine

隔離病房《ㄍㄜˊㄌㄧˊㄅㄧㄥˋㄈㄤˊ》
an isolation ward

隔開《ㄍㄜˊㄎㄞ》
to separate; to set apart; to partition

隔閡《ㄍㄜˊㄏㄜˊ》
no meeting of minds; a mental barrier

隔間《ㄍㄜˊㄐㄧㄢ》
a partition

隔絕《ㄍㄜˊㄐㄩㄝˊ》
blocked or obstructed; separated; to cut off; to isolate

隔牆有耳《ㄍㄜˊㄑㄧㄤˊㄧㄡˇㄦˇ》
(literally) There are ears on the other side of the wall. —It's difficult to keep a secret. 或 Beware of eavesdroppers.

隔靴搔癢《ㄍㄜˊㄒㄩㄝㄙㄠㄧㄤˇ》
(literally) to scratch an itching foot with the boot on —not to the point; having no effect; to attempt an ineffective solution

隔肢《ㄍㄜˊ·ㄓ》
① to titillate ② to give someone a hard time

隔肢窩《ㄍㄜˊ·ㄓㄨㄛ》
the armpit

隔山《ㄍㄜˊㄕㄢ》
the relationship between half brothers and sisters by the same father

隔扇《ㄍㄜˊㄕㄢˋ》
a paper or wooden partition

隔日《ㄍㄜˊㄖˋ》
① the next day or the day after next ② every other day

隔熱《ㄍㄜˊㄖㄜˋ》
(construction) heat insulation

隔宿《ㄍㄜˊㄙㄨˋ》
after a night; overnight

隔岸《ㄍㄜˊㄢˋ》
on the other side of the river, sea, etc.

隔岸觀火《ㄍㄜˊㄢˋㄍㄨㄢㄏㄨㄛˇ》
(literally) to watch a fire on the other side of the river —to be indifferent; to show no concern

隔夜《ㄍㄜˊㄧㄝˋ》
after a night; last night

隔音《ㄍㄜˊㄧㄣ》
soundproof: 這是一間隔音室。This is a soundproof room.

隔音板《ㄍㄜˊㄧㄣㄅㄢˇ》
an acoustic tile; an acoustic board

【隕】 6635
　　　　ㄩㄣˇ yeun yun
1. to fall
2. to die

隕滅《ㄩㄣˇㄇㄧㄝˋ》
① to fall from outer space and burn up ② to meet one's death; to perish

隕命《ㄩㄣˇㄇㄧㄥˋ》
to die 亦作「殞命」

隕涕《ㄩㄣˇㄊㄧˋ》
tears falling

隕鐵《ㄩㄣˇㄊㄧㄝˇ》
meteoric iron

隕落《ㄩㄣˇㄌㄨㄛˋ》
① (said of a meteorite, etc.) to fall from the sky or outer space ② (said of a famous or influential person) to pass away; to die

隕星《ㄩㄣˇㄒㄧㄥ》
(astronomy) a meteor; a meteoroid that has entered the earth's atmosphere

隕石《ㄩㄣˇㄕˊ》
a meteorite; a fallen meteoroid; a mass of stone or metal that has reached the earth from outer space

隕泗《ㄩㄣˇㄙˋ》
to shed tears

隕越《ㄩㄣˇㄩㄝˋ》
① to topple and fall down ②

to fulfill one's duties improperly or erroneously

【隖】 6636
　　　　ㄨ wuh wù
1. a parapet; a low wall
2. a structure sloping toward the middle on all sides, as a dock

【隘】 6637
　　　　ㄞˋ ay ài
1. a strategic pass; a strategic point
2. narrow
3. urgent
4. destitute

隘路《ㄞˋㄌㄨˋ》
a narrow road; a road flanked by water or streams

隘口《ㄞˋㄎㄡˇ》
a (mountain) pass

隘塞《ㄞˋㄙㄜˋ》
a strategic pass or point

隘險《ㄞˋㄒㄧㄢˇ》
of great strategic value

【隙】 6638
　　　　(隟) ㄒㄧˋ shih xì
1. a crack; a fissure; a crevice
2. a grudge; a dislike; a dispute; a quarrel; a complaint
3. spare time; leisure
4. an opportunity; a loophole
5. an important passageway or corridor, as the Berlin Corridor

隙地《ㄒㄧˋㄉㄧˋ》
a vacant lot or space; an uncultivated land or tract

隙駒《ㄒㄧˋㄐㄩ》
How time flies!

隙罅《ㄒㄧˋㄒㄧㄚˋ》
a crack, crevice, or fissure: 杯子上有一條隙罅。There was a crack in the cup.

【隗】 6639
　　　　ㄨㄟˇ woei wěi
1. high; lofty
2. a Chinese family name

十一畫

【際】 6640
　　　　ㄐㄧˋ jih jì
1. (to occur) at the time or on the occasion of
2. a border or boundary; an edge
3. by the side of; beside
4. in the middle; between; among

〔**阜部**〕

5. opportunity; fortune or luck

際畔 (ㄐㄧˋ ㄆㄢˋ)
along the border; bordering on

際會 (ㄐㄧˋ ㄏㄨㄟˋ)
① to meet; to encounter ② a happenstance

際此 (ㄐㄧˋ ㄘˇ)
at a time like this; on such an occasion: 際此佳期特向你祝賀 I send you my best wishes on this happy occasion.

際遇 (ㄐㄧˋ ㄩˋ)
① opportunity; chance ② what one has experienced or encountered in one's life

際涯 (ㄐㄧˋ ㄧㄚˊ)
a margin; an outer limit

【障】 6641
　ㄓㄤˋ janq zhàng
1. to separate; to screen; a barrier; a screen
2. a dike; an embankment
3. to defend; to guard; to shield
4. to guarantee
5. to hinder; to obstruct

障蔽 (ㄓㄤˋ ㄅㄧˋ)
to screen; to obstruct

障礙 (ㄓㄤˋ ㄞˋ)
① obstacles; barriers; obstructions: 有勇氣就無障礙。 Courage knows no obstacle. ② a malfunction; a handicap: 視力不好是學生的障礙。 Poor eyesight is a handicap to a student.

障礙競走 (ㄓㄤˋ ㄞˋ ㄐㄧㄥˋ ㄗㄡˇ)
the game of walking over a prepared course with artificial obstructions

障礙物 (ㄓㄤˋ ㄞˋ ㄨˋ)
an obstacle; an obstruction; anything that hinders

障翳 (ㄓㄤˋ ㄧˋ)
① a wooden fan carried in procession ② to conceal or screen

障眼法 (ㄓㄤˋ ㄧㄢˇ ㄈㄚˇ)
① legerdemain ② a cover-up; camouflage

十二畫

【隤】 6642
　(隤) ㄊㄨㄟˊ twei tuí
1. to fall in ruins; to collapse

2. (said of horses) tired and jaded

【鄰】 6643
　(鄰) ㄌㄧㄣˊ lin lín
1. a neighbor: 愛你的鄰居像愛自己一樣。 Love your neighbors as yourself.
2. neighboring; nearby: 他住在隣近村內。 He lives in the neighboring village.

十三畫

【隨】 6644
　ㄙㄨㄟˊ swei suí
1. to follow; to trace; to come after
2. to listen to; to submit to; to comply with
3. to let (it go, it be, etc.)
4. to accompany: 雷隨閃電而來。 Thunder accompanies lightning.
5. to resemble; to look like
6. a Chinese family name

隨波逐流 (ㄙㄨㄟˊ ㄅㄛ ㄓㄨˊ ㄌㄧㄡˊ)
① to follow the currents in sailing ② to speak and behave as others do without views of his own

隨報分送 (ㄙㄨㄟˊ ㄅㄠˋ ㄈㄣ ㄙㄨㄥˋ)
to be distributed gratis along with the newspaper

隨筆 (ㄙㄨㄟˊ ㄅㄧˇ)
to write as one's thought rambles; literary rambles; miscellaneous writings; jottings

隨便 (ㄙㄨㄟˊ ㄅㄧㄢˋ)
① as you like; as you see fit; as you please: 隨便你去做。 You can do as you like. ② casual; careless: 他待人很隨便。 He is very casual with other people.

隨票附送 (ㄙㄨㄟˊ ㄆㄧㄠˋ ㄈㄨˋ ㄙㄨㄥˋ)
to be distributed gratis along with the ticket

隨片登臺 (ㄙㄨㄟˊ ㄆㄧㄢˋ ㄉㄥ ㄊㄞˊ)
(said of a leading actor or actress) to appear on stage in person on the premiere of a movie

隨分 (ㄙㄨㄟˊ ㄈㄣˋ)
① to be content with one's lot ② (to do things) within the limits of one's strength or resources ③ to contribute

one's share as part of a present

隨方就圓 (ㄙㄨㄟˊ ㄈㄤ ㄐㄧㄡˋ ㄩㄢˊ)
easygoing; adaptable; accommodating; easy to get along with

隨風轉舵 (ㄙㄨㄟˊ ㄈㄥ ㄓㄨㄢˇ ㄉㄨㄛˋ) or
① to take action as opportunity arises ② irresolution

隨風兒倒 (ㄙㄨㄟˊ ㄈㄥ ㄦ ㄉㄠˇ)
(literally) to turn with the wind—without any views or ideas of one's own

隨帶 (ㄙㄨㄟˊ ㄉㄞˋ)
to carry about; to take along: 除信以外隨您書籍兩包。 Accompanying the letter are two parcels of books.

隨到隨考 (ㄙㄨㄟˊ ㄉㄠˋ ㄙㄨㄟˊ ㄎㄠˇ)
to undergo a test as soon as one arrives

隨地 (ㄙㄨㄟˊ ㄉㄧˋ)
any place

隨地吐痰 (ㄙㄨㄟˊ ㄉㄧˋ ㄊㄨˇ ㄊㄢˊ)
to spit freely at any place

隨地小便 (ㄙㄨㄟˊ ㄉㄧˋ ㄒㄧㄠˇ ㄅㄧㄢˋ)
to urinate freely at any place

隨同 (ㄙㄨㄟˊ ㄊㄨㄥˊ)
to follow or accompany; together with

隨來隨去 (ㄙㄨㄟˊ ㄌㄞˊ ㄙㄨㄟˊ ㄑㄩˋ)
Some people are arriving, and others are leaving.

隨高就低 (ㄙㄨㄟˊ ㄍㄠ ㄐㄧㄡˋ ㄉㄧ)
to adapt to circumstances

隨口 (ㄙㄨㄟˊ ㄎㄡˇ)
to slip out of one's tongue without much thought: 他隨口答覆了她。 He gave her a casual answer.

隨和 (ㄙㄨㄟˊ ㄏㄜˋ)
① (ㄙㄨㄟˊ ㄏㄜˊ) priceless treasures (隨侯珠 and 卞和璧)
② (ㄙㄨㄟˊ ㄏㄜˋ) to repeat what others are saying
③ (ㄙㄨㄟˊ ㄏㄜˊ) easygoing; amiable: 她是個隨和的女孩。 She is an amiable girl.

隨後 (ㄙㄨㄟˊ ㄏㄡˋ)
immediately afterward; right off; in no time at all; right after

隨宜 (ㄙㄨㄟˊ ㄧˊ)
to follow one's father or elder brother on a tour of

official duty

隨機教學 (ㄙㄨㄟ ㄐㄧ ㄐㄧㄠ ㄒㄩㄝ)
to teach whenever and wherever opportunity presents itself (as teaching names of animals in a zoo)

隨機應變 (ㄙㄨㄟ ㄐㄧ ㄧㄥ ㄅㄧㄢ)
to adapt oneself quickly to the changing circumstances

隨即 (ㄙㄨㄟ ㄐㄧ)
right away; promptly; immediately; soon afterward: 她說完áæ即離去。 She left right away after saying something.

隨叫隨到 (ㄙㄨㄟ ㄐㄧㄠ ㄙㄨㄟ ㄉㄠ)
(said of goods or service) to arrive as soon as it is ordered by telephone call; to be on call at any hour

隨軍記者 (ㄙㄨㄟ ㄐㄩㄣ ㄐㄧ ㄓㄜ)
a war correspondent

隨喜 (ㄙㄨㄟ ㄒㄧ)
① to visit temples or shrines ② (Buddhism) to feel happy when one sees others doing good

隨心所欲 (ㄙㄨㄟ ㄒㄧㄣ ㄙㄨㄛ ㄩ)
to do anything one's heart dictates

隨鄉入鄉 (ㄙㄨㄟ ㄒㄧㄤ ㄖㄨ ㄒㄧㄤ)
In a strange land, do as the natives do. 或 When in Rome, do as the Romans do.

隨想曲 (ㄙㄨㄟ ㄒㄧㄤ ㄑㄩ)
(music) caprice; *capriccio*

隨行 (ㄙㄨㄟ ㄒㄧㄥ)
to follow or accompany someone on a trip

隨行人員 (ㄙㄨㄟ ㄒㄧㄥ ㄖㄣ ㄩㄢ)
an entourage; a suite; attendants or aides accompanying a VIP on a tour; retinues

隨着 (ㄙㄨㄟ ·ㄓㄜ)
along with; in the wake of; in pace with: 我願隨着你去。 I'll go along with you.

隨珠彈雀 (ㄙㄨㄟ ㄓㄨ ㄊㄢ ㄑㄩㄝ)
(literally) to kill a bird with a precious pearl—to gain a trifle at great cost

隨衆 (ㄙㄨㄟ ㄓㄨㄥ)
to follow the crowd

隨處 (ㄙㄨㄟ ㄔㄨ)
everywhere; at all places: 他們隨處都去。 They go every-

where.

隨時 (ㄙㄨㄟ ㄕ)
at all times; anytime

隨時制宜 (ㄙㄨㄟ ㄕ ㄓ ㄧ)
to change tactics as a situation demands; to act according to circumstances

隨時隨地 (ㄙㄨㄟ ㄕ ㄙㄨㄟ ㄉㄧ)
at all times and places; anytime and anyplace; wherever and whenever

隨侍 (ㄙㄨㄟ ㄕ)
① to wait upon ② an orderly; a personal attendant

隨侍在側 (ㄙㄨㄟ ㄕ ㄗㄞ ㄘㄜ)
to be by the side (of a sick elder, usually one's parent) —an expression usually appearing in a funeral notice

隨手 (ㄙㄨㄟ ㄕㄡ)
at hand; readily; immediately: 請隨手關門。 Please shut the door after you.

隨身 (ㄙㄨㄟ ㄕㄣ)
to carry something with one; to take something with one; to carry about: 警察可以隨身帶槍。 The policemen can take guns with them.

隨身東西 (ㄙㄨㄟ ㄕㄣ ㄉㄨㄥ ·ㄒㄧ)
things that one carries with him

隨身聽 (ㄙㄨㄟ ㄕㄣ ㄊㄧㄥ)
a walkman

隨身衣服 (ㄙㄨㄟ ㄕㄣ ㄧ ·ㄈㄨ)
clothes for change one takes along during a trip

隨聲附和 (ㄙㄨㄟ ㄕㄥ ㄈㄨ ㄏㄜ)
to echo another's utterances without ideas or views of one's own; to chime in with others

隨順 (ㄙㄨㄟ ㄕㄨㄣ)
to accord or comply with

隨從 (ㄙㄨㄟ ㄘㄨㄥ)
an entourage; aides; attendants

隨從武官 (ㄙㄨㄟ ㄘㄨㄥ ㄨ ㄍㄨㄢ)
an aide-de-camp

隨俗 (ㄙㄨㄟ ㄙㄨ)
to act according to the prevailing customs or practices: 入境隨俗。 When in Rome, do as the Romans do.

隨俗浮沈 (ㄙㄨㄟ ㄙㄨ ㄈㄨ ㄔㄣ)
(literally) to drift along with the world—without

ideas or ambition of one's own

隨隨便便 (ㄙㄨㄟ ㄙㄨㄟ ㄅㄧㄢ ㄅㄧㄢ)
easygoing; casual; sloppy

隨宜 (ㄙㄨㄟ ㄧ)
to comply with propriety

隨意 (ㄙㄨㄟ ㄧ)
according to your wish; as you like it; as you please; to have no restraint; to act as one pleases 參看「隨便①」: 隨意拿吧！ Take as many as you please.

隨意畫 (ㄙㄨㄟ ㄧ ㄏㄨㄚ)
freehand drawing

隨意肌 (ㄙㄨㄟ ㄧ ㄐㄧ)
voluntary muscles

隨遇平衡 (ㄙㄨㄟ ㄩ ㄆㄧㄥ ㄏㄥ)
(physics) indifferent or neutral equilibrium

隨遇而安 (ㄙㄨㄟ ㄩ ㄦ ㄢ)
to feel at ease under all circumstances: 他隨遇而安。 He feels at ease under all circumstances.

隨員 (ㄙㄨㄟ ㄩㄢ)
an entourage; a retinue; aides on a tour 亦作「隨行人員」

隨緣 (ㄙㄨㄟ ㄩㄢ)
(Buddhism) ① one's activities resulting from the outer circumstances ② to do things in accordance with one's situation

〔阜 部〕

【隧】 6645
ㄙㄨㄟ suey suì
1. an underground passage; a tunnel
2. to go round and round
3. (in ancient China) a tower on the wall to watch signal fires

隧道 (ㄙㄨㄟ ㄉㄠ)
a tunnel: 這火車通過隧道。 The train passed through a tunnel.

【隩】 6646
ㄩ yuh yù
(又讀 ㄠ aw ào)
1. a bend of a stream; a cove
2. warm
3. inhabitable land

【險】
ㄒㄧㄢ shean xiǎn
1. dangerous; danger
2. obstructed; obstruct
3. a strategic pass

【阜部】

4.cunning; mean and crafty; sinister

5.nearly; almost; within an ace of: 他險遭不幸。He came within an ace of death.

險詖(ㄒㄧㄢˇ ㄅㄧˋ)
① vile; mean ② fawning, obsequiousness

險灘(ㄒㄧㄢˇ ㄊㄢ)
a dangerous shoal; rapids

險固(ㄒㄧㄢˇ ㄍㄨˋ)
strategic and impregnable

險巇(ㄒㄧㄢˇ ㄐㄧ)
(said of terrain, roads, etc.) difficult; hazardous

險境(ㄒㄧㄢˇ ㄐㄧㄥˋ)
a dangerous situation

險句(ㄒㄧㄢˇ ㄐㄩ)
a sentence whose construction is out of the ordinary or peculiar

險譎(ㄒㄧㄢˇ ㄐㄩㄝˊ)
cunning and vicious; crafty and mean

險峻(ㄒㄧㄢˇ ㄐㄩㄣˋ)
(said of terrain) of highly strategic significance; (said of hills, etc.)precipitous

險詐(ㄒㄧㄢˇ ㄒㄧ)or 險巇(ㄒㄧㄢˇ ㄒㄧ)
dangerous; danger(s)

險些(ㄒㄧㄢˇ ㄒㄧㄝ)or 險些兒(ㄒㄧㄢˇ ㄒㄧㄝ)
nearly; almost: 他險些兒死了。He was almost dead.

險象環生(ㄒㄧㄢˇ ㄒㄧㄤˋ ㄏㄨㄢˊ ㄕㄥ)
dangers lurking on all sides; to be beset with danger; signs of danger appearing everywhere

險詐(ㄒㄧㄢˇ ㄓㄚˋ)
treacherous; treachery; sinister and crafty

險症(ㄒㄧㄢˇ ㄓㄥˋ)
a serious disease; a severe illness

險勝(ㄒㄧㄢˇ ㄕㄥˋ)
to win by a narrow margin

險遭不測(ㄒㄧㄢˇ ㄗㄠ ㄅㄨˋ ㄘㄜˋ)
to escape death by a hair's breadth

險遭毒手(ㄒㄧㄢˇ ㄗㄠ ㄉㄨˊ ㄕㄡˇ)
to have a narrow escape from assassination, murder, attack, etc.

險阻(ㄒㄧㄢˇ ㄗㄨˇ)or 險盈(ㄒㄧㄢˇ ㄗㄥ)
hazardous; dangerous (mountain passes, etc.); precarious (situations, etc.); difficult (terrain)

險惡(ㄒㄧㄢˇ ㄜˋ)
① dangerous; perilous; ominous; precarious ② devious; diabolic; mean; sinister: 他居心險惡。He had sinister intentions.

險巇(ㄒㄧㄢˇ ㄧ)
dangerous; strategic

險易(ㄒㄧㄢˇ ㄧˋ)
① difficult and easy ② disturbance and peace

險要(ㄒㄧㄢˇ ㄧㄠˋ)
(said of a place) strategic and capable of being easily defended

險語(ㄒㄧㄢˇ ㄩˇ)
sensational remarks

險韻(ㄒㄧㄢˇ ㄩㄣˋ)
to rhyme with obscure words; difficult rhyme

十四畫

【隱】 6648
ㄧㄣˇ yǐn　yìn

1. hidden; concealed; secret; mysterious

2. dark; obscure; not evident or obvious

3. to retire; to reject public life; to live like a hermit

4. painful; grievous

5. a riddle

6. destitute; poor

7. to examine and study

8. a low wall

9. a Chinese family name

隱比(ㄧㄣˇ ㄅㄧˇ)
metaphor 亦作「暗喻」

隱蔽(ㄧㄣˇ ㄅㄧˋ)
to conceal; to take cover; to cover up

隱沒(ㄧㄣˇ ㄇㄛˋ)
① to pass unnoticed by the public ② to fade; to disappear: 他的身影隱沒在黑暗中。His figure faded into the darkness.

隱瞞(ㄧㄣˇ ㄇㄢˊ)
to hide the truth; to cover up: 我沒什麼好隱瞞的。I have nothing to hide.

隱秘(ㄧㄣˇ ㄇㄧˋ)
① to conceal; to hide ② a secret

隱名(ㄧㄣˇ ㄇㄧㄥˊ)
to remain anonymous; to conceal one's name

隱伏(ㄧㄣˇ ㄈㄨˊ)
to lie concealed(or hidden); to lie low

隱遁(ㄧㄣˇ ㄉㄨㄣˋ)
to retire from public life; to live in reclusion

隱慝(ㄧㄣˇ ㄊㄜˋ)
a hidden crime; unrevealed guilt; some secret wickedness

隱聽(ㄧㄣˇ ㄊㄧㄥ)
to keep quiet and listen; to eavesdrop

隱退(ㄧㄣˇ ㄊㄨㄟˋ)
to retire; retirement: 他已隱退了。He has retired from the world.

隱痛(ㄧㄣˇ ㄊㄨㄥˋ)
hidden sorrow or pain

隱匿(ㄧㄣˇ ㄋㄧˋ)
to conceal; to hide: 他隱匿在山中。His hideaway is in the mountains.

隱宮(ㄧㄣˇ ㄍㄨㄥ)
castration (as a form of punishment in ancient times)

隱花果(ㄧㄣˇ ㄏㄨㄚ ㄍㄨㄛˇ)
syconium, such as a fig

隱花植物(ㄧㄣˇ ㄏㄨㄚ ㄓˊ ㄨˋ)
the cryptogam

隱諱(ㄧㄣˇ ㄏㄨㄟˋ)
① taboo (on the parent's or emperor's personal name) ② to avoid mentioning; to cover up

隱晦(ㄧㄣˇ ㄏㄨㄟˋ)
obscure; ambiguous

隱患(ㄧㄣˇ ㄏㄨㄢˋ)
hidden dangers; latent dangers; lurking perils

隱疾(ㄧㄣˇ ㄐㄧˊ)
① ailments beneath one's garment ② ailments one wants to keep to oneself, as syphilis, impotence, etc.

隱居(ㄧㄣˇ ㄐㄩ)
to retire from public life; to live in seclusion

隱君子(ㄧㄣˇ ㄐㄩㄣ ㄗˇ)
a retired scholar

隱情(ㄧㄣˇ ㄑㄧㄥˊ)
secrets; things which cannot be revealed to others; facts one wishes to hide

隱修 (ㄧㄣˇ ㄒㄧㄡ)
an anchorite

隱顯墨水 (ㄧㄣˇ ㄒㄧㄢˇ ㄇㄛˋ ㄕㄨㄟˇ)
invisible ink; sympathetic ink

隱形人 (ㄧㄣˇ ㄒㄧㄥˊ ㄖㄣˊ)
an invisible man

隱形眼鏡 (ㄧㄣˇ ㄒㄧㄥˊ ㄧㄢˇ ㄐㄧㄥˋ)
contact lenses

隱性 (ㄧㄣˇ ㄒㄧㄥˋ)
(genetics) recessive

隱姓埋名 (ㄧㄣˇ ㄒㄧㄥˋ ㄇㄞˊ ㄇㄧㄥˊ)
to live incognito; to live in obscurity; to live as a hermit

隱者 (ㄧㄣˇ ㄓㄜˇ)
a recluse; a hermit

隱士 (ㄧㄣˇ ㄕˋ)
a retired scholar; a recluse

隱身術 (ㄧㄣˇ ㄕㄣ ㄕㄨˋ) or 隱身法 (ㄧㄣˇ ㄕㄣ ㄈㄚˇ)
the magic of making oneself invisible

隱忍 (ㄧㄣˇ ㄖㄣˇ)
to bear insults, effrontery, grievances, etc. with patience; to forbear; to bottle up one's resentment

隱惻 (ㄧㄣˇ ㄘㄜˋ)
commiseration or sympathy

隱藏 (ㄧㄣˇ ㄘㄤˊ)
to hide; to conceal

隱私 (ㄧㄣˇ ㄙ)
one's secrets; private matters one wants to hide

隱私權 (ㄧㄣˇ ㄙ ㄑㄩㄢˊ)
privacy

隱惡揚善 (ㄧㄣˇ ㄜˋ ㄧㄤˊ ㄕㄢˋ)
to cover up another's bad deeds and praise his virtues

隱逸 (ㄧㄣˇ ㄧˋ)
a recluse; a retired person

隱憂 (ㄧㄣˇ ㄧㄡ)
hidden or latent worries; lurking dangers

隱隱作痛 (ㄧㄣˇ ㄧㄣˇ ㄗㄨㄛˋ ㄊㄨㄥˋ)
to feel dull pain

隱語 (ㄧㄣˇ ㄩˇ)
parables; riddles

隱喻 (ㄧㄣˇ ㄩˋ)
a metaphor

隱約 (ㄧㄣˇ ㄩㄝ) or 隱隱約約 (ㄧㄣˇ ㄧㄣˇ ㄩㄝ ㄩㄝ)
indistinct; obscure; ambiguous; abstruse

【隰】 6649
ㄒㄧˊ shyi xí
1. low, marshy land
2. newly opened farmland
3. a Chinese family name

【隮】 6650
ㄐㄧ jī jí
1. to rise up; to ascend
2. a rainbow
3. to fall; to topple

十五畫

【隳】 6651
ㄏㄨㄟ huei huī
to destroy; to ruin; to break

十六畫

【隴】 6652
ㄌㄨㄥˇ loong lǒng
1. another name of Kansu (甘肅) Province
2. a mound 亦作「壟」
3. prosperous
4. a Chinese family name

隴畝 (ㄌㄨㄥˇ ㄇㄨˇ)
a rural community; the farm

隴海鐵路 (ㄌㄨㄥˇ ㄏㄞˇ ㄊㄧㄝˇ ㄌㄨˋ)
the Lung-Hai Railway, from Lanchow, Kansu (甘肅蘭州), to Lienyünkang, Kiangsu (江蘇連雲港, formerly known as 海州)

隶 部
ㄉㄞˋ day dài

九畫

【隸】 6653
ㄌㄧˋ lih lì
1. to be subordinate to; inferior; to belong or attach to
2. servants; slaves; underlings
3. a type of Chinese calligraphy
4. to practice; to learn
5. a Chinese family name

隸書 (ㄌㄧˋ ㄕㄨ) or 隸字 (ㄌㄧˋ ㄗˋ)
a clerical style of Chinese calligraphy; official script, an ancient style of calligraphy current in the Han

---

Dynasty (206 B.C.—A.D. 220), simplified from *Hsiao-chuan* (小篆)

隸屬 (ㄌㄧˋ ㄕㄨˇ)
to be attached to; subordinate to; under the jurisdiction or command of

隸人 (ㄌㄧˋ ㄖㄣˊ)
① convicts ② petty officials

隸圉 (ㄌㄧˋ ㄩˇ)
servants; underlings

隹 部
ㄓㄨㄟ juei zhuī

【隹】 6654
ㄓㄨㄟ juei zhuī
a general name of short-tailed birds, such as pigeons

二畫

【隻】 6655
ㄓ jy zhī
1. a numerary adjunct for a hen, pigeon, bird, ox, goat, hand, foot, etc.: 她買了一隻雞. She bought a chicken.
2. single; alone; one of a pair: 他隻身前來. He came alone.
3. odd (number)

隻立 (ㄓ ㄌㄧˋ)
to stand alone

隻輪不反 (ㄓ ㄌㄨㄣˊ ㄅㄨˋ ㄈㄢˇ)
(literally) not a single chariot returned—routed

隻雞絮酒 (ㄓ ㄐㄧ ㄒㄩˋ ㄐㄧㄡˇ)
(an expression used in writing mourning for the death of a friend) sacrifice offered to the dead

隻句 (ㄓ ㄐㄩˋ)
a single sentence; a brief note

隻手 (ㄓ ㄕㄡˇ)
single-handed

隻身 (ㄓ ㄕㄣ)
alone; all by oneself: 他隻身到台北. He went to Taipei alone. 他隻身在外. He was away from home all by himself.

隻日 (ㄓ ㄖˋ)
odd days of a lunar month

隻字（ㄓˊ ㄗˋ）
a single word or character; a very brief note: 隻字無誤。 Not a single character is wrong.

隻字片紙（ㄓˊ ㄗˋ ㄆㄧㄢˋ ㄓˇ）
a very brief note or letter

隻言片語（ㄓˊ ㄧㄢˊ ㄆㄧㄢˋ ㄩˇ）
a few words: 她未留下隻言片語。She left behind not even a few words.

隻眼（ㄓˊ ㄧㄢˇ）
① one-eyed—(figuratively) a discerning viewpoint ② an original idea; a fresh view

隻影（ㄓˊ ㄧㄥˇ）
all alone; all by oneself

【隼】 6656 ㄓㄨㄣˇ joen zhǔn（又讀 ㄙㄨㄣˇ soen sǔn）
1. an aquiline nose
2. a hawk; a falcon

三畫

【雀】 6657 ㄑㄩㄝˋ chiueh què（酷音 ㄑㄧㄠˇ cheau qiāo）
1. a general name of small birds, as sparrows, chickadees, etc.
2. freckled

雀斑（ㄑㄩㄝˋ ㄅㄢ）
freckles: 她的臉上有雀斑。She has a freckled face.

雀屏中選（ㄑㄩㄝˋ ㄆㄧㄥˊ ㄓㄨㄥ ㄒㄩㄢˇ）or 雀屏中目（ㄑㄩㄝˋ ㄆㄧㄥˊ ㄓㄨㄥ ㄇㄨˋ）
to be selected as someone's son-in-law (a reference to the founding emperor of the Tang Dynasty who won the hand of his queen by hitting the eyes of two peacocks painted on screen doors in an archery contest)

雀麥（ㄑㄩㄝˋ ㄇㄞˋ）
Bromus japonicus, a variety of oats

雀盲（ㄑㄩㄝˋ ㄇㄤˊ）or 雀瞽（ㄑㄩㄝˋ ㄍㄨˇ）
night blindness; nyctalopia

雀立（ㄑㄩㄝˋ ㄌㄧˋ）
to hop around

雀羅（ㄑㄩㄝˋ ㄌㄨㄛˊ）
a net for catching birds

雀息（ㄑㄩㄝˋ ㄒㄧˊ）

to remain quiet; to remain silent

雀戰（ㄑㄩㄝˋ ㄓㄢˋ）
to play a game of mah-jong

雀巢鳩佔（ㄑㄩㄝˋ ㄔㄠˊ ㄐㄧㄡ ㄓㄢˋ）
(literally) The sparrow's nest is occupied by a pigeon. —to usurp other's position, property, etc.

雀舌（ㄑㄩㄝˋ ㄕㄜˊ）
name of a kind of tender tea leaves

雀鼠之爭（ㄑㄩㄝˋ ㄕㄨˇ ㄓ ㄓㄥ）
a lawsuit; a dispute

雀噪（ㄑㄩㄝˋ ㄗㄠˋ）
noisy and vociferous

雀躍（ㄑㄩㄝˋ ㄩㄝˋ）
to jump up with joy; greatly excited with joy: 他們聽到這個消息雀躍不已。They jumped for joy at the news.

四畫

【雄】 6658 ㄒㄩㄥˊ shyong xióng
1. male; masculine; virile
2. a person or state having great power and influence
3. heroic; brave; strong; martial; ambitious
4. to win; to triumph; victory
5. to scold others with insulting words
6. a Chinese family name

雄霸一方（ㄒㄩㄥˊ ㄅㄚˋ ㄧ ㄈㄤ）or 雄據一方（ㄒㄩㄥˊ ㄐㄩˋ ㄧ ㄈㄤ）
(said of warlords, contending princes, etc.) to hold a part of the country and to exercise undisputed authority

雄辯（ㄒㄩㄥˊ ㄅㄧㄢˋ）
a forceful presentation of one's points in a debate; eloquence: 事實勝於雄辯。Facts speak louder than eloquent words.

雄辯滔滔（ㄒㄩㄥˊ ㄅㄧㄢˋ ㄊㄠ ㄊㄠ）
to argue eloquently

雄兵（ㄒㄩㄥˊ ㄅㄧㄥ）
crack troops; powerful armies

雄飛（ㄒㄩㄥˊ ㄈㄟ）
to strive for bigger and better things

雄風（ㄒㄩㄥˊ ㄈㄥ）

an awe-inspiring air; a gallant and stately manner

雄圖（ㄒㄩㄥˊ ㄊㄨˊ）or 雄略（ㄒㄩㄥˊ ㄌㄩㄝˋ）
an ambitious scheme; a great aspiration

雄豪（ㄒㄩㄥˊ ㄏㄠˊ）
① heroes or powerful persons ② ambitious and warlike; martial

雄厚（ㄒㄩㄥˊ ㄏㄡˋ）
ample; plentiful; rich; abundant; substantial or very considerable (strength, wealth, etc.): 他的資金雄厚。He has abundant funds.

雄花（ㄒㄩㄥˊ ㄏㄨㄚ）
(botany) a male flower; a staminate flower

雄渾（ㄒㄩㄥˊ ㄏㄨㄣˊ）
powerful; grand; grandiose

雄黃（ㄒㄩㄥˊ ㄏㄨㄤˊ）
realgar

雄黃酒（ㄒㄩㄥˊ ㄏㄨㄤˊ ㄐㄧㄡˇ）
liquor with a small amount of realgar to be drunk on the Dragon Boat Festival so that one can avoid snake and insect poisoning the year round

雄雞（ㄒㄩㄥˊ ㄐㄧ）
a cock; a male chicken

雄赳赳（ㄒㄩㄥˊ ㄐㄧㄡ ㄐㄧㄡ）
imposing; looking brave and resolute; valiantly

雄劍（ㄒㄩㄥˊ ㄐㄧㄢˋ）
one of a pair of famous swords in ancient China

雄健（ㄒㄩㄥˊ ㄐㄧㄢˋ）
powerful; vigorous; strapping; very healthy, virile and energetic

雄將（ㄒㄩㄥˊ ㄐㄧㄤˋ）
a top-notch soldier or general; a man of great physical strength

雄氣（ㄒㄩㄥˊ ㄑㄧˋ）
a gallant or heroic disposition

雄器（ㄒㄩㄥˊ ㄑㄧˋ）
(botany) antheridia

雄心（ㄒㄩㄥˊ ㄒㄧㄣ）
ambition; great expectations

雄心勃勃（ㄒㄩㄥˊ ㄒㄧㄣ ㄅㄛˊ ㄅㄛˊ）
very ambitious

雄心壯志（ㄒㄩㄥˊ ㄒㄧㄣ ㄓㄨㄤˋ ㄓˋ）

high hopes and great ambition; lofty ideals and high goals; lofty aspirations and great ideals

雄心未死(ㄒㄩㄥˊ ㄒㄧㄣ ㄨㄟˇ ㄙˇ)
undying ambition; not to give up yet

雄偉(ㄒㄩㄥˊ ㄨㄟˇ)
imposing and overpowering

雄峙(ㄒㄩㄥˊ ㄓˋ)
to stand imposingly

雄鎮(ㄒㄩㄥˊ ㄓㄣˋ)
a strategic city which can be easily defended

雄長(ㄒㄩㄥˊ ㄓㄤˇ)
hegemony

雄壯(ㄒㄩㄥˊ ㄓㄨㄤˋ)
majestic; virile; powerful; strong

雄師(ㄒㄩㄥˊ ㄕ)
crack troops; a powerful army 亦作雄兵」

雄視(ㄒㄩㄥˊ ㄕˋ)
to dominate (in a certain field of achievement)

雄勝(ㄒㄩㄥˊ ㄕㄥˋ)
a strategic pass, position, etc.

雄蕊(ㄒㄩㄥˊ ㄖㄨㄟˇ)
(botany) the stamen

雄姿(ㄒㄩㄥˊ ㄗ)
a dashing look; a manly form; a brave appearance; the look of audacity and prowess

雄才大略(ㄒㄩㄥˊ ㄘㄞˊ ㄉㄚˋ ㄌㄩㄝˋ)
(said of a ruler) extremely capable

雄兒(ㄒㄩㄥˊ ㄦˊ)
a man among men; a hero

雄偉(ㄒㄩㄥˊ ㄨㄟˇ)
grandeur; majestic; stately; imposing; magnificent

【雁】 6659
(鴈)(ㄧㄢˋ yann yàn)
the wild goose

雁帛(ㄧㄢˋ ㄅㄛˊ)
letters; correspondence

雁門(ㄧㄢˋ ㄇㄣˊ)
name of several places in Shansi, Shensi, Honan and Kiangsu

雁杳魚沉(ㄧㄢˋ ㄧㄠˇ ㄩˊ ㄔㄣˊ)
without news or letters; to have lost contact

雁來紅(ㄧㄢˋ ㄌㄞˊ ㄏㄨㄥˊ)
the Chinese amaranth

雁行(ㄧㄢˋ ㄏㄤˊ)
①to walk like flying wild geese, one after another ② brothers

雁折翼(ㄧㄢˋ ㄓㄜˊ ㄧˋ)
the death of a brother

雁戶(ㄧㄢˋ ㄏㄨˋ)
a transient resident

雁序(ㄧㄢˋ ㄒㄩˋ)
brothers

雁陣(ㄧㄢˋ ㄓㄣˋ)
wild geese flying in good order, like a military deployment

雁齒(ㄧㄢˋ ㄔˇ)
things laid out in a neat row or in good order

雁字(ㄧㄢˋ ㄗˋ)
characters formed by flying wild geese (as "一" or "人")

雁足傳書(ㄧㄢˋ ㄗㄨˊ ㄔㄨㄢˊ ㄕㄨ)
to bring a message or letter

【雅】 6660
(ㄧㄚˇ yea yǎ)
1. refined; polished; sophisticated; not common or vulgar
2. elegant; graceful
3. usually; often; frequently; much
4. name of an ancient musical instrument
5. friendship; acquaintance
6. (now rarely) a wine vessel
7. (a polite term) your
8. a Chinese family name

雅步(ㄧㄚˇ ㄅㄨˋ)
leisurely and graceful steps

雅痞(ㄧㄚˇ ㄆㄧˇ)
Yuppie or Yuppy (a young, ambitious, and well-educated city-dweller who has a professional career and an affluent lifestyle)

雅美族(ㄧㄚˇ ㄇㄟˇ ㄗㄨˊ)
the Yamis, an aborigine tribe on Orchid Island (Lan-yü) off the eastern coast of Taiwan

雅典(ㄧㄚˇ ㄉㄧㄢˇ)
Athens, capital of Greece

雅典娜(ㄧㄚˇ ㄉㄧㄢˇ ㄋㄚˋ)
Athena

雅典主義(ㄧㄚˇ ㄉㄧㄢˇ ㄓㄨˇ ㄧˋ)
Atticism, or atticism

雅利安族(ㄧㄚˇ ㄌㄧˋ ㄢ ㄗㄨˊ)
the Aryans

雅量(ㄧㄚˇ ㄌㄧㄤˋ)
① magnanimity; generous; broad-mindedness ② a great capacity for drinking

雅魯藏布江(ㄧㄚˇ ㄌㄨˇ ㄗㄤˋ ㄅㄨˋ ㄐㄧㄤ)
the Brahmaputra River

雅歌(ㄧㄚˇ ㄍㄜ)
①to sing highbrow songs ② (in the Bible) the Song of Solomon

雅故(ㄧㄚˇ ㄍㄨˋ)
① an old friend ② usually

雅觀(ㄧㄚˇ ㄍㄨㄢ)
graceful and elegant in appearance; propriety in conduct

雅庫特人(ㄧㄚˇ ㄎㄨˋ ㄊㄜˋ ㄖㄣˊ)
the Yakuts

雅庫次克(ㄧㄚˇ ㄎㄨˋ ㄘˋ ㄎㄜˋ)
Yakutsk, U.S.S.R.

雅號(ㄧㄚˇ ㄏㄠˋ)
(a polite expression) your name

雅懷(ㄧㄚˇ ㄏㄨㄞˊ)
a generous heart; refined taste and disposition

雅誨(ㄧㄚˇ ㄏㄨㄟˋ) or 雅教(ㄧㄚˇ ㄐㄧㄠˋ)
(a polite expression used in letters) your instruction or advice; your esteemed opinion

雅集(ㄧㄚˇ ㄐㄧˊ)
a gathering of men of letters

雅鑒(ㄧㄚˇ ㄐㄧㄢˋ)
(a polite expression) for your perusal

雅趣(ㄧㄚˇ ㄑㄩˋ)
refined tastes

雅興(ㄧㄚˇ ㄒㄧㄥˋ)
enthusiasm in refined pursuits

雅馴(ㄧㄚˇ ㄒㄩㄣˋ)
(said of writing or remarks) polished, refined or elegant

雅致(ㄧㄚˇ ㄓˋ)
① refined tastes; refinement ② fine; delicate; elegant; tasteful

雅正(ㄧㄚˇ ㄓㄥˋ)
① graceful and upright ② a polite expression written on one's own calligraphic work presented to a friend as a gift) Please point out my shortcomings.

〔隹部〕

〔隹部〕

雅囑(ㄧㄚˇ ㄓㄨˇ)
(a polite expression) your orders or advice

雅士(ㄧㄚˇ ㄕˋ)or 雅人(ㄧㄚˇ ㄖㄣˊ)
a refined scholar; a person of refined tastes

雅事(ㄧㄚˇ ㄕˋ)
refined activities of the intelligentsia

雅人深致(ㄧㄚˇ ㄖㄣˊ ㄕㄣ ㄓˋ)
a sophisticated person with profound thoughts

雅賊(ㄧㄚˇ ㄗㄟˊ)
a thief who steals only books and works of art

雅座(ㄧㄚˇ ㄗㄨㄛˋ)
a nicely fixed chamber or room in a restaurant for customers who desire privacy

雅俗(ㄧㄚˇ ㄙㄨˊ)
the refined and the vulgar; the sophisticated and the simple-minded

雅俗共賞(ㄧㄚˇ ㄙㄨˊ ㄍㄨㄥˋ ㄕㄤˇ)
(said of art, performances, etc.) to appeal to both the sophisticated and the simple-minded

雅素(ㄧㄚˇ ㄙㄨˋ)
①personal background ②old friendship ③virtue in simplicity

雅愛(ㄧㄚˇ ㄞˋ)
(a polite expression) your patronage; your help: 多謝雅愛。 Thanks for your patronage (or help).

雅爾達會議(ㄧㄚˇ ㄦˇ ㄉㄚˊ ㄏㄨㄟˋ ㄧˋ)
the Yalta Conference among Roosevelt, Churchill and Stalin, held on February 4, 1945

雅意(ㄧㄚˇ ㄧˋ)
your ideas or views

雅游(ㄧㄚˇ ㄧㄡˊ)
very sociable; easy to get along with people

雅言(ㄧㄚˇ ㄧㄢˊ)
①well-intentioned criticism; honest advice ②things one often talks about

雅玩(ㄧㄚˇ ㄨㄢˊ)
①refined pastimes of the intelligentsia ②a polite expression in presenting a curio, etc. to a friend

雅望(ㄧㄚˇ ㄨㄤˋ)
your spotless fame

雅樂(ㄧㄚˇ ㄩㄝˋ)
①(in ancient China) ceremonial music ②Chinese classical music

雅馴(ㄧㄚˇ ㄒㄩㄣˋ)
refined or sophisticated taste

【集】   6661
ㄐㄧˊ jyí jí

1. to assemble; to collect; to gather together; to concentrate
2. a collection of works by one or more authors; to compile; to edit
3. achievements
4. a fair; a periodical market

集部(ㄐㄧˊ ㄅㄨˋ)
the fourth section of *Encyclopedia Sinica*, which contains literary works

集大成(ㄐㄧˊ ㄉㄚˋ ㄔㄥˊ)
a theory, etc. representing a generalization of many views or ideas; eclectic

集體(ㄐㄧˊ ㄊㄧˇ)
collective

集體農場(ㄐㄧˊ ㄊㄧˇ ㄋㄨㄥˊ ㄔㄤˇ)
a collective farm

集體領導(ㄐㄧˊ ㄊㄧˇ ㄌㄧㄥˇ ㄉㄠˇ)
collective leadership

集體管理(ㄐㄧˊ ㄊㄧˇ ㄍㄨㄢˇ ㄌㄧˇ)
mass management

集體經濟(ㄐㄧˊ ㄊㄧˇ ㄐㄧㄥ ㄐㄧˋ)
collective economy

集體決定(ㄐㄧˊ ㄊㄧˇ ㄐㄩㄝˊ ㄉㄧㄥˋ)
group decision

集體創作(ㄐㄧˊ ㄊㄧˇ ㄔㄨㄤˋ ㄗㄨㄛˋ)
a collective(literary or artistic)work; collective creation

集體安全(ㄐㄧˊ ㄊㄧˇ ㄢ ㄑㄩㄢˊ)
collective security

集體研究(ㄐㄧˊ ㄊㄧˇ ㄧㄢˊ ㄐㄧㄡˋ)
team research

集團(ㄐㄧˊ ㄊㄨㄢˊ)
an organization; a body of people; a bloc; a faction; a clique

集團結婚(ㄐㄧˊ ㄊㄨㄢˊ ㄐㄧㄝˊ ㄏㄨㄣ)
a mass wedding; a wedding ceremony either held at a court of law or under the sponsorship of a civic or military organization, in which many couples are

joined in wedlock

集團軍(ㄐㄧˊ ㄊㄨㄢˊ ㄐㄩㄣ)
an army (a military outfit which consists of more than two corps)

集股(ㄐㄧˊ ㄍㄨˇ)
to collect capital (in order to establish a business)

集刊(ㄐㄧˊ ㄎㄢ)
collected papers (of an academic institution)

集合(ㄐㄧˊ ㄏㄜˊ)
to assemble; to gathered together; to muster

集合名詞(ㄐㄧˊ ㄏㄜˊ ㄇㄧㄥˊ ㄘˊ)
a collective noun

集合體(ㄐㄧˊ ㄏㄜˊ ㄊㄧˇ)
(said of minerals) an aggregate

集會(ㄐㄧˊ ㄏㄨㄟˋ)
a meeting; a conference; an assemblage; an assembly

集會結社(ㄐㄧˊ ㄏㄨㄟˋ ㄐㄧㄝˊ ㄕㄜˋ)
to assemble and form an organization, society, etc.

集會自由(ㄐㄧˊ ㄏㄨㄟˋ ㄗˋ ㄧㄡˊ)
freedom of assembly

集結(ㄐㄧˊ ㄐㄧㄝˊ)
to concentrate (troops)

集錦(ㄐㄧˊ ㄐㄧㄣˇ)
a collection of homogeneous passages from various literary pieces; a hodgepodge

集句(ㄐㄧˊ ㄐㄩˋ)
to cull lines here and there from a poet's work and piece them together into a new poem

集聚(ㄐㄧˊ ㄐㄩˋ)
to collect or gather together: 一群人集聚在街角。A crowd gathered on the corner.

集權(ㄐㄧˊ ㄑㄩㄢˊ)
centralization of authority; concentration of power

集訓(ㄐㄧˊ ㄒㄩㄣˋ)
to train many people at the same place and same time; a camp training

集注(ㄐㄧˊ ㄓㄨˋ)
①to focus ②variorum

集中(ㄐㄧˊ ㄓㄨㄥ)
①to concentrate; to center; to centralize: 他集中心力在工作上。He concentrated his mind on ·his work. ②to gather

集中營 (ㄐㄧ ㄓㄨㄥ ㄧㄥˊ)
a concentration camp

集產主義 (ㄐㄧˊ ㄔㄢˇ ㄓㄨˇ ㄧˋ)
collectivism

集市 (ㄐㄧˊ ㄕˋ)
a periodic market

集少成多 (ㄐㄧˊ ㄕㄠˇ ㄔㄥˊ ㄉㄨㄛ)
Many a little makes a mickle.

集上 (ㄐㄧˊ ˙ㄕㄤ)
on the market

集資 (ㄐㄧˊ ㄗ)
to raise funds; to collect money; to pool resources

集子 (ㄐㄧˊ ˙ㄗ)
a collection; collected works; an anthology: 這本集子很不錯。 This collection is very good.

集思廣益 (ㄐㄧˊ ㄙ ㄍㄨㄤˇ ㄧˋ)
to canvass various opinions and benefit from them

集散地 (ㄐㄧˊ ㄙㄢˋ ㄉㄧˋ)
a commercial center; a commercial port

集議 (ㄐㄧˊ ㄧˋ)
to meet and discuss; to hold a conference

集腋成裘 (ㄐㄧˊ ㄧㄝˋ ㄔㄥˊ ㄑㄧㄡˊ)
Small resources pooled together can accomplish big things. 或 Many a little makes a mickle.

集郵 (ㄐㄧˊ ㄧㄡˊ)
philately; stamp collection

集郵簿 (ㄐㄧˊ ㄧㄡˊ ㄅㄨˋ)
a stamp album

集郵家 (ㄐㄧˊ ㄧㄡˊ ㄐㄧㄚ)
a philatelist or stamp collector

集於一身 (ㄐㄧˊ ㄩˊ ㄧ ㄕㄣ)
to center on one person, as powers, etc.

【雇】 6662
 ㄍㄨˋ guh gù
to employ or hire

雇不到 (ㄍㄨˋ ㄅㄨˋ ㄉㄠˋ)
unable to hire or employ —either because of low pay or shortage of labor supply

雇不起 (ㄍㄨˋ ㄅㄨˋ ㄑㄧˇ)
cannot afford to hire: 他雇不起他Λ。 He couldn't afford to hire a servant.

雇農 (ㄍㄨˋ ㄋㄨㄥˊ)
hired laborers on the farm; a hired farm hand

雇工 (ㄍㄨˋ ㄍㄨㄥ)
① a hired laborer: 他做臨時雇工。 He worked for hire. ② to hire a laborer

雇主 (ㄍㄨˋ ㄓㄨˇ)
the employer

雇車 (ㄍㄨˋ ㄔㄜ)
to hire a cab, truck, etc. together with its driver

雇船 (ㄍㄨˋ ㄔㄨㄢˊ)
to charter or hire a boat

雇員 (ㄍㄨˋ ㄩㄢˊ)
an auxiliary employee of very low rank in a government office

雇傭 (ㄍㄨˋ ㄩㄥ)
hired or employed

五畫

【雍】 6663
 ㄩㄥ iong yōng
1. harmonious; harmony; peaceful; union
2. name of various places or states throughout the dynasties
3. to block up; to obstruct
4. a Chinese family name

雍睦 (ㄩㄥ ㄇㄨˋ)
harmonious or friendly

雍和 (ㄩㄥ ㄏㄜˊ)
harmony

雍正 (ㄩㄥ ㄓㄥˋ)
the reigning title of the third emperor of the Ching Dynasty

雍容 (ㄩㄥ ㄖㄨㄥˊ)
a majestic, stately or imposing appearance

雍容華貴 (ㄩㄥ ㄖㄨㄥˊ ㄏㄨㄚˊ ㄍㄨㄟˋ)
(said of a woman) graceful and poised; regal

雍容自得 (ㄩㄥ ㄖㄨㄥˊ ㄗˋ ㄉㄜˊ)
poised; in the peace of mind

雍閼 (ㄩㄥ ㄜˋ)
to block or stop up; to obstruct

雍熙 (ㄩㄥ ㄒㄧ)
harmonious; peaceful

【雉】 6664
 ㄓˋ jyh zhì
1. a pheasant
2. a unit of volume measure in ancient China (about 30' square by 10')

雉媒 (ㄓˋ ㄇㄟˊ)

a domesticated pheasant used as a decoy in pheasant hunting

雉堞 (ㄓˋ ㄉㄧㄝˊ)
a parapet with embrasures; crenelation

雉雞 (ㄓˋ ㄐㄧ)
a pheasant; a tartar pheasant

雉經 (ㄓˋ ㄐㄧㄥ)
to commit suicide by hanging

【雊】 6665
 ㄍㄡˋ gow gòu
the crow of a male pheasant

【雌】 6666
 ㄘ tsy cī
1. female; feminine; woman-like; soft (voice, etc.)
2. weak; retiring
3. the vanquished; defeated
4. to scold
5. to expose or show (the teeth) 亦作「齜」

雌風 (ㄘ ㄈㄥ)
① evil practice or custom ② the tantrum of a virago or shrew

雌伏 (ㄘ ㄈㄨˊ)
to lie low; not ambitious; retiring; withdrawing; not aggressive

雌懦 (ㄘ ㄋㄨㄛˋ)
weak-minded; cowardly

雌老虎 (ㄘ ㄌㄠˇ ㄏㄨˇ)
① a tigress ② (colloquial) a loud-mouthed shrew, fishwife or virago 亦作「母老虎」

雌花 (ㄘ ㄏㄨㄚ)
a pistillate flower

雌黃 (ㄘ ㄏㄨㄤˊ)
① orpiment (As₂S₃) ② to make changes in writing ③ to criticize without grounds; to malign 參看「信口雌黃」

雌性 (ㄘ ㄒㄧㄥˋ)
female

雌雄 (ㄘ ㄒㄩㄥˊ)
① the female and the male ② the victor and the loser: 讓我們決一雌雄。 Let's have a showdown. 或 Let's fight a decisive battle. ③ things that form a pair—as precious swords in ancient China

雌雄莫辨 (ㄘ ㄒㄩㄥˊ ㄇㄛˋ ㄅㄧㄢˋ)
unable to distinguish the sex

〔隹部〕

identity

雌雄淘汰(ㄘ ㄒㄩㄥˊ ㄊㄠˊ ㄊㄞˋ)
sexual selection

雌雄同體(ㄘ ㄒㄩㄥˊ ㄊㄨㄥˊ ㄊㄧˇ)
hermaphrodite

雌雄同株(ㄘ ㄒㄩㄥˊ ㄊㄨㄥˊ ㄓㄨ)
monoecious; monoecism

雌雄同劍(ㄘ ㄒㄩㄥˊ ㄊㄨㄥˊ ㄐㄧㄢˋ)
the name of a pair of pre-cious swords in ancient China

雌雄異體(ㄘ ㄒㄩㄥˊ ㄧˋ ㄊㄧˇ)
gonochorism

雌雄異株(ㄘ ㄒㄩㄥˊ ㄧˋ ㄓㄨ)
dioecious

雌蕊(ㄘ ㄖㄨㄟˇ)
a pistil

雌威(ㄘ ㄨㄟ)
the tantrum of a shrew

【雋】6667
1. ㄐㄩㄣˋ jiunn jùn
1. good-looking
2. talented; outstanding;
extraordinary

雋拔(ㄐㄩㄣˋ ㄅㄚˊ)
outstandingly talented

雋楚(ㄐㄩㄣˋ ㄔㄨˇ)
outstanding; extraordinary;
preeminence

雋譽(ㄐㄩㄣˋ ㄩˋ)
high fame or good reputa-tion

【雋】6667
2. ㄐㄩㄢˋ jiuann juàn
1. fat meat
2. meaningful
3. a Chinese family name

雋永(ㄐㄩㄣˋ ㄩㄥˇ)
(said of remarks or writ-ings) very interesting or intriguing; meaningful

【雎】6668
ㄐㄩ jiu jū
1. a kind of waterfowl (雎鳩)
which observes fidelity in
sex life, probably the os-prey
2. (now rarely) to hesitate; to
avoid

六畫

【雒】6669
ㄌㄨㄛˋ luoh luò
1. a black horse with white
mane
2. to brand
3. name of a river

4. an owl

八畫

【雕】6670
ㄉㄧㄠ diau diāo
1. to engrave; to carve or cut,
as in sculpture
2. an eagle; a hawk
3. to exhaust; to weaken

雕板(ㄉㄧㄠ ㄅㄢˇ)
to cut blocks of wood for
printing (first started in the
Sui (隋) Dynasty)

雕梁畫棟(ㄉㄧㄠ ㄌㄧㄤˊ ㄏㄨㄚˋ ㄉㄨㄥˋ)
carved beams and painted
rafters—a richly ornamented
building

雕龍(ㄉㄧㄠ ㄌㄨㄥˊ)
(literally) the carving of
dragons—a highly embel-lished literary style

雕戈(ㄉㄧㄠ ㄍㄜ)
a carved lance or engraved
spear

雕肝琢腎(ㄉㄧㄠ ㄍㄢ ㄓㄨㄛˊ ㄕㄣˋ)
to exhaust physical and
mental energy

雕弓(ㄉㄧㄠ ㄍㄨㄥ)
a painted or ornamented
bow

雕刻(ㄉㄧㄠ ㄎㄜˋ)
sculpture; to engrave

雕花(ㄉㄧㄠ ㄏㄨㄚ)
to engrave figures or pic-tures

雕漆(ㄉㄧㄠ ㄑㄧ)
to engrave or carve on lac-quer ware

雕像(ㄉㄧㄠ ㄒㄧㄤˋ)
① a sculptured statue ② por-trayal of a person

雕琢(ㄉㄧㄠ ㄓㄨㄛˊ)
① to cut and polish (gems)
② to polish a piece of writ-ing; to write in an ornate
style

雕蟲小技(ㄉㄧㄠ ㄔㄨㄥˊ ㄒㄧㄠˇ ㄐㄧˋ)
a petty skill or craft; a skill
which has no significant val-ue

雕蟲篆(ㄉㄧㄠ ㄔㄨㄥˊ ㄓㄨㄢˋ)
a type of calligraphy featur-ing characters twisting and
turning like worms

雕蟲篆刻(ㄉㄧㄠ ㄔㄨㄥˊ ㄓㄨㄢˋ ㄎㄜˋ)
(a self-derogatory expres-

sion) skill in writing poetic
prose

雕塑(ㄉㄧㄠ ㄙㄨˋ)
① sculpture; to cut wood or
clay for a statue or idol ②
(figuratively) to paint a pic-ture (of something or some-body)

雕雲(ㄉㄧㄠ ㄩㄣˊ)
propitious clouds; clouds
portending good fortune

【雠】6671
ㄔㄡˊ chour chóu
a pair of birds

九畫

【雖】6672
ㄙㄨㄟ suei suī
(又讀ㄙㄨㄟ swei suí)
1. although; even though; even
if; supposing
2. to push away; to dismiss
3. only
4. (now rarely) a lizard-like
reptile

雖敗猶榮(ㄙㄨㄟ ㄅㄞˋ ㄧㄡˊ ㄖㄨㄥˊ)
to feel proud even in defeat

雖說(ㄙㄨㄟ ㄕㄨㄛ)
even though; although

雖然(ㄙㄨㄟ ㄖㄢˊ)
even though; although; in
spite of; even if

雖則(ㄙㄨㄟ ㄗㄜˊ)
although; even if; still; 雖則
他不來，我也不介意。I won't
mind even if he doesn't
come.

十畫

【雙】6673
ㄕㄨㄤ shuang shuāng
1. a pair; a brace; a couple;
persons or things that come
in pairs: 他有一雙新襪子。He
has a new pair of socks.
2. two; both; even (as distinct
from odd)

雙倍(ㄕㄨㄤ ㄅㄟˋ)
double; twofold; twice the
amount or number: 十爲五之
雙倍。Ten is the double of
five.

雙胞胎(ㄕㄨㄤ ㄅㄠ ㄊㄞ)
twins

雙邊貿易(ㄕㄨㄤ ㄅㄧㄢ ㄇㄠˋ ㄧˋ)
bilateral trade; two-way

trade

雙面(ㄕㄨㄤ ㄇㄧㄢˋ)
two-sided; double-edged;
double-faced; reversible

雙名(ㄕㄨㄤ ㄇㄧㄥˊ)
a given name consists of
two characters

雙目失明(ㄕㄨㄤ ㄇㄨˋ ㄕ ㄇㄧㄥˊ)
to be blind in both eyes

雙分兒(ㄕㄨㄤ ㄈㄣ ㄦ)
double shares; double the
amount; twice as much

雙飛(ㄕㄨㄤ ㄈㄟ)
flying in pairs—close union
as man and wife who are
very much in love

雙方(ㄕㄨㄤ ㄈㄤ)
both parties or sides (in a
dispute, an agreement, etc.)

雙方同意(ㄕㄨㄤ ㄈㄤ ㄊㄨㄥˊ ㄧˋ)
mutual consent

雙峯駝(ㄕㄨㄤ ㄈㄥ ㄊㄨㄛˊ)
a double-humped camel; the
Bactrian camel

雙幅(ㄕㄨㄤ ㄈㄨˊ)
(said of fabrics or piece
goods) of double standard
width

雙打(ㄕㄨㄤ ㄉㄚˇ)
to play in doubles (as tennis); doubles: 男女混合雙打
mixed doubles

雙瞳剪水(ㄕㄨㄤ ㄊㄨㄥˊ ㄐㄧㄢ ㄕㄨㄟˇ)
clear, beautiful eyes of a
pretty girl

雙鯉(ㄕㄨㄤ ㄌㄧˇ)
letters

雙料(ㄕㄨㄤ ㄌㄧㄠˋ)
articles, products built with
added strength, durability,
etc. by using better and
more raw materials

雙掛號(ㄕㄨㄤ ㄍㄨㄚˋ ㄏㄠˋ)
registered mail with return
receipt

雙軌(ㄕㄨㄤ ㄍㄨㄟˇ)
double-tracked (railway);
double tracks: 雙軌鐵路 a
railway with a double track

雙軌制(ㄕㄨㄤ ㄍㄨㄟˇ ㄓ)
(education) the double-track
system

雙關(ㄕㄨㄤ ㄍㄨㄢ)
ambiguous; subject to two
different interpretations: 一
語雙關 a phrase with a dou-
ble meaning

雙關語(ㄕㄨㄤ ㄍㄨㄢ ㄩˇ)
a double entendre; a pun

雙管齊下(ㄕㄨㄤ ㄍㄨㄢˇ ㄑㄧˊ ㄒㄧㄚˋ)
①to do two things simultaneously in order to attain an
objective; a double-barreled
move ②ambiguous; subject
to two different interpretations

雙款(ㄕㄨㄤ ㄎㄨㄢˇ)
(said of paintings, calligraphy, etc.) with both "upper"
and "lower" inscriptions (i.e.
both the names of the recipient and the artist)

雙號(ㄕㄨㄤ ㄏㄠˋ)
(said of tickets, seats, etc.)
an even number

雙簧(ㄕㄨㄤ ㄏㄨㄤˊ)
a kind of variety show
featuring two performers,
one of whom speaks while
the other acts out the gestures at the same time; a
two-man comic show

雙簧管(ㄕㄨㄤ ㄏㄨㄤˊ ㄍㄨㄢˇ)
(music) an oboe

雙頰(ㄕㄨㄤ ㄐㄧㄚˊ)
both cheeks: 這小孩雙頰通紅。
The boy has rosy cheeks.

雙腳(ㄕㄨㄤ ㄐㄧㄠˇ)
both feet; the two feet

雙肩(ㄕㄨㄤ ㄐㄧㄢ)
both shoulders; the two
shoulders

雙棲(ㄕㄨㄤ ㄑㄧ)
to live together as man and
wife

雙親(ㄕㄨㄤ ㄑㄧㄣ)
one's parents: 他的雙親很富
有。His parents are very
rich.

雙曲線(ㄕㄨㄤ ㄑㄩ ㄒㄧㄢˋ)
(mathematics) a hyperbola

雙全(ㄕㄨㄤ ㄑㄩㄢˊ)
①both (parents) alive ②
both intact; possessing both:
他智勇雙全。He possesses
both intelligence and bravery.

雙喜臨門(ㄕㄨㄤ ㄒㄧ ㄌㄧㄣˊ ㄇㄣˊ)
to have simultaneously two
happy events in a family
(such as a son getting married on the father's birthday)或 A double blessing
has descended upon the

house.

雙下巴(ㄕㄨㄤ ㄒㄧㄚˋ ㄅㄚ)
a double chin

雙薪家庭(ㄕㄨㄤ ㄒㄧㄣ ㄐㄧㄚ ㄊㄧㄥˊ)
two-paycheck families

雙響(ㄕㄨㄤ ㄒㄧㄤˇ)
name of a kind of fire
cracker which soars like a
rocket and explodes with
two blasts 亦作「二踢腳」

雙餉(ㄕㄨㄤ ㄒㄧㄤˇ)
double pay for soldiers

雙向溝通(ㄕㄨㄤ ㄒㄧㄤˋ ㄍㄡ ㄊㄨㄥ)
two-way communication

雙向交通(ㄕㄨㄤ ㄒㄧㄤˋ ㄐㄧㄠ ㄊㄨㄥ)
two-way traffic

雙姓(ㄕㄨㄤ ㄒㄧㄥˋ)
a family name which con-
sists of two characters

雙週刊(ㄕㄨㄤ ㄓㄡ ㄎㄢ)
a fortnightly; a biweekly

雙翅類(ㄕㄨㄤ ㄔˋ ㄌㄟˋ)
(zoology) the Diptera

雙城記(ㄕㄨㄤ ㄔㄥˊ ㄐㄧˋ)
A Tale of Two Cities, by
Charles Dickens

雙脣音(ㄕㄨㄤ ㄔㄨㄣˊ ㄧㄣ)
bilabial consonants

雙重(ㄕㄨㄤ ㄔㄨㄥˊ)
double; dual; twofold: 它起
雙重作用。It served a dual
purpose.

雙重標準(ㄕㄨㄤ ㄔㄨㄥˊ ㄅㄧㄠ ㄓㄨㄣˇ)
double standard

雙重國籍(ㄕㄨㄤ ㄔㄨㄥˊ ㄍㄨㄛˊ ㄐㄧˊ)
dual nationality

雙重人格(ㄕㄨㄤ ㄔㄨㄥˊ ㄖㄣˊ ㄍㄜˊ)
(psychology) a dual personality; a split personality; a
dual nature

雙十節(ㄕㄨㄤ ㄕˊ ㄐㄧㄝˊ)
the "Double Tenth", October
10, the National Day of the
Republic of China

雙殺(ㄕㄨㄤ ㄕㄚ)
(baseball) double play

雙手(ㄕㄨㄤ ㄕㄡˇ)
the two hands; both hands

雙手萬能(ㄕㄨㄤ ㄕㄡˇ ㄨㄢˋ ㄋㄥˊ)
With two hands, one can
work miracles.

雙身子(ㄕㄨㄤ ㄕㄣ ㄗ)
a pregnant woman

雙生(ㄕㄨㄤ ㄕㄥ)
twin; twins: 這兩個學生是雙
生兄弟。The two students are

〔隹
部〕

〔隹部〕

twin brothers.

雙聲疊韻（ㄕㄨㄤ ㄕㄥ ㄉㄧㄝˊ ㄩㄣˋ）
alliteration and repetition in rhyme, such as 祈求 and 叮嚀

雙數（ㄕㄨㄤ ㄕㄨˋ）
an even number 亦作「偶數」

雙雙對對（ㄕㄨㄤ ㄕㄨㄤ ㄉㄨㄟˋ ㄉㄨㄟˋ）
in pairs and couples: 他們雙雙對對地進來。 They came in pairs.

雙日（ㄕㄨㄤ ㄖˋ）
even days

雙人房（ㄕㄨㄤ ㄖㄣˊ ㄈㄤˊ）
a double room; a twin room

雙人床（ㄕㄨㄤ ㄖㄣˊ ㄔㄨㄤˊ）
a double bed

雙人舞（ㄕㄨㄤ ㄖㄣˊ ㄨˇ）
a dance for two people; pas de deux

雙子星（ㄕㄨㄤ ㄗˇ ㄒㄧㄥ）or 雙子宮（ㄕㄨㄤ ㄗˇ ㄍㄨㄥ）or 雙子座（ㄕㄨㄤ ㄗˇ ㄗㄨㄛˋ）
(astronomy) Gemini

雙子葉植物（ㄕㄨㄤ ㄗˇ ㄧㄝˋ ㄓˊ ㄨˋ）
(botany) a dicotyledon

雙層（ㄕㄨㄤ ㄘㄥˊ）
double layers; double decks

雙層牀（ㄕㄨㄤ ㄘㄥˊ ㄔㄨㄤˊ）
a double-decked bunk

雙宿雙飛（ㄕㄨㄤ ㄙㄨˋ ㄕㄨㄤ ㄈㄟ）
to live like man and wife; to sleep and move together

雙蛾（ㄕㄨㄤ ㄜˊ）
eyebrows of a woman

雙翼飛機（ㄕㄨㄤ ㄧˋ ㄈㄟ ㄐㄧ）
a biplane

雙眼皮兒（ㄕㄨㄤ ㄧㄢˇ ㄆㄧˊ ㄦˊ）
the upper eyelid which has a double fold at the lower edge, a common feature among Occidentals

雙氧水（ㄕㄨㄤ ㄧㄤˋ ㄕㄨㄟˇ）
hydrogen peroxide

雙亡（ㄕㄨㄤ ㄨㄤˊ）
(said of one's parents or of a couple) Both are dead.

雙魚座（ㄕㄨㄤ ㄩˊ ㄗㄨㄛˋ）
(astronomy) Pisces

雙月刊（ㄕㄨㄤ ㄩㄝˋ ㄎㄢ）
a bimonthly

【雛】 6674
ㄔㄨˊ chwu chú

1. a chick
2. a very young bird—a fledgling
3. a small kid or toddler

雛鳳（ㄔㄨˊ ㄈㄥˋ）
bright and promising children

雛鳥（ㄔㄨˊ ㄋㄧㄠˇ）
a very young bird—a fledgling

雛雞（ㄔㄨˊ ㄐㄧ）
a chick; a chicken

雛妓（ㄔㄨˊ ㄐㄧˋ）
a very young prostitute

雛菊（ㄔㄨˊ ㄐㄩˊ）
a daisy

雛形（ㄔㄨˊ ㄒㄧㄥˊ）
a miniature form; a scaled-down model of anything; an embryonic form

雛兒（ㄔㄨˊ ㄦˊ）
① a very young prostitute ② an inexperienced young man; a novice ③ a young girl

雛鴨（ㄔㄨˊ ㄧㄚ）
a duckling

【雜】 6675
ㄗㄚˊ tzar zá

1. to mix; to blend; mixed; blended
2. miscellaneous
3. motley; medley
4. petty and numerous

雜拌兒（ㄗㄚˊ ㄅㄢˋ ㄦˊ）
mixed nuts; sweetmeats and sundries (served in New Year holidays)

雜八湊兒（ㄗㄚˊ ㄅㄚ ㄘㄡˋ ㄦˊ）
a motley of different things; a collection of varied things

雜牌（ㄗㄚˊ ㄆㄞˊ）
a less known and inferior brand

雜評（ㄗㄚˊ ㄆㄧㄥˊ）
(journals, newspapers, etc.) a short commentary; a leaderette

雜麪（ㄗㄚˊ ㄇㄧㄢˋ）
noodles made of flour of mixed grains

雜費（ㄗㄚˊ ㄈㄟˋ）
miscellaneous expenses; sundry charges

雜沓（ㄗㄚˊ ㄊㄚˋ）
confused or disorderly

雜遝（ㄗㄚˊ ㄊㄚˋ）
numerous; many

雜談（ㄗㄚˊ ㄊㄢˊ）
a chat; a rambling talk; a random talk

雜念（ㄗㄚˊ ㄋㄧㄢˋ）
distracting thoughts

雜流（ㄗㄚˊ ㄌㄧㄡˊ）
① (formerly) petty officials ② (formerly) people dealing in commerce and trade

雜糧（ㄗㄚˊ ㄌㄧㄤˊ）
miscellaneous grain crops, as oat, millet, etc. (as opposed to rice and wheat which are staple foods)

雜亂（ㄗㄚˊ ㄌㄨㄢˋ）
confused and disorderly; to be jumbled

雜亂無章（ㄗㄚˊ ㄌㄨㄢˋ ㄨˊ ㄓㄤ）
motley; disorderly; in utter confusion; in a great mess

雜感（ㄗㄚˊ ㄍㄢˇ）
rambling observations; random thoughts

雜合菜（ㄗㄚˊ ㄏㄜˊ ㄘㄞˋ）
a dish prepared by mixing or cooking the leftovers of a previous dinner or feast

雜貨（ㄗㄚˊ ㄏㄨㄛˋ）
groceries; sundry goods

雜貨店（ㄗㄚˊ ㄏㄨㄛˋ ㄉㄧㄢˋ）
a sundry store; a grocery; a corner drugstore

雜貨商（ㄗㄚˊ ㄏㄨㄛˋ ㄕㄤ）
a sundriesman

雜燴（ㄗㄚˊ ㄏㄨㄟˋ）
a dish of mixed food items

雜婚（ㄗㄚˊ ㄏㄨㄣ）
intermarriage

雜記（ㄗㄚˊ ㄐㄧˋ）
a miscellany; miscellaneous notes; random notes; jottings

雜技（ㄗㄚˊ ㄐㄧˋ）
a variety of juggling skills; a vaudeville; an acrobatic feat

雜技團（ㄗㄚˊ ㄐㄧˋ ㄊㄨㄢˊ）
an acrobatic troupe

雜家（ㄗㄚˊ ㄐㄧㄚ）
one of the nine schools of learning in ancient China, which combined the various schools of thoughts

雜交（ㄗㄚˊ ㄐㄧㄠ）
① (biology) to hybridize; to cross ② hybridization; crossbreed; a cross; interbreeding ③ promiscuity

雜居（ㄗㄚˊ ㄐㄩ）or 雜處（ㄗㄚˊ ㄔㄨˋ）
the living together of differ-

ent races or classes of people

雜劇(ㄗㄚˊ ㄐㄩˋ)
a variety show; a comedy or farce

雜七雜八(ㄗㄚˊ ㄑㄧ ㄗㄚˊ ㄅㄚ)or 雜七八拉(ㄗㄚˊ ㄑㄧ ㄅㄚ ㄌㄚ)
a motley; a jumble of various things; odds and ends

雜項(ㄗㄚˊ ㄒㄧㄤˋ)
miscellaneous items; (said of people) of different backgrounds and occupations

雜性花(ㄗㄚˊ ㄒㄧㄥˋ ㄏㄨㄚ)
a polygamous flower

雜學(ㄗㄚˊ ㄒㄩㄝˊ)
miscellaneous learning —unorthodox or unconventional learning

雜質(ㄗㄚˊ ㄓˊ)
impurities

雜誌(ㄗㄚˊ ㄓˋ)
a magazine; a periodical; a journal

雜種(ㄗㄚˊ ㄓㄨㄥˇ)
①a mixed breed; a hybrid ②(in ancient China) a foreign race or tribe ③a bastard; son of a bitch

雜史(ㄗㄚˊ ㄕˇ)
a personal recording of a single incident or of happenings during a given period

雜耍(ㄗㄚˊ ㄕㄨㄚˇ)
juggler's feats; a vaudeville or variety show

雜稅(ㄗㄚˊ ㄕㄨㄟˋ)
miscellaneous taxes; irregular taxes

雜糅(ㄗㄚˊ ㄖㄡˊ)
the mixing or blending together of a variety of things

雜然(ㄗㄚˊ ㄖㄢˊ)
all; unanimously

雜錄(ㄗㄚˊ ㄌㄨˋ)
notes or records of miscellaneous and petty incidents, episodes, etc.

雜亂(ㄗㄚˊ ㄌㄨㄢˋ)
disorderly and confused; motley

雜草(ㄗㄚˊ ㄘㄠˇ)
weeds: 這花園雜草叢生. The garden was covered with weeds.

---

the mixing or assorting (especially impromptu) of miscellaneous things together which usually don't have a central theme

雜錯(ㄗㄚˊ ㄘㄨㄛˋ)
mixed 亦作「雜厝」

雜耍(ㄗㄚˊ ㄕㄨㄚˇ)
feats displayed in a vaudeville or variety show

雜色(ㄗㄚˊ ㄙㄜˋ)
variegated; parti-colored; motley

雜碎(ㄗㄚˊ ·ㄙㄨㄟ)
①complicated and trifling ②the internal organs of cattle or lambs as a dish ③chop suey, or chop sooy ④conscience; the true nature of a person

雜役(ㄗㄚˊ ㄧˋ)
odd jobs; chores

雜音(ㄗㄚˊ ㄧㄣ)
noises; (recording) humming or other unwanted sounds

雜樣(ㄗㄚˊ ㄧㄤˋ)
to mix together different types of things

雜務(ㄗㄚˊ ㄨˋ)
chores; miscellaneous duties

雜物(ㄗㄚˊ ㄨˋ)
miscellaneous articles or objects; odds and ends

雜文學(ㄗㄚˊ ㄨㄣˊ ㄒㄩㄝˊ)
(literally) miscellaneous literature, as narratives, commentaries, etc.

雜院兒(ㄗㄚˊ ㄩㄢˋ ㄦ)
a cluster of houses sharing a common courtyard and inhabited by a number of families

【巂】6676
ㄙㄨㄟ soei suí
name of an old town in today's Szechwan Province

【雞】6677
(雞) ㄐㄧ ji jī
a chicken, a hen; a cock; a fowl

雞巴(ㄐㄧ ·ㄅㄚ)
(colloquial) the penis

雞皮(ㄐㄧ ㄆㄧˊ)
(figuratively) the shriveled skin of the aged

雞皮疙瘩(ㄐㄧ ㄆㄧˊ ㄍㄜ ·ㄉㄚ)
goose pimples; goose flesh

雞皮鶴髮(ㄐㄧ ㄆㄧˊ ㄏㄜˋ ㄈㄚˇ)
(said of the aged) with shriveled skin and hoary-headed

雞毛帚(ㄐㄧ ㄇㄠˊ ㄓㄡˇ)
a chicken-feather duster 亦作「雞毛撢子」

雞毛蒜皮(ㄐㄧ ㄇㄠˊ ㄙㄨㄢˋ ㄆㄧˊ)
(literally) chicken feathers and pieces of garlic skin —petty or trifling things

雞鳴狗盜(ㄐㄧ ㄇㄧㄥˊ ㄍㄡˇ ㄉㄠˋ)
(ability to) crow like a cock and snatch like a dog — small tricks; various kinds of talent or skill useful in emergency

雞飛蛋打(ㄐㄧ ㄈㄟ ㄉㄢˋ ㄉㄚˇ)
(literally) The hen has flown away and the eggs have been broken.—Everything's lost.

雞坊(ㄐㄧ ㄈㄤˊ)
a chicken farm; a pen for raising chickens; a chicken coop

雞蛋(ㄐㄧ ㄉㄢˋ)or 雞卵(ㄐㄧ ㄌㄨㄢˇ)
a hen's egg

雞蛋碰石頭(ㄐㄧ ㄉㄢˋ ㄆㄥˋ ㄕˊ ㄊㄡˊ)
like an egg hitting a rock —to attack someone much stronger than oneself

雞蛋裏挑骨頭(ㄐㄧ ㄉㄢˋ ㄌㄧˇ ㄊㄧㄠ ㄍㄨˇ ㄊㄡˊ)
to look for a bone in an egg —to look for a flaw where there is none; to find fault on purpose; to nitpick

雞蛋糕(ㄐㄧ ㄉㄢˋ ㄍㄠ)
sponge cake

雞蛋黃(ㄐㄧ ㄉㄢˋ ㄏㄨㄤˊ)
the yolk of a hen's egg

雞蛋青(ㄐㄧ ㄉㄢˋ ㄑㄧㄥ)
the white of a hen's egg

雞頭(ㄐㄧ ㄊㄡˊ)
(botany) a popular name of seeds of euryale ferox (芡實)

雞頭肉(ㄐㄧ ㄊㄡˊ ㄖㄡˋ)
a young woman's breasts

雞湯(ㄐㄧ ㄊㄤ)
chicken soup

雞啼(ㄐㄧ ㄊㄧˊ)
the crowing of cocks; cock-crow. 他雞啼即起。 He was up at cockcrow.

雞腿(ㄐㄧ ㄊㄨㄟˇ)
drumsticks (chicken's legs)

[隹部]

〔隹部〕

雞肋(ㄐㄧ ㄌㄟˋ)
① tasteless; meaningless; something one is reluctant to give up although it's both tasteless and meaningless ② to be weak physically

雞零狗碎
pieces and bits; piecemeal

雞籠(ㄐㄧ ㄌㄨㄥˊ)
a basket for fowls; a fowl coop

雞冠(ㄐㄧ ㄍㄨㄢ)
the cockscomb

雞冠花(ㄐㄧ ㄍㄨㄢ ㄏㄨㄚ)
(botany) a cockscomb

雞冠石(ㄐㄧ ㄍㄨㄢ ㄕˊ)
(mineral) realgar

雞口牛後(ㄐㄧ ㄎㄡˇ ㄋㄧㄡˊ ㄏㄡˋ)
(literally) It's better to be the bill of a chicken than the anus of an ox.—The king of a small country is preferable to a prime minister of an empire. 或 It's better to be the boss of a small group than the top lieutenant in a large organization. 或 It is better to reign in hell than serve in heaven.

雞叫(ㄐㄧ ㄐㄧㄠˋ)
(said of a cock) to crow; (said of a hen) to cackle

雞姦
sodomy; to bugger

雞棲(ㄐㄧ ㄑㄧ)
the place where chickens are raised

雞犬不寧(ㄐㄧ ㄑㄩㄢˇ ㄅㄨˋ ㄋㄧㄥˊ)
(literally) Not even the chickens and dogs are left in peace.—great disturbance; a pandemonium

雞犬不留(ㄐㄧ ㄑㄩㄢˇ ㄅㄨˋ ㄌㄧㄡˊ)
(literally) Not even a chicken or dog is left alive. —to give no quarter; to kill all

雞犬不驚(ㄐㄧ ㄑㄩㄢˇ ㄅㄨˋ ㄐㄧㄥ)
(literally) Not even a single chicken or dog is disturbed.—peaceful and quiet

雞犬相聞(ㄐㄧ ㄑㄩㄢˇ ㄒㄧㄤ ㄨㄣˊ)
to live nearby or in the neighborhood

雞犬升天(ㄐㄧ ㄑㄩㄢˇ ㄕㄥ ㄊㄧㄢ)或
雞犬皆仙(ㄐㄧ ㄑㄩㄢˇ ㄐㄧㄝ ㄒㄧㄢ)
(literally) Even chickens

and dogs ascended to the heaven after their master became an immortal.—the rise of a powerful person's underlings

雞心(ㄐㄧ ㄒㄧㄣ)
a jewel shaped like a chicken's heart

雞胸(ㄐㄧ ㄒㄩㄥ)或雞胸脯兒(ㄐㄧ ㄒㄩㄥ ㄈㄨˊㄦ)
human chest shaped like a chicken's

雞汁(ㄐㄧ ㄓ)
broth prepared by steaming chicken

雞胗(ㄐㄧ ㄓㄣˊ)
the gizzard of a chicken

雞吵鵝鬥(ㄐㄧ ㄔㄠˇ ㄜˊ ㄉㄡˋ)
to fight noisily and incessantly

雞尸牛從(ㄐㄧ ㄕ ㄋㄧㄡˊ ㄘㄨㄥˊ)
better to be a dog's head than a lion's tail—better to lead in a small position than to take a back seat under a great leader 參看「雞口牛後」

雞肉(ㄐㄧ ㄖㄡˋ)
chicken (as food)

雞子(ㄐㄧ ㄗˇ)
a chick

雞子兒(ㄐㄧ ㄗˇㄦ)
the hen's egg

雞兒(ㄐㄧㄦ)
a chicken

雞眼(ㄐㄧ ㄧㄢˇ)
corns (on the feet)

雞窩(ㄐㄧ ㄨㄛ)
a chicken coop

雞尾酒(ㄐㄧ ㄨㄟˇ ㄐㄧㄡˇ)
cocktail

雞尾酒會(ㄐㄧ ㄨㄟˇ ㄐㄧㄡˇ ㄏㄨㄟˋ)
a cocktail party

雞瘟(ㄐㄧ ㄨㄣ)
chicken plague

【雝】 6678
ㄩㄥ iong yōng
harmonious; peaceful

十一畫

【離】 6679
ㄌㄧˊ li lí

1. to leave; to depart; to separate; separation: 他離開巴黎到紐約去。He left Paris for New York.

2. to defy; to go against

3. distant from; apart from: 月球與地球距離甚遠。The moon is distant from the earth.

4. to run into; to meet with

5. to act in pair

6. (said of light) bright

7. a Chinese family name

離別(ㄌㄧˊ ㄅㄧㄝˊ)
to say good-bye; to leave; to separate; separation; parting

離不開(ㄌㄧˊ ㄅㄨˋ ㄎㄞ)
① cannot do without; unable to separate from ② cannot get away—too busy

離不開手兒(ㄌㄧˊ ㄅㄨˋ ㄎㄞ ㄕㄡˇㄦ)或
離不開身兒(ㄌㄧˊ ㄅㄨˋ ㄎㄞ ㄕㄣㄦ)
not having a free hand —very busy

離叛(ㄌㄧˊ ㄆㄢˋ)
to rebel; to turn one's back to; to walk out on

離披(ㄌㄧˊ ㄆㄧ)
scattered; dispersed

離譜(ㄌㄧˊ ㄆㄨˇ)
too far away from what is normal or acceptable; far off the beam

離得了(ㄌㄧˊ ㄉㄜ ㄌㄧㄠˇ)或離得開(ㄌㄧˊ ㄉㄜ ㄎㄞ)
① able to do without ② can leave

離地(ㄌㄧˊ ㄉㄧˋ)
① to leave the ground; to rise from the ground; to soar into the air ② above the ground

離題(ㄌㄧˊ ㄊㄧˊ)
to depart from the topic; to digress; digression

離離(ㄌㄧˊ ㄌㄧˊ)
① lushly; luxuriantly; in rich clusters ② not to attend personally

離宮(ㄌㄧˊ ㄍㄨㄥ)
① a temporary abode for an emperor on a tour ② name of a constellation

離開(ㄌㄧˊ ㄎㄞ)
to separate from; to leave; to depart; to keep away from; to deviate from

離合(ㄌㄧˊ ㄏㄜˊ)
separation and reunion

離合器(ㄌㄧˊ ㄏㄜˊ ㄑㄧˋ)
the clutch (of a motorcycle)

離恨(ㄌㄧˊ ㄏㄣˋ)
parting grief

離婚(ㄌㄧㄏㄨㄣ)
to divorce; a divorce

離婚者(ㄌㄧㄏㄨㄣㄓㄜˇ)
(said of a woman) a divorcée;
(said of a man) a divorcé

離婚證(ㄌㄧㄏㄨㄣㄓㄥˋ)
a certificate of divorce

離家(ㄌㄧㄐㄧㄚ)
to leave home; to be away
from home; to depart from
home

離間(ㄌㄧㄐㄧㄢ)
to drive a wedge between;
to alienate (allies, etc.); to
sow discord

離經叛道(ㄌㄧㄐㄧㄥㄆㄢˋㄉㄠˋ)
to rebel against orthodox
teachings

離境(ㄌㄧㄐㄧㄥˋ)
to leave a country or place

離境簽證(ㄌㄧㄐㄧㄥˋㄑㄧㄢㄓㄥˋ)
an exit visa

離奇(ㄌㄧㄑㄧˊ)
odd; fantastic; strange;
intriguing: 這是件很離奇的事
兒。It's a very odd business.

離棄(ㄌㄧㄑㄧˋ)
to abandon; to desert: 他離棄
了他的妻兒。He abandoned
his wife and children.

離情別緒(ㄌㄧㄑㄧㄥˊㄅㄧㄝˊㄒㄩˋ)
the sad feelings at separation; parting sorrows

離去(ㄌㄧㄑㄩˋ)
to leave; to go away; to
depart: 我的打字員已離去。My
typist has left me.

離群索居(ㄌㄧㄑㄩㄣˊㄙㄨㄛˇㄐㄩ)
to leave one's friends and
live alone

離析(ㄌㄧㄒㄧ)
to disintegrate (as a regime,
etc.)

離席(ㄌㄧㄒㄧˊ)
to leave or withdraw a dinner party, conference, etc.

離心離德(ㄌㄧㄒㄧㄣㄌㄧㄉㄜˊ)
(said of many people) each
going his own way; lacking
unity

離心力(ㄌㄧㄒㄧㄣㄌㄧˋ)
① centrifugal force ② factors which give rise to disloyalty

離心角(ㄌㄧㄒㄧㄣㄐㄧㄠˇ)
an eccentric angle

離心器(ㄌㄧㄒㄧㄣㄑㄧˋ)
a centrifuge; a centrifugal
machine 亦作「離心機」

離鄉背井(ㄌㄧㄒㄧㄤㄅㄟˋㄐㄧㄥˇ)
to travel to a distant land;
to stay far away from home
亦作「背井離鄉」

離職(ㄌㄧㄓˊ)
①to leave or resign from
one's office ②to retire from
one's office

離愁(ㄌㄧㄔㄡˊ)
parting sorrow or grief; sadness at separation

離任(ㄌㄧㄖㄣˋ)
to leave one's post

離子(ㄌㄧㄗˇ)
an ion

離座(ㄌㄧㄗㄨㄛˋ)
to leave one's seat

離騷(ㄌㄧㄙㄠ)
the title of a long poem
authored by Chü Yüan (屈
原) of the state of Chu (楚)
during the Epoch of Warring
States in which Chü Yüan
vented his grievances for
being disparaged and discarded by the king

離散(ㄌㄧㄙㄢˇ)
separated and scattered;
dispersed

離貳(ㄌㄧㄦˋ)
to harbor a rebellious heart

離異(ㄌㄧㄧˋ)
to separate; to divorce: 他們
已經離異。They have been
divorced.

【難】 6680
1. ㄋㄢˊ nan nán
1. difficult; not easy; hard
2. unable; not in a position to
3. unpleasant; not good

難保(ㄋㄢˊㄅㄠˇ)
①difficult to judge; hard to
say; unable to guarantee: 今
天確保下不了雨。It's hard to
say that it won't rain today.
②difficult to hold (a city,
position, etc.); hard to guard
or keep

難辦(ㄋㄢˊㄅㄢˋ)
difficult to manage or operate

難憑(ㄋㄢˊㄆㄧㄥˊ)
cannot be relied upon; unreliable; cannot be accepted

as evidence; cannot be taken
as truth

難買賣(ㄋㄢˊㄇㄞˇㄈㄥˋㄇㄞˋ)
to make things difficult for
somebody; to give someone
a hard time

難免(ㄋㄢˊㄇㄧㄢˇ)
can hardly avoid; inescapable; inevitable: 犯錯是難免
的。Mistakes can hardly be
avoided.

難分難捨(ㄋㄢˊㄈㄣㄋㄢˊㄕㄜˇ)
(said of a couple in love)
very reluctant to separate 亦
作「難捨難分」

難打交道(ㄋㄢˊㄉㄚˇㄐㄧㄠ．ㄉㄠ)
hard to deal wih; difficult to
get along with

難得(ㄋㄢˊㄉㄜˊ)
①rare; hard to get; hard to
come by: 它是本難得的書。It's
a rare book.② fortunate;
lucky ③rarely; seldom: 我難
得碰見他。I rarely met him.

難倒(ㄋㄢˊㄉㄠˇ)
to confound; to daunt; to
baffle; to beat

難道(ㄋㄢˊㄉㄠˋ)or 難道說(ㄋㄢˊㄉㄠˋ
ㄕㄨㄛ)
Is it possible…? 或Do you
really mean to say…?

難當(ㄋㄢˊㄉㄤ)
①hard to shoulder (such a
responsibility, etc.) ②hard
to endure; unbearable

難度(ㄋㄢˊㄉㄨˋ)
degree of difficulty; difficulty: 這種動作難度很大。This
action is extremely difficult.

難懂(ㄋㄢˊㄉㄨㄥˇ)
hard to understand; difficult
to comprehend

難逃法網(ㄋㄢˊㄊㄠˊㄈㄚˇㄨㄤˇ)
It's hard to escape the dragnet of law. 或Crime does
not pay.

難題(ㄋㄢˊㄊㄧˊ)
a hard nut to crack; a tough
problem; a puzzle

難聽(ㄋㄢˊㄊㄧㄥ)
①unpleasant to hear (often
referring to vulgar or abusive expressions, etc.); to
grate on the ear ②offensive;
coarse ③scandalous

難耐(ㄋㄢˊㄋㄞˋ)
unable to endure; unbearable

（隹部）

難能可貴(ㄋㄢ ㄋㄥ ㄎㄜ ㄍㄨㄟ)
rare and commendable (merits, achievements, etc.)

難過(ㄋㄢ ㄍㄨㄛ)
① to feel uneasy; to feel bad; to feel sorry: 我對她的不幸感到難過. I felt sorry about her misfortune.② hard to endure or bear; uncomfortable ③ difficult; hard

難怪(ㄋㄢ ㄍㄨㄞ)
① cannot hold responsible for ② no wonder that; it's understandable that: 難怪他做了此事. No wonder he should have done it.

難關(ㄋㄢ ㄍㄨㄢ)or(ㄋㄢ ㄍㄨㄢ)
an impasse; an obstacle or obstruction difficult to overcome; a difficult situation; a crisis; a juncture of great difficulty; straits: 他們終於度過難關. They finally tided over a crisis.

難管(ㄋㄢ ㄍㄨㄢ)
difficult to govern; hard to rule or restrain

難堪(ㄋㄢ ㄎㄢ)
① to embarrass; embarrassment ② intolerable; unbearable

難看(ㄋㄢ ㄎㄢ)
① bad-looking; not pleasant to the eye; ugly; offensive; repulsive ② embarrassing; awkward

難解(ㄋㄢ ㄐㄧㄝ)
difficult to understand; incomprehensible; hard to solve

難解難分(ㄋㄢ ㄐㄧㄝ ㄋㄢ ㄈㄣ)
① difficult to separate ② to be locked together (in a struggle)

難講(ㄋㄢ ㄐㄧㄤ)
hard to say; difficult to predict: 很難講那一個比較好. It's hard to say which is better.

難兄難弟(ㄋㄢ ㄒㄩㄥ ㄋㄢ ㄉㄧ)
brothers who are equally talented

難治(ㄋㄢ ㄓ)
difficult to cure

難吃(ㄋㄢ ㄔ)
unbearable to palate; unpalatable; tasting bad

hard to deal with

難產(ㄋㄢ ㄔㄢ)
① (medicine) difficult labor; dystocia ② hard to come into being or materialize

難成(ㄋㄢ ㄔㄥ)
difficult to accomplish or succeed

難處(ㄋㄢ ㄔㄨ)
① (ㄋㄢ ㄔㄨ) hard to get along with
② (ㄋㄢ ˙ㄔㄨ) difficult points; problems: 她有她的難處. She has her problems.

難事(ㄋㄢ ㄕ)
a difficult task; something not easy to manage; a difficult matter

難受(ㄋㄢ ㄕㄡ)
① to feel bad; to feel sorry ② unbearable; intolerable ③ to suffer pain; to feel unwell

難上加難(ㄋㄢ ㄕㄤ ㄐㄧㄚ ㄋㄢ)or難上難(ㄋㄢ ㄕㄤ ㄋㄢ)
most difficult; almost impossible

難說(ㄋㄢ ㄕㄨㄛ)
① hard to say or predict ② difficult to speak out (for fear of embarrassing or paining others, etc.) ③ not easy to express with words

難說話(ㄋㄢ ㄕㄨㄛ ㄏㄨㄚ)
(said of a person) hard to deal with; very strict with subordinates

難字(ㄋㄢ ㄗ)
a difficult word; a big word; hard words

難走(ㄋㄢ ㄗㄡ)
(said of a road) tortuous; difficult to negotiate

難色(ㄋㄢ ㄙㄜ)
an expression of reluctance or unwillingness: 他面有難色. He showed an expression of reluctance.

難以(ㄋㄢ ㄧ)
difficult; hard to: 她很難以取悅. She is hard to please.

難以逆料(ㄋㄢ ㄧ ㄋㄧ ㄌㄧㄠ)
hard to predict

難以相信(ㄋㄢ ㄧ ㄒㄧㄤ ㄒㄧㄣ)or難信(ㄋㄢ ㄒㄧㄣ)
incredible; difficult to believe; hard to believe 亦作

「難以置信」

難以相處(ㄋㄢ ㄧ ㄒㄧㄤ ㄔㄨ)
hard to get along with

難以形容(ㄋㄢ ㄧ ㄒㄧㄥ ㄖㄨㄥ)
indescribable; beyond description

難以出口(ㄋㄢ ㄧ ㄔㄨ ㄎㄡ)
difficult to speak out one's mind (for various reasons)

難以為繼(ㄋㄢ ㄧ ㄨㄟ ㄐㄧ)
hard to carry on; difficult to continue

難言之隱(ㄋㄢ ㄧㄢ ㄓ ㄧㄣ)
secrets or problems one doesn't want to reveal

難為(ㄋㄢ ㄨㄟ)
① (ㄋㄢ ㄨㄟ) difficult to perform or manage
② (ㄋㄢ ˙ㄨㄟ) ⓐ to put (someone) in a spot; to make matters difficult for someone; to press ⓑ Thanks for the trouble you have taken.ⓒ an expression to comfort someone who has had some very unpleasant experience

難為情(ㄋㄢ ㄨㄟ ㄑㄧㄥ)
to feel ashamed, uneasy or embarrassed; bashful: 她好難為情. She is rather bashful.

難聞(ㄋㄢ ㄨㄣ)
stinking; malodorous

難忘(ㄋㄢ ㄨㄤ)
difficult to forget; unforgettable

【難】 6680
2. ㄋㄢ nán nàn

1. disaster; calamity; misfortune
2. to rebuke; to reprove; to reprimand
3. to discountenance

難不倒(ㄋㄢ ㄅㄨ ㄉㄠ)or難不倒(ㄋㄢ ˙ㄅㄨ ㄉㄠ)
will not be beaten (by a problem or question); cannot beat or corner someone (with a question or task)

難民(ㄋㄢ ㄇㄧㄣ)
refugees

難民收容所(ㄋㄢ ㄇㄧㄣ ㄕㄡ ㄖㄨㄥ ㄙㄨㄛ)
a haven or shelter for refugees; a refugee camp or center 亦作「難民營」

難童(ㄋㄢ ㄊㄨㄥ)
a refugee child

難兄難弟 (ㄋㄢˊ ㄒㄩㄥ ㄋㄢˊ ㄉㄧˋ)
fellow sufferers

難住了 (ㄋㄢˊ ·ㄓㄨˋ·ㄌㄜ)
to be unable to answer a question or to do a task that is too difficult

難友 (ㄋㄢˊ ㄧㄡˇ)
a fellow sufferer

雨 部
（ㄩˇ yeu yǔ）

【雨】 6681
1. ㄩˇ yeu yǔ
rain; rainy

雨布 (ㄩˇ ㄅㄨˋ)
waterproof cloth

雨棚 (ㄩˇ ㄆㄥˊ)
a rainshed

雨帽 (ㄩˇ ㄇㄠˋ)
a rain hat; a rain cap

雨沐風餐 (ㄩˇ ㄇㄨˋ ㄈㄥ ㄘㄢ)
(literally) to bathe in the rain and eat meals in the wind—to toil rain or shine

雨滴 (ㄩˇ ㄉㄧ) or 雨點兒 (ㄩˇ ㄉㄧㄢˇ ㄦ)
raindrops

雨天 (ㄩˇ ㄊㄧㄢ)
a rainy day: 那天是雨天。It was rainy that day.

雨立 (ㄩˇ ㄌㄧˋ)
to stand in the rain

雨林 (ㄩˇ ㄌㄧㄣˊ)
rain trees; a rainforest

雨淋日曬 (ㄩˇ ㄌㄧㄣˊ ㄖˋ ㄕㄞˋ)
wear and tear of the weather; exposure to the elements

雨量 (ㄩˇ ㄌㄧㄤˋ)
(meteorology) rainfall; the amount of rainfall or precipitation

雨量計 (ㄩˇ ㄌㄧㄤˋ ㄐㄧˋ)
a rain gauge; a udometer

雨露 (ㄩˇ ㄌㄨˋ)
favors and kindness; benevolence

雨果 (ㄩˇ ㄍㄨㄛˇ)
Victor Marie Hugo (1802-1885), French poet, novelist and dramatist

雨過天青 (ㄩˇ ㄍㄨㄛˋ ㄊㄧㄢ ㄑㄧㄥ) or 雨過天晴 (ㄩˇ ㄍㄨㄛˋ ㄊㄧㄢ ㄑㄧㄥˊ)
(literally) When the rain is

over, the sky clears up. 或 After a storm comes a calm. —When the incident (or confusion) is over, everything goes back to normal.

雨後春筍 (ㄩˇ ㄏㄡˋ ㄔㄨㄣ ㄙㄨㄣˇ)
to mushroom like bamboo shoots after rain

雨後送傘 (ㄩˇ ㄏㄡˋ ㄙㄨㄥˋ ㄙㄢˇ)
(literally) to give someone an umbrella after the rain is over—to give untimely help

雨花臺 (ㄩˇ ㄏㄨㄚ ㄊㄞˊ)
name of a spot in suburban Nanking, noted for its colorful pebbles

雨季 (ㄩˇ ㄐㄧˋ)
the rainy season; the monsoon

雨脚 (ㄩˇ ㄐㄧㄠˇ)
dense raindrops

雨具 (ㄩˇ ㄐㄩˋ)
things for wet weather—umbrellas, raincoats, galoshes, etc.

雨泣 (ㄩˇ ㄑㄧˋ)
tears falling down like rain

雨鞋 (ㄩˇ ㄒㄧㄝˊ)
rainshoes; galoshes

雨靴 (ㄩˇ ㄒㄩㄝ)
oiled or rubber boots for wet weather; galoshes

雨珠 (ㄩˇ ㄓㄨ)
raindrops

雨師 (ㄩˇ ㄕ)
the rain god

雨水 (ㄩˇ ㄕㄨㄟˇ)
①rain water ②one of 24 climatic periods in the lunar calendar, which falls on February 19 or 20

雨字頭兒 (ㄩˇ ㄗˋ ㄊㄡˊ ㄦ)
a Chinese character topped by the radical 雨, as 霖, 電, 雷, etc.

雨傘 (ㄩˇ ㄙㄢˇ)
an umbrella

雨散雲收 (ㄩˇ ㄙㄢˇ ㄩㄣˊ ㄕㄡ)
① (literally) The rain stops and the sky clears up. ② to separate, as friends ③ afterwards (after sexual intercourse)

雨衣 (ㄩˇ ㄧ)
a raincoat

雨意 (ㄩˇ ㄧˋ)
signs indicating rain; signs

which is about to rain: 現在頗有雨意。Now it looks like rain.

雨雲 (ㄩˇ ㄩㄣˊ)
rain clouds

【雨】 6681
2. ㄩˋ yuh yù
to rain down; to pour down

雨淚 (ㄩˋ ㄌㄟˋ)
tears pouring down like rain

三畫

【雩】 6682
1. ㄩˊ yu yú
to pray for rain; the sacrifice for the rain god

雩壇 (ㄩˊ ㄊㄢˊ)
a stand or platform where praying for rain is conducted

雩祭 (ㄩˊ ㄐㄧˋ)
a sacrifice or ritual in praying for rain

【雩】 6682
2. ㄩˋ yuh yù
the rainbow

【雪】 6683
1. ㄒㄩㄝˇ sheue xuě
1. snow: 山上積雪很深。The mountains are deep in snow.
2. to clean; to wash or wipe away

雪崩 (ㄒㄩㄝˇ ㄅㄥ)
a snowslide; an avalanche of snow

雪片 (ㄒㄩㄝˇ ㄆㄧㄢˋ)
①snowflakes ②to come in like an avalanche

雪盲 (ㄒㄩㄝˇ ㄇㄤˊ)
snow blindness

雪膚 (ㄒㄩㄝˇ ㄈㄨ)
a snow-white skin

雪地冰天 (ㄒㄩㄝˇ ㄉㄧˋ ㄅㄧㄥ ㄊㄧㄢ)
a land of snow and ice; a frozen land

雪堆 (ㄒㄩㄝˇ ㄉㄨㄟ)
a snowbank; a snowdrift

雪泥鴻爪 (ㄒㄩㄝˇ ㄋㄧˊ ㄏㄨㄥˊ ㄓㄠˇ)
(literally) talon marks on the snow—traces of past events

雪虐風饕 (ㄒㄩㄝˇ ㄋㄩㄝˋ ㄈㄥ ㄊㄠ)
heavy snows and high winds —extreme cold

雪萊 (ㄒㄩㄝˇ ㄌㄞˊ)
Percy Bysshe Shelley (1792-1822), British poet

【雨 部】

雪梨(ㄒㄩㄝ ㄌㄧ)
① Sidney, Australia ② a kind of pear

雪裏紅(ㄒㄩㄝ ㄌㄧ ㄏㄨㄥ)or 雪裏蕻(ㄒㄩㄝ ㄌㄧ ㄏㄨㄥ)
(botany) Brassica juncea, potherb mustard

雪裏青(ㄒㄩㄝ ㄌㄧ ㄑㄧㄥ)
an ilex 亦作「多青」

雪花(ㄒㄩㄝ ㄏㄨㄚ)
snowflakes

雪花膏(ㄒㄩㄝ ㄏㄨㄚ ㄍㄠ)
any kind of vanishing face-cream 亦作「面霜」

雪花石膏(ㄒㄩㄝ ㄏㄨㄚ ㄕ ㄍㄠ)
(mineral) alabaster 亦作「純白石膏」

雪肌(ㄒㄩㄝ ㄐㄧ)
a snow-white skin 參看「雪膚」

雪茄(ㄒㄩㄝ ㄐㄧㄚ)
cigars

雪窖冰天(ㄒㄩㄝ ㄐㄧㄠ ㄅㄧㄥ ㄊㄧㄢ)
a snow-and-ice-locked land

雪景(ㄒㄩㄝ ㄐㄧㄥ)
a landscape of snow; a snow scene

雪橇(ㄒㄩㄝ ㄑㄧㄠ)
a sled; a toboggan; a sledge; a sleigh (a transportation vehicle on the snow-covered ground)

雪球(ㄒㄩㄝ ㄑㄧㄡ)
① a snowball ② as in 擲雪球—to snowball

雪青(ㄒㄩㄝ ㄑㄧㄥ)
lilac 亦作「淡紫色」

雪鞋(ㄒㄩㄝ ㄒㄧㄝ)
snowshoes

雪線(ㄒㄩㄝ ㄒㄧㄢ)
the snow line

雪中高士(ㄒㄩㄝ ㄓㄨㄥ ㄍㄠ ㄕ)or 雪中君子(ㄒㄩㄝ ㄓㄨㄥ ㄐㄩㄣ ㄗ)
a poetic name of plum blossoms (梅花)

雪中送炭(ㄒㄩㄝ ㄓㄨㄥ ㄙㄨㄥ ㄊㄢ)
to give timely assistance; to send things which are in urgent need, as food for hungry refugees

雪車(ㄒㄩㄝ ㄔㄜ)or 雪橇(ㄒㄩㄝ ㄑㄧㄠ)
a sledge; a sled; a sleigh

雪鋤(ㄒㄩㄝ ㄔㄨ)
a snowplow

雪窗(ㄒㄩㄝ ㄔㄨㄤ)
(literally) to study by the window lighted by reflection of snow—very diligent in study

雪山(ㄒㄩㄝ ㄕㄢ)
① a snow-capped mountain ② the Snow Mountains, in New Guinea

雪上加霜(ㄒㄩㄝ ㄕㄤ ㄐㄧㄚ ㄕㄨㄤ)
(literally) to add frost to snow—disasters coming one after another in succession

雪人(ㄒㄩㄝ ㄖㄣ)
① Abominable Snowman, the legendary snowman in the Himalayas; the yeti ② a human figure made out of snow

雪壓霜欺(ㄒㄩㄝ ㄧㄚ ㄕㄨㄤ ㄑㄧ)
to be slighted and insulted by all

雪鴝(ㄒㄩㄝ ㄨ)
a snowbird

6683
【雪】　2.(ㄒㄩㄝ shiueh xue)
（又讀 ㄒㄩㄝ sheue xue)

1. snow-white; snowy
2. to avenge; to wipe out grievances

雪白(ㄒㄩㄝ ㄅㄞ)
snow-white; snowy

雪亮(ㄒㄩㄝ ㄌㄧㄤ)
bright as snow; shiny: 人民的眼睛是雪亮的。People's eyes are as bright as snow.

雪恨(ㄒㄩㄝ ㄏㄣ)
to avenge one's grudge; to avenge wrongs done to one; to avenge oneself on; to avenge

雪恥(ㄒㄩㄝ ㄔ)or(ㄒㄩㄝ ㄕ)
to wipe out a shame; to avenge an insult or humiliation

雪恥復國(ㄒㄩㄝ ㄔ ㄈㄨ ㄍㄨㄛ)
to wipe out national shame and recover the fatherland

雪冤(ㄒㄩㄝ ㄩㄢ)or(ㄒㄩㄝ ㄩㄢ)
to wipe out grievances; to vindicate oneself; to clear oneself of a false charge; to redress a wrong

四畫

【雯】6684
ㄨㄣ wen wén
the coloring on the clouds

【雰】6685
ㄈㄣ fen fēn
mist; fog

【雱】6686
ㄆㄤ parng páng
snowing heavily

【雲】6687
ㄩㄣ yun yún

1. clouds
2. a cloud of; a large number of
3. short for Yunnan Province
4. a Chinese family name

雲豹(ㄩㄣ ㄅㄠ)
a clouded leopard

雲鬢(ㄩㄣ ㄅㄧㄣ)
the hairdo of a beautiful woman—like floating clouds

雲片糕(ㄩㄣ ㄆㄧㄢ ㄍㄠ)
a kind of Chinese dessert made of rice in the shape of rectangular thin strips

雲杪(ㄩㄣ ㄇㄧㄠ)
distant and high

雲母(ㄩㄣ ㄇㄨ)
mica

雲房(ㄩㄣ ㄈㄤ)
chambers or cabins where Buddhist monks live

雲端(ㄩㄣ ㄉㄨㄢ)
in the clouds

雲梯(ㄩㄣ ㄊㄧ)
a scaling ladder

雲天(ㄩㄣ ㄊㄧㄢ)
clouds and sky—high above

雲天高誼(ㄩㄣ ㄊㄧㄢ ㄍㄠ ㄧ)
(your) great kindness and friendship (used mostly in correspondence)

雲吞(ㄩㄣ ㄊㄨㄣ)
Chinese ravioli; stuffed dumplings with delicate flour wrapping 亦作「餛飩」

雲南(ㄩㄣ ㄋㄢ)
Yunnan Province, Southwestern China

雲南起義(ㄩㄣ ㄋㄢ ㄑㄧ ㄧ)
the military uprising against Yüan Shih-kai (袁世凱) in 1915 led by General Tsai O (蔡鍔) in Yunnan

雲霓(ㄩㄣ ㄋㄧ)
clouds and rainbows—which give promise of rain in a

〔雨部〕

drought

雲泥(ㄩㄣˊ ㄋㄧˊ)
clouds and mud—great difference in social standing

雲量(ㄩㄣˊ ㄌㄧㄤˋ)
(meteorology) cloudiness; cloud amount; cloud cover

雲羅(ㄩㄣˊ ㄌㄨㄛˊ)
dense clouds

雲龍風虎(ㄩㄣˊ ㄌㄨㄥˊ ㄈㄥ ㄏㄨˇ)
A great leader attracts capable followers.

雲岡石窟(ㄩㄣˊ ㄍㄤ ㄕˊ ㄎㄨ)
a number of grottos stretching about half a kilometer long at Yunkang, Shansi Province, containing thousands of Buddha statues of various sizes carved over a period of about 100 years between the 4th and the 5th centuries

雲貴(ㄩㄣˊ ㄍㄨㄟˋ)
Yunnan and Kweichow provinces

雲貴高原(ㄩㄣˊ ㄍㄨㄟˋ ㄍㄠ ㄩㄢˊ)
the Yunnan-Kweichow Plateau

雲開見日(ㄩㄣˊ ㄎㄞ ㄐㄧㄢˋ ㄖˋ)
(literally) When the clouds part, one sees the sun.—a turn of fortune for the better

雲海(ㄩㄣˊ ㄏㄞˇ)
a sea of clouds

雲漢(ㄩㄣˊ ㄏㄢˋ)
the Milky Way

雲鬢(ㄩㄣˊ ㄅㄧㄣˋ)
the beautiful hairdo of an attractive woman

雲集(ㄩㄣˊ ㄐㄧˊ)
to congregate; to gather; to flock together; to come together in crowds

雲際(ㄩㄣˊ ㄐㄧˋ)
in the clouds

雲髻(ㄩㄣˊ ㄐㄧˋ)
women's hair; a lady's hair-coil

雲譎波詭(ㄩㄣˊ ㄐㄩㄝˊ ㄅㄛ ㄍㄨㄟˇ)
the unpredictable, ever-changing nature of things

雲起龍驤(ㄩㄣˊ ㄑㄧˇ ㄌㄨㄥˊ ㄒㄧㄤ)
(said of heroes, rebels, etc.) rising up in time of social upheavals

雲氣(ㄩㄣˊ ㄑㄧˋ)

thin, floating clouds

雲衢(ㄩㄣˊ ㄑㄩˊ)or 雲路(ㄩㄣˊ ㄌㄨˋ)
high official ranks

雲雀(ㄩㄣˊ ㄑㄩㄝˋ)
a skylark; a meadow lark

雲霄(ㄩㄣˊ ㄒㄧㄠ)
① clouds ② one who is unmoved by monetary gains or high positions; a person of high virtue

雲簫(ㄩㄣˊ ㄒㄧㄠ)
a kind of panpipe

雲霄(ㄩㄣˊ ㄒㄧㄠ)
①the sky—very high; 爆竹聲震徹雲霄。The cracking noise of firecracker resounded to the skies.②name of a county in Fukien

雲霄飛車(ㄩㄣˊ ㄒㄧㄠ ㄈㄟ ㄔㄜ)
a roller coaster

雲消霧散(ㄩㄣˊ ㄒㄧㄠ ㄨˋ ㄙㄢˋ)
(literally) clouds dissipating and fog melting away—The troubles are over.

雲行雨施(ㄩㄣˊ ㄒㄧㄥˊ ㄩˇ ㄕ)
(said of a ruler) to be benevolent to the people

雲蒸霞蔚(ㄩㄣˊ ㄓㄥ ㄒㄧㄚˊ ㄨㄟˋ)
radiant, colorful and flourishing

雲中白鶴(ㄩㄣˊ ㄓㄨㄥ ㄅㄞˊ ㄏㄜˋ)
a man of unimpeachable integrity

雲收雨散(ㄩㄣˊ ㄕㄡ ㄩˇ ㄙㄢˋ)
① separation; dispersion ② the end of sexual intercourse

雲杉(ㄩㄣˊ ㄕㄢ)
a spruce fir

雲彩(ㄩㄣˊ ˙ㄘㄞ)
clouds illuminated by the rising or setting sun

雲層(ㄩㄣˊ ㄘㄥˊ)
layers of clouds

雲遊(ㄩㄣˊ ㄧㄡˊ)
to travel without a destination; to wander about

雲煙(ㄩㄣˊ ㄧㄢ)
clouds and smog

雲煙過眼(ㄩㄣˊ ㄧㄢ ㄍㄨㄛˋ ㄧㄢˇ)
(literally) clouds and smoke that float past the eyes — transient glories; things having no lasting value

雲霧(ㄩㄣˊ ㄨˋ)
clouds and fog—obscure

places

雲雨(ㄩㄣˊ ㄩˇ)
① grace and favor ② sexual intercourse; making love

雲雨巫山(ㄩㄣˊ ㄩˇ ㄨ ㄕㄢ)
(figuratively) The couple are enraptured with love.

五畫

【零】6688
ㄌㄧㄥˊ líng
1. zero; nil; nought
2. a fraction; fractional; remainder
3. to flow down
4. a light rain; drizzle

零賣(ㄌㄧㄥˊ ㄇㄞˋ)
① retail sales ② to sell by the piece or in small quantities

零分(ㄌㄧㄥˊ ㄈㄣ)
① (grading examination papers) zero; no marks ② (sports) scoreless

零丁(ㄌㄧㄥˊ ㄉㄧㄥ)
left alone without company; solitary; lonely 亦作「伶仃」

零丁孤苦(ㄌㄧㄥˊ ㄉㄧㄥ ㄍㄨ ㄎㄨˇ)
solitary; lonely; without friends or relatives

零度(ㄌㄧㄥˊ ㄉㄨˋ)
zero; nought degrees: 昨晚氣溫降到零度。The temperature fell to zero last night.

零頭(ㄌㄧㄥˊ ˙ㄊㄡ)
① oddments (a sum which together with a much larger round figure makes the whole) ② small bits of cloth good only for patching clothes, etc.

零零碎碎(ㄌㄧㄥˊ ㄌㄧㄥˊ ㄙㄨㄟˋ ㄙㄨㄟˋ)
fragmented; piecemeal

零零落落(ㄌㄧㄥˊ ㄌㄧㄥˊ ㄌㄨㄛˋ ㄌㄨㄛˋ)or 零落落(ㄌㄧㄥˊ ㄌㄨㄛˋ ㄌㄨㄛˋ)
① desolate and scattered; dilapidated; run-down ② withered and fallen

零亂(ㄌㄧㄥˊ ㄌㄨㄢˋ)
disorderly; in confusion; in disorder: 桌子很零亂。The table was in disorder.

零股(ㄌㄧㄥˊ ㄍㄨˇ)
(stock exchange) ① odd lots ② a small band of (stragglers or guerrillas separated

〔雨部〕

from the main force)

零工(ㄌㄧㄥ ㄍㄨㄥ)
①odd jobs; short-term hired labor ②an odd-job man; a casual laborer

零花(ㄌㄧㄥ ㄏㄨㄚ)
(said of money) for every-day expenses, such as buying a bus ticket or a pack of cigarettes, etc.; incidental expenses

零件(ㄌㄧㄥ ㄐㄧㄢ)
(said of machines) compo-nent parts; spare parts

零錢(ㄌㄧㄥ ㄑㄧㄢ)
small change; petty cash; odd change

零星(ㄌㄧㄥ ㄒㄧㄥ)
①fragmented; fractional; not as a whole ②scattered

零食(ㄌㄧㄥ ㄕ)
snacks; refreshments: 他一直吃零食，所以他老是超重。He's forever snacking and will always be overweight.

零時(ㄌㄧㄥ ㄕ)
zero hour

零售(ㄌㄧㄥ ㄕㄡ)
retail sales; to sell by retail

零售店(ㄌㄧㄥ ㄕㄡ ㄉㄧㄢ)
a retail shop; a sundry store

零售商(ㄌㄧㄥ ㄕㄡ ㄕㄤ)
a retailer

零數(ㄌㄧㄥ ㄕㄨ)
oddments

零嘴(ㄌㄧㄥ ㄗㄨㄟ)
snacks 參看「零食」

零存整付(ㄌㄧㄥ ㄘㄨㄣ ㄓㄥ ㄈㄨ)
(banking) to deposit small sums of money every day, week, or month and to draw out both principal and inter-est in a lump sum when the specified time comes up

零散(ㄌㄧㄥ ㄙㄢ)
scattered: 農舍零散分佈在各處。Farmhouses are scattered here and there.

零碎(ㄌㄧㄥ ·ㄙㄨㄟ)
fragments; fragmentary; fractions; fractional; odds and ends

零兒(ㄌㄧㄥ ㄦ)
oddments

零用(ㄌㄧㄥ ㄩㄥ)
①(said of money) for every-day expenses of a non-

descript nature ②pocket money

零用錢(ㄌㄧㄥ ㄩㄥ ㄑㄧㄢ)
pocket money

雷 6689
ㄌㄟ lei léi

1. thunder: 遠處在打雷。It's thundering in the distance.
2. a mine (an explosive): 車子觸爆地雷。The car struck a mine.
3. a Chinese family name

雷劈(ㄌㄟ ㄆㄧ)
to be struck by lightning (or thunder)

雷鳴(ㄌㄟ ㄇㄧㄥ)
①roars of thunder; thunder-peal ②very loud sounds; thunderous: 他們的表演受到雷鳴般的掌聲。Their perfor-mance met with thunderous applause.

雷達(ㄌㄟ ㄉㄚ)
a radar

雷達網(ㄌㄟ ㄉㄚ ㄨㄤ)
a radar network

雷電(ㄌㄟ ㄉㄧㄢ)
lightning and thunder

雷電交加(ㄌㄟ ㄉㄧㄢ ㄐㄧㄠ ㄐㄧㄚ)
It's thundering and lighten-ing.

雷動(ㄌㄟ ㄉㄨㄥ)
(said of cheers, applause, etc.) thunderous: 運動場上歡聲雷動。There are thunderous cheers in the playground.

雷頭風(ㄌㄟ ㄊㄡ ㄈㄥ)
the initial severity of a new boss, which often tapers off as time goes by

雷霆(ㄌㄟ ㄊㄧㄥ)
①great wrath; a great fury; a rage ②overwhelming or overpowering

雷霆萬鈞(ㄌㄟ ㄊㄧㄥ ㄨㄢ ㄐㄩㄣ)
overwhelming or overpower-ing (power, strength, etc.); extremely powerful

雷同(ㄌㄟ ㄊㄨㄥ)
similar; identical; exactly the same: 金子的顏色和黃銅雷同。Gold is similar to brass in color.

雷鳥(ㄌㄟ ㄋㄧㄠ)
a thunderbird (in the mythology of some North America Indians)

雷厲風行(ㄌㄟ ㄌㄧ ㄈㄥ ㄒㄧㄥ)
to enforce a law or rule with speed and great deter-mination; to take drastic measures

雷管(ㄌㄟ ㄍㄨㄢ)
a percussion cap; a detona-tor

雷公(ㄌㄟ ㄍㄨㄥ)
the thunder god

雷汞(ㄌㄟ ㄍㄨㄥ)or雷酸汞(ㄌㄟ ㄙㄨㄢ ㄍㄨㄥ)
fulminating mercury

雷虎小組(ㄌㄟ ㄏㄨ ㄒㄧㄠ ㄗㄨ)
the Thunder Tigers, a dare-devil aerobatic team of the Chinese Air Force

雷擊(ㄌㄟ ㄐㄧ)
to be electrocuted by light-ning accidentally; to be struck by lightning

雷州半島(ㄌㄟ ㄓㄡ ㄅㄢ ㄉㄠ)
the Leichou Peninsula in southwest Kwangtung

雷震(ㄌㄟ ㄓㄣ)
thunderclaps

雷陣(ㄌㄟ ㄓㄣ)
a continuous peal of rolling thunder

雷陣雨(ㄌㄟ ㄓㄣ ㄩ)
a thundershower

雷池(ㄌㄟ ㄔ)
①name of a lake in An-hwei Province ②(figurative-ly) the utmost limit: 他不敢越雷池一步。He doesn't dare to transgress the utmost limit.

雷師(ㄌㄟ ㄕ)
the thunder god

雷射(ㄌㄟ ㄕㄜ)
a laser

雷射唱片(ㄌㄟ ㄕㄜ ㄔㄤ ㄆㄧㄢ)
a compact disc (CD)

雷射唱機(ㄌㄟ ㄕㄜ ㄔㄤ ㄐㄧ)
a CD player

雷聲(ㄌㄟ ㄕㄥ)
a thunderclap; thunder: 閃電過後，就是雷聲。After the lightning came the thunder.

雷聲大，雨點小(ㄌㄟ ㄕㄥ ㄉㄚ ㄩ ㄉㄧㄢ ㄒㄧㄠ)
to talk a great deal about something with little or no follow-up action

雷雨(ㄌㄟ ㄩ)

【電】 6690
ㄉㄧㄢˋ diann diàn
1. electricity; power
2. short for cable or telegram

電波(ㄉㄧㄢˋㄅㄛ)
electric waves

電報(ㄉㄧㄢˋㄅㄠˋ)
a cable; a telegram; to wire:
我發一通電報給他。I sent a
telegram to him.

電報費(ㄉㄧㄢˋㄅㄠˋㄈㄟˋ)
a cable charge; a telegram
fee

電報掛號(ㄉㄧㄢˋㄅㄠˋㄍㄨㄚˋ《ㄏㄠˋ》)
a cable address

電報機(ㄉㄧㄢˋㄅㄠˋㄐㄧ)
a telegraph transmitter or
receiver: 誰發明電報機? Who
invented the telegraph transmitter?

電報局(ㄉㄧㄢˋㄅㄠˋㄐㄩˊ)
a telegraph office

電報轉發機(ㄉㄧㄢˋㄅㄠˋㄓㄨㄢˇㄈㄚ
ㄐㄧ)
a telegraph repeater

電表(ㄉㄧㄢˋㄅㄧㄠˇ)
① any meter for measuring
electricity, such as an ammeter or a voltmeter ② a
kilowatt-hour meter

電冰箱(ㄉㄧㄢˋㄅㄧㄥㄒㄧㄤ)or電氣
冰箱(ㄉㄧㄢˋㄑㄧˋㄅㄧㄥㄒㄧㄤ)
a refrigerator; an ice box 亦
作「冰箱」

電瓶(ㄉㄧㄢˋㄆㄧㄥˊ)
a storage battery; an accumulator

電碼(ㄉㄧㄢˋㄇㄚˇ)
the code (of a cable); a
cipher

電碼簿(ㄉㄧㄢˋㄇㄚˇㄅㄨˋ)or電碼本
(ㄉㄧㄢˋㄇㄚˇㄅㄣˇ)
a code book

電鰻(ㄉㄧㄢˋㄇㄢˊ)
Gymnotus electricus, an electric eel

電門(ㄉㄧㄢˋㄇㄣˊ)
a switch for electric current;
a switch 亦作「開關」: 電門發
生故障。The switch was out of
order.

電木(ㄉㄧㄢˋㄇㄨˋ)
(chemistry) bakelite

電費(ㄉㄧㄢˋㄈㄟˋ)
a power rate; a power bill

---

a thunderstorm

to rush to a place like a
flash

電覆(ㄉㄧㄢˋㄈㄨˋ)
to cable a reply

電導(ㄉㄧㄢˋㄉㄠˇ)
conductivity

電導體(ㄉㄧㄢˋㄉㄠˇㄊㄧˇ)
an electric conductor

電燈(ㄉㄧㄢˋㄉㄥ)
electric lights or lamps

電燈泡(ㄉㄧㄢˋㄉㄥㄆㄠˋ)
① an electric bulb ② (colloquial) an unwanted third party who accompanies a court-
ing pair

電鍍(ㄉㄧㄢˋㄉㄨˋ)
electroplate

電動(ㄉㄧㄢˋㄉㄨㄥˋ)
powered by electricity

電動刮鬍刀(ㄉㄧㄢˋㄉㄨㄥˋㄍㄨㄚㄏㄨˊ
ㄉㄠ)
a shaver; an electric shaver

電動機(ㄉㄧㄢˋㄉㄨㄥˋㄐㄧ)
an electric motor; an induction motor

電動車(ㄉㄧㄢˋㄉㄨㄥˋㄔㄜ)
an electric motor car; an
electric driven vehicle

電動玩具(ㄉㄧㄢˋㄉㄨㄥˋㄨㄢˊㄐㄩˋ)
① a battery-powered toy ②
a video game; a TV game; a
computer game

電臺(ㄉㄧㄢˋㄊㄞˊ)
a radio station

電毯(ㄉㄧㄢˋㄊㄢˇ)
an electric blanket

電燙(ㄉㄧㄢˋㄊㄤˋ)
to wave or curl hair by electricity

電梯(ㄉㄧㄢˋㄊㄧ)
an electric lift; an elevator

電筒(ㄉㄧㄢˋㄊㄨㄥˇ)
a flashlight

電腦(ㄉㄧㄢˋㄋㄠˇ)
a computer; an electronic
computer; an electronic
brain

電腦指令(ㄉㄧㄢˋㄋㄠˇㄓˇㄌㄧㄥˋ)
computer instructions

電腦製圖(ㄉㄧㄢˋㄋㄠˇㄓˋㄊㄨˊ)
computer cartography

電腦終端機(ㄉㄧㄢˋㄋㄠˇㄓㄨㄥㄉㄨㄢ
ㄐㄧ)
a computer terminal

電腦程式(ㄉㄧㄢˋㄋㄠˇㄔㄥˊㄕˋ)
a computer program

電腦設備(ㄉㄧㄢˋㄋㄠˇㄕㄜˋㄅㄟˋ)

---

computer installation

電腦擇偶(ㄉㄧㄢˋㄋㄠˇㄗㄜˊㄡˇ)
computer dating

電腦印表機(ㄉㄧㄢˋㄋㄠˇㄧㄣˋㄅㄧㄠˇ
ㄐㄧ)
a computer printer

電腦語言(ㄉㄧㄢˋㄋㄠˇㄩˇㄧㄢˊ)
computer language

電能(ㄉㄧㄢˋㄋㄥˊ)
electric energy

電鈕(ㄉㄧㄢˋㄋㄧㄡˇ)
a button that controls electric currents

電纜(ㄉㄧㄢˋㄌㄢˇ)
a cable (usually submarine)

電離(ㄉㄧㄢˋㄌㄧˊ)
electrolytic dissociation

電力(ㄉㄧㄢˋㄌㄧˋ)
electric power

電力公司(ㄉㄧㄢˋㄌㄧˋㄍㄨㄥㄙ)
a power company

電力學(ㄉㄧㄢˋㄌㄧˋㄒㄩㄝˊ)
electrodynamics

電療法(ㄉㄧㄢˋㄌㄧㄠˊㄈㄚˇ)
electrotherapy

電料行(ㄉㄧㄢˋㄌㄧㄠˋㄏㄤˊ)
a store selling electric appliances or accessories

電流(ㄉㄧㄢˋㄌㄧㄡˊ)
an electric current

電流計(ㄉㄧㄢˋㄌㄧㄡˊㄐㄧˋ)
a galvanometer

電聯車(ㄉㄧㄢˋㄌㄧㄢˊㄔㄜ)
an electric multiple unit rail-
car (EMUR)

電鈴(ㄉㄧㄢˋㄌㄧㄥˊ)
an electric bell; a buzzer

電令(ㄉㄧㄢˋㄌㄧㄥˋ)
to transmit orders by cable
or telegram

電爐(ㄉㄧㄢˋㄌㄨˊ)
an electric stove; a hot plate

電路(ㄉㄧㄢˋㄌㄨˋ)
an electric circuit

電杆(ㄉㄧㄢˋㄍㄢ)
poles for electric wires

電感(ㄉㄧㄢˋㄍㄢˇ)
electric induction

電鍋(ㄉㄧㄢˋㄍㄨㄛ)
an electric rice cooker

電光(ㄉㄧㄢˋㄍㄨㄤ)
electric light; a flash of
lightning

電光石火(ㄉㄧㄢˋㄍㄨㄤㄕˊㄏㄨㄛˇ)
anything that vanishes in a
flash

〔雨部〕

〔雨部〕

電工(ㄉㄧㄢˋ ㄍㄨㄥ)
① an electrician ② electric-engineering

電工技術(ㄉㄧㄢˋ ㄍㄨㄥ ㄐㄧˋ ㄕㄨˋ)
electrotechnics

電烤箱(ㄉㄧㄢˋ ㄎㄠˇ ㄒㄧㄤ)
an electric oven

電賀(ㄉㄧㄢˋ ㄏㄜˋ)
to congratulate by cable

電荷(ㄉㄧㄢˋ ㄏㄜˊ)
an electric charge

電銲 or 電焊(ㄉㄧㄢˋ ㄏㄢˋ)
electric welding; electric soldering

電焊棒(ㄉㄧㄢˋ ㄏㄢˋ ㄅㄤˋ)
a soldering iron

電弧(ㄉㄧㄢˋ ㄏㄨˊ)
an electric arc

電花(ㄉㄧㄢˋ ㄏㄨㄚ)
electric sparks

電話(ㄉㄧㄢˋ ㄏㄨㄚˋ)
telephone; phone

電話簿(ㄉㄧㄢˋ ㄏㄨㄚˋ ㄅㄨˋ)
a telephone directory; a telephone book

電話分機(ㄉㄧㄢˋ ㄏㄨㄚˋ ㄈㄣ ㄐㄧ)
a telephone extension

電話亭(ㄉㄧㄢˋ ㄏㄨㄚˋ ㄊㄧㄥˊ)
a telephone booth

電話號碼(ㄉㄧㄢˋ ㄏㄨㄚˋ ㄏㄠˋ ㄇㄚˇ)
a telephone number

電話會議(ㄉㄧㄢˋ ㄏㄨㄚˋ ㄏㄨㄟˋ ㄧˋ)
a telecon

電話機(ㄉㄧㄢˋ ㄏㄨㄚˋ ㄐㄧ)
a telephone set

電話接線生(ㄉㄧㄢˋ ㄏㄨㄚˋ ㄐㄧㄝ ㄒㄧㄢˋ ㄕㄥ)
a telephone operator

電話交換機(ㄉㄧㄢˋ ㄏㄨㄚˋ ㄐㄧㄠ ㄏㄨㄢˋ ㄐㄧ)
a telephone switchboard

電話局(ㄉㄧㄢˋ ㄏㄨㄚˋ ㄐㄩˊ)
a telephone office

電話用戶(ㄉㄧㄢˋ ㄏㄨㄚˋ ㄩㄥˋ ㄏㄨˋ)
a telephone subscriber

電化教育(ㄉㄧㄢˋ ㄏㄨㄚˋ ㄐㄧㄠˋ ㄩˋ)
audio-visual education

電匯(ㄉㄧㄢˋ ㄏㄨㄟˋ)
T/T (telegraphic transfer)

電機(ㄉㄧㄢˋ ㄐㄧ)
electrical machinery

電機工程(ㄉㄧㄢˋ ㄐㄧ ㄍㄨㄥ ㄔㄥˊ)
electrical engineering: 他主修電機工程。 He majors in electrical engineering.

電機系(ㄉㄧㄢˋ ㄐㄧ ㄒㄧˋ)
the department of electrical engineering in a college

電極(ㄉㄧㄢˋ ㄐㄧˊ)
an electrode

電擊(ㄉㄧㄢˋ ㄐㄧˊ)
an electric shock; struck by lightning

電吉他(ㄉㄧㄢˋ ㄐㄧˊ ㄊㄚ)
an electric guitar

電解(ㄉㄧㄢˋ ㄐㄧㄝˇ)
electrolysis

電解質(ㄉㄧㄢˋ ㄐㄧㄝˇ ㄓˊ)or 電解液(ㄉㄧㄢˋ ㄐㄧㄝˇ ㄧㄝˋ)
an electrolyte

電鍵(ㄉㄧㄢˋ ㄐㄧㄢˋ)
a switch (for connecting or shutting off electric current)

電晶體(ㄉㄧㄢˋ ㄐㄧㄥ ㄊㄧˇ)
a transistor

電晶體收音機(ㄉㄧㄢˋ ㄐㄧㄥ ㄊㄧˇ ㄕㄡ ㄧㄣ ㄐㄧ)
a transistor radio

電鋸(ㄉㄧㄢˋ ㄐㄩˋ)
an electric saw

電氣(ㄉㄧㄢˋ ㄑㄧˋ)
electric

電氣化(ㄉㄧㄢˋ ㄑㄧˋ ㄏㄨㄚˋ)
electrification; to electrify

電氣設備(ㄉㄧㄢˋ ㄑㄧˋ ㄕㄜˋ ㄅㄟˋ)
electrical equipment

電氣用品(ㄉㄧㄢˋ ㄑㄧˋ ㄩㄥˋ ㄆㄧㄣˇ)or 電器(ㄉㄧㄢˋ ㄑㄧˋ)
electric appliances

電請(ㄉㄧㄢˋ ㄑㄧㄥˇ)
to invite by telegram

電線(ㄉㄧㄢˋ ㄒㄧㄢˋ)
electric wires: 電線能輸送電流。 Electric wires carry electricity.

電線走火(ㄉㄧㄢˋ ㄒㄧㄢˋ ㄗㄡˇ ㄏㄨㄛˇ)
a short circuit

電信(ㄉㄧㄢˋ ㄒㄧㄣˋ)
telecommunications

電信局(ㄉㄧㄢˋ ㄒㄧㄣˋ ㄐㄩˊ)
① a telephone and telegraph office ② Directorate General of Telecommunications under the Ministry of Communications

電信業務(ㄉㄧㄢˋ ㄒㄧㄣˋ ㄧㄝˋ ㄨˋ)
telecommunication service

電刑(ㄉㄧㄢˋ ㄒㄧㄥˊ)
electrocution (of criminals); death by electric chair

電訊(ㄉㄧㄢˋ ㄒㄩㄣˋ)
telecommunications; wire communications

電訊局(ㄉㄧㄢˋ ㄒㄩㄣˋ ㄐㄩˊ)
the office of telecommunications

電鐘(ㄉㄧㄢˋ ㄓㄨㄥ)
an electric clock

電池(ㄉㄧㄢˋ ㄔˊ)
an electric battery; a dry cell

電插頭(ㄉㄧㄢˋ ㄔㄚ ㄊㄡˊ)
a wire plug

電插座(ㄉㄧㄢˋ ㄔㄚ ㄗㄨㄛˋ)
a wire socket

電車(ㄉㄧㄢˋ ㄔㄜ)
a tramcar; a streetcar; a trolley car: 他乘電車上下班。 He rides on a streetcar to and from work.

電擎(ㄉㄧㄢˋ ㄑㄧㄥˊ)
with great speed, like lightning

電場(ㄉㄧㄢˋ ㄔㄤˇ)
an electric field

電廠(ㄉㄧㄢˋ ㄔㄤˇ)
a power plant

電唱頭(ㄉㄧㄢˋ ㄔㄤˋ ㄊㄡˊ)
a pickup

電唱機(ㄉㄧㄢˋ ㄔㄤˋ ㄐㄧ)
an electric phonograph; a record player

電傳打字電報機(ㄉㄧㄢˋ ㄔㄨㄢˊ ㄉㄚˇ ㄗˋ ㄉㄧㄢˋ ㄅㄠˋ ㄐㄧ)
a teletypewriter

電石(ㄉㄧㄢˋ ㄕˊ)
calcium carbide or carbide

電石氣(ㄉㄧㄢˋ ㄕˊ ㄑㄧˋ)
acetylene

電示(ㄉㄧㄢˋ ㄕˋ)
to instruct by cable or telegram

電勢(ㄉㄧㄢˋ ㄕˋ)
electric potential 亦作「電位」

電視(ㄉㄧㄢˋ ㄕˋ)
television; TV; 你看了電視上的賽船節目嗎? Did you see the boat race on (the) television?

電視播送機(ㄉㄧㄢˋ ㄕˋ ㄅㄛ ㄙㄨㄥˋ ㄐㄧ)
a television transmitter

電視頻道(ㄉㄧㄢˋ ㄕˋ ㄆㄧㄣˊ ㄉㄠˋ)
television channel

電視臺(ㄉㄧㄢˋ ㄕˋ ㄊㄞˊ)
a television station

電視連續劇(ㄉㄧㄢˋ ㄕˋ ㄌㄧㄢˊ ㄒㄩˋ ㄐㄩˋ)
a soap opera

電視錄影(ㄉㄧㄢㄕㄌㄨㄒㄧㄥ)
video recording

電視廣播(ㄉㄧㄢㄕㄍㄨㄤㄅㄛ)
a videocast

電視機(ㄉㄧㄢㄕㄐㄧ)
a TV set; a television
receiving set: 黑白電視機比彩
色的便宜。A black-and-white
TV is cheaper than a color
set.

電視節目(ㄉㄧㄢㄕㄐㄧㄝㄇㄨ)
a TV program

電視劇(ㄉㄧㄢㄕㄐㄩ)
a teleplay

電視轉播(ㄉㄧㄢㄕㄓㄨㄢㄅㄛ)
a television relay

電視採訪(ㄉㄧㄢㄕㄘㄞㄈㄤ)
a televised interview

電視遊樂器(ㄉㄧㄢㄕㄧㄡㄌㄜㄑㄧ)
a video game

電視演說(ㄉㄧㄢㄕㄧㄢㄕㄨㄛ)
a televised speech

電視影片(ㄉㄧㄢㄕㄧㄥㄆㄧㄢ)
a telefilm

電視網(ㄉㄧㄢㄕㄨㄤ)
a television network

電扇(ㄉㄧㄢㄕㄢ)or 電風扇(ㄉㄧㄢ
ㄈㄥㄕㄢ)
an electric fan: 他想買的是冷
氣，不是電扇。What he wants
to buy is an air conditioner,
not an electric fan.

電熱(ㄉㄧㄢㄖㄜ)
electric heat

電熱器(ㄉㄧㄢㄖㄜㄑㄧ)
an electric heater or radiator

電容器(ㄉㄧㄢㄖㄨㄥㄑㄧ)
a capacitor

電子(ㄉㄧㄢㄗ)
an electron

電子翻譯機(ㄉㄧㄢㄗㄈㄢㄧㄐㄧ)
an electronic translator

電子計算機(ㄉㄧㄢㄗㄐㄧㄙㄨㄢㄐㄧ)
an electronic computer

電子計算中心(ㄉㄧㄢㄗㄐㄧㄙㄨㄢ
ㄓㄨㄥㄒㄧㄣ)
a computing center

電子琴(ㄉㄧㄢㄗㄑㄧㄣ)
an eletronic organ

電子顯微鏡(ㄉㄧㄢㄗㄒㄧㄢㄨㄟ
ㄐㄧㄥ)
an electron microscope; an
electronic microscope

電子音樂(ㄉㄧㄢㄗㄧㄣㄩㄝ)
electron music

電阻(ㄉㄧㄢㄗㄨ)
(electricity) resistance

電磁(ㄉㄧㄢㄘ)
electromagnetism

電磁鐵(ㄉㄧㄢㄘㄊㄧㄝ)
electromagnetic steel

電磁爐(ㄉㄧㄢㄘㄌㄨ)
an induction cooker

電磁學(ㄉㄧㄢㄘㄒㄩㄝ)
electromagnetics

電磁石(ㄉㄧㄢㄘㄕ)
an electromagnet

電椅(ㄉㄧㄢㄧ)
the electric chair

電壓(ㄉㄧㄢㄧㄚ)
voltage

電壓計(ㄉㄧㄢㄧㄚㄐㄧ)
a voltmeter

電邀(ㄉㄧㄢㄧㄠ)
to invite by cable or telegram

電眼(ㄉㄧㄢㄧㄢ)
an electric eye; a magic eye

電影(ㄉㄧㄢㄧㄥ)
movies; motion pictures: 下
午看電影去吧。Let's go to the
movies this afternoon.

電影明星(ㄉㄧㄢㄧㄥㄇㄧㄥㄒㄧㄥ)
a movie star

電影圖書館(ㄉㄧㄢㄧㄥㄊㄨㄕㄨㄍㄨㄢ)
a film library

電影界(ㄉㄧㄢㄧㄥㄐㄧㄝ)
the moviedom; the filmdom

電影劇本(ㄉㄧㄢㄧㄥㄐㄩㄅㄣ)
a screenplay

電影製片廠(ㄉㄧㄢㄧㄥㄓㄆㄧㄢㄔㄤ)
a movie studio

電影製片人(ㄉㄧㄢㄧㄥㄓㄆㄧㄢㄖㄣ)
a movie producer

電影字幕(ㄉㄧㄢㄧㄥㄗㄇㄨ)
a film caption

電影演員(ㄉㄧㄢㄧㄥㄧㄢㄩㄢ)
a movie actor or actress; a
cinemactor or cinemactress

電影音樂(ㄉㄧㄢㄧㄥㄧㄣㄩㄝ)
film music

電影院(ㄉㄧㄢㄧㄥㄩㄢ)
a movie theater; a cinema

電位(ㄉㄧㄢㄨㄟ)
electric potential

電位器(ㄉㄧㄢㄨㄟㄑㄧ)
a potentiometer

電網(ㄉㄧㄢㄨㄤ)
a net or fence connected

with electric current

電魚(ㄉㄧㄢㄩ)
①to fish by electricity ②
Narke japonica, a flatfish

電源(ㄉㄧㄢㄩㄢ)
the source of electricity

電熨斗(ㄉㄧㄢㄩㄣㄉㄡ)
an electric iron

【雹】 ㄅㄠ baur báo 6691
(讀音 ㄅㄛ bor bó)
hail; a hailstone

雹子(ㄅㄠ·ㄗ)
hail; a hailstone

六畫

【需】 ㄒㄩ shiu xū 6692
1. to need; to require; to
demand
2. expenses; provisions; needs;
necessaries
3. hesitation; delay

需款(ㄒㄩㄎㄨㄢ)
to need money; in need of
money

需求(ㄒㄩㄑㄧㄡ)
to need; to require; needs;
demands: 他的需求不多。He
does not need much.

需次(ㄒㄩㄘ)
to wait for an official
appointment

需才孔亟(ㄒㄩㄘㄞㄎㄨㄥㄐㄧ)
to urgently need persons of
ability or talent

需要(ㄒㄩㄧㄠ)
to need or require; needs or
requirements

需要品(ㄒㄩㄧㄠㄆㄧㄣ)
necessities; essentials

需要額(ㄒㄩㄧㄠㄜ)
the amount needed

七畫

【震】 ㄓㄣ jenn zhèn 6693
1. to shake; to tremble, as an
earthquake
2. to excite; to shock
3. scared; terrified
4. (now rarely) thunder; a
thunderclap
5. the 4th of the Eight Diagrams

〔雨
部〕

〔雨部〕

震幅(ㄓㄣ ㄈㄨ)
the amplitude of an earth-quake

震悼(ㄓㄣ ㄉㄠ)
to be shocked and grieved

震旦(ㄓㄣ ㄉㄢ)
the ancient Indian name of China

震動(ㄓㄣ ㄉㄨㄥ)or 震撼(ㄓㄣ ㄏㄢ)
①to vibrate; to shake; to move: 雷聲震動山谷。The thunder shook the valley. ②to be shocked or shaken

震天駭地(ㄓㄣ ㄊㄧㄢ ㄏㄞ ㄉㄧ)
terrifying; tremendously shocking; world-shaking

震盪(ㄓㄣ ㄉㄤ)
a loud thunderclap; a sudden peal of thunder

震怒(ㄓㄣ ㄋㄨ)
greatly infuriated; wrath; rage

震慄(ㄓㄣ ㄌㄧ)
trembling from fear

震古鑠今(ㄓㄣ ㄍㄨ ㄕㄨㄛ ㄐㄧㄣ)
(said of a great achievement, etc.) unprecedented; peerless

震宮(ㄓㄣ ㄍㄨㄥ)
the palace of a prince

震恐(ㄓㄣ ㄎㄨㄥ)
to be shocked

震駭(ㄓㄣ ㄏㄞ)
greatly terrified or shocked; stunned

震撼(ㄓㄣ ㄏㄢ)
to shake; shaken

震悸(ㄓㄣ ㄐㄧ)
terrified; shocked

震驚(ㄓㄣ ㄐㄧㄥ)
greatly surprised

震懼(ㄓㄣ ㄐㄩ)
terrified; in trepidation

震懾(ㄓㄣ ㄓㄜ)
to awe; to frighten

震災(ㄓㄣ ㄗㄞ)
a disaster caused by an earthquake

震耳欲聾(ㄓㄣ ㄦ ㄩ ㄌㄨㄥ)
deafening; ear-splitting (sound, voice, etc.)

震央(ㄓㄣ ㄧㄤ)or 震源(ㄓㄣ ㄩㄢ)
an epicenter; a focus

【霄】6694
ㄒㄧㄠ　shiau　xiāo
1. the sky
2. night
3. to exhaust; to dissolve
4. clouds or mist

霄漢(ㄒㄧㄠ ㄏㄢ)
the sky; the firmament

霄壤(ㄒㄧㄠ ㄖㄤ)
heaven and earth

霄壤之分(ㄒㄧㄠ ㄖㄤ ㄓㄜ ㄈㄣ)or 霄壤之別(ㄒㄧㄠ ㄖㄤ ㄓㄜ ㄅㄧㄝ)
as far apart as heaven and earth; poles apart

霄外(ㄒㄧㄠ ㄨㄞ)
beyond the sky or clouds

【霆】6695
ㄊㄧㄥ　tyng　tíng
a sudden peal of thunder; a thunderbolt

霆擊(ㄊㄧㄥ ㄐㄧ)
as quickly as lightning

【霈】6696
ㄆㄟ　pey　pèi
1. rains; torrential rains
2. favors; good graces

霈然(ㄆㄟ ㄖㄢ)
copious; plentiful

【霉】6697
ㄇㄟ　mei　méi
musty; moldy; mold; mildewed; mildew

霉天(ㄇㄟ ㄊㄧㄢ)
the rainy season

霉爛(ㄇㄟ ㄌㄢ)
moldy and rotten

霉菌(ㄇㄟ ㄐㄩㄣ)
mold; mildew

霉氣(ㄇㄟ ㄑㄧ)
①a moldy smell; musty ②bad luck or fortune: 我一星期來霉氣不斷。I've had bad luck all week.

八畫

【霍】6698
ㄏㄨㄛ　huoh　huò
1. very rapidly; in a flash; suddenly
2. a Chinese family name

霍地(ㄏㄨㄛ ㄉㄧ)
suddenly; very quickly: 他霍地立起身來。He suddenly stood up.

霍亂(ㄏㄨㄛ ㄌㄨㄢ)
cholera

霍光(ㄏㄨㄛ ㄍㄨㄤ)
Huo Kuang, one of the greatest generals in the Western Han Dynasty

霍霍(ㄏㄨㄛ ㄏㄨㄛ)
①rapidly ②the sound of grinding or sharpening knives, etc. ③bright; brilliant; sparkling

霍去病(ㄏㄨㄛ ㄑㄩ ㄅㄧㄥ)
Huo Chü-ping, a famous general in the Western Han Dynasty

霍霍(ㄏㄨㄛ ㄖㄢ)
①lightning ②at lightning speed

霍然(ㄏㄨㄛ ㄖㄢ)
①rapidly; suddenly ②(said of an illness) to be cured quickly

【霎】6699
ㄕㄚ　shah　shà
1. an instant; in the twinkle of an eye—a very short time
2. a slight rain; drizzle

霎時(ㄕㄚ ㄕ)or 霎時間(ㄕㄚ ㄕ ㄐㄧㄢ)
in a very short while or moment; in a split second; in a jiffy

霎霎(ㄕㄚ ㄕㄚ)
①the sound of falling rain ②chilly air; cold winds

霎眼(ㄕㄚ ㄧㄢ)
to wink

【霏】6700
ㄈㄟ　fei　fēi
the falling of snow and rain

霏霏(ㄈㄟ ㄈㄟ)
to whirl around in confusion; to fly all over

【霑】6701
ㄓㄢ　jan　zhān
1. soaked; to become wet or damp; to moisten
2. to receive (benefits, etc.)

霑沐(ㄓㄢ ㄇㄨ)
to receive favors

霑染(ㄓㄢ ㄖㄢ)
①to get affected by a communicable disease ②to gain a small advantage

霑醉(ㄓㄢ ㄗㄨㄟ)
dead drunk

霑恩(ㄓㄢ ㄣ)
to be granted special favors; to be indebted to

【霓】6702
ㄋㄧ　ni　ní
a rainbow; a colored cloud

覓虹燈(ㄋㄧˊ ㄏㄨㄥˊ ㄉㄥ)
the neon light

覓裳舞(ㄋㄧˊ ㄔㄤˊ ㄨˇ)
name of a dance in the Tang Dynasty; a dance in which the female dancers wear colorful costumes

覓裳羽衣曲(ㄋㄧˊ ㄔㄤˊ ㄩˇ ㄧ ㄑㄩˇ)
name of a tune composed by Emperor Ming of the Tang Dynasty

【霖】 6703 ㄌㄧㄣˊ lin lín
a copious rain falling continuously; a continuous heavy rain

霖霖(ㄌㄧˊㄌㄧㄣˊ)
incessant raining

霖雨(ㄌㄧˊㄩˇ)
①a pouring rain ②graces; favors; benevolence

九畫

【霜】 6704 ㄕㄨㄤ shuang shuāng
1. frost; hoarfrost
2. white and powdery—like hoarfrost
3. coolness; indifference; grave
4. virtuous; pure and clean

霜鬢(ㄕㄨㄤ ㄅㄧㄣˋ)
hoary hair on the temples

霜毛(ㄕㄨㄤ ㄇㄠˊ)
pure, white feathers

霜鋒(ㄕㄨㄤ ㄈㄥ)
sharp, gleaming blades

霜刀(ㄕㄨㄤ ㄉㄠ)
a sharp, shining knife

霜臺(ㄕㄨㄤ ㄊㄞˊ)
a respectful reference to an imperial censor 亦作「御史臺」

霜天(ㄕㄨㄤ ㄊㄧㄢ)
a bleak sky (in cold weather)

霜害(ㄕㄨㄤ ㄏㄞˋ)
damage to farm crops caused by frost; frostbite; frost injury; 受霜害的農作物 frostbitten crops

霜降(ㄕㄨㄤ ㄐㄧㄤˋ)
one of the 24 climatic periods in the lunar calendar, which begins from October 23 or 24

霜期(ㄕㄨㄤ ㄑㄧˊ)
(meteorology) the frost season

霜淇淋(ㄕㄨㄤ ㄑㄧˊㄌㄧㄣˊ)
soft ice cream

霜雪(ㄕㄨㄤ ㄒㄩㄝˋ)
①frost and snow ②snow-white

霜準(ㄕㄨㄤ ㄓㄨㄣˇ)
severe laws or regulations

霜刃(ㄕㄨㄤ ㄖㄣˋ)
a sharp edged sword or knife

霜操(ㄕㄨㄤ ㄘㄠ)
moral uprightness; incorruptibility

霜草(ㄕㄨㄤ ㄘㄠˇ)
white grass

霜葉(ㄕㄨㄤ ㄧㄝˋ)
leaves turning white

霜威(ㄕㄨㄤ ㄨㄟ)
gravity and severity; awe

霜月(ㄕㄨㄤ ㄩㄝˋ)
the seventh moon in the lunar calendar

【霞】 6705 ㄒㄧㄚˊ shya xiá
colored, low-hanging clouds; rosy clouds

霞帔(ㄒㄧㄚˊ ㄆㄟˋ)
①an embroidered scarf or cape for a woman of noble rank in ancient times ②robes, etc. of a Taoist monk ③a beautiful dancing dress

霞光(ㄒㄧㄚˊ ㄍㄨㄤ)
rays of morning or evening sunlight

霞蔚(ㄒㄧㄚˊ ㄨㄟˋ)
splendid; magnificent

【霝】 6706 ㄌㄧㄥˊ ling líng
1. rain; rainfall
2. to fall

十一畫

【霧】 6707 ㄨˋ wuh wù
fog; mist; vapor

霧約(ㄨˋ ㄩㄝ)
to retire from public life; to live as a recluse

霧鬢風鬟(ㄨˋ ㄅㄧㄣˋ ㄈㄥ ㄏㄨㄢˊ)
beautiful tresses of a woman

霧裏看花(ㄨˋ ㄌㄧˇ ㄎㄢˋ ㄏㄨㄚ)
(literally) to look at flowers in a fog—failing eyesight of the aged

霧縠(ㄨˋ ㄏㄨˊ)
gossamer; a piece of extremely thin silk

霧氣(ㄨˋ ㄑㄧˋ)
fog or mist

霧塞(ㄨˋ ㄙㄞ)
obscured; mentally blinded

霧散(ㄨˋ ㄙㄢˇ)
to disperse like mist or fog

【霪】 6708 ㄧㄣˊ yn yín
to rain for a long time

霪雨(ㄧㄣˊ ㄩˇ)
an incessant rain: 霪雨爲災。An incessant rain becomes disastrous.

十二畫

【霰】 6709 ㄒㄧㄢˇ shiann xiǎn
sleet; snow and rain

霰彈(ㄒㄧㄢˇ ㄉㄢˋ)
a case shot; a canister shot

霰石(ㄒㄧㄢˇ ㄕˊ)
aragonite

【霤】 6710 (霤) ㄌㄧㄡˋ liow liù
1. the dripping of water (rain, etc.) from the eaves
2. eaves

【露】 6711 1. ㄌㄨˋ luh lù
1. dew
2. uncovered; exposed; to show; to reveal; to betray
3. a cold, soothing and aromatic drink; beverages distilled from flowers, fruit or leaves
4. a Chinese family name

露布(ㄌㄨˋ ㄅㄨˋ)or 露板(ㄌㄨˋ ㄅㄢˇ)or 露版(ㄌㄨˋ ㄅㄢˇ)
①an unsealed letter or imperial edict ②a message reporting a military victory

露封(ㄌㄨˋ ㄈㄥ)
an unsealed letter

露地(ㄌㄨˋ ㄉㄧˋ)
an open field

露點(ㄌㄨˋ ㄉㄧㄢˇ)
(meteorology)the dew point

露臺(ㄌㄨˋ ㄊㄞˊ)
a topless balcony or terrace where emperors observed

〔雨 部〕

〔雨部〕

heavenly phenomena in ancient times

露頭(ㄌㄨˋ ㄊㄡˊ)
①to take off a hat and lay bare the top of a head ②(mineralogy) an outcrop 亦作「露苗」

露頭角(ㄌㄨˋ ㄊㄡˊ ㄐㄧㄠˇ)or(ㄌㄨˋ ㄊㄡˊ ㄐㄧㄠˋ)
(said of a young person) beginning to show ability or talent; budding

露袒(ㄌㄨˋ ㄊㄢˇ)
(said of the human body) exposed or uncovered; naked

露體(ㄌㄨˋ ㄊㄧˇ)
naked; in the nude; in the altogether

露天(ㄌㄨˋ ㄊㄧㄢ)
open air; outdoor

露天電影院(ㄌㄨˋ ㄊㄧㄢ ㄉㄧㄢˋ ㄧㄥˇ ㄩㄢˋ)
an open-air cinema (or movie theater)

露天學校(ㄌㄨˋ ㄊㄧㄢ ㄒㄩㄝˊ ㄒㄧㄠˋ)
an open-air school

露立(ㄌㄨˋ ㄌㄧˋ)
①to stand outdoors ②with no place to live in

露骨(ㄌㄨˋ ㄍㄨˇ)
(said of remarks, etc.) without reserve or tact; candid; outspoken; thinly veiled; undisguised

露井(ㄌㄨˋ ㄐㄧㄥˇ)
an uncovered well

露禽(ㄌㄨˋ ㄑㄧㄣˊ)
a crane (a kind of bird)

露止(ㄌㄨˋ ㄓˇ)
to sleep outdoors 亦作「露宿」

露珠(ㄌㄨˋ ㄓㄨ)
dewdrops: 樹葉上有露珠。There were dewdrops on the leaves.

露車(ㄌㄨˋ ㄔㄜ)
a topless cart

露水(ㄌㄨˋ ㄕㄨㄟˇ)
dew: 草為露水所沾溼。The grass was wet with dew.

露水夫妻(ㄌㄨˋ ㄕㄨㄟˇ ㄈㄨ ㄑㄧ)
a couple living together without being married

露水珠兒(ㄌㄨˋ ㄕㄨㄟˇ ㄓㄨ ㄦ)
dewdrops 亦作「露珠」

露次(ㄌㄨˋ ㄘˋ)
to station (troops, etc.) in the open air 亦作「露宿」

露宿(ㄌㄨˋ ㄙㄨˋ)
to stay overnight in an open field

露宿風餐(ㄌㄨˋ ㄙㄨˋ ㄈㄥ ㄘㄢ)
(literally) to sleep in the open air and eat in the wind —the hardships of a traveler

露營(ㄌㄨˋ ㄧㄥˊ)
to camp; to bivouac; an open-air camping; a jamboree; a camporee

露尾藏頭(ㄌㄨˋ ㄨㄟˇ ㄘㄤˊ ㄊㄡˊ)
①to act clandestinely ②The more one tries to cover, the more one reveals.

【露】 6711
2. ㄌㄨˋ lòu
to appear; to emerge; to show: 他的臉上露出怒容。Anger showed in his face.

露白(ㄌㄨˋ ㄅㄞˊ)
to show money, valuables, etc. one carries unintentionally

露苗(ㄌㄨˋ ㄇㄧㄠˊ)
①to sprout; to put forth ②imminent (occurrence of something)

露面(ㄌㄨˋ ㄇㄧㄢˋ)
to show up; to appear in public; to show one's face; to make an appearance

露風(ㄌㄨˋ ㄈㄥ)
to divulge; to become known

露鋒芒(ㄌㄨˋ ㄈㄥ ㄇㄤˊ)
to make one's aggressiveness or talent felt

露頭(兒)(ㄌㄨˋ ㄊㄡˊ ㄦ)
to appear

露臉(ㄌㄨˋ ㄌㄧㄢˇ)
①successful; with flying colors ②to show one's face; to appear

露怯(ㄌㄨˋ ㄑㄧㄝˋ)
to appear clumsy (in manners); (usually said of the country people) to show one's ignorance

露相(ㄌㄨˋ ㄒㄧㄤˋ)
to show one's true form or colors

露齒(ㄌㄨˋ ㄔˇ)
to show one's teeth

露出破綻(ㄌㄨˋ ㄔㄨ ㄆㄛˋ ㄓㄢˋ)
to show one's slip; to belie

露出馬腳(ㄌㄨˋ ㄔㄨ ㄇㄚˇ·ㄐㄧㄠ)or露

馬腳(ㄌㄨˋ ㄇㄚˇ ㄐㄧㄠˇ)
to reveal one's true form or character; to show the cloven hoof; to reveal slips or leave loopholes in one's story

露出真相(ㄌㄨˋ ㄔㄨ ㄓㄣ ㄒㄧㄤˋ)
to give one away

露才(ㄌㄨˋ ㄘㄞˊ)
to display one's talent or knowledge

露財(ㄌㄨˋ ㄘㄞˊ)
to show wealth unintentionally

露一手(ㄌㄨˋ ㄧ ㄕㄡˇ)
to make an exhibition of one's skills; to show off; to display one's skills or cleverness

十三畫

【霹】 6712
ㄆㄧ pi pī
thunders; a sudden peal of thunder

霹雷(ㄆㄧ ㄌㄟˊ)
a sudden peal of thunder

霹靂(ㄆㄧ ㄌㄧˋ)
a sudden peal of thunder; a thunderclap; a thunderbolt

霹靂火(ㄆㄧ ㄌㄧˋ ㄏㄨㄛˇ)
a person with a very low boiling point; a rash and impatient person; a hotspur

霹靂車(ㄆㄧ ㄌㄧˋ ㄔㄜ)
carts equipped with rock-throwing catapults for attacking fortresses in ancient times

霹靂手(ㄆㄧ ㄌㄧˋ ㄕㄡˇ)
a judge capable of making fast decisions and judgments

霹靂舞(ㄆㄧ ㄌㄧˋ ㄨˇ)
break dance

【霸】 6713
(霸) ㄅㄚˋ bah bò
1. to dominate; to rule by might rather than right
2. a feudal lord; a chief or leader; an oppressor
3. something in which one is specially talented or gifted outstanding

霸道(ㄅㄚˋ ㄉㄠˋ)
①(ㄅㄚˋ ㄉㄠˋ) to rule by might and tact instead of right and

〔雨
部〕

virtue; to throw one's weight or to bully around; over-bearing; high-handed

②(ㄅㄚ·ㄌㄧㄠ) a strong or heavy dosage (of medicine)

霸略(ㄅㄚ ㄌㄩㄝ)
the strategy or scheme of a tyrant

霸功(ㄅㄚ ㄍㄨㄥ)
hegemony; hegemonic achievements

霸據(ㄅㄚ ㄐㄩ)
to occupy by force

霸氣(ㄅㄚ ㄑㄧ)
aggressiveness

霸權(ㄅㄚ ㄑㄩㄢ)
the authority of a powerful feudal prince; hegemony

霸者(ㄅㄚ ㄓㄜ)
an oppressor; a tyrant

霸佔(ㄅㄚ ㄓㄢ)
to occupy or take by force

霸主(ㄅㄚ ㄓㄨ)
①a powerful chief of the princes of the Epoch of Spring and Autumn (722-484 B.C.) ②an overlord; a hegemon

霸術(ㄅㄚ ㄕㄨ)
Machiavellianism

霸業(ㄅㄚ ㄧㄝ)
the achievement, career, etc. of a powerful head of feudal lords

霸王(ㄅㄚ ㄨㄤ)
①the leader of feudal lords ②the supreme chief or leader

【霶】 6714
(霶) ㄆㄤ pang pāng
to rain cats and dogs

霶霈
to rain hard; a heavy rain

十四畫

【霽】 6715
ㄐㄧ jih jì
①to stop raining; to clear up after rain or snow; 雨霽。The rain is over.
②to stop being angry

霽範(ㄐㄧ ㄈㄢ)
a mild and moderate manner

霽色(ㄐㄧ ㄙㄜ)
①mild and pleasant expres-

sion ②(said of the sky after rain) clear and blue

霽威(ㄐㄧ ㄨㄟ)
to stop being angry; to stop anger

霽月(ㄐㄧ ㄩㄝ)
①a clear moon after rain; an unclouded moon ②open-minded

【霾】 6716
ㄇㄞ mai mái
1. cloudy; misty or foggy; haze: 他在一個陰霾的日子離去。He left on a cloudy day.
2. a duststorm

十六畫

【靂】 6717
ㄌㄧ lih lì
as in 霹靂—a sudden peal of thunder

【霭】 6718
ㄞ ae ǎi
1. mild; amiable; peaceful; kind; amiable; friendly
2. cloudy; haze; mist
3. a Chinese family name

靄靄(ㄞˇ)
①luxuriant growth ②numerous ③cloudy—thick and dusky

【靆】 6719
ㄉㄞ day dài
as in 靆靆, 參看「靆」

【靈】 6720
ㄌㄧㄥ ling líng
1. the spirit; the soul
2. a fairy; an elf
3. anything pertaining to the deceased
4. wonderful; a wonder
5. mysterious; supernatural; divine
6. clever; nimble; sharp; with quick reflexes: 他的耳朵很靈。He has sharp ears.
7. good; excellent; efficacious; effective; to work: 這藥還不靈? Does this medicine work?
8. witchcraft
9. a Chinese family name

靈便(ㄌㄧㄥ ㄅㄧㄢ)
①nimble; adroit; dexterous ②convenient; easy to handle; handy

靈牌(ㄌㄧㄥ ㄆㄞ)
a spirit tablet; an ancestral tablet

靈媒(ㄌㄧㄥ ㄇㄟ)
spirit mediumship

靈敏(ㄌㄧㄥ ㄇㄧㄣ)
adroitness; dexterity; sensitive; clever; skillful; active; acute; nimble

靈妃(ㄌㄧㄥ ㄈㄟ)
a woman immortal

靈旛(ㄌㄧㄥ ㄈㄢ)
a streamer borne by the eldest son of the deceased at a funeral

靈府(ㄌㄧㄥ ㄈㄨ)
①the source of one's spirit —the mind, or brain ②one of the five sage emperors in ancient times to rule the earth

靈丹(ㄌㄧㄥ ㄉㄢ)or 靈丹妙藥(ㄌㄧㄥ ㄉㄢ ㄇㄧㄠ ㄧㄠ)
a wonder drug; a panacea; a drug with high efficacy

靈臺(ㄌㄧㄥ ㄊㄞ)
①the source of one's spirit —the mind or brain ②a balcony or terrace where ancient emperors watched heavenly phenomena ③name of a county in Kansu Province

靈透(ㄌㄧㄥ ㄊㄡ)
clever and bright; active, energetic and lovable 亦作「伶透」

靈堂(ㄌㄧㄥ ㄊㄤ)
a hall where the body of the deceased is placed during the funeral service; a mourning hall

靈通(ㄌㄧㄥ ㄊㄨㄥ)
①(said of news, messages, etc.) to spread fast; to pass with great speed ②having quick access to information; well-informed

靈童(ㄌㄧㄥ ㄊㄨㄥ)
(Taoism) an immortal who appears in the form of a boy; an immortal boy

靈感(ㄌㄧㄥ ㄍㄢ)
①inspiration ②the faculty of telepathy

靈根(ㄌㄧㄥ ㄍㄣ)
①morality; virtue ②the body ③the tongue

靈骨塔(ㄌㄧㄥ ㄍㄨ ㄊㄚ)
a pagoda-shaped ossuary or ossuarium

〔青部〕

靈光(ㄌㄧㄥˊ ㄍㄨㄤ)
①(Buddhism) the natural inclination or goodness in a person ②strange light; divine light ③(Shanghai dialect) wonderful; good; excellent

靈光殿(ㄌㄧㄥˊ ㄍㄨㄤ ㄉㄧㄢˋ)
①name of an imperial hall in the Han Dynasty which survived many calamities ②a person or thing which survives continuous disasters

靈龕(ㄌㄧㄥˊ ㄎㄢ)
a niche, jar or shrine where the remains of a deceased person are contained

靈活(ㄌㄧㄥˊ ㄏㄨㄛˊ)
energetic, active and clever; quick-witted; quick-minded; flexible; nimble: 這位學生腦筋靈活. The student is quick-witted.

靈魂(ㄌㄧㄥˊ ㄏㄨㄣˊ)
the soul; the spirit

靈魂論(ㄌㄧㄥˊ ㄏㄨㄣˊ ㄌㄨㄣˋ)
animism

靈機一動(ㄌㄧㄥˊ ㄐㄧ ㄧ ㄉㄨㄥˋ)
to have a brainstorm; to have a brain wave; to dawn on one suddenly

靈界(ㄌㄧㄥˊ ㄐㄧㄝˋ)
(Buddhism) the realm of departed spirits

靈柩(ㄌㄧㄥˊ ㄐㄧㄡˋ)
a coffin containing a corpse; a bier

靈均(ㄌㄧㄥˊ ㄐㄩㄣ)
another name of Chü Yüan (屈原), an aggrieved poet-official of Chu in ancient China

靈祇(ㄌㄧㄥˊ ㄑㄧˊ)
gods; deities

靈氣(ㄌㄧㄥˊ ㄑㄧˋ)
(said of beautiful mountains) spiritual influence

靈巧(ㄌㄧㄥˊ ㄑㄧㄠˇ)
①clever; ingenious; nimble: 她有一雙靈巧的手. She has a pair of clever hands. ②cute; lovable: 她真是個靈巧可愛的女孩子. She is such a cute girl.

靈前(ㄌㄧㄥˊ ㄑㄧㄢˊ)
before the spirit of the deceased; in front of the tab-

---

let honoring the deceased

靈犀一點通(ㄌㄧㄥˊ ㄒㄧ ㄧ ㄉㄧㄢˇ ㄊㄨㄥ)
a meeting of minds; mental rapport

靈效(ㄌㄧㄥˊ ㄒㄧㄠˋ)
(usually said of drugs, etc.) with unbelievable efficacy or curing power

靈脩(ㄌㄧㄥˊ ㄒㄧㄡ)
the king

靈秀(ㄌㄧㄥˊ ㄒㄧㄡˋ)
refined, elegant and exquisite

靈心慧性(ㄌㄧㄥˊ ㄒㄧㄣ ㄏㄨㄟˋ ㄒㄧㄥˋ)
intelligent and talented

靈性(ㄌㄧㄥˊ ㄒㄧㄥˋ)
intelligence, or a natural gift

靈芝(ㄌㄧㄥˊ ㄓ)
Ganoderma lucidum, a kind of dark brownish and hard fungus, which is supposed to possess supernatural powers

靈車(ㄌㄧㄥˊ ㄔㄜ)
a hearse; a funeral carriage

靈櫬(ㄌㄧㄥˊ ㄔㄣˋ)
a coffin

靈牀(ㄌㄧㄥˊ ㄔㄨㄤˊ)
a bier; a spirit bed

靈爽(ㄌㄧㄥˊ ㄕㄨㄤˇ)
gods and deities

靈肉(ㄌㄧㄥˊ ㄖㄡˋ)
the soul and the flesh; the soul and the body

靈人(ㄌㄧㄥˊ ㄖㄣˊ)
an immortal being

靈草(ㄌㄧㄥˊ ㄘㄠˇ)
a kind of fungus regarded as an elixir of life in ancient times

靈異(ㄌㄧㄥˊ ㄧˋ)
strange; mysterious; occult: 靈魂論是靈異之學. Animism is an occult science.

靈藥(ㄌㄧㄥˊ ㄧㄠˋ)
wonderful drugs; magic draughts

靈驗(ㄌㄧㄥˊ ㄧㄢˋ)
①(said of a prediction, or prophecy) to come true; with unbelievable accuracy ②(said of a drug, etc.) with uncanny or unbelievable efficacy

靈位(ㄌㄧㄥˊ ㄨㄟˋ)
a tablet inscribed with the name of the deceased (for

---

worshiping, etc.)

靈雨(ㄌㄧㄥˊ ㄩˇ)
a timely rain

十七畫

【靉】 6721
ㄞˋ ay ài
參看「靉靆」

靉靆(ㄞˋ ㄉㄞˋ)
①cloudy ②glasses or spectacles ③unclear; obscure; indistinct

青 部
ㄑㄧㄥ ching qīng

【青】 6722
ㄑㄧㄥ ching qīng
1. green; blue; black
2. green grass
3. not ripe
4. young; youth; youthful
5. the skin of bamboo
6. as in 蛋青—the white of an egg
7. short for Tsinghai Province or Tsingtao
8. a Chinese family name

青白眼(ㄑㄧㄥ ㄅㄞˊ ㄧㄢˇ)
to esteem or look down

青幫(ㄑㄧㄥ ㄅㄤ)
a secret society founded by Chen Yüan (陳圓) toward the last years of the Ching Dynasty

青萍(ㄑㄧㄥ ㄆㄧㄥˊ)
①green duckweeds ②name of a treasured sword

青梅(ㄑㄧㄥ ㄇㄟˊ)
green plums; unripened plums

青梅竹馬(ㄑㄧㄥ ㄇㄟˊ ㄓㄨˊ ㄇㄚˇ)
green plums and a bamboo horse—the innocent affection between a boy and a girl in their childhood

青黴素(ㄑㄧㄥ ㄇㄟˊ ㄙㄨˋ)
penicillin 亦作「盤尼西林」

青盲(ㄑㄧㄥ ㄇㄤˊ)
①green-blindness; eyesight which cannot recognize green color ②glaucoma

青苗(ㄑㄧㄥ ㄇㄧㄠˊ)

rice seedlings: 這些青苗長得很好。The rice seedlings grow well.

青苗法〈ㄑㄧㄥ ㄇㄧㄠˊ ㄈㄚˇ〉
a loan program introduced by Prime Minister Wang An-shih(王安石) of the northern Sung Dynasty, under which farmers would get the government loan when they planted rice seedlings and would make repayment after a harvest, plus a 20 percent interest

青面獠牙〈ㄑㄧㄥ ㄇㄧㄢˋ ㄌㄧㄠˊ ㄧㄚˊ〉
green-faced and long-toothed —to have a fierce look on one's face

青黛〈ㄑㄧㄥ ㄉㄞˋ〉or **青靛**〈ㄑㄧㄥ ㄉㄧㄢˋ〉
name of a Chinese medicine, mostly for external use

青島〈ㄑㄧㄥ ㄉㄠˇ〉
Tsingtao, a port-and-resort in Shantung Province

青燈〈ㄑㄧㄥ ㄉㄥ〉
oil lamps

青苔〈ㄑㄧㄥ ㄊㄞˊ〉
green moss (lichen): 石頭長滿了青苔。The stones are covered with moss.

青天〈ㄑㄧㄥ ㄊㄧㄢ〉
①the blue sky ②(in old China) an incorruptible and wise judge; an upright official

青天白日〈ㄑㄧㄥ ㄊㄧㄢ ㄅㄞˊ ㄖˋ〉
blue sky and white sun—a fine day; in broad daylight

青天白日滿地紅旗〈ㄑㄧㄥ ㄊㄧㄢ ㄅㄞˊ ㄖˋ ㄇㄢˇ ㄉㄧˋ ㄏㄨㄥˊ ㄑㄧˊ〉
the national flag of the Republic of China

青天白日旗〈ㄑㄧㄥ ㄊㄧㄢ ㄅㄞˊ ㄖˋ ㄑㄧˊ〉
the flag of blue sky and white sun—the flag of the Kuomintang

青天霹靂〈ㄑㄧㄥ ㄊㄧㄢ ㄆㄧ ㄌㄧˋ〉
a bolt from the blue

青銅〈ㄑㄧㄥ ㄊㄨㄥˊ〉
bronze

青銅時代〈ㄑㄧㄥ ㄊㄨㄥˊ ㄕˊ ㄉㄞˋ〉
the Bronze Age

青光眼〈ㄑㄧㄥ ㄍㄨㄤ ㄧㄢˇ〉
glaucoma 亦作「青光障」or「青盲」

medical practice

青鳥〈ㄑㄧㄥ ㄋㄧㄠˇ〉
①a bird messenger of Fairy God-Mother(西王母)—a messenger ②*The Blue Bird* by Maurice Maeterlinck

青年〈ㄑㄧㄥ ㄋㄧㄢˊ〉
youthful people; youths; young people; young men or women

青年團〈ㄑㄧㄥ ㄋㄧㄢˊ ㄊㄨㄢˊ〉
①a youth corps ②China Youth Corps

青年會〈ㄑㄧㄥ ㄋㄧㄢˊ ㄏㄨㄟˋ〉
YMCA (Young Men's Christian Association)參看「女青年會」

青年軍〈ㄑㄧㄥ ㄋㄧㄢˊ ㄐㄩㄣ〉
military units formed by student volunteers from the end of the Sino-Japanese War of 1937-1945

青睞〈ㄑㄧㄥ ㄌㄞˋ〉
a look of joy; favor; preference; high regard

青樓〈ㄑㄧㄥ ㄌㄡˊ〉
①a brothel—(figuratively) prostitutes ②a mansion in ancient times ③the abode of a beauty

青驪〈ㄑㄧㄥ ㄌㄧˊ〉
a dark horse; a black horse

青帘〈ㄑㄧㄥ ㄌㄧㄢˊ〉
the streamer of a wineshop

青蓮〈ㄑㄧㄥ ㄌㄧㄢˊ〉
utpala, the blue lotus, to the shape of whose leaves Buddha's eyes are likened

青蓮居士〈ㄑㄧㄥ ㄌㄧㄢˊ ㄐㄩ ㄕˋ〉
another name of Li Po(李白), a great Chinese poet

青果〈ㄑㄧㄥ ㄍㄨㄛˇ〉
①fresh fruits ②an olive

青光眼〈ㄑㄧㄥ ㄍㄨㄤ ㄧㄢˇ〉
glaucoma 參看「青內障」

青宮〈ㄑㄧㄥ ㄍㄨㄥ〉
the palace of a prince 亦作「東宮」

青海〈ㄑㄧㄥ ㄏㄞˇ〉
①Tsinghai (or Chinghai) Province, China ②Koko Nor, a lake in Tsinghai

青蒿〈ㄑㄧㄥ ㄏㄠ〉
Artemisia apiacea, a grassy-plant of the chrysanthemum family with pale yellow and aromatic blossoms in au-

tumn

青黃不接〈ㄑㄧㄥ ㄏㄨㄤˊ ㄅㄨˋ ㄐㄧㄝ〉
(literally) The old grain is used up before the harvest of the new crop.—a period of insufficiency to tide over; temporary shortage

青紅皂白〈ㄑㄧㄥ ㄏㄨㄥˊ ㄗㄠˋ ㄅㄞˊ〉
(literally) different colors —right and wrong; the truth about an event

青及〈ㄑㄧㄥ ㄐㄧˊ〉
to be honored by your perusal (a conventional phrase used in correspondence)亦作「青覽」

青椒〈ㄑㄧㄥ ㄐㄧㄠ〉
green cayenne pepper

青簡〈ㄑㄧㄥ ㄐㄧㄢˇ〉
books

青衿or **青襟**〈ㄑㄧㄥ ㄐㄧㄣ〉
①the blue collar of a student's dress in ancient China —(figuratively) a student ②a young man

青筋〈ㄑㄧㄥ ㄐㄧㄣ〉
blue veins

青〈ㄑㄧㄥ〉
green; blue

青杏〈ㄑㄧㄥ ㄒㄧㄥˋ〉
a green apricot—not ripe yet

青州從事〈ㄑㄧㄥ ㄓㄡ ㄘㄨㄥˊ ㄕˋ〉
fine wine

青竹絲〈ㄑㄧㄥ ㄓㄨˊ ㄙ〉
Trimeresurus gramineus, a kind of very venomous snake

青塚〈ㄑㄧㄥ ㄓㄨㄥˇ〉
the tomb of Wang Chao-chün(王昭君), a famed beauty of the Han Dynasty, in present Inner Mongolia (Suiyüan)

青出於藍〈ㄑㄧㄥ ㄔㄨ ㄩˊ ㄌㄢˊ〉
to surpass one's master or teacher in learning

青春〈ㄑㄧㄥ ㄔㄨㄣ〉
①one's youth; young adulthood: 他們充滿青春活力。They are bursting with youthful vigor. ②age (in asking a youth): 她青春幾何? How young (or old) is she?

青春痘〈ㄑㄧㄥ ㄔㄨㄣ ㄉㄡˋ〉or **青春怱**〈ㄑㄧㄥ ㄔㄨㄣ ㄓˋ〉
acne

〔青部〕

青春期（くㄥㄔㄨㄣㄑㄧˊ）
adolescence; puberty; teens

青春腺（くㄥㄔㄨㄣㄒㄧㄢˋ）
reproductive glands

青史（くㄥㄕˇ）
①history: 他的名字將永垂青史。 His name will go down in the annals of history. ②a Chinese double name

青少年（くㄥㄕㄠˋㄋㄧㄢˊ）
teenagers; youngsters

青少年問題（くㄥㄕㄠˋㄋㄧㄢˊㄨㄣˋㄊㄧˊ）
the problems of adolescent

青衿（くㄥㄐㄧㄣ）
①clothes worn by low-rank officials ②(Chinese opera) a leading female role

青山（くㄥㄕㄢ）
a green hill: 留得青山在, 不怕沒柴燒。 While there is a life, there is a hope.

青山綠水（くㄥㄕㄢㄌㄩˋㄕㄨㄟˇ）
blue mountains and green water—a charming natural scene

青紫（くㄥㄗˇ）
①purple and blue (bruises) ②the purple silk ribbons and blue silk ribbons attached to an official seal; (figuratively) officials of high rank

青菜（くㄥㄘㄞˋ）
vegetables; the greens

青草（くㄥㄘㄠˇ）
green grass

青翠（くㄥㄘㄨㄟˋ）
fresh green; verdant

青蔥（くㄥㄘㄨㄥ）
verdant; fresh green

青絲（くㄥㄙ）
①black hair (of a woman or girl) ②sliced preserved plums used as dressing on food (usually sweet)

青娥（くㄥㄜˊ）
young girls

青蛾（くㄥㄜˊ）
eyebrows

青衣（くㄥㄧ）
①clothes of the poor in ancient China ②everyday clothes ③(Chinese opera) a leading female role

青衣祭酒（くㄥㄧㄐㄧˋㄐㄧㄡˇ）

(Chinese opera) the most accomplished female role player

青眼（くㄥㄧㄢˇ）
preference; high regard; favor

青烏術（くㄥㄨ ㄕㄨˋ）
geomancy

青蛙（くㄥㄨㄚ）
a frog

青魚（くㄥㄩˊ）
a mackerel

青玉（くㄥㄩˋ）
a sapphire

青雲（くㄥㄩㄣˊ）
①high in virtue or position ②retirement ③the sky

青雲直上（くㄥㄩㄣˊㄓˊㄕㄤˋ）
to soar higher and higher in one's career

青雲志（くㄥㄩㄣˊㄓˋ）
great ambition; high and noble ambition or aspiration: 願君能達青雲志。 May you fulfill your great ambition.

五畫

【靖】 6723
ㄐㄧㄥˋ jìng jìng
1. peaceful; still; tranquil; quiet
2. to pacify; to quell (an uprising, etc.); to tranquilize
3. to order
4. to praise in public
5. a Chinese family name

靖邊（ㄐㄧㄥˋㄅㄧㄢ）
①to pacify or safeguard the border ②name of a county in Shensi Province

靖難（ㄐㄧㄥˋㄋㄢˋ）
①to stabilize a dangerous situation, etc.; to pacify ②a historical episode during the reign of Emperor 建文 of the Ming Dynasty when the capital was taken by the emperor's uncle who later on usurped the throne

靖亂（ㄐㄧㄥˋㄌㄨㄢˋ）
to quell uprisings; to put down a rebellion

靖國（ㄐㄧㄥˋㄍㄨㄛˊ）
to pacify the nation; to restore order in the country

靖言（ㄐㄧㄥˋㄧㄢˊ）
insincere words; sweet talk; flattery

七畫

【靚】 6724
ㄐㄧㄥˋ jìng jìng
1. to ornament; to doll up
2. still; quiet; tranquil

靚妝 or 靚粧 or 靚糚（ㄐㄧㄥˋㄓㄨㄤ）
(said of a woman) fully dressed and ornamented

靚衣（ㄐㄧㄥˋㄧ）
beautiful dresses, jewels, etc.

八畫

【靜】 6725
ㄐㄧㄥˋ jìng jìng
1. still; motionless; quiet(ly); calm; tranquility; silent: 請安靜。 Please be quiet.
2. peaceful; harmonious; serene
3. virtuous; chaste

靜僻（ㄐㄧㄥˋㄆㄧˋ）
quiet or out-of-the-way (spots, places, etc.)

靜默（ㄐㄧㄥˋㄇㄛˋ）
①silence; to become silent: 他是一位辭默寡言的人。 He is a man of silence. ②to mourn in silence

靜脈（ㄐㄧㄥˋㄇㄞˋ）
veins

靜脈曲張（ㄐㄧㄥˋㄇㄞˋㄑㄩㄓㄤ）
varix; varicosity

靜脈注射（ㄐㄧㄥˋㄇㄞˋㄓㄨˋㄕㄜˋ）
intravenous injection

靜美（ㄐㄧㄥˋㄇㄟˇ）
(art) static beauty

靜謐（ㄐㄧㄥˋㄇㄧˋ）
quiet; still; tranquil

靜穆（ㄐㄧㄥˋㄇㄨˋ）
solemn and quiet

靜電（ㄐㄧㄥˋㄉㄧㄢˋ）
static electricity

靜電感應（ㄐㄧㄥˋㄉㄧㄢˋㄍㄢˇㄧㄥˋ）
electrostatic induction

靜電場（ㄐㄧㄥˋㄉㄧㄢˋㄔㄤˇ）
an electrostatic field

靜態（ㄐㄧㄥˋㄊㄞˋ）
a motionless state; the state of stillness; a stationary state

靜聽（ㄐㄧㄥˋㄊㄧㄥ）
to listen quietly

靜力學(ㄐㄧㄥˋ ㄌㄧˋ ㄒㄩㄝˊ)
statics

靜觀(ㄐㄧㄥˋ ㄍㄨㄢ)
to observe quietly

靜觀自得(ㄍㄨㄢ ㄗˋ ㄉㄜˊ)
Everything comes to one
who waits.

靜候(ㄐㄧㄥˋ ㄏㄡˋ)
to await quietly

靜寂(ㄐㄧㄥˋ ㄐㄧˊ)
calm; quiet; tranquility

靜極思動(ㄐㄧㄥˋ ㄐㄧˊ ㄙ ㄉㄨㄥˋ)
When one remains idle for
too long, he thinks of taking
an active role in life.

靜地(ㄐㄧㄥˋ ㄐㄧㄥˋ·ㄉㄜ)
quietly; calmly; silently

靜兒(ㄐㄧㄥˋ ㄦˊ)
quiet; silent

靜居思過(ㄐㄧㄥˋ ㄐㄩ ㄙ ㄍㄨㄛˋ)
to live in seclusion and
make self-examination

靜悄悄(ㄐㄧㄥˋ ㄑㄧㄠˇㄑㄧㄠˇ)
quietly; stealthily; very
quiet: 教室靜悄悄的。It was
very quiet in the classroom.

靜修(ㄐㄧㄥˋ ㄒㄧㄡ)
to study, train, or discipline
(oneself) without being disturbed by what's going on
outside

靜心(ㄐㄧㄥˋ ㄒㄧㄣ)
to calm one's mind; a peaceful mind

靜止(ㄐㄧㄥˋ ㄓˇ)
motionless; static; rest; at a
standstill: 光陰不是永遠靜止
的。Time is never at a standstill.

靜舍(ㄐㄧㄥˋ ㄕㄜˋ)
① a Buddhist temple ② a
quiet house

靜水(ㄐㄧㄥˋ ㄕㄨㄟˇ)
still water; stagnant water

靜若處女，動若脫兔(ㄐㄧㄥˋ ㄖㄨㄛˋ ㄔㄨˇ
ㄋㄩˇ ，ㄉㄨㄥˋ ㄖㄨㄛˋ ㄊㄨㄛ ㄊㄨˋ)
Deliberate in counsel,
prompt in action.

靜字(ㄐㄧㄥˋ ㄗˋ)
an adjective

靜坐(ㄐㄧㄥˋ ㄗㄨㄛˋ)
to sit still with a peaceful
mind; to sit still as a form
of therapy

靜坐示威(ㄐㄧㄥˋ ㄗㄨㄛˋ ㄕˋ ㄨㄟ)or
靜坐抗議(ㄐㄧㄥˋ ㄗㄨㄛˋ ㄎㄤˋ ㄧˋ)

to sit in; a sit-in demonstration; a sit-in protest

靜思(ㄐㄧㄥˋ ㄙ)
to think or contemplate quietly; to meditate

靜以制動(ㄐㄧㄥˋ ㄧˇ ㄓˋ ㄉㄨㄥˋ)
to beat action by inaction

靜夜(ㄐㄧㄥˋ ㄧㄝˋ)
a silent night; in the still of
the night: 我喜歡在靜夜沈思，I
like to meditate in the still
of the night.

靜養(ㄐㄧㄥˋ ㄧㄤˇ)
to rest or convalesce without disturbance; to recuperate in quiet surroundings

靜物畫(ㄐㄧㄥˋ ㄨˋ ㄏㄨㄚˋ)
(painting) still life

【靛】 6726
ㄉㄧㄢˋ diann diàn
indigo; any blue dyes; indigo
color

靛白(ㄉㄧㄢˋ ㄅㄞˊ)
indigo white

靛藍(ㄉㄧㄢˋ ㄌㄢˊ)
indigo blue

靛精(ㄉㄧㄢˋ ㄐㄧㄥ)
indigotin

靛青(ㄉㄧㄢˋ ㄑㄧㄥ)
indigo—a blue dye obtained
from various plants

靛油(ㄉㄧㄢˋ ㄧㄡˊ)
aniline oil

十畫

【靝】 6727
ㄊㄧㄢ tian tiān
(Taoism) the heaven

非 部
ㄈㄟ fei fēi

【非】 6728
ㄈㄟ fei fēi
1. negative; not; not to be;
non-: 細菌非肉眼所能見。
Germs cannot be seen by the
naked eye.
2. faults; mistakes; evils;
wrong: 他要文過飾非。He
tries to cover up his mistakes.
3. to object; to refute; to con-

sider as wrong; to censure;
to blame
4. short for Africa

非賣品(ㄈㄟ ㄇㄞˋ ㄆㄧㄣˇ)
items not for sale: 所有物品
都是非賣品。All these items
are not for sale.

非美活動委員會(ㄈㄟ ㄇㄟˇ ㄏㄨㄛˊ
ㄉㄨㄥˋ ㄨㄟˇ ㄩㄢˊ ㄏㄨㄟˋ)
House Committee on Un-
American Activities

非命(ㄈㄟ ㄇㄧㄥˋ)
① death by accident or violence: 他死於非命。He died a
violent death. ② a refutation
on fatalism

非法(ㄈㄟ ㄈㄚˇ)
illegal; unlawful; illicit

非法罷工(ㄈㄟ ㄈㄚˇ ㄅㄚˋ ㄍㄨㄥ)
an illegal strike

非法翻印(ㄈㄟ ㄈㄚˇ ㄈㄢ ㄧㄣˋ)
to pirate

非法集會(ㄈㄟ ㄈㄚˇ ㄐㄧˊ ㄏㄨㄟˋ)
an illegal assembly

非法拘留(ㄈㄟ ㄈㄚˇ ㄐㄩ ㄌㄧㄡˊ)
illegal detention

非法行為(ㄈㄟ ㄈㄚˇ ㄒㄧㄥˊ ㄨㄟˊ)
illegal acts

非法佔領(ㄈㄟ ㄈㄚˇ ㄓㄢˋ ㄌㄧㄥˇ)
illegal occupation

非法持有(ㄈㄟ ㄈㄚˇ ㄔˊ ㄧㄡˇ)
illegal possession

非法收入(ㄈㄟ ㄈㄚˇ ㄕㄡ ㄖㄨˋ)
illicit income

非法遊行示威(ㄈㄟ ㄈㄚˇ ㄧㄡˊ ㄒㄧㄥˊ
ㄕˋ ㄨㄟ)
an illegal demonstration

非非之想(ㄈㄟ ㄈㄟ ㄓ ㄒㄧㄤˇ)
wishful thinking

非肥皂(ㄈㄟ ㄈㄟˊ ㄗㄠˋ)
detergent

非凡(ㄈㄟ ㄈㄢˊ)
extraordinary; remarkable;
uncommon; outstanding: 他
最後獲得非凡的成功。He
finally achieved extraordinary success.

非分(ㄈㄟ ㄈㄣˋ)
undeserved; beyond the
scope of duty or position;
presumptuous: 我不想知道他
的非分要求。I do not want to
know his presumptuous
demands.

非分之想(ㄈㄟ ㄈㄣˋ ㄓ ㄒㄧㄤˇ)
a thought or desire entirely

〔非
部〕

〔非部〕

not on a par with or within one's ability, position, duty, etc. to harbor; an improper thought or desire

非得(ㄈㄟ ㄉㄜˊ)
must; to have to; to have no other alternative but to...: 做這種事得仔細才行。You must be careful when you do this job.

非導體(ㄈㄟ ㄉㄠˇ ㄊㄧˇ)
nonconductors

非但(ㄈㄟ ㄉㄢˋ)or非止(ㄈㄟ ㄓˇ)
not only

非獨(ㄈㄟ ㄉㄨˊ)
not only; not merely

非同小可(ㄈㄟ ㄊㄨㄥˊ ㄒㄧㄠˇ ㄎㄜˇ)
tremendously important; no small matter; very serious; having grave consequences

非難(ㄈㄟ ㄋㄢˊ)
to blame; to dispute; to censure; to criticize; to reproach

非類(ㄈㄟ ㄌㄟˋ)
①gangsters; robbers; bandits ②people not of the same race

非禮(ㄈㄟ ㄌㄧˇ)
①improper ②to assault a woman sexually

非驢非馬(ㄈㄟ ㄌㄩˊ ㄈㄟ ㄇㄚˇ)
neither an ass nor a horse —grotesque; unlike anything; to imitate unsuccessfully

非官方(ㄈㄟ ㄍㄨㄢ ㄈㄤ)or非官式(ㄈㄟ ㄍㄨㄢ ㄕˋ)
unofficial

非婚生子女(ㄈㄟ ㄏㄨㄣ ㄕㄥ ㄗˇ ㄋㄩˇ)
illegitimate children

非計(ㄈㄟ ㄐㄧˋ)
not a good idea; a poor plan

非冀(ㄈㄟ ㄐㄧˋ)
a hope beyond one's reach; a wild hope

非交戰國(ㄈㄟ ㄐㄧㄠ ㄓㄢˋ ㄍㄨㄛˊ)
a nonbelligerent

非金屬(ㄈㄟ ㄐㄧㄣ ㄕㄨˇ)
nonmetals

非晶體(ㄈㄟ ㄐㄧㄥ ㄊㄧˇ)
amorphous

非君莫屬(ㄈㄟ ㄐㄩㄣ ㄇㄛˋ ㄕㄨˇ)
Only you can fill the post.

非軍事化(ㄈㄟ ㄐㄩㄣ ㄕˋ ㄏㄨㄚˋ)
to demilitarize

非軍事區(ㄈㄟ ㄐㄩㄣ ㄕˋ ㄑㄩ)
a demilitarized zone

非軍事人員(ㄈㄟ ㄐㄩㄣ ㄕˋ ㄖㄣˊ ㄩㄢˊ)
civilian personnel

非笑(ㄈㄟ ㄒㄧㄠˋ)
to ridicule; to laugh at

非刑(ㄈㄟ ㄒㄧㄥˊ)
torture; punishment not specified in the law: 獄卒非刑拷打囚犯。The jailer tortured the prisoner brutally.

非支群島(ㄈㄟ ㄓ ㄑㄩㄣˊ ㄉㄠˇ)
the Fiji Islands 亦作「飛枝群島」

非洲(ㄈㄟ ㄓㄡ)
Africa

非戰鬥員(ㄈㄟ ㄓㄢˋ ㄉㄡˋ ㄩㄢˊ)
noncombatants

非戰公約(ㄈㄟ ㄓㄢˋ ㄍㄨㄥ ㄩㄝ)
①an antiwar pact; a treaty renouncing the use of force ②the General Treaty of the Renunciation of War signed in 1928

非正式(ㄈㄟ ㄓㄥˋ ㄕˋ)
informal; unofficial: 宴會要穿什麼衣服—正式或非正式的? What dress should we wear —formal or informal?

非正式訪問(ㄈㄟ ㄓㄥˋ ㄕˋ ㄈㄤˇ ㄨㄣˋ)
an informal (or unofficial) visit

非池中物(ㄈㄟ ㄔˊ ㄓㄨㄥ ㄨˋ)
one who has a promising future

非常(ㄈㄟ ㄔㄤˊ)
①extraordinary; emergency; unusual ②very; highly; terribly; simply: 他的表演非常精彩。His performance was simply wonderful.

非常時期(ㄈㄟ ㄔㄤˊ ㄕˊ ㄑㄧ)
time of emergency

非常識(ㄈㄟ ㄔㄤˊ ㄕˋ)
silly; absurd; nonsensical; lack of common sense

非常手段(ㄈㄟ ㄔㄤˊ ㄕㄡˇ ㄉㄨㄢˋ)or非常方式(ㄈㄟ ㄔㄤˊ ㄈㄤ ㄕˋ)
emergency measures

非常上訴(ㄈㄟ ㄔㄤˊ ㄕㄤˋ ㄙㄨˋ)
an extraordinary appeal (initiated by the procurator general of the Supreme Court)

非常人(ㄈㄟ ㄔㄤˊ ㄖㄣˊ)
an extraordinary person; an outstanding person

非時(ㄈㄟ ㄕˊ)
wrong timing; not the proper time

非人(ㄈㄟ ㄖㄣˊ)
①a bad man; a ruffian; a villain ②not the right man ③inhuman

非人待遇(ㄈㄟ ㄖㄣˊ ㄉㄞˋ ㄩˋ)
inhuman treatment

非人生活(ㄈㄟ ㄖㄣˊ ㄕㄥ ㄏㄨㄛˊ)
a miserable life; the life of beasts of burden: 那裏的難民過着非人生活。The fugitives there live a miserable life.

非此不可(ㄈㄟ ㄘˇ ㄅㄨˋ ㄎㄜˇ)
Nothing else will do. 或 There's no alternative. 或 This is the only way.

非議(ㄈㄟ ㄧˋ)
to censure; to dispute; to reproach

非也(ㄈㄟ ㄧㄝˇ)
This is not so.

非楊即墨(ㄈㄟ ㄧㄤˊ ㄐㄧˊ ㄇㄛˋ)
to have to be either this or that

非我莫屬(ㄈㄟ ㄨㄛˇ ㄇㄛˋ ㄕㄨˇ)
I, and I alone, am qualified for, or deserve, (the position).

非我族類(ㄈㄟ ㄨㄛˇ ㄗㄨˊ ㄌㄟˋ)
not one among us—aliens

非望(ㄈㄟ ㄨㄤˋ)
a wild hope or desire

七畫

【靠】 6729
ㄎㄠˋ kaw kào
1. to rely on; to depend on
2. to lean on: 把梯子靠在牆上。Lean the ladder against the wall.
3. near to; bordering on; to keep to (the left or the right), as in driving: 所有的行人一律靠右走。All pedestrians should keep to the right.
4. (Chinese opera) make-believe armor worn by actors

靠背(ㄎㄠˋ ㄅㄟˋ)
the back of a chair

靠背椅(ㄎㄠˋ ㄅㄟˋ ㄧˇ)
a chair with a high back

靠邊兒(ㄎㄠˋ ㄅㄧㄢ ㄦˊ)or靠邊(ㄎㄠˋ ㄅㄧㄢ)

ㄅㄞ
①to keep to the right or left side (of the road): 請靠邊兒站。Please stand aside. 行人靠邊走。Pedestrians keep to the side of the road. ②reasonable; near the truth

靠不住(ㄎㄠˋ ㄅㄨˋ ㄓㄨˋ)
not dependable; not to be trusted; not reliable

靠得住(ㄎㄠˋ ㄉㄜˊ ㄓㄨˋ)
dependable; can be trusted; reliable

靠墊(ㄎㄠˋ ㄉㄧㄢˋ)
a (back) cushion

靠天吃飯(ㄎㄠˋ ㄊㄧㄢ ㄔ ㄈㄢˋ)
to depend on heaven for food—to leave everything to fate

靠攏(ㄎㄠˋ ㄌㄨㄥˇ)
①to shorten the distance; to sit or stand closer: 向前靠攏! Close ranks! ②to shift allegiance to a new master; to tergiversate

靠攏分子(ㄎㄠˋ ㄌㄨㄥˇ ㄈㄣ ˙ㄗ)
a turncoat; a tergiversator: 我們鄙視靠攏分子。We despise tergiversators.

靠近(ㄎㄠˋ ㄐㄧㄣˋ)
①near to; in the neighborhood of ②to approach; to draw nearer

靠枕(ㄎㄠˋ ㄓㄣˇ)
a pillow; a cushion

靠山(ㄎㄠˋ ㄕㄢ)
a person from whom one draws his influence; a supporter in high position; someone to lean on; a backer; a patron; a helper; a protector

靠山吃山,靠水吃水(ㄎㄠˋ ㄕㄢ ㄔ ㄕㄢ ,ㄎㄠˋ ㄕㄨㄟˇ ㄔ ㄕㄨㄟˇ)
to make a living in one's given circumstances

靠自己(ㄎㄠˋ ㄗˋ ㄐㄧˇ)
to rely on oneself; independent

靠子(ㄎㄠˋ ˙ㄗ)
①something to lean on ②embroidered make-believe armor worn by warriors in Chinese opera

靠岸(ㄎㄠˋ ㄢˋ)
to draw alongside the shore, quay or pier; to pull in to

the shore

靠椅(ㄎㄠˋ ㄧˇ)
an easy chair; a lounge chair

十一畫

【靡】 6730　ㄇㄧ˙ mi　mǐ
1. to disperse; to scatter; to divide; blown away by the wind
2. to lean with pressure
3. not; no; negative
4. tiny; petty; small
5. wonderful; good; excellent

靡敝(ㄇㄧˊ ㄅㄧˋ)
decline; to get weak; emaciated

靡靡(ㄇㄧˊ ㄇㄧˊ)
①lewd; licentious ②delayed; procrastinating ③slowly

靡靡之音(ㄇㄧˊ ㄇㄧˊ ㄓ ㄧㄣ)
lewd music or songs; decadent music

靡麗(ㄇㄧˊ ㄌㄧˋ)
extravagant

靡有孑遺(ㄇㄧˊ ㄧㄡˇ ㄐㄧㄝˊ ㄧˊ)
not a person left; all have died off; no survivor

靡顏膩理(ㄇㄧˊ ㄧㄢˊ ㄋㄧˋ ㄌㄧˇ)
beautiful and fair-skinned

【靡】 6730　ㄇㄧ˙ mi　mí
1. to waste; extravagant: 他過著奢靡的生活。He lived an extravagant life.
2. to rot

靡費(ㄇㄧˊ ㄈㄟˋ)
to waste; extravagant; wasteful 亦作「糜費」

面 部
ㄇㄧㄢˋ miann miàn

【面】 6731
ㄇㄧㄢˋ miann miàn
1. the face of a person
2. the surface; the top; the face
3. a side; a direction; an aspect
4. extent; range; scale; scope
5. to face or confront; to look
6. face-to-face; in or to one's

face; personally; directly
7. (mathematics) a plane
8. to indicate something flat

面壁(ㄇㄧㄢˋ ㄅㄧˋ)
①to face the wall ②to do nothing; to waste time ③(Zen Buddhism) to face the wall and meditate

面稟(ㄇㄧㄢˋ ㄅㄧㄥˇ)
to report to a superior or an elder in person

面部(ㄇㄧㄢˋ ㄅㄨˋ)
the face; facial

面不改色(ㄇㄧㄢˋ ㄅㄨˋ ㄍㄞˇ ㄙㄜˋ)
not to change color; to remain composed; without batting an eyelid

面皰(ㄇㄧㄢˋ ㄆㄠˋ)
pimples; acne; comedos

面盆(ㄇㄧㄢˋ ㄆㄣˊ)
a wash basin

面龐(ㄇㄧㄢˋ ㄆㄤˊ)
facial appearance; facial features: 我弟弟有個圓圓的面龐。My younger brother has a round face.

面皮(ㄇㄧㄢˋ ㄆㄧˊ)
①face-skin; face ②fine leather covering the exterior of a bag, case, etc.

面皮薄(ㄇㄧㄢˋ ㄆㄧˊ ㄅㄛˊ)
sensitive; with a sharp sense of shame

面皮厚(ㄇㄧㄢˋ ㄆㄧˊ ㄏㄡˋ)
shameless; brazen; thick-skinned

面貌(ㄇㄧㄢˋ ㄇㄠˋ)
appearance; features of a person; face; looks

面面(ㄇㄧㄢˋ ㄇㄧㄢˋ)
(from) all sides or angles

面面(ㄇㄧㄢˋ ㄇㄧㄢˋ ㄐㄩˋ)
a comprehensive analysis; an exhaustive description

面面俱到(ㄇㄧㄢˋ ㄇㄧㄢˋ ㄐㄩˋ ㄉㄠˋ)
well considered in every respect

面面相覷(ㄇㄧㄢˋ ㄇㄧㄢˋ ㄒㄧㄤ ㄑㄩˋ)
to look at each other in fear, not knowing what to do; to gaze at each other in speechless despair

面命(ㄇㄧㄢˋ ㄇㄧㄥˋ)
to instruct or charge someone face to face

面目(ㄇㄧㄢˋ ㄇㄨˋ)
face; features; looks; appear-

［面部］

面目清秀 (ㄇㄧㄢ ㄇㄨ ㄑㄧㄥ ㄒㄧㄡ)
ance; countenance: 這小女孩面目清秀。The little girl has a delicate appearance.

面目可憎 (ㄇㄧㄢ ㄇㄨ ㄎㄜˇ ㄗㄥ)
abominable (in looks); ugly; repulsive in appearance

面目全非 (ㄇㄧㄢ ㄇㄨ ㄑㄩㄢˊ ㄈㄟ)
Everything's changed beyond recognition.

面目猙獰 (ㄇㄧㄢ ㄇㄨ ㄓㄥ ㄋㄧㄥˊ)
sinister in appearance

面目一新 (ㄇㄧㄢ ㄇㄨ ㄧˋ ㄒㄧㄣ)
a brand-new look; to present a completely new appearance; to assume a new aspect

面縛 (ㄇㄧㄢ ㄈㄨˊ)
to tie hands behind the back

面帶病容 (ㄇㄧㄢ ㄉㄞˋ ㄅㄧㄥˋ ㄖㄨㄥˊ)
One's face shows a sickly countenance.

面帶愁容 (ㄇㄧㄢ ㄉㄞˋ ㄔㄡˊ ㄖㄨㄥˊ)
sad-faced; a woeful look

面豆 (ㄇㄧㄢ ㄉㄡˋ)
smallpox 亦作「天花」

面對 (ㄇㄧㄢ ㄉㄨㄟˋ)
to face (a person, situation, direction or object); to confront; opposite; facing: 我們要面對現實。We must face reality.

面對面 (ㄇㄧㄢ ㄉㄨㄟˋ ㄇㄧㄢ)
face-to-face; vis-à-vis

面談 (ㄇㄧㄢ ㄊㄢˊ)
to talk face-to-face; to take up a matter with somebody personally; to interview

面託 (ㄇㄧㄢ ㄊㄨㄛ)
to ask someone to do something in person

面團團 (ㄇㄧㄢ ㄊㄨㄢˊ ㄊㄨㄢˊ)
a full round face

面嫩 (ㄇㄧㄢ ㄋㄣˋ)
timid; sensitive

面臨 (ㄇㄧㄢ ㄌㄧㄣˊ)
to be faced with; to be confronted with; to be up against: 我們面臨了一個新的問題。A new problem confronted us.

面告 (ㄇㄧㄢ ㄍㄠˋ)
to tell in person

面寬 (ㄇㄧㄢ ˙ㄎㄨㄢ)
latitude; width; breadth

面孔 (ㄇㄧㄢ ㄎㄨㄥˇ)
the face (of a person)

面和心不和 (ㄇㄧㄢ ㄏㄜˊ ㄒㄧㄣ ㄅㄨˋ ㄏㄜˊ)
to remain friendly in appearance but estranged at heart

面會 (ㄇㄧㄢ ㄏㄨㄟˋ)
to meet

面黃肌瘦 (ㄇㄧㄢ ㄏㄨㄤˊ ㄐㄧ ㄕㄡˋ)
thin and sickly in appearance; an emaciated look; sallow and emaciated

面紅 (ㄇㄧㄢ ㄏㄨㄥˊ)
to blush

面紅耳赤 (ㄇㄧㄢ ㄏㄨㄥˊ ㄦˇ ㄔˋ)
to blush; to flush (either because of shame or anger): 她因羞愧而面紅耳赤。She flushed with shame.

面積 (ㄇㄧㄢ ㄐㄧ)
area

面頰 (ㄇㄧㄢ ㄐㄧㄚˊ)
cheeks

面交 (ㄇㄧㄢ ㄐㄧㄠ)
① to deliver (something) to the recipient in person ② an acquaintance

面巾 (ㄇㄧㄢ ㄐㄧㄣ)
① a face towel ② a piece of cloth covering the face of the dead

面巾紙 (ㄇㄧㄢ ㄐㄧㄣ ㄓˇ) or 面紙 (ㄇㄧㄢ ㄓˇ)
face tissues

面具 (ㄇㄧㄢ ㄐㄩˋ)
a mask; a face: 這位警察戴着防毒面具。The policeman is wearing a gas mask.

面前 (ㄇㄧㄢ ㄑㄧㄢˊ)
in front of; in the presence of; before

面壁 (ㄇㄧㄢ ㄅㄧˋ)
to face a wall (and see nothing)—unlearned

面請 (ㄇㄧㄢ ㄑㄧㄥˇ)
to request in person

面洽 (ㄇㄧㄢ ㄑㄧㄚˋ) or (ㄇㄧㄢ ㄑㄧˋ)
to meet and talk it over; to take up a matter with someone personally

面謝 (ㄇㄧㄢ ㄒㄧㄝˋ)
to thank in person

面向 (ㄇㄧㄢ ㄒㄧㄤˋ)
to face (a certain direction, a person or object): 那房子面向街道。The house faces the street.

面相學 (ㄇㄧㄢ ㄒㄧㄤˋ ㄒㄩㄝˊ)
physiognomy

面值 (ㄇㄧㄢ ㄓˊ)
① par value; face value; nominal value ② denomination

面折 (ㄇㄧㄢ ㄓㄜˊ) or 面斥 (ㄇㄧㄢ ㄔˋ) 面責 (ㄇㄧㄢ ㄗㄜˊ)
to scold a person to his face

面罩 (ㄇㄧㄢ ㄓㄠˋ)
a face guard

面囑 (ㄇㄧㄢ ㄓㄨˇ)
to tell a subordinate or junior in person

面陳 (ㄇㄧㄢ ㄔㄣˊ)
to report in person; to deliver something to a superior in person

面試 (ㄇㄧㄢ ㄕˋ)
an oral quiz; an audition; an interview

面紗 (ㄇㄧㄢ ㄕㄚ)
a veil (for women)

面首 (ㄇㄧㄢ ㄕㄡˇ)
a catamite

面授機宜 (ㄇㄧㄢ ㄕㄡˋ ㄐㄧ ㄧˊ)
personally instruct somebody on the line of action to pursue; personally tell someone how to do something; to give confidential briefing

面善 (ㄇㄧㄢ ㄕㄢˋ)
① to look familiar: 她很面善。Her face seems familiar. ② to look kind-hearted

面善心險 (ㄇㄧㄢ ㄕㄢˋ ㄒㄧㄣ ㄒㄧㄢˇ) or 面善心惡 (ㄇㄧㄢ ㄕㄢˋ ㄒㄧㄣ ㄜˋ)
a wolf in sheep's clothing

面商 (ㄇㄧㄢ ㄕㄤ)
to meet in person and talk it over; to consult personally

面上無光 (ㄇㄧㄢ ㄕㄤˋ ㄨˊ ㄍㄨㄤ)
loss of prestige

面生 (ㄇㄧㄢ ㄕㄥ)
(said of a person) unfamiliar; to have not met before: 這女人面生得很。I don't think I've seen this woman before.

面熟 (ㄇㄧㄢ ㄕㄡˊ)
to look familiar

面霜 (ㄇㄧㄢ ㄕㄨㄤ)
cream

面如土色 (ㄇㄧㄢ ㄖㄨˊ ㄊㄨˇ ㄙㄜˋ)
to look ashen; to look pale: 小男孩嚇得面如土色。The little boy turned pale with fright.

容(ㄇㄧㄢˊ ㄖㄨㄥˊ)
countenance; face

子(ㄇㄧㄢˊ ㄗˇ)
①honor; one's face (in the figurative sense); 他不給我面子。He won't do me the honor. ②the outside or facing of a garment

奏(ㄇㄧㄢˊ ㄗㄡˋ)
to report to the emperor in person

辭(ㄇㄧㄢˊ ㄘˊ)
①to decline in person ②to go to say good-bye to somebody; to take leave of somebody

從(ㄇㄧㄢˊ ㄘㄨㄥˊ)
to feign obedience

色(ㄇㄧㄢˊ ㄙㄜˋ)
①one's facial complexion: 她的面色紅潤。She is ruddy-cheeked. ②facial expression

色蒼白(ㄇㄧㄢˊ ㄙㄜˋ ㄘㄤ ㄅㄞˊ)
to look pale

額(ㄇㄧㄢˊ ㄜˊ)
(economics) denomination

議(ㄇㄧㄢˊ ㄧˋ)
face-to-face negotiations; to negotiate face to face

謁(ㄇㄧㄢˊ ㄧㄝˋ)
to call on a superior or an elder

邀(ㄇㄧㄢˊ ㄧㄠ)
to invite in person

有難色(ㄇㄧㄢˊ ㄧㄡˇ ㄋㄢˊ ㄙㄜˋ)
to look reluctant

有菜色(ㄇㄧㄢˊ ㄧㄡˇ ㄘㄞˋ ㄙㄜˋ)
to look pale or pallid

無人色(ㄇㄧㄢˊ ㄨˊ ㄖㄣˊ ㄙㄜˋ)
to look extremely scared; to look ghastly pale

晤(ㄇㄧㄢˊ ㄨˋ)
to meet in person

諭(ㄇㄧㄢˊ ㄩˋ)
instructions or exhortations given in person; to give orders in person

譽(ㄇㄧㄢˊ ㄩˋ)
to praise a person in his presence

七畫

【覥】6732
1. ㄊㄧㄢˇ tean tiǎn
ashamed and embarrassed

---

ashamed and embarrassed

覥臉(ㄊㄧㄢˇ ㄌㄧㄢˇ)
shameless; to brazen it out

覥(ㄊㄧㄢˇ)
to blush for shame; to come to blush with shame

覥(ㄊㄧㄢˇ)
shameless

【覥】6732
2. ㄇㄧㄢˇ mean miǎn
shy; timid

覥覥(ㄇㄧㄢˇ ㄇㄧㄢˇ)
shy; timid; bashful: 她在生人面前羞得覥覥。She's shy with strangers.

十二畫

【䩩】6733
ㄏㄨㄟˋ huey huì
to wash one's face

十四畫

【靨】6734
ㄧㄝˋ yeh yè
dimples in the face

靨輔 or 靨輔(ㄧㄝˋ ㄈㄨˇ)
dimples in the face

革 部
《ㄍㄜˊ ger gé

【革】6735
1. 《ㄍㄜˊ ger gé
1. hides stripped of hair; skin; leather
2. to get rid of; to eliminate
3. to change; to reform; to renovate
4. (now rarely) human skin
5. Chinese percussion musical instruments
6. armor
7. soldiers
8. one of the Eight Diagrams
9. a Chinese family name

革面革心(《ㄍㄜˊ ㄇㄧㄢˋ 《ㄍㄜˊ ㄒㄧㄣ)
to repent and reform oneself inside out

革命(《ㄍㄜˊ ㄇㄧㄥˋ)
a revolution (political, economic, etc.)

革命黨(《ㄍㄜˊ ㄇㄧㄥˋ ㄉㄤˇ)
a revolutionary political party

革命軍(《ㄍㄜˊ ㄇㄧㄥˋ ㄐㄩㄣ)
the revolutionary army; the revolutionary forces

革命先烈紀念日(《ㄍㄜˊ ㄇㄧㄥˋ ㄒㄧㄢ ㄌㄧㄝˋ ㄐㄧˋ ㄋㄧㄢˋ ㄖˋ)
Revolutionary Martyrs' Day on March 29

革退(《ㄍㄜˊ ㄊㄨㄟˋ)
to dismiss; to fire; dishonorable discharge

革囊(《ㄍㄜˊ ㄋㄤˊ)
①a leather bag ②the human body

革履(《ㄍㄜˊ ㄌㄩˇ)
leather shoes

革故鼎新(《ㄍㄜˊ 《ㄨˋ ㄉㄧㄥˇ ㄒㄧㄣ)
to rid the old bane and reform

革心(《ㄍㄜˊ ㄒㄧㄣ)
to repent

革新(《ㄍㄜˊ ㄒㄧㄣ)
to reform; to renovate; innovation

革新運動(《ㄍㄜˊ ㄒㄧㄣ ㄩㄣˋ ㄉㄨㄥˋ)
a reformation movement

革職(《ㄍㄜˊ ㄓˊ)
to fire; a dishonorable discharge; to dismiss

革除(《ㄍㄜˊ ㄔㄨˊ)
①to rid; to eliminate (ills, etc.); to abolish ②to expel; to dismiss

【革】6735
2. ㄐㄧˊ jyi jí
urgent; dangerous

二畫

【釘】6736
ㄉㄧㄥ ding dīng
1. to mend the soles of shoes
2. a patch

四畫

【靳】6737
ㄐㄧㄣˋ jinn jìn
1. ornamental trappings under the neck of a horse
2. stingy
3. a Chinese family name

【靴】6738
ㄒㄩㄝ shiue xuē
boots

靴底(ㄒㄩㄝ ㄉㄧˇ)
soles of boots

靴子(ㄒㄩㄝ ·ㄗ)
boots: 他的靴子是用橡膠做的。
His boots are made of rubber.

【靶】 6739
ㄅㄚˇ baa bǎ
1. the target
2. the splashboard of a chariot

靶機(ㄅㄚˇ ㄐㄧ)
a drone (a pilotless plane for target shooting)

靶心(ㄅㄚˇ ㄒㄧㄣ)
bull's-eye

靶場(ㄅㄚˇ ㄔㄤˇ)
a firing range; a shooting range

靶子(ㄅㄚˇ ·ㄗ)
a target: 他的箭沒有射中靶子。His arrow missed the target.

【靷】 6740
ㄧㄣˇ yiin yǐn
the leather belts that connect a cart with the horse, etc.

【靸】 6741
1. ㄙㄚˇ saa sǎ
a child's shoes

靸鞋(ㄙㄚˇ ㄒㄧㄝˊ)
slippers

【靸】 6741
2. ㄊㄚˇ ta tǎ
to wear (shoes) in a casual way

五畫

【鞅】 6742
1. ㄧㄤ yeang yǎng
（又讀）1. ㄧㄤ iang yǎng
1. a martingale; a halter
2. a horse

鞅掌(ㄧㄤ ㄓㄤˇ)
weariness; all-bustled; to be overburdened

鞅鞅(ㄧ ㄤ ㄧ ㄤ)
discontentedly 亦作「怏怏」

【靺】 6743
ㄇㄛˋ moh mò
1. stockings
2. the Tungusic tribe

靺鞨(ㄇㄛˋ ㄏㄜˊ)
①the Tungusic tribe in ancient China ②name of a precious stone

【靼】 6744
ㄉㄚˊ dar dá
1. as in 韃靼—the Tartars
2. soft leather

六畫

【鞍】 6745
ㄢ an ān
a saddle, a saddle-like terrain or thing

鞍轡(ㄢ ㄆㄟˋ)
saddles and reins

鞍馬(ㄢ ㄇㄚˇ)
①(gymnastics) a pommel horse; a side horse ②saddle and horse

鞍馬勞頓(ㄢ ㄇㄚˇ ㄌㄠˊ ㄉㄨㄣˋ)
tired because of long travel on horseback; travel-worn

鞍子(ㄢ ·ㄗ)
a saddle

【鞋】 6746
ㄒㄧㄝˊ shye xié
shoes; footwear

鞋拔子(ㄒㄧㄝˊ ㄅㄚˊ ·ㄗ)
a shoehorn; a shoe lifter: 我穿鞋要用鞋拔子。I have to use a shoe lifter to put on my shoes.

鞋幫(ㄒㄧㄝˊ ㄅㄤ)
the sides of a shoe

鞋面(ㄒㄧㄝˊ ㄇㄧㄢˋ)
the vamp

鞋帶(ㄒㄧㄝˊ ㄉㄞˋ)
a shoestring; a shoelace

鞋底(ㄒㄧㄝˊ ㄉㄧˇ)or 鞋底子(ㄒㄧㄝˊ ㄉㄧˇ ·ㄗ)
the sole of a shoe: 這隻鞋的鞋底有一個洞。There is a hole in the sole of this shoe.

鞋店(ㄒㄧㄝˊ ㄉㄧㄢˋ)
a shoeshop

鞋童(ㄒㄧㄝˊ ㄊㄨㄥˊ)
a shoeshine boy

鞋墊(ㄒㄧㄝˊ ㄉㄧㄢˋ)
a shoepad; an insole

鞋跟(ㄒㄧㄝˊ ㄍㄣ)
the heel of a shoe

鞋扣(ㄒㄧㄝˊ ㄎㄡˋ)
shoe buckle

鞋匠(ㄒㄧㄝˊ ㄐㄧㄤˋ)
a shoemaker; a cobbler: 這位作家曾當過鞋匠。The writer had been a shoemaker.

鞋楦子(ㄒㄧㄝˊ ㄒㄩㄢˋ ·ㄗ)
a last; a shoe tree

鞋刷子(ㄒㄧㄝˊ ㄕㄨㄚ ·ㄗ)
a shoebrush

鞋油(ㄒㄧㄝˊ ㄧㄡˊ)
shoe polish

鞋襪(ㄒㄧㄝˊ ㄨㄚˋ)
shoes and socks

【鞏】 6747
ㄍㄨㄥˇ goong gǒng
1. to tie or bind with thongs
2. secure; firm; strong; to guard; to secure; to strengthen
3. a Chinese family name

鞏膜(ㄍㄨㄥˇ ㄇㄛˊ)
(anatomy) sclera

鞏固(ㄍㄨㄥˇ ㄍㄨˋ)
①strong; secure; well guarded ②to consolidate (one's position, strength, etc.)

七畫

【鞘】 6748
ㄑㄧㄠˋ chiaw qiào
a scabbard; a sheath

八畫

【鞠】 6749
ㄐㄩˊ jyu jú
1. to bow; a bow (as a gesture of respect)
2. a ball; a leather ball
3. to nourish; to raise or rear
4. young; tender
5. high
6. to exhaust
7. to admonish; to warn; to caution
8. to make judicial investigation
9. a Chinese family name

鞠躬(ㄐㄩˊ ㄍㄨㄥ)
to bow; a bow (as a gesture of respect): 主人鞠躬迎客。The host bowed his guest in.

鞠躬盡瘁，死而後已(ㄐㄩˊ ㄍㄨㄥ ㄐㄧㄣˋ ㄘㄨㄟˋ, ㄙˇ ㄦˊ ㄏㄡˋ ㄧˇ)
to devote oneself to the task until one's death; to concentrate on one's task till one's heart stops beating

鞠子(ㄐㄩˊ ·ㄗ)
a little child

鞠養(ㄐㄩˊ ㄧㄤˇ)or 鞠育(ㄐㄩˊ ㄩˋ)
to raise or rear kids

九畫

【鞭】 6750
ㄅㄧㄢ bian biān
1. a whip; a lash; to whip or lash; to flagellate; to flog
2. an ancient weapon shaped like a whip
3. a string of firecrackers

鞭背(ㄅㄧㄢ ㄅㄟ)
to whip the back as a form of punishment in ancient times

鞭辟(ㄅㄧㄢ ㄆㄧˋ)
to urge and encourage

鞭辟入裏(ㄅㄧㄢ ㄆㄧˋ ㄖㄨˋ ㄌㄧˇ)
deep-cutting; incisive; penetrating; trenchant

鞭炮(ㄅㄧㄢ ㄆㄠˋ)
(a long string of) firecrackers: 孩子們在燃放鞭炮。
The children are letting off firecrackers.

鞭扑(ㄅㄧㄢ ㄆㄨ)
to whip; to lash or chastise

鞭毛(ㄅㄧㄢ ㄇㄠˊ)
(biology) flagellum

鞭打(ㄅㄧㄢ ㄉㄚˇ)
to flog with a whip; to flagellate: 他屢次鞭打這個男孩。
He gave the boy repeated floggings.

鞭笞(ㄅㄧㄢ ㄔ)
to flog with a whip; to flagellate; to castigate

鞭刑(ㄅㄧㄢ ㄒㄧㄥˊ)
flogging

鞭笞(ㄅㄧㄢ ㄔ)
①to flog with a whip: 他毫無怨恨地接受了鞭笞。He took the whipping without a murmur. ②to urge or goad along

鞭長莫及(ㄅㄧㄢ ㄔㄤˊ ㄇㄛˋ ㄐㄧˊ)
beyond one's influence; beyond one's reach; out of range

鞭楚(ㄅㄧㄢ ㄔㄨˇ)
to whip; to flog; to flagellate

鞭箠 or 鞭捶(ㄅㄧㄢ ㄔㄨㄟˊ)
to flog with a whip

鞭尸(ㄅㄧㄢ ㄕ)
to give vent to one's hatred by whipping the body of a dead enemy or tyrant

鞭子(ㄅㄧㄢ ˙ㄗ)

a whip; a lash: 該拿鞭子抽他一頓。He wants the whiplash.

鞭策(ㄅㄧㄢ ㄘㄜˋ)
①a horsewhip ②to urge or goad on; to encourage: 我們應該經常鞭策自己，努力讀書。We should constantly urge ourselves on to study hard.

【鞦】 6751
ㄑㄧㄡ chiou qiū
1. a swing
2. a crupper
3. traces

鞦韆(ㄑㄧㄡ ㄑㄧㄢ)
a swing: 小孩子在邊鞦韆。The children were playing on the swings.

【鞧】 6752
ㄑㄧㄡ chiou qiū
a crupper

【鞨】 6753
ㄏㄜˊ her hé
as in 靺鞨—the Tungusic tribe in ancient China

鞨(ㄏㄜˊ)
a turban

【鞫】 6754
ㄐㄩ jyu jū
1. to question criminals
2. extreme poverty

【鞬】 6755
ㄐㄧㄢ jian jiān
1. a quiver (for arrows) on a horse
2. to store; to keep and collect

十畫

【韝】 6756
ㄍㄡ gou gōu
the armlet and glove of a falconer

鞲鞴(ㄍㄡ ㄅㄟˋ)
a piston

【鞳】 6757
ㄊㄚ tah tà
the sound of bells and drums

【鞴】 6758
ㄅㄟˋ bey bèi
as in 鞲鞴—a piston

鞴馬(ㄅㄟˋ ㄇㄚˇ)
to ride a horse

【鞶】 6759
ㄆㄢˊ parn pán
a large belt

十一畫

【鞺】 6760
ㄊㄤ tarng táng
the sound of drums

鞺鞳(ㄊㄤ ㄊㄚˋ)
the sound of bells and drums

十三畫

【韃】 6761
ㄉㄚˊ dar dá
Tartars

韃靼(ㄉㄚˊ ㄉㄚˊ)
Tartars

韃靼海峽(ㄉㄚˊ ㄉㄚˊ ㄏㄞˇ ㄒㄧㄚˊ)
Tatar Strait

【韁】 6762
ㄐㄧㄤ jiang jiāng
same as 繮—reins

十五畫

【韆】 6763
ㄑㄧㄢ chian qiān
as in 鞦韆—a swing

十七畫

【韉】 6764
ㄐㄧㄢ jian jiān
saddle cloth

韋 部
ㄨㄟˊ wei wéi

【韋】 6765
ㄨㄟˊ wei wéi
1. tanned leather; leather
2. a Chinese family name

韋伯斯特(ㄨㄟˊ ㄅㄛˊ ㄙ ㄊㄜˋ)
Noah Webster, 1758-1843, American lexicographer and essayist

韋編(ㄨㄟˊ ㄅㄧㄢ)
(before the invention of paper in China) a book consisting of bamboo slabs strung together with leather strings

韋編三絕(ㄨㄟˊ ㄅㄧㄢ ㄙㄢ ㄐㄩㄝˊ)
to study diligently

韋布(ㄨㄟˊ ㄅㄨˋ)
leather girdles and coarse cloth—the dress of com-

moners

韋帶（ㄨㄟ ㄉㄞˋ）
a leather girdle worn by a commoner

韋馱（ㄨㄟ ㄊㄨㄛˊ）
a Buddhist god whose job is to keep evils away and to guard the temple; Skanda

韋氏音標（ㄨㄟˊ ㄕˋ ㄧㄣ ㄅㄧㄠ）
phonetic symbols adopted in Webster's dictionaries

韋衣（ㄨㄟˊ ㄧ）
① hunting clothes ② simple clothes

三畫

【韌】 6766
ㄖㄣˋ renn rèn
soft but tough; elastic; pliable but strong; tenacious

韌皮（ㄖㄣˋ ㄆㄧˊ）
the bast (of a tree)

韌帶（ㄖㄣˋ ㄉㄞˋ）
(physiology) ligaments

韌度（ㄖㄣˋ ㄉㄨˋ）
resilience

韌性（ㄖㄣˋ ㄒㄧㄥˋ）
tenacity

五畫

【靫】 6767
ㄈㄨˊ fwu fú
a leather garment worn during sacrificial rituals in ancient times

八畫

【韓】 6768
ㄏㄢˊ harn hán
1. a fence
2. name of two feudal states in the late Chou Dynasty
3. short for the Republic of Korea
4. a Chinese family name

韓非（ㄏㄢˊ ㄈㄟ）
Han Fei, a famous legalist (? -234 B.C.) during the Epoch of Warring States

韓非子（ㄏㄢˊ ㄈㄟ ㄗˇ）
title of a 20-volume work by Han Fei (韓非)

韓柳（ㄏㄢˊ ㄌㄧㄡˇ）
Han Yü (韓愈) and Liu

Tzung-yüan (柳宗元), two leading writers of the Tang Dynasty

韓國（ㄏㄢˊ ㄍㄨㄛˊ）
① the Republic of Korea ② the state of Han in the Epoch of Spring and Autumn ③ the state of Han in the Epoch of Warring States

韓信（ㄏㄢˊ ㄒㄧㄣˋ）
Han Hsin, a famous general who helped found the Western Han Dynasty

韓戰（ㄏㄢˊ ㄓㄢˋ）
the Korean War (1950-1953)

韓世忠（ㄏㄢˊ ㄕˋ ㄓㄨㄥ）
Han Shih-chung (1089-1151), a famous general of the Sung Dynasty

韓愈（ㄏㄢˊ ㄩˋ）
Han Yu (768-824), a literary giant in the Tang Dynasty

【韔】 6769
ㄔㄤˋ chanq chàng
1. a wrapper or case for bow
2. to sheathe a bow; to put a bow in its case

九畫

【韙】 6770
ㄨㄟˇ woei wěi
right; proper; propriety

十畫

【韜】 6771
ㄊㄠ tau tāo
1. scabbards or sheaths for blades or swords
2. military strategy; tactics
3. to conceal
4. to idle

韜筆（ㄊㄠ ㄅㄧˇ）
to let the pen idle—to write no more

韜略（ㄊㄠ ㄌㄩㄝˋ）
military strategy or tactics

韜光（ㄊㄠ ㄍㄨㄤ）
① to conceal one's talents, gifts, etc. ② name of a learned Buddhist monk in the Tang Dynasty

韜光養晦（ㄊㄠ ㄍㄨㄤ ㄧㄤˇ ㄏㄨㄟˋ）
to conceal one's ability and hide one's time

韜弓（ㄊㄠ ㄍㄨㄥ）

to sheathe a bow; to put a bow in its case

韜晦（ㄊㄠ ㄏㄨㄟˋ）
to obscure; oblivion; to hide one's true capacities or intentions

【韞】 6772
ㄩㄣˋ yunn yùn
to conceal; to hide (one's talents, etc.)

韞櫝 or 韞匵（ㄩㄣˋ ㄉㄨˊ）
(said of a talented person) to live like a recluse; to prefer to be a commoner

---

韭 部
ㄐㄧㄡˇ jeou jiǔ

【韭】 6773
（韭）ㄐㄧㄡˇ jeou jiǔ
scallions; leeks; Chinese chives

韭花（ㄐㄧㄡˇ ㄏㄨㄚ）or 韭菜花（ㄐㄧㄡˇ ㄘㄞˋ ㄏㄨㄚ）
blossoms of leeks or scallions, edible when tender

韭黃（ㄐㄧㄡˇ ㄏㄨㄤˊ）
yellow, tender leeks or scallions

韭菜（ㄐㄧㄡˇ ㄘㄞˋ）
leeks or scallions

音 部
ㄧㄣ in yīn

【音】 6774
ㄧㄣ in yīn
1. sound; voice
2. tone; accent; timbre
3. a musical note
4. (usually used in correspondence) news; information; tidings: 他帶來佳音. He brought welcome news.

音波（ㄧㄣ ㄅㄛ）
sound waves 亦作「聲波」

音爆（ㄧㄣ ㄅㄠˋ）
a sonic boom: 我早上聽到了音爆。I heard the sonic boom this morning.

音標（ㄧㄣ ㄅㄧㄠ）

phonetic signs (or symbols)

音標文字(一ㄅㄧㄠˋㄇㄣˊㄗ丶)
phonetic transcription;
phonography

音變(一ㄅㄧㄢˋ)
change of intonation of
words in a sentence for
emphasis, etc.

音符(一ㄈㄨˊ)
(music) notes: 高音符我唱不
來. I can't sing the high
notes.

音帶(一ㄉㄞˋ)
the vocal cords

音調(一ㄉㄧㄠˋ)
① the pitch of a sound; tone:
她用高音調唱歌. She sings at
a high pitch. ② musical
pitch according to the standard of ancient pitch pipes

音量(一ㄌㄧㄤ丶)
the volume (of sound)

音律(一ㄌㄩ丶)
temperament

音高(一ㄍㄠ)
(music) pitch

音階(一ㄐㄧㄝ)
musical scale

音節(一ㄐㄧㄝˊ)
a syllable: "China" 是個兩音
節的字. "China" is a word
of two syllables.

音強(一ㄑㄧㄤˊ)
the loudness of a sound

音信(一ㄒㄧㄣˋ)or 音訊(一ㄒㄩㄣ丶)
news; information; tidings;
messages: 我一直沒有他的音
信. I have had no news from
him.

音響(一ㄒㄧㄤˇ)
① audio ② sound; acoustics

音響電子琴(一ㄒㄧㄤˇㄉㄧㄢˋㄗˇㄑㄧㄣˊ)
a synthesizer

音響效果(一ㄒㄧㄤˇㄒㄧㄠˋㄍㄨㄛˇ)
sound effect

音訊(一ㄒㄩㄣ丶)
letters; news

音訓(一ㄒㄩㄣˋ)
to teach the pronunciation
of a word and explain its
meaning

音質(一ㄓˊ)
tonality; tone quality

音叉(一ㄔㄚ)
a tuning fork

音塵(一ㄔㄣˊ)
traces; whereabouts

音長(一ㄔㄤˊ)
(phonetics) length

音程(一ㄔㄥˊ)
(music) interval

音書(一ㄕㄨ)
letters; correspondence;
information or news

音容(一ㄖㄨㄥˊ)
voice and countenance

音容宛在(一ㄖㄨㄥˊㄨㄢˇㄗㄞˋ)
(a conventional written
expression referring to the
deceased in a funeral rite)
His or her voice and appearance seem to be still with
us.

音色(一ㄙㄜ丶)or 音品(一ㄆㄧㄣˇ)
timbre (of a sound or
voice); tone color

音速(一ㄙㄨ丶)
the speed of sound (about
1,087 ft. per second or 738
miles per hour)

音素(一ㄙㄨ丶)
sound elements; phonemes

音義(一ㄧˋ)
pronunciation and meaning

音譯(一ㄧˋ)
transliteration by sound
rather than meaning (as 布
爾喬亞 for "bourgeois")

音問(一ㄨㄣ丶)
news or information; letter
or correspondence

音域(一ㄩˋ)
(music) the range; the compass; the register

音樂(一ㄩㄝˋ)
music: 他們隨音樂跳舞. They
danced to the music.

音樂比賽(一ㄩㄝˋㄅㄧˇㄙㄞˋ)
a musical competition

音樂電視(節目)(一ㄩㄝˋㄉㄧㄢˋㄕ
ㄐㄧㄝˊㄇㄨˋ)
MTV (Music Television)

音樂會(一ㄩㄝˋㄏㄨㄟ丶)
a concert; a musical recital

音樂家(一ㄩㄝˋㄐㄧㄚ)
a musician

音樂節(一ㄩㄝˋㄐㄧㄝˊ)
Music Day on April 5

音樂系(一ㄩㄝˋㄒㄧˋ)
the department of music in
college

音樂演奏(一ㄩㄝˋㄧㄢˇㄗㄡˋ)
a musical performance

音樂院(一ㄩㄝˋㄩㄢˋ)or 音樂學院
(一ㄩㄝˋㄒㄩㄝˊㄩㄢˋ)
a conservatory of music; the
academy of music

音韻(一ㄩㄣ丶)
a rhyme

音韻學(一ㄩㄣ丶ㄒㄩㄝˊ)
phonology

四畫

【韵】6775
(韻)ㄩㄣˋ yunn　yùn
1. rhyme
2. harmony

【歆】6776
ㄒㄧㄣ shin　xīn
1. to inhale; to smell
2. to envy
3. sacrificial food
4. to move; to touch
5. to admire

歆羨(ㄒㄧㄣㄒㄧㄢˋ)
to envy

五畫

【韶】6777
ㄕㄠˊ shaur　sháo
1. the music during the time of
the sage emperor Shun (舜)
2. beautiful; excellent; harmonious
3. continuous

韶光(ㄕㄠˊㄍㄨㄤ)or 韶華(ㄕㄠˊㄏㄨㄚˊ)
① beautiful scenes in the
spring: 韶華不再. Springtime
waits for no man. ② best
years of one's life—youth

韶秀(ㄕㄠˊㄒㄧㄡˋ)
good-looking and handsome

韶山(ㄕㄠˊㄕㄢ)
Shaoshan, a mountain in
Hunan Province

十畫

【韻】6778
ㄩㄣˋ yunn　yùn
1. rhymes
2. harmony of sound
3. refined; sophisticated; polished; elegant
4. vowels

韻母(ㄩㄣˋㄇㄨˇ)
vowel—an open sound

〔頁部〕

produced by the voice

韻母(ㄩㄣ ㄇㄨˇ)
vowel—a symbol representing an open sound produced by the voice

韻律(ㄩㄣ ㄌㄩˋ)
meter; rhythm; rhyme scheme

韻律舞(ㄩㄣ ㄌㄩˋ ㄨˇ)
an aerobic dance

韻腳(ㄩㄣ ㄐㄧㄠˇ)
rhyme at the end of a line of poetry

韻致(ㄩㄣ ㄓˋ)
a manner; a poise; a style

韻事(ㄩㄣ ㄕˋ)
a romantic incident of an intellectual which smacks of refined taste and elegant style; a romantic affair: 張先生的韻事極多。Mr. Chang's romantic affairs are numerous.

韻書(ㄩㄣ ㄕㄨ)
books listing characters grouped under various rhymes; a dictionary of rhymes

韻味(ㄩㄣ ㄨㄟˋ)
refined and sophisticated taste; lingering charm; lasting appeal

韻文(ㄩㄣ ㄨㄣˊ)
a rhymed composition; verse: 韻文不一定就是好詩。Not all verse is great poetry.

韻語(ㄩㄣ ㄩˇ)
① rhymed sentences or phrases ② a refined remark

十三畫

〔響〕 6779
ㄒㄧㄤˇ sheang xiǎng
1. a report; a sound; an echo; a noise: 我聽到一聲炮響。I heard a report of a cannon.
2. (said of sound) loud or high: 馬達聲太響了。The motor's too loud (or noisy).
3. to make a sound; to sound; to ring: 門鈴響了。The doorbell rang.

響馬(ㄒㄧㄤˇ ㄇㄚˇ)
mounted highwaymen in North China—so called for shooting a sounding arrow as a signal for action

響動(ㄒㄧㄤˇ ㄉㄨㄥˋ)
sound of something tumultuous

響亮(ㄒㄧㄤˇ ㄌㄧㄤˋ)
① sonorous; loud and clear; stentorian: 別用空洞而響亮的文句。Don't use phrases of empty sonorousness. ② straightforward

響鈴(兒)(ㄒㄧㄤˇ ㄌㄧㄥˊ ㄦ)
a bell

響箭(ㄒㄧㄤˇ ㄐㄧㄢˋ)
sounding arrows, used in old days as signals

響徹(ㄒㄧㄤˇ ㄔㄜˋ)
to resound through; to reverberate through: 勝利的歌聲響徹雲霄。Songs of victory resound through the skies.

響聲(ㄒㄧㄤˇ ㄕㄥ)
a sound; an echo; a noise: 聽不見響聲了。No more sound was heard.

響應(ㄒㄧㄤˇ ㄧㄥˋ)
to echo in support; to respond favorably; to rise in support

響尾蛇(ㄒㄧㄤˇ ㄨㄟˇ ㄕㄜˊ)
the rattlesnake; the sidewinder

響尾蛇飛彈(ㄒㄧㄤˇ ㄨㄟˇ ㄕㄜˊ ㄈㄟ ㄉㄢˋ)
(military) a sidewinder

頁 部
ㄧㄝˋ yeh yè

〔頁〕 6780
ㄧㄝˋ yeh yè
a page (in books, etc.); a sheet (of paper, etc.): 他撕下一頁。He tore one of the pages.

頁邊(ㄧㄝˋ ㄅㄧㄢ)
the margin

頁碼(ㄧㄝˋ ㄇㄚˇ)
the page number

頁次(ㄧㄝˋ ㄘˋ)
the page number

頁岩(ㄧㄝˋ ㄧㄢˊ)
shale

二畫

〔頂〕 6781
ㄉㄧㄥˇ diing dǐng
1. the top of anything
2. the crown of the head
3. topmost; extremely; very: 這本手冊頂有用的。The handbook is very useful.
4. to carry (a weight) on one's head; to push the head against; to wear on the head
5. to gore; to butt: 這牛不會頂人的。This bull does not gore people.
6. to push up; to prop up
7. to cope with; to stand up to
8. to substitute: 教練叫我頂替那投手。The coach told me to substitute for that pitcher.
9. to equal; to be equivalent to
10. to offend intentionally; to retort; to turn down: 他頂了他的母親幾句。He said a few words to his mother in retort.
11. used as a unit

頂拜(ㄉㄧㄥˇ ㄅㄞˋ)
to kneel down and kowtow

頂讓(ㄉㄧㄥˇ ㄖㄤˋ)
to buy a shop from another person after it has been liquidated

頂批(ㄉㄧㄥˇ ㄆㄧ)
running commentaries on the upper margin of the pages in a Chinese book

頂名(ㄉㄧㄥˇ ㄇㄧㄥˊ)
to assume someone's name with the intent to cheat

頂風(ㄉㄧㄥˇ ㄈㄥ)
① to move against the wind: 他們頂風而行。They walk against the wind. ② a head wind

頂峰(ㄉㄧㄥˇ ㄈㄥ)
the peak; the summit; the pinnacle

頂大(ㄉㄧㄥˇ ㄉㄚˋ)
the largest

頂戴(ㄉㄧㄥˇ ㄉㄞˋ)
① to salute or pay respects to ② (Ching Dynasty) the color and quality of the bead on the ceremonial hat of an official, which indicates the wearer's rank ③ to wear on one's head

頂點(ㄉㄧㄥˇ ㄉㄧㄢˇ)
the pinnacle; the topmost;

the top (of a hill); the utmost; the apex; the zenith; the acme: 他曾經達到了名氣的頂點。He was once on the pinnacle of fame.

頂多(ㄉㄧㄥˇ ㄉㄨㄛ)
at (the) most; at best

頂端(ㄉㄧㄥˇ ㄉㄨㄢ)
the top; the peak; the apex

頂頭(ㄉㄧㄥˇ ㄊㄡˊ)
① the top; a superior officer
② the opposite; the end

頂頭上司(ㄉㄧㄥˇ ㄊㄡˊ ㄕㄤˋ ㄙ)
the immediate boss

頂替(ㄉㄧㄥˇ ㄊㄧˋ)
① to assume someone's name with the intent to cheat ② to represent someone; to take someone's place: 主席走了誰來頂替他？Who's going to take the chairman's place after he leaves?

頂天立地(ㄉㄧㄥˇ ㄊㄧㄢ ㄌㄧˋ ㄉㄧˋ)
(literally) with one's feet planted on the ground and head supporting the sky—independent and indomitable

頂禮膜拜(ㄉㄧㄥˇ ㄌㄧˇ ㄇㄛˊ ㄅㄞˋ)
to bow and kneel in worship; to pay homage to

頂缸(ㄉㄧㄥˇ ㄍㄤ)
to take the blame for someone else

頂骨(ㄉㄧㄥˇ ㄍㄨˇ)
parietal bones

頂瓜瓜 or 頂呱呱(ㄉㄧㄥˇ ㄍㄨㄚ ㄍㄨㄚ)
topmost; the top; the best; excellent; first-rate: 他的英文真是頂呱呱的。His English is indeed excellent.

頂好(ㄉㄧㄥˇ ㄏㄠˇ)
the best; the first; the topmost; good; excellent; wonderful: 近來天氣頂好的。The weather has been wonderful.

頂角(ㄉㄧㄥˇ ㄐㄧㄠ)
(mathematics) a vertical angle; a vertex angle

頂尖(ㄉㄧㄥˇ ㄐㄧㄢ)
the peak; the highest point; the top; the best: 他在班上的成績是頂尖的。He is at the top of his class.

頂針(ㄉㄧㄥˇ ㄓㄣ)
a thimble

頂真(ㄉㄧㄥˇ ㄓㄣ)
to do something in a serious manner; to take something seriously: 我只是在開玩笑，別太頂真了。I am only joking; don't take it too seriously.

頂住(ㄉㄧㄥˇ ㄓㄨˋ)
to support with the head; to brace or strengthen something with a support

頂撞(ㄉㄧㄥˇ ㄓㄨㄤˋ)
to offend or dispute with words; to talk back; to contradict (one's elder or superior): 他公然頂撞我。He contradicted me openly.

頂踵(ㄉㄧㄥˇ ㄓㄨㄥˇ)
from head to heel

頂少(ㄉㄧㄥˇ ㄕㄠˇ)
at least

頂上(ㄉㄧㄥˇ ㄕㄤˋ)
① on the top; the highest point ② the best; top-grade

頂上功夫(ㄉㄧㄥˇ ㄕㄤˋ ㄍㄨㄥ ㄈㄨ)
the work at the top of the head—the work of the barber

頂嘴(ㄉㄧㄥˇ ㄗㄨㄟˇ)
① to quarrel ② to argue with a superior or an elder; to reply defiantly; to answer (or talk) back: 不要頂嘴，否則我就處罰你。Don't answer (me) back, or I'll punish you.

頂罪(ㄉㄧㄥˇ ㄗㄨㄟˋ)
to act as a fall guy; to be a scapegoat; to receive punishment for another person

頂罪者(ㄉㄧㄥˇ ㄗㄨㄟˋ ㄓㄜˇ)
a whipping boy 亦作「代人受過者」

頂喪駕靈(ㄉㄧㄥˇ ㄙㄤ ㄐㄧㄚˋ ㄌㄧㄥˊ)
(said of the sons of the deceased) to carry streamers and protect the spirit of their father or mother beside the coffin in a funeral procession

頂芽(ㄉㄧㄥˇ ㄧㄚˊ)
(botany) a terminal bud

【頃】 6782
ㄑㄧㄥˇ chiing qǐng
1. a moment; an instant; just; just now
2. a hundred *mu* (畝) —10,000 square meters
3. to lean toward one side; to

---

incline

頃步(ㄑㄧㄥˇ ㄅㄨˋ)
half a step

頃刻(ㄑㄧㄥˇ ㄎㄜˋ)
in a short moment: 他頃刻就來。He will be here in less than a moment.

頃刻之間(ㄑㄧㄥˇ ㄎㄜˋ ㄓ ㄐㄧㄢ)
in a twinkling; in an instant

頃者(ㄑㄧㄥˇ ㄓㄜˇ)
just now; a short while ago

三畫

【項】 6783
ㄒㄧㄤˋ shiang xiàng
1. the back of the neck; the nape
2. the back of a cap or crown
3. an item; an article; a matter; a kind; a class
4. funds; a sum of money
5. (mathematics) a term
6. a Chinese family name

項背相望(ㄒㄧㄤˋ ㄅㄟˋ ㄒㄧㄤ ㄨㄤˋ)
to walk in an unbroken procession; one after another in close succession

項目(ㄒㄧㄤˋ ㄇㄨˋ)
an item; an article (in an agreement, etc.)

項鍊(ㄒㄧㄤˋ ㄌㄧㄢˋ)
a necklace

項領(ㄒㄧㄤˋ ㄌㄧㄥˇ)
① the large neck ② strategic positions or places

項圈(ㄒㄧㄤˋ ㄑㄩㄢ)
a collar; a necklace

項下(ㄒㄧㄤˋ ㄒㄧㄚˋ)
under a certain article or item

項莊舞劍，意在沛公(ㄒㄧㄤˋ ㄓㄨㄤ ㄨˇ ㄐㄧㄢˋ，ㄧˋ ㄗㄞˋ ㄆㄟˋ ㄍㄨㄥ)
Hsiang Chuang performed the sword dance as a cover for his attempt on Liu Pang's life.—to act with a hidden motive

項羽(ㄒㄧㄤˋ ㄩˇ) or 項籍(ㄒㄧㄤˋ ㄐㄧ)
Hsiang Yü, a great warrior who contested the throne with the founding emperor of the Western Han Dynasty and lost

【順】 6784
ㄕㄨㄣˋ shuenn shùn
1. to follow; to submit to; obe-

〔頁部〕

dient; to cause to surrender; to fall in with: 他順從了多數的決定。He submitted to the majority decision

2. in the same direction as; with; along: 船隨流而下。The ship went downstream.

3. agreeable; favorable; comfortable; happy; 她的聲音很順耳。Her voice is agreeable on the ear.

4. to arrange; to put in order

5. convenient; smooth

6. to take the opportunity to

順便(ㄕㄨㄣˋ ㄅㄧㄢˋ)
at one's convenience; (to do something) while on one's way to perform a major work; without taking extra trouble: 我可以順便做完它。I can finish doing it without taking extra trouble.

順民(ㄕㄨㄣˋ ㄇㄧㄣˊ)
① the people who surrender to their new lord ② people who leave their fate to heaven

順命(ㄕㄨㄣˋ ㄇㄧㄥˋ)
① to obey orders ② to leave one's fate to heaven; resigned to one's fate

順風(ㄕㄨㄣˋ ㄈㄥ)
① to move with the wind: 祝你一路順風。May you have a pleasant journey. 或 *Bon voyage.* ② good luck ③ a favorable wind; a tail wind

順風轉舵(ㄕㄨㄣˋ ㄈㄥ ㄓㄨㄢˇ ㄉㄨㄛˋ)
to trim one's sails; to take one's cue from changing conditions

順風扯旗(ㄕㄨㄣˋ ㄈㄥ ㄔㄜˇ ㄑㄧˊ)
to do an undertaking at an opportune moment

順風吹火(ㄕㄨㄣˋ ㄈㄥ ㄔㄨㄟ ㄏㄨㄛˇ)
to do a job made easy by outside help

順風而呼(ㄕㄨㄣˋ ㄈㄥ ㄦˊ ㄏㄨ)
to promote a public cause; to champion a cause that enjoys popular support

順風耳(ㄕㄨㄣˋ ㄈㄥ ㄦˇ)
① an old-fashioned loudspeaker ② (in Chinese mythology) ears that could hear sounds miles away; a clairaudient ③ a well-informed person: 他是我們這個社區的順

風耳。He is a well-informed man in our community.

順道(ㄕㄨㄣˋ ㄉㄠˋ)
① to obey good reasons ② to do something on the way to a place, which requires no additional travel

順當(ㄕㄨㄣˋ ㄉㄤ)
without a hitch; easy and smooth: 一切進行順當。Everything went off without a hitch.

順條順理(ㄕㄨㄣˋ ㄊㄧㄠˊ ㄕㄨㄣˋ ㄌㄧˇ)
pliant; obedient; to go along; to comply

順天者昌，逆天者亡(ㄕㄨㄣˋ ㄊㄧㄢ ㄓㄜˇ ㄔㄤ, ㄋㄧˋ ㄊㄧㄢ ㄓㄜˇ ㄨㄤˊ)
(said of rulers) Those who obey the mandate of heaven will prosper, while those who defy it will perish.

順天應人(ㄕㄨㄣˋ ㄊㄧㄢ ㄧㄥˋ ㄖㄣˊ)
(said of a monarch) to follow the mandate of heaven and comply with the wishes of the people

順理(ㄕㄨㄣˋ ㄌㄧˇ)
reasonable; logical

順理成章(ㄕㄨㄣˋ ㄌㄧˇ ㄔㄥˊ ㄓㄤ)
logical; as a matter of course

順利(ㄕㄨㄣˋ ㄌㄧˋ)
(going) smoothly; easy (going); having no trouble; encountering no difficulties; without a hitch: 會議正順利進行。The meeting is going on smoothly.

順流(ㄕㄨㄣˋ ㄌㄧㄡˊ)
① going with the (water) current: 他順流游泳。He swam with the current. ② to do things properly or according to reason

順溜(ㄕㄨㄣˋ ㄌㄧㄡ)
① easy and amiable ② kind and peaceful ③ without any hindrance; smooth

順路(ㄕㄨㄣˋ ㄌㄨˋ)
in passing; while on the way; direct route: 到學校這麼走不順路。This is not the direct route to school.

順竿兒爬(ㄕㄨㄣˋ ㄍㄢ ㄦ ㄆㄚˊ)
to fawn; to act as a yes-man; to fall readily in with other people's wishes

順口(ㄕㄨㄣˋ ㄎㄡˇ)
① to speak without much thought; to slip out of one's tongue; to talk casually: 他也不想想就順口說了。He spoke without thinking. ② easy to speak, read or sing ③ to suit one's taste: 這些點心我吃得很順口。I like the taste of these desserts.

順口溜(ㄕㄨㄣˋ ㄎㄡˇ ㄌㄧㄡ)
doggerel; a jingle

順候(ㄕㄨㄣˋ ㄏㄡˋ)
(used in the conclusion of a letter, roughly equivalent to) with best wishes or regards

順化(ㄕㄨㄣˋ ㄏㄨㄚˋ)
① to obey the law of nature ② Hue, old capital of Vietnam

順境(ㄕㄨㄣˋ ㄐㄧㄥˋ)
in easy circumstances; in favorable circumstances: 處順境之人不可志得意滿。One should not be complacent in easy circumstances.

順其自然(ㄕㄨㄣˋ ㄑㄧˊ ㄗˋ ㄖㄢˊ)
to let nature take its course; in accordance with its natural tendency

順情順理(ㄕㄨㄣˋ ㄑㄧㄥˊ ㄕㄨㄣˋ ㄌㄧˇ)
in accordance with propriety and reason

順心(ㄕㄨㄣˋ ㄒㄧㄣ)
satisfactorily; gratifying: 他最近過得很順心。He spent his life satisfactorily recently.

順序(ㄕㄨㄣˋ ㄒㄩˋ)
according to right order; sequence

順治(ㄕㄨㄣˋ ㄓˋ)
the reigning title of the first emperor of the Ching Dynasty

順差(ㄕㄨㄣˋ ㄔㄚ)
favorable balance; surplus

順暢(ㄕㄨㄣˋ ㄔㄤˋ)
smooth; unhindered

順時(ㄕㄨㄣˋ ㄕˊ)
① on time ② to be in luck

順事(ㄕㄨㄣˋ ㄕˋ)
matters that one is happy to talk about; matters that make one leap with joy

順適(ㄕㄨㄣˋ ㄕˋ)
(said of one's manner) casual, composed, or natural

順勢(ㄕㄨㄣˋ ㄕˋ)
to take advantage of an opportunity (as provided by an opponent's reckless move)

順手(ㄕㄨㄣˋ ㄕㄡˇ)
①smooth (operation); easy (going): 事情辦得相當順手。It was done quite smoothly. ② to do something without extra trouble ③handy; conveniently

順手牽羊(ㄕㄨㄣˋ ㄕㄡˇ ㄑㄧㄢ ㄧㄤˊ)
to steal something in passing; to steal something without premeditation because the article in question happens to be conveniently located when one chances to see it; to pick up something on the sly

順守(ㄕㄨㄣˋ ㄕㄡˇ)
just to carry on according to former practices

順水(ㄕㄨㄣˋ ㄕㄨㄟˇ)
(to sail) with the stream or current; downstream: 順水游泳或划船都不難。It is easy to swim or row downstream.

順水推舟(ㄕㄨㄣˋ ㄕㄨㄟˇ ㄊㄨㄟ ㄓㄡ)
to approve something that is sure to succeed; to render help where it is scarcely needed; to make use of an opportunity to gain one's end

順水人情(ㄕㄨㄣˋ ㄕㄨㄟˇ ㄖㄣˊ ㄑㄧㄥˊ)
to do someone a favor without causing oneself any trouble; a favor done at little cost to oneself

順嘴兒(ㄕㄨㄣˋ ㄗㄨㄟˇㄦ)
to speak casually without much thought; to slip out of one's tongue

順從(ㄕㄨㄣˋ ㄘㄨㄥˊ)
①to obey; obedient; to comply ②(psychology) submission

順俗(ㄕㄨㄣˋ ㄙㄨˊ)
to act according to the customs; to go with the crowd

順遂(ㄕㄨㄣˋ ㄙㄨㄟˋ)
without a hitch or obstruction; very smooth or easy going; in satisfactory circumstances

順耳(ㄕㄨㄣˋ ㄦˇ)
pleasant to the ear

順延(ㄕㄨㄣˋ ㄧㄢˊ)
to postpone for one day, and another day, and so on, in case of necessity (as in the case of poor weather upsetting a games schedule); to put off until another time: 他們把遠足順延到下個月。They put off the outing till next month.

順眼(ㄕㄨㄣˋ ㄧㄢˇ)
to please the eye; pleasant to the eye: 他看起來挺順眼的。He pleases the eye.

順應(ㄕㄨㄣˋ ㄧㄥˋ)
to adjust (to changes)

順應潮流(ㄕㄨㄣˋ ㄧㄥˋ ㄔㄠˊ ㄌㄧㄡˊ)
to conform to modern trends

順應時代(ㄕㄨㄣˋ ㄧㄥˋ ㄕˊ ㄉㄞˋ)
to conform to the times

【頇】6785
ㄏㄢ han hān
as in 顢頇-stupid and incompetent; foolish and slow

【須】6786
ㄒㄩ shiu xū
1. to have to; must; to need: 他必須很努力。He has to make a great effort.
2. necessary; proper
3. probably
4. a beard
5. a moment; a while
6. to wait for
7. to stop at
8. a Chinese family name

須得(ㄒㄩ ㄉㄜˊ)
must have; should have

須待(ㄒㄩ ㄉㄞˋ)
①to have to wait until⋯ ② to expect; to look forward to

須當(ㄒㄩ ㄉㄤ)
must: 此事須當如此。You must do it like this.

須知(ㄒㄩ ㄓ)
①to have to know; should know ②that which is essential to know—common knowledge; to note

須要(ㄒㄩ ㄧㄠˋ)
to have to; must: 你須要趕快去。You must go quickly.

須臾(ㄒㄩ ㄩˊ)
in an instant; a short while or moment: 他們須臾不可分離。They cannot do without

each other even for a short moment.

四畫

【頌】6787
ㄙㄨㄥˋ sonq sòng
1. to praise; to acclaim; an accolade; to extol; to eulogize; to laud
2. a hymn to something; a composition in praise of some achievements, etc.; an ode; a eulogy; a paean
3. a section in The Book of Poetry 詩經

頌美(ㄙㄨㄥˋ ㄇㄟˇ)
to praise the achievements of others; to acclaim

頌德碑(ㄙㄨㄥˋ ㄉㄜˊ ㄅㄟ)
a stone tablet with inscriptions in praise of the achievements in the administration of an official

頌歌(ㄙㄨㄥˋ ㄍㄜ)
hymns; odes

頌聲載道(ㄙㄨㄥˋ ㄕㄥ ㄗㄞˋ ㄉㄠˋ)
praises all along the way—popular support

頌讚(ㄙㄨㄥˋ ㄗㄢˋ)
to praise; acclaim; an accolade

頌詞(ㄙㄨㄥˋ ㄘˊ)
a message of praise, congratulations or felicitations; a eulogy; a complimentary address; a speech delivered by an ambassador on presentation of his credentials

頌揚(ㄙㄨㄥˋ ㄧㄤˊ)
to praise; to acclaim; to eulogize; to laud; to extol: 無私,是值得頌揚的。Unselfishness is laudable.

【頎】6788
ㄑㄧˊ chyi qí
tall (physical build)

頎然(ㄑㄧˊ ㄖㄢˊ)
tall

【頏】6789
ㄏㄤˊ harng háng
as in 頡頏-to match; to contest; birds flying up and down; well-matched

【預】6790
ㄩˋ yuh yù
1. beforehand; previously; in advance: 我們預先商量一下。

Let's have a talk about it in advance.
2. to prepare; to make ready; reserve (funds, troops, etc.)
3. to take part in

〔頁部〕

預備(ㄩˋ ㄅㄟˋ)
to prepare; to get ready beforehand; preparatory; 你們預備好了嗎? Are you all ready?

預備兵(ㄩˋ ㄅㄟˋ ㄅㄧㄥ)
reservists

預備會議(ㄩˋ ㄅㄟˋ ㄏㄨㄟˋ ㄧˋ)
a preparatory meeting or conference

預備金(ㄩˋ ㄅㄟˋ ㄐㄧㄣ)
reserve funds; budget allowance

預備軍官(ㄩˋ ㄅㄟˋ ㄐㄩㄣ ㄍㄨㄢ)
a reserve officer; an officer on the reserve list

預備役(ㄩˋ ㄅㄟˋ ㄧˋ)
reserve service

預報(ㄩˋ ㄅㄠˋ)
a forecast; an advance notice or announcement: 根據天氣預報, 明天是晴天。According to the weather forecast tomorrow will be fine.

預(ㄩˋ ㄅㄨˇ)
to augur; to foretell; to predict: 這件事情的結果如何尚難預卜。The consequence of this thing is hard to predict.

預謀(ㄩˋ ㄇㄡˊ)
to scheme or plan beforehand; premeditated (manslaughter, etc.)

預防(ㄩˋ ㄈㄤˊ)
to prevent beforehand; to nip in the bud; to prepare against; to forestall; prevention: 預防勝於治療。Prevention is better than cure.

預防注射(ㄩˋ ㄈㄤˊ ㄓㄨˋ ㄕㄜˋ)
preventive inoculation

預防醫學(ㄩˋ ㄈㄤˊ ㄧ ㄒㄩㄝˊ)
preventive medicine

預付(ㄩˋ ㄈㄨˋ)
to pay in advance

預付費用(ㄩˋ ㄈㄨˋ ㄈㄟˋ ㄩㄥˋ)
prepaid expenses

預付利息(ㄩˋ ㄈㄨˋ ㄌㄧˋ ㄒㄧ)
prepaid interest

預定(ㄩˋ ㄉㄧㄥˋ)
① to reserve (seats, rooms, etc.) 參看「預訂」② to set (a date, etc.); to be scheduled

預訂(ㄩˋ ㄉㄧㄥˋ)
to subscribe or order in advance; to place an order; to book; to reserve: 房間這全預訂一空。All rooms are reserved.

預力混凝土(ㄩˋ ㄌㄧˋ ㄏㄨㄣˋ ㄋㄧㄥˊ ㄊㄨˇ)
prestressed concrete

預料(ㄩˋ ㄌㄧㄠˋ)
to predict; to surmise; to anticipate; to expect: 沒有人預料到會有驟雨。Nobody expected the shower.

預留(ㄩˋ ㄌㄧㄡˊ)
to put aside for later use; to keep something in reserve

預告(ㄩˋ ㄍㄠˋ)
to inform or notify beforehand; advance notice; to herald; to preannounce

預告片(ㄩˋ ㄍㄠˋ ㄆㄧㄢˋ)
(motion picture) a trailer

預購(ㄩˋ ㄍㄡˋ)
to purchase in advance

預感(ㄩˋ ㄍㄢˇ)
① a premonition; a presentiment: 我有不祥的預感。I have a bad presentiment. ② to have a premonition

預科(ㄩˋ ㄎㄜ)
a preparatory course

預計(ㄩˋ ㄐㄧˋ)
to estimate; to surmise; to calculate in advance

預計成本(ㄩˋ ㄐㄧˋ ㄔㄥˊ ㄅㄣˇ)
predetermined costs

預計收入(ㄩˋ ㄐㄧˋ ㄕㄡ ㄖㄨˋ)
anticipated revenue

預借(ㄩˋ ㄐㄧㄝˋ)
to borrow or draw money (or one's salary) in advance

預繳(ㄩˋ ㄐㄧㄠˇ)
to pay (taxes, etc.) in advance

預見(ㄩˋ ㄐㄧㄢˋ)
to anticipate; to envision; to foresee; foresight; prevision: 這結果是可以預見的。This result can be predicted.

預期(ㄩˋ ㄑㄧˊ)
to expect; to estimate; to anticipate: 結果和預期的相符。The results are consistent with expectations.

預習(ㄩˋ ㄒㄧˊ)
①(said of students) to prepare lessons before class ② to rehearse or drill; rehearsal or drill

預先(ㄩˋ ㄒㄧㄢ)
beforehand; in advance: 你應好預先聲明。You'd better state it explicitly beforehand.

預想(ㄩˋ ㄒㄧㄤˇ)
to anticipate; to expect

預選(ㄩˋ ㄒㄩㄢˇ)
① a preliminary selection o contest ② primaries (in th U.S. presidential election etc.)

預支(ㄩˋ ㄓ)
to draw (salary) in advanc

預支費用(ㄩˋ ㄓ ㄈㄟˋ ㄩㄥˋ)
prepaid expenses

預知(ㄩˋ ㄓ)
to know beforehand or i advance; a fore-knowledge

預兆(ㄩˋ ㄓㄠˋ)
an omen; premonition; presage; a sign; a harbinger 這是吉祥的預兆。It is an auspicious omen.

預展(ㄩˋ ㄓㄢˇ)
a preview (of an exhibition

預政(ㄩˋ ㄓㄥˋ)
to take an active part i politics

預鑄混凝土(ㄩˋ ㄓㄨˋ ㄏㄨㄣˋ ㄋㄧㄥˊ ㄊㄨˇ)
precast concrete

預鑄式房屋(ㄩˋ ㄓㄨˋ ㄕˋ ㄈㄤˊ ㄨ)
a prefabricated house; a fab

預祝(ㄩˋ ㄓㄨˋ)
to congratulate (victory o success) beforehand

預產期(ㄩˋ ㄔㄢˇ ㄑㄧ)
(medicine) the estimate date of childbirth (E.D.C.)

預示(ㄩˋ ㄕˋ)
to betoken; to indicate

預審(ㄩˋ ㄕㄣˇ)
a preliminary trial; a inquest

預測(ㄩˋ ㄘㄜˋ)
to predict; to make a fore cast; prediction: 並非所有的 天氣預測都準確。Not all th predictions about the weath er will come true.

預賽(ㄩˋ ㄙㄞˋ)

a preliminary competition; an elimination contest; a trial match

預算
an estimate; a budget; to calculate in advance: 每人都應該有自己的預算。Everybody must have a budget of his own.

預算案(ㄩㄙㄨㄢˋ ㄢˋ)
the budget as a bill in the assembly

預言(ㄩˋ ㄧㄢˊ)
① prophecy; a prediction; a forecast: 有些人自稱有預言的本能。Some people claim to have natural powers of prediction. ② to predict; to foretell

預言家(ㄩˋ ㄧㄢˊ ㄐㄧㄚ)
a prophet; a fortuneteller

預演(ㄩˋ ㄧㄢˇ)
a preview; a rehearsal: 我們預演之後見面。We'll meet after rehearsal.

預聞(ㄩˋ ㄨㄣˊ)
to participate in; to interfere with

預約(ㄩˋ ㄩㄝ)
a preliminary agreement; to preengage; to subscribe for a book that is to be published; to make an appointment

預約掛號(ㄩˋ ㄩㄝ ㄍㄨㄚˋ ㄏㄠˋ)
to have an appointment with a doctor

【頑】 6791
ㄨㄢˊ　wán
1. stupid; dull; ignorant
2. obstinate; stubborn
3. recalcitrant; unruly; defiant
4. to play
5. naughty or impish

頑皮(ㄨㄢˊ ㄆㄧˊ)
naughty or impish (children)

頑民(ㄨㄢˊ ㄇㄧㄣˊ)
unruly or ungovernable people; refractory people

頑鈍(ㄨㄢˊ ㄉㄨㄣˋ)
① foolish; stupid; dull ② a person without principles; a shameless person

頑童(ㄨㄢˊ ㄊㄨㄥˊ)
naughty or unruly children; an urchin

頑劣(ㄨㄢˊ ㄌㄧㄝˋ)
stubborn and stupid; good-for-nothing

頑懦矗立(ㄨㄢˊ ㄌㄧㄢˊ ㄗㄨㄥˇ ㄌㄧˋ)
to lead the people toward virtuous ways

頑梗(ㄨㄢˊ ㄍㄥˇ)
foolishly stubborn or obstinate; perverse; pigheaded

頑固(ㄨㄢˊ ㄍㄨˋ)
① stubborn; obstinate; headstrong: 他像騾子一樣頑固。He is as stubborn as a mule. ② ultraconservative

頑固份子(ㄨㄢˊ ㄍㄨˋ ㄈㄣˋ ㄗˇ)
die-hards

頑抗(ㄨㄢˊ ㄎㄤˋ)
to resist stubbornly; stubborn resistance

頑健(ㄨㄢˊ ㄐㄧㄢˋ)
(I'm) still healthy and strong—a polite expression: 頑健如故。I am in good health as usual.

頑強(ㄨㄢˊ ㄑㄧㄤˊ)
stubborn; obstinacy; tenacious

頑癬(ㄨㄢˊ ㄒㄧㄢˇ)
ringworm that is difficult to cure; stubborn dermatitis

頑石(ㄨㄢˊ ㄕˊ)
unpolished stones or coarse rocks

頑石點頭(ㄨㄢˊ ㄕˊ ㄉㄧㄢˇ ㄊㄡˊ)
(said of statements or teachings) so persuasive and moving that even the rocks nod in agreement

頑耍(ㄨㄢˊ ㄕㄨㄚˇ)
to play; to romp about: 他們正在院子裡頑耍。They are romping about in the yard.

【頒】 6792
ㄅㄢ　bān
1. to bestow on; to grant; to confer on
2. to proclaim; to make public; to promulgate
3. to distribute; to send out

頒布(ㄅㄢ ㄅㄨˋ)
to proclaim or promulgate (laws or regulations, orders, etc.): 國王頒布了一項命令。The king promulgated a decree.

頒發(ㄅㄢ ㄈㄚ)
to bestow; to award or distribute (prizes, etc.)

頒獎(ㄅㄢ ㄐㄧㄤˇ)
to hand out an award or prize

頒行(ㄅㄢ ㄒㄧㄥˊ)
to promulgate and enforce; to make public and put into practice

頒賜(ㄅㄢ ㄘˋ)
to confer (honors or degrees) on someone

【頓】 6793
1. ㄉㄨㄣˋ　duenn　dùn
1. to stop or halt; to pause
2. to kowtow
3. to stamp (the foot)
4. to arrange; to put in order
5. a time; a turn
6. immediately; promptly
7. to be tired; to fall apart
8. to be broken
9. a Chinese family name

頓巴敦橡園(ㄉㄨㄣˋ ㄅㄚ ㄉㄨㄣˋ ㄒㄧㄤˋ ㄩㄢˊ)
the Dumbarton Oaks, an estate in the District of Columbia

頓巴敦橡園會議(ㄉㄨㄣˋ ㄅㄚ ㄉㄨㄣˋ ㄒㄧㄤˋ ㄩㄢˊ ㄏㄨㄟˋ ㄧˋ)
the Dumbarton Oaks Conference—It was held at the Dumbarton Oaks to discuss proposals for creation of the United Nations, August — October, 1944.

頓筆(ㄉㄨㄣˋ ㄅㄧˇ)
① to stop writing ② to pause in writing

頓開茅塞(ㄉㄨㄣˋ ㄎㄞ ㄇㄠˊ ㄙㄜˋ)
suddenly see the light; suddenly come to an understanding

頓口無言(ㄉㄨㄣˋ ㄎㄡˇ ㄨˊ ㄧㄢˊ)
to have nothing to say in reply; to be completely silenced

頓河(ㄉㄨㄣˋ ㄏㄜˊ)
the Don River, in European U.S.S.R.

頓號(ㄉㄨㄣˋ ㄏㄠˋ)
a punctuation mark "、" indicating a very brief pause in reading

頓躓(ㄉㄨㄣˋ ㄓˋ)
① to trip over something and fall ② in dire straits

頓時(ㄉㄨㄣˋ ㄕˊ)

immediately; promptly.

頓首(ㄉㄨㄣˇ ㄕㄡˇ)
to make a ceremonious nod;
to kowtow

頓足(ㄉㄨㄣˇ ㄗㄨˊ)or 頓腳(ㄉㄨㄣˇ ㄐㄧㄠˇ)
to stamp one's foot

頓足捶胸(ㄉㄨㄣˇ ㄗㄨˊ ㄔㄨㄟˊ ㄒㄩㄥ)
to stamp one's foot and hit
one's breast

頓挫(ㄉㄨㄣˇ ㄘㄨㄛˋ)
① to encounter failure; to
receive a setback ② (said of
musical notes) rising and
falling

頓悟(ㄉㄨㄣˇ ㄨˋ)
to realize suddenly; to come
to a sudden realization

【頓】 6793
2. ㄉㄨˊ dwu dú
as in 冒頓(ㄇㄛˋ ㄉㄨˊ)—name of
a Tartar chieftain in the
early Western Han Dynasty

【頍】 6794
ㄎㄨㄟˇ koei kuǐ
to raise one's head

五畫

【領】 6795
ㄌㄧㄥˇ liing lǐng
1. the neck
2. the collar; the neckband: 他
抓住我的衣領。He took me by
the collar.
3. a piece of clothing
4. to lead; to head; to guide; to
usher: 把客人領到大廳去。
Usher the guests into the
hall.
5. to receive; to get: 他已經領了
養老金。He has received his
pension.
6. to understand
7. (now rarely) to manage; to
operate

領班(ㄌㄧㄥˇ ㄅㄢ)
the leader of a team; a head-
man; a foreman

領兵(ㄌㄧㄥˇ ㄅㄧㄥ)
① to lead troops ② a military officer

領帶(ㄌㄧㄥˇ ㄉㄞˋ)
① a necktie ② to lead

領帶夾(ㄌㄧㄥˇ ㄉㄞˋ ㄐㄧㄚ)
a tie clip

領導(ㄌㄧㄥˇ ㄉㄠˇ)
① to lead; leadership: 誰將領

導這個班? Who is going to
lead this class? ② a guide

領導有方(ㄌㄧㄥˇ ㄉㄠˇ ㄧㄡˇ ㄈㄤ)
to lead correctly; wise
leadership

領道(ㄌㄧㄥˇ ㄉㄠˋ)
to lead the way

領單(ㄌㄧㄥˇ ㄉㄢ)
a slip of paper which enti-
tles the bearer to get something

領隊(ㄌㄧㄥˇ ㄉㄨㄟˋ)
the leader of a team or
group; to lead a group: 這支
探險隊由周先生領隊。The
expedition was led by Mr.
Chou.

領頭(ㄌㄧㄥˇ ㄊㄡˊ)
to initiate; to start; to begin;
to lead; to make a be-
ginning; to be the first to
do something: 我領頭, 大家
跟着唱吧! I'll lead off, please
join in.

領土(ㄌㄧㄥˇ ㄊㄨˇ)or 領地(ㄌㄧㄥˇ ㄉㄧˋ)
territory

領土完整(ㄌㄧㄥˇ ㄊㄨˇ ㄨㄢˊ ㄓㄥˇ)
territorial integrity: 我們要保
衛國家的領土完整。We'll safe-
guard our country's territorial integrity.

領路(ㄌㄧㄥˇ ㄌㄨˋ)
to lead the way

領略(ㄌㄧㄥˇ ㄌㄩㄝˋ)
to understand; to taste; to
experience; to appreciate

領港(ㄌㄧㄥˇ ㄍㄤˇ)
a pilot (in a port)

領口(ㄌㄧㄥˇ ㄎㄡˇ)
the collar of a garment; the
neckband

領款(ㄌㄧㄥˇ ㄎㄨㄢˇ)
to receive funds; to draw
money

領空(ㄌㄧㄥˇ ㄎㄨㄥ)
territorial air; an aerial
domain

領海(ㄌㄧㄥˇ ㄏㄞˇ)
territorial waters or seas

領航(ㄌㄧㄥˇ ㄏㄤˊ)
to navigate; navigation; to
pilot

領航員(ㄌㄧㄥˇ ㄏㄤˊ ㄩㄢˊ)
a navigator; a pilot

領回(ㄌㄧㄥˇ ㄏㄨㄟˊ)
to get back; to take back

領會(ㄌㄧㄥˇ ㄏㄨㄟˋ)

to understand; to appreciat
我還沒有領會你的意思。I sta
don't understand what yo
mean.

領結(ㄌㄧㄥˇ ㄐㄧㄝˊ)
the loop of a necktie; a bo
tie

領教(ㄌㄧㄥˇ ㄐㄧㄠˋ)
① to be taught; to ge
instruction ② (a polit
expression) to have receive
your reply ③ thanks; muc
obliged ④ (sarcastically)
experience or encounter
to ask advice

領巾(ㄌㄧㄥˇ ㄐㄧㄣ)
a scarf

領獎(ㄌㄧㄥˇ ㄐㄧㄤˇ)
to receive an award or priz

領情(ㄌㄧㄥˇ ㄑㄧㄥˊ)
to appreciate favors give
to feel grateful to somebod
你的好意我十分領情。I
very grateful to you fo
your kindness.

領取(ㄌㄧㄥˇ ㄑㄩˇ)
to get; to receive

領悉(ㄌㄧㄥˇ ㄒㄧ)
to have learned (an expre
sion used in letters)

領洗(ㄌㄧㄥˇ ㄒㄧˇ)
to be baptized; to receiv
baptism: 他領洗成為羅馬天
教徒。He was baptized
Roman Catholic.

領謝(ㄌㄧㄥˇ ㄒㄧㄝˋ)
to receive with thanks

領袖(ㄌㄧㄥˇ ㄒㄧㄡˋ)
a leader; the leading figure

領袖慾(ㄌㄧㄥˇ ㄒㄧㄡˋ ㄩˋ)
the desire or drive to be
leader

領先(ㄌㄧㄥˇ ㄒㄧㄢ)
① to lead; to walk ahead ②
the lead; the first place o
position: 他在賽跑中領先。H
took the lead in the race.

領銜(ㄌㄧㄥˇ ㄒㄧㄢˊ)
① the first to sign in a lis
of signatures ② to be th
first on a name list ③ t
play the lead in a film: 這部
電影由他領銜主演。He playe
the lead in this film.

領薪水(ㄌㄧㄥˇ ㄒㄧㄣ ㄕㄨㄟˇ)
to receive pay; to get salary
to get the pay check

【頷章】(ㄐㄧㄥ ㄓㄤ)
insignia on the collars of military uniforms; collar badges

頷事(ㄐㄧㄥ ㄕ)
(diplomacy)a consul

頷事館(ㄐㄧㄥ ㄕ《ㄨㄢ)
a consulate

頷事裁判權(ㄐㄧㄥ ㄕ ㄘㄞ ㄆㄢ ㄑㄩㄢ)
consular jurisdiction

頷受(ㄐㄧㄥ ㄕㄡ)
to receive; to enjoy (your favors, etc.)

頷賞(ㄐㄧㄥ ㄕㄤ)
to receive a reward

頷水(ㄐㄧㄥ ㄕㄨㄟ)
① inland waters ②territorial waters; territorial sea

頷子(ㄐㄧㄥ ㄗ)
the collar or neck of a garment

頷座員(ㄐㄧㄥ ㄗㄨㄛ ㄩㄢ)
an usher in a theater or concert hall

頷罪(ㄐㄧㄥ ㄗㄨㄟ)
to admit guilt; to plead guilty

頷養(ㄐㄧㄥ ㄧㄤ)
to adopt (a child)

頷悟(ㄐㄧㄥ ㄨ)
to understand; to comprehend

頷域(ㄐㄧㄥ ㄩ)
① a domain; a realm; the territory of a nation: 領域廣大。 The domain is vast. ② a realm; a field; a sphere; a domain

【頗】 6796
. ㄆㄛ po pō
. somewhat
. quite; very; fairly; considerably; rather
. a Chinese family name

頗表同情(ㄆㄛ ㄅㄧㄠˇ ㄊㄨㄥ ㄑㄧㄥ)
rather sympathetic; to sympathize considerably

頗多(ㄆㄛ ㄉㄨㄛ)
rather many; many

頗好(ㄆㄛ ㄏㄠˇ)
rather good; good

頗佳(ㄆㄛ ㄐㄧㄚ)
rather good; fairly good

頗久(ㄆㄛ ㄐㄧㄡˇ)
for quite a while

頗想(ㄆㄛ ㄒㄧㄤˇ)

to be rather inclined to do something

頷知一二(ㄉㄧㄢˇ ㄓ ㄧ ㄦ)
(literally)to know one or two things (about it) —to know it rather well: 他對歌劇頷知一二。He knows opera rather well.

頷重(ㄉㄧㄢˇ ㄓㄨㄥˋ)
rather heavy; fairly heavy: 這本書頗重。The book is rather heavy.

頷有(ㄉㄧㄢˇ ㄧㄡˇ)
to have a lot of (dough, etc.); to be very much like (his/her ways, etc.); a lot of: 我頗有同感。I feel the same way as you do.

頷為滿意(ㄉㄧㄢˇ ㄨㄟˊ ㄇㄢˇ ㄧ)
rather or much satisfied; very contented: 我對你的解釋頗為滿意。I am much satisfied with your explanation.

頷欲(ㄆㄛ ㄩ)
rather intend to do something

【頗】 6796
. ㄆㄛ po pō
inclined to one side; unjustly

六畫

【頰】 6797
. ㄐㄧㄚ jya jiá
to deduct; to omit

【頰】 6797
. ㄒㄧㄝ shye xié
(又讀 ㄐㄧㄝ jye jié)
to fly up

頰頡(ㄒㄧㄝˊ)
①to match; to contest: 從未有人能與他頰頡。He never met his match. ②(said of birds)to fly high and low; haughty; conceited

【頦】 6798
. ㄏㄞ hair hái
(又讀 ㄎㄜ ke kē
ㄎㄜˇ ker kě)
the chin

【頫】 6799
. ㄈㄨ fuu fǔ
with one's chin down; to bow one's head

【頠】 6800
. ㄨㄟ woei wěi
quiet; tranquil

【頝】 6801
ㄒㄩ shiu xū
a term of address for elder sisters in the state of Chu (楚) in ancient China

七畫

【頤】 6802
. ㄧ yi yí
1. the cheeks
2. to nourish; to rear; to take care of oneself
3. a Chinese family name

頤和園(ㄏㄜˊ ㄩㄢˊ)
the Yi-ho Garden (or the Summer Palace) built by Empress Dowager Tzu Hsi (慈禧) at the end of the Ching Dynasty, where the summer palace was located: 頤和園是著名的觀光勝地。The Yi-ho Garden is a famous tourist resort.

頤指(ㄓˇ)
to signify one's intentions to servants or subordinates by merely twisting the cheeks

頤指氣使(ㄓˇ ㄑㄧ ㄕˇ)
to order about; to be extremely bossy: 他的妻子喜歡頤指氣使。He has a very bossy wife.

頤神(ㄕㄣˊ)
to rest one's mind; to have a mental relaxation

頤養(ㄧˇ ㄧㄤˇ)
to nourish; to keep fit; to take care of oneself; to recuperate

【頭】 6803
. ㄊㄡˊ tour tóu
1. the head: 他打我的頭。He hit me on the head.
2. the top; the first; first; the beginning
3. the chief; the boss; the leader; the head (of a group)
4. the two ends (of anything); a side; an aspect
5. a head (of cattle, etc.)
6. an auxiliary, as a suffix

頭版(ㄊㄡˊ ㄅㄢˇ)
①the front page (of a newspaper) ②the first edition

頭部(ㄊㄡˊ ㄅㄨ)
the head

頭破血流(ㄊㄡˊ ㄆㄛ ㄒㄧㄝˇ ㄌㄧㄡˊ)

【頁 部】

〔頁部〕

with one's head broken and bleeding(as a result of a savage beating)

頭皮(ㄊㄡ ㄆㄧˊ)
the scalp

頭皮屑(ㄊㄡ ㄆㄧˊ ㄒㄧㄝˋ)
dandruff

頭毛(ㄊㄡ ㄇㄠˊ)
the hair

頭名(ㄊㄡ ㄇㄧㄥˊ)
the first(in an examination, contest, etc.)

頭目(ㄊㄡ ㄇㄨˋ)
a chief; a leader; a ringleader; a chieftain; the head of a group

頭髮(ㄊㄡ ˙ㄈㄚ)
hair on the head: 她留頭髮。She is letting her hair grow.

頭風(ㄊㄡ ㄈㄥ)
a headache

頭戴式耳機(ㄊㄡ ㄉㄞˋ ㄕˋ ㄦˇ ㄐㄧ)
a headband receiver

頭道(ㄊㄡ ㄉㄠˋ)
①the first time ②the first (course or dish in a feast)

頭燈(ㄊㄡ ㄉㄥ)
(mining)a head lamp

頭等(ㄊㄡ ㄉㄥˇ)
first class; the best quality

頭等艙(ㄊㄡ ㄉㄥˇ ㄘㄤ)
a first-class cabin

頭頂(ㄊㄡ ㄉㄧㄥˇ)
①the top of one's head ②to wear or support with one's head

頭胎(ㄊㄡ ㄊㄞ)
the firstborn

頭套(ㄊㄡ ㄊㄠˋ)
an actor's headgear

頭頭是道(ㄊㄡ ㄊㄡ ㄕˋ ㄉㄠˋ)
logically(arranged and narrated); systematically and orderly(stated); clearly and reasonably(presented)

頭疼(ㄊㄡ ㄊㄥˊ)
(to have a)headache

頭挑(ㄊㄡ ㄊㄧㄠ)
the choicest; the best choice

頭童齒豁(ㄊㄡ ㄊㄨㄥˊ ㄔˇ ㄏㄨㄛˋ)
bald head and teeth gone—old

頭痛(ㄊㄡ ㄊㄨㄥˋ)
a headache: 這孩子真讓我頭痛。This boy is a headache

for me.

頭痛醫頭，腳痛醫腳(ㄊㄡ ㄊㄨㄥˋ ㄧ ㄊㄡ，ㄐㄧㄠˇ ㄊㄨㄥˋ ㄧ ㄐㄧㄠˇ)
to treat only where the pain is—not to find the source of a disease; a superficial way of doing things; to deal with problems on an ad hoc basis

頭腦(ㄊㄡ ㄋㄠˇ)
①brains; mind: 他頭腦簡單。He is simple-minded. ②main threads; clues: 他的話讓我摸不著頭腦。I cannot grasp the main threads of his words. ③the chief or boss

頭腦不清(ㄊㄡ ㄋㄠˇ ㄅㄨˋ ㄑㄧㄥ)
mixed-up; muddleheaded

頭腦清醒(ㄊㄡ ㄋㄠˇ ㄑㄧㄥ ㄒㄧㄥˇ)
clearheaded; with an alert mind

頭裏(ㄊㄡ ˙ㄌㄧ)
①earlier; before(with reference to time) ②in front; ahead: 請讓頭走，我馬上就來。Please go ahead. I will be there soon.

頭臉(ㄊㄡ ㄌㄧㄢˇ)
one's appearance or features

頭領(ㄊㄡ ㄌㄧㄥˇ)
the leader

頭顱(ㄊㄡ ㄌㄨˊ)
the head

頭路(ㄊㄡ ㄌㄨˋ)
①a clue; a main thread ②one's occupation; one's job ③access

頭蓋骨(ㄊㄡ ㄍㄞˋ《ㄞˇ》or 頭骨(ㄍㄨˇ)
(anatomy) the skull; the cranium

頭會箕斂(ㄊㄡ ㄎㄨㄞˋ ㄐㄧ ㄌㄧㄢˇ)
heavy taxation

頭盔(ㄊㄡ ㄎㄨㄟ)
a helmet: 消防隊員戴皮製頭盔。Firemen wear leather helmets.

頭號(ㄊㄡ ㄏㄠˋ)
①number one; principal; leading; arch(enemy) ②the best ③the largest

頭條新聞(ㄊㄡ ㄊㄧㄠˊ ㄒㄧㄣ ㄨㄣˊ)
headline news; the leading story in a paper

頭昏(ㄊㄡ ㄏㄨㄣ)
dizzy; giddy; 他突然感到頭昏。He felt dizzy suddenly.

頭昏腦脹(ㄊㄡ ㄏㄨㄣ ㄋㄠˇ ㄓㄤˋ)
to feel dizzy and have a headache

頭昏眼花(ㄊㄡ ㄏㄨㄣ ㄧㄢˇ ㄏㄨㄚ)
dizzy

頭家(ㄊㄡ ㄐㄧㄚ)
the operator of a gambling joint

頭巾(ㄊㄡ ㄐㄧㄣ)
a turban; a kerchief

頭獎(ㄊㄡ ㄐㄧㄤˇ)
the first prize

頭角(ㄊㄡ ㄐㄩㄝˊ)
①a lead or clue ②looks of a promising youth; brilliance (of a young person); talent

頭角崢嶸(ㄊㄡ ㄐㄩㄝˊ ㄓㄥ ㄖㄨㄥˊ)
outstanding

頭屑(ㄊㄡ ㄒㄧㄝˋ)
dandruff

頭銜(ㄊㄡ ㄒㄧㄢˊ)
the official title of a person

頭緒(ㄊㄡ ㄒㄩˋ)
①leads or clues; main clues (said of a complicated affair) ②ways or means ③ systematical; sequence

頭緒繁多(ㄊㄡ ㄒㄩˋ ㄈㄢˊ ㄉㄨㄛ)
numerous leads and clues; confusing

頭陣(ㄊㄡ ㄓㄣˋ)
①the first battle ②the beginning of anything

頭脹(ㄊㄡ ㄓㄤˋ)
to feel heavy in the head

頭重腳輕(ㄊㄡ ㄓㄨㄥˋ ㄐㄧㄠˇ ㄑㄧㄥ)
top-heavy

頭蝨(ㄊㄡ ㄕ)
head lice; Pediculus humanus capitis

頭上(ㄊㄡ ㄕㄤˋ)
on the head; on top

頭生兒(ㄊㄡ ㄕㄥ ㄦ)
the firstborn

頭水貨(ㄊㄡ ㄕㄨㄟˇ ㄏㄨㄛˋ)
goods of the best quality

頭子(ㄊㄡ ˙ㄗ)
①the best; the winner ②the leader (of bandits, rebels etc.)參看「頭目」: 土匪頭子已被絞死。The bandit chief has been hanged.

頭遭(ㄊㄡ ㄗㄠ)or 頭一遭(ㄊㄡ ㄧ ㄗㄠ)
the first time: 我頭一遭受騙時非常生氣。I was very angry when I was cheated the first

time.

頭足異處
(ㄊㄡ ㄗㄨˊ ㄧˋ ㄔㄨˋ)
(literally) with one's head and feet in different places—beheaded

頭彩 (ㄊㄡˊ ㄘㄞˇ)
the first prize in a lottery

頭寸 (ㄊㄡˊ ㄘㄨㄣˋ)
cash; money supply

頭兒 (ㄊㄡˊ ㄦ)
① the head: 他是我們這隊的頭兒。He is the head of our team. ② the boss ③ the ends ④ extremes

頭一回 (ㄊㄡˊ ㄧ ㄏㄨㄟˊ)
for the first time: 他生平頭一回看到海。He saw the sea for the first time in his life.

頭油 (ㄊㄡˊ ㄧㄡˊ)
hair tonic or oil

頭尾 (ㄊㄡˊ ㄨㄟˇ)
① head and tail—beginning and end ② a Chinese dish with the head and tail of a fish cooked in soybean sauce and sugar

頭暈 (ㄊㄡˊ ㄩㄣ)
dizzy; giddy; dizziness

頭暈眼花 (ㄊㄡˊ ㄩㄣ ㄧㄢˇ ㄏㄨㄚ)
dizzy of head and dim of eyes

【頭】 6803
ㄊㄡ •ㄊㄡ •tou tou
1. a suffix indicating positions or directions
2. as a suffix to certain verbs to indicate the worthiness

【頰】 6804
ㄐㄧㄚˊ jya jiá
the cheeks: 這小孩雙頰緋紅。The boy has rosy cheeks.

頰輔 (ㄐㄧㄚˊ ㄈㄨˇ)
flesh on the cheeks

頰骨 (ㄐㄧㄚˊ ㄍㄨˇ)
the cheekbone

頰上添毫 (ㄐㄧㄚˊ ㄕㄤˋ ㄊㄧㄢ ㄏㄠˊ)
(literally) to make a portrait come alive by adding some hair on the cheeks—to give a magic touch to a literary piece; to add the punch line

【頷】 6805
ㄏㄢˋ hann hàn
1. the chin; the jaws
2. a slight nod of the head

頷聯 (ㄏㄢˋ ㄌㄧㄢˊ)
(in a poem of eight lines) the third and fourth lines which

form a couplet

領首 (ㄌㄧㄥˇ ㄕㄡˇ)
to nod the head—a sign of approval: 他領首表示贊成。He nodded approval (or in approval or approvingly).

領首示意 (ㄌㄧㄥˇ ㄕㄡˇ ㄕˋ ㄧˋ)
to give a nod as a signal

【頵】 6806
ㄐㄩㄣ jiun jūn
large-headed; top-heavy

【頸】 6807
ㄐㄧㄥˇ jing jǐng
the neck; the throat: 她的頸子戴著金鍊。She wore a gold chain around the neck.

頸聯 (ㄐㄧㄥˇ ㄌㄧㄢˊ)
(in a poem of eight lines) the fifth and sixth lines of a poem which form a couplet

頸項 (ㄐㄧㄥˇ ㄒㄧㄤˋ)
the front and back of the neck

頸枕 (ㄐㄧㄥˇ ㄓㄣˇ)
(machinery) bearing

【頹】 6808
ㄊㄨㄟˊ twei tuí
1. to crumble; disintegrated; ruined; dilapidated; to collapse
2. weakened; withered; emaciated; declining; decadent
3. bald
4. to descend; to cascade down
5. a Chinese family name

頹波 (ㄊㄨㄟˊ ㄅㄛ)
water cascading—declining; worsening; deteriorating

頹敗 (ㄊㄨㄟˊ ㄅㄞˋ)
degenerating; decadent; depraved

頹記 (ㄊㄨㄟˊ ㄑㄧˋ)
to sink and become ruined; dilapidated

頹廢 (ㄊㄨㄟˊ ㄈㄟˋ)
① ruined; weakened; decadent ② low-spirited; depressed

頹廢派 (ㄊㄨㄟˊ ㄈㄟˋ ㄆㄞˋ)
the decadents

頹廢主義 (ㄊㄨㄟˊ ㄈㄟˋ ㄓㄨˇ ㄧˋ)
decadentism

頹放 (ㄊㄨㄟˊ ㄈㄤˋ)
slovenly; unconventional; bohemian; cynical

頹風 (ㄊㄨㄟˊ ㄈㄥ)
depraved or decadent cus-

toms; corruptive practices; moral degeneracy

頹唐 (ㄊㄨㄟˊ ㄊㄤˊ)
dispirited; decrepit; failing

頹替 (ㄊㄨㄟˊ ㄊㄧˋ)
falling apart; ruined; to disintegrate or deteriorate

頹齡 (ㄊㄨㄟˊ ㄌㄧㄥˊ)
closing years of one's life; the declining years

頹勢 (ㄊㄨㄟˊ ㄕˋ)
a declining tendency: 他試著去挽回頹勢。He tried to turn the tide in his favor.

頹然 (ㄊㄨㄟˊ ㄖㄢˊ)
submissive; pliant .

頹喪 (ㄊㄨㄟˊ ㄙㄤˋ)
beaten; ruined; discouraged: 勿因一次失敗而頹喪，再試試看。Don't let one failure discourage you. Try again.

頹陽 (ㄊㄨㄟˊ ㄧㄤˊ)
the setting sun

頹運 (ㄊㄨㄟˊ ㄩㄣˋ)
declining fortune

【頻】 6809
ㄆㄧㄣˊ pyn pín
1. incessant; successive; continuous; frequently or repeatedly
2. urgent; precarious
3. same as 顰—to knit the brows
4. frequency

頻頻 (ㄆㄧㄣˊ ㄆㄧㄣˊ)
incessantly; repeatedly; continuously; frequently: 她對他頻頻招手。She waved her hand to him again and again.

頻煩 or 頻繁 (ㄆㄧㄣˊ ㄈㄢˊ)
frequent; incessant; busy

頻道 (ㄆㄧㄣˊ ㄉㄠˋ)
(television) a channel

頻年 (ㄆㄧㄣˊ ㄋㄧㄢˊ)
years in a row; successive years; year after year

頻率 (ㄆㄧㄣˊ ㄌㄩˋ)
frequency

頻數 (ㄆㄧㄣˊ ㄕㄨˋ)
repeatedly; incessantly; frequently

頻仍 (ㄆㄧㄣˊ ㄖㄥˊ)
frequently; often: 中國過去外患頻仍。China was subject to repeated foreign aggression.

頻蹙 (ㄆㄧㄣˊ ㄘㄨˋ)

a woebegone look; looking sad

八畫

（頁部）

【頗】 6810 ㄎㄜ ke kē

a drop or droplet; a grain; a pill; a numeral adjunct for (bombs, bullets, etc.): 天上有幾顆星。There are a few stars in the sky.

顆粒(ㄎㄜ ㄌㄧˋ)
a drop; a grain; a bead

【頦】 6811 ㄘㄨㄟˊ tsuey cuí

as in 顦顇—haggard (from grief or anxiety)

九畫

【額】 6812 ㄜˊ er é

1. the forehead
2. a fixed amount, value, number, etc.; a quota
3. a horizontal tablet
4. a Chinese family name

額面(ㄜ ㄇㄧㄢˋ)
face value (of a banknote, bond, etc.)

額面價格(ㄜ ㄇㄧㄢˋ ㄐㄧㄚˋ ㄍㄜˊ)
face value

額非爾士峯(ㄜ ㄈㄟㄦˇ ㄕ ㄈㄥ)
Mt. Everest

額定(ㄜ ㄉㄧㄥˋ)
specified(numbers or amounts); rated

額定人數(ㄜ ㄉㄧㄥˋ ㄖㄣˊ ㄕㄨˋ)
the maximum number of persons allowed; the stipulated number of personnel

額頭(ㄜ ㄊㄡˊ)
the forehead

額骨(ㄜ ㄍㄨˇ)
the frontal bone

額黃(ㄜ ㄏㄨㄤˊ)
(said of women in ancient times) to paint the forehead yellow as makeup

額角(ㄜ ㄐㄧㄠˇ)
the temples

額手(ㄜ ㄕㄡˇ)
to raise the hand to the forehead—a gesture of respect or congratulations

額手稱慶(ㄜ ㄕㄡˇ ㄔㄥ ㄑㄧㄥˋ)
to put one's hand on one's forehead in jubilation; to be overjoyed

額數(ㄜ ㄕㄨˋ)
the fixed figure, amount, number, etc.

額外(ㄜ ㄨㄞˋ)
extra; beyond the set amount, figure, number or quota

額外費用(ㄜ ㄨㄞˋ ㄈㄟˋ ㄩㄥˋ)
extraneous expenses

額外收入(ㄜ ㄨㄞˋ ㄕㄡ ㄖㄨˋ)
extra income: 我去年都沒有額外收入。I did not have any extra income last year.

【顋】 6813 （腮）ㄙㄞ sai sāi
the cheeks

顋幫子(ㄙㄞ ㄅㄤ˙ ㄗ)or 顋頰(ㄙㄞ ㄐㄧㄚˊ)
the cheeks

【題】 6814 ㄊㄧˊ tyi tí

1. the forehead
2. a sign; a signal
3. a subject; the title of a composition or speech
4. commentaries; notes
5. to sign; to write; to inscribe
6. the end; the top
7. the ornamental woodwork under the eaves of public buildings
8. a Chinese family name

題跋(ㄊㄧˊ ㄅㄚˊ)
a colophon; notes or commentaries in a book, painting or calligraphy; prefaces and postscripts

題筆(ㄊㄧˊ ㄅㄧˇ)
to write: 他很早便開始靠題筆為生。He began to earn his living by writing early.

題壁(ㄊㄧˊ ㄅㄧˋ)
to write on the wall

題品(ㄊㄧˊ ㄆㄧㄣˇ)or 題評(ㄊㄧˊ ㄆㄧㄥˊ)
to comment on; to criticize

題名(ㄊㄧˊ ㄇㄧㄥˊ)
①to inscribe one's name; to autograph ②to name a work; to entitle

題名錄(ㄊㄧˊ ㄇㄧㄥˊ ㄌㄨˋ)
①a roster of successful candidates who participated in the same civil service examination in former times ②a

book for recording names

題目(ㄊㄧˊ ㄇㄨˋ)
①the subject or title of a composition or speech; a theme or heading ②a question or problem(especially in a test)

題款(ㄊㄧˊ ㄎㄨㄢˇ)
(on a scroll) the date and the name of a writer and the person it is dedicated to

題畫(ㄊㄧˊ ㄏㄨㄚˋ)
to write on a painting

題解(ㄊㄧˊ ㄐㄧㄝˇ)
①explanatory notes on the title or background of a book ②keys to exercises or problems

題簽(ㄊㄧˊ ㄑㄧㄢ)
to write the title on a book

題詩(ㄊㄧˊ ㄕ)
to write verses on something

題署(ㄊㄧˊ ㄕㄨˇ)
to write on scrolls of couplets or horizontal tablets

題字(ㄊㄧˊ ㄗˋ)
to write on something; an inscription; an autograph

題辭 or 題詞(ㄊㄧˊ ㄘˊ)
①complimentary verses or prose inserted at the beginning of a book by a person other than the author; a foreword ②an inscription; a dedication ③to write a few words of encouragement, appreciation or commemoration; to inscribe

題材(ㄊㄧˊ ㄘㄞˊ)
material constituting the main theme of an article, composition, etc.: 這是寫繁本的好題材。This is good material for a play.

題額(ㄊㄧˊ ㄜˊ)
to write on a horizontal tablet

題外(ㄊㄧˊ ㄨㄞˋ)
beyond the subject being discussed

【頷】 6815 ㄏㄜˊ hé

1. the jowl; the cheek bones; jaws
2. high-cheekboned
3. reverence

頷骨(ㄏㄜˊ ㄍㄨˇ)

the jawbones; maxillary
bones

顎下腺(ㄜˋ ㄒ丨ㄚˋ ㄒ丨ㄢˋ)
the submaxillary gland

【顏】 6816 ㄧㄢˊ yan yán

1. face (physically); countenance; features
2. reputation; prestige; face
(figuratively): 他竟厚顏說出
此話。He has the face to say
that.
3. dyes; colors: 他用明亮的顏色
來畫它。He painted it with
bright colors.
4. a Chinese family name

顏面(丨ㄢˊ ㄇ丨ㄢˋ)
①face; honor: 他必須顧全顏
面。He has to save face. ②
countenance; face

顏料(丨ㄢˊ ㄌ丨ㄠˋ)
dyestuffs; pigments

顏厚(丨ㄢˊ ㄏㄡˋ)
①thick-skinned; unblushing;
brazen ②(figuratively) face
thickened because of feeling
shame—shame-faced

顏回(丨ㄢˊ ㄏㄨㄟˊ)
Yen Hui (521–490B.C.), one
of the most respected disciples of Confucius

顏筋柳骨(丨ㄢˊ ㄐ丨ㄣ ㄌ丨ㄡˇ ㄍㄨˇ)
the sinews of Yen Chen-
ching (顏眞卿) and the
bones of Liu Kung-chüan
(柳公權), (Yen and Liu were
both famous calligraphers in
the Tang Dynasty)—calligraphy of the highest order

顏之推(丨ㄢˊ ㄓ ㄊㄨㄟ)
Yen Chih-tui (531-?), a
famous writer-official

顏眞卿(丨ㄢˊ ㄓㄣ ㄑ丨ㄥ)
Yen Chen-ching (708-784), a
famous general-calligrapher
in the Tang Dynasty

顏氏家訓(丨ㄢˊ ㄕˋ ㄐ丨ㄚ ㄒㄩㄣˋ)
a work by Yen Chih-tui (顏
之推) dealing with the discipline of one's own mind and
the family

顏色(丨ㄢˊ ㄙㄜˋ)or(丨ㄢˊ·ㄕㄞ)
①color; hue; pigment ②
countenance; facial expression ③a lesson: 給他一點顏
色看看。Teach him a lesson.

顏色自若(丨ㄢˊ ㄙㄜˋ ㄗˋ ㄖㄨㄛˋ)
to be composed with the

---

face unchanged

【顒】 6817 ㄩㄥˊ yong yóng

1. severe
2. great; large
3. large-headed

【顓】 6818 ㄓㄨㄢ juan zhuān

1. cautious
2. stupid; dull; ignorant
3. a Chinese family name

顓頊(ㄓㄨㄢ ㄒㄩˋ)
name of an emperor in
ancient China, a grandson of
the Yellow Emperor (黃帝)

十畫

【顗】 6819 丨ˇ yii yǐ

quiet; tranquil; solemn

【願】 6820 ㄩㄢˋ yuann yuàn

1. to be willing; to be desirous
of; to hope; to wish
2. anything one wishes or
desires; an ambition or aspiration: 他終於如願以償。
Finally he had his wishes
fulfilled.
3. a vow
4. to think

願天下有情人皆成眷屬(ㄩㄢˋ
ㄊ丨ㄢ ㄒ丨ㄚˋ 丨ㄡˇ ㄑ丨ㄥˊ ㄖㄣˊ ㄐ丨ㄝ
ㄔㄥˊ ㄐㄩㄢˋ ㄕㄨˇ)
May all lovers unite in marriage!

願海(ㄩㄢˋ ㄏㄞˇ)
a profound wish

願心(ㄩㄢˋ ㄒ丨ㄣ)
①the wish of Buddha to
save all people and the wish
of all the faithful to become
Buddha ②a vow

願意(ㄩㄢˋ 丨ˋ)
①to be willing ②to like; to
want ③to approve of

願望(ㄩㄢˋ ㄨㄤˋ)
one's wish, aspiration; what
one's heart desires: 和平是全
世界人類的共同願望。Peace is
the common aspirations of
the world's people.

【顙】 6821 ㄙㄤˇ saang sǎng

1. the forehead
2. to kowtow

【顚】 6822 ㄉ丨ㄢ dian diān

---

1. the top; the highest spot; the
head
2. to fall; to topple; to upset
3. to jolt; to bump
4. upside down
5. mad; lunatic

顚簸(ㄉ丨ㄢ ㄅㄛˇ)
to shake; to joggle or jolt; to
bump; to toss

顚沛(ㄉ丨ㄢ ㄆㄟˋ)or顚頓(ㄉ丨ㄢ
ㄉㄨㄣˋ)
①to fall ②(figuratively) to
be desperate; to fail in one's
attempt

顚沛流離(ㄉ丨ㄢ ㄆㄟˋ ㄌ丨ㄡˊ ㄌ丨ˊ)or
顚連(ㄉ丨ㄢ ㄌ丨ㄢˊ)
(said of refugees) suffering
deprivations and hardships;
running around without a
roof over one's head; to lead
a vagrant life

顚仆(ㄉ丨ㄢ ㄆㄨˊ)
to fall down

顚撲不破(ㄉ丨ㄢ ㄆㄨ ㄅㄨˋ ㄆㄛˋ)
(said of theories) irrefutable; absolutely right: 世界上
沒有顚撲不破的真理。There is
no irrefutable truth in the
world.

顚末(ㄉ丨ㄢ ㄇㄛˋ)
from the beginning to the
end

顚毛(ㄉ丨ㄢ ㄇㄠˊ)
hair on top of head

顚覆(ㄉ丨ㄢ ㄈㄨˋ)
to topple; to subvert; subver-
sion

顚倒(ㄉ丨ㄢ ㄉㄠˇ)or顚顚倒倒(ㄉ丨ㄢ
ㄉ丨ㄢ ㄉㄠˇ ㄉㄠˇ)
①upside down; to reverse;
to transpose; to invert: 他把
圖畫掛顚倒了。He hung the
picture upside down. ②men-
tally deranged; infatuated;
lunatic; confused; disordered:
我爲我表妹神魂顚倒。I was in-
fatuated with my cousin.

顚倒是非(ㄉ丨ㄢ ㄉㄠˇ ㄕˋ ㄈㄟ)or顚倒
黑白(ㄉ丨ㄢ ㄉㄠˇ ㄏㄟ ㄅㄞˊ)
to confuse justice and injustice; to distort truth; to twist
facts

顚來倒去(ㄉ丨ㄢ ㄌㄞˊ ㄉㄠˇ ㄑㄩˋ)
①to lack orderliness or cohesion of thought; all jumbled up ②over and over

顚鸞倒鳳(ㄉ丨ㄢ ㄌㄨㄢˊ ㄉㄠˇ ㄈㄥˋ)

〔頁
部〕

【頁部】

the ecstasy of a couple in the act of making love

顛狂 or 癲狂 (ㄉㄧㄢ ㄨㄤˊ)
mad; lunatic; crazy

顛躓 (ㄉㄧㄢ ㄓˋ)
to fall down

顛三倒四 (ㄉㄧㄢ ㄙㄢ ㄉㄠˇ ㄙˋ)
① in total disorder; topsy-turvy; all in confusion ② lunatic; insane

【類】 6823 ㄌㄟˋ ley lèi
1. a species; a kind; a class; a race; a group; a category
2. similar; alike
3. (now rarely) good; virtue
4. a kind of wildcat
5. (now rarely) biased; prejudiced
6. a Chinese family name

類比 (ㄌㄟˋ ㄅㄧˇ)
(logic) analogy

類別 (ㄌㄟˋ ㄅㄧㄝˊ)
classification; categorization

類篇 (ㄌㄟˋ ㄆㄧㄢ)
one of the oldest and largest dictionaries in China compiled by Szu-Ma Kuang (司馬光) and others, containing 53,165 characters

類推 (ㄌㄟˋ ㄊㄨㄟ)
to reason by analogy; to draw analogies

類同 (ㄌㄟˋ ㄊㄨㄥˊ)
similar to; alike

類固醇 (ㄌㄟˋ ㄍㄨˋ ㄔㄨㄣˊ)
steroid

類化 (ㄌㄟˋ ㄏㄨㄚˋ)
(psychology) apprehension

類皆如此 (ㄌㄟˋ ㄐㄧㄝ ㄖㄨˊ ㄘˇ)
similar in kind; in like way

類聚 (ㄌㄟˋ ㄐㄩˋ)
Birds of the same feather flock together.

類型 (ㄌㄟˋ ㄒㄧㄥˊ)
a type; a category: 像他那一類型的人不可信賴. Men of his type are not to be trusted.

類書 (ㄌㄟˋ ㄕㄨ)
any reference book with entries arranged in the form of a dictionary or according to subjects

類人猿 (ㄌㄟˋ ㄖㄣˊ ㄩㄢˊ)
an anthropoid

類似 (ㄌㄟˋ ㄙˋ)
to resemble; similar to; like;

to be analogous to: 人的心臟類似唧筒. The human heart is analogous to a pump.

類似點 (ㄌㄟˋ ㄙˋ ㄉㄧㄢˇ)
similarities

【顖】 6824 ㄒㄧㄣˋ shinn hsìn
the part of the human head from the top to the forehead

十一畫

【顢】 6825 ㄇㄢ man mán
careless, ignorant and stupid

顢頇 (ㄇㄢ ㄏㄢ)
① careless ② ignorant and stupid

十二畫

【顧】 6826 ㄍㄨˋ guh gù
1. to look at; to gaze
2. to turn the head around and look
3. to attend to; to mind; to care for; to concern oneself about; to regard; to look after
4. to visit; to call on
5. however; but; nevertheless
6. indeed; really
7. a Chinese family name

顧不得 (ㄍㄨˋ ㄅㄨˋ ㄉㄜˊ)
unable to take care of; to have to disregard

顧不了 (ㄍㄨˋ ㄅㄨˋ ㄌㄧㄠˇ)
unable to look after

顧不過來 (ㄍㄨˋ ㄅㄨˋ ㄍㄨㄛˋ ㄌㄞˊ)
unable to take care of (so many things)

顧盼 (ㄍㄨˋ ㄆㄢˋ)
to look around

顧盼生姿 (ㄍㄨˋ ㄆㄢˋ ㄕㄥ ㄗ)
to look around charmingly

顧盼自雄 (ㄍㄨˋ ㄆㄢˋ ㄗˋ ㄒㄩㄥˊ)
complacent; proud and satisfied; to look down upon the world

顧名子 (ㄍㄨˋ ㄇㄧㄥˊ ˙ㄗ)
① to care for one's face or reputation ② to value friendship; unwilling to embarrass others

顧名思義 (ㄍㄨˋ ㄇㄧㄥˊ ㄙ ㄧˋ)
(literally) to see the name and think of the meaning;

as a term suggests—self-explanatory; self-evident

顧得過來 (ㄍㄨˋ ㄉㄜˊ ㄍㄨㄛˋ ㄌㄞˊ)
able to take care of

顧到 (ㄍㄨˋ ㄉㄠˋ)
to take something into consideration: 失敗的可能性已被顧到了. The possibility of failure has been taken into consideration.

顧念 (ㄍㄨˋ ㄋㄧㄢˋ)
① to care for; to be worried about ② to think of with affection

顧臉面 (ㄍㄨˋ ㄌㄧㄢˇ ㄇㄧㄢˋ)
to have regard for one's face, reputation or respectability

顧慮 (ㄍㄨˋ ㄌㄩˋ)
to show concern about; misgivings; concern; scruple: 我們對他的教學能力有所顧慮. We had misgivings about his ability to teach.

顧客 (ㄍㄨˋ ㄎㄜˋ) or 顧主 (ㄍㄨˋ ㄓㄨˇ)
customers; patrons; clients: 顧客至上. The customer is king.

顧愷之 (ㄍㄨˋ ㄎㄞˇ ㄓ)
Ku Kai-chih, circa 345-411, a famous painter in the Tsin (晉) Dynasty

顧及 (ㄍㄨˋ ㄐㄧˊ)
in consideration of; in view of; to care about; to attend to; to take something into consideration: 他無暇顧及此事. He has no time to attend to the matter.

顧忌 (ㄍㄨˋ ㄐㄧˋ)
misgivings; scruple; fear: 他做此事毫無顧忌. He did it without scruple.

顧前不顧後 (ㄍㄨˋ ㄑㄧㄢˊ ㄅㄨˋ ㄍㄨˋ ㄏㄡˋ)
to act with no regard for the consequences; to see only one aspect of a matter; to act rashly

顧曲周郎 (ㄍㄨˋ ㄑㄩ ㄓㄡ ㄌㄤˊ)
a music connoisseur

顧全 (ㄍㄨˋ ㄑㄩㄢˊ)
to have consideration for and take care to preserve

顧全面子 (ㄍㄨˋ ㄑㄩㄢˊ ㄇㄧㄢˋ ˙ㄗ)
to save somebody's face; to spare somebody's feelings

顧全大局《ㄍㄨㄑㄩㄢㄉㄚˋㄐㄩˊ》
in the interest of the whole;
for the sake of the country,
organization, etc.; to take
the situation as a whole into
consideration

顧惜《ㄍㄨˋㄒㄧˊ》
to value; to care for

顧恤《ㄍㄨˋㄒㄩˋ》
to care for; to sympathize
with

顧主《ㄍㄨˋㄓㄨˇ》
a customer; a patron; a client; clientele: 我們設法讓顧主
完全滿意。We try to give our
clients complete satisfaction.

顧左右而言他《ㄍㄨˋㄗㄨㄛˇㄧㄡˋㄦˊㄧㄢ ㄊㄚ》
to evade a question

顧此失彼《ㄍㄨˋㄘˇㄕ ㄅㄧˇ》
to take care of one thing
and miss the other

顧炎武《ㄍㄨˋㄧㄢˊㄨˇ》
Ku Yen-wu, 1613-1682, a
famous scholar in the clos-
ing years of the Ming
Dynasty, also known as Ku
Ting-lin (顧亭林)

顧影《ㄍㄨˋㄧㄥˇ》
complacent

顧影自憐《ㄍㄨˋㄧㄥˇㄗˋ ㄌㄧㄢˊ》
(literally) to look at one's
shadow and fall in love with
oneself — narcissism; self-
glorification; to look at
one's shadow and lament
one's lot

顧問《ㄍㄨˋㄨㄣˋ》
an advisor; a consultant; a
counsellor

【纇】 6827 ㄌㄟˋ ley lèi
1. blemish
2. fierce; recalcitrant

【顥】 6828 ㄏㄠˋ haw hào
1. bright; luminous
2. (said of hair) hoary or white
3. very great; very large

【顦】 6829 (憔) ㄑㄧㄠˊ chyau qiáo
haggard

顦顇《ㄑㄧㄠˊㄘㄨㄟˋ》
haggard as a result of grief,
etc.

十三畫

【顫】 6830 ㄓㄢˋ chann chàn
(又讀 ㄓㄢˋ jann zhàn)
to tremble; to shake; to
shiver; to quiver; to vibrate

顫筆《ㄓㄢˋㄅㄧˇ》
(Chinese calligraphy) to
write with the hand shaking
in order to gain forcefulness
in the strokes

顫抖《ㄓㄢˋㄉㄡˇ》
to tremble; to shiver; to
shake; to quiver

顫動《ㄓㄢˋㄉㄨㄥˋ》
to shake; to tremble; to
quiver; to shiver; to vibrate:
樹葉在微風中顫動。The leaves
quivered in the breeze.

顫悠悠《ㄓㄢˋㄧㄡ ㄧㄡ》
trembling; shaky; flickering

顫巍巍《ㄓㄢˋㄨㄟˊㄨㄟˊ》or 顫顫巍巍
《ㄓㄢˋ·ㄓㄢ ㄨㄟˊㄨㄟˊ》
shaking; shivering; tottering;
faltering

十四畫

【顯】 6831 ㄒㄧㄢˇ shean xiǎn
1. evident; manifest; clear
2. high-positioned; eminent;
prominent
3. well-known; renowned; famed;
reputed
4. to expose; to make known;
to display; to show; to manifest
5. a prefix referring to one's
forebears

顯妣《ㄒㄧㄢˇㄅㄧˇ》
my late mother

顯明《ㄒㄧㄢˇㄇㄧㄥˊ》
evident; clear; remarkable

顯達《ㄒㄧㄢˇㄉㄚˊ》
to attain high office; to
achieve prominence in officialdom

顯得《ㄒㄧㄢˇ·ㄉㄜ》
to look; to seem; to appear:
他顯得有不舒服。He seems
a bit unwell.

顯靈《ㄒㄧㄢˇㄌㄧㄥˊ》
omens, etc. given by the soul
of a dead person; a divine
manifestation; an epiphany

顯露《ㄒㄧㄢˇㄌㄨˋ》
to appear; to show; to mani-

fest; to unveil: 她臉上顯露出
輕蔑的笑容。A contemptuous
smile appeared on her face.

顯露頭角《ㄒㄧㄢˇㄌㄨˋㄊㄡˊㄐㄧㄠˇ》
to show one's promise

顯貴《ㄒㄧㄢˇㄍㄨㄟˋ》
bigwigs; eminent personages:
他專門結交顯貴。He associat-
ed with eminent personages
exclusively.

顯官《ㄒㄧㄢˇㄍㄨㄢ》
a ranking or high official

顯考《ㄒㄧㄢˇㄎㄠˇ》
my late father

顯赫《ㄒㄧㄢˇㄏㄜˋ》
outstanding; illustrious;
powerful; mighty; prominent;
renowned; glorious: 他有聲勢
顯赫。He has a powerful
influence.

顯花植物《ㄒㄧㄢˇㄏㄨㄚ ㄓˊㄨˋ》
a flowering plant; a phaner-
ogam

顯豁《ㄒㄧㄢˇㄏㄨㄛˋ》
evident; clear; conspicuous

顯懷《ㄒㄧㄢˇㄏㄨㄞˊ》
a state of pregnancy which
is already visible

顯晦《ㄒㄧㄢˇㄏㄨㄟˋ》
the luminous and the
obscure, brightness and
darkness

顯宦《ㄒㄧㄢˇㄏㄨㄢˋ》
a ranking or high official

顯見《ㄒㄧㄢˇㄐㄧㄢˋ》
It is evident that....

顯爵《ㄒㄧㄢˇㄐㄩㄝˊ》
a high government position

顯親《ㄒㄧㄢˇㄑㄧㄣ》
① to glorify one's parents ②
powerful relatives

顯顯《ㄒㄧㄢˇㄒㄧㄢˇ》
bright and brilliant; illustrious

顯現《ㄒㄧㄢˇㄒㄧㄢˋ》
to appear; to reveal

顯像《ㄒㄧㄢˇㄒㄧㄤˋ》
(photography) to develop

顯像電話《ㄒㄧㄢˇㄒㄧㄤˋㄉㄧㄢˋㄏㄨㄚˋ》
a video phone

顯像液《ㄒㄧㄢˇㄒㄧㄤˋㄧㄝˋ》
(photography) developer

顯形兒《ㄒㄧㄢˇㄒㄧㄥˊㄦ》
(said of apparitions or
spirits) to appear in human
form; to show one's true

〔風部〕

form or colors

顯性(ㄒㄧㄢˇ ㄒㄧㄥˋ)
(biology) dominance

顯性基因(ㄒㄧㄢˇ ㄒㄧㄥˋ ㄐㄧ ㄧㄣ)
a dominant gene

顯學(ㄒㄧㄢˇ ㄒㄩㄝˊ)
practical learning (referring to Confucianism and Mohism)

顯者(ㄒㄧㄢˇ ㄓㄜˇ)
a dignitary; the eminent ones

顯着(ㄒㄧㄢˇ ㄓㄜ˙)
①to appear; to seem ②to feel; to cause to feel

顯章(ㄒㄧㄢˇ ㄓㄤ)
to make clear; to clarify; to state with honesty

顯著(ㄒㄧㄢˇ ㄓㄨ)
evident; clear; notable; eye-catching; marked; remarkable; outstanding: 學生進步顯著。The students have made marked progress.

顯著特徵(ㄒㄧㄢˇ ㄓㄨ ㄊㄜˋ ㄓ)
a marked feature

顯敞(ㄒㄧㄢˇ ㄔㄤˇ)
spacious

顯出(ㄒㄧㄢˇ ㄔㄨ)
to appear; to show (in contrast)

顯示(ㄒㄧㄢˇ ㄕˋ)
to indicate; to show; to reveal; to demonstrate

顯身手(ㄒㄧㄢˇ ㄕㄣ ㄕㄡˇ)
to show one's talent or skill

顯聖(ㄒㄧㄢˇ ㄕㄥˋ)
to make evident a divine presence or power

顯然(ㄒㄧㄢˇ ㄖㄢˊ)
evident; clearly visible; obvious; apparent: 顯然他已改變意向。Apparently he has changed his mind.

顯祖(ㄒㄧㄢˇ ㄗㄨˇ)
one's forebears

顯而易見(ㄒㄧㄢˇ ㄦˊ ㄧˋ ㄐㄧㄢˋ)
evidently; apparently

顯要(ㄒㄧㄢˇ ㄧㄠˋ)
bigwigs; notables; VIPs (very important persons)

顯眼(ㄒㄧㄢˇ ㄧㄢˇ)
conspicuous; striking; eye-catching: 把它放在顯眼的地方。Put it in a conspicuous place.

顯揚(ㄒㄧㄢˇ ㄧㄤˊ)
to cite; to commend; to praise; to acclaim

顯影(ㄒㄧㄢˇ ㄧㄥˇ)
(cinematography) to develop

顯微膠片(ㄒㄧㄢˇ ㄨㄟ ㄐㄧㄠ ㄆㄧㄢˋ)
microfilm

顯微鏡(ㄒㄧㄢˇ ㄨㄟ ㄐㄧㄥˋ)
a microscope

顯微外科(ㄒㄧㄢˇ ㄨㄟ ㄨㄞ ㄎㄜ)
microsurgery

【顬】6832
ㄖㄨˊ ru rú
參看「顳顬」

十五畫

【顰】6833
ㄆㄧㄣˊ pyn pín
to frown; to knit one's brows

顰眉(ㄆㄧㄣˊ ㄇㄟˊ)
to knit the brows

顰蹙(ㄆㄧㄣˊ ㄘㄨˋ)
a look of grief, sorrow or anxiety; a glum look

十六畫

【顱】6834
ㄌㄨˊ lu lú
1. the skull
2. the head
3. the forehead

顱骨(ㄌㄨˊ ㄍㄨˇ)
the skull; the parietal bone

十八畫

【顴】6835
ㄑㄩㄢˊ chyuan quán
the cheekbone

顴骨(ㄑㄩㄢˊ ㄍㄨˇ)
the cheekbone; the malar bone; the malar: 她的顴骨突起。She has prominent cheek bones.

【顳】6836
ㄋㄧㄝˋ nieh niè
the temple

顳顬(ㄋㄧㄝˋ ㄖㄨˊ)
(physiology) the temple

風 部
ㄈㄥ feng fēng

【風】6837
1. ㄈㄥ feng fēng
1. wind; a gust; breeze; a gale
2. education; influence
3. customs; practices; a fad, fashion; fashionable
4. a scene
5. a style; a manner; deportment; taste
6. fame; reputation
7. rumor
8. ailments supposedly caused by wind and dampness 參看「風濕」

風波(ㄈㄥ ㄅㄛ)
disputes; quarrels; disturbances; restlessness

風伯(ㄈㄥ ㄅㄛˊ)or風師(ㄈㄥ ㄕ)
the god of wind

風暴(ㄈㄥ ㄅㄠˋ)
a storm; a windstorm

風標(ㄈㄥ ㄅㄧㄠ)
①a wind sock or wind cone; a weathercock ②a typical personal style

風平浪靜(ㄈㄥ ㄆㄧㄥˊ ㄌㄤˋ ㄐㄧㄥˋ)
a calm and unruffled sea; calm and tranquil: 暴風雨過後，海上風平浪靜。After the storm the sea was calm.

風馬牛不相及(ㄈㄥ ㄇㄚˇ ㄋㄧㄡˊ ㄅㄨˋ ㄒㄧㄤ ㄐㄧˊ)
things entirely not related; irrelevant

風媒花(ㄈㄥ ㄇㄟˊ ㄏㄨㄚ)
an anemophilous flower

風貌(ㄈㄥ ㄇㄠˋ)
①style and features ②a view; a scene

風帽(ㄈㄥ ㄇㄠˋ)
a hood; a cowl-like hat worn in winter

風靡一時(ㄈㄥ ㄇㄧˇ ㄧˋ ㄕˊ)
to become a fad or vogue of the time; to become fashionable for a time

風木(ㄈㄥ ㄇㄨˋ)or風樹(ㄈㄥ ㄕㄨˋ)
to regret that one failed to take good care of his parents while they were alive

風帆(ㄈㄥ ㄈㄢ)
a sailboat

風範(ㄈㄥ ㄈㄢ)
① appearance; an air; a manner ② a model; a paragon

風風雨雨(ㄈㄥ ㄈㄥ ㄩˇ ㄩˇ)
① storms; winds and rains ② rumors being rife; gossips going the rounds

風德(ㄈㄥ ㄉㄜˊ)
to exert moral influence

風度(ㄈㄥ ㄉㄨˋ)
a manner; poise; bearing; carriage

風度翩翩(ㄈㄥ ㄉㄨˋ ㄆㄧㄢ ㄆㄧㄢ)
(said of a young man) graceful bearing or carriage

風動(ㄈㄥ ㄉㄨㄥˋ)
to receive popular response or wide support

風頭(ㄈㄥ ˙ㄊㄡ)
① a situation; circumstances; the trend of events (as affecting a person) ② the way the wind blows ③ popularity, distinction or prominence (of a person of accomplishment); the limelight: 她似乎很愛出風頭。She seems fond of the limelight.

風頭甚健(ㄈㄥ ㄊㄡ ㄕㄣˋ ㄐㄧㄢˋ)
very popular; enjoying great distinction

風調雨順(ㄈㄥ ㄊㄧㄠˊ ㄩˇ ㄕㄨㄣˋ)
favorable weather (for raising crops); a timely wind and rain

風土誌(ㄈㄥ ㄊㄨˇ ㄓˋ)
a record of local customs, tradition, etc.

風土人情(ㄈㄥ ㄊㄨˇ ㄖㄣˊ ㄑㄧㄥˊ)
local customs and practices

風浪(ㄈㄥ ㄌㄤˋ)
① wind and waves at sea ② a storm (in the figurative sense): 他是個久經風浪的人。He has weathered many a storm.

風裏來，雨裏去(ㄈㄥ ㄌㄧˇ ㄌㄞˊ，ㄩˇ ㄌㄧˇ ㄑㄩˋ)
to come in the wind and go in the rain—to accomplish one's task even in the teeth of wind and rain

風力(ㄈㄥ ㄌㄧˋ)
the force of the wind; wind

power

風力表(ㄈㄥ ㄌㄧˋ ㄅㄧㄠˇ)
a wind gauge; an anemometer

風流(ㄈㄥ ㄌㄧㄡˊ)
① elegant style; a refined taste; intellectually sophisticated ② to have a weakness for women

風流倜儻(ㄈㄥ ㄌㄧㄡˊ ㄊㄧˋ ㄊㄤˇ)
casual and elegant bearing; charming; dashing

風流債(ㄈㄥ ㄌㄧㄡˊ ㄓㄞˋ)
predestined romantic ties between a man and a woman

風流事(ㄈㄥ ㄌㄧㄡˊ ㄕˋ)
① an affair; a romance; a romantic episode ② poetic pursuits

風流罪過(ㄈㄥ ㄌㄧㄡˊ ㄗㄨㄟˋ ㄍㄨㄛˋ)
blemishes; small defects

風流雲散(ㄈㄥ ㄌㄧㄡˊ ㄩㄣˊ ㄙㄢˋ)
① to dissipate to nothing; to vanish without a trace ② (said of old companions) separated and dispersed

風流韻事(ㄈㄥ ㄌㄧㄡˊ ㄩㄣˋ ㄕˋ)
a romantic affair; gaieties

風涼(ㄈㄥ ㄌㄧㄤˊ)
cool

風涼話(ㄈㄥ ㄌㄧㄤˊ ㄏㄨㄚˋ)
irresponsible and satiric remarks; sarcastic comments: 我討厭他的風涼話。I hate his sarcastic comments.

風鈴(ㄈㄥ ㄌㄧㄥˊ)
aeolian bells (hung on the eaves of pagodas or temple buildings)

風鈴草(ㄈㄥ ㄌㄧㄥˊ ㄘㄠˇ)
Canterbury bells; bellflowers

風格(ㄈㄥ ㄍㄜˊ)
a style: 風格即其人。The style is the man.

風概(ㄈㄥ ㄍㄞˋ)
bearing and magnanimity

風乾(ㄈㄥ ㄍㄢ)
to dry in the shade by air or wind; to air-dry

風骨(ㄈㄥ ㄍㄨˇ)
① incorruptibility; moral fortitude; the strength of character ② the vigor of style

風光(ㄈㄥ ㄍㄨㄤ)
① scenery ② elegant style or taste ③ glory; good reputa-

tion

風口(ㄈㄥ ㄎㄡˇ)
a place where there is a draught

風和日暖(ㄈㄥ ㄏㄜˊ ㄖˋ ㄋㄨㄢˇ)or 風和日麗(ㄈㄥ ㄏㄜˊ ㄖˋ ㄌㄧˋ)
the bright sunshine and gentle breezes; warm and sunny weather

風寒(ㄈㄥ ㄏㄢˊ)
a cold; flu; a chill: 大夫說她是受了風寒。The doctor said that she has caught a chill.

風花雪月(ㄈㄥ ㄏㄨㄚ ㄒㄩㄝˇ ㄩㄝˋ)
wind, flowers, snow and the moon—all ingredients for a gay life; love affairs

風華(ㄈㄥ ㄏㄨㄚˊ)
elegance and talent; grace

風華絕代(ㄈㄥ ㄏㄨㄚˊ ㄐㄩㄝˊ ㄉㄞˋ)
unsurpassed elegance and intellectual brilliance

風化(ㄈㄥ ㄏㄨㄚˋ)
① customs and cultural influence; decency ② (chemistry) efflorescence ③ erosion by the elements

風化區(ㄈㄥ ㄏㄨㄚˋ ㄑㄩ)
a district of loose women

風化作用(ㄈㄥ ㄏㄨㄚˋ ㄗㄨㄛˋ ㄩㄥˋ)
(chemistry) efflorescence

風化罪(ㄈㄥ ㄏㄨㄚˋ ㄗㄨㄟˋ)
an offense against public morals

風紀(ㄈㄥ ㄐㄧˋ)
discipline (of students, troops, etc.); general moral standards

風節(ㄈㄥ ㄐㄧㄝˊ)
moral fortitude

風教(ㄈㄥ ㄐㄧㄠˋ)
customs and cultural influence

風景(ㄈㄥ ㄐㄧㄥˇ)
scenery; a landscape

風景畫(ㄈㄥ ㄐㄧㄥˇ ㄏㄨㄚˋ)
a landscape

風景區(ㄈㄥ ㄐㄧㄥˇ ㄑㄩ)
scenic spots

風鏡(ㄈㄥ ㄐㄧㄥˋ)
goggles

風捲殘雲(ㄈㄥ ㄐㄩㄢˇ ㄘㄢˊ ㄩㄣˊ)
like wind sweeping away clouds—to make a clean sweep of something

風起雲湧(ㄈㄥ ㄑㄧˇ ㄩㄣˊ ㄩㄥˇ)

like rising winds and surging clouds—popular support; an enthusiastic response

風氣(ㄈㄥㄑㄧ)
①customs; a general mood; common practices; general environment or circumstances; traditions ②air; manner; bearing

風氣未開(ㄈㄥㄑㄧㄨㄟㄎㄞ)
comparatively primitive or simple in customs; uncivilized; culturally backward

風琴(ㄈㄥㄑㄧㄣ)
(a musical instrument) an organ

風情(ㄈㄥㄑㄧㄥ)
①romantic feelings ②flirtatious expressions; coquetry: 她善於賣弄風情。 She is good at playing the coquetry. ③fine taste; refined feelings

風趣(ㄈㄥㄑㄩ)
interesting; funny; humorous; witty; wit; a sense of humor: 他說話很風趣。 He is a witty talker.

風險(ㄈㄥㄒㄧㄢ)
risk; danger: 從事探險的人必須不怕風險。 Those who take exploration must fear no dangers.

風信(ㄈㄥㄒㄧㄣ)
the season and direction of wind

風信器(ㄈㄥㄒㄧㄣㄑㄧ)
a wind cone

風信子(ㄈㄥㄒㄧㄣㄗ)
(botany)a hyacinth 亦作「洋水仙」

風箱(ㄈㄥㄒㄧㄤ)
bellows; a wind chest

風向(ㄈㄥㄒㄧㄤ)
the direction of wind

風行(ㄈㄥㄒㄧㄥ)
to become fashionable; to be popular: 這首歌曾經風行一時。 The song had a great vogue at one time.

風行草偃(ㄈㄥㄒㄧㄥㄘㄠㄧㄢ)
(literally) When the wind blows, the grass bends.—the influence of moral teaching

風行一時(ㄈㄥㄒㄧㄥㄧㄕ)
to be fashionable for a certain duration; to become a fad of the time

風穴(ㄈㄥㄒㄩㄝ)
where the wind comes from

風致(ㄈㄥㄓ)
appearance; manner and bearing; poise: 風致極佳。 One's appearance and bearing are excellent.

風疹(ㄈㄥㄓㄣ)
rubeola; rubella; German measles; urticaria

風箏(ㄈㄥㄓㄥ)
a kite: 那些孩子們在廣場上放風箏。 Those children were flying kites in the square.

風燭(ㄈㄥㄓㄨ)or 風中殘燭(ㄈㄥㄓㄨㄥㄘㄢㄓㄨ)
a lighted candle in the wind —old and ailing

風燭殘年(ㄈㄥㄓㄨㄘㄢㄋㄧㄢ)
old and ailing like a candle guttering in the wind—old age; in the closing years of one's life

風馳電掣(ㄈㄥㄔㄉㄧㄢㄔㄜ)
to whip along as fast as wind and lightning

風車(ㄈㄥㄔㄜ)
①a windmill ②a kind of toy wheel which turns by the power of wind ③a winnower

風車花(ㄈㄥㄔㄜㄏㄨㄚ)
a passionflower 亦作「西番蓮」

風潮(ㄈㄥㄔㄠ)
①directions of wind and tide ②disturbance, upheaval; a storm; unrest

風塵(ㄈㄥㄔㄣ)
①hardships of traveling around ②confusion of the world ③the world of prostitution

風塵僕僕(ㄈㄥㄔㄣㄆㄨㄆㄨ)
dust-covered and tired from traveling; to be travel-worn and weary

風塵女郎(ㄈㄥㄔㄣㄋㄩㄌㄤ)
a prostitute; a call girl

風成岩(ㄈㄥㄔㄥㄧㄢ)
(geology)aeolian rocks

風吹草動(ㄈㄥㄔㄨㄟㄘㄠㄉㄨㄥ)
the rustle of leaves in the wind—slight commotion; disquiet; slight disturbance

風傳(ㄈㄥㄔㄨㄢ)
①It is said that.... 或It is

rumored that.... ②hearsay; rumor

風濕(ㄈㄥㄕ)
rheumatism

風沙(ㄈㄥㄕㄚ)
a sandy wind; a sandstorm

風扇(ㄈㄥㄕㄢ)
①a fan ②an electric fan

風伸(ㄈㄥㄕㄣ)
①the god of wind; Aeolus ②poise; bearing; manner

風尚(ㄈㄥㄕㄤ)
fashion; a custom, a vogue; a fad; taste of the time

風聲(ㄈㄥㄕㄥ)
①news; rumor;·information 你聽到戰爭的風聲沒有? Have you got news of the war? ② (now rarely) teaching

風聲鶴唳(ㄈㄥㄕㄥㄏㄜㄌㄧ)
to sense danger everywhere; very scared and jittery; to be afraid of one's own shadow

風水(ㄈㄥㄕㄨㄟ)
fengshui—the direction and surroundings of a house or tomb, supposed to have an influence on the fortune of a family and their offsprings a geomantic omen: 他很會看風水。 He is good at practicing geomancy.

風水先生(ㄈㄥㄕㄨㄟㄒㄧㄢㄕㄥ)
a geomancer

風霜(ㄈㄥㄕㄨㄤ)
①wind and frost—hard ships; suffering (usually referring to traveling) ②severe; severity ③time honored

風姿(ㄈㄥㄗ)
looks; graceful bearing

風姿綽約(ㄈㄥㄗㄔㄨㄛㄩㄝ)
(said of a woman) charming poise and graceful bearing

風災(ㄈㄥㄗㄞ)
disaster caused by strong winds, typhoons, etc.

風采(ㄈㄥㄘㄞ)
an elegant manner and appearance; fine deportment graceful bearing

風操(ㄈㄥㄘㄠ)
style, character and behavior

風餐露宿(ㄈㄥㄘㄢㄌㄨㄙㄨ)

(literally) to eat in the wind and sleep in the open air —the hardships of traveling or fieldwork

風從(ㄈㄥ ㄘㄨㄥˊ)
to follow or obey (a popular leader) willingly

風絲(ㄈㄥ ㄙ)
slight breezes; zephyrs

風騷(ㄈㄥ ㄙㄠ)
①(said of women) seductive; flirtatious; coquettish ②refinement in literary works; literary excellence

風掃落葉(ㄈㄥ ㄙㄠˇ ㄌㄨㄛˋ ㄧㄝˋ)
(literally) like wind sweeping away the fallen leaves —irresistible

風俗(ㄈㄥ ㄙㄨˊ)
customs; accepted practices

風俗習慣(ㄈㄥ ㄙㄨˊ ㄒㄧˊ ㄍㄨㄢˋ)
customs and habits

風速(ㄈㄥ ㄙㄨˋ)
wind velocity (or speed)

風衣(ㄈㄥ ㄧ)
a thin, usually waterproof, overcoat for warding off wind and rain

風雅(ㄈㄥ ㄧㄚˇ)
①matters pertaining to writing of poems or other literary works; refinement ②graceful, tasteful; refined: 他的舉止風雅。 He has refined manners.

風謠(ㄈㄥ ㄧㄠˊ)
customs and ditties

風言風語(ㄈㄥ ㄧㄢˊ ㄈㄥ ㄩˇ)or 風言霧語(ㄈㄥ ㄧㄢˊ ㄨˋ ㄩˇ)
groundless, satiric remarks; gossips; slanderous gossips: 風言風語，不聽也罷。 You might as well not listen to the slanderous gossips.

風物(ㄈㄥ ㄨˋ)
sights; scenes; scenery

風味(ㄈㄥ ㄨㄟˋ)
①the bearing and taste of a person ②elegance ③the taste and style of food

風聞(ㄈㄥ ㄨㄣˊ)
rumored; according to unconfirmed reports; to get wind of

風雨(ㄈㄥ ㄩˇ)
wind and rain; the elements —trials and hardships

風雨表(ㄈㄥ ㄩˇ ㄅㄧㄠˇ)
a barometer 亦作「氣壓計」

風雨飄搖(ㄈㄥ ㄩˇ ㄆㄧㄠ ㄧㄠˊ)
precarious; critical (times)

風雨同舟(ㄈㄥ ㄩˇ ㄊㄨㄥˊ ㄓㄡ)
to be in the same boat; sharing a common fate

風雨淒淒(ㄈㄥ ㄩˇ ㄑㄧ ㄑㄧ)
dejection or gloom one feels in time of incessant wind and rain

風雨如晦，雞鳴不已(ㄈㄥ ㄩˇ ㄖㄨˊ ㄏㄨㄟˋ，ㄐㄧ ㄇㄧㄥˊ ㄅㄨˋ ㄧˇ)
(figuratively) to remain sober when the rest of the world is in confusion; to think of the just in times of stress (詩經·國風·風雨)

風雨無阻(ㄈㄥ ㄩˇ ㄨˊ ㄗㄨˇ)
to take place on schedule regardless of weather changes; rain or shine: 我們明天一定到那裏，風雨無阻。We will be there tomorrow, rain or shine.

風月(ㄈㄥ ㄩㄝˋ)
①matters concerning love; seductive arts of a woman ②easy and random (talks, etc.)

風月場中(ㄈㄥ ㄩㄝˋ ㄔㄤˇ ㄓㄨㄥ)
places of debauchery or sensuality; the world of carnal pleasure

風月無邊(ㄈㄥ ㄩㄝˋ ㄨˊ ㄅㄧㄢ)
①The wonders of natural beauty are boundless. ②An amorous affair knows no limits.

風雲(ㄈㄥ ㄩㄣˊ)
①wind and clouds ②unpredictable changes ③high-positioned; high and exalted; imposing

風雲變色(ㄈㄥ ㄩㄣˊ ㄅㄧㄢˋ ㄙㄜˋ)
(said of a disaster) catastrophic; drastic change of a political situation

風雲際會(ㄈㄥ ㄩㄣˊ ㄐㄧˋ ㄏㄨㄟˋ)
the gathering of heroes or talented persons

風雲人物(ㄈㄥ ㄩㄣˊ ㄖㄣˊ ㄨˋ)
a heroic figure; a famed personage; one who is constantly in the news; a man of the hour

風韻(ㄈㄥ ㄩㄣˋ)
charms; poise and bearing

風韻猶存(ㄈㄥ ㄩㄣˋ ㄧㄡˊ ㄘㄨㄣˊ)
(said of a middle-aged woman) to look still attractive

〔風〕 6837
2. ㄈㄥ feng fēng
1. to announce; to make known
2. to ridicule; to satirize
3. to blow

五畫

〔颯〕 6838
ㄙㄚˋ sah sà
1. the sound of wind; rustling
2. weakened; failing; declining

颯沓(ㄙㄚˋ ㄊㄚˋ)
①crowded; numerous; abundant ②flying in a flock

颯遝(ㄙㄚˋ ㄊㄚˋ)
(said of sound) roaring and reverberating

颯然(ㄙㄚˋ ㄖㄢˊ)
the sound of wind

颯颯(ㄙㄚˋ ㄙㄚˋ)
①the swishing sound of wind ②the pattering sound of rain

〔颱〕 6839
ㄊㄞˊ tair tái
a typhoon; a hurricane

颱風(ㄊㄞˊ ㄈㄥ)
a typhoon; a hurricane

颱風警報(ㄊㄞˊ ㄈㄥ ㄐㄧㄥˇ ㄅㄠˋ)
a typhoon warning

颱風眼(ㄊㄞˊ ㄈㄥ ㄧㄢˇ)
a typhoon eye

六畫

〔颳〕 6840
ㄍㄨㄚ gua guā
wind blowing; to blow

颳風(ㄍㄨㄚ ㄈㄥ)
wind blowing

八畫

〔颶〕 6841
ㄐㄩˋ jiuh jù
a hurricane; a gale; strong gusts at sea; a cyclone

颶風(ㄐㄩˋ ㄈㄥ)
a hurricane; a gale; a cyclone

〔風部〕

〔飛部〕

九畫

【颺】 6842 l た yang yáng
1. blown or tossed about by the wind; to float
2. to fly or blow away
3. to scatter; to spread

颺帆 or 揚帆 (l た ㄷㄢ)
to set sail

十畫

【颼】 6843 ㄙㄨ sou sōu
1. blown about by wind
2. the swishing sound of a fast-flying object, as an arrow

【颻】 6844 l ㄠ yaw yáo
waving and drifting with the wind

十一畫

【飄】 6845 ㄆl ㄠ piau piāo
1. to blow; to float (in the air); to waft; to move with the wind: 風飄葉落。The wind blows and the leaves fall from the trees.
2. a cyclone; a whirling wind
3. to float; to drift (on the water) 亦作「漂」; 樹葉在水上飄流著。Leaves were floating on the water.

飄泊 or 飄蕩 (ㄆl ㄠ ㄅㄛ)
to drift about—with no fixed lodging place; to wander: 他在異鄉飄泊了三年。He wandered aimlessly in a strange land for three years.

飄布 (ㄆl ㄠ ㄅㄨ)
an identification badge made of cloth issued by secret societies to their members

飄蓬 (ㄆl ㄠ ㄆㄥ)
①scattered; dispersed ②to drift about alone

飄飄 (ㄆl ㄠ ㄆl ㄠ)
①lightly; airily ②wind blowing to be driven; to wander

飄飄然 (ㄆl ㄠ ㄆl ㄠ ㄖㄢ)
feeling slightly comfortably dizzy, as after a light drink; complacent; self-satisfaction; having a feeling of euphoria or elation; light-footed

飄飄欲仙 (ㄆl ㄠ ㄆl ㄠ ㄩ ㄒl ㄢ)
light, airy, comfortable, complacent

飄風 (ㄆl ㄠ ㄈㄥ)
①a violent wind ②a whirl-wind; a cyclone

飄帶 (ㄆl ㄠ ㄉㄞ)
long bands or ribbons attached to clothes, hats, etc.

飄蕩 or 漂蕩 (ㄆl ㄠ ㄉㄤ)
to drift along without fixed lodging or to float: 小船隨波飄蕩。The boat floated off with the tide.

飄流 (ㄆl ㄠ ㄌl ㄡ)
①to drift; to float ②to knock about; to wander aimlessly

飄零 (ㄆl ㄠ ㄌl ㄥ)
①(said of leaves and plants) falling and withering ②to drift about alone; wandering; homeless

飄落 (ㄆl ㄠ ㄌㄨㄛ)
to fall down slowly in the air

飄忽 (ㄆl ㄠ ㄏㄨ)
①to float in the air hither and thither ②to have no fixed address ③light and speedy

飄忽不定 (ㄆl ㄠ ㄏㄨ ㄅㄨ ㄉl ㄥ)
to drift from place to place: 他的行蹤飄忽不定。He drifted from place to place.

飄疾 (ㄆl ㄠ ㄐl)
quickly; rapidly

飄零 (ㄆl ㄠ ㄒ)
withering and dilapidated

飄雪 (ㄆl ㄠ ㄒㄩㄝ)
snowflakes falling

飄然 (ㄆl ㄠ ㄖㄢ)
gracefully; airily; flying

飄散 (ㄆl ㄠ ㄙㄢ)
dispersed and flying about

飄逸 (ㄆl ㄠ l)
elegant; high, stately and graceful: 他的神采飄逸。He has an elegant bearing.

飄搖 (ㄆl ㄠ l ㄠ)
①to dance and toss about

in the wind ②precarious; unsteady

飄洋 (ㄆl ㄠ l ㄤ)
to take a sea voyage

飄揚 (ㄆl ㄠ l ㄤ)
to be blown about in the wind; to flutter

十二畫

【飆】 6846 (飇) ㄅl ㄠ biau biāo
violent winds; gales

飆車 (ㄅl ㄠ ㄔㄜ)
to speed a car or a motor-cycle

飛 部
ㄈㄟ fei fēi

【飛】 6847 ㄈㄟ fei fēi
1. to fly; to flit: 我們自倫敦飛抵巴黎。We flew from London to Paris.
2. quickly; rapidly
3. high, as a bridge
4. to hang in the air; in the air

飛報 (ㄈㄟ ㄅㄠ)
to report by a fleet messenger; an express message; an urgent dispatch

飛奔 (ㄈㄟ ㄅㄣ) or 飛跑 (ㄈㄟ ㄆㄠ)
to run very fast; to fly: 他沿路飛奔。He flew down the road.

飛盤 (ㄈㄟ ㄆㄢ)
a Frisbee

飛蓬 (ㄈㄟ ㄆㄥ)
①Erigeron acris, a species of raspberry ②to drift or toss in the wind—uncertain or unsteady ③(said of hair) disheveled

飛瀑 (ㄈㄟ ㄆㄨ)
a waterfall; a cascade; a cat-aract

飛沫 (ㄈㄟ ㄇㄛ)
droplets (of a waterfall or from other sputtering sources)

飛毛腿 (ㄈㄟ ㄇㄠ ㄊㄨㄟ)
a fast runner; fleet-footed

飛刀 (ㄈㄟ ㄉㄠ)

〔飛 部〕

①to wield the knife ②a flying knife

飛彈(ㄈㄟ ㄉㄢ)
①a stray bullet or shell ②a missile

飛碟(ㄈㄟ ㄉㄧㄝˊ)
a flying saucer; an unidentified flying object (UFO)

飛短流長
short rumors; malicious gossips; 她太喜歡飛短流長。She is too fond of gossip.

飛騰(ㄈㄟ ㄊㄥˊ)
①to fly high (as one's fortune) ②to soar (as prices)

飛梯(ㄈㄟ ㄊㄧ)
a kind of ladder used in ancient times for attacking the enemy by scaling the city wall

飛艇(ㄈㄟ ㄊㄧㄥˇ)
an airship; a flying boat

飛鳥(ㄈㄟ ㄋㄧㄠˇ)
flying birds

飛來橫禍(ㄈㄟ ㄌㄞˊ ㄏㄥˋ ㄏㄨㄛˋ)or 飛禍(ㄈㄟ ㄏㄨㄛˋ)
sudden, unexpected calamity or misfortune

飛來艷福(ㄈㄟ ㄌㄞˊ ㄧㄢˋ ㄈㄨˊ)
an unexpected romance or affair with a beauty

飛梁(ㄈㄟ ㄌㄧㄤˊ)
a single-span bridge

飛輪(ㄈㄟ ㄌㄨㄣˊ)
①a balance wheel; a flywheel ②a sprocket wheel

飛快(ㄈㄟ ㄎㄨㄞˋ)
①fast; rapidly; with lightning speed; at full speed ②extremely sharp

飛黃騰達(ㄈㄟ ㄏㄨㄤˊ ㄊㄥˊ ㄉㄚˊ)
to make rapid advances in one's career; to ride on the crest of one's success

飛機(ㄈㄟ ㄐㄧ)
an airplane; a plane; 他們搭飛機去香港。They went to Hong Kong by plane.

飛機棚(ㄈㄟ ㄐㄧ ㄆㄥˊ)or 飛機庫(ㄈㄟ ㄐㄧ ㄎㄨˋ)
a hangar

飛機場(ㄈㄟ ㄐㄧ ㄔㄤˇ)
an airport; an airfield; an airdrome

飛機失事(ㄈㄟ ㄐㄧ ㄕ ㄕˋ)
an air accident; a plane

---

crash

飛騎(ㄈㄟ ㄑㄧˊ)
light cavalry

飛劍(ㄈㄟ ㄐㄧㄢˋ)
(in Chinese legend) a sword which can take the life of a person miles away; a flying sword

飛濺(ㄈㄟ ㄐㄧㄢˋ)
to sputter; to splash: 浪花飛濺到岩石上。The waves splashed on the rock.

飛將軍(ㄈㄟ ㄐㄧㄤ ㄐㄩㄣ)or 飛將(ㄈㄟ ㄐㄧㄤ)
①the nickname of Li Kuang (李廣), one of the greatest generals in the Han Dynasty ②an ace pilot

飛禽(ㄈㄟ ㄑㄧㄣˊ)
birds

飛禽走獸(ㄈㄟ ㄑㄧㄣˊ ㄗㄡˇ ㄕㄡˋ)
birds and beasts

飛泉(ㄈㄟ ㄑㄩㄢˊ)
leaping fountains; a geyser; a cliffside spring

飛檄(ㄈㄟ ㄒㄧˊ)
to issue a manifesto

飛翔(ㄈㄟ ㄒㄧㄤˊ)
to fly; to glide in the air; to hover in the air

飛行(ㄈㄟ ㄒㄧㄥˊ)
to fly, as a plane; flight; flying: 飛行是鳥類天生的能力。Flight is natural to birds.

飛行家(ㄈㄟ ㄒㄧㄥˊ ㄐㄧㄚ)
a flyer

飛行甲板(ㄈㄟ ㄒㄧㄥˊ ㄐㄧㄚˇ ㄅㄢˇ)
a flight deck

飛行員(ㄈㄟ ㄒㄧㄥˊ ㄩㄢˊ)
the pilot of a plane

飛雪(ㄈㄟ ㄒㄩㄝˇ)
the falling snow

飛針走線(ㄈㄟ ㄓㄣ ㄗㄡˇ ㄒㄧㄢˋ)
to sew quickly

飛漲(ㄈㄟ ㄓㄤˇ)
(said of prices) to soar rapidly; to skyrocket

飛馳(ㄈㄟ ㄔˊ)
to speed along; 時間飛馳而過。The time sped quickly by.

飛船(ㄈㄟ ㄔㄨㄢˊ)
an airship

飛蟲(ㄈㄟ ㄔㄨㄥˊ)
flying insects

飛石(ㄈㄟ ㄕˊ)

---

stone missiles used in ancient warfare

飛矢(ㄈㄟ ㄕˇ)
a flying arrow

飛砂走石(ㄈㄟ ㄕㄚ ㄗㄡˇ ㄕˊ)
sand and stones flying all about—a very strong wind

飛昇(ㄈㄟ ㄕㄥ)
to soar; to ascend

飛聲騰實(ㄈㄟ ㄕㄥ ㄊㄥˊ ㄕˊ)
excellent in fame as in substance

飛鼠(ㄈㄟ ㄕㄨˇ)
①a bat ②a squirrel glider

飛賊(ㄈㄟ ㄗㄟˊ)
①a thief capable of acrobatic feats; a nimble-footed burglar; a cat burglar ②an intruding enemy airman; an air marauder

飛走(ㄈㄟ ㄗㄡˇ)
①birds and beasts ②to fly away

飛速(ㄈㄟ ㄙㄨˋ)
urgent; quickly; at full speed: 我們的重工業正飛速發展。Our heavy industry is progressing quickly.

飛送(ㄈㄟ ㄙㄨㄥˋ)
to send by an express courier

飛蛾(ㄈㄟ ㄜˊ)
the flying moth; the moth

飛蛾赴火(ㄈㄟ ㄜˊ ㄈㄨˋ ㄏㄨㄛˇ)or 飛蛾投火(ㄈㄟ ㄜˊ ㄊㄡˊ ㄏㄨㄛˇ)or 飛蛾撲火(ㄈㄟ ㄜˊ ㄆㄨ ㄏㄨㄛˇ)
(literally) The flying moth is forever attracted by the flame;—to dig one's own grave; to flirt with death

飛檐(ㄈㄟ ㄧㄢˊ)
the up-turned eaves on the corners of a roof

飛檐走壁(ㄈㄟ ㄧㄢˊ ㄗㄡˇ ㄅㄧˋ)
(said of swordsmen, etc. in old Chinese novels) to leap onto roofs and vault over walls; to fly on eaves and walk on walls—acrobatic feats

飛眼(ㄈㄟ ㄧㄢˇ)
to speak with the eyes; to make eyes; to ogle

飛燕(ㄈㄟ ㄧㄢˋ)
①nimble and quick ②Flying Swallow—name of a queen in the Han Dynasty, a

famous skinny beauty

飛揚（ㄈㄟ ㄧㄤ）
to rise up and flutter, as a flag; to float in the air, as music; to fly about, as dust: 到處飛揚着歡樂的笑聲。Laughter was floating in the air.

飛揚跋扈（ㄈㄟ ㄧㄤ ㄅㄚˊ ㄏㄨˋ）
unruly and haughty

飛鷹走狗（ㄈㄟ ㄧㄥ ㄗㄡˇ ㄍㄡˇ）
to release falcons and unleash dogs—hunting

飛舞（ㄈㄟ ㄨˇ）
① to dance in the wind: 雪花在空中飛舞。Snowflakes are dancing in the air. ② to flutter: 蝴蝶在花叢中翩然飛舞。Butterflies fluttered from flower to flower.

飛吻（ㄈㄟ ㄨㄣˇ）
to throw someone a kiss

飛魚（ㄈㄟ ㄩˊ）
a flying fish; a skipjack

飛魚飛彈（ㄈㄟ ㄩˊ ㄈㄟ ㄉㄢˋ）
(military) an Exocet

飛語（ㄈㄟ ㄩˇ）
groundless words; rumors

飛躍（ㄈㄟ ㄩㄝˋ）
by leaps and bounds; advancing rapidly

十二畫

【飜】6848
（翻）ㄈㄢ　fan　fān
to turn over

食 部
ㄕˊ shyr shí

【食】6849
1. ㄕˊ shyr shí
1. to eat
2. food; meal
3. livelihood; living
4. (an old usage) salary; pay
5. same as 蝕—eclipse

食不甘味（ㄕˊ ㄅㄨˋ ㄍㄢ ㄨㄟˋ）or 食不知味（ㄕˊ ㄅㄨˋ ㄓ ㄨㄟˋ）
to eat food but without knowing its taste—deep anxiety, grief, etc.

食不果腹（ㄕˊ ㄅㄨˋ ㄍㄨㄛˇ ㄈㄨˋ）
to have not enough to eat

食不厭精（ㄕˊ ㄅㄨˋ ㄧㄢˋ ㄐㄧㄥ）
to be meticulous about fine food

食品（ㄕˊ ㄆㄧㄣˇ）
foods; food items; foodstuffs: 穀類和肉都是食品。Grain and meat are foodstuffs.

食品防腐劑（ㄕˊ ㄆㄧㄣˇ ㄈㄤˊ ㄈㄨˇ ㄐㄧˋ）
food disinfectant

食品店（ㄕˊ ㄆㄧㄣˇ ㄉㄧㄢˋ）
a store for selling food items; a food store; a confectionary; a bakery

食品加工（ㄕˊ ㄆㄧㄣˇ ㄐㄧㄚ ㄍㄨㄥ）
food processing

食譜（ㄕˊ ㄆㄨˇ）
a cookbook; a collection of recipes: 請把食譜借給我。Please lend me your cookbook.

食毛踐土（ㄕˊ ㄇㄠˊ ㄐㄧㄢˋ ㄊㄨˇ）
to live on the land and eat what it produces

食米（ㄕˊ ㄇㄧˇ）
rice (husked): 大部分中國人以食米爲生。Most Chinese live on rice.

食俸（ㄕˊ ㄈㄥˋ）
① the salary of a public official ② to be in government service

食道（ㄕˊ ㄉㄠˋ）
① the ways of eating; table manners ② the route for transporting foodstuffs ③ the gullet; the esophagus

食道癌（ㄕˊ ㄉㄠˋ ㄞˊ）
esophageal cancer; carcinoma esophagi

食道炎（ㄕˊ ㄉㄠˋ ㄧㄢˊ）
esophagitis

食堂（ㄕˊ ㄊㄤˊ）
a mess hall; the restaurant

食糖（ㄕˊ ㄊㄤˊ）
sugar

食料（ㄕˊ ㄌㄧㄠˋ）
edibles; foodstuffs; eatables

食糧（ㄕˊ ㄌㄧㄤˊ）
foodstuffs; food grain; provisions: 我們冬季的食糧夠嗎？Have we enough provisions for the winter?

食量（ㄕˊ ㄌㄧㄤˋ）
the quantity of food one consumes; appetite

食祿（ㄕˊ ㄌㄨˋ）
① to draw government pay; to be in public service ② the salary of an official

食古不化（ㄕˊ ㄍㄨˇ ㄅㄨˋ ㄏㄨㄚˋ）
to read a lot of classics without digestion; to be pedantic

食管（ㄕˊ ㄍㄨㄢˇ）
the esophagus 亦作「食道」

食客（ㄕˊ ㄎㄜˋ）
dependent-advisors under a leader in ancient times, especially during the Epoch of Warring States; a person sponging on an aristocrat

食後（ㄕˊ ㄏㄡˋ）
after meal

食火鷄（ㄕˊ ㄏㄨㄛˇ ㄐㄧ）
the cassowary

食具（ㄕˊ ㄐㄩˋ）
a table service (such as bowls, etc.)

食前（ㄕˊ ㄑㄧㄢˊ）
before meal

食指（ㄕˊ ㄓˇ）
the index finger

食指浩繁（ㄕˊ ㄓˇ ㄏㄠˋ ㄈㄢˊ）
many mouths to feed

食蟲動物（ㄕˊ ㄔㄨㄥˊ ㄉㄨㄥˋ ㄨˋ）
an insectivore; insectivorous animals

食蟲類（ㄕˊ ㄔㄨㄥˊ ㄌㄟˋ）
the insectivora

食蟲植物（ㄕˊ ㄔㄨㄥˊ ㄓˊ ㄨˋ）
an insectivore; insectivorous plants

食少事繁（ㄕˊ ㄕㄠˇ ㄕˋ ㄈㄢˊ）
to eat little and work a lot—won't be able to last long

食肉動物（ㄕˊ ㄖㄡˋ ㄉㄨㄥˋ ㄨˋ）
the carnivore

食肉類（ㄕˊ ㄖㄡˋ ㄌㄟˋ）
the carnivora

食肉寢皮（ㄕˊ ㄖㄡˋ ㄑㄧㄣˇ ㄆㄧˊ）
(literally) to eat an enemy's flesh and sleep on his hide—deep hatred for an enemy

carnivorous animals

食草動物（ㄕˊ ㄘㄠˇ ㄉㄨㄥˋ ㄨˋ）
herbivorous animals; herbivores

食草獸（ㄕˊ ㄘㄠˇ ㄕㄡˋ）
herbivorous animals

食色性也（ㄕˊ ㄙㄜˋ ㄒㄧㄥˋ ㄧㄝˇ）
The desire for food and sex is part of human nature.

食宿(ㄕ ㄙㄨ)
board and lodging; bed and
board

食而不化(ㄕ ㄦ ㄅㄨ ㄏㄨㄚˋ)
to eat without digesting—to
read without real compre-
hension

食蟻獸(ㄕ ㄧˇ ㄕㄡˋ)
the anteater; the Ameisenbär

食邑(ㄕ ㄧˋ)
a fief granted to a meritorious person in ancient times

食油(ㄕ ㄧㄡˊ)
edible oil

食鹽(ㄕ ㄧㄢˊ)
kitchen salt; table salt

食言(ㄕ ㄧㄢˊ)
to break one's words or
promise

食言而肥(ㄕ ㄧㄢˊ ㄦ ㄈㄟˊ)
to grow fat by eating one's
words—to break a promise

食無求飽(ㄕ ㄨˊ ㄑㄧㄡˊ ㄅㄠˇ)
to practice pertinence in eating habits

食物(ㄕ ㄨˋ)
eatables; provisions; foodstuffs: 牛奶是有價值的食物。
Milk is a valuable food.

食物配給(ㄕ ㄨˋ ㄆㄟˋ ㄐㄧˇ)
a ration of foodstuffs; food
rationing

食物療法(ㄕ ㄨˋ ㄌㄧㄠˊ ㄈㄚˇ)
dietotherapy

食物鏈(ㄕ ㄨˋ ㄌㄧㄢˋ)
a food chain

食物過敏(ㄕ ㄨˋ ㄍㄨㄛˋ ㄇㄧㄣˇ)
food allergy

食物中毒(ㄕ ㄨˋ ㄓㄨㄥ ㄉㄨˊ)
food poisoning

食慾(ㄕ ㄩˋ)
appetite: 這盤菜能促進你的食
慾。The dish will whet your
appetite.

食慾不振(ㄕ ㄩˋ ㄅㄨ ㄓㄣˋ)
a poor appetite; lack of
appetite: 他今天食慾不振。He
has a poor appetite today.

食玉炊桂(ㄕ ㄩˋ ㄔㄨㄟ ㄍㄨㄟˋ)
the high living costs

食用(ㄕ ㄩㄥˋ)
①edible ②living expenses

食用動物(ㄕ ㄩㄥˋ ㄉㄨㄥˋ ㄨˋ)
meat animals

食用植物(ㄕ ㄩㄥˋ ㄓˊ ㄨˋ)
edible plants; vegetables

【食】6849
2.(飼)ㄙˋ syh sì
to feed

二畫

【飢】6850
ㄐㄧ ji jī
1. hungry; hunger; starving;
famine
2. a Chinese family name

飢不擇食(ㄐㄧ ㄅㄨˋ ㄗㄜˊ ㄕ)
(both literally and figuratively) When one is hungry,
one is not particular about
what he is going to eat. 或
Hunger is the best sauce.

飢民(ㄐㄧ ㄇㄧㄣˊ)
starved people; famished
people

飢渴(ㄐㄧ ㄎㄜˇ)
hungry and thirsty: 她覺得飢
渴。She was feeling hungry
and thirsty.

飢困(ㄐㄧ ㄎㄨㄣˋ)
to be beset by hunger and
poverty

飢寒交迫(ㄐㄧ ㄏㄢˊ ㄐㄧㄠ ㄆㄛˋ)
to suffer from hunger and
cold

飢荒(ㄐㄧ ㄏㄨㄤ)
famine: 千萬人死於飢荒。
Thousands died of famine.

飢饉(ㄐㄧ ㄐㄧㄣˇ)
famine

飢驅(ㄐㄧ ㄑㄩ)
driven by hunger—to toil for
a living

飢者易為食(ㄐㄧ ㄓㄜˇ ㄧˋ ㄨㄟˊ ㄕ)
A hungry person would eat
whatever food that is available.

飢腸轆轆(ㄐㄧ ㄔㄤˊ ㄌㄨˋ ㄌㄨˋ)
to feel very hungry

飢色(ㄐㄧ ㄙㄜˋ)
a hungry look

飢餓(ㄐㄧ ㄜˋ)
hunger; hungry; starvation:
所有人都感到飢餓。All the
people felt hungry.

【飣】6851
ㄉㄧㄥˋ ding dìng
1. food items for the display
purpose only
2. flowery language without
substance

【飡】6852
(餐)ㄘㄢ tsan cān

---

a meal; to eat

三畫

【飧】6853
(飱)ㄙㄨㄣ suen sūn
1. cooked food
2. supper
3. to mix cooked rice with
water

四畫

【飩】6854
ㄊㄨㄣˊ twen tún
as in 餛飩—stuffed dump-
lings

【飪】6855
(餁)ㄖㄣˋ renn rèn
to cook

【飭】6856
ㄔˋ chyh chì
1. severe
2. reverent; respectful; careful
3. to manage; to make ready;
to keep in order
4. to order; to instruct or
direct

飭辦(ㄔˋ ㄅㄢˋ)
to instruct a subordinate to
do something

飭拿(ㄔˋ ㄋㄚˊ)
to give orders for the arrest
of: 警方飭拿竊賊。The police
warrant the arrest of robbers.

飭勵(ㄔˋ ㄌㄧˋ)
to exhort; to instruct and
encourage 亦作「敕勵」

飭令(ㄔˋ ㄌㄧㄥˋ)
to order; to instruct or
direct

飭交(ㄔˋ ㄐㄧㄠ)
to order someone to dis-
patch forward; to deliver

飭知(ㄔˋ ㄓ)
to inform or notify a subordinate or a lower agency: 他
已飭知下屬。He has made
orders known to all the subordinates.

飭查(ㄔˋ ㄔㄚˊ)
to order an investigation: 警
長已飭查此案。The sheriff or-
dered an investigation of the
case.

飭屬(ㄔˋ ㄕㄨˇ)
to order subordinates (to do

〔食
部〕

〔食

部〕

something)

飲遵(ㄧㄣˇ ㄗㄨㄣ)
(said of orders) to be obeyed

【飲】 6857
1. ㄧㄣˇ yiin yǐn

1. to drink
2. drinks: 冷飲 cold drinks 熱飲 hot drinks
3. to swallow (insult, anger, etc.)
4. to be hit (by a bullet, an arrow, etc.)

飲彈(ㄧㄣˇ ㄉㄢˋ)
to be hit by bullets: 他飲彈身亡。He was killed by a bullet.

飲料(ㄧㄣˇ ㄌㄧㄠˋ)
beverages; drinks (usually referring to soft drinks)

飲恨(ㄧㄣˇ ㄏㄣˋ)
①to swallow grievances; to harbor a grudge: 他飲恨而終。He died with a grievance in his heart. ②to be defeated in a competition or contest

飲酒(ㄧㄣˇ ㄐㄧㄡˇ)
to drink wine or liquor

飲泣(ㄧㄣˇ ㄑㄧˋ)
to weep in deep sorrow

飲血(ㄧㄣˇ ㄒㄧㄝˇ)
①to weep in deep sorrow ②to drink blood, as savages do

飲鴆止渴(ㄧㄣˇ ㄓㄣˋ ㄓˇ ㄎㄜˇ)
(literally) to drink poison in order to quench one's thirst —shortsightedness 或 A moment's relief or pleasure can bring endless sufferings to come.

飲茶(ㄧㄣˇ ㄔㄚˊ)
①to drink tea ②(in Kwangtung) to drink tea along with refreshments

飲醇自醉(ㄧㄣˇ ㄔㄨㄣˊ ㄗˋ ㄗㄨㄟˋ)
to win other's support or heart with one's virtue

飲食(ㄧㄣˇ ㄕˊ)
to drink and eat; drink and food: 醫生給病人規定飲食。The doctor put the patient on a diet.

飲食店(ㄧㄣˇ ㄕˊ ㄉㄧㄢˋ)
a small restaurant; an eatery

飲食男女(ㄧㄣˇ ㄕˊ ㄋㄢˊ ㄋㄩˇ)

food and drink and sex —man's major desire

飲食業(ㄧㄣˇ ㄕˊ ㄧㄝˋ)
the catering trade; the restaurant business

飲食無味(ㄧㄣˇ ㄕˊ ㄨˊ ㄨㄟˋ)
to have no appetite for food or drink

飲食衛生(ㄧㄣˇ ㄕˊ ㄨㄟˋ ㄕㄥ)
dietetic hygiene

飲水(ㄧㄣˇ ㄕㄨㄟˇ)
①drinking water ② to drink water

飲水機(ㄧㄣˇ ㄕㄨㄟˇ ㄐㄧ)
a water fountain; a drinking fountain

飲水思源(ㄧㄣˇ ㄕㄨㄟˇ ㄙ ㄩㄢˊ)
(literally) When one drinks water, one thinks of its source.—grateful for favors received; not to forget one's origin

飲醉(ㄧㄣˇ ㄗㄨㄟˋ)
to get drunk

飲用(ㄧㄣˇ ㄩㄥˋ)
to drink: 此水不可飲用。The water is not drinkable.

【飲】 6857
2. ㄧㄣˋ yinn yìn
to make animals drink

飲馬(ㄧㄣˋ ㄇㄚˇ)
to water a horse

【飫】 6858
ㄩˋ yuh yù
1. surfeited; glutted
2. to grant; to confer
3. to feast
4. to eat or drink to repletion

飫聞(ㄩˋ ㄨㄣˊ)
to have heard enough—not again

【飯】 6859
ㄈㄢˋ fann fàn
1. cooked rice; cooked grain for food
2. a meal: 飯前洗手。Wash your hands before you have a meal.
3. to feed
4. a profession; a means of living: 這口飯不容易吃。It is difficult to earn this kind of a living.

飯票(ㄈㄢˋ ㄆㄧㄠˋ)
①a food coupon ②(slang) a husband

飯鋪(ㄈㄢˋ ㄆㄨˋ)
a restaurant; a store selling

cooked rice only

飯店(ㄈㄢˋ ㄉㄧㄢˋ)
①a restaurant ②a hotel

飯攤(ㄈㄢˋ ㄊㄢ)
a food stall; a food stand

飯廳(ㄈㄢˋ ㄊㄧㄥ)
a dining room; a mess hall

飯桶(ㄈㄢˋ ㄊㄨㄥˇ)
①a tub for storing cooked rice ②a good-for-nothing; a stupid or clumsy fellow

飯來開口(ㄈㄢˋ ㄌㄞˊ ㄎㄞ ㄎㄡˇ)or 飯來張口(ㄈㄢˋ ㄌㄞˊ ㄓㄤ ㄎㄡˇ)
to eat but not to work; to live like a parasite; to have only to open one's mouth to be fed—to live an easy life, with everything provided

飯粒(ㄈㄢˋ ㄌㄧˋ)
a grain of cooked rice

飯量(ㄈㄢˋ ㄌㄧㄤˋ)
an appetite; capacity for eating: 他的飯量比你小。He eats less than you do.

飯落兒(ㄈㄢˋ ㄌㄨㄛˋ ㄦ)
a means of living

飯鍋(ㄈㄢˋ ㄍㄨㄛ)
a pot for cooking rice

飯館(ㄈㄢˋ ㄍㄨㄢˇ)
a restaurant

飯盒(ㄈㄢˋ ㄏㄜˊ)
a lunch box; a rice container; a mess tin

飯後(ㄈㄢˋ ㄏㄡˋ)
after meals: 飯後要刷牙。Brush your teeth after meals.

飯局(ㄈㄢˋ ㄐㄩˊ)
a luncheon or dinner party; a feast: 他下星期有兩個飯局。He has two dinner parties next week.

飯前(ㄈㄢˋ ㄑㄧㄢˊ)
before meals: 我們在飯前洗手。We wash our hands before meals.

飯桌(ㄈㄢˋ ㄓㄨㄛ)
a dining table

飯匙倩(ㄈㄢˋ ㄔˊ ㄑㄧㄢˋ)
a trimerous snake, a very venomous snake, found in the mountains of Taiwan

飯食(ㄈㄢˋ ㄕˊ)
①food and meals: 那兒的飯食挺不錯的。I got fine food there. ②to eat rice as staple food

飯菜(ㄈㄢˋ ㄘㄞˋ)
① dishes to go with rice ② a meal; a repast; food

飯碗(ㄈㄢˋ ㄨㄢˇ)
① a rice bowl ②(slang) one's job: 他上個月丟了飯碗. He lost his job last month.

五畫

【飼】 6860
ㄙ syh sì

to feed; to raise (domesticated animals): 他飼養許多羊. He raises a large number of sheep.

飼兔(ㄙ ㄊㄨˋ)
① domesticated rabbits ② to feed rabbits

飼料(ㄙ ㄌㄧㄠˋ)
animal feed; fodder; forage: 放些飼料到倉裏. Put some fodder in the bins.

飼養(ㄙ ㄧㄤˇ)
to raise; to breed: 你用什麼飼養禽獸? What do you feed your poultry on?

【飴】 6861
ㄧˊ yi yí

1. syrup; jellylike sugar made from grains
2. delicious; tasty
3. delicacies
4. to give as a gift; to present

【飽】 6862
ㄅㄠˇ bao bǎo

1. to eat to the full; surfeited
2. satisfied
3. full; plump
4. fully; to the full

飽的的(ㄅㄠˇ ㄅㄠˇ ㄉㄜ˙)
stuffed with food; glutted; surfeited

飽滿(ㄅㄠˇ ㄇㄢˇ)
well-stacked (figures, etc.); full; plump: 他給我看顆粒飽滿的小麥. He showed me the plump wheat.

飽暖(ㄅㄠˇ ㄋㄨㄢˇ)
well-fed and well-clad; more than enough to eat and wear

飽暖思淫慾(ㄅㄠˇ ㄋㄨㄢˇ ㄙ ㄧㄣˊ ㄩˋ)
Debauchery is a common vice among the wealthy.

飽嗝(ㄅㄠˇ ㄍㄜˊ)
flatulence after a solid meal; a hiccup

飽看(ㄅㄠˇ ㄎㄢˋ)
to read or look at to one's heart's content; to feast one's eyes on

飽和(ㄅㄠˇ ㄏㄜˊ)
saturation; saturated: 舊車買賣的市場已趨飽和. The market for used cars is saturated.

飽和點(ㄅㄠˇ ㄏㄜˊ ㄉㄧㄢˇ)
the saturation point

飽和脂肪酸(ㄅㄠˇ ㄏㄜˊ ㄓ ㄈㄤˊ ㄙㄨㄢ)
saturated fatty acid

飽經風霜(ㄅㄠˇ ㄐㄧㄥ ㄈㄥ ㄕㄨㄤ)
① weather-beaten ② to have experienced the vicissitudes of life or have experienced the hardships of life

飽經世故(ㄅㄠˇ ㄐㄧㄥ ㄕˋ ㄍㄨˋ)
well-experienced in the ways of the world

飽學(ㄅㄠˇ ㄒㄩㄝˊ)
well-versed; well-learned or widely-read: 他父親是個飽學鴻儒之士. His father is a well-read, learned literate.

飽學之士(ㄅㄠˇ ㄒㄩㄝˊ ㄓ ㄕˋ)
a learned scholar; an erudite person

飽脹(ㄅㄠˇ ㄓㄤˋ)
glutted; surfeited to the bursting point

飽吃(ㄅㄠˇ ㄔ)or飽餐(ㄅㄠˇ ㄘㄢ)
to eat to one's heart's content; to glut

飽嘗(ㄅㄠˇ ㄔㄤˊ)
to experience or taste (bitterness, hardships, etc.) to the fullest extent: 他飽嘗人生的苦樂. He fully tasted all the sweets and bitters of life.

飽食煖衣(ㄅㄠˇ ㄕˊ ㄋㄨㄢˇ ㄧ)
well-fed and well-clad

飽食終日(ㄅㄠˇ ㄕˊ ㄓㄨㄥ ㄖˋ)
well-fed all day (without doing anything worthwhile)

飽受(ㄅㄠˇ ㄕㄡˋ)
to suffer (insult, grievances, etc.) to the fullest extent: 在車禍中, 她飽受虛驚. She suffered from nervous fears in the car accident.

飽人不知餓人饑(ㄅㄠˇ ㄖㄣˊ ㄅㄨˋ ㄓ ㄜˋ ㄖㄣˊ ㄐㄧ)or飽漢不知餓漢饑
(ㄅㄠˇ ㄏㄢˋ ㄅㄨˋ ㄓ ㄜˋ ㄏㄢˋ ㄐㄧ)
(literally) He who is well-fed does not know what

hunger is like.—He who is in comfortable circumstances does not know the bitterness of misfortune.

飽私囊(ㄅㄠˇ ㄙ ㄋㄤˊ)
to embezzle public funds

飽以老拳(ㄅㄠˇ ㄧˇ ㄌㄠˇ ㄑㄩㄢˊ)
to give someone a sound beating or slugging

【飾】 6863
ㄕˋ shyh shì

1. to ornament; to decorate; to polish (writing); to adorn: 他的言詞需要潤飾. His speech needs polishing.
2. ornamentation; decorations
3. to excuse oneself on a pretext, etc.; to fake
4. clothing and dresses
5. to whitewash; to deceive; to cover up
6. to play the role of; to act the part of

飾非(ㄕˋ ㄈㄟ)
to hide and gloss over one's faults

飾過(ㄕˋ ㄍㄨㄛˋ)
to hide and gloss over one's mistakes; to whitewash: 報告書極力為他飾過. The report whitewashed him.

飾終(ㄕˋ ㄓㄨㄥ)
funeral rites

飾詞(ㄕˋ ㄘˊ)or飾辭(ㄕˋ ㄘˊ)
① an excuse; a pretext ② to polish a piece of writing

飾物(ㄕˋ ㄨˋ)
adornments; decorations; ornaments: 她的房間滿是飾物. Her room is crowded with ornaments.

飾偽(ㄕˋ ㄨㄟˇ)
to fake; to make or copy something in order to deceive

六畫

【餂】 6864
ㄊㄧㄢˇ tean tiǎn

to obtain by hook—to entice or bait with flatteries

【餃】 6865
ㄐㄧㄠˇ jeau jiǎo

stuffed dumplings; ravioli

餃子(ㄐㄧㄠˇ ㄗ˙)
stuffed dumplings; ravioli

〔食部〕

【餈】 6866
（粢）ㄘ tsyr cí
rice cakes

【餉】 6867
ㄒㄧㄤ sheang xiàng
1. pay, provisions, rations, etc. for the military or the police
2. to entertain with food; to feast; to present food as a gift

餉賓（ㄒㄧㄤ ㄅㄧㄣ）or 餉客（ㄒㄧㄤ ㄎㄜˋ）
to entertain guests with food

餉錢（ㄒㄧㄤ ㄑㄧㄢˊ）
a soldier's pay

餉銀（ㄒㄧㄤ ㄧㄣˊ）
military expenditure; a serviceman's pay

【養】 6868
1. ㄧㄤˇ yeang yàng
1. to grow; to raise; to breed; to rear; to bring up
2. to support or keep (a family, etc.)
3. to give birth to: 她養了一個女兒。She gave birth to a girl.
4. to nourish; to cultivate (one's mind, etc.)
5. to educate
6. to nurse (a wound or illness)
7. oxygen 亦作「氧」
8. a Chinese family name

養兵（ㄧㄤ ㄅㄧㄥ）
to maintain and train soldiers (in preparation for war)

養兵千日，用在一朝（ㄧㄤ ㄅㄧㄥ ㄑㄧㄢ ㄖˋ，ㄩㄥˋ ㄗㄞˋ ㄧ ㄓㄠ）
(literally) to maintain an army for a thousand days to use it for a moment

養病（ㄧㄤ ㄅㄧㄥˋ）
①to convalesce; to recuperate; to nurse a disease: 他的父親在家養病。His father is recuperating at home. ②convalescence; recuperation

養母（ㄧㄤ ㄇㄨˇ）
a foster mother

養分（ㄧㄤ ㄈㄣ）
the amount of nutritious substance in a given food item; nutrition

養蜂（ㄧㄤ ㄈㄥ）
to raise or keep bees; to engage in apiculture

養蜂場（ㄧㄤ ㄈㄥ ㄔㄤˇ）
an apiary; a bee yard

養蜂業（ㄧㄤ ㄈㄥ ㄧㄝˋ）
apiculture business

養父（ㄧㄤ ㄈㄨˋ）
a foster father

養父母（ㄧㄤ ㄈㄨˋ ㄇㄨˇ）
foster parents

養禽室（ㄧㄤ ㄑㄧㄣˊ ㄕˋ）
an aviary 亦作「鳥舍」

養女（ㄧㄤ ㄋㄩˇ）
an adopted daughter; a foster daughter

養樂多（ㄧㄤ ㄌㄜˋ ㄉㄨㄛ）
the trademark of a yogurt preparation

養老（ㄧㄤ ㄌㄠˇ）
①(said of persons) to retire and enjoy the fruit of one's work in the past ②to provide for the aged

養老保險（ㄧㄤ ㄌㄠˇ ㄅㄠˇ ㄒㄧㄢˇ）
endowment insurance

養老費（ㄧㄤ ㄌㄠˇ ㄈㄟˋ）
money saved up for old age

養老金（ㄧㄤ ㄌㄠˇ ㄐㄧㄣ）
an old age pension: 他退休後靠養老金過活。He lived on a pension after his retirement.

養老院（ㄧㄤ ㄌㄠˇ ㄩㄢˋ）
a home for destitute old people

養料（ㄧㄤ ㄌㄧㄠˋ）
nutrition; nutritious value

養廉（ㄧㄤ ㄌㄧㄢˊ）
①an old name of salary for public officials ②expenses for supporting or maintaining a living

養路（ㄧㄤ ㄌㄨˋ）
highway or railroad maintenance

養路隊（ㄧㄤ ㄌㄨˋ ㄉㄨㄟˋ）
a road gang; a road maintenance crew

養路稅（ㄧㄤ ㄌㄨˋ ㄕㄨㄟˋ）
highway maintenance tax

養漢（ㄧㄤ ㄏㄢˋ）
(said of a woman) to have extramarital affairs

養虎傷身（ㄧㄤ ㄏㄨˇ ㄕㄤ ㄕㄣ）
(literally) to raise a tiger which will injure its feeder later on—to keep a bad subordinate who will one day bring ruin to his protector

養虎遺患（ㄧㄤ ㄏㄨˇ ㄧˊ ㄏㄨㄢˋ）
To keep a tiger is to invite calamity.—Appeasement brings disaster.

養護（ㄧㄤ ㄏㄨˋ）
①to rear and educate kids ②to maintain; to conserve

養活（ㄧㄤ ˙ㄏㄨㄛ）
①to support or keep (a family or somebody): 他獨力養活一個大家庭。He alone supports a big family. ②to rear; to bring up

養晦（ㄧㄤ ㄏㄨㄟˋ）
to live in retirement and wait for the opportune moment to stage a comeback

養雞（ㄧㄤ ㄐㄧ）
to raise chickens

養雞場（ㄧㄤ ㄐㄧ ㄔㄤˇ）
a chicken farm

養家（ㄧㄤ ㄐㄧㄚ）
to support one's family

養家費（ㄧㄤ ㄐㄧㄚ ㄈㄟˋ）
a family support allowance given to an employee sent away for an assignment which calls for his long absence from home

養家活口（ㄧㄤ ㄐㄧㄚ ㄏㄨㄛˊ ㄎㄡˇ）
to support one's family

養精蓄銳（ㄧㄤ ㄐㄧㄥ ㄒㄩˋ ㄖㄨㄟˋ）
to nourish and discipline one's stamina; to nurse one's strength (in preparation for a challenging task ahead)

養氣（ㄧㄤ ㄑㄧˋ）
①oxygen ②to cultivate and discipline one's capacity for greatness

養媳（ㄧㄤ ㄒㄧˊ）
a daughter-in-law who is brought up in her future husband's home until she comes of age and formally gets married

養心（ㄧㄤ ㄒㄧㄣ）
to cultivate mental calm; to nourish the mind

養性（ㄧㄤ ㄒㄧㄥˋ）
to discipline one's temperament

養殖（ㄧㄤ ㄓˊ）
to breed (aquatics)

養殖漁業（ㄧㄤ ㄓˊ ㄩˊ ㄧㄝˋ）

【食部】

piscilculture

養志(一尤 ㄓ)
①to ennoble one's aspirations ②to be obedient to one's parents; to be a dutiful son

養眞(一尤 ㄓㄣ)
to discipline one's temperament

養珠(一尤 ㄓㄨ)
cultured pearls

養豬(一尤)
to raise hogs or pigs

養豬場(一尤 ㄓㄨ ㄔㄤ)
a pig farm

養成(一尤 ㄔㄥ)
to discipline and train; to cultivate (good habits. etc.); to develop (bad habits, etc.); 我們要養成良好的習慣. We should cultivate good habits.

養成所(一尤 ㄔㄥ ㄙㄨㄛ)
a training school; a training seminar

養贍(一尤 ㄕㄢ)
to support (parents or a family)

養神(一尤 ㄕㄣ)
to have mental relaxation; to give one's mental faculty a rest; 他正在閉目養神呢! He is sitting in repose with his eyes closed.

養傷(一尤 ㄕㄤ)
to nurse one's injuries or wounds

養生(一尤 ㄕㄥ)
to preserve one's health; to keep in good condition

養生之道(一尤 ㄕㄥ ㄓ ㄉㄠ)
a regimen; the formula of healthy living

養生送死(一尤 ㄕㄥ ㄙㄨㄥ ㄙ)or(一尤 ㄕㄥ ㄙㄨㄥ ㄙ)
to support one's parents when they are alive and to look after their funeral arrangement upon their death (which is the duty of a son)

養子(一尤 ㄗ)
①a foster or an adopted son ②to bring up children

養尊處優(一尤 ㄗㄨㄣ ㄔㄨ 一ㄡ)
to live in luxury (or clover); to enjoy high rank and live at ease and in comfort

養蠶(一尤 ㄘㄢ)
to engage in sericulture

養疴 or 養痾(一尤 ㄎㄜ)
to undergo a period of recuperation or convalescence 參看「養病」

養而不敎(一尤 ㄦ ㄅㄨˋ ㄐ一ㄠ)
to bear children without educating them

養兒防老(一尤 ㄦ ㄈㄤ ㄌㄠ)
to raise sons as insurance against the insecurity of old age

養魚(一尤 ㄩ)
to breed fish; to engage in piscilculture

養魚池(一尤 ㄩ ㄔ)
a fishpond

養育(一尤 ㄩ)
to rear; to raise and educate; 養育兒女並非易事. It is not easy to rear children.

養癰遺患(一尤 ㄩㄥ 一 ㄏㄨㄢ)
(literally) A wound not treated in time will cause great trouble afterwards. —Appeasement will bring greater disasters afterwards.

【養】 6868
2. 一尤 yang yáng
to support one's parents

【餌】 6869
ㄦ eel ěr
1. to bait; to entice; bait
2. cakes
3. food
4. to eat

餌敵(ㄦ ㄉ一)
to set up a trap for the enemy

【餁】 6870
ㄖㄣ renn rèn
same as 飪—to cook

【餅】 6871
(餅) ㄅ一ㄥ biing bǐng
1. cakes; biscuits; pastry
2. anything round and flat, as a disc

七畫

【餐】 6872
1. ㄘㄢ tsan cān
1. a meal; 我們一日吃三餐. We take three meals a day.
2. to eat
3. food

餐費(ㄘㄢ ㄈㄟ)

boarding expense; a food bill

餐風宿露(ㄘㄢ ㄈㄥ ㄙㄨˋ ㄌㄨˋ)
(literally) to eat in the wind and sleep in the dew—hardships of traveling in old times 參看「風餐露宿」

餐廳(ㄘㄢ ㄊ一ㄥ)
a restaurant; a dining hall; a mess hall

餐後演說(ㄘㄢ ㄏㄡ 一ㄢ ㄕㄨㄛ)
an after-dinner speech

餐巾(ㄘㄢ ㄐ一ㄣ)
a napkin

餐具(ㄘㄢ ㄐㄩ)
a dinner set; tableware; a dinner-service

餐券(ㄘㄢ ㄑㄩㄢ)
a meal coupon; a meal ticket

餐車(ㄘㄢ ㄔㄜ)
a diner; a dining car

餐飲業(ㄘㄢ 一ㄣ 一ㄝ)
restaurants, bars, coffee houses and tearooms

【餑】 6873
cakes; fancy baked foods

餑餑(ㄅㄛ ·ㄅㄛ)
cakes; tarts and other pastry foods

【餒】 6874
ㄋㄟ neei něi
1. to starve; hungry
2. decay or decomposition of fish
3. lacking in confidence, courage, etc.; disheartened; dispirited

【餓】 6875
ㄜ eh è
1. hungry; hunger
2. greedy; covetous
3. to starve

餓不死(ㄜ ㄅㄨˋ ㄙ)
won't starve; cannot be starved to death

餓莩 or 餓殍(ㄜ ㄆ一ㄠ)
persons starved to death; bodies of famine victims

餓倒(ㄜ ㄉㄠ)
to collapse from hunger

餓了(ㄜ ·ㄌㄜ)
hungry; 她餓得餓了. She was feeling hungry.

餓狼(ㄜ ㄌㄤ)
a greedy and covetous per-

【食
部】

son

餓鬼(さ ㄍㄨㄟ)
①a person who is always
hungry ②a person who eats
piggishly

餓漢(さ ㄏㄢ)
a starving or hungry man

餓虎撲食(さ ㄏㄨ ㄆㄨ ㄕ)
to seize fiercely—like a hungry tiger

餓壞了(さ ㄏㄨㄞ ㄌㄜ)
to be starving: 我餓壞了! 何
時進餐? I'm starving. What
time is dinner?

餓死(さ ㄙ)or餓殺(さ ㄕㄚ)
to die of hunger; to be
starved to death: 很多人餓死
了。A lot of people were
starved to death.

【餔】6876
　　ㄅㄨ bu bū
1. to eat
2. time for supper
3. sunset

餔啜(ㄅㄨ ㄔㄨㄛ)
to eat and drink

餔時(ㄅㄨ ㄕ)
evening; late afternoon;
suppertime 亦作「晡時」

【餖】6877
　　ㄉㄡ dow dòu
food items set out for show,
not to be eaten

餖飣(ㄉㄡ ㄉㄧㄥ)
①food items set out for
show ②showy and flashy
expressions in writings

【餗】6878
　　ㄙㄨ suh sù
food in a caldron or tripod

【餘】6879
　　ㄩ yu yú
1. remaining; the remnant or
remainder; the rest
2. a surplus; an overplus; an
excess
3. a balance
4. a complement of a number
or figure; odd
5. after

餘波(ㄩ ㄅㄛ)
aftermaths; the swell after a
storm; a postlude

餘波蕩漾(ㄩ ㄅㄛ ㄉㄤ ㄧㄤ)
The effect (of a major
event) is still being felt.

餘黨(ㄩ ㄉㄤ)
remnants of an outlawed

faction or disbanded gang

餘地(ㄩ ㄉㄧ)
a spare space; an alternative; elbowroom; leeway: 還
有改進的餘地。There is some
room for improvement.

餘桃(ㄩ ㄊㄠ)
male homosexuality

餘孽(ㄩ ㄋㄧㄝ)
remnants of rebel groups,
secret societies, etc.; surviving supporters of an evil
cause

餘年(ㄩ ㄋㄧㄢ)
the remaining years of one's
life: 餘年可數。One's failing
years are numbered.

餘利(ㄩ ㄌㄧ)
a profit; net profit

餘力(ㄩ ㄌㄧ)
strength or energy to spare

餘糧(ㄩ ㄌㄧㄤ)
surplus grain

餘論(ㄩ ㄌㄨㄣ)
①unfinished comments ②an
epilogue, etc.

餘割(ㄍㄜ)
(mathematics) a cosecant

餘可類推(ㄩ ㄎㄜ ㄌㄟ ㄊㄨㄟ)
The rest may be inferred by
analogy.

餘款(ㄩ ㄎㄨㄢ)
remaining funds; a favorable
balance; surplus funds

餘暉 or 餘輝(ㄩ ㄏㄨㄟ)
twilight at sunset

餘悸(ㄩ ㄐㄧ)
a lingering shock or fear: 她
至今仍心有餘悸。She still has
a lingering fear until now.

餘角(ㄩ ㄐㄧㄠ)
(mathematics) a complement
of an angle; a complemen-
tary angle

餘燼(ㄩ ㄐㄧㄣ)
①ashes; embers ②defeated
and dispersed troops

餘切(ㄩ ㄑㄧㄝ)
(mathematics) a cotangent

餘錢(ㄩ ㄑㄧㄢ)
spare money; surplus funds:
你有沒有餘錢可借? Do you
have any spare money to
lend?

餘慶(ㄩ ㄑㄧㄥ)
①blessings left to one's children ②the name of counties

in Kweichow (貴州) and
Heilungkiang (黑龍江) prov-
inces

餘暇(ㄩ ㄒㄧㄚ)
spare time; leisure; free
time: 我沒有餘暇。I have no
spare time.

餘下的(ㄩ ㄒㄧㄚ ㄉㄜ)
the remainder; the remaining; the rest

餘閒(ㄩ ㄒㄧㄢ)
spare time; leisure

餘弦(ㄩ ㄒㄧㄢ)
(mathematics) a cosine

餘剩(ㄩ ㄒㄧㄥ)
a surplus; an overplus; a
profit

餘香(ㄩ ㄒㄧㄤ)
lingering fragrance

餘興(ㄩ ㄒㄧㄥ)
①an entertainment program
arranged for a gathering ②
a lingering interest; a wish
to prolong a pleasant amusement

餘震(ㄩ ㄓㄣ)
aftershocks in the wake of a
strong earthquake

餘事(ㄩ ㄕ)
①unfinished tasks ②extra
tasks or matters ③matters
of secondary importance

餘生(ㄩ ㄕㄥ)
①the remaining years of
one's life; old age ②a survival (after a disaster)

餘剩(ㄩ ㄕㄥ)
the remainder; the residue

餘數(ㄩ ㄕㄨ)
① the balance ②(math-
ematics) the complement of
a number ③(mathematics)
the residue; the remainder

餘熱(ㄩ ㄖㄜ)
decay heat

餘子(ㄩ ㄗ)
①the others; the rest: 餘子碌
碌。The rest are common
place. ②children by a con
cubine

餘存(ㄩ ㄘㄨㄣ)
a balance; the remainder

餘額(ㄩ ㄜ)

① a surplus amount; a remaining sum; a balance: 餘額不多。The balance is not much. ②vacancies to be filled

餘音嫋嫋(ㄩㄣㄧㄠˇㄋㄧㄠˇ)
The enchanting notes persist long after the musicians bowed out.

餘音繞梁(ㄩㄧㄖㄠˋㄌㄧㄤˊ)
The thrilling voice keeps reverberating in the air after the vocalist has stopped singing.

餘蔭(ㄩˊㄧㄣˋ)
blessings left to one's children

餘映(ㄩˊㄧㄥˋ)
calamity or misfortune which makes itself felt long after the seed was sown

餘外(ㄩˊㄨㄞˋ)
over and above; in addition

餘威(ㄩˊㄨㄟ)
the influence or power of someone that remains after his death

餘味(ㄩˊㄨㄟˋ)
pleasant memories; delicious taste one feels afterward; an aftertaste

餘裕(ㄩˊㄩˋ)
① more than enough; abundant; very well-to-do; ample; plenty ②(said of action)freely and without any constraint

餘勇可賈(ㄩˊㄩㄥˇㄎㄜˇㄍㄨˇ)
with courage to spare; very courageous or brave

八畫

【餅】6880
(餅) ㄅㄧㄥˇ biing bǐng
cakes; cookies; biscuits; pastries; pies; dumplings: 吃一點水果餅吧! Have some fruit pies.

anything roundish, as a disc

餅乾(ㄅㄧㄥˇㄍㄢ)
biscuits or crackers

餡(ㄅㄧㄥˇㄒㄧㄢˊ)
the filling of a pie

餌(ㄅㄧㄥˇㄦˊ)
steamed cakes of rice or wheat flour

【餚】6881
ㄧㄠˊ yau yáo
dishes and foods

【餛】6882
ㄏㄨㄣˊ hwen hún
stuffed dumplings with delicate flour wrapping; ravioli

餛飩(ㄏㄨㄣˊ·ㄊㄨㄣ)
stuffed dumplings with delicate flour wrapping; ravioli

【餞】6883
ㄐㄧㄢˋ jiann jiàn
1. a farewell dinner or luncheon
2. to send off; to convoy
3. to present as a gift
4. preserves; jam: 她很喜歡吃蜜餞。She likes to eat preserves very much.

餞別(ㄐㄧㄢˋㄅㄧㄝˊ)or餞行(ㄐㄧㄢˋㄒㄧㄥˊ)
to entertain a parting friend with a feast or a farewell dinner: 我們下週要為朋友餞行。We'll give our friend a farewell dinner next week.

餞春(ㄐㄧㄢˋㄔㄨㄣ)
(a Chinese custom) a feast to bid farewell to spring toward the end of the season

【餡】6884
ㄒㄧㄢˋ shiann xiàn
anything serving as stuffing for dumplings, etc.

stuffing: 這些餃子餡兒聞起來好香。The stuffing of these dumplings smells good.

餡兒(ㄒㄧㄢˋㄦ)

餡餅(ㄒㄧㄢˋㄅㄧㄥˇ)
a kind of broiled-and-baked meat pie; a pasty

【餧】6885
ㄨㄟˋ wey wèi
same as 餵—to feed

【館】6886
(舘) ㄍㄨㄢˇ goan guǎn
1. a house; a guesthouse; a hotel
2. to stay or lodge
3. an official residence
4. an embassy; a legation; a consulate
5. a place for cultural activities
6. premises
7. a school (in former times)
8. a suffix for a library, teahouse, restaurant, theater,

etc.

館兒(ㄍㄨㄢˇㄦ)
a restaurant; a teahouse; a wineshop

館閣(ㄍㄨㄢˇㄍㄜˊ)
another name of 翰林, an official in charge of academic affairs in former times

館閣氣(ㄍㄨㄢˇㄍㄜˊㄑㄧˋ)
flowery, ornamental but a little stale literary style

館長(ㄍㄨㄢˇㄓㄤˇ)
a superintendent; a curator; the head of a library or an institute, etc.: 這個圖書館的館長工作很努力。The head of the library works very hard.

館舍(ㄍㄨㄢˇㄕㄜˋ)
a guesthouse: 館舍幽雅。The guesthouse is quiet and tasteful.

餖子(ㄍㄨㄢˇㄗ)
① a restaurant: 我們常上館子。We often dine in a restaurant. ② a theater

【餜】6887
ㄍㄨㄛˇ guoo guǒ
cakes, dumplings, etc.

餜子(ㄍㄨㄛˇㄗ)
twisted fritters 亦作「油條」

【餟】6888
ㄓㄨㄟˋ juey zhuì
a libation

九畫

【餮】6889
ㄊㄧㄝˇ tieh tiě
as in 饕餮
1. a legendary fierce animal
2. a greedy and gluttonous person

【餱】6890
ㄏㄡˊ hour hóu
dry provisions

餱糧(ㄏㄡˊㄌㄧㄤˊ)
dry provisions

【餬】6891
ㄏㄨˊ hwu hú
1. congee; porridge; gruel
2. paste

餬口(ㄏㄨˊㄎㄡˇ)
just to make ends meet; to make a bare living; to eke out one's livelihood

餬紙(ㄏㄨˊㄓˇ)
① to paste paper ②paper

for pasting

【餳】 6892　ㄒㄧㄥˊ shyng xíng
1. malt sugar or syrup
2. sticky
3. poor or dull (eyesight)

【餵】 6893　(餧) ㄨㄟˋ wey wèi
to feed; to raise

餵奶(ㄨㄟˋ ㄋㄞˇ)
to feed a baby with milk; to
breast-feed: 她堅持要自己餵
奶。She insisted on breast-
feeding her own child.

餵牲口(ㄨㄟˋ ㄕㄥ ㄎㄡˇ)
to raise or feed domestic
animals

餵養(ㄨㄟˋ ㄧㄤˇ)
to raise; to rear; to keep

十畫

【餿】 6894　ㄙㄡ sou sóu
1. decayed; rotten; stale; ran-
cid; spoiled: 菜餿了。The dish
has spoiled.
2. lousy; foul

餿腿(ㄙㄡ ㄊㄨㄟˇ)
to do a lot of legwork in
vain

餿主意(ㄙㄡ ㄓㄨˇ ㄧˋ)
a lousy idea: 這是誰的餿主
意? Whose rotten (or lousy)
idea is this?

餿臭(ㄙㄡ ㄔㄡˋ)
rotten and smelly

餿酸(ㄙㄡ ㄙㄨㄢ)
stale

【餼】 6895　ㄒㄧˋ shih xì
1. to present as a gift
2. animals; animals for sacrifices
3. grains; rice
4. animal feed; fodder

餼牢(ㄒㄧˋ ㄌㄠˊ)
animals; animals for sacrifices

餼廩(ㄒㄧˋ ㄌㄧㄣˇ)
(in ancient China) grain allowances for salaried graduates

餼羊(ㄒㄧˋ ㄧㄤˊ)
sheep for sacrifices

【餾】 6896　ㄌㄧㄡˊ liow liú
1. to steam

2. distilled (water)

【餻】 6897　(糕) ㄍㄠ gau gāo
cakes; dumplings

【餽】 6898
(饋) ㄎㄨㄟˋ kuey kuì
1. to offer food to a superior
2. to present as a gift

十一畫

【饅】 6899　ㄇㄢˊ man mán
stuffed or unstuffed dumplings; steamed buns; steamed
bread

饅頭(ㄇㄢˊ ˙ㄊㄡ)
steamed dumplings

【饈】 6900　ㄒㄧㄡ shiou xiū
1. to eat; a meal
2. to offer; to offer as tribute
3. delicious food; a delicacy; a
dainty

【饉】 6901　ㄐㄧㄣˇ jiin jǐn
as in 饑饉—famine; hunger

十二畫

【饋】 6902　ㄎㄨㄟˋ kuey kuì
1. to offer food to a superior
2. to send someone a present;
to present as a gift

饋貧糧(ㄎㄨㄟˋ ㄆㄧㄣˊ ㄌㄧㄤˊ)
①food for the poor② (fig-
uratively) knowledge for the
ignorant

饋糧(ㄎㄨㄟˋ ㄌㄧㄤˊ)
to send provisions

饋路(ㄎㄨㄟˋ ㄌㄨˋ)
a route for military supplies

饋食(ㄎㄨㄟˋ ㄕˊ)
(in ancient China) to offer
cooked food as sacrifices

饌人(ㄓㄨㄢˋ ㄖㄣˊ)
a cook

饋贈(ㄎㄨㄟˋ ㄗㄥˋ)
to present (a gift); to make
a present of something

【饌】 6903　ㄓㄨㄢˋ juann zhuàn
1. to prepare food
2. food and drink; dainties
3. to eat and drink

饌具(ㄓㄨㄢˋ ㄐㄩˋ)
food vessels: 饌具齊備。Food

vessels are complete.

【饑】 6904　ㄐㄧ ji jī
1. a year of famine
2. hunger; hungry

饑溺(ㄐㄧ ㄋㄧˋ)
extreme sufferings among
the masses

饑寒交迫(ㄐㄧ ㄏㄢˊ ㄐㄧㄠ ㄆㄛˋ)
to suffer from both the cold
and hunger

饑荒(ㄐㄧ ㄏㄨㄤ)
famine

饑饉(ㄐㄧ ㄐㄧㄣˇ)
starvation; famine

饑歉(ㄐㄧ ㄑㄧㄢˋ)
famine; scarcity

饑驅(ㄐㄧ ㄑㄩ)
driven by hunger or famine

【饒】 6905　ㄖㄠˊ rau ráo
1. abundant; plentiful; full or
fertile
2. to give something extra as
a gift; to let somebody have
something into the bargain
3. to forgive; to spare; to have
mercy; to let somebody off
4. lenient; liberal
5. (now rarely) even though; in
spite of the fact that; wha
ever
6. a Chinese family name

饒命(ㄖㄠˊ ㄇㄧㄥˋ)
to spare a life

饒富(ㄖㄠˊ ㄈㄨˋ)
affluence; abundant; plent
ful

饒多(ㄖㄠˊ ㄉㄨㄛ)
affluence

饒舌(ㄖㄠˊ ㄕㄜˊ)
loquacious; talkative; garr
lous; voluble

饒恕(ㄖㄠˊ ㄕㄨˋ)
to forgive; to pardon: 他偷
已被饒恕。He was forgive
for stealing the money.

饒人(ㄖㄠˊ ㄖㄣˊ)
①to forgive another perso
他不輕易饒人。He is not
man who forgives easily.
to give the other guy a wa
out

饒讓(ㄖㄠˊ ㄖㄤˋ)
to forgive; to be tolerant o
lenient

饒益(ㄖㄠˊ ㄧˋ)

abundance; wealthy; a surplus

饒沃(ㄖㄠ ㄨㄛ)
fertile: 臺灣是饒沃之地。Taiwan is a piece of fertile land.

饒裕(ㄖㄠ ㄩ)
abundance; affluence

【饍】6906
(膳) ㄕㄢ shann shàn
1. a meal
2. to eat; to board

【餾】6907
(餾) ㄌㄧㄡ liow liú
1. to steam
2. to distill

十三畫

【饗】6908
ㄒㄧㄤ sheang xiǎng
1. to dine and wine guests; to give a big party or a banquet
2. a sacrificial ceremony

饗宴(ㄒㄧㄤ ㄧㄢ)
a feast

【饔】6909
ㄩㄥ iong yōng
1. cooked food
2. breakfast
3. slaughtered animals

饔牲(ㄩㄥ ㄕㄥ)
to present slaughtered or live animals to another

饔飱(ㄩㄥ ㄙㄨㄣ)
breakfast and supper

饔飱不繼(ㄩㄥ ㄙㄨㄣ ㄅㄨ ㄐㄧ)
discontinuation of supper after breakfast—poverty-stricken

【饕】6910
ㄊㄠ tau tāo
1. name of a legendary ferocious animal
2. a fierce person
3. a greedy and gluttonous person

饕餮(ㄊㄠ ㄊㄧㄝ)or饕餮之徒(ㄊㄠ ㄊㄧㄝ ㄓ ㄊㄨ)
① gluttons; greedy persons ②
name of ancient barbarian tribes

【饘】6911
ㄓㄢ jan zhān
thick congee or porridge

饘粥(ㄓㄢ ㄓㄡ)or(ㄓㄢ ㄓㄡ)

---

congee; porridge

十四畫

【饜】6912
ㄧㄢ yann yàn
1. full-stomached; sufficient; surfeited; satiated
2. to partake plentifully of

饜食(ㄧㄢ ㄕ)
to eat to repletion

饜事(ㄧㄢ ㄕ)
plenty to do; busy

饜足(ㄧㄢ ㄗㄨ)
surfeited; satiated

饜飫(ㄧㄢ ㄩ)
to eat to repletion; to glut

十六畫

【饃】6913
(饝) ㄇㄛ mo mó
steamed dumplings

饃饃(ㄇㄛ ˙ㄇㄛ)
steamed dumplings

十七畫

【饞】6914
ㄔㄢ charn chán
piggish; gluttonous; greedy

饞癆(ㄔㄢ ㄌㄠ)
① to be piggish about good food ② lecherous; lewd

饞涎欲滴(ㄔㄢ ㄒㄧㄢ ㄩ ㄉㄧ)
(said of mouth) to water; to drool over; to covet

饞嘴(ㄔㄢ ㄗㄨㄟ)
gluttonous

首 部
ㄕㄡ shoou shǒu

【首】6915
ㄕㄡ shoou shǒu
1. the head
2. the king; the emperor; the chief; the leader
3. the first; the beginning: 他搭首班車去台中。He took the first bus to Taichung.
4. a (poem, song, etc.): 請爲我們唱一首歌。Sing a song for us.

首謀(ㄕㄡ ㄇㄡ)
the first and chief planner; the mastermind; the ring-leader

首犯(ㄕㄡ ㄈㄢ)
the ringleader; the principal criminal

首度(ㄕㄡ ㄉㄨ)
(said of a sports team) to meet another team for the first game

首府(ㄕㄡ ㄈㄨ)
the capital city: 倫敦是英國的首府。London is the capital city of England.

首當其衝(ㄕㄡ ㄉㄤ ㄑㄧ ㄔㄨㄥ)
the first to bear the brunt of

首都(ㄕㄡ ㄉㄨ)
the (national) capital: 華盛頓爲美國首都。Washington, D. C. is the capital of the U.S.

首途(ㄕㄡ ㄊㄨ)or首道(ㄕㄡ ㄊㄠ)
to start on one's way; to embark on a journey

首推(ㄕㄡ ㄊㄨㄟ)
to consider (a person) first

首腦(ㄕㄡ ㄋㄠ)or首腦人物(ㄕㄡ ㄋㄠ ㄖㄣ ㄨ)
the chief; the boss; the key member; the mastermind

首難(ㄕㄡ ㄋㄢ)
the first to start an uprising

首領(ㄕㄡ ㄌㄧㄥ)
① the leader; the chief: 他是我的首領。He is my chief. ② head and neck

首輪放映(ㄕㄡ ㄌㄨㄣ ㄈㄤ ㄧㄥ)
first runs

首告(ㄕㄡ ㄍㄠ)
① the informer; the squeaker ② the first to

首功(ㄕㄡ ㄍㄨㄥ)
① merit for the number of enemy soldiers one has beheaded ② the first merit; the most merited

首肯(ㄕㄡ ㄎㄣ)
to nod one's head in approval; to approve

首揆(ㄕㄡ ㄎㄨㄟ)or首相(ㄕㄡ ㄒㄧㄤ)
the premier; the prime minister: 大家向首相歡呼。The people cheered the premier.

首級(ㄕㄡ ㄐㄧ)
the human head

首屆(ㄕㄡ ㄐㄧㄝ)

【香部】

the first (conference, assembly, etc.)

首七 (ㄕㄡˇ ㄑㄧ)
the 7th day after a person's death

首妻 (ㄕㄡˇ ㄑㄧ)
one's first wife; one's legal wife (as distinct from concubines)

首屈一指 (ㄕㄡˇ ㄑㄩ ㄧ ㄓˇ)
the foremost; second to none; the best: 他是我國首屈一指的詩人。 He is our foremost poet.

首席 (ㄕㄡˇ ㄒㄧˊ)
the highest-ranking; the highest-positioned; the senior

首席代表 (ㄕㄡˇ ㄒㄧˊ ㄉㄞˋ ㄅㄧㄠˇ)
the chief delegate

首席女高音 (ㄕㄡˇ ㄒㄧˊ ㄋㄩˇ ㄍㄠ ㄧㄣ)
the chief soprano

首席女主角 (ㄕㄡˇ ㄒㄧˊ ㄋㄩˇ ㄓㄨˇ ㄐㄩㄝˊ)
the premiere (the leading lady in an opera)

首席檢察官 (ㄕㄡˇ ㄒㄧˊ ㄐㄧㄢˇ ㄔㄚˊ ㄍㄨㄢ)
the chief procurator

首席小提琴手 (ㄕㄡˇ ㄒㄧˊ ㄒㄧㄠˇ ㄊㄧˊ ㄑㄧㄣˊ ㄕㄡˇ)
the concertmaster

首先 (ㄕㄡˇ ㄒㄧㄢ)
the very first; at first; first of all: 首先要盡你自己的義務。 Do your own duty first of all.

首選 (ㄕㄡˇ ㄒㄩㄢˇ)
① the best among the successful candidates under the old civil service examination system ② preliminary elections

首長 (ㄕㄡˇ ㄓㄤˇ)
the chief (of a tribe, bureau, department, ministry, etc.); the leading cadre; the senior officer

首倡 (ㄕㄡˇ ㄔㄤˋ)
the first to advocate; to initiate; to pioneer; to originate: 這計劃是誰首倡的? With whom did the scheme originate?

首唱 (ㄕㄡˇ ㄔㄤˋ)
① the first to advocate ② (in a poem-composing contest) the first to complete a poem

首創 (ㄕㄡˇ ㄔㄨㄤˋ)

to found; to start; to initiate

首位 (ㄕㄡˇ ㄨㄟˋ)

首飾 (ㄕㄡˇ ㄕˋ)
jewelry; ornaments; trinkets

首善之區 (ㄕㄡˇ ㄕㄢˋ ㄓ ㄑㄩ)
the national capital

首鼠兩端 (ㄕㄡˇ ㄕㄨˇ ㄌㄧㄤˇ ㄉㄨㄢ)
procrastinating; vacillating; hesitating

首任 (ㄕㄡˇ ㄖㄣˋ)
the first to be appointed to an office

首如飛蓬 (ㄕㄡˇ ㄖㄨˊ ㄈㄟ ㄆㄥˊ)
disheveled hair; hair like the flying artemisia; hair like a rebellious floor-mopper

首遭敗績 (ㄕㄡˇ ㄗㄠ ㄅㄞˋ ㄐㄧ)
to suffer the first defeat

首座 (ㄕㄡˇ ㄗㄨㄛˋ)
① the first seat; the highest ranking or positioned ② the senior monk in a Buddhist sanctuary

首從 (ㄕㄡˇ ㄘㄨㄥˊ)or(ㄕㄡˇ ㄗㄨㄥ)
the ringleader and the followers; the principal and the accessory

首次 (ㄕㄡˇ ㄘˋ)
the first time: 我首次見到她是五年以前。I first met her five years ago.

首惡 (ㄕㄡˇ ㄜˋ)
the principal (criminal); the ringleader

首義 (ㄕㄡˇ ㄧˋ)
the first to rise up against tyranny, etc.

首頁 (ㄕㄡˇ ㄧㄝˋ)
the first page; page number one; the title page

首要 (ㄕㄡˇ ㄧㄠˋ)
of the first importance; first of all; chief

首要條件 (ㄕㄡˇ ㄧㄠˋ ㄊㄧㄠˊ ㄐㄧㄢˋ)
the number one condition; a prerequisite; the most important

首映 (ㄕㄡˇ ㄧㄥˋ)
the premiere (of a movie)

首尾 (ㄕㄡˇ ㄨㄟˇ)
① the head and the tail; the beginning and the end ② from beginning to end

首尾相應 (ㄕㄡˇ ㄨㄟˇ ㄒㄧㄤ ㄧㄥˋ)
head and tail (or beginning and end) corresponding with each other

首位 (ㄕㄡˇ ㄨㄟˋ)
① the place of honor ② the first place

二畫

【逵】 6916
ㄎㄨㄟˊ kwei kuí
1. a road; a path
2. as in 鍾馗—the name of a Taoist immortal, famous for catching evil spirits

八畫

【馘】 6917
(聝) 《ㄍㄨㄛˊ gwo guó
to count the number of enemy troops one killed by the number of the left ears cut from the bodies

香 部
ㄒㄧㄤ shiang xiāng

【香】 6918
ㄒㄧㄤ shiang xiāng
1. sweet-smelling; fragrant; aromatic; balmy
2. tasty; delicious
3. fair; beautiful
4. incense; spice; balm

香餑餑兒 (ㄒㄧㄤ ㄅㄛ ㄅㄛ ㄦ)
① a beloved person ② a welcome thing

香檳 or 香賓 (ㄒㄧㄤ ㄅㄧㄣ)
champagne

香噴噴的 (ㄒㄧㄤ ㄆㄣ ㄆㄣ ㄉㄜ)
smelling very good; sweet-smelling

香片 (ㄒㄧㄤ ㄆㄧㄢˋ)
jasmine tea: 我喜歡香片甚於紅茶。I like jasmine tea better than black tea.

香妃 (ㄒㄧㄤ ㄈㄟ)
a Muslim concubine of Emperor Kao Tsung of the Ching Dynasty

香粉 (ㄒㄧㄤ ㄈㄣˇ)
cosmetic powder

香楓 (ㄒㄧㄤ ㄈㄥ)
a kind of liquidambar; a sweet gum

香馥馥 (ㄒㄧㄤ ㄈㄨˋ ㄈㄨˋ)

sweet-smelling; fragrant

香袋(ㄒㄧㄤ ㄉㄞˋ)
a sachet; a small perfumed bag

香稻(ㄒㄧㄤ ㄉㄠˋ)
rice (a poetic term)

香燈(ㄒㄧㄤ ㄉㄥ)
incense sticks and lamps burning on an altar

香甜(ㄒㄧㄤ ㄊㄧㄢˊ)
① sweet; delicious ②(to sleep) soundly

香囊(ㄒㄧㄤ ㄋㄤˊ)
a sachet

香紙紙馬(ㄒㄧㄤ ㄓˇ ㄓˇ ㄇㄚˇ)or 香燭
楮馬(ㄒㄧㄤ ㄓㄨˊ ㄔㄨˇ ㄇㄚˇ)
incense, candles and paper horses—materials for worship and sacrifices for the dead

香料(ㄒㄧㄤ ㄌㄧㄠˋ) 她在小甜餅上加
spice; balm: 香料。She adds spice to cookies.

香奩(ㄒㄧㄤ ㄌㄧㄢˊ)
women's toiletries

香爐(ㄒㄧㄤ ㄌㄨˊ)
a thurible; a censer

香港(ㄒㄧㄤ ㄍㄤˇ)
Hong Kong, or Hongkong:
香港是遠東的貿易中心。Hong Kong is the commercial center of the Far East.

香港腳(ㄒㄧㄤ ㄍㄤˇ ㄐㄧㄠˇ)
Hongkong foot; athlete's foot

香菇(ㄒㄧㄤ ㄍㄨ)
a kind of edible mushroom grown on wooden logs

香瓜(ㄒㄧㄤ ㄍㄨㄚ)
a muskmelon; a cantaloupe:
這香瓜味道甚美。This cantaloupe is delicious.

香閨(ㄒㄧㄤ ㄍㄨㄟ)
a lady's chamber

香客(ㄒㄧㄤ ㄎㄜˋ)
visitors to temples; pilgrims:
很多香客去耶路撒冷。Many pilgrims went to Jerusalem.

香荷包(ㄒㄧㄤ ㄏㄜˊ ㄅㄠ)
a kind of sachet

香花(ㄒㄧㄤ ㄏㄨㄚ)
fragrant flowers

香火(ㄒㄧㄤ ㄏㄨㄛˇ)
① incense burned and candles lighted in honor of a

deity, an ancestor, etc. ② an oath; a vow

香火因緣(ㄒㄧㄤ ㄏㄨㄛˇ ㄧㄣ ㄩㄢˊ)
brotherhood based on an oath made in one's previous life; deep mental accord between friends

香灰(ㄒㄧㄤ ㄏㄨㄟ)
ashes of incense

香會(ㄒㄧㄤ ㄏㄨㄟˋ)
a group of pilgrims from various walks of people such as acrobats, stilts-walkers, tailors, food vendors, etc.

香蕉(ㄒㄧㄤ ㄐㄧㄠ)
a banana

香蕉皮(ㄒㄧㄤ ㄐㄧㄠ ㄆㄧˊ)
banana peelings

香精(ㄒㄧㄤ ㄐㄧㄥ)
essence

香氣(ㄒㄧㄤ ㄑㄧˋ)
a sweet smell; a pleasant odor; fragrance; aroma: 玫瑰花香襲宜人。These roses have delightful fragrance.

香錢(ㄒㄧㄤ ㄑㄧㄢˊ)
cash contributions by visitors to a temple

香消玉殞(ㄒㄧㄤ ㄒㄧㄠ ㄩˋ ㄩㄣˇ)
(literally) The fragrance is gone and the jade is fallen.
—The beauty is dead.

香燭(ㄒㄧㄤ ㄓㄨˊ)
incense and candles—materials for the altar

香巢(ㄒㄧㄤ ㄔㄠˊ)
a brothel; a house of ill fame

香腸(ㄒㄧㄤ ㄔㄤˊ)
sausage

香串(ㄒㄧㄤ ㄔㄨㄢˋ)
a rosary made of fragrant material

香椿頭(ㄒㄧㄤ ㄔㄨㄣ ㄊㄡˊ)
cedar shoots

香山居士(ㄒㄧㄤ ㄕㄢ ㄐㄩ ㄕˋ)
a nickname of the Tang Dynasty poet Pai Chü-i(白居易)

香水(ㄒㄧㄤ ㄕㄨㄟˇ)
perfume; scent: 她用了過多的香水。She uses too much scent.

香肉(ㄒㄧㄤ ㄖㄡˋ)
(euphemism) dog meat

香澤(ㄒㄧㄤ ㄗㄜˊ)
perfumed hair oil

香皂(ㄒㄧㄤ ㄗㄠˋ)
perfumed soap; toilet soap:
我買了一塊香皂。I bought a cake of toilet soap.

香菜(ㄒㄧㄤ ㄘㄞˋ)
parsley

香草(ㄒㄧㄤ ㄘㄠˇ)
① vanilla ② a fragrant herb

香草美人(ㄒㄧㄤ ㄘㄠˇ ㄇㄟˇ ㄖㄣˊ)
a loyal vassal and his lord
(from a metaphor in 離騷)

香酥雞(ㄒㄧㄤ ㄙㄨ ㄐㄧ)
crisp fried chicken

香案(ㄒㄧㄤ ㄢˋ)
a long altar on which incense burners are placed; an incense table

香油(ㄒㄧㄤ ㄧㄡˊ)
① perfumed oil; aromatic oil
② sesame oil

香煙(ㄒㄧㄤ ㄧㄢ)
① cigarettes ② continuity of the family line: 他家香煙絕了。His family line died out.
③ smoke of burning incense

香豔(ㄒㄧㄤ ㄧㄢˋ)
full of glamor; glamorous; amorous

香豔故事(ㄒㄧㄤ ㄧㄢˋ ㄍㄨˋ ㄕˋ)or 香豔小說(ㄒㄧㄤ ㄧㄢˋ ㄒㄧㄠˇ ㄕㄨㄛ)
a love story

香味(ㄒㄧㄤ ㄨㄟˋ)
spicy taste; aromatic flavor

香櫞(ㄒㄧㄤ ㄩㄢˊ)
a kind of fragrant but inedible citron 亦稱「佛手柑」

香雲紗(ㄒㄧㄤ ㄩㄣˊ ㄕㄚ)
silk fabric with a thin film of lacquer on the surface, manufactured in Kwangtung and used as summer dress material

九畫

【馥】 6919
ㄈㄨˋ fuh fù
fragrance; aroma

馥郁(ㄈㄨˋ ㄩˋ)
powerfully fragrant

十一畫

【馨】 6920
ㄒㄧㄣ shin xīn
(又讀 ㄒㄧㄥ shing xīng)

〔香部〕

〔馬部〕

fragrance or aroma (especially that which comes from afar)

馨香(ㄒㄧㄣ ㄒㄧㄤ)
fragrance; aroma

馬 部

ㄇㄚ maa mǎ

【馬】 6921
ㄇㄚ maa mǎ

1. a horse: 人有失錯, 馬有漏蹄. Men all make mistakes; horses all stumble.
2. a Chinese family name

馬背(ㄇㄚ ㄅㄟ)
horseback: 他騎在馬背上。He is on horseback.

馬寶(ㄇㄚ ㄅㄠ)
bezoar of a horse (used as medicine)

馬棒(ㄇㄚ ㄅㄤ)
a short club for driving a horse

馬錶 or 馬表(ㄇㄚ ㄅㄧㄠ)
a pocket watch; a stopwatch: 馬錶壞了。The stopwatch will not work.

馬鞭子(ㄇㄚ ㄅㄧㄢ ㄗ)
a horsewhip

馬弁(ㄇㄚ ㄅㄧㄢ)
bodyguards or orderlies of ranking officers in former times

馬不停蹄(ㄇㄚ ㄅㄨˋ ㄊㄧㄥ ㄊㄧˊ)
to travel on horseback without stop—to do something without stop or a single halt

馬棚(ㄇㄚ ㄆㄥ)
a stable

馬匹(ㄇㄚ ㄆㄧ)
horses; horseflesh: 他是個鑑別馬匹的行家。He's a good judge of horseflesh.

馬屁大王(ㄇㄚ ㄆㄧˋ ㄉㄚˋ ㄨㄤ)
a sycophant; a flatterer

馬屁精(ㄇㄚ ㄆㄧˋ ㄐㄧㄥ)
a flatterer; a toady

馬屁之用大矣哉(ㄇㄚ ㄆㄧˋ ㄓ ㄩㄥˋ ㄉㄚˋ ㄧˇ ㄗㄞ)
Flattery is everything.

馬票(ㄇㄚ ㄆㄧㄠ)
a pari-mutuel ticket

馬馬虎虎(ㄇㄚ ㄇㄚ ㄏㄨ ㄏㄨ)or 馬虎(ㄇㄚ ㄏㄨ)
① perfunctory; careless; sloppy; slovenly ② not very good; so-so

馬販子(ㄇㄚ ㄈㄢˋ ㄗ)
a horse dealer; a horse-coper

馬糞(ㄇㄚ ㄈㄣˋ)
horse dung

馬糞紙(ㄇㄚ ㄈㄣˋ ㄓ)
a kind of coarse cardboard; strawboard

馬房(ㄇㄚ ㄈㄤ)
a stable

馬夫(ㄇㄚ ˙ㄈㄨ)
a groom: 馬夫餵食廐中的馬。The groom fed the horses in the stable.

馬達(ㄇㄚ ㄉㄚˊ)
a motor

馬達加斯加(ㄇㄚ ㄉㄚˊ ㄐㄧㄚ ㄙ ㄐㄧㄚ)
Madagascar

馬德拉斯(ㄇㄚ ㄉㄜˊ ㄌㄚ ㄙ)
Madras, an Indian port

馬德里(ㄇㄚ ㄉㄜˊ ㄌㄧˇ)
Madrid, the capital of Spain

馬刀(ㄇㄚ ㄉㄠ)
a saber

馬到成功(ㄇㄚ ㄉㄠˋ ㄔㄥˊ ㄍㄨㄥ)
to be accomplished quickly and easily; with immediate success

馬燈(ㄇㄚ ㄉㄥ)
a barn lantern

馬蹬(ㄇㄚ ㄉㄥˋ)
a stirrup

馬丁路得(ㄇㄚ ㄉㄧㄥ ㄌㄨˋ ㄉㄜˊ)
Martin Luther, 1483-1546, the founder of the Protestant movement

馬隊(ㄇㄚ ㄉㄨㄟˋ)
mounted troops; cavalry troops

馬太福音(ㄇㄚ ㄊㄞˋ ㄈㄨˊ ㄧㄣ)
the Gospel of Matthew

馬蹄(ㄇㄚ ㄊㄧˊ)
① hoofs of a horse ② a horseshoe

馬蹄表(ㄇㄚ ㄊㄧˊ ㄅㄧㄠˇ)
a desk clock; a table clock

馬蹄鐵(ㄇㄚ ㄊㄧˊ ㄊㄧㄝˇ)
a horseshoe

馬蹄袖(ㄇㄚ ㄊㄧˊ ㄒㄧㄡˋ)
sleeves with a flapper for

the protection of a horse rider's hand holding the rein against cold

馬蹄形(ㄇㄚ ㄊㄧˊ ㄒㄧㄥˊ)
the shape of a hoof; U-shaped

馬蹄銀(ㄇㄚ ㄊㄧˊ ㄧㄣˊ)
silver ingots in the shape of a horseshoe

馬桶(ㄇㄚ ㄊㄨㄥˇ)
a chamber pot; a close-stool; a nightstool

馬尼拉(ㄇㄚ ㄋㄧˊ ㄌㄚ)
Manila, the capital of Philippines 亦作「馬尼剌」

馬拉加共和國(ㄇㄚ ㄌㄚ ㄐㄧㄚ ㄍㄨㄥˋ ㄏㄜˊ ㄍㄨㄛˊ)
the Malagasy Republic

馬拉松(ㄇㄚ ㄌㄚ ㄙㄨㄥ)
① marathon ② Marathon

馬拉威共和國(ㄇㄚ ㄌㄚ ㄨㄟ ㄍㄨㄥˋ ㄏㄜˊ ㄍㄨㄛˊ)
the Republic of Malawi

馬勒(ㄇㄚ ㄌㄜˋ)
the bit of a horse

馬來半島(ㄇㄚ ㄌㄞˊ ㄅㄢˋ ㄉㄠˇ)
the Malay Peninsula

馬來羣島(ㄇㄚ ㄌㄞˊ ㄑㄩㄣˊ ㄉㄠˇ)
the Malay Archipelago

馬來西亞(ㄇㄚ ㄌㄞˊ ㄒㄧ ㄧㄚˇ)
Malaysia; Malaysian: 他太太是馬來西亞人。His wife comes from Malaysia.

馬來人(ㄇㄚ ㄌㄞˊ ㄖㄣˊ)
a Malay; the Malays

馬來亞(ㄇㄚ ㄌㄞˊ ㄧㄚˇ)
Malaya, a state of Malaysia

馬來語(ㄇㄚ ㄌㄞˊ ㄩˇ)
the Malay language; Malay: 他說馬來語。He speaks Malay.

馬力(ㄇㄚ ㄌㄧˋ)
horsepower

馬利蘭(ㄇㄚ ㄌㄧˋ ㄌㄢˊ)
the state of Maryland, U.S.A.

馬利共和國(ㄇㄚ ㄌㄧˋ ㄍㄨㄥˋ ㄏㄜˊ ㄍㄨㄛˊ)
the Republic of Mali

馬利亞(ㄇㄚ ㄌㄧˋ ㄧㄚˇ)
Mary; the Virgin Mary 亦作「瑪利亞」

馬鬃(ㄇㄚ ㄌㄧㄝˋ)
a mane: 那匹馬的馬鬃稀少。That horse has a thin mane.

馬列主義(ㄇㄚ ㄌㄧㄝˋ ㄓㄨˇ ㄧˋ)or 馬克斯列寧主義(ㄇㄚ ㄎㄜˋ ㄙ ㄌㄧㄝˋ

馬部

ㄇㄚˇ ㄇㄨㄤ ㄧ）
Marxism-Leninism

馬六甲海峽 (ㄇㄚˇ ㄌㄧㄡˋ ㄐㄧㄚˇ ㄏㄞˇ ㄒㄧㄚˊ)
the Strait of Malacca 亦作
「馬六甲海峽」

馬鈴薯 (ㄇㄚˇ ㄌㄧㄥˊ ㄕㄨˊ)
a potato: 馬鈴薯長在地下。
Potatoes grow under the ground.

馬路 (ㄇㄚˇ ㄌㄨˋ)
a street; a highway; a road:
你穿越馬路時要小心。Be careful when you cross streets.

馬路如虎口 (ㄇㄚˇ ㄌㄨˋ ㄖㄨˊ ㄏㄨˇ ㄎㄡˇ)
The street is as dangerous
as a tiger.— Beware of
traffic accidents.

馬絡頭 (ㄇㄚˇ ㄌㄨㄛˋ ㄊㄡˊ)
a halter

馬哥字羅 (ㄇㄚˇ ㄍㄜ ㄗˋ ㄌㄨㄛˊ)
Marco Polo, C. 1254 - 1324,
Italian traveler who stayed
in China for 23 years

馬革裹屍 (ㄇㄚˇ ㄍㄜˊ ㄍㄨㄛˇ ㄕ)
to have the corpse wrapped
in horsehide—to die in battle

馬褂 (ㄇㄚˇ ㄍㄨㄚˋ)
the ceremonial jacket of a
mandarin

馬關條約 (ㄇㄚˇ ㄍㄨㄢ ㄊㄧㄠˊ ㄩㄝ)
the Treaty of Shimonoseki,
1895, under which Taiwan
and the Pescadores were
ceded to Japan by the Manchu government

馬公 (ㄇㄚˇ ㄍㄨㄥ)
Makung, a harbor of the
Pescadores: 我們在早晨到達
馬公。We arrived at Makung in
the morning.

馬可尼 (ㄇㄚˇ ㄎㄜˇ ㄋㄧˊ)
Marchese Guglielmo Marconi, 1874-1937, Italian inventor

馬克 (ㄇㄚˇ ㄎㄜˋ)
a Deutsche mark; an ostmark; a mark

馬克白 (ㄇㄚˇ ㄎㄜˋ ㄅㄞˊ)
Macbeth, a tragedy

馬克吐溫 (ㄇㄚˇ ㄎㄜˋ ㄊㄨˇ ㄨㄣ)
Mark Twain, 1835-1910,
American writer

馬克斯 (ㄇㄚˇ ㄎㄜˋ ㄙ)
Karl Marx, 1818-1883, German philosopher

馬克斯主義 (ㄇㄚˇ ㄎㄜˋ ㄙ ㄓㄨˇ ㄧˋ)
Marxism, the system of economic and political thought
developed by Karl Marx

馬口鐵 (ㄇㄚˇ ㄎㄡˇ ㄊㄧㄝˇ)
tinplate 亦作「洋鐵」

馬褲 (ㄇㄚˇ ㄎㄨˋ)
riding breeches

馬後砲 (ㄇㄚˇ ㄏㄡˋ ㄆㄠˋ)
①belated action: 我這個建議
也許是馬後砲。My suggestion
may already be too late. ②
I-told-you-so! remarks

馬虎 (ㄇㄚˇ ·ㄏㄨ)
careless; casual: 這個年輕人
做事較馬虎。This young man
is a rather careless fellow.

馬蜞 (ㄇㄚˇ ㄏㄨㄤ)
a horseleech

馬甲 (ㄇㄚˇ ㄐㄧㄚˇ)
①armor for a horse ②
(Shanghai dialect) a vest

馬腳 (ㄇㄚˇ ㄐㄧㄠˇ)
one's concealed true character

馬廐 (ㄇㄚˇ ㄐㄧㄡˋ)
a stable

馬具 (ㄇㄚˇ ㄐㄩˋ)
horse gear; riding gear

馬其頓 (ㄇㄚˇ ㄑㄧˊ ㄉㄨㄣˋ)
Macedonia

馬球 (ㄇㄚˇ ㄑㄧㄡˊ)
polo: 你會玩馬球嗎? Do you
know how to play polo?

馬戲 (ㄇㄚˇ ㄒㄧˋ)
a circus show; a circus

馬戲團 (ㄇㄚˇ ㄒㄧˋ ㄊㄨㄢˊ)
a circus troupe; a circus

馬歇爾計劃 (ㄇㄚˇ ㄒㄧㄝ ㄦˇ ㄐㄧˋ ㄏㄨㄚˋ)
the Marshall Plan

馬靴 (ㄇㄚˇ ㄒㄩㄝ)
jackboots; riding boots: 他買
了一雙新馬靴。He bought a
pair of new jackboots.

馬掌 (ㄇㄚˇ ㄓㄤˇ)
a horseshoe

馬齒徒增 (ㄇㄚˇ ㄔˇ ㄊㄨˊ ㄗㄥ)
(literally) like a horse that
grows only in the number of
teeth—having accomplished
nothing despite one's advanced age (usually a polite
expression)

馬車 (ㄇㄚˇ ㄔㄜ)
a carriage; a coach; a landau: 汽車已取代了四輪馬車。
Automobiles have taken the
place of carriages.

馬氏文通 (ㄇㄚˇ ㄕˋ ㄨㄣˊ ㄊㄨㄥ)
title of a book by Ma
Chien-chung (馬建中) in the
late 19th century, in which
Chinese grammar was discussed for the first time

馬首是瞻 (ㄇㄚˇ ㄕㄡˇ ㄕˋ ㄓㄢ)
to follow someone; to look
on someone as an example

馬上 (ㄇㄚˇ ㄕㄤˋ)
①on horseback ②right
away; at once; immediately;
without delay: 我離開之後,他
馬上就到。He arrived immediately after I left.

馬衛 (ㄇㄚˇ ㄕㄨˋ)
horsemanship

馬祖 (ㄇㄚˇ ㄗㄨˇ)
①the goddess of the sea
much worshiped in Taiwan
and the southern China
coast 亦作「媽祖」② the
Matsu Islands (off the Fukien coast)

馬鬃 (ㄇㄚˇ ㄗㄨㄥ)
a mane; horsehair

馬槽 (ㄇㄚˇ ㄘㄠˊ)
a manger

馬嘶 (ㄇㄚˇ ㄙ)
to neigh; a neigh

馬賽 (ㄇㄚˇ ㄙㄞˋ)
Marseilles, a French port: 馬
賽是法國第二大城市。Marseilles is the second largest
city in France.

馬賽克 (ㄇㄚˇ ㄙㄞˋ ㄎㄜˋ)
(architecture) mosaic

馬鞍子 (ㄇㄚˇ ㄢ·ㄗ)
a saddle

馬爾地夫 (ㄇㄚˇ ㄦˇ ㄉㄧˋ ㄈㄨ)
the Maldive Islands

馬爾他 (ㄇㄚˇ ㄦˇ ㄊㄚ)
Malta, an island in the
Mediterranean between
Sicily and Africa

馬爾薩斯 (ㄇㄚˇ ㄦˇ ㄙㄚˋ ㄙ)
Thomas Robert Malthus,
1766-1834, English economist:
馬爾薩斯以人口論聞名。Malthus was famous for his
Essay on Population.

馬醫 (ㄇㄚˇ ㄧ)
a horse doctor; a veterinarian

馬衣 (ㄇㄚˇ ㄧ)

horsecloth

馬雅文化 (ㄇㄚˇ ㄧㄚˇ ㄨㄣˊ ㄏㄨㄚˋ)
Maya civilization

馬仰人翻 (ㄇㄚˇ ㄧㄤˇ ㄖㄣˊ ㄈㄢ)
The rider falls as the horse rears in fright.—There is panic.

馬尾 (ㄇㄚˇ ㄨㄟˇ)
①a horsetail ②name of a harbor in Fukien

馬援 (ㄇㄚˇ ㄩㄢˊ)
Ma Yüan, 14 B.C.—49 A.D., a famous general of the Han Dynasty

二畫

【馭】 6922
ㄩˋ yuh yù
1. to drive (a carriage, chariot, etc.)
2. to govern; to rule; to control
3. a driver

【馮】 6923
ㄈㄥˊ ferng féng
a Chinese family name

馮婦 (ㄈㄥˊ ㄈㄨˋ)
①Feng Fu, a man in Tsin, famous for his skill in seizing tigers ②as in 重作馮婦—a role one has played before; something one is called upon to do again

馮夷 (ㄈㄥˊ ㄧˊ)
the water god in charge of the Yellow River 亦作「河伯」

【馮】 6923
ㄆㄧㄥˊ pyng píng
1. to gallop
2. by dint of; on the strength of 亦作「憑」

馮河 (ㄆㄧㄥˊ ㄏㄜˊ)
(literally) to cross a river without a boat—to be reckless

馮虛御風 (ㄆㄧㄥˊ ㄒㄩ ㄩˋ ㄈㄥ)
to tread thin air and sail by wind (a feat attributed to immortals)

三畫

【馱】 6924
1. ㄊㄨㄛˊ two tuó
to carry (a load) on the back

馱不動 (ㄊㄨㄛˊ ㄅㄨˋ ㄉㄨㄥˋ)
too heavy to carry on the

---

back

馱著 (ㄊㄨㄛˊ ˙ㄓㄜ)
carrying (a load) on the back

【馱】 6924
2. ㄉㄨㄛˋ duoh duò
a load carried by a pack animal

【馳】 6925
ㄔˊ chyr chí
1. to go swiftly; to fleet; to rush; to speed: 一架飛機由天空飛馳而過. A plane fleeted across the sky.
2. to exert; to exercise
3. to spread; to propagate

馳辯 (ㄔˊ ㄅㄧㄢˋ)
to exert the gift of speech; to exercise one's eloquence

馳馬 (ㄔˊ ㄇㄚˇ)
to go swiftly on horseback

馳名 (ㄔˊ ㄇㄧㄥˊ)
①to spread one's fame ②famous; well-known; renowned: 一大群人向那馳名的英雄歡呼. A great crowd of people greeted the famous hero.

馳名中外 (ㄔˊ ㄇㄧㄥˊ ㄓㄨㄥ ㄨㄞˋ)
renowned at home and abroad

馳年 (ㄔˊ ㄋㄧㄢˊ)
the fleeting years

馳念 (ㄔˊ ㄋㄧㄢˋ) or 馳思 (ㄔˊ ㄙ) or 馳系 (ㄔˊ ㄒㄧˋ)
to let one's thoughts run to (somebody or something missed)

馳驅 (ㄔˊ ㄑㄩ)
①to move swiftly; to fleet; to rush; to speed ②to run errands; to serve others ③to race horses and whip them

馳檄 (ㄔˊ ㄒㄧˊ)
to speed the mobilization order

馳騁 (ㄔˊ ㄔㄥˇ)
①to rush about on horseback ②to play an active part in

馳驛 (ㄔˊ ㄧˋ)
(said of government officials on official tour in ancient times) to travel speedily from post to post along a designated route

---

to move swiftly; to speed; to run after (empty fame, power, money, etc.)

【馴】 6926
ㄒㄩㄣˊ shyun xún
(又讀 ㄒㄩㄣˊ shiunn xún)
1. tame
2. mild; docile; obedient; well-bred
3. gradual
4. to tame; to put under control; to break (an animal)

馴伏 (ㄒㄩㄣˊ ㄈㄨˊ)
to tame; to subdue; to break in; subdued; obedient: 這老虎終被馴服了. The tiger was finally broken in.

馴良 (ㄒㄩㄣˊ ㄌㄧㄤˊ)
docile; obedient; tractable; gentle

馴鹿 (ㄒㄩㄣˊ ㄌㄨˋ)
a reindeer

馴和 (ㄒㄩㄣˊ ㄏㄜˊ)
mild; good-natured; gentle: 這男孩有馴和的性情. The boy has a gentle spirit (or nature).

馴行 (ㄒㄩㄣˊ ㄒㄧㄥˊ)
good deeds

馴至 (ㄒㄩㄣˊ ㄓˋ)
(said of a situation) to develop gradually; to come by degrees

馴獅人 (ㄒㄩㄣˊ ㄕ ㄖㄣˊ)
a lion tamer

馴獸師 (ㄒㄩㄣˊ ㄕㄡˋ ㄕ)
an animal tamer

馴善 (ㄒㄩㄣˊ ㄕㄢˋ)
good-natured; mild; gentle

馴順 (ㄒㄩㄣˊ ㄕㄨㄣˋ)
obedient; docile; tractable: 她騎著一匹馴順的馬. She rides a docile horse.

馴養 (ㄒㄩㄣˊ ㄧㄤˇ)
to raise (animals); to domesticate (animals); to tame: 象可以馴養以供表演之用. Elephants can be tamed for show.

【馵】 6927
ㄓㄨˋ juh zhù
a horse with the hind left leg white

四畫

【駁】 6928
ㄅㄛ bor bó
1. variegated; parti-colored
2. mixed; impure; jumbled
3. to rebut; to dispute; to refute; to disprove; 真理不怕人駁. Truth fears no refutation.
4. to transport; to ship; to load and unload

駁辯(ㄅㄛ ㄅㄧㄢ)
to argue; to dispute; to debate

駁倒(ㄅㄛ ㄉㄠ)
to defeat in a debate

駁回(ㄅㄛ ㄏㄨㄟ)
to reject; to turn down; to overrule(an appeal, request, etc.); 他駁回這項控告. He rejected the accusation.

駁回上訴(ㄅㄛ ㄏㄨㄟ ㄕㄤ ㄙㄨ)
to reject an appeal

駁詰(ㄅㄛ ㄐㄧㄝ)
to question persistently

駁正(ㄅㄛ ㄓㄥ)
to correct by argument

駁斥(ㄅㄛ ㄔ)
①to refute; to rebut; to disprove; to contradict ②to reject(an appeal)

駁船(ㄅㄛ ㄔㄨㄢ)
a lighter(in a harbor, etc.)亦作「搬運船」

駁雜(ㄅㄛ ㄗㄚ)or駁錯(ㄅㄛ ㄘㄨㄛ)
mixed; impure

駁色(ㄅㄛ ㄙㄜ)
variegated; parti-colored

駁議(ㄅㄛ ㄧ)
to dispute; to refute

駁運(ㄅㄛ ㄩㄣ)
to transport; to ship

【駃】 6929
ㄐㄩㄝ jyue jué
a hybrid horse

駃騠(ㄐㄩㄝ ㄊㄧ)
a hybrid horse(the product of a donkey after mating a stallion)

五畫

【駐】 6930
ㄓㄨ juh zhù
1. to halt
2. to remain temporarily; to station(troops, diplomatic representatives, etc.)

駐蹕(ㄓㄨ ㄅㄧ)
the emperor's lodging when traveling

駐兵(ㄓㄨ ㄅㄧㄥ)
to station troops

駐防(ㄓㄨ ㄈㄤ)
to garrison (a place)

駐地(ㄓㄨ ㄉㄧ)
a place where a particular military unit is stationed

駐屯(ㄓㄨ ㄊㄨㄣ)
(said of troops) to be stationed at

駐華大使(ㄓㄨ ㄏㄨㄚ ㄉㄚ ㄕ)
an ambassador to China: 他奉派為駐華大使. He was appointed ambassador to China.

駐華大使館(ㄓㄨ ㄏㄨㄚ ㄉㄚ ㄕ ㄍㄨㄢ)
an embassy in China

駐節(ㄓㄨ ㄐㄧㄝ)
(said of diplomats) to be stationed in a country

駐軍(ㄓㄨ ㄐㄩㄣ)
①to station troops ②an occupation force ③a garrison; garrison troops

駐紮(ㄓㄨ ㄓㄚ)
(said of troops) to be stationed at

駐守(ㄓㄨ ㄕㄡ)
to station troops at a place for defense purpose: 他們被派駐守臺南. They were stationed at Tainan.

駐顏(ㄓㄨ ㄧㄢ)
to preserve a youthful complexion

駐顏有術(ㄓㄨ ㄧㄢ ㄧㄡ ㄕㄨ)
(said of a woman) to possess the secret of preserving a youthful complexion

【駑】 6931
ㄋㄨ nu nú
1. an old, worn-out horse; a jade; a hack
2. incompetent; stupid; good-for-nothing

駑馬(ㄋㄨ ㄇㄚ)
an old, worn-out horse; a jade; a hack

駑馬戀棧豆(ㄋㄨ ㄇㄚ ㄌㄧㄢ ㄓㄢ ㄉㄡ)
(literally) a jaded horse hankering after its stall—an incompetent man clinging to a good position

駑鈍(ㄋㄨ ㄉㄨㄣ)
incompetent; incapable

駑駘(ㄋㄨ ㄊㄞ)
an old, worn-out horse; a jade; a hack

駑鉛(ㄋㄨ ㄑㄧㄢ)
mediocre

駑(ㄋㄨ ㄒㄧㄚ)
inferior

駑散(ㄋㄨ ㄙㄢ)
inferior; mediocre

【駒】 6932
ㄐㄩ jiu jū
1. a young and fleet-footed horse; a foal; a colt
2. (figuratively) the sun

駒光(ㄐㄩ ㄍㄨㄤ)
fleeting time

駒隙(ㄐㄩ ㄒㄧ)
fleeting time

駒齒(ㄐㄩ ㄔ)
milk teeth—youth

駒影(ㄐㄩ ㄧㄥ)
fleeting time

【駔】 6933
1. ㄗㄤ tzaang zǎng
1. a strong horse
2. a horse broker

【駔】 6933
2. ㄗㄨ tzuh zú
a swift horse; a fine horse

【駔】 6933
3. ㄘㄤ tsaang cāng
參看「駔子」

駔子(ㄘㄤ ˙ㄗ)
a rascal; a ruffian; a mean person

【駕】 6934
ㄐㄧㄚ jiah jià
1. to ride; to drive; to pilot: 你會駕車嗎? Can you drive a car?
2. to excel; to surpass
3. to yoke; to put the horses to the carriage
4. vehicles
5. an honorific epithet
6. to control; to reign or rule
7. the emperor

駕崩(ㄐㄧㄚ ㄅㄥ)
(said of the emperor) to pass away

駕臨(ㄐㄧㄚ ㄌㄧㄣ)
to give(our humble place) the honor of your visit

駕機(ㄐㄧㄚ ㄐㄧ)
to pilot a plane

駕輕就熟(ㄐㄧㄚ ㄑㄧㄥ ㄐㄧㄡ ㄕㄨ)
(literally) to drive a light

〔馬部〕

【馬部】

carriage through a familiar road—to do a task with ease

駕車(ㄐㄧㄚˋ ㄔㄜ)
to drive a vehicle

駕駛(ㄐㄧㄚˋ ㄕˇ)
①to drive (automobiles); to pilot (aircraft); to steer (boats): 小心駕駛. Drive with caution. ②a driver: 他是個莽撞的駕駛. He is a reckless driver.

駕駛執照(ㄐㄧㄚˋ ㄕˇ ㄓˊ ㄓㄠˋ)
a driver's license

駕駛員(ㄐㄧㄚˋ ㄕˇ ㄩㄢˊ)
a driver; a pilot: 駕駛員降下飛機. The pilot landed the airplane.

駕霧騰雲(ㄐㄧㄚˋ ㄨˋ ㄊㄥˊ ㄩㄣˊ)
to ride mist and float on clouds (as immortals do)

駕馭(ㄐㄧㄚˋ ㄩˋ)
①to drive (horse-drawn vehicles) ②to control; to tame; to maneuver; to direct: 這些馬好駕馭. These horses are hard to control.

駕御(ㄐㄧㄚˋ ㄩˋ)
to exercise control; to be at the helms

【駘】 6935
ㄊㄞˊ tair tái
1. a worn-out horse; a jade
2. weary; exhausted; jaded
3. incompetent

【駙】 6936
ㄈㄨˋ fuh fù
1. extra horses harnessed by the side of the team
2. swift

駙馬(ㄈㄨˋ ㄇㄚˇ)
①an ancient official title ②imperial son-in-law

【駛】 6937
ㄕˇ shyy shǐ
1. (said of vehicles) to run; (said of vessels) to sail: 你會駕駛船嗎? Can you sail a boat?
2. fast; fleeting

駛回(ㄕˇ ㄏㄨㄟˊ)
(said of vessels or vehicles) to return; to sail back; to go back

駛近(ㄕˇ ㄐㄧㄣˋ)
(said of vehicles or vessels) to approach

駛行(ㄕˇ ㄒㄧㄥˊ)
(said of vessels or vehicles)

to go; to run; to sail: 該船順風駛行. The ship ran before the wind.

駛船(ㄕˇ ㄔㄨㄢˊ)
to sail a ship: 孩子們正在學習駛船. The boys are learning to sail.

【駝】 6938
ㄊㄨㄛˊ two tuó
1. a camel: 駱駝被人稱爲沙漠之舟. A camel is called a ship of the desert.
2. hunchbacked
3. to carry on the back
4. to pay

駝背(ㄊㄨㄛˊ ㄅㄟˋ)
hunchbacked; humpbacked

駝峯(ㄊㄨㄛˊ ㄈㄥ)
the hump of a camel

駝鳥(ㄊㄨㄛˊ ㄋㄧㄠˇ)
an ostrich: 駝鳥不會飛. Ostriches cannot fly.

駝絨(ㄊㄨㄛˊ ㄖㄨㄥˊ)
①camel's hair ②fabric made of camel's hair

駝子(ㄊㄨㄛˊ ˙ㄗ)
a humpbacked person; a humpback; a hunchback

【駟】 6939
ㄙˋ syh sì
1. a team of four horses
2. horses
3. four
4. name of a star

駟不及舌(ㄙˋ ㄅㄨˋ ㄐㄧˊ ㄕㄜˊ)
Even a team of four horses cannot overtake and recover what is already said.

駟馬難追(ㄙˋ ㄇㄚˇ ㄋㄢˊ ㄓㄨㄟ)
Even with a team of four horses, it is difficult to overtake carelessly uttered words. 一言既出，駟馬難追. When a word has once left the lips, the swiftest horse cannot overtake it.

駟馬高車(ㄙˋ ㄇㄚˇ ㄍㄠ ㄔㄜ)
a high carriage drawn by a team of four horses—(figuratively) vehicles of the rich

六畫

【駭】 6940
ㄏㄞˋ hay hài
1. to terrify; to frighten; to startle; to scare; to amaze; to surprise: 這消息使我們大爲

驚駭. The news greatly surprised us.
2. to marvel; to wonder

駭怕(ㄏㄞˋ ㄆㄚˋ)
scared; frightened: 此次地震你驚怕嗎? Were you frightened by the earthquake?

駭浪(ㄏㄞˋ ㄌㄤˋ)
awful waves; fearful billows

駭怪(ㄏㄞˋ ㄍㄨㄞˋ)
to be shocked; to be astonished; to marvel and wonder

駭汗(ㄏㄞˋ ㄏㄢˋ)
to perspire as a result of fright

駭人聽聞(ㄏㄞˋ ㄖㄣˊ ㄊㄧㄥ ㄨㄣˊ)
(said of atrocities, crimes, etc.) frightening; blood-curdling; shocking (news)

駭愕(ㄏㄞˋ ㄜˋ)
to be amazed; to be flabbergasted: 我對他的行爲感到駭愕. I was amazed at his conduct.

駭異(ㄏㄞˋ ㄧˋ)
surprised; amazed

駭悅(ㄏㄞˋ ㄩㄝˋ)
to marvel

【駱】 6941
ㄌㄨㄛˋ luoh luò
1. a white horse (or steed) with black mane
2. a camel
3. a Chinese family name

駱賓王(ㄌㄨㄛˋ ㄅㄧㄣ ㄨㄤˊ)
Lo Pin-wang, ?-684, an early Tang Dynasty man of letters, noted for his denunciation of Empress Wu in a manifesto

駱馬(ㄌㄨㄛˋ ㄇㄚˇ)
(zoology) a llama

駱駝(ㄌㄨㄛˋ ㄊㄨㄛˊ)
a camel

駱駝隊(ㄌㄨㄛˋ ㄊㄨㄛˊ ㄉㄨㄟˋ)
a camel train; a caravan of camels

駱駝絨(ㄌㄨㄛˋ ㄊㄨㄛˊ ㄖㄨㄥˊ)
①camel's hair ②fabric made of camel's hair

【駬】 6942
ㄦˇ eel ěr
name of a legendary swift horse

【駁】 6943
ㄅㄛˊ bor bó
1. a kind of fierce animal
2. mixed; impure

s.to refute 亦作「駁」

【駢】 6944 ㄆㄧㄢˊ pyan pián
a. a pair of horses
s. to stand or lie side by side
參看「駢」

七畫

【騁】 6945 ㄔㄥˇ cheeng chǎng
a. to go swiftly; to speed
s. to exert; to unfold; to develop
s. to give free play to; to lend wings to

騁步(ㄔㄥˇ ㄅㄨˋ)
to rush; to speed

騁目(ㄔㄥˇ ㄇㄨˋ)
to look as far as the eyes can see

騁能(ㄔㄥˇ ㄋㄥˊ)
to give full display to one's abilities

騁懷(ㄔㄥˇ ㄏㄨㄞˊ)
to feel elated; to feel brimming happiness; to have one's heart filled with joy

騁志(ㄔㄥˇ ㄓˋ)
to lend wings to one's ambition

騁馳(ㄔㄥˇ ㄔˊ)
(said of a person or animal)
to go at full speed

騁望(ㄔㄥˇ ㄨㄤˋ)
to look as far as one can see

【駿】 6946 ㄐㄩㄣˋ jiunn jùn
a. a fine horse; a swift horse
b. great; large
s. swift; speedy
s. rigorous; stringent 亦作「峻」
s. outstanding

駿奔(ㄐㄩㄣˋ ㄅㄣ)
to speed; to rush

駿馬(ㄐㄩㄣˋ ㄇㄚˇ)
a fine horse

駿命(ㄐㄩㄣˋ ㄇㄧㄥˋ)
the great appointment — Heaven's will

駿發(ㄐㄩㄣˋ ㄈㄚˋ)
swift success in life

駿骨(ㄐㄩㄣˋ ㄍㄨˇ)
①a talented person ②a fine horse

駿驥(ㄐㄩㄣˋ ㄐㄧˋ)

a fine horse

駿足(ㄐㄩㄣˋ ㄗㄨˊ)
①a fine horse ②a talented person

駿逸(ㄐㄩㄣˋ ㄧˋ)
distinguished; outstanding; surpassing 亦作「俊逸」

【騂】 6947 ㄒㄧㄥ shing xīng
red

【駭】 6948 ㄞˊ air ái
stupid; foolish

【駸】 6949 ㄑㄧㄣ chin qīn
galloping; speeding

【駻】 6950 ㄏㄢˋ hann hàn
1. wild (horses); fierce
2. a saddle

駻馬(ㄏㄢˋ ㄇㄚˇ)
an untamed horse; a fierce-tempered horse

八畫

【騎】 6951 ㄑㄧˊ chyi qí
(名詞讀音 ㄐㄧˋ jih jì)
to ride (a horse, etc.); to sit astride on: 你會騎馬嗎? Can you ride?

騎兵(ㄑㄧˊ ㄅㄧㄥ)or(ㄐㄧˋ ㄅㄧㄥ)
cavalry; mounted troops

騎馬(ㄑㄧˊ ㄇㄚˇ)
to ride a horse: 他每天早晨騎馬。 He rides every morning.

騎馬布(ㄑㄧˊ ㄇㄚˇ ㄅㄨˋ)
a hygienic band

騎馬找馬(ㄑㄧˊ ㄇㄚˇ ㄓㄠˇ ㄇㄚˇ)
(literally) to ride a horse while looking for another one — to hold a temporary position while seeking a better job

騎縫(ㄑㄧˊ ㄈㄥˋ)
the edges of two separate sheets of a document (on which a seal is to be stamped with part of the impression on each of the two sheets)

騎樓(ㄑㄧˊ ㄌㄡˊ)
an arcade (a covered avenue)

騎驢(ㄑㄧˊ ㄌㄩˊ)
①to ride a donkey ②intermediary exploitation

騎驢覓驢(ㄑㄧˊ ㄌㄩˊ ㄇㄧˋ ㄌㄩˊ)
(literally) to seek a donkey while riding one — to forget what one already has

騎驢找馬(ㄑㄧˊ ㄌㄩˊ ㄓㄠˇ ㄇㄚˇ)
(literally) to ride a donkey as one seeks a horse — to maintain a job while looking for a better one

騎寇(ㄑㄧˊ ㄎㄡˋ)
mounted bandits; invading enemy cavalry

騎虎難下(ㄑㄧˊ ㄏㄨˇ ㄋㄢˊ ㄒㄧㄚˋ)
(literally) unable to get down from the tiger's back — in a position from which there is no easy retreat; unable to stop or quit; to have no way to back down

騎虎之勢(ㄑㄧˊ ㄏㄨˇ ㄓ ㄕˋ)
an awkward position from which there is no retreat

騎牆(ㄑㄧˊ ㄑㄧㄤˊ)
to sit on the fence; uncommitted between two opposing forces

騎牆派(ㄑㄧˊ ㄑㄧㄤˊ ㄆㄞˋ)
fence-sitters; a timeserver; an opportunist

騎師(ㄑㄧˊ ㄕ)
a jockey

騎士(ㄑㄧˊ ㄕˋ)
①a knight ②a horseback rider

騎射(ㄑㄧˊ ㄕㄜˋ)
horsemanship and archery

騎術(ㄑㄧˊ ㄕㄨˋ)
equitation; horsemanship

騎從(ㄐㄧˋ ㄗㄨㄥˋ)
aides and servants on horseback

【駢】 6952 ㄆㄧㄢˊ pyan pián
(駢) ㄆㄧㄢˊ
1. a pair of horses
2. to stand, lie, or go side by side

駢比(ㄆㄧㄢˊ ㄅㄧˇ)
contiguous

駢枝(ㄆㄧㄢˊ ㄇㄨˇ ㄑㄧˊ)
a superfluity; a redundancy

駢體文(ㄆㄧㄢˊ ㄊㄧˇ ㄨㄣˊ)or駢文
(ㄆㄧㄢˊ ㄨㄣˊ)
a euphuistically antithetic style of writing prevalent in the 6th and 7th centuries A.D.

駢儷(ㄆㄧㄢˊ ㄌㄧˋ)

馬
部

（馬部）

the antithesis of four-word and six-word clauses or sentences which was in vogue in the 6th and 7th centuries A. D.

駢鄰(ㄆㄧㄢˊㄌㄧㄣˊ)
a next-door neighbor; side by side

駢肩(ㄆㄧㄢˊㄐㄧㄢ)
shoulders beside shoulders —crowded

駢四儷六(ㄆㄧㄢˊㄙˋㄌㄧˋㄌㄧㄡˋ)
antithesis of four-word and six-word sentences prevalent in the 6th and 7th centuries A.D.

【騏】 6953 ㄑㄧˊ chyi qí
1. a dark-blue horse
2. a fine horse
3. dark blue

騏驎 or 麒麟(ㄑㄧˊㄌㄧㄣˊ)
name of a fabulous animal

騏驥(ㄑㄧˊㄐㄧˋ)
a legendary fine horse (said capable of covering 1,000 *li* in a day)

【騄】 6954 ㄌㄨˋ luh lù
name of a legendary swift horse

騄駬 or 綠耳(ㄌㄨˋㄦˇ)
name of a legendary swift horse

【騅】 6955 ㄓㄨㄟ juei zhuī
a piebald horse

【騐】 6956 ㄧㄢˋ yann yàn
(驗) to test

九畫

【騖】 6957 ㄨˋ wuh wù
1. to rush; to speed
2. unrestrained; uninhibited

騖外(ㄨˋㄨㄞˋ)
to depart from one's proper role

騖遠(ㄨˋㄩㄢˇ)
impractically ambitious; overambitious

【騙】 6958 ㄆㄧㄢˋ piann piàn
1. to cheat; to defraud; to swindle; to deceive
2. to get by fraud

---

a fraud; a swindle; a trick; a chicanery; a deception; a hoax; a racket: 這只是個騙局, 別太認眞。It is only a hoax. Don't take it seriously.

騙錢(ㄆㄧㄢˋㄑㄧㄢˊ)
to cheat a person out of money; to get money by fraud

騙取(ㄆㄧㄢˋㄑㄩˇ)
to obtain by fraud; to cheat: 他騙取我的錢。He cheated me out of money.

騙取選票(ㄆㄧㄢˋㄑㄩˇㄒㄩㄢˇㄆㄧㄠˋ)
to wangle votes

騙術(ㄆㄧㄢˋㄕㄨˋ)
a trick; a ruse; a stratagem; wiles

騙人(ㄆㄧㄢˋㄖㄣˊ)
to cheat others; to defraud others; to swindle others; to lie

騙子(ㄆㄧㄢˋ·ㄗ)
a swindler; a cheat; a confidence man; a racketeer; an impostor; a fraud

騙嘴(ㄆㄧㄢˋㄗㄨㄟˇ) or 騙吃(ㄆㄧㄢˋㄔ)
to get food by fraud or trickery

騙財(ㄆㄧㄢˋㄘㄞˊ)
to get money by fraud or trickery

騙案(ㄆㄧㄢˋㄢˋ)
a case of fraud

【騣】 6959 (鬃) ㄗㄨㄥ tzong zōng
a mane

【騤】 6960 ㄎㄨㄟˊ kwei kuí
(said of a horse) lively; vigorous; strong

【騠】 6961 ㄊㄧˊ tyi tí
a hybrid horse produced by mating a donkey with a stallion

【騞】 6962 ㄏㄨㄛˋ huoh huò
the sound of a knife cutting something

十畫

【騫】 6963 ㄑㄧㄢ chian qiān
1. to raise high; to uplift

---

2. to soar; to fly; to rise
3. to pull up
4. frightened

騫騰(ㄑㄧㄢㄊㄥˊ)
to soar high or go up (especially in officialdom)

騫舉(ㄑㄧㄢㄐㄩˇ)
to soar

騫旗斬將(ㄑㄧㄢㄑㄧˊㄓㄢˇㄐㄧㄤˋ)
to pull up enemy flags and behead enemy generals on the battlefield

【騭】 6964 ㄓˋ jyh zhì
1. a stallion
2. to go up; to rise
3. predestined

【騰】 6965 ㄊㄥˊ terng téng
1. to prance; to rear; to leap; to jump
2. to go up; to rise; to fly; to soar
3. to turn over; to surrender; to transfer

騰馬(ㄊㄥˊㄇㄚˇ)
a stallion

騰達(ㄊㄥˊㄉㄚˊ)
to prosper; to thrive

騰騰(ㄊㄥˊㄊㄥˊ)
① soaring; rising ② drunk; asleep ③ slowly

騰郡(ㄊㄥˊㄐㄩㄣˋ)
① to transfer ② to move something to make room

騰貴(ㄊㄥˊㄍㄨㄟˋ)
(said of prices) to skyrocket

騰空(ㄊㄥˊㄎㄨㄥ)
to fly in the sky; to soar

騰捷(ㄊㄥˊㄐㄧㄝˊ)
to fly swiftly; to flit

騰蛟起鳳(ㄊㄥˊㄐㄧㄠㄑㄧˇㄈㄥˋ)
(literally) a flying dragon and soaring phoenix—(figuratively) genius

騰笑(ㄊㄥˊㄒㄧㄠˋ)
to arouse laughter

騰驤(ㄊㄥˊㄒㄧㄤ)
to leap high; to prance

騰閃(ㄊㄥˊㄕㄢˇ)
to dodge; to ward off; to evade

騰躍(ㄊㄥˊㄩㄝˋ)
① to prance; to be lively; to be active ②(said of prices) to skyrocket

騰雲駕霧(ㄊㄥˊㄩㄣˊㄐㄧㄚˋㄨˋ)

①to sail clouds and ride mist (as immortals do) ②fast; quick

【騷】 6966 ㄙㄠ sau sāo

1. to disturb; to agitate
2. to worry; to feel concerned
3. ill-smelling; stinking
4. (colloquial) amorous; erotic

騷動(ㄙㄠ ㄉㄨㄥˋ)
disturbance; unrest; upheaval; commotion; tumult: 群眾騷動起來。The crowd was in unrest.

騷體(ㄙㄠ ㄊㄧˇ)
poetic style in the tradition of 離騷 by Chü Yüan (屈原)

騷女人(ㄙㄠ ㄋㄩˇ ㄖㄣˊ)
a woman of loose morals; an erotic woman

騷老頭兒(ㄙㄠ ㄌㄠˇ ㄊㄡˊ ㄦ)
(colloquial) an old man with strong sexual desire; an old wolf

騷亂(ㄙㄠ ㄌㄨㄢˋ)
disturbance; unrest; upheaval; agitation; tumult

騷客(ㄙㄠ ㄎㄜˋ)or 騷人(ㄙㄠ ㄖㄣˊ)
騷人墨客(ㄙㄠ ㄖㄣˊ ㄇㄛˋ ㄎㄜˋ)
a poet; a bard

騷屑(ㄙㄠ ㄒㄧㄝˋ)
the whistling sound of wind

騷擾(ㄙㄠ ㄖㄠˇ)
to disturb; to harass; to agitate

騷然(ㄙㄠ ㄖㄢˊ)
disturbed; tumultuous; agitated; in commotion; an uproar: 天下騷然。The whole country was thrown into an uproar.

【騶】 6967 ㄗㄡ tzou zōu

1. an official in charge of driving carriages
2. a mounted escort

騶卒(ㄗㄡ ㄗㄨˊ)
①a servant ②a groom

騶從(ㄗㄡ ㄗㄨㄥˋ)
the escort of a nobleman

【騮】 6968 ㄌㄧㄡˊ liou liú
a legendary fine horse

十一畫

【騾】 6969 ㄌㄨㄛˊ luo luó

a mule

騾馬(ㄌㄨㄛˊ ㄇㄚˇ)
a mule

騾夫(ㄌㄨㄛˊ ㄈㄨ)
a muleteer; a muleman

騾車(ㄌㄨㄛˊ ㄔㄜ)
a mule cart

騾子(ㄌㄨㄛˊ ㄗ˙)
①a mule ②a stubborn person

【驁】 6970 ㄠˋ aur áo

1. a fine horse
2. an untamed horse
3. proud; haughty; arrogant

驁放(ㄠˋ ㄈㄤˋ)
very haughty and unrestrained

【驀】 6971 ㄇㄛ˙ moh mò

1. sudden; abrupt
2. to mount the horse

驀地(ㄇㄛˋ ㄉㄧˋ)
suddenly; all of a sudden

驀忽(ㄇㄛˋ ㄏㄨˊ)
suddenly; all of a sudden

驀然(ㄇㄛˋ ㄖㄢˊ)
suddenly; all of a sudden

【驂】 6972 ㄘㄢ tsan cān
the two outside horses of a team of four

驂乘(ㄘㄢ ㄕㄥˋ)
(in ancient China) three persons sat in one chariot, the driver sat between the other two, the first one sitting by his left was a senior or the director, the third one sitting in his right was called 驂乘 the third one in the chariot) 亦作「陪乘」

【驃】 6973 ㄆㄧㄠ piaw piào

1. a horse with a yellowish white color
2. valiant
3. galloping

驃騎(ㄆㄧㄠ ㄐㄧˋ)
an ancient title of general rank

【驄】 6974 ㄘㄨㄥ tsong cōng
a horse with a bluish white color

【驅】 6975 ㄑㄩ chiu qū

1. to go before others
2. to drive; to urge
3. to expel
4. to command

驅鬼(ㄑㄩ ㄍㄨㄟˇ)
to exorcise evil spirits

驅遣(ㄑㄩ ㄑㄧㄢˇ)
①to send away (a person so as to get rid of him) ②to order (a person) about

驅邪(ㄑㄩ ㄒㄧㄝˊ)
to expel evil; to keep evil spirits away

驅逐(ㄑㄩ ㄓㄨˊ)
to drive out; to get rid of; to expel: 敵人被驅逐出城。The enemy were driven out of the city.

驅逐機(ㄑㄩ ㄓㄨˊ ㄐㄧ)
a pursuit plane

驅逐艦(ㄑㄩ ㄓㄨˊ ㄐㄧㄢˋ)
a destroyer

驅馳(ㄑㄩ ㄔˊ)
to run about busily (for others)

驅車(ㄑㄩ ㄔㄜ)
to drive a carriage or car

驅除(ㄑㄩ ㄔㄨˊ)
to drive out; to get rid of; to eliminate

驅蟲劑(ㄑㄩ ㄔㄨㄥˊ ㄐㄧˋ)or 驅蟲藥(ㄑㄩ ㄔㄨㄥˊ ㄧㄠˋ)
a helminthic; an anthelmintic; an insect repellent; vermifuge

驅使(ㄑㄩ ㄕˇ)
to order (a person) about: 你沒有權力驅使我。You have no right to order me about.

驅策(ㄑㄩ ㄘㄜˋ)
①to urge; to spur: 他驅策同仁們更加努力。He urged (on) the crew to greater efforts. ②to order (a person) about

驅散(ㄑㄩ ㄙㄢˋ)
to disperse by force; to scatter; to dispel: 陽光驅散了薄霧。The sun dispelled the mist.

十二畫

【驕】 6976 ㄐㄧㄠ jiau jiāo

1. untamed; intractable; disobedient
2. proud; haughty; arrogant; overbearing

〔馬部〕

【馬部】

3. severe; harsh; intense

驕兵必敗(ㄐㄧㄠ ㄅㄧㄥ ㄅㄧˋ ㄅㄞˋ)
An army which is cocksure about its invincibility is doomed to defeat.

驕敵(ㄐㄧㄠ ㄉㄧˊ)
①to underestimate the enemy ②an enemy who is excessively self-confident

驕態(ㄐㄧㄠ ㄊㄞˋ)
proud bearing; a haughty manner; an overbearing attitude

驕橫(ㄐㄧㄠ ㄏㄥˋ)
arrogant and high-handed

驕驕(ㄐㄧㄠ ㄐㄧㄠ)
(said of grass, weeds, etc.) luxuriant and tall

驕蹇(ㄐㄧㄠ ㄐㄧㄢˇ)
proud and disrespectful

驕矜(ㄐㄧㄠ ㄐㄧㄣ)
(literary language) puffed up; conceited; self-important; proud; haughty

驕狎(ㄐㄧㄠ ㄒㄧㄚˊ)
to treat with haughty disrespect

驕者必敗(ㄐㄧㄠ ㄓㄜˇ ㄅㄧˋ ㄅㄞˋ)
Pride goes before a fall.

驕戰(ㄐㄧㄠ ㄓㄢˋ)
Relying on one's own force, one fights fiercely.

驕奢(ㄐㄧㄠ ㄕㄜ)
pride and extravagance

驕奢淫佚(ㄐㄧㄠ ㄕㄜ ㄧㄣˊ ㄧˋ)
pride, luxury, dissolute and self-indulgence—characteristics that tend to mark the life of the wealthy or the powerful

驕人(ㄐㄧㄠ ㄖㄣˊ)
①a successful flatterer ②to try to impress people; to show off ③the proud

驕子(ㄐㄧㄠ ㄗˇ)
a proud favorite (of Heaven, etc.)

驕恣(ㄐㄧㄠ ㄗˋ)
proud and unruly

驕縱(ㄐㄧㄠ ㄗㄨㄥˋ)
disregardful of all authority; proud and unruly

驕色(ㄐㄧㄠ ㄙㄜˋ)
a haughty expression; a proud look

驕傲(ㄐㄧㄠ ㄠˋ)
proud; haughty; disdainful;

pride: 不要驕傲自滿。Don't be full of pride and conceit.

驕兒(ㄐㄧㄠ ㄦˊ)
a beloved son

驕易(ㄐㄧㄠ ㄧˋ)
to treat with disrespect

驕陽(ㄐㄧㄠ ㄧㄤˊ)
the intense sunshine; the hot sunshine

驕盈(ㄐㄧㄠ ㄧㄥˊ)
proud and self-complacent

【驊】6977
ㄏㄨㄚˊ hwa huá
name of a legendary fine horse

【騧】(ㄍㄨㄚ ㄍㄨㄚˇ)
name of a legendary fine horse

【驍】6978
ㄒㄧㄠ shiau xiǎo
1. having courage and agility; brave; valiant
2. a fine horse

驍悍(ㄒㄧㄠ ㄏㄢˋ)
brave and fierce

驍騎(ㄒㄧㄠ ㄐㄧˋ)
brave and fierce cavalry

驍將(ㄒㄧㄠ ㄐㄧㄤˋ)
a valiant general

驍雄(ㄒㄧㄠ ㄒㄩㄥˊ)
capable and ambitious

驍衛(ㄒㄧㄠ ㄨㄟˋ)
the imperial guards

驍勇(ㄒㄧㄠ ㄩㄥˇ)
brave and skillful in fighting

【駰】6979
ㄌㄧㄣ lin lín
(said of horses) piebald

【騮】6980
(騩) ㄌㄧㄡˊ liou liú
name of a legendary fine horse

十三畫

【驗】6981
(験) ㄧㄢˋ yann yàn
1. to test; to examine; to analyze
2. to produce an effect: 這藥效靈驗。The medicine has produced an effect.
3. to verify; to prove

驗明(ㄧㄢˋ ㄇㄧㄥˊ)
to ascertain by a test or examination

驗明正身(ㄧㄢˋ ㄇㄧㄥˊ ㄓㄥˋ ㄕㄣ)
to make a positive identification of a criminal before execution

驗方(ㄧㄢˋ ㄈㄤ)
effective medical prescriptions

驗放(ㄧㄢˋ ㄈㄤˋ)
(said of a customs office or checkpoint) to allow shipment of goods to pass after checking the contents

驗電器(ㄧㄢˋ ㄉㄧㄢˋ ㄑㄧˋ)
an electroscope

驗痰(ㄧㄢˋ ㄊㄢˊ)
to examine sputum under the microscope

驗尿(ㄧㄢˋ ㄋㄧㄠˋ)
a urine test; urinalysis

驗光(ㄧㄢˋ ㄍㄨㄤ)
optometry

驗看(ㄧㄢˋ ㄎㄢˋ)
to examine; to take a close look

驗勘(ㄧㄢˋ ㄎㄢ)
to investigate; to inspect

驗訖(ㄧㄢˋ ㄑㄧˋ)
"examined" (a note stamped on or attached to finished products)

驗槍(ㄧㄢˋ ㄑㄧㄤ)
(military) to inspect arms

驗血(ㄧㄢˋ ㄒㄩㄝˋ)
a blood test

驗屍(ㄧㄢˋ ㄕ)
a post-mortem examination; an autopsy

驗屍官(ㄧㄢˋ ㄕ ㄍㄨㄢ)
a coroner

驗濕器(ㄧㄢˋ ㄕ ㄑㄧˋ)
a hygroscope

驗收(ㄧㄢˋ ㄕㄡ)
to accept (goods, buildings, etc.) after ascertaining that the quality or quantity meets requirements

驗傷(ㄧㄢˋ ㄕㄤ)
to examine an injury by competent authorities of law

驗算(ㄧㄢˋ ㄙㄨㄢˋ)
to check computations

【驚】6982
ㄐㄧㄥ jing jīng
1. to startle; to surprise; to amaze; to astound; to alarm; to flabbergast; to dumbfound; to terrify; to frighten
2. afraid; frightened; scared

fearful; terrified

3. to marvel; to be surprised; to be amazed

驚怕(ㄐㄧㄥ ㄆㄚˋ)
scared; afraid; fearful

驚風(ㄐㄧㄥ ㄈㄥ)
(Chinese medicine) convulsions or spasms suffered by a convalescent child

驚駭駭浪(ㄐㄧㄥ ㄈㄥ ㄏㄞˋ ㄌㄤˋ)
fearful winds and terrific billows

驚服(ㄐㄧㄥ ㄈㄨˊ)
to marvel at and acknowledge the superiority of someone

驚倒(ㄐㄧㄥ ㄉㄠˇ)
to collapse from fright

驚動(ㄐㄧㄥ ㄉㄨㄥˋ)
① to astonish; to startle; to stir up; to alarm ② to bother; to disturb; to trouble

驚濤駭浪(ㄐㄧㄥ ㄊㄠˊ ㄏㄞˋ ㄌㄤˋ)
(said of the sea) churning; furious; choppy; mountainous waves

驚歎(ㄐㄧㄥ ㄊㄢˋ)
to marvel; to exclaim

驚歎號(ㄐㄧㄥ ㄊㄢˋ ㄏㄠˋ)
an exclamation mark; an exclamation point

驚堂木(ㄐㄧㄥ ㄊㄤˊ ㄇㄨˋ)
a wooden block used by a judge in former times to maintain order in the court

驚天地, 泣鬼神(ㄐㄧㄥ ㄊㄧㄢ ㄉㄧˋ, ㄑㄧˋ ㄍㄨㄟˇ ㄕㄣˊ)
(said of heroism, etc.) to startle the universe and move the gods

驚天動地(ㄐㄧㄥ ㄊㄧㄢ ㄉㄨㄥˋ ㄉㄧˋ)
to startle even the universe; earth-shaking; world-shaking

驚怪(ㄐㄧㄥ ㄍㄨㄞˋ)
to marvel; to be amazed and puzzled

驚弓之鳥(ㄐㄧㄥ ㄍㄨㄥ ㄓ ㄋㄧㄠˇ)
(literally) a bird frightened by the bow—a person seized with fear because of some frightening experience encountered in the past; scared as a rabbit

驚恐(ㄐㄧㄥ ㄎㄨㄥˇ)
scared; afraid; fearful

驚駭(ㄐㄧㄥ ㄏㄞˋ)
frightened; terrified; terror-

stricken: 這受驚駭的孩子跑回家。The terrified child ran home.

驚汗(ㄐㄧㄥ ㄏㄢˋ)
perspiration of fear; cold perspiration

驚魂(ㄐㄧㄥ ㄏㄨㄣˊ)
a frightened mind

驚魂未定(ㄐㄧㄥ ㄏㄨㄣˊ ㄨㄟˋ ㄉㄧㄥˋ)
not yet become calm or normal from a fright; not yet recovered from astonishment; still badly shaken: 我還驚魂未定。I haven't yet recovered from my astonishment.

驚慌(ㄐㄧㄥ ㄏㄨㄤ)
to lose one's head from terror; to be frightened and confused; to panic

驚惶失措(ㄐㄧㄥ ㄏㄨㄤˊ ㄕ ㄘㄨㄛˋ)
to lose one's head from fear; terrified and not knowing what to do; to panic

驚鴻(ㄐㄧㄥ ㄏㄨㄥˊ)
a woman with an amazing grace

驚鴻一瞥(ㄐㄧㄥ ㄏㄨㄥˊ ㄧ ㄆㄧㄝˋ)
to have a fleeting glimpse of a beauty

驚悸(ㄐㄧㄥ ㄐㄧˋ)
quickened heartbeat due to fear

驚叫(ㄐㄧㄥ ㄐㄧㄠˋ)
to cry in fear; to scream

驚懼(ㄐㄧㄥ ㄐㄩˋ)
scared; afraid; fearful

驚奇(ㄐㄧㄥ ㄑㄧˊ)
to be surprised; to marvel

驚喜(ㄐㄧㄥ ㄒㄧˇ)
pleasantly surprised

驚嚇(ㄐㄧㄥ ㄒㄧㄚˋ)
to frighten; to scare; to alarm suddenly

驚險(ㄐㄧㄥ ㄒㄧㄢˇ)
alarmingly dangerous; breathtaking; thrilling: 那真是一個驚險的場面。That's really a thrilling scene.

驚心(ㄐㄧㄥ ㄒㄧㄣ)
to be shaken; to be frightened

驚心動魄(ㄐㄧㄥ ㄒㄧㄣ ㄉㄨㄥˋ ㄆㄛˋ)
heart-shaking; soul-stirring; horrified

驚醒(ㄐㄧㄥ ㄒㄧㄥˇ)
to cause to wake up with a

startle

驚蟄(ㄐㄧㄥ ㄓㄜˊ)or(ㄐㄧㄥ ㄓˊ)
one of the 24 climatic periods into which the lunar year is divided (beginning from March 5 or 6)

驚視(ㄐㄧㄥ ㄕˋ)
to look at in surprise

驚世駭俗(ㄐㄧㄥ ㄕˋ ㄏㄞˋ ㄙㄨˊ)
to astound the world with an extraordinary idea, etc.

驚擾(ㄐㄧㄥ ㄖㄠˇ)
to disturb; to cause trouble to others

驚人(ㄐㄧㄥ ㄖㄣˊ)
surprising; astonishing; astounding; startling; amazing; sensational: 多麼驚人的消息! What startling news!

驚走(ㄐㄧㄥ ㄗㄡˇ)
① to run away in a fright ② to scare away: 狗把賊驚走。The dog scared the thief away.

驚座(ㄐㄧㄥ ㄗㄨㄛˋ)
to amaze fellow guests; to cause raised eyebrows among those present

驚愕(ㄐㄧㄥ ㄜˋ)
to be astonished; to be astounded; to be dumbfounded; to be flabbergasted

驚疑(ㄐㄧㄥ ㄧˊ)
fearful and apprehensive; afraid and anxious; suspicious from fear

驚異(ㄐㄧㄥ ㄧˋ)
to be surprised; to be amazed; to marvel: 我們對他的成功感到驚異。We are marveled at his success.

驚訝(ㄐㄧㄥ ㄧㄚˋ)
to be surprised; to be amazed; to marvel

【驛】 6983
(ㄧˋ) yih yì
a station where couriers rested in former times; a courier station

驛馬車(ㄧˋ ㄇㄚˇ ㄔㄜ)
a stagecoach

驛亭(ㄧˋ ㄊㄧㄥˊ)
a station where couriers rested in former times; a courier station; a post house

驛吏(ㄧˋ ㄌㄧˋ)
officers in charge of a

〔骨部〕

courier station 亦作「驛丞」

驛館(ㄧˋ ㄍㄨㄢˇ)
a post house

驛騎(ㄧˋ ㄐㄧˋ)
horses kept at a courier station in former times

驛站(ㄧˋ ㄓㄢˋ)
a courier station; a post (where formerly couriers changed horses or rested)

驛車(ㄧˋ ㄔㄜ)
courier carts at a post house in former times

驛丞(ㄧˋ ㄔㄥˊ)
an official in charge of a courier station

驛使(ㄧˋ ㄕˇ)
a courier

十四畫

【驟】 6984
ㄗㄡˋ tzow zòu
1. to gallop
2. swift; sudden: 狂風驟起。A strong wind struck all of a sudden.
3. frequent

驟降(ㄗㄡˋ ㄐㄧㄤˋ)
a rapid fall (of snow)

驟至(ㄗㄡˋ ㄓˋ)
to arrive suddenly; to come without warning

驟然(ㄗㄡˋ ㄖㄢˊ)
suddenly: 驟然下起雨來了。All of a sudden it began to rain.

驟雨(ㄗㄡˋ ㄩˇ)
a sudden rainstorm

十六畫

【驢】 6985
ㄌㄩˊ liu lú
an ass; a donkey

驢蒙虎皮(ㄌㄩˊ ㄇㄥˊ ㄏㄨˇ ㄆㄧˊ)
a donkey in a tiger's skin —an empty show of strength

驢鳴狗吠(ㄌㄩˊ ㄇㄧㄥˊ ㄍㄡˇ ㄈㄟˋ)
asses braying and dogs barking—a poor style of writing

驢年馬月(ㄌㄩˊ ㄋㄧㄢˊ ㄇㄚˇ ㄩㄝˋ)
a time that will never come

驢騾(ㄌㄩˊ ㄌㄨㄛˊ)
donkeys as draft animals

驢臉(ㄌㄩˊ ㄌㄧㄢˇ)
a donkey's face—a long face

驢叫(ㄌㄩˊ ㄐㄧㄠˋ)
a donkey's bray—a loud, unpleasant voice

驢駒子(ㄌㄩˊ ㄐㄩ˙)
a young donkey; the foal of a donkey

驢車(ㄌㄩˊ ㄔㄜ)
a donkey cart

驢脣不對馬嘴(ㄌㄩˊ ㄔㄨㄣˊ ㄅㄨˊ ㄉㄨㄟˋ ㄇㄚˇ ㄗㄨㄟˇ)
(literally) A donkey's lips do not match a horse's mouth.— incongruous; irrelevant

驢子(ㄌㄩˊ ˙ㄗ)or **驢兒**(ㄌㄩˊ ㄦˊ)
a donkey; an ass

【驥】 6986
ㄐㄧˋ jih jì
1. a very fast horse
2. a man of outstanding ability; a great man

驥子龍文(ㄐㄧˋ ㄗˇ ㄌㄨㄥˊ ㄨㄣˊ)
outstanding children of a family

驥足(ㄐㄧˋ ㄗㄨˊ)
a great talent

驥尾(ㄐㄧˋ ㄨㄟˇ)
on the coattails of a great man

十七畫

【驤】 6987
ㄒㄧㄤ shiang xiāng
1. a horse with the right hind leg white
2. to uplift
3. galloping with a raised head

驤騰(ㄒㄧㄤ ㄊㄥˊ)
to gallop forward; to advance with determination

驤首(ㄒㄧㄤ ㄕㄡˇ)
to raise the head proudly

十八畫

【驩】 6988
ㄏㄨㄢ huan huān
to have joy

十九畫

【驪】 6989
ㄌㄧˊ li lí
1. a black horse
2. to drive a carriage drawn

by two horses

驪龍(ㄌㄧˊ ㄌㄨㄥˊ)
a black dragon

驪歌(ㄌㄧˊ ㄍㄜ)
a song of farewell (from a farewell poem entitled 驪駒)

驪姬(ㄌㄧˊ ㄐㄧ)
name of a princess during the Epoch of Spring and Autumn

驪駕(ㄌㄧˊ ㄐㄧㄚˋ)
to drive a carriage drawn by two horses

驪駒(ㄌㄧˊ ㄐㄩ)
①a black horse ② the title of a farewell poem

驪珠(ㄌㄧˊ ㄓㄨ)
a pearl supposedly held under the jaw of a black dragon

驪山老母(ㄌㄧˊ ㄕㄢ ㄌㄠˇ ㄇㄨˇ)
name of a female immortal

骨 部
ㄍㄨˇ guu gǔ

【骨】 6990
1. ㄍㄨˇ guu gǔ
1. a bone: 他跌斷了肋骨。He broke his rib bone.
2. a framework; a frame; a skeleton: 研究一下房子的骨架。Study the frame of a house.

骨牌(ㄍㄨˇ ㄆㄞˊ)
dominoes or similar pieces used in mahjong, etc.

骨牌理論(ㄍㄨˇ ㄆㄞˊ ㄌㄧˇ ㄌㄨㄣˋ)
the domino theory—the theory that if one act or event is allowed to take place a succession of similar acts or events will follow

骨盤(ㄍㄨˇ ㄆㄢˊ)or **骨盆**(ㄍㄨˇ ㄆㄣˊ)
(anatomy) the pelvis

骨膜炎(ㄍㄨˇ ㄇㄛˊ ㄧㄢˊ)
periostitis

骨法(ㄍㄨˇ ㄈㄚˇ)
①a frame (of the body) ② phrenological features ③ (calligraphy) forcefulness of strokes

骨肥(ㄍㄨˇ ㄈㄟˊ)
fertilizer made from animal

bones; bone meal

骨董(ㄍㄨˇ ㄉㄨㄥˇ)
curios; antique objects

骨炭(ㄍㄨˇ ㄊㄢˋ)
boneblack; animal charcoal

骨鏡(ㄍㄨˇ ㄐㄧㄥˋ)
osteoscope

骨力(ㄍㄨˇ ㄌㄧˋ)
forcefulness of calligraphic strokes

骨立(ㄍㄨˇ ㄌㄧˋ)
skinny; bony

骨瘤(ㄍㄨˇ ㄌㄧㄡˊ)
an osteoma

骨骼 or 骨格(ㄍㄨˇ ㄍㄜˊ)
a frame of the body; a skeleton

骨幹(ㄍㄨˇ ㄍㄢˋ)
①(anatomy) a diaphysis ② the backbone; a mainstay: 這種人是國家的骨幹。Such men are the backbone of the country.

骨鯁 or 骨骾(ㄍㄨˇ ㄍㄥˇ)
honest; upright; outspoken

骨鯁在喉(ㄍㄨˇ ㄍㄥˇ ㄗㄞˋ ㄏㄡˊ)
to have a fishbone caught in one's throat—to have opinions one cannot but express

骨科(ㄍㄨˇ ㄎㄜ)
osteopathy

骨科醫生(ㄍㄨˇ ㄎㄜ ㄧ ㄕㄥ)
an osteopath

骨灰(ㄍㄨˇ ㄏㄨㄟ)
bone ashes

骨架(ㄍㄨˇ ㄐㄧㄚˋ)
a framework; a frame; a skeleton

骨節(ㄍㄨˇ ㄐㄧㄝˊ)or 骨關節(ㄍㄨˇ ㄍㄨㄢ ㄐㄧㄝˊ)
joints (of bones)

骨節痛(ㄍㄨˇ ㄐㄧㄝˊ ㄊㄨㄥˋ)
gout

骨節炎(ㄍㄨˇ ㄐㄧㄝˊ ㄧㄢˊ)
osteoarthritis

骨氣(ㄍㄨˇ ㄑㄧˋ)
fortitude; backbone; pluck; guts; grit; spirit; courage: 他是一個有骨氣的人。He is a man of backbone.

骨相學(ㄍㄨˇ ㄒㄧㄤˋ ㄒㄩㄝˊ)
phrenology

骨學(ㄍㄨˇ ㄒㄩㄝˊ)
osteology

骨質(ㄍㄨˇ ㄓˊ)
osseous tissue

骨折(ㄍㄨˇ ㄓㄜˊ)
a bone fracture

骨瘦如柴(ㄍㄨˇ ㄕㄡˋ ㄖㄨˊ ㄔㄞˊ)
thin and emaciated; very skinny; as thin as a stick; all bone and skin; to be reduced to a skeleton

骨肉(ㄍㄨˇ ㄖㄡˋ)or (ㄍㄨˇ ㄖㄡˋ)
one's own flesh and blood —blood relations

骨肉之情(ㄍㄨˇ ㄖㄡˋ ㄓ ㄑㄧㄥˊ)
love of one's own flesh and blood

骨肉至親(ㄍㄨˇ ㄖㄡˋ ㄓˋ ㄑㄧㄣ)
blood relations

骨軟筋酥(ㄍㄨˇ ㄖㄨㄢˇ ㄐㄧㄣ ㄙㄨ)
unnerved; enervated; un-manned

骨子(ㄍㄨˇ ㄗ)
a framework; a frame, a skeleton

骨子裏頭(ㄍㄨˇ ㄗ ㄌㄧˇ ㄊㄡ)
①in one's innermost nature; at heart ②in substance; fundamentally

骨刺(ㄍㄨˇ ㄘˋ)
(pathology) a bony spur; a bony projection or exostosis

骨髓(ㄍㄨˇ ㄙㄨㄟˇ)
marrow: 他被凍得透到骨髓。He was frozen to the marrow.

骨髓炎(ㄍㄨˇ ㄙㄨㄟˇ ㄧㄢˊ)
osteomyelitis

骨炎(ㄍㄨˇ ㄧㄢˊ)
osteitis

骨癌(ㄍㄨˇ ㄞˊ)
cancer in the bone: 他死於骨癌。He died of the cancer in the bone.

【骨】 6990
2.《ㄍㄨˊ》gú
a bone (in some colloquial phrases)

骨頭架子(ㄍㄨˇ ㄊㄡˊ ㄐㄧㄚˋ ㄗ)
①a frame (of the body); a skeleton ②a skinny person; a bag of bones 亦作「瘦皮猴」

骨碌(ㄍㄨˇ ㄌㄨ)
rolling; to turn round and round: 他從床上一骨碌爬起來。

He rolls out of bed.

【骨】 6990
3.《ㄍㄨ》gu
an alternative pronunciation of 骨 (《ㄍㄨˇ》) used in some phrases

骨朵兒(ㄍㄨ ㄉㄨㄛ ㄦ)
a bud

三畫

【骭】 6991
《ㄍㄢˇ》gann gàn
the shinbone

【骫】 6992
《ㄨㄟˇ》woei wěi
to bend; to twist

四畫

【骰】 6993
1. 《ㄕㄞˇ》shae shǎi
dice; to dice

骰花兒(ㄕㄞˇ ㄏㄨㄚ ㄦ)
spots on a dice

骰子(ㄕㄞˇ ㄗ)or 骰兒(ㄕㄞˇ ㄦ)
dice

【骰】 6993
2. 《ㄊㄡˊ》tour tóu
a literary pronunciation of 骰 (ㄕㄞˇ)

骰子令(ㄊㄡˊ ㄗ ㄌㄧㄥˋ)
(at a banquet) obligation to drink imposed on someone by throwing dice

骰子選(ㄊㄡˊ ㄗ ㄒㄩㄢˇ)
a game basically similar to backgammon

【骯】 6994
ㄤ ang āng
dirty; filthy; foul

骯髒(ㄤ ㄗㄤ)
dirty; filthy

五畫

【骷】 6995
ㄎㄨ ku kū
a human skeleton

骷髏(ㄎㄨ ㄌㄡˊ)
a human skeleton

六畫

【骻】 6996
ㄎㄨㄚˋ kuah kuà
the waist bone

〔骨部〕

【骸】 6997 ㄏㄞˊ hair hái
1. the shinbone
2. a skeleton

骸骨(ㄏㄞˊ ㄍㄨˇ)
a skeleton

【骼】 6998 ㄍㄜˊ ger gé
a bone; a skeleton

七畫

【骾】 6999 ㄍㄥˇ geeng gěng
a fishbone, etc., stuck in the throat 亦作「鯁」

八畫

【髀】 7000 ㄅㄧˋ bih bì
1. buttocks
2. the hipbone; the innominate bone

髀骨(ㄅㄧˋ ㄍㄨˇ)
the hipbone; the innominate bone

髀肉復生(ㄅㄧˋ ㄖㄡˋ ㄈㄨˋ ㄕㄥ)
having put on flesh again at the buttocks (an expression of regret at a long absence from horseback, where a soldier is supposed to belong)

【髁】 7001 ㄎㄜˊ ke kē
1. the hipbone; the innominate bone
2. the kneecap; the kneepan

十一畫

【髏】 7002 ㄌㄡˊ lou lóu
as in 骷髏—a human skeleton

十三畫

【髒】 7003 ㄗㄤ tzang zāng
dirty; filthy; 軟布易髒。Soft clothes dirty easily.

髒東西(ㄗㄤ ㄉㄨㄥ˙ㄒㄧ)
a dirty thing; filth

髒土(ㄗㄤ ㄊㄨˇ)
dirty soil

髒兮兮的(ㄗㄤ ㄒㄧ ㄒㄧ ˙ㄉㄜ)
very much soiled; very dirty;
把你髒兮兮的臉洗一洗。Wash your dirty face.

髒心(ㄗㄤ ㄒㄧㄣ)
an impure heart; a dirty mind

髒病(ㄗㄤ ㄅㄧㄥˋ)
venereal disease

髒瘡(ㄗㄤ ㄔㄨㄤ)
syphilitic lesions of the skin

髒字(ㄗㄤ ㄗˋ)or 髒字眼兒(ㄗㄤ ㄗˋ ㄧㄢˇ)
an obscene word; a swear-word; a profane word

【髓】 7004 ㄙㄨㄟˇ soei suǐ
marrow; pith; essence: 簡潔乃機智之精髓。Brevity is the marrow and pith of wit.

【體】 7005 ㄊㄧˇ tii tǐ
1. the body
2. shape; form
3. an entity; a unit
4. a style; a fashion; a system
5. substance; essence
6. theory (as opposed to practice)

體魄(ㄊㄧˇ ㄆㄛˋ)
the human body as the source of strength: 他的體魄強壯結實。His physical form is strong and stout.

體貌(ㄊㄧˇ ㄇㄠˋ)
①a figure and face ②decorum; propriety

體面(ㄊㄧˇ ㄇㄧㄢˋ)
①honor; dignity; face: 東方人很講體面。Face is very important to Oriental peoples. ②appearing good; looking elegant

體罰(ㄊㄧˇ ㄈㄚˊ)
corporal punishment

體法(ㄊㄧˇ ㄈㄚˇ)
an established mode or style

體範(ㄊㄧˇ ㄈㄢˋ)
a model; a pattern: 這學生是勤勉的體範。This student is a model of diligence.

體大思精(ㄊㄧˇ ㄉㄚˋ ㄙ ㄐㄧㄥ)
(said of a book) extensive in scope and penetrating in thought

體態(ㄊㄧˇ ㄊㄞˋ)
①outward form; an exterior look ②a manner, deport-ment, or a carriage (of a woman): 她體態優雅。She has a graceful carriage.

體態輕盈(ㄊㄧˇ ㄊㄞˋ ㄑㄧㄥ ㄧㄥˊ)
(said of a woman) with a charming sprightly carriage

體貼(ㄊㄧˇ ㄊㄧㄝ)
kind; considerate; thoughtful

體統(ㄊㄧˇ ㄊㄨㄥˇ)
①a system; an organized whole ②propriety in conduct

體能(ㄊㄧˇ ㄋㄥˊ)
physical agility; stamina

體念(ㄊㄧˇ ㄋㄧㄢˋ)
to be understanding; to make allowance for; to be sympathetic toward

體力(ㄊㄧˇ ㄌㄧˋ)
physical strength; stamina: 這年輕人缺乏體力。The youth lacks stamina.

體力勞動(ㄊㄧˇ ㄌㄧˋ ㄌㄠˊ ㄉㄨㄥˋ)
physical or manual labor

體例(ㄊㄧˇ ㄌㄧˋ)
general form

體諒(ㄊㄧˇ ㄌㄧㄤˋ)
to be understanding or sympathetic toward; to be considerate for: 我的父親是很體諒人的。My father is quite understanding.

體格(ㄊㄧˇ ㄍㄜˊ)
physique: 他是一個體格強壯的男人。He is a man of strong physique.

體格檢查(ㄊㄧˇ ㄍㄜˊ ㄐㄧㄢˇ ㄔㄚˊ)
a physical examination

體高(ㄊㄧˇ ㄍㄠ)
height (of a person)

體會(ㄊㄧˇ ㄏㄨㄟˋ)
to understand through something beyond the intellect; to comprehend intuitively

體積(ㄊㄧˇ ㄐㄧ)
volume (of a solid)

體己(ㄊㄧˇ ㄐㄧ˙)
①private; personal ②confidential

體系(ㄊㄧˇ ㄒㄧˋ)
a system (of thoughts, etc.); orderliness

體現(ㄊㄧˇ ㄒㄧㄢˋ)
to embody; to incarnate; to reflect; to express

體行(ㄊㄧˇ ㄒㄧㄥˊ)
to embody in one's own

actions

刑(ㄒㄧㄥˊ)
corporal punishment meted out by a court of law in former times

型(ㄒㄧㄥˊ)
an external physical appearance; (physical) build

血(ㄒㄩㄝˋ)
to be considerate of and sympathize with

質(ㄓˊ)
a bodily constitution; a physical make-up

制(ㄓˋ)
a system of rules; a system

裁(ㄘㄞˊ)
a style in art; a layout

脹系數(ㄓㄤˋ ㄒㄧˋ ㄕㄨˋ)
a coefficient of cubical expansion

重(ㄓㄨㄥˋ)
body weight

察(ㄔㄚˊ)
①to examine or investigate with intensive personal attention ②to be understanding or sympathetic toward

式(ㄕˋ)
a mode; a style

認(ㄖㄣˋ)
to perceive intuitively

裁(ㄘㄞˊ)
a form or a style (of writing): 那個作家用簡潔的體裁寫作。The author writes in a concise style.

操(ㄘㄠ)
gymnastics; calisthenics

操選手(ㄘㄠ ㄒㄩㄢˇ ㄕㄡˇ)
a gymnast

①an outline; a summary; the gist: 體要鮮明。The substance and outline are clear. ②concise; terse; succinct

to experience firsthand; firsthand experience

無完膚(ㄨˊ ㄨㄢˊ ㄈㄨ)
injured all over the body (often used figuratively for damage inflicted by verbal attacks): 這男孩被打得體無完膚。The boy was injured all over the body.

外受精(ㄨㄞˋ ㄕㄡˋ ㄐㄧㄥ)

(anatomy) external fertilization

體位(ㄊㄧˇ ㄨㄟˋ)
the grade of a draftee's physical fitness

體味(ㄊㄧˇ ㄨㄟˋ)
to appreciate; to savor

體溫(ㄊㄧˇ ㄨㄣ)
body temperature: 他的體溫在上升。His temperature is going up.

體溫計(ㄊㄧˇ ㄨㄣ ㄐㄧˋ)
a clinical thermometer

體育(ㄊㄧˇ ㄩˋ)
①physical education ②athletics: 他擅長體育。He is good at athletics.

體育道德(ㄊㄧˇ ㄩˋ ㄉㄠˋ ㄉㄜˊ)
sportsmanship

體育館(ㄊㄧˇ ㄩˋ ㄍㄨㄢˇ)
a gymnasium; an indoor stadium

體育會(ㄊㄧˇ ㄩˋ ㄏㄨㄟˋ)
an athletic club

體育記者(ㄊㄧˇ ㄩˋ ㄐㄧˋ ㄓㄜˇ)
a sportswriter

體育家(ㄊㄧˇ ㄩˋ ㄐㄧㄚ)
a physical educator

體育節(ㄊㄧˇ ㄩˋ ㄐㄧㄝˊ)
Athletics Day (September 9)

體育系(ㄊㄧˇ ㄩˋ ㄒㄧˋ)
the department of physical education (in a college)

體育場(ㄊㄧˇ ㄩˋ ㄔㄤˇ)
a stadium; a play ground

體育用品(ㄊㄧˇ ㄩˋ ㄩㄥˋ ㄆㄧㄣˇ)
sports goods; sports requisites 亦作「體育用品」

體用(ㄊㄧˇ ㄩㄥˋ)
theory and practice

髑 7006
ㄉㄨˊ dwu dú
the human skull

髑髏(ㄉㄨˊ ㄌㄡˊ)
the human skull

十四畫

髕 7007
ㄅㄧㄣˋ binn bìn
the kneecap; the kneepan

髕腳(ㄅㄧㄣˋ ㄐㄧㄠˇ)
an ancient punishment of cutting off the kneecap

高 部
《ㄍㄠ gau gāo》

【高】 7008
《ㄍㄠ gau gāo》
1. high; tall: 那是一座很高的塔。That's a very high tower.
2. of a high level or degree; above the average
3. lofty
4. a Chinese family name

高不可攀(ㄍㄠ ㄅㄨˋ ㄎㄜˇ ㄆㄢ)
too high to be reached (both literally and figuratively)

高不成低不就(ㄍㄠ ㄅㄨˋ ㄔㄥˊ ㄉㄧ ㄅㄨˋ ㄐㄧㄡˋ)
unable to find a mate or employment because the object available is either beyond one's reach or below one's minimum expectations

高攀(ㄍㄠ ㄆㄢ)
①to climb high ②to cultivate friendship with the socially elevated

高朋滿座(ㄍㄠ ㄆㄥˊ ㄇㄢˇ ㄗㄨㄛˋ)
All the seats are occupied by distinguished guests.

高帽(ㄍㄠ ㄇㄠˋ)or高帽子(ㄍㄠ ㄇㄠˋ ㄗ)
flattery; soft soap: 別被她的高帽所騙。Don't be deceived by her flattery.

高門(ㄍㄠ ㄇㄣˊ)
an illustrious family

高錳酸鉀(ㄍㄠ ㄇㄥˇ ㄙㄨㄢ ㄐㄧㄚˇ)
potassium permanganate

高妙(ㄍㄠ ㄇㄧㄠˋ)
exquisite; excellent

高棉(ㄍㄠ ㄇㄧㄢˊ)
Cambodia

高明(ㄍㄠ ㄇㄧㄥˊ)
①clever; wise; superior: 這個方法一點也不高明。This method is not clever at all. ②an expert; a master; a qualified person

高名(ㄍㄠ ㄇㄧㄥˊ)
fame; renown; great reputation

高發(ㄍㄠ ㄈㄚ)
(in former times) to pass the civil service examination

〔高
部〕

高飛球《ㄍㄠ ㄈㄟ ㄑㄧㄡ》
(baseball) fly

高飛遠走《ㄍㄠ ㄈㄟ ㄩㄢ ㄗㄡ》
to abscond

高峰《ㄍㄠ ㄈㄥ》
the peak; the summit; the culmination; the climax: 他現在人緣達頂高峰。He is at the climax of his popularity.

高風《ㄍㄠ ㄈㄥ》
noble character

高風亮節《ㄍㄠ ㄈㄥ ㄌㄧㄤ ㄐㄧㄝ》
noble character and incorruptible principle

高大《ㄍㄠ ㄉㄚ》
tall and big; colossal

高蹈《ㄍㄠ ㄉㄠ》
① to go on a long journey
② to be aloof from the world

高蹈派《ㄍㄠ ㄉㄠ ㄆㄞ》
the Parnassians (in French literature)

高蛋白《ㄍㄠ ㄉㄢ ㄅㄞ》
high protein

高檔《ㄍㄠ ㄉㄤ》
(dialect) the top grade; superior quality

高等《ㄍㄠ ㄉㄥ》
high or advanced (in the grade)

高等法院《ㄍㄠ ㄉㄥ ㄈㄚ ㄩㄢ》
the High Court: 囚犯被帶到高等法院候審。The prisoner was brought to the High Court for trial.

高等代數《ㄍㄠ ㄉㄥ ㄉㄞ ㄕㄨ》
higher algebra

高等動物《ㄍㄠ ㄉㄥ ㄉㄨㄥ ㄨ》
higher animals

高等考試《ㄍㄠ ㄉㄥ ㄎㄠ ㄕ》
the Higher Civil Service Examination in the country

高等教育《ㄍㄠ ㄉㄥ ㄐㄧㄠ ㄩ》
higher education

高等小學《ㄍㄠ ㄉㄥ ㄒㄧㄠ ㄒㄩㄝ》or 高小《ㄍㄠ ㄒㄧㄠ》
senior primary school which consists of the fifth and sixth grades

高等植物《ㄍㄠ ㄉㄥ ㄓ ㄨ》
higher plants

高等文官《ㄍㄠ ㄉㄥ ㄨㄣ ㄍㄨㄢ》
a high civil official

高低《ㄍㄠ ㄉㄧ》
① height ② a sense of propriety; discretion ③ (dialect) on any account; simply ④ (dialect) at last; after all ⑤ relative superiority or inferiority

高低不平《ㄍㄠ ㄉㄧ ㄅㄨ ㄆㄧㄥ》
uneven; rugged; irregular

高地《ㄍㄠ ㄉㄧ》
high ground; uplands

高第《ㄍㄠ ㄉㄧ》
a high place on the list of successful examinees

高調《ㄍㄠ ㄉㄧㄠ》
① a high-pitched note ② high-sounding (but impractical) assertions

高度《ㄍㄠ ㄉㄨ》
① an altitude; a height; an elevation: 這座山的高度是多少? What is the height of the mountain? ② highly; great

高度表《ㄍㄠ ㄉㄨ ㄅㄧㄠ》
an altimeter

高段《ㄍㄠ ㄉㄨㄢ》
(said of chess masters, judo experts, etc.) top-grade

高塔《ㄍㄠ ㄊㄚ》
a high tower; a high steeple

高擡貴手《ㄍㄠ ㄊㄞ ㄍㄨㄟ ㄕㄡ》
(literally) Raise your noble hands.—Please be merciful.

高擡身價《ㄍㄠ ㄊㄞ ㄕㄣ ㄐㄧㄚ》
to put a high price on oneself

高談闊論《ㄍㄠ ㄊㄢ ㄎㄨㄛ ㄌㄨㄣ》
to talk freely; to talk in a lively atmosphere

高湯《ㄍㄠ ㄊㄤ》
① consommé ② thin soup

高堂《ㄍㄠ ㄊㄤ》
① a hall with a high ceiling ② parents

高徒《ㄍㄠ ㄊㄨ》
(your) esteemed student

高能《ㄍㄠ ㄋㄥ》
having outstanding competence; very capable

高年《ㄍㄠ ㄋㄧㄢ》
advanced in age; aged

高樓大廈《ㄍㄠ ㄌㄡ ㄉㄚ ㄒㄧㄚ》or 高《ㄍㄠ ㄌㄡ ㄉㄚ ㄒㄧㄚ》
tall buildings; skyscrapers

高欄《ㄍㄠ ㄌㄢ》
the high hurdles

高麗《ㄍㄠ ㄌㄧ》
a former name of Korea

高麗棒子《ㄍㄠ ㄌㄧ ㄅㄤ ㄗ》
(offensive) a Korean

高麗參《ㄍㄠ ㄌㄧ ㄕㄣ》
ginseng 亦作「人參」: 高麗參貴。The ginseng is very expensive.

高麗人《ㄍㄠ ㄌㄧ ㄖㄣ》
a Korean

高利貸《ㄍㄠ ㄌㄧ ㄉㄞ》
usury: 那商人放高利貸。The merchant lent money at usury.

高利率政策《ㄍㄠ ㄌㄧ ㄌㄩ ㄓㄥ ㄘㄜ》
high interest policy

高硫酸《ㄍㄠ ㄌㄧㄡ ㄙㄨㄢ》
persulfuric acid

高粱《ㄍㄠ ㄌㄧㄤ》
kaoliang; sorghum; kafir

高粱酒《ㄍㄠ ㄌㄧㄤ ㄐㄧㄡ》
kaoliang wine

高齡《ㄍㄠ ㄌㄧㄥ》
advanced age; great age; old age

高盧《ㄍㄠ ㄌㄨ》
Gaul

高論《ㄍㄠ ㄌㄨㄣ》
an outstanding statement; original remarks; brilliant ideas

高歌《ㄍㄠ ㄍㄜ》
to sing aloud

高箇子 or 高個子《ㄍㄠ ㄍㄜ ㄗ》
a tall person: 他是個高箇子。He is a tall man.

高低低《ㄍㄠ ㄍㄠ ㄉㄧ ㄉㄧ》
uneven; rugged

高高在上《ㄍㄠ ㄍㄠ ㄗㄞ ㄕㄤ》
(literally) situated high above—(figuratively) lofty; aloof

高跟鞋《ㄍㄠ ㄍㄣ ㄒㄧㄝ》
high-heeled shoes

高崗《ㄍㄠ ㄍㄤ》
the peak or summit; a high mountain

高掛《ㄍㄠ ㄍㄨㄚ》
hanging high; suspended high

高貴《ㄍㄠ ㄍㄨㄟ》
noble; exalted

高官厚祿《ㄍㄠ ㄍㄨㄢ ㄏㄡ ㄌㄨ》
a high position and fat salary

高功能《ㄍㄠ ㄍㄨㄥ ㄋㄥ》

high-performance; high performance

科技產品《ㄍㄠ ㄐㄧˋ ㄔㄢˇ ㄆㄧㄣˇ》
a high-tech product

亢《ㄍㄠ ㄎㄤˋ》
proud and indomitable

空《ㄍㄠ ㄎㄨㄥ》
high altitude; upper air

呼《ㄍㄠ ㄏㄨ》
to shout; to call out aloud

級《ㄍㄠ ㄐㄧˊ》
①a high grade; a high class; superior ②advanced (courses)

級中學《ㄍㄠ ㄐㄧˊ ㄓㄨㄥ ㄒㄩㄝˊ》or 高中
a senior middle school; a senior high school

級參謀《ㄍㄠ ㄐㄧˊ ㄘㄢ ㄇㄡˊ》
a high staff officer; a top-grade counselor

誼《ㄍㄠ ㄐㄧˋ》
exalted ideals

髻《ㄍㄠ ㄐㄧˋ》
a kind of tall coiffure

加索《ㄍㄠ ㄐㄧㄚ ㄙㄨㄛˇ》
Caucasus; Caucasia

價《ㄍㄠ ㄐㄧㄚˋ》
a high price; an exorbitant price: 他以高價售出他的房子。
He has sold his house at a high price.

價收購《ㄍㄠ ㄐㄧㄚˋ ㄕㄡ ㄍㄡˋ》
to buy (usually from private individuals) for a high price

架鐵路《ㄍㄠ ㄐㄧㄚˋ ㄊㄧㄝˇ ㄌㄨˋ》
an elevated railroad

架橋《ㄍㄠ ㄐㄧㄚˋ ㄑㄧㄠˊ》
a viaduct

階層《ㄍㄠ ㄐㄧㄝ》
high rank; top rank

階人物《ㄍㄠ ㄐㄧㄝ ㄖㄣˊ ㄨˋ》
persons of high rank

節《ㄍㄠ ㄐㄧㄝˊ》
great moral fortitude; incorruptibility

潔《ㄍㄠ ㄐㄧㄝˊ》
noble and pure; exalted and immaculate

就《ㄍㄠ ㄐㄧㄡˋ》
opportunity for a high or higher position, a good or better employment, etc.

見《ㄍㄠ ㄐㄧㄢˋ》
your esteemed opinion or advice: 對於此事您有何高見?

What is your esteemed opinion of this matter?

高車《ㄍㄠ ㄔㄜ》
①name of an ancient tribe in what is Mongolia today ②a high-canopied chariot of ancient times

高攀《ㄍㄠ ㄆㄢ》
①to raise high; to uplift ②to become a hermit

高峻《ㄍㄠ ㄐㄩㄣˋ》
precipitous; steep: 此山高峻。
This mountain is steep.

高氣壓《ㄍㄠ ㄑㄧˋ ㄧㄚ》
high atmospheric pressure

高峭《ㄍㄠ ㄑㄧㄠˋ》
precipitous; high and steep

高蹺《ㄍㄠ ㄑㄧㄠ》
stilts

高強《ㄍㄠ ㄑㄧㄤˊ》
surpassing; outstanding; superior

高情《ㄍㄠ ㄑㄧㄥˊ》
your kindness; your thoughtfulness

高下《ㄍㄠ ㄒㄧㄚˋ》
superiority and inferiority

高效率《ㄍㄠ ㄒㄧㄠˋ ㄌㄩˋ》
high-efficiency

高薪《ㄍㄠ ㄒㄧㄣ》
high pay; a handsome salary: 他支領高薪。He receives a high salary.

高行《ㄍㄠ ㄒㄧㄥ》
noble conduct

高興《ㄍㄠ ㄒㄧㄥˋ》or 高高興興
《ㄍㄠ ㄍㄠ ㄒㄧㄥˋ ㄒㄧㄥˋ》
glad; elated; delighted: 很高興看到你。I am delighted to see you.

高血糖症《ㄍㄠ ㄒㄩㄝˇ ㄊㄤˊ ㄓㄥˋ》
(pathology) hyperglycemia

高血壓《ㄍㄠ ㄒㄩㄝˇ ㄧㄚ》
high blood pressure; hypertension

高軒《ㄍㄠ ㄒㄩㄢ》
a large, spacious vehicle

高懸《ㄍㄠ ㄒㄩㄢˊ》
to hang high

高雄《ㄍㄠ ㄒㄩㄥˊ》
Kaohsiung, a port city in southern Taiwan

高著兒《ㄍㄠ ㄓㄠ ㄦ》
a very clever sort of stratagem or scheme; a clever move 亦作「高招」

高瞻遠矚《ㄍㄠ ㄓㄢ ㄩㄢˇ ㄓㄨˋ》
farseeing; provident; far-sighted

高枕無憂《ㄍㄠ ㄓㄣˇ ㄨˊ ㄧㄡ》
to sleep in peace; to be free from worries

高漲《ㄍㄠ ㄓㄤˇ》
(said of a price or the water level) to rise

高掌遠蹠《ㄍㄠ ㄓㄤˇ ㄩㄢˇ ㄓˊ》
①wide open ②having great ambitions

高蹈《ㄍㄠ ㄓㄠˋ》
noble conduct

高中《ㄍㄠ ㄓㄨㄥ》
①《ㄍㄠ ㄓㄨㄥ》a senior high school
②《ㄍㄠ ㄓㄨㄥˋ》to pass an examination

高超《ㄍㄠ ㄔㄠ》
surpassing; outstanding; exalted; superior; superb

高潮《ㄍㄠ ㄔㄠˊ》
①a high tide ②a climax: 劇情漸入高潮。The plot is reaching a dramatic climax.

高敞《ㄍㄠ ㄔㄤˇ》
(said of buildings, etc.) tall and spacious: 這些建築物很高敞。These buildings were tall and spacious.

高唱入雲《ㄍㄠ ㄔㄤˋ ㄖㄨˋ ㄩㄣˊ》
(literally) to sing in a very high pitch or with very great intensity—to be very much talked about; on everybody's lips

高處《ㄍㄠ ㄔㄨˋ》
a high place; altitudes

高士《ㄍㄠ ㄕˋ》
a man with a noble character

高視闊步《ㄍㄠ ㄕˋ ㄎㄨㄛˋ ㄅㄨˋ》
①having uncommon dignity ②proud; disdainful; to stalk: 一個年輕人高視闊步走出房來。A young man stalks out of the room.

高射砲《ㄍㄠ ㄕㄜˋ ㄆㄠˋ》
an antiaircraft gun; an ack-ack

高燒《ㄍㄠ ㄕㄠ ㄦ》
a high fever: 他發高燒。He has a high fever.

高手《ㄍㄠ ㄕㄡˇ》
a master (in a skill, trade, etc.); an expert: 他是下棋的

〔髟部〕

高手。He is a master of chess.

高壽《ㄍㄠ ㄕㄡ》
①advanced age; old age; great age ②your age (in addressing an aged person)

高山病《ㄍㄠ ㄕㄢ ㄅ|ㄥ》
mountain sickness; altitude sickness

高山流水《ㄍㄠ ㄕㄢ ㄌ|ㄡ ㄕㄨㄟ》
(literally) high mountains and flowing waters—sympathetic interaction between two minds, from the story of the musician Po Ya (伯牙) and his friend Chung Tzuchi (鍾子期) who knew his mind was on high mountains and flowing waters merely by listening to his music

高山景行《ㄍㄠ ㄕㄢ ㄐ|ㄥ|ㄥ》
to admire great virtue

高山植物《ㄍㄠ ㄕㄢ ㄓˊ ㄨˋ》
an alpine plant

高山族《ㄍㄠ ㄕㄢ ㄗㄨˊ》
the aborigines of Taiwan

高山仰止《ㄍㄠ ㄕㄢ |ㄤˇ ㄓˇ》
The mountain is so high that one looks up to it with awe. —(figuratively) A man of virtue is so great that one looks up to him awfully.

高深《ㄍㄠ ㄕㄣ》
recondite; abstruse; profound; deep; advanced; lofty

高尚《ㄍㄠ ㄕㄤˋ》
①noble; exalted ②(said of pursuits, entertainments, etc.) high-class; refined; respectable

高陞《ㄍㄠ ㄕㄥ》
to get a promotion; to be promoted

高聲大笑《ㄍㄠ ㄕㄥ ㄉㄚˋ ㄒ|ㄠˋ》
to roar with laughter

高聲朗誦《ㄍㄠ ㄕㄥ ㄌㄤˇ ㄙㄨㄥˋ》
to recite aloud: 他高聲朗誦這首長詩。He recited the long poem aloud.

高熱《ㄍㄠ ㄖㄜˋ》
a high temperature; a high fever: 她發高熱。She has a high fever.

高人《ㄍㄠ ㄖㄣˊ》
a man of lofty character 亦作「高士」②an expert; a person of superior talent or

ability; a master

高人一等《ㄍㄠ ㄖㄣˊ | ㄉㄥˇ》
a cut above other people

高人一籌《ㄍㄠ ㄖㄣˊ | ㄔㄡˊ》
a notch better than average people

高姿態《ㄍㄠ ㄗ ㄊㄞˋ》
a lofty stance

高足《ㄍㄠ ㄗㄨˊ》or 高足弟子《ㄍㄠ ㄗㄨˊ ㄉ|ˋ ㄗˇ》or 高弟《ㄍㄠ ㄉ|ˋ》
(an honorific term) your capable student; your brilliant disciple

高祖《ㄍㄠ ㄗㄨˇ》
①one's great-great-grandfather ②one's ancestor ③the founder of a dynasty

高祖母《ㄍㄠ ㄗㄨˇ ㄇㄨˇ》
one's great-great-grandmother

高祖父《ㄍㄠ ㄗㄨˇ ㄈㄨˋ》
one's great-great-grandfather

高蹤《ㄍㄠ ㄗㄨㄥ》
noble deeds

高才生《ㄍㄠ ㄘㄞˊ ㄕㄥ》
a bright and excellent student

高僧《ㄍㄠ ㄙㄥ》
a high-ranking monk; a prelate; a learned monk

高速《ㄍㄠ ㄙㄨˋ》
high speed

高速公路《ㄍㄠ ㄙㄨˋ ㄍㄨㄥ ㄌㄨˋ》
an expressway; a freeway; a motorway

高聳《ㄍㄠ ㄙㄨㄥˇ》
to tower; to rise high

高額《ㄍㄠ ㄜˊ》
a large sum; a large amount (of money) 亦作「鉅額」

高矮《ㄍㄠ ㄞˇ》
stature; height; high and low

高傲《ㄍㄠ ㄠˋ》
proud; overbearing; haughty

高昂《ㄍㄠ ㄤˊ》
(said of prices, morale, etc.) rising high

高爾夫球《ㄍㄠ ㄦˇ ㄈㄨ ㄑ|ㄡˊ》
golf

高爾夫球棒《ㄍㄠ ㄦˇ ㄈㄨ ㄑ|ㄡˊ ㄅㄤˋ》
golf clubs

高爾夫球僮《ㄍㄠ ㄦˇ ㄈㄨ ㄑ|ㄡˊ ㄊㄨㄥˊ》
a caddie

高爾夫球場《ㄍㄠ ㄦˇ ㄈㄨ ㄑ|ㄡˊ ㄔㄤˇ》
a golf course; a golf links

高爾基《ㄍㄠ ㄦˇ ㄐ|》
Maxim Gorki, 1868-19: Russian writer

高義 or 高誼《ㄍㄠ |ˋ》
a great friendship; a gre kindness

高壓電線《ㄍㄠ |ㄚ ㄉ|ㄢˋ ㄒ|ㄢˋ》
高壓線《ㄍㄠ |ㄚ ㄒ|ㄢˋ》
a high-tension wire

高壓政策《ㄍㄠ |ㄚ ㄓㄥˋ ㄘㄜˋ》
a high-handed policy

高壓手段《ㄍㄠ |ㄚ ㄕㄡˇ ㄉㄨㄢˋ》
high-handed measures; tyrannical measures

高牙大纛《ㄍㄠ |ㄚˊ ㄉㄚˋ ㄉㄠˋ》
flags and emblems of a hi official

高雅《ㄍㄠ |ㄚˇ》
elegant; noble and gracef refined

高眼《ㄍㄠ |ㄢˇ》
keen foresight; vision

高音《ㄍㄠ |ㄣ》
①high tones; treble ②soprano or tenor

高臥《ㄍㄠ ㄨㄛˋ》
to live in peace and ease; be free from anxiety; sleep soundly

高位《ㄍㄠ ㄨㄟˋ》
a high position: 他在銀行居高位。He holds a high po tion in a bank.

高溫《ㄍㄠ ㄨㄣ》
a high temperature

高溫計《ㄍㄠ ㄨㄣ ㄐ|ˋ》
a pyrometer

高文典冊《ㄍㄠ ㄨㄣˊ ㄉ|ㄢˇ ㄘㄜˋ》
major administrative do ments of the imperial cou

高原《ㄍㄠ ㄩㄢˊ》
highlands; plateaus

髟 部
ㄅ|ㄠ biau biāo

三畫

【髟】 7009
ㄅ|ㄠ kuen kūn

1. an ancient punishment shaving the hair

to shear trees

鉗（ㄑㄧㄢˊ ㄑㄧˊ）
ancient punishments of shaving the hair and chaining the neck

【髢】7010
（ㄊㄧˋ tìh tì）
wearing false hair

四畫

【髣】7011
（ㄈㄤˇ faang fǎng）
like; similar

髣髴 or 彷彿（ㄈㄤˇ ㄈㄨˊ）
①like; similar ②seem; as if

【髯】7012
（髯）（ㄖㄢˊ ran rán）
whiskers

虯髯（ㄑㄧㄡˊ ㄖㄢˊ）
a heavily bearded man

絡腮胡（ㄌㄨㄛˋ ㄙㄞ ㄏㄨˊ）
a heavily bearded fellow

髯口（ㄖㄢˊ ㄎㄡˇ）
artificial whiskers worn by actors in Peiking opera

美髯（ㄇㄟˇ ㄖㄢˊ）
bearded old man; an old man

髯翁（ㄖㄢˊ ㄨㄥ）
nickname of the Sung Dynasty poet Su Shih (蘇軾), who was heavily bearded

【髦】7013
（ㄇㄠˊ mau máo）
children's hair style with front hair covering the forehead

髦頭（ㄇㄠˊ ㄊㄡˊ）
the mane

英髦（ㄧㄥ ㄇㄠˊ）
man of talent

俊髦（ㄐㄩㄣˋ ㄇㄠˊ）
man of talent

髦士（ㄇㄠˊ ㄕˋ）
man of talent; a man of superior character

五畫

【髫】7014
（ㄊㄧㄠˊ tyau tiáo）
children's hair style with hair hanging down the forehead

髫齒（ㄊㄧㄠˊ ㄔˇ）
youngster; a child

髫年（ㄊㄧㄠˊ ㄋㄧㄢˊ）
childhood; youth

髫齔（ㄊㄧㄠˊ ㄔㄣˋ）
childhood; youth

【髪】7015
（ㄈㄚˇ faa fǎ）
1. hair (covering human heads)
2. a hairbreadth; a hair's breadth

髪匪（ㄈㄚˇ ㄈㄟˇ）
the Taiping rebels of the late Ching Dynasty who grew long hair

髪膚（ㄈㄚˇ ㄈㄨ）
one's hair and skin

髪短心長（ㄈㄚˇ ㄉㄨㄢˇ ㄒㄧㄣ ㄔㄤˊ）
(literally) to have sparse hair and an intelligent mind —old and wise

髪蠟（ㄈㄚˇ ㄌㄚˋ）
pomade

髪際（ㄈㄚˇ ㄐㄧˋ）
hairline

髪髻（ㄈㄚˇ ㄐㄧˋ）
hair tied in a knot

髪夾（ㄈㄚˇ ㄐㄧㄚ）
a hairpin; a bobby pin

髪膠（ㄈㄚˇ ㄐㄧㄠ）
hair spray; fixture for hair

髪妻（ㄈㄚˇ ㄑㄧ）
one's first wife

髪型（ㄈㄚˇ ㄒㄧㄥˊ）or 髪式（ㄈㄚˇ ㄕˋ）
a hair style; a hairdo; a coiffure

髪指（ㄈㄚˇ ㄓˇ）
so angry that the hair rises; to boil with anger: 他的暴行令人髪指。His atrocities made one boil with anger.

髪針（ㄈㄚˇ ㄓㄣ）
a hairpin

髪刷（ㄈㄚˇ ㄕㄨㄚ）
a hairbrush

髪油（ㄈㄚˇ ㄧㄡˊ）
hair oil; pomade: 他塗髪油。He puts pomade on the hair.

髪網（ㄈㄚˇ ㄨㄤˇ）
a hair net

【髴】7016
（ㄈㄨˊ fwu fú）
as in 髣髴—like; similar

【髥】7017
（ㄖㄢˊ ran rán）
same as 髯—whiskers

【髭】7018
（ㄗ tzy zi）
moustaches

髭鬚（ㄗ ㄒㄩ）
moustaches and beards

六畫

【髻】7019
（ㄐㄧˋ jìh jì）
a coiffure with a topknot

【髹】7020
（ㄒㄧㄡ shiou xiū）
1. a kind of dark-red paint
2. to paint or lacquer (articles)

七畫

【鬁】7021
（ㄌㄧˋ lih lì）
as in 鬎鬁—favus

【鬃】7022
（ㄓㄨㄚˊ jua zhuó）
women's headdresses in mourning

鬃髻（ㄓㄨㄚˊ ㄐㄧˋ）
a kind of hairdo worn by young girls and maid servants in former times

八畫

【鬆】7023
（ㄙㄨㄥ song sōng）
1. loose; lax; slack
2. to relax: 放鬆你的肌肉。Relax your muscles.
3. to loosen: 螺絲釘鬆了。The screw has loosened.
4. soft; light

鬆綁（ㄙㄨㄥ ㄅㄤˇ）
to untie, undo, or unfasten someone or something tied

鬆動（ㄙㄨㄥ ·ㄉㄨㄥ）or 鬆通（ㄙㄨㄥ ·ㄊㄨㄥ）
①to become less crowded ②not hard up; well-off ③to become relaxed or flexible

鬆土機（ㄙㄨㄥ ㄊㄨˇ ㄐㄧ）
a scarifier

鬆口氣（ㄙㄨㄥ ㄎㄡˇ ㄑㄧˋ）
to relax for a while; to get a breathing spell

鬆開（ㄙㄨㄥ ㄎㄞ）
to loosen

鬆緊（ㄙㄨㄥ ㄐㄧㄣˇ）
tension and relaxation

鬆緊帶（ㄙㄨㄥ ㄐㄧㄣˇ ㄉㄞˋ）
an elastic cord, string, band, etc.

鬆勁（ㄙㄨㄥ ㄐㄧㄣˋ）or 鬆勁兒（ㄙㄨㄥ

〔髟部〕

【鬥
部】

ㄐㄧㄠㄦ
to slack; to loose strength

鬆懈(ㄙㄨㄥ ㄒㄧㄝˋ)
to relax efforts, attention, etc.: 你不能鬆懈,要繼續努力。 You must not relax in your efforts.

鬆心(ㄙㄨㄥ ㄒㄧㄣ)
carefree

鬆性(ㄙㄨㄥ ㄒㄧㄥˋ)
(physics) porosity

鬆弛(ㄙㄨㄥ ㄔˊ)
①relaxed; flabby ②lax; slack: 繩子鬆弛了。The rope was slack.

鬆手(ㄙㄨㄥ ㄕㄡˇ)
to let go the hands; to relax the hold

鬆頓(ㄙㄨㄥ ㄖㄨㄢˋ)
loose and soft

鬆脆(ㄙㄨㄥ ㄘㄨㄟˋ)
(said of food) crisp and soft

鬆散(ㄙㄨㄥ ㄙㄢˇ)
incompact; not solid; loosely arranged: 文章結構鬆散。The article is loosely organized.

鬆鬆垮垮(ㄙㄨㄥ ㄙㄨㄥ ㄎㄨㄚˇ ㄎㄨㄚˇ)
to behave in a lax way; to be slack and perfunctory

【鬈】 7024
ㄑㄩㄢˊ chyuan quán
1. fine hair
2. curled hair

鬈髮(ㄑㄩㄢˊ ㄈㄚˇ)
crimps

鬈曲(ㄑㄩㄢˊ ㄑㄩ)
to crinkle; to curl 亦作「捲曲」

【鬃】 7025
ㄗㄨㄥ tzong zōng
1. the topknot of a lady's headdress
2. the mane: 那匹馬鬃稀。That horse has a thin mane.
3. a bristle

鬃毛(ㄗㄨㄥ ㄇㄠˊ)
a horse mane

九畫

【鬎】 7026
ㄌㄚˋ lah là
favus

鬎鬁(ㄌㄚˋ ㄌㄧˋ)
favus

鬎鬁頭(ㄌㄚˋ ㄌㄧˋ ㄊㄡˊ)
a scalp affected with favus

【鬍】 7027
ㄏㄨˊ hwu hú
beard

鬍鬚(ㄏㄨˊ ㄒㄩ)
beard

鬍子(ㄏㄨˊ ㄗ˙)
beard

十畫

【鬑】 7028
ㄌㄧㄢˊ lian lián
hair hanging down the temples

鬑鬖(ㄌㄧㄢˊ ㄙㄢ)
having sparse hair on the temples

【鬐】 7029
ㄑㄧˊ chyi qí
1. the mane
2. fins 亦作「鰭」

【鬒】 7030
ㄓㄣˇ jeen zhěn
having dark, glossy hair

十一畫

【鬘】 7031
ㄇㄢˊ man mán
(said of hair) fair

十二畫

【鬚】 7032
ㄒㄩ shiu xū
1. beard; whiskers
2. whiskers (of a cat, etc.)
3. an awn

鬚眉(ㄒㄩ ㄇㄟˊ)
①beard and eyebrows ②men

鬚髮(ㄒㄩ ㄈㄚˇ)
beard and hair

鬚根(ㄒㄩ ㄍㄣ)
fine rootlets of plants; fibrous roots

鬚生(ㄒㄩ ㄕㄥ)
a bearded character (in Chinese opera)

鬚髯如戟(ㄒㄩ ㄖㄢˊ ㄖㄨˊ ㄐㄧˇ)
beard bristling like halberds

十三畫

【鬟】 7033
ㄏㄨㄢˊ hwan huán
1. to dress the hair in a coiled knot

2. a female servant; a maid

鬟髻(ㄏㄨㄢˊ ㄐㄧˋ)
a woman's coiffure with topknot

十四畫

【鬢】 7034
ㄅㄧㄣˋ binn bìn
hair on the temples

鬢斑(ㄅㄧㄣˋ ㄅㄢ)
hair turning gray at the temples

鬢邊(ㄅㄧㄣˋ ㄅㄧㄢ)
temples (behind the forehead)

鬢毛(ㄅㄧㄣˋ ㄇㄠˊ)
hair on the temples

鬢髮(ㄅㄧㄣˋ ㄈㄚˇ)
hair on the temples

鬢亂釵橫(ㄅㄧㄣˋ ㄌㄨㄢˋ ㄔㄞ ㄏㄥˊ)
hair in disorder and hairpin out of place (said of woman upon getting out of bed)

鬢角 or 鬢脚(ㄅㄧㄣˋ ㄐㄧㄠˇ)
temples (beside the ears)

鬢霜(ㄅㄧㄣˋ ㄕㄨㄤ)
temples covered with white hair

十五畫

【鬣】 7035
ㄌㄧㄝˋ lieh liè
1. long beard; long whiskers
2. the mane
3. fins

鬣狗(ㄌㄧㄝˋ ㄍㄡˇ)
a hyena or a hyaena 亦作「狼」

鬥　部
ㄉㄡˋ dow dòu

【鬥】 7036
ㄉㄡˋ dow dòu
same as 鬭—to struggle

四畫

【鬧】 7037
ㄉㄡˋ dow dòu
same as 鬭—to struggle

五畫

【鬧】 7038
ㄋㄠ naw nào

to disturb; to agitate; to trouble

to have or experience (disasters, sickness, etc.)

noisy; uproarious, stormy; clamorous

鬧彆扭 (ㄋㄠ ㄅㄧㄝˋ ㄋㄧㄡˇ)
to act peevishly; to show resentment; to be dissatisfied; to bicker, to be at odds: 他們又在鬧彆扭。They are bickering again.

鬧病 (ㄋㄠ ㄅㄧㄥˋ)
to get sick; to fall ill

鬧不清 (ㄋㄠ ㄅㄨˋ ㄑㄧㄥ)
unable to tell apart; unable to distinguish

鬧脾氣 (ㄋㄠ ㄆㄧˊ ㄑㄧˋ)
to show temper; to get into a temper

鬧翻 (ㄋㄠ ㄈㄢ)
to fall out with somebody: 那兩個人鬧翻了。The two men fell out.

鬧翻天 (ㄋㄠ ㄈㄢ ㄊㄧㄢ)
to raise a hell of a noise; to raise a rumpus

鬧房 (ㄋㄠ ㄈㄤˊ)
rough horseplay at weddings; to play practical jokes on the newlyweds on the wedding night 參看「鬧新房」

鬧風潮 (ㄋㄠ ㄈㄥ ˙ㄔㄠ)
to stir up a public commotion

鬧肚子 (ㄋㄠ ㄉㄨˋ ˙ㄗ)
to have loose bowels: 他鬧肚子。He has loose bowels.

鬧亂子 (ㄋㄠ ㄌㄨㄢˋ ˙ㄗ)
to start trouble; to create disturbances

鬧革命 (ㄋㄠ ㄍㄜˊ ㄇㄧㄥˋ)
to make revolution; to rise in revolution

鬧個不休 (ㄋㄠ ˙ㄍㄜ ㄅㄨˋ ㄒㄧㄡ)
to have a ceaseless storm or dispute; to cause trouble or harass persistently

鬧鬼 (ㄋㄠ ㄍㄨㄟˇ)
①(said of a house, etc.) haunted ②to play tricks behind somebody's back; to use underhand means

鬧耗子 (ㄋㄠ ㄏㄠˋ ˙ㄗ)
infested with rats

鬧轟轟 (ㄋㄠ ㄏㄨㄥ ㄏㄨㄥ)
① arousing intense excitement; sensational; very exciting ②uproarious; clamorous; noisy

鬧饑荒 (ㄋㄠ ㄐㄧ ˙ㄏㄨㄤ)
to have a famine

鬧家務 (ㄋㄠ ㄐㄧㄚ ˙ㄨ)
to have a domestic disturbance

鬧酒 (ㄋㄠ ㄐㄧㄡˇ)
to start a drinking bout; to engage in a drunken brawl; to behave ridiculously when drunk

鬧情緒 (ㄋㄠ ㄑㄧㄥˊ ㄒㄩˋ)
to be in a bad mood; to be in low spirits

鬧窮 (ㄋㄠ ㄑㄩㄥˊ)
to be poor; to be in lack of money or funds

鬧戲 (ㄋㄠ ㄒㄧˋ)
a farce 亦作「鬧劇」

鬧笑話 (ㄋㄠ ㄒㄧㄠˋ ㄏㄨㄚˋ)
to arouse ridicule; to make oneself a laughing stock

鬧新房 (ㄋㄠ ㄒㄧㄣ ㄈㄤˊ)
rough horseplay at a wedding; to play practical jokes on the newlyweds in the bridal chamber

鬧性子 (ㄋㄠ ㄒㄧㄥˋ ˙ㄗ)
to go into a temper

鬧學潮 (ㄋㄠ ㄒㄩㄝˊ ˙ㄔㄠ)
to incite the student riot or demonstration on or outside the school campus

鬧著玩兒 (ㄋㄠ ˙ㄓㄜ ㄨㄢˊ ㄦ)
to raise hell just for fun or joke

鬧鐘 (ㄋㄠ ㄓㄨㄥ)
an alarm clock: 鬧鐘壞了。The alarm clock is out of order.

鬧事 (ㄋㄠ ㄕˋ)
to cause trouble or uproar; to raise hell

鬧市 (ㄋㄠ ㄕˋ)
a busy shopping district

鬧熱 (ㄋㄠ ㄖㄜˋ)
full of noisy bustle

鬧嚷嚷 (ㄋㄠ ㄖㄤˇ ㄖㄤˇ)
noisy; clamorous

鬧賊 (ㄋㄠ ㄗㄟˊ)
to be visited by burglars

鬧意見 (ㄋㄠ ㄧˋ ㄐㄧㄢˋ)
to have differences of opinion; to have disputes

六畫

【鬨】 7039
ㄏㄨㄥ hong hòng

1. to be boisterous or uproarious; uproar; clamor; noise
2. a dispute; a quarrel

鬨堂 (ㄏㄨㄥ ㄊㄤˊ)
to fill a room with roars of laughter; to bring the house down

八畫

【鬩】 7040
ㄒㄧˋ shih xì
to quarrel; to conflict

鬩牆 (ㄒㄧˋ ㄑㄧㄤˊ)
to quarrel within the family; an intramural fight

十畫

【鬪】 7041
(鬥) ㄉㄡˋ dow dòu
to struggle

十四畫

【鬬】 7042
ㄉㄡˋ dow dòu

to struggle; to fight; to contend; to conflict; to vie; to compete; quarrelsomeness

鬬不過 (ㄉㄡˋ ㄅㄨˋ ㄍㄨㄛˋ)
unable to win in the struggle; can't be able to fight against

鬬牌 (ㄉㄡˋ ㄆㄞˊ)
to play cards: 來鬬牌吧。Let's play cards.

鬬富 (ㄉㄡˋ ㄈㄨˋ)
to vie in wealth

鬬牛 (ㄉㄡˋ ㄋㄧㄡˊ)
a bullfight

鬬牛者 (ㄉㄡˋ ㄋㄧㄡˊ ㄓㄜˇ)or鬬牛士 (ㄉㄡˋ ㄋㄧㄡˊ ㄕˋ)
a bullfighter; a matador

鬬牛場 (ㄉㄡˋ ㄋㄧㄡˊ ㄔㄤˇ)
a bullring

鬬弄 (ㄉㄡˋ ㄋㄨㄥˋ)

① to seduce; to flirt with ② to play jokes; to make fun of

鬥狠 or 鬥很（ㄉㄡ ㄏㄣˇ）
to compete in ferocities

鬥話（ㄉㄡ ㄏㄨㄚˋ）
to argue; to debate

鬥雞（ㄉㄡ ㄐㄧ）
a cockfight; cockfighting

鬥雞眼（ㄉㄡ ㄐㄧ ㄧㄢˇ）
crossed eyes; convergent strabismus

鬥勁（ㄉㄡ ㄐㄧㄥˋ）
to compete in strength

鬥氣（ㄉㄡ ㄑㄧˋ）
to quarrel on emotional grounds

鬥巧（ㄉㄡ ㄑㄧㄠˇ）
① by chance; by coincidence; accidentally 亦作「鬥巧」: 我鬥巧遇到他。I met him by chance. ② to compete in skill or ingenuity

鬥趣（ㄉㄡ ㄑㄩˋ）
to joke

鬥拳（ㄉㄡ ㄑㄩㄢˊ）
boxing: 你喜歡鬥拳嗎? Do you like boxing?

鬥蟋蟀（ㄉㄡ ㄒㄧ ㄕㄨㄞˋ）or 鬥促織（ㄉㄡ ㄘㄨˋ ㄓ）
a cricketfight

鬥閑氣（ㄉㄡ ㄒㄧㄢˊ ㄑㄧˋ）
to quarrel about trifles

鬥志（ㄉㄡ ㄓˋ）
pugnacious spirit; fighting spirit; the determination to compete or fight

鬥智（ㄉㄡ ㄓˋ）
a battle of wits; a contest of wits

鬥智不鬥力（ㄉㄡ ㄓˋ ㄅㄨˋ ㄉㄡ ㄌㄧˋ）
to fight a battle of wits, not of limbs

鬥爭（ㄉㄡ ㄓㄥ）
struggle; conflict; strife

鬥嘴（ㄉㄡ ㄗㄨㄟˇ）or 鬥口（ㄉㄡ ㄎㄡˇ）
to quarrel; to wrangle; to squabble

鬥殴（ㄉㄡ ㄡ）
to have a fight; to fight; to brawl: 孩子們在鬥殴。The boys are fighting.

鬥鵪鶉（ㄉㄡ ㄢ ㄔㄨㄣˊ）
a quailfight

鬥鴨（ㄉㄡ ㄧㄚ）
a duckfight

中欄

十六畫

【鬮】　7043
ㄐㄧㄡ jiōu jiū
lots (to be drawn)

鬮兒（ㄐㄧㄡㄦ）
lots (to be drawn)

鬯 部
彳尤 chanq chàng

【鬯】　7044
彳尤 chanq chàng
1. sacrificial spirits; herb-flavored spirits
2. same as 暢—unobstructed

鬯酒（彳尤 ㄐㄧㄡˇ）
sacrificial spirits

十九畫

【鬱】　7045
ㄩˋ yuh yù
1. a tulip
2. a plum (*Prunus japonica*)
3. held in check; pent-up; stagnant
4. luxuriant; lush

鬱悶（ㄩˋ ㄇㄣˋ）
to have pent-up emotions or thoughts

鬱陶（ㄩˋ ㄊㄠˊ）
melancholy; pensive; sad; anxiously

鬱積（ㄩˋ ㄐㄧ）
pent-up (feelings); to smolder: 仇恨鬱積在他心頭。Hatred smolders in his bosom.

鬱結（ㄩˋ ㄐㄧㄝˊ）or 鬱塞（ㄩˋ ㄙㄜˋ）
to suffer from pent-up feelings

鬱金（ㄩˋ ㄐㄧㄣ）
Curcuma longa, a kind of fragrant herb

鬱金香（ㄩˋ ㄐㄧㄣ ㄒㄧㄤ）
a tulip: 這裏的鬱金香在五月開花。Tulips bloom here in May.

鬱沈沈（ㄩˋ ㄔㄣˊ ㄔㄣˊ）
depressed; despondent; dejected; low-spirited

鬱悒（ㄩˋ ㄧˋ）
melancholy; pensive; sad

鬱蓊（ㄩˋ ㄨㄥˇ）
luxuriant; lush

鬱郁（ㄩˋ ㄩˋ）
fragrant; sweet-smelling

鬱鬱不樂（ㄩˋ ㄩˋ ㄅㄨˋ ㄌㄜˋ）
despondent; dejected; depressed; low-spirited

鬱鬱寡歡（ㄩˋ ㄩˋ ㄍㄨㄚˇ ㄏㄨㄢ）
to mope; to feel low; one's spirits droop

鬲 部
ㄌㄧˋ lih lì

【鬲】　7046
1.《ㄜˊ ger gé
1. name of an ancient state
2. name of an ancient sage
3. same as 隔

【鬲】　7046
2. ㄌㄧˋ lih lì
a kind of caldron

十二畫

【鬻】　7047
ㄩˋ yuh yù
1. to sell
2. to bring up
3. young; childish

鬻子（ㄩˋ ㄗˇ）
① a merchant; a trader ② young child ③ to sell one's own children

鬻文（ㄩˋ ㄨㄣˊ）
to write for pay: 他鬻文為生。He makes a living by writing.

鬻獄（ㄩˋ ㄩˋ）
to accept bribes from litigants

鬼 部
《ㄨㄟ goei guǐ

【鬼】　7048
《ㄨㄟ goei guǐ
1. spirits; ghosts; demons; devils
2. cunning; crafty; wily; deceitful

3. sinister; dark; evil; a dirty trick, work, etc.

鬼魔（ㄍㄨㄟ ㄇㄛˊ）
evil spirits; demons

鬼魅（ㄍㄨㄟ ㄇㄟˋ）
bogies; goblins; monsters

鬼門關（ㄍㄨㄟ ㄇㄣˊ ㄍㄨㄢ）
the gate to the land of ghosts; the gate of hell

鬼迷心竅（ㄍㄨㄟ ㄇㄧˊ ㄒㄧㄣ ㄑㄧㄠˋ）
to be possessed; to be obsessed

鬼斧神工（ㄍㄨㄟ ㄈㄨˇ ㄕㄣˊ ㄍㄨㄥ）
prodigious workmanship

鬼道（ㄍㄨㄟ ㄉㄠˋ）
magic; wizardry; sorcery

鬼點子（ㄍㄨㄟ ㄉㄧㄢˇ ㄗ˙）
wicked ideas; tricks

鬼胎（ㄍㄨㄟ ㄊㄞ）
an evil plot; a dark scheme: 他心懷鬼胎。He harbored sinister designs.

鬼頭風（ㄍㄨㄟ ㄊㄡˊ ㄈㄥ）
a tornado; a twister; a whirlwind

鬼頭鬼腦（ㄍㄨㄟ ㄊㄡˊ ㄍㄨㄟ ㄋㄠˇ）
①crafty and sinister; evil and shrewd; secretive ②hiding and peeping

鬼剃頭（ㄍㄨㄟ ㄊㄧˋ ㄊㄡˊ）
a kind of balding disease

鬼臉（ㄍㄨㄟ ㄌㄧㄢˇ）
a grimace; to grimace: 小丑向孩子們做鬼臉。The clown grimaced at the children.

鬼錄（ㄍㄨㄟ ㄌㄨˋ）
a register or roll of the dead

鬼怪（ㄍㄨㄟ ㄍㄨㄞˋ）
monsters; goblins; bogies; ghosts

鬼鬼祟祟（ㄍㄨㄟ ㄍㄨㄟ ㄙㄨㄟˋ ㄙㄨㄟˋ）
stealthy; furtive; sneaky; clandestine; surreptitious; secretive

鬼工（ㄍㄨㄟ ㄍㄨㄥ）
prodigious skill; marvelous workmanship

鬼哭狼號（ㄍㄨㄟ ㄎㄨ ㄌㄤˊ ㄏㄠˊ）or 鬼哭神號（ㄍㄨㄟ ㄎㄨ ㄕㄣˊ ㄏㄠˊ）
to give dreary cries and screams

鬼話（ㄍㄨㄟ ㄏㄨㄚˋ）
false words; lies; nonsense

鬼話連篇（ㄍㄨㄟ ㄏㄨㄚˋ ㄌㄧㄢˊ ㄆㄧㄢ）
to tell a whole series of lies; to lie from start to finish; to talk nonsense throughout

鬼畫符（ㄍㄨㄟ ㄏㄨㄚˋ ㄈㄨˊ）
①a very poor work of calligraphy; awful calligraphy ②a hypocritical talk

鬼火（ㄍㄨㄟ ㄏㄨㄛˇ）
a jack-o'-lantern; a will-o'-the-wisp

鬼魂（ㄍㄨㄟ ㄏㄨㄣˊ）
ghosts; spirits of the dead; apparitions

鬼混（ㄍㄨㄟ ㄏㄨㄣˋ）
to spend days in an idle, slovenly way; to hang around; to fool around

鬼機伶兒（ㄍㄨㄟ ㄐㄧ ㄌㄧㄥˊ）
cleverness; sly

鬼節（ㄍㄨㄟ ㄐㄧㄝˊ）
the Ghosts' Festival (the 15th of the 7th lunar month)

鬼黠（ㄍㄨㄟ ㄒㄧㄚˊ）
cunning; crafty; shrewd; wily; sly: 那孩子可鬼黠了。The kid is very shrewd.

鬼主意（ㄍㄨㄟ ㄓㄨˇ ㄧˋ）
a crafty idea; a dark scheme

鬼出電入（ㄍㄨㄟ ㄔㄨ ㄉㄧㄢˋ ㄖㄨˋ）
to move in and out with lightning speed and wizardly elusiveness

鬼使神差（ㄍㄨㄟ ㄕˇ ㄕㄣˊ ㄔㄞ）
to do something inexplicably as if manipulated by supernatural beings

鬼市（ㄍㄨㄟ ㄕˋ）
a secret market with business done after dark

鬼神（ㄍㄨㄟ ㄕㄣˊ）
ghosts and deities; spirits and gods; spiritual beings

鬼子（ㄍㄨㄟ ㄗ˙）
a devil or monster (a term of abuse for foreigners)

鬼才（ㄍㄨㄟ ㄘㄞˊ）
a genius in an unorthodox way

鬼聰明（ㄍㄨㄟ ㄘㄨㄥ ㄇㄧㄥˊ）
petty cleverness

鬼祟（ㄍㄨㄟ ㄙㄨㄟˋ）
①misfortunes brought by evil spirits ②stealthy; clandestine

鬼物（ㄍㄨㄟ ㄨˋ）
evil spirits; devils; demons; ghosts

鬼蜮伎倆（ㄍㄨㄟ ㄩˋ ㄐㄧˋ ㄌㄧㄤˇ）
dirty underhand tricks

四畫

【魁】7049
ㄎㄨㄟ kwei kuí
1. the chief; the head; the leader
2. tall; big; great

魁北克（ㄎㄨㄟ ㄅㄟˇ ㄎㄜˋ）
Quebec, a province in Canada

魁杓（ㄎㄨㄟ ㄅㄧㄠ）
the second star of the Dipper

魁柄（ㄎㄨㄟ ㄅㄧㄥˋ）
the reins of government

魁甲（ㄎㄨㄟ ㄐㄧㄚˇ）
the top candidate in the national civil service examination in former times

魁星（ㄎㄨㄟ ㄒㄧㄥ）
the god of literature

魁士（ㄎㄨㄟ ㄕˋ）
an eminent scholar

魁首（ㄎㄨㄟ ㄕㄡˇ）
①the first on the list of successful candidates in the former civil service examination ②the leader; the chief; the head

魁梧（ㄎㄨㄟ ㄨˊ）or 魁岸（ㄎㄨㄟ ㄢˋ）or 魁偉（ㄎㄨㄟ ㄨㄟˇ）
tall and robust; husky

【魂】7050
ㄏㄨㄣˊ hwen hún
a soul; a spirit

魂不附體（ㄏㄨㄣˊ ㄅㄨˋ ㄈㄨˋ ㄊㄧˇ）
frightened out of one's wits

魂魄（ㄏㄨㄣˊ ㄆㄛˋ）
a soul

魂飛魄散（ㄏㄨㄣˊ ㄈㄟ ㄆㄛˋ ㄙㄢˋ）
①frightened out of one's senses; frightened out of one's wits ②as good as dead

魂飛天外（ㄏㄨㄣˊ ㄈㄟ ㄊㄧㄢ ㄨㄞˋ）
①frightened out of one's senses; frightened out of one's wits ②completely carried away by passion; infatuated

魂靈（ㄏㄨㄣˊ ㄌㄧㄥˊ）
a soul 亦作「靈魂」

魂銷（ㄏㄨㄣˊ ㄒㄧㄠ）
spellbound; infatuated; bewitched

（鬼部）

〔魚部〕

五畫

【魄】 7051
ㄆㄛˋ poh pò
1. (Taoism) vigor; animation; life
2. form; shape; body
3. the dark part of the moon

魄力(ㄆㄛˋ ㄌㄧˋ)
guts; decisiveness; the ability to make major decisions promptly; courage to plunge ahead in big things: 他沒有魄力。He has no guts.

魄散(ㄆㄛˋ ㄙㄢˋ)
unnerved; unmanned

【魄】 7051
2. ㄊㄨㄛˋ tuoh tò
used in the phrase 落魄—dispirited; out of luck

【魅】 7052
ㄇㄟˋ mey mèi
1. a mischievous spirit; a goblin; an elf
2. to charm; to mislead

魅力(ㄇㄟˋ ㄌㄧˋ)
glamor; sexiness; attractiveness; spell; charm; charisma

魅惑(ㄇㄟˋ ㄏㄨㄛˋ)
to bedevil; to bewitch; to captivate

八畫

【魍】 7053
ㄨㄤˇ woang wǎng
a kind of monster

魍魎(ㄨㄤˇ ㄌㄧㄤˇ)
a kind of monster

【魎】 7054
ㄌㄧㄤˇ leang liǎng
a kind of monster

【魏】 7055
ㄨㄟˋ wey wèi
1. lofty; stately; magnificent
2. name of a kingdom during the Epoch of Warring States, and another in the 3rd century A.D.
3. a Chinese family name

魏碑(ㄨㄟˋ ㄅㄟ)
stone tablets of the Northern Wei Dynasty, noted for the vigorous calligraphy carved on them, the rubbings of which are used as models among calligraphers

魏闕(ㄨㄟˋ ㄑㄩㄝˋ)
the gate of the imperial palace

魏徵(ㄨㄟˋ ㄓㄥ)
Wei Cheng, 580-643, a famous statesman during the heyday of the Tang Dynasty

魏武帝(ㄨㄟˋ ㄨˇ ㄉㄧˋ)
the title of Tsao Tsao (曹操) as emperor

魏文帝(ㄨㄟˋ ㄨㄣˊ ㄉㄧˋ)
the title of Tsao Pi (曹丕), eldest son of Tsao Tsao (曹操) as emperor

【魆】 7056
(魆) ㄩˋ yuh yù
a fabulous creature which supposedly hurts human beings by casting sand out of its mouth

十一畫

【魑】 7057
ㄔ chy chī
a mountain demon resembling a tiger

魑魅(ㄔ ㄇㄟˋ)
evil spirits; demons

魑魅魍魎(ㄔ ㄇㄟˋ ㄨㄤˇ ㄌㄧㄤˇ)
all sorts of monsters and goblins

【魔】 7058
ㄇㄛˊ mo mó
a wizard; a witch; a demon; a devil

魔法(ㄇㄛˊ ㄈㄚˇ)
magic; wizardry; sorcery; witchcraft

魔道(ㄇㄛˊ ㄉㄠˋ)
evil principles of courses

魔力(ㄇㄛˊ ㄌㄧˋ)
magic power; wizardly ability; charm; spell

魔鬼(ㄇㄛˊ ㄍㄨㄟˇ)
devils; demons; evil spirits

魔掌(ㄇㄛˊ ㄓㄤˇ)
devil's clutches; evil hands

魔障(ㄇㄛˊ ㄓㄤˋ)
(Buddhism) evil obstacles on the way to truth

魔術(ㄇㄛˊ ㄕㄨˋ)
magic; wizardry; witchcraft; sorcery

魔術方塊(ㄇㄛˊ ㄕㄨˋ ㄈㄤ ㄎㄨㄞˋ)
a magic square

魔術家(ㄇㄛˊ ㄕㄨˋ ㄐㄧㄚ)
a magician

魔王(ㄇㄛˊ ㄨㄤˊ)
the Devil; Satan; Prince of Darkness

十四畫

【魘】 7059
ㄧㄢˇ yean yǎn
a nightmare: 我昨夜夢魘。I had a nightmare last night.

魘魅(ㄧㄢˇ ㄇㄟˋ)
to kill by magic, witchcraft or voodoo

魚 部
ㄩˊ yu yú

【魚】 7060
ㄩˊ yu yú
fish

魚白色(ㄩˊ ㄅㄞˊ ㄙㄜˋ)
silver-gray (like the belly of a fish)

魚鰾(ㄩˊ ㄅㄧㄠˋ)
the air bladder of a fish; a swimming bladder

魚片(ㄩˊ ㄆㄧㄢˋ)or 魚片兒(ㄩˊ ㄆㄧㄢˋ)
slices of fish meat; a fish fillet

魚米之鄉(ㄩˊ ㄇㄧˇ ㄓ ㄒㄧㄤ)
land of agriculture and fishery; land of plenty

魚苗(ㄩˊ ㄇㄧㄠˊ)
fry (of fish)

魚目混珠(ㄩˊ ㄇㄨˋ ㄏㄨㄣˋ ㄓㄨ)
(literally) to pass fish eyes as pearls—① to masquerade ② to offer something bogus

魚販(ㄩˊ ㄈㄢˋ)
a fishmonger

魚封(ㄩˊ ㄈㄥ)
letters; epistles

魚肚(ㄩˊ ㄉㄨˋ)
fish maws used as food

魚肚白(ㄩˊ ㄉㄨˋ ㄅㄞˊ)
silver-gray (like the belly of a fish)—gray dawn

魚塘(ㄩˊ ㄊㄤˊ)
a fishpond

魚雷(ㄩˊ ㄌㄟˊ)
a torpedo

魚雷艇(ㄩˊ ㄌㄟˊ ㄊㄧㄥˇ)

魚雷(ㄩˊ ㄌㄟˊ)
a torpedo boat

魚類(ㄩˊ ㄌㄟˋ)
fishes; Pisces

魚類學(ㄩˊ ㄌㄟˋ ㄒㄩㄝˊ)
ichthyology

魚爛而亡(ㄩˊ ㄌㄢˋ ㄦˊ ㄨㄤˊ)
(said of a country) to fall because of internal strife

魚鱗(ㄩˊ ㄌㄧㄣˊ)
scales (of fish)

魚鱗天兒(ㄩˊ ㄌㄧㄣˊ ㄊㄧㄢ ㄦˊ)
a mackerel sky

魚鱗癬(ㄩˊ ㄌㄧㄣˊ ㄒㄧㄢˇ)
ichthyosis

魚卵(ㄩˊ ㄌㄨㄢˇ)
roe; spawn

魚卵石(ㄩˊ ㄌㄨㄢˇ ㄕˊ)
oolite

魚龍(ㄩˊ ㄌㄨㄥˊ)
an ichthyosaur

魚龍混雜(ㄩˊ ㄌㄨㄥˊ ㄏㄨㄣˋ ㄗㄚˊ)
Fish and dragons jumbled together. —various kinds of people mixed up; a mixed lot

魚鈎(ㄩˊ ㄍㄡ)
a fishhook

魚狗(ㄩˊ ㄍㄡˇ)or魚虎(ㄩˊ ㄏㄨˇ)
Alcedo bengalensis, a species of kingfisher

魚竿(ㄩˊ ㄍㄢ)
a fishing rod; a fish pole

魚肝油(ㄩˊ ㄍㄢ ㄧㄡˊ)
cod-liver oil

魚缸(ㄩˊ ㄍㄤ)
a fish globe

魚罟(ㄩˊ ㄍㄨˇ)
a fishnet; a fishing net

魚骨(ㄩˊ ㄍㄨˇ)
fishbones

魚鼓(ㄩˊ ㄍㄨˇ)
a wooden drum (in a Buddhist temple, etc.)

魚貫(ㄩˊ ㄍㄨㄢˋ)
in a column; in procession; to proceed one by one

魚口(ㄩˊ ㄎㄡˇ)or魚口打(ㄩˊ ㄎㄡˇ ㄉㄚˇ)
bubo

魚膾(ㄩˊ ㄎㄨㄞˋ)
a dish prepared from slices of fish

魚化石(ㄩˊ ㄏㄨㄚˋ ㄕˊ)
ichthyolite

魚箋(ㄩˊ ㄐㄧㄢ)
letter paper; stationery

魚鰭(ㄩˊ ㄑㄧˊ)
fins

魚群(ㄩˊ ㄑㄩㄣˊ)
a shoal of fish

魚蝦(ㄩˊ ㄒㄧㄚ)
fish and shrimps

魚腥味(ㄩˊ ㄒㄧㄥ ㄨㄟˋ)
a fishy smell

魚玄機(ㄩˊ ㄒㄩㄢˊ ㄐㄧ)
a talented woman of the Tang Dynasty whose poems are famous

魚質龍文(ㄩˊ ㄓˊ ㄌㄨㄥˊ ㄨㄣˊ)
(literally) a dragon in outward marks but a fish in essence thing with an impressive appearance

魚池(ㄩˊ ㄔˊ)
a fishpond: 一隻青蛙跳入魚池. A frog jumped into the fishpond.

魚翅(ㄩˊ ㄔˋ)
shark's fins, a delicacy on a Chinese menu

魚叉(ㄩˊ ㄔㄚ)
a harpoon; a gaff; a fish spear

魚沈雁杳(ㄩˊ ㄔㄣˊ ㄧㄢˋ ㄧㄠˇ)
heard of no more (like a fish that dives and never surfaces or a wild duck that departs and never returns)

魚市(ㄩˊ ㄕˋ)
a fish market: 他上魚市買魚去. He went to the fish market to buy fish.

魚生(ㄩˊ ㄕㄥ)
raw fish in fine cuts

魚水和諧(ㄩˊ ㄕㄨㄟˇ ㄏㄜˊ ㄒㄧㄝˊ)
(said of a married couple) to live in harmony like fish and water

魚肉(ㄩˊ ㄖㄡˋ)
①fish and meat ②victims of oppression ③to oppress; to bully: 好的統治者不會魚肉貧民. A good ruler will not oppress the poor.

魚肉鄉民(ㄩˊ ㄖㄡˋ ㄒㄧㄤ ㄇㄧㄣˊ)
to oppress the people

魚子(ㄩˊ ㄗˇ)
spawn; roe

魚子醬(ㄩˊ ㄗˇ ㄐㄧㄤˋ)
caviar

魚刺(ㄩˊ ㄘˋ)
fishbones

魚鬆(ㄩˊ ㄙㄨㄥ)
dried fish floss

魚餌(ㄩˊ ㄦˇ)
fish bait

魚游釜中(ㄩˊ ㄧㄡˊ ㄈㄨˇ ㄓㄨㄥ)
(literally) to be a fish swimming in the cooking pot—to have one's days numbered; to be doomed

魚鹽(ㄩˊ ㄧㄢˊ)
fish and salt—marine resources

魚鹽之利(ㄩˊ ㄧㄢˊ ㄓ ㄌㄧˋ)
gain from marine resources

魚眼石(ㄩˊ ㄧㄢˇ ㄕˊ)
apophyllite

魚雁(ㄩˊ ㄧㄢˋ)
letters; epistles

魚雁鮮通(ㄩˊ ㄧㄢˋ ㄒㄧㄢ ㄊㄨㄥ)
hardly write to one another

魚秧(ㄩˊ ㄧㄤ)
fry (of fish)亦作「魚栽」

魚鷹(ㄩˊ ㄧㄥ)
a kind of sea bird

魚尾板(ㄩˊ ㄨㄟˇ ㄅㄢˇ)
a fishplate

魚尾紋(ㄩˊ ㄨㄟˇ ㄨㄣˊ)
crow's-feet

魚丸子(ㄩˊ ㄨㄢˊ ˙ㄗ)
a fish ball; a fish cake

魚塭(ㄩˊ ㄨㄣ)
a fish farm

魚網(ㄩˊ ㄨㄤˇ)
a fishnet; a fishing net: 他們用魚網捕魚. They caught fish with a fishing net.

魚與熊掌(ㄩˊ ㄩˇ ㄒㄩㄥˊ ㄓㄤˇ)
unable to make up one's mind as to which of two desirable things to choose

三畫

【虹】 7061
ㄏㄨㄥˊ hong hóng
rays

虹魚(ㄏㄨㄥˊ ㄩˊ)
a skate

四畫

【魷】 7062
ㄧㄡˊ you yóu
a cuttlefish

魷魚(ㄧㄡˊ ㄩˊ)
a cuttlefish

〔魚部〕

〔魚部〕

【魯】 7063 ㄌㄨˇ luu lǔ
1. stupid; dull
2. vulgar
3. name of an ancient kingdom in what is today's Shantung; an alternative name of Shantung
4. a Chinese family name

魯般 or 魯班(ㄌㄨˇ ㄅㄢ)
another name of Kung-Shu Pan (公輸班), a master carpenter in the kingdom of Lu (魯)during the Epoch of Spring and Autumn

魯般尺 or 魯班尺(ㄌㄨˇ ㄅㄢ ㄔˇ)
a carpenter's square

魯壁(ㄌㄨˇ ㄅㄧˋ)
the walls of Confucius's home (from which a number of classics were later discovered)

魯濱遜飄流記(ㄌㄨˇ ㄅㄧㄣ ㄒㄩㄣˋ ㄆㄧㄠ ㄌㄧㄡˊ ㄐㄧˋ)
Robinson Crusoe, by Daniel Defoe, 1659?-1731

魯莽(ㄌㄨˇ ㄇㄤˇ)
①rude; disrespectful; ill-mannered; uncivil; discourteous ②rash; careless

魯殿靈光(ㄌㄨˇ ㄉㄧㄢˋ ㄌㄧㄥˊ ㄍㄨㄤ)
①the only remaining embodiment of past glory ②the sole survivor among elder scholars of virtue or among statesmen commanding respect

魯鈍(ㄌㄨˇ ㄉㄨㄣˋ)
dull; slow-witted

魯男子(ㄌㄨˇ ㄋㄢˊ ㄗˇ)
men unmoved by feminine charms

魯凱(ㄌㄨˇ ㄎㄞˇ)
the Rukai tribe among the aborigines in Taiwan

魯仲連(ㄌㄨˇ ㄓㄨㄥˋ ㄌㄧㄢˊ)
①Lu Chung-lien, a person in the Epoch of Warring States, skilled in mediating ②a mediator

魯人(ㄌㄨˇ ㄖㄣˊ)
①a slow-witted person; a dullard ②a native of the kingdom of Lu(魯); a native of Shantung

魯衛之政(ㄌㄨˇ ㄨㄟˋ ㄓ ㄓㄥˋ)
things very much alike

魯魚亥豕(ㄌㄨˇ ㄩˊ ㄏㄞˋ ㄕˇ)
(literally) the confusion of 魯 with 魚 and of 亥 with 豕 —copying or typographical errors

【魴】 7064 ㄈㄤˊ farng fáng
the freshwater bream

五畫

【鮎】 7065 ㄋㄧㄢˊ nian nián
Parasilurus asotus, a kind of slippery long fish

【鮑】 7066 ㄅㄠˋ baw bào
1. an abalone
2. salted fish
3. a Chinese family name

鮑叔牙(ㄅㄠˋ ㄕㄨˊ ㄧㄚˊ)
Pao Shu-ya, a statesman in the Epoch of Spring and Autumn, known for his great friendship for Kuan Chung(管仲)

鮑魚(ㄅㄠˋ ㄩˊ)
①an abalone 亦作「石決明」
②salted fish

鮑魚之肆(ㄅㄠˋ ㄩˊ ㄓ ㄙˋ)
a market for salted fish—an objectionable environment

【鮒】 7067 ㄈㄨˋ fuh fù
a gold carp; a crucian carp

六畫

【鮫】 7068 ㄐㄧㄠ jiau jiāo
a shark

鮫魚(ㄐㄧㄠ ㄩˊ)
a shark

【鮪】 7069 ㄨㄟˇ woei wěi
a tuna

鮪釣(ㄨㄟˇ ㄉㄧㄠˋ)
a tuna liner

【鮭】 7070 ㄍㄨㄟ guei guī
a salmon

【鮮】 7071 1. ㄒㄧㄢ shian xiān
1. fresh; new: 這肉不太新鮮。
This meat is not very fresh.
2. delicious; tasty
3. bright; attractive: 這件裙子顏色太鮮豔。This skirt is too

bright.

鮮卑(ㄒㄧㄢ ㄅㄟ)
a tribe of the Tungusic people in Manchuria and eastern Mongolia from 2nd to 7th century A.D.

鮮眉亮眼(ㄒㄧㄢ ㄇㄟˊ ㄌㄧㄤˋ ㄧㄢˇ)
distinct eyebrows and bright eyes—a good-looking face

鮮美(ㄒㄧㄢ ㄇㄟˇ)
fresh and delicious

鮮明(ㄒㄧㄢ ㄇㄧㄥˊ)
①sharp; distinct ②bright-colored

鮮嫩(ㄒㄧㄢ ㄋㄨㄣˋ)
fresh and tender

鮮果(ㄒㄧㄢ ㄍㄨㄛˇ)
fresh fruit: 你喜歡吃鮮果嗎?
Do you like fresh fruit?

鮮花(ㄒㄧㄢ ㄏㄨㄚ)
fresh flowers: 李小姐喜歡鮮花。Miss Lee likes fresh flowers.

鮮活(ㄒㄧㄢ ㄏㄨㄛˊ)
fresh and lively

鮮貨(ㄒㄧㄢ ㄏㄨㄛˋ)
fresh batches of fruit or vegetables

鮮紅(ㄒㄧㄢ ㄏㄨㄥˊ)
bright red

鮮血(ㄒㄧㄢ ㄒㄩㄝˋ)
fresh blood; blood

鮮血淋漓(ㄒㄧㄢ ㄒㄩㄝˋ ㄌㄧㄣˊ ㄌㄧˊ)
drenched with blood; blood dripping

鮮食(ㄒㄧㄢ ㄕˊ)
①fresh food ②to eat fresh food

鮮肉(ㄒㄧㄢ ㄖㄡˋ)
fresh meat

鮮豔(ㄒㄧㄢ ㄧㄢˋ)
bright-colored; resplendent

鮮豔奪目(ㄒㄧㄢ ㄧㄢˋ ㄉㄨㄛˊ ㄇㄨˋ)
attractively bright-colored; resplendent

鮮味(ㄒㄧㄢ ㄨㄟˋ)
fresh flavor

鮮于(ㄒㄧㄢ ㄩˊ)
a double Chinese family name

fish fresh from water; fresh fish

【鮮】 7071 2. ㄒㄧㄢˇ shean xiǎn
rare; few; seldom

【羊民】（ㄒㄧㄤˊ ㄇㄧㄣˊ）
① an orphan ② underprivileged people

羊少（ㄒㄧㄤˊ ㄕㄠˇ）
rare; few

羊羊（ㄒㄧㄤˊ ㄒㄧㄤˊ）
seldom to have; rare

【鯗】 7072
ㄒㄧㄤˇ sheang xiǎng
dried and salted fish

七畫

【鯀】 7073
ㄍㄨㄣˇ goen gǔn
. name of a kind of fish
. father of the legendary ruler, Yü(禹)

【鯇】 7074
ㄏㄨㄢˊ huenn hún
a grass carp

【鯁】 7075
ㄍㄥˇ geeng gěng
. a fishbone stuck in the throat
. honest; straightforward

鯁直（ㄍㄥˇ ㄓˊ）
honest; straightforward; outspoken

【鯉】 7076
ㄌㄧˇ lii lǐ
. a carp
. letters; epistles

鯉庭（ㄌㄧˇ ㄊㄧㄥˊ）
receiving instructions from one's father

鯉素（ㄌㄧˇ ㄙㄨˋ）
letters

鯉魚（ㄌㄧˇ ㄩˊ）
a common carp: 在日本鯉魚象徵勇氣。In Japan a carp symbolizes courage.

鯉魚跳龍門（ㄌㄧˇ ㄩˊ ㄊㄧㄠˋ ㄌㄨㄥˊ ㄇㄣˊ）
to succeed in the civil service examination in former times

【鯊】 7077
ㄕㄚ sha shā
a shark

鯊魚（ㄕㄚ ㄩˊ）
a shark 亦作「沙魚」

鯊魚皮（ㄕㄚ ㄩˊ ㄆㄧˊ）
sharkskin

八畫

【鯤】 7078
ㄎㄨㄣ kuen kūn

. a kind of legendary fish said to be thousands of miles long
2. spawn; roe

【鯡】 7079
ㄈㄟ fei fēi
a herring

【鯖】 7080
ㄑㄧㄥ ching qīng
a mackerel

【鯛】 7081
ㄉㄧㄠ diau diāo
a sea bream; a porgy; a scup

【鯨】 7082
ㄐㄧㄥ jing jīng
a whale

鯨波（ㄐㄧㄥ ㄅㄛ）
huge waves in the ocean

鯨吞蠶食（ㄐㄧㄥ ㄊㄨㄣ ㄘㄢˊ ㄕˊ）
aggression by engulfing and nibbling processes

鯨類（ㄐㄧㄥ ㄌㄟˋ）
whales

鯨油（ㄐㄧㄥ ㄧㄡˊ）
whale oil

鯨魚（ㄐㄧㄥ ㄩˊ）
a whale

【鯪】 7083
ㄌㄧㄥ ling líng
. a legendary fish
2. a dace

【鯫】 7084
ㄗㄡ tzou zōu
. a small fish
2. small

九畫

【鯽】 7085
ㄐㄧˋ jih jì
a gold carp

鮂魚（ㄐㄧˋ ㄩˊ）
a gold carp

【鰈】 7086
ㄉㄧㄝˊ dye dié
a sole (fish)

【鯿】 7087
ㄅㄧㄢ bian biān
a freshwash bream

【鰌】 7088
（鰍）ㄑㄧㄡ chiou qiū
a loach

【鰒】 7089
ㄈㄨˋ fuh fù
an abalone 亦作「鮑魚」or「石決明」

【鰍】 7090
ㄑㄧㄡ chiou qiū
a loach

【鰓】 7091
ㄙㄞ sai sāi
gills (of fish): 魚和蝌蚪有鰓。Fish and tadpoles have gills.

十畫

【鰥】 7092
ㄍㄨㄢ guan guān
1. a kind of huge predatory fish
2. a widower
3. a bachelor

鰥夫（ㄍㄨㄢ ㄈㄨ）
① a widower ② a bachelor

鰥寡（ㄍㄨㄢ ㄍㄨㄚˇ）
① old widowers and widows ② old bachelors and spinsters

鰥寡孤獨（ㄍㄨㄢ ㄍㄨㄚˇ ㄍㄨ ㄉㄨˊ）
those who have no wives, husbands, parents or children

鰥棍兒（ㄍㄨㄢ ㄍㄨㄣˋ ㄦ）
a bachelor

【鰜】 7093
ㄐㄧㄢ jian jiān
a sole (fish)

鰜鰈（ㄐㄧㄢ ㄉㄧㄝˊ）
a couple in love

【鰮】 7094
ㄨㄣ uen wēn
a sardine

【鰭】 7095
ㄑㄧˊ chyi qí
fins

【鰣】 7096
ㄕˊ shyr shí
a reeves shad; a hilsa herring

【�692】 7097
ㄧㄠ yau yáo
the nautilus; the ray

十一畫

【鰻】 7098
ㄇㄢˊ man mán
an eel

【鱈】 7099
ㄒㄩㄝˊ sheue xué
a cod: 鱈魚是主要的食用魚之一。Cod is one of the chief food fishes.

【鰲】 7100
（鼇）ㄠˊ aur áo
a sea-tortoise

鰲頭（ㄠˊ ㄊㄡˊ）

the top successful candidate in the civil service examination in former times

【鰱】 7101
ㄌㄧㄢˊ lian lián
a silver carp

【鰾】 7102
ㄅㄧㄠˋ biau biào
1. the maw of a fish; the air bladder; the swimming bladder
2. fish glue

鰾膠 (ㄅㄧㄠˋ ㄐㄧㄠ)
fish glue

【鱅】 7103
ㄩㄥ yong yóng
a bighead

【鰹】 7104
ㄐㄧㄢ jian jiān
a bonito

十二畫

【鱔】 7105
ㄕㄢˋ shann shàn
an eel; a moray eel; 鱔魚看起來像蛇。 An eel looks like a snake.

【鱖】 7106
ㄐㄩㄝˊ jyue jué
(又讀 ㄍㄨㄟˋ guey guì)
Mandarinfish

【鱗】 7107
ㄌㄧㄣˊ lin lín
scales (of fish)

鱗包 (ㄌㄧㄣˊ ㄅㄠ)
(botany) a scale

鱗片 (ㄌㄧㄣˊ ㄆㄧㄢˋ)
①scales (of fish, etc.) ②a bud scale

鱗鱗 (ㄌㄧㄣˊ ㄌㄧㄣˊ)
ripples

鱗淪 (ㄌㄧㄣˊ ㄌㄨㄣˊ)
ripple-like

鱗鴻 (ㄌㄧㄣˊ ㄏㄨㄥˊ)
letters; epistles

鱗集 (ㄌㄧㄣˊ ㄐㄧˊ)
to flock together; to assemble

鱗甲 (ㄌㄧㄣˊ ㄐㄧㄚˇ)
hard scales (of crocodiles, etc.)

鱗介 (ㄌㄧㄣˊ ㄐㄧㄝˋ)
fishes and mollusks; fishery products

鱗莖 (ㄌㄧㄣˊ ㄐㄧㄥ)
(botany) a bulb 亦作「球莖」

鱗屑癬 (ㄌㄧㄣˊ ㄒㄧㄝˋ ㄒㄧㄢˇ)
ringworm

鱗爪 (ㄌㄧㄣˊ ㄓㄠˇ)
(literally) scales and claws —minutiae; trifles

鱗傷 (ㄌㄧㄣˊ ㄕㄤ)
wounds or injuries all over the body

鱗次櫛比 (ㄌㄧㄣˊ ㄘˋ ㄐㄧㄝˊ ㄅㄧˇ)
(said of houses or buildings) systematically arranged like scales of a fish or teeth of a comb; row upon row

鱗萃 (ㄌㄧㄣˊ ㄘㄨㄟˋ)
to herd together; to flock together

【鱘】 7108
ㄒㄩㄣˊ shyun xún
a sturgeon

十三畫

【鱟】 7109
ㄏㄡˋ how hòu
a king crab

【鱣】 7110
ㄓㄢ jan zhān
Acipenser mikadoi, a kind of sturgeon

【鱔】 7110
ㄕㄢˋ shann shàn
an eel

十五畫

【鱵】 7111
ㄓㄣ jen zhēn
a saury

十六畫

【鱸】 7112
ㄌㄨˊ lu lú
perch; bass

鱸魚 (ㄌㄨˊ ㄩˊ)
the sea bass

【鱷】 7113
ㄜˋ eh è
a crocodile; an alligator

鱷魚 (ㄜˋ ㄩˊ)
a crocodile; an alligator

二十二畫

【鱻】 7114
(鮮) ㄒㄧㄢ shian xiān
fresh; tasty

鳥 部
ㄋㄧㄠˇ neau niǎo

【鳥】 7115
ㄋㄧㄠˇ neau niǎo
a bird

鳥媒花 (ㄋㄧㄠˇ ㄇㄟˊ ㄏㄨㄚ)
ornithophilous flowers

鳥面鵠形 (ㄋㄧㄠˇ ㄇㄧㄢˋ ㄏㄨˊ ㄒㄧㄥˊ)
gaunt and emaciated from hunger

鳥糞 (ㄋㄧㄠˇ ㄈㄣˋ)
bird droppings

鳥道 (ㄋㄧㄠˇ ㄉㄠˋ)
a path wide enough only for a bird to pass—a precipitous path

鳥蛋 (ㄋㄧㄠˇ ㄉㄢˋ) or 鳥卵 (ㄋㄧㄠˇ ㄌㄨㄢˇ)
bird's eggs

鳥類 (ㄋㄧㄠˇ ㄌㄟˋ)
birds

鳥類學 (ㄋㄧㄠˇ ㄌㄟˋ ㄒㄩㄝˊ)
ornithology

鳥類學家 (ㄋㄧㄠˇ ㄌㄟˋ ㄒㄩㄝˊ ㄐㄧㄚ)
an ornithologist

鳥籠 (ㄋㄧㄠˇ ㄌㄨㄥˊ)
a birdcage

鳥革翬飛 (ㄋㄧㄠˇ ㄍㄜˊ ㄏㄨㄟ ㄈㄟ)
(said of buildings) graceful and handsome like a bird spreading its wings or a pheasant showing off its resplendent feathers in flight

鳥瞰 (ㄋㄧㄠˇ ㄎㄢˋ)
①to have a bird's-eye view ②an aerial view, a bird's-eye view

鳥喙 (ㄋㄧㄠˇ ㄏㄨㄟˋ)
a beak

鳥集鱗萃 (ㄋㄧㄠˇ ㄐㄧˊ ㄌㄧㄣˊ ㄘㄨㄟˋ)
to gather in large numbers like birds or fishes; to flock together

鳥盡弓藏 (ㄋㄧㄠˇ ㄐㄧㄣˋ ㄍㄨㄥ ㄘㄤˊ)
(literally) to put away the bow when the birds are gone—to discharge a worthy official in times of peace

鳥舉 (ㄋㄧㄠˇ ㄐㄩˇ)
to act as quickly as a bird takes off

鳥槍(ㄋㄧㄠˇㄑㄧㄤ)
a fowling piece

鳥之將死，其鳴也悲(ㄋㄧㄠˇ
ㄓㄐㄧㄤㄙㄙˇ ㄑㄧˊㄇㄧㄥˊㄧㄝˇㄅㄟ)
(literally) When a bird is
about to die, its songs are
pathetic.—A man's last
words are sincere.

鳥爪(ㄋㄧㄠˇㄓㄠˇ)
① bird's talons ② fine, delicate human finger tips

鳥篆(ㄋㄧㄠˇㄓㄨㄢˋ)or鳥籀(ㄋㄧㄠˇ
ㄓㄡˋ)
an ancient form of Chinese
characters shaped like bird
tracks

鳥巢(ㄋㄧㄠˇㄔㄠˊ)or鳥窠(ㄋㄧㄠˇㄎㄜ)
a bird's nest

鳥蟲書(ㄋㄧㄠˇㄔㄨㄥˊㄕㄨ)
one of the six forms of
Chinese characters estab-
lished by Wang Mang(王莽)

鳥銃(ㄋㄧㄠˇㄔㄨㄥˋ)
a fowling piece

鳥獸(ㄋㄧㄠˇㄕㄡˋ)
birds and beasts

鳥獸行(ㄋㄧㄠˇㄕㄡˋㄒㄧㄥˊ)
beastly conduct; incestuous
scandal

鳥獸散(ㄋㄧㄠˇㄕㄡˋㄙㄢˋ)
to disperse in confusion like
birds or beasts

鳥葬(ㄋㄧㄠˇㄗㄤˋ)
exposure of a corpse to
birds of prey

鳥嘴(ㄋㄧㄠˇㄗㄨㄟˇ)
a beak; a bill

鳥彝(ㄋㄧㄠˇㄧˊ)
cups engraved with designs
of birds

鳥窩(ㄋㄧㄠˇㄨㄛ)
a bird's nest

鳥胃(ㄋㄧㄠˇㄨㄟˋ)
a gizzard

鳥為食亡，人為財死(ㄋㄧㄠˇㄨㄟˊ
ㄕˊㄨㄤˊ ㄖㄣˊㄨㄟˊㄘㄞˊㄙˇ)
(a Chinese proverb) Birds
die in pursuit of food, and
human beings die in pursuit
of wealth. 亦作「人為財死,鳥
為食亡」

鳥王(ㄋㄧㄠˇㄨㄤˊ)
the king of birds—phoenix

鳥語(ㄋㄧㄠˇㄩˇ)or鳥言(ㄋㄧㄠˇㄧㄢˊ)
① birds' songs or chirps ②
foreign languages

鳥語花香(ㄋㄧㄠˇㄩˇㄏㄨㄚㄒㄧㄤ)
birds singing and flowers
radiating fragrance—the joyous scene in spring

鳥園(ㄋㄧㄠˇㄩㄢˊ)
an aviary

二畫

【鳧】 7116
　　ㄈㄨˊ fwu fú
a wild duck

鳧脛雖短(ㄈㄨˊㄐㄧㄥˋㄙㄨㄟㄉㄨㄢˇ)
(literally) It is hard to
lengthen a duck's legs.—One
should be contented with
what one has.

鳧趨雀躍(ㄈㄨˊㄑㄩㄑㄩㄝˋㄩㄝˋ)
to dance with excitement; to
jump about for joy

鳧水(ㄈㄨˊㄕㄨㄟˇ)
to swim 亦作「游泳」；他鳧水
過河。He swam across the
river.

鳧藻之士(ㄈㄨˊㄗㄠˇㄓㄕˋ)
a man in a right environ-
ment (like wild ducks
among duckweed)

鳧燕雖飛(ㄈㄨˊㄧㄢˋㄙㄨㄟㄈㄟ)or鳧
乙(ㄈㄨˊㄧˇ)or鳧燕(ㄈㄨˊㄧㄢˋ)
(literally) It's hard to distinguish between high-flying
wild ducks and swallows.
—things easily confused

【鳩】 7117
　　ㄐㄧㄡ jiou jiū
1. a pigeon; a dove
2. to collect; to assemble

鳩摩羅什(ㄐㄧㄡㄇㄛˊㄌㄨㄛˊㄕˊ)
Kumarajiva, name of a Buddhist monk from Central
Asia who translated a number of Buddhist scriptures
into Chinese in the 5th century

鳩民(ㄐㄧㄡㄇㄧㄣˊ)
to assemble people peace-
fully

鳩斂(ㄐㄧㄡㄌㄧㄢˋ)
to collect taxes

鳩工(ㄐㄧㄡㄍㄨㄥ)
to assemble workmen

鳩工庀材(ㄐㄧㄡㄍㄨㄥㄆㄧˇㄘㄞˊ)
to assemble workmen and
procure materials (in preparation for a construction
job)

鳩合(ㄐㄧㄡㄏㄜˊ)
to gather together; to assemble

鳩集(ㄐㄧㄡㄐㄧˊ)or鳩聚(ㄐㄧㄡㄐㄩˋ)
to assemble; to gather

鳩居(ㄐㄧㄡㄐㄩ)
my humble house

鳩形鵠面(ㄐㄧㄡㄒㄧㄥˊㄏㄨˊㄇㄧㄢˋ)
gaunt and emaciated from
malnutrition

鳩胸(ㄐㄧㄡㄒㄩㄥ)
a pigeon breast; pigeon-
breasted

鳩占鵲巢(ㄐㄧㄡㄓㄢˋㄑㄩㄝˋㄔㄠˊ)
(literally) a pigeon in a
magpie's nest—enjoying the
fruits of others' without having worked hard; to usurp
what is another's

鳩杖(ㄐㄧㄡㄓㄤˋ)
a staff with a pigeon-like
handle (presented to the
aged as a token of respect)

鳩拙(ㄐㄧㄡㄓㄨㄛˊ)
(a self-depreciatory term)
stupid as a pigeon

鳩眾(ㄐㄧㄡㄓㄨㄥˋ)
to assemble a big crowd

鳩率(ㄐㄧㄡㄕㄨㄞˋ)
to assemble and lead

三畫

【鳲】 7118
　　ㄕ shy shī
a cuckoo

鳲鳩(ㄕㄐㄧㄡ)
① a cuckoo; a turtledove ②
a poem in *The Book of Odes*
(詩經)

【鳳】 7119
　　ㄈㄥˋ feng fèng
Feng—a male phoenix

鳳毛(ㄈㄥˋㄇㄠˊ)
a fine son taking after his
father

鳳毛麟角(ㄈㄥˋㄇㄠˊㄌㄧㄣˊㄐㄧㄠˇ)
the feathers of a phoenix
and the horn of a unicorn
—rare treasures or talents;
something extremely rare

鳳鳴朝陽(ㄈㄥˋㄇㄧㄥˊㄓㄠㄧㄤˊ)
(literally) the phoenix singing to the sun—capable men
born in the right time
(whose talents are employed
by a wise ruler instead of

（鳥部）

〔鳥部〕

being buried)

鳳邸(ㄈㄥ ㄉㄧˇ)
the emperor's abode where he lived before his accession to the throne

鳳蝶(ㄈㄥ ㄉㄧㄝˊ)
Papilio xuthus, a kind of butterfly

鳳頭鞋(ㄈㄥ ㄊㄡˊ ㄒㄧㄝˊ)
shoes with the tip adorned with the image of a phoenix (formerly worn by women)

鳳鳥不至(ㄈㄥ ㄋㄧㄠˇ ㄅㄨˋ ㄓˋ)
(literally) The Feng bird does not come.—There are no wise men in the government. 或 There is no wise king or emperor in the court.

鳳輦(ㄈㄥ ㄋㄧㄢˇ)
① the imperial carriage ② the carriage of an immortal

鳳梨(ㄈㄥ ㄌㄧˊ)
a pineapple

鳳閣龍樓(ㄈㄥ ㄍㄜˊ ㄌㄨㄥˊ ㄌㄡˊ)
the imperial palace

鳳冠(ㄈㄥ ㄍㄨㄢ)
a kind of headgear for a lady (especially for a bride) in former times

鳳冠霞帔(ㄈㄥ ㄍㄨㄢ ㄒㄧㄚˊ ㄆㄟˋ)
the headgear and dress of a lady or bride in former times

鳳凰(ㄈㄥ ㄏㄨㄤˊ)
Feng-huang—phoenixes (鳳 being male and 凰 being female)

鳳凰木(ㄈㄥ ㄏㄨㄤˊ ㄇㄨˋ)
Delonix regia, a flame tree

鳳凰來儀(ㄈㄥ ㄏㄨㄤˊ ㄌㄞˊ ㄧˊ)
the phoenix coming and showing a gentle air—a good omen

鳳凰于飛(ㄈㄥ ㄏㄨㄤˊ ㄩˊ ㄈㄟ)
a couple of phoenixes on the wing—happy marriage

鳳駕(ㄈㄥ ㄐㄧㄚˋ)
the imperial carriage

鳳舉(ㄈㄥ ㄐㄩˇ)
① to soar high; to rise to a high position ② the travel of a courtier on an imperial assignment ③ the flight of an immortal

鳳旗(ㄈㄥ ㄑㄧˊ)
the imperial flag

鳳翹(ㄈㄥ ㄑㄧㄠˊ)
① a kind of headgear for women ② formerly, women's shoes adorned with the embroidered images of phoenixes

鳳求凰(ㄈㄥ ㄑㄧㄡˊ ㄏㄨㄤˊ)
courtship

鳳闕(ㄈㄥ ㄑㄩㄝˋ)
the gate of the imperial palace

鳳仙花(ㄈㄥ ㄒㄧㄢ ㄏㄨㄚ)
a balsam; a garden balsam

鳳穴(ㄈㄥ ㄒㄩㄝˋ)
a cultural center

鳳詔(ㄈㄥ ㄓㄠˋ)
the imperial mandate; the imperial decree

鳳池(ㄈㄥ ㄔˊ)or 鳳沼(ㄈㄥ ㄓㄠˇ)
① a position enjoying the trust of the emperor ② an ancient government agency vested with broad powers

鳳雛(ㄈㄥ ㄔㄨˊ)
(literally) a young phoenix—a capable young man; a talented person

鳳山(ㄈㄥ ㄕㄢ)
Fengshan, a city in Taiwan

鳳生鳳兒(ㄈㄥ ㄕㄥ ㄈㄥ ㄦˊ)
a fine son born of a fine father

鳳藻(ㄈㄥ ㄗㄠˇ)
beautiful expressions

鳳髓龍肝(ㄈㄥ ㄙㄨㄟˇ ㄌㄨㄥˊ ㄍㄢ)
(figuratively)rare delicacies

鳳尾蕉(ㄈㄥ ㄨㄟˇ ㄐㄧㄠ)or 鳳尾松(ㄈㄥ ㄨㄟˇ ㄙㄨㄥ)
a cycad

鳳尾草(ㄈㄥ ㄨㄟˇ ㄘㄠˇ)
ferns

鳳尾魚(ㄈㄥ ㄨㄟˇ ㄩˊ)
a long-tailed anchovy

【鳴】　7120
　　　ㄇㄧㄥˊ ming míng
1. (said of birds) to sing; to chirp; to warble; (said of cocks) to crow
2. the notes of birds
3. to make sounds; to sound

鳴不平(ㄇㄧㄥˊ ㄅㄨˋ ㄆㄧㄥˊ)
to voice grievances; to complain against injustice

鳴砲示慶(ㄇㄧㄥˊ ㄆㄠˋ ㄕˋ ㄑㄧㄥˋ)
to salute by setting off fire-crackers or by firing cannons

鳴放(ㄇㄧㄥˊ ㄈㄤˋ)
the airing of views (through posters, meetings or other media)

鳴鳳(ㄇㄧㄥˊ ㄈㄥˋ)
(literally) a singing phoenix—something of rare beauty or value

鳴笛(ㄇㄧㄥˊ ㄉㄧˊ)
to blow a whistle; to signal with a siren

鳴鏑(ㄇㄧㄥˊ ㄉㄧˊ)
arrows that give a particular sound when shot (used to signal commands to an army in ancient times)

鳴蜩(ㄇㄧㄥˊ ㄊㄧㄠˊ)
Graptopsaltria colorata, a kind of cicada

鳴鑼聚衆(ㄇㄧㄥˊ ㄌㄨㄛˊ ㄐㄩˋ ㄓㄨㄥˋ)
to beat the gong to assemble people

鳴鑾(ㄇㄧㄥˊ ㄌㄨㄢˊ)
the emperor's journey

鳴鼓(ㄇㄧㄥˊ ㄍㄨˇ)
to beat the drum

鳴鼓而攻(ㄇㄧㄥˊ ㄍㄨˇ ㄦˊ ㄍㄨㄥ)
to attack while beating the drum; to stage an open attack or condemnation

鳴管(ㄇㄧㄥˊ ㄍㄨㄢˇ)
(said of birds) syrinxes

鳴鳩(ㄇㄧㄥˊ ㄐㄧㄡ)
a pigeon; a dove

鳴金收兵(ㄇㄧㄥˊ ㄐㄧㄣ ㄕㄡ ㄅㄧㄥ)
to beat the gong to call back the troops; to with draw the troops from the battle

鳴禽類(ㄇㄧㄥˊ ㄑㄧㄣˊ ㄌㄟˋ)
the oscines

鳴琴而治(ㄇㄧㄥˊ ㄑㄧㄣˊ ㄦˊ ㄓˋ)
to rule by enlightenment; to rule by minimum interference with the people

鳴槍(ㄇㄧㄥˊ ㄑㄧㄤ)
to fire rifles into the air (as a warning to a mob, rioters etc.)

鳴謝(ㄇㄧㄥˊ ㄒㄧㄝˋ)
to express gratitude

鳴寃(ㄇㄧㄥˊ ㄩㄢ)
to complain of unfairness; to air grievances

【鳶】　7121
　　ㄩㄢ iuan yuán
1. a kite; a hawk

2. a kite (a toy)

鳶飛魚躍(ㄩㄢ ㄈㄟ ㄩˊ ㄩㄝˋ)
kites flying and fishes jumping—natural freedom of
things in the universe

鳶尾科(ㄩㄢ ㄨㄟˇ ㄎㄜ)
(botany) the iris family

四畫

【鴆】 7122
ㄓㄣˋ jenn jenn
1. a kind of venomous bird
2. poisoned wine

鴆媒(ㄓˋ ㄇㄟˊ)
to slander; to libel

鴆毒(ㄓˋ ㄉㄨˊ)
① poison; venom ② to slander; to harm by devious
means

鴆酒(ㄓˋ ㄐㄧㄡˇ)
poisoned wine

【鴇】 7123
ㄅㄠˇ bao bao
1. *Otis dybowskii*, a bird resembling the wild goose
2. a prostitute
3. a procuress

鴇母(ㄅㄠˇ ㄇㄨˇ)
a procuress

鴇兒(ㄅㄠˇ ㄦˊ)
① a prostitute ② a procuress

【鴉】 7124
ㄧㄚ ia yā
a crow; a raven: 天下烏鴉一
般黑. Crows are black the
whole world over.

鴉鬢(ㄧㄚ ㄅㄧㄣˋ)
the raven black hair of a
woman

鴉片(ㄧㄚ ㄆㄧㄢˋ)
opium

鴉片戰爭(ㄧㄚ ㄆㄧㄢˋ ㄓㄢˋ ㄓㄥ)
the Opium War (1839-1842)

鴉片煙(ㄧㄚ ㄆㄧㄢˋ ㄧㄢ)
opium: (to be smoked)

鴉片煙鬼(ㄧㄚ ㄆㄧㄢˋ ㄧㄢ ㄍㄨㄟˇ)
an addict to opium smoking;
an opium addict

鴉片煙館(ㄧㄚ ㄆㄧㄢˋ ㄧㄢ ㄍㄨㄢˇ)
an opium den

鴉片煙癮(ㄧㄚ ㄆㄧㄢˋ ㄧㄢ ㄧㄣˇ)
addiction to opium smoking;
opium addiction

鴉默雀靜兒(ㄧㄚ ㄇㄛˋ ㄑㄩㄝˋ
ㄐㄧㄥˋ ㄦˊ)
so quiet that not a voice can

be heard

鴉鳴鵲噪(ㄧㄚ ㄇㄧㄥˊ ㄑㄩㄝˋ ㄗㄠˋ)
full of confused voices

鴉雀亂(ㄧㄚ ㄑㄩㄝˋ ㄌㄨㄢˋ)
utter disorder

鴉鬟(ㄧㄚ ㄏㄨㄢˊ)or 鴉頭
a female servant; a maid 亦
作「丫鬟」or「丫頭」

鴉鬟(ㄧㄚ ㄏㄨㄢˊ)
a glossy headdress of a
woman

鴉雀無聲(ㄧㄚ ㄑㄩㄝˋ ㄨˊ ㄕㄥ)or 鴉雀
無閒(ㄧㄚ ㄑㄩㄝˋ ㄨˊ ㄨㄣˊ)
so quiet that not a single
voice can be heard

鴉巢生鳳(ㄧㄚ ㄔㄠˊ ㄕㄥ ㄈㄥˋ)
(literally) a phoenix born in
a crow's nest—a distin-
guished man from a humble
family

鴉嘴鋤(ㄧㄚ ㄗㄨㄟˇ ㄔㄨˊ)
a mattock

鴉色(ㄧㄚ ㄙㄜˋ)
reddish blue

【鴃】 7125
(鵙) ㄐㄩㄝˊ jyue jué
a shrike; a butcherbird

鴃舌(ㄐㄩㄝˊ ㄕㄜˊ)
languages of barbarians

【鴈】 7126
ㄧㄢˋ yann yàn
1. same as 雁—a wild goose
2. same as 贗—bogus; forged,
etc.

五畫

【鴒】 7127
ㄌㄧㄥˊ ling líng
a wagtail

【鴕】 7128
ㄊㄨㄛˊ two tuó
an ostrich

鴕鳥(ㄊㄨㄛˊ ㄋㄧㄠˇ)
an ostrich

【鴛】 7129
ㄩㄢ iuan yuān
the male mandarin duck

鴛夢重溫(ㄩㄢ ㄇㄥˋ ㄔㄨㄥˊ ㄨㄣ)
reunion of the old lovers
after a long separation; to
rekindle old flame of love

鴛侶(ㄩㄢ ㄌㄩˇ)
a spouse

鴛機(ㄩㄢ ㄐㄧ)
an embroidery kit

鴛綺(ㄩㄢ ㄑㄧˇ)

magnificent fabrics

鴛釵(ㄩㄢ ㄔㄞ)
a kind of hairpin for women

鴛鴦(ㄩㄢ ㄧㄤ)
mandarin ducks, which
always live in pairs—a symbol of lovers

鴛鴦被(ㄩㄢ ㄧㄤ ㄅㄟˋ)or 鴛被
bedding for a couple; double
bedding

鴛鴦梅(ㄩㄢ ㄧㄤ ㄇㄟˊ)
plums hanging in pairs from
the same footstalks

鴛鴦桃(ㄩㄢ ㄧㄤ ㄊㄠˊ)
a kind of peach

鴛鴦蝴蝶派(ㄩㄢ ㄧㄤ ㄏㄨˊ ㄉㄧㄝˊ ㄆㄞˋ)
literature characterized by
shallow love stories

鴛鴦劍(ㄩㄢ ㄧㄤ ㄐㄧㄢˋ)
swords made in pairs

鴛鴦戲水(ㄩㄢ ㄧㄤ ㄒㄧˋ ㄕㄨㄟˇ)
(literally) mandarin ducks
playing in the water—lovemaking

鴛鴦枕(ㄩㄢ ㄧㄤ ㄓㄣˇ)
a double pillow (for the
newly married)

鴛鴦草(ㄩㄢ ㄧㄤ ㄘㄠˇ)
a kind of herb

鴛鴦瓦(ㄩㄢ ㄧㄤ ㄨㄚˇ)
mandarin duck roof-tiles
—roof-tiles in pairs

【鴞】 7130
ㄒㄧㄠ shiau xiāo
an owl

鴞科(ㄒㄧㄠ ㄎㄜ)
the owl family

鴞炙(ㄒㄧㄠ ㄓˋ)
to expect a roast owl—to
count the chickens before
they are hatched

【鴟】 7131
ㄔ chy chī
1. a kite
2. an owl
3. winecups

鴟吻(ㄔ ㄨㄣˇ)
a kind of roof ornament

鴟目虎吻(ㄔ ㄇㄨˋ ㄏㄨˇ ㄨㄣˇ)
(literally) an owl's eyes and
a tiger's lips—a very fierce-
looking face

鴟顧(ㄔ ㄍㄨˋ)
to look back without mov-
ing the body like an owl

鴟梟(ㄒㄧ ㄒㄧㄠ)

〔鳥
部〕

〔鳥部〕

an owl

鴟鴞（ㄔ ㄒㄧㄠ）
①an owl ②a canto in *The Book of Odes* (詩經)

鴟峙
to form an abominable or brutal opposition

鴟張
stretched wings of an owl—brutal oppressors

鴟視
to watch with greed or avarice

鴟蹲
to squat like an owl

鴟夷
a leather bag

鴟尾（ㄔ ㄨㄟˇ）or 鴟吻（ㄔ ㄨㄣˇ）
a kind of ornament on the roof ridge

【鴣】 7132
《ㄨ gu gū
a kind of pigeon, as in 鷓鴣—a partridge; a francolin

鴝鴣《ㄨ ㄨ》
a kind of pigeon

【鴦】 7133
| � 七 iang yāng
the female mandarin duck
參看「鴛」

【鴨】 7134
|Ｙ ia yā
a duck

鴨蛋（|Ｙ ㄉㄢˋ）
①a duck's egg ②(slang) scoreless; zero

鴨蛋臉兒（|Ｙ ㄉㄢˋ ㄌ|ㄢˇ）
an oval face (regarded as an ideal shape for a woman's face)

鴨蛋圓兒（|Ｙ ㄉㄢˋ ㄩㄢˊ）
egg-shaped; oval

鴨爐（|Ｙ ㄌㄨˊ）
a censer or thurible (so named because they were often shaped like ducks)

鴨綠江（|Ｙ ㄌㄨˋ ㄐ|ㄤ）
the Yalu River

鴨黃（|Ｙ ㄏㄨㄤˊ）
a duckling 亦作「小鴨」

鴨腳（|Ｙ ㄐ|ㄠˇ）
①a duck's feet ②gingko or ginkgo (so named because the tree leaf looks like the duck's webbed foot)

鴨叫（|Ｙ ㄐ|ㄠˋ）
quacks of the duck

an owl

鴨掌（|Ｙ ㄓㄤˇ）
webs on duck's feet

鴨翅席（|Ｙ ㄔˋ ㄒ|ˊ）
a banquet featuring ducks and fish fins

鴨舌帽（|Ｙ ㄕㄜˊ ㄇㄠˋ）
a cap with a visor

鴨絨（|Ｙ ㄖㄨㄥˊ）
down on a duck's abdomen

鴨子（|Ｙ·ㄗ）
a duck

鴨子房兒（|Ｙ·ㄗ ㄈㄤˊ兒）
a duckhouse

鴨子兒（|Ｙ·ㄗ 兒）
a duck's egg

鴨嘴筆（|Ｙ ㄗㄨㄟˇ ㄅ|ˇ）
a drawing pen; a ruling pen

鴨嘴獸（|Ｙ ㄗㄨㄟˇ ㄕㄡˋ）
an ornithorhynchus; a duck-bill; a platypus

鴨兒梨（|Ｙ兒 ㄌ|ˊ）
a kind of pear

【鴥】 7135
ㄩˋ yuh yù
flying rapidly; flitting

【鴝】 7136
<ㄩˊ chyu qú
a species of myna (or mynah, minah)

鴝鵒〈ㄩˊ ㄩˋ〉
a species of myna (or mynah, minah)

六畫

【鴿】 7137
《ㄜ ge gē
a pigeon; a dove

鴿派（《ㄜ ㄆㄞˋ）
the doves (persons who support a peaceful policy)

鴿棚（《ㄜ ㄆㄥˊ）or 鴿籠（《ㄜ ㄌㄨㄥˊ）
a pigeon house

鴿雛兒（《ㄜ ㄔㄨˊ兒）
a young pigeon

鴿子（《ㄜ·ㄗ）
a pigeon

鴿子傳書（《ㄜ·ㄗ ㄔㄨㄢˊ ㄕㄨ）
transmission of messages by homing pigeons

【鴟】 7138
ㄐ|ㄠˇ jiau jiǎo
Nycticorax prasinosceles, a kind of water bird

鴟鴿（ㄐ|ㄠˇ ㄐ|ㄥˋ）
Nycticorax prasinosceles, a

kind of water bird

【鴻】 7139
ㄏㄨㄥˊ horng hóng
1. a wild swan; a wild goose
2. great; huge; large

鴻博（ㄏㄨㄥˊ ㄅㄛˊ）
marked by extensive learning; erudite

鴻寶（ㄏㄨㄥˊ ㄅㄠˇ）
a secret collection of rare books

鴻筆（ㄏㄨㄥˊ ㄅ|ˇ）
a great pen—(figuratively) a great literary style

鴻毛（ㄏㄨㄥˊ ㄇㄠˊ）
swan's down—something very light or insignificant

鴻門宴（ㄏㄨㄥˊ ㄇㄣˊ |ㄢˋ）
a banquet held by Hsiang Yü (項羽) for his rival Liu Pang (劉邦) at Hung-men (鴻門) in which attempt was made on the guest's life but foiled, an event often referred to in describing similar situations

鴻名（ㄏㄨㄥˊ ㄇ|ㄥˊ）
great reputation; great fame

鴻飛冥冥（ㄏㄨㄥˊ ㄈㄟ ㄇ|ㄥˊ ㄇ|ㄥˊ）
to run away without leaving any trace behind

鴻範（ㄏㄨㄥˊ ㄈㄢˋ）
a great plan or enterprise

鴻福齊天（ㄏㄨㄥˊ ㄈㄨˊ ㄑ|ˊ ㄊ|ㄢ）
One's vast happiness is as high as the heaven.

鴻都（ㄏㄨㄥˊ ㄉㄨ）
a library (in the Han Dynasty)

鴻洞（ㄏㄨㄥˊ ㄉㄨㄥˋ）
①profound; deep ②joined together; blended; to merge with

鴻圖（ㄏㄨㄥˊ ㄊㄨˊ）
①a great plan; a great enterprise; a great undertaking ②a great domain

鴻烈（ㄏㄨㄥˊ ㄌ|ㄝˋ）
great exploits

鴻臚（ㄏㄨㄥˊ ㄌㄨˊ）
an ancient official title

鴻溝（ㄏㄨㄥˊ ㄍㄡ）
①the river that separated the domain of Hsiang Yü (項羽) from that of Liu Pang (劉邦) ②a border; a boundary ③a gulf

【鴻】(ㄏㄨㄥˊ ㄏㄨˊ)
a wild swan

鴻鵠之志(ㄏㄨㄥˊ ㄏㄨˊ ㄓ ㄓˋ)
great ambition

鴻基(ㄏㄨㄥˊ ㄐㄧ)
foundation of a great undertaking

鴻漸(ㄏㄨㄥˊ ㄐㄧㄢˋ)
gradual promotion on the ladder of officialdom; gradual rise in one's career

鴻禧(ㄏㄨㄥˊ ㄒㄧˇ)
great felicity

鴻緒(ㄏㄨㄥˊ ㄒㄩˋ)
the throne; imperial succession

鴻志(ㄏㄨㄥˊ ㄓˋ)
great ambition

鴻爪(ㄏㄨㄥˊ ㄓㄠˇ)
traces that one leaves behind

鴻鐘(ㄏㄨㄥˊ ㄓㄨㄥ)
a great bell

鴻儒(ㄏㄨㄥˊ ㄖㄨˊ)or 鴻生(ㄏㄨㄥˊ ㄕㄥ)
a man of great scholarship; a man of extensive learning

鴻藻(ㄏㄨㄥˊ ㄗㄠˇ)
great writing

鴻材(ㄏㄨㄥˊ ㄘㄞˊ)
a great literary style

鴻嗷(ㄏㄨㄥˊ ㄠˊ)
moans of a starving crowd

鴻案(ㄏㄨㄥˊ ㄢˋ)
mutual respect between husband and wife, from the story of Liang Hung (梁鴻), whose wife, when attending on him, always held the tray as high as the eyebrows

鴻恩(ㄏㄨㄥˊ ㄣ)
great favor or kindness

鴻儀(ㄏㄨㄥˊ ㄧˊ)
① your valued present ② your honorable appearance

鴻業(ㄏㄨㄥˊ ㄧㄝˋ)
achievements of a ruler

鴻猷(ㄏㄨㄥˊ ㄧㄡˊ)
great plans

鴻雁 or 鴻鴈(ㄏㄨㄥˊ ㄧㄢˋ)
wild swans and geese—refugees

鴻雁傳書(ㄏㄨㄥˊ ㄧㄢˋ ㄔㄨㄢˊ ㄕㄨ)
to deliver messages by wild swans

鴻雁哀鳴(ㄏㄨㄥˊ ㄧㄢˋ ㄞ ㄇㄧㄥˊ)
The refugees are moaning sorrowfully.

鴻文(ㄏㄨㄥˊ ㄨㄣˊ)
great writing

【鷃】 7140
ㄧㄢˇ yann yǒn
a species of quail

鷃雀(ㄧㄢˇ ㄑㄩㄝˋ)
a species of quail

【鵃】 7141
ㄓㄡ jou zhōu
as in 鶻鵃—Treron permagna, a kind of pigeon

【鴽】 7142
ㄖㄨˊ ru rú
Trunix blakistoni, a kind of quail

【鴷】 7143
ㄌㄧㄝˋ lieh liè
a woodpecker

【鴰】 7144
ㄍㄨㄚ gua guā
as in 老鴰—the crow

【鵂】
ㄒㄧㄡ shiou xiū
an owl

鵂鶹(ㄒㄧㄡ ㄌㄧㄡˊ)
an owl

七畫

【鸚】 7146
ㄩˋ yuh yù
as in 鸚鵡—myna (or mynah)

【鵑】 7147
ㄐㄩㄢ jiuan juān
as in 杜鵑—① the cuckoo ② an azalea

【鶟】 7148
ㄊㄨˊ tu tú
a kind of water bird

鶟鶦(ㄊㄨˊ ㄑㄧˊ)
a kind of water bird

【鵓】 7149
ㄅㄛ bor bó
a kind of pigeon

鵓鴣(ㄅㄛˊ ㄍㄨ)
a pigeon

鵓鴿(ㄅㄛˊ ㄍㄜ)
a kind of pigeon

【鵌】 7150
ㄊㄨ twu tú
a kind of bird which shares its nest with rats

【鵜】 7151
ㄊㄧˊ tyi tí
a pelican

鵜鶘(ㄊㄧˊ ㄏㄨˊ)
a pelican

鵜鴂(ㄊㄧˊ ㄐㄩㄝˊ)
a cuckoo

【鵝】 7152
(鵞, 鵝) ㄜˊ er é
a goose; a gander

鵝毛(ㄜˊ ㄇㄠˊ)
goose feathers

鵝毛被(ㄜˊ ㄇㄠˊ ㄅㄟˋ)
bedding stuffed with goose down

鵝毛筆(ㄜˊ ㄇㄠˊ ㄅㄧˇ)
a quill pen

鵝毛管(ㄜˊ ㄇㄠˊ ㄍㄨㄢˇ)
a goose quill

鵝毛雪(ㄜˊ ㄇㄠˊ ㄒㄩㄝˇ)
heavy snow

鵝蛋臉兒(ㄜˊ ㄉㄢˋ ㄌㄧㄢˇ ㄦ)
an egg-shaped face; an oval face

鵝梨(ㄜˊ ㄌㄧˊ)
a kind of pear grown in Hsüan City (宣城), Anhwei Province

鵝翎扇(ㄜˊ ㄌㄧㄥˊ ㄕㄢˋ)
a goose-feather fan

鵝鑾鼻(ㄜˊ ㄌㄨㄢˊ ㄅㄧˊ)
name of the southernmost cape of Taiwan

鵝卵石(ㄜˊ ㄌㄨㄢˇ ㄕˊ)
pebbles

鵝湖之會(ㄜˊ ㄏㄨˊ ㄓ ㄏㄨㄟˋ)
a meeting between Sung Dynasty Confucian scholars Chu Hsi (朱熹) and Lu Chiu-yüan (陸九淵) at O-hu (鵝湖), a hill in Kiangsi, to discuss their differences

鵝黄(ㄜˊ ㄏㄨㄤˊ)
the fine yellow of the gosling

鵝叫(ㄜˊ ㄐㄧㄠˋ)
cackles of geese

鵝行鴨步(ㄜˊ ㄒㄧㄥˊ ㄧㄚ ㄅㄨˋ)
to walk at the slow pace of geese or ducks

鵝掌(ㄜˊ ㄓㄤˇ)
webbed feet of the goose

鵝準(ㄜˊ ㄓㄨㄣˇ)
the crest of a gander

鵝絨(ㄜˊ ㄖㄨㄥˊ)
down of a goose

【鵠】 7153
1. ㄏㄨˊ hwu hú
1. a swan
2. standing erect; standing quietly

鵠面鳩形(ㄏㄨˊ ㄇㄧㄢˋ ㄐㄧㄡ ㄒㄧㄥˊ)
emaciated from hunger

【鳥部】

鵠髮（ㄏㄨˊ ㄈㄚˋ）
gray hair; white hair

鵠立
to stand on the lookout

鵠候
to await eagerly

鵠企（ㄏㄨˊ ㄑㄧˋ）or 鵠望（ㄏㄨˊ ㄨㄤ）
to expect, or anticipate, eagerly

鵠侍
to attend upon respectfully

【鵠】 7153
2.《ㄍㄨˇ guu guu》
a target

鵠的 的（ㄉㄧˋ）or 鵠子（ㄍㄨˇ ㄗ）
the target; the bull's-eye

【鵡】 7154
ㄨˇ wuu wu
as in 鸚鵡—a parrot

八畫

【鵬】 7155
ㄆㄥˊ perng péng
Peng, a fabulous bird supposed to be the greatest of all kinds, comparable to the roc

鵬圖（ㄆㄥˊ ㄊㄨˊ）
great ambition

鵬搏（ㄆㄥˊ ㄅㄛˊ）
to strive for greatness

鵬鯤（ㄆㄥˊ ㄎㄨㄣ）
①a the greatest thing ②a very great personage

鵬舉（ㄆㄥˊ ㄐㄩˇ）
①to push ahead toward an objective ②another name of Yüeh Fei (岳飛) of the Sung Dynasty

鵬程萬里（ㄆㄥˊ ㄔㄥˊ ㄨㄢˋ ㄌㄧˇ）
(literally) a journey of 10,000 miles faced by the roc —of great promise

鵬鷃（ㄆㄥˊ ㄧㄢˋ）
as different in size as the roc is from the quail

【鵩】 7156
ㄈㄨˊ fwu fú
a buzzard; a vulture

鵩鳥（ㄈㄨˊ ㄋㄧㄠˇ）
a buzzard; a vulture

【鵪】 7157
ㄢ an ǎn
a quail

鵪鶉（ㄢ ㄔㄨㄣˊ）
a quail

【鵰】 7158
ㄉㄧㄠ diau diāo
a bird of prey; a vulture 亦作「鵰」

【鵾】 7159
ㄎㄨㄣ kuen kūn
a bird resembling the crane

鵾雞（ㄎㄨㄣ ㄐㄧ）
①a bird resembling the crane ②a phoenix

【鵲】 7160
ㄑㄩㄝˋ chiueh què
(又讀 ㄑㄧㄠˊ cheau qiáo)
a magpie

鵲報（ㄑㄩㄝˋ ㄅㄠˋ）or 鵲報喜（ㄑㄩㄝˋ ㄅㄠˋ ㄒㄧˇ）
the magpie's lucky chirp—a good omen

鵲起（ㄑㄩㄝˋ ㄑㄧˇ）
to rise at an opportune time

鵲橋（ㄑㄩㄝˋ ㄑㄧㄠˊ）
(in folklore) the bridge of magpies, which Weaving Maid (織女) supposedly crosses to meet Cowherd (牛郎) on the 7th of the 7th lunar month

鵲笑鳩舞（ㄑㄩㄝˋ ㄒㄧㄠˋ ㄐㄧㄡ ㄨˇ）
(literally) Magpies laugh and pigeons dance.—All are happy and merry.

鵲巢鳩占 or 鵲巢鳩佔（ㄑㄩㄝˋ ㄔㄠˊ ㄐㄧㄡ ㄓㄢˋ）
(literally) The magpie's nest is occupied by the pigeon. —illegal occupation of another's place

鵲噪（ㄑㄩㄝˋ ㄗㄠˋ）
the chattering of magpies

【鵷】 7161
ㄩㄢ iuan yuān
參看「鵷雛」

鵷行（ㄩㄢ ㄒㄧㄥˊ）
courtiers as a collective body

鵷雛（ㄩㄢ ㄔㄨˊ）
a bird resembling the legendary phoenix

【鵮】 7162
ㄑㄧㄢ chian qiān
1. to peck
2. to ridicule; to deride

【鶉】 7163
ㄔㄨㄣˊ chwen chún
a quail

鶉雞類（ㄔㄨㄣˊ ㄐㄧ ㄌㄟˋ）
Gallinaceae

鶉居（ㄔㄨㄣˊ ㄐㄩ）
to be without a fixed home

鶉衣百結（ㄔㄨㄣˊ ㄧ ㄅㄞˇ ㄐㄧㄝˊ）
coarse clothes with many patches

【鶄】 7164
ㄐㄧㄥ jing jīng
Mycticorax prasinosceles, a kind of water bird

【鶊】 7165
ㄍㄥ geng gēng
as in 鶬鶊—an oriole

九畫

【鶘】 7166
ㄏㄨˊ hwu hú
as in 鵜鶘—a pelican

【鶖】 7167
ㄑㄧㄡ chiou qiú
a marabou, a kind of water bird

【鶚】 7168
ㄜˋ eh è
an osprey; a water hawk

鶚表（ㄜˋ ㄅㄧㄠˇ）
a letter of recommendation

鶚薦（ㄜˋ ㄐㄧㄢˋ）
to recommend (a person)

鶚眙（ㄜˋ ㄧˊ）
frightened; scared

鶚視（ㄜˋ ㄕˋ）
to look fiercely

鶚書（ㄜˋ ㄕㄨ）
a letter of recommendation

【鶡】 7169
ㄏㄜˊ her hé
1. a sort of nightingale
2. a sort of pheasant

鶡旦（ㄏㄜˊ ㄉㄢˋ）
Pteropus pselaphon

鶡冠（ㄏㄜˊ ㄍㄨㄢ）
a kind of cap worn by ancient warriors or by hermits

鶡雞（ㄏㄜˊ ㄐㄧ）
a sort of pheasant

【鶩】 7170
ㄨˋ wuh wu
ducks

鶩舲（ㄨˋ ㄌㄧㄥˊ）
a small boat

【鶒】 7171
ㄔˋ chyh chì
a kind of water bird

【鶗】 7172
ㄊㄧˊ tyi tí
a cuckoo

賜鴃(ㄊㄧˊ ㄐㄩㄝˊ)
a cuckoo

十畫

【鶴】 ⁷¹⁷³ ㄏㄜˋ heh hè
(語音 ㄏㄠˊ haur hào)

a crane

鶴板(ㄏㄜˋ ㄅㄢˇ)
an imperial edict calling on the capable to volunteer for government service

鶴鳴之士(ㄏㄜˋ ㄇㄧㄥˊ ㄓ ㄕˋ)
a scholar widely admired for both virtue and learning

鶴髮(ㄏㄜˋ ㄈㄚˇ)
white hair

鶴髮童顏(ㄏㄜˋ ㄈㄚˇ ㄊㄨㄥˊ ㄧㄢˊ)
a hoary head with a youthful face

鶴髮雞皮(ㄏㄜˋ ㄈㄚˇ ㄐㄧ ㄆㄧˊ)
a hoary head with wrinkled skin

鶴頂紅(ㄏㄜˋ ㄉㄧㄥˇ ㄏㄨㄥˊ)
a fleshy knob on the head of a crane (said to be poisonous)

鶴立(ㄏㄜˋ ㄌㄧˋ)or鶴望(ㄏㄜˋ ㄨㄤˋ)
to expect, or await, eagerly

鶴立雞羣(ㄏㄜˋ ㄌㄧˋ ㄐㄧ ㄑㄩㄣˊ)
(literally) a crane standing among chickens — far surpassing the others; to stand head and shoulders over others

鶴唳(ㄏㄜˋ ㄌㄧˋ)
the cries of cranes

鶴列(ㄏㄜˋ ㄌㄧㄝˋ)
to array troops in orderly formations

鶴林(ㄏㄜˋ ㄌㄧㄣˊ)
Buddhist or Taoist temples

鶴宮(ㄏㄜˋ ㄍㄨㄥ)
the palace of the crown prince

鶴駕(ㄏㄜˋ ㄐㄧㄚˋ)
①the carriage of the crown prince ②the whereabouts of an immortal

鶴金梅(ㄏㄜˋ ㄐㄧㄣ ㄇㄟˊ)
(botany) silverweed

鶴禁(ㄏㄜˋ ㄐㄧㄣˋ)
the palace of the crown prince

鶴膝(ㄏㄜˋ ㄒㄧ)

---

a warning of danger

鶴企(ㄏㄜˋ ㄑㄧˇ)
waiting for or looking forward in eagerness

鶴膝(ㄏㄜˋ ㄒㄧ)
①a slender spear ②(in poetic composition) the defect of an identical tone occurring in the 5th and the 15th words

鶴軒(ㄏㄜˋ ㄒㄩㄢ)
(a polite expression referring to oneself) an incompetent person holding a high position

鶴氅(ㄏㄜˋ ㄔㄤˇ)
a coat made of feathers

鶴壽(ㄏㄜˋ ㄕㄡˋ)or鶴算(ㄏㄜˋ ㄙㄨㄢˋ)
longevity

鶴觴(ㄏㄜˋ ㄕㄤ)
good wine from a distant source

鶴書(ㄏㄜˋ ㄕㄨ)
an imperial summons for a hermit

鶴嘴鋤(ㄏㄜˋ ㄗㄨㄟˇ ㄔㄨˊ)
a mattock; a pickaxe

鶴尊(ㄏㄜˋ ㄗㄨㄣ)
a kind of wine container

鶴馭(ㄏㄜˋ ㄩˋ)
the carriage of an immortal

【鶬】 ⁷¹⁷⁴ ㄘㄤ tsang cang
an oriole

鶬鶊(ㄘㄤ ㄍㄥ)
an oriole

【鷪】 ⁷¹⁷⁵ ㄧㄥ ing yíng
a greenfinch; a Chinese oriole

鶯啼燕語(ㄧㄥ ㄊㄧˊ ㄧㄢˋ ㄩˇ)
Orioles sing and swallows chatter. (a phrase descriptive of a fine spring day)

鶯歌(ㄧㄥ ㄍㄜ)
songs of the oriole

鶯谷(ㄧㄥ ㄍㄨˇ)
talented but remaining in obscurity (like an oriole hidden in a valley)

鶯簧(ㄧㄥ ㄏㄨㄤˊ)or鶯舌(ㄧㄥ ㄕㄜˊ)
the melodious warble of the oriole

鶯遷(ㄧㄥ ㄑㄧㄢ)
to be promoted, or move into a new residence (an expression of congratula-

---

tion)

鶯聲燕語(ㄧㄥ ㄕㄥ ㄧㄢˋ ㄩˇ)
(literally) like an oriole singing and a swallow talking—the pleasant effect of a woman's speech

鶯梭(ㄧㄥ ㄙㄨㄛ)
orioles flitting

鶯鶯燕燕(ㄧㄥ ㄧㄥ ㄧㄢˋ ㄧㄢˋ)
a crowd of women chattering together pleasantly

【鷀】 ⁷¹⁷⁶ ㄘˊ tsyr cí
as in 鸕鷀—a cormorant

【鶺】 ⁷¹⁷⁷ ㄐㄧˊ jyi jí
a wagtail

鶺鴒 or 脊令(ㄐㄧ ㄌㄧㄥˊ)
a wagtail

【鶌】 ⁷¹⁷⁸ 1.《ㄍㄨ guu gǔ
Treron permagna, a kind of pigeon

鶌鶪(ㄍㄨ ㄊㄨ)
a wild duck

鶌鴡(ㄍㄨ ㄐㄩ)or 鶌鵙(ㄍㄨ ㄐㄩ)
Treron pe8magna, a kind of pigeon

【鶥】 ⁷¹⁷⁸ 2.ㄏㄨˊ hwu hú
a kind of bird of prey

鶻突(ㄏㄨˊ ㄊㄨ)
muddleheaded; confused

鶻侖(ㄏㄨˊ ㄌㄨㄣˊ)
whole 亦作「囫圇」

鶻軍(ㄏㄨˊ ㄐㄩㄣ)
a swift army

【鶼】 ⁷¹⁷⁹ ㄐㄧㄢ jian jiān
a fabulous bird having only one wing so that a pair must unite in order to fly

鶼鰈(ㄐㄧㄢ ㄉㄧㄝˊ)
birds and fishes that move in pairs—a devoted couple

【鷁】 ⁷¹⁸⁰ ㄧˋ yih yì
a fabulous sea bird

鷁首(ㄧˋ ㄕㄡˇ)
the bow of a boat

【鶹】 ⁷¹⁸¹ ㄌㄧㄡˊ liou liú
as in 鵂鶹—the owl

【鷂】 ⁷¹⁸² ㄧㄠˋ yaw yào
a hawk; a sparrow hawk

鷂子(ㄧㄠˋ ˙ㄗ)

〔鳥部〕

【鳥部】

① a sparrow hawk ② a kite (a toy)

鷂子翻身(一幺·アゼ アゝ)
a hawk's turn (a fast bodily motion in Chinese pugilism)

鷂鷹(一幺 一ㄥ)
a hawk; a sparrow hawk

【鷃】 7183　一马 yann yàn
a quail

鷃雀(一马くㄩㄝ)
quails and sparrows; small birds

【鷇】 7184　ㄎㄡ kow kòu
fledglings

鷇食(ㄎㄡ ㄕˊ)
to live on the help of others (like fledglings)

鷇音(ㄎㄡ 一ㄣ)
(literally) the chirping of fledglings—divergent opinions

【鷄】 7185　(雞) ㄐㄧ jī jí
fowls

十一畫

【鷓】 7186　ㄓㄜ jeh zhè
a partridge

鷓鴣(ㄓㄜ ㄍㄨ)
a partridge; a francolin

鷓鴣菜(ㄓㄜ ㄍㄨ ㄘㄞˋ)
① digenea simplex ② Chinese medicine made from this sea plant as a parasiticide for children

【鷖】 7187　一 yi
1. a gull
2. dark blue
3. a phoenix

【鷗】 7188　ㄡ ou ōu
a gull

鷗波(ㄡ ㄅㄛ)
to lead the free and leisurely life of a hermit (like that of a gull among the waves)

鷗盟(ㄡ ㄇㄥˊ)
(literally) to live with gulls as if they were one's sworn companions—to live a hermit's life

鷗鷺忘機(ㄡ ㄌㄨˋ ㄨㄤˋ ㄐㄧ)
(said of a hermit) so much

in harmony with nature that the water birds are not frightened away by his presence

【鷙】 7189　ㄓˋ jyh zhì
1. birds of prey
2. fierce; cruel; violent

鷙猛(ㄓˋ ㄇㄥˇ)
fierce; cruel; ruthless

鷙鳥(ㄓˋ 一ㄠˇ)
birds of prey

鷙勇(ㄓˋ ㄩㄥˇ)
fierce and brave

【鸔】 7190　ㄓㄨㄛˊ jwo zhuó
a kind of water bird

十二畫

【鷥】 7191　ㄙ sy sī
an egret

【鷦】 7192　ㄐㄧㄠ jiau jiāo
a wren

鷦鷯(ㄐㄧㄠ ㄌㄧㄠˊ)
a wren; the tailorbird

鷦鷯一枝(ㄐㄧㄠ ㄌㄧㄠˊ 一 ㄓ)
(literally) just one twig for the wren to perch on—any humble position

【鷯】 7193　ㄌㄧㄠˊ liau liáo
as in 鷦鷯—a wren

【鷩】 7194　ㄅㄧˋ bih bì
a kind of pheasant

鷩雉(ㄅㄧˋ ㄓˋ)
a kind of pheasant

【鷫】 7195　ㄙㄨˋ suh sù
a kind of wild swan

【鷲】 7196　ㄐㄧㄡˋ jiow jiù
a vulture

【鷸】 7197　ㄩˋ yuh yù
a snipe

鷸蚌相爭(ㄩˋ ㄅㄤˋ ㄒㄧㄤ ㄓㄥ)
(literally) the fight between the snipe and the clam (with both ending up as captives of the fisherman)—a quarrel which benefits only a third party

鷸冠(ㄩˋ ㄍㄨㄢ)
a kind of ancient cap a-

dorned with snipe feathers

【鷺】 7198　ㄌㄨˋ luh lù
Egretta garzetta, an egret

鷺序(ㄌㄨˋ ㄒㄩˋ)
orderly formation of egrets flying—distinct order of seniority in officialdom

鷺鷥(ㄌㄨˋ ㄙ)
an egret

十三畫

【鷸】 7199　ㄒㄩㄝˊ shyue xué
a tanager

鷽鳩(ㄒㄩㄝˊ ㄐㄧㄡ)
a kind of pigeon

鷽鳩笑鵬(ㄒㄩㄝˊ ㄐㄧㄡ ㄒㄧㄠˋ ㄆㄥˊ)
(literally) the pigeon laughing at the roc—ignorance of one's own limitations

【鷳】 7200　ㄕㄨˇ shuu shǔ
a blackbird

【鸂】 7201　ㄒㄧ shi xī
a kind of water bird resembling the mandarin duck

鸂鶒(ㄒㄧ ㄔˋ)
a kind of water bird resembling the mandarin duck

【鸇】 7202　ㄓㄢ jan zhān
a kind of bird of prey

【鷹】 7203　一ㄥ ing yīng
a hawk; an eagle; a falcon

鷹鼻鷂眼(一ㄥ ㄅㄧˊ 一ㄠˋ 一ㄢˇ)
the nose and eyes of a hawk—an avaricious look

鷹瞵鶚視(一ㄥ ㄌㄧㄣˊ ㄜˋ ㄕˋ)
to look at something or someone fiercely

鷹鉤鼻子(一ㄥ ㄍㄡ ㄅㄧˊ·ㄗ)
an aquiline nose

鷹架(一ㄥ ㄐㄧㄚˋ)
a scaffold (for supporting workmen and building materials)

鷹犬(一ㄥ ㄑㄩㄢˇ)
① falcons and dogs used in hunting ② hired ruffians; rapacious underlings

鷹爪(一ㄥ ㄓㄠˇ)
① talons (or claws) of a falcon, hawk, etc. ② a kind of young tea leaves

鷹鸇(ㄧㄥ ㄓㄢ)
powerful men

鷹師(ㄧㄥ ㄕ)
a falconer

鷹視(ㄧㄥ ㄕˋ)
a fierce look

鷹式飛彈(ㄧㄥ ㄈㄟ ㄉㄢˋ)
the Hawk missiles

鷹隼(ㄧㄥ ㄙㄨㄣˇ)or(ㄧㄥ ㄓㄨㄣˇ)
hawks and falcons—cruel or
fierce people

鷹洋(ㄧㄥ ㄧㄤˊ)
a Mexican silver dollar

鷹揚(ㄧㄥ ㄧㄤˊ)
powerful, or outstanding
(like a soaring falcon)

鷹揚宴(ㄧㄥ ㄧㄤˊ ㄧㄢ)
a banquet for celebration
following announcement of
the results of a local examination under the military
service examination system
of the Ching Dynasty

十六畫

【鸕】 7204
ㄌㄨˊ luu lú
a cormorant

鸕鷀(ㄌㄨˊ ㄘ)
a cormorant

十七畫

【鸚】 7205
ㄧㄥ ing yīng
a parrot

鸚哥(ㄧㄥ ㄍㄜ)
a parrot

鸚哥鼻(ㄧㄥ ㄍㄜ ㄅㄧˊ)
a hooked nose

鸚哥綠(ㄧㄥ ㄍㄜ ㄌㄩˋ)or 鸚綠(ㄧㄥ ㄌㄩˋ)
green of the parrot

鸚鵡(ㄧㄥ ㄨˇ)
a parrot

鸚鵡杯(ㄧㄥ ㄨˇ ㄅㄟ)
a cup made of a kind of spiral shell

鸚鵡螺(ㄧㄥ ㄨˇ ㄌㄨㄛˊ)
a nautilus (a kind of mollusk)

鸚鵡學舌(ㄧㄥ ㄨˇ ㄒㄩㄝˊ ㄕㄜˊ)
to parrot another's statement, theory, etc.

十八畫

【鸛】 7206
ㄍㄨㄢ guann guàn
a stork

鸛雀(ㄍㄨㄢ ㄑㄩㄝˋ)
a stork

【鸜】 7207
ㄑㄩ chyu qú
a species of myna (or
mynah)

鸜鵒(ㄑㄩ ㄩˋ)
Aethiopsar cristatellus, a
species of myna (or mynah)

十九畫

【鸝】 7208
ㄌㄧˊ lí
as in 黃鸝—a Chinese oriole

【鸞】 7209
ㄌㄨㄢˊ luan luán
1. a luan (a fabulous bird
related to the phoenix)
2. the bells at horses' bits

鸞鳳鳳泊(ㄌㄨㄢˊ ㄈㄥˋ ㄈㄣ ㄅㄛˊ)
①fine calligraphy ②separa-
tion of husband and wife

鸞鳳(ㄌㄨㄢˊ ㄈㄥˋ)
①a married couple ②a
luan (a fabulous bird) and a
phoenix—(figuratively)
good beings ③handsome;
gallant

鸞鳳和鳴(ㄌㄨㄢˊ ㄈㄥˋ ㄏㄜˊ ㄇㄧㄥˊ)
harmony in marriage

鸞帶(ㄌㄨㄢˊ ㄉㄞˋ)
a kind of dressing band
worn by players in Chinese
opera

鸞刀(ㄌㄨㄢˊ ㄉㄠ)
a sword adorned with bells

鸞鶴(ㄌㄨㄢˊ ㄏㄜˋ)
a luan (a fabulous bird) and
a crane which immortals
supposedly ride about

鸞交鳳友(ㄌㄨㄢˊ ㄐㄧㄠ ㄈㄥˋ ㄧㄡˇ)
a couple deeply in love

鸞箋(ㄌㄨㄢˊ ㄐㄧㄢ)
tinted letter paper

鸞車(ㄌㄨㄢˊ ㄔㄜ)
an imperial carriage

鸞旗(ㄌㄨㄢˊ ㄑㄧˊ)
an imperial flag

鸞翔鳳集(ㄌㄨㄢˊ ㄒㄧㄤˊ ㄈㄥˋ ㄐㄧˊ)
gathering together of tal-

ented men

鸞翔鳳翥(ㄌㄨㄢˊ ㄒㄧㄤˊ ㄈㄥˋ ㄓㄨˋ)
fine calligraphy

鸞帚(ㄌㄨㄢˊ ㄓㄡˇ)
a kind of broom

鸞輅(ㄌㄨㄢˊ ㄌㄨˋ)
an itinerary of the emperor
on tour

鸞輿(ㄌㄨㄢˊ ㄩˊ)
an imperial sedan chair

鹵 部
ㄌㄨˇ luu lǔ

【鹵】 7210
ㄌㄨˇ luu lǔ
1. alkaline or saline soil
2. natural salt
3. rude; unrefined 亦作「魯」
4. to capture; to seize 亦作「擄」

鹵莽(ㄌㄨˇ ㄇㄤˇ)
rude; rash; foolhardy: 他是個
鹵莽的傢伙。He is a rude fel-
low.

鹵莽滅裂(ㄌㄨˇ ㄇㄤˇ ㄇㄧㄝˋ ㄌㄧㄝˋ)
careless and haphazard;
crude; coarse

鹵掠 or 擄掠(ㄌㄨˇ ㄌㄩㄝˋ)
to plunder; to seize; to capture

鹵鹼(ㄌㄨˇ ㄐㄧㄢˇ)or 鹵鹽(ㄌㄨˇ ㄧㄢˊ)
alkali

鹵水(ㄌㄨˇ ㄕㄨㄟˇ)
alkaline, or saline ground
water

鹵素(ㄌㄨˇ ㄙㄨˋ)
halogen

鹵味(ㄌㄨˇ ㄨㄟˋ)
①pot-stewed fowl, meat,
etc. served cold ②a salty
taste; saltiness

九畫

【鹹】 7211
ㄒㄧㄢˊ shyan xián
saltish; salty; briny; salted:
這湯太鹹了。The soup is too
salty.

鹹蛋(ㄒㄧㄢˊ ㄉㄢˋ)
salted eggs

鹹海(ㄒㄧㄢˊ ㄏㄞˇ)
Lake Aral

［鹵部］

鹹湖(ㄒㄧㄢˊㄏㄨˊ)or鹹水湖(ㄒㄧㄢˊㄕㄨㄟˇㄏㄨˊ)
salt lakes

鹹鷄子兒(ㄒㄧㄢˊㄐㄧㄗㄦ)
brined hen's eggs

鹹津(ㄒㄧㄢˊㄐㄧㄣ)
a salty taste; saltiness

鹹津津兒(ㄒㄧㄢˊㄐㄧㄣㄐㄧㄣㄦ)or鹹津津的(ㄒㄧㄢˊㄐㄧㄣㄐㄧㄣㄉㄜ)
salty

鹹潟(ㄒㄧㄢˊㄒㄧˋ)
salt land

鹹水(ㄒㄧㄢˊㄕㄨㄟˇ)
saline water; salt water

鹹水妹(ㄒㄧㄢˊㄕㄨㄟˇㄇㄟˋ)
(Cantonese dialect) prostitutes who do business exclusively with foreigners

鹹水魚(ㄒㄧㄢˊㄕㄨㄟˇㄩˊ)
salt-water fish

鹹肉(ㄒㄧㄢˊㄖㄡˋ)
salted meat

鹹肉莊(ㄒㄧㄢˊㄖㄡˋㄓㄨㄤ)
(Shanghai dialect) an unlicensed brothel

鹹菜(ㄒㄧㄢˊㄘㄞˋ)
pickled vegetables; pickles

鹹酸(ㄒㄧㄢˊㄙㄨㄢ)
salty and sour at the same time

鹹鴨蛋(ㄒㄧㄢˊㄧㄚㄉㄢˋ)
salted duck's eggs

鹹鹹(ㄒㄧㄢˊㄒㄧㄢˊ)
a salty taste; saltiness

鹹魚(ㄒㄧㄢˊㄩˊ)
salted fish

十畫

【鹺】 7212　ㄘㄨㄛˊ tswo cuó
1. briny; salty
2. salt

鹺使(ㄘㄨㄛˊㄕˇ)
(Ching Dynasty) an official in charge of the salt industry in a given area; a salt commissioner 亦作「鹽運使」

【鹻】 7213　(鹼)ㄐㄧㄢˇ jean jiǎn
alkali

十三畫

【鹼】 7214　(鹼)ㄐㄧㄢˇ jean jiǎn

lye; alkali

鹼地(ㄐㄧㄢˇㄉㄧˋ)
alkaline soil

鹼度(ㄐㄧㄢˇㄉㄨˋ)
basicity

鹼化(ㄐㄧㄢˇㄏㄨㄚˋ)
saponification

鹼金屬(ㄐㄧㄢˇㄐㄧㄣㄕㄨˇ)
alkali metal

鹼性(ㄐㄧㄢˇㄒㄧㄥˋ)
alkalinity

鹼性反應(ㄐㄧㄢˇㄒㄧㄥˋㄈㄢˇㄧㄥ)
alkaline reaction

鹼性鹽(ㄐㄧㄢˇㄒㄧㄥˋㄧㄢˊ)
basic salt

鹼石灰(ㄐㄧㄢˇㄕˊㄏㄨㄟ)
soda-lime

十四畫

【鹽】 7215　1. ㄧㄢˊ yan yán
common salt; salt; 請把鹽遞給我。Pass me the salt, please.

鹽巴(ㄧㄢˊㄅㄚ)
(dialect)salt; common salt

鹽民(ㄧㄢˊㄇㄧㄣˊ)
the population engaged in the salt industry

鹽法(ㄧㄢˊㄈㄚˇ)
laws governing the salt industry; salt laws

鹽鐵(ㄧㄢˊㄊㄧㄝˇ)
manufacture of salt and iron (a basic industry in ancient times)

鹽田(ㄧㄢˊㄊㄧㄢˊ)
a salt garden; a salt pond

鹽類(ㄧㄢˊㄌㄟˋ)
(chemistry) salt

鹽滷(ㄧㄢˊㄌㄨˇ)
a kind of thick brine; bittern

鹽湖(ㄧㄢˊㄏㄨˊ)
salt lakes

鹽花(ㄧㄢˊㄏㄨㄚ)
fine grains of salt

鹽基(ㄧㄢˊㄐㄧ)
(chemistry) a base; a hydroxyl radical

鹽價(ㄧㄢˊㄐㄧㄚˋ)
the price of salt

鹽井(ㄧㄢˊㄐㄧㄥˇ)
a salt well

鹽區(ㄧㄢˊㄑㄩ)
districts for administration

of the salt industry

鹽泉(ㄧㄢˊㄑㄩㄢˊ)
a brine spring

鹽梟(ㄧㄢˊㄒㄧㄠ)
an illegal salt dealer

鹽政(ㄧㄢˊㄓㄥˋ)
administration of the salt industry; salt administration

鹽池(ㄧㄢˊㄔˊ)
a salt pond

鹽場(ㄧㄢˊㄔㄤˇ)or鹽坼(ㄧㄢˊㄔㄜˋ)
a salt farm; a salt field; a saltworks

鹽場公署(ㄧㄢˊㄔㄤˇㄍㄨㄥㄕㄨˋ)
the saltworks administration (a government agency in charge of salt manufacture in a given district in the early years of the Republic)

鹽商(ㄧㄢˊㄕㄤ)
salt merchants; salt dealers

鹽水(ㄧㄢˊㄕㄨㄟˇ)
salt solution; salt water; brine

鹽水灌腸(ㄧㄢˊㄕㄨㄟˇㄍㄨㄢˋㄔㄤˊ)
salt enema

鹽水注射(ㄧㄢˊㄕㄨㄟˇㄓㄨˋㄕㄜˋ)
a salt injection

鹽稅(ㄧㄢˊㄕㄨㄟˋ)
salt tax; salt gabelle

鹽竈(ㄧㄢˊㄗㄠˋ)
a stove for boiling brine (in salt manufacture)

鹽酸(ㄧㄢˊㄙㄨㄢ)
hydrochloric acid

鹽務(ㄧㄢˊㄨˋ)
administration of the salt industry

鹽味(ㄧㄢˊㄨㄟˋ)
a salty taste; saltiness

鹽運使(ㄧㄢˊㄩㄣˋㄕˇ)
(in former times) an official in charge of the salt industry in given area; a salt commissioner

【鹽】 7215　2. ㄧㄢˋ yann yàn
1. to salt
2. to envy

鹿 部
（ㄌㄨ luh lù）

【鹿】 7216
（ㄌㄨ luh lù）
a deer; a stag; a doe

鹿皮（ㄌㄨ ㄆㄧˊ）
deerskin

鹿皮冠（ㄌㄨ ㄆㄧˊ 《ㄨㄢ）or 鹿巾（ㄌㄨ ㄐㄧㄣ）
the costume customarily worn by a hermit

鹿鳴宴（ㄌㄨ ㄇㄧㄥˊ ㄧㄢˋ）
a celebration party following success in the local examination under the former civil service examination system

鹿特丹（ㄌㄨ ㄊㄜˋ ㄉㄢ）
Rotterdam, Holland

鹿駭（ㄌㄨ ㄏㄞˋ）
frightened like a deer

鹿角（ㄌㄨ ㄐㄧㄠˇ）
antlers

鹿筋（ㄌㄨ ㄐㄧㄣ）
deer's sinews (regarded as a delicacy)

鹿肉（ㄌㄨ ㄖㄡˋ）
venison

鹿茸（ㄌㄨ ㄖㄨㄥˊ）
young antlers (regarded as a very valuable medicine)

鹿死不擇音（蔭）（ㄌㄨ ㄙˇ ㄅㄨˋ ㄗㄜˊ ㄧㄣ）
A dying deer does not choose a shade.—A desperate man will resort to anything.

鹿死誰手（ㄌㄨ ㄙˇ ㄕㄟˊ ㄕㄡˇ）
(literally) Who is to kill the deer?—Who will win?

鹿兒島（ㄌㄨ ㄦˊ ㄉㄠˇ）
Kagoshima, a Japanese island

鹿尾（ㄌㄨ ㄨㄟˇ）
a deer's tail (a rare delicacy)

鹿苑（ㄌㄨ ㄩㄢˋ）
a deer garden

二畫

【麀】 7217
（ㄧㄡ iou yōu）
a female deer; a doe

麀鹿（ㄧㄡ ㄌㄨˋ）
a female deer; a doe

【麂】 7218
（ㄐㄧˇ jii jǐ）
Moschus chinensis, an animal resembling the deer but without antlers

四畫

【麃】 7219
（ㄅㄧㄠ biau biāo）
to till the land; to weed

麃麃（ㄅㄧㄠ ㄅㄧㄠ）
having a martial appearance

【麃】 7219.2
（麅）ㄆㄠˊ paur páo
a species of roe

五畫

【麈】 7220
（ㄓㄨ juu zhù）
1. a kind of deer
2. to whisk; to dust

麈談（ㄓㄨ ㄊㄢˊ）
to converse or talk leisurely while holding a duster

麈尾（ㄓㄨ ㄨㄟˇ）
a duster

【麅】 7221
（ㄆㄠˊ paur páo）
a species of roe

六畫

【麋】 7222
（ㄇㄧˊ mi mí）
Alces machlis, a kind of deer

麋沸（ㄇㄧˊ ㄈㄟˋ）
disturbance; chaos; unrest

麋繁（ㄇㄧˊ ㄍㄠˇ）
old; aged

麋鹿（ㄇㄧˊ ㄌㄨˋ）
①(animal) the elk and the deer ②(figuratively) a rude person

七畫

【麐】 7223
（麟）ㄌㄧㄣˊ lin lín
the female of a fabulous animal resembling a deer

【麇】 7224
（麕）ㄐㄩㄣ jiun jūn
a species of roe deer

八畫

【麑】 7225
（ㄋㄧˊ ni ní）
a young deer; a fawn

麑鹿（ㄋㄧˊ ㄌㄨˋ）
a young deer; a fawn

麑裘（ㄋㄧˊ ㄑㄧㄡˊ）
fawn's furs

【麒】 7226
（ㄑㄧˊ chyi qí）
the male of a fabulous animal resembling the deer

麒麟（ㄑㄧˊ ㄌㄧㄣˊ）
Chi-lin, a fabulous animal resembling the deer said to appear only in time of peace and prosperity

麒麟楦（ㄑㄧˊ ㄌㄧㄣˊ ㄒㄩㄢˋ）
something impressive in appearance only

麒麟座（ㄑㄧˊ ㄌㄧㄣˊ ㄗㄨㄛˋ）
(astronomy) Monoceros

麒麟兒（ㄑㄧˊ ㄌㄧㄣˊ ㄦ）
a wonder child; an infant prodigy

【麓】 7227
（ㄌㄨ luh lù）
the foot of a hill or mountain

【麗】 7228
（ㄌㄧˋ lih lì）
1. beautiful; elegant; fine; magnificent
2. to hang
3. same as 儷—dual; double

麗風（ㄌㄧˋ ㄈㄥ）
a northwest wind

麗服（ㄌㄧˋ ㄈㄨˊ）
beautiful dress

麗都（ㄌㄧˋ ㄉㄨ）
beautiful; fine

麗譙（ㄌㄧˋ ㄑㄧㄠˊ）
a magnificent tower

麗質（ㄌㄧˋ ㄓˊ）
beauty (especially feminine)

麗曜（ㄌㄧˋ ㄧㄠˋ）
pleasing in appearance; good-looking

麗日光天（ㄌㄧˋ ㄖˋ 《ㄨㄤ ㄊㄧㄢ）
a beautiful, bright day

麗人（ㄌㄧˋ ㄖㄣˊ）
a beautiful woman; a beauty;

【麗】

a belle 亦作「美人」

麗澤（ㄌㄧ ㄗㄜˊ）
benefits derivable from mutual contact between friends

麗藻（ㄌㄧ ㄗㄠˇ）
fine language; flowery words

麗辭（ㄌㄧ ㄘˊ）
flowery language; elegant phrases

麗文（ㄌㄧ ㄨㄣˊ）
elegant writing

麗月（ㄌㄧ ㄩㄝˋ）
the second lunar month

【麕】ㄐㄩㄣ jiun jūn
a species of roe

麕（ㄐㄩㄣ ㄐㄧ）
to herd together; to flock together; to gather

十畫

【麝】 7230　ㄕㄜˋ sheh shè
a musk deer

麝墨（ㄕㄜˋ ㄇㄛˋ）
sweet-smelling ink

麝牛（ㄕㄜˋ ㄋㄧㄡˊ）
a musk ox

麝香（ㄕㄜˋ ㄒㄧㄤ）
musk

麝月（ㄕㄜˋ ㄩㄝˋ）
the moon

十一畫

【麞】 7231　ㄓㄤ jang zhāng
Moschus chinloo, a deer-like animal

麞頭鼠目（ㄓㄤ ㄊㄡˊ ㄕㄨˇ ㄇㄨˋ）
a roe's head and a mouse's eyes—a mean physiognomy

十二畫

【麟】 7232　ㄌㄧㄣˊ lin lín
the female of a fabulous animal resembling the deer

麟鳳（ㄌㄧㄣˊ ㄈㄥˋ）
①rare treasures ②persons of rare virtue

麟牒（ㄌㄧㄣˊ ㄉㄧㄝˊ）
the genealogy of the royal household

麟藻（ㄌㄧㄣˊ ㄗㄠˇ）
the imperial secretariat of the Tang Dynasty

麟麟（ㄌㄧㄣˊ ㄌㄧㄣˊ）
bright; brilliant

麟閣（ㄌㄧㄣˊ ㄍㄜˊ）
the place where images of meritorious subjects were displayed during the Han Dynasty 亦作「麒麟閣」

麟角（ㄌㄧㄣˊ ㄐㄧㄠˇ）or 麟角鳳毛（ㄌㄧㄣˊ ㄐㄧㄠˇ ㄈㄥˋ ㄇㄠˊ）
rare things

麟經（ㄌㄧㄣˊ ㄐㄧㄥ）or 麟史（ㄌㄧㄣˊ ㄕˇ）
the Spring and Autumn Annals by Confucius

麟趾（ㄌㄧㄣˊ ㄓˇ）
accomplished children

麟兒（ㄌㄧㄣˊ ㄦˊ）
a fine son

二十二畫

【麤】 7233　ㄘㄨ（粗）tsu cū
coarse; rough

麥 部
ㄇㄛˋ moh mò

【麥】 7234　ㄇㄞˋ may mài（ㄇㄛˋ moh mò）
1. wheat; barley; oats
2. a Chinese family name

麥餅（ㄇㄞˋ ㄅㄧㄥˇ）
wheaten cake

麥片（ㄇㄞˋ ㄆㄧㄢˋ）
oatmeal

麥芒（ㄇㄞˋ ㄇㄤˊ）
beards or awns of barley, oats, etc.

麥苗（ㄇㄞˋ ㄇㄧㄠˊ）
young wheat, barley, etc.

麥飯豆羹（ㄇㄞˋ ㄈㄢˋ ㄉㄡˋ ㄍㄥ）
coarse meals of a farming family

麥粉（ㄇㄞˋ ㄈㄣˇ）
flour

麥麩（ㄇㄞˋ ㄈㄨ）
wheat bran

麥地那（ㄇㄞˋ ㄉㄧˋ ㄋㄚˋ）
Medina, Saudi Arabia

麥多（ㄇㄞˋ ㄉㄨㄛ）or 麥門冬（ㄇㄞˋ ㄇㄣˊ ㄉㄨㄥ）
Liriope graminifolia, a medicinal herb

麥田（ㄇㄞˋ ㄊㄧㄢˊ）
wheatland; a wheat field

麥浪（ㄇㄞˋ ㄌㄤˋ）
the wavy motion of wheat, etc., in the field when winds blow

麥卡圖（ㄇㄞˋ ㄎㄚˇ ㄊㄨˊ）
Gerhardus Mercator, 1512-1594, Flemish geographer

麥克風（ㄇㄞˋ ㄎㄜˋ ㄈㄥ）
a microphone: 他正在試麥克風。He is testing the microphone.

麥克阿瑟（ㄇㄞˋ ㄎㄜˋ ㄚ ㄙㄜˋ）
Douglas MacArthur, 1880-1964, American general

麥加（ㄇㄞˋ ㄐㄧㄚ）
Mecca, Saudi Arabia

麥稭（ㄇㄞˋ ㄐㄧㄝ）
wheat straw; stalks of wheat, etc.

麥角病（ㄇㄞˋ ㄐㄧㄠˇ ㄅㄧㄥˋ）
ergot—a disease of rye and other cereals in which the grains are replaced by blackish fungous growths

麥角菌（ㄇㄞˋ ㄐㄧㄠˇ ㄐㄩㄣ）
ergot—any fungus producing 麥角

麥酒（ㄇㄞˋ ㄐㄧㄡˇ）
beer 亦作「啤酒」；喝麥酒要連泡沫喝。Drink beer with the froth.

麥秀黍油（ㄇㄞˋ ㄒㄧㄡˋ ㄕㄨˇ ㄧㄡˊ）
The wheat and the corn grow but the fatherland is no more.

麥哲倫（ㄇㄞˋ ㄓㄜˊ ㄌㄨㄣˊ）
Ferdinand Magellan (c. 1480-1521), Portuguese navigator

麥哲倫海峽（ㄇㄞˋ ㄓㄜˊ ㄌㄨㄣˊ ㄏㄞˇ ㄒㄧㄚˊ）
Strait of Magellan, a strait near the south tip of South America

麥場（ㄇㄞˋ ㄔㄤˊ）
a wheat-thrashing floor

麥子（ㄇㄞˋ ˙ㄗ）
wheat; barley

麥穗（ㄇㄞˋ ㄙㄨㄟˋ）
ears of wheat, etc.

【麥】（left margin）部

麥芽(ㄇㄞˋ ㄧㄚˊ)
malt

麥芽糖(ㄇㄞˋ ㄧㄚˊ ㄊㄤˊ)
malt sugar; maltose

麥芽酵素(ㄇㄞˋ ㄧㄚˊ ㄐㄧㄠˋ ㄙㄨˋ)
maltase

四畫

【麩】 7235
ㄈㄨ fu fú
bran

麩質(ㄈㄨ ㄓˊ)
gluten

麩酸(ㄈㄨ ㄙㄨㄢ)
glutamic acid

【麪】 7236
(麵) ㄇㄧㄢˋ miann
miàn

1. flour
2. dough
3. noodles

麪包(ㄇㄧㄢˋ ㄅㄠ)
bread

麪包店(ㄇㄧㄢˋ ㄅㄠ ㄉㄧㄢˋ)
a bakery

麪包屑(ㄇㄧㄢˋ ㄅㄠ ㄒㄧㄝˋ)
crumbs of bread

麪包師(ㄇㄧㄢˋ ㄅㄠ ㄕ)
a baker

麪包樹(ㄇㄧㄢˋ ㄅㄠ ㄕㄨˋ)
a breadfruit tree

麪粉(ㄇㄧㄢˋ ㄈㄣˇ)
flour; 我們用麪粉做成麪包。
We make flour into bread.

麪粉廠(ㄇㄧㄢˋ ㄈㄣˇ ㄔㄤˇ)
a flour mill

麪條(ㄇㄧㄢˋ ㄊㄧㄠˊ)
noodles; spaghetti; vermicelli

麪糰(ㄇㄧㄢˋ ㄊㄨㄢˊ)
dough

麪糊(ㄇㄧㄢˋ ㄏㄨˊ)
flour paste

麪筋(ㄇㄧㄢˋ ㄐㄧㄣ)
gluten of flour

麪杖(ㄇㄧㄢˋ ㄓㄤˋ)
a rolling pin 亦作「擀麪杖」

麪茶(ㄇㄧㄢˋ ㄔㄚˊ)
porridge made by mixing roasted flour in boiling water

麪食(ㄇㄧㄢˋ ㄕˊ)
wheaten foods; pastry

六畫

【麯】 7237
(麴) ㄑㄩ chyu qū
a ferment for brewing

【麰】 7238
ㄇㄡˊ mou móu
barley: 啤酒是麰製成的。Beer is made from barley.

八畫

【麴】 7239
(麯) ㄑㄩ chyu qū
yeast; a ferment for brewing: 麴是一種發酵劑。Yeast is a ferment.

麴黴(ㄑㄩ ㄇㄟˊ)or 麴菌(ㄑㄩ ㄐㄩㄣˋ)
aspergilli (especially those with enzymes capable of effecting fermentation)

麴糵(ㄑㄩ ㄋㄧㄝˋ)
① the yeast and the malt—a ferment for brewing ② brewed spirits

麴監(ㄑㄩ ㄐㄧㄢ)
an official in charge of wines and liquors

麴錢(ㄑㄩ ㄑㄧㄢˊ)
the tax paid by brewers

麴秀才(ㄑㄩ ㄒㄧㄡˋ ㄘㄞˊ)or 麴生(ㄑㄩ ㄕㄥ) or 麴君(ㄑㄩ ㄐㄩㄣ)
wine; liquor

麴院(ㄑㄩ ㄩㄢˋ)
a brewery

九畫

【麵】 7240
(麪) ㄇㄧㄢˋ miann
miàn
flour; noodles

麻 部
ㄇㄚˊ ma má

【麻】 7241
ㄇㄚˊ ma má
1. hemp; jute; ramie; sisal; flax
2. sesame
3. numb; torpid
4. a tingle; to tingle
5. pockmarked
6. rough
7. pitted; spotty

麻痺(ㄇㄚˊ ㄅㄧˋ)

paralysis; palsy; numbness: 他的左腳麻痺了。His left leg is paralyzed.

麻布(ㄇㄚˊ ㄅㄨˋ)
hempen fabrics; gunny; linen

麻面(ㄇㄚˊ ㄇㄧㄢˋ)
a pockmarked face

麻木(ㄇㄚˊ ㄇㄨˋ)
paralyzed; numbed; palsied

麻木不仁(ㄇㄚˊ ㄇㄨˋ ㄅㄨˋ ㄖㄣˊ)
numbed; paralyzed; unsympathetic; unfeeling

麻煩(ㄇㄚˊ ㄈㄢˊ)
① troublesome: 這事真麻煩。This thing is really troublesome. ② trouble ③ to bother: 這點小事不要去麻煩老師了。Don't bother our teacher with such trifles.

麻袋(ㄇㄚˊ ㄉㄞˋ)
a jute bag; a hemp bag; a gunny-bag

麻刀(ㄇㄚˊ ㄉㄠ)or 麻擣(ㄇㄚˊ ㄉㄠˇ)
hemp chopped up for strengthening mortar

麻俐(ㄇㄚˊ ㄌㄧˋ)
quick; swift; agile

麻六甲(ㄇㄚˊ ㄌㄧㄡˋ ㄐㄧㄚˇ)
Malacca

麻六甲海峽(ㄇㄚˊ ㄌㄧㄡˋ ㄐㄧㄚˇ ㄏㄞˇ ㄒㄧㄚˊ)
Strait of Malacca, a strait between Sumatra and the Malay Peninsula

麻臉(ㄇㄚˊ ㄌㄧㄢˇ)
a pockmarked face

麻姑(ㄇㄚˊ ㄍㄨ)
① name of a mountain in Kiangsi ② name of a female immortal

麻胡(ㄇㄚˊ ㄏㄨˊ)
① a pockmarked, bearded man ② 參看「麻虎子」

麻虎子(ㄇㄚˊ ㄏㄨˇ ˙ㄗ)
a goblin often mentioned to scare children

麻黃(ㄇㄚˊ ㄏㄨㄤˊ)
Ephedra sinica, a medical herb; a horsetail

麻稭(ㄇㄚˊ ㄐㄧㄝ)
hemp stalks

麻醬(ㄇㄚˊ ㄐㄧㄤˋ)
sesame paste

麻將牌(ㄇㄚˊ ㄐㄧㄤˋ ㄆㄞˊ)
mah-jong pieces

麻雀(ㄇㄚˊ ㄑㄩㄝˋ)

〔麻部〕

（黃 部）

① a sparrow ② mah-jong

麻雀雖小，五臟俱全 (ㄇㄚˊ ㄑㄩㄝˋ ㄙㄨㄟ ㄒㄧㄠˇ，ㄨˇ ㄗㄤˋ ㄐㄩˋ ㄑㄩㄢˊ)
Although the sparrow is small, it has all the vital organs—small but complete

麻鞋 (ㄇㄚˊ ㄒㄧㄝ)
hempen sandals

麻線 (ㄇㄚˊ ㄒㄧㄢˋ)
linen threads

麻織品 (ㄇㄚˊ ㄓˋ ㄆㄧㄣˇ)
linen fabrics

麻疹 (ㄇㄚˊ ㄓㄣˇ)
(medicine) measles: 麻疹是小孩子生的病。Measles is a children's disease.

麻繩 (ㄇㄚˊ ㄕㄥˊ)
hemp cordage; hemp rope: 他抓住麻繩。He grasps the hemp rope.

麻省理工學院 (ㄇㄚˊ ㄕㄥˇ ㄌㄧˇ ㄍㄨㄥ ㄒㄩㄝˊ ㄩㄢˋ)
Massachusetts Institute of Technology(MIT)

麻子 (ㄇㄚˊ ·ㄗ)
① a pockmarked person ② pockmarks

麻醉 (ㄇㄚˊ ㄗㄨㄟˋ)
① to anesthetize ② to dope; to drug

麻醉劑 (ㄇㄚˊ ㄗㄨㄟˋ ㄐㄧˋ) or 麻藥 (ㄇㄚˊ ㄧㄠˋ)
① an anesthetic ② narcotics; drugs; dopes

麻醉藥品 (ㄇㄚˊ ㄗㄨㄟˋ ㄧㄠˋ ㄆㄧㄣˇ)
narcotics

麻薩諸塞州 (ㄇㄚˊ ㄙㄚˋ ㄓㄨ ㄙㄜˋ ㄓㄡ)
the state of Massachusetts, U. S. A.

麻衣 (ㄇㄚˊ ㄧ)
① hemp mourning garments; gunny garments worn as mourning dress by the children and wife of the deceased ② a robe of hemp

麻衣相法 (ㄇㄚˊ ㄧ ㄒㄧㄤˋ ㄈㄚˇ)
a system of physiognomy said to originate from a Taoist in the Sung Dynasty

麻油 (ㄇㄚˊ ㄧㄡˊ)
sesame oil

三畫

【麼】 7242
  1. ㄇㄜ　mo mó
1. tiny

2. a special particle found in dramatic dialogues

【麼】 7242
  2.(麼・嗎)・ㄇㄚ　ma
a final interrogative particle

【麼】 7242
  3. ㄇㄚˊ ma má
a particle used in the phrase 「幹麼」(why): 你來此幹麼? Why are you coming here?

【麼】 7242
  4.・ㄇㄜ　・me me
a particle used in the interrogative phrase 「甚麼」(what): 甚麼事情? What is the matter?

四畫

【麾】 7243
  1. ㄏㄨㄟ huei hui
1. a flag; a banner; a standard
2. to command; to lead

麾旗 (ㄏㄨㄟ ㄑㄧˊ)
flags; banners

麾軍 (ㄏㄨㄟ ㄐㄩㄣ)
to lead an army

麾下 (ㄏㄨㄟ ㄒㄧㄚˋ)
① under a general's command ② sir (in addressing a general)

黃 部
ㄏㄨㄤˊ hwang huáng

【黃】 7244
  ㄏㄨㄤˊ hwang huáng
1. yellow
2. a Chinese family name

黃白花貓 (ㄏㄨㄤˊ ㄅㄞˊ ㄏㄨㄚ ㄇㄠ)
(usually said of cats, dogs, etc.) white with yellow spots

黃柏 (ㄏㄨㄤˊ ㄅㄛˊ) or 黃檗 (ㄏㄨㄤˊ ㄅㄛˋ)
Phellodendron amurense, a kind of oak, whose bark is used in Chinese medicine

黃包車 (ㄏㄨㄤˊ ㄅㄠ ㄔㄜ)
a ricksha

黃榜 (ㄏㄨㄤˊ ㄅㄤˇ)
an imperial edict

黃埔軍官學校 (ㄏㄨㄤˊ ㄅㄨˇ ㄐㄩㄣ ㄍㄨㄢ ㄒㄩㄝˊ ㄒㄧㄠˋ)
Whampoa Military Academy
(the cradle of the military leaders of China)

黃袍 (ㄏㄨㄤˊ ㄆㄠˊ)
① high-ranking Buddhist monks (marked by their yellow robes) ② the imperial robe

黃袍加身 (ㄏㄨㄤˊ ㄆㄠˊ ㄐㄧㄚ ㄕㄣ)
to be made emperor (a reference to Chao Kuang-yi (趙匡胤), who was put to the throne by the rebellious troops under his command)

黃皮書 (ㄏㄨㄤˊ ㄆㄧˊ ㄕㄨ)
a yellow book

黃浦灘 (ㄏㄨㄤˊ ㄆㄨˇ ㄊㄢ)
Shanghai (an alternative name): 她在黃浦灘長大。She grew up in Shanghai.

黃麻 (ㄏㄨㄤˊ ㄇㄚˊ)
jute

黃馬褂 (ㄏㄨㄤˊ ㄇㄚˇ ㄍㄨㄚˋ)
a costume of the mandarins often bestowed by the emperor as a special favor

黃梅 (ㄏㄨㄤˊ ㄇㄟˊ)
① ripe plums ② name of county in Hupeh Province

黃梅調 (ㄏㄨㄤˊ ㄇㄟˊ ㄉㄧㄠˋ)
a popular folk melody originated from 黃梅 (name) revived by Hong Kong film makers

黃梅天氣 (ㄏㄨㄤˊ ㄇㄟˊ ㄊㄧㄢ ㄑㄧˋ)
the weather when plums ripen; early summer weather, usually rainy

黃梅雨 (ㄏㄨㄤˊ ㄇㄟˊ ㄩˇ)
early summer rain

黃毛丫頭 (ㄏㄨㄤˊ ㄇㄠˊ ㄧㄚ ·ㄊㄡ)
a fledgling little girl

黃門 (ㄏㄨㄤˊ ㄇㄣˊ)
① a yellow palace gate ② eunuch

黃米 (ㄏㄨㄤˊ ㄇㄧˇ)
① coarse rice ② millet: 黃米粥很美味。Millet porridge is delicious.

黃米麵 (ㄏㄨㄤˊ ㄇㄧˇ ㄇㄧㄢˋ)
millet flour

黃髮垂髫 (ㄏㄨㄤˊ ㄈㄚˇ ㄔㄨㄟˊ ㄊㄧㄠˊ)
the aged and the young

黃扉 (ㄏㄨㄤˊ ㄈㄟ)
the prime minister's abode

黃蜂 (ㄏㄨㄤˊ ㄈㄥ)
wasps

黃道吉日 (ㄏㄨㄤˊ ㄉㄠˋ ㄐㄧˊ ㄖˋ)
a lucky day

黃豆(ㄏㄨㄤ ㄉㄡ)
soybean: 醬油是用黃豆製造的。
Sauce is made from soybeans.

黃豆芽(ㄏㄨㄤ ㄉㄡ ㄧㄚ)
soybean sprouts

黃膽病(ㄏㄨㄤ ㄉㄢ ㄅㄧㄥ)or 黃疸
(ㄏㄨㄤ ㄉㄢ)
jaundice; icterus: 她患了黃膽病。She suffers from jaundice.

黃帝(ㄏㄨㄤ ㄉㄧ)
Huang Ti, or the Yellow Emperor, a legendary ruler

黃湯(ㄏㄨㄤ ㄊㄤ)
wine: 他灌了不少黃湯。He has taken a lot of wine.

黃鐵礦(ㄏㄨㄤ ㄊㄧㄝ ㄎㄨㄤ)
pyrites

黃天(ㄏㄨㄤ ㄊㄧㄢ)
the name assumed by Chang Chiao (張角), the leader of the Yellow Turban Rebels (黃巾賊) at the close of the Eastern Han Dynasty

黃庭堅(ㄏㄨㄤ ㄊㄧㄥ ㄐㄧㄢ)
Huang Ting-chien (1045-1105), a famed poet and calligrapher

黃土(ㄏㄨㄤ ㄊㄨ)
loess

黃土泥(ㄏㄨㄤ ㄊㄨ ㄋㄧ)
muddy loess

黃童(ㄏㄨㄤ ㄊㄨㄥ)
a child; a youngster

黃銅(ㄏㄨㄤ ㄊㄨㄥ)
brass

黃銅礦(ㄏㄨㄤ ㄊㄨㄥ ㄎㄨㄤ)
chalcopyrite

黃牛(ㄏㄨㄤ ㄋㄧㄡ)
①a common Chinese ox ② a scalper of tickets, etc. ③ (slang) to fail to appear on an appointment; to fail to show up; to break a promise: 他今天又黃牛了。He fails to show up again today.

黃牛票(ㄏㄨㄤ ㄋㄧㄡ ㄆㄧㄠ)
scalped tickets

黃蠟(ㄏㄨㄤ ㄌㄚ)
beeswax

黃老(ㄏㄨㄤ ㄌㄠ)
①Huang Ti (黃帝) and Lao-tzu (老子) ②Taoism

黃鸝(ㄏㄨㄤ ㄌㄧ)
the oriole

黃曆(ㄏㄨㄤ ㄌㄧ)
(colloquial) an almanac

黃連(ㄏㄨㄤ ㄌㄧㄢ)
Coptis chinensis, whose bitter seeds are used in Chinese medicine

黃連樹下彈琴(ㄏㄨㄤ ㄌㄧㄢ ㄕㄨ ㄒㄧㄚ ㄊㄢ ㄑㄧㄣ)
(figuratively) to seek pleasure under adverse circumstances

黃臉婆(ㄏㄨㄤ ㄌㄧㄢ ㄆㄛ)
the yellow-faced woman—my wife

黃磷(ㄏㄨㄤ ㄌㄧㄣ)
yellow phosphorus

黃粱(ㄏㄨㄤ ㄌㄧㄤ)
a variety of millet

黃粱夢(ㄏㄨㄤ ㄌㄧㄤ ㄇㄥ)
an evanescent dream(from the story of a man who had all sorts of wonderful experiences in a dream only to discover that he had just dozed off briefly while having his millet cooked)

黃落(ㄏㄨㄤ ㄌㄨㄛ)
(said of vegetation in autumn) yellow and bare

黃龍府(ㄏㄨㄤ ㄌㄨㄥ ㄈㄨ)
an administrative district set up in part of what is today's Inner Mongolia and Manchuria by the Tungusic invaders in the 11th and 12th centuries

黃瓜(ㄏㄨㄤ ㄍㄨㄚ)
a cucumber

黃冠(ㄏㄨㄤ ㄍㄨㄢ)
①a Taoist priest ②costumes of farmers

黃口孺子(ㄏㄨㄤ ㄎㄡ ㄖㄨ ㄗ)
a sucking child; a baby

黃河(ㄏㄨㄤ ㄏㄜ)
the Yellow River

黃河流域(ㄏㄨㄤ ㄏㄜ ㄌㄧㄡ ㄩ)
the Yellow River Valley

黃河水澄清(ㄏㄨㄤ ㄏㄜ ㄕㄨㄟ ㄔㄥ ㄑㄧㄥ)
the clearing of the Yellow River—an impossibility (because the turbulent water carries large amount of sands from the upperstream)

黃海(ㄏㄨㄤ ㄏㄞ)
the Yellow Sea

黃花(ㄏㄨㄤ ㄏㄨㄚ)
a chrysanthemum: 她很喜歡

黃花。She is very fond of chrysanthemums.

黃花崗(ㄏㄨㄤ ㄏㄨㄚ ㄍㄤ)
Huanghuakang, a knoll outside Canton

黃花崗七十二烈士(ㄏㄨㄤ ㄏㄨㄚ ㄍㄤ ㄑㄧ ㄕ ㄦ ㄌㄧㄝ ㄕ)
the 72 Revolutionary Martyrs of Huanghuakang (who lost their lives on March 29, 1911, in an attempt to capture Canton and were buried at 黃花崗)

黃花閨女(ㄏㄨㄤ ㄏㄨㄚ ㄍㄨㄟ ㄋㄩ)
a virgin

黃花九輪草(ㄏㄨㄤ ㄏㄨㄚ ㄐㄧㄡ ㄌㄨㄣ ㄘㄠ)
polyanthus

黃花魚(ㄏㄨㄤ ㄏㄨㄚ ㄩ)
a labrus

黃禍(ㄏㄨㄤ ㄏㄨㄛ)
the yellow peril

黃昏(ㄏㄨㄤ ㄏㄨㄣ)
dusk: 在黃昏時燈光亮了起來。The lights go on at dusk.

黃酒(ㄏㄨㄤ ㄐㄧㄡ)
①same as 紹興酒—wine from Shaohsing (紹興) ② a kind of yellowish rice wine brewed in Taiwan

黃巾(ㄏㄨㄤ ㄐㄧㄣ)
the Yellow Turban Rebels at the close of the Eastern Han Dynasty

黃金(ㄏㄨㄤ ㄐㄧㄣ)
gold: 過去人們常以黃金付帳。People used to pay in gold.

黃金海岸(ㄏㄨㄤ ㄐㄧㄣ ㄏㄞ ㄢ)
Gold Coast, Africa

黃金時代(ㄏㄨㄤ ㄐㄧㄣ ㄕ ㄉㄞ)
the golden age

黃卷青燈(ㄏㄨㄤ ㄐㄩㄢ ㄑㄧㄥ ㄉㄥ)
the Buddhist scriptures and lamps for the Buddhist altar—the life or abode of a Buddhist

黃絹幼婦(ㄏㄨㄤ ㄐㄩㄢ ㄧㄡ ㄈㄨ)
a popular code for the phrase 絕妙 (extremely exquisite)

黃旗紫蓋(ㄏㄨㄤ ㄑㄧ ㄗ ㄍㄞ)
a symbol, or spirit, of the emperor

黃鉛礦(ㄏㄨㄤ ㄑㄧㄢ ㄎㄨㄤ)
mimetite

黃麴毒素(ㄏㄨㄤ ㄑㄩ ㄉㄨ ㄙㄨ)
aflatoxin

〔黃部〕

【黍部】

黃雀(ㄏㄨㄤ ㄑㄩㄝ)
a titmouse

黃泉(ㄏㄨㄤ ㄑㄩㄢ)
Hades

黃銅鑛(ㄏㄨㄤ ㄊㄨㄥ ㄎㄨㄤ)
stannite

黃癬(ㄏㄨㄤ ㄒㄩㄢ)
favus

黃興(ㄏㄨㄤ ㄒㄧㄥ)
Huang Hsing, 1872-1916, a leader of the Chinese National Revolution

黃鐘(ㄏㄨㄤ ㄓㄨㄥ)
one of the notes in traditional Chinese music

黃種人(ㄏㄨㄤ ㄓㄨㄥ ㄖㄣ)
the yellow race; the Mongolian race

黃巢(ㄏㄨㄤ ㄔㄠ)
Huang Chao, the bloodthirsty leader of a rebellion at the time of Hsi Tzung (僖宗) during the Tang Dynasty

黃澄澄(ㄏㄨㄤ ㄔㄥ ㄔㄥ)
glistening yellow; golden

黃石公園(ㄏㄨㄤ ㄕ ㄍㄨㄥ ㄩㄢ)
Yellowstone National Park, U.S.A.

黃砂(ㄏㄨㄤ ㄕㄚ)
yellow soil; loess

黃鼠(ㄏㄨㄤ ㄕㄨ)
a kind of desert gopher

黃鼠狼(ㄏㄨㄤ ㄕㄨ ㄌㄤ)
a weasel 亦作「鼬」

黃水瘡(ㄏㄨㄤ ㄕㄨㄟ ㄔㄨㄤ)
eczema

黃熱病(ㄏㄨㄤ ㄖㄜ ㄅㄧㄥ)
yellow fever

黃色(ㄏㄨㄤ ㄙㄜ)
①yellow②decadent; obscene; pornographic

黃色小說(ㄏㄨㄤ ㄙㄜ ㄒㄧㄠ ㄕㄨㄛ)
a sex novel; a pornographic novel

黃色新聞(ㄏㄨㄤ ㄙㄜ ㄒㄧㄣ ㄨㄣ)
① yellow journalism ② sex news

黃色炸藥(ㄏㄨㄤ ㄙㄜ ㄓㄚ ㄧㄠ)
trinitrotoluene (TNT)

黃色書刊(ㄏㄨㄤ ㄙㄜ ㄕㄨ ㄎㄢ)
pornographic books and periodicals

黃芽菜(ㄏㄨㄤ ㄧㄚ ㄘㄞ)
a celery cabbage

黃油(ㄏㄨㄤ ㄧㄡ)
① butter oil ② tallow

黃楊木(ㄏㄨㄤ ㄧㄤ ㄇㄨ)
boxwood

黃鶯(ㄏㄨㄤ ㄧㄥ)
an oriole

黃魚(ㄏㄨㄤ ㄩ)
a yellow croaker

黃玉(ㄏㄨㄤ ㄩ)
topaz

五畫

【黈】 7245
ㄊㄡˇ toou tǒu
1. yellow
2. to increase

十三畫

【黌】 7246
ㄏㄨㄥˊ horng hóng
a school

黌門(ㄏㄨㄥ ㄇㄣ)
a school

黌教(ㄏㄨㄥ ㄐㄧㄠ)
schooling

黌舍(ㄏㄨㄥ ㄕㄜ)or黌宇(ㄏㄨㄥ ㄩ)
a school building

黍 部
ㄕㄨ shuu shǔ

【黍】 7247
ㄕㄨ shuu shǔ
a variety of millet

黍米(ㄕㄨ ㄇㄧ)
grain of 黍 (a variety of millet); millet grain

黍谷生春(ㄕㄨ ㄍㄨ ㄕㄥ ㄔㄨㄣ)
the advent of spring in the cold Shu-ku Hills—a change for the better of a needy life

黍稷(ㄕㄨ ㄐㄧ)
a variety of millet

黍子(ㄕㄨˇ ㄗ)
a variety of millet

黍油麥秀(ㄕㄨ ㄧㄡ ㄇㄞ ㄒㄧㄡ)
The grains grow luxuriantly among the ruins of the former capital.

三畫

【黎】 7248
ㄌㄧˊ líi
1. many; numerous
2. black; dark
3. the aborigines of Hainan
4. a Chinese family name

黎巴嫩(ㄌㄧ ㄅㄚ ㄋㄣ)
Lebanon

黎苗(ㄌㄧ ㄇㄧㄠ)
the people; the common people

黎民(ㄌㄧ ㄇㄧㄣ)or黎首(ㄌㄧ ㄕㄡ)or黎庶(ㄌㄧ ㄕㄨ)
the multitude; the common people

黎明(ㄌㄧ ㄇㄧㄥ)
dawn; daybreak: 他黎明即起。He got up at dawn.

黎老(ㄌㄧ ㄌㄠ)
an aged person

黎黑(ㄌㄧ ㄏㄟ)
black; dark

黎元洪(ㄌㄧ ㄩㄢ ㄏㄨㄥ)
Li Yüan-hung, 1864-1928, a general serving under the Manchu rulers, who joined the National Revolution and was later made president of the Republic

五畫

【黏】 7249
ㄋㄧㄢˊ nian nián
1. to stick
2. sticky; glutinous; gluey; adhesive; clammy; viscid

黏不住(ㄋㄧㄢ ㄅㄨ ㄓㄨ)
to fail to stick or adhere: 這郵票黏不住。The stamp won't stick.

黏膜(ㄋㄧㄢ ㄇㄛ)
the mucous membrane

黏米(ㄋㄧㄢ ㄇㄧ)
glutinous rice

黏度(ㄋㄧㄢ ㄉㄨ)
(chemistry) viscosity

黏貼(ㄋㄧㄢ ㄊㄧㄝ)
to glue; to paste; to stick: 這些郵票都黏貼在一起。These stamps have stuck together.

黏土(ㄋㄧㄢ ㄊㄨ)
clay: 磚是用黏土做的。Bricks are made of clay.

黏土細工(ㄋㄧㄢ ㄊㄨ ㄒㄧ ㄍㄨㄥ)
clay work

黏力(ㄋㄧㄢ ㄌㄧ)

adhesive power; viscosity

黏合劑(ㄐㄧㄚˊ ㄏㄜˊ ㄐㄧ)
adhesives

黏糊糊兒(ㄐㄧㄢˊ ㄏㄨˊ ㄏㄨˋ ㄦ˙-ㄎㄜ)
pasty; sticky; glutinous

黏涎子(ㄐㄧㄢˊ ㄒㄧㄢˊ ˙ㄗ)
slaver; slobber

黏性(ㄐㄧㄢˊ ㄒㄧㄥˋ)
viscosity

黏著(ㄐㄧㄢˊ ˙ㄓㄜ)
to stick; to adhere: 黏膠黏住那男孩的頭髮。Gum adhered to the boy's hair.

黏著(ㄓㄢ ㄓㄨˊˋ)
to stick together; to adhere

黏液(ㄐㄧㄢˊ ㄧㄝˋ)
viscous liquid; mucus; mucilage

黏油(ㄐㄧㄢˊ ㄧㄡ)
sticky oil; heavy oil

黑 部
ㄏㄜ heh hè

【黑】　7250
ㄏㄟ hei hēi
(讀音 ㄏㄜ heh hè)

1. black; dark: 這是個黑夜。It is a black night.
2. evil; sinister; gloomy: 未來似乎充滿了黑暗。The future seemed filled with gloom.

黑白(ㄏㄟ ㄅㄞˊ)
black and white—right and wrong, good and bad, etc.

黑白片(ㄏㄟ ㄅㄞˊ ㄆㄧㄢˋ)
black-and-white photos or films

黑白分明(ㄏㄟ ㄅㄞˊ ㄈㄣ ㄇㄧㄥˊ)
①right and wrong clearly distinguished ②the sharp contrast between black and white

黑白花兒(ㄏㄟ ㄅㄞˊ ㄏㄨㄚ ㄦ)
(said of animals) covered with spots of white and black; white with black spots; piebald

黑斑(ㄏㄟ ㄅㄢ)
dark spots; black specks

黑板(ㄏㄟ ㄅㄢˇ)
a blackboard

黑板刷(ㄏㄟ ㄅㄢˇ ㄕㄨㄚ)

an eraser; a wiper 亦作「黑板擦」

黑不溜俅(ㄏㄟ ㄅㄨˋ ㄌㄧㄡ ㄑㄧㄡˊ)
swarthy; dark; black

黑煤(ㄏㄟ ㄇㄟˊ)
coal: 我們缺黑煤。We are short of coal.

黑莓(ㄏㄟ ㄇㄟˊ)
a blackberry

黑眉烏嘴(ㄏㄟ ㄇㄟˊ ㄨ ㄗㄨㄟˇ)
dark or filthy (said of a face or anything that is dirty looking)

黑眸(ㄏㄟ ㄇㄡˊ)
the black pupil of the eye

黑麵包(ㄏㄟ ㄇㄧㄢˋ ㄅㄠ)
black bread; rye bread

黑名單(ㄏㄟ ㄇㄧㄥˊ ㄉㄢ)
a blacklist

黑幕(ㄏㄟ ㄇㄨˋ)
what is done under cover; a dark secret

黑道日(ㄏㄟ ㄉㄠˋ ㄖˋ)
an unlucky day

黑道人物(ㄏㄟ ㄉㄠˋ ㄖㄣˊ ㄨˋ)
a gangster; an underworld figure

黑店(ㄏㄟ ㄉㄧㄢˋ)
an inn that kills and robs lodgers

黑洞(ㄏㄟ ㄉㄨㄥˋ)
(astronomy) a black hole

黑洞洞(ㄏㄟ ㄉㄨㄥˋ ㄉㄨㄥˋ)
very dark

黑陶文化(ㄏㄟ ㄊㄠˊ ㄨㄣˊ ㄏㄨㄚˋ)
Black-Pottery Culture

黑炭(ㄏㄟ ㄊㄢˋ)
charcoal

黑體字(ㄏㄟ ㄊㄧˇ ㄗ)
boldface type

黑尿病(ㄏㄟ ㄋㄧㄠˋ ㄅㄧㄥˋ)
blackwater fever

黑奴(ㄏㄟ ㄋㄨˊ)
Negro slaves

黑龍江(ㄏㄟ ㄌㄨㄥˊ ㄐㄧㄤ)
①the Amur River ②Heilungkiang (a province in Manchuria)

黑格爾(ㄏㄟ ㄍㄜˊ ㄦˇ)
Georg Wilhelm Friedrich Hegel, 1770-1831, German philosopher

黑咕隆咚(ㄏㄟ ㄍㄨ ㄌㄨㄥˊ ㄉㄨㄥ)
very dark; gloomy; pitch-dark

黑寡婦(ㄏㄟ ㄍㄨㄚˇ ㄈㄨˋ)

a black widow (a poisonous spider)

黑鍋(ㄏㄟ ㄍㄨㄛ)
a blackened pot— (figuratively) a wrong; an injustice 參看「背黑鍋」

黑口(ㄏㄟ ㄎㄡˇ)
the black croaker

黑盒子(ㄏㄟ ㄏㄜˊ ˙ㄗ)
a cockpit voice recorder

黑海(ㄏㄟ ㄏㄞˇ)
the Black Sea

黑話(ㄏㄟ ㄏㄨㄚˋ)
argot; secret jargon of thieves, etc.

黑貨(ㄏㄟ ㄏㄨㄛˋ)
①stolen goods; smugglers' goods: 他們如何得到黑貨?How did they get the stolen goods? ②opium

黑錢(ㄏㄟ ㄑㄧㄢˊ)
(slang) underhand payment; bribery

黑漆漆(ㄏㄟ ㄑㄧ ㄑㄧ)
pitch-dark; very dark: 屋子裏黑漆漆的。The room was pitch-dark.

黑心(ㄏㄟ ㄒㄧㄣ)
a black heart; an evil heart

黑心肝(ㄏㄟ ㄒㄧㄣ ㄍㄢ)
an ungrateful person

黑猩猩(ㄏㄟ ㄒㄧㄥ ㄒㄧㄥ)
a chimpanzee

黑熊(ㄏㄟ ㄒㄩㄥˊ)
a black bear

黑痣(ㄏㄟ ㄓˋ)
a mole (on the skin)

黑種(ㄏㄟ ㄓㄨㄥˇ)or黑種人(ㄏㄟ ㄓㄨㄥˇ ㄖㄣˊ)
the black race

黑船(ㄏㄟ ㄔㄨㄢˊ)
a pirate ship

黑市(ㄏㄟ ㄕˋ)
a black market

黑社會(ㄏㄟ ㄕㄜˋ ㄏㄨㄟˋ)
underworld society; the underworld; gangsterdom: 黑社會中鮮有壽終者。Natural death is a rarity in gangsterdom.

黑手(ㄏㄟ ㄕㄡˇ)
a vicious backstage manipulator

黑手黨(ㄏㄟ ㄕㄡˇ ㄉㄤˇ)
the Black Hand; the Mafia

〔黑部〕

黑人(ㄏㄟ ㄖㄣˊ)
a Negro; a black: 他是個黑人。He is a Negro.

黑棗(ㄏㄟ ㄗㄠˇ)
dateplum persimmon (*Diospyros lotus*)

黑死病(ㄏㄟ ㄙˇ ㄅㄧㄥˋ)
the Black Death

黑色(ㄏㄟ ㄙㄜˋ)
black

黑色火藥(ㄏㄟ ㄙㄜˋ ㄏㄨㄛˇ ㄧㄠˋ)
black powder; gunpowder

黑色素(ㄏㄟ ㄙㄜˋ ㄙㄨˋ)
melanin

黑暗(ㄏㄟ ㄢˋ)
darkness; dark: 不要讓小孩睡在黑暗裏。Don't leave the child alone in the dark.

黑暗時代(ㄏㄟ ㄢˋ ㄕˊ ㄉㄞˋ)
the dark ages

黑暗世界(ㄏㄟ ㄢˋ ㄕˋ ㄐㄧㄝˋ)
a dark world—a world without justice

黑壓壓(ㄏㄟ ㄧㄚ ㄧㄚ)
extremely crowded; a dense or dark mass of

黑夜(ㄏㄟ ㄧㄝˋ)
a dark night; night

黑黝黝(ㄏㄟ ㄧㄡˇ ㄧㄡˇ)
① shiny black ② dim; dark: 這房間黑黝黝的。This room is dark.

黑煙(ㄏㄟ ㄧㄢ)
① black smoke ② opium

黑影(ㄏㄟ ㄧㄥˇ)
a dark shadow; a shadow

黑五類(ㄏㄟ ㄨˇ ㄌㄟˋ)
The five black categories of the Mao era—landlords, rich farmers, counter revolutionaries, rightists and criminals)

三畫

【黓】 7251
ㄧˋ yih yì
black

四畫

【黔】 7252
ㄑㄧㄢˊ chyan qián
1. black
2. Kweichow (an alternative name)

黔黎(ㄑㄧㄢˊ ㄌㄧˊ)

the common people

黔驢技窮(ㄑㄧㄢˊ ㄌㄩˊ ㄐㄧˋ ㄑㄩㄥˊ)
the Kweichow donkey at the end of its resourcefulness—a person who has exposed his limited ability (from the story of a donkey brought to Kweichow which the tiger first feared but soon overpowered after discovering that it could only bray and kick)

黔首(ㄑㄧㄢˊ ㄕㄡˇ)
the people; the multitude

【默】 7253
ㄇㄛˋ mon mò
1. speechless; silent
2. quiet; still

默不作聲(ㄇㄛˋ ㄅㄨˋ ㄗㄨㄛˋ ㄕㄥ)
to keep silence; to keep quiet; to refuse to speak

默片(ㄇㄛˋ ㄆㄧㄢˋ)
a silent movie

默默(ㄇㄛˋ ㄇㄛˋ)
① quietly; silently ② secretly; in one's heart

默默無言(ㄇㄛˋ ㄇㄛˋ ㄨˊ ㄧㄢˊ)
wordless; speechless; silent; in silence: 他默默無言地走了。He silently went away.

默默無聞(ㄇㄛˋ ㄇㄛˋ ㄨˊ ㄨㄣˊ)
obscure; unknown to the public; without getting public attention: 他一生默默無聞。He remains obscure all his life.

默禱(ㄇㄛˋ ㄉㄠˇ)
to pray silently: 她默禱上帝賜助。She prayed silently to God for help.

默讀(ㄇㄛˋ ㄉㄨˊ)
to read silently

默念(ㄇㄛˋ ㄋㄧㄢˋ)
① to repeat (a passage, etc.) silently inside the mind ② to ponder or think

默記(ㄇㄛˋ ㄐㄧˋ)
silently remember

默劇(ㄇㄛˋ ㄐㄩˋ)
pantomime 亦作「啞劇」

默契(ㄇㄛˋ ㄑㄧˋ)
a tacit understanding; an implicit agreement; a secret agreement

默寫(ㄇㄛˋ ㄒㄧㄝˇ)or 默書(ㄇㄛˋ ㄕㄨ)
to write from memory

默許(ㄇㄛˋ ㄒㄩˇ)

tacit permission

默識(ㄇㄛˋ ㄓˋ)
to memorize silently

默然(ㄇㄛˋ ㄖㄢˊ)
silently; in silence: 我們數分鐘默然無語。We passed several minutes in silence.

默認(ㄇㄛˋ ㄖㄣˋ)
tacit consent, confession or approval; to pass over something in silence: 他默認此事。He passed over the matter in silence.

默坐(ㄇㄛˋ ㄗㄨㄛˋ)
to sit in silence: 她默坐。She sits in silence.

默誦(ㄇㄛˋ ㄙㄨㄥˋ)
① to read silently ② to repeat (a passage, etc.) silently

默哀(ㄇㄛˋ ㄞ)
to stand in silent tribute

五畫

【點】 7254
ㄉㄧㄢˇ dean diǎn
1.a dot; a spot; a speck
2.a point: 請說要點! Come to the point, please.
3.a drop; a small amount; a little: 請給我一點點。Please give me a little.
4.snacks; refreshments
5.hours
6.to dot; to mark
7.to instruct; to teach
8.to check; to examine; to investigate; to review
9.to light; to ignite: 請將火點着。Light the fire, please.
10.to select; to pick out
11.to nod (the head): 他走過時向我點頭。He nodded to me as he passed.
12.to touch; to point at

點撥(ㄉㄧㄢˇ ㄅㄛ)
① to teach; to instruct ② to instigate

點播(ㄉㄧㄢˇ ㄅㄛ)
(agriculture) dibble seeding; dibbling

點兵(ㄉㄧㄢˇ ㄅㄧㄥ)
(in the army) to gather men for a roll call

點不着(ㄉㄧㄢˇ ㄅㄨˋ ㄓㄠˊ)
incapable of being lighted; incapable of igniting

點破(ㄉㄧㄢ ㄆㄛ)
to unravel (a mystery, etc.);
to point out

點卯(ㄉㄧㄢ ㄇㄠ)
to call the roll (of officials
in former times)

點名(ㄉㄧㄢ ㄇㄧㄥ)
①to call the roll; to make a
roll call ②to mention somebody by name

點名簿(ㄉㄧㄢ ㄇㄧㄥ ㄅㄨ)or 點名冊
a roll (of names)

點到為止(ㄉㄧㄢ ㄉㄠ ㄨㄟ ㄓ)
to go through the motions

點燈(ㄉㄧㄢ ㄉㄥ)
to light lamps: 需要我點燈嗎?
Shall I light the lamp?

點滴(ㄉㄧㄢ ㄉㄧ)
①drops; small amounts; a
bit ②(medicine) an intra-
venous drip

點滴歸公(ㄉㄧㄢ ㄉㄧ ㄍㄨㄟ ㄍㄨㄥ)
Every particle of the revenues goes into the state
coffers.—very honest

點點(ㄉㄧㄢ ㄉㄧㄢ)
①small and numerous ②to
have a snack ③to supply
punctuation marks

點定(ㄉㄧㄢ ㄉㄧㄥ)
to make corrections in writings

點頭(ㄉㄧㄢ ㄊㄡ)or 點點頭
to nod: 她點頭並微笑。She
nodded and smiled.

點頭哈腰(ㄉㄧㄢ ㄊㄡ ㄏㄚ ㄧㄠ)
to say hello

點鐵成金(ㄉㄧㄢ ㄊㄧㄝ ㄔㄥ ㄐㄧㄣ)
to transform common metal
into gold—to make a poor
writing into a literary
masterpiece by skillful
retouching

點鬼簿(ㄉㄧㄢ ㄍㄨㄟ ㄅㄨ)
a roll of ghosts (a term deri-
sively applied to the writings of the Tang Dynasty
writer Yang Chiung (楊炯),
which abounded in names of
ancients)

點勘(ㄉㄧㄢ ㄎㄢ)
to collate

點號(ㄉㄧㄢ ㄏㄠ)
a comma and the pause
mark 、

點翰林(ㄉㄧㄢ ㄏㄢ ㄌㄧㄣ)
to be chosen as a member of
翰林院

點化(ㄉㄧㄢ ㄏㄨㄚ)
to enlighten; to point out the
correct path

點火(ㄉㄧㄢ ㄏㄨㄛ)
to light a fire: 請點火。Light
the fire, please.

點交(ㄉㄧㄢ ㄐㄧㄠ)
to hand over (articles) after
a checkup

點檢(ㄉㄧㄢ ㄐㄧㄢ)
to check or inspect (articles) one by one: 他點檢所有
物品。He checked all articles
one by one.

點金成鐵(ㄉㄧㄢ ㄐㄧㄣ ㄔㄥ ㄊㄧㄝ)
to damage the beauty of the
original work (through ill-
advised changes or corrections)

點將(ㄉㄧㄢ ㄐㄧㄤ)
to make a roll call of officers

點睛(ㄉㄧㄢ ㄐㄧㄥ)
(said of writing) to provide
striking key points; to write
the punch line

點清(ㄉㄧㄢ ㄑㄧㄥ)
to count accurately

點戲(ㄉㄧㄢ ㄒㄧ)
(Peking opera) to select
from a list the performances
one desires to see

點心(ㄉㄧㄢ ㄒㄧㄣ)
snacks; refreshments: 我們在
那吃點心。We had a snack
there.

點醒(ㄉㄧㄢ ㄒㄧㄥ)
to point out someone's
errors and make him realize
them

點穴(ㄉㄧㄢ ㄒㄩㄝ)
①(Chinese boxing) to at-
tack a vital point ②to select the site of a grave
through geomancy, etc.

點著(ㄉㄧㄢ ㄓㄠ)
to have lighted or ignited

點綴(ㄉㄧㄢ ㄓㄨㄟ)
to provide decorative accessories; to embellish

點鐘(ㄉㄧㄢ ㄓㄨㄥ)
hours; o'clock

點唱(ㄉㄧㄢ ㄔㄤ)
(said of a music audience,

etc.) to select one's desired
numbers or songs for the
performers to sing or play

點穿(ㄉㄧㄢ ㄔㄨㄢ)
to unravel (a mystery, etc.)

點石成金(ㄉㄧㄢ ㄕ ㄔㄥ ㄐㄧㄣ)
①to turn stone into gold
(by merely touching it) ②
(figuratively) to make sentences or a composition perfect

點收(ㄉㄧㄢ ㄕㄡ)
to check and accept (articles that are delivered or
handed over)

點首(ㄉㄧㄢ ㄕㄡ)
to nod: 他點首表示同意。He
nodded in agreement.

點數
①(ㄉㄧㄢ ㄕㄨ) the number of
points; a score
②(ㄉㄧㄢ ㄕㄨ) to count the
number of articles or the
amount of money

點燃(ㄉㄧㄢ ㄖㄢ)
to light; to kindle; to ignite

點字(ㄉㄧㄢ ㄗ)
Braille

點子(ㄉㄧㄢ ˙ㄗ)
①a dot; a spot; a speck ②a
little; a bit ③a key point ④
ideas: 這男孩點子很多。The
boy is full of ideas.

點菜(ㄉㄧㄢ ㄘㄞ)
to order favorite dishes at a
restaurant

點竄(ㄉㄧㄢ ㄘㄨㄢ)
to alter phrases in (a composition)

點兒(ㄉㄧㄢㄦ)
①a little; a bit ②a dot; a
spot ③a punctuation point
④a drop

點眼藥(ㄉㄧㄢ ㄧㄢ ㄧㄠ)
to apply eye lotion

【黛】　7255
　　　　ㄉㄞˋ dày
1. a bluish-black material used
by ancient women to
blacken their eyebrows
2. a beauty

黛眉(ㄉㄞ ㄇㄟ)
①to blacken the eyebrows
②blackened eyebrows of
women

黛螺(ㄉㄞ ㄌㄨㄛ)
①a kind of green paint in

【黑部】

〔黑部〕

Chinese painting ② a woman's blackened eyebrows and spiral headdress

黛綠（カㄞˋ ㄌㄩˋ）
①a beauty in full dress ② dark green

黛鬢（カㄞˋ ㄈㄣˋ）
glossy dark hair of women

黛蛾（カㄞˋ ㄜˊ）
beautiful eyebrows of a woman

黛奧辛 or 戴奧辛（カㄞˋ ㄠˋ ㄒㄧㄣ）
dioxin

【黜】 7256　ㄔㄨˋ chuh chù
1. to reject; to dismiss
2. to dismiss; to degrade; to demote

黜免（ㄔㄨˋ ㄇㄧㄢˇ）
to dismiss from office; to remove from office

黜退（ㄔㄨˋ ㄊㄨㄟˋ）
to dismiss; to send away

黜華崇實（ㄔㄨˋ ㄏㄨㄚˊ ㄔㄨㄥˊ ㄕˊ）
to reject luxury and uphold simplicity

黜陟（ㄔㄨˋ ㄓˋ）
demotion and promotion

黜斥（ㄔㄨˋ ㄔˋ）
to dispel; to reject; to keep away

黜升（ㄔㄨˋ ㄕㄥ）
demotion and promotion

【黝】 7257　ㄧㄡˇ yeou yǒu
bluish black

黝黑（ㄧㄡˇ ㄏㄟ）
(said of a complexion) dark; swarthy

黝堊（ㄧㄡˇ ㄜˋ）
①black pillars and white walls ② to decorate with both white paint and black paint

黝黝（ㄧㄡˇ ㄧㄡˇ）
gloomy; dark

六畫

【點】 7258　ㄒㄧㄚˇ shya xiǎ
1. smart; clever; shrewd
2. crafty; cunning; artful; wily

點吏（ㄒㄧㄚˇ ㄌㄧˋ）
a crafty evil official

點慧（ㄒㄧㄚˇ ㄏㄨㄟˋ）
clever; smart; shrewd: 她是個

點慧的女孩子。She is a very clever girl.

點智（ㄒㄧㄚˇ ㄓˋ）
clever; smart; shrewd; crafty

點鼠（ㄒㄧㄚˇ ㄕㄨˇ）
①a cunning rat ②a cunning person

【黟】 7259　ㄧ yi yī
1. ebony
2. dark; black

八畫

【黥】 7260　ㄑㄧㄥˊ chyng qíng
ancient punishment of tattooing the face; branding

黥面（ㄑㄧㄥˊ ㄇㄧㄢˋ）or 黥首（ㄑㄧㄥˊ ㄕㄡˇ）
ancient punishment of tattooing the face

【黧】 7261　ㄌㄧˊ li lí
dark yellow; sallow

黧黑（ㄌㄧˊ ㄏㄟ）
(said of a complexion) dark: 他的膚色黧黑。He has a dark complexion.

黧黃（ㄌㄧˊ ㄏㄨㄤˊ）
①dark yellow; sallow ② an oriole

黧雞（ㄌㄧˊ ㄐㄧ）
the look of worry, cunning, jealousy, or hatred revealed through one's eyes

黧鶯（ㄌㄧˊ ㄧㄥ）
a kind of oriole

【黨】 7262　ㄉㄤˇ daang dǎng
1. a party; a faction; a clique; a gang; an association
2. relatives
3. a community of 500 families (in ancient times)
4. to take sides; to associate; to be a partizan
5. as in 鄉黨—village

黨部（ㄉㄤˇ ㄅㄨˋ）
the headquarters of a political party

黨派（ㄉㄤˇ ㄆㄞˋ）
factions; parties; cliques: 這個國家有許多黨派。There are many parties in this country.

黨派政治（ㄉㄤˇ ㄆㄞˋ ㄓㄥˋ ㄓˋ）
party politics

黨費（ㄉㄤˇ ㄈㄟˋ）

membership dues paid to a political party

黨代表（ㄉㄤˇ ㄉㄞˋ ㄅㄧㄠˇ）
a party representative

黨徒（ㄉㄤˇ ㄊㄨˊ）
followers; parties and their members (a derogatory expression)

黨同伐異（ㄉㄤˇ ㄊㄨㄥˊ ㄈㄚˊ ㄧˋ）
to unite with those who agree and fight those who differ

黨歌（ㄉㄤˇ ㄍㄜ）
the song of a political party

黨綱（ㄉㄤˇ ㄍㄤ）
the platform of a political party

黨錮（ㄉㄤˇ ㄍㄨˋ）
interdiction of party activities by confinement of partisans, etc.

黨國（ㄉㄤˇ ㄍㄨㄛˊ）
the party and the nation: 他忠於黨國。He is royal to the party and the nation.

黨國元老（ㄉㄤˇ ㄍㄨㄛˊ ㄩㄢˊ ㄌㄠˇ）
an elder statesman of the party and the nation

黨棍（ㄉㄤˇ ㄍㄨㄣˋ）
a dirty politician who uses his party membership as a means of promoting self-interest

黨魁（ㄉㄤˇ ㄎㄨㄟˊ）
a party boss; a party chieftain: 他是共和黨的黨魁。He is the boss of the Republican Party.

黨禍（ㄉㄤˇ ㄏㄨㄛˋ）
disasters resulting from partisanship

黨徽（ㄉㄤˇ ㄏㄨㄟ）
the emblem of a political party

黨籍（ㄉㄤˇ ㄐㄧˊ）
a party affiliation

黨紀（ㄉㄤˇ ㄐㄧˋ）
party discipline

黨見（ㄉㄤˇ ㄐㄧㄢˋ）
sentiments of a party, clique, etc.

黨禁（ㄉㄤˇ ㄐㄧㄣˋ）
interdiction of party activities by confinement of partisans, etc.

黨旗（ㄉㄤˇ ㄑㄧˊ）
the flag of a political party

黨性(カオ ㄒ丨ㄥ)
loyalty to the party

黨章(カオ ㄓㄤ)
the constitution of a political party

黨爭(カオ ㄓㄥ)
a factional fight; a partisan war

黨政(カオ ㄓㄥ)
the party and the government administration

黨證(カオ ㄓㄥ)
a membership card of a political party

黨人(カオ ㄖㄣ)
partisans

黨義(カオ 丨)
principles of a party

黨務(カオ ㄨ)
party affairs

黨外(カオ ㄨㄞ)
outside the party

黨羽(カオ ㄩ)
adherents or followers (especially of a condemned leader); members of a clique

黨與(カオ ㄩ)
fellow partisans

黨員(カオ ㄩㄢ)
a party member; a partisan

【黝】7263
丨ㄨ yuh yù
yellowish black

【黯】7264
丨ㄢ yean yǎn
bluish black

九畫

【黯】7265
ㄢ ann àn
1. very dark; pitch-dark: 這房間太黯, This room is too dark.
2. miserable; dismal

黯淡無光(ㄢ カㄢ ㄨ ㄍㄨㄤ)
gloomy; somber; dismal

黯然消魂(ㄢ ㄖㄢ ㄒ丨ㄠ ㄏㄨㄣ)
deeply affected (as by the sorrow of parting)

黯然失色(ㄢ ㄖㄢ ㄕ ㄙㄜ)
to appear very dull or poor in comparison; to be outshone; to be eclipsed

黯然神傷(ㄢ ㄖㄢ ㄕㄣ ㄕㄤ)
to feel dejected; to feel depressed

黲慘(ㄘㄢ ㄘㄢ)
gloomy; dismal

黲黮(ㄊㄢ)
gloomy; somber; sad

【黮】7266 1.ㄊㄢ taan tǒn
pitch-dark; pitch-black

【黮】7266 2.ㄕㄣ shenn shèn
a mulberry

十一畫

【黪】7267
ㄘㄢ tsaan cǒn
light bluish dark

黪白(ㄘㄢ ㄅㄞ)
gray

黪淡(ㄘㄢ ㄉㄢ)
gloomy; dull

【黴】7268
ㄇㄟ mei méi
1. mold; mildew; must
2. germs; bacteria
3. fungi
4. dirty; dingy

黴毒(ㄇㄟ ㄉㄨ)
syphilis 亦作「梅毒」

黴爛(ㄇㄟ ㄌㄢ)
decaying and mildew-covered

黴菌(ㄇㄟ ㄐㄩㄣ)
①fungi; mold fungi ②germs; bacteria

十三畫

【黵】7269
ㄉㄢ daan dàn
to tattoo the face

黵面(ㄉㄢ ㄇ丨ㄢ)
an ancient punishment of tattooing a criminal's face

十四畫

【黡】7270
丨ㄢ yean yǎn
black moles (on the skin)

十五畫

【黷】7271
ㄉㄨ dwu dú
1. to tarnish
2. to be rash about
3. to corrupt

黷武(ㄉㄨ ㄨ)
to use military might rashly; to be trigger-happy

黹 部
ㄓ jyy zhǐ

【黹】7272
ㄓ jyy zhǐ
embroidery; needlework

五畫

【黼】7273
ㄈㄨ fwu fǔ
a kind of embroidered design on ancient sacrificial robes; a kind of sacrificial robes

七畫

【黼】7274
ㄈㄨ fuu fǔ
a kind of ancient sacrificial robes embroidered with hatchets

黼黻(ㄈㄨ ㄈㄨ)
axes embroidered on an official's robe as a symbol of distinction

黽 部
ㄇ丨ㄣ miin mǐn

【黽】7275
ㄇ丨ㄣ miin mǐn
to strive; to endeavor

黽勉(ㄇ丨ㄣ ㄇ丨ㄢ)
to strive; to endeavor; to exert oneself

四畫

【黿】7276
ㄩㄢ yuan yuán
a kind of large turtle

黿鳴鱉應(ㄩㄢ ㄇ丨ㄥ ㄅ丨ㄝ 丨ㄥ)
(literally) The small turtle responds as the large turtle calls.—The lord and his vassals get along quite well.

〔黹·黽部〕

五畫

【鼂】 7277
ㄔㄠ ㄔㄠ chaur chǎo
1. a kind of sea turtle
2. a Chinese family name

六畫

【鼃】 7278
(蛙) ㄨㄚ ua wā
a frog

八畫

【鼅】 7279
(蜘) ㄓ jy zhī
a spider

十一畫

【鰲】 7280
ㄠ aur áo
a huge sea turtle

鰲背負山
My indebtedness to you is
as great as the load of a
mountain to a turtle. 參看「鰲
戴」

鰲抃
to clap and dance with joy

鰲峯 (ㄈㄥ)or 鰲禁 (ㄐㄧㄣ)or 鰲
署 (ㄕㄨ)or 鰲頭 (ㄊㄡ)
the highly revered center for
men of letters 亦作「翰苑」

鰲戴
to feel indebted (used in expressing one's gratitude)

鰲頭 or 鰲頭 (ㄊㄡ)
the top successful candidate
in a civil service examination under the former system

十二畫

【鱉】 7281
(鱉) ㄅㄧㄝ bie biē
Trionyx sinensis, a kind of
fresh-water turtle 亦作「甲魚」

鱉縮頭 (ㄙㄨㄛ ㄊㄡ)
to hide oneself from danger
(as a turtle withdraws its
head under its shell); to
behave cowardly

【鼉】 7282
ㄊㄨㄛ two tuó

---

a kind of water lizard (whose
skin was often used to make
drums)

鼉更 (ㄍㄥ)
to beat the watches (with
drums)

鼉鼓 (ㄍㄨ)
①drums made of the skins
of large water lizards;
lizard-skin drums ②to beat
the watches with drums

鼎 部
ㄉㄧㄥ diing dǐng

【鼎】 7283
ㄉㄧㄥ diing dǐng
1. a huge tripod of bronze
with two ears; a heavy
three-legged caldron or sacrificial vessel
2. vigorous; thriving; flourishing
3. involving three parts or
things; triangular

鼎沸 (ㄈㄟ)
tumultuous; boiling; hubbub;
noisy and confused

鼎臣 (ㄔㄣ)
the three chief ministers of
the state (in ancient times)

鼎鼎大名 (ㄉㄧㄥ ㄉㄧㄥ ㄉㄚ ㄇㄧㄥ)
renowned; famous; illustrious; celebrated; a great reputation

鼎鼐 (ㄋㄞ)
the office of the prime minister; premiership

鼎力 (ㄌㄧ)
①great strength; herculean
strength ②your kind effort

鼎力玉成 (ㄌㄧ ㄩ ㄔㄥ)
to help accomplish this
small task with your great
power (in complimenting
another for a help sought or
rendered)

鼎立 (ㄌㄧ)
(said of rival groups, etc.)
to develop a triangular balance of power

鼎革 (ㄍㄜ)
(said of dynastic changes)
replacement of the old by

---

the new

鼎湖 (ㄏㄨ)
an emperor's death

鼎鑊 (ㄏㄨㄛ)
①a caldron used as a cooking vessel in ancient times
②to cook an offending minister in a caldron, one of the
severest punishments in
ancient times

鼎甲 (ㄐㄧㄚ)
the three top candidates in
the imperial examination
under the former civil service examination system

鼎席 (ㄒㄧ)
the office of a minister

鼎新 (ㄒㄧㄣ)
to renew

鼎姓 (ㄒㄧㄥ)
a great clan

鼎峙 (ㄓ)
to form a triangular balance
of power

鼎折足 (ㄓㄜ ㄗㄨ)
a tripod with a broken leg
—a minister who ruins the
state

鼎鐘 (ㄓㄨㄥ)
bells or vessels engraved
with inscriptions honoring
worthy men

鼎臣 (ㄔㄣ)
important courtiers; high
ministers

鼎食 (ㄕ)
food of the nobility

鼎士 (ㄕ)
a strong man; a man of
great strength

鼎盛 (ㄕㄥ)
in a period of great prosperity; prosperous; thriving; vigorous; flourishing

鼎足 (ㄗㄨ)
①a triangular situation; a
triangular balance of power
②the three top ministers of
a state in ancient times

鼎足而三 (ㄗㄨ ㄦ ㄙㄢ)
divided into three rival
groups; developing into a
triangular balance of power

鼎族 (ㄗㄨ)
a great clan 亦作「鼎姓」

鼎俎 (ㄗㄨ)
①a prime minister; a pre-

mier ② vessels holding sacrificial animals; cooking vessels

鼎彝(ㄉㄧㄥˇ ㄧˊ)
sacrificial vessels engraved with inscriptions in honor of worthy men

鼎業(ㄉㄧㄥˇ ㄧㄝˋ)
a ruler's achievements

鼎言(ㄉㄧㄥˇ ㄧㄢˊ)
words of importance; important statements

鼎位(ㄉㄧㄥˇ ㄨㄟˋ)
the office of the prime minister; premiership

鼎運(ㄉㄧㄥˇ ㄩㄣˋ)or 鼎祚(ㄉㄧㄥˇ ㄗㄨㄛˋ)
the destiny of the nation

二畫

【鼐】 7284
ㄋㄞ nay nǎi
a huge tripod caldron

【鼏】 7285
ㄇㄧˋ mih mì
the cover of a tripod caldron

三畫

【鼒】 7286
ㄗ tzy zī
a tripod with a small opening on the top

鼓 部
《ㄨˇ guu gǔ

【鼓】 7287
《ㄨˇ guu gǔ
1. drums
2. to drum; to beat a drum
3. to vibrate; to quiver
4. to rouse; to stir up; to instigate

鼓盆(《ㄨˇ ㄆㄣˊ)or 鼓盆之戚(《ㄨˇ ㄆㄣˊ ㄓ ㄑㄧ)
to pound on a tub—to be bereaved of one's wife

鼓鼙(《ㄨˇ ㄆㄧˊ)
a kind of military drum

鼓膜(《ㄨˇ ㄇㄛˋ)
the eardrum; the tympanic

membrane

鼓風爐(《ㄨˇ ㄈㄥ ㄌㄨˊ)
a blast furnace

鼓腹(《ㄨˇ ㄈㄨˋ)
① well-fed and unoccupied; eating well and living well
② to beat one's belly as a drum

鼓刀(《ㄨˇ ㄉㄠ)
to manipulate the knife—to slaughter animals

鼓動(《ㄨˇ ㄉㄨㄥˋ)
to instigate; to rouse; to incite; to stir up; to excite

鼓樓(《ㄨˇ ㄌㄡˊ)
a drum tower

鼓浪嶼(《ㄨˇ ㄌㄤˋ ㄩˇ)
Kulangyu, an islet facing Amoy, Fukien

鼓勵(《ㄨˇ ㄌㄧˋ)
to encourage; to hearten: 英文老師講得多話鼓勵我們。Our English teacher said a lot to encourage us.

鼓號樂隊(《ㄨˇ ㄏㄠˋ ㄩㄝˋ ㄉㄨㄟˋ)
a drum and bugle band

鼓惑(《ㄨˇ ㄏㄨㄛˋ)
to instigate; to induce to go astray

鼓角(《ㄨˇ ㄐㄩㄝˊ)
drums and horns (especially in the army)

鼓起勇氣(《ㄨˇ ㄑㄧˇ ㄩㄥˇ ㄑㄧˋ)
to pluck up courage

鼓掌(《ㄨˇ ㄓㄤˇ)
to clap the hands; to give applause: 他們鼓掌歡迎他。They clapped their hands to welcome him.

鼓脹(《ㄨˇ ㄓㄤˋ)
bloating (of the abdomen, etc.); tympanites; to bloat

鼓吹(《ㄨˇ ㄔㄨㄟ)
①(《ㄨˇ ㄔㄨㄟ) to advocate; to uphold; to promote; to propagate: 他鼓吹多建學校。He advocates building more schools.
②(《ㄨˇ ㄔㄨㄟ)a kind of ancient court music

鼓舌如簧(《ㄨˇ ㄕㄜˊ ㄖㄨˊ ㄏㄨㄤˊ)
to wag one's tongue (for honeyed words, malicious gossip, etc.)

鼓手(《ㄨˇ ㄕㄡˇ)
a drum player; a drummer: 少年鼓手擊鼓。The boy drum-

mer beat a drum.

鼓聲(《ㄨˇ ㄕㄥ)
drumbeats

鼓譟 or 鼓噪(《ㄨˇ ㄗㄠˋ)
to raise an uproar; to be uproarious: 聽衆鼓譟起來。The audience are uproarious.

鼓兒詞(《ㄨˇ ㄦˊ ㄘˊ)
a form of folk entertainment with singing accompanied by drums

鼓翼(《ㄨˇ ㄧˋ)
to flap the wings: 鳥正鼓翼飛翔。The bird was flapping its wings.

鼓舞(《ㄨˇ ㄨˇ)
① to rouse; to inspire; to stir up; to excite; to spur on: 成功鼓舞我們做出更大的努力。Success inspires us to greater efforts. ② to dance for joy; to rejoice

鼓舞士氣(《ㄨˇ ㄨˇ ㄕˋ ㄑㄧˋ)
to enhance troop morale; to cheer up troops: 他們唱歌鼓舞士氣。They sing to cheer up troops.

鼓樂喧天(《ㄨˇ ㄩㄝˋ ㄒㄩㄢ ㄊㄧㄢ)
Loud music fills the air.

五畫

【鼕】 7288
ㄉㄨㄥ dong dōng
the rattle of drums

六畫

【鼗】 7289
ㄊㄠˊ taur táo
a kind of small hand-drum with two swinging knobs (that can strike the face of the drum being twirled)

八畫

【鼙】 7290
ㄆㄧˊ pyi pí
a kind of war drum

鼙(ㄆㄧˊ 《ㄨˇ)
a kind of war drum

【鼠·鼻部】

鼠 部
ㄕㄨ shuu **shǔ**

【鼠】 7291
ㄕㄨ shuu shǔ
a mouse; a rat: 老鼠吱吱叫。
A mouse squeaks.

鼠輩(ㄕㄨ ㄅㄟ)
a mean fellow

鼠目(ㄕㄨ ㄇㄨ)
①small, protruding eyes ②
lacking foresight; short-
sighted

鼠目寸光(ㄕㄨ ㄇㄨ ㄘㄨㄣ ㄍㄨㄤ)
lacking foresight; short-
sighted

鼠膽(ㄕㄨ ㄉㄢ)
cowardice

鼠肚雞腸(ㄕㄨ ㄉㄨ ㄐㄧ ㄔㄤ)
(literally) a rat's stomach
and a chicken's bowels
—narrow-mindedness

鼠遁(ㄕㄨ ㄉㄨㄣ)
to flee helter-skelter like a
rat

鼠狼(ㄕㄨ ㄌㄤ)
a weasel 亦作「鼬鼠」

鼠肝蟲臂(ㄕㄨ ㄍㄢ ㄔㄨㄥ ㄅㄧ)
(literally) a rat's liver and
an insect's limbs—things of
very little value

鼠口不出象牙(ㄕㄨ ㄎㄡ ㄅㄨ ㄔㄨ
ㄒㄧㄤ ㄧㄚ)
(figuratively) to utter nothing but dirty words

鼠洞(ㄕㄨ ㄉㄨㄥ)or鼠穴(ㄕㄨ ㄒㄩㄝ)
a rat hole

鼠灰色(ㄕㄨ ㄏㄨㄟ ㄙㄜ)
dark gray

鼠技(ㄕㄨ ㄐㄧ)
(literally) a rat's ability
—limited talents; versatile
but not impressive 或 Jack
of all trades but master of
none.

鼠竊狗盜(ㄕㄨ ㄑㄧㄝ ㄍㄡ ㄉㄠ)
(figuratively) petty thieves
and small-time robbers

鼠蹊(ㄕㄨ ㄒㄧ)
the groin

鼠子(ㄕㄨ ㄗ)
a mean fellow

鼠攘狼奔(ㄕㄨ ㄖㄤ ㄌㄤ ㄅㄣ)
to run away in all directions

鼠竄(ㄕㄨ ㄘㄨㄢ)
to run away like frightened
rats: 敵軍抱頭鼠竄。Our en-
emies run away like frightened rats.

鼠思(ㄕㄨ ㄙ)
to be pensive

鼠疫(ㄕㄨ ㄧ)
a bubonic plague; a pestilence

鼠疫菌(ㄕㄨ ㄧ ㄐㄩㄣ)
plague bacilli

鼠牙雀角(ㄕㄨ ㄧㄚ ㄑㄩㄝ ㄐㄩㄝ)
(figuratively) to carry on a
lawsuit; to litigate

鼠眼(ㄕㄨ ㄧㄢ)
①small, protruding eyes ②
lack of foresight

鼠尾草(ㄕㄨ ㄨㄟ ㄘㄠ)
Salvia japonica, a kind of
medical herb

五畫

【鼬】 7292
ㄧㄡ yow yòu
a weasel

鼬鼠(ㄧㄡ ㄕㄨ)
a weasel

【鼪】 7293
ㄕㄥ sheng shēng
a weasel

七畫

【鼯】 7294
ㄨ wu wú
a flying squirrel

鼯鼠(ㄨ ㄕㄨ)
a flying squirrel

鼯鼠技窮(ㄨ ㄕㄨ ㄐㄧ ㄑㄩㄥ)
at one's wit's end: 他幾乎鼯
鼠技窮。He was almost at his
wit's end.

九畫

【鼴】 7295
ㄧㄢ yean yǎn
a mole (a burrowing ani-
mal)

十畫

【鼹】 7296
ㄒㄧ shi xi
a mouse

【鼺】 7297
ㄌㄟ yean yǎn
Mogera wogura wogura, a
kind of insectivorous rodent

鼻 部
ㄅㄧ byi **bí**

【鼻】 7298
ㄅㄧ byi **bí**
1. a nose
2. before any others; first

鼻峯(ㄅㄧ ㄈㄥ)
the bridge of the (human)
nose

鼻竇炎(ㄅㄧ ㄉㄡ ㄧㄢ)
sinusitis

鼻塌嘴歪(ㄅㄧ ㄊㄚ ㄗㄨㄟ ㄨㄞ)
(literally) a snub nose and a
wry mouth—a very ugly face

鼻頭(ㄅㄧ ㄊㄡ)
a nose

鼻涕(ㄅㄧ ㄊㄧ)
nasal mucus; snivel; nasal
drips

鼻牛兒(ㄅㄧ ㄋㄧㄡ ㄦ)
nose wax; nose dirt

鼻梁兒(ㄅㄧ ㄌㄧㄤ ㄦ)
the bridge of the nose

鼻孔(ㄅㄧ ㄎㄨㄥ)
nostrils

鼻尖(ㄅㄧ ㄐㄧㄢ)
the tip of the nose

鼻腔(ㄅㄧ ㄑㄧㄤ)
the nasal cavity

鼻青臉腫(ㄅㄧ ㄑㄧㄥ ㄌㄧㄢ ㄓㄨㄥ)
a bloody nose and a swollen
face—bruised in the face: 他
摔得鼻青臉腫。He fell and
bruised his face.

鼻息(ㄅㄧ ㄒㄧ)
the breath

鼻息如雷(ㄅㄧ ㄒㄧ ㄖㄨ ㄌㄟ)
to snort or snore terribly

鼻血(ㄅㄧ ㄒㄧㄝ)
nosebleed; nasal hemorrhage

鼻準(ㄅㄧ ㄓㄨㄣ)
the tip of the nose

鼻子(ㄅㄧ ·ㄗ)
a nose

鼻子眼兒(ㄅ|ˊ·ㄦ ㄧㄢˇ|ㄦ)
nostrils

鼻祖(ㄅ|ˊ ㄗㄨˇ)
a founder; an originator

鼻塞(ㄅ|ˊ ㄙㄜˋ)
to have a stuffy nose; nasal congestion

鼻煙(ㄅ|ˊ |ㄢ)
snuff (a kind of tobacco); to snuff

鼻煙壺(ㄅ|ˊ |ㄢ ㄏㄨˊ)
a snuff bottle

鼻咽癌(ㄅ|ˊ |ㄢ |ˊ)
nasopharyngeal carcinoma

鼻炎(ㄅ|ˊ |ㄢˊ)
nasal catarrh: 他能治好你的鼻炎. He can cure your nasal catarrh.

鼻癌(ㄅ|ˊ |ˊ)
nasopharyngeal cancer

鼻音(ㄅ|ˊ |ㄣ)
(phonetics) nasal sounds; nasals

三畫

【鼾】 7299
ㄏㄢ han hān
to snore

鼾聲如雷(ㄏㄢ ㄕㄥ ㄖㄨˊ ㄌㄟˊ)
to snore terribly

鼾睡(ㄏㄢ ㄕㄨㄟˋ)
a heavy sleep with snoring

五畫

【齁】 7300
ㄏㄡ hou hōu
1. snoring; snorting
2. (sickeningly) sweet or salty

十畫

【齅】 7301
(嗅) ㄒ|ㄡˋ shiow xiù
to smell

十三畫

【齈】 7302
ㄋㄨㄥˊ nong nóng
a kind of nasal ailment characterized by abundance of snivel

齊 部
ㄑ|ˊ chyi qi

【齊】 7303
　　1. ㄑ|ˊ chyi qi
1. equal; uniform; to be on a level
2. name of an ancient feudal state
3. name of a dynasty
4. to set in order
5. a Chinese family name

齊備(ㄑ|ˊ ㄅㄟˋ)
everything complete; everything ready

齊步(ㄑ|ˊ ㄅㄨˋ)
in step; uniform steps

齊眉(ㄑ|ˊ ㄇㄟˊ)
respect between husband and wife—referring to the story of Liang Hung (梁鴻) and Meng Kuang(孟光)

齊民(ㄑ|ˊ ㄇ|ㄣˊ)
the masses; the multitude; the common people; the ordinary people

齊名(ㄑ|ˊ ㄇ|ㄥˊ)
equally well-known; equal in fame

齊大非偶(ㄑ|ˊ ㄉㄚˋ ㄈㄟ ㄡˇ)
(said of a family as possible future in-laws) too rich to be a good match

齊東野語(ㄑ|ˊ ㄉㄨㄥ |ㄝˇ ㄩˇ)
unreliable talk

齊頭並進(ㄑ|ˊ ㄊㄡˊ ㄅ|ㄥˋ ㄐ|ㄣˋ)
to go ahead together; to march together; to do something simultaneously; to do two or more things at once

齊年(ㄑ|ˊ ㄋ|ㄢˊ)
of the same age: 他們齊年. They are of the same age.

齊國(ㄑ|ˊ ㄍㄨㄛˊ)
the ancient state of Chi in what is today's Shantung

齊桓公(ㄑ|ˊ ㄏㄨㄢˊ ㄍㄨㄥ)or 齊桓(ㄑ|ˊ ㄏㄨㄢˊ)
a powerful ruler till 643 B.C. of the ancient state of Chi (齊) during the Epoch of Warring States

齊集(ㄑ|ˊ ㄐ|ˊ)

all assembled: 學生們在禮堂齊集. The students were all assembled in the school hall.

齊家(ㄑ|ˊ ㄐ|ㄚ)
to govern one's family; to regulate one's family

齊齊哈爾(ㄑ|ˊ ㄑ|ˊ ㄏㄚ ㄦˇ)
Tsitsihar (or Lungkiang), Manchuria

齊驅(ㄑ|ˊ ㄑㄩ)
to advance abreast—to be equal in ability

齊全(ㄑ|ˊ ㄑㄩㄢˊ)
everything complete; nothing missing; all in readiness: 我希望一切齊全. I hope nothing is missing.

齊心(ㄑ|ˊ ㄒ|ㄣ)
of one mind: 如果我們齊心,一切事情就好辦了. When we are of one mind, everything becomes easy.

齊整(ㄑ|ˊ ㄓㄥˇ)
orderly; tidy; neat

齊齒(ㄑ|ˊ ㄔˇ)
① of the same age ② (traditional Chinese phonetics) a final beginning with an unrounded high front vowel (ia, ian, etc.)

齊楚(ㄑ|ˊ ㄔㄨˇ)
① orderly; tidy ② Chi and Chu, two important feudal states in the Epoch of Warring States

齊聲(ㄑ|ˊ ㄕㄥ)
in unison; with one voice

齊人之福(ㄑ|ˊ ㄖㄣˊ ㄓ ㄈㄨˊ)
to have more than one wife; to have a concubine: 那商人享齊人之福. The merchant has more than one wife.

齊一(ㄑ|ˊ|)
uniform; equal

【齋】 7303
　　2.(齊) ㄓㄞ jai zhāi
pious; respectful; chaste

齋莊(ㄓㄞ ㄓㄨㄤ)
respectful; sober; serious

齋宿(ㄓㄞ ㄙㄨˋ)
to show piety by passing the night in fasting·

齋糠(ㄓㄞ ㄙㄨˋ)
grave and respectful

【齊】 7303
　　3. ㄗ tzy zī
1. the lower edge of a garment

〔齒
部〕

2. same as 粢—sacrificial grain
齊盛(ㄗ ㄔㄥˊ)
sacrifices offered
齊衰(ㄗ ㄘㄨㄞ)
dress worn for the second
degree of mourning

三畫

【齋】 7304
(齋) ㄓㄞ jāi zhāi
1. pious; respectful; chaste;
pure
2. to abstain from meat; to
fast
3. to purify oneself
4. to provide Buddhist monks
with meals
5. a room for study; a study; a
school
6. a vegetarian meal
齋飯(ㄓㄞ ㄈㄢˋ)
a vegetarian meal for a
Buddhist monk
齋壇(ㄓㄞ ㄊㄢˊ)
an altar for Buddhist worship
齋堂(ㄓㄞ ㄊㄤˊ)
a dining room in a Buddhist
temple
齋戒(ㄓㄞ ㄐㄧㄝˋ)
to abstain from meat, wine,
etc. (when offering sacrifices to gods); to fast
齋戒沐浴(ㄓㄞ ㄐㄧㄝˋ ㄇㄨˋ ㄩˋ)
to purify oneself by observing abstinent rules and bathing
齋醮(ㄓㄞ ㄐㄧㄠˋ)
to perform a Buddhist service
齋心(ㄓㄞ ㄒㄧㄣ)
to purify the mind
齋主(ㄓㄞ ㄓㄨˇ)
the host at a Buddhist vegetarian dinner
齋舍(ㄓㄞ ㄕㄜˋ)or齋屋(ㄓㄞ ㄨ)
①a room for fasting ②a
study ③a school
齋僧(ㄓㄞ ㄙㄥ)
to provide Buddhist monks
with meals
齋月(ㄓㄞ ㄩㄝˋ)
①(Buddhism) the first, fifth
and ninth lunar months ②
(Islam) Ramadan; the month
of fast

七畫

【齎】 7305
1.(賫, 賷) ㄐㄧ jī jī
1. to present; to offer
2. to harbor; to have in one's
mind; to entertain
齎盜糧(ㄐㄧ ㄉㄠˋ ㄌㄧㄤˊ)
(figuratively) to become the
unwitting tool of the enemy
齎恨(ㄐㄧ ㄏㄣˋ)
to harbor hatred; to entertain a grudge
齎志(ㄐㄧ ㄓˋ)
to cherish unfulfilled ambitions
齎咨(ㄐㄧ ㄗ)
an exclamation
齎送(ㄐㄧ ㄙㄨㄥˋ)
to present; to offer
【齎】 7305
2. ㄗ tzy zī
same as 資—wealth; estates

九畫

【齏】 7306
ㄐㄧ jī jī
1. pulverized; powdered
2. seasonings in powdered
form
齏粉(ㄐㄧ ㄈㄣˇ)
①fine powder; powdered;
pulverized ②to be completely annihilated; to run the
greatest risk; to raze to the
ground
齏糟(ㄐㄧ ㄗㄠ)
minute and complicated

齒 部
ㄔˇ chyy chǐ

【齒】 7307
ㄔˇ chyy chǐ
1. teeth: 他拔掉兩顆牙齒。He
had two teeth pulled.
2. age
3. to speak of; to mention: 不
足掛齒。Don't mention it.
4. a tooth-like part of anything
齒髮(ㄔˇ ㄈㄚ)

one's tooth and hair—one's
age
齒蠹(ㄔˇ ㄉㄨˋ)
tooth decay
齒痛(ㄔˇ ㄊㄨㄥˋ)
toothache
齒冷(ㄔˇ ㄌㄥˇ)
to scorn; to ridicule; to jeer
齒輪(ㄔˇ ㄌㄨㄣˊ)
a cogwheel; a gear wheel; a
gear
齒垢(ㄔˇ ㄍㄡˋ)
tartar (on the teeth)
齒根(ㄔˇ ㄍㄣ)
the root of a tooth
齒軌(ㄔˇ ㄍㄨㄟˇ)
a rack railway
齒冠(ㄔˇ ㄍㄨㄢ)
the crown of a tooth
齒科(ㄔˇ ㄎㄜ)
dentistry: 他主修齒科。He is a
dentistry major.
齒寒(ㄔˇ ㄏㄢˊ)
(said of either of two interdependent beings) to suffer
due to failure of the other
齒及(ㄔˇ ㄐㄧˊ)
to mention (something not
worth mentioning)
齒擊(ㄔˇ ㄐㄧˊ)
to clatter the teeth in trembling
齒決(ㄔˇ ㄐㄩㄝˊ)
to bite off with the teeth
齒腔(ㄔˇ ㄑㄧㄤ)
the gum of the tooth
齒齲(ㄔˇ ㄑㄩˇ)
tooth decay
齒質(ㄔˇ ㄓˋ)
dentine
齒讓(ㄔˇ ㄖㄤˋ)
to yield to seniors
齒如編貝(ㄔˇ ㄖㄨˊ ㄅㄧㄢ ㄅㄟˋ)or齒如
齊貝(ㄔˇ ㄖㄨˊ ㄑㄧˊ ㄅㄟˋ)
very beautiful teeth
齒次(ㄔˇ ㄘˋ)
order of seniority
齒髓(ㄔˇ ㄙㄨㄟˇ)
pulp of the tooth
齒兒(ㄔˇ ㄦˊ)
teeth (of a comb, a saw,
etc.)
齒牙餘論(ㄔˇ ㄧㄚˊ ㄩˊ ㄌㄨㄣˋ)
to praise others
齒音(ㄔˇ ㄧㄣ)

〔龍部〕

(phonetics) dental sounds; dentals

齗【一ㄣ】
gums (of the teeth)

齗危【一ㄨㄟ】
very old age (with teeth about to fall out)

齗吻【一ㄨㄣ】
teeth and lips

齗亡舌存【ㄔ ㄨㄤ ㄕㄜ ㄘㄨㄣ】
(literally) After the teeth have fallen out, the tongue remains.—The strong is more likely to fall than the weak.

齜齔【ㄊㄠ ㄔㄣ】
to shed the milk teeth

齠容【ㄊㄠ ㄖㄨㄥ】
a youthful look

二畫

【齔】 7308
ㄔㄣ chenn chèn
1. to have milk teeth replaced with permanent teeth
2. children

三畫

【齕】 7309
ㄏㄜ her hé
to gnaw; to munch

齕吞【ㄏㄜ ㄊㄨㄣ】
to swallow without mastication

四畫

【齗】 7310
一ㄣ yn yín
1. gums (of the teeth)
2. to dispute

齗齗【一ㄣ 一ㄣ】
disputing

五畫

【齟】 7311
ㄐㄩ jeu jǔ
irregular teeth

齟齬【ㄐㄩ ㄩ】
①irregular teeth ②to have discord; to disagree

【齠】 7312
ㄊㄠ tyau tiáo
to shed the milk teeth

齠年【ㄊㄠ ㄋ一ㄢ】or 齠齡【ㄊㄠ ㄌ一ㄥ】
the age of shedding the milk teeth—childhood

【齡】 7313
ㄌ一ㄥ ling líng
age; years: 他們是學齡兒童。
They are school-age children.

【齣】 7314
ㄔㄨ chu chū
1. a chapter (of old-style novels)
2. a numeric adjunct for plays

【齜】 7315
ㄗ tzy zī
1. to open the mouth and show the teeth
2. uneven teeth

齜牙【ㄗ 一ㄚ】
to open the mouth and show the teeth

六畫

【齦】 7316
一ㄣ yn yín
gums (of the teeth)

【齧】 7317
【嚙,囓】ㄋ一ㄝ nieh niè
to gnaw; to bite

齧臂【ㄋ一ㄝ ㄅ一】
to bite one's arm as a sign of determination (as in taking the oath of brotherhood, etc.)

齧斷【ㄋ一ㄝ ㄉㄨㄢ】
to bite off

齧齒類【ㄋ一ㄝ ㄔ ㄌㄟ】
rodents

齧噬【ㄋ一ㄝ ㄕ】
to bite; to gnaw: 恐懼齧噬他的心靈。Fear is gnawing his heart.

【齩】 7318
【咬】一ㄠ yeau yǎo
to bite: 這狗齩他一口。The dog bit him.

七畫

【齪】 7319
ㄔㄨㄛ chuoh chuò
as in 齷齪—①narrow; small ②dirty

【齬】 7320
ㄩ yeu yǔ

as in 齟齬—①uneven teeth ②to disagree; to have discord

九畫

【齷】 7321
ㄨㄛ woh wò
參看「齷齪」

齷齪【ㄨㄛ ㄔㄨㄛ】
①narrow; small ②dirty

【齲】 7322
ㄑㄩ cheu qǔ
tooth decay

齲齒【ㄑㄩ ㄔ】
a decayed tooth; a carious tooth

【齶】 7323
ㄜ eh è
the roof of the mouth; the palate

十畫

【齹】 7324
【齝】ㄔ chy chí
irregular teeth; uneven teeth

龍 部
ㄌㄨㄥ long lóng

【龍】 7325
ㄌㄨㄥ long lóng
1. a dragon
2. of the emperor; imperial
3. a huge extinct reptile
4. a Chinese family name

龍幣【ㄌㄨㄥ ㄅ一】
the silver dollar coin, 8 taels in weight, minted by Emperor Wu in the Han Dynasty

龍牌【ㄌㄨㄥ ㄆㄞ】
an imperial tablet (kept in schools, government offices, etc., during the Ching Dynasty, to which students or officials were required to pay their respect)

龍袍【ㄌㄨㄥ ㄆㄠ】
an imperial robe

龍蟠鳳逸【ㄌㄨㄥ ㄆㄢ ㄈㄥ 一】
exceedingly talented (persons)

〔龍部〕

龍蟠虎踞(ㄌㄨㄥˊ ㄆㄢˊ ㄏㄨˇ ㄐㄩ)
like a dragon that coils and a tiger that crouches—impressive terrain

龍馬(ㄌㄨㄥˊ ㄇㄚˇ)
(figuratively) aged but vigorous; old but strong

龍脈(ㄌㄨㄥˊ ㄇㄞˋ)
a winding mountain range

龍門(ㄌㄨㄥˊ ㄇㄣˊ)
fame; success; glory

龍門造像(ㄌㄨㄥˊ ㄇㄣˊ ㄗㄠˋ ㄒㄧㄤˋ)
stones images of Buddha cut into the cliff at Lungmen (龍門), Honan, during the 6th century

龍目(ㄌㄨㄥˊ ㄇㄨˋ)
①the emperor's eyes ②(botany) longan

龍飛(ㄌㄨㄥˊ ㄈㄟ)
to ascend the throne

龍飛榜(ㄌㄨㄥˊ ㄈㄟ ㄅㄤˇ)
the first list of officials selected after an emperor's accession

龍飛鳳舞(ㄌㄨㄥˊ ㄈㄟ ㄈㄥˋ ㄨˇ)
(literally) like dragons flying and phoenixes dancing—vivid and vigorous flourishes in calligraphy

龍鳳(ㄌㄨㄥˊ ㄈㄥˋ)
①fine offspring; excellent children ②men of wisdom ③a noble look ④man and woman ⑤dragon and phoenix

龍鳳餅(ㄌㄨㄥˊ ㄈㄥˋ ㄅㄧㄥˇ)
cake presented to the bride's family by the bridegroom's

龍鳳帖(ㄌㄨㄥˊ ㄈㄥˋ ㄊㄧㄝˇ)
betrothal cards 亦作「結婚證書」

龍鳳相配(ㄌㄨㄥˊ ㄈㄥˋ ㄒㄧㄤ ㄆㄟˋ)
union of a dragon and a phoenix (a congratulatory phrase on the occasion of a wedding)

龍鳳呈祥(ㄌㄨㄥˊ ㄈㄥˋ ㄔㄥˊ ㄒㄧㄤˊ)
prosperity brought by the dragon and the phoenix—in extremely good fortune

龍膽紫(ㄌㄨㄥˊ ㄉㄢˇ ㄗˇ)
gentian violet

龍燈(ㄌㄨㄥˊ ㄉㄥ)
a lantern shaped like a dragon

龍邸(ㄌㄨㄥˊ ㄉㄧˇ)
the emperor's abode prior to

his accession

龍套(ㄌㄨㄥˊ ㄊㄠˋ)
①a kind of costume in Chinese opera ②a character in such a costume in Chinese opera—a role that requires neither acting nor singing ③a very insignificant role: 他只是個跑龍套的。He plays an insignificant role.

龍頭(ㄌㄨㄥˊ ㄊㄡˊ)
①a faucet; a tap; a cock ②the top successful candidate in the imperial examination under the former civil service examination system ③the leader of a sect, secret society, etc.

龍頭蛇尾(ㄌㄨㄥˊ ㄊㄡˊ ㄕㄜˊ ㄨㄟˇ)
(literally) to have a dragon's head and a snake's tail—to dwindle away to nothing after an initial display of strength

龍潭虎穴(ㄌㄨㄥˊ ㄊㄢˊ ㄏㄨˇ ㄒㄩㄝˋ)
(literally) the dragon's lake and the tiger's den—places of extreme danger

龍騰虎躍(ㄌㄨㄥˊ ㄊㄥˊ ㄏㄨˇ ㄩㄝˋ)
dragons rising and tigers leaping—a scene of bustling activity

龍跳虎臥(ㄌㄨㄥˊ ㄊㄧㄠˋ ㄏㄨˇ ㄨㄛˋ)
(literally) the dragon dancing and the tiger lurking—a free and vigorous style of writing

龍庭(ㄌㄨㄥˊ ㄊㄧㄥˊ)
①the imperial court ②the facial features of a noble man

龍腦(ㄌㄨㄥˊ ㄋㄠˇ)
Borneo camphor; borneol

龍樓鳳閣(ㄌㄨㄥˊ ㄌㄡˊ ㄈㄥˋ ㄍㄜˊ)
the emperor's abode; the imperial palace

龍鱗(ㄌㄨㄥˊ ㄌㄧㄣˊ)
①neatly arranged ②(figuratively) the grandeur of the king

龍肝鳳髓(ㄌㄨㄥˊ ㄍㄢ ㄈㄥˋ ㄙㄨㄟˇ)
rare delicacies

龍骨(ㄌㄨㄥˊ ㄍㄨˇ)
①a keel (of a boat) ②fossiles of animals supposed to be dragons' bones

龍其(ㄌㄨㄥˊ ㄍㄨㄥˋ)

an imperial emblem

龍宮(ㄌㄨㄥˊ ㄍㄨㄥ)
the palace of the sea god

龍葵(ㄌㄨㄥˊ ㄎㄨㄟˊ)
(botany) black nightshade

龍虎山(ㄌㄨㄥˊ ㄏㄨˇ ㄕㄢ)
name of a mountain in Kiangsi, the holy land of Taoists

龍江(ㄌㄨㄥˊ ㄐㄧㄤ)
Lungkiang (or Tsitsihar), Manchuria

龍井茶(ㄌㄨㄥˊ ㄐㄧㄥˇ ㄔㄚˊ)
a kind of green tea produced at Hangchow, Chekiang

龍駒(ㄌㄨㄥˊ ㄐㄩ)
①a fine horse ②talented youth

龍捲風(ㄌㄨㄥˊ ㄐㄩㄢˇ ㄈㄥ)
a tornado; a cyclone; a twister

龍潛(ㄌㄨㄥˊ ㄑㄧㄢˊ)
(said of a prospective emperor) to wait for accession

龍蝦(ㄌㄨㄥˊ ㄒㄧㄚ)
a lobster

龍涎(ㄌㄨㄥˊ ㄒㄧㄢˊ)or 龍涎香(ㄌㄨㄥˊ ㄒㄧㄢˊ ㄒㄧㄤ)
ambergris, found in sperm whales, used in perfumes

龍虎步(ㄌㄨㄥˊ ㄒㄧˇ ㄏㄨˇ ㄅㄨˋ)
(literally) to prance in a dragon-like manner and pace in a tiger-like manner—an imposing air; a dignified manner; an awe-inspiring carriage

龍驤虎視(ㄌㄨㄥˊ ㄒㄧㄤ ㄏㄨˇ ㄕˋ)
(literally) to prance like the dragon and glance like the tiger—to cherish great ambitions

龍行虎步(ㄌㄨㄥˊ ㄒㄧㄥˊ ㄏㄨˇ ㄅㄨˋ)
the dignified manner of an emperor

龍性(ㄌㄨㄥˊ ㄒㄧㄥˋ)
recalcitrance; unmanageability; intractability

龍鬚菜(ㄌㄨㄥˊ ㄒㄩ ㄘㄞˋ)
Asparagus schoberioides

龍穴(ㄌㄨㄥˊ ㄒㄩㄝˋ)
(geomancy) an ideal site for a grave

龍舟(ㄌㄨㄥˊ ㄓㄡ)or 龍船(ㄌㄨㄥˊ ㄔㄨㄢˊ)
a dragon-shaped racing boat

（for use on the Dragon-Boat Festival); a dragon boat

龍舟競渡 (カㄨㄥˊ ㄓㄡ ㄐㄧㄥˋ ㄉㄨˋ)
a dragon-boat race (the major event on the Dragon-Boat Festival on the 5th of the 5th lunar month)

龍章 (カㄨㄥˊ ㄓㄤ)
① an imperial emblem ② the emperor's calligraphy

龍章鳳姿 (カㄨㄥˊ ㄓㄤ ㄈㄥˋ ㄗ)
a noble and handsome appearance

龍爭虎鬥 (カㄨㄥˊ ㄓㄥ ㄏㄨˇ ㄉㄨˋ)
a fierce battle between giants

龍種 (カㄨㄥˊ ㄓㄨㄥˇ)
the dragon's seed—descendants of an emperor

龍牀 (カㄨㄥˊ ㄔㄨㄤˊ)
the emperor's bed

龍蛇 (カㄨㄥˊ ㄕㄜˊ)
① men of extraordinary talent ② strokes in cursive calligraphy ③ weapons

龍蛇混雜 (カㄨㄥˊ ㄕㄜˊ ㄏㄨㄣˋ ㄗㄚˊ)
the wise and the unwise huddled together

龍山寺 (カㄨㄥˊ ㄕㄢ ㄙˋ)
Lung Shan Temple, an old temple in Taipei, Taiwan

龍生龍, 鳳生鳳 (カㄨㄥˊ ㄕㄥ カㄨㄥˊ, ㄈㄥˋ ㄕㄥ ㄈㄥˋ)
Like father, like son.

龍牙草 (カㄨㄥˊ ㄧㄚˊ ㄘㄠˇ)
(botany) an agrimony

龍顏 (カㄨㄥˊ ㄧㄢˊ)
the noble face of the emperor

龍顏大悅 (カㄨㄥˊ ㄧㄢˊ ㄉㄚˋ ㄩㄝˋ)
The emperor looks greatly pleased. 或 The imperial countenance shows great pleasure.

龍眼 (カㄨㄥˊ ㄧㄢˇ)
longan

龍吟虎嘯 (カㄨㄥˊ ㄧㄣˊ ㄏㄨˇ ㄒㄧㄠˋ)
the howl of dragons mingled with the roar of tigers; awe-inspiring roars (as of winds, waves, etc.)

龍洋 (カㄨㄥˊ ㄧㄤˊ)
a kind of silver coin minted

toward the close of the Ching Dynasty

龍陽君 (カㄨㄥˊ ㄧㄤˊ ㄐㄩㄣ)
a catamite

龍文 (カㄨㄥˊ ㄨㄣˊ)
① a fine horse ② fine writing ③ a fine dragon

龍王 (カㄨㄥˊ ㄨㄤˊ) or 龍王爺 (カㄨㄥˊ ㄨㄤˊ ㄧㄝˊ)
the sea god

龍馭上賓 (カㄨㄥˊ ㄩˋ ㄕㄤˋ ㄅㄧㄣ)
The emperor has passed away.

龍驤鳳鳴 (カㄨㄥˊ ㄩˋ ㄈㄥˋ ㄇㄧㄥˊ)
(said of the intellect) bright; brilliant

六畫

【龔】 7326
《ㄍㄨㄥ　gong gōng》
1. reverential 亦作「恭」
2. a Chinese family name

【龕】 7327
《ㄎㄢ　kan kān》
a niche for an idol

龜 部
《ㄍㄨㄟ　guei guī》

【龜】 7328
1. 《ㄍㄨㄟ　guei guī》
a tortoise; a turtle

龜貝 (《ㄍㄨㄟ ㄅㄟˋ)
tortoise shell used as money in ancient times

龜版 (《ㄍㄨㄟ ㄅㄢˇ)
tortoiseshell

龜頭 (《ㄍㄨㄟ ㄊㄡˊ)
the glans penis; the glans

龜奴 (《ㄍㄨㄟ ㄋㄨˊ)
a servant in a brothel

龜鶴 (《ㄍㄨㄟ ㄏㄜˋ)
very old age

龜甲 (《ㄍㄨㄟ ㄐㄧㄚˇ)
tortoiseshell

龜甲獸骨文字 (《ㄍㄨㄟ ㄐㄧㄚˇ ㄕㄡˋ 《ㄨˇ ㄨㄣˊ)
the oracle-bone characters

龜鑑 (《ㄍㄨㄟ ㄐㄧㄢˋ) or 龜鏡 (《ㄍㄨㄟ ㄐㄧㄥˋ)
divination and retrospection

龜兆 (《ㄍㄨㄟ ㄓㄠˋ)
① marks on seared tortoise shell used for divination in ancient times ② omens

龜坼 (《ㄍㄨㄟ ㄔㄜˋ)
cracks in the soil due to drought

龜筮 (《ㄍㄨㄟ ㄕˋ)
divination

龜玉 (《ㄍㄨㄟ ㄩˋ)
a treasure

【龜】 7328
2. 《ㄐㄩㄣ　jiun jūn》
chapped; cracked

龜裂 (ㄐㄩㄣ ㄌㄧㄝˋ)
chapped; cracked: 花瓶掉落而龜裂 A vase fell and cracked.

【龜】 7328
3. 《ㄑㄧㄡ　chiou qiū》
used in 龜茲

龜茲 (ㄑㄧㄡ ㄘˊ)
a country in Central Asia during the Han Dynasty

龠 部
《ㄩㄝ　yueh yuè》

【龠】 7329
《ㄩㄝ　yueh yuè》
1. a kind of flute
2. a kind of measuring vessel

五畫

【龢】 7330
《和》 《ㄏㄜˊ　her hé》
harmonious; peaceful

九畫

【龥】 7331
《籲》 《ㄩˋ　yuh yù》
to call for; to make an appeal for

國語注音符號索引

編　法：本索引係照單字讀音，按國語注音符號順序編列，其讀音相同
　　　　者，再按部首順序。單字後註明單字編號。

用　法：遇有僅知讀音不悉字形之單字，可按國語注音符號，查出索引
　　　　中單字，再根據單字編號，查出書內單字及這一單字為首所組
　　　　成的詞語。

MANDARIN PHONETIC SYMBOL INDEX

In this index the characters are arranged according to their
respective MPS transcriptions. Characters with the same pronunciation are arranged according to their respective radicals. The figure to the right of each character is its identification number
under which the character can be found in the body of the dictionary.

If the dictionary user knows the pronunciation of the character
he is looking for but is unfamiliar with its strokes, he can find it in
the index according to its MPS transcription. Using the identification number as a guide, he can locate in the dictionary the character and the entries beneath it.

注音	單字	字號	注音	單字	字號	注音	單字	字號	注音	單字	字號	注音	單字	字號	注音	單字	字號	注音	單字	字號
				菠	4965		跛	5858		背	4646		(鮑)			幫	1345
				鉢	6353	ㄅㄛˋ	亳	70		胃	4740		鮑	7066		帮	1345
				盂	6353		北	458		倍	5052	ㄅㄢ	扳	1806		(幫)	
ㄅㄚ	八	311		(鉢)			播	2043		被	5397		搬	1993		梆	2472
	叭	537		缽	6353		擘	2071		褙	5438		斑	2153		浜	2880
	吧	586		(缽)			簸	4210		貝	5747		瘢	2154		邦	6175
	巴	1302	ㄅㄛˊ	鉑	6873		薄	5111		輩	6002		班	3654		榜	2547
	扒	1793		伯	113		薜	5131		邶	6185		癍	3671		膀	3305
	捌	1891		勃	428		蘗	5168		鋇	6395		般	4802		綁	4345
	疤	3595		博	487	•ㄅㄛ	蔔	5081		鞴	6758		頒	6792		膀	4718
	笆	4089		帛	1318	ㄅㄞ	掰	1942	ㄅㄠ	剝	398	ㄅㄢˇ	坂	814	ㄅㄤˇ	傍	235
	耙	4520		搏	1977	ㄅㄞˊ	白	3692		包	451		板	2365		旁	2178
	芭	4850		柏	2394	ㄅㄞˊ	伯	113		炮	3185		版	3302		棒	2480
	犯	5724		欂	2645		捭	1900		炰	3185		鈑	4804		磅	3898
ㄅㄚˊ	八	311		泊	2827		擺	2087		(炮)			舨	5253		膀	4718
	拔	1848		淿	2881		柏	2394		胞	4652		闆	6565		蚌	5199
	茇	4896		渤	2963		百	3693		苞	4871		阪	6587		蒡	5655
	跋	5851		濼	3135		襬	5467		褒	5441	ㄅㄢˋ	伴	116		鎊	6457
	鈸	6340		犮	3339	ㄅㄞˋ	拜	1856		襃	5453		半	479	ㄅㄥ	崩	1247
ㄅㄚˇ	把	1818		白	3692		敗	2131		薄	5111		扮	1803		繃	4433
	鈀	6329		百	3693		稗	4011		雹	6691		拌	1841		綳	4433
	靶	6739		碚	3922		粺	4251	ㄅㄠˇ	保	176		瓣	3520		(繃)	
ㄅㄚˋ	壩	895		箔	4142	ㄅㄟ	卑	482		堡	849		絆	4321		甭	3549
	把	1818		簿	4207		埤	842		寶	1156		辦	6042	ㄅㄥˇ	繃	4433
	灞	3166		粿	4268		悲	1622		寶	1156	ㄅㄣ	奔	932		綳	4433
	爸	3291		脖	4685		掭	1970		(寶)			奔	932		(繃)	
	罷	4505		膞	4723		杯	2357		葆	5022		(奔)			榜	2547
	耙	4581		舶	4809		盃	3719		褓	5436		犇	3330		繃	4433
	霸	5478		荸	4950		碑	3874		飽	6862		賁	5773		綳	4433
	覇	6713		葧	5081		背	4646		鴇	7123	ㄅㄣˇ	本	2333		(繃)	
•ㄅㄚ	吧	586		薄	5111	ㄅㄟ	北	458	ㄅㄠˋ	報	848		畚	3138		蹦	5923
	罷	4505		踣	5889	ㄅㄟˋ	倍	194		抱	1826		苯	4880		进	6106
ㄅㄛ	剝	1270		鈸	6340		備	239		暴	2276	ㄅㄣˋ	奔	932		进	6106
	嶓	2031		鉑	6349		孛	1081		瀑	3277		奔	932		(进)	
	播	2043		鎛	6462		悖	1589		爆	3277		(奔)		ㄅㄧ	屄	1191
	波	2839		雹	6691		憊	1712		菢	4991		笨	4097		逼	6116
	玻	3426		駁	6928		焙	3208		豹	5735	ㄅㄤ	傍	235	ㄅㄧˊ	荸	4950
	番	3575		駮	6943		狽	3357		趵	5846					鼻	7298
	般	4802	ㄅㄛˋ	簸	4210		碚	3880		鮑	6347				ㄅㄧˇ	匕	456
							糒	4256		鑤	6347					妣	966

	彼	1461	革	4989	標	2581	汴	2788	餅	6871		怕	1526
	比	2731	蔥	5061	熛	3248	緶	4398	餅	6880	·ㄆㄚ	杷	2363
	秕	3986	蓽	5079	森	3370	辡	4455	並	19		琶	3458
	筆	4109	蔽	5089	臕	4751	變	5695	併	189	ㄆㄛ	坡	820
	鄙	6224	薜	5131	臕	4751	辨	6043	併	189		波	2839
ㄅㄧˇ	俾	187	神	5422	(臕)		辯	6045	(併)			潑	3072
	啤	723	裨	5459	標	6489	辯	6046	井	1351		陂	6596
	壁	882	髲	5509	鏢	6518	遍	6123	抨	2008		頗	6796
	婢	1023	詖	5556	飆	6846	儐	277	柄	2393	ㄆㄛˊ	婆	1015
	嬖	1059	費	5768	飇	6846	彬	1453	病	3607		皤	3708
	幣	1343	賁	5773	(飆)		放	2120	竝	4076		繁	4428
	庇	1361	跛	5858	麃	7219	斌	2151	哺	2249		鄱	6234
	弊	1414	躃	5916	婊	1028	檳	2626	通	6088	ㄆㄛˇ	叵	544
	弼	1435	蹕	5941	表	5375	濱	3131	餔	6876		頗	6796
	必	1497	蹕	5947	褾	5424	瀕	3146	不	8		拍	2337
	愎	1639	辟	6039	鏢	6433	繽	4458	醭	6290		朴	2337
	愊	1642	逼	6116	鰾	7102	豳	5733	卜	488		泊	2822
	拂	1834	避	6156	砭	3851	賓	5785	哺	637		珀	3422
	敝	2133	邲	6183	箯	4156	賔	5785	捕	1892		破	3854
	繁	2148	鄙	6224	邊	4229	(賔)		補	5415		粕	4238
	比	2731	鉍	6361	編	4389	邪	6173	不	8		迫	6068
	怭	2732	閟	6532	蝙	5268	儐	277	佈	125		廹	6068
	泌	2829	閣	6541	邊	6166	擯	2077	埠	841		(迫)	
	湢	2994	陛	6605	鞭	6750	殯	2713	布	1307		醱	6292
	狴	3355	牌	7000	編	7087	臏	4748	怖	1525		魄	7056
	璧	3503	璧	7194	區	471	髕	7007	步	2684		拍	1840
	畁	3559	愍	7281	扁	1783	髕	7034	篰	4194	ㄆㄞ	俳	183
	畢	3573	鷩	7281	稨	4017	兵	316	簿	4214		徘	1475
	瘠	3636	(鷩)		窆	4049	冰	335	部	6206		排	1923
	皕	3704	別	372	藊	5025	并	1351					牌	3303
	睥	3782	覽	5929	蝙	5268	丙	16	**ㄆ**		ㄆㄞˊ	簰	4192
	碧	3887	蹩	5939	褊	5433	屏	1198	注音	單字 字號		派	287
	祕	3936	躄	3675	貶	5764	昺	2237				湃	297
	祕	3936	癟	3675	便	164	昺	2237	ㄆㄚ	葩	5011	鎩	182
	(祕)		(癟)		卞	489	(昺)			趴	5845	ㄆㄟ	披	182
	箅	4146	鷩	1438	弁	1410	柄	2393	ㄆㄚˊ	扒	1793		胚	465
	篦	4173	彪	1454	偏	1483	炳	3187		爬	3285		醅	627
	篳	4181	標	2018	忭	1512	秉	3982		琶	3458	ㄆㄟˊ	培	83
	臂	4740	杓	2345	抃	1810	稟	4007		耙	4581		婓	542
	芘	4884			昪	2236	邴	6186	ㄆㄚˋ	帕	1312		賠	579

邳	6184	磐	3903	硼	3872	陂	6596	片	3301	瓶	3526
陪	6613	胖	4648	彭	1455	陴	6618	篇	4162	瓶	3526
ㄆㄟ		般	4802	朋	2316	鼙	7290	翩	4554	(瓶)	
佩	141	蟠	5320	棚	2486	**ㄆㄧ**		蒲	5025	秤	3992
被	1310	肇	6759	澎	3090	仳	98	**ㄆㄧㄢ**		砰	4479
旆	2181	**ㄆㄢ**		硼	3872	劈	411	便	164	萍	4881
沛	2807	判	371	蓬	4184	匹	470	楩	2537	蘋	4982
珮	3437	叛	524	膨	4731	否	566	胼	4689	蘋	5164
醅	6034	拌	1841	瓻	4832	仳	1359	胼	4689	評	5555
配	6249	拚	1853	蓬	5063	庀	3587	(胼)		耕	6001
霈	6696	泮	2843	鬅	7155	疕	3630	諞	5624	馮	6923
ㄆㄠ		胖	3564	**ㄆㄥ**		痞	3672	鶣	5902	**ㄆㄨ**	
拋	1840	盼	3745	捧	1898	苤	4899	骿	6944	仆	77
抛	1840	襻	5472	**ㄆㄥ**		僻	268	骿	6952	扑	1792
(拋)		**ㄆㄣ**		碰	3879	屁	1187	**ㄆㄧㄢ**		撲	2046
泡	2841	噴	761	掽	3879	澼	3109	褊	5624	痡	3629
胈	4681	歕	2675	(砰)		甓	3534	匾	1483	鋪	6410
ㄆㄠ		**ㄆㄣ**		**ㄆㄧ**		甓	5686	片	3301	僕	256
刨	373	湓	2980	丕	13	辟	6039	遍	6123	匍	453
匏	454	盆	3717	劈	411	闢	6579	騙	6958	蔔	1340
咆	602	**ㄆㄤ**		匹	470	**ㄆㄧㄢ**		**ㄆㄧㄣ**		朴	2337
庖	1365	兵	27	批	1808	撇	2034	姘	1018	樸	2587
炮	3185	滂	3018	披	1828	瞥	3815	姘	1018	濮	3128
袍	5392	磅	3898	砒	3848	**ㄆㄧㄝ**		(姘)		璞	3498
麃	7219	雱	6714	紕	4292	撇	2034	拼	1924	脯	4680
ㄆㄠ		**ㄆㄤ**		被	5397	苤	4899	拼	1924	莆	4945
跑	7221	傍	235	霹	6712	**ㄆㄧㄠ**		(拼)		菩	4986
跑	5854	庬	507	啤	658	漂	3041	**ㄆㄧㄣ**		葡	5006
ㄆㄠ		尨	1175	埤	842	飄	6845	嬪	5164	蒲	5037
泡	2841	龐	1403	枇	2362	嫖	1048	貧	5753	蒲	5038
炮	3185	彷	1459	毗	2733	瓢	3519	頻	6809	蹼	5937
疱	3612	傍	1487	琵	3457	標	2018	顰	6833	酺	6267
皰	3710	旁	2178	疲	3599	**ㄆㄧㄠ**		**ㄆㄧㄣ**		醭	6290
砲	3859	旁	2178	皮	3709	殍	2701	品	621	**ㄆㄨ**	
藏	3920	(旁)		紕	4292	漂	3041	牝	3311	圃	795
ㄆㄡ		膀	4718	罷	4505	瞟	3803	聘	4601	埔	838
抔	1817	螃	5291	羆	4508	縹	4424	**ㄆㄧㄥ**		普	2255
掊	1919	逄	6083	脾	4699	莩	4942	乒	34	浦	2885
裒	5411	**ㄆㄤ**		蚍	5203	剽	407	娉	1003	溥	3006
ㄆㄡ		胖	4648	神	5422	漂	3041	坪	828	譜	5681
剖	394	**ㄆㄥ**		貔	5744	票	3948	屏	1198		
掊	1919	怦	1529	郫	6207	驃	6973	平	1349		
部	3525	抨	1827	鈹	6362	偏	221	憑	1710		
ㄆㄢ		澎	3090			扁	1783	枰	2419		
攀	2093	烹	3202					洴	2919		
潘	3074	砰	3852								
番	3575										
ㄆㄢ											
繁	2552										
盤	3732										

注音	單字	字號
ㄆㄨ	錯	6499
	暴	2276
	曝	2296
	瀑	3138
	舖	4791
	鋪	6410

ㄇ

注音	單字	字號
ㄇㄚ	媽	1043
ㄇㄚˊ	痲	3635
	蔴	5088
	蟆	5313
	麻	7241
	麼	7242
ㄇㄚˇ	嗎	709
	瑪	3482
	碼	3895
	螞	5296
	鎷	6471
	馬	6921
ㄇㄚˋ	禡	3963
	罵	4504
•ㄇㄚ	嗎	709
	蟆	5313
	麼	7242
	麼	7242
	(麼)	
ㄇㄛ	摸	2017
ㄇㄛˊ	摩	2022
	摹	2023
	模	2584
	磨	3904
	模	4265
	膜	4725
	蘑	5153
	謨	5666
	饃	6913
	饝	6913
	(饝)	

注音	單字	字號
	魔	7058
	麼	7242
ㄇㄛˇ	抹	1830
ㄇㄛˋ	嚜	747
	墨	878
	寞	1141
	抹	1830
	末	2332
	歿	2693
	歿	2693
	(歿)	
	沒	2803
	沫	2808
	漠	3049
	瘼	3664
	礳	3904
	秣	3994
	脈	4671
	脉	4671
	(脉)	
	鰵	4671
	(脉)	
	膜	4725
	茉	4897
	莫	4944
	袜	5394
	貉	5740
	(貉)	
	貘	5745
	陌	6600
	驀	6743
	蓦	6971
	麥	7234
	默	7253
•ㄇㄛ	麼	7242
ㄇㄞˊ	埋	834
	霾	6716
ㄇㄞˇ	買	5765
	脈	4671

注音	單字	字號
	脉	4671
	(脉)	
	鰵	4671
	(脉)	
	賣	5794
	邁	6159
ㄇㄟ	麥	7234
	媒	1032
	魅	1256
	枚	2378
	梅	2458
	楣	2527
	沒	2803
	湄	2976
	煤	3223
	玫	3413
	眉	3754
	苺	4894
	莓	4935
	羋	6215
	霉	6697
	黴	7268
ㄇㄟˇ	每	2727
	浼	2893
	美	4515
	鎂	6449
ㄇㄟˋ	妹	973
	媚	1033
	寐	1137
	昧	2226
	沬	2809
	瑁	3463
	眛	3758
	袂	5379
	謎	5648
	魅	7052
ㄇㄠ	摸	2017
	貓	5743
	貓	5743
	(貓)	

注音	單字	字號
ㄇㄠˊ	旄	2182
	毛	2735
	氂	2742
	矛	3826
	茅	4889
	茆	4890
	蝥	5279
	孟	5317
	錨	6436
	髦	7013
ㄇㄠˇ	卯	495
	昴	2231
	泖	2834
ㄇㄠˋ	冒	325
	帽	1329
	懋	1732
	旄	2182
	楙	2518
	瑁	3463
	眊	3750
	瞀	3795
	耄	4570
	毛	4859
	茂	4886
	袤	5395
	貌	5741
	貿	5772
ㄇㄡˊ	牟	3312
	眸	3768
	繆	4434
	謀	5640
	鍪	6443
	麰	7238
ㄇㄡˇ	某	3313
	牡	3313
ㄇㄡˋ	瞀	3795
	茂	4886
	袤	5395
ㄇㄢ	埋	834
	樠	2586

注音	單字	字號
	邊	3054
	瞞	3802
	蔓	5069
	蠻	5354
	謾	5663
	蹣	5915
	顢	6825
	矇	6899
	鬘	7031
	鰻	7098
ㄇㄢˇ	滿	3037
	嬤	1050
ㄇㄢˋ	慢	1334
	慢	1674
	曼	2308
	漫	3054
	縵	4420
	蔓	5069
	謾	5663
	鏝	6486
	墁	6486
	(鏝)	
ㄇㄣ	悶	1619
	燜	3262
ㄇㄣˊ	們	198
	捫	1901
	燜	3262
	門	6529
ㄇㄣˋ	悶	1619
	懣	1736
	燜	3262
•ㄇㄣ	們	198
ㄇㄤ	厖	507
	忙	2749
	育	3742
	硭	3869
	芒	4838
	茫	4906
	邙	6170

注音	單字	字號
	鉈	6408
ㄇㄤ	梓	2604
	淯	3070
	莽	4947
	莽	4947
	(莽)	
	蟒	5319
ㄇㄤˊ	尨	1175
	嫇	1346
	幪	1741
	懞	1743
	(懞)	
	曚	2293
	朦	2326
	檬	2328
	氓	2747
	濛	3123
	蕄	3533
	亡	3553
	盟	3723
	甍	3728
	(甍)	
	曚	3826
	朦	3829
	萌	4982
	蒙	5037
	虻	5196
ㄇㄥˇ	夢	1086
	孟	1089
	咪	61
ㄇㄧ	醚	3807
ㄇㄧˊ	彌	1430
	獼	3153

ㄇㄧˊ
獼 3403 ／ 彌 3971 ／ 糜 4259 ／ 縻 4427 ／ 蘼 5176 ／ 謎 5648 ／ 迷 6073 ／ 醚 6281 ／ 醾 6299 ／ 麋 6730 ／ 麑 7222

ㄇㄧˇ
弭 1429 ／ 敉 2124 ／ 眯 3765 ／ 米 4233 ／ 羋 4513 ／ 靡 6730

ㄇㄧˋ
冪 333 ／ 宓 1110 ／ 密 1130 ／ 汨 2780 ／ 泌 2829 ／ 祕 3936 ／ 秘 3936 ／ (祕) 3936 ／ 蜜 5251 ／ 覓 5483 ／ 覔 5483 ／ (覓) 5483 ／ 謐 5654 ／ 嗎 7285

ㄇㄧㄝ
乜 38 ／ 咩 646

ㄇㄧㄝˊ
滅 3020 ／ 篾 4183 ／ 蔑 4183 ／ 蔑 5068 ／ 薎 5068 ／ (薎) 5359

ㄇㄧㄠˊ
描 1949 ／ 瞄 3793 ／ 苗 4868

ㄇㄧㄠˇ
杪 2355 ／ 淼 2954 ／ 渺 2973 ／ 眇 3748 ／ 秒 3985 ／ 緲 4391 ／ 藐 5140 ／ 邈 6165

ㄇㄧㄠˋ
妙 964 ／ 廟 4028 ／ 繆 4434 ／ 繆 4434

ㄇㄧㄡˊ
繆 4434 ／ 繆 5668

ㄇㄧㄢˊ
棉 2477 ／ 眠 3759 ／ 綿 4391 ／ 緜 4400

ㄇㄧㄢˇ
丏 9 ／ 免 299 ／ 冕 328 ／ 勉 431 ／ 娩 1014 ／ 愐 1632 ／ 沔 2800 ／ 湎 2978 ／ 眄 3747 ／ 緬 4392 ／ 腼 4714 ／ 靦 6732 ／ 面 6731 ／ 麪 7236 ／ 麵 7240

ㄇㄧㄣˊ
岷 1222 ／ 忞 1521 ／ 旻 2209 ／ 民 2748 ／ 珉 3421 ／ 緡 4386 ／ 緍 4386 ／ 閩 6547

ㄇㄧㄣˇ
愍 1647 ／ 憫 1705 ／ 抿 1854 ／ 敏 2127 ／ 泯 2844 ／ 湣 2972 ／ 澠 3100 ／ 皿 3714 ／ 閔 6539 ／ 黽 7275

ㄇㄧㄥˊ
冥 331 ／ 名 556 ／ 明 2217 ／ 暝 2272 ／ 溟 3001 ／ 瞑 3799 ／ 茗 4902 ／ 螟 5297 ／ 酩 6257 ／ 銘 6375 ／ 鳴 7120

ㄇㄧㄥˇ
皿 3714 ／ 瞑 3799 ／ 茗 4902 ／ 酩 6257

ㄇㄧㄥˋ
命 599

ㄇㄨˊ
模 2584 ／ 摹 3386

ㄇㄨˇ
姆 976 ／ 拇 1835 ／ 母 2726 ／ 牡 3313 ／ 畝 3568 ／ 鉧 6344

ㄇㄨˋ
募 440 ／ 墓 866 ／ 幕 1335 ／ 慕 1693 ／ 暮 2274 ／ 木 2330 ／ 沐 2799 ／ 牧 3316 ／ 目 3739 ／ 睦 3784 ／ 穆 4028 ／ 繆 4434 ／ 苜 4870 ／ 莫 4944 ／ 鉬 6363

ㄈㄟ
扉 1788 ／ 緋 ／ 菲 4970 ／ 蜚 5250 ／ 霏 6700 ／ 非 6728 ／ 飛 6847 ／ 鯡 7079

ㄈㄟˊ
肥 4633 ／ 腓 4701

ㄈㄟˇ
匪 465 ／ 悱 1597 ／ 斐 2152 ／ 朏 2318 ／ 棐 2491 ／ 榧 2562 ／ 篚 4168 ／ 翡 4550 ／ 菲 4970 ／ 蜚 5250 ／ 誹 5603

ㄈㄟˋ
吠 565 ／ 廢 1398 ／ 佛 1533 ／ 沸 2814 ／ 狒 3350 ／ 痱 3633 ／ 疿 3633 ／ 肺 4642 ／ 芾 4861 ／ 費 5768

ㄈ

注音	單字	字號
ㄈㄚ	伐	110
	法	2832
	發	3690
ㄈㄚˊ	乏	33
	伐	110
	法	2832
	砝	3853
	筏	4114
	罰	4501
	閥	6545
ㄈㄚˇ	法	2832
	灋	2832
	(法)	
ㄈㄚˋ	髮	7015
	法	2832
	琺	3453
ㄈㄛˊ	佛	137
ㄈㄟ	啡	652
	妃	957

ㄈㄡˊ
浮 2890 ／ 罘 4493 ／ 芣 4843 ／ 否 566 ／ 缶 4476

ㄈㄢ
帆 1308 ／ 杬 1308 ／ (帆) 1341 ／ 幡 4376 ／ 旛 2192 ／ 番 3575 ／ 繙 4441 ／ 翻 4562 ／ 蕃 5090 ／ 飜 6848

ㄈㄢˊ
凡 347 ／ 帆 1308 ／ 帆 1308 ／ (帆) ／ 樊 2579 ／ 煩 3226 ／ 燔 3256 ／ 璠 3500 ／ 礬 3918 ／ 繁 4428 ／ 緐 4428 ／ (繁) ／ 膰 4734 ／ 蕃 5090 ／ 蘩 5149 ／ 蘗 5171 ／ 蹯 5932 ／ 釩 6319

ㄈㄢˇ
反 520 ／ 返 ／ 梵 2465 ／ (棑)

ㄈㄢˋ
氾 2764 ／ 汎 2769 ／ 泛 2838 ／ 犯 3340 ／ 范 4108 ／ 範 4161 ／ 范 4887 ／ 販 5755 ／ 飯 6859

ㄈㄣ
分 359 ／ 吩 567

	單字	字號
	菜	2490
	氛	2751
	紛	4299
	芬	4848
	棻	4960
	雰	6685
ㄈㄣˊ	墳	881
	粉	2369
	棼	2492
	汾	2789
	焚	3211
	黂	4521
	黂	5098
	黂	5773
ㄈㄣˇ		4235
ㄈㄣˋ	分	359
	份	359
	(分)	
	噴	761
	奮	948
	忿	1520
	憤	1719
	糞	4260
ㄈㄤ	坊	811
	妨	969
	方	2174
	枋	2370
	肪	4635
	芳	4855
ㄈㄤˊ	妨	969
	房	1781
	肪	4635
	防	6590
	魴	7064
ㄈㄤˇ	仿	102
	倣	102
	(仿)	
	彷	1459
	昉	2214
	紡	4300

	單字	字號
	舫	4803
	訪	5539
	髣	7011
ㄈㄤˋ	放	2119
ㄈㄥ	丰	22
	封	1159
	峯	1230
	楓	2515
	澧	3161
	烽	3201
	瘋	3643
	葑	5002
	蜂	5236
	鑫	5350
	豐	5719
	酆	6242
	鋒	6404
	風	6837
ㄈㄥˊ	縫	4416
	逢	6103
	馮	6923
	唪	668
ㄈㄥˇ	俸	185
	奉	931
	縫	4416
	諷	5636
	風	6837
	鳳	7119
ㄈㄨ	夫	919
	孵	1093
	敷	2142
	枹	2389
	柎	2392
	膚	4724
	跗	5848
	駙	5856
	郛	6227
	鈇	6332
	麩	7235
ㄈㄨˊ	伏	109

	單字	字號
	伻	174
	匐	455
	夫	919
	孚	1080
	祓	1314
	幅	1328
	弗	1421
	彿	1465
	彿	1533
	扶	1804
	拂	1834
	服	2317
	枹	2389
	桴	2451
	氟	2752
	洑	2852
	浮	2890
	涪	2910
	祓	3934
	福	3956
	符	4101
	籇	4151
	紱	4310
	紼	4313
	縛	4408
	罘	4493
	艴	4827
	芙	4839
	茀	4861
	苻	4883
	莆	4895
	茯	4907
	荸	4942
	蕨	4962
	蚨	5208
	蜉	5244
	蝠	5275
	袱	5400
	輻	6010
	郛	6196

	單字	字號
	鼓	6767
	鬴	7016
	鳧	7116
	鵬	7156
	黻	7273
ㄈㄨˇ	俯	181
	府	1368
	拊	1839
	撫	2042
	斧	2166
	父	3290
	甫	3547
	簠	4203
	脯	4680
	腐	4695
	腑	4696
	莆	4945
	輔	5991
	釜	6314
	頫	6799
	黼	7274
ㄈㄨˋ	仆	77
	付	86
	傅	234
	副	399
	咐	606
	婦	1024
	富	1136
	復	1485
	服	2317
	父	3290
	柎	3935
	腹	4711
	蕷	5281
	蝮	5283
	複	5432
	覆	5476
	赴	5518
	負	5748
	賦	5796

	單字	字號
	賻	5802
	赴	5829
	輹	6013
	阜	6582
	附	6597
	覆	6919
	駙	6936
	鮒	7067
	鰒	7089

ㄉ

注音	單字	字號
ㄉㄚ	搭	1988
	答	4119
	耷	4592
	褡	5447
ㄉㄚˊ	妲	970
	怛	1528
	打	1794
	瘩	3656
	答	4119
	縫	4450
	達	6130
	粗	6744
	韃	6761
ㄉㄚˇ	打	1794
ㄉㄚˋ	大	916
ㄉㄚ˙	瘩	3656
	縫	4450
ㄉㄜ	得	1476
	德	1493
ㄉㄜ˙	得	1476
	的	3696
	襶	5471
ㄉㄞ	呆	584
	呆	1466
	獃	3383
ㄉㄞˇ	歹	2691
	逮	6107
ㄉㄞˋ	代	91

	單字	字號
	大	916
	岱	1220
	帶	1325
	待	1466
	怠	1545
	戴	1775
	殆	2695
	玳	3420
	袋	5471
	襶	5471
	貸	5766
	迨	6066
	逮	6107
	靆	6719
	黛	7255
ㄉㄟ	得	1476
ㄉㄠ	刀	356
	叨	528
	切	1498
	剟	4798
ㄉㄠˇ	倒	199
	導	1167
	島	1232
	搗	1982
	擣	2075
	禱	3972
ㄉㄠˋ	倒	199
	到	377
	導	1167
	幬	1344
	悼	1602
	燾	3274
	盜	3727
	稻	4022
	纛	4473
	翿	4978
	蹈	5907
	道	6129
ㄉㄡ	兜	304

	筼	4182	(膽)	7269		簦	4202	(迪)		経	4336
	都	6214		黵 7269		鐙	5714		適 6144		蠹 4574
ㄉㄡˇ	抖	1821	ㄉㄢˋ	但 123		鐙	6496		鏑 6480		婕 5265
	斗	2156		咴 661	ㄉㄥˇ	戥	1768	ㄉㄧˇ	底 1364		蝶 5286
	蚪	5201		噉 661		等	4113		抵 1829		褋 5451
	陡	6608		(啖)	ㄉㄥˋ	凳	350		柢 2406		諜 5623
ㄉㄡˋ	痘	3623		彈 1437		橙	350		氐 2747		跌 5852
	竇	4070		憚 1701		(凳)			牴 3320		蹀 5901
	脰	4682		憺 1722		嶝	1271		砥 3849		迭 6069
	荳	4954		擔 2059		澄	3088		舐 5504		鰈 7086
	讀	5692		旦 2199		磴	3691		觝 5548	ㄉㄧㄠ	凋 341
	豆	5710		氮 2759		櫈	3691		邸 6187		习 357
	逗	6095		淡 2931		(凳)		ㄉㄧˋ	地 810		叼 529
	餖	6877		澹 3110		瞪	3810		娣 1012		彫 1451
	鬥	7036		癉 3670		磴	3909		帝 1320		碉 3876
	鬩	7037		石 3841		蹬	5930		弟 1324		貂 5738
	鬮	7041		菪 4985		鄧	6230		棣 2487		雕 6670
	鬭	7042		蛋 5220		鐙	6496		的 3696		鯛 7081
ㄉㄢ	丹	25		蜑 5247	ㄉㄧ	低	127		睇 3774		鵰 7158
	偁	275		蜑 5587		提	1951		禘 3962	ㄉㄧㄠˇ	弔 1420
	單	701	ㄉㄤ	噹 760		氐	2747		第 4102		吊 1420
	擔	2059		璫 3506		滴	3033		締 4385		(弔)
	担	2059		當 3582		羝	4522		蒂 5028		掉 1920
	(擔)			襠 5460		隄	6626		蔕 5070		調 5605
	殫	2710		鐺 6507		堤	6626		螮 5304		釣 6320
	眈	3749	ㄉㄤˇ	擋 2061		(隄)			螮 5304		銚 6376
	簞	4198		攩 2107	ㄉㄧˊ	嫡	1051		(蝃)	ㄉㄧㄡ	丟 18
	耽	4593		檔 2610		敵	2141		諦 5628		銩 6388
	躭	4595		當 3582		滌	3030		遞 6137	ㄉㄧㄢ	顛 1286
	聃	4595		讜 5705		狄	3344	ㄉㄧㄝ	爹 3292		掂 1910
	(耼)			黨 7262		的	3696	ㄉㄧㄝˊ	喋 685		攧 2105
	軂	5962	ㄉㄤˋ	宕 1109		笛	4096		慄 1628		滇 3021
	鄲	6235		擋 2061		羅	4272		昳 2234		顛 3686
	酖	6251		檔 2610		翟	4547		牒 3517		顛 3686
ㄉㄢˇ	撣	2050		當 3582		荻	4930		疊 3586	ㄉㄧㄢˇ	典 319
	揮	2050		盪 3737		覿	5498		叠 3586		碘 3881
	(撢)			蕩 5104		覿	5891		(疊)		點 7254
	疸	3601	ㄉㄥ	燈 3250		蹢	5922		昳 3757	ㄉㄧㄢˋ	佃 122
	膽	4736		登 3689		迪	6067		碟 3892		垫 873
	胆	4736					廸	6067				奠 942

	店	1366
	惦	1616
	殿	2721
	淀	2914
	澱	3107
	玷	3419
	甸	3556
	痁	3613
	簟	4199
	鈿	6342
	電	6690
	靛	6726
ㄉㄧㄥ	丁	2
	仃	75
	叮	538
	奵	3410
	町	3557
	疔	3591
	耵	3740
	釘	6313
	靪	6736
ㄉㄧㄥˇ	酊	6246
	頂	6781
	鼎	7283
ㄉㄧㄥˋ	定	1114
	碇	3878
	訂	5516
	釘	6386
	錠	6424
	飣	6851
ㄉㄨ	督	3787
	都	6214
	闍	6566
ㄉㄨˊ	櫝	2632
	毒	2729
	瀆	3136
	牘	3307
	犢	3335
	獨	3391
	碡	3883

注音	單字	字號
	轟	4473
	讀	5692
	頓	6793
	髑	7006
	髏	7271
ㄉㄨˇ	堵	854
	睹	3790
	篤	4170
	肚	4626
	覩	5489
	賭	5799
ㄉㄨˋ	妒	961
	妬	961
	(妒)	
	度	1369
	斁	2146
	杜	2349
	渡	2960
	肚	4626
	蠧	5353
	蠹(蠧)	5353
	鍍	6438
ㄉㄨㄛ	哆	624
	多	909
ㄉㄨㄛˊ	多	909
	奪	945
	掇	1914
	敠	2135
	裰	5421
	鐸	6506
ㄉㄨㄛˇ	朵	2339
	朵(朵)	2339
	躱	5963
ㄉㄨㄛˋ	剁	380
	咄	601
	墮	880
	度	1369
	惰	1625
	柮	2415
	柁	2418
	舵	4808
	踱	5873
	蹀	5898
ㄉㄨㄟ	駄	6924
	堆	847
	兌	298
	對	1166
	憝	1715
	憞	1737
	敦	2138
	碓	3877
	隊	6632
ㄉㄨㄢ	端	4083
	崭	4578
ㄉㄨㄢˇ	短	3836
	斷	2173
	段	2716
	緞	4382
	鍛	6441
	煅	6441
	(鍛)	
ㄉㄨㄣ	墩	879
	惇	1607
	敦	2138
	燉	5928
	肫	3751
	疊	5945
ㄉㄨㄣˋ	噸	757
	沌	2797
	坉	3179
	燉	3253
	盾	3752
	遁	6117
	遯	6146
	鈍	6334
	頓	6793
ㄉㄨㄥ	多	334
	哆	596
	東	2360
	涷	5264
	擊	7288
ㄉㄨㄥˇ	懂	1723
	董	5008
ㄉㄨㄥˋ	凍	343
	動	433
	峒	1226
	恫	1561
	棟	2485
	洞	2859
	胴	4663
	涷	5264

ㄊ

注音	單字	字號
ㄊㄚ	他	84
	塌	857
	她	953
	它	1099
	牠	3314
	褟	5448
	趿	5850
	鉈	6359
	鞑	6741
ㄊㄚˊ	塔	860
	嗒	710
	拓	1847
	搨	1992
	達	2051
	榻	2549
	沓	2806
	澾	3056
	獺	3401
	踏	5883
	蹋	5911
	躂	5946
	達	6130
	遝	6136
	遢	6140
	錔	6469
	闒	6569
	闟	6581
	鞳	6757
ㄊㄜˋ	忒	1501
	牠	3314
	忒	1501
	忑	1503
	慝	1685
	特	3321
	鈇	6394
ㄊㄞ	胎	4647
ㄊㄞˊ	苔	4866
	台	540
	擡	2073
	抬	2073
	(擡)	
	炲	2420
	檯	2625
	臺	4771
	苔	4866
	邰	6181
	颱	6839
ㄊㄞˊ	駘	6935
ㄊㄞˋ	太	918
	態	1668
	汰	2783
	泰	2849
	鈦	6330
ㄊㄠ	叨	528
	慆	1664
	桃	1868
	掏	1917
	搯	1996
	滔	3024
	濤	3124
	絛	4342
	絲	4435
	謟	5661
	韜	6771
	饕	6910
ㄊㄠˊ	桃	2440
	洮	2869
	淘	2925
	濤	3124
	燾	3274
	翻	4566
	萄	4976
	逃	6079
	陶	6620
	叟	7289
ㄊㄠˇ	討	5520
ㄊㄠˋ	套	939
ㄊㄡ	偷	231
	投	1819
	頭	6803
	骰	6993
ㄊㄡˇ	斜	7245
ㄊㄡˋ	透	4771
·ㄊㄡ	頭	6803
ㄊㄢˇ	坦	816
ㄊㄢˋ	忝	1548
	探	1930
	攤	2103
	灘	3164
	癱	3609
	貪	5756
ㄊㄢˊ	壇	885
	彈	1437
	叠	2280
	檀	2607
	潭	3081
	澹	3110
	痰	3632
	罈	4484
	罎	4488
	藫	5146
	談	5608
	譚	5679
	郯	6209
ㄊㄢˇ	坦	822
	忐	1502
	毯	2739
	袒	5393
	黮	7266
ㄊㄢˋ	嘆	2668
	歎	2668
	(歎)	
	炭	3190
	碳	3890
ㄊㄤ	湯	2989
	蹚	5918
	鏜	6485
	唐	644
	堂	845
	塘	862
	搪	1994
	棠	2488
	糖	4258
	膛	4729
	螗	5290
	螳	5306
	醣	6283
	鏜	6760
ㄊㄤˇ	倘	202
	帑	1311
	惝	1615
	淌	2920
	燙	5964
ㄊㄤˋ	趟	5841
ㄊㄥ	滕	3028
	疼	3605
	籐	4220
	謄	4414

	單字 字號		單字 字號		單字 字號	單字 字號		單字 字號	單字 字號
	滕 4727		逖 6094	闐 6567	葵 5026	薜 5158		筒 4117
	藤 5147		錫 6393	忝 1522	魄 7051	箇 4127
	螣 5649	去ㄧㄝ	鬄 7010	殄 2696	推 1933	罎 4818
去ㄧ	騰 6965		帖 1313	潠 2929	隤 6642	筒 4904
	剔 393		怗 1540	腆 4690	頹 6808	酮 6261
去ㄧˊ	梯 2466		貼 5769	舔 4790	腿 4717	銅 6371
	踢 5888	去ㄧㄝˊ	帖 1313	覥 5487	蛻 5233	桶 2454
	啼 673		鐵 6504	覥 6732	退 6076	筒 4117
	提 1951	去ㄧㄝˇ	帖 1313	餂 6864	湍 2979	統 4337
	媞 3959		饕 6889	(餂)	團 804	慟 1677
	稊 4002	去ㄧㄠˊ	桃 1553	廳 1405	摶 2013	痛 3622
	綈 4347		挑 1868	汀 2766	槫 4270	衕 5364
	緹 4396		桃 3947	聽 4612	彖 1442	
	鵜 4919	去ㄧㄠ	佻 144	亭 68	吞 563
	鷈 5904		條 2463	停 225	啍 2288
	鶗 5914		苕 4867	婷 1030	囤 788
	醍 6277		蜩 5257	庭 1374	屯 1208
	隄 6626		調 5605	廷 1407	臀 4739
	堤 6626		迢 6062	渟 2957	芚 4849
	(隄)		磬 7014	筳 4133	豚 5723
	題 6814		鼗 7312	蜓 5241	鈍 6854
	騠 6961	去ㄧㄠˇ	挑 1868	霆 6695	余 2763
	鵜 7151		窕 4051	挺 1884	褪 5444
	鶙 7172		朓 2321	梃 2457	恫 1561
去ㄧˇ	體 7005		眺 3770	町 3557	痌 3616
去ㄧˋ	体 184		糶 4274	艇 4813	通 6097
	倜 205	去ㄧㄠˋ	朓 4665	錠 6402	仝 95
	剃 386		跳 3979	聽 4612	佟 140
	嚏 767	去ㄧㄢ	天 917	禿 3979	僮 264
	屜 1199		添 2949	(禿)	同 553
	屟 1199		薕 6727	鵚 7148	峒 1226
	(屜)	去ㄧㄢˊ	恬 1563	凸 352	彤 1447
	弟 1424		湉 2997	圖 803	瞳 2284
	悌 1583		甜 3538	塗 861	朣 2327
	惕 1609		田 3551	屠 1201	桐 2445
	揥 2089		畋 3562	徒 1475	橦 2603
	替 2310		鈿 6342	途 4006	潼 3084
	殢 2708			突 4044	氃 3389
	涕 2902			荼 4931	瞳 3809
	薙 5124				童 4079

ㄋ

注音	單字	字號
ㄋㄚ	那	6174
ㄋㄚ	南	486
	拿	1874
	挐	1874
	(拿)	
ㄋㄚˇ	哪	645
	那	6174
ㄋㄚˋ	吶	573
	娜	1009
	捺	1905
	納	4288
	衲	5380
	訥	5537
	那	6174
	鈉	6333
•ㄋㄚ	哪	645
ㄋㄜ	訥	5537
•ㄋㄜ	呢	587
ㄋㄞˇ	乃	28
	奶	951
	氖	4831
	迺	6085
ㄋㄞˋ	奈	930
	柰	2412

ㄋㄞˋ

單字	字號
耐	4576
褦	5443
褦	7284

ㄋㄟˊ

單字	字號
那	6174
餒	6874

ㄋㄟˋ

單字	字號
内	307
那	6174

ㄋㄠˊ

單字	字號
孬	1539
撓	2035
橈	2597
猱	3375
譨	5680
鐃	6494

ㄋㄠˇ

單字	字號
堖	1626
瑙	3468
腦	4704

ㄋㄠˋ

單字	字號
淖	2921
鬧	7038

ㄋㄡˋ

單字	字號
耨	4588

ㄋㄢˊ

單字	字號
南	486
喃	678
枏	2367
楠	2367
(枏)	
男	3555
諵	5621
難	6680

ㄋㄢˇ

單字	字號
腩	4712
赧	5823
難	6680

ㄋㄣˋ

單字	字號
嫩	1054

ㄋㄤˊ

單字	字號
囊	780

ㄋㄤˇ

單字	字號
攮	2112

ㄋㄤˋ

單字	字號
囊	2299

ㄋㄥˊ

單字	字號
能	4666

ㄋㄥˋ

單字	字號
㑚	3119

ㄋㄧˊ

單字	字號
倪	212
呢	587
妮	971
尼	1183
怩	1532
泥	2842
猊	3364
霓	4758
蜺	5266
輗	5994
覔	6702
齯	7225

ㄋㄧˇ

單字	字號
你	115
妳	985
擬	2076
旎	2186
薾	3971

ㄋㄧˋ

單字	字號
匿	472
慝	1620
暱	2278
昵	2278
(暱)	
泥	2842
溺	3013
睨	3783
膩	4732
衵	5381
逆	6081

ㄋㄧㄝ

單字	字號
捏	1895
捏	1895
(捏)	
捻	1908
苶	4879

ㄋㄧㄝˇ

單字	字號
囁	776
孽	1096
蘖	1096
(蘖)	
糱	2638
涅	2895
湼	2895
(湼)	
蘖	4273
糱	4273

ㄋㄧㄢˊ

單字	字號
拈	1836
粘	4239
鮎	7065
黏	7249
捻	1908
撚	2037
攆	2092
碾	3894
輦	6000
輾	6014

ㄋㄧㄢˋ

單字	字號
唸	669
廿	1409
念	1518
您	1596

ㄋㄧㄤˊ

單字	字號
娘	1007
孃	1007
(娘)	
釀	6297
凝	345

ㄋㄧㄥˊ

單字	字號
嚀	765
寧	1143
擰	2082
檸	2620
獰	3397
甯	3550
擰	2082

ㄋㄧㄥˋ

單字	字號
佞	139
擰	2082
濘	3119
甯	3550

ㄋㄧㄠˇ

單字	字號
嬲	1065
嫋	1065
(嬝)	1067
蔦	5076
裊	5406
鳥	7115

ㄋㄧㄠˋ

單字	字號
尿	1185
溺	3013

ㄋㄧㄡ

單字	字號
妞	963
牛	3310

ㄋㄧㄡˇ

單字	字號
忸	1514
扭	1802
狃	3346
紐	4289
鈕	6336
杻	5357
謬	5668

ㄋㄧㄢ

單字	字號
蔫	5083
年	1350

ㄋㄨㄛ

單字	字號
按	1881
娜	1009
愞	686
獳	1734
搦	1990
糯	4269
稬	4269
(糯)	
穤	4269
(糯)	
諾	5639

ㄋㄨㄢˇ

單字	字號
暖	2270
煖	3220

ㄋㄨㄥˊ

單字	字號
儂	270
濃	3115
檂	4034
膿	4735
農	6049
醲	6294
鱱	7302

ㄋㄨㄥˋ

單字	字號
弄	1411

ㄋㄩˇ

單字	字號
女	949
釹	6322
衄	1514
恧	1574
朒	5357

ㄋㄩㄝˋ

單字	字號
㰦	3648
虐	5181
謔	5647

ㄌ

注音	單字	字號
ㄌㄚ	喇	681
	拉	1838
ㄌㄚˊ	剌	391
	拉	1838
ㄌㄚˇ	喇	2205
ㄌㄚˋ	喇	681
	剌	391
	瘌	3646

單字	字號
腊	4700
臘	4750
落	5000
蠟	5343
辣	6041
鑞	6517
鬎	7026

ㄌㄚ・／ㄌㄛ・

單字	字號
啦	664
咯	614

ㄌㄜˋ／ㄌㄛˋ

單字	字號
餎	5443
仂	74
勒	432
垃	827
扐	1887
樂	2571
泐	2826
肋	4621

ㄌㄞˊ

單字	字號
了	46
來	149
峽	1248
徠	1481
淶	2944
萊	4979
郲	6212
錸	6416

ㄌㄞˋ

單字	字號
瀨	3151
癩	3680
睞	3778
籟	4223
賚	5787
賴	5800

ㄌㄟˇ／ㄌㄟˋ

單字	字號
勒	432
擂	2054
累	4307
縲	4421
纍	4466
蔂	4487
蠃	5179
鐳	6508

ㄌㄟ	雷	6689	ㄌㄡ	僂	250	ㄌㄤ	廊	1385		罹	4506		吏	560	ㄌㄧㄝ	冽	338
	儡	283		嘍	729		榔	2539		藜	5143		唳	650		列	368
	壘	891		婁	1019		浪	2887		蘺	5175		慄	1660		劣	420
	磊	3901		摟	2007		狼	3356		蜊	5240		戾	1779		捩	1899
	累	4307		樓	2580		琅	3442		蝄	5344		曆	2282		洌	2853
	耒	4579		蔞	5082		瑯	3479		褵	5450		栗	2426		烈	3194
	蕾	5114		螻	5308		稂	4004		貍	5742		櫟	2629		獵	3398
	蘱	5145		髏	7002		莨	4953		醨	6286		櫪	2634		裂	5403
ㄌㄟ	誄	5577	ㄌㄡ	摟	2007		蜋	5246		鱺	6309		歷	2689		趔	5837
	擂	2054	ㄌㄡ	簍	4193		郎	5300		離	6679		溧	2813		躐	5951
	淚	2926	ㄌㄡ	漏	3043		跟	5878		驪	6989		瀝	2904		鬣	7035
	泪	2926		瘻	3662		郎	6199		鸝	7208		澟	3007		裂	7143
	(淚)			鏤	6490		鋃	6400		黎	7248		瀝	3148	ㄌㄧㄠ	撩	2044
	累	4307		陋	6599	ㄌㄤ	朗	2322		鑫	7261		痢	3625	ㄌㄧㄠ	僚	258
	纇	4467	•ㄌㄡ	嘍	729	ㄌㄤ	狼	3205	ㄌㄧ	俚	175		癘	3673		嘹	743
	肋	4621	ㄌㄢ	婪	1025		閬	6549		哩	633		礫	3916		寮	1147
	酹	6266		嵐	1258	ㄌㄤ	浪	2887		娌	1004		礪	3917		寥	1153
	類	6823		闌	2095		閬	6549		悝	1591		立	4073		寮	1172
	顆	6827		爛	2155	ㄌㄥ	楞	2520		李	2340		笠	4095		憭	1684
ㄌㄠ	撈	2028		欄	2641		稜	4010		浬	2886		粒	4237		憀	1707
ㄌㄠ	勞	438		瀾	3158		薐	5121		澧	3103		糲	4271		撩	2044
	嘮	736		籃	4217	ㄌㄥ	冷	337		理	3441		苙	4892		澄	3069
	撈	2028		藍	5137	ㄌㄥ	愣	1634		禮	3970		荔	4903		潦	3079
	牢	3315		蘭	5172		楞	2520		蠡	5344		苈	4929		猭	3388
	癆	3668		鑑	5464	ㄌㄧ	哩	633		裏	5410		莉	4946		療	3665
	醪	6287		襴	5470	ㄌㄧ	釐	1047		裡	5410		蒞	5060		繚	4439
ㄌㄠ	佬	158		讕	5698		梨	2475		(裏)			蠣	5346		聊	4598
	姥			闌	6564		梨	2475		豊	5715		詈	5549		遼	6155
	潦	3079	ㄌㄢ	懶	1740		(梨)			邐	6168		櫟	6036		鐐	6495
	老	4568		攬	2111		犛	2742		體	6293		酈	6243		鷯	7193
	銠	6383		擥	2111		漓	3044		里	6305		隸	6653	ㄌㄧㄠ	了	46
ㄌㄠ	勞	438		(攬)			蔾	3066		鯉	6396		麗	6717		憭	1707
	嘮	1708		欖	2649		棃	3326		鯉	7076		黧	7021		燎	3252
	潦	3079		纜	4475		犁	3326	ㄌㄧ	例	151		鬲	7228		瞭	3811
	澇	3094		覽	5497		(棃)			例	171		麗	7246		蟟	5066
	烙	3200	ㄌㄢ	濫	3126		犛	3334		儷	374	ㄌㄧ	裏	5410		蟟	5326
	絡	4331		爛	3158		狸	3359	•ㄌㄧ	力	417		儷	190		釕	6318
	落	5000		爛	3281		璃	3490		勵	445	ㄌㄧㄝ	咧	607	ㄌㄧㄠ	廖	1388
	酪	6258		纜	4475		籬	4230		屬	513	ㄌㄧㄝ	咧	607		撂	2021
ㄌㄡ	摟	2007						縭	4417								料	2157

第一欄

	字	號
	燎	3252
	瞭	3811
	鐐	6495
ㄌㄧㄠ		
ㄌㄧㄡ	溜	3003
	劉	412
	旒	2189
	榴	2550
	流	2875
	瀏	3141
	琉	3438
	留	3569
	畱	3569
	(留)	
	瘤	3658
	瘤	7101
	(瘤)	
	硫	3863
	硫	3863
	(硫)	
	遛	6135
	鎦	6500
	鶹	6968
	驑	6980
	鷚	7181
ㄌㄧㄡ	柳	2399
	綹	4364
ㄌㄧㄡ	六	313
	溜	3003
	遛	6135
	霤	6710
	餾	6710
	(餾)	
	餾	6896
	鎦	6907
ㄌㄧㄢ	憐	469
	奩	469
	(奩)	
	帘	1315
	廉	1384
	怜	1538

第二欄

	字	號
	憐	1698
	漣	3050
	濂	3114
	璉	3491
	簾	4212
	聯	4604
	蓮	5064
	薕	5173
	褳	5671
	連	6104
	鎌	6470
	鐮	6503
	鬑	7028
	鰱	7101
ㄌㄧㄢ	臉	4743
ㄌㄧㄢ	戀	1748
	斂	2147
	楝	2522
	歛	2677
	殮	2712
	瀲	3159
	煉	3218
	練	4395
	鍊	6435
	鏈	6478
ㄌㄧㄣ	鱗	1268
	林	2375
	淋	2924
	燐	3255
	琳	3459
	璘	3496
	痳	3634
	臨	3814
	磷	3910
	臨	4763
	轔	6025
	遴	6148
	鄰	6233
	隣	6643

第三欄

	字	號
	霖	6703
	驎	6979
	鱗	7107
	膦	7223
	麟	7232
ㄌㄧㄣ	凜	344
	廩	1401
	懍	1727
	檁	2617
	澟	3117
ㄌㄧㄣ	吝	562
	淋	2924
	磷	3910
	蘭	5152
	賃	5774
	躪	5959
ㄌㄧㄤ	梁	2456
	涼	2916
	梁	4246
	粱	4247
	糧	4267
	良	4824
	踉	5246
	諒	5614
	跟	5878
	粮	6004
	量	6308
ㄌㄧㄤ	倆	190
	兩	309
	魎	7054
ㄌㄧㄤ	亮	69
	倞	195
	喨	697
	晾	2263
	諒	5614
	跟	5878
	輛	5996
	量	6308
ㄌㄧㄥ	拾	1845
ㄌㄧㄥ	令	92

第四欄

	字	號
	伶	117
	凌	342
	囹	792
	岭	1219
	怜	1538
	櫺	2640
	泠	2837
	淩	2935
	玲	3418
	瓴	3523
	綾	4369
	羚	4523
	翎	4542
	聆	4597
	舲	4805
	苓	4865
	菱	4987
	蛉	5219
	輪	5976
	輘	5995
	酃	6241
	醽	6298
	鈴	6341
	陵	6619
	零	6688
	霝	6706
	靈	6720
	鯪	7083
	鴒	7127
	齡	7313
ㄌㄧㄥ	嶺	1278
	領	6795
ㄌㄧㄥ	令	92
	另	532
ㄌㄨ	嚕	5614
ㄌㄨ	廬	1402
	爐	2636
	瀘	3145
	爐	3280
	盧	3735

第五欄

	字	號
	纑	4468
	纑	4489
	臚	4752
	臚	4822
	蘆	5160
	轤	6035
	鑪	6519
	顱	6834
	鱸	7112
	鱺	7204
ㄌㄨ	擄	2055
	櫓	2630
	櫓	2630
	(櫓)	
	澢	3064
	虜	5187
	魯	7063
	鹵	7210
ㄌㄨ	僇	253
	六	313
	勠	442
	录	1441
	戮	1772
	淥	2934
	漉	3040
	潞	3076
	璐	3501
	碌	3873
	祿	3952
	簏	4186
	籙	4221
	綠	4354
	菉	4990
	蓼	5066
	角	5500
	賂	5775
	路	5871
	輅	5985
	轆	6021
	逯	6114

第六欄

	字	號
	醁	6275
	錄	6418
	陸	6622
	露	6711
	騄	6954
	鷺	7198
	鹿	7216
	麓	7227
ㄌㄨㄛ	捋	1887
ㄌㄨㄛ	囉	779
	玀	3404
	籮	4231
	羅	4509
	蘿	5177
	螺	5307
	覶	5495
	覼	5495
	(覼)	
	邏	6167
	鑼	6524
	驘	6969
ㄌㄨㄛ	攞	2055
	屢	4754
	臝	5187
	臝	5336
	裸	5420
ㄌㄨㄛ	咯	614
	洛	2860
	濼	3135
	烙	3200
	珞	3431
	絡	4331
	落	5000
	酪	6258
	雒	6669
	駱	6941

繃	4447	蛄	5216	錮	6430	蜾	5262	倌	193
缸	4477	舺	5503	雇	6662	裹	5427	冠	329
罡	4494	蛄	5982	顧	6826	課	6887	官	1112
肛	4627	轂	6016	《ㄨㄚ		過	6124	棺	2498
鋼	6414	辜	6038	刮	375	《ㄨㄞ		泰	3649
《尢ˇ		酤	6255	括	1860	乖	35	矜	3827
岡	1216	鈷	6358	栝	2424	拐	1842	綸	4365
崗	1241	骨	6990	瓜	3516	枴	2382	堯	4938
港	2967	鴣	7132	筈	4120	夬	920	觀	5499
《尢ˋ		骨	6990	聒	4599	怪	1535	關	6574
虹	5195	《ㄨˇ		蝸	5287	儈	233	鰥	7092
《ㄥ		古	530	适	6078	圭	808	《ㄨㄢˇ	
庚	1367	蝦	730	颳	6840	歸	2690	琯	3461
更	2304	殼	2542	鴰	7144	溈	3095	筦	4126
便	2888	榾	2563	《ㄨㄚˇ		珪	3435	管	4149
杭	3988	汩	2781	寡	1144	瑰	3480	脘	4675
稉	3988	牯	3318	卦	493	皈	3514	舘	4938
(稉)		罟	3738	掛	1928	皈	3699	館	6886
粳	4248	瞽	3818	挂	1928	規	5482	《ㄨㄢˋ	
羹	4533	穀	4018	(掛)		邽	6194	冠	329
耕	4582	罟	4495	絓	4327	閨	6546	慣	1675
廣	5792	羖	4519	罣	4497	鮭	7070	摜	2006
鶊	7165	股	4631	褂	5431	龜	7328	灌	3162
《ㄥˇ		臌	4745	詿	5582	匭	466	盥	3733
哽	639	蕎	5058	《ㄨㄛ		宄	1098	祼	3953
埂	836	蠱	5348	渦	2965	晷	2261	罐	4490
梗	2462	詁	5547	蝸	5314	癸	3688	觀	5499
綆	4348	谷	5706	過	6124	簋	4190	貫	5757
耿	4594	賈	5779	郭	6208	詭	5569	鸛	7206
骾	6999	轂	6016	鍋	6437	軌	5968	《ㄨㄣ	
鯁	7075	鈷	6358	國	797	鬼	7048	滾	3036
《ㄥˋ		骨	6990	幗	1336	《ㄨㄟˋ		滾	3036
互	56	鴣	7153	摑	2005	劊	413	(滾)	
更	2304	鶻	7178	虢	5190	會	2312	袞	5388
《ㄨ		鼓	7287	馘	6917	桂	2439	賨	5398
估	114	《ㄨˋ		膕	6917	檜	2612	鯀	7073
呱	591	估	114	(膕)		櫃	2624	棍	2479
咕	594	僱	265	《ㄨㄛˇ		洴	3027	《ㄨㄤ	
姑	981	固	793	果	2377	瞶	3812	光	2877
孤	1087	故	2122	椁	2504	貴	5763	洸	2877
沽	114	梏	2460	槨	2504	跪	5867	胱	4662
菰	4141	糖	3637	(槨)		鱖	7106	廣	1399
苽	4900			猓	3368			獷	3399
菇	4967			菓	4995				
菰	4968								

注音	單字	字號
ㄎㄚ	咖	60..
ㄎㄚˇ	卡	49..
	咳	61..
ㄎㄞˇ	略	67..
ㄎㄜ	刻	38..
	柯	2408
	棵	2499
	珂	3422
	疴	3602
	胢	3602
	(疴)	
	瞌	3800

	礚	3900		愾	1678		闞	6576	ㄎㄨ	楛	2519		藭	5191		鯤	7078
	科	3984		楷	2533	ㄎㄢˋ	勘	435		苦	4874		閫	6575		鵾	7159
	稞	4013		豈	5712		看	3755	ㄎㄨˋ	庫	1373	ㄎㄨㄟˊ	㚟	906	ㄎㄨㄣˇ	壼	902
	窠	4869		鎧	6453		瞰	3824		矻	3843		奎	933		悃	1579
	蝌	5269		鎧	6463		闞	6576		袴	5399		揆	1946		捆	1886
	軻	5980		闓	6570	ㄎㄣ	啃	666		絝	5399		暌	2271		綑	4351
	鈳	6365	ㄎㄞˋ	愒	1631		墾	883		(袴)			睽	3791		閫	6548
	頦	6798		愾	1659		懇	1731		褲	5449		葵	5017	ㄎㄨㄣˋ	困	787
	顆	6810		慨	1678		肯	4637		酷	6264		逵	6110		睏	3775
	髁	7001		欬	2653		肎	4637	ㄎㄨㄚ	夸	926		馗	6916	ㄎㄨㄤ	匡	463
ㄎㄜ	咳	616	ㄎㄠ	尻	1182		(肯)			姱	995		騤	6960		恇	1562
	欬	2653		拷	1871		肯	4637		誇	5579		魁	7049		框	2443
	殼	2719		栲	2430		(肯)		ㄎㄨㄚˇ	垮	833	ㄎㄨㄟˇ	傀	233		筐	4116
	㲉	2719		烤	3198	ㄎㄣˋ	掯	1679	ㄎㄨㄚˋ	胯	4660		跬	5869		誆	5581
	(殼)			考	4569	ㄎㄤ	穅	4264		跨	5860		頍	6794		狂	3343
	売	2719		攷	4569		扛	1798	ㄎㄨㄛˋ	廓	1390	ㄎㄨㄟˋ	犄	6996		誑	5585
	(殼)			(考)		ㄎㄤˊ	扛	1679		括	1860		喟	695	ㄎㄨㄤˋ	壙	890
	頦	6798	ㄎㄠˇ	犒	3332	ㄎㄤˇ	亢	61		擴	2086		愧	1654		曠	2295
ㄎㄜˊ	可	539		銬	6380		伉	104		闊	6562		媿	1654		框	2443
	坷	823		靠	6729		抗	1820	ㄎㄨㄞ	擓	2068		(愧)			況	2821
ㄎㄜˋ	渴	2970	ㄎㄡ	摳	2014		炕	3178		囧	4778		憒	1704		況	2821
	克	297	ㄎㄡˇ	口	527		鈧	6327		膾	5036		潰	3087		(況)	
	刻	384	ㄎㄡˋ	叩	533	ㄎㄤˋ	傾	249		儈	273		簣	4201		眶	3767
	剋	390		寇	1135		坑	819		創	413		聵	4610		礦	3919
	可	539		扣	1797		硜	3865		塊	855		蕢	5100		纊	4463
	喀	721		蔻	5065		鏗	6482		快	1510		饋	6898		貺	5767
	客	1117		釦	6323		阬	6585		旝	2193		餽	6902		鄺	6240
	恪	1560		瞉	7184		肯	4637		會	2312	ㄎㄨㄢ	寬	1152		鑛	6516
	溘	3000	ㄎㄢ	刊	362		肎	4637		檜	2612	ㄎㄨㄢˇ	款	2657	ㄎㄨㄥ	悾	1603
	緙	4399		勘	435		(肯)			澮	3104		欵	2657		空	4042
	課	5600		堪	850		尻	378		獪	3392		(款)			崆	4147
ㄎㄞ	揩	1961		戡	1766		哭	634		蒯	4136		歀	4066	ㄎㄨㄥˇ	孔	1076
	開	6533		看	3755		枯	2380		膾	4737	ㄎㄨㄣ	坤	821		恐	1567
ㄎㄞˇ	凱	349		龕	7327		窟	4055		蒯	5036		崑	1238	ㄎㄨㄥˋ	控	1931
	剴	403	ㄎㄢˇ	侃	148		骷	6995		郐	6238		昆	2212		空	4042
	嘅	726		坎	817		剈	378		蕢	1283		琨	3450			
	嘅	726		檻	2623		哭	634		盔	3725		蚰	5229			ㄏ
	(嘅)			歁	2661		枯	2380	ㄎㄨㄟ	恢	1591		褌	5434			
	愷	1658		砍	3847		窟	4055		盔	3725		錕	6429	注音	單字	字號
				輡	6029		骷	6995		窺	4064		髡	7009	ㄏㄚ	嗃	758
															ㄏㄚ	哈	626
															ㄏㄚˊ	蛤	5225

蝦 5280	赫 5824	鎬 3707	捍 1890	**ㄏㄥˋ**	戽 1780
ㄏㄚˊ	郝 6198	耗 4584	撼 2052	橫 2606	扈 1787
哈 626	鶴 7173	號 5188	旱 2207	**ㄏㄨ**	楛 2519
ㄏㄜ	黑 7250	郻 6220	暵 2277	乎 32	滬 3029
喝 693	**ㄏㄞ**	鎬 6464	汗 2772	呼 598	瓠 3513
訶 5543	孩 1088	顥 6828	漢 3053	忽 1519	祜 3093
ㄏㄜˊ	還 6161	駒 7300	瀚 3147	惚 1612	笏 409
何 132	頦 6798	侯 160	翰 4558	戲 1774	護 5689
劾 426	骸 6997	喉 683	菡 4984	欻 2660	**ㄏㄨㄚ**
合 547	**ㄏㄞˇ**	猴 3376	軒 5737	歑 2670	嘩 73
和 604	海 2891	矦 3833	銲 6411	滹 2953	花 485
曷 2305	醢 6284	篌 4165	釬 6411	虖 5184	華 496
核 2428	亥 63	餱 6890	(銲)	囫 790	**ㄏㄨㄚˊ**
河 2816	咳 1124	吼 577	頷 6805	壺 901	划 36
涸 2912	氦 2756	候 203	頔 6950	弧 1426	劃 40
盍 3721	駭 6940	厚 508	**ㄏㄣˊ**	斛 2158	嘩 73
盒 3724	**ㄏㄟ**	后 557	痕 3620	槲 2984	滑 302
禾 3978	嘿 747	後 1472	**ㄏㄣˇ**	湖 3349	猾 338
紇 4284	黑 7250	逅 6080	很 1468	狐 3371	譁 567
翮 4557	**ㄏㄠ**	鍭 7109	狠 3352	瑚 3472	豁 570
荷 4927	嚆 764	**ㄏㄢ**	**ㄏㄣˋ**	糊 4252	驊 697
蓋 5049	蒿 5043	啣 1717	恨 1558	縠 4403	**ㄏㄨㄚˋ**
褐 5435	薅 5112	蚶 5214	**ㄏㄤ**	胡 4654	劃 40
覈 5477	呵 742	酣 6254	夯 924	葫 5012	化 45
貉 5740	嚄 762	頇 6785	杭 2356	蝴 5285	樺 258
餄 6385	壕 889	骭 7299	**ㄏㄤˊ**	瑚 5369	畫 357
閡 6543	濠 2737	函 355	桁 2432	縠 5510	華 496
閤 6544	號 5188	含 568	沆 2796	醐 6278	話 557
闔 6571	蠔 5340	寒 1138	航 4801	觳 6891	豁 570
鞨 6753	豪 5728	嵅 1250	行 5360	鵠 7027	**ㄏㄨㄛˊ**
騔 7169	貉 5740	鹹 2541	迒 6061	鶘 7153	活 287
齕 7309	鶴 7173	汗 2772	頏 6789	鶻 7166	夥 91
齘 7330	**ㄏㄠˇ**	涵 2911	桁 2432	鶻 7178	火 632
ㄏㄜˇ	郝 6198	邯 6180	沆 2796	**ㄏㄨˇ**	**ㄏㄨㄛˇ**
和 604	好 954	韓 6768	**ㄏㄥ**	唬 667	和 60
喝 693	昊 2215	喊 684	亨 65	滸 3035	鈥 88
嚇 766	晧 2252	罕 4492	哼 638	琥 3203	**ㄏㄨㄛˋ**
奭 947	浩 2883	闞 6576	**ㄏㄥˊ**	虎 5180	惑 162
荷 4927	滈 2912	悍 1586	恆 1551	**ㄏㄨˋ**	或 176
菏 5707	祜 3098	憾 1721	恒 1551	互 53	檴 208
賀 5771	灝 3165	扞 1796	(恆)	怙 1527	獲 339
	皓 3702		桁 2432	戶 1777	嬳 384
			橫 2606		
			珩 3433		
			蘅 5159		
			衡 5372		

單字	字號	單字	字號	單字	字號	單字	字號	單字	字號	單字	字號
者	3844	煥	3268	桓	2446	渾	2975	翃	4540	(羿)	4143
禍	3955	應	5196	環	3504	溷	3012	荭	5023	箕	4431
穫	4036	誨	5597	繯	4448	諢	5626	虹	5195	羈	4511
虇	5157	賄	5776	還	6161	鯇	7074	訌	5523	肌	4622
蠖	5342	ㄏㄨㄟ 匯	467	鐶	6445	ㄏㄨㄤ 肓	4625	閎	6535	蒺	5178
豁	5707	卉	481	鐶	6505	荒	4920	鴻	7139	覉	5479
貨	5754	卉	481	闤	6580	鳳	348	黌	7246	羈	5480
雘	6510	(卉)		鬟	7033	ㄏㄨㄥ 徨	1484	ㄏㄨㄥ 哄	623	畸	5508
霍	6698	喙	690	ㄏㄨㄢ 浣	2882	惶	1630	ㄏㄨㄥ 汞	2778	譏	5672
騞	6962	彗	1443	㳠	3118	湟	2990	閧	7039	跡	5863
ㄏㄨㄞ 徊	1470	彙	1445	緩	4390	潢	3077			蹟	5925
懷	1739	恚	1569	ㄏㄨㄢ 喚	691	煌	3217	**ㄐ**		蹐	5949
槐	2558	惠	1623	奂	935	璜	3497	注音　單字　字號		迹	6074
淮	2939	慧	1689	宦	1121	皇	3698	ㄐㄧ 乩	42	隮	6650
踝	5884	晦	2251	幻	1355	磺	3911	几	346	雞	6677
壞	893	橞	2565	患	1594	篁	4160	咭	694	飢	6850
ㄏㄨㄟ 徽	1495	濊	3116	換	1958	簧	4206	唧	694	饑	6904
恢	1557	燴	3270	摜	2066	蝗	5271	(嘰)		鷄	7185
揮	1963	穢	4033	渙	2955	蟥	5318	嘰	738	賷	7305
撝	2049	篲	4197	漶	3063	遑	6126	基	844	賷	7305
暉	2266	繢	4443	煥	3224	黃	7244	奇	929	(賷)	
灰	3172	繪	4565	瘓	3644	幌	1333	姬	1005	賚	7305
翬	4553	蕙	5097	豢	5727	怳	1536	屐	1196	齎	7306
虺	5196	薈	5117	頔	6026	恍	1555	稘	1255	ㄐㄧ 亝	59
褘	5437	橞	5323	逭	6113	晃	2242	幾	1358	伋	106
詼	5576	誨	5597	婚	1022	諱	5650	期	2325	即	504
輝	5997	諱	5632	悟	1614	晃	2242	朞	2325	即	504
隳	6243	賄	5776	昏	2218	ㄏㄨㄥ 哄	623	(期)		(即)	
麾	7243	闠	6577	昬	5018	烘	3197	機	2605	及	518
回	784	禂	6733	閽	6556	薨	5128	激	3112	吃	549
ㄏㄨㄟ 徊	1470	懳	1747	ㄏㄨㄣ 混	2945	訇	5519	犄	3328	吉	551
洄	2850	歠	2680	渾	2975	轟	6030	璣	3499	咭	694
茴	4910	蘆	5702	瑚	3473	紅	7061	畸	3581	唧	694
蛔	5222	譅	5746	餛	6882	ㄏㄨㄥ 宏	1108	畿	3583	(嘰)	
迴	6072	譅	5746	魂	7050	弘	1422	磯	3908	嫉	1045
廻	6072	(羅)		ㄏㄨㄢ 恩	1670	泓	2831	禨	3969	寂	1132
(迴)		轠	6988	惃	1670	洪	2865	稽	4023	发	1213
ㄏㄨㄟ 悔	1584	寳	1154	(恩)		紅	4283	積	4029		
會	2312			混	2945	紘	4293	笄	4121		
毀	2722							笄	4121		

較	5983	驚	7196	簡	4200	間	6534	蓋	5138	涇	2894
轎	6024	兼	320	簡	4200	閒	6538	觀	5493	睛	3777
醮	6291	堅	846	(簡)		餞	6883	臁	5816	杭	3988
ㄐㄧㄡ		奸	952	繭	4453	**ㄐㄧㄣ**		近	6056	(杭)	
啾	674	姦	992	蠒	4551	今	79	進	6109	梗	3988
噍	748	尖	1170	褟	5458	巾	1305	靳	6737	梗	4248
揪	1962	戔	1762	謇	5652	斤	2164	**ㄐㄧㄤ**		精	4249
摻	1962	械	2510	譾	5691	津	2861	僵	266	經	4350
(揪)		殲	2714	研	5861	矜	3827	姜	987	耕	4582
摎	2015	湔	2981	研	5861	祲	3950	將	1162	莖	4936
樛	2582	漸	3062	(研)		禁	3954	疆	2711	菁	4969
湫	2988	煎	3229	甕	5908	筋	4118	江	2776	荊	4994
究	4039	健	3331	鐧	6498	衿	5386	漿	3067	荊	4994
糺	4276	監	3731	鰜	7213	襟	5461	韁	3584	(荊)	
糾	4277	箋	4138	臉	7214	劤	5501	韁	4447	鷩	6982
赳	5828	(箋)		件	100	金	6310	薑	5122	鯨	7082
摎	6022	緘	4380	**ㄐㄧㄢ**		**ㄐㄧㄣ**		螿	5310	鶄	7164
圖	7043	縑	4406	健	226	僅	251	豆	5711	**ㄐㄧㄥ**	
		肩	4634	偺	263	儘	281	韁	6762	井	55
鳩	7117	艱	4825	儉	274	卺	502	**ㄐㄧㄤ**		儆	272
ㄐㄧㄡ		菅	4957	劍	414	廑	1389	奬	946	剄	387
久	29	蒹	5040	建	1408	槿	2573	槳	2570	憬	1703
九	39	間	6534	檻	2623	殣	2706	蔣	5074	景	2256
灸	3173	閒	6538	健	2741	瑾	3487	講	5657	環	3495
玖	3412	鍵	6755	澗	3062	緊	4375	匠	462	警	5685
糺	4276	鰜	6764	潤	3078	菫	4993	將	1162	阱	6589
糾	4277	鰜	7093	濺	3134	覲	5493	觀	5493	頸	6807
韭	5032	鰹	7179	監	3731	謹	5670	強	1434	倞	195
赳	5828	**ㄐㄧㄢ**		箭	4155	錦	6427	強	1434	清	340
酒	6250	俊	274	腱	4708	饉	6901	(強)		勁	427
韭	261	剪	400	艦	4820	**ㄐㄧㄣ**		彊	1434	境	870
ㄐㄧㄡ		戩	1769	荐	4926	勁	427	(強)		徑	1474
僦	590	揀	1944	薦	5127	噤	750	洚	2903	敬	2139
咎	1177	揀	2067	見	5481	搢	1984	糨	4266	淨	2937
就	1387	柬	2410	諫	5630	晉	2241	糨	4266	痙	3624
殿	2128	檢	2615	賤	5795	晉	2241	(糨)		竟	4077
救	2407	減	2959	踐	5881	(晉)		絳	4338	競	4084
柩	2449	瞼	3817	鍵	6446	浸	2892	醬	6288	脛	4676
柏	3593	筧	4137	鐧	6498	燼	3275	降	6601	逕	6092
疚	4039			鑑	6512	瑨	3485	京	67	鏡	6488
究	4773			鑒	6513	盡	3730	兢	305	靖	6723
臼	4781					禁	3954	旌	2185		
舅	4785					縉	4409	晶	2260		
舊											

		字	字號		字	字號		字	字號		字	字號		字	字號		字	字號
		靚	6724		筥	4125		厥	511	ㄐㄩㄝ	倨	200		郡	6201		其	317
		靜	6725		籧	4228		噘	756	ㄐㄩㄢ	圈	799		雋	6667		奇	929
ㄐㄩ		俱	182		舉	4784		嗺	774		娟	1010		駿	6946		歧	1214
		居	1188		舉	4784		孒	1075		悁	1580	ㄐㄩㄥ	侷	1784		崎	1237
		崌	1249		(舉)			崛	1243		捐	1893		侷	1784		旂	2179
		拘	1852		莒	4934		憰	1749		涓	2899		洞	2822		旗	2190
		据	1902		蹫	5900		抉	1813		蠲	5349		炯	3186		期	2325
		沮	2810		鉏	6348		掘	1922		身	5960		烱	3186		枝	2376
		狙	3351		齟	7311		撅	2109		鐫	6502		(炯)			棋	2478
		琚	3447	ㄐㄩ	侶	182		橛	2455		鵑	7147		窘	4054		棊	2478
		疽	3604		侷	210		桷	2460	ㄐㄩㄢ	卷	499		絅	4322		(棋)	
		痀	3610		具	318		決	2786		捲	1907		迥	6064		歧	2685
		罝	4496		劇	410		決	2786	ㄐㄩㄢ	倦	209		逈	6084		淇	2951
		苴	4878		句	531		(決)			卷	499					琦	3449
		蒩	4972		屨	1206		爛	3282		圈	799					琪	3451
		菹	5031		巨	1296		爵	3289		悁	1580		**ㄑ**			畦	3570
		裾	5430		懼	1744		玃	3390		狷	3358	注音	單字	字號		畿	3583
		趄	5833		拒	1846		珏	3414		睊	3773	˙ㄑ	㟄	659		碁	3884
		車	5966		据	1902		玨	3416		睠	3789	ㄑㄧ	七	3		祁	3926
		鋦	6405		據	2063		玨	3416		絹	4343		妻	974		祇	3930
		鋸	6413		沮	2810		(玨)			鄄	6219		崎	1237		祈	3931
		雎	6668		炬	3184		璺	3821		雋	6667		悽	1604		祺	3951
		駒	6932		瞿	3819		絕	3819	ㄐㄩㄣ	君	791		惄	1691		萁	4373
ㄐㄩ		侷	163		秬	3996		腳	4687		困	561		憰	1691		耆	4571
		局	1186		窶	4065		腳	4707		均	815		(惄)			臍	4749
		揭	1896		簴	4213		蕨	5101		鈞	3712		戚	1763		萁	4974
		掬	1937		聚	4602		蕞	5109		軍	5969		敧	2114		齊	5135
		桔	2447		苣	4893		蠼	5355		鈞	6337		期	2325		蕲	5154
		橘	2600		虡	5189		覺	5496		額	6806		柒	2390		蠐	5337
		臼	4774		距	5551		角	5502		麕	7224		栖	2497		跂	5425
		菊	4958		足	5844		觖	5536		麏	7229		欺	2659		錡	6425
		踘	5876		距	5859		譎	5675		龜	7328		沏	2805		頎	6788
		鼳	6749		踞	5885	ㄐㄩㄝ	蹶	5934	ㄐㄩㄣ	俊	168		淒	2923		騎	6951
		鞫	6754		遽	6157		缺	6929		峻	1233		溪	3009		騏	6953
ㄐㄩ		咀	600		醵	6295		鱖	7106		捃	1885		漆	3042		鬐	7029
		枸	2388		鉅	6345		鴂	7125		浚	2879		緀	4980		鰭	7099
		柜	2403		鋸	6413		缺	7125		濬	3129		萋	5617		麒	7099
		欅	2643		颶	6841		(鴂)			畯	3579		郪	6211		齊	7303
		沮	2810	ㄐㄩㄝ	撅	2026					竣	4080				ㄑㄧ	乞	4
		矩	3834	ㄐㄩㄝ	倔	200	ㄐㄩㄝ	蹶	5934		菌	4959	ㄑㄧ	七	3		啟	66

啟	660	ㄑㄧㄝˋ 切	360	殼	2719	千	475	綮	2569	蹡	5921
(啓)		契	936	殻	2719	嵌	1257	欠	2650	鎗	6460
屺	1211	妾	975	(殼)		慳	1648	歉	2666	錆	6483
杞	2350	怯	1534	壳	2719	掔	1680	縴	4422	鏹	6484
棨	2489	愜	1643	(殼)		扦	1800	茜	4842	ㄑㄧㄤˊ 嬙	1061
綺	4366	慊	1662	竅	4069	牽	1943	茜	4922	強	1434
檠	4374	挈	1875	翹	4561	奉	2002	蒨	5054	强	1434
豈	5712	揭	2313	誚	5589	搴	2019	ㄑㄧㄣ 侵	162	(強)	
起	5830	竊	4072	譙	5678	牽	3324	嶔	1274	彊	1434
ㄑㄧˇ		篋	4164	鞘	6748	簽	4211	欽	2658	(強)	
企	103	蹊	5890	ㄑㄧㄡ 丘	15	籤	4226	衾	5385	戕	1761
器	751	鍥	6442	楸	2534	韱	4226	親	5490	檣	2616
契	936	ㄑㄧㄠ 撬	2045	秋	3983	(籤)		駸	6949	牆	3300
妻	974	敲	2140	秌	3983	芊	4834	ㄑㄧㄣˊ 勤	441	墻	3300
慼	1713	橇	2596	(秋)		襄	5446	勲	1730	(牆)	
慽	1713	硗	3912	蚯	5211	謙	5656	擒	2062	嬙	5123
(慼)		蹺	5935	邱	6182	遷	6151	檎	2613	ㄑㄧㄤˇ 強	1434
棄	2476	蹻	5936	鞦	6751	鉛	6351	琴	3456	强	1434
弃	2476	鍫	6444	鞧	6752	阡	6583	禽	3977	(強)	
(棄)		鍬	6454	鰍	7088	韆	6763	秦	3989	彊	1434
氣	2753	ㄑㄧㄠˊ 僑	255	鰍	7090	騫	6963	芩	4846	(強)	
汽	2794	喬	700	鶖	7167	鵮	7162	芹	4858	搶	1989
泣	2840	嶠	1272	龜	7328	ㄑㄧㄢˊ 乾	44	螓	5295	襁	5454
砌	3846	憔	1700	ㄑㄧㄡˊ 仇	78	前	392	衾	5385	褓	5454
磧	3906	樵	2588	囚	782	拑	1843	罩	5475	(襁)	
繢	4383	橋	2598	毬	2738	掮	1936	ㄑㄧㄣˇ 寢	1145	鏹	6484
葺	5020	瞧	3261	求	2767	潛	3073	撳	2032	ㄑㄧㄥ 嗆	705
訖	5526	瞧	3813	泅	2828	箝	4148	沁	2790	餂	1771
跂	5849	翹	4561	球	3440	虔	5182	ㄑㄧㄤ 嗆	705	熗	3238
迄	6051	蕎	5094	虬	5192	鈐	6335	戧	1771	蹌	5912
ㄑㄧㄚ 穄	659	譙	5678	虯	5193	鉗	6350	搶	1989	蹡	5921
掐	1918	顦	6829	蝤	5278	錢	6426	槍	2557	傾	249
ㄑㄧㄚˇ 卡	491	ㄑㄧㄠˇ 巧	1295	裘	5414	黔	7252	瑲	3484	卿	505
ㄑㄧㄚˇ 卡	491	悄	1581	賕	5786	纏	4460	羌	4514	氫	2757
ㄑㄧㄚˊ 恰	1564	愀	1637	述	6091	譴	5689	(羌)		清	3261
洽	2872	雀	6657	逎	6128	遣	6141	羌	4517	蜻	5261
ㄑㄧㄝ 切	360	鵲	7160	酋	6247	倩	211	腔	4697	輕	5992
ㄑㄧㄝˊ 伽	121	ㄑㄧㄠˋ 俏	170	ㄑㄧㄡˇ 糗	4255	塹	868	蜣	5255	青	6722
茄	4888	峭	1229	ㄑㄧㄢ 仟	89	慊	1662	蹌	5912	鯖	7080
且	12	撬	2045	僉	252					ㄑㄧㄥˊ 情	1606

第一欄

繫 2070
晴 2259
顈 7260
〈ㄑㄧㄥˇ〉
請 5610
頃 6782
〈ㄑㄧㄥˋ〉
慶 1696
磬 3905
綮 4374
馨 4481
親 5490
謦 5665
〈ㄑㄩ〉
區 473
屈 1190
嘔 1265
敺 2144
曲 2302
祛 2805
軀 3819
袪 3940
胠 4653
姐 5217
蚰 5228
袪 5396
詘 5559
趨 5842
軀 5965
驅 6975
〈ㄑㄩˊ〉
劬 424
渠 2962
璩 3507
蘧 3685
翟 3819
籧 4228
絇 4305
胊 4656
菣 5108
蕖 5167
蚰 5228
衢 5373
鴝 7136

第二欄

鸛 7207
麴 7237
麯 7239
〈ㄑㄩˇ〉
取 522
娶 1017
曲 2302
齲 7322
去 514
漆 3042
覷 5494
覰 5494
（覰）
覷 5494
趣 6558
〈ㄑㄩㄝ〉
缺 4478
闕 6572
〈ㄑㄩㄝˊ〉
闋 3663
〈ㄑㄩㄝˋ〉
卻 503
却 503
（卻）
恪 1534
恪 1560
愨 1686
榷 1972
權 2561
殼 2719
毃 2719
（殼）
壳 2719
（殼）
確 3870
碏 3882
確 3893
觳 5510
闋 6563
闕 6572
雀 6657
鵲 7160

第三欄

〈ㄑㄩㄢ〉
圈 799
弮 1430
惓 1588
棬 2496
〈ㄑㄩㄢˊ〉
全 308
卷 499
惓 1610
拳 1873
權 2647
泉 2848
牷 3322
痊 3618
筌 4111
蜷 4924
蟤 5260
詮 5570
踡 5887
醛 6282
銓 6373
顴 6835
〈ㄑㄩㄢˇ〉
犬 3338
畎 3563
綣 4356
〈ㄑㄩㄢˋ〉
券 376
勸 446
逡 6102
〈ㄑㄩㄣˊ〉
群 4526
（羣）
裙 5408
〈ㄑㄩㄥ〉
穹 4041
芎 4837
〈ㄑㄩㄥˊ〉
嬛 1062
惸 1635
煢 3233
瓊 3512
穹 4041
窮 4061
筇 4110

第四欄

芎 4837
窮 5151
蛩 5226
邛 6171

注音	單字	字號
ㄒㄧ	僖	257
	兮	314
	吸	574
	唏	643
	嘻	744
	奚	941
	嬉	1055
	巇	1281
	希	1309
	徯	1489
	恓	1554
	悉	1593
	扱	1807
	攜	2100
	携	2100
	（攜）	
	摡	2100
	（攜）	
	擕	2100
ㄒㄧ	晞	2248
	晰	2257
	晳	2258
	曦	2297
	析	2371
	栖	2423
	棲	2497
	欄	2590
	欷	2656
	浠	2917
	溪	3009
	烯	3207

第五欄

熙 3234
熹 3257
熺 3257
（熹）
犀 3327
犧 3336
睳 3570
皙 3862
禧 3967
稀 4000
羲 4530
膝 4726
螅 5248
蠵 5315
西 5473
觿 5513
謑 5708
谿 5709
豨 5729
蹊 5910
醯 6289
釐 6309
鎎 7201
關 7296
熄 1039
席 1323
息 1575
惜 1617
昔 2220
檄 2608
熄 3237
習 4544
腊 4700
蓆 5047
褵 5428
襲 5469
覡 5486
錫 6428

第六欄

〈ㄒㄧˇ〉
喜 692
屣 1203
徙 1479
憙 1714
枲 2384
洒 2855
洗 2856
璽 3508
禧 3967
葸 5019
蓰 5087
縰 5321
蒠 5644
〈ㄒㄧˋ〉
係 480
卅 480
夕 907
戲 1774
戯 1774
（戲）
歙 2672
汐 2771
潟 3075
盻 3745
矽 3842
禊 3958
夐 4040
系 4309
細 4452
綯 4452
繫 4546
肸 4641
舄 4780
舃 4780
（舄）
郤 6204
隙 6638
隟 6638
（隙）
餼 6895

	(攝)	解 5505	笑 4093	嫌 1046	現 3439
ㄒㄧㄚ 瞎 3797	搚 2100	謝 5658	肖 4623	嫻 1056	綫 4378
蝦 5280	(攝)	躞 5956	酵 6263	嫻 1056	線 4381
ㄒㄧㄚˊ 俠 178	斜 2159	邂 6160	ㄒㄧㄡ 休 111	(嫻)	縣 4402
匣 464	絜 4341	ㄒㄧㄠ 削 389	修 180	弦 1425	羨 4527
峽 1234	纈 4462	哮 635	庥 1371	械 2510	腺 4713
挾 1889	脅 4670	嚚 777	羞 4524	涎 2900	莧 4941
暇 2265	衺 5383	宵 1126	脩 4678	痃 3609	見 5481
押 2401	諧 5629	枵 2383	貅 5739	癇 3669	蜆 5718
洽 2872	邪 6176	梟 2464	饈 6900	絃 4318	鞻 6032
狎 3347	鞋 6746	消 2897	鬏 7020	舷 4810	限 6602
狹 3360	頡 6797	瀟 3149	鵂 7145	誠 5645	霰 6709
瑕 3467	ㄒㄧㄝˇ 寫 1151	硝 3867	ㄒㄧㄡˋ 宿 1131	賢 5793	餡 6884
牽 4795	血 5356	簫 4208	朽 2338	賢 5817	ㄒㄧㄣ 心 1496
轄 6017	ㄒㄧㄝˋ 卸 500	綃 4346	嗅 704	銜 6378	炘 1515
遐 6127	寫 1151	蕭 5102	宿 1131	閑 6537	新 2171
鍻 6458	屑 1197	蛸 5231	岫 1217	閒 6538	昕 2221
霞 6705	廨 1400	蟰 5347	溴 3011	鹹 7211	欣 2652
點 7258	懈 1725	逍 6086	秀 3980	ㄒㄧㄢˇ (毨) 1173	歆 2664
ㄒㄧㄚˋ 下 7	械 2467	銷 6392	繡 4444	毨 1173	炘 3180
嚇 766	楔 2517	霄 6694	繡 4444	(毨)	芯 4851
夏 904	樹 2544	驍 6978	(繡)	(獮) 1276	莘 4937
廈 1383	泄 2824	鴞 7130	臭 4766	洒 2855	薪 5129
暇 2265	淺 2864	ㄒㄧㄠˊ 學 1094	袖 5390	冼 2856	訢 5535
罅 4482	漢 2991	烄 3294	銹 6412	燹 3273	辛 6037
ㄒㄧㄝ 些 57	潟 3101	ㄒㄧㄠˇ 小 1168	鏽 6497	獮 3395	鋅 6401
歇 2663	瀉 3139	曉 2285	顀 7301	玁 3405	鑫 6520
蠍 5273	瀉 3153	筱 4130	ㄒㄧㄢ 仙 87	玁 3405	歆 6776
蠍 5335	變 3272	篠 4180	先 295	(玁)	馨 6920
ㄒㄧㄝˊ 偕 223	解 3393	謏 5653	纖 1071	獬 3683	ㄒㄧㄣˊ 尋 1165
勰 443	絏 4329	儌 240	掀 1911	蘚 5170	ㄒㄧㄣˋ 信 179
協 485	絏 4329	哮 635	暹 2279	蜆 5238	囟 785
叶 545	(絏)	嘯 737	祆 3928	跣 5866	焮 3209
協 1565	薤 5126	孝 1083	纖 4472	銑 6372	芯 4851
挾 1889	蟹 5328	效 2123	蹮 5955	險 6647	舋 6300
擷 2085	蟹 5328	効 2123	銛 6377	顯 6831	顖 6824
攜 2100	(蟹)	敩 2149	鮮 7071	鮮 7071	ㄒㄧㄤ 厢 1382
携 2100	褻 5456	校 2429	鑫 7114	ㄒㄧㄢˋ 峴 1231	湘 2985
(攜)	褻 5456	歊 2674	ㄒㄧㄢˊ 咸 617	憲 1718	相 3744
撷 2100	(褻)		啣 662	獻 3402	

注音	單字	字號	注音	單字	字號	注音	單字	字號	注音	單字	字號	注音	單字	字號	注音	單字	字號
丁|尤	箱	4154		形	1448	丁ㄩ	昫	2233		黌	7199		煮	3203		迅	6052
	緗	4384		形	1448		栩	2425		雪	6683		薰	3236		遜	6132
	纕	4471		(形)			湑	2993		鱈	7099		燻	3236		馴	6926
	缸	4800		硎	3871		煦	3231	丁ㄩㄝ	削	389		(薰)		丁ㄩㄥ	兄	291
	薌	5119		行	5360		許	5541		穴	4038		獯	3396		兇	294
	襄	5455		邢	6177		詡	5563		血	5356		爋	4059		凶	351
	鄉	6221		邢	6189	丁ㄩ	勗	434		雪	6683		纁	4461		匈	452
	鑲	6522		鉶	6419		勖	434	丁ㄩㄢ	喧	696		葷	5018		恟	1556
	香	6918		陘	6604		(勗)			嬛	1062		薰	5134		洶	2871
	驤	6987		餳	6892		卹	501		宣	1118		醺	6296		胸	4664
丁|尤	庠	1370	丁|ㄥ	擤	2081		壻	899		揎	1971	丁ㄩㄣ	尋	1165		胷	4664
	祥	3946		省	3753		婿	899		暄	2264		峋	1225		(胸)	
	翔	4545		醒	6276		(壻)			瑄	3465		巡	1291		詾	5538
	詳	5574	丁|ㄥ	倖	201		序	1363		翾	4564		巡	1291	丁ㄩㄥ	熊	3235
	降	6601		姓	983		恤	1559		萱	4997		(巡)			雄	6658
丁|尤	享	66		幸	1352		慉	1665		諼	5620		徇	1467	丁ㄩㄥ	夐	905
	想	1644		性	1531		敘	2125		誼	5625		循	1486			
	響	6779		悻	1600		敍	2125		軒	5970		恂	1550		业	
	餉	6867		杏	2344		(敘)		丁ㄩㄢ	懸	1742		揗	2033			
	饟	6908		興	4783		叙	2125		旋	2184		旬	2202	注音	單字	字號
	鯗	7072		荇	4925		(敍)			漩	3052		洵	2870	业	之	30
丁|尤	像	254		莕	4932		旭	2203		玄	3406		潯	3083		卮	494
	向	559		行	5360		洫	2863		璇	3489		珣	3436		巵	1867
	嚮	769	丁ㄩ	吁	548		滀	3058		璿	3510		紃	4280		指	1985
	巷	1303		噓	735		畜	3567		縣	4402		荀	4915		支	2113
	橡	2290		墟	874		絮	4340		還	6161		蕈	5105		枝	2376
	橡	2601		戌	1754		緒	4379	丁ㄩㄢ	癬	3683		詢	5564		梔	2461
	相	3744		歔	2673		續	4464		選	6152		巡	6053		栀	2461
	象	5725		盱	3741		芧	4845	丁ㄩㄢ	旋	2184		巡	6053		(梔)	
	鄉	6221		繻	4457		蓄	5046		渲	2968		(巡)			氏	2746
	項	6783		胥	4643		馘	5781		漩	3052		郇	6191		汁	2765
丁|ㄥ	惺	1636		蓿	5067		酗	6252		炫	3183		馴	6926		知	3831
	星	2223		虛	5185	丁ㄩㄝ	噱	756		眩	3760	丁ㄩㄣ	異	1304		祇	3930
	猩	3374		許	5531		薛	5125		絢	4332		徇	1467		祗	3938
	腥	4703		需	6692		靴	6738		衒	5362		殉	2699		織	4437
	興	4783		須	6786	丁ㄩㄝ	學	1094		鉉	6346		汛	2777		肢	4632
	馨	6920		嬃	6801		尋	1165		鏇	6475		蕈	5106		脈	4658
丁|ㄥ	騂	6947		顬	7032		遑	5879	丁ㄩㄣ	勛	444		訊	5522		脂	4668
	刑	364	丁ㄩ	徐	1473					壎	887		訓	5524		芝	4840
	型	832								曛	2294					蜘	5249
																隻	6655

业					
福 7279	寅 1140	輊 5988	鰲 5301	療 3661	軸 5977
值 208	峙 1227	遲 6147	遮 6145	砦 3858	[业ㄞ] 帶 1317
執 843	峽 1316	郅 6190	[业ㄜ] 哲 636	這 6096	肘 4624
姪 994	幟 1339	銍 6379	[业ㄜ] 懾 1682	招 1855	[业ㄢ] 青 326
指 1867	彘 1444	鑕 6515	儋 1745	昭 2228	兕 589
摭 2011	志 1504	陟 6607	折 1822	朝 2324	宙 1113
擲 2084	忮 1511	雉 6664	摘 2004	着 3776	晝 2247
植 2500	懥 1733	鷙 6964	摺 2016	著 5003	甃 3528
殖 2702	摯 2024	鸞 7189	磔 3899	釗 6315	皺 3713
直 3743	智 2262	[业ㄚ] 扎 1791	[业ㄜ] 翟 4547	着 3776	箒 4216
熱 4426	治 2819	扡 1872	蜇 5239	找 1809	簉 4216
職 4609	滯 3031	揸 1967	蟄 5312	沼 2817	(簉)
蟄 5312	炙 3181	查 2411	褶 5451	爪 3284	紂 4279
質 5797	時 3571	植 2514	謫 5667	兆 293	綯 4405
跖 5855	東 3590	渣 2961	[业ㄜ] 讁 5694	召 536	青 4645
蹠 5920	峙 3621	割 408	輒 5989	旐 2188	占 490
蹢 5922	痓 3627	扎 1791	轍 6005	罩 2287	旃 2180
躑 5952	知 3831	札 2334	轍 6023	棹 2502	氈 2745
[业] 只 534	秩 3993	[业ㄜ] 炸 3189	[业ㄜ] 者 4572	櫂 2627	毡 2745
咫 612	稚 4009	箚 4150	赭 5825	炤 3191	(氈)
址 813	樨 4009	紮 4304	緒 6450	照 3232	氊 2745
徵 1491	(稚)	紮 4304	宅 1102	笊 4090	(氈)
恉 1578	窒 4050	(紮)	柘 2400	罩 4498	氊 2745
指 1867	袟 4324	銅 6440	浙 2878	肇 4618	(氈)
旨 2200	緻 4397	閘 6540	蔗 5071	詔 5554	沾 2820
枳 2381	置 4500	[业ㄚ] 貶 3761	這 6096	趙 5838	瞻 3816
止 2681	腟 4730	乍 31	鷓 7186	[业ㄡ] 周 588	覘 5484
沚 2804	至 4769	[业ㄜ] 吒 555	[业ㄡ] 着 3776	啁 653	詹 5575
砥 3849	致 4770	咋 603	著 5003	州 1290	邅 6162
祇 3930	(致)	[业ㄞ] 咤 608	齊 7303	洲 2868	霑 6701
祉 3932	蛭 5227	搾 1979	齋 7304	整 3736	饘 6911
紙 4295	製 5429	柵 2416	(齋) 7304	粥 4242	鱣 7110
耆 4571	誌 5584	榨 2546	[业ㄞ] 宅 1102	舟 4797	鸇 7202
正 4856	識 5677	炸 3189	擇 2060	賙 5788	[业ㄢ] 展 1195
趾 5847	豸 5734	[业ㄞ] 痄 3614	翟 4547	輖 5986	嶄 1267
黹 5979	質 5797	笮 4107	[业ㄞ] 窄 4048	週 6108	搌 2001
酯 6259	贄 5806	蚱 5213	[业ㄞ] 債 246	鵃 7141	斬 2168
阯 6591	顜 5953	[业ㄜ] 蜡 5252	寨 1149	[业ㄢ] 妯 972	琖 3444
黹 7272		[业ㄞ] 詐 5552		舳 4806	盞 3728
[业] 制 381		折 1822			輾 6014
					[业ㄞ] 佔 131
					占 490

	1		2		3		4		5		6
	戰 1773		畛 5975		崢 1244		豬 5732		苧 4875		霻 7190
	暫 2275		鬒 7030		征 1463		邾 6195		著 5003	业ㄨㄞ	拽 1869
	棧 2484	业ㄣ	振 1880		徵 1491		銖 6374	业ㄨㄚ	蛀 5215		跩 5874
	湛 2986		揕 1952		徰 1537	业ㄨ	尤 2335	业ㄨㄞ	註 5545		跩 1869
	站 4074		朕 2320		挣 1925		燭 3271		鑄 6511	业ㄨㄟ	椎 2501
	綻 4367		枕 2373		楨 2528		竹 4085		罺 6927		追 6075
	蘸 5174		瑱 3481		正 2682		竺 4086		駐 6930		錐 6420
	醮 5926		賑 5783		烝 3195	业ㄨㄚ	筑 4115	业ㄨㄚ	抓 1816		佳 6654
	顫 6830		酖 6251		爭 3286		築 4166		揭 2053		騅 6955
业ㄣ	偵 229		鎭 6465		猙 3365		軸 4806		罜 7022	业ㄨㄟ	墜 876
	振 1880		陣 6617		癥 3679	业ㄨㄛ	躅 5943	业ㄨㄞ	爪 3284		惴 1627
	斟 2161		震 6693		睁 3781		軸 5977	业ㄨㄛ	捉 1888		綴 4362
	椹 2508		鴆 7122		筝 4139		逐 6090		桌 2436		縋 4404
	楨 2528	业尢	張 1433		蒸 5039	业ㄨ	主 26		棹 2502		贅 5807
	榛 2540		彰 1456		靜 5611		囑 781		涿 2913		餟 6888
	珍 3425		樟 2577		貞 5749		屬 1207	业ㄨㄛ	卓 484	业ㄨㄢ	專 1161
	甄 3527		漳 3059		鉦 6355		拄 1833		啄 1833		甎 3530
	眞 3762		獐 3387		錚 6423		渚 2956		拙 1851		塼 3530
	真 3762		璋 3493	业ㄥ	拯 1859		煮 3228		撾 2074		(甎)
	(眞) 3762		章 4078		整 2145		麈 3228		斫 2167		磚 3907
	砧 3850		蟑 5316	业ㄥ	幀 1330		(煮)		斮 2169		尚 4578
	禎 3960		鄣 6229		挣 1925		曙 3825		斲 2172		顓 6818
	禛 3964		鼚 7231		政 2121		貯 5759	业ㄨㄢ	斵 2172	业ㄨㄢ	轉 775
	箴 4158	业尢	掌 1940		正 2682		塵 7220		梲 2468		轉 6020
	朕 4657		漲 3060		症 3608	业ㄨ	佇 124		椓 2506		傳 244
	臻 5045		長 6528		証 5561		住 128		浞 2905		撰 2047
	診 5544	业尢	丈 4		證 5674		助 421		濁 3113		璱 3466
	貞 5749		仗 85		鄭 6231		宁 1100		濯 3127		篆 4163
	針 6316		嶂 1266	业ㄨ	侏 153		杼 2364		灼 3174		籑 4192
	鍼 6447		帳 1324		朱 2336		柱 2409		焯 3210		賺 5801
	鱵 7111		幛 1338		株 2427		祝 2414		琢 3446		轉 6020
业ㄣ	枕 2373		杖 2348		橥 2639		注 2845	业ㄨㄣ	着 3776		饌 6903
	疹 3565		漲 3060		洙 2857		炷 3188		镯 4449	业ㄨㄣ	窀 4048
	珍 3603		瘴 3659		潴 3154		祝 3942		茁 4885		肫 4636
	稹 4024		脹 4688		珠 3432		妤 4075		著 5003		諄 5607
	紾 4314		賬 5798		硃 3860		筯 4129	业ㄨㄣ	诼 5613		迬 6060
	縝 4412		長 6528		茱 4908		箸 4157		踔 5893	业ㄨㄣ	准 339
	朕 4657		障 6641		蛛 5223		粥 4242		酌 6248		準 3004
	診 5544	业ㄥ	丁 2		誅 5578		紵 4316	业ㄨ尢	鐲 6501		隼 6656
					諸 5637		書 4552			业ㄨ尢	妝

單字	字號
业ㄨㄤ	
庄	1360
椿	2575
粧	4244
莊	4933
业ㄨㄤ	
裝	5416
僮	264
壯	898
戆	1750
撞	2039
狀	3342
业ㄨㄥ	
中	21
伀	1516
忠	1517
忠	3716
終	4319
蟲	5309
衷	5382
鍾	6448
鐘	6493
业ㄨㄥ	
家	332
塚	858
種	4014
腫	4705
踵	5899
业ㄨㄥ	
中	21
仲	97
眾	3772
種	4014
眾	5358
重	6306

彳

注音	單字	字號
彳	吃	549
	喫	549
	(吃)	
	嗤	719
	媸	1041
	摛	2009
	痴	3641
	癡	3676
	眵	3771
	笞	4098
	絺	4344
	蚩	5209
	螭	5303
	郗	6203
	魑	7057
	鴟	7131
彳	侘	7324
	垞	459
	圻	875
	尺	1180
	弛	1423
	持	1865
	池	2773
	篪	2819
	箎	4174
	箎	4174
	(箎)	
	茬	4891
	跰	5886
	馳	6925
彳	侈	150
	呎	585
	尺	1180
	恥	1577
	耻	4596
	蚇	5210
	褫	5445
	豉	5713
	齒	7307
彳	傺	248
	勅	429
	叱	541
	啻	672
	彳	1458
	敕	2129
	斥	2165
	熾	3249
	眙	3756
	翅	4539
	赤	5821
	趷	5864
	頳	5879
	飭	6856
	鶒	7171
彳ㄚ	叉	517
	嗏	702
	差	1298
	扠	1801
	扱	1807
	插	1954
	挿	1954
	(插)	
	杈	2342
	番	4776
彳ㄚ	察	1142
	搽	1981
	查	2411
	槎	2559
	碴	3891
	茶	4878
	茶	4912
彳ㄚ	叉	517
彳ㄚ	佽	155
	剎	379
	剎	379
	(剎)	
	妊	997
	妊	997
	(妊)	
	岔	1212
	差	1298
	杈	2342
	汊	2768
	杈	5377
	詫	5567
彳ㄜ	車	5966
彳ㄜ	尺	1180
	扯	1805
	撦	2041
	坼	824
	徹	1492
	拆	1837
	犁	1941
	撤	2030
	澈	3089
	轍	6023
彳ㄞ	差	1298
	拆	1837
	釵	6325
彳ㄞ	儕	280
	柴	2413
	茈	4882
	豺	5736
	蒫	4951
	瘥	3655
	蠆	5334
彳ㄠ	弨	1427
	抄	1812
	超	5834
	鈔	6331
彳ㄠ	嘲	739
	巢	1292
	晁	2243
	朝	2324
	潮	3082
	吵	7277
彳ㄠ	吵	572
	炒	3182
	鈔	6331
彳ㄡ	抽	1831
	搐	1973
	犨	3337
	瘳	3660
	篘	4177
	紬	4308
	仇	78
彳ㄡ	傳	279
	幬	1344
	惆	1605
	愁	1646
	疇	3585
	稠	4012
	籌	4218
	紬	4308
	綢	4355
	裯	5423
	鯈	5697
	鯈	5697
	(鯈)	
	躊	5948
	酬	6260
	雔	6671
彳ㄡ	丑	11
	瞅	3792
	醜	6279
彳ㄡ	臭	4766
彳ㄢ	攙	2098
	襜	5463
	單	701
	嬋	1057
	孱	1091
	巉	1282
	廛	1393
	欃	2644
	毚	2734
	潺	3085
	澶	3111
	瀍	3143
	禪	3968
	纏	4465
	蟬	5324
	蟾	5332
	讒	5699
	饞	5699
	(饞)	
	劖	406
	產	3541
	葴	5091
	諂	5606
	鏟	6487
	闡	6578
彳ㄢ	懺	1743
	羼	4535
	顫	6830
彳ㄣ	嗔	712
	捵	1904
	琛	3445
	瞋	3796
	郴	6210
彳ㄣ	塵	867
	宸	1128
	忱	1513
	晨	2253
	橙	2599
	沈	2798
	沉	2798
	(沈)	
	臣	4759
	蔯	5085
	諶	5635
	辰	6047
	陳	6617
彳ㄣ	櫬	2635
	稱	4015
	襯	5468
	讖	5701
	趁	5832
	趂	5832
	(趂)	
	齔	7308
彳ㄤ	倀	188
	倡	207
	娼	1026
	昌	2216
	猖	2814
	菖	4963
	閶	6553

注音	字	碼
（ㄕ續）	栻	2422
	氏	2746
	遾	3105
	示	3923
	筮	4128
	耆	4571
	紙	4788
	鳖	5301
	視	5485
	試	5565
	臂	5586
	諡	5618
	諟	5646
	謚	5662
	識	5677
	弒	5713
	貰	5760
	軾	5984
	逝	6087
	適	6144
	釋	6304
	鈰	6360
	飾	6863
•ㄕ	匙	459
ㄕㄚ	挲	1878
	殺	2718
	沙	2802
	煞	3230
	痧	3626
	砂	3845
	紗	4294
	莎	4948
	裟	5417
	鎩	6476
	鯊	7077
ㄕㄚˊ	嗄	670
ㄕㄚˇ	傻	276
	儍	276
	（傻）	
ㄕㄚˋ	嗄	703
	廈	1383
	歃	2665
	煞	3230
	翣	4140
	萐	4549
	霎	6699
ㄕㄜ	奢	943
	畲	3577
	賒	5784
ㄕㄜˊ	什	72
	佘	134
	折	1822
	揲	1966
	甚	3537
	舌	4786
	蛇	5218
	虵	5218
	（蛇）	
	闍	6566
ㄕㄜˇ	捨	1897
	舍	4787
ㄕㄜˋ	射	1160
	拾	1864
	攝	2101
	歙	2672
	涉	2896
	社	3925
	舍	5001
	設	5540
	赦	5822
	麝	7230
ㄕㄞ	篩	4172
ㄕㄞˇ	色	4826
	骰	6993
ㄕㄞˋ	曬	2300
	晒	2300
	（曬）	
	殺	2718
ㄕㄟˊ	誰	5601
ㄕㄠ	弨	1431
	捎	1894
	梢	2470
	燒	3254
	稍	3999
	筲	4131
	箾	4176
	艄	4195
	蛸	5231
ㄕㄠˊ	勺	447
	杓	2345
	芍	4836
	韶	6777
ㄕㄠˇ	少	1169
ㄕㄠˋ	劭	425
	哨	632
	少	1169
	捎	1894
	潲	3093
	紹	4312
	邵	6179
ㄕㄡ	收	2115
ㄕㄡˊ	熟	3243
ㄕㄡˇ	守	3104
	手	1789
	首	6915
ㄕㄡˋ	受	523
	售	891
	壽	903
	授	1913
	狩	3354
	獸	3400
	瘦	3652
	綬	4357
ㄕㄢ	刪	979
	姍	979
	山	1209
	扇	1786
	搧	1991
	杉	2341
	潸	3086
	煽	3239
	珊	3424
	羴	4531
	羶	4532
	膻	4747
	舢	4799
	芟	4841
	苫	4876
	衫	5376
	跚	5857
ㄕㄢˇ	彡	6326
	閃	6531
	陝	6612
ㄕㄢˋ	單	701
	嬗	1060
	扇	1786
	掞	1926
	擅	2057
	汕	2770
	疝	3594
	禪	3968
	繕	4438
	膳	4733
	蟮	5327
	蟺	5330
	訕	5525
	贍	5813
	赸	5831
	鄯	6232
	饍	6906
	鱔	7105
	鐥	7110
ㄕㄣ	伸	118
	參	515
	呻	597
	娠	1011
•ㄕㄣ	深	2943
	椮	3260
	甡	3540
	申	3554
	砷	3855
	紳	4311
	莘	4937
	葠	5007
	蔘	5007
	（蔘）	
	詵	5580
	身	5960
	鉮	6367
ㄕㄣˊ	神	3943
ㄕㄣˇ	哂	622
	嬸	1069
	審	1150
	沈	2798
	瀋	3140
	矧	3832
	諗	5616
	讅	5693
ㄕㄣˋ	慎	1661
	滲	3032
	甚	3537
	脤	4684
	腎	4694
	葚	5004
	蜃	5237
	矤	7266
ㄕㄤ	裮	247
	商	655
	殤	2707
	湯	2989
	觴	5511
ㄕㄤˇ	上	6
	晌	2244
	賞	5790
ㄕㄤˋ	上	6
	尚	1171
	裳	5425
ㄕㄥ	勝	437
	升	476
	昇	2213
	牲	3319
	生	3539
	甥	3542
	笙	4094
	聲	4606
	陞	6606
	鉎	7293
ㄕㄥˇ	澠	3100
	繩	4445
	省	3753
	眚	3763
ㄕㄥˋ	乘	36
	剩	401
	勝	437
	嵊	1263
	晟	2245
	盛	3727
	聖	4600
	賸	4746
	貹	5805
ㄕㄨ	姝	988
	抒	1815
	摴	2020
	攄	2091
	書	2306
	梳	2473
	梳	2473
	樗	2578
	樞	2583
	殊	2700
	殳	2715
	洙	2857
	疏	3588
	疎	3588
	（疏）	
	疏	3588

注音	單字	字號
ㄕㄨ	(疏)	
	紓	4291
	舒	4789
	蔬	5077
	輸	6009
	叔	521
	塾	869
	熟	1090
	淑	2922
	熟	3243
	秫	3997
	菽	4973
	贖	5818
ㄕㄨˇ	屬	1207
	數	2143
	暑	2268
	署	4502
	薯	5133
	藷	5165
	蜀	5235
	鸀	7200
	黍	7247
	鼠	7291
ㄕㄨˋ	倏	196
	墅	871
	庶	1376
	恕	1568
	戍	1755
	數	2143
	曙	2291
	束	2351
	樹	2595
	流	2811
	漱	3057
	澍	3091
	疏	3588
	署	4502
	術	5363
	袒	5407
	豎	5717

注音	單字	字號
	刷	382
ㄕㄨㄚ	耍	4577
	刷	382
ㄕㄨㄛ	說	5598
	妁	955
	帥	1319
	搠	1999
	數	2143
	朔	2319
	槊	2553
	爍	3278
	碩	3889
ㄕㄨㄞ	芍	4836
	蜂	5311
	鑠	6514
	挼	6561
	衰	5378
ㄕㄨㄞˇ	甩	3546
	帥	1319
	率	3407
	蜂	5311
ㄕㄨㄟˊ	誰	5601
	水	2761
ㄕㄨㄟˋ	悅	1321
	睡	3779
	稅	4001
	蛻	5233
	說	5598
	栓	1862
	栓	2421
	問	6530
ㄕㄨㄢ	涮	2952
ㄕㄨㄣˇ	吮	569
	楯	2536
	盾	3752
	瞬	3807
	舜	4794
	順	6784
ㄕㄨㄤ	孀	1070

注音	單字	字號
	瀧	3152
	雙	6673
	霜	6704
	爽	3295

ㄖ

注音	單字	字號
ㄖ	日	2198
ㄖㄜ	喏	686
	惹	4873
	熱	3245
	爇	3279
ㄖㄠ	蕘	5096
	饒	6905
ㄖㄠˇ	擾	2088
	繞	6150
ㄖㄡ	揉	1948
	柔	2397
	蹂	5903
	糅	6011
	肉	4619
ㄖㄢ	然	3215
	燃	3251
	髯	7012
	髯	7017
ㄖㄢˇ	冉	322
	染	2396
	苒	4864
ㄖㄣ	人	71
	仁	73
	任	101
	壬	897
	紝	4297
	紝	4297
	(紝)	
ㄖㄣˇ	忍	1500
	稔	4008

注音	單字	字號
	荏	4918
ㄖㄣˋ	切	88
	任	101
	刃	358
	妊	960
	恁	1566
	紉	4286
	紉	4297
	紝	5384
	袵	5405
	訒	5530
	認	5583
	靭	5971
	韌	6766
	餁	6855
	餁	6870
ㄖㄤ	嚷	773
	攘	2097
	瓤	3521
	瀼	3973
	穰	4037
	禳	4471
ㄖㄤˇ	嚷	773
	壤	894
	攘	2097
ㄖㄤˋ	讓	5700
ㄖㄥ	扔	1795
ㄖㄥˊ	仍	81
	礽	3924
ㄖㄨ	儒	278
	嚅	763
	如	956
	孺	1095
	濡	3125
	茹	4914
	襦	5465
	顬	6832
ㄖㄨˊ	駑	7142

注音	單字	字號
ㄖㄨˋ	乳	43
	汝	2775
	辱	6048
	入	306
	洳	2867
	溽	3015
	縟	4413
	肉	4619
	茹	4914
	蓐	5050
	褥	5442
	辱	6048
	鈮	6390
ㄖㄨㄛ	按	1881
ㄖㄨㄛˊ	婼	219
	弱	1432
	蒻	4442
	箬	4153
	篛	4178
	若	4873
	蒻	5055
ㄖㄨㄟ	緌	4372
	蕤	5103
	蕊	5726
	蕊	5093
	枘	2374
	汭	2782
	瑞	3471
	睿	3794
	芮	4852
	蚋	5202
	蜹	5267
	銳	6391
	頠	5276
	蠕	5341
	軟	5974
	頓	6012
	阮	6588
ㄖㄨㄥˊ	橤	3329

注音	單字	字號
ㄖㄨㄣ	潤	3080
	閏	6536
ㄖㄨㄥ	容	1129
	嵘	1277
	戎	1756
	榕	2538
	榮	2551
	毯	2736
	溶	3240
	熔	3240
	絨	4334
	羢	4525
	肜	4630
	茸	4913
	蓉	5048
	融	5338
	鎔	6459
ㄖㄨㄥˇ	宂	1101
	氄	2744

ㄗ

注音	單字	字號
ㄗ	吱	578
	咨	610
	姿	999
	孜	1082
	孳	1092
	淄	2915
	滋	3022
	粢	4241
	緇	4370
	茲	4909
	菑	4961
	葘	4961
	(葘)	
	諮	5631
	貲	5761
	資	5777
	趑	5836

注音	單字	字號
	輞	5993
	鏎	6422
	鎡	6456
	髭	7020
	嶵	7286
	齊	7303
	齎	7305
	齜	7315
ㄗˇ	仔	82
	姉	977
	姊	977
	(姊)	
	子	1073
	梓	2459
	滓	3025
	秭	3995
	第	4100
	籽	4234
	紫	4306
	籽	4580
	茈	4882
	訾	5546
	訿	5560
ㄗˋ	訶	395
	字	1078
	态	1572
	漬	3055
	牸	3323
	眥	3764
	眦	3764
	(眥)	
	栽	4667
	自	4764
ㄗㄚ	匝	460
	咂	595
	紮	4304
	紮	4304
	(紮)	
	臜	4757
ㄗㄚˊ	拶	1863

注音	單字	字號
	椊	2448
	砸	3856
	雜	6675
ㄗㄜˊ	則	385
	咋	603
	嘖	732
	幘	1337
	擇	2060
	澤	3106
	笮	4048
	笮	4107
	簀	4189
	舴	4807
	責	5758
	賊	5780
	齰	5810
ㄗㄜ˙	迮	6071
ㄗㄜ˙	怎	1542
ㄗㄟˋ	仄	76
	昃	2211
ㄗㄞ	哉	627
	栽	2438
	災	3175
	灾	3175
	(災)	
	㞢	3175
	蓄	4961
	蕾	4961
	(蕾)	
ㄗㄞˇ	仔	82
	宰	1123
	崽	1254
	載	5987
ㄗㄞˋ	再	324
	在	806
	載	5987
	賊	5780
ㄗㄠˊ	糟	4263
	蹧	5924

注音	單字	字號
	遭	6142
ㄗㄠˊ	鑿	6527
ㄗㄠˇ	早	2201
	棗	2481
	澡	3102
	繰	4454
	藻	5156
	蚤	5207
ㄗㄠˋ	噪	753
	慥	1676
	燥	3269
	皁	3694
	皂	3695
	竈	4071
	灶	4071
	(竈)	
ㄗㄡ	箃	4191
	諏	5684
	躁	5942
	造	6101
	掫	1939
	緅	4371
	諏	5612
	譖	5651
	鄒	6222
	鄹	6239
	陬	6614
	騶	6967
	鯫	7084
ㄗㄡˇ	走	5827
	奏	934
	揍	1950
	驟	6984
ㄗㄢ	簪	4205
ㄗㄢˊ	咱	615
ㄗㄢˇ	拶	1863
	揝	1969
	攢	2102
	昝	2235
	椊	2448

注音	單字	字號
ㄗㄢˋ	趙	5843
	暫	2275
	讚	5703
	贊	5811
ㄗㄣ	鏨	6244
	簪	6491
ㄗㄣˇ	響	4205
ㄗㄣˇ	怎	1542
ㄗㄢˊ	諎	5676
ㄗㄤ	牂	3299
	臢	4757
	臧	4762
	賍	5782
	臟	5815
	牂	7003
ㄗㄤˇ	駔	6933
	奘	938
	臟	4755
	葬	5013
	藏	5139
ㄗㄥ	增	877
	憎	1699
	曾	2309
	繒	3839
	繪	4436
ㄗㄥˋ	甑	3532
	繒	4436
	贈	5809
ㄗㄨˊ	租	3990
	卒	483
	捽	1906
	族	2187
	鏃	2566
	足	5844
	鏃	6474
ㄗㄨˇ	俎	169
	祖	3937
	組	4320
	組	5557
	阻	6592

注音	單字	字號
ㄗㄨˋ	詛	6933
	作	138
	嗺	749
ㄗㄨㄛˊ	作	138
	捽	1906
	昨	2227
ㄗㄨㄛˇ	佐	129
	左	1294
	撮	2048
ㄗㄨㄛˋ	作	138
	做	224
	坐	818
	座	1372
	作	1523
	柞	2404
	祚	3941
	胙	4649
	酢	6253
	繫	6527
	阼	6593
ㄗㄨㄟ	嘴	740
	崒	2254
	最	2311
	罪	4499
	檇	5099
	皋	6040
	醉	6272
ㄗㄨㄢ	鑽	6525
	纂	4192
	纂	4456
	鑽	4474
	鑽	6525
ㄗㄨㄣ	尊	1164
	樽	2593
	罇	4483
	遵	6149
ㄗㄨㄣˇ	撙	2036

注音	單字	字號
ㄗㄨㄥ	宗	1111
	從	1480
	棕	2507
	椶	2507
	(棕)	
	縱	4418
	蓯	5010
	踪	5896
	蹤	5919
	騣	6959
	鬉	7025
ㄗㄨㄥˇ	傯	227
	總	4425
ㄗㄨㄥˋ	從	1480
	從	1480
	(從)	
	鬃	4253
	椶	4253
	(椶)	
	綜	4353
	縱	4418

ㄘ

注音	單字	字號
ㄘ	差	1298
	态	1572
	疵	3615
	雌	6666
ㄘˊ	慈	1666
	瓷	3524
	疵	3615
	磁	3896
	祠	3944
	粢	4241
	茨	4905
	茲	4909
	詞	5558
	辭	6044
	鶿	6866
	鷀	7176

注音	單字	字號
	鴜(鷀)	7176
ㄘ	此	2683
	泚	2835
	玼	3423
ㄘ	伺	119
	刺	383
	廁	1381
	次	2651
	賜	5789
ㄘㄚ	擦	2078
ㄘㄜ	側	228
	册	323
	厠	1381
	惻	1638
	測	2969
	策	4122
	筴	4132
ㄘㄞ	猜	3367
ㄘㄞ	才	1790
	材	2346
	纔	4469
	裁	5402
	財	5751
ㄘㄞ	彩	1452
	採	1929
	睬	3786
	綵	4363
	曬	5865
	踩	5894
	采	6302
ㄘㄞ	菜	4964
	蔡	5073
	采	6302
ㄘㄠ	操	2058
	糙	4261
ㄘㄠ	嘈	727
	曹	2307
	槽	2574
	漕	3048

注音	單字	字號
ㄘㄢ	鱝	5302
	慚	1724
	岑	4829
	草	4917
ㄘㄢ	磋	1676
	湊	2977
	湊	2977
	(湊)	
	勝	4702
ㄘㄢ	䎁	6007
	參	515
	餐	6872
	驂	6972
	慙	1688
	憯	1688
	(憯)	
ㄘㄢ	殘	2703
	蠶	5351
ㄘㄢ	慘	1673
	憯	1709
	黲	7267
ㄘㄤ	㜗	3267
	璨	3505
	粲	4245
ㄘㄣ	參	515
ㄘㄣ	岑	1215
	涔	2901
	倉	191
	傖	237
	滄	3019
	艙	4817
	蒼	5042
	鶬	7174
ㄘㄤ	藏	5139
ㄘㄤ	駔	6933
	層	1204
	噌	1269
	曾	2309
ㄘㄥ	蹭	5931

注音	單字	字號
ㄘㄨ	粗	4236
	皻	7233
ㄘㄨ	徂	1464
	殂	2698
ㄘㄨ	促	166
	卒	483
	猝	3369
	簇	4187
	蔟	5086
	趣	5840
	齪	5891
	鼀	5917
	蔟	5927
	蹴	5933
	顣	5938
	醋	6274
ㄘㄨㄛ	搓	1980
	撮	2048
	磋	3897
	莎	4949
	鹺	5909
ㄘㄨㄛ	嵯	1264
	痤	3631
	瘥	3655
	矬	3835
	鹾	7212
ㄘㄨㄛ	遳	3483
	脞	4683
ㄘㄨㄛ	剉	388
	厝	510
	挫	1879
	措	1934
	撮	2048
	莝	4952
	銼	6409
	錯	6431
	催	241
	崔	1239
	璀	2012
	榱	2548

注音	單字	字號
	繀	4407
	衰	5378
ㄘㄨㄟ	璀	3488
ㄘㄨㄟ	崒	659
	焠	1601
	檇	2596
	漼	2740
	淬	2938
	瘁	3640
	粹	4250
	翠	4548
	脆	4669
	胦	4669
	(脆)	
	脺	4693
	膵	4693
ㄘㄨㄟ	萃	4975
	領	6811
ㄘㄨㄢ	攅	2099
	余	2763
	頹	5958
ㄘㄨㄢ	攥	2102
	爨	3283
ㄘㄨㄢ	竄	4068
	蕞	4169
ㄘㄨㄣ	村	2347
	皴	3711
	邨	6178
	存	1079
	蹲	5928
ㄘㄨㄣ	忖	1507
	时	552
	寸	1157
ㄘㄨㄥ	囱	789
	從	1480
	悤	1549
	匆	1549
	(怱)	
	悤	1595

注音	單字	字號
	椶	1576
	璁	3486
	璁	3494
	聰	4605
	蔥	5027
	蔥	5075
	鏓	6477
	驄	6974
ㄘㄨㄥ	叢	526
	從	1480
	丛	1480
	(從)	
	淙	2928
	琮	3455

ㄙ		
注音	單字	字號
ㄙ	司	546
	嘶	741
	廝	1394
	思	1544
	斯	2038
	斯	2170
	澌	3096
	私	3981
	絲	4339
	緦	4387
	罳	4503
	螄	5292
	鍶	6451
	鷥	7191
ㄙˇ	死	2692
ㄙ	伺	119
	似	120

注音	單字	字號
	巳	1301
	廁	1381
	柶	2417
	汜	2774
	泗	2833
	祀	3927
	禩	3966
	笥	4099
	耜	4585
	肆	4616
	賜	5789
	食	6849
	飼	6860
	駟	6939
ㄙㄚ	仨	94
	撒	2029
ㄙㄚ	撒	2029
	洒	2855
	灑	3163
	靸	6741
ㄙㄚ	卅	478
	薩	5132
	跶	5850
	颯	6838
ㄙㄜ	嗇	706
	圾	812
	塞	863
	澀	3121
	溮	3121
	(澀)	
	惡	3462
	穡	4032
	色	4826
	鎩	6387
ㄙㄞ	塞	863
	腮	4716
	顋	6813
	鰓	7091
ㄙㄞ	塞	863

注音	單字	字號
ㄙㄞ	賽	5804
ㄙㄠ	搔	1978
	繰	4432
	繰	4454
	縢	4744
	艘	4816
	騷	6966
ㄙㄠˇ	嫂	1038
	掃	1912
	掃	1912
	(掃)	
ㄙㄠˋ	掃	1912
	掃	1912
	(掃)	
	臊	4744
ㄙㄡ	嗖	680
	廋	1386
	搜	1987
	溲	3010
	蒐	5033
	鎪	6843
	餿	6894
ㄙㄡˇ	叟	525
	嗽	725
	擻	2090
	瞍	3798
	藪	5150
ㄙㄡˋ	嗽	724
	漱	3057
ㄙㄢ	三	5
	參	515
ㄙㄢ	叄	238
	散	2137
	糝	4262
	繖	4440
ㄙㄢˋ	散	2137
ㄙㄣ	森	2493
ㄙㄤ	喪	699
	桑	2437
ㄙㄤˇ	嗓	711

注音	單字	字號
	顙	6821
ㄙㄤˋ	磉	609
ㄙㄥ	僧	262
ㄙㄨ	甦	3543
	穌	4026
	蘇	5162
	酥	6256
ㄙㄨˊ	俗	173
ㄙㄨˋ	嗦	707
	塑	859
	夙	910
	宿	1131
	愫	1656
	愬	1671
	泝	2836
	涑	2898
	溯	3008
	簌	4185
	粟	4240
	素	4302
	縮	4419
	蓿	4617
	膆	4722
	蔌	5067
	蕀	5080
	訴	5542
	謖	5660
	速	6100
	遡	6139
	餗	6878
	鷫	7195
ㄙㄨㄛ	唆	641
	娑	1006
	抄	1878
	杪	2452
	梭	2471
	簑	4179
	縮	4419
	莎	4948

注音	單字	字號
	莎	4949
	蓑	5051
ㄙㄨㄛˇ	索	4303
ㄙㄨㄛˋ	嗩	708
	所	1782
	琑	3478
	索	4303
	鎖	6455
	鎖	6492
ㄙㄨㄟ	睢	3780
	綏	4349
	荽	4928
	雖	6672
	綏	4349
	遂	6118
	隋	6631
	濉	6644
	雖	6672
ㄙㄨㄟˇ	繐	6676
	髓	7004
	歲	2688
ㄙㄨㄟˋ	燧	3265
	碎	3875
	祟	3945
	穗	4031
	術	5363
	誶	5602
	遂	6118
	邃	6164
	隧	6645
ㄙㄨㄢ	痠	3628
	酸	6265
ㄙㄨㄢˇ	篹	4192
	筭	4135
	算	4144
	蒜	5035
ㄙㄨㄢˋ	算	4144
ㄙㄨㄣ	孫	1089
	孫	3382
ㄙㄨㄣ	飱	5044
	殢	6853

注音	單字	字號
	殢	6853
	(殢)	
ㄙㄨㄣˇ	損	1975
	榫	2545
	筍	4112
	笋	4112
	(筍)	
	簨	4204
	隼	6656
ㄙㄨㄣˋ	遜	6132
ㄙㄨㄥ	崧	1246
	嵩	1261
	松	1516
	松	2366
	淞	2930
	鬆	7023
ㄙㄨㄥˇ	悚	1587
	慫	1687
	竦	4081
	聳	4607
ㄙㄨㄥˋ	宋	1106
	訟	5532
	誦	5596
	送	6077
	頌	6787

ㄚ

注音	單字	字號
ㄚ	啊	657
	腌	4692
	阿	6594
ㄚˊ	嗄	703
ㄚˇ	啊	6417
	阿	6594
ㄚ˙	啊	657

ㄛ

注音	單字	字號
ㄛ	喔	688
ㄛˊ	哦	631

	殢	6853
•ㄛ	呵	593

ㄜ

注音	單字	字號
ㄜ	婀	1016
	屙	1200
	痾	3602
	痾	3602
	(痾)	
	阿	6594
ㄜˊ	俄	167
	哦	631
	娥	1013
	峨	1228
	我	4943
	蛾	5234
	訛	5533
	鵝	5682
	鋨	6398
	額	6812
	鵝	7152
	鵞	7152
	(鵝)	
	䲨	7152
	(鵝)	
ㄜˇ	惡	1624
	我	1759
	猗	3363
ㄜˋ	俄	167
	厄	506
	呃	582
	堊	752
	崿	1260
	惡	1624
	愕	1633
	戹	1778
	扼	1824
	搤	1824
	(扼)	

注音	單字	字號
ㄜˋ	夕	2691
	(歹)	
	腭	4715
	尊	4999
	諤	5627
	軶	5973
	遏	6125
	鄂	6216
	鍔	6439
	閼	6554
	阨	6586
	阸	6598
	顎	6815
	餓	6875
	鑩	7113
	鶚	7168
	鰐	7323

ㄝ

注音	單字	字號
ㄝ	誒	5599

ㄞ

注音	單字	字號
ㄞ	哀	620
	哎	628
	唉	642
	埃	837
	挨	1876
ㄞˊ	呆	584
	挨	1876
	捱	1903
	獃	3383
	癌	3667
	皚	3706
	騃	6948
ㄞˇ	噯	759
	欸	2655
	毐	2728
	矮	3837

ㄞ		
囍	5155
彋	6718
噯	759
嬡	1063
愛	1653
曖	2289
瑷	3502
僾	3885
曖	3915
艾	4830
薆	5115
隘	6637
靉	6721

ㄟ		
注音	單字	字號
ㄟ	欸	2655

ㄠ		
注音	單字	字號
ㄠ	凹	353
	熬	3244
	嗷	722
	嗸	722
	(嗷)	
	敖	2130
	熬	3244
	獒	3385
	璈	3492
	翱	4556
	翶	4563
	鰲	4608
	鼇	5305
	警	5664
	遨	6143
	鏖	6479
	鏖	6481
	鷔	6970
	鰲	7100

ㄠ		
竈	7280
媼	1042
拗	1849
襖	5462
傲	243
坳	825
奧	1726
拗	1849
敖	2130
澳	3108
懊	3266
隩	6646

ㄡ		
注音	單字	字號
ㄡ	毆	2144
	歐	2669
	毆	2724
	漚	3046
	甌	3529
	謳	5669
	鷗	7188
	偶	230
	嘔	731
	耦	4587
	藕	5142
	嘔	731
	慪	1683
	漚	3046

ㄢ		
注音	單字	字號
ㄢ	安	1105
	庵	1375
	盦	3734
	菴	4988
	諳	5633
	鞍	6745
	鶴	7157

	俺	186
	岸	1223
	按	1866
	暗	2269
	案	2435
	犴	3341
	萻	4988
	闇	6559
	黯	7265

ㄣ		
注音	單字	字號
ㄣ	恩	1573
ㄣ ㄣ	嗯	716
	嗯	716
	嗯	716
	摁	1997

ㄤ		
注音	單字	字號
ㄤ	腌	4692
	航	6994
ㄤ ㄤ	昂	2210
	盎	3722

ㄦ		
注音	單字	字號
ㄦ	兒	300
	洏	2876
	而	4575
	胹	4673
ㄦ	洱	2866
	爾	3296
	珥	3430
	耳	4590
	邇	6163
	鉺	6382
	餌	6869
	輯	6942

	二	49
	貳	5762

ㄧ		
注音	單字	字號
ㄧ	一	1
	伊	105
	依	157
	咿	619
	噫	754
	壹	900
	揖	1953
	欹	2662
	漪	3051
	猗	3363
	禕	3961
	繄	4429
	翳	4559
	衣	5374
	醫	6285
	鷖	7187
	黟	7259
ㄧˊ	一	1
	儀	269
	匜	461
	咦	609
	圯	809
	夷	925
	姨	993
	宜	1116
	彝	1446
	彞	1446
	(彝)	
	怡	1530
	沂	2791
	洟	2858
	疑	3589
	痍	3617
	眙	3756
	眱	3766

	移	3998
	簃	4188
	胰	4661
	臣	4760
	蓂	4919
	蛇	5218
	訑	5529
	詒	5553
	誼	5604
	跠	5752
	貽	5770
	迤	6054
	迻	6082
	遺	6154
	頤	6802
	鮿	6861
ㄧˇ	乙	37
	以	93
	倚	204
	已	1300
	庋	1785
	旖	2191
	椅	2503
	檥	2618
	矣	3830
	艤	4819
	苡	4872
	苢	4901
	蟻	5331
	蜻	5895
	轙	6028
	迤	6054
	釓	6311
	釔	6366
	鈘	6381
	頠	6819
ㄧˋ	一	1
	亦	64
	佁	90

	佚	136
	佾	146
	億	271
	刈	361
	劓	416
	嘒	778
	奕	937
	射	1160
	屹	1210
	嶧	1275
	奕	1413
	弋	1415
	役	1460
	悒	1585
	意	1650
	憶	1720
	懌	1728
	懿	1746
	齸	1746
	(齸)	
	抑	1823
	拽	1869
	挹	1882
	掖	1923
	斁	2146
	易	2219
	映	2234
	晹	2286
	曳	2303
	代	2354
	枻	2391
	殪	2709
	毅	2723
	泄	2825
	浥	2884
	液	2909
	溢	3005
	熠	3242
	異	3574

異(異) 3574	押 1832	曳 2303	繇 4430	楢 2523	荾 4939
疫 3597	椏 2505	業 2526	肴 4640	油 2815	誘 5588
瘞 3657	鴉 7124	液 2909	謠 5659	游 2974	柚 6303
益 3720	ㄧㄚˊ 枒 2372	燁 3263	軺 5978	猶 3373	鼬 7292
瞖 3806	涯 2908	腋 4691	遙 6134	猷 3377	ㄧㄢ 咽 618
繶 4415	牙 4860	葉 5001	銚 6376	由 3552	奄 928
繹 4451	芽 4860	謁 5641	陶 6620	疣 3598	嫣 1052
義 4528	妌 5205	鄴 6237	餚 6881	繇 4430	崦 1251
羿 4537	衙 5367	醬 6734	鰩 7097	猶 5095	懕 1735
翊 4541	ㄧㄚˇ 亞 58	頁 6780	ㄧㄠ 咬 613	蚰 5212	懨 1735
翌 4543	啞 665	ㄧㄞ 崖 1240	夭 921	蝤 5277	(懨) 1735
翳 4559	雅 6660	吚 554	杳 2359	輶 6008	殷 2717
翼 4560	ㄧㄚˋ 亞 58	夭 921	歾 2694	逌 6105	湮 2948
肄 4615	姬 1027	妖 962	窅 4046	遊 6121	烟 3199
肊 4620	掗 1957	幺 1354	窈 4047	郵 6213	焉 3204
腋 4691	訝 5534	么 1354	窅 4778	鈾 6357	煙 3222
臆 4742	軋 5967	(幺) 1354	皎 7318	蚘 7062	燕 3258
薏 5120	迓 6057	徼 1494	ㄧㄠˇ 拗 1849	ㄧㄡ 卣 492	胭 4659
藝 5144	˙ㄧㄚ 唷 581	祅 3929	曜 2293	友 519	腌 4692
鎴 5259	ㄧㄛ 唷 663	腰 4706	樂 2571	有 2315	臙 4753
衣 5374	ㄧㄝ 喍 746	蘨 5021	燿 3276	櫾 2567	蔫 4971
裔 5412	掖 1923	要 5474	耀 4567	懮 3246	蔫 5083
裛 5418	耶 4591	邀 6158	葯 5030	楥 3246	鄢 6225
詣 5562	揶 1968	嶢 851	藥 5148	牖 3306	醃 6269
誼 5604	椰 2512	姚 986	要 5474	羑 4516	閹 6554
議 5683	爺 3293	崤 1245	躍 5950	莠 4939	閼 6555
譯 5687	邪 3443	嶢 1273	鑰 6521	酉 6245	嚴 772
肔 5752	耶 4591	徭 1488	鎬 6844	銪 6384	妍 996
軼 5981	邪 6176	搖 1983	鷂 7182	黝 7257	妍 996
逸 6112	ㄧㄝˇ 也 41	殽 2720	ㄧㄡ 優 284	ㄧㄡˋ 佑 130	(妍) 996
邑 6169	冶 336	洮 2869	幽 1357	侑 154	岩 1224
鎰 6466	野 6307	淆 2918	悠 1592	又 516	巖 1287
鐿 6509	咽 618	爻 3294	憂 1694	右 543	延 1406
驛 6983	夜 911	猇 3378	攸 2116	囿 794	戼 2025
鷁 7180	射 1160	傛 3378	滺 3065	宥 1120	檐 2609
黓 7251	拽 1869	(猺)	燢 3266	幼 1356	沿 2823
ㄧㄚ 丫 20	掖 1923	猺 3477	櫌 4589	有 2315	炎 3176
呀 581	摩 2083	窯 4062	麀 7217	柚 2402	焰 3216
壓 886	曄 2283	窯 4062	ㄧㄡˊ 尤 1174	祐 3933	燄 3216
		(窯)	犰 2177		(焰) 3216

畬	3576	域	840	谷	5706	說	5598	怨	1547	韻	6778
盂	3715	嫗	1049	豫	5730	越	5835	愿	1672	ㄩㄥ 傭	242
禺	3976	寓	1139	遇	6120	躍	5950	掾	1947	塘	872
竽	4060	尉	1163	遹	6153	軏	5972	瑗	3474	壅	884
腴	4087	峪	1235	郁	6188	鉞	6352	苑	4863	庸	1378
臾	4709	彧	1450	鈺	6356	鑰	6521	院	6609	慵	1681
舁	4775	御	1482	闇	6557	閱	6551	願	6820	擁	2056
舁	4777	愈	1649	陼	6646	龠	7329	量	2267	邕	3160
與	4782	慾	1692	雨	6681	ㄩㄢ 冤	330	黿	2760	灉	3684
萸	5024	拗	1849	雩	6682	冤	330	贇	5812	臃	4741
虞	5186	昱	2230	預	6790	(冤)		ㄩㄣ 云	52	邕	6172
褕	5440	棫	2495	飫	6858	嬡	1050	勻	448	鄘	6226
覦	5488	欲	2654	取	6922	淵	2942	昀	2222	雍	6663
諛	5622	毓	2730	欝	7045	薦	7121	畇	4124	雝	6678
踰	5897	汨	2781	蒉	7047	篤	7129	紜	4296	饔	6909
輿	6015	浴	2889	魆	7056	鴛	7161	耘	4583	ㄩㄥˊ 傭	242
輩	6031	煜	3221	馭	7135	ㄩㄢˊ 元	290	芸	4857	喁	676
逾	6115	熨	3247	遹	7146	原	509	蒷	5110	塘	872
隅	6625	燠	3266	鷸	7197	員	629	雲	6687	庸	1378
隅	6627	獄	3384	鬻	7263	園	801	ㄩㄣˇ 允	289	慵	1681
雩	6682	玉	3408	顝	7331	圓	802	殞	2705	顒	6817
餘	6879	瘉	3647	ㄩㄝ 曰	2301	ㄩㄢˇ 援	1965	狁	3345	鰫	7103
魚	7060	癒	3674	ㄩㄝ 約	4282	沅	2792	磒	3902	ㄩㄥˇ 俑	172
ㄩ 予	47	矞	3828	刖	367	湲	2992	隕	6635	勇	430
傴	245	禦	3965	岳	1280	源	2999	ㄩㄣˋ 孕	1077	壅	884
圉	796	禹	3976	嶽	1280	爰	3287	惲	1629	憑	1667
宇	1103	籲	4225	悅	1582	猿	3379	慍	1657	擁	2056
嶼	1279	籲	4232	戉	1753	猨	3379	量	2267	永	2762
庾	1380	聿	4614	曜	2293	(猿)		熨	3247	泳	2847
瑀	3475	育	4639	月	2314	緣	4388	縕	4410	涌	2907
禹	3975	與	4782	樂	2571	芫	4847	蘊	5163	湧	2983
窳	4063	芋	4835	樾	2592	苑	4863	蘊	5163	甬	3548
羽	4536	蔚	5072	淪	3157	蚖	5289	(蘊)		臃	4741
與	4782	菀	5113	籥	4227	螈	5293	運	6122	蛹	5232
語	5591	蜮	5258	粵	4243	袁	5387	鄆	6217	詠	5550
鋙	6406	裕	5413	耀	5030	轅	6018	醞	6280	咏	5550
雨	6681	語	5591	藥	5148	鵷	7276	韞	6772	(詠)	
齬	7320	論	5619			ㄩㄢ 遠	6138	韻	6775	ㄩㄥˋ 踊	5880
ㄩˋ 喻	698	譽	5690			ㄩㄢ 媛	1034			用	3545

國語羅馬字索引

編　法：本索引係照單字讀音，按國語羅馬字字母順序編列。其讀音相同者，再按部首順序。單字後註明單字編號。

用　法：遇有僅知讀音不悉字形之單字，可按國語羅馬字字母查出索引中單字，再根據單字編號，查出書內單字及這一單字為首所組成的詞語。

GWOYEU ROMATZYH INDEX

In this index the characters are arranged according to the alphabetical order of Gwoyeu Romatzyh. Characters with the same pronunciation are arranged according to their respective radicals. The figure to the right of each character is its identification number under which the character can be found in the body of the dictionary.

If the dictionary user knows the pronunciation of the character he is looking for but is unfamiliar with its strokes, he can find it in the index according to the alphabetical order of Gwoyeu Romatzyh. Using the identification number as a guide, he can locate in the dictionary the character and the entries beneath it.

A

注音	單字	字號
a	啊	657
	腌	4692
	阿	6594
·a	啊	657
aan	俺	186
ae	嗳	759
	欸	2655
	毐	2728
	矮	3837
	藹	5155
	靄	6718
ah	錒	6417
	阿	6594
ai	哀	620
	唉	628
	唉	642
	埃	837
	挨	1876
air	呆	584
	挨	1876
	捱	1903
	獃	3383
	癌	3667
	皚	3706
	騃	6948
an	安	1105
	庵	1375
	盦	3734
	菴	4988
	諳	5633
	鞍	6745
	鵪	7157
ang	腌	4692
	肮	6994
ann	岸	1223
	按	1866
	暗	2269
	案	2435
	犴	3341
	庵	4988
	闇	6559
	黯	7265
anq	盎	3722
ao	遌	1042
	拗	1849
	襖	5462
ar	嗄	703
arng	昂	2210
au	凹	353
	熬	3244
aur	嗷	722
	謷	722
	(嗷)	
	敖	2130
	熬	3244
	癸	3385
	璈	3492
	翱	4556
	翶	4563
	鰲	4608
	螯	5305
	鷔	5664
	遨	6143
	鏊	6479
	鏖	6481
	驁	6970
	鼇	7100
	鼈	7280
aw	傲	243
	坳	825
	奧	944
	懊	1726
	拗	1849
	敖	2130
	澳	3108
	澚	3266
	隩	6646
ay	嗳	759
	嫒	1063
	愛	1653
	璦	2289
	礙	3885
	凝	3915
	艾	4830
	薆	5115
	隘	6637
	靉	6721

B

注音	單字	字號
ba	八	311
	叭	537
	吧	586
	巴	1302
	扒	1793
	捌	1891
	疤	3595
	笆	4089
	粑	4520
	芭	4850
	豝	5724
·ba	吧	586
	罷	4505
baa	把	1818
	鈀	6329
	靶	6739
baan	坂	2365
	版	3302
	版	4804
	蝂	5253
	闆	6565
	阪	7280
baang	榜	2547
	牓	3305
	綁	4345
bae	伯	113
	捭	1900
	擺	2087
	柏	2394
	百	3693
	襬	5467
bah	壩	895
	把	1818
	灞	3166
	爸	3291
	罷	4505
	耙	4581
	覇	5478
	霸	6713
bai	掰	1942
bair	白	3692
ban	扳	1806
	攽	1993
	班	2153
	瘢	2154
	班	3434
	斒	3654
	瘢	3671
	般	4802
	頒	6792
bang	傍	235
	幫	1345
	幇	1345
	(幫)	
	梆	2472
	浜	2880
	邦	6175
bann	伴	116
	半	479
	扮	1803
	拌	1841
	瓣	3520
	絆	4321
	辦	6042
banq	膀	4718
	傍	235
	棒	2480
	磅	3898
	膀	4718
	蚌	5199
	謗	5655
	鎊	6457
bao	保	176
	堡	849
	寶	1156
	寳	1156
	(寶)	
	葆	5022
	褓	5436
	飽	6862
	鴇	7123
bar	八	311
	拔	1848
	茇	4896
	跋	5851
	鈸	6340
bau	剝	398
	包	451
	炮	3185
	炰	3185
	(炮)	
	胞	4652
	苞	4871
	褒	5441
	襃	5453
baur	薄	5111
	雹	6691
baw	報	848
	抱	1826
	暴	2276
	瀑	3138
	爆	3277
	苞	4991
	豹	5735
	釣	5846
	鉋	6347
	鑤	6347
	(鉋)	
	鎊	7066
bay	拜	1856
	敗	2131
	稗	4011
	粺	4251
bean	匾	471
	扁	1783
	稨	4049
	藊	5025
	褊	5268
	編	5433
	貶	5764
beau	婊	1028
	表	5375
	裱	5424
	錶	6433
beei	北	458
been	奔	940
	本	2333
	畚	4880
beeng	繃	4433
	絣	4433
	(繃)	
bei	卑	482
	悲	1622
	揹	1970
	杯	2357
	盃	3719
	碑	3874
	背	4646
ben	奔	932
	奙	932
	(奔)	

犇 3330	bian 逼 6116	bie 憋 1711	篦 4181	(昺)	旛 1270
賁 5773	砭 3851	鱉 7281	臂 4740	柄 2393	撥 2031
錛 6434	碥 4156	鼈 7281	苾 4884	炳 3187	播 2043
beng 崩 1247	邊 4229	(鼈)	萆 4989	秉 3982	波 2839
繃 4433	編 4389	biee 彆 3675	蓖 5061	稟 4007	玻 3426
綳 4433	編 5268	癟 3675	蓽 5079	邴 6186	番 3575
(繃)	邊 6166	(彆)	蔽 5089	餅 6871	般 4802
benn 奔 932	鞭 6750	bieh 別 1438	薜 5131	餅 6880	菠 4965
奔 932	編 7087	bih 俾 187	裨 5422	bin 儐 277	鉢 6353
(奔)	biann 便 164	啚 723	襞 5459	彬 1453	缽 6353
笨 4097	卞 489	壁 882	駕 5509	份 2120	(缽)
benq 榜 2547	弁 1410	婢 1023	詖 5556	斌 2151	盋 6353
繃 4433	徧 1473	弼 1059	費 5768	檳 2626	(鉢)
綳 4433	忭 1512	幣 1343	賁 5773	濱 3131	•bo 葡 5081
(繃)	抃 1810	庇 1361	跛 5858	瀕 3146	boh 亳 70
蹦 5923	昪 2236	弊 1414	蹕 5916	繽 4458	北 458
迸 6106	汴 2788	弱 1435	觱 5941	豳 5733	播 2043
迸 6106	緶 4398	必 1497	躄 5947	賓 5785	檗 2071
(迸)	辡 4455	愎 1639	辟 6039	寅 5785	薄 5111
berng 甭 3549	變 5695	福 1642	邲 6116	(賓)	薜 5131
bey 倍 194	辨 6043	拂 1834	避 6156	bing 兵 316	薇 5168
備 239	辦 6045	敝 2133	邲 6183	冰 335	boo 簸 4210
孛 1081	辯 6046	斃 2148	鄙 6224	并 1351	簸 5858
悖 1589	遍 6123	比 2731	鈚 6361	binn 儐 277	bor 伯 113
憊 1712	biau 彪 1454	毖 2732	閉 6532	擯 2077	勃 428
焙 3208	標 2018	泌 2829	閟 6541	殯 2713	博 487
狽 3357	杓 2345	淠 2994	陛 6605	臏 4748	帛 1318
碚 3880	標 2581	牸 3355	髀 7000	鬢 7007	搏 1977
糒 4256	熛 3248	璧 3503	鷩 7194	髩 7034	柏 2394
背 4646	森 3370	畀 3559	bii 七 456	binq 並 19	檘 2645
臂 4740	膘 4751	畢 3573	妣 966	併 189	泊 2827
蓓 5052	膘 4751	痹 3636	彼 1461	併 189	淳 2881
被 5397	(膘)	痞 3704	比 2731	(併)	渤 2963
褙 5438	鏢 6489	睥 3782	秕 3986	并 1351	濼 3135
貝 5747	鑣 6518	碧 3887	筆 4109	抨 2008	犮 3339
輩 6002	飆 6846	祕 3936	鄙 6224	柄 2393	白 3692
邶 6185	麃 6846	秘 3936	biing 丙 16	病 3607	百 3693
鋇 6395	(飆)	(祕)	屏 1198	竝 4075	礴 3922
鞴 6758	麃 7219	算 4146	昺 2237	bo 剝 398	
bi 屄 1191	biaw 縹 7102	箆 4173	昞 2237		

		C					
箔 4142		注音	單字	字號	詫 5567	樵 2644	cheang 強 1434
簿 4207			chai		差 1298	轟 2734	強 1434
檗 4268		·ch	啐 659		拆 1837	潺 3085	(強)
脖 4685		cha	叉 517	chair	釵 6325	澶 3111	疆 1434
膊 4723			嗏 702		儕 280	瀍 3143	(強)
舶 4809			差 1298		柴 2413	禪 3968	搶 1989
孛 5081			扠 1801		茝 4882	纏 4465	襁 5454
葡 5111			扱 1807		豺 5736	蟬 5324	襁 5454
踣 5889			插 1954	chan	攙 2098	蟾 5332	(強)
鈸 6340			插 1954		襜 5463	饞 5699	鏹 6484
鉑 6349			(插)	chang	伥 188	饞 6914	cheau 巧 1295
鎛 6462			杈 2342		倀 207	charng 倡 282	怊 1581
雹 6691			臿 4776		娼 1026	嘗 733	悄 1637
駁 6928		chaa	叉 517		昌 2216	場 853	雀 6657
駮 6943		chaan	剒 406		猖 3362	嫦 1053	chee 尺 1180
鵓 7149			產 3541		菖 4963	常 1327	扯 1805
bu 晡 2249			葳 5091	chann	閶 6553	徜 1478	撦 2041
通 6088			謟 5606		懺 1743	腸 4710	cheeng 懲 2015
鋪 6876			鑔 6487		屬 4535	萇 4977	逞 6099
buh 不 8		chaang	閛 6578	chanq	顫 6830	裳 5425	騁 6945
佈 125	chaang	場 853			倡 207	長 6528	cheh 坼 824
埠 841		廠 1396			唱 649	chau 弨 1427	徹 1492
布 1307		惝 1615			悵 1598	抄 1812	拆 1837
怖 1525		敞 2134			暢 2273	超 5834	掣 1931
步 2684		昶 2232			韔 6769	鈔 6331	撤 2030
篰 4194		氅 2743	chao		吵 572	chaw 嘲 739	澈 3089
簿 4214	chae	蒫 4951			炒 3182	巢 1292	轍 6023
部 6206	chah	侘 155	char		察 1981	晁 2243	chen 嗔 712
buu 卜 488		剎 379			搽 2411	朝 2324	cherng 捵 1904
哺 637		剎 379			查 2411	潮 3082	琛 3445
捕 1892		(剎)			楂 2559	晁 7277	瞋 6210
補 5415		姹 997	chay		碴 4878	鈔 3655	撐 2027
bwu 不 8		妊 997			苴 4878	臺 5334	撐 2027
醭 6290		(姹)	che		茶 4912	cheng 車 5966	(撐)
bye 別 372		岔 1212	charn		單 701	chea 卡 491	樘 2611
蹩 5929		差 1298			嬋 1057	chean 淺 2947	篖 3309
蹾 5939		杈 2342			孱 1091	繨 4460	琤 3448
byi 荸 4950		汊 2768			巉 1282	譂 5689	瞠 3804
鼻 7298		杈 5377			廛 1393	遭 6141	

chenn 稱 4015	chern 塵 867	cherng 丞 17
蟶 5329	宸 1128	乘 36
赬 5826	忱 1513	呈 570
鐺 6507	晨 2253	城 835
櫬 2635	橙 2599	懲 1738
稱 4015	沈 2798	成 1757
襯 5468	沉 2798	承 1825
識 5701	(沈)	晟 2245
趁 5832	臣 4759	根 2483
趂 5832	蔯 5085	橙 2599
(趁)	諶 5635	澄 3088
鮟 7308	辰 6047	澂 3099
chenq 秤 3992	陳 6617	
稱 4015		
cheou 糢 4255		

盛 3726	僉 252	塹 868	怯 1534	起 5830	龜 7328
程 4005	千 475	傔 1662	愜 1643	chiin 寢 1145	chiu 區 473
裎 5409	嵌 1257	槧 2569	慊 1662	chiing 請 5610	屈 1190
誠 5592	愆 1648	欠 2650	挈 1875	頃 6782	嶇 1265
郕 6205	掔 1680	歉 2666	揭 2313	chin 侵 162	敺 2144
醒 6262	扦 1800	綪 4422	竊 4072	嵌 1274	曲 2302
cheu 取 522	掔 2002	茜 4922	篋 4164	欽 2658	呿 2805
娶 1017	搴 2019	蒨 5054	踥 5890	衾 5385	瞿 3819
曲 2302	牽 3324	chianq 嗆 705	鍥 6442	親 5490	祛 3940
鸝 7322	簽 4211	戧 1771	chih 企 103	駸 6949	胠 4653
cheuan 犬 3338	籤 4226	熗 3238	器 751	ching 傾 249	蛆 5217
畎 3563	籤 4226	蹌 5912	契 936	卿 505	蛐 5228
綣 4356	(籤)	chiau 撬 2045	妻 974	氫 2757	袪 5396
chi 七 3	芊 4834	敲 2140	慼 1713	清 2946	詘 5559
妻 974	褰 5446	橇 2596	憩 1713	蜻 5261	趨 5842
崎 1237	謙 5656	磽 3912	(慼)	輕 5992	軀 5965
悽 1604	遷 6151	蹺 5935	棄 2476	青 6722	驅 6975
惑 1691	鉛 6351	蹻 6444	弃 2476	鯖 7080	chiuan 圈 799
懨 1691	阡 6583	鍬 6454	(棄)	chinn 撳 2032	棬 1430
(慼)	韆 6763	chiaw 俏 170	氣 2753	沁 2790	悛 1588
戚 1763	騫 6963	峭 1229	汽 2794	chinq 慶 1696	椦 2496
敧 2114	鵮 7162	撬 2045	泣 2840	磬 3905	chiuann 券 376
期 2325	chiang 嗆 705	殼 2719	砌 3846	綮 4374	勸 446
柒 2390	戕 1771	殻 2719	磧 3906	罄 4481	缺 4478
栖 2423	搶 1989	(殼)	緝 4383	親 5490	chiue 闕 6572
棲 2497	槍 2557	壳 2719	葺 5020	謦 5665	chiueh 卻 503
欺 2659	瑲 3484	(殻)	訖 5526	chiong 穹 4041	却 503
沏 2805	羌 4514	竅 4069	跂 5849	芎 4837	(卻)
凄 2923	羗 4514	翹 4561	迄 6051	chiou 丘 15	怯 1534
溪 3009	(羌)	誚 5589	chii 乞 40	楸 2534	恪 1560
漆 3042	羌 4517	譙 5678	啓 660	秋 3983	愨 1686
緝 4383	腔 4697	鞘 6748	啟 660	秌 3983	榷 1972
妻 4980	蜣 5255	chie 切 360	(啓)	(秋)	權 2561
淇 5617	蹌 5912	chiee 且 12	屺 1211	蚯 5211	殼 2719
郪 6211	蹡 5921	chieh 切 360	杞 2350	邱 6182	(殼)
·chi 崒 659	鎗 6460	契 936	棨 2489	鞦 6751	壳 2719
chia 挿 1918	鏘 6483	妾 975	稽 4023	鞧 6752	(殻)
chiah 恰 1564	鐘 6484		綺 4366	鰍 7088	确 3870
洽 2872	chiann 倩 211		綮 4374	鰌 7090	碏 3882
chian 仟 89			豈 5712	鶖 7167	

碻 3893	chorng 崇 1236	竄 4053	褼 5439	蛴 5245	(強) 1434
轂 5510	种 3987	(窗)	chwan 傳 244	蟛 5940	彊 1434
闄 6563	蟲 5325	膧 4053	椽 2511	躇 5944	戕 1761
闟 6572	重 6306	(窗)	船 4812	躇 5954	檣 2616
雀 6657	chou 抽 1831	chuanq 創 404	遄 6119	組 6348	牆 3300
鵲 7160	搐 1973	愴 1655	chwang 幢 1342	鋤 6407	墻 3300
chiuh 去 514	篘 3337	愴 6573	牀 3297	除 6611	(墻)
漆 3042	搐 3660	chuann 串 23	床 3297	雛 6674	蕃 5123
虩 5494	紬 4308	釧 6324	(牀)	chy 吃 549	僑 255
覷 5494	chour 仇 78	chuay 嘬 749	chwei 倕 197	喫 549	喬 700
(覷)	儔 279	踹 5905	垂 826	(吃)	嶠 1272
覷 5494	嬦 1344	chuei 吹 575	捶 1938	嗤 719	憔 1700
(覷)	惆 1605	炊 3177	搥 1986	媸 1041	樵 2588
趣 5840	愁 1646	chuen 春 2225	椎 2501	摛 2009	橋 2598
闃 6558	疇 3585	椿 2513	槌 2556	痴 3641	瞧 3813
chiun 逡 6102	稠 4012	chuh 亍 50	箠 4145	癡 3676	翹 4561
chŏai 揣 1960	籌 4218	傗 184	菙 5015	眵 3771	蕎 5094
choan 端 689	綢 4308	怵 1541	錘 6421	笞 4098	譙 5678
舛 4793	綢 4355	搐 1995	鎚 6461	絺 4344	顦 6829
choang 闖 6573	裯 5423	歜 2679	陲 6616	蚩 5209	伽 121
choen 惷 5345	錘 5697	奮 3567	chwen 淳 2941	螭 5303	茄 4888
憲 5345	鐘 5697	矗 3823	純 4290	都 6203	傑 248
(蠢)	(錘)	絀 4315	脣 4677	魑 7057	勮 429
踳 5906	躊 5948	處 5183	唇 4677	鴟 7131	吡 541
chong 充 292	酬 6260	觸 5512	(脣)	耆 7324	笡 672
充 292	鮋 6671	黜 7256	蒓 5059	chya 卡 491	彳 1458
(充)	chow 臭 4766	畜 1776	蒪 5078	chyan 乾 392	敕 2129
仲 1508	chu 出 354	chuo 啜 671	醇 6271	扦 1843	斥 2165
憧 1702	初 369	chuoh 戳 2679	鶉 7163	搴 1936	熾 3249
沖 2801	韵 7314	綽 4368	chwu 儲 285	潛 3073	眙 3756
沖 2801	欻 2660	輟 5999	幮 1347	箝 4148	翅 4539
(沖)	chua 搋 1974	醊 6273	厨 1392	虔 5182	赤 5821
舂 4779	chuai 揣 1289	齪 7319	橱 2633	鈐 6335	趐 5879
衝 5368	chuan 穿 4043	chuu 儲 285	櫥 2633	鉗 6350	飭 6856
chonq 衡 5368	chuang 創 404	杵 2361	(櫥)	錢 6426	鶒 7171
銃 6370	瘡 3651	楚 2525	滁 3016	黔 7252	chyi 七 3
choong 龍 1155	窗 4053	楮 2532	篨 4175	chyang 強 1434	其 317
choou 丑 11	窗 4053	礎 3914	蒢 4586	強 1434	奇 929
眈 3792	(窗)	處 5183	躇 4862		
醜 6279			蹰 5062		
			chyang 嬙 1061		
			強 1434		
			強 1434		

注音	單字	字號
	岐	1214
	崎	1237
	旂	2179
	旗	2190
	期	2325
	枝	2376
	棋	2478
	基	2478
	(棋)	
	歧	2685
	淇	2951
	琦	3449
	琪	3451
	畦	3570
	畿	3583
	碁	3884
	祁	3926
	祇	3930
	祈	3931
	祺	3951
	萁	4373
	耆	4571
	臍	4749
	其	4974
	齊	5135
	蘄	5154
	蠐	5485
	跂	5849
	錡	6425
	頎	6788
	騎	6951
	騏	6953
	鬐	7029
	鰭	7095
	麒	7226
	齊	7303
hyn	勤	441
	勍	1730
	擒	2062
	檎	2613

注音	單字	字號
	琴	3456
	禽	3977
	秦	3989
	芩	4846
	芹	4858
	螓	5295
	衾	5385
	覃	5475
chyng	情	1606
	擎	2070
	晴	2259
	黥	7260
chyong	嬛	1062
	惸	1606
	煢	3233
	瓊	3512
	穹	4041
	窮	4061
	筇	4110
	芎	4837
	蛩	5151
	跫	5226
	邛	6171
chyou	仇	78
	囚	782
	毬	2738
	求	2767
	泅	2828
	球	3440
	虬	5192
	蚯	5193
	蝤	5278
	裘	5414
	賕	5786
	遒	6091
	逎	6128
	酋	6247
chyr	匙	459
	墀	875

注音	單字	字號
	尺	1180
	弛	1423
	持	1865
	池	2773
	治	2819
	篪	4174
	箎	4174
	(箎)	
	荎	4891
	踟	5886
	遲	6147
	馳	6925
chyu	劬	424
	氍	2962
	璩	3507
	蘧	3685
	瞿	3819
	籧	4228
	絇	4305
	胸	4656
	胠	5108
	蓬	5167
	蛐	5228
	衢	5373
	鴝	7136
	鸜	7207
	鼩	7237
	麯	7237
	麴	7237
chyuan	全	308
	卷	499
	惓	1610
	拳	1873
	權	2647
	泉	2848
	痊	3322
	瘁	3618
	荃	4111
	萲	4924
	蜷	5260
	詮	5570

注音	單字	字號
	踏	5887
	醛	6282
	銓	6373
	顴	6835
	鬈	7024
chyue	闋	3663
chyun	羣	4526
	群	4526
	(羣)	
	裙	5408
chyy	侈	150
	呎	585
	尺	1180
	恥	1577
	耻	4596
	蚇	5210
	褫	5445
	豉	5713
	齒	7307

D

注音	單字	字號
da	搭	1988
	答	4119
	耷	4592
•da	搭	5447
	瘩	3656
	繨	4450
daa	打	1794
daan	撢	2050
	撣	2050
	(撣)	
	疸	3601
	膽	4736
	胆	4736
	(膽)	
	黵	7269
daang	擋	2061
	攙	2107
	檔	2610

注音	單字	字號
	當	3582
	讜	5705
	黨	7262
dae	歹	2691
	逮	6107
dah	大	916
dai	呆	584
	待	1466
	獃	3383
dan	丹	25
	儋	275
	單	701
	擔	2059
	担	2059
	(擔)	
	殫	2710
	眈	3749
	簞	4198
	耽	4593
	聃	4595
	聸	4595
	(聸)	
	舥	5962
	鄲	6235
	酖	6251
dang	噹	760
	當	3582
	襠	5460
	鐺	6507
dann	但	123
	啖	661
	噉	661
	(啖)	
	彈	1437
	憚	1701
	憺	1722
	擔	2059
	旦	2199
	氮	2759

注音	單字	字號
	淡	2931
	澹	3110
	癉	3670
	石	3841
	萏	4985
	蛋	5220
	蜑	5247
	誕	5587
	鉭	6364
danq	宕	1109
	擋	2061
	檔	2610
	當	3582
	邆	3737
	瀁	5104
dao	倒	199
	導	1167
	島	1232
	搗	1982
	擣	2075
	禱	3972
dar	妲	970
	怛	1528
	打	1794
	瘩	3656
	答	4119
	繨	4450
	達	6130
	靼	6744
	韃	6761
dau	刀	356
	叨	528
	忉	1498
	舠	4798
daw	倒	199
	到	377
	導	1167
	幬	1344
	悼	1602
	纛	3274

音	字	號
	盜	3727
	稻	4022
	纛	4473
	翿	4566
	薅	4978
	蹈	5907
	道	6129
day	代	91
	大	916
	岱	1220
	帶	1325
	待	1466
	怠	1545
	戴	1775
	殆	2695
	玳	3420
	袋	5391
	襶	5471
	貸	5766
	迨	6066
	逮	6107
	駘	6719
	黛	7255
•de	得	1476
	的	3696
	襶	5471
dean	典	319
	碘	3881
	點	7254
deei	得	1476
deeng	戥	1768
	等	4113
deng	燈	3250
	登	4202
	瞪	5714
	鐙	6496
denq	凳	350
	橙	350
	(凳)	

音	字	號
	嶝	1271
	澄	3088
	凳	3691
	橙	3691
	(凳)	
	瞪	3810
	磴	3909
	鄧	6230
	鐙	6496
der	得	1476
	德	1493
di	低	127
	提	1951
	氐	2747
	滴	3033
	羝	4522
	隄	6626
	堤	6626
	(隄)	
dian	顛	1286
	掂	1910
	攧	2105
	滇	3021
	顛	3686
	顛	6822
diann	佃	122
	坫	873
	奠	942
	店	1366
	惦	1616
	殿	2721
	淀	2914
	澱	3107
	玷	3419
	甸	3556
	坫	3613
	簟	4199
	鈿	6342
	電	6690

音	字	號
	靛	6726
diau	凋	341
	习	357
	叨	529
	彫	1451
	碉	3876
	貂	5738
	雕	6670
	鯛	7081
	鵰	7158
diaw	弔	1420
	吊	1420
	(弔)	
	掉	1920
	調	5605
	釣	6320
	銚	6376
die	爹	3292
dih	地	810
	娣	1012
	帝	1320
	弟	1424
	棣	2487
	的	3696
	睇	3774
	締	3962
	第	4102
	綈	4385
	蒂	5028
	蔕	5070
	螲	5304
	蝃	5304
	(螲)	
	諦	5628
	遞	6137
dii	底	1364
	抵	1829
	柢	2406
	氐	2747
	牴	3320

音	字	號
	砥	3849
	舐	5504
	詆	5548
	邸	6187
	酊	6246
	頂	6781
	鼎	7283
ding	丁	2
	仃	75
	叮	538
	玎	3410
	町	3557
	疔	3591
	盯	3740
	釘	6313
	釘	6736
dinq	定	1114
	碇	3878
	訂	5516
	釘	6313
	錠	6424
	釘	6851
diou	丟	18
	銩	6388
doan	短	3836
doen	躉	3751
dong	多	334
	哆	596
	東	2360
	鶇	5264
	鼕	7288
	(東)	
donq	凍	343
	動	433
	峒	1226
	恫	1561
	棟	2485
	洞	2859
	胴	4663
	腖	5264

音	字	號
doong	懂	1723
	董	5008
doou	抖	1821
	斗	2156
	蚪	5201
	陡	6608
dou	兜	304
	篼	4182
	都	6214
dow	痘	3623
	竇	4070
	脰	4682
	荳	4954
	讀	5692
	豆	6095
	逗	6877
	鬥	7036
	閗	7037
	鬦	7042
	鬪	7042
du	督	3787
	都	6214
	闍	6566
duan	端	4083
	耑	4578
duann	斷	2173
	段	2716
	緞	4382
	煅	6441
	煅	6441
	(鍛)	
duei	堆	847
duen	墩	879
	惇	1607
	敦	2138
	燉	3253
	蹲	5928
duenn	頓	757
	沌	2797

音	字	號
	屯	3179
	炖	3253
	盾	3752
	遁	6117
	鈍	6334
	頓	6793
duey	兌	298
	對	1166
	憝	1715
	懟	1737
	敦	2138
	碓	3877
	隊	6632
duh	妒	961
	妬	961
	(妒)	
	度	1369
	斁	2146
	杜	2349
	渡	3928
	肚	4626
	蠹	5353
	蠧	5353
	(蠹)	
	鍍	6438
duo	多	624
	夛	909
	剟	380
	咄	601
	墮	880
	度	1369
	惰	1625
	柮	2415
	柁	2418
	舵	4808
	踱	5873
	跥	5898
	軃	6924
duoo	桑	2339

注音	單字	字號
duu	朵	2339
	(朵)	
	躲	5963
	埵	854
	睹	3790
	篤	4170
	肚	4626
	覩	5489
	睹	5799
dwo	多	909
	奪	945
	掇	1914
	裰	2135
	裰	5421
	鐸	6506
dwu	櫝	2632
	毒	2729
	瀆	3136
	牘	3307
	犢	3835
	獨	3391
	碡	3883
	纛	4473
	讀	5692
	頓	6793
	髑	7006
	黷	7271
dye	喋	685
	慄	1628
	昳	2234
	牒	3304
	耋	3517
	疊	3586
	曡	3586
	(疊)	
	眣	3757
	碟	3892
	絰	4336
	蜇	4574
	蹀	5265

注音	單字	字號
	蝶	5286
	褶	5451
	諜	5623
	跌	5852
	喋	5901
	迭	6069
	軼	7086
dyi	嫡	1051
	敵	2141
	滌	3030
	狄	3344
	的	3696
	笛	4096
	糴	4272
	翟	4547
	荻	4930
	覿	5498
	跡	5891
	蹢	5922
	迪	6067
	廸	6067
	(迪)	
	適	6144
	鏑	6480

E

注音	單字	字號
e	烔	1016
	屙	1200
	痾	3602
	疴	3602
	(疴)	
	阿	6594
	惡	1624
	我	1759
ee	猗	3363
	洱	2866
eel	爾	3296
	珥	3430
	耳	4590

注音	單字	字號
	邇	6163
	鉺	6382
	餌	6869
	駬	6942
een	嗯	716
eh	俄	167
	厄	506
	呃	582
	壓	752
	崿	1260
	惡	1624
	愕	1633
	屄	1778
	扼	1824
	扼	1824
	(扼)	
	歹	2691
	夕	2691
	(歹)	
	腭	4715
	咢	4999
	諤	5627
	範	5973
	遏	6125
	鄂	6216
	鍔	6439
	關	6554
	陌	6586
	呃	6598
	頸	6815
	餓	6875
	鱷	7113
	翡	7168
	鱷	7323
êh	誒	5599
ell	二	49
	貳	5762
en	恩	1573
enn	嗯	716
	摁	1997

注音	單字	字號
er	俄	167
	哦	631
	娥	1013
	峨	1228
	莪	4943
	蛾	5234
	訛	5533
	譌	5682
	鋨	6398
	額	6812
	鵝	7152
	鷲	7152
	(鵝)	
	皒	7152
	(鵝)	
erl	兒	300
	洏	2876
	而	4575
	胹	4673
ern	嗯	716
ey	欸	2655

F

注音	單字	字號
fa	伐	110
	法	2832
	發	3690
faa	法	2832
	灋	2832
	(法)	
	髮	7015
faan	反	520
	翻	6058
faang	仿	102
	倣	102
	(仿)	
	彷	1459
	昉	2214
	紡	4300
	紡	4803

注音	單字	字號
	訪	5539
	髣	7011
fah	法	2832
	琺	3453
	帆	1308
	帆	1308
	(帆)	
	幡	1341
	旛	2192
	番	3575
	緔	4441
	翻	4562
	番	5090
	飜	6848
fang	坊	811
	妨	969
	方	2174
	枋	2370
	肪	4635
	芳	4673
fanq	梵	2465
	氾	2764
	汎	2769
	泛	2838
	犯	3340
	范	4108
	範	4887
	販	5755
	飯	6859
fann	放	2119
far	乏	33
	伐	110
	法	2832
	砝	3853
	筏	4114
	罰	4501
	閥	6545
farn	凡	347
	帆	1308

注音	單字	字號
	帆	1308
	(帆)	
	樊	2579
	煩	3226
	燔	3256
	璠	3500
	蕃	3918
	繁	4428
	蘩	4428
	(繁)	
	膰	4734
	蕃	5090
	藩	5149
	繁	5171
	蹯	5932
	釩	6319
farng	妨	969
	房	1781
	肪	4635
	防	4590
	魴	7064
feei	匪	465
	悱	1597
	斐	2152
	朏	2318
	棐	2491
	榧	4168
	翡	4550
	菲	4970
	蜚	5250
	誹	5603
	粉	4255
feen	啡	668
feeng	啡	652
fei	妃	957
	扉	1788
	緋	4376
	菲	4970
	蜚	5250

注音	單字	字號
fei	霏	6700
	非	6728
	飛	6847
	鯡	7079
feir	淝	2927
	肥	4633
	腓	4701
fen	分	359
	昐	567
	蚡	2490
	氛	2751
	紛	4299
	芬	4848
	蕡	4960
	雰	6685
feng	丰	22
	封	1159
	峯	1230
	楓	2515
	灃	3161
	烽	3201
	瘋	3643
	葑	5002
	蜂	5236
	酆	5350
	豐	5719
	鄷	6242
	鋒	6404
	風	6837
fenn	分	359
	份	359
	(分)	
	僨	761
	奮	948
	忿	1520
	憤	1719
	糞	4260
fenq	俸	185
	奉	931
	縫	4416
	諷	5636
	風	6837
	鳳	7119
fern	墳	881
	枌	2369
	棻	2492
	汾	2789
	焚	3211
	豶	4521
	黂	5098
	蕡	5773
ferng	逢	4416
	蓬	6103
	馮	6923
fey	吠	565
	廢	1398
	狒	1533
	沸	2814
	疿	3350
	痱	3633
	(痱)	3633
	肺	4642
	芾	4861
	費	5768
foou	否	566
	缶	4476
for	佛	137
four	浮	2890
	罘	4493
	苯	4843
fu	夫	919
	孵	1093
	敷	2142
	枹	2389
	柎	2392
	膚	4724
	趺	5848
	跗	5856
	郙	6227
	鈇	6332
	麩	7235
fuh	仆	77
	付	86
	傅	234
	副	399
	咐	606
	婦	1024
	富	1136
	復	1485
	服	2317
	父	3290
	柎	3935
	腹	4711
	蝮	5281
	複	5283
	蝜	5432
	覆	5476
	訃	5748
	負	5796
	賻	5802
	赴	5829
	輹	6013
	阜	6582
	附	6597
	馥	6919
	鮒	6936
	鮒	7067
	鰒	7089
fuu	俯	181
	府	1368
	拊	1839
	撫	2042
	斧	2166
	枎	2389
	柎	2392
	父	3290
	甫	3547
	簠	4203
	腑	4680
	腐	4695
	脯	4696
	甫	4945
	輔	5991
	釜	6314
	頫	6799
	黼	7274
fwu	伏	109
	俘	174
	匐	455
	夫	919
	孚	1080
	帗	1314
	幅	1328
	弗	1421
	彿	1465
	佛	1533
	扶	1804
	拂	1834
	服	2317
	枹	2389
	桴	2451
	氟	2752
	洑	2852
	浮	2890
	涪	2910
	祓	3934
	福	3956
	符	4101
	箙	4151
	紱	4310
	紼	4313
	縛	4408
	罦	4827
	芙	4839
	苻	4861
	苻	4883
	莩	4895
	茯	4907
	葍	4942
	菔	4962
	蚨	5208
	蜉	5244
	蝠	5275
	袚	5400
	輻	6010
	郛	6196
	紼	6767
	髴	7016
	鳧	7116
	鵩	7156
	韍	7273

G

注音	單字	字號
ga	咖	605
	嘎	2204
gaan	感	1652
	擀	2065
	敢	2136
	桿	2474
	橄	2591
	澉	3097
	稈	4003
	簳	4215
	趕	5839
gaang	筻	1216
	崗	1241
	港	2967
gae	改	2117
gah	尬	1176
gai	垓	4316
	荄	4930
	該	5573
	賅	5778
	陔	6603
gan	乾	44
	乾	44
	(乾)	
	尷	1178
	干	1348
	杆	2353
	柑	2398
	泔	2830
	玕	3411
	甘	3536
	疳	3600
	竿	4088
	肝	4628
gang	剛	396
	岡	1216
	崗	1241
	杠	2352
	綱	4360
	堽	4447
	缸	4477
	罡	4494
	肛	4627
	鋼	6414
gann	幹	2474
	旰	2206
	骭	2541
	淦	2933
	灨	3169
	紺	4317
	贛	5820
ganq	戇	2560
	虹	5195
gao	搞	2003
	攪	2108
	杲	2358
	槁	2554
	藁	2554
	(槁)	
	稿	4019
	稿	4019
	(稿)	
	縞	4411
	鎬	6464

羅馬字	字	編號
gar	軋	5967
	钆	6312
gau	樏	2543
	皋	3700
	皐	3700
	(皋)	
	睪	3788
	睪	3788
	(睪)	
	篙	4171
	糕	4257
	羔	4518
	膏	4721
	皐	4767
	餻	6897
	高	7008
gaw	告	580
	膏	4721
	誥	5595
	郜	6197
	鋯	6397
gay	丐	10
	概	2568
	槩	2568
	(概)	
	溉	3045
	蓋	5029
	蓋	5049
	(蓋)	
	鈣	6338
ge	割	402
	咯	614
	哥	630
	戈	1751
	擱	2079
	歌	2667
	牁	3298
	疙	3592

羅馬字	字	編號
	紇	4284
	胳	4629
	茖	4992
	鴿	7137
gee	笴	4105
	舸	4811
	葛	5005
	蓋	5049
geei	給	4333
geen	艮	4823
geeng	哽	639
	埂	836
	梗	2462
	綆	4348
	耿	6999
	鯁	7075
geh	個	192
	各	550
	洛	3861
	箇	4152
	虼	5197
	鉻	6389
gen	根	2431
	跟	5862
geng	庚	1367
	更	2304
	浭	2888
	杭	3988
	粳	3988
	(杭)	
	粳	4248
	藁	4533
	耕	4582
	鶊	7165
genn	瓦	56
	艮	4823
	茛	4921

羅馬字	字	編號
genq	亙	56
	更	2304
ger	咯	614
	喀	715
	格	2433
	楁	2564
	膈	4720
	葛	5005
	蛤	5225
	緪	6027
	郃	6193
	鎘	6472
	閣	6542
	閤	6544
	隔	6634
	革	6735
	骼	6998
	鬲	7046
goa	寡	1144
goai	拐	1842
	枴	2382
goan	琯	3461
	筦	4126
	管	4149
	脘	4675
	舘	4792
	莞	4938
	館	6886
goang	廣	1399
	獷	3399
goei	匭	466
	宄	1098
	晷	2261
	癸	3688
	簋	4190
	詭	5569
	軌	5968
	鬼	7048
goen	滾	3036
	渷	3036

羅馬字	字	編號
	(滾)	
	袞	5388
	衮	5398
	鯀	7073
gong	供	156
	公	312
	功	418
	宮	1122
	工	1293
	弓	1418
	恭	1576
	攻	2118
	紅	4283
	肱	4638
	蚣	5206
	觥	5506
	躬	5961
	襲	7326
gonq	供	156
	共	315
	貢	5750
goong	拱	1861
	栱	2450
	珙	2778
	珙	3429
	鞏	6747
goou	枸	2388
	狗	3348
	耉	4573
	耇	4573
	(耇)	
	苟	4898
gou	勾	449
	句	531
	枸	2388
	溝	3002
	篝	4167
	緱	4394
	鈎	6339
	鉤	6354

羅馬字	字	編號
gow	耩	6756
	講	327
	勾	449
	垢	831
	夠	912
	够	912
	(夠)	
	姤	990
	媾	1044
	彀	1436
	搆	1976
	構	2555
	覯	5492
	詬	5568
	購	5803
	逅	6133
	遘	6133
	雊	6665
gu	估	114
	呱	591
	咕	594
	姑	981
	孤	1087
	沽	2818
	箍	4141
	苽	4900
	菇	4967
	菰	4968
	蛄	5216
	觚	5503
	罛	5982
	轂	6016
	辜	6038
	酤	6255
	鈷	6358
	骨	6990
	鴣	7132
gua	刮	375
	括	1860
	栝	2424

羅馬字	字	編號
	瓜	3516
	筈	4120
	聒	5287
	适	6078
	颳	6840
	鴰	7144
guah	卦	493
	掛	1928
	挂	1928
	(掛)	
	絓	4327
	罣	4497
	褂	5431
	詿	5582
guai	乖	35
	倌	193
guan	冠	329
	官	1112
	棺	2498
	瘝	3649
	矜	3827
	綸	4365
	莞	4938
	觀	5499
	關	6574
	鰥	7092
guang	光	296
	洸	2877
	胱	4662
guann	冠	329
	慣	1675
	摜	2006
	灌	3162
	盥	3733
	祼	4490
	罐	4490
	觀	5499
	貫	5757
	鸛	7206

注音	單字	字號
guanq	枕	2441
	甎	5585
	逛	6098
guay	夬	920
	怪	1535
guei	傀	233
	圭	808
	歸	2690
	溈	3095
	珪	3435
	瑰	3480
	瘣	3514
	皈	3699
	規	5482
	邽	6194
	閨	6546
	鮭	7070
	龜	7328
guenn	椢	2479
guey	劊	413
	會	2312
	桂	2439
	檜	2612
	櫃	2624
	洭	3027
	瞶	3812
	貴	5763
	跪	5867
	鱖	7106
guh	估	114
	傴	265
	固	793
	故	2122
	梏	2460
	痼	3637
	錮	6430
	雇	6662
	顧	6826
guo	渦	2965
	蟈	5314
	過	6124
	郭	6208
	鍋	6437
guoh	過	6124
guoo	果	2377
	椁	2504
	槨	2504
	(椁)	
	猓	3368
	菓	4995
	蜾	5262
	裹	5427
	課	6887
guu	古	530
	抿	730
	榖	2542
	榾	2563
	汩	2781
	岵	3318
	盬	3738
	瞽	3818
	穀	4018
	罟	4495
	羖	4519
	股	4631
	膄	4745
	菩	5058
	蠱	5348
	詁	5547
	谷	5706
	賈	5779
	穀	6016
	鈷	6358
	骨	6990
	鴣	7153
	鶻	7178
	鼓	7287
gwo	國	797
	幗	1336
	摑	2005
	虢	5190
	膕	6917
	膕	6917
	(膕)	
gwu	骨	6990

H

注音	單字	字號
ha	哈	626
haa	哈	626
haan	喊	684
	罕	4492
	闞	6576
hae	海	2891
	醢	6284
hair	孩	1088
	還	6161
	頦	6798
	骸	6997
han	憨	1717
	蚶	5214
	酣	6254
	頇	6785
	鼾	7299
hang	夯	924
hann	悍	1586
	憾	1721
	扞	1796
	撼	2052
	旱	2207
	暵	2277
	汗	2772
	漢	3053
	瀚	3147
	翰	4558
	菡	4984
	釬	5737
	銲	6411
	釺	6411
	(銲)	
	頷	6805
	驛	6950
hanq	桁	2432
	沆	2796
hao	好	954
	郝	6198
har	蛤	5225
	蝦	5280
harn	函	355
	含	568
	寒	1138
	嵌	1250
	斡	2541
	汗	2772
	涵	2911
	邯	6180
	韓	6768
harng	杭	2356
	桁	2432
	沆	2796
	航	5360
	迒	6061
	頏	6789
hau	嘩	742
	嚆	764
	薅	5043
	蔊	5112
haur	嗥	762
	嚎	889
	毫	2737
	濠	3122
	號	5188
	蠔	5340
	豪	5728
	貉	5740
	鶴	7173
haw	好	954
	昊	2215
	晧	2252
	浩	2883
	淏	2912
	澔	3098
	灝	3165
	皓	3702
	皞	3707
	耗	4584
	號	5188
	郜	6198
	鎬	6464
	顥	6828
hay	亥	63
	咳	616
	害	1124
	氦	2756
	駭	6940
he	呵	593
	喝	693
	訶	5543
heen	很	1468
	狠	3352
heh	和	604
	喝	693
	嚇	766
	爽	947
	荷	4927
	豁	5707
	賀	5771
	赫	5824
	郝	6198
	鶴	7173
hei	嘿	747
	黑	7250
heng	亨	65
	哼	638
henn	恨	1558
henq	橫	2606
her	何	132
	劤	426
	合	547
	和	604
	曷	2305
	核	2428
	河	2816
	涸	2912
	盍	3721
	盒	3724
	禾	3978
	紇	4284
	翮	4557
	荷	4927
	蓋	5049
	褐	5435
	藹	5477
	貉	5740
	餄	6385
	闔	6543
	闐	6544
	闔	6571
	鞨	6753
	鷛	7169
	魺	7309
	龢	7330
hern	痕	3620
herng	恆	1551
	恒	1551
	(恆)	
	桁	2432
	橫	2606
	珩	3433
	衡	5159
	衡	5372
hm	嗅	758
hoan	浣	3118
	澣	3118
	縓	4390
hoang	幌	1333
	恍	1536

	恍	1555		餱	6890		患	1594		卉	480		惑	1621		環	3504
hoen	晃	2242	how	侯	203		换	1958		(卉)			或	1760		繯	4448
	諕	5650		厚	508		擐	2066		喙	690		擭	2080		還	6161
hoei	混	2945		后	557		涣	2955		彗	1443		濩	3132		鍰	6445
hoei	悔	1584		後	1472		渙	3063		彙	1445		獲	3394		鐶	6505
	會	2312		逅	6080		焕	3224		恚	1569		檴	3840		闌	6580
	毁	2722		鱟	7109		焕	3644		惠	1623		眷	3844		鬟	7033
	燬	3268	hu	乎	32		黎	5727		慧	1689		禍	3955	hwang	凰	348
	虺	5196		呼	598		顜	6026		晦	2251		穫	4036		徨	1484
	誨	5597		忽	1519		逭	6113		會	2312		藿	5157		惶	1630
	賄	5776		惚	1612	huanq	晃	2242		槥	2565		蠖	5342		湟	2990
hong	哄	623		戲	1774	huay	壞	893		濊	3116		豁	5707		潢	3077
	烘	3197		欻	2660	huei	徽	1495		繪	3270		貨	5754		煌	3217
	薨	5128		歘	2670		恢	1557		穢	4033		鑊	6510		璜	3497
	訇	5519		淴	2953		揮	1963		蕙	4197		霍	6698		皇	3698
	轟	6030		滹	3034		撝	2049		繢	4443		騞	6962		磺	3911
	虹	7061		虖	5184		暉	2266		繪	4446	huoo	伙	112		篁	4160
honq	汞	2778	hua	嘩	734		灰	3172		翙	4565		夥	915		簧	4206
	閧	7039		花	4854		翬	4553		蟪	5097		火	3171		蝗	5271
hoong	哄	623		華	4966		虺	5196		蕙	5117		鈥	6328		蟥	5318
hoou	吼	577	huah	化	457		褌	5437		總	5323	huu	唬	667		遑	6126
horng	宏	1108		樺	2589		詼	5576		諱	5597		滸	3035		黃	7244
	弘	1422		畫	3578		輝	5997		譓	5632		琥	3452	hwei	回	784
	泓	2831		華	4966		隳	6651		賄	5776		虎	5180		徊	1470
	洪	2865		話	5572		麾	7243		闠	6577	hwa	划	365		洄	2850
	紅	4283	huan	懽	1747	huen	婚	1022		饋	6733		劃	409		茴	4910
	紘	4293		歡	2680		惛	1614	huh	互	53		嘩	734		蚘	5222
	翃	4540		讙	5702		昏	2218		怙	1527		滑	3023		迴	6072
	荭	5023		貛	5746		童	5018		戶	1777		猾	3381		廻	6072
	虹	5195		貛	5746		闇	6556		扈	1780		華	4966		(迴)	
	訌	5523		(貛)		huenn	恩	1670		嫮	1787		譁	5673	hwen	混	2945
	閎	6535		驩	6988		恒	1670		梏	2519		豁	5707		渾	2975
	鴻	7139	huang	慌	1663		(恩)			滬	3029		驊	6977		琿	3473
	黌	7246		肓	4625		混	2945		瓠	3518	hwai	徊	1470		餛	6882
hou	齁	7300		荒	4920		渾	2975		祜	3939		懷	2558		魂	7050
hour	侯	683	huann	喚	691		溷	3012		笏	4091		槐	2939	hwo	活	2873
	猴	3376		奐	935		諢	5626		護	5688	hwan	寰	1154	hwu	囫	790
	疾	3833		宦	1121		舷	7074		豁	5707		桓	2446		壺	901
	篌	4165		幻	1355	huo	卉	480	huoh	堅	888					弧	1426
																斛	2158

單字	字號
槲	2572
湖	2984
狐	3349
猢	3371
瑚	3472
糊	4252
縠	4403
胡	4654
葫	5012
蝴	5285
衚	5369
觳	5510
醐	6278
餬	6891
鬍	7027
鵠	7153
鶘	7166
鶻	7178

I

注音	單字	字號
i	一	1
	伊	105
	依	157
	咿	619
	噫	754
	壹	900
	揖	1953
	欹	2662
	漪	3051
	猗	3363
	禕	3961
	繄	4429
	翳	4559
	衣	5374
	醫	6285
	鷖	7187
	黟	7259
ia	丫	20
	呀	581
	壓	886
	押	1832
	椏	2505
	鴉	7124
	鴨	7134
·ia	呀	581
ian	咽	618
	奄	928
	殗	1052
	崦	1251
	惡	1735
	懨	1735
	(惡)	
	殷	2717
	淹	2948
	烟	3199
	焉	3204
	煙	3222
	燕	3258
	胭	4659
	腌	4692
	臙	4753
	菸	4971
	蔫	5083
	郾	6225
	醃	6269
	閹	6554
	闇	6555
iang	央	923
	泱	2697
	決	2846
	秧	3991
	鞅	6742
	薵	7133
iau	吆	554
	夭	921
	妖	962
	幺	1354
	么	1354

注音	單字	字號
	(幺)	
	徵	1494
	祆	3929
	腰	4706
	葽	5021
	要	5474
	邀	6158
ie	噎	746
	掖	884
	耶	4591
in	暗	687
	因	786
	姻	998
	愔	1641
	慇	1669
	殷	2717
	氤	2754
	湮	2987
	瘖	3645
	瘞	3957
	絪	4335
	茵	4911
	諲	5643
	銦	6386
	闉	6561
	陰	6615
	陻	6624
	堙	6624
	(陻)	
	音	6774
ing	娛	1036
	嬰	1066
	應	1729
	攖	2096
	櫻	2642
	瑛	3469
	瓔	3515
	纓	4470
	罃	4480
	罌	4486

注音	單字	字號
	庸	4738
	英	4877
	鶯	7175
	盧	7203
	鸚	7205
io	唷	663
iong	傭	242
	埇	872
	塎	1378
	廱	1404
	慵	1681
	擁	2056
	邕	3160
	雍	3684
	臃	3684
	邕	6172
	鄘	6226
	雍	6663
	雝	6678
	廱	6909
iou	優	284
	幽	1357
	悠	1592
	憂	1694
	攸	2116
	悠	3065
	煤	3266
	繇	4589
	膺	7217
iu	游	2932
	瘀	3638
	紆	4281
	迂	6050
iuan	冤	330
	冤	330
	(冤)	
	嫚	1050
	淵	2942
	鳶	7121

注音	單字	字號
	駕	7129
	鴶	7161
iue	曰	2301
	約	4282
iun	暈	2267
	氳	2760
	贇	5812

J

注音	單字	字號
ja	扎	1791
	挓	1872
	揸	1967
	查	2411
	植	2514
	渣	2914
jaa	貶	3761
jaan	展	1195
	斬	1267
	搌	2001
	斬	2168
	瑧	3444
	盞	3728
	輾	6014
jaang	掌	1940
jang	漲	3060
	長	6528
jae	窄	4048
jah	乍	31
	吒	555
	咋	603
	咤	608
	搾	1979
	柵	2416
	榨	2231
	炸	3189
	痄	3614
	笮	4107
	蚱	5213
	蜡	5252

注音	單字	字號
	詐	5552
jai	摘	2004
	齊	7303
	齋	7304
	(齋)	
jair	宅	1102
	擇	2060
	翟	4547
jan	占	489
	旃	2180
	氈	2745
	氊	2745
	(氈)	
	氈	2745
	(氈)	
	沾	2820
	瞻	3816
	覘	5484
	詹	5575
	遭	6162
	霑	6701
	饘	6911
	鐘	7110
	鷓	7202
jang	張	1433
	彰	1456
	樟	2577
	漳	3059
	獐	3387
	璋	3493
	章	4078
	蟑	5316
	鄣	6229
	鱆	7231
jann	佔	475
	占	490
	戰	1773
	暫	2275
	棧	2484

Rom.	字	No.	字	No.	字	No.	字	No.	字	No.	Rom.	字	No.
	湛	2986	召	536	簡	4200	餃	6865	診	5544		症	3608
	站	4074	族	2188	簡	4200	jee 者	4572	貞	5749		証	5561
	綻	4367	翟	2287	(簡)		赭	5825	針	6316		證	5674
	蘸	5174	棹	2502	繭	4453	鍺	6450	鍼	6447		鄭	5231
	醮	5926	權	2627	鵑	4551	枕	2373	鱵	7111	jeong 侗	1784
	顫	6830	炤	3191	禂	5458	jeen 畛	3565	丁	2		洞	2822
janq 丈	4	照	3232	謇	5652	疹	3603	崢	1244		炯	3186
仗	85	笊	4090	謇	5691	稹	4024	征	1463		烔	3186
嶂	1266	罩	4498	趼	5861	縝	4314	徵	1491		(烔)	
帳	1324	肇	4618	趼	5861	軫	4412	怔	1537		窘	4054
幛	1338	詔	5554	(趼)		胗	4657	掙	1925		絅	4322
杖	2348	趙	5838	蹇	5908	診	5544	楨	2528		迥	6064
漲	3060	jay 債	246	鐧	6498	稹	5975	正	2682		迴	6084
瘴	3659	寨	1149	鹻	7213	鬒	7030	烝	3195	jeou 久	29
脹	4688	療	3661	鹼	7214	jeeng 抮	1859	爭	3286		九	39
賬	5798	砦	3858	jeang 獎	946	整	2145	猙	3365		灸	3173
長	6528	je 折	1822	槳	2570	jeh 宅	1102	癥	3679		玖	3412
障	6641	蟄	5301	蔣	5074	柘	2400	睜	3781		糺	4276
jao 找	1809	遮	6145	講	5657	浙	2878	箏	4139		糾	4277
沼	2817	·je 着	3776	jeau 佻	145	蔗	5071	蒸	5039		韭	5032
爪	3284	jea 假	216	儌	260	這	6096	諍	5611		赳	5828
jar 劄	408	夏	904	剿	405	鷓	7186	貞	5749		酒	6250
扎	1791	岬	1218	(剿)		jen 偵	229	鉦	6355		韭	6773
札	2334	嶭	2160	徼	1494	振	1880	錚	6423	jer 哲	636
炸	3189	積	2614	撟	2040	斟	2161	jenn 振	1880		悊	1682
箚	4150	甲	3553	攪	2108	椹	2508	揕	1952		偖	1745
紮	4304	胛	3571	湫	2988	楨	2528	朕	2320		折	1822
紮	4304	賈	5779	狡	3353	榛	2540	枕	2373		摘	2004
(紮)		鉀	6343	皎	3701	珍	3425	塡	3481		摺	2016
鍘	6440	jean 俴	274	矯	3838	甄	3527	賑	5783		磔	3899
閘	6540	剪	400	筊	4123	真	3762	酖	6251		矺	4547
jau 招	1855	戩	1769	絞	4330	真	3762	鎭	6465		蜇	5239
昭	2228	揀	1944	繳	4449	(真)		陣	6610		蟄	5312
朝	2324	撿	2067	脚	4687	砧	3850	陳	6617		褶	5451
著	3776	柬	2410	脚	4707	禎	3964	震	6693		謫	5667
釗	6315	檢	2615	角	5500	禛	3964	鴆	7122		讁	5694
jaur 着	3776	減	2959	鷮	5936	箴	4158	jenq 幀	1330		輒	5989
著	5003	瞼	3817	較	5983	胗	4657	掙	1925		轍	6005
jaw 兆	293	筧	4137	鉸	6369	臻	4772	政	2121		轍	6023
							蓁	5045	正	2682	jeu 咀	600

jih　伎 108｜寰 321｜劑 415｜妓 959｜季 1085｜寄 1133｜忌 1499｜悸 1599｜技 1811｜旡 2196｜既 2197｜(既)｜臮 2281｜洎 2851｜濟 3039｜濟 3123｜祭 3949｜稷 4020｜蔡 4030｜紀 4278｜繫 4452｜繼 4459｜罽 4507｜芰 4853｜薊 5118｜薺 5135｜覬 5491｜計 5515｜記 5528｜跽 5877｜際 6640｜霽 6715｜騎 6951｜驥 6986｜鬐 7019｜郟 7085

jii　几 346｜己 1299｜幾 1358｜庋 1362｜戟 1765｜戰 1765｜(戰)｜掎 1916｜撛 2072｜濟 3123｜給 4333｜脊 4672｜蟣 5322｜踦 5895｜麂 7218

jiin　僅 251｜儘 281｜卺 502｜廑 1389｜槿 2573｜瑾 3487｜緊 4375｜堇 4993｜覲 5493｜謹 5670｜錦 6427｜饉 6901

jiing　井 55｜儆 272｜剄 387｜憬 1703｜景 2256｜璟 3495｜警 5685｜阱 6589｜頸 6807

jin　今 79｜巾 1305｜斤 2164｜津 2861｜矜 3827｜祲 3950｜禁 3954｜筋 4118｜衿 5461｜觔 5501｜金 6310

jing　京 67｜兢 305｜旌 2185｜晶 2260｜涇 2894｜睛 3777｜杭 3988｜梗 3988｜(杭)｜梗 4248｜精 4249｜經 4350｜耕 4582｜莖 4936｜菁 4969｜荊 4994｜荆 4994｜(荆)｜驚 6982｜鯨 7082｜鶄 7164

jinn　勁 427｜搢 1984｜晉 2241｜晋 2241｜(晋)｜浸 2892｜燼 3275｜璶 3485｜盡 3730｜禁 3954｜縉 4409｜藎 5138｜覲 5493｜瑨 5816｜近 6056｜進 6109｜斳 6737

jinq　倞 195｜凈 340｜勁 427｜境 870｜徑 1474｜敬 2139｜淨 2937｜痙 3624｜竟 4077｜競 4084｜脛 4676｜逕 6092｜鏡 6488｜靖 6723｜靚 6724｜靜 6725

jiu　俱 182｜居 1188｜崌 1249｜拘 1852｜据 1902｜沮 2810｜狙 3351｜琚 3447｜疽 3604｜痀 3610｜罝 4496｜苴 4878｜菹 4972｜葅 5031｜裾 5430｜趄 5833｜車 5966｜鋦 6405｜雎 6668｜駒 6932

jiong　局 1784

jiou　啾 748｜揪 1962｜揫 1962｜(揪)｜撢 2015｜摎 2582｜湫 2988｜究 4039｜糺 4276｜糾 4277｜赳 5828｜轇 6022｜鬮 7043｜鳩 7117

jiow　僦 261｜咎 590｜就 1177｜廏 1387｜救 2128｜樞 2407｜柩 2449｜疚 3593｜究 4039｜臼 4773｜舅 4781｜舊 4785｜鷲 7196

jiuan　圈 799｜娟 1010｜悁 1580｜捐 1893｜涓 2899｜罥 5349｜身 5960｜錈 6502｜鵑 7147

jiuann　倦 209｜卷 499｜圈 799｜狷 3358｜睠 3773｜睊 3789｜絹 4343｜鄄 6219｜雋 6667

jiue　撅 2026

jiueh　倔 200

jiuh　俱 182｜偈 210｜具 318｜劇 410｜句 531｜屨 1206｜巨 1296｜懼 1744｜拒 1846｜据 1902｜據 2063｜沮 2810｜炬 3184｜璩 3819｜秬 3996｜窶 4065｜窶 4213｜聚 4602｜苣 4893｜虡 5189｜詎 5551｜足 5844｜距 5859｜踞 5885｜遽 6157｜醵 6295｜鉅 6345｜鋸 6413

jiun	颶	6841		椶	3772		檏	2639		撞	2039		駐	6930		鐲	6501
	君	561		種	4014		洙	2857	狀	3342	juay	捉	1888		鸜	7190
	困	791		宗	5358		澍	3154	juay	拽	1869		桌	2436	jwu	尤	2335
	均	815		重	6306		珠	3432	juei	椎	2501		棹	2502		爝	3271
	麕	3712	joong	蒙	332		硃	3860		追	6075		涿	2913		竹	4085
	軍	5969		塚	858		茱	4908		錐	6420		主	26		竺	4086
	鈞	6337		種	4014		蛛	5223		隹	6654		囑	781		筑	4115
	頵	6806		腫	4705		誅	5578		騅	6955		屬	1207		築	4166
	麇	7224		踵	5899		諸	5637	juen	密	4045		拄	1833		軸	5943
	麏	7229	joou	帚	1317		豬	5732		肫	4636		渚	2956		躅	5977
	麕	7328		肘	4624		邾	6195		諄	5607		煮	3228		逐	6090
jiunn	俊	168	jou	周	588		銖	6374		迍	6060		麥	3228	jy	之	30
	峻	1233		喌	653	jua	抓	1816	juey	墜	876		(煮)			厃	494
	捃	1885		州	1290		撾	2053		惴	1627		矚	3825		指	1867
	浚	2879		洲	2868		檛	7022		縋	4362		貯	5759		揩	1893
	濬	3129		盩	3736	juai	拽	1869		綴	4401		躅	7220		支	2113
	晙	3579		粥	4242	juan	專	1161		贅	5807		卓	484		枝	2376
	竣	4080		舟	4797		甎	3530		饌	6888		啄	654		梔	2461
	菌	4959		啁	5788		塼	3530	juh	仔	124		拙	1851		梔	2461
	郡	6201		輈	5986		(甎)			住	128		擢	2074		(梔)	
	雋	6667		週	6108		磚	3907		助	421		斫	2167		氏	2746
	駿	6946		鵃	7141		耑	4578		宁	1100		斮	2169		汁	2765
joa	爪	3284	jour	妯	972		顓	6818		杼	2365		斷	2172		知	3831
joai	跩	5874		舳	4806	juang	妝	965		柱	2409		斲	2172		祇	3930
joan	喎	775		胄	326		庄	1360		梲	2414		(斷)			祇	3938
	轉	6020	jow	咒	589		椿	2575		注	2845		梲	2468		織	4437
joen	准	339		宙	1113		粧	4244		炷	3188		琢	2506		胑	4632
	準	3004		晝	2247		莊	4933		祝	3942		涿	2905		胝	4668
	隼	6656		鼄	3528	juann	裝	5416		竚	4075		濁	3113		脂	4668
jong	中	21		籒	3713	juann	傳	244		筋	4129		濯	3127		芝	4840
	伀	1516		籀	4216		撰	2047		箸	4157		灼	3174		蜘	5249
	忠	1517		籀	4216		璇	3466		粥	4242		焯	3210		隻	6655
	盅	3716		(籀)			篆	4163		紵	4316		琢	3446		跱	7279
	終	4319		紂	4279		蠢	4192		耆	4552		着	3776	jya	夾	927
	螽	5309		縐	4405		賺	5801		芧	4875		繳	4449		恝	1764
	衷	5382		青	4645		轉	5893		著	5003		出	4885		戛	1764
	鍾	6448	ju	侏	153	juanq	饌	6903		蛀	5215		著	5003		(戛)	
	鐘	6493		朱	2336		僮	264		註	5545		諑	5613		筴	4132
jonq	中	21		株	2427		壯	898		鑄	6511		踱	5893			
	仲	97					戀	1750		罻	6927		酌	6248			

莢	4940	裕	5401	識	5677	籍	4219	jyue		jyy		
蛺	5230	許	5521	豸	5734	級	4298	倔	200	只	534	
袷	5401	詰	5571	質	5797	脊	4672	厥	511	咫	612	
裌	5419	頡	6797	贄	5806	蒺	5041	噱	756	址	813	
跲	5870	jyh		躓	5953	蕺	5130	嚼	774	徵	1491	
郟	6200	制	381	輊	5988	藉	5136	孓	1075	恉	1578	
鋏	6403	實	1140	運	6147	蹐	5892	崛	1243	指	1867	
頰	6797	時	1227	邿	6190	蹟	5913	復	1749	旨	2200	
頰	6804	帙	1316	鋕	6379	輯	6006	抉	1813	枳	2381	
jyau		幟	1339	鑕	6515	集	6661	掘	1922	止	2681	
嚼	774	麎	1444	陟	6607	革	6735	攫	2109	沚	2804	
jye		志	1504	雉	6664	鶺	7177	橛	2455	砥	3849	
偈	217	忮	1511	騭	6964	jyr		桷	2460	祇	3930	
傑	236	懥	1733	鷙	7189	值	208	決	2786	祉	3932	
劫	423	摯	2024	氎	59	執	843	決	2786	紙	4295	
刦	423	智	2262	伋	106	姪	994	(決)		耆	4571	
(刦)		桎	2444	卽	504	指	1867	爝	3282	芷	4856	
婕	1021	治	2819	即	504	摭	2011	爵	3289	趾	5847	
孒	1074	滯	3031	(卽)		擲	2084	玃	3390	軹	5979	
嵑	1253	炙	3181	及	518	植	2500	玦	3414	酯	6259	
截	1770	時	3571	吃	549	殖	2702	珏	3416	阯	6291	
拮	1858	寔	3590	吉	551	直	3743	玨	3416	黹	7272	
捷	1909	痔	3621	唧	694	繫	4426	(玨)				
揵	1909	痣	3627	喞	694	職	4609	瞿	3821			
(捷)		知	3831	(喞)		蟄	5312	絕	4328			
擷	2085	秩	3993	嫉	1045	質	5797	脚	4687			
杰	2379	稚	4009	寂	1132	跖	5855	腳	4707			
桀	2434	穉	4009	岌	1213	蹠	5920	蕨	5101			
桔	2447	(稚)		急	1546	蹢	5922	蕗	5109			
楬	2530	窒	4050	戢	1767	躑	5952	蹻	5355			
櫛	2631	絷	4324	擊	2069	jyu		覺	5496			
潔	3071	織	4397	棘	2482	侷	163	角	5500			
癤	3678	置	4500	極	2531	局	1186	觖	5502			
瞜	3785	膣	4730	檝	2619	掲	1896	訣	5675			
碣	3888	至	4769	瀀	2704	掬	1937	譎	5934			
碣	4082	致	4770	汲	2785	桔	2447	駃	6929			
簲	4140	致	4770	疾	3606	橘	2600	鱖	7106			
節	4159	(致)		瘠	3653	臼	4774	鳩	7125			
結	4326	蛭	5227	笈	4092	菊	4958	缺	7125			
絜	4341	製	5429			蜀	5876	(鳩)				
羯	4529	誌	5584			鞫	6749					
卿	5288					鞠	6754					

K

注音	單字	字號
ka	咖	605
kaa	卡	491
	咳	616
kaan	侃	148
	坎	817
	檻	2623
	欿	2661
	砍	3847
	輱	6029
	闞	6576
kaang	慷	1679
kae	凱	349
	剀	403
	嘅	726
	嘅	726
	(嘅)	

注音	單字	字號
	愷	1658
	慨	1678
	楷	2533
	豈	5712
	鍇	6453
	鎧	6463
	闓	6570
kah	喀	675
kai	揩	1961
	開	6533
kan	刊	362
	勘	435
	堪	850
	栽	1766
	看	3755
	龕	7327
kang	康	1377
	慷	1679
	糠	4264
kann	勘	435
	看	3755
	瞰	3808
	闞	3824
	闞	6576
kanq	亢	61
	伉	104
	抗	1820
	炕	3178
	鈧	6327
kao	拷	1871
	栲	2430
	烤	3198
	考	4569
	攷	4569
	(考)	
karng	扛	1798
kau	尻	1182
kaw	犒	3332
	銬	6380
	靠	6729

注音	單字	字號
kay	愒	1631
	愾	1659
	慨	1678
	欬	2653
ke	刻	384
	柯	2408
	棵	2499
	珂	3422
	苛	3602
	桐	3602
	(珂)	
	瞌	3800
	磕	3900
	科	3984
	棵	4013
	窠	4056
	苛	4869
	蝌	5269
	軻	5980
	鈳	6365
	頦	6798
	顆	6810
	髁	7001
kee	可	539
	坷	823
	渴	2970
keen	啃	666
	墾	883
	懇	1731
	肯	4637
	肎	4637
	(肯)	
koei	肯	4637
	(肯)	
keeng	肯	4637
	肎	4637
	(肯)	
keh	克	297

注音	單字	字號
	刻	384
	剋	390
	可	539
	嗑	721
	客	1117
	恪	1560
	溘	3000
	絆	4399
	課	5600
keng	傾	249
	坑	819
	硻	3865
	鏗	6482
	阬	6585
kenn	根	5404
ker	咳	616
	欬	2653
	殼	2719
	殳	2719
	(殼)	
	壳	2719
	(殼)	
	頃	6798
koa	垮	833
koai	擓	2068
	佮	4778
koan	刪	5036
	款	2657
	欵	2657
	(款)	
	窽	4066
	傀	233
koei	哇	5869
	頄	6794
koen	臺	902
	悃	1579
	捆	1886
	綑	4351
	閫	6548
kong	悾	1603

注音	單字	字號
	空	4042
	箜	4147
konq	控	1931
	空	4042
koong	孔	1076
	恐	1567
koou	口	527
kou	摳	2014
kow	叩	533
	寇	1135
	扣	1797
	叩	5065
	釦	6323
	彀	7184
ku	刳	378
	哭	634
	枯	2380
	窟	4055
	骷	6995
kua	夸	926
	侉	995
	胯	5579
kuah	胯	4660
	跨	5860
	刳	6996
kuan	寬	1152
kuang	匡	463
	框	1562
	框	2443
	誆	4116
	誑	5581
kuanq	壙	890
	曠	2295
	框	2443
	況	2821
	況	2821
	(況)	
	眶	3767
	礦	3919
	纊	4463

注音	單字	字號
	貺	5767
	鄺	6240
	鑛	6516
kuay	儈	273
	創	413
	塊	855
	快	1510
	旝	2193
	會	2312
	檜	2612
	澮	3104
	獪	3392
	筷	4737
	膾	5036
	郐	6238
kuei	歸	1283
	悝	1591
	盔	3725
	窺	4064
	巋	5191
	闚	6575
kuen	坤	821
	堃	1238
	昆	2212
	琨	3450
	蚰	5229
	緄	5434
	錕	6429
	髡	7009
	鯤	7078
	鵾	7159
kuenn	困	2295
	睏	2443
kuey	夬	468
	喟	695
	愧	1654
	媿	1654
	(媿)	
	憒	1704

注音	單字	字號
	潰	3087
	蕢	4201
	聵	4610
	簣	5100
	饋	6898
	匱	6902
kuh	庫	1373
	砍	3843
	袴	5399
	綺	5399
	(袴)	
	褲	5449
	酷	6264
kuoh	廓	1390
	括	1860
	擴	2086
	闊	6562
kuu	桍	2519
	苦	4874
	絝	3343
	誇	5585
kwang	狂	3343
	誆	5585
	閫	6575
kwei	奎	928
	蘬	5191
	闚	6575
	奎	933
	揆	1946
	暌	2271
	楑	3791
	葵	5017
	逵	6110
	馗	6916
	騤	6960
	魁	7049

L

注音	單字	字號
la	剌	391
	拉	1838
	旯	2205
·la	啦	664
laa	喇	681
laan	懶	1740

	攬	2111		浪	2887		賚	5787		雷	6689	lhu	嚕	768		怜	1538

以下按原書分欄逐錄：

第一欄

	攬 2111
	擥 2111
	(攬)
	欖 2649
	纜 4475
	覽 5497
aang	朗 2322
	烺 3205
	閬 6549
lah	剌 391
	瘌 3646
	臘 4700
	臈 4750
	落 5000
	蠟 5343
	辣 6041
	鑞 6517
	鬎 7026
lai	來 149
	峽 1248
	徠 1481
	淶 2944
	萊 4979
	郲 6212
	鉃 6416
lan	婪 1025
	嵐 1258
	攔 2095
	斕 2155
	欄 2641
	瀾 3158
	籃 4217
	藍 5137
	蘭 5172
	襤 5464
	襴 5470
	讕 5698
	闌 6564
lang	廊 1385
	榔 2539

第二欄

	浪 2887
	狼 3356
	琅 3442
	瑯 3479
	稂 4004
	莨 4953
	蜋 5246
	螂 5300
	踉 5878
	郎 6199
	鋃 6400
lann	濫 3126
	瀾 3158
	爛 3281
	欚 4475
lanq	浪 2887
	閬 6549
lao	佬 158
	姥 991
	潦 3079
	老 4568
	銠 6383
lau	勞 438
	哰 736
	撈 2028
	牢 3315
	髝 3668
	嫪 6287
law	勞 438
	憦 1708
	潦 3079
	澇 3094
	烙 3200
	絡 4331
	落 5000
	酪 6258
lay	瀨 3151
	癩 3680
	睞 3778
	賴 4223

第三欄

	賚 5787
	賴 5800
le	襰 5443
·le	了 46
lea	倆 190
	臉 4743
leang	倆 190
	兩 309
	魎 7054
leau	了 46
	憭 1707
	燎 3252
	膫 3811
	蓼 5066
	蟟 5326
	釕 6318
leei	儡 283
	壘 891
	磊 3901
	累 4307
	耒 4579
	蕾 5114
	蘲 5145
	誄 5577
leeng	冷 337
leh	仂 74
	勒 432
	垃 827
	扐 1887
	樂 2571
	泐 2826
	肋 4621
lei	累 4307
	縲 4421
	纍 4466
	儽 4487
	羸 4534
	蔂 5179
	鐳 6508

第四欄

	雷 6689
leng	楞 2520
	稜 4010
	穄 5121
lenq	愣 1634
	楞 2520
leou	柳 2399
	綹 4364
leu	侶 161
	呂 583
	婁 1019
	屢 1202
	履 1205
	捋 1887
	旅 2183
	梠 2469
	縷 4423
	膂 4719
	褸 5452
	鋁 6399
leuan	孿 1072
ley	擂 2054
	淚 2926
	泪 2926
	(淚)
	累 4307
	類 4467
	肋 4621
	酹 6266
	類 6823
	類 6827
lha	喇 681
lhau	拉 1838
	撈 2028
lhei	勒 432
lhi	哩 633
lhiau	撩 2044
lhing	拎 1845
lhiou	溜 3003
lhou	摟 2007

第五欄

lhu	嚕 768
	擼 1915
	曘 779
lhuen	捋 1887
lhuo	攄 2104
li	釐 1047
	棃 2475
	梨 2475
	(棃)
	犛 2742
	漓 3044
	藜 3066
	犛 3326
	犁 3326
	(犛)
	釐 3334
	狸 3359
	璃 3490
	離 4230
	縭 4417
	罹 4506
	藜 5143
	蘺 5175
	蜊 5240
	蠡 5344
	褵 5450
	貍 5742
	驪 6286
	鱺 6309
	釐 6679
	驪 6989
	鸝 7208
	黎 7261
·li	裏 5410
lian	奩 469
	奩 469
	(奩)

第六欄

	怜 1538
	憐 1698
	連 3050
	濂 3114
	璉 3491
	簾 4212
	聯 4604
	蓮 5064
	薕 5173
	襝 5457
	謰 5671
	連 6104
	鎌 6470
	鐮 6503
	鬑 7028
	鰱 7101
liang	梁 2456
	涼 2916
	粱 4246
	糧 4267
	良 4824
	娘 5246
	諒 5614
	踉 5878
	輬 6004
	量 6308
liann	戀 1748
	斂 2147
	楝 2522
	歛 2677
	殮 2712
	瀲 3159
	煉 3218
	練 4395
	鍊 6435
	鏈 6478
lianq	亮 69
	倞 195
	喨 697

暸 2263	蠡 7035	隸 6653	臨 4763	齡 7313	閭 6550
諒 5614	梨 7143	曆 6717	轔 6025	linn 吝 562	驢 6985
踉 5878	lih 例 151	黧 7021	遴 6148	淋 2924	luan 孌 1097
輛 5996	例 171	萬 7046	鄰 6233	磷 3910	孿 2106
量 6308	儷 286	麗 7228	鱗 6643	閵 5152	liueh 掠 1927
liau 僚 258	利 374	lii 俚 175	霖 6703	藺 5774	略 3572
嘹 743	力 417	哩 633	驎 6979	躪 5959	畧 3572
寮 1147	勵 445	娌 1004	鱗 7107	linq 令 92	(略)
寮 1153	屬 513	悝 1591	吝 7223	另 532	liuh 律 1471
寮 1172	吏 560	李 2340	麟 7232	liou 劉 412	慮 1695
憭 1684	唳 650	浬 2886	ling 令 92	旒 2189	氯 2758
憿 1707	慄 1660	澧 3103	伶 117	榴 2550	濾 3137
撩 2044	戾 1779	理 3441	凌 342	流 2875	率 3407
潦 3069	曆 2282	禮 3970	囹 792	瀏 3141	綠 4354
潦 3079	栗 2426	藶 5344	岭 1219	琉 3438	菉 4990
燎 3388	櫟 2629	裏 5410	怜 1538	留 3569	•lo 咯 614
療 3665	櫪 2634	裡 5410	櫺 2640	雷 3569	loan 卵 498
繚 4439	歷 2689	(裏)	泠 2837	(留)	long 嚨 771
聊 4598	沴 2813	豊 5715	淩 2935	瘤 3658	攏 2094
遼 6155	浺 2904	邐 6168	玲 3418	癉 3658	瞳 2298
鐐 6495	溧 3007	體 6293	瓴 3523	(瘤)	朧 2329
鷯 7193	溧 3148	里 6305	綾 4369	硫 3863	櫳 2637
liaw 廖 1388	痢 3625	鋰 6396	羚 4523	硫 3863	礱 2637
撂 2021	癧 3673	鯉 7076	翎 4542	(硫)	(櫳)
料 2157	礫 3916	liin 凜 344	聆 4597	遛 6135	瀧 3152
燎 3252	礪 3917	廩 1401	鈴 4805	鎦 6500	瓏 3513
瞭 3811	立 4073	懍 1727	苓 4865	駵 6968	癃 3666
鐐 6495	笠 4095	檁 2617	菱 4987	驑 6980	矓 3822
lie 咧 607	粒 4237	澟 3117	蛉 5219	鶹 7181	礲 3921
liee 咧 607	蠣 4271	liing 嶺 1278	輪 5976	liow 六 313	窿 4067
lieh 列 338	芷 4892	領 6795	綾 5995	溜 3003	籠 4224
列 368	荔 4903	lin 嶙 1268	鄲 6241	遛 6135	聾 4613
劣 420	苙 4929	林 2375	醽 6298	霤 6710	蘢 5166
捩 1899	莉 4946	淋 2924	鈴 6341	霤 6710	隆 6628
洌 2853	蒞 5060	燐 3255	陵 6619	(雷)	龍 7325
烈 3194	蠣 5346	琳 3459	零 6688	籠 6896	lonq 弄 1411
獵 3398	詈 5549	璘 3496	霝 6706	鏴 6907	衖 5365
裂 5403	蟀 6033	痳 3634	靈 6720	liu 婁 1019	loong 壟 892
趔 5837	蟶 6036	瞵 3814	鯪 7083	樓 2628	攏 2094
躐 5951	鄝 6243	磷 3910	鴒 7127	嫠 3662	籠 4224

	字	號		字	號		字	號		字	號		字	號		字	號
loou	隴	6652		圇	798		籮	4231		麻	7241		盲	3742		茂	4886
	擻	2007		崙	1242		羅	4509		麼	7242		硭	3869		袤	5395
	篓	4193		掄	1915		蘿	5177	·ma	嗎	709		芒	4838		貌	5741
lou	僂	250		淪	2936		螺	5307		蟆	5313		茫	4906		貿	5772
	嘍	729		綸	4365		覼	5495		麼	7242		邙	6170	may	脈	4671
	蔞	1019		論	5615		覼	5495		麼	7242		鋩	6408		衇	4671
	摟	2007		輪	6003		(覼)		mann			mann	嫚	1050		(脈)	
	樓	2580	luenn	論	5615		邏	6167	maa	嗎	709		嫚	1334		脉	4671
	蔞	5082	luh	六	313		鑼	6524		瑪	3482		慢	1674		(脈)	
	螻	5308		勠	442		騾	6969		碼	3895		曼	2308		賣	5794
	髏	7002		录	1441	luoh	咯	614		螞	5296		漫	3054		邁	6159
·lou	嘍	729		戮	1772		洛	2860		鎷	6471		縵	4420		麥	7234
low	漏	3043		淥	2934		濼	3135		馬	6921		蔓	5069	mean	麼	7242
	瘻	3662		漉	3040		烙	3200	maan	滿	3037		謾	5663		丏	9
	鏤	6490		潞	3076		犖	3333	maang	樠	2604		鏝	6486		免	299
	陋	6599		璐	3501		珞	3431		澷	3070		墁	6486		免	299
	露	6711		碌	3873		絡	4331		莽	4947		(鏝)			(免)	
lu	盧	1402		祿	3952		落	5000		莽	4947	mao	卯	495		冕	328
	壚	2636		鹿	4186		酪	6258		(莽)			昂	2231		勉	431
	瀘	3145		簏	4221		雒	6669		蟒	5319		泖	2834		娩	1014
	爐	3280		綠	4354		駱	6941	mae	買	5765		庬	2182		愐	1632
	盧	3735	luoo	菉	4990	luoo	蠃	4754	mah	榪	3963		毛	2735		沔	2800
	纑	4468		蓼	5066		臝	5187		罵	4504		氂	2742		湎	2978
	罏	4489		角	5500		贏	5336	mai	埋	834		矛	3826		眄	3747
	臚	4752		賂	5775		裸	5420		霾	6716		茅	4889		緬	4392
	轤	4822		路	5871	luu	摞	2055	man	埋	834		茆	4890		腼	4714
	蘆	5160		輅	5985		櫚	2630		樠	2586		鰲	5279		靦	6732
	轤	6035		轆	6021		欏	2630		漫	3054		蝥	5317	meau	杪	2954
	鑪	6519		逯	6114		(櫚)			瞞	3802		錨	6436		渺	2973
	顱	6834		醁	6275		瀂	3064		蔓	5069		髦	7013		眇	3748
	鑪	7112		錄	6418		臝	5187		蕒	5354	maw	冒	325		秒	3985
	鸕	7204		陸	6622		魯	7063		謾	5663		帽	1329		緲	4391
luan	欒	1285		露	6711		鹵	7210		蹣	5915		懋	1732		藐	5140
	欒	2648		騄	6954					顢	6825		庬	2182		邈	6165
	灤	3168		鷺	7198	**M**				饅	6899		楙	2518	meei	每	2727
	孿	4756		鹿	7216					鏋	7031		瑁	3463		浼	2893
	鑾	6526		麓	7227	注音	單字	字號		鰻	7098		眊	3750		美	4515
	鸞	7209	luo	囉	779	ma	痲	3635	mang	厖	507		督	3795		鎂	6449
luann	亂	45		玀	3404		蔴	5088		忙	1506		耄	4570	meeng	懵	1741
luen	倫	213					蟆	5313		氓	2749		芼	4859			

羅馬字	字	號碼
	猛	3366
	艋	4815
	蜢	5254
	蠓	5339
	錳	6432
mei	媒	1032
	媚	1256
	枚	2378
	梅	2458
	楣	2527
	沒	2803
	湄	2976
	煤	3223
	玫	3413
	眉	3754
	莓	4894
	莓	4935
	郿	6215
	霉	6697
	黴	7268
men	們	198
	捫	1901
	穈	4025
	門	6529
·men	們	198
meng	㡛	1175
	幪	1346
	幪	1741
	懞	1741
	(懞)	
	曚	2292
	朦	2328
	檬	2621
	氓	2793
	濛	3120
	甍	3531
	亡	3558
	盟	3729
	瞢	3805
	矒	3820
	鑝	4821
	萌	4981
	蒙	5034
	虻	5198
	甿	5284
menn	悶	1619
	懣	1736
menq	夢	3262
	孟	1084
mey	妹	973
	媚	1033
	寐	1137
	昧	2809
	珻	3463
	眛	3758
	袂	5379
	謎	5648
	魅	7052
mha	媽	1043
mhau	摸	2017
	貓	5743
	猫	5743
	(貓)	
mhen	悶	1619
	懣	3262
mheng	矒	3820
mhi	咪	611
	瞇	3801
mhie	乜	38
	吽	646
	芈	4513
mho	摸	2017
mi	彌	1439
	瀰	3156
	獼	3403
	禰	3971
	麋	4259
	麋	4427
	薜	5176
	謎	5648
	迷	6073
	醚	6281
	醾	6299
	麋	6730
	蘗	7222
mian	㟃	2477
	眠	3759
	綿	4372
	縣	4400
	瞑	3799
	面	6731
	麪	7236
	麵	7240
miau	描	1949
	瞄	3793
	苗	4868
miaw	妙	964
	廟	1395
	繆	4434
mieh	滅	3020
	篾	4183
	蔑	4183
	(蔑)	
	茂	5068
	蔑	5068
	(蔑)	
	蠛	5359
mih	幕	333
	宓	1110
	密	1130
	汨	2780
	泌	2829
	祕	3936
	秘	3936
	(祕)	
	蜜	5251
	覓	5483
	鼏	5483
	(覓)	
	鹽	5654
	厹	7285
mii	弭	1429
	枚	2124
	眯	3765
	米	4233
	羋	6730
miin	憫	1647
	憫	1705
	抿	1854
	敏	2127
	泯	2844
	湣	2972
	澠	3100
	皿	3714
	閔	6539
	閩	6547
	黽	7275
miing	皿	3714
	瞑	3799
	茗	4902
min	酩	6257
	岷	1222
	忞	1521
	旻	2209
	民	2748
	珉	3421
	緡	4386
	緡	4386
	(緡)	
	閩	6547
ming	冥	
	名	556
	明	2217
	瞑	2272
	溟	3001
	瞑	3799
	茗	4902
	螟	5297
	酩	6257
	銘	6375
	鳴	7120
minq	命	599
miow	瞑	2272
	繆	4434
mo	摩	2022
	摩	2023
	模	2584
	磨	3904
	糢	4265
	膜	4725
	蘑	5153
	謨	5666
	饃	6913
	饃	6913
	(饝)	
	魔	7058
	麿	7242
moh	嘿	747
	墨	878
	寞	1141
	抹	1830
	末	2332
	歿	2693
	歿	2693
	(歿)	
	沒	2803
	沫	2808
	漠	3049
	瞙	3664
	磨	3904
	秣	3994
	脈	4671
	貃	4671
	(貊)	
	脈	4671
	(脈)	
	膜	4725
	茉	4896
	莫	4946
	袜	5398
	貉	5740
	貃	5740
	(貉)	
	貘	5740
	陌	6600
	驀	6970
	麥	7230
	默	7250
moo	抹	1830
moou	某	2398
mou	牡	3313
	牟	3312
	眸	3768
	繆	4434
	謀	5640
	鍪	6443
	麰	7238
	瞀	
mow	茂	4886
	麥	5395
mu	模	2584
	獏	3386
muh	募	440
	墓	866
	幕	1335
	幕	1693
	幕	2274
	木	2330
	沐	2799
	牧	3316
	目	
	睦	
	穆	4028
	繆	4434
	苜	4870

注音	單字	字號
	莫	4944
	鉬	6363
muu	姆	976
	拇	1835
	母	2726
	牡	3313
	畝	3568
	鉧	6344

N

注音	單字	字號
na	南	486
	拿	1874
	拏	1874
	(拿)	
·na	哪	645
·naa	哪	645
	那	6174
naan	腩	4712
	報	5823
naang	攮	2112
	囊	2299
nae	乃	28
	奶	951
	氖	2750
	艿	4831
	廼	6085
nah	呐	573
	娜	1009
	捺	1905
	納	4288
	衲	5380
	訥	6174
	鈉	6333
nan	南	486
	喃	678
	枏	2367
	楠	2367
	(枏)	

注音	單字	字號
	男	3555
	諵	5621
	難	6680
nang	囔	780
nann	難	6680
nao	惱	1626
	瑙	3468
	腦	4704
nau	恢	1539
	撓	2035
	橈	2597
	猱	3375
	蟯	5680
	鐃	6494
naw	淖	2921
	鬧	7038
nay	奈	930
	柰	2412
	耐	4576
	褦	5443
	鼐	7284
·ne	呢	587
nean	捻	1908
	撚	2037
	撐	2092
	碾	3894
	輦	5994
	輾	6014
neau	嬝	1065
	娟	1065
	(嬝)	
	嫋	1067
	蔦	5076
	裊	5076
	鳥	7115
neei	那	6174
	餒	6874
neh	訥	5537
neng	能	4666
nenn	嫩	1054

注音	單字	字號
nenq	濘	3119
neou	忸	1514
	扭	1802
	扭	3346
	紐	4289
	鈕	6336
neu	女	949
	釹	6322
ney	內	307
	那	6174
	那	6174
nha	薾	5083
nhian	蔫	5083
nhie	捏	1895
	揑	1895
	(捏)	
	捻	1908
nhiou	妞	963
ni	倪	212
	呢	587
	妮	971
	尼	1183
	怩	1532
	泥	2842
	猊	3364
	霓	4758
	蚭	5266
	輗	5994
	覽	6702
	霓	7225
nian	年	1350
	拈	1836
	粘	4239
	鮎	7065
	黏	7113
niang	娘	1007
	孃	1007
	(娘)	
niann	唸	669
	廿	1409
	念	1518

注音	單字	字號
nianq	釀	6297
niaw	尿	1185
	溺	3013
	茶	4879
nie	乜	38
nieh	囁	776
	孽	1096
	蘗	1096
	(蘗)	
	齧	2638
	涅	2895
	湼	2895
	(涅)	
	蘖	4273
	臬	4273
	(蘖)	
	嵲	4611
	槷	4765
	齧	4768
	躡	5161
	躡	5161
	(躡)	
	蘗	5169
	躠	5957
	鎳	6467
	鑷	6523
	闑	6568
niueh	隉	6630
	顳	6836
niuh	齧	7317
	囓	7317
	(齧)	
nih	匿	472
	怒	1620
nong	儂	270
	濃	3115
	穠	4034
	膿	4735
	農	6049

注音	單字	字號
	溺	3013
	睨	3783
	膩	4732
	祂	5381
	逆	6081
nii	你	115
	妳	985
	擬	2076
	旎	2186
	禰	3971
niing	擰	2082
nin	您	1596
ning	凝	345
	嚀	765
	寧	1143
	擰	2082
	檸	2620
	獰	3397
	甯	3550
ninq	佞	139
	擰	2082
	濘	3119
	甯	3550
niou	牛	3310
niow	拗	1849
	忸	5357
	謬	5668
niueh	瘧	3648
	虐	5181
	謔	5647
niuh	衄	1514
	恧	1574
	衄	5357
noan	暖	2270
	煖	2278
	昵	2278
	(暖)	
	泥	2842

注音	單字	字號
	溺	3013
	睨	3783
	膩	4732
nonq	弄	1411
now	犏	4588
nu	奴	950
	孥	1086
	笯	4104
	駑	6931
nuh	怒	1543
nuo	娜	1009
	挪	1877
	挼	1881
nuoh	唦	686
	懦	1734
	撋	1990
	糯	4269
	稬	4269
	(糯)	
	穤	4269
	(糯)	
	諾	5639
nuoo	娜	1009
nuu	努	422
	弩	1428
	笯	3857

注音	單字	字號
	醵	6294
	黷	7302

O

注音	單字	字號
o	喔	688
·o	呵	593
oou	偶	230
	嘔	731
	耦	4587
	藕	5142
or	哦	631
ou	毆	2144
	歐	2669
	毆	2724
	漚	3046
	甌	3529

注音	單字	字號
ow	謳	5669
	鷗	7188
	嘔	731
	慪	1683
	漚	3046

P

注音	單字	字號
pa	葩	5011
	趴	5845
·pa	杷	2363
	琶	3458
pah	帕	1312
	怕	1526
pai	拍	1844
	俳	183
	徘	1477
	排	1921
	牌	3303
	簰	4196
pan	攀	2093
	潘	3074
	番	3575
pang	乒	27
	滂	3018
	磅	3898
	雱	6714
pann	判	371
	叛	524
	拚	1841
	拼	1853
	泮	2843
	畔	3564
	盼	3746
	襻	5472
panq	胖	4648
pao	跑	5854
par	扒	1793
	爬	3285
	琶	3458

注音	單字	字號
	耙	4581
parn	槃	2552
	盤	3732
	磐	3903
	胖	4648
	般	4802
	蟠	6759
parng	傍	235
	庬	507
	尨	1175
	龐	1403
	彷	1459
	徬	1487
	旁	2178
	雱	2178
	(旁)	
	膀	4718
	螃	5291
	逄	6083
pau	雹	6686
	拋	1840
	抛	1840
	(拋)	
	泡	2841
	脬	4681
paur	刨	454
	咆	602
	庖	1365
	炮	3185
	袍	5392
	麃	7219
	卷	7221
paw	泡	2841
	炮	3185
	疱	3612
	庖	3710
	砲	3859
	礮	3920

注音	單字	字號
pay	派	2874
	湃	2971
	錄	6452
pean	編	5624
	摽	2018
	殍	2701
	漂	3041
	標	3803
	縹	4424
	苹	4942
peeng	捧	1898
pei	披	1828
	胚	4651
	醅	6270
peir	培	839
	裴	5426
	賠	5791
	邳	6184
	陪	6613
pen	噴	761
	默	2675
peng	怦	1529
	抨	1827
	澎	3090
	烹	3202
	砰	3852
	硼	3872
	碰	3879
	掽	3879
	(碰)	
pern	滋	2980
	盆	3717
perng	彭	1455
	朋	2316
	棚	2486
	澎	3090
	硼	3872
	蓬	4184
	膨	4731
	芃	4832

注音	單字	字號
	蓬	5063
	鵬	7155
pey	佩	141
	帔	1310
	施	2181
	沛	2807
	珮	3437
	轡	6034
	配	6249
	霈	6696
pi	丕	13
	劈	411
	匹	470
	批	1808
	披	1828
	砒	3848
	紕	4292
	被	5397
	霹	6712
pian	偏	221
	扁	1783
	片	3301
	篇	4162
	翩	4554
	萹	5025
	編	1483
	片	3301
piann	遍	6123
	騙	6958
piau	漂	3041
	飄	6845
piaw	剽	407
	漂	3041
	票	6973
pie	撇	2034
	瞥	3815
piee	撇	2034
	苤	4899
pih	僻	268

注音	單字	字號
	屁	1187
	辮	2064
	澼	3019
	甓	3534
	襞	5686
	辟	6039
	闢	6579
	優	98
	劈	411
	匹	470
	否	566
	庀	1359
	疋	3587
	痞	3672
piin	品	621
pin	姘	1018
	姘	1018
	(姘)	
	拼	1924
	(拼)	
ping	乒	34
	娉	1003
	牝	3311
pinn	聘	4601
	聘	4601
pinq	坡	820
po	波	2839
	潑	3072
	陂	6596
	頗	6796
poh	拍	1844
	朴	2337
	泊	2827
	珀	3427
	破	3854
	粕	4238
	迫	6068

注音	單字	字號
	廹	6068
	(迫)	
	醭	6292
	魄	7051
poo	回	544
	頗	6796
poou	剖	394
	掊	1919
por	婆	1015
	皤	3703
	繁	4428
	鄱	6234
	抔	1817
	掊	1919
	裒	4899
pu	仆	
	扑	1792
	撲	2046
	痡	3629
	鋪	6410
puh	曝	2276
	曝	2276
	瀑	3130
	舖	4791
	鋪	6410
puu	圃	795
	誧	838
	普	2255
	浦	2885
	溥	3006
	譜	5681
	錯	6499
pwu	僕	256
	匍	453
	幞	453
	朴	2337
	模	2587
	濮	3128
	璞	3498

注音	單字	字號
	脯	4680
	莆	4945
	菩	4986
	葡	5006
	蒲	5037
	蒲	5038
	蹼	5937
	醭	6267
	醭	6290
	釙	6317
pyan	便	164
	楩	2537
	胼	4689
	腁	4689
	(胼)	
	諞	5624
	蹁	5902
	骿	6944
	駢	6952
pyau	嫖	1048
	瓢	3519
pyi	啤	658
	埤	842
	枇	2362
	毗	2733
	琵	3457
	疲	3599
	皮	3709
	紕	4292
	罷	4505
	羆	4508
	脾	4699
	蚍	5203
	神	5422
	貔	5744
	郫	6207
	鈹	6362
	陴	6596
	陴	6618
	鼙	7290

注音	單字	字號
pyn	熉	1068
	蘋	5164
	貧	5753
	頻	6809
	顰	6833
pyng	坪	828
	屏	1198
	平	1349
	憑	1710
	枰	2419
	洴	2919
	瓶	3526
	瓶	3526
	(瓶)	
	秤	3992
	輧	4479
	萃	4881
	萍	4982
	蘋	5164
	評	5555
	耕	6001
	馮	6923

R

注音	單字	字號
raan	冉	322
	染	2396
raang	嚷	773
	壤	894
	攘	2097
ran	然	3215
	燃	3251
	髯	7012
	髯	7017
rang	攘	2097
	瓤	3521
	禳	3973
	穰	4037
	纕	4471

注音	單字	字號
ranq	讓	5700
rao	擾	2088
	嬈	5096
	饒	6905
	繞	4442
raw	遶	6150
ree	喏	686
	惹	1645
	若	1500
	稔	4008
	紝	4297
	紝	4297
	(紝)	
	荏	4918
reh	熱	3245
	蓺	3279
ren	人	71
	仁	73
	任	101
	壬	897
	紝	4297
	紝	4297
	(紝)	
reng	仍	81
	礽	3924
renn	仞	88
	再	4864
	任	101
	刃	358
	妊	960
	恁	1566
	紉	4286
	袵	5384
	衽	5405
	訒	5530
	認	5583
	靭	5971
	韌	6766
	飪	6855
	餁	6870

注音	單字	字號
rhang	嚷	773
rheng	扔	1795
roan	蝡	5276
	蠕	5341
	軟	5974
	輭	6012
	阮	6588
roei	蕊	5093
rong	容	1129
	蝾	1277
	戎	1756
	榕	2538
	榮	2551
	毧	2736
	溶	3014
	熔	3240
	絨	4334
	羢	4525
	肜	4630
	茸	4913
	蓉	5048
	融	5294
	蠑	5338
	鎔	6459
roong	冗	1101
	氄	2744
roou	糅	4254
rou	鞣	1948
	柔	2397
	蹂	5903
	縣	6011
	肉	4619
ru	儒	278
	嚅	763
	如	956
	嬬	1095
	濡	3125
	茹	4914

注音	單字	字號
ruei	挼	3544
	綏	4377
	荽	5103
	桵	5726
ruen	稕	3329
	潤	3080
ruenn	閏	6536
	枘	2782
ruey	叡	2374
	汭	2782
	瑞	3471
	睿	3794
	芮	4852
	蚋	5202
	蜹	5267
	銳	6391
ruh	入	306
	洳	2867
	溽	3015
	縟	4413
	肉	4619
	茹	4914
	蓐	5050
	褥	5442
	辱	6048
	鋤	6390
ruo	挼	1881
ruoh	偌	219
	弱	1432
	蒻	3279
	箬	4153
	篛	4178
	若	4873
	蒻	5055
ruu	乳	43
	汝	2775
	辱	6048
ryh	日	2198
	S	

注音	單字	字號
sa	仨	94
	撒	2029
saa	撒	2029
	洒	2855
	灑	3163
	靸	6741
saan	傘	238
	散	2137
	糝	4262
	繖	4440
	嗓	711
saang	顙	6821
sah	卅	478
	薩	5132
	跋	5850
	颯	6838
sai	塞	863
	腮	4716
	顋	6813
	鰓	7091
san	三	5
	參	515
sang	喪	699
	桑	2437
sann	散	2137
sanq	喪	699
sao	嫂	1038
	掃	1912
	掃	1912
	(掃)	
sau	搔	1978
	繅	4432
	繰	4454
	臊	4744
	艘	4816
	騷	6966
saw	掃	1912
	埽	1912

第一欄

羅馬字	字	號碼
	(掃)	
	臊	4744
say	塞	863
	賽	5804
seh	嗇	706
	圾	812
	塞	863
	澀	3121
	濇	3121
	(澀)	
	瑟	3462
	穡	4032
	色	4826
	鉋	6387
sen	森	2493
seng	僧	262
sha	抄	1878
	殺	2718
	沙	2802
	煞	3230
	痧	3626
	砂	3845
	紗	4294
	莎	4948
	娑	5417
	鎩	6476
	鯊	7077
shaa	傻	276
	傻	276
	(傻)	
shaan	閃	6531
	陝	6612
shaang	上	6
	晌	2244
	賞	5790
	色	4826
shae	殼	6993
shah	嗄	703
	廈	1383
	歃	2665

第二欄

羅馬字	字	號碼
	煞	3230
	箑	4140
	霎	4549
	簁	6699
shai	篩	4172
shan	刪	370
	姍	979
	山	1209
	扇	1786
	搧	1991
	杉	2341
	潸	3086
	煽	3239
	珊	3424
	善	4531
	羶	4532
	膻	4747
	舢	4799
	芟	4841
	苫	4876
	衫	5376
	珊	5857
	釤	6326
shang	傷	247
	商	655
	殤	2707
	湯	2989
	觴	5511
	裳	5425
·shang		
shann	善	679
	單	701
	嬗	1060
	扇	1786
	掞	1926
	擅	2057
	汕	2770
	疝	3594
	禪	3967
	繕	4438
	膳	4733

第三欄

羅馬字	字	號碼
	蟮	5327
shean	蟺	5330
	訕	5525
	贍	5813
	赸	5831
	鄯	6232
	饍	6906
	鱔	7105
	鱓	7110
shanq	上	6
	尙	1171
	少	1169
shao	哨	670
shar	弰	1431
shau	捎	1894
	梢	2470
	燒	3254
	稍	3999
	筲	4131
	箱	4176
sheang	筲	4195
	艄	4814
	蛸	5231
shaur	与	447
	杓	2345
	勺	4836
sheau	韶	6777
shaw	劭	425
	哨	632
	少	1169
	捎	1894
	潲	3093
shay	紹	4312
	邵	6179
	曬	2300
	晒	2300
	(曬)	
	殺	2718
she	奢	943
	畬	3577

第四欄

羅馬字	字	號碼
	賒	5784
shean	弰	1173
	赸	1173
	(赸)	
	瞼	1276
	洒	2855
	洗	2856
	燹	3273
	獮	3395
	獫	3405
	獶	3405
	(玁)	
	癬	3683
	薛	5170
	蜆	5238
	跣	5866
	銑	6372
	險	6647
	顯	6831
sheang	鮮	7071
	享	66
	想	1644
	響	6779
	餉	6867
	饗	6908
	鱻	7072
sheau	小	1168
	曉	2285
	筱	4130
	篠	4180
shee	謏	5653
	捨	1897
	舍	4787
sheen	晒	622
	嬸	1069
	審	1150
	沈	2798
	瀋	3140
	矧	3832
	諗	5616

第五欄

羅馬字	字	號碼
sheeng	謄	5693
	省	3753
	眚	3763
sheh	射	1160
	拾	1864
	攝	2101
	歙	2672
	涉	2896
	社	3925
	舍	4787
	葉	5001
	設	5540
	赦	5822
	麝	7230
sheir	誰	5601
shen	伸	118
	參	515
	呻	597
	娠	1011
	深	2943
	桑	3260
	姓	3540
	申	3554
	砷	3855
	紳	4311
	莘	4937
	葆	5007
	蔘	5007
	身	5960
	鉮	6367
sheng	勝	437
	升	476
	牲	3319
	生	3539
	甥	3542
	笙	4094
	聲	4606

第六欄

羅馬字	字	號碼
	陞	6606
	陹	7293
shenn	慎	1661
	渗	3032
	甚	3537
	脤	4684
	腎	4694
	葚	5004
	蜃	7266
shenq	乘	36
	剩	401
	勝	437
	嵊	1263
	晟	2245
	盛	3726
	聖	4600
	膡	4746
	賸	5805
sheou	宿	1131
	朽	2338
	什	72
	佘	134
	折	1822
sher	揲	1966
	甚	3537
	舌	4786
	蛇	5218
	虵	5218
	(蛇)	
	闍	6566
shern	神	3943
	澠	3100
	繩	4445
sheu	恂	2233
	栩	2478
	湑	2925
	煦	3231
	許	5541
	詡	5563

rom	字	no.	rom	字	no.	rom	字	no.	rom	字	no.
	諲	5634		熻	3257		鋊	6377		象	5725
	鄶	6236		(熹)			鮮	7071		鄉	6221
sheuan	辭	3683		犀	3327	shiang	廂	1382		餉	6783
	選	6152		鑴	3336		湘	2985	shiau	削	389
sheue	雪	6683		畦	3570		相	3744		哮	635
	鱈	7099		皙	3705		箱	4154		嚣	777
shi	偦	257		硒	3862		緗	4384		宵	1126
	分	314		禧	3966		纕	4471		枵	2383
	吸	574		稀	4000		紅	4800		梟	2464
	唏	643		羲	4530		薌	5119		消	2897
	嘻	744		膝	4726		襄	5455		瀟	3149
	奚	941		斯	5248		鄉	6221		硝	3867
	嬉	1055		螄	5315		鑲	6522		蕭	4208
	巇	1281		蟴	5352		香	6918		綃	4346
	希	1309		西	5473		驤	6987		蕭	5102
	徯	1489		觿	5513	shiann	峴	1231		蛸	5231
	恓	1554		谿	5708		憲	1718		蠨	5347
	悉	1593		豀	5709		獻	3402		逍	6086
	扱	1807		蹊	5729		現	3439		銷	6392
	攜	2100		蹊	5910		綫	4378		霄	6694
	携	2100		醯	6289		線	4381		驍	6978
	(攜)	2100		鼶	6309		縣	4402		鴞	7130
	携	2100		鸂	7201		羨	4527		哮	635
	(攜)	2100		黦	7296		腺	4713		嘘	737
	携	2100	shia	睲	3797		莧	4941		孝	1083
	(攜)	2100		蝦	5280		見	5481		效	2123
	晞	2248	shiah	下	7		賺	5718		効	2123
	晰	2257		嚇	766		艦	5718		(效)	
	晢	2258		夏	904		檻	6602		敩	2149
	曦	2297		廈	1383		限	6602		校	2429
	析	2371		暇	2265		陷	6621		歊	2674
	栖	2423		砷	4482		靃	6709		笑	4093
	棲	2497	shian	仙	87		餡	6884		肖	4623
	楥	2590		先	295	shiang	像	254		酵	6263
	歙	2656		孅	1071		向	559	shie	些	57
	淅	2917		掀	1911		嚮	769		歇	2663
	溪	3009		祅	3928		巷	1303		蝎	5273
	烯	3207		纖	4472		橡	2290		蠍	5335
	熙	3234		躚	5955		橡	2601	shiee	寫	1151
	熹	3257					相	3744		血	5356

rom	字	no.	rom	字	no.	rom	字	no.
shieh	卸	500		矽	3842	shiing	悻	1636
	寫	1151		禊	3958		擤	2081
	屑	1197		穸	4040		省	3753
	廨	1400		系	4275		醒	6276
	懈	1725		細	4309	shin	心	1496
	械	2467		繫	4452		忻	1515
	楔	2517		蠡	4546		新	2171
	樹	2544		肸	4641		昕	2221
	泄	2824		易	4780		欣	2652
	洩	2864		舄	4780		歆	2664
	渫	2991		(易)				
	澥	3101		郤	6204			
	瀉	3139		陜	6638			
	瀣	3153		隙	6638			
	燮	3272		(隙)				
	絜	3393		餏	6895			
	紲	4329		闟	7040			
	絏	4329	shii	喜	692			
	(紲)			屣	1203			
	薤	5126		徙	1479			
	蟹	5328		憙	1714			
	蠏	5328		枲	2384			
	(蟹)			洒	2855			
	褻	5456		洗	2856			
	褻	5456		璽	3508			
	(褻)			禧	3967			
	解	5505		葸	5019			
	謝	5658		蓰	5087			
	邂	5956		嬉	5321			
	邂	6160		禧	5644			
shih	係	165	shiing					
	卌	481						
	夕	907						
	戲	1774						
	戲	1774						
	(戲)							
	歆	2672						
	汐	2771						
	潟	3075						
	昐	3745						

炘	3180	匈	4664	顳	7032	(絞)		shoei 水	2761	shuah 刷	382
芯	4851	(胸)		shiuan 喧	696	敫	2125	shoen 吭	569	shuai 摔	2010
莘	4937	shionq 夐	5538	嬛	1062	旭	2203	楯	2536	衰	5378
薪	5129	敻	905	宣	1118	洫	2863	盾	3752	拴	1862
新	5535	shiou 休	111	揎	1971	漵	3058	shoou 守	1104	栓	2421
辛	6037	修	180	暄	2264	畜	3567	首	6915	閂	6530
鋅	6401	庥	1371	瑄	3465	絮	4340	shou 收	2115	shuang 孀	1070
鑫	6520	羞	4524	翧	4564	緒	4379	shour 熟	3243	瀧	3152
歆	6776	脩	4678	萱	4997	續	4464	show 受	523	雙	6673
馨	6920	貅	5739	護	5620	芧	4845	售	647	霜	6704
shing 惺	1636	饈	6900	誼	5625	蓄	5046	壽	903	shuann 涮	2952
星	2223	鵂	7020	軒	5970	賉	5781	授	1913	帥	1319
猩	3374	鳩	7145	shiuann 旋	2184	酗	6252	狩	3354	率	3407
腥	4703	shiow 嗅	704	渲	2968	shiun 勳	444	獸	3400	shuay 蟀	5311
興	4783	宿	1131	漩	3052	壎	887	瘦	3652	shuenn 瞬	3807
馨	6920	岫	1217	炫	3183	曛	2294	綬	4357	舜	6784
醒	6947	溴	3011	眩	3760	熏	3203	shu 姝	988	順	6791
shinn 信	179	秀	3980	絢	4332	燻	3236	抒	1815	shuey 悅	1321
囟	785	繡	4444	衒	5362	燻	3236	摴	2020	睡	3779
伈	3209	綉	4444	鉉	6346	(熏)		攄	2091	稅	4001
芯	4851	(繡)		鏇	6475	獯	3396	書	2306	蛻	5233
釁	6300	臭	4766	shiue 噱	756	窨	4059	梳	2473	說	5598
顖	6824	袖	5390	薛	5125	纁	4461	梳	2473	shuh 倏	196
shinq 倖	201	銹	6412	靴	6738	罃	5018	(梳)		墅	871
姓	983	鏽	6497	shiueh 削	389	薫	5134	樞	2578	庶	1376
幸	1352	鼬	7301	穴	4038	醺	6296	樞	2583	恕	1568
性	1531	shiu 吁	548	血	5356	shiunn 巽	1304	殊	2700	戍	1755
悻	1600	嘘	735	shiuh 雪	6683	徇	1467	殳	2715	數	2143
杏	2344	墟	874	勗	434	殉	2699	洙	2857	曙	2394
興	4783	戌	1754	(勗)		汛	2777	疏	3588	束	2351
荇	4925	歔	2673	卹	501	蕈	5106	疎	3588	樹	2595
莕	4932	盱	3741	壻	899	訊	5522	(疏)		沭	2811
行	5360	繻	4457	壻	899	訓	5524	疏	3588	漱	3057
shiong 兄	294	胥	4643	序	1363	迅	5652	(疏)		澍	3091
兇	351	蓿	5067	恤	1559	遜	6132	紓	4291	疏	3588
匈	452	盧	5185	慉	1665	馴	6926	舒	4789	署	5363
恟	1556	許	5531	絞	2125	shoa 耍	4577	蔬	5077	術	5407
洶	2871	需	6692	叙	2125	shoai 用	3546	輸	6009	竪	5717
胸	4664	須	6786			shoang 爽	3295	shua 刷	382	述	6070
		婿	6801								

Rom.	字	No.	Rom.	字	No.	Rom.	字	No.	Rom.	字	No.	Rom.	字	No.	Rom.	字	No.
shuo	說	5598		獅	3380		衙	6378		嗜	714		橄	2608	shyu	徐	1473
shuoh	妁	955		絁	4325		閑	6537		嚙	755		熄	3237	shyuan	懸	1742
	帥	1319		蓍	5057		閒	6538		士	896		習	4544		旋	2184
	搠	1999		虱	5194		鹹	7211		奭	947		腊	4700		漩	3052
	數	2143		蝨	5282	shyang	庠	1370		室	1119		蓆	5047		玄	3406
	朔	2319		詩	5566		祥	3946		市	1306		褐	5428		璇	3489
	槊	2553		鳾	7118		翔	4545		式	1416		襲	5469		璿	3510
	爍	3278	·shy	匙	459		詳	5574		弒	1417		覷	5486		縣	4402
	碩	3889	shya	俠	178		降	6601		恃	1552		錫	6428	shyue	還	6161
	妁	4836		匣	464	shyau	斅	1094		拭	1857		隰	6649		學	1094
	蜙	5311		峽	1234		交	3294		是	2229	shyn	尋	1165		蘖	5879
	鑠	6514		挾	1889	shye	偕	223		柿	2387	shyng	刑	364		鷽	7199
shuu	屬	1207		暇	2265		勰	443		枾	2422		型	832	shyun	尋	1165
	數	2143		枒	2401		協	485		氏	2746		形	1448		咰	1225
	暑	2268		洽	2872		叶	545		澨	3105		形	1448		巡	1291
	署	4502		狎	3347		協	1565		示	3923		(形)			巡	1291
	薯	4593		狹	3360		挾	1889		筮	4128		硎	3871		(巡)	
	藷	5165		瑕	3467		擷	2085		耆	4571		行	5360		徇	1467
	蜀	5235		傘	4795		擷	2100		舐	4788		邢	6177		循	1486
	鷫	7200		轄	6017		(擷)			螫	5301		邢	6189		恂	1550
	黍	7247		遐	6127		攜	2100		視	5485		鉶	6419		撏	2033
	鼠	7291		鎋	6458		(攜)			試	5565		陘	6604		旬	2202
shwei	誰	5601		霞	6705		攜	2100		誓	5586		餳	6892		洵	2870
shwu	叔	521		黠	7258		(攜)			諡	5618	shyong	熊	3235		潯	3083
	塾	869	shyan	咸	617		携	2100		諟	5646		雄	6658		珣	3436
	孰	1090		卿	662		(攜)			謚	5662	shyr	什	72		紃	4280
	淑	2922		嫌	1046		斜	2159		識	5677		十	474		荀	4915
	熟	3243		嫻	1056		絜	4341		豉	5713		實	1148		蕈	5105
	秫	3997		嫺	1056		纈	4462		貰	5760		射	1160		詢	5564
	菽	4973		(嫻)			脅	4670		賦	5984		拾	1864		巡	6053
	贖	5818		弦	1425		亥	5383		逝	6087		時	2240		巡	6053
shy	失	922		械	2510		諧	5629		適	6144		峕	2240		(巡)	
	尸	1179		涎	2900		邪	6176		釋	6304		(時)			郇	6191
	屍	1193		孩	3609		鞋	6746		鈰	6360		湜	2982		馴	6926
	師	1322		癇	3669		頡	6797		飾	6863		石	3841		鱏	7108
	拾	1864		絃	4318	shyh	世	14	shyi	媳	1039		碩	3889	shyy	使	147
	施	2176		骸	4810		事	48		席	1575		蒔	5053		史	978
	濕	3133		誠	5645		仕	83		惜	1617		蝕	5270		始	978
	溼	3133		賢	5793		使	147		昔	2220		食	6849		屎	1194
	(濕)			賢	5817		侍	152					鰣	7096			
							勢	439									

	字	號		字	號		字	號		字	號		字	號		字	號
	弛	1423		餿	6894		涷	2898	sy	司	546	ta	他	84	tair	台	540
	矢	3829	sow	嗽	724		溯	3008		嘶	741		塌	857		擡	2073
	豕	5722		漱	3057		簌	4185		廝	1394		她	953		抬	2073
	駛	6937	su	甦	3543		粟	4240		思	1544		它	1099		(檯)	
soan	篅	4192		穌	4026		素	4302		撕	2038		牠	3314		枱	2420
soei	襜	6676		蘇	5162		縮	4419		斯	2170		褟	5448		檯	2625
	髓	7004		酥	6256		虪	4617		澌	3096		趿	5850		臺	4771
soen	損	1975	suan	痠	3628		膆	4722		私	3981		鉈	6359		苔	4866
	槫	2545		酸	6265		宿	5067		絲	4339		鎉	6741		邰	6181
	筍	4112	suann	筭	4135		蔌	5080		緦	4387	taa	塔	4387		鲐	6839
	(筍)	4112		算	4144		觫	5507		罳	4503	taan	坦	822		駘	6935
	簨	4204		蒜	5035		訴	5542		螄	5292		忐	1502	tan	坍	816
	隼	6656	suei	睢	3780		謖	5660		鍶	6451		毯	2739		怹	1548
song	崧	1246		綏	4349		速	6100		鷥	7191		袒	5393		探	1930
	嵩	1261		葰	4928		遡	6139	syh	伺	119		罎	7266		灘	2103
	忪	1516		雖	6672		餗	6878		似	120	taang	倘	202		攤	3164
	松	2366	suen	孫	1089		鷫	7195		俟	177		帑	1311		貪	3687
	淞	2930		猻	3382	suo	唆	641		兕	302		惝	1615		貪	5756
	鬆	7023		蓀	5044		娑	1006		嗣	718		淌	2920	tang	湯	2898
sonq	宋	1106		殉	6853		挲	1878		四	783		躺	5964		鏜	5918
	訟	5532		殉	6853		桫	2452		姒	982	tah	嗒	710		鐋	6485
	誦	5596		(殉)			桫	2471	tah	寺	1158		拓	1847	tann	探	1930
	送		suenn	巽	6132		簑	4179		巳	1301		撻	1992		歎	2668
	頌	6787	suey	歲	2688		縮	4419		廁	1381		撻	2051		嘆	2668
soong	悚	1587		燧	3265		莎	4948		柶	2417		榻	2549		(歎)	
	愯	1687		碎	3875		莎	4949		汜	2774		杳	2806		炭	3190
	竦	4081		泉	3945		蓑	5051		泗	2833		澾	3056		碳	3890
	鏉	4607		穗	4031	suoo	嗩	708		祀	3927		獺	3401	tanq	燙	3259
soou	叟	525		襚	5363		所	1782		禩	3966		踏	5883		趟	5841
	嗾	725	suh	誶	5602		瑣	3478		笥	4099		蹋	5911	tao	討	5520
	擻	2090		邃	6118		索	4303		耜	4585		蹬	5946	tarn	壇	885
	瞍	3798		遂	6164		鎖	6455		肆	4616		達	6130		彈	1437
	藪	5150		隧	6645		鎖	6492		賜	5789		遝	6136		疊	2280
sou	嗖	680	suh	嗦	707	swei	綏	4349		食	6849		邋	6140		檀	2607
	廋	1386		塑	859		遂	6118		飼	6860		錔	6469		潭	3081
	搜	1987		夙	910		隋	6631		駟	6939		闥	6581		澹	3110
	溲	3010		宿	1131		雖	6644	syy	死	2692		鞳	6757		痰	3633
	蒐	5033		愫	1656	swo	索	4303		**ㄊ**		tai	胎	4647		蟫	4488
	颼	6843		愬	1671	swu	俗	173	注音	單字	字號		苔	4866		藫	5146
				泝	2836												

音	字	號	音	字	號	音	字	號
	覃	5475	tay	太	918	tiaw	胱	2321
	談	5608		態	1668		眺	3770
	譚	5679		汰	2783		糶	4274
	郯	6209		泰	2849		朓	4665
arng	唐	644		鈦	6330		跳	5872
	堂	845	te	式	1501	tie	帖	1313
	塘	862		忚	3314		怗	1540
	搪	1994		忝	1522		貼	5769
	棠	2488		殄	2696	tiec	帖	1313
	糖	4258		洟	2929		鐵	6504
	膛	4729		腆	4690	tieh	帖	1313
	螗	5290		舔	4790		餮	6889
	螳	5306		蜆	5487	tih	倜	184
	醣	6283		覥	6732		偍	205
	鏜	6485		餂	6864		剃	386
	饟	6760	teau	挑	1868		嚏	767
tau	叨	528		窕	4051		雁	1199
	慆	1664	teh	忒	1501		厔	1199
	挑	1868		忑	1503		(雁)	
	掏	2996		慝	1685		弟	1424
	搯	1996		特	3321		俤	1583
	滔	3024		鈦	6394		昜	1609
	濤	3124	terng	滕	3028		瑅	2089
	條	4342		疼	3605		普	2310
	絛	4435		籐	4220		殢	2708
	詔	5661		縢	4414		涕	2902
	韜	6771		螣	4727		薙	5124
	饕	6910		藤	5147		逖	6094
taur	桃	2440		謄	5649		錦	6393
	檮	2622		騰	6965		髰	7010
	洮	2869	ti	剔	393	ting	體	7005
	淘	2925		梯	2466	tiing	挺	1884
	濤	3124		踢	5888		梃	2457
	燾	3274	tian	天	917		町	3557
	翿	4566		添	2949		艇	4813
	萄	4976		蘺	6727		鋌	6402
	逃	6079	tiann	瑱	3481		聽	1405
	陶	6620	tiau	佻	1553		汀	2766
	醱	7289		挑	1868		聽	4612
taw	夋	939		祧	3947	tinq	聽	4612

音	字	號	音	字	號	音	字	號
toei	腿	4717		㬢	1709	tsaur	嘈	727
toen	籴	2763		黔	7267		曹	2307
	恫	1561	tsaang	駔	6933		槽	2574
tong	炳	3616	tsae	彩	1452		漕	3048
	通	6097		採	1929		螬	5302
tonq	慟	1677		睬	3786		艚	1676
	痛	3622		綵	4363	tsay	菜	4964
	衕	5364		踩	5894		蔡	5073
toong	桶	2454	tsai	采	6302		采	6302
	筒	4117		猜	3367	tseh	側	228
	統	4337	tsair	才	1790		冊	323
toou	疰	7245		材	2346		廁	1381
torng	仝	95		縗	4469		惻	1638
	佟	140		裁	5402		測	2969
	僮	264		財	5751		策	4122
	同	553	tsan	參	515		筴	4132
	峒	1226	tsang	倉	237	tsen	參	515
	彤	1447		滄	3019	tseng	噌	5931
	曈	2284		艙	4817	tsern	岑	1215
	朣	2327		蒼	5042		涔	2901
	桐	2445		鶬	7174	tserng	層	1204
	橦	2603	tsann	燦	3265		嶒	1269
	潼	3084		璨	3488		曾	2309
	罿	3389		粲	4245	tsoei	璀	3488
	瞳	3809	tsao	慅	1724	tsoen	付	1507
	童	4079		艸	4829	tsong	団	789
	筒	4117		草	4917		從	1480
	苘	4127	tsarn	慚	1688		忽	1549
	罏	4818		慙	1688		匆	1549
	茼	4904		(慚)			(忽)	
	酮	6261		殘	2703		怱	1595
	銅	6371		蠶	5351		樅	2576
tou	偷	231	tsarng	藏	5139		琮	3486
tou	頭	6803	tsau	操	2058		璁	3494
tour	投	1819		糙	4261		聰	4605
	頭	6803					蓯	5027
	骰	6993					蔥	5075
tow	透	6089					鏦	6477
tsa	擦	2078					驄	6974
tsaan	慘	1673				tsorng	叢	526

	從	1480
	从	1480
	(從)	
	淙	2928
	琮	3455
tsow	湊	2977
	湊	2977
	(湊)	
	腠	4702
	輳	6007
tsu	粗	4236
	麤	7233
tsuan	攛	2099
	余	2763
	氽	5958
tsuann	篡	3283
	竄	4068
	墓	4169
tsuei	催	241
	崔	1239
	摧	2012
	榱	2548
	縗	4407
	衰	5378
tsuen	村	2347
	皴	3711
	邨	6178
tsuenn	吋	522
	寸	1157
tsuey	崒	659
	悴	1601
	槯	2596
	漼	2740
	淬	2938
	瘁	3640
	粹	4250
	翠	4548
	脆	4669
	脃	4669
	(脆)	

	臎	4693
	膵	4693
	(膵)	
	萃	4975
	頜	6811
tsuh	促	166
	卒	483
	猝	3369
	簇	4187
	蔟	5086
	趣	5840
	踆	5891
	氎	5917
	臧	5927
	戳	5933
	鑸	5938
	醋	6274
tsuo	搓	1980
	撮	2048
	磋	3897
	莎	4949
	蹉	5909
tsuoh	剟	388
	厝	510
	挫	1879
	措	1934
	撮	2048
	莖	4952
	鑹	6409
	錯	6431
tsuoo	瑳	3483
	胙	4683
tswan	攢	2102
tswen	存	1079
	蹲	5928
	蹉	1264
tswo	痤	3631
	瘥	3655
	矬	3835
	鹾	7212

tswu	租	1464
	俎	2698
tsy	差	1298
	恣	1572
	疵	3615
	雌	6666
tsyh	伺	119
	刺	383
	廁	1381
	次	2651
	賜	5789
tsyr	慈	1666
	瓷	3524
	疵	3615
	磁	3896
	祠	3944
	茦	4241
	茨	4905
	茲	4909
	詞	6044
	鶿	7176
	鷀	7176
	(鶿)	
tsyy	此	2683
	泚	2835
	玼	3423
tu	禿	3979
	秃	3979
	(禿)	
	鵣	7148
tuan	湍	2102
tuann	彖	1442
tuei	推	1933
tuen	吞	563
	暾	2288
tuenn	褪	5444
	蜕	5233
	退	6076

tuh	兔	301
	兔	301
	(兔)	
	吐	558
	莵	4955
tuo	佗	133
	它	1099
	托	1799
	拖	1850
	扡	1850
	(拖)	
	扡	3314
	脱	4679
	託	5527
tuoh	唾	651
	拓	1847
	柝	2405
	籜	4222
	薄	5158
	魄	7051
tuoo	妥	968
	度	1379
	楕	2602
tuu	吐	558
	土	805
	釷	6321
twan	團	804
	摶	2013
	糰	4270
twei	瀆	6642
	頹	6808
twen	国	788
	屯	1208
	臀	4739
	芚	4849
	豚	5723
	魨	6854
two	佗	133
	柁	2418
	橐	2594

	沱	2812
	紽	4323
	酡	5529
	跎	5853
	陀	6595
	駝	6924
	駞	6938
	鮀	7128
	鼉	7282
twu	凸	352
	圖	803
	塗	861
	屠	1201
	徒	1475
	稌	4006
	突	4044
	荼	4931
	英	5026
	途	6093
	酴	6268
	餘	7150
tyan	壥	864
	恬	1563
	甛	2997
	滇	3021
	甜	3538
	田	3551
	畋	3562
	鈿	6342
	闐	6567
tyau	佻	144
	條	2463
	笤	4106
	苕	4867
	蜩	5257
	調	5605
	迢	6062
	磬	7014
	齠	7312
tyi	啼	673

	提	195
	禔	395
	稊	400
	綈	434
	緹	439
	黃	491
	蹄	590
	蹏	591
	醍	627
	隄	662
	堤	662
	(隄)	
tyng	題	681
	鬌	715
	鶗	717
	亭	
	停	
	婷	
	庭	137
	廷	140
	渟	
	筳	413
	蜓	
	霆	
tza	匝	
	咂	59
	紮	430
	紥	
	(紮)	
	臢	
tzaan	拶	
	攢	
	趲	210
	咎	
	桫	
tzaang	駔	
tzae	仔	
	宰	

第一欄

注音	單字	字號
zai	惠	1254
	載	5987
	哉	627
	栽	2438
	災	3175
	灾(災)	3175
	栽(災)	3175
	薔	4961
	薔(薔)	4961
zan	簪	4205
ang	牂	3299
	臟	4757
	臧	4762
	牂	5782
	臟	5815
	牂	7003
ann	暫	2275
	讚	5703
	贊	6244
	鏨	6491
anq	笑	938
	臟	4755
	葬	5013
	藏	5139
zao	早	2201
	棗	2481
	澡	3102
	繰	4454
	藻	5156
	蚤	5207
ar	拶	1863
	栌	2448
	砸	3856
	雜	6675
arn	咱	615
au	糟	4263

第二欄

注音	單字	字號
zaur	蹧	5924
	遭	6142
zaw	鑿	6527
	噪	753
	慥	1676
	燥	3269
	皁	3694
	皂	3695
	竈	4071
	灶(竈)	4071
	簉	4191
	譟	5684
	躁	5942
	造	6101
zay	再	324
	在	806
	載	5987
zee	怎	1542
zeen	怎	1542
zeh	仄	76
zeir	昃	2211
	賊	5780
zen	簪	4205
zeng	增	877
	憎	1699
	曾	2309
	熷	3839
	繒	4436
	譜	5676
zenn	甑	3532
	繒	4436
	贈	5809
zer	則	385
	咋	603
	嘖	732
	幘	1337
	擇	2060
	澤	3106
	穸	4048

第三欄

注音	單字	字號
	笮	4107
	簀	4189
	莋	4807
	責	5758
	賊	5780
	賾	5810
tzoan	迮	6071
	篹	4192
	纂	4456
	鑚	4474
	鑚	6525
tzoei	嘴	740
tzoen	樽	2036
tzong	宗	1111
	從	1480
	椶	2507
	椶(椶)	2507
	縱	4418
	葼	5010
	踪	5896
	蹤	5919
	鬷	6959
	鬃	7025
tzong	從	1480
	從	1480
	(從)	
	棕	4253
	椶(棕)	4253
	綜	4353
	縱	4418
tzoong	偬	227
	總	4425
tzoou	走	603
	諏	5612
	鄒	6222

第四欄

注音	單字	字號
tzou	鄋	6239
	陬	6614
	騶	6967
	鯫	7084
tzow	奏	934
	揍	1950
	驟	6984
tzu	租	3990
tzuan	鑽	6525
	揝	1969
	擇	2110
	鑽	6525
tzuen	尊	1164
	樽	2593
	繜	4483
	鐏	6149
tzuey	晬	2254
	最	2311
	罪	4499
	纂	5099
	皋	6040
	醉	6272
tzuh	組	6933
tzuo	作	138
	嘬	749
tzuoh	作	138
	做	224
	坐	818
	座	1372
	怍	1523
	柞	2404
	胙	3941
	酢	4649
	酢	6253
	鑿	6527
tzuoo	佐	129
	左	1294
	撮	2048
tzuu	組	169

第五欄

注音	單字	字號
tzwo	作	138
	昨	2227
tzwu	卒	483
	捽	1906
	族	2187
	械	2566
	足	5844
	鏃	6474
tzy	吱	578
	咨	610
	姿	999
	孜	1082
	孳	1092
	淄	2915
	滋	3022
	棄	4241
	緇	4370
	茲	4909
	菑	4961
	菑(菑)	4961
	諮	5631
	貲	5761
	資	5777
	趑	5836
	輜	5993
	錙	6422
	鎡	6456
	髭	7018
	觜	7286
	齊	7303
	齋	7305
	齜	7315
tzyh	制	395
	字	1078

第六欄

注音	單字	字號
	恣	1572
	漬	3055
	秄	3323
	眥	3764
	眦(眥)	3764
	栽	4667
	自	4764
tzyy	仔	82
	姊	977
	姉(姊)	977
	子	1073
	梓	2459
	滓	3025
	秭	3995
	第	4100
	籽	4234
	紫	4306
	秄	4580
	茈	4882
	訾	5546
	訿	5560

U

注音	單字	字號
u	嗚	713
	圬	807
	屋	1192
	巫	1297
	惡	1624
	扵	2175
	汚	2779
	汚(汚)	2779
	汙(汚)	2779
	烏	3193
	誣	5593

第一欄

注音	單字	字號
ua	鄔	6223
	呱	591
	哇	625
	媧	1035
	挖	1870
	窪	4058
	蛙	5221
	鼃	7278
·ua	哇	625
uai	歪	2687
uan	剜	397
	彎	1440
	灣	3167
	婉	5263
	豌	5716
uang	汪	2784
uei	倭	214
	偎	220
	委	984
	威	1000
	葳	1252
	微	1490
	椳	2509
	溾	2995
	煨	3225
	薆	4983
	蕤	5016
	逶	6111
uen	隈	6629
	溫	2998
	温	2998
	(溫)	3650
	韞	6019
	鰮	7094
ueng	嗡	720
	翁	4538
uo	倭	214
	渦	2965
	窩	4057

第二欄

萬 4998

W

注音	單字	字號
wa	娃	1001
wah	瓦	3522
	袜	5394
	襪	5466
wan	丸	24
	刓	366
	完	1107
	烷	3206
	玩	3415
	紈	4285
	芄	4833
	頑	6791
wang	亡	60
	忘	1505
	王	3409
wann	惋	1608
	曼	2308
	玩	3415
	翫	4555
	腕	4698
	萬	4996
	万	4996
	(萬)	5069
	妄	958
wanq	往	1462
	忘	1505
	旺	2208
	望	2323
	王	3409
way	外	908
wei	危	497
	唯	648
	圍	800

第三欄

注音	單字	字號
	蒐	1262
	巋	1284
	唯	1326
	幃	1331
	微	1490
	惟	1618
	桅	2442
	濰	3130
	為	3192
	爲	3288
	維	4358
	薇	5116
	違	6131
wen	闈	6560
	韋	6765
	文	2150
	紋	4287
	聞	4603
	蚊	5200
	螡	5299
	雯	6684
wenn	問	656
	扤	1814
	搵	1998
	文	2150
	汶	2787
	璺	3511
	紊	4301
wenq	璺	3533
	璺	4485
wey	位	126
	偽	259
	味	592
	喂	677
	尉	1690
	未	2331
	渭	2966
	濊	3116

第四欄

注音	單字	字號
	為	3192
	爲	3288
	畏	3561
	胃	4644
	蔚	5072
	蝟	5274
	衛	5370
	衞	5371
	謂	5642
	遺	6154
	餧	6885
	餵	6893
	魏	7055
woa	瓦	3522
woan	婑	1014
	婉	1020
	宛	1115
	挽	1883
	晚	2246
	浣	2882
	涴	3118
	琬	3454
	腕	3580
	皖	3703
	盌	3723
	碗	3886
	椀	3886
	綰	4359
	莞	4938
	莬	4956
	踠	5882
	輓	5990
woang	往	1462
	惘	1611
	枉	2368
	網	4361
	罔	4491
	蜿	5256
	輞	5998

第五欄

注音	單字	字號
	魍	7053
woei	偉	218
	僞	259
	唯	648
	委	984
	娓	1002
	尾	1184
	洧	2862
	煒	3219
	狠	3372
	瑋	3464
	痏	3619
	痿	3639
	緯	4393
	葦	5141
	蔿	5609
	隗	6639
	韙	6770
	頠	6800
	骫	6992
	魂	7069
woen	刎	363
	吻	576
	穩	4035
	脗	4686
woeng	滃	3017
	蓊	5056
woh	偓	222
	幄	1332
	握	1959
	斡	2162
	沃	2793
	涴	2950
	渥	2964
	臥	4761
	齷	7321
woo	我	1759
	吳	571

第六欄

注音	單字	字號
	吾	579
	巫	1297
	无	2195
	梧	2453
	毋	2725
	浯	2906
	無	3214
	蕪	5107
	蜈	5243
	誣	5593
	鼯	7294
wuh	務	436
	勿	450
	塢	865
	婺	1031
	寤	1146
	悟	1590
	惡	1624
	戊	2250
	杌	2343
	物	3317
	誤	5594
	逜	6059
	鎢	6468
	阢	6584
	隖	6638
	霧	6707
	鶩	6957
	騖	7170
wuu	五	
	仵	
	伍	
	侮	
	午	472
	嫵	745
	潕	
	斌	
	(斌)	

圉 796	膌 4661	披 1923	裏 5418	蚓 5204	澄 3142	
宇 1103	臣 4760	敭 2146	詣 5562	隱 6648	瀅 3150	
峿 1279	羨 4919	易 2219	誼 5604	靷 6740	濚 3155	
庚 1380	蛇 5218	映 2234	議 5683	飲 6857	熒 3241	
敔 2132	訑 5529	曀 2286	譯 5687	yiing 影 1457	營 3264	
瑀 3475	詒 5553	曳 2354	她 5981	景 2256	瑩 3476	
禹 3975	誼 5604	代 2391	逸 6112	穎 3068	盈 3718	
窳 4063	貤 5752	枻 2709	邑 6169	癭 3681	榮 4401	
羽 4536	貽 5770	毅 2723	鎰 6466	潁 4027	螢 5277	
與 4782	迆 6054	泄 2824	鐿 6509	穎 4027	蠅 5333	
語 5591	迻 6082	洟 2825	驛 7180	(穎) 4027	蠃 5814	
鋙 6406	遺 6154	浥 2884	黓 7251	郢 6202	傭 6055	
雨 6681	頤 6681	液 2909	yii 乙 37	yinn 印 496	yong 俑 242	
齬 7320	飴 6861	溢 3005	以 93	膺 1391	喁 676	
yeuan 遠 6138	yih 一 1	燡 3242	倚 204	憖 1716	墉 872	
yeun 尤 289	亦 64	異 3574	已 1300	罃 4059	庸 1378	
殞 2705	仡 90	異 3574	扆 1785	胤 4655	慵 1681	
狁 3345	佚 136	(異) 3574	旖 2191	蔭 6615	顒 6817	
碩 3902	佾 146	疫 3597	椅 2503	飲 6857	用 3545	
隕 6635	億 271	瘞 3657	檹 2618	yinq 媵 1040		you 尤 1174
yi 一 1	刈 361	益 3720	矣 3830	應 1729		狖 2177
儀 269	剆 416	瞖 3806	艤 4819	映 2224		楢 2523
匜 461	嗌 778	繾 4415	苢 4872	硬 3866		油 2815
咦 609	奕 937	繹 4451	蟻 5331	迎 6055		游 2974
圯 809	射 1160	義 4528	踦 5895	yn 吟 564		猶 3377
夷 925	屹 1210	羿 4537	輢 6028	垠 829		由 3552
姨 993	嶧 1275	翊 4543	迤 6054	夤 914		柚 3598
宜 1116	弈 1413	翌 4559	迆 6063	寅 1134		繇 4430
彝 1446	弋 1415	翼 4560	钇 6311	淫 2940		蚰 5095
彜 1446	役 1460	肄 4615	釔 6366	狺 3361		蝣 5277
(彝) 1446	悒 1585	肊 4620	鈘 6381	鄞 6368		輶 6008
怡 1530	意 1650	腋 4691	顗 6819	銀 6368		逌 6105
沂 2791	憶 1720	臆 4742	yiin 尹 1181	嚚 6708		遊 6121
潩 2858	懌 1728	薏 5120	引 1419	龂 7310		郵 6213
疑 3589	懿 1746	藝 5144	檃 2646	齦 7316		銪 6357
痍 3617	懿 1746	蜴 5259	釿 2671	yng 塋 856		魷 7062
眙 3756	(懿) 1746	衣 5374	螠 3682	嬴 1064		yow 佑 130
眱 3766	抑 1823	裔 5412		楹 2535		
移 3998	拽 1869			熒 3026		
簃 4188	挹 1882					

侑 154	孟 3715	猨 3379	燿 4567	玉 3408	鬱 7045	
又 516	禺 3976	(猿)	葯 5030	瘉 3647	鷸 7047	
右 543	繇 4060	緣 4388	藥 5148	癒 3674	鬻 7056	
囿 794	竽 4087	芫 4847	說 5598	矞 3828	軟 7135	
宥 1120	腴 4709	苑 4863	越 5835	禦 3965	鴥 7146	
幼 1356	與 4775	蝯 5289	躍 5950	禺 3976	鬮 7197	
有 2315	舁 4777	螈 5293	軏 5972	籞 4225	鸒 7263	
柚 2402	與 4782	袁 5387	鉞 6352	籲 4232	齀 7331	
祐 3933	萸 5024	轅 6018	鑰 6521	聿 4614	yun　云 52	
莠 4939	虞 5186	黿 7276	閱 6551	育 4639	勻 448	
誘 5588	褕 5440	yuann　媛 1034	兪 7329	與 4782	昀 2222	
釉 6303	覦 5488	怨 1547	yuh　喻 698	芋 4835	筠 4124	
鼬 7292	諛 5622	願 1672	域 840	蔚 5072	紜 4296	
yu　予 47	踰 5897	掾 1947	嫗 1049	菀 5113	耘 4583	
于 51	輿 6015	苑 4863	寓 1163	蜮 5139	芸 4857	
余 135	轝 6031	遠 6138	峪 1235	裕 5413	蕓 5110	
俞 310	逾 6115	院 6609	或 1450	語 5591	雲 6687	
妤 967	隃 6625	顠 6820	御 1482	諭 5619	yunn　孕 1077	
娛 1008	隅 6627	yueh　刖 367	愈 1649	譽 5690	惲 1629	
崳 1259	雩 6682	岳 1221	慾 1692	谷 5706	慍 1657	
愉 1640	餘 6879	悅 1582	拗 1849	豫 5730	暈 2267	
愚 1651	魚 7060	戉 1753	昱 2230	遇 6120	熨 3247	
揄 1945	yuan　元 290	曜 2293	棫 2495	遹 6153	縕 4410	
於 2175	原 509	月 2314	欲 2654	郁 6188	蘊 5163	
旗 2194	員 629	樂 2571	籲 2730	鈺 6356	蘊 5163	
楡 2521	圓 801	橬 2592	汩 2781	閾 6557	(蘊)	
楱 2524	圜 802	瀹 3157	浴 2889	隩 6646	運 6122	
歟 2678	援 1965	禴 3974	煜 3221	雨 6681	鄆 6217	
渝 2958	沅 2792	籥 4227	熨 3247	雩 6682	醞 6280	
漁 3038	湲 2992	粵 4243	燠 3266	預 6790	韞 6772	
瑜 3470	源 2999		獄 3384	飫 6858	韵 6775	
璵 3509	爰 3287			馭 6922	韻 6778	
畬 3576	猿 3379					

聯合國華語注音符號索引

編 法：本索引係照單字讀音，按聯合國華語注音符號順序編列。其讀
　　　　音相同者，再按部首順序。單字後註明單字編號。

用 法：遇有僅知讀音不悉字形之單字，可按聯合國華語注音查出索引
　　　　中單字，再根據單字編號，查出書內單字及這一單字為首所組
　　　　成的詞語。

U. N. MANDARIN PHONETIC
SYMBOL INDEX

In this index the characters are arranged according to the
alphabetical order of U. N. MPS. Characters with the same pronunciation are arranged according to their respective radicals. The
figure to the right of each character is its identification number
under which the character can be found in the body of the dictionary.

If the dictionary user knows the pronunciation of the character
he is looking for but is unfamiliar with its strokes, he can find it in
the index according to the alphabetical order of U.N.MPS. Using
the identification number as a guide, he can locate in the dictionary the character and the entries beneath it.

A

注音	單字	字號
ā	啊	657
	腌	4692
	阿	6594
á	嗄	703
à	錒	6417
	阿	6594
a	啊	657
āi	哀	620
	哎	628
	唉	642
	埃	837
	挨	1876
ái	呆	584
	挨	1876
	捱	1903
	獃	3383
	癌	3667
	皚	3706
	騃	6948
ǎi	噯	759
	欸	2655
	毒	2728
	矮	3837
	藹	5155
	靄	6718
ài	嗳	759
	嬡	1063
	愛	1653
	曖	2289
	璦	3502
	碍	3885
	礙	3915
	艾	4830
	薆	5115
	隘	5710
	靉	6721
ān	安	1105

注音	單字	字號
	庵	1375
	盦	3734
	菴	4988
	諳	5633
	鞍	6745
	鵪	7157
ǎn	俺	186
àn	岸	1223
	按	1866
	暗	2269
	案	2435
	犴	3341
	菴	4988
	闇	6559
	黯	7265
āng	腌	4692
	骯	6994
áng	昂	2210
àng	盎	3722
āo	凹	353
	熬	3244
áo	嗷	722
	謷(嗷)	722
	敖	2130
	熬	3244
	獒	3385
	璈	3492
	翱	4556
	翺	4563
	鰲	4608
	螯	5305
	鼇	5664
	遨	6143
	鏊	6479
	鏖	6481
	驁	6970
	鰲	7100
	鼇	7280

注音	單字	字號
ǎo	媼	1042
	拗	1849
	襖	5462
ào	傲	243
	坳	825
	奧	1726
	拗	1849
	墺	2130
	澳	3108
	懊	3266
	隩	6646

B

注音	單字	字號
bā	八	311
	叭	537
	吧	586
	巴	1302
	扒	1793
	捌	1891
	疤	3595
	笆	4089
	粑	4520
	芭	4850
	豝	5724
bá	八	311
	拔	1848
	茇	4896
	跋	5851
	釛	6340
bǎ	把	1818
	鈀	6329
	靶	6739
bà	壩	895
	把	1818
	灞	3166
	爸	3291
	罷	4505

注音	單字	字號
	耙	4581
	霸	5478
	覇	6713
ba	吧	586
	罷	4505
bāi	掰	1942
bái	白	3692
bǎi	伯	113
	捭	1900
	擺	2087
	柏	2394
	百	3693
	襬	5467
bài	拜	1856
	敗	2131
	稗	4011
	粺	4251
bān	扳	1806
	搬	1993
	斑	2153
	媥	2154
	班	3434
	瘢	3671
	般	4802
	頒	6792
bǎn	坂	814
	板	2365
	版	3302
	舨	4804
	蝂	6565
	阪	6587
bàn	伴	116
	半	479
	扮	1803
	拌	1841
	瓣	2958
	絆	4321
	辦	6042

注音	單字	字號
bāng	傍	235
	幫	1345
	帮(幫)	1345
	梆	2472
	浜	2880
	邦	6175
bǎng	榜	2547
	膀	3305
	綁	4345
	膀	4718
bàng	傍	235
	旁	2178
	棒	2480
	磅	3898
	膀	4718
	蚌	5199
	謗	5655
	鎊	6457
bāo	剝	398
	包	451
	炮	3185
	炰(炮)	3185
	胞	4652
	苞	4871
	褒	5441
	褒	5453
báo	薄	5111
	雹	6691
bǎo	保	5253
	堡	849
	寶	1156
	寶(寶)	1156
	葆	5022
	褓	5436
	鴇	6862
	鴇	7123
bao	報	848

注音	單字	字號
	抱	1826
	暴	2276
	瀑	3138
	爆	3277
	菢	4991
	豹	5735
	趵	5846
	鉋	6347
	鑤(鉋)	6347
	鮑	7066
bēi	卑	482
	埤	842
	悲	1622
	揹	1970
	杯	2357
	盃	3719
	碑	3874
	背	4646
bēi	北	458
bèi	倍	194
	備	239
	孛	1081
	悖	1589
	憊	1712
	焙	3208
	狽	3357
	碚	3880
	糒	4256
	背	4646
	臂	4740
	蓓	5052
	被	5397
	褙	5438
	貝	5747
	輩	6002
	邶	6185
	鋇	6395
	鞴	6758

注音	字	頁碼
bēn	奔	932
	奔	932
	(奔)	
	犇	3330
	賁	5773
	錛	6434
běn	畚	940
	本	2333
	奔	3566
	苯	4880
bèn	奔	932
	奔	932
	(奔)	
	笨	4097
běng	崩	1247
	繃	4433
	繃	4433
	(繃)	
béng beng	甭	3549
	繃	4433
	繃	4433
	(繃)	
bèng	榜	2547
	繃	4433
	繃	4433
	(繃)	
	蹦	5923
	迸	6106
	迸	6106
	(迸)	
bī	屄	1191
	逼	6116
bí	荸	4950
	鼻	7298
bǐ	匕	456
	妣	966
	彼	1461
	比	2731
	秕	3986
	筆	4109
bì	俾	187
	啤	723
	壁	882
	婢	1023
	嬖	1059
	幣	1343
	庇	1361
	弊	1414
	弼	1423
	必	1497
	復	1639
	愊	1642
	拂	1834
	敝	2133
	斃	2148
	比	2731
	毖	2732
	泌	2829
	溫	2994
	狴	3355
	璧	3503
	畀	3559
	畢	3573
	痹	3636
	皕	3704
	睥	3782
	碧	3887
	祕	3936
	祕	3936
	(祕)	
	算	4146
	箆	4173
	篳	4181
	臂	4740
	苾	4884
	荸	4989
	蓖	5061
	蓽	5079
	蔽	5089
	薜	5131
	襬	5422
	襞	5459
	觱	5509
	詖	5556
	費	5768
	賁	5773
	跛	5858
	躄	5916
	蹕	5941
	蹕	5947
	辟	6039
	逼	6116
	避	6156
	邲	6183
	鄙	6224
	鉍	6361
	閉	6532
	閟	6541
	陛	6605
	髀	7000
	縶	7194
biān	砭	3851
	籩	4156
	邊	4229
	編	4389
	蝙	5268
	邊	6166
	鞭	6750
	鯿	7087
biǎn	匾	471
	扁	1783
	稨	4017
	窆	4049
	萹	5025
	蝙	5268
	褊	5433
	貶	5764
biàn	便	164
	卞	1410
	弁	1410
	徧	1483
	忭	1512
	抃	1810
	昪	2236
	汴	2788
	緶	4398
	辡	4455
	變	5695
	辨	6043
	辮	6045
	辯	6046
	遍	6123
biāo	彪	1454
	標	2018
	杓	2345
	標	2581
	穮	3248
	猋	3370
	臕	4751
	膘	4751
	鏢	6489
	鑣	6518
	飆	6846
	飇	6846
	麃	7219
biǎo	婊	1028
	表	5375
	裱	5424
	錶	6433
biào	鰾	7102
biē	憋	1711
	鱉	7281
	鼈	7281
	(鱉)	
bié	別	372
	蹩	5929
	蹩	5939
biě	癟	3675
	癟	3675
	(癟)	
biè	彆	1438
bīn	儐	277
	彬	1453
	攽	2120
	斌	2151
	檳	2626
	濱	3131
	瀕	3146
	繽	4458
	豳	5733
	賓	5785
	賓	5785
	(賓)	
	邠	6173
bìn	儐	277
	擯	2077
	殯	2713
	臏	4748
	鬢	7007
	鬂	7034
bīng	兵	316
	冰	335
	并	1351
bǐng	丙	16
	屏	1198
	昺	2237
	昞	2237
	(昺)	
	柄	2393
	炳	3187
	秉	3982
	稟	4007
	邴	6186
	餅	6871
	餅	6880
bìng	並	19
	併	189
	併	189
	(併)	
	并	1351
	摒	2008
	柄	2393
	病	3607
	垃	4076
bō	剝	398
	蟠	1270
	撥	2031
	播	2043
	波	2839
	玻	3426
	番	3575
	般	4802
	菠	4965
	鉢	6353
	盋	6353
	(鉢)	
	鉢	6353
	(鉢)	
bó	僰	6873
	伯	113
	勃	428
	博	487
	帛	1318
	搏	1977
	柏	2394
	槔	2645
	泊	2827
	淳	2881
	渤	2963
	澡	3135
	犮	3339
	白	3692
	百	3693
	礴	3922
	箔	4142
	簿	4207
	粕	4268
	脖	4685

注音	單字	字號
	膊	4723
	舶	4809
	孛	4950
	葡	5081
bǒ	薄	5111
	踣	5889
	鈸	6340
	鉑	6349
	鎛	6462
	雹	6691
	駁	6928
	駮	6943
	鵓	7149
	簸	4210
	跛	5858
bò	亳	70
	北	458
	播	2043
	擘	2071
	簸	4210
	薄	5111
	薜	5131
	蘗	5168
bo	蔔	5081
	啵	2249
bū	通	6088
	餔	6876
bú	不	8
	醭	6290
bǔ	卜	488
	哺	637
	捕	1892
	補	5415
bù	不	8
	佈	125
	埠	841
	布	1307
	怖	1525
	步	2684
	節	4194
	簿	4214
	部	6206

C

注音	單字	字號
cā	擦	2078
cāi	猜	3367
cái	才	1790
	材	2346
	纔	4469
	裁	5402
	財	5751
cǎi	彩	1452
	採	1929
	睬	3786
	綵	4363
	跴	5865
	踩	5894
	采	6302
cài	菜	4964
	蔡	5073
	采	6302
cān	參	515
	飡	6852
	餐	6872
	驂	6972
cán	慚	1688
	慙	1688
	(慚)	
	殘	2703
	蠶	5351
cǎn	慘	1673
	憯	1709
	黲	7267
càn	燦	3267
	璨	3505
	粲	4245
cāng	倉	191
	傖	237
	滄	3019
	艙	4817
	蒼	5042
	鶬	7174
cáng	藏	5139
cǎng	驅	6933
cāo	操	2058
	糙	4261
cáo	嘈	727
	曹	2307
	槽	2574
	漕	3048
	螬	5302
cǎo	懆	1724
	艸	4829
	草	4917
cào	愺	1676
cè	側	228
	冊	323
	厠	1381
	側	1638
	測	2969
	策	4122
	筴	4132
cēn	參	515
cén	岑	1215
	涔	2901
céng	層	1204
	嶒	1269
	曾	2309
cèng	蹭	5931
chā	叉	517
	喳	702
	差	1298
	扠	1801
	扱	1807
	插	1954
	插	1954
	(插)	
	杈	2342
	臿	4776
chá	察	1142
	搽	1981
	查	2411
	槎	2559
	碴	3891
	苴	4878
	茶	4912
chǎ	叉	517
chà	侘	155
	剎	379
	刹	379
	(刹)	
	妊	997
	姹	997
	(妊)	
	岔	1212
chāi	差	1298
	杈	2342
	汊	2768
	拆	1837
	釵	6325
chái	儕	280
	柴	2413
	芷	4882
	豺	5736
	茝	4951
chài	瘥	3655
	蠆	5334
chān	攙	2098
	襜	5463
chán	單	701
	嬋	1057
	孱	1091
	纏	1282
	廛	1393
	欃	2644
	毚	2734
	潯	3085
	澢	3111
	瀇	3143
	禪	3968
	纏	4465
	蟬	5324
	蟷	5332
	讒	5699
	饞	6914
	鑱	6487
	闡	6578
chǎn	產	3541
	藏	5091
	諂	5606
	鏟	6487
	闡	6578
chàn	懺	1743
	屩	4535
	顫	6830
chāng	倀	188
	倡	1026
	昌	2216
	娼	3362
	菖	4963
	閶	6553
cháng	償	282
	甞	733
	場	853
	嫦	1053
	常	1327
	徜	1478
	腸	4710
	萇	4977
	裳	5425
	長	6528
chǎng	場	853
	廠	1396
	敞	2134
	昶	2232
chàng	鼚	2743
	倡	207
	唱	649
	悵	1598
	暢	2273
	韔	6769
	韔	7044
chāo	弨	1427
	抄	1812
	超	5834
	鈔	6331
cháo	巢	1292
	晁	2243
	朝	2324
	潮	3082
	鼂	7277
chǎo	吵	572
	炒	3182
	鈔	6331
chē	車	5966
chě	尺	1180
	扯	1805
	撦	2041
chè	徹	1492
	坼	824
	拆	1837
	掣	1941
	撤	2030
	澈	3089
	轍	6023
chēn	嗔	712
	抻	1904
	琛	3445
	賝	3796
	郴	6210
chén	塵	867
	宸	1128
	忱	1513
	晨	2253

橙	2599	盛	3726			遲	6147	chǒng 寵	1155	篎	4175	遄	6119
沈	2798	程	4005			馳	6925	chòng 衝	5368	勮	4586	chuǎn 喘	689
沉	2798	裎	5409	chǐ 侈	150			銃	6370	郪	4862	舛	4793
(沈)		誠	5592	呎	585	chōu 抽	1831			藜	5062	串	23
臣	4759	郕	6205	尺	1180	搐	1973			蛼	5245	釧	6324
蔯	5085	chéng 酲	6262	恥	1577	犨	3337			蟻	5940	chuàng 創	404
塵	5635	逞	1738	耻	1577	摎	3660			躇	5954	瘡	3651
辰	6047	騁	6099	蚇	5210	篘	4177			鉏	6348	窗	4053
陳	6617	騁	6945	褫	5445	紬	4308			鋤	6407	窻	4053
chèn 襯	2635	chèng 秤	3992	豉	5713	chóu 仇	78			除	6611	(窗)	4053
稱	4015	稱	4015	齒	7307	儔	279			雛	6674	牕	4053
襯	5468	chī 吃	549	chì 傺	248	幬	1344	chǔ 儲	285	chuáng 幢	1342
讖	5701	喫	549	勅	429	惆	1605	杵	2361	淋	3297
趁	5832	(吃)		叱	541	愁	1646	楚	2525	床	3297
趂	5832	齒	719	啻	672	疇	3585	楮	2532	(牀)	3297
(趁)		燀	1041	彳	1458	稠	4012	礎	3914	闖	6573
chēng 鐺	7308	摛	2009	敕	2129	籌	4218	處	5183	chuàng 創	404
撐	2027	痴	3641	斥	2165	紬	4308	褚	5439	愴	1655
撐	2027	癡	3676	熾	3249	綢	4355	chù 亍	50	闖	6573
(撐)		胎	3771	眙	3756	裯	5423	俶	184	chuī 吹	575
樘	2611	笞	4098	翅	4539	讎	5697	怵	1541	炊	3177
竀	3309	絺	4344	赤	5821	讐	5697	搐	1995	chuí 倕	197
琤	3448	蚩	5209	趐	5864	(讐)		歜	2676	垂	826
瞠	3804	螭	5303	逞	5879	躊	5948	畜	3567	捶	1938
稱	4015	郗	6203	飭	6856	酬	6260	矗	3823	搥	1986
鏿	5329	鵄	7057	鶒	7171	雠	6671	絀	4315	椎	2501
檉	5826	蚩	7131	chōng 充	292	chǒu 丑	11	處	5183	槌	2556
鏳	6507	蠢	7324	充	292	吜	3792	觸	5512	箠	4145
chéng 丞	17	chí 匙	459	(充)		醜	6279	黜	7256	菙	5015
乘	36	墀	875	仲	1508	chòu 臭	4766	chuā 欻	2660	錘	6421
呈	570	尺	1180	憧	1702	chū 出	354	揣	1974	鎚	6461
城	835	弛	1423	沖	2801	初	369	chuāi 揣	749	陲	6616
懲	1738	持	1865	沖	2801	貙	7314	chuài 踹	5905	chūn 春	2225
成	1757	池	2773	(沖)		chú 儲	1347	chuān 川	1289	椿	2513
承	1825	治	2819	春	4779	幮	1392	穿	4043	淳	2941
晟	2245	篪	4174	衝	5368	櫥	2633	chuán 傳	244	純	4290
根	2483	篪	4174	chóng 崇	1236	櫉	2633	椽	2511	脣	4677
橙	2599	茌	4891	种	3987	(櫥)		(椽)			
澄	3088	跑	5886	蟲	5325	滁	3016	船	4812		
澂	3099			重	6306						

注音	單字	字號
chún	唇	4677
	(脣)	
	純	5059
	尊	5078
	醇	6271
	鶉	7163
chūn	惷	5345
	惷	5345
	(蠢)	
	賰	5906
chuō	戳	1776
chuò	啜	671
	惙	1613
	歠	2679
	綽	4368
	輟	5999
	醊	6273
	醱	7319
cī	差	1298
	恣	1572
	疵	3615
	雌	6666
cí	慈	1666
	姿	3524
	疵	3615
	磁	3896
	祠	3944
	茨	4905
	茲	4909
	詞	5558
	辭	6044
	薋	6866
	粢	4241
	(薋)	
	鶿	7176
	鷥	7176
	(鷀)	
cǐ	此	2683
	泚	2835
	玼	3423
cì	伺	119
	刺	383
	刷	1381
	次	2651
	賜	5789
	刏	789
cóng	從	1480
	忩	1549
	匆	1549
	(怱)	
	悤	1595
	樅	2576
	璁	3486
	瑽	3494
	聰	4605
	蔥	5027
	蓯	5075
	鏓	6477
cóng	叢	526
cóng	從	1480
	从	1480
	(從)	
	淙	2928
	琮	3455
còu	湊	2977
	湊	2977
	(湊)	
	腠	4702
	賨	6007
cū	粗	4236
	麤	7233
cú	徂	1464
	殂	2698
cù	促	166
	卒	483
	猝	3369
	簇	4187
	蔟	5086
	趣	5840
	跐	5891
	齏	5917
	蹴	5927
	蹙	5933
	覷	5938
	醋	6274
cuān	攛	2099
	汆	2763
	躥	5958
cuán	攢	2102
	欑	3283
	爨	4068
cuī	催	241
	崔	1239
	推	2012
	榱	2548
	縗	4407
	衰	4411
cuǐ	璀	3488
cuì	啐	659
	悴	1601
	橇	2596
	毳	2740
	淬	2938
	瘁	3640
	粹	4250
	翠	4548
	脆	4669
	膬	4669
	(脆)	
	膵	4693
	膵	4693
	(膵)	
	萃	4975
	顇	6811
cūn	村	2347
	皴	3711
	邨	6178
cún	存	1079
	蹲	5928
cǔn	忖	1507
cùn	吋	552
	寸	1157
cuō	搓	1980
	撮	2048
	磋	3897
	莎	4949
	蹉	5909
cuó	嵯	1264
	痤	3631
	瘥	3655
	矬	3835
	鹺	7212
cuǒ	瑳	3483
	脞	4683
cuò	剉	388
	厝	510
	挫	1879
	措	1934
	撮	2048
	莝	4952
	銼	6409
	錯	6431

D

注音	單字	字號
dā	搭	1988
	答	4119
	耷	4592
	褡	5447
dá	妲	970
	怛	1528
	打	1794
	瘩	3656
	答	4119
	繨	4450
	達	6130
	韃	6744
dān	丹	25
	儋	275
	單	701
	擔	2059
	担	2059
	(擔)	
	殫	2710
	眈	3749
	簞	4198
	耽	4593
	聃	4595
	聸	4595
	(聃)	
	馱	5962
	鄲	6235
	酖	6251
dǎ	打	1794
dà	大	916
da	瘩	3656
	繨	4450
dāi	呆	584
	待	1466
	獃	3383
dǎi	歹	2691
	逮	6107
	代	91
dài	大	916
	岱	1220
	帶	1325
	待	1466
	怠	1545
	戴	1775
	殆	2695
	玳	3420
	袋	5391
	襶	5471
	貸	5766
	迨	6066
	逮	6107
	靆	6719
	黛	7255
dǎn	撢	2050
	撣	2050
	(撢)	
	疸	3601
	膽	4736
	胆	4736
	(膽)	
	黵	7269
dàn	但	123
	啖	661
	噉	661
	(啖)	
	彈	1437
	憚	1701
	儋	1722
	擔	2059
	亶	2199
	氮	2759
	淡	2931
	澹	3110
	憺	3670
	石	3841
	萏	4985
	蛋	5247
	蜑	5247
	誕	5587
	紞	6364
dāng	噹	760
	璫	3506
	當	5460
	鐺	6507
dǎng	擋	2061
	攩	2107
	欓	2610
	當	3582
	讜	5705
	黨	7262

拼音	字	號	拼音	字	號	拼音	字	號
dàng	宕	1109	dèng	戥	1768	dǐ	底	1364
	襠	2061		等	4113		抵	1829
	檔	2610	dèng	凳	350		柢	2406
	當	3582		橙	350		氐	2747
	盪	3737		(凳)			牴	3320
	蕩	5104		嶝	1271		砥	3849
dāo	刀	356		澄	3088		舴	5504
	叨	528		磴	3691		詆	5548
	忉	1498		櫈	3691		邸	6187
	初	4798		(凳)		dì	地	810
dǎo	倒	199	dì	瞪	3810		娣	1012
	導	1167		磴	3909		帝	1320
	島	1232		蹬	5930		弟	1424
	搗	1982		鄧	6230		棣	2487
	擣	2075		鐙	6496		的	3696
	禱	3972	dī	低	127		睇	3774
dào	倒	199		提	1951		禘	3962
	到	377		氐	2747		第	4102
	導	1167		滴	3033		締	4385
	幬	1344		瓻	4522		蒂	5028
	悼	1602		隄	6626		蔕	5070
	燾	3274		堤	6626		螮	5304
	盜	3727		(隄)			螲	5304
	稻	4022	dí	嫡	1051		(締)	
	纛	4473		敵	2141		諦	5628
	翿	4566		滌	3344		遞	6137
	菿	4978		狄	3344	diān	顛	1286
	蹈	5907		的	3696		掂	1910
	道	6129		笛	4096		攧	2105
dé	得	1476		糴	4272		滇	3021
	德	1493		翟	4547		癲	3686
de	得	1476		荻	4930		巔	6822
	的	3696		覿	5498	diǎn	典	319
	襶	5471		跡	5891		碘	3881
děi	得	1476		蹢	5922		點	7254
dèng	燈	3250		迪	6067	diàn	佃	122
	登	3689		廸	6067		坫	873
	簦	4202		(迪)			奠	942
	璒	5714		邁	6144		店	1366
	鐙	6496		鏑	6480		惦	1616

拼音	字	號	拼音	字	號	拼音	字	號
	殿	2721		蝶	5286		胴	4663
	淀	2914		褶	5451		腖	5264
	澱	3107		諜	5623	dōu	兜	304
	玷	3419		跌	5852		蔸	4182
	旬	3556		蹀	5901		都	6214
	店	3613		迭	6069	dǒu	斗	2156
	簟	4199		鰈	7086		蚪	5201
	鈿	6342	dīng	丁	2		陡	6608
	電	6690		仃	75	dòu	痘	3623
	靛	6726		叮	538		竇	4070
diāo	凋	341		玎	3410		脰	4682
	刁	357		町	3557		荳	5692
	叼	529		疔	3591		豆	5710
	彫	1451		盯	3740		逗	6095
	碉	3876		釘	6313		餖	6877
	貂	5738		酊	6736		鬥	7036
	雕	6670	dǐng	酊	6246		閗	7037
	鯛	7081		頂	6781		鬦	7041
	鵰	7158		鼎	7283		鬬	7042
diào	弔	1420	dìng	定	1114	dū	督	3787
	吊	1420		碇	3878		都	6214
	(弔)			訂	5516		闍	6566
	掉	1920		釘	6313	dú	櫝	2632
	調	5605		錠	6424		毒	2729
	釣	6320		飣	6320		瀆	3136
	銚	6376	diū	丟	18		牘	3335
diē	爹	3292		銩	6388		犢	3335
dié	喋	685	dōng	冬	334		獨	3391
	揲	1628		咚	596		碡	3883
	昳	2234		東	2360		瓄	4473
	牒	3304		崠	5264		讀	5692
	瓞	3517		鼕	7288		頓	6793
	疊	3586	dǒng	懂	1723		髑	7006
	叠	3586		董	5008		黷	7271
	(疊)		dòng	凍	343	dǔ	堵	854
	昳	3757		動	433		睹	3790
	碟	3892		峒	1226		篤	4170
	絰	4336		恫	2485		肚	4626
	蝶	5265		棟	2859			

注音	單字	字號
dù	覩	5489
	睹	5799
	妒	961
	妬	961
	(妒)	
	度	1369
	斁	2146
	杜	2349
	渡	2960
	肚	4626
	蠹	5353
	蠧	5353
	(蠹)	
	鍍	6438
duān	端	4083
	耑	4578
duǎn	短	3836
duàn	斷	2173
	段	2716
	緞	4382
	鍛	6441
	煅	6441
	(鍛)	
duī	堆	847
duì	兑	298
	對	1166
	懟	1715
	憝	1737
	敦	2138
	碓	3877
	隊	6632
dūn	墩	879
	惇	1607
	敦	2138
	燉	3253
	蹲	5928
dǔn	盹	3751
dùn	噸	757
	沌	2797

注音	單字	字號
	屯	3179
	燉	3253
	盾	3752
	遁	6117
	遯	6146
	鈍	6334
	頓	6793
duō	哆	624
	多	909
duó	多	909
	奪	945
	掇	1914
	敠	2135
	裰	5421
	鐸	6506
duǒ	朵	2339
	朶	2339
	(朵)	
	躱	5963
duò	剁	380
	咄	601
	墮	880
	度	1369
	惰	1625
	柮	2415
	柁	2418
	舵	4808
	踱	5873
	跺	5898
	馱	6924

注音	單字	字號
é	哦	631
	娥	1013
	峨	1228
	莪	4943
	蛾	5234
	訛	5682
	鋨	6398
	額	6812
	鵝	7152
	䳘	7152
	(鵝)	
	鵞	7152
	(鵝)	
ě	惡	1624
	我	1759
	猗	3363
è	厄	506
	呃	582
	堊	752
	崿	1260
	惡	1624
	愕	1633
	戹	1778
	扼	1824
	搤	1824
	(扼)	
	歹	2691
	歺	2691
	(歹)	

E

注音	單字	字號
ê	婀	1016
	屙	1200
	痾	3602
	疴	3602
	(疴)	
	阿	6594
é	俄	167

注音	單字	字號
è	吃	6598
	顎	6815
	餓	6875
	鱷	7113
	鶚	7168
	齶	7323
ê	誒	5599
è	欸	2655
ēn	恩	1573
én	嗯	716
ěn	嗯	716
èn	嗯	716
	摁	1997
ér	兒	300
	洏	2876
	而	4575
	胹	4673
ěr	洱	2866
	爾	3296
	珥	3430
	耳	4590
	邇	6163
	鉺	6382
	餌	6869
	駬	6942
èr	二	49
	貳	5762

F

注音	單字	字號
fā	伐	110
	法	2832
	發	3690
fá	乏	33
	伐	110
	法	2832
	砝	4114
	筏	4501

注音	單字	字號
	閥	6545
fǎ	法	2832
	灋	2832
	(法)	
fà	髮	7015
	法	2832
	琺	3453
fān	帆	1308
	帆	1308
	(帆)	
	幡	1341
	旛	1882
	番	3575
	繙	4441
	翻	4562
	蕃	5090
	襎	6848
fán	凡	347
	帆	1308
	帆	1308
	(帆)	
	樊	2579
	煩	3226
	燔	3256
	璠	3500
	礬	3918
	繁	4428
	緐	4428
	(繁)	
fǎn	反	520
	返	6058
fàn	梵	2465
	氾	2764
	汎	2769

注音	單字	字號
fàn	泛	2838
	犯	3340
	笵	4108
	範	4161
	范	4887
	販	5755
	飯	6859
fāng	坊	811
	妨	969
	方	2174
	枋	2370
	肪	4635
	芳	4855
fáng	妨	969
	房	1781
	肪	4635
	防	6590
	魴	7064
fǎng	仿	102
	俲	102
	(仿)	
	彷	1459
	昉	2214
	紡	4300
	舫	4803
	訪	5539
	髣	7011
fàng	放	2119
fēi	啡	652
	妃	957
	扉	1788
	緋	4376
	菲	4970
	蜚	5250
	霏	6700
	非	6728
	飛	6847
	鯡	7079
féi	淝	2927
	肥	4633

注音	單字	字號
fēi	腓	4701
	匪	465
	俳	1597
	斐	2152
	朏	2318
	棐	2491
	榧	2562
	篚	4168
	翡	4550
	菲	4970
	蜚	5250
	誹	5603
fèi	吠	565
	廢	1398
	佛	1533
	沸	2814
	狒	3350
	疿	3633
	痱	3633
	(痱)	
	肺	4642
	芾	4861
	費	5768
fēn	分	359
	吩	567
	菜	2490
	氛	2751
	紛	4299
	芬	4848
	棻	4960
	雰	6685
fén	墳	881
	棼	2369
	棼	2492
	汾	2789
	焚	3211
	粉	4521
	黃	5098
	賁	5773
fěn	粉	4235

注音	單字	字號
fèn	分	359
	份	359
	(分)	
	噴	761
	奮	948
	忿	1520
	憤	1719
	糞	4260
fēng	丰	22
	封	1159
	峯	1230
	楓	2515
	灃	3161
	烽	3201
	瘋	3643
	葑	5002
	蜂	5236
	蘴	5350
	豐	5719
	酆	6242
	鋒	6404
	風	6837
féng	縫	4416
	逢	6103
	馮	6923
fěng	唪	668
	俸	185
fèng	奉	931
	縫	4416
	諷	5636
	風	6837
	鳳	7119
fó	佛	137
fóu	浮	2890
fǒu	否	566
	缶	4476
fū	夫	919
	孵	1093

注音	單字	字號
	敷	2142
	枹	2389
	柎	2392
	膚	4724
	趺	5848
	跗	6227
	鈇	6332
	麩	7235
fú	伏	109
	俘	174
	匍	455
	夫	1080
	岐	1314
	幅	1328
	弗	1421
	彿	1465
	佛	1533
	扶	1804
	拂	1834
	服	2317
	枹	2389
	桴	2451
	氟	2752
	洑	2852
	浮	2890
	涪	2910
	祓	3934
	福	3956
	符	4101
	籤	4151
	紱	4310
	紼	4313
	縛	4408
	罘	4493
	艴	4827
	芙	4839
	苻	4861
	茀	4883

注音	單字	字號
	甫	4895
	茯	4907
	莩	4942
	蕨	4962
	蚨	5208
	蜉	5244
	蝠	5275
	袚	5400
	輻	6010
	郛	6196
	馱	6767
	髯	7016
	鳧	7116
	鵩	7156
	黻	7273
fǔ	俯	181
	府	1368
	拊	1839
	撫	2042
	斧	2166
	父	3290
	甫	3547
	簠	4203
	脯	4680
	腐	4695
	腑	4696
	莆	4945
	輔	5991
	釜	6314
	頫	6799
	黼	7274
fù	仆	77
	付	86
	傅	234
	副	399
	咐	606
	婦	1024
	富	1136
	復	1485
	服	2317

注音	單字	字號
	父	3290
	祔	3935
	腹	4711
	蝮	5281
	蝮	5283
	複	5432
	覆	5476
	訃	5518
	負	5748
	賦	5802
	賻	5802
	赴	5829
	複	6013
	阜	6582
	附	6597
	馥	6919
	駙	6936
	鮒	7067
	鰒	7089

注音	單字	字號
G		
gā	咖	605
gá	尜	2204
	軋	5967
	釓	6312
	鎶	6415
gǎ	尬	1176
gāi	垓	830
	荄	4916
	該	5573
	賅	5778
	陔	6603
gǎi	改	2117
gài	丐	10
	概	2568
	槩	2568
	(槩)	
	溉	3045

注音	單字	字號
	蓋	5029
	蓋	5049
	盍	5049
	(蓋)	
gān	鈣	6338
	乾	44
	乾	44
	(乾)	
	鳶	1178
	干	1348
	杆	2353
	柑	2398
	泔	3411
	玕	3536
	疳	3600
	竿	4088
	肝	4628
gǎn	感	1652
	擀	2065
	敢	2136
	桿	2474
	橄	2591
	澉	3097
	稈	4003
	趕	5839
gàn	幹	1353
	旰	2206
	紺	2541
	淦	2933
	灨	3169
	紺	4317
	贛	5820
	骭	6991
gāng	剛	396
	岡	1216
	崗	1241
	杠	2352
	綱	4360

	字	字號		字	字號		字	字號		字	字號		字	字號		字	字號
	棺	2498		皈	3699		鹹	6917		嶭	1250	hǎo	嘷	742		釳	4284
	療	3649		規	5482		鹹	6917		犴	2541		噑	762		閡	4557
	矜	3827		邦	6194		(鹹)			汗	2772		壕	889		荷	4927
	綸	4365		閨	6546	guǒ	果	2377		涵	2911		毫	2737		蓋	5049
	莞	4938		鮭	7070		椁	2504		邯	6180		濠	3122		褐	5435
	觀	5499		龜	7328		槨	2504		韓	6768		號	5188		覈	5477
guǎn	鱹	7092	guǐ	胿	466		(椁)		hàn	喊	684		蠔	5340		貉	5740
	琯	3461		匭	1098		猓	3368		罕	4492		豪	5728		餄	6385
	筦	4126		晷	2261		菓	4995		闞	6576		貉	5740		閡	6543
	管	4149		癸	3688		蜾	5262	hàn	悍	1586		鶴	7173		閤	6544
	脘	4675		蠡	4190		裹	5427		憾	1721	hǎo	好	954		閨	6571
	館	4792		詭	5569		餜	6887		扦	1796		郝	6198		鞨	6753
	莞	4938		軌	5968	guò	過	6124		捍	1890	hào	好	954		鶡	7169
	館	6886		鬼	7048					撼	2052		昊	2215		鹖	7309
guàn	冠	329	guì	劊	413		**H**			旱	2207		晧	2252		齕	7330
	慣	1675		會	2312	注音	單字	字號		暵	2277		浩	2883	hè	龢	604
	摜	2006		桂	2439	hā	哈	626		汗	2772		淏	2912		喝	693
	灌	3162		檜	2612	há	蛤	5225		漢	3053		澔	3098		嚇	766
	盥	3733		櫃	2624		蝦	5280		瀚	3147		灝	3165		奭	947
	裸	3953		洼	3027	hǎ	哈	626		翰	4558		皓	3702		荷	4927
	罐	4490		瞶	3812	hái	孩	1088		菡	4984		皜	3707		豁	5707
	觀	5499		貴	5763		還	6161		釺	5737		耗	4584		賀	5771
	貫	5757		跪	5867		頦	6798		銲	6411		號	5188		赫	5771
	鸛	7206		鱖	7106		骸	6997		釬	6411		郜	6220		郝	6198
guāng	光	296	gǔn	滾	3036	hǎi	海	2891		(銲)			鎬	6464		鶴	7173
	洸	2877		滾	3036		醢	6284		頷	6805		顥	6828	hēi	黑	7250
	胱	4662		(滾)		hài	亥	63		顄	6950	hē	呵	593		嘿	747
guǎng	廣	1399		袞	5388		咳	616	hāng	夯	924		喝	693		黑	7250
	獷	3399		裒	5398		害	1124	háng	杭	2356		訶	5543	hén	痕	3620
guàng	桄	2441		鮌	7073		氦	2756		桁	2432	hé	何	132	hěn	很	1468
	逛	5585	gùn	棍	2479		駭	6940		沆	2796		劾	426		狠	3352
	逛	6098	guō	渦	2965	hān	憨	1717		航	4801		合	547	hèn	恨	1558
guī	傀	233		堝	5314		蚶	5214		行	5360		和	604	hēng	亨	65
	圭	808		過	6124		酣	6254		迒	6061		核	2428		哼	638
	歸	2690		郭	6208		頇	6785		頏	6789		河	2816	héng	哼	1551
	潙	3095	guó	國	797		鼾	7299	hàng	桁	2432		涸	2912		恒	1551
	珪	3435		幗	1336	hán	函	355		沆	2796		盉	3721		(恆)	
	瑰	3480		摑	2005		含	568	hāo	嚆	764		盒	3724		桁	2432
	瓌	3514		虢	5190		寒	1138		蒿	5043		禾	3978		横	2606
										薅	5112					珩	3433

拼音	字	號	拼音	字	號	拼音	字	號	拼音	字	號	拼音	字	號	拼音	字	號
	蘅	5159	hū	乎	32		厴	1787		環	3504		逳	6126		喙	690
	衡	5372		呼	598		桔	2519		繯	4448		黃	7244		彗	1443
hèng	橫	2606		忽	1519		滬	3029		還	6161	huǎng	幌	1333		彚	1445
hm	噷	758		惚	1612		軤	3518		鍰	6445		恍	1536		恚	1569
hōng	哄	623		戲	1774		祜	3939		鐶	6505		慌	1555		惠	1623
	烘	3197		欻	2660		笏	4091		闤	6580		晃	2242		慧	1689
	薨	5128		歑	2817		護	5688		鬟	7033		謊	5650		晦	2251
	訇	5519		淴	2953	huā	嘩	734	huǎn	浣	2882	huàng	晃	2242		會	2312
	轟	6030		滹	3034		花	4854		澣	3118	huī	徽	1495		樻	2565
	訌	7061		虖	5184		華	4966		緩	4390		恢	1557		濊	3116
hóng	宏	1108	hú	囫	790	huá	划	365	huàn	喚	691		揮	1963		燴	3270
	弘	1422		壺	901		劃	409		奐	935		撝	2049		穢	4033
	泓	2831		弧	1426		嘩	734		宦	1121		暉	2266		篲	4197
	洪	2865		斛	2158		滑	3023		幻	1355		灰	4553		繢	4443
	紅	4283		槲	2572		猾	3381		患	1594		虺	5196		繪	4446
	紘	4293		湖	2984		華	4966		換	1958		褘	5437		翽	4565
	翃	4540		狐	3349		譁	5673		摜	2066		詼	5576		蕙	5097
	荭	5023		猢	3371		豁	5707		渙	2955		輝	5997		蕢	5117
	虹	5195		糊	4252		驊	6977		漶	3063		隳	6651		螝	5323
	訌	5523		縠	4403	huà	劃	409		煥	3224		麾	7243		誨	5597
	閎	6535		胡	4654		化	457		瘓	3644	huí	回	784		諱	5632
	鴻	7139		葫	5012		樺	2589		豢	5727		徊	1470		賄	5776
	黌	7246		蝴	5285		畫	3578		轘	6026		洄	2850		闠	6577
hǒng	哄	623		衚	5369		華	4966		逭	6113		茴	4910		靧	6733
hòng	汞	2778		縠	5510		話	5572	huāng	慌	1663		蛔	5222	hūn	婚	1022
	閧	7039		醐	6278	huái	徊	1470		肓	4625		迴	6072		惛	1614
hōu	齁	7300		餬	6891		懷	1739		荒	4920		廻	6072		昏	2218
hóu	侯	160		鶻	7027		槐	2558		凰	348		(迴)			葷	5018
	喉	683		鵠	7153		淮	2939	huáng	徨	1484	huǐ	悔	1584		闇	6556
	猴	3376		鶘	7166		踝	5884		惶	1630		會	2312	hún	混	2945
	疾	3833	hǔ	唬	667	huài	壞	893		湟	2990		毀	2722		渾	2975
	葔	4165		濬	3035	huān	懽	1747		潢	3077		燬	5196		琿	3473
	餱	6890		琥	3452		歡	2680		煌	3217		譭	5597		餛	6882
hǒu	吼	577		虎	5180		讙	5702		璜	3497		賄	5776		魂	7050
hòu	候	203	hù	互	53		貛	5746		皇	3698	huì	匯	467	hùn	混	2945
	厚	508		怙	1527		獾	5746		磺	3911		卉	480		慁	1670
	后	557		戶	1777		(貛)			簧	4206		卉	480		悃	1670
	後	1472	huàn	冱	1780		驩	6988		蝗	5271		(卉)			(惽)	
	逅	6080		戶	1777	huán	寰	1154		蟥	5318					混	2945
	鱟	7109		冱	1780		桓	2446								渾	2975

注音	單字	字號
	溷	3012
huō	嚄	5626
	豁	7074
huó	豁	5707
huó	活	2873
huǒ	伙	112
	夥	915
	火	3171
	鈥	6328
huò	和	604
	嚄	888
	惑	1621
	或	1760
	獲	2080
	濩	3132
	獲	3394
	蠖	3840
	舂	3844
	禍	3955
	穫	4036
	矆	5157
	瀖	5342
	豁	5707
	貨	5754
	鑊	6510
	霍	6698
	騞	6962

J

注音	單字	字號
jī	乩	42
	几	346
	唧	694
	唧	694
	(唧)	
	嘰	738
	基	844
	奇	929
	姬	1005
	屐	1196
	稽	1255
	幾	1358
	期	2325
	朞	2325
	(期)	
	機	2605
	激	3112
	犄	3328
	璣	3499
	畸	3581
	畿	3583
	磯	3908
	禨	3969
	稽	4023
	積	4029
	笄	4121
	笄	4121
	(笄)	
	箕	4143
	績	4431
	羈	4510
	羇	4511
	肌	4622
	齏	5178
	羈	5479
	羈	5480
	觭	5508
	譏	5672
	跡	5863
	蹟	5925
	躋	5949
	迹	6074
	隮	6650
	雞	6677
	飢	6850
	饑	6904
	雞	7185
	賫	7305
	賫	7305
	(賫)	
	賫	7305
	(賫)	
	齏	7306
jí	亟	59
	伋	106
	卽	504
	即	504
	(卽)	
	及	518
	吃	549
	吉	551
	唧	694
	唧	694
	(唧)	
	嫉	1045
	寂	1132
	岌	1213
	急	1546
	戟	2069
	棘	2482
	楫	2529
	極	2531
	檝	2619
	殛	2704
	汲	2785
	疾	3606
	瘠	3653
	瘵	4092
	籍	4219
	級	4298
	脊	5041
	蒺	5130
	藉	5136
	踖	5892
	蹐	5913
	輯	6006
	集	6661
	革	6735
	鶺	7177
jǐ	几	346
	己	1299
	幾	1358
	庋	1362
	戟	1765
	戟	1765
	(戟)	
	掎	1916
	擠	2072
	濟	3123
	給	4333
	脊	4672
	蟣	5322
	踦	5895
	麂	7218
jì	伎	108
	冀	321
	劑	415
	妓	959
	季	1085
	寄	1133
	忌	1499
	悸	1599
	技	1811
	旡	2196
	旣	2197
	既	2197
	(旣)	
	暨	2281
	洎	2851
	漈	3039
	濟	3123
	祭	3949
	稷	4020
	稷	4030
	紀	4278
	繫	4452
	繼	4459
	闃	4507
	芰	4853
	薊	5118
	霽	5135
	覬	5491
	計	5515
	記	5528
	跽	5877
	際	6640
	霽	6715
	騎	6951
	驥	6986
	髻	7018
	鄉	7085
jiā	伽	121
	佳	143
	傢	232
	加	419
	嘉	728
	夾	927
	家	1127
	枷	2386
	珈	3428
	痂	3611
	笳	4103
	葭	5014
	袈	5389
	豭	5731
	迦	6065
	鎵	6473
jiá	夾	927
	恝	1570
	戛	1764
	戛	1764
	(戛)	
	筴	4132
	荚	4940
	莢	5230
	袷	5401
	袷	5419
	跲	5870
	郟	6200
	鋏	6403
	頰	6797
	頰	6804
jiǎ	假	216
	夏	904
	岬	2081
	斝	2160
	檟	2614
	甲	3553
	胛	4650
	賈	5779
	鉀	6343
jià	假	216
	價	267
	夾	927
	嫁	1037
	架	2385
	稼	2934
	駕	6934
jiān	兼	320
	堅	846
	奸	952
	姦	992
	尖	1170
	戔	1284
	搛	2510
	殲	2714
	漸	2981
	湔	3062
	煎	3229
	犍	3731
	監	3731
	箋	4138
	籛	4138
	(箋)	
	緘	4380
	縑	4406
	肩	4634

睍	4825	建	1408	將	1162	徼	1494	街	5366	解	5505
音	4957	檻	2623	強	1434	播	2040	階	6633	**jiè** 介	80
蒹	5040	键	2741	強	1434	攪	2108	**jié** 偈	217	借	206
間	6534	漸	3062	(強)	1434	湫	2988	傑	236	屆	1189
閒	6538	澗	3078	彊	1434	疚	3353	劫	423	戒	1758
鹼	6755	濺	3134	(強)	1434	皎	3701	刼	423	械	2467
鶄	6764	监	3731	洚	2903	矯	3838	(刼)	423	玠	3417
鰹	7093	箭	4155	糡	4266	姣	4123	婕	1021	界	3560
鰹	7104	腱	4708	糨	4266	絞	4330	孑	1074	疥	3596
鶺	7179	艦	4820	(糨)	4266	繳	4449	嵑	1253	芥	4844
jiǎn 俭	274	荐	4926	絳	4338	脚	4687	截	1770	藉	5136
剪	400	薦	5127	醤	6288	腳	4707	拮	1858	解	5505
戬	1769	見	5481	降	6601	角	5500	捷	1909	誡	5590
揀	1944	諫	5630	**jiāo** 交	62	蹻	5936	捷	1909	**jīn** 今	79
撿	2067	賤	5795	嚼	748	較	5983	(捷)	1909	巾	1305
柬	2410	踐	5881	姣	989	鉸	6865	擷	2085	斤	2164
檢	2615	鍵	6446	嬌	1058	餃	6865	杰	2379	津	2861
減	2959	銅	6498	憍	1697	**jiào** 叫	535	桀	2434	矜	3827
瞼	3817	鑑	6512	教	2126	嚼	748	桔	2447	祲	3950
筧	4137	鑒	6513	椒	2494	嶠	1272	楬	2530	禁	3954
簡	4200	間	6534	澆	3092	徼	1494	櫛	2631	筋	4118
簡	4200	閒	6538	焦	3213	播	2040	潔	3678	衿	5386
(簡)	4200	餞	6883	燋	3261	教	2126	睫	3785	襟	5461
繭	4453	**jiāng** 僵	266	礁	3913	斠	2163	碣	3888	觔	5501
蕑	4551	姜	987	膠	4728	校	2429	竭	4082	金	6310
裥	5458	將	1162	茭	4923	窖	4052	箪	4140	**jǐn** 僅	251
謇	5652	殭	2711	蕉	5092	覺	5496	節	4159	儘	281
譾	5691	江	2776	蛟	5224	訓	5517	結	4326	巹	502
趼	5861	漿	3067	跤	5875	較	5983	絜	4341	廑	1389
趼	5861	疆	3584	郊	6192	轎	6024	羯	4529	槿	2573
(趼)		繮	4447	驕	6976	醮	6291	迦	5288	瑾	2706
蹇	5908	薑	5122	鮫	7068	**jiē** 偕	223	袷	5401	瑾	3487
鐗	6498	螿	5310	鵁	7138	喈	682	訐	5521	緊	4375
鰜	7213	豇	5711	鷦	7192	嗟	717	詰		菫	4993
鹼	7214	**jiǎng** 奖	946	嘮	774	揭	1964	頡	6797	覲	5493
jiàn 件	100	奬	2570	**jiǎo** 佼	145	癤	3678	**jiě** 姊	977	謹	5670
健	226	蒋	5074	僥	260	皆	3697	姉	977	錦	6427
僭	263	講	5657	剿	405	稭	4016	(姉)		饉	6901
俭	274	**jiàng** 匠	462	勦	405	結	4326	姐	980	**jìn** 劤	427
剑	414			(剿)						嚌	750

注音	單字	字號
	訣	5536
	譎	5675
	蕨	5934
	駃	6929
	鱖	7106
	鴃	7125
	(鴃)	7125
juě juè	蕨	5934
	倔	200
jūn	君	561
	困	791
	均	815
	鞫	3712
	軍	5969
	鈞	6337
	頵	6806
	麇	7224
	麏	7229
	龜	7328
jùn	俊	168
	峻	1233
	捃	1885
	浚	2879
	濬	3129
	晙	3579
	竣	4080
	菌	4959
	郡	6201
	雋	6667
	駿	6946

K

注音	單字	字號
kā	咖	605
kǎ	卡	491
	咳	616
kà	喀	675
kāi	揩	1961

注音	單字	字號
	開	6533
kǎi	凱	349
	剴	403
	嘅	726
	嘅	726
	(嘅)	
	愷	1658
	慨	1678
	楷	2533
	豈	5712
	鍇	6453
	鎧	6463
	闓	6570
kǎi	愒	1631
	愾	1659
	慨	1678
	欬	2653
kān	刊	362
	勘	435
	堪	850
	戡	1766
	看	3755
	龕	7327
kǎn	侃	148
	坎	817
	檻	2623
	歁	2661
	砍	3847
	輡	6029
	闞	6576
kàn	勘	435
	看	3755
	瞰	3808
	矙	3824
	闞	6576

注音	單字	字號
kàng	亢	61
	伉	104
	抗	1820
	坑	3178
	鈧	6327
kāo	尻	1182
kǎo	拷	1871
	栲	2430
	烤	3198
	考	4569
	攷	4569
	(考)	
kào	犒	3332
	銬	6380
	靠	6729
kè	刻	384
kē	柯	2408
	棵	2499
	珂	3422
	疴	3602
	痾	3602
	(疴)	
	瞌	3800
	磕	3900
	科	3984
	稞	4013
	窠	4056
	苛	5269
	蚵	5269
	軻	5980
	鈳	6365
	頦	6798
	顆	6810
	髁	7001

注音	單字	字號
kè	克	297
	刻	384
	剋	390
	可	539
	嗑	721
	客	1117
	恪	1560
	溘	3000
	緙	4399
	課	5600
kěn	啃	666
	墾	883
	懇	1731
	肯	4637
	(肯)	
kěn	肯	4637
	(肯)	
kèn	根	5404
kēng	傾	249
	坑	819
	硜	3865
	鏗	6482
	阬	6585
kēng	肯	4637
	耳	4637
	(肯)	
ké	宵	4637
kè	渴	2970
ké	咳	616
	欬	2653
	殼	2719
	売	2719
	(殼)	2719
	殼	2719
kōng	空	4042
	箜	4147
kǒng	孔	1076
	恐	1567
kòng	控	1931

注音	單字	字號
	(殼)	6798
	頦	
kōu	摳	2014
kǒu	口	527
	叩	533
kòu	寇	1135
	扣	1797
	蔻	5065
	釦	6323
	彀	7184
kū	刳	378
	哭	634
	枯	2380
	窟	4055
	骷	6995
	酷	2519
kǔ	苦	4874
kù	庫	1373
	矻	3843
	袴	5399
	綺	5399
	(袴)	
	褲	5449
	酷	6264
kuā	夸	926
	姱	995
	誇	5579
kuǎ	垮	833
kuà	胯	4660
	跨	5860
	骻	6996
kuǎi	擓	2068
	舀	4778
kuài	儈	273
	劊	413
	塊	855
	快	1510
	旝	2193
	會	2312
	檜	2612

注音	單字	字號
	澮	3104
	渝	3392
	裌	4136
	膾	4737
	劊	5036
	郐	6238
kuān	寬	1152
kuǎn	款	2657
	欵	2657
	(款)	
	窾	4066
kuāng	匡	463
	恇	1562
	框	2443
	筐	2443
	誆	5581
kuáng	狂	3343
	誑	5585
kuàng	壙	890
	曠	2295
	框	2443
	況	2821
	況	2821
	(況)	
	眶	3767
	礦	3919
	纊	4463
	貺	5247
	鄺	6240
	鑛	6516
kuī	巋	1283
	悝	1591
	盔	3725
	窺	4064
	虧	5191
	闚	6575
	夔	906
	奎	933
	揆	1946
	暌	2271

音	字	字號		音	字	字號
kuî	睽	3791	kuò	廓	1390
	葵	5017		括	1860
	逵	6110		擴	2086
	馗	6916		闊	6562
	騤	6960			
	魁	7049		**L**	
kuǐ	傀	233	注音	單字	字號
	跬	5869	lā	喇	681
	頍	6794		拉	1838
kuì	匱	468		剌	391
	喟	695		拉	1838
	愧	1654		旯	2205
	媿	1654	lá	喇	681
	(愧)			剌	391
	憒	1704		瘌	3646
	潰	3087		臘	4700
	簣	4201		臈	4750
	聵	4610		落	5000
	蕢	5100		蠟	5343
	餽	6898		辣	6041
	饋	6902		鑞	6517
kūn	坤	821		鬎	7026
	崑	1238	la	啦	664
	昆	2212	lái	來	149
	琨	3450		崍	1248
	蚰	5229		徠	1481
	裈	5434		淶	2944
	錕	6429		萊	4979
	髡	7009		郲	6212
	鯤	7078		錸	6416
	鵾	7159	lài	瀨	3151
kǔn	壼	902		癩	3680
	悃	1579		睞	3778
	捆	1886		賴	4223
	綑	4351		賚	5787
	閫	6548		賴	5800
kùn	困	787	lán	婪	1025
	睏	3775		嵐	1258
				攔	2095
				爛	2155

字	字號		音	字	字號		音	字	字號		音	字	字號		音	字	字號
欄	2641		lāo	嘮	736		lèi	累	4307			蜊	5240
讕	3158			撈	2028			耒	4579			蠡	5344
籃	4217			牢	3315			蕾	5114			褵	5450
藍	5137			髈	3668			蘽	5145			貍	5742
蘭	5172			醪	6287			誄	5577			醨	6286
襤	5464	lǎo	佬	158		lèi	擂	2054			籬	6309
襴	5470		姥	991			淚	2926			離	6679
斕	5698		潦	3079			泪	2926			驪	6989
闌	6564		老	4568			(淚)				酈	7248
lǎn 懶	1740		銠	6383			累	4307			黎	7261
攬	2111	lào	勞	438			類	4467		lǐ	俚	175
欖	2111		憥	1708			肋	4621			哩	633
欖	2649		潦	3079			酹	6266			娌	1004
鑭	4475		涝	3094			類	6823			悝	1591
覽	5497		烙	3200			類	6823			李	2886
làn 濫	3126		絡	4331		léng	楞	2520			澧	3103
瀾	3158		落	5000			稜	4010			理	3441
爛	3281		酪	6258			薐	5121			禮	3970
纜	4475	lē	襇	5443		lěng	冷	337			蠡	5344
láng 廊	1385	lè	仂	74			愣	1634			裏	5410
榔	2539		勒	432			楞	2520			裡	5410
浪	2887		垃	827		lī	哩	633			(裏)	
狼	3356		捋	1887		lí	釐	1047			豊	5715
琅	3442		樂	2571			黎	2475			逦	6168
瑯	3479		泐	2826			梨	2475			體	6293
稂	4621		肋	4621			(棃)				里	6305
莨	4953	le	了	46			犛	2742			鋰	7076
蜋	5246	lēi	勒	432			漓	3066			鯉	7076
螂	5300		擂	2054			犛	3326		lì	例	151
踉	5878		累	4307			梨	3326			俐	171
郎	6199	léi	縲	4421			(犛)				儷	286
鋃	6400		纍	4466			犛	3334			利	374
lǎng 朗	2322		羸	4487			璃	3490			力	417
烺	3205		蘽	4534			籬	4230			勵	513
閬	6549		纍	5179			縭	4417			厲	560
làng 浪	2887		鐳	6508			羅	4506			唳	650
閬	6549		雷	6689			藜	5143			慄	1660
lāo 撈	2028	lěi	儡	283			蠡	5175				
lǎo 勞	438		壘	891								
			磊	3901								

	戾	1779		怜	1538		魘	7054	lié	咧	607		磷	3910	liú	劉	412
	曆	2282		憐	1698	liàng	亮	69	liè	咧	607		闌	5152		旒	2189
	栗	2426		連	3050		僚	195		冽	338		賁	5774		榴	2550
	櫟	2629		濂	3114		喨	697		列	368		躪	5959		流	2875
	櫪	2634		璉	3491		晾	2263		劣	420	líng	拾	1845		瀏	3141
	歷	2689		亷	4212		諒	5614		捩	1899	líng	令	92		琉	3438
	沴	2813		聯	4604		踉	5878		洌	2853		伶	117		留	3569
	涖	2904		蓮	5064		輛	5996		烈	3194		凌	342		畱	3569
	溧	3007		蓝	5173		量	6308		獵	3398		囹	792		(留)	
	瀝	3148		褳	5457	liǎo	撩	2044		裂	5403		岭	1219		瘤	3658
	癘	3625		謰	5671	liào	僚	258		趔	5837		怜	1538		瘤	3658
	癧	3673		連	6104		嘹	743		躐	5951		櫺	2640		(瘤)	
	礫	3916		鎌	6470		寥	1147		鬣	7035		泠	2837		硫	3863
	礪	3917		鐮	6503		寮	1153		鬛	7143		淩	2935		硫	3863
	立	4073		繿	7028		尥	1172	lín	嶙	1268		玲	3418		(硫)	
	笠	4095		縺	7101		憭	1684		林	2375		瓴	3523		遛	6135
lián	粒	4237	liàn	臉	4743		憭	1707		淋	2924		綾	4369		鎦	6500
liàn	糲	4271	liǎn	戀	1748		撩	2044		燐	3255		羚	4523		騮	6968
	苈	4892		斂	2147		潦	3069		琳	3459		翎	4542		驑	6980
	荔	4903		楝	2522		潦	3079		璘	3496		聆	4597		鰡	7181
	莅	4929		歛	2677		獠	3388		痲	3634		舲	4805	liǔ	柳	2399
	莉	4946		殮	2712		膋	3665		瞵	3814		苓	4865		絡	4364
	蒞	5060		潋	3159		繚	4439		磷	3910		菱	4987	liù	六	313
	蛎	5346		煉	3218		聊	4598		臨	4763		蛉	5219		溜	3003
	詈	5549		練	4395		遼	6155		繗	6025		蛉	5976		遛	6135
	躒	6033		鍊	6435		鐐	6495		遴	6148		輘	5995		蔖	6710
	轢	6036		鏈	6478		镣	7193		邻	6233		酃	6241		蕾	6710
liáng	酈	6243	liáng	梁	2456	liǎo	了	46		隣	6643		醽	6298		(蕾)	
	隸	6653		涼	2916		憭	1707		霖	6703		鈴	6341		餾	6896
	靂	6717		梁	4246		燎	3252		驎	6979		陵	6619		餾	6907
	鬲	7021		粮	4247		嘹	3811		鱗	7107		零	6688	lo	咯	614
	鬲	7046		糧	4267		蓼	5066		麐	7223		靈	6706	lóng	嚨	771
	麗	7228		良	4824		蟟	5193		麟	7232		霝	6720		攏	2094
li	裏	5410		踉	5246		釕	6318	lǐn	凜	3326		鯪	7083		嚨	2298
liǎ	倆	190		踉	5878	liào	廖	1388		廪	1401		鴒	7127		朧	2329
lián	奩	469		辌	6004		撂	2021		懍	1727		齡	7313		櫳	2637
	(匲)	469		量	6308		料	2157		檁	2617	lǐng	嶺	1278		礲	2637
	帘	1315	liǎng	倆	190		燎	3252		澟	3117		領	6795		(櫳)	
	廉	1384		兩	309		瞭	3811	lìn	吝	562	lìng	令	92		瀧	3152
							鐐	6495		淋	2924	liū	溜	3003		瓏	3513

注音	單字	字號
	癃	3666
	曨	3822
	礱	3921
	窿	4067
	篭	4224
	罿	4613
	蘢	5166
	隆	6628
lóng	龍	7325
	壟	892
	攏	2094
	籠	4224
	隴	6652
lòng	弄	1411
	衖	5365
lōu	摟	2007
lóu	僂	250
	嘍	729
	婁	1019
	摟	2007
	樓	1772
	蔞	5082
	螻	5308
	髏	7002
lǒu	摟	2007
	簍	4193
lòu	漏	3043
	瘻	3662
	鏤	6490
	陋	6599
	露	6711
lou	嘍	729
lū	嚕	768
lú	盧	1402
	櫨	2636
	瀘	3145
	爐	3280
	盧	3735
	籚	4468
	纑	4489
	臚	4752
	轤	4822
	蘆	5160
	轤	6035
	鑪	6519
	顱	6834
	鱸	7112
	鸕	7204
lǔ	擄	2055
	櫓	2630
	樐	2630
	(櫓)	
	滷	3064
	虜	5187
	魯	7063
	鹵	7210
lù	僇	253
	六	313
	勎	442
	氯	1441
	戮	1772
	淥	2934
	漉	3040
	潞	3076
	璐	3501
	碌	3873
	祿	3952
	簏	4186
	簶	4221
	綠	4354
	菉	4990
	蓼	5066
	角	5775
	路	5871
	輅	5985
	轆	6021
	逯	6114
	醁	6275
	錄	6418
	陸	6622
	露	6711
	騄	6954
	鷺	7198
	鹿	7216
lú	麓	7227
	婁	1019
	櫚	2628
	攄	3662
	閭	6550
	鑪	6985
lǚ	侶	161
	呂	583
	婁	1019
	屢	1205
	履	1205
	拎	1887
	旅	2183
	梠	2469
	縷	4423
	膂	4719
	褸	5452
	鋁	6399
lǜ	律	1471
	慮	1695
	氯	2758
	濾	3137
	率	3407
	綠	4354
	葎	4990
luán	孿	1285
	攣	2648
	灤	3168
	臠	5336
	鸞	6526
	鑾	7209
luǎn	卵	498
luàn	亂	45
luán	孌	1097
	攣	2106
lüǎn	變	1072
lüè	掠	1927
	略	3572
	畧	3572
	(略)	
lún	掄	1915
	倫	213
	圇	798
	崙	1242
	掄	1915
	淪	2936
	綸	4365
	論	5615
	輪	6003
lùn	論	5615
luō	囉	779
	拎	1887
	攞	2104
	玀	3404
	籮	4231
	羅	4509
	蘿	5177
	螺	5307
	覼	5495
	覶	5495
	(覶)	
	邏	6167
	鑼	6524
	驒	6969
luó	攞	2055
	嬴	4754
	臝	5187
	蠃	5336
	裸	5420
luǒ	咯	614
	洛	2860
	濼	3135
	烙	3200
	犖	3333
luò	珞	3431
	絡	4331
	落	5000
	酪	6258
	雒	6669
	輅	6941

M

注音	單字	字號
mā	媽	1043
má	痲	3635
	麻	5088
	蟆	5313
	麻	7241
	麼	7242
mǎ	嗎	709
	瑪	3482
	禡	3895
	螞	5296
	鎷	6471
	馬	6921
mà	禡	3963
	罵	4504
ma	嗎	709
	蟆	5313
	麼	7242
	麼	7242
	(麼)	
mái	埋	834
	霾	6716
mǎi	買	5765
mài	脈	4671
	脉	4671
	(脈)	
	霢	4671
	(脈)	
	賣	5794
	邁	6159
	麥	7234
mán	埋	834
	横	2586
	漫	3054
	瞞	3802
	蔓	5069
	縵	5354
	謾	5663
	蹣	5915
	顢	6825
	饅	6899
	鬘	7031
	鰻	7098
mǎn	滿	3037
màn	嫚	1050
	慢	1674
	曼	2308
	漫	3054
	縵	4420
	蔓	5069
	謾	5663
	鏝	6486
	墁	6486
	(墁)	
máng	厖	507
	忙	1506
	氓	2749
	盲	3869
	芒	4838
	茫	4947
	硭	3070
	莽	4947
mǎng	漭	3070
	蟒	4947
	(蟒)	
	蝱	5319
māo	摸	2017
	貓	5743

注音	字	號碼
máo	猫 (貓)	5743
	旄	2182
	毛	2735
	髦	2742
	矛	3826
	茅	4889
	茆	4890
	蝥	5279
	蟊	5317
	錨	6436
	氂	7013
	莓	4894
	苺	4935
	酈	6215
	霉	6697
	徽	7268
mǎo	卯	495
	昴	2231
	卯	2834
mào	冒	325
	帽	1329
	愗	1732
	旄	2182
	楙	2518
	瑁	3463
	眊	3750
	瞀	3795
	芼	4570
	芼	4859
	茂	4886
	袤	5395
	貌	5741
	貿	5772
me	麼	7242
méi	媒	1032
	帽	1256
	枚	2378
	梅	2458
	楣	2527
	沒	2803
	湄	2976
	煤	3223
	玫	3413
	眉	3754
měi	每	2727
	渼	2893
	美	4515
	鎂	6449
mèi	妹	973
	媚	1033
	寐	1137
	昧	2226
	沬	2809
	珇	3463
	眛	3758
	袂	5379
	謎	5648
	魅	7052
mēn	悶	1619
	焖	3262
mén	們	198
	捫	1901
	摩	4025
	門	6529
mèn	悶	1619
	懑	1736
men	們	198
mēng	朦	3820
méng	尨	1175
	蠓	1346
	懵	1741
	慒 (懵)	1741
	曚	2292
	朦	2328
	檬	2621
	氓	2749
	濛	3120
	氂	3531
	虻	3558
	盟	3729
	甍	3805
	瞢	3820
	矇	4821
	萌	4981
	蒙	5034
	虻	5198
	宀	5284
měng	懵	1741
	猛	3366
	艋	4815
	蜢	5254
	蠓	5339
	鋩	6432
mèng	夢	913
	孟	1084
mǐ	咪	611
	眯	3801
mí	彌	1439
	瀰	3156
	獼	3403
	禰	3971
	縻	4259
	麋	4427
	蘪	5176
	謎	5648
	迷	6073
	醚	6281
	釄	6299
	麛	6730
	麋	7222
mǐ	弭	1429
	枚	2124
	眯	3765
	米	4233
	芈	4513
	麛	6730
mì	冪	333
	宓	1110
	密	1130
	汩	2780
	泌	2829
	祕	3936
	秘 (祕)	3936
	蜜	5251
	覓	5483
	冪 (覓)	5483
	譴	5654
	痲	7285
mián	棉	2477
	眠	3759
	綿	4372
	緜	4400
miǎn	丏	9
	免	299
	冕	328
	勉	431
	娩	1014
	悃	1632
	沔	2800
	湎	2978
	眄	3747
	緬	4392
	腼	4714
	靦	6732
miàn	瞑	3799
	面	6731
	麪	7236
	麵	7240
miáo	描	1949
	瞄	3793
	苗	4868
miǎo	杪	2355
	淼	2954
	渺	2973
	眇	3748
	秒	3985
	緲	4391
	藐	5140
	邈	6165
miào	妙	964
	廟	1395
	繆	4434
miē	乜	38
	咩	646
	半	4513
miè	滅	3020
	蔑	4183
	篾 (篾)	4183
	蔑	5068
	蔑 (蔑)	5068
	嵼	5359
mín	岷	1222
	忞	1521
	旻	2209
	民	2748
	珉	3421
	緡	4386
	緍 (緡)	4386
	閩	6547
mǐn	憫	1647
	愍	1705
	抿	1854
	敏	2127
	泯	2844
	湣	2972
	渳	3100
	皿	3714
	閔	6539
	閩	6547
	黽	7275
míng	冥	331
	名	556
	明	2217
	暝	2272
	溟	3001
	瞑	3799
	蓂	4902
	螟	5297
	酩	6257
	銘	6375
	鳴	7120
mǐng	皿	3714
	瞑	3799
	茗	4902
	酩	6257
mìng	命	599
	暝	2272
miù	繆	4434
	謬	5668
mō	摸	2017
mó	摩	2022
	劘	2023
	模	2584
	磨	3904
	糢	4725
	膜	4725
	蘑	5153
	謨	5666
	饃	6913
	饝 (饝)	6913
	魔	7058
	麼	7242
mǒ	抹	1830
mò	嘿	747
	墨	878
	寞	1141
	抹	1830
	末	2332
	歿	2693
	歿 (歿)	2693

（第一欄）

音	字	字號
	沒	2803
	沫	2808
	漠	3049
	寞	3664
	磨	3904
	秣	3994
	脈	4671
	䘑	4671
	(脈)	
	脉	4671
	(脈)	
	膜	4725
	茉	4897
	莫	4944
	袜	5394
	絡	5740
	貊	5740
	(貉)	
	蟆	5745
	陌	6600
	駢	6743
	冪	6971
	麥	7234
	默	7253
móu	牟	3312
	眸	3768
	繆	4434
	謀	5640
	鍪	6443
	鶜	7238
mǒu	某	2395
	牡	3313
mòu	瞀	3795
	茂	4886
	袤	5395
mú	模	2584
	氁	3386
mǔ	姆	976
	拇	1835
	母	2726

（第二欄）

音	字	字號
	牡	3313
	畝	3568
	鉧	6344
mù	募	440
	墓	866
	幕	1335
	慕	1693
	慕	2274
	木	2330
	沐	2799
	牧	3316
	目	3739
	睦	3784
	穆	4028
	繆	4434
	苜	4870
	莫	4944
	鉬	6363

N

注音	單字	字號
nā	那	6174
ná	南	486
	拿	1874
	拏	1874
	(拿)	
nǎ	哪	645
	那	6174
nà	呐	573
	娜	1009
	捺	1905
	納	4288
	衲	5380
	訥	5537
	那	6174
	鈉	6333
	哪	645
na	哪	645
nǎi	乃	28
	奶	951

（第三欄）

音	字	字號
	氖	2750
	芿	4831
	迺	6085
nài	奈	930
	柰	2412
	耐	4576
	褦	5443
	鼐	7284
nán	南	486
	喃	678
	枏	2367
	楠	2367
	(枏)	
	男	3555
	諵	5621
	難	6680
nǎn	腩	4712
	䫚	5823
nàn	難	6680
nāng	囊	780
náng	灢	2112
	曩	2299
nāo	憹	1539
	撓	2035
	橈	2597
	猱	3375
	譊	5680
	鐃	6494
nǎo	惱	1626
	瑙	3468
	腦	4704
nào	淖	2921
	鬧	7038
nè	訥	5537
ne	呢	587
nèi	那	6174
	餒	6874
nèi	內	307
	那	6174
nèn	嫩	1054

（第四欄）

音	字	字號
néng	能	4666
	澤	3119
ní	倪	212
	呢	587
	妮	971
	尼	1183
	怩	1532
	泥	2842
	猊	3364
	霓	4758
	蚭	5266
	輗	5994
	覽	6702
	齯	7225
nǐ	你	115
	妳	985
	擬	2076
	旎	2186
	禰	3971
nì	匿	472
	惄	1620
	暱	2278
	昵	2278
	(暱)	
	泥	2842
	溺	3013
	睨	3783
	膩	4732
	袒	5381
	逆	6081
niān	蔫	5083
nián	年	1350
	拈	1836
	粘	4239
	鮎	7065
	黏	7249
niǎn	捻	1908
	撚	2037
	撑	2092
	碾	3894

（第五欄）

音	字	字號
niáng	娘	1007
	孃	1007
	(娘)	
niàng	釀	6297
niǎo	嬈	1065
	嫋	1065
	(嫋)	
	嬝	1067
	蔦	5076
	裊	5406
	鳥	7115
niào	尿	1185
	溺	3013
nie	捏	1895
	揑	1895
	(捏)	
niè	捻	1908
	苶	4879
	乜	38
	囁	776
	孽	1096
	蘖	1096
	(蘗)	
	躡	2638
	涅	2895
	湼	2895
	(涅)	
	蘗	4273
	糱	4273
	(蘖)	
	臬	4611
	臲	4765
	鎳	4768
	蘖	5161
	糱	5161

（第六欄）

音	字	字號
	蘖	6000
	蠥	6014
	齧	5169
	齧	5957
	鎘	6467
	鑷	6523
	闑	6568
	隉	6630
	顳	6836
	齧	7317
	嚙	7317
	(齧)	
	囓	7317
	(齧)	
nín	您	1596
níng	凝	345
	寧	765
	嚀	1143
	擰	2082
	檸	2620
	獰	3550
	甯	3550
nǐng	擰	2082
nìng	佞	139
	擰	2082
	濘	3119
	甯	3550
niú	妞	963
	牛	3310
	忸	1514
	扭	1802
	狃	4289
	紐	6336
	鈕	5357
	謬	5668
niù	拗	1849
	妞	963
nóng	儂	270
	濃	4031
	穠	4034
	膿	4735

注音	單字	字號		注音	單字	字號		注音	單字	字號
	農	6049		ō	喔	688		pān	攀	2093
	醲	6294		ó	哦	631			潘	3074
	齈	7302		o	呵	593			番	3575
nòng	弄	1411		ōu	敺	2144		pán	槃	2552
nòu	耨	4588			歐	2669			盤	3732
nú	奴	950			毆	2724			磐	3903
	孥	1086			漚	3046			胖	4648
	笯	4104			甌	3529			般	4802
	駑	6931			謳	5669			蟠	5320
nǔ	努	422			鷗	7188			繁	6759
	弩	1428		ǒu	偶	230		pàn	判	371
	砮	3857			嘔	731			叛	524
nù	怒	1543			耦	4587			拌	1841
nǚ	女	949			藕	5142			拚	1853
	釹	6322		òu	嘔	731			泮	1853
nǜ	衄	1514			慪	1683			胖	3564
	恧	1574			漚	3046			盼	3746
	朒	5357							襻	5472
nuǎn	暖	2270		**P**				pāng	乓	27
	煖	3220		注音	單字	字號			滂	3018
nüè	瘧	3648		pā	葩	5011			磅	3898
	虐	5181			趴	5845			雱	6714
	謔	5647			扒	1793		páng	傍	235
nuó	娜	1009			爬	3285			厖	507
	挪	1877			琶	3458			尨	1175
	捼	1881			杷	4581			龐	1403
	娜	1009		pā	帕	1312			彷	1459
nuò	喏	686			怕	1526			旁	2178
	懦	1734		pa	杷	2363			荺	2178
	搦	1990			琶	3458			(旁)	
	糯	4269		pāi	拍	1844			膀	4718
	稬	4269		pái	俳	183			螃	5291
	(糯)				徘	1477			逄	6083
	穤	4269			排	1921			雱	6714
	(糯)				牌	3303		pàng	胖	4648
	諾	5639			箄	4196		pāo	拋	1840
				pài	派	2874			抛	1840
O					湃	2971			(拋)	
注音	單字	字號			鎁	6452			泡	2841

注音	單字	字號		注音	單字	字號		注音	單字	字號
	脬	4681			砰	3852			鈹	6362
pāo	刨	373			硼	3872			陂	6596
	匏	454		péng	彭	1455			陴	6618
pāo	咆	602			朋	2316			鼙	7290
	庖	1365			棚	2486		pǐ	仳	98
	炮	3185			澎	3090			劈	411
	袍	5392			硼	3872			匹	470
	爮	7219			篷	4184			否	566
	麭	7221			膨	4731			庀	1359
páo	跑	5854			瓩	4832			疋	3587
pào	泡	2841			蓬	5063			痞	3630
	炮	3185			鵬	7155			癖	3672
	疱	3612		pěng	捧	1898			苤	4899
	皰	3710		pèng	椪	3879		pì	僻	268
	砲	3859			搕	3879			屁	1187
	礮	3920			(碰)				澼	3109
pēi	坯	1828		pī	丕	13			甓	3534
	胚	4651			劈	411			譬	5686
	醅	6270			匹	470			闢	6039
péi	培	839			批	1808			闢	6579
	裴	5426			披	1828		pian	偏	221
	賠	5791			砒	3848			扁	1783
	邳	6184			紕	4292			片	3301
	陪	6613			被	5397			篇	4162
pèi	佩	141			霹	6712			翩	4554
	妃	1310		pí	啤	658			萹	5025
	旆	2181			埤	842		pián	便	164
	沛	2807			枇	2362			楩	2537
	珮	3437			毗	2733			胼	4689
	轡	6034			琵	3457			腁	4689
	配	6249			疲	3599			(胼)	
	霈	6696			皮	3709			諞	5624
pēn	噴	761			紕	4292			蹁	5902
	歕	2675			罷	4505			駢	6944
	溢	2980			羆	4508			骿	6952
pén	盆	3717			脾	4699		pián	諞	5624
pěng	怦	1529			蚍	5203		piàn	徧	1483
	抨	1827			裨	5422			片	3301
	澎	3090			豼	5744			遍	6123
	烹	3202			郫	6207				

注音	單字	字號
piàn	骗	6958
piāo	漂	3041
piáo	嫖	1048
	瓢	3519
piǎo	摽	2018
	殍	2701
	漂	3041
	縹	3803
	縹	4424
	莩	4942
piào	剽	407
	漂	3041
	票	3948
	驃	6973
piē	撇	2034
	瞥	3815
piě	撇	2034
	苤	4899
pīn	姘	1018
	姘	1018
	(姘)	
	拼	1924
	拼	1924
	(拼)	
pín	嫔	1068
	蘋	5164
	嬪	5753
	频	6809
	颦	6833
pǐn	品	621
pìn	牝	3311
	聘	4601
pīng	乒	34
	娉	1003
píng	坪	828
	屏	1198
	平	1349
	憑	1710
	枰	2419
	洪	2919
	瓶	3526
	瓶	3526
	(瓶)	
	秤	3992
	絣	4479
	苹	4881
	萍	4982
	蘋	5164
	評	5555
	帡	6001
píng	馮	6923
pìng	聘	4601
pō	坡	820
	波	2839
	泼	3072
	陂	6596
	颇	6796
pó	婆	1015
	嬷	3708
	繁	4428
pǒ	叵	544
	颇	6796
pò	拍	1844
	朴	2337
	泊	2827
	珀	3854
	破	3854
	粕	4238
	迫	6068
	迫	6068
	(迫)	
	酸	6292
	魄	7051
pōu	抔	1817
	掊	1919
	裒	5411
pǒu	剖	394
	掊	1919
	瓿	3525
pū	仆	77
	扑	1792
	撲	2046
	痡	3629
	鋪	6410
pú	僕	256
	匐	453
	蟆	1340
	朴	2337
	樸	2497
	濮	3128
	璞	3498
	脯	4680
	莆	4945
	菩	4986
	葡	5006
	蒲	5037
	蒱	5038
	蹼	5937
	醭	6267
	醵	6290
	釙	6317
pǔ	圃	795
	埔	838
	普	2255
	浦	2885
	溥	3006
	譜	5681
	鐠	6499
pù	暴	2276
	曝	2296
	瀑	3138
	舗	4791
	鋪	6410
qī	妻	974
	崎	1237
	悽	1604
	慽	1691
	慼	1691
	(慼)	
	戚	1763
	攲	2114
	期	2325
	柒	2390
	栖	2423
	棲	2497
	欺	2659
	沏	2805
	淒	2923
	溪	3009
	漆	3042
	緝	4383
	萋	4980
	萁	5617
	郪	6211
qí	七	3
	七	317
	其	929
	奇	1214
	崎	1237
	旂	2179
	旗	2190
	期	2325
	枝	2376
	棋	2478
	棊	2478
	(棋)	
	歧	2685
	淇	2951
	琦	3449
	琪	3451
	畦	3570
	畿	3583
	碁	3884
	祁	3926
	祇	3930
	祈	3931
	祺	3951
	耆	4373
	蓍	4571
	臍	4749
	萁	4974
	齊	5135
	蘄	5154
	蠐	5337
	跂	5849
	錡	6425
	頎	6788
	騎	6951
	騏	6953
	鬐	7029
	鰭	7095
	麒	7226
	齊	7303
qǐ	乞	40
	启	660
	啟	660
	(啟)	
	屺	1211
	杞	2350
	棨	4023
	綺	4366
	綮	4374
	豈	5712
	起	5830
qì	企	103
	器	751
	契	936
	妻	974
	愒	1713
	愒	1713
	(愒)	
	棄	2476
	弃	2476
	(棄)	
	氣	2753
	汽	2794
	泣	2840
	砌	3846
	磧	3906
	緝	4383
	葺	5020
	訖	5526
	跂	5849
	迄	6051
qi	啐	659
qiā	掐	1918
	扴	491
	卡	491
qiǎ	卡	491
qià	恰	1564
	洽	2872
qiān	仟	89
	佥	252
	剑	475
	嵌	1257
	慊	1648
	悭	1680
	扦	1800
	搴	2002
	撁	2019
	牽	3324
	簽	4211
	篯	4226
	籤	4226
	(籤)	
	芊	5151
	褰	5411
	謙	6151
	遷	6151
	鉛	6583
	阡	6583
	韆	6763

Q

注音	單字	字號
q	啐	659
qī	七	3

qián	鷺 6963		鎗 6460		蟜 1272		篋 4164		綮 4374	裘 5414
	鷤 7162		鏘 6483		憔 1700		踥 5890		磬 4481	賕 5786
	乾 44		鏹 6484		樵 2588		鍥 6442		親 5490	逑 6091
	前 392	**qiáng**	嫱 1061		橋 2598	**qīn**	侵 162		警 5665	逑 6128
	拑 1843		強 1434		瞧 3813		嶔 1274	**qióng**	穹 4041	酋 6247
	搯 1936		強 1434		翹 4561		欽 2658		芎 4837	**qiú** 樛 4255
	潛 3073		(強)		蕎 5094		衾 5385	**qióng**	嬛 1062	**qú** 區 473
	箝 4148		彊 1434		譙 5678		親 5490		憌 1635	屈 1190
	虔 5182		(強)		顦 6829		駸 6949		煢 3233	嶇 1265
	鈐 6335		戕 1761	**qiǎo**	巧 1295	**qín**	勤 441		瓊 3512	敺 2144
	鉗 6350		檣 2616		悄 1581		懃 1730		穹 4041	曲 2302
	錢 6426		牆 3300		愀 1637		擒 2062		窮 4061	泃 2805
	黔 7252		墻 3300		雀 6657		檎 2613		筇 4110	瞿 3819
qiǎn	淺 2947		(墻)		鵲 7160		琴 3456		芎 4837	祛 3940
	繾 4460		蔷 5123	**qiào**	俏 170		禽 3977		藑 5151	胠 4653
	譴 5689	**qiǎng**	強 1434		峭 1229		秦 3989		蛩 5226	蛆 5217
	遣 6141		強 1434		撬 2045		芩 4846		跫 5868	蛐 5228
qiàn	倩 211		(強)		殼 2719		芹 4858		邛 6171	祛 5396
	塹 868		彊 1434		壳 2719		螓 5295	**qiū**	丘 15	詘 5559
	嗛 1662		(強)		(殼)		衾 5385		楸 2534	趨 5842
	槧 2569		搶 1989		殳 2719		覃 5475		秋 3983	驅 5965
	欠 2650		襁 5454		(殼)	**qǐn**	寢 1145		秌 3983	鰸 6975
	歉 2666		襁 5454		皽 4069	**qìn**	撳 2032		(秋)	**qú** 劬 424
	縴 4422		(褓)		翹 4561		沁 2790		蚯 5211	渠 2962
	芡 4842		鏹 6484		誚 5589	**qīng**	傾 249		邱 6182	璩 3507
	茜 4922	**qiàng**	嗆 705		譙 5678		卿 505		鞦 6751	癯 3685
	傔 5054		戧 1771		鞘 6748		氫 2757		鰌 6752	瞿 3819
qiāng	嗆 705		熗 3238	**qiē**	切 360		清 2946		鰍 7088	籧 4228
	戧 1771		蹌 5912	**qié**	伽 121		蜻 5261		鰍 7090	約 4305
	搶 1989		蹡 5921		茄 4888		輕 5992		鶖 7167	朐 4656
	槍 2557	**qiāo**	撬 2045	**qiě**	且 12		青 6722		龜 7328	蕖 5108
	瑲 3484		敲 2140	**qiè**	切 360		鯖 7080	**qiú**	仇 78	蘧 5167
	羌 4514		橇 2596		挈 936	**qíng**	情 1606		囚 782	蛐 5228
	羗 4514		硗 3912		妾 975		擎 2070		毬 2738	衢 5373
	(羌)		蹺 5935		怯 1534		晴 2259		求 2767	鴝 7136
	羟 4517		蹻 5936		愜 1643		黥 7260		泅 2828	鸜 7207
	腔 4697		鍫 6444		慊 1662	**qǐng**	請 5610		球 3440	麯 7237
	蜣 5255		鍬 6454		緳 1875		頃 6782		虬 5192	麴 7239
	蹌 5912	**qiáo**	僑 255		揭 2313	**qìng**	慶 1696		虯 5193	**qǔ** 取 522
	蹡 5921		700		竊 4072		磬 3905		蝤 5278	娶 1017

注音	單字	字號
	曲	2302
	鼩	7322
qù	去	514
	漆	3042
	覷	5494
	覻	5494
	(覷)	5494
	覰	5494
	(覷)	
	趣	5840
	闃	6558
quān	圈	799
	弮	1430
	悛	1588
	棬	2496
quán	全	308
	卷	499
	惓	1610
	拳	1873
	權	2647
	泉	2848
	痊	3322
	瘁	3618
	筌	4111
	荃	4924
	蜷	5260
	詮	5570
	踡	5887
	醛	6282
	銓	6373
	顴	6835
	鬈	7024
quǎn	犬	3338
	畎	3563
	綣	4356
quàn	券	376
	勸	446
quē	缺	4478
	闕	6572
qué	瘸	3663

注音	單字	字號
què	卻	503
	却	503
	(卻)	
	怯	1534
	恪	1560
	愨	1686
	榷	1972
	権	2561
	殼	2719
	売	2719
	(殼)	
	殼	2719
	(殼)	
	确	3870
	碏	3882
	確	3893
	礐	5510
	闋	6563
	闕	6572
	雀	6657
	鵲	7160
qūn	逡	6102
qún	羣	4526
	群	4526
	(羣)	
	裙	5408

R

注音	單字	字號
rán	然	3215
	燃	3251
	髯	7012
	髥	7017
rǎn	冉	322
	染	2396
	苒	4864
rāng	嚷	2097
ráng	瓤	3521
	禳	3973

注音	單字	字號
	穰	4037
	繢	4471
rǎng	嚷	773
	壤	894
	攘	2097
	讓	5700
ráo	蕘	5096
	饒	6905
	撓	2088
rào	繞	4442
	遶	6150
rě	喏	686
	惹	1645
rè	若	4873
	熱	3245
	燕	3279
rén	人	71
	仁	73
	任	101
	壬	897
	紝	4297
	紝	4297
	(紝)	
	忍	1500
	稔	4008
	荏	4918
	仞	88
rèn	任	101
	刃	358
	妊	960
	恁	1566
	紉	4286
	紝	4297
	紝	4297
	(紝)	
	衽	5384
	袵	5405
	訒	5530
	認	5583
	軔	5971

注音	單字	字號
	韌	6766
	飪	6855
	餁	6870
rēng	扔	1795
réng	仍	81
	礽	3924
rì	日	2198
róng	容	1129
	蠑	1277
	戎	1756
	榕	2538
	榮	2551
	毧	2736
	溶	3014
	熔	3240
	絨	4334
	狨	4525
	肜	4630
	茸	4913
	蓉	5048
	融	5294
	螎	5338
	鎔	6459
rǒng	冗	1101
	氄	2744
róu	揉	1948
	柔	2397
	蹂	5903
	糅	6011
ròu	肉	4619
rú	儒	278
	嚅	763
	如	956
	孺	1095
	濡	3125
	茹	4914
	襦	5465
	顬	6832
	鴽	7142

注音	單字	字號
rǔ	乳	43
	汝	2775
	辱	6048
rù	入	306
	洳	2867
	溽	3015
	縟	4413
	肉	4619
	茹	4914
	蓐	5050
	褥	5442
	辱	6048
	鈮	6390
	蝡	5341
ruǎn	蝡	5341
	軟	5974
	輭	6012
	阮	6588
ruí	甤	3544
	緌	5103
	蕤	5726
	蕊	5093
ruǐ	蕊	5093
ruì	柄	2374
	汭	2782
	瑞	3471
	睿	4852
	芮	4929
	蚋	5202
	蚋	5267
	銳	6391
	叡	219

注音	單字	字號
rún	犉	3329
rùn	潤	3080
	閏	6536
ruó	挼	1881
ruò	偌	219
	弱	1432
	爇	3279
	箬	4153
	篛	4178

注音	單字	字號
	若	4873
	翺	5050

S

注音	單字	字號
sā	仨	94
	撒	2029
sǎ	撒	2029
	洒	4413
	灑	4914
	靸	6741
sà	卅	478
	薩	5132
	趿	5850
	颯	6838
sāi	塞	4716
	腮	6813
	顋	7059
sài	塞	863
	賽	5804
sān	三	5
	參	515
	叁	238
	散	2137
	毿	4262
	繖	4440
sàn	散	2137
	喪	699
sāng	桑	2511
	嗓	699
	顙	6821
sàng	喪	699
são	搔	1978
	繰	4432
	繰	4504
	臊	4816
	騷	6966
sǎo	嫂	1038

shǐ 弛 1423	逝 6087	輸 6009	shuāi 摔 2010	sī 司 546	松 2366
矢 3829	適 6144	shú 叔 521	衰 5378	嘶 741	淞 2930
豕 5722	釋 6304	塾 869	shuǎi 甩 3546	廝 1394	鬆 7023
駛 6937	鈰 6360	孰 1090	shuài 帥 1319	思 1544	sóng 悚 1587
shì 世 14	飾 6863	淑 2922	率 3407	斯 2038	慫 1687
事 48	shí 匙 459	熟 3243	蟀 5311	斯 2170	竦 4081
仕 83	收 2115	菽 3997	shuān 拴 1862	澌 3096	聳 4607
使 147	shóu 熟 3243	菽 4973	栓 2536	私 3981	sòng 宋 1106
侍 152	shǒu 守 1104	shǔ 屬 1207	閂 6530	絲 4339	訟 5532
勢 439	手 1789	數 2143	shuàn 涮 2952	緦 4387	誦 5596
嗜 714	首 6915	暑 2268	shuāng 孀 1070	罳 4503	送 6077
嗜 755	shòu 受 523	署 4502	瀧 3152	螄 5292	頌 6787
士 896	售 647	薯 5133	雙 6673	鍶 6451	sōu 嗖 680
奭 947	壽 903	蓿 5165	霜 6704	鷥 7191	廋 1386
室 1119	授 1913	蜀 5235	shuǎng 爽 3295	sǐ 死 2692	搜 1987
市 1306	狩 3354	騎 7200	shuí 誰 5601	sì 伺 119	溲 3010
式 1416	獸 3400	黍 7247	shuǐ 水 2761	似 120	蒐 5033
弒 1417	瘦 3652	鼠 7291	帨 1321	俟 177	颼 6843
恃 1552	綬 4357	shù 倏 196	睡 3779	兕 302	餿 6894
拭 1857	shū 姝 988	墅 871	稅 4001	嗣 718	叟 525
是 2229	抒 1815	庶 1376	蛻 5233	四 783	sóu 嗽 725
柿 2387	摅 2020	恕 1568	說 5598	姒 982	擻 3798
柸 2422	攄 2091	戍 1755	shǔn 吮 569	寺 1158	藪 5150
氏 2746	書 2306	數 2143	楯 2536	巳 1301	sǒu 嗾 724
適 3105	梳 2473	曙 2291	盾 3752	廝 1381	漱 3057
示 3923	梳 2473	束 2351	shùn 瞬 3807	栖 2417	甦 3543
筮 4128	(梳)	樹 2595	舜 4794	汜 2774	sū 穌 4026
耆 4571	樗 2578	沭 2811	順 5894	祀 3833	蘇 5162
舐 4788	樞 2583	漱 3057	shuō 說 5598	祀 3927	酥 6256
螫 5301	殊 2700	澍 3091	shuò 妁 955	禩 3966	sú 俗 173
視 5485	父 2715	疏 3588	帥 1319	笥 4099	sù 嗉 859
試 5565	洙 2857	署 4502	搠 1999	耜 4585	塑 859
誓 5586	疏 3588	術 5363	數 2143	肆 4616	夙 910
諡 5618	疏 3588	桓 5407	朔 2319	賜 5789	宿 1131
諟 5646	(疏)	竪 5717	槊 2553	食 6849	愫 1687
謚 5662	疎 3588	述 6070	爍 3278	飼 6860	愬
識 5677	(疏)	shuā 刷 382	碩 3889	駟 6939	泝
豉 5713	紓 4291	shuǎ 耍 4577	丐 4836	sōng 崧 1246	涑 2898
貰 5760	舒 4789	shuà 刷 382	蟀 5311	嵩 1261	溯 3008
賦 5984	蔬 5077		鑠 6514	松 1516	

注音	單字	字號
sù	蔌	4185
	粟	4240
	素	4302
	縮	4419
	膆	4617
	愫	4722
	蓿	5067
	藗	5080
	訴	5542
	謖	5660
	速	6100
	遡	6139
	餗	6878
	麤	7195
suān	痠	3628
	酸	6265
suán	璿	4192
suàn	蒜	4135
	算	4144
	蒜	5035
suī	睢	3780
	綏	4349
	夊	4928
	雖	6672
suí	綏	4349
	遂	6118
	隋	6633
	雖	6672
	濉	6676
	隨	7004
suì	歲	2688
	燧	3265
	碎	3875
	祟	3945
	穗	4031
	術	5363
	誶	5602
	遂	6118
sūn	遜	6164
	隬	6645
	孫	1089
	猻	3382
	蓀	5044
	殙	6853
	殨	6853
sǔn	損	1975
	榫	2545
	筍	4112
	笋	4112
	(筍)	4112
sùn	簨	4204
	隼	6656
	潠	6132
suō	唆	641
	娑	1006
	挱	1878
	挲	2452
	梭	2471
	簑	4179
	縮	4419
	莎	4948
	莎	4949
	蓑	5051
	索	4436
suó	嗦	708
suǒ	所	1782
	瑣	3478
	索	4303
	鎖	6455
	鎍	6492

Ｔ

注音	單字	字號
tā	他	84
	塌	857
	她	953
	它	1099
	牠	3314
	祂	5448
	趿	5850
	鉈	6359
	鈒	6741
tǎ	塔	860
	嗒	710
tà	拓	1847
	搨	1992
	縫	2051
	榻	2549
	嗒	2806
	濕	3056
	獺	3401
	踏	5883
	踹	5911
	躂	6130
	遢	6136
	邋	6140
	錫	6469
	闒	6569
	鞳	6757
tái	胎	4647
	苔	4866
	台	540
	擡	2073
	抬	2073
	枱	2420
	檯	2625
	臺	4771
	苔	4866
	邰	6181
	颱	6839
	駘	6935
tài	太	918
	態	1668
	汰	2783
	泰	2849
	鈦	6330
tān	坍	816
	怹	1548
	探	1930
	攤	2103
	灘	3164
	癱	3687
	貪	5756
tán	彈	1437
	曇	2280
	檀	2607
	潭	3081
	澹	3110
	痰	3632
	罈	4484
	蠶	4488
	藫	5146
	罩	5475
	談	5608
	譚	5679
	郯	6209
tǎn	坦	822
	忐	1502
	毯	2739
	袒	5393
	驒	7266
tàn	探	1930
	歎	2668
	嘆	2668
	炭	3190
	碳	3890
tāng	湯	2989
	蹚	5918
	鏜	6485
táng	唐	644
	堂	845
	塘	862
	搪	1994
	棠	2488
	糖	4258
	膛	4729
	螗	5290
	螳	5306
	醣	6283
	鐺	6485
	鞺	6760
tǎng	倘	202
	帑	1311
	惝	1615
	淌	2920
	躺	5964
tàng	燙	3259
	趟	5841
tāo	叨	528
	慆	1664
	挑	1868
	掏	1917
	搯	1996
	滔	3024
	濤	3124
	絛	4342
	縧	4435
	謟	5661
	韜	6771
	饕	6910
táo	桃	2440
	檮	2622
	洮	2869
	淘	2925
	濤	3124
	藋	3274
	萄	4976
	逃	6079
	陶	6620
	鼗	7289
tǎo	討	5520
tào	套	939
tè	忒	1501
	牠	3314
	忒	1501
	忑	1503
	慝	1685
	特	3321
	鋱	6394
téng	滕	3028
	疼	4220
	籐	4414
	縢	4727
	藤	5147
	謄	5649
	騰	6965
tī	剔	393
	梯	2466
	踢	5888
tí	啼	673
	提	1951
	媞	3959
	稊	4002
	綈	4347
	緹	4396
	羬	4919
	蹄	5904
	鶗	5914
	醍	6277
	隄	6626
	堤	6626
	(隄)	6626
	題	6814
	騠	6961
	鵜	7151
	鶗	7172
tǐ	體	7005
tì	倜	184
	偶	205

注音	單字	字號
	剃	386
	嚏	767
	雁	1199
	雁	1199
	(雁)	
	弟	1424
	悌	1583
	惕	1609
	遞	2089
	替	2310
	殢	2708
	俶	2902
	褅	5124
	逖	6094
	錫	6393
	髰	7010
tiān	天	917
	添	2949
	韉	6227
tián	塡	864
	恬	1563
	湉	2997
	滇	3021
	甜	3538
	田	3551
	畋	3562
	鈿	6342
	闐	6567
tiǎn	忝	1522
	殄	2696
	湎	2929
	腆	4690
	舔	4790
	覥	5487
	靦	6732
	餂	6864
tiàn	瑱	3481
tiāo	佻	1553
	挑	1868
	祧	3947

注音	單字	字號
tiáo	佻	144
	條	2463
	笤	4106
	苕	4867
	蜩	5257
	調	5605
	迢	6062
	磬	7014
	髫	7312
tiǎo	挑	1868
	窕	4051
tiào	朓	2321
	眺	3770
	糶	4274
	脁	4665
	跳	5872
tiē	帖	1313
	怗	1540
	貼	5769
tiě	帖	1313
	鐵	6504
tiè	帖	1313
	餮	6889
tīng	聽	1405
	汀	2766
	聽	4612
tíng	亭	68
	停	225
	婷	1030
	庭	1374
	廷	1407
	渟	2957
	筳	4133
	蜓	5241
	霆	6695
tǐng	侹	1884
	挺	2457
	町	3557
	艇	4813
	鋌	6402

注音	單字	字號
tìng	聽	4612
	恫	1561
tōng	痌	3616
	通	6097
tóng	仝	95
	佟	140
	僮	264
	同	553
	峒	1226
	彤	1447
	曈	2284
	朣	2327
	桐	2445
	橦	2603
	潼	3084
	瞳	3809
	童	4079
	筒	4117
	箐	4127
	艟	4818
	茼	4904
	酮	6261
	銅	6371
tǒng	桶	2454
	筒	4117
	統	4337
tòng	慟	1677
	痛	3622
	衕	3374
tōu	偷	231
tóu	投	1819
	頭	6803
	骰	6993
	蚪	7245
tòu	透	6089
tou	頭	6803
tū	禿	3979
	禿	3979
	(禿)	

注音	單字	字號
tú	鵌	7148
	凸	352
	圖	803
	塗	861
	屠	1201
	徒	1475
	稌	4006
	突	4044
	荼	4931
	途	6093
	酴	6268
	醄	7150
tǔ	吐	558
	土	805
	釷	6321
tù	兔	301
	兔	301
	(兔)	
	吐	558
	菟	4955
tuān	湍	2979
tuán	團	804
	摶	2013
	糰	4270
	彖	1442
tuī	推	1933
tuí	頹	6642
	蕷	4717
	蛻	5233
	退	6076
tūn	吞	563
	暾	2288
	囤	788
tún	屯	1208
	臀	4739
	芚	4849
	豚	5723
	魨	6854

注音	單字	字號
tùn	褪	2763
	褪	5444
tuō	佗	133
	它	1099
	托	1799
	拖	1850
	扡	1850
	牠	3314
	脫	4679
	託	5527
	佗	133
tuó	柁	2418
	橐	2594
	沱	2812
	砣	4323
	舵	5529
	跎	5853
	陀	6595
	馱	6924
	駝	6938
	鴕	7128
	鼉	7282
tuǒ	妥	968
	庹	1379
	橢	2602
tuò	唾	651
	拓	1847
	柝	2405
	籜	4222
	蘀	5158
	魄	7051

W

注音	單字	字號
wā	呱	591
	哇	625
	媧	1035
	挖	1870
	窪	4058

注音	單字	字號
	蛙	5221
	鼃	7278
wá	娃	1001
wǎ	瓦	3522
wà	瓦	3522
	袜	5394
	襪	5466
wa	哇	625
wāi	歪	2687
	崴	908
wǎi	剜	397
	彎	1440
	灣	3167
	蜿	5263
	豌	5716
wán	丸	24
	刓	366
	完	1107
	烷	3200
	玩	3415
	紈	4833
	頑	6793
wǎn	婠	1014
	娩	1020
	宛	1115
	挽	1883
	晚	2244
	浣	2883
	涴	3118
	琬	3453
	皖	3725
	盌	3884
	碗	3388
	(碗)	
	綰	435
	莞	
	菀	

注音	單字	字號
	踠	5882
	輓	5990
wàn	悗	1608
	曼	2308
	玩	3415
	翫	4555
	腕	4698
	萬	4996
	万	4996
	(萬)	
	蔓	5069
wāng	汪	2784
wáng	亡	60
	忘	1505
	王	3409
wǎng	往	1462
	惘	1611
	枉	2368
	網	4361
	罔	4491
	蛧	5256
	輞	5998
	魍	7053
wàng	妄	958
	往	1462
	忘	1505
	旺	2208
	望	2323
	朢	2326
	王	3409
wēi	倭	214
	偎	220
	委	984
	威	1000
	崴	1252
	微	1490
	椳	2509
	溾	2995
	煨	3225
	萎	4983

注音	單字	字號
	葳	5016
	逶	6111
	隈	6629
wéi	危	497
	唯	648
	圍	800
	嵬	1262
	巍	1284
	帷	1326
	韡	1331
	微	1490
	惟	1618
	桅	2442
	濰	3130
	為	3192
	爲	3288
	維	4358
	薇	5116
	違	6131
	闈	6560
	韋	6765
	偉	218
	僞	259
wěi	唯	648
	委	984
	娓	1002
	尾	1184
	洧	2862
	煒	3219
	猥	3464
	瑋	3464
	痏	3619
	痿	3639
	緯	4393
	葦	5009
	薳	5141
	諉	5609
	隗	6639
	韙	6770
	顡	6800

注音	單字	字號
	歔	6992
	鮪	7069
wèi	位	126
	味	592
	喂	677
	尉	1163
	慰	1690
	未	2331
	渭	2966
	濊	3116
	為	3192
	爲	3288
	畏	3561
	胃	4644
	蔚	5072
	蝟	5274
	衛	5370
	衞	5371
	謂	5642
	遺	6154
	餧	6885
	餵	6893
	魏	7055
wēn	溫	2998
	溫	2998
	(溫)	
	瘟	3650
	轀	6019
wén	文	2150
	紋	4287
	聞	4603
	蚊	5200
	螡	5299
	雯	6684
wěn	刎	363
	吻	576
	穩	4035
	脗	4686

注音	單字	字號
wèn	問	656
	抆	1814
	搵	1998
	文	2150
	汶	2787
	璺	3511
	紊	4301
	聞	4603
wēng	嗡	720
	翁	4538
wěng	滃	3017
	蓊	5056
wèng	甕	3533
	罋	4485
wǒ	倭	214
	渦	2965
	窩	4057
	萵	4998
wǒ	我	1759
wò	偓	222
	喔	688
	握	1332
	幄	1959
	斡	7055
	沃	2793
	涴	2950
	渥	2964
	臥	4761
	齷	7321
wū	嗚	713
	圬	807
	屋	1192
	巫	1297
	惡	1624
	於	2175
	污	2779
	汙	2779
	(污)	
	汚	2779
	(污)	

注音	單字	字號
	烏	3193
	誣	5593
	鄔	6223
	吳	571
wú	吾	579
	巫	1297
	无	2195
	梧	2453
	毋	2725
	浯	2906
	無	3214
	蕪	5107
	蜈	5243
	誣	5593
	鼯	7294
wǔ	五	54
	仵	99
	伍	107
	侮	159
	午	477
	嫵	745
	斌	1029
	憮	1029
	(憮)	
	廡	1397
	忤	1509
	捂	1706
	搗	2000
	武	2686
	牾	3325
	舞	4796
	鵡	7154
wù	兀	438
	務	436
	勿	450
	塢	865
	婺	1031
	寤	1146
	悟	1590
	惡	1624

注音	單字	字號
	戊	1752
	晤	2250
	杌	2343
	物	3317
	誤	5594
	迕	6059
	鋈	6468
	阢	6584
	隖	6636
	霧	6707
	鶩	6957
	鶩	7170

X

注音	單字	字號
xī	僖	257
	兮	314
	吸	574
	唏	643
	嘻	941
	奚	944
	嬉	1055
	巇	1281
	希	1309
	徯	1489
	恓	1554
	悉	1807
	扱	1807
	攜	2100
	攜	2100
	(攜)	
	攜	2100
	(攜)	
	攜	2100
	(攜)	
	晞	2248
	晰	2257
	晳	2258
	曦	2297
	析	2371

	字	號		字	號		字	號		字	號		字	號		字	號
	栖	2423		習	4544		舄	4780		銛	6377	xiàn	顯	6831		飴	6867
	楼	2497		腊	4700		(舄)			鮮	7071		鮮	7071		饗	6908
	檞	2590		蓆	5047		郤	6204		卨	7114		峴	1231		驤	7072
	欷	2656		裼	5428		隙	6638	xián	咸	617		憲	1718	xiàng	像	254
	浙	2917		襲	5469		隙	6638		啣	662		獻	3402		向	559
	溪	3009		覡	5486		(隙)			嫌	1046		現	3439		嚮	769
	烯	3207		錫	6428		鵗	6895		嫻	1056		綫	4378		巷	1303
	熙	3234		隰	6649		閡	7040		嫺	1056		線	4381		曏	2290
	熹	3257	xǐ	喜	692	xiā	瞎	3797		(嫻)			縣	4402		橡	2601
	(熹)	3257		屣	1203		蝦	5280		弦	1425		羨	4527		相	3744
	犀	3327		徙	1479	xiá	俠	178		械	2510		腺	4713		象	5725
	犧	3336		憙	1714		匣	464		涎	2900		莧	4941		項	6783
	畦	3570		枲	2384		峽	1234		痃	3609		見	5481	xiāo	削	389
	皙	3705		洒	2855		挾	1889		癇	3669		豏	5718		哮	635
	硒	3862		洗	2856		暇	2265		絃	4318		艦	6032		嘵	777
	禧	3967		璽	3508		柙	2401		舷	4810		限	6621		宵	1126
	稀	4000		禧	3967		洽	3347		誠	5645		霰	6709		枵	2383
	羲	4530		蕙	5019		狎	3360		賢	5793		餡	6884		梟	2464
	膝	4726		蓰	5087		瑕	3467		賢	5817	xiāng	廂	1382		消	2897
	蜥	5248		蟢	5321		盫	4795		衘	6378		湘	2985		瀟	3149
	蟋	5315		諰	5644		磍	6017		閑	6537		相	3744		硝	3867
	禊	5352	xì	係	165		遐	6127		閒	6538		箱	4208		簫	4208
	西	5473		卌	480		鍜	6458		鹹	7211		緗	4384		綃	4346
	爔	5513		夕	907		霞	6705	xiǎn	尟	1173		纕	4471		蕭	5102
	溪	5708		戲	1774		黠	7258		尠	1173		舡	4800		蛸	5231
	谿	5709		戱	1774	xià	下	7		(尠)			薌	5119		蠨	5347
	豨	5729		(戲)			嚇	766		嶮	1276		襄	5455		逍	6086
	蹊	5910		歙	2672		夏	904		洒	2855		鄉	6221		銷	6392
	醯	6289		汐	2771		廈	1383		洗	2856		鑲	6522		霄	6976
	蠵	6309		潟	3075		暇	2265		燹	3395		香	6918		驍	6978
	鸂	7201		盻	3745		罅	4482		獮	3405		驤	6987		鴞	7130
	鸂	7296		矽	3842	xiān	仙	87		玁	3405	xiáng	庠	1370	xiǎo	斅	5190
xī	媳	1039		禊	3958		先	295		(玁)			祥	3946		爻	交
	席	1323		罗	4040		娺	1071		險	3683		翔	4545	xiǎo	小	1168
	息	1575		系	4275		掀	1911		蘚	5170		詳	5574		曉	2285
	惜	1617		細	4309		暹	2279		蜆	5238		降	6601		筱	4130
	昔	2220		繫	4546		祆	3928	xiǎng	跣	5866	xiǎng	享	66		篠	4180
	熸	2608		舾	4641		纖	4472		銑	6372		想	1644		謏	5653
	熄	3237		舄	4780		躚	5955		險	6647		響	6779	xiào	俲	

哮 635	血 5356	薪 5129	性 1531	袖 5390	(敘)
嘯 737	**xiè** 卸 500	訢 5535	悻 1600	銹 6412	敍 2125
孝 1083	寫 1151	辛 6037	杏 2344	鏽 6497	(敘)
效 2123	屑 1197	鋅 6401	興 4783	髹 7301	旭 2203
効 2123	屧 1400	鑫 6520	荇 4925	**xū** 吁 548	洫 2863
(效)	解 1725	歆 6776	莕 4932	嘘 735	淢 3058
斅 2149	械 2467	馨 6920	行 5360	壚 874	畜 3567
校 2429	楔 2517	**xín** 尋 1165	**xiōng** 兄 291	戌 1754	絮 4340
歊 2674	樹 2544	**xìn** 信 179	兇 294	戲 2673	緒 4379
笑 4093	泄 2824	凶 785	凶 351	盱 3741	續 4464
肖 4623	洩 2864	焮 3209	匈 452	繻 4457	芌 4845
酵 6263	澥 2991	芯 4851	恟 1556	胥 4643	蓄 5046
xiē 些 57	潟 3101	**xīng** 釁 6300	洶 2871	蓿 5067	賉 5781
歇 2663	瀉 3139	頯 6824	胸 4664	虚 5185	酗 6252
蝎 5273	灂 3153	惺 1636	訩 4664 (胸)	許 5531	**xuān** 喧 696
蠍 5335	爕 3272	星 2223	訩 5538	需 6692	宣 1118
xié 偕 223	絜 3393	猩 3374	**xióng** 熊 3235	須 6786	揎 1971
鯁 443	綫 4329	腥 4703	雄 6658	婿 6801	暄 2264
協 485	繳 4329 (綫)	興 4783	**xiòng** 敻 905	鬚 7032	瑄 3465
叶 545	薤 5126	馨 6920	**xiū** 休 111	**xú** 徐 1473	翾 4564
協 1565	蟹 5328	**xíng** 騂 6947	修 180	**xǔ** 昫 2233	萱 4997
挾 1889	蠏 5328 (蟹)	刑 364	庥 1371	栩 2425	諼 5620
擷 2085	褻 5456	型 832	羞 4524	滸 2993	誼 5625
攜 2100	褻 5456 (褻)	形 1448	脩 4678	煦 3231	軒 5970
擕 2100 (擷)	解 5505	形 1448 (形)	貅 5739	許 5541	**xuán** 懸 1742
攜 2100 (擕)	謝 5658	硎 3871	饈 6900	詡 5563	旋 2184
携 2100 (擕)	邂 5956	行 5360	髹 7020	諝 5634	漩 3052
斜 2159	邂 6160	邢 6177	鵂 7145	鄦 6236	玄 3406
絜 4341	**xīn** 心 1496	邢 6189	**xiǔ** 宿 1131	**xù** 敘 434	璇 3489
纈 4462	忻 1515	鋞 6419	朽 2338	勗 434 (勗)	璿 3510
脅 4670	新 2171	陘 6604	**xiù** 嗅 704	卹 501	縣 4402
夋 5383	昕 2221	**xǐng** 惺 1636	宿 1131	壻 899	還 6161
諧 5629	欣 2652	擤 2081	岫 1217	婿 899 (壻)	**xuǎn** 癬 3683
邪 6176	歆 2664	省 3753	溴 3011	序 1363	(癬) 6152
鞋 6746	炘 3180	醒 6276	秀 3980	恤 1559	**xuàn** 旋 2184
頡 6797	芯 4851	**xìng** 倖 201	繡 4444	愇 1665	渲 2968
xiě 寫 1151	莘 4937	姓 983	綉 4444 (繡)	絮 2125	漩 3052
		幸 1352	臭 4766	叙 2125	炫 3183
					眩 3760

注音	單字	字號
	絢	4332
	衒	5362
	鉉	6346
	鏇	6475
xuē	噱	756
	薛	5125
	靴	6738
xué	學	1094
	尋	1165
	覶	5879
	鱟	7199
xuě	雪	6683
	鱈	7099
xuè	削	389
	穴	4038
	血	5356
	雪	6683
xūn	勳	444
	塤	887
	曛	2294
	薰	3203
	薰	3236
	爋	3236
	(熏)	
	獯	3396
	窨	4059
	纁	4461
	薰	5018
	薰	5134
	醺	6296
xún	尋	1165
	峋	1225
	巡	1291
	廵	1291
	(巡)	
	徇	1467
	循	1486
	恂	1550
	撏	2033
	旬	2202

注音	單字	字號
	洵	2870
	潯	3083
	珣	3436
	紃	4280
	荀	4915
	蕁	5105
	詢	5564
	巡	6053
	廵	6053
	(巡)	
	郇	6191
	馴	6926
	鱘	7108
xùn	巽	1304
	徇	1467
	殉	2699
	汛	2777
	蕈	5106
	訊	5522
	訓	5524
	迅	6052
	遜	6132
	馴	6926

Y

注音	單字	字號
yā	ㄚ	20
	呀	581
	壓	886
	押	1832
	椏	2505
	鴉	7124
	鴨	7134
yá	牙	2372
	枒	2908
	牙	3308
	芽	4860
	蚜	5205
	衙	5367

注音	單字	字號
yǎ	亞	58
	啞	665
	雅	6660
	亞	58
	婭	1027
	掗	1957
	訝	5534
	軋	5967
	迓	6057
ya	呀	581
yái	崖	1240
yān	咽	618
	奄	928
	嫣	1052
	崦	1251
	懕	1735
	(懕)	1735
	殷	2717
	淹	2948
	烟	3199
	焉	3204
	煙	3222
	燕	3258
	胭	4659
	腌	4692
	臙	4753
	菸	4971
	蔫	5083
	鄢	6225
	醃	6269
	閹	6554
	閼	6555
yán	嚴	772
	妍	996
	姸	996
	(妍)	
	岩	1224
	巖	1287
	延	1406

注音	單字	字號
	罕	2025
	檐	2609
	沿	2823
	炎	3176
	焰	3216
	燄	3216
	(焰)	
	癌	3667
	研	3864
	硏	3864
	(研)	
	筵	4134
	簷	4209
	綖	4352
	蜒	5242
	言	6552
	閻	6552
	顏	6816
	鹽	7215
yǎn	偃	215
	儼	287
	兗	303
	奄	928
	巘	1288
	弇	1412
	掩	1935
	掩	1956
	沇	2795
	渷	2996
	演	3047
	琰	3460
	甗	3535
	眼	3769
	蝘	5272
	衍	5361
	郾	5618
	魘	7059
	黤	7264
	黶	7270
	黶	7295

注音	單字	字號
	饜	7297
yàn	厭	512
	咽	640
	唁	640
	堰	852
	宴	1125
	彥	1449
	晏	2239
	沿	2823
	灩	3170
	灩	3170
	(灩)	
	炎	3212
	焰	3216
	燄	3216
	(焰)	
	燕	3258
	硯	3868
	艷	4828
	諺	5638
	讌	5704
	艷	5720
	豔	5721
	贗	5808
	贗	5819
	贗	6301
	雁	6912
	駮	6956
	驗	6981
	鳽	7126
	鷃	7140
	鷰	7183
	鶠	7215
yāng	央	923
	泱	2697
	殃	2846
	秧	3991

注音	單字	字號
	軼	6742
	蕎	7133
yáng	伴	142
	徉	1469
	揚	1955
	暘	2238
	楊	2516
	洋	2854
	烊	3196
	煬	3642
	羊	4512
	陽	6623
	颺	6842
yǎng	仰	96
	氧	2755
	瀁	3144
	癢	3677
	痒	3677
	(癢)	
	軼	6742
	養	6868
	怏	1571
	樣	2585
	漾	3061
	煬	3227
	養	6868
yāo	吆	554
	夭	921
	妖	937
	幺	1354
	么	1354
	(幺)	
	徼	1494
	祅	2011
	腰	4201
	葽	5082
	要	5474
	邀	6158

yīn
鋇 6386
闇 6561
陰 6615
隉 6624
嫛 6624
(陰)
音 6774

yín
吟 564
垠 829
夤 914
寅 1134
淫 2940
狺 3361
鄞 6368
銀 6368
霪 6708
齗 7310
顤 7316

yǐn
尹 1181
引 1419
梁 2646
飲 2671
癮 3682
蚓 5204
隱 6648
靷 6740
飲 6857

yìn
印 496
廕 1391
憖 1716
窨 4059
胤 4655
蔭 5084
陰 6615
飲 6857

yīng
媖 1036
嬰 1066
應 1729
攖 2096
櫻 2642

瑛 3469
瓔 3515
纓 4470
蓉 4480
罌 4486
膺 4738
英 4877
鸚 7175
鷹 7203
鸚 7205

yíng
堡 856
穎 1064
楹 2535
榮 3026
濴 3142
濙 3150
瀅 3155
灷 3241
營 3264
臺 3476
盈 3718
縈 4401
螢 5298
蠅 5333
贏 5814
迎 6055
影 1457

yǐng
景 2256
穎 3068
瘿 3681
穎 4027
穎 4027
(穎)
郢 6202
膡 1040

yìng
應 1729
映 2224
硬 3866
迎 6055
哂 663

yōng
傭 242
墉 872
鄄 884
庸 1378
雁 1404
慵 1681
擁 2056
邅 3160
邅 3684
瞳 4741
邕 6172
郵 6226
雍 6663
雕 6678
費 6909

yóng
傭 242
嗈 676
墉 872
庸 1378
慵 1681
顒 6817
鯖 7103

yǒng
俑 172
勇 430
埋 884
憑 1667
擁 2056
永 2762
泳 2847
涌 2907
湧 2983
甬 3548
臃 4741
蛹 5232
詠 5550
咏 5550
(詠)
踊 5880

yòng
用 3545

yōu
優 284

幽 1357
悠 1592
憂 1694
攸 2116
懲 3065
煲 3266
蕘 4589
麀 7217

yóu
尤 1174
斿 2177
楢 2523
油 2815
游 2974
猶 3373
猷 3377
由 3552
疣 3598
蕕 4430
蕕 5095
蚰 5212
蝣 5277
輶 6008
道 6105
遊 6121
郵 6213
鈾 6357
魷 7062

yǒu
卣 492
友 519
有 2315
柚 2567
掫 3246
樬 3246
(櫾)
牖 3306
羑 4516
莠 4939
酉 6245
銪 6384
黝 7257

yòu
佑 130
侑 154
又 516
右 543
囿 794
宥 1120
幼 1356
有 2315
柚 2402
祐 3933
莠 4939
誘 5588
釉 6303
幽 7292

yū
淤 2932
瘀 3638
紆 4281
迂 6050
餘 6879
魚 7060

yú
予 47
于 51
余 135
俞 310
妤 967
娛 1008
嵎 1259
愉 1640
愚 1651
揄 1945
於 2175
旟 2194
楡 2521
楱 2524
歟 2678
(歟)
漁 3038
瑜 3470
璵 3509
畬 3576
盂 3715
禹 3976

窬 4060
竽 4087
腴 4709
臾 4775
舁 4777
與 4782
萸 5024
虞 5186
褕 5440
覦 5488
諛 5622
踰 5897
輿 6015
轝 6115
隃 6625
隅 6627
雩 6682
餘 6879
魚 7060

yǔ
予 47
僂 245
圉 796
嶼 1279
庾 1380
敔 2132
瑀 3975
窳 4063
羽 4536
與 4782
語 5591
鋙 6408
雨 6681
齬 7320

yù
喅 698
域 840
飫 1049
寓 1139

(第一欄)

字	字號
尉	1163
峪	1235
或	1450
御	1482
愈	1649
慾	1692
拗	1849
昱	2230
棫	2495
欲	2654
毓	2730
汩	2781
浴	3221
煜	3221
熨	3247
燠	3266
獄	3384
玉	3408
瘉	3647
癒	3675
鬻	3828
禦	3965
禹	3976
籲	4225
龥	4232
聿	4614
育	4639
與	4782
芋	4835
蔚	5072
萮	5113
域	5258
裕	5591
諭	5619
譽	5690
谷	5706
豫	5730
遇	6120
遹	6153

(第二欄)

字	字號
郁	6188
鈺	6356
闋	6557
陳	6646
雨	6681
雩	6682
預	6790
馭	6858
馯	6922
鬱	7045
鷖	7047
鵒	7056
龥	7135
鴥	7135
鴮	7146
鵒	7197
黦	7263
顳	7331

yuān

字	字號
冤	330
冤	330
(冤)	
嫄	1050
淵	2942
鳶	7121
鴛	7129
鶵	7161

yuán

字	字號
元	290
原	509
員	629
園	801
圓	802
援	1965
沅	2792
湲	2992
源	2999
爰	3287
猿	3379
猨	3379
(猿)	
緣	4388
芫	4847
苑	4863
蝯	5289
蟓	5293
袁	5387
轅	6018
黿	7276
遠	6138

yuàn

字	字號
媛	1034
怨	1547
愿	1672
掾	1947
瑗	3474
苑	4863
遠	6138
院	6609
願	6820

yuē

字	字號
曰	2301
約	4282
刖	367

yuè

字	字號
岳	1280
嶽	1280
悅	1582
戉	1753
曜	2293
月	2314
樂	2571
樾	2592
瀹	3157
籥	3974
爚	4227
粵	4243
耀	4567
蒻	5148
說	5598
越	5835
躍	5950
軏	5972
鉞	6352
鑰	6521
閼	6551
龠	7329

yūn

字	字號
暈	2267
氳	2760
贇	5812

yún

字	字號
云	52
勻	448
昀	2222
筠	4124
紜	4296
耘	4583
芸	4857
薯	5110
雲	6687

yǔn

字	字號
允	289
殞	2705
狁	3345
磒	3902
隕	6635

yùn

字	字號
孕	1077
惲	1629
慍	1657
暈	2267
熨	3247
縕	4410
蘊	5163
藴	5163
(蘊)	
運	6122
鄆	6217
醖	6280
韗	6772
韵	6775
韻	6778

Z

注音	單字	字號
zā	匝	460
	咂	595
	紮	4304
	紥	4304
	(紮)	
	臜	4757
zá	拶	1863
	桚	2448
	砸	6675
	雜	6675
zāi	哉	627
	栽	2438
	災	3175
	菑	3175
	(災)	
	灾	3175
	(災)	
	菑	4961
	甾	4961
	(菑)	
zǎi	仔	82
	宰	1123
	崽	1254
	載	5987
zài	再	324
	在	806
	載	5987
zān	簪	4205
zán	咱	615
zǎn	拶	1863
	揝	1969
	攢	2102
	昝	2235
	桚	2448
	趲	5843
zàn	暫	2275
	讚	5703
	贊	5811
	酂	6244
	瓚	6491
	饡	3299
	臢	4757

zāng

字	字號
臧	4762
賍	5782
臟	5815
髒	7003
駔	6933

zàng

字	字號
奘	938
臟	4755
葬	5013
藏	5139

zāo

字	字號
糟	4263
蹧	5924
遭	6142

záo

字	字號
鑿	6527

zǎo

字	字號
早	2201
棗	2481
澡	3102
繰	4454
藻	5156
蚤	5207

zào

字	字號
唣	753
慅	1676
燥	3269
皁	3694
皂	3695
竈	4071
灶	4071
(竈)	
籠	4191
譟	5684
躁	5942
造	6101

zé

字	字號
則	385
咋	603
嘖	732
幘	1337
擇	2060
澤	3106
窄	4048
笮	4107
簀	4189

	字	號		字	號		字	號		字	號		字	號		字	號
	酢	4807		吒	608		崭	1267		長	6528		讁	5667	zhěn	枕	2373
	責	5758		搾	1979		搌	2001		障	6641		讆	5694		畛	3565
	賊	5780		柵	2416		斬	2168	zhāo	招	1855		輒	5989		疹	3603
	讀	5810		榨	2546		琖	3444		昭	2228		轍	6005		稹	4024
zé	迮	6071		炸	3189		盏	3728		朝	2324		轍	6023		紾	4314
zě	怎	1542		痄	3614		輾	6014		着	3776	zhě	者	4572		縝	4412
zè	仄	76		笮	4107	zhàn	佔	131		著	5003		赭	5825		胗	5544
	昃	2211		蚱	5213		占	490		釗	6315		鍺	6450		畛	5975
zéi	賊	5780		蜡	5252		戰	1773	zháo	着	3776	zhè	宅	1102		鬒	7030
zēn	簪	4205		詐	5552		暫	2275		著	5003		柘	2400	zhèn	振	1880
zěn	怎	1542	zhāi	摘	2004		棧	2484	zhǎo	找	1809		浙	2878		偡	1952
zèn	譖	5676		齊	7303		湛	2986		沼	2817		蔗	5071		朕	2320
zēng	增	877		齋	7304		站	—		爪	3284		這	6096		枕	2373
	憎	1699		斋	7304		綻	4367	zhào	兆	293		鷓	7186		瑱	3481
	曾	2309		(齋)			蘸	5174		召	536	zhe	着	3776		賑	5783
	繒	3839	zhái	宅	1102		覽	5926		旐	2188		著	5003		酖	6251
	繪	4436		擇	2060		顫	6830	zhào	翟	2287	zhěi	這	6096		鎭	6465
zèng	甑	3532		翟	4547	zhāng	張	1433		棹	2502	zhēn	偵	229		陣	6610
	繒	4436		窄	4048		彰	1456		權	2627		振	1880		震	6617
	贈	5809	zhài	責	246		樟	3059		炤	3191		斟	2161		鴆	6693
zhā	扎	1791		寨	1149		獐	3387		照	3232		楨	2508		鴆	7122
	挓	1872		瘵	3661		璋	3493		笊	4090		榛	2528	zhēng	丁	2
	摣	1967		砦	3858		章	4078		罩	4498		榛	2540		崢	1244
	查	2411	zhān	占	490		蟑	5316		肇	4618		珍	3425		征	1463
	楂	2514		痟	2180		鄣	6229		詔	5554		甄	3527		徵	1491
	渣	2961		甎	2745		麞	7231		趙	5838		眞	3762		佂	1537
zhǎ	劄	408		氈	2745	zhǎng	掌	1940	zhē	折	1822		真	3762		挣	1925
	扎	1791		(氊)			漲	3060		螫	5301		(眞)			楨	2528
	札	2334		毡	2745		長	6528		遮	6145		砧	—		正	2682
	炸	3189		(氈)		zhàng	丈	4	zhé	哲	636		禎	3960		烝	3195
	箚	4150		沾	2820		仗	85		悊	1682		禛	3964		爭	3286
	楂	4304		瞻	3816		嶂	1266		讋	1745		箴	4158		猙	3679
	樝	4304		觛	5484		帳	1324		摺	1822		臻	4772		睜	3781
	(柤)			詹	5575		幛	1338		摘	2004		蓁	5045		箏	4139
	鍘	6440		遭	6162		杖	2348		摺	2016		診	5544		蒸	5039
	閘	6540		霑	6701		漲	3060		磔	3899		貞	5749		諍	5611
zhǎ	眨	3761		鱣	6911		瘴	3659		翟	4547		針	6316		貞	5749
zhà	乍	31		鑸	7110		脹	4688		蜇	5239		鍼	6447		諍	5611
	吒	555		鸇	7202		賬	5798		蟄	5312		鍼	7111		貞	5749
	咋	603	zhǎn	展	1195					褶	5451					鉦	6355

zhěng 錚 6423	殖 2702	摯 2024	騺 7189	晝 2247	責 3228
拯 1859	直 3743	智 2262	隲 21	縐 3528	(煮)
整 2145	縶 4426	桎 2444	zhōng 中 21	皺 3713	曙 3825
zhèng 幀 1330	職 4609	治 2819	忪 1516	籀 4216	貯 5759
掙 1925	蟄 5312	滯 3031	忠 1517	籒 4216	麈 7220
政 2121	質 5797	炙 3181	盅 3716	(籒)	zhù 佇 124
正 2682	跖 5855	時 3571	終 4319	紂 4279	住 128
症 3608	蹠 5920	寘 3590	螽 5309	綢 4405	助 421
証 5561	躑 5922	痔 3621	衷 5382	胄 4645	宁 1100
證 5674	躅 5952	痣 3627	鍾 6448	zhū 侏 153	杼 2364
鄭 6231	zhǐ 只 534	知 3831	鐘 6493	朱 2336	柱 2409
zhī 之 30	咫 612	zhòng 冢 332	zhōng 冢 332	株 2427	柷 2414
厄 494	址 813	塚 858	塚 858	櫫 2639	注 2845
指 1867	徵 1491	種 4014	種 4014	洙 2857	炷 3188
揸 1985	恉 1578	腫 4705	腫 4705	瀦 3154	祝 3942
支 2113	指 1867	踵 5899	踵 5899	珠 3432	筋 4075
枝 2376	旨 2200	zhòng 中 21	zhòng 中 21	硃 3860	箸 4129
梔 2461	枳 2381	仲 97	仲 97	茱 4908	筯 4157
栀 2461	止 2681	眾 3772	眾 3772	蛛 5223	粥 4242
氏 2746	沚 2804	種 4014	種 4014	誅 5578	紵 4316
汁 2765	砥 3849	衆 5358	衆 5358	諸 5637	翥 4552
知 3831	祇 3930	重 6306	重 6306	豬 5732	苧 4875
祇 3930	祉 3932	zhōu 周 588	zhōu 周 588	邾 6195	著 5003
祗 3938	紙 4295	喌 653	喌 653	銖 6374	蛀 5215
織 4437	耆 4571	州 1290	州 1290	zhú 尢 2335	註 5545
肢 4632	芷 4856	洲 2868	洲 2868	燭 3271	鑄 6511
胑 4658	趾 5847	盩 3736	盩 3736	竹 4085	翬 6927
脂 4668	軹 5979	粥 4242	粥 4242	竺 4115	駐 6930
芝 4840	酯 6259	舟 4797	舟 4797	筑 4115	zhuā 抓 1816
蜘 5249	阯 6591	賙 5788	賙 5788	築 4166	撾 2053
隻 6655	黹 7272	輈 5986	輈 5986	舳 4806	髽 7022
緇 7279	zhǐ 制 381	週 6108	週 6108	蠋 5943	zhuǎ 爪 3284
zhí 值 208	寘 1140	鵃 7141	鵃 7141	軸 5977	zhuāi 拽 1869
執 843	峙 1227	zhóu 妯 972	zhóu 妯 972	逐 6190	zhuài 跩 5874
姪 994	幟 1316	軸 5977	軸 5977	zhǔ 主 26	拽 1869
指 1867	幟 1339	zhòu 帚 1317	zhòu 帚 1317	囑 781	zhuān 專 1161
摭 2011	廌 1444	肘 4624	肘 4624	屬 1207	甎 3530
擲 2084	志 1504	zhòu 胄 326	zhòu 胄 326	拄 1833	塼 3530
植 2500	忮 1511	咒 589	咒 589	渚 2956	(甎)
	懥 1733	宙 1113	宙 1113	煮 3228	磚 3907

附錄㈠國語注音符號與各式羅馬拼音對照表

一、聲母

國語注音符號 Mandarin Phonetic Symbols	威妥瑪式 Wade System	國語羅馬字 Gwoyeu Romatzyh	聯合國華語注音符號 U.N. Mandarin Phonetic Symbols	國語注音符號 Mandarin Phonetic Symbols	威妥瑪式 Wade System	國語羅馬字 Gwoyeu Romatzyh	聯合國華語注音符號 U.N. Mandarin Phonetic Symbols
ㄅ	p	b	b	ㄏ	h	h	h
ㄆ	p'	p	p	ㄐ	ch(i)	j(i)	j
ㄇ	m	m	m	ㄑ	ch'(i)	ch(i)	q
ㄈ	f	f	f	(广)		(gn)	
(万)		(v)		ㄒ	hs	sh(i)	x
ㄉ	t	d	d	ㄓ	ch	j	zh
ㄊ	t'	t	t	ㄔ	ch'	ch	ch
ㄋ	n	n	n	ㄕ	sh	sh	sh
ㄌ	l	l	l	ㄖ	j	r	r
ㄍ	k	g	g	ㄗ	tz, ts-	tz	z
ㄎ	k'	k	k	ㄘ	tz', ts'-	ts	c
(兀)		(ng)		ㄙ	sz, ss, s-	s	s

二、韻母

國語注音符號 Mandarin Phonetic Symbols	威妥瑪式 Wade System	國語羅馬字 Gwoyeu Romatzyh	聯合國華語注音符號 U.N. Mandarin Phonetic Symbols	國語注音符號 Mandarin Phonetic Symbols	威妥瑪式 Wade System	國語羅馬字 Gwoyeu Romatzyh	聯合國華語注音符號 U.N. Mandarin Phonetic Symbols
(帀)	-u, -ih	y		ㄧㄡ	yu, -iu	iou	iou
ㄚ	a	a	a	ㄧㄢ	yen, -ian	ian	ian
ㄛ	o	o	o	ㄧㄣ	yin, -in	in	in
ㄜ	o(ê)	e	e	ㄧㄤ	yang, -iang	iang	iang
ㄝ	ê	ê	ê	ㄧㄥ	ying, -ing	ing	ing
ㄞ	ai	ai	ai				
ㄟ	ei	ei	ei	ㄨ	wu, -u	u	u
ㄠ	ao	au	ao	ㄨㄚ	wa, -ua	ua	ua
ㄡ	ou	ou	ou	ㄨㄛ	wo, -uo	uo	uo
ㄢ	an	an	an	ㄨㄞ	wai, -uai	uai	uai
ㄣ	ên	en	en	ㄨㄟ	wei, -ui(-uei)	uei	uei
ㄤ	ang	ang	ang	ㄨㄢ	wan, -uan	uan	uan
ㄥ	êng	eng	eng	ㄨㄣ	wên, -un	uen	uen
ㄦ	êrh	el	er	ㄨㄤ	wang, -uang	uang	uang
				ㄨㄥ	wêng, -ung	ueng, -ong	ueng, -ong
ㄧ	i	i	i				
ㄧㄚ	ya, -ia	ia	ia	ㄩ	yü, -ü	iu	ü
ㄧㄛ	io	io		ㄩㄝ	yüeh, -üeh	iue	üe
ㄧㄝ	yeh, -ieh	ie	ie	ㄩㄢ	yüan, -üan	iuan	üan
ㄧㄞ	yai	iai	iai	ㄩㄣ	yün, -ün	iun	ün
ㄧㄠ	yao, -iao	iao	iao	ㄩㄥ	yün, -iung	iong	iong

三、聲調

式名　調類	國語注音符號 Mandarin Phonetic Symbols	威妥瑪式 Wade System	聯合國華語注音符號 U. N. Mandarin Phonetic Symbols	註:國語羅馬字條例複雜,於附錄㈢說明。
陰平	無號(可用"-"代表)	1	ˉ	
陽平	ˊ	2	ˊ	
上聲	ˇ	3	ˇ	
去聲	ˋ	4	ˋ	
輕聲	•	5	無號	

附錄(二)國語羅馬字聲調

(1)陰平

	l	ㄧ i	ㄨ u	ㄩ iu
(ω)	-y			
ㄚ	a	ㄧㄚ ia	ㄨㄚ ua	
ㄛ	o	ㄧㄛ io	ㄨㄛ uo	
ㄜ	e			
ㄝ	ê	ㄧㄝ iê		ㄩㄝ iue
ㄞ	ai	ㄧㄞ iai	ㄨㄞ uai	
ㄟ	ei		ㄨㄟ uei	
ㄠ	au	ㄧㄠ iau		
ㄡ	ou	ㄧㄡ iou		
ㄢ	an	ㄧㄢ ian	ㄨㄢ uan	ㄩㄢ iuan
ㄣ	en	ㄧㄣ in	ㄨㄣ uen	ㄩㄣ iun
ㄤ	ang	ㄧㄤ iang	ㄨㄤ uang	
ㄥ	eng	ㄧㄥ ing	ㄨㄥ ueng	
-ㄨㄥ	-ong	ㄩㄥ iong		
ㄦ(-ㄦ)	el(-l)			

註：聲母如果是 m, n, l, r 等濁音就在聲母後加h，如mhau(貓)、nhiou(妞)、lhiou(溜)、rheng(扔)。

(2)陽平

	l	ㄧ yi	ㄨ wu	ㄩ yu
(ω)	-yr			
ㄚ	ar	ㄧㄚ ya	ㄨㄚ wa	
ㄛ	or		ㄨㄛ wo	
ㄜ	er			
ㄝ	êr	ㄧㄝ ye		ㄩㄝ yue
ㄞ	air	ㄧㄞ yai	ㄨㄞ wai	
ㄟ	eir		ㄨㄟ wei	
ㄠ	aur	ㄧㄠ yau		
ㄡ	our	ㄧㄡ you		
ㄢ	arn	ㄧㄢ yan	ㄨㄢ wan	ㄩㄢ yuan
ㄣ	ern	ㄧㄣ yn	ㄨㄣ wen	ㄩㄣ yun
ㄤ	arng	ㄧㄤ yang	ㄨㄤ wang	
ㄥ	erng	ㄧㄥ yng		
-ㄨㄥ	-orng	ㄩㄥ yong		
ㄦ(-ㄦ)	erl(-r)			

註：聲母如果是 m, n, l, r 就用基本形式，如mau(毛)、niou(牛)、liou(流)、ren(人)。

(3)上聲

	l	ㄧ yii,-ii	ㄨ wuu,-uu	ㄩ yeu,-eu
(ω)	-yy			
ㄚ	aa	ㄧㄚ yea,-ea	ㄨㄚ woa,-oa	
ㄛ	oo		ㄨㄛ woo,-uoo	
ㄜ	ee			
ㄝ	êê	ㄧㄝ yee,-iee		ㄩㄝ eue
ㄞ	ae		ㄨㄞ woai,-oai	
ㄟ	eei		ㄨㄟ woei,-oei	
ㄠ	ao	ㄧㄠ yeau,-eau		
ㄡ	oou	ㄧㄡ yeou,-eou		
ㄢ	aan	ㄧㄢ yean,-ean	ㄨㄢ woan,-oan	ㄩㄢ yeuan,-euan
ㄣ	een	ㄧㄣ yiin,-iin	ㄨㄣ woen,-oen	ㄩㄣ yeun,-eun
ㄤ	aang	ㄧㄤ yeang,-eang	ㄨㄤ woang,-oang	
ㄥ	eeng	ㄧㄥ yiing,-iing	ㄨㄥ woeng	
-ㄨㄥ	-oong	ㄩㄥ yeong,-eong		
ㄦ(-ㄦ)	eel(-l)			

(4)去聲

	l	ㄧ yih,-ih	ㄨ wuh,-uh	ㄩ yuh,-iuh
(ω)	-yh			
ㄚ	ah	ㄧㄚ yah,-iah	ㄨㄚ wah,-uah	
ㄛ	oh		ㄨㄛ woh,-woh	
ㄜ	eh			
ㄝ	êh	ㄧㄝ yeh,-ieh		ㄩㄝ yueh,-iueh
ㄞ	ay		ㄨㄞ way,-uay	
ㄟ	ey		ㄨㄟ wey,-uey	
ㄠ	aw	ㄧㄠ yaw,-iaw		
ㄡ	ow	ㄧㄡ yow,-iow		
ㄢ	ann	ㄧㄢ yann,-iann	ㄨㄢ wann,-uann	ㄩㄢ yuann,-iuann
ㄣ	enn	ㄧㄣ yinn,-irinn	ㄨㄣ wenn,-uenn	ㄩㄣ yunn,-iunn
ㄤ	anq	ㄧㄤ yanq,-ianq	ㄨㄤ wanq,-uanq	
ㄥ	enq	ㄧㄥ yinq,-inq	ㄨㄥ wenq	
-ㄨㄥ	-onq	ㄩㄥ yonq,-ionq		
ㄦ(-ㄦ)	ell(-l)			

(5)輕聲

國語羅馬字的輕聲，以用基本形式為原則。如果是會話教科書，要確切標出輕聲，可以在字前點上"."。

附錄㈢國語注音符號第一式與第二式對照表

國語注音符號第一式				國語注音符號第二式			
一、聲母							
唇　　音	ㄅ	ㄆ	ㄇ	ㄈ	b	p	m	f
舌尖音	ㄉ	ㄊ	ㄋ	ㄌ	d	t	n	l
舌根音	ㄍ	ㄎ	ㄏ		g	k	h	
舌面音	ㄐ	ㄑ	ㄒ		j(i)	ch(i)	sh(i)	
翹舌音	ㄓ	ㄔ	ㄕ	ㄖ	j	ch	sh	r
舌齒音	ㄗ	ㄘ	ㄙ		tz	ts	s	
二、韻母							
單　韻 ①	(帀)				r, z			
單　韻 ②	ㄧ	ㄨ	ㄩ		i, yi	u, wu	iu, yu	
單　韻 ③	ㄚ	ㄛ	ㄜ	ㄝ	a	o	e	ê
複　韻	ㄞ	ㄟ	ㄠ	ㄡ	ai	ei	au	ou
聲隨韻	ㄢ	ㄣ	ㄤ	ㄥ	an	en	ang	eng
捲舌韻	ㄦ				er			
三、結合韻母(前有聲母時用)							
齊齒呼	ㄧㄚ	ㄧㄛ	ㄧㄝ		ia	io	ie	
	ㄧㄞ	ㄧㄠ	ㄧㄡ		iai	iau	iou	
	ㄧㄢ	ㄧㄣ	ㄧㄤ	ㄧㄥ	ian	in	iang	ing
合口呼	ㄨㄚ	ㄨㄛ	ㄨㄞ	ㄨㄟ	ua	uo	uai	uei
	ㄨㄢ	ㄨㄣ	ㄨㄤ	ㄨㄥ	uan	uen	uang	ung
撮口呼	ㄩㄝ	ㄩㄢ	ㄩㄣ	ㄩㄥ	iue	iuan	iun	iung
四、聲調							
陰平聲	(不加)				－			
陽平聲	ˊ				ˊ			
上　　聲	ˇ				ˇ			
去　　聲	ˋ				ˋ			
輕　　聲	˙				(不加)			

附錄㈣國音兒化韻表

中華新韻六兒附韻目	韻內所含			等呼	併入之韻	變入之韻	略　　　　　例
一颯兒 (ㄚㄦ)	ㄚㄦ						法兒(ㄈㄚㄦ)　難兒(ㄋㄚㄦ)　塔兒(ㄊㄚㄦ)　那兒(ㄋㄚㄦ)
					ㄞㄦ ㄢㄦ		呆兒(ㄉㄞㄦ)　孩兒(ㄏㄞㄦ)　矮兒(ㄞㄦ)　菜兒(ㄘㄞㄦ) 竿兒(ㄍㄢㄦ)　盤兒(ㄆㄢㄦ)　桿兒(ㄍㄢㄦ)　罈兒(ㄊㄢㄦ)
	ㄧㄚㄦ						蝦兒(ㄒㄧㄚㄦ)　芽兒(ㄧㄚㄦ)　價兒(ㄐㄧㄚㄦ)　價兒(ㄐㄧㄚㄦ)
					ㄧㄞㄦ ㄧㄢㄦ		煙兒(ㄧㄢㄦ)　段兒(ㄍㄨㄢㄦ)　簾兒(ㄌㄧㄢㄦ)　脚兒(ㄐㄧㄠㄦ)
			ㄨㄚㄦ				窪兒(ㄨㄚㄦ)　滑兒(ㄏㄨㄚㄦ)　爪兒(ㄓㄨㄚㄦ)　話兒(ㄏㄨㄚㄦ)
					ㄨㄞㄦ ㄨㄢㄦ		快兒(ㄎㄨㄞㄦ)　懷兒(ㄏㄨㄞㄦ)　枴兒(ㄍㄨㄞㄦ)　塊兒(ㄎㄨㄞㄦ) 灣兒(ㄨㄢㄦ)　丸兒(ㄨㄢㄦ)　碗兒(ㄨㄢㄦ)　段兒(ㄉㄨㄢㄦ)
				ㄩㄚㄦ		ㄩㄢㄦ	圈兒(ㄑㄩㄢㄦ)　園兒(ㄩㄢㄦ)　蓮兒(ㄌㄩㄢㄦ)　院兒(ㄩㄢㄦ)
二颯兒 (ㄛㄦ)	ㄛㄦ						坡兒(ㄆㄛㄦ)　靜兒(ㄛㄦ)　抹兒(ㄇㄛㄦ)　破兒(ㄆㄛㄦ)
			ㄨㄛㄦ				窩兒(ㄨㄛㄦ)　國兒(ㄍㄨㄛㄦ)　夥兒(ㄏㄨㄛㄦ)　座兒(ㄗㄨㄛㄦ)
三颯兒 (ㄜㄦ)	ㄜㄦ						鴿兒(ㄍㄜㄦ)　盒兒(ㄏㄜㄦ)　個兒(ㄍㄜㄦ)
					ㄓㄦ ㄟㄦ ㄣㄦ		枝兒(ㄓㄦ)　絲兒(ㄙㄦ)　紙兒(ㄓㄦ)　翅兒(ㄔㄦ) 赫兒(ㄏㄜㄦ)　洞兒(ㄉㄦ)　子兒(ㄗㄦ)　字兒(ㄗㄦ) 碑兒(ㄅㄟㄦ)　蕾兒(ㄌㄟㄦ) 根兒(ㄍㄣㄦ)　門兒(ㄇㄣㄦ)　本兒(ㄅㄣㄦ)　悶兒(ㄇㄣㄦ)
	ㄧㄜㄦ					ㄧㄝㄦ	街兒(ㄐㄧㄝㄦ)　茶兒(ㄔㄚㄦ)　帖兒(ㄊㄧㄝㄦ)　葉兒(ㄧㄝㄦ)
					ㄧㄦ ㄧㄢㄦ		滴兒(ㄉㄧㄦ)　鼻兒(ㄅㄧㄦ)　底兒(ㄉㄧㄦ)　氣兒(ㄑㄧㄦ) 今兒(ㄐㄧㄣㄦ)　緊兒(ㄐㄧㄣㄦ)　信兒(ㄒㄧㄣㄦ)
			ㄨㄜㄦ			ㄨㄝㄦ	堆兒(ㄉㄨㄟㄦ)　回兒(ㄏㄨㄟㄦ)　鬼兒(ㄍㄨㄟㄦ)　味兒(ㄨㄟㄦ)
					ㄨㄣㄦ		村兒(ㄘㄨㄣㄦ)　尊兒(ㄗㄨㄣㄦ)　純兒(ㄔㄨㄣㄦ)　根兒(ㄍㄨㄣㄦ)
				ㄩㄜㄦ		ㄩㄝㄦ	月兒(ㄩㄝㄦ)
					ㄩㄣㄦ ㄩㄣㄦ		駒兒(ㄐㄩㄦ)　菊兒(ㄐㄩㄦ)　曲兒(ㄑㄩㄦ) 句兒(ㄐㄩㄦ) 運兒(ㄩㄣㄦ)
四颯兒 (ㄠㄦ)	ㄠㄦ						梟兒(ㄠㄦ)　桃兒(ㄊㄠㄦ)　襲兒(ㄗㄠㄦ)　道兒(ㄉㄠㄦ)
	ㄧㄠㄦ						鷂兒(ㄧㄠㄦ)　橋兒(ㄑㄧㄠㄦ)　鳥兒(ㄋㄧㄠㄦ)　票兒(ㄆㄧㄠㄦ)
五颯兒 (ㄡㄦ)	ㄡㄦ						鉤兒(ㄍㄡㄦ)　頭兒(ㄊㄡㄦ)　口兒(ㄎㄡㄦ)　豆兒(ㄉㄡㄦ)
	ㄧㄡㄦ						妞兒(ㄋㄧㄡㄦ)　牛兒(ㄋㄧㄡㄦ)　酒兒(ㄐㄧㄡㄦ)　袖兒(ㄒㄧㄡㄦ)
六颯兒 (ㄤㄦ)	ㄤㄦ						缸兒(ㄍㄤㄦ)　忙兒(ㄇㄤㄦ)　牆兒(ㄘㄤㄦ)　杖兒(ㄓㄤㄦ)
	ㄧㄤㄦ						箱兒(ㄒㄧㄤㄦ)　羊兒(ㄧㄤㄦ)　響兒(ㄒㄧㄤㄦ)　亮兒(ㄌㄧㄤㄦ)
			ㄨㄤㄦ				裝兒(ㄓㄨㄤㄦ)　黃兒(ㄏㄨㄤㄦ)　網兒(ㄨㄤㄦ)　框兒(ㄎㄨㄤㄦ)
七颯兒 (ㄥㄦ)	ㄥㄦ						蜂兒(ㄈㄥㄦ)　繩兒(ㄕㄥㄦ)　捧兒(ㄆㄥㄦ)　梟兒(ㄍㄥㄦ)
	ㄧㄥㄦ						釘兒(ㄉㄧㄥㄦ)　明兒(ㄇㄧㄥㄦ)　弁兒(ㄅㄧㄥㄦ)　杏兒(ㄒㄧㄥㄦ)
			ㄨㄥㄦ				翁兒(ㄨㄥㄦ)
八颯兒 ㄨㄥㄦ (ㄩㄥㄦ)	一ㄨ ㄥㄦ						虫兒(ㄔㄨㄥㄦ)　鳳兒(ㄈㄥㄦ)　孔兒(ㄎㄨㄥㄦ)　洞兒(ㄉㄨㄥㄦ)
			ㄩㄥㄦ				熊兒(ㄒㄩㄥㄦ)
九颯兒 (ㄨㄦ)				ㄨㄦ			珠兒(ㄓㄨㄦ)　雛兒(ㄔㄨㄦ)　鼓兒(ㄍㄨㄦ)　兔兒(ㄊㄨㄦ)
	開口	齊齒	合口	撮口			

	國語注音符號第一式				聯合國華語注音			
一、聲母								
唇 音	ㄅ	ㄆ	ㄇ	ㄈ	b	p	m	f
舌 尖 音	ㄉ	ㄊ	ㄋ	ㄌ	d	t	n	l
舌 根 音	ㄍ	ㄎ	ㄏ		g	k	h	
舌 面 音	ㄐ	ㄑ	ㄒ		j	q	x	
翹 舌 音	ㄓ	ㄔ	ㄕ	ㄖ	zh	ch	sh	r
舌 齒 音	ㄗ	ㄘ	ㄙ		z	c	s	
二、韻母								
單 韻 ①	(帀)							
單 韻 ②	ㄧ	ㄨ	ㄩ		i	u	ü	
單 韻 ③	ㄚ	ㄛ	ㄜ	ㄝ	a	o	e	ê
複 韻	ㄞ	ㄟ	ㄠ	ㄡ	ai	ei	ao	ou
聲 隨 韻	ㄢ	ㄣ	ㄤ	ㄥ	an	en	ang	eng
捲 舌 韻	ㄦ				er			
三、結合韻母(前有聲母時用)								
齊 齒 呼	ㄧㄚ	ㄧㄛ	ㄧㄝ		ia		ie	
	ㄧㄞ	ㄧㄠ	ㄧㄡ			iao	iou	
	ㄧㄢ	ㄧㄣ	ㄧㄤ	ㄧㄥ	ian	in	iang	ing
合 口 呼	ㄨㄚ	ㄨㄛ	ㄨㄞ	ㄨㄟ	ua	uo	uai	uei
	ㄨㄢ	ㄨㄣ	ㄨㄤ	ㄨㄥ	uan	uen	uang	ueng
撮 口 呼	ㄩㄝ	ㄩㄢ	ㄩㄣ	ㄩㄥ	üe	üan	ün	iong
四、聲調								
陰 平 聲	(不加)							
陽 平 聲	ˊ							
上 聲	ˇ							
去 聲	ˋ							
輕 聲	˙				˙(或不加)			

※聯合國華語注音(漢語注音)補充說明

(1)「ㄓ(知)、ㄔ(蚩)、ㄕ(詩)、ㄖ(日)、ㄗ(資)、ㄘ(雌)、ㄙ(思)」等七個音節的韻母是i,即:知、蚩、詩、日、資、雌、思等字拼作zhi, chi, shi, ri, zi, ci, si。

(2)韻母ㄦ寫成er,用做韻尾的時候寫成r。例如:「兒童」拼作ertong,「花兒」拼作huar。

(3)韻母ㄝ單用的時候寫成ê。

(4)i, ia, ie, iao, iou, ian, in, iang, ing, iong等韻母,前面沒有聲母的時候,寫成:yi(衣), ya(呀), ye(耶), yao(腰), you(憂), yan(煙), yin(因), yang(央), ying(英), yong(擁)。

(5)u, ua, uo, uai, uan, uen, uang, ueng等韻母,前面沒有聲母的時候,寫成:wu(烏), wa(蛙), wo(窩), wai(歪), wei(威), wan(彎), wen(溫), wang(汪), weng(翁)。

(6)ü, üe, üan, ün等韻母,前面沒有聲母的時候,寫成:yu(迂), yue(約), yuan(冤), yun(暈);ü上兩點也省略。若跟聲母j,q, x拼的時候,ü上兩點也省略:ju(居), qu(區), xu(虛),ü是跟聲母n,l拼的時候,仍然寫成:nü(女), lü(呂)。

(7)iou, uei, uen前面加聲母的時候,寫成:iu, ui, un。例如:niu(牛), gui(歸), lun(論)。

(8)在給華語注音的時候,為了使拼式簡短,ng可以省作ŋ。

The Twenty-four Solar Terms

APPROXIMATE DATES		THE SOLAR TERMS		ZODIACAL POSITION OF THE SUN
Feb.	5	立　春	Spring begins	Aquarius
〃	19	雨　水	Rain water	Pisces
Mar.	5	驚　蟄	Excited insects	〃
〃	20	春　分	Vernal equinox	Aries
Apr.	5	清　明	Clear and bright	〃
〃	20	穀　雨	Grain rains	Taurus
May	5	立　夏	Summer begins	〃
〃	21	小　滿	Grain fills	Gemini
June	6	芒　種	Grain in ear	〃
〃	21	夏　至	Summer solstice	Cancer
July	7	小　暑	Slight heat	〃
〃	23	大　暑	Great heat	Leo
Aug.	7	立　秋	Autumn begins	〃
〃	23	處　暑	Limit of heat	Virgo
Sep.	8	白　露	White dew	〃
〃	23	秋　分	Autumnal equinox	Libra
Oct.	8	寒　露	Cold dew	〃
〃	23	霜　降	Hoar frost descends	Scorpio
Nov.	7	立　冬	Winter begins	〃
〃	22	小　雪	Little snow	Sagittarius
Dec.	7	大　雪	Heavy snow	〃
〃	21	冬　至	Winter solstice	Capricorn
Jan.	6	小　寒	Little cold	〃
〃	21	大　寒	Severe cold	Aquarius

Ordinary and Literary Names for the Months

1	正　月	春王，		元月，	青陽，	三陽，	孟陽，	
2	二　月	中和，		杏月，		如月，	花朝，	
3	三　月	桃月，		上巳，		寒食，		
4	四　月	清和，		麥秋，	槐月，	梅月，		*The literary names*
5	五　月	榴月，	蒲月，	天中，		滿月，	端月，	*follow those used*
6	六　月	荷月，	伏月，	天貺，				*colloquially, which*
7	七　月	桐月，		巧月，	中元，	蘭月，		*are given in the*
8	八　月	桂月，		中秋，				*second column.*
9	九　月	菊秋，		菊月，		重陽，		
10	十　月	陽春，		小陽春，				
11	十 一 月	葭月，	冬月，	冬仲月，	長至，			
12	十 二 月	臘月，		嘉平，		清祀，		

編輯經過

一九八五年春，遠東編審委員會決定將梁實秋先生主編之最新實用漢英辭典擴充增編，並成立擴編小組，指定本人綜理其事，余受命之後，立即著手籌備，並全力以赴，以免隕越。又擴編人員除原有遠東編審委員當然參加外，同時另行邀請各大專院校教授及百餘位優秀同學參加查證、校訂等工作。

一九八七年秋，擴編小組完成初稿，為慎重審核初稿起見，另行設立編審小組，分三班制，日夜加班，假日亦然，期能於最短時間內完成。

一九八七年十一月三日，梁實秋先生逝世，吾人痛失導師，惟編審方針依舊，同仁更加全力以赴，務期擴編工作按原定計畫完成。遇有疑難，統由編審委員會及主編張芳杰先生及總審定朱良箴先生會同詳加審核訂正。

擴編期間，路瑞教授就原典提多建議，彌足珍貴。陳如一先生提「師丈」一詞，經梁實秋教授指示收入本典。其他專家學者亦相繼提供寶貴意見，吾人獲益良多，至為感謝。意見既多，爭議之處在所難免。其中最引起爭議者，則為冠詞。部分英語教師力主在英文「可數名詞」前加 a，在機關名稱前加 the，如公共汽車 a bus；父親 a father；台灣銀行 the Bank of Taiwan。部分專家認為加冠詞誤導讀者，如：他坐公共汽車上學。He goes to school by bus. 讀者不能在 bus 前加 a；兒子叫父親Father，絕不會在Father前加a；台灣銀行大門上方的英文名稱Bank of Taiwan, 不是The Bank of Taiwan, 至於在英文句子中該加冠詞或不加冠詞，乃屬英文法領域。擴編小組同仁斟酌各方意見，決定在英文「可數名詞」前加 a，在機關名稱前不加 the。定義說明部分及例句，則依據文法及習慣用法加冠詞或不加冠詞。至於人名、地名，有主張用威妥瑪氏拼音法，有主張用國語羅馬拼音法，有主張用聯合國華語拼音法。我們慎重研究後，決定保留現有拼法，不加更改；為便於讀者查閱，在附錄部分增列「專有名詞拼音對照表」。

為適應一般讀者及大、中學生攜帶輕便需要，編審會將遠東漢英大辭典加以精簡，縮小版本，酌量刪除部分詞條、例句及附錄。謹此說明。

近年來，編校人員所遭遇困難殊多，終能一一克服。對此種任勞任怨之精神，余感激至深。惟編校工作浩繁，疏漏之處在所難免，尚祈　海內外專家學者不吝指教為幸。

鄧樂然　謹識
一九九一年十一月

新字新詞補充

新字新詞補充